2020

The International WHO'S WHO

2020

The International WHO'S WHO

83rd Edition

VOLUME 1: A–K

Routledge
Taylor & Francis Group
LONDON AND NEW YORK

Eighty-third edition published 2019
by Routledge
2 Park Square, Milton Park, Abingdon, Oxon., OX14 4RN, United Kingdom

and by Routledge
52 Vanderbilt Avenue, New York, NY 10017, USA

www.routledge.com

Routledge is an imprint of the Taylor & Francis Group, an informa business

First published 1935

ISBN: 978-0-367-13558-4 (The Set)
ISBN: 978-0-367-27813-7 (Volume 1)
ISSN: 0074-9613

Typeset in Frome by Data Standards Limited

Editorial Director: Paul Kelly
Editorial Researchers: Denize Rodricks (Senior Team Leader), Shubha Banerjee (Team Leader), Meer Hussain (Senior Editorial Researcher), Nitya Arora (Editorial Researcher), Saumya Bhasin (Editorial Researcher), Aakanksha Saklani (Editorial Researcher), Sreerupa Sen (Editorial Researcher)
Consulting Editors: Sue Leckey, Justin Lewis
Editorial Assistant: Lucy Pritchard

PUBLISHER'S NOTE

The *International Who's Who* has been published annually since 1935 and provides biographical information on the most famous and talented men and women in the world today. We select the entries entirely on merit and our books are recognized by librarians in every country as a standard reference source in its field. We wish to make it clear that the Europa Biographical Reference Series has no connection with any other business purporting to produce a publication with the same title or a similar title to ours.

FOREWORD TO THE 83rd EDITION

This is the 83rd edition of THE INTERNATIONAL WHO'S WHO, which since its first publication in 1935 has become the standard reference work on the world's most famous and influential personalities. Now in two volumes, the current edition includes details of the lives and achievements of 25,000 of the world's leading men and women.

In compiling THE INTERNATIONAL WHO'S WHO, our aim is to create a reference work that answers the needs of readers seeking information on the lives of our most gifted and significant contemporaries. We choose the entries entirely on merit and for their continuing interest and importance, adding many hundreds to the selection on a regular basis. Some are household names in every continent. Others are noted for their contributions in specialized fields or for their role in the political, economic, social or cultural life of their particular countries. The scope and diversity of the work is reflected in the range of activities represented, which includes architecture, art, business, cinema, diplomacy, engineering, fashion, journalism, law, literature, medicine, music, photography, politics, science, sport, technology and theatre.

Entrants are sent questionnaires so that they may have an opportunity to make necessary additions and amendments to their biographical details. Supplementary research is continually conducted by the Editors and the Europa editorial department to ensure that the work is as up-to-date as possible upon publication. Valuable assistance is also provided by consultants and experts in particular fields or with specialized knowledge of certain countries.

The introduction contains a list of abbreviations and international telephone codes. The names of entrants whose death has been reported over the past year are included in the Obituary. There is also a section on Reigning Royal Families.

The biographical information contained in this 83rd edition, as well as information on past entrants, deceased entrants and entrants from the wide range of other Europa biographical sources, is provided online in WORLD WHO'S WHO. Using the product's sophisticated search functions, researchers can easily and quickly access the rich biographical data in the comprehensive Europa biographical database. As well, online users can take advantage of the quarterly updating cycle that ensures the data is as current as possible. Details of this resource are available at www.worldwhoswho.com.

Not many countries have their own who's who, and not all national who's whos are published annually. THE INTERNATIONAL WHO'S WHO 2020 represents a library of information from all countries that is not found elsewhere and is unrivalled in its balance and coverage.

May 2019

ALPHABETIZATION KEY

The list of names is alphabetical, with the entrants listed under surnames. If part of an entrant's first given name is in parentheses, this will not affect his or her alphabetical listing.

All names beginning Mc and Mac are treated as though they began Mac, e.g. McDowell before Mace, MacFarlane after McFadyen, Machen before McHenry.

Names with Arabic prefixes are normally listed after the prefix except when requested by the entrant. In the case of surnames beginning De, Des, Du, van or von the entries are normally found under the prefix. Names beginning St are listed as if they began Saint, e.g. St Arnaud after Sainsbury. As a general rule Chinese names are alphabetized under the last name.

In the case of an entrant whose name is spelt in a variety of ways, who is known by a pseudonym or best known by another name, a cross reference is provided, e.g.:

Fayrouz (see Fairuz).

Le Carré, John (see Cornwell, David John Moore).

Lloyd, Chris(tine) Marie Evert (see Evert, Chris(tine) Marie).

ABBREVIATIONS

AAA	Agricultural Adjustment Administration
AAAS	American Association for the Advancement of Science
AAF	Army Air Force
AASA	Associate of the Australian Society of Accountants
AB	Bachelor of Arts; Aktiebolag; Alberta
ABA	American Bar Association
AC	Companion of the Order of Australia
ACA	Associate of the Institute of Chartered Accountants
ACCA	Associate of the Association of Certified Accountants
Acad.	Academy; Académie
Accad.	Accademia
accred	accredited
ACIS	Associate of the Chartered Institute of Secretaries
ACP	American College of Physicians
ACS	American Chemical Society
ACT	Australian Capital Territory
ADC	Aide-de-camp
Adm.	Admiral
Admin(.)	Administrative; Administration; Administrator
AE	Air Efficiency Award
AERE	Atomic Energy Research Establishment
AF	Air Force
AFC	Air Force Cross
ADB	African Development Bank
affil.	affiliated
AFL	American Federation of Labor
AFM	Air Force Medal
AG	Aktiengesellschaft (Joint Stock Company)
Agric.	Agriculture
a.i.	ad interim
AIA	Associate of the Institute of Actuaries; American Institute of Architects
AIAA	American Institute of Aeronautics and Astronautics
AIB	Associate of the Institute of Bankers
AICC	All-India Congress Committee
AICE	Associate of the Institute of Civil Engineers
AIChE	American Institute of Chemical Engineers
AIDS	Acquired Immune Deficiency Syndrome
AIEE	American Institute of Electrical Engineers
AIME	American Institute of Mining Engineers; Associate of the Institution of Mining Engineers
AIMechE	Associate of the Institution of Mechanical Engineers
AIR	All-India Radio
AK	Alaska; Knight of the Order of Australia
Akad.	Akademie
AL	Alabama
Ala	Alabama
ALS	Associate of the Linnaean Society
Alt.	Alternate
AM	Alpes Maritimes; Albert Medal; Master of Arts; Member of the Order of Australia
Amb.	Ambassador
AMICE	Associate Member of the Institution of Civil Engineers
AMIEE	Associate Member of the Institution of Electrical Engineers
AMIMechE	Associate Member of the Institution of Mechanical Engineers
ANC	African National Congress
ANU	Australian National University
AO	Officer of the Order of Australia
AP	Andhra Pradesh
Apdo	Apartado
APEC	Asia and Pacific Economic Co-operation
approx.	approximately
appt	appointment
apptd	appointed
apt	apartment
AR	Arkansas
ARA	Associate of the Royal Academy
ARAM	Associate of the Royal Academy of Music
ARAS	Associate of the Royal Astronomical Society
ARC	Agriculture Research Council
ARCA	Associate of the Royal College of Art
ARCM	Associate of the Royal College of Music
ARCO	Associate of the Royal College of Organists
ARCS	Associate of the Royal College of Science
ARIBA	Associate of the Royal Institute of British Architects
Ariz.	Arizona
Ark.	Arkansas
ARSA	Associate of the Royal Scottish Academy; Associate of the Royal Society of Arts
ASEAN	Association of South-East Asian Nations
ASLIB	Association of Special Libraries and Information Bureaux
ASME	American Society of Mechanical Engineers
Asoc.	Asociación
Ass.	Assembly
Asscn	Association
Assoc.	Associate
ASSR	Autonomous Soviet Socialist Republic
Asst	Assistant
ATV	Associated Television
Aug.	August
autobiog.	autobiography
AZ	Arizona
b.	born
BA	Bachelor of Arts; British Airways
BAAS	British Association for the Advancement of Science
BAFTA	British Academy of Film and Television Arts
BAgr	Bachelor of Agriculture
BAgrSc	Bachelor of Agricultural Science
BAO	Bachelor of Obstetrics
BAOR	British Army of the Rhine
BArch	Bachelor of Architecture
Bart	Baronet
BAS	Bachelor in Agricultural Science
BASc	Bachelor of Applied Science
BBA	Bachelor of Business Administration
BBC	British Broadcasting Corporation
BC	British Columbia
BCC	British Council of Churches
BCE	Bachelor of Civil Engineering
BChir	Bachelor of Surgery
BCL	Bachelor of Civil Law; Bachelor of Canon Law
BCom(m)	Bachelor of Commerce
BCS	Bachelor of Commercial Sciences
BD	Bachelor of Divinity
Bd	Board
BDS	Bachelor of Dental Surgery
BE	Bachelor of Education; Bachelor of Engineering
BEA	British European Airways
BEcons	Bachelor of Economics
BEd	Bachelor of Education
Beds.	Bedfordshire
BEE	Bachelor of Electrical Engineering
BEM	British Empire Medal
BEng	Bachelor of Engineering
Berks.	Berkshire
BFA	Bachelor of Fine Arts
BFI	British Film Institute
BIM	British Institute of Management
biog.	biography
BIS	Bank for International Settlements
BL	Bachelor of Laws
BLA	Bachelor of Landscape Architecture
Bldg	Building
BLit(t)	Bachelor of Letters; Bachelor of Literature
BLL	Bachelor of Laws
BLS	Bachelor in Library Science
blvd	boulevard
BM	Bachelor of Medicine
BMA	British Medical Association
BMus	Bachelor of Music
Bn	Battalion
BNOC	British National Oil Corporation
BOAC	British Overseas Airways Corporation
BP	Boîte Postale
BPA	Bachelor of Public Administration
BPharm	Batchelor of Pharmacy
BPhil	Bachelor of Philosophy
Br.	Branch
Brig.	Brigadier
BS	Bachelor of Science; Bachelor of Surgery
BSA	Bachelor of Scientific Agriculture
BSc	Bachelor of Science
Bt	Baronet
Bucks.	Buckinghamshire
c.	child; children; circa
CA	California; Chartered Accountant
Calif.	California
Cambs.	Cambridgeshire
Cand.	Candidate; Candidature
Cantab.	of Cambridge University
Capt.	Captain
Cards.	Cardiganshire
CB	Companion of the (Order of the) Bath
CBC	Canadian Broadcasting Corporation
CBE	Commander of the (Order of the) British Empire
CBI	Confederation of British Industry
CBiol	Chartered Biologist
CBIM	Companion of the British Institute of Management
CBS	Columbia Broadcasting System
CC	Companion of the Order of Canada

CChem	Chartered Chemist
CCMI	Companion of the Chartered Management Institute (formerly CIMgt)
CCP	Chinese Communist Party
CD	Canadian Forces Decoration; Commander Order of Distinction
Cdre	Commodore
CDU	Christlich-Demokratische Union
CE	Civil Engineer; Chartered Engineer
CEAO	Communauté Economique de l'Afrique de l'Ouest
Cen.	Central
CEng	Chartered Engineer
CENTO	Central Treaty Organization
CEO	Chief Executive Officer
CERN	Conseil (now Organisation) Européen(ne) pour la Recherche Nucléaire
CFR	Commander of the Federal Republic of Nigeria
CGM	Conspicuous Gallantry Medal
CGT	Confédération Général du Travail
CH	Companion of Honour
Chair.	Chairman; Chairwoman; Chairperson
CHB	Companion of Honour of Barbados
ChB	Bachelor of Surgery
Chem.	Chemistry
ChM	Master of Surgery
CI	Channel Islands
CIA	Central Intelligence Agency
Cia	Compagnia (Company)
Cía	Compañía (Company)
CID	Criminal Investigation Department
CIE	Companion of the (Order of the) Indian Empire
Cie	Compagnie (Company)
CIEE	Companion of the Institution of Electrical Engineers
CIMgt	Companion of the Institute of Management (now CCMI)
C-in-C	Commander-in-Chief
CIO	Congress of Industrial Organizations
CIOMS	Council of International Organizations of Medical Science
CIS	Commonwealth of Independent States
CLD	Doctor of Civil Law (USA)
CLit	Companion of Literature
CM	Canada Medal; Master in Surgery
CMEA	Council for Mutual Economic Assistance
CMG	Companion of (the Order of) St Michael and St George
CNAA	Council for National Academic Awards
CNRS	Centre National de la Recherche Scientifique
CO	Colorado; Commanding Officer
Co.	Company; County
COI	Central Office of Information
Col	Colonel
Coll.	College
Colo	Colorado
COMECON	Council for Mutual Economic Assistance
COMESA	Common Market for Eastern and Southern Asia
Comm.	Commission
Commdg	Commanding
Commdr	Commander; Commandeur
Commdt	Commandant
Commr	Commissioner
CON	Commander of Order of Nigeria
Conf.	Conference
Confed.	Confederation
Conn.	Connecticut
Contrib.	Contributor; contribution
COO	Chief Operating Officer
Corp.	Corporate
Corpn	Corporation
Corresp.	Correspondent; Corresponding
CP	Communist Party; Caixa Postal (Post Office Box)
CPA	Certified Public Accountant; Commonwealth Parliamentary Association
CPhys	Chartered Physicist
CPP	Convention People's Party (Ghana)
CPPCC	Chinese People's Political Consultative Conference
CPSU	Communist Party of the Soviet Union
cr.	created
CSc	Candidate of Sciences
CSCE	Conference on Security and Co-operation in Europe
CSI	Companion of the (Order of the) Star of India
CSIRO	Commonwealth Scientific and Industrial Research Organization
CSSR	Czechoslovak Socialist Republic
CStJ	Commander of (the Order of) St John of Jerusalem
CT	Connecticut
Cttee	Committee
CUNY	City University of New York
CV	Commanditaire Vennootschap
CVO	Commander of the Royal Victorian Order
d.	daughter(s)
DArch	Doctor of Architecture
DB	Bachelor of Divinity
DBA	Doctor of Business Administration
DBE	Dame Commander of (the Order of) the British Empire
DC	District of Columbia
DCE	Doctor of Civil Engineering
DCL	Doctor of Civil Law; Doctor of Canon Law
DCM	Distinguished Conduct Medal
DCMG	Dame Commander of (the Order of) St Michael and St George
DCnL	Doctor of Canon Law
DComm	Doctor of Commerce
DCS	Doctor of Commercial Sciences
DCT	Doctor of Christian Theology
DCVO	Dame Commander of the Royal Victorian Order
DD	Doctor of Divinity
DDR	Deutsche Demokratische Republik (German Democratic Republic)
DDS	Doctor of Dental Surgery
DE	Delaware
Dec.	December
DEcon	Doctor of Economics
DEd	Doctor of Education
DEFRA	Department for Environment, Food and Rural Affairs
Del.	Delegate; Delegation; Delaware
Denbighs.	Denbighshire
DenD	Docteur en Droit
DenM	Docteur en Medicine
DEng	Doctor of Engineering
Dep.	Deputy
Dept	Department
DES	Department of Education and Science
Desig.	Designate
DèsL	Docteur ès Lettres
DèsSc	Docteur ès Sciences
Devt	Development
DF	Distrito Federal
DFA	Doctor of Fine Arts; Diploma of Fine Arts
DFC	Distinguished Flying Cross
DFM	Distinguished Flying Medal
DH	Doctor of Humanities
DHist	Doctor of History
DHL	Doctor of Hebrew Literature
DHSS	Department of Health and Social Security
DHumLitt	Doctor of Humane Letters
DIC	Diploma of Imperial College
DipAD	Diploma in Art and Design
DipAgr	Diploma in Agriculture
DipArch	Diploma in Architecture
DipEd	Diploma in Education
DipEng	Diploma in Engineering
DipMus	Diploma in Music
DipScEconSc	Diploma of Social and Economic Science
DipTh	Doctor of Theology
Dir	Director
Dist	District
DIur	Doctor of Law
DIurUtr	Doctor of both Civil and Canon Law
Div.	Division; divisional
DJur	Doctor of Law
DK	Most Esteemed Family (Malaysia)
DL	Deputy Lieutenant
DLit(t)	Doctor of Letters; Doctor of Literature
DLS	Doctor of Library Science
DM	Doctor of Medicine (Oxford)
DMD	Doctor of Dental Medicine
DMedSc	Doctor of Medical Science
DMilSc	Doctor of Military Science
DMunSci	Doctor of Municipal Science
DMS	Director of Medical Services
DMus	Doctor of Music
DMV	Doctor of Veterinary Medicine
DO	Doctor of Ophthalmology
DPH	Diploma in Public Health
DPhil	Doctor of Philosophy
DPM	Diploma in Psychological Medicine
DPS	Doctor of Public Service
Dr	Doctor
DrAgr	Doctor of Agriculture
DrIng	Doctor of Engineering
DrIur	Doctor of Laws
DrMed	Doctor of Medicine
DrOecPol	Doctor of Political Economy
DrOecPubl	Doctor of (Public) Economy
DrPhilNat	Doctor of Natural Philosophy
Dr rer. nat	Doctor of Natural Sciences
Dr rer. pol	Doctor of Political Science
DrSc(i)	Doctor of Sciences
DrScNat	Doctor of Natural Sciences
DS	Doctor of Science
DSC	Distinguished Service Cross
DSc(i)	Doctor of Sciences
DScS	Doctor of Social Science
DSM	Distinguished Service Medal
DSO	Companion of the Distinguished Service Order
DSocSc	Doctor of Social Science
DST	Doctor of Sacred Theology
DTech	Doctor of Technology
DTechSc(i)	Doctor of Technical Sciences
DTheol	Doctor of Theology
DTM	Diploma in Tropical Medicine
DTM&H	Diploma in Tropical Medicine and Hygiene
DUP	Diploma of the University of Paris
DUniv	Doctor of the University

E	East; Eastern
EBRD	European Bank for Reconstruction and Development
EC	European Commission; European Community
ECA	Economic Co-operation Administration; Economic Commission for Africa
ECAFE	Economic Commission for Asia and the Far East
ECE	Economic Commission for Europe
ECLA	Economic Commission for Latin America
ECLAC	Economic Commission for Latin America and the Caribbean
ECO	Economic Co-operation Organization
Econ.	Economic
Econs	Economics
ECOSOC	Economic and Social Council
ECSC	European Coal and Steel Community
ECWA	Economic Commission for Western Asia
ed	educated; edited
Ed.	Editor
ED	Efficiency Decoration; Doctor of Engineering (USA)
EdD	Doctor of Education
Edin.	Edinburgh
EdM	Master of Education
Edn	Edition
Educ.	Education
EEC	European Economic Community
EFTA	European Free Trade Association
eh	Ehrenhalben (Honorary)
EIB	European Investment Bank
EM	Edward Medal; Master of Engineering (USA)
Emer.	Emerita; Emeritus
Eng	Engineering
EngD	Doctor of Engineering
ENO	English National Opera
EPLF	Eritrean People's Liberation Front
ESA	European Space Agency
ESCAP	Economic and Social Commission for Asia and the Pacific
ESCWA	Economic and Social Commission for Western Asia
est.	established
ETH	Eidgenössische Technische Hochschule (Swiss Federal Institute of Technology)
Ets	Etablissements
EU	European Union
EURATOM	European Atomic Energy Community
Exec.	Executive
Exhbn	Exhibition
Ext.	Extension
f.	founded
FAA	Fellow of Australian Academy of Science
FAAS	Fellow of the American Association for the Advancement of Science
FAATS	Fellow of the Australian Academy of Technological Sciences
FACC	Fellow of the American College of Cardiology
FACCA	Fellow of the Association of Certified and Corporate Accountants
FACE	Fellow of the Australian College of Education
FACP	Fellow of American College of Physicians
FACS	Fellow of the American College of Surgeons
FAHA	Fellow Australian Academy of the Humanities
FAIA	Fellow of the American Institute of Architects
FAIAS	Fellow of the Australian Institute of Agricultural Science
FAIM	Fellow of the Australian Institute of Management
FAO	Food and Agriculture Organization
FAS	Fellow of the Antiquarian Society
FASE	Fellow of Antiquarian Society, Edinburgh
FASSA	Fellow Academy of Social Sciences of Australia
FBA	Fellow of the British Academy
FBI	Federal Bureau of Investigation
FBIM	Fellow of the British Institute of Management
FBIP	Fellow of the British Institute of Physics
FCA	Fellow of the Institute of Chartered Accountants
FCAE	Fellow Canadian Academy of Engineering
FCGI	Fellow of the City and Guilds of London Institute
FCIA	Fellow of the Chartered Institute of Arbitrators
FCIB	Fellow of the Chartered Institute of Bankers
FCIC	Fellow of the Chemical Institute of Canada
FCIM	Fellow of the Chartered Institute of Management
FCIS	Fellow of the Chartered Institute of Secretaries
FCMA	Fellow of the Chartered Institute of Management Accountants
FCO	Foreign and Commonwealth Office
FCSD	Fellow of the Chartered Society of Designers
FCT	Federal Capital Territory
FCWA	Fellow of the Institute of Cost and Works Accountants (now FCMA)
FDGB	Freier Deutscher Gewerkschaftsbund
FDP	Freier Demokratische Partei
Feb.	February
Fed.	Federation; Federal
FEng	Fellow(ship) of Engineering
FFCM	Fellow of the Faculty of Community Medicine
FFPHM	Fellow of the Faculty of Public Health Medicine
FGS	Fellow of the Geological Society
FGSM	Fellow of the Guildhall School of Music
FIA	Fellow of the Institute of Actuaries
FIAL	Fellow of the International Institute of Arts and Letters
FIAM	Fellow of the International Academy of Management
FIAMS	Fellow of the Indian Academy of Medical Sciences
FIAP	Fellow of the Institution of Analysts and Programmers
FIArb	Fellow of the Institute of Arbitrators
FIB	Fellow of the Institute of Bankers
FIBA	Fellow of the Institute of Banking Associations
FIBiol	Fellow of the Institute of Biologists
FICE	Fellow of the Institution of Civil Engineers
FIChemE	Fellow of the Institute of Chemical Engineers
FID	Fellow of the Institute of Directors
FIE	Fellow of the Institute of Engineers
FIEE	Fellow of the Institution of Electrical Engineers
FIEEE	Fellow of the Institute of Electrical and Electronics Engineers
FIFA	Fédération Internationale de Football Association
FIJ	Fellow of the Institute of Journalists
FilLic	Licentiate in Philosophy
FIM	Fellow of the Institute of Metallurgists
FIME	Fellow of the Institute of Mining Engineers
FIMechE	Fellow of the Institute of Mechanical Engineers
FIMI	Fellow of the Institute of the Motor Industry
FInstF	Fellow of the Institute of Fuel
FInstM	Fellow of the Institute of Marketing
FInstP	Fellow of the Institute of Physics
FInstPet	Fellow of the Institute of Petroleum
FIPM	Fellow of the Institute of Personnel Management
FIRE	Fellow of the Institution of Radio Engineers
FITD	Fellow of the Institute of Training and Development
FL	Florida
Fla	Florida
FLA	Fellow of the Library Association
FLN	Front de Libération Nationale
FLS	Fellow of the Linnaean Society
FMedSci	Fellow of the Academy of Medical Sciences
fmr(ly)	former(ly)
FNI	Fellow of the National Institute of Sciences of India
FNZIA	Fellow of the New Zealand Institute of Architects
FRACP	Fellow of the Royal Australasian College of Physicians
FRACS	Fellow of the Royal Australasian College of Surgeons
FRAeS	Fellow of the Royal Aeronautical Society
FRAI	Fellow of the Royal Anthropological Institute
FRAIA	Fellow of the Royal Australian Institute of Architects
FRAIC	Fellow of the Royal Architectural Institute of Canada
FRAM	Fellow of the Royal Academy of Music
FRAS	Fellow of the Royal Astronomical Society; Fellow of the Royal Asiatic Society
FRBS	Fellow of the Royal Society of British Sculptors
FRCA	Fellow of the Royal College of Anaesthetists
FRCM	Fellow of the Royal College of Music
FRCO	Fellow of the Royal College of Organists
FRCOG	Fellow of the Royal College of Obstetricians and Gynaecologists
FRCP	Fellow of the Royal College of Physicians
FRCPE	Fellow of the Royal College of Physicians, Edinburgh
FRCPGlas	Fellow of the Royal College of Physicians (Glasgow)
FRCPI	Fellow of the Royal College of Physicians of Ireland
FRCPath	Fellow Royal College of Pathologists
FRCR	Fellow Royal College of Radiology
FRCS	Fellow of the Royal College of Surgeons
FRCSE	Fellow of the Royal College of Surgeons, Edinburgh
FRCVS	Fellow of the Royal College of Veterinary Surgeons
FREconS	Fellow of the Royal Economic Society
FREng	Fellow of the Royal Academy of Engineering
FRES	Fellow of the Royal Entomological Society
FRFPS	Fellow of the Royal Faculty of Physicians and Surgeons
FRG	Federal Republic of Germany
FRGS	Fellow of the Royal Geographical Society
FRHistS	Fellow of the Royal Historical Society
FRHortS	Fellow of the Royal Horticultural Society
FRIBA	Fellow of the Royal Institute of British Architects
FRIC	Fellow of the Royal Institute of Chemists
FRICS	Fellow of the Royal Institute of Chartered Surveyors
FRMetS	Fellow of the Royal Meteorological Society
FRNCM	Fellow of the Royal Northern College of Music
FRPS	Fellow of the Royal Photographic Society
FRS	Fellow of the Royal Society
FRSA	Fellow of the Royal Society of Arts
FRSAMD	Fellow of the Royal Scottish Academy of Music and Drama
FRSC	Fellow of the Royal Society of Canada; Fellow of the Royal Society of Chemistry
FRSE	Fellow of the Royal Society of Edinburgh
FRSL	Fellow of the Royal Society of Literature
FRSM	Fellow of the Royal Society of Medicine
FRSNZ	Fellow of the Royal Society of New Zealand
FRSS	Fellow of the Royal Statistical Society
FRSSA	Fellow of the Royal Society of South Africa
FRTS	Fellow of the Royal Television Society
FSA	Fellow of the Society of Antiquaries
FSIAD	Fellow of the Society of Industrial Artists and Designers
FTI	Fellow of the Textile Institute
FTS	Fellow of Technological Sciences
FWAAS	Fellow of the World Academy of Arts and Sciences
FZS	Fellow of the Zoological Society
GA	Georgia
Ga	Georgia
GATT	General Agreement on Tariffs and Trade
GB	Great Britain

ABBREVIATIONS

GBE	Knight (or Dame) Grand Cross of (the Order of) the British Empire
GC	George Cross
GCB	Knight Grand Cross of (the Order of) the Bath
GCIE	Knight Grand Commander of (the Order of) the Indian Empire
GCMG	Knight (or Dame) Grand Cross of (the Order of) St Michael and St George
GCSI	Knight Grand Commander of (the Order of) the Star of India
GCVO	Knight (or Dame) Grand Cross of the Royal Victorian Order
GDR	German Democratic Republic
Gen.	General
GHQ	General Headquarters
GLA	Greater London Authority
Glam.	Glamorganshire
GLC	Greater London Council
Glos.	Gloucestershire
GM	George Medal
GmbH	Gesellschaft mit beschränkter Haftung (Limited Liability Company)
GOC	General Officer Commanding
GOC-in-C	General Officer Commanding-in-Chief
Gov.	Governor
Govt	Government
GPO	General Post Office
Grad.	Graduate
GRSM	Graduate of the Royal School of Music
GSO	General Staff Officer
Hants.	Hampshire
hc	honoris causa
HE	His Eminence; His (or Her) Excellency
Herefords.	Herefordshire
Herts.	Hertfordshire
HH	His (or Her) Highness
HI	Hawaii
HIV	human immunodeficiency virus
HLD	Doctor of Humane Letters
HM	His (or Her) Majesty
HMS	His (or Her) Majesty's Ship
Hon.	Honorary; Honourable
Hons	Honours
Hosp.	Hospital
HQ	Headquarters
HRH	His (or Her) Royal Highness
HSH	His (or Her) Serene Highness
HSP	Hungarian Socialist Party
HSWP	Hungarian Socialist Workers' Party
Hunts.	Huntingdonshire
IA	Iowa
Ia	Iowa
IAAF	International Association of Athletics Federations
IAEA	International Atomic Energy Agency
IATA	International Air Transport Association
IBA	Independent Broadcasting Authority
IBRD	International Bank for Reconstruction and Development (World Bank)
ICAO	International Civil Aviation Organization
ICC	International Chamber of Commerce
ICE	Institution of Civil Engineers
ICEM	Intergovernmental Committee for European Migration
ICFTU	International Confederation of Free Trade Unions
ICI	Imperial Chemical Industries
ICOM	International Council of Museums
ICRC	International Committee for the Red Cross
ICS	Indian Civil Service
ICSID	International Centre for Settlement of Investment Disputes
ICSU	International Council of Scientific Unions
ID	Idaho
Ida	Idaho
IDA	International Development Association
IDB	Inter-American Development Bank
IEA	International Energy Agency
IEE	Institution of Electrical Engineers
IEEE	Institution of Electrical and Electronic Engineers
IFAD	International Fund for Agricultural Development
IFC	International Finance Corporation
IGAD	Intergovernmental Authority on Development
IISS	International Institute for Strategic Studies
IL	Illinois
Ill.	Illinois
ILO	International Labour Organization
IMCO	Inter-Governmental Maritime Consultative Organization
IMechE	Institution of Mechanical Engineers
IMF	International Monetary Fund
IMO	International Maritime Organization
IN	Indiana
Inc.	Incorporated
Ind.	Indiana; Independent
Insp.	Inspector
Inst.	Institute; Institution
Int.	International
INTERPOL	International Criminal Police Organization
INTUC	Indian National Trades Union Congress
IOC	International Olympic Committee
IPU	Inter-Parliamentary Union
ISO	Companion of the Imperial Service Order
ITA	Independent Television Authority
ITU	International Telecommunications Union
ITV	Independent Television
IUPAC	International Union of Pure and Applied Chemistry
IUPAP	International Union of Pure and Applied Physics
Jan.	January
JCB	Bachelor of Canon Law
JCD	Doctor of Canon Law
JD	Doctor of Jurisprudence
JMK	Johan Mangku Negara (Malaysia)
JP	Justice of the Peace
Jr	Junior
JSD	Doctor of Juristic Science
Jt(ly)	Joint(ly)
JUD	Juris utriusque Doctor (Doctor of both Civil and Canon Law)
JuD	Doctor of Law
JUDr	Juris utriusque Doctor (Doctor of both Civil and Canon Law); Doctor of Law
Kan.	Kansas
KBE	Knight Commander of (the Order of) the British Empire
KC	King's Counsel
KCB	Knight Commander of (the Order of) the Bath
KCIE	Knight Commander of (the Order of) the Indian Empire
KCMG	Knight Commander of (the Order of) St Michael and St George
KCSI	Knight Commander of (the Order of) the Star of India
KCVO	Knight Commander of the Royal Victorian Order
KG	Royal Knight of the Most Noble Order of the Garter
KGB	Committee of State Security (USSR)
KK	Kaien Kaisha
KLM	Koninklijke Luchtvaart Maatschappij (Royal Dutch Airlines)
KNZM	Knight of the New Zealand Order of Merit
KP	Knight of (the Order of) St Patrick
KS	Kansas
KStJ	Knight of (the Order of) St John of Jerusalem
KT	Knight of (the Order of) the Thistle
Kt	Knight
KY	Kentucky
Ky	Kentucky
LA	Louisiana; Los Angeles
La	Louisiana
Lab.	Laboratory
Lancs.	Lancashire
LDP	Liberal Democratic Party
LDS	Licentiate in Dental Surgery
Legis.	Legislative
Leics.	Leicestershire
LenD	Licencié en Droit
LèsL	Licencié ès Lettres
LèsSc	Licencié ès Sciences
LG	Lady of (the Order of) the Garter
LHD	Doctor of Humane Letters
LI	Long Island
LicenDer	Licenciado en Derecho
LicenFil	Licenciado en Filosofía
LicMed	Licentiate in Medicine
Lincs.	Lincolnshire
LittD	Doctor of Letters
LLB	Bachelor of Laws
LLC	Limited Liability Company
LLD	Doctor of Laws
LLL	Licentiate of Laws
LLM	Master of Laws
LLP	Limited Liability Partnership
LM	Licentiate of Medicine; Licentiate Midwifery
LN	League of Nations
LPh	Licentiate of Philosophy
LRAM	Licentiate of the Royal Academy of Music
LRCP	Licentiate of the Royal College of Physicians
LSE	London School of Economics and Political Science
Lt	Lieutenant
Ltd	Limited
Ltda	Limitada
LTh	Licentiate in Theology
LVO	Lieutenant, Royal Victorian Order
m.	married; marriage; metre(s)
MA	Massachusetts; Master of Arts
MAgr	Master of Agriculture (USA)
Maj.	Major
MALD	Master of Arts in Law and Diplomacy
Man.	Management; Manager; Managing; Manitoba
MArch	Master of Architecture
Mass	Massachusetts
Math.	Mathematics; Mathematical
MB	Bachelor of Medicine; Manitoba
MBA	Master of Business Administration
MBE	Member of (the Order of) the British Empire
MBS	Master of Business Studies
MC	Military Cross
MCC	Marylebone Cricket Club
MCE	Master of Civil Engineering

ABBREVIATIONS

MCh	Master of Surgery
MChD	Master of Dental Surgery
MCL	Master of Civil Law
MCom(m)	Master of Commerce
MCP	Master of City Planning
MD	Maryland; Doctor of Medicine
Md	Maryland
MDiv	Master of Divinity
MDS	Master of Dental Surgery
ME	Maine; Myalgic Encephalomyelitis
Me	Maine
MEconSc	Master of Economic Sciences
MEd	Master in Education
mem.	member
MEng	Master of Engineering (Dublin)
MEP	Member of European Parliament
MFA	Master of Fine Arts
Mfg	Manufacturing
Mfrs	Manufacturers
Mgr	Monseigneur; Monsignor
MI	Michigan; Marshall Islands
MIA	Master of International Affairs
MICE	Member of the Institution of Civil Engineers
MIChemE	Member of the Institution of Chemical Engineers
Mich.	Michigan
Middx	Middlesex
MIEE	Member of the Institution of Electrical Engineers
Mil.	Military
MIMarE	Member of the Institute of Marine Engineers
MIMechE	Member of the Institution of Mechanical Engineers
MIMinE	Member of the Institution of Mining Engineers
Minn.	Minnesota
MInstT	Member of the Institute of Transport
Miss.	Mississippi
MIStructE	Member of the Institution of Structural Engineers
MIT	Massachusetts Institute of Technology
MJ	Master of Jurisprudence
MLA	Member of the Legislative Assembly; Master of Landscape Architecture
MLC	Member of the Legislative Council
MM	Military Medal
MLitt	Master in Letters
MM	Military Medal
MMus	Master of Music
MN	Minnesota
MNOC	Movement of Non-Aligned Countries
MO	Missouri
Mo.	Missouri
MOH	Medical Officer of Health
Mon.	Monmouthshire
Mont.	Montana
Movt	Movement
MP	Member of Parliament; Madhya Pradesh
MPA	Master of Public Administration (Harvard)
MPh	Master of Philosophy (USA)
MPhil	Master of Philosophy
MPolSci	Master of Political Science
MPP	Member of Provincial Parliament (Canada)
MRAS	Member of the Royal Asiatic Society
MRC	Medical Research Council
MRCP	Member of the Royal College of Physicians
MRCPE	Member of the Royal College of Physicians, Edinburgh
MRCS	Member of the Royal College of Surgeons
MRCSE	Member of the Royal College of Surgeons, Edinburgh
MRCVS	Member of the Royal College of Veterinary Surgeons
MRI	Member of the Royal Institution
MRIA	Member of the Royal Irish Academy
MRIC	Member of the Royal Institute of Chemistry
MRP	Mouvement Républicain Populaire
MS	Mississippi; Master of Science; Master of Surgery
MSc	Master of Science
MScS	Master of Social Science
MSP	Member Scottish Parliament
MT	Montana
MTS	Master of Theological Studies
MUDr	Doctor of Medicine
MusB(ac)	Bachelor of Music
MusD(oc)	Doctor of Music
MusM	Master of Music (Cambridge)
MVD	Master of Veterinary Medicine
MVO	Member of the Royal Victorian Order
MW	Master of Wine
N	North; Northern
NAS	National Academy of Sciences (USA)
NASA	National Aeronautics and Space Administration
Nat.	National
NATO	North Atlantic Treaty Organization
Naz.	Nazionale
NB	New Brunswick
NBC	National Broadcasting Corporation
NC	North Carolina
ND	North Dakota
NE	Nebraska; North East
NEA	National Endowment for the Arts
Neb.	Nebraska
NEDC	National Economic Development Council
NERC	Natural Environment Research Council
Nev.	Nevada
NF	Newfoundland
NGO	Non-Governmental Organization
NH	New Hampshire
NHS	National Health Service
NI	Northern Ireland
NIH	National Institutes of Health
NJ	New Jersey
NL	Newfoundland and Labrador
NM	New Mexico
Northants.	Northamptonshire
Notts.	Nottinghamshire
Nov.	November
NPC	National People's Congress
nr	near
NRC	Nuclear Research Council
NS	Nova Scotia
NSF	National Science Foundation
NSW	New South Wales
NT	Northern Territory
NU	Nunavut Territory
NV	Naamloze Vennootschap; Nevada
NW	North West
NWT	North West Territories
NY	New York (State)
NZ	New Zealand
NZIC	New Zealand Institute of Chemistry
O	Ohio
OAPEC	Organization of Arab Petroleum Exporting Countries
OAS	Organization of American States
OAU	Organization of African Unity
OBE	Officer of (the Order of) the British Empire
OC	Officer of the Order of Canada
Oct.	October
OE	Order of Excellence (Guyana)
OECD	Organisation for Economic Co-operation and Development
OEEC	Organization for European Economic Co-operation
OFS	Orange Free State
OH	Ohio
OHCHR	Office of the United Nations High Commissioner for Human Rights
OIC	Organization of the Islamic Conference
OJ	Order of Jamaica
OK	Oklahoma
Okla	Oklahoma
OM	Member of the Order of Merit
ON	Ontario; Order of Nigeria
Ont.	Ontario
ONZ	Order of New Zealand
OP	Ordo Praedicatorum (Dominicans)
OPCW	Organization for the Prohibition of Chemical Weapons
OPEC	Organization of the Petroleum Exporting Countries
OPM	Office of Production Management
OQ	Officer National Order of Québec
OR	Oregon
Ore.	Oregon
Org.	Organization
OSB	Order of St Benedict
OSCE	Organization for Security and Co-operation in Europe
Oxon.	of Oxford University; Oxfordshire
PA	Pennsylvania
Pa	Pennsylvania
Parl.	Parliament; Parliamentary
PC	Privy Councillor
PCC	Provincial Congress Committee
PdB	Bachelor of Pedagogy
PdD	Doctor of Pedagogy
PdM	Master of Pedagogy
PDS	Partei des Demokratischen Sozialismus
PE	Prince Edward Island
PEI	Prince Edward Island
Pembs.	Pembrokeshire
PEN	Poets, Playwrights, Essayists and Novelists (Club)
Perm.	Permanent
PGCE	Postgraduate Certificate in Education
PhB	Bachelor of Philosophy
PhD(r)	Doctor of Philosophy
PharmD	Docteur en Pharmacie
Phila	Philadelphia
PhL	Licentiate of Philosophy
PLA	People's Liberation Army; Port of London Authority
PLC	Public Limited Company
PLO	Palestine Liberation Organization
PMB	Private Mail Bag
pnr	partner
PO(B)	Post Office (Box)
POW	Prisoner of War
PPR	Polish Workers' Party
PPRA	Past President of the Royal Academy
PQ	Province of Québec
PR	Puerto Rico
PRA	President of the Royal Academy

Pref.	Prefecture
Prep.	Preparatory
Pres.	President
PRI	President of the Royal Institute (of Painters in Water Colours)
PRIBA	President of the Royal Institute of British Architects
Prin.	Principal
Priv Doz	Privat Dozent (recognized teacher not on the regular staff)
PRO	Public Relations Officer
Proc.	Proceedings
prod.	producer
Prof.	Professor
Propr	Proprietor
Prov.	Province; Provincial
PRS	President of the Royal Society
PRSA	President of the Royal Scottish Academy
PSM	Panglima Setia Mahota
Pty	Proprietary
Publ.(s)	Publication(s)
Publr	Publisher
Pvt.	Private
PZPR	Polish United Workers' Party
QC	Québec; Queen's Counsel
QGM	Queen's Gallantry Medal
Qld	Queensland
QPM	Queen's Police Medal
QSO	Queen's Service Order
q.v.	quod vide (to which refer)
RA	Royal Academy; Royal Academician; Royal Artillery
RAAF	Royal Australian Air Force
RAC	Royal Armoured Corps
RACP	Royal Australasian College of Physicians
RADA	Royal Academy of Dramatic Art
RAF	Royal Air Force
RAFVR	Royal Air Force Volunteer Reserve
RAM	Royal Academy of Music
RAMC	Royal Army Medical Corps
RAOC	Royal Army Ordnance Corps
RC	Roman Catholic
RCA	Radio Corporation of America; Royal Canadian Academy; Royal College of Art
RCAF	Royal Canadian Air Force
RCM	Royal College of Music
RCP	Romanian Communist Party
RCP	Royal College of Physicians
RCPI	Royal College of Physicians of Ireland
Regt	Regiment
REME	Royal Electric and Mechanical Engineers
Rep.	Representative; represented
Repub.	Republic
resgnd	resigned
retd	retired
Rev.	Reverend
RI	Rhode Island
RIBA	Royal Institute of British Architects
RMA	Royal Military Academy
RN	Royal Navy
RNR	Royal Naval Reserve
RNVR	Royal Naval Volunteer Reserve
RNZAF	Royal New Zealand Air Force
RP	Member Royal Society of Portrait Painters
RPR	Rassemblement pour la République
RSA	Royal Scottish Academy; Royal Society of Arts
RSC	Royal Shakespeare Company; Royal Society of Canada
RSDr	Doctor of Social Sciences
RSFSR	Russian Soviet Federative Socialist Republic
RSL	Royal Society of Literature
Rt Hon.	Right Honourable
Rt Rev.	Right Reverend
RVO	Royal Victorian Order
RWS	Royal Society of Painters in Water Colours
s.	son(s)
S	South; Southern
SA	Sociedad Anónima; Société Anonyme; South Africa; South Australia
SAARC	South Asian Association for Regional Co-operation
SADC	South African Development Community
SAE	Society of Aeronautical Engineers
Salop.	Shropshire
SALT	Strategic Arms Limitation Treaty
Sask.	Saskatchewan
SB	Bachelor of Science (USA)
SC	Senior Counsel; South Carolina
SCAP	Supreme Command Allied Powers
ScB	Bachelor of Science
ScD	Doctor of Science
SD	South Dakota
SDak	South Dakota
SDLP	Social and Democratic Liberal Party
SDP	Social Democratic Party
SE	South East
SEATO	South East Asia Treaty Organization
Sec.	Secretary
SEC	Securities and Exchange Commission
Secr.	Secretariat
SED	Sozialistische Einheitspartei Deutschlands (Socialist Unity Party of the German Democratic Republic)
Sept.	September
S-et-O	Seine-et-Oise
SHAEF	Supreme Headquarters Allied Expeditionary Force
SHAPE	Supreme Headquarters Allied Powers in Europe
SJ	Society of Jesus (Jesuits)
SJD	Doctor of Juristic Science
SK	Saskatchewan
SLD	Social and Liberal Democrats
SM	Master of Science
SOAS	School of Oriental and African Studies
Soc.	Society; Société
SpA	Societá per Azioni
SPD	Sozialdemokratische Partei Deutschlands
Sr	Senior
SRC	Science Research Council
SRL	Societé a responsabilité
SSM	Seria Seta Mahkota (Malaysia)
SSR	Soviet Socialist Republic
St	Saint
Staffs.	Staffordshire
STB	Bachelor of Sacred Theology
STD	Doctor of Sacred Theology
STL	Licentiate of Sacred Theology
STM	Master of Sacred Theology
str.	strasse
Supt	Superintendent
SW	South West
SWAPO	South West Africa People's Organization
TA	Territorial Army
TD	Teachta Dála (member of the Dáil); Territorial Decoration
Tech.	Technical; Technology
Temp.	Temporary
Tenn.	Tennessee
Tex.	Texas
ThB	Bachelor of Theology
ThD	Doctor of Theology
THDr	Doctor of Theology
ThM	Master of Theology
TN	Tennessee
Trans.	Translation; Translator
Treas.	Treasurer
TU(C)	Trades Union (Congress)
TV	television
TX	Texas
UAE	United Arab Emirates
UAR	United Arab Republic
UCLA	University of California at Los Angeles
UDEAC	L'Union Douanière et Economique de l'Afrique Centrale
UDR	Union des Démocrates pour la République
UED	University Education Diploma
UK	United Kingdom (of Great Britain and Northern Ireland)
UKAEA	United Kingdom Atomic Energy Authority
UMIST	University of Manchester Institute of Science and Technology
UMNO	United Malays National Organization
UN(O)	United Nations (Organization)
UNA	United Nations Association
UNCED	United Nations Council for Education and Development
UNCHS	United Nations Centre for Human Settlements (Habitat)
UNCTAD	United Nations Conference on Trade and Development
UNDCP	United Nations International Drug Control Programme
UNDP	United Nations Development Programme
UNDRO	United Nations Disaster Relief Office
UNEF	United Nations Emergency Force
UNEP	United Nations Environment Programme
UNESCO	United Nations Educational, Scientific and Cultural Organisation
UNFPA	United Nations Population Fund
UNHCR	United Nations High Commissioner for Refugees
UNICEF	United Nations International Children's Emergency Fund
UNIDO	United Nations Industrial Development Organization
UNIFEM	United Nations Development Fund for Women
UNITAR	United Nations Institute for Training and Research
Univ.	University
UNKRA	United Nations Korean Relief Administration
UNRRA	United Nations Relief and Rehabilitation Administration
UNRWA	United Nations Relief and Works Agency
UNU	United Nations University
UP	United Provinces; Uttar Pradesh
UPU	Universal Postal Union
Urb.	Urbanizacion
US	United States
USA	United States of America
USAAF	United States Army Air Force
USAF	United States Air Force
USAID	United States Agency for International Development
USN	United States Navy
USNR	United States Navy Reserve
USPHS	United States Public Health Service
USS	United States Ship
USSR	Union of Soviet Socialist Republics

UT	Utah
UWI	University of the West Indies
VA	Virginia
Va	Virginia
VC	Victoria Cross
VI	(US) Virgin Islands
Vic.	Victoria
Vol.(s)	Volume(s)
VSO	Voluntary Services Overseas
VT	Vermont
Vt	Vermont
W	West; Western
WA	Washington (State); Western Australia
Warwicks.	Warwickshire
Wash.	Washington (State)
WCC	World Council of Churches
WCT	World Championship Tennis
WEU	Western European Union
WFP	World Food Programme
WFTU	World Federation of Trade Unions
WHO	World Health Organization
WI	Wisconsin
Wilts.	Wiltshire
WIPO	World Intellectual Property Organization
Wis.	Wisconsin
WMO	World Meteorological Organization
WNO	Welsh National Opera
Worcs.	Worcestershire
WRAC	Women's Royal Army Corps
WRNS	Women's Royal Naval Service
WTO	World Trade Organization
WV	West Virginia
WVa	West Virginia
WWF	World Wildlife Fund
WY	Wyoming
Wyo.	Wyoming
YMCA	Young Men's Christian Association
Yorks.	Yorkshire
YT	Yukon Territory
YWCA	Young Women's Christian Association

INTERNATIONAL TELEPHONE CODES

To make international calls to telephone and fax numbers listed in the book, dial the international code of the country from which you are calling, followed by the appropriate country code for the organization you wish to call (listed below), followed by the area code (if applicable) and telephone or fax number listed in the entry.

	Country code
Abkhazia	7
Afghanistan	93
Åland Islands	358
Albania	355
Algeria	213
American Samoa	1 684
Andorra	376
Angola	244
Anguilla	1 264
Antigua and Barbuda	1 268
Argentina	54
Armenia	374
Aruba	297
Ascension Island	247
Australia	61
Austria	43
Azerbaijan	994
Bahamas	1 242
Bahrain	973
Bangladesh	880
Barbados	1 246
Belarus	375
Belgium	32
Belize	501
Benin	229
Bermuda	1 441
Bhutan	975
Bolivia	591
Bonaire	599
Bosnia and Herzegovina	387
Botswana	267
Brazil	55
British Indian Ocean Territory (Diego Garcia)	246
British Virgin Islands	1 284
Brunei	673
Bulgaria	359
Burkina Faso	226
Burundi	257
Cabo Verde	238
Cambodia	855
Cameroon	237
Canada	1
Cayman Islands	1 345
Central African Republic	236
Ceuta	34
Chad	235
Chile	56
China, People's Republic	86
Christmas Island	61
Cocos (Keeling) Islands	61
Colombia	57
Comoros	269
Congo, Democratic Republic	243
Congo, Republic	242
Cook Islands	682
Costa Rica	506
Côte d'Ivoire	225
Croatia	385
Cuba	53
Curaçao	599
Cyprus	357
Czech Republic	420
Denmark	45
Djibouti	253
Dominica	1 767
Dominican Republic	1 809
Ecuador	593

	Country code
Egypt	20
El Salvador	503
Equatorial Guinea	240
Eritrea	291
Estonia	372
Ethiopia	251
Falkland Islands	500
Faroe Islands	298
Fiji	679
Finland	358
France	33
French Guiana	594
French Polynesia	689
Gabon	241
Gambia	220
Georgia	995
Germany	49
Ghana	233
Gibraltar	350
Greece	30
Greenland	299
Grenada	1 473
Guadeloupe	590
Guam	1 671
Guatemala	502
Guernsey	44
Guinea	224
Guinea-Bissau	245
Guyana	592
Haiti	509
Honduras	504
Hong Kong	852
Hungary	36
Iceland	354
India	91
Indonesia	62
Iran	98
Iraq	964
Ireland	353
Isle of Man	44
Israel	972
Italy	39
Jamaica	1 876
Japan	81
Jersey	44
Jordan	962
Kazakhstan	7
Kenya	254
Kiribati	686
Korea, Democratic People's Republic (North Korea)	850
Korea, Republic (South Korea)	82
Kosovo	381*
Kuwait	965
Kyrgyzstan	996
Laos	856
Latvia	371
Lebanon	961
Lesotho	266
Liberia	231
Libya	218
Liechtenstein	423
Lithuania	370
Luxembourg	352
Macao	853
Madagascar	261
Malawi	265
Malaysia	60

	Country code
Maldives	960
Mali	223
Malta	356
Marshall Islands	692
Martinique	596
Mauritania	222
Mauritius	230
Mayotte	262
Melilla	34
Mexico	52
Micronesia, Federated States	691
Moldova	373
Monaco	377
Mongolia	976
Montenegro	382
Montserrat	1 664
Morocco	212
Mozambique	258
Myanmar	95
Nagornyi Karabakh	374
Namibia	264
Nauru	674
Nepal	977
Netherlands	31
New Caledonia	687
New Zealand	64
Nicaragua	505
Niger	227
Nigeria	234
Niue	683
Norfolk Island	672
North Macedonia	389
Northern Mariana Islands	1 670
Norway	47
Oman	968
Pakistan	92
Palau	680
Palestinian Territories	970 or 972
Panama	507
Papua New Guinea	675
Paraguay	595
Peru	51
Philippines	63
Pitcairn Islands	872
Poland	48
Portugal	351
Puerto Rico	1 787
Qatar	974
Réunion	262
Romania	40
Russian Federation	7
Rwanda	250
Saba	599
Saint-Barthélemy	590
Saint Christopher and Nevis	1 869
Saint Helena	290
Saint Lucia	1 758
Saint-Martin	590
Saint Pierre and Miquelon	508
Saint Vincent and the Grenadines	1 784
Samoa	685
San Marino	378
São Tomé and Príncipe	239
Saudi Arabia	966
Senegal	221
Serbia	381
Seychelles	248
Sierra Leone	232
Singapore	65
Sint Eustatius	1721
Sint Maarten	1721
Slovakia	421
Slovenia	386
Solomon Islands	677
Somalia	252
South Africa	27
South Ossetia	7
South Sudan	211
Spain	34
Sri Lanka	94
Sudan	249
Suriname	597
Svalbard	47
Swaziland	268
Sweden	46
Switzerland	41
Syria	963
Taiwan	886
Tajikistan	992
Tanzania	255
Thailand	66
Timor-Leste	670
Togo	228
Tokelau	690
Tonga	676
Transnistria	373
Trinidad and Tobago	1 868
Tristan da Cunha	290
Tunisia	216
Turkey	90
'Turkish Republic of Northern Cyprus'	90 392
Turkmenistan	993
Turks and Caicos Islands	1 649
Tuvalu	688
Uganda	256
Ukraine	380
United Arab Emirates	971
United Kingdom	44
United States of America	1
United States Virgin Islands	1 340
Uruguay	598
Uzbekistan	998
Vanuatu	678
Vatican City	39
Venezuela	58
Viet Nam	84
Wallis and Futuna Islands	681
Yemen	967
Zambia	260
Zimbabwe	263

* Mobile telephone numbers for Kosovo use either the country code for Monaco (377) or the country code for Slovenia (386).

Note: Telephone and fax numbers using the Inmarsat ocean region code 870 are listed in full. No country or area code is required, but it is necessary to precede the number with the international access code of the country from which the call is made.

REIGNING ROYAL FAMILIES OF THE WORLD

Biographical entries of most of the reigning monarchs and of certain other members of the reigning royal families will be found in their appropriate alphabetical order in the biographical section of this book. The name under which they can be found in the text of the book will be listed in this section in bold type.

BAHRAIN

Reigning King

HM SHEIKH HAMAD BIN ISA AL-**KHALIFA**; b. 28 January 1950; succeeded 6 March 1999 as Ruler of Bahrain on the death of his father, Sheikh Isa bin Sulman al-Khalifa; acceded as Amir 6 March 1999; proclaimed King 14 February 2002; married 9 October 1968, Shaikha Sabeeka bint Ibrahim al-Khalifa; three sons, one daughter; four sons, four daughters with his three other wives.

Crown Prince

HRH Sheikh Salman bin Hamad bin Isa al-**Khalifa**, b. 21 October 1969; married Hala bint D'aij al-Khalifa (died 2018); two sons, two daughters.

Parents of the King

Sheikh Isa bin Salman Al Khalifa, b. 3 June 1931, died 6 March 1999; succeeded to the throne December 1961, on the death of his father, Sheikh Salman bin Hamad Al Khalifa; married 8 May 1949, Shaikha Hessa bint Salman Al Khalifa (b. 1933); six sons, six daughters.

BELGIUM

Reigning King

HM KING **PHILIPPE** I; b. 15 April 1960; succeeded to the throne 21 July 2013, on the abdication of his father, King Albert II; married 4 December 1999, Mathilde Marie Christiane Ghislaine d'Udekem d'Acoz (Queen Mathilde) (b. 20 January 1973).

Children of the King

HRH Princess Elisabeth, Duchess of Brabant, b. 25 October 2001.

HRH Prince Gabriel, b. 20 August 2003.

HRH Prince Emmanuel, b. 4 October 2005.

HRH Princess Eléonore, b. 16 April 2008.

Brother and Sister of the King

Princess Astrid, b. 5 June 1962; married 22 September 1984, Archduke Lorenz; son, Prince Amedeo, b. February 1986; daughter, Princess Maria Laura, b. August 1988; son, Prince Joachim, b. December 1991; daughter, Princess Louisa-Maria, b. October 1995; daughter, Princess Laetitia Maria, b. 23 April 2003.

Prince Laurent, b. 19 October 1963; married 12 April 2003, Claire Coombs; daughter, Princess Louise, b. February 2004; son, Prince Aymeric, b. December 2005; son, Prince Nicolas, b. December 2005.

Parents of the King

King Albert II, b. 6 June 1934; succeeded to the throne 9 August 1993, on the death of his brother, King Baudouin I; married 2 July 1959, Donna Paola Ruffo di Calabria (Queen Paola) (b. 11 September 1937); abdicated 21 July 2013 in favour of his son, Crown Prince Philippe; three children.

BHUTAN

The Druk Gyalpo (Dragon King)

HM DASHO JIGME KHESAR NAMGYAL **WANGCHUCK**; b. 21 February 1980; succeeded to the throne 14 December 2006, on the abdication of his father, the Druk Gyalpo Jigme Singye Wangchuk.

Crown Prince

HRH Crown Prince Jigme Namgyel Wangchuck, Druk Gyalsey (Dragon Prince) of Bhutan, b. 5 February 2016.

Brothers and Sisters of the King

HRH Princess Chimi Yangzom Wangchuck, b. 10 January 1980.

HRH Princess Sonam Dechen Wangchuck, b. 5 August 1981.

HRH Princess Dechen Yangzom Wangchuck, b. 2 December 1981.

HRH Princess Kesang Choden Wangchuck, b. 23 January 1982.

HRH Prince Jigyel Ugyen Wangchuck, b. 16 July 1984.

HRH Prince Khamsum Singye Wangchuck, b. 6 October 1985.

HRH Prince Jigme Dorji Wangchuck, b. 14 April 1986.

HRH Princess Euphelma Choden Wangchuck, b. 6 June 1993.

HRH Prince Ugyen Jigme Wangchuck, b. 11 November 1994.

Parents of the King

King Jigme Singye **Wangchuck**, b. 11 November 1955; succeeded to the throne 24 July 1972; crowned 2 June 1974; abdicated 14 December 2006; married Queen Ashi Tshering Yandon Wangchuck (b. 21 June 1959); two sons, one daughter; three sons, four daughters with his three other wives.

BRUNEI

Reigning Sultan and Yang di-Pertuan

HM Sultan Haji HASSANAL **BOLKIAH MU'IZUDDIN WADDAULAH**; b. 15 July 1946; succeeded as 29th Sultan 5 October 1967, on the abdication of his father, Sultan Haji Omar Ali Saifuddien II; crowned 1 August 1968; married 29 July 1965, HM Raja Isteri Pengiran Anak Hajjah Saleha; two sons, four daughters; also married 28 October 1981, Mariam Abd Aziz (divorced 2003); two sons, two daughters; also married 19 August 2005, HRH Pengiran Isteri Azrinaz Mazhar Hakim (divorced 2010); one son, one daughter.

Crown Prince

HRH Prince Haji al-**Muhtadee Billah**, b. 17 February 1974; proclaimed Crown Prince 10 August 1998; married 9 September 2004, HRH Pengiran Anak Isteri Pengiran Anak Sarah binti Pengiran Salleh Ab Rahaman; two sons, one daughter.

Brothers of the Sultan

HRH Prince Mohamed **Bolkiah**, b. 27 August 1947.

HRH Prince Haji Sufri Bolkiah, b. 31 July 1951.

HRH Prince Haji Jefri **Bolkiah**, b. 6 November 1954.

CAMBODIA

Reigning King

KING **NORODOM SIHAMONI**; b. 14 May 1953; appointed King by the Royal Council of the Throne October 2004, following the abdication of his father, the late King Norodom Sihanouk.

Brothers and Sisters of the King

Princess Buppha Devi, b. 8 January 1943.

Prince Yuvaneath, b. 17 October 1943.

Prince **Norodom Ranariddh**, b. 2 January 1944.

Prince Ravivong, b. 1944, died 1973.

Prince Chakrapong, b. 21 October 1945.

Prince Naradipo, b. 10 February 1946, died 1976.

Princess Soriya Roeungsey, b. 1947, died 1976.

Princess Kantha Bopha, b. 1948, died 14 December 1952.

Prince Khemanourak, b. 1949, died 1975.

Princess Botum Bopha, b. 1951, died 1976.

Princess Socheata, b. 1953, died 1975.

Prince Narindrapong, b. 18 September 1954, died 8 October 2003.

Princess Arunrasmy, b. 2 October 1955.

Parents of the King

King Norodom Sihanouk, b. 31 October 1922, died 15 October 2012; elected King 1941; abdicated 1955; took oath of fidelity to vacant throne 1960; elected Head of State 1960, on the death of his father; deposed 1970; elected as King 24 September 1993; abdicated October 2004; married Queen Norodom Monineath Sihanouk.

DENMARK

Reigning Queen

HM QUEEN **MARGRETHE II**; b. 16 April 1940; succeeded to the throne 14 January 1972, on the death of her father, King Frederik IX; married 10 June 1967, Count Henri Marie Jean André de Laborde de Monpezat (HRH

Prince Consort Henrik, renounced title of Prince Consort to become HRH Prince Henrik of Denmark 1 January 2016) (b. 11 June 1934, died 13 February 2018).

Children of the Queen

HRH Crown Prince **Frederik André Henrik Christian**, b. 26 May 1968; married 14 May 2004, Mary Elizabeth Donaldson (HRH Crown Princess Mary Elizabeth) (b. 5 February 1972); son, HRH Prince Christian Valdemar Henri John, b. 15 October 2005; daughter, HRH Princess Isabella Henrietta Ingrid Margrethe, b. 21 April 2007; son, HRH Prince Vincent Frederik Minik Alexander, b. 8 January 2011; daughter, HRH Princess Josephine Sophia Ivalo Mathilda, b. 8 January 2011.

HRH Prince Joachim Holger Waldemar Christian, b. 7 June 1969; married 1st 18 November 1995, Alexandra Christina Manley (Alexandra Christina, Countess of Frederiksborg) (b. 30 June 1964) (divorced 2005); son, HH Prince Nikolai William Alexander Frederik, b. 28 August 1999; son, HH Prince Felix Henrik Valdemar Christian, b. 22 July 2002; married 2nd 24 May 2008, Marie Cavallier (Princess Marie of Denmark); son, HH Prince Henrik Carl Joachim Alain, b. 4 May 2009; daughter, HH Princess Athena Marguerite Françoise Marie, b. 24 January 2012.

Sisters of the Queen

HRH Princess Benedikte Astrid Ingeborg Ingrid, b. 29 April 1944; married 3 February 1968, Prince Richard zu Sayn-Wittgenstein-Berleburg (b. 29 October 1934); son, Prince Gustav, b. 12 January 1969; daughter, Countess von Pfeil und Klein-Ellguth (formerly Princess Alexandra), b. 20 November 1970, (married, two children); daughter, Princess Nathalie, b. 2 May 1975, (married, one son).

HM Queen Anne-Marie Dagmar Ingrid of the Hellenes, b. 30 August 1946; married 18 September 1964, HM King **Constantine II** of the Hellenes (b. 2 June 1940); daughter, Princess Alexia, b. 10 July 1965, (married, four children); son, Prince Pavlos, b. 20 May 1967, (married, five children); son, Prince Nikolaos, b. 1 October 1969, (married); daughter, Princess Theodora, b. 9 June 1983; son, Prince Philippos, b. 26 April 1986.

Parents of the Queen

King Frederik IX, b. 11 March 1899 (son of King Christian X and Queen Alexandrine), died 14 January 1972; married 24 May 1935, Princess Ingrid of Sweden (b. 28 March 1910, died 7 November 2000).

ESWATINI

Reigning Monarch

KING **MSWATI III**; b. 19 April 1968; proclaimed Crown Prince September 1983, following the death of his father the previous year; installed as head of state 25 April 1986.

Father of the King

King Sobhuza II, b. 22 July 1899, died 21 August 1982; 210 children with 70 wives.

JAPAN

Reigning Emperor

His Imperial Majesty EMPEROR **NARUHITO**; b. 23 February 1960; succeeded to the throne 1 May 2019, on the abdication of his father, Emperor Akihito; married 9 June 1993, Masako Owada (Empress Masako) (b. 9 December 1963).

Daughter of the Emperor

Princess Aiko (Toshi-no-miya), b. 1 December 2001

Brother and Sister of the Emperor

The Crown Prince **Fumihito**, b. 30 November 1965; married 29 June 1990, Kiko Kawashima (The Crown Princess Kiko) (b. 11 September 1966); daughter, Princess Mako, b. 23 October 1991; daughter, Princess Kako, b. 29 December 1994; son, Prince Hisahito, b. 6 September 2006.

Sayako Kuroda (fmrly Nori-no-miya, then Princess Sayako), b. 18 April 1969; married 15 November 2005 (relinquished Imperial claim), Yoshiki Kuroda (b. 17 April 1965).

Parents of the Emperor

Emperor Akihito, b. 23 December 1933; abdicated 30 April 2019; married 10 April 1959, Empress Michiko (b. 20 October 1934); three children.

JORDAN

Reigning King

KING **ABDULLAH II IBN AL-HUSSEIN**; b. 30 January 1962; succeeded to the throne 7 February 1999, on the death of his father, King Hussein Ibn Talal; married 10 June 1993, Rania al-Yassin (Queen **Rania al-Abdullah**) (b. 31 August 1970).

Children of the King

HRH Crown Prince Hussein, b. 28 June 1994.

HRH Princess Iman, b. 27 September 1996.

HRH Princess Salma, b. 26 September 2000.

HRH Prince Hashem, b. 30 January 2005.

Brothers and Sisters of the King

Princess Alia, b. 13 February 1956; married 1st 11 July 1977, Nasser Wasfi Mirza (divorced 1983); son, Prince Hussein Mirza, b. 12 February 1981; married 2nd 30 July 1988, Mohammad Farid as-Saleh; son, Talal as-Saleh, b. 12 September 1989; son, Abdel Hamid as-Saleh, b. 15 November 1991.

Prince Feisal, b. 11 October 1963; married 1st 10 August 1987, Alia at-Tabaa (Princess Alia) (divorced April 2008); daughter, Princess Ayah, b. 11 February 1990; son, Prince Omar, b. 22 October 1993; daughter, Princess Aisha, b. 27 March 1996; daughter, Princess Sarah, b. 27 March 1996; married 2nd 24 May 2010, Sara Qabbani (Princess Sara) (divorced 14 September 2013); married 3rd 4 January 2014, Zeina Lubbadeh (Princess Zeina); son, Prince Abdullah bin Feisal, b. 17 February 2016; son Prince Mohammad bin Feisal, b. 8 April 2017.

Princess Zein, b. 23 April 1968; married 3 August 1989, Majdi Farid as-Saleh; son, Jaafar as-Saleh, b. 9 November 1990; daughter, Jumana as-Saleh; adopted daughter, Tahani al-Shahwa.

Princess Aisha, b. 23 April 1968; married 1st 26 July 1990, Zeid Juma'a (divorced); son, Aoun Juma'a, b. 27 May 1992; daughter, Muna Juma'a, b. 18 July 1996; married 2nd 27 January 2016, Ashraf (fmrly Edward) Banayoti (divorced 1 July 2016).

Princess Haya bint al-Hussein, b. 3 May 1974; married 10 April 2004, Sheikh Muhammad bin Rashid al-Maktoum (Ruler of Dubai); daughter, Sheikha Al Jalila, b. 2 December 2007; son, Sheikh Zayed, b. 7 January 2012.

Prince Ali, b. 23 December 1975; married 23 April 2004, Rym Brahimi; daughter, Princess Jalilah, b. 16 September 2005; son, Prince Abdullah, b. 19 March 2007.

Prince Hamzah, b. 29 March 1980; named Crown Prince of Jordan 1999 (title rescinded by King Abdullah 2004); married 1st 29 August 2003 (official wedding 27 May 2004), Princess Noor bint Asem Ben Nayef (divorced 9 September 2009); daughter, Princess Haya, b. 18 April 2007; married 2nd 12 January 2012, Princess Basmah Bani Ahmad; daughter, Princess Zein, b. 3 November 2012; daughter, Princess Zein, b. 3 November 2012; daughter, Princess Noor, b. 5 July 2014; daughter, Princess Badiya, b. 8 April 2016; daughter, Princess Nafisa, b. 7 February 2018.

Prince Hashim, b. 10 June 1981; married 15 April 2006, Fahdah Mohammed Abu Neyan; daughter, Princess Haalah, b. 6 April 2007; daughter, Princess Rayet, b. 4 July 2008; daughter, Princess Fatima al-Alia, b. 5 November 2011; son, Prince Hussein Haidara, b. 15 June 2015.

Princess Iman, b. 24 April 1983; married 22 March 2013, Zaid Azmi Mirza; son, Omar Mirza, b. 8 October 2014.

Princess Raiyah, b. 9 February 1986.

Parents of the King

King Hussein ibn Talal, b. 14 November 1935, died 7 February 1999; married 1st Dina bint Abdelhamid (Queen Dina) (divorced), one child; married 2nd Antoinette Gardner (Princess Muna) (divorced 1972), four children; married 3rd Alia Toukan (Queen Alia) (deceased), two children; married 4th Lisa Najeeb Halaby (**Queen Noor**) (b. 23 August 1951), four children.

KUWAIT

Reigning Emir

SHEIKH SABAH AL-AHMAD AL-JABER AS-**SABAH**; b. 16 June 1929; married Fatuwah bint Salman as-Sabah (died 1990); four children (two deceased); succeeded as Emir 29 January 2006, following the abdication of Sheikh Saad al-Abdullah as-Salim as-Sabah.

Crown Prince

HH Sheikh Nawaf al-Ahmad al-Jaber as-**Sabah**, b. 25 June 1937; married Sharifa Sulaiman Al-Jasem Al-Ghanim; four sons, one daughter; proclaimed Crown Prince 20 February 2006.

Children of the Emir

Sheikh Nasser Bin Sabah Al-Ahmad Al-Sabah, b. 27 April 1948.

Sheikh Hamed Al-Ahmad Al-Sabah.

Sheikh Ahmed Al-Sabah, died 1969.

Sheikha Salwa Al-Sabah, died 23 June 2002.

Father of the Emir

Sheikh Ahmad Al-Jaber Al-Sabah, b. 1885, died 29 January 1950; appointed tenth ruler of Kuwait 1921, following the death of his uncle, the ninth ruler of Kuwait Sheikh Salem Al-Sabah.

LESOTHO

Reigning King

KING **LETSIE III**; b. 17 July 1963; installed as King 12 November 1990, abdicated 25 January 1995, reinstalled 7 February 1996, following the death of his father, King Moshoeshoe II on 15 January, crowned 31 October 1997; married 18 February 2000, Karabo Anna Mots'oeneng (Queen 'Masenate Mohato Bereng Seeiso).

Children of the King

Princess Senate Mary Mohato Seeiso, b. 7 October 2001.

Princess 'MaSeeiso Mohato Seeiso, b. 20 November 2004.

Crown Prince Lerotholi Mohato **Seeiso, b. 18 April 2007.**

Parents of the King

Moshoeshoe II, b. 2 May 1938, died 15 January 1996; married Tabitha 'Masentle Lerotholi Mojela (Queen 'Mamohato of Lesotho) (b. 28 April 1941), three children.

LIECHTENSTEIN

Reigning Prince

HSH PRINCE **HANS-ADAM II**, Duke of Troppau and Jägerndorf, Count of Rietberg; b. 14 February 1945; succeeded 13 November 1989, on the death of his father, Prince Franz Josef II; married 30 July 1967, Countess Marie Aglaë Kinsky von Wchinitz und Tettau (Princess Marie) (b. 14 April 1940).

Children of the Prince

Hereditary Prince **Alois Philipp Maria**, b. 11 June 1968; appointed permanent representative 15 August 2004, performing the duties of Head of State from that time; married 3 July 1993, Duchess Sophie of Bavaria (b. 28 October 1967); son, Prince Joseph Wenzel, b. 24 May 1995; daughter, Princess Marie Caroline, b. 17 October 1996; son, Prince Georg, b. 20 April 1999; son, Prince Nikolaus, b. 6 December 2000.

Prince Maximilian, b. 16 May 1969; married 29 January 2000, Angela Gisela Brown; son, Prince Alfons, b. 18 May 2001.

Prince Constantin, b. 15 March 1972; married 18 July 1999, Countess Marie Kalnoky; son, Prince Moritz, b. 27 May 2003; daughter, Princess Georgina, b. 23 July 2005; son Prince Benedikt, b. 18 May 2008.

Princess Tatjana, b. 10 April 1973; married 5 June 1999, Philipp von Lattorff; son, Lukas, b. 13 May 2000; daughter, Elisabeth, b. 25 January 2002; daughter, Marie Teresa, b. 18 January 2004; daughter, Camilla, b. 14 November 2005; daughter, Anna, b. 3 August 2007; daughter, Sophia, b. 30 October 2009; son, Maximilian, b. 17 December 2011.

Brothers and Sisters of the Prince

Prince Philipp, b. 19 August 1946; married 11 September 1971, Isabelle de l'Arbre de Malander; son, Prince Alexander, b. 19 May 1972; son, Prince Wenzeslaus, b. 12 May 1974; son, Prince Rudolf, b. 7 September 1975.

Prince Nikolaus, b. 24 October 1947; married 20 March 1982, Princess Margaretha of Luxembourg (b. 15 May 1957); son, Prince Leopold Emmanuel, b. 20 May 1984 (deceased); daughter, Princess Maria-Annunciata, b. 12 May 1985; daughter, Princess Marie-Astrid, b. 26 June 1987; son, Prince Joseph-Emmanuel, b. 7 May 1989.

Princess Nora, b. 31 October 1950; married 11 June 1988, Vicente Marques de Mariño (died 22 July 2002); daughter, María Teresa, b. 21 November 1992.

Prince Wenzel, b. 19 November 1962, died 28 February 1991.

LUXEMBOURG

Reigning Monarch

HRH GRAND DUKE **HENRI ALBERT FÉLIX MARIE GUILLAUME**; b. 16 April 1955; succeeded 7 October 2000, on the abdication of his father, Grand Duke Jean; married 14 February 1981, Maria Teresa Mestre y Batista-Falla, b. 22 March 1956.

Children of the Grand Duke

HRH Prince **Guillaume Jean Joseph Marie**, b. 11 November 1981; proclaimed Hereditary Grand Duke of Luxembourg 18 December 2000; married 20 October 2012, Countess Stéphanie de Lannoy, 18 February 1984.

Prince Félix Léopold Marie Guillaume, b. 3 June 1984; married 21 September 2013, Claire Margareta Lademacher (Princess Claire), b. 21 March 1985; daughter, Princess Amalia of Nassau, b. 15 June 2014.

Prince Louis Xavier Marie Guillaume, b. 3 August 1986; married 29 September 2006, Tessy Antony, b. 28 October 1985 (divorced 4 April 2019); son, Prince Gabriel, b. 12 March 2006; son, Prince Noah, b. 21 September 2007.

Princess Alexandra Joséphine Teresa Charlotte Marie Wilhelmine, b. 16 February 1991.

Prince Sébastien Henri Marie Guillaume, b. 16 April 1992.

Brothers and Sisters of the Grand Duke

Archduchess Marie-Astrid of Austria, b. 17 February 1954; married 6 February 1982, Carl Christian of Habsburg Lorraine, Archduke of Austria; daughter, Archduchess Marie-Christine Anne Astrid Zita Charlotte of Austria, b. 31 July 1983; son, Archduke Imre, b. 8 December 1985; son, Archduke Christophe, b. 2 February 1988; son, Archduke Alexander, b. 26 September 1990; daughter, Archduchess Gabriella, b. 26 March 1994.

Prince Jean, b. 15 May 1957; married 1st 27 May 1987, Hélène Suzanne Vestur (divorced 2004); daughter, Marie-Gabrielle, b. 8 December 1986; son, Constantin Jean Philippe, b. 22 July 1988; son, Wenceslas, b. 17 November 1990; son, Carl-Johann, b. 15 August 1992; married 2nd 18 March 2009, Diane de Guerre.

Princess Margaretha, b. 15 May 1957; married 20 March 1982, Prince Nikolaus of Liechtenstein (b. 24 October 1947); son, Prince Leopold Emmanuel, b. 20 May 1984 (deceased); daughter, Princess Maria-Annunciata, b. 12 May 1985; daughter, Princess Marie-Astrid, b. 26 June 1987; son, Prince Joseph-Emmanuel, b. 7 May 1989.

Prince Guillaume, b. 1 May 1963; married 24 September 1994, Sibilla Sandra Weiller (y Torlonia) (b. 12 June 1968); son, Prince Paul-Louis, b. 4 March 1998; son, Prince Léopold, b. 2 May 2000; daughter, Princess Charlotte, b. 2 May 2000; son, Prince Jean, b. 13 July 2004.

Parents of the Grand Duke

Grand Duke Jean Benoit Guillaume Marie Robert Louis Antoine Adolphe Marc d'Aviano, b. 5 January 1921, died 23 April 2019; married 9 April 1953, Joséphine Charlotte, Princess of Belgium (b. 11 October 1927, died 10 January 2005).

MALAYSIA

Yang di-Pertuan Agong (Supreme Head of State)

HM The Sultan of **Pahang**, Abdullah Ri'ayatuddin al-Mustafa Billah Shah ibni Sultan Ahmad Shah al-Musta'in Billah.; b. 30 July 1959; elected as 16th Yang di-Pertuan Agong 24 January 2019, took office 31 January 2019.

Timbalan Yang di-Pertuan Agong (Deputy Supreme Head of State)

HRH The Sultan of **Perak**, Tuanku Nazrin Muizzuddin Shah ibni al-Marhum Sultan Azlan Muhibuddin Shah.

The Hereditary Rulers

There are nine hereditary rulers who qualify for and elect the positions of Yang di-Pertuan Agong and Timbalan Yang di-Pertuan Agong.

The Yang di-Pertuan Besar of **Negeri Sembilan**, Tuanku Muhriz ibni al-Marhum Tunku Munawir.

HRH The Sultan of **Selangor**, Tuanku Sharafuddin Idris Shah Salahuddin Abdul Aziz Shah.

HRH Tuanku Syed Sirajuddin al-Marhum Syed Putra Jamalullail, The Raja of **Perlis**.

HRH The Sultan of **Terengganu**, Tuanku Mizan Zainal Abidin.

HRH The Sultan of **Kedah**, Tuanku Haji Abdul Halim Mu'adzam Shah ibni al-Marhum Sultan Badlishah.

HRH The Sultan of **Kelantan**, Tengku Muhammad Faris Petra ibni Sultan Ismail Petra, Sultan Muhammad V.

HRH The Sultan of **Johor**, Sultan Ibrahim Ismail ibni al-Marhum Sultan Mahmud Iskandar.

MONACO

Reigning Monarch

HSH PRINCE **ALBERT II**, Albert Alexandre Louis Pierre Grimaldi; b. 14 March 1958; succeeded 6 April 2005, on the death of his father, Prince Rainier III; daughter (Jazmin Grace Grimaldi, b. 4 March 1992) with Tamara Rotolo; son (Alexandre Coste, b. 24 August 2003) with Nicole Coste; married 2 July 2011, Charlene Lynette Wittstock (Charlene, Princess of Monaco), b. 25 January 1978; daughter, Princess Gabriella, b. 10 December 2014; son, Prince Jacques, b. 10 December 2014.

Sisters of the Prince

Princess Caroline Louise Marguerite, b. 23 January 1957; married 1st 28 June 1978, Philippe Junot (divorced 1980, marriage annulled 1992); married 2nd 29 December 1983, Stefano Casiraghi (died 3 October 1990); son, Andrea Albert Pierre, b. 8 June 1984; daughter, Charlotte Marie

Pomeline, b. 3 August 1986; son, Pierre Rainier Stefano, b. 5 September 1987; married 3rd 23 January 1999, Prince Ernst August of Hanover; stepson, Prince Ernst August of Hanover, b. 19 July 1983, stepson, Prince Christian of Hanover, b. 1 June 1985; daughter, Princess Alexandra of Hanover, b. 20 July 1999.

Princess Stéphanie Marie Elisabeth, b. 1 February 1965; married 1st 1 July 1995, Daniel Ducruet (divorced 1996); son, Louis Robert Paul, b. 26 November 1992; daughter, Pauline Grace Maguy, b. 4 May 1994; daughter, Camille Marie Kelly Gottlieb, b. 15 July 1998; married 2nd 10 September 2003, Adans Lopez Peres (divorced 2004).

Parents of the Prince

HSH Prince Rainier III, Rainier Louis Henri Maxence Bertrand Grimaldi, b. 31 May 1923, died 6 April 2005; married 18 April 1956, Grace Patricia Kelly (b. 12 November 1929, died 14 September 1982).

MOROCCO

Reigning King

HM KING **MOHAMMED VI**; b. 21 August 1963; succeeded to the throne 23 July 1999, on the death of his father, King Hassan II; married 21 March 2002, HRH Princess Lalla Salma Bennani (b. 10 May 1978).

Children of the King

HRH Crown Prince Moulay Hassan, b. 8 May 2003.

HRH Princess Lalla Khadija, b. 28 February 2007.

Brothers and Sisters of the King

HRH Princess Lalla Meryem, b. 26 August 1962; married 15 September 1984, Fouad Filali (divorced 1999); daughter, Lalla Soukaïna, b. 30 April 1986; son, Moulay Idriss, b. 11 July 1988.

HRH Princess Lalla Asma, b. 29 September 1965; married 5 November 1986, Khalid Bouchentouf; son, Moulay Yazid, b. 25 July 1988; daughter, Lalla Nuhaila, b. 29 May 1992.

HRH Princess Lalla Hasna, b. 19 November 1967; married 13 December 1991, Khalid Benharbit; daughter, Lalla Oumaïma, b. 15 December 1995; daughter, Lalla Oulaya, b. 20 October 1997.

HRH Prince Moulay Rachid, b. 20 June 1970; married 15 June 2014, Oum Kalthum Boufarès; son, Moulay Ahmed, b. 23 June 2016.

Parents of the King

HM King Hassan II, b. 9 July 1929, died 23 July 1999; married 1st 1961, Lalla Latifa Hammou (five children); married 2nd 1961, Lalla Fatima bint Qaid Amhourok.

THE NETHERLANDS

Reigning King

HM KING **WILLEM-ALEXANDER** CLAUS GEORGE FERDINAND; b. 27 April 1967; succeeded to the throne 30 April 2013, on the abdication of his mother, Queen Beatrix (now HRH Princess **Beatrix**); married 2 February 2002, Máxima Zorreguieta Cerruti (b. 17 May 1971); daughter, HRH Princess Catharina-Amalia Beatrix Carmen Victoria, b. 7 December 2003; daughter, HRH Princess Alexia Juliana Marcella Laurentien, b. 26 June 2005; daughter, HRH Ariane Wilhelmina Máxima Inés, b. 10 April 2007.

Brothers of the King

HRH Prince (Johan) Friso Bernhard Christiaan David, b. 25 September 1968, died 12 August 2013; married 24 April 2004 (relinquished right to the throne and membership of the Royal House), Mabel Wisse Smit; daughter, Countess Luana, b. 26 March 2005; daughter, Countess Zaria, b. 18 June 2006.

HRH Prince Constantijn Christof Frederik Aschwin, b. 11 October 1969; married 17 May 2001, Laurentien Brinkhorst (b. 25 May 1966); daughter, Countess Eloise, b. 8 June 2002; son, Count Claus-Casimir, b. 21 March 2004; daughter, Countess Leonore, b. 3 June 2006.

Parents of the King

HRH Princess **Beatrix** of The Netherlands, b. 31 January 1938; married 10 March 1966, Prince Claus George Willem Otto Frederik Geert Jonkheer van Amsberg (b. 6 September 1926, died 6 October 2002).

NORWAY

Reigning King

HM KING **HARALD V**; b. 21 February 1937; succeeded to the throne 17 January 1991, on the death of his father, King Olav V; sworn in 21 January 1991; married 29 August 1968, Sonja Haraldsen (HM Queen Sonja) (b. 4 July 1937).

Children of the King

Princess Märtha Louise, b. 22 September 1971; married 24 May 2002, Ari Mikael Behn (formerly Ari Mikael Bjørshol, b. 30 September 1972); daughter, Maud Angelica Behn, b. 29 April 2003; daughter, Leah Isadora Behn, b. 8 April 2005; daughter, Emma Tallulah Behn, b. 29 September 2008.

HRH Crown Prince **Haakon**, b. 20 July 1973; married 25 August 2001, Mette-Marit Tjessem Høiby (HRH Crown Princess Mette-Marit) (b. 19 August 1973); stepson, Marius Borg Høiby, b. 13 January 1997; daughter, HRH Princess Ingrid Alexandra, b. 21 January 2004; son, HH Prince Sverre Magnus, b. 3 December 2005.

Sisters of the King

Princess Ragnhild, b. 9 June 1930, died 16 September 2012; married 15 May 1953, Erling Lorentzen; three children.

Princess Astrid, b. 12 February 1932; married 12 January 1961, Johan Martin Ferner (b. Johan Martin Jacobsen, 22 July 1927, died 24 January 2015); five children.

Parents of the King

King Olav V, b. 2 July 1903, died 17 January 1991; married 21 March 1929 Princess Märtha of Sweden (b. 28 March 1901, died 5 April 1954).

OMAN

Reigning Sultan

SULTAN **QABOOS BIN SAID AS-SAID**; b. 18 November 1940; assumed power 23 July 1970, after deposing his father, Sultan Said bin Taimur (b. 13 August 1910, died 19 October 1972); married 1976, Sayyidah Nawwal bint Tariq (divorced 1977).

QATAR

Reigning Amir

HH SHEIKH TAMIM BIN HAMAD BIN KHALIFA ATH-**THANI**; b. 3 June 1980; proclaimed heir apparent 8 August 2003, succeeded to the throne 25 June 2013 on the abdication of his father; married 1st 8 January 2005, Sheikha Jawahar bint Hamad bin Sohaim ath-Thani; married 2nd 3 March 2009, Sheikha Anoud bint Mana Al-Hajri; married 3rd 25 February 2014, Sheikha Noora bint Hathal al-Dosari.

Children of the Amir by His First Wife

HE Sheikha Almayassa bint Tamim ath-Thani, b. 2006

HE Sheikh Hamad bin Tamim ath-Thani, b. 2008

HE Sheikha Aisha bint Tamim ath-Thani, b. 2010

HE Sheikh Jassim bin Tamim ath-Thani, b. 2012

Children of the Amir by His Second Wife

HE Sheikha Nayla bint Tamim ath-Thani, b. 27 May 2010

HE Sheikh Abdullah bin Tamim ath-Thani, b. 29 September 2012

HE Sheikha Rodha bint Tamim bin Hamad ath-Thani, b. January 2014

HE Sheikh Al-Qaqa bin Tamim bin Hamad ath-Thani, b. 3rd October 2015

Children of the Amir by His Third Wife

HE Sheikh Joa'an bin Tamim bin Hamad ath-Thani, b. 27 March 2015

HE Sheikh Mohammed bin Tamim bin Hamad ath-Thani, b. 17 July 2017

HE Sheikh Fahad bin Tamim bin Hamad ath-Thani, b. 16 June 2018

Parents of the Amir

HH Sheikh Hamad bin Khalifa ath-**Thani**, b. 1 January 1952; assumed power 27 June 1995, after deposing his father, Sheikh Khalifa bin Hamad ath-Thani (b. 17 September 1932), abdicated 25 June 2013 in favour of his son, HH Sheikh Tamim bin Hamad bin Khalifa ath-Thani; married 1st Sheikha Mariam bint Muhammad ath-Thani (two sons, six daughters); married 2nd Sheikha Mozah bint Nasser al-Missned (five sons, two daughters); married 3rd Sheikha Noora bint Khalid ath-Thani (four sons, five daughters).

SAMOA

O le Ao o le Malo (Head of State)

HH Tuimaleali'ifano Va'aletoa **Sualauvi II**; b. 29 April 1947; elected Head of State 30 June 2017; married HH Masiofo Fa'amausili Leinafo.

SAUDI ARABIA

Reigning King

HM KING SALMAN IBN ABD AL-AZIZ AS-**SA'UD**; b. 13 December 1935; succeeded to the throne, 23 January 2015, on the death of his half-brother, King Abdullah.

Crown Prince

HRH Muhammad ibn Salman ibn Abd al-Aziz as-**Sa'ud**, b. 31 August 1985; son of King Salman ibn Abd al-Aziz as-Sa'ud; married Sara bint Mashoodr bin Abdulaziz as-Sa'ud; appointed Deputy Crown Prince 29 April 2017; appointed Crown Prince 21 June 2017.

Brothers of the King include

King Saud ibn Abd al-Aziz as-Sa'ud, b. 15 January 1902, acceded 9 November 1953 (following the death of his father, King Abd al-Aziz as-Sa'ud), relinquished the throne 2 November 1964, died 24 January 1969.

King Faisal ibn Abd al-Aziz as-Sa'ud, b. April 1906, acceded 2 November 1964, died 25 March 1975; children include son, Prince Sa'ud al-Faisal as-**Sa'ud**, b. 1941; son, Prince Turki al-Faisal ibn Abd al-Aziz as-**Sa'ud**, b. 15 February 1945.

HRH Prince Mohammed ibn Abd al-Aziz as-Sa'ud, b. 4 March 1910, died 25 November 1988.

King Khalid ibn Abd al-Aziz as-Sa'ud, b. 13 February 1913, acceded 25 March 1975, died 13 June 1982.

King Fahd ibn Abd al-Aziz as-**Sa'ud**, b. 16 March 1921, acceded 13 June 1982, died 1 August 2005.

King Abdullah ibn Abd al-Aziz as-**Sa'ud**, b. 1 August 1924, acceded 1 August 2005, died 23 January 2015.

HRH Crown Prince Sultan ibn Abd al-Aziz as-**Sa'ud**, b. 5 January 1928, died 22 October 2011; children include son, HRH Prince Bandar ibn Sultan ibn Abd al-Aziz as-**Sa'ud**, b. 2 March 1949.

HRH Prince Talal ibn Abd al-Aziz as-**Sa'ud**, b. 15 August 1931, died 22 December 2018; children include son, Prince Walid ibn **Talal**.

HRH Prince Nayef ibn Abd al-Aziz as-**Sa'ud**, b. 1934, died 16 June 2012; children include son, Prince Muhammad ibn Nayef ibn Abd al-Aziz as-**Sa'ud**.

HRH Prince Muqrin ibn Abd al-Aziz as-**Sa'ud**, b. 15 September 1945.

SPAIN

Reigning King

HM KING **FELIPE VI**; b. 30 January 1968; succeeded to the throne 19 June 2014 on the abdication of his father; married 22 May 2004, HRH Princess Letizia Ortiz Rocasolano (HM Queen Letizia) (b. 15 September 1972).

Children of the King

HRH Princess Leonor, The Princess of **Asturias**, Princess of Viana, Princess of Girona, Duchess of Montblanc, Countess of Cervera and Lady of Balaguer, b. 31 October 2005.

HRH Princess (Infanta) Sofía, b. 29 April 2007.

Sisters of the King

HRH Princess (Infanta) Elena, b. 20 December 1963; married 18 March 1995, Don Jaime de Marichalar y Sáenz de Tejada (divorced 21 January 2010); son, Felipe Juan Froilán de Todos los Santos, b. 17 July 1998; daughter, Victoria Federica, b. 9 September 2000.

HRH Princess (Infanta) Cristina, b. 13 June 1965; married 4 October 1997, Iñaki Urdangarin (b. 15 January 1968); son, Juan Valentín, b. 29 September 1999; son, Pablo Nicolás Sebastián, b. 6 December 2000; son, Miguel, b. 30 April 2002; daughter, Irene, b. 5 June 2005.

Parents of the King

HM King **Juan Carlos I** b. 5 January 1938; succeeded to the throne 22 November 1975, abdicated 19 June 2014 in favour of his son HRH Prince Felipe, The Prince of Asturias; married 14 May 1962, Princess Sofía of Greece (HM Queen Sofía) (b. 2 November 1938, daughter of the late King Paul of the Hellenes and Queen Frederica).

SWEDEN

Reigning King

HM KING **CARL XVI GUSTAF**; b. 30 April 1946; succeeded to the throne 15 September 1973, on the death of his grandfather, King Gustaf VI Adolf; married 19 June 1976, Silvia Renate Sommerlath (HM Queen **Silvia**) (b. 23 December 1943).

Children of the King

HRH Crown Princess **Victoria Ingrid Alice Désirée**, Duchess of Västergötland, b. 14 July 1977; married 19 June 2010, Olof Daniel Westling Bernadotte (Prince Daniel, Duke of Västergötland), b. 15 September 1973; daughter, Princess Estelle, Duchess of Östergötland, b. 23 February 2012; son, Prince Oscar, Duke of Skåne, b. 2 March 2016.

HRH Prince Carl Philip Edmund Bertil, Duke of Varmland, b. 13 May 1979; married 13 June 2015, Sofia Kristina Hellqvist, b. 6 December 1984; son, Prince Alexander, Duke of Södermanland, b. 19 April 2016; son, Prince Gabriel, b. 31 August 2017.

HRH Princess Madeleine Thérèse Amelie Josephine, Duchess of Hälsingland and Gästrikland, b. 10 June 1982; married 8 June 2013, Christopher O'Neill, b. 27 June 1974; daughter, Princess Leonore, Duchess of Gotland, b. 20 February 2014; son, Prince Nicolas, Duke of Ångermanland, b. 15 June 2015; daughter, Princess Adrienne of Sweden, Duchess of Blekinge, b. 9 March 2018 .

Sisters of the King

Princess Margaretha, b. 31 October 1934; married 30 June 1964, John Ambler (b. 6 June 1924, died 31 May 2008); daughter, Sibylla Louise, b. 14 April 1965; son, Charles Edward, b. 14 July 1966; son, James Patrick, b. 10 June 1969.

Princess Birgitta, b. 19 January 1937; married 25 May 1961, Prince Johann Georg of Hohenzollern (b. 31 July 1932); son, Carl Christian, b. 5 April 1962; daughter, Désirée, b. 27 November 1963; son, Hubertus, b. 10 June 1966.

Princess Désirée, b. 2 June 1938; married 5 June 1964, Baron Nils-August Otto Carl Niclas Silfverschiöld (b. 31 May 1934, died 11 April 2017); son, Carl Otto Edmund, b. 22 March 1965; daughter, Kristina Louise Ewa Madeleine, b. 29 September 1966; daughter, Hélène Ingeborg Sibylla, b. 20 September 1968.

Princess Christina, b. 3 August 1943; married 15 June 1974, Tord Magnuson (b. 7 April 1941); son, Carl Gustaf Victor, b. 8 August 1975; son, Tord Oscar Fredrik, b. 20 June 1977; son, Victor Edmund Lennart, b. 10 September 1980.

Parents of the King

Prince Gustaf Adolf, Duke of Västerbotten, b. 22 April 1906, died 26 January 1947; married 20 October 1932, Sibylla, Princess of Saxe-Coburg and Gotha (b. 18 January 1908, died 28 November 1972).

THAILAND

Reigning King

HM KING **MAHA VAJIRALONGKORN**, (King Rama X); b. 28 July 1952; proclaimed Crown Prince 28 December 1972; succeeded to the throne 1 December 2016, shortly after the death of his father, King Bhumibol Adulyadej (Rama IX); crowned 4 May 2019; married 1st 3 January 1977, Mom Luang Soamsawali Kitiyakara (b. 13 July 1957) (divorced 1991); two daughters; married 2nd 1994 Yuvadhida Polpraserth (divorced 1996); four sons, one daughter (no royal claim); married 3rd 10 February 2001, Mom Srirasmi Mahidol na Ayudhya (HRH Princess Srirasmi, The Royal Consort) (b. 9 December 1971) (divorced December 2014); one son; married 4th 1 May 2019 Suthida Tidjai (b. 3 June 1978).

Children of the King

Princess Bajrakitiyabha, b. 7 December 1978

HRH Princess Siriwanwari Nariratana, b. 8 January 1987 (elevated status by royal command 15 June 2005).

HRH Prince Teepangkorn Rasmichoti, b. 29 April 2005.

Sisters of the King

Princess Ubol Ratana, b. 5 April 1951; married August 1972, Peter Ladd Jensen (relinquished royal claim) (divorced 1998); daughter, Khun Ploypailin, b. 12 February 1981; son, Khun Poomi, b. 16 August 1983, died 26 December 2004; daughter, Khun Sirikittiya, b. 18 March 1985.

HRH Princess Maha Chakri Sirindhorn, b. 2 April 1955.

HRH Princess **Chulabhorn**, b. 4 July 1957; married 7 January 1982, Flight Lieutenant Virayuth Didyasarin (divorced 1984); daughter, Princess Siribhachudabhorn, b. 8 October 1982; daughter, Princess Aditayadornkitikhun, b. 5 May 1984.

Parents of the King

HM King Bhumibol Adulyadej (King Rama IX), b. 5 December 1927, died 13 October 2016; succeeded to the throne 9 June 1946, on the death of his brother, King Ananda Mahidol; crowned 5 May 1950; married 28 April 1950, Mom Rajawongse Sirikit Kitiyakara (Queen Sirikit) (b. 12 August 1932).

TONGA

Reigning King

HM KING **Tupou VI**; b. 12 July 1959; proclaimed Crown Prince 11 September 2006; succeeded to the throne 18 March 2012, on the death of his elder brother, King George Tupou V; married 11 December 1982, Nanasipau'u Vaea (Princess Nanasipau'u).

Children of the King

Princess Latufuipeka Tuku'aho, b. 17 November 1983.

Crown Prince Tupouto'a 'Ulukalala, b. 17 September 1985, married 12 July 2012, Sinaitakala Fakafanua (b. 1987); son, Prince Taufa'ahau Manumataongo, b. 10 May 2013; daughter, Princess Halaevalu Mata'aho, b. 12 July 2014.

Prince Viliami Tuku'aho, The Prince Ata, b. 27 April 1988.

Brothers and Sister of the King

King George Tupuo V; b. 4 May 1948, died 18 March 2012; succeeded to the throne 10 September 2006; daughter 'Ilima Lei Fifita Tohi, b. 1974.

HRH Princess Salote Mafile'o Pilolevu Tuku'aho Tuita, Princess Regent, b. 17 November 1951; married 21 July 1976, Captain Ma'ulupekotofa Tuita (known as Honourable Tuita) (four daughters, one adopted son).

HRH Prince Fatafehi Alaivahamama'o Tuku'aho (known as Honourable Matu), b. 17 December 1954, died 17 February 2004; married (relinquished royal claim).

Parents of the King

King **Taufa'ahau Tupou IV**, b. 4 July 1918, died 10 September 2006; succeeded to the throne 15 December 1965; married 1947, Princess Halaevalu Mata'aho 'Ahome'e (Queen Halaevalu Mata'aho) (b. 29 May 1926, died 19 February 2017).

UNITED ARAB EMIRATES

Reigning Rulers

Ruler of Abu Dhabi: HH Sheikh KHALIFA BIN ZAYED AN-**NAHYAN**; b. 1948; succeeded to the throne 2 November 2004; married 1964 Sheikha Shamsa bint Suhail Al Mazrouei; two sons, six daughters.

Ruler of Dubai: HH Sheikh MUHAMMAD BIN RASHID AL-**MAKTOUM**; b. 15 July 1949; succeeded to the throne 4 January 2006; married 2nd 10 April 2004, HRH Princess Haya bint al-Hussein of Jordan; daughter, Al-Jalila, b. 2 December 2007; son, Zayed, b. 7 January 2012.

Ruler of Sharjah: HH Sheikh SULTAN BIN MUHAMMAD AL-**QASIMI**; b. 6 July 1939; succeeded to the throne 25 January 1972.

Ruler of Ras al-Khaimah: HH Sheikh SAUD IBN SAQR AL-**QASIMI**; b. 10 February 1956; succeeded to the throne 27 October 2010.

Ruler of Umm al-Qaiwain: HH Sheikh SAUD BIN RASHID AL-**MU'ALLA**; b. 1 October 1952; succeeded to the throne 2 January 2009.

Ruler of Ajman: HH Sheikh HUMAID BIN RASHID AN-**NUAIMI**; b. 1931; succeeded to the throne 6 September 1981.

Ruler of Fujairah: HH Sheikh HAMAD BIN MUHAMMAD ASH-**SHARQI**; b. 25 May 1948; succeeded to the throne 18 September 1974.

UNITED KINGDOM

Reigning Queen

HM QUEEN **ELIZABETH II**; b. 21 April 1926; succeeded to the throne 6 February 1952, on the death of her father, King George VI; crowned 2 June 1953; married 20 November 1947, HRH Prince Philip, Duke of **Edinburgh**, Earl of Merioneth, Baron Greenwich, KG, KT, OM, GBE, AC, QSO (b. 10 June 1921), son of Prince Andrew of Greece and Princess Alice of Battenberg (Mountbatten).

Children of the Queen

HRH Prince Charles Philip Arthur George, The Prince of **Wales**, Duke of Cornwall, Duke of Rothesay, Earl of Chester, Earl of Carrick, Baron Renfrew, Lord of the Isles and Great Steward of Scotland, KG, KT, GCB, OM, AK, QSO, ADC (heir-apparent), b. 14 November 1948; married 1st 29 July 1981, Lady Diana Frances Spencer (The Princess of Wales) (divorced 1996, died 31 August 1997); son, HRH Prince **William** Arthur Philip Louis of Wales (HRH The Duke of **Cambridge**), b. 21 June 1982; married 29 April 2011, Catherine Elizabeth Middleton (HRH The Duchess of **Cambridge**) (son, HRH Prince George Alexander Louis of Cambridge, b. 22 July 2013; daughter, HRH Princess Charlotte Elizabeth Diana, b. 2 May 2015); son, HRH Prince Louis Arthur Charles of Cambridge, b. 23 April 2018); son, HRH Prince Henry Charles Albert David of Wales (HRH The Duke of Sussex), b. 15 September 1984; married 19 May 2018, Rachel Meghan Markle (HRH The Duchess of Sussex) (son, HRH Archie Harrison Mountbatten-Windsor, b. 6 May 2019); married 2nd 9 April 2005, Camilla Parker Bowles (HRH The Duchess of **Cornwall**) (b. 17 July 1947).

HRH Princess Anne Elizabeth Alice Louise, The Princess **Royal**, KG, KT, GCVO, QSO, b. 15 August 1950; married 1st 14 November 1973, Captain Mark Phillips (divorced 1992); son, Peter Mark Andrew Phillips, b. 15 November 1977; daughter, Zara Anne Elizabeth Phillips, b. 15 May 1981; married 2nd 12 December 1992, Vice-Admiral Timothy Laurence, CB, MVO, ADC.

HRH Prince Andrew Albert Christian Edward, The Duke of **York**, Earl of Inverness, Baron Killyleagh, KS, KCVO, ADC, b. 19 February 1960; married 23 July 1986, Sarah Ferguson (The Duchess of York) (b. 15 October 1959) (divorced 1996); daughter, Princess Beatrice Elizabeth Mary of York, b. 8 August 1988; daughter, Princess Eugenie Victoria Helena of York, b. 23 March 1990; married 12 October 2018, Jack Christopher Stamp Brooksbank.

HRH Prince Edward Antony Richard Louis, The Earl of **Wessex**, KS, KCVO, ADC, b. 10 March 1964; married 19 June 1999, Sophie Rhys-Jones (HRH The Countess of Wessex) (b. 20 January 1965); daughter, Lady Louise Alice Elizabeth Mary Windsor, b. 8 November 2003; son, James Alexander Philip Theo, Viscount Severn, b. 17 December 2007.

Parents of the Queen

King George VI, b. 14 December 1895 (son of King George V and Queen Mary), died 6 February 1952; married 26 April 1923, Lady Elizabeth Angela Marguerite Bowes-Lyon (Queen Elizabeth The Queen Mother) (b. 4 August 1900, died 30 March 2002).

Sister of the Queen

Princess Margaret Rose, Countess of Snowdon, CI, GCVO, b. 21 August 1930, died 9 February 2002; married 6 May 1960, Antony Armstrong-Jones (Earl of Snowdon, GCVO) (divorced 1978, died 13 January 2017); son, David Albert Charles, Viscount Linley, b. 3 November 1961, (married, two children); daughter, Lady Sarah Frances Elizabeth Chatto (née Armstrong-Jones), b. 1 May 1964, (married, two children).

The full titles of Queen Elizabeth II are as follows:

United Kingdom

"Elizabeth the Second, by the Grace of God, of the United Kingdom of Great Britain and Northern Ireland and of Her other Realms and Territories Queen, Head of the Commonwealth, Defender of the Faith."

Canada

"Elizabeth the Second, by the Grace of God, of the United Kingdom, Canada and Her other Realms and Territories Queen, Head of the Commonwealth, Defender of the Faith."

Australia

"Elizabeth the Second, by the Grace of God, Queen of Australia and Her other Realms and Territories, Head of the Commonwealth."

New Zealand

"Elizabeth the Second, by the Grace of God, Queen of New Zealand and Her other Realms and Territories, Head of the Commonwealth, Defender of the Faith."

Jamaica

"Elizabeth the Second, by the Grace of God, Queen of Jamaica and of Her other Realms and Territories Queen, Head of the Commonwealth."

Barbados

"Elizabeth the Second, by the Grace of God, Queen of Barbados and of Her other Realms and Territories, Head of the Commonwealth."

The Bahamas

"Elizabeth the Second, by the Grace of God, Queen of the Commonwealth of The Bahamas and of Her other Realms and Territories, Head of the Commonwealth."

Grenada

"Elizabeth the Second, by the Grace of God, Queen of the United Kingdom of Great Britain and Northern Ireland and of Grenada and Her other Realms and Territories, Head of the Commonwealth."

Papua New Guinea

"Elizabeth the Second, Queen of Papua New Guinea and of Her other Realms and Territories, Head of the Commonwealth."

Solomon Islands

"Elizabeth the Second, by the Grace of God, Queen of the Solomon Islands and of Her other Realms and Territories, Head of the Commonwealth."

Tuvalu

"Elizabeth the Second, by the Grace of God, Queen of Tuvalu and of Her other Realms and Territories, Head of the Commonwealth."

Saint Lucia

"Elizabeth the Second, by the Grace of God, Queen of Saint Lucia and of Her other Realms and Territories, Head of the Commonwealth."

Saint Vincent and the Grenadines

"Elizabeth the Second, by the Grace of God, Queen of Saint Vincent and the Grenadines and of Her other Realms and Territories, Head of the Commonwealth."

Belize

"Elizabeth the Second, by the Grace of God, Queen of Belize and of Her other Realms and Territories, Head of the Commonwealth."

Antigua and Barbuda

"Elizabeth the Second, by the Grace of God, Queen of Antigua and Barbuda and of Her other Realms and Territories, Head of the Commonwealth."

Saint Christopher and Nevis

"Elizabeth the Second, by the Grace of God, Queen of Saint Christopher and Nevis and of Her other Realms and Territories, Head of the Commonwealth."

The Republics of India, Ghana, Cyprus, Tanzania, Uganda, Kenya, Zambia, Malawi, Singapore, Botswana, Guyana, Nauru, The Gambia, Sierra Leone, Bangladesh, Sri Lanka, Malta, Trinidad and Tobago, Seychelles, Dominica, Kiribati, Vanuatu, Maldives, Namibia, Mauritius, South Africa, Fiji, Pakistan, Cameroon and Mozambique, together with the Federation of Malaysia, the Kingdom of Lesotho, the Kingdom of Eswatini, the Kingdom of Tonga, the Independent State of Samoa and the Sultanate of Brunei, recognize the Queen as "Head of the Commonwealth".

OBITUARY

Abalakin, Victor Kuz'mich	23 April 2018
Adji, Boukary	4 July 2018
Ahlmark, Per	8 June 2018
Alexander, Meena	21 November 2018
Alexeeva, Ludmilla	8 December 2018
Alferov, Zhores Ivanovich	1 March 2019
Allen, Paul Gardner	15 October 2018
Alsop, William Allen	12 May 2018
Ambartsumyan, Sergey Aleksandrovich	4 August 2018
Amissah-Arthur, Kwesi Bekoe	29 June 2018
Anderson, John Anthony	13 November 2018
Andersson, Bibi	14 April 2019
Annan, Kofi Atta	18 August 2018
Arens, Moshe	7 January 2019
Ashdown Of Norton Sub-Hamdon, Jeremy John Durham (Paddy) Ashdown	22 December 2018
Ashida, Jun	20 October 2018
Atiyah, Michael Francis	11 January 2019
Atkinson, Harry Hindmarsh	30 December 2018
Ayales Esna, Edgar	25 April 2018
Aznavour, Charles	1 October 2018
Azuma, Takamitsu	18 June 2015
Baker, Russell Wayne	21 January 2019
Barenblatt, Grigory Isaakovich	22 June 2018
Baring, Arnulf Martin	2 March 2019
Barnard, Eric Albert	23 May 2018
Beckett, Wendy	26 December 2018
Behmen, Alija	1 August 2018
Belotserkovsky, Oleg Mikhailovich	15 July 2015
Belshaw, Cyril Shirley	20 November 2018
Benetton, Carlo	10 July 2018
Bennet, Douglas (Doug) Joseph, Jr	10 June 2018
Bertolucci, Bernardo	26 November 2018
Betancur Cuartas, Belisario	7 December 2018
Billington, James Hadley	20 November 2018
Bitov, Andrei Georgevich	3 December 2018
Bjurström, Per Gunnar	4 September 2017
Blom-Cooper, Louis Jacques	19 September 2018
Bodman, Samuel Wright, III	7 September 2018
Bondurant, Stuart	26 May 2018
Bonner, John Tyler	7 February 2019
Bor, Naci	2018
Botha, Roelof Frederik (Pik)	12 October 2018
Bott, Martin Harold Phillips	20 October 2018
Bourgain, Jean	22 December 2018
Brenner, Sydney	5 April 2019
Briggs, Winslow Russell	11 February 2019
Broecker, Wallace (Wally) Smith	19 February 2019
Browne-Wilkinson, Nicolas Christopher Henry Browne-Wilkinson	25 July 2018
Brown, Harold	4 January 2019
Buldakov, Aleksey Ivanovich	3 April 2019
Bunin, Igor Mikhailovich	12 May 2018
Bush, George Herbert Walker	30 November 2018
Buthelezi, Manas	20 April 2016
Cagiati, Andrea	2018
Calder, John Mackenzie	13 August 2018
Campbell, Allan McCulloch	19 April 2018
Campbell, Roderick Samuel Fisher	22 March 2018
Caputo, Dante	20 June 2018
Carlsson, Arvid	29 June 2018
Carlucci, Frank Charles	3 June 2018
Carrick, John Leslie	18 May 2018
Carrington, Peter Alexander Rupert Carrington	10 July 2018
Casida, John Edward	30 June 2018
Castrillón Hoyos, Darío	18 May 2018
Cavalli-Sforza, Luigi Luca	31 August 2018
Chadwick, Peter	12 August 2018
Channing, Carol	15 January 2019
Chatterjee, Somnath	13 August 2018
Chen, Jinhua	2 July 2016
Chew, Geoffrey Foucar	11 April 2019
Chiladze, Tamaz	28 September 2018
Chisholm, Samuel Hewlings	9 July 2018
Cho, Yang-ho	7 April 2019
Chung, Sze-yuen	14 November 2018
Ciry, Michel	26 December 2018
Coates, Anne Voase	8 May 2018
Conway, Jill Ker	1 June 2018
Cortazzi, (Henry Arthur) Hugh	14 August 2018
Cox, Robert Warburton	9 October 2018
Daneliya, Georgiy Nikolayevich	4 April 2019
Danneels, Godfried	14 March 2019
Dassault, Serge	28 May 2018
De Cecco, Marcello	3 March 2016
Denholm, Ian (John Ferguson)	15 May 2018
Dewost, Jean-Louis	2 March 2019
Dianov, Evgeny Mikhailovich	30 January 2019
Djuhar, Sutanto	2 July 2018
Dlamini, Barnabas Sibusiso	28 September 2018
Donald, Alan (Ewen)	14 July 2018
Donen, Stanley	21 February 2019
Do, Muoi	1 October 2018
Dore, Ronald Philip	13 November 2018
Doruk, Mustafa	1 July 2017
Drach, Ivan Fyodorovich	19 June 2018
Dwurnik, Edward	28 October 2018
Eberle, James Henry Fuller	17 May 2018
Eibl-Eibesfeldt, Irenäus	2 June 2018
Eichelbaum, (Johann) Thomas	31 October 2018
Eigen, Manfred	6 February 2019
Elliott, Roger James	16 May 2018
Ellison, Harlan Jay	27 June 2018
Elverding, Peter A. F. W.	31 August 2017
Enwezor, Okwui	15 March 2019
Eskola, Antti Aarre	6 September 2018
Falcam, Leo A.	12 February 2018
Farquhar, John William	22 August 2018
Feast, Michael William	1 April 2019
Feher, George	28 November 2017
Feng, Lanrui	28 February 2019
Fernandes, George	29 January 2019
Fettweis, Günter Bernhard Leo	31 October 2018
Finney, Albert	7 February 2019
Fletcher, Neville Horner	1 October 2017
Fornés, María Irene	30 October 2018
Frängsmyr, Tore	28 August 2017
Franklin, Aretha	16 August 2018
Fraser, William Kerr	13 September 2018
Freeman, Michael Alexander Reykers	14 September 2017
Frère, Albert Pol Oscar Ghislain	3 December 2018
Froment-Meurice, Henri	2 July 2018
Funai, Tetsuro	4 July 2017
Galmot, Yves	3 October 2017
Ganz, Bruno	16 February 2019
Gaombalet, Célestin-Leroy	19 December 2017
García Pérez, Alan Gabriel Ludwig	17 April 2019
Gardner, Richard Newton	15 February 2019
Georgievski, Ljubiša	6 December 2018
Gidada, Negaso	27 April 2019
Giacconi, Riccardo	9 December 2018
Gibbs, Roger Geoffrey	3 October 2018
Gielen, Michael Andreas	8 March 2019
Gill, Anthony (Keith)	6 August 2018
Giri, Tulsi	18 December 2018
Gizenga, Antoine	24 February 2019
Glauber, Roy J.	26 December 2018
Glazer, Nathan	19 January 2019
Goldman, William	16 November 2018
Gomes, Daniel	11 December 2017
Govorukhin, Stanislav Sergeyevich	14 June 2018
Grassle, J. Frederick	6 July 2018
Greengard, Paul	13 April 2019
Gurirab, Theo-Ben	14 July 2018
Habgood, John Stapylton Habgood	6 March 2019
Hall, Donald Andrew	23 June 2018
Hanson, John Gilbert	13 January 2017
Hargrove, Roy Anthony	2 November 2018
Harkianakis, Stylianos	25 March 2019
Hasselmo, Nils	23 January 2019
Hercus, Luise Anna	15 April 2018
Hernández Colón, Rafael	2 May 2019
Hiller, Susan	28 January 2019
Hollings, Ernest (Fritz)	6 April 2019
Holtzman, Wayne Harold	23 January 2019
Hooley, Christopher	13 December 2018
Ho, Tao	29 March 2019
Hultqvist, Bengt Karl Gustaf	24 February 2019
Hurford, Peter John	3 March 2019
Hush, Noel Sydney	20 March 2019
Imry, Yoseph	29 May 2018
Indiana, Robert	19 May 2018

OBITUARY

Isayev, Alexander Sergeyevich	30 August 2018
Ishizaka, Kimishige	6 July 2018
Islam, Syed Ashraful	3 January 2019
Ismail, Amat	16 October 2018
Israelachvili, Jacob Nissim	20 September 2018
Jahn, Robert George	15 November 2017
Jayawardena, Amarananda Somasiri	29 May 2018
Jean Benoît Guillaume Marie Robert Louis Antoine Adolphe Marc D'Aviano, Grand Duke of Luxembourg	23 April 2019
Jeffrey, Robin Campbell	4 November 2018
Jin, Yong	30 October 2018
Jory, Edward John	4 September 2016
Jowell, Tessa Jane Helen Douglas Jowell	12 May 2018
Kalpokas, Donald Masike'Vanua	20 March 2019
Kao, Charles K.	23 September 2018
Karunanidhi, Muthuvel 'Kalaignar'	7 August 2018
Kashio, Kazuo	18 June 2018
Kates, Robert William	21 April 2018
Khadjiev, Salambek Naibovich	2018
Kim, Jong-pil	23 June 2018
Kim, Yong-chun	16 August 2018
Kinkel, Klaus	4 March 2019
Klug, Aaron	20 November 2018
Knussen, (Stuart) Oliver	8 July 2018
Kobzon, Iosif Davydovich	30 August 2018
Kok, Willem (Wim)	20 October 2018
Koltai, Ralph	15 December 2018
Koo, Bon-moo	20 May 2018
Kopelson, Arnold	8 October 2018
Krauthammer, Charles	21 June 2018
Krueger, Alan Bennett	16 March 2019
Kubuabola, Jone Yavala	16 September 2018
Küçük, İrsen	10 March 2019
Kutz, Kazimierz	18 December 2018
Labrie, Fernand	17 January 2019
Lacey, Richard Westgarth	3 February 2019
Lagerfeld, Karl Otto	19 February 2019
Lance, James Waldo	20 February 2019
Lange, Hermann	28 July 2018
Lanzmann, Claude	5 July 2018
Laqueur, Walter	30 September 2018
Lebed, Aleksey Ivanovich	27 April 2019
Lederman, Leon M.	3 October 2018
Lee, Stan	12 November 2018
Leibinger, Berthold	16 October 2018
Levi, Isaac	25 December 2018
Levy, Andrea	14 February 2019
Lewis, Bernard	19 May 2018
Likhachev, Vasily Nikolayevich	8 April 2019
Ling, Jiefang	15 December 2018
Lin, Yu-Lin	9 June 2018
Li, Rui	16 February 2019
List, Roland	26 January 2019
Liu, Dongdong	25 February 2015
López-Ibor, Juan José	12 January 2015
Louly, Mohamed Mahmoud Ould Ahmed	16 March 2019
Loutfy, Aly	27 May 2018
Lugar, Richard (Dick) Green	28 April 2019
Lukianenko, Levko (Hryhorovych)	7 July 2018
Mcbride, William Griffith	27 June 2018
Mccain, John Sidney, III	25 August 2018
Mcgee, Liam E.	13 February 2015
Mccomb, Leonard William Joseph	19 June 2018
Macdonald, Donald Stovel	14 October 2018
Magowan, Peter Alden	27 January 2019
Manani Magaya, Alison	24 August 2015
Mao, Zhiyong	4 March 2019
Marchionne, Sergio	25 July 2018
Marshall, (Carole) Penny	17 December 2018
Martini-Urdaneta, Alberto	5 July 2017
Martre, Henri Jean François	3 July 2018
Masol, Vitaliy Andreyevich	21 September 2018
Matsushita, Yasuo	20 July 2018
Maurício, Armindo Cipriano	28 September 2016
Medelci, Mourad	28 January 2019
Medvedev, Zhores Aleksandrovich	15 November 2018
Meinwald, Jerrold	23 April 2018
Melchett, Peter Robert Henry Mond	29 August 2018
Mendelsohn, John	7 January 2019
Mensah, Joseph Henry	12 July 2018
Merwin, W(illiam) S(tanley)	15 March 2019
Metzger, Henry	20 November 2018
Mirrlees, James Alexander	29 August 2018
Mitchell, Arthur Adam, Jr	19 September 2018
Mojaddedi, Sibghatullah	11 February 2019
Monory, Jacques	17 October 2018
Moore, Gerald Ernest	24 March 2018
Morley, Malcolm	2 June 2018
Mosonyi, György	29 May 2018
Moureaux, Philippe	15 December 2018
Mroudjaé, Ali	2 May 2019
Munk, Walter Heinrich	8 February 2019
Murphy, Thomas (Tom)	15 May 2018
Murray, Leslie (Les) Allan	29 April 2019
Mwape, Lupando Augustine Festus K.	21 January 2019
Myerson, Jacob M.	7 July 2018
Nagare, Masayuki	7 July 2018
Naipaul, V(idiadhar) S(urajprasad)	11 August 2018
Nakai, Hiroshi	22 April 2017
Nakanishi, Koji	28 March 2019
Namphy, Henri	26 June 2018
Nanterme, Pierre	31 January 2019
Neild, Robert Ralph	18 December 2018
Nekrošius, Eimuntas	20 November 2018
Newton, John Oswald	26 September 2016
Nishikawa, Koichiro	28 November 2018
Noakes, Michael	30 May 2018
Norwich, John Julius Cooper	1 June 2018
Nott, Peter John	20 August 2018
Novozhilov, Genrikh Vasilievich	28 April 2019
Obando Y Bravo, Miguel	3 June 2018
O'Brien Quinn, James Aiden	28 December 2018
Ollila, Esko Juhani	1 December 2018
Olszewski, Jan Ferdynand	7 February 2019
Omar, Abu Hassan Bin Haj	8 September 2018
Omar, Napsiah binti	16 April 2018
Orrego Vicuña, Francisco	2 October 2018
Orszulik, Alojzy	21 February 2019
Osbaldeston, Gordon Francis	6 March 2019
Oz, Amos	28 December 2018
Parrikar, Manohar	17 March 2019
Peart, (William) Stanley	14 March 2019
Pérez-Llorca, José Pedro	6 March 2019
Peters, Wallace	December 2018
Petkoff Malec, Teodoro	31 October 2018
Petre, Zoe	1 September 2017
Piat, Jean	18 September 2018
Pieronek, Tadeusz	27 December 2018
Pieroth, Elmar	31 August 2018
Pihl, Jüri	3 February 2019
Pintilie, Lucian	16 May 2018
Powers, William C., Jr	10 March 2019
Previn, André George	28 February 2019
Rabin, Oskar Yakovlevich	7 November 2018
Rajeswar, Thanjavelu	13 January 2018
Ramazani Baya, Raymond	1 January 2019
Reino, Fernando	15 April 2018
René, (France) Albert	27 February 2019
Rétoré, Guy	15 December 2018
Reuber, Grant Louis	7 July 2018
Reyes López, Juan Francisco	10 January 2019
Reynolds, Burt	6 September 2018
Reynolds, Peter William John	19 October 2017
Richter, Burton	18 July 2018
Riddell, Clayton (Clay) H.	15 September 2018
Rindler, Wolfgang	8 February 2019
Ripa Di Meana, Carlo	2 March 2018
Robuchon, Joël	6 August 2018
Roche, (Eamonn) Kevin	1 March 2019
Rodríguez Araque, Ali	19 November 2018
Roeg, Nicolas Jack	23 November 2018
Rogers, James E., Jr	17 December 2018
Rogers, T. Gary	2 May 2017
Röller, Wolfgang	9 March 2018
Rose, Clive (Martin)	17 April 2019
Roth, Philip Milton	22 May 2018
Rowland, (John) David	18 February 2019
Rowlinson, John Shipley	15 August 2018
Rozhdestvensky, Gennady Nikolayevich	16 June 2018
Rubenstein, Edward	19 March 2019
Ryman, Robert	8 February 2019
Sahnoun, Mohamed	20 September 2018
Sakaiya, Taichi	8 February 2019
Salakhitdinov, Makhmud	27 April 2018
Sanyal, Meera H.	11 January 2019
Sa'ud, Talal bin Abd al-Aziz al-	22 December 2018
Schieffer, Rudolf	15 September 2018
Schroder, Bruno Lionel	20 February 2019
Screech, Michael Andrew	1 June 2018
Sebastián Aguilar, Fernando	24 January 2019
Semikhatov, Mikhail Alexandrovich	28 November 2018
Sen, Mrinal	30 December 2018
Severino, Rodolfo	19 April 2019
Shagari, Shehu Usman Aliu	28 December 2018
Shahrudi, Sayed Mahmoud Hashemi	24 December 2018
Shange, Ntozake	27 October 2018
Sheng, Zhongguo	7 September 2018
Shimogaichi, Yoichi	25 October 2017
Shimomura, Osamu	19 October 2018
Shipley, Walter Vincent	11 January 2019

Shmarov, Valery Nikolayevich	14 October 2018
Shock, Maurice	7 July 2018
Sidhu, Shivinder Singh	25 October 2018
Simms, David John	24 June 2018
Simon, Neil	26 August 2018
Singh, Bhishma Narain	1 August 2018
Sioufas, Dimitris	11 January 2019
Skou, Jens Christian	28 May 2018
Smith, David Cecil	29 June 2018
Stanley, Eric Gerald	21 June 2018
Starobinski, Jean	4 March 2019
Stein, Elias M.	23 December 2018
Steitz, Thomas A.	9 October 2018
Stepin, Vyacheslav Semenovich	14 December 2018
Stoltenberg, Thorvald	13 July 2018
Street, Laurence Whistler	21 June 2018
Strunk, Klaus Albert	7 September 2018
Swinnerton-Dyer, (Henry) Peter Francis	26 December 2018
Swire, Adrian (Christopher)	24 August 2018
Sy, Henry, Sr	19 January 2019
Szabo, Denis	13 October 2018
Tadros, Tharwat Fouad	23 May 2018
Talling, J(ohn) F(rancis)	20 June 2017
Tauran, Jean-Louis Pierre	5 July 2018
Taylor, Paul B.	29 August 2018
Thacker, Charles (Chuck) P.	12 June 2017
Thomson, John Adam	3 June 2018
Thomson, Peter William	20 June 2018
Thorne León, Jaime	5 April 2018
Thouless, David James	6 April 2019
Thurau, Klaus Walther Christian	1 November 2018
Tian, Congming	6 December 2017
Tiwari, Narayan Dutt	18 October 2018
Tomlinson, Mel Alexander	5 February 2019
Tomur, Dawamat	19 December 2018
Tran, Dai Quang	21 September 2018
Ty, George S. K. (Siao Kian)	23 November 2018
Ullsten, Ola	28 May 2018
Urbain, Robert	9 November 2018
Vajpayee, Atal Bihari	16 August 2018
Van Caenegem, Raoul Charles	15 June 2018
Varda, Agnès	29 March 2019
Venturi, Robert	18 September 2018
Verba, Sidney	4 March 2019
Verstraete, Marc	16 August 2018
Viénot, Marc	28 January 2019
Vincent of Coleshill, Richard (Frederick) Vincent	8 September 2018
Virilio, Paul	10 September 2018
von der Dunk, Hermann Walther	22 August 2018
Wald, Patricia McGowan	12 January 2019
Walker, Alan Cyril	20 November 2017
Wang, Charles B.	21 October 2018
Wang, Guangying	29 October 2018
Wang, Ruilin	8 December 2018
Ward, Ian Macmillan	5 November 2018
Warnock, (Helen) Mary Warnock	20 March 2019
Wasserman, Robert Harold	23 May 2018
Weatherall, David John	8 December 2018
Wellershoff, Dieter	15 June 2018
White, Guy Kendall	22 May 2018
Widjaja, Eka Tjipta	26 January 2019
Wilson, Michael H.	10 February 2019
Winkler, Hans Günter	9 July 2018
Winters, Robert Cushing	3 December 2018
Wofford, Harris Llewellyn	21 January 2019
Wolde-Giorgis, Girma	15 December 2018
Wolfe, Thomas (Tom) Kennerly, Jr	14 May 2018
Xiao, Yang	19 April 2019
Xing, Shizhong	11 March 2019
Yakovlev, Veniamin Fedorovich	24 July 2018
Yang, Zhiguang	14 May 2016
Yarrow, Eric Grant	22 September 2018
Yasuoka, Okiharu	19 April 2019
Yemelyanov, Stanislav Vasilevich	15 November 2018
Yonekura, Hiromasa	16 November 2018
Yu, Min	16 January 2019
Yursky, Sergei Yurievich	8 February 2019
Zachau, Hans G.	17 December 2017
Zakharchenko, Aleksandr Vladimirovich	31 August 2018
Zhang, Shoucheng	1 December 2018
Zhu, Xu	15 September 2018

THE INTERNATIONAL WHO'S WHO

2020

A

AARON, David L., MA; American diplomatist and academic; b. 21 Aug. 1938, Chicago, Ill.; m. Chloe W. Aaron; one c.; ed Occidental Coll. and Woodrow Wilson School of Public and Int. Affairs, Princeton Univ.; entered Foreign Service 1962, served as Political and Econ. Officer, Embassy in Guayaquil, Ecuador, Int. Relations Officer, Dept of State 1964–66, Political Officer, NATO, Paris 1966, then served with Arms Control and Disarmament Agency; Sr Staff mem. Nat. Security Council 1972–74, Legis. Asst to Senator Walter Mondale 1974–75, Task Force Leader, Senate Select Cttee on Intelligence 1975–76, mem. staff, Carter-Mondale presidential campaign, Transition Dir with Nat. Security Council and CIA 1976–77, Deputy Asst to Pres. for Nat. Security Affairs 1977–81; Vice-Pres. Oppenheimer & Co. Inc. 1981–85, Dir Oppenheimer Int. 1984; Sr Adviser, Mondale presidential campaign; writer and lecturer, Lantz-Harris Agency 1985–93; consultant, 20th Century Fund 1990–92, Sr Fellow 1992–93; US Rep. to OECD 1993, US Special Envoy for Cryptography 1996, Under-Sec. of Commerce for Int. Trade 1997–2001; Sr Int. Advisor, Int. Trade Practice Group, Dorsey & Whitney LLP (law firm) 2001–03; joined RAND Corpn as Director of the Center for Middle East Public Policy 2003, served on RAND-Qatar Policy Inst. Bd of Overseers, then Sr Fellow; Dr hc (Occidental Coll.); Nat. Defense Medal. *Television:* The Gulf War (script), Miracle on 44th Street: The Action Studio (script). *Publications include:* State Scarlet 1987, Agent of Influence 1989, Crossing by Night 1993; articles in newspapers and journals.

ABADI, Haider Jawad Kathem al-, BEng, PhD; Iraqi politician; b. 1952, Baghdad; m.; three c.; ed Baghdad Univ. of Tech., Univ. of Manchester, UK; joined Islamic Dawa Party 1967; in exile in UK until 2003 (worked in transport sector as industry adviser and business consultant), returned to Iraq 2003; Minister of Communications in Iraqi Governing Council 2003; Adviser to Prime Minister 2005; mem. Council of Reps (Parl.) 2005–, Chair. Economy, Investment and Reconstruction Cttee 2005, Finance Cttee 2013, Deputy Speaker 2014; Prime Minister 2014–18; mem. Iraq Petroleum Advisory Cttee (participated in Iraq Petroleum Confs 2009–12). *E-mail:* albadi2@hotmail.com (office).

ABAGA NCHAMA, Lucas, DEA; Equatorial Guinean economist, central banker and politician; b. 4 March 1961, Ebebiyín, Río Muni; m.; three c.; ed Univ. Jean Monnet, St Etienne and Univ. Lyon II, France; joined Banque des Etats de l'Afrique Centrale (BEAC) 1998, with Bata br. 1999–2003, Pres., BEAC Audit Cttee 2007–08, Dir-Gen. of Operations 2008, Gov. BEAC 2010–17; Dir-Gen. of Economy, Ministry of Economy and Trade 2003–06; Sec.-Gen., Ministry of Finance and the Budget 2006–08, Minister of Finance and the Budget 2018–19; Commdr, Order of Valour (Cameroon) 2017. *Address:* c/o Ministry of Finance and the Budget, Malabo, Equatorial Guinea (office).

A-BAKI, Ivonne, BA, BArch, MPA; Ecuadorean diplomatist and artist; b. Guayaquil; m. Sammi A-Baki; two s. one d.; ed Univ. of Paris (Sorbonne), France, Harvard Univ., USA; fmr Dir Conflict Man. Group, Harvard Univ., del. to confs in Geneva 1984, Lausanne 1985; Adviser to Pres. on Ecuador–Peru peace negotiations –1998; Consul-Gen., then Hon. Consul in Lebanon; Consul-Gen. in Boston, Mass; apptd Amb. to USA 1999; unsuccessful cand. for Pres. of Ecuador 2002; Minister of Foreign Trade, Industrialization, Fishing and Competition 2003–05; Pres. Andean Parl., Bogotá, Colombia 2007–09; UNESCO Goodwill Amb. 2010–; apptd Ecuadorean negotiator for Yasuní-ITT Initiative and Pres.'s special envoy in charge of preserving the Yasuni National Park and Head, YNP Foundation; painter, numerous exhbns in museums, galleries and pvt. collections in Europe, N and S America and Middle East; f. Harvard Foundation for the Arts; Artist-in-Residence, Harvard Univ. 1991–98; Pres. Arts and Community Renewal Coalition, Boston, Beyond Boundaries Foundation; Founder Galapagos Conservancy Foundation; Order of Merit, Honorato Vasquez Order; numerous other awards.

ABAL MEDINA, Juan Manuel, Jr, PhD; Argentine political scientist, politician, writer and academic; b. 5 May 1968, Buenos Aires; s. of Juan Manuel Abal Medina and Cristina Moldes; m. Guillermina Koch; three d.; ed Univ. of Buenos Aires, Latin American Social Sciences Inst., Mexico; fmr Lecturer, Univ. of Buenos Aires, Nat. Univ. of Quilmes, Univ. of San Andrés; Dir Nat. Public Admin Inst. 2000–01; fmr Visiting Researcher, Dept of Govt, Georgetown Univ., USA; Political and Legis. Dir for Mayor of Buenos Aires 2001, Dir of Strategic Planning 2003–05; Under-Sec. of Public Man. and Adviser to Pres. 2005–07, Sec. of Cabinet and Public Man. 2008–09, Sec. of Public Man. 2009–11, Communications Sec. Jan.–Dec. 2011, Chief, Cabinet of Ministers 2011–13; Amb. to ALADI and MERCOSUR 2014; mem. Senate 2014–; Sec. of Int. Affairs, Partido Justicialista. *Publications include:* El federalismo electoral argentino 2001, Los partidos políticos: ¿un mal necesario? 2004, Evaluando el desempeño democrático de las instituciones políticas argentinas 2007; numerous articles in political science journals. *Address:* Senado, Congreso de la Nación, Avenida Rivadavia 1864, C1033AAV Buenos Aires, Argentina (office). *Telephone:* (11) 4010-3000 (office). *E-mail:* juan.abalmedina@senado.gov.ar (office). *Website:* www.senado.gov.ar (office).

ABALKHAIL, Sheikh Mohamed Ali, BA; Saudi Arabian government official and financial executive; b. 30 Oct. 1932, Buraidah; s. of Ali Abdullah Abalkhail and Fatima Abdulaziz Othaim; m. 1966; two s. two d.; ed Cairo Univ., Egypt; began career as Asst Dir of Office of Minister of Communications, later Dir; Dir-Gen. of Inst. of Public Admin; Deputy Minister of Finance and Nat. Econ., then Vice-Minister, Minister of State, Minister for Finance and Nat. Econ. 1975–95; fmr Chair. Riyadh Bank; Chair. Centre for Econ. and Man. Studies; mem. JP Morgan Int. Council; decorations from Belgium, Egypt, France, Niger, Pakistan, Saudi Arabia, Sudan, Germany, Morocco, Spain; Lifetime Achievement Award, Arab Economic Forum 2013. *Leisure interests:* reading, sports. *Address:* PO Box 943, Riyadh 11421 (office); PO Box 287, Riyadh 11411, Saudi Arabia. *Telephone:* (1) 478-1722 (office). *Fax:* (1) 478-1904 (office). *E-mail:* mabakhail@sanadco.com (office).

ABASSI, Houcine; Tunisian trade unionist; b. 19 Aug. 1947, Sbikha; m.; four c.; early career as teacher; joined Union Générale Tunisienne du Travail (Tunisian Gen. Labour Union, UGTT) 1973, various roles including mem., Gen. Union of Supervisors 1983, mem., Regional Labour Union, Kairouan 1997, Sec.-Gen., Regional Labour Union, Kairouan 2002, mem. Exec. Bd, responsible for Legislation and Study Dept 2006, Sec.-Gen., UGTT 2011–17; as leader of UGTT took part in Tunisian Nat. Dialogue Quartet, involved in negotiations to rebuild democracy following Tunisian Revolution 2011; Perm. Mem. Exec. Bd, Int. Trade Union Confed.; Pres. Arab Union Confed.; Dr hc (Dōshisha Univ.); Commdr, Ordre de la République tunisienne, Commdr, Légion d'honneur; German Africa Foundation Award 2015, Nobel Peace Prize 2015 (co-recipient as part of Tunisian Nat. Dialogue Quartet). *Address:* c/o Union Générale Tunisienne du Travail, 29 place Muhammad Ali, 1000 Tunis, Tunisia (office). *Telephone:* (71) 332-400 (office). *Fax:* (71) 354-114 (office). *E-mail:* ugtt.tunis@email.ati.tn (office). *Website:* www.ugtt.org.tn (office).

ABAZA, Mohammed Maher, BSc; Egyptian engineer, business executive and fmr politician; b. 12 March 1930, Sharkia; s. of Muhamed Osman Abazah; m. Ezdehar Abo El-Ela 1955; one s. one d.; ed Cairo Univ. and studies in W Germany and Sweden; engineer, Dept of Hydroelectric Power, Ministry of Public Works 1951–64; several sr positions in Egyptian Electricity Authority 1964–73; First Under-Sec. of State, Ministry of Electricity and Energy 1975–80, Minister of Electricity and Energy 1980–99; fmr Chair. MIDTAP Co., MIDOR Electricity Co., Petrosport Co., Emarat Misr Co.; mem. Bd EMG Co.; Pres. Int. Asscn for Electricity Generation, Transmission and Distribution (Afro-Asian region) 1996–99; mem. numerous nat. and int. scientific cttees; mem. World Energy Council, IEEE, Thomas Alva Edison Foundation, Int. Council on Large Electrical Systems (CIGRE), Int. Conf. on Electricity Distribution (CIRED); The Greatest Nile Medal, Golden Medal of Distinction, Order of the Repub. (First Class, Egypt, France, Poland, Niger), Royal Order of the Polar Star (Grand Cross, Sweden), Grand Cross of the Order of Merit (FRG, Italy), Order of the Grand Cross (Italy), Cross of the Order of Merit (Italy), Grand Cross of the Order of Merit (First Class) (Finland), Order of the State (First Class, Yugoslavia), Order of Merit (Greece), Order of the State (First Class, Syria, Cen. African Repub.). *Publications include:* several articles in trade journals and for int. confs. *Leisure interests:* philately, photography, reading, swimming. *Address:* c/o MIDTAP Co., 22 El Badia Street, Heliopolis, Cairo; 8 Taha Hussein Street, Zamalek, Cairo, Egypt (home). *E-mail:* midtap@midtap.com.eg.

ABBAS, Mahmud, (Abu Mazen), PhD; Palestinian politician and head of state; *President;* b. 26 March 1935, Safad, Galilea; m. Amina Abbas; three s.; ed Damascus Univ., Syria, Moscow Univ., Russia; civil servant, UAE –1967; co-f. Fatah (largest political party in The Palestine Nat. Liberation Movt), mem. Cen. Cttee 1964–; elected to Palestine Liberation Org. (PLO) Exec. Cttee 1980, Head Pan-Arab and Int. Affairs Dept 1984, Sec.-Gen. PLO Exec. Cttee 1996–2004, Chair. 2004–; Exec. Pres. Palestinian Nat. Authority (PNA), known internationally as Palestinian Authority (PA) 2005–; participated in Middle East Peace Conf., Washington, DC and in Norwegian-mediated peace talks with Israel. *Publications:* more than 60 books, including The Other Side: the Secret Relationship Between Nazism and Zionism. *Address:* Office of the President, Ramallah, Palestinian Territories. *E-mail:* fateh@fateh.org. *Website:* president.ps.

ABBAS, Tan Sri Dato' Seri Shamsul Azhar, MSc; Malaysian oil industry executive; *Chairman, MMC Corporation Berhad;* ed Universiti Sains Malaysia, Univ. of Pennsylvania; fmr Chair. Malaysia Nat. Trust Fund; joined Petronas 1974, served in several sr positions, including Vice-Pres. Oil Business, Vice-Pres. Petrochemicals, Vice-Pres. Exploration (Upstream) and Vice-Pres. Maritime and Logistics, Man. Dir MISC (Petronas subsidiary) 2010–11, Chair. Petronas Carigali Sdn Berhad 2010–15 and Chair. Petronas Maritime Services Sdn Berhad, Pres. and CEO Petroliam Nasional Berhad (Petronas) 2010–15, Acting Chair. 2011–12, Dir Petronas Gas 2015–17, Acting Chair. Petronas Dagangan Berhad (also, mem. Bd of Dirs); Sr Ind. Dir (non-exec.), ENRA Group Berhad 2015–; Chair. MMC Corporation Berhad 2015–; PSE Kinsale Energy Ltd, PSE Seven Head Ltd, AET Tanker Holdings Sdn Berhad; fmr Pro-Chancellor Universiti Teknologi PETRONAS; mem. Bd of Trustees Razak School of Government (RSOG). *Address:* MMC Corporation Berhad, Ground Floor, Wisma Budiman, Persiaran Raja Chulan, 50200 Kuala Lumpur, Malaysia (office); ENRA Group Berhad, D2-U3-10, Block D2, Solaris Dutamas, No.1, Jalan Dutamas 1, Kuala Lumpur 50480, Malaysia (office). *Telephone:* (3) 20711000 (office); (3) 23003555 (office). *Fax:* (3) 20261921 (office); (3) 23003550 (office). *E-mail:* corporatecomm@mmc.com.my (office); info@enra.my (office). *Website:* www.mmc.com.my (office); www.enra.my (office).

ABBASI, Sardar Mehtab Ahmad Khan, LLB; Pakistani politician; b. 15 Dec. 1952, Malkot, Abbottabad; mem. Khyber Pakhtunkhwa Provincial Ass. 1986–2014; Chief Minister of Khyber-Pakhtunkhwa 1997–99; Senator 2003–08 (resgnd); mem. Nat. Ass. for NA-17 Abbottabad-I 2008–13; Fed. Minister for Railways 2008; Opposition Leader, Khyber Pakhtunkhwa Prov. Ass. 2013–14 (resgnd); Gov. of Khyber Pakhtunkhwa 2014–16 (resgnd); mem. and fmr Sr Vice-Pres. Pakistan Muslim League—Nawaz.

ABBASI, Shahid Khaqan, BS; Pakistani engineer, businessman and politician; b. 27 Dec. 1958, Karachi; s. of Khaqan Abbasi; m.; three s.; ed Lawrence Coll., Murree, Univ. of California, Los Angeles, George Washington Univ., USA; began his career as electrical engineer working in USA and Saudi Arabia; mem. Pakistan Muslim League—N (PML—N); mem. Nat. Ass. of Pakistan (Constituency NA-36) 1988–2002, (Constituency NA-50) 2008–18; apptd Parl. Sec. of Defence 1993, fmr Chair. Standing Cttee of Nat. Ass. on Defence; Chair. Pakistan Int. Airlines 1997–99; Founder and Chair. Airblue Ltd 2003–07, later COO; Minister Of Commerce March–May 2008, Minister for Petroleum and Natural Resources 2013–17, Minister of Planning and Devt 2017, Minister of Energy 2017; Prime Minister 2017–18, Chair. Econ. Coordination Cttee 2017. *Address:* c/o Pakistan Muslim League—N, 20H St 10, F-8/3, Islamabad, Pakistan (office). *Telephone:* (51) 2852662 (office). *Fax:* (51) 2852663 (office). *E-mail:* info@pmln.org (office). *Website:* pmln.org.

ABBASI, Zafar Mahmood; Pakistani naval officer; *Chief of Naval Staff* ed Pakistan Naval Acad., Britannia Royal Naval Coll., UK, Royal Australian Naval Coll., Nat. Defence Univ.; joined Pakistan Navy 1978; commissioned as Lt 1981, later joined Submarine Branch, received specialization in underwater warfare and surface warfare from USA; CO, PNS Khaiber 2001–03, commanded 21st Mine Squadron and 25th Destroyer Squadron 2005–07, promoted to the rank of Commodore with one-star 2008, Asst Chief of Naval Staff (ACNS), Operations, then ACNS, Plans 2008–10, fmr Chief Inspector; Commdt, Pakistan Naval Acad. 2010–11, also Dir-Gen. Maritime Security Agency; promoted to Flag officer commanding 2013, apptd Commdr of the Karachi Coast 2013, Commdr Pakistan Fleet 2014; Vice-Chief of Naval Staff June–Oct. 2017, Chief of Naval Staff 2017–; Nishan-i-Imtiaz. *E-mail:* webmaster@paknavy.gov.pk (office). *Website:* www.paknavy.gov.pk.

ABBOTT, Gregory (Greg) Wayne, BBA, JD; American lawyer, judge and politician; *Governor of Texas;* b. 13 Nov. 1957, Wichita Falls, Tex.; s. of Calvin Roger and Doris Lacristia (Jacks) Abbott; m. Cecilia Therese Phalen 1982; one d.; ed Univ. of Texas, Vanderbilt Univ. Law School; called to the Bar, Tex. 1985; Attorney, Butler & Binion, Houston, Tex. 1984–92; Trial Judge, 129th State Dist Court, Houston 1992–96; Justice, Texas Supreme Court 1996–2001; Attorney-Gen. State of Texas 2002–15; Gov. of Texas 2015–; mem. Texas Asscn of State Judges, Houston Young Lawyers Asscn, Houston Bar Asscn; Republican; Houston Bar Asscn Outstanding Young Lawyer 1994. *Address:* Office of the Governor, State Capitol, POB 12428, Austin, TX 78711-2428, USA (office). *Telephone:* (512) 463-2000 (office). *Fax:* (512) 463-1849 (office). *Website:* www.governor.state.tx.us (office).

ABBOTT, Hon. Anthony (Tony) John, LLB, MA; Australian politician; b. 14 Nov. 1957, London, England; m. Margaret Abbott; three d.; ed Univ. of Sydney, Univ. of Oxford, UK; began career as journalist and feature writer for The Bulletin and The Australian; Press Sec. and Political Adviser to John Hewson (Leader of the Opposition) 1990–93; Exec. Dir Australians for Constitutional Monarchy 1993–94; mem. House of Reps (Liberal) for Warringah 1994–, Parl. Sec. to Minister for Employment, Educ., Training and Youth Affairs 1996–98, also Leader of the House and Minister assisting the Prime Minister for Public Service 2001–03, Leader of the Opposition 2009–13, Prime Minister of Australia 2013–15; Minister for Employment, Workplace Relations and Small Business 2001, Minister for Health and Ageing 2003–07, Shadow Minister for Families, Community Services, Indigenous Affairs and the Voluntary Sector 2007–09; mem. Liberal Party of Australia, Leader 2009–15. *Publications include:* The Minimal Monarchy 1995, How to Win the Constitutional War 1997. *Address:* c/o Department of the Prime Minister and Cabinet, 1 National Circuit, Barton, ACT 2600, Australia (office). *Telephone:* (2) 6271-5111 (office). *Fax:* (2) 6271-5414 (office). *Website:* www.dpmc.gov.au (office); www.tonyabbott.com.au.

ABBOUD, A(lfred) Robert, AB, LLB, MBA; American banker and business executive; *President, A. Robert Abboud and Company;* b. 29 May 1929, Boston, Mass.; s. of Alfred Abboud and Victoria Abboud; m. Joan Grover Abboud 1955; one s. two d.; ed Harvard Coll., Harvard Law School, Harvard Business School; Asst Cashier, Int. Dept, First Nat. Bank of Chicago 1960, Asst Vice-Pres. Int. 1962, Vice-Pres. 1964, Sr Vice-Pres. 1969, Exec. Vice-Pres. 1972, Vice-Chair. 1973, Deputy Chair. of Bd 1974–75, Chair. of Bd 1975–80; Pres., COO and Dir Occidental Petroleum Corpn 1980–84; Pres. A. Robert Abboud and Co. (pvt. investment co.), Fox Grove, Ill. 1984–; Chair. Braeburn Capital Inc. 1984–92; Chair. and CEO First City Bancorp of Tex. Inc., Houston 1988–91, First City Nat. Bank of Houston 1988–91; Co-Chair. and Ind. Lead Dir Ivanhoe Energy Inc., Vancouver 2006–; fmr mem. Bd of Dirs AAR Corpn, Dir Cities Service, ICN Biomedicals, ICN Pharmaceuticals, Inland Steel Co., AMOCO, Hartmarx Corpn, Alberto-Culver Co.; Bronze Star, Purple Heart, US Marine Corps 1952; Baker Scholar, Harvard Business School 1958. *Publications include:* Introduction of US Commercial Paper in Foreign Markets: Premature and Perilous? 1970, A Proposed Course for US Trade and Investment Policies 1971, A Proposal to Help Reverse the Narrowing Balance in the US Balance of Trade 1971, The Outlook for a New Monetary System 1971, Opportunities for Foreign Banks in Singapore 1971, The International Competitiveness of US Banks and the US Economy 1972, Money in the Bank: How Safe Is It? 1988. *Address:* A. Robert Abboud & Co., 960 II Route 22, Suite 212, Fox River Grove, IL 60021 (office); 209 Braeburn Road, Barrington Hills, IL 60010, USA (home). *Telephone:* (847) 639-0101 (office); (847) 658-4808 (home). *Fax:* (847) 639-0233 (office). *E-mail:* araco@mc.net (office).

ABD AL-AZIZ, Muhammad Imhamid; Libyan government official; fmr mem. Perm. Mission of Libya to UN, New York; fmr Sr Crime Prevention and Criminal Justice Officer, UN Centre for Int. Crime Prevention, Vienna; Minister of Int. Co-operation 2012–13, Deputy Minister of Foreign Affairs –2013, Minister of Foreign Affairs and Int. Co-operation 2013–14.

ABDALLAH MANIRAKIZA, Hon. Tabu; Burundian politician; *Deputy Secretary-General, Economic Community for Central African States;* b. 6 Oct. 1956, Rumonge; m. Bertille Kabura; three s. one d.; spent 32 years in exile in Switzerland and Rwanda; returned to Burundi 2006; Dir of Budget and State Control, Ministry of Finance Nov. 2006–Feb. 2007, Minister of Planning 2007–10, Sr Adviser to Pres., Minister of Planning and Reconstruction 2010–12, of Finance and Planning for Econ. Devt 2012–16; led team of observers from Int. Conf. on the Great Lakes Region to S Sudan to observe independence referendum 2011; Deputy Sec.-Gen. Econ. Community for Central African States 2016–; mem. Conseil nat. pour la défense de la démocratie—Forces pour la défense de la démocratie; Diplomatic Award, BEN TV 2012. *Publications:* Step By Step On My Way 2018, On My Way Back Home 2018. *Address:* Economic Community of Central African States, PO Box 2112, Libreville, Gabon (office). *Telephone:* 01-44-47-31 (office). *E-mail:* ta.manirakiza@genie.africa (office). *Website:* www.ceeac-eccas.org (office).

ABDALLAHI, Sidi Ould Cheikh; Mauritanian politician and fmr head of state; b. 1938, Aleg; m. Khatou Mint El Boukhari; three s. one d.; ed École normale supérieure William Ponty, Senegal, Univ. of Dakar, Senegal and Univ. of Grenoble, France; Dir of Planning, Second Plan for the Econ. and Social Devt of Mauritania 1968–71; served in several govt positions including Minister of State for Nat. Economy 1971–78; Econ. Adviser, Kuwait Fund for Arab Econ. Devt, Kuwait 1982–85, Head of Econs and Finance, Niger Div. 1989–2003; Minister of Hydraulics and Energy 1986–87, of Fisheries and Maritime Economy 1987–89; Pres. of Mauritania 2007–08 (ousted in coup).

ABDEL-RAHMAN YOUSSEF, Ali, BSc, MSc, PhD; Egyptian construction engineer, academic, fmr university administrator and business executive; *Chairman, Engineering Consultation Office (E.C.O.);* ed Cairo Univ., McGill Univ. and Univ. of New Brunswick, Canada; instructor, Dept of Construction Eng, Cairo Univ. 1974–76, Asst Prof. 1976–81, Assoc. Prof. 1981–86, Prof. of Concrete Construction Design 1986–, Dir of Construction Eng Lab., Faculty of Eng 1991–, Vice-Dean of Educ. and Student Affairs 1995–2001, Dean Faculty of Eng 2001–04, Pres. Cairo Univ. 2004–08; Chair. Engineering Consultation Office (E.C.O.); Chair. Centre for Support of Architectural and Eng Designs; mem. Scientific Cttee Housing and Building Nat. Research Centre; State Prize for Eng Sciences 1985. *Address:* Engineering Consultation Office (E.C.O.), 3 Kambeez Street, Dokki, Giza, Egypt (office). *Telephone:* (2) 37492580 (office). *Fax:* (2) 37480227 (office). *E-mail:* eco_ar@aliabdelrahman.com (office). *Website:* aliabdelrahman.com (office).

ABDELA'ALI, Fawzi, BA, MA; Libyan lawyer and politician; b. 1971, Misrata; ed Univ. of Garyounis, Inst. of Higher Educ.; worked as a prosecutor at Misrata Cen. Court; fmr militia leader in Misrata; mem. Transitional Nat. Ass. 2011; Minister of the Interior 2011–12 (resgnd); Ind. *Address:* c/o Ministry of the Interior, Tripoli, Libya.

ABDELAZIZ, Maged Abdelfattah; Egyptian diplomatist and UN official; b. 1954; m.; one d.; ed Ain Shams Univ. School of Law; joined diplomatic service 1979, served in several positions in Ministry of Foreign Affairs including Int. Orgs Div., Legal and Treaties Dept 1979–83 (Head 1987–89), Second and First Sec., Perm. Mission to UN, New York 1983–87, Political Counsellor in charge of Middle East, Arab-Soviet Relations, Int. Orgs and Disarmament, Embassy in Moscow 1989–93, Head, Specialized Agencies Dept, Multilateral Sector, Ministry of Foreign Affairs 1993–95, Political Counsellor, Office of Perm. Rep. to UN, New York 1995–97, Prin. Rep. in all disarmament issues 1997–99, Deputy Perm. Rep. to UN 1997–99, Co-ordinator, Del. during membership on Security Council 1996–97, apptd Rep. in Expert Group, UN Sec.-Gen., UN Register for Conventional Arms 1997, apptd Chair. Disarmament Comm. 1999, Diplomatic Adviser and Official Spokesman of Pres. 1999–2005; Amb. and Perm. Rep. to UN, New York 2005–12; Special Adviser to the UN Sec.-Gen. on Africa 2012–18.

ABDELKERIM, Mahamat Nour; Chadian fmr rebel leader and government official; b. eastern Chad; trained in French mil. schools; f. Rally for Democracy and Liberty (RDL) 2005; fmr rebel leader of United Front for Democratic Change (FUC), signed peace deal with Govt 2006; Minister of Nat. Defence March–Dec. 2007 (dismissed); took refuge in Libyan embassy. *Address:* c/o Ministry of National Defence, BP 916, N'Djamena, Chad.

ABDELMAHMOUT, Issa Mahamat; Chadian politician; *Minister of Finance and the Budget;* ed Univ. de Poitiers, Univ. de Tours; long career in Ministry of Finance and the Budget, including as Inspector, Gen. Inspectorate of Finances, Div. Man. (Financial Control), Deputy Inspector Gen. of State 2017–18, Minister of Finance and the Budget 2018–. *Publication:* Tchad: Comment sortir de la crise économique: causes, conséquences et solutions 2017. *Address:* Ministry of Finance and the Budget, BP 144, N'Djamena, Chad (office). *Telephone:* 98639818 (mobile) (office). *E-mail:* contact@finances.gouv.td (office). *Website:* finances.gouv.td (office).

ABDENUR, Roberto, BSc, LLB; Brazilian diplomatist (retd); b. 5 May 1942, Rio de Janeiro; m.; three c.; ed London School of Econs, UK, Pontifical Catholic Univ. of Rio de Janeiro; joined Ministry of External Relations 1964, with Div. of Communications and Archives 1964–65, Trade Policy Div. 1966–67, Acting Head of Tech. Section of Analysis and Planning 1968, Sec. for Policy Planning 1968, Staff of Cabinet of Minister of External Relations 1969, Asst to Sec.-Gen. 1975–78, in charge of econ. and trade matters at Ministry 1979–84, Sec.-Gen. (Deputy Minister) of External Relations 1993–95, Deputy Consulate Gen. then Consulate Gen. in London 1969–73, First Sec., Embassy in Washington, DC 1973–75, Amb. to Ecuador 1985–88, to China 1989–93, to Germany 1995–2002, to Austria 2002–03, to USA 2004–06 (retd); Exec. Vice-Pres. Instituto Brasileiro de Ética Concorrencial—ETCO (Brazilian Inst. for Ethics in Competition) –2014, now mem. Advisory Bd. *Address:* c/o Instituto Brasileiro de Ética Concorrencial, Rua Viradouro 63, CEP 04538-110 São Paulo SP, Brazil (office). *Website:* www.etco.org.br (office).

ABDESSALEM, Rafik Ben, BA, PhD; Tunisian politician; b. 1968; m. Soumaya Ghannouchi; ed Mohammed V Univ., Rabat, Morocco, Univ. of Westminster, UK; mem. Exec. Office, Union Générale des Etudiants de Tunisie (UGET) 1987–90; in exile in Morocco and later in London during rule of Zine el Abidine Ben Ali; f. Maghreb Center for Research and Translation, London; Chair. London Platform for Dialogue; fmr Visiting Scholar, Oxford Centre for Islamic Studies; Sr Researcher and Head of Research and Studies Office, Al Jazeera Centre for

Studies, Doha; Minister of Foreign Affairs 2011–13; mem. Hizb al-Nahdah (now Parti de la Renaissance/Hizb al-Nahdah), fmr mem. party bureau in exile, mem. Political Bureau, mem. Exec. Bureau in charge of media 2001–07; mem. Shura council. *Publications include:* La religion, la laïcité et la démocratie, Les États Unis d'Amérique entre la force dure et la force douce, Les réformes islamiques et la modernité; regular contributor to Asharq Al-Awsat (int. Arabic daily newspaper). *Address:* Parti de la Renaissance/Hizb al-Nahdah, rue Elless, ave Muhammad V, Montplaisir, 1073 Tunis, Tunisia (office). *Telephone:* (71) 900-907 (office). *Fax:* (71) 901-679 (office). *E-mail:* webmaster@nahdha.tn (office). *Website:* www.ennahdha .tn (office).

ABDIĆ, Fikret 'Babo' (Papa); Bosnia and Herzegovina/Croatian politician and business executive; b. 29 Sept. 1939, Donja Vidovska, Velika Kladuša; one d.; Dir Agrokomerc co. 1980s; charged with fraud in Fmr Yugoslavia 1987, convicted, sentenced to two years' imprisonment, acquitted on appeal 1989; Co-founder (with Alijah Izetbegović), Party of Democratic Action (PDA); set up autonomous region of W Bosnia in defiance of Cen. Govt in Sarajevo 1993, his forces were crushed by Pres. Izetbegović 1995; fled to Croatia in 1995, f. pvt. food co.; f. political party Democratic People's Union (DNZ) 1996; accused of war crimes by Bosnia 2001; extradition to Bosnia repeatedly refused by Croatian Govt on account of his Croatian citizenship; sentenced by Croatian court to 20 years' imprisonment for war crimes committed during Bosnian war 1993–95 July 2002, reduced on appeal to 15 years' imprisonment, released March 2012; permitted by Bosnian Election Comm. to run for Muslim post in three-man inter-ethnic presidency while still in prison Oct. 2002.

ABDILDIN, Serikbolsyn Abdildayevich, DEcon; Kazakhstani politician; *Chairman, Kazakstan Kommunistik Partiyasy (CPK—Communist Party of Kazakhstan);* b. 25 Nov. 1937, Kyzylkesek, Semipalatinsk; m. Abdildina Laura; one s. one d.; ed Kazakh Nat. Agric. Univ., KasGoz Post-Grad. Coll.; mem. CP of Soviet Union 1964–91; Minister of Agric. 1985–87; mem. Kazakstan Kommunistik Partiyasy (CPK—CP of Kazakhstan) 1981–91, First Sec. (Leader) 1991–2010, Chair. 2010–; Deputy Supreme Council 1985–94, Deputy in Majlis (Nat. Ass.) 1999–2004, First Speaker 1991–94; joined Socialist Party of Kazakhstan (SPK) 1993; unsuccessful cand. in Kazakh presidential elections 1999; joined Democratic Choice of Kazakhstan (DCK—opposition movt) 2001; Deputy Chair. Union of CP 2004–; Prof., Kazakh Nat. Agric. Univ. 1995–. *Publications:* more than 200 scientific publs 1964–2011. *Leisure interests:* fishing, hunting. *Address:* 114 Pushkin Street, Almaty (office); Communist Party of Kazakhstan, 010000 Nur-Sultan, Beibitshilik kosh. 27/49, Kazakhstan (office). *Telephone:* (7172) 21-32-97 (office); (7017) 22-42-49 (home). *Fax:* (7172) 21-32-97 (office). *E-mail:* pravdakz@ list.ru (office).

ÄBDIQALİQOVA, Gülşara Nawşaqızı, PhD; Kazakhstani politician; *Secretary, Ministry of Labour and Social Protection;* b. 15 May 1965; ed Jambıl Technological Inst. of Light and Food Industries; Sr Insp. and Head of Dept, Qızılorda Regional Dept of Social Security 1987–94; consultant, Cttee of Supreme Council of Repub. of Kazakhstan on social protection of the population 1994–95; worked in Ministry of Labour and Social Protection as Chief of Dept, Deputy Head, Head of Pensions Man., Deputy Dir of Social Welfare Dept, Dir of Dept of Social Security and Social Assistance, Dir of Dept of Pensions and Regulation Incomes 1995–2003; Deputy Minister of Labour and Social Protection 2003–05, 2006–07; Chair. JSC Life Insurance Co.– State Annuity Co. 2005–06; Sec., Ministry of Labour and Social Protection 2007–08, 2015–; Adviser to Pres. of Kazakhstan 2008–09, 2009–12; Chair. Nat. Comm. for Women, Family and Demographic Policy under Pres. of Kazakhstan 2008–09; Minister of Labour and Social Protection 2009–12; Deputy Prime Minister, responsible for Human Devt 2014. *Address:* Ministry of Labor and Social Protection of Population, 010000 Nur-Sultan, Mangilik El Street 8, House of the Ministries, Front Door 6, Kazakhstan (office). *Telephone:* (7172) 74-37-23 (office). *E-mail:* kense@enbek.gov.kz (office). *Website:* www.enbek.gov.kz (office).

ÄBDIRAHMANOV, Qairat Qudaibergenulı; Kazakhstani diplomatist; b. 21 April 1964, Panfilov, Taldıqorğan Oblast (now Jarkent, Almatı Oblast), Kazakh SSR, USSR; m. Maira Äbdirahmanova; two c.; ed Kazakh State Nat. Univ.; joined Ministry of Foreign Affairs as Third Sec. in Europe Dept 1993, Deputy Chief, then Chief of Asia Dept 1994–98, also served as Deputy Dir Asia, Middle East and Africa Dept and as Dir Dept of Europe and the Americas, Dir Dept of Bilateral Co-operation 1998–99, Deputy Minister of Foreign Affairs 1999–2001, Deputy Chief of Mission and Minister-Counsellor in London 2001–03, Amb. to Israel 2003–06, Deputy Minister of Foreign Affairs 2006–07, Amb. to Austria and Perm. Rep. to Int. Orgs in Vienna 2007–08, Amb. and Perm. Rep. to OSCE, Vienna 2008–11, Chair. Perm. Council 2010, Amb. to Austria and Perm. Rep. to Int. Orgs, Vienna 2011–14, Amb. and Perm. Rep. to UN, New York 2014–16, Minister of Foreign Affairs 2016–18. *Address:* c/o Ministry of Foreign Affairs, 010000 Nur-Sultan, D. Kunaev kösh. 31, Kazakhstan (office).

ABDIU, Fehmi, DrIur; Albanian judge and academic; b. 5 Jan. 1944, Dibra; m.; two c.; ed Faculty of Law, Tirana Univ., Teachers' Training School, Peshkopi; Judge, Fieri Dist Court 1968–73, Deputy Chief 1974–77, Chief 1977–85; Chief, Tirana Dist Court 1989–90; Judge, Supreme Court 1985–89, Deputy Chief 1990–92; mem. Parl. 1991–98; mem. Constitutional Court 1998–2010, Pres. 1998–2004; Dean, Faculty of Law, Illyria Univ., Tirana; Golden Order Naim Frashëri 2004. *Publications include:* The Politic According to the Constitution and Laws, Constitution and the Constitutional Court of the Republic of Albania, The Constitution, the Law and the Justice, Civil Action During Criminal Process. *Address:* Bulevard "Zhan D'Ark" Pallati 4, Ap. 1, Kati 9, Albania (home). *Telephone:* (5) 422-8125 (home).

ABDOOL KARIM, Quarraisha, BS, MS, PhD; South African epidemiologist and academic; *Professor of Epidemiology, Mailman School of Public Health, Columbia University;* b. 28 March 1960, Durban, KwaZulu-Natal; m. Prof. Salim Safurdeen Abdool Karim; ed Univ. of the Witwatersrand, Univ. of Durban-Westville, Columbia Univ., USA, Univ. of Pretoria, Univ. of Natal; Prof., Centre for the AIDS Programme of Research in South Africa (CAPRISA), Nelson R. Mandela School of Medicine, Univ. of KwaZulu-Natal, currently Assoc. Scientific Dir; also currently Prof. in Clinical Epidemiology, Mailman School of Public Health, Columbia Univ.; Visiting Scientist, Massachusetts Gen. Hosp.; Visiting Lecturer, Harvard Univ.; Chair. South African Nat. AIDS Council Prevention Tech. Task Team; mem. UNAIDS Scientific Expert Panel, Scientific Advisor to Exec. Dir of UNAIDS, New Specialist Amb. for UNAIDS 2017–; mem. Advisory Bd, Higher Educ. and Training HIV/AIDS Programme (HEAIDS); mem. Scientific Advisory Bd, US Pres.'s Emergency Plan for AIDS Relief (PEPFAR), Chair. PEPFAR Adolescent Girls and Young Women Expert Working Group; mem. HIV Centre Strategic Advisory Cttee, NIH OAR Microbicides Planning Group; mem. Editorial Bd, HIV Clinical Trials, AIDS, JIAS; mem. Acad. of Science of South Africa; Foreign Assoc. mem. US Nat. Acad. of Medicine; Fellow, African Acad. of Sciences (Vice-Pres., Southern African Region), Royal Soc. of South Africa, Acad. of Sciences for the Developing World (fmrly Third World Acad. of Sciences—TWAS); Order of Mapungubwe (Bronze); TWAS-Lenovo Science Prize, SAMRC Scientific Merit Award, Science-for-Society Gold Medal, ASSAF Award, African Union Kwame Nkrumah Science Award, L'Oréal-UNESCO Award for Women in Science (Africa and the Arab States) 2016. *Achievements include:* most important scientific contribution to HIV prevention is CAPRISA 004 tenofovir gel trial which demonstrated effectiveness of coitally-applied tenofovir gel in preventing HIV and HSV-2 acquisition in women; has played key role in building science base in southern Africa through the Columbia Univ.–Southern African Fogarty AIDS Int. Training and Research Programme since 1998. *Publications include:* several books and book chapters and more than 170 peer-reviewed papers in professional journals. *Address:* PH18, Mailman School of Public Health, Columbia University, 720 West 168th Street, New York, NY 10032, USA (office). *Telephone:* (212) 305-9081 (office). *Fax:* (212) 305-9080 (office). *E-mail:* qa4@columbia.edu (office). *Website:* www.mailman.columbia.edu (office).

ABDOU MADI, Mohamed; Comoran politician and diplomatist; b. 1956, Mjamaoue; m.; five c.; ed Algeria, Poland; tax insp., Moroni 1988; convicted of fraud, served sentence as a domestic servant; Perm. Sec., CTRAP (org. funded by UNDP to implement reforms in civil service) –1994; Sec.-Gen. Rassemblement pour la Démocratie et le Renouveau (RDR); Prime Minister of the Comoros 1994, also responsible for Public Works; Minister of Justice, Public Affairs, Employment, Professional Training, Admin. Decentralization and Institutional Reform 1998; Adviser, Embassy in Madagascar 2000; joined govt of Anjouan leader Colonel Mohamed Bacar 2007, govt removed from office by combined Comoros and African Union Force 2008.

ABDOULFATAH CHARIF, Mohamed Bakri Ben, LenD; Comoran lawyer, diplomatist and politician; *Vice-President, Supreme Court;* ed Univ. of Garyounis, Benghazi, Libya; fmr teacher of Arabic; fmr Pres. Tribunal de Première Instance, Fomboni; Sec.-Gen., Ministry of Justice 1992, Pres., Tribunal de Mohéli 1996; took part in drafting of new Constitution 1999; mem. Cour Constitutionelle (Constitutional Court) 2004–06; Amb. to Libya 2006–11; Minister of External Relations and Co-operation, with responsibility for the Diaspora and Francophone and Arab Relations 2011–13, Minister-in-Charge of Finance and Budget and Minister of Justice 2015; fmr advisor to Supreme Court, apptd Vice-Pres. 2016.

ABDRASHITOV, Vadim Yusupovich; Russian film director; b. 19 Jan. 1945, Kharkov, Ukraine; s. of Yusup Sh. Abdrashitov and Galina Abdrashitov; m. Natella G. Toidze; one s. one d.; ed Moscow State Inst. of Cinematography (VGIK); mem. Russian Film Acad., Russian Union of Cinematographers; Order of the Fatherland, Fourth Class 2006; RSFSR State Prize 1984, State Prize of the USSR 1991, People's Artist of Russia 1996. *Films include:* Witness for the Defence (USSR Riga Prize) 1977, The Turning 1978, Foxhunting 1980, The Train Has Stopped 1982, The Parade of the Planets 1984, Plumbum, or a Dangerous Game (Gold Medal, Venice Festival 1987) 1986, The Servant (Alfred Bauer Prize 1989) 1988, Armavir 1991, The Play for a Passenger (Silver Bear Award, Berlin Festival 1995) 1995, Time of the Dancer 1997, Magnetic Storms 2003. *Address:* 119270 Moscow, 3d. Frunzenskaya 9, Apt 211, Russia. *Telephone:* (495) 242-35-54.

ABDRISAEV, Baktybek, PhD; Kyrgyzstani diplomatist, scientist and academic; b. 17 April 1958, Bishkek; s. of Dyushen Abdrisaev and Kalicha Jakypova; m. Cholpon Akmatalieva; two c.; ed Bishkek Polytechnical Inst. (now Kyrgyz Tech. Univ.), Inst. of Electronics, Acad. of Sciences of Belarus; Jr Scientific Fellow, Bishkek Polytechnical Inst. 1980–84, Sr Scientific Fellow 1987–88; Scientific Fellow, Inst. of Physics, Acad. of Sciences of Kyrgyz Repub. 1988–91, Sr Scientific Fellow 1991–92; staff expert, Pres.'s Dept of Int. Relations 1992–93, Head of Dept 1993–96; mem. Parl. 1995–2000; Amb. to USA and Canada 1996–2005; currently Lecturer, Utah Valley Univ., USA; mem. European Acad. of Natural Sciences 2004–, Russian Acad. of Natural Sciences 2005–; Hon. Prof., Int. Univ. of Kyrgyzstan 2006; Union of Youth of Kyrgyzstan Scientific Achievement Award 1992. *Publications include:* Kyrgyzstan's Voice in Washington 2005; more than 100 scientific articles and presentations on applied optics, diplomacy and sustainable mountain development. *Leisure interests:* hiking, table tennis. *Address:* Utah Valley University, Department of History and Political Science, 800 West University Parkway, Orem, UT 84058, USA (office). *Telephone:* (801) 863-8351 (office). *Fax:* (801) 863-7013 (office). *E-mail:* abdrisba@uvu.edu (office). *Website:* www.uvu.edu (office).

ABDUL, Paula Julie; American singer and choreographer; b. 19 June 1962, San Fernando, Calif.; d. of Harry Abdul and Lorraine Abdul; m. 1st Emilio Estevez 1992 (divorced 1994); m. 2nd Brad Beckerman 1996 (divorced 1998); ed Van Nuys High School, Northridge Coll. California State Univ.; choreographer, LA Laker basketball cheerleaders; choreographer for several bands, including Duran Duran, Toto, The Pointer Sisters, ZZ Top; scenes in films Bull Durham, Coming To America, The Waiting Game, The Doors, Touched By Evil, Junior High School; City of Crime video (from film Dragnet); worldwide performances as singer include tours throughout USA, UK, Japan and Far East; f. Co Dance (dance co.); series judge, various TV series including: American Idol: The Search for a Superstar 2002–09, The X Factor (USA) 2011–12, So You Think You Can Dance 2014–; Rolling Stone Award for Best Female Singer 1989, American Music Awards for Favorite Pop/Rock Female Vocalist 1989, 1992, Billboard Magazine Top Female Pop Album 1990, Grammy Award for Best Music Video (for Opposites Attract) 1991, Starlight Foundation Humanitarian of the Year, Los Angeles 1992. *Choreography includes:* pop videos: The Jacksons and Mick Jagger's Torture, George Michael's Monkey, Janet Jackson's Control, Nasty (MTV Video Award for best choreography 1987), When I Think Of You, What Have You Done For Me Lately; television: Dolly Parton Christmas Special, Tracey Ullman Show (Emmy Award for best choreography) 1989. *Television includes:* as series judge: American

Idol: The Search for a Superstar 2002–09, Live to Dance 2011, The X Factor (USA version) 2011–12, So You Think You Can Dance (Australian version) 2014, (USA version) 2015–16. *Recordings include:* albums: Forever Your Girl 1989, Shut Up And Dance (The Dance Mixes) 1990, Spellbound 1991, Head Over Heels 1995, Greatest Hits 2000. *Website:* www.paulaabdul.com.

ABDUL HADI, Mahdi, PhD; Palestinian research institute director; *Chairman, Palestinian Academic Society for the Study of International Affairs (PASSIA);* ed Bradford Univ., UK; Co-Founder and Ed. Al-Fajr daily newspaper 1972–74; Co-Founder and Gen. Sec. Council for Higher Educ. in the West Bank 1977–80; Founder and Pres. Arab Thought Forum, Jerusalem 1977–81; special adviser to Ministry of Occupied Land Affairs, Amman, Jordan 1985–86; Founder and Chair., Bd of Trustees, Palestinian Academic Soc. for Study of Int. Affairs (PASSIA) 1987–; Co-Founder, Black Sea Univ. Foundation, Bucharest 1990, Jerusalem National Cttee 1992, EuroMeSCo Network 1995; mem. Arab Thought Forum, Amman 2002; mem. Christian Dialogue in Beirut 2000, Jerusalem Arab Council, Palestinian Council for Justice and Peace, Asscn of Palestinian Policy Research Insts; mem. Bd of Trustees, Yasser Arafat Foundation, Cairo 2009–. *Publications:* Awakening Sleeping Horses 2000; numerous articles, monographs and essays in newspapers and journals. *Address:* Palestinian Academic Society for the Study of International Affairs (PASSIA), 13, Hind Al-Husseini Street, Alley 2, Wadi Al-Joz, POB 19545, Jerusalem, Israel (office). *Telephone:* 2-6264426 (office). *Fax:* 2-6282819 (office). *E-mail:* passia@passia.org (office). *Website:* www.passia.org (office).

ABDUL-JABBAR, Kareem; American basketball coach, writer and fmr professional basketball player; b. (Ferdinand Lewis Alcindor, Jr), 16 April 1947, New York; s. of Lewis Alcindor and Cora Alcindor; ed Power Memorial High School, Univ. of California, Los Angeles; graduated as the leading scorer in UCLA history (2,325 points); played for Nat. Basketball Asscn (NBA) Milwaukee Bucks 1969–75, for NBA Los Angeles Lakers 1975–89; All NBA First Team 1971–74, 1976–77, 1980–81, 1984, 1986; NBA All-Defensive First Team 1974–75, 1979–81; retd from game 1989; Asst Coach Alchesay High School (Whiteriver, AZ) 1999–2000; Asst Coach NBA LA Clippers 2000; Asst Coach NBA Indiana Pacers 2002; Head Coach USBLs Oklahoma Storm 2002; Asst Coach Los Angeles Lakers 2005; NBA career records include: most minutes (57,446), most points (33,387), most field goals made (15,837), most field goals attempted (28,307), most blocks (3,189); first player in NBA history to play 20 seasons; 1,560 games played; 18 NBA All-Star games played; named Cultural Amb. for US 2012; All-City 1963–65, All-American 1963–65, Consensus All-American 1963–65, First Team All-America 1967, 1968, 1969, Nat. Player of the Year 1967, 1969, Nat. Collegiate Athletic Asscn (NCAA) Tournament Most Outstanding Player 1967, 1968, 1969, Naismith Award Winner 1969, NBA Rookie of the Year 1970, NBA Most Valuable Player—MVP 1971, 1972, 1974, 1976, 1977, 1980, NBA Finals MVP 1971, 1975, Sports Illustrated Sportsman of the Year 1985, elected to Basketball's Hall of Fame 1995, Presidential Medal of Freedom 2016. *Publications include:* Giant Steps (with Peter Knobler) 1983, Kareem (with Mignon McCarthy) 1990, On the Shoulders of Giants: My Journey Through the Harlem Renaissance (with Raymond Obstfeld) 2007, What Color Is My World? The Lost History of African American Inventors (with Raymond Obstfeld) 2012. *Website:* kareemabduljabbar.com.

ABDUL JALIL, Mustafa Mohammed; Libyan politician and judge; b. 1952, Al Bayda; ed Dept of Shari'a and Law, Arabic Language and Islamic Studies Faculty, Univ. of Libya; apptd Asst to Sec. of Public Prosecutor, Al Bayda, before being apptd a judge in 1978; Pres. Court of Appeals, then Pres. of the Court, Al Bayda 2002–07; Minister of Justice (under Col Gaddafi) 2007–11, resgnd after being sent to Benghazi to negotiate the release of hostages taken by rebels 21 Feb. 2011; Chair. Nat. Transitional Council of Libya March 2011–Aug. 2012; trial before a military court in connection with the killing of former interior minister Abdel-Fattah Younis announced 2013.

ABDUL-RAHMAN, Tan Sri Datuk Omar, PhD, MVD, MRCVS, FASc; Malaysian professor of veterinary pathology and university administrator; b. 9 Nov. 1932, Kota Bharu, Kelantan; three c.; ed Sydney and Queensland Univs, Australia and Univ. of Cambridge, UK; Demonstrator in Veterinary Pathology, Queensland Univ. 1959; Veterinary Research Officer, Veterinary Research Inst., Ipoh 1960–67, Sr Research Officer 1967–70, Deputy Dir 1971–72; Foundation Prof. and Dean, Faculty of Veterinary Medicine and Animal Sciences, Universiti Putra Malaysia 1972–78, Prof. of Veterinary Pathology 1982–2001, Deputy Vice-Chancellor 1982–84; apptd Pres. Malaysian Scientific Asscn 1984, currently Adviser; fmr Pres. Asscn of Veterinary Surgeons Malaysia–Singapore; mem. Nat. Council for Scientific Research and Devt, Malaysia, Nat. Comm. for UNESCO, Nat. Devt Planning Cttee of Malaysia 1984; Adviser to Prime Minister on Science and Tech. 1985–2001; Exec. Chair. Venture Capital for Tech. Acquisition 2001–07; apptd Pres. and CEO Malaysia Univ. of Science and Tech. (MUST); Founding Chair. Commonwealth Partnership for Tech. Man. (CPTM); Founding Pres. and Sr Fellow, Malaysian Acad. of Sciences; Pres. Malaysian Asscn of Professional Speakers 2006–; Founding Chair. Malaysian Tech. Devt Corpn, Tech. Park Malaysia Corpn; Founding Jt Chair. Malaysian Industry-Govt Group for High Tech.; Founding Fellow, Islamic Acad. of Sciences; Fellow, Acad. of Sciences for the Third World; mem. Editorial Advisory Bd Tropical Veterinarian (journal) 1983–; Exec. Chair. Kumpulan Modal Perdana Sdn Bhd; mem. Bd of Dirs OSK Ventures Int. Bhd, Green Packet Bhd, Encorp Bhd, Kotra Industries Bhd, Great Wall Plastic Industries Bhd, BCT Tech. Bhd; Hon. Fellow, Nat. Acad. of Sciences of Kyrgyz Repub.; Dr hc (Stirling) 1986, (Melbourne), (Guelph), (Bristol), (Queensland); Asean Achievement Award (Science) 1993, Fook Ying Tung South East Asia Prize 1998, Tun Abdul Razak Award (Int. Category) 2000; Darjah Mulia Seri Melaka (state award), Johan Setia Mahkota, Johan Mangku Negara and Panglima Setia Mahkota (fed. awards). *Publications include:* over 100 publs on science and tech. *Address:* c/o MUST Ehsan Foundation, Malaysia University of Science and Technology, Unit GL33 (Ground Floor), Block C, Kelana Square, 17, Jalan SS7/26, 47301 Petaling Jaya, Selangor D.E; Malaysian Association of Professional Speakers, c/o Suite 47-4, 4th Floor, PJ Highway Centre, Jalan 51/205, 46050 Petaling Jaya, Selangor, Malaysia. *E-mail:* info@maps.org.my (home).

ABDULAI, Yesufu Seyyid Momoh; Nigerian economist and international organization official; b. 19 June 1940, Auchi; s. of Momoh Abdulai and Haijia Fatimah Abdulai; m. Zene Makonnen Abdulai 1982; three s. one d.; ed Mount Allison Univ. and McGill Univ., Canada; taught econs in Canada; Tech. Asst to Exec. Dir (Africa Group I), World Bank Group, Washington, DC 1971–73, Adviser to Exec. Dir 1973–78, Alternate Exec. Dir for Africa Group 1 1978–80, Exec. Dir 1980–82, Vice-Chair. Jt Audit Cttee Exec. Bd 1980–82; Chair. Jt Secr. African Exec. Dirs of World Bank Group and the IMF 1975–77; Man. Dir and CEO Fed. Mortgage Bank of Nigeria 1982–83; Dir-Gen. OPEC Fund for Int. Devt 1983–2003; mem. Prize Cttee, Arab Gulf Programme for UN Devt Orgs (AGFUND) Int. Prize for Pioneering Devt Projects; Grand Decoration of Honour (Austria) 2004. *Leisure interests:* sport, reading, photography, listening to music.

ABDULATIPOV, Ramazan Gadzhimuradovich, DPhilSc; Russian/Dagestan politician, diplomatist and university administrator; b. 4 Aug. 1946, Guerguta, Dagestan; m.; two s. one d.; ed Dagestan State Univ.; mem. CPSU 1973–91; CP work 1974–76; Sr Teacher, Dagestan Pedagogical Inst. 1975–76; Head of Murmansk Higher School of Marine Eng 1978–87; Head of Sector, Div. of Int. Relations of CPSU Cen. Cttee 1988–90; RSFSR People's Deputy 1990–93, Chair. Council of Nationalities 1990–93; elected to Council of Fed. 1993, Deputy Chair. 1994–96; mem. State Duma 1995–97; Deputy Prime Minister 1997–98, Minister of Nat. Policy 1998–99; Rep. of Saratov Region in Council of Fed. 2000–05; Amb. to Tajikistan 2005–08; Pres. Ass. of Peoples of Russia 1998–; Pres. of Dagestan 2013–17; Rector Moscow State Univ. of Culture and Arts; participant in numerous peace-making missions on N Caucasus; Pres. Fed. of UNESCO Clubs in Russia; mem. Russian Acad. of Natural Sciences. *Publications:* Lenin's Policy of Internationalism in USSR, Internationalism and the Spiritual and Moral Development of the Peoples of Dagestan, What is the Essence of Your Being?, Power and Conscience, Nature and Paradoxes of National Consciousness Authority of Sense, Ethnic Question and State Structure of Russia: From Cran Tower to the Kremlin Gates, Inscriptions. *Leisure interests:* painting, aphoristic poetry.

ABDULLA, Ahmed; Maldivian newspaper publisher, fmr politician and fmr diplomatist; b. 26 Sept. 1949, Malé; s. of Abdullah Hassan and Hawwa Fulhu; m. Ameena Abdulla; one s. three d.; Asst Clerk/Calligrapher, Viyafaari Miadhu daily newspaper 1965–66; primary school teacher, English and Dhivehi Aliya School 1966–68; Asst to the Ed., Vaguthu daily newspaper 1966–68; Clerk, Ministry of Educ. 1967–68; Clerk, Prime Minister's Office 1968; Sec., Minister Bureau, Ministry of Health 1968–69, Minister Bureau, Ministry of Educ. 1969–72; Asst to the Sec., Prime Minister's Office 1972–73; Third Sec., Embassy in Colombo 1973–75; Asst to the Minister of Transport 1975–77; Under-Sec., Ministry of External Affairs 1977–78, Perm. Mission of Maldives to UN, New York 1977–78, Sr Under-Sec., Ministry of External Affairs 1979, Head of Embassy in Colombo 1979–86, High Commr to Sri Lanka 1986–88 (also accred to India, Pakistan, Bangladesh and as Amb. to Nepal and Bhutan) 1988–95; Minister of Health 1993–2004; mem. Parl. 1995–2009; Minister of Information, Arts and Culture 2004–05; Acting Minister of Foreign Affairs 2005; Minister of Environment, Energy and Water 2005–08 (resgnd); mem. Maldivian Democratic Party 2010; Founder, Owner and Chair. Miadhu News (newspaper) 1995–2013. *Leisure interests:* calligraphy, reading, sports fishing, badminton, swimming. *Address:* G. Mescot, Lonuziyaarai Magu, Malé (home); c/o Miadhu News, G. Maple Leaf, Ameenee Magu, Malé, Maldives. *Telephone:* 3322557 (home); 3320700. *Fax:* 3321504 (home); 3320500. *E-mail:* admin@miadhu.com.mv. *Website:* www.miadhu.mv.

ABDULLAH, Abdullah, DMed; Afghan ophthalmologist and politician; *Chief Executive (Prime Minister);* b. 5 Sept. 1960, second dist of Karte Parwan, Kabul; s. of Ghulam Muhayuddine Khan and Siddiqa Muhayuddine Khan; m.; one s. three d.; ed Naderia High School, Faculty of Medicine, Kabul Univ.; completed training in ophthalmology 1983, subsequently served as a specialist at Noor Eye Hosp., Kabul; went to Pakistan during Soviet occupation to care for Afghan refugee families at Sayed Jamal-U-Din Hosp. 1984; joined the Afghan Freedom Fighters 1985, served as caretaker in charge of health affairs for Panjshir Valley resistance front; became an adviser and close companion of Ahmad Shah Massoud; Mujahidin activist, Jamiat-i-Islami group; Sr Spokesman, Defence Ministry 1992–96; Deputy Minister of Foreign Affairs, Northern Alliance 1999, caretaker Minister of Foreign Ministry for the officially recognized govt-in-exile of the Islamic Repub. of Afghanistan from 1999 until the collapse of the Taliban 2001; participated in Future of Afghanistan Govt Talks, Bonn Nov. 2001; Minister of Foreign Affairs, Afghan Interim Authority Dec. 2001–June 2002, Afghan Transitional Authority 2002–04, of Afghanistan 2004–06; Sec.-Gen. Massoud Foundation 2006–09; cand. in presidential election 2009 (withdrew from runoff election Nov. 2009); Chief Exec. (Prime Minister) of Afghanistan 29 Sept. 2014–; f. Coalition for Change and Hope (now National Coalition of Afghanistan) 2009. *Leisure interests:* music, swimming, ping-pong. *Address:* Office of Special Assistant to the Chief Executive of the Islamic Republic of Afghanistan, Kabul, Afghanistan (office). *E-mail:* a.z.anwari@ceo.gov.af (office). *Website:* ceo.gov.af/en (office).

ABDULLAH, Burhanuddin, BAgric, MA; Indonesian economist and fmr central banker; b. 10 July 1947, Garut, West Java; m. Ike Juliawati; ed School of Agric., Tanjungsari, Padjadjaran Univ. Bandung, Michigan State Univ., USA; joined Bank Indonesia 1979, worked in Credit Dept 1981, later with Econ. Research and Statistics Dept, then Personal Asst to Gov.; joined IMF, Washington, DC 1989, Asst Exec. Dir 1990–93; Head Econ. Co-operation and Int. Trade Div., Indonesia 1993–95; Deputy Dir for Int. Affairs 1995–96; Deputy Dir Econ. Research and Monetary Policy Dept 1996–98; Deputy Gov. Bank Indonesia 2000–03, Gov. 2003–08, also Gov of IMF for Indonesia; Co-ordinating Minister of Econ. Affairs June–Aug. 2001; Chair. Advisory Bd, Padjadjaran University Alumni Asscn 2003–08, Indonesian Economists Asscn 2003–09, Centre for Microfinance Studies & Devt 2010; Gen. Leader, Magazine KARSA 2011; Chair. Multipurpose Co-operative Enterprises 'Mataholang' 2011, Indonesian Co-operative Soc. 2011; Penerima Bintang Mahaputra Utama Republik Indonesia 2007; Hon. DEcon (Univ. of Diponegoro) 2006; Dr hc (Univ. of Padjadjaran, Bandung) 2007; Best Central Bank Gov., Global Finance, Washington, DC 2007, Joon S. Moon Best Alumni of Michigan State Univ. 2007. *Address:* Jl. Tirtayasa X No. 1, Kebayoran Baru, South Jakarta 12160, Indonesia (home).

ABDULLAH, Farooq, MB; Indian physician and politician; b. 21 Oct. 1937, Srinagar, Kashmir; s. of Sheikh Mohammad Abdullah and Begum Abdullah; m. Mollie Abdullah 1968; one s. (Omar Farooq Abdullah) three d.; ed S.M.S. Medical Coll., Jaipur, Rajasthan; mem. Lok Sabha (lower house of Parl.) 1980–82, for

Srinagar constituency 2009–14; mem. Jammu and Kashmir Legis. Ass. 1982–90, 1996–2002, Dec. 2008–Feb. 2009; Minister of Health 1983–87, of New and Renewable Energy 2009–14; Chief Minister, Jammu and Kashmir 1983–90, 1996–2002, 2002–08; mem. Rajya Sabha (upper house of Parl.) 2002–08, Feb.–May 2009; Pres. State Cen. Labour Union, Jammu and Kashmir Nat. Conf.; Chair. Jammu and Kashmir Muslim Auquaf Trust, Sher-i-Kashmir Nat. Medical Inst. Trust, Sher-i-Kashmir Inst. of Medical Sciences; Gen. Sec. Indo-Arab Friendship Soc., Nat. Integration Council; Patron Jammu and Kashmir Nat. Conf.; mem. India Int. Centre; Leader, Jammu and Kashmir Nat. Conf. Parl. Party; Pres. J and K Cricket Asscn; Hon. DLitt. (Aligarh Muslim Univ.); Nat. Solidarity Award 1998, Eminent Personality of the Year, Indian Medical Asscn 1999, Dr B.C. Roy Nat. Award 1999. *Leisure interests:* golf, photography, gardening, music. *Address:* Ministry of New and Renewable Energy, Block 14, CGO Complex, Lodhi Road, New Delhi 110 003 (office); 40, Gupkar Road, Srinagar, India (home). *Telephone:* (11) 24361298 (office); (194) 2452540 (home). *Fax:* (11) 24361830 (office); (194) 2452120 (home). *E-mail:* farooq_abdullah@rediffmail.com (home); secymnes@nic .in (office). *Website:* mnes.nic.in (office).

ABDULLAH, Shri Omar Farooq, BCom; Indian politician; *President, Jammu and Kashmir National Conference (JKNC);* b. 10 March 1970, Rochford, Essex, UK; s. of Farooq Abdullah and Mollie Abdullah; m. Payal Abdullah; two s.; ed Sydenham Coll., Mumbai; Pres. Youth Nat. Conf.; elected to Lok Sabha (Parl.) 1998, re-elected 1999, 2004; Pres. Jammu and Kashmir Nat. Conf. 2002–; mem. Parl. for Srinagar constituency (Nat. Conf. Party) 1998; mem. Cttee of Transport and Tourism, Consultative Cttee, Ministry of Tourism 1998–99; Minister of State for Commerce and Industry 1999–2001, for External Affairs 2001–02; Chief Minister of Jammu and Kashmir 2009–15; mem. Jammu and Kashmir Legis. Ass. (Jammu and Kashmir Nat. Conf.) from 28-Beerwah constituency 2014–. *Leisure interests:* tennis, skiing, swimming, squash, biking. *Address:* Jammu and Kashmir National Conference (JKNC), Mujahid Manzil, Nawa-i-Subh Complex Zero Bridge, Srinagar 190 002, India (office). *Telephone:* (194) 2452326 (office). *E-mail:* contact@jknc.in (office). *Website:* www.jknc.in (office); www .jklegislativeassembly.nic.in (office).

ABDULLAH, Dato' Saifuddin bin, BA; Malaysian politician; *Minister of Foreign Affairs;* b. 27 Jan. 1961; m. Norlin Shamsul Bahri; one d.; ed Malay Coll. Kuala Kangsar, Universiti Malaya; fmr Pres. Malaysian Youth Council; fmr mem. UN Sec. Gen.'s High-Level Panel on Youth Employment; Consultant, Econ. and Social Comm. for Asia and the Pacific (ESCAP); Jt-Sec. Bosnia Action Front; mem. Parl. (UMNO) for Temerloh 2008–13, for Indera Mahkota (PKR) 2018–; Chief Sec. Pakatan Harapan (Alliance of Hope) 2015–; CEO Global Movt of Moderates Foundation (GMM); Dir (Strategic and Social Devt), Institut Darul Ehsan; fmr Deputy Minister of Higher Educ.; Minister of Foreign Affairs 2018–; fmr mem. United Malay Nat. Org. (UMNO), fmr mem. UMNO Supreme Council; mem. Parti Keadilan Rakyat (PKR, People's Justice Party) 2015–. *Publications:* eight books, including New Politics: Multiracial and Moderate Malaysian Democracy 2017. *Address:* Ministry of Foreign Affairs, Aras 3, Wisma Putra, Presint 2, Pusat Pentadbiran Kerajaan Persekutuan, 62602 Putrajaya, Malaysia (office). *Telephone:* (3) 88874000 (office). *Fax:* (3) 88891717 (office). *E-mail:* anifah@kln.gov .my (office). *Website:* www.kln.gov.my (office); www.saifuddinabdullah.com.my.

ABDULLAH, Yousuf bin Alawi bin; Omani government minister and diplomatist; *Minister responsible for Foreign Affairs;* b. 1942, Salalah; s. of Abdullah bin Alawi; ed Egypt, univ. studies in political science, UK; joined Diplomatic Service 1970, Second Sec., Ministry of Foreign Affairs 1972, postings to Cairo and Beirut, Amb. to Lebanon 1973, Under-Sec., Ministry of Foreign Affairs 1974, Minister of State 1982, Minister responsible for Foreign Affairs 1997–; First Grade Sultan Qaboos Decoration, Order of Merit, Egypt, Officier, Légion d'honneur, Grand Decoration of Honour (Austria), Cavaliere Grande Croce (Italy) and other foreign decorations. *Address:* Ministry of Foreign Affairs, PO Box 252, Muscat 112, Oman (office). *Telephone:* 24699453 (office). *Fax:* 24696141 (office). *E-mail:* info@mofa.gov .om (office). *Website:* www.mofa.gov.om (office).

ABDULLAH II IBN AL-HUSSEIN, HM King of Jordan, GCB, GCMG; head of state and army officer; b. 30 Jan. 1962, Amman; s. of King Hussein Ibn Talal and Princess Muna al-Hussein; m. Rania al-Yassin 1993 (Queen Rania); two s. two d.; ed Islamic Educ. Coll., St Edmund's School, Surrey, UK, Deerfield Acad., USA, Sandhurst Mil. Acad. and Univ. of Oxford, UK; succeeded to the throne 7 Feb. 1999; commissioned Second Lt 1981, Reconnaissance Troop Leader 13th/18th Bn Royal Hussars (British Army), FRG and England; rank of First Lt 1984; Platoon Commdr and Co. second-in-command 40th Armoured Brigade, Jordan, Commdr Tank Co. 91st Armoured Brigade 1985–86 (rank of Capt.); Tactics Instructor Helicopter Anti-Tank Wing 1986–87; undertook advanced studies in int. affairs at School of Foreign Service, Georgetown Univ., Washington, DC 1987–88; Company Commdr 17th Tank Bn, 2nd Guards Brigade then Bn second-in-command (rank of Maj.) 1989; attended Command and Staff Coll., Camberley, UK 1990; Armour Rep. Office of the Insp.-Gen. 1991, Commdr 2nd Armoured Car Regt, 40th Brigade (rank of Lt Col) 1992; promoted to rank of Col 1993; Deputy Commdr Jordanian Special Forces Jan.–June 1994; promoted to the rank of Brig. 1994 and assumed command of Royal Jordanian Special Forces; Commdr of Special Operations Command 1997–; Pres. Jordan Nat. Football Fed.; Hon. Pres. Int. Tourism Golden Rudder Soc.; Head Nat. Cttee for Tourism and Archaeological Film Production 1997–; Grand Master, Order of al-Hussein bin Ali, Grand Master, Supreme Order of the Renaissance, Order of the Star of Jordan, Grand Master, Order of the Star of Jordan, Grand Master, Order of Independence; Hon. KCVO 1984, Kt Grand Cross 1987, with Grand Cordon 2001, Order of Merit of the Italian Repub., Grand Cordon 1993, then Collar 1999, Order of the Chrysanthemum (Japan), Grand Cross, Order of the House of Orange (Netherlands) 1994, Grand Cross, Order of Naval Merit, with White Distinctive (Spain) 1995, Grand Cross, Order of Aeronautical Merit, with White Distinctive (Spain) 1999, Collar, Order of al-Khalifa of Bahrain 1999, Extraordinary Grade, Order of Merit of Lebanon 1999, Order of the Grand Conqueror, First Class (Libya) 1999, Grand Cross, Order of the White Eagle (Poland) 1999, Kt, Grand Order of Mugunghwa (South Korea) 1999, Grand Cross with Collar, Order of Isabel the Catholic (Spain) 1999, Grand Cross with Collar, Royal Norwegian Order of St Olav 2000, Grand Star of the Decoration of Honour for Services to the Repub. of Austria 2001, Grand Cross, Order of the Bath, Military Class (GCB) 2001, Grand Cross Special Class, Order of Merit of the FRG 2002, Order of Prince Yaroslav the Wise, First Class (Ukraine) 2002, Kt, Order of the Seraphim (Sweden) 2003, Collar, Order of the Star of Romania 2005, Grand Cross, Order of the Netherlands Lion 2006, Grand Cross with Collar, Order of Charles III (Spain) 2006, Grand Collar, Order of Prince Henry (Portugal) 2008, Collar of the Royal Family Order of the Crown of Brunei (DKMB) 2008, Medal for the Tenth Anniversary of the Capital Astana (Kazakhstan) 2008, Grand Collar, Order of Saint James of the Sword (Portugal) 2009, Order of Merit, First Class (Ukraine) 2011, Order of the White Lion, First Class (Czech Repub.) 2015, Kt Grand Cordon, Order of Leopold (Belgium) 2016, Templeton Prize 2018. *Leisure interests:* car racing (fmr Jordanian Nat. Rally Racing Champion), water sports, scuba diving, collecting ancient weapons and armaments. *Address:* Royal Hashemite Court, Amman, Jordan. *Website:* www.kingabdullah.jo.

ABDULLAYEV, Ixtiyor; Uzbekistani lawyer and government official; b. 22 May 1966, Uchko'prik Dist, Farg'ona Viloyat, Uzbek SSR, USSR; ed Perm State Univ.; Judge, Farg'ona City Criminal Court 1988–90, Acting Chair. 1993–95; Chief Consultant, Farg'ona Viloyat Justice Dept 1990–93; Chair. Farg'ona Viloyat Court 1995–97; Citizen and Amnesty Officer, Office of State Adviser for Coordination of Law Enforcement and Control Agencies 1997–2000; Chair. Andijon Viloyat Criminal Court 2000–01; Deputy State Advisor to Pres. on coordination of law enforcement and supervisory activities 2001–02, State Advisor to Pres. 2006–09, 2009–15; First Deputy Minister of Justice 2002–06; Dir, Inst. for Monitoring Current Legislation 2007–09; mem. Senate (upper house of Oliy Majlis, parl.) 2010–15; Prosecutor-Gen. 2015–18; Chair., State Security Service (Davlat Xavfsizlik Xizmati) 2018–19. *Address:* c/o Davlat Xavfsizlik Xizmati, Tashkent, Matbuotchilar ko'ch. 9, Uzbekistan (office).

ABDURIXIT, Abdulahat; Chinese politician; b. March 1942, Yining, Xinjiang; ed Xinjiang Eng Coll.; joined CCP 1960; engineer then Vice-Pres. Xinjiang Uygur Autonomous Region Construction Survey and Design Acad., Vice-Dir Xinjiang Uygur Autonomous Region Planning Comm.; Vice-Chair. Xinjiang Uygur Autonomous Region 1965–93; Chair. Xinjiang Uygur Autonomous Region 1993–2003; apptd Vice-Sec. CCP Xinjiang Uygur Autonomous Region Cttee 1993; mem. CCP 15th Cen. Cttee 1997–2002, 16th Cen. Cttee 2002–07, 17th Cen. Cttee 2007–12; Chair. Regional People's Congress, Xinjiang 2003–08; Vice-Chair. 11th CPPCC Nat. Cttee 2008–13; Pres. Chinese–African People's Friendship Asscn. *Address:* Chinese–African People's Friendship Association, 1 Taijichang Street, Beijing 100740, People's Republic of China. *Telephone:* (10) 6513103. *Fax:* (10) 85114769. *E-mail:* info@capfa.org.cn. *Website:* www.capfa.org.cn.

ABDYGULOV, Tolkunbek, MA, PhD; Kyrgyzstani economist and banking executive; *Chairman, National Bank of the Kyrgyz Republic;* b. 7 July 1976, Bokonbayevo, Tonskiy Dist, Yssyk-Kul Oblast, Kyrgyz SSR, USSR; ed Int. Univ. of Kyrgyzstan, Nagoya Univ., Japan, Texas Southern Univ., USA, Econ. Inst. of the Nat. Acad. of Science of the Kyrgyz Repub.; Economist, Directorate on Investments and Tech. Assistance Coordination (DITAC), Nat. Bank of the Kyrgyz Repub. 1997–2000, Sr Economist 2000–01, Lead Economist 2001–03, apptd Lead Economist Financial Div. 2005, Chief Economist, Project Implementation Unit 2005–06; apptd Dir of Public Foundation, Information Future 2006; Consultant, Financial and Private Sector Devt Dept, Eastern Europe and Cen. Asia Unit, World Bank 2007–08; apptd Sr Lecturer, Econs Dept, American Univ. of Cen. Asia 2008; Expert of Econ. Sector, Econ. and Social Policy Dept, Exec. Office, Pres. of Kyrgyz Repub. 2008–09, Head of Strategies and Program Service, Cen. Agency of Kyrgyz Repub. on Devt, Investments and Innovations 2009–10, apptd Acting State Sec., Ministry of Econ. Regulation 2010, Head, Economy and Strategic Devt Dept, Exec. Office of Govt of Kyrgyz Repub. 2010–12, Head, Economy and Investment Dept 2012–14; Chair. Nat. Bank of the Kyrgyz Repub. 2014–Aug. 2017, Dec. 2017–; First Deputy Prime Minister Aug. 2017–Dec. 2017; mem. Bd of Govs IMF; Nat. Prize for the Young Scientists-Akyl Tirek 2013. *Address:* National Bank of the Kyrgyz Republic, 720001 Bishkek, 168 Chuy Avenue, Kyrgyzstan (office). *Telephone:* (312) 61-04-86 (office). *E-mail:* mail@nbkr.kg (office). *Website:* www.nbkr.kg (office).

ABDYKARIMOV, Oralbai; Kazakhstani politician; b. 18 Dec. 1944, Kievka, Karaganda region; m. Abdykarimova Jamal; three s. one d.; ed Alma-Ata Higher CPSU School, Karaganda State Univ.; leading posts in Komsomol and CP organs of Kazakhstan; Deputy Head, then Head of Admin. Office of Pres. of Kazakhstan; Chair. Mazhilis (Parl.); Chair. Higher Disciplinary Council, State Comm. for Fight with Corruption; mem. Senate (Parl.), Chair. of Senate 1999–2004; Sec. of State and presidential adviser 2004–07; Chair. Nur Otan party public council on fighting corruption 2007; fmr mem. Security Council of Kazakhstan; Order Barys. *Address:* Senat, 010000 Nur-Sultan, Abay d-ly 33, Parliament House, Kazakhstan (office). *E-mail:* smimazh@parlam.kz (office). *Website:* www.parlam.kz (office).

ABDYLDAYEV, Erlan; Kyrgyzstani diplomatist, consultant and academic; b. 21 July 1966, Almatı, Kazakh SSR, USSR; m.; one s. one d.; ed Moscow State Inst. of Int. Relations; Asst, Dept of the Socialist Asian Countries, Ministry of Foreign Affairs, USSR 1989, Attaché and Third Sec., Embassy of USSR, later of Russia, in Beijing, People's Repub. of China 1989–94; expert consultant, Int. Dept of the Presidential Admin 1994–97; First Deputy Foreign Minister 1997–2001, Amb. to People's Repub. of China 2001–05; expert, Inst. of Public Policy, Bishkek 2005–; Country Dir for Kyrgyzstan, Inst. for War and Peace Reporting 2007–; Minister of Foreign Affairs 2012–18; Order of Friendship 2017; Dr hc (Moscow State Inst. of Int. Relations) 2012.

ABE, Nobuyasu; Japanese diplomatist, research institute director and fmr UN official; b. 9 Sept. 1945, Akita; m. Akiko Sugawara; two s.; ed Univ. of Tokyo, Amherst Coll., USA; entered Foreign Service 1967, has held variety of positions in fields of arms control and disarmament; served in Embassy in Washington, DC 1969–71, Pvt. Sec. to Foreign Minister Toshio Kimura 1974, to Kiichi Miyazawa 1974–76, in Perm. Mission to Int. Orgs, Geneva 1977–79, in Embassy in Tel-Aviv 1979–81, Dir of Policy Planning 1984–86, Perm. Mission to UN, New York 1987–90, 1996–97, Embassy in Manila 1990–92, Consul-Gen., Consulate Gen. in Boston 1994–96, Dir-Gen. for Arms Control and Science Affairs 1997–99, Amb. to Int. Orgs, Vienna 1999–2001, to Saudi Arabia 2001–03, UN Under-Sec.-Gen. for Disarmament Affairs, New York 2003–06, Amb. to Switzerland 2006–08, then Dir Center for the Promotion of Disarmament and Non-Proliferation, Japan Inst. of Int. Affairs –2014; Commr Japan Atomic Energy Comm. 2014–17; mem. UN Sec.-Gen.'s Advisory Bd on Disarmament Matters; mem. Bd of Trustees, UN Inst. for

Disarmament Research; mem. Geneva Centre for Security Policy, IISS 1984–, Advisory Bd, Int. Comm. for Nuclear Nonproliferation and Disarmament 2008–10; mem. Council, United Nations Univ. 2010–; Int. Fellow, Weatherhead Center for Int. Affairs, Harvard Univ. 1986–87; Visiting Prof., Doshisha Univ. 2010, Akita Int. Univ. 2011–. *Address:* c/o Atomic Energy Commission, Central Government Building No.4 (7F), 3-1-1 Kasumigaseki, Chiyoda-ku, Tokyo 100-8970, Japan (office). *Telephone:* (3) 3581-6690 (office). *Fax:* (3) 3581-9828 (office).

ABE, Shinzō, LLB; Japanese politician; *Prime Minister;* s. of Shintaro Abe; grandson of Nobusuke Kishi; ed Faculty of Law, Seikei Univ., Univ. of Southern California, USA; began career with Kobe Steel Ltd –1982; Exec. Asst to Minister for Foreign Affairs 1982–87; apptd Pvt. Sec. to Chair. of Gen. Council, LDP 1987, Pvt. Sec. to Sec.-Gen. 1987–93, Dir of LDP Social Affairs Div. 1999–2000, Sec.-Gen. 2003–04, Acting Sec.-Gen. 2004, Pres. 2006–07, 2012–; mem. House of Reps (Yamaguchi Pref., 4th Electoral Dist) 1993–, mem. Standing Cttee on Foreign Affairs 1993–99, on Health and Welfare 1999–2000, on Security 1999–2000; Deputy Chief Cabinet Sec. 2000–01, 2001–03, Chief Cabinet Sec. 2005–06, Prime Minister 2006–07 (resgnd), 2012–. *Publications include:* Utsukushii Kuni E (Toward a Beautiful Country) 2006. *Address:* Prime Minister's Office, 1-6-1, Nagata-cho, Chiyoda-ku, Tokyo 100-8968 (office); Liberal-Democratic Party, 1-11-23, Nagata-cho, Chiyoda-ku, Tokyo 100-8910, Japan (office). *Telephone:* (3) 3581-2361 (office); (3) 3581-6211 (office). *Fax:* (3) 3581-1910 (office); (3) 5511-8855 (office). *E-mail:* koho@ldp.jimin.or.jp (office). *Website:* www.kantei.go.jp; www.jimin.jp (office).

ABED, Sir Fazle Hasan, Kt, KCMG; Bangladeshi business executive and foundation executive; *Founder and Chairperson, BRAC;* b. 1936; ed Univ. of Dhaka, Univ. of Glasgow, UK; Sr Corp. Exec., Shell Oil, Chittagong early 1970s; left job and went to London, UK to devote himself to Bangladesh's War of Independence; helped initiate campaign called Help Bangladesh to organize funds for the war effort in Bangladesh; returned to newly ind. Bangladesh and established BRAC (fmrly Bangladesh Rural Advancement Cttee) to rehabilitate returning refugees in a remote area in a northeastern dist of the country 1972, currently Chair.; Chair., Bd of Dirs, BRAC Bank Ltd 2013–; apptd by UN Sec.-Gen. Ban Ki-moon to Eminent Persons Group for Least Developed Countries 2010; Dr hc (Yale Univ.) 2007, (Columbia Univ.) 2008, (Univ. of Oxford) 2009, (Rikkyo Univ.) 2009, (Univ. of Bath) 2010, (Univ. of Manchester) 2012; Ramon Magsaysay Award for Community Leadership 1980, UNICEF's Maurice Pate Award 1992, Olof Palme Award 2001, Schwab Foundation Social Entrepreneurship Award 2002, Gates Award for Global Health 2004, UNDP Mahbub ul Haq Award for Outstanding Contribution in Human Development 2004, Palli Karma Sahayak Foundation Award for Lifetime Achievement in Social Development and Poverty Alleviation 2007, Henry R. Kravis Prize in Leadership 2007, Inaugural Clinton Global Citizen Award 2007, David Rockefeller Bridging Leadership Award 2008, Conrad Hilton Foundation Humanitarian Award 2009, WISE Prize 2011, Open Society Prize 2013, World Food Prize 2015, Lego Prize 2018. *Address:* BRAC Centre, 75 Mohakhali, Dhaka 1212, Bangladesh (office). *Telephone:* (2) 9881265 (office). *Fax:* (2) 8823542 (office). *E-mail:* info@brac.net (office). *Website:* www.brac.net (office).

ABED DE ZAVALA, Sheila R.; Paraguayan lawyer, environmentalist and politician; *Founder and Executive Director, Instituto de Derecho y Economía Ambiental (IDEA), Paraguay;* m. Carlos Zuccolillo; five c.; ed Universidad Nacional de Asunción, Université de Limoges; Environmental Law & Policy Prof. in the Masters Programme on Environmental Eng, Universidad Nacional de Asunción; Founder and Exec. Dir IDEA (Instituto de Derecho y Economía Ambiental), Asunción, Paraguay 1996–; past Gen. Co-ordinator Alianza Regional para Políticas de Conservación en América Latina y el Caribe (Regional Alliance for Conservation Policies in Latin America and the Caribbean); Chair. Comm. on Environmental Law, Int. Union for Conservation of Nature; Minister of Justice and Labour 2013–15; mem. Grupo Zapallar on Trade and Environment (South American coalition of NGOs and individual mems); has represented the Paraguayan Govt before UN Framework Convention on Climate Change; has represented civil society in Biodiversity and Ramsar Conventions. *Publications:* co-author of eight publs.

ABEGEBRIEL, Agus Maftuh; Indonesian academic and diplomatist; *Ambassador to Saudi Arabia;* fmr mem. Faculty of Shariah and Law of State, Islamic University Sunan Kalijaga, Yogyakarta, also fmr Dir Siyasa Research Inst.; Amb. to Saudi Arabia (also accred to OIC) 2016–. *Address:* Embassy of Indonesia, PO Box 94343, Riyadh 11693, Saudi Arabia (office). *Telephone:* (11) 488-2800 (office). *Fax:* (11) 488-2966 (office). *E-mail:* kbri.riyadh@gmail.com (office). *Website:* riyadh.kemlu.go.id (office).

ABEL, Caroline; Seychelles economist and central banker; *Governor, Central Bank of Seychelles;* d. of Antoine Abel; ed Univ. of Leeds, Univ. of Glasgow, UK; began career as economist with Social Security Fund; joined Central Bank of Seychelles as Sr Bank Clerk 1994–96, Research Officer, Dept of Research and Statistics 1999, becoming Sr Research Officer and Dir of Research, Head of Div. for Policy, Market Operations and Statistics 2006–10, Deputy Gov. 2010–11, First Deputy Gov. 2011–12, Gov. Central Bank of Seychelles (first female) 2012–. *Address:* Office of the Governor, Central Bank of Seychelles, Independence Avenue, POB 701, Victoria, Seychelles (office). *Telephone:* 4282000 (office). *Fax:* 4226035 (office). *E-mail:* enquiries@cbs.sc (office). *Website:* www.cbs.sc (office).

ABEL, Edward William, CBE, PhD, DSc; British chemist and academic; *Professor Emeritus of Inorganic Chemistry, University of Exeter;* b. 3 Dec. 1931, Mid-Glamorgan, Wales; s. of Sydney J. Abel and Donna Maria Grabham; m. Margaret R. Edwards 1960; one s. one d.; ed Bridgend Grammar School, Glamorgan, Univ. Coll. Cardiff and Northern Polytechnic, London; Research Fellow, Imperial Coll. London 1957–59; Lecturer and Reader, Univ. of Bristol 1959–71; Prof. of Inorganic Chem., Univ. of Exeter 1972–97, Deputy Vice-Chancellor 1991–94, now Prof. Emer.; Visiting Prof., Univ. of British Columbia 1970, Univ. of Japan 1971, Tech. Univ. of Brunswick 1973, ANU, Canberra 1990; mem. Council, RSC 1978–82, 1983–2002, Pres. RSC 1996–98, Ed.-in-Chief Tutorial Chemistry Texts (ten vols) 1999; Chair. Scientific Affairs Bd, Univ. Grants Cttee 1986–89; Hon. Fellow, Univ. of Cardiff 1999; Hon. DUniv (London Metropolitan Univ.); Hon. DSc (Exeter) 2000, (Univ. of Glamorgan); Tilden Medal, RSC 1981. *Publications:* Organometallic Chemistry Vols 1–25 (ed.) 1970–95, Comprehensive Organometallic Chemistry I (ed.) (nine vols) 1984, II (14 vols) 1995. *Leisure interest:* gardening. *Address:* 1A Rosebarn Avenue, Exeter, Devon, EX4 6DY, England (home). *Telephone:* (1392) 270272 (home). *E-mail:* mea@rosebarn.eclipse.co.uk (home).

ABELA, Carmelo; Maltese politician; *Minister for Foreign Affairs and Trade Promotion;* b. 10 Feb. 1972, Zejtun; m. Melanie Abela; two c.; ed Univ. of Malta; Man., Mid-Med Bank Ltd/HSBC Bank Malta PLC 1990–2014; mem. Zejtun Local Council 1994–96; mem. House of Reps (parl.) 2006–, Deputy Speaker 2003–10, Govt Whip 2013–14; Minister for Home Affairs and Nat. Security 2014–17, Govt Spokesman in Prime Minister's Office 2014, Minister for Foreign Affairs and Trade Promotion 2017–; mem. Parl. Ass. of Org. for Security and Cooperation in Europe (OSCE) 2013–16; mem. Partit Laburista (Labour Party). *Address:* Ministry for Foreign Affairs and Trade Promotion, Palazzo Parisio, Merchants Street, Valletta VLT 1171, Malta (office). *Telephone:* 21242191 (office). *Fax:* 21236604 (office). *E-mail:* info.mfa@gov.mt (office). *Website:* foreignaffairs.gov.mt (office); carmeloabela.org.

ABELA, George, BA, LLD, M. Juris (European Law), KUOM; Maltese lawyer, politician and fmr head of state; b. 22 April 1948, Qormi; s. of George Abela and Ludgarda Abela (née Debono); m. Margaret Abela 1976; one s. one d.; ed Univ. of Malta; fmr attorney in pvt. practice, specializing in civil, commercial and industrial law; legal consultant to Gen. Workers' Union 1975–2000; fmr legal adviser to Medical Asscn of Malta; Pres. Qormi FC –1982, Pres. Malta Football Asscn 1982–92; Deputy Leader in charge of Party Affairs, Malta Labour Party 1992–96; legal adviser to Prime Minister of Malta 1996–97; fmr Dir Cen. Bank of Malta; fmr Exec. Dir Bank of Valletta PLC; fmr arbitrator, Court of Arbitrator for Sports, Lausanne; Pres. of Malta 2009–14. *Address:* c/o Office of the President, The Palace, Valletta VLT, 1190 (office); Margherita, Triq Il-Melh, Marsascala MSK, 3113, Malta (home). *Telephone:* 2163928 (home). *E-mail:* gabela0404@gmail.com (home).

ABELE, John E., BS; American medical device industry executive (retd); m. Mary Abele; three c.; ed Amherst Coll.; several exec. positions with medical device firms in 1960s including with Advanced Instruments Inc.; joined Medi-tech 1969 then f. Cooper Scientific 1970 and acquired Medi-tech, Pres. 1970–83, helped develop, manufacture and market first steerable catheter; co-f. (with Peter Nicholas) Boston Scientific Corpn 1979, Chair. 1979–95, Vice-Chair. and Founder, Office of the Chair. 1995–96 (retd); Founder Chair. Argosy Foundation (pvt. family foundation) 1997–; Founding Chair. FIRST (For Inspiration and Recognition of Science and Tech.) Foundation 2002–10, apptd Vice-Chair. 2010; mem. and Hon. Fellow, Soc. of Interventional Radiology. *Address:* c/o Argosy Foundation, 555 East Wells Street, Suite 1650, Milwaukee, WI 53202, USA. *Website:* www.argosyfnd.org.

ABERBACH, David, BA, BSc, MLitt, DPhil; British academic; *Professor of Jewish Studies, McGill University;* b. 17 Oct. 1953, London; s. of Prof. Moshe Aberbach and Rose Aberbach (née Firsht); m. Mimi Skelker 1980; three d.; ed Talmudical Acad. of Baltimore, USA, Univ. Coll., London, Univ. of Oxford, Tavistock Clinic, Open Univ.; fmr Lecturer, Univs of Oxford and Cambridge, Leo Baeck Coll. and Cornell Univ., USA 1982–86; Visiting Asst Prof., McGill Univ., Canada 1986–87, Assoc. Prof., Dept of Jewish Studies 1987–2006, Prof. 2006–; Visiting Prof., Univ. Coll. London 1992–93, 1998, 2001–02, 2008–09; Academic Visitor, Sociology Dept, LSE 1992–93, 1994–98, 2001–03, Govt Dept, LSE 2004, 2006, 2008–10, Humanities Center, Harvard Univ. 2010–12, Weatherhead Center for Int. Affairs and Kennedy Center for Int. Devt, Harvard Univ. 2013; Visiting Sr Fellow, Dept of Int. Devt, LSE 2013–18. *Radio:* broadcasts based on book on charisma (BBC World Service). *Publications include:* At the Handles of the Lock: Themes in the Fiction of S. J. Agnon 1984, Bialik 1988, Surviving Trauma: Loss, Literature and Psychoanalysis 1989, Realism, Caricature and Bias: The Fiction of Mendele Mocher Sefarim 1993, Imperialism and Biblical Prophecy 750–500 BCE 1993, Charisma in Politics, Religion and the Media: Private Trauma, Public Ideals 1996, Revolutionary Hebrew, Empire and Crisis 1998, The Roman-Jewish Wars and Hebrew Cultural Nationalism (co-author) 2000, Major Turning Points in Jewish Intellectual History 2003, C. N. Bialik: Selected Poems (ed.) 2004, Jewish Cultural Nationalism: Origins and Influences 2008, Moshe Aberbach, Jewish Education and History: Continuity, Crisis and Change (ed.) 2009, The European Jews, Patriotism and the Liberal State 1789–1939 2012, National Poetry, Empires and War 2015, The Bible and the 'Holy Poor' 2018, Nationalism, War, and Jewish Education 2018, Literature and Poverty: From the Hebrew Bible to the Second World War 2019; articles in British Journal of Sociology, Commentary, Comparative Literature Studies, Ethnic and Racial Studies, The Journal of Politics, Culture and Society, Prooftexts, Hebrew Union Coll. Annual, Harvard Theological Review, International History Review, International Journal of Psycho-Analysis, Journal of Modern Jewish Studies, Nations and Nationalism, Polin, TLS, THES and others. *Leisure interests:* cinema, gardening, painting, coastal path hiking. *Address:* Department of Jewish Studies, McGill University, Leacock Building, 855 Sherbrooke W, Montreal, PQ H3A 2T7, Canada (office); 32 Ravenshurst Avenue, London, NW4 4EG, England (home). *Telephone:* (514) 398-5009 (office). *Website:* www.mcgill.ca/jewishstudies/faculty/aberbach (office).

ABERCROMBIE, Neil, BA, MA, PhD; American politician and fmr state governor; b. 26 June 1938, Buffalo, NY; s. of G. Donald Abercrombie and Vera June Abercrombie (née Giersdorf); m. Dr Nancie Ellen Caraway 1981; ed Williamsville High School (now Williamsville South High School), Union Coll., Schenectady, NY, Univ. of Hawaii, Mānoa; variety of jobs when young including as waiter at Chuck's Steak House, Waikiki, locker desk clerk at Cen. YMCA, custodian at Mother Rice Preschool, construction apprentice programme dir; fmr elementary school teacher and coll. lecturer; unsuccessful cand. for Democratic nomination to US Senate 1970; mem. Hawaii State House of Reps 1975–79, Hawaii State Senate 1980–86; mem. US House of Reps, Washington, DC for 1st Congressional Dist of Hawaii 1986–87 (special election), 1991–2010 (resgnd to run in Hawaii gubernatorial election Feb. 2010); mem. Honolulu City Council 1988–90; Gov. of Hawaii 2011–14; Democrat. *Publication:* Blood of Patriots (novel, with Richard Hoyt) 1996. *Leisure interests:* weightlifting, walking Kanoa, visiting family. *Address:* c/o Executive Chambers, State Capitol, 415 South Beretania Street, Honolulu, HI 96813, USA (office). *Website:* www.neilabercrombie.com.

ABEYWARDENA, Vajira; Sri Lankan politician; *Minister of Home Affairs;* b. 2 Sept. 1960; m.; ed Mahinda Coll., Univ. of Moratuwa; mem. Sri Lanka Parl. (Galle Dist) 1994–2010, 2015–, Minister of Public Admin, Man. and Reforms 2001–04, Minister of Home Affairs 2015–; mem. United Nat. Party, currently Chair. Provincial Council and Local Authorities Nat. Sub-Cttee. *Address:* Ministry of Home Affairs, Independence Square, Colombo 7 (office); No. 3, 34th Lane, Queens Road, Colombo 3, Sri Lanka (home). *Telephone:* (11) 2682900 (office). *Fax:* (11) 2683665 (office). *E-mail:* secretary-ha@pubad.gov.lk (office); abeywardena_v@parliament.lk.

ABHISIT, Vejjajiva (Mark), BA, MPhil, LLB; Thai economist and politician; *Leader Democrat Party (Prachatipat);* b. 3 Aug. 1964, Newcastle-upon-Tyne, England; s. of Dr Athasit Vejjajiva and Dr Sodsai Vejjajiva; m. Dr Pimpen Sakuntabhai; two c.; ed Eton Coll., Univ. of Oxford, UK, Ramkhamhaeng Univ.; fmr Lecturer, Chulachomklao Royal Mil. Acad. and Faculty of Econs, Thammasat Univ.; mem. Parl. (Democrat) for Bangkok 1992–2001, Democrat Party List 2001–06, Democrat Party List Zone 6 2007–; Govt Spokesperson 1992–94, Deputy-Sec. to the Prime Minister for Political Affairs 1994, Chair. House Educ. Affairs Cttee 1995, Cttee to Consider the Nat. Educ. Bill of 1999 1998; Minister to the Prime Minister's Office 2001; Deputy Leader Democrat Party (Prachatipat) 1999, Leader 2005–; Prime Minister 2008–11; Leader of the Opposition 2011–13; Kt Grand Cordon of the Most Noble Order of the Crown of Thailand 1998, Kt Grand Cordon (Special Class) of the Most Exalted Order of the White Elephant 1999. *Address:* Democrat Party (Prachatipat), 67 Thanon Setsiri, Samsen Nai, Phyathai, Bangkok 10400, Thailand (office). *Website:* www.opm.go.th (office); www.democrat.or.th (office); www.abhisit.org.

ABIHAGGLE, Carlos Enrique, MA; Argentine economist, academic, diplomatist and government official; b. 20 March 1945, Mendoza; ed Escuela Domingo Bombal, Escuela Superior de Comercio Martin Zapata, Universidad Naciónal de Cuyo, Univ. of Pennsylvania, USA; Prov. Senator 1983–87; Nat. Del. 1993–97; Gen. Supt for Irrigation, Mendoza 1999; fmr Minister for Work and Public Services; Chair., Latin-American Network of Basin Orgs (LANBO) 1999–2000; Amb. to Chile 2003–07; apptd Sec. of Int. Relations and Regional Integration, Universidad Nacional de Cuyo 2008; presenter, Pensar en positivo (TV programme) 2008; Founder TM Group Latinoamerica 2008; Founder website ar.espaciodeahorro.com (presents food price information for consumers) 2014; Gran Cruz de la Orden al Merito (Chile) 2007. *Television:* Pensar en Positivo. *Publication:* The Economic Impact of Viticulture in the Argentine. *Website:* ar.espaciodeahorro.com (office).

ABIL, Iolu Johnson, MBE; Ni-Vanuatu politician and fmr head of state; b. 1942, Tanna; s. of George Yavinian; ed Onesua High School, Loughborough Int. Co-operative Coll., UK, Univ. of the South Pacific, Suva, Fiji; Co-operative Inspector, British Nat. Service, Port Vila 1964; with New Hebrides Co-operative Dept 1964–80; fmr Sec., Ministry of Lands; interim Ombudsman of Vanuatu 2004–05; fmr Chair. Air Vanuatu; Pres. of Vanuatu 2009–14; ordained as Elder, Presbyterian Church 1975; mem. Vanuaaku Pati (Our Land Party), fmr Vice-Pres. *Address:* c/o Office of the President, PMB 100, Port Vila, Vanuatu.

ABILDAYEV, Bolot; Kyrgyzstani business executive and fmr government official; *General Director, Gazprom Neft Asia;* b. 6 Sept. 1963; ed Kyrgyz State Univ., Voznesensky Leningrad Inst. of Finance and Econs; Vice-Pres. Kyrgyz Commodity Exchange 1991–93; Chief Insp. State Tax Inspectorate 1996; joined Ministry of Finance 1999, Dir Cen. Treasury 2001, Minister of Finance 2002–05; Gen. Dir Gazprom Neft Asia 2006–, Gazprom Kyrgyzstan 2014–. *Address:* Gazprom Kyrgyzstan, 1/2 Gorky St., Bishkek 720005, Kyrgyzstan (office). *Telephone:* (312) 53-00-35 (office). *Fax:* (312) 53-00-33 (office). *E-mail:* delo@gazprom.kg (office). *Website:* www.gazprom.com/about/subsidiaries/list-items/kyrgyzstan/ (office).

ABILOV, Geldimyrat; Turkmenistani fmr central banker; First Deputy Chair. Türkmenistanyň Merkezi Banky (Cen. Bank of Turkmenistan) 2005–07, Chair. 2007–08; Rep. of Turkmenistan at World Bank and Asian Devt Bank. *Address:* c/o Central Bank of Turkmenistan, 744000 Aşgabat, Bitarap Türkmenistan köç. 36, Turkmenistan. *E-mail:* merkezb2@online.tm.

ABIRACHED, Robert; French writer and academic; *Professor Emeritus, University of Paris X;* b. 25 Aug. 1930, Beirut, Lebanon; m. Marie-France de Bailliencourt 1974; one s. one d.; ed Lycée Louis-le-Grand and École Normale Supérieure, Paris; Attaché, CNRS 1960–64; Drama Critic, Nouvel Observateur 1964–66; Literary and Drama Critic, La Nouvelle Revue Française 1956–72; Lecturer, later Prof., Univ. of Caen 1969–81; Prof. and Dir Dept of Drama, Univ. of Paris X 1988–99, Prof. Emer. 1999–; Prof., Conservatoire nat. supérieur d'art dramatique 1993–97; Dir Theatre and Exhbns, Ministry of Culture 1981–88; Pres. Int. Festival of Francophones, Limoges 1990–2000, Observatory of Cultural Politics, Grenoble, 1991–2001; Docteur d'Etat ès Lettres; Officier, Légion d'honneur; Commdr, Ordre nat. du Mérite, des Arts et des Lettres, des Palmes académiques; Prix Sainte-Beuve 1962. *Plays include:* Tu connais la musique? 1972, Giacomo Casanova comédien (in Italian) 1997. *Television includes:* La Consultation, Agnès, Agnès, Le dernier mot 1973. *Publications include:* Casanova ou la dissipation (essay) 1961, l'Emerveillée (novel) 1963, Tu connais la musique? (play) 1971, La crise du personnage dans le théâtre moderne (essay) 1978, Le théâtre et le Prince tome I: L'Embellie 1992, La décentralisation théâtrale (four vols) (ed.) 1992–95, Le Théâtre et le Prince tome II: Un système fatigué 2005, Le théâtre en France au XXme siècle (essay and anthology) 2011. *Address:* 4 rue Robert-Turquan, 75016 Paris, France (home). *Telephone:* 1-45-25-24-87 (home). *E-mail:* robert.abirached@orange.fr (home).

ABIZAID, Gen. John, MA; American army officer (retd) and diplomatist; *Ambassador to Saudi Arabia;* b. 1 April 1951, Redwood City, Calif.; m.; three c.; ed US Mil. Acad., West Point, Harvard Univ., Univ. of Jordan; began career with 82nd Air Airborne Div., Fort Bragg, N Carolina, led Ranger rifle co. during invasion of Grenada 1983, led 1st Infantry Div., 504th Parachute Infantry Regt, Commdt US Mil. Acad., Asst to Chair. of Jt Chiefs of Staff 1993, fmr Dir of Strategic Plans and Policy, Jt Staff, later Dir of Jt Staff. Deputy Commdr, then Commdr for Combined Forces Command, US Cen. Command 2003–07 (retd); Sr Pnr, JPA Partners LLC (consulting firm), Gardnerville, Nev. 2007–; Annenberg Distinguished Visiting Fellow, Hoover Inst., Stanford Univ. 2007; Amb. to Saudi Arabia 2019–; mem. Bd of Dirs USAA (financial services firm) 2007–, RPM International Inc. 2008–; Distinguished Chair of the Combating Terrorism Center, US Military Acad., West Point; Montgomery Fellow, Dartmouth Coll. 2008; mem. Council on Foreign Relations, IISS; Hon. Officer of the Order of Australia; Legion of Merit, Gold Cross, Honour of the Bundeswehr; Defense Distinguished Service Medal, Army Distinguished Service Medal, Bronze Star Medal. *Address:* USEmbassy, PO Box 94309, Riyadh 11693, Saudi Arabia (office). *Telephone:* (11) 488-3800 (office). *Fax:* (11) 488-7360 (office). *Website:* sa.usembassy.gov (office).

ABLAZA, Gerardo C., Jr, AB, MBA; Philippine telecommunications industry executive; *President and CEO, Manila Water Company, Inc.;* b. 1953; ed De La Salle Univ., Coll. of Business Admin, Univ. of Philippines; began career at Unilever; several positions at Citibank NA 1983–97 including Country Business Man. for Philippines and Guam 1996–97 and Vice-Pres. Citibank NA Singapore for Consumer Banking; joined Ayala Corpn, assigned to Globe Telecom Inc. as Exec. Vice-Pres. and COO 1997, Pres. and CEO 1998–2009, mem. Man. Cttee, Ayala Corpn, also Sr Man. Dir and Chair. Innove Communications (subsidiary); Pres. and CEO Manila Water Company, Inc. 2010–; mem. Bd of Dirs Bank of The Philippine Islands 2001–; Dir Ho Chi Minh City Infrastructure Investment Jt Stock Co. 2016; Asia Business Leadership Award and CEO Choice of the Year Award, TNT 2004, Citi Distinguished Alumni Award for Leadership and Ingenuity 2013. *Address:* Manila Water Company, Inc., MWSS Administration Building 489, Katipunan Road, Balara, Quezon City 1105, Philippines (office). *Telephone:* (632) 917-5900 (office). *E-mail:* info@manilawater.com (office). *Website:* www.manilawater.com (office).

ÄBLYAZOV, Muxtar Qabılulı; Kazakhstani fmr banker and politician; b. 16 May 1963, Galkino, Southern Kazakhstan Oblast (now Turkistan Oblast) Kazakh SSR, USSR; m. Alma Shalabaeva; two s. two d.; est. Astana Holding (multi-sector pvt. holding co.) 1993; acquired shares in Bank TuranAlem (later known as BTA Bank) 1998; apptd Head of state-owned Kazakhstan Electricity Grid Operating Co. 1997; Minister for Energy, Industry and Trade 1998–99; co-f. Democratic Choice of Kazakhstan opposition political movt 2001; convicted of "abusing official powers as a minister" and sentenced to six years in prison, released from prison on condition that he renounce politics May 2003; moved to Moscow to rebuild business interests 2003; Chair. BTA Bank 2005–09; accused of money laundering and fraud March 2009, fled to London, UK. *Address:* 40 boulevard des Nations, BP 351, 69962 Corbas Cedex, France. *Website:* mukhtarablyazov.org.

ABNEY, David P., BBA; American business executive; *Chairman and CEO, UPS Inc.;* b. Greenwood, Miss.; m. Sherry Abney; ed Delta State Univ.; began career as a part-time package loader while at univ.; began career at United Parcel Service (UPS) at facility in Greenwood, Miss. 1974, fmr Pres. SonicAir, Pres. UPS International 2003–07, COO UPS Inc. 2007–14, CEO 2014–, Chair. 2016–; mem. Bd of Dirs, Allied Waste Industries, Inc. 2008–, Johnson Controls, Air Couriers Conf. of America, Southern Center for Int. Studies, Coalition of Service Industries, Cargo Network Services, Business Roundtable, Delta State Univ. Alumni Foundation; Chair. World Affairs Council of Atlanta; mem. President's Export Council; Trustee, The UPS Foundation; Professionalism in Services/Support Man. Award, Int. Asscn of Services Man. *Address:* UPS Inc., 55 Glenlake Parkway NE, Atlanta, GA 30328, USA (office). *Telephone:* (404) 828-6000 (office). *Fax:* (404) 828-6562 (office). *E-mail:* info@ups.com (office). *Website:* www.ups.com (office).

ABO AUF, Ezzat; Egyptian actor, fmr doctor and fmr musician; b. 21 Aug. 1948; m. Fatima Abo Auf (died 2012); one s. one d.; ed Al Azhar Univ. Faculty of Medicine, Cairo; worked as gynaecologist for five years; fmr professional musician, bands include 4M (with four sisters) 1979–91; acting debut in film Ice Cream in Golem 1992; Pres. Cairo Int. Film Festival 2006–12, Egyptian Actors Union; mem. Les Petits Chats band, Black Coats band. *Television:* host of several popular TV shows including talk show Cairo Today (Al Qahira Al Yom). *Films include:* Strawberry War 1992, Traffic Light 1994, Birds of Darkness 1995, Ismailia Back and Forth 1995, Assassination 1996, Searching for Tut Ankh Amun 1996, The Land of Fear 1998, A Woman's Destiny 1999, The Lovers 1999, The Red Book 2000, Let Go 2004, One of the People 2006, Baby Doll's Night 2007, El Zamahlaweya 2008, Bobos 2009, Omar and Salma 2 2009, Omar and Salma 3 2012, Game Over 2012, Al Me'adeya 2013, Paparazzi 2015, Under Table 2016.

ĀBOLTIŅA, Solvita; Latvian politician; b. 19 Feb. 1963, Ogre, Latvian SSR; m. Jānis Āboltiņš; two c.; ed Rīga Secondary School No. 5, Faculty of Law, Univ. of Latvia; worked for jt stock co. Latvijas kultūrpreces 1979–93; joined Ministry of Foreign Affairs 1993, Sr Officer, Consular Dept 1993–95, Head of Consular and Legal Affairs Div. 1995, Dir Consular Dept 1995–2002; mem. Saeima (Parl.) 2002–, Chair. Legal Affairs Cttee 2002–04, Deputy Chair. (Speaker) of the Saeima 2009–10, Chair. (Speaker) 2010–14; legal adviser, Ministry of Foreign Affairs July–Dec. 2004; Minister of Justice 2004–06; mem. Jaunais laiks (New Era) party 2002–11, Chair. 2008–10; mem. Vienotība (Unity) party 2011–, Chair. 2011–16. *Address:* Vienotība (Unity), Zigfrīda Annas Meierovica bulvāris 12-3, Rīga 1050, Latvia (office). *Telephone:* 6720-5472 (office). *E-mail:* birojs@vienotiba.lv (office); sekretare@vienotiba.lv (office). *Website:* www.vienotiba.lv (office).

ABOUMRAD, Daniel Hajj; Mexican telecommunications executive; *CEO, América Móvil SAB de CV;* b. 1966, Mexico City; s.-in-law of Carlos Slim Helú; ed Anáhuac Univ.; Dir, América Móvil SAB de CV, CEO 2000–; CEO Hulera Euzkadi SAB de CV; mem. Bd of Dirs Carso Global Telecom, América Telecom, Grupo Carso SA de CV, Radiomóvil Dipsa SAB de CV, Teléfonos de México (Telmex). *Address:* América Móvil SAB de CV, Lago Zurich 245, Edificio Telcel, Col. Granada Ampliación, CP 11529 Mexico City, DF, Mexico (office). *Telephone:* (55) 2581-4449 (office). *Fax:* (55) 2581-4422 (office). *E-mail:* info@americamovil.com (office). *Website:* www.americamovil.com (office).

ABOUTRIKA, Mohamed, BPhil; Egyptian professsional footballer (retd); b. 7 Nov. 1978; m.; two c.; ed Cairo Univ.; midfield player; played with Tersana youth team 1990–97, with sr team 1997–2004; striker, Al Ahly Football Club 2004–13; mem. Egyptian Nat. Football Team 2001–13, tournaments include Confed. of African Football (CAF) African Cup of Nations 2006 (scored winning goal in penalty shootout), CAF Champions League 2006 (top scorer of tournament), FIFA Club World Championship 2006 (top scorer), Egyptian League 2006 (top scorer), African Cup of Nations 2008 (scored winning goal in final); UN World Food Programme Amb. Against Hunger; named Best Player in Egypt 2004, 2005, 2006,

2007, Africa Best Player of the Year 2006, 2008, 2012, 2013, BBC African Footballer of the Year 2008. *Address:* c/o Egyptian Football Association, 5 Gabalaya Street, Gezira El Borg Post Office, Cairo, Egypt (office). *Website:* www.efa.com.eg (office).

ABOUYOUB, Hassan; Moroccan politician and diplomatist; *Ambassador to Italy;* b. 18 May 1952; joined Ministry of Commerce and Industry, then Dir of Int. Trade 1980, Minister of External Trade and Minister of Foreign Investment and Tourism 1990–93; elected mem. Parl. 1993; Amb. to Saudi Arabia 1994–95; Minister of Agric. 1995–97; Amb. responsible for trade negotiations 1998; Amb. to France 1999–2006; apptd Amb.-at-Large and Chief Foreign Policy Adviser to King Mohamed VI of Morocco 2006; directed Morocco's accession to GATT and its trade negotiations with EU, participated in conclusion of Uruguay Round, helped organize Marrakesh Ministerial Conf.; Hon. Chair. SIDA-Entreprises Maroc 2006–; Amb. to Italy 2010–, then apptd Perm. Rep. to FAO, IFAD and WFP 2011, also accred as Amb. to San Marino, Malta and Albania 2011–; mem. Bd of Advisors, Global Panel Foundation. *Address:* Embassy of Morocco, Via Lazzaro Spallanzani 8–10, 00161 Rome, Italy (office). *Telephone:* (06) 4402524 (office). *Fax:* (06) 44004458 (office). *E-mail:* sifamaroma@ambaciatadelmarocco.it (office). *Website:* www.ambasciatadelmarocco.it (office).

ABOVA, Tamara, DJur; Russian professor of law; *Head, Centre of Civil Studies, Civil Law, Civil and Arbitration Procedure Department, Institute of State and Law, Russian Academy of Sciences;* b. 18 Nov. 1927, Sumy, Ukrainian SSR, USSR; m. (divorced); one s.; ed Moscow Law Univ.; Sr Consultant, USSR Ministry of Transport 1959–64; Sr Researcher 1964, Head of Div. 1987, later Head of Centre of Civil Studies, Civil Law, Civil and Arbitration Procedure Dept, Inst. of State and Law, Russian Acad. of Sciences; Arbitrator, Int. Commercial Arbitration Court, Chamber of Commerce and Industry, Vice-Chair. Arbitrator, Maritime Arbitration Comm. 2006–; mem. Scientific-Consultative Council, Supreme State Arbitration Court of Russian Fed.; Expert Council on Civil Legislation in State Duma (Parl.) of Russian Fed.; participant in USSR and Russian Women's Movt; Honoured Scientist of the Russian Fed. 2006, Top Lawyer of the Year 2014. *Publications:* more than 150 works on civil law, civil procedure, arbitration etc. *Leisure interests:* music, theatre, art exhbns. *Address:* Centre for Civil Studies, Institute of State and Law, 119991 Moscow, Znamenka str. 10, Russia (office). *Telephone:* (495) 691-17-09 (office). *Fax:* (495) 691-85-74 (office). *E-mail:* igpran@igpran.ru (office).

ABRAHAM, E(dward) Spencer, JD; American consultant and fmr politician; *Chairman and CEO, The Abraham Group LLC;* b. 12 June 1952, East Lansing, Mich.; s. of Eddie Abraham and Juliette Sear Abraham; m. Jane Abraham; three c.; ed Michigan State Univ., Harvard Law School; attorney, Lansing, Mich. 1980–; Prof., Thomas M. Cooley Law School, Lansing 1981–; Chair. Mich. Republican Party 1983–90; Chair. Mich. Del. Republican Nat. Convention 1984; Chair. Presidential Inaugural Cttee, Mich. 1985; Deputy Chief of Staff to Vice-Pres. Dan Quayle 1991–93; Co-Chair. Nat. Republican Congressional Cttee 1991–93; Counsel to Canfield, Paddock and Stone 1993–94; Senator from Mich. 1995–2001; US Sec. of Energy 2001–04 (resgnd); Founder, Chair. and CEO The Abraham Group LLC (consulting firm), Washington, DC 2004–; Chair. and CEO Abraham & Roetzel LLC; fmr Chair. (non-exec.) AREVA, Inc.; mem. Bd of Dirs Occidental Petroleum, Ind. Vice-Chair. 2013–; mem. Bd of Dirs, PBF Energy Inc., NRG Energy, Inc. 2012–, Two Harbors Investment Corpn 2014–, Uranium Energy Corpn 2015–; Chair. Advisory Bd Lynx Global Realty Asset Fund Onshore LLC, Uranium Energy Corpn; fmr Dir, GenOn Energy, Inc., ICx Technologies; mem. Bd or Advisory Cttee, Sindicatum Sustainable Resources, C3; Trustee, Churchill Center; Distinguished Visiting Fellow, Hoover Inst., Stanford Univ. –2008, Co-Chair. Cttee for Justice 2005–08; mem. Electricity Advisory Bd (also Sec.) 2001; mem. Mich., American and DC Bar Asscns; Co-founder Federalist Soc. *Publication:* Lights Out!: Ten Myths About (and Real Solutions to) America's Energy Crisis (co-author) 2010. *Address:* The Abraham Group LLC, 600 Fourteenth Street, NW, Suite 500, Washington, DC 20005 (office); Areva Inc., 4800 Hampden Lane, Suite 1100, Bethesda, MD 20814, USA (office). *Telephone:* (202) 393-7700 (Abraham Group) (office). *Fax:* (202) 393-7701 (Abraham Group) (office). *Website:* www.abrahamgroupllc.com (office).

ABRAHAM, F(ahrid) Murray; American actor; b. 24 Oct. 1939, Pittsburgh, Pa; m. Kate Hannan 1962; two c.; ed Univ. of Texas; Prof., Brooklyn Coll. 1985–; Dir No Smoking Please, Time & Space Ltd Theatre, New York; numerous Broadway plays, musicals, TV appearances and films; Obie Award (for Uncle Vanya) 1984, Golden Globe Award 1985, Los Angeles Film Critics Award 1985, William Shakespeare Award for Classical Theatre, Shakespeare Theatre Company 2012. *Films include:* Amadeus (Acad. Award 1985) 1985, The Name of the Rose 1987, Russicum 1987, Slipstream, Hard Rain, Personal Choice, Eye of the Widow 1989, An Innocent Man 1990, Mobsters 1991, Bonfire of the Vanities 1991, By The Sword 1992, Last Action Hero 1993, Surviving the Game 1994, Nostradamus 1994, Mighty Aphrodite 1995, Children of the Revolution 1996, Mimic 1997, Star Trek IX 1998, Falcone 1999, Muppets from Space 1999, Finding Forrester 2000, I cavalieri che fecero l'impresa 2001, 13 Ghosts 2001, Joshua 2002, The Bridge of San Luis Rey 2004, And Quietly Flows the Don 2004, Peperoni ripieni e pesci in faccia 2004, A House Divided 2006, The Stone Merchant 2006, Perestroika 2007, Come le formiche 2007, Carnera: The Walking Mountain 2008, Language of the Enemy 2008, Perestroika 2009, Barbarossa: Siege Lord 2009, The Unseen World 2010, September Eleven 1683 2012, Goltzius and the Pelican Company 2012, Inside Llewyn Davis 2013, The Grand Budapest Hotel 2014, The Mystery of Dante 2014, A Little Game 2014; narrator Herman Melville, Damned in Paradise 1985, OBS 1985. *Stage appearances:* The Wonderful Ice Cream Suit 1965, The Man in the Glass Booth 1968, 6 Rms Rivvu 1972, Bad Habits 1974, The Ritz 1976, Landscape of the Body 1977, The Master and Margarita 1978, Teibele and Her Demon 1979, King Lear 1981, Frankie and Johnny in the Clair de lune 1987, A Month in the Country 1995. *Television includes:* Dream West 1986, The Betrothed 1989, Largo Desolato 1990, A Season of Giants 1991, The First Circle 1992, Il Caso Dozier 1993, Journey to the Center of the Earth 1993, Larry McMurtry's Dead Man's Walk 1996, Color of Justice 1997, Esther 1999, Noah's Ark 1999, Excellent Cadavers 1999, The Darkling 2000, Dead Lawyers 2004, The Final Inquiry 2006, Shark Swarm 2008, Beauty and the Beast 2012, Homeland (series) 2012–. *Address:* c/o IMG Artists, 4111 West Alameda Avenue, Suite 509, Burbank, CA 91505, USA.

ABRAHAM, Ronny; French judge and professor of international law; *Judge, International Court of Justice;* b. 5 Sept. 1951, Alexandria, Egypt; ed Univ. of Paris II, Inst. d'Études Politiques, Ecole Nat. d'Admin, Paris; Prof., Inst. d'Études Politiques, Paris –1998; Assoc. Prof., Univ. of Paris X, Nanterre 1997–2003; Assoc. Prof. of Public Int. Law and Human Rights, Univ. of Paris II, Panthéon-Assas 2004–; Admin. Tribunal Judge 1978–85, 1987–88; Asst Dir Office of Legal Affairs, Ministry of Foreign Affairs 1986–87, Dir of Legal Affairs 1998–; Maître des requêtes 1988–2000; Counseiller d'État 2000–; Govt Commr within the judicial system 1989–98; Judge, Int. Court of Justice, The Hague 2005–, Pres. 2015–18; Rep. of France to many cases before Int. Court of Justice, European Court of Human Rights, Court of Justice of the EC and int. arbitral tribunals; mem. Cttee of Experts for the Improvement of Procedures for the Protection of Human Rights 1986–98, Chair. 1987–2004; Chair. Jt Consultative Cttee OECD 1994–98; Del. to UN Gen. Ass. 1998–2004; Chair. French Del. to Ass. of States Parties to Rome Statute of Int. Criminal Court 2002–04; Head of French Del. to Cen. Comm. for Navigation of the Rhine 1998–, Chair. 2002–03; mem. Bd Soc. française pout le droit int.; mem. European Group of Public Law. *Publications:* numerous books, papers and articles in professional journals on int. and European law. *Address:* International Court of Justice, Peace Palace, Carnegieplein 2, 2517 KJ, The Hague, The Netherlands (office); Université Panthéon Assas, 12 place Panthéon, 75005 Paris, France (office). *Telephone:* (70) 302-23-23 (The Hague) (office); 1-44-41-57-00 (Paris) (office). *Fax:* (70) 364-99-28 (The Hague) (office). *E-mail:* info@icj-cij.org (office). *Website:* www.icj-cij.org (office); www.u-paris2.fr (office).

ABRAHAMSEN, Egil, MSc, DTech; Norwegian fmr engineer and business executive; b. 7 Feb. 1923, Hvaler; s. of Anker Christian Abrahamsen and Aagot Abrahamsen (née Kjoelberg); m. Randi B. Wiborg 1951 (died 2002); one s. two d.; ed Polytechnical Univ. of Norway, Univ. of California, Berkeley, USA, Durham Univ. and Newcastle Univ., UK; Surveyor, Det Norske Veritas 1952–54, Sr Surveyor 1954–57, Prin. Surveyor 1957–75, Deputy Pres. 1966, Vice-Pres. 1967, Pres. 1967–85; Ed. European Shipbuilding 1955–60; Chair. and mem. numerous cttees; Chair. Bd of A/S Veda 1967–70, Bd of Dirs A.S. Computas 1967–83, The Abrahamsen Cttee 1984–86, Norsk Hydro 1985–92; Chair. Norwegian Telecom 1980–95, Royal Caribbean Cruise Line A/S (RCCL) 1985–89, OPAK 1985–2005, I.M. Skaugen 1990–99, Eikland 1990–99, Kosmos 1988–92, IKO Group 1988–92; Innovation 1990–2004; mem. Bd Den Norske Creditbank 1983–88; Kt Commdr, Order of the Lion (Finland) 1983, Commdr, Order of St Olav (Norway) 1987, Chevalier, Légion d'honneur 1987, Ordre nat. du Mérite 1990, and numerous other decorations. *Leisure interests:* skiing, tennis. *Address:* Borgenveien 50, 0373 Oslo, Norway (home). *Telephone:* 91-71-40-05 (home); 22-49-18-78 (home). *Fax:* 22-49-93-02 (home). *E-mail:* egiab@online.no.

ABRAHAMSON, Lt-Gen. (retd) James Alan; American air force officer (retd) and business executive; *Chairman, Center for the Advancement of Science in Space (CASIS);* b. 19 May 1933, Williston, ND; s. of Norval S. Abrahamson and Thelma B. Helle; m. Barbara Jean Northcott 1959 (died 1985); one s. one d.; ed Massachusetts Inst. of Tech. and Univ. of Oklahoma; commissioned USAF 1955, Lt-Gen. 1982, Gen. 1987; Flight Instructor, Bryan AF Base, Tex. 1957–59; Spacecraft Project Officer Vela Nuclear Detection Satellite Programme, LAAF Station 1961–64; Fighter Pilot, Tactical Air Command 1964; Astronaut USAF Manned Orbiting Lab. 1967–69; mem. staff, Nat. Aeronautics and Space Council, White House 1969–71; Commdr 4950th Test Wing USAF 1973–74; Insp.-Gen. AF Systems Command 1974–76; Dir F-16 Fighter Programme 1976–80; Deputy Chief of Staff for Systems, Andrews AF Base, Md 1980–81; Assoc. Admin. for Space Transportation System, NASA HQ 1981–84; Dir Strategic Defence Initiative Org. 1984–89; Pres. Transportation Sector, Exec. Vice-Pres. for Devt, Hughes Aircraft Co. 1989–92; Chair. Oracle Corpn 1992–95; Lecturer in Astronautics, AIAA 1993; moved to International Air Safety LLC, Washington, DC 1995; Founder and currently Chair. and CEO StratCom International LLC; Chair. Center for the Advancement of Science in Space (CASIS) 2014–; mem. Nat. Advisory Bd Childhelp USA; numerous awards and medals. *Leisure interests:* sports, music, poetry. *Address:* CASIS, 6905 North Wickham Road, Suite 500, Melbourne, FL 32940, USA (office). *Telephone:* (321) 253-5101 (office). *Fax:* (321) 757-6126 (office). *Website:* www.iss-casis.org (office).

ABRAHAMYAN, Hovik Argami, CandMedSci; Armenian politician; b. 24 Jan. 1958, Mkhchyan, Ararat Marz, Armenian SSR, USSR; m.; three c.; ed Yerevan Automobile Road Vocational Coll., Yerevan Inst. of Nat. Economy, trained in burns surgery at Moscow Surgery Inst.; mil. service in Soviet Army 1977–79; Div. Head, Burastan Cognac Factory 1990–91; Dir Artashat Wine and Cognac Factory 1991–95; mem. Republican Party of Armenia, mem. Exec. Bd; mem. Nat. Ass. (Azgayin Zhoghov—Parl.) first convocation 1995–99, re-elected for Constituency No. 17, Ashtarak 2008–, Chair. (Speaker) 2008–11 (resgnd), 2012–14; Chair. Artashat City Council Exec. Cttee 1995–96; Mayor of Artashat 1996–98; Marzpet (Gov.) of Ararat 1998–2000; Minister of Regional Admin and Urban Devt Co-ordination 2000–01, of Regional Admin 2001–02, of Regional Admin and Infrastructure Co-ordination 2002–05, of Territorial Admin endowed with functions of Co-ordinating Minister 2005–07; mem. Security Council 2005–; Deputy Prime Minister and Minister of Territorial Admin 2007–08; Sec.-Gen. Presidential Staff April–Sept. 2008; election campaign Man., Republican Party of Armenia (HHK) 2011–; Prime Minister of Armenia 2014–16 (resgnd); Chair. Yerevan State Econs Univ. Bd; mem. Yerevan State Univ. Bd; Order of 'Mesrop Mashtots' for services to the Repub. of Artsakh (Nagornyi Karabakh); Anania Shirakatsi Medal, Prime Minister's Commemorative Medal, Marshall Baghramyan Medal, Fridtjof Nansen Commemorative Gold Medal, Golden Medal of the Parl. of Greece, Golden Medal of the Theatrical Figures, IPA CIS Gold Medal, Commemorative Medal of Russian SFS Border Guard Dept in the Repub. of Armenia, First Grade Medal 'For Services Contributed to the Motherland' 2012. *Address:* c/o Office of the Prime Minister, 0010 Yerevan, Hanrapetutyun Hraparak, Government Building 1, Armenia. *E-mail:* hotline@gov.am.

ABRAMOV, Alexander G., PhD; Russian physicist and business executive; *Chairman, Evraz Group;* b. 1959; m.; three c.; ed Moscow Inst. of Physics and Tech.; worked at Inst. of High Temperatures, USSR (now Russian) Acad. of Sciences; f. EvrazMetal (predecessor of Evraz) 1992, mem. Original Group, Chair. and CEO Evraz Group –Jan. 2006, Chair. Jan.–May 2006, mem. (non-exec.) Bd May 2006–08, Chair. Evraz Group 2008–, currently CEO Evraz Invest; Bureau mem. Council of Entrepreneurs, Council of Entrepreneurs set up by Govt of Russian Fed. *Address:* Evraz Group SA, 1 Allée Scheffer, 2520 Luxembourg (office); EvrazHolding OOO, 127006 Moscow, ul. Dolgorukovskaya 15, Bldgs 4 and 5, Russia (office). *Telephone:* (495) 234-46-31 (Moscow) (office). *Fax:* (495) 232-13-59 (Moscow) (office). *E-mail:* info@evraz.com (office). *Website:* www.evraz.com (office).

ABRAMOVIĆ, Marina; Serbian performance artist; b. 30 Nov. 1946, Belgrade, Yugoslavia (now Serbia); d. of Vojin Abramović and Danica Rosić; m. 1st Neša Paripović (divorced); m. 2nd Paolo Canevari (divorced); ed Acad. of Fine Arts, Belgrade, Acad. of Fine Arts, Zagreb; Lecturer, Acad. of Fine Arts, Novi Sad 1973–75; Prof. for Performance Art, Hochschule für Bildende Kunst, Braunschweig, Germany 1994–2001; now based in New York; f. Marina Abramović Inst. for Preservation of Performance Art; Dr hc (Art Inst. of Chicago) 2004; Hon. Dr of Arts (Univ. of Plymouth, UK) 2009, (Instituto Superior de Arte, Cuba) 2012; Golden Lion, 47th Venice Biennale 1997, Niedersächsicher Kunstpreis 2003, Best Show in a Commercial Gallery Award, Int. Asscn of Art Critics 2003, Austrian Decoration for Science and Art 2008, Cultural Leadership Award, American Fed. of Arts 2011, '13 July' Lifetime Achievement Awards, Podgorica, Montenegro 2012, Berliner Bear 2012. *Publication:* Walk Through Walls: A Memoir 2016. *Address:* c/o Sean Kelly Gallery, 528 West 29th Street, New York, NY 10001-1308, USA. *Telephone:* (212) 239-1181. *Fax:* (212) 239-2467. *E-mail:* contact@mai-hudson.org (office). *Website:* mai.art (office).

ABRAMOVICH, Roman Arkadyevich; Russian/Israeli business executive and politician; b. 24 Aug. 1966, Saratov, Russian SFSR, USSR; s. of Arkadii Nakhimovich Abramovich and Irina Vassilyevna Abramovich; m. 1st Olga Yuryevna Lysova 1987 (divorced 1990); m. 2nd Irina Vyacheslavovna Malandina 1991 (divorced 2007); two s. three d.; partner Dariya 'Dasha' Zhukova; one s. one d.; ed Industrial Inst., Ukhta, Komi, Moscow Gubkin Inst. of Oil and Gas; f. cos Supertechnologiya-Shishmarev, Elita, Petroltrans, GID, NPR 1992–95; Head of Moscow Office, Runicom SA, Switzerland 1993–96; Co-f. (with the late Boris Berezovskii) Jt Stock Co. P.K. Trust 1995; f. cos Mekong, Centurion-M, Agrofert, Multitrust, Oilimpex, Sibreal, Forneft, Servet, Branko, Vektor-A 1995–96; Founder and Dir-Gen. Runicom Ltd, Gibraltar 1997–99; Dir Moscow br., Sibneft 1996–97, Dir Sibneft 1996–2005; acquired major interest in Evraz Group SA (steel and mining cos) 2006; mem. State Duma 1998–2000; Gov. of Chukot Autonomous Okrug 2000–08 (resignation rejected by Pres. Putin 2007, accepted 3 July 2008), Head of Govt 2001–08, Chair. Dist Duma, Chukot Autonomous Okrug 2008–13; Owner, Chelsea Football Club (UK) 2003–; Prin. Owner, Millhouse LLC pvt. investment co.; Order of Honour 2006; named by Ekspert (Russian business magazine) as Person of the Year (jtly) 2003. *Address:* Evraz Group SA, 121353 Moscow, str. Belovezhskaya, 4, Block B, Russia (office). *Telephone:* (495) 363-19-63 (office). *Website:* www.evraz.com (office).

ABRAMS, Hon. Elliott, BA, MSc (Econ), JD; American lawyer, diplomatist, writer and fmr government official; *Special Representative for Venezuela, Council on Foreign Relations;* b. 24 Jan. 1948, New York; s. of Joseph Abrams and Mildred Abrams; m. Rachel Abrams (deceased); three c.; ed Harvard Coll., Harvard Law School, London School of Econs, UK; Chief of Staff, Special Counsel for Senator Daniel P. Moynihan 1977–79; Asst Sec. of State for Int. Org. Affairs 1981, for Human Rights and Humanitarian Affairs 1981–85, for Inter-American Affairs 1985–89; Sr Fellow, Hudson Inst. 1990–96; Pres. Ethics and Public Policy Center 1996–2001; Special Asst to Pres. of US, The White House and Sr Dir for Democracy, Human Rights and Int. Operations 2001–02, Special Asst to Pres. and Sr Dir for Near East and North African Affairs 2002–05, Deputy Asst to Pres. and Deputy Nat. Security Advisor for Global Democracy Strategy 2005–09; Sr Fellow for Middle Eastern Studies, Council on Foreign Relations 2009–, Special Rep. for Venezuela 2019–; mem. Faculty, Edmund A. Walsh School of Foreign Service, Georgetown Univ.; mem. US Holocaust Memorial Council 2009–14; mem. US Comm. on Int. Religious Freedom 1999–2001 (Chair. 2000–01), 2012–14; mem. Bd of Dirs Nat. Endowment for Democracy 2014–; Grand Cross, Order of the Sun (Peru) 2001; Sec. of State's Distinguished Service Award 1988, Scholar-Statesman Award, Washington Inst. for Near East Policy 2012. *Publications include:* Undue Process: A Story of How Political Differences are Turned into Crimes 1993, Security and Sacrifice: Isolation, Intervention, and American Foreign Policy 1995, Faith or Fear: How Jews Can Survive in a Christian America 1997, Honor Among Nations: Intangible Interests and Foreign Policy 1998, Close Calls: Intervention, Terrorism, Missile Defence, and "Just War" Today 1998, Secularism, Spirituality, and the Future of American Jewry 1999, The Influence of Faith 2001, Democracy – How Direct?: Views from the Founding Era and the Polling Era 2002, Tested By Zion: The Bush Administration and the Israeli–Palestinian Conflict 2013; numerous articles in journals and magazines, including The Weekly Standard. *Address:* Council on Foreign Relations, 58 East 68th Street, New York, NY 10065, USA (office). *Telephone:* (212) 434-9400 (office). *Fax:* (212) 434-9800 (office). *E-mail:* ZShapiro@cfr.org (office); eabrams@cfr.org (office). *Website:* www.cfr.org/americas/venezuela (office).

ABRAMS, J(effrey) J(acob); American film director, producer, writer and actor; b. 27 June 1966, New York City; s. of Gerald W. Abrams and Carol Ann Abrams; m. Katie McGrath; three c.; ed Sarah Lawrence Coll.; co-f. Bad Robot (production co.) 2001; also composes film music. *Productions include:* Exec. Producer, Dir, Writer: (TV series) Felicity 1998–2002, Alias 2001–06, Lost 2004–10 (Emmy award for Outstanding Directing for a Drama Series 2005, Producers Guild of America award for Best TV Series, Drama 2006); Exec. Producer: (TV series): What About Brian 2006, Six Degrees 2006, Boundaries 2008, Person of Interest 2011–15, Alcatraz 2012, Revolution 2012–14, Almost Human 2013–14, Believe 2014; (TV film) Dead People 2015; Exec. Producer and Writer: (film) Forever Young 1992; (TV series) Fringe 2008–13; Producer, Writer, Actor: (film) Regarding Henry 1991; Producer: (films) The Pallbearer 1996, Cloverfield 2008, Mission: Impossible – Rogue Nation 2015, Star Trek Beyond 2016; Writer and Producer: (film) Joy Ride 2001; Writer and Dir: (films) Impossible III 2006, Super 8 2011; Writer: (screenplays) Gone Fishin' 1997, Armageddon 1998; Producer and Dir: (films) Star Trek 2009, Star Trek Into Darkness 2013; Producer, Writer and Dir: (film) Star Wars: The Force Awakens 2015; Actor: (films) Six Degrees of Separation 1993, Diabolique 1996, The Suburbans 1999. *Address:* Bad Robot Productions, 1261 Olympic Blvd, Santa Monica, CA 90404, USA (office). *Telephone:* (310) 664-3456 (office). *Website:* www.badrobot.com (office).

ABRAMS, Norman, AB, JD; American lawyer, academic and university administrator; *Distinguished Professor Emeritus of Law, University of California, Los Angeles;* b. 1933, Chicago, Ill.; ed Univ. of Chicago; Ed.-in-Chief, University of Chicago Law Review while a student; fmr Assoc. in Law, Columbia Univ. Law School; Research Assoc. and Dir Harvard-Brandeis Cooperative Research for Israel's Legal Devt, Harvard Law School –1959; mem. staff, UCLA 1959–, on leave from UCLA serving as Special Asst to US Attorney Gen. in Criminal Div., US Dept of Justice 1966–67, now Distinguished Prof. Emer., UCLA School of Law, Assoc. Dean of Law School 1989–91, Vice-Chancellor of Academic Personnel 1991–2001, Interim Dean of Law School 2003–04, Acting Chancellor, UCLA 2006–07 (retd); Lifetime Distinguished Service Award, UCLA Emeriti Asscn 2012. *Publications include:* Evidence: Cases and Materials (ninth edn, co-author with Berger, Mansfield and Weinstein), Anti-Terrorism and Criminal Enforcement (fourth edn) 2012, Federal Criminal Law and Its Enforcement (fifth edn, with Beale and Klein) 2010. *Address:* c/o UCLA Law School, 385 Charles E. Young Drive East, 1242 Law Building, Los Angeles, CA 90095-1405, USA (office). *E-mail:* abrams@law.ucla.edu (office). *Website:* www.law.ucla.edu (office).

ABRAMSKY, Dame Jennifer (Jenny) Gita, DBE, CBE, BA; British radio producer, editor and broadcasting industry executive; *Chair, Governing Body, Royal Academy of Music;* b. 7 Oct. 1946; d. of Chimen Abramsky and Miriam Abramsky (née Nirenstein); m. Alasdair D. MacDuff Liddell 1976 (died 2012); one s. one d.; ed Holland Park School and Univ. of East Anglia; joined BBC Radio as Programme Operations Asst 1969, Producer, The World at One 1973, Ed. PM 1978–81, Producer Radio Four Budget Programmes 1979–86, The World at One 1981–86, Ed. Today programme 1986–87, News and Current Affairs Radio 1987–93, est. Radio Four News FM 1991, Controller BBC Radio Five Live 1993–96, Dir Continuous News Services, BBC (including Radio Five Live, BBC News 24, BBC World Service, BBC News Online, Ceefax) 1996–98, Dir BBC Radio 1998–2000, BBC Radio and Music 2000–06, Head, Audio and Music Group 2006–08, also in charge of BBC Radio Drama and Popular Music TV 2007–08, mem. Exec. Bd; Chair., Heritage Lottery Fund and Nat. Heritage Memorial Fund 2008–14; Chair., Governing Body, Royal Acad. of Music 2014–; Chair. Univ. of London 2008–; News Int. Visiting Prof. of Broadcast Media, Exeter Coll., Oxford 2002; mem. Econ. and Social Research Council 1992–96, Editorial Bd British Journalism Review 1993–; Vice-Chair. Digital Radio Devt Bureau 2002–08, RAM; mem. Bd of Dirs Hampstead Theatre 2003–, Chair. 2005–; mem. Bd of Govs BFI 2000–06; Gov. Royal Ballet; Trustee, Shakespeare Schools Festival, Central School of Ballet; Radio Acad. Fellowship 1998; Fellow, Central School of Speech and Drama; Hon. Prof., Thames Valley Univ. 1994, Hon. RAM 2002; Hon. MA (Salford) 1997, Dr hc (Westminster), (East Anglia), Hon. DCL (Kent) 2011; Woman of Distinction, Jewish Care 1990, Sony Radio Acad. Award 1995. *Leisure interests:* theatre, music. *Address:* Royal Academy of Music, Marylebone Road, London, NW1 5HT, England (office). *Telephone:* (20) 7873-7373 (office). *Website:* www.ram.ac.uk (office).

ABRAMSON, Jill Ellen, BA; American journalist, newspaper editor and academic; *Senior Lecturer, Department of English, Harvard University;* b. 1954; d. of Norman L. Abramson and Dovie Abramson; m. Henry Griggs; two c.; ed Harvard Univ.; covered 1976 US presidential election for Time Magazine; Editorial Consultant, The American Lawyer 1976; Ed.-in-Chief, Legal Times, Washington, DC 1986–88; Deputy Bureau Chief and investigative reporter, Wall Street Journal 1988–97; joined New York Times 1997, Enterprise Ed., Washington Bureau 1997–99, Washington Ed. 1999–2000, Washington Bureau Chief 2000–03, News Man. Ed. 2003–11, Exec. Ed. 2011–14; currently Sr Lecturer, Dept of English, Harvard Univ.; apptd columnist, Guardian US 2016; Nat. Press Club Award 1992. *Publications include:* Where They Are Now 1986, Strange Justice (with Jane Mayer) 1994, The Puppy Diaries: Raising a Dog Named Scout 2011, Merchants of Truth: The Business of News and the Fight for Facts 2019. *Address:* Barker Center 065, 12 Quincy Street, Cambridge, MA 02138, USA (office). *Telephone:* (617) 495-9862 (office). *E-mail:* abramson@fas.harvard.edu (office). *Website:* english.fas.harvard.edu (office).

ABRASZEWSKI, Andrzej, MA, LLD; Polish diplomatist and international organization official; b. 4 Jan. 1938, Paradyz; s. of Antoni Abraszewski and Maria Zaleska; m. Teresa Zagorska; one s.; ed Cen. School for Foreign Service, Warsaw and Copernicus Univ., Toruń; researcher, Polish Inst. for Int. Affairs, Warsaw 1962–71; Sec. Polish Nat. Cttee on the 25th anniversary of the UN 1970; Counsellor to the Minister for Foreign Affairs, Dept of Int. Orgs, Ministry of Foreign Affairs 1971–83; mem. Polish del. to UN Gen. Ass. 1971–90, with rank of Amb. 2001–, mem. Ad Hoc Working Group on UN's programme and budget machinery 1975, mem. Advisory Cttee on Admin. and Budgetary Questions 1977–82, 2001–09, Vice-Chair. 2006–07, Vice-Chair. Admin. and Budgetary Cttee of Gen. Ass. 1979, Chair. 1982, mem. Cttee on Contribs 1983–88 (Vice-Chair. 1987–88), 2010–, Cttee for Programmes and Co-ordination (Vice-Chair. 1989, Chair. 1990); Asst to Deputy Minister for Foreign Affairs 1984–90; mem. UN Jt Inspection Unit 1991–2000, Vice-Chair. 1993, 1998, Chair. 1994, UN Secr. consultant on results-based management 2011; Prize of the Minister for Foreign Affairs, Prize of the Minister of Finance. *Publications:* various publs on UN affairs, including Reform of the United Nations: a progress report 2000, Financing of the United Nations 2007, paper on results-based management 2011. *Leisure interests:* boating, skiing, swimming. *Address:* United Nations Advisory Committee on Contributions, New York, NY 10017, USA (office); Adriatycka 3, 02-761 Warsaw, Poland (home). *Telephone:* (212) 963-5306 (office). *Fax:* (212) 963-1943 (office). *E-mail:* abraszewski@un.org (office). *Website:* www.polandun.org (office); www.un.org/en/ga/contributions (office).

ABREHE, Berhane, MS; Eritrean civil engineer and politician; ed Univ. of Illinois, USA; Acting Minister of Land, Water and Environment 1998; Dir of Macroenonomic Policy, Office of the Pres. 1993–2001; Minister of Finance 2001–12; mem. Bd of Govs, African Devt Bank Group, Eritrea, Eastern and Southern African Trade and Devt Bank. *Address:* c/o Ministry of Finance, POB 896, Asmara, Eritrea (office).

ABREU, Alcinda António de; Mozambican politician; b. 13 Oct. 1953, Nova-Sofala; ed Universidad Eduardo Mondlane, Univs of Johannesburg and London; Deputy Gen. Sec. Organização da Juventude Moçambicana 1977–91; mem. Parl. 1977–94; Minister of Social Welfare Co-ordination 1994–97, of Foreign Affairs and Co-operation 2005–08, of Environmental Affairs (now Minister of Environmental Co-ordination) 2008–15; apptd by FRELIMO as mem. Nat. Elections Comms responsible for organizing municipal elections in 1998 and general election 1999; elected to Political Cttee, FRELIMO 2002–.

ABRIAL, Gen. Stéphane; French consultant and fmr air force officer; *Chairman, Musée de l'Air et de l'Espace;* b. 7 Sept. 1954, Condom-en-Armagnac (Gers); m. Michaela Abrial; two c.; ed École de l'Air, US Air War Coll., Montgomery, Institut des hautes études de défense nationale, Paris; began mil. service 1973, exchange programme in USAF Acad., graduated from French Air Force Acad. 1975, completed pilot training 1976, extensive experience as fighter pilot and operational commdr, served in unit of German Luftwaffe 1981–84, in unit of Greek Air Force 1988, took part in liberation of Kuwait as commdr of French Air Force's 5th Fighter Wing during Operation Desert Storm 1990–91, served at NATO Int. Mil. Staff in Brussels 1996–99, several appointments to pvt. offices of French Prime Minister and Pres., went on to serve as head of French air defence and air operations, Air Force Chief of Staff 2006–09; Supreme Allied Commdr Transformation, NATO 2009–12 (first European apptd permanently as head of a NATO strategic command); Adviser to Jean-Paul Herteman, Chair. and CEO of Safran 2013; Chair. Musée de l'Air et de l'Espace 2014–; Grand Officier, Légion d'honneur, Officier, Ordre nat. du Mérite, Croix de guerre des théâtres d'opérations extérieures with star, Croix du Combattant, Médaille de l'Aéronautique, Overseas Medal with two bars, Commdr, US Legion of Merit, Verdienstkreuz der Bundeswehr (Silver), German Sports Badge (Mil. version in Bronze), Order of Abdulaziz al Saud (Saudi Arabia) (Superior Class), Kuwait Liberation Medal (Saudi Arabia), Kuwait Liberation Medal (Kuwait), Officer, Order of Aeronautical Merit (Brazil), Santos-Dumont Medal of Merit (Medalha do Mérito Santos Dumont), Brazilian Air Force; Hon. DSc (Old Dominion Univ.) 2011; Distinguished Leadership Award, Atlantic Council 2010. *Address:* Musée de l'Air et de l'Espace, Aéroport de Paris, 93350 Le Bourget, France (office). *Telephone:* 1-49-92-70-00 (office). *Website:* www.museeairespace.fr (office).

ABRIL, Victoria; Spanish actress; b. (Victoria Mérida Rojas), 14 July 1959, Madrid; m. 1st Gustavo Laube 1977–82 (divorced); m. 2nd Pierre Edelman (divorced); two s. *Theatre includes:* Obras de Mihura, Company Tirso de Molina 1977, Viernes, día de libertad, Company L. Prendes 1977, Nuit d'Ivresse, Paris 1986. *Films include:* Obsesión 1975, Robin and Marian 1975, Caperucita Roja 1975, Cambio de Sexo 1975, La Bien Plantada 1976, Doña Perfecta 1976, Esposa y Amante 1977, La Muchacha de las Bragas de Oro 1979, Asesinato en el Comité Central 1981, La Guerrillera 1981, La Colmena 1982, La batalla del Porro 1982, Le Bastard 1982, La Lune dans le Caniveau 1982, Sem Sombra de pecado 1982, J'ai Epousé un Ombre 1982, Rio Abajo 1982, Bajo el Signo de Piscis 1983, Le Voyage 1983, Las Bicicletas son para el Verano 1983, L'Addition 1983, Rouge George 1983, La noche más Hermosa 1984, Padre Nuestro 1984, After Dark 1984, L'Addition 1984, La Hora Bruja 1985, Tiempo de Silencio 1985, Max mon Amour 1985, Vado e Torno 1985, El Lute 1987, El Placer de Matar 1987, Barrios Altos 1987, El Juego más Divertido 1987, Ada dans la Jungle 1988, Baton Rouge 1988, Sandino 1989, Átame! 1989, A solas Contigo 1990, Amantes 1990, High Heels 1992, Lovers (Silver Bear for Best Actress, Berlin Film Festival) 1992, Intruso 1993, Kika 1993, Jimmy Hollywood 1994, Casque Bleu 1994, Nadie Hablará de Nosotras Cuandro Hayamas Muerto (Best Actress, Cannes) 1995, Gazon Maudit 1996, Freedomfighters 1996, La femme du cosmonaute 1998, Between Your Legs 1999, Mon Père, Ma Mère, Mes Frères et Mes Soeurs 1999, 101 Reykjavik 2001, Sin Noticias de Dios 2002, Don't Tempt Me 2003, Incautos 2003, El Septimo Día 2004, Cause Toujours 2004, Incautos 2004, Escuela de Seduccion 2004, Les gens honnêtes vivent en France 2005, Carne de Neón (short) 2005, Tirante el Blanco (aka The Maidens' Conspiracy) 2006, Les Aristos 2006, El Camino de los Ingleses (aka Summer Rain) 2006, 48 heures par jour 2008, Mejor que nunca 2008, Leur morale... et la nôtre 2008, Solo quiero caminar 2008, Musée haut, musée bas 2008, Man on Asphalt 2012, Mince alors! 2012, Madres Libres 2016, Born to Win 2016. *Television includes:* Los libros (series) 1974, La barraca (mini-series) 1979, Estudio 1 (series) 1982, Télévision de chambre: Sous le signe du poisson (film) 1984, La huella del crimen: El crimen del Capitán Sánchez (film) 1985, Los pazos de Ulloa (mini-series) 1985, La mujer de tu vida: La mujer lunática (film) 1990, Riders of the Dawn (series) 1990, X Femmes (series) 2009, Myster Mocky présente (series short) 2009, Le grand restaurant (film) 2010, Clem (series) 2010–17, Les beaux mecs (series) 2011, Hospital Central (series) 2011, La chanson du dimanche (series) 2011, Sin identidad (series) 2014–15, Capitaine Marleau (series) 2016. *Address:* c/o Alsira García-Maroto, Gran Via 63–3° izda, 28013 Madrid, Spain.

ABRIL-MARTORELL HERNÁNDEZ, Fernando, BA, BS; Spanish business executive; *CEO, Indra Sistemas, SA;* s. of Fernando Abril Martorell; ed Instituto Católico de Administración y Dirección de Empresas-ICADE; began career with JP Morgan; Gen. Man. Corp. Finance, Telefónica SA 1997–99, Pres. Telefónica Publicidad e Información (TPI) 1998–2000, COO Telefónica SA 2000, mem. Bd of Dirs 2000–03, Man. Dir 2001–03; Man. Dir and CEO Grupo Credit Suisse España 2005–10, Sr Adviser 2011; Deputy CEO and CFO Promotora de Informaciones, SA 2010–11, CEO 2012–15; CEO Indra Sistemas, SA 2015–; mem. Bd of Dirs ENCE Energía y Celulosa SA, Telefonica Brasil SA. *Address:* Indra Sistemas, SA, Avda Bruselas #35, Parque Empresarial Arroyo de la Vega., Alcobendas, Madrid, Spain (home). *Telephone:* (91) 4805000 (office). *Fax:* (91) 4805080 (office). *E-mail:* indra@indracompany.com (office). *Website:* www.indracompany.com (office).

ABRIL Y CASTELLÓ, HE Cardinal Santos; Spanish ecclesiastic and diplomatist; b. 21 Sept. 1935, Alfambra; ed Pontifical Ecclesiastical Acad., Rome; ordained priest, Diocese of Teruel (Albarracín) 1960; worked in Pakistan, Turkey and Second Section of the Secr. of State in Rome; apptd Titular Archbishop of Tamada 1985; Apostolic Nuncio to Bolivia 1985–89; Apostolic Pro-Nuncio to Cameroun (also accred to Gabon and Equatorial Guinea) 1989–96; Apostolic Nuncio to Yugoslavia 1996–2000, to Argentina 2000–03, to Slovenia 2003–11 (also accred to Bosnia and Herzegovina 2003–05 and Macedonia 2003–11); Vice-Chamberlain of the Apostolic Chamber 2011–12; mem. Congregation for Bishops 2011–; Archpriest of the Basilica di Santa Maria Maggiore 2011–16; cr. Cardinal (Cardinal-Deacon of San Ponziano) 2012; participated in Papal Conclave 2013. *Address:* c/o Palazzo Apostolico, 00120 Città del Vaticano, Rome, Italy (office).

ABSALON, Julien; French mountain biker; b. 16 Aug. 1980, St Amé; m. Emilie; winner World Jr Championships, Mont St Anne 1998, U23 Category, European Championships 2001, 2002; winner World Cup 2003, 2006, 2007, 2008, 2009; Gold Medal, World Championships 2004, 2005, 2006, 2007, 2014; Gold Medal, Olympic Games 2004, 2008; winner, European Championships 2006, 2013, 2014, 2015, 2016; winner French Championships 2006, 2014, 2015, 2016. *Leisure interests:* snowboarding, paragliding, motocross. *E-mail:* athlet-go@wanadoo.fr. *Website:* www.absalon-julien.com.

ABU-GHAZALEH, Haifa Shaker, BA, MA, PhD; Jordanian psychologist and politician; *Special Representative to Civil Society for the Secretary-General, League of Arab States;* m.; one s. two d.; ed Ein Shams Univ., Cairo, Egypt, Univ. of Jordan, Jesuit Univ., Beirut; held several prominent govt positions, including as Adviser to Minister and Gen. Dir for Foreign Relations, Ministry of Educ. 1968–95; Pres. Gen. Fed. of Jordanian Women 1994–96; Regional Project Co-ordinator for UNIFEM, Regional Programme Dir for Arab States Regional Office, UNIFEM 1998–2007, also served as Arab Region Focal Point for the UN for NGO Forum on Women, Beijing 1995 1993–95; Senator to Upper House of Parl. 2007–10; Gen. Sec. Nat. Council for Family Affairs 2007–11; Minister of Tourism and Antiquities 2011; currently Special Rep. to Civil Society for the League of Arab States Sec.-Gen.; Co-founder Gen. Fed. of Jordanian Women; Founder-mem. Women Workers Asscn 2004; Jordanian Rep. and Exec. mem. Arab Women Org. 2008; Exec. Bd mem. Arab Family Org. 2008; mem. Bd of Trustees, Center for Women's Studies, Univ. of Jordan 2006; mem. Bd Royal Comm. 'We Are All Jordan-Kalona Al-Ardun' 2006, Nat. Council for Family Affairs 2007, Nat. Cttee for Women's Affairs 2008; mem. ICT Royal Cttee 2006; Int. mem. Sheikh Sebeka Gender Award Foundation; numerous int. and regional women leadership awards, including awards from Omani Ministry of Social Affairs and Gen. Fed. of Jordanian Women, Women's Leadership Award, Ministry of Educ. 2001, Women's Leadership Award, Ministry of Social Devt (Oman) 2006, UNIFEM Lifetime Achievement Award for Exceptional Services and Commitment 2007, Humanitarian Aid Club 2007, Ministry of Manpower and Migration Award for Egypt 2007, Sheika Sabika Bint Ibrahim Al-Khalifa Award 2007, UN Econ. and Social Comm. for Western Asia (ESCWA) Award 2007, Teaching Excellence Medal from HM King Abdalla 2009, Achievement Award for Exceptional Services, Jordan Tourism Union 2011, Achievement Award for Exceptional Services, Ministry of Tourism and Antiquities 2011. *Television:* wrote, produced and presented a weekly vocational and educational programme for Jordan TV, also a weekly programme, Window on Modern Education, for Jordan TV. *Publications:* numerous books including Teacher's Guide Book 1982, Student's Guide to Secondary & Higher Education 1983, General Principles of Social Defense 1983, Information to Education 1984, Counseling & Guidance Guide 1985, Measurement & Education 1985, Teacher's Guide Book for School Health Education (six parts) 1990, Me & My Career (four parts) 1991, Guide Book for Kindergarten Teacher (two parts) 1994, Guide Book for Early Child Development (four parts) 1995, Gender & Development: A Resource Book 1998, Al-Kashif in Gender & Development 1999, Gender and Youth, Training Manual 2005, The Contribution of NGOs to Beijing+10 2005, Arab Women, Beijing and Beyond 2007, CEDAW KIT (UNIFEM) 2007, Team Leader and Expert of CRC Indicators 2009, Arab Women CEDAW+30 2009, CEDAW Indicators 2009; articles in int. journals including Women for Women; papers presented at numerous int. forums, including several Nat. Women's Machineries in the Arab World, Oxford Research Group, Wilton Park Conf. Forum, Govt of Jordan, ABA, UN Foundation, Women for Peace Int. Org., Inst. of Diplomacy, Abu Dhabi, UNESCO, Japanese Univ., Tokyo, American Univ., Washington, DC and Finnish Adult Educ. Org. *Address:* Office of the Secretary General, League of Arab States, Secretariat, PO Box 11642, Tahrir Square, Cairo, Egypt (office). *Telephone:* (2) 5752966 (office); (6) 5532834 (home); 79-5578678 (mobile). *Fax:* (2) 5740331 (office); (6) 5532938 (home). *E-mail:* hifa.abu@gmail.com; haifa.nhdra@gmail.com (home). *Website:* www.lasportal.org (office); haifaag.com.

ABU GHAZALEH, Mohammad; Palestinian business executive; *Chairman and CEO, Fresh Del Monte Produce Inc.;* Man. Dir Metico 1967–86; Pres. and CEO United Trading Co. 1986–96; acquired Fresh Del Monte Produce, Inc. 1996, Chair. and CEO 1996–; Chair. and CEO IAT Group, Inc. 1997–2010; Chair. Royal Jordanian Air Acad.; Dir Jordan Kuwait Bank 2004–11, Int. Gen. Insurance Co. Ltd (fmr Chair.), United Cable Co. Inc., Bank Misr Liban, Amwal Invest. *Address:* Fresh Del Monte Produce, Inc., POB 149222, Coral Gables, FL 33114-9222, USA (office). *Telephone:* (305) 520-8400 (office). *Fax:* (305) 567-0320 (office). *E-mail:* mabu-ghazaleh@freshdelmonte.com (office). *Website:* www.freshdelmonte.com (office).

ABU-GHAZALEH, Talal; Palestinian/Jordanian management consultant and intellectual property expert; *Chairman of the Management Board, Talal Abu-Ghazaleh Organization;* b. 22 April 1938, Jaffa; m. Nuha Salameh; two s. two d.; ed American Univ. of Beirut; Founder and Chair. Man. Bd Talal Abu-Ghazaleh Int. (TAGI) (now Talal Abu-Ghazaleh Org.) (mem. firm of Grant Thornton Int.), regional holding group of professional firms operating through 34 offices in Arab World and comprising, among others Talal Abu-Ghazaleh & Co. (TAGCO), Abu-Ghazaleh Consultancy & Co. (AGCOC), Al-Dar Consulting Co. (ADCO), Talal Abu-Ghazaleh Assocs Ltd (TAGA), Arab Int. Projects Co. (AIPC), The First Projects Man. Co. (FPMC), Talal Abu-Ghazaleh Int. Man. Inc. (TAGIMI), TMP Agents, Arab Bureau for Legal Services (ABLE), Al-Dar Gen. Trading Co. (ADTCO); mem. Senator (upper house of Jordanian Parl.) 2010–11, 2016–; Chair. Arab Knowledge Man. Soc. (fmrly Arab Man. Soc.) 1989–, Jordanian Nat. Orchestra Asscn 2014–; Chair. CEO4Green, Jordan 2015, Hon. Council of Consortium for Sustainable Urbanization, USA 2015; Amb. of Tourism and the Sustainable Devt Goals, World Tourism Org. 2017–; mem. Bretton Woods Cttee 2014, UN Social Impact Fund High Level Advisory Bd 2017, Advisory Bd, INSEAD Global Talent Competitiveness Index, France 2017; Hon. mem. Kuwaiti Asscn of Accountants and Auditors, Kuwait 2017; Chevalier, Légion d'honneur 1985, numerous decorations from Tunisia, Kuwait, Bahrain and Jordan; Hon. DHumLitt (Canisius Coll. Buffalo, NY) 1988, Hon. PhD (Bethlehem Univ.) 2014, (Mutah Univ.) 2015, (Jerash Univ., Jordan) 2016. *Publications:* Taxation in the Arab Countries, The Abu-Ghazaleh English–Arabic Dictionary of Accounting, Trade Mark Laws in the Arab Countries. *Address:* Talal Abu-Ghazaleh Organization, Building No. 26, Prince Shaker bin Zaid Street, Shmeisani, PO Box 921100, Amman 11192, Jordan (office). *Telephone:* (6) 5100 900 (office). *Fax:* (6) 5100 901 (office). *E-mail:* jordan@agip.com (office). *Website:* www.tagi.com (office).

ABU-HAMMOUR, Muhammed, MA, PhD; Jordanian economist and government official; b. 1961, Salt; m.; two s. two d.; ed Yarmouk Univ., Univ. of Jordan, Univ. of Surrey, UK; Researcher, Public Finance Div., Cen. Bank of Jordan 1987–91, Chief, External Economy and Balance of Payments Div. 1992–94, Chief, Public Finance Div. 1997–98; Adviser to Minister of Finance 1998–2000, Vice-Chair. Evaluation of Monetary, Financial and Econ. Situations Cttee 1999–; Chair. Fiscal Monitoring Unit 1999, Sec. Gen., Ministry of Finance 2000–03; Minister of Industry and Trade July–Oct. 2003; Minister of Finance 2003–05, 2009–11; Chair. Exec. Privatization Comm. 2005–09; mem. Bd of Dirs, Jordan Phosphate Mines Co., Jordan Nat. Bank, The Jordanian Hashemite Fund for Human Devt; fmr mem. Bd of Dirs, Jordan Telecom, Royal Jordanian, Arab Bank, Social Security Corpn, Nat. Resources Investment and Devt Corpn, Deposit Insurance Corpn, Jordan Petroleum Refinery Co. Ltd; part-time lecturer to grad. students in Econs, Univ. of Jordan 1998–; Minister of Finance of the Year in the Middle East, Euromoney Emerging Markets magazine, Washington, DC 2004. *Publications:* Property Tax in Jordan 1987, Factors Affecting Debt Service Ratio in Jordan 1988, The Impact of Financial Assistance and External Loans on Balance of Payments and Money Supply 1989, The Impact of Budget Deficit on GNP, BOP and Money Supply in Jordan 1990, The Instruments of Islamic Internal Debt 1992, Attracting Foreign Direct Investment in Jordan 1993, Measuring Taxable Capacity and Tax Effort in Jordan 1998. *Address:* c/o Ministry of Finance, PO Box 85, Amman 11118, Jordan.

ABU-JABER, Diana, BA, MA, PhD; Jordanian/American author and academic; *Professor of English, Portland State University;* b. 1960, Syracuse, NY; ed State Univ. of New York, Oswego and Binghamton, Univ. of Windsor, Canada; Visiting Asst Prof. in English, Iowa State Univ. 1990; Asst Prof. of English, Univ. of Oregon 1990–95; Prof. of English, Portland State Univ. 1996–, currently Writer-in-Residence, Dept of English; Nat. Endowment for the Arts Writing Fellowship 1994–96, Int. Writers Nat. Endowment for the Arts Fellowship in Fiction 1996–98, Fulbright Research Award, Amman, Jordan 1996. *Radio:* frequent contrib. to Nat. Public Radio. *Publications include:* fiction: Arabian Jazz (Oregon Book Award 1994) 1993, Crescent (PEN Center USA Award for Literary Fiction 2004, Before Columbus Foundation American Book Award 2004, Willamette Writers Northwest Distinguished Author Award 2004) 2003, Origin (Arab-American Book Award 2008, Florida Book Award Bronze Medal 2008) 2007, Birds of Paradise (Arab-American National Book Award 2012) 2011; non-fiction: The Language of Baklava (Northwest Bookseller's Award 2005) 2005, Life Without a Recipe: A Memoir 2016; contrib. of short fiction to many journals including Northwest Review, Left Bank, Story, Many Mountains Moving, Kenyon Review, Salt Hill Journal, Middle East Report, Tin House Magazine, Good Housekeeping magazine, Flyway Literary Magazine, Southern Review. *Address:* c/o Miriam Feuerle and Kate Gannon, Lyceum Agency, 915 SE 35th Avenue, #205, Portland, OR 97214, USA (office); Department of English, Stratford Hall Room 202, Portland State University, Portland, OR 97207, USA (office). *Telephone:* (503) 467-4622 (office); (503) 267-2918 (office). *Website:* www.lyceumagency.com (office); www.english.pdx.edu (office); www.dianaabujaber.com. *Fax:* (503) 725-3554 (office). *E-mail:* abujaber@pdx.edu (office); abujaber@aol.com.

ABU-LAHOM, Rashid Aboud Sharian; Yemeni politician; *Minister of Finance;* Minister of Finance 2019–. *Address:* Ministry of Finance, POB 190, San'a, Yemen (office). *Telephone:* (1) 260365 (office). *Fax:* (1) 263040 (office). *E-mail:* support@mofyemen.net (office). *Website:* www.mof.gov.ye (office).

ABU MAZEN (see ABBAS, Mahmud).

ABU-NIMAH, Hasan; Jordanian diplomatist; b. 11 Sept. 1935, Battir, Jerusalem; s. of Abdul Rahim Abu-Nimah and Fatima Othman Oweinah; m. Samira Al-Najjar; three c.; ed Al-Ummah Coll., Bethlehem, American Univ. of Beirut, Birkbeck Coll., London; fmr political commentator, Amman Broadcasting Service and Lecturer, Teacher Training Centre, Ramallah, Jordan; Third Sec., Embassy, Kuwait 1965–67, Second Sec., Embassy, Iraq 1967–70, First Sec. in USA 1970–72, with Foreign Ministry, Amman 1972–73, Counsellor, Embassy, UK 1973–77, Amb. to Belgium (also accred to Netherlands and Luxembourg) 1978–90, to Italy 1990–95; Perm. Rep. to UN 1995–2000; Dir Royal Inst. for Inter-Faith Studies 2004–14; currently adviser to Prince El-Hassan bin Talal; contribs to Electronic Intifada and Electronic Iraq (online publs), Green Left Weekly 2003, The Daily Star, Al-Rai; weekly articles in The Jordan Times and Al-Ghad; Order of Grand Cross of Crown of Belgium, Order of Independence of Jordan, Grade I, Order of the Star of Jordan (Al-Kawkab), Medal of Pope Paul VI, Order of Grand Cross of Merit, Italy. *Leisure interests:* hunting, reading, researching, writing. *Address:* PO Box 132, Jubeihah, Amman 11941, Jordan (home). *Telephone:* (9626) 461-8051 (office); (9626) 534-1360 (home). *Fax:* (9626) 461-8053 (office). *E-mail:* abunimah@nol.com.jo (home).

ABU SULAYMAN, Muna, BA, MA; Saudi Arabian broadcaster; b. 16 May 1973, Philadelphia, Pa, USA; d. of Dr Abdulhamid Abu Sulayman; divorced; two d.; ed King Abdulaziz Univ., Int. Islamic Univ. Malaysia, George Mason Univ., USA, King Saud Univ., Riyadh; Lecturer in English Dept, King Saud Univ. 1997–2004; Co-host Kalam Nawaem (Softly Speaking), Middle East Broadcasting Centre 2002–07; Exec. Man. of Strategic Studies and Research Initiatives 2004–06; Exec. Dir and Sec.-Gen. Alwaleed Bin Talal Foundation 2006–12; f. range of fashion and accessories; mem. Bd Muslim Women's Fund, Soliya, Meedan Volunteer Dir for Friends of Saudi Arabia Asscn 2004–; mem. Advisory Bd Peaceful Families Project, Gem Schools; mem. Saudi Media Asscn; best known as the first Saudi woman to appear on non-government global TV; Saudi UN Goodwill Amb., UNDP (first Saudi woman) 2005; Global Amb. for Silatech (social initiative to create jobs and econ. opportunities for young people in the Arab world) 2013–; Young Global Leader, World Econ. Forum 2004. *Television includes:* co-host, Kalam Nawaem (Softly Speaking), MBC-TV 2002–07. *Address:* Silatech, PO Box 34111, Doha, Qatar. *Telephone:* 4499-4800; 5-44244118 (mobile). *Fax:* 4472-7651. *E-mail:* info@munaabusulayman.com; info@silatech.com. *Website:* www.silatech.com; www.munaabusulayman.com; www.facebook.com/Muna.Abusulayman.Page.

ABUBAKAR, Gen. (retd) Abdulsalami; Nigerian international official, fmr head of state and army officer; b. 13 June 1942, Minna; m. Fati Lami Abubakar; six c.; ed Minna, Bida, Kaduna, Tech. Inst., Kaduna; joined Nigerian Army 1963, with UN peacekeeping force in Lebanon 1978–79, Chief of Defence Staff and Chair. Jt Chiefs of Staff of the Armed Forces 1993–98, fmrly active in Cttee of W African Chiefs of Staff; Commdr in Chief 1998; Head of Govt of Nigeria 1998–99; apptd UN Special Envoy to Democratic Repub. of the Congo 2000; Head of Commonwealth Observer Mission to Oversee Zimbabwe's Parl. Elections 2000, Mission to Monitor Pres. Elections in Zimbabwe March 2002. *Publication:* Nigeria: A new beginning 1998.

ABULGAZIYEV, Mukhammetkaly; Kyrgyzstani agronomist, government official and politician; *Prime Minister;* b. 20 Jan. 1968, Kochkor Dist, Naryn Oblast, Kyrgyz SSR, USSR; ed K.I. Scriabin Agricultural Inst., Faculty of Econs and Business, Int. Univ. of Kyrgyzstan; Deputy Dir of Finance, Kyrgyzstan agro-industrial co. 1994–95; Exec. Dir Azhar LLC, Bishkek 1995–97; Expert, Dept of State Fund lending support to small and medium-sized enterprises 1997–98; with Employment Office of Dir of the Population, Pervomaisky Dist, Bishkek 1998–99; Dir Dept of Employment of the Population in Bishkek 1999–2003; Head of Internal Audit, Social Fund of the Kyrgyz Repub. 2003, Head of Chui Oblast Man. of Social Fund of the Kyrgyz Repub. 2003–07, Head of Social Fund of Kyrgyz Repub. apparatus 2007–09, Deputy Chair. Social Fund of Kyrgyz Repub. 2009–10, Chair. 2010–16; First Deputy Prime Minister 2016–17, Acting Prime Minister 22–26 Aug. 2017, Prime Minister 2018–; Adviser to the Pres. 2017–18; Diplomas of Ministry of Labour and Social Protection, Chui Oblast State Admin, Mayor of Bishkek, Cen. Cttee of Trade Unions; Badges: 'Excellence in the Social Fund of the Kyrgyz Repub.', 'Excellence in Internal Revenue Service'; Medal 'For Distinction in Mil. Service' II Degree; Memorial Construction of the Sarcophagus (at Chernobyl Nuclear Power Plant, Ukrainian SSR); Rep. of 'Combat Brotherhood Without Borders' in the Kyrgyz Repub. (Kyrgyzstan Chernobyl catastrophe liquidators). *Address:* Office of the Government, 720003 Bishkek, Dom Pravitelstva, Kyrgyzstan (office). *Telephone:* (312) 62-53-78 (office). *E-mail:* ps@mail.gov.kg (office). *Website:* www.gov.kg (office).

ABUOM, Agnes, BS, PhD; Kenyan international organisation official; *Moderator, Central Committee, World Council of Churches;* b. Nandi Hills, Northwest Kenya; m.; two d.; ed Univ. of Nairobi, Univ. of Uppsala, Sweden; Africa Pres., WCC 1999–2006, later served on Exec. Cttee, Moderator, Central Cttee 2013–, represents Anglican Church of Kenya; also serves as devt consultant for National Council of Churches of Kenya, All Africa Conference of Churches, Nairobi Peace Initiative and other orgs; Co-Pres. of Religions for Peace and Nat. Council of Churches of Kenya; Founder-Dir Taabco Research and Devt Consultants 1997–2018. *Address:* World Council of Churches, 150 route de Ferney, Postfach 2100, 1211 Geneva 2, Switzerland (office). *Telephone:* 227916111 (office). *Fax:* 227910361 (office). *E-mail:* info@wcc-coe.org (office). *Website:* www.oikoumene.org (office).

ABUZAYD, Karen Koning, MA; American UN official; *Special Adviser on the Summit on Addressing Large Movements of Refugees and Migrants, United Nations;* b. 21 Aug. 1941, Youngstown, Ohio; m. Abdul Abu Zayd 1969; two c.; ed DePauw Univ., McGill Univ., Canada; fmr Lecturer in Political Science and Islamic Studies, Makerere Univ., Uganda and Juba Univ., Sudan; joined UNHCR 1981, worked on various emergencies across Africa, served as UNHCR Chief of Mission during Bosnian war, Chef du Cabinet to High Commr Sadako Ogata, and Regional Rep. to USA and Caribbean 1981–2000, Deputy Commr-Gen. UNRWA 2000–05, Commr-Gen. 2005–10, Commr, Ind. Int. Comm. of Inquiry on the Syrian Arab Republic, OHCHR, Geneva 2011–16, Special Adviser on the UN Summit on Addressing Large Movements of Refugees and Migrants 2016–; Peace Prize of the UN Asscn in Spain (ANUE) 2011. *Address:* Summit on Addressing Large Movements of Refugees and Migrants, Office of the United Nations High Commissioner for Human Rights, Palais des Nations, 1211 Geneva 10, Switzerland (office). *Website:* www.ohchr.org (office).

ABYKAYEV, Nurtai Abykayevich; Kazakhstani diplomatist and government official; *Chairman of the National Security Committee;* b. 15 May 1947, Jambul (now Taraz), Almaty Oblast; m.; three c.; ed S.M. Kirov Ural Polytech. Inst., Alma-Ata (Almaty) Higher CP School; has rank of Amb.; engineer, Almaty factory of heavy machine construction 1972–76; CP functionary 1976–88; First Sec. of Cen. Cttee 1988–89; Asst to First Sec., Cen. Cttee CP of Kazakh SSR 1989–90; Head Adm. of Pres. and Prime Minister of Repub. of Kazakhstan, mem. Nat. Security Cttee 1990–95, Chair. 1999–2000, 2010–; Amb. to UK (also accred to Denmark, Norway and Sweden) 1995–96; First Asst to Pres. of Kazakhstan 1996–99, fmr Head of Presidential Admin; First Deputy Minister of Foreign Affairs 1999; Amb. to Russian Fed. 2002–03, 2007–09; First Vice-Minister of Foreign Affairs 2009–10; Chair. of Senate 2004–07; Head of Secretariat, Congress of Leaders of World and Traditional Religions. *Address:* National Security Committee, Nur-Sultan, Kazakhstan (office). *Telephone:* (717-2) 32-50-50 (office). *E-mail:* press@knb.kz (office). *Website:* www.knb.kz (office).

ACCARDO, Salvatore; Italian violinist and conductor; b. 26 Sept. 1941, Turin; s. of Vincenzo Accardo and Ines Nea Accardo; m. Resy Corsi 1973; ed Conservatorio S. Pietro a Majella, Naples and Chigiana Acad., Siena; first professional recital 1954; won First Prize, Geneva Competition aged 15 and First Prize, Paganini Competition aged 17; repertoire includes concertos by Bartók, Beethoven, Berg, Brahms, Bruch, Paganini, Penderecki, Prokofiev, Saint-Saëns, Sibelius, Stravinsky and Tchaikovsky; plays with world's leading conductors and orchestras, including Amsterdam Concertgebouw, Berlin Philharmonic, Boston Symphony, Chicago Symphony, Cleveland, La Scala, Milan, Santa Cecilia, Rome, BBC Symphony, London Symphony and Philharmonia; also appears as soloist/dir with the English, Scottish and Netherlands Chamber Orchestras; Artistic Dir Naples Festival; Cavaliere di Gran Croce 1982; Commdr, Order of Cultural Merit (Monaco) 1999; numerous music prizes include Caecilia Prize (Brussels) and Italian Critics' Prize for recording of the Six Paganini Concertos and Diapason d'Or for recording of the Sibelius Concerto. *Recordings include:* the Paganini Concertos and Caprices (Deutsche Grammophon), concertos by Beethoven and Brahms, complete works for violin and orchestra by Bruch, concertos by Mendelssohn, Dvořák, Sibelius and Tchaikovsky (Philips/Phonogram). *Publications:* Edn Paganini Sixth Concerto, Paganini: Variations on "Carmagnola". *Leisure interests:*

hi-fi, electronics, sport, cooking. *Address:* c/o Adriana Armaroli. *Telephone:* (02) 49434974; 347-0767387 (mobile). *E-mail:* management@salvatoreaccardo.it. *Website:* www.salvatoreaccardo.it.

ACCOYER, Bernard; French physician and politician; b. 12 Aug. 1945, Lyons (Rhône); m. Charlotte Marie Jacquier 1971; three c.; head of clinic, specialising in Oto-Rhino-Laryngology (Ear, Nose and Throat) 1976; Mayor and mem. Municipal Council, Annecy-le-Vieux (Haute-Savoie) 1989–2016; mem. Conseil Général, Haute-Savoie 1992–98; mem. Assemblée Nationale (Haute-Savoie (1ère)) 1993– (re-elected 1997, 2002, 2007, 2012), Pres. Assemblée Nationale 2007–12; First Vice-Chair. Union pour un Mouvement Populaire Parl. Group 2002–04, Chair. 2004–07, party became Les Républicains 2015, Sec.-Gen. 2016–; National Order of Merit. *Address:* Les Républicains, 238 rue de Vaugirard, 75015 Paris, France. *E-mail:* baccoyer@assemblee-nationale.fr (office); bernard.accoyer@wanadoo.fr (home). *Website:* www.republicains.fr.

ACEVEDO FLORES, Carlos Gerardo, PhD; Salvadorean central banker and fmr academic; *President, Banco Central de Reserva de El Salvador;* ed Instituto Libre de Filosofía y Ciencias Sociales-Universidad Iberoamericana, Mexico, Vanderbilt Univ., Duke Univ., Boulder Econs Inst., USA; Prof., Dept of Philosophy, Univ. Centroamericana José Simeón Cañas, San Salvador 1984–91, Prof. of Econs 1994, Prof. of Organizational Environment 2007–10; Teaching Asst, Vanderbilt Univ. 1996–98; Sr Analyst, Investigation Dept, Banco Central de Reserva de El Salvador 1998–99, Pres. Banco Central de Reserva de El Salvador 2009–; Prof., Inst. of Business Admin, Instituto Superior de Economía y Administración de Empresas (ISEADE), San Salvador 1999–2010; Prof. of Monetary and Fiscal Policy, School of Econs and Business (ESEN), San Salvador 2000–01; Prof. of Econs and Int. Business Ethics, Universidad Francisco Gavidia, San Salvador 2006–08; Prof. of Econ. Theory, Univ. Dr Jose Matias Delgado, Antiguo Cuscatlán 2007–10; Section Man., Macroeconomics Dept, Fundación Salvadoreña para el Desarrollo Económico y Social (FUSADES) 1999–2004; Deputy Coordinator, Human Devt Report on El Salvador, UNDP 2004–09. *Address:* Office of the President, Banco Central de Reserva de El Salvador, Alameda Juan Pablo II, entre 15 y 17 Avda Norte, Apdo 01-106, San Salvador, El Salvador (office). *Telephone:* 2281-8000 (office). *Fax:* 2281-8011 (office). *E-mail:* info@bcr.gob.sv (office). *Website:* www.bcr.gob.sv (office).

ACHAARI, Mohammad; Moroccan writer; b. 1951, Moulay Idriss Zerhoun; ed Mohammed V Univ.; fmr contrib. to several Moroccan newspapers including Al-Alam, Al Ittihad Al Ichtiraki; mem. Union des Écrivains du Maroc (Moroccan Union of Writers) 1975–, Pres. 1989–96; Sec.-Gen. Syndicat nat. de l'agriculture 1979–84; Bureau Chief, Al Ittihad Al Ichtiraki (daily newspaper) 1983–98; elected mem. Majlis al-Nuab (Parl.) 1997; Minister of Culture 1998, Minister of Culture and of Communications 2000, 2002–07; mem. Union socialiste des forces populaires, mem. Political Bureau; mem. Syndicat nat. de la Presse, Fondation Mohammed V pour la Solidarité. *Publications include:* six collections of poetry, short-story collection; El Jardin de la Soledad/The Garden of Solitude (collected poems in English and Spanish translation) 2005, White Wings in Her Feet 2008, Yabab La Yaqtul Ahadan 2010, Kitab Al Shathayah 2011; novels: South of the Soul, The Arch and the Butterfly (co-recipient Int. Prize for Arabic Fiction 2011) 2010.

ACHAKZAI, Mehmood Khan, MSc; Pakistani politician and mechanical engineer; *Chairman, Pashtoonkhwa Milli Awami Party;* b. 14 Dec. 1948, Gulistan, Balochistan Prov.; s. of Abdul Samad Khan Achakzai; brother of Mohammad Khan Achakzai; m.; five c.; ed Univ. of Eng and Tech., Peshawar; elected to Provincial Ass. of Balochistan 1973; Chair. Pashtoonkhwa Milli Awami Party (Pashtun nationalist party based in Balochistan); mem. Nat. Ass. three times from Qilla Abdullah and also from Quetta; Chair. Pakistan Oppressed Nations Movt; Leader All Parties Democratic Alliance. *Address:* Pashtoonkhwa Milli Awami Party, Club Road, Quetta, Balochistan, Pakistan (office). *Telephone:* (81) 2839500 (office). *E-mail:* owaisjan@pmap.info (office).

ACHAKZAI, Mohammad Khan; Pakistani economist and politician; b. 1938, Qila Abdullah Dist, Balochistan Prov.; s. of Abdul Samad Khan Achakzai; brother of Mehmood Khan Achakzai; ed Jamia Millia Coll., Delhi, India, Forman Christian Coll., Lahore, Harvard Univ., USA, Univ. of Glasgow, UK; started career as lecturer of econs, Government Coll., Quetta 1960; Asst Prof., economics dept, Balochistan Univ.; joined the Planning Comm. of Pakistan, retired as Chief Economist; affiliated with Pashtoonkhwa Milli Awami Party; Gov. of Balochistan 2013–18. *Address:* c/o Governor House, Zarghoon Road, Quetta, Balochistan, Pakistan (office).

ACHARYA, Gyan Chandra, BA, MA; Nepalese diplomatist, government official and UN official; b. 20 Nov. 1960, Kathmandu; m.; two c.; ed Tribhuvan Univ.; joined Foreign Service as Section Officer 1983, served in European Div., Ministry of Foreign Affairs 1983–86, Second Sec., Embassy in Cairo 1986–91, served in UN and Int. Orgs Div., Ministry of Foreign Affairs and Office of the Foreign Sec. 1991–95, First Sec./Counsellor, Embassy in Berlin 1995–98, Jt Sec. (Dir-Gen.), Econ. Relations and Coordination Div. April–Sept. 1998, Spokesman of the Ministry of Foreign Affairs and Jt Sec. (Dir-Gen.) Europe-American Div./S Asia and SAARC Div. 1998–2003, Amb. to Switzerland and Amb. and Perm. Rep. to UN Office and WTO, Geneva 2003–07, Foreign Sec. of Nepal 2007–09, Amb. and Perm. Rep. to UN, New York 2009–12; Under-Sec.-Gen. and High Rep. of the Sec.-Gen. for the Least Developed Countries, Landlocked Developing Countries and Small Island Developing States, UN 2012–17. *Address:* c/o Office of the High Representative for the Least Developed Countries, Landlocked Developing Countries and the Small Island Developing States (UN-OHRLLS), United Nations, Room S-770, New York, NY 10017, USA (office).

ACHARYA, Madhu Raman; Nepalese diplomatist and UN official; b. 24 Feb. 1957, Udavapur; m.; two c.; ed Tribhuvan Univ., Kathmandu; Asst Lecturer, Tribhuvan Univ. 1982–83; Section Officer, Ministry of Home Affairs 1983–90; Asst Sec., Ministry of Finance 1990–93, Under-Sec. of Finance 1993–96; Jt Sec., Ministry of Foreign Affairs 1996–97, Deputy Chief of Mission, Embassy in New Delhi 1997–98, Amb. to Bangladesh 1998–2001, Foreign Sec. 2001–05, Amb. and Perm. Rep. to UN, New York 2005–09, Chair. Fourth Cttee (Special Political and Decolonization) for 61st session of Gen. Ass. 2006, apptd Dir UN Assistance Mission for Iraq (UNAMI) 2010; apptd Exec. Dir South Asia Centre for Policy Studies (SACEPS); head of panel commissioned to suggest ways to Foreign Ministry's organisation and services 2015. *Publications:* several books, including Nepal Culture Shift!: Reinventing Culture in the Himalayan Kingdom 2002, Business of Bureaucracy.

ACHARYA, Padmanabha Balakrishna, BA, BCom, LLB; Indian politician; *Governor of Nagaland;* b. 8 Oct. 1931, Udupi, Karnataka; s. of Shri Balakrishna and Smt Radha; m. Kavita Acharya; three s. one d.; ed Mahatma Gandhi Memorial Coll., Udupi, Mumbai Univ.; mem. All-Indian Student Council 1951–77, Nat. Pres. 1995–2000; Founder and Sec.-Gen. Student Experience in Inter-state Living (student exchange programme) 1967–; Founder and Gen. Sec. Indian Nat. Fellowship Centre (non-govt org.) 1975; mem. Senate, Mumbai Univ., mem. Academic Council 1988–91, mem. Exec. Council 1981–91; various roles with Mumbai Educational Trust including Treas., Sec., Chair. and Pres.; Gov. of Nagaland 2014–, also of Tripura 2014–15, of Assam 2015–16, of Arunachal Pradesh Jan.–Sept. 2017; mem. Bharatiya Janata Party (BJP) 1980–, Pres., BJP NW Dist 1987, mem. Cttee, Mumbai BJP 1989, mem. BJP Nat. Exec. 1991. *Address:* Office of the Governor, Raj Bhavan, Kohima 797 001, Nagaland, India (office). *Telephone:* (370) 2242917 (office). *Fax:* (370) 2242898 (office). *E-mail:* rajbhavankohima@nic.in (office). *Website:* www.rajbhavan.nagaland.gov.in (office).

ACHIDI ACHU, Simon; Cameroonian politician; b. 5 Nov. 1934, Santa Mbu; ed Cameroon Protestant Coll., Bali, Yaoundé Univ., Univ. of Besançon, France, Nat. School of Magistracy, Yaoundé; worked as agricultural Asst, Cameroon Devt Corpn before entering univ.; fmr interpreter, Presidency, Yaoundé, Chief Accountant, Widikum Council, Pres. N W Prov. Co-operative Union Ltd; Minister-del. in charge of State Reforms 1971; Minister of Justice and Keeper of the Seals 1972–75; worked in pvt. business 1975–88; mem. Parl. (Rassemblement démocratique du peuple camerounais) 1988–92; Prime Minister of Cameroon 1992–96; mem. CPDM; Chair. Société Nationale d'Investissement (Nat. Investment Corpn) 2003; mem. Senate 2013–, Vice-Pres. of Senate 2013–17. *Leisure interests:* farming, football. *Address:* The Senate, Yaoundé, Cameroon (office). *Telephone:* 22222–0484 (office). *Fax:* 22223-5475 (office). *Website:* www.assnat.cm (office).

ACHLEITNER, Paul; Austrian business executive; *Chairman of the Supervisory Board, Deutsche Bank AG;* b. 1956; ed Univ. of St Gallen, Switzerland, Harvard Business School, USA; Man., Strategy Consulting, Bain & Co., Boston, USA 1984–88; Vice-Pres., Mergers and Acquisitions, Goldman Sachs & Co., New York, USA 1988–89, Exec. Dir, Investment Banking, Goldman Sachs International, London, UK 1989–94, Chair. and Partner (Goldman Sachs Group), Goldman Sachs & Co. OHG, Frankfurt 1994–99; mem. Man. Bd, Allianz SE (formely Allianz AG) 2000–12; Chair. Supervisory Bd, Deutsche Bank AG 2012–; mem. Supervisory Bd, Bayer AG, Daimler AG, RWE AG; mem. Shareholders' Cttee, Henkel AG & Co. KGaA. *Address:* Deutsche Bank AG, Taunusanlage 12, 60262 Frankfurt am Main, Germany (office). *Telephone:* (69) 910000 (office). *Fax:* (69) 91034225 (office). *E-mail:* info@db.com (office). *Website:* www.db.com (office).

ACHUTHANANDAN, V(elikkakathu) S(ankaran); Indian politician; b. 20 Oct. 1923, Punnapra, Alappuzha, Kerala; s. of Sri. Sankaran and Smt. Accamma; m. K. Vasumathy; one s. one d.; joined State Congress 1938; elected mem. Kerala Legis. Ass. 1967, 1970, 1991, 2001, 2006, mem. for Malampuzha constituency, Palghat Dist 2006–; Leader of Opposition 1992–96, 2001–06; mem. Communist Party of India (CPI) 1940; imprisoned for five and a half years during so-called Freedom Struggle period and went underground for a further four and half years, mem. State Secr. of CPI 1957–, left CPI Nat. Council, formed Communist Party of India (Marxist) CPI(M) 1964, Sec. Kerala CPI(M) 1980–92; apptd mem. Politburo 1985–2009; Chief Minister of Kerala 2006–11. *Leisure interest:* reading. *Address:* Kerala State Committee, AKG Centre, A. Raghavan Road, Thiruvananthapuram 695 034, India (office). *Telephone:* (47) 12305731 (office). *Fax:* (47) 12307141 (office). *E-mail:* cpmkerala@asianetindia.com (office). *Website:* www.cpimkerala.org (office).

ACIEW, Akec Khoc; South Sudanese physician and diplomatist; b. 1 Jan. 1956, Bor Co., Jangelei State; ed Rumbek Secondary School, Khartoum, Univ. of Khartoum, medical training in Minnesota, USA; interned at different hosps 1980, moved back to Juba in the South to become a practitioner at Juba Teaching Hosp.; transferred to Primary Health Care Dept, Ministry of Health in Southern Sudan 1982, responsible for training community health workers, nurses and midwives; nominated to go to France 1983, specialized in paediatrics and medical statistics; returned to Sudan to help those in need during political conflict; joined Sudan People's Liberation Army (SPLA) 1986, appointed Dir of SPLA Medical Corps; with Sudan Rehabilitation and Relief Agency as a regional co-ordinator of Northern Upper Nile, Nasir 1989–90; dispatched to France as Rep. of Sudan People's Liberation Movt 1991–2003, trained and worked as a clinical haematologist; medical training in Minnesota, USA 2004–06; recalled as part of the power-sharing arrangements in Comprehensive Peace Agreement 2006; Amb. in Govt of Nat. Unity (GONU) 2006, Deputy Perm. Rep., Perm. Mission of Sudan to UN, New York 2007–08, Chargé d'affaires a.i., Embassy in Washington, DC 2008–10, participated in Declaration of Independence of Repub. of South Sudan 9 July 2011, Amb. of South Sudan to USA 2012–14.

ACKEREN, Robert Van; German filmmaker, screenwriter and producer; b. 22 Dec. 1946, Berlin; s. of Max Van Ackeren and Hildegard Van Ackeren; Prof. of TV and Film, Acad. of Media Arts, Cologne; German Film Prize, Ernst Lubitsch Prize, Federal Film Prize (FRG), Max Ophüls Prize, Prix Celuloide, Premio Incontri Int., Prix Cinedecouverte, El Premio Cid, Prix L'âge d'or. *Films:* Einer weiss mehr 1964, Wham 1965, Sticky Fingers 1966, Nou Nou 1967, Ja und Nein 1968, Für immer und ewig 1969, Blondie's No. 1 1971, Küss mich, Fremder 1972, Harlis 1973, Der letzte Schrei 1975, Belcanto 1977, Das andere Lächeln 1978, Die Reinheit des Herzens 1980, Deutschland Privat 1981, Die flambierte Frau 1983, Die Tigerin 1985, Die Venusfalle 1987, Die Wahre Geschichte von Männern und Frauen 1992, Deutschland privat - Im Land der bunten Träume 2007. *Address:* Kurfürstendamm 132A, 10711 Berlin, Germany (home).

ACKERMAN, F. Duane, BS, MS, MBA; American telecommunications industry executive (retd); *Chairman Emeritus, BellSouth Corporation;* b. 1942, Plant City, Fla; m. Kappy Ackerman; four c.; ed Rollins Coll., Massachusetts Inst. of Tech.;

joined Southern Bell Telephone and Telegraph Co. 1964, various posts with BellSouth Group, including Pres. and CEO, BellSouth Telecommunications 1992–95, Vice-Chair. and COO, BellSouth Corpn 1995–97, Pres., CEO 1997–98, Chair. and CEO 1998–2006 (retd) 1996–2005, now Chair. Emer.; fmr Chair. Nat. Council on Competitiveness, Georgia Research Alliance; fmr Vice-Chair. Nat. Security Telecommunications Advisory Cttee; mem. Bd of Dirs Home Depot 2007–15, United Parcel Service of America, Inc. 2007–15, Allstate Corpn 1999–2015; fmr mem. Pres.'s Council of Advisors on Science and Tech.; fmr mem. US Homeland Security Advisory Council; Trustee, Rollins Coll.; fmr Gov. Soc. of Sloan Fellows, MIT.

ACKERMAN, Raymond, BCom; South African business executive; *Adviser, Pick 'n Pay Group;* b. 10 March 1931, Cape Town; s. of Gus Ackerman; m. Wendy Ackerman; four c.; ed Bishops Diocesan Coll., Univ. of KwaZulu-Natal; trainee man., Greatermans Group 1951; f. Pick 'n Pay Group (retail group) 1967, Chair. 1967–2010, Adviser 2010–; f. The Raymond Ackerman Acad. of Entrepreneurial Devt, Grad. School of Business, Univ. of Cape Town 2005; Founder Ackerman Family Educational Trust; Melvin Jones Fellow, Lions Clubs Int. 1999; Paul Harris Fellow, Rotary Int; Dr hc (Rhodes Univ.) 1986, (Univ. of Cape Town) 2001, (Univ. of Kwazulu-Natal) 2009; Outstanding Young South African Award 1965, Business Achiever of the Year, Herald Times 1994, Businessman of the Year Award 1994, Outstanding Business Leadership for Commitment to Improving the Quality of Life in South Africa 1996, Pioneer Award, South Africa Council of Shopping Centres 2001, Woodrow Wilson Centre Award 2008, David Rockefeller Bridging Leadership in Africa Award, Synergos Inst. 2010, Lifetime Achiever Award, Sunday Times, Protea Award, Asscn of Marketers, Humanitarian Award, B'nai B'rith, Man of the Year Award, Millennium Achievement Award, Inst. of Marketing Man. *Publications include:* Hearing Grasshoppers Jump: The Story of Raymond Ackerman (co-author) 2001, A Sprat to Catch a Mackerel: Key Principles to Build Your Business (autobiography) 2010. *Address:* Pick 'n Pay Group, 101 Rosmead Avenue, Kenilworth, Cape Town 7708, South Africa (office). *Telephone:* (21) 6581000 (office). *Fax:* (21) 7970314 (office). *Website:* www.picknpay.co.za (office).

ACKERMAN, Valerie (Val) B.; American lawyer, sports executive and fmr basketball player; *Commissioner, Big East Conference;* b. 7 Nov. 1959, Lakewood Township, New Jersey; m. Charlie Rappaport; two d.; ed Univ. of Virginia, Univ. of California, Los Angeles; fmr professional basketball player in France; Assoc., Simpson Thacher & Bartlett (law firm), New York 1986–88; Attorney and Sr Exec., Nat. Basketball Asscn 1988–96; mem. Bd of Dirs, USA Basketball 1990–, Pres. 2005–08; Commr Big East Conf. (split from American Athletic Conf.) 2013–; Founding Pres. Women's Nat. Basketball Asscn 1996–2005; mem. Exec. Cttee Naismith Memorial Basketball Hall of Fame; mem. Bd of Dirs, Girls Inc., NYC Sports Devt Corpn; mem. Nat. Bd of Trustees for March of Dimes; mem. Adjunct Faculty, MS in Sports Man. Program, Columbia Univ. 2009–, has taught Leadership and Personnel Man.; contributing columnist for espnw.com; Brandweek Co-Marketer of the Year Award (co-recipient) 1997, Exec. of the Year Award, New Jersey Sportswriters Asscn 1997, March of Dimes Sports Achievement Award 1997, inducted into GTE Academic All-America Hall of Fame 1999, Outstanding Mother Award, Nat. Mother's Day Cttee 2002, Silver Anniversary Award, Nat. Collegiate Athletic Asscn 2006, Women of Distinction Diploma, IOC 2008, John Bunn Lifetime Achievement Award, Naismith Memorial Basketball Hall of Fame 2008, inducted into Women's Basketball Hall of Fame's Class of 2011, Champion in Sports Business, Sports Business Journal 2011. *Address:* The Big East Conference, 655 Third Avenue, New York, NY 10017, USA (office). *Telephone:* (646) 663-3444 (office). *Fax:* (646) 848-8304 (office). *E-mail:* vackerman@bigeast.com (office). *Website:* www.bigeast.com (office).

ACKERMANN, Haider; Colombian fashion designer; b. 29 March 1971, Santa Fé de Bogotá; adopted aged nine months by a French Alsatian family; ed Acad. of Fine Arts, Antwerp, Belgium; spent his childhood in Ethiopia, Chad, Algeria and France before family moved to the Netherlands; went to Belgium and enrolled in Acad. of Fine Arts, Antwerp 1994 then worked as an intern at John Galliano's Paris offices; asst to Wim Neels (fmr acad. teacher) and worked on Belgian designer's men's and womenswear collections; presented his first collection in Paris 2001; hired as Head Designer for Ruffo Research, commissioned to design two collections (Spring-Summer and Autumn-Winter 2003) while continuing to produce his own line; signed partnership with fashion group bvba "32" 2005, split into two ind. cos 2013; one of the designers approached to succeed Galliano at Dior; Creative Dir Berluti 2016–18; Swiss Textiles Award 2004. *Address:* Atelier Haider Ackermann, Populierenlaan 34, 2020 Antwerp, Belgium (office); c/o Michèle Montagne, 184 rue Saint-Maur, 75010 Paris, France (office). *Telephone:* (3) 821-60-75 (office); 1-42-03-91-00 (office). *Fax:* (3) 828-43-64 (office); 1-42-03-12-22 (office). *E-mail:* info@haiderackermann.be (office); press@michelemontagne.com (office). *Website:* haiderackermann.be.

ACKERMANN, Ronny; German professional skier; b. 6 May 1977; winner, Gundersen and Sprint Disciplines, World Cup, Trondheim, Norway 2004; second, Gundersen Discipline, World Cup, Oberhof, Germany 2004; winner Sprint Discipline, World Cup, Ruhpolding, Germany 2005; second, Sprint Discipline, World Cup, Seefeld, Austria 2005, third, Gundersen Discipline 2005; second, Mass Start, World Cup, Sapporo, Japan 2005; winner, Gundersen Discipline, World Ski Championships, Oberstdorf, Germany 2005; third, Sprint Discipline, World Cup, Lahti, Finland 2005; second, Gundersen Discipline, World Cup, Lahti 2005; third, Gundersen Discipline, World Cup, Oslo, Norway 2005; third, Sprint Discipline, World Cup, Oslo 2005; mem. Rhoener WSV Dermbach skiing club. *Address:* c/o Martina Reichel, Deutsche Sport-Marketing GmbH, Schaumainkai 91, 60596 Frankfurt am Main, Germany. *Telephone:* (69) 695801-11 (home). *Fax:* (69) 695801-30 (home). *E-mail:* martina.reichel@dsm-olympia.de. *Website:* www.ronnyackermann.de.

ACKLAND, Joss (Sidney Edmond Jocelyn), CBE; British actor; b. 29 Feb. 1928, London; s. of Norman Ackland and Ruth Izod; m. Rosemary Jean Kirkcaldy 1951 (died 2002); two s. (one deceased) five d.; ed Dame Alice Owens School, Cen. School of Speech Training and Dramatic Art; has worked in theatre since 1945; repertory includes Stratford-upon-Avon, Arts Theatre, Buxton, Croydon, The Embassy, Coventry, Oxford, Pitlochry, USA, Yugoslavia, USSR, Ireland; tea planter in Cen. Africa 1954–57; disc jockey in Cape Town 1955–57; mem. Old Vic Theatre Co. 1958–61; Artistic Dir Mermaid Theatre 1961–63; Dir The Plough and the Stars; Amb. for Motor Neurone Disease; mem. Drug Helpline, Amnesty Int; Hon. Fellow, Central School of Speech and Drama. *Theatre roles include:* Falstaff in Henry IV, Parts I and II, Hook and Darling in Peter Pan, Clarence Darrow in Never the Sinner, Mitch in A Streetcar Named Desire, Brassbound in Captain Brassbound's Conversion, Sir in The Dresser (nat. tour), Petruchio in The Taming of the Shrew (nat. tour), Gaev in The Cherry Orchard, Gus in Hotel in Amsterdam, Sam in Collaborators, Ill in The Visit, Eustace Perrin State in The Madras House, John Tarleton in Misalliance, Weller Martin in The Gin Game, Captain Shotover in Heartbreak House, Lear in King Lear at the Old Vic, London 2013. *West End musical roles include:* Squeezum in Lock Up Your Daughters, Romain Gary in Jean Seburg, Jorrocks in Jorrocks, Frederic in A Little Night Music, Perón in Evita, Captain Hook and Mr Darling in Peter Pan – the Musical. *Films include:* Seven Days to Noon 1949, Crescendo 1969, The House That Dripped Blood, Villain, Great Expectations, The Four Musketeers, Royal Flash, England Made Me, Lady Jane 1984, A Zed and Two Noughts 1985, The Sicilian 1986, To Kill a Priest 1987, White Mischief 1988, Lethal Weapon II, The Hunt for Red October, To Forget Palermo, Tre Colonne in Cronaca 1989, The Object of Beauty, The Sheltering Desert, The Bridge, A Murder of Quality 1990, Voices in the Garden 1992, Georgino, Occhio Pinocchio 1993, Nowhere to Run 1993, The Bible, Miracle on 34th Street, Mad Dogs and Englishmen, A Kid at the Court of King Arthur, Citizen X 1994, Daisies in December, Till the End of Time, Surviving Picasso, Deadly Voyage 1995, Swept from the Sea 1996, Firelight 1997, Game of Mirrors, Son of Sandokan, Milk, Passion of Mind 1998, Mumbo Jumbo 2000, No Good Deed 2001, K19: The Widowmaker 2002, I'll Be There 2002, A Different Loyalty 2004, Asylum 2005, These Foolish Things 2006, How About You... 2007, Flawless 2007, The Boy with Chocolate Fingers (short) 2011, The Stain (short) (voice) 2011, Prisoners of the Sun 2013, The Portrait (short) 2014, Katherine of Alexandria 2014, Aeris (short; narrator) 2014. *Radio roles include:* Macbeth in Macbeth, The King in The King and I, Honoré Lachailles in Gigi, God in The Little World of Don Camillo, Victor Hugo in Les Misérables, The Dog in Investigations of a Dog, Socrates in The Trial and Death of Socrates 2008, Big Daddy in Cat on a Hot Tin Roof 2008. *Television includes:* The Indian Tales of Rudyard Kipling (series) 1964, Play for Today (series) – The Lie 1970, – The Bankrupt 1972, – Access to the Children 1973, When We Are Married (film) 1987, The Man Who Lived at the Ritz (film) 1991, The Barretts of Wimpole Street (film) 1982, Shadowlands (film) 1985, A Woman Named Jackie (mini-series) 1991, First and Last (film) 1989, They Do It with Mirrors (film) 1991, Deadly Voyage (film) 1996, Tales from the Madhouse (mini-series) – Barabbas 2000, Gioco di specchi (film) 2000, Othello (film) 2001, Lionheart: The Crusade (film) 2003, Henry VIII (film) 2003, Icon (film) 2005, Midsomer Murders (series) – Vixen's Run 2006, Above and Beyond (mini-series) 2006, Moscow Zero, Hogfather (film) 2006, Kingdom (series) 2007, Crusoe (series) 2008–10, Pinocchio (film) 2010. *Publications include:* I Must Be in There Somewhere (autobiog.) 1989, My Better Half and Me (with Rosemary Ackland) 2009. *Leisure interests:* writing, painting, reading, 32 grandchildren, 10 great-grandchildren. *Address:* c/o Paul Pearson, 18 Leamore Street, London, W6 0JZ, England (office). *Telephone:* (20) 8748-1478 (office). *E-mail:* joss@converged.net.au (office).

ACKROYD, Norman, CBE, RA, FRCA; British artist; b. 26 March 1938, Leeds, Yorks., England; s. of Albert Ackroyd and Clara Briggs; m. 1st Sylvia Buckland 1963 (divorced 1975); two d.; m. 2nd Penelope Hughes-Stanton 1978; one s. one d.; ed Cockburn High School, Leeds, Leeds Coll. of Art, Royal Coll. of Art, London; Tutor in Etching, Cen. School of Art and Design 1965–93; Prof. of Etching, Univ. of Indiana, USA 1970; Prof. of Etching, Univ. of the Arts, London 1994–; comms include: Haringey West Indian Cultural Centre 1986, Lloyds Bank Tech. Centre, London 1990, Tetrapak, Heathrow 1991, Freshfields, London 1992, British Airways, Birmingham Int. Airport—Eurohub 1993, British Embassy, Moscow 2000, Lazard, London 2003, Great Portland Estates, London 2008, Sainsbury Lab., Univ. of Cambridge 2010; elected Royal Academician 1991; Sr Fellow, RCA 2000; works featured in various public collections world-wide, including Albertina Museum, Vienna, Art Inst. of Chicago, Arts Council of GB, British Council, British Museum, London, Cleveland Museum of Art, Fogg Art Museum, Harvard, Musée d'Art et d'Histoire, Geneva, Museum of Fine Arts, Boston, Museum of Modern Art, New York, Nat. Gallery of Art, Washington, DC, Nat. Gallery of Canada, Nat. Gallery of Norway, Nat. Gallery of Scotland, Nat. Gallery of South Africa, Queensland Art Gallery, Rijksmuseum, Amsterdam, The Royal Collection, Windsor Castle, Stedelijk, Amsterdam, Tate Gallery, London, Utah Museum of Fine Art; lives in Bermondsey, London; British Int. Print Biennale Prize 1974, 1982, Royal Soc. of Etchers and Engravers Award 1984, 1985, Bronze Medal, Frechen, Germany 1986. *Television includes:* BBC documentaries 1980, 2006, Artists in Print (Etching) 1981, A Prospect of Rivers 1988, What Do Artists Do All Day? 2013. *Publications include:* Landscapes and Figures, Etchings (with William McIlvanney) 1973, The Pictish Coast (with Douglas Dunn) 1988, St Kilda: The Furthest Island 1989, Windrush 1990. *Leisure interests:* British history, archaeology, cricket. *Address:* c/o Zillah Bell Gallery, 5 Kirkgate, Thirsk, North Yorks., YO7 1PQ, England. *Telephone:* (1845) 522479. *E-mail:* norman@normanackroyd.com; info@zillahbellgallery.co.uk. *Website:* www.normanackroyd.com; www.zillahbellgallery.co.uk.

ACKROYD, Peter, CBE, MA, FRSL; British writer; b. 5 Oct. 1949, London; s. of Graham Ackroyd and Audrey Whiteside; ed St Benedict's School, Ealing, Clare Coll., Cambridge and Yale Univ., USA; Literary Ed. The Spectator 1973–77, Jt Man. Ed. 1978–82; Chief Book Reviewer, The Times 1986–; Mellon Fellow, Yale Univ.; Hon. Fellow, Clare Coll., Cambridge 2008, Hon. Fellow, RIBA 2009; Hon. DLitt (Univ. of Exeter), (London Guildhall), (City Univ.), (Univ. Coll., London), (Brunel Univ.) 2006. *Play:* The Mystery of Charles Dickens 2000. *Television:* Charles Dickens (BBC 2), Peter Ackroyd's London (BBC 2) 2004, The Romantics (BBC 2) 2006, London Visions (Artsworld) 2007, Peter Ackroyd's Venice (BBC 2) 2009. *Publications include:* fiction: The Great Fire of London 1982, The Last Testament of Oscar Wilde (Somerset Maugham Prize 1984) 1983, Hawksmoor (Whitbread Award for Fiction 1986, Guardian Fiction Award 1986) 1985, Chatterton 1987, First Light 1989, English Music 1992, The House of Doctor Dee 1993, Dan Leno and the Limehouse Golem 1994, Milton in America 1996, The Plato Papers 1999, The Clerkenwell Tales (short stories) 2003, The Lambs of London 2004, The Fall of Troy 2006, The Casebook of Victor Frankenstein 2009, The Canterbury Tales: A Retelling 2009, The Death of King Arthur: The Immortal

Legend 2010, Three Brothers 2013; non-fiction: Notes for a New Culture 1976, Dressing Up: Transvestism and Drag: The History of an Obsession 1979, Ezra Pound and His World 1980, T. S. Eliot (RSL W. H. Heinemann Award 1985, Whitbread Award for Biography 1985) 1984, Dickens 1990, Introduction to Dickens 1991, Blake 1995, The Life of Thomas More 1998, London: The Biography 2000, Dickens: Public Life and Private Passion 2002, The Collection 2002, Albion: The Origins of the English Imagination 2002, Illustrated London 2003, The Beginning: Voyages Through Time (juvenile) 2003, Chaucer 2004, Shakespeare: The Biography 2005, Brief Lives: Newton 2006, Thames: Sacred River 2007, Poe: A Life Cut Short 2008, Venice: Pure City 2009, The English Ghost: Spectres through Time 2010, London Under 2011, The History of England (Vol. 1 Foundation 2011, Vol. 2 Tudors 2013, Vol. 3 Civil War 2014, Vol. 4 Revolution 2016, Vol. 5 Dominion 2018), Wilkie Collins 2012, London: The Concise Biography 2012, Charlie Chaplin 2014, Alfred Hitchcock 2015, Queer City 2017; poetry: London Lickpenny 1973, Country Life 1978, The Diversions of Purley 1987. *Address:* c/o Susijn Agency Ltd, 820 Harrow Road, London, NW10 5JU, England (office). *Telephone:* (20) 8968-7435 (office). *E-mail:* info@thesusijnagency.com (office). *Website:* www.thesusijnagency.com/PeterAckroyd.htm (office).

ACLAND, Sir Antony (Arthur), KG, GCMG, GCVO; British fmr diplomatist; b. 12 March 1930, London; s. of Brig. P. B. E. Acland; m. 1st Clare Anne Verdon 1956 (died 1984); two s. one d.; m. 2nd Jennifer McGougan (née Dyke) 1987; ed Eton Coll., Christ Church, Oxford; joined diplomatic service 1953, at Middle East Centre for Arab Studies 1954, served in Dubai 1955, Kuwait 1956, at Foreign Office 1958–62, Asst Pvt. Sec. to Sec. of State 1959–62, mem. UK Mission to UN 1962–66, Head of Chancery, Mission in Geneva 1966–68, at FCO 1968, Head of Arabian Dept 1970–72, Prin. Pvt. Sec. to Foreign and Commonwealth Sec. 1972–75, Amb. to Luxembourg 1975–77, to Spain 1977–79, Deputy Under-Sec. of State 1980–82, Perm. Under-Sec. of State and Head of Diplomatic Service 1982–86, Amb. to USA 1986–91; Provost of Eton 1991–2000; Chancellor, Order of St Michael and St George 1994–2005; Dir Shell Transport and Trading 1991–2000, Booker PLC 1992–99; Chair. Council of the Ditchley Foundation 1991–96, Tidy Britain Group 1991–96 (Pres. 1996–2002); Pres. Exmoor Soc. 2007; Trustee, Nat. Portrait Gallery 1991–99, Esmée Fairbairn Foundation 1991–2005; Hon. DCL (Exeter) 1988, (William and Mary Coll., USA) 1990, (Reading) 1991. *Leisure interests:* country pursuits, reading. *Address:* Staddon Farm, nr Winsford, Minehead, Somerset, TA24 7HY, England (home). *Telephone:* (1643) 831489 (home).

ACOGNY, Germaine; Senegalese/French dancer, choreographer and teacher; *Artistic Director, L'École des sables;* b. 28 June 1944, Porto Novo, Benin; m. Helmut Vogt; moved to France 1962, returned to Dakar to found pvt. professional dance studio; Dir Mudra Africa Int. Dance School, Dakar 1977–82; worked in Brussels with Maurice Béjart; dancer, choreographer with Peter Gabriel (q.v.) 1984; first solo performance Sahel 1984; collaborated with drummer Arona N'Diaye to stage Ye'ou, the Awakening 1985; performance at World of Music and Dance Festival 1993; co-f. (with Helmut Vogt) Studio-Ecole-Ballet-Theatre of the Third World, Toulouse, France; f. The School of Sands (L'École des sables maison int. de danse), Toubab Dialaw, Senegal 1995, Artistic Dir 2015–; f. Jant Bi Dance Co.; Artistic Dir Dance Section, Afrique en Créations/AFAA (French Asscn for Artistic Action) 1997–2000; also Artistic Dir Contemporary African Dance Competition; Tchourai Solo 2001–08, Fagaala (with Kota Yamazaki) 2003–04, organiser of annual three-month workshop for African dancers and choreographers; Chevalier, Ordre nat. du Merite, Officier des Arts et des Lettres 2009, Chevalier, Ordre Nat. du Lion (Senegal), Commdr, Ordre des Arts et Lettres, 2009, Commdr des Arts et des Lettres (Senegal) 2012; London Dance and Performance Award for Ye'ou, the Awakening 1991, Foundation for Contemporary Performance Arts Award 2005, Bessie Award 2007. *Dance includes:* Ye'ou, the Awakening 1985, Sahel 1987, Afrique, ce corps memorable 1990, Yewa, Eau Sublime, for dance Biennale Lyon 1994, Z 1995, Le coq est mort (The Rooster is Dead) 2001, Tchourai 2001, Fagaala 2004, Waxtaan (with Patrick Acogny) 2006, Opéra du Sahel 2007 (tour to Africa 2009), Les écailles de la mémoire (Scales of Memory) 2008, Songook Yaakaar 2010, A un endroit du début Solo (with Mikael Serre) 2015. *Television includes:* Regard de Femmes, Double Je (Pivot), Ecole des Sables (documentary), Tchourai (documentary). *Publications include:* African Dance 1980, Tchourai 2005. *Address:* Jant-Bi/L'École des sables, BP 22626, Toubab Dialaw, 15523 Dakar-Ponty, Senegal (office). *Telephone:* (33) 8363619 (office). *Fax:* (33) 8363619 (office). *E-mail:* jantbi@gmail.com (office); germaine.acogny@jantbi.org. *Website:* www.jantbi.org (office).

ACOSTA MONTALVÁN, Iván Adolfo, LLM; Nicaraguan government official and international organization official; *Minister of Finance and Public Credit;* joined Ministry of Finance and Public Credit 2007, positions held include Gen. Sec., Vice-Minister of Finance and Public Credit, Minister of Finance and Public Credit 2012–; Deputy Gov. Banco Centroamericano de Integracion Economica; Gov. for Nicaragua, World Bank, Inter-American Devt Bank. *Address:* Ministry of Finance and Public Credit, Frente a la Asamblea Nacional, Apdo 2170, Managua, Nicaragua (office). *Telephone:* 2222-7061 (office). *Fax:* 2222-6430 (office). *E-mail:* webmaster@mhcp.gob.ni (office). *Website:* www.hacienda.gob.ni (office).

ACOSTA, Carlos, CBE; Cuban/British ballet dancer and choreographer; b. (Carlos Yunior Acosta Quesada), 2 June 1973, Havana; m. Charlotte Acosta; one d.; ed Nat. Ballet School of Cuba; guest appearances with numerous int. ballet cos 1989–91; guest dancer, English Nat. Ballet 1991–92; dancer, Nat. Ballet of Cuba 1992–93; Prin. Dancer, Houston Ballet 1993–; joined The Royal Ballet, London 1998, Prin. Guest Artist 2003–16; Founder Acosta Danza, Cuba 2016; Prix de Lausanne Gold Medal 1990, Spanish Vegnale Dance Prix 1990, Grand Prix and Gold Medal, Fourth Annual Ballet Competition, Paris 1990, Grand Prix, Third Juvenile Dance Competition 1991, Dance Fellowship, Princess Grace Foundation (USA) 1995, Int. Critics' Prize Chile, Nat. Dance Awards Best Male Dancer 2004, Outstanding Achievement in Dance, Laurence Olivier Awards 2007, Prix Benois de la Danse 2008. *Performances include:* English Nat. Ballet: Polovtsian Dances from Prince Igor 1991, The Nutcracker 1992, Cinderella 1992; Nat. Ballet of Cuba: Giselle 1994, Don Quixote 1994, Swan Lake 1994; Houston Ballet: The Nutcracker 1993, Swan Lake, La Bayadère, Don Quixote; Royal Ballet: In the middle, somewhat elevated 1998, Raymonda, La Fille mal gardée, My Brother, My Sisters, Giselle, Rhapsody, Le Corsaire, The Nutcracker 2000, Coppelia 2000, Shadowplay 2000, Don Quixote 2001, 2013, Apollo 2002, Tocororo 2003, La Fille mal gardée 2005, Romeo and Juliet 2012, Swan Lake 2012, Manon 2014, Carmen 2015. *Publication:* No Way Home: A Cuban Dancer's Story (biog.) 2007, Pig's Foot (novel) 2013. *Address:* c/o Carlos Acosta Management, Aviation House, 1–7 Sussex Road, Haywards Heath, West Sussex, RH16 4DZ, England (office). *Telephone:* (1444) 450901 (office). *E-mail:* rupert.rohan@validworldwide.com (office); info@carlosacosta.com (office). *Website:* www.carlosacosta.com.

ACOSTA, (Rene) Alexander, AB, JD; American lawyer, university administrator and government official; *Secretary of Labor;* b. 16 Jan. 1969, Miami; m. Jan Williams; two c.; ed Harvard Coll., Harvard Law School; law clerk to Judge Samuel Alito, US Court of Appeals for the Third Circuit 1994–95; private legal practice with Kirkland & Ellis, Washington, DC; fmr law teacher, George Mason School of Law; Sr Fellow, Ethics and Public Policy Center 1998–2000; Asst Attorney Gen. for Civil Rights 2003–05; US Attorney for Southern Dist of Florida 2005–09; Dean, Florida Int. Univ. Coll. of Law 2009–17; Sec. of Labor 2017–; mem. Nat. Labor Relations Bd 2002–03; mem. Florida Innocence Comm., Florida Supreme Court Comm. on Professionalism, Comm. for Hispanic Rights and Responsibilities; Republican. *Address:* US Department of Labor, 200 Constitution Ave. NW, Washington, DC 20210, USA (office). *Telephone:* (866) 487-2365 (office). *Website:* www.dol.gov (office).

ACQUAVELLA, William; American art dealer and gallery owner; *Owner, Acquavella Galleries;* s. of late Nicholas Acquavella (founder of Acquavella Galleries) and Edythe Acquavella; m. Donna Acquavella; two s. one d.; ed Westminster School, Simsbury, Conn., Washington and Lee Univ., Lexington, Va; began by working for his father at Acquavella Galleries 1960, has sold major paintings and sculpture to pvt. collectors and museums world-wide, gallery has presented exhbns of Claude Monet, Edgar Degas, Paul Cézanne, Alfred Sisley, Pierre-Auguste Renoir, Camille Pissarro, Amedeo Modigliani, Pierre Bonnard, Yves Tanguy, Fernand Léger, Pablo Picasso, Henri Matisse, Robert Rauschenberg, Lyonel Feininger, Alberto Giacometti, Joan Miró, Lucian Freud and James Rosenquist; fmr Pres. Art Dealers Asscn of America; mem. Bd Westminster School. *Leisure interests:* tennis, golf, skiing. *Address:* Acquavella Galleries, Inc., 18 East 79th Street (between Madison and Fifth Avenues), New York, NY 10075, USA (office). *Telephone:* (212) 734-6300 (office). *Fax:* (212) 794-9394 (office). *E-mail:* info@acquavellagalleries.com (office). *Website:* www.acquavellagalleries.com (office).

ACUIL, Awut Deng, BA; South Sudanese politician; *Minister of Gender and Social Development;* b. Tonj; d. of Rek Dinka and Agar Dinka; widowed; seven c.; ed US International Univ., Kenya; refugee in Kenya; mem. Sudanese People's Liberation Movt's negotiating delegation at Intergovernmental Authority on Devt peace talks 2002; Minister of Labour and Public Service 2010–11, of Gender and Social Development 2013–; co-f. Sudanese Women's Asscn, Nairobi, Sudanese Women's Voice for Peace, Sudanese Catholic Bishops Regional Conf.; est. Pankar (peace and good governance grassroots initiative); mem. Inst. for Inclusive Security's Women Waging Peace Network 1999–; InterAction Humanitarian Award 2002, Vital Voices Global Leadership Award 2007. *Address:* Ministry of Gender and Social Development, Ministries Complex, Juba, South Sudan (office). *Telephone:* 126925801 (office). *E-mail:* mgswragoss@gmail.com (office).

ACZÉL, János D., PhD, FRSC; Canadian (b. Hungarian) mathematician and academic; *Distinguished Professor Emeritus and Adjunct Professor, Department of Pure Mathematics, University of Waterloo;* b. 26 Dec. 1924, Budapest; s. of Dezső Aczél and Irén Aczél; m. Susan Kende 1946; two d.; ed D. Berzsenyi High School, Univ. of Budapest; teaching asst, Univ. of Budapest 1946–48; Statistician, Metal Workers' Trade Union, Budapest 1948; Asst Prof., Univ. of Szeged 1948–50; Assoc. Prof. and Dept Head, Tech. Univ., Miskolc 1950–52; Dept Head, Assoc. Prof. then Prof., L. Kossuth Univ., Debrecen 1952–65; Prof., Dept of Pure Math., Univ. of Waterloo, Ont., Canada 1965–, Distinguished Prof. 1969–93, Distinguished Prof. Emer. and Adjunct Prof. 1993–; many visiting professorships and fellowships, N America, Europe, Africa, Asia and Australia 1963–; Chair. Int. Symposia on Functional Equations 1962–96, Hon. Chair. 1997–; mem. Canadian Math. Soc., American Math. Soc., New York Acad. of Science; Fellow, Royal Soc. of Canada 1971 (Convener Math. Div. 1974–75, Chair. Acad. of Science Editorial Cttee 1977–78); Foreign Fellow, Hungarian Acad. of Sciences 1990; donor, L. Fejér-J. Aczél Scholarship, Univ. of Waterloo, donor Susan and János Aczél Scholarship; Dr hc (Karlsruhe) 1990, (Graz) 1995, (Katowice) 1996, (Miskolc) 1999, (Debrecen) 2003; M. Beke Award, J. Bolyai Math. Soc. 1961, Award of Hungarian Acad. of Sciences 1962, Cajal Medal, Nat. Research Council of Spain 1988, Kampé de Feriet Award, Int. Conf. on Information Processing and Man. of Uncertainty in Knowledge-Based Systems 2004. *Publications:* more than 300 articles and ten books, including Lectures on Functional Equations and their Applications 1966 (republished 2006), A Short Course on Functional Equations Based upon Recent Applications to the Social and Behavioral Sciences 1987, Functional Equations in Several Variables (with J. Dhombres) 1989, (enlarged Russian trans. 2003); Hon. Ed.-in-Chief Aequationes Math; Ed. Theory and Decision Library, Series B and seven int. mathematical journals. *Leisure interests:* reading, swimming, walking. *Address:* Department of Pure Mathematics, University of Waterloo, Waterloo, ON N2L 3G1, Canada (office). *Telephone:* (519) 888-4567, ext. 36140 (office). *Fax:* (519) 725-0160 (office). *E-mail:* jdaczel@math.uwaterloo.ca (office). *Website:* www.math.uwaterloo.ca (office).

ADABASHYAN, Aleksander Artemovich; Russian scriptwriter, artist and actor; b. 8 March 1945, Moscow; m. Shadrina Yekaterina Igorevna; two d.; ed Moscow (Stroganov) Higher School of Art and Design; began career as art dir working with Nikita Mikhalkov (q.v.). *Films include:* At Home Among Strangers, A Stranger at Home (art dir) 1975, The Slave of Love (artistic designer) 1976, Trans-Siberian Express 1978, Five Evenings (actor) 1979, Several Days in the Life of Oblomov 1980, Kinsfolk 1982, Mado, Poste Restante (dir) 1992, Unfinished Piece for Mechanical Piano (scriptwriter/co-scriptwriter) 1997, The President and His Niece (actor) 2000. *Address:* Novy Arbat str. 31, Apt 36, 121099 Moscow, Russia. *Telephone:* (495) 205-00-89.

ADACHI, Naoki, LLB; Japanese business executive; *Chairman, Toppan Printing Company Ltd;* ed Chuo Univ.; joined Sales Dept, Toppan Printing Co. Ltd 1962, has held several exec. positions including Man. Dir 1995–97, Sr Man. Dir 1997–98, Vice-Pres. 1998–2000, Pres. and CEO 2000–10, Chair. 2010–, mem. Bd of Dirs

2005–; mem. Bd of Dirs Toppan Forms Co., Ltd 2000–, Toyo Ink SC Holdings Co., Ltd 2008–, Daiichi Sankyo Co., Ltd 2015–. *Address:* Toppan Printing Company Ltd, 1, Kanda Izumi-cho, Chiyoda-ku, Tokyo, 101-0024, Japan (office). *Telephone:* (3) 3835-5111 (office). *Fax:* (3) 3835-0674 (office). *Website:* www.toppan.co.jp (office).

ADADA, Rodolphe; Republic of the Congo politician and diplomatist; b. 28 April 1946; joined Cen. Cttee of Congolese Labour Party (PCT) 1972; Minister of Mines and Energy 1977–84, of Mines and Oil 1984–89, of Secondary and Higher Educ., in charge of Scientific Research 1989–91, of Foreign Affairs and Cooperation 1997–2007, promoted to rank of Minister of State for Foreign Affairs 2005; elected to Nat. Ass. as PCT cand. in first constituency of Ouenze, 5th arrondissement of Brazzaville 2002–; Jt African Union-UN Special Rep. in Darfur 2007–09; Minister of State for Industrial Devt and the Promotion of the Pvt. Sector 2009–12, Minister of State for Transport, Civil Aviation and Maritime Trade 2012–16.

ADAM, Lt-Gen. Anbaree Abdul Sattar; Maldivian army officer (retd), politician and diplomatist; m. Ihusaana Ahmed; two s. one d.; fmr Dir and Dir-Gen. of Nat. Security, Minister of State for Defence and Nat. Security 1993–96, Chief of Staff of Nat. Security Services (NSS), and Deputy C-in-C of NSS and of Police 1996–2004; first resident High Commr to India (also accred to Nepal and Bhutan) 2004–10; fmr Chair. Air Maldives; Green Diplomatist Award, Diplomatic Endeavour and Action Neology Award, Lifetime Diplomacy Award in the area of Diplomacy and International Relations, Garden Global Leadership Award for Diplomacy, Peace and International Understanding Award, Inst. of UN and UNESCO Studies (IUNUS) 2008.

ADAM, Azeema, MA, PhD; Maldivian economist and banker; *Envoy of Maldives, United Nations;* b. 22 Nov. 1971; ed Univ. of Leicester, UK, Univ. of Canberra, Australia; Research Officer, Econ. Research and Statistics Div., Maldives Monetary Authority (MMA) 1991–95, Officer-in-Charge 1999–2000, Asst Man. July–Oct. 2000, Deputy Man. 2001–04, Man. 2004–06, Exec. Dir, Monetary Policy and Research Div. 2006–13 (on study leave 2008–11), Asst Gov. and Chief Economist, Monetary Policy, Research and Statistics 2013–14, Gov. 2014–17 (resgnd); Envoy on Financing for Devt, Perm. Mission of Maldives to UN and other Int. Orgs., Geneva 2018–. *Address:* Permanent Mission of the Republic of Maldives to the United Nations and other International Organizations in Geneva, Rue de Varembé 7, 1202 Genève, Switzerland (office). *Telephone:* 225523777 (office). *Fax:* 227326339 (office). *E-mail:* info@maldivesmission.ch (office). *Website:* maldivesmission.ch.

ADAM, Jean-Paul, MA; Seychelles politician; *Minister of Health and Social Affairs;* ed Univ. of Manchester, Univ. of Sheffield, UK; worked as language asst, Bordeaux, France 2000; joined Ministry of Foreign Affairs 2001, becoming Protocol Officer and later Second Sec. 2001–05; Dir, Presidential Affairs, Office of the Pres. 2005–06, Dir-Gen. 2006–07, Prin. Sec. 2007–09, Sec. of State in Office of the Pres. 2009; Minister of Foreign Affairs 2010–15, of Finance, Trade and the Blue Economy 2015–16, of Health and Social Affairs 2016–; Trustee, Seychelles Univ. Foundation. *Address:* Ministry of Health and Social Affairs, POB 52, Mont Fleuri, Seychelles (office). *Telephone:* 4388000 (office). *Fax:* 4226042 (office). *Website:* www.moh.gov.sc (office).

ADAM, Robert, RIBA, FRSA; British architect; *Director, ADAM Architecture;* b. 10 April 1948, Dorset; s. of R. Wilson Adam and Margaret Adam; m. Sarah J. Chalcraft 1970; one s. one d.; ed Canford School and Regent Street Polytechnic (now Univ. of Westminster); Co-founder ADAM Architecture (fmrly Robert Adam Architects) 1986, Dir 2000–; Founder and Chair. Popular Housing Group 1995–2003; Chair. INTBAU 2000–12, Chair. UK Chapter 2009–; Founder and Chair. Coll. Of Chapters; mem. Planning and Urban Design Group, RIBA 1995–2012, mem. Council RIBA 1999–2002, Hon. Sec. 2001–03, Trustee RIBA Trust 2003–; Chair. Faculty of Fine Art, British School at Rome 1993–97 (mem. 1989), Vice-Chair. Council 1997–99; mem. Architecture Club Cttee 1987–, English Heritage London Advisory Group 1996–2002; Academician, Acad. of Urbanism 2006–; mem. Design Review Panel, Design Council 2012–, Comm. for Architecture and the Built Environment 1999–2003; lectures including tours in USA, Russia and China; Trustee Maria Nobrega Charitable Trust 2003–; contrib. to numerous TV and radio programmes; Hon. Fellow, Royal Incorporation of Architects in Scotland 2014–; numerous awards including Bannister Fletcher Prize 1973, Rome Scholarship 1973–74, Commendation, London Borough of Richmond-upon-Thames Conservation and Design Awards Scheme 1991, Winner, Copper Roofing Competition Copper Devt Assoc. 1995, Elmbridge Borough Council Design/Conservation Award 1998, RIBA Southern Region Nat. Housebuilder Design Award, Best Partnership Devt Commendation for 2000, Marsh Country Life Awards 2001, What House? Awards 2013, City of Winchester Trust Award 2013. *Projects include:* new country houses in Hants., Cambridge, Yorks., S Oxon., Glos., Wilts., Bucks., Dorset; restaurant and display buildings, new villages for the Duchy of Cornwall, Shepton Mallet and Midsomer Norton, new town centre, Rocester, Staffs., village extension in Trowse, nr Norwich, master plan for St Andrew's Hosp., Northampton, master plan for new dist, Leith Scotland, new co. HQ, Dogmersfield Park, Humanities Library, Univ. of Oxford, new library for Ashmolean Museum, Oxford, Solar House, W Sussex, Millennium Pavilion Pvt. Estate, Hants., new offices, Piccadilly, London, William Wake House, Northampton. *Works in public collections:* V&A Contemporary Furniture Collection (Pembroke table for Alma Furniture Co.), RIBA Drawings Collection Tower of the Orders. *Publications include:* Classical Architecture: A Complete Handbook 1990, Buildings by Design 1994, The 7 Sins of Architects 2010, New Classicists: Robert Adam, The Search for a Modern Classicism 2010, The Globalisation of Modern Architecture 2012, Identifying Trends in Masterplanning: A Typographical Classification System (Urban Design Int.) 2013, The Country House Ideal: Recent Work by ADAM Architecture 2015; contrib.: Urban Identity: Learning from Place 2011, Doha, Qatar: Architecture and Globalisation in the Persian Gulf Region 2013, The Architectural Capriccio 2014; numerous articles in nat. newspapers, magazines and journals. *Address:* ADAM Architecture, Old Hyde House, 75 Hyde Street, Winchester, SO23 7DW, England (office). *Telephone:* (1962) 843843 (office). *Fax:* (1962) 843303 (office). *E-mail:* contact@adamarchitecture.com (office). *Website:* www.adamarchitecture.com (office).

ADAMI, Franco; Italian sculptor; b. 19 Nov. 1933, Pisa; s. of Toscano Adami and Giuseppina Bertoncini; m. Jacqueline Sylvius; one s. two d.; ed Leonardo da Vinci Inst., Pisa, Scuola d'Arte, Cascina and School of Fine Arts, Florence; Sculpture Prize of Cascina 1957, Prix Fernand Dupré for sculpture (France) 1981, Prix Charles Oulmont, Fondation de France 1987. *Leisure interests:* antiques. *Address:* Via del Vicinato 13, Pontestrada, 55045 Piatrasanta, Italy; 250 rue du Faubourg Saint-Antoine, 75012 Paris, France. *Telephone:* (058) 471317. *Fax:* (058) 471317. *Website:* francoadami.wordpress.com.

ADAMISHIN, Anatoly Leonidovich, CandHistSc; Russian diplomatist, fmr politician and business consultant; *Co-President, Association of Euro-Atlantic Co-operation;* b. 11 Oct. 1934, Kiev, Ukrainian SSR; m. Svetlana Adamishina; one d.; ed Moscow State Univ.; joined diplomatic service 1957, Third, then Second Sec., Embassy in Rome 1959–65, Counsellor in First European Countries Dept, Ministry of Foreign Affairs 1965–71, Counsellor in Dept of Gen. Int. Problems 1973–78, Head of First European Dept 1978–86; Deputy Minister of Foreign Affairs 1986–90, mem. of Collegium, Ministry of Foreign Affairs 1979; mem. State Duma (Parl.) 1993–95, First Deputy Minister 1992–94; Pres. USSR Comm. for UNESCO 1987–90; USSR (now Russian) Amb. to Italy 1990–92, to UK 1994–97; Minister for Co-operation with CIS Countries 1997–98; Vice-Pres. Systema Corpn 1998–2004; currently Co-Pres. Asscn of Euro-Atlantic Co-operation; Head of Chair and Prof., Russian Acad. of State Service 1998; mem. Yabloko 2004–; several decorations from USSR, including Red Banner; Grand Cross (Italy) 1992. *Television:* Diplomat's Notes (series) 2003. *Publications:* The Decline and Revival of the Great Power (La Plejade Award, Rome 1995, Best Publication of the Year, International Life, Moscow 2000) 1993, The White Sun of Angola 2001. *Leisure interests:* classical music, opera, tennis. *Address:* Association of Euro-Atlantic Co-operation, 119034 Moscow, 3 ul. Prechistenka (office); Apt 170, 2/1 Kutuzovski, Moscow, Russia (home). *Telephone:* (495) 203-62-71 (office); (495) 243-53-81 (home). *Fax:* (495) 230-22-29 (office); (495) 243-53-81 (home). *E-mail:* aeac@mail.ru (office); adamishin@dialup.ptt.ru (home). *Website:* aeac.narod.ru (office).

ADAMKUS, Valdas; Lithuanian politician and fmr head of state; b. (Voldemaras Adamkavičius), 3 Nov. 1926, Kaunas; m. Alma Adamkienė; ed Munich Univ., Univ. of Ill., Ill. Inst. of Tech.; resistance movt, World War II; left Lithuania; on staff World YMCA, Sec.-Gen. and Chair. Chief Physical Training and Sports Cttee; emigrated to USA 1949; worked in Chicago sports car factory, draftsman eng co.; f. Academic Sports Club of American Lithuanians 1951; Chair. Bd of Santara Cen. of Lithuanian Students in USA 1957–58; Vice-Chair., Chair. Santara-Sviesa Fed. of Lithuanian Émigrés 1958–67; mem. Bd Lithuanian Community in USA 1961–64; Deputy Chair. Cen. Bd, mem., Chair. American Lithuanian Community; Chair. Org. Cttee World Lithuanian Games 1983; fmr Head Scientific Research Cen. Environment Protection Agency, Admin. for Mid-West Regions Environment Protection Agency, USA, active participation in political life of Lithuania 1993–; Pres. of Lithuania 1998–2002, 2004–09; UNESCO Goodwill Amb. for the Construction of Knowledge Socs 2003–; mem. Club of Madrid; Hon. mem. The Int. Raoul Wallenberg Foundation; Grand Cross of the Order of Falcon (Iceland) 1998, Grand Cross of the Order of St Olof (Norway) 1998, First Class, Order of Yaroslav the Wise (Ukraine) 1998, Collar and Grand Cross of the Order of Mary's Land (Estonia) 1999, Grand Cross of the Order of the Saviour (Greece) 1999, Collar and Grand Cross of the Order for Service (Italy) 1999, Order of the White Eagle (Poland) 1999, Grand Cross of the Order for Service (Malta) 1999, Grand Cross of the Order for Service (Hungary) 1999, Grand Cross of the Order of Friendship (Kazakhstan) 2000, Collar and Grand Cross of the Order of Three Stars (Latvia) 2001, Grand Cross, Légion d'honneur 2001, Collar of the Order of the Star of Romania 2001, Order of St Meshrop Mashtots (Armenia) 2002, Collar and Grand Cross of the Order of the White Rose (Finland) 2002, Order of Special Merit (Uzbekistan) 2002, Order of Vytautas the Great with Golden Collar 2003, Golden Collar and Grand Cross of the Order of the White Star (Estonia) 2004, Order of Isabel the Catholic with Collar (Spain) 2005, Special Class of the Grand Cross of the Order for Service (Germany) 2005, Grand Cross of the Order of Leopold (Belgium) 2006, Grand Cross, Order of the Bath (UK) 2006, First Class of the Order for Merits (Ukraine) 2006, Order 'Mother Theresa' (Albania) 2007, Grand Cordon of the Supreme Order of the Chrysanthemum (Japan) 2007, St George's Victory Order (Georgia) 2007, Grand Cross of the Order of the Lion (Netherlands) 2008, Collar of the Order of the Merit (Chile) 2008, Grand Star of the Decoration for Services to the Repub. 2009, Order of Stara Planina (Bulgaria) 2009; Dr hc (Vilnius) 1989, (Indiana St Joseph Coll.) 1991, (Northwestern Univ.) 1994, (Kaunas, American Catholic Univs) 1998, (Lithuanian Agricultural Univ., Illinois Inst. of Tech.) 1999, (Lev Gumilev Euro-Asian Univ. Kazakhstan) 2000, (De Paul Univ., Chicago, Law Univ. of Lithuania) 2001, (Vytautas Magnus Univ., Lithuania) 2002, (Lithuanian Acad. of Physical Educ.) 2004, (Yerevan State Univ., Armenia, Baku State Univ., Azerbaijan) 2006, (Donetsk Univ., Ukraine) 2006, (Univ. of Notre Dame, USA) 2007, Nicolaus Copernicus Univ., Poland) 2007, Tallinn Univ., Estonia) 2008, (Univ. of Chile) 2008, (Klaipėda Univ.) 2008, John Paul II Catholic Univ., Poland) 2009, ISM Univ. of Man. and Econs) 2009; Pres.'s Award for Distinguished Fed. Civilian Service 1985, Gold Medal, US Environment Protection Agency, US Distinguished Service Award, Int. Environmental Award 1988, St Andrew 'Dialogue of Civilisation' Prize Laureate (Russia) 2002, European of the Year 2007. *Website:* www.adamkus.lt.

ADAMS, Amy; American actress; b. 20 Aug. 1974, Vicenza, Italy; d. of Richard Adams and Kathryn Adams (née Hicken); m. Darren Le Gallo 2015; one d.; began performing career as dancer, Boulder's Dinner Theatre and Country Dinner Playhouse, Minneapolis. *Films:* Drop Dead Gorgeous 1999, Psycho Beach Party 2000, The Chromium Hook (short) 2000, Cruel Intentions 2 2000, The Slaughter Rule 2002, Pumpkin 2002, Serving Sara 2002, Catch Me if You Can 2002, The Last Run 2004, Junebug (Nat. Soc. of Film Critics Award for Best Supporting Actress, San Francisco Film Critics Circle Award for Best Supporting Actress, Southeastern Film Critics Asscn Award for Best Supporting Actress) 2005, The Wedding Date 2005, Standing Still 2005, Talladega Nights: The Ballad of Ricky Bobby 2006, Pennies (short) 2006, Tenacious D in The Pick of Destiny 2006, The Ex 2006, Underdog (voice) 2007, Enchanted (Saturn Award for Best Actress) 2007, Charlie Wilson's War 2007, Sunshine Cleaning 2008, Miss Pettigrew Lives for a Day 2008, Doubt 2008, Night at the Museum 2 2009, Julie & Julia 2009, Moonlight Serenade 2009, Leap Year 2010, Love & Distrust 2010, The Fighter (Detroit Film Critics Soc. Award for Best Supporting Actress, Las Vegas Film Critics Soc. Award for Best

Supporting Actress) 2010, The Muppets 2011, On the Road 2012, The Master 2012, Trouble with the Curve 2012, Man of Steel 2013, American Hustle (Golden Globe Award for Best Actress in a Motion Picture, Comedy or Musical, Screen Actors Guild Award for Outstanding Performance by a Cast in a Motion Picture 2014) 2013, Lullaby 2014, Big Eyes (Golden Globe Award for Actress in a Motion Picture (Musical or Comedy) 2015) 2014, Batman v. Superman: Dawn of Justice 2016, Arrival 2016, Nocturnal Animals 2016, Justice League 2017, Vice 2018. *Television:* The Peter Principle (film) 2000, That '70s Show (series) 2000, Charmed (series) 2000, Zoe, Duncan, Jack & Jane (series) 2000, Providence (series) 2000, Buffy the Vampire Slayer (series) 2000, Smallville (series) 2001, The West Wing (series) 2002, King of the Hill (series) 2004, Dr. Vegas (series) 2004, The Office (series) 2005–06, Sharp Objects (series) (Critics' Choice TV Award for Best Actress in a Movie/Mini series) 2018. *Address:* c/o Brillstein Entertainment Partners, 9150 Wilshire Blvd, Suite 350, Beverly Hills, CA 90212, USA (office). *Telephone:* (310) 275-6135 (office). *Website:* www.bepmedia.com (office).

ADAMS, Bryan, OC; Canadian/British rock singer, songwriter, musician (guitar) and photographer; b. 5 Nov. 1959, Kingston, Ont.; pnr Alicia Grimaldi; two d.; numerous world-wide tours; 15 Juno Awards, Recording Artist of the Decade, Canada, Grammy Award, American Music Award, Gov.-Gen's Performing Arts Award for Lifetime Artistic Achievement 2010, Special Int. Award, Ivor Novello Awards 2016. *Recordings:* albums: Bryan Adams 1980, You Want It You Got It 1981, Cuts Like A Knife 1983, Reckless 1984, Into The Fire 1987, Waking Up The Neighbours 1991, So Far So Good 1992, Live! Live! Live! 1995, 18 'Til I Die 1996, MTV Unplugged 1987, On A Day Like Today 1998, The Best Of Me 2000, Spirit: Stallion of Cimarron (film soundtrack) 2002, Room Service 2004, 11 2008, Bare Bones 2010, Tracks of My Years 2014, Get Up! 2015. *Publications:* Bryan Adams: The Official Biography 1995, Made in Canada (photographs by Bryan Adams). *Address:* The Leighton-Pope Organisation, 8 Glenthorne Mews, 115a Glenthorne Road, Hammersmith, London, W6 0LJ, England (office); 425 Carrall Street, Suite 520, Vancouver, BC V6B 6E3, Canada (office). *Telephone:* (20) 8741-4453 (office). *Fax:* (20) 8741-4289 (office). *E-mail:* info@l-po.com (office); info@bryanadams.com (office). *Website:* www.bryanadams.com.

ADAMS, Gerard (Gerry); Northern Irish politician and author; b. 6 Oct. 1948, Belfast; s. of Gerry Adams, Sr and Annie Hannaway; m. Colette McCardle 1971; three c.; ed St Mary's Christian Brothers School, Belfast; worked as a barman; Founder-mem. NI Civil Rights Asscn; mem. Belfast Housing Action Cttee; interned in Long Kesh March 1972; released to take part in secret London talks between Sec. of State for NI and Irish Republican Army (IRA) July 1972; re-arrested 1973, attempted to escape from Maze Prison, sentenced to 18 months' imprisonment, released Feb. 1977; charged with membership of Provisional IRA Feb. 1978, freed after seven months because of insufficient evidence for conviction; Vice-Pres. Sinn Féin 1978–83, Pres. 1983–2018; MP for Belfast West 1983–92, 1997–2011; mem. NI Ass. for Belfast West 1998–2010 (Ass. suspended 11 Feb. 2000 and 14 Oct. 2002); involved in peace negotiations with British Govt 1988–94; TD (mem. Dáil Éireann, Irish Parl.) for Louth 2011–; Thorr Award, Switzerland 1995. *Publications:* Falls Memory 1982, The Politics of Irish Freedom 1986, A Pathway to Peace 1988, Cage 11 (autobiog.) 1990, Who Fears to Speak...? 1991 (revised edn 2001), The Street and Other Stories 1993, Selected Writings 1994, Free Ireland: Towards a Lasting Peace 1995, Our Day Will Come (autobiog.) 1996, Before the Dawn (autobiog.) 1996, An Irish Voice 1997, An Irish Journal 2001, Hope and History 2003, A Farther Shore 2005, The New Ireland: A Vision For The Future 2005, An Irish Eye 2007, My Little Book of Tweets 2016.

ADAMS, Jan, AO, PSM, BEcons (Hons), LLB (Hons); Australian diplomatist and government official; b. Wodonga, Vic.; m.; one c.; ed Monash Univ., Melbourne; worked in OECD Environment and Trade Directorates, Paris, France; Adviser to Minister for Trade and Minister for Industry, Science and Tech., Senator Peter Cook 1993–96; joined Dept of Foreign Affairs and Trade (DFAT) as Asst Sec., APEC Br. 1999, Minister Counsellor (Trade), Washington, DC 2000–04, Amb. for the Environment and Amb. for Climate Change 2005–08, First Asst Sec., Free Trade Agreement Div. 2008–13, Deputy Sec. with responsibility for Trade and Econ. Issues 2013–16, Amb. to People's Repub. of China 2016–19; Public Service Medal 2007. *Address:* Embassy of Australia, 21 Dong Zhi Men Wai Dajie, San Li Tun, Beijing 100600, People's Republic of China (office). *Telephone:* (10) 51404111 (office). *Fax:* (10) 51404204 (office). *E-mail:* pubaff.beijing@dfat.gov.au (office). *Website:* www.china.embassy.gov.au (office).

ADAMS, John Coolidge; American composer and conductor; b. 15 Feb. 1947, Worcester, Mass; m. Deborah O'Grady; one s.; ed Harvard Univ.; appearances as clarinettist and conductor; Head, Composition Dept, San Francisco Conservatory of Music 1971–81; advisor on new music, San Francisco Symphony Orchestra 1978–82, Composer-in-Residence 1982–85; Creative Advisor, St Paul Chamber Orchestra 1988–89; Creative Chair, Los Angeles Philharmonic Orchestra 2009–; Guggenheim Fellowship 1982, Fellow, BAC&S 2005; Fellow American Acad. of Arts and Sciences 1997, American Acad. of Arts and Letters 1997; Dr hc (Yale Univ.) 2013, (Harvard Univ.) 2012, (Univ. of Cambridge), (Northwestern Univ.), (Juilliard School), (RAM) 2015; Chevalier, Ordre des Arts et des Lettres; Harvard Arts Medal 2007, Opera News Award 2008, Nat. Endowment for the Arts Opera Award 2009, Erasmus Prize 2019, Cyril Magnin Award for Outstanding Achievement in the Arts, California Gov.'s Award for Lifetime Achievement in the Arts. *Film:* as composer: Io sono l'amore 2009, Call Me by Your Name 2017. *Compositions include:* opera and stage works: Nixon in China (Grammy Award for Best Contemporary Composition 1989) 1987, The Death of Klinghoffer 1991, I Was Looking at the Ceiling and Then I Saw the Sky 1995, El Niño 1999, Doctor Atomic 2004, A Flowering Tree, 2006, The Gospel According to the Other Mary 2012, Girls of the Golden West 2017; orchestral works: Shaker Loops 1978, Common Tones in Simple Time 1979, Harmonium 1980, Grand Pianola Music 1981–82, Harmonielehre 1984–85, The Chairman Dances 1985, Short Ride in a Fast Machine 1986, Tromba Lontana 1986, Fearful Symmetries 1988, The Wound-Dresser 1989, Eros Piano 1989, El Dorado (Grammy Award for Best Contemporary Composition 1998) 1991, Violin Concerto (Grawemeyer Award for Music Composition 1995) 1993, Gnarly Buttons 1996, A Flowering Tree 2008; chamber and ensemble works: Christian Zeal and Activity 1973, China Gates 1977, Phrygian Gates 1977, Chamber Symphony (Royal Philharmonic Soc. Music Award for Best Chamber Composition 1994) 1992, John's Book of Alleged Dances 1994, Road Movies 1995, Naïve and Sentimental Music 1998, El Niño 2000, Guide to Strange Places 2001, On the Transmigration of Souls (Pulitzer Prize for Music 2003, Grammy Awards for Best Classical Album, Best Orchestral Performance, Best Classical Contemporary Composition 2005, Classical BRIT Award for Contemporary Music 2005) 2002, The Dharma at Big Sur 2003, My Father Knew Charles Ives (Classical BRIT Award for Contemporary Composer 2007) 2003, Doctor Atomic Symphony (British Composer Award for Best Int. Composition 2009) 2005, Son of Chamber Symphony 2007, City Noir 2009, Absolute Jest 2012, Saxophone Concerto 2013, Scheherazade.2 2014, Must the Devil Have All the Good Tunes? (concerto for piano and orchestra) 2018. *Publications:* Hallelujah Junction (memoir) (Northern California Book Award for Creative Nonfiction) 2008; contribs to New York Times Book Review, New Yorker. *Address:* HarrisonParrott, The Ark, Talgarth Road, London, W6 8BJ, England (office). *E-mail:* (20) 7229-9166 (office). *Website:* www.harrisonparrott.com (office); www.earbox.com.

ADAMS, Kirby, BS, MBA; American/Australian steel industry executive; b. Atlanta, Ga; ed Auburn Univ., Univ. of Virginia; Head of Strategy, Armco Inc., Nat. Supply Div., Houston, Tex. 1979–81; series of roles heading operating divs and leading planning, strategy, M&A, and restructuring, including acquisition and spin off of TIMET, NL Industries Inc., Houston and New York City 1981–89; Pres. and CEO Titanium Metals Corpn Inc. (TIMET), Pittsburgh/Denver 1989–95; Pres. and CEO BHP Ltd, Melbourne, Australia 1995–99, Founding Man. Dir and CEO BHP Steel, Melbourne, Australia 2000–02, Pres. BHP Service Cos, Exec. Gen. Man., Corp. Strategy and Business Devt; Sr Man., BlueScope Steel, Melbourne, Australia 2002–07, led BlueScope Steel through demerger from BHP-Billiton and an IPO; CEO Corus Group PLC, UK 2009–10, mem. Exec. Cttee and Bd Tata Steel Europe Ltd and Tata Steel Ltd; mem. Bd Business Council of Australia 2002–07; mem. Int. Iron and Steel Inst. 2000–07 (fmr Chair. and Vice-Chair.); fmr Chair. Titanium Devt Asscn; cr. Indian jt venture with Tata Steel 2006; mem. Bd of Dirs TTR (Trans-Tasman Resources Ltd) 2012–; Trustee, Darden School Foundation, Univ. of Virginia Darden School of Business 2014–17; IISI Silver Medal for steel industry safety leadership. *Leisure interests:* swimming, skiing, physical fitness, travel, architecture.

ADAMS, Michael W. W., BSc, PhD; British biochemist and academic; *Distinguished Research Professor, Department of Biochemistry and Molecular Engineering, University of Georgia;* ed Univ. of London, UK; spent two years in post-doctoral research at Purdue Univ.; joined Exxon Research and Engineering Co. 1981; joined Dept of Biochemistry and Molecular Biology, Univ. of Georgia, 1987, currently Distinguished Research Prof.; mem. American Acad. of Microbiology 2003–; Charles Thom Award, Soc. of Industrial Microbiology 2010, World Technology Award (Energy) 2013. *Publications include:* has edited seven books; more than 300 papers in professional journals. *Address:* Department of Biochemistry and Molecular Biology, B122 Life Sciences Building, University of Georgia, Athens, GA 30602, USA (office). *Telephone:* (706) 542-2060 (office); (706) 542-1909 (Lab.) (office). *Fax:* (706) 542-1738 (office). *E-mail:* adams@bmb.uga.edu (office). *Website:* www.bmb.uga.edu (office); adams.bmb.uga.edu (office).

ADAMS, Paul Nicholas, BA; British business executive; b. 12 March 1953, Manchester, England; s. of Peter Charles Adams and Joan Adams; m.; one s. two d.; ed Culford School and Ealing Coll.; began career with Shell UK; Marketing Dir Beecham Int. 1983–86; Vice-Pres. of Marketing for Europe, Pepsi-Cola Int. 1986–91, also Man. Dir Pepsi Cola France and Area Vice-Pres. for Scandinavia; joined British American Tobacco PLC 1991, Regional Dir for Asia Pacific 1991–99, for Europe 1999–2001, Man. Dir 2002–03, Chief Exec. 2004–11; mem. Exec. Cttee Transatlantic Business Dialogue, Trilateral Comm.; Founding mem. Global Business Leaders Alliance Against Counterfeiting. *Leisure interests:* family, theatre, rugby, shooting. *Address:* c/o British American Tobacco PLC, Globe House, 4 Temple Place, London, WC2R 2PG, England. *E-mail:* info@bat.com.

ADAMS, Phillip Andrew, AO, AM, FAHA, FRSA; Australian writer, broadcaster and filmmaker; b. 12 July 1939; m. 1st (divorced); three d.; m. 2nd Patrice Newell; one d.; ed Eltham High School; columnist and critic 1956–; Chair. Film, Radio and TV Bd 1972–75; Founder-mem. Australia Council 1972–75; Vic. Govt Rep., Australian Children's TV Foundation 1981–87; Pres. Vic. Council for Arts 1982–86; Chair. Australian Film Inst. 1975–80, Australian Film Comm. 1983–90, Comm. for the Future 1985–90, Nat. Australia Day Council 1992–96; Foundation Chair., Australian Centre for Social Innovation 2009–; mem. Bd Ausflag 1990–, Cttee for the Centenary of Fed. 1994; worked with Families in Distress 1985–, Montsalvat Artists' Soc. 1986–, CARE Australia 1995–97; Sr ANZAC Fellow 1981; mem. Bd Nat. Museum of Australia 1996–97, Festival of Ideas 1999; mem. Council, Adelaide Festival 1996; Hon. FAHA 2008; Hon. DUniv (Griffith Univ.) 1998, (Univ. of South Australia) 2004; Hon. DLitt (Edith Cowan Univ.) 2003, (Univ. of Sydney), (Macquarie Univ.) 2013; Dr hc (Macquarie Univ.) 2013, (Australian Film Television and Radio School) 2015; Raymond Longford Award 1981, Australian Arts Award 1987, Australian Humanist of the Year 1987, CSICOP Award for Responsibility in Media (New York) 1996, Australian Republican of the Year 2006, Human Rights and Equal Opportunity Comm. Human Rights Medal 2006, Media Hall of Fame 2014. *Films include:* Jack and Jill: A Postscript 1970, The Naked Bunyip 1971, The Adventures of Barry McKenzie 1972, Don's Party 1975, The Getting of Wisdom 1976, Grendel Grendel Grendel 1980, We of the Never Never 1982, Lonely Hearts 1982, Fighting Back 1983. *Radio includes:* Compere, Late Night Live (ABC). *Television includes:* Death and Destiny, Short and Sweet (ABC), Adams' Australia (BBC), The Big Question, Face the Press (SBS). *Publications include:* Adams with Added Enzymes 1970, The Unspeakable Adams 1977, More Unspeakable Adams 1979, The Uncensored Adams 1981, The Inflammable Adams 1983, Adams Versus God 1985, Harold Cazneaux: The Quiet Observer (co-author) 1994, Classic Columns 1994, The Penguin Book of Australian Jokes (co-author) 1994, The Penguin Book of Jokes from Cyberspace (co-author) 1995, The Big Questions (co-author) 1996, The Penguin Book of More Australian Jokes 1996, Kookaburra 1996, Emperors of the Air 1997, Retreat from Tolerance? 1997, More Big Questions (co-author) 1998, The Penguin Book of Schoolyard Jokes (co-author) 1998, A Billion Voices 1999, The Penguin Book of All New Australian Jokes (co-author) 2000, Adams Ark 2004, Adams vs. God: The Rematch 2007, Backstage Politics 2011, Bedtime Stories 2012, Tales From My 21 Years at RN's Late Night Live 2012. *Leisure interests:*

archaeology, reading. *Address:* c/o Radio National, ABC, GPO Box 9994, Sydney, NSW 2001, Australia. *E-mail:* philadams@ozemail.com.au.

ADAMS, Valerie; New Zealand athlete; b. 6 Oct. 1984, Rotorua; m. Bertrand Vili (divorced 2010); shot putter; Olympic Champion, World Champion and Commonwealth record-holder, having thrown a distance of 20.56m; won World Youth Championships 2001; World Jr Champion 2002; Silver Medal, Commonwealth Games, Manchester 2002; Bronze Medal, World Championships, Helsinki 2005, Gold Medal, World Championships, Osaka 2007, Gold Medal, World Championships, Berlin 2009, Gold Medal, World Championships, Daegu 2013, Gold Medal, World Championships, Moscow 2013; finished second at World Athletics Final; Gold Medal, Commonwealth Games, Melbourne 2006; broke Oceania record in winning her first World Indoor Title in Valencia 2008 (throw of 20.19m); Gold Medal, Olympic Games, Beijing 2008, London 2012; New Zealand Sportswoman of the Year 2006–12, New Zealand Sports Award of the Year 2008, IAAF World Athlete of the Year 2014.

ADANI, Gautam S.; Indian business executive; *Executive Chairman, Adani Group;* b. 24 June 1962, Ahmedabad; s. of Shantilal Adani and Shantaben Adani; m. Priti Adani; two s.; ed CN Vidyalay School, Ahmedabad; began career in diamond trade, Mahindra Bros, Mumbai 1978; f. plastics factory, Ahmedabad 1981; f. Adani Group 1988 with interests in commodities trading, power generation, coal mining and agric., currently Exec. Chair.; mem. Bd of Dirs Adani Energy Ltd, Adani Enterprises Ltd, Adani Petronet (Dahej) Port Pvt. Ltd, Adani Welspun Exploration Ltd, Adani Wilmar Ltd, Jain Int. Trade Org. Ltd; Chair. and Man. Dir Mundra Port and Special Econ. Zone Ltd; Excellence in Man. Award 2006. *Leisure interest:* yoga. *Address:* Adani House, Near Mithakhali Six Roads, Navarangpura, Ahmedabad 380 009 (office); Adani House, Plot No 83, Sector 32, Institutional Area, Gurgaon 122 001, India (office). *Telephone:* (79) 25555555 (Ahmedabad) (office). *Fax:* (79) 26565500 (Ahmedabad) (office). *Website:* www.adani.com (office).

ADCOCK, Fleur, OBE, CNZM, MA, FRSL; British writer; b. 10 Feb. 1934, Papakura, New Zealand; d. of Cyril John Adcock and Irene Robinson; m. 1st Alistair Teariki Campbell 1952 (divorced 1958); two s.; m. 2nd Barry Crump 1962 (divorced 1966); ed Victoria Univ., Wellington; Asst Lecturer, Univ. of Otago 1958, Asst Librarian 1959–61; with Alexander Turnbull Library 1962; with FCO 1963–79; freelance writer 1979–; Northern Arts Fellowship in Literature, Newcastle and Durham Univs 1979–81; Eastern Arts Fellowship, Univ. of East Anglia 1984; Writer-in-Residence, Univ. of Adelaide, New Zealand 1986; mem. Poetry Soc.; Festival of Wellington Poetry Award 1961, New Zealand State Literary Fund Award 1964, Buckland Award 1967, 1979, Jessie MacKay Award 1968, 1972, Cholmondeley Award 1976, New Zealand Nat. Book Award 1984, Arts Council Writers' Award 1988, Queen's Gold Medal for Poetry 2006. *Publications include:* The Eye of the Hurricane 1964, Tigers 1967, High Tide in the Garden 1971, The Scenic Route 1974, The Inner Harbour 1979, Below Loughrigg 1979, The Oxford Book of Contemporary New Zealand Poetry (ed.) 1982, Selected Poems 1983, The Virgin and the Nightingale: Medieval Latin Poems 1983, Hotspur: A Ballad for Music 1986, The Incident Book 1986, The Faber Book of 20th Century Women's Poetry 1987, Orient Express: Poems by Grete Tartler (trans.) 1989, Time Zones 1991, Letters from Darkness: Poems by Daniela Crasnaru (trans.) 1991, High Primas and the Archpoet (ed. and trans.) 1994, The Oxford Book of Creatures (ed. with Jacqueline Simms) 1995, Looking Back 1997, Poems 1960–2000 (Queen's Gold Medal for Poetry 2006) 2000, Dragon Talk 2010, Glass Wings 2013, The Land Ballot 2015, Hoard 2017. *Address:* 14 Lincoln Road, London, N2 9DL, England (home). *Telephone:* (20) 8444-7881 (home).

ADDIS, Richard James, MA; British writer, journalist and entrepreneur; *Chairman and Editor-in-Chief, The Day;* b. 23 Aug. 1956, Malacca, Malaysia; s. of Richard Thomas Addis and Jane Addis; m. Eunice Minogue 1983 (divorced 2000); one s. two d.; two s. by Helen Slater; ed Rugby School, Downing Coll., Cambridge; Asst Ed. Evening Standard 1985–89; Deputy Ed. Sunday Telegraph 1989–91; Exec. Ed. Daily Mail 1991–95; Ed. Daily Express 1995–98, The Express on Sunday 1996–98; Ed. Mail on Sunday Review 1998–99; Ed. The Globe and Mail, Toronto 1999–2002; Ed. Financial Times Weekend 2002–06; Ed.-in-Chief Newsweek Europe 2014–15; Founder and Man. Dir Shakeup Media, London 2006; Founder, Chair. and Ed.-in-Chief, The Day, London 2010–. *Leisure interests:* herb-surfing, portacenere. *E-mail:* richard@theday.co.uk (office). *Website:* www.theday.co.uk (office).

ADDISON, Mark Eric, CB, MA, MBA, PhD; British fmr civil servant; b. 22 Jan. 1951; s. of Sydney Robert James Addison and Prudence Margaret Addison (née Russell); m. Lucinda Clare Booth 1987; ed Marlborough Coll., St John's Coll., Cambridge, City Univ. and Imperial Coll., London; with Dept of Employment 1978–95, Pvt. Sec. to Parl. Under-Sec. of State 1982, Pvt. Sec. to Prime Minister 1985–88; Regional Dir London Training Agency 1988–91, Dir Finance and Resource Man. 1991–94; Dir Safety Policy Health and Safety Exec. 1994–97; Dir Better Regulation Unit, Office of Public Service 1997–98; Chief Exec. Crown Prosecution Service 1998–2001; Dir-Gen. Operations and Service Delivery, Dept for Environment, Food and Rural Affairs 2001–05, Acting Perm. Sec. 2005, Interim Chief Exec. Rural Payments Agency 2006; Chair., Nursing and Midwifery Council 2012–14, Dorset County Hosp. NHS Foundation Trust 2016–, State Honours Cttee 2017–; Vice-Chair. Charity for Civil Servants 2016–; mem. Advisory Cttee on Business Appointments 2012–17. *Leisure interests:* British motorbikes, our garden and wildflower meadow in Dorset. *Telephone:* 7788-190209 (mobile). *E-mail:* mark@addisonbooth.com.

ADDO-KUFUOR, Kwame, MA, BChir, FRCP; Ghanaian politician and physician; *Chairman, Social Security and National Insurance Trust;* b. 14 July 1940, Kumasi, Ashanti Region; m. Rosemary Addo-Kufuor; three c.; ed Achimota School, Univ. Coll. Medical Hosp., London, Univ. of Cambridge and Middlesex Medical School Hosp., UK; worked at several hosps including W Suffolk Gen. Hosp., Bury St Edmunds, St Charles Hosp., London, Oldchurch Hosp., Essex, St Helier Hosp., London 1970s; fmr Medical Dir, Kufuor Clinic, Kumasi; fmr Inspector of Examinations for Final Bachelor of Medicine, Univ. of Ghana Medical School; fmr Chair. of Operations, Prisons Council of Ghana; elected mem. Parl. (NPP—New Patriotic Party) for Manhyia, served on House Cttee, Health Cttee, Cttee on Selection; Chair. Cabinet Cttee on Governance; fmr Shadow Minister of Health; fmr Acting Minister of Interior; Minister of Defence 2001–07, of Interior 2008–09; Chair. Social Security and Nat. Insurance Trust 2017–; currently Lecturer (part-time), Dept of Medicine, School of Medical Sciences (KNUST); fmr mem. NPP Nat. Council and Chair. Health Cttee; fmr Chair. Jesus Coll. Cambridge UN Students Asscn; fmr Pres. Ghana Medical Asscn; fmr Rep. for W Africa to Confed. of African Medical Asscns; Hon. Sec. Medical Students Asscn, Jesus Coll., Cambridge. *Publications:* Safe Motherhood in the Upper West Region of Ghana (ed.); several articles in medical journals. *Leisure interests:* music, gardening, football, swimming, watching boxing. *Address:* 95 Obenesu Crescent, East Contonments, Accra, (home); Social Security and National Insurance Trust, PO Box MB 149, Accra, Ghana (office). *Telephone:* (21) 777797 (home); (02) 225135 (office). *Fax:* (21) 773951 (home). *E-mail:* contactcentre@ssnit.org.gh (office). *Website:* www.ssnit.org.gh (office).

ADEANG, David Waiau; Nauruan lawyer and politician; *Minister assisting the President and Minister of Finance;* b. 24 Nov. 1969; s. of Kennan Adeang (fmr Pres. of Nauru); MP for Ubenide constituency 2001–, Speaker of Parl. March–April 2008; Minister of Finance May–Aug. 2003, of Foreign Affairs and Justice June–Oct. 2004, of Foreign Affairs and Finance Oct. 2004–07, of Finance, Sustainable Devt and Justice 2013–16, Minister assisting the Pres., Minister of Finance and Sustainable Devt, also of Justice and Border Control, of Multicultural Affairs, of Eigigu Holdings Corpn, and of Nauru Air Corpn 2016–; Founding mem. Naoero Amo (Nauru First Party) 2003–. *Address:* Ministry of Finance, Government Offices, Yaren, Nauru (office). *Telephone:* 557-3133 (office). *E-mail:* minister.finance@naurugov.nr (office). *Website:* naurugov.nr (office).

ADEBAYO, Cornelius Olatunji; Nigerian academic and politician; b. 24 Feb. 1941, Oke-Onigbin, Kwara State; ed Barewa Coll., Zaria, Ahmadu Bello Univ., Zaria, Univ. of Ghana, Legon; Lecturer in English, Univ. of Ife (now Obafemi Awolowo Univ.) 1969–73; Founding Head, Dept of Humanities, Kwara State Coll. of Tech. (now Kwara State Polytechnic) 1973; Commr for Educ., later for Information and Econ. Devt, Kwara State 1975–78; Senator (Unity Party of Nigeria) 1979; Gov. of Kwara State 1983; mem. Nat. Democratic Coalition (NADECO, pro-democracy group) in 1990s, detained in Calabar Prison 1996, in exile in Canada 1996, served as Canada Rep. NADECO-Abroad 1998; Federal Minister of Communications 2003–06, of Works 2006, of Transport 2007, of Defence 2012.

ADEEB, Ahmed, BA, MBA; Maldivian economist, business executive and politician; b. (Ahmed Adeeb Abdul Ghafoor), 11 April 1982, Malé; m. Fathimath Liushar 2006; one s. one d.; ed Staffordshire Univ., UK, Edith Cowan Univ., Australia; worked at Maldives Customs Services 2001–04; COO Millennium Capital Management 2008–10; Treas., Maldives Nat. Chamber of Commerce and Industries 2008–10, Pres. 2010–11; Acting Minister of Fisheries and Agriculture Feb.–March 2012, Minister of Tourism 2012–15; Vice-Pres. of Maldives July–Nov. 2015; Vice-Pres. Progressive Party of Maldives 2013; arrested on charge of high treason 2015.

ADELE, MBE; British singer and songwriter; b. (Adele Laurie Blue Adkins), 5 May 1988, London; m. Simon Konecki 2016; one s.; ed BRIT School for Performing Arts and Tech.; professional solo artist 2008–; tours in UK, USA, Canada; worked with Jim Abiss, Eg White and Mark Ronson; recorded with the Raconteurs, sang with Burt Bacharach at BBC Electric Proms 2008; Critics' Choice Award, BRIT Awards 2008, BRIT Awards for Best British Female Solo Artist 2012, 2016, Grammy Awards for Best Female Pop Vocal Performance 2008, for Best New Artist 2008, for Record of the Year 2012, 2017, for Song of the Year 2012, 2017, for Best Pop Solo Performance 2012, 2017, for Best Short Form Music Video 2012, for Best Pop Solo Performance 2013, for Best Song Written for Visual Media (for Skyfall) 2014, Songwriter of the Year, Ivor Novello Awards 2012, Ivor Novello Award for Most Performed Work of 2011 (for Rolling in the Deep) 2012, Golden Globe Award for Best Original Song in a Motion Picture (for Skyfall) 2013, Academy Award for Best Original Song (with Paul Epworth) (for Skyfall) 2013, BRIT Award for Best British Single (for Hello) 2016, BRIT Awards for Global Success 2016, 2017, Songwriter of the Year, Ivor Novello Awards 2016, Billboard Music Awards for Top Artist 2016, for Top Female Artist 2016, for Top Billboard 200 Artist 2016, for Top Selling Song (Hello) 2016, for Top Radio Song (Hello) 2016. *Television:* Ushi Says: Hi 2001, Saturday Night Live 2008, Ugly Betty 2009. *Recordings include:* albums: 19 2008, 21 (Grammy Awards for Album of the Year 2012, for Best Pop Vocal Album 2012, Mastercard British Album of the Year, BRIT Awards 2012, Billboard Music Award for Top Pop Album 2013) 2011, 25 (BRIT Award for British Album of the Year 2016, Billboard Music Award for Top 200 Album 2016, Grammy Award for Album of the Year 2017) 2015. *Address:* c/o XL Recordings, 1 Codrington Mews, London, W11 2EH, England. *E-mail:* info@septembermanagement.com. *Website:* www.xlrecordings.com; www.adele.tv.

ADELI, Seyed Muhammad Hossein, PhD; Iranian economist, banker and diplomatist; *Chairman and CEO, Ravand Institute for Economic and International Studies;* b. 1952, Ahwaz; m. Khadijeh Aryan; two s. one d.; ed Tehran Business School, Univ. of Tehran, California Coast Univ., USA, Jamia Millia Islamia; temp. Attaché in Canada 1979–80, Dir-Gen. of Econ. Affairs, Ministry of Foreign Affairs 1982–86, Amb. to Japan 1987–89; Gov. Bank Markazi Iran (Cen. Bank of Iran) 1990–95; Amb. to Canada 1995–99, Deputy Minister for Econ. Affairs, Ministry of Foreign Affairs 1999–2004, Amb. to UK 2005; Founder, Chair. and CEO Ravand Inst. for Econ. and Int. Studies (think-tank), Tehran; Chair. Amin Investment Bank 2000–11; Sec.-Gen. Gas Exporting Countries Forum (GECF) 2014–; Order of the Rising Sun (Japan) 2014. *Leisure interest:* reading. *Address:* Ravand Institute for Economic and International Studies, Unit 6-2, 1479 Jam Building, Vali-e Asr Avenue, Tehran, 19668-43116, Iran (office). *Telephone:* (21) 22019734 (office). *Fax:* (21) 22019735 (office). *E-mail:* contact@ravandinstitute.com (office). *Website:* www.ravandinstitute.com (office).

ADELMAN, David L, BA, JD, MPA; American attorney and fmr diplomatist; *Partner, Reed Smith LLP;* b. 24 May 1964, New York; s. of Nelson Adelman and Donna Adelman; m. Caroline Aronovitz Adelman; three c.; ed Georgia State Univ., Univs of Georgia, Emory; began career as Staff Attorney, Law Dept, State of Georgia, later Asst Attorney-Gen. 1991–93; Assoc., then partner Sutherland Asbill and Brennan LLP 1994–2010, appointed to and Evidence Cttee, State Bar of Georgia; State Senator, Georgia Gen. Ass. 2002–10; Democratic Whip in Georgia

Senate 2004–10, elected Chair. Georgia Code Revision Comm. 2005; Instructor, School of Public and Int. Affairs, Univ. of Georgia 2005, 2007; Chair. Senate Urban Affairs Cttee 2007–10; Amb. to Singapore 2010–13; Head of Govt Affairs for Asia Pacific, Goldman Sachs Group 2013–15; Partner, Reed Smith LLP 2015–; Advisor, Legis. Advisory Cttee, State Bar of Georgia 2003–05, Judiciary Cttee 2005–09; mem. Courts Future Cttee, State Bar of Georgia 2003–05, Evidence Study Cttee 2003–08, Dist of Columbia Bar Asscn, State Bar of Georgia, Federal Bar Asscn, Atlanta Bar Asscn, Decatur-DeKalb Bar Asscn; mem. Bd of Visitors, Emory Univ.; Bd mem. Georgia Wilderness Inst., Anti-Defamation League, American Jewish Cttee, Emory Public Interest Cttee, Druid Hills Civic Asscn, Women's Resource Centre to End Domestic Violence, Health Students Taking Action Together; Merit Badge Counsellor for Boy Scout Troop 18; Legis. Leadership Award, Gov. Council on Disabilities 2004, Hope Award, Partnership Against Domestic Violence 2004, Pro-Choice Men Cook Award, NARAL Pro-choice 2004, Sighted Guide Award, Nat. Fed. of Blind, Georgia 2005, Thomas B. Murphy Award, Young Democrats of Georgia 2006, Star of Life Award, Georgia Asscn of Emergency Medical Services 2007, 2008, Environmental Leadership Award, League of Conservation Voters 2008, Champion of Change Award, Women's Resource Centre to End Domestic Violence 2010, Legislator of the Year, Multiple Sclerosis Soc. Georgia. *Address:* Reed Smith LLP, 599 Lexington Avenue, 22nd Floor, New York, NY 10022, USA (office). *Telephone:* (212) 902-0300 (office). *E-mail:* dadelman@reedsmith.com (office). *Website:* www.reedsmith.com (office).

ADELMAN, Kenneth Lee, PhD; American consultant and fmr government official; b. 9 June 1946, Chicago, Ill.; s. of Harry Adelman and Corinne Unger; m. Carol Craigle 1971; two d.; ed Grinnell Coll., Georgetown Univ.; with US Dept of Commerce 1968–70; Special Asst, VISTA, Washington, DC 1970–72; Liaison Officer, AID 1975–76; Asst to Sec. of Defense 1975–77; Sr Political Scientist, Stanford Research Inst., Arlington, Va 1977–81; Amb. and Deputy Perm. Rep. to UN, New York 1981–83; Dir Arms Control and Disarmament Agency (ACDA) 1983–88; Vice-Pres. Inst. of Contemporary Studies 1988–; mem. Defense Policy Bd Advisory Cttee; Sr Counselor, Edelman Public Relations, Washington, DC; Co-Founder (with wife) Movers & Shakespeares (consultancy) 1997, currently Vice-Pres.; fmr Exec. Dir USA for Innovation; mem. Exec. Bd Noel Foundation; mem. Advisory Bd Princeton Review; Sec., Bd of Trustees, Freedom House; mem. Bd Shakespeare Theatre, Washington, DC; Instructor in Shakespeare, Georgetown Univ. 1977–79; taught at George Washington Univ.; Co-Host Tech Cen. Station; mem. Cttee on the Present Danger. *Publications:* The Great Universal Embrace 1989, The Defense Revolution (with Norman Augustine) 1990, Shakespeare in Charge: The Bard's Guide to Leading and Succeeding on the Business Stage (with Norman Augustine) 1999, Reagan at Reykjavik: Forty-Eight Hours 2014; numerous articles in newspapers, magazines and professional journals. *Address:* Movers and Shakespeares, 4018 North 27th Street, Arlington, VA 22207, USA (office). *Telephone:* (703) 525-0100 (office). *Website:* www.moversandshakespeares.com (office).

ADELSOHN, Ulf, LLB; Swedish politician and business executive; b. 4 Oct. 1941, Stockholm; s. of Oskar Adelsohn and Margareta Adelsohn; m. Lena Liljeroth 1981; one s. one d.; legal adviser, Real Estate Co., Stockholm City 1968–70; Man.'s Asst, Swedish Confed. of Professional Asscns 1970–73; Commr, Street and Traffic Dept, Stockholm City Admin 1973–76; Mayor and Finance Commr 1976–79; Minister for Transport and Communications 1979–81; mem. Riksdagen (Parl.) 1982–88; Leader Moderata Samlingspartiet (Conservative Party) 1981–86; County Gov. of Stockholm 1992–2001; Chair. Luftfartsverket (Civil Aviation Authority) 1992–2002, Skansen (open air museum) 1998–2004; Chair. Swedish Railways 2002–11 (resgnd), Swedish Hotel and Restaurants Asscn 2001; Sr Adviser, Stockholm Chamber of Commerce, Ogilvy; King's Medal of the 12th Dimension with Ribbon of the Order of the Seraphims. *Publications:* Torsten Kreuger, Sanningen på väg (Torsten Kreuger, Truth on its Way) 1972, Kommunalmän: Hur skulle ni göra om det vore era egna pengar? (Local Politicians: What Would You Do If It Was Your Money?) 1978, Ulf Adelsohn Partiledare 1981–86 (Leader of the Party 1981–86) 1987, Priset för ett liv (The Price for a Life) 1991. *Leisure interests:* ice hockey, tennis. *Address:* Moderata samlingspartiet, POB 2080, 103 12 Stockholm, Sweden (office). *Website:* moderaterna.se (office).

ADEMI, Arber, DrIur; Macedonian lawyer, academic and politician; *Minister of Education and Science;* b. 25 Sept. 1985, Kumanovo, Macedonia, Yugoslavia; m.; two c.; ed Goce Delčev Gymnasium, Kumanovo, State Univ., Tetovo, Univ. of Tirana, Albania; part-time Asst, Faculty of Law, State Univ., Tetovo 2009–10, part-time Asst, Faculty of Business Admin 2009–12, Vice-Dean for Educational Affairs 2009–12, full-time Asst, Faculty of Law 2010–; consultant to Minister of Labour and Social Policy April–Oct. 2010; mem. team of experts drafting changes to legislation on balanced regional devt 2013–; mem. working group meeting on drafting of new Law on Admin. Gen. Procedure 2013–; Deputy Prime Minister, responsible for European Affairs 2016–17; Deputy Minister of Educ. and Science 2017–18, Minister of Educ. and Science 2018–; has attended numerous scientific confs. *Publications:* numerous scientific papers in professional journals. *Leisure interests:* literature, theatre. *Address:* Ministry of Education and Science, 1000 Skopje, ul. Kiril i Metodij 54, North Macedonia (office). *Website:* www.mon.gov.mk (office).

ADENUGA, Mike Adeniyi Agbolade Ishola, BSc, MBA; Nigerian business executive; *Chairman and CEO, Globacom Ltd;* b. 29 April 1953, Ijebu Igbo, Ogun; s. of Michael Agbolade Adenuga, Sr and Juliana Oyindamola Adenuga; m.; seven c.; ed Northwestern Univ., Pace Univ., USA; Founder Chair. and CEO Globacom Ltd (mobile telecommunications network) 2003–; Chair. Conoil Plc; Owner, Equitorial Trust Bank Ltd (acquired by Sterling Bank Plc 2011), acquired majority shares in Sterling Bank Plc 2011; Officer, Order of the Niger, Commdr, Order of the Niger. *Leisure interest:* soccer. *Address:* Globacom Ltd, Mike Adenuga Towers, 1 Mike Adenuga Close, Off Adeola Odeku, Victoria Island, Lagos, Nigeria (office). *Telephone:* (805) 0020121 (office). *E-mail:* mikeadenuga@consultant.com. *Website:* www.gloworld.com (office).

ADEOSUN, Kemi, BSc; Nigerian accountant, politician and fmr investment banker; *Chairman, Africa Export-Import Bank;* b. 1967, London, England; m. Niyi Adeosun; ed Univ. of East London, Univ. of London; Accounting Asst, British Telecom PLC, London 1989–90; Sr Auditor, Goodman Jones (chartered accountants), London 1990–93; Internal Audit Man., London Underground Ltd 1994–95; Internal Audit Man., Prism Consulting 1996–2000; Sr Man., Global Risk Management Solutions, PriceWaterhouseCoopers, London 2000–02; Man. Dir, Chapel Hill Denham Management (investment bank), Lagos 2002–10; Man. Dir, Quo Vadis Partnership 2010–11; Finance Commr, Ogun State Govt, SW Nigeria 2011–15; Minister of Finance 2015–18 (resgnd); Chair. Bd of Govs., ECOWAS Bank for Investment and Devt 2015–; Chair. Africa Export-Import Bank 2018–; mem. Inst. of Chartered Accountants Nigeria, Inst. of Chartered Accountants England and Wales. *Address:* Africa Export-Import Bank, 2 (B) El-Maahad El-Eshteraky Street, Heliopolis, Cairo 11341, Egypt (office). *Telephone:* (2) 24564100 (office). *E-mail:* mail@afreximbank.com (office). *Website:* www.afreximbank.com (office).

ÁDER, János, DrIur; Hungarian politician and head of state; *President;* b. 9 May 1959, Csorna, Győr-Moson-Sopron Co.; m. Anita Herczegh; one s. three d.; ed Révai Miklós Grammar School, Győr, Eötvös Loránd Univ., Budapest; law clerk, Budapest Dist VI Council 1983–84; researcher, Inst. of Sociology, Hungarian Acad. of Sciences 1986–90; joined Fed. of Young Democrats (Fidesz) 1988, mem. Nat. Election Cttee 1989, campaign chief for 1990 parliamentary elections and for both parliamentary and local elections in 1994, Chair. Steering Cttee 1992–93, party Vice-Pres. 1993–2002, Exec. Vice-Pres. 1995–97, 1999–2000, 2001–02, Parl. Group Leader 2002–06; mem. Parl. 1990–98, Deputy Speaker of Nat. Ass. and mem. House Cttee 1997–98, 2006–12, Speaker, Nat. Ass. 1998–2002; mem. European Parl. 2009–12; Pres. of Hungary 2012–. *Leisure interests:* angling, soccer. *Address:* Office of the President, 1014 Budapest, Sándor-Palace, Szent György tér 1–2 (office); Office of the President, 1536 Budapest, Pf. 227, Hungary. *Telephone:* (1) 224-5000 (office). *Fax:* (1) 224-5039 (office). *E-mail:* sajto@keh.hu (office). *Website:* www.keh.hu (office).

ADÈS, Thomas Joseph Edmund, MA, MPhil; British composer, pianist and conductor; b. 1 March 1971, London; s. of Timothy Adès and Dawn Adès; ed Univ. Coll. School, Guildhall School of Music, King's Coll., Cambridge, St John's Coll., Cambridge; solo recitalist with Composers Ensemble 1992; PLG Young Concert Artists Platform concert at Purcell Room 1993; Composer-in-Asscn, Hallé Orchestra 1993–95; Lecturer, Univ. of Manchester 1993–94; Fellow Commoner in Creative Arts, Trinity Coll., Cambridge 1995–97; Benjamin Britten Prof. of Music, RAM 1997–99; Musical Dir Birmingham Contemporary Music Group 1998–2000; Artistic Dir Aldeburgh Festival 1999–2008; R. and B. Debs Composer Chair., Carnegie Hall, New York 2007–08; conducted BBC Symphony Orchestra at BBC Proms 2013; Artistic Partner, Boston Symphony Orchestra 2016–; coaches Piano and Chamber Music annually at Int. Musicians Seminar, Prussia Cove; Lutine Prize, GSM 1986, winner, Paris Rostrum, for best piece by composer under 30 1994, Royal Philharmonic Prize 1997, Elise L. Stoeger Prize 1996, Salzburg Easter Festival Prize 1999, Hindemith Prize 2001, ISCM Young Composers Award 2002, Musical America Award for Composer of the Year 2011, Léonie Sonning Music Prize 2015. *Compositions include:* Five Eliot Landscapes 1990, Chamber Symphony 1990, Catch 1991, Darkness Visible 1992, Under Hamelin Hill 1992, Fool's Rhymes 1992, Still Sorrowing 1993, Life Story 1993, Living Toys 1993, . . . but all shall be well 1993, Sonata da Caccia 1994, The Origin of the Harp 1994, Arcadiana (Ernst von Siemens Prize) 1994, Powder Her Face 1995, Traced Overhead 1995–96, These Premises are Alarmed 1996, Asyla (Royal Philharmonic Soc. Award for Large-scale Composition 1997, Grawemeyer Prize 1999) 1997, Concerto Conciso 1997–98, America (A Prophecy) 1999, January Writ 1999, Piano Quintet 2000, Brahms 2001, The Tempest (Olivier Award for outstanding achievement in opera 2005, Royal Philharmonic Soc. award for large-scale composition 2005) 2004, Three Studies from Couperin 2006, Tevot (Royal Philharmonic Soc. Award for large-scale composition) 2007, The Four Quarters (British Composer Award for Best Chamber Music 2012) 2011, Totentanz for mezzo-soprano, baritone and orchestra 2013, The Exterminating Angel 2016. *Recordings include:* American Counterpoint (American Classics Series) 2010, Busoni: Piano Concerto, Turnadot Suite, Sarabande and Cortège 2010, Stravinsky: Complete Music for Violin & Piano 2010, The Importance of Being Earnest 2014, The Tempest (Contemporary category, Gramophone Awards 2010, DVD of production from Metropolitan Opera awarded Diapason d'Or de l'année 2013, Best Opera recording, Grammy Awards 2014, Music DVD Recording of the Year, ECHO Klassik Awards 2014). *Television includes:* Music for the 21st Century: Thomas Adès (Channel 4), Powder Her Face (Channel 4). *Address:* IMG Artists, LLC, Carnegie Hall Tower, 152 West 57th Street, 5th Floor, New York, NY 10019-3433, USA (office). *E-mail:* aelsesser@imgartists.com (office). *Website:* thomasades .com.

ADESIDA, Ilesanmi, BS, MS, PhD, FIEEE; American (b. Nigerian) electrical engineer, academic and university administrator; *Professor Emeritus, University of Illinois at Urbana-Champaign;* b. 1949; ed Univ. of California, Berkeley; worked briefly at Cornell Univ. and then as univ. admin. in Nigeria; joined faculty, Univ. of Illinois at Urbana-Champaign 1987, Prof., Beckman Inst. of Advanced Science and Tech. 1994–, Donald Biggar Willett Prof. of Eng, Dept of Electrical and Computer Eng 2003–, Dir Micro and Nanotechnology Lab. 2000–05, Dir Center for Nanoscale Science and Tech. 2003–12, Interim Dean, Coll. of Eng 2005–06, Dean 2006–12, Vice-Chancellor for Academic Affairs and Provost, Univ. of Illinois 2012–15, now Prof. Emer.; mem. Bd of Dirs FLUOR Corpn 2007–11; mem. Nat. Acad. of Eng, Minerals, Metals and Materials Soc., Materials Research Soc., Soc. for Eng Educ.; Fellow, IEEE 1998, AAAS 2003, American Vacuum Soc. 2004, Optical Soc. of America 2004; Pres. IEEE Electron Devices Soc. 2006–07, mem. IEEE David Sarnoff Award Cttee 2006–; attained US citizenship 2002; Student Presidential Award, Electron Microscopy Society of America EMSA 1978, Oakley-Kunde Award for Excellence in Undergraduate Education, Univ. of Illinois 1994, Electron Devices Society Distinguished Service Award 2011, Functional Materials John Bardeen Award 2016. *Publications include:* numerous scientific papers in professional journals on applications of advanced semiconductor processing and in manufacturing of high-speed microelectronic devices and circuits. *Address:* Micro and Nanotechnology Laboratory, University of Illinois, 208 N Wright Street, Urbana, IL 61801, USA (office). *Telephone:* (217) 333-3097 (office). *Fax:* (217) 244-6375 (office). *E-mail:* iadesida@illinois.edu (office); mntl@illinois.edu. *Website:* mntl.illinois.edu (office).

ADESINA, Akinwumi Ayodeji; Nigerian agricultural economist and international banker; *President, African Development Bank;* b. 1960, Ogun State; m.

Grace Adesina; two c.; ed Univ. of Ife (now Obafemi Awolowo Univ.), Purdue Univ., USA; Asst Prin. Economist, Int. Crops Research Inst. for the Semi-Arid Tropics 1988–90; Prin. Economist and Coordinator of West Africa Rice Econs Task Force, West Africa Rice Devt Asscn 1990–95; Prin. Economist and Social Science Research Co-ordinator, Int. Inst. of Tropical Agric. 1995–98; Sr Scientist, Rockefeller Foundation 1998, Rep. for Southern African 1999–2003, Assoc. Dir for Food Security 2003–08; Vice-Pres., Policy and Partnerships Alliance for Green Revolution in Africa –2011; Federal Minister of Agric. and Natural Resources 2011–15; Pres. African Devt Bank 2015–; Pres. African Asscn of Agricultural Econs 2008–10; apptd by UN Sec.-Gen. Ban Ki-moon as one of the 17 global leaders to spearhead the Millennium Devt Goals; Hon. DHumLitt (Franklin and Marshall Coll.) 2010; YARA Prize 2007, Council for Agricultural Science and Tech. Borlaug CAST Award 2010, Forbes African Person of the Year 2013, World Food Prize 2017. *Address:* African Development Bank, Immeuble du Centre de Commerce International d'Abidjan, ave Jean-Paul II, 01 BP 1387, Abidjan 01, Côte d'Ivoire (office). *Telephone:* 225-20-26-1 (office). *E-mail:* afdb@afdb.org (office). *Website:* www.afdb.org (office).

ADESINA, Segun, DEd; Nigerian professor of education; *Vice-President, African University Institute;* b. 5 Jan. 1941, Abeokuta, Ogun State; s. of Samuel Adesina and Georgiette Adesina; m. 1968; five c.; ed Loyola Coll., Nigerian Coll. of Arts, Science and Tech., Univ. of Ife and Northern Illinois and Columbia Univs, USA; history tutor, Loyola Coll. 1965–66; Asst Lecturer in Educ., Univ. of Lagos Coll. of Educ. 1967–69, Lecturer 1969–75; Sr Lecturer, Univ. of Lagos Faculty of Educ. 1975–77, Assoc. Prof. 1977–78, Prof. of Educ. 1988–2000, now Dir Inst. of Educ.; fmr Prof. of Educ., Ilorin Univ.; Visiting Prof. and Provost, Univ. of Ife, Adeyemi Coll. of Educ., Ondo 1984–85; Exec. Sec. Nigerian Educational Research Council 1987; Adviser on Educ. UN Office, Geneva 1975–76; consultant, UNESCO, Senegal 1984; Vice-Pres. African Univ. Inst., Imeko, Ogun State 2005–; Fellow, Nigerian Inst. of Admin. Man.; Assoc., Inst. of Personnel Man.; mem. Nigerian Inst. of Man., Presidential Cttee on Brain Drain; Obamoyegun of Ondo; Bajiki of Afon; Okonomo of Imeko. *Publications:* Primary Education in Nigeria: A Book of Readings, Planning and Educational Development in Nigeria (co-ed.) 1978, The Development of Modern Education in Nigeria 1988, Growth Without Development: Nigeria's Educational Experience 1914–2004 2006, Universal Basic Education in Nigeria: Prospects and Challenges 2007. *Leisure interest:* Gospel music. *Address:* PO Box 41, Abeokuta, Nigeria (home). *Telephone:* (803) 5638515 (mobile) (office); (39) 232226 (home); (803) 4388120 (mobile) (home).

ADEWOYE, Omoniyi, PhD; Nigerian academic and fmr politician; b. 27 Oct. 1939, Inisa, Osun State; s. of Chief James Woye and Victoria Fadunke Woye; m. Margaret Titilayo 1967; five d.; ed Kiriji Memorial Coll., Igbajo, Univ. of Ibadan, Univ. of London, UK, Columbia Univ., USA; Lecturer in History, Univ. of Ibadan 1968–75, Sr Lecturer 1975, Prof. of History 1984–2000, Vice-Chancellor 1996–2000, Prof. Emer. 2005–; Commr for Econ. Devt, Western State 1975–76; Commr for Finance and Econ. Devt, Oyo State 1976–77; Fed. Commr for Econ. Devt 1977–79; First Chair. Council of Ministers, Econ. Community of W African States 1977–78; Chair. Council of Ministers, Nigerian–Niger Jt Comm. 1977–78; Consultant to Econ. Comm. for Africa on Econ. Integration in W Africa 1982–83; Hon. Treas. Historical Soc. of Nigeria 1972–77; Woodrow Wilson Dissertation Scholarship (Columbia Univ.) 1967, Afgrad Fellowship (USA) 1964–68; Chair. Bd of Fellows, Osun Anglican Community 2005–; Order of the Federal Republic of Nigeria 2006. *Publications include:* The Legal Profession in Nigeria 1865–1962 1977, The Judicial System in Southern Nigeria 1854–1954 1977, Law and the Management of Change 2003; numerous articles on law and development in Africa. *Leisure interests:* gardening, reading, writing, music. *Address:* University of Ibadan, PO Box 7321, Ibadan, Nigeria. *Telephone:* 806019706 (office); 8042117560 (home). *E-mail:* omoniyiadewoye@yahoo.com.

ADHANOM GHEBREYESUS, Tedros, MSc, PhD; Ethiopian immunologist, politician and international organization executive; *Director-General, World Health Organisation;* m.; four s. one d.; ed Asmara Univ., Univ. of London, Univ. of Nottingham, UK; fmr Head, Tigray Regional Health Bureau; served in various technical posts in Ministry of Health, becoming Minister of State for Health 2004–05, Minister of Health 2005–12; Minister of Foreign Affairs 2012–16; Chair. Fourth Conf. of Ministers of Health of the African Union 2009–; fmr Chair. Global Fund Against AIDS, Tuberculosis and Malaria 2009–11, Roll Back Malaria, UNAIDS Programme Coordination Board 2009; Co-Chair. Partnership for Maternal, Newborn and Child Health 2005–09; Dir-Gen. WHO 2017–; fmr Chair. Bd of Dirs Addis Ababa Univ.; mem. High Level Taskforce on Innovative Int. Financing for Health Systems 2009; fmr mem. Bd Global Alliance for Vaccines and Immunization; co-f. (with Yale Univ. Global Health Leadership Inst.) Ethiopian Hospital Alliance for Quality 2011; Del. Harvard School of Public Health Forum 2012; Hon. Fellow, London School of Hygiene and Tropical Medicine 2012; American Soc. of Tropical Medicine and Hygiene Young Investigator Award 1999, Ethiopian Public Health Asscn Young Researcher Award 2003, Jimmy and Rosalynn Carter Humanitarian Award 2011, Yale Univ. Stanley T. Woodward Lectureship 2012, Women Deliver Award for Perseverance 2016. *Address:* World Health Organization (WHO), 20 ave Appia, 1211 Geneva 27, Switzerland (office). *Telephone:* 227912111 (office). *Fax:* 227913111 (office). *E-mail:* info@who.int (office). *Website:* www.who.int (office).

ADHIKARI, Ram Prashad, MCom; Nepalese banking executive; b. Saping, Kabhrepalanchok; worked in Nepal Rastra Bank for 30 years, worked as Chief Man. at various branch offices as well as in FOREX Div., becoming Exec. Dir Research Dept (retd); Sr Economist, South East Asian Central Banks (SEACEN) Centre, Kuala Lumpur, Malaysia 1997–2000; Chair. Rastriya Banijya Bank, Kathmandu 2009–11, apptd Man. Dir 2011. *Publications include:* Fiscal Consolidation in the SEACEN Countries, Economic Interdependence Among the Asian Countries; has published several articles on foreign exchange, foreign trade, govt finance and monetary policies.

ADHIN, (Michael) Ashwin Satyandre, MSc; Suriname politician; *Vice-President;* b. 10 June 1980, Paramaribo; m. Gracella Mahabier; ed Delft Univ., The Netherlands; early career as Project Man. for several telecommunications cos in Suriname; Prof., Anton de Kom Univ. 2005–12; Minister of Educ. and Community Devt 2013–15; mem. Nat. Ass. for Paramaribo 2015–; Vice-Pres. of Suriname 2015–; Chair. Culturele Unie Suriname 2011–13; mem. Nat. Democratic Party. *Leisure interests:* music, yoga. *Address:* Office of the Vice-President, Dr Sophie Redmondstraat 118, Frank Essed Gebouw, Paramaribo, Suriname (office). *Telephone:* 474805 (office). *Fax:* 472917 (office). *E-mail:* kabinet@vicepresident.gov.sr (office). *Website:* www.gov.sr/kabinet-van-de-vice-president.aspx (office).

ADIE, Kathryn (Kate), CBE, OBE, BA; British journalist, broadcaster and author; b. 19 Sept. 1945; d. of Babe Dunnett (née Issit) and adopted d. of John Wilfrid Adie and Maud Adie (née Fambely); ed Sunderland Church High School, Univ. of Newcastle; technician and producer BBC Radio 1969–76; reporter BBC TV South 1977–78, BBC TV News 1979–81, corresp. 1982–89, Chief News Corresp. 1989–2003, currently presenter, From Our Own Correspondent, BBC Radio 4; freelance journalist, broadcaster and TV presenter 2003–; Visiting Fellow, Univ. of Bournemouth 1998–; Hon. Prof., Sunderland Univ. 1995, Hon. Fellow, Royal Holloway, Univ. of London 1996, Freeman of Sunderland 1990; Hon. MA (Bath) 1987, (Newcastle) 1990, Hon. DLitt (City Univ.) 1989, (Loughborough) 1991, (Sunderland) 1993, (Robert Gordon) 1996, (Nottingham) 1998, (Nottingham Trent) 1998, Hon. MUniv (Open Univ.) 1996; Royal TV Soc. News Award 1981, 1987, Monte Carlo Int. News Award 1981, 1990, BAFTA Richard Dimbleby Award 1989. *Publications include:* The Kindness of Strangers (autobiography) 2002, Corsets to Camouflage: Women and War 2003, Nobody's Child: The Lives of Abandoned Children 2005, Into Danger 2008, Fighting on the Home Front: The Legacy of Women in World War One 2013. *Address:* POB 317, Brentford, London, TW8 8WX, England (office). *Telephone:* (20) 8838-2871 (office).

ADIKOESOEMO, Soegiarto; Indonesian business executive; *President Commissioner, AKR Corporindo Tbk;* b. 1938; m.; three c.; Founder AKR Corporindo Tbk, Pres. Dir 1982–92, Pres. Commr 1992–, also Pres. Commr PT Arthakencana Rayatama 1992–, PT Arjuna Utama Kimia 2007–, PT Andahanesa Abadi 2004–, PT AKR Niaga Indonesia 2012–; Chair. and Legal Rep. Khalista (Liuzhou) Chemical Industries Ltd 2004–; Pres. Dir/ Legal Counsel Guangxi (Guigang) AKR Container Port Co. Ltd 2006–, AKR (Guigang) Port Co. Ltd 2006–, AKR (Guigang) Transshipment Port Co. Ltd 2006–, AKR (Guangxi) Coal Trading Co. Ltd 2008–; Vice-Pres. Commr PT Sorini Towa Berlian Corporindo. *Address:* PT AKR Corporindo Tbk, Wisma AKR, Lt 7-8, Jl Panjang No 5, Kebon Jeruk, Jakarta, Indonesia (office). *Telephone:* (21) 5311588 (office). *Website:* www.akr.co.id (office).

ADING, Jack; Marshall Islands accountant and politician; b. 1 Sept. 1960, Ujelang Atoll; m. Luren Loeak; seven c.; ed Eastern Arizona Coll., USA, Hawaii Pacific Univ.; Accounting Technician, Sr Citizen Program, Marshall Islands Ministry of Social Services 1981–83; Accountant, Marshall Islands Housing Authority 1983–87; Asst to Chief of Housing and Home Improvement, Majuro 1987–89, Chief of Housing and Home Improvement 1989; Accountant, Pacific Resources for Educ. and Learning, Hawaii 1994–2006; mem. Nitijela (Parl.) from Enewetak/Ujelang 2007–; Minister of Finance 2008–12, 2014–16; mem. United People's Party (UPP). *Address:* Nitijela, Parliament Building, POB 24, MH 96960, Majuro, The Marshall Islands (office). *Telephone:* (625) 3678 (office). *Fax:* (692) 6253687 (office). *Website:* rmiparliament.org (office).

ADITYANATH, Yogi, BSc; Indian priest and politician; *Chief Minister of Uttar Pradesh;* b. (Ajay Mohan Bish), 5 June 1972; ed Hemwati Nandan Bahuguna Garhwal Univ.; joined Ayodhya Ram temple movement 1990s, becoming Mahant (Chief priest) of Gorakhnath Math (temple) 1994; mem. Lok Sabha (lower house of parl.) for Gorakhpur 1998–; Founder Hindu Yuva Vahini (militant youth org.) 2002; Chief Minister of Uttar Pradesh 2017–; mem. Bharatiya Janata Party (BJP) 1991–. *Address:* Lal Bahadur Shastri Bhawan, Lucknow 226001, Uttar Pradesh, India (office). *Telephone:* (522) 2239296 (office). *Fax:* (522) 2239573 (office). *E-mail:* cmup@nic.in (office). *Website:* upcmo.up.nic.in (office).

ADJAYE, David, OBE, MA; British/Tanzanian architect; *Principal, Adjaye Associates;* b. 1966, Dar-es-Salaam, Tanzania; ed Royal Coll. of Art; reformed studio as Adjaye/Associates 2000–; fmr Lecturer at RCA, Visiting Prof., Princeton Prof. School of Architecture, Louis Kahn Visiting Prof., Univ. of Pennsylvania, Kenzo Tange Prof. in Architecture, Harvard Grad. School of Design, Unit Tutor, Architectural Asscn, London; Chartered Mem., RIBA; Sr Fellow, Design Futures Council; Hon. Fellow, AIA, Foreign Hon. Mem., American Acad. of Arts and Letters; RIBA First Prize Bronze Medal 1993, Design Miami/Year of the Artist 2011. *Radio:* hosted BBC Radio programme which featured an interview with Oscar Neimeyer, also interviewed Indian architect Charles Correa 2005. *Television:* co-presented two TV series of Dreamspaces for BBC (six-part series on modern architecture); presented BBC documentary Building Africa: The Architecture of a Continent 2005. *Publications:* Houses: Recycling, Reconfiguring, Rebuilding 2005, Making Public Buildings 2006. *Address:* Adjaye Associates, The Edison, 223–231 Old Marylebone Road, London, NW1 5QT, England (office). *Telephone:* (20) 7258-6140 (office). *Fax:* (20) 7258-6148 (office). *Website:* www.adjaye.com (office).

ADKERSON, Richard C., BS, MBA; American business executive; *President, CEO and Vice-Chairman, Freeport-McMoRan Inc.;* b. 1947; ed Mississippi State Univ., Advanced Man. Program of Harvard Business School; Professional Accounting Fellow, SEC, Washington, DC and a Presidential Exchange Exec. 1976–78; Pnr and Man. Dir Arthur Andersen & Co. –1989 (headed Worldwide Oil and Gas Industry Practice); joined Freeport-McMoRan Inc. 1989, Pres. and CEO McMoRan Exploration Co. 1998–2004, Chief Financial Officer, Freeport-McMoRan Inc. 2000–03, CEO 2003–, Pres. 2008–, Vice-Chair. 2013–, Co-Chair. McMoRan Exploration Co. 1998–2013; Pres. Mississippi State Univ. Foundation Bd of Dirs, Chair. State of the Future capital campaign, mem. University's Advisory Bds for the Coll. of Business and Industry and the Agribusiness Inst.; Chair. Int. Council on Mining and Metals; mem. Exec. Bd Int. Copper Asscn, M.D. Anderson Cancer Center Bd of Visitors, Business Council of New Orleans and the River Region, Devt Bd of Fellowship of Christian Athletes of New Orleans, Bd of New Orleans Police and Justice Foundation, Louisiana State Univ. Ourso Coll. of Business Exec. Bd of Advisors, Xavier Univ. Pres.'s Council, New Orleans Baptist Theological Seminary Foundation Bd; Trustee, The Nat. World War II Museum; Dr hc (Mississippi State Univ.) 2010; Outstanding Accounting Alumnus of Mississippi State Univ. 1989, Outstanding Alumnus of Mississippi State Univ.'s Coll. of Business and Industry 1991, Richard C. Adkerson School of Accountancy est. by Mississippi State Univ. in his honour, inducted into American Mining Hall of Fame 2010, Nat. Alumnus of the Year, Mississippi State Univ. 2011, Charles F.

Rand Memorial Award, American Inst. of Mining, Metallurgical and Petroleum Engineers 2011, Exec. of the Year, W. P. Carey School of Business Dean's Council, Arizona State Univ. 2011. *Address:* Freeport-McMoRan Inc., One North Central Avenue, Phoenix, AZ 85004-4414, USA (office). *Telephone:* (602) 366-8100 (office). *E-mail:* info@fcx.com (office). *Website:* www.fcx.com (office).

ADKISSON, Perry Lee, PhD; American entomologist and academic; *Distinguished Professor Emeritus of Entomology and Chancellor Emeritus, Texas A&M University;* b. 11 March 1929, Hickman, Ark.; s. of Robert L. Adkisson and Imogene Adkisson (née Perry); m. 1st Frances Rozelle 1956 (died 1995); one d.; m. 2nd Gloria Ray 1998; ed Univ. of Arkansas, Kansas State Univ., Harvard Univ.; Asst Prof. of Entomology, Univ. of Missouri 1956–58; Assoc. Prof. of Entomology Texas A&M Univ. 1958–63, Prof. of Entomology 1963–67, Head Dept of Entomology 1967–78, apptd Distinguished Prof. of Entomology 1967, currently Distinguished Prof. Emer., Vice-Pres. for Agric. and Renewable Resources 1978–80, Deputy Chancellor for Agric. 1980–83, Deputy Chancellor 1983–86, Chancellor 1986–91, Chancellor Emer. 1991–, Regent's Prof. 1991–95; Consultant Int. AEC, Vienna 1969–74; Chair. Texas Pesticide Advisory Comm. 1972; mem. Panel on Integrated Pest Control FAO, Rome 1971–78; mem. NAS, Governing Bd Int. Crop Research Inst. for Semi-Arid Tropics 1982–88, Standing Cttee for Int. Plant Protection Congresses 1984–, Texas Science and Tech. Council 1986–88, Advisory Cttee, Export-Import Bank of the US 1987; Alexander Von Humboldt Award 1980, Distinguished Service Award, American Inst. of Biological Sciences 1987, Distinguished Alumni Award (Ark. Univ.) 1990, Wolfe Prize in Agric. 1994–95, World Food Prize 1997, Medallion Alumni Award, Kansas State Univ. 1999 and numerous other awards. *Publications include:* Controlling Cotton's Insect Pests: A New System 1982; several papers on insect diapause and other entomological topics. *Leisure interests:* gardening, fishing. *Address:* The Reed House, 1 Reed Drive, College Station, TX 77843, USA (home). *Telephone:* (409) 845-2516 (home).

ADLER, Julius, AB, MS, PhD, FAAS; American biologist, biochemist and professor of biochemistry; *Professor Emeritus, Department of Biochemistry, University of Wisconsin;* b. 30 April 1930, Edelfingen, Germany; s. of Adolf Adler and Irma Stern; m. Hildegard Wohl 1963; one s. one d.; ed Harvard Univ., Univ. of Wisconsin; emigrated to USA 1938, naturalized US citizen 1943; Postdoctoral Fellow, Washington Univ., St Louis 1957–59, Stanford Univ. 1959–60; Asst Prof., Depts of Biochemistry and Genetics, Univ. of Wisconsin 1960–63, Assoc. Prof. 1963–66, Prof. 1966–96, Prof. Emer. 1997–, Edwin Bret Hart Prof. 1972; Steenbock Prof. of Microbiological Sciences 1982–92; mem. American Acad. of Arts and Sciences, American Philosophical Soc., NAS, Wisconsin Acad. of Sciences, Arts and Letters; Fellow, American Acad. of Microbiology, Wisconsin Acad. of Sciences, Arts, and Letters 1996; Behring Lecturer, Philips Univ. of Marburg 1989, Hartman-Müller Memorial Lecturer, Univ. of Zürich 1984; Dr hc (Tübingen) 1987, (Regensburg) 1995; Selman A. Waksman Microbiology Award, NAS 1980, Otto-Warburg Medal, German Soc. of Biological Chem. 1986, Hilldale Award, Univ. of Wisconsin 1988, R.H. Wright Award, Simon Fraser Univ. 1988, Abbott-American Soc. for Microbiology Lifetime Achievement Award 1995, William C. Rose Award, American Soc. for Biochemistry and Molecular Biology 1996. *Publications include:* research papers on the behaviour of simple organisms, especially bacteria, research on the behaviour of fruit flies. *Address:* 457C Biochemistry Addition, Department of Biochemistry, 433 Babcock Drive, University of Wisconsin, Madison, WI 53706-1544 (office); 1234 Wellesley Road, Madison, WI 53705, USA (home). *Telephone:* (608) 262-3693 (office). *E-mail:* adler@biochem.wisc.edu (office). *Website:* www.biochem.wisc.edu (office).

ADLEŠIĆ, Đurđa; Croatian politician; b. 18 April 1960, Bjelovar; m.; one c.; ed Univ. of Zagreb; Founder-mem. Hrvatska socijalno liberalna stranka (HSLS—Croatian Social Liberal Party) 1990–2011, Vice-Pres. 2000–06, Pres. 2006–09; mem. Sabor (Parl.) 1995–2011, mem. Cttee for Family, Youth and Sports, Cttee for War Veterans, Pres. HSLS Group of Deputies 1998–2011, Vice-Pres. Sabor 2004–08; Mayor of Bjelovar 2001–08; Deputy Prime Minister 2008–11; unsuccessful cand. in presidential election 2005; fmr Vice-Pres. Comm. for Determining the Victims of War.

ADLINGTON, Rebecca (Becky), OBE; British swimmer; b. 17 Feb. 1989, Mansfield, Notts.; d. of Steve Adlington and Kay Adlington; m. Harry Needs 2014; one d.; ed The Brunts School, Mansfield; began swimming with Sherwood Colliery Swimming Club; selected for Nottinghamshire County Swim Squad (Nova Centurion); European Championships (long course), Budapest 2006: silver medal, 800m freestyle, Budapest 2010: gold medal, 400m freestyle, bronze medal, 4×200m freestyle; World Championships (short course), Manchester 2008: gold medal, 800m freestyle, silver medal, 4×200m freestyle; Olympic Games, Beijing 2008: gold medal, 400m freestyle, 800m freestyle; World Championships (long course), Rome 2009: bronze medal, 400m freestyle, 4×200m freestyle, Shanghai 2011: gold medal, 800m freestyle, silver medal, 400m freestyle; Commonwealth Games, Delhi 2010 (competed for England): gold medal, 400m freestyle, 800m freestyle, bronze medal, 200m freestyle, 4×200m freestyle; Olympic Games, London 2012: bronze medal, 400m freestyle, 800m freestyle; first British swimmer to win two Olympic gold medals since 1908 and GB's most successful Olympic swimmer in 100 years; coach: Bill Furniss; Amb. for the Encephalitis Soc.; retd from all competitive swimming Feb. 2013; named by Sports Journalists' Asscn of GB as Sportswoman of the Year 2008, 2011, voted third in BBC's Sports Personality of the Year Award 2008, Laureus World Sports Awards Breakthrough of the Year Award 2008, Sherwood Swimming Baths in Mansfield renamed the Rebecca Adlington Swimming Centre following refurbishment 2010.

ADOLFO; American fashion designer; b. (Adolfo F. Sardiña), 15 Feb. 1933, Cardenas, Matanzas, Cuba; ed St Ignacio de Loyola Jesuit School, Havana; served in Cuban Army; apprentice, Cristóbal Balenciaga millinery salon, Paris 1950–52; apprentice millinery designer, Bergdorf Goodman, New York 1953–54; designer Emme (milliners), New York 1954–62; worked as unpaid apprentice, Chanel, New York summers of 1957, 1966; Owner and Head Designer, Adolfo Inc., New York 1962–93; f. Adolfo Enterprises (licensing firm) 1993; Designer, Adolfo Menswear Inc. and Adolfo Scarves Inc., New York 1978; created perfume line for Frances Denny, New York 1979; f. Adolfo F. Sardiña Trust; mem. Council, Fashion Designers of America 1982. *Address:* Adolfo Inc., 60 East 42nd Street, Suite 1138, New York, NY 10165, USA (office). *Telephone:* (212) 682-1977 (office). *Website:* adolfo.com (office).

ADOUKI, Martin, DJur; Republic of the Congo diplomatist; b. 8 April 1942, Makoua; ed Bordeaux and Paris Univs and Int. Inst. of Public Admin., Paris; Information Officer for the Group of African, Caribbean and Pacific Countries (ACP) in Brussels and attended negotiations between the ACP and the EEC; fmrly Lecturer in Law at the Marien Ngouabi Univ., Brazzaville and later Special Adviser to the Prime Minister; Perm. Rep. to the UN 1985–94, to UN Security Council 1986–87, Pres. UN Security Council 1986–87, Chair. UN African Group Sept. 1986, Rep. of Chair. of OAU to UN 1986–87, Head Congo Del. to 43rd Session of Gen. Ass. 1988; mem. of the Zone of Peace and Co-operation in the South Atlantic 1988–90, mem. Del. of UN Special Cttee on the Verification of Elections in Namibia 1989, Vice-Pres. UN Gen. Ass. (44th Session) 1989; Observer on the Gen. Elections in Nicaragua Feb. 1990, Head Del. to World Summit for Children Sept. 1990; Chair. 4th Cttee of 45th Session of Gen. Ass. 1990–91; apptd Amb. and Diplomatic Adviser to Pres. 1998.

ADRIANO, Dino, FCCA, FCIM; British business executive; *Trustee, The Sainsbury Archive;* b. 24 April 1943, London; s. of Dante Adriano and Yole Adriano; m. Susan Rivett 1996; two d.; ed Strand Grammar School and Highgate Coll.; articled clerk, George W. Spencer & Co., Chartered Accountants 1959–64; joined J. Sainsbury plc 1964, trainee, Accounting Dept 1964–65, Financial Accounts Dept 1965–73, Br. Financial Control Man. 1973–80, Gen. Man. Homebase 1981–86, Area Dir, Sainsbury's Central and Western Area 1986–89, Man. Dir Homebase 1989–95, Chair. 1991–96, Asst Man. Dir J. Sainsbury plc 1995–96, Deputy Chief Exec. 1996–97; Deputy Chair. Shaw's Supermarkets Inc. 1994, Chair. 1994–96; Dir, Giant Food Inc. 1994–96, Laura Ashley plc 1996–98; Chair. Bd Govs, Thames Valley Univ. 2004–09; Trustee, Oxfam 1990–96, 1998–2004, Adviser on Retail Matters 1996–98, 2004–06, Vice-Chair. 2001–04; Trustee, WRVS 2001–07, The Sainsbury Archive 2007–, Sainsbury Veterans Welfare Scheme 2007–, Chartered Inst. of Marketing 2015–; Hon. DUniv (Thames Valley) 2009. *Leisure interests:* opera, music, soccer, cookery. *E-mail:* dino.adriano@lineone.net (office).

ADVANI, Lal Krishna; Indian politician, fmr journalist and social worker; b. 8 Nov. 1927, Karachi (now in Pakistan); s. of Kishinchand Advani and Gyani Advani; m. Kamala Jagtiani 1965; one s. one d.; ed D.G. Nat. Coll., Hyderabad, Sind, Govt Law Coll., Mumbai; joined Rashtriya Swayam Sevak Sangh (RSS, social work org.) 1942, Sec. of Karachi br. 1947; joined Bharatiya Jana Sangh (BJS) 1951, party work in Rajasthan –1958, Sec. Delhi State Jana Sangh 1958–63, Pres. Delhi State Jana Sangh 1970–72, All India Jana Sangh 1973, re-elected 1974, 1975, Bharatiya Janata Party (BJP) 1986–91, 1993–98; mem. Bharatiya Jana Sangh 1951–77; Vice-Pres. Delhi State Jana Sangh 1965–67; elected mem. Rajya Sabha (Parl.) 1970, 1976, 1982, 1988, 1991, 1998, 1999, 2004, 2009–, Deputy Prime Minister 1999–2004, Leader of Opposition Jan.–April 1980, Lok Sabha 1991–93, 2004–10, mem. Parl. Cttee on Public Undertakings 1972–74, 1981–82, Gen. Purposes Cttee 1980–85, Cttee on Subordinate Legislation 1984–86, 1987–89; Minister for Information and Broadcasting 1977–79, of Kashmir Affairs 1998–99, of Home Affairs 1999–2004, of Coal and Mines (Additional Charge) July–Aug. 2002, of Personnel, Pensions and Public Grievances (Additional Charge) 2003–04; Chair. Delhi Metropolitan Council 1967–70; Gen. Sec. Bharatiya Janata Party 1977–80, 1980–86; Jt Sec. Rajasthan State Jana Sangh 1952–57; mem. Delhi Metropolitan Council 1966–70, Inter-Governmental Conf. on Communication Policies in Asia and Oceania, Kuala Lampur 1977; Indian Del. at UNESCO Gen. Conf. 1978; Leader, Jana Sangh Group in Interim Metropolitan Council 1966–67; Indian Parl. Del. to Strasbourg 1991; mem. Cen. Exec. of BJS 1966; Jt Ed. BJS paper Organizer 1960–67; Outstanding Parliamentarian Award 1999. *Publications include:* A Prisoner's Scrap-Book, The People Betrayed. *Leisure interests:* theatre, cinema, books, sports, music. *Address:* 26 Tughlak Crescent, New Delhi 110 011 (office); 1835/16, Kasturbhai Block, Din Dayal Bhawan, J. P. Chowk, Khanpur, Ahmedabad (home); 30 Prithviraj Raj Road, New Delhi 110 003, India (home). *Telephone:* (11) 23001700 (office); (11) 23794124 (New Delhi) (home). *Fax:* (11) 23001762 (office); (11) 23012791 (office); (11) 23017419 (New Delhi) (home). *E-mail:* advanilk@sansad.nic.in (office). *Website:* www.bjp.org (office); www.lkadvani.in (home).

ADVANI, Pankaj Arjan, BCom; Indian professional snooker player; b. 24 July 1985, Pune, Maharashtra; ed Frank Anthony Public School, Bangalore, Mahaveer Jain Coll., Bangalore; spent early years in Kuwait before moving to Bangalore; trained in snooker by fmr nat. snooker champion Arvind Savur; won Indian Jr Billiards Championship 2000, 2001, 2003, 2005, Indian Jr Snooker Championship 2003, 2005; professional 2003–; won first world championship title at Int. Billiards and Snooker Fed. (IBSF) World Snooker Championship, China 2003; other wins include IBSF World Billiards Championship, Malta 2005, Bangalore 2008, Leeds, UK 2009, 2012, Asian Billiards Championship 2005, 2008 (only player to have won title twice), 2009, 2010, 2012, 6 Red Snooker Pentangular Team Championship, Pakistan 2008, Australian Open Billiards Championship, Melbourne 2008 (first Indian winner); gold medal, Men's English Billiards, Asian Games, Doha 2006, Guangzhou 2010; bronze medal, Men's English Billiards, Asian Indoor Games, Ho Chi Minh City 2009; Nat. Billiards and Snooker Champion 2009; won IBSF World 6-Red Snooker Championship on debut 2014; only player ever to win professional world titles in both the long and short formats of snooker (15-red standard and 6-red) and both formats of English billiards (time and point); helped India win first ever World Team Billiards Championship, Glasgow, UK 2014; announced relinquishing snooker tour card to concentrate on billiards career Sept. 2014; numerous awards, including Sports Star Sportsperson of the Year 2003, Indo-American Young Achiever's Award 2003, Arjuna Award 2004, Rajeev Gandhi Award 2004, Hero India Sports Award 2004, Bangalore Univ. Sportsperson of the Year 2005, Sports Writers' Asscn of Bangalore Award 2005, Senior Sportsperson of the Year 2005, Vision of India's Int. Indian Award 2005, Rajiv Gandhi Khel Ratna Award 2006, Kempegowda Award, Karnataka 2007, Rajyotsava Award (Karnataka's highest civilian award) 2007, Padma Shri Award 2009. *Address:* c/o Karnataka State Billiards Association, 5/1 Miller Tank Bed Area, Jasma Bhavan Road, Bangalore 560 052, India. *Telephone:* (80) 43223222 (office); (80) 22269970 (office). *Fax:* (80) 22257315 (office). *E-mail:* contact@ksba.in (office); ksba_blr@dataone.in (office). *Website:* www.ksba.in (office).

ADYRKHAYEVA, Svetlana Dzantemirovna; Russian/Ossetian ballerina and ballet teacher; *Director, Svetlana Adyrkhayeva Ballet Studio;* b. 12 May 1938,

Khumalag, North Ossetia; d. of Taissya Gougkayeva and Dzantemir Adyrkhayev; m. Alexey Zakalinsky 1966; one d.; ed Leningrad Choreographic School, Theatre Acad. of Russia; danced with Glinka Theatre of Opera and Ballet, Chelyabinsk 1955–58; with Odessa Opera and Ballet 1958–60; dancer at Bolshoi Theatre 1960–88, Balletmaster-Repetiteur 2001–; Dir Svetlana Adyrkhayeva Ballet Studio, Moscow; USSR People's Artist 1984. *Principal parts include:* Odette-Odile, Princess Florine, Woman of the Bronze Mountain (Prokofiev's Stone Flower), Zarema (Asafiev's Fountain of Bakhchisaray), Mehmene Banu (Melikov's Legend of Love), Aegina (Khatchaturyan's Spartacus), Kitri (Minkus's Don Quixote). *Leisure interests:* reading, travelling. *Address:* 121099 Moscow, 1st Smolensky per. 9, Apt 74, Russia. *Telephone:* (495) 241-13-62.

AEBISCHER, Patrick, MD, DrMed; Swiss medical scientist, academic, university administrator and entrepreneur; *Professor Emeritus, École Polytechnique Fédérale de Lausanne;* b. 22 Nov. 1954, Fribourg; s. of Emile Aebischer (known as Yoki) and Joan Aebischer (née O'Boyle); m.; two c.; ed Univs of Geneva and Fribourg; Research Scientist, Asst, Assoc. Prof. of Medical Sciences, Brown Univ., USA 1984–92, Chair. Section of Artificial Organs, Biomaterials and Cellular Tech., Div. of Biology and Medicine 1991; Prof. and Dir, Surgical Research Div. and Gene Therapy Centre, Univ. Hosp. of Lausanne 1992–99; Pres. and Prof. of Neurosciences and Head of Neurodegenerative Disease Lab., École Polytechnique Fédérale de Lausanne (one of the two Swiss Fed. Insts of Tech.) 2000–16, Prof. Emer. 2017–; f. CytoTherapeutics Inc. 1989, Modex Therapeutics Inc. 1996, Amazentis SA (start-up companies) 2007; mem. Bd of Dirs Lonza Group 2008– (also Vice-Chair. 2014–), Nestlé Health Science 2011–; Pres. and Chair. Advisory Bd, Novartis Venture Funds 2014–; Sr Pnr NanoDimension 2017–; Dir (non-Exec.) Logitech Int. SA 2016–, Renovo Group PLC, Inspired Capital PLC, IsoTis NV, IsoTis Orthobiologics, IsoTis SA, StemCells Inc.; mem. Advisory Bd Coursera Inc. 2012–; mem. Biomedical Sciences Int. Advisors Council 2013–; mem. Bd World Econ. Forum 2013–16, Montreux Jazz Festival, Verbier Festival; mem. Scientific Advisory Bd Voyager Therapeutics Inc. 2016–, Anecova SA, Link Medicine Corp., Oxford Biomedica PLC; mem. Bd of Trustees Jacobs Foundation 2017–; Fellow, Swiss Nat. Science Foundation 1984–86, Swiss Acad. for the Medical Sciences 1998, American Inst. for Medical and Biological Eng Sciences 2000, Swiss Eng Acad. 2009; Hon. Doctorate (Univ. de Montréal) 2011, (Korea Advanced Inst. of Science and Tech.) 2016; Kolff Award (Young Investigator Award, American Soc. for Artificial Internal Organs), New York 1987, Robert Bing Award, Swiss Acad. of Medicine 1994, Pfizer Foundation Award for Clinical Neurosciences 1997. *Publications include:* numerous papers in professional journals on the development of cell and gene transfer approaches for the treatment of neurodegenerative diseases. *Address:* École Polytechnique Fédérale de Lausanne, Centre Est, Station 1, 1015 Lausanne (office); Laboratoire d'étude sur la Neurodégénérescence, École Polytechnique Fédérale de Lausanne, EPFL SV BMI LEN, Bâtiment AI, Station 19, 1015 Lausanne, Switzerland (office). *Telephone:* (2169) 37001 (office); (2169) 39505 (office). *E-mail:* patrick.aebischer@epfl.ch (office). *Website:* people.epfl.ch/patrick.aebischer (office); len.epfl.ch (office).

AFANASIEV, Evgeny Vladimirovich; Russian diplomatist; b. 25 May 1947, Rostov-on-Don, USSR; m.; one s. three d.; ed Moscow State Inst. of Int. Relations; joined Ministry of Foreign Affairs of USSR 1970, Attaché, USSR Embassy in Beijing 1970–75, Attaché, First Far Eastern Dept, Ministry of Foreign Affairs 1975–76, Third Sec., Second Sec., First Sec., USSR Embassy in Washington, DC 1976–84, First Sec., First Far Eastern Dept, Ministry of Foreign Affairs 1984–85, Chief Asst to Deputy Foreign Minister in charge of Asian and Pacific Affairs 1985–87, Counsellor, Secr. of Minister of Foreign Affairs 1987, Counsellor, USSR/Russian Fed. Embassy in Washington, DC 1987–92, First Deputy Dir Gen., First Asia and Pacific Bureau, Ministry of Foreign Affairs 1992–94, Dir First Asian Dept 1994–97, Amb. to South Korea 1997–2001, Dir First Asian Dept 2001–04, Amb. to Thailand and Perm. Rep. of Russia to ESCAP 2004–10, Dir Human Resources Dept (mem. of Collegium), Ministry of Foreign Affairs 2010–12, Amb. to Japan 2012–18; Order of Friendship.

AFASH, Mohamed Nagy Ismail ('Gedo'); Egyptian professional footballer; b. 30 Oct. 1984, Damanhur, Beheira; attacking midfielder/striker; started career at Hosh Essa Sports Centre 2001–02; played for teams Ala'ab Damanhour 2002–05, Al-Ittihad Al Sakandary 2005–10, Al-Ahly 2010– (won Egyptian Premier League 2010/11, 2013/14, Egyptian Super Cup 2010, 2014, CAF Champions League 2012, 2013, CAF Super Cup 2013, 2014), Hull City (loan) 2013–14 (runner-up, Football League Championship 2012–13); debut with Egyptian Nat. Football Team 2009, took part in African Cup of Nations 2010 (mem. of winning team and top scorer of the tournament). *Address:* Egyptian Football Association, 5 Gabalaya Street, Gezira El Borg Post Office, Cairo, Egypt (office). *Telephone:* (2) 27351793 (office). *E-mail:* efa_football@hotmail.com (office). *Website:* www.efa.com.eg (office).

AFEEF, Hassan; Maldivian politician; m. Farhath Afeef; MP for Thaa Atoll, Shadow Home Minister; Leader, Maldivian Democratic Party Parl. Group –2009, currently mem.; Political Adviser to Pres. 2009–10; Minister of Home Affairs 2010–12; fmr mem. Judicial Services Comm.; arrested by Coup Police Feb. 2013. *Address:* Maldivian Democratic Party (MDP), H. Sharaashaa, 2nd Floor, Sosun Magu, Malé 20-059, Maldives (office). *Telephone:* 3340044 (office). *Fax:* 3322960 (office). *E-mail:* secretariat@mdp.org.mv (office); minhah@dhivenhinet.net.mv (office). *Website:* www.mdp.org.mv (office).

AFEWERKI, Issaias; Eritrean head of state; *President;* b. 2 Feb. 1946, Asmara; m. Saba Haile; three c.; trained as engineer; joined Eritrean Liberation Front (ELF) 1966, mil. training in China 1966, Leader of fourth regional area ELF 1968, Gen. Commdr ELF 1969; Founding mem. Eritrean People's Liberation Front (now People's Front for Democracy and Justice—PFDJ 1977), fmr Asst Sec.-Gen., Sec.-Gen. 1987, currently Leader; Chair. State Council, Nat. Ass.; Sec. Gen. Provisional Govt of Eritrea 1991; assumed power May 1991; elected Pres. of Eritrea by Nat. Ass. 1993–. *Address:* Office of the President, PO Box 257, Asmara, Eritrea (office). *Telephone:* (1) 122132 (office). *Fax:* (1) 125123 (office).

AFFANDI RAJA MOHAMED NOOR, Datuk Raja Mohamed; Malaysian army officer; *Chief of Defence Forces;* b. 20 June 1957, Kampung Raja, Terengganu State; m. Datin Norlida Abdul Mubin; one s. three d.; ed Officer Cadet School, Port Dickson, mil. insts in Australia and Pakistan; commissioned as Second Lt, Corps of the Royal Malay Regiment (RAMD) 1977, later becoming platoon leader, co. commdr, field commdr, Chief Instructor, Pusasda Army Basic Training Centre, Commanding Officer, 8 RAMD Bn, Mil. Asst to Deputy Chief of Army, Asst Chief of Staff and Chief of Planning and Devt (Div. 2), Chief of Field Office (Army) 2008–09, Armed Forces Chief of Staff 2009–13, Army Chief 2013–16, Chief of Defence Forces Dec. 2016–; attained rank of Lt-Gen. 2008, Gen. 2013. *Leisure interests:* reading, sports, golf. *Address:* Malaysian Armed Forces Headquarters, Wisma Pertahanan, Wilayah Persekutuan, Kuala Lumpur 50634, Malaysia (office). *Telephone:* (3) 26921333 (office). *Fax:* (3) 26911757 (office). *E-mail:* sk.komlek@mod.gov.my (office). *Website:* www.mafhq.mil.my (office).

AFFLECK, Ben; American actor and director; b. 15 Aug. 1972, Berkeley; brother of Casey Affleck; m. Jennifer Garner 2005 (divorced 2017); one s. two d. *Films include:* School Ties 1992, Buffy the Vampire Slayer, Dazed and Confused, Mallrats 1995, Glory Daze, Office Killer, Chasing Amy 1997, Going All the Way 1997, Good Will Hunting (also screenplay with Matt Damon q.v., Acad. Award and Golden Globe for Best Original Screenplay 1997) 1997, Phantoms 1998, Armageddon 1998, Shakespeare in Love 1998, Reindeer Games 1999, Forces of Nature 1999, Dogma 1999, Daddy and Them 1999, The Boiler Room 1999, 200 Cigarettes 1999, Bounce 2000, The Third Wheel (also producer) 2000, Pearl Harbor 2001, The Sum of All Fears 2002, Changing Lanes 2002, Daredevil 2003, Gigli 2003, Paycheck 2003, Jersey Girl 2004, Surviving Christmas 2004, Man About Town 2006, Hollywoodland 2006, Smokin' Aces 2006, Gone Baby Gone (dir, writer and producer) 2007, He's Just Not That Into You 2009, State of Play 2009, Extract 2009, The Company Men 2010, The Town (dir and writer) 2010, Argo (dir Golden Globe Award for Best Dir 2013, Outstanding Directorial Achievement in Feature Film, Directors Guild of America 2013, BAFTA Award for Best Dir 2013) 2012, To the Wonder 2012, Gone Girl 2014, Batman v Superman: Dawn of Justice 2016, The Accountant 2016, Justice League 2017. *Television includes:* Voyage of the Mimi, Against the Grain, Lifestories: Families in Crisis, Hands of a Stranger, Daddy. *Address:* c/o Grant, Tani Barash & Altman, LL, 9100 Wilshire Blvd, Suite 1000W, Beverly Hills, CA 90212, USA.

AFFLECK, Casey; American actor, director and producer; b. (Caleb Casey McGuire Affleck), 12 Aug. 1975, Falmouth, Mass; s. of Timothy Byers Affleck and Christopher Anne (née Boldt); brother of Ben Affleck; m. Summer Phoenix 2006 (divorced 2016); two s.; ed Columbia Univ. *Films include:* To Die For 1995, Race the Sun 1996, Chasing Amy 1997, Good Will Hunting 1997, Desert Blue 1998, 200 Cigarettes 1999, The Book of Charles (dir) 1999, Drowning Mona 2000, Hamlet 2000, Committed 2000, Attention Shoppers 2000, American Pie 2 2001, Soul Survivors 2001, Gerry 2002, Ocean's Twelve 2004, Lonesome Jim 2005, The Last Kiss 2006, Gone Baby Gone 2007, The Assassination of Jesse James by the Coward Robert Ford (Satellite Award for Best Supporting Actor–Motion Picture 2007) 2007, I'm Still Here (also dir, producer, writer, cinematographer, ed.) 2010, The Killer Inside Me 2010, Tower Heist 2011, Ain't Them Bodies Saints 2013, Out of the Furnace 2013, Interstellar 2014, Manchester by the Sea (Golden Globe Award for Best Actor–Motion Picture Drama 2016, Boston Soc. of Film Critics for Best Actor 2016, Broadcast Film Critics Asscn for Best Actor 2016, Chicago Film Critics Asscn for Best Actor 2016, Critics' Choice Movie Award for Best Actor 2016, Gotham Award 2016, Acad. Award for Best Actor 2017, BAFTA for Leading Actor 2017) 2016, The Finest Hours 2016, Triple 9 2016, A Ghost Story 2017. *Television includes:* Lemon Sky (film) 1988, The Kennedys of Massachusetts (mini-series) 1990, All Grown Up (producer) 2003. *Address:* WME Entertainment, 9601 Wilshire Blvd, 3rd Floor, Beverly Hills, CA 90210-5213, USA (office). *Telephone:* (310) 285-9000 (office). *Fax:* (310) 248-2020 (office). *Website:* www.wmeentertainment.com (office).

AFRIDI, Sahibzada Mohammad Shahid Khan, (Shahid Afridi); Pakistani professional cricketer (retd); b. 1 March 1980, Khyber Agency, Federally Administered Tribal Areas; m. Nadia; four d.; all-rounder; right-handed batsman; leg-break googly bowler; played for Karachi 1995–2010, Pakistan 1996–2011 (Capt. 2010–11), Habib Bank Ltd 1997–2009, MCC 2001, Leics. 2001, Derbyshire 2003, Griqualand West 2003–04, Kent 2004, Ireland 2006, Sind 2007–08, Deccan Chargers 2008, South Australia 2009–10, Southern Redbacks 2010, Hants. 2011–, Melbourne Renegades 2011–, Dhaka Gladiators 2011–, Ruhuna Royals 2012, Asia XI, ICC World XI; First-class debut: 1995/96; Test debut: Pakistan v Australia, Karachi 22–26 Oct. 1998; One-Day Int. (ODI) debut: Kenya v Pakistan, Nairobi (Aga) 2 Oct. 1996; T20I debut: England v Pakistan, Bristol 28 Aug. 2006; played in 27 Tests (48 wickets, 1,716 runs), 398 ODI matches (395 wickets, 8,064 runs), 98 T20I matches (97 wickets, 1,405 runs); announced retirement from all forms of int. cricket Feb. 2011; Amb. fifth Blind Cricket World Cup, Pakistan Blind Cricket Council (PBCC); Sitara-i-Imtiaz 2018. *Address:* c/o Pakistan Cricket Board, Gaddafi Stadium, Lahore 54600, Pakistan. *Telephone:* (42) 571-7231. *Fax:* (42) 571-1860. *E-mail:* info@pcboard.com.pk. *Website:* www.pcboard.com.pk/home.html.

AGA KHAN IV, HH Prince Shah Karim al-Hussaini, Spiritual Leader and Imam of Ismaili Muslims, KBE, BA; British; b. 13 Dec. 1936, Creux-de-Genthod, Geneva, Switzerland; s. of Prince Aly Salomon Khan and Princess Tajuddawlah Aly Khan (late Viscountess Camrose, née Joan Barbara Yarde-Buller); m. 1st Sarah Frances Croker-Poole (Begum Salimah Aga Khan) 1969 (divorced 1995); two s. one d.; m. 2nd Princess Gabriele zu Leiningen (Begum Inaara Aga Khan) 1998 (separated 2011); one s.; ed Le Rosey, Switzerland, Harvard Univ., USA; became Aga Khan on the death of his grandfather Sir Sultan Mahomed Shah, Aga Khan III, GCSI, GCIE, GCVO 1957; granted title of His Highness by Queen Elizabeth II 1957, of His Royal Highness by the Shah of Iran 1959; Founder and Chair. Aga Khan Foundation 1967, Aga Khan Award for Architecture 1977–, Inst. of Ismaili Studies 1977–, Aga Khan Fund for Econ. Devt, Geneva 1984, Aga Khan Trust for Culture 1988, Aga Khan Agency for Microfinance 2005–; Founder and Chancellor Aga Khan Univ., Pakistan 1983–, Univ. of Central Asia (Tekeli, Kazakhstan, Naryn, Kyrgyzstan and Khorugh, Tajikistan) 2001–; Founder Pres. Yacht Club Costa Smeralda, Sardinia; mem. Royal Yacht Squadron 1982–; Assoc. Foreign mem. Acad. des Beaux-Arts 2008; Foreign mem., Class of Humanities, Lisbon Acad. of Sciences 2009; Hon. Col, 6th Lancers, Pakistani Army 1970; Hon. Citizen of the Town of Kisumu (Kenya) 1981, of Lahore (Pakistan) 1980, of Granada (Spain) 1991, of the City of Samarqand (and Key to the City) 1992, of the Islamic Ummah of Timbuktu (Mali) 2003, of Dar es Salaam (Tanzania) 2005, of the Municipality of Timbuktu 2008; Hon. Prof., Univ. of Osh, Kyrgyzstan 2002; Hon.

Fellow, Coll. of Physicians and Surgeons of Pakistan 1985; Hon. FRIBA 1991; Hon. mem. Pakistan Medical Asscn 1981, AIA 1992; Foreign Hon. mem. American Acad. of Arts and Sciences 1996; Hon. Canadian citizenship 2009; Commdr, Ordre du Mérite Mauritanien 1960; Grand Croix, Ordre du Prince Henry du Gouvernement Portugais 1960; Ordre Nat. de la Côte d'Ivoire 1965, de la Haute-Volta 1965; Ordre Nat. Malgache 1966; Ordre du Croissant Vert des Comores 1966; Grand Cordon, Ordre du Tadj de l'Empire d'Iran 1967; Nishan-i-Imtiaz (Pakistan) 1970; Cavaliere di Gran Croce dell'Ordine al Merito della Repubblica (Italy) 1977; Grand Officier, Ordre Nat. du Lion (Senegal) 1982; Nishan-e-Pakistan (Pakistan) 1983; Grand Cordon of Ouissam-al Arch (Morocco) 1986; Cavaliere del Lavoro (Italy) 1988; Commdr, Légion d'honneur 1990; Gran Cruz del Orden del Mérito Civil (Spain) 1991; Grand Croix, Order of Merit (Portugal) 1998; Order of Friendship (Tajikistan) 1998; Order of Bahrain (First Class) 2003; Hon. CC 2004; Grã-Cruz da Ordem Militar de Cristo (Portugal) 2005; Chief of the Order of the Golden Heart (Kenya) 2007; Grand Cross, Nat. Order of Mali 2008; Grand Mécène (Grand Patron) and Grand Donateur (Grand Donor), Paris 2009; Commdr des Arts et des Lettres 2010, Order of Danaker (Kyrgyzstan) 2016; Hon. LLD (Peshawar Univ.) 1967, (Univ. of Sind) 1970, (McGill Univ.) 1983, (McMaster Univ.) 1987, (Univ. of Wales) 1993, (Brown Univ.) 1996, (Toronto) 2004, (Nat. Univ. of Ireland) 2008, (Harvard) 2008, (Alberta) 2009; Hon. DLitt (London) 1989; Hon. DHumLitt (American Univ. of Beirut) 2005, (American Univ. in Çairo) 2006; Hon. DD (Cambridge) 2009; Hon. DUniv (Ottawa) 2012; Dr hc (Évora, Portugal) 2006, (Univ. of Sankore, Mali) 2008; Hon. Dr of Sacred Letters (Toronto) 2013; Key to the City of Karachi, Pakistan 1981, The Gold Mercury International 'Ad Personam' Award (UK) 1982, Thomas Jefferson Memorial Foundation Medal in Architecture, Univ. of Virginia 1984, AIA Honor Award 1984, La Medalla de Oro del Consejo Superior de Colegios de Arquitectos, Spain 1987, Médaille d'Argent, Acad. d'Architecture, Paris 1991, Huésped de Honor de Granada, Spain 1991; Key to the City of Lisbon 1996, Hadrian Award, World Monuments Fund (USA) 1996, Gold Medal, City of Granada (Spain) 1998; Insignia of Honour, Union Int. des Architectes 2001, Archon Award, Int. Nursing Honour Soc., Sigma Theta Tau International 2001, State Award of Peace and Progress (Kazakhstan) 2002, Vincent Scully Prize, Nat. Building Museum (USA) 2005, Die Quadriga (Germany) 2005, Andrew Carnegie Medal of Philanthropy (UK) 2005, Key to the City of Ottawa 2005, Tolerance Prize, Evangelical Acad. of Tutzing 2006, Royal Toledo Foundation (Real Fundación de Toledo) Award 2006, 10th annual Peter O'Sullevan Award at the Savoy, London 2006, Honoured Educator of the Repub. of Kazakhstan 2008, Key to the City of Austin, Tex. 2008, Philanthropic Entrepreneur of the Year, Le Nouvel Économiste, Paris 2009, One of The 500 Most Influential Muslims in the World, Royal Islamic Strategic Studies Centre (Jordan) 2009, 2010, 2011, 2012, 2013, ULI J.C. Nichols Prize for Visionaries in Urban Devt, Los Angeles 2011, UCSF Medal, Univ. of California, San Francisco 2011, ITBA Special Recognition Award, Co. Kildare, Ireland 2012, David Rockefeller Bridging Leadership Award 2012, Gold Medal, Royal Architectural Inst. of Canada 2013, 2013 North–South Prize of the Council of Europe 2014, Address to the Parl. of Canada 2014, Citation by Inst. of Architects, Pakistan 2014, Padma Vibhushan (India) 2015. *Leisure interests:* breeding racehorses, yachting, skiing. *Address:* Aiglemont, 60270 Gouvieux, France.

AGAFANGEL, His Eminence (Savvin Alexey Mikhailovich), Metropolitan of Odessa and Izmail, Kand.Theol; Ukrainian Orthodox ecclesiastic; b. 2 Sept. 1938, Burdino, Lipetsk Region; s. of Savvin Mikhail Petrovick and Savvina Marpha Federovna; ed Odessa Seminary, Moscow Theological Acad.; took monastic vows 1965; ordained as archimandrite 1967; Rector Odessa Seminary 1967–75; Bishop of Vinnitsa and Bratslav 1975–81; ordained as Archbishop 1981, Archbishop of Vinnitsa and Bratslav 1981–89; ordained as Metropolitan 1989, Metropolitan of Vinnitsa and Bratslav 1989–92; Metropolitan of Odessa and Izmail 1992–; People's Deputy of Ukraine 1990–94; Rector Odessa Seminary 1993–98; rep. of Russian Orthodox Church in Ukraine; Dr hc (Kiev) 1995; Order of the Holy Cross (Jerusalem Patriarchate) 1981, Order of Friendship of Peoples 2003; UN Peace Medal 1988, Ukrainian President's Award, 2nd Rank 1999, 1st Rank 2003, Imperial Culture Award, Union of Writers of Russia 2005. *Address:* Monastery of the Dormition, Mayatchny pereulok 6, Odessa 65038, Ukraine (home). *Telephone:* (48) 746-3037 (home).

AGAM, Tan Sri Hasmy, BA, MA; Malaysian diplomatist; b. 3 Feb. 1944, Malacca; m.; two d.; ed Univ. of Malaya, Kuala Lumpur, Fletcher School of Law and Diplomacy, Tufts Univ., USA; joined Foreign Ministry as Asst Sec. 1968, various positions in Ministry and in missions in Saigon, Washington, DC, Hanoi and London; seconded to Nat. Inst. of Public Admin as Head, Centre for Int. Relations and Diplomacy 1981; Amb. to Libya (also accred to Malta) 1986–88, to France (also accred to Portugal) 1990–92; Alt. Perm. Rep. to UN, Alt. Del. to Security Council 1988–90; Dir-Gen. Relations with ASEAN, Foreign Ministry 1993, Deputy Sec.-Gen. for Int. Orgs and Multilateral Econs 1994–96; Alt. Perm. Rep. to UN 1996–98, apptd Perm. Rep. 1998; mem. Sec.-Gen.'s Advisory Bd on Disarmament Matters; currently Exec. Chair. Institute of Diplomacy and Foreign Relations (IDFR), Ministry of Foreign Affairs; Chair. Human Rights Commission of Malaysia (SUHAKAM) 2010–13; Adjunct Prof., Northern Univ. of Malaysia, Int. Islamic Univ. Malaysia, Nat. Univ. of Malaysia; Panglima Setia Mahkota, Panglima Jasa Negara, Darjah Mulia Seri Melaka, Johan Setia Mahkota, Kesatria Mangku Negara.

AGAM, Yaacov; Israeli artist; b. (Jacob Gipstein), 1928, Rishon Le-zion; s. of Yehoshua Gibstein; m. Clila Agam 1954; two s. one d.; ed Bezalel School of Art, Jerusalem, Atelier d'art abstrait, Paris; Guest Lecturer, Harvard Univ. 1968; travelling retrospective exhbn Paris (Nat. Museum of Modern Art), Amsterdam, Düsseldorf, Tel-Aviv 1972–73; Chevalier, l'Ordre des Arts et Lettres 1974; Hon. DPhil (Tel Aviv Univ.) 1975; Prize for Artistic Research, Sao Paulo, Brazil 1963, Medal of the Council of Europe 1977, Jan Amos Comenius Medal, UNESCO 1996. *Films:* as producer: Recherches et inventions 1956, Le désert chante 1957. *Publications:* 36 books covering his non-verbal visual learning method (visual alphabet). *Address:* 26 rue Boulard, Paris 75014, France. *Telephone:* 1-43-22-00-88.

AGANBEGYAN, Abel Gezevich, LLD; Russian/Armenian economist; *Head of the Department, Economic Theory and Policy, Russian Presidential Academy of National Economy and Public Administration (RANEPA);* b. 8 Oct. 1932, Tbilisi, Georgia; s. of Galina A. Aganbegyan; m. Zoya V. Kupriyanova 1953; one s. one d.; ed Moscow State Econ. Inst.; mem. CPSU 1956–91; Economist, Gen. Econ. Dept, State Cttee for Labour and Wages 1955–61; Head of Lab., Inst. of Econs and Industrial Eng, Siberian Branch of USSR Acad. of Sciences 1961–67, Dir Inst. of Econs and Industrial Eng 1967–85; Prof. of Econs, Novosibirsk State Univ.; Prof. Acad. of Nat. Econ.; Chair. Cttee for Study of Productive Forces and Natural Resources 1965; Rector, Acad. of Nat. Economy 1989–2002; currently Head of Dept, Econ. Theory and Policy, Russian Presidential Acad. of Nat. Economy and Public Admin (RANEPA); mem. Presidium; Chair. All-Union Club of Managers; Corresp. mem. USSR (now Russian) Acad. of Sciences 1964, mem. 1974, Acad.-Sec., Dept of Econ. 1986–89; fmr Hon. Pres. Int. Economic Asscn; Foreign mem. Bulgarian and Hungarian Acads. of Sciences; Hon. mem. Int. Econometric Soc.; Corresp. FBA; two Orders of Lenin; Dr. hc (Alicante, Łódź, Barcelona, Seoul, London). *Publications:* Wages and Salaries in the USSR 1959, On the Application of Mathematics and Electronic Machinery in Planning 1961, Some Questions of Monopoly Price Theory with Reference to the USA 1961, Economical-Mathematical Analysis of Input-Output Tables in USSR 1968, System of Models of National Economy Planning 1972, Management of the Socialist Enterprises 1979, Management and Efficiency: USSR Economy in 1981–85 1981, Siberia—not by Hearsay (with Z. Ibragimova) 1981, Economic Methods in Planned Management (with D. Kazakevich) 1985, Enterprise: Managing Scientific and Technological Progress (with V. Rechin) 1986; The Challenge: Economics of Perestroika 1987, Moving the Mountain: Inside Perestroika 1989, Measures and Stages of Improving USSR Economy 1991, Socio-Economic Development of Russia 2003. *Address:* Department of Economic Theory and Policy, RANEPA, 119571, Moscow, Vernadsky Prospekt, 82, Russia (office). *Telephone:* (495) 433-25-72 (office). *Fax:* (499) 270-29-72 (office). *E-mail:* aganbegyan@ranepa.ru (office). *Website:* www.ranepa.ru (office).

AĞAOĞLU, Adalet; Turkish writer; b. 23 Oct. 1929, Ankara; d. of Mustafa Sümer and İsmet Sümer; m. Halim Ağaoğlu 1954; ed Univ. of Ankara; worked for Türkiye Radyo Televizyon Kurumu (TRT) 1953–73; freelance writer 1973–; Co-founder Arena Theatre Co.; Hon. PhD (Anadolu Univ.) 1998, Dr hc (Ohio State Univ.) 1998; TDK Theatre Award 1974, Pres. of the Turkish Repub. Grand Prize for Culture and the Arts 1995. *Publications include:* (in Turkish) novels: Lying Down to Die 1973, The Fine Rose of My Mind 1976, A Wedding Night (Sedat Simavi Literature Award 1979, Orhan Kemal Novel Award 1980, Madaralı Novel Award 1980) 1979, The End of Summer 1980, A Few People 1984, Migration Cleansing 1985, No... 1987, Cold in Spirit 1991, A Romantic Viennese Summer (Aydın Doğan Novel Award 1997) 1993, Dert Dinleme Uzmanı 2014; short stories: High Tension (Sait Faik Prize 1975) 1974, The First Sound of Silence 1978, Come On, Let's Go 1982, Ways to Defend Life 1997; essays: Crossing 1986, My Life at Night 1992, Encounters 1993, Other Encounters 1996; plays: Three Plays (Prize of Turkish Language Inst.) 1956, Playing Mum and Dad 1964, Bingo 1967, The Crack in The Roof 1969, The Death of a Hero 1973, Cocoons 1973, The Song that Wrote Itself 1977, Plays 1982, Too Far Too Close (Is Bankasi Grand Award for the Theatre 1991) 1991, The Story of the Wall 1992, The Poem and the Fly 1992. *Leisure interests:* reading, writing. *Address:* Piyasa Cad, Bülbül Sok, 10/5 Ceviz Apt, Büyükdere, Istanbul, Turkey. *Telephone:* (1) 1422636.

AGARWAL, Anil; Indian business executive; *Executive Chairman, Vedanta Resources plc;* b. 1954, Patna, Bihar; m. Kiran Gupta; one s. one d.; f. Sterlite Gold Ltd (now Sterlite Industries) 1976, fmrly CEO, later Man. Dir, Chair. 2004–, mem. Remuneration Cttee; currently Chair. and Man. Dir, Vedanta Resources plc (diversified metals and mining group) after Sterlite acquired Shamsher Sterling, CEO 1979–2005, Exec. Chair. 2005–; Chair. (non-exec.) Sterlite Technologies Ltd 2006–; mem. Bd of Dirs BALCO, HZL, Vedanta Alumina Ltd, Copper Mines of Tasmania Pty Ltd; Entrepreneur of the Year, Ernst & Young 2008, Lifetime Achievement Award, Mining Journal 2009, Business Leader Award, Economic Times 2012, Entrepreneur of the Year, Asian Awards 2016. *Address:* Vedanta House, 75 Nehru Road, Vile Parle (East), Mumbai 400 099, India (office). *Telephone:* (22) 66461000 (office). *Fax:* (22) 66461451 (office). *Website:* www.vedantaresources.com (office).

AGARWAL, Bina, PhD; Indian economist and academic; *Professor of Development Economics and Environment, University of Manchester;* b. Jabalpur; ed Univ. of Delhi, Univ. of Cambridge, UK, Delhi School of Econs; Research Assoc., Council for Social Devt 1972–74; Visiting Fellow, Inst. of Devt Studies, Univ. of Sussex, UK 1978–79, Research Fellow, Science Policy Research Unit 1979–80; Assoc. Prof. of Econs, Inst. of Econ. Growth, Univ. of Delhi 1981–88, Prof. 1988–, Dir Inst. of Econ. Growth 2009–12, Head, Population Research Centre 1996–98, 2002–04, 2009–11; Prof. of Devt Econs and Environment, Univ. of Manchester, UK 2012–; Fellow, Bunting Inst., Radcliffe Coll., USA 1989–91; Visiting Prof., Harvard Univ. Cttee on Degrees in Women's Studies 1991–92, First Daniel H.H. Ingalls Visiting Prof. March–Sept. 1999, Visiting Research Fellow, Ash Inst., Kennedy School of Govt 2006–07, Hon. Visiting Fellow March–Dec. 2008; Visiting Scholar, Inst. for Advanced Study, Princeton 1995; Visiting Prof., School of Natural Resources and Environment, Univ. of Michigan 2003; Visiting Prof., Coll. of Liberal Arts, Univ. of Minnesota May–June 2004, Visiting Prof. and Winton Chair Holder 2004; Global Visiting Prof., New York Univ.; Hirschorn Visiting Prof., Barnard Coll., Columbia Univ. Dec. 2001; Pres. Int. Asscn for Feminist Econs 2004 (Vice-Pres. and Bd mem. 1999–2002); Pres. Int. Soc. for Ecological Economics 2010–; Vice-Pres. Int. Econ. Asscn 2002–05; Research Assoc., Council for Social Devt, Delhi, mem. Exec. Cttee 1999–2002; Founder-mem. Ankur (Delhi-based NGO conducting non-formal education in Delhi's slums) 1981; Founder-mem. Exec. Cttee Int. Soc. for Ecological Econs, Delhi 2000–05, Indian Asscn of Women's Studies 1984–86, 1998–2000; mem. Five Year Plans 1988–89, 1996, 2001, 2005–06; mem. Organizing Cttee XI to XIV World Congresses 1995–2004; mem. Bd of Dirs, UN Research Inst. for Social Devt 2009–; mem. Research Advisory Cttee on Women's Studies, Indian Council for Social Science Research, New Delhi 1987–89, Research Advisory Cttee on Women and Agricultural Modernisation, Indian Council of Agricultural Research 1987–88, Tech. Mission on Drinking Water and Related Water Man., Ministry of Science and Tech. 1987–89, Expert Group on Structural Adjustment & Women, Commonwealth Secretariat, London 1988–89, Advisory Cttee, Female-Headed Households, Population Council, New York 1989–92, Harvard Centre for Population and Devt Studies 1990–91, Advisory Cttee on Research Priorities for the Educ. of Girls and Women in Africa, African Acad. of

Sciences (Kenya) 1992–94; mem. Advisory Cttee, UNDP Human Devt Report on Poverty 1997, Steering Cttee, Int. Union for Conservation of Nature Comm. for Environmental, Econ. and Social Policy 1997–99 (mem. Exec. Cttee 1999–2002), Governing Body of Global Devt Network: 2000–06, Advisory Bd, Pradan (non-governmental org. promoting self-help groups and income generating activities in rural central India) 2000–06, Indo-European Union Round Table 2001–04, Advisory Bd, FAO, Rome 2002– (mem. Steering Cttee 2007), Cttee for Devt Policy, UN Econ. and Social Council 2007–, Think Tank of Feminist Economists for 11th Plan 2007; mem. Accad. Nazionale dei Lincei; Padma Shri, Pres. of India 2008; Officier, Ordre du Mérite agricole 2017; Dr hc (Inst. of Social Studies, The Hague) 2007, (Univ. of Antwerp) 2011; Malcolm Adisheshiah Award for distinguished contribs to devt studies 2002, Ramesh Chandra Award for outstanding contribs to agricultural econs 2005, Leontief Award, Global Devt and Environment Inst., Tufts Univ., USA 2010, Balzan Prize 2017, Louis Malassis Int. Scientist Prize 2017. *Publications include:* Mechanization in Indian Agriculture 1983, Cold Hearths and Barren Slopes: The Woodfuel Crisis in the Third World 1986, Structures of Patriarchy: State, Community and Household in Modernizing Asia (ed.) 1988, Women, Poverty and Ideology in Asia: Contradictory Pressures, Uneasy Resolutions (co-ed.) 1989, Women and Work in the World Economy 1991, A Field of One's Own: Gender and Land Rights in South Asia 1994 (Ananda Kentish Coomaraswamy Book Prize 1996, Edgar Graham Book Prize 1996, K. H. Batheja Award 1995–96), Psychology, Rationality and Economic Behaviour: Challenging Assumptions (co-ed.) 2005, Capabilities, Freedom and Equality: Amartyr Sen's Work from a Gender Perspective (co-ed.) 2006, Gender and Green Governance 2010, Gender Challenges (three-vol. compendium of author's selected papers) 2016; numerous articles in learned journals on property rights, environment, agricultural technology, poverty, political economy of gender and related topics. *Leisure interests:* writing poetry, painting, reading literature and biography, nature walks, movies. *Address:* School of Environment, University of Manchester, IDPM, School of Environment, Arthur Lewis Building, Oxford Road, Manchester, M13 9PL, England (office); Institute of Economic Growth, University Enclave, University of Delhi, Delhi 110 007, India (office). *Telephone:* (11) 27667250 (Delhi) (office). *E-mail:* bina.agarwal@manchester.ac.uk (office); bbina.india@gmail.com (home). *Website:* www.seed.manchester.ac.uk (office); www.iegindia.org (office); www.binaagarwal.com.

AGARWAL, Sudarshan, LLB; Indian lawyer and politician (retd); b. 19 June 1931, Ludhiana; m. Usha Agarwal; one s. one d.; Chief Returning Officer, Indian presidential election 1982, 1992; Sec.-Gen. Rajya Sabha 1981–93; Gov. of Uttaranchal (now Uttarakhand) 2003–07, of Sikkim 2007–08; currently involved in community work; participated in several parl. confs and int. goodwill dels world-wide; mem. and Past Pres. Rotary Club of Delhi, Dist Gov. Rotary International, mem. Bd of Dirs, mem. and Chair. several Rotary International Cttees, Chair. Rotary Foundation (India) 1992–2002, Trustee, Rotary Service to Humanity Awards Trust; mem. Nat. Human Rights Comm. 1998–2000; Chair. Uttaranchal State Red Cross Soc. and State Child Welfare Council; Pres. Delhi Gymkhana Club 1986–88; Pres. Emer. Rotary Blood Bank & Eye Care Centre; Patron Him Jyoti School, Chief Patron IMA Blood Bank, Dehradun; Hon. DSc (Gurukul Univ., Uttaranchal); Rotary Foundation Citation for Meritorious Service and Rotary Foundation Distinguished Service Award. *Leisure interest:* gardening. *Address:* Rotary Blood Bank, 57 Tughlakabad Institutional Area, New Delhi, 110 062 (office); C-312, Defence Colony, New Delhi, 110 024, India (home). *Telephone:* (11) 29054065 (office); (11) 24332676 (home). *Fax:* (11) 26056333 (office). *E-mail:* sud .agarwal@gmail.com (home). *Website:* www.rotarybloodbank.org (office); www .himjyotischool.org (office).

AGASSI, Andre; American professional tennis player (retd); b. 29 April 1970, Las Vegas, Nev.; s. of Mike Agassi and Elizabeth Agassi; m. 1st Brooke Shields (q.v.) 1997 (divorced 1999); m. 2nd Steffi Graf (q.v.); one s.; coached from age 13 by Nick Bollettieri, strength coach Gil Reyes; turned professional 1986; semi-finalist, French Open 1988, US Open 1988, 1989; mem. US team that defeated Australia in Davis Cup Final 1990; defeated Stefan Edberg to win inaugural ATP World Championship, Frankfurt 1991; finalist French Open 1990, 1991, US Open 1990, 1995, 2002, Wimbledon 1999; won Wimbledon 1992, US Open 1994, 1999, Canadian Open 1995, Australian Open 1995, 2000, 2001, 2003, French Open 1999; winner Olympic Games tennis tournaments 1996; Asscn of Tennis Professionals World Champion 1990; fifth player to win all four Grand Slam titles; winner of 59 singles titles and one doubles title; retd 2006; f. Andre Agassi Charitable Foundation to help at-risk youth in Las Vegas 1994; f. Agassi Enterprises, Inc.; named by Longines as their brand amb. 2007; announced three-year partnership with Jacobs Creek winemakers 2012; with Gil Reyes introduced own line of fitness equipment, BILT By Agassi and Reyes 2012; cr. the Canyon-Agassi Charter School Facilities Fund; has appeared in numerous TV commercials. *Publication:* Open (autobiog.) 2009. *Address:* Andre Agassi Charitable Foundation, 1120 North Town Center Drive, Suite 160, Las Vegas, NV 89169, USA. *Telephone:* (702) 227-5700. *Fax:* (702) 866-2928. *E-mail:* info@agassi.net. *Website:* www.andreagassi.com; www.agassifoundation.org; www.atpworldtour .com/Tennis/Players/Ag/A/Andre-Agassi.aspx.

AGASSI, Shai, BSc; Israeli business executive; b. April 1968, Tel-Aviv; s. of Reuven Agassi; m.; two s.; ed Technion (Israeli Inst. of Tech.); computer programmer, Army Intelligence, Israeli Army; f. QuickSoft (software distribution co.) 1990, Menahel Inc. 1991, TopManage 1992, QuickSoft Media 1994; f. TopTier Software 1992, Chair. 1996–99, Chief Exec. 1999–2001; Chief Exec. SAP Portals (later SAP Markets) 2001–02, mem. Exec. Bd SAP AG, Walldorf 2002–07, Top Tech. Developer 2003; Pres. Product and Tech. Group 2003–07, consultant 2007–; resgnd his position to pursue interests in alternative energy and climate change; Founder Better Place (fmrly Project Better Place) 2007, CEO 2007–12; CEO Newrgy 2014–15. *Leisure interest:* reading technology books. *Address:* c/o Better Place, 1070 Arastradero Road, Suite 220, Palo Alto, CA 94304, USA. *E-mail:* information@betterplace.com. *Website:* www.betterplace.com.

AĞBAL, Naci; Turkish civil servant and politician; b. 1 Jan. 1968, Bayburt; m.; two c.; ed İstanbul Univ., Univ. of Exeter, UK; joined Inspection Bd, Ministry of Finance 1989, becoming Finance Inspector 1993, Dept Man., Gen. Directorate of Revenues 2003, Dir-Gen. of Budget and Financial Control 2007, Under-Sec., Ministry of Finance 2009–15, Minister of Finance 2015–18; mem. Grand Nat. Ass. (parl.) for Bayburt 2015–; mem. Council of Higher Educ. (YÖK) 2008; mem. Bd of Trustees, Ahmet Yesevi Univ. 2008–; mem. Justice and Devt Party. *Address:* c/o Ministry of Finance, Maliye Bakanlığı, Dikmen Cad. 06450, Ankara, Turkey (office).

AGBÉNONCI, Aurélien, LLM; Benin politician and fmr UN official; *Minister of Foreign Affairs and Co-operation;* b. 1958; m.; two c.; ed Univ. de Dakar, Senegal, Univ. Paris X Nanterre, France; worked in Faculty of Law, Univ. Paris X Nanterre; fmr Sr Programme Coordinator and Chief of Staff, Pan-African Social Prospects Centre, Benin; several years with UN in positions throughout Africa, including as UNDP Deputy Resident Rep. in Cameroon 1996–99, in Côte d'Ivoire 1999–2003, UN Resident Coordinator and UNDP Resident Rep. in Congo 2003–08, in Rwanda 2008–11, Humanitarian Coordinator, UN Resident Coordinator and UNDP Resident Rep. in Mali 2012–13, Deputy Special Rep. of the Sec.-Gen. for UN Multidimensional Integrated Stabilization Mission in Central African Repub. (MINUSCA) 2014–16; Minister of Foreign Affairs and Co-operation 2016–. *Address:* Ministry of Foreign Affairs and Co-operation, Zone Résidentielle, route de l'Aéroport, 06 BP 318, Cotonou, Benin (office). *Telephone:* 21-30-09-06 (office). *Fax:* 21-38-19-70 (office). *E-mail:* infos@maebenin.bj (office). *Website:* www .diplomatie.gouv.bj (office).

AGBOYIBO, (Apollinaire) Yawovi; Togolese politician and lawyer; b. 31 Dec. 1943; ed in Togo, Senegal, France and Côte d'Ivoire; fmr Head of Nat. Human Rights Comm.; Leader, Action Cttee for Renewal (CAR) party 1991–2008, Hon. Pres. 2010–, jailed for six months for defaming Togolese Prime Minister Aug. 2001, freed as gesture of appeasement March 2002; cand. in presidential elections 2003, 2010; led inter-Togolese dialogue in Burkina Faso helping to broker agreement to form a power-sharing cabinet Aug. 2006; Prime Minister of Togo Sept. 2006–07. *Address:* Comité d'action pour le Renouveau (CAR), 58 ave du 24 janvier, BP06, Lomé, Togo (office). *Telephone:* 222-05-66 (office). *Fax:* 221-62-54 (office). *E-mail:* yagboyibo@bibway.com (office).

AGHILI, Shadmehr; Iranian singer, musician, composer, producer and actor; b. 27 Jan. 1973, Tehran; ed Tehran Conservatory of Music; singer and writer of popular songs; emigrated to Canada, now lives in Los Angeles; live concert, Las Vegas Dec. 2014. *Film:* Par e Parvaz (also composed soundtrack). *Recordings include:* albums: Bahar e Man 1997, Fasl e Ashenayi 1998, Mosaafer 1998, Dehati 1999, Mashgh e Sokoot 1999, Naghmeha ye Mashreghi 1999, Par e Parvaz 2001, Doori o Pashimani 2003, Khiali Nist 2003, Adam Foroush 2004, Popcorn 2005, Taghdir 2009, Tarafdaar 2012, Tajrobeh Kon 2016. *Website:* www.shadmehr.info.

AGIUS, Carmel (Lino) A., BA, LLD; Maltese international judge; b. 18 Aug. 1945, Sliema; s. of Anthony Buttigieg and Josephine Buttigieg; m. Tanya Said; two d.; ed Univ. of Malta; called to the Bar Jan. 1970; Legal Adviser, Bank of Valletta 1976–77; appointed Magistrate 1977; Presiding Judge, Maltese Court of Appeal, Criminal Court and Constitutional Court 1977–2001; mem. Perm. Court of Arbitration, The Hague 1999–2008; Judge, Criminal Division, Int. Criminal Tribunal for fmr Yugoslavia (ICTY) 2001–17, Presiding Judge, Trial Chamber II 2003–10, Vice-Pres. ICTY 2011–15, Pres. 2015–17; Maltese Rep., Central Council of Int. Asscn of Judges 1989–2001; Head, Maltese Del., UN Comm. on Crime Prevention and Criminal Justice, Vienna 1990–2001; Govt of Malta Rep., UN Preparatory Cttee on proposed Perm. Int. Criminal Court 1996–98; co-Founder and Lecturer, Inst. of Criminology, Univ. of Malta, Pro-Chancellor, Univ. of Malta 1996–99; Ed. Mediterranean Journal of Human Rights 1998–2004; Nat. Order of Merit of Malta 2015.

AGIUS, Marcus Ambrose Paul, MA, MBA; British business executive and investment banker; *Chairman, PA Consulting Group;* b. 22 July 1946, Walton-on-Thames; s. of Alfred Victor Louis Benedict Agius and Ena Eleanora Alberta Agius (née Hueffer); m. Kate Juliette de Rothschild 1971; two d.; ed Trinity Hall, Univ. of Cambridge, Harvard Business School, USA; worked with Vickers PLC 1968–70; joined Lazard Brothers and Co. Ltd subsequently Lazard London 1972, Chair. 2001–06, Deputy Chair. Lazard LLC 2002–06; Chair. Barclays PLC 2007–12; Dir (non-exec.) Exbury Gardens Ltd 1977–, BAA (British Airports Authority) PLC 1995–2006 (Deputy Chair. 1998–2002 and Chair. 2002–06); Sr Ind. Dir BBC 2006–12; Chair. BBA (British Business Amb.) 2010–12; mem. Advisory Council, The City UK 2010–12; Exec. Cttee IIEB (Interim International Exec. Bd), Takeover panel 2010–12; Trustee, Royal Botanic Gardens, Kew 2006–09; Chair. Bd of Trustees, The Royal Botanic Gardens, Kew 2009–; Chair. Foundation and Friends, Royal Botanic Gardens, Kew 2004–; Chair. PA Consulting Group 2014–. *Leisure interests:* gardening, shooting, skiing, fine art, sailing. *Address:* PA Consulting Group, 7th Floor, 10 Bressenden Place, London, SW1E 5DN, England (office). *Telephone:* (20) 7333-5281 (office). *E-mail:* office@marcus-agius.com (office); colleen.cornfield@paconsulting.com (office). *Website:* www.paconsulting .com (office).

AGLUKKAQ, The Hon. Leona; Canadian politician; b. 28 June 1967; fmr Asst Deputy Minister of Human Resources, Regional Govt of Nunavut; fmr Minister of Health and Social Services and Minister Responsible for Status of Women, Exec. Council of Nunavut; Deputy Clerk, Nunavut Legis. Ass. 2000–02, mem. Legis. Ass. 2004–08; mem. Parl. for Nunavut 2008–15; Minister for Health 2008–13, Minister of Environment, Minister of Canadian Northern Econ. Devt Agency and Minister for Arctic Council 2013–15; mem. Conservative Party of Canada. *Address:* Conservative Party of Canada, 130 Albert Street, Suite 1720, Ottawa, ON K1P 5G4, Canada (office). *Telephone:* (613) 755-2000 (office). *Fax:* (613) 755-2001 (office). *E-mail:* info@conservative.ca (office). *Website:* www.conservative.ca (office).

AGNELO, HE Cardinal Geraldo Majella; Brazilian ecclesiastic; *Archbishop Emeritus of São Salvador da Bahía;* b. 19 Oct. 1933, Juiz de Fora; s. of Antônio Agnelo and Silvia Spagnolo Agnelo; ordained priest 1957; elected Bishop of Toledo 1978; Bishop of Londrina 1982; resgnd 1991; Archbishop of São Salvador da Bahía 1999–2011, Archbishop Emer. 2011–; cr. Cardinal (Cardinal-Priest of San Gregorio Magno alla Magliana Nuova) 2001. *Address:* Archdiocese of São Salvador da Bahía, Rua Martin Afonso de Souza 270, 40100–050 Salvador, Bahía (office); Avenida Cardeal da Silva 26, Casa 33, 40220–140 Salvador, Bahía, Brazil (home). *Telephone:* (71) 328-6699 (office); (71) 331-2738 (home). *Fax:* (71) 328-0068 (office); (71) 261-5243 (home). *E-mail:* contato@arquidiocesedesalvador.org.br (office).

AGNEW, Jonathan Geoffrey William, MA; British banker; b. 30 July 1941, Windsor, Berks.; s. of Sir Geoffrey William Gerald Agnew and Hon. Doreen Maud Jessel; m. 1st Hon. Agneta Joanna Middleton Campbell 1966 (divorced 1985); one s. two d.; m. 2nd Marie-Claire Dreesmann 1990; one s. one d.; ed Eton Coll. and Trinity Coll., Cambridge; with The Economist 1964–65, IBRD 1965–67; with Hill Samuel & Co. 1967–73, Dir 1971; Morgan Stanley & Co. 1973–82, Man. Dir 1977; with J.G.W. Agnew & Co. 1983–86; Chief Exec. ISRO 1986; with Kleinwort Benson Group PLC 1987–93, Chief Exec. 1989–93; Chair. Limit PLC 1993–2000, Henderson Geared Income & Growth Trust PLC 1995–2003, Gerrard Group PLC 1999–2000, LMS Capital plc 2006–10, The Cayenne Trust PLC 2006–15, Ashmore Global Opportunities Ltd 2007–13, Fleet Mortgages Ltd 2014–; Dir (non-exec.) Thos. Agnew & Sons Ltd 1969–2008, Thos. Agnew & Sons (Holdings) Ltd 2008–13, Jarvis PLC 2003–04; Dir (non-exec.) Nationwide Building Soc. 1997–2007, Deputy Chair. (non-exec.) 1999–2002, Chair. 2002–07; Dir (non-exec.) Beazley PLC 2002–12, Chair. 2003–12; Dir Soditic Ltd 2001–04; Sr Ind. Dir Rightmove PLC 2006–15; mem. Council Lloyd's 1995–99. *Address:* Flat E, 51 Eaton Square, London, SW1W 9BE, England (home). *Telephone:* 7714-243891 (mobile) (home); (20) 7235-7589 (home). *E-mail:* jgwagnew@yahoo.co.uk (home).

AGNEW, (Morland Herbert) Julian, MA; British art dealer; b. 20 Sept. 1943, London; s. of Sir Geoffrey William Gerald Agnew and Hon. Doreen Maud Jessel, CB, CMG; m. 1st Elizabeth Margaret Moncrieff Mitchell 1973 (divorced 1992); one s. two d.; m. 2nd Victoria Burn Callander 1993 (divorced 2013); one s.; ed Eton Coll., Trinity Coll., Cambridge; joined Thomas Agnew & Sons Ltd 1965, Dir 1968, Man. Dir 1987–92, Chair. 1992–2013; Pres. British Antique Dealers Asscn 1979–81; Chair. Soc. of London Art Dealers 1986–90; Chair. Friends of the Courtauld Inst. 2002–05, Trustee 2006–; Pres. Evelyn Trust, Cambridge. *Leisure interests:* art, theatre, opera, music, books, golf. *Address:* Flat 111, Howard House, Dolphin Square, London, SW1V 3PE (home); Egmere Farm House, Egmere, nr Walsingham, Norfolk, England (home).

AGNEW, Sir Rudolph (Ion Joseph), Kt, FRSA; British business executive; b. 12 March 1934; s. of Rudolph John Agnew and Pamela Geraldine Agnew (née Campbell); m. Whitney Warren 1980; ed Downside School; Commissioned Officer, 8th King's Royal Irish Hussars 1953–57; joined Consolidated Gold Fields PLC 1957, apptd Exec. Dir 1973, Deputy Chair. 1978–82, Group Chief Exec. 1978–89, Chair. 1983–89, mem. Cttee of Man. Dirs 1986–89; Chief Exec. Amey Roadstone Corpn 1974–78, Chair. 1974–77; Chair. and CEO TVS Entertainment 1990–93; apptd Chair. Stena Int. BV (fmrly Sealink Stena Line) 1990, Federated Aggregates PLC 1991–95, Bona Shipholding Ltd, Bermuda 1993–98, LASMO PLC 1994–2000, Redland PLC 1995–97, Star Mining Corpn 1995–98; Jt Chair. Global Stone Corpn (Canada) 1993–94; Dir (non-exec.) New London PLC 1985–96, Standard Chartered PLC 1988–97, Newmount Mining Corpn, USA 1989–98, Hanson PLC 1989–91; Vice-Pres. Nat. Asscn of Boys Clubs; mem. Council WWF (UK) 1989– (Trustee 1983–89); Fellow, Game Conservancy. *Leisure interest:* shooting. *Address:* 7 Eccleston Street, London, SW1X 9LX, England.

AGOL, Ian, BS, PhD; American mathematician and academic; *Professor, University of California, Berkeley;* b. 13 May 1970; ed California Inst. of Tech., Univ. of California, San Diego; Visiting Research Asst Prof., Univ. of California, Davis 1998–2000; Postdoctoral Fellow, Univ. of Melbourne, Australia 2000–01; Asst Prof., Univ. of Illinois, Chicago 2001–04, Assoc. Prof. 2004–06, Prof. 2006–07; Assoc. Prof., Univ. of California, Berkeley 2007–12, Prof. 2012–, Miller Prof. 2012, Simons Fellow 2013; Ed. Journal of Topology, Forum of Mathematics; Sloan Fellow 2003, Guggenheim Fellow 2005, Speaker, ICM 2006, Madrid 2006, Clay Research Award (co-recipient) 2009, Simons Sabbatical Fellowship 2012, Senior Berwick Prize, London Math. Soc. 2012, Oswald Veblen Prize in Geometry (co-recipient) 2013, Plenary Speaker, ICM, Seoul 2014, Breakthrough Prize in Math. (co-recipient) 2016. *Publications:* numerous papers in professional journals on the topology of three-dimensional manifolds. *Address:* University of California, Berkeley, 970 Evans Hall #3840, Berkeley, CA 94720-3840, USA (office). *Telephone:* (510) 642-4377 (office). *E-mail:* ianagol@math.berkeley.edu (office). *Website:* math.berkeley.edu (office).

AGON, Jean-Paul; French business executive; *Chairman and CEO, L'Oréal Group;* b. 6 July 1956, Paris; three c.; ed Hautes Etudes Commerciales; joined L'Oréal Paris Group and worked in sales and marketing 1978–81, Gen. Man. Consumer Products Div., Greece 1981–86, Gen. Man. L'Oréal Paris 1986–89, Int. Man. Dir Luxury Products Div., Biotherm 1989–94, Gen. Man. L'Oréal Germany 1994–97, Man. Dir L'Oréal Group's Asia zone 1997–2001, Pres. and CEO L'Oréal USA 2001–06, CEO L'Oréal 2006–11, Chair. and CEO 2011–. *Address:* L'Oréal SA, 41 rue Martre, 92117 Clichy Cedex, France (office). *Telephone:* 1-47-56-70-00 (office). *Fax:* 1-47-56-80-02 (office). *E-mail:* info@loreal.com (office). *Website:* www.loreal.com (office).

AGOPYAN, Vahan, PhD; Brazilian/Armenian academic and engineer; *Rector, Universidade de São Paulo (USP);* b. 8 Dec. 1951, Istanbul, Turkey; ed Escola Politécnica da USP, King's Coll. London; Full Prof. in Materials and Components of Civil Construction, Escola Politécnica da Universidade de São Paulo (USP) 1991, Vice-Rector, Postgraduate Studies 2010–14, Deputy Rector 2014–18, Rector 2018–; Vice-Pres. Int. Council for Research and Innovation in Bldg and Construction; Adviser, Inst. of Engineering, Mauá Inst. of Tech., Brazilian Council of Sustainable Construction; mem. Bd of Trustees, (IPEN) Nuclear and Energy Research Inst., São Paulo Research Foundation (FAPESP); Eminent Engineer of the Year, Inst. of Eng 2004. *Address:* Universidade de São Paulo, Rua da Reitoria, 374 Cidade Universitária, 05508-220 São Paulo, SP, Brazil (office). *Telephone:* (11) 3091-3500 (office). *E-mail:* imprensa@usp.br (office). *Website:* www.reitoria.usp.br (office).

AGOSTINI, Giacomo (Ago); Italian motorcyclist; b. 16 June 1942, Brescia; s. of Aurelio Agostini and Maria Vittoria; m. Maria Agostini; one s. one d.; rode for Morini 1961–64; understudy to Mike Hailwood at MV Augusta 1965, number one rider 1966–73, 1976–77; rode for Yamaha 1974–76; 311 wins; a record 122 Grand Prix wins (54 at 350 cc, 68 at 500 cc); 12 Isle of Man TT wins (350 cc: 1966, 1967, 1968, 1969, 1970, 1972; 500 cc: 1967, 1968, 1969, 1970, 1971, 1972); 18 Italian championship wins; a record 15 World Championship wins (350 cc: 1968, 1969, 1970, 1971, 1972, 1973, 1974; 500 cc: 1966, 1967, 1968, 1969, 1970, 1971, 1972, 1975); shares (with Mike Hailwood) record for most races won in a season (19 in 1970); AMA Motorcycle Hall of Fame 1999, named Grand Prix Legend, Fédération Internationale de Motocyclisme (FIM) 2000.

AGOVAKA, Peter Shanel; Solomon Islands politician; *Minister of Communication and Aviation;* b. 1 Nov. 1959, Bemuta Village, Guadalcanal Prov.; ed North Sydney Inst. of Eng, Australia; fmr Community Affairs Officer, Gold Ridge Mining Ltd; MP for Cen. Guadalcanal 2006–; Minister for Provincial Govt and Constituency Devt April–May 2006, for Commerce, Industries and Employment 2006–07, of Foreign Affairs 2010–12, Minister for Police, Nat. Security and Correctional Services 2014–15, of Communication and Aviation 2015–; Leader, Ind. MPs Jan.–Sept. 2008. *Address:* Ministry of Communication and Aviation, POB G8, Honiara, Solomon Islands (office). *Telephone:* 36720 (office). *Fax:* 36220 (office).

AGRE, Peter C., BA, MD; American physician, molecular biologist and academic; *Director, Johns Hopkins Malaria Research Institute;* b. 1949, Northfield, Minn.; ed Theodore Roosevelt High School, Minneapolis, Augsburg Coll., Minneapolis, Johns Hopkins Univ., Baltimore; Fellow, Univ. of North Carolina 1974–81; Fellow, Depts of Medicine and Cell Biology, Johns Hopkins Univ., Baltimore, Md 1981–2005, Prof. of Biological Chem. 1993–2005; Vice-Chancellor, Science and Tech. of Chem. and Public Policy Studies and Prof. of Cell Biology and Public Policy Studies, Duke Univ. Medical Center 2005–08, mem. Chancellor's Science Advisory Council 2006–07; Prof. and Dir Johns Hopkins Malaria Research Inst. 2008–; mem. NAS 2000–, American Acad. of Arts and Sciences 2003–, AAAS (mem. Bd Dirs, Pres.-Elect 2007–08, Pres. 2009); Founding mem. Scientists and Engineers for America (mem. Bd of Advisors); numerous hon. doctorates; Nobel Prize in Chem. (co-recipient) for his discovery of aquaporins 2003, Distinguished Eagle Scout Award. *Publications include:* numerous specialist papers. *Leisure interest:* cross-country skiing (participated in the Vasaloppet ski race). *Address:* E5143 Bloomberg School of Public Health, Baltimore, MD 21205, USA (office). *Telephone:* (443) 287-8745 (office). *Fax:* (410) 955-0105 (office). *E-mail:* malaria@jhsph.edu (office). *Website:* malaria.jhsph.edu (office).

AGREST, Diana, DipArch, FAIA; American architect, urban designer and filmmaker; *Co-founder and Partner, Agrest and Gandelsonas Architects;* b. 1945, Buenos Aires, Argentina; m. Mario Gandelsonas; ed Univ. of Buenos Aires, École Pratique des Hautes Études and Centre du Recherche d'Urbanisme, Paris, France; Prof., Columbia, Princeton and Yale Univs, USA 1973–96; currently Prof. of Architecture, Cooper Union, New York; Partner (with husband), Agrest and Gandelsonas Architects, New York; f. Diana Agrest Architectural Firm, New York; Fellow, Inst. for Architecture and Urban Studies, New York 1972–84; Design Excellence Award, AIA NY State 2002, Design Excellence Award, AIA New York City 2002, Design Merit Award, Soc. of Registered Architects 2002, Masterwork Award, Municipal Art Soc. 2002, NY State Council on the Arts Grant 2003, AIA Brunner Award Grant 2004. *Architectural and urban design works include:* Melrose Community Center, New York, urban design for Shanghai, People's Repub. of China, plan for West Midtown Manhattan, New York, farm in Sagaponack, NY, house in Sagaponack, farm in Uruguay, Des Moines Vision Plaza, Ia, duplex on Central Park West, Manhattan, house in Majorca, Spain. *Film:* The Making of an Avant-Garde: The Institute for Architecture and Urban Studies 1967–1984 (writer, dir and producer), premiered at Museum of Modern Art, New York 2013. *Publications include:* A Romance with the City: The Work of Irwin S. Chanin, Architecture from Without: Theoretical Framings for a Critical Perspective 1991, Agrest and Gandelsonas Works (co-author) 1995, The Sex of Architecture (co-ed.) 1996; articles on architecture in numerous int. publs. *Leisure interest:* film-making. *Address:* Agrest and Gandelsonas Architects, 636 Broadway, Suite 1105, New York, NY 10012 (office); Irwin S. Chanin School of Architecture, Cooper Union, 30 Cooper Square, New York, NY 10003, USA. *Telephone:* (212) 625-3800 (A&G) (office); (212) 353-4100 (Cooper). *Fax:* (212) 965-8830 (A&G) (office); (212) 353-4327 (Cooper). *E-mail:* office@ag-architects.com (office); agrest@cooper.edu. *Website:* www.ag-architects.com (office); www.cooper.edu/architecture.

AGUAD BEILY, Oscar Raúl, LLB; Argentine lawyer and politician; *Minister of Defence;* b. 7 May 1950, Córdoba; s. of Raúl Aguad and Hilda Beily; m. María Dolores Albarenque 1976; five d.; ed Nat. Univ. of Córdoba; Chief of Staff to Mayor of Córdoba Ramón Mestre 1983; Sec., Govt of the Municipality of Córdoba 1983–91; f. Amparo Legal (legal assistance office) 1994; Minister of Institutional Affairs and Social Devt of Córdoba Prov. 1995–99; Federal Comptroller, City of Corrientes 1999–2001; Federal Comptroller, Corrientes Prov. Mar–Dec. 2001; mem. Chamber of Deputies (Parl.) from Córdoba Prov. 2005–; Minister of Communications 2015–17; Minister of Defence 2017–; fmr mem. Bd of Dirs La Voz del Interior (daily newspaper), Univ. of Córdoba Foundation; mem. Unión Cívica Radical (UCR). *Address:* Ministry of Defence, Azopardo 250, C1328ADB Buenos Aires, Argentina (office). *Telephone:* (11) 4346-8800 (office). *E-mail:* consultas@mindef.gob.ar (office). *Website:* www.mindef.gov.ar (office).

AGUADO, Victor M., MSc, MEng; Spanish engineer, aviation industry executive and fmr international organization official; b. 9 June 1953, Palencia; m. Paloma Sierra de Aguado; one s. two d.; ed Polytechnic Univ., Madrid, MIT, USA; student trainee, Lufthansa 1975; Aeronautical Engineer in Spanish Air Force 1977–78; Systems Engineer in civil and mil. air traffic man., Mitre Corpn, Boston, USA 1978–83; Programme Dir, Civil Aviation Authority, Madrid 1983–84; Exec. Adviser to Sec. of State for Aerospace and Telecommunications Affairs 1984–85, Chair. Inter-Govt Task Force on major aerospace programmes 1984–85, Deputy Dir-Gen. for Industry 1985–88, Dir-Gen. and Head of Cabinet of Sec. of State for Defence 1988–90; apptd CEO ISDEFE SA Systems Engineering and Consulting Co., Madrid 1990; Air Navigation Commr, ICAO, Montréal 1993, becoming Pres. of Air Navigation Comm. 1996–2000; Dir-Gen. Eurocontrol (European Org. for the Safety of Air Navigation), Brussels 2001–07; mem. Special Corps of Aeronautical Engineers of Civil Aviation Authority; fmr mem. Bd of Trustees ISDEFE, HISPASAT (satellite communications operator), INSA (aerospace Eng); fmr mem. Bd of Govs, Flight Safety Foundation, Virginia, USA; Grand Cross of the Aeronautical Order of Merit; Global NavCom '97 Laurel Award, American Legion Award.

AGÜERO DE CORRALES, Mireya, LLB, BA; Honduran diplomatist and politician; *Chancellor of the Republic;* m. Hector Luis Corrales; four c.; joined Consular Service 1981, Foreign Service 1983, held various positions including

Head, Dept of Int. Politics and Head, Interamerican Affairs Dept within Directorate of Foreign Policy, Dir of Central American Affairs and mem. Advisory Bd for Minister of Foreign Affairs, Vice-Minister of Foreign Affairs 2010–13, Minister of Foreign Affairs 2013–15 (resgnd), Chancellor of the Republic 2014–; has participated in numerous forums and negotiation processes within UN, OAS, Central American Integration System and Central America–EU round tables; Area Coordinator for Foreign Policy, Juan Manuel Galvez Centre for Political, Econ. and Social Studies; fmr Campus Dir, Catholic Univ. of Honduras, Prof. of Law 1993; fmr mem. Int. Law Comm. of Bar Asscn of Honduras; Order of Merit, rank of Grand Cross (Chile) 2011, Order of Francisco Morazan, Grade of Grand Cross, Silver Plate 2012. *Website:* www.sre.gob.hn (office).

AGÜERO LARA, María Dolores, LLM; Honduran lawyer and politician; *Secretary of Foreign Affairs and International Co-operation;* b. 1982; m. Felipe Antonio Young 2015; ed Univ. Nacional Autónoma de Honduras, Univ. of Chile, Heidelberg Univ.; began career as Legal Asst, Honduran Private Business Council (COHEP); fmr Assoc., López Rodezno (law firm); joined Secr. (Ministry) of Foreign Affairs 2010, entered Diplomatic and Consular Service of Honduras 2013, roles include Legal Adviser on Investment Promotion and Trade, Dir of Integration in Foreign Policy Directorate, mem. Organizing Cttee of 'Honduras is Open for Business' (econ. conf.) 2011; Presidential Commr for Integration and Rep. for Honduras to Central American Integration System (SICA) Exec. Cttee; Rep. and Spokesperson, Central American Security Comm.; Deputy Sec. of Foreign Affairs 2015–17, Sec. (Minister) of Foreign Affairs and Int. Co-operation 2017–. *Address:* Secretariat of Foreign Affairs and International Co-operation, Centro Cívico Gubernamental, Antigua Casa Presidencial, Blvd Kuwait, Contiguo a la Corte Suprema de Justicia, Tegucigalpa, Honduras (office). *Telephone:* 2236-0300 (office). *E-mail:* cancilleria.honduras@gmail.com (office). *Website:* www.sre.gob.hn (office).

AGUIAR-BRANCO, José Pedro Correia de; Portuguese lawyer and politician; *Founding Director, José Pedro Aguiar-Branco;* b. 18 July 1957; ed Univ. de Coimbra, Institut d'études politiques de Bordeaux, France; Founding Dir José Pedro Aguiar-Branco (legal practice) 2003–; mem. Assembleia da República (Parl.) 2005–; Minister of Justice 2004–05, of Nat. Defence 2011–15; mem. Partido Social Democrata (PSD), Chair. PSD Parl. Group 1996–99, 2009–10; mem. Nat. Directorate, Portuguese Asscn of Young Lawyers (APJA) 1987–89 (Vice-Pres. 1988–91, Pres. 1991–94); mem. Portuguese Bar Asscn (Pres. Porto Div. 2002–04). *Address:* José Pedro Aguiar-Branco, Rua José Falcão 110, 4050-315 Porto, Portugal (office). *Telephone:* (220) 122100 (office). *Fax:* (220) 122101 (office). *E-mail:* info@jpab.pt (office). *Website:* www.jpab.pt (office).

AGUIAR CUNHA, Paulo Guilherme; Brazilian engineer, academic and business executive; *Chairman Emeritus, Ultrapar Holdings;* b. 1 March 1940, Rio de Janeiro; ed Pontifícia Universidade Católica do Rio de Janeiro; Prof. of Eng, Pontifícia Universidade Católica do Rio de Janeiro and at Fed. Univ. of Rio de Janeiro 1963–66; joined Ultrapar 1967, Vice-Pres. 1973–81, CEO 1981–2007, Chair. Ultrapar Holdings 1998–2018, Chair. Emer. 2018–; mem. Bd of Dirs Monteiro Aranha 1997–; Pres. Brazilian Asscn of Tech. Standards (ABNT), Instituto Brasileiro de Petróleo; fmr Pres. IEDI (Research Inst. for Industrial Devt), currently mem. Bd of Dirs; mem. CMN (Nat. Monetary Council), Bd of BNDESPAR (subsidiary of BNDES), Consulting Bd of Brazilian Chemical Industries Asscn (ABIQUIM), Bd of Superior Council of Economy, Consultative Council for Industry of Federação das Indústrias do Estado de São Paulo (FIESP), Bd of Insper (fmrly IBMEC), IPT (Technological Research Inst.), Bd of Superior Strategic Council of FIESP 2008–. *Address:* Ultrapar Holdings, Avenida Brigadeiro Luiz Antônio 1343, São Paulo 01317-910, Brazil (office). *Telephone:* (11) 3177-7014 (office). *Fax:* (11) 3177-6107 (office). *E-mail:* info@ultra.com.br (office). *Website:* www.ultra.com.br (office).

AGUILAR MARMOLEJO, María de los Dolores, MA, PhD; Mexican international organization executive; *Director-General, Inter-American Children's Institute (IIN-OAS);* b. 1966; ed Universidad La Salle, México, Univ. of Santiago de Compostela, Spain; extensive experience as a teacher; has worked with Univ. of Anahuac and Technological Univ. of Mexico; currently Prof. of Basic Educ., with grad. studies in philosophy, Universidad La Salle, México; recognized instructor in workshops and adviser on schoolwork consultancy; lectures on issues of family, children, health, educ., policy and organizational devt, among others; mem. Partido Acción Nacional (Nat. Action Party—PAN) 1984–, cand. for various elective offices at local level; Deputy to Fed. Dist Legis. Ass. 1997–2000; worked for Nat. System for Integral Devt of the Family 2001–08, served as adviser to Directorate-Gen., Deputy Dir Care Unit to the Vulnerable Population and CEO for Child Welfare; participated in design of 'Diagnóstico de la Familia Mexicana' basic tool for the analysis, design and implementation of public policies on the family 2003–05; Dir-Gen. Inter-American Children's Inst. (IIN-OAS) 2008–. *Address:* Inter-American Children's Institute, Avenida 8 de Octubre 2904, Montevideo 11600, Uruguay (office). *Telephone:* (2) 487-2150 (office). *Fax:* (2) 487-3242 (office). *E-mail:* direcciongral@iinoea.org (office). *Website:* www.iin.oea.org (office).

AGUILAR MONTOYA, Rocío; Costa Rican lawyer and politician; *Minister of Finance;* b. 14 Dec. 1956, Escazu, San José; d. of José Joaquin Aguilar Monge and Dona Gilda Maria Montoya Alvarado; m. Rómulo Picado Chacón; three c.; ed Univ. of Costa Rica, Escuela Libre de Derecho, Central American Inst. of Business Admin (INCAE); worked for Banco Banex 1981–2001, becoming Corp. Dir; Dir, Nat. Council for Supervision of the Financial System (Conassif) 2002; Technical Sec., Nat. Council of Concessions 2002–05; Contralora Gen. (Comptroller Gen.) of the Repub. 2005–12; Partner (Financial Services and Infrastructure), Deloitte Consulting 2015–18; Head, Gen. Superintendency of Financial Insts (Sugef) March–May 2018; Minister of Finance 2018–; mem. Costa Rican Banking Asscn 1999–2000, Costa Rican Devt Asscn 1999–2005. *Address:* Ministry of Finance, Edif. Antigüo Banco Anglo, Avda 2a, Calle 3a, San José, Costa Rica (office). *Telephone:* 2284-5000 (office). *Fax:* 2255-4874 (office). *E-mail:* comunicacionmh@hacienda.go.cr (office). *Website:* www.hacienda.go.cr (office).

AGUILERA, Christina Maria; American singer; b. 18 Dec. 1980, Staten Island, New York; m. Jordan Bratman 2005 (divorced); one s. one d.; appeared on US Star Search TV talent show aged eight; joined cast of The New Mickey Mouse Club aged 12; worldwide promotional touring 1997–; solo artist 1998–; coach and judge, The Voice (US TV show) 2011–13, 2015, 2016; apptd WFP Amb. Against Hunger; Grammy Award for Best New Artist 2000, American Latino Media Arts (ALMA) Award for Best New Entertainer 2000, Billboard Award for Female Vocalist of the Year 2000, Q Award (for Dirrty) 2003, Grammy Awards for Best Female Pop Vocal Performance (for Beautiful) 2004, (for Ain't No Other Man) 2007, for Best Pop Duo/Group Performance (for Say Something, with A Great Big World) 2015, MTV Europe Music Award for Best Female Artist 2006, Special Achievement Award, ALMA Awards 2012, George McGovern Leadership Award 2012. *Film:* Burlesque 2010, The Emoji Movie 2017, Zoe 2018. *Recordings include:* albums: Christina Aguilera 1999, Mi Reflejo (Billboard Latin Music Award for Best Pop Album of the Year 2001) 2000, My Kind Of Christmas 2000, Just Be Free 2001, Stripped 2002, Back to Basics 2006, Bi-On-Ic 2010, Lotus 2012, Liberation 2018. *Address:* c/o Irving Azoff, Azoff Music Management, LLC, 1100 Glendon Avenue, Suite 2000, Los Angeles, CA 90024, USA (office). *Website:* www.christinaaguilera.com.

AGUILERA, Isabel, MBA; Spanish business executive; *President, Twindocs International Services;* b. 1961, Seville; two c.; ed Univ. of Seville, Instituto de Empressa; studied architecture and urban planning; Dir of Distribution and Marketing Communications Compaq Spain 1985–88; Marketing Man. Hewlett-Packard Spain 1989–95; with Airtel 1995–97; Man. Dir for Spain, Portugal and Italy, Dell Computer SA 1997–2002; COO and mem. Man. Cttee NH Hoteles 2002–06; Man. Dir Google Spain and Portugal 2006–08; Pres. General Electric Spain and Portugal 2008–09; Pres. Twindocs Int. Services 2011–; Chair. Social Council, Univ. of Seville 2011–; mem. Bd of Dirs Indra Sitemas 2005–, Banco Mare Nostrum, SA 2013–, Aegón España, Egasa XXI, SA; fmr Int. Dir Instituto de Empresa. *Address:* Twindocs International Services, c/Bari 39, 1ª planta Plaza, Zaragoza 50197, Spain (office). *Website:* www.twindocs.com/EN (office).

AGUIRRE, Eduardo, Jr, BS; American banker, government official and fmr diplomatist; *Chairman and CEO, Atlantic Partners Group LLC;* b. 30 July 1946, Cuba; m. Maria Teresa Aguirre; one s. one d.; ed Louisiana State Univ., American Bankers Asscn's Nat. Commercial Lending Grad. School; emigrated from Cuba aged 15; apptd to Nat. Comm. for Employment Policy; apptd to State Bar of Tex. as non-attorney Dir 1990; mem. Bd of Regents Univ. of Houston System for a six-year term, Chair. 1996–98; fmr Pres. Int. Pvt. Banking, Bank of America; fmr Vice-Chair. and COO Export-Import Bank of the US (Ex-Im Bank), Acting Chair. for one year; Dir of US Citizenship and Immigration Services, Dept of Homeland Security 2003–05; has served on numerous professional and civic bds, including Tex. Children's Hosp., Tex. Bar Foundation, Operación Pedro Pan Foundation, Bankers Asscn for Finance and Trade, Houston chapters of the American Red Cross and the Salvation Army; Amb. to Spain 2005–09; Chair. and CEO Atlantic Partners Group LLC 2009–; mem. Bd of Dirs Greater Houston Partnership, BBVA Compass Bancshares, Inc. 2009–, Tex. Children's Hospital; mem. Royal Acad. of the Sea 2007–. mem. International Advisory Council, APCO Worldwide; Hon. mem. Foundation for Spanish Royal Acad. of the Sea 2007; Order of Hilal-i-Quaid-i-Azam (Pakistan), Grand Officer, Order of José Matías Delgado (El Salvador), Grand Officer, Order of Christopher Columbus (Dominican Repub.), Grand Cross of the First Class of the Pontifical Equestrian Order of St. Gregory the Great (The Holy See), Order of Isabella the Catholic Grand Cross (Spain); numerous other decorations from Spain, Andorra and Rwanda; Dr hc (Univ. of Connecticut, Univ. of Houston, Universidad Tecnológica de Santiago, Dominican Repub.); Ellis Island Medal of Honor, Americanism Medal, The Daughters of the American Revolution 2004. *Telephone:* (281) 556-0753. *E-mail:* eaguirre@atlanticpartners.us.

AGUIRRE SACASA, Francisco Zavier, BSc, MA; Nicaraguan politician; ed Georgetown and Harvard Univs, USA; mem. Int. Advisory Bd, Panamerican Agric. School; joined World Bank 1969, Chief of Chile, Ecuador and Peru Div., Latin America and Caribbean Region 1977–83, Chief of Trade, Finance and Industry Div., Eastern and Southern Africa Region 1983–86, Asst-Dir Agric. Projects, Latin America and Caribbean Region 1986–87, Sr Adviser to Vice-Pres., Latin America and Caribbean Region 1987–88, Dir External Affairs Dept 1988–90, Dir Cen. Africa and Indian Ocean Dept (Africa Regional Office) 1990–95, Dir Operations Evaluation Dept 1995–97; Amb. to USA and Canada 1997–2002; Minister of Foreign Affairs 1997–2002; Sec. of Int. Affairs, Constitutional Liberal Party (PLC) –2012 (resgnd); unsuccessful presidential cand. 2006, vice-presidential cand. 2011. *Publications include:* contribs to The Boston Globe, The Christian Science Monitor, The Wall Street Journal, The Washington Post, The Washington Times, La Prensa.

AGUIRRE URIOSTE, Luis Fernando, MSc, PhD; Bolivian biologist, conservationist and academic; *Researcher and Professor, Centre for Biodiversity and Genetics, Universidad Mayor de San Simon;* ed Universidad Mayor de San Andres, La Paz, Antwerp Univ., Belgium; f. Bolivian Bat Conservation Programme of BIOTA (one of four major programmes at Centro de Estudios en Biologia Teorica y Aplicada) to protect bats through educ. and practical habitat conservation throughout Bolivia; currently Researcher and Prof., Centre for Biodiversity and Genetics, Universidad Mayor de San Simon; mem. Scientific Advisory Bd Bat Conservation International, Network of Educators of Conservation Biology (AMNH), Int. Union for Conservation of Nature Chiropteran Specialist Group; Assoc. Ed. Acta Chiropterologica, Mastozoologia Neotropical, Revista Boliviana de Ecologia, Ecologia en Bolivia; reviewer for several int. scientific journals, including Conservation Biology, Biotropica, Acta Chiropterologica, Ecography, Journal of Tropical Ecology, Journal of Mammalogy; Pres. Asociacion Boliviana de Investigadores de Mamiferos 2005–; Adjunct Researcher, Center for Environmental Research and Conservation, Columbia Univ., New York, USA 2006–; Devt Cooperation Prize, Belgian Cooperation Program 2005, Oliver P. Person Award, American Soc. of Mammalogists 2006, Whitley Award in memory of Daniel Kelly, Rufford Maurice Laing Foundation 2007. *Publications:* more than 30 scientific papers in professional journals. *Address:* Centro de Biodiversidad y Genética, Universidad Mayor de San Simón, Calle Sucre y parque la Torre, Cochabamba, Bolivia (office). *Telephone:* (4) 4231765 (office). *E-mail:* laguirre@fcyt.umss.edu.bo (office). *Website:* umss.academia.edu/Departments/Centro_de_Biodiversidad_y_Genetica (office).

ÁGÚSTSSON, Helgi; Icelandic diplomatist (retd); b. 16 Oct. 1941, Reykjavik; s. of Ágúst H. Pétursson and Helga Jóhannesdóttir; m. Hervör Jónasdóttir 1963; three s. one d.; ed Commercial Coll. of Iceland and Univ. of Iceland; joined Ministry for Foreign Affairs 1970; First Sec. and Counsellor, London 1973–77; Dir Defence Div.

Ministry for Foreign Affairs and Icelandic Chair. US–Icelandic Defence Council 1979; Minister-Counsellor, Washington, DC 1983–87; Deputy Perm. Sec., Ministry for Foreign Affairs 1987; Amb. to UK 1989–94; Perm. Sec., Ministry for Foreign Affairs 1995–99; Amb. to Denmark 1998–99, to USA 2002–06; Chief of Protocol, Ministry of Foreign Affairs –2009 (retd); apptd Chair. Save the Children (Iceland) 2009; fmr Pres. Icelandic Basketball Fed.; Hon. GCVO; Grand Cross, Order of Dannebrog, Kt Commdr of White Rose, Grand Cross of Mérito Civil, Kt Commdr of Pole Star, Grand Cross, Order of the Falcon, Grand Cross Oranje-Nassau Order, Grand Cross Norwegian Service Order, Grand Cross IMR. *Leisure interests:* salmon fishing, music, chess, theatre.

AGUT BONSFILLS, Joaquim, BSc, MBA; Spanish media executive; *Director-General, CIRSA Gaming Corporation;* ed Univ. Polytécnica de Catalunya, Barcelona, Univ. de Navarra; joined Synthese SA as Dir of Business Devt, Barcelona, Gen. Man. 1980; worked for family-owned co. Agut SA (later acquired by Gen. Electric) 1982; various sr positions with Gen. Electric (GE), including Vice-Pres. and Gen. Man. of Marketing and Sales, Pres. and CEO GE Power Controls, Pres. and CEO GE Nat. Exec. for Spain and Portugal, Chair. Pan European GE Quality Council, Leader of European Corp. Exec. Council (CEC); Chair. Terra Networks –2000; Exec. Chair. Terra Lycos (following merger of Terra and Lycos 2000) 2000–04; Chair. and CEO Endemol Group 2004–06; Dir-Gen., CIRSA Gaming Corpn 2006–; Young Businessman of the Year Award 1984. *Address:* CIRSA, Edificio CIRSA, Carretera de Castellar, 298, 08226 Barcelona, Spain (office). *Telephone:* (93) 7396700 (office). *E-mail:* cirsa@cirsa.com (office). *Website:* www.cirsa.com (office).

AGUTTER, Jennifer (Jenny) Ann, OBE; British actress and dancer; b. 20 Dec. 1952, Taunton, Somerset, England; d. of Derek Brodie Agutter and Catherine Agutter (née Lynam); m. Johan Tham 1990; one s.; ed Elmhurst Ballet School; film debut in East of Sudan 1964; has appeared in numerous TV films, dramas and series and on stage with RSC and Nat. Theatre. *Plays include:* The Tempest, Spring Awakening, Hedda Gabler, Betrayal, The Unified Field, Breaking the Code, Love's Labour's Lost, Peter Pan. *Films include:* Ballerina 1964, Gates of Paradise 1967, Star 1968, I Start Counting 1969, The Railway Children 1969, Walkabout, Logan's Run 1975, The Eagle Has Landed, Equus, The Man in the Iron Mask, Riddle of the Sands, Sweet William, The Survivor 1980, An American Werewolf in London 1981, Secret Places 1983, Dark Tower 1987, King of the Wind 1989, Child's Play 2 1991, Freddie as Fro 7 1993, Blue Juice 1995, English Places, English Faces 1996, The Parole Officer 2001, At Dawning 2001, Number One, Longing. Number Two, Regret 2004, Heroes and Villains 2006, Irina Palm 2007, The Magic Door (video) 2007, Intercom (short) 2008, Act of God 2009, Glorious 39 2009, Burke and Hare 2010, Golden Brown 2011, Avengers Assemble 2012, Outside Bet 2012, Captain America: The Winter Soldier 2014, Queen of the Desert 2015, Tin 2015. *Television includes:* Amy 1980, Not a Penny More, Not a Penny Less 1990, The Good Guys, Puss in Boots 1991, Love Hurts 1994, Heartbeat 1994, September 1995, 1996, The Buccaneers 1995, And The Beat Goes On 1996, A Respectable Trade 1997, Bramwell 1998, The Railway Children 2000, Spooks (series) 2002–03, The Alan Clark Diaries (series) 2004–06, The Invisibles (series) 2008, Monday Monday (series) 2009, Call the Midwife (series) 2012–. *Publication:* Snap 1983. *Leisure interest:* photography. *Address:* c/o Ken McReddie Associates Ltd, 11 Connaught Place, London, W2 2ET, England. *Telephone:* (20) 7439-1456. *Fax:* (20) 7734-6530. *E-mail:* email@kenmcreddie.com. *Website:* www.kenmcreddie.com; www.jennyagutter.net.

AGYEMAN, Julian, BSc, MA, PhD, FRSA, FRGS; British environmental social scientist and academic; *Professor, Department of Urban and Environmental Policy and Planning, Tufts University;* b. Beverley, East Yorks., England; ed Durham Univ., Newcastle Univ., Middlesex Univ., Univ. of London; taught geography at a secondary school in Carlisle, Cumbria; Environmental Policy Adviser, Notting Dale Urban Studies Centre, London, later in local govt in London Boroughs of Lambeth and Islington; consulted and taught environmental policy at London South Bank Univ.; Co-founder Black Environmental Network 1988, Chair. –1994; Co-founder Local Environment: The International Journal of Justice and Sustainability 1996, currently Ed.-in-Chief; ran a consulting firm in London specializing in communicating environmental and sustainable solutions to local govts, not-for-profit orgs and businesses 1992–98; Prof., Dept of Urban and Environmental Policy and Planning, Tufts Univ. 1999–; Contributing Ed., Environment: Science and Policy for Sustainable Development; Sr Scholar, Center for Humans and Nature, Chicago; mem. Editorial Bd, Australian Journal of Environmental Education; Series Ed. Just Sustainabilities: Policy, Planning and Practice; Series Co-Ed. Routledge Equity, Justice and the Sustainable City; Outstanding Faculty Contrib. to Grad. Studies Award, Tufts Univ. Grad. Student Council 2005, Benton H Box Award 2015, Cambridge (Mass) Food Hero Fellow 2015. *Publications include:* Local Environmental Policies and Strategies (co-ed.) 1994, People, Plants and Places 1995, Just Sustainabilities: Development in an Unequal World (co-ed.) 2003, Sustainable Communities and the Challenge of Environmental Justice 2005, The New Countryside? Ethnicity, Nation and Exclusion in Contemporary Rural Britain (co-ed.) 2006, Speaking for Ourselves: Environmental Justice in Canada (2009), Environmental Justice in the Former Soviet Union (co-ed.) 2009, Environmental Inequalities Beyond Borders: Local Perspectives on Global Injustices (co-ed.) 2011, Cultivating Food Justice: Race, Class and Sustainability (co-ed.) 2011, Introducing Just Sustainabilities: Policy, Planning and Practice 2013, Incomplete Streets: Processes, Practices, and Possibilities (co-ed.) 2014, Sharing Cities: A Case for Truly Smart and Sustainable Cities (co-author with Duncan McLaren) 2015; more than 160 other publs, including book chapters, peer-reviewed articles, published conf. presentations, published reports, book reviews, newspaper articles, op-eds and articles in professional journals and magazines. *Address:* Department of Urban and Environmental Policy and Planning, Tufts University, 97 Talbot Avenue, Medford, MA 02155, USA (office). *Telephone:* (617) 627-3394 (office); (617) 627-4017 (office). *Fax:* (617) 627-3377 (office). *E-mail:* julian.agyeman@tufts.edu (office). *Website:* julianagyeman.com (office).

AHADI, Anwar al-Haq, BA, MA, MBA, PhD; Afghan banker, politician and academic; *Chairman, New National Front of Afghanistan;* b. 12 Aug. 1951, Jigdalai, Sarobi Dist; s. of Abdul Haq; m. 2nd Fatima Gailani; ed Hibibiya High School, American Univ. of Beirut, Lebanon, Northwestern Univ., Chicago, USA; fmr mem. of staff Continental Bank of Chicago; joined Afghan Mellat Party (Afghan Social Democratic Party) 1969, elected to Supreme Council 1987, 1990, Pres. 1995–2016; Chair. New Nat. Front of Afghanistan 2016–; Asst Prof. of Political Sciences, Carlton Univ. 1984; Banking Dir, Continental Elona Bank, Chicago 1985–87; Prof. of Political Sciences, Providence Univ. 1987–2002; Gov. Da Afghanistan Bank (Cen. Bank of Afghanistan) 2002–04; Minister of Finance 2004–09, of the Economy 2009, of Commerce and Industry 2009–13.

AHARONOV, Yakir, BSc, PhD; Israeli physicist and academic; *Professor of Theoretical Physics and James J. Farley Professor of Natural Philosophy, Chapman University;* b. 28 Aug. 1932, Haifa; ed Technion (Israel Inst. of Tech.), Haifa, Univ. of Bristol, UK; Research Assoc., Brandeis Univ., Waltham, Mass, USA 1960–61; Asst Prof., Yeshiva Univ., USA 1961–64, Assoc. Prof. 1964–67, Prof. 1967–73; Prof. of Physics, Tel-Aviv Univ. 1967–73, Prof. Emer. 1973–; Distinguished Prof., Univ. of South Carolina, USA 1973–2006; Prof., George Mason Univ. 2006–08; Prof. of Theoretical Physics, Schmid Coll. of Science, Dept of Physics, Computational Science and Engineering, Chapman Univ., Calif., also James J. Farley Prof. of Natural Philosophy 2008–; Chair. in Theoretical Physics, Univ. of South Carolina; Alex Maguy-Glass Chair in Theoretical Physics, Tel-Aviv Univ.; Van Vleck Lecturer, Univ. of Minnesota 2000; Pres. Iyar, Israeli Inst. for Advanced Research; mem. Israeli Nat. Acad. of Science 1990, NAS 1993–; Fellow, American Physical Soc. 1981, Patron, Perimeter Inst. for Theoretical Physics; Hon. DSc (Technion – Israel Inst. of Tech.) 1992, (Univ. of South Carolina) 1992, (Univ. of Bristol) 1997; Hon. DUniv (Buenos Aires) 1999; Weizmann Prize in Physics 1984, Rothschild Prize in Physics 1984, Miller Research Professorship Award, Berkeley 1988–89, Israeli Nat. Prize in Physics 1989, Elliot Cresson Medal 1991, Distinguished Scientist Gov. Award, South Carolina 1993, Hewlett-Packard Europhysics Prize 1995, Wolf Prize in Physics (co-recipient) 1998. *Publications:* more than 170 papers in learned journals. *Address:* Chapman University, Schmid College of Science, Department of Physics, Computational Science and Engineering, One University Drive, Orange, CA 92866, USA (office). *Telephone:* (714) 289-2052 (office). *Fax:* (714) 289-2041 (office). *E-mail:* aharonov@chapman.edu (office); yakir@post.tau.ac.il. *Website:* www.chapman.edu/our-faculty/yakir-aharonov (office); www.tau.ac.il/~yakir.

AHERN, Bertie; Irish accountant and politician; b. 12 Sept. 1951, Dublin; s. of Cornelius Ahern and Julia Ahern (née Hourihane); m. Miriam Patricia Kelly 1975 (separated); two d.; ed Rathmines Coll. of Commerce (now Dublin Inst. of Tech.), Univ. Coll., Dublin; TD (Fianna Fáil Party) for Dublin-Finglas 1977–81, Dublin Cen. 1981–2011, Pres. Fianna Fáil 1994–2011; mem. Dublin City Council 1978–88, Lord Mayor 1986–87; Asst Chief Whip 1980–81; Fianna Fáil Spokesman on Youth Affairs 1981–82; Govt Chief Whip and Minister of State, Depts of the Taoiseach and of Defence March–Dec. 1982; Opposition Chief Whip 1982–84; Fianna Fáil Front Bench Spokesman on Labour 1984–87; Minister for Labour 1987–91, for Finance 1991–94, for Industry and Commerce Jan. 1993; Tánaiste (Deputy Prime Minister) and Minister for Arts, Culture and the Gaeltacht Nov.–Dec. 1994; Leader of the Opposition 1994–97; Taoiseach (Prime Minister of Ireland) 1997–2008 (resgnd); Pres. European Council Jan.–June 2004; mem. Bd, Co-operation Ireland 2008, World Solar Foundation; mem. Agenda Council on Conflict Resolution; Sr Advisor to the Int. Advisory Council of the Harvard Int. Negotiation Program; mem. Bd of Govs IMF 1991–94, World Bank 1991–94; Chair. European Investment Bank 1991–92, Dublin Millennium Cttee 1988, Int. Forestry Fund 2010, Bougainville Referendum Comm. 2018; mem. advisory Bd Parker Green Int.; fmr mem. Bd of Govs Univ. Coll. Dublin, Dublin Port and Docks Bd, Eastern Health Bd, Dublin Chamber of Commerce; Hon. Adjunct Prof. of Mediation and Conflict Intervention, School of Business and Law, NUI Maynooth Hon. DIur (Washington Coll., Chestertown, MD) 2015; Grand Cross, Order of Merit with Star and Sash (Germany) 1991. *Publications:* Bertie Ahern: The Autobiography 2009. *Leisure interests:* sports, reading. *Address:* Drumcondra Business Centre, 120 Upper Drumcondra Road, Drumcondra, Dublin 7, Republic of Ireland (office). *Website:* www.bertieahernoffice.com.

AHERN, Dermot, BCL; Irish politician; b. Feb. 1955, Drogheda, Co. Louth; s. of Jeremiah Ahern and Gertrude Alice Ahern (née McGarrity); m. Maeve Coleman; two d.; ed Marist Coll., Dundalk, Univ. Coll., Dublin, Inc. Law Soc. of Ireland; solicitor 1976–; mem. Louth Co. Council 1979–91; mem. Fianna Fáil 1987–; mem. Dáil Éireann for Louth constituency 1987–2011, mem. various parl. cttees; Asst Govt Whip 1988–91; Minister of State at Depts of the Taoiseach and Defence, Govt Chief Whip 1991–92; Minister for Social, Community and Family Affairs 1997–2002, for Communications, Marine and Natural Resources 2002–04, Minister for Foreign Affairs 2004–08, Minister for Justice, Equality and Law Reform 2008–11; mem. British-Irish Parl. Body 1991–97 (Co-Chair. 1993–95).

AHLSTRÖM, Krister Harry, BSc, MSc; Finnish business executive; *Senior Adviser and Investing Partner, Desigence Oy;* b. 29 Aug. 1940, Helsinki; s. of Harry F. Ahlström and Asta A. Ahlström (née Seege); m. Anja I. Artto 1974; one s. four d.; ed Helsinki Univ. of Technology; Product Engineer, Gen. Man. and mem. Bd of Man. Oy Wärtsilä Ab 1966–81; Dir and mem. Exec. Bd A. Ahlström Corpn 1981–82, Pres. and CEO 1982–98, Chair. 1998–99; Sr Adviser and Investing Partner, Desigence Oy, Helsinki 1995–; fmr Vice-Chair. Stora Enso Oyj, Chair. 2012–; Chair. Nordea Securities; Chair. Confed. Finnish Employers 1986–92, Fed. of Finnish Metal, Eng and Electrotechnical Industries 1992–96, Orgalime (Organisme de Liaison des Industries Métalliques Européennes), Brussels 1994–96; Chair. Research Inst. of Finnish Economy; mem. Advisory Bd Procuritas AB; mem. Swedish Royal Acad. of Eng Sciences; Bergsråd (hon. title awarded by Pres. of Finland); granted title of Ikiteekkarin 2012; Hon. DrTech; Dr hc (Arts). *Leisure interests:* sailing (world winner 8mR 1975), skiing. *Address:* Desigence Oy, Lemuntie 3-5 B, 00510 Helsinki (office); Kvarnvägen 2A2, 00140 Helsinki, Finland (home). *Telephone:* (93) 505280 (office); 500-500788 (mobile) (home). *Fax:* (93) 5052899 (office); (9) 625560 (home). *Website:* www.desigence.com (office).

AHLUWALIA, Montek Singh, BA, MA, MPhil; Indian economist and government official; b. 24 Nov. 1943, New Delhi; s. of Jagmohan Singh and Push J. M. Singh; m. Dr Isher Judge Ahluwalia; two c.; ed Univ. of Delhi, Magdalen Coll. and St Antony's Coll., Oxford, UK; Economist, World Bank, Washington, DC, USA 1968–71, Deputy Div. Chief, Public Finance Div. 1971–72, Chief of Income Distribution Div., Devt Research Centre 1972–79, Dir Ind. Evaluation Office 2001–04; Econ. Advisor, Dept of Econ. Affairs, Ministry of Finance 1979–85;

Additional Sec. to Prime Minister 1985–88, Special Sec. to Prime Minister 1988–90; Sec. of Commerce 1990–91; Sec., Dept of Econ. Affairs, Ministry of Finance 1991–93, Finance Sec. 1993–98; mem. Econ. Advisory Council to Prime Minister 1998–2001; Deputy Chair. Planning Comm. 2004–14 (resgnd); Hon. Fellow, Magdalen Coll., Oxford; Hon. DCL (Oxford) 2008; Hon. DSc (Indian Inst. of Tech., Roorkee) 2011, (Indian School of Mines) 2013; Sikh of the Year Award 2008, EDGE Education Personality of the Year Award 2009, Padma Vibhushan 2011. *Publications include:* Re-distribution with Growth: An Approach to Policy (co-author) 1975, Reforming the Global Financial Architecture 2000; book chapters and several articles on various aspects of the Indian economy in academic journals. *Leisure interest:* playing golf. *Address:* c/o Planning Commission, Yojana Bhavan, Parliament Street, New Delhi 110 001 India. *E-mail:* dch@nic.in.

AHMAD, Kazi Rakibuddin, BSc, MSc, MBA; Bangladeshi government official and civil servant (retd); b. 2 Dec. 1943, Jessore Dist; m.; two d.; ed Univ. of Dhaka, Boston Univ., USA, Harvard Univ., USA, Georgetown Univ., USA; joined Civil Service of Pakistan in 1960s; took part in War of Independence 1971 as Sub-Divisional Officer, Brahmanbaria; Deputy Sec. and Zonal Admin. Officer under First Bangladesh Govt then Deputy Commr of Comilla; fmr Econ. Minister, Embassy in Tokyo, Jt Sec., Cabinet Div.; Educ. Sec. 2000–03; Parl. Sec. –2003; Chief Election Commr 2012–17; Chair. Bangladesh Chemical Industries Corpn, Trading Corpn of Bangladesh; Dir-Gen. NGO Affairs Bureau.

AHMAD OF WIMBLEDON, Baron (Life Peer), cr. 2011, of Wimbledon in the London Borough of Merton; **Tariq Ahmad;** British politician and business executive; *Minister of State for the Commonwealth and United Nations;* b. 3 April 1968, London; m.; two s. one d.; joined Natwest's Grad. Man. programme 1991, worked in a variety of frontline and strategic roles, including Head of Marketing, Sponsorship and Branding for NatWest's capital markets Div. –2000; worked as part of Exec. Man. team for US-based fund manager Alliance Bernstein 2000–04; joined Sucden Financial, London 2004, served on Exec. Cttee and as Dir of Marketing and Corp. Strategy; Assoc., Inst. of Financial Services; Councillor, Wimbledon, London Borough of Merton 2002–, Cabinet Mem. for Environment and Transport 2006–08, for Community Safety & Engagement 2008–09; Deputy Chair. London Councils' Transport and Environment Cttee 2006–08; Conservative Party Parl. cand. in Croydon North 2005; Vice-Chair. Conservative Party with responsibilities for Cities 2008–10; worked for AMYA nat. youth org. in various nat. roles, including Sec. responsible for Educ. and Training, Health and Sport, as well as Community and Charities, Vice-Pres. 1999–2008; Gov., Wimbledon Park Primary School 2001–06; Lord in Waiting 2012–14; Under-Sec. of State, Communities and Local Govt 2014–15, Minister for Countering Extremism 2015–16, for Transport (Minister for Aviation) 2015–17; Minister of State for the Commonwealth and UN 2017–. *Address:* Foreign and Commonwealth Office, King Charles Street, London, SW1A 2AH (office); House of Lords, Westminster, London, SW1A 0PW, England (office). *Telephone:* (300) 330-3000; (20) 7008-1500 (office). *E-mail:* ahmadt@parliament.uk (office). *Website:* www.gov.uk/government/organisations/foreign-commonwealth-office (office).

AHMADINEJAD, Mahmoud, PhD; Iranian politician and fmr head of state; b. 28 Oct. 1956, Garmsar; ed Iran Univ. of Science and Tech. (IUST); joined Islamic Revolutionary Guards Corps 1986; Prof. of Civil Eng, IUST 1989–; Adviser for Cultural Affairs to Minister of Culture and Higher Educ. 1993; fmr Vice-Gov., then Gov. Maku and Khoy; Gov.-Gen. Ardabil prov. 1993–97; Mayor of Tehran 2003–05; Pres. of Iran 2005–13; interim Minister of Petroleum May–June 2011; mem. Cen. Council, Islamic Soc. of Engineers; mem. Iran Tunnel Soc., Iran Civil Eng Soc. *Publications include:* numerous articles on political, social, cultural and economic topics. *Website:* www.ahmadinejad.ir.

AHMADZAI, Abdullah, BIT; Afghan civil servant; *Country Representative, The Asia Foundation;* b. 1975, Qarabagh Dist, Kabul Prov.; ed Brains Degree Coll., Peshawar, Pakistan, workshop certificates from Harvard Univ. and Int. Foundation for Electoral Services, USA; actively involved with Afghanistan Constitution Comm. mandated by the 2001 Bonn Agreement to draft a new constitution 2003–04; Kuchies Liaison Officer, Nat. Area Man., Nat. Head of Field Operations, Chief of Operations Counterpart, Chief of Operations, in Jt Election Man. Body and Ind. Election Comm. 2004–06, Chief Electoral Officer and CEO Ind. Election Comm. 2010–13; Sr Nat. Capacity Building Adviser, later Deputy Chief of Party, later Chief of Party, The Asia Foundation 2006–09, Deputy Country Rep. 2012–14, Country Rep. 2015–; Vice-Pres. ASPIRE (Afghanistan Logistic Services co.) 2009; attended numerous workshops in India and UAE on governance. *Address:* The Asia Foundation, PO Box 175, Kabul, Afghanistan (office). *Telephone:* 793-606042 (mobile). *E-mail:* abdullah.ahmadzai@asiafoundation.org (office). *Website:* asiafoundation.org (office).

AHMAR, Lt-Gen. Ali Mohsin al; Yemeni army officer and government official; *Vice-President;* b. 20 June 1945, Sanhan; commissioned as Lt in Mechanized Forces of Republican Guard 1966; attained rank of Col 1979, Commdr of an Armoured Brigade 1979, Mil. Sec. 1983, Commdr, 1st Armoured Div. 1987–2011, Commdr, North-Western Mil. Dist 2011–12; Adviser to Pres. for defence and security affairs 2012; fled Yemen following Houthi takeover 2014, returned to lead mil. operation in Hajja Prov. Dec. 2015; Deputy Chief Commdr of Yemen armed forces 2016– (based in Saudi Arabia); Vice-Pres. of Yemen 2016–.

AHMED, Abdulrahman Sulaiman al-, BAdminSci, MA; Saudi Arabian diplomatist; *Ambassador to Belgium and the European Union;* b. 17 Nov. 1963; m.; four c.; ed St John's Univ., New York, USA, Inst. of Diplomatic Studies, Riyadh, King Saud Univ.; joined Ministry of Foreign Affairs (MFA) as Attaché and ranked in diplomatic corps 1987, worked at Perm. Mission to UN, New York 1994–2001, including follow-up meetings of Security Council, UN First Cttee on Int. Security and Disarmament Issues and UN Sixth Cttee on Legal Issues, worked in Ministry Agency for Consular Affairs for Bilateral Relations (Western Admin), followed by Multilateral Relations, Int. Orgs Admin serving as Chargé d'affaires a.i. for numerous periods at Perm. Mission to UN, New York, Gen. Man. for Unions and Groups Admins 2009–14, Amb. to Belgium and EU, Brussels 2014–; mem. Faculty (part-time), Inst. of Diplomatic Studies, MFA, Riyadh 2005–; Founding mem. Saudi Political Sciences Asscn. *Address:* Delegation of Saudi Arabia, Avenue Louise 326, 1050 Brussels, Belgium (office). *Telephone:* (2) 649-20-44 (office). *Fax:* (2) 646-85-38 (office). *E-mail:* beemb@mofa.gov.sa (office). *Website:* embassies.mofa.gov.sa/sites/Belgium/EN/BrusselsDelegation (office).

AHMED, Abiy, PhD; Ethiopian politician and fmr army officer; *Prime Minister;* b. 15 Aug. 1976, Beshasha, Oromia Region; s. of Ahmed Ali and Tezeta Wolde; m. Zinash Tayachew; three d.; ed Microlink Information Tech. Coll., Addis Ababa, Greenwich Univ., London, Addis Ababa Univ. Inst. for Peace and Security Studies; joined Ethiopian Nat. Defence Force 1993, served in Army Signals Corps; deployed as mem. UN Peacekeeping Force (UNAMIR), Kigali, Rwanda 1995; retd from army with rank of Lt-Col; co-f. Ethiopian Information Network Security Agency (INSA) 2007, Acting Dir 2008–10; mem. House of Peoples' Reps (lower house of parl.) 2010–; fmr Dir Oromia Housing and Urban Devt Office; Minister of Science and Tech. 2015; Deputy Pres., Oromia Region –2018; Prime Minister 2018–; mem. Ethiopian People's Revolutionary Democratic Front (EPRDF) 1991–, mem. Exec. Cttee, Chair. Exec. Cttee 2018–; mem. Oromo People's Democratic Org. (OPDO—changed name to Oromo Democratic Party (ODP) 2018) 1991–, Head of OPDO Secr. 2017–, Chair. ODP 2018–. *Address:* Office of the Prime Minister, POB 1013, Addis Ababa, Ethiopia (office). *Telephone:* (11) 1552044 (office). *Fax:* (11) 1552020 (office). *Website:* www.ethiopia.gov.et (office).

AHMED, Al-Dirdiri Mohamed, LLM; Sudanese lawyer and politician; *Minister of Foreign Affairs;* b. 22 Nov. 1975, En Nahud City, Northern Kordofan State; m.; four c.; ed Univ. of Khartoum, Univ. of London, Oxford Univ.; Prof. of Int. Law, Univ. of Khartoum; served as rapporteur to constitutional amendment comm. that drafted Sudanese constitution 2005; legal rep. of Sudan in border dispute over Abyei at Perm. Court of Arbitration, The Hague 2008–09; fmr Chargé d'affaires, embassy in Nairobi; Amb. and mem. Sudanese Del. during negotiations on South Sudan's right for self-determination; Minister of Foreign Affairs 2018–; currently mem. Nat. Congress Party; fmr Dir Int. Law and Admin. Affairs. *Publication:* African Borders and Secession in International Law. *Address:* Ministry of Foreign Affairs, University St, POB 873, Khartoum, Sudan (office). *Telephone:* (183) 772756 (office). *E-mail:* mfaweb@mofa.gov.sd (office). *Website:* www.mofa.gov.sd (office).

AHMED, Aneesa; Maldivian politician (retd) and organization official; *President, Hope for Women;* b. 29 Sept. 1949, Malé; divorced; one s. one d.; ed studied nursing in India and Australia; staff nurse, Govt Hosp., Malé 1973–77, Sister-in-Charge 1978–80; mem. People's Special Majlis 1979–85, 1993–97, apptd by Pres. 1997–99, mem. People's Majlis for Mulaku Atoll 1999–2009, Leader Parl. Group Dhivehi Rayyithunge Party 2006–09, Deputy Speaker of People's Majlis 2008–09; Under-Sec., Ministry of Foreign Affairs 1980–81; Asst to Exec. Sec., Pres.'s Office 1981–82, Presidential Aide 1982–89, Sr Presidential Aide 1989–92, Dir-Gen. Foreign Relations, Pres.'s Office 1992–98; Deputy Minister of Women's Affairs and Social Security 1998–2002, Minister of Women's Affairs, Family Devt and Social Security 2002–04, of Health 2004–05, of the Pres.'s Office 2005–08; Founder and Pres. Hope for Women (NGO) 2010–; Humphrey Fellow, Pennsylvania State Univ., USA 1985–86; Int. Women of Courage Award, US Dept of State 2012. *Leisure interests:* reading, walking. *Address:* Hope for Women, M. Veyla Villa, Ruvaagu Magu, Malé (office); M Lonuveli, Raiveri Hingun, Malé 20-02, Maldives (home). *Telephone:* 3326566 (home). *E-mail:* hope@hopeforwomen.org.mv (office). *Website:* hopeforwomen.org.mv (office).

AHMED, Azleen; Maldivian politician; Minister of Education –2016, of Home Affairs 2016–18; Pres. Local Govt Authority 2017–, Comm. on State Asset Recovery 2017–; mem. Progressive Party of Maldives. *Address:* c/o Ministry of Home Affairs, Velaanaage Bldg, 10th Floor, Ameer Ahmed Magu, Malé 20-096, Maldives (office).

AHMED, Azzam al-, BA; Palestinian politician; b. 1947, Jenin; m.; three c.; ed Baghdad Univ., Iraq; Head, Gen. Union of Palestinian Students (GUPS) in Iraq 1971–74, Deputy Head GUPS Exec. Cttee 1974–80; Palestine Liberation Org. (PLO) Rep. to Iraq 1979–94; joined Fatah 1989, served in several sr positions, mem. Revolutionary Council 1989; mem. Parl. 1996–; Minister of Public Works 1996–2003, Minister of Telecommunications and IT 2003, Head, Fatah bloc in Palestinian Legis. Council –2007; Deputy Prime Minister March–June 2007; mem. Fatah Cen. Cttee; mem. Exec. Cttee, PLO 2018–. *Address:* c/o Fatah (Harakat at-Tahrir al-Watani al-Filastin—Palestine National Liberation Movement), Gaza, Palestinian Autonomous Areas.

AHMED, Fakhruddin, BA, MA, PhD; Bangladeshi economist and civil servant (retd) and fmr central banker; b. 1 May 1940, Munshiganj, British India; s. of Dr Mohiuddin Ahmed and Firoza Akhter Khatun; m. Neena Ahmed; one s.; ed Dhaka Univ., Williams Coll., USA, Princeton Univ., USA; began career as Lecturer in Econs, Dhaka Univ.; served in Civil Service of Pakistan and in Govt of Bangladesh –1978, lastly as Jt Sec., Econ. Relations Div., Ministry of Finance; several sr positions at World Bank, Washington, DC, USA 1978–2001; Gov. Bangladesh Bank 2001–05; Chair. Palli Karma-Sahayak Foundation (apex fund) 2005–07; Hon. Chief Adviser of Caretaker Govt of Bangladesh, in charge of Cabinet Div., of Ministry of Establishment, of Ministry of Home Affairs and of Election Comm. Secr. 2007–08, Hon. Chief Adviser, in charge of Cabinet Div. of Ministry of Establishment and Ministry of Information 2008–09.

AHMED, Maj. Hafizuddin, BA (Hons), MA; Bangladeshi army officer (retd) and politician; b. 29 Oct. 1944, Lalmohan, Bhola; s. of Dr Azharuddin Ahmed; ed Brojomohun Coll., Barisal, Univ. of Dhaka, Pakistan Mil. Acad., Kakul, Abbottabad; joined Mohammedan Sporting Club (Dhaka) 1964; selected for Nat. Football Team of Pakistan 1967–70; commissioned in Pakistan Army 1968, joined Armoured Corps and was posted to 1 East Bengal Regt, rank of Capt., took part in Bangladesh Liberation War 1970–71, rank of Maj. in Bangladesh Army 1971; entered politics as an ind. cand. from Bhola; mem. Parl. for Bhola-3 1986–; mem. Standing Cttee and Vice-Chair. Bangladesh Jatiyotabadi Dal (Bangladesh Nationalist Party), apptd Sec.-Gen. of faction Oct. 2007; fmr Minister of Water Resources, of Commerce; arrested several times 2011, 2012, 2013. *Publications include:* Gourobangone 2004, Roktebheja Ekattor 2007. *Address:* Bangladesh Jatiyotabadi Dal (Bangladesh Nationalist Party), 28/1 Naya Paltan, VIP Road, Dhaka 1000, Bangladesh (office). *Telephone:* (2) 8351929 (office). *Fax:* (2) 8318678 (office). *E-mail:* bnpbd@e-fsbd.net (office). *Website:* www.bnpbd.org (office).

AHMED, Jameel Yusuf; Pakistani civil servant and business executive; *Chairman, TPL Direct Insurance Ltd;* b. 10 May 1946, Hyderabad Deccan, India; s. of Yusuf Ahmed and of Amina Yusuf; m.; one s. two d.; ed Karachi Polytechnic Inst.; industrialist in paper cone mfg co. 1969; Founder Citizen Police Liaison Cttee (CPLC) Reporting Cell (est. to restore confidence in police service) 1989, Co-Chief CPLC 1990–96, Chief 1996–2003; currently Chair. TPL Direct Insurance Ltd; mem. Bd of Govs Karachi Public Transport and Social Educ. Soc. (KPTC) 1999; mem. Advisory Bd Interior Div., Fed. Ministry of the Interior 2000; Hon. Sec. Bd of Govs Al-Murtaza School Network Charitable Trust 1989, Chair. Steering Cttee Professional Devt Centre, Al-Murtaza 2001–; mem. Steering Cttee NGO Resource Centre, Aga Khan Foundation 2001–; Founder and Trustee Panah Women's Shelter 2001–; fmr Chair. All Pakistan Paper Cone Mfrs Asscn; Dir Asia Crime Prevention Foundation, Japan; mem. Advisory Council, Fellowship Fund for Pakistan, Woodrow Wilson International Centre for Scholars 2004–; Sitara-e-Shujaat 1992, Mulla Asghar Memorial Int. Award for Excellence in Educ. 2002. *Address:* Office of the Chairman, TPL Direct Insurance Ltd, 172-B, 2nd Floor, Najeeb Centre, Block-2, P.E.C.H.S., Karachi (office); 37-L/1, Block-6, PECHS, Karachi, Pakistan (home). *Telephone:* (21) 111000301 (office); (21) 4546428 (home). *E-mail:* juchief@hotmail.com (home). *Website:* tplinsurance.com (office).

AHMED, Khurshid, BA, LLB; Pakistani trade union official; *General Secretary, Pakistan Workers Federation;* b. 13 July 1936, Lahore; s. of Bashid Ahmad Dar and Naseem Ahmed (née Begum); m. Sahaira Nasreen; two s. four d.; active in trade union movt in Pakistan 1956–; Chair. Bukhtiar Memorial Computer Training Centre, Lahore, Faisalabad, Gujranwala and Hyderabad; Vice-Pres. ILO Conf., Geneva 1986; currently Gen. Sec. Pakistan Workers Fed. and Pakistan Wapda Hydroelectric Cen. Labour Union; mem. Pakistan Tripartite Cttee, Pakistan Workers Labour Comm., Nat. Industrial Relations Comm.; Sec. and Trustee Bukhtiar Labour Welfare Trust; Ed. Pak Workers. Pakistan Workers journal; elected mem. ILO Governing Body, Geneva since early 1970s; Rep., Int. Workers Group; Sitara Imtaz of Pakistan. *Publications include:* (in Urdu) Trade Union Struggle in Pakistan, Trade Union Struggle of WAPDA Workers, International Labour Organisation, The Challenge of the 21st Century and the Role of the Working Class of Pakistan, Socio-Economic Problems Facing the Working Class of the Country, Responsibility of the Labour Movement of Pakistan; (in English) Dignity of Labour, Journalism on Labour Issues, History of Labour Movement in Pakistan; regular contrib. to nat. press on current labour issues. *Address:* Sadiq Colony, Mumtaz Street, Ghari Shau, Lahore, Pakistan (home). *Telephone:* (42) 6363097 (home). *E-mail:* gs@pwf.org.pk (office). *Website:* www.pwf.org.pk (office).

AHMED, Mahmud Yayale, MA, BA; Nigerian civil servant and government official; b. 15 April 1952, Shira, Bauchi State; s. of Mallam Ahmadu; m.; seven c.; ed Ahmadu Bello Univ., Zaria; began his civil service career in Bauchi State 1977; served as Vice-Prin., Makurdi community secondary school; Deputy Sec., Ministry of Animal Health and Forestry Resources 1982–83; Acting Perm. Sec., Ministry of Rural Devt and Cooperatives 1983–84; based at Ministry of Finance and Econ. Planning 1984–86; joined Fed. Civil Service 1986, served in various posts including Admin. Officer I, Sec. CIPBS, Dir Finance and Accounts, Perm. Sec. and Head of Service of the Fed. 2000–07; Minister of Defence 2007–08; Sec. to the Govt of the Fed. 2008–; Chair. Bd Jos Electricity Distribution Co. 2013–, Industrial and General Insurance PLC 2016– (Dir 2014–); Ind. Dir Erin Energy Corpn 2017–; fmr mem. Council, Bauchi Coll. of Arts and Science, Coll. of Educ., Azare, Coll. of Legal and Islamic Studies, Misau; Ajiyan Katagum, Akowonio of Idanre Kingdom; Hon. LLD (Abuja), (Fed. Univ. of Tech.), Hon. DLit (Bayero Univ., Kano), (Univ. of Benin), (Univ. of Usmanu Danfodiyo Univ.), Dr hc (Novena Univ.), (Igbinedion Univ.). *Address:* c/o Office of the Head of State, New Federal Secretariat Complex, Shehu Shagari Way, Central Area District, Abuja, Nigeria (office). *Telephone:* (9) 5233536 (office). *Website:* www.statehouse.gov.ng (office).

AHMED, Gen. Moeen Uddin; Bangladeshi army officer (retd); b. 21 Jan. 1953, Chittagong; m. Begum Naznin Moeen; one s. one d.; ed Defence Services Command and Staff Coll., Mirpur, US Army Command and Staff Coll., Harvard Univ., Centre for Security Studies of Hawaii, USA; began mil. service 1975, fmr positions include Weapons Training Officer, Platoon Commdr Bangladesh Mil. Acad., Brigade Maj., Infantry Brigade, Grade One Staff Officer, Mil. Operations Directorate, Army HQ, Col Infantry Div., Directing Staff Defence Services Command and Staff Coll., Sr Instructor Army Wing, later Chief Instructor, Commdt School of Infantry and Tactics, Mil. Sec. and Master Gen. of Ordnance, Army HQ, rank of Lt-Gen. 2005, Chief of Army Staff 2005–09, rank of Gen.; fmr Defence Adviser, High Comm. in Pakistan; served with UN Assistance Mission for Rwanda (UNAMIR); Force Commdr's Commendation, US Forces Commendation.

AHMED, Mohamed Jameel, PhD; Maldivian lawyer and politician; b. 13 Oct. 1969, Fuvamulah; m. Haulath Faheem; three c.; ed School of Oriental and African Studies, Univ. of London, UK, Int. Islamic Univ., Malaysia; Minister of Justice 2005–07, of Civil Aviation and Telecommunications 2008–09, of Home Affairs 2012–13; running mate of Progressive Party of Maldives presidential cand. Abdullah Yameen 2013; Vice-Pres. of the Maldives 2013–15; Founder-mem. New Maldives Group; Sr mem. Japan Int. Co-operation Agency Alumni Soc., Maldives. *Address:* Progressive Party of Maldives, Henveiru, Thema, Malé, Maldives (office). *Telephone:* 3303838 (office). *Fax:* 3330524 (office). *E-mail:* info@ppm.mv (office). *Website:* www.ppm.mv (office).

AHMED, Adm. Mohammad Nizamuddin; Bangladeshi naval officer; *Chief of Naval Staff;* b. 1960, Madaripur; s. of M. A. Rashid and Fazilatunnesa Ahmed; m. Nazmun Nahar; two s.; ed Madaripur Nazimuddin Govt Coll., Marshal Tito Naval Acad., Yugoslavia; joined Navy 1979, served at Naval HQ in various positions, including Dir Personnel Services, Naval HQ, Sec. to Navy Chief, Instructor, Naval Acad. and TAS School, Dir of Operations, Coast Guard HQ, Deputy Pres. ISSB, Commdr, Chittagong Naval Command, apptd Chair. Chittagong Port Authority 2012, Patuakhali Payra Port Authority 2013, Chief of Naval Staff 2016–; Osamanyo Sheba Padak, Shadhinota Padak 2016, Bangladesh Coast Guard Medal. *Address:* Naval Headquarters, Banani, Dhaka 1213, Bangladesh (office). *Telephone:* (2) 9836141 (office). *Fax:* (2) 9836270 (office). *E-mail:* info@navy.mil.bd (office). *Website:* www.navy.mil.bd (office).

AHMED, Moudud, MA; Bangladeshi barrister and politician; b. 24 May 1940, Noakhali, Bengal Presidency, British India; s. of Bara Moulana; m. Hasna Jasimuddin; two s.; ed Dhaka Univ.; fmr Gen. Sec. East Pakistan House, UK; took active part in struggle for independence, organizing External Publicity Div. of Bangladesh Govt in exile; Ed. Bangladesh (weekly); lawyer, Bangladesh Supreme Court 1972–74; Gen. Sec. Cttee for Civil Liberties Legal Aid 1974; imprisoned during State of Emergency 1974; Head, Bangladesh del. to 32nd Session UN Gen. Ass. 1977; Adviser to Pres. 1977; mem. Bangladesh Nationalist Party 1978–84, 1996–, Jatiya Party 1984–96; Minister of Communications 1985–86, Deputy Prime Minister in charge of Ministry of Industries 1986–88, Prime Minister and Minister of Industry 1988–89, Vice-Pres. 1989–90; under house arrest 1990–91, imprisoned Dec. 1991, later released; Minister of Law, Justice and Parl. Affairs 2001–06; Visiting Prof., Elliott School of Int. Affairs, George Washington Univ. 1997; Visiting Fellow, South Asian Inst. of Heidelberg Univ., Harvard Univ. Centre for Int. Affairs, Univ. of Oxford, UK; mem. Elliott School Int. Council. *Publications include:* Chaloman Itihas; Bangladesh Contemporary Events and Documents, Bangladesh Constitutional Quest for Autonomy 1979, Bangladesh: Era of Sheikh Mujibur Rahman 1983, Democracy and the Challenge of Development: A Study of Politics and Military Interventions in Bangladesh 1995, South Asia: Crisis of Development – The Case of Bangladesh 2003, Shongshod-e Ja Bolechhi 2006, Emergency and the Aftermath: 2007–2008 2014. *Address:* Islam Chamber, 9th floor, 125/A, Motijheel C/A, Dhaka 1000, Bangladesh (office). *Telephone:* (2) 9888694 (home).

AHMED, Naseer, MA; Maldivian banking executive and economist; *Governor, Maldives Monetary Authority;* b. 31 Oct. 1975, Malé; ed Curtin Univ., Australia, Williams Coll., USA; part-time lecturer, Maldives Nat. Univ. 2005–06; Man. Maldives Monetary Authority 2008–11, Gov. 2017–; State Minister, Ministry of Finance April–Dec. 2011, Public Financial Man. Consultant 2016–17; Man. Dir White Shell 2010–15; CEO Capital Market Devt Authority 2015–16. *Address:* Majeedhee Bldg, Boduthakurufaanu Magu, Malé 20-182, Maldives (office). *Telephone:* 3314940 (office). *Fax:* 3323862 (office). *E-mail:* mail@mma.gov.mv (office). *Website:* www.mma.gov.mv (office).

AHMED, Salahuddin, BSc, MA, LLM; Bangladeshi lawyer and government official; b. 8 Feb. 1948, Dhaka; ed London School of Econs, UK, Dhaka Univ., Colombia Univ., USA; Asst Prof., Dept of Econs, Dhaka Univ. 1971–77, Asst Prof., Inst. of Business Admin 1980–83; began practising law 1980, lawyer at High Court 1982–2008; Assoc. Counsel, Dr Kamal Hossain & Assocs (law firm), Dhaka –2008; Additional Attorney-Gen. 2007–08, Attorney-Gen. 2008–09 (resgnd); mem. Supreme Court Bar Asscn, Human Rights Bangladesh, South Asian Asscn for Regional Co-operation in Law, Bangladesh Chapter, Governing Council of South Asian Inst. of Advanced Legal and Human Rights Studies. *Address:* c/o South Asian Institute of Advanced Legal and Human Rights Studies, House No. 55 (Ground Floor), Road No. 5, Dhanmondi Residential Area, Dhaka 1205, Bangladesh. *Telephone:* (2) 9613603. *E-mail:* info@sails-law.org. *Website:* www.sails-law.org.

AHMED, Salehuddin, MA, PhD; Bangladeshi central banker (retd) and academic; *Professor, Business School, BRAC University;* b. 1 Jan. 1949; m. Parveen Ahmed; one s. one d.; ed Dhaka Univ., McMaster Univ., Canada; Lecturer in Econs, Dhaka Univ. 1970; joined civil service and served in various admin. capacities, including in Centre on Integrated Rural Devt for Asia and the Pacific, Dhaka; fmr Dir-Gen. Bangladesh Acad. for Rural Devt, Comilla, Non-Governmental Org. Affairs Bureau of Office of the Prime Minister; Man. Dir Palli Karma Sahayak Foundation (apex funding agency of macro-credit operations in Bangladesh) 1996–2005; Gov. and Chair. Bangladesh Bank (cen. bank) 2005–09; mem. Rating Cttee Credit Rating Agency of Bangladesh Ltd (CRAB); Prof., Business School, North South Univ. 2009–14, BRAC Univ. 2014–; Distinguished Alumni Award, McMaster Univ. 2006. *Publications:* more than 38 books and 92 reports and journal articles. *Leisure interests:* listening to music, watching TV movies, travelling. *Address:* BRAC University Business School, Room UB 20603, Building 2, 66, Mohakhli, Dhaka 1212 (office); Apartment 4, Silicon Point, Plot 311, Road 10, Block D, Bashundhara Residential Area, Dhaka 1212, Bangladesh (home). *Telephone:* (2) 9844051 (Ext. 4058) (office); (2) 55037340 (home). *E-mail:* asalehuddin@bracu.ac.bd (office); asalehuddin@gmail.com. *Website:* www.bracu.ac.bd (office).

AHMED, Shahabuddin, BA, MA; Bangladeshi judge and fmr head of state; b. 1 Feb. 1930, Pemai of Kendua, Greater Mymensingh Dist; s. of Talukder Risat A. Bhuiyan (deceased); m. Anowara Begum; two s. three d.; ed Dhaka Univ., Lahore Civil Service Acad., Univ. of Oxford, UK; joined Civil Service of Pakistan 1954 as Sub-Div. Officer, later Additional Deputy Commr; transferred to Judicial Br. 1960; fmr Additional Dist and Sessions Judge, Dhaka and Barisal; fmr Dist and Sessions Judge, Comilla and Chittagong; fmr Registrar High Court of E Pakistan; elevated to High Court Bench 1972; apptd Judge of Appellate Div., Supreme Court of Bangladesh 1980; Chief Justice 1990, 1991–95; Chair. Labour Appellate Tribunal 1973–74, Bangladesh Red Cross Soc. 1978–82, Comm. of Inquiry into police shootings of students 1983, Nat. Pay Comm. 1984; Vice-Pres. League of Red Cross and Red Crescent Soc., Geneva, Switzerland; Acting Pres. of Bangladesh 1990–91, Pres. 1996–2001; Hon. Master, Hon. Soc. of Gray's Inn, London.

AHMED, Sheikh Sharif Sheikh; Somali politician and fmr head of state; b. 25 July 1964, Middle Shabelle region; m.; two c.; ed Sheikh Sufi Inst., Kordufan Univ., Sudan, Open Univ., Libya; fmr teacher, Juba Secondary School, Mogadishu; elected to head local court in Jowhar 2002, Head of Islamic Courts Union 2002–06; fled to Kenya 2007, returned under UN peace agreements with transitional government 2008; Chair. Alliance for the Re-liberation of Somalia –2009; Pres. of Somalia 2009–12; cand. in presidential election 2017.

AHMED, Sufyan, BA, MSc; Ethiopian government official; b. 1 May 1958, Eastern Hararghe; m.; one d.; ed Addis Ababa Univ.; Coll. Instructor, Jimma Coll. of Agric. and Addis Ababa Univ. 1983–93; d Head of Trade Bureau, Oromiya State 1993; Commr, Ethiopian Customs Authority 1993–95; Minister of Finance 1995–2001, Minister of Finance and Econ. Devt 2001–15; mem. Bd of Govs African Development Bank, Eastern and Southern African Trade and Development Bank (PTA Bank) 2013–; mem. Oromo People's Democratic Org. (OPDO).

AHMED, Air Chief Marshal (retd) Tanvir Mehmood, MSc; Pakistani air force officer (retd); b. 1 Feb. 1952; m.; four c.; ed Pakistan Air Force (PAF) Public School, Sargodha, PAF Acad., Risalpur, Turkish Air War Coll. and Nat. Defence Coll.,

Islamabad; joined Pakistan Air Force (PAF) and took fighter and operational conversion courses, qualified flying instructor and combat commdr on fighter aircraft, commanded Fighter Squadron, F-16s Flg Wing, PAF Base, Sargodha and PAF Acad., Risalpur, Deputy Dir in Operations Br., Personal Staff Officer to two Air Chiefs, Dir F-16 project, Sr Air Staff Officer at Northern Air Command, Peshawar and Dir-Gen. Air Weapons Complex, Wah, served as Deputy Chief Air Staff Admin and Operations; served in UAE Air Force as fighter instructor pilot; Vice-Chief of Air Staff 2003–06, Chief of Air Staff 2006–09; Sitara-i-Basalat, Sitara-i-Imtiaz (Mil.), Hilal-i-Imtiaz (Mil.), Nishan-e-Imtiaz (Mil.).

AHMED, Vice-Adm. (retd) Zahir Uddin; Bangladeshi naval officer (retd); *Chairman, Western Maritime Academy;* b. 1957, Kapasia upazilla under Gazipur Dist; s. of Shafiuddin Ahmed; m. Shabnam Ahmed; one s. one d.; ed Britannia Royal Naval Coll., Dartmouth, UK, various univ. courses in The Netherlands, Pakistan, China and USA, Defence Services Command and Staff Coll., Dhaka, US Naval War Coll., Newport, RI (class valedictorian), Nat. Defence Coll., Mirpur; joined Bangladesh Navy (BN) as an Officer Cadet 1976; mem. pioneer batch of BN; completed specialization in Navigation and Direction (ND) from Pakistan; first CO frigate BNS Bangabandhu; also commanded BN frigates BNS Umar Farooq, BNS Abu Bakar; served as Cdre Commdg BN Flotilla (COMBAN) and as Cdre Commdg Chittagong (COMCHIT) to command BN Fleet and Chittagong Area Command, respectively; performed duty of Commdt Bangladesh Marine Acad. and Dir Gen. Bangladesh Coast Guard; Chief of the Naval Staff 2009–13; Chair. Western Maritime Acad. 2014–; promoted to rank of Vice-Adm. 2009; Chief of the Naval Staff Commendation. *Address:* Western Maritime Academy, Uttara, Dhaka 1207, Bangladesh. *Telephone:* (2) 8963534 (office). *E-mail:* info@wma-bd.com (office). *Website:* www.wma-bd.com (office).

AHMED, Zainab, BSc, MBA; Nigerian politician and accountant; *Minister of Finance;* b. 16 June 1960; ed Ahmadu Bello Univ., Ogun State Univ., Queen Amina Coll.; fmr Audit Trainee Egunjobi Suleiman & Co. Chartered Accountants; Accountant II Ministry of Finance, Kaduna State Govt 1982–84, Accountant I 1984; joined Nigerian Telecommunications Ltd (NITEL) 1985, first apptd Sr Officer (Finance), later promoted to Deputy Gen. Man. (Corporate Treasury) –2002; Acting Chief Finance Officer, Nigerian Mobile Telecommunications Ltd (MTEL) 2002–09; Man. Dir Kaduna Industrial and Finance Co. Ltd (KIFC) 2009–10; Exec. Sec., Nigeria Extractive Industries Transparency Initiative (NEITI) 2010–18, mem. Bd of Dirs –2018; Minister of State, Budget and Nat. Planning 2015–18; Minister of Finance 2018–; mem., Chartered Inst. of Man. Taxation, Nigerian Inst. of Man.; Fellow, Asscn of Nat. Accountants of Nigeria, Inst. of Company and Commercial Accountants. *Address:* Federal Ministry of Finance, Central Business District, Ahmadu Bello Way, Central Area, PMB 14, Garki, Abuja Nigeria (office). *Telephone:* (9) 2346290 (office).

AHMETAJ, Arben, PhD; Albanian politician; b. 28 June 1969, Gjirokastër; m. Albina Mançka; two d.; ed Univ. of Tirana, Univ. of Bucharest, Romania, Univ. of Kentucky, USA; fmr Lecturer, Univ. of Tirana; fmr Fiscal Affairs Adviser, American Bank of Albania; several roles within Ministry of Finance, Dir-Gen., Gen. Directorate of Taxes, Adviser to the Minister of Finance 1992–93, Chief of Cabinet, Ministry of Finance 1997–98; Deputy Minister for European Integration 2004–05; Deputy Minister of Energy and Industry 2003–05; Minister of Finance 2016–May 2017, Aug. 2017–Dec. 2018; mem. Kuvendi Popullor (Parl.) for Korca 2009–, mem. Econ. and Financial Cttee; mem. Partia Socialiste e Shqipërisë (Socialist Party of Albania). *Address:* c/o Ministry of Finance, Bulevardi Dëshmorët e Kombit 3, 1010 Tirana, Albania.

AHMETAJ, Mimoza; Kosovo diplomatist, politician and fmr dentist; b. 1 Oct. 1971; m. Ferid Koçani; three c.; ed Univ. Clinical Dentistry Centre of Kosovo, Prishtina; medical doctor of dentistry, specializing in orthodontics; worked at Council for the Defence of Human Rights 1993–98; worked at Office of Special Rep. of Sec.-Gen. at UN Interim Admin Mission in Kosovo (UNMIK) 1999–2001; mem. Kosovo Ass. (Parl.) as mem. of Partia Demokratike e Kosovës (PDK—Democratic Party of Kosovo) 2007–10; Adviser to Prime Minister Hashim Thaçi during his premiership 2008–14; Amb. to Slovenia 2012–13, to Belgium (also accred to EU, NATO and Luxembourg) 2014–16; Minister of European Integration 2017.

AHMETI, Ali, (Abaz Gjuka); Macedonian politician and educator; *Chairman, Bashkimi Demokratik për Integrim / Demokratska Unija za Integracija (BDI—Democratic Union for Integration);* b. 4 Jan. 1959, Zajas, Kičevo municipality, Socialist Repub. of Macedonia, Socialist Fed. Repub. of Yugoslavia; m.; one s. one d.; ed Univ. of Prishtina, Kosovo; political activist as student; imprisoned for taking part in demonstrations by Kosovo Albanians 1981; gained political support from Nat. Movt for the Liberation of Kosovo, elected mem. Council 1986; granted asylum in Switzerland 1986; active in dissident People's Movt of Kosovo throughout 1980s; one of leaders of student and miners protests against Milosevic Govt 1988–89; elected mem. of leadership of Nat. Movt of Kosovo 1988, re-elected 1993; one of main organizers of protests of the Albanian diaspora in Europe 1989–90; lived in Switzerland 1993–2001; Founding mem. Ushtria Çlirimtare e Kosovës (UÇK—Kosovo Liberation Army) 1996, elected mem. of main HQ of UÇK 1998; elected Supreme Commdr and Rep. of Ushtria Çlirimtare e Kombëtare (UÇK—M—Nat. Liberation Army) 2001, placed on list of people unwelcome in USA because of terrorist activities and proclaimed persona non grata in Switzerland and other countries June 2001; following signing of Ohrid Agreement in Aug. 2001 and decomposition of UÇK—M in Sept. 2001, was engaged in political process of implementation of this Agreement; named as leader of Co-ordination Council which unified all Albanian political parties in Macedonia, and the former structures of UÇK—M; Co-founder Bashkimi Demokratik për Integrim/Demokratska Unija za Integracija (BDI—Democratic Union for Integration) 1999, Chair. 2002–; elected mem. Parl. 2002; formed multi-ethnic coalition Govt with Za Makedonija Zaedno (Together for Macedonia) coalition 2002–06, and as part of coalition led by Vnatrešno-Makedonska Revolucionerna Organizacija-Demokratska Partija za Makedonsko Nacionalno Edinstvo (Internal Macedonian Revolutionary Org.-Democratic Party for Macedonian Nat. Unity) 2008–. *Address:* Bashkimi Demokratik për Integrim, 1200 Tetova, Reçicë e vogël, Rruga 170 No. 2 (office); Assembly (Sobranie), 1000 Skopje, Stojan Andov, 11 Oktomvri bb, North Macedonia (office). *Telephone:* (4) 4334398 (office). *Fax:* (4) 4334397 (office). *E-mail:* cabinet@bdi.mk (office). *Website:* www.bdi.mk (office).

AHMETI, Shpend, MPA; Kosovo politician; *Mayor of Prishtina;* b. 18 April 1978, Prishtina, Socialist Autonomous Province of Kosovo, Socialist Repub. of Serbia, Socialist Fed. Repub. of Yugoslavia; m. Ardiana Gjinolli; two c.; ed American Univ. in Bulgaria, Blagoevgrad, Harvard Univ. Kennedy School of Govt, USA; senator, then Pres. Student Govt, American Univ. in Bulgaria 1999–2002; worked for World Bank on Kosovo's Public Expenditure Review, and for EBRD; Founder and fmr Exec. Dir GAP Inst. of Advanced Studies; fmr Leader, Frymë e Re (New Spirit Party), merged into Vetëvendosje!—Self-Determination!), Vice-Chair. Vetëvendosje! —2018; Prof. of Public Policy and Int. Econ. Policy, American Univ. in Kosovo 2005–14; Mayor of Prishtina 2014–; mem. and Chair. Partia Social Demokrate e Kosovës (PSD—Social Democratic Party of Kosovo) 2018–; several awards, including World Bank Spot Award and one from European Debating Championships. *Address:* Prishtina (Prishtinë)/Priština Municipality Administration, Rruga UÇK 2, 10000 Prishtina (office); Partia Socialdemokrate e Kosovës, 10000 Prishtina, Rruga Gustav Meyer 1, Kosovo (office). *Telephone:* (38) 234944 (Municipality) (office); (38) 225645 (PSD) (office). *E-mail:* info@prishtina-komuna.org (office); info@psd-ks.org (office). *Website:* kk.rks-gov.net/prishtine (office).

AHN, Chong-ghee, BA, MA; South Korean diplomatist; *Ambassador to Belgium, Luxembourg and the European Union;* b. 21 Jan. 1957; m.; one s.; ed Seoul Nat. Univ., Georgetown Univ., USA; joined Ministry of Foreign Affairs 1982, Second Sec., Embassy in Washington, DC 1991–93, First Sec., Embassy in La Paz, Bolivia 1993–96, Aide to the Vice-Minister of Foreign Affairs 1996–98, Counsellor, Perm. Mission to UN Office and other Int. Orgs, Geneva 1998–2002, Dir for Admin. Man. and Legal Affairs, Ministry of Foreign Affairs and Trade Jan.–Dec. 2002, Dir WTO Div., Multilateral Trade Bureau Dec. 2002–04, Counsellor, Embassy in Washington, DC 2004–07, Deputy Dir-Gen., Bilateral Trade Bureau, Ministry of Foreign Affairs and Trade 2007–08, Dir-Gen. 2008–11, Consul-Gen. in Shanghai 2011–13, Deputy Minister for Econ. Affairs, Ministry of Foreign Affairs 2013–15, Amb. to Belgium (also accred to Luxembourg and to Perm. Mission to EU, Brussels) 2015–; Order of Service Merit (Red Stripes) 2009. *Address:* Mission of Republic of Korea to the European Union, Chaussée de la Hulpe 173–175, 1170 Brussels (Watermael-Boitsfort), Belgium (office). *Telephone:* (2) 675-57-77 (office). *Fax:* (2) 675-52-21 (office). *E-mail:* eukorea@mofa.go.kr (office). *Website:* bel.mofa.go.kr (office).

AHN, Choong-yong, BA, MA, PhD; South Korean economist and academic; *Chaired Professor, Graduate School of International Studies, Chung-Ang University;* ed Kyung-Pook Nat. Univ., Univ. of Hawaii and Ohio State Univ., USA; Prof. of Econs, Chung-Ang Univ. 1974–2006, Distinguished Prof., Grad. School of Int. Studies 2006–09, Chaired Prof. 2009–; consultant to World Bank 1978–88, also adviser to Fed. of Korean Industries 1980 and Bank of Korea 1984–87; UNIDO Chief Tech. Adviser to Govt of Malaysia 1990–93; Chair. Chohung Bank 1999–2002; Chair. APEC Econ. Cttee 2002–05; Chair. Korean Nat. Cttee for Pacific Econ. Co-operation (KOPEC) 2001; Pres. Korea Inst. for Int. Econ. Policy 2002–05; apptd Foreign Investment Ombudsman, Korea Trade-Investment Promotion Agency (KOTRA) 2006; mem. Presidential Econ. Advisory Council 2002–05, Presidential Council on Nat. Competitiveness 2008–, Regulatory Reform Cttee 2009–10 (Chair. 2010–); mem. Editorial Bd Global Asia (journal); Pres. Korea Econometric Soc. 1991–93, Korea Int. Econs Asscn 1994–95, Devt Econs Asscn 1997–98, Asscn of Trade and Industry Studies 2000–01; mem. Bd of Dirs Korea Electric Power Corpn 2014–; Hon. Gov. Gangwon Prov. 2014–; Economist of the Year, Maeil Business Newspaper 1984, Okita Saburo Policy Research Award, Nat. Inst. of Research Investment of Japan 2000, Academic Excellence Award, Chung-Ang Univ. 2001, Free Economy Publication Award, Fed. of Korean Industries 2002. *Publications include:* India-Korea Dialogue for A 21st Century Partnership (co-ed.) 2012; numerous articles and newspapers in journals. *Address:* Graduate School of International Studies, 84, Heukseok-Ro, Dongjak-Gu, Seoul 156-756, Republic of Korea (office). *Telephone:* (2) 820-5624 (office). *E-mail:* cyahn@cau.ac.kr (office). *Website:* ggs.cau.ac.kr (office).

AHN, Ho-young; South Korean diplomatist, government official and academic; b. 5 July 1956; m.; two s.; ed Seoul Nat. Univ., Grad. School of Georgetown Univ., Washington, DC, USA; joined Ministry of Foreign Affairs 1978, Second Sec., Embassy in New Delhi 1984–90, First Sec., Embassy in Washington, DC 1990–93, Dir Treaties Div. II, Treaties Bureau, Ministry of Foreign Affairs 1993–94, Dir Int. Trade Div. III, Int. Trade Bureau 1994–96, Counsellor for Korean Del. to OECD, Paris 1996–98, Counsellor for Korean Perm. Del. to WTO, Geneva 1998–2002, Dir Int. Trade Law Div., Office of the Minister for Trade 2002–03, Dir-Gen. Multilateral Trade Bureau, Ministry of Foreign Affairs and Trade (MOFAT) 2003–04; Dir-Gen. Econ. Co-operation Bureau, Ministry of Finance and Economy 2004–06; Adjunct Prof. of Law and Diplomacy, Korea Univ. 2006–08; Deputy Minister for Trade, MOFAT 2008–11, also Pres.'s Sherpa for G-20 and G8 outreach meetings, Amb. to Belgium and Head of Korean Mission to EU, Brussels 2011–12, First Vice-Minister of Foreign Affairs and Trade 2012–13, Amb. to USA 2013–17; Yeongsan Diplomat Award 2018.

AHN, Hyun-soo, (Viktor Ahn); Russian (b. South Korean) short-track speed skater; b. 23 Nov. 1985, Seoul; ed Korea Nat. Sport Univ.; began speed skating at Myungji Elementary School aged eight; debut for S Korea, Olympic Games, Salt Lake City, USA 2002; bronze medal, 500m, World Championships, Beijing 2005; silver medal, 1000m and Overall, World Championships, Montreal 2002, 1000m, Warsaw 2003, 1000m and 5000m Relay, Beijing 2005; gold medal, 5000m Relay, World Championships, Montreal 2002, 1500m, 5000m Relay and Overall 2003, 1000m, 1500m, 5000m Relay and Overall, World Championships, Gothenburg 2004, 1500m and Overall, World Championships, Beijing 2005, 1000m, 1500m, World Championships, Minneapolis 2006; World Cup ranking: third, 500m and 1000m 2002/03, second, 1500m 2002/03, 500m 2003/05, 1000m and 1500m 2004/05, 1000m 2005/06, first, 1000m and 1500m 2003/04, 500m and 1500m 2005/06, third, Overall 2004/05, second, Overall 2002/03, first, Overall 2003/04, 2005/06; bronze medal, 500m, Olympic Games, Turin 2006; gold medal, 1000m, 1500m and 5000m relay, Olympic Games, Turin 2006; Russian citizenship 2011, now competes for Russia; gold medal, 500m, 1000m, 5000m relay, Olympic Games, Sochi 2014, bronze medal, 1500m; became short-track speed skater with the most Olympic medals (8), tied with Apolo Anton Ohno, and short-track speed skater with the most Olympic Gold medals (6); now coaches short track for Russian team. *Leisure interest:* watching movies. *Address:* c/o Russian Skating Union, Moscow 119991,

Luzhnetskaya nab. 8, Office 230, Russian Federation. *Telephone:* (495) 725-46-76. *Fax:* (495) 637-02-37. *E-mail:* info@russkating.ru. *Website:* www.russkating.ru.

AHO, Esko Tapani, MScS; Finnish business executive and fmr politician; b. 20 May 1954, Veteli; s. of Kauko Kaleva Aho and Laura Kyllikki (née Harjupatana) Aho; m. Kirsti Hannele Söderkultalahti 1980; two s. one d.; ed Univ. of Helsinki; Chair. Youth Org. of the Centre Party 1974–80, Chair. Finnish Centre Party (KESK) 1990–2002; Political Sec. to Minister of Foreign Affairs 1979–80; Trade Agent, Kannus 1980; mem. Parl. 1983–2003; Prime Minister of Finland 1991–95; unsuccessful cand. for Pres. of Finland 2000; Lecturer, Harvard Univ., USA 2000, Sr Fellow Mossavar-Rahmani Center for Business and Govt, Harvard Kennedy School 2012–14; Pres. Finnish Nat. Fund for Research and Devt (SITRA) 2004–08; Exec. Vice-Pres. of Corp. Relations and Responsibility, Nokia Corpn 2008–12, mem. Exec. Bd 2009–12; Vice-Chair. Tech. Industries of Finland 2009, Liberal Int. 1994–2002, Finnish Olympic Cttee 1997–2000; Chair. Finnish Ski Asscn 1996–2000; mem. Bd of Dirs Fortum Corpn 2006, Russian Venture Co. 2007; mem. Club de Madrid, Science and Tech. in Soc. Forum, InterAction Council, Fondation Sophia Antipolis. *Leisure interests:* literature, tennis, theatre.

AHOOMEY-ZUNU, Arthème Kwesi Séléagodji, LLM; Togolese lawyer and politician; b. 1 Dec. 1958, Lomé; Admin. Sec., Nat. Comm. on Human Rights 1988–94; mem. Assemblée Nat. (Parl.), mem. Comm. on Human Rights 1994–99; mem. Ind. Nat. Electoral Comm. 1993–2005, Pres. 2000–02; Minister of Territorial Admin 2006–07; Sec.-Gen., Presidency of the Repub. 2008–12; Minister of Trade and Pvt. Sector Promotion 2011–12; Prime Minister 2012–15; Founder-mem. Convergence Patriotique Panafricaine. *Address:* Union pour la République, 572 rue Pydal Tokoin Wuiti, BP 1208, Lomé, Togo (office). *Telephone:* 22-26-04-95 (office). *Fax:* 22-61-00-33 (office). *E-mail:* rpttogo@yahoo.fr (office). *Website:* www.unir-le-togo.com (office).

AHOUSSOU-KOUADIO, Jeannot, LLM, MBA; Côte d'Ivoirian lawyer and politician; *Minister of State in the Office of the President;* b. 6 March 1951, Raviart, Tie-N'Diekro Dist; m.; six c.; ed Abidjan Univ., Rennes Univ., France; Bureau mem. Mouvement des Etudiants et Elèves de Côte d'Ivoire (MEECI), Lycée Classique de Bouaké 1970, MEECI Faculty of Law 1975–77; Pres. Asscn des Elèves et Etudiants, Didievi 1975–77; Consultant and Trainer, Nat. Inst. of Perm. Devt (INPP) 1979–80; mem. Bar, Abidjan 1981–; Municipal Councillor, Didievi 1985–90; Deputy Mayor, Attécoubé 1990–95; Councillor, city of Abidjan 1995–2000; mem. Econ. and Social Council of Côte d'Ivoire 1999; mem. Assemblée Nationale (Parl.) for Didievi/Tie-N'Diekro constituency 2000–; Minister of Industry and the Private Sector 2002–05; campaign dir for Henri Konan Bédié during first round of 2010 presidential election, and for Alassane Ouattara during second round; Pres. Asscn of Deputies and Execs of Grand Centre, PDCI (Democratic Party of Côte d'Ivoire) 2010; Minister of State, Keeper of the Seals and Minister of Justice 2010–12, Prime Minister March–Nov. 2012, Minister of State in the Office of the Pres. 2013–; Chair. Regional Council of the region of the Aries 2013; Pres. Ass. of Regions and Districts of Côte d'Ivoire 2013; mem. Parti démocratique de la Côte d'Ivoire—Rassemblement démocratique africain (PDCI—RDA), mem. Political Bureau and Deputy Sec.-Gen. for Legal Affairs, Vice-Pres. PDCI 2014; Grand Officer de l'rdre nat. *Leisure interests:* reading, travelling. *Address:* Office of the President, 01 BP 1366, Abidjan 01, Côte d'Ivoire (office). *Telephone:* 22-47-74-47 (office). *Fax:* 20-21-14-25 (office). *E-mail:* j_ahoussou@yahoo.fr. *Website:* www.cotedivoirepr.ci (office).

AHRENDS, Peter, AADipl, RIBA; British architect (retd); b. 30 April 1933, Berlin, Germany; s. of Steffen Bruno Ahrends and Margarete Marie Sophie Ahrends (née Visino); m. Elizabeth Robertson 1954; two d.; ed King Edward VII School, Johannesburg, Architectural Asscn, London; research into decoration in Islamic Architecture 1956; Visiting Critic and/or External Examiner Kumasi Univ., Architectural Asscn School of Architecture, Nova Scotia Tech. Univ., Univ. of Strathclyde; with Steffen Ahrends & Partners, Johannesburg 1957–58; with Denys Lasdun & Partners 1959–60; with Julian Keable & Partners; teacher, Architectural Asscn School of Architecture 1960–61; f. Ahrends, Burton and Koralek Architects 1961, Partner and Dir 1961–2009 (retd); Visiting Prof., Kingston Polytechnic 1983–84; teacher and conducted workshops Architectural Asscn School of Architecture, Canterbury Art School, Univ. of Edinburgh, Winter School, Edinburgh, Plymouth Polytechnic, Plymouth Art School; Prof., Bartlett School of Architecture and Planning, Univ. Coll. London 1986–89; mem. RIBA, Design Council; Chair. UK Architects Against Apartheid 1988–93; Design Adviser, London Devt Agency; RIBA Good Design in Housing Award 1977, RIBA Architecture Award 1978, 1993, 1996, 1999, Structural Steel Design Award 1980, Structural Steel Design Commendation 1993; RIAI Architecture Award 1999, Gulbenkian Museum of the Year Award 1999, Designs on Democracy Competition Winner. *Publications include:* Ahrends, Burton & Koralek, Architects (monograph) 1991; collaborations: The Architecture of ABK 2002; numerous articles in professional journals. *Leisure interests:* architecture and architecture-related interests. *Address:* c/o ABK Architects Dublin, 34 Lower Leeson Street, Dublin 2, Ireland (office).

AHRENDTS, Angela, DBE, BA; American retail executive; b. 12 June 1960, New Palestine, Ind.; d. of Richard Ahrendts and Jean Ahrendts; m. Gregg Couch; three c.; ed Ball State Univ., Muncie, Ind.; Pres. Donna Karan International 1989–96; Exec. Vice-Pres. Henri Bendel 1996–98; Vice-Pres. Merchandising and Design, Liz Claiborne Inc. 1998–99, Sr Vice-Pres. Corp. Merchandising and Group Pres. for Modern Brands 1999–2002, Exec. Vice-Pres. 2002–05; Exec. Dir Burberry Group plc 2006–13, CEO 2006–13 (resgnd); Sr Vice-Pres., Retail and Online Stores, Apple, Inc. 2014–19; mem. Business Advisory Group, Prime Minister's Office, UK 2010–16; Hon. Fellow, Shenkar Coll. of Eng and Design 2011; Hon. LHD (Ball State Univ., Muncie, Ind.) 2010; Medal of Honor, St George's Soc. of New York 2011. *Address:* c/o Apple, 1 Infinite Loop, Cupertino, CA 95014, USA.

AHRWEILER, Hélène, DenHist, DèsL; French/Greek university professor and administrator; *Professor Emeritus, University of Paris (Sorbonne);* b. 28 Aug. 1926, Athens, Greece; d. of Nicolas Glykatzi and Calliroe Psaltides; m. Jacques Ahrweiler 1958; one d.; ed Univ. of Athens, Univ. of Paris (Sorbonne); Research Worker CNRS 1955–67, Head of Research 1964–67; apptd Prof., Univ. of Paris (Sorbonne) 1967, now Prof. Emer.; Pres. Univ. de Paris I 1976–81; Rector Acad., Chancellor Univs of Paris 1982–89; Chair. and Pres. Terra Foundation for the Arts, Chicago; Sec.-Gen. Int. Cttee of Historical Sciences 1980–90; Vice-Pres. Conseil d'Orientation du Centre Georges Pompidou 1975–89, Conseil Supérieur de l'Education Nationale 1983–89; Pres. Centre Georges Pompidou 1989–91; Pres. Comité d'Ethique des Sciences, CNRS 1994; Pres. Admin Council, European Cultural Centre of Delphi, Nat. Theatre, Athens; Pres. Asscn Int. Dimitri Chostakovitch; mem. Greek, British, Belgian, German and Bulgarian Acads; Hon. Pres. Asscn of Int. Byzantine Studies; Commdr de la Légion d'honneur, Grand Croix Ordre nat. du Mérite, Commdr des Arts et des Lettres, Officier des Palmes académiques; numerous foreign decorations; Dr hc (London, New York, Belgrade, Harvard, Lima, New Brunswick, Athens Social Science Univ., American Univ. of Paris, Haifa, Thessaloniki, Fribourg, Univ. of Creta). *Publications include:* Byzance et la Mer 1966, Etudes sur les structures administratives et sociales de Byzance 1971, l'Idéologie politique de l'empire byzantin 1975, Byzance: les pays et les territoires 1976, Geographica 1981, The Making of Europe 2000, Les Européens 2001, Why Byzantium 2009, Marathônia and Ethnika 2011; four vols of poetry in Greek; contribs to numerous books. *Leisure interests:* tennis, swimming. *Address:* 28 rue Guynemer, 75006 Paris, France (home). *Telephone:* 1-42-22-98-47 (home). *Fax:* 1-45-44-46-49 (home).

AHSAN, Chaudhry Aitzaz; Pakistani barrister, writer, human rights activist and politician; b. 27 Sept. 1945, Murree, Punjab; ed Aitchison Coll. and Government Coll., Lahore, Univ. of Cambridge, UK; called to the Bar, Gray's Inn, London 1967; came first in Cen. Superior Services examination but refused to join govt service during mil. rule of Gen. Ayub Khan; currently Sr Advocate, Supreme Court; Pres. Supreme Court Bar Asscn; fought cases in defence of Benazir Bhutto 2001 and fmr Prime Minister Nawaz Sharif, successfully represented Chief Justice Iftikhar Mohammad Chaudhry in Supreme Court of Pakistan 2007; began political career 1970s; mem. Pakistan People's Party (PPP); elected to Punjab Ass. and inducted into prov. cabinet, Minister of Information, Planning and Devt 1977 (resgnd); expelled from PPP; became an active leader of Movt for the Restoration of Democracy (MRD) following coup by Gen. Mohammad Zia-ul-Haq, rejoined PPP during martial law period, jailed several times as political prisoner without trial for active participation in MRD movt; mem. Nat. Ass. from Lahore (PPP) 1988–92, 2002– (also from Bahawalnagar in S. Punjab 2002–), mem. Standing Cttee on Interior, Standing Cttee on Public Accounts; elected to Senate 1994, Leader of House and Leader of Opposition 1996–99; Fed. Minister for Law and Justice, Interior, Narcotics Control 1988–90; has been under arrest periodically for involvement in effort to restore Iftikhar Mohammad Chaudhry as Chief Justice of Pakistan following suspension of constitution and removal of Chief Justice Chaudhry from the bench by Pres. Pervez Musharraf 2007; Founder and Vice-Pres. Human Rights Comm. of Pakistan; Asian Human Rights Defender Award, Asian Human Rights Comm., Hong Kong 2008, Award for Distinction in Int. Law and Affairs, New York State Bar Asscn 2008. *Publications:* The Indus Saga and the Making of Pakistan (also Urdu trans., Sindh Sagar Aur Qyam-e-Pakistan), Divided by Democracy (with Lord Meghnad Desai). *Address:* c/o Pakistan People's Party, 8 Street 19, F-8/2, Islamabad, Pakistan.

AHTISAARI, Martti; Finnish diplomatist and fmr head of state; *Chairman, Crisis Management Initiative;* b. 23 June 1937, Viipuri; s. of Oiva Ahtisaari and Tyyne Ahtisaari; m. Eeva Irmeli Hyvärinen 1968; one s.; ed Univ. of Oulu; joined Finnish Ministry for Foreign Affairs 1965, worked in various positions in Ministry's Bureau for Tech. Cooperation 1965–72, Asst Dir 1971–72; Deputy Dir Ministry for Foreign Affairs, Dept for Int. Devt Co-operation 1972–73; mem. Govt Advisory Cttee on Trade and Industrialisation Affairs of Developing Countries 1971–73; Amb. to Tanzania 1973–76 (also accred to Zambia, Somalia and Mozambique 1975–76); mem. Senate of UN Inst. for Namibia 1975–76; UN Commr for Namibia 1977–81, Special Rep. of Sec.-Gen. for Namibia 1978; Under-Sec. of State in charge of Int. Devt Co-operation, Ministry for Foreign Affairs 1984–86; UN Envoy, Head of operation monitoring Namibia's transition to independence 1989–90, Sr Envoy, participated in peace-making efforts in fmr Yugoslavia 1992–93; Pres. of Finland 1994–2000; EU's Special Envoy on Crisis in Kosovo 1999, Special Envoy of the Sec.-Gen. of the UN for the Future Status Process for Kosovo 2005–08; mem. observer group on Austrian Govt's human rights record 2000; Co-Insp. of IRA arms dumps 2000–01; Head of UN fact-finding mission into Israeli operation in Jenin refugee camp 2002; Chair. Int. Crisis Group –2004; mem. Bd War-torn Societies Project Int., Balkan Children and Youth Foundation; mem. Open Soc. Inst. Int. Adviser's Group, Exec. Bd of Int. Inst. for Democracy and Electoral Assistance –2003, Jt Advisers' Group Soros Foundations; Chair. Global Action Council of Int. Youth Foundation, Int. Bd WSP Int., founder and Chair. Crisis Man. Initiative, Helsinki 2000–; Co-Chair. EastWest Inst. –2005; Chair. Supervisory Bd Finnish Nat. Opera; mem. The Elders 2009–18, Elder Emer. 2018–; mem. Bd of Trustees, Averett Univ., Inter Press Service Int. Asscn; mem. Steering Cttee Northern Research Forum; Patron Koeppler Appeal; mem. Bd of Dirs Elcoteq SE, UPM-Kymmene, Naantali Music Festival, EUSTORY; Hon. Chair. Pro Baltica Forum, Advisory Cttee of Eurasia Foundation, Int. Cttee of Vyborg Library; Hon. Trustee, American-Scandinavian Foundation, Hon. AO 2002, Order of the Companion of Oliver Tambo 2004, Golden Medal of Independence (Republic of Kosovo) 2009; Dr hc (Univ. of Oulu) 1989, (Bentley Coll., Waltham, Mass) 1990, (Kasetsart Univ., Bangkok) 1995, (Univ. of Turku) 1995, (Helsinki School of Econs and Business Admin) 1996, (Univ. of Palermo, Argentina) 1997, (Univ. of Helsinki) 1997, 2006, (Univ. of Moscow (MGIMO)) 1997, (Kyiv) 1998, (Univ. of Tech., Espoo) 1998, (Univ. of Namibia) 2000, (Columbia Univ.) 2000, (Univ. of Jyväskylä) 2000, (Averett Coll.) 2001, (American Univ., Bulgaria) 2005, (Univ. of Helsinki) 2006, (Univ. of St Gallen) 2007, (Hosei Univ.) 2008, (Univ. Coll. London) 2008, (Univ. of Kuopio) 2010, (Univ. of Eastern Finland) 2010; Franklin D. Roosevelt Four Freedoms Award 2000, Hessen Peace Prize 2000, J. William Fulbright Award for Int. Understanding 2000, European Centre for Common Ground European Peacebuilder Award 2003, European Foundation for Culture Euro-Atlantic Bridge Prize 2003, American-Scandinavian Foundation Golden Medal 2006, Friends of the UN Common Humanity Award 2006, Manfred Wörner Medal, German Ministry of Defence 2007, Geuzenmedal, Geuzen Resistance 1940–1945 Foundation 2008, Delta Prize for Global Understanding, Univ. of Georgia and Delta Air Lines 2008, Chair.'s Award of Int. Crisis Group for outstanding contributions to conflict prevention and resolution in Europe, Asia and Africa 2008, Félix Houphouët-Boigny Peace Prize, UNESCO 2008, Nobel Peace Prize 2008, Open Society Prize, Central European Univ. 2009,

Arts and Letters Award, Finlandia Foundation 2010. *Leisure interests:* golf, music, reading. *Address:* Crisis Management Initiative, Eteläranta 12, 2nd Floor, 00130 Helsinki, Finland (office). *Telephone:* (9) 4242810 (office). *Fax:* (9) 42428110 (office). *E-mail:* cmi.helsinki@cmi.fi (office). *Website:* www.cmi.fi (office).

AHUJA, Sanjiv, BE, MS; Indian telecommunications industry executive; *Chairman and CEO, Augere Ltd;* b. 1956; ed Delhi Univ., Columbia Univ., USA; various exec. positions at IBM, including head of telecommunications software div. 1990s; fmr Pres. then COO Telcordia Technologies; CEO Comstellar Technologies –2003; COO Orange 2003–04, CEO 2004–07, Chair. Orange UK 2007–08; Chair. and CEO Augere Ltd 2009–; CEO LightSquared Inc. 2010–12, currently Chair.; Founder and Chair. Eaton Telecom Infrastructure; apptd Dir (non-exec.) Telenor SA 2009; fmr Dir (non-exec.) Cadbury Schweppes plc 2006–08; mem. Man. Cttee France Telecom Group; Partner Redwood Venture Partners. *Address:* Augere Ltd, Fifth Floor, 55 Baker Street, London, W1U 8AN, England (office). *Telephone:* (20) 7467-3940 (office). *Fax:* (20) 7467-3941 (office). *E-mail:* enquiries@augereholdings.com (office). *Website:* augereholdings.com (office).

AI, Weiwei; Chinese artist and social activist; *Artistic Director, China Art Archive and Warehouse;* b. 1957, Beijing; s. of Ai Qing; m. Lu Qing; ed Beijing Film Acad.; freelance curator, cultural adviser, architect and social critic; Co-founder art group The Stars 1979; Co-founder, with the late Hans van Dijk and Frank Uytterhaegen, loft-gallery China Art Archive and Warehouse (CAAW), Beijing 1998, currently Artistic Dir; f. FAKE Design 1999; collaborated with Swiss firm Herzog de Meuron as architectural consultant for Olympic Stadium ('Bird's Nest') for 2008 Olympic Games in Beijing; outspoken critic of Govt's human rights record; detained by authorities for alleged evasion of taxes and destroying evidence and held in a secret location April 2011, arrest prompted global campaign for his release, released on bail after pleading guilty June 2011; exhibited as part of the German Pavilion at 55th Int. Art Exhbn, Venice Biennale 2013; Hon. Prof., Berlin Univ. of the Arts 2011 Lifetime Achievement Award, Chinese Contemporary Art Awards 2008, Appraisers Asscn Award for Excellence in Arts 2013, Amnesty Int. Amb. of Conscience Award (co-recipient) 2015, Marina Kellen French Outstanding Contributions to the Arts Award, National Arts Awards 2018. *Address:* China Art Archive and Warehouse, PO Box 100102-43, Beijing 100102, People's Republic of China (office). *Telephone:* (10) 84565152 (office). *Fax:* (10) 84565154 (office). *E-mail:* mail@caaw.com.cn (office). *Website:* www.archivesandwarehouse.com (office); aiweiwei.com.

AIDA, Takefumi, PhD; Japanese architect and academic; b. 5 June 1937, Tokyo; s. of Takeshi Aida and Chiyo Aida; m. Kazuko Aida 1966; one s. one d.; ed School of Architecture, Waseda Univ., Tokyo; qualified architect 1967; Prof., Shibaura Inst. of Tech., Tokyo 1976–2000, Prof. and Dean Dept of Architecture and Eng 1991–94; major works include: Memorial at Iwo-Jima Island, Tokyo 1983, Toy Block House X, Shibuya, Tokyo 1984, Tokyo War Dead Memorial Park, Bunkyo, Tokyo 1988, Saito Memorial Hall, Shibaura Inst. of Tech., Tokyo 1990, Community Centre, Kawasato 1993, Funeral Hall, Mizuho 1998, Nenseiji Temple 2001; Japan Architects Asscn Annual Prize for Newcomers 1982, 2nd Prize Int. Doll's House Competition 1983, The 12th Award for Landscaping Architecture, The JIA Twenty-five Year Award 2007. *Publications include:* Architecture Note, Toy Block Houses 1984, Toy Block House X 1986, Takefumi Aida Buildings and Projects 1990, The Works of Takefumi Aida 1998, The Collected Edition of Takefumi Aida 1998, Words of an Architect 2014. *Leisure interest:* Shogi. *Address:* 1-3-2 Okubo, Shinjuku-ku, Tokyo 169-0072, Japan (home). *Fax:* (3) 3209-7960 (home). *E-mail:* t-aida@kt.rim.or.jp (office); t-aida@aida-doi-architects.co.jp (office). *Website:* www.aida-doi-architects.co.jp (office).

AIDARBEKOV, Chingiz Azamatovich; Kyrgyzstani politician and diplomatist; *Minister of Foreign Affairs;* b. 27 Oct. 1977, Kyrgyz SSR; ed Int. Univ., Kyrgyz-Russian Slavic Univ.; Attaché, Ministry of Foreign Affairs, Third Sec. of CIS Dept 2001, Second Sec. 2001–03, First Sec. 2003–05, Chargé d'affaires, Embassy in Uzbekistan 2005–08, Counsellor, Embassy in Turkmenistan 2008–10; Deputy Head of Foreign Policy, Dept of the Pres. 2011; Head of Int. Relations and Protocol, Exec. Office of Parl. 2012–16; Amb. to Japan 2016–18; Minister of Foreign Affairs 2018–. *Address:* Ministry of Foreign Affairs, 720040 Bishkek, bul. Erkindik 57, Kyrgyzstan (office). *Telephone:* (312) 62-05-45 (office). *Fax:* (312) 66-05-01 (office). *E-mail:* gendep@mofa.kg (office). *Website:* www.mfa.gov.kg (office).

AIDEED, Hussein Mohamed Farrah; Somali/American politician; b. 16 Aug. 1962, Beledweyne, Mudug Region, Somalia; s. of Gen. Mohamed Farah Aideed (died 1996); mem. Habr Gedir clan; m. 1st; m. 2nd 1995; one d.; m. 3rd (divorced); one d.; ed Covina High School, Covina, Calif.; emigrated to USA 1978, obtained US citizenship; joined US Marine Corps Reserve 1987, attained position of Corporal; translator, US-led peacekeeping force in Somalia 1992; public works clerk, Water Supply and Roads Maintenance Dept, W Covina City Hall, Southern Calif. –1995; returned to Somalia 1995; led reorganization of clan militia and armed conquest of Baidoa 1995; Leader Somali Nat. Alliance 1996–; Co-Chair. Somali Reconciliation and Restoration Council; participated in peace talks on future of Somalia, Nairobi, Kenya 2002; imprisoned in Nairobi on charges of failing to pay debts 2002; Deputy Prime Minister 2005–07 (dismissed); Minister of Internal Affairs 2005–07, of Public Works and Housing 2007–08; defected to Asmara, Eritrea.

AIELLO, Danny; American actor; b. 20 June 1933, New York; s. of Daniel Louis Aiello and Frances Pietrocova; m. Sandy Cohen 1955; three s. one d. *Theatre includes:* Lamppost Reunion 1975 (Theatre World Award), Gemini 1977 (Obie Award 1977), Hurlyburly 1985. *Films include:* Bang the Drum Slowly 1973, The Godfather II 1976, Once Upon a Time in America 1984, The Purple Rose of Cairo 1985, Moonstruck 1987, Do the Right Thing 1989 (Boston Critics Award, Chicago Critics Award, LA Critics Award, all for Best Supporting Actor), Harlem Nights 1989, Jacob's Ladder 1990, Once Around 1991, Hudson Hawk 1991, The Closer 1991, 29th Street 1991, Mistress 1992, Ruby 1992, The Pickle 1992, The Cemetery Club 1992, The Professional 1994, Prêt-a-Porter 1994, Léon 1994, City Hall 1995, Power of Attorney 1995, Two Days in the Valley 1996, Mojave Moon 1996, Two Much 1996, A Brooklyn State of Mind 1997, Bring Me the Head of Mavis Davis 1998, Wilbur Falls 1998, 18 Shades of Dust 1999, Mambo Cafe 2000, Prince of Central Park 2000, Dinner Rush 2000, Off Key 2001, The Russian Job 2002, Marcus Timberwolf 2002, The Last Request 2002, Mail Order Bride 2003, Zeyda and the Hitman 2004, Brooklyn Lobster 2005, Lucky Number Slevin 2006, The Last Request 2006, The Shoemaker 2006, Stiffs 2010, Dolly Baby 2013, Henry & Me 2014, Reach Me 2014, The Neighborhood 2017. *Television includes:* The Preppie Murder 1989, A Family of Strangers 1993 (Emmy Award), The Last Don (mini-series) 1997, Dellaventura (series) 1997, The Last Don II (mini-series) 1998. *Music includes:* albums: I Just Wanted To Hear the Words 2004, Live from Atlantic City 2008, My Christmas Song for You 2010. *Publications include:* I Only Know Who I Am When I Am Somebody Else: My Life on the Street, On the Stage, and in the Movies 2014. *Address:* c/o Tracey Miller and Associates Inc., 2610 Fire Road, Egg Harbor Township, NJ 08234, USA. *Telephone:* (609) 383-2323. *E-mail:* info@tmapublicity.com. *Website:* www.tmapublicity.com; www.dannyaiello.com.

AIGRAIN, Jacques, PhD; Swiss/French business executive; b. 1954; m., two c.; ed Dauphine Univ., Sorbonne; joined JP Morgan 1981, served as co-head of investment banking client coverage, fmr mem. Man. Cttee; joined Swiss Reinsurance Co. (Swiss Re) as Head, Financial Services Business Group and mem. Exec. Bd Cttee 2001, CEO 2004–09, currently mem. Bd of Dirs; Chair. LCH.Clearnet Group Ltd 2010–15; Partner and Man. Dir Warburg Pincus LPP 2013–16, Sr Adviser 2016–; mem. Supervisory Bd Deutsche Lufthansa, Swiss International Airlines; mem. Bd of Dirs Resolution; mem. Financial Industry Advisory Bd, Apax Partners LLP. *Website:* www.warburgpincus.com (office).

AIKEN, Linda H., PhD, FAAN, FRCN, RN; American nurse, sociologist and academic; *Claire M. Fagin Leadership Professor in Nursing, Professor of Sociology and Director, Center for Health Outcomes and Policy Research, University of Pennsylvania;* b. 29 July 1943, Roanoke, Va; d. of William Jordan and Betty Philips Harman (née Warner); one s. one d.; ed Univ. of Florida, Univ. of Texas, Univ. of Wisconsin; nurse, Univ. of Florida Medical Center 1964–65, Instructor, Coll. of Nursing 1966–67; Instructor, School of Nursing, Univ. of Missouri 1967–70, Clinical Nurse Specialist 1967–70; Lecturer, School of Nursing, Univ. of Wisconsin 1973–74; Program Officer, Robert Wood Johnson Foundation 1974–76, Dir of Research 1976–79, Asst Vice-Pres. 1979–81, Vice-Pres. 1981–87; Claire M. Fagin Leadership Prof. in Nursing and Prof. of Sociology and Dir Center for Health Outcomes and Policy Research, Univ. of Pennsylvania 1988–; mem. Pres. Clinton's Nat. Health Care Reform Task Force 1993; Commr Physician Payment Review Comm. Nat. Advisory Council, US Agency for Health Care Policy and Research; Assoc. Ed. Journal of Health and Social Behaviour 1979–81; Fellow and Past Pres. American Acad. of Nursing 1978, Inst. of Medecine 1982, Nat. Acad. of Social Insurance 1989; Fellow, American Acad. of Arts and Sciences 1998; numerous awards including Jessie M. Scott Award, American Nurses Asscn 1984, 2002, Nurse Scientist of the Year Award 1991, Distinguished Pathfinder Research Award 2001, Barbara Thoman Curtis Award, Individual Codman Award, Jt Comm. on Accreditation of Healthcare Orgs 2003, Sackler Award for Sustained Nat. Leadership in Health Research 2006, Graham Prize for Health Services Research, Baxter Int. Foundation 2006, Amb., Research!America's Rogers Soc. for Global Health Research 2009, HRH Princess Muna Al-Hussein Award for Significant Contribs to Health Care Across Borders 2010, Velji Global Health Project of the Year Award, Consortium of Univs for Global Health 2013, Gustav O. Lienhard Award, Inst. of Medicine, NAS 2014. *Publications:* Nursing in the 1980s: Crises, Challenges, Opportunities (ed.) 1982, Evaluation Studies Review Annual (co-ed.) 1985, Applications of Social Science to Clinical Medicine and Health Policy (co-ed.) 1986, Charting Nursing's Future (co-ed.) 1991, Hospital Restructuring in North America and Europe 1997, Advances in Hospital Outcomes Research 1998, Accounting for Variation in Hospital Outcomes: Cross-National Study 1999, International Nursing Migration (co-ed.) 2007; contribs to professional journals. *Address:* University of Pennsylvania School of Nursing, Room 387 Fagin Hall, 418 Curie Blvd, Philadelphia, PA 19104-4217 (office); 2209 Lombard Street, Philadelphia, PA 19146-1107, USA (home). *Telephone:* (215) 898-9759 (office). *Fax:* (215) 573-2062 (office). *E-mail:* laiken@nursing.upenn.edu (office). *Website:* www.nursing.upenn.edu/faculty/profile.asp?pid=107 (office).

AILLAGON, Jean Jacques; French politician and cultural official; b. 2 Oct. 1946, Metz; s. of Charles Aillagon and Anne-Marie Louis; two c.; ed Univs of Toulouse and Nanterre; Prof. of History and Geography, Lycée de Tulle 1973–76; Deputy Dir Ecole Nat. Supérieure des Beaux-Arts 1978–82; Admin. Musée Nat. d'Art Moderne (Centre Pompidou) 1982–85; Asst to Dir of Cultural Affairs of City of Paris 1985–88; Del.-Gen. for Cultural Programmes of City of Paris 1988–93; Dir-Gen. Vidéothèque de Paris 1992–93; Dir of Cultural Affairs of City of Paris 1993–96; Pres. Centre Georges Pompidou 1996–2002; Minister of Culture and Communication 2002–04; Pres. and Dir-Gen. TV5 Monde 2005–06; Dir Palazzo Grassi, Venice April–Aug. 2007; Pres. Château de Versailles 2007–11; Pres. comm. organizing year 2000 celebrations 1999–2001; Artistic Dir Commissariat for France–Egypt Year 1996–98; Pres. Les Arts Décoratifs (private arts devt org.) 2013; mem. Mouvement Démocrate (MoDem), mem. Exec. Bureau 2016–; Chevalier, Ordre Nat. du Mérite, des Palmes académiques, Commdr Légion d'honneur 2016. *Website:* jean-jacques-aillagon.typepad.fr (office).

AILLERET, François; French government official; *President, École des Neurosciences de Paris-Île-de-France;* b. 7 June 1937; s. of Pierre Ailleret and Denise Nodé-Langlois; m. Chantal Flinois 1963; four c.; ed École Polytechnique, École Nationale des Ponts et Chausseés; served in Algeria and Côte d'Ivoire in early 1960s; various appointments at Paris Airport 1967–80; joined Electricité de France (EdF) 1980, Deputy Dir-Gen. 1987, Dir-Gen. 1994–96, Vice-Pres. 1996, Pres. EdF Int. 1996–2003, Hon. CEO 2003–; Pres. Int. Union of Electricity Producers and Distributors (UNIPEDE) 1997–2000; Admin. Pechiney 1996–2003; currently Pres. Asscn Française de Normalisation (AFNOR) 2002–11; Chair. French Energy Council 1998–2004; mem. Conseil Economique et Social (Nat.) 1999–2010; Pres., Conseil d'Admin, Institut Pasteur 2005–11, École des Neurosciences de Paris-Île-de-France 2011–; Commdr, Légion d'honneur, Commdr, Ordre nat. du Mérite, Croix de la Valeur militaire. *Address:* EdF, 151 boulevard Haussmann, 75008 Paris (office); 22 rue Rouelle, 75015 Paris, France (home). *Telephone:* 1-40-42-26-70 (office). *Fax:* 1-40-42-77-78 (office). *E-mail:* francois.ailleret@edf.fr (office). *Website:* www.paris-neuroscience.fr (office).

AIMÉE, Anouk; French actress; b. (Françoise Dreyfus), 27 April 1932, Paris; d. of Henry Dreyfus and Geneviève Durand; m. 2nd Nico Papatakis 1951; one d.; m. 3rd Pierre Barouh 1966; m. 4th Albert Finney 1970 (divorced 1978); ed Ecole de la rue Milton, Paris, Ecole de Barbezieux, Pensionnat de Bandd, Inst. de Megève and Cours Bauer-Therond; film and TV actress 1955–; Commdr des Arts et des Lettres,

Golden Globe Award 1968, Prix Féminin, Cannes. *Theatre includes:* Sud 1954, Love Letters 1990, 1994. *Films include:* Les mauvaises rencontres 1955, Tous peuvent me tuer 1957, Pot bouille 1957, Montparnasse 19 1957, La tête contre les murs 1958, Les drageurs 1959, La dolce vita, Le farceur, Lola, Les amours de Paris, L'imprévu 1960, Quel Notre Dame 1960, Le jugement dernier 1961, Sodome et Gomorrhe 1961, Les grands chemins 1962, Education sentimentale 1962, Huit et demi 1962, Un homme et une femme 1966, Un soir un train 1967, The Appointment 1968, Model Shop 1968, Justine 1968, Si c'était à refaire 1976, Mon premier amour 1978, Salto nel vuoto 1979, La tragédie d'un homme ridicule 1981, Qu'est-ce qui fait courir David? 1982, Le Général de l'armée morte 1983, Vive la vie 1984, Le succès à tout prix 1984, Un homme et une femme: vingt ans déjà 1986, Docteur Norman Bethune 1992, Les Marmottes 1993, Les Cent et une nuits 1995, Prêt-à-porter 1995, Une pour toutes 2000, La Petite prairie aux bouleaux 2003, Ils se mariérent et eurent beaucoup d'enfants 2004, De particulier à particulier 2006. *Television:* Une page d'amour 1979, L'Île bleue 2001, Des voix dans le jardin, Napoléon 2002, Claude Lelouch, on s'aimera (narrator) 2007. *Leisure interests:* reading, life, human rights. *Address:* c/o Artmédia, 20 avenue Rapp, 75007 Paris, France (home).

AINSLEY, John Mark; British singer (tenor); b. 9 July 1953, Crewe, Cheshire; s. of John Alwyn Ainsley and Dorothy Sylvia Ainsley (née Anderson); partner William Whitehead; ed Royal Grammar School, Worcester, Madgalen Coll., Oxford; debut in Stravinsky's Mass, Royal Festival Hall 1984; many concert performances from 1985 with Taverner Consort, New London Consort and London Baroque; appearances in Mozart Masses at The Vienna Konzerthaus with Heinz Holliger, Handel's Saul at Göttingen with John Eliot Gardiner, Mozart Requiem under Yehudi Menuhin at Gstaad and Pulcinella at the Barbican under Jeffrey Tate; other concerts with Ulster Orchestra and Bournemouth Sinfonietta; debut in USA at Lincoln Center in Bach's B Minor Mass with Christopher Hogwood 1990; opera debut at the Innsbruck Festival in Scarlatti's Gli Equivoci nel Sembiante, at ENO in the Return of Ulysses 1989; title role in Méhul's Joseph for Dutch Radio, Handel's Acis in Stuttgart and Solomon for Radio France under Leopold Hager; has sung Mozart's Tamino for Opera Northern Ireland and Ferrando for Glyndebourne Touring Opera; sang Ferrando at Glyndebourne 1992, Don Ottavio 1994, Haydn's The Seasons with the London Classical Players; BBC Proms Concerts, London 1993, Stravinsky concert under Andrew Davis at Royal Festival Hall 1997, Monteverdi's Orfeo for Munich Opera Festival 1999, Jupiter in Semele for ENO 1999, Bach's St Matthew Passion at BBC Proms 2002, Skuratov in From the House of the Dead for Amsterdam, Vienna and Aix en Provence Festivals, 2007, Captain Vere in Billy Budd for Frankfurt Opera 2007, Emilio in Partenope for ENO 2008, title role in Idomeneo and Bazajet in Tamerlano for Munich Opera Festival 2008, Captain Vere in Billy Budd at Glyndebourne Festival 2010, De Nederlandse Opera 2011; Visiting Prof., RAM; Grammy Award for Best Opera Recording 1995, Munich Festival Prize 1999, Royal Philharmonic Soc. Singer Award 2007. *Recordings include:* Purcell, Odes (with Trevor Pinnock) 1988, Handel's Nisi Dominus (under Simon Preston) 1989, Handel, Saul 1991, Handel, Acis and Galatea 1993, Blow, Fairest Work of Happy Nature 1993, Great Baroque Arias (with the King's Consort) 1994, Handel, Jephtha 1994, Zelenka, Lamentations of Jeremiah 1994, Finzi, Dies Natalis and Intimations 1996, Warlock, Curlew Capriol Serenade Songs 1997, Mozart, Requiem 1998, Mozart, Songs 1998, Ireland, Songs 1999, Mozart's C Minor Mass (with Christopher Hogwood) 1999, Quilter, Songs 2000, Vaughan Williams, Songs 2000, L'invitation au voyage 2006, Finzi, Intimations of Immortality 2009, Grainger, Jungle Book and Other Choral Works 2011, Britten: War Requiem (BBC Music Magazine Choral Award 2014). *Address:* c/o Tim Menah, Askonas Holt Limited, 15 Fetter Lane, London, EC4V 1BW, England (office). *Telephone:* (20) 7400-1700 (office). *Fax:* (20) 7400-1799 (office). *E-mail:* tim.menah@askonasholt.co.uk (office). *Website:* www.askonasholt.co.uk (office).

AINSLIE, Sir Charles Benedict (Ben), Kt, CBE; British sailor; *Team Principal and Skipper, Ineos Team UK;* b. 5 Feb. 1977, Macclesfield, Cheshire; s. of Roddy Ainslie (skipper of 'Second Life' in first Whitbread Round the World Race 1973–74) and Susan Ainslie; m. Georgie Ainslie 2014; one d.; ed Peter Symonds Coll., Winchester, Hants.; began sailing in Restronguet Creek, Cornwall aged eight; competitive results include Laser Radial European Champion 1993, Laser Radial World Champion 1993, Youth World Champion 1995, Laser European Champion 1996, 1998, 1999, 2000, Laser World Champion 1998, 1999, Finn European Champion 2002, 2003, Finn World Champion 2002, 2003, 2004 (first Briton to win three consecutive Finn titles), 2005, 2008, 2012 (most successful Finn sailor ever), ISAF Open Match Racing World Championship 2010; four gold medals in successive Olympic Games (Laser Class, Sydney 2000, Finn Class, Athens 2004, Finn Class, Beijing 2008, Finn Class, London 2012), also won silver medal in Laser Class at Atlanta Olympic Games 1996; joined Team New Zealand in late 2004 to compete in America's Cup 2007; won 34th America's Cup as tactician with Oracle Team, USA 2013; launched Ben Ainslie Racing Ltd 2013; Team Principal and Skipper, Land Rover BAR 2014–, competed in 35th America's Cup, Bermuda 2017; Team Principal and Skipper, Ineos Team UK 2018–, British challenger for the 36th America's Cup 2021; Hon. mem. Royal Cornwall Yacht Club, Stokes Bay Sailing Club, Restronguet Sailing Club, Hayling Island Sailing Club; Hon. degree in Sports Science (Univ. Coll. of Chichester), Hon. degree (Univ. of Portsmouth); British Young Sailor of the Year 1995, British Yachtsman of the Year 1995, 1999, 2000, 2002, Sports Writers' Assen Best Int. Newcomer 1996, Int. Sailing Fed. (ISAF) World Sailor of the Year 1998, 2002, 2008, 2012. *Leisure interests:* cycling, flying, football, cricket, golf. *Address:* Ineos Team UK, The Camber, East Street, Portsmouth, PO1 2JJ, England (office). *Telephone:* (23) 9228-7814 (home). *E-mail:* media@ineosteamuk.com (office). *Website:* www.ineosteamuk.com (office); www.benainslie.com.

AINSWORTH, Robert (Bob) William; British politician; b. 19 June 1952, Coventry, Warwicks.; m. Gloria Ainsworth; two d.; worked for Jaguar Cars, Coventry; held various positions in trade union and Labour movt including Shop Steward, Sec. of Jt Shop Steward Cttee, Sheet Metal Workers Union Br. Pres., Constituency Labour Party Chair.; City Councillor, Coventry 1984–92; MP (Labour) for Coventry North East 1992–2015, apptd Whip 1995, Lord Commr of HM Treasury (Govt Whip) 1997–2001, Parl. Under-Sec. at Dept for Environment, Transport and the Regions Jan.–June 2001, Home Office Minister with responsibility for Drugs and Organized Crime 2001–03, Govt Deputy Chief Whip 2003–07, Minister for the Armed Forces 2007–09, Sec. of State for Defence 2009–10. *Address:* Bayley House, 22–23 Bayley Lane, Coventry, CV1 5RJ, England (office). *Telephone:* (2476) 226707 (office). *Fax:* (2476) 433401 (office).

AIREY, Dawn Elizabeth, MA, FRSA, FRTS; British media executive; *Senior Vice-President, Europe, the Middle East and Africa, Yahoo! Inc.;* b. 15 Nov. 1960, Preston, Lancs.; one d.; ed Kelly Coll., Girton Coll. Cambridge; with Cen. TV 1985–93; ITV Network Centre 1993–94; Channel 4 1994–96; Channel 5 1996–2002, Chief Exec. 2000–02; Man. Dir Sky Networks 2002–06; CEO Iostar (TV production and distribution co.) April 2007 (resgnd); Dir of Global Content, ITV 2007–08, mem. Bd of Dirs 2008; Chair. and CEO Channel 5 Broadcasting Ltd 2008–10; Pres. CLT-UFA UK TV, RTL Group, London 2010–13; Sr Vice-Pres., Europe, the Middle East and Africa, Yahoo! Inc. 2013–; fmr Chair. The Grierson Trust, National Youth Theatre; Fellow, Royal TV Soc. 1998, Vice-Pres. 2002–; mem. Bd of Dirs Thomas Cook PLC, British Library; Exec. Chair. Media Guardian Edinburgh Int. TV Festival 2001–06; mem. Bd Int. Emmy Awards; Olswang Business Woman of the Year 2000. *Leisure interests:* cinema, tennis. *Address:* Yahoo! EMEA Ltd, 5–7 Point Village, North Wall Quay, Dublin 1, Ireland (office). *Telephone:* (1) 8663100 (office). *Fax:* (1) 8663101 (office). *Website:* www.yahoo.com (office).

AIRLIE, 13th Earl of; **David George Patrick Coke Ogilvy,** KT, GCVO, PC, RVO; British business executive; b. 17 May 1926, London; s. of 12th Earl of Airlie, KT, GCVO, MC and Lady Alexandra Marie Bridget Coke; m. Virginia Fortune Ryan 1952; three s. three d.; ed Eton Coll.; Chair. Schroders PLC 1977–84, Ashdown Investment Trust Ltd 1968–84, J. Henry Schroder Bank AG (Switzerland) 1977–84, Baring Stratton Investment Trust PLC 1986–2000; Chair. Gen. Accident Fire and Life Assurance Corpn PLC 1987–97; Dir J. Henry Schroder Wagg & Co. Ltd 1961–84, Schroder, Darling and Co. Holdings Ltd (Australia) 1977–84, Schroder Inc. (USA) 1977–84, Schroder Int. Ltd 1973–84, Scottish & Newcastle Breweries PLC 1969–83; Dir Royal Bank of Scotland Group PLC 1983–93; Lord Chamberlain of the Queen's Household 1984–97; Lord Lt of Angus 1989–2001; Capt.-Gen. of Royal Co. of Archers 2004–; Chancellor, Univ. of Abertay, Dundee 1994–; Chair. Historic Royal Palaces 1998–2002; Pres. Nat. Trust for Scotland 1998–2002; Gov. Nuffield Hosps; Hon. Pres. Scout Assen in Scotland 1988–2002, JP Angus 1990; Hon. LLD (Dundee) 1990. *Telephone:* (1575) 570108; (1575) 540231 (home). *Fax:* (1575) 540223 (office); (1575) 540570109; (1575) 540400 (home). *E-mail:* office@airlieestates.com (office). *Website:* www.airlieestates.com (office). *Address:* Airlie House, Cortachy, Kirriemuir, Angus, DD8 4LY, Scotland (home); 36 Sloane Court West, London, SW3 4TB, England (home).

AISI, Robert Guba, OBE, LLB; Papua New Guinea lawyer, business executive and fmr diplomatist; *Executive General Manager–External Relations, ExxonMobil Papua New Guinea Ltd;* m. Susan Iamonama Aisi; four c.; ed Univ. of Papua New Guinea, postgraduate studies at Legal Training Inst., Int. Inst. of Public Admin, France; admitted to Bar, Nat. and Supreme Courts 1980, Victorian Bar, Australia 1987, served with Australian law firms based in Papua New Guinea; served with Exec. Br. (Legal Affairs) of UNESCO; Prin. Legal Officer, City of Port Moresby Governing Authority 1986–90; Prin. Legal Officer and Deputy Comm. Sec., Electricity Comm. 1990–92; Partner, Posman Kua Aisi Lawyers 1998–2001; Councillor (later Visiting Lecturer), Papua New Guinea Legal Training Inst. –2002; Amb. and Perm. Rep. to UN, New York 2002–15, apptd Chair. Special Cttee on Decolonization 2004, Asian States Regional Group 2004; Exec. Gen. Man.–External Relations, ExxonMobil Papua New Guinea Ltd 2015–; fmr Pres. Business Council Papua New Guinea; mem. Australia-Papua New Guinea Business Council; Hon. Consul to South Africa. *Website:* pnglng.com (office).

AISSAMI, Tareck Zaidan el; Venezuelan lawyer and politician; b. 12 Nov. 1974, El Vigía, Mérida; s. of Zaidan el Amin el Aissami; m.; two c.; ed Univ. of the Andes (ULA); became involved in politics whilst at univ., becoming Pres. ULA student union; mem. Nat. Ass. for Mérida state 2006–07, Vice-Pres., Standing Cttee on Family, Women and Youth; Vice-Minister of Citizen Security, Ministry of the Interior 2007–08; Minister of the Interior and Justice 2008–12; Gov. of Aragua state 2012–17; Exec. Vice-Pres. of Venezuela 2017–18; mem. United Socialist Party, Vice-Pres. for Andes region 2011–13, for Central-Western region 2013–. *Website:* Tareck.psuv.org.ve (office).

AITMATOV, Ilghiz Torokulovich, PhD, DTechSc; Kyrgyzstani geologist; *Director, Institute of Physics and Mechanics of Rocks, Kyrgyz National Academy of Sciences;* b. 8 Feb. 1931, Frunze (now Bishkek); s. of Torokul Aitmatov and Naghima Aitmatova (née Abdulvaliyeva); m. Rosalia Jamankulovna Jenchuraeva 1961; one s. two d.; ed Moscow Inst. of Geological Survey, USSR Acad. of Sciences, Inst. of Mining; foreman, engineer, head anti-avalanche surveillance service, Kyrgyz Geological Dept 1954–57; doctoral studies USSR Acad. of Sciences, Inst. of Mining (Moscow) 1957–60; jr researcher, Head of Lab., Deputy Dir Inst. of Physics and Mechanics of Rocks, Kyrgyz Nat. Acad. of Sciences, Head of Lab. 1960–68, Deputy Dir 1968–79, Dir 1970–88, Pres. 1990–94, Dir 1994–, Academician-Sec., Dept of Physical, Math. and Earth Sciences 1988–90, Pres. Kyrgyz Acad. of Sciences 1990–93; Corresp. mem. Kyrgyz Nat. Acad. of Sciences 1986, mem. 1988–; mem. Political Council, People's Republican Party of Kyrgyzstan 1992–95; mem. Parl. (Supreme Council) of Kyrgyz Repub. 1990–91; mem. Pres. Council 1990–94; mem. Russian Acad. of Mining Sciences, Int. Engineering Acad. and other int. acads.; Kyrgyzstan SSR State Prize 1984, USSR State Prize 1989, Merited Worker of Science of Kyrgyzstan; other medals and awards. *Achievements include:* Scientific Discovery Phenomena of Saltatory Release of Residual Stresses in Rocks (co-author) 1998. *Publications:* more than 250 papers on rock and mass geomechanics, including seven monographs, 15 inventions and one scientific discovery. *Address:* 98 ul. Toktoghula, Apartment 9, 720000 Bishkek (home); Institute of Physics and Mechanics of Rocks, National Academy of Sciences, ul. O. Mederova 98, 720035 Bishek, Kyrgyzstan (office). *Telephone:* (312) 54-11-15 (office); (312) 66-21-89 (home). *Fax:* (312) 54-11-17 (office); (312) 68-00-47 (home). *E-mail:* ifmgp@yandex.ru (office); djam@freenet.kg (home).

AIZAWA, Masuo, MSc, BE, DEng, PhD; Japanese research institute director and academic; *Professor Emeritus, Faculty of Engineering, Tokyo Institute of Technology;* b. 1942, Yokohama; ed Yokohama Nat. Univ., Grad. School of Science and Eng, Tokyo Inst. of Tech.; Research Assoc., Chemical Resources Lab., Tokyo Inst. of Tech. 1971–80; Assoc. Prof., Inst. of Material Science, Tsukuba Univ. 1980–86;

Assoc. Prof., Faculty of Eng, Tokyo Inst. of Tech. 1986, Prof. 1986–94, Dean of Faculty of Bioscience and Biotechnology 1994–96, 1998–2000, Vice-Pres. Tokyo Inst. of Tech. 2000–01, Pres. 2001–07, Prof. Emer. 2007–; Advising Prof., Shanghai Jiaotong Univ. 2003–; Pres. Japan Asscn of Nat. Univs 2005–07, Electrochemical Soc. of Japan, Int. Soc. of Molecular Electronics and Biocomputing, Intelligent Materials Forum; fmr Vice-Pres. Chemical Soc. of Japan, Japan Univ. Accreditation Asscn; Exec. mem. Council for Science and Tech. Policy, Cabinet Office 2006–13; Counsellor to Pres., Japan Science and Technology Agency 2013–; mem. Science Council of Japan, Cen. Council for Educ.; Chemical Soc. of Japan Award 1997, Electrochemical Soc. Award 2003, 2005, Int. Chemical Sensors Award. *Address:* Tokyo Institute of Technology, 2 Chome-12-1 Ookayama, Meguro, Tokyo 152-8550, Japan (office). *Telephone:* (3) 3726-1111 (office). *Website:* www.titech.ac.jp (office).

AJIBOLA, Hon. Prince Bola, LLB; Nigerian lawyer and judge; b. 22 March 1934, Lagos; s. of Oba A. S. Ajibola and Adikatu Ashakun Ajibola; m. Olu Ajibola 1961; three s. two d.; ed Holborn Coll. of Law, London Univ., UK; called to the English Bar (Lincoln's Inn) 1962; Prin. Partner, Bola Ajibola & Co., Lagos, Ikeja, Abeokuta and Kaduna, specializing in commercial law and int. arbitration; fmr Attorney-Gen. and Fed. Minister of Justice; Temporary Pres. UN Gen. Ass., 17th Special Session on Narcotic Drugs 1990; Chair. Task Force for Revision of the Laws of the Fed. 1990, Gen. Council of the Bar, Disciplinary Cttee of the Bar, Advisory Cttee on the Prerogative of Mercy; Founder and Pres. African Concern 1996–; Founder Islamic Movt for Africa 1996; Judge and Vice-Pres. IBRD Tribunal, Washington, DC 1995; Vice-Pres. Inst. of Int. Business Law and Practice, Paris, Int. Contractual Relations Comm., ICC; Chair. Body of Sr Advocates of Nigeria 1986–, Body of Benchers (also life mem.) 1989–90; Nat. Chair. World Peace Through Law Centre; Ed. Nigeria's Treaties in Force 1970–1990, All Nigeria Law Reports 1961–90; Ed.-in-Chief, Justice; Gen. Ed. Fed. Ministry of Justice Law Review Series (seven vols); Fellow, Chartered Inst. of Arbitrators, Nigerian Inst. of Advanced Legal Studies; mem. Nigerian Bar Asscn (Pres. 1984–85), African Bar Asscn, Int. Bar Asscn, Asscn of World Lawyers, ICC, Commonwealth Law Asscn, World Arbitration Inst., Soc. for the Reform of Criminal Law, Nigerian Inst. of Int. Affairs; mem. Nigerian del. to UN Gen. Ass. 1986, Int. Court of Justice, The Hague 1991–94; mem. Nigeria Police Council, Int. Law Comm., Perm. Court of Arbitration, The Hague, ICC Court of Arbitration, Int. Maritime Arbitration Comm., Paris, Panel of Int. Arbitrators, London Inst. of Arbitrators, Int. Advisory Cttee of World Arbitration Inst., USA; Hon. LLD (Buckingham) 1996; Outstanding Citizen Merit Award, Ogun State of Nigeria 1986. *Publications:* Principles of Arbitration 1980, The Law and Settlement of Commercial Disputes 1984, Law Development and Administration in Nigeria 1987, Integration of the African Continent Through Law 1988, Banking Frauds and Other Financial Malpractices in Nigeria 1989, Women and Children under Nigerian Law 1990, Scheme Relating to Mutual Assistance in Criminal Matters and the Control of Criminal Activities within Africa and numerous other books on other legal topics. *Address:* Bola Ajibola & Co., 52, Allen Avenue, 1st Floor, Ikeja. Lagos, Nigeria (office). *Telephone:* (office). *Fax:* 234-1-2700970 (office). *E-mail:* info@bolaajibolaandco.com (office); bolaajibolaandco@yahoo.com. *Website:* www.bolaajibolaandco.com.

AJODHIA, Jules Rattankoemar; Suriname politician; b. 27 Jan. 1945, Wanica Dist; m. Lucia Kamlawatie Baldew; one s. two d.; ed Univ. of Suriname; Minister of Justice 1988–90; Vice-Pres. 1991–96, 2000–05; Vice-Pres. of Suriname –2005; fmr Vice-Chair. Verenigde Hervormings Partij (VHP) (Progressive Reform Party); mem. Nat. Ass.; Grand Officer of the Hon. Order of the Yellow Star. *Address:* Verenigde Hervormings Partij, Mr. J. Lachmonstraat 130, Paramaribo, Suriname (office). *Telephone:* 494497 (office). *Fax:* 463939 (office). *E-mail:* info@vhp.sr (office). *Website:* www.vhp.sr (office).

AKADIRI, Saliou; Benin diplomatist and politician; b. 1950, Issaba, Pobè, Plateau Département; m.; c.; ed Univ. of Dahomey (now Nat. Univ. of Benin), Centre de Formation et de Perfectionnement des Cadres de l'Admin Publique et Privée (now Ecole Nat. d'Admin et de Magistrature), Institut Int. d'Admin Publique and Univ. of Paris 1 (Sorbonne), France; held numerous positions with Ministry of Foreign Affairs, including as Asst Man., later Man. and Dir, Central Admin Dept, First Counsellor, later Minister-Counsellor, Embassy in Paris 1987–96, Chef de Cabinet to Dir-Gen., Agence Intergouvernementale de la Francophonie, Org. Int. de la Francophonie, Paris 1998–2006, Minister of Foreign Affairs, African Integration, Francophone Affairs and Beninois Abroad 2015–16; Sec.-Gen., Syndicat Nat. des Diplomates et assimilés du Bénin 1978–83; Founding mem. Asscn de Développement du Dist de Pobè 1986; Vice-Pres. Asscn pour le Développement Economique, Social et Culturel de l'Ouémé 1986; First Vice-Pres., Comité Révolutionnaire d'Admin, Cotonou V Dist 1982–84; Mayor of Pobè 2008–; mem. Parti du Renouveau Démocratique –2013; Founding Pres. Union des Forces de Progrès (UFP) 2014; Officier, Ordre Nat. du mérite Français. *Address:* Office of the Mayor, Pobè, Benin (office).

AKAGAWA, Jiro; Japanese writer; b. 29 Feb. 1948, Fukuoka; m. Fumiko Serita 1973; one d.; ed Toho-gakuen High School; fmr proofreader for Japan Soc. of Mechanical Engineers; mem. Japanese Mystery Writers' Asscn 1977–; Kadokawa Publishing Book Award 1980. *Publications include:* more than 500 works including novels: Ghost Train (All Yomimono New Mystery Writers' Prize) 1976, The School Festival for the Dead 1977, The Deduction of Tortoise-shell Holmes 1978, High School Girl with a Machine Gun 1978, The Requiem Dedicated to the Bad Wife 1980, Virgin Road 1983, Chizuko's Younger Sister 1989, The Ghost Story of the Hitokoizaka-Slope 1995, The Ball at Castle Dracula 2008, Calico Cat Holmes' Tea Party 2008, Yurei Basu Tsua: AI Ni Omakase 1 2011, A Detective Story, Two, Incident in the Bedroom Suburb, Voice From Heaven, Sailor Suit, Machine Gun. *Leisure interests:* classical music, watching movies. *Address:* 40-16-201 Ohyama-cho, Sibuya-ku, Tokyo 151-0065, Japan (home).

AKALAITIS, JoAnne, BA; American theatre director and academic; *Wallace Benjamin Flint and L. May Hawver Flint Professor Emerita of Drama, Bard College;* b. 29 June 1932, Chicago, Ill.; d. of Clement Akalaitis and Estelle Mattis; m. Philip Glass 1965 (divorced 1974); one s. one d.; ed Univ. of Chicago, Stanford Univ. Grad. School; Artistic Dir New York Shakespeare Festival 1991–92; Wallace Benjamin Flint and L. May Hawver Flint Prof. of Theater, Bard Coll. 2003–12, now Wallace Benjamin Flint and L. May Hawver Flint Prof. Emer. of Drama; Rockefeller Playwright Fellow; Rosamund Gilder Fellow; Guggenheim Fellow 1978; Co-founder Mabou Mines (avant-garde theatre co.), New York 1970; recipient of five Obies for distinguished direction, Edwin Booth Award, Rosamund Gilder Award for Outstanding Achievement in Theatre. *Works directed include:* Beckett's Cascando 1976, Dressed Like an Egg 1977, Dead End Kids 1980, A History of Nuclear Power (writer and dir of play and film), Request Concert (Drama Desk Award) 1981, The Photographer 1983, Beckett's Endgame 1984, Genet's The Balcony 1985, Green Card (writer and dir) 1986, Greg Büchner's Leon & Lena (and Lenz) 1987, Genet's The Screens 1987, Cymbeline 1989, 'Tis Pity She's a Whore 1992, Henry IV (Pts I & II) 1991, Woyzeck 1992, In the Summer House 1993. *Publication:* Green Card. *Leisure interest:* cooking. *Telephone:* (845) 758-7936. *E-mail:* akalaiti@bard.edu. *Website:* www.bard.edu/academics/programs/arts.

AKAMATSU, Hirotaka; Japanese politician; *Vice-Speaker, House of Representatives;* b. 3 May 1948, Aichi Pref.; ed Waseda Univ.; began career with Nippon Express 1971; mem. Aichi Prefectural Ass. (three terms) 1979; mem. Social Democratic Party –1996, apptd Sec.-Gen. 1993; mem. House of Reps (for Aichi No. 5 constituency) 1990–, Vice-Speaker 2012–14, 2017–; Minister of Agric., Forestry and Fisheries 2009–10; Chair. several cttees including Cttee on Foreign Affairs 2004–05, mem. Fundamental Nat. Policies Cttee; mem. Democratic Party of Japan 1996–, Vice-Pres., Chair. Election Campaign Cttee 2009. *Address:* House of Representatives, 1-7-1 Nagatacho, Chiyoda-ku, Tokyo 100-0014, Japan (office). *Telephone:* (3) 3581-5111 (office). *Website:* www.shugiin.go.jp (office); go-akamatsu.com.

AKAMATSU, Ryoko; Japanese academic, diplomatist and civil servant; *President, Japanese Association of International Women's Rights;* b. 24 Aug. 1929, Osaka; d. of Rinsaku Akamatsu and Asaka Akamatsu; ed Tsuda Coll. and Univ. of Tokyo; joined Ministry of Labour 1955, Dir Women Workers' Div. 1970–72; Dir-Gen. Yamanashi Labour Standard Bureau 1975–78; Counsellor in charge of Women's Affairs, Prime Minister's Office 1978–79; Minister, Perm. Mission to UN, New York 1979–82; Dir-Gen. Women's Bureau, Ministry of Labour 1982–85; Amb. to Uruguay 1986–89; Pres. Japan Inst. of Workers' Evolution 1989–93; Prof., Bunkyo Gakuin Univ. 1992–2003; Minister of Educ., Science, Culture and Sports 1993–94; currently Pres. Japanese Asscn of International Women's Rights; Councillor, Asian Women's Fund; Grand Cordon of the Order of the Rising Sun 2003. *Publications include:* Girls Be Ambitious (autobiography) 1990, Beautiful Uruguay 1990, Enacting Laws of Equal Employment Opportunity for Men and Women 2003. *Leisure interests:* reading, swimming, listening to classical music. *E-mail:* info@jaiwr.org (office). *Website:* www.jaiwr.org (office).

AKAR, Gen. Hulusi; Turkish military commander and government official; *Minister of National Defence;* b. 1 Jan. 1952, Kayseri; m. Şule Akar; two c.; ed Army War Coll., Armed Forces Staff Coll., Middle East Tech. Univ., Ankara Univ., Boğaziçi Univ.; joined Turkish Armed Forces as Infantry Officer 1972, Cadet Platoon Leader and Data Processing Officer, Turkish Mil. Acad. 1976–80, becoming Co. Commdr and Section Chief at various units and HQ including Turkish Gen. Staff, posted abroad as Staff Officer in Intelligence Div. at AFSOUTH HQ, Naples, Italy 1990–93, Mil. Asst to Land Forces Commdr 1993–94, to Commdr of Turkish Armed Forces 1994–97, Commdr, Turkish Brigade, Zenica, Bosnia 1997–98, Commdr, Internal Security Brigade 1998–2000, Chief of Plans and Policy, AFSOUTH HQ, Naples 2000–02, Commdr of Land Forces Logistics 2007–09, Commdr of NRDC-T and 3rd Turkish Corps 2009–11, Deputy Chief of Turkish Gen. Staff 2011–13, Commdr, Turkish Land Forces 2013–15, Chief of Gen. Staff 2015–18; Minister of Nat. Defence 2018–; attained rank of Brig. 1998, Maj.-Gen. 2002, Lt 2007, Gen. 2011; numerous awards including Distinguished Service Medal, Armed Forces Medal of Honour, Kosovo KFOR Operations NATO Medal, Korean Nat. Security Merit Medal, US Order of Merit, Kazakhstan Armed Forces 20th Anniversary Medal, Kyrgyzstan Armed Forces Gen. Staff Distinguished Service Medal. *Address:* Ministry of National Defence, Milli Savunma Bakanlığı, 06100 Ankara, Turkey (office). *Telephone:* (312) 4026100 (office). *Fax:* (312) 4184737 (office). *Website:* www.msb.gov.tr (office).

AKASAKA, Kiyotaka, MA; Japanese diplomatist and UN official; *President, Foreign Press Center/Japan;* b. 24 Aug. 1948, Osaka; ed Kyoto Univ. and Trinity Coll., Cambridge, UK; joined Foreign Ministry 1971, held several posts at Secr. of GATT 1988–91, WHO 1993–97, Deputy Dir-Gen. Multilateral Co-operation Dept, Ministry of Foreign Affairs 1997–2000, Amb. and Perm. Rep., UN, New York 2000–01, Consul-Gen., Embassy in Sao Paulo 2001–03, Deputy Sec.-Gen. OECD 2003–07, Under-Sec.-Gen., Dept of Communications and Public Information, UN 2007–12; Pres. Foreign Press Center/Japan 2012–; Rep. to Kyoto Conf. on Climate Change 1997; Vice-Chair. Prep. Cttee World Summit on Sustainable Devt, Johannesburg 2002. *Publications:* The GATT and the Uruguay Round Negotiations; The Cartagena Protocol on Biosafety and numerous journal articles on trade, the environment and sustainable devt. *Address:* Foreign Press Center/Japan, 6F Nippon Press Center Building, 2-2-1, Uchisaiwaicho, Chiyoda-ku, Tokyo, 100-0011, Japan (office). *Telephone:* (3) 3501-3401 (office). *Fax:* (3) 3501-3622 (office). *E-mail:* ma@fpcjpn.or.jp (office). *Website:* fpcj.jp (office).

AKASAKI, Isamu, DrEng; Japanese physicist and academic; *Lifetime Professor, Meijo University;* b. 30 Jan. 1929, Kagoshima Pref.; ed Kyoto and Nagoya Univs; Research Scientist, Kobe Kogyo Corpn (now Fujitsu Ltd) 1952–59; Research Assoc., Asst Prof. and Assoc. Prof., Dept of Electronics, Nagoya Univ. 1959–64, Prof. 1981–92, Project Leader, Research and Devt of GaN-based blue light-emitting diodes, sponsored by Japan Science and Tech. (JST) Agency 1987–90, Prof. Emer. 1992–, Univ. Prof. 2004, Research Fellow, Akasaki Research Centre 2001–, Akasaki Inst. opened 2006; Head of Basic Research Lab. 4, Matsushita Research Inst. Tokyo, Inc. 1964–74, Gen. Man. Semiconductor Dept 1974–81; Prof., Meijo Univ. 1992–, Project Leader, Research and Devt of GaN-based Short-Wavelength Semiconductor Laser Diode, sponsored by JST 1993–99, Project Leader, High-Tech Research Centre for Nitride Semiconductors, sponsored by MEXT 1996–2004, Dir Research Centre for Nitride Semiconductors 2004–, Lifetime Prof. 2010–; Visiting Prof., Research Centre for Interface Quantum Electronics, Hokkaido Univ. 1995–96; Project Leader, Japan Soc. for the Promotion of Science's Research for the Future programme 1996–2001; Chair. R&D Strategic Cttee on the Wireless Devices Based on Nitride Semiconductors, sponsored by METI 2003–06; mem. NAS; Foreign Assoc., US Nat. Acad. of Eng 2008; Fellow, IEEE 1999; Medal with Purple Ribbon 1997, Order of the Rising Sun,

Gold Rays with Neck Ribbon 2002, Person of Cultural Merit 2004, Order of Culture 2011; Dr hc (Univ. of Montpellier II) 1999, (Linkoping Univ.) 2001; Japanese Asscn for Crystal Growth Award 1989, Chu-Nichi Culture Prize 1991, Technological Contrib. Award, Japanese Asscn for Crystal Growth in commemoration of its 20th anniversary 1994, Heinrich Welker Gold Medal, Int. Symposium on Compound Semiconductors 1995, Eng Achievement Award, IEEE/Lasers Electro-Optics Soc. 1996, Inoue Harushige Award, JST Agency 1998, C&C the Nippon Electric Co. Corpn 1998, Laudise Prize, Int. Org. for Crystal Growth 1998, IEEE Jack A. Morton Award 1998, Rank Prize, Rank Prize Foundation 1998, Gordon E. Moore Award, Electrochemical Soc. 1999, Toray Science and Tech. Prize, Toray Science Foundation 1999, Asahi Prize, Asahi Shinbun Cultural Foundation 2001, Outstanding Achievement Award, Japan Soc. of Applied Physics 2002, Fujihara Prize, Fujihara Foundation of Science 2002, Takeda Award, Takeda Foundation 2002, Pres.'s Award, Science Council of Japan 2003, Solid State Devices and Materials Award 2003, Tokai TV Culture Prize 2004, John Bardeen Award, Minerals, Metals and Materials Soc. 2006, Outstanding Achievement Award, Japanese Asscn for Crystal Growth 2006, Hon. Lifetime Achievement Award, 162nd Research Cttee on Wide Bandgap Semiconductor Photonic and Electronic Devices, Japan Soc. for the Promotion of Science 2007, Kyoto Prize in Advanced Tech., Inamori Foundation 2009, IEEE Edison Medal 2011, Special Award for Intellectual Property Activities, JST Agency 2011, Minami-Nippon Culture Prize-Hon. Prize 2011, Nobel Prize in Physics (co-recipient with Hiroshi Amano and Shuji Nakamura for the invention of blue light-emitting diodes—LEDs) 2014, Charles Stark Draper Prize, Nat. Acad. of Eng (co-recipient) 2015. *Achievements include:* known for inventing the bright gallium nitride (GaN) p-n junction blue LED in 1989 and subsequently the high-brightness GaN blue LED. *Publications:* numerous papers in professional journals. *Address:* Graduate School of Science and Engineering, 1-501 Shiogamaguchi, Tempaku-ku, Nagoya 468-8502, Japan (office). *Telephone:* (52) 832-1151 (switchboard) (office). *E-mail:* kouhou@ccmails.meijo-u.ac.jp (office). *Website:* www.meijo-u.ac.jp/english/academics/sci_tech/materials/laboratory.html (office).

AKAYEV, Askar Akayevich, DTech; Kyrgyzstani politician and physicist; *Professor and Senior Researcher, Prigogine Institute for Mathematical Investigations of Complex Systems, Lomonosov Moscow State University;* b. 10 Nov. 1944, Kyzyl-Bairak Kemin Dist; s. of Akai Tokoyev and Ossel Tokoyeva; m. Mairam Akayeva 1970; two s. two d.; ed Leningrad Inst. of Precise Mechanics and Optics; Prof., Frunze (now Bishkek) Polytechnical Inst. 1972–73, Chair. 1976–86; Prof., Inst. of Precise Mechanics and Optics 1973–76; Head of Science Dept, Cen. Cttee, Kyrgyz CP 1986–87; mem. CPSU 1981–91 (resgnd); fmr mem. Cen. Cttee Kyrgyz CP, Vice-Pres.; fmr Pres. Kyrgyz SSR; Pres. Kyrgyz SSR Acad. of Sciences 1987–90; fmr mem. CPSU Constitutional Compliance Cttee; fmr mem. USSR Supreme Soviet Cttee on Econ. Reform 1991; Exec. Pres. Kyrgyz SSR 1990, Pres. of Kyrgyzstan 1990–2005; Prof. and Sr Researcher, Prigogine Inst. for Math. Investigations of Complex Systems, Lomonosov Moscow State Univ. 2005–; Academician, Int. Acad. of Informatization, Canada 1997; Hon. Academician, Int. Eng Acad., Int. Acad. of Creation 1996; Grand Cross (First Class), Order of the White Double Cross (Slovakia) 2003; Albert Einstein Award 1999, Devotion to Peace and Good Award, Russia 2000, WIPO Gold Medal 2001, Elizabeth Haub Award for Environmental Diplomacy 2003, Gold Kondratieff Medal, Int. N.D. Kondratieff Foundation 2012. *Publications:* Methods of Data Optical Processing 1992, Diplomacy of the Silk Road 1999, The Memorable Decade 2001, Kyrgyz Statehood and the National Epos 'Manas' 2002, The Difficult Road to Democracy 2002; more than 80 articles on radiophysics and politics. *Leisure interests:* travelling with the family, mountain skiing, mountaineering. *Address:* Lomonosov Moscow State University, 119991 Moscow, GSP-1, Leninskie Gory, Russian Federation (office). *Telephone:* (495) 939-10-00 (office). *Fax:* (495) 939-01-26 (office). *E-mail:* office@akaev.kg (office); mmf@mech.math.msu.su (office). *Website:* www.msu.ru (office).

AKBARUDDIN, Syed, MA; Indian diplomatist; *Permanent Representative to UN;* b. 27 April 1960; s. of S Bashiruddin and Dr Zeba Bashiruddin; m. Padma; two c.; joined Indian Foreign Service 1985, served in Riyadh and Cairo, First Sec. (in-charge of UN Security Council Reform and Peace-Keeping), Perm. Mission to UN, New York 1995–98, Consul-Gen. Jeddah, Saudi Arabia 2000–04, Dir Foreign Sec.'s Office 2004–05, Jt-Sec. (Div. of External Publicity and Public Diplomacy), Ministry of External Affairs, New Delhi 2012–15, Additional-Sec. April–Sept. 2015, Chief Coordinator India–Africa Forum Summit 2015, Perm. Rep. to UN 2016–, fmr Counsellor, Indian High Comm., Islamabad, Pakistan; Head of External Relations and Policy Coordination Unit and Special Asst to Dir-Gen., Int. Atomic Energy Agency (IAEA), Vienna 2006–11. *Address:* Permanent Mission of India, 235 E 43rd Street, New York, NY 10017, USA (office). *Telephone:* (212) 490-9660 (office). *Fax:* (212) 490-9656 (office). *E-mail:* india@un.int (office). *Website:* www.pminewyork.org (office).

AKÇA, Halil İbrahim, MA; Turkish diplomatist and international organization official; *Secretary-General, Economic Cooperation Organization;* b. 1963, Sivas; m.; three c.; ed Istanbul Tech. Univ., Univ. of Delaware, USA; Deputy Expert, Devlet Planlama Teşkilatı (State Planning Org.) 1989–96, Planning Expert (Communications Sector and Project Analysis) 1996, Deputy Under-Sec. 2002–08, Under-Sec. Jan.–June 2009; Adviser to Minister of Finance 1996–97; Head of Tech. Del., 'Turkish Repub. of Northern Cyprus' 2002–08; Amb. to 'Turkish Repub. of Northern Cyprus' 2011–15; Sec.-Gen., Econ. Cooperation Org. 2015–; mem. Bd of Dirs Retirement Fund of Repub. of Turkey 1997, Turkish Development Bank 2002–08; mem. Exec. Bd e-Transformation Turkey Project. *Address:* Economic Cooperation Organization, 1 Golbou Alley, Kamranieh Street, POB 14155-6176, Tehran, Iran (office). *Telephone:* (21) 22831733 (office). *Fax:* (21) 22831732 (office). *E-mail:* registry@ecosecretariat.org (office). *Website:* www.ecosecretariat.org (office).

AKÇAM, Zechariah, BA, MA; Turkish diplomatist; *Ambassador to Indonesia;* b. 1968, Çukurçayır, Balıkesir-Savastepe Co.; m.; two c.; ed Savastepe Imam Hatip High School, Univ. of Ankara, George Washington Univ., American Univ., USA, School of Int. Service, Ankara, Catholic Univ. of America, USA, Bilkent Univ.; worked as researcher-trainee, Near Eastern Div., Library of Congress, Washington, DC; attended seminars at Nat. Security Coll., Coll. of Europe, Bruges, World Bank Inst., Cicero Foundation, Paris, Harvard Kennedy School of Govt; expert, EU Directorate Gen., Under-Secr. of Foreign Trade 1997; mem. Parl. (AK Party) for İzmir 2002–07; Vice-Pres. of External Relations, Ministry of Foreign Affairs 2007–12, Amb. to Indonesia 2012–. *Address:* Embassy of Turkey, Jalan H.R. Rasuna Said, Kav. 1, Kuningan, Jakarta 12950, Indonesia (office). *Telephone:* (21) 5256250 (office). *Fax:* (21) 5226056 (office). *E-mail:* embassy.jakarta@mfa.gov.tr (office). *Website:* jakarta.emb.mfa.gov.tr (office).

AKÇAPAR, Burak, DrIur; Turkish academic and diplomatist; *Ambassador to India;* m. Dr Şebnem Köşer Akçapar; one s.; ed academic degree and exec. training programmes at various colls and univs in Turkey, Germany and USA as well as at Turkish Diplomatic Acad.; served at Missions in Qatar (Deputy Chief of Mission, Embassy in Doha) and Germany (Vice-Consul in Hamburg) and twice at Int. Security and Disarmament Dept, Ministry of Foreign Affairs (MFA) 1988–97, Defence Planning and Operations Div., NATO Int. Staff 1997–2002, Head of Planning Dept, Directorate Gen. for Policy Planning, MFA 2002–04, 2008–09, First Political Counsellor, Embassy in Washington, DC 2004–06, Deputy Chief of Mission 2006–08, Deputy Dir Gen. for Political Affairs focusing on South Asia, MFA 2009–11, Turkish mem. of Int. Contact Group on Afghanistan and Co-Chair. Working Group on Regional Co-operation, Amb. to India (also accred to Nepal and the Maldives) 2011–; Hon. Dr of Diplomacy and Int. Relations (India); NATO Award for Excellence 2002. *Publications:* The International Law of Conventional Arms Control in Europe 1996, Turkey's New European Era 2006, People's Mission to the Ottoman Empire: M.A. Ansari and the Indian Medical Mission, 1912–13 2014; three book chapters on arms control and int. defence co-operation; numerous academic articles and papers on a range of int. issues. *Address:* Embassy of Turkey, 50N Nyaya Marg, Chanakyapuri, New Delhi 110 021, India (office). *Telephone:* (11) 26889054 (office). *Fax:* (11) 24101974 (office). *E-mail:* embassy.newdelhi@mfa.gov.tr (office). *Website:* yenidelhi.be.mfa.gov.tr (office); www.akcapar.com.

AKCHURIN, Renat Suleymanovich, DrMed; Russian cardiovascular surgeon; *Professor and Head, Department of Cardiovascular Surgery, Moscow Institute of Clinical Cardiology;* b. 2 April 1946, Andijan, Uzbekistan; s. of Akchurin Suleyman Safievich and Akchurina Tazkira Kiyamovna; m. Natalya Pavlovna Akchurina; two s.; ed Inst. of Medicine (now Seehenov Acad. of Medicine); gen. practitioner, polyclinics 1970–73; Ordinator, Jr, Sr Researcher, Inst. of Clinical and Experimental Medicine 1973–84; worked at Baylor Univ., Texas, USA 1984; Surgeon, Prof. and Head of Dept of Cardiovascular Surgery, Moscow Inst. of Clinical Cardiology 1984–; mem. Bd of Dirs, Int. Surgical Soc. of M. DeBakey, Scientific Council of World Soc. Angiologists, Presidium of Rossiyskogo Soc. for Cardiovascular Surgery; mem. European Soc. for Cardiovascular Surgery; Corresp. mem. Russian Acad. of Medical Sciences 1997, Russian Acad. of Science; Hon. mem. Acad. of Sciences of Tatarstan Repub.; Order of Merit (Russia) 1996, Order of the Eagle (Third Class) 1997, Order of the Commodore (Peru) 2000; USSR State Prize 1982, Russian Fed. State Prize 2001, Russian Govt Prize for research and achievement in the field of surgery 2003. *Achievements include:* performed first heart and lung transplantation operations in USSR; performs about 100 bypass operations a year, performed a bypass operation on Pres. Yeltsin 1996; patented several inventions of medical instruments. *Publications include:* more than 300 scientific papers and articles. *Leisure interests:* music, sports, hunting, cooking. *Address:* Institute of Clinical Cardiology, 121552 Moscow, Cherepkovskaya str. 15A, Russia (office). *Telephone:* (499) 140-93-36 (office); (499) 149-17-08 (office). *E-mail:* rsakchurin@list.ru (office); 3ko@list.ru (office).

AKEIL, Ahmad Abdallah al-; Saudi Arabian banker; Chair. Arab Bank for Econ. Devt in Africa (Banque arabe pour le développement économique en Afrique—BADEA); Chair. SANAD Cooperative Insurance and Reinsurance; mem. Bd of Dirs Arab Nat. Bank. *Address:* Arab Bank for Economic Development in Africa, Sayed Abd ar-Rahman el-Mahdi Street, PO Box 2640, Khartoum 11111, Sudan (office). *Telephone:* (1) 83773646 (office). *Fax:* (1) 83770600 (office). *E-mail:* badea@badea.org (office). *Website:* www.badea.org (office).

AKENSON, Donald Harman, BA, MEd, PhD, DLitt, DHum, FRSA, FRSC, FRHistS; Canadian historian and academic; *Douglas Professor of Canadian and Colonial History, Queen's University, Kingston;* b. 22 May 1941, Minneapolis, Minn., USA; s. of Donald Nels Akenson and Fern L. Harman Akenson; ed Yale Univ., Harvard Univ.; Allston Burr Sr Tutor, Dunster House, Harvard Coll. 1966–67; Assoc. Prof. of History, Queen's Univ., Kingston, Ont. 1970–74, Prof. 1974–, currently Douglas Prof. of Canadian and Colonial History; Beamish Research Prof., Inst. of Irish Studies, Univ. of Liverpool 1998–2002; Guggenheim Fellow 1984–85; Hon. DLitt (McMaster) 1995, (Guelph) 2000, Hon. DHumLitt (Lethbridge) 1996, Hon. LLD (Regina) 2002, Dr hc (Queens Univ. Belfast) 2008, (Victoria Univ., Wellington, New Zealand) 2010; Chalmers Prize 1985, Landon Prize 1987, Grawemeyer World Peace Prize 1993, Molson Laureate 1996 and numerous other awards. *Publications include:* The Irish Education Experiment 1970, The Church of Ireland: Ecclesiastical Reform and Revolution 1800–1885 1971, Education and Enmity: The Control of Schooling in Northern Ireland 1920–50 1973, The United States and Ireland 1973, A Mirror to Kathleen's Face: Education in Independent Ireland 1922–60 1975, Local Poets and Social History: James Orr, Bard of Ballycarry 1977, Between Two Revolutions: Islandmagee, Co. Antrim 1798–1920 1979, A Protestant in Purgatory: Richard Whately: Archbishop of Dublin 1981, The Irish in Ontario: A Study of Rural History 1984, Being Had: Historians, Evidence and the Irish in North America 1985, The Life and Times of Ogle Gowan 1986, Small Differences: Irish Catholics and Irish Protestants, 1815–1921 1988, Half the World from Home: Perspectives on the Irish in New Zealand 1990, Occasional Papers on the Irish in South Africa 1991, God's Peoples: Covenant and Land in South Africa, Israel and Ulster 1992, The Irish Diaspora, A Primer 1993, Conor: A Biography of Conor Cruise O'Brien 1994, If the Irish Ran the World: Montserrat 1630–1730, Surpassing Wonder: The Invention of the Bible and the Talmuds 1998, Saint Saul: A Skeleton Key to the Historical Jesus 2000, Intolerance: The E. Coli of the Human Mind 2004, An Irish History of Civilization (two vols) 2006, Some Family – The Mormons and How Humanity Keeps Track of Itself 2007, Ireland, Sweden and the Great European Migration 1815–1914 2011, Discovering the End of Time: Irish Evangelicals in the Age of Daniel O'Connell 2016; novels: The Lazar House Notebooks 1981, Brotherhood Week in Belfast 1984, The Orangeman: The Edgerston Audit 1987, At Face Value: The Life and Times of Eliza McCormack 1990. *Address:* Department of History, Queen's

University, Kingston, ON, K7L 3N6, Canada (office). *Telephone:* (613) 533-2150 (office). *E-mail:* 8da8@queensu.ca (office). *Website:* www.queensu.ca/history (office).

AKERLOF, George Arthur, BA, PhD; American economist and academic; *Daniel E. Koshland, Senior Distinguished Professor Emeritus of Economics, University of California, Berkeley;* b. 17 June 1940, New Haven, Conn.; m. Janet L. Yellen; one s.; ed Massachusetts Inst. Tech., Yale Univ.; Asst Prof., Univ. of Calif., Berkeley 1966–70, Assoc. Prof. 1970–77, Prof. 1977–78, Daniel E. Koshland, Sr. Distinguished Prof. of Econs 1980, currently Prof. Emer.; Faculty, McCourt School of Public Policy, Georgetown Univ. 2014–; Visiting Prof., Indian Statistical Inst. 1967–68; Research Assoc., Harvard Univ. 1969; Sr Staff Economist, Pres.'s Council of Econ. Advisers 1973–74; Visiting Research Economist, Special Studies Section, Bd of Govs of the Fed. Reserve System 1977–78; Cassel Prof. with respect to Money and Banking, LSE 1978–80; Sr Fellow, The Brookings Inst. 1994–; Vice-Pres. American Econ. Asscn; mem. Bd of Dirs Nat. Bureau for Economic Research 1997–; Assoc. Ed. several journals on econs; Guggenheim Fellow; Fellow, Econometric Soc., American Acad. of Arts and Sciences, Inst. for Policy Reform; Dr hc (Univ. of Zurich) 2000; Ely Lecturer, American Econ. Asscn 1990, Fisher-Shultz Lecturer, World Congress of the Econometrics Soc. 1995, Harry Johnson Lecturer, Royal Econ. Asscn 1997, Henry George Lecturer, Univ. of Scranton 1998, Gunnar Myrdal Lecturer (Centenary of Birth) 1998, Henry George Lecturer, Williams Coll. 1999, Woodward Lecturer, Univ. of British Columbia 1999, Nobel Memorial Prize in Economic Sciences 2001 (jt recipient); numerous other awards and prizes. *Publications:* An Economic Theorist's Book of Tales 1984, Animal Spirits: How Human Psychology Drives the Economy, and Why It Matters for Global Capitalism (with Robert Shiller) 2009. *Address:* Department of Economics, 530 Evans Hall, #3880, University of California, Berkeley, CA 94720-3880, USA (office). *Telephone:* (510) 642-5837 (office). *Fax:* (510) 642-6615 (office). *E-mail:* akerlof@econ.berkeley.edu (office). *Website:* elsa.berkeley.edu/~akerlof (office).

AKERMANN, Markus; Swiss business executive; b. 25 Jan. 1947; ed Univ. of St Gallen, Univ. of Sheffield, UK; with Swiss Banking Corpn 1975–78; joined Holcim Ltd 1978, served in posts including Latin America Area Man. 1987, mem. Exec. Cttee 1993–2002, mem. Bd of Dirs and CEO 2002–12 (retd), Dir 2012–, Chair. Man. Bd Holcim Foundation; CEO ACC Acquisition LLC; mem. Bd of Dirs ACC Ltd, India, Ambuja Cements Ltd 2006–12, Holcim Ecuador SA 2002–13, Holcim (Vietnam) Ltd; mem. Global Holcim Innovation Prize Jury 2012. *Address:* Holcim Group Support Ltd, Hagenholzstrasse 85, 8050 Zurich, Switzerland (office). *Telephone:* (58) 858-58-58 (office). *Fax:* (58) 858-58-59 (office). *E-mail:* info@holcim.com (office). *Website:* www.holcim.com (office).

AKERS-JONES, Sir David, KBE, CMG, JP, MA; British civil servant (retd); b. 14 April 1927, Worthing, Sussex; s. of Walter George Jones and Dorothy Jones; m. Jane Spickernell 1951 (died 2002); one s. (deceased) one d.; ed Worthing High School and Brasenose Coll., Oxford; with British India Steam Navigation Co. 1945–49; Malayan Civil Service 1954–57; Hong Kong Civil Service 1957–86, Sec. for New Territories and for Dist Admin, Hong Kong Govt 1973–85, Chief Sec. 1985–86; Acting Gov. Hong Kong 1986–87; Hong Kong Affairs Adviser to China 1993–97; Chair. Nat. Mutual Asia Hong Kong (later AXA China Region) 1988–2001, Hong Kong Housing Authority 1988–93, Global Asset Man. Hong Kong 1988; Dir Hysan Devt Co. Ltd, The Mingly Corpn Ltd; Vice-Pres. WWF Hong Kong 1995–, Hong Kong Girl Guides; columnist, The Standard; Hon. Pres. Outward Bound Trust (Hong Kong) 1986–; Hon. mem. RICS; Hon. DCL (Kent Univ.) 1987; Hon. LLD (Chinese Univ. of Hong Kong) 1988; Hon. DScS (City Univ., Hong Kong) 1993; Grand Bauhinia Medal (Hong Kong) 2003. *Publication:* Feeling the Stones: Reminiscences 2004. *Leisure interests:* painting, gardening, walking, music. *Address:* Flat 1, Floor 25, Bamboo Grove, 80 Kennedy Road, Hong Kong Special Administrative Region, People's Republic of China (home). *Telephone:* (852) 2491-9319 (office); (852) 2491-9319 (home). *Fax:* (852) 2491-1300 (home). *E-mail:* akersjon@pacific.net.hk (home).

AKERSON, Daniel F., BSc (Eng), MSc (Econs); American business executive; *Vice-Chairman and Special Advisor, The Carlyle Group;* ed US Naval Acad., London School of Econs, UK; held several key posts at MCI Communications Corpn 1983–93, including Exec. Vice-Pres. and Chief Financial Officer 1987–90, Pres. and COO 1992–93; Gen. Partner, Forstmann Little & Co. (pvt. equity firm) 1993; Chair. and CEO General Instrument Co. 1993–95; Chair. Nextel Communications, Inc. 1996–2001, CEO 1996–99; Chair. and CEO XO Communications, Inc. 1999–2003; mem. Exec. Cttee, Man. Dir and Head of Global Buyout, The Carlyle Group, Washington, DC 2003–10, Vice-Chair. and Special Advisor 2014–; apptd mem. Bd of Dirs General Motors Co. 2009, CEO 2010–14, Chair. 2011–14; mem. Bd of Dirs US Naval Acad. Foundation, Tsinghua Univ. School and Econs and Man. Advisory Bd, Int. Business Leaders Advisory Council of Shanghai; mem. Business Council; T.C. and Elizabeth Cooke Business Medallion, Coll. of William & Mary 2004, Distinguished Grad. Award, US Naval Acad. 2012. *Address:* The Carlyle Group, 1001 Pennsylvania Avenue, NW, Washington, DC 20004-2505, USA (office). *Telephone:* (202) 729-5626 (office). *Fax:* (202) 347-1818 (office). *Website:* www.carlyle.com (office).

ÅKESSON, Eva, PhD; Swedish professor of chemical physics and university administrator; *Vice-Chancellor, Uppsala University;* b. 30 Dec. 1961, Ängelholm; ed Umeå Univ.; post-doctoral researcher, Univ. of Minnesota, USA; selected as Sr Researcher by Research Council in the field of photochemical reaction mechanisms 1996; Researcher, Lund Univ. from 1996, also worked as a teacher and Dir of Studies, Vice-Rector Lund Univ. 2003–08, Deputy Vice-Chancellor 2009–11; Rectrix Magnifica (Vice-Chancellor), Uppsala Univ. 2012–; mem. CSN (Cen. Bd for Student Aid), Kristianstad Univ. Coll., Swedish Inst., Nat. Cttee for Chem.; Titular mem. IUPAC Cttee on Chem. Educ. 2005–; Chair. Int. Expert Panels for Evaluating Leadership and Governance of Educ., Univ. of Helsinki 2008, Aalto School of Science 2011. *Publications:* numerous papers in professional journals in the field of femtochemistry, using ultrafast spectroscopy to follow chemical reactions and dynamics. *Address:* Universitetsledningens kansli S:t Olofsg. 10B, Box 256, 751 05 Uppsala, Sweden (office). *Telephone:* (18) 471-33-10 (office). *Fax:* (18) 471-16-40 (office). *E-mail:* rektor@uu.se (office). *Website:* www.uu.se (office).

AKHALAIA, Bachana (Bacho); Georgian lawyer and government official; b. 24 Oct. 1980, Zugdidi; s. of Roland Akhalaia; ed Faculty of Law, Tbilisi State Univ.; Project Co-ordinator, Liberty Inst. (non-govt org.) 2003–04; Deputy Public Defender (Ombudsman) 2004–05; Head of Penitentiary Dept, Ministry of Justice 2005–08; Deputy Minister of Defence 2008–09, Minister of Defence 2009–12, of Internal Affairs July–Sept. 2012; arrested Nov. 2012, accused of exceeding official powers, illegal confinement and torture, acquitted July 2013, sentenced to 45 months' imprisonment on charges of abuse of office Oct. 2013, pardoned by outgoing Pres. Mikheil Saakashvili Nov. 2013, pardon subsequently appealed, further charges of abuse of power presented Nov. 2013, acquittal upheld on two charges Dec. 2013 and March 2014, remained in preventative detention awaiting further trial Aug. 2014, sentenced to seven years and six months in jail in a case involving prisoner beatings and a fatal shooting in 2006 Oct. 2014.

AKHMETOV, Danial Kenzhetayevich, BEng, BEcons; Kazakhstani politician; *President, Athletics Federation of Kazakhstan;* b. 15 June 1954, Pavlodar; m.; two c.; ed Pavlodar Industry Inst.; fmr racing cyclist; fmr Deputy Prime Minister and Minister of Industry, Energy, Transport and Communications; Akim (Gov.) Pavlodar Oblast 1995–97, 2001–03; Akim (Gov.) Northern Kazakhstan Oblast 1997–99; Deputy, then First Deputy Prime Minister 1999–2001; Prime Minister of Kazakhstan 2003–07 (resgnd); Minister of Defence 2007–09; Head Environmental Energy Co. 2010; Minister of Energy and Infrastructure 2012–14; Akim (Gov.) East Kazakhstan Oblast 2014–; Pres. Athletics Federation of Kazakhstan 2018–. *Address:* Athletics Federation of Kazakhstan, Astana, Dostyk 3 (office); Eastern Kazakhstan Akim, 070019 Oskemen, M.Gorky Street, 40, Kazakhstan. *Telephone:* (7172) 52-42-36. *E-mail:* info@kazathletics.kz; chancellery@akimvko.gov.kz. *Website:* kazathletics.kz; www.akimvko.gov.kz.

AKHMETOV, Rinat Leonidovych, BA; Ukrainian business executive; *President, System Capital Management;* b. 21 Sept. 1966, Donetsk; m. Liliya Smirnova; two s.; ed Donetsk State Univ.; f. Donetsk City Bank; Head, Donetsk Industrial Group (conglomerate of steel and mining cos); Founder, Pres. and prin. shareholder, System Capital Management (holding co. with controlling shares in more than 90 cos); Owner and Pres. Shakhtar Donetsk football club 1996–; Deputy (Partiya Rehioniv—Party of the Regions), Verkhovna Rada (Supreme Council) 2007–12; Founder Foundation for Devt of Ukraine 2005, Foundation for Effective Governance, Kyiv 2007 (shut down amid protests against him Jan. 2014); Hon. Citizen of Donetsk 2006; Chevalier of the Miner's Glory Medal, Honoured Worker of Fitness and Sports of Ukraine 1999, Chevalier of Order of Merit (Third Class) 2002, (Second Class) 2004, (First Class) 2006, Sitara-e-Pakistan for Merits to Pakistan 2007, Order of Prince Yaroslav the Wise (Fifth Class) 2010; Donetsk Citizens' Recognition Prize, Donetsk City Council 2008. *Address:* JSC System Capital Management, 83001 Donetsk, Pushkinsky Business Centre, vul. Maryinska 1, Ukraine (office). *Telephone:* (62) 381-50-36 (office). *Fax:* (62) 381-50-06 (office); (62) 381-50-50 (office). *E-mail:* scm@scm.com.ua (office). *Website:* www.scm.com.ua (office); www.scmholding.com (office); www.shakhtar.com.

AKHTAR, Muhammad, MSc, PhD, FRS; British/Pakistani biochemist and academic; b. 23 Feb. 1933, Punjab, India; s. of Muhammad Azeem Chaudhry; m. Monika E. Schürmann 1963; two s.; ed Govt Coll. Sargodha, Govt Coll. Lahore, Univ. of Punjab and Imperial Coll., London; Research Scientist, Research Inst. for Medicine and Chem., Cambridge, Mass, USA 1959–63; Lecturer in Biochemistry, Univ. of Southampton 1963–66, Sr Lecturer 1966–68, Reader 1968–73, Prof. 1973–98, Head, Dept of Biochemistry 1978–93, Chair. School of Biochemical and Physiological Sciences 1983–87, Prof. Emer. of Biochemistry 1998–; fmr Dir Gen. and Prof., School of Biological Sciences, Univ. of the Punjab; Distinguished Nat. Prof., Higher Education Comm., Islamabad 2004–; Chair. School of Biochemical and Physiological Sciences 1983–87, Inst. of Biomolecular Sciences 1989–90; Dir SERC Molecular Recognition Centre 1990–94; Founding Fellow, Third World Acad. of Sciences 1984, Treasurer, mem. Council 1993–97, Vice-Pres. 1997–2003; Foreign Fellow, Pakistan Acad. of Sciences 2000; mem. Council Royal Soc. 1983–85; mem. Biochemical Soc. Cttee 1983–86; Hon. Fellow, Univ. Coll. London 2010; Hon. DSc (Karachi Univ.) 2000; Sitara-I-Imtiaz (Pakistan), Flintoff Medal, Royal Soc. of Chem. 1993, Third World Acad. of Sciences Medal 1996. *Publications:* numerous articles in biochemical and chemical journals. *Address:* Biological Sciences, University of Southampton, Southampton, SO17 1BJ, England (office); University of the Punjab, Quaid-e-Azam Campus, PO Box 54590, Lahore, Pakistan (office). *Telephone:* (23) 8076-7718 (Southampton) (office); (42) 99231099 (Lahore) (office). *Fax:* (42) 99231101 (Lahore) (office). *E-mail:* ma3@soton.ac.uk (office). *Website:* www.pu.edu.pk (office).

AKHTAR, Shamshad, BA, MA, MSc, PhD; Pakistani economist, UN official, government official and fmr central banker; b. 1954, Hyderabad, Sindh Prov.; ed Univ. of Punjab, Quaid-e-Azam Univ., Univ. of Sussex and Paisley Coll. of Tech. (now Univ. of Paisley), UK, Harvard Univ., USA; briefly worked at planning offices in Pakistan at Fed. and Sindh Govt levels; economist, World Bank mission in Pakistan 1980–90; Sr then Prin. Financial Sector Specialist, Asian Devt Bank (ADB) 1990–98; Man. and Coordinator for APEC Finance Ministers' Group 1998–2001, Dir Govt Finance and Trade Div. for East and Cen. Asia Dept, then Deputy Dir-Gen. South East Asia Dept 2001–04, Dir-Gen. 2004–05; Gov. (first woman) State Bank of Pakistan 2006–09, also Gov. of the IMF for Pakistan; Special Sr Adviser, Office of the Pres. 2009; Vice-Pres., Middle East and North Africa, World Bank 2009–12; Minister of Finance, Revenue and Econ. Affairs (in caretaker govt) June–Aug. 2018; Exec. Sec., ESCAP, UN 2013–15; Visiting Fellow, Harvard Univ. Dept of Econs 1987; Best Cen. Bank Gov. in Asia, Emerging Markets newspaper 2007, Cen. Bank Gov. of the Year in Asia, Banker Magazine 2008. *Publications include:* numerous papers on econs and finance. *Address:* c/o Ministry of Finance, Revenue and Economic Affairs, Blk C, Pakistan Secretariat, Islamabad, Pakistan (office).

AKHTAR, Tasleem, MBBS, DCh, MRCP FRCP; Pakistani paediatrician, medical research officer and academic; b. 1 Sept. 1944, Village Jhanda, Tehsil Dist; m.; one s. one d.; ed Khyber Medical Coll., Univ. of Peshawar, Royal Coll. of Physicians, London, UK, Royal Coll. of Physicians and Surgeons, Edinburgh, UK; est. Neonatal Unit, Khyber Medical Coll. (now Khyber Medical Univ.) 1976, Sr Medical Research Officer Pakistan Medical Research Council (PMRC) Research Centre 1979–80, Research Dir 1980, Exec. Dir PMRC 1994–2004, Chair. 1996–99, currently Prof. Emer., Consultant and Supervisor, Master in Health Research Programme; Dir Prov. Health Services Acad., Dept of Health, Govt of North-West Frontier Prov. (NWFP) 1999–2000; Chief of Research and Academic Advancement,

Fatima Memorial Coll. of Medicine and Surgery, Lahore, currently Sr Tech. Advisor, Policy and Research, Nur Foundation; Gen. Sec. Pakistan Paediatric Asscn, NWFP Br. (PPA–NWFP) 1980–82, 1984–86, Pres. 1982–84, Vice-Pres. PPA Centre 1990; Chief Ed. Pakistan Journal of Medical Research, PMRC; Asst Ed. Pakistan Paediatric Journal, Lahore; mem. Hosp. Monitoring Cttee, Ministry of Health; mem. Governing Bd Nat. Inst. of Health, Islamabad; mem. Bd of Dirs NWFP Health Foundation, The Network for Consumer Protection; mem. Forum on Telemedicine in Pakistan, Tech. Resource Mobilization Unit 2001–02; American Public Health Asscn Award for Most Successful Int. Collaboration 1997, Tamgha-e- Imtiaz 2012. *Address:* Nur Center for Research and Policy, 4th Floor, College Building, Fatima Memorial Hospital, Shadman, Lahore, Pakistan (office). *Telephone:* 111-555-600 (office). *E-mail:* info@nurfoundation.org (office); akhtar_tasleem@hotmail.com. *Website:* nurfoundation.org (office).

AKHUNDZADA, Hibatullah; Afghan guerrilla leader; *Leader, Taliban;* b. 1961, Panjwayi Dist, Kandahar Prov.; worked as mem. Dept Promotion of Virtue and the Prevention of Vice police, Farah Prov. 1996, later Instructor, Jihadi Madrasa; fmr Chief Justice, Shari'ah Courts, Islamic Emirate of Afghanistan; Deputy Leader, Taliban 2015–16, Supreme Commdr 2016–.

AKIHITO, HIM The Emperor Emeritus of Japan, KG, GCVO; b. 23 Dec. 1933, Tokyo; s. of Emperor Hirohito and of Empress Nagako; m. Michiko Shoda 1959; two s. (including HIM Emperor Naruhito) one d.; ed Gakushuin schools and Faculty of Politics and Econs, Gakushuin Univ.; official investiture as Crown Prince 1952; succeeded 7 Jan. 1989; crowned 12 Nov. 1990; abdicated 30 April 2019; has undertaken visits to numerous countries and travelled widely throughout Japan; Hon. Pres. or Patron, Asian Games 1958, Int. Sports Games for the Disabled 1964, Eleventh Pacific Science Congress 1966, Japan World Exposition 1970, Int. Skill Contest for the Disabled 1981; mem. Ichthyological Soc. of Japan; Foreign mem. Linnean Soc. of London 1980, Hon. mem. 1986; Research Assoc., Australian Museum; Hon. Sec. Int. Conf. on Indo-Pacific Fish 1985; Hon. mem. Zoological Soc. of London 1992, Research Inst. for Natural Science of Argentina 1997; Collar and Grand Cordon, Supreme Order of the Chrysanthemum, Grand Cordon, Order of the Rising Sun with the Paulownia Blossoms (Grand Cordon, Order of the Paulownia Flowers from 2003), Grand Cordon, Order of the Sacred Treasure, Order of Culture; Order of the Supreme Sun (Afghanistan), Grand Star, Decoration for Services to the Repub. of Austria, Collar, Order of al-Khalifa (Bahrain), Grand Cordon, Order of Leopold (Belgium), Presidential Order (Botswana), Grand Collar, Order of the Southern Cross (Brazil), Grand Cordon, Order of Valour (Cameroon), Grand Collar, Order of the Merit of Chile, Grand Collar, Order of the Cross of Boyaca (Colombia), Grand Cordon, Nat. Order of the Leopard (Democratic Repub. of the Congo/Zaïre), Grand Cordon, Nat. Order of the Ivory Coast, Order of the White Lion, 1st Class (Civil Div.) with Collar Chain (Czech Repub.), Kt Grand Cross, Order of the Elephant (Denmark) 1953, Grand Collar, Order of the Nile (Egypt), The Collar of the Cross, Order of the Cross of Terra Mariana (Estonia), Grand Collar, Order of Solomon (Ethiopia), Grand Cross with Collar, Order of the White Rose (Finland), Grand Croix, Légion d'honneur, Grand Cross, Special Class, Order of Merit of the FRG, Grand Kt, Order of the Repub. of Gambia, Grand Cross, Order of the Redeemer (Greece), Grand Cross with Chain, Order of Merit of the Repub. of Hungary, Grand Cross with Collar, Order of the Falcon (Iceland), Star of Adipurna, 1st Class (Indonesia), Grand Cross with Cordon, Order of Merit of the Italian Repub., Collar, Order of al-Hussein bin Ali (Jordan), Order of the Golden Eagle (Kazakhstan), Order of the Golden Heart (Kenya), Collar, Order of Mubarak the Great (Kuwait), Kt Grand Cross with Chain, Order of the Three Stars (Latvia), Kt Grand Band, Order of the Star of Africa (Liberia), Kt Grand Band, Order of the Pioneers of the Repub. (Liberia), Great Grand Cross with Collar, Order of Vytautas the Great (Lithuania), Kt, Order of the Gold Lion of the House of Nassau (Luxembourg), Grand Kt, Order of the Lion (Malawi), Order of the Crown of the Realm (Malaysia), Grand Cordon, Nat. Order of Mali, Grand Collar, Order of the Aztec Eagle (Mexico), Grand Collar, Order of Muhammad (Morocco), Kt, Order of Ojaswi Rajanya (Nepal), Kt Grand Cross, Order of the Netherlands Lion, Grand Cordon, Order of the Fed. Repub. (Nigeria), Grand Cross with Collar, Royal Norwegian Order of St Olav, Order of Oman, Superior Class, Nishan-e-Pakistan, 1st Class, Gold Collar, Order of Manuel Amador Guerrero (Panama), Grand Cross in Brilliants, Order of the Sun (Peru), Chief Kt, Philippine Legion of Honour, Order of the White Eagle (Poland), Grand Collar, Order of St James of the Sword (Portugal), Grand Collar, Order of Prince Henry (Portugal), Collar of Independence (Qatar), Badr Chain (Saudi Arabia), Grand Cordon, Order of the Lion (Senegal), Grand Cross in Gold, Order of Good Hope (South Africa), Kt, Order of the Golden Fleece (Spain), Collar, Order of Charles III (Spain), Kt with Collar, Royal Order of the Seraphim (Sweden), The Most Auspicious Order of the Rajamitrabhorn (Thailand), The Most Illustrious Order of the Royal House of Chakri (Thailand), Order of Prince Yaroslav the Wise, First Class (Ukraine), Collar of the Fed. (UAE), Queen Elizabeth II Coronation Medal; hon. degree from Uppsala Univ., Sweden 2007; Golden Medal of Merit of the Japanese Red Cross, Golden Medal of Hon. mem., King Charles II Medal of the Royal Soc., London; a newly described goby named *Exyrias akihito* in his honour 2005. *Publications:* numerous papers in the journal of the Ichthyological Soc. of Japan and others in the journal Science and the journal Nature. *Leisure interests:* taxonomic study of gobiid fish, natural history and conservation, history, tennis. *Address:* The Imperial Palace, 1-1 Chiyoda, Chiyoda-ku, Tokyo 100, Japan. *Telephone:* (3) 32131111.

AKIL, Hakkı, BA; Turkish diplomatist and consultant; b. 5 Jan. 1953, Kargı/Çorum; m.; one c.; ed Univ. of Bordeaux and Ecole Nationale d'Admin, France; joined Ministry of Foreign Affairs (MFA) 1979, Third Sec., Legal Dept of Consular Services 1979–82, Second Sec., Embassy in Damascus 1982–84, Vice-Consul, then Consul, Consulate Gen. in Paris 1984–87, studies in Paris 1987–89, Head of Section, Gen. Directorate of Econ. Relations with the Middle East and Energy-related Topics, MFA 1989–90, Counsellor for Political Affairs, Embassy in Paris 1990–94, Head of Section, Relations Dept of the Caucasus 1994–95, Head of Dept of Policy Planning 1995–96, Deputy Perm. Rep. to WTO, Chair. Cttee for Admin Budget and Finance, Dir of Pension Funds and Savings Cttee 1996–2000, Head of Dept of Energy, MFA 2000–01, Deputy Dir of Cases Related to Energy, Environment and Water, MFA 2001–04, Chair. Budget Cttee, Charter Secr. of Energy 2001–04, Chair. Working Group on Trade and Transit in Energy Charter 2004–05, Amb. to Turkmenistan 2005–08, to UAE 2008–09, Deputy Asst Sec. of State for Econ. Affairs, MFA (G-20 Sherpa for Turkey) 2009–11, Amb. to Italy 2011–14, to France 2014–16; Chief Advidor to the Chair., Çalık Holding 2016–. *Address:* Çalık Holding A.S., Büyükdere Caddesi 163, 34394Şişli, Istanbul, Turkey (office). *Telephone:* (212) 3065000 (office). *Fax:* (212) 3065600 (office). *E-mail:* info@calik.com (office). *Website:* www.calik.com (office).

AKIMOV, Maksim Alekseyevich; Russian politician; *Deputy Chairman of Government;* b. 1 March 1970, Maloyaroslavets, Kaluga Oblast, Russian SFSR, USSR; m.; two s.; ed Tsiolkovskii Kaluga State Pedagogical Univ.; began career as secondary school history teacher 1993–94; CEO FineArt Audit 1994–96; Chair. Kaluga Regional Securities Market Comm. 1996–97; Deputy Dir, Economy and Industry Dept, Kaluga Oblast govt 1997–2001; First Deputy Chair., State Property Cttee, Kaluga Oblast 2001–04; Minister of Econ. Devt, Kaluga regional govt 2004; First Deputy Mayor, later Mayor of Kaluga 2004–07; Deputy Gov., Kaluga Oblast 2007–12; Deputy Chief of Govt Staff of Russian Fed. 2012–18; Deputy Chair. of Govt 2018–; Chair. Bd of Dirs OAO Russian Railways (OJSC RZD) 2018–; Order of Alexander Nevsky 2014, Special Merit Medal of Kaluga Oblast 2017. *Address:* Office of the Government, 103274 Moscow, Krasnopresnenskaya nab. 2, Russia (office). *Telephone:* (495) 985-42-80 (office). *Fax:* (495) 605-53-62 (office). *E-mail:* duty_press@aprf.gov.ru (office). *Website:* government.ru (office).

AKINCI, Mustafa; Turkish-Cypriot politician; *President, 'Turkish Republic of Northern Cyprus';* b. 28 Dec. 1947, Limassol; m.; three d.; ed Middle East Technical Univ., Ankara; mem. Turkish Cypriot Constituent Ass. 1975; Mayor of N Nicosia 1976–90; Founding Pres., Union of Turkish Cypriot Municipalities 1983–; Leader, Communal Liberation Party (TKP) 1987–2001; mem. Ass. of Repub. (Turkish Cypriot Parl.) 1993–2009; Deputy Prime Minister and Minister of Tourism 1999–2001; Founding mem. and Leader, Peace and Democracy Movt 2003 (merged with Communal Liberation Party to form Communal Democracy Party 2007); Pres. 'Turkish Repub. of N Cyprus' 2015–; Europa Nostra Medal of Honour (jt recipient) 2003. *Publication:* Belediye Başkanlığı'nda 14 Yıl' (14 Years as Mayor) 2010. *Address:* Office of the President, Şht Selahattin Sonat Sok, Lefkoşa (Nicosia), Mersin 10, Turkey (office). *Telephone:* 2283444 (office). *Fax:* 2272252 (office). *E-mail:* info@kktcb.org (office). *Website:* www.kktcb.org (office); www.mustafaakinci.com.

AKINKUGBE, Oladipo Olujimi, Atobase of Ife, Babalofin of Ijebu-Igbo, Adingbuwa of Ondo, Ikolaba Balogun Basegun of Ibadan, MD, DPhil, DTM&H, FRCP, FAS, CON; Nigerian professor of medicine; *Professor Emeritus, College of Medicine, University of Ibadan;* b. 17 July 1933, Ondo; s. of Chief Odofin David Akinkugbe and Chief (Mrs) Grace Akinkugbe; m. Dr Folasade Dina 1965; two s.; ed Govt Coll., Ibadan, Univ. Coll., Ibadan, Univs of London, Liverpool and Oxford, UK; Lecturer in Medicine, Univ. of Ibadan 1964–66, Sr Lecturer 1966–68, Prof. 1968–95, Prof. Emer. 1996–, Dean of Medicine 1970–74, Chair. of Cttee of Deans 1972–74, mem. Council 1971–74; Visiting Prof. of Medicine, Harvard Univ. 1974–75; Principal, Univ. Coll., Ilorin 1975–77; Vice-Chancellor Univ. of Ilorin 1977–78, Ahmadu Bello Univ. 1978–79; Pro-Chancellor and Chair. Council, Port Harcourt Univ. 1986–90; Pres. Nigerian Asscn of Nephrology 1987–89, Nigerian Hypertension Soc. 1992–95; mem. Scientific Advisory Panel, CIBA Foundation, Council of Int. Soc. of Hypertension, WHO Expert Cttees on Cardiovascular Diseases, Smoking Control, Professional and Tech. Educ. of Medical and Auxiliary Personnel, Sr Consultant 1983–84, WHO Advisory Cttee on Health Research 1990; currently Chair. Premier Medicaid Int.; Visiting Fellow, Balliol Coll., Oxford 1981–82; Visiting Prof. of Medicine, Univ. of Oxford 1981–82; mem. Bd of Trustees, Obafemi Awolowo Foundation, Nigerian Heartcare Foundation 1994–, Chair. 2000– (also mem. Governing Council), Nigerian Educare Trust 1995, The Social Sciences and Reproductive Health Research Network 1996, Ajumogobia Science Foundation; Chair. Bd of Man., Univ. Coll. Hosp., Ibadan 2000–04; Pres. African Heart Network 2001; Founding Pres. Nigerian Soc. for Information, Arts and Culture 2001–; Patron Sickle Cell Asscn of Nigeria; mem. several editorial bds; Fellow, Nigerian Acad. of Science; Hon. Fellow, Univ. of Ibadan 1998; Nigerian Nat. Order of Merit 1997, Commdr, Order of the Niger 1979, Order of the Fed. Repub. of Nigeria 2004, Officier, Ordre Nat. de la République de Côte d'Ivoire; Hon. DSc (Ilorin) 1982, (Fed. Univ. Tech. Akure) 1994, (Port-Harcourt) 1997, (Ogun State Univ.) 1998; Searle Distinguished Research Award 1989, Life Achievement Award, Nigerian Acad. of Science 2004, Boehringer Ingelheim Award, Int. Soc. of Hypertension 2004. *Publications include:* High Blood Pressure in the African 1972, Priorities in National Health Planning (ed.) 1974, Hypertension in Africa (ed.) 1975, Cardiovascular Diseases in Africa (ed.) 1976, Clinical Medicine in the Tropics – Cardiovascular Disease 1986, Nigeria's Health in the 90s (co-ed.) 1996, A Compendium of Clinical Medicine (ed.) 1999; numerous papers on hypertension and renal disease. *Leisure interests:* bird-watching, music, gardening. *Address:* College of Medicine, University of Ibadan, Ibadan, Oyo State (office); The Little Summit, Olubadan Aleshinloye Way, Iyaganku, Ibadan (home); Premier Medicaid International, Olive House N6/53, Fajuyi Road, PO Box 29259, Secretariat Post Office, Adamasingba, Ibadan, Nigeria (office). *Telephone:* (2) 2410052 (office); (3) 7866956 (mobile). *Fax:* (2) 2410052 (office). *E-mail:* p_medicaid@yahoo.co.uk (office); info@premiermedicaid.com.ng (office). *Website:* www.premiermedicaid.com.ng (office).

AKIŞEV, Daniyar; Kazakhstani economist and central banker; b. 25 May 1976, Almaty; ed Kazakh State Acad. of Man.; Sr Economist, Cen. Asian Stock Exchange 1995–96; Chief Economist, Research and Statistics Dept, Nat. Bank of Kazakhstan 1996–98, Head, Financial Insts and Markets Research Office 1998–2001, Deputy Dir of Research and Statistical Analysis Dept 2002–03, Dir Research and Statistical Analysis Dept 2003–07, Deputy Gov., Nat. Bank of Kazakhstan 2007–14; Head of Social and Econ. Monitoring Dept, Exec. Office of the President 2014–15, Acting Aide to President of Kazakhstan Aug.–Nov. 2015; Gov. Nat. Bank of Kazakhstan 2015–19; Honored Employee of Nat. Bank of Kazakhstan 2006. *Address:* c/o National Bank of Kazakhstan, 050040 Almaty, Koktem-3 21, Kazakhstan (office).

AKIYA, Einosuke; Japanese religious leader; *Counsellor, Soka Gakkai International;* b. 15 July 1930, Tokyo; s. of Jubei Akiya and Yuki Akiya; m. Akiko Ishida 1957; two s.; ed Waseda Univ.; with Soka Gakkai 1951–, Young Men's Div. Chief 1956–59, Youth Div. Chief 1959–66, Dir 1961–62, Vice-Gen. Dir 1962–67, Gen. Admin. 1967–70, Vice-Pres. 1970–81, Pres. 1981–2006, Chair. Exec. Guidance Conf. 2006–; Ed.-in-Chief Seikyo Shimbun 1968, Rep. Dir 1975–81, Pres. 1987–90,

Exec. Adviser 1990–2006; Gen. Dir Soka Gakkai Int. 1981–92, Exec. Counsellor 1992–95, Deputy Pres. 1995–2007, Counsellor 2007–. *Leisure interests:* reading, music, theatre. *Address:* Soka Gakkai, 32 Shinano-machi, Shinjuku-ku, Tokyo 160-8583, Japan (office). *Telephone:* (3) 3353-7111 (office). *Website:* www.sgi.org (office).

AKIYAMA, Kotaro; Japanese newspaper executive; Man. Ed. Asahi Shimbun –2005, apptd Pres. and CEO and Rep. Dir Asahi Shimbun Co. 2005, Chair. Compliance Cttee 2006; apptd Ind. Dir TV Asahi Corpn 2006, NSK (Japanese Newspaper Publrs and Eds Asscn, Chair. –2013); Pres. Mihou Sangyo K.K; Chair. Asahi Shinbun Bunka Zaidan Foundation.

AKIYAMA, Yoshihisa; Japanese business executive; b. 1931; Chair. Kansai Electric Power Co. –2010, Chair. Kansai Econ. Fed. (Kankeiren); Chair. Kansai Asscn of Corp. Execs 1994–95; Chair. IIS Japan (non-profit making org.), Asscn for Commemorative Events of 1300th Anniversary of Nara Heijo-kyo Capital, Research Inst. of Innovative Tech. for Earth, Osaka Wan Bay Area Kaihatsu Suishin Kiko Foundation, Kinkichiku Chijo Digital Hoso Jikken Jkyogikai; Pres. Akiyama Tosoten, Y.K.; mem. or fmr mem. Bd of Dirs, Nippon Life Insurance Co., Japan Airlines Co. Ltd, Japan Productivity Centre for Socio-Econ. Devt; Corp. Auditor, Japan Airlines Corpn. *Address:* c/o Kansai Electric Power Company, 6-16 Nakanoshima 3-chome, Kita-ku, Osaka 530-8270, Japan.

AKODJÈNOU, Arnauld Antoine, PhD; Benin diplomatist and UN official; *Deputy Special Representative of the Secretary-General, United Nations Multidimensional Integrated Stabilization Mission in Mali (MINUSMA);* b. 27 Oct. 1950; m.; three c.; ed Univ. of Benin, Cotonou, Inst. of Int. Relations of Cameroon, Yaoundé, Grad. Inst. of Int. Studies, Geneva; Political Science Researcher, World Social Prospects Asscn and UNITAR, Geneva 1982–86; Assoc. Social Services Officer, UNHCR, Djibouti 1986–95; Chief of Bureau, Unit of Burundi and Rwanda 1995–97, also various positions in Regional Bureau for Africa, covering Great Lakes, W Africa and Cen. Africa; UNHCR Rep. in Mali 1999–2000, in Sierra Leone 2000–03; Regional Coordinator for Liberia and Côte d'Ivoire, Accra, Ghana 2003; Dir of Emergency and Security Services, UNHCR HQ, Geneva 2003–05; Dir Div. of Operational Services 2005–09; Inspector Gen. UNHCR 2009–11; Deputy Special Rep. of Sec.-Gen., UN Operation in Côte d'Ivoire (UNOCI) 2011–14, UN Multidimensional Integrated Stabilization Mission in Mali (MINUSMA) 2014–. *Address:* Multidimensional Integrated Stabilization Mission in Mali (MINUSMA), Bamako, Mali (office). *Website:* www.un.org/en/peacekeeping/missions/minusma/ (office).

AKOL AJAWIN, Lam, PhD; South Sudanese engineer and politician; *Leader, Sudan People's Liberation Movement—Democratic Change;* b. 15 July 1950, Dongula; m.; three c.; ed Univ. of Khartoum, Heriot-Watt Univ. and Imperial Coll. London, UK; mem. African Nationalists Front (ANF) 1970–75; Teaching Asst, Univ. of Khartoum 1976–80, Lecturer in Chemical Eng 1980–86 (also mem. Exec. Cttee, Teacher's Union 1984–86); Lecturer (part-time), Faculty of Science and Tech., Univ. of Gezira 1982–84; Chair. Port Sudan oil refinery 1985–86; joined Sudan People's Liberation Army (SPLA) 1986, Zonal Commdr of North Upper Nile 1987–88, of Southern Blue Nile 1990–91, Dir SPLM Office of Co-ordination and External Relations 1988–90, SPLM Chief Negotiator in peace talks 1988–91, Chair. SPLM-United 1994–2003; participated in armed rebellion with Dr Riek Machar that split the rebel movt; signed Fashoda Agreement with Sudanese Govt 1997; Minister of Transport 1998–2002; Minister of Foreign Affairs 2005–07, of Cabinet Affairs 2007; Founder and Leader, Sudan People's Liberation Movt—Democratic Change 2009–; mem. Sudanese Eng Soc. 1975–, American Inst. of Chemical Engineers 1980–; Founding mem. Sudan African Congress (SAC) 1985, Sudan Rural Solidarity 1986, Justice Party 2002; Hon. Dr rer. pol (Juba Univ.) 1999. *Publications:* SPLM/SPLA: Inside an African Revolution 2001, SPLM/SPLA: The Nasir Declaration 2003, Southern Sudan: Colonialism, Resistance, and Autonomy 2007. *Address:* Sudan People's Liberation Movement—Democratic Change, Juba, South Sudan (office). *E-mail:* info@splmtoday.com (office). *Website:* www.splmtoday.com (office).

ARORA, Nikesh, BElecEng, MBA; American (b. Indian) chartered financial analyst and business executive; b. 9 Feb. 1968, India; m. Ayesha Thapar; ed Inst. of Tech., Banaras Hindu Univ. (now Indian Inst. of Tech.), Varanasi, Boston Coll., Northeastern Univ.; Vice-Pres., Finance, Fidelity Investments 1992–97; Vice-Pres., Putnam Investments 1997–2000; CEO T-Motion PLC 2000–01; Chief Marketing Officer, T-Mobile Europe 2001–04; Pres., EMEA Sales, Marketing & Partnerships, Google Inc. 2004–11, Sr Vice-Pres. and Chief Business Officer 2011–13; Vice-Chair. SoftBank Corpn (renamed SoftBank Group Corpn 2015) 2014–16, CEO SoftBank Internet and Media, Inc. (currently SB Group US, Inc.) 2014–16, Dir Sprint Corpn 2014–, Rep. Dir, Pres. and COO, SoftBank Group Corpn 2015–16; Chair. Yahoo Japan Corpn 2015–, mem. Bd of Advisors, SoftBank Group Corpn 2016–; mem. Bd of Dirs, The Harlem Children's Zone 2013–, Tipping Point Community 2014–. *Address:* SoftBank Group Corporation, 1-9-1 Higashi-shimbashi, Minato-ku, Tokyo 105-7303, Japan (office); Sprint Corporation, 6200 Sprint Parkway, Overland Park, KS 66251, USA (office). *Telephone:* (3) 6889-2000 (Tokyo) (office); (703) 433-4000 (Overland Park) (office). *E-mail:* info@softbank.jp (office); boardinquiries@sprint.com (office). *Website:* www.softbank.jp/en/corp (office); www.sprint.com (office).

AKRAM, Wasim (see WASIM, Akram).

AKŞENER, Meral, PhD; Turkish politician; *Chair, İyi Partisi (Good Party);* b. 18 July 1956, İzmit, Kocaeli; m. Tuncer Akşener; one c.; ed Istanbul Univ., Marmara Univ. Social Sciences Inst.; began career as teacher 1979–82; Research Asst, Yıldız Tech. Univ. 1982; fmr Lecturer, Kocaeli Univ. and Marmara Univ.; mem. Grand Nat. Ass. (Parl.) (True Path Party) 1995–2002, (Nationalist Movt Party) 2007–15, Deputy Speaker 2007–15; Minister of the Interior 1996–97; mem. Doğru Yol Partisi (True Path Party) 1995–2001, Milliyetçi Hareket Partisi (Nationalist Movt Party) 2001–16 (expelled); Founding Chair. İyi Partisi (Good Party) 2017–; f. Zübeyda Hanım Foundation for Families of Martyrs; cand. in presidential election 2018. *Address:* İyi Partisi, Mustafa Kemal Mah. 2120, Cad. No. 9, 06520 Çankaya, Ankara, Turkey (office). *Telephone:* (312) 4080808 (office). *Website:* iyiparti.org.tr (office); meralaksener.com.tr.

AKSU, Abdülkadir; Turkish politician; *Deputy Chairman, Justice and Development Party (Adalet ve Kalkınma Partisi);* b. 12 Oct. 1944, Diyarbakır; m.; two c.; ed Ankara Univ.; trainee clerk in Diarbekir 1968; Deputy Dist Gov. in Gench, Akchadaa, Doanshehir; Dist Gov. of Kanak 1970; reserve mil. officer in Askale 1971–73; Dist Gov. of Sarakaya 1973–76; Chief of Police, Malatya 1976–77; Gov. of Kahramanmarash 1977–78; Gov. of Rize 1980; Cen. Gov. 1980; Gov. of Gaziantep 1984–87; elected MP (Motherland Party) 1987; Minister of Internal Affairs 1989–91, 2002–07 (resgnd); State Minister for GAP; joined Welfare Party 1996, later Vice-Chair.; joined Justice and Devt Party (Adalet ve Kalkınma Partisi), currently First Deputy Chair.; mem. Int. Inst. for Security and Cooperation; Union of Journalists Bureaucrat of the Year 1986, Siyaset Magazine Policy Maker of the Year 2002, Siyaset Magazine Minister of the Year 2002–03. *Address:* Justice and Development Party (Adalet ve Kalkınma Partisi), Söğütözü Caddesi 6, Çankaya, Ankara, Turkey (office). *Telephone:* (312) 2045000 (office). *Fax:* (312) 2045044 (office). *E-mail:* rte@akparti.org.tr (office). *Website:* www.akparti.org.tr (office).

AKSYONOV, Sergei Valeryevich; Russian business executive and politician; *Head of the Republic and Chairman of the Council of Ministers, Republic of Crimea;* b. 26 Nov. 1972, Bălţi, Moldovan SSR, USSR; two c.; moved to Crimea 1989, enrolled in a coll. for Soviet mil. engineers shortly before the collapse of the Soviet Union, refused to swear an oath of allegiance to Ukraine; graduated from Higher Mil.-Political Construction Coll., Simferopol 1993; Deputy Dir Ellada (food products co.) 1993–98; Deputy Dir Asteriks co. 1998–2001; Deputy Dir Eskada co. 2001–14; mem. Russkaya Obshchina Kryma (Russian Community of Crimea) 2008–, Grazhdanskii Aktiv Kryma (Civic Action of Crimea) 2008–; developed Russkoye Yedinstvo (Russian Unity) party 2008–09, Leader 2009–; Co-Pres. Co-ordinating Council, Za Russkoye Yedinstvo v Krymu! (For Russian Unity in Crimea!) 2009–14, State Council 2014–; Deputy (Russkoye Yedinstvo), Supreme Council of Crimea 2010–14, State Council 2014–; *de facto* Prime Minister of the self-declared 'Republic of Crimea' Feb.–March 2014, Chair. Council of Ministers, Repub. of Crimea March 2014–, Head of the Repub. of Crimea April 2014–; warrant for his arrest issued by Shevchenko Dist court of Kiev March 2014; put on Canadian, EU and US sanction lists; Head of Crimea's Greco-Roman wrestling org. *Address:* Office of the Head of the Republic, 295005 Simferopol, pr. Kirova 13, Crimea, Russian Federation (office). *Telephone:* (652) 54-45-42 (office). *E-mail:* sovmin@rk.gov.ru (office). *Website:* rk.gov.ru (office).

AKSYUCHITS, Viktor Vladimirovich; Russian politician and Orthodox philosopher; *President, Russian Universities Foundation;* b. 27 Aug. 1949, Vardantsy, Minsk region, USSR (now Belarus); m. 2nd; five c.; ed Riga Navigation School, Moscow State Univ.; served in navy 1969–72; mem. CPSU 1971–78; seasonal worker in Siberia and Far East 1978–88; Founder Orthodox Unity Church; ed Vybor (journal); Chair. Duma (Bd) of Political Council, Russian Christian Democratic Movt 1990–98; Chair. Orthodox Brotherhood Resurrection 1990–96; People's Deputy of Russia 1990–93; mem. Duma of Russian People's Congress 1992–96; Lecturer, State Acad. of Slavic Culture 1996–2003; adviser to Deputy Prime Minister Boris Nemtsov 1997–98; Chair. Bd of Dirs, Orthodox Social Service Foundation 2000–09; Pres. Russian Univs Foundation. *Publications:* seven books on Christian philosophy, theology and philosophy of history, including Cross Grace, Russia's Mission 2009; numerous articles on political science and cultural studies. *Address:* 119517 Moscow, Matveevskaya, 10-2-234, Russia (home). *Telephone:* (985) 991-56-69 (home). *E-mail:* aksyu@mail.ru (office).

AKUFO-ADDO, Nana Addo Dankwa, BSc (Econs); Ghanaian politician, lawyer and head of state; *President;* b. 29 March 1944, Accra; s. of Edward Akufo-Addo (fmr Chief Justice and Pres. Second Repub.) and Adeline Akufo-Addo; m. Rebecca Akufo-Addo (née Griffiths-Randolph); five c.; ed Lancing Coll., Sussex, UK, Univ. of Ghana, Legon; called to English Bar (Middle Temple) 1971, Ghanaian Bar 1975; Assoc. Counsel, Coudert Freres (US law firm), Paris office, France 1971–75; Jr mem. U. V. Campbell 1975–79; Sr Partner and Co-Founder Prempeh & Co.; Gen. Sec. People's Movt for Freedom and Justice 1977–78; mem. Gen. Legal Council 1991–96, Gen. Council, Ghana Bar Asscn 1991–96 (Vice-Pres. Greater Accra Regional Br. 1991–96); Founder and first Chair. Ghana Cttee on Human and People's Rights; mem. Nat. Council and Nat. Exec. Cttee, New Patriotic Party (NPP) 1992–2000; mem. Parl. (NPP) for Abuakwa constituency 1996–2000, Chair. NPP Internal Affairs Cttee, NPP Legal and Constitutional Affairs Cttee, Sec. NPP Political Cttee, Sec. NPP Policy Advisory Cttee 1996, Standing Cttee on Subsidiary Legislation 1997–2001; Ranking Minority mem. Parl.'s Select Cttee on Constitutional, Legal and Parl. Affairs 1997–2001; Minister of Foreign Affairs 2000–07; NPP cand. for Pres. of Ghana 2008, 2012; Pres. of Ghana 2017–; Chair. Commonwealth Observer Mission for South African elections 2014; Chair. DHL, Ghana Ltd, Kinesec Communications Co. Ltd; Hon. Fellow, Legon Hall, Univ. of Ghana. *Leisure interests:* listening to music, sports. *Address:* Office of the President, Flagstaff House, Liberation Crescent, Accra, Ghana (office). *Telephone:* (30) 2666997 (office). *E-mail:* contact@presidency.gov.gh (office). *Website:* www.presidency.gov.gh (office).

AKUNIN, Boris, (Anna Borisova); Russian (b. Georgian) writer; b. (Grigory Shalvovich Chkhartishvili), 20 May 1956, Georgia; ed Moscow State Univ.; Deputy Ed.-in-Chief Inostrannaya Literatura (magazine) –2000; Ed.-in-Chief, Anthology of Japanese Literature (20 vols); Chair. Exec. Bd Pushkin Library (Soros Foundation). *Publications include:* fiction: Azazel 1998, Winter Queen 1998, Turkish Gambit 1998, Leviathan 1998, The State Counsellor 1999, Jack of Spades 1999, The Seagull 2000, The Coronation 2000, Pelagia and the White Bulldog 2000, Fairy Tales for Idiots 2000, Lover of Death Vol. One 2001, Lover of Death Vol. Two 2001, Pelagia and the Black Monk 2001, Pelagia and the Red Rooster 2003, The Diamond Chariot 2003, F.M. 2006, Falcon and the Swallow 2009, All the World's a Stage 2009, The Black City 2012; non-fiction: The Writer and Suicide 1999, Cemetery Tales 2004; as Anna Borisova: There 2007, The Idea-Man 2009, Vremena goda 2011; contrib. to numerous reviews and criticisms, numerous trans of Japanese, American and English literature. *Address:* c/o Linda Michaels Ltd, PO Box 567, 344 Main Street, Lakeville, CT 06039-0567, USA (office). *Website:* www.boris-akunin.com (office).

AL-NAQI, Abbas Ali, BComm; Kuwaiti government official and international organization official; *Secretary-General, Organization of Arab Petroleum Exporting Countries;* b. 1947; ed Kuwait Univ., Univ. of Southern California, USA; Financial Accountant, State Budget, Ministry of Finance and Oil 1971–75,

Controller, Oil and Gas Marketing, Ministry of Oil 1975–81, Controller, Int. Relations and Orgs Dept 1981–84, Dir Econ. Planning and Analysis Dept 1984–89, Dir Oil Accounting and Financial Analysis Dept 1989–94, Asst Under-Sec. for Econ. Affairs 1994–2007, Under-Sec. 2007–08; Sec.-Gen. Org. of Arab Petroleum Exporting Countries (OAPEC) 2008–, mem. Exec. Bd representing Kuwait 2000–08; Chair. Kuwaiti Nat. Cttee for UN Convention on Climate Change 1994–; Vice-Pres. representing Asia, Second UN Convention on Climate Change 1996; Head of Jt Exec. Cttee, Aramco Overseas Co. 2000–02; mem. Bd of Dirs Arab Maritime Petroleum Transport Co. 1977–96, Kuwait Nat. Petroleum Co. 1995–98, Kuwait Oil Co. 1998–2002, Arab Petroleum Investments Corpn 1996–, Kuwait Gulf Oil Co. 2004–07, Kuwait Nat. Petroleum Corpn 2007–; mem. UN Cttee for Sustainable Devt, Kuwait Accountant Soc. *Address:* Organization of Arab Petroleum Exporting Countries, PO Box 20501, Safat 13066, Kuwait (office). *Telephone:* 24959000 (office). *Fax:* 24959755 (office). *E-mail:* oateefa@oapecorg.org (office). *Website:* www.oapecorg.org (office).

ALABBAR, Mohammed Ali Rashid, BA; United Arab Emirates government official and business executive; *Chairman, Emaar Properties;* b. 1963; ed Albers School of Business and Econs at Seattle Univ., USA; served as Dir-Gen. Dept of Econ. Devt; Chair. Emaar Properties PJSC (real estate co.) 1997–; Vice-Chair. Dubai Aluminium Co. Ltd (DUBAL) 1992–2003, Dubai World Trade Centre 1992–2002; Chair. Emcredit (first ind. credit information co. in UAE); f. and Chair. Africa Middle East Resources (AMER, mining co.); currently also Sr Aide to Ruler of Dubai and Vice-Pres./Prime Minister of UAE, Sheikh Mohammed bin Rashid al-Maktoum; mem. Dubai Exec. Council; fmr Chair. UAE Golf Asscn (now Emirates Golf Fed.); Dr hc (Seattle Univ.) 2007; Arabian Business Businessman of the Year 2011; Arab Bankers' Asscn of N America Achievement Award 2012. *Address:* Emaar Properties PJSC, PO Box 9440, Dubai (office); Dubai Executive Council, Emirates Towers Building, 20th Floor, Sheikh Zayed Road, 72233 Dubai, United Arab Emirates (office). *Telephone:* (4) 330-2111 (office). *Fax:* (4) 330-2999 (office). *E-mail:* pe@tec.gov.ae (office); info@alabbar.info. *Website:* dubai.ae/en/pages/default.aspx (office); www.alabbar.info; www.emaar.com.

ALAGIAH, George, OBE; British journalist, broadcaster and writer; *Presenter, Six O'Clock News and World News Today, British Broadcasting Corporation (BBC);* b. 22 Nov. 1955, Sri Lanka; m. Frances Robathan; two s.; ed St John's Coll., Portsmouth and Univ. of Durham; family moved to Ghana 1960; worked in print journalism for South Magazine 1982–89; joined the BBC 1989, Leading Foreign Corresp. specializing in Africa and the developing world, BBC's Africa Corresp., Johannesburg 1994–98, Presenter The World News on BBC 4 2002, Presenter BBC Six O'Clock News 2003–, World News Today (rebranded as GMT with George Alagiah 2010) 2006–, BBC World; has interviewed many internationally prominent figures; has contributed to The Guardian, Daily Telegraph, The Independent and Daily Express newspapers; Bd mem. Royal Shakespeare Co.; Patron NAZ Project, Parenting UK 2000–, Fairtrade Foundation 2002–09; Critics' Award and Golden Nymph Award, Monte Carlo TV Festival 1992, Best Int. Report, Royal TV Soc. 1993, Best TV Journalist Award, Amnesty Int. 1994, One World Broadcasting Trust Award 1994, James Cameron Memorial Trust Award 1995, Bayeux Award for War Reporting 1996, Media Personality of the Year, Ethnic Minority Media Awards 1998, BAFTA Award (part of BBC Team) for coverage of Kosovo conflict 2000, Asian Award for Outstanding Achievement in TV 2010. *Publications include:* A Passage to Africa 2001, The Day That Shook the World, A Home from Home (autobiography) 2006. *Address:* BBC News, Broadcasting House, London, W1A 1AA, England (office). *Telephone:* (20) 8743-8000 (office). *Fax:* (20) 8743-7882 (office). *Website:* www.bbc.co.uk (office).

ALAGNA, Roberto; French singer (tenor); b. 7 June 1963, Clichy-sous-Bois; m. 1st Florence Lancien (deceased); one d.; m. 2nd Angela Gheorghiu 1996 (divorced 2013); m. 3rd Aleksandra Kurzak 2015; one d.; ed studied in Paris, France and Italy; debut as Alfredo in La Traviata, Glyndebourne Touring Opera at Plymouth 1988; Met, New York debut as Rodolfo 1996; appearances worldwide at Covent Garden, London, Monte Carlo, Vienna Staatsoper, Théâtre du Châtelet, Paris, La Scala, Milan, Chicago and at the New York Met; repertoire includes Rodolfo (La Bohème), Edgard (Lucia di Lammermoor), Rigoletto, L'Elisir d'amore, Roméo, Don Carlos, Roberto Devereux, Duke of Mantua, Don Carlos, Alfredo, L'Amico Fritz, La Rondine, Faust, Des Grieux (Manon Lescaut); Chevalier, Ordre des Arts et des Lettres 1996, Officier, Ordre des Arts et des Lettres 2002, Officier, National Order of Merit 2003; winner, Pavarotti Competition 1988, Personalité Musicale de l'Année 1994, Laurence Olivier Award for Outstanding Achievement in Opera 1995, Lyric Artist of the Year, Victoires de la Musique Awards 1997, 2004, Vermeil Medal of the City of Paris 2001. *Recordings include:* Duets and Arias (with Angela Gheorghiu), La Bohème 1996, Don Carlos 1996, La Rondine 1997, My Life is an Opera 2014, Malèna 2016. *Address:* Theateragentur Dr Germinal Hilbert, Maximilianstrasse 22, 80539 Munich, Germany (office). *Telephone:* (89) 2907470 (office). *Fax:* (89) 29074790 (office). *E-mail:* agentur@hilbert.de (office). *Website:* www.hilbert.de (office); www.robertoalagna.net/en.

ALAINI, Mohsin Ahmed; Yemeni politician and diplomatist; b. 20 Oct. 1932, Bani Bahloul, N Yemen; m. Aziza Abulahom 1962; two s. two d.; ed Faculty of Law, Cairo Univ. and the Sorbonne, Paris; schoolteacher, Aden 1958–60; Int. Confed. of Arab Trade Unions 1960–62; Minister of Foreign Affairs, Yemeni Repub. Sept.–Dec. 1962, 1974–80; Perm. Rep. to UN 1962–65, 1965–66, 1967–69; Minister of Foreign Affairs May–July 1965; Prime Minister Nov.–Dec. 1967, 1974–80; Amb. to USSR 1968–70; Prime Minister, Minister of Foreign Affairs Feb. 1971, 1971–72, 1974–75; Amb. to France Aug.–Sept. 1974, 1975–76, to UK 1973–74, to FRG 1982–84, to USA 1984–97; Perm. Rep. to UN, New York 1980–82; apptd Deputy Chair. Consultative Council 1997. *Publications include:* Battles and Conspiracies against Yemen 1957, Fifty Years of Mounting Sands (autobiog.) 2000. *Leisure interests:* reading, exercising. *Address:* 8 Wissa Wassif Street, Giza, Cairo, Egypt (home). *Telephone:* (2) 5702423 (Cairo). *Fax:* (2) 5762423 (Cairo) (home).

ALAK, Julio César; Argentine lawyer and politician; b. 9 Jan. 1958, Benito Juárez; m.; three c.; ed Univ. of La Plata; practised as a lawyer in La Plata; mem. Partido Justicialista (PJ), Pres. La Plata Br. 1988; Mayor of La Plata 1991–2007; mem. Bd of Dirs, Aerolíneas Argentinas and Austral Lineas Aereas 2008–, Pres. 2008–09; Minister of Justice and Human Rights 2009–15.

ALAKIJA, Folorunsho; Nigerian business executive; *Vice-Chairman, Famfa Oil Limited;* b. 15 July 1951, Lagos; m. Modupe Alakija 1976; four s.; ed Pitman's Central Coll., American Coll. in London, UK; started career as Sec., International Merchant Bank of Nigeria (now defunct); launched fashion label Supreme Stitches; attained Oil Prospecting Licence for Famfa Oil Ltd 1993, currently Vice-Chair.; currently also Man. Dir Rose of Sharon Group (Rose of Sharon Prints and Promotions Ltd, Digital Reality Prints Ltd); Founder-Pres. Rose of Sharon Foundation 2008–; Vice-Chair. Nat. Heritage Council and Endowment for the Arts 2013–; Best Designer in Nigeria 1986. *Publication:* Growing With the Hand That Gives the Rose 2011. *Address:* Famfa Oil Limited, 290A Ajose Adeogun Street, Victoria Island, Lagos, Nigeria (office). *Telephone:* (1) 7747979 (office). *Fax:* (1) 2710933 (office). *E-mail:* admin@famfa.com (office). *Website:* www.famfa.com (office); theroseofsharonfoundation.org (office).

ALAM, Mahbubey, BA, MA, LLB; Bangladeshi lawyer and government official; *Attorney-General;* b. 17 Feb. 1949, Mouchhamandra; ed Dhaka Univ., Inst. of Constitutional and Parl. Studies, New Delhi, India, City Law Coll., Dhaka; enrolled as advocate and started practice at Dhaka Court 1973, enrolled on High Court 1975, on Appellate Div. of Supreme Court 1980, as Sr Advocate, Appellate Div., Supreme Court of Bangladesh 1998; Additional Attorney-Gen. of Bangladesh 1998–2001, Attorney-Gen. 2009–; mem. Bangladesh Supreme Court Bar Asscn, Gen. Sec. 1993–94, Pres. 2005–06; mem. Bangladesh Bar Council 2004–. *Address:* Office of the Attorney-General, Bangladesh Supreme Court, Dhaka 1000, Bangladesh (office). *Telephone:* (2) 9562868 (office). *E-mail:* info@minlaw.gov.bd (office). *Website:* www.lawjusticediv.gov.bd/static/attorny_general.php (office).

ALAM, Shah Mahboob, MA; Pakistani civil servant and business executive; ed Karachi Univ., Nat. Inst. of Public Admin, Coll., Lahore; officer of BPS-21, Govt of Pakistan; has served in sr security positions in Sindh and Balochistan; also served on deputation in Ministry of Foreign Affairs for eight years; Dir-Gen. Office of the Nat. Security Adviser to the Prime Minister –2008; apptd Exec. Dir (Security), Oil and Gas Devt Co. Ltd 2008, later CEO and Man. Dir. *Address:* c/o Oil and Gas Development Co. Ltd, OGDCL House, Plot No. 3, Jinnah Avenue, Blue Area, Islamabad, Pakistan.

ALAPAYEV, Marat O.; Kyrgyzstani fmr central banker; m.; two c.; fmr Lecturer, Dept of Political Economy, Osh Pedagogical Teacher Training Coll.; worked as a broker in the securities market; Chair. Bakai Bank 1998–2006; Head, Cttee of Dirs Manas Int. Airport 2005–06; Acting Chair. Nat. Bank of the Kyrgyz Repub. (Kyrgyz Respublikasynyn Uluttuk Banky) April 2006, Chair. from 2006. *Address:* c/o Kyrgyz Respublikasynyn Uluttuk Banky, 720040 Bishkek, Umetaliyeva 101, Kyrgyzstan. *E-mail:* mail@nbkr.kg.

ALARCÓN DE QUESADA, Ricardo; Cuban diplomatist and politician; b. 21 May 1937; s. of Roberto Alarcón de Quesada; m. Margarita Maza (died 2008); one d.; ed Univ. de Habana; Head of Student Section, Prov. Office of 26 July Revolutionary Movt 1957–59; Pres. Univ. Students' Fed., Sec. Union of Young Communists; Dir for Regional Policies (Latin America), Ministry of Foreign Affairs 1962–66; mem. Governing Council of Inst. for Int. Politics, Ministry of Foreign Affairs, Deputy Minister of Foreign Affairs 1978, mem. Tech. Advisory Council 1980; Perm. Rep. of Cuba to the UN 1966–78; Pres. UNDP 1976–77; Alt. mem. Cen. Cttee of CP of Cuba 1980–2013, mem. Politburo 1992–2013; Minister of Foreign Affairs 1992–93; Pres. Nat. Ass. of People's Power 1993–2013.

ALARCÓN MANTILLA, Luis Fernando, MSc, PhD; Colombian politician and engineer; b. Aug. 1951, Bucaramanga; m.; ed Univ. of the Andes, Massachusetts Inst. of Tech.; engineer with Mejía Millan y Perry Ltd and Prof. of Civil Eng Univ. of the Andes 1980–83, currently mem. Bd of Dirs; Head of Public Investment Unit, Nat. Dept of Planning 1983–84; Dir-Gen. of Budget, Ministry of Finance and Public Credit 1984–86; economist, Inter-American Devt Bank (IDB), Washington, DC 1986; Vice-Minister, Ministry of Finance and Public Credit 1986–87, Minister of Finance and Public Credit 1987–91; fmr Pres. Flota Mercante Grancolombiana SA, Asscn of Pension Fund Admins and Unemployment, Asofondos of Colombia; Man. Dir, Petrocolombia; CEO Asociación Colombiana de Administradoras de Fondos de Pensiones y Cesantía-Asofondos de Colo; Gen. Man. Electrical Interconnection SA-ISA; Chair. and CEO Grupo Empresarial ISA; Co-Chair. World Econ. Forum on Latin America 2010; mem. of Governing Council for Foreign Trade, Bd of Banco de la República, Nat. Council for Econ. and Social Policy 1987; Chair. Flota Mercante Grancolombiana; mem. Bd of Dirs Banco de Bogota, Colombia Stock Exchange, Petrocolombia SA, Co. of Electric Energy Transmission Paulista, INTERNEXA, Avianca, Bavaria, Caracol SA, Cafesalud, Valores Bavaria and Caracol TV.

ALARCON RIVERA, Fabián Ernesto, PhD; Ecuadorean politician; b. 14 April 1947, Quito; s. of Dr Fabián Alarcón Falconi and Maria Antonieta Rivera Larrea; m. Lucía Peña Ochoa 1976; two s. one d.; ed Pontifical Catholic Univ.; councillor, Quito 1969; fmr Prefect of Pinchincha Prov. 1984–88; Pres. of Congress 1991–92, 1995–97; fmr Deputy to Congress (three times), fmr Speaker of Congress (three times); represented Ecuador in Inter-American Congress of Lawyers in Brazil, Puerto Rico and Quito; mem. Patriotic People's Party, American Fed. of Lawyers; Acting Pres. of Ecuador 6–10 Feb. 1997, Pres. of Ecuador 1997–98; arrested on charges of illegally hiring personnel 1999, released 2005; mem. Frente Radical Alfarista, Leader 2002; fmr Pres. Law School Asscn.

ALARIE, Pierre, MPA; Canadian business executive and diplomatist; *Ambassador to Mexico;* m. Catherine Genois; two s. one d.; ed Coll. of Europe, Bruges, Belgium; joined Dept of External Affairs 1982, served as Trade Desk Officer with European Bureau, served abroad as Second Sec. in Lagos, Nigeria and as First Sec. in Santiago, Chile; returned to pvt. sector 1991; Vice-Pres., Business Devt, Bombardier's Transportation Group 1991–93; Vice-Pres., Business Devt, SNC-Lavalin International, Mexico City 1994; Man. Dir, Latin America, real estate subsidiary of Caisse de Dépôt et Placement du Québec –1998; Country Rep. in Mexico City, Bank of Nova Scotia 1998–2004; Dir, Mergers and Acquisitions, Hydro-Québec International 2004–05; adviser to several Canadian cos 2006–09; Vice-Pres., Business Devt and Sales, Canadian Commercial Corpn, Ottawa 2009–15; Amb. to Mexico 2015–. *Address:* Embassy of Canada, Schiller 529, Col. Bosque de Chapultepec (Polanco), Del. Miguel Hidalgo, 11580 México DF, Mexico (office). *Telephone:* (55) 5724-7900 (office). *Fax:* (55) 5724-7980 (office). *E-mail:*

mex@international.gc.ca (office). *Website:* www.canadainternational.gc.ca/mexico-mexique (office).

ALASANIA, Irakli, LLB; Georgian diplomatist and politician; b. 21 Dec. 1973, Batumi, Ajara ASSR, Georgian SSR, USSR; s. of Gen. Mamia Alasania; m. Natia Panjikidze; two c.; ed Tbilisi State Univ., Georgian Acad. of Security, Stanford Univ. Graduate School of Business; with Ministry of State Security 1994–98; with Ministry of Foreign Affairs 1998–2001, postings include Embassies in Washington, DC, Ottawa and Mexico City; Head, Directorate for Security Issues, Nat. Security Council 2001–02, Deputy Sec. 2004–05; First Deputy Minister of State Security 2002–04, of Defence March–July 2004; Special Rep. for Abkhazia and Head of de jure Govt, Abkhazia Autonomous Repub. 2005–06, Special Rep. for Abkhazia negotiations 2005–; adviser to Pres. of Georgia on Conflict Resolution 2006; Amb. and Perm. Rep. to UN, New York 2006–08 (resgnd); joined Republican and New Rights parties in Alliance for Georgia Feb. 2009, Chair. 2009–10, Founder and Leader Chveni Sakartvelo-Davisuphali Demokratebi (ChS-DD—Our Georgia-Free Democrats) party as part of the alliance July 2009–16, alliance cand. in Tbilisi mayoral elections May 2010, announced break-up of alliance June 2010, one of three co-founding parties of Qartuli Ocneba (Georgian Dream) Political Coalition Feb. 2012; Minister of Defence 2012–14, announced 'temporary withdrawal' from political life Oct. 2016, currently Sr Partner at SP Consulting 2016–. *Address:* SP Consulting, 1729 King Street, Suite 100, Alexandria, VA, USA (office). *Telephone:* (703) 684-8400 (office). *E-mail:* info@spconsulting.com (office). *Website:* sp2lc.com/partners/ambassador-irakli-alasania/ (office).

ALBA, Jessica Marie; American actress and model; b. 28 April 1981, Pomona, Calif.; d. of Mark Alba and Catherine Alba (née Jensen); m. Cash Warren 2008; two d.; ed David Mamet's Atlantic Theater Co.; took first acting class aged 12, signed by agent 1994; Founder The Honest Company (makes chemical-free products); Choice Actress Teen Choice Award, Saturn Award for Best Actress on Television, ALMA Award for Breakthrough Actress of the Year 2001, Superstar of Tomorrow, Young Hollywood Awards 2005. *Films include:* Camp Nowhere 1994, Venus Rising 1995, P.U.N.K.S. (video) 1999, Never Been Kissed 1999, Idle Hands 1999, Paranoid 2000, The Sleeping Dictionary 2003, Honey 2003, Sin City 2005, Fantastic Four 2005, Into the Blue 2005, The Ten 2007, Fantastic 4: Rise of the Silver Surfer (Favourite Female Movie Star, Nickelodeon Kids' Choice Awards 2008) 2007, Good Luck Chuck 2007, Bill 2007, Awake 2007, The Eye 2008, The Love Guru 2008, The Killer Inside Me 2010, Valentine's Day 2010, Machete 2010, An Invisible Sign 2010, Little Fockers 2010, Spy Kids: All the Time in the World in 4D 2011, A.C.O.D. 2013, Escape from Planet Earth (voice) 2013, Machete Kills 2013, Sin City: A Dame to Kill For 2014, Stretch 2014, Lessons in Love 2014, Barely Lethal 2015, Entourage 2015. *Television includes:* Flipper (series) 1995–98, Dark Angel (series) 2000–02, The Spoils of Babylon (mini-series) 2014. *Leisure interests:* swimming and scuba diving, playing golf, cooking, Harley Davidson motorcycles. *Address:* c/o Patrick Whitesell, WME Entertainment, 9601 Wilshire Boulevard, Beverly Hills, CA 90210-5213, USA (office).

ALBACETE CARREIRA, Alfonso; Spanish painter; b. 14 March 1950, Málaga; s. of Alfonso Albacete and María Carreira; m. Luisa Gómez 1986; one s. one d.; studied painting, with Juan Bonafé and architecture; studied painting Valencia 1969, then in Paris; first one-man exhbn, Madrid 1972; first exhbn USA, Center for Contemporary Art, Chicago 1989; works included in numerous collections of contemporary art including Chase Manhattan Bank, New York, White House Collection, Washington, Collection Dobe, Zurich, Museo Reina Sofia, Madrid. *Leisure interests:* botany, architecture. *Address:* Vegap, Centro de Madrid, Gran Vía 16, 5 planta, 28013 Madrid, Spain (office); Joaquín Maruía López, 23–7° C, 28015 Madrid, Spain (office). *Telephone:* (91) 5326632 (office); (91) 5491140 (office). *Fax:* (91) 5315398 (office). *E-mail:* infomad@vegap.es (office). *Website:* www.vegap.es (office).

ALBANESE, Thomas (Tom), BS, MS; American mining industry executive; b. 9 Sept. 1957, New Jersey; m. Mary Ross; two d.; ed Univ. of Alaska, Fairbanks; COO Nerco Minerals –1993, Gen. Man. Rio Tinto plc Greens Creek mine (after acquisition of Nerco by Rio Tinto), Admiralty Island, Alaska 1993–95, Group Exploration Exec., London 1995–98, Vice-Pres. Eng and Tech. Services, Kennecott Utah Copper 1998–2000, CEO Industrial Minerals Group, Rio Tinto 2000–04, CEO Copper Group and Head, Exploration, London 2004, Dir Group Resources, Rio Tinto Group, Melbourne –2006, mem. Bd of Dirs Rio Tinto plc and Rio Tinto Ltd 2006–13, Chief Exec. Rio Tinto Group 2007–13; CEO Vedanta Resources PLC 2014–17; mem. Bd of Dirs, Palabora Mining Co. 2004–06, Ivanhoe Mines 2006–07, Franco-Nevada Corpn 2018–; mem. Exec. Cttee Int. Copper Asscn 2004–06. *Address:* c/o Nevada Cooper, Inc., 61 E Pursel Lane PO Box 1640, Yerington, NV 89447, USA.

ALBANEZ DE ESCOBAR, Ana Vilma; Salvadorean economist and politician; b. 2 March 1954, San Salvador; m. Carlos Patricio Escobar; one d.; ed Universidad Centroamericana 'José Simeón Cañas'; fmr Project Man. USAID; fmr Prof. of French; Pres. Salvadorean Inst. of Social Security 1999–2003; Vice-Pres. of El Salvador (first woman) 2004–09; mem. Alianza Republicana Nacionalista (ARENA) party; mem. Asamblea Legislativa for San Salvador (ARENA) 2012–; mem. Trifinio Trinational Comm. *Address:* Asamblea Legislativa, San Salvador, El Salvador (office). *E-mail:* anav.escobar@asamblea.gob.sv (office). *Website:* www.asamblea.gob.sv (office).

ALBAR, Datuk Seri Syed Hamid bin Syed Jaafar; Malaysian politician; *Chairman, Suruhanjaya Pengangkutan Awam Darat (Land Public Transport Commission);* b. 15 Jan. 1944; mem. BN-UMNO Party; mem. Parl. for Kota Tinggi; Minister in the Prime Minister's Dept and Minister of Law *c.* 1993; Minister of Defence *c.* 1997; Minister of Foreign Affairs *c.* 1999–2008; Minister of Home Affairs and Internal Security 2008–09; Chair. Land Public Transport Comm. 2010–. *Website:* www.spad.gov.my.

ALBARN, Damon, OBE; British singer, musician (keyboards) and songwriter; b. 23 March 1968, Whitechapel, London; s. of Keith Albarn and Hazel Albarn; ed Stanway Comprehensive, Colchester, East 15 Drama School, Debden; mem. and lead singer, Blur (fmrly named Seymour) 1989–; live appearances and tours worldwide; Founder-mem. and Musical Dir of 'virtual band', Gorillaz 1998–, collaborating with numerous guest artists; Founder-mem. The Good The Bad and The Queen 2006–; other collaborations include Michael Nyman, Massive Attack, Bobby Womack, De La Soul, Africa Express; with Blur: Brit Awards for Best Single, Best Video, Best Album, Best Band 1995, for Outstanding Contrib. to Music 2012, Best Alternative Band, Smash Hits Awards 1994, Best Band and Best Live Act, NME Awards 1995, Best Act in the World Today, Q Awards 1999, Best Band, Best Single (Tender), NME Awards 2000, NME Award for Best Live Event (Blur at Hyde Park) 2010; with Gorillaz: Q Awards for Best Video, for Best Producer 2005, Digital Music Award for Top Online Band, for Best Use of Digital Platforms 2005, MTV Europe Music Award for Best Group 2005, Grammy Award for Best Pop Collaboration with Vocals (for Feel Good Inc.) 2006, NME John Peel Music Innovation Award 2006, Ivor Novello Award for Songwriter of the Year 2006, Q Inspiration Award 2007, Brit Award for British Group 2018; other: Ivor Novello Awards – Best Songwriters (shared with Noel Gallagher) 1996, PRS for Music Heritage Award 2009, Inspiration Award, MOJO Awards 2009, Lifetime Achievement Award, Ivor Novello Awards 2016; with Africa Express: Songlines Music Award for Best Group 2016. *Film:* Face 1997. *DVDs include:* with Gorillaz: Phase One: Celebrity Take Down 2002, Phase Two: Slow Boat to Hades 2006. *Compositions:* wrote film scores for Ravenous (with Michael Nyman) 1998, Ordinary Decent Criminal 1999, 101 Reykjavík (with Einar Örn Benediktsson) 2000; wrote theatre score for Monkey: Journey to the West 2007; wrote libretto and score for opera Dr Dee 2011, for musical wonder.land 2016. *Recordings include:* albums: with Blur: Leisure 1991, Modern Life Is Rubbish 1993, Parklife (Best Album, Q Awards 1994, Best Album, Best Single, Best British Video, BRIT Awards 1995, Best Album, NME Awards 1995) 1994, The Great Escape (Best Album, Q Awards 1995) 1995, Blur 1997, 13 1999, The Best Of Blur 2000, Think Tank (Best Album, Q Awards 2003, Best Album, South Bank Show Awards 2003) 2003, Midlife 2009, The Magic Whip 2015; with Gorillaz: Gorillaz 2001, G-Sides 2002, Laika Come Home 2002, Demon Days 2005, D-Sides 2007, Plastic Beach 2010, The Fall 2011, Dr Dee 2012, Humanz 2017, The Now Now 2018; solo: Mali Music (various contributors) 2002, Democrazy 2003, Everyday Robots 2014; with The Good The Bad and The Queen: The Good The Bad and The Queen 2007; with DRC Music: Kinshasa One Two 2011; with Rocket Juice and the Moon: Rocket Juice and the Moon 2012; with Africa Express: Maison des Jeunes 2013, In C Mali 2014, The Orchestra of Syrian Musicians and Guests 2016. *Leisure interests:* football, taekwondo. *Address:* c/o Eleven Management, Suite B, Park House, 206–208 Latimer Road, London, W10 6QY, England (office). *Telephone:* (20) 8749-1177 (office). *E-mail:* info@elevenmgmt.com (office). *Website:* elevenmgmt.com (office); www.blur.co.uk; www.gorillaz.com; www.thegoodthebadandthequeen.com; www.damonalbarnmusic.com.

ALBAYRAK, Berat, BA, MA, PhD; Turkish business executive and politician; *Minister of Treasury and Finance;* b. 21 Feb. 1978, Istanbul; s. of Sadık Albayrak; son-in-law of Pres. Recep Tayyip Erdoğan; m. Esra Erdoğan 2004; three c.; ed Istanbul Univ., New York Pace Univ. Lubin School of Business; joined Çalık Holding (business conglomerate) 1999, Financial Dir, Çalık Holding USA 2002, Country Man, Çalık Holding USA 2004, Deputy Chief Financial Officer, Çalık Holding 2006–07, CEO 2007–13; fmr lecturer in banking and finance, Marmara Univ.; mem. Grand Nat. Ass. (Parl.) (AKP) for Istanbul I 2015–18; Minister of Energy and Natural Resources 2015–18; Minister of Treasury and Finance 2018–, Deputy Chair. Turkey Wealth Fund 2018–; mem. Adalet ve Kalkınma Partisi (AKP, Justice and Devt Party), mem. AKP Central Exec. Cttee. *Address:* Ministry of Treasury and Finance, Maliye Bakanlığı, Dikmen Cad. 06450, Ankara, Turkey (office). *Telephone:* (312) 4152900 (office). *Fax:* (312) 4257816 (office). *E-mail:* bilgi@sgb.gov.tr (office). *Website:* www.maliye.gov.tr (office).

ALBERT II, HSH Prince of Monaco (Albert Alexandre Louis Pierre Grimaldi), BA; b. 14 March 1958; s. of Prince Rainier III of Monaco and Princess Grace (née Kelly); one s. with Nicole Coste one d. with Tamara Rotolo; m. Princess Charlene of Monaco (fmr South African swimmer Charlene Wittstock) 2011; one s. one d. (twins); ed Albert I High School, Amherst Coll., Mass, USA; ranked as 1st Class Ensign (Sub-Capt.); Pres. Monegasque Del. to Gen. Ass., UN 1993–; Chair. of several sports feds and cttees; Chair. Organizing Cttee, Monte Carlo Int. Television Festival 1988–; Deputy Chair. Princess Grace Foundation of Monaco; named Prince Regent of Monaco 31 March 2005, became Sovereign Prince of Monaco upon death of father Prince Rainier III 6 April 2005, enthroned 12 July 2005; Hon. Pres. Int. Athletic Foundation, Int. Modern Pentathlon Union, World Beach Volleyball, Hon. Citizen of Fort Worth 2000, Hon. Chair. Jeune Chambre Economique, Monaco Aide et Présence, Hon. mem. St Petersburg Naval Ass., Int. Inst. for Human Rights, Hon. Prof. of Int. Studies, Tarrant County Coll., Fort Worth 2000; Grand Cross, Order of Grimaldi 1958, Grand Officier, Nat. Order of the Lion of Senegal 1977, Grand Cross 2012; Grand Cross, Order of Saint-Charles 1979, Kt Grand Cross, Equestrian Order of the Holy Sepulchre of Jerusalem 1983, Grand Officier, Légion d'honneur 1984, Col of the Carabineers 1986, Chevalier, Order of Malta 1989, Grand Officer, Mérite Int. du Sang 1994, Grand Cross, Nat. Order of Merit 1997, Grand Cross, Nat. Order of Niger 1998, Grand Cross of the Jordanian Renaissance (Nahdah Medal) 2000, Grand Collar of the Order of Jose Simeon Cañas (El Salvador) 2002, Grand Cross of the Order of Vasco Núñez de Balboa (Panama) 2002, Grand Cross, Order of the Sun of Peru 2003, Grand Cross, Order Juan Mora Fernandez (Costa Rica) 2003, Order of Stara Planina (Bulgaria) 2004, Kt Grand Cross with Grand Cordon of the Order of Merit of the Italian Repub. 2005, Grand Croix, Légion d'honneur 2006, Grand Prix Humanitaire de France 2007, Commdr, Ordre des Palmes académiques 2009, Kt Grand Cross, Grand Order of King Tomislav (Croatia) 2009, 1st Class decoration of the Order of Stara Planina (Bulgaria) 2011, Grand Cordon of the Supreme Order of the Renaissance (Jordan) 2011, Grand Cordon, Order of Merit (Lebanon) 2011, Grand Officer, Nat. Order of Burkina Faso 2012, Grand Cross, Order of Vytautas the Great (Lithuania) 2012, Grand Cross, Nat. Order of Mali 2012, Order of Merit of the Repub. of Poland (First Class) 2012, Kt Grand Cross, Order of Prince Danilo I, Collar of the Order of Merit of Malta, Recipient of the 70th Birthday Badge Medal of King Carl XVI Gustaf (Sweden) 2016; Dr hc (Pontifical Univ., Maynooth) 1996; Zayed Int. Prize – Category 1: Global leadership in environment and sustainable devt 2014. *Address:* Palais Princier, BP 518, MC 98015, Monaco. *Website:* www.palais.mc.

ALBERT II, Former King of the Belgians Albert Félix Humbert Théodore Christian Eugéne Marie; b. 6 June 1934, Brussels; s. of King Léopold III and Queen Astrid (fmrly Princess of Sweden); m. Donna Paola Ruffo di Calabria 1959; two s. HM King Philippe I, Prince Laurent, one d. Princess Astrid; fmrly Prince of

Liège; succeeded to the throne 9 Aug. 1993, on the death of his brother King Baudouin I, abdicated 21 July 2013 in favour of his son Crown Prince Philippe; Pres. Caisse Générale d'Epargne et de Retraite 1954–92; Pres. Belgian Office of Foreign Trade 1962–93; Pres. Belgian Red Cross 1958–93; Grand Cordon of the Order of Leopold, Grand Master of the Order of Leopold 1993–2012, Order of the African Star, Royal Order of the Lion, Order of the Crown, Order of Leopold II, Great Star of Honour for Services to the Repub. of Austria 1958, Cordon of the Order of Stara Planina (Bulgaria) 2003, GCVO, Grand Cross, Order of the Dannebrog (Denmark), Kt of the Order of the Elephant (Denmark), Collar of the Order of the Cross of Terra Mariana (Estonia) 2008, Grand Cross of the Order of the White Rose (Finland) 2004, Grand Cross, Special Class, Order of Merit of the FRG, Grand Cross, Order of the Redeemer (Greece), Grand Cross with Chain, Order of Merit of the Repub. of Hungary, Civilian Class, Kt of the Collar of the Equestrian Order of the Holy Sepulchre of Jerusalem 1995, Kt Grand Cross of the Order of the Falcon (Iceland) 1979, Kt Grand Cross of the Order of Merit of the Italian Repub. 1973, Kt Grand Cross with Collar of the Order of Merit of the Italian Repub. 1998, Collar of the Order of the Chrysanthemum (Japan), Commdr, Grand Cross with Chain of the Order of Three Stars (Latvia) 2007, Golden Collar of the Order of Vytautas the Great (Lithuania), Kt of the Order of the Gold Lion of the House of Nassau (Luxembourg), Kt Grand Cross of the Order of St Charles (Monaco) 1957, Special Class of the Order of the Mohammedi (Morocco), Kt Grand Cross of the Order of the Netherlands Lion, Kt Grand Cross of the Order of Orange-Nassau, Grand Cross with Collar of the Order of St Olav (Norway), Kt Grand Cross of the Order of the White Eagle (Poland), Grand Cordon of the Mil. Order of Aviz (Portugal) 1985, Grand Collar of the Order of the Infante Dom Henrique 1999, Sash (Collar) of the Order of the Star of Romania 2009, Sash (Collar) of the Order of the Golden Fleece (Spain) 1994, Grand Cross of the Order of Charles III 1977, Kt with Collar of the Order of the Seraphim (Sweden), Bailiff and Kt Grand Cross of Honour and Devotion of the Sovereign Mil. Order of Malta, Kt of the Order of the Golden Fleece (House of Habsburg), Kt of the Order of Saint Michael (House of Bourbon), Kt of the Order of the Most Holy Annunciation, Kt Grand Cross of the Order of Sts Maurice and Lazarus; Dr hc (Catholic Univ. of Leuven, Saint Louis Univ., Baguio City, Ghent Univ., Free Univ. of Brussels, Catholic Univ. of Mons, Polytechnic Faculty of Mons). *Address:* The Royal Palace, Rue Brederode 16, 1000 Brussels, Belgium. *Telephone:* (2) 551-20-20. *Website:* www.monarchie.be.

ALBERTI, Sir (Kurt) George Matthew Mayer, MA, DPhil, FRCP; British physician; b. 27 Sept. 1937, Koblenz, Germany; s. of William Peter Matthew Alberti and Edith Elizabeth Alberti; m. 1st 1964; m. 2nd Stephanie Anne Amiel 1998; three s.; ed Univ. of Oxford; Research Fellow, Harvard Univ. 1966–69; Research Officer, Univ. of Oxford 1969–73; Prof. of Chemical Pathology, Univ. of Southampton 1973–78; Prof. of Clinical Biochemistry and Metabolic Medicine, Univ. of Newcastle 1978–85, Prof. of Medicine 1985–2002, Dean 1995–97; Prof. of Metabolic Medicine, Imperial Coll. London 1999–2002; Sr Research Investigator, Imperial Coll. 2015–; Nat. Dir for Emergency Access, Dept of Health 2002–09; Chair. King's Coll. Hospital 2011– March 2015, Visiting Prof. 2013–; Dir Research and Devt, Northern and Yorkshire Regional Health Authority 1992–95; Chair. Diabetes UK; Pres. Royal Coll. of Physicians 1997–2002; Fellow, Acad. of Medicine, Singapore, Hong Kong, Coll. of Physicians, Sri Lanka, Thailand, South Africa; Hon. DMed (Århus), (Southampton) 2000, (Athens) 2002; Hon. DSc (Cranfield) 2005, (Warwick) 2005, (Northumbria) 2011. *Publications:* Ed. International Textbook of Diabetes Mellitus 1997 and more than 1,100 papers, reviews and ed books. *Leisure interests:* jogging, hillwalking, crime fiction, opera. *Address:* King's College Hospital, Denmark Hill, London, SE5 9RS (office); Department of Endocrinology, St Mary's Hospital, London, W2 1NY (office); 57 Lancaster Avenue, West Norwood, London, SE27 9EL, England (home). *Telephone:* (20) 3299-9000 (office). *Fax:* (20) 3299-3445 (office). *E-mail:* george.alberti@nhs.net.

ALBERTSSON, Per-Åke, BSc, PhD; Swedish biochemist and academic; *Professor Emeritus, Department of Biochemistry and Structural Biology, Lund University;* b. 19 March 1930, Skurup; s. of Albert Olsson and Frideborg Olsson; m. 1st Elisabet Godberg 1955 (divorced 1978); five s. one d.; m. 2nd Charlotte Erlanson 1978; three d.; ed Swedish High School, Ystad and Univs of Lund and Uppsala; Docent, Biochemistry, Univ. of Uppsala 1960, Lecturer 1963–65; Prof. of Biochemistry, Univ. of Umeå 1965–75; Prof. of Biochemistry, Lund Univ. 1975–95, then Prof. Emer., Dept of Biochemistry and Structural Biology; Research Zoologist, UCLA 1961–62; Visiting Prof., Stanford Univ. 1972–73, Univ. of Calif., Berkeley 1982–83; mem. Swedish Acad. of Sciences, Swedish Acad. of Eng Sciences, Royal Physiographic Soc. of Lund, Röda Kapellet (symphonic band), City Council of Lund 1991–94; Bd mem. Lunds Energi AB 1994–98, Thylabisco AB 2007–; Gold Medal, Swedish Acad. of Eng Sciences, Gold Medal, Swedish Chemical Soc., Norblad-Ekstrand Medal, Bror Holmberg Medal. *Publications include:* Partition of Cell Particles and Macromolecules 1960 (third edn 1986), Livets uppkomst 1968; more 170 scientific publs in journals. *Leisure interest:* playing music with flute and recorders. *Address:* Lund University, Department of Biochemistry and Structural Biology, Box 124, 22100 Lund, Sweden (office). *Telephone:* (46) 222-8190 (office). *Fax:* (46) 222-4116 (office). *E-mail:* Per-Ake.Albertsson@biochemistry.lu.se (office). *Website:* www.mps.lu.se (office).

ALBERY, Tim; British theatre and opera director; b. 20 May 1952; began career in theatre and turned to opera in 1980s; numerous productions for Royal Opera House, ENO, Opera North, Scottish Opera, others. *Plays directed include:* War Crimes 1981, Secret Gardens 1983, Venice Preserv'd 1983, Hedda Gabler 1984, The Princess of Cleves 1985, Mary Stuart 1988, As You Like It 1989, Berenice 1990, Wallenstein 1993, Macbeth 1996, Attempts on Her Life 1997, Nathan the Wise 2004. *Operas directed include:* (for ENO) Billy Budd 1988, Beatrice and Benedict 1990, Peter Grimes 1991, Lohengrin 1993, From the House of the Dead 1997, La Bohème 2000, War and Peace 2001, Boris Godunov 2008; (for Opera North) The Midsummer Marriage 1985, The Trojans 1986, La Finta Giardiniera 1989, Don Giovanni 1991, Don Carlos 1992, Luisa Miller 1995 Così fan tutte 1997, Katya Kabanova 1999, Così fan tutte 2004, One Touch of Venus 2004, 2005, Croesus 2007, Macbeth 2008; (for Welsh Nat. Opera) The Trojans 1987, Nabucco 1995; (for Scottish Opera) The Midsummer Marriage 1988, The Trojans 1990, Fidelio 1994, The Ring Cycle 2003, Don Giovanni 2006; (for Australian Opera) The Marriage of Figaro 1992; (for Netherlands Opera) Benvenuto Cellini 1991, La Wally 1993, Beatrice and Benedict 2001; (for Bayerische Staatsoper) Peter Grimes 1993, Simon Boccanegra 1995, Ariadne Auf Naxos 1996; (for Batignano Festival, Italy) The Turn of the Screw 1983; (for Bregenz Festival, Austria) La Wally 1990; (for Royal Opera House) Cherubin 1994, The Flying Dutchman 2009, Tannhäuser 2010, 2016; (for Metropolitan Opera, New York) Midsummer Night's Dream 1996, The Merry Widow 2000; (for Minnesota Opera) Passion 2004; (for Canadian Opera Company, Toronto) Rodelinda 2005, Gotterdämmerung 2006, War and Peace 2008; (for Reisopera, Netherlands) Nabucco 2008; (for Luminato Festival, Toronto) The Children's Crusade 2009, Prima Donna 2010; (for Dallas Opera) Otello 2009; (for Sadler's Wells, London) Prima Donna 2010; (for Santa Fe Opera) The Magic Flute 2010; Grimes on the Beach (for Aldeburgh Festival) 2013. *Address:* c/o Harriet Cruickshank, Cruickshank Cazenove, 97 Old South Lambeth Road, London, SW8 1XU, England (office). *Telephone:* (20) 7735-2933 (office). *Fax:* (20) 7582-6405 (office). *E-mail:* office@cruickshankcazenove.com (office).

ALBRIGHT, Madeleine Korbel, BA, MA, PhD; American international affairs adviser, fmr diplomatist and fmr government official; *Chairman, Albright Stonebridge Group;* b. 15 May 1937, Prague, Czechoslovakia; d. of Joseph Korbel and Anna Speeglova; m. Joseph Albright 1959 (divorced 1983); three d.; ed Wellesley Coll. and Columbia Univ.; Prof. of Int. Affairs, Georgetown Univ. 1982–83; Head, Center for Nat. Policy 1985–93; chief legis. asst to Democratic Senator Edmund Muskie 1976–78; mem. Nat. Security Council staff in Carter Admin 1978–81; adviser to Democrat cands Geraldine Ferraro 1984 and Michael Dukakis 1988; Perm. Rep. to UN 1993–97 (first foreign-born holder of this post); Sec. of State (first female) 1997–2001; Co-founder and Chair. The Albright Group LLC (now Albright Stonebridge Group) 2001–, also Chair. Albright Capital Management (affiliated investment advisory firm); Chair. Nat. Democratic Inst. for Int. Affairs, Washington, DC 2001–; Chair. PEW Global Attitudes Project; Pres. Truman Scholarship Foundation; mem. Bd NY Stock Exchange; mem. Council on Foreign Relations, American Political Science Asscn, American Asscn for Advancement of Slavic Studies; Presidential Medal of Freedom 2012. *Publications include:* Poland: The Role of the Press in Political Change 1983, Madam Secretary: A Memoir 2003, The Mighty and the Almighty: Reflections on Faith, God and World Affairs 2006, Memo to the President Elect 2008, Read My Pins 2009, Prague Winter: A Personal Story of Remembrance and War 1937–1948 2012, Fascism: A Warning 2018; numerous articles. *Address:* Albright Stonebridge Group, 601 Thirteenth Street, NW, 10th Floor, Washington, DC 20005, USA (office). *Telephone:* (202) 759-5100 (office). *Fax:* (202) 759-5101 (office). *Website:* www.albrightstonebridge.com (office).

ALBUQUERQUE, Maria Luís, MEconSc; Portuguese economist and politician; b. 16 Sept. 1967, Braga; m.; three c.; ed Univ. Lusíada, Lisbon, Univ. Técnica de Lisboa; served for several years within Ministry of Finance, including as Sr Adviser, Directorate-Gen. of Treasury and Finance 1996–99, Adviser to Sec. of State for Treasury and Finance 2001, Dir, Dept of Financial Man. 2001–07, Head, Centre for Markets and Treasury Man., Inst. of Treasury and Public Credit 2007–11; Sec. of State for Treasury and Finance 2011–12, Sec. of the Treasury 2012–13, Minister of State and of Finance 2013–15; Lecturer, Univ. Lusíada, Inst. of Econs and Man. and Setúbal Univ. Moderna 1991–2006; mem. Partido Social Democrata (PSD).

ALBURQUERQUE DE CASTRO, Rafael, DJur; Dominican Republic politician; b. 14 June 1940, Santo Domingo; s. of Rafael Alburquerque Zayas-Bazán and Dona Mercedes de Castro; m. Martha Montes de Oca 1970; two d.; ed Univ. of Santo Domingo, Sorbonne, Université de Paris, France; Minister of Labour 1991–2000; Vice-Pres. of Dominican Repub. 2004–12. *Publications include:* Legislación del Trabajo 1985, La subordinación jurídica en la era digital 2002. *Website:* rafaelalburquerque.com.

ALCALA, Proceso Jaraza, BSc; Philippine politician; b. 2 July 1955, Trento; s. of Hermilando Ka Eming C. Alcala; m. Corazon Asuncion Maaño; three c.; ed Luzonian Univ. Foundation (now Enverga Univ.); mem. House of Reps (lower house of parl.) for Quezon Prov. Second Dist 2004–10, Vice-Chair. Agric. and Food Cttee, Public Works and Highways Cttee; Sec. (Minister) of Agric. 2010–16; fmr Trustee, Tanim Kalikasan (environmental org.), Barangay Pagdalagan, City of San Fernando; mem. Lucena City Fisheries and Agric. Council; Lifetime mem., Philippine Inst. of Civil Engineers; mem. Liberal Party; Hon. DTech (Pampanga Agric. Coll.) 2013; Quezon Medalya ng Karangalan for Environmental Protection, Prov. of Quezon 2003.

ALCHAAR, Mohamed Nedal, PhD; Syrian/American economist, academic and government official; b. 1956, Aleppo; divorced; one s. one d.; ed Univ. of Aleppo, George Washington Univ., USA; fmr Dir of Market Performance Analysis, Fed. Nat. Mortgage Asscn (Fannie Mae), Washington, DC, USA; fmr Vice-Pres. Johnson & Higgins (insurance brokers), Washington, DC; Prof., Faculty of Econs, Univ. of Aleppo 1996–2001; fmr Prof. of Econs and Finance, George Washington Univ.; mem. People's Council of Syria 2003–07; Sec.-Gen. Accounting and Auditing Org. for Islamic Financial Insts 2009–11; Minister of Economy and Trade and Chair. Higher Investment Council 2011–12; keynote speaker at more than 100 confs world-wide; placed under EU sanctions on grounds that he briefly served as a Syrian government minister 2012, sanctions ruled as void by European Court, Luxembourg 2014; Prize of HH Sheikh Mohammed Bin Rashid al-Maktoum for Banking Excellence 2006. *Publications:* numerous books, including Fundamentals of Banking Operations, Financial Markets, Economic Inquiries; articles on finance, monetary policy and exchange rate analysis.

ALCKMIN, Geraldo José Rodrigues; Brazilian fmr anaesthesiologist and politician; b. 7 Nov. 1952, Pindamonhangaba, São Paulo; s. of Geraldo José Rodrigues Alckmin and Miriam Penteado; m. Maria Lúcia Ribeiro Alckmin 1979; three c. (one deceased); ed Universidade de Taubaté Medical School; began political career as City Councillor, Pindamonhangaba 1973–77, Mayor of Pindamonhangaba 1976–82; State Congressman 1982–86; Fed. Congressman 1983–94, author of Law Project that became the 'Customer Defence Code'; Co-founder Brazilian Social Democracy Party (Partido da Social Democracia Brasileira—PSDB) 1988, Pres. in State of São Paulo 1991–94; Vice-Gov., State of São Paulo 1994–2001, Gov. 2001–06, 2011–18; Sec. of Devt, State of São Paulo 2009–10; PSDB cand. in presidential elections Oct. 2006, Oct. 2018. *Address:* c/o Partido da Social Democracia Brasileira, Av. Indianópolis, 1123, Moema, 04063-002 São Paulo, Brazil. *Telephone:* (11) 5078-4545. *Fax:* (11) 5078-4545. *E-mail:* faleconosco@psdb-sp.org.br. *Website:* www.psdb-sp.org.br.

ALDA, Alan, BS; American actor, director, screenwriter and author; b. (Alphonso Joseph D'Abruzzo), 28 Jan. 1936, New York, NY; s. of Robert Alda and Joan Browne; m. Arlene Weiss 1957; three d.; ed Fordham Univ.; performed with Second City 1963; Trustee Museum of TV and Radio, Rockefeller Foundation; Presidential Appointee, Nat. Comm. for Observance of Int. Women's Year 1976; Co-Chair. Nat. ERA Countdown Campaign 1982; Co-f. Alan Alda Center for Communicating Science, Stony Brook Univ. 2017; Fellow, American Acad. of Arts and Sciences 2006; Dr hc (Saint Peter's Univ.) 1974, (Fordham Univ.) 1978, (Drew Univ.) 1979, (Wesleyan Univ.) 1983, (Long Island Univ.) 2004, (Carnegie Mellon Univ.) 2015, (Univ. of Dundee) 2017; six Emmy Awards (Best Actor, Best Supporting Actor, Best Dir and Best Writer), six Golden Globe Awards for Best (TV) Actor, three Dirs' Guild of America Awards, Writers' Guild Award, seven People's Choice Awards, Humanitas Award for Writing, elected to TV Acad. Hall of Fame 1994, Screen Actors Guild Lifetime Achievement Award 2019. *Broadway appearances include:* The Owl and the Pussycat, Purlie Victorious, Fair Game for Lovers, The Apple Tree, Our Town (London) 1991, Jake's Women 1992, Glengarry Glen Ross (Drama Desk Award for Outstanding Ensemble Performance) 2005, Love Letters 2014, and others. *Films include:* Gone Are the Days! 1963, Paper Lion 1968, The Extraordinary Seaman 1968, The Moonshine War 1970, Jenny 1970, The Mephisto Waltz 1971, To Kill a Clown 1972, California Suite 1978, Same Time Next Year 1978, The Seduction of Joe Tynan (also wrote screenplay) 1979, Crimes and Misdemeanours (D.W. Griffith Award, New York Film Critics' Award) 1989, Whispers in the Dark 1992, And the Band Played On 1993, Manhattan Murder Mystery 1993, White Mile 1994, Canadian Bacon 1995, Everybody Says I Love You 1996, Murder at 1600 1997, Mad City 1997, The Object of My Affection 1998, What Women Want 2000, The Aviator 2004, Resurrecting the Champ 2007, Diminished Capacity 2008, Flash of Genius 2008, Nothing But the Truth 2008, Tower Heist 2011, Wanderlust 2012, The Longest Ride 2015, Bridge of Spies 2015; actor, dir, writer of The Four Seasons 1981, Sweet Liberty 1986, A New Life 1987, Betsy's Wedding 1990. *Television includes:* The Glass House 1972, M*A*S*H (five Golden Globe Awards) 1972–83, Tune in America 1975, Kill Me If You Can (film) 1977, E.R. 1999, Club Land 2001, The Killing Yard 2001, The West Wing (series) 2004–06, 30 Rock 2009–10, The Big C (series) 2011–13, The Blacklist (series) 2013–14; devised series We'll Get By 1975; Fair Game for Lovers (Theatre World Award); And The Band Played On 1993, White Mile 1994, Jake's Women (film) 1996, ER 1999, The West Wing (series) (Primetime Emmy Award for Outstanding Supporting Actor in a Drama Series 2006) 2004–06, The Big C (series) 2011–13, The Blacklist 2013–14, Horace and Pete 2016, Ray Donovan 2018–19. *Publications include:* Never Have Your Dog Stuffed (memoir) 2006, Things I Overheard While Talking to Myself 2007, If I Understood You, Would I Have This Look On My Face? 2017. *Website:* www.alanalda.com.

ALDER, Berni Julian, PhD; American theoretical physicist; *Professor Emeritus of Applied Science, University of California, Davis;* b. 9 Sept. 1925, Duisburg, Germany; s. of Ludwig Alder and Ottilie Gottschalk; m. Esther Romella Berger 1956; two s. one d.; ed Univ. of California, Berkeley and California Inst. of Tech.; Instructor, Univ. of Calif., Berkeley 1951–54; Theoretical Physicist, Univ. of Calif. Lawrence Livermore Nat. Lab. 1955–93; Prof. of Applied Science, Univ. of California, Davis 1987–93, Prof. Emer. 1993–; NSF Sr Post Doctoral Fellow, Weizman Inst. (Israel) and Univ. of Rome 1963–64; Van der Waals Prof., Univ. of Amsterdam 1971; Guggenheim Fellow, Univ. of Cambridge, UK and Leiden, Netherlands 1954–55; Assoc. Prof., Univ. of Paris 1972; Hinshelwood Prof., Univ. of Oxford 1986; Lorentz Prof., Univ. of Leiden 1990; G.N. Lewis Lecturer 1984, Kistiakowsky Lecturer 1990, Royal Soc. Lecturer 1991, Grad. Lecturer 2000; Ed. Journal of Computational Physics; mem. NAS; Fellow, Japanese Promotion of Science 1989, American Physics Soc.; ACS Hildebrand Award 1985, Berni J. Alder Prize est. by European Physical Soc. 1999, IUPAP Boltzmann Prize 2002, Nat. Medal of Science 2009. *Publications include:* Methods of Computational Physics 1963, many chapters in books and articles in journals. *Leisure interests:* hiking, skiing, gardening. *Address:* Lawrence Livermore National Laboratory, PO Box 808, Livermore, CA 94551-0808 (office); 1245 Contra Costa Drive, El Cerrito, CA 94530, USA (home). *Telephone:* (925) 422-4384 (office); (510) 231-0137. *Fax:* (925) 422-6594 (office). *E-mail:* alder1@llnl.gov (office). *Website:* www.llnl.gov (office).

ALDER, Jens, BSc, MBA; Swiss business executive; *Chairman, Alpiq Holding AG;* b. 1957; ed Swiss Fed. Inst. of Tech. (ETH), Zürich, INSEAD, Fontainebleau, France; trained as electrical engineer; began career with Standard Telephon & Radio AG; various exec. positions Alcatel STR AG, Motor Columbus AG, Alcatel Schweiz AG; Head of Network Services Business Unit and mem. Man. Bd Swisscom AG 1998–99, CEO 1999–2006; Pres. and CEO TDC A/S 2006–08, Adviser 2008; Chair. Supervisory Bd, RTX Telecom A/S 2010–14, mobilcom-debitel AG; Chair. IWB Industrielle Werke Basel 2010–15, BG Ingenieurs Conseils 2011–15, Goldbach Group AG 2013–18, Alpiq Holding AG 2015–; mem. Bd of Dirs CA Technologies 2011–; Pres. Schweizerische Gesellschaft für Konjunkturforschung; mem. Man. Bd Swiss Information and Telecommunications Tech. Asscn (SICTA), Swiss Employers' Fed. *Leisure interest:* skiing. *Address:* Alpiq Holding AG, Ch. de Mornex 10, 1003 Lausanne, Switzerland (office). *Telephone:* 213412111 (office). *E-mail:* info@alpiq.com (office). *Website:* www.alpiq.com (office).

ALDERDICE OF KNOCK, Baron (Life Peer), cr. 1996, of Knock, in the City of Belfast; **John Thomas Alderdice,** MB, BCh, BAO, FRCPsych, KCFO; British/Irish politician, academician and psychiatrist (retd); *Director, Centre for the Resolution of Intractable Conflict, Harris Manchester College, University of Oxford;* b. 28 March 1955, Lurgan, Co. Antrim, Northern Ireland; s. of Rev. David Alderdice and Helena Alderdice (née Shields); m. Joan Margaret (née Hill) 1977; two s. one d.; ed Ballymena Acad., Queen's Univ., Belfast; Royal Coll. of Psychiatrists; Consultant Psychiatrist in Psychotherapy, Eastern Health and Social Services Bd/Belfast Health & Social Care Trust (EHSSB/BH&SCT) 1988–2010; Dir Northern Ireland Inst. of Human Relations 1991–94; Exec. Medical Dir, S and E Belfast Health and Social Services Trust 1993–97; mem. Alliance Party of Northern Ireland 1978–2004, mem. Exec. Cttee 1984–98, Chair. Policy Cttee 1985–87, Vice-Chair. 1987, Leader 1987–98; contested Belfast E 1987, 1992, Northern Ireland European Parl. elections 1989; Councillor, Belfast City Council 1989–97; Leader of Del. to Inter-Party and Inter-Govt Talks on Future of Northern Ireland 1991–98; Leader of Del. at Forum for Peace and Reconciliation (Dublin Castle) 1994–96; mem. Northern Ireland Forum for Political Dialogue 1996–98; Vice-Pres. European Liberal Democrat and Reform Party 1999–2003, Exec. Cttee mem. 1987–2003, Treas. 1995–99; Vice-Pres. Liberal Int. 1992–99, Deputy Pres. 1999–2005, Pres. 2005–09, Hon. Pres. 2015–, Chair. Human Rights Cttee 1999–2005; mem. House of Lords 1996–, Convenor Liberal Democrat Parliamentary Party 2010–14; mem. Northern Ireland Ass. (Belfast E) 1998–2002, Speaker 1998–2004 (Ass. suspended Oct. 2002–May 2007); Commr, Ind. Monitoring Comm. 2003–11; Visiting Prof., Dept of Psychiatry, Univ. of Virginia 2006–10; Sr Research Fellow and Dir, Centre for Resolution of Intractable Conflict, Harris Manchester Coll., Oxford 2012–; Chair. World Fed. of Scientists' Perm. Monitoring Panel on Motivation for Terrorism 2008–17; Pres. ARTIS (Europe) Ltd, Westminster Pastoral Foundation; Vice Pres. and Dir, Int. Dialogue Initiative; Adviser, Oxford Research Group; mem. Editorial Bd of Psychoanalytic Psychotherapy, Advisory Bd, Centre for Reform; Trustee, Ulster Museum 1993–97, Nat. Liberal Club 2010– (Chair. Bd of Trustees 2011–14); mem. UK Cttee on Standards in Public Life 2010–16; Sr Research Fellow, Harris Manchester Coll., Univ., of Oxford 2012; Chair, Centre for Democracy and Peace Building 2014–; Clinical Prof., Dept of Psychiatry, Univ. of Maryland, Baltimore 2016–; Hon. Lecturer/Sr Lecturer, Faculty of Medicine, Queen's Univ. Belfast 1991–99, Hon. Prof., Faculty of Medicine, Univ. of San Marcos, Lima (Peru) 1999; Hon. DLitt (Univ. of East London) 2008, Hon. LLD (Robert Gordon Univ., Scotland) 2009, Hon. DUniv (The Open Univ., UK) 2014, Hon. LLD (Queen's Univ., Kingston, Ontario, Canada) 2017, Hon. DHL (Universidad de America, Bogota, Colombia) 2018; W. Averell Harriman Award for Democracy 1998, John F. Kennedy Profiles in Courage Award 1998, Silver Medal of Congress of Peru 1999, Medal of Honour of Peru Coll. of Medicine 1999, Extraordinary Meritorious Service to Psychoanalysis, Int. Psychoanalytical Asscn 2005, Ettore Majorana Erice Prize, World Fed. of Scientists 2005, Liberal Int., Prize for Freedom 2015. *Publications include:* articles on psychology of religious fundamentalism, radicalization, terrorism and violent political conflict, large group phenomena, first nation people. *Leisure interests:* music, singing, gastronomy, travel. *Address:* Harris Manchester College, Mansfield Road, Oxford, OX1 3TD (office); House of Lords, Westminster, London, SW1A 0PW, England (office). *Telephone:* (1865) 618081 (Oxford) (office); (20) 7219-5050 (London) (office). *E-mail:* john.alderdice@hmc.ox.ac.uk (office); alderdicej@parliament.uk (office). *Website:* www.parliament.uk/biographies/lords/john-alderdice/26850 (office); www.lordalderdice.com.

ALDERS, Johannes Gerardus Maria (Hans); Dutch fmr politician and business executive; *President Commissioner, ProRail;* b. 17 Dec. 1952, Nijmegen; m. Noes Alders 1972 (died 2005); one d.; ed vocational school; fmr jr man. in an employment agency; mem. Gelderland Prov. Ass. 1978, Leader Partij van de Arbeid (PvdA) Group 1979; elected mem. Parl. 1982, Sec. PvdA Parl. Group 1987–89; Minister of Housing, Physical Planning and the Environment 1989–94; Commr of the Queen, Prov. of Groningen 1996–2007; Pres. Energie-Nederland 2007–, Pensioenfonds Zorg en Welzijn; Pres. Commr ProRail 2014–; also Pres. Supervisory Bd Univ. Medical Center Groningen; mem. Bd of Dirs Lysias Consulting Group, Nat. Foundation Sporttotalisator; mem. Bd of Legal Aid Assistance, Ministry of Justice. *Address:* ProRail Publiekscontacten, Postbus 2038, 3500 GA, Utrecht, The Netherlands (office). *E-mail:* info@prorail.nl (office). *Website:* www.prorail.nl (office).

ALDERTON, Clive, LVO; British diplomatist; *Principal Private Secretary to TRH The Prince of Wales and The Duchess of Cornwall;* m. Catriona Canning; one s. one d.; posted to Embassy in Warsaw 1988–90, UK Perm. Representation to EU, Brussels 1990–93, Desk Officer, Far Eastern Dept, FCO 1993–96, Head of Indo-China Section, SEAD 1996–98, Head of Chancery and Deputy Head of Mission, High Comm. in Singapore 1998–2003, Consul-Gen., Lille, France 2004–06, Pvt. Sec. to Their Royal Highnesses The Prince of Wales and The Duchess of Cornwall 2006–12, Amb. to Morocco (also accred to Mauritania) 2012–15; Prin. Pvt. Sec. to TRH The Prince of Wales and The Duchess of Cornwall 2015–. *Address:* Clarence House, London, SW1A 1BA, England (office). *Website:* www.princeofwales.gov.uk (office); www.princeofwales.gov.uk/the-duchess-of-cornwall (office).

ALDINGER, William F., III, BA, JD; American business executive; b. 25 June 1947, Brooklyn, New York; s. of William F. Aldinger; m. Alberta Aldinger; four c.; ed Baruch Coll., City Coll., Brooklyn Law School; with US Trust Co. 1969–75; with Citibank Corpn 1975–86; Exec. Vice-Pres. Wells Fargo Bank 1986–92, Vice-Chair. 1992–94; Pres. and CEO Hongkong and Shanghai Banking Corpn (HSBC) (fmrly Household Int.) 1994–96, Chair. and CEO 1996–2005, Pres. and CEO HSBC North America Holdings Inc. 2004–05 (retd); Pres. and CEO Capmark Financial Group 2006–08, Consultant 2008–; mem. Bd of Dirs Children's Memorial Medical Centre, Children's Memorial Hosp., Children's Memorial Foundation, Business Advisory Council, Chicago Urban League, Evanston Northwestern Healthcare; Trustee, Northwestern Univ., J.L. Kellogg Grad. School of Man., Orchestral Asscn, Chicago Symphony Orchestra, Baruch Coll. Fund, Museum of Science and Industry, Chicago; mem. New York Bar, Chicago Club; Dr hc (Baruch Coll.) 2005; inducted into Chicago Business Hall of Fame 2002, Builder Award, Casa Cen.Community 2003, Distinguished Alumnus Award, Baruch Coll. 2004, Adam Smith Business Citizen Medal 2004, Harold H. Hines Award, United Negro Coll. Fund 2004. *Address:* c/o Capmark Financial Group, 116 Welsh Road, Horsham, PA 19044, USA.

ALDOSHIN, Sergey Mikhailovich, DChem; Russian chemist and academic; *Director, Institute of Problems of Chemical Physics;* b. 2 March 1953, Krasny Pochinki, Kadom Dist; ed Rostov State Univ.; Dir Inst. of Problems of Chemical Physics, Chernogolovka 1997–; Prof. and Dean of Faculty of Physical-Chemical Eng, Moscow State Univ.; mem. Presidium, Russian Acad. of Sciences; Gold Medal for Contrib. to World Science and Int. Collaboration 2003, Russian Fed. Govt Award in Science and Eng. *Publications:* numerous scientific papers. *Address:* Institute of Problems of Chemical Physics, 1 Semenov av., 142432 Chernogolovka, Moscow Region, Russia (office). *Telephone:* (495) 993-57-07 (office). *Fax:* (496) 52-25-636 (office). *E-mail:* aldoshin@icp.ac.ru (office). *Website:* www.icp.ac.ru (office).

ALDRIN, (Edwin Eugene) 'Buzz', Jr, DSc; American astronaut, author and scientist; *Chairman, Starcraft Enterprises;* b. 20 Jan. 1930, Montclair, NJ; s. of Col Edwin E. Aldrin and Marion Moon; m. 1st (divorced 1978); two s. one d.; m. 2nd Lois Driggs Cannon 1988; ed US Mil. Acad. and Massachusetts Inst. of Tech.; fmr mem. USAF; completed pilot training 1952; flew combat missions during Korean War; later became aerial gunnery instructor, Nellis Air Force Base, Nev.; attended

Squadron Officers' School at Air Univ., Maxwell Air Force Base, Ala; later Flight Commdr 36th Tactical Fighter Wing, Bitburg, Germany; completed astronautics studies at MIT 1963; selected by NASA as astronaut 1963; Gemini Target Office, Air Force Space Systems Div., LA, Calif. 1963; later assigned to Manned Spacecraft Center, Houston, Tex.; pilot of backup crew for Gemini IX mission 1966; pilot for Gemini XII 1966; backup command module pilot for Apollo VIII; lunar module pilot for Apollo XI, landed on the moon 20 July 1969; Commdt Aerospace Research Pilot School 1971–72; Scientific Consultant, Beverly Hills Oil Co., LA; Chair. Starcraft Enterprises 1988–, Starcraft Boosters Inc. 1996–, ShareSpace Foundation 1998–, Nat. Space Soc.; Fellow, American Inst. of Aeronautics and Astronautics; retd from USAF 1972; Pres. Research & Eng Consultants Inc. 1972–; consultant to JRW, Jet Propulsion Lab.; Hon. mem. Royal Aeronautical Soc.; several hon. degrees; Medal of Freedom, USA and numerous other awards. *Publications:* First on the Moon: A Voyage with Neil Armstrong (with Michael Collins) 1970, Return to Earth (with Wayne Warga) 1974, Men From Earth (with Malcolm McConnell) 1989, Encounter with Tiber (with John Barnes) 1996, The Return (with John Barnes) 2000, Reaching for the Moon 2005, Magnificent Desolation 2009, Mission to Mars: My Vision for Space Exploration 2013. *Leisure interests:* scuba diving, snow skiing, star gazing. *Address:* 10380 Wilshire Blvd, Suite 703, Los Angeles, CA 90024, USA (office). *Telephone:* (310) 278-0384 (office); (310) 278-0384 (home). *Fax:* (310) 278-0388 (office); (310) 278-0388 (home). *E-mail:* starbuzz2@aol.com (office). *Website:* www.buzzaldrin.com (office).

ALEKPEROV, Vagit Yusufovich, DEcon; Russian/Azerbaijani business executive; *President, Lukoil;* b. 1 Sept. 1950, Baku, Azerbaijan; m.; one s.; ed Azizbekov Inst. of Oil and Chem., Azerbaijan; worked in oil industry in Azerbaijan and Western Siberia 1968–75; worked as engineer for Kasporneft, Surgutneftegaz, Bashneft cos 1975–84; Dir Kogalymneftegas (oil-extraction co.) 1984–90; Deputy, then First Deputy Minister of Oil and Gas Industry of USSR 1990–91; Chair. Bd Imperial Bank, Petrocommerce Bank; Founder, mem. Bd of Dirs and Pres. PJSC Lukoil 1993–, Chair. 1993–2000, currently Chair. Man. Cttee; Deputy Chair. Oil Exporters Union of Russia; Vice-Pres. Int. Oil Consortium; mem. Russian Acad. of Natural Sciences; awarded four orders and eight medals; winner of two Russian Govt prizes. *Publication:* Vertical Integrated Oil Companies in Russia. *Leisure interests:* travel, spending time with family and friends. *Address:* PJSC Lukoil, 101000 Moscow, Sretenskii bulv. 11, Russia (office). *Telephone:* (495) 627-44-44 (office). *Fax:* (495) 625-70-16 (office). *E-mail:* pr@lukoil.com (office); DepKadry@lukoil.com (office). *Website:* www.lukoil.com (office).

ALEKSANDROV, Aleksandr Pavlovich, PhD; Russian cosmonaut and pilot; b. 20 Feb. 1943, Moscow; m. Natalia Valentinovna Aleksandrova; one s. one d.; ed Baumann Tech. Inst., Moscow; mem. CPSU 1970; after service in Soviet Army started work with Space Programme 1964–; took part in elaboration of control system of spacecraft, Cosmonaut 1978–, participated in Soyuz-T and Salyut programmes; successfully completed 149-day flight to Salyut-7 orbital station with V. A. Lyakhov 1983 and effected spacewalk, July 1987, with A. Victorenko and M. Fares; joined Yurii Romanenko in space, returned to Earth Dec. 1987; completed 160-day flight on Mir Space Station; Chief, Dept of Crew Training and Extra Vehicular Activity at Energya design and production firm; Chief, NPO Energia Cosmonaut Group 1993–96; Chief, Flight Test Directorate, RKK Energiya im. S.P. Koroleva OAO 1996–2006, currently adviser to Pres.; mem. Extra Vehicular Activity Cttee, IAF 1994–; Academician, Int. Informatization Acad. 1997; Hero of Soviet Union 1983, 1987, Hero of Syria, two Orders of Lenin, Pilot-Cosmonaut of the USSR, Medal 'For Merit in Space Exploration' (Russian Fed.). *Address:* Office of the President, RKK Energiya im. S.P. Koroleva OAO, 141070 Korolev, ul. Lenina 4A, Moskovskaya Oblast (office); 129515 Moscow, Khovanskaya str. 3, 27, Russia. *Telephone:* (495) 513-72-48 (office); (495) 215-56-19 (home). *Fax:* (495) 513-61-38 (office). *E-mail:* post@rsce.ru (office). *Website:* www.energia.ru (office).

ALEKSASHENKO, Sergey Vladimirovich, BA, PhD; Russian investment banker, academic and fmr government official; *Director of Macroeconomic Research, Higher School of Economics, National Research University;* b. 23 Dec. 1959, Likino-Dulevo, Moscow Region; m.; two c.; ed Moscow State Univ.; mem. of staff, Moscow Inst. of Econs and Math., USSR Acad. of Sciences 1986–90; leading expert, USSR State Comm. on Econ. Reform; Exec. Dir Inst. of Russian Union of Industrialists and Entrepreneurs 1991–93, Dir-Gen. 1995; Deputy Minister of Finance 1993–95; Pres. Russian Foreign Exchange Market Asscn 1995; Dir-Gen. Expert Univ. RSPP 1995, mem. Scientific Council 1995; First Deputy Chair. Cen. Bank of Russian Fed. 1995–98; Chair. Audit Comm.; Chair. Asscn of Current Stock Exchanges of Russia 1995–; First Deputy Chair. Observation Council Savings Bank 1996–99; Head of Centre of Devt Analytical Group 1999–; Deputy Dir-Gen. Interros (holding co.) 2000–04, Man. Dir 2004; Pres. Antanta Capital Investment Group 2004; Man. Dir and Head of Moscow Rep. Office, Merrill Lynch Investment Bank 2006–08; Dir of Macroeconomic Research, Higher School of Econs, Nat. Research Univ. 2008–; mem. Bd of Dirs OJSC Aeroflot 2008–, Russian National Reserve Bank 2009–; fmr Scholar-in-Residence, Econ. Policy Program, Carnegie Moscow Center; fmr mem. Advisory Council to Chair. of Cen. Bank, Expert Council, Accounts Chamber of Russian Fed.; Hon. Prof., Jilin Univ., China 1997. *Publications include:* Battle for the Rouble, Alma Mater; over 100 publs on fiscal and econ. matters. *Leisure interests:* photography, diving. *Address:* Higher School of Economics, Moscow 109028, Office E 302, 11 Pokrovskiy Bulvar, Russia (office). *Telephone:* (495) 771-3254 (office). *Fax:* (495) 771-3254 (office). *E-mail:* aleksashenko@hse.ru (office). *Website:* www.hse.ru/en (office).

ALEKSEEV, Aleksander Yuryevich, PhD; Russian diplomatist and politician; b. 20 Aug. 1946, Moscow; m.; one d.; ed Moscow Inst. of Int. Relations; diplomatic posts abroad, including in India and in Ministry of Foreign Affairs of USSR and Russian Fed. 1969–92, Head of Directorate of Western and South Asia, Ministry of Foreign Affairs 1992–93, Amb. to Pakistan 1993–98, Dir Third Asian Dept, Ministry of Foreign Affairs 1998–2001, Perm. Rep. to OSCE, Vienna 2001–04; Deputy Minister of Foreign Affairs 2004–07, apptd Amb. and Perm. Rep. to Council of Europe, Strasbourg 2007; govt awards.

ALEKSISHVILI, Aleksi (Alex), (Lekso), MA (Public Policy), MA (Econ); Georgian politician and government adviser; *Chairman, Policy and Management Consulting Group;* b. 21 Feb. 1974, Tbilisi; m. (divorced); one s. one d.; ed Duke Univ., N Carolina, USA, Tbilisi State Univ.; mem. Faculty of Econ. Relations, Tbilisi State Univ. 1991–96; fmr Deputy Minister of Finance and First-Deputy Minister of Finance; Pres. Young Economists Soc. of Georgia 1994–2001; Minister of Econ. Devt 2004–05; Minister of Finance 2005–07; Gov. for Georgia, IMF and World Bank 2005; mem. Bd of Dirs Nat. Bank of Georgia 2007–08; Chair. UN Comm. on Sustainable Devt 2005–06; Chair. Policy and Management Consulting Group 2007–; PIDP Fellow 2002–04. *Address:* PMCG LLC, 61 Aghmashenebeli Avenue, 4th Floor, 0102 Tbilisi, Georgia (office). *Telephone:* (322) 92-11-71 (office). *E-mail:* a.aleksishvili@pmcg.ge (office). *Website:* www.pmcg-i.com (office).

ALEMÁN GURDIÁN, Juan Daniel, PhD; Guatemalan/Salvadorean (b. Nicaraguan) lawyer, international organization official and academic; b. 28 Aug. 1956, Leon, Nicaragua; m. Silvia Elizabeth Cáceres Vettorazzi; two s.; ed Universidad Rafael Landívar, Guatemala, Univ. of Navarre, Pamplona, Spain; moved to Guatemala City and became Guatemalan citizen 1973; Pres. Law Students' Asscn 1978–79; participated in summer seminars in Univs of London, UK and Nice, France; began professional career as Tax Dept Man., Peat Marwick & Mitchell (law firm), Guatemala; began career as Univ. Lecturer in Faculty of Law, Universidad Rafael Landívar, later held Chair of Int. Public Law and Business Law; also taught Int. Econ. Law at Inst. of Int. Relations, Universidad Francisco Marroquin, Guatemala, later became its Dir; apptd Adjoint Sec.-Gen. Cen. American Econ. Integration Secr. (SIECA), Guatemala City 1991; left office in SIECA to fill Policy Secr. of Presidency of Repub. of Guatemala; granted incorporation as advocate and notary of Repub. of Nicaragua 1994; moved to San Salvador to serve as Corp. Advocate of SIGMA/Q group (Cen. American co.) 1995, served as Sec., Bd and mem. Strategic Cttee; Visiting Prof. of Business Ethics, Escuela Superior de Negocios (ESEN), El Salvador 2001; granted Salvadoran nationality 2001; authorized to practise as lawyer and notary in El Salvador 2004; Sec.-Gen. Cen. American Integration System (Sistema de la Integración Centroamericana—SICA) 2009–13; mem. Chamber of Industry of Guatemala, Training Centre of Guatemala (TAYASAL); Sec., Bd Centre for Nat. Econ. Research of Guatemala (CIEN); Founding mem., Dir and Chair. Cttee of Legal Studies, Salvadoran Foundation for Econ. and Social Devt (FUSADES). *Publications include:* regular contrib. to specialized publs.

ALEMÁN HEALY, José Miguel, BA, JD; Panamanian lawyer and fmr government official; *Partner, Arias, Alemán & Mora;* b. 8 May 1956, Panamá City; m. Victoria Dutari Martinelli de Alemán; two s.; ed Ripon Coll., Wis., Tulane Univ., USA; admitted to Bar 1981; Vice-Pres. Panamanian Bar Asscn 1990–91; Chair. Fourth Annual Lawyers Congress 1990; Vice-Minister of Govt and Justice 1991, Minister of Foreign Affairs 1999–2002; unsuccessful cand. for Pres. (Vision of the Country) 2004; currently Pnr, Arias, Alemán & Mora (law firm); mem. Nat. Council of Foreign Relations (Consejo Nacional de Relaciones Exteriores) 2009–16; mem. Bd of Dirs Aramo Fiduciary Services Inc., Multi Credit Bank Inc., Compañia Nacional de Seguros, SA, Banex Int. SA, Costa Rica. *Address:* Arias, Alemán & Mora, 50th Street and 74th Street Building, 16th Floor, POB 0830-1580, Panamá 9, Panama (office). *Telephone:* 270-1011 (office). *Fax:* 270-0174 (office). *E-mail:* jaleman@aramolaw.com (office). *Website:* www.aramolaw.com (office).

ALEMÁN LACAYO, Arnoldo; Nicaraguan lawyer, politician and fmr head of state; b. 23 Jan. 1946, Managua; s. of Arnoldo Alemán Sandoval; m. 1st Maria Dolores Cardenal Vargas (died 1989); two s. two d.; m. 2nd Maria Fernanda Flores Lanzas; one s. two d.; ed Nat. Autonomous Univ. of Leon; fmr Leader pro-Somoza Liberal Student Youth Org. during 1960s; served as lawyer 1968–79; imprisoned for alleged counter-revolutionary activity 1980, placed under house arrest 1989; Mayor of Managua 1990–95; Gen. Sec. Partido Liberal Constitucionalista 1990–91, 1993–96; Pres. Fed. of Cen. American Municipalities 1993–95; Leader, Liberal Party Alliance 1996; Pres. of Nicaragua 1997–2001; sentenced to 20 years' imprisonment for corruption Dec. 2003, sentence overturned 2009; Pres. Asociación de Cafetaleros de Managua 1983–90, Unión de Cafetaleros de Nicaragua 1986–90, Federación de Municipios de América Cen. 1992–93, Federación Municipal de Ciudades de Centroamérica 1993–95; Vice-Pres. Unión de Productores Agropecuarios de Nicaragua 1986–90; mem. Consejo Superior de la Empresa Privada 1988–90; Orden Nacional al Mérito, Colombia, Orden de Isabel la Católica, Spain.

ALEMANNO, Gianni, BEng; Italian politician; *Secretary, National Movement for Sovereignty;* b. 3 March 1958, Bari; m. Isabella Rauti; one s.; ed Univ. of Rome; Prov. Sec., Fronte della Gioventù di Roma 1982; Sec., Movimento Sociale Italiano Youth Div. 1988; fmr mem. Exec. Bd Alleanza Nazionale, becoming Nat. Coordinator for Econ. and Social Policy and Vice-Pres., Pres. Rome Div. 2007–; mem. Lazio Regional Council 1990, becoming Vice-Pres. Industrial, Commercial and Trades Comm.; mem. Chamber of Deputies (Parl.) 1994–; Minister of Agric. and Forestry 2001–06; unsuccessful cand. for Mayor of Rome 2006, Mayor of Rome 2008–13; Pres. Euro-Mediterranean Conf. on Fisheries and Agric. 2003; Pres. Fondazione Nuova Italia 2006; f. Area (monthly journal); Dir Aspen Institut Italia; mem. Popolo della Libertà 2009–13; f. Italy First 2013–14, also Pres.; mem. Fratelli d'Italia (Brothers of Italy) 2014–15, Nat. Action 2015–17, Movimento Nazionale per la Sovranità (Nat. Movement for Sovereignty) 2017– (also Sec.); mem. Club alpino italiano; Hon. mem. Kadima World Italia. *Publication:* Intervista sulla destra sociale 2002. *Leisure interest:* mountaineering. *Address:* National Movement for Sovereignity, Via Giovanni Paisiello 40, 00198 Rome, Italy (office). *Telephone:* (06) 85357599 (office). *E-mail:* info@movimento-nazionale.it (office). *Website:* www.movimento-nazionale.it (office); www.duepuntozero.alemanno.it.

ALEMANY, Ellen, BA, MBA; American business executive; *CEO, CIT Group Inc.;* m. Jack Alemany; three c.; ed Fordham Univ.; began banking career at Chase Manhattan Bank, Sr Lender in Operations, Structured Trade, and the Media and Electronics Dept 1977–87; with Citigroup 1987–2007, held several sr positions including Exec. Vice-Pres. for Commercial Lending Group (including CitiCapital, Commercial Markets Group, Commercial Real Estate Group), mem. Bd of Dirs Citigroup N.A. and CEO Global Transaction Services –2007, mem. Citigroup's Operating Cttee; CEO Royal Bank of Scotland Group's RBS Americas, Citizens Financial Group 2007–08, Chair. and CEO Citizens Financial Group and RBS Americas 2008–13 (retd), mem. Royal Bank of Scotland Group's Global Exec. Cttee 2008–13; mem. Bd of Dirs CIT Group Inc. 2014–, CEO 2016–; mem. Fed. Advisory Council 2008, Financial Services Roundtable 2008, Clearing House Payments Co. 2009; mem. Bd Center for Discovery, March of Dimes New York Div.; mem. Providence Coll. Business Advisory Council. *Address:* CIT Group Inc., 11 West

42nd Street, New York, NY 10036, USA (office). *Telephone:* (212) 461-5200 (office). *Website:* www.cit.com (office).

ALENCHERRY, HE Cardinal George, PhD; Indian ecclesiastic and academic; *Major Archbishop of Ernakulam-Angamaly (Syro-Malabarese);* b. 19 April 1945, Thuruthy, Changanacherry; ed Pontifical Ecclesiastical Seminary of St Joseph, Alwaye, Institut Catholique de Paris, France; ordained priest 1972; served as Sec. of Archeparch of Changanacherry and Asst Pastor of the Cathedral, as well as Dir of Sunday Schools in the archeparchy; apptd Dir of Centre for Catechesis, Oriental Pastoral Centre; then directed Pastoral Orientation Centre, Cochin, inter-ritual, of the Kerala Catholic Bishops' Conf.; served as a Prof. of Pastoral Counselling and Systematic Theology, Faculty of Paurastya Vidyapitham, Pontifical Oriental Inst. of Religious Studies, Vadavathoor, Kottayam, and at Pontifical Inst. of Theology and Philosophy, Alwaye, St Thomas Apostolic Seminary; Vicar-Gen. of the archeparchy 1996–97; Bishop of Thuckalay (Syro-Malabarese) 1996–2011, Major Archbishop of Ernakulam-Angamaly (Syro-Malabarese) 2011–; cr. Cardinal (Cardinal-Priest of San Bernardo alle Terme) 2012; Patriarch of Mar Thoma Nasranis and the Gate of All India; participated in Papal Conclave (one of four cardinal-electors from outside the Latin Church) 2013; fmr Sec. of Synod of Bishops, Syro-Malabar Church; fmr Chair. Syro-Malabar Major Archiepiscopal Comm. for Catechism, Comm. for the Laity of the Catholic Bishops' Conf. of India. *Address:* Major Archbishop's House, PO Box 2580, Broadway, Ernakulam Kochi 682 031, Kerala, India (office). *Telephone:* (484) 2352629 (office); (484) 2352906 (office). *Fax:* (484) 2355010 (office); (484) 2366028 (office). *E-mail:* cardinal@ ernakulamarchdiocese.org (office). *Website:* www.ernakulamarchdiocese.org (office).

ALESHIN, Boris S.; Russian business executive and fmr politician; *Chairman, Ramport;* b. 3 March 1955; ed Moscow Physics and Tech. Inst.; held several positions at Scientific Research Inst. of Automatic Systems, including Lead Engineer, Sr Researcher, Chief of Sector, Chief of Lab., Head of Div. 1982–90; Commercial Dir State Scientific Research Inst. of Aviation Systems 1990–98, Sales Dir 1998–2000; Chair. State Cttee for Standardization and Metrology 2001–03; Deputy Prime Minister responsible for Industrial Policy 2003–04; Chair. Comm. on Export Control of Russian Fed. 2003–04; Head of Rosprom (Fed. Agency for Industry) 2004–07; Pres. and Deputy Chair. AvtoVAZ (Volga Automobile Plant) OAO 2007, Chair. GM-AVTOVAZ Jt Venture 2008–09; Gen. Dir N.E. Zhukovsky Central Aerohydrodynamic Inst. 2009–15; currently Chair. Ramport; mem. Man. Bd JSCB Novikombank; Assoc. Mem. Russian Acad. of Sciences fmr Chair. Russian-Uzbek Govt Comm.; Moscow Medal, State Prize of Russian Fed. in Science and Eng. *Address:* Ramport, 140187 Moscow, Zhukovsky, Narkomvod Str., building 23, Russia (office). *Telephone:* (495) 232-01-39 (office). *Fax:* (495) 232-01-39 (office). *E-mail:* info@ramport.aero (office). *Website:* www.ramport.aero (office).

ALESKEROV, Shamil, PhD; Azerbaijani government official and international organization official; b. 29 March 1946, Baku; m. Nabinna Alaskarova; two c.; ed Azerbaijan Oil and Chemistry Inst.; Engineer, Sr Engineer, Jr Research Fellow, Azerbaijan Energy Research and Devt Inst., USSR Ministry of Energy, Baku 1968–78; Industrial Devt Officer, Dept for Projects and Program Devt, Secr. UNIDO, Vienna 1981–87; Deputy Dir-Gen., State Foreign Trade Asscn 1988–92; Chief of Div., Dept of Int. Econ. Relations, Ministry of Foreign Affairs 1992–94, Deputy Head 1996–97; Sr Consultant (econ. service), Office of Pres. 1994–96; Asst to Sec.-Gen. (projects coordinator), Org. of Black Sea Econ. Cooperation 1997–2000; Deputy Sec.-Gen. and Dir, Dept of Energy, Minerals and Environment, ECO 2000–06, Sec.-Gen. ECO 2012–15; Amb.-at-Large for energy cooperation and regional econ. orgs, Ministry of Foreign Affairs 2006–09; Deputy Perm. Rep., Perm. Mission to Int. Orgs in Vienna (UN, UNIDO, IAEA, OSCE) 2009–12.

ALEXANDER, (Andrew) Lamar, BA, JD; American politician; *Senator from Tennessee;* b. 3 July 1940, Maryville, Tenn.; s. of Andrew Lamar Alexander and Genevra F. Rankin; m. Leslee K. (Honey) Buhler 1969; two s. two d.; ed Vanderbilt and New York Univs; mem. Bar of La. and Tenn.; law clerk to presiding justice, US Court of Appeals (5th Circuit), New Orleans; Assoc., Fowler, Rountree, Fowler & Robertson (law firm), Knoxville 1965; Legis. Asst to Senator Howard Baker, US Senate, Washington, DC 1967–68; Exec. Asst to Bryce Harlow, White House Congressional Liaison Office 1969–70; Pnr, Dearborn & Ewing (law firm), Nashville 1971–78; Gov. of Tenn. 1979–87; Chair. Leadership Inst., Belmont Coll., Nashville 1987–88; Pres. Univ. of Tennessee 1988–90; Sec. of Educ. 1991–93; Counsel, Baker, Donelson, Bearman and Caldwell (law firm) 1993–98; in pvt. legal practice 1999–; Senator from Tenn. 2003–, Chair. Senate Republican Conf. 2007–12; mem. Pres.'s Task Force on Federalism; Chair. Nat. Govs Asscn 1985–86, Pres.'s Comm. on Americans Outdoors 1985–87, Republican Satellite Exchange Network 1993–95; mem. Bd of Dirs Corporate Child Care Inc., Nashville, Martin Marietta Corpn Bethesda, Md; Chair. Republican Neighborhood Meeting 1993; Republican; numerous awards, including Award of Appreciation, Southern Asscn of Student Financial Aid Admins 2010, Certificate of Appreciation, Citizens for Fort Campbell 2010, Award for Distinguished Public Service, Inst. of Electrical and Electronics Engineers Inc., USA 2010, Spirit of Enterprise Award, US Chamber of Commerce 2010, Corridor Champion Award, Tennessee Valley Corridor 2010, Pres.'s Award, Nat. Music Publrs' Asscn 2010, Distinguished Leadership Award, Nuclear Infrastructure Council 2010, Thomas Jefferson Award, Int. Foodservice Distributors Asscn 2010, Spirit of Enterprise Award, US Chamber of Commerce 2011, Guardian of Small Business Award, Nat. Fed. of Ind. Business 2012. *Publications:* seven books, including Steps Along the Way 1986, Six Months Off 1988, We Know What We Do 1995. *Leisure interest:* piano. *Address:* 455 Dirksen Senate Office Building, Washington, DC 20510 (office); 3322 West End Avenue, #120, Nashville, TN 37203, USA. *Telephone:* (202) 224-4944 (office); (615) 736-5129. *Fax:* (202) 228-3398 (office); (615) 269-4803. *Website:* www .alexander.senate.gov/public (office); www.lamaralexander.com.

ALEXANDER, Anthony J., BS, LLB, JD; American lawyer and business executive; b. 1951, Akron, Ohio; m. Becky Alexander; four s.; ed Univ. of Akron, Harvard Univ. Law School, Massachusetts Inst. of Tech.; fmr Dir, COO and Head of UK Operations, Hanson PLC; Exec. Ohio Edison Co. (merged with other utility cos into FirstEnergy Corpn 1997) 1972–89, Vice-Pres., Gen. Counsel 1989–91, Sr Vice-Pres., Gen. Counsel 1991–96, Exec. Vice-Pres., Gen. Counsel 1996–97, currently mem. Bd of Dirs; Exec. Vice-Pres., Gen. Counsel FirstEnergy Corpn 1999–2000, Pres. 2000–01, COO 2001–04, Dir 2002–15, Acting CEO 2003–04, Pres. and CEO 2004–15; Exec. Vice-Pres. and Gen. Counsel Toledo Edison 1997–2000; Exec. Vice-Pres. and Gen. Counsel Pennsylvania Power Co. 1999–2000, Pres. 2000–, CEO 2004–; Pres. Cleveland Electric Illuminating Co. 2000–, CEO 2004–; Pres. Pennsylvania Electric Co. 2002–, CEO 2004–; Pres. and CEO Metropolitan Edison Co. 2004–; CEO, Pres. and Man. of JCP and Transition Funding LLC 2004–; mem. Bd of Dirs Team NEO, Ohio Electric Utility Inst., Asscn of Edison Illuminating Cos, Inc.; mem. Republican Nat. Cttee's Team 100 2000; apptd to US Energy Dept Transition Team by Pres. George W. Bush 2000; currently Vice-Chair. Greater Akron Chamber; Dir-at-Large Nat. Asscn of Mfrs; Dir Nuclear Energy Inst.; mem. Ohio Business Roundtable; mem. Bd of Trustees Akron Tomorrow, Team NEO; Dr Frank L. Simonetti Distinguished Business Alumni Award, Univ. of Akron. *Address:* FirstEnergy Corporation, 76 South Main Street, Akron, OH 44308, USA (office). *Telephone:* (800) 633-4766 (office). *Fax:* (330) 384-3866 (office). *E-mail:* thowson@firstenergycorp.com (office). *Website:* www.firstenergycorp.com (office).

ALEXANDER, Bill, BA; British theatre director; b. (William Alexander Paterson), 23 Feb. 1948, Hunstanton, Norfolk, England; s. of Bill Paterson and Rosemary Paterson; m. Juliet Harmer 1978; two d.; ed St Lawrence Coll. Ramsgate and Keele Univ.; began career at Bristol Old Vic directing Shakespeare and the classics and contemporary drama; joined RSC 1977, Assoc. Dir 1978–91, Hon. Assoc. Artistic Dir 1991–; productions for RSC include: Tartuffe, Richard III 1984, Volpone, The Accrington Pals, Clay, Captain Swing, School of Night, A Midsummer Night's Dream, The Merry Wives of Windsor; other theatre work at Nottingham Playhouse, Royal Court Theatre, Victory Theatre, New York and Shakespeare Theatre, Washington, DC; Artistic Dir Birmingham Repertory Co. 1993–2000, productions include: Othello, The Snowman, Macbeth, Dr Jekyll and Mr Hyde, The Alchemist, Awake and Sing, The Way of the World, Divine Right, The Merchant of Venice, Old Times, Frozen, Hamlet, The Tempest, The Four Alice Bakers, Jumpers, Nativity (co-author) 1999, Quarantine 2000, Twelfth Night 2000, An Enemy of the People (Theatre Clwyd) 2002, Frozen, Mappa Mundi (Royal Nat. Theatre) 2002, The Importance of Being Earnest (Northampton) 2002, Titus Andronicus (RSC) 2003, King Lear (RSC) 2004, The School of Night (Mark Taper Forum, Los Angeles) 2008, Glamour (Nottingham Playhouse) 2009; Olivier Award for Dir of the Year 1986. *Film:* The Snowman 1998. *Leisure interest:* tennis. *Address:* Rose Cottage, Tunley, Glos., GL7 6LP, England (home). *Telephone:* (1285) 760555 (office). *Fax:* (1285) 760494 (office). *E-mail:* bill2juliet@btinternet.com (office).

ALEXANDER, Christopher, BS, MS, PhD; British architect, academic, consultant, writer and builder; *Professor in the Graduate School and Professor Emeritus of Architecture, University of California, Berkeley;* b. 4 Oct. 1936, Vienna, Austria; m. Margaret Moore 2008; two d.; ed Oundle, Trinity Coll., Cambridge, Harvard Univ.; fmrly with Center for Cognitive Studies, Harvard Univ., with Jt Center for Urban Studies, Harvard Univ. and MIT 1959–63; Prof. of Architecture, Univ. of Calif., Berkeley 1963, now Prof. Emer., Research Prof. in the Humanities 1965, Prof. in Grad. School, 1998–; Visiting Fellow, Rockefeller Foundation Villa Serbelloni 1965; Founder and Pres., Center for Environmental Structure 1967–2015; Trustee, Prince of Wales's Inst. for Architecture 1991–97; Chair. Bd of Dirs PatternLanguage.com, Berkeley, Calif. 1999–2006; Fellow, Harvard Univ. 1961–64, American Acad. of Arts and Sciences 1996; mem. Swedish Royal Acad. 1980–; Best Bldg in Japan Award 1985, Seaside Prize 1994, Nat. Building Museum Vincent Scully Prize 2009, Global Award for Sustainable Architecture 2014, numerous other awards and prizes. *Major works include:* 35 bldgs of New Eishin Univ., Tokyo, Linz Café, Linz, village school, Gujarat, low-cost housing in Mexico and Peru, Shelter for the Homeless, San José, numerous pvt. houses and public bldgs on four continents; Center for Environmental Structure has undertaken around 200 projects, including town and community planning world-wide. *Publications include:* Notes on the Synthesis of Form 1964, The Oregon Experiment 1975, A Pattern Language 1977, The Timeless Way of Building 1979, The Linz Café 1981, A New Theory of Urban Design 1984, The Nature of Order (four vols): The Phenomenon of Life 2001, The Luminous Ground 2003, The Process of Creating Life 2004, A Vision of the Living World 2005, The Battle for the Life and Beauty of the Earth 2012; more than 200 articles in design journals. *Address:* The Center for Environmental Structure, 2701 Shasta Road, Berkeley, CA 94708, USA (office); Meadow Lodge, Binsted, nr Arundel, West Sussex, BN18 0LQ, England (home). *Telephone:* (510) 841-6166 (office). *Website:* www.patternlanguage.com (office); www.livingneighborhoods.org (office).

ALEXANDER, Clifford L., Jr, BA, LLD; American lawyer and fmr government official; *President, Alexander & Associates, Inc.;* b. 21 Sept. 1933, Harlem, New York; s. of Clifford Alexander and Edith Alexander (née McAllister); m. Adele Logan Alexander 1959; one s. one d.; ed Harvard and Yale Univs; practised as lawyer in New York, Partner, Verner, Liipfert, Bernhard, McPherson and Alexander (law firm); Asst Dist Attorney, New York Co. 1959; Exec. Dir Manhattanville-Hamilton-Grange Neighborhood Conservation Project 1961–62, Harlem Youth Opportunities Unlimited; Foreign Affairs Officer, Nat. Security Council Staff 1963–64; Deputy Special Asst, later Deputy Special Counsel to Pres. Lyndon Johnson 1964–67; Chair. Equal Employment Opportunity Comm. 1967–69 (resgnd); mem. Comm. for Observance of Human Rights 1968; Special Amb. to Swaziland 1968; Partner, Arnold & Porter (law firm); news commentator and host, Cliff Alexander–Black on White TV programme 1971–74; Prof. of Law, Howard Univ. 1973–74; US Sec. of the Army, Washington, DC 1977–81; Founder-Pres. Alexander & Assocs Inc. 1981–; Adjunct Prof., Georgetown Univ.; Prof., Howard Univ.; Chair. Moody's Corpn –2003; fmr Chair. and CEO Dun & Bradstreet Corpn; mem. Bd of Dirs Mexican-American Legal Defense and Educ. Fund, Dreyfus Third Century Fund Inc., MCI Corpn, Dreyfus Common Stock Fund, Dreyfus Tax Exempt Fund; fmr mem. Bd of Overseers Harvard Univ.; Trustee, Atlanta Univ.; fmr mem. Bd of Govs American Stock Exchange; mem. ABA, DC Bar Asscn, Community and Friends Bd, Kennedy Center; Hon. LLD (Univ. of Maryland, Atlanta Univ., Morgan State Univ., Wake Forest Univ.); Frederick Douglass Award. *Address:* Alexander & Associates, Inc., 400 C Street, NE, Washington, DC 20002-5818 (office); 512 A Street, SE, Washington, DC 20003-1139, USA (home). *Telephone:* (202) 546-0111 (office).

ALEXANDER, Sir Daniel (Danny) Grian, Kt, BA (Hons); British banking executive and fmr politician; *Vice-President and Corporate Secretary, Asian Infrastructure Investment Bank;* b. 15 May 1972, Edinburgh, Scotland; s. of Dion Ralph Alexander and Jane Alexander; m. Rebecca Hoar 2005; two d.; ed Lochaber High School, Fort William, St Anne's Coll., Oxford; worked as a press officer for Scottish Liberal Democrats 1993–94; Dir of Communications, European Movt 1996–99; Head of Communications, Britain in Europe 1999–2003; Head of Communications, Cairngorms Nat. Park Authority 2003–05; mem. Parl. for Inverness, Nairn, Badenoch and Strathspey 2005–15; Liberal Democrat Spokesperson for Work and Pensions, especially disabled people 2005–07; Whip 2006–07; Shadow Chancellor of the Duchy of Lancaster (Spokesperson for Social Exclusion) 2007; Shadow Sec. of State for Work and Pensions 2007–08; Chief of Staff to Nick Clegg as Leader of Liberal Democrats 2007–10; Chair. Liberal Democrat Manifesto Group 2007–10; led Liberal Democrat team in negotiations that resulted in formation of a Coalition Govt with the Conservative Party May 2010; Sec. of State for Scotland (and provided ministerial support to Deputy Prime Minister) May 2010; Chief Sec. to the Treasury 2010–15; Vice-Pres. and Corp. Sec., Asian Infrastructure Investment Bank 2016–; Trustee, Chance to Shine; Hon. Fellow, St Anne's Coll. Oxford. *Leisure interests:* hill-walking, fishing, cricket, travel, sports of all kinds. *Address:* Asian Infrastructure Investment Bank, 9B Financial Street, Beijing 100033, People's Republic of China (office). *E-mail:* secretariat@aiib.org (office). *Website:* www.aiib.org (office).

ALEXANDER, Douglas Garven, LLB, MA; British solicitor and politician; b. 26 Oct. 1967, Glasgow, Scotland; s. of Douglas N. Alexander; brother of Wendy Alexander MSP; m. Jacqueline Christian; one s. one d.; ed Park Mains High School, Erskine, Lester B. Pearson United World Coll. of the Pacific, Vancouver, Canada, Univ. of Edinburgh, Univ. of Pennsylvania, USA; press steward, Michael Dukakis US presidential campaign and staff mem. of Democratic Senator, USA 1988; Parl. Researcher and speech writer for Gordon Brown MP 1990; qualified as solicitor 1993; unsuccessful cand. in Perth and Kinross by-election 1995, Perth Gen. Election 1997; mem. Parl. for Paisley South (following by-election) 1997–2005, for Paisley and Renfrewshire South 2005–15; Minister for E-Commerce and Competitiveness, Dept of Trade and Industry 2001–02; Minister of State, Cabinet Office 2002–04; Minister for the Cabinet Office and Chancellor of the Duchy of Lancaster 2003–04; Minister of State, Trade, Investment and Foreign Affairs, FCO and Dept of Trade and Industry 2004–05; Minister of State for Europe, FCO 2005–06; Sec. of State for Transport and for Scotland 2006–07, for Int. Devt 2007–10; Shadow Sec. of State for Int. Devt May–Oct. 2010, for Work and Pensions 2010–11, Shadow Foreign Sec. 2011–15; mem. Nat. Exec. Cttee, Labour Party; Gen. Election Campaign Co-ordinator 1999–2001, 2007–13, Chair. of Gen. Election Strategy 2013–15. *Address:* c/o 2014 Mile End Mill, Abbey Mill Business Centre, Seedhill Road, Paisley, PA1 1JS, Scotland. *E-mail:* dalexandermp@talk21.com. *Website:* www.douglasalexander.org.uk.

ALEXANDER, Héctor, MA, PhD; Panamanian economist, academic and politician; ed Univ. of Panama, Univ. of Chicago and Univ. of St Thomas, USA, Catholic Univ. of Chile; Prof. of Microeconomics, Analysis and Project Evaluation, Faculty of Econs, Univ. of Panama; Prof. of Accounting and Microeconomics, Panama Canal Coll.; mem. Tech. Comm. for Incentives to Exports, Ministry of Commerce and Industries; Expositor, Seminar on Economy for Journalists, organized by Repub. Nat. Bank 1976; fmr Minister of Planning and Political Economy; fmr Minister for External Relations; fmr Minister of Property and Treasury; fmr Minister in charge of Commerce and Industry; Sub-Gerente, Zona Libre de Colón; Minister of the Economy and Finance 2007–12; currently Dean of Postgraduate Studies, Universidad Católica Santa María La Antigua; Econ. Adviser, Superior Direction, Interoceanica Regional Authority (ARI), Dir of Tech. Planning; mem. of team that negotiated Torrijos-Carter Treaty concerning econ. position of Panama; Finance Minister of the Year/Americas, The Banker magazine 2009. *E-mail:* halexander@usma.ac.pa.

ALEXANDER, Hon. Jane; American actress, producer, author and conservationist; b. (Jane Seyferth Quigley), 28 Oct. 1939, Boston, Mass; d. of Thomas Bartlett and Ruth Quigley; m. 1st Robert Alexander 1962 (divorced 1969); one s.; m. 2nd Edwin Sherin 1975; ed Sarah Lawrence Coll., Univ. of Edinburgh, UK; Guest Artist-in-Residence, Oklahoma Arts Inst. 1982; Chair. Nat. Endowment for Arts 1994–97; Francis Eppes Prof., Florida State Univ. 2002–04; mem. Bd of Dirs Women's Action for Nuclear Disarmament 1981–88, Film Forum 1985–90, Nat. Stroke Asscn 1984–91, American Birding Asscn 2007–; mem. Global Advisory Group, BirdLife Int.; mem. Bd of Trustees, Wildlife Conservation Soc. 1997–2007, The MacDowell Colony 1997–2008, Arts International 2000–05, Bd Nat. Audubon Soc. 2012–; Jane Alexander Global Wildlife Amb., Indianapolis Prize, Indianapolis Zoo 2012; Co-Chair. Conservation Council, Panthera; Hon. DFA (The Juilliard School) 1994, (North Carolina School of Arts) 1994, (The New School of Social Research) 1996, (Smith Coll.) 1999, (Pa State Univ.) 2000, Hon. PhD (Univ. of Pennsylvania) 1995, (Duke Univ.) 1996, (Coll. of the Atlantic) 2011 and numerous other hon. degrees; Lifetime Achievement Award, Americans for Arts 1999, Harry S. Truman Award for Public Service 1999, Directors' Guild of America Award 2002, Indianapolis Prize and numerous other awards. *Broadway appearances include:* The Great White Hope (Tony Award 1969) 1968–69, Find Your Way Home 1974, Hamlet 1975, The Heiress 1976, Goodbye Fidel 1980, Night of the Iguana 1988, Shadowlands 1990–91, The Visit 1992, The Sisters Rosensweig 1993, Honour 1998. *Other stage appearances include:* Antony and Cleopatra 1981, Hedda Gabler 1981, Approaching Zanzibar 1989, The Cherry Orchard 2000, Mourning Becomes Electra 2002, Rose and Walsh 2003, Chasing Manet 2009, A Moon to Dance By 2010, The Lady from Dubuque 2012. *Films include:* The Great White Hope 1970, All the President's Men 1976, Kramer vs. Kramer 1979, Brubaker 1980, Sweet Country 1986, Glory 1989, The Cider House Rules 1999, Sunshine State 2002, The Ring 2002, Fur: An Imaginary Portrait of Diane Arbus 2006, Feast of Love 2007, Gigantic 2008, The Unborn 2009, Terminator Salvation 2009, Dream House 2011, Mr. Morgan's Last Love 2012. *Television includes:* Eleanor and Franklin 1976, Playing for Time (Emmy Award) 1980, Kennedy's Children 1981, A Marriage: Georgia O'Keeffe and Alfred Stieglitz 1991, Stay the Night 1992, The Jenifer Estess Story 2001, Carry Me Home 2004, Warm Springs (Emmy Award) 2005, Tell Me You Love Me 2007, The Good Wife (series) 2011, William and Kate: A Royal Romance 2011; 30 others. *Publications include:* The Bluefish Cookbook (with Greta Jacobs) 1979, (co-trans.) The Master Builder (Henrik Ibsen), Command Performance: An Actress in the Theater of Politics 2000, Wild Things, Wild Places, Adventurous Tales of Wildlife and Conservation on Planet Earth 2016, 2017. *Leisure interest:* bird watching. *Address:* c/o David Kalodner, WME Entertainment, 11 Madison Avenue, New York, NY 10019, USA (office). *E-mail:* info@wmeentertainment.com (office); info@barkingdogentertainment.net (office).

ALEXANDER, Jonathan James Graham, DPhil, FBA, FSA; British/American art historian and academic; *Sherman Fairchild Professor Emeritus of Fine Arts, New York University;* b. 20 Aug. 1935, London, England; s. of Arthur Ronald Brown and Frederica Emma Graham; m. 1st Mary Davey 1974 (divorced 1994); one s.; m. 2nd Serita Winthrop 1996 (divorced 2001); ed Magdalen Coll., Oxford; Asst, Dept of Western Manuscripts, Bodleian Library, Oxford 1963–71; Lecturer, History of Art Dept, Univ. of Manchester 1971–73, Reader 1973–87; Prof. of Fine Arts, Inst. of Fine Arts, New York Univ. 1988–2002, Sherman Fairchild Prof. of Fine Arts 2002–11, Emer. 2011–; Lyell Reader in Bibliography, Univ. of Oxford 1982–83; Sandars Lecturer, Univ. of Cambridge 1984–85; Visiting Prof., Univ. Coll. London 1991–92; Fellow, Medieval Acad. of America 1999; John Simon Guggenheim Memorial Foundation Fellowship 1995–96, Distinguished Visiting Fellowship, La Trobe Univ., Melbourne, Australia 1997; Visiting Fellow, All Souls Coll., Oxford 1998; J. Clawson Mills Fellow, Metropolitan Museum of Art, New York 2002; Samuel H. Kress Prof., Center for Advanced Study in the Visual Arts, Nat. Gallery of Art, Washington, DC 2004–05; Panizzi Lectures, British Library, London 2007–08; Hon. Fellow, Pierpont Morgan Library 1995; Prix Minda de Gunzburg 1987. *Publications include:* Illuminated Manuscripts in the Bodleian Library, Oxford (with Otto Pächt) (three vols) 1966, 1970, 1973, Italian Illuminated Manuscripts in the library of Major J. R. Abbey (with A. C. de la Mare) 1969, Norman Illumination at Mont St Michel *c.* 966–1100 1970, The Master of Mary of Burgundy, A Book of Hours 1970, Italian Renaissance Illuminations 1977, Insular Manuscripts 6th–9th Century 1978, The Decorated Letter 1978, Illuminated Manuscripts in Oxford College Libraries, Age of Chivalry (co-ed.), Art in Plantagenet England 1200–1400 1987, Medieval Illuminators and their Methods of Work 1993, The Painted Page: Italian Renaissance Book Illumination 1450–1550 (ed.) 1994, The Townley Lectionary (introduction) 1997, Studies in Italian Manuscript Illumination 2002; articles in Burlington Magazine, Arte Veneta, Pantheon, Art Bulletin etc. *Leisure interests:* music, gardening. *Address:* Institute of Fine Arts, 1 East 78th Street, New York, NY 10075, USA (office). *Telephone:* (212) 992-5876 (office). *Fax:* (212) 992-5807 (office). *Website:* www.ifa.nyu.edu (office).

ALEXANDER, Wendy, MA, MBA, FRSA; British university administrator and fmr politician; *Vice-Principal (International), University of Dundee;* b. 27 June 1963, Glasgow, Scotland; d. Reverend Douglas N. Alexander and Joyce O. Alexander; m. Brian Ashcroft; two c.; ed Park Mains High School, Erskine, Pearson Coll., Canada, Univ. of Glasgow, Univ. of Warwick and Institut Européen d'Admin des Affaires (INSEAD), France; fmr consultant with Booz Allen & Hamilton (now Booz & Co.); apptd Special Adviser to Sec. of State for Scotland 1997; MSP (Labour) for Paisley N 1999–2011, Minister for Communities 1999–2000, for Enterprise and Lifelong Learning 2000–01, for Enterprise, Transport and Lifelong Learning 2001–02, Chair. Finance Cttee 2006–07, Chair. Scotland Bill Cttee 2010–11, mem. Economy and Energy Cttee, co-convenor Cross-Party Group in Scottish Parl. for Scottish Economy, Leader, Scottish Labour Party 2007–08 (resgnd), mem. Scottish Parl. 1999–2011; Visiting Prof., Univ. of Strathclyde Business School 2002–12; columnist, Daily Record newspaper 2007; apptd Assoc. Dean, Degree Programmes and Career Services, London Business School 2012; Vice-Prin. (Int.) Univ. of Dundee 2015–; mem. Royal Soc. for the Protection of Birds, Amnesty International, Aldersgate Group, Edinburgh 2016; Scottish Politician of the Year (Channel 4) 2000, Johnnie Walker Award (Scottish Politician of the Year) 2005, Womansphere Global Award honoree 2013; Dr hc (Strathclyde) 2007, (West of Scotland) 2012. *Publications include:* First Ladies of Medicine 1986; contribs to The World is Ill Divided: Women's Work in Scotland 1992, The State and the Nations 1996, The Ethnicity Reader 1997, New Gender Agenda 2000, Chasing the Tartan Tiger 2003, New Wealth for Old Nations (co-ed.) 2003, Donald Dewar, Scotland's First First Minister (ed.) 2005. *Leisure interests:* ornithology, Scottish Islands. *Address:* University of Dundee, Nethergate, Dundee, DD1 4HN, Scotland (office). *Telephone:* (13) 8238-3171 (office). *E-mail:* m.z.hendry@dundee.ac.uk (office). *Website:* www.dundee.ac.uk.

ALEXANDER II KARAĐORĐEVIC, HRH Crown Prince of Serbia; b. 17 July 1945, London, England; s. of HM King Peter II of Yugoslavia and HRH Princess Alexandra of the Hellenes and Denmark; m. 1st HRH Princess Maria da Gloria of Orléans and Bragança 1972 (divorced 1983); m. 2nd Katherine Batis 1985; three s.; ed Le Rosey, Switzerland, Gordonstoun, Scotland, Culver Mil. Acad., USA, Royal Mil. Acad., UK; commissioned in British Army, 16th/5th The Queen's Royal Lancers, rank of Acting Capt. 1971, British Army Ski Champion 1972; business exec. working in Rio de Janeiro, New York, Chicago and London; in exile from birth, visited Belgrade for the first time Oct. 1991, est. residence in The Royal Palace, Belgrade 2001. *Leisure interests:* skiing, scuba diving, underwater photography, family. *Address:* The Royal Palace, 11040 Belgrade, Serbia (home). *Telephone:* (11) 3064000 (office). *Fax:* (11) 3064040 (office). *E-mail:* office@dvor.rs (office). *Website:* www.royalfamily.org (office).

ALEXANDRA, HRH Princess (see Ogilvy, HRH Princess Alexandra).

ALEXANDRE, Boniface; Haitian judge and politician; b. 31 July 1936; three c.; fmr lawyer with Cabinet Lamarre; Judge, Supreme Court during 1990s, Chief Justice 2002–04; Acting Pres. 2004–06; currently Lecturer, Port-au-Prince; Hon. Citizen of Lafayette, La, USA 2003.

ALEXEEV, Dmitri Konstantinovich; Russian pianist; *Professor of Advanced Piano, Royal College of Music;* b. 10 Aug. 1947, Moscow; s. of Konstantin Alekseyev and Gertrude Bolotina; m. Tatiana Sarkisova 1970; one d.; ed Moscow Conservatoire; studied under Dmitri Bashkirov; performs regularly in Russia, in UK and throughout Europe and USA and has toured Japan, Australia etc.; has performed with orchestras including Berlin Philharmonic, Chicago Symphony Orchestra, Philadelphia Orchestra, Royal Concertgebouw Orchestra of Amsterdam, London Symphony Orchestra, London Philharmonic Orchestra, Philharmonia Orchestra, Royal Philharmonic, BBC Symphony Orchestra, Orchestre de Paris, Israel Philharmonic and the Munich Bavarian Radio Orchestra; worked with Ashkenazy, Boulez, Dorati, Gatti, Gergiev, Giulini, Jansons, Muti, Pappano, Rozhdestvensky, Salonen, Svetlanov, Temirkanov, Rostropovich, Lynn Harrell, Yuri Bashmet, Joshua Bell, Nicolai Gedda, Elisabeth Soderstrom and Barbara Hendricks; world premiere of Penderecki's Piano Sextet, Vienna Musikverein 2000, premiere of Penderecki's Piano Concerto under the baton of the composer, Beijing Festival 2002; Artistic Dir Leeds Int. Recital Series 2008–09; apptd Prof. of Piano, Royal Coll. of Music, London 2005, Prof. of Advanced Piano 2013–; prizewinner, Int. Marguerite Long Competition, Paris 1969, Int. George Enescu Competition, Bucharest 1970, Int. Tchaikovsky Competition, Moscow 1974, 5th Leeds Int. Piano Competition 1975 and other int. competitions; Edison Award (Netherlands) for his recording of the complete Rachmaninov Preludes. *Recordings:* works by Bach, Brahms, Chopin, Grieg, Liszt, Medtner, Prokofiev, Rachmaninov, Schumann, Shostakovich, Scriabin, Glazunov, Gershwin and Hindemith. *Address:* IMG Artists, The Light Box, 111 Power Road, London, W4 5PY, England (office); Royal College of Music, Prince Consort Road, London, SW7 2BS England (office). *Telephone:* (20) 7957-5800 (office); (20) 7591-4300 (office). *Fax:* (20) 7957-5801 (office). *E-mail:* artistseurope@imgartists.com (office); dmitri .alexeev@rcm.ac.uk (office). *Website:* www.imgartists.com (office); www.rcm.ac.uk/ keyboard (office).

ALEXEYEV, Nikolay Gennadyevich; Russian conductor; *Principal Conductor, St Petersburg Philharmonic Orchestra;* b. 1 May 1956, Leningrad; s. of Gennady Nikolayevich Alexeyev and Tamara Andreyevna Alexeyeva; m. Nina Yefimovna Alexeyeva; two s.; ed Glinka Choir School, St Petersburg State Conservatory; Chief Conductor Ulyanovsk Philharmonic Orchestra 1983–2001; Prin. Guest Conductor Zagreb Philharmonic and Estonian Nat. Symphony 1994–97; Artistic Dir and Prin. Conductor Estonian Nat. Symphony Orchestra 2000–10; Assoc. Prin. Conductor St Petersburg Philharmonic Orchestra 2000–, now Prin. Conductor; currently Dir Symphonic Dept of St Petersburg State Conservatory; performs with leading orchestras, including Symphony Orchestra, Moscow, Russian Nat. Orchestra, Moscow Philharmonic; tours in Europe, USA, Japan; Order of the White Star, Third Class 2006, People's Artist of the Russian Federation 2007; Prize Int. H. von Karajan Music Competition 1982, Int. V. Talikh Competition 1985, Cultural Award of Repub. of Estonia 2010, St Petersburg Govt Prize 2017. *Address:* c/o Andres Siitan Artists Management, Käokeele tee 20-2 Alliku, Saue vald 76403, Estonia (office); St Petersburg Philharmonia, Mikhailovskaya str. 2, St Petersburg, Russia (office). *Telephone:* 689-4468 (office); (812) 931-98-71 (office); (812) 271-04-90 (home). *E-mail:* info@asartists.com (office); mail@philharmonia.spb.ru (office). *Website:* www.asartists.com (office); www.philharmonia.spb.ru (office).

ALEXIEVICH, Svetlana; Belarusian journalist and writer; b. 31 May 1948, Ivano-Frankovsk, Ukraine; ed Minsk Univ.; worked as journalist on local newspaper in early 1970s; Kurt Tucholsky Prize, Swedish PEN Club, Stockholm 1996, Andrej Sinjavskij Prize, Moscow 1997, Triumph Prize 1998, European Understanding Prize for contrib. to a better understanding among European nations 1998, 'Témoin du Monde', Paris 1999, Erich Maria Remarque Peace Prize (Germany) 2001, Nat. Book Critics' Circle Award, New York 2006, Oxfam Novib PEN Award 2007, Nobel Prize for Literature 2015. *Publications include:* non-fiction: Aposhniya svedki. kniga nedzitsyachyh raskaza? 1985, U voyny ne zhenskoe litso (trans. as War's Unwomanly Face) 1985, Tsinkovye mal'chiki (trans. as Zinky Boys: Soviet Voices from a Forgotten War) 1990, Zacharavanyya smertsu (Enchanted with Death) 1993, Poslednie svideteli (The Last Witnesses) 1985, Charnobyl'skaya malitva (trans. as Chernobyl Prayer: A Chronicle of the Future) 1997, Vremja second chènd (Second-hand Time: The Demise of the Red (Wo)man) (Bronze Medal Arthur Ross Book Award 2017) 2013. *Address:* c/o Galina Dursthoff, Marsiliusstr. 70, 50937 Cologne, Germany (office). *Telephone:* (221) 444254 (office). *Fax:* (221) 4600053 (office). *E-mail:* galina@dursthoff.de (office); svett_al@hotmail.com. *Website:* www.dursthoff.de (office); alexievich.info.

ALEXIS, Francis, LLM, PhD; Grenadian politician, author and lawyer; b. 3 Oct. 1947, Grenada; s. of John Everest Alexis and Anastasia Omega Alexis; m. Margaret de Bique 1973; three d.; ed Grenada Boys' Secondary School, Univ. of West Indies, Hugh Wooding Law School and Univ. of Cambridge; fmr clerk, Jonas Brown & Hubbards Ltd, Grenada; later civil servant, Grenada; Sr Lecturer in Law and Deputy Dean, Faculty of Law, Univ. of West Indies; barrister-at-law, Grenada; MP 1984–; Minister of Labour, Co-operatives, Social Security and Local Govt 1984–87; Attorney-Gen. and Minister of Legal Affairs and Labour 1987; Opposition MP 1987–90; Founder-mem. and Deputy Leader New Nat. Party 1986, Nat. Democratic Congress 1987–95; Attorney-Gen. and Minister of Legal Affairs and Local Govt 1990–95; Acting Prime Minister on various occasions 1990–95; Leader Govt Business, House of Reps in Parl. 1990–95, Grenada Nat. Del. to Commonwealth Parl. Asscn UK 1986, to Windward Islands Political Union Talks 1991–92, to UN Gen. Ass. 1993, Canada 1994; Father of House of Reps in Parl. 1995–; Founder-mem., Leader Democratic Labour Party, now People's Labour Movement 1995–2008; Vice-Pres. Grenada Bar Asscn 1997–98, fmr Pres. *Publications:* Commonwealth Caribbean Legal Essays 1981, Changing Caribbean Constitutions 1983, H. Aubrey Fraser: Eminent Caribbean Jurist 1985, The Constitution and You 1991; articles in law journals. *Leisure interests:* reading, writing, music. *Address:* St Paul's, St George's, Grenada (home). *Telephone:* 440-2378 (home).

ALEXIS, Jacques-Edouard, MSc; Haitian politician and university rector; b. 21 Sept. 1947, Gonaïves; m.; five c.; ed Faculty of Agronomics and Veterinary Medicine, State Univ. of Haïti, Laval Univ.; Prof., Univ. of Quisqueya 1990, Rector, 1990–96, Co-ordinator, Office of Institutional Devt 2003–05; Minister of Nat. Educ., Youth and Sport 1996–99, of Culture 1997–99, of the Interior and Local Govt 1999–2001; Prime Minister 1998–2001, 2006–08; Pres. Educ. et Société Foundation 2001.

ALFANO, Angelino; Italian lawyer and politician; b. 31 Oct. 1970, Agrigento; ed Catholic Univ. of Sacro Cuore, Milan; mem. Sicilian Regional Ass. 1996–2001; mem. Camera dei Deputati (Parl.) for Sicily 1 constituency 2001–13, for Piemonte 1 constituency 2013–; Regional Sec., Forza Italia 2005–08; Sec. Popolo della Libertà party 2011–13; Minister of Justice 2008–11, Vice-Pres., Council of Ministers 2013–14, Minister of Interior 2013–16, of Foreign Affairs 2016–18; Pres. Nuovo Centrodestra 2014–; Chairperson-in-Office OSCE Jan.–June 2018.

ALFARO ESTRIPEAUT, Roberto; Panamanian business executive and fmr diplomatist; m.; five c.; ed George Washington Univ., USA, Inst. of Higher Studies in Admin, Venezuela, Canal Zone Coll., Center for Studies of Insurance Admin; CEO Financiera de Seguros, SA 1981–97; Gen. Man. Financeria de Seguros SA 1994–97; Pres. Bd of Dirs Aseguradora La Unión 1997–99; Gen. Man. Proexport Int. Devt Inc. 1998–99; Treasurer Bd of Dirs, Corporación Panameña de Energia SA 1998–99; Vice-Minister of Commerce and Industry, Govt of Panama 1990–91, Minister 1991–94; Amb. to Italy 2000–02, to USA 2003–04; Sr Partner, Interglobal Busisness Brokers; Pres. Asscn of Panamanian Business Exec. 2008; currently Dir, World Youth Day Cttee; mem. Bd of Dirs Canal Bank, SA. *Address:* Panamanian Association of Business Executives, Panama City, Panama. *Telephone:* 204-1500. *Website:* apede.org.

ALFARO MAYKALL, Laura, BA, MA, PhD; Costa Rican economist, academic and government official; *Warren Alpert Professor of Business Administration, Harvard Business School;* ed Universidad de Costa Rica, Pontificia Universidad Católica de Chile, Univ. of California, Los Angeles, USA; Econ. Consultant, Consejeros Económicos y Financieros, San José 1990–92; Asst Prof. of Business Admin, Harvard Business School, USA 1999–2004, Assoc. Prof. 2004–10, Warren Alpert Prof. of Business Admin, Business, Govt and Int. Economy Unit 2013–, also Faculty Assoc., Harvard Weatherhead Center for Int. Affairs; Minister of Nat. Planning and Econ. Policy 2010–12; Faculty Research Assoc., Nat. Bureau of Econ. Research; Non-resident Fellow, OECD 2009–10; mem. American Econ. Asscn, Latin America and Caribbean Econ. Asscn; mem. Policy Cttee, David Rockefeller Center for Latin American Studies; named Young Global Leader by World Econ. Forum 2008. *Publications:* numerous articles in academic journals. *Address:* Morgan Hall 293, Soldiers Field, Boston, MA 02163, USA (office). *Telephone:* (617) 495-7981 (office). *Website:* www.hbs.edu (office).

ALFIE, Isaac; Uruguayan economist, academic and politician; *Professor of Economics and Public Finance, Universidad de Montevideo;* b. 27 April 1962, Montevideo; m.; two c.; ed Universidad de la República; fmr Lecturer, Universidad de la República, Universidad ORT, Universidad de Belgrano, Argentina; Dir of Macroeconomic Programming, Ministry of Economy 2000, Macroeconomic Policy Adviser –2003; Minister of Economy and Finance 2003–05; Gov. and Exec. Dir for Uruguay, Inter-American Devt Bank (IDB); Senator (Partido Colorado) 2005–10; currently Prof. of Econs and Public Finance, Universidad de Montevideo, also Asst Prof., Dept of Econs, Universidad de la República; Latin American Finance Minister of the Year, Emerging Markets (financial website) 2004. *Address:* Faculty of Business Studies and Economics, Universidad de Montevideo, Dr. Prudencio de Pena 2544, 11100 Montevideo 11600, Uruguay (office). *E-mail:* ialfie@um.edu.uy (office). *Website:* fcee.um.edu.uy (office).

ALFREÐSDÓTTIR, Lilja Dögg, MEconSc; Icelandic economist and politician; b. 4 Oct. 1973; m. Magnus Óskar Hafsteinsson; two c.; ed Univ. of Iceland, Columbia Univ., USA; Adviser with IMF, Washington, DC 2010–13; Asst Dir, Office of Int. Relations and Gen. Secr., Icelandic Central Bank 2013–16; seconded to Prime Minister's Office as temporary Project Man. 2014–15; Minister of Foreign Affairs 2016–17; mem. Progressive Party.

ALGABID, Hamid; Niger lawyer and politician; *Chairman, Rassemblement pour la démocratie et le progrès—Djamaa (RDP);* b. 1941, Tamont; m.; five c.; ed Abidjan Univ.; Sec.-Gen. of Finance 1974–79; Country Administrator, Econ. Community of West African States 1975–76, Islamic Devt Bank 1976–79; Sec. of State for Foreign Affairs and Cooperation 1979–81; Minister of Trade 1981–82, of Trade and Transport 1982–83; Minister Del. for Finance 1983; Prime Minister of Niger 1983–88; Sec.-Gen. Org. of the Islamic Conf. 1989–96; Chair. Rassemblement pour la démocratie et le progrès—Djamaa (RDP) 1997–; unsuccessful presidential cand. 1999, 2004; mem. Assemblée nationale 1999–; Pres. High Council of Territorial Collectivities (HCCT) 2004–10; apptd Amb.-at-Large 2011. *Address:* Rassemblement pour la démocratie et le progrès—Djamaa (RDP), pl. Toumo, Niamey, Niger (office). *Telephone:* 20-74-23-82 (office).

ALGAYEROVA, Olga, MA, MBA; Slovak diplomatist and international organization official; *Executive Secretary, United Nations Economic Commission for Europe;* b. 1959; ed Malta Univ., Open Univ. Business School, UK, Bratislava Business School, Univ. of Economics; Head of Representation of Slovak Repub., Compensacion y Comercio SA, Barcelona 1991–93; Exec. Dir, Transtrade sro 1993–95; Head, Export Dept, Slovakofarma, Hlohovec 1995–2002; Corp. Export Man., Zentiva International AS 2003–06; State Sec., Ministry of Foreign Affairs 2006–10; Pres. Slovak Millennium Devt Goals 2010–17; Adviser, Office of the Prime Minister 2012–16; Perm. Rep. to Int. Orgs in Vienna 2012–17; Exec. Sec., UN Econ. Comm. for Europe (ECE) 2017–. *Leisure interests:* sport (fmr Czechoslovakia jr rep. in volleyball), tennis, squash, skiing. *Address:* United Nations Economic Commission for Europe, Palais des Nations, 1211 Geneva 10, Switzerland (office). *Telephone:* 229171234 (office). *Fax:* 229170505 (office). *E-mail:* info.ece@unece.org (office). *Website:* www.unece.org (office); www .algayerova.sk.

ALHAKIM, Mohamed Ali, BA, MS, PhD; Iraqi diplomatist, government official and fmr business executive; *Minister of Foreign Affairs;* b. July 1952, Najaf; ed Baghdad Univ., Univ. of Birmingham, Univ. of Southern California; taught graduate and undergraduate courses in Man. and Tech., USA 1980–88; consultant and worldwide dir at several int. business and tech. cos 1986–2003; Deputy Sec.-Gen. Iraq Governing Council 2003–04; Amb., Ministry of Foreign Affairs 2004; Deputy Sec.-Gen. Arab League for Political Affairs 2004; Minister of Telecommunications in Iraqi transitional Govt 2004–05; Acting Minister of Finance while Minister of Finance negotiated Iraq's debt relief with Paris Club, IMF and IBRD (World Bank) 2004–05; mem. Iraqi Nat. Ass. (INA) 2005–06, mem. Foreign Relations Sub-cttee, represented INA at several int. confs; Sr Political and Econ. Adviser to Vice-Pres. of Iraq Adel Abdel Mahdi 2004–10; Amb. and Dir of several depts, Ministry of Foreign Affairs 2006–10: European Dept, Arab Dept including the Arab League, Policy Planning Amb. and Perm. Rep. to UN and other Int. Orgs, Geneva 2010–13, represented Iraq at all UN Orgs and Agencies, including Human Rights Council, WTO, WHO, Conf. on Disarmament, chaired Arab Ambassadors Group, Geneva 2011, Asian Ambassadors Group 2011, Vice-Pres. UNCTAD Conf. from Asian Group 2010, 2012, Vice-Pres. Int. Biological Weapon Conf. from the Asian Group 2012, represented Asian Mem. of States Region at Human Rights Consultative Group 2012, mem. Presidents P6, Conf. on Disarmament 2013, Amb. and Perm. Rep. to UN, New York 2013–17, Undersecretary-Gen. of UN and Exec.

Sec. UN Econ. and Social Comm. for Western Asia (ESCWA) 2017–18; Minister of Foreign Affairs 2018–. *Address:* Ministry of Foreign Affairs, opp. State Organization for Roads and Bridges, Karradat Mariam, Baghdad, Iraq (office). *Telephone:* (1) 537-0091 (office). *E-mail:* press@iraqmfamail.com (office). *Website:* www.mofa.gov.iq (office).

ALHEGELAN, Sheikh Faisal Abdul Aziz; Saudi Arabian diplomatist; b. 7 Oct. 1929, Jeddah; s. of Sheikh Abdul Aziz Al-Hegelan and Fatima Al-Eissa; m. Nouha Tarazi 1961; three s.; ed Faculty of Law, Fouad Univ., Cairo; with Ministry of Foreign Affairs 1952–54, served in Embassy in Washington, DC 1954–58, Chief of Protocol in Ministry 1958–60; Political Adviser to HM King Sa'ud 1960–61; Amb. to Spain 1961–68, to Venezuela and Argentina 1968–75, to Denmark 1975–76, to UK 1976–79, to USA 1979–83, to France 1996–2003; Minister of State and mem. Council of Ministers (Saudi Arabia) April–Sept. 1984, of Health 1984–96; Chair. Bd of Dirs Saudi Red Crescent Soc. 1984–, Saudi Anti-Smoking Soc. 1985–; Chair. Bd of Trustees, Saudi Council for Health Specialties 1992–; Order of King Abdulaziz, Gran Cruz Cordon of King Abdul Aziz, Order of Isabela la Católica (Spain), Gran Cordón, Orden del Libertador (Venezuela), Grande Oficial, Orden Riobranco (Brazil), May Grand Decoration (Argentina); Hon. KBE. *Leisure interests:* bridge, golf.

ALHENDAWI, Ahmad, BA; Jordanian international organization official and UN official; *Secretary-General, World Organization of the Scout Movement;* b. 20 May 1984; ed Institut Européen, Al-Balqa Applied Univ.; Youth Policy Adviser to Arab League and Officer, Technical Secr. of the Arab Youth and Sports Ministers' Council 2009–12; apptd Team Leader, World Bank-funded programme to League of Arab States on institutional devt to strengthen Arab policy and participation 2012; Envoy of UN Sec.-Gen. on Youth 2013–17; Sec.-Gen., World Org. of the Scouts Movement 2017–; also served as Team Leader for Nat. Youth Policy Project, Iraq, Youth Programme Assoc., UN Population Fund (UNFPA), Iraq, Emergency Programme Officer, Save the Children, Regional Consultant for projects of Danish Youth Council in Middle East and North Africa; Co-founder All Jordan Youth Comm., Youth for Democracy Network, Jordanian Comm. for Democratic (also Head), International Youth Council, New York. *Address:* World Organization of the Scout Movement, Suite 3, Level 17, Menara Sentral Vista, 150 Jalan Sultan Abdul Samad Brickfields, 50470 Kuala Lumpur, Malaysia (office). *Telephone:* (3) 22769000 (office). *Fax:* ((3) 22769089 (office). *E-mail:* worldbureau@scout.org (office). *Website:* www.scout.org (office).

ALI, Abdiweli Mohamed, BA, MA, PhD; Somali economist and politician; ed Somali Nat. Univ., Vanderbilt Univ., George Mason Univ., Kennedy School of Govt, Harvard Univ., USA; Dir Excise Tax Dept, Ministry of Finance, Mogadishu 1985–86, Asst Dir Research and Statistics 1988–91; Adjunct Prof. of Econs, Northern Virginia Community Coll., Alexandria 1993–98, Teaching Fellow, John F. Kennedy School of Govt, Harvard Univ. 1998–99, Teaching Fellow, Harvard Inst. for Int. Devt 1999; Assoc. Prof. of Econs, Niagara Univ. 2003–11; Deputy Prime Minister and Minister of Planning and Int. Co-operation 2010–11, Prime Minister and Minister of Planning and Int. Co-operation 2011–12; Pres., autonomous Puntland State of Somalia 2014–19; fmr consultant to UNDP; Consultant, African Econ. Research Consortium, Nairobi, Kenya 2005–; mem. American Econ. Assn, Southern Econ. Assn, Atlantic Econ. Soc., Public Choice Soc., Assn of Private Enterprise Educ.; Excellence in Research Award, Coll. of Business Admin, Niagara Univ. 2004, 2006, Best Article Award, Atlantic Economic Journal 2002. *Publications:* numerous articles in econ. journals.

ALI, Hon. Abdullahi Jama; Somali central banker; Gov. Cen. Bank of Somalia 2011–13, 2015–. *Address:* Office of the Governor, Central Bank of Somalia, 1 Villa Somalia, Mogadishu, Somalia (office). *Telephone:* (1) 657733 (office). *Fax:* (1) 215026 (office). *Website:* www.somalbanca.org (office).

ALI, Adel Abdulla, MBA; Bahraini airline industry executive; *Founder and CEO, Air Arabia;* ed Univ. of Manchester, UK, Marlhurst Univ., Oregon, USA; 20-year career with British Airways, including several sr regional posts, becoming Gen. Man. for Middle East and N Africa; Vice-Pres. of Commercial and Customer Service, Gulf Air 2001–03; f. Air Arabia 2003, mem. Bd of Dirs and Group CEO 2003–; Chair. Sharjah Information Systems Assocs, Alpha Sharjah Catering; several awards, including Aviation Business Magazine Airline CEO of the Year 2007, Low Cost Airline CEO of the Year 2007, 2008, 2009, 2010, Best Business Man for the Year 2011. *Leisure interest:* cooking. *Address:* Air Arabia Head Quarters, Sharjah Freight Center (Cargo), near Sharjah International Airport, PO Box 132, Sharjah, United Arab Emirates (office). *Telephone:* (6) 5088888 (office). *Fax:* (6) 5580244 (office). *E-mail:* contactus@airarabia.com (office). *Website:* www.airarabia.com (office).

ALI, Tan Sri Datuk Ahmad Tajuddin, BSc, PhD; Malaysian engineer; *President, Academy of Sciences Malaysia;* ed Malay Coll. Kuala Kangsar, Universiti Putra Malaysia, King's Coll. and Queen Mary Coll., London, UK, Harvard Business School, USA; began career as Asst Engineer, Nat. Electricity Bd of Malaya 1973, Sr Research Officer, Tun Ismail Atomic Research Centre 1977–83; Field Expert, IAEA 1985–88; Deputy Dir-Gen., Nuclear Energy Unit of Prime Minister's Dept 1983–89; Dir-Gen., Standards and Industrial Research Inst. of Malaysia 1989–96; Chair. and CEO Tenaga Nasional Berhad 1996–2000; Chair. Energy Comm. of Malaysia 2010–; Pres. Acad. of Sciences Malaysia 2011–; Chair. Gas Malaysia Sdn Bhd 2001–04, UEM Group Berhad 2007–, UEM Land Holdings Berhad 2008–, Malaysian Oxygen Berhad, Malaysian Standards and Accreditation Council; Adjunct Prof., Univ. Utara Malaysia; mem. Governing Council, Int. Org. for Standardization, Geneva, Switzerland; Co-Chair. (Industry), Malaysian Industry–Govt Group for High Tech.; mem. Int. Advisory Council, Universiti Tenaga Nasional, APEC Business Advisory Council (ABAC), Governing Council of Int. Inst. of Applied Systems Analysis, Laxenburg, Austria; mem. Bd of Govs Malay Coll. Kuala Kangsar; Fellow, Inst. of Engineers Malaysia, Asean Fed. of Eng Orgs; Dato' Paduka Maharaja Perlis by Raja of Perlis 1993; Hon. DSc (Universiti Putra Malaysia) 2000, (Universiti Malaysia Terengganu) 2009, Hon. DEng (Universiti Tenaga Nasional) 2008; Award for Outstanding Contribution to the Eng Profession, Inst. of Engineers Malaysia 1996, Prominent Player Award, Construction Industry Devt Bd Malaysia 2009. *Address:* Akademi Sains Malaysia, 902-4 Jalan Tun Ismail, 50480 Kuala Lumpur, Malaysia (office). *Telephone:* (3) 26949898 (office). *Fax:* (3) 26945858 (office). *E-mail:* admin@akademisains.gov.my (office). *Website:* www.akademisains.gov.my (office).

ALI, Ahmed Thasmeen, BA, MA; Maldivian politician; b. 1967; m. Visam Ali; ed Univ. of Warwick, UK, American Univ., Cairo, Egypt; mem. Dhivehi Rayyithunge Party (DRP—Maldivian People's Party), Deputy Leader 2008–10, Pres. 2010–13; elected mem. People's Majlis (Parl.) for Baa Atoll 1990s, currently for Kendhoo Constituency, fmr Deputy Speaker, Leader of DRP Parl. Group 2009–; fmr Deputy Dir Ministry of Trade and Industry; Minister of Home Affairs 2005–07, of Atolls Devt 2007–08; vice-presidential running mate of Maumoon Abdul Gayoom in presidential election Oct. 2008; Chair. Bd Dirs Dhiraagu 2005–; Regional Rep. CPA; presidential cand. of DRP 2010. *Address:* Dhivehi Rayyithunge Party, Irufa, Faashanaakilege Magu, Galolhu, Malé, Maldives (office). *Telephone:* 3320456 (office). *Fax:* 3344774 (office).

ALI, Aires Bonifácio; Mozambican politician; b. 6 Dec. 1955; teacher, Frelimo Secondary School, Namaacha –1976; Dir Francisco Manyanga Secondary School, Maputo 1977; Prov. Dir of Educ. and Culture, Nampula 1980–86; Head, Minister of Educ.'s Office 1989–90; Nat. Dir School Social Welfare Programmes 1991–92; Gov. Niassa Prov. 1995–2000, Inhambane Prov. 2000–04; Minister of Educ. and Culture 2005–10; Prime Minister 2010–12.

ALI, Amadou; Cameroonian politician; *Deputy Prime Minister;* b. 1943, Kolofata; m.; three c.; ed Nat. School of Admin and Magistracy, Int. Inst. of Public Admin, France; First Deputy Sr Divisional Office, Ngaoundéré 1971–72; Dir of Territorial Organization, Ministry of Territorial Administration 1972–74; Sec.-Gen., Ministry of Public Service 1974–82; Del.-Gen. for Tourism 1982–83; Del.-Gen. for Nat. Gendarmerie 1983–85; Sec. of State for Defence in charge of Nat. Gendarmerie 1985–96; Sec.-Gen. at the Presidency with the rank and prerogatives of a Minister, concurrently Sec. of State for Defence 1996–97; Minister–del. at the Presidency in charge of Defense 1997–2001; Sr Minister in charge of Justice 2001–04; Deputy Prime Minister 2004–, also Minister-del. at the Presidency in charge of Relations with the Assemblies; mem. Rassemblement démocratique du peuple camerounais (RDPC); Commdr, Légion d'honneur, Ordre de la Valeur. *Address:* c/o Office of the Prime Minister, Yaoundé, Cameroon (office). *Telephone:* 223-8005 (office). *Fax:* 223-5735 (office). *Website:* www.spm.gov.cm (office).

ALI, Anwar, MSc; Pakistani nuclear physicist, academic and administrator; b. 1943, Lahore; ed Univ. of Punjab, Govt Coll., Lahore, Univ. of Birmingham, UK; worked as Dir at Dr A.Q. Khan Research Labs (KRL, fmr Eng Research Lab.); joined Pakistan Atomic Energy Comm. (PAEC) as Asst Scientific Officer 1967, mem. (Tech.) 2001–09, Chair. 2006–09; Research Scientist and Prof. of Nuclear Eng, Pakistan Inst. of Eng and Applied Sciences 2009; Sitara-i-Imtiaz 1998, Hilal-e-Imtiaz 1998, Nishan-i-Imtiaz 2016; Hon. DPhil 2009; Chagai Medal 1998, Pres.'s Medal for Pride of Performance 2003, Special Commendation from Chief of Army Staff and Chair. Jt Chiefs of Staff Cttee. *Achievements include:* one of pioneers of PAEC's Uranium Enrichment Project-706, Kahuta Research Labs; played key role in formative years of Nat. Defence Complex in developing guidance and control system for Shaheen-I rocket; mem. team of scientists and engineers who carried out nuclear tests at Ras Koh Hills, Chagai region 1998. *Address:* c/oPakistan Institute of Engineering and Applied Sciences, PO Nilore, Islamabad, Pakistan (office).

ALI, Datuk Hamidon; Malaysian diplomatist and UN official; b. 22 Jan. 1950, Tangkak, Johor; m. Datin Amy Low Abdulah; two s.; ed Monash Univ., Australia, Harvard Univ., USA; worked as Minister Counsellor, Embassy in Tokyo, First Sec., Embassy in Beijing, Second Sec., Embassy in Paris; held several positions at Ministry of Foreign Affairs, including Under-Sec. for Econs, Prin. Asst Sec. for Maritime and the Environment, and Prin. Asst Sec. for the Inspectorate; Under-Sec. I in-charge of multilateral and regional issues, including APEC and Indian Ocean Rim Assn for Regional Cooperation 1991–96; Perm. Rep. to UN, Geneva 1996–2001, also accred to WTO and UN Conf. on Disarmament; High Commr to Singapore 2001–03; Amb. to Indonesia 2003–05, Amb. and Perm. Rep. to UN, New York 2005–11; apptd Vice-Pres. UNICEF 2008; Pres. ECOSOC 2010–11; apptd Chair. Nat. Authority Chemical Weapons Convention (CWC) 2012; Chair. UN, Population Award Cttee; fmr Chair. 5th Cttee (Man. and Budgetary) of 62nd Session of UN Gen. Ass.; served as Chair. Co-ordinating Bureau of the Non-Aligned Movement and the ASEAN New York Cttee; Vice-Chair. UN Forum on Forests 2006–07; fmr Co-ordinator of the Asian Group on Human Rights; fmr Chair. OIC Group, Group of Representatives of G15, Commonwealth Group of Developing Countries in WTO, Asian Group in UNCTAD, Asia-Pacific Group in ILO; fmr mem. Advisory Bd South-North Development Monitor (published by the Third World Network); chaired the 'Friends of Dr. Supachai' group in run-up to selection of Dr Supachai Panichpakdi as Dir-Gen. of WTO; Commdr, Order of Bernado O'Higgins (Chile) 1994; Darjah Panglima Jasa Negara (PJN) from King of Malaysia (carries the title Datuk), Darjah Kebesaran Setia Mahkota Kelantan Yang Amat Terbilang (SPSK) from Sultan of Kelantan (carries the title Dato), Darjah Yang Mulia Mahkota Johor (DPMJ) from Sultan of Johor (carries the title Dato'), Kesatria Mangku Negara (KMN) from King of Malaysia 1995, Darjah Indera Mahkota Pahang (DIMP) from Sultan of Pahang (carries the title Dato') 2001. *Address:* Ministry of Foreign Affairs (Kementerian Luar Negeri), Aras 3, Wisma Putra, Pusat Pentadbiran Kerajaan Persekutuan, Presint 2, 62602 Putrajaya, Malaysia (office).

ALI, Hatem; Syrian actor and film and television director; b. 2 June 1962; fmr Lecturer, Higher Inst. of Dramatic Arts, Damascus; has directed numerous films for cinema and TV, including 30-episode TV drama series El-malek Farouk (King Farouq) 2007. *Plays directed include:* Mat Thalath Marrat (Dead Three Times), Ahl Al Hawa (People of Instincts), Albareha, Alyawm Waghadan (Yesterday, Today and Tomorrow). *Plays written include:* Mawt Modares Al Tariekh Al Agouz (Death of the Old History Teacher), Hadath Wama Lam Yahdouth (What Happened and What Didn't), Tholatheyet Al Hesar (Blockade trilogy). *Films include:* as actor: Daerat Al Nar (Circle of Fire), Hegrat Al Qalb Ila Al Qalb, Al Gawareh, Al Ragol S (Mr. S), Abou Kamel; as dir: Al Oshak (The Lovers), Shaghaf (Passion), Silina 2009, Al Layl Al-Tawil (The Long Night) 2009 (Taormina Int. Film Festival Golden Tauro 2009). *Television series include:* as dir: Safar (Travelling), Al Fosoul Al Arbaa'a (The Four Seasons) (first and second parts), Maraya 98 1998, Maraya 99 1999, Aelati Wa Ana (My Family and I) 2000, Al Zier

Salem 2000, Salah Al Din 2001, Sakr Quraish (Quraish Hawk) 2002, Rabea Qurtoba (Córdoba Spring) 2003, Al Taghrieba Al Felastineya (Adonia Award for Best Dir 2004) 2003, Ahlam Kabiera (Big Dreams) 2004, Molouk Al Tawaef (Adonia Award for Best Dir, Silver Work Award, Tunisia Festival) 2005, Asey Addame' (Hard to Loosen a Tear) 2005, Ala Toul Al Ayam (All the Days) 2006, Al Malek Farouk (King Farouk) 2007, Seraa Ala El Remal 2008, Omar ibn al-Khattab 2012, Underground 2013; as writer: Muaziek, Qous Qazah (Rainbow), Al Qelaa (The Castle). *Address:* c/o Syrian National Film Organization, Rawda, Damascus, Syria. *Telephone:* (11) 3334201. *Website:* www.damascusfest.com; www.hatemali.com.

ALI, Mahershala, BA, MFA; American actor; b. (Mahershalalhashbaz Gilmore), 16 Feb. 1974, Oakland, Calif.; s. of Phillip Gilmore and Willicia Gilmore; m. Amatus Sami-Karim 2013; one d.; ed St Mary's Coll., New York Univ. *Television includes:* series: Crossing Jordan 2001–02, Haunted 2002, NYPD Blue 2002, CSI: Crime Scene Investigation 2003, The Handler 2003, Threat Matrix 2003–04, The 4400 2004–07, Lie to Me 2009, Treme 2011–12, Alphas 2011–12, House of Cards 2013–16, Luke Cage 2016, True Detective 2019. *Films include:* Making Revolution 2003, The Curious Case of Benjamin Button 2008, Crossing Over 2008, Predators 2010, The Place Beyond the Pines 2012, Go for Sisters 2013, Kicks 2016, Free State of Jones 2016, Hidden Figures 2016, Moonlight (Critics' Choice Movie Award for Best Supporting Actor 2016, Screen Actors Guild Award for Outstanding Performance by a Male Actor in a Supporting Role 2016, Acad. Award for Best Supporting Actor 2017) 2016, Roxanne Roxanne 2017, Green Book (North Texas Film Critics Asscn Award for Best Supporting Actor 2018, Critics' Choice Movie Awards for Best Supporting Actor 2018, Golden Globe Award for Best Supporting Actor in a Motion Picture 2019, Screen Actors Guild Award Outstanding Performance by a Male Actor in a Supporting Role 2019, Acad. Award for Actor in a Supporting Role 2019) 2018, Spider-Man: Into the Spider-Verse 2018, Alita: Battle Angel 2019.

ALI, M'Madi Ahamada; Comoran diplomatist and politician; fmr Consul, Consulate in Nairobi, Kenya; apptd Minister of Justice and Islamic Affairs 2006; apptd Chief of Staff to the Presidency in charge of Defence 2011.

ALI, Rt Hon. Gen. Moses, LLB; Ugandan lawyer, politician and army officer; *Second Deputy Prime Minister and Deputy Leader of Government Business in Parliament;* b. 5 April 1939, Meliaderi, Atabo Parish, Pakele Div., Adjumani Dist; ed Old Kampala Sr Secondary School, Staff Coll., Camberley and Holborn Coll., London, UK, Makerere Univ., Law Devt Centre, Kampala; mil. training as Cadet Officer and Paratrooper Instructor; Officer-in-Charge, Uganda Paratrooper School 1969–71, apptd Commdt 1971; Minister of Prov. Educ. 1973, of Youth, Culture and Sports –1990; charged with plotting terrorist activities, acquitted 1991, rejoined cabinet 1994; served as Minister of Finance, Second Deputy Prime Minister and Minister of Tourism, Trade and Antiquities; Minister of Internal Affairs 2000; MP for East Moyo Co., Adjumani Dist 2001–06, 2011–; rank of Lt-Gen. 2003, promoted to a four-star Gen. in Uganda People's Defence Force 2012; First Deputy Prime Minister and Minister of Disaster Preparedness and Refugees –2006; Third Deputy Prime Minister and Deputy Leader of Govt Business in Parl. 2011–15, Second Deputy Prime Minister and Deputy Leader of Govt Business 2015–; fmr Chair. W Nile Parl. Group; fmr Vice-Chair. Nat. Resistance Movt; fmr Gov. African Devt Bank; fmr Chair. Cabinet Econ. Cttee, Islamic Devt Bank of Govs, Fed. of Uganda Football Asscn, Cen. Tender Bd; fmr mem. Nat. Resistance Council, Moyo Dist, Uganda Council, Islamic Univ., Appointment Cttee of Uganda Parl.; fmr Del. to Constitutent Ass. for E Moyo Dist; Distinguished Service Order, Mil. Cross, Operational and Repub. Medal. *Address:* Office of the Prime Minister, Plot 9-11, Apollo Kagwa Road, PO Box 341, Kampala, Uganda (office). *Telephone:* (41) 7770500 (office). *Fax:* (41) 4341139 (office). *E-mail:* ps@opm.go.ug (office). *Website:* www.opm.go.ug (office).

ALI, Brig.-Gen. Muhammad Nasser Ahmad, MA; Yemeni army officer and government official; has held numerous positions in Yemeni army, including Chair. for Admin. Affairs, 20th Infantry Brigade, Deputy Chair. Supplement Div., Ministry of Defence, Dir of Supplement, Dir of Logistics and Supply; Minister of Defence 2006–14; Medal of Unity (May 22), Medal of Courage, Medal of Duty, Medal of Sincerity.

ALI, Mohammad Shamsher, BSc, MSc, PhD; Bangladeshi physicist, academic and organization official; *Professor Emeritus, Southeast University;* b. 9 Nov. 1937, Bheramara, Kushtia; s. of Amir Ali and Rahima Khatun; m. Saqeba Ali; two s.; ed Rajshahi Govt Coll., Univs of Dhaka, Univs of Manchester, UK; Scientific Officer, Atomic Energy Comm. 1961–65, Sr Scientific Officer 1965–69, Prin. Scientific Officer 1970–75, Chief Scientific Officer 1976–82; Dir Atomic Energy Centre, Dhaka 1970–78; Prof. of Physics, Univ. of Dhaka 1982–2006; Founder-Vice-Chancellor Bangladesh Open Univ. 1992–96; Founder-Vice-Chancellor, Southeast Univ., Dhaka 2002–10, now Prof. Emer.; Pres. Bangladesh Acad. of Sciences 2004–12; Vice-Pres. Asscn of Acads of Sciences in Asia 2004–10, 2014–16; mem. Advisory Cttee, Bangladesh Atomic Energy Comm. 1977–87; Sr Assoc., Int. Centre for Theoretical Physics, Trieste; Gen. Sec. Bangladesh Asscn of Scientists and Scientific Professions 1978–81; Dir Int. Distance Educ. Accreditation League, Philippines 2011–; Life mem. Asiatic Soc. of Bangladesh, Bangladesh Math. Soc.; mem. New York Acad. of Sciences, Pugwash Group, American Physical Soc., Inter-Acad. Panel on Int. Issues (exec. mem. 2003–09), Fed. of Asian Scientific Acads and Socs, Regional Cttee of Int. Council for Science (Asia and the Pacific) 2006–09, Nat. Council of Science and Tech.; Fellow, Bangladesh Acad. of Sciences (Pres. 2004–12), TWAS (The World Acad. of Sciences for the Developing World) (also mem. Exec. Council for Central and South Asia 2019–(22)), Islamic World Acad. of Sciences (Jordan, mem. Council 1989–94), Bangladesh Physical Soc., Bangla Acad.; Hon. Prof. of Physics, Dhaka Univ. 1973–, Hon. mem. World Innovation Foundation 2006, Hon. Fellow, Hon. Assoc., Abdus Salam Int. Centre for Theoretical Physics, Trieste; Hari Prasanna Roy Gold Medal, Univ. of Dhaka 1974, Gold Medal, Bangladesh Acad. of Sciences 1985, Third World Network of Scientific Orgs Award 1990, J.C. Bose Gold Medal, Mother Teresa Gold Medal, Khan Bahadur Ahsanullah Gold Medal 2004, Lifetime Achievement Award in Higher Educ. Leadership, Int. Univ. Leadership Colloquium (Malaysia), TWAS-ROCASA Award 2013. *Film:* Science Learning at Home: The Hand that Rocks the Cradle Rules the World (documentary) 1985. *Publications include:* as co-author: The Culture of Science in Bangladesh 1983, Poverty and Technology 1986, Scientific Indications in the Holy Quran 1990, Muslim Contributions to Science and Technology 1996; as author: Aladdin's Real Lamp: Science and Technology, Islam Science and Culture, Making Math Fun; more than 70 research papers on nuclear and hypernuclear physics. *Leisure interests:* catching fish, reading poetry and literature, listening to music, travelling. *Address:* House # 28, Road # 4, Dhanmondi R/A, Dhaka 1209, Bangladesh (home). *Telephone:* 1819-253931 (mobile) (office). *E-mail:* msali_37@yahoo.com (home); m.shamsher.ali.37@gmail.com (home). *Website:* mshamsherali.com.

ALI, Mustafa, BFA; Syrian sculptor; b. 1956, Latakia; ed Plastic Arts Centre, Minor Arts Centre, Faculty of Fine Arts, Univ. of Damascus, Faculty of Fine Arts, Carrara, Italy; known for elegant, monumental sculptures, widely collected in the Arab world for nearly three decades; mem. Syndicates of Fine Arts, Arab Plastic Artists Union; mem. Higher Cttee for Acquisition, Ministry of Culture; works have been displayed at exhbns in Canada, N Africa, Lebanon, Jordan, Syria and France; works held in Ministry of Culture, Syria, Public Palace, Damascus, Nat. Museum, Syria, Contemporary Art Museum, Syria, Contemporary Art Museum, Jordan, Al Sharjah Museum, UAE, Deir Mar Musa Monastery, Al Nabek; Bronze Prize, Sharjah Biennial 1992, Gold Prize, Lattakia Biennial 1997, Emmar Int. Art Symposium Prize 2007, Winner Arab World Inst. Competition 2008. *Monuments designed include:* Int. Damascus Fair Tower of Memory, Umayyad Square Monument (with Ihsan Intabi), Syrian Gate in Mediterranean Olympiad, Pari, Italy. *Address:* Mustafa Ali Gallery-Art Foundation, PO Box 14225, Damascus, Syria (office). *Telephone:* (11) 5440236 (office). *Fax:* (11) 5421988 (office). *E-mail:* m-ali@scs-net.org (office).

ALI, Dato Paduka Serbinibin Haji; Brunei diplomatist and civil servant; *Ambassador to Belgium;* b. 10 April 1955; m.; four c.; joined Foreign Service early 1980s, with Embassies in Singapore 1982–84, Bangkok 1984–85, Tokyo 1989–92; Asst Dir Protocol and Consular Affairs Dept, Ministry of Foreign Affairs 1985–86, Deputy Dir 1986–89, Deputy Dir Multilateral Econs Dept 1992–96, Dir 1997–98, Dir of Politics (Asia and Pacific Affairs) 1996–97; Deputy Exec. Dir APEC Secr., Singapore Jan.–Dec. 1999, Exec. Dir 1999–2001; Perm. Rep. to UN, New York 2001; Perm. Sec., Ministry of Health *c.* 2007; mem. Del. to Co-ordinators Meeting, Movt of Non-Aligned Countries; attended ministerial-level meetings of OIC, APEC and ASEAN; currently Amb. to Belgium. *Address:* Embassy of Brunei Darussalam, 238 Avenue F. D. Roosevelt, 1050 Brussels, Belgium (office). *Telephone:* (2) 675-08-78 (office). *Fax:* (2) 672-93-58 (office). *E-mail:* serbini.ali@mfa.gov.bn (office); info@bruneiembassy.be (office). *Website:* bruneiembassy.be (office).

ALI, Shahid, BAcc (Hons), MMan, MBA; Maldivian consultant and business executive; *Managing Director, State Trading Organization Plc;* ed Int. Islamic Univ., Malaysia, Australian Nat. Univ.; experienced in business man. finance, investment appraisals and project man. since early 1990s; worked in several projects for multilateral agencies including World Bank, Asian Devt Bank and UNDP; held various Govt positions, including Deputy Dir, Ministry of Finance and Treasury; Man. Dir and Non-Ind. Exec. Dir State Trading Org. Plc 2008–; Sir Roland Wilson Award for Best MBA Student, ANU 2006. *Address:* State Trading Organization Plc, STO Building, Boduthakurufaanu Magu, Maafannu, Malé 20-345, Maldives (office). *Telephone:* 3344333 (office). *Fax:* 3344334 (office). *E-mail:* info@stomaldives.net (office). *Website:* www.stomaldives.com (office).

ALI, Tariq; British (b. Pakistani) political activist, writer and filmmaker; b. 21 Oct. 1943, Lahore, Pakistan; pnr Susan Watkins; one s. two d.; ed Punjab Univ., Univ. of Oxford; Editorial Dir Verso 1999–; mem. Editorial Bd New Left Review 1982–; mem. Fourth International. *Publications include:* fiction: Redemption 1990, Shadows of the Pomegranate Tree 1992, Fear of Mirrors 1998, The Book of Saladin 1999, The Stone Woman 2000, The Illustrious Corpse 2003, A Sultan in Palermo 2005, Night of the Golden Butterfly 2010; non-fiction: The Thoughts of Chairman Harold (compiler) 1967, The New Revolutionaries: A Handbook of the International Radical Left (ed.) 1969, Pakistan: Military Rule or People's Power? 1970, The Coming British Revolution 1972, Chile: Lessons of the Coup: Which Way to Workers' Power? (with Gerry Hedley) 1974, 1968 and After: Inside the Revolution 1978, Trotsky for Beginners 1980, Can Pakistan Survive? 1983, What is Stalinism? (ed.) 1984, The Stalinist Legacy: Its Impact on Twentieth-Century World Politics (ed.) 1984, An Indian Dynasty: The Story of the Nehru-Gandhi Family 1985, Street Fighting Years: An Autobiography of the Sixties 1987, Revolution from Above: Where is the Soviet Union Going? 1988, Moscow Gold (with Howard Brenton) 1990, 1968: Marching in the Streets (with Susan Watkins) 1998, Ugly Rumours (with Howard Brenton) 1998, Masters of the Universe?: NATO's Balkan Crusade (ed.) 2000, The Clash of Fundamentalisms: Crusades, Jihads and Modernity 2002, The Clash of Fundamentalisms: Bush in Babylon: Recolonising Iraq 2003, Rough Music 2005, Conversations with Edward Said 2006, Pirates of the Caribbean: Axis of Hope 2006, The Leopard and the Fox 2007, A Banker for All Seasons: Crooks and Cheats Inc. 2007, The Assassination 2008, The Duel: Pakistan on the Flight Path of American Power 2009, The Protocols of the Elders of Sodom 2009, The Obama Syndrome 2010, On History: Tariq Ali and Oliver Stone in Conversation 2011, The Extreme Centre: A Warning 2015; contribs to periodicals, including London Review of Books. *Address:* c/o Verso, 6 Meard Street, London, W1F 0EG, England (office). *E-mail:* tariq.ali3@btinternet.com (office). *Website:* www.tariqali.org.

ALI, Zine al Abidine Ben; Tunisian politician and fmr head of state; b. 3 Sept. 1936, Hammam Sousse; m. Leila Ben Ali; three c.; ed as grad. in electronics, Saint-Cyr Mil. Acad., France, Chalons-sur-Marne School of Artillery, France, Special School of Intelligence and Security, USA; Head of Mil. Security 1958–74; Mil. and Naval Attaché, Rabat, Morocco 1974–77; mem. of Cabinet for Minister of Nat. Defence, Dir-Gen. Nat. Security 1977–80; Amb. to Poland 1980–84; Sec. of State for Nat. Security 1984–85, Minister of the Interior 1986–87, Minister of State for the Interior May–Nov. 1987, Pres. of Tunisia 1987–2011 (forced to step down and flee to Saudi Arabia); mem. politbureau of Parti Socialiste Destourien (PSD) 1986, Sec.-Gen. PSD 1986, Chair. Rassemblement Constitutionnel Démocratique (RCD); Order of Merit of Bourguiba, Order of Independence, Order of the Repub., several foreign orders. *Leisure interests:* computers, music, sports.

ALI AL-MADANI, Ahmad Mohamed, BA, MA, PhD; Saudi Arabian development banker; b. 13 April 1934, Medina; s. of Mohamed Ali and Amina Ali; m. Ghada Mahmood Masri 1968; one s. three d.; ed Cairo Univ., Egypt, Univ. of

Michigan and State Univ. of New York, Albany, USA; Dir Scientific and Islamic Inst., Aden 1958–59; Deputy Rector, King Abdul Aziz Univ., Jeddah 1967–72; Deputy Minister of Educ. for Tech. Affairs 1972–75; Pres. Islamic Devt Bank 1975–93, 1995–2016, also Chair. Bd of Exec. Dirs; Sec.-Gen. Muslim World League 1993–95; mem. King Abdul Aziz Univ. Council, King Saud Univ., Oil and Minerals Univ., Islamic Univ., Imam Mohammed Ben Saud Univ.; mem. Admin. Bd Saudi Credit Bank, Saudi Fund for Devt; King Faisal Int. Prize for Service to Islam 2005. *Publications:* numerous articles and working papers on Islamic econs, banking and educ. *Leisure interests:* cycling, walking. *Address:* c/o Islamic Development Bank, PO Box 5925, Jeddah 21432, Saudi Arabia (office).

ALIBEK, Ken, MD, PhD, ScD; American (b. Kazakhstani) industrial biotechnologist and academic; b. (Kanatzhan Alibekov), 1950, Kauchuk, Kazakh SSR; s. of Bayzak Alibekov and Rosa Alibekov; m. Lena Yemesheva 1976; four c.; ed Tomsk Medical Inst.; fmr mem. CP; cadet intern in mil. section of Tomsk Medical Inst. 1973; Jr Lt, later Sr Lt in Soviet Army, attained rank of Col 1987; mem. staff E European Scientific Br., Inst. of Applied Biochemistry, Omutninsk, Sr Scientist Siberian Br., Berdsk 1976; Deputy Dir (later Dir) Stepnogorsk Biological Research Centre, Deputy Chief Biopreparat Biosafety Div. 1987, First Deputy Chief 1988, working for Soviet Union's offensive biological weapons programme; Dir Biomash 1990–91; visited American mil. and research sites 1991; defected to USA 1992, debriefed by US mil. on Soviet and Russian biological weapons programme, consultant to NIH and numerous US Govt agencies in fields of industrial tech., medical microbiology, biological weapons defence and biological weapons non-proliferation; Pres. and Chief Scientific Officer AFG Biosolutions Inc.; Founder, Pres. and CEO MaxWell Biocorporation LLC 2006–; Distinguished Prof., George Mason Univ. –2006; Sr Fellow, Centre for Advanced Defense Studies; returned to Astana, Kazakhstan 2010, apptd Prof., Dept of Chem. and Biology, School of Science and Tech., Nazarbayev Univ. 2010, also Vice-Dean for Research; apptd CEO Nat. Medical Holding JSC, Astana 2013; Hon. DSc 1988. *Publications include:* Biohazard (autobiog. with Stephen Handelman) 2000, Jane's Chem-Bio Handbook 2002, Biological Weapons 2003, Biological and Chemical Terrorism: A Guide for Healthcare Providers and First Responders 2003, Bioterrorism and Infectious Agents: A New Dilemma for the 21st Century (ed) 2005, New and Evolving Infections of the 21st Century 2009; numerous articles in professional journals. *Address:* c/o School of Science and Technology, Nazarbayev University, 53 Kabanbay batyr Avenue, Nur-Sultan 010000, Kazakhstan (office).

ALIĆ, Muhidin, LLB; Bosnia and Herzegovina politician; b. 14 Sept. 1960, Šije, Tešanj Prov.; m.; two c.; ed high school in Doboj, Sarajevo Univ.; served in Bosnia and Herzegovina Army, then several positions in police force; fmr Sec. Tešanj Municipal Council; fmr Asst Minister of Justice, Minister of Labour, Social Policy and Refugees, Minister of Interior, Zenica-Doboj Canton Govt; Minister of Internal Affairs, Fed. of Bosnia and Herzegovina 2006–11.

ALIER, Abel, LLM; South Sudanese politician and judge; b. 1933, Bor Dist, Upper Nile Prov.; s. of Kwai Alier and Anaai Alier; m. Siama Fatma Bilal 1970; one d.; ed Univ. of Khartoum and Yale Univ., USA; fmr advocate; Dist Judge in El Obeid, Wad Medani and Khartoum –1965; participant in Round Table Conf. and mem. Twelve Man Cttee to Study the Southern Problem 1965; mem. Constitution Comms 1966–67, 1968; fmr mem. Law Reform Comm. and Southern Front; Minister of Supply and Internal Trade 1969–70; Minister of Works 1970–71; Minister of Southern Affairs 1971–72; Vice-Pres. of Sudan 1971–82; Minister of Construction and Public Works 1983–85; fmr Chair. Nat. Elections Comm.; mem. Panel of Arbitrators, Perm. Court of Int. Arbitration, The Hague 1988–; apptd head nat. cttee to investigate death of John Garang 2005; Pres. Supreme Exec. Council for the South 1972–78, 1980–81; mem. Political Bureau, Sudanese Socialist Union; mem. Bd of Dirs Industrial Planning Corpn, Nat. Scholarship Bd; Hon. LLD (Khartoum) 1978. *Publications include:* Regional Autonomy for the South 1970, The Visit of President Nyerere to the Southern Region 1974 1975, Peace and Development in the Southern Region 1977, Southern Sudan: Too Many Agreements Dishonoured 1999, Excesses in Human Rights Violations 2002. *Leisure interests:* tennis, athletics, reading, history and literature. *Address:* c/o National Election Commission, Altayef South Kenana Sugar Co., Khartoum, Sudan (office).

ALIERTA IZUEL, César, LLB, MBA; Spanish telecommunications executive; b. 5 May 1945, Zaragoza; ed Univ. of Zaragoza, Columbia Univ., New York, USA; fmr stockbroker; Gen. Man. Capital Markets Div., Banco Urquijo, Madrid 1970–85; Founder and Chair. Beta Capital 1985–96; Chair. Spanish Financial Analysts' Assen 1991; Chair. Tabacalera SA 1996–99, Co-Chair. Altadis Group (following merger with French group Seita) 1999–2000; mem. Bd of Dirs, Telefónica SA 1997–, Exec. Chair. and CEO 2000–16; mem. Bd of Dirs, China Unicom, Telecom Italia; Ind. Bd mem., Chair. Remuneration Cttee and mem. Nominations Cttee of the Bd of Dirs of International Consolidated Airlines Group (co. resulting from merger of Iberia and British Airways) 2010–; mem. Columbia Business School Bd of Overseers; Chair. Social Bd of UnED (nat. Long Distance Spanish Univ.), Business Council for Competitiveness 2011–; Gov. European Foundation for Quality Man.; fmr mem. Bd of Dirs and Standing Cttee Madrid Stock Exchange; charged with insider trading related to sales in 1997 of Tabacalera shares July 2005; The Global Spanish Entrepreneur, Spanish/US Chamber of Commerce in recognition of Telefónica Group's success in joining the New York Dow Jones Global Titans 50 index 2005, Americas Soc. Gold Medal 2010. *Address:* Telefónica SA, Gran Vía 28, 28013 Madrid, Spain (office). *Telephone:* (91) 584-0306 (office). *Fax:* (91) 531-9347 (office). *E-mail:* info@telefonica.com (office). *Website:* www .telefonica.com (office).

ALIMOV, Rashid; Tajikistani politician, diplomatist and international organization official; *Secretary-General, Shanghai Cooperation Organization;* b. 1953; m.; two c.; ed Tajik Univ.; Chair. Trade Union Cttee Tajik Univ. 1975–77; head of group of lecturers, Cen. Comsomol Cttee of Tajik SSR, instructor, regional and city CP cttees, Dushanbe; mem. Div. of Propaganda, First Sec. Frunze Regional Cttee of Tajikistan CP 1988–89, Second Sec. Dushanbe City CP Cttee 1989; Chair. Comm. on Problems of Youth, Supreme Soviet of Tajikistan 1989–91; State Counsellor to fmr Pres. Nabiyev 1990–92; Minister of Foreign Affairs of Tajikistan 1992–94; Perm. Rep. to UN, New York 1994, Deputy Pres. of the Ass. 1999–2000; Amb. to China 2005–15; Sec.-Gen., Shanghai Cooperation Organization, Beijing 2016–. *Address:* Shanghai Cooperation Organization, Liangmaqiao Road 41, Chaoyang District, Beijing, People's Republic of China (office). *Telephone:* (10) 65329807 (office). *Fax:* (10) 65329808 (office). *E-mail:* sco@sectsco.org (office). *Website:* www.sectsco.org (office).

ALINGTON, William Hildebrand, MArch; New Zealand architect; b. 18 Nov. 1929, Wellington; s. of Edward Hugh Alington and Beatrice McCrie Alington; m. Margaret Hilda Broadhead 1955 (deceased); one s. two d.; ed Hutt Valley High School, School of Architecture, Auckland Univ. Coll., School of Architecture Univ. of Illinois; architectural cadet and architect, Head Office Ministry of Works, Wellington 1950–65; architect, London Office of Robert Matthew & Johnson-Marshall 1956–57; Pnr, Gabites & Beard 1965–71, Gabites Toomath Beard Wilson & Pnrs 1971–72, Gabites Alington & Edmondson 1972–79, Gabites Porter & Pnrs 1978–83; Sr Pnr, Alington Group Architects 1984–; Asst Ed. NZIA Journal 1964–69; Pres. Architectural Centre 1970–72; Hon. Lecturer, Victoria Univ. of Wellington School of Architecture 1975–85, Tutor 1986–2003; Vice-Pres. and Br. Chair. New Zealand Inst. of Architects 1977–79, mem. Council 1965–79; mem. Wellington Anglican Diocesan Synod 1972–90; New Zealand Inst. of Architects Award 1972, 1975, 1976, 1977, 2001, 2007. *Publications:* numerous articles in specialist journals. *Leisure interests:* gardening, painting, church government. *Address:* 60 Homewood Crescent, Wellington, New Zealand. *Telephone:* (4) 476-8495. *Fax:* (4) 476-8495 (home). *E-mail:* alington@xtra.co.nz (home).

ALINGUÉ, Jean Bawoyeu; Chadian politician; b. 18 Aug. 1937, N'Djamena; s. of Marc Bawoyeu Alingué and Tabita Poureng; m. Esther Azina 1960; three s. four d.; fmr Pres. of Nat. Ass.; Prime Minister of Chad 1991–92; Minister of Justice and Keeper of the Seals 2008–10, of Posts and Information and Communications Technologies 2010–13; Chair. Union pour la Démocratie et la République; Presidential Cand. for elections 2001.

ALIREZA, Abdullah ibn Ahmed Zainal, BA; Saudi Arabian business executive and politician; ed Whittier Coll. and Harvard Business School, USA; fmr adviser to Supreme Econ. Council; fmr Chair. Jeddah Chamber of Commerce and Industry; fmr Cabinet Minister without Portfolio; Minister of Commerce and Industry 2008–11; fmr Chair. Saudi Arabian Standards Org., Comm. for Devt of Industrial Cities & Tech. Zones; headed team that negotiated Saudi Arabia's accession to WTO; mem. or fmr mem. Bd of Dirs, Gen. Investment Fund, Supreme Comm. for Tourism, General Org. for Mil. Industries, King Abdulaziz and his Companions for the Gifted; mem. Human Resource and Devt Fund. *Address:* c/o Ministry of Commerce and Industry, PO Box 1774, Airport Road, Riyadh 11162, Saudi Arabia. *E-mail:* public-relation@commerce.gov.sa.

ALIREZA, Yusuf Abdulla Yusuf Akbar; American (b. Bahraini) business executive; b. Aug. 1970, Bahrain; ed Georgetown Univ. School of Foreign Service; joined Goldman Sachs, New York 1992, moved to London 1997, held positions in fixed-income sales and hedge fund sales, Partner 2004, later Head of EMEA Sales and Structuring Efforts –2008, moved to Hong Kong to lead Goldman's Asia Pacific Securities Div. 2008, Co-Pres. Asia (excluding Japan) and mem. Global Man. Cttee –2012; Exec. Dir and CEO Noble Group Ltd, Hong Kong 2012–16 (resgnd); mem. Global Bd of Room to Read.

ALITALO, Kari K., MD, DrMedSci; Finnish molecular biologist, medical researcher and academic; *Academy Professor of Molecular Biology of Cancer, University of Helsinki;* b. 21 May 1952, Kuopio; ed Univ. of Helsinki; postdoctoral studies at Univ. of Washington, Seattle 1981–83, Univ. of California, San Francisco, USA 1983–86; Prof. of Medical Biochemistry in Finland 1986–87; Research Prof., Finnish Cancer Inst. 1987–88; Prof. of Cancer Biology, Finnish Acad. of Sciences 1988–93, Research Prof. 1993–; Dir Molecular/Cancer Biology Research Program 1999–2000, Acad. of Finland Centre of Excellence in Cancer Biology 2000–13; Acad. Prof. of Molecular Biology of Cancer, Univ. of Helsinki 1993–, Dir Centre of Excellence on Translational Cancer Biology, Faculty of Medicine; Dir Wihuri Research Inst. 2013–; mem. Academia Europaea, Swedish Royal Acad. of Sciences 2012; Foreign mem. NAS; Prix Leopold Griffuel (France) 2002, Nordic Prize, Eric Fernström Foundation 2005, Louis-Jeantet Prize for Medicine (Switzerland) 2006, InBev-Baillet Latour Health Prize (Belgium) 2009, Dr H.P. Heineken Prize for Medicine 2014. *Publications:* more than 550 published papers in professional journals. *Address:* Molecular Cancer Biology Program Biomedicum Helsinki, PO Box 63, Haartmaninkatu 8, University of Helsinki, 00014 Helsinki, Finland (office). *Telephone:* (2) 941-25511 (office). *Fax:* (2) 941-25510 (office). *E-mail:* kari.alitalo@helsinki.fi (office). *Website:* research.med .helsinki.fi/cancerbio/alitalo (office).

ALITO, Samuel A., Jr, AB, JD; American judge; *Associate Justice, Supreme Court;* b. 1 April 1950, Trenton, NJ; s. of Samuel Alito, Sr and Rose Fradusco; m. Martha-Ann Bomgardner 1985; one s. one d.; ed Princeton Univ. and Yale Law School; law clerk, Third Circuit US Court of Appeals 1976–77; Asst US Attorney 1977–81; Asst to US Solicitor Gen., Washington, DC 1981–85; Deputy Asst US Attorney Gen. 1985–87; US Attorney, Dist of New Jersey 1987–90; Judge, Third Circuit US Court of Appeals 1990–2005; nominated by Pres. George W. Bush for Assoc. Justice on US Supreme Court Oct. 2005, confirmed 2006; fmr Ed. Yale Law Journal. *Address:* Supreme Court of the United States, 1 First Street, NE, Washington, DC 20543, USA (office). *Telephone:* (202) 479-3211 (office). *Fax:* (202) 479-3021 (office). *Website:* www.supremecourtus.gov (office).

ALIVISATOS, A(rmand) Paul, BSc (Hons), PhD; American chemist and academic; *Professor of Chemistry and Samsung Distinguished Professor in Nanoscience and Nanotechnology Research, University of California, Berkeley;* b. 12 Nov. 1959, Chicago, Ill.; ed Univ. of Chicago, Univ. of California, Berkeley; family moved to Athens, Greece 1970, returned to USA late 1970s; postdoctoral fellow, AT&T Bell Labs 1986–88; mem. Faculty, Univ. of California, Berkeley 1988–, currently Prof. of Chem. and Materials Science & Eng and Samsung Distinguished Prof. in Nanoscience and Nanotechnology Research; Sr mem. Tech. Staff, Lawrence Berkeley Nat. Lab., Dir Materials Sciences Div. 2002–08, Assoc. Lab. Dir for Physical Sciences 2005–08, Deputy Dir Lab. 2008–09, Dir Lab. 2009–; Ed. Nano Letters; mem. NAS 2004, American Acad. of Arts and Sciences 2004; Fellow, American Physical Soc., AAAS; Presidential Young Investigator Award, Alfred P. Sloan Foundation Fellowship, ACS Exxon Solid State Chem. Fellowship, Coblentz Award 1994, Wilson Prize, Harvard Univ., Outstanding Young Investigator Award, Materials Research Soc. 1995, Dept of Energy Award for Sustained Outstanding Research in Materials Chem. 1997, ACS Award in Colloid and

Surface Chem. 2004, Rank Prize 2006, Distinguished Alumni Award, Univ. of Chicago 2006, Eni Italgas Prize for Energy and Environment 2006, Ernest Orlando Lawrence Award 2007, Kavli Distinguished Lectureship in Nanoscience, Materials Research Soc. 2008, Linus Pauling Award 2011, Von Hippel Award, Materials Research Soc. 2011, Wolf Foundation Prize in Chem. (shared with Charles Lieber) for his contribs to nanochemistry 2012. *Publications:* numerous papers in professional journals on the structural, thermodynamic, optical and electrical properties of colloidal inorganic nanocrystals. *Address:* D-43A Hildebrand, MC 1460, Department of Chemistry, University of California, Berkeley, CA 94720-1460, USA (office). *Telephone:* (510) 643-7371 (office); 510-642-2148 (Lab.) (office). *Fax:* (510) 642-6911 (office). *E-mail:* paul.alivisatos@berkeley.edu (office). *Website:* chemistry.berkeley.edu (office); www.cchem.berkeley.edu/pagrp (office).

ÄLIYEV, İlhäm Heydar oğlu, BA, PhD; Azerbaijani business executive, politician and head of state; *President;* b. 24 Dec. 1961, Baku, Azerbaijan SSR, USSR; s. of Heydar Äliyev, fmr Pres. of Azerbaijan; m. Mehriban Pashayeva; three c.; ed Moscow State Univ. of Int. Relations; lecturer, Moscow State Univ. of Int. Relations 1985–90; engaged in commercial activity in Moscow and İstanbul 1991–94; First Vice-Pres. State Oil Co. of the Azerbaijani Repub. (SOCAR) 1994–2003; mem. Parl. 1995–2003; Deputy Chair. Yeni Azerbaijan (New Azerbaijan) party 1999–2001, First Deputy Chair. 2001–; Prime Minister of Azerbaijan Aug. 2003; Pres. of Azerbaijan Oct. 2003–; Pres. Nat. Olympic Cttee 1997–; Leader Azerbaijani Parl. Del. to Council of Europe Parl. Ass. (PACE) 2001–03; Hon. Prof. L.N. Gumilev Eurasian Nat. Univ., Kazakhstan, Univ. of Nat. and World Economy, Bulgaria, Moscow State Univ. 2008, Belarusian State Univ., Magtymguly Turkmenistan State Univ.; Order of Heydar Äliyev, Order of Şeykülislam (Azerbaijan), Ven. Sergius of Radonezh Order of Russian Orthodox Church (First Degree), Order of Holy Prince Daniel of Moscow, (First Degree), Kt Grand Cross, Order of Three Stars (Latvia), Order of Honour (Georgia) 2003, Order of the Star of Romania 2004, Order of King Abdul Aziz al-Sa'ud (Saudi Arabia) 2005, Grand Croix, Légion d'honneur 2007, Order of Prince Yaroslav The Wise (First Degree) (Ukraine) 2008, Grand Cross, Order of Merit (Poland) 2008, Order of Mubarak Al-Kabeer (Kuwait) 2009, Gold Medal of Greek Parl. 2009, Order of Glory and Honour (First Degree) (Russia) 2010, Order of the Repub. of Serbia 2013, First Class of the Order of State of Repub. of Turkey 2013, Order of Liberty (Ukraine) 2013; Dr hc (Lincoln Univ., USA, Moscow State Univ., Bilkent Univ., Turkey, Nat. Acad. of Taxes, Ukraine, Petroleum and Gas Univ. of Ploieşti, Romania, Kyung Hee Univ., South Korea, Jordan Univ., Corvinus Univ. of Budapest, Hungary, Kyiv Taras Shevchenko Nat. Univ., Ukraine, Baku State Univ., Ankara Univ., Turkey, Çukurova Univ., Turkey); PACE Medal 2004, Ihsan Dogramacı Prize for Int. Relations for Peace (Turkey), Supreme Order of the Hall of Fame FILA 'Legend of Sport', Order of Glory of the Int. Confed. of Sport Orgs of CIS countries, Order of Glory 'Great Cordon', Int. Mil. Sport Council. *Address:* Office of the President, 1066 Baku, İstiqlaliyyät küç. 19, Azerbaijan (office). *Telephone:* (12) 492-53-81 (office). *Fax:* (12) 492-35-43 (office). *E-mail:* office@apparat.gov.az (office). *Website:* www.president.az (office); www.ilham-aliyev.com.

ALIYEV, Mukhu Gimbatovich, PhD; Russian/Dagestan politician; b. 6 Aug. 1940, Tanusi, Dagestan; m.; two c.; ed Dagestan State Univ.; began career as teacher, then Head, Nizhne-Gakvarinskaya Secondary School; Sec., Comsomol Cttee, Dagestan State Univ. 1964–66; First Sec., Makhachkala City Comsomol Cttee 1969–72, Makhachkala Dist CPSU Cttee 1972–85; Bureau Head, Dagestan Div. CPSU Cttee 1985–90; First Sec., Dagestan Repub. CPSU Cttee 1990–91; mem. Supreme Soviet of Dagestan (parl.), Vice-Chair. 1991–95; Chair. Econs Cttee, Repub. of Dagestan 1992–94; Chair. People's Ass., Repub. of Dagestan 1999–2006; Pres. of Dagestan 2006–10; mem. Council of Feds of Russia 1995, Deputy Chair. Cttee on Foreign Affairs 1995–2001; fmr mem. Parl. Ass., CIS and Council of Europe; Labour Red Banner 1976, Badge of Honour 1981, For Services to Motherland, class IV 2000, class III 2005. *Publications:* Dagestan Republic: Priorities of National Policy 1996, Unity and Integrity of Dagestan Republic as a Constitutional Principle 1998, Searching for Consent 2002; numerous articles in magazines and journals. *Address:* 33/1a Korkmasov Street, 367005 Makhachkala, Dagestan, Russia (home). *Telephone:* (8722) 67-04-96 (home).

ÄLIYEVA, Mehriban Arif qızı, PhD; Azerbaijani physician and politician; *First Lady and First Vice-President;* b. (Mehriban Pashayeva), 26 Aug. 1964, Baku, Azerbaijan SSR, USSR; d. of Arif Pashayev and Aida Imanguliyeva; m. İlhäm Heydar oğlu Äliyev (q.v.) 1983; one s. two d.; ed Secondary School No. 23, N. Narimanov Azerbaijan State Medical Univ., I.M. Sechenov First Moscow State Medical Inst.; worked at Eye Diseases Research Inst., Moscow 1988–92; est. Azerbaijan–Irs magazine (published in Azerbaijani, English and Russian) 1996; mem. Yeni Azärbaycan Partiyası (New Azerbaijan Party 2004)–, Deputy Chair. 2013–; mem. Nat. Ass. for Xazar Constituency No. 14 2005–17; First Lady of Azerbaijan 2003–; First Vice-Pres. 2017–; Pres. Gymnastics Fed. of Azerbaijan 2002–, Heydar Aliyev Foundation 2004–; Chair. Azerbaijan Culture Foundation; mem. Exec. Cttee, Nat. Olympic Cttee of Azerbaijan 2004–; Chair. Organizing Cttee, 2015 European Games 2013–15; Goodwill Amb. for UNESCO 2004–, ISESCO (Islamic Educational, Scientific and Cultural Org.) 2006–; Hon. Prof., I.M. Sechenov First Moscow State Medical Univ.; Heydar Aliyev Order; Chevalier, Légion d'honneur; Hon. Diploma of the State of Kuwait; Hilal-e-Pakistan; Order of Merit (Poland); Sretenjski Orden (Serbia); Dr hc (Veliko Tarnovo Univ., Bulgaria, Israel Medical Acad.); Olympic Excellence special hon. award from Int. Olympic Acad., UN Population Fund Diploma, WHO Prize, UNESCO Mozart Medal. *Address:* Office of the President, 1066 Baku, İstiqlaliyyät küç. 19, Azerbaijan (office). *Telephone:* (12) 492-53-81 (office). *Fax:* (12) 492-35-43 (office). *E-mail:* office@apparat.gov.az (office). *Website:* www.president.az (office); www.mehriban-aliyeva.az.

ALJOVÍN GAZZANI, Cayetana, MBA; Peruvian lawyer, public servant, journalist and politician; b. 6 Sept. 1966, Lima; d. of Javier Aljovín Swayne and Lucy Gazzani Bosworth; m. 1st Sergio Salinas Rivas; m. 2nd Fritz Du Bois Freund (died 2014); ed Pontifical Catholic Univ. of Peru, Univ. Adolfo Ibáñez, Chile; Advisor and mem. Council of Ministers Secr. of State Modernization 1996; Sec. Gen., Ministry of Economy and Finance 1998; consultant for IDB, COSUDE, Nextel Peru 2000–06; Vice Minister of Communications 2006–08; Exec. Dir Proinversión (Private Investment Promotion Agency) 2008; fmr Dir of Regulatory Affairs, BellSouth Peru; Partner, Estudio Miranda & Amado Abogados (law firm); Man. of Corp. Affairs and Dir of Regulatory Affairs, Communications and Institutional Relations, Gas Natural de Lima and Callao-Cálidda 2011–12; Gen. Man. Llorente & Cuenca (consultancy) 2011–12; journalist and presenter, Radio Programas del Perú and Panamericana Televisión 2012–; Minister of Devt and Social Inclusion 2016–17; Minister of Energy and Mines 2017–18; Minister of Foreign Affairs Jan.–April 2018; Prof. of Telecommunications Law, Pontifical Catholic Univ. of Peru 2012–, Peruvian Univ. of Applied Sciences, Nat. Univ. of San Marcos, San Martín de Porres Univ. 2012–; Chair. Communications Cttee, Nat. Mining, Petroleum and Energy Soc. 2011; fmr Gen. Man. Procapitales (Asscn of Companies Promoting Capital Markets); Exec. Vice Pres. Nat. Confed. of Private Business Insts (CONFIEP); fmr Dir Lima Stock Exchange; fmr mem. Telecommunications Privatization Cttee, Comm. for the Promotion of Private Investment (COPRI); fmr mem. Bd of Dirs Office of Insts and State Orgs (OIOE). *Address:* c/o Ministry of Foreign Affairs, Jirón Lampa 535, Lima 1, Peru (office).

ALKAN, Ali; Turkish judge; *Chief Justice, Supreme Court of Appeals;* b. 9 Feb. 1950, Kızılcahamam, Ankara Prov.; m.; one c.; ed Ankara Univ. Faculty of Law; mil. service as reserve officer, Antalya; began career as judge nominee in Ankara, later serving as judge in Pervari, Çayıralan and Haymana; fmr Judge, Ankara Commercial Court and Chair. Judicial Comm. on Justice; mem. Supreme Court of Appeals 1997–, Pres. 13th Civil Law Chamber of Supreme Court 2009–12, Chief Justice, Supreme Court of Appeals 2012–. *Address:* Office of the Chief Justice, Supreme Court of Appeals, Atatürk Bulvarı No 1, Bakanlıklar, 06658 Ankara, Turkey (office). *Telephone:* (312) 4161000 (office). *E-mail:* iletisim@yargitay.gov.tr (office). *Website:* www.yargitay.gov.tr (office).

ALKATIRI, Mari bin Amude; Timor-Leste politician; b. 26 Nov. 1949, Dili; m. Marina Ribeiro; three c.; fmr chartered surveyor; est. Movt for the Liberation of East Timor (Timor-Leste) 1970; Co-Founder and Sec.-Gen. Frente Revolucionário do Timor Leste Independente—Fretilin (Revolutionary Front for an Ind. Timor-Leste) 1974–; lived in political exile, teaching in Mozambique –1999; Minister for Econs in Transitional Admin; Prime Minister of Timor-Leste 2002–06, 2017–18, also Minister for Economy and Devt, later Minister for Devt and the Environment 2002–06; Gran Cruz, Ordem do Infante D. Henrique de Portugal 2016. *Address:* c/o Office of the Prime Minister, Palácio do Governo, Av. Presidente Nicolau Lobato, Dili, Timor-Leste (office).

ALKHANOV, Alu; Russian (Chechen) politician and government official; b. 20 Jan. 1947, Taldykorgan Prov., Kazakhstan; m.; three c.; ed Transport Police School, Belarus, USSR Interior Ministry Acad.; joined Soviet Militsiya service 1983; served in various positions in Ministry of the Interior, Chechen—Nokchi Repub.; Chief of Transport Police Dept 1995–96, of Shakhty Transport Police, Rostov Region 1997–2000, of Groznyi Transport Police 2000–03; Minister of the Interior, Chechen—Nokchi Repub. 2003–04; Pres. of Chechen—Nokchi Repub. 2004–07; Deputy Minister of Justice 2007, in charge of penitentiary system 2010; Order of Courage 1996, Order of Merit for the Fatherland, 4th class 2007, Order of Honour 2011.

ALLAM, Magdi Cristiano; Italian (b. Egyptian) journalist, editor, author and politician; b. 22 April 1952, Cairo, Egypt; s. of Muhammad Allam and Safeya Allam; m.; two c.; m. 2nd Valentina Colombo; two s. one d.; ed Catholic Coll. of Comboni Sisters, Cairo, Salesian Coll., La Sapienza Univ., Rome; began journalistic career 1978, worked for several Italian publs, including nat. daily newspaper La Repubblica; joined Corriere della Sera 2003, Deputy Dir –2008, currently op-ed. columnist, ad personam Asst Publr and Deputy Ed.; Arab and Islamic affairs commentator; appears frequently on nat. TV news shows; mem. Unione di Centro (UdC—Union of the Centre) 2008–10; mem. European Parl., Brussels (Group of the European People's Party (Christian Democrats) 2009–11, Europe of Freedom and Democracy Group 2001–14) 2009–14; Regional Councillor, Basilicata 2010–; Founder-mem. Io amo l'Italia (ALI, originally Protagonisti per l'Europa Cristiana—Protagonists for Christian Europe) 2010–14; mem. Fratelli d'Italia – Alleanza Nazionale (FdI-AN—Brothers of Italy Nat. Alliance) 2014–; converted from Islam to Christianity during the Vatican's Easter vigil service 2008, announced his abandonment of the Catholic Church March 2013; co-recipient Dan David Prize, Tel-Aviv Univ. (Israel) 2006, Prix St-Vincent in journalism, Ambrogino the City of Milan, Mass Media Award, American Jewish Cttee. *Publications include:* Vincere la paura (Winning Fear), Diary of Islam 2002, Bin Laden in Italy 2002, Saddam: The Secret History of a Dictator 2003, Kamikaze Made in Europe: Can the West Defeat the Islamic Terrorists? 2004, Overcoming Fear 2005, I Love Italy, But Do Italians? 2006, Viva Israele 2007, Thank You Jesus: My Conversion from Islam to Catholicism 2008, Christian Europe Free 2009; numerous other books and articles on relations between Western culture and values and the Islamic world. *Address:* c/o Fratelli d'Italia—Alleanza Nazionale, Via Quattro Cantoni 16, 00184 Rome, Italy (office). *Telephone:* (06) 4880690 (office). *Fax:* (06) 48907931 (office). *E-mail:* info@fratelli-italia.it (office). *Website:* www.fratelli-italia.it (office).

ALLAMAND ZAVALA, Andrés; Chilean lawyer and politician; b. 7 Feb. 1956, Santiago; s. of Miguel Allamand Madaune and Margarita Zavala Pintos; m. Bárbara Lyon (divorced); four c. (one deceased); ed Saint George's Coll., Santiago, Univ. of Chile; f. own legal practice 1980s; f. Movimiento Unión Nacional 1983, becoming Sec.-Gen.; co-f. Renovación Nacional 1987, Sec.-Gen. 1988–90, Pres. 1990–96; mem. Cámara de Diputados (lower house of parl.) for Las Condes, Vitacura y Lo Barnechea Dist 1994–98; mem. Senado (upper house of parl.) for Décima Región Norte 2006–11, Pres. Labour and Social Welfare Cttee 2008; Pres. Instituto Libertad 1996–98; with IDB, Washington, DC 1998–2000; Dean, School of Govt, Univ. Adolfo Ibáñez, Santiago 2002–07, apptd Dir of Devt 2001; Minister of Nat. Defence 2011–12; Sec.-Gen. Unión de Partidos de America Latina 1990–97. *Publications include:* La Travesía del Desierto 1999, La política importa. Democracia y desarrollo en América Latina (co-author) 2003, El Desalojo 2007, La Estrella y el Arco Iris (co-author) 2010, La Salida. Cómo derrotar a la Nueva Mayoría en 2017 2016.

ALLAN, Sir Alexander (Alex) Claud Stuart, Kt, KCB, BA (Hons), MSc; British civil servant; b. 9 Feb. 1951; s. of Lord Allan of Kilmahew and Maureen Catherine Flower Stuart-Clark; m. 1st Katie Christine Clemson 1978 (died 2007); m. 2nd Sarah Stacey 2012; ed Harrow School, Clare Coll., Cambridge, Univ. Coll., London; with HM Customs and Excise 1973–76, HM Treasury 1976–92, Prin. Pvt. Sec. to

Chancellor of the Exchequer 1986–89; secondments in Australia 1983–84; Under-Sec. for Int. Finance 1989–90, for Public Expenditure Policy, 1990–92; Prin. Pvt. Sec. to the Prime Minister 1992–97; High Commr in Australia 1997–2000; e-Envoy, Cabinet Office 1999–2000; Perm. Sec., Dept for Constitutional Affairs, later Ministry of Justice 2004–07; Chair. Jt Intelligence Cttee and Professional Head of Intelligence Analysis, Cabinet Office 2007–11; Prime Minister's Ind. Adviser on Ministerial Interests 2011–; mem. Selection Panel for QC Appointments 2011–, Advisory Cttee on Business Appointments 2011–, Advisory Bd of the Oxford Internet Inst. 2011–; Trustee, Treloar Trust 2011–; carried out Review of Records Man. in Govt 2014. *Publication:* Records Review – Sir Alex Allan 2014. *Leisure interests:* sailing, Grateful Dead music, cycling, computers, bridge. *Address:* 3 St Peter's Wharf, Chiswick Mall, London, W6 9UD, England. *Telephone:* (20) 8741-2770. *E-mail:* alex@whitegum.com. *Website:* www.whitegum.com.

ALLAN, John, BA; British business executive; *President, Confederation of British Industry;* b. Aug. 1948; ed Univ. of Edinburgh; began career with Lever Brothers and Bristol-Myers in various marketing roles; Retail Dir for Marketing, Buying and Retail Operations, Fine Fare (subsidiary of ABF) for eight years; Divisional CEO, BET for nine years; CEO Ocean Group plc 1994–2000, then CEO Exel following merger with NFC to form Exel plc 2000, Exel acquired by Deutsche Post 2005, mem. Bd, Deutsche Post, responsible for managing integration and Logistics Div., Chief Financial Officer, Deutsche Post 2007–09 (retd); Chair. Dixons Retail 2009–14 (merged with Carphone Warehouse to form Dixons Carphone 2014), Deputy Chair. and Sr Ind. Dir, Dixons Carphone 2014–15; Chair. Barratt Developments plc 2014–, London First 2015–; mem. Bd of Dirs and Chair. (non-exec.), Tesco plc 2015–; Pres. CBI 2018–; Regent Univ. of Edinburgh 2012–; fmr Chair. Samsonite; Dir (non-exec.), Royal Mail –2015; fmr Dir (non-exec.), Worldpay (fmr Chair.), National Grid, PHS Group, Hamleys, and others. *Address:* Office of the Chairman, Tesco plc, New Tesco House, PO Box 18, Delamare Road, Cheshunt, Herts., EN8 9SL (office); Confederation of British Industry, Cannon Place, 78 Cannon Street, London, EC4N 6HN, England (office). *Telephone:* (1992) 632222 (office); (20) 7379-7400 (CBI) (office). *Fax:* (1992) 644962 (office); (20) 7379-7200 (CBI) (office). *E-mail:* john.allan@tesco.com (office); enquiries@cbi.org.uk (home). *Website:* www.tesco.com (office); www.cbi.org.uk (office).

ALLAN, M. Elyse, BA, MBA; Canadian (b. American) business executive; m. Don Allan; one s.; ed Dartmouth Coll., Amos Tuck School of Business; began career at General Electric (GE) as consultant in Corp. Marketing Consulting Services group, Bridgeport, Conn. 1984; moved to Canada as Man. Customer Service Program, GE Canada 1988, later Marketing Man. GE Commercial and Industrial Lighting; Dir of Marketing Ont. Hydro; Pres. and CEO Toronto Bd of Trade (first woman) 1995–2004; Pres. and CEO GE Canada 2004–18; Chair. Bd of Dirs Providence Healthcare; Dir Brookfield Asset Man. Inc. 2015–; mem. Nat. Round Table on the Environment and the Economy 2005–; mem. Bd of Dirs Public Policy Forum, Canadian Council of Chief Execs; mem. Bd of Govs Canadian Council on Unity; fmr mem. Bd of Visitors, Rockefeller Centre for Public Policy; mem. Order of Canada 2014; Dr hc (Ryerson Univ.) 2005; Woman of Distinction (business), YWCA 2012.

ALLARD, A. Wayne, DMV; American veterinarian and fmr politician; *Vice-President for Government Relations, American Motorcyclist Association;* b. 2 Dec. 1943, Colorado; s. of Amos W. Allard and S. Jean Stewart; m. Joan Malcolm 1967; two d.; ed Colorado State Univ.; early career as veterinarian, Allard Animal Hosp.; mem. Colo State Senate (Republican) 1982–91, Chair. Health, Environment and Insts Cttee, Chair. Senate Majority Caucus; mem. US House of Reps from 4th Dist, Colo 1991–96, mem. House Agric. Cttee 1991–96, House Small Business Cttee 1991–92, House Interior and Insular Affairs Cttee 1991–92, House Cttee on Cttees 1991–94, House Budget Cttee 1993–96, House Natural Resources Cttee 1993–96, Jt Cttee on Reorganization of Congress 1993–96, Chair. House Sub-Cttee of Agric. Conservation, Forest and Water 1995–96; Senator from Colo 1997–2009 (retd), mem. Banking, Urban Affairs Cttee 1997–2009, Environment and Public Works Cttee 1997–2009, Intelligence Select Cttee 1997–2009, Armed Services Cttee and numerous other cttees; Vice-Pres. for Govt Relations, American Motorcyclist Asscn, Washington, DC 2011–; Founder and Man. Partner, Wayne Allard Assocs, LLC; Founder and CEO Prion Research Inst.; fmr health officer, Loveland, Colo; fmr mem. Regional Advisory Council on Veterinarian Medicine, W Interstate Comm. on Higher Educ., Colo Low-Level Radioactive Waste Advisory Cttee; Chair. United Way; Founding mem. American Veterinary Medical Asscn (AVMA), Colo Veterinarian Medicine Asscn, Larimer Co. Veterinarian Medicine Asscn; mem. Bd Veterinarian Practitioners (Charter mem.), American Animal Hosp. Asscn, Nat. Conf. State Legislatures (Vice-Chair. Human Resources Cttee 1987); mem. Loveland Chamber of Commerce; Fort Collins Lions Club Future Citizen of Tomorrow Award and Scholarship 1962, One of Top Four Colorado 4-H mems in Leadership Guardian Advisory Cttee for NFIB 1963, Honor Alumnus, Colorado State Univ. (CSU) 1990, Honoree, George H. Glover Gallery of Distinguished Faculty and Alumni of CSU 1992, CSU Alumni Charles A. Lory Public Service Award 1999, AMVA Pres.'s Award 1999, George E. Brown, Jr Congressional Honor Award for Leadership in Imaging and Geospatial Information 1999, AVMA Meritorious Service Award 2006. *Address:* American Motorcyclist Association, 101 Constitution Avenue NW, Suite 800W, Washington, DC 20001, USA (office). *Telephone:* (202) 742-4301 (office). *Fax:* (202) 742-4282 (office). *Website:* www .americanmotorcyclist.com (office).

ALLARDT, Erik Anders, MA, PhD; Finnish university chancellor and sociologist; *Professor of Sociology, University of Helsinki;* b. 9 Aug. 1925, Helsinki; s. of Arvid Allardt and Marita Allardt (née Heikel); m. Sagi Nylander 1947; one s. two d.; ed Univ. of Helsinki, Columbia Univ., New York, USA; Prof. of Sociology, Univ. of Helsinki 1958–, Dean of the Faculty of Social Sciences 1969–70; Pres. Acad. of Finland 1986–91; Chancellor of the Åbo Acad. Univ. 1992–94; mem. European Science Foundation Exec. Council 1987–92, Vice-Pres. 1990–92; mem. Bd Scandinavia-Japan Sasakawa Foundation 1987–96; Founder-mem. Academia Europaea 1988–; Fellow, Woodrow Wilson Int. Center for Scholars 1978–79; Visiting Prof. numerous countries and univs; Commdr of the Swedish Order of the Northern Star; Grand Cross Knight, Icelandic Order of the Falcon 1997; Dr hc (Stockholm) 1978, (Åbo Akademi) 1978, (Uppsala) 1984, (Bergen) 1996, (Copenhagen) 2000. *Publications:* (with Rokkan) Mass Politics: Studies in Political Sociology 1970, Att Ha, Att Älska, Att Vara. Om Välfärd i Norden 1975, Implications of the Ethnic Revival in Modern, Industrialized Society 1979, (with Lysgaard and Sørensen) Sociologin i Sverige, vetenskap, miljö och organisation 1988, The History of the Social Sciences in Finland 1997. *Leisure interest:* playing with grandchildren. *Address:* Department of Sociology, PB 18, 00014 University of Helsinki, Helsinki (office); Unionsgatan 45B 40, 00170 Helsinki, Finland (home). *Telephone:* (9) 19123963 (office); (9) 1354550 (home). *Fax:* (9) 19123967 (office). *E-mail:* erik.allardt@helsinki.fi (office).

ALLAWI, Ali Abdel-Amir, SB, MBA; Iraqi business executive, government official and academic; b. Dec. 1947; ed Massachusetts Inst. of Tech. and Harvard Business School, USA; fmr consultant to World Bank and Head, Pan-Arab investment co.; Prof., Univ. of Oxford, UK –2003; Minister of Trade and Minister of Defence, Interim Iraq Governing Council 2003–04, Minister of Finance, Iraqi Transitional Govt 2005–06, then Sr Adviser to Prime Minister of Iraq; Sr Assoc. Mem., St Antony's Coll., Oxford; Sr Fellow, Princeton Univ. 2008–09; Sr Visiting Fellow, Carr Center, Kennedy School of Govt, Harvard Univ. 2009–10; Visiting Research Prof., Middle East Inst., Nat. Univ. of Singapore 2013–14; mem. United Iraqi Alliance; Hon. Fellow, Inst. for Arab and Islamic Studies, Exeter Univ., UK; Robert and Joanna Bendetson Global Public Diplomacy Award, Inst. for Global Leadership, Tufts Univ. 2007. *Publications:* The Occupation of Iraq: Winning the War, Losing the Peace 2007, The Crisis of Islamic Civilization 2009, King Faisal I of Iraq 2013. *E-mail:* ali@aliallawi.com. *Website:* www.aliallawi.com.

ALLAWI, Ayad, MSc, DrMed; Iraqi neurologist and politician; b. 1945; ed Baghdad Univ., Univ. of London, UK; from prominent Shia family in Baghdad; fmr mem. Ba'ath Party; left Iraq 1971 going first to Beirut then London; survived assassination attempt 1978; formed Iraqi Nat. Accord dissident group 1990, involved in attempted coup against Saddam Hussein 1996; fmr consultant to UNDP, WHO, UNICEF; apptd mem. Iraqi Governing Council 2003, Chair. Security Cttee 2003–04; Interim Prime Minister of Iraq 2004–05; Leader, Iraqi Nat. Movt (Iraqiya) 2010; Vice-Pres. of Iraq 2014–15.

ALLÈGRE, Claude Jean, PhD; French professor of earth sciences and politician; *Professor Emeritus, Université Paris Diderot-Paris;* b. 31 March 1937, Paris; s. of Prof. Roger Allègre and Lucette Allègre (née Hugoueneq); m. Claude Blanche Simon 1967; three s. one d.; ed Lycées Saint-Maur and Saint-Louis, Faculté des Sciences, Paris; Asst, Univ. de Paris 1962–68; Dir of Lab. of Geochemistry and Cosmochemistry, Univ. de Paris VI and VII 1967–2006, Prof. Emer. 2006–; Asst Physician, Inst. de Physique du Globe 1968–70, Dir 1976–86; Chair-Prof. of Earth Sciences Univ. de Paris VII 1970–2006; joined Socialist Party 1973, mem. Steering Cttee 1987, Exec. Cttee 1990; Prof. of Earth Sciences, MIT 1975–76; Vernadsky Lecturer, Univ. of Moscow 1986; A.D. White Prof.-at-Large, Cornell Univ. 1987–92, USA; Special Adviser to Lionel Jospin 1988–92; mem. European Parl. 1989–94; Regional Councillor, Languedoc-Roussillon 1992; Minister of Nat. Educ., Research and Tech. 1997–2000; science columnist, CPAC, Nat. Ass. 2001–02; Pres. Admin. Council of Bureau de Recherches Géologiques et Minières 1993–97; Foreign mem. NAS, Royal Soc. 2002, Acad. of Sciences of India 2006; mem. Bd of Dirs Ipsos Group 2002; mem. Meteoritical Soc. 1980, American Geophysical Union 1984, Geochemical Soc. and European Asscn for Geochemistry 1990, Institut Universitaire de France 1992, French Acad. of Sciences 1995–, Geological Soc. of America 1998, Institut de Physique du Globe; Hon. mem. American Acad. of Arts and Sciences 1988, European Geosciences Union 1992, European Geophysical Soc. 1992, Trinity Hon. Lecturer, San Antonio, Tex. 1992, Geochemical Soc. of London 1994, Boston Philosophical Soc., Hon. Prof., China Univ. of Geosciences, Beijing 1999; Commdr, Légion d'honneur, Ordre des Palmes académiques; Grand Cross, Order of Merit (Germany); Commdr, Order of Southern Cross (Brazil); Dr hc (Cardiff Univ.) 1997, (Univ. of Bristol) 1998, (Free Univ. of Brussels) 1998, (Imperial Coll. London) 2001, (Univ. of Rome 3) 2003; Crafoord Prize 1986, Goldsmith Medal, Geochemical Soc. of America 1986, Wollaston Medal, Geological Soc. of London 1987, Arthur Day-Gold Medal, Geological Soc. of America 1988, CNRS 1994, William Bowie Medal 1995, Holmes Medal of the European Geosciences Union 1995, Bowie Medal, American Geophysical Union 1995. *Publications include:* L'Ecume de la terre 1983, De la pierre à l'étoile 1985, Les fureurs de la terre 1987, Economiser la planète 1990, Introduction à une histoire naturelle 1992, L'Age des savoires 1993, Ecologie des villes, ecologie des champs 1993, L'Etat de la planète 1994, La défaite de platon 1995, Questions de France 1996, Dieu face à la science 1997, Toute vérité est bonne à dire 2000, Vive L'école libre 2000, Histoires de terre 2001, Galilée 2002, Géologie isotopique 2005, Le Défi du monde (co-author) 2006, Ma vérité sur la planète 2007, La science et la vie, journal d'un anti-panurge 2008, La Science est le défi du XXIe siècle 2009, L'Imposture climatique 2010. *Address:* Institut de physique du globe, Round 24, BP 89, 4, place Jussieu, 75252 Paris Cedex 05 (office); Université Paris Diderot, 5 rue Thomas-Mann, 75013 Paris, France (office). *Telephone:* 1-57-27-57-27 (Institut de physique du globe) (office). *Fax:* 1-44-27-37-52 (Université Paris Diderot-Paris) (office). *Website:* www.academie-sciences.fr (office); www.univ-paris-diderot.fr (office).

ALLÈGRE, Maurice Marie, LenD; French engineer, research co-ordinator and business executive; b. 16 Feb. 1933, Antibes; s. of Guy Allègre and Renée-Lise Bermond; m. Catherine Pierre 1962; one s. one d.; ed Ecole Polytechnique, Ecole Nat. Supérieure des Mines and Ecole Nat. Supérieure du Pétrole et des Moteurs, Faculté de Droit; Engineer, Direction des Carburants, Ministry of Industry 1957–62; Dir Mines de l'Organisme Saharien 1962–64; Tech. Adviser to Ministry of Finance and Econ. Affairs 1965–67; Délégué à l'Informatique and Pres. Inst. de Recherche d'Informatique et d'Automatique 1968–74; Chief of Nickel Mission to New Caledonia 1975; Asst Dir-Gen. Inst. Français du Pétrole 1976–81; Pres. and Dir-Gen. ISIS 1976–81; Pres. FRANLAB, COFLEXIP 1976–81; Pres. Agence Nat. de Valorisation et de la Recherche (ANVAR) 1982–84; Dir Scientific and Tech. Devt, Ministry of Research and Tech. 1982–84; Dir-Gen. Bureau de Recherches Géologiques et Minières 1984–88, Pres. 1988–92; Pres. Agence Nationale pour la Gestion des Déchets Radioactifs (ANDRA—Nat. Agency for Man. of Radioactive Waste) 1993–98; Pres. Sicav Vauban 1998–2000; Pres. AGRER Asscn 1998; int. consultant on energy policy and radioactive waste 1998–; mem. ASPO France; Chevalier, Légion d'honneur, Officier, Ordre nat. du Mérite. *Leisure interests:* photography, skiing, sailing. *Address:* Maurice Allègre Conseils, 85 rue de Sèvres,

75006 Paris; 50 boulevard d'Aguillon, 06600 Antibes, France. *Telephone:* 1-45-44-94-51 (office).

ALLEN, Sir Geoffrey, Kt, PhD, FRS, FREng, FRSC, FInstP, FIM; British polymer scientist and university administrator (retd); b. 29 Oct. 1928, Clay Cross, Derbyshire, England; s. of John James Allen and Marjorie Allen; m. Valerie Frances Duckworth 1972; one d.; ed Clay Cross Tupton Hall Grammar School, Univ. of Leeds; Postdoctoral Fellow, Nat. Research Council, Canada 1952–54; Lecturer, Univ. of Manchester 1955–65, Prof. of Chemical Physics 1965–75; Prof. of Polymer Science, Imperial Coll. of Science and Tech., Univ. of London 1975–76, Prof. of Chemical Tech. 1976–81; Fellow, Imperial Coll. 1986, UMIST 1994; Adviser, Kobe Steel Ltd 1990–2005; Chair. Science Research Council 1977–81; Head of Research, Unilever PLC 1981–90, Dir of Unilever responsible for Research and Eng 1982–90; Dir (non-exec.) Courtaulds 1987–93; Pres. PRI, SCI 1990–92; mem. Nat. Consumer Council 1993–96; Vice-Pres. Royal Soc. 1991–93; Chancellor, Univ. of East Anglia 1994–2003; mem. Royal Comm. on Environmental Protection 1994–2000; Pres. Inst. of Materials 1994–95; Visiting Fellow, Robinson Coll., Cambridge 1980–; Fellow, Royal Acad. of Eng; Hon. FCGI, Hon. FIM, Hon. FIChemE; Hon. MSc (Manchester), Hon. DSc (Durham, E Anglia) 1984, (Bath, Bradford, Keele, Loughborough) 1985, (Essex, Leeds) 1986, (Cranfield) 1988, (Surrey) 1989, (North London) 1999, Dr hc (Open Univ.). *Leisure interests:* opera, walking, talking. *Address:* Flat 6.12, St Johns Building, 79 Marsham Street, London, SW1P 4SB, England (home). *Telephone:* (20) 3583-5630 (home). *E-mail:* sir.geoffrey@tiscali.co.uk.

ALLEN, George, BA, JD; American business executive and fmr politician; *President, George Allen Strategies LLC;* b. 8 March 1952; s. of George Herbert Allen and Henrietta Lumbroso; m. 1st Anne Patrice Rubel 1979 (divorced 1983); m. 2nd Susan Allen (née Brown); three c.; ed Univs of California, Virginia; mem. Va House of Dels 1982–90; mem. US House of Reps, Washington, DC 1991–94; Gov. of Va 1994–98; Senator from Va 2000–07, Chair. Senate High Tech Task Force 2001; currently Pres. George Allen Strategies LLC; f. American Energy Freedom Centre 2009; Reagan Ranch Presidential Scholar, Young America's Foundation 2007–, also mem. Bd of Govs; mem. Bd of Dirs Lee Technologies, nanoTox, Hillsdale Group, Xybernaut 1998, Commonwealth Biotechnologies 1998–2006; f. Appalachian School of Law, currently mem. Bd of Trustees; mem. Bd of Advisors Com-Net Ericsson 2000; mem. 'Small b' Business Cttee; Pnr, Business Expansion and Relocation Team, McGuireWoods LLP 1998; Republican; Jefferson Scholar, American Legis. Exchange Council 1998. *Publication:* What Washington Can Learn From the World of Sports 2010. *Address:* George Allen Strategies LLC, 717 Princess Street, Alexandria, VA 22314, USA (office). *Telephone:* (571) 970-4636 (office). *Website:* www.georgeallenstrategies.com (office); www.yaf.org/TheReaganRanch.aspx (office); www.georgeallen.com.

ALLEN, Dame Ingrid Victoria, DBE, DL, MD, DSc, FRCPath, FMedSci, MRIA; British professor of neuropathology; *Professor Emerita and Honorary Professor, Queen's University, Belfast;* b. 30 July 1932, Belfast; d. of Robert Allen and Doris V. Allen (née Shaw); m. 1st Alan Watson Barnes 1972 (died 1987); m. 2nd John Thompson 1996; ed Ashleigh House School, Belfast, Cheltenham Ladies Coll., Queen's Univ. Belfast; House Officer Royal Victoria Hosp. (RVH), Belfast 1957–58, Sr Registrar 1964–65; Musgrave Research Fellow, Tutor in Pathology, Calvert Research Fellow, Queen's Univ., Belfast (QUB) 1958–64; Sr Lecturer and Consultant in Neuropathology, QUB/RVH 1966–78, Reader and Consultant 1978–79, Prof. 1979–97, Prof. Emer. and Hon. Prof. 1997–; Head NI Regional Neuropathology Service 1979–97; mem. MRC 1988–94; Dir for Research and Devt Health and Personal Social Services, NI 1997–2002; Visiting Prof., Univ. of Ulster 1997–; visiting professorships in India, Singapore, Chicago, Maryland, Malaysia and Bosnia; Vice-Pres. Int. Soc. of Neuropathology 1988–92; Fellow, Royal Coll. of Pathologists, Vice-Pres. 1993–96; fmr mem. Cttee on Women in Science and Tech., Office of Public Service and Science; mem. numerous editorial bds and bds of medical research charities; Hon. Fellow, Int. Soc. of Neuropathology 1997. *Publications include:* Greenfield's Neuropathology 1984, McAlpine's Multiple Sclerosis (contrib.) 1990; numerous articles in learned journals on neuropathology, demyelinating diseases, neurovirology, neuro-oncology and biomedical research and devt. *Leisure interests:* reading, sailing, escaping to an island off the NW coast of Ireland. *Address:* Room 113, School of Biology and Biochemistry, Medical Biology Centre, Queen's University Belfast, 97 Lisburn Road, Belfast, BT9 7BL (office); 95 Malone Road, Belfast, BT9 6SP, Northern Ireland (home). *Telephone:* (28) 9027-2116 (office); (28) 9066-6662 (home). *Fax:* (28) 9023-6505; (28) 9033-5877 (office). *E-mail:* i.allen@qub.ac.uk (office); ingrid.allen@btinternet.com (home). *Website:* www.qub.ac.uk (office); www.profingridallen.co.uk/.

ALLEN, Gen. John R., BSc, MSc, MA; American military officer (retd); *Special Presidential Envoy for the Global Coalition to Counter ISIL;* b. Fort Belvoir, Va; ed US Naval Acad., Annapolis, Md, Nat. War Coll., Georgetown Univ., Washington, DC; commissioned in US Marine Corps 1976, serving first as Platoon and Rifle Co. Commdr, 2nd Bn, 8th Marines 1976, Operations Officer, 3rd Bn, 4th Marines, Fleet Marine Force 1985; Lecturer, Political Science Dept, US Naval Acad., also Jump Officer and Jump Master 1988; Dir Infantry Officer Course, The Basic School 1990–92, Commdr 1999–2001; Div. G-3 Operations Officer for 2nd Marine Div. 1994, subsequently assumed command of 2nd Bn, 4th Marines (took part in Operation Sea Signal, Caribbean 1994 and Operation Jt Endeavor, Balkans 1995–96); Sr ADC to Commdt of Marine Corps 1996; Deputy Commdt, US Naval Acad. 2001–02, Commdt of Midshipmen in 2002; Prin. Dir for Asian and Pacific Affairs, Office of US Sec. of Defense 2003–06; Deputy Commdg Gen., II Marine Expeditionary Force and Commdg Gen., 2nd Marine Expeditionary Brigade 2006–08 (took part in Operation Iraqi Freedom as Deputy Commdg Gen. of Multi-Nat. Forces West); Deputy Commdr, US Cen. Command, MacDill Air Force Base, Tampa, Fla 2008–11, Acting Commdr June–Aug. 2010; nominated as Special Asst on Afghanistan and Iraq to Chair. of Jt Chiefs of Staff May 2011; Commdr Int. Security Assistance Force (ISAF) and Commdr US Forces Afghanistan (USFOR-A) 2011–13; Special Presidential Envoy for the Global Coalition to Counter ISIL (Islamic State of Iraq and the Levant) 2014–; attained rank of Brig.-Gen. 2003, Maj.-Gen. 2007, Lt-Gen. 2008, Gen. 2011; fmr term mem. Council on Foreign Relations; numerous mil. awards including Defense Distinguished Service Medal, Legion of Merit with three award stars, Navy and Marine Corps Commendation Medal with three award stars, Global War on Terrorism Service Medal, Nat. Defense Service Medal with two service stars; Meritorious Service Medal (Mongolia), First Class, Gold Medal of the Polish Armed Forces, Order of the Resplendent Banner with Special Cravat (Taiwan). *Address:* Department of State, 2201 C Street, NW, Washington, DC 20520, USA (office). *Telephone:* (202) 647-4000 (office). *Fax:* (202) 647-6738 (office). *Website:* www.state.gov/s/seci/ (office).

ALLEN, John Robert Lawrence, DSc, FRS, FGS, FSA; British geologist, sedimentologist and academic; *Professor Emeritus, University of Reading;* b. 25 Oct. 1932; s. of George Eustace Allen and Alice Josephine (née Formby); m. Jean Mary Wood 1960; four s. one d.; ed St Philip's Grammar School, Birmingham, Univ. of Sheffield; mem. staff, Univ. of Reading 1959–, Prof. of Geology 1972–89, of Sedimentology 1989–93, apptd. Research Prof. Postgrad. Research Inst. for Sedimentology 1993, now Prof. Emer., Visiting Prof. in Archaeology; Assoc. mem. Royal Belgian Acad. of Sciences; Hon. LLD (Sheffield), Hon. DSc (Reading); Lyell Medal, Geological Soc. 1980, David Linton Award, British Geomorphological Research Group 1983, Twenhofel Medal, Soc. of Econ. Paleontologists and Minerologists 1987, G.K. Warren Prize, NAS, USA 1990, Sorby Medal, Int. Asscn of Sedimentologists 1994, Penrose Medal, Geological Soc. of America 1996. *Publications:* Current Ripples 1968, Physical Processes of Sedimentation 1970, Sedimentary Structures 1982, Principles of Physical Sedimentology 1985; numerous contribs to professional journals. *Leisure interests:* cooking, music, opera, pottery, walking. *Address:* 17C Whiteknights Road, Reading, Berks., RG6 7BY, England (home). *Telephone:* (118) 926-4621 (home); (118) 378-6352 (office). *E-mail:* j.r.l.allen@reading.ac.uk (office). *Website:* www.reading.ac.uk/archaeology/about/staff/j-r-l-allen.aspx (office).

ALLEN, John Walter, MA, FRSE; British physicist and academic; *Professor Emeritus of Solid State Physics, University of St Andrews;* b. 7 March 1928, Birmingham, England; s. of Walter Allen and Beryl Parsons; m. 1st Mavis Williamson 1956 (died 1972); m. 2nd Hania Szawelska 1981; one s.; ed King Edward's School, Birmingham, Sidney Sussex Coll., Cambridge; RAF Educ. Br. 1949–51; staff scientist, Ericsson Telephones, Nottingham 1951–56; Royal Naval Scientific Service, Services Electronics Research Lab. 1956–68; Visiting Prof., Stanford Univ., USA 1964–66; Tullis Russell Fellow, Univ. of St Andrews 1968–72, Reader in Physics, Dir of Wolfson Inst. of Luminescence 1972–81, Prof. of Solid State Physics 1980–93, Prof. Emer. 1993–; Hon. DSc (St Andrews). *Publications:* some 130 papers in scientific journals including the first account of a practical light-emitting diode 1962. *Leisure interests:* archaeology, traditional dance. *Address:* School of Physics and Astronomy, University of St Andrews, North Haugh, St Andrews, Fife, KY16 9AJ (office); 2 Dempster Terrace, St Andrews, Fife, KY16 9QQ, Scotland (home). *Telephone:* (1334) 463029 (office); (1334) 474163 (home). *Fax:* (1334) 463104 (office). *E-mail:* jwa@st-and.ac.uk (office). *Website:* www.st-andrews.ac.uk/physics (office).

ALLEN, Sir Patrick Linton, ON, GCMG, CD, PhD; Jamaican administrator, teacher, ecclesiastic and government official; *Governor-General;* b. 7 Feb. 1951, Portland; s. of Ferdinand Allen and Christina Allen; m. Patricia; three c.; ed Moneague Teachers Coll., Andrews Univ., USA; Prin., Robins Bay Primary School 1976–78, Hillside Primary School 1978–80; ordained Seventh Day Adventist pastor 1989; Asst Registrar, Andrews Univ. 1996–98; Pres. Cen. Jamaica Conf. of Seventh Day Adventists 1998–2000, West Indies Union of Seventh Day Adventists 2000–; Gov.-Gen. of Jamaica 2009–; Dr hc (Northern Caribbean Univ.). *Leisure interests:* badminton, athletics, basketball, cricket. *Address:* Office of the Governor-General, King's House, Hope Road, Kingston 10, Jamaica (office). *Telephone:* 927-6424 (office). *Fax:* 978-6025 (office). *E-mail:* kingshouse@kingshouse.gov.jm (office). *Website:* www.kingshousejamaica.gov.jm (office).

ALLEN, Richard V.; American academic, international business consultant and fmr government official; *Senior Counselor, APCO Worldwide Inc.;* b. 1 Jan. 1936, Collingswood, NJ; s. of C. Carroll Allen, Sr and Magdalen Buchman; m. Patricia Ann Mason 1957; three s. four d.; ed Notre Dame Univ. and Univ. of Munich; helped found Cen. for Strategic and Int. Studies, Georgetown Univ. 1962; Consultant and fmr Prof., Hoover Inst., Stanford Univ.; with Nat. Security Council 1968–69; mem. Ronald Reagan's staff, campaigns 1976, Bd Govs Ronald Reagan Presidential Foundation 1985; Pres. Richard V. Allen Co., Washington 1982–90, Chair. 1991–; Head Nat. Security Council and Nat. Security Adviser 1981–82; Chair. Fed. Capital Bank 1987; Sr Council for Foreign Policy and Nat. Security Affairs, Repub. Nat. Cttee 1982–88; mem. Bd of Dirs Xsirius Inc. 1991–92; Distinguished Fellow and Chair. Asian Studies Center, The Heritage Foundation 1982; Chair. German-American Tricentenial Foundation 1983; Founding mem. US Nat. Cttee for Pacific Basin 1984; Sr Fellow, Hoover Inst. 1983–; mem. Advisory Bd Catholic Campaign for America 1993–, Nixon Center, Center for Strategic and Int. Studies; mem. Republican Congressional Policy Advisory Bd 1998–, Nat. Security Advisory Group, Defense Policy Bd, Council for Foreign Relations; currently Sr Counselor, APCO Worldwide Inc. (consulting firm), Washington, DC; mem. Advisory Council, Nat. Republican Inst. for Int. Affairs; mem. Bd of Trustees, Intercollegiate Studies Inst., Council on Foreign Relations, Int. Crisis Group; Hon. Fellow in Politics, St. Margaret's Coll., Univ. of Otago; Order of Diplomatic Merit Ganghwa (Repub. of Korea) 1982; Kt Commdr's Cross (FRG) 1983; Order of Brilliant Star (Repub. of China) 1986; Sovereign Mil. Order of Kts of Malta 1987; hon. degrees (Hanover Coll.) 1981, (Korea Univ.) 1982, Pepperdine Univ. *Publications:* numerous books on political and economic affairs including Peace or Peaceful Coexistence 1966, Communism and Democracy: Theory and Action 1967. *Address:* APCO Worldwide, 1615 L Street, Suite 900, NW, Washington, DC 20036-5623, USA (office). *Telephone:* (202) 778-1000 (office). *Fax:* (202) 466-6002 (office). *E-mail:* information@apcoworldwide.com (office). *Website:* www.apcoworldwide.com (office).

ALLEN, Samuel R., BA; American business executive; *Chairman and CEO, Deere & Co.;* b. 1953, Sumter, SC; ed Purdue Univ., West Lafayette, Ind.; joined Deere & Co. (collectively called John Deere) 1975, worked in Consumer Products Div., Worldwide Construction and Forestry Div., John Deere Power Systems, and Worldwide Agricultural Div., including managing operations in Latin America, China and East Asia, and Australia, has served as a sr officer of co. since 2001, with additional responsibilities in human resources, industrial relations, and John Deere Credit's global operations, Pres., Worldwide Construction and Forestry Div.–June 2009, responsible for global operations of John Deere Power Systems, for Deere's intelligent mobile equipment technologies and for Deere's advanced tech. and eng, mem. Bd of Dirs June 2009–, Pres. and COO Deere & Co. June–Aug. 2009, Pres. and CEO Aug. 2009–10, Chair. and CEO Feb. 2010–; Chair. Council on Competitiveness 2010–; apptd mem. Bd of Dirs Whirlpool Corpn 2010 (currently Presiding Dir). *Address:* Deere & Co. World Headquarters, One John Deere Place, Moline, IL 61265, USA (office). *Telephone:* (309) 765-8000 (office). *Fax:* (309) 765-5671 (office). *E-mail:* GoldenKennethB@JohnDeere.com (office). *Website:* www.deere.com (office).

ALLEN, Sharon; American business executive; b. 7 Oct. 1951, Kimberly, Ida; ed Univ. of Idaho; fmrly in charge of Portland office, Deloitte & Touche USA LLP, later mem. Bd of Dirs Deloitte & Touche USA LLP and Man. Pnr, Deloitte US Firms' Pacific Southwest practice, Los Angeles, Chair. (first woman) Deloitte & Touche USA LLP, served on Client Service Standards Task Force, Pnr Admissions Cttee and in many other cttee capacities 2003–11; mem. Bd of Dirs Los Angeles Area Chamber of Commerce, United Way of Greater Los Angeles, Ind. Colls of Southern Calif., YMCA of Metropolitan Los Angeles; Dr hc (Univ. of Idaho) 2004; numerous awards for business and community leadership.

ALLEN, Sir Thomas Boaz, Kt, CBE, MA, FRCM, FRAM; British singer (baritone); *Chancellor, Durham University;* b. 10 Sept. 1944, Seaham Harbour, Co. Durham; s. of Thomas Boaz Allen and Florence Allen; m. 1st Margaret Holley 1968 (divorced 1986); one s.; m. 2nd Jeannie Gordon Lascelles 1988; one step-s. one step-d.; ed Robert Richardson Grammar School, Ryhope, Royal Coll. of Music, London, Univs of Newcastle, Birmingham and Durham; Prin. Baritone, Welsh Nat. Opera 1969–72, Royal Opera House, Covent Garden 1972–78; freelance opera singer 1978–, singing at Glyndebourne Opera 1973, ENO, London Coliseum 1986, La Scala 1987, Chicago Lyric Opera 1990, Royal Albert Hall 2000, London Proms 2002, Royal Opera House, Covent Garden 2003, Metropolitan Opera, New York 2005; Prince Consort Prof., Royal Coll. of Music 1994; Hambro Visiting Prof. of Opera, Univ. of Oxford 2000–01; Pres. British Youth Opera 2000–; Patron Samling Foundation, Music in Hosps, Oxford Lieder Festival, Kathleen Ferrier Awards; Chancellor, Durham Univ. 2011–; performances include: Die Zauberflöte 1973, Le Nozze di Figaro 1974, Così fan tutte 1975, 2010, 2012, Don Giovanni 1977, The Cunning Little Vixen 1977, Simon Boccanegra, Billy Budd, La Bohème, L'Elisir d'Amore, Faust, Albert Herring, Die Fledermaus, La Traviata, A Midsummer Night's Dream, Gianni Schicchi 2008, Der Rosenkavalier 2009–10, Die Meistersinger von Nürnberg 2010, Hänsel und Gretel 2010–11, Il turco in Italia 2011, Il barbiere di Siviglia 2011; Albert Herring (as producer) 2002; Dir Così fan tutte, Samling Opera, The Sage, Gateshead 2005, Le nozze di Figaro 2006, Il barbiere di Siviglia 2007, Der Rosenkavalier 2009, Il turco in Italia 2009, Gianni Schicchi 2010; Vice-Pres. Durham Univ. Choral Soc.; Artist-in-Residence Royal Coll. of Music 2018–; Hon. Patron, Durham Cathedral Choir Asscn; Hon. Fellow, Univ. of Sunderland, Jesus Coll., Oxford; Hon. mem. RAM; Hon. MA (Newcastle) 1984, Hon. DMus (Durham) 1988, (Birmingham) 2004; Queen's Prize 1967, Gulbenkian Fellow 1968, Royal Philharmonic Soc. BBC Radio 3 Listeners' Award 2004, Bayerischer Kammersänger, Bavarian State Opera, Queen's Medal for Music 2013. *Recordings:* numerous including: Duruflé, Requiem and Four Motets 1987, Duparc, Songs 1989, Duruflé and Fauré, Requiems 1998, Songs My Father Taught Me 2002, More Songs My Father Taught Me 2003. *Film:* Mrs Henderson Presents 2005, The Real Don Giovanni 2009. *Publication:* Foreign Parts: A Singer's Journal 1993. *Leisure interests:* painting, drawing, ornithology, golf, fishing. *Address:* Askonas Holt Ltd, 15 Fetter Lane, London, EC4V 1BN, England (office); Durham University Executive Office, Palatine Centre, Stockton Road, Durham, DH1 3LE, England. *Telephone:* (20) 7400-1700 (office); (20) 7400-1799 (office). *E-mail:* info@askonasholt.co.uk (office). *Website:* www.askonasholt.co.uk (office); www.dur.ac.uk/about/governance/senior/chancellor.

ALLEN, Tim; American actor and comedian; b. (Timothy Alan Dick), 13 June 1953, Denver; m. 1st Laura Diebel (divorced); one d.; m. 2nd Jane Hadjuk 2006; ed Western Mich. Univ., Univ. of Detroit; fmr creative dir for advertising agency, Detroit; debut as comedian on Showtime Comedy Club All Stars 1988; presenter, Annual Golden Globe Awards 1999, 2003, 2007, 2011; Favorite Comedy Actor, People's Choice Award for Favorite Male Performer in a New TV Series 1992, People's Choice Award for Favorite Male TV Performer 1993–99, People's Choice Award for Favorite Comedy Motion Picture Actor 1995, Kids' Choice Awards Hall of Fame Award 1996, Annie Award for Outstanding Individual Achievement for Voice Acting by a Male Performer in an Animated Feature Production 1999, named a Disney Legend for his work on the Toy Story and The Santa Clause franchises 1999, received a Star on the Hollywood Walk of Fame at 6898 Hollywood Blvd 2004. *Films include:* Comedy's Dirtiest Dozen, The Santa Clause 1994, Toy Story (voice) 1995, Meet Wally Sparks 1997, Jungle 2 Jungle 1997, For Richer or Poorer 1997, Galaxy Quest 1999, Toy Story 2 (voice) 2000, Buzz Lightyear of Star Command: The Adventure Begins 2000, Who is Cletis Tout? 2001, Joe Somebody 2001, Big Trouble 2002, The Santa Clause 2 2002, Christmas with the Kranks 2004, The Shaggy Dog 2006, Zoom 2006, The Santa Clause 3: The Escape Clause 2006, Wild Hogs 2007, Redbelt 2008, My Dad's Six Wives 2009, Crazy on the Outside 2010, Toy Story 3 (voice) 2010, Chimpanzee (narrator) 2012, The Penguin King 2012, 3 Geezers! 2013. *Television includes:* Home Improvement (series) (TV Guide Award for Favorite Actor in a Comedy 1999) 1991–99, Tim Allen: Men Are Pigs 1990, Tim Allen Rewrites America (specials), Showtime Comedy Club All-Stars II 1988, Jimmy Neutron: Win, Lose and Kaboom (voice) 2004, Last Man Standing (TV Guide Award for Favorite Comeback 2012) 2011–, Toy Story of Terror! (voice) 2013, Toy Story That Time Forgot (voice) 2014. *Publications:* Don't Stand Too Close to a Naked Man 1994, I'm Not Really Here 1996. *Address:* c/o Messina Baker Entertainment, 955 Carrillo Drive, Suite 100, Los Angeles, CA 90048, USA (office). *Telephone:* (323) 954-8600 (office). *Website:* ideaexchange.timallen.com; www.timallen.com.

ALLEN, Woody; American actor, writer, producer and director; b. (Allen Stewart Konigsberg), 1 Dec. 1935, Brooklyn, NY; s. of Martin Konigsberg and Nettie Konigsberg (née Cherry); m. 1st Harlene Rosen 1956 (divorced 1962); m. 2nd Louise Lasser 1966 (divorced 1970); m. 3rd Soon-Yi Previn 1997; two adopted d.; one s. with Mia Farrow (q.v.); ed City Coll. of New York and New York Univ.; made his debut as a performer in 1961 at the Duplex in Greenwich Village; has performed in a variety of nightclubs across the USA; produced the play Don't Drink the Water 1966, Morosco Theater 1966, Broadhurst Theatre 1969; made his Broadway debut as Allan Felix in Play it Again, Sam, which he also wrote; during the 1950s wrote for TV performers Herb Shriner 1953, Sid Caesar 1957, Art Carney 1958–59, Jack Paar and Carol Channing, also wrote for the Tonight Show and the Gary Moore Show; Dr hc (Universitat Pompeu Fabra, Spain) 2007; Laurel Award for Screen Writing Achievement 1987, D.W. Griffith Award 1996, Directors Guild of America Lifetime Achievement Award 1996, San Sebastian Film Festival Donosti a Prize 2004, Cecil B DeMille Award, Golden Globe Awards, Hollywood Foreign Press Association 2013. *Plays include:* Don't Drink the Water 1966, The Floating Lightbulb 1981, Death Defying Acts (one act) 1995. *Opera:* as producer: Gianni Schicchi, Los Angeles Opera 2008. *Films include:* What's New Pussycat? 1965, Casino Royale 1967, What's Up, Tiger Lily? 1967, Take the Money and Run 1969, Bananas 1971, Everything You Always Wanted to Know About Sex 1972, Play it Again, Sam 1972, Sleeper 1973, Love and Death 1976, The Front 1976, Annie Hall (Acad. Awards for Best Dir and Best Writer 1978, BAFTA Film Awards for Best Screenplay and Best Direction 1978) 1977, Interiors 1978, Manhattan (BAFTA Film Award for Best Screenplay – Original 1980) 1979, Stardust Memories 1980, A Midsummer Night's Sex Comedy 1982, Zelig 1983, Broadway Danny Rose (BAFTA Film Award for Best Screenplay – Original 1985) 1984, The Purple Rose of Cairo (BAFTA Film Awards for Best Film and Best Screenplay – Original 1986, Golden Globe Award for Best Screenplay 1986) 1985, Hannah and Her Sisters (BAFTA Film Award for Best Direction 1987, Acad. Award for Best Writing, Screenplay Written Directly for the Screen 1987) 1986, Radio Days 1987, September 1987, Another Woman 1988, Oedipus Wrecks 1989, Crimes and Misdemeanors 1989, Alice 1990, Scenes from a Mall 1991, Shadows and Fog 1991, Husbands and Wives (BAFTA Award Film Award for Best Screenplay – Original 1993) 1992, Manhattan Murder Mystery 1993, Bullets Over Broadway 1995, Mighty Aphrodite 1995, Everyone Says I Love You 1996, Deconstructing Harry 1997, Celebrity 1998, Antz (voice only) 1998, Wild Man Blues 1998, Stuck on You 1998, Company Men 1999, Sweet and Lowdown 1999, Small Town Crooks 2000, The Curse of the Jade Scorpion 2001, Hail Sid Caesar! 2001, Hollywood Ending 2002, Anything Else 2003, Melinda and Melinda 2004, Match Point 2005, Scoop 2006, Cassandra's Dream 2007, Vicky Cristina Barcelona 2008, Whatever Works 2009, You Will Meet a Tall Dark Stranger 2010, Midnight in Paris (Golden Globe Award for Best Screenplay 2012, Acad. Award for Best Writing, Screenplay Written Directly for the Screen 2012) 2011, To Rome With Love 2012, Blue Jasmine 2013, Magic in the Moonlight 2014, Irrational Man 2015, Café Society 2016, Wonder Wheel 2017. *Television:* Sounds from a Town I Love 2001, Crisis in Six Scenes 2016. *Publications include:* Getting Even 1971, Without Feathers 1975, Side Effects 1980, The Complete Prose 1994, Telling Tales (contrib. to charity anthology) 2004, Mere Anarchy 2007, The Insanity Defense 2007; contribs to Playboy and New Yorker. *Leisure interests:* chocolate milk shakes, poker, chess, baseball; also a noted clarinettist. *Address:* 930 Fifth Avenue, New York, NY 10021, USA.

ALLEN OF KENSINGTON, Baron (Life Peer), cr. 2013, of Kensington in the Royal Borough of Kensington and Chelsea; **Charles Lamb Allen,** Kt, CBE, FRSA, FCMA; British business executive and broadcaster; *Chairman, Global Radio Group;* b. 4 Jan. 1957; accountant, British Steel 1974–79; Deputy Audit Man. Gallaghers PLC 1979–82; Dir Man. Services Grandmet Int. Services Ltd 1982–85, Group Man. Dir Compass Vending, Grandmet Innovations Ltd 1986–87, Man. Dir Grandmet Int. Services Ltd 1987–88, Man. Dir Compass Group Ltd 1988–91, Chief Exec. Leisure Div., Granada Group 1991–92; Chair. Granada Leisure and Services 1993–2000, CEO LWT (following takeover by Granada) 1994–96 (Chair. 1996), CEO Granada Group PLC 1996–2000, Chair. GMTV 1996–2000, Jt Deputy Chair. Granada Compass PLC 2000, Exec. Chair. Granada PLC 2000–03, CEO ITV PLC (after merger of Granada and Carlton) 2003–07; Chair. Global Radio Group (Heart, Capital, Classic FM, LBC, Gold, XFM, Choice) 2007–; Chair. (non-exec.) EMI Music 2008–10, CEO 2010–11; Chair. Exec. Bd of the Labour Party 2012–15; Chair. Manchester Commonwealth Games 2002–, British Red Cross 2012–13, 2 Sisters Food Group 2011–, ISS A/S 2013–; Chair. Bd of Trustees, Join In Trust 2012–16; Advisory Chair., Moelis & Company (ind. investment bank) 2016–; Chief Adviser, Home Office 2006–08; Sr Adviser, Goldman Sachs Capital Partners 2008–15; Owner, Grandmet Management Ltd (consultancy); mem. Bd of Dirs (non-exec.) Tesco plc 1999–2010, Endemol 2008–13, Virgin Media 2008–13, GET A/S 2009–14; mem. London 2012 Ltd (effort to bring 2012 Olympics to London) 2002–06, London Organising Cttee of the Olympic and Paralympics Games (LOCOG) 2006–14, Manchester 2002 Ltd 2002–03; Hon. DBA (Manchester Metropolitan) 1999, (Salford) 2002; named as Mayor of the Olympic Village, London for the duration of the Games May 2012. *Leisure interests:* visual and performing arts, int. travel and cultures. *Address:* Global Radio Group, 30 Leicester Square, London, WC2H 7LA (office); House of Lords, Westminster, London, SW1A 0PW, England. *Telephone:* (20) 7766-6000 (office); (20) 7219-5353. *Fax:* (20) 7766-6111 (office). *E-mail:* info@thisisglobal.com (office). *Website:* www.thisisglobal.com (office).

ALLENDE, Isabel; Chilean/American writer, journalist and academic; b. 2 Aug. 1942, Lima, Peru; d. of Tomás Allende and Francisca Llona Barros; m. 1st Miguel Frias 1962; one s. one d.; m. 2nd William Gordon 1988 (separated 2015); journalist, Paula women's magazine 1967–74, Mampato children's magazine 1969–74, TV shows and film documentaries 1970–74, El Nacional newspaper, Caracas, Venezuela 1975–84; taught literature at Montclair State Coll., NJ 1985, Univ. of Virginia, Charlottesville 1988, Univ. of California, Berkeley 1989; Goodwill Amb. for Hans Christian Andersen Bicentenary 2004; lecture tours in USA and Europe, speech tours in univs and cols, numerous literature workshops; mem. Academia de Artes y Ciencias, Puerto Rico 1995, Academia de la Lengua, Chile 1989, American Acad. of Arts and Letters 2004; Hon. Citizen of Austin, Tex. USA 1995; Hon. Prof. of Literature, Univ. of Chile 1991; Hon. mem. Acad. of Devt and Peace, Austria 2000; Chevalier, Ordre des Arts et Lettres 1994, Condecoracion Gabriela Mistral (Chile) 1994; Hon. DLitt (New York State Univ.) 1991, (Bates Coll., USA) 1994, (Dominican Coll., USA) 1994, (Columbia Coll., USA) 1996; Hon. DHumLitt (Florida Atlantic Univ.) 1996; Dr hc (Lawrence Univ., USA) 2000, (Mills Coll., USA) 2000, (Illinois Wesleyan Univ.) 2002, (Harvard Univ., USA) 2014, (Univ. of Santiago, Chile) 2015; Best Novel of the Year (Chile) 1983, Panorama Literario Award (Chile) 1983, Author of the Year (Germany) 1984, Book of the Year (Germany) 1984, Grand Prix d'Evasion Award (France) 1984, Point de Mire Award, Belgian Radio and TV 1985, Best Novel (Mexico) 1985, Author of the Year (Germany) 1986, Quality Paperback Book Club New Voice (USA) 1986, Premio

Literario Colima Award (Mexico) 1986, XV Premio Internazionale I Migliori Dell'Anno (Italy) 1987, Mulheres Best Foreign Novel Award (Portugal) 1987, Quimera Libros (Chile) 1987, Book of the Year (Switzerland) 1987, Library Journal's Best Book (USA) 1988, Before Columbus Foundation Award (USA) 1988, Freedom to Write Pen Club (USA) 1991, XLI Bancarella Literary Award (Italy) 1993, Ind. Foreign Fiction Award (UK) 1993, Brandeis Univ. Major Book Collection Award (USA) 1993, Marin Women's Hall of Fame (USA) 1994, Feminist of the Year Award, The Feminist Majority Foundation (USA) 1994, Read About Me Literary Award (USA) 1996, Critics' Choice Award (USA) 1996, Books to Remember Award, American Library Asscn 1996, Gift of HOPE Award, HOPE Educ. and Leadership Fund (USA) 1996, Harold Washington Literary Award, City of Chicago 1996, Malaparte Award, Amici di Capri (Italy) 1998, Donna Città Di Roma Literary Award (Italy) 1998, Dorothy and Lillian Gish Prize (USA) 1998, Sara Lee Frontrunner Award (USA) 1998, GEMS Women of the Year Award (USA) 1999, Donna Dell'Anno 1999 Award (Italy) 1999, Books to Remember, The New York Public Library WILLA Literary Award 2000, Excellence in Int. Literature and Arts Award (USA) 2002, The Celebration of Books Amb. Award (USA) 2002, Int. Women's Forum Award (Mexico) 2002, Nopal Award, Cal Poly Pomona (USA) 2003, Cyril Magnin Lifetime Achievement Award (USA) 2003, Premios Iberoamericano de Letrasjose Donoso (Chile) 2003, Premio Personalidad Distinguida, Universidad del Pacifico (Chile) 2004, Commonwealth Award of Distinguished Service for Literature (USA) 2004, Premio Nacional de Literatura 2010, Presidential Medal of Freedom (US) 2014, Lifetime Achievement Award, PEN Center 2016, Anisfield-Wolf Book Award for Lifetime Achievement 2017, Medal for Distinguished Contribution to American Letters, Nat. Book Foundation 2018. *Plays:* El Embajador 1971, La balada del medio pelo 1973, Los siete espejos 1974. *Publications:* La casa de los espíritus (novel, trans. as The House of the Spirits) 1982, La gorda de porcelana (juvenile short stories) 1983, De amor y de sombra (novel, trans. as Of Love and Shadows) 1984, Cuentos de Eva Luna (short stories, trans. as Stories of Eva Luna) 1989, El plan infinito (novel, trans. as The Infinite Plan) 1991, Paula (memoir) 1994, Afrodita (trans. as Aphrodite) 1998, Hija de la fortuna (novel, trans. as Daughter of Fortune) 1999, Retrato en sepia (novel, trans. as Portrait in Sepia) 2000, La ciudad de las bestias (juvenile novel, trans. as City of the Beasts) 2002, Mi país inventado (memoir, trans. as My Invented Country) (Latino Literacy Now Award for Best Biography 2004) 2003, El reino del dragón de oro (juvenile novel, trans. as Kingdom of the Golden Dragon) (Latino Literacy Now Award for Best Young Adult Fiction 2004) 2003, El Zorro (novel) 2005, El Bosque de los Pigmeos (juvenile novel, trans. as Forest of the Pygmies) 2005, Inés del alma mía (novel, trans. as Inés of My Soul) 2006, La Suma de los Días (memoirs, trans. as The Sum of Our Days) 2007, La Isla Bajo el Mar (novel, trans. as Island Beneath the Sea) 2009, El Cuaderno de Maya (trans. as Maya's Notebook) 2011, El Juego de Ripper (trans. as Ripper) 2014, El Amante Japonés (trans. as The Japanese Lover) 2015, Más Allá Del Invierno (trans. as In The Midst Of Winter) 2017. *Address:* Carmen Balcells, Diagonal 580, Barcelona 21, Spain (office); 116 Caledonia Street, Sausalito, CA 94965, USA (office). *Website:* www.agenciabalcells.com (office); www.isabelallende.com. *Fax:* (415) 332-1313 (office). *E-mail:* assistant@isabelallende.com (office).

ALLENDE, Jorge Eduardo, PhD; Chilean biochemist, molecular biologist and academic; *Professor of Biochemistry and Molecular Biology, Instituto de Ciencias Biomédicas, University of Chile;* b. 11 Nov. 1934, Cartago, Costa Rica; s. of Octavio Allende and Amparo Rivera; m. Catherine C. Connelly 1961; three s. one d.; ed Louisiana State, Rockefeller and Yale Univs, USA; Research Assoc., Lab. of Prof. Fritz Lipmann at Rockefeller Univ. 1961–62; Asst Prof., Dept of Biochemistry, Univ. of Chile 1963–68, Assoc. Prof. 1968–71, Prof. of Biochemistry and Molecular Biology 1972–, also First Dir; Pres. Pan American Asscn of Biochemical Socs 1976; mem. Exec. Cttee Int. Union of Biochemistry 1982–91, Int. Cell Research Org. 1976–; mem. Exec. Bd Int. Council of Scientific Unions 1986–90; Regional Co-ordinator Latin American Network of Biological Sciences 1975–97; mem. UNESCO Int. Scientific Advisory Bd 1996; Chair. Advisory Comm. on Health Research, Pan-American Health Org. 1999–2003; Co-ordinator Science Educ. Program, Inter-Academy Panel; Foreign Assoc. Inst. of Medicine, NAS 1992, NAS 2001; Fogarty Scholar-in-Residence, NIH, USA; Founder-mem. Latin American Acad. of Sciences; mem. Chilean Acad. of Sciences, Pres. 1991–94; Fellow, Third World Acad. of Sciences, Vice-Pres. 2004–06; Hon. mem. Chilean Acad. of Medicine; Grand Cross of Scientific Merit (Brazil) 2002; Dr hc (Buenos Aires) 1993; Chilean Nat. Prize in Natural Sciences 1992, Purkwa Prize, French Acad. of Sciences 2007, Rector Medal Juvenal Hernandez Jaque 2013, Foundation Award KONEX of Argentina 2013. *Publications:* more than 140 research articles in learned journals, 25 articles on science policy and science educ. *Leisure interests:* music, reading, swimming. *Address:* Program de Biol. Cel. y Mol., Inst. Cs. Biomed., Facultad de Medicina, Universidad de Chile, Casilla 70086, Santiago 7, Chile (office). *Telephone:* (2) 678-6255 (office). *Fax:* (2) 737-6320 (office). *E-mail:* Jallende@uchile.cl (office). *Website:* icbm.cl (office).

ALLERT, Richard (Rick) Hugh, AO; Australian financial executive; ed Kings Coll., Adelaide; Carroll Winter & Co. Chartered Accountants 1959–60; joined Peat Marwick Mitchell & Co. 1960, Pnr 1973–79; Sr Partner, Allert Heard & Co. Chartered Accountants 1979–89; Chair. Southcorp 1989–2002; apptd Dir Coles Myer Ltd (renamed Coles Group Ltd 2006) 1995, Chair. 2002–07; Chair. Tourism Australia 2007–12, AXA Asia Pacific Holdings Ltd, AustralAsia Railway Corpn, Nat. Wine Centre, Aboriginal Foundation of South Australia Inc., Performing Arts Bd, Australia Council; Dir Australian Business Arts Foundation; fmr Chair. Voyages Hotels & Resorts Pty Ltd, Pembroke School Foundation; fmr Nat. Pres. Nat. Heart Foundation of Australia; fmr Deputy Chair. South Australian Devt Council, Adelaide Football Club Ltd; fmr Bd mem. Northern Territory Devt Corpn, Northern Territory Trade Devt Zone, South Australian Oil and Gas Corpn; fmr Commr South Australian Health Comm.; fmr mem. Review of Business Taxation (Ralph Cttee), Singapore Australia Business Alliance Forum; Fellow, Inst. of Chartered Accountants (Australia); AM 1997; Hon. DUniv (Univ. of S Australia) 2000; Centenary Medal 2001, Ernst & Young Champion of Entrepreneurship Award, Cen. Region 2011.

ALLEY, Kirstie; American actress; b. 12 Jan. 1951, Wichita, Kan.; m. Parker Stevenson (divorced 1997); one s. one d.; People's Choice Award 1998. *Films include:* Star Trek II, The Wrath of Khan 1982, One More Chance, Blind Date, Champions 1983, Runaway 1984, Summer School 1987, Look Who's Talking Too 1990, Madhouse 1990, Look Who's Talking Now 1993, David's Mother (TV film) 1994, Village of the Damned 1995, It Takes Two 1995, Sticks and Stones 1996, Nevada 1996, For Richer or Poorer 1997, Deconstructing Harry 1997, Toothless 1997, Drop Dead Gorgeous 1999, The Mao Game 1999, Back By Midnight 2004, Syrup 2013, Accidental Love 2015. *Stage appearances include:* Cat on a Hot Tin Roof, Answers. *Television includes:* Cheers 1987–93, Veronica's Closet 1997, Blonde 2001, Salem Witch Trials (mini-series) 2002, Profoundly Normal 2003, Family Sins 2003, While I Was Gone 2004, Fat Actress (series) 2005, The Minister of Divine (film) 2007, Write & Wrong (film) 2007, The Minister of Divine (film) 2007, The Manzanis (film) 2012, Baby Sellers (film) 2013, Kirstie (series) 2013–14, Hot in Cleveland (series) 2013–14 and numerous other TV films and series. *Address:* Jason Weinberg and Associates, 122 East 25th Street, 2nd Floor, New York, NY 10010, USA.

ALLEY, Richard B., BSc, MSc, PhD; American geologist and academic; *Evan Pugh Professor of Geosciences, Pennsylvania State University;* b. 18 Aug. 1957; ed Ohio State Univ., Univ. of Wisconsin; Postdoctoral Research Asst, Univ. of Wisconsin-Madison 1987–88; Asst Prof., Dept of Geosciences and Coll. of Earth and Mineral Sciences Environment Inst., Pennsylvania State Univ. 1988–92, Assoc. Prof. 1992–96, Prof. 1996–, Evan Pugh Prof. of Geosciences 2000–; three field seasons in Antarctica (geology 1978, glaciology 1984, 1985), eight in Greenland (glaciology 1985, 1989–92, glacial geology 2003 and twice in 2005), three in Alaska (glaciology 1995, 2000, 2002), two in Utah (geology 1979, 1981), one in Wyoming (glacial geology 2008), much work (many months in total) at Nat. Ice Core Lab., Denver, Colo; mem. NAS 2008; Foreign mem. Royal Soc. 2014; Fellow, American Acad. of Arts and Sciences 2010, AAAS, American Geophysical Union, Geological Soc. of America; Dr hc (Univ. of Wisconsin); Faculty Scholar Medal, Pennsylvania State Univ., also Eisenhower Award and Coll. of Earth and Mineral Sciences Wilson Teaching Award, Mitchell Innovative Teaching Award and Faculty Mentoring Award; Heinz Award; Revelle Medal, American Geophysical Union, also Horton Award (Hydrology Section), Emiliani Lecturer (Paleo. Section), Nye Lecturer (Cryospheric Sciences Section) and Bjerknes Lecturer (Atmospheric Sciences Section); Louis Agassiz Medal (Cryospheric Section), European Geosciences Union, Schneider Award for Science Communication, Public Service Award, Geological Soc. of America, also Easterbrook Award of their Quaternary Geology and Geomorphology Section; Award for Outstanding Contrib. to Public Understanding of the Geosciences, American Geological Inst., Distinguished Geographer Award, Pennsylvania Geographical Soc., Sustained Achievement Award, Renewable Natural Resources Foundation, D&L Packard Fellowship, Presidential Young Investigator Award, G. Comer Mentorship, Seligman Crystal, Int. Glaciological Soc. 2005, Tyler Prize for Environmental Achievement 2009, Heinz Award 2012, Friend of the Planet Award, Nat. Center for Science Educ. 2014, Wollaston Medal 2017. *Publications include:* Rocking the Parks: Geological Stories of the National Parks 1999, The West Antarctic Ice Sheet: Behavior and Environment (co-ed.) 2001, The Two-Mile Time Machine: Ice Cores, Abrupt Climate Change, and Our Future (Nat. Phi Beta Kappa Science Book Award, Choice Award 2001) 2000, Abrupt Climate Change: Inevitable Surprises (co-author) 2002, Earth: The Operators' Manual 2011, The Fate of Greenland (co-author) 2011; more than 220 papers in scientific journals on glaciology, ice sheet stability and palaeoclimates from ice cores. *Address:* Department of Geosciences, Penn State University, 517B Deike Building, University Park, PA 16802, USA (office). *Telephone:* (814) 863-1700 (office). *Fax:* (814) 863-7823 (office). *E-mail:* rba6@psu.edu (office); ralley@essc.psu.edu (office). *Website:* www.geosc.psu.edu (office).

ALLEYNE, Sir George, Kt, MD, FRCP; Barbadian physician and UN official; b. 7 Oct. 1932, Barbados; s. of Clinton Alleyne and Eileen Alleyne (née Gaskin); m. Sylvan I. Chen 1958; two s. one d.; ed Harrison Coll., Univ. of the West Indies; Sr Resident, Univ. Hosp. of the West Indies 1963; Research Fellow, Tropical Metabolism Research Unit, Jamaica 1964–72; Prof. of Medicine, Univ. of the W Indies 1972–81, Chair. Dept of Medicine 1976–81; Head Research Unit, Pan American Health Org. 1981–83, Dir Health Programmes 1982–90, Asst Dir 1990–95, Dir 1995–2003, Dir Emer. 2003–; Special Envoy of the UN Sec.-Gen. for HIV/AIDS in the Caribbean 2003–10; Chancellor Univ. of the West Indies 2003–17, then Chancellor Emer.; Order of the Caribbean Community 2001; Hon. DSc (Univ. of the West Indies) 1988. *Publications include:* The Importance of Health: A Caribbean Perspective 1989, Public Health for All 1991, Health and Tourism 1992; over 100 articles in major scientific research journals. *Leisure interests:* gardening, reading. *Address:* Pan American Health Organization, 525 23rd Street, NW, Washington, DC 20037, USA (office). *Telephone:* (202) 974-3057 (office). *Fax:* (202) 974-3677 (office). *E-mail:* alleyned@paho.org (office).

ALLFORD, Simon, BA, DipArch, RIBA; British architect; *Partner, Allford Hall Monaghan Morris;* b. 27 July 1961, London; s. of David Allford and Margaret Beryl Allford (née Roebuck); ed Hampstead Comprehensive School, Sheffield Univ., The Bartlett School of Architecture, Univ. Coll. London; with Nicholas Grimshaw 1983–85, BDP 1986–89; Partner, Allford Hall Monaghan Morris 1989–; Lecturer, Univ. Coll. London 1987–; mem. Architectural Asscn Council 1996–, Hon. Sec. 1991–2001, Hon. Treas. 2001–05; Vice-Pres. RIBA 2005–11; Chair. Architecture Foundation 2013–; Trustee, Architecture Asscn Foundation 2013–; writer, critic, teacher, judge, adviser, trustee and commentator on architectural subjects; over 30 RIBA Awards, eight Housing Design Awards, eight BCI Awards, three BCO Awards, 11 Civic Trust Awards, four AIA Awards, four MIPIM Awards, two WAF Awards, numerous Practice Awards, including Architect's Journal and Building magazine Practice of the Year 2013. *Recent projects include:* The Angel, Tea and Yellow Buildings, Adelaide Wharf, the Saatchi Gallery and Chobham Acad., transformation of Burntwood School, Wandsworth (RIBA Stirling Prize 2015), St John Bosco School, Battersea, 240 Blackfriars, Univ. of Amsterdam's Roetersei-land campus, new Google HQ, King's Cross, London, The White Collar Factory, London, Elephant Park, London, primary school, Alconbury Weald, shop at Barbican Arts Centre, three mixed use projects on Regent Street for the Crown Estate, and other large urban projects in London and USA. *Publications include:* manual: The Architecture and Office of Allford Hall Monaghan Morris. *Leisure interests:* architecture, Sheffield Wednesday Football Club. *Address:* Allford Hall Monaghan Morris, 2nd Floor, Block C, Morelands, 5–23 Old Street, London EC1V 9HL (office); 232 Bickenhall Mansions, Bickenhall Street, London, W1U 6BW, England (home). *Telephone:* (20) 7251-5261 (office); (20) 7487-5391 (home). *Fax:*

(20) 7251-5123 (office). *E-mail:* sallford@ahmm.co.uk (office). *Website:* www.ahmm .co.uk (office).

ALLI, Baron (Life Peer), cr. 1998, of Norbury in the London Borough of Croydon; **Waheed Alli;** British media executive and politician; b. 16 Nov. 1964; ed Norbury Manor School, Stanley Tech. Coll.; created Planet 24 Productions Ltd (fmrly 24 Hour Productions) with pnr Charlie Parsons, Jt Man. Dir 1992–99; mem. House of Lords 1998– (Labour); Man. Dir Carlton Productions 1998–2000; Chair. Asos PLC –2012; mem. Bd of Dirs Castaway Television Productions Ltd, BM Creative Management Ltd, Olga TV Ltd, Silvergate Investments Ltd (investment company), Silvergate Retail Ltd, Silvergate Media Ltd, Silvergate PPL Ltd, Silvergate Media Holdings Ltd, Vampire Squid Productions Ltd, Monkey WTB Ltd, Fairytale HD Ltd, QAM Building Management Ltd, Castaway Holdings Ltd; Pres. National Youth Theatre; apptd Vice-Pres. UNICEF UK 2003; Chancellor, De Montfort Univ. 2006–16; Trustee, Crimestoppers, Charlie Parsons Foundation; Stonewall Award 2008. *Address:* House of Lords, London, SW1A 0PW, England (office). *Telephone:* (20) 7219-5353 (office). *Fax:* (20) 7219-5979 (office). *E-mail:* contactholmember@parliament.uk (office).

ALLIANCE, Baron (Life Peer), cr. 2004, of Manchester in the County of Greater Manchester; **David Alliance,** CBE, CBIM, FRSA; British business executive; b. June 1932, Kashan, Iran; m. (divorced); three c.; first acquisition, Thomas Hoghton (Oswaldtwistle) 1956; acquired Spirella 1968, then Vantona Ltd, 1975 to form Vantona Group 1975; acquired Carrington Viyella to form Vantona Viyella 1983, Nottingham Mfg 1985, Coats Patons to form Coats Viyella 1986; Group Chief Exec. Coats Viyella 1975–90, Chair. 1989–99; Chair. N. Brown Group (mail order firm) 1968–2012 (now mem. Bd of Dirs), Tootal Group PLC 1991–99; Gov. Tel-Aviv Univ. 1989–; Fellow, Royal Soc. for the Encouragement of Arts, Mfrs and Commerce; Fellow, City and Guilds of London Inst.; mem. Prince's Youth Business Trust, Council for Industry and Higher Educ., Univ. of Manchester Foundation, Wiseman Inst.; mem. Liberal-Democrat Party; Hon. Fellow, UMIST, Shenkar Coll. of Textile Tech. and Fashion; Hon. FCGI 1991; Hon. LLD (Manchester) 1989, (Liverpool) 1996; Hon. DSc (Heriot-Watt) 1991. *Address:* House of Lords, Westminster, London, SW1A 0PW, England.

ALLIES, Edgar Robin (Bob), OBE, MA, DipArch, RIBA, RIAS, FRSA; British architect; *Partner, Allies and Morrison Architects;* b. 5 Sept. 1953, Singapore; s. of Edgar Martyn and Lily Maud; m. Jill Franklin; one s. one d.; ed Reading School, Univ. of Edinburgh; est. Allies and Morrison Architects with Graham Morrison 1983, Partner 1983–; Lecturer, Univ. of Cambridge 1984–88; George Simpson Visiting Prof., Univ. of Edinburgh 1995; Visiting Prof., Univ. of Bath 1996–99; mem. Faculty of Fine Arts, British School of Rome, Italy 1997–2002; Kea Distinguished Visiting Prof., Univ. of Maryland, USA 1999; Chair. The Brick Awards 2009–12, Design South East Review Panel 2014–; Visiting Prof. Univ. of Reading 2016–; mem. Council Architectural Asscn 2004–07, CABE Nat. Design Review Panel 2006–18, RIBA Awards Group 2009–11, London Mayor's Design Advisory Group 2012–16; Rome Scholar in Architecture 1981–82; Medal for Architecture, Edin. Architectural Asscn 1977, Building Awards Architectural Practice of the Year 2004, Building Design Architect of the Year Award 2007, the practice has won 35 RIBA Awards. *Publications include:* Model Futures 1983, Allies and Morrison 1996, Cultivating the City: London Before and After 2012 2009, Allies and Morrison, Vol. 1 2012, The Fabric of Place 2013, Allies and Morrison, Vol. 2 2018. *Leisure interest:* contemporary music. *Address:* Allies and Morrison, 85 Southwark Street, London, SE1 0HX (office); 12 Well Road, London, NW3 1LH, England (home). *Telephone:* (20) 7921-0100 (office). *Fax:* (20) 7921-0101 (office). *E-mail:* boballies@alliesandmorrison.com (office). *Website:* www .alliesandmorrison.com (office).

ALLIK, Jüri, PhD; Estonian psychologist and academic; *Professor of Experimental Psychology and Head, Department of Psychology, University of Tartu;* b. 3 March 1949, Tallinn; s. of Karl Allik and Niina Raudsepp; m. Anu Realo; one s. two d.; ed Moscow Univ., Russia, Tampere Univ., Finland; Prof. of Psychophysics, Univ. of Tartu 1992–2002, Dean, Faculty of Social Sciences 1996–2001, Prof. of Experimental Psychology and Head, Dept of Psychology 2002–; Chair. Estonian Science Foundation 2003–09; Pres. Estonian Psychological Asscn 1988–94, Vice-Pres. 1994–2001; Ed. Trames; Assoc. Ed. European Journal of Personality 2004–09; mem. Estonian Acad. of Sciences; Foreign mem. Finnish Acad. of Science and Letters 1997, Academia Europaea 2014; Order of the White Star, 4th Class (Estonia); Nat. Science Award 1998, 2005. *Publications:* The Five-Factor Model of Personality Across Cultures (co-ed.) 2002; numerous articles in scientific journals on visual perception, comparative study of collectivism vs individualism, the works of Sigmund Freud, and history of psychology. *Address:* Department of Psychology, University of Tartu, Näituse 2, Tartu 50409, Estonia (office). *Telephone:* (7) 372-5184277 (office). *Fax:* (7) 375900 (office). *E-mail:* juri.allik@ut.ee (office); jyri@ psych.ut.ee (office). *Website:* www.psych.ut.ee/~jyri (office).

ALLIOT-MARIE, Michèle, MA, DenD, DenScPol; French lawyer and politician; b. 10 Sept. 1946, Villeneuve-le-Roi, Val-de-Marne; d. of Bernard Marie and Renée Leyko; m. Michel Alliot (divorced); partner, Patrick Ollier; ed Faculté de Droit et des Sciences Econ. de Paris, Faculté des Lettres de Paris-Sorbonne, Univ. de Paris I; Asst Lecturer, Faculté de Droit et des Sciences Econ. de Paris then at Univ. de Paris I 1970–84, Sr Lecturer in Econs and Man. 1984–; Tech. Adviser to Minister of Social Affairs 1972–73, Adviser to Minister of Overseas Territories 1973–74, to Jr Minister for Tourism March–Sept. 1974, Tech. Adviser to Jr Minister for Univs 1974–76, Chef de Cabinet to Jr Minister for Univs then to Minister for Univs 1976–78; Dir, later Pres.-Dir Gen. UTA-Indemnité 1979–84; adviser on Admin. and Public Service Issues, RPR 1981–84, Asst Sec.-Gen. Legal Advisory Cttee 1984, mem. Cen. Cttee 1984, Exec. Cttee 1985, Nat. Sec. for Educ. and Research 1985; Deputy for Pyrénées-Atlantiques (RPR) 1986, 1988–93, 1995–2002, 2007–12; Sec. of State in charge of schools, Ministry of Educ. 1986–88; Nat. Sec. RPR (Research and Planning) 1988–90, Asst Sec.-Gen. (Foreign Relations) 1990–92; Municipal Councillor for Ciboure 1983–89, for Biarritz 1989–91; mem. European Parl. (UDF-RPR) 1989; Minister for Youth and Sports 1993–95; mem. and First Vice-Pres. Regional Council of Pyrénées-Atlantiques 1995–2001; Mayor of Saint-Jean-de-Luz 1995–2002, Deputy Mayor 2002–; Nat. Sec. RPR for Social Affairs 1997, mem. Political Cttee 1998, Nat. Sec. in charge of elections 1999, Pres. RPR 1999–2002 (party dissolved), Vice-Pres. Union for a Popular Movement 2009–; Minister of Defence and Veterans' Affairs 2002–07, of the Interior, Overseas Possessions and Territorial Collectivities 2007–09, of Justice and Keeper of the Seals 2009–10, of Foreign and European Affairs 2010–11 (resgnd); mem. Political Cttee Alliance pour la France 1998; fmr Pres. Comm. for Defence of Rights and Freedoms, Foundation for Voluntary Orgs; Commdr de l'Etoile équatoriale (Gabon), de l'Etoile d'Anjouan (Comoros), du Mérite de l'Educ. Nat. (Côte d'Ivoire), Ordre de la République (Egypt), Palmes Magistrales (First Class) (Peru). *Publications include:* L'actionnariat des salariés 1975, La Décision politique: attention une république peut en cacher une autre 1983, La Grande peur des classes moyennes 1996, La République des irresponsables 1999.

ALLIS, C. David, BS, MS, PhD; American biochemist, geneticist, microbiologist and academic; *Tri-Institutional Professor, Joy and Jack Fishman Professor and Head of Laboratory of Chromatin Biology and Epigenetics, The Rockefeller University;* b. 22 March 1951; ed Univ. of Cincinnati, Indiana Univ.; Postdoctoral Fellow, Univ. of Rochester 1978–81, Marie and Joseph Wilson Prof. of Biology and Prof. of Oncology 1995–98; Asst Prof., then Assoc. Prof., then Full Prof., Dept of Biochemistry and Cell Biology, Baylor Coll. of Medicine 1981–90; Prof., Dept of Biology, Syracuse Univ. 1990–95; Harry F. Byrd, Jr Prof. of Biochemistry and Molecular Genetics, Prof. of Microbiology and mem. Center for Cell Signaling, Univ. of Virginia Health System 1998–2003; Tri-Institutional Prof., Joy and Jack Fishman Prof. and Head of Lab. of Chromatin Biology and Epigenetics, The Rockefeller Univ. 2003–; mem. NAS, American Acad. of Arts and Sciences; Dickson Prize in Biomedical Sciences 2002, Massry Prize 2003, Gairdner Foundation Int. Award 2007, ASBMB-Merck Award 2008, Lewis S. Rosenstiel Award 2011, Japan Prize (co-recipient) 2014, Breakthrough Prize in Life Sciences (co-recipient) 2015, Albert Lasker Basic Medical Research Award 2018. *Publications:* numerous papers in professional journals. *Address:* The Rockefeller University, 1230 York Avenue, New York, NY 10065, USA (office). *Telephone:* (212) 327-8000 (switchboard) (office). *Fax:* (212) 327-7974 (office). *E-mail:* c.david.allis@rockefeller.edu (office). *Website:* lab.rockefeller.edu/allis (office).

ALLISON, Graham Tillett, Jr, AB, MA, PhD; American academic and fmr government official; *Douglas Dillon Professor of Government, Harvard University;* b. 23 March 1940, Charlotte, NC; s. of Graham T. Allison, Sr and Virginia Wright; m. Elisabeth K. Smith 1968; ed Davidson Coll., Harvard Univ., Univ. of Oxford, UK; Instructor of Govt, Harvard Univ. 1967–68, Asst Prof. of Govt 1968–70, Assoc. Prof. of Politics 1970–72, Prof. of Politics 1972–93, Assoc. Dean and Chair. Public Policy Program, John F. Kennedy School of Govt 1975–77, Dean and Don K. Price Prof. of Politics 1977–89, Douglas Dillon Prof. of Govt 1989–, Dir Belfer Center for Science and Int. Affairs, John F. Kennedy School of Govt 1995–2017; Asst Sec. of Defense for Policy and Plans, Dept of Defense, Washington, DC 1993–94; numerous professional appointments; Hon. DPhil (Uppsala Univ.) 1979, Hon. DLaws (Davidson Coll.) 1985, (Univ. of North Carolina, Wilmington) 1992; Dept of Defense Distinguished Public Service Medal (twice). *Publications include:* Essence of Decision: Explaining the Cuban Missile Crisis 1971, Sharing International Responsibilities: A Report to the Trilateral Commission 1983; co-author: Hawks, Doves and Owls: An Agenda for Avoiding Nuclear War 1985, Fateful Visions: Avoiding Nuclear Catastrophe 1988, Windows of Opportunity: From Cold War to Peaceful Competition 1989, Window of Opportunity: The Grand Bargain for Democracy in the Soviet Union 1991, Beyond Cold War to Trilateral Cooperation in the Asia-Pacific Region 1992, Avoiding Nuclear Anarchy 1996, America's Achilles Heel: Nuclear, Biological, and Chemical Terrorism and Covert Attack 1998, Catastrophic Terrorism 1998, Realizing Human Rights: Moving from Inspiration to Impact 2000, Nuclear Terrorism: The Ultimate Preventable Catastrophe 2004, Lee Kuan Yew: The Grand Master's Insights on China, the United States, and the World (co-author) 2013, Destined for War: Can America and China Escape Thucydides's Trap? 2017. *Leisure interests:* fishing, tennis. *Address:* John F. Kennedy School of Government, 79 JFK Street, Cambridge, MA 02138 (office); 69 Pinehurst Road, Belmont, MA 02478-1502, USA (home). *Telephone:* (617) 496-6099 (office). *Fax:* (617) 495-1905 (office). *E-mail:* graham_allison@ harvard.edu (office). *Website:* www.hks.harvard.edu (office).

ALLISON, James Patrick, BS, PhD; American immunologist and academic; *Professor and Chair of Immunology and Executive Director, Immunology Platform, M.D. Anderson Cancer Center, University of Texas;* b. 7 Aug. 1948, Alice, Tex.; m. Malinda Bell; ed Univ. of Texas; Asst Biochemist and Asst Prof., Univ. of Texas 1977–83, Adjunct Prof. of Zoology 1979–84, Prof. and Chair of Immunology and Exec. Dir, Immunology Platform, M.D. Anderson Cancer Center 2012–, also Vivian L. Smith Distinguished Chair in Immunology 2013–; Visiting Scholar, Dept of Pathology, Stanford Univ. 1983–84; Prof. of Immunology, Univ. of California, Berkeley 1985–2004, also Dir, Cancer Research Lab. 1985–2004, Interim Head, Div. of Immunology 1987–89, Head, Div. of Immunology 1989–97; David H. Koch Chair of Immunologic Studies, Memorial Sloan-Kettering Cancer Center and Chair., Immunology Program 2004–12, also Dir Ludwig Center for Cancer 2007–12; Investigator, Howard Hughes Medical Inst. 2004–12; Consultant, Becton-Dickinson Immunocytometry Systems, Inc. 1984; mem. Editorial Bd Development Immunology 1989; Reviewing Ed. Science 1985–87; Assoc. Ed. Journal of Immunology 1987, International Immunology 1988; Fellow, AAAS, American Acad. of Microbiology 1997; mem. NAS, American Asscn of Immunologists, American Asscn of Cancer Research, Inst. of Medicine; Centeon Award for Innovative Breakthroughs in Immunology 2001, Dana Foundation Award in Human Immunology Research, American Asscn of Immunologists 2008, C. Chester Stock Award for Distinguished Achievement in Biomedical Research, Memorial Sloan-Kettering Cancer Center 2008, Richard V. Smalley, MD Memorial Lectureship Award, Int. Soc. for Biological Therapy of Cancer 2010, Breakthrough Achievements in Translational Cancer Research, American Skin Asscn 2011, Advancement of Cancer Research Award, Gilda's Club 2011, Lloyd J. Old Award in Cancer Immunology, AACR-CRI 2013, Breakthrough Prize in Life Sciences (jt winner) 2014, Canada Gairdner Int. Award 2014, Szent-Györgyi Prize for Progress in Cancer Research 2014, Harvey Prize, Technion, Israel (jt winner) 2014, Lasker~DeBakey Clinical Medical Research Award, Lasker Foundation 2015, Balzan Prize 2017, Albany Medical Center Prize in Medicine and Biomedical Research 2018, Nobel Prize in Physiology or Medicine (jt winner) 2018. *Address:* University of Texas M.D. Anderson Cancer Center, 1515 Holcombe Boulevard, Houston, TX 77030, USA (office). *Telephone:* (713) 792-2121 (office). *Fax:* (713) 790-1529 (office). *E-mail:* jallison@mdanderson.org (office). *Website:* faculty .mdanderson.org/James_Allison/Default.asp (office).

ALLISON, Robert J., Jr, BSc; American petroleum industry executive; *Chairman Emeritus, Anadarko Petroleum Corporation;* b. 29 Jan. 1939; m. Carolyn Allison; three c.; ed Kansas Univ.; various sr positions with Amoco Production Co. 1959–73; Vice-Pres. of Operations, Anadarko Production Co. (now Anadarko Petroleum Corpn) 1973–76, mem. Bd of Dirs 1976–, Pres. 1976–79, CEO 1979–2002, Chair. 1986–2005 (resgnd), Chair. Emer. 2005–; mem. Bd of Dirs American Petroleum Inst., US Oil & Gas Asscn; mem. Nat. Petroleum Council, Soc. of Petroleum Engineers, Natural Gas Supply Asscn; Dir Freeport-McMoran Copper & Gold; mem. All-American Wildcatters 1991, Chair. 1999–2000; Assoc. mem. Univ. Cancer Foundation, Univ. of Texas M. D. Anderson Cancer Center; Trustee United Way of Texas Gulf Coast; Dir Spindletop (fmr Pres. and Chair.); mem. Bd of Dirs N. Harris Montgomery Community Coll. Dist Foundation, Sam Houston Area Council, Boy Scouts of America; Offshore Energy Center Pinnacle Award 2002. *Address:* c/o Board of Directors, Anadarko Petroleum Corporation, 1201 Lake Robbins Drive, The Woodlands, TX 77380, USA (office). *Website:* www.anadarko.com (office).

ALLISON-MADUEKE, Diezani, BSc, MBA; Nigerian architect, government official and international organization official; b. 6 Dec. 1960, Port Harcourt; m. Allison Madueke 1999; ed Howard Univ., Washington, DC, USA, Univ. of Cambridge, UK; fmr Architectural Intern, Charles Szoradi Architects, Washington, DC; fmr Project Engineer, American Interior Builders, Washington, DC; fmr Design Coordinator, Furman Construction Man. Inc., Rockville, Md; fmr Project Man., Facilities Planning and Devt Dept, Howard Univ.; Head of Projects Unit, Shell Petroleum Devt Co. of Nigeria Ltd, Lagos 1993–96, Head of Corporate Issues Man. 1996–2007; Minister of Transportation 2007–08, of Mines and Steel Devt 2008–10, of Petroleum Resources 2010–15; Pres. OPEC 2014–15; extradited in UK on charges of money laundering 2015; Dr hc (Nigerian Defence Acad., Kaduna) 2011.

ALLOUACHE, Merzak; Algerian film director and screenwriter; b. 6 Oct. 1944, Algiers; s. of Omar Allouache and Fatma Allouache; m. Lazib Anissa 1962; one d.; ed Institut des hautes études cinématographiques, Office de Radiodiffusion-Télévision Française, France; worked in Nat. Inst. of Cinema, Algiers, later in Inst. of Film, Paris; after return to Algeria worked as Adviser, Ministry of Culture; Silver Prize, Moscow Festival; Tanit d'Or Prize, Carthage 1979. *Films include:* Our Agrarian Revolution (documentary) 1973, Omar Gatlato, Les aventures d'un héros, L'homme qui regardait les fenêtres 1982, Bab El-Oued City 1994, Lumière et Compagnie 1995, Salut Cousin! 1996, Dans la décapotable 1996, Alger–Beyrouth: Pour Mémoire 1998, Pepe Carvalho: La Solitude du Manager (TV) 1999, À bicyclette (TV) 2001, L'Autre Monde 2001, Chouchou 2003, Bab el seb 2005, Tamanrasset (Premio Signis, Cagliari) 2008, Harragas 2009, Normal! (Best Arab Narrative Film Award, Doha Tribeca Film Festival) 2011, The Repentant 2012, The Rooftops 2013. *Publication:* Bab El-Oued (novel) 1994.

ALMADA LÓPEZ, Carlos Fernando, MBA, PhD; Mexican diplomatist; *Ambassador to Japan;* ed Autonomous Univ. of Sinaloa, Univ. of Law, Econs and Social Sciences, Paris, France; fmr sr official at Ministry of Energy and Ministry of the Interior; fmr Dir-Gen. of Social Communication of the Presidency; fmr Dir Centre for Studies in Public Policy, Nat. Inst. of Public Admin, later Vice-Pres. for Int. Affairs; fmr Head of Exec. Office of Gov. of Nuevo Leon and Under-Sec. of Communications and Transport; fmr Dir-Gen., Int. Inst. of Admin. Sciences, Brussels; Co-ordinator of Int. Affairs, Govt of Nuevo Leon; fmr Sec. of Admin, State Govt of Mexico; fmr Amb. to Portugal, Amb. to Japan 2015–. *Address:* Embassy of Mexico, 2-15-1, Nagata-cho, Chiyoda-ku, Tokyo 100-0014, Japan (office). *Telephone:* (3) 3581-1131 (office). *Fax:* (3) 3581-4058 (office). *E-mail:* calmada@sre.gob.mx (office); infojpn@sre.gob.mx (office); embajadamexicojapon@sre.gob.mx (office). *Website:* embamex.sre.gob.mx/japon (office).

ALMAGRO LEMES, Luis Leonardo; Uruguayan lawyer, diplomatist and politician; *Secretary-General, Organization of American States;* b. 1 June 1963; ed Univ. de la República, Montevideo; Rep. of Uruguay to UNESCO, Paris 1988; Pres. Int. Co-operation Cttee, Junta Nacional de Prevención del Tráfico Ilícito y Uso Abusivo de Drogas 1989–91; First Sec. (Commerce), Embassy in Iran 1991–96; with Directorate-Gen. for Political Affairs 1996; Nat. Co-ordinator, Grupo de Valdivia 1997–98; Sec., Embassy in Berlin 1998–2003; Dir of Int. Affairs, Ministry of Livestock, Agric. and Fishing 2005–07; Amb. to People's Repub. of China 2007–10; Minister of Foreign Affairs 2010–15; elected Senator 2014; mem. União de Nações Sul-Americanas (Union of South American Nations) Del. to Venezuela 2014; Sec.-Gen. OAS 2015–; mem. Movimiento de Participación Popular. *Address:* Organization of American States, 17th Street and Constitution Avenue, NW, Washington, DC 20006-4499, USA (office). *Telephone:* (202) 370-5000 (office). *Fax:* (202) 458-3967 (office). *E-mail:* pacontreras@oas.org (office). *Website:* www.oas.org (office).

ALMODÓVAR, Pedro; Spanish film director and screenwriter; b. 25 Sept. 1949, Calzada de Calatrava, Ciudad Real, Castilla La Mancha; fronted a rock band; worked at Telefónica for ten years; started career with full-length super-8 films; made 16mm short films 1974–83; f. El Deseo SA (film production co.); Pres. of Jury, Cannes Film Festival 2017; Foreign hon. mem. American Academy of Arts and Sciences 2001; Dr hc (Howard Univ.) 2009, (Univ. of Oxford) 2016; Prince of Asturias Award for the Arts 2006. *Films include:* Film político 1974, Dos putas, o historia de amor que termina en boda 1974, El Sueño, o la estrella 1975, Homenaje 1975, La caída de Sódoma 1975, Blancor 1975, Sea caritativo 1976, Muerte en la carretera 1976, Sexo va, sexo viene 1977, Salomé 1978, ¡Folle... folle... fólleme Tim! 1978, Pepe, Luci, Bom y otras chicas del montón 1980, Laberinto de pasiones 1982, Entre tinieblas 1983, ¿Qué he hecho yo para merecer esto? 1985, Matador 1986, La ley del deseo 1987, Mujeres al borde de un ataque de nervios (Felix Award) 1988, ¡Átame! 1990, Tacones lejanos 1991, Kika 1993, La flor de mi secreto 1995, Carne trémula 1997, Todo sobre mi madre (Acad. Award for Best Foreign Language Film) 1999, Hable con ella (BAFTA Award for Best Film not in the English language 2003, Acad. Award for Best Original Screenplay 2003) 2002, La mala educación 2004, Volver (Best Foreign Film Nat. Bd of Review 2006, Goya Award for Best Film, Best Dir 2007, Best Foreign Film, London Film Critics' Circle Awards 2007) 2006, Los abrazos rotos 2009, La piel que habito 2011, I'm So Excited 2013, Julieta 2016. *Publications include:* Fuego en las entrañas 1982, The Patty Diphusa Stories and Other Writings 1992. *Address:* c/o El Deseo SA, Ruiz Perelló 15, Madrid 28028, Spain (office).

ALMUNIA AMANN, Joaquín; Spanish economist, politician and fmr EU official; b. 17 June 1948, Bilbao; m.; two c.; ed Univ. of Deusto; Economist, Council Bureau of the Spanish Chambers of Commerce, Brussels 1972–75; Chief Economist, Unión General de Trabajadores (trade union) 1976–79; mem. Parl. 1979–2004, Spokesperson, Socialist Parl. Group 1994–97; mem. Fed. Cttee of the Spanish Socialist Workers' Party (Partido Socialista Obrero Español—PSOE) 1979–, Leader of the PSOE 1997–2000; Minister of Employment and Social Security 1982–86, of Public Admin 1986–91; Socialist cand. for Prime Minister 2000; EU Commr for Econ. and Monetary Affairs 2004–10, for Competition 2010–14, EC Vice-Pres. 2010–14. *Publication:* Memorias Políticas 2001. *Address:* c/o European Commission, Rue de la Loi 200, BERL 11/238, 1049 Brussels, Belgium (office).

ALOGOSKOUFIS, Georgios, MSc, PhD; Greek economist, academic and politician; b. 17 Oct. 1955, Athens; m. Dika Agapitidou; one s. two d.; ed Univ. of Athens, London School of Econs, UK; Research Assoc., Hellenic Observatory, LSE 1985–2001; Lecturer in Econs, Birkbeck Coll., Univ. of London 1988–92, Reader in Econs 1989–90; Prof. of Econs, Athens Univ. of Econs and Business 1990–; Research Fellow, Centre for Econ. Policy Research, London 1994–98; Counsellor, EC 1989–90, World Bank 1991–92; Pres. Council of Financial Experts (SOE), Ministry of Nat. Economy 1992–93; Pres. Inst. of Econ. Studies 1994–96; elected mem. Parl. 1996, mem. Parl. Cttee for Econ. Relations 1996–2004, Parl. Speaker for Political Economy 1997–2004; Minister of the Economy and Finance 2004–09; mem. Exec. Bd European Econ. Asscn 1994–98; Sayers Prize, Univ. of London 1981. *Publications:* External Constraints on Macroeconomic Policy: The European Experience 1991, The Crisis of Economic Policy 1994, Unemployment: Choices for Europe, Monitoring European Integration 5 1995, La Drachme: du Phoenix à l'euro (Acad. of Athens Prize) 2002, Greece after the Crisis 2009. *Leisure interests:* music, tennis. *E-mail:* athina@alogoskoufis.gr. *Website:* www.alogoskoufis.gr; www.aueb.gr.

ALOIS PHILIPP MARIA, HSH The Hereditary Prince of Liechtenstein, Count Rietberg, LLM; Liechtenstein royal; *Permanent Representative of the Head of State;* b. 11 June 1968, Zurich, Switzerland; s. of Prince Hans-Adam II and Princess Marie of Liechtenstein; m. HRH Duchess Sophie in Bavaria, Princess of Bavaria, now also Hereditary Princess of Liechtenstein and Countess of Rietberg 1993; three s. one d.; ed Liechtenstein Grammar School, Royal Mil. Acad., Sandhurst, UK, Salzburg Univ., Austria; heir to the throne of Liechtenstein; commissioned Second Lt, Coldstream Guards, Hong Kong and London 1988; swore Oath of Allegiance to Constitution alongside his father 1990; worked for auditing firm, London 1993–96; returned to live in Vaduz and given responsibility for various sections of the royal assets; apptd Perm. Rep. (Regent) for exercising his father's sovereign powers 15 Aug. 2004; Grand Star, Order of Merit of the Principality of Liechtenstein; Grand Decoration of Honour in Gold with Sash for Services to the Repub. of Austria 2000, King Bhumibol Adulyadej Diamond Jubilee Medal (Thailand) 2006, Sovereign Mil. Order of Malta, Grand Cross pro Merito Melitensi – Civilian Special Class 2011, King Willem-Alexander I of The Netherlands Investiture Medal 2013, Recipient of the 70th Birthday Badge Medal of King Carl XVI Gustaf (Sweden) 2016. *Address:* Fürstenhaus von Liechtenstein, Schloss Vaduz, Vaduz 9490, Liechtenstein (office). *Telephone:* 2381200 (office). *Fax:* 2381201 (office). *E-mail:* se@sfl.li (office). *Website:* www.fuerstenhaus.li/en/princely-house/hereditary-prince-alois (office).

ALOKO, Muhammad Eshaq; Afghan lawyer and government official; b. 1935, Kandahar; m.; two s. one d.; ed Mil. High School and Mil. Acad., Kabul, also studied law and admin in FRG; lived in Germany and worked at Ministry of Justice, Hamburg 1980s to early 2000s; worked as intelligence officer for fmr Pres. Mohammed Daoud Khan; First Deputy Attorney-Gen. and Pres. Comm. for Guantanamo Detainees –2008, Attorney-Gen. 2008–14. *Publications include:* Daud Khan de KGB pa lamunu ke, Jalalabad Naghmey, Puti-e-Tubi, Saharona che Amali Nashu.

ALOMAR, Raphaël; French banker and business executive; b. 28 July 1941, Tourcoing; s. of Raphaël Alomar and Jeanne Alomar (née Broutin); m. Nicole Labrunie 1964; three s.; ed Sorbonne, Paris, Ecole des Hautes Etudes Commerciales and Ecole Nationale d'Admin (ENA); Sec.-Gen. Etablissements Broutin 1966–69; Adviser to Gen. Man. Société Générale 1969–86; Prof. of Corp. Financial Man., ENA 1974–82, Pres. Alumni Asscn 1984–96; Assoc. Gen. Man. Cie de Navigation Mixte and of Via Banque 1986–93; Gov. Council of Europe Devt Bank 1993–2011; Officier, Légion d'honneur, Commdr, Order of Isabella the Catholic, Commdr, Order of the Lion of Finland. *Publication:* Financing Business Development 1981. *Address:* c/o Council of Europe Development Bank, 55 avenue Kléber, 75116 Paris, France.

ALONEFTIS, Andreas P., MBA, ADipC, FAIA, ACIS; Cypriot business executive and fmr government official; b. 24 Aug. 1945, Nicosia; s. of Polycarpos Aloneftis and Charitini Aloneftis; m. Nedi Georghiades 1967; one s. one d.; ed New York Inst. of Finance Coll. of New York Stock Exchange, Southern Methodist Univ., Harvard Univ., USA, Henley Management Coll., UK, Chartered Inst. for Securities and Investment, UK; served in Nat. Guard 1964–66; served 16 years in Cyprus Devt Bank; Gen. Man. and Chief Exec. Officer, Cyprus Investment and Securities Corpn Ltd (CISCO) 1982–88; Minister of Defence 1988–93; Gen. Man. ALICO (Cyprus) 1993–95; Man. Dir CYPRIALIFE Ltd 1995–99; Gen. Man. Insurance, Cyprus Popular Bank Group 1999–2001; Chair. and CEO Allied Capital Ltd 2001–16; Exec. Vice-Chair. Alliance Reinsurance Co. Ltd 2002–08; Chair. Bd of Govs Cyprus Broadcasting Corpn 2003–06; Business Man./Dir IKOS CIF Ltd 2005–11; Pres. Asscn of Int. Accountants 2007–09; mem. Bd of Dirs Flagstone Alliance Insurance and Reinsurance plc 2008–10; mem. Bd of Govs, Cyprus Int. Inst. of Management 2016–; Open Fellowship, Southern Methodist Univ. 1978, Salzburg Seminar Fellow 1984, Paul Harris Fellow; Fulbright Grantee 1977–78. *Publications:* numerous articles, working papers and monographs. *Leisure interests:* jogging, reading, cinema, travelling. *Address:* 10 Kastellorizo Street, Aglantzia, Nicosia 2108, Cyprus (home). *Telephone:* (22) 817970 (home). *E-mail:* alonefan@cytanet.com.cy (home).

ALONSO DÍAZ, Fernando; Spanish racing driver; b. 29 July 1981, Oviedo, Asturias; s. of José Luis Alonso; m. Raquel del Rosario 2006; ed Santo Ángel de la Guarda; began competing on karting circuit at early age, winner of several karting championships at local, regional, nat. and int. levels; first victory came in Pola Liviana 1988; World Jr Karting Champion 1996; moved to open-wheel cars 1999, Spanish Nissan Open Series Champion 1999; Formula One debut at Australian Grand Prix 2001; with Renault team 2002–06, 2008–09, with McLaren team 2007, with Ferrari team 2010–14, with McLaren-Honda team 2015–; winner Hungarian Grand Prix 2003, Chinese Grand Prix 2005, San Marino Grand Prix 2005, German Grand Prix 2005, European Grand Prix 2005, French Grand Prix 2005, Bahrain Grand Prix 2005, 2006, Malaysian Grand Prix 2005, 2007, 2012, British Grand Prix 2006, Australian Grand Prix 2006, Canadian Grand Prix 2006, Japanese Grand Prix 2006, Monaco Grand Prix 2006, 2007, Spanish Grand Prix 2006, Singapore Grand Prix 2008, Japanese Grand Prix 2008, Bahrain Grand Prix 2010, German Grand Prix 2010, Italian Grand Prix 2010, Singapore Grand Prix 2010, Korean Grand Prix 2010, British Grand Prix 2011, Malaysian Grand Prix 2012, European Grand Prix 2012, German Grand Prix 2012, Chinese Grand Prix 2013, Spanish Grand Prix 2013; winner Formula One Drivers' Championship 2005, 2006, finished third 2007, second 2010; mem. Bd of Dirs Grand Prix Drivers' Asscn; Premio Príncipe de Asturias 2005. *Leisure interests:* cycling, football, tennis. *Website:* en.hondaracingf1.com (office); www.fernandoalonso.com.

ALOR KUOL, Deng; South Sudanese politician; s. of Deng Majiok; fmr Commdr, Sudan People's Liberation Army (SPLA); attended peace talks in Nairobi 1994; fmr Minister of Cabinet Affairs, Minister of Foreign Affairs 2007, fmr Minister of Regional Co-operation; Minister of Foreign Affairs, Govt of S Sudan (following independence) 2011, of Cabinet Affairs 2013 (suspended June 2013), of Foreign Affairs and International Co-operation 2016–18; arrested on charges of coup plotting Dec. 2013 (later released into Kenyan custody); took part in Intra-SPLM Party Dialogue Arusha II (Phase Two), Arusha, Tanzania Jan. 2015; mem. Sudan People's Liberation Movt (SPLM).

ALOS, Albert, BSc, DrEng; Spanish electronic engineer, academic and fmr university administrator; *Professor Emeritus, Pan-Atlantic University;* b. 17 Sept. 1939, Barcelona; ed School of Eng, Univ. of Bilbao; Lecturer in Electrical Eng, Univ. of Ife, Lagos and Ibadan, Nigeria 1967–93; Co-founder Lagos Business School (now part of Pan-Atlantic Univ.) 1991, Dean 1993–2004, Vice-Chancellor Pan-Atlantic Univ. 2002–09, now Prof. Emer.; Chair. Ikota Educational Foundation; fmr mem. Vision 2010 Cttee; Dir of Research, Inst. for Work and Family Integration; Project Dir, Ikota Educ. Foundation; Fellow, Inst. of Dirs, Acad. of Eng, Soc. for Corp. Governance; Founding mem. Nigerian Econ. Summit Group; IEEE Award 1986, Nat. Univs Comm. Award for Dedication and Exemplary Leadership 2003, Dir Devt Award, Inst. of Dirs Nigeria 2003, Distinguished Lecturer Award, Nigerian Soc. of Engineers 2005, Award as a Great Alumnus, Univ. of Ibadan 2009, Comm. of Vice-Chancellors Award for leadership role in pvt. univs 2011, Exemplary Leadership Award, Soc. for Corp. Governance 2016. *Publications include:* The Pains & Gains of Growth: Case Studies on Entrepreneurship, Not by Chance: Memories of Lagos Business School, Sowing the Seed. *Leisure interests:* reading, tennis. *Address:* Pan-Atlantic University, Km 49, Lagos-Epe Express Way, Ajah, Lagos (office); 35 Adeola Hopewell Street, Victoria Island, Lagos, Nigeria (home). *Telephone:* 802-5014624 (mobile) (office); 802-7780670 (mobile) (home). *E-mail:* aalos@lbs.edu.ng (office). *Website:* www.lbs.edu.ng/sites/faculty_research/alos_albert (office); www.pau.edu.ng (office).

ALPER, Howard, OC, PhD, FRSC; Canadian chemist and academic; *Distinguished University Professor, University of Ottawa;* b. 17 Oct. 1941, Montreal, Quebec; s. of Max Alper and Frema Alper; m. Anne Fairhurst 1966; two d.; ed Sir George Williams Univ., McGill Univ.; NATO Postdoctoral Fellow, Princeton Univ. 1967–68; Asst Prof., State Univ. of New York at Binghamton 1968–71, Assoc. Prof. 1971–74; Assoc. Prof., Univ. of Ottawa 1975–77, Prof. 1977–, Chair. Dept of Chem. 1982–85, 1988–91, 1991–94, Asst Vice-Pres. (Research) 1995–96, Vice-Pres. (Research) 1997–2006, currently Distinguished Univ. Prof.; Pres. RSC 2001–03; Co-Chair. IAP-The Global Network of Science Acads 2006–; Chair. Govt of Canada's Science, Tech. and Innovation Council 2007–, Int. Advisory Bd, Chair. Knowledge Economy Network 2011–, Science Advisory Comm., World Econ. Forum; Vice-Chair. RIKEN Advisory Comm. 2008–; Assoc. Fellow, TWAS-Acads of Sciences of the Developing World 2003; Corresp. mem. Mexican Acad. of Sciences 2009; Titular mem. European Acad. of Arts, Sciences and Humanities; Hon. Fellow, Chemical Inst. of Canada, 2006, Chemical Research Soc. of India 2006; Hon. mem. Colombia Acad. of Sciences 2011, Hon. Foreign mem. Chemical Soc. of Japan 2013; Officier, Ordre nat. du Mérite 2002, Commdr, Order of Merit of the Republic of Italy 2014; Chemical Inst. of Canada Inorganic Chem. Award 1980, Catalysis Award 1984, Guggenheim Fellowship 1985–86, Killam Research Fellow 1986–88, Alfred Bader Award in Organic Chem. 1990, Commemorative Medal (125th Anniversary of Canada) 1992, E.W.R. Steacie Award 1993, Urgel-Archambault Prize in Physical Sciences, Math. and Eng (ACFAS) 1996, Chemical Inst. of Canada Medal 1997, Bell Canada Forum Award 1998, Gerhard Herzberg Gold Medal in Science and Eng 2000, Le Sueur Memorial Award 2002, Chemical Inst. of Canada Montreal Medal 2003. *Publications include:* more than 540 papers and more than 32 patents in the area of organometallic chem. and catalysis. *Address:* Department of Chemistry, University of Ottawa, 10 Marie Curie, D'Iorio 402, Ottawa, ON K1N 6N5, Canada (office). *Telephone:* (613) 562-5189 (office). *Fax:* (613) 562-5871 (office). *E-mail:* howard.alper@uottawa.ca (office). *Website:* www.chem.uottawa.ca (office).

ALPERN, Robert J., BA, MD; American nephrologist, academic and university administrator; *Ensign Professor of Medicine (Nephrology) and Dean, School of Medicine, Yale University;* b. 3 Nov. 1950; m. Patricia Preisig; two c.; ed Northwestern Univ., Univ. of Chicago, Columbia Presbyterian, Univ. of California, San Francisco; intern in internal medicine, Columbia Univ. 1976–77, resident in internal medicine 1977–79; Fellow in Nephrology and Renal Physiology, Univ. of California Cardiovascular Research Inst., San Francisco 1979–82, Asst Prof. of Internal Medicine, Univ. of California, San Francisco 1982; Assoc. Prof., Texas SW Medical Center, Dallas 1987–90, Chief of Nephrology 1987–98, Prof. of Medicine 1990–2004, Ruth W. and Milton P. Levy Sr Prof. of Molecular Nephrology 1994–2004, also Dean, Texas SW Medical Center 1998–2004; Ensign Prof. of Medicine and Dean, School of Medicine, Yale Univ. 2004–; mem. American Soc. of Clinical Investigation, Asscn of American Physicians, Inst. of Medicine 2007–, American Soc. of Nephrology (Pres. 2000–01), Int. Soc. of Nephrology, Soc. of Gen. Physiology, American Physiological Soc., American Heart Asscn; mem. Advisory Council Nat. Inst. of Diabetes and Digestive and Kidney Diseases; mem. Bd of Dirs, Abbott Laboratories 2008–; SW Medical Center Outstanding Teaching Award 1999, American Soc. of Nephrology John P. Peters Award 2008. *Publications:* numerous scientific articles and book chapters. *Address:* Office of the Dean, Yale School of Medicine, PO Box 208055, 333 Cedar Street, New Haven, CT 06510, USA (office). *Telephone:* (203) 785-4672 (office). *E-mail:* robert.alpern@yale.edu (office). *Website:* medicine.yale.edu/intmed/people/robert_alpern-1.profile (office).

ALPERT, Herb; American musician (trumpet), songwriter and record industry executive; b. 31 March 1935, Los Angeles, Calif.; s. of Louis Alpert and Tillie Goldberg; m. 1st Sharon Mae Lubin 1956 (divorced); two c.; m. 2nd Lani Hall; one d.; ed Univ. of Southern California; f. Herb Alpert and the Tijuana Brass 1962; Co-owner and fmr Pres. Carnival record co., later renamed A&M Record Co., Co-Chair. 1962–94; Founder and Co-Chair. Almo Sounds 1994–2002; f. Herb Alpert Foundation 1988; Lifetime Achievement Award (non-performer), Rock and Roll Hall of Fame Foundation 2005, Nat. Medal of Arts 2012. *Recordings include:* albums: The Lonely Bull 1962, Tijuana Brass 1963, Tijuana Brass Vol. 2 1963, South Of The Border 1964, Whipped Cream & Other Delights 1965, Going Places 1965, What Now My Love 1965, S.R.O. 1966, Sounds Like Us 1967, Herb Alpert's Ninth 1967, Beat Of The Brass 1968, Christmas Album 1968, Warm 1969, The Brass Are Comin' 1969, Summertime 1971, Solid Brass 1972, Four Sider 1973, You Smile, The Song Begins 1974, Coney Island 1975, Just You And Me 1976, Herb Alpert/Hugh Masekela 1978, Rise 1979, Keep Your Eyes On Me 1979, Beyond 1980, Magic Man 1981, Fandango 1982, Blow Your Own Horn 1983, Noche De Amor 1983, Bullish 1984, Wild Romance 1985, Keep Your Eye On Me 1987, Under A Spanish Moon 1988, My Abstract Heart 1989, North On South Street 1991, Midnight Sun 1992, Second Wind 1996, Passion Dance 1997, Colors 1999, Definitive Hits 2001, Lost Treasures 2005, Whipped Cream & Other Delights Rewhipped 2006, Anything Goes (with Lani Hall) 2009, I Feel You (with Lani Hall) 2011, Steppin' Out (Grammy Award for Best Pop Instrumental Album 2014) 2013, Come Fly With Me 2015. *Address:* Herb Alpert Foundation, 1414 Sixth Street, Santa Monica, CA 90401, USA. *Telephone:* (424) 272-7082. *Website:* www.herbalpert.com; www.herbalpertfoundation.org.

ALPERT, Joseph Stephen, MD; American physician and university administrator; *Professor of Medicine, Arizona Sarver Heart Center, University of Arizona;* b. 1 Feb. 1942, New Haven, Conn.; s. of Zelly C. Alpert and Beatrice A. Kopsofsky; m. Helle Mathiasen 1965; one s. one d.; ed Yale and Harvard Univs; Instructor in Medicine, Peter Bent Brigham Hosp., Harvard Univ. 1973–74; Lt-Commdr, USN, Dir Coronary Care Unit, San Diego Naval Hosp. and Asst Prof. of Medicine, Univ. of Calif., San Diego 1974–76; Dir Levine Cardiac Unit and Asst Prof. of Medicine, Peter Bent Brigham Hosp. and Harvard Univ. 1976–78; Dir Div. of Cardiovascular Medicine and Edward Budnitz Prof. of Cardiovascular Medicine, Univ. of Massachusetts Medical School 1978–92, Chair. Medicine Dept 1992–2006, Robert S. and Irene P. Flinn Prof. of Medicine 1992; Budnitz Prof. of Cardiovascular Medicine 1988–92; Chair. of Medicine Dept, Univ. of Ariz. 1992–2006 Prof. of Medicine, Arizona Sarver Heart Center 1992–; Fulbright Fellow, Copenhagen 1963–64; US Public Health Service Fellow, Harvard and Copenhagen 1966–67; NIH Special Fellow, Harvard 1972–74; Fellow, American Coll. of Physicians, American Coll. of Cardiology (Trustee 1996–2001), American Heart Asscn Clinical Council (Vice-Chair. 1991–92, Chair. 1993–95), American Coll. of Chest Physicians; mem. American Bd of Internal Medicine, Bd of Trustees 2001–03; Ed.-in-Chief, American Journal of Medicine 2005–; Gold Medal of Univ. of Copenhagen and other awards, including Gifted Teacher Award, American Coll. of Cardiology 2004. *Publications include:* The Heart Attack Handbook 1978, Physiopathology of the Cardiovascular System 1984, Modern Coronary Care 1990, Diagnostic Atlas of the Heart 1994, Cardiology for the Primary Care Physician 1998, Valvular Heart Disease 2000; co-author of other books including: Manual of Coronary Care 1978, Manual of Cardiovascular Diagnosis and Therapy 2003; author of more than 400 articles in scientific journals. *Leisure interests:* poetry, music, swimming, cycling, cooking, travel. *Address:* Department of Medicine, 6th Floor, Room 6334, Arizona Health Sciences Center, 1501 North Campbell Avenue, Tucson, AZ 85724-5035 (office); 3440 E Cathedral Rock Circle, Tucson, AZ 85718, USA (home). *Telephone:* (520) 405-8338 (office). *E-mail:* jalpert@email.arizona.edu (office). *Website:* heart.arizona.edu (office); medicine.arizona.edu (office).

ALPHANDÉRY, Edmond, DèsSc; French economist, politician and business executive; b. 2 Sept. 1943, Avignon; m. Laurence Alphandéry; one s.; ed Inst. d'études politiques de Paris, Univ. of Chicago, USA; Lecturer, Faculty of Law, Univ. d'Aix en Provence and Univ. Paris IX Dauphine 1969–71; Sr Lecturer and Dean of Faculty of Econ. Science, Univ. de Nantes 1972–74; Assoc. Prof., Univ. of Pittsburgh, USA 1975; Prof. of Econs, Univ. of Paris II 1975–93; elected Deputy to Nat. Ass. for Maine and Loire 1978–93, also Vice-Pres. then Pres. Gen. Council of Maine and Loire; mem. Finance Comm., Nat. Ass. 1979–93; Head of Investigatory Mission into European Econ. and Monetary Union 1991; Minister of the Economy 1993–95; Chair. Council of Ministers of the Economy and Finance, EU, Brussels 1995; Chair. Electricité de France (EDF) 1995–98; Founding Pres. Euro 50 Group 1999–; Chair. Supervisory Bd, CNP (Caisse Nat. de Prévoyance) Assurances SA 1998–2007, Chair. Bd of Dirs 2007–12; Chair. Centre des Professions Financières –2013, Centre for European Policy Studies, Brussels 2014–16; mem. Advisory Bd Banque de France 1996–, RWE 1997–2002, Supervisory Bd Bayernwerk AG 1997–98; Sr Adviser, Nomura Securities France; Dir (non-voting), Crédit Agricole Indosuez (fmrly Calyon) 2002–15; Dir, GDF Suez 2003–; mem. Consultative Cttee A.T. Kearney France 2013–; Fulbright Award 1967–68. *Publications:* Les politiques de stabilisation (co-author) 1974, Cours d'analyse macroéconomique 1976, Analyse monétaire approfondie 1978, 1986: Le piège 1985, La réforme obligée, sous le soleil de l'Euro 2000. *Address:* Banque Nomura France, 7 place d'Iéna, 75116 Paris, France (office). *Telephone:* 1-53-89-30-97 (office). *E-mail:* edmond.alphandery@yahoo.fr (office).

ALSHAMMAR, (Malin) Therese; Swedish swimmer; b. 26 Aug. 1977, Solna Municipality, Stockholm Co.; d. of Krister Alshammar and Britt-Marie Smedh; pnr Johan Wallberg; one s.; won three Olympic medals, 25 World Championship medals and 43 European Championship medals; European Championships (long course), Seville 1997: bronze medal, 50m freestyle, silver medal, 4×100m freestyle, Istanbul 1999: gold medal, 4×100m medley, silver medal, 50m freestyle, 4×100m freestyle, Helsinki 2000: gold medal, 50m freestyle, 100m freestyle, 4×100m freestyle, 4×100m medley, Berlin 2002: gold medal, 50m freestyle, silver medal, 4×100m freestyle, 4×100m medley, Madrid 2004: gold medal, 50m freestyle, Budapest 2006: gold medal, 50m butterfly, silver medal, 50m freestyle, Eindhoven 2008: bronze medal, 50m freestyle, Budapest 2010: gold medal, 50m butterfly, 50m freestyle, silver medal, 4×100m medley, bronze medal, 4×100m freestyle, 100m butterfly; European Championships (short course), Sheffield 1998: silver medal, 50m backstroke, 4×50m medley, Lisbon 1999: gold medal, 50m freestyle, 100m freestyle, 4×50m freestyle, 4×50m medley, Valencia 2000: gold medal, 50m freestyle, 100m freestyle, 4×50m freestyle, 4×50m medley, Antwerp 2001: gold medal, 50m butterfly, 4×50m freestyle, 4×50m medley, silver medal, 50m freestyle, Riesa 2002: gold medal, 4×50m freestyle, 4×50m medley, Trieste 2005: silver medal, 4×50m freestyle, bronze medal, 4×50m medley, Helsinki 2006: gold medal, 50m butterfly, 4×50m freestyle, silver medal, 50m freestyle, 4×50m medley; Olympic Games, Sydney 2000: silver medal, 50m freestyle, 100m freestyle, bronze medal, 4×100m freestyle; World Championships (long course), Fukuoka 2001: silver medal, 50m freestyle, 50m butterfly, Montreal 2005: bronze medal, 50m butterfly, Melbourne 2007: gold medal, 50m butterfly, silver medal, 50m freestyle, Rome 2009: silver medal, 50m freestyle, Shanghai 2011: gold medal, 50m freestyle, silver medal, 50m butterfly; World Championships (short course), Gothenburg 1997: bronze medal, 4×100m freestyle, Hong Kong 1999: bronze medal, 4×100m medley, Athens 2000: gold medal, 50m freestyle, 100m freestyle, 4×100m freestyle, 4×100m medley, Moscow 2002: gold medal, 50m freestyle, 100m freestyle, 4×100m freestyle, 4×100m medley, Indianapolis 2004: silver medal, 4×100m freestyle, bronze medal, 50m freestyle, Shanghai 2006: gold medal, 50m butterfly, silver medal, 50m freestyle, bronze medal, 4×100m freestyle, Dubai 2010: gold medal, 50m butterfly, silver medal, 100m butterfly; personal bests (long course): 50m freestyle 23.88s 2009, 100m freestyle 53.58s 2009, 50m backstroke 29.22s 2005, 50m butterfly 25.07s (world record) 2009, 100m butterfly 57.55s 2010; personal bests (short course): 50m freestyle 23.27s 2009, 100m freestyle 52.17s 2000, 50m backstroke 26.62s 2009, 100m backstroke 57.43s 2009, 50m butterfly 24.46s (world record) 2009, 100m butterfly 55.53s 2010, 100m individual medley 58.51s 2009; clubs: Sundbybergs IK, Stockholmspolisens IF, Järfälla SS –1992, SK Neptun 1993–95, 1996–2008, Helsingborgs SS 1996, Nebraska Cornhuskers 1997–99, Täby Sim 2008–; coach: Johan Wallberg; Female World Cup Overall Winner 2005/06–2007, 2010–11, FINA Swimmer of the Year 2010. *Film appearance:* The Crawl (documentary short) 2004. *Television appearances:* Time Out (series) 2003, M2A – Mission to Athens (series documentary) 2003, Nyhetsmorgon (series) 2008–11, Skavlan (series) 2010. *Address:* c/o Täby Sim, Simhallen, 183 34 Täby, Sweden. *Telephone:* (8) 768-15-44. *E-mail:* kansli@tabysim.se. *Website:* www.tabysim.se.

ALSHAYA, Mohammed Abdul Aziz, BA, MBA; Kuwaiti retail executive; *Executive Chairman, Alshaya Group;* ed Kuwait Univ., Wharton School, Univ. of Pennsylvania, USA; began career working at Mothercare (retailer) in UK for three months; joined Alshaya Group in 1980s, worked in franchise div., then CEO M. H. Alshaya Co. Retail Div. 1990–93, Exec. Chair. 1993–99, CEO Alshaya Group 1999–2002, Exec. Chair. 2002–; Chair. Mabanee (real estate co.); mem. Bd of Trustees Arab Thought Foundation, Mentor Foundation (Int.); mem. Bd of Overseers, Wharton School, Univ. of Pa; mem. Kuwaiti Supreme Council of Planning and Devt; mem. Foreign Direct Investment Council of Turkey; Retail CEO of the Year, CEO Middle East Magazine 2010. *Address:* Alshaya Group, PO Box 181, Safat 13002 (office); Alshaya Group, Pepsi Cola Street, behind Mercedes-Benz Garage, Shuwaikh, Kuwait (office). *Telephone:* 22242000 (office). *Fax:* 24842891 (office). *E-mail:* info@alshaya.com (office). *Website:* www.alshaya.com (office).

ALSOP, Marin, MusM; American violinist and conductor; *Music Director, Baltimore Symphony Orchestra;* b. 16 Oct. 1956, New York; d. of Keith LaMar Alsop and Ruth Alsop (née Condell); m. Kristin Jurkscheit Auden; one s.; ed began piano studies aged two, violin studies aged five; Juilliard Pre-Coll., Yale Univ. and Juilliard School of Music; freelance violinist with New York Symphony Orchestra, Mostly Mozart, New York Chamber Symphony, American Composers Orchestra, several Broadway shows 1976–79; began conducting studies with Carl Bamberger 1979, Harold Farberman 1985; f. String Fever (14-piece swing band) 1981; Founder and Dir Concordia Orchestra 1984–; debut with London Symphony Orchestra 1988; Assoc. Conductor Richmond Symphony 1988; studied with Leonard Bernstein, Seiji Ozawa and Gustav Meier, Tanglewood Music Center 1989; Music Dir Eugene Symphony, Ore. 1989–96, Conductor Laureate 1996–; Music Dir Long Island Philharmonic 1990–96; debut with Philadelphia Orchestra and Los Angeles Philharmonic 1990; Artistic Dir Cabrillo Festival of Contemporary Music 1992–2016; Music Dir Colorado Symphony, Denver 1993–2005; debut Schleswig Holstein Music Festival 1993; Creative Conductor Chair. St Louis Symphony Orchestra 1996–98; Prin. Guest Conductor, Royal Scottish Nat. Symphony 1999–; Prin. Guest Conductor, City of London Sinfonia 1999–; Prin. Conductor Bournemouth Symphony Orchestra (first woman to head UK symphony orchestra) 2001–07; Music Dir Baltimore Symphony Orchestra 2007–; apptd Prin. Conductor, São Paulo Symphony Orchestra 2012, Music Dir 2013–; Chief Conductor, ORF Vienna Radio Symphony Orchestra (2019–); Dir of Graduate Conducting, Peabody Inst., Johns Hopkins Univ. 2015–; guest teacher/artist, Nat. Orchestral Inst. 1991–2001, Oberlin Coll. 1998, Interlochen Center for the Arts 1998, Curtis Inst. 1998; Fellow, American Acad. of Arts and Sciences; Hon. RAM 2012, Hon. mem. Royal Philharmonic Soc. 2014, Hon. Fellow, Newnham Coll. Cambridge 2017; Hon. DLitt (Gonzaga Univ.) 1995, (Univ. of Minnesota) 2009; Leonard Bernstein Conducting Fellow, Tanglewood Music Festival 1988, 1989, Stokowski Conducting Competition 1988, Koussevitzky Conducting Prize 1989, ASCAP Award for Adventuresome Programming of Contemporary Music 1991, Univ. of Colorado Distinguished Service Award 1997, State of Colorado Gov.'s Award for Excellence in the Arts 1998, Royal Philharmonic Soc. Conducting Award 2003, Gramophone Artist of the Year 2003, Classical BRIT Award for Female Artist of the Year 2005, MacArthur Fellow and Grant 2005, MacArthur Genius Award 2005, Royal Philharmonic Soc. BBC Radio 3 Listeners' Award 2006, Musical America Award for Conductor of the Year 2009, Crystal Award 2019. *Achievements include:* first woman to conduct the orchestra at La Scala, Concertgebouw Orchestra 2007; est. Orchkids after-school programme in inner city Baltimore 2008; first woman to conduct Last Night of the BBC Promenade Concerts, London 2013. *Recordings include:* Fever Pitch, Fanfares for the Uncommon Woman, Saint-Saens, Blue Monday, Victory Stride, Fiddle Concerto for Violin and Orchestra, Gorgon, Music of Edward Collins, Too Hot to Handel, Barber Vols I–IV, Passion Wheels, Tchaikovsky Symphony No. 4, Bernstein Chichester Psalms, Brahms cycle with London Philharmonic, Barber cycle with Royal Scottish Nat. Orchestra, John Adams' Nixon in China, Bernstein's Mass. *Address:* c/o David V. Foster, Opus 3 Artists, 470 Park Avenue South, 9th Floor North, New York, NY 10016, USA (office); Intermusica Artists Management Ltd, Crystal Wharf, 36 Graham Street, London, N1 8GJ, England (office). *Telephone:* (212) 584-7568 (Opus 3) (office). *E-mail:* rachel@rachelbowron.com (office); dfoster@opus3artists.com (office); marinalsop@aol.com. *Website:* www.opus3artists.com (office); www.intermusica.co.uk (office); www.marinalsop.com.

ALSTON, Philip G., BComm, LLM, JSD; Australian academic; *John Norton Pomeroy Professor of Law, New York University;* b. 23 Jan. 1950, Melbourne; brother of Richard Alston; ed Univ. of Melbourne, Univ. of California, Berkeley, USA; Chief of Staff to Cabinet Minister, Australia, 1974–75; Human Rights Officer, UN Centre for Human Rights 1978–84; Lecturer and Visiting Prof., Harvard Law School 1984–89, 1993; Assoc. Prof. of Int. Law, Fletcher School of Law and Diplomacy, Tufts Univ., Boston 1985–89; Prof. of Law and Foundation Dir, Centre for Int. and Public Law, ANU 1989–95; Helen L. Deroy Visiting Prof. of Law, Univ. of Mich. 1993; Prof. of Int. Law, European Univ. Inst. 1996–2001, Co-Dir Acad. of European Law 1996–2001, Head of Law Dept 1997–98; Visiting Prof., Woodruff Chair of Int. Law, Univ. of Georgia 2000–01; John Norton Pomeroy Prof. of Law, School of Law, New York Univ. 2001–; Sr Legal Adviser to UNICEF 1984–92; Discrimination Commr for ACT 1992–94; rapporteur, UN Cttee on Econ., Social and Cultural Rights, 1987–90, Chair. 1991–98, UN Special Rapporteur on Extrajudicial, Summary or Arbitrary Executions 2004–10, Special Rapporteur on extreme poverty and human rights, UN Human Rights Council 2014–; rapporteur, Meeting of Chairs of UN Human Rights Treaty Bodies, 1988, 1990, 1992, 1997–98, Chair. 1990, 1993, 1997–98; mem. Tech. Advisory Group, UN study on Impact of Armed Conflict on Children 1995–97; ind. expert reporting on effectiveness of UN Human Rights Bodies, reports submitted 1989, 1993, 1997; Co-Ed. Australian Yearbook of Int. Law 1991–96, Ed.-in-Chief, European Journal of International Law 1996–2007; Series Co-Ed. Collected Courses of the Academy of European Law 1998–; Chair. Coordinating Cttee for UN Human Rights Special Procedures 2005–06. *Publications include:* The Future of UN Human Rights Treaty Monitoring (co-ed.) 2000, International Human Rights in Context: Law, Politics, Morals (with H. Steiner) 2000, Peoples' Rights (ed. and contrib.) 2001, Economic and Social Rights: A Bibliography 2005, The United Nations and Human Rights: A Critical Appraisal (ed. and contrib.) 2005, Human Rights and Development (ed.) 2005, Neglected Rights 2006; over 100 articles in journals on law and human rights. *Address:* Vanderbilt Hall, Room 305, New York University School of Law, 40 Washington Square South, New York, NY 10012-1099, USA (office). *Telephone:* (212) 998-6173 (office). *E-mail:* philip.alston@nyu.edu (office). *Website:* www.law.nyu.edu (office).

ALSTON, Hon. Richard Kenneth Robert, BA, BCom, MBA, LLM, AO; Australian diplomatist, politician and business executive; *Chairman, Waratah Group;* b. 19 Dec. 1941, brother of Philip Alston; m. Margaret Mary Alston; two c.; ed Xavier Coll., Univ. of Melbourne, Monash Univ.; Senator for Vic. 1986–2004; Shadow Minister for Communications 1989–90, for Social Security, Child Care and Retirement Incomes 1990–92, for Social Security, Child Care and Superannuation 1992, for Superannuation and Child Care and Shadow Minister Assisting Leader on Social Policy 1992–93, for Communications and the Arts 1994–96; Minister for Communications and the Arts 1996–2003, for Information Tech. 1998–2003; High Commr to UK 2005–08; Chair. TFS Corpn 2011–12 (resgnd); Chair. Waratah Group 2013–; Adjunct Prof., Faculty of Information Tech., Bond Univ., Queensland 2004–; Nat. Chair. Australian Council for Overseas Aid 1978–83; Chair. Afghan-Australia Council 1987–90; Fed. Pres. UNA of Australia 1977–79, Liberal Party of Australia 2014–; mem. Bd of Dirs Chime Communications plc 2008–; mem. Int. Advisory Bd CQS(UK) LLP 2008–; Gov. Nat. Gallery of Australia Foundation; mem. Bell Shakespeare Foundation, Melba Foundation; Fellow, Inst. of Dirs 1983–88; Centenary Medal 2001. *Leisure interests:* Aboriginal art, modern literature, Oriental rugs, jogging, reading, pumping iron. *Address:* Office of the Chairman, Waratah Group, 177 Parramatta Road, Auburn, NSW 2144 (office); Liberal Party of Australia, PO Box 6004, Kingston, ACT 2604, Australia (office). *Telephone:* (2) 8064-2923 (office); (2) 6273-2564 (Liberal Party of Australia) (office). *Fax:* (2) 9748-1050 (office); (2) 6273-1534 (Liberal Party of Australia) (office). *E-mail:* libadm@liberal.org.au (office). *Website:* www.waratahgroup.com (office); www.liberal.org.au (office).

ALTANKHUYAG, Norovyn; Mongolian politician; b. 1958, Ulaangom, Uvs Prov.; ed Mongolian State Univ., Inst. of Man. Devt, Humboldt Univ., Germany; Lecturer, Mongolian State Univ. 1981–91; apptd Sec., MSDP 1990, Vice-Chair. 1994–96, Sec.-Gen. 1999; mem. Mongolian Great Khural 1996–2000, 2001–, Acting Prime Minister Oct. 2009, Chief Deputy Prime Minister –2012, Prime Minister 2012–14; Minister of Agric. and Industry April–July 1998, Acting Minister 1998–99; Minister of Finance and Economy 2004–06; Chair. Songinohayrhan Democratic Party (DP) 2000–01, Sec.-Gen. DP 2001.

ALTBACH, Philip G., AB, AM, PhD; American professor of education, researcher and author; *Research Professor and Director, Center for International Higher Education, Lynch School of Education, Boston College;* b. 3 May 1941, Chicago, Ill.; s. of Milton Altbach and Josephine Huebsch; m. Edith Hoshino 1962; two s.; ed Univ. of Chicago; Lecturer on Educ., Harvard Univ. 1965–67, also Postdoctoral Fellow; Asst Prof., Assoc. Prof., Dept of Educational Policy Studies, Univ. of Wisconsin, Madison 1967–75; Prof., Dept of Educational Org., Admin and Policy, State Univ. of New York, Buffalo 1975, Chair. 1985–88, Dir Comparative Educ. Center 1978–94, Chair. Dept of Social Foundations 1978–82, Adjunct Prof., School of Information and Library Studies 1982, Adjunct Prof., Dept of Sociology 1991; Project Dir NSF study of higher educ. in newly industrializing countries 1988–90; Research Prof., Lynch School of Educ., Boston Coll. 1994–, J. Donald Monan SJ Prof. of Higher Educ. 1995–2013, Dir Centre for Int. Higher Educ. 1995–; Chair. Int. Advisory Council, Graduate School of Educ., Shanghai Jiao Tong Univ.; Fulbright Research Prof., Univ. of Bombay 1968; Visiting Prof., Moscow State Univ. 1982, Univ. of Malaya 1983, School of Educ., Stanford Univ. 1988–89, Institut de Sciences Politiques, Paris, Univ. of Mumbai, India; Guest Prof., Inst. of

Higher Educ., Peking Univ., China; Onwell Fellow, Univ. of Hong Kong; Sr Scholar, Taiwan Govt; Visiting Fellow, Hoover Inst., Stanford Univ. 1988–89; Sr Assoc. Carnegie Foundation for Advancement of Teaching 1992–96; N American Ed. Higher Education 1976–92, Educational Policy 1989–2005; Founding Ed. Educational Policy 1985–2004; Ed. Comparative Education Review 1978–88, International Higher Education 1994–, Review of Higher Education 1996–2004; Assoc. Ed. American Education Research Journal 2008–; Fellow, German Academic Exchange Service, Nat. Science Council of Taiwan, Japan Soc. for Promotion of Science; Consultant, Rockefeller Foundation; Distinguished Scholar Leader, Fulbright New Century Scholars Programme 2004–06; Howard Bowen Distinguished Career Achievement Award, Asscn for the Study of Higher Educ. 2009, Lifetime Career Award, Higher Educ. Group of the Comparative and Int. Educ. Society 2010. *Publications include:* Turmoil and Transition: The International Imperative in Higher Education, Comparative Higher Education, Student Politics in America, International Comparison of Academic Salaries: An Exporatory Study (co-author), The Decline of the Guru: The Academic Profession in the Third World (ed), Private Higher Education: A Global Revolution (co-ed) 2005, International Handbook of Higher Education (co-ed) 2006, Higher Education in the New Century: Global Challenges and Innovative Ideas (co-ed) 2007, Tradition and Transition: The International Imperative in Higher Education 2007, World Class Worldwide: Transforming Research Universities in Asia and Latin America (co-ed) 2008, Trends in Global Higher Education: Tracking an Academic Revolution (co-author) 2009, Leadership for World-Class Universities: Challenges for Developing Countries (ed) 2011, The Road to Academic Excellence: The Making of World Class Research Universities (co-ed) 2011, Paying the Professoriate: A Global Comparison of Compensation and Contracts (co-ed) 2012, The Global Future of Higher Education and the Academic Profession: The BRICs and the United States (co-ed) 2013, The International Imperative in Higher Education 2013; author or co-author of numerous articles in professional journals etc. *Address:* Campion Hall, Room 101, Lynch School of Education, Boston College, 140 Commonwealth Avenue, Chestnut Hill, MA 02467, USA (office). *Telephone:* (617) 552-4236 (office). *Fax:* (617) 552-0812 (office). *E-mail:* philip.altbach@bc.edu (office). *Website:* www.bc.edu/research/cihe/about/pga.html (office).

ALTER, Harvey J., BA, MD; American physician, infectious disease specialist and academic; *Chief, Infectious Disease Section and Associate Director of Research Department, Department of Transfusion Medicine, Warren Magnuson Clinical Center, National Institutes of Health;* ed Univ. of Rochester, NY, Strong Memorial Hosp., Rochester, Nat. Insts of Health, Bethesda, MD, Univ. of Washington Hosp. System, Seattle, Washington, Georgetown Univ. Hosp., Washington, DC; Instructor in Medicine, Georgetown Univ. School of Medicine 1966–68, Asst Prof. of Medicine 1968–69, Clinical Asst Prof. of Medicine 1969–71, Clinical Assoc. Prof. of Medicine 1971–88, Clinical Prof. of Medicine 1988–; Adjunct Prof., Southwest Foundation for Biomedical Research, San Antonio, TX 1986–; on Faculty, Clinical Research Training Program, NIH 1988–, currently Chief, Infectious Disease Section and Assoc. Dir Research Dept, Transfusion Medicine Warren Magnuson Clinical Center; mem. Scientific Advisory Bd Acrometrix Corpn 1999–; ISBT Liason to Int. Consortium for Blood Safety 2000–; mem. Interagency HCV Working Group 2000–, Scientific Advisory Bd Blood Centers of the Pacific 2000–, Scientific Advisory Bd Hepatitis B Foundation 2002–; Ad Hoc Consultant to Food and Drug Admin (FDA) and Blood Products Advisory Comm. 1997–, Review Panel USAID 1998, FDA Cttee on Emerging Infectious Agents 1999–; Assoc. Ed. Transfusion Medicine Reviews 1986–, Journal of Viral Hepatitis 1994–; Section Ed. 'Hepatology Highlights', Hepatology 2001–; mem. NAS 2002–, Inst. of Medicine 2002–, American Fed. for Clinical Research, American Soc. of Hematology, Int. Soc. of Hematology, Int. Soc. of Blood Transfusion, American Asscn of Blood Banks, Mid-Altantic Asscn of Blood Banks, American Asscn for the Study of Liver Diseases, Asscn of American Physicians; Fellow, American Coll. of Physicians, American Soc. of Internal Medicine; Distinguished Service Medal, USPHS 1977, NIH Directors Award 1986, Emily Cooley Award and Lectureship, American Asscn of Blood Banks 1987, Stanley Davidson Lecturer, Royal Coll. of Physicians, Scotland 1990, Karl Lansteiner Award, American Asscn of Blood Banks 1992, Leon Schiff State of Art Lectureship, American Asscn for the Study of Liver Diseases 1996, Emil von Behring Award Lectureship, Int. Soc. of Blood Transfusion 1996, James Blundell Prize, British Blood Transfusion Service 1999, Laboratory Public Service Nat. Leadership Award 1999, Year 2000 World Health Day Award, American Asscn for World Health 2000, Distinguished Scientist Award, Hepatitis B Foundation 2000, Albert Lasker Award for Clinical Medical Research 2000, Scientific Achievement Award, Hepatitis Foundation International 2001, George Hoyt Whipple Award/Lectureship, U. Roch. 2001, Seymour Kalter Lectureship, Southwest Foundation for Biomedical Research 2001, Presidential Award, Int. Soc. for Blood Transfusion 2002, Distinguished Scientist Award, American Liver Foundation 2002, Canada Gairdner Int. Award 2013. *Publications:* numerous articles in scientific journals. *Address:* National Institutes of Health, Warren G. Magunson Clinical Center, Department of Transfusion Medicine, 10 Center Drive, MSC-1184 Building 10, Room 1C711, Bethesda, MD 20892, USA (office). *Telephone:* (301) 496-8393 (office). *Fax:* (301) 402-2965 (office). *E-mail:* halter@dtm.cc.nih.gov (office). *Website:* www.cc.nih.gov (office).

ALTHER, Lisa, BA; American writer, academic and journalist; b. (Elisabeth Greene Reed), 23 July 1944, Kingsport, Tenn.; d. of John Shelton Reed and Alice Greene Reed; ed Wellesley Coll.; editorial asst, Atheneum Publrs, New York 1967–68; freelance writer 1968–; Lecturer, St Michael's Coll., Winooski, Vt 1980–81; Basler Chair, East Tennessee State Univ. 1999–2000. *Publications include:* Kinflicks 1975, Original Sins 1980, Other Women 1984, Bedrock 1990, Birdman and the Dancer 1993, Five Minutes in Heaven 1995, Kinfolks 2007, Washed in the Blood 2011, Blood Feud 2012, Stormy Weather and Other Stories 2012, About Women 2015; contrib. to periodicals. *Address:* c/o Martha Kaplan Agency, 115 West 29th Street, New York, NY 10001, USA (office). *Telephone:* (212) 279-7134 (office). *Fax:* (212) 279-6251 (office). *E-mail:* kaplanagency@sprynet.com (office); lisaalther@lisaalther.com (office). *Website:* www.lisaalther.com.

ALTMAIER, Peter; German politician; *Federal Minister for Economic Affairs and Energy;* b. 18 June 1958, Ensdorf, Saar; ed Univ. of the Saarland, Saarbrücken; joined Junge Union (CDU youth org.) 1974, State Chair., Saarland Junge Union 1988–90; joined CDU 1976, District Chair., Saarlouis CDU 2000–08, Deputy State Chair., Saarland CDU 2011–; Research Asst, European Inst., Univ. of the Saarland 1988–90; Civil Servant, European Comm. 1990–94, Gen. Sec., EEC Admin Comm. on Social Security for Migrant Workers 1993–94; mem. Bundestag (Parl.) 1994–, Legal adviser to CDU/CSU Parl. Group 2004–05, First Parl. State Sec., CDU/CSU Parl. Group 2009–12; Parl. State Sec., Fed. Ministry of the Interior 2005–09; Fed. Minister for the Environment, Nature Conservation and Nuclear Safety 2012–13; Head of Fed. Chancellery and Fed. Minister for Special Tasks 2013–18, Acting Minister of Finance 2017–18, Fed. Minister for Econ. Affairs and Energy 2018–; Pres. Europa-Union Deutschland 2006–11. *Address:* Federal Ministry of Economic Affairs and Energy, Scharnhorststr. 34–37, 10115 Berlin, Germany (office). *Telephone:* (30) 186150 (office). *Fax:* (30) 186157010 (office). *E-mail:* kontakt@bmwi.bund.de (office). *Website:* www.bmwi.de (home); www.peteraltmaier.de.

ALTMAN, Stuart Harold, BBA, MA, PhD; American health policy researcher, economist and academic; *Sol C. Chaikin Professor of National Health Policy, Heller School for Social Policy and Management, Brandeis University;* b. 8 Aug. 1937, Bronx, New York; s. of Sidney Altman and Florence Altman; m. Diane Kleinberg 1959; three d.; ed City Coll. of New York, Univ. of California, Los Angeles; Labor Market Economist, Fed. Reserve Bd 1962–64; Econ. Consultant and Manpower Economist, Office of US Asst Sec. of Defense, Washington, DC 1964–66; Asst Prof. of Econs, Brown Univ. 1966–68, Assoc. Prof. 1968–70; Univ. Fellow and Dir of Health Studies, Urban Inst. 1970–71; Deputy Admin., Office of Health, Cost of Living Council, US Dept of Health, Educ. and Welfare 1973–74, Deputy Asst Sec. for Planning and Evaluation (Health) 1971–76; Visiting Lecturer, Grad. School of Public Policy, Univ. of Calif., Berkeley 1976–77; Sol C. Chaikin Prof. of Nat. Health Policy, Heller School, Brandeis Univ. 1977–, Dean 1977–92, Co-Chair. Advisory Bd, Schneider Insts for Health Policy, Interim Pres. Brandeis Univ. 1990–91; Chair. Prospective Payment Assessment Comm., US Congress 1984–96, Advisory Bd, Mass Savings Lives Program, Commonwealth Fund 1988–89; Pres. Asscn for Health Services Research 1983–85, Nat. Foundation Health Services Research 1985–86; Chair. Health Industry Forum, Council on Health Care Econs and Policy; Co-Chair. Health Care Task Force for Commonwealth of Mass 2000–04; mem. Bd of Dirs Lincare Holdings Inc. 2001–; mem. NAS Inst. of Medicine 1996–; mem. Bd Robert Wood Johnson Clinical Scholars 1977–83, Beth Israel Hosp., Brookline, Mass 1979–91, Tufts New England Medical Center 2002–; fmr mem. Pres. Clinton's Health Policy Transition Team; Hon. Fellow, American Coll. of Health Care Execs 1996–97; Dr hc (Brandeis Univ., Rush Univ.); Special Recognition Award, American Asscn of Medical Colls 1996–97, Distinguished Investigator's Award, Acad. Health 2004. *Publications include:* The Growing Physician Surplus: Will it Benefit or Bankrupt the U.S. Health System? 1982, Ambulatory Care: Problems of Cost and Access (with others) 1983, Will the Medicare Prospective Payment System Succeed? Technical Adjustments Can Make the Difference 1986, Competition and Compassion: Conflicting Roles for Public Hospitals 1989, Strategic Choices for a Changing Health Care System 1996, The Future US Healthcare System: Who Will Care for the Poor and Uninsured? 1997, Regulating Managed Care: Theory, Practice and Future Options 1999, America's Health Care SAFETY NET: Intact but Endangered 2000, Policies for an Aging Society 2002. *Leisure interests:* sailing, cross-country skiing, boating, tennis, golf. *Address:* Heller School for Social Policy and Management, Brandeis University, 415 South Street, MS 035, Waltham, MA 02454-9110 (office); 11 Bakers Hill Road, Weston, MA 02493, USA (home). *Telephone:* (781) 736-3803 (office); (781) 891-9144 (home). *E-mail:* altman@brandeis.edu (office). *Website:* heller.brandeis.edu (office).

ALTMANN, Rev. Dr Walter, PhD; Brazilian ecclesiastic and international organization executive; *Professor of Systematic Theology, Theological College;* b. 4 Feb. 1944, Porto Alegre; s. of Friedhold Altmann and Ricarda Altmann (née Sättler); m. Madalena Zwetsch Altmann; four d.; ed studied theology in São Leopoldo, Brazil, Buenos Aires, Argentina and Univ. of Hamburg, Germany; parish pastor, Ijui, southern Brazil 1972–74; Prof. of Systematic Theology, Theological Coll., São Leopoldo 1974–2002, 2011–, Head of Theological Coll. 1981–87; Dir Ecumenical Inst. for Postgraduate Studies 1989–94; Pres. Consejo Latinoamericano de Iglesias (Latin American Council of Churches) 1995–2001; Second Vice-Pres., Evangelical Church of the Lutheran Confession in Brazil 1990–94, Vice-Pres. 1998–2002, Pres. 2002–10; mem. Council of Lutheran World Fed. 2003–06; Moderator Cen. Cttee, WCC 2006–13; Award of Merit (category: Theological Reflection), Associated Church Press (ACP) 1990. *Publications include:* more than ten books, including Der Begriff der Tradition bei Karl Rahner 1974, Luther and Liberation, A Latin American Perspective 1992, Nossa fé e suas razões: O Credo Apostólico – história, mensagem, atualidade 2004, Palavra a seu Tempo 2010, Maravilhoso Presente 2010; 180 articles on Martin Luther, Latin American theology, ethics and ecumenism; hundreds of articles in specialized magazines and reviews in Portuguese, Spanish, German and English, among others. *Address:* Theological College, Rua Pastor Rodolfo Saenger, 284 São Leopoldo RS, Brazil (office). *Telephone:* (51) 3592-6835 (office). *Fax:* (51) 3592-6835 (office). *E-mail:* waltmann@sinos.net (office); walteraltmann@msn.com.

ALTON, Roger Martin; British journalist; b. 20 Dec. 1947, Oxford; s. of Reggie Alton and Jeanine Alton; m. (divorced); one d.; ed Clifton Coll., Exeter Coll., Oxford; grad. trainee, Liverpool Post, then Gen. Reporter and Deputy Features Ed. 1969–74; Sub-Ed. News The Guardian 1974–76, Chief Sub-Ed. News 1976–81, Deputy Sports Ed. 1981–85, Arts Ed. 1985–90, Weekend Magazine Ed. 1990–93, Features Ed. 1993–96, Asst Ed. 1996–98, Ed. The Observer (British Press Award for Newspaper of the Year 2007) 1998–2007, The Independent 2008–10; Exec. Ed. The Times 2010–15; writes sport column for The Spectator 2008–; Editor of the Year, What the Papers Say Awards 2000, GQ Editor of the Year 2005. *Leisure interests:* mountaineering, skiing, films, sports. *Address:* The Spectator, 22 Old Queen Street, London, SW1H 9HP, England (office). *Telephone:* (20) 7961-0200 (office). *Website:* www.spectator.co.uk/author/roger-alton.

ALTSCHUL, Stephen F., PhD; American mathematician; *Senior Investigator, Computational Biology Branch, National Center for Biotechnology Information;* b. 28 Feb. 1957; ed Harvard Coll. and Massachusetts Inst. of Tech.; Guest, Rockefeller Univ., New York 1977–78, Guest Investigator 1984–86; NSF Grad. Fellow, MIT 1981–84; Research Asst, Univ. of N Carolina 1986–87; Postdoctoral Fellow, Nat. Inst. of Diabetes, and Digestive and Kidney Diseases/Math. Research Br., Bethesda, MD 1987–89; Staff Fellow, Nat. Library of Medicine/Nat. Center for

Biotechnology Information, Bethesda 1989–91, Sr Staff Fellow 1991–94, Sr Investigator, Computational Biology Br. 1994–, Chair. 1996–98; Adjunct Prof., Univ. of Maryland 2002–07; mem. Advisory Bd Genome Biology 1999–2010; Fellow, American Coll. of Medical Informatics 2001; Pehr Edman Award, Int. Asscn for Protein Structure Analysis and Proteomics 2004. *Publications:* numerous articles in scientific journals. *Address:* Computational Biology Branch, National Center for Biotechnology Information, National Library of Medicine, National Institutes of Health, Bethesda, MD 20894, USA (office). *Telephone:* (301) 435-7803 (office). *Fax:* (301) 480-2288 (office). *E-mail:* altschul@ncbi.nlm.nih.gov (office). *Website:* www.ncbi.nlm.nih.gov (office).

ALTYNBAYEV, General (retd) Mukhtar; Kazakhstani air force officer (retd) and politician; b. 10 Dec. 1945, Karaganda; m. Gulbanu Rahimbaevna Altynbayeva; one s.; ed Karaganda Aviation Centre, Armavir Air Defence Mil. School, G.K. Jukov Air Defence Mil. Acad.; started career as miner, Karaganda 1962–66; graduated pilot school 1964; became pilot-cadet Kinnel-Cherkassy Aviation Training Centre 1965; held various mil. command positions including Flight Commdr, Squadron Commdr, Deputy Commdr of training regiment 1972–75, apptd Commdr of a fighter's regiment Ural Dist 1979; Deputy Div. Commdr then Commdr of Air Defence Div., Turkestan Mil. Dist 1985–88, Commdr of Air Defence Corps 1992; apptd Air Defence Commdr and Deputy Defence Minister 1992, Air Forces Commdr 1993, Minister of Defence 1996, 2001–06, Acting Minister of Defence June 2009; mem. Senate 2010–, mem. Int. Affairs, Defense and Security Cttee. *Address:* Senate (Senat), 010000 Nur-Sultan, Abay d-ly 33, Parliament House, Kazakhstan (office). *Telephone:* (7172) 74-72-39 (office). *Fax:* (7172) 24-26-19 (office). *Website:* www.parlam.kz (office).

ALVA, Margaret, BA, BL; Indian lawyer, social worker, trade unionist and politician; b. 14 April 1942, Mangalore, Karnataka; d. of Shri P. A. Nazareth and Elizabeth L. Nazareth; m. Niranjan Alva 1964; three s. one d.; ed Mount Carmel Coll. and Govt Law Coll., Bangalore; Gen. Sec., All India Catholic Univ. Fed. 1961; Jt Sec., Govt Law Coll. Students' Union 1963–64; State Convenor, Karnataka Pradesh Congress Women's Front 1972–73, Congress Party (now Indian Nat. Congress) Standing Cttee on Information and Broadcasting 1975–76; MP 1974–2004; elected to Rajya Sabha (Council of States) 1974–98, Deputy Chief Whip Congress Party 1993–95, Gen. Sec. –2008 (resgnd); Union Minister of State for Parl. Affairs 1984–85, for Youth Affairs, Sports, Women and Child Devt 1985–89, for Personnel, Public Grievances and Pensions 1991 (with additional charge of Parl. Affairs 1993–96); mem. 13th Lok Sabha 1999 (mem. Panel of Chairmen), Cttee on Transport and Tourism 1999–2000, House Cttee 1999–2000, Gen. Purposes Cttee 1999–2000; Chair. Cttee on Empowerment of Women 2000–01; mem. Consultative Cttee, Ministry of Tourism 2000–04; Gov. of Uttarakhand 2009–12, of Rajasthan 2012–14, of Goa July–Aug. 2014, of Gujarat July–Aug. 2014; Spokesperson, Congress Parl. Party; Pres. Delhi YWCA 1975–78, World Women Parliamentarians for Peace 1986–88; Founder-Pres. Karuna (NGO working for women and children); mem. Indian Del. to UN Conf., Mexico 1975, UN Gen. Ass. 1976; mem. All India Congress Cttee, Int. Fed. of Women Lawyers, Nat. Children's Bd 1977–78, Nat. Adult Educ. Bd 1978–79, IPU Coordinating Cttee of Women Parliamentarians 2000–; Hon. DLitt (Mysore) 1989; Mahila Siromani Award 1991, Rajiv Gandhi Excellence Award 1991, Dr T.M.A. Pai Foundation Outstanding Konkani Award 1991, Global Leadership Award, Vital Voices Global Partnership 2007. *Leisure interests:* painting, music, drama, travel. *Address:* 11 Milton Street, Cooke Town, Bangalore 560 001, India (home). *Telephone:* (80) 5469799 (home).

ALVA CASTRO, Luis; Peruvian politician and economist; b. 17 Feb. 1942, Trujillo; ed Univ. Nacional de Trujillo and Univ. Inca Garcilaso de la Vega; fmr Dir Corporación de Desarrollo Económico y Social de la Libertad; Deputy for Libertad; has held various posts in Partido Aprista Peruano including Sec.-Gen. of Northern Regional Org., mem. Political Comm. and Nat. Sec. for Electoral Matters; Chair. Nat. Planning Comm. of Partido Aprista Peruano; Second Vice-Pres. of Repub. 1985–90, Pres. Council of Ministers (Prime Minister) 1985–90, Minister of Economy and Finance 1985–87, of the Interior 2007–08 (resgnd); re-elected to Congress 2000–11, Pres. of the Congress 2009–10; Pres. Comm. for Integration and Inter-parl. Relations 2001–02; Pres. Econ. Comm. 2001–06; Pres. Andean Parl. Aug.–Dec. 2001, Vice-Pres. 2002–07. *Publications:* La Necesidad del Cambio, Manejo Presupuestal del Perú, En Defensa del Pueblo, Endeudamiento Externo del Perú, Deuda Externa: Un reto para los Latinoamericanos and other books and essays. *Address:* Partido Aprista Peruano, Av Alfonso Ugarte N° 1012, Breña, Peru (office). *Telephone:* (1) 2931943 (office). *E-mail:* info@apra.org.pe (office). *Website:* www.apra.org.pe (office).

ALVARADO QUESADA, Carlos, MSc, MA; Costa Rican novelist, politician and head of state; *President;* b. 14 Jan. 1980, San José; s. of Alejandro Alvarado Induni and Adelia Quesada Alvarado; m. Claudia Dobles Camargo; one s.; ed Univ. of Costa Rica, Univ. of Sussex Inst. of Devt Studies; Adviser to Partido Acción Ciudadana parl. group, Legis. Ass. (parl.) 2006–10; Asst Brand Man., Procter & Gamble, Panama 2011–12; Prof., School of Sciences of Collective Communication, Univ. of Costa Rica and School of Journalism, Univ. Latina de Costa Rica; Communication Dir for presidential campaign of Luis Guillermo Solís 2014; Minister of Labour and Social Security 2016–17; Pres. of Costa Rica 2018–; mem. Partido Acción Ciudadana (PAC). *Publications include:* Transcripciones Infieles (short stories) 2006, La historia de Cornelius Brown (novel) (Premio Joven Creación de la Editorial Costa Rica) 2007, Las Posesiones (novel) 2012, Temporada en Brighton (novel) 2015. *Address:* Casa Presidencial, Zapote, Apdo 520, 2010 San José, Costa Rica (office). *Telephone:* 2207-9100 (office). *Fax:* 2253-9078 (office). *E-mail:* sugerencias@presidencia.go.cr (office). *Website:* www.presidencia.go.cr (office).

ALVAREZ, Aida, BA; American journalist and fmr government official; b. Aguadilla, Puerto Rico; ed Harvard Univ.; fmr news reporter and presenter, Metromedia TV, New York; fmr reporter, New York Post; fmr mem. New York City Charter Revision Comm.; fmr Vice-Pres. New York City Health and Hosps Corpn; investment banker, First Boston Corpn New York, San Francisco 1986–93; Dir Office Fed. Housing Enterprise Oversight 1993–97; Dir US Small Business Admin, Washington, DC 1997–2001; Chair. Latino Community Foundation of San Francisco; mem. Bd of Overseers, Harvard Univ. 2000–; mem. Bd of Dirs UnionBanCal Corpn 2004–, Wal-Mart Stores Inc. 2006–; mem. Diversity Advisory Bd Deloitte & Touche LLP; Trustee Latino Community Foundation; fmr mem. Bd of Dirs Nat. Hispanic Leadership Agenda, New York Community Trust, Nat. Civic League; fmr Chair. Bd Municipal Assistance Corpn/Victim Services Agency, New York; NY State Chair. Gore Presidential Campaign 1988; Nat. Co-Chair. Women's Cttee Clinton Presidential Campaign 1992; mem. Pres. Econ. Transition Team 1992; official spokeswoman for Senator John Kerry during 2004 US presidential elections; Hon. LLD (Iona Coll.) 1985; Front Page Award 1982, Assoc. Press Award for Excellence 1982.

ALVAREZ, Carlos Alberto (Chaco); Argentine politician and international organization official; b. 26 Dec. 1948, Buenos Aires; m. Liliana Chiernajowsky; one s. three d.; ed Mariano Acosta Coll., Univ. of Buenos Aires; Assessor, Regional Econ. Cttee of Nat. Senate 1983–89; Deputy to Nat. Ass. (Partido Justicialista) for Fed. Capital 1989–93, 1997–99; left Partido Justicialista and f. Partido Movimento por la Democracia y la Justicia Social (MODEJUSO) 1990; f. Frente Grande; Pres. Frente Grande Bloc in Nat. Constitutional Convention 1994; Founder, Leader Frente del País Solidario—FREPASO 1994–2001; Vice-Pres. of Argentina 1999–2000 (resgnd); Pres. Cttee of Perm. Reps, Mercosur 2005–09; Sec.-Gen. Latin American Integration Asscn 2011–17.

ALVAREZ, Ralph, BBA; American business executive; *Executive Chairman, Skylark Co. Ltd;* b. 1955, Cuba; ed Univ. of Miami; worked for Burger King Corpn 1977–89, held several exec. positions including Man. Dir Burger King Spain, Pres. Burger King Canada, Regional Vice-Pres. for Florida Region; Corp. Vice-Pres. and Div. Vice-Pres.—Florida, Wendy's International Inc. 1990–94; joined McDonald's 1994, several exec. positions including Pres. McDonald's Mexico, Chief Operations Officer and Pres. Cen. Div., McDonald's USA, Pres. McDonald's N America 2005–06, mem. Bd of Dirs, Pres. and COO McDonald's Corpn 2006–09; Exec. Chair. Skylark Co. Ltd (restaurant chain owner), Tokyo 2013–; mem. Bd of Dirs Eli Lilly and Co. 2009–, Dunkin' Donuts 2012–, Lowes Cos Inc.; serves on Pres.'s Council and Int. Advisory Bd, Univ. of Miami, Fla; fmr Pres. Ronald McDonald House Charities, Mexico; mem. Bd of Trustees, Field Museum, Chicago. *Address:* Office of the Executive Chairman, Skylark Co. Ltd, 1-25-8, Nishikubo, Musashino, Tokyo 180-0013, Japan (office). *Website:* www.skylark.co.jp (office).

ÁLVAREZ ÁLVAREZ, José Antonio, MA, MBA; Spanish banking executive; *CEO, Santander Group;* b. 1960, León; ed Univ. of Chicago, USA; joined Santander 2002, Exec. Vice-Pres. of Financial Man. and Investor Relations Div. (Chief Financial Officer) 2004–14, mem. Bd of Dirs and CEO Santander Group 2015–, mem. Bd of Dirs, Banco Santander (Brasil) SA, SAM Investments Holdings Ltd, fmr Dir, Santander Consumer Finance, SA, fmr mem. Supervisory Bd, Santander Consumer AG, Santander Consumer Holding GmbH, Santander Holdings USA, Inc., Bank Zachodni WBK; fmr Dir Bolsas y Mercados Españoles. *Address:* Santander Group, City Avenida de Cantabria s/n, 28660 Boadilla del Monte, Madrid, Spain (office). *Telephone:* (90) 2112211 (office). *E-mail:* comunicacion@gruposantander.com (office). *Website:* www.santander.com (office).

ÁLVAREZ MARTÍNEZ, HE Cardinal Francisco, DCL; Spanish ecclesiastic; *Archbishop Emeritus of Toledo;* b. 14 July 1925, Santa Eulalia de Ferroñes; ordained priest 1950; consecrated Bishop of Tarazona 1973; Bishop of Calahorra and La Calzada 1976–89, of Orihuela 1989–95; Archbishop of Toledo 1995–2002, Archbishop Emer. 2002–; Apostolic Admin. of Cuenca 1996; cr. Cardinal-Priest, S. Maria "Regina Pacis" a Monte Verde 2001. *Address:* Archdiocese of Toledo, Arco de Palacio 2, 45002 Toledo, Spain (office). *Telephone:* (25) 224100 (office); (25) 223439 (home). *Fax:* (25) 222639 (office); (25) 222771 (home). *E-mail:* arztoletan@planalfa.es (office). *Website:* www.architoledo.org (office).

ÁLVAREZ-PALLETE LÓPEZ, José María; Spanish business executive; *Chairman and CEO, Telefónica SA;* b. 12 Dec. 1963, Madrid; ed Complutense Univ. of Madrid, Free Univ. of Brussels, Belgium, Instituto Panamericano de Alta Dirección de Empresa, Mexico City; began career with Arthur Young 1987; with Benito & Monjardín/Kidder, Peabody & Co. 1988–95; Head of Investor Relations and Studies Dept, Cementos Portland (Cemex) 1995–96, Financial Man. for Spain 1996–98, Gen. Man. for Admin and Finance, responsible for Cemex Groups interests in Indonesia and mem. Bd, Cemex Asia Ltd 1998–99; Gen. Man. of Corp. Finance, Telefónica, SA 1999–2002, Chair. and CEO 2002–06, Man. Dir Telefónica Latin America 2006–09, Chair. and CEO Telefónica Latin America 2009–11, Chair. and CEO Telefonica Europe 2011–12, COO Telefónica, SA 2012–16, mem. Bd of Dirs, Chair. and CEO 2016–, mem. Exec. Cttee; Hon. mem. Carlos III Foundation Latin-American Forum 2003; CFO Europe Best Practice Award (category of Mergers and Acquisitions 2000), CFO Europe Magazine (The Economist Group) 2001, 'Forum de Alta Dirección' Golden Master 2007, Best Business Leader, El Economista 2011, Award of Excellence, Asscn of Telecommunication Tech. Engineers 2013, Medalla Sorolla, Hispanic Soc. of America 2014, recognized by Latin Trade as Innovative Corp. Leader of the Year, Bravo Business Awards 2014. *Address:* Telefónica SA, Gran Vía 28, 28013 Madrid, Spain (office). *Telephone:* (91) 584-0306 (office). *Fax:* (91) 531-9347 (office). *E-mail:* info@telefonica.com (office). *Website:* www.telefonica.com (office).

ÁLVAREZ RENDUELES, José Ramón, LLM, PhD; Spanish fmr central banker, business executive and university professor; *Chairman and President, ArcelorMittal España SA;* b. 17 June 1940, Gijón; s. of Ramón Alvarez Medina; m. Eugenia Villar 1964; four s. one d.; State Economist 1964; rank of Full Prof. in Public Finance 1973; Head of Econ. Studies in Planning Comm. 1969; Dir Inst. of Econ. Devt 1973; Tech. Sec.-Gen., Ministry of Finance 1973–75, Under-Sec. for Econ. Affairs 1975–76; Sec. of State for Econ. Affairs 1977–78; Gov. Bank of Spain 1978–84; Chair. COFIR 1988–93, Productos Pirelli 1986–, Peugeot España 1996; Chair. and Pres. Aceralia Corporacion Siderurgica SA (merged into Arcelor 2001, became part of ArcelorMittal 2006), ArcelorMittal España SA 1997–; Pres. Prince of Asturias Foundation 1996–2008; Gran Cruz Mérito Civil, Gran Cruz Isabel la Católica, Legión d'Honneur (France). *Publications:* Valoración actual de la imposición sobre consumo 1971, La Hacienda pública y el medio ambiente 1973. *Leisure interests:* golf, music, literature, lawn tennis. *Address:* ArcelorMittal España SA, Lugar Residencia la Granda S/N, 33440 Gozón, Principality of Asturias (office); Peguerinos 12-F, 28035 Madrid, Spain (home). *Telephone:* (98) 5187000 (office). *Fax:* (98) 5126088 (office). *E-mail:* comunicaespana@arcelormittal.com (office). *Website:* flateurope.arcelormittal.com (office).

ALVI, Arif-ur-Rehman, BDS; Pakistani politician, head of state and fmr dentist; *President;* b. 29 Aug. 1949, Karachi; s. of Habib-ur-Rehman Elahi Alvi; m. Samina Alvi; four c.; ed De Montmorency Coll. of Dentistry, Lahore, Univ. of Michigan, Univ. of Pacific, San Francisco; practised as dentist in Karachi; f. Alvi Dental Hosp., Karachi; fmr Dean of Orthodontics, Coll. of Physicians and Surgeons of Pakistan; Pres., Pakistan Dental Asscn 1997–2001, Pakistan Asscn of Orthodontists 2005, Asia Pacific Dental Fed. 2006–07; Councillor, World Dental Fed. 2007–13; Founding mem. Pakistan Tehreek-e-Insaf (PTI, Pakistan Movement for Justice) 1996, mem. PTI Cen. Exec. Cttee, Pres., PTI Sindh 1997–2001, Central Vice Pres. 2001–06, PTI Sec.-Gen. 2006–13; mem. Nat. Ass. (PTI) from Karachi 2013–18; Pres. of Pakistan 2018–. *Address:* Office of the President, Aiwan-e-Sadr, Islamabad, Pakistan (office). *Telephone:* (51) 9010100 (office). *Fax:* (51) 9208046 (office). *E-mail:* protocol@president.gov.pk (office). *Website:* www.presidentofpakistan.gov.pk (office).

ALWARD, David Nathan, BA, MA; Canadian politician; *Consul-General to Boston;* b. 2 Dec. 1959, Beverly, Mass, USA; s. of Rev. Ford Alward and Jean Alward; m. Rhonda Alward; two s.; ed Bryan Coll., Dayton, Tenn., USA; civil servant with Fed. Govt 1982–96; self-employed as human resource devt and community devt consultant 1996–99; owner of small family cattle farm, Riceville, NB; MLA for Woodstock electoral dist 1999–, mem. Select Cttee to Review Appointments by Lt-Gov.-in-Council, Select Cttee on Pvt. Passenger Automobile Insurance; NB Minister of Agric., Fisheries and Aquaculture 2003–06; Premier of NB 2010–14, also Minister of Intergovernmental Affairs 2010–14; mem. Progressive Conservative Party of NB, Leader 2008–14; Consul-Gen. to Boston 2015–. *Address:* Consulate-General of Canada, 3 Copley Place, Suite 400, Boston, MA 02116, USA (office). *Telephone:* (617) 247-5100 (office). *Fax:* (617) 247-5190 (office). *E-mail:* bostn@international.gc.ca. *Website:* www.can-am.gc.ca/boston.

ALWARD, Peter Andrew Ulrich; British classical music consultant; b. 20 Nov. 1950, London; s. of Herbert Andrew Alward and Marion Evelyne Schreiber; ed Bryanston School, Guildhall School of Music and Drama; worked for Simrock Music Publrs 1968–70; EMI Records UK 1970–74, European Co-ordinator EMI Classical Div. (Munich) 1975–83, Exec. Producer for all EMI recordings with Herbert von Karajan 1976–89, Man. (UK) Artists and Repertoire 1983, Int. Dir A&R 1985, Vice-Pres. 1989, Sr Vice-Pres. 1997, Pres. EMI Classics 2002–04; mem. Royal Opera House Covent Garden Opera Advisory Bd 1998–99; mem. Bd Trustees Young Concert Artists Trust 1999–2004; mem. Artistic Cttee, Herbert von Karajan Stiftung 2003–10; mem. European Advisory Bd, The Cleveland Orchestra 2009–11; Trustee, Masterclass Media Foundation 2006–15; mem. Editorial Advisory Bd, BBC Music 2006–16; Dir (non-exec.) Royal Opera House Enterprises 2007–16, Opera Rara 2009–11; mem. Kuratorium Salzburg Int. Stiftung Mozarteum 2008–13; consultant, Bavarian Radio Symphony Orchestra record label 2008–; Jury Pres. ARD Piano Competition Munich 2011; Jury Vice-Pres. Santander Piano Competition 2012; Jury mem. Salzburg Festival/Nestlé Young Conductors Award 2010–; Intendant and Man. Dir Osterfestspiele Salzburg (Salzburg Easter Festival) 2010–15; Ring of the City of Salzburg; Gramophone Special Achievement Award 2004. *Leisure interests:* classical music, painting and sculpture, theatre, books, collecting stage and costume designs, cooking, travelling. *Address:* 24 Midway, Walton-on-Thames, Surrey, KT12 3HZ, England (home). *Telephone:* (1932) 226741 (home). *E-mail:* peter@wotan844.fsnet.co.uk (home).

ALZAHID, Sheikh; **Issam;** Saudi Arabian business executive; *Chairman, Alzahid Group of Companies;* Chair. Alzahid Group of Companies (f. by Alzahid Family as Alzahid Construction 1951), significant interests in mining, logistics, oil and gas, manufacturing, information technology, foodstuffs, retail and many other sectors. *Address:* Alzahid Group Headquarters, Silver Tower Street, Al-Khobar 31952, Eastern Saudi Arabia (office). *Telephone:* (3) 8656323 (office). *Fax:* (3) 8950948 (office). *E-mail:* chairman@alzahidgroup.com (office). *Website:* www.alzahidgroup.com (office).

AMADOU, Hama; Niger politician; b. 1950; m.; three c.; ed Ecole nationale d'administration, Niamey, École nationale d'administration, France; started career as regional inspector of customs in Zinder and Maradi 1972–74; Deputy Prefect of Agadez 1978–80, Gen. Secr. Zinder prefecture 1980; fmr Head of Ministry of Information; fmr Man. Dir Niger Broadcasting Bd; fmr Pvt. Sec. to Pres. Seyni Kountche and Pres. Ali Saibou; Prime Minister of Niger 1995–96, 2000–07; Sec.-Gen. Mouvement national pour une société de développement—Nassara 2001–09; arrested on corruption charges 2008, imprisoned and released on health reasons 2009; went into exile in France, returned to Niger 2010; Founder and Pres. Mouvement Démocratique Nigérien (Moden) 2010–; unsuccessful cand. (Moden) for Pres. of Niger 2011; mem. Nat. Ass. (Parl.) 2011–, Pres. Nat. Ass. 2011–14; cand. in presidential election 2016. *Address:* c/o National Assembly, pl. de la Concertation, BP 12234, Niamey, Niger (office).

AMAN, Dato' Sri Anifah bin Haji, BA; Malaysian politician; b. 16 Nov. 1953, Keningau, Sabah; m. Siti Rubiah Abdul Samad; three s.; ed Univ. of Buckingham, UK; Cttee mem., Beaufort Div., Malay Nat. Org. (UMNO) 1991–94, Treasurer 1994–99, Head of Kimanis Div. 2004–; mem. Parl. for Beaufort 1999–; Deputy Minister of Primary Industries 1999–2004, of Plantation Industries and Commodities 2004–08; Minister of Foreign Affairs 2009–18; fmr Man. Sabah Football M-League Team; fmr Vice-Pres., Exec. Cttee mem. and Council mem., Football Asscn of Malaysia; fmr Pres. Sabah Football Asscn; Ahli Setia Darjah Kinabalu 1994, Panglima Gemilang Darjah Kinabalu 1998, Darjah Mahkota Pahang 2004; Special Award of Leadership for Sports, Ministry of Culture 1996. *Leisure interests:* football, golf. *Address:* United Malays National Organization, Menara Dato' Onn, 38th Floor, Jalan Tun Ismail, 50480 Kuala Lumpur, Malaysia (office). *Telephone:* (3) 40429511 (office). *Fax:* (3) 40412358 (office). *E-mail:* email@umno.net.my (office). *Website:* www.umno-online.my (office).

AMAN, Air Marshal Sohail, BSc, MSc, MA; Pakistani air force officer; b. 10 June 1959, Lahore; m.; four c.; ed Pakistan Air Force (PAF) War Coll., Kings College, London, UK, PAF Air War Coll.; commissioned in Gen. Duty Pilots br. of Pakistan Air Force 1980, has held several operational positions, including Chief Flying Instructor F-16, CCS, commanded a Fighter Squadron, Combat Commanders School and Fighter Base, has also held several staff positions, including Dir of Operations, Dir of Plans, Asst Chief of Air Staff (Operations), Air Officer Commanding, Central Air Command, Deputy Chief of Air Staff (Training/Operations) –2015, Chief of Air Staff 2015–18; Patron-in-Chief Ski Fed. of Pakistan; Nishan-e-Imtiaz (Order of Excellence), Hilal-e-Imtiaz (Crescent of Excellence), Sitara-e-Imtiaz (Star of Excellence), Tamgha-i-Imtiaz (Medal of Excellence), US Legion of Merit 2018. *Address:* c/o Pakistan Air Force Air Headquarters, E9, 44230 Islamabad, Pakistan (office). *Telephone:* (51) 9507751 (office). *Fax:* (51) 9260868 (office). *E-mail:* mediaaffair@paf.gov.pk (office). *Website:* www.paf.gov.pk (office).

AMANI, Michel N'Guessan; Côte d'Ivoirian politician; b. 1957, Messoukro; fmr teacher of history and geography in various secondary schools in Bouaké, Botro and Bodokro; Sec.-Gen. Front Populaire Ivoirien (FPI) for Bouaké 1990–92, Fed.-Sec. for Centre region 1992; Minister of Nat. Educ. 2000–07, of Defence 2007–11.

AMANN, Ronald, MSocSc, PhD, FRSA, ACSS; British academic and civil servant (retd); *Professor Emeritus of Comparative Politics, University of Birmingham;* b. 21 Aug. 1943, North Shields; s. of George Amann and Elizabeth Towell; m. Susan Peters 1965; two s. one d.; ed Heaton Grammar School, Newcastle-upon-Tyne and Univ. of Birmingham; Consultant, OECD and Research Assoc. 1965–69; Lecturer, Sr Lecturer in Soviet Science Policy, Univ. of Birmingham 1969–83, Dir Centre for Russian and East European Studies (CREES) 1983–89, Prof. of Comparative Politics 1986–, now Prof. Emer., Dean Faculty of Commerce and Social Science 1989–91, Pro-Vice-Chancellor 1991–94; Chief Exec. and Deputy Chair. Econ. and Social Science Research Council (ESRC) 1994–99; Dir-Gen. Centre for Man. and Policy Studies, Cabinet Office 1999–2002; Chair. Centre for Research on Innovation and Competition, Univ. of Manchester; Visiting Fellow, Osteuropa Inst. Munich 1975; Specialist Adviser, House of Commons Select Cttee on Science and Tech. 1976, mem. Steering Cttee, Centre for the Analysis of Risk and Regulation, LSE; Founding Academician, Acad. of Learned Socs. for the Social Services 1999; ind. mem. West Midlands Police Authority 2007–12. *Publications:* co-author: Science Policy in the USSR 1969, The Technological Level of Soviet Industry 1977, Industrial Innovation in the Soviet Union 1982, Technical Progress and Soviet Economic Development 1986. *Leisure interests:* walking, modern jazz, cricket. *Address:* 26 Spring Road, Edgbaston, Birmingham, B15 2HA, England (home). *Telephone:* (121) 440-6186 (home).

AMANO, Hiroshi, BE, ME, DE, FInstP; Japanese physicist and academic; *Professor, Nagoya University;* b. 11 Sept. 1960, Hamamatsu; ed Nagoya Univ.; Research Assoc., Nagoya Univ. 1988–92, Prof. 2010–; Asst Prof., Meijo Univ. 1992–98, Assoc. Prof. 1998–2002, Prof. 2002–10; mem. SPIE, American Physical Soc., Optical Soc. of America, Japan Soc. for Applied Physics; Special Award, Fifth Optoelectronics Conf. 1994, IEEE/LEOS Eng Achievement Award 1996, APEX/JJAP Editorial Contrib. Award, Japan Soc. of Applied Physics 2014, Nobel Prize for Physics (co-recipient with Isamu Akasaki and Shuji Nakamura for the invention of blue light-emitting diodes (LEDs)) 2014. *Publications:* Wide Bandgap Semiconductors 2007, Nitrides with Nonpolar Surfaces (co-author) 2008, Frontier of Ultra-High Efficiency Solar Cells and Their Materials 2011, Bandgap Enginnering, Section Two – Current Status of Light Source LED 2011, III-Nitride Based Light Emitting Diodes and Applications, Introduction Part A. Progress and Prospect of Growth of Wide-Band-Gap III-Nitrides 2013; numerous papers in professional journals. *Address:* Graduate School of Engineering, Department of Electrical Engineering and Computer Science, Furo-cho, Chikusa-ku, Nagoya 464-8601, Japan (office). *E-mail:* amano@nuee.nagoya-u.ac.jp (office). *Website:* www.nuee.nagoya-u.ac.jp (office).

AMANO, Mari; Japanese diplomatist and international organization executive; *Secretary-General, Asian Productivity Organization;* m.; three d.; ed Univ. of Tokyo, Hertford Coll., Oxford, UK; career diplomat for over 30 years in Ministry of Foreign Affairs, posts have included service in Econ. Affairs Bureau, Ministry of Foreign Affairs 1980–84, Embassy in Kuwait 1984–87, Perm. Mission to OECD, Paris 1987–92, Minister at Embassies in Thailand 1994–96, USA 1996–98, Deputy Dir-Gen. in Multilateral Co-operation Dept, Ministry of Foreign Affairs 2000–01, Chief Negotiator for Trade Related Investment Measures in Uruguay Round 2000–03, Consul Gen., Houston, Tex. 2001–04; Deputy Exec. Dir Korean Peninsula Energy Devt Org. (KEDO) Secr. 2004–07; Deputy Sec.-Gen. OECD, in charge of Devt Cluster and Policy Coherence dossier 2007–11; Amb. and Perm. Rep. of Japan to Conf. on Disarmament 2011–13; Sec.-Gen. Asian Productivity Org., Tokyo 2013–. *Address:* Asian Productivity Organization, Leaf Square Hongo Building, 2F 1-24-1 Hongo, Bunkyo-ku, Tokyo 113-0033, Japan (office). *Telephone:* (3) 3830-0411 (office). *Fax:* (3) 5840-5322 (office). *E-mail:* apo@apo-tokyo.org (office). *Website:* www.apo-tokyo.org (office).

AMANO, Yukiya; Japanese diplomatist and international organization official; *Director General, International Atomic Energy Agency;* b. 9 May 1947, Kanagawa Pref.; m.; ed Univ. of Tokyo, Univ. of Franche-Comté, France, Univ. of Nice, France; joined Ministry of Foreign Affairs 1972, postings include embassies in Vientiane, Washington, DC and Brussels, Dir for Research Coordination and Sr Research Fellow, Japan Inst. of Int. Affairs 1988–90, Dir Nuclear Science Div., Ministry of Foreign Affairs 1993–94, also Dir Nuclear Energy Div., Counselor, Japanese Del. to Conf. on Disarmament, Geneva, Switzerland 1994–97, Consul Gen., Marseille, France 1997–99, Deputy Dir-Gen. for Arms Control and Scientific Affairs 1999–2000, Dir-Gen. Disarmament, Nonproliferation and Science Dept 2002–05, Perm. Rep. and Amb. to Int. Orgs, UN, Vienna 2005–09; mem. for Japan, IAEA Bd of Govs 2005–09, Chair. IAEA Bd of Govs 2005–06, Dir-Gen. IAEA 2009–; Chair. G7 Nuclear Safety Group 2000; Lecturer in Int. Politics, Yamanashi Univ. 1991–92; Fellow, Weatherhead Center for Int. Affairs, Harvard Univ. 2001; Visiting Scholar, Monterey Inst. of Int. Studies, USA 2001–02. *Publications:* Sea Dumping of Liquid Radioactive Waste by Russia 1994; several articles on nuclear non-proliferation and nuclear disarmament. *Address:* Office of the Director General, International Atomic Energy Agency, PO Box 100, Wagramer Strasse 5, 1400 Vienna, Austria (office). *Telephone:* (1) 26000 (office). *Fax:* (1) 26007 (office). *E-mail:* official.mail@iaea.org (office). *Website:* www.iaea.org (office).

AMANPOUR, Christiane, CBE, AB; British journalist and broadcasting correspondent; *Chief International Correspondent, CNN;* b. 12 Jan. 1958, London; d. of Mohammad Amanpour and Patricia Amanpour; m. James Rubin 1998; one s.; ed primary school in Tehran, Iran, Holy Cross Convent and New Hall School, UK, Univ. of Rhode Island, USA; radio producer/USA Asst, BBC Radio, London

1980–82; radio reporter, WBRU, Brown Univ., USA 1981–83; electronic graphics designer, WJAR, Providence, RI 1983; Asst, CNN Int. Assignment Desk, Atlanta, Ga 1983, news writer, CNN, Atlanta 1984–86, reporter/producer, CNN, New York 1987–90, Int. Corresp., CNN 1990–94, Sr Int. Corresp. 1994–96, Chief Int. Corresp. 1996–2010, 2011–, also host of nightly global affairs programme, Amanpour 2009–; Anchor, This Week, ABC News 2010–11, Global Affairs Anchor 2011–; UNESCO Goodwill Amb. for Freedom of Expression and Journalist Safety 2015; mem. Bd of Dirs Cttee to Protect Journalists; Fellow, Soc. of Professional Journalists, American Academy of Arts and Sciences 2010; Hon. Citizen of Sarajevo 2006; Hon. mem. Graduating Class of Harvard Coll. 2010; Hon. Bd mem. Daniel Pearl Foundation; Hon. DHumLitt (Emory Univ.) 1997, (Northwestern Univ.) 2010; Dr hc (Univ. of Rhode Island), (Univ. of Michigan) 2006, (Smith Coll.) 2008, (Georgia State Univ.) 2010, (Amherst Coll.) 2012, (Univ. of Southern California) 2012; three Dupont-Columbia Awards 1986–96, eleven News and Documentary Emmy Awards, four George Foster Peabody Awards, Women, Men and Media Breakthrough Award 1991, Livingston Award for Young Journalists 1992, George Polk Award for Television Reporting 1993, 1996, named Woman of the Year by New York Chapter of Women in Cable and Telecommunications 1994, Courage in Journalism Award, Int. Women's Media Foundation 1994, Nymphe d'Honneur, Monte Carlo Television Festival 1997, Univ. of Missouri Honor Award for Distinguished Service to Journalism 1999, Courage in Journalism Award, Worldfest-Houston Int. Film Festival Gold Award, Livingston Award for Young Journalists, Edward R. Murrow Award for Distinguished Achievement in Broadcast Journalism 2002, Goldsmith Career Award for Excellence in Journalism, Kennedy School of Govt, Harvard Univ. 2002, Sigma Chi Award (SDX) for her reports from Goma, Zaïre, WorldFest-Houston Int. Film Festival Gold Award, Persian Woman of the Year 2007, The Fourth Estate Award, Nat. Press Club 2008, Walter Cronkite Award for Excellence in Journalism, Walter Cronkite School of Journalism and Mass Communication 2011, inducted into Cable Hall of Fame 2015. *Leisure interests:* reading, riding, tennis, swimming, sky diving. *Address:* CNN, 16 Great Marlborough Street, London, W1F 7HS, England (office). *E-mail:* amanpour@cnn.com (office); info@abcnews.go.com (office). *Website:* edition.cnn.com/shows/amanpour (office); abcnews.go.com/ThisWeek (office).

AMARAL, Sérgio Silva do, LLB, MPolSci; Brazilian diplomatist; *Ambassador to USA;* b. 1 June 1944, São Paulo; s. of Pedro Augusto do Amaral and Maria Aparecida Silva do Amaral; divorced; four c.; ed Universidade de São Paulo, Université Paris 1 Panthéon-Sorbonne, France; fmr Chair., Foreign Trade Council of Ministers (CAMEX), Brazilian Devt Bank (BNDES), Brazil-China Business Council (CBBC); worked as an attorney at Felsberg and Assocs.; Sec. for Int. Affairs Ministry of Foreign Affairs 1988–90; Counsellor, Embassy of Brazil, Washington 1984, Minister-Counsellor 1991, Amb. to UK 1999–2001, to France 2003–05, to USA 2016–; Perm. Rep. to OECD 2003; Exec. Sec. Ministry of the Environment 1993; Head of Cabinet Ministry of Finance 1994, Head of Dept, Social Communication 1995; Minister of State for Devt, Industry and Foreign Trade 2001–03; fmr Asst Prof. of Int. Relations, Univ. of Brasilia; Alt. Gov., IMF, World Bank; Alt. Rep., GATT; Dir, Center for American Studies, FAAP; mem. Bd of Dirs Strategic Council of the Industry Fed. of São Paulo; mem. Bd WWF Brazil; Grand Officer, Order of Merit Armed Forces, Order of Aeronautical Merit, Order of Naval Merit, Légion d'Honneur, France, Grand Cross of the Order of Rio Branco, Grand Cross of the Order of Judicial Merit, Great Cross of Scientific Merit, Grand Cross of the Aztec Order of Mexico, Great Cordon of the Order of the Sacred Treasure, Japan, Grand Cross of the Order of the Rep. of Italy, Grand Cross of the Order of Merit of the Portuguese Rep. *Address:* Embassy of Brazil, 3006 Massachusetts Ave, NW, Washington, DC 20008, USA (office). *Telephone:* (202) 238-2700 (office). *Fax:* (202) 238-2827 (office). *E-mail:* press.washington@itamaraty.gov.br (office). *Website:* washington.itamaraty.gov.br (office).

AMARATUNGA, John Anthony Emmanuel; Sri Lankan lawyer and politician; b. 21 May 1940, Colombo; m.; ed Colombo Law Coll., Aquinas Coll. of Higher Studies, St Joseph's Coll., Colombo, De Mazenod Coll., Kandana; mem. Parl. for Gampaha (United Nat. Party) 1978–, apptd Chief Opposition Whip 2010; apptd Deputy Minister of Finance and Planning 1988, Acting Minister of Finance and Planning 1988; Minister of State 1989–90, of Prov. Councils 1990, of Home Affairs and Prov. Councils 1993, of Interior and Christian Affairs 2001–04; mem. del. to UN Gen. Ass. 2010. *Address:* Parliament of Sri Lanka, Sri Jayewardenepura Kotte (office); No. 88, Negombo Road, Kandana, Sri Lanka (home). *Telephone:* (11) 2777100 (office). *Fax:* (11) 2777564 (office). *E-mail:* webmaster@parliament.lk (office). *Website:* www.parliament.lk (office).

AMARI, Akira; Japanese politician; *Minister in charge of Economic Revitalization and of Total Reform of Social Security and Tax, and Minister of State for Economic and Fiscal Policy;* b. 27 Aug. 1948, Atsugi, Kanagawa; ed Pref. Sr High School, Atsugi, Keio Univ. Law School; worked for Sony Corpn 1972–74; mem. House of Reps of New Liberal Club for Ninami-Kanto, for Kanagawa Pref. 13th Dist 1983–; subsequently joined LDP, Sr Dir LDP Commerce and Industry Panel 1990–95, Chair. 1995; Parl. Vice-Minister of Int. Trade and Industry 1989; Deputy Sec.-Gen. LDP 1999–2001, Chief Deputy Sec.-Gen. 2001; Minister of Labour 1998–99; Chair. House Budget Cttee 2004–05; Minister of Economy, Trade and Industry 2006–08; Minister of State for Regulatory Reform, Admin. Reform and Civil Service Reform 2008–09; Minister in charge of Econ. Revitalization and of Total Reform of Social Security and Tax, and Minister of State for Econ. and Fiscal Policy 2012–; mem. Japan-Korea Parliamentarians' Union, Japan-China Friendship Parliamentarians' Union. *Leisure interest:* collecting antiques. *Address:* Cabinet Office 1-6-1, Nagata-cho, Chiyoda-ku, Tokyo 100-8968 (office); Liberal-Democratic Party (LDP), 1-11-23, Nagata-cho, Chiyoda-ku, Tokyo 100-8910, Japan (office). *Telephone:* (3) 5253-2111 (office); (3) 3581-6211 (office). *E-mail:* koho@ldp.jimin.or.jp (office). *Website:* www.cao.go.jp (office); www.jimin.jp (office); www.amari-akira.com.

AMARJARGAL, Rinchinnyamyn, MEcons; Mongolian politician; b. 1961, Ulaanbaatar; m.; one s.; ed Moscow Inst. of Econs, Univ. of Bradford, UK; officer, Cen. Council of Mongolian Trade Unions 1982–83; Lecturer, Mil. Acad. and Tech. Univ. 1983–91; Dir Econs Coll., Ulan Bator 1991–96; MP 1996–99, 2004–; Minister and Acting Minister of External Relations April–Dec. 1998, Prime Minister of Mongolia 1999–2000; apptd Chair. Mongolian Nat. Democratic Party 1999–2000, fmr mem. Gen. Council; mem. Democratic Party 2000–; f. Amarjargal Foundation 2001; Dr hc (Bradford) 2000. *Address:* c/o Democratic Party, Democratic Party Central Bldg, Sükhbaataryn Talbai 8, Sükhbaatar District, Ulan Bator, Mongolia. *Telephone:* (11) 262055. *Fax:* (11) 312810. *Website:* www.demparty.mn; www.amarjargal.org.

AMARKHIL, Zia ul-Haq; Afghan government official; Dir Field Operations Dept, Ind. Election Comm. (IEC) –2012, Sec. IEC Secr. and Chief Electoral Officer 2012–14.

AMARYN, Uladzimir Viktaravich; Belarusian economist and politician; b. 1961, Minsk; m.; two s.; ed Belarusian State Econ. Univ., Acad. of Public Admin, Minsk; served several years with Ministry of Finance including as Head of Fiscal Policy 2001–06, Deputy Minister of Finance 2006–08, First Deputy Minister of Finance 2008–14, Minister of Finance 2014–18. *Address:* c/o Ministry of Finance, 220010 Minsk, vul. Savetskaya 7, Belarus (office).

AMATO, HE Cardinal Angelo, SDB; Italian ecclesiastic and academic; *Prefect of the Congregation for the Causes of Saints;* b. 8 June 1938, Molfetta; ed Salesian high school, Pontifical Salesian Univ., Rome (licenciate in philosophy), Pontifical Gregorian Univ., Rome; entered the Salesians of St John Bosco, after completing novitiate at Salesian high school; ordained a priest 1967; began teaching at Pontifical Salesian Univ. as an asst 1972; Fellow, Ecumenical Patriarchate of Constantinople, Thessaloniki, Greece, at monastery Orthodox Moní Vlatádon, home of Inst. of Patriarchal Patristic Studies 1978–79; spent sabbatical year in Washington, DC, USA studying theology of religions 1988; currently Prof. of Dogmatics at Pontifical Salesian Univ., Dean of Faculty of Theology 1981–87, 1993–97; served as consultor to Congregation for the Doctrine of the Faith and Pontifical Council for Promoting Christian Unity as well as for Congregation for Bishops; Sec. Congregation for the Doctrine of the Faith 2002–08; Titular Archbishop of Sila 2003–; served as a consultor to the Pontifical Councils for Christian Unity and Interreligious Dialogue; mem. Congregation for Divine Worship and the Discipline of the Sacraments; Prefect of the Congregation for the Causes of Saints 2008–; mem. Congregation for the Doctrine of the Faith 2010–; cr. Cardinal (Cardinal-Deacon of S. Maria in Aquiro) 2010; participated in Papal Conclave 2013. *Address:* Palazzo delle Congregazioni, Piazza Pio XII 10, 00193 Rome, Italy (office). *Telephone:* (06) 69884247 (office). *Fax:* (06) 69881935 (office). *Website:* www.vatican.va/roman_curia/congregations/csaints (office).

AMATO, Giuliano, LLB, LLM; Italian politician, academic and university administrator; *Professor Emeritus, European University Institute, Italy;* b. 13 May 1938, Turin; ed Univ. of Pisa, Sant'Anna School of Advanced Studies, Columbia Univ., USA; Prof. of Italian and Comparative Constitutional Law, Univ. of Rome 1975–97, later Prof. Emer.; joined Italian Socialist Party (PSI) 1958, mem. Cen. Cttee 1978–94, Nat. Deputy Sec. 1988–92, Leader –2000, Asst Sec.; mem. Camera dei Deputati for Turin-Novara-Vercelli 1983, 1987–93; Under-Sec. of State, Presidency of Council of Ministers 1983–87, Vice-Pres. Council of Ministers and Minister of the Treasury 1987–89; Deputy Prime Minister of Italy 1987–88, Prime Minister 1992–93, 2000–01; Pres. Italian Antitrust Authority 1994–97; foreign debt negotiator for Albanian Govt 1991–92; Minister for Constitutional Reforms 1998–99; Minister for Treasury 1999–2000; Vice-Pres. EU Special Convention on Pan-European Constitution 2001–06; Senator for Grosseto 2001–06; Minister of Internal Affairs 2006–08; Chair. Istituto della Enciclopedia Italiana 2009–13; Prof. Emer. European Univ. Inst., Italy 2013–; Pres. Sant'Anna School of Advanced Studies 2012–13; Judge, Constitutional Court 2013–; mem. Partito Democratico 2007–; Foreign Hon. mem. American Acad. of Arts and Sciences 2001. *Publications:* Antitrust and the Bounds of Power 1997, Tornare al Futuro 2001, Dialoghi post-secolari 2006, Un altro mondo è possibile? Parole per capire e per cambiare 2006, Genèse et destinée de la Constitution européenne 2007, Il gioco delle pensioni: rien ne va plus? 2007. *Address:* European University Institute, Department of Law, Via Bolognese 156, 50139 Florence, Italy (office). *Website:* www.eui.eu/DepartmentsAndCentres/Law (office).

AMATONG, Juanita Dy, BSc, MA; Philippine economist, academic and public finance expert; b. 23 March 1935, Bindoy, Negros Oriental; d. of Eking Dy and Felisa Anuling; m. Ernesto S. Amatong; two s. two d.; ed Silliman Univ., Dumaguete City, Maxwell School of Public Admin and Citizenship, Syracuse Univ. NY, USA; Asst Prof., Silliman Univ. 1961–63; Lecturer, Andres Bonifacio Coll., Zamboanga del Norte, Philippines 1968–71; Sr Financial Analyst, Ministry of Finance 1971–83; Special Asst to Prime Minister 1984–86; economist, IMF, Washington, DC 1985–89; Asst Sec. (Minister) of Finance 1986–95, Under-Sec. (Deputy Minister) of Finance 1992–95, 2001–03, Sec. (Minister) of Finance 2003–05; Exec. Asst Cen. Bank of Philippines (Bangko Sentral ng Pilipinas, BSP) 1984–86, mem. Monetary Bd 2005–11; mem. Faculty, School of Business Man. Educ. and Grad. School Program, Andres Bonifacio Coll. 2013–; Resident Consultant, Govt Myanmar Consultancy 1992; Exec. Dir, Alt. Exec. Dir, Adviser to Exec. Dir World Bank, IFC and Multilateral Investment Guarantee Agency, Washington, DC 1995–98; consultant, Chemonics International 1998–2000; Man. Pnr, Resource and Measures Assoc. Co. 1999–2000; Professorial Lecturer, School of Public Admin, Univ. of the Philippines; mem. Faculty, School of Business Man. Educ. and Grad. School Program, Andres Bonifacio Coll. 2013–; mem. Devt Budget Coordinating Cttee, Policy Governing Bd Targeted Interventions for Econ. Reforms and Governance (TIERG) 2004, Policy Advisory Bd Cities Alliance, World Bank (IBRD) 2005; Chair. Bd of Trustees, Silliman Univ., Chair. Silliman Univ. Medical Foundation Center Inc.; mem. Bd Trustees, Bantay Katarungan (NGO on sentinel of justice) 2000–; Officer, Philippine Legion of Honor 1998; Outstanding Silliman Univ. Alumnus 1977, First Woman Exec. Dir World Bank Group, Philippine Centennial 1998, Living Treasure in the Philippines (Nat. Cttee on the Centennial of Feminist Movement of the Philippines) 2005, Outstanding Negrense in Govt Service (Prov. of Negros Oriental) 2005. *Publications include:* Decontrol and its Effects, Taxation of Capital Gains in Developing Countries, The Revenue Importance of Lotteries, The Reconciliation of Government Transaction Statistics: National Accounts, Commission on Audit and Office of Budget and Management Reports 1987, Local Government Fiscal and Financial Management Best Practices (ed.) 2005. *Leisure interests:* reading, painting, cooking. *Address:* 21 Masambahin Street, Teacher's Village, Dilliman, Quezon City 1100, Philippines (home). *Telephone:* (2) 9224647 (home).

AMBANI, Anil Dhirubai, BSc, MBA; Indian business executive; *Chairman, Reliance Group;* b. 4 June 1959, Mumbai; s. of Shri Dhirubhai Hirachand Ambani and Kokilaben Dhirubhai Ambani; brother of Mukesh Ambani; m. Tina Ambani; two s.; ed Univ. of Bombay (now Mumbai), Wharton School, Univ. of Pennsylvania, USA; apptd Co-CEO Reliance Industries Ltd 1983, then Vice-Chair., Man. Dir, apptd Chair. Reliance Group (cr. after division of Reliance Industries Ltd and comprising Reliance Communications, Reliance Capital, Reliance Infrastructure and Reliance Power) 2006–, mem. Bd of Dirs Reliance Europe Ltd; mem. Bd of Dirs and Vice-Chair. Indian Petrochemicals Corpn Ltd –2005 (resgnd); mem. Rajya Sabha (upper house of Parl.) 2004–06; Chair. Bd Govs Nat. Safety Council; Co-founder Indian School of Business, Hyderabad; Co-Chair. India-China CEO Forum; mem. Bd of Govs Indian Inst. of Man., Ahmedabad, Indian Inst. of Tech., Kanpur; mem. US-India CEO Forum; mem. Bd of Overseers, Wharton School; mem. President's Global Council, New York Univ.; mem. Advisory Bd Warwick Business School, UK; est. Kokilaben Dhirubhai Ambani Hospital, Mumbai; Business India Businessman of the Year 1997, Indian Alumni Award, Wharton India Econ. Forum 2001, Bombay Man. Asscn Entrepreneur of the Decade Award 2002, CEO of the Year, Platts Global Energy Awards 2004, Businessman of the Year, The Times of India 2006. *Leisure interests:* long-distance running, football. *Address:* Reliance Centre, 19 Walchand Hirachand Marg, Ballard Estate, Mumbai 400 001, India (office). *Telephone:* (22) 30375522 (office). *Fax:* (22) 30375577 (office). *E-mail:* anil.ambani@relianceada.com (office). *Website:* www.relianceada.com (office).

AMBANI, Mukesh D., BChemEng, MBA; Indian business executive; *Chairman and Managing Director, Reliance Industries Limited;* b. 19 April 1957, Colony of Aden, Yemen; s. of Dhirubhai Hirachand Ambani and Kokilaben Dhirubhai Ambani; brother of Anil D. Ambani; m. Nita Ambani; two s. one d.; ed Univ. Inst. of Chemical Tech., Mumbai, Stanford Univ., USA; joined family-owned Reliance Industries Ltd (India's largest pvt. co.) 1981, Man. Dir 1986–, Chair. 2002–, Chair. Reliance Retail Ltd, also mem. Bd of Dirs Reliance Europe Ltd, Reliance Infotel Broadband Services Ltd, Reliance Foundation, IMG Reliance Pvt. Ltd; Chair. Indian Petrochemicals Corpn Ltd, FLAG Telecom; Owner Indian Premier League team Mumbai Indians; Chair. Bd of Trustees, Indian Inst. of Software Eng; Chair. Bd of Govs Indian Inst. of Man., Bangalore, Pandit Deendayal Petroleum Univ., Gandhinagar; Vice-Chair. Exec. Cttee World Business Council for Sustainable Devt 2008; mem. Bd of Dirs Bank of America Corpn (first non-American); mem. Prime Minister's Advisory Council on Trade and Industry, Bd Govs of Nat. Council of Applied Econ. Research, Advisory Council of the Indian Banks Asscn, Millennium Devt Goals Advocacy Group constituted by the UN, Foundation Bd of World Econ. Forum, Indo-USA CEOs Forum, Advisory Council for the Grad. School of Business, Stanford Univ.; mem. Advisory Council of the Indian Inst. of Tech., Mumbai, Governing Bd of Public Health Foundation of India; mem. Int. Advisory Bd, Citigroup, Nat. Bd of Kuwait, Brookings; Dr hc (Maharaja Sayajirao Univ.) 2007; numerous awards including Global Leader for Tomorrow, World Econ. Forum, Switzerland 1994, Business India Businessman of the Year Award 1997, Distinguished Alumnus of the Decade, Univ. of Mumbai 1999, Ernst & Young Entrepreneur of the Year Award 2000, Dean's Medal, Univ. of Pennsylvania School of Eng and Applied Science 2010, Dwight D. Eisenhower Global Leadership Award, The Business Council for Int. Understanding 2010, Entrepreneur of the Decade, All India Management Asscn 2013, Othmer Gold Medal, Chemical Heritage Foundation (USA) 2016. *Leisure interests:* movies, cricket. *Address:* Reliance Industries Ltd, 3rd Floor, Maker Chamber IV, 222 Nariman Point, Mumbai 400 021, India (office). *Telephone:* (22) 22785000 (office). *Fax:* (22) 22870303 (office). *E-mail:* M_Ambani@ril.com (office). *Website:* www.ril.com (office).

AMBONGO BESUNGU, Rev. Fridolin; Democratic Republic of the Congo ecclesiastic; *Archbishop of Kinshasa;* b. 24 Jan. 1960, Boto; ed Saint Eugène de Mazenod Inst., Alphonsian Acad.; ordained priest, Order of Friars Minor Capuchin 1988; Bishop of Bokungu-Ikela 2004–18; Apostolic Admin. of Kole 2008–15, of Mbandaka-Bikoro 2016; Archbishop of Mbandaka-Bikoro 2016–18; Coadjutor Archbishop of Kinshasa 2018; Archbishop of Kinshasa 2019–. *Address:* Archdiocese of Kinshasa, Archeveche, 2 Avenue de l'Universite, Quartier Mososo, Cummune Limete, Kinshasa 1, Democratic Republic of the Congo (office). *Telephone:* (82) 2992036 (office). *E-mail:* archikinchancellerie@gmail.com (office). *Website:* www.archikin-online.org (office).

AMBROS, Victor R., PhD; American molecular biologist and academic; *Silverman Professor of Natural Sciences, Program of Molecular Medicine, University of Massachusetts Medical School;* b. 1 Dec. 1953, Hanover, NH; ed Massachusetts Inst. of Tech.; Research Asst, MIT Center for Cancer Research 1975–76, Grad. Research Asst 1976–79; Chaim Weizmann Postdoctoral Fellow 1979; American Cancer Soc. Postdoctoral Fellow 1980–81; NIH Postdoctoral Fellow 1982–84; Asst Prof., Dept of Cellular and Developmental Biology, Harvard Univ. 1985–88, Assoc. Prof. 1988–92; Assoc. Prof., Biological Sciences, Dartmouth Coll. 1992–96, Prof. 1996–2001, Prof. of Genetics, Dartmouth Medical School 2001–07; Prof., Program in Molecular Medicine, Univ. of Massachusetts Medical School 2008–, currently Silverman Prof. of Natural Sciences, Program of Molecular Medicine, Co-Dir RNA Therapeutics Inst.; mem. NAS 2007; Newcomb Cleveland Prize (co-recipient), AAAS 2003, Gene Knudson Lecturer in Molecular Genetics, Oregon State Univ. 2003, Lewis S. Rosenstiel Award in Basic Medical Science, Brandeis Univ. (co-recipient) 2006, Medal for Outstanding Contribs in the Past 15 Years, Genetics Soc. of America 2006, Jack M. Buchanan Medal, MIT 2006, Benjamin Franklin Medal in Life Sciences (co-recipient) 2008, Albert Lasker Basic Medical Research Award (co-recipient) 2008, Gairdner Foundation Int. Award (co-recipient) 2008, Warren Triennial Prize (co-recipient), Massachusetts Gen. Hosp. 2008, Dickson Prize, Univ. of Pittsburgh 2009, Horwitz Prize, Columbia Univ. (co-recipient) 2009, Massry Award (co-recipient) 2009, Dr Paul Janssen Award for Biomedical Research, Johnson & Johnson (co-recipient) 2012, Keio Medical Science Prize, Keio Univ. (co-recipient) 2013, Gruber Genetics Prize (co-recipient) 2014, Wolf Prize in Medicine (co-recipient) 2014, Breakthrough Prize in Life Sciences (co-recipient) 2015. *Achievements include:* discoverer of first known microRNA. *Publications:* numerous papers in professional journals. *Address:* Program in Molecular Medicine, University of Massachusetts Medical School, Biotech Two, Suite 306, 373 Plantation Street, Worcester, MA 01605, USA (office). *Telephone:* (508) 856-6380 (office). *E-mail:* victor.ambros@umassmed.edu (office). *Website:* www.umassmed.edu/ambroslab (office).

AMBROSE, The Hon. Rona, PC, BA, MA; Canadian politician; b. 15 March 1969, Valley View, Alberta; m. Bruce Ambrose; ed Univs of Victoria and Alberta; fmr political columnist; fmr owner Ambrose Consulting Ltd; fmr Sr Intergovernmental Officer, Int. and Intergovernmental Relations Dept, Govt of Alberta; MP for Edmonton-Spruce Grove 2004–15, for Sturgeon River–Parkland 2015–; Sr Intergovernmental Affairs Critic, Conservative Official Opposition 2004, later Int. Trade Critic; Minister of the Environment 2006–07; Pres. of the Queen's Privy Council for Canada, Minister of Intergovernmental Affairs and Minister of Western Econ. Diversification 2007–08, Minister of Labour 2008–10, of Public Works and Govt Services, also for Status of Women 2010–13, of Health 2013–15; Vice-Chair. Treasury Bd Cttee 2008–. *Address:* Conservative Party of Canada, 130 Albert Street, Suite 1720, Ottawa, ON K1P 5G4, Canada (office). *Telephone:* (613) 755-2000 (office). *Fax:* (613) 755-2001 (office). *E-mail:* info@conservative.ca (office); rona.ambrose.c1a@parl.gc.ca (office). *Website:* www.conservative.ca (office); www.ronaambrose.com.

AMEER, Ibrahim; Maldivian politician; *Minister of Finance;* fmr Fulbright Scholar; Minister of Finance 2018–; mem. Maldivian Democratic Party; mem. Bd of Govs., Islamic Development Bank. *Address:* Ministry of Finance, Ameenee Magu, Block 379, Malé 20379, Maldives (office). *Telephone:* 3328790 (office). *Fax:* 3324432 (office). *E-mail:* admin@finance.gov.mv (office). *Website:* www.finance.gov.mv (office).

AMELING, Elisabeth (Elly) Sara; Dutch singer; b. 8 Feb. 1938, Rotterdam; m. Arnold W. Beider 1964; ed studied singing with Jo Bollekamp, with Jacoba and Sam Dresden and with Bodi Rapp, studied French art song with Pierre Bernac; recitals in Europe, SA, Japan; debut in USA 1968, annual tours of USA and Canada 1968–, farewell tour 1995; sang with Concertgebouw Orchestra, New Philharmonic Orchestra, BBC Symphony Orchestra, Berlin Philharmonic, Cincinnati Symphony, San Francisco Symphony, Toronto Symphony, Chicago Symphony; has appeared in Mozart Festival, Washington, DC 1974, Caramoor Festival 1974, Art Song Festival, Princeton, NJ 1974; retired from recital stage in 1995, now teaches selected masterclasses; Kt, Order of Orange-Nassau 1971, Order of the Netherlands Lion 2008; Dr hc (Univ. of BC) 1981, (Westminister Choir Coll., Princeton, NJ) 1985, (Cleveland Inst. of Music) 1986, (Shenandoah Univ.) 1988; First Prize, Concours Int. de Musique, Geneva, Grand Prix du Disque, Edison Prize, Preis der Deutschen Schallplattenkritik, Stereo Review Record of the Year Award. *Recordings include:* Mozart Concert, Handel Concert, Cantatas (Bach), Mörike Lieder (Wolf), Aimez-vous Handel?, Aimez-vous Mozart?, Christmas Oratorio (Bach), Symphony No. 2 (Mahler), Te Deum (Bruckner), Italienisches Liederbuch (Wolf).

AMELIO, William J., BChemEng, MA; American business executive; *CEO, Avnet Inc;* b. 25 Nov. 1957; m. Jamie Amelio; ed Lehigh Univ., Sloan Master's Program at Stanford Univ.; with IBM 1979–97, held several Sr Man. positions, including Gen. Man. of Operations for IBM's Personal Computing Div.; Pres. and CEO Honeywell's transportation and power-systems divs, and Head of turbocharging-systems business at Allied Signal Inc. (predecessor of Honeywell International Inc.) 1997–2000; Exec. Vice-Pres. and COO NCR Corpn's Retail and Financial Group 2000–01; Sr Vice-Pres. Asia-Pacific and Japan, Dell Inc. 2001–05; Pres. and CEO Lenovo Group Ltd 2005–09 (resgnd), special adviser to Bd 2009; Pres. and CEO CHC Helicopter, Richmond, BC, Canada 2010–15; CEO, mem. Bd Avnet Inc. 2016–; co-f. (with his wife) and Chair. Caring for Cambodia. *Address:* 2211 South 47th Street, Phoenix, AZ, 85034, USA (office). *Telephone:* (480) 643-2000 (office). *Fax:* (480) 643-7199 (office). *Website:* www.avnet.com.

AMENÁBAR, Alejandro; Spanish/Chilean film director; b. 31 March 1973, Santiago, Chile; ed Complutense Univ., Madrid. *Films:* Head (short film) 1991, Himenóptero (short film) (Best Short Film, Elche Festival, Alicante, Carabanchel Festival, Madrid) 1992, Luna (short film) (Luis García Berlanga Award for Best Script, AICA Award for Best Soundtrack) 1995, Tésis (Thesis) 1996, Abre los Ojos (Open Your Eyes) 1997, The Others 2001, Vanilla Sky (writer) 2001, El Soñador (writer and producer) 2004, Mar adentro (The Sea Inside) (Best Foreign Language Film, Nat. Bd of Review, Best Dir, Best Film, Goya Awards 2005, Best Foreign Film, Ind. Spirit Awards 2005, Grand Prix of Jury, Int. Venice Film Festival 2004, Best Foreign Language Film, Acad. Awards 2005) 2004, Agora 2009; composer: Al Lado del Atlas 1994, Allanamiento de Morada 1998, La lengua de las mariposas 1999, Nadie conoce a Nadie 1999. *Television:* Un viaje mar adentro 2005. *Website:* www.clubcultura.com/clubcine/clubcineastas/amenabar/index.htm.

AMER, Tarek Hassan Nour El Din; Egyptian banking executive and central banker; *Governor, Central Bank of Egypt;* held several managerial positions in Citibank, Egyptian American Bank, Bank of America, Bank of Credit and Commerce working in Middle East and North Africa; Chair. Nat. Bank of Egypt (NBE) 2008–13, apptd CEO and Man. Dir NBE (UK) Ltd 2013; Deputy Gov. Cen. Bank of Egypt 2008–13, Gov. 2015–, also mem. Bd of Dirs; fmr Pres. Fed. of Egyptian Banks; fmr Vice-Chair., Banque Misr, Egypt, Arab Int. Bank, Egyptian Banking Inst.; Gen. Man. Banks of Bahrain and Kuwait. *Address:* Central Bank of Egypt, 31 Sharia Qasr el-Nil, Cairo, Egypt (office). *Telephone:* (2) 27702770 (office). *Fax:* (2) 25976081 (office). *E-mail:* info@cbe.org.eg (office). *Website:* www.cbe.org.eg (office).

AMERASINGHE, Chittharanjan Felix, PhD, LLD; Sri Lankan lawyer and judge; b. 2 March 1933, Colombo; s. of Samson Felix Amerasinghe, OBE and Mary Victorine Abeyesundere; m. Wimala Nalini Pieris 1964; one s. two d.; ed Royal Coll., Trinity Hall, Cambridge, UK, Harvard Univ. Law School, USA; Supervisor in Law, Trinity Hall, Cambridge 1955–57; Jr Exec., Caltex Oil Co., Colombo 1959–61; Lecturer in Law, Univ. of Ceylon 1962–65, Sr Lecturer 1965–68, Reader 1968–69, Prof. of Law 1969–71; Counsel, World Bank 1970–75, Sr Counsel 1975–81, Exec. Sec., World Bank Admin. Tribunal 1981–96; Judge, UN Tribunal, New York 1997–2000, Commonwealth Int. Arbitral Tribunal 1999–2002; Consultant in Int. Law, Govt of Ceylon 1963–70; mem. Ceylon Govt Comm. on Local Govt 1969; Adjunct Prof. of Int. Law, School of Law, American Univ. 1991–93; mem. Panel of Arbitrators and Conciliators, Law of the Sea Convention, Int. Centre for Settlement of Investment Disputes, Panel of UN Compensation Comm. for Kuwait; Exec. Council mem. American Soc. of Int. Law 1980–83; Assoc. mem. Inst. de Droit

Int. 1981–87, mem. 1987–; mem. Int. Law Asscn 1986–; mem. Sr Editorial Bd, Project on Governing Rules of Int. Law, American Soc. of Int. Law; mem. Hon. Cttee Int. Inst. of Human Rights 1968–; mem. Advisory Bd Int. Inst. of Environmental Law 1987–98, Sri Lanka Journal of Int. Law 1989–, Int. Orgs Law Review 2004–; Sr Fellow (Visiting), Trinity Hall, Cambridge 1996–97; Trinity Hall Law Studentship 1956–59, Research Fellowship, Harvard Univ. Law School 1957–58; Hon. Prof. of Int. Law, Univ. of Colombo 1991–94; Henry Arthur Thomas Classical Award, Univ. of Cambridge 1953, Angus Classical Prize 1953, Clement Davies Prize for Law 1955, Major Scholar and Prizeman, Trinity Hall, Cambridge 1953–56, Yorke Prize 1964, Certificate of Merit, American Soc. of Int. Law 1988–89. *Publications include:* Some Aspects of the Actio Iniuriarum in Roman-Dutch Law 1966, State Responsibility for Injuries to Aliens 1967, Defamation and Other Injuries in Roman-Dutch Law 1968, Studies in International Law 1969, The Doctrines of Sovereignty and Separation of Powers in the Law of Ceylon 1970, The Law of the International Civil Service (two vols) 1988, Documents on International Administrative Tribunals 1989, Case Law of the World Bank Administrative Tribunal (three vols) 1989, 1991, 1994, Local Remedies in International Law 1990, 2003, Principles of the Institutional Law of International Organizations 1996, 2005, Jurisdiction of International Tribunals 2003, Evidence in International Litigation 2005, Diplomatic Protection 2008; articles in leading law and int. law journals. *Leisure interests:* classical and classical jazz music, art, artifacts, philately, photography, walking. *Address:* 6100 Robinwood Road, Bethesda, MD 20817, USA (home). *Telephone:* (301) 229-2766 (home). *Fax:* (301) 229-4151 (home).

AMES, Bruce Nathan, BA, PhD, FAAS; American biochemist and academic; *Professor, Graduate School, Department of Biochemistry and Molecular Biology, University of California, Berkeley;* b. 16 Dec. 1928, New York; s. of Dr M. U. Ames and Dorothy Andres Ames; m. Dr Giovanna Ferro-Luzzi 1960; one s. one d.; ed Cornell Univ. and California Inst. of Tech., Nat. Inst. of Health, Maryland; Postdoctoral Fellow, NIH 1953–54, Biochemist 1954–60; NSF Fellow, Labs of F. C. Crick, Cambridge and F. Jacob, Paris 1961; Chief Section of Microbial Genetics, Lab. of Molecular Biology, NIH 1962–67; Prof. of Biochemistry and Molecular Biology, Univ. of California, Berkeley 1968–, Dir Nat. Inst. of Environmental Health Sciences Centre 1979–, Chair. Dept of Biochemistry 1983–89; Sr Research Scientist, Children's Hosp. Oakland Research Inst. 1968–; Fellow, Acad. of Toxicological Sciences 1992, American Acad. of Microbiology 1992; mem. Nat. Cancer Advisory Bd 1976–82, NAS, American Acad. of Arts and Sciences, American Aging Asscn, AAAS, ACS, American Coll. of Toxicology, American Soc. of Biochemistry and Molecular Biology, American Soc. of Nutritional Sciences, Environmental Mutagen Soc., Gerontological Soc. of America, Mitochondrial Medicine Soc., Molecular Medicine Soc., New York Acad. of Science, Oxygen Soc., Soc. for Free Radical Research, Soc. of Toxicology; Foreign mem., Royal Swedish Acad. of Sciences 1989; Hon. Foreign mem. Japan Cancer Asscn 1987, Hon. mem. Japan Pharmaceutical Soc. 1998; Dr hc (Tufts Univ.) 1987, (Univ. of Bologna) 1989; ACS Eli Lilly Award 1964, Arthur Flemming Award 1966, Rosenstiel Award 1976, Fed. of American Socs. for Experimental Biology Award 1976, Wankel Award 1978, John Scott Medal 1979, Bolton L. Corson Medal 1980, New Brunswick Lectureship Award, American Soc. for Microbiology 1980, Gen. Motors Cancer Research Fund Charles S. Mott Prize 1983, Gairdner Foundation Award 1983, Tyler Prize for Environmental Achievement 1985, ACS Spencer Award 1986, Roger G. Williams Award in Preventive Nutrition 1989, Gold Medal American Inst. of Chemists 1991, Glenn Foundation Prize 1992, shared Japan Prize 1997, Nat. Medal of Science 1998, Linus Pauling Prize for Health Research 2001, Lifetime Achievement Award of American Soc. for Microbiology 2001, Thomas Hunt Morgan Medal, Genetics Soc. of America 2004, M.S. Rose Award, American Soc. for Nutrition/CRN 2008, George C. Marshall Founders Award 2008, elected to Orthomolecular Medicine Hall of Fame 2010, SOT Lifetime Achievement Award 2012. *Achievements include:* invented Ames test which identifies possible carcinogens by studying their mutagenic effect on bacteria. *Publications include:* more than 500 scientific papers in areas of operons, biochemical genetics, histidine biosynthesis, mutagenesis, detection of environmental carcinogens and mutagens, oxygen radicals as a cause of aging and degenerative diseases, anti-carcinogens, micronutrient deficiency. *Address:* Children's Hospital Oakland Research Institute, 5700 Martin Luther King Jr. Way, Oakland, CA 94609-1673 (office); University of California, Berkeley, Department of Biochemistry and Molecular Biology, 142 LSA, Room 3200, Berkeley, CA 94720-3200 (office); 1324 Spruce Street, Berkeley, CA 94709, USA (home). *Telephone:* (510) 450-7625 (office). *Fax:* (510) 597-7128 (office). *E-mail:* bames@chori.org (office). *Website:* mcb.berkeley .edu (office); www.bruceames.org (office).

AMES, Roger; Trinidad and Tobago music company executive; *CEO, International, Ticketmaster Inc.;* b. 1949; with EMI UK 1975–79; mem. staff, A & R Dept, Phonogram, PolyGram UK 1979–83, Chair. and CEO PolyGram UK 1991–94, Group Exec. and Vice-Pres. PolyGram Int. Ltd 1996–99, Pres. PolyGram Music Group 1996–99; Gen. Man. London Records 1983, later Man. Dir, purchased back-catalogue of Factory Records; Pres. Warner Music Int. 1999, Chair. and CEO Warner Music Group 1999–2004; Sr Advisor, Time Warner, EMI Music 2005–07; Pres. EMI Music, North America 2007–08, Pres. EMI Music, UK Jan.–May 2008; CEO, Int., Ticketmaster Inc. 2009–; Advisor, Ingenious VCT Funds. *Address:* Ticketmaster UK, 48 Leicester Square, London, WC2H 7LR, England (office). *Telephone:* (20) 7344-4000 (office). *Fax:* (20) 7915-0411 (office). *Website:* www .ticketmaster.co.uk (office).

AMEY, Julian Nigel Robert, MA; British charitable trust administrator and fmr civil servant; *CEO, Institute of Healthcare Engineering and Estate Management;* b. 19 June 1949; s. of Robert Amey and Diana Amey (née Coles); m. Ann Victoria Brenchley 1972; three d.; ed Wellingborough School, Magdalene Coll., Cambridge; Dir Int. Sales and Marketing Longman Group Ltd 1985–89; Exec. Dir BBC English World Service 1989–94; seconded to Dept of Trade and Industry 1994–96; Dir-Gen. Canning House 1996–2001; Pnr, The English Place 2001–; CEO Chartered Inst. of Building Services Engineers 2001–06, Trinity Coll., London 2006–09, Imperial Soc. of Teachers of Dancing 2009–11, Inst. of Healthcare Eng and Estate Man. 2012–; Chair. Anglo-Chilean Soc.; Gov. Bath Spa Univ.; fmr mem. Ilha da Uniao Samba School. *Publications include:* Spanish Business Directory 1979, Portuguese Business Dictionary 1981. *Leisure interests:* cricket, tennis, travel. *Address:* Institute of Healthcare Engineering and Estate Management, 2 Abingdon House, Cumberland Business Centre, Northumberland Road, Portsmouth, Hants., PO5 1DS, England (office). *Telephone:* (23) 9282-3186 (office). *Fax:* (23) 9281-5927 (office). *E-mail:* julian.amey@iheem.org.uk (office). *Website:* www.iheem.org.uk (office).

AMIGO VALLEJO, HE Cardinal Carlos, OFM; Spanish ecclesiastic; *Archbishop Emeritus of Seville;* b. 23 Aug. 1934, Medina de Rioseca, Valladolid; ed Faculty of Medicine, Univ. of Valladolid, Cen. Univ. of Madrid; joined Order of Friars Minor (Franciscans); ordained priest in Rome 1960; provincial of Franciscan Prov. of Santiago 1970; Archbishop of Tangier, Morocco 1973–82; consecrated, Church of San Francisco el Grande, Madrid, 1974; acted as mediator to resolve conflicts in Algeria, Libya, Morocco, Mauritania and Tunisia 1976–82; Metropolitan Archbishop of Seville 1982–2009, Archbishop Emer. 2009–; cr. Cardinal (Cardinal-Priest of Santa Maria in Monserrato degli Spagnoli) 2003; participated in Papal Conclave 2005, 2013; Pres. 5th Centennial of the Evangelization of America 1984, High Bishops of Spain 1993, 1996–, Episcopal Comm. of Missions and Cooperation with Churches 1999, Episcopal Comm. of Spanish Episcopal Conf. 2002; del. to Ordinary Ass. of World Synod of Bishops, Vatican City 1977, 1983, 1994, Gen. Conf. of Latin American Episcopate, Dominican Repub. 1992; mem. Exec. Cttee Spanish Episcopal Conf. 1984, Pontifical Comm. for Latin America 1990, 1995, 2000–, Pontifical Council for Health 2002–, Acads of Buenas Letras, Medicina and Belles Artes of Seville; apptd Special Envoy, San Juan de Puerto Rico 2012; fmr mem. Nat. Comm. for 5th Centennial, Cttee of Experts of Universal Exhbn; Orden al Mérito de los Padres de la Patria Dominicana (Dominican Repub.) 1995; Hon. PhD (Tech. Univ. of Cibao, Dominican Repub.) 1995, Hon. Academician, Royal Acad. of Veterinary Sciences, Seville; Silver Medal of Repub. of Panama 2000, Gold Medal, Royal Acad. of Veterinary Sciences 2008, Seville, Adoptive Son of the Prov. of Seville 2011. *Address:* Arzobispado de Sevilla, Pza. Virgen de los Reyes s/n, Apartado 6, 41080, Seville, Spain (office). *Website:* www .diocesisdesevilla.org (office).

AMINE, Souef Mohamed al-; Comoran politician, diplomatist and UN official; *Minister of Foreign Affairs, International Cooperation and Francophonie;* b. 28 July 1962, Moroni; m.; three s. one d.; Amb. to Egypt (also accred to Arab League) 1995–98, Deputy Foreign Minister 1998, Minister of Foreign Affairs Int. Cooperation and Francophonie 1999–2002, 2017–, Minister of State, Minister of Foreign Affairs, Co-operation, Francophone Affairs, with responsibility for Comorans Abroad 2002–05, Amb. and Perm. Rep. to UN, New York 2006–07; Head of Liaison Office of UN Hybrid Mission of the African Union in Darfur (UNAMID), Khartoum, Nyala (South Darfur) and El fasher (Darfur North) 2011–15, Head of UN Multidimensional Integrated Stabilization Mission in Mali (MINUSMA) Regional Office in Gao, Mali 2015–17, worked with UN Dept of Peacekeeping Operations; fmr Ed. La Lettre de Beit-Salam. *Publications:* Les Comores en Mouvement 2008, Les Grands Défis de la politique étrangère des Comores 2009. *Leisure interests:* Oriental culture, African music. *Address:* Ministry of Foreign Affairs, International Cooperation and Francophonie, BP 428, Moroni, The Comoros (office). *Telephone:* 7732306 (office). *Fax:* 7732108 (office). *E-mail:* mirex@snpt.km (office). *Website:* www.diplomatie.gouv.km (office).

AMINU, Jibril Muhammed, PhD, FRCP; Nigerian diplomatist, physician and academic; b. 14 Aug. 1939, Song, Adamawa State; m.; nine c.; ed Ahmadu Bello Univ., Univ. of Ibadan, Royal Postgraduate Medical School, London; Consultant in Medicine, Sr Lecturer, Sub-Dean of Clinical Studies, Univ. of Ibadan Medical School 1973–75; Exec. Sec., Nat. Univs Comm. 1975–79; Prof. of Medicine, specializing in Cardiology and Hypertension, Univ. of Maiduguri 1979–95, Univ. Vice-Chancellor 1980–85; Visiting Prof. of Medicine, Coll. of Medicine, Howard Univ., Washington, DC 1979–80; Minister of Educ. 1985–89, of Petroleum and Mineral Resources 1989–92; Del. to Nigerian Nat. Constitutional Conf. 1994–95; Amb. to USA 1999–2003; Senator for Adamawa Central (People's Democratic Party) 2003–11, Chair. Senate Cttee on Foreign Affairs; Pres. African Petroleum Producers Asscn 1991, OPEC Conf. 1991–92; Chair. First Meeting of Ministers of Educ. in Sub-Saharan Africa; Vice-Pres. for Africa of Third World Acad. of Sciences Network of Scientific Orgs; Foundation mem. Bd of Trustees, People's Democratic Party of Nigeria 1998; Fellow, Nigerian Acad. of Science 1972, W African Coll. of Physicians 1980, Nigerian Postgraduate Medical Coll. 2004, African Acad. of Science; mem. World Bank Preparatory Cttee on Educ. for All, Jornitien 1990; Ordre National de la Légion d'Honneur 1998, Commdr of the Order (Niger); Hon. DSc (Univ. of Maiduguri) 2005; Bobaselu of The Source 2010. *Publications include:* Quality and Stress in Nigerian Education 1986, Observations 1987. *E-mail:* jubrilaminu@yahoo.com (office).

AMIS, Martin Louis, BA; British writer; b. 25 Aug. 1949, Oxford; s. of Kingsley Amis and Hilary Bardwell; m. 1st Antonia Phillips 1984 (divorced 1996); m. 2nd Isabel Fonseca 1998; five c.; ed Exeter Coll., Oxford; Asst Ed., TLS 1971, Fiction and Poetry Ed. TLS 1974–75; Asst Literary Ed., New Statesman 1975–77, Literary Ed. 1977–79; apptd special writer for The Observer newspaper 1980; Prof., Centre for New Writing, Univ. of Manchester 2007–11; Galaxy Nat. Book Award for Outstanding Achievement 2010. *Publications:* fiction: The Rachel Papers (Somerset Maugham Award 1974) 1973, Dead Babies 1975, new edn as Dark Secrets 1977, Success 1978, Other People: A Mystery Story 1981, Money: A Suicide Note 1984, Einstein's Monsters (short stories) 1987, London Fields 1989, Time's Arrow, or, the Nature of the Offence 1991, God's Dice 1995, The Information 1995, Night Train 1997, Heavy Water and Other Stories 1999, Yellow Dog 2003, The Last Days of Muhammad Atta (short stories, novella, essay) 2006, House of Meetings (novella) 2006, The Pregnant Widow 2010, Lionel Asbo 2012, The Zone of Interest 2014; non-fiction: My Oxford (with others) 1977, Invasion of the Space Invaders 1982, The Moronic Inferno and Other Visits to America 1986, Visiting Mrs Nabokov and Other Excursions 1993, Experience: A Memoir (James Tait Black Memorial Prize for Biography 2001) 2000, The War Against Cliché (essays and reviews 1971–2000) 2001, Koba the Dread: Laughter and Twenty Million 2002, The Second Plane 2008, The Rub of Time: Bellow, Nabokov, Hitchens, Travolta, Trump. Essays and Reportage 2017; contrib. to many publs. *Leisure interests:* tennis, chess, snooker. *Address:* Wylie Agency (UK) Ltd, 17 Bedford Square, London, WC1B 3JA, England (office). *Telephone:* (20) 7908-5900 (office). *Fax:* (20) 7908-5901 (office). *E-mail:* mail@wylieagency.co.uk (office).

AMMANN, Karl; Swiss wildlife photographer, journalist, author and conservationist; b. 1948, St Gallen; ed St Gallen Grad. School of Econs, Cornell Univ., USA; moved to Kenya to start work with Intercontinental Hotels 1974, spent six months helping Zaïre Govt organize 'The Rumble in the Jungle' boxing match between George Foreman and Muhammad Ali 1974; moved to Cairo to manage hotel 1978; spent two years in Masai Mara Game Reserve to do research for first photographic title, Cheetah 1980; set up eco-tourism camp in Masai Mara 1983, camp in Virunga Mountains, Rwanda 1986, sold camps to concentrate on photography; Media Asia Advertising Award 1991, BBC Wildlife Photographer of the Year, World in Our Hands Award 1996–2000, Dolly Green Award for Artistic Achievement, Genesis Awards 1997, Chimfunshi Pal award in recognition of his work to raise awareness of plight of chimpanzees 1999, Special Genesis Award for media work in exposing bushmeat crisis 2000, Winner, Landscape and Nature category, American Photo, Special Contest Issue No. 5, a Time Magazine Hero of the Environment 2007, Brigitte Bardot Int. Genesis Award 2008. *Achievements include:* undertook first investigative expedition in Africa looking into apes orphaned by bushmeat trade 1992; initiated campaign with European Zoo Assoc. leading to a 2m.-signature petition being presented to European Parl. 1995; has also produced images of a hitherto unknown ape Bili Ape. *Television:* documentary: The Cairo Connection (broadcast on SABC2's 50/50) (Environmental Journalist of the Year, South African Broadcasting Corpn 2008). *Publications include:* Cheetah 1984, The Hunters and the Hunted 1989, Die Grossen Menschenaffen (photography) 1992, Masai Mara 1993, Gorillas 1998, Little Bull: Growing Up in Africa's Elephant Kingdom 1998, Orangutan Odyssey (photography) 1999, The Great Apes and Humans (co-author) 2001, Great Ape Odyssey (photography) 2002, Eating Apes (with Dale Peterson) (Science Book of the Year, The Economist and Discovery Magazine) 2003, Consuming Nature (photography) 2005. *E-mail:* karl@karlammann.ch (office). *Website:* www.karlammann.com (office).

AMMON, Niels Peter Georg; German diplomatist; b. 23 Feb. 1952, Frankfurt; m. Marliese Heimann; two d.; ed Freie Universität Berlin, Inst. for Operations Research, Diplomatic School, Bonn; joined Foreign Service 1978, served in Embassy in London 1980–82, in Dakar 1982–85, served at Fed. Minister of Foreign Affairs, Bonn 1985–89, served in Embassy in New Delhi 1989–91, mem. Policy Planning Staff 1991–96, Head of Policy Planning Staff in Pres.'s Office 1996–99, EC Minister, Embassy in Washington, DC 1999–2001, Dir-Gen. for EC Affairs and Sustainable Devt, Fed. Ministry of Foreign Affairs, Berlin 2003–05, also G8-Sous Sherpa, Amb. to France 2007–08, State Sec., Fed. Ministry of Foreign Affairs 2008–11, Amb. to USA 2011–14, to UK 2014–18. *Leisure interests:* working out, hiking, listening to the music of Bob Dylan.

AMOAKO, Kingsley Y., BA, MA, PhD; Ghanaian economist; *President, African Center for Economic Transformation;* b. 13 Sept. 1944, Accra; ed Univ. of Ghana, Univ. of California, Berkeley, USA; with IBRD from the 1970s, Dir Dept of Educ. and Social Policy 1993–95; UN Under-Sec.-Gen. and Exec. Sec. Econ. Comm. for Africa (ECA) 1995–2005; Distinguished African Scholar, Woodrow Wilson Int. Center 2006; Founder and Pres. African Center for Econ. Transformation, Accra 2006–; mem. Policy Advisory Bd DATA (debt, AIDS, trade, Africa); Dr hc (Addis Ababa Univ.) 2003, (Kwame Nkrumah Univ. of Science and Tech., Kumasi) 2005. *Address:* African Center for Economic Transformation, 50 Liberation Road, Ridge Residential Area, Accra, Ghana (office); African Center for Economic Transformation, 1776 K Street, NW, Suite 200, Washington, DC 20006, USA (office). *E-mail:* info@acetforafrica.org (office). *Website:* acetforafrica.org (office).

AMON, Angelika, BS, PhD; Austrian/American molecular and cell biologist and academic; *Professor of Biology and Kathleen and Curtis Marble Professor in Cancer Research, Massachusetts Institute of Technology;* b. 1967, Austria; m.; two d.; ed Univ. of Vienna, Research Inst. of Molecular Pathology; Amon Lab began at Whitehead Inst. 1996–99, lab moved to Center for Cancer Research, MIT (now known as Koch Inst. for Integrative Cancer Research) 1999–, currently Prof. of Biology and Kathleen and Curtis Marble Prof. in Cancer Research; HHMI Investigator, Howard Hughes Medical Inst. 2000–; Foreign Assoc., European Molecular Biology Org.; mem. American Acad. of Microbiology, NAS 2010–, American Acad. of Arts and Sciences 2017–; NAS Award in Molecular Biology, Paul Marks Prize for Cancer Research, Memorial Sloan-Kettering Cancer Center, Alan T. Waterman Award, NSF, Eli Lilly Young Investigator Award, Presidential Early Career Award for Scientists and Engineers, (PECASE), Genetics Soc. of America Medal, Ira Herskowitz Award, Genetics Soc. of America, ASBMB Amgen Award, American Soc. for Biochemistry and Molecular Biology, Ernst Jung Prize (co-recipient) 2013, Vanderbilt Prize in Biomedical Science 2018, Breakthrough Prize in Life Sciences 2019, Vilcek Prize in Biomedical Science 2019. *Publications:* numerous papers in professional journals. *Address:* Room 76–561, Koch Institute for Integrative Cancer Research, Massachusetts Institute of Technology, 500 Main Street, Building 76, Cambridge, MA 02139-4307, USA (office). *Telephone:* (617) 258-8964 (office); (617) 258-6559 (office). *Fax:* (617) 258-6558 (office). *E-mail:* angelika@mit.edu (office). *Website:* biology.mit.edu/people/angelika_amon (office); ki.mit.edu/people/faculty/amon (office).

AMON TANOH, Marcel; Côte d'Ivoirian politician; *Minister of Foreign Affairs;* b. 25 Nov. 1951; m.; four c.; ed Univ. d'Abidjan, Univ. Paris VIII; Sec.-Gen. Cocody Town Hall, Abidjan 1980–83; Dir-Gen. Société ivoirienne de confection et diffusion (SICD), Paris 1983–86; Pres. African Commodity Trading Co., London 1986–92; CEO Société d'import-export de produits agricoles et de marchandises (Siepam), Abidjan 1986–96; Dir Société Agro-Industrielle de Soubré (cocoa export business) 1989–94; Dir-Gen. Société ERF (Etudes et recherche de financement) 1996; Minister of Transport Aug.–Nov. 2002, of Tourism 2003–05, of Construction, Urban Affairs and Housing 2005; Cabinet Dir Presidency of the Repub. 2011–17; Minister of Foreign Affairs 2017–; mem. Rassemblement des Républicains (RDR). *Address:* Ministry of Foreign Affairs, Bloc Ministériel, blvd Angoulvant, BP V109, Abidjan, Côte d'Ivoire (office). *Telephone:* 20-22-71-50 (office). *Fax:* 20-33-23-08 (office). *E-mail:* infos@mae.ci (office). *Website:* www.mae.ci (office).

AMORIM, Celso Luiz Nunes; Brazilian diplomatist and politician; b. 3 June 1942, Santos, São Paulo; s. of Vicente Matheus Amorim and Beatriz Nunes Amorim; m. Ana Maria Amorim; three s. one d.; ed Rio Branco Inst., Diplomatic Acad. Vienna and London School of Econs; Lecturer in Portuguese, Rio Branco Inst. 1976; apptd Lecturer, Dept of Political Science and Int. Relations, Univ. of Brasília 1977; Dir-Gen. EMBRAFILME (Brazilian Film Corpn) 1979–82; Deputy Head of Mission, The Hague 1982–85; Perm. Rep. to UN, GATT and Conf. on Disarmament, Geneva 1991–93 (Pres. 2000), to UN and WTO 1999–2001; Sec. for Int. Affairs, Ministry of Science and Tech. 1987–88; Dir-Gen. for Cultural Affairs, Ministry of Foreign Affairs 1989–90, for Econ. Affairs 1990–91, Sec.-Gen. 1993, Minister of Foreign Affairs 1993–94, 2003–11, of Defence 2011–15; Perm. Rep. to UN, New York 1995–99; Amb. to UK 2001–02; Chair. UN Security Council Resolution Sanctions Cttee on Kosovo 1998–99, UN Security Council Panels on Iraq 1999, Governing Body ILO 2000, Council for Trade in Services, WTO 2001; Perm. mem. Dept of Int. Affairs, Inst. of Advanced Studies, Univ. of São Paulo; mem. Canberra Comm. on Elimination of Nuclear Weapons 1966, Int. Task Force on Security Council Peace Enforcement 1997; Foreign Policy Asscn Medal (USA) 1999. *Publications include:* several works on political theory, int. relations, cultural policies and subjects connected with science and tech. *Leisure interests:* reading, travel, art, cinema.

AMOS, Daniel (Dan) Paul, BS; American insurance industry executive; *Chairman and CEO, Aflac Inc.;* b. 13 Aug. 1951, Pensacola, Fla; s. of Paul Amos (Co-founder of Aflac Inc.); ed Univ. of Georgia; joined Aflac Inc. 1973, Sales Dept 1973–83, Pres. 1983–87, COO 1987–90, CEO Aflac Inc. and mem. Bd of Dirs 1990–, Chair. 2001–; mem. Bd of Dirs Synovus Financial Corpn, Southern Co.; mem. Bd of Trustees, Children's Healthcare of Atlanta, House of Mercy of Columbus; fmr mem. Consumer Affairs Advisory Cttee, Securities and Exchange Comm.; fmr Chair. Japan America Soc. of Georgia, Univ. of Georgia Foundation; Dr Martin Luther King Jr Unity Award, Anti-Defamation League's Torch of Liberty Award. *Address:* Aflac Worldwide Headquarters, 1932 Wynnton Road, Columbus, GA 31999, USA (office). *Telephone:* (706) 323-3431 (office); (800) 992-3522 (office). *Fax:* (706) 324-6330 (office). *Website:* www.aflac.com (office).

AMOS, Paul S., II, BEcons, MBA, JD; American business executive; *President, Aflac Inc.;* s. of Daniel P. Amos; ed Duke Univ., Emory Univ., Tulane Univ.; fmrly worked in corp. legal div., Skadden, Arps, Slate, Meagher & Flom (merger and acquisitions firm), Washington, DC; served as state sales co-ordinator for Aflac's Georgia-North operations, Exec. Vice-Pres. of US Operations 2005–06, COO 2006–07, COO Aflac US 2006–, Pres. Aflac Inc. 2007–, also mem. Bd of Dirs; mem. Bd of Dirs Winship Cancer Center at Emory Univ., Turner School of Business at Columbus State Univ., Make-a-Wish Foundation of Southwest Georgia; mem. Bd of Trustees, Georgia Research Alliance, Bd of Visitors, Duke Univ. Divinity School, Water Contingency Task Force of Gov. Sonny Perdue of Ga. *Address:* Aflac Worldwide Headquarters, 1932 Wynnton Road, Columbus, GA 31999, USA (office). *Telephone:* (706) 323-3431 (office); (800) 992-3522 (office). *Fax:* (706) 324-6330 (office). *E-mail:* info@aflac.com (office). *Website:* www.aflac.com (office).

AMOS, Rt Hon. the Baroness (Life Peer), cr. 1997, of Brondesbury in the London Borough of Brent; **Valerie Ann Amos**, CH, MA; British politician, diplomatist and UN official; b. 13 March 1954, Guyana; d. of E. Michael Amos and Eunice V. Amos; ed Univs of Warwick, Birmingham and East Anglia; Race Relations Adviser, London Borough of Lambeth 1981–83; Women's Adviser, London Borough of Camden 1983–85; Head of Training and Devt, London Borough of Hackney 1985–87, Head of Man. Services 1988–89; Chief Exec. Equal Opportunities Comm. 1989–94; Dir Fraser Bernard 1994–98; Govt Whip 1998–2001; Parl. Under-Sec. of State, FCO 2001–03; Sec. of State for Int. Devt 2003; mem. (non-affiliated), House of Lords 1997–, Leader 2003–07, leave of absence 2010–; High Commr to Australia 2009–10; Under-Sec.-Gen. for Humanitarian Affairs and Emergency Relief Coordinator, UN, New York 2010–15; Commr Fulbright Comm. 2009; Dir Hampstead Theatre 1992–98; Chair. Royal African Soc. 2007–; Deputy Chair. Runnymede Trust 1990–98; Fellow, Centre for Corp. Reputation, Univ. of Oxford 2007–; Dir (non-exec.), Travant Capital Partners 2007–; fmr Dir (non-exec.), Univ. Coll. London Hospitals Trust; fmr Chair. Afiya Trust, Bd of Govs, Royal Coll. of Nursing Inst.; mem. Advisory Cttee Centre for Educ. Devt Appraisal and Research, Univ. of Warwick 1991–98, Gen. Advisory Council BBC, King's Fund Coll. Cttee 1992–98, Council Inst. of Employment Studies 1993–98, Advisory Bd Global Health Group, Univ. of San Francisco; Trustee, Women's Therapy Centre 1989–; fmr Trustee, Inst. of Public Policy Research, VSO; Hon. Prof., Thames Valley Univ. 1995; Hon. LLD (Warwick) 2000, (Staffordshire) 2000, (Manchester) 2001, (Leicester) 2006, (Bradford) 2007, (Birmingham) 2008, (Stirling) 2010. *Leisure interest:* cricket. *Address:* House of Lords, Westminster, London, SW1A 0PW, England. *Website:* www.parliament.uk/biographies/lords/baroness-amos/3477.

AMOUDI, Sheikh; **Mohammed Hussein Ali Al-**; Saudi Arabian/Ethiopian business executive; *Chairman, Corral Petroleum Holdings;* b. 21 July 1946, Dessie, Ethiopia; m. Sofia Saleh Al Amoudi; eight c.; emigrated to Saudi Arabia became a Saudi citizen 1965; f. construction co. consortium, Mohammed International Development Research and Organization Companies (MIDROC), built nationwide underground oil storage complex 1988, acquired Yanbu Steel 2000; substantial business interests in Ethiopia, also owns oil refineries in Morocco and Sweden; involved also in mining, agriculture, hotels, hospitals, finance, operations and maintenance; holding and operating cos Corral Petroleum Holdings (investment portfolio includes Preem Petroleum, Sweden, Svenska Petroleum & Exploration, SAMIR, Naft Services Co. (Saudi Arabia), Fortuna Holdings (Lebanon) and MIDROC; detained on corruption charges 2017, released 2018; Order of the Polar Star (Sweden); Hon. PhD (Addis Ababa Univ.); honoured jtly by World Bank and US State Dept for his work in supporting African development 1997, King Saud Univ. Gold Medal from King Abdullah 2009, honoured at 19th Arab Economic Forum Summit in Beirut with special reference to his commitment to sustainable development 2011. *Address:* Corral Petroleum Holdings AB, Warfvinges väg 45, 112 80 Stockholm, Sweden (office). *Telephone:* (10) 450-10-00 (Stockholm) (office). *E-mail:* info@preem.se (office). *Website:* www.preem.se (office); www.sheikhmohammedalamoudi.info.

AMOYAL, Pierre Alain Wilfred; French violinist and academic; *University Professor in Violin, University Mozarteum;* b. 22 June 1949, Paris; s. of Dr Wilfred Amoyal and Vera Amoyal (née Popravka); m. 2nd Leslie Chabot 1988; ed Cours d'Etat, Vanves, Conservatoire Nat. Supérieur de Musique, Univ. of Southern California, USA; studied with Jascha Heifetz; invited by Sir Georg Solti to perform Berg's violin concerto with Orchestre de Paris 1971 and by Pierre Boulez to perform Schoenberg's Concerto with Orchestre de Paris 1977; recital debut at Carnegie Hall 1985; numerous performances worldwide with orchestras including Berlin Philharmonic, Vienna Symphony Orchestra, Filarmonica della Scala, Milan, Royal Philharmonic, New Philarmonia, Orchestre Nat. de France, Residentie-Orkest, The Hague; Prof. of Violin, Conservatoire Nat. Supérieur de

Musique, Paris 1977–88, Lausanne Conservatory 1987; Univ. Prof. in Violin, Univ. Mozarteum, Salzburg 2013–; Co-founder (with Alexis Weissenberg) and Artistic Dir Lausanne Summer Music Acad. 1991–; f. Camerata of Lausanne 2002, ensemble orchestra of young musicians; mem. Jury, Singapore Int. Violin Competition 2015; Chevalier, Ordre des Arts et des Lettres 1985, Chevalier, Ordre Nat. du Mérite 1995; First Prize, Conservatoire de Versailles 1960, Conservatoire Nat. Supérieur de Musique, Paris 1962, for chamber music, Conservatoire Nat. Supérieur de Musique, Prix Ginette Neveu, Prix Paganini, Prix Enesco 1970, Grand Prix du Disque 1974, 1977, Prix du Rayonnement de la Fondation Vaudoise pour la Promotion et la Création artistique 2002, Prix de Lausanne 2006. *Recordings include:* Symphonie espagnole (Lalo), Violin Concerto (Mendelssohn), Concertos No. 1 and 2 and Two Sonatas (Prokofiev), Tartini's concertos, Third Concerto, Havanaise and Rondo Capriccioso (Saint-Saëns), Concerto No. 1 (Bruch), Concerto (Glazunov), Sonatas (Fauré), Horn Trio (Brahms), Concertos (Mozart), Concerto (Sibelius), Concerto (Tchaikovsky), Sonatas (Brahms), Concerto (Schoenberg), works of Albert Huybrechts 2009. *Leisure interests:* photography, literature, sport. *Address:* University Mozarteum, Mirabellplatz 1, 5020 Salzburg, Austria (office). *E-mail:* pierre@amoyal.com. *Website:* www.amoyal.com; www.uni-mozarteum.at (office).

AMPUERO ESPINOZA, Roberto, BA, MA, PhD; Chilean novelist, university professor and politician; *Minister of Foreign Affairs;* b. 20 Feb. 1953, Valparaíso; s. of Roberto Ampuero Brule and Angelica Espinoza; m. 1st Margarita Flores, one s.; m. 2nd Ana Lucrecia Rivera Schwarz, one s. one d.; ed Univ. of Chile, Karl Marx Univ., Leipzig, Humboldt Univ., Berlin; mem. Chilean Communist Youth –1976; lived in exile in Cuba 1973–79, East Germany 1979–83; returned to Chile 1993; lived in Stockholm 1997–2000; columnist, El Mercurio (daily newspaper) 2009, New York Times Syndicate, La Tercera; Amb. to Mexico 2011; fmr Prof., Dept of Spanish and Portuguese, Univ. of Iowa; Minister of Culture 2013–14, Minister of Foreign Affairs 2018–; Dir Fundación Avanza Chile; Visiting Prof. Finis Terrae Univ.; currently Sr Fellow, Fundación para el Progreso (FPP); Fellow Civitella Ranieri Foundation, Italy; fmr Fellow, International Writing Program, Univ. of Iowa, USA. *Publications include:* ¿Quién mató a Cristián Kustermann? (Who Killed Cristián Kusterman?) (El Mercurio Revista del Libro Prize 1993) 1993, Boleros en La Habana (Boleros in Havana) 1994, El alemán de Atacama (The German of Atacama) 1996, El hombre golondrina (The Swallow Man) 1997, Nuestros años verde olivo (Our Olive Green Years) 1999, La guerra de los duraznos (The War of the Peaches) 2001, Los amantes de Estocolmo (The Stockholm Lovers) 2003, Cita en el Azul Profundo (Appointment at the Azul Profundo) 2004, Halcones de la noche (Nighthawks) 2005, La Historia como conjetura: La narrativa de Jorge Edwards (The Story as Conjecture: The narrative of Jorge Edwards) (essay) 2006, Pasiones griegas (Greek Passions) 2006, El caso Neruda (The Neruda Case) 2008, La otra mujer (The Other Woman) 2010, Bahía de los misterios (Bay of Mysteries) 2013, El Ultimo Tango de Salvador Allende (The Last Tango of Salvador Allende) 2014. *Address:* Ministry of Foreign Affairs, Teatinos 180, Santiago, Chile (office). *Telephone:* (2) 2827-4200 (office). *Website:* www.minrel.gov.cl (office).

AMR, Mohamed Kamal Ali; Egyptian diplomatist and government official; b. 1 Dec. 1942; Counsellor, Embassy in Washington, DC 1990s; fmr Amb. to Saudi Arabia; fmr Perm. Rep. to World Bank; represented Egypt in several African orgs; Minister of Foreign Affairs 2011–13.

AMRANAND, Piyasvasti, BA (Hons), MSc, PhD; Thai civil servant and business executive; *Independent Director and Chairman, PTT Public Company Limited;* b. 11 July 1953, Bangkok; m. Anik Wichiancharoen; ed Brasenose Coll., Oxford and London School of Econs, UK; played role in deregulating and privatizing several energy-related state enterprises including PTT and power generation business during 1990s; Sec.-Gen., Nat. Energy Policy Office 2001–02; Deputy Perm. Sec., Office of the Perm. Sec., Prime Minister's Office 2002–03; Exec. Chair. Kasikorn Asset Management Co. Ltd 2003–06; Minister of Energy 2006–08; Pres. Thai Airways International Public Co. Ltd 2009–12; Ind. Dir and Chair. PTT Public Co. Ltd 2014–; Ind. Dir, Bangkok Aviation Fuel Services PLC 1995–2006, Muang Thai Insurance Public Co. Ltd –2006, Kasikornbank Public Co. Ltd 2013–; Dir, The Ruang Khao Global Balanced Fund, Fuel Pipeline Transportation Ltd 1996–; Chair. Energy for Environment Foundation; Dir Accreditation Programme, Thai Inst. of Dirs 2005. *Address:* PTT Public Co. Ltd, 555 Vibhavadi Rangsit Road, Chatuchak, Bangkok 10900, Thailand (office). *Telephone:* (2) 537-2000 (office). *Fax:* (2) 537-3499 (office). *E-mail:* info@pttplc.com (office). *Website:* www.pttplc .com (office).

AMUDUN, Niyaz; Chinese party and government official; *Chairman, Standing Committee of Xinjiang Uygur Autonomous Regional People's Congress;* b. 1932, Xinjiang Uygur Autonomous Region, Luntai; joined CCP 1953; Sec. CCP Autonomous Prefectural Cttee, Xinjiang Uygur Autonomous Region, Korla 1955–60; mem. CCP Autonomous County Cttee, Secr. Xinjiang Uygur Autonomous Region, Luntai 1960–62; Deputy Dir Commerce Dept, Xinjiang Uygur Autonomous Region 1962–66, Supply and Marketing Cooperatives 1962–66; Mayor Urumqi City, Xinjiang Uygur Autonomous Region 1966–67; Deputy Sec. CCP Autonomous City Cttee, Urumqi City 1973–78, Sec. 1973–78; Deputy to 4th NPC 1975, Vice-Chair. Ethnic Affairs Cttee 1978–83; Vice-Chair. Govt of Xinjiang Uygur Autonomous Region 1979–83; Chair. Standing Cttee of Xinjiang Uygur Autonomous Region People's Congress 1983–; Deputy Sec. CCP Xinjiang Uygur Autonomous Region Cttee 1985–, Sec. Political Science and Law Cttee 1985–; Chair. Xinjiang Uygur Autonomous Regional 8th People's Congress 1985, Standing Cttee of 7th Xinjiang People's Congress 1989–93, of 8th Xinjiang Uygur Autonomous Regional People's Congress 1993–; Del., 13th CCP Nat. Congress 1987, 15th Nat. Congress 1997–2002; Deputy, 8th NPC 1993–98; mem. Cen. Comm. for Discipline Inspection, CCP Cen. Cttee. *Address:* Standing Committee of Xinjiang Uygur Autonomous Region People's Congress, Urumqi, People's Republic of China.

AMUM OKECH, Pagan; South Sudanese politician; b. 3 Jan. 1959, Malakal; joined Sudan People's Liberation Army (SPLA) 1983, served as mil. and civilian admin., Malakal, Bahr al-Ghazal, Melut, apptd civilian admin., Kapoeta 1991, fmr commdr SPLM/A operations in eastern Sudan, fmr mem. SPLM negotiating team for CPA (Comprehensive Peace Agreement), Sec.-Gen. SPLM 2005–13 (suspended July 2013); Minister of Peace and CPA Implementation 2011–15; fmr Diplomatic Affairs Adviser to Pres. of Sudan; fmr Sec.-Gen. Nat. Democratic Alliance; in exile in USA since 2015.

AMUNUGAMA, Sarath Leelananda Bandara, PhD; Sri Lankan politician, civil servant and newspaper executive; b. 10 July 1939; m.; ed Trinity Coll., Kandy, Univ. of Ceylon; fmr govt agent in Kandy Dist; fmr Dir of Information; fmr Perm. Sec. to Ministry of Information and Broadcasting; worked as int. civil servant for UNESCO HQ, Paris, France; fmr Spokesman for People's Alliance (PA); MP (United People's Freedom Alliance) for Mahanuwara, Kandy Dist 1994–; Minister of Northern Rehabilitation 2000, of Culture 2000, of Finance –2005, of Public Admin and Home Affairs 2005–07, of Enterprise Devt and Investment Promotion 2007–09, of Public Admin and Home Affairs and Deputy Minister of Finance and Planning 2009–10, Hon. Sr Minister of Int. Monetary Co-operation and Deputy Minister of Finance and Planning 2010, Acting Minister of Skills Development and Technology 2018, Minister of Foreign Affairs Oct.–Dec. 2018; Chair. The Associated Newspapers of Ceylon Ltd. *Address:* Citizens For Sarath, 50, Kande Veediya, Kandy (office); 50/1 Siripa Road, Colombo 05, Sri Lanka (home). *Telephone:* (81) 4949580 (office); (81) 2499703; (77) 3489388 (mobile); (11) 2586789. *E-mail:* amunugama_s@parliament.lk (office); cypher@mea.gov.lk (office). *Website:* www .parliament.lk/en/members-of-parliament/directory-of-members/viewMember/57 (office).

AMUSÁTEGUI DE LA CIERVA, José María; Spanish banker; b. 12 March 1932, San Roque; s. of Antonio Amusátegui de la Cierva and Dolores Amusátegui de la Cierva; m. 1st Maria Luz; m. 2nd Amalia de León 1988 (divorced); six c.; ed Colegio de Huérfanos de la Armada and Univ. of Madrid; state lawyer, Minister of Finance, Gerona 1959–70; joined Instituto Nacional de Industria 1963, Vice-Chair. 1970; Sec., Bd of Dirs Boada Altos Hornos de Vizcaya 1967; Deputy Chair. Prodinsa 1974; Chair. Catalan Devt Bank 1975, Intelsa 1975–80, Astilleros Españoles 1980; Pres. Spanish Shipyard, Dir Naval Div. 1980; Deputy Chair. Instituto Nacional de Hidrocarburos 1981; Chair. Campsa 1982; Man. Dir and Deputy Chair. Banco Hispano Americano 1985, Chair. 1991–99, also Pres.; Dir Union Fenosa SA 1991–93, Pres. 1993, currently Hon. Chair. and mem. Exec. Cttee; Chair. Banco Cen. Hispano 1992–99; Pres. Banco Vitalicio de Espana SA de Seguros (acquired by La Estrella, SA de Seguros y Reaseguros 2010) from 1993; Co-Chair. Banco Santander Cen. Hispanoamericano (BSCH, now Banco Santander Cen. Hispano SA) 1999–2002, Hon. Chair. 2002–; Grand Cross of Civil Merit. *Leisure interests:* motorcycling, astronomy, botany. *Address:* Banco Vitalicio de Espana SA de Seguros, Paseo de Gracia 11, 08007 Barcelona (office); Unión Fenosa SA, Avenida de San Luis, 28033 Madrid, Spain (office). *Telephone:* (93) 4840100 (Barcelona) (office); (91) 5676000 (Madrid) (office). *Fax:* (91) 5718246 (Madrid) (office). *Website:* www.generali.es (office).

AN, Zhendong; Chinese government official and engineer; b. 5 Sept. 1930, Tangshan, Hebei Prov.; ed Hebei Engineering Coll.; engineer, Railway Admin, Electric Power Div., Heilongjiang Prov., Qiqihar City 1952–58; engineer, Heilongjiang Silicon Rectifier Factory, Harbin City 1963–67; Engineer, Deputy Factory Dir Harbin Rectifier Equipment Factory 1967–81; Chief Engineer, 2nd Light Industry Bureau 1981–82; joined Jiusan Soc. 1981, Vice-Chair. 6th, 7th, 8th, 9th and 10th Cen. Cttee; Vice-Gov. Heilongjiang 1983–90; Vice-Chair. Standing Cttee Heilongjiang Prov. People's Congress 1990–93; mem. 6th NPC 1983–88, 7th NPC 1988–93, 8th NPC 1993–98; mem. 9th CPPCC Nat. Cttee, Standing Cttee 1998–2003, Vice-Chair. (Heilongjiang Prov.) 2003–08; Vice-Pres. Chinese Package Soc.; Dir Chinese Industry Econ. Soc.; named Model Worker of Special Grade of Harbin, Model Worker of Heilongjiang Prov. *Achievements include:* inventions of: Signal and Radio Telephone in Railroad Cars 1958, Fire-fighting Automatic System in Cities 1963, Explosion-proof Rectifier Equipment in Coal Mines 1973, Power Factor Electricity Regulator 1976.

AN QIYUAN, BEng; Chinese government official and fmr geologist; b. July 1933, Lingtong Co., Shaanxi Prov.; ed Dept of Geology, Northwest China Univ.; joined CCP 1953; leader geological team of Songliao Petroleum Prospecting Bureau 1958–59; Dir of Oil Mine and Chief, Underground Operation Section of 1st HQ Oil Extracting in Daqing 1964–65; Dir Petroleum Geophysics Prospecting Bureau, Ministry of Petroleum 1973–77; Deputy Dir State Seismological Bureau 1977–80, Dir 1982–88; mem. Standing Cttee CCP Shaanxi Prov. Cttee, Sec. CCP Xian Municipal Cttee 1988; mem. Standing Cttee CPPCC Comm. for Inspecting Discipline 1992–94; Sec. CCP Shaanxi Prov. Cttee 1994–97; Chair. CPPCC Shaanxi Prov. Cttee 1998–2003; mem. 9th CPPCC Nat. Cttee 1998–2003. *Publications:* Developing Shaanxi Province and Enriching the People by Grasping the Keystone and Fulfilment. *Leisure interest:* reading.

ANAND, Viswanathan (Vishy), BCom; Indian chess grandmaster; b. 11 Dec. 1969, Mayiladuthurai, Tamil Nadu; s. of Krishnamurthy Viswanathan and Susheela Viswanathan; m. Aruna Anand 1996; one s.; ed Loyola Coll., Chennai; started playing chess aged six; won Nat. Sub-Jr Chess Championship aged 14 1983; youngest Indian to achieve title of Int. Master aged 15 1984; nat. chess champion aged 16 1985; World Jr Chess Champion and Grandmaster (first Indian holder) 1988; won World Chess Fed. (FIDE) World Chess Championships 2000–02, undisputed World Champion 2007–13, apptd Continental Asst for Asia, also Councillor, Planning and Devt Comm. 2019–; tournament victories include Asian Jr Chess Championship, Coimbatore 1984, Asian Jr Chess Championship, Hong Kong 1985, World Jr Chess Championship (first Indian winner) 1987, FIDE World Chess Championship (first Indian winner) 2000, Corus Chess Tournament 2003, 2004, 2006, FIDE World Championship Tournament, Mexico City 2007, Grenkeleasing Rapid Championship 2007, Linares Chess Tournament 2007, 2008, FIDE World Chess Championships 2008, 2010, 2012, GRENKE Chess Classic Baden-Baden 2013, World Chess Championship Candidates Tournament 2014, Bilbao Masters (Grand Slam) 2014, 6th London Chess Classic 2014, Zurich Chess Challenge 2015, Leon Chess Masters Rapid Tournament 2016, St Louis Champions Tournament 2016; mem. Bd of Dirs Olympic Gold Quest 2010–; Padma Shri 1987, Padma Bhushan 2000, Padma Vibhushan 2007, Russian Order of Friendship 2014; Rajiv Gandhi Khel Ratna Award 1991–92, Chess Oscars 1997, 1998, 2003 and 2004, named Indian Sportsperson of the Year 2012. *Publication:* My Best Games of Chess 1998. *Address:* c/o Kuruvilla Abraham, TNQ Sponsorship (India) Pvt. Ltd, 28 Anna Enclave, Injambakkam, Chennai 699 941, India (office). *E-mail:* mail@tnq.in (office). *Website:* tnq.in (office).

ANANDASANGAREE, Veerasingham; Sri Lankan politician; *President, Tamil United Liberation Front;* b. 15 June 1933, Point Pedro; s. of S. Veerasingham and Ratnam; m.; four c.; ed Sri Somaskanda Coll., Christian Coll. Atchuvely, Hartley

Coll., Zahira Coll.; teacher, Hindu Coll., Jaffna, Poonakri MMV, Kotelawela GTM School, Ratmalana, Christ King Coll., Ja-Ela 1953–59; Chair. Karaichi Village Council 1965–68, Karaichi Town Council 1968–69; practised as lawyer 1967–83; mem. Ceylon Parl. 1970–83, Sri Lanka Parl. 2000–04; joined All Ceylon Tamil Congress 1966, Youth Front Pres. 1970; joined Tamil United Front (later Tamil United Liberation Front), Propaganda Sec., Tamil United Liberation Front 1976–83, mem. Politburo 1983–93, Sr Vice-Pres. 1993–2002, Acting Pres. 1998–2001, Pres. 2002–; UNESCO Madanjeet Singh Prize 2006. *Address:* Tamil United Liberation Front, 5/3A Wijayaba Mawatha, Kalubowila, Dehiwala, Colombo, Sri Lanka (office). *Telephone:* (11) 2552372 (office). *E-mail:* tulfsl@yahoo.com (office). *Website:* tamilunitedliberationfront.org (office); anandasangary.com (office).

ANANIASHVILI, Nina Gedevanovna; Georgian/Russian ballet dancer; *Artistic Director, State Ballet of Georgia;* b. 28 March 1963, Tbilisi; d. of Gedevan Ananiashvili and Lia Gogolashvili; m. Gregory Vashadze 1988; one s. one d.; ed State Choreographic Schools of Georgia and Bolshoi Theatre, Russia; Prima Ballerina, Bolshoi Ballet, Moscow 1981–, Prin., American Ballet Theater 1993–2009; has performed on tour world-wide with New York City Ballet, Royal Ballet, Royal Danish Ballet, Kirov Ballet, Royal Swedish Ballet, Ballet de Monte Carlo, The Munich Ballet, La Scala Ballet, Houston Ballet, Boston Ballet, Tokyo Ballet and others; Prima Ballerina and Artistic Dir, State Ballet of Georgia 2004–, ballets staged include classical works and ballets by Balanchine, Ashton, Bournonville and Kylián; tours to USA 2007, 2008, 2010, Edinburgh Int. Festival 2008 and Japan 2012; apptd UN Goodwill Amb. in Georgia 2007; Order for Outstanding Service to Fatherland (Russia) 2000, Order of Honour (Georgia) 2003, Presidential Order of Light (Georgia) 2010, Order of the Star of Italian Solidarity 2011; numerous awards including Gold Medal, Varna Int. Competition (Bulgaria) 1980, Grand Prix, Moscow Int. Competition 1981, Gold Medal, Moscow Int. Competition 1984, Grand Prix, Int. Ballet Competition, Jackson 1986, People's Artist of Repub. of Georgia 1989, Triumph Prize for achievement in art 1992, State Prize of Georgia 1993, People's Artist of Russia 1995, Zurab Anjaparidze and Rustaveli State Prize 1993, State Prize of the Russian Federation—For the Merit to the Fatherland 2001, Dance Magazine Award for Outstanding Achievement 2002. *Dance:* over 100 roles including Giselle, Odette/Odile (Swan Lake), Aurora (Sleeping Beauty), Raimonda, Juliet (Romeo and Juliet), Nikya (La Bayadère), Kitri (Don Quixote). *Leisure interests:* antique books, modern painting. *Address:* State Ballet of Georgia, Tbilisi Opera and Ballet Theatre, 0108 Tbilisi, Rustaveli Ave. 25, Georgia (office); 119270 Moscow, Frunzenskaya nab. 46, Apt. 79, Russia. *E-mail:* ballet@comtv.ru (office). *Website:* www.opera.ge (office); www.ananiashvili.com.

ANASTASE, Roberta Alma; Romanian politician and sociologist; b. 27 March 1976, Ploieşti; m. Victor Farca 2013; one s.; ed postgraduate studies in Political Science and European Studies; mem. Democratic Party (now Democratic Liberal Party) 1991–, served in turn as Vice-Pres. Youth Org., mem. Nat. Political Bureau and Head of Prahova Br., currently Exec. Sec. for Int. Relations; mem. Camera Deputaţilor (Chamber of Deputies) for Prahova constituency 2004–07, for 11th Electoral Dist of Prahova (Ploiesti-Vest) 2008–, Chair. (first woman) 2008–12; Observer, European Parl. 2005–07, mem. European Parl. (European People's Party–European Democrats) 2007–08, served as European Parl. Rapporteur for the Black Sea Synergy; represented Romania at Miss Universe competition 1996. *Address:* Camera Deputaţilor (Chamber of Deputies), Palatul Parlamentului, 050563 Bucharest, Palatul Parlamentului, str. Izvor 2–4, Sector 5, Romania (office). *Telephone:* (21) 3160300 (office). *Fax:* (21) 4141111 (office). *E-mail:* roberta.anastase@cdep.ro (office). *Website:* www.cdep.ro (office).

ANASTASIADES, Nikos; Cypriot politician, lawyer and head of state; *President;* b. 1946, Limassol; m. Andri Moustakoudes; two d.; ed Univ. of Athens, Univ. of London, UK; practising lawyer, Limassol 1972–; Dist Sec. Youth Org. of Dimokratikos Synagermos (DISY—Democratic Rally Party) 1976–85 (Pres. 1987–90), Vice-Pres. DISY 1985–86, 1990–93, Parl. Leader DISY 1993–97, Deputy Pres. 1995–97, Pres. 1997–2013; mem. Parl. 1981–2013, Speaker, House of Reps 1996–2001; Pres. of Cyprus 2013–. *Address:* Office of the President, Presidential Palace, Dem. Severis Avenue, 1400 Nicosia (office); Dimokratikos Synagermos, PO Box 25303, 25 Pindarou Street, 1061 Nicosia, Cyprus (office). *Telephone:* 22867400 (office); 22883000 (office). *Fax:* 22753821 (office); 22867594 (office). *E-mail:* president@presidency.gov.cy; disy@disy.org.cy (office). *Website:* www.cyprus.gov.cy (office); www.disy.org.cy (office).

ANAYA, Rudolfo, MA; American academic and author; *Professor Emeritus, University of New Mexico;* b. 30 Oct. 1937, Pastura, New Mexico; s. of Martin Anaya and Rafaelita Mares; m. Patricia Lawless 1966; ed Albuquerque High School, Browning Business School, Univ. of New Mexico; teacher, Albuquerque public schools 1963–70; Dir Counseling Center, Univ. of Albuquerque 1971–73; Lecturer, Univ. Anahuac, Mexico City 1974; Prof., Dept of Language and Literature, Univ. of New Mexico 1974–93, Prof. Emer. 1993–; Founder, Ed. Blue Mesa Review 1989–93; Martin Luther King, Jr/César Chávez, Rosa Parks Visiting Prof., Univ. of Michigan, Ann Arbor 1996; currently Assoc. Ed. The American Book Review; Bd Contributing Ed. The Americas Review; Advisory Ed. Great Plains Quarterly; f. PEN-NM, Teachers of English and Chicano Language Arts 1991; Founder, Pres. NM Rio Grande Writers Asscn; mem. Bd Before Columbus Foundation; mem. Nat. Asscn of Chicano Studies, Modern Language Asscn of America, Nat. Council of Teachers of English, Trinity Forum, La Academia Soc., La Compania de Teatro de Albuquerque, Multi-Ethnic Literary Asscn, Before Columbus Foundation, Santa Fe Writers Co-op; Fellow, Nat. Chicano Council on Higher Educ. 1978–79; Hon. DHumLitt (Albuquerque) 1981, (Marycrest Coll.) 1984, (New England) 1992, (Calif. Lutheran Univ.) 1994, (New Hampshire) 1997, Hon. PhD (Santa Fe) 1991, Hon. DLitt (New Hampshire) 1996; recipient of numerous awards, including Nat. Endowment for the Arts Fellowship 1980, New Mexico Gov.'s Award for Excellence and Achievement in Literature 1980, W.K. Kellogg Foundation Fellowship 1983–86, New Mexico Eminent Scholar Award 1989, Rockefeller Foundation Residency Bellagio, Italy 1991, Excellence in the Humanities Award, New Mexico Endowment for the Humanities 1995, Tomás Rivera Mexican American Children's Book Awards 1995, 2000, Distinguished Achievement Award, Western Literature Asscn 1997, Ariz. Adult Authors Award, Arizona Library Asscn 2000, Wallace Stegner Award Center of the American West 2001, Nat. Medal of Arts 2001, Nat. Asscn of Chicano/Chicana Studies Scholar 2002. *Plays include:* Billy the Kid, Who Killed Don José?, Matachines, Angie, Ay, Compadre, The Farolitos of Christmas, Rosalinda 2013. *Films include:* Bless Me, Ultima 2012. *Publications include:* Bless Me, Ultima (Premio Quinto Sol Award 1971) 1972, Heart of Aztlan 1976, Tortuga (American Book Award, Before Columbus Foundation 1979) 1979, Cuentos: Tales from the Hispanic Southwest (trans.) 1980, The Silence of the Llano (short stories) 1982, The Legend of La Llorona 1984, The Adventures of Juan Chicaspatas (poem) 1985, A Chicano in China 1986, Lord of the Dawn, The Legend of Quetzalcoatl 1987, Alburquerque (PEN-WEST Fiction Award 1993) 1992, The Anaya Reader (anthology) 1994, Zia Summer 1995, The Farolitos of Christmas (children's fiction) 1995, Jalamanta, A Message from the Desert 1996, Rio Grande Fall 1996, Maya's Children (children's fiction) 1997, Descansos: An Interrupted Journey (with Estevan Arellano and Denise Chávez) 1997, Isis in the Heart 1998, Shaman Winter 1999, Farolitos for Abuelo (children's fiction) 1999, My Land Sings 1999, Roadrunner's Dance 2000, Elegy for Cesar Chavez 2000, The Santero's Miracle (children's fiction) 2004, Serafina's Stories 2004, Jemez Spring 2005, The Man who Could Fly and other stories 2006, Curse of the ChupaCabra 2006, First Tortilla 2007, ChupaCabra and the Roswell UFO (children's fiction) 2008, Randy Lopez Goes Home 2011, How Hollyhocks Came to New Mexico 2012, How Chile Came to New Mexico 2013, The Old Man's Love Story 2013; short stories in literary magazines in USA and internationally; has also edited various collections of short stories. *Leisure interests:* reading, travel, apple orchards. *Address:* 5324 Cañada Vista NW, Albuquerque, NM 87120-2412, USA (home).

ANCRAM, 13th Marquis of Lothian; **Michael Andrew Foster Jude Kerr,** PC, QC, DL, LLB, MA; British politician; b. 7 July 1945; s. of 12th Marquess of Lothian and Antonella, Marchioness of Lothian; m. Lady Jane Fitzalan-Howard 1975; two d.; ed Ampleforth, Christ Church Coll., Oxford, Univ. of Edinburgh; fmr columnist, Daily Telegraph (Manchester edn); partner in tenanted arable farm; called to Scottish Bar 1970, practised law 1970–79; MP for Berwickshire and East Lothian Feb.–Oct. 1974, for Edinburgh S 1979–87, for Devizes 1992–2010, mem. House of Commons Energy Select Cttee 1979–83; Parl. Under-Sec. of State, Scottish Office 1983–87, Parl. Under-Sec., NI Office 1993–94, Minister of State 1994–97; Shadow Cabinet Spokesman for Constitutional Affairs 1997–98, Shadow Sec. of State for Foreign and Commonwealth Affairs 2001–05, for Int. Affairs 2003–04, for Defence 2005; Vice-Chair. Conservative Party in Scotland 1975–80, Chair. 1980–83, Chair. Conservative Party 1998–2001, Deputy Leader 2001–05; Chair. Northern Corp. Communications 1989–91, Global Strategy Forum 2006–, MEC International Ltd; Dir CSM Parl. Consultants 1988–92; mem. Bd Scottish Homes 1988–90, Intelligence and Security Cttee 2006–10, 2011–; apptd Chair. Le Cercle 2012; Trustee Mitsubishi UFJ Trust, Oxford Foundation. *Publications:* pamphlets: Still a Conservative 2006, Dancing with Wolves 2008, Farewell to Drift 2010. *Leisure interests:* skiing, fishing, photography, folk-singing. *Address:* House of Lords, London, SW1A 0PW (office); 30 Smith Square, London, SW1P 3HF, England (home). *Telephone:* (20) 7219-5353 (office). *Fax:* (20) 7219-5979 (office). *E-mail:* lothianm@parliament.uk (office); mancram@hotmail.com (home).

ANDERS, Edward, MA, PhD; American professor of chemistry; *Horace B. Horton Professor Emeritus, University of Chicago;* b. (Edward Alperovitch), 21 June 1926, Liepaja, Latvia; s. of Adolph Alperovitch and Erica Leventals; m. Joan Elizabeth Fleming 1955; one s. one d.; ed Univ. of Munich, Germany, Columbia Univ.; Instructor in Chem., Univ. of Ill. at Urbana 1954–55; Asst Prof. of Chem., Univ. of Chicago 1955–60, Assoc. Prof. 1960–62, Prof. 1960–73, Horace B. Horton Prof. of Physical Sciences 1973–91, Prof. Emer. 1991–; Visiting Prof., Calif. Inst. of Tech. 1960, Univ. of Berne 1963–64, 1970, 1978, 1980–81, 1983, 1987–88, 1989–90; Research Assoc., Field Museum of Natural History 1968–91; Fellow, American Acad. of Arts and Sciences 1973–; mem. NAS 1974–; Assoc., Royal Astronomical Soc., UK 1974–; Fairchild Distinguished Scholar, Calif. Inst. of Tech. 1992–93; Hon. DChem (Latvian Acad. of Sciences) 2000; Cleveland Prize, AAAS 1959, Smith Medal, NAS 1971, Leonard Medal, Meteoritical Soc. 1974, Goldschmidt Medal, Geochemical Soc. 1990, Kuiper Prize, American Astronomical Soc. 1991, Hess Medal (American Geophysical Union) 1995. *Publications:* over 260 articles in scientific journals. *Leisure interests:* classical music, hiking, photography. *Address:* c/o Department of Chemistry, University of Chicago, 5735 South Ellis Avenue, Chicago, IL 60637, USA.

ANDERSEN, Ib; Danish ballet dancer; *Artistic Director, Ballet Arizona;* b. 14 Dec. 1954, Copenhagen; s. of Ingolf Andersen and Anna Andersen; ballet dancer, Royal Danish Ballet 1973–80, Prin. Dancer 1975–80; Prin. Dancer, New York City Ballet 1980–94; Ballet Master, Pittsburgh Ballet Theater 1997; Artistic Dir Ballet Ariz. 2000–; mem. Balanchine Trust; Nijinsky Prize, Gold Medallion of Merit Award, Nat. Soc. of Arts and Letters 2006. *Address:* Ballet Arizona, 2835 E Washington Street, Phoenix, AZ 85034, USA (office). *Telephone:* (602) 381-0184 (office). *Fax:* (602) 381-0189 (office). *E-mail:* questions@balletaz.org (office). *Website:* www.balletaz.org (office).

ANDERSEN, Nils Smedegaard, MSc; Danish business executive; b. 8 July 1958, Århus; ed Århus Univ.; began career as Sales Dir Tuborg International, becoming Man. Dir of several Carlsberg and Tuborg cos, mem. group man. 1999–2007, CEO Carlsberg A/S 2001–07; mem. Bd Dirs, A.P. Møller-Maersk A/S 2005–16, Partner and Group CEO 2007–16; mem. European Round Table of Industrialists 2001–; Co-Chair. EU-Russia Industrialists' Round Table 2007–; mem. Bd Dirs, William Demant Holding A/S, Oticon A/S; Kt's Cross, Order of the Dannebrog 2010. *Address:* c/o A.P. Møller-Mærsk A/S, Esplanaden 50, 1098 Copenhagen K, Denmark. *E-mail:* info@maersk.com.

ANDERSEN, Ronald Max, BS, MS, PhD; American sociologist and academic; *Wasserman Professor Emeritus, Department of Health Policy and Management, School of Public Health, University of California, Los Angeles;* b. 15 Feb. 1939, Omaha, Neb.; s. of Max Adolph Andersen and Evangeline Dorothy Andersen (née Wobbe); m. Diane Borella 1965; one d.; ed Univ. of Santa Clara, Purdue Univ.; Research Assoc. Purdue Farm Cardiac Project, Dept of Sociology, Purdue Univ. 1962–63; Assoc. Study Dir Nat. Opinion Research Center, Univ. of Chicago 1963–66, Research Assoc. Center for Health Admin. Studies 1963–77; Instructor, Grad. School of Business, Univ. of Chicago 1966–68, Asst Prof. 1968–72, Asst Prof., Dept of Sociology 1970–72, Assoc. Prof. Grad. School of Business, then Prof. 1974–90, Assoc. Dir Center for Health Admin. Studies 1977–80, Dir Grad.

Program in Health Admin. 1980–90; Chair. Editorial Bd Health Administration Press, Chicago 1980–83, 1988–; Wasserman Prof. of Health Services and Prof. of Sociology, UCLA School of Public Health 1991–2006, Chair. Dept of Health Services 1993–96, 2000–03, Wasserman Prof. Emer. 2004–; mem. Royal Soc. of Science, Uppsala; mem. numerous cttees, advisory panels etc.; mem. American Sociological Asscn, American Statistical Asscn, American Public Health Asscn; Fellow, Inst. of Medicine; Dr hc (Purdue Univ.); Baxter Allegiance Prize 1999, Distinguished Investigator Award Asscn for Health Services Research, Leo G. Reeder Award for Distinguished Service to Medical Sociology. *Publications:* author, co-author, ed. and co-ed. of numerous books, monographs, book chapters and articles in professional journals. *Address:* Department of Health Services, UCLA School of Public Health, Box 951772, 31-293C CHS, 10833 Le Conte Avenue, Los Angeles, CA 90095-1772 (office); 10724 Wilshire Boulevard, Apartment 312, Los Angeles, CA 90024-4453, USA (home). *Telephone:* (310) 206-1810 (office). *Fax:* (310) 825-3317 (office). *E-mail:* randerse@ucla.edu (office). *Website:* people.healthsciences.ucla.edu/institution/personnel?personnel_id=112445 (office).

ANDERSEN, Torkild, MSc, DPhil; Danish physicist and academic; *Professor Emeritus of Physics, University of Århus;* b. 19 June 1934, Randers; m. Inger Bloch-Petersen 1957; one s. one d.; ed Tech. Univ., Copenhagen; Industrial Chemist 1958–59; Asst and Assoc. Prof. of Chem., Univ. of Århus 1959–71, Prof. of Physics (Atomic Physics) 1971–2001, Prof. Emer. 2001–; Postdoctoral Fellow, Univ. of Cambridge, UK 1961–63, Univ. of Lyon, France 1968; Visiting Prof., Univ. of Colorado, USA 1984–85, Flinders Univ., S Australia 1988, 1994; mem. Bd Carlsberg Foundation 1996–2004; Advisor for Lundbeck Foundation 2005–11; mem. Royal Danish Acad. of Sciences and Letters (Kongelige Danske Videnskabernes Selskab) 1979–; N. Bjerrum Prize 1972, Univ. of Århus Science Faculty Prize 2006. *Publications include:* over 200 scientific contribs to chemistry and physics journals. *Address:* Institute of Physics and Astronomy, University of Århus, Nordre. Ringgade, 8000 Århus C (office); 38 Lyngvej, 8600 Silkeborg, Denmark (home). *Telephone:* 87-15-56-83 (office). *E-mail:* fystor@phys.au.dk (office).

ANDERSON, Bradbury (Brad) H., BA; American retail executive; b. 1950, Sheridan, Wyo.; m. Janet Anderson; two s.; ed Waldorf Coll., Forest City, Ia, Univ. of Denver; began career as commissioned salesman, Sound of Music Inc. (predecessor to Best Buy), various man. positions, Best Buy Co., Inc. 1973, including Vice-Pres. 1981–86, Exec. Vice-Pres. 1986–91, mem. Bd of Dirs 1986–2010, Pres. and COO 1991–2002, Vice-Chair. 2001–09, CEO 2002–09, Dir and mem. Finance and Investment Policy Cttee 2013–16; mem. Bd of Dirs, Best Buy Children's Foundation, Junior Achievement Inc. 2000–, Nat. Junior Achievement, Int. Mass Retail Asscn, Retail Industry Leaders' Asscn, American Film Inst., General Mills Inc. 2007–18, Carlson Companies Inc. 2009–, Waste Management, Inc. 2011–, LightHaus Logic Inc. 2013–; mem. Waldorf Coll. Bd of Regents 1998–; Trustee, Minnesota Public Radio Inc., Mayo Clinic 2009–, Mayo Clinic, Rochester, NY 2009–; Waldorf Coll. Alumni Distinguished Service Award 1997, Retail Merchandiser Retail Exec. of the Year 2002. *Leisure interests:* cycling, reading biographies, theatre, music. *Address:* c/o Best Buy Co., Inc., Corporate Headquarters, 7601 Penn Avenue South, Richfield, MN 55423, USA. *E-mail:* info@bestbuy.com.

ANDERSON, Campbell McCheyne, BEcons; Australian business executive; b. 17 Sept. 1941, Sydney; s. of Allen Taylor Anderson and Ethel Catherine Rundle; m. Sandra Maclean Harper 1965; two s. one d.; ed Armidale School, NSW, Univ. of Sydney; audit clerk, Priestley and Morris 1958–59; with Boral Ltd 1962–69; Gen. Man. then Man. Dir Reef Oil and Basin Oil 1969–72; with Burmah Oil Australia Ltd 1972–73, New York 1973–74, Div. Dir, then Chief Financial Officer, Burmah Oil Trading Ltd, UK 1974–75, Dir 1975–76, Exec. Dir Burmah Oil Co. Ltd 1976–82, Man. Dir Burmah Oil PLC 1982–85; Man. Dir Renison Goldfields Consolidated Ltd 1985, Man. Dir and CEO 1986–93, Dir Consolidated Gold Fields PLC 1985–89; Chair. Ampolex Ltd 1991–96, Dir 1996–97; Man. Dir North Ltd 1994–98; Chair. Energy Resources Australia Ltd 1994–98; Pres. Business Council of Australia 1999–2000; Chair. Southern Pacific Petroleum 2001–07; Pres. Australia/Japan Soc. of Vic. 1995–98; mem. Bd of Dirs Aviva Australia Holdings Ltd 1999–2009, IBJ Bank Australia 1999–2003, Reconciliation Australia 2001–07, ThoroughVisioN 2004; Assoc., Australian Soc. of Certified Practising Accountants; mem. Sentient Council 2001. *Leisure interests:* golf, shooting, horse racing, swimming. *Address:* 77 Drumalbyn Road, Bellevue Hill, NSW 2023, Australia. *Telephone:* (4) 1751-2187. *Fax:* (2) 9327-5035.

ANDERSON, Christopher (Chris), BEcons; Australian journalist; b. 9 Dec. 1944; s. of C. F. Anderson and L. A. Anderson; m. Gabriella Douglas 1969; one s. one d.; ed Picton High School, NSW, Univ. of Sydney, Columbia Univ., USA; journalist and political commentator 1962–76; Deputy Ed., later Ed., The Sun-Herald 1976–79; Deputy Ed., later Ed., Sydney Morning Herald 1980–83, Ed.-in-Chief 1983–88; Man. Dir and Group Ed. Dir John Fairfax Ltd 1987–90, Chief Exec. 1990–91; Man. Ed. Australian Broadcasting Corpn 1993–95; Chief Exec. TV New Zealand Ltd 1995–97; CEO Optus Communications 1997–2004; served as adviser to Packer family on their media interests 2004–09; mem. Bd Publishing and Broadcasting Ltd, Foxtel, Austrade 2004–07; Andrew Olle Media Lecturer 2004. *Leisure interests:* cricket, reading.

ANDERSON, Donald Thomas, AO, BSc, PhD, DSc, FRS; Australian biologist and academic; *Professor Emeritus of Biology, University of Sydney;* b. 29 Dec. 1931, Eton, Berks., England; s. of Thomas Anderson and Flora Anderson; m. Joanne T. Claridge 1960; one s.; ed Univ. of London, UK, Univ. of Sydney; Lecturer in Zoology, Univ. of Sydney 1958–63, Sr Lecturer 1963–68, Reader 1968–72, apptd Prof. 1972, Challis Prof. of Biology 1984–91, Prof. Emer. 1992–; Visiting Prof., King's Coll., London 1970; Kowalevsky Medal 2001. *Publications include:* Embryology and Phylogeny in Annelids and Arthropods 1973, Barnacles 1994, Atlas of Invertebrate Anatomy 1996, Invertebrate Zoology 1998, 2001. *Leisure interests:* photography, gardening. *Address:* 5 Angophora Close, Wamberal, NSW 2260, Australia (home). *Telephone:* (2) 4311-6598 (home). *E-mail:* dtjta@ozemail.com.au (office).

ANDERSON, Gillian, BFA; American actress; b. 9 Aug. 1968, Chicago, Ill.; d. of Edward Anderson and Rosemary Anderson; m. 1st Errol Clyde Klotz (divorced); one d.; m. 2nd Julian Ozanne 2004 (divorced 2006); two s.; ed DePaul Univ., Chicago, Goodman Theater School, Chicago; worked at Nat. Theatre, London; appeared in two off-Broadway productions; Golden Globe Awards 1995, 1997, Screen Actors' Guild Awards 1996, 1997, Emmy Award 1997. *Theatre includes:* Absent Friends (Manhattan Theater Club) (Theater World Award 1991) 1991, The Philanthropist (Along Wharf Theater) 1992, What the Night is For (Comedy Theatre, London, Whatsonstage.com Theatregoers' Choice Best Actress Award 2003) 2002, The Sweetest Swing in Baseball (Royal Court Theatre, London) 2004, A Doll's House (Donmar Warehouse, London) 2009, We Are One: A celebration of tribal peoples (Apollo Theatre, London) 2010, A Streetcar Named Desire (Young Vic, London, Evening Standard Award for Best Actress) 2014. *Films include:* Three at Once 1986, A Matter of Choice 1988, The Turning 1992, Princess Mononoke (voice, English-language version) 1997, Chicago Cab 1998, The X-Files 1998, The Mighty 1998, Playing By Heart 1998, The House of Mirth 2000, The Mighty Celt 2005, Tristram Shandy: A Cock and Bull Story 2005, The Last King of Scotland 2006, Straightheads 2007, The X Files: I Want to Believe 2008, How to Lose Friends & Alienate People 2008, Boogie Woogie 2009, Johnny English Reborn 2011, Shadow Dancer 2012, L'enfant d'en haut 2012, Mr. Morgan's Last Love 2012, Robot Overlords 2015. *Television includes:* Home Fire Burning (film) 1992, The X-Files 1993–2002, 2016–, When Planes Go Down (film) 1996, Future Fantastic (series presenter, BBC), Bleak House (series, BBC) 2005, Any Human Heart (series) 2010, The Crimson Petal and the White (mini-series) 2011, Moby Dick (series) 2011, Great Expectations (series, BBC) 2011, Hannibal (NBC) 2013, 2015, The Fall (series, BBC) 2013, 2014, American Gods 2017–. *Address:* 10100 Santa Monica Blvd, Suite 1300, Los Angeles, CA 90067-4003, USA. *Website:* www.gilliananderson.ws.

ANDERSON, James (Jimmy) Michael, OBE; British professional cricketer; b. 30 July 1982, Burnley, Lancashire; m. Daniella Anderson (neé Lloyd); two d.; ed St Theodore's RC High School, Burnley; left-handed batsman, right arm fast medium bowler; teams: Lancashire 2002–, England 2002–, Auckland 2007–08; First-class debut 2002; ODI debut: England vs Australia, Melbourne 15 Dec. 2002; Test debut: England vs Zimbabwe, Lord's 22–24 May 2003; T20I debut: England vs Australia, Sydney 9 Jan. 2007; played in 143 Tests (to Sept. 2018), scored 1,150 runs and took 564 wickets (average 26.84) with 26 five-wicket and three 10-wicket performances, best bowling of 11/71 against Pakistan in Nottingham 2010; played in 194 ODIs (to March 2015), scored 273 runs and took 269 wickets (average 29.22) with 2 five-wicket performances, best bowling of 5/23 against South Africa in Port Elizabeth 2009; played 19 T20Is (to Nov. 2009), took 18 wickets (average 30.66), best bowling of 3/23 against Netherlands in Lord's 2009; played 234 First-Class matches (to July 2018), scored 1766 runs and took 909 wickets (average 25.40) with 44 five-wicket and six ten-wicket performances, best bowling of 7/42; youngest player to take hat-trick for Lancashire 2003; leading Test wicket-taker among fast bowlers with 564 wickets; most wickets for England in both Tests and ODIs; first English bowler to reach 400 and 500 wickets in Tests; highest 10th-wicket Test batting partnership of 198 runs with Joe Root against India 2014; launched first collection with luxury menswear brand Chess London 2014; f. The Numbers Collection (wines under Wine Cellar Club); Freedom of Burnley 2012. *Films:* Exec. Producer: Warriors (Documentary film) 2015. *Radio:* Host Not Just Cricket, BBC Radio 5 Live (with Graeme Swann and Greg James). *Address:* c/o Nicola Barrigan, M&C Saatchi Merlin, 36 Golden Square, London, W1F 9EE, England (office); England and Wales Cricket Board, Lord's Cricket Ground, London, NW8 8QZ, England (office). *Telephone:* (20) 7259-1460 (Nicola Barrigan) (office); (20) 7432-1200 (office). *E-mail:* Nicola.Barrigan@mcsaatchimerlin.com (office). *Website:* www.mcsaatchimerlin.com (office); www.ecb.co.uk (office); www.jamesanderson613.com. *Fax:* (20) 7286-5583 (office).

ANDERSON, John Duncan, AO, MA; Australian fmr politician; b. 14 Nov. 1956, Sydney; s. of D. A. Anderson; m. Julia Gillian Robertson 1987; five c.; ed Kings School, Parramatta, St Paul's Coll., Univ. of Sydney; fmr farmer and grazier; MP for Gwydir, NSW 1989–2007; Deputy Leader Nat. Party of Australia 1993–99, Leader 1999–2005; Shadow Minister for Primary Industry 1993–96; Minister for Primary Industries and Energy 1996–98, for Transport and Regional Devt 1997–2005, Deputy Prime Minister 1999–2005 (resgnd). *Leisure interests:* farming, shooting, reading, photography, motoring. *Address:* 206 Conadilly Street, Gunnedah, NSW 2380, Australia (home).

ANDERSON, June, BA; American singer (soprano); b. 30 Dec. 1952, Boston, Mass; ed Yale Univ.; debut with New York City Opera in the Magic Flute 1978, European debut as Semiramide at Rome Opera; performances at most major opera houses in USA and Europe, for companies including Metropolitan Opera, New York, Milwaukee Florentine Opera, San Diego Opera, Seattle Opera, Chicago Lyric Opera, Royal Opera, London, La Scala, Milan, Opéra de Paris, Teatro Colon, Buenos Aires, Gran Teatre del Liceu, Barcelona, Wiener Staatsoper, La Fenice, Venice; has worked with conductors including Leonard Bernstein, James Conlon, Charles Dutoit, Daniele Gatti, James Levine, Zubin Mehta, Riccardo Muti, Seiji Ozawa; Commdr, Ordre des Arts et des Lettres; Bellini d'Oro Prize, Grammy Award for Best Classical Album (for Bernstein: Candide) 1991. *Roles include:* Queen of the Night in The Magic Flute, New York City Opera 1978, title role in Lucia di Lammermoor, Milwaukee Florentine Opera 1982 and Chicago 1990, Gulnara in Il Corsaro, San Diego Opera Verdi Festival 1982, I Puritani, Edmonton Opera 1982–83, title role in Semiramide, Rome Opera 1982–83 and Metropolitan Opera 1990, Rosina in The Barber of Seville, Seattle Opera and Teatro Massimo 1982–83, Cunégonde in Candide 1989, Metropolitan Opera debut as Gilda in Rigoletto 1989, title role in Luisa Miller, La Fenice, Venice 2006; Dialogues des Carmélites at Opéra de Nice and Salome at Opéra Royal de Wallonie 2011, Adams' Nixon in China at Théâtre du Châtelet, Paris 2012; concert and oratorio vocalist: Chicago Pops Orchestra, Handel Festival Kennedy Center, Denver Symphony, St Louis Symphony, Cincinnati Symphony, Maracaibo (Venezuela) Symphony; first Messa di Requiem by Verdi in Paris 2007; concerts/recitals/festivals in Canada, France, Palestine and Israel 2012. *Address:* Bettina Brentano, 44, rue Barbet de Jouy, 75007 Paris, France (office). *E-mail:* contact@oia-brentano.com (office). *Website:* www.oia-brentano.com (office); www.june-anderson.com.

ANDERSON, Laurie P., MFA; American performance artist, musician (keyboards, violin) and writer; b. 5 June 1947, Wayne, Ill.; d. of Arthur T. Anderson and Mary Louise Anderson (née Rowland); m. Lou Reed 2008 (died 2013); ed Columbia

Univ., Barnard Coll.; instructor in Art History, City Coll., CUNY 1973–75; freelance critic, Art News, Art Forum; composer and performer in multi-media exhbns; Artist-in-Residence, ZBS Media 1974, NASA 2002–04; Distinguished Artist-In-Residence, Experimental Media and Performing Arts Center, Rensselaer Polytechnic Inst. 2012–; fmr Artist-In-Residence High Performance Rodeo, Calgary, Alberta, UCLA Center for the Art of Performance; residencies at Yaddo (retreat for writers and artists) 2011, 2012, 2014, American Acad. in Rome; Guest Dir Brighton Festival, UK 2016; Guggenheim Fellow 1983; Dr hc (Art Inst. of Chicago), (Philadelphia Coll. of the Arts); Gish Prize 2007, Pratt Inst. Honorary Legends Award 2011, Yaddo Artist Medal 2015. *Film performances:* Carmen, Personal Service Announcements, Beautiful Red Dress, Talk Normal, Alive From Off Center, What You Mean We?, Language Is A Virus, This Is The Picture, Sharkey's Day, Dear Reader, Home of the Brave (writer, dir, performer) 1986, Puppet Motel (CD-ROM) 1995, Heart of a Dog 2015. *Recordings include:* O Superman 1981, Big Science 1982, United States 1983, Mister Heartbreak 1984, Strange Angels 1989, Bright Red 1994, The Ugly One With The Jewels And Other Stories 1995, Life on a String 2001, Live At Town Hall, New York City 2002, Homeland 2010; film scores: Home Of The Brave 1986, Swimming To Cambodia, Monster In A Box. *Publications include:* The Package 1971, October 1972, Transportation, Transportation 1973, The Rose and the Stone 1974, Notebook 1976, Artifacts at the End of a Decade 1981, Typisch Frac 1981, United States 1984, Empty Places: A Performance 1989, Laurie Anderson's Postcard Book 1990, Stories from the Nerve Bible 1993, Night Life 2007. *Address:* Curtis R. Priem Experimental Media and Performing Arts Center, Rensselaer Polytechnic Institute, 110 8th Street, Troy, NY 12180, USA (office). *Telephone:* (518) 276-3921 (office). *E-mail:* studio@difficultmusic.com (office). *Website:* empac.rpi.edu (office); www.laurieanderson.com.

ANDERSON, Paul G. (Pete), BS; American business executive; ed Truman Univ.; managed and worked for three cooperative orgs in Kan. 1976–87; joined Farmers Commodities Corpn 1987, developed and was Div. Man. Integrated Marketing Program –1995; with FCStone since 1987, Vice-Pres. of Operations 1995–99, Pres. and CEO 1999–2009, Pres. INTL FCStone Inc. (following merger with International Assets Holding Corpn) 2009–12, also fmr Vice-Chair., Dir 2012–; Past Pres. Kansas Cooperative Council; Past Founding Chair. Arthur Capper Cooperative Center, Kansas State Univ.; mem. Bd of Dirs Associated Benefits Corpn; mem. Nat. Council of Farmer Cooperatives, Nat. Feed and Grain Asscn and several other state asscns. *Address:* INTL FCStone Inc., 708 Third Avenue, 15th Floor, New York, NY 10017, USA (office). *Telephone:* (212) 485-3500 (office). *Fax:* (212) 485-3505 (office). *E-mail:* info@intlfcstone.com (office). *Website:* www.intlfcstone.com (office).

ANDERSON, Paul M., BS, MBA; Australian business executive; b. 1 April 1945, USA; m. Kathy Anderson; two d.; ed Univ. of Washington, Stanford Univ., USA; joined Ford Motor Co. 1969, Planning Man. 1972–74; Dir Corp. Planning, Texas Eastern Corpn 1977–80, Pres. Texas Eastern Synfuels Inc. and Project Dir Tri-State Synfuels Co. 1980–82, Vice-Pres. Planning and Eng, Texas Eastern Corpn 1982–85, Sr Vice-Pres. Financial and Diversified Operations 1985–90; Vice-Pres. Finance and Chief Finance Officer Inland Steel Industries Inc. 1990–91; Exec. Vice-Pres., then Pres. Panhandle Eastern Pipe Line Co. 1991–93; Pres. and CEO PanEnergy Corpn 1995–97, Chair. 1997, Dir, Pres., COO Duke Energy Corpn (after merger between Duke Power and PanEnergy Corpn 1997) 1997–98, Chair. and CEO 2003–07; Man. Dir and CEO Broken Hill Pty Co. Ltd (later BHP Ltd, now BHP-Billiton) 1998–2002; mem. Bd of Dirs BAE Systems PLC, Spectra Energy (Chair. 2007–09), BP plc 2010–. *Publications include:* Analysis of Faulted Power Systems 1973, Power System Control and Stability 1977, Subsynchronous Resonance in Power Systems (co-author) 1990, Series Compensation of Power Systems 1996. *Leisure interest:* motorcycling. *Address:* c/o Board of Directors, BP plc, 1 St. James's Square, London, SW1Y 4PD, England.

ANDERSON, Paul S., BS, PhD; American chemist; b. 3 Feb. 1938, Concord, Vt; ed Univs of Vermont and New Hampshire; Postdoctoral appointment with Prof. Meinwaid at Cornell Univ., NY; joined Merck Sharp & Dohme Research Labs 1964, Sr Research Chemist, Medicinal Chem. Dept 1964–69, Research Fellow 1969–73, Sr Research Fellow 1973–75, Assoc. Dir Medicinal Chem. Dept 1975–79, Sr Dir 1979–80, Exec. Dir 1980–88, Vice-Pres. for Chem. at West Point research facility 1988–94 (retd); worked in DuPont-Merck Pharmaceuticals Co. (became Dupont Pharmaceuticals Co. 1998) 1994–98, Sr Vice-Pres. for Chemical and Physical Sciences 1998–2001, co. acquired by Bristol-Myers Squibb 2001, Vice-Pres. Drug Discovery, Bristol-Myers Squibb 2001–02; Chair. Medicinal Chem. Div., ACS 1987, Gordon Research Conf. on Medicinal Chem. 1991; Pres. ACS 1997; mem. Bd Dirs, MDS, Inc., Albany Molecular Research, Inc. 2002–, Chemical Heritage Foundation; Trustee, Gordon Research Confs; mem. Scientific Advisory Bd Vertex Pharmaceuticals, Inc. 2004–; mem. NIH Study Section on Bioorganic Chem. and Natural Products 1985–88, Chair. 1988–89; fmr mem. NIH Nat. Advisory Gen. Medicinal Sciences Council, Nat. Research Council, Bd on Chemical Sciences and Tech.; Founding mem. Exec. Advisory Council Univ. of Kansas School of Pharmacy; Hon. DSc (Univ. of Vermont, Univ. of Montpelier) 1998; Hon. DChem (Univ. of New Hampshire) 2001; ACS (Philadelphia Section) Award 1992, ACS E.B. Hershberg Award 1995, ACS Award in Industrial Chem. 2001, Perkin Medal, Soc. for Chemical Industry 2002, Nat. Acad. of Sciences Award for Chem. in Service to Soc. 2003, ACS Priestley Medal 2006.

ANDERSON, Paul Thomas; American film director, screenwriter and producer; b. 26 June 1970, Studio City, Calif.; s. of Ernie Anderson; partner Maya Rudolph 2001–; one s. two d.; ed Montclair Coll. Prep. High School; began career as production asst on TV films. *Films include:* The Dirk Diggler Story (short) 1988, Cigarettes and Coffee (short) 1993, Hard Eight 1996, Boogie Nights (Best New Filmmaker, Boston Soc. of Film Critics, New Generation Award, Los Angeles Film Critics Asscn, Metro Media Award, Toronto Int. Film Festival) 1997, Flagpole Special (short) 1998, Magnolia (Best Dir and Best Screenplay, Toronto Film Critics Asscn 1999, Golden Bear, Berlin Film Festival 2000) 1999, Punch-Drunk Love (Best Dir, Cannes Film Festival, Best Director, Toronto Film Critics Asscn) 2002, Couch (short) 2002, Blossoms and Blood 2003, There Will Be Blood (Best Dir, Los Angeles Film Critics Asscn, Silver Bear for Best Dir, Berlin Film Festival 2008, Dir of the Year, London Critics Circle Film Awards 2008) 2007, The Master (Best Dir, Los Angeles Film Critics Asscn, Silver Lion for Best Dir, Venice Int. Film Festival) 2012, Inherent Vice (Best Adapted Screenplay, Nat. Bd of Review and San Francisco Film Critics' Circle Awards) 2014. *Music videos:* Try by Michael Penn 1997, Across the Universe by Fiona Apple 1998, Fast as You Can by Fiona Apple 1999, Save Me by Aimee Mann 1999, Limp by Fiona Apple 2000, Paper Bag by Fiona Apple 2000, Here We Go by Jon Brion 2002, Hot Knife by Fiona Apple 2013. *Address:* c/o Creative Artists Agency, 2000 Avenue of the Stars, Los Angeles, CA 90067, USA (office). *Telephone:* (424) 288-2000 (office). *Fax:* (424) 288-2900 (office). *Website:* www.caa.com (office).

ANDERSON, Porter Warren, Jr, BA, MA, PhD; American microbiologist and academic; *Professor Emeritus of Pediatrics, University of Rochester;* b. 1 Jan. 1937, Corinth, Miss.; ed Sidney Lanier High School, Emory Univ., Harvard Univ.; Research Trainee, Oak Ridge Nat. Lab. 1957; Asst Chemist, Tropical Research Dept, United Fruit Co., Honduras 1959–61; mem. Faculty, Dept of Chem., Stillman Coll., Tuscaloosa, Ala 1966–68; Research Assoc., Children's Hosp. Medical Center, Boston 1968–77; Asst Prof., Harvard Univ. 1972–75, Assoc. Prof. 1975–77; Assoc. Prof., Dept of Pediatrics and Microbiology, Univ. of Rochester School of Medicine and Dentistry, NY 1977–87, Prof. 1987–95, now Prof. Emer. of Pediatrics; apptd Sr Lecturer, Harvard Medical School 2006; mem. NAS 2010; Fellow, American Acad. of Microbiology 2011; Albert Lasker Clinical Research Award 1996. *Publications include:* nine issued patents and three patent applications pending. *Address:* c/o University of Rochester Medical Center, Department of Pediatrics, 601 Elmwood Avenue, Rochester, NY 14642; 914 Grande Avenue, PO Box 378492, Key Largo, FL 33037, USA.

ANDERSON, Reid Bryce; Canadian ballet director; b. 1 April 1949, New Westminster, BC; ed Dolores Kirkwood Acad., Burnaby, Royal Ballet School, London, UK; Prin. Dancer, Stuttgart Ballet 1969–83, Ballet Master 1983–85, Artistic Dir 1996–2018; Artistic Dir Ballet of British Columbia 1987–89, Nat. Ballet of Canada 1989–96; has staged John Cranko's works for Royal Ballet, Paris Opera Ballet, American Ballet Theatre, Royal Danish Ballet, Ballet of the Teatro alla Scala in Milan, Australian Ballet, Deutsche Staatsoper in Berlin, Hamburg Ballett, Teatro Colon in Buenos Aires, Boston Ballet, San Francisco Ballet, Rome Opera Ballet, Norwegian Nat. Ballet, Nat. Ballet of China, Ballet of the Vienna State Opera, San Francisco Ballet, Tokyo Ballet; Bundesverdienstkreuz; John Cranko Prize 1989, 1996, Deutscher Tanzpreis 2006, Dir of the Year, Dance Europe magazine 2006, Verdienstmedaille of Baden-Wurttemberg 2009, Staufermedaille (Gold) 2018, Die Ehrenmitglieder der Staatstheater Stuttgart 2018.

ANDERSON, Richard H., BA, JD; American airline industry executive; *Executive Chairman, Delta Air Lines, Inc.;* b. Galveston, Tex.; m. Susan Anderson; ed Univ. of Houston, Clear Lake, South Texas Coll. of Law; joined Continental Airlines 1987, served as Staff Vice-Pres. and Deputy Gen. Counsel; joined Northwest Airlines 1990, served as Sr Vice-Pres., Tech. Operations and Airport Affairs, Exec. Vice-Pres., COO and CEO 2001–04; Exec. Vice-Pres. UnitedHealth Group 2004–07, also served as Pres. Commercial Markets Group; mem. Bd of Dirs and CEO Delta Air Lines, Inc. 2007–16 (merged with Northwest Airlines 2010), Exec. Chair. 2016–; Chair. Airlines for America (fmrly Air Transport Asscn of America), Bd of Govs, Int. Air Transport Asscn 2013–14; mem. Bd of Dirs, Medtronic, Inc., Cargill; Chevalier, Légion d'honneur 2011; Airline Strategy Award for Executive Leadership, Airline Business magazine and Spencer Stuart global exec. search firm 2010, The Sandra Taub Humanitarian Award, Breast Cancer Research Foundation 2011. *Address:* Delta Air Lines Inc., PO Box 20706, 1030 Delta Blvd, Atlanta, GA 30320-6001, USA (office). *Telephone:* (404) 715-2600 (office). *Fax:* (404) 715-5042 (office). *E-mail:* info@delta.com (office). *Website:* www.delta.com (office).

ANDERSON, Robert Geoffrey William, BSc, MA, DPhil, FRSE; British academic and museum director; *President and CEO, Science History Institute;* b. 2 May 1944, London; s. of Herbert Patrick Anderson and Kathleen Diana Burns; m. 1st Margaret Elizabeth Callis Lea 1973; two s.; m. 2nd Jane Virginia Portal; ed Woodhouse School, London, St John's Coll., Oxford (Casberd Exhibitioner); Asst Keeper, Royal Scottish Museum, Edinburgh 1970–75, Dir 1984–85; Asst Keeper, Science Museum, London 1975–80, Keeper 1980–84; Dir Nat. Museums of Scotland 1985–92; Dir British Museum, London 1992–2002; Curator, School of Advanced Study, Univ. of London 1994–2002, Bd mem. Warburg Inst. 1993–97; Vice-Pres. and Fellow, Clare Hall, Cambridge 2009–13, Fellow Emer. 2013–; Visiting Fellow, Inst. for Advanced Study, Princeton, USA 2002–03, Centre for Research in Arts, Social Sciences and Humanities, Univ. of Cambridge 2003, Churchill Coll. 2003–04, Corpus Christi Coll. 2004–05; Pres. British Soc. for the History of Science 1988–90, Scientific Instrument Comm. of the Int. Union of the History and Philosophy of Science 1982–97, Asscn of Ind. Libraries 2003–16; Pres. and CEO Chemical Heritage Foundation (now Science History Inst.), Philadelphia, USA 2017–; mem. Editorial Bd, Ambix, Annals of Science, Journal of the History of Collecting; Chair. Soc. for History of Alchemy and Chem. 2007–; mem. Bd of Dirs, Dutch Nat. Science Museum, Boerhaave Museum, Leiden 1995–99; mem. Bd of Visitors, Inst. for Advanced Study in Humanities, Univ. of Edinburgh 1987–2000, Museum of History of Science, Univ. of Oxford 2002–; mem. Int. Acad. of History of Science 2002; Hon. FSA (Scotland) 1991; Hon. Fellow, St John's Coll. Oxford 2002; Commdr des Arts et des Lettres 2002; Hon. DSc (Edinburgh) 1995, (Durham) 1998; ACS Dexter Award 1986, Paul Bunge Prize 2016. *Publications include:* The Playfair Collection 1978, Science in India 1982, Science, Medicine and Dissent (ed.) 1987, A New Museum for Scotland (ed.) 1990, Joseph Black: A Bibliography (with G. Fyffe) 1992, Making Instruments Count 1993, The Great Court at the British Museum 2000, Enlightening the British: Knowledge, Discovery and the Museum in the Eighteenth Century (ed.) 2003, The Correspondence of Joseph Black 2012, Cradle of Chemistry (ed.) 2015. *Leisure interest:* books. *Address:* Science History Institute, 315 Chestnut Street, Philadelphia, PA 19106, USA (office); Clare Hall, University of Cambridge, Herschel Road, Cambridge, CB3 9AL, England (office). *Telephone:* (215)-925-2222 (Philadelphia) (office); (1223) 328049 (Cambridge) (office). *E-mail:* carbon@sciencehistory.org (office). *Website:* www.sciencehistory.org (office); www.clarehall.cam.ac.uk (office).

ANDERSON, Sir Roy Malcolm, Kt, CBiol, PhD, DIC, FRS, FRSB, FMedSci, FIBiol, ARCS; British scientist, academic and fmr university administrator; *Professor of Infectious Disease Epidemiology, Imperial College London;* b. 12 April 1947, Herts.; s. of James Anderson and Betty Watson-Weatherburn; m. 1st Dr Mary Joan Mitchell 1975 (divorced 1989); m. 2nd Claire Baron 1990 (divorced

2013); m. 3rd Janet Louise Meyrick 2014; ed Duncombe School, Bengeo, Richard Hale School, Hertford, Imperial Coll., London; IBM Research Fellow, Univ. of Oxford 1971–73; Lecturer, King's Coll., London 1973–77; Lecturer, Imperial Coll. 1977–80, Reader 1980–82, Prof. 1982–93, Head of Dept of Biology 1984–93; Chair. Dept of Infectious Disease Epidemiology, Imperial Coll. Faculty of Medicine, Univ. of London 2000–08, 2009–, Prof. of Infectious Disease Epidemiology 2007–, Rector, Imperial Coll. London 2008–10; Linacre Prof. of Zoology, Univ. of Oxford 1993–2000, Head of Dept of Zoology 1993–98, Dir Wellcome Trust Centre for Epidemiology of Infectious Diseases 1994–2000; seconded to Ministry of Defence as Chief Scientific Adviser 2003–07; Visiting Prof., McGill Univ. 1982–; Alexander Langmuir Visiting Prof., Harvard Univ. 1990–; Genentech Visiting Prof., Univ. of Washington 1998; James McLaughlin Visiting Prof., Univ. of Texas 1999; Nuffield Medal Lecturer, Royal Soc. of Medicine 2002; Chair. Science Advisory Council, Dept for Environment, Food and Rural Affairs (Defra) 2004–; mem. Natural Environment Research Council (NERC) 1988–91 (Chair. Services and Facilities Cttee 1989–90); mem. Advisory Council on Science and Tech. (ACOST) 1989–93 (Chair. Standing Cttee on Environment 1990–93); mem. Council, Royal Soc. 1989–91, Zoological Soc. 1988–90, Royal Soc. of Tropical Medicine and Hygiene 1989–92; mem. Court, London School of Hygiene and Tropical Medicine 1993–2003; mem. Spongiform Encephalopathy Advisory Cttee 1998–2003; Dir (non-exec.) GlaxoSmithKline 2007–, Imperial Coll. Healthcare NHS Trust 2008–09; mem. Science Advisory Bd, IMS 1997–99, deCode 1998–2002, Bill and Melinda Gates Foundation Initiative on Grand Challenges in Global Health 2003–11, Partnership for Child Devt 2012–, WHO Neglected Tropical Diseases Programme 2008–12; Dir London Centre for Neglected Tropical Disease Research 2012–; mem. Int. Advisory Bd Hakluyt & Co. Ltd; Chair. Oxford Biologica Ltd (fmrly IBHSC Ltd) 1999–2001; Chair. Int. Advisory Panel, PTT Public Co. Ltd, Thailand; mem. Eng and Physical Sciences Research Council (EPSRC) 2004–08; mem. Govt's China Task Force 2009–12; Trustee, The Wellcome Trust 1991–92 (Gov. 1992–2000), Natural History Museum 2008–; Fellow, Royal Soc. of Tropical Medicine and Hygiene; Fellow, Merton Coll., Oxford 1993–2000; Gov., Inst. of Govt 2008–; Foreign mem. Inst. of Medicine, NAS 2000–, French Acad. of Sciences 2010–; mem. Advisory Bd, Singapore Nat. Research Foundation 2009–13, Nat. Science and Tech. Devt Agency, Thailand 2009–, Bio-Int. Advisory Panel, Malaysia 2009–; Hon. FRCPath 2000–, Hon. Fellow, Royal Agricultural Soc. 2002, Hon. FRSS 2002–, Hon. MRCP, Hon. Fellow Linacre Coll., Oxford 1993; Hon. DSc (East Anglia) 1997, (Stirling) 1998, (Aberdeen) 2009; Zoological Soc. Scientific Medal 1982, Huxley Memorial Medal 1983, C.A. Wright Memorial Medal 1986, David Starr Jordan Medal 1986, Chalmers Medal 1988, Weldon Medal 1989, John Hill Grundy Medal 1990, Frink Medal 1993, Joseph Smadel Lecture and Medal, Infectious Diseases Soc. of America 1994, Distinguished Statistical Ecologist Award 1998, Distinguished Parasitologist Award, American Soc. of Parasitology 1999. *Publications:* Population Dynamics of Infectious Disease Agents: Theory and Applications (ed.) 1982, Population Biology of Infectious Diseases (co-ed. with R. M. May) 1982, Infectious Diseases of Humans: Dynamics and Control (with R. M. May) 1991. *Leisure interests:* hill walking, croquet, natural history, photography. *Address:* Department of Infectious Disease Epidemiology, Imperial College London, St Mary's Campus, Norfolk Place, London, W2 1PG, England (office). *Telephone:* (20) 7594-3399 (office). *E-mail:* roy.anderson@imperial.ac.uk (office). *Website:* www3.imperial.ac.uk (office).

ANDERSON, Ruth, BA; British professional business services executive; b. Enniskillen, Northern Ireland; ed Univ. of Bradford; joined KPMG LLP (UK unit of KPMG) 1976, apptd Partner 1989, mem. Bd Dirs (first woman on bd of large professional services firm in UK) 1998–2004, Vice-Chair. 2005–09; mem. Bd of Dirs Ocado Group PLC 2010–, Travis Perkins plc 2011–, Coats Group plc 2014–, The Royal Parks; Trustee The Eve Appeal, Duke of Edinburgh's Award. *Leisure interests:* theatre, cinema, gardening.

ANDERSON, Wesley (Wes) Wales; American film director; b. 1 May 1969, Houston, Tex.; ed St John's School, Univ. of Tex.; Best New Filmmaker Award, MTV Movie Awards 1996. *Films include:* dir, writer, producer: Bottle Rocket (short) 1994, Bottle Rocket 1996, Rushmore (Best Dir, Ind. Spirit Awards, New Generation Award, Los Angeles Film Critics Asscn) 1998, The Royal Tenenbaums 2001, The Life Aquatic with Steve Zissou 2004, The Darjeeling Limited 2007, Fantastic Mr Fox 2009, Moonrise Kingdom 2012, The Grand Budapest Hotel (Screenwriter of the Year, London Critics' Circle 2015, Golden Globe Award for Best Motion Picture – Musical or Comedy 2015, BAFTA Award for Best Original Screenplay 2015) 2014; producer: The Squid and the Whale 2005. *Address:* c/o United Talent Agency Inc., 9560 Wilshire Blvd, Suite. 500, Beverly Hills, CA 90212, USA (office). *Telephone:* (310) 273-6700 (office). *Website:* www.unitedtalent .com (office); www.wesanderson.org.

ANDERSON, Sir (William) Eric (Kinloch), Kt, KT, MA, MLitt, DLitt, FRSE; British educationalist; b. 27 May 1936, Edinburgh, Scotland; s. of W. J. Kinloch Anderson and Margaret Harper; m. Anne Elizabeth Mason 1960; one s. one d.; ed George Watson's Coll., Univ. of St Andrews, Balliol Coll., Oxford; Asst Master, Fettes Coll., Edinburgh 1960–64, 1966–70, Gordonstoun School 1964–66; Headmaster, Abingdon School 1970–75, Shrewsbury School 1975–80, Eton Coll. 1980–94, Provost 2000–09; Rector, Lincoln Coll. Oxford 1994–2000; mem. Visiting Cttee of Memorial Church, Harvard 2001–07; Trustee, Nat. Heritage Memorial Fund 1996–98 (Chair. 1998–2001), Royal Collection Fund 2000–06, Shakespeare Birthplace Trust 2001–, Abbotsford Trust 2012–16; Chair. Cumberland Lodge 1997–2009; Visitor, Harris Manchester Coll., Oxford 2001–; Hon. DLitt (St Andrews, Hull, Siena, Birmingham, Aberdeen). *Publications include:* The Journal of Walter Scott (ed.) 1972, The Percy Letters (Vol. IX) 1988, The Sayings of Sir Walter Scott 1995, About Eton 2010, Sir Walter's Wit and Wisdom 2013, Sir Walter's Verse 2013, Sir Walter's Tales 2015; articles and reviews. *Leisure interests:* theatre, golf. *Address:* The Homestead, Kingham, OX7 6YA, England (office). *E-mail:* anderson1616@btinternet.com (home).

ANDERSSON, Bertil, BSc, MSc, PhD, DSc; Swedish biochemist, academic and university administrator; *President Emeritus, Nanyang Technological University;* b. 1948, Finspång, Östergötland; ed Umeå Univ., Lund Univ.; apptd Prof. of Biochemistry, Stockholm Univ. 1986, Head of Dept of Biochemistry, then Dean of Faculty of Chemical Sciences 1996–2003; Rector (Pres.) Linköping Univ. 1999–2003, apptd Prof. of Biochemistry 2004, currently Prof. Emer.; Adjunct Prof., Umeå Univ.; Visiting Prof. and Fellow, Imperial Coll. London, UK; Chief Exec. European Science Foundation, Strasbourg 2004–07; Provost, Nanyang Technological Univ. 2007–11, Pres. 2011–17, Pres. Emeritus 2018–; mem. Nobel Cttee for Chem. (Chair. 1997) 1989–97, Nobel Foundation 2000–06 (also mem. Bd of Trustees 2006–10); Vice-Pres. Research Advisory Bd European Comm. (EURAB) 2004–07; Chair. Global Alliance of Technological Univs; Swedish Rep. of Fed. of European Biochemical Socs 1988–90; mem. Bd Swedish Agricultural and Forestry Research Council –Chem. 1989–96, Swedish Natural Science Research Council 1991–98; Chair. Swedish Biochemical Soc. 1988–90, Swedish Nat. Cttee for Biochemistry and Molecular Biology 1991–94; mem. Forskningsforum (Forum for Swedish Science) 2001–03; Adviser to Swedish Govt on new research funding mechanisms 2003–04, to Swedish Ministry for Science and Educ. 2003, 2006–09; mem. Bd Kalmar Univ. Coll. 2004–07, Körber Foundation, Hamburg 2005–, Governing Bd Singapore Centre on Environmental Life Sciences Eng, Bd Building and Construction Authority, A*STAR Singapore (Govt agency for nat. scientific research and devt); fmr mem. Royal Swedish Acad. of Sciences, Australian Acad. of Sciences, Academia Europaea; Fellow Singapore National Academy of Science 2016–; Hon. Pro-Chancellor SRM Univ., Andhra Pradesh, India; Dr hc from several univs, including Hebrew Univ. of Jerusalem, Israel and Univ. of New South Wales, Australia; Wilhelm Exner Medal 2011, Medal for Educational Merit, World Cultural Council 2013, Meritorious Service Medal, Govt of Singapore 2017. *Publications:* more than 300 papers in professional journals on photosynthesis research, biological membranes, protein and membrane purification, light stress in plants, also several articles devoted to popular sciences and science policy. *Address:* Nanyang Technological University, SBS-01s-45e, 50 Nanyang Avenue, Singapore 639798 (office). *Telephone:* 65923670 (office). *E-mail:* bertil.andersson@ ntu.edu.sg (office). *Website:* www.ntu.edu.sg (office).

ANDERSSON, Göran Bror (Benny); Swedish composer and musician (keyboards); b. 16 Dec. 1946, Stockholm; m. 1st Frida Lyngstad 1978 (divorced 1981); m. 2nd Mona Nörklit 1981; two s. one d.; keyboard player and songwriter, the Hep Stars 1964–69; songwriter with Björn Ulvæus 1966–; partner in production with Ulvæus at Polar Music 1971; mem. pop group, ABBA 1972–82; winner, Eurovision Song Contest 1974; worldwide tours; concerts include Royal Performance, Stockholm 1976, Royal Albert Hall, London 1977, UNICEF concert, New York 1979, Wembley Arena 1979; reunion with ABBA, Swedish TV This Is Your Life 1986; continued writing and producing with Ulvæus 1982–; produced musical Mamma Mia! with Ulvæus, West End, London 1999–; Founder and bandleader, BAO (Benny Anderssons Orkester) and Benny Andersson Band 2001–; also composer for many other artists including Gemini, Ainbusk, Josefin Nilsson; mem., Royal Swedish Acad. of Music 2007; Dr hc (Stockholm Univ. Faculty of Humanities) 2007, (Luleå Tekniska Univ. Faculty of Humanities and Social Sciences) 2012; World Music Award for Best Selling Swedish Artist 1993, Ivor Novello Special International Award (with Björn Ulvaeus) 2002, inducted into Rock and Roll Hall of Fame (with ABBA) 2010. *Films:* as composer: ABBA: The Movie (also performer) 1977, Mio in the Land of Faraway 1987, Songs from the Second Floor 2000, You, the Living 2007, Mamma Mia! 2008, Palme (Guildbagge Award 2013) 2012. *Compositions include:* ABBA songs (with Ulvaeus); musicals: Chess (with lyrics by Tim Rice) 1983, Kristina Från Duvemåla (based on Vilhelm Moberg's epic novels, Utvandrarna) 1995, Mamma Mia! (with Ulvaeus) 1999. *Recordings include:* albums: with the Hep Stars: We and Our Cadillac 1965, The Hep Stars 1966, Jul med Hep Stars 1967, It's Been a Long Long Time 1968, Songs We Sang 68 1968; with Ulvaeus: Lycka 1970; with ABBA: Ring Ring 1973, Waterloo 1974, ABBA 1975, Greatest Hits 1976, Arrival 1977, The Album 1978, Voulez-Vous 1979, Greatest Hits Vol. 2 1979, Super Trouper 1980, The Visitors 1981, The Singles: The First Ten Years 1982, Thank You For The Music 1983, Absolute ABBA 1988, ABBA Gold 1992, More ABBA Gold 1993, Forever Gold 1998, The Definitive Collection 2001; with BAO: Benny Anderssons orkester 2001, BAO! 2004, BAO 3 2007, Story of a Heart 2009, O klang och jubeltid 2011, Tomten har åkt hem 2012; solo: Piano 2017; singles include: with ABBA: Ring Ring 1973, Waterloo 1974, Mamma Mia 1975, Dancing Queen 1976, Fernando 1976, Money Money Money 1976, Knowing Me Knowing You 1977, The Name Of The Game 1977, Take A Chance On Me 1978, Summer Night City 1978, Chiquitita 1979, Does Your Mother Know? 1979, Angel Eyes/Voulez-Vous 1979, Gimme Gimme Gimme (A Man After Midnight) 1979, I Have A Dream 1979, The Winner Takes It All 1980, Super Trouper 1980, On And On And On 1981, Lay All Your Love On Me 1981, One Of Us 1981, When All Is Said And Done 1982, Head Over Heels 1982, The Day Before You Came 1982, Under Attack 1982, Thank You For The Music 1983. *Publication:* Mamma Mia! How Can I Resist You? (with Björn Ulvaeus and Judy Craymer) 2006. *Address:* c/o Mono Music AB, Stockholm (office); Södra Brobänken 41A, 111 49 Stockholm, Sweden. *Telephone:* (8) 555-19-600 (office). *E-mail:* info@ monomusic.se (office). *Website:* www.monomusic.se (office); www.abbasite.com; www.bennyanderssonband.com; www.bennyanderssonorkester.se.

ANDERSSON, Harriet; Swedish actress; b. 14 Feb. 1932, Stockholm; began career in chorus at Oscars Theatre; subsequently appeared in reviews and then started serious dramatic career at Malmö City Theatre 1953; now appears regularly at Kunigliga Dramatiska Teatern, Stockholm; Swedish Film Asscn plaque. *Films include:* Summer with Monica 1953, Sawdust and Tinsel 1953, Women's Dreams 1955, Dreams of a Summer Night 1955, Through a Glass Darkly (German Film Critics' Grand Prize) 1961, Siska 1962, Dream of Happiness 1963, One Sunday in September 1963, All Those Women 1964, To Love (Best Actress Award, Venice Film Festival) 1964, Loving Couples 1964, For the Sake of Friendship 1965, Vine Bridge 1965, Adventure Starts Here 1965, Stimulantia 1965–66, Rooftree 1966, The Serpent 1966, The Deadly Affair 1967, The Girls 1968, Anna 1970, Cries and Whispers 1972, The Stake, Happy End 1999, Dogville 2003. *Television includes:* Kaspar i Nudådalen (series) 2001, Stora teatern (mini-series) 2002, Belinder auktioner (series) 2003, Swedenhielms (film) 2003, The Sandhamn Murders (series) 2010, Fjällbackamorden: Havet ger, havet tar (film) 2013. *Theatre includes:* Anne Frank in The Diary of Anne Frank, Ophelia in Hamlet, The Beggar's Opera and plays by Chekhov. *Address:* c/o Sandrew Film & Theater AB, Box 5612, 114 86 Stockholm, Sweden.

ANDERSSON, Leif, PhD; Swedish biochemist and academic; *Professor of Functional Genomics, Uppsala University;* currently Prof. of Functional Genomics, Uppsala Univ.; Guest Prof., Molecular Animal Genetics, Swedish Univ. of Agricultural Science; mem. Royal Swedish Soc. for Agric. and Forestry, Royal

Swedish Acad. of Sciences, Royal Physiographic Soc.; Foreign mem. NAS; Wolf Prize in Agric. (co-recipient) 2014. *Publications:* numerous papers in professional journals. *Address:* Department of Medical Biochemistry and Microbiology, Biomedical Centre, Uppsala University, Box 597, 751 24 Uppsala, Sweden (office). *Telephone:* (18) 471-4904 (office). *Fax:* (18) 471-4833 (office). *E-mail:* leif.andersson@imbim.uu.se (office). *Website:* www.imbim.uu.se/forskning/anderssonresearch.html (office); www.imbim.uu.se/Research/+Genomics/Andersson_Leif (office).

ANDERSSON, Leif Christer Leander, MD, PhD; Finnish pathologist and academic; *Professor Emeritus of Pathology, University of Helsinki;* b. 24 March 1944, Esse; s. of Herman Alfons Andersson and Elvi Alina Häll; m. Nea Margareta Gustavson 1971 (died 2003); one s. two d.; ed Univ. of Helsinki; Visiting Investigator, Univ. of Uppsala, Sweden 1975–76, Scripps Clinic and Research Inst., La Jolla, Calif., USA 1989–90; Prof. of Pathology, Univ. of Helsinki 1981–, now Emer.; Research Prof., Finnish Acad. of Science 1987–92; Prof. of Pathology, Karolinska Inst., Stockholm, Sweden 1996–2000, Head of Pathology, Karolinska Hosp. 1997, Foreign Adjunct Prof. 2004–; Head of Diagnostics, Div. of Pathology and Medical Genetics, Helsinki Univ. Hosp. 2002–03; Chair. Finnish Cancer Inst. 2003–11; Pres. Finnish Soc. of Sciences and Letters, Helsinki 2007–10; ERC Panel mem. 2007–13; Kt, First Class, Order of the White Rose of Finland 1992, Commdr, Order of the Lion of Finland 2009; Anders Jahres Medical Prize, Univ. of Oslo 1981, Finska Läkaresällskapets Prize 1985, E.J. Nyström Prize, Finnish Soc. of Sciences and Letters 2003, Runeberg Prize 2007, Liv och Hälsa Prize 2012. *Publications:* more than 380 original publs on cell biology, membrane glycoproteins, immunology, haematology, oncology and pathology. *Leisure interest:* happy jazz. *Address:* Department of Pathology, Haartman Institute, University of Helsinki, PO Box 21 (Haartmaninkatu 3), 00014 Helsinki, Finland (office). *Telephone:* 50-4482790 (mobile) (office). *Fax:* (9) 1912-6675 (office). *E-mail:* leif.andersson@helsinki.fi (office). *Website:* www.hi.helsinki.fi/english/about/pathology.html (office).

ANDERSSON, (Eva) Magdalena, BSc; Swedish economist and politician; *Minister for Finance;* b. 23 Jan. 1967, Uppsala; m. Prof. Richard Friberg; two c.; ed Katedralskolan, Uppsala, Stockholm School of Econs, Inst. for Advanced Studies, Vienna, Austria, Harvard Univ., USA; teacher (part-time), Stockholm School of Econs 1994; Political Adviser, Prime Minister's Office 1996–98, Dir of Planning 1998–2004; Sec. of State, Ministry of Finance 2004–06; mem. Social Democratic Parl. party group 2007–09; Deputy Dir-Gen., Swedish Tax Agency 2009–12; Domestic Policy Adviser to party Chair. 2009–12; mem. Swedish Social Democratic Party, Econ. Policy Spokesperson 2012–14; Minister for Finance 2014–; mem. Bd Policy Network 2005–09. *Address:* Ministry of Finance, Jakobsgatan 24, 103 33 Stockholm, Sweden (office). *Telephone:* (8) 405-10-00 (office). *Fax:* (8) 21-73-86 (office). *E-mail:* finansdepartementet.registrator@regeringskansliet.se (office). *Website:* www.regeringen.se/sveriges-regering/finansdepartementet (office); www.socialdemokraterna.se/magdalenaandersson.

ANDET-KOYARA, Marie-Noëlle; Central African Republic agronomist and politician; *Minister of Defence;* b. 14 Dec. 1955; divorced; five c.; ed Institut universitaire de technologie agronomique et forestière, Mbaïki, Bureau pour le développement et la production agricole, France; trained as agronomist with Compagnie ivoirienne pour le développement des textiles (CIDT), Côte d'Ivoire; began career as Head, Action des femmes rurales, Ouham-Pendé Region 1980, becoming Head of Extension Service; Head of Village Asscn, Société centrafricaine de développement agricole (SOCADA) 1982, Agricultural Trainer for Central and Eastern Regions, SOCADA 1983–86, Head of Training Dept, SOCADA 1985–97, Head of Training and Devt 1987–90; Dir Savannah Food Devt Project and Rep., African Devt Foundation 1990–93; Minister of Agric. and Rural Promotion, also Minister for Advancement of Women 1993–96; Rep. to FAO, Cape Verde (now Cabo Verde) 1996–2001, Burkina Faso 2001–07, Côte d'Ivoire 2007–13; Minister of Rural Devt 2013–14, Minister of State in charge of Public Works and Planning 2014–15, Minister of Defence (first woman) Jan.–Oct. 2015, 2017–. *Address:* Ministry of Defence, Bangui, Central African Republic (office). *Telephone:* 21-61-00-25 (office).

ANDO, Hiroyasu; Japanese diplomatist and government official; *President, The Japan Foundation;* b. 22 Nov. 1944, Kanagawa Pref., Tokyo; ed Faculty of Literature, Univ. of Tokyo, studies in USA; joined Ministry of Foreign Affairs 1970, held several posts including Asst Gen. Man. for Econ. Transactions, Sec. of the First Minister, Asst Gen. Man. for Countries of Asia 1986–88, Counsellor, Embassy in London, UK 1988, Dir, Overseas Establishments Div., Ministry of Foreign Affairs 1992–94, Deputy Dir-Gen. Econs Affairs Bureau 1994–96; Pvt. Sec. to Prime Minister 1996; Deputy Dir-Gen. Asian Affairs Bureau, Ministry of Foreign Affairs 1996–99, Envoy Extraordinary and Minister Plenipotentiary, Embassy in Washington, DC 1999–2002, Dir-Gen. Middle Eastern and African Affairs Bureau 2002–03, Consul-Gen. 2003–06, Asst Chief Cabinet Sec. 2006–08, Amb. to Italy (also accred to Albania) 2008–11; Pres. The Japan Foundation 2011–. *Address:* The Japan Foundation, 4-4-1 Yotsuya, Shinjuku-ku, Tokyo 160-0004, Japan (office). *Telephone:* (3) 5369-6075 (office). *Fax:* (3) 5369-6044 (office). *E-mail:* jf-toiawase@jpf.go.jp (office). *Website:* www.jpf.go.jp (office).

ANDO, Tadao; Japanese architect; b. 13 Sept. 1941, Osaka; m. Yumiko Kato 1970; one c.; fmr professional boxer; taught himself architecture by observing bldgs in Africa, America, Europe; Founder and Dir Tadao Ando Architect and Assocs 1969–; Prof., Univ. of Tokyo 1997–2003, Prof. Emer. 2003–; Visiting Prof., Columbia, Harvard, Yale Univs, USA; Hon. mem. AIA, American Acad. of Arts and Letters, Royal Acad. of Arts; Chevalier de l'Ordre des Arts et des Lettres 1995, Officier de l'Ordre des Arts et des Lettres 1997, Order of Culture 2010, Commdr, Order of Art and Letters (France) 2013, Grand Officer, Order of the Star (Italy) 2013; Gold Medal of Architecture, French Acad. 1989, Carlsberg Architecture Prize 1992, Japan Art Acad. Prize 1993, Asahi Prize 1994, Pritzker Prize 1995, Imperial Praemium Prize 1996, RIBA Royal Gold Medal 1997, Gold Medal, American Inst. of Architects 1997, Kyoto Prize 2002, Gold Medal, International Union of Architects 2005, Neutra Medal for Professional Excellence, Cal Poly Pomona Coll. of Environmental Design 2012, John F. Kennedy Center Gold Medal in the Arts 2010, Shimpei Goto Award 2010, Isamu Noguchi Award 2016. *Works include:* Tomishima House, Osaka 1973, Uno House, Kyoto 1974, Tatsumi House, Osaka 1975, Bansho House, Aichi Prefecture 1976, Wall House (Matsumoto House), Hyōgo Prefecture 1977, Okusu House, Tokyo 1978, Matsutani House, Kyoto 1979, Fuku House, Wakayama Prefecture 1980, Bansho House Addition, Aichi Prefecture 1981, Ishii House, Shizuoka Prefecture 1982, Bigi Atelier, Tokyo 1983, Rokko Housing nr Osaka 1983, Uejo House, Osaka Prefecture 1984, Atelier Yoshie Inaba, Tokyo 1985, TS Building, Osaka 1986, Karaza Theater, Tokyo 1987, Church on the Water, Hokkaido 1988, Morozoff P & P Studio, Kobe 1989, the Church of Light, Osaka 1989, Garden of Fine Arts Osaka 1990, Museum of Literature, Hyōgo 1991, Water Temple, Osaka 1991, Benesse House, Kagawa 1992, Vitra Seminar House, Weil am Rhein 1993, Suntory Museum, Osaka 1994, Naoshima Contemporary Art Museum, Kagawa 1995, Asahi Beer Oyamazaki Villa Museum of Art, Kyoto Prefecture 1995, Shanghai Pusan Ferry Terminal, Osaka 1996, Museum of Gojo Culture & Annex, Nara Prefecture 1997, Daikoku Denki Headquarters Building, Aichi Prefecture 1998, Church of the Light Sunday School, Osaka Prefecture 1999, Rockfield Shizuoka Factory, Shizuoka 2000, Teatro Armani-Armani World Headquarters, Milan 2001, Modern Art Museum of Fort Worth, Texas, USA 2002, Piccadilly Gardens, Manchester, UK 2003, Langen Foundation, Neuss, Germany 2004, Morimoto (restaurant), Manhattan, USA 2005, Omotesando Hills, Jingumae 4-Chome, Tokyo 2006, 21 21 Design Sight, Tokyo 2007, Glass House, Seopjikoji, South Korea 2008, Gate of Creation, Universidad de Monterrey, Monterrey, Mexico 2009, Capella Niseko Resort and Residences, Hokkaido Prefecture 2010, Kaminoge Station, Tokyu Corpn, Tokyo 2011, Akita Museum of Art, Akita 2012, Hansol Museum, Wonju, South Korea 2013, Jaeneung Culture Center, Seol, South Korea 2015, school for Benetton, Northern Italy. *Publications include:* Tadao Ando 1981, Tadao Ando: Buildings, Project, Writings 1984. *Address:* Tadao Ando Architect and Associates, 5-23 Toyosaki, 2-chome, Kita-ku, Osaka 531, Japan (office). *Website:* www.tadao-ando.com.

ANDOR, László, MA; Hungarian economist, politician and fmr EU official; b. 1966, Zalaegerszeg; m. Erika Varsányi; two c.; ed Zrínyi Miklós Gimnázium, Zalaegerszeg, Karl Marx Univ. (now the Corvinus Univ. of Budapest), George Washington Univ., Washington, DC, USA, Univ. of Manchester, UK (British Council Fellow); researcher, Politikatörténeti Intézet (political research inst.); Fellowship, Dept of Political Science, Univ. of Oslo, Norway 1992, Dept of War Studies, King's Coll., London, UK 1995, Netherlands Inst. for Advanced Study in the Humanities and Social Sciences, Wassenaar 2001–02; fmr Visiting Fulbright Scholar, Rutgers Univ., USA; Assoc. Prof., Dept of Econ. Policy, Budapest Univ. of Econ. Sciences, King Sigismund Coll.; mem. econ. policy advisory bd to Prime Minister Ferenc Gyurcsány 2003–05; mem. Bd Econ. Section of Hungarian Socialist Party 2003–; mem. Bd of Dirs EBRD 2005–09; Commr for Employment, Social Affairs and Inclusion, EC, Brussels 2010–14; Ed. leftist Hungarian quarterly social science journal, Eszmélet (Consciousness) 1993–; Széchenyi Professorship Grant 2000–03. *Publications include:* Market Failure: Structural Adjustment in Eastern Europe (co-author) 1998, Hungary on the Road to the European Union: Transition in Blue 2000. *Address:* c/o European Commission, 200 Rue de la Loi, 1049 Brussels, Belgium.

ANDOV, Stojan; Macedonian economist and politician; b. 1935; ed Skopje Univ., Belgrade Univ.; Co-Founder and mem. Exec. Bd Liberal Party of Macedonia 1990; Deputy Chair. Repub. Exec. Cttee; mem. Union Veche (Parl.) of Yugoslavia; took part in negotiations between Yugoslavia and EC; Amb. of Yugoslavia to Iraq; Del. to Nat. Ass. Repub. of Macedonia 1990–, Chair. 1990–96, Pres. Nat. Ass. 2000–02; Acting Pres. of Macedonia Oct. 1995–Jan. 1996; Head, Reform Forces of Macedonia-Liberal Party faction, Co-Chair. 1996. *Address:* Sobranje, 1000 Skopje, 11 Oktombri bb, North Macedonia (office). *Telephone:* (2) 112255 (office). *Fax:* (2) 237947 (office). *E-mail:* sgjorgi@assembly.gov.uk (office). *Website:* www.assembly.gov.mk/sobranje.

ANDRADE, Maria, BSc, MSc, PhD; Cabo Verde plant scientist; *Research Scientist, International Potato Center;* b. 1958, São Filipe Fogo, Cape Verde Islands (now Cabo Verde); ed Univ. of Arizona and North Carolina State Univ., USA; taught high school maths and science for two years in Cape Verde before being identified by USAID to study agronomy in USA with support from an African American Inst. scholarship; joined Int. Inst. for Tropical Agric. and worked in Southern Africa; began breeding research with Vitamin A-enriched orange-fleshed sweet potato (OFSP) in drought-prone areas of sub-Saharan Africa 1997; currently Research Scientist, Int. Potato Center (Centro Internacional de la Papa), Lima, Peru; World Food Prize (co-recipient) 2016. *Address:* Centro Internacional de la Papa, Avenida La Molina 1895, La Molina, Apartado Postal 1558, Lima, Peru (office). *Telephone:* 3496017 (office). *E-mail:* cip@cgiar.org (office). *Website:* cipotato.org (office).

ANDRÁSFALVY, Bertalan, PhD, DSc; Hungarian politician, ethnographer and academic; *Professor Emeritus, University of Pécs;* b. 17 Nov. 1931, Sopron; s. of Károly Andrásfalvy and Judit Mezey; m. Mária Gere; three s.; ed Budapest Univ. of Arts and Sciences; with Museum of Szekszárd 1955, Transdanubian Research Inst. of the Hungarian Acad. of Sciences 1960–76, Archives of Baranya Co. and Museum of Pécs –1985; Exec., later Dept Head Ethnographic Research Group, Hungarian Acad. of Sciences; Assoc. Prof., Univ. of Pécs 1989–93, Prof. 1993–2001, Prof. Emer. 2001–; mem. Cttee Hungarian Democratic Forum; mem. of Parl. 1990–94; Minister of Culture and Public Educ. 1990–93; Hon. mem. Finnish Literature Soc.; Grand Silver Medal with Ribbon (Austria), Order of Merit Medium Cross with Star (Hungary), Grosse Verdienstkreutz (Germany), Grand Cross of Lion's Order of Knighthood (Finland); Eriksson Prize of the Swedish Royal Acad., István Győrffy Memorial Medal of Hungarian Ethnographic Soc. *Publications:* Contrasting Value Orientation of Peasant Communities, Die traditionelle Bewirtschaftung der Überschwemmungsgebiete in Ungarn, European Culture of the Hungarian People, Vom 'Nutzen' der Volkskunst und der Volkskunde, Duna-Drava Nemzeti Park (co-author) 2001, Folyamatok es Fordulopontok (co-author) 2003, Hagyomany es Jovendo: Nepismereti Tanulmanyok 2004. *Leisure interest:* gardening. *E-mail:* bercimari@gmail.com.

ANDRE, Carl; American sculptor; b. 16 Sept. 1935, Quincy, Mass; s. of George H. Andre and Margaret M. Andre (née Johnson); m. Ana Mendieta 1985 (deceased); ed Phillips Acad.; served in US Army 1955–56; moved to New York 1957; worked as freight brakeman and conductor on Pennsylvania Railroad 1960–64; first public exhbn 1964; numerous public collections in USA and Europe; Fellow, John Simon Guggenheim Memorial Foundation 1984; f. Carl Andre and Mellissa L.

Kretschmer Foundation; Roswitha Haftmann Foundation Prize 2011. *Address:* PO Box 100, New York, NY 10276; 300 Mercer Street, Apt 34E, New York, NY 10003-6778, USA. *E-mail:* camkfoundation@melissakretschmer.com; carlandremelissalkretschmerfound@verizon.net. *Website:* www.carlandre.net.

ANDREA, Pat; Dutch artist; b. 25 June 1942, The Hague; s. of Kees Andrea and Metty Naezer; m. 1st Cecile Hessels 1966 (divorced 1983); m. 2nd Cristina Ruiz Guiñazu 1993; three s. one d.; ed Royal Acad. of Fine Arts, The Hague; paints in figurative style, focusing on personal deformities, people in dramatic situations, sex and violence in suspense; represented in MOMA, New York, Centre Pompidou, Paris and Frissiras Museum, Athens; Prof. Ecole Nat. Supérieur des Beaux Arts, Paris 1998–, Corresp. Académie des Beaux Arts Institut de France; Royal Subsidy for painting 1963, 1972; Jacob Maris Prize 1968. *Films include:* (with Fred Compain) Du crime consideré comme un des Beaux Arts 1981, Journal de Patagonie 1985, (with Marie Binet) L'aventure Pat Andrea 2002, (with Jorge Amat) La puñalada Pat Andrea 2004. *Publications include:* (with H. P. de Boer) Nederlands gebarenboekje 1979, 2004, (with J. Cortazar) La Puñalada 1982, Pat Andrea: conversations avec Pierre Sterckx 1993. *Address:* 52 avenue F.V.Raspail, 94110 Arcueil, France (office). *Telephone:* (1) 45-47-89-08 (office). *Fax:* (1) 45-47-89-08 (office).

ANDREAS, G(lenn) Allen, BA, JD; American business executive (retd); *President and CEO Galaco Capital LLC;* b. 22 June 1943, Cedar Rapids, Ia; s. of Glenn Allen Andreas and Vera Irene Yates; m. Toni Kay Hibma 1964; one s. two d.; ed Valparaiso Univ., Ind., Valparaiso Univ. School of Law; attorney, US Treasury Dept 1969–73; with Legal Dept, Archer Daniels Midland Co. 1973–86, Treasurer 1986–89, Chief Financial Officer of European Operations 1989–94, Vice-Pres. and Counsel to Exec. Cttee 1994–96, mem. Office of CEO 1996–97, Pres. and CEO 1997–99, Chair. and CEO 1999–2006, Chair. 2006–07; Chair. and CEO, Galaco Capital LLC; mem. World Econ. Forum, Bretton Woods Cttee, Trilateral Comm., Bd McCombie Group, LLC; mem. European Advisory Bd, Carlyle Group. *Leisure interest:* golf. *Address:* Galaco Capital LLC, 748 60th Street, St Oakland, CA 94609, USA.

ANDREESSEN, Marc Lowell, BS; American entrepreneur, business executive and software engineer; *Partner, Andreessen Horowitz;* b. 9 July 1971, Cedar Falls, Ia; m. Laura Arrillaga 2006; ed Univ. of Illinois, Urbana-Champaign; raised in New Lisbon, Wis.; undergraduate intern at IBM, Austin, Tex. for one summer; also worked at Nat. Center for Supercomputing Applications, Univ. of Illinois, Urbana-Champaign, co-created, with Eric Bina, Mosaic (first widely-used web browser) 1993; moved to Calif. to work at Enterprise Integration Technologies 1993; Co-founder, with Jim Clark, and Vice-Pres. of Tech., Mosaic Communications Corpn (name later changed to Netscape Communications), distributed the Netscape Navigator web browser 1994, Mosaic source code licensed by Microsoft from Spyglass, Inc. (offshoot of Univ. of Illinois) to create Internet Explorer web browser; Netscape acquired by AOL 1999, Chief Tech. Officer 1999–2001; left Netscape to form Loudcloud (services-based Web hosting co.) 2001, sold hosting business to EDS and renamed Opsware 2003, Chair. 2003–07 (co. bought by Hewlett-Packard 2007); co-f. Ning (provides platform for social-networking websites); investor in Digg (social news website), Plazes, Netvibes, CastTV and Twitter; launched RockMelt browser project 2010; mem. Bd of Dirs Facebook, eBay, Hewlett-Packard, Bump, TinyCo, Mixed Media Labs; fmr mem. Bd of Dirs Open Media Network; Co-founder, with Ben Horowitz, Andreessen Horowitz venture capital firm 2009–, acquired a stake in Skype Ltd 2009, Kno, Inc. (digital education platform co.); one of only six inductees in World Wide Web Hall of Fame announced at first int. Conf. on World Wide Web 1994, featured on the cover of TIME magazine 1996, 1998 and other publs, Queen Elizabeth Prize for Eng (co-recipient) 2013. *Address:* Andreessen Horowitz, 2865 Sand Hill Road, Suite 101, Menlo Park, CA 94025, USA (office). *E-mail:* pmarcablog@gmail.com (office); a16z@theoutcastagency.com (office). *Website:* a16z.com (office); blog.pmarca.com.

ANDREEV, Aleksandr Fyodorovich, DrPhysSc; Russian physicist and academic; *Vice-President, Russian Academy of Sciences;* b. 10 Dec. 1939, Leningrad; s. of Fyodor Andreev and Nina Andreeva; m. Tamara Turok 1960; one d.; ed Moscow Physico-Tech. Inst.; Jr then Sr Researcher, Moscow Physico-Tech. Inst. 1964–79, Prof. 1979–; Deputy Dir Kapitza Inst. for Physical Problems, USSR Acad. of Sciences 1984–91, Dir 1991–; Corresp. mem. USSR (now Russian) Acad. of Sciences 1981–87, Full mem. 1987, Vice-Pres. 1991–2013, currently Fellow, fmr Chair. Research Council on Low-Temperature Physics, mem. Gen. Physics and Astronomy Section, Branch of Physical Sciences; Lorentz Prof., Univ. of Leiden 1992; Ed.-in-Chief Priroda 1993–, Register of Experimental and Theoretical Physics 1997–; Chair. Comm. for State Scientific Stipends; Foreign mem. Finnish Acad. of Science and Letters 2002, Georgian Acad. of Sciences 2002, Polish Acad. of Sciences 2005, National Acad. of Sciences of Ukraine 2008; mem. Scientific Council, Int. Centre of Theoretical Physics 1996–2003; Lomonosov Prize, USSR Acad. of Sciences 1984, Lenin Prize 1986, Carus-Medaille de Deutschen Akad. der Naturforscher Leopoldina, Carus-Preis der Stadt Schweinfurt 1987, Simon Memorial Prize (UK) 1995, Kapitza Gold Medal, Russian Acad. of Sciences 1999, Ind. Prize Triumph 2003, Int. Pomeranchuk Prize 2004, John Bardeen Int. Prize 2006, Demidov Prize, Russian Acad. of Sciences 2011. *Address:* Academy of Sciences, Kapitza Institute for Physical Problems, 119334 Moscow, Kosygin Street 2, Russia (office). *Telephone:* (495) 137-32-48 (office). *Fax:* (495) 651-21-25 (office). *E-mail:* andreev@kapitza.ras.ru (office). *Website:* www.kapitza.ras.ru (office).

ANDREJEVS, Georgs, DMed; Latvian politician, diplomatist, physician and scientist; b. 30 Oct. 1932, Tukums; m. Anita Andrejeva; one s. one d.; ed Latvian Medical Inst.; paramedic, Rīga first aid station 1953–59; Head of Dept, P. Stradiņs Clinic, Rīga 1959–62, Asst 1962–64, teacher 1964–74; Asst Prof., Head Dept of Surgery, Chief Anaesthesiologist and Reanimatologist of Ministry of Health 1962–92; Head of Dept and Prof., Rīga Inst. of Medicine 1974–90; Head of Dept, Latvian Acad. of Medicine 1994–95; Founder Latvijas ceļš (Latvian Way) party 1993; mem. Latvian People's Front; Deputy to Latvian Repub. Supreme Council; Sec. Comm. for Foreign Affairs of Supreme Council; Minister of Foreign Affairs 1992–94; mem. Saima (Parl.) 1993–95; Amb. to Canada 1995–98, to Council of Europe 1998–2004; Chair. Council of Europe Ministers Deputies 2000–01, Council of Europe Cttee of Ministers Working Party on Co-operation between the Council of Europe and the EU 2001–03; mem. European Parl. (Group of the Alliance of Liberals and Democrats for Europe) 2004–09, Vice-Chair. Cttee on the Environment, Public Health and Food Safety 2007–09, mem. Del. to EU-Armenia, EU-Azerbaijan and EU-Georgia Parl. Cooperation Cttees 2004–09, Substitute mem. Del. to EU-Croatia Jt Parl. Cttee 2004–09; mem. Latvian Acad. of Sciences 1995–, European Asscn of Anaesthesiologists 1997–; Fellow, Royal Coll. of Anaesthetists, UK 1995; doyen d'âge, Council of Europe diplomatic corps; Commdr, Order of the Three Stars. *Address:* Akmenu iela 15, 1048 Rīga, Latvia.

ANDREOLI, Kathleen Gainor; American professor of nursing and university administrator; *Dean Emerita, College of Nursing, Rush University;* b. 22 Sept. 1935, Albany, New York; d. of John Edward Gainor and Edmunda Ringelmann Gainor; m. Thomas Eugene Andreoli 1960 (divorced); one s. two d.; ed Georgetown Univ. and Vanderbilt Univ. School of Nursing and Univ. of Alabama School of Nursing, Birmingham; Staff Nurse, Albany Hosp. Medical Center, New York 1957; instructor, various schools of nursing 1957–70; Educational Dir, Physician Asst Program, Dept of Medicine, School of Medicine, Univ. of Alabama 1970–75, subsequently Asst Prof. then Assoc. Prof. of Nursing 1970–79, Prof. of Nursing 1979; Prof. of Nursing, Special Asst to Pres. for Educational Affairs, Univ. of Texas Health Science Center, Houston 1979–82, Vice-Pres. for Educational Services, Interprofessional Educ. and Int. Programs 1983–87; Vice-Pres. Nursing Affairs and John L. and Helen Kellogg Dean of Coll. of Nursing Rush Univ., Chicago 1987–2005, Dean Emer. 2005–; Ed. Heart and Lung, Journal of Total Care 1971; mem. Bd of Dirs American Asscn of Colleges of Nursing 1998–2000; mem. Nat. Advisory Nursing Council V.H.A. 1992, Advisory Bd Robert Wood Johnson Clinic Nursing School Program, Visiting Cttee Vanderbilt Univ. School of Nursing, Editorial/Advisory Bd The Nursing Spectrum 1996–, Advisory Bd Major Diseases: Diabetes Mellitus and Hypertension 1999, numerous other bodies; mem. Inst. of Medicine of NAS, Inst. of Medicine of Chicago; Fellow, American Acad. of Nursing; Founders Award, NC Heart Asscn 1970, Distinguished Alumni Awards, Vanderbilt Univ. and Univ. of Alabama, Birmingham, Sigma Theta Tau Dean's Award 2003, GE Healthcare-American Asscn of Critical Care Nursing Pioneering Spirit Award 2009, Visionary Leadership Award 2010; numerous other awards. *Publications include:* Comprehensive Cardiac Care (co-author) 1983; numerous articles in professional journals. *Leisure interests:* music, art, reading, bicycling, travelling. *Address:* Rush University Medical Center, 600 South Paulina Street, Suite 1080, Chicago, IL 60612-3806 (office); 1212 South Lake Shore Drive, Chicago, IL 60605-2402, USA (home). *Telephone:* (312) 942-7117 (office); (312) 266-8338 (home). *Fax:* (312) 942-3043 (office). *E-mail:* Kathleen_G_Andreoli@rush.edu (office). *Website:* www.rushu.rush.edu/nursing (office).

ANDREOTTI, Lamberto, BS, MSc; American pharmaceutical industry executive; b. 6 July 1950, Rome; s. of Giulio Andreotti and Livia Danese; ed Univ. of Rome, Italy, Massachusetts Inst. of Tech.; held various sr roles at Farmitalia Carlo Erba, KABI Pharmacia and then at Pharmacia & Upjohn –1998; Vice-Pres. and Gen. Man., Italy and European Oncology, Bristol-Myers Squibb 1998–2000, Pres., Europe 2000–02, Sr Vice-Pres. and Pres., International 2002–05, Pres. and COO Bristol-Myers Squibb 2005–10, mem. Bd of Dirs 2009–, CEO 2010–15, Chair. Bd of Dirs 2015–17; Sr Adviser EW Healthcare Partners 2017–; mem. Bd of Dirs, DowDuPont Inc. 2012–, UniCredit SpA 2018–, American-Italian Cancer Foundation. *Address:* EW Healthcare Partners, 280 Park Avenue, 27th Floor E, New York, NY 10017, USA (office). *Telephone:* (646) 429-1251 (office). *Fax:* (212) 922-0551 (office). *E-mail:* newyork@ewhealthcare.com (office). *Website:* www.ewhealthcare.com (office).

ANDRESEN, Brit, MArch; Norwegian architect and academic; *Architect/Practice Professor, Brit Andresen Architect, University New Castle;* m. Peter O'Gorman (deceased); ed Univ. of Trondheim; awarded scholarship to study housing in The Netherlands; won competition to co-design Burrell Museum (with John Meunier and Barry Gasson), Glasgow, UK; fmr part-time teacher of architecture, Univ. of Cambridge and Architectural Asscn, UK; Prof. of Architecture, Univ. of Queensland, Australia 1978–2010, Prof. Emer. 2010–; Practice Prof., Univ. New Castle; fmr Asst Prof., UCLA, USA; Tutor, Glenn Murcutt Int. Master Class, Sydney 2006; Co-founder Andresen O'Gorman Architects (with Peter O'Gorman); Life Fellow, Royal Australian Inst. of Architects (RAIA); RAIA Gold Medal (first woman to receive medal) 2002. *Architectural works include:* Burrell Museum (Glasgow), Rosebery House (Brisbane), Ocean View House (Mt Mee), Mooloomba House (Point Lookout), Forest House (Indooroopilly), Moreton Bay Houses (Wynnum), Booran House (Minjerriba Island), Apt.4 Dornoch Tce (Highgate Hill). *Television:* In the Mind of the Architect. *Publications include:* articles on architecture in professional journals and architectural projects on websites: umemagazine.com No. 22, Vols 1 and 2, sedimentarycity.com. *Address:* School of Architecture, University of Queensland, Brisbane, Queensland 4072, Australia (office). *Telephone:* (7) 3365-3537 (office). *E-mail:* b.andresen@uq.edu.au (office).

ANDRETTI, Mario; American business executive and fmr racing driver; b. 28 Feb. 1940, Montona, Italy; s. of Alvise Andretti and Rina Andretti; m. Dee Ann Hoch 1961; two s. one d.; began racing career in Nazareth, Pa aged 19; Indy Car Nat. Champion 1965, 1966, 1969, 1984; winner of Daytona 500 1967; winner of 12 Hours of Sebring 1967, 1970, 1972; winner of Indianapolis 500 1969; USAC Nat. Dirt Track Champion 1974; Formula One World Champion 1978; winner of Int. Race of Champions 1979; all-time Indy Car lap leader (7,595); all-time leader in Indy Car pole positions won (67); oldest race winner in recorded Indy Car history; retd from active driving 1994; Commendatore, Order of Merit; Driver of the Year 1967, 1978, 1984, Driver of the Quarter Century 1992, Driver of the Century 1999–2000, FIA Gold Medal for Motor Sport 2007, Library of Congress Living Legend 2008, inducted in 20 nat. and int. halls of fame. *Achievements include:* 111 career wins, 52 Indy Car victories (USAC & CART), 12 Formula One victories (FIA), 9 Sprint Car victories (USAC), 9 Midget victories (ARDC, NASCAR & USAC), 7 Formula 5000 victories (SCCA/USAC), 7 World Sports Car victories (FIA), 5 Dirt Track victories (USAC), 4 Three-Quarter Midget victories (ATQMRA), 3 IROC victories, 2 stock car victories (NASCAR & USAC), 1 non-championship race. *Publications include:* Mario Andretti: A Driving Passion (biog.), Andretti (biog.). *Leisure interests:* flying ultralight, snowmobiling, tennis, opera. *Telephone:* (248) 335-3535 (office). *Fax:* (248) 335-3352 (office). *E-mail:* jc@sportsmanagementnetwork.com (office). *Website:* www.sportsmanagementnetwork.com (office); www.marioandretti.com.

ANDREW, Christopher Robert (Rob), MBE, MA; British professional rugby union coach and fmr professional rugby union player; *CEO and Director, Sussex*

County Cricket Club; b. 18 Feb. 1963, Richmond, Yorks.; m. Sara Andrew 1989; two d.; ed Univ. of Cambridge; chartered surveyor; fly-half; fmr mem. Middlesbrough, Cambridge Univ., Nottingham, Gordon (Sydney, Australia) clubs; mem. Wasps Club 1987–91, 1992–96, Capt. until 1989–90; with Toulouse 1991–92, Barbarians, Newcastle 1996–; int. debut England versus Romania 1985; Five Nations debut England versus France 1985; Capt. England team, England versus Romania, Bucharest 1989; mem. Grand Slam winning team 1991, 1992; record-holder for drop goals in ints; retd from int. rugby 1995, returned 1997–99; Devt Dir Newcastle Rugby Football Club 1996–2006; Elite Rugby Dir Rugby Football Union 2006–11, Dir of Operations 2011–16; CEO and Dir Sussex County Cricket Club 2017–; fmr Assoc. Dir DTZ Debenham Thorpe; Hon. Pres. Wooden Spoon. *Publication:* A Game and a Half 1995. *Leisure interests:* gardening, pushing a pram, golf. *Address:* Sussex Cricket Limited – The 1st Central County Ground, Eaton Road, Hove BN3 3AN, England (office). *Telephone:* (84) 4264-0202 (office). *Website:* www.sussexcricket.co.uk.

ANDREWS, Anthony; British actor; b. 12 Jan. 1948, Hampstead, London; s. of Stanley Thomas Andrews and Geraldine Agnes (née Cooper); m. Georgina Simpson 1971; one s. two d.; ed Royal Masonic School, Herts.; started acting 1967. *TV appearances include:* Doomwatch, Woodstock 1972, A Day Out, Follyfoot, Fortunes of Nigel 1973, The Pallisers, David Copperfield 1974, Upstairs, Downstairs 1975, French Without Tears, The Country Wife, Much Ado About Nothing 1977, Danger UXB 1978, Romeo and Juliet 1979, Brideshead Revisited (British Acad. TV Award for Best Actor 1982, Golden Globe Award for Best Performance by an Actor in a Mini-Series 1983) 1981, Ivanhoe 1982, The Scarlet Pimpernel 1983, Columbo 1988, The Strange Case of Dr. Jekyll and Mr. Hyde 1989, Hands of a Murderer 1990, Lost in Siberia 1990, The Law Lord 1991, Jewels 1992, Ruth Rendell's Heartstones, Mothertime, David Copperfield 2000, Love in a Cold Climate (mini-series) 2001, Cambridge Spies (mini-series) 2003, Birdsong (mini-series) 2012, The Syndicate (mini-series) 2015. *Films Include:* The Scarlet Pimpernel, Under the Volcano, A War of the Children, Take Me High 1973, Operation Daybreak 1975, Les Adolescents 1976, The Holcroft Covenant 1986, Second Victory 1987, Woman He Loved 1988, The Lighthorsemen 1988, Hannah's War 1988, Lost in Siberia (also producer) 1990, Haunted (also co-producer) 1995, Last Night 2007, The King's Speech 2010. *Plays:* 40 Years On, A Midsummer Night's Dream, Romeo and Juliet, One of Us 1986, Coming into Land 1986, Dragon Variation, Tima and the Conways, My Fair Lady 2003–04, The Woman in White 2005, The Letter 2007, Bully Boy 2011.

ANDREWS, John Hamilton, AO, MArch, FTS, RIBA; Australian architect; b. 29 Oct. 1933, Sydney, NSW; s. of K. Andrews; m. Rosemary Randall 1958; four s.; ed North Sydney Boys' High School, Univ. of Sydney, Harvard Univ., USA; in pvt. practice, Toronto, Canada 1962, Sydney 1970–; f. John Andrews Architects (now John Andrews International Pty Ltd), Toronto 1962; mem. staff, Univ. of Toronto School of Architecture 1962–67, Chair. and Prof. of Architecture 1967–69; Chair. Architecture and Design Comm., Australia Council 1980–83, Founding Chair. Design Arts Bd 1983–88; Architectural Juror, Australian Archives Nat. HQ Bldg 1979, Parl. House Competition 1979–80, The Peak, Hong Kong 1983, Hawaii Loa Coll. 1986, Gov. Gen.'s Medals, Canada 1986; mem. Visual Arts Bd, Australia Council 1977–80, Bd mem. 1988–90, RIBA; Assoc., NZ Inst. of Architects; Foundation mem. Australian Acad. of Design 1990; Fellow, Royal Architectural Inst. of Canada; Life Fellow, Royal Australian Inst. of Architects; Hon. FAIA; Hon. DArch (Sydney) 1980; Centennial Medal (Canada) 1967, Massey Medal (Canada) 1967, Arnold Brunner Award, American Acad. of Arts and Letters 1971, American Inst. of Architects Honour Award 1973, Gold Medal, Royal Australian Inst. of Architects 1980, Advance Australia Award 1982, Sulman Medal (Australia) 1983, Design Excellence 25 Year Award, Ontario Asscn of Architecture, Scarborough Coll. 1989. *Publication:* Architecture: A Performing Art 1982. *Leisure interests:* fly fishing, surfing. *Address:* Colleton, Cargo Road, Orange, NSW 2800, Australia (home). *Telephone:* (2) 6365-6223 (office). *Fax:* (2) 6365-6211 (office).

ANDREWS, Dame Julie Elizabeth, DBE; British actress and singer; b. (Julia Wells), 1 Oct. 1935, Walton-on-Thames, Surrey; m. 1st Tony Walton 1959 (divorced 1968); one d.; m. 2nd Blake Edwards 1969 (died 2010); one step-s. one step-d. and two adopted d.; ed voice lessons with Lillian Stiles-Allen; first stage appearance aged 12 as singer, London Hippodrome; played in revues and concert tours; debut in Starlight Roof, London Hippodrome 1947; work for UN Devt Fund for Women; three Golden Globe Awards 1964, 1965, Emmy Award 1987, BAFTA Award 1989, Kennedy Center Honor 2001, Screen Actors' Guild Lifetime Achievement Award 2006. *Theatre includes:* Starlight Roof (London Hippodrome) 1947, Cinderella (London Palladium), The Boy Friend (Broadway) 1954, My Fair Lady 1956–60, Camelot (Broadway) 1960–62, Putting it Together 1993, Victor, Victoria 1995–96. *Films include:* Mary Poppins (Academy Award for Best Actress 1964) 1963, The Americanization of Emily 1964, The Sound of Music 1964, Hawaii 1965, Torn Curtain 1966, Thoroughly Modern Millie 1966, Star! 1967, Darling Lili 1970, The Tamarind Seed 1973, 10 1979, Little Miss Marker 1980, S.O.B. 1980, Victor/Victoria 1981, The Man Who Loved Women 1983, That's Life 1986, Duet For One 1986, The Sound of Christmas (TV) 1987, Our Sons (TV) 1991, Relative Values 1999, The Princess Diaries 2001, Shrek 2 (voice) 2004, The Princess Diaries 2: Royal Engagement 2004, The Cat That Looked at a King 2004, Shrek the Third (voice) 2007, Enchanted (voice) 2007, The Tooth Fairy 2010, Shrek Forever After (voice) 2010, Despicable Me (voice) 2010. *TV appearances include:* High Tor 1956, The Julie Andrews Hour 1972–73, Great Performances Live in Concert 1990, The Julie Show (ABC) 1992, Eloise at the Plaza 2003, Eloise at Christmastime 2003. *Recordings include:* albums: My Fair Lady (Broadway cast recording) 1956, The Lass With The Delicate Air 1957, Julie Andrews Sings 1958, Rose Marie 1958, Camelot (Broadway cast recording) 1960, Don't Go In The Lion's Cage Tonight 1962, Heartrending Ballads and Raucous Ditties 1962, Julie & Carol at Carnegie Hall (with Carol Burnett) 1962, Mary Poppins (film soundtrack) 1964, The Sound Of Music (film soundtrack) 1965, A Christmas Treasure 1968, Star! 1968, Darling Lili 1969, TV's Fair Julie 1972, The Secret of Christmas 1977, Christmas With Julie Andrews 1982, Love Me Tender 1983, Broadway's Fair Julie 1984, Love Julie 1989, At The Lincoln Center (with Carol Burnett) 1989, The King And I (studio cast) 1992, Broadway: The Music of Richard Rodgers 1994, Here I'll Stay: The Words of Alan Jay Lerner 1996, Nobody Sings It Better 1996. *Publications include:* Mandy (as Julie Andrews Edwards) 1972, Last of the Really Great Whangdoodles 1973, The Great American Mousical (as Julie Andrews Edwards, with Emma Walton Hamilton) 2006, Home (autobiog.) 2008. *Leisure interests:* skiing, riding. *Address:* WME Entertainment, 9601 Wilshire Boulevard, 3rd Floor, Beverly Hills, CA 90210, USA (office). *Telephone:* (310) 850-4550 (office); (310) 285-9000 (office). *Fax:* (310) 248-5650 (office); (310) 285-9010 (office). *E-mail:* jcolbert@wmeentertainment.com (office); ndavid@wmeentertainment.com (office). *Website:* www.wmeentertainment.com (office).

ANDREWS, Kevin, BA, LLB, LLM; Australian lawyer and politician; b. 9 Nov. 1955, Sale, Vic.; m. Margaret Andrews; four c.; ed Univ. of Melbourne, Monash Univ.; Research Solicitor, Law Inst. of Victoria 1980–81, Co-ordinator, Continuing Legal Educ. 1981–83; Assoc. to Hon. Sir James Gobbo, Supreme Court of Vic. 1983–85; Barrister-at-Law, Vic. 1985–91; mem. House of Reps for Menzies, Vic. 1991–; Minister for Ageing 2001–03, Minister for Employment and Workplace Relations 2003–07, Minister Assisting the Prime Minister for the Public Service 2003–07, Minister for Immigration and Citizenship Jan.–Dec. 2007, Minister for Social Services 2013–14, Minister of Defence 2014–15; mem. Liberal Party of Australia. *Address:* c/o Department of Defence, Russell Offices, Russell Drive, Campbell, Canberra, ACT 2600, Australia (office). *Website:* kevinandrews.com.au.

ANDREWS, Nancy Catherine, BS, MS, MD, PhD; American physician, biologist and academic; *Vice-Chancellor and Dean, School of Medicine, Duke University;* b. 29 Nov. 1958, Syracuse, NY; d. of William Shankland Andrews and Virginia Helen Andrews (née Rogers); m. Bernard Mathey-Prevot; one s. one d.; ed Yale Univ., Massachusetts Inst. of Tech., Harvard Medical School; joined faculty of Harvard Univ. Medical School 1991, becoming Leland Fikes Prof. of Pediatrics 2003, George Richards Minot Prof. of Pediatrics 2006, Dean for Basic Sciences and Grad. Studies 2003–07; Investigator, Howard Hughes Medical Inst. 1993–2006; Attending Physician in Hematology and Oncology, Children's Hosp., Boston 1991–2003; fmr Distinguished Physician, Dana-Farber Cancer Inst., Boston; Vice Chancellor for Academic Affairs and Dean, School of Medicine, Duke Univ. 2007–; Pres. American Soc. of Clinical Investigation 2008–09; mem. NAS Inst. of Medicine 2006–; mem. American Acad. of Arts and Sciences 2007–, Fellow 2006–; Samuel Rosenthal Prize for Excellence in Academic Pediatrics 1998, American Fed. for Medical Research Foundation Outstanding Investigator Award in Basic Science 2000, Soc. for Pediatric Research E. Mead Johnson Award 2002, Harvard Medical School Dean's Leadership Award for Advancement of Women 2004. *Publications include:* over 100 peer-reviewed articles and 23 book chapters. *Address:* Dean's Suite, DUMC 2927, Duke University School of Medicine, Davison Building, 200 Trent Drive, Durham, NC 27710, USA (office). *Telephone:* (919) 684-8111 (office). *Fax:* (919) 684-0208 (office). *E-mail:* nancy.andrews@duke.edu (office). *Website:* medschool.duke.edu (office).

ANDREYCHENKO, Uladzimir Pavlovich; Belarusian agronomist and politician; *Chairman (Speaker), House of Representatives (Palata Predstaviteley);* b. 1949, Maryanovo, Lioznenskiy Dist, Vitebsk (Viciebsk) Oblast, Belarusian SSR, USSR; ed Velikoluk Agricultural Inst., Minsk Higher Party School; early career as technician, Pobeda Sotsializma Agricultural Collective Farm, Verkhnedvinsiy Dist, Vitebsk Oblast 1968; served in Soviet Army 1968–70; agronomist, Lioznenskiy Dist Agricultural Tech. Centre 1970–72; Instructor and Leader, Organizational Dept, Lioznenskiy Dist Cttee Br. Komsomol (Communist Youth League) 1972–74; Instructor, Lioznenskiy Dist Cttee, CP of Belarus 1974–75; Sec., Party Cttee, Akademenki Soviet Farm and Chair. Danukalov Lioznenskiy Collective Farm 1975–81; Sr Agric. Man. Lioznenskiy Dist Exec. Cttee 1981–85, Chair. 1985–87; First Sec., Verkhnedvinskiy Dist Cttee, CP of Belarus 1987–91; Deputy Chair., later Chair., Cttee for Agric. and Supplies, Vitebsk Oblast Exec. Cttee 1991–94, Chair. Vitebsk Oblast Exec. Cttee 1994–2008; Deputy, 12th Supreme Soviet of BSSR (Parl.) 1991–94 (dissolved under new constitution of 1994); mem. first, second and third terms, Council of the Repub. (Soviet Respubliki) 1996–2000, 2000–04, 2004–08, Chair. (Speaker) House of Reps (Palata Predstaviteley) Oct. 2008–; First Deputy Chair. Parl. Ass., Union State of Belarus and Russia 2008–, also mem. Higher State Council of Union Govt; Order of the Fatherland (III Degree, Second Class), Honoured Scholar of Belarusian SSR, Honoured Agricultural Worker of the Repub. of Belarus; Hon. Diplomas of the Supreme Council of BSSR, Nat. Ass. of Belarus, Council of Ministers of Belarus. *Address:* Office of the Chairman, Palata Predstaviteley (House of Representatives), 220010 Minsk, vul. Savetskaya 11, Belarus (office). *Telephone:* (17) 222-32-62 (office). *Fax:* (17) 327-37-84 (office). *E-mail:* kc1@house.gov.by (office). *Website:* house.gov.by (office).

ANDREYEV, Vladimir Alekseyevich; Russian actor, stage director and academic; *President, Vermolova Theatre;* b. 27 Aug. 1930; m. Natalia Selezneva; one s. one d.; ed State Inst. of Theatre Arts Cinema (GITIS); actor with Yermolova Theatre Moscow 1952–70, Dir 1970–85, 1990–; teaches concurrently at GITIS, Prof. 1978–; Chief Dir of Maly Theatre, Moscow 1985–88; fmr Head, Dept of Acting, Russian Acad. of Theatre Arts (fmr Chair. Drama Faculty); Pres. Vermolova Theatre 2012–; mem. CPSU 1962–92, Int. Acad. of Theatre, Russian Acad. of Theatre Arts; USSR People's Artist 1985; Stanislavsky State Prize 1980, 1993, State Prize of Russia 1990, Govt Prize for Theatre Arts 1994, 2001. *Roles include:* Aleksey in V. Rozov's It's High Time!, Vasilkov in Ostrovsky's Crazy Money, Golubkov in Bulgakov's Flight, Sattarov in Valeyev's I Give You Life, Dorogin in Zorin's Lost Story, Writer in Bunin's Grammar of Love, Nikita in Chekhov's One Big Small Drama. *Productions include:* Vampilov's plays: Last Summer in Chulimsk and The Duck Hunt; Money for Mary (based on a work by V. Rasputin), The Shore (based on Yuriy Bondarev's novel), Uncle Vanya, Three Sisters (Chekhov). *Publications:* I Remember with an Open Heart, One Endless Plot. *Leisure interests* fine art, architecture, football, politics. *Address:* Russian Academy of Theatre Arts, 103888 Moscow, 6, Maly Kislovsky pereulok (office); Tverskaya 9-60, 125009 Moscow, Russia (home). *Telephone:* (495) 691-91-92 (office); (495) 629-48-57 (home). *Fax:* (495) 690-05-97 (office). *E-mail:* yermolova@theatre.ru; info@gitis.net (office). *Website:* www.gitis.net (office); www.ermolova.theatre.ru (office).

ANDRIAMANJATO, Ny Hasina; Malagasy mathematician and politician; *President, Antananarivo Municipal Authority;* s. of Richard Andriamanjato; m.; three c.; ed Lomonosov State Univ., Moscow, Russia; mem. Cttee for Econ. and Social Recovery 1992; Minister for Post and Telecommunications 1993–2002; mem. Congress Party for Malagasy Independence; unsuccessful ind. cand. in presidential election Dec. 2006; Gen. Co-ordinator, Admin., Financial, Econ. and Infrastructure and Urban Affairs, Antananarivo Town Hall –2009; Minister of Foreign Affairs (following coup d'état) 2009–10, also Deputy Prime Minister 2009–10 (resgnd); currently Minister of Posts, Telecommunications and New Technologies; Pres. Délégation spéciale de la ville d'Antananarivo (municipal authority) 2014–. *Leisure interests:* playing the piano. *Address:* Commune urbaine d'Antananarivo, 4, rue Fernand Kasanga, Tsimbazaza, BP 1279, 101 Antananarivo, Madagascar (office). *Telephone:* (32) 1150185 (office). *Fax:* (20) 2234115 (office). *E-mail:* cua.spm@gmail.com (office).

ANDRIAMBOLOLONA, Vonintsalama Sehenosoa, MEconSci; Malagasy economist and politician; ed Univ. of Antananarivo, Ecole nat. des services du Trésor, Marnes la Vallée, France, IMF Inst., Washington, Int. Devt Law Inst., Rome, UNCTAD, Geneva; joined Ministry of Finance, Budget and Planning 1977, becoming Dir, Treasury Dept 1996–2003, Sec.-Gen., Ministry of Finance and Budget 2009–15, Minister of Finance and the Budget (first female) 2017–19; Alt. Gov., World Bank 2014–15; Alt. Authorizing Officer, European Devt Fund 2014–15; Chair., Privatization Cttee of nat. banks Bankin'ny Tantsaha Mpamokatra (BTM) and Banky Fampandrosoana ny Varotra (BFV); fmr Dir Banque Centrale de Madagascar, Aéroports de Madagascar, BFV/Société Générale, Société d'Exploitation du Port du Toamasina. *Address:* c/o Ministry of Finance and the Budget, BP 61, Antaninarenina, Antananarivo, Madagascar (office).

ANDRIANTSITOHAINA, Naina; Malagasy business executive and politician; *Minister of Foreign Affairs;* b. 1963; s. of Jean-Charles Andriantsitohaina and Ginette Rabesahala; m. Carole Andrianony; four c.; ed Univ. Orléans-la-Source; Dir-Gen. Prochimad SA 1989–; CEO Ultima Media (press group) 2003–; Chair. Groupe Andriantsitohaina (family business) 2009–; Chair. Banque de Madagascar et de l'Océan Indien (BMOI) 2011–; Co-founder Dujardin Delacour & Cie (communications agency) 2011–; CEO Nouvelle imprimerie des arts graphiques (NIAG) 2015–; Pres. Syndicat des Industries de Madagascar (SIM) 2001–05, Groupement des Entreprises de Madagascar (GEM) (employers' orgs) 2005–11; adviser to Prime Minister 2002–04; Minister of Foreign Affairs 2019–. *Address:* Ministry of Foreign Affairs, rue Andriamifidy, Anosy, BP 836, Antananarivo 101, Madagascar (office). *Telephone:* (20) 2221196 (office). *Fax:* (20) 2234484 (office). *E-mail:* contact@mae.gov.mg (office). *Website:* mae.gov.mg (office).

ANDRIKIENĖ, Laima Liucija, DEcon; Lithuanian politician and academic; b. 1 Jan. 1958, Druskininkai; m. (husband deceased); one s.; ed Druskininkai Secondary School, Druskininkai Seven-Year Music School, Vilnius State Univ., Univ. of Manchester, UK; engineer, Computing Centre, Lithuanian Research Inst. of Agricultural Econs 1980–82, Researcher, Sr Researcher 1982–88; British Council Post-Doctoral Fellow, Univ. of Manchester 1988–89; Asst to Deputy Chair. Council of Ministers, Lithuanian SSR 1989–90; Deputy, Supreme Soviet 1990; signatory to Act on Re-establishment of Ind. State of Lithuania 1990; mem. Independence Party 1990–92; mem. Seimas (Parl.) 1992–2000, mem. Foreign Affairs Cttee, Vice-Chair. June–Oct. 2000, European Affairs Cttee 1998–2000; Co-founder Homeland Union Party (Lithuanian Conservatives) 1993, mem. Bd 1993–98; Minister of Trade and Industry 1996, of European Affairs 1996–98; Head, Lithuanian Parl. Del. to Baltic Ass. 1998–2000 (Chair. Presidium 1998–99, 2000); Founder and Chair. Homeland People's Party 1999–2001; mem. Union of the Right 2001–03, Homeland Union 2003–; Chair. Bd Laitenis UAB, Vilnius 2001–03; consultant, Asscn of Lithuanian Chambers of Commerce, Industry and Crafts 2002–; Assoc. Prof., Dept of Political Science, Law Univ. of Lithuania 2002–04, Dir Inst. of EU Policy and Man. 2002–03, Dean Faculty of Public Man. 2003–04; mem. European Parl. (Group of the European People's Party (Christian Democrats) and European Democrats) 2004–, Vice-Chair. Sub-cttee on Human Rights, mem. Cttee on Int. Trade, Del. to Euronest Parl. Ass.; Pew Fellowship Scholar, School of Foreign Service, Georgetown Univ., Washington, DC, USA 1996; Grand Officier, Ordre nat. du Mérite 1997, Cross of Commdr of the Order of the Lithuanian Grand Duke Gediminas 2004; Dr hc (Kingston Univ.) 2007; Independence Medal of Repub. of Lithuania 2000, Medal of the Baltic Ass. 2003, Golden Sign of Honour, Confed. of Lithuanian Industrialists 2008. *Publications include:* more than 60 articles and academic monographs on foreign policy, EU policies and man., interest groups and lobbying, econ. reform, agricultural econs and human rights. *Address:* European Parliament, Bâtiment Altiero Spinelli, ASP 11E153, 60 rue Wiertz, 1047 Brussels, Belgium (office); 8/26 Liejyklos Street, 01120 Vilnius, Lithuania. *Telephone:* (5) 212-2360; 699-05062 (Mobile). *Fax:* (2) 284-9858 (office). *E-mail:* laimaliucija.andrikiene@europarl.europa.eu (office); info@laimaandrikiene.lt. *Website:* www.europarl.europa.eu (office); www.eppgroup.eu; www.laimaandrikiene.lt.

ANDRIUKAITIS, Vytenis Povilas, MD; Lithuanian physician, politician and EU official; *Commissioner for Health and Food Safety, European Commission;* b. 9 Aug. 1951, Yakut ASSR (now Repub. of Sakha—Yakutiya), Russian SFSR, USSR; m. Irena Meižytė; two s. one d.; ed Kaunas 24th High School, Kaunas Medical Inst., Univ. of Vilnius, Mil. Hosp., Riga dist, Moscow Bakulev Cardiovascular Inst., USSR; family deported to Siberia June 1941, allowed to return 1958; surgeon at Kaunas 3rd Hosp. 1975–76, at Cen. Hosp., Ignalina dist 1976–84; surgeon 1984–; Cardiac Surgeon, Heart Surgery Centre, Republican Clinical Hosp., Vilnius 1985–93; Lecturer, State Environmental Health Centre 2006–08; participant in anti-Soviet underground from 1969, participated in underground Social Democratic Circle activities from 1976, studied in underground of Antanas Strazdas humanitarian thought and self-education univ. 1975–82, arrested and questioned by KGB 1976; supported restoration of Lietuvos socialdemokratų partija (LSDP—Social Democratic Party of Lithuania) 1988–89, mem. LSDP and mem. Lithuanian Reform Movt, Deputy Chair. LSDP 1989–99, 2001, Chair. 1999–2001; Deputy of Lithuanian Repub. to Supreme Soviet 1990–92; signatory of Independence Act of Ind. Lithuania; co-author of Constitution of Repub. of Lithuania 1990–92 (adopted 1992); mem. Del. of Baltic Ass. of Parl. of Lithuania 1990–2004; mem. Parl. 1992–2014, Elder Deputy of LSDP Group; mem. Del. to Council of Europe Parl. Ass. of Lithuanian Parl. 1994–96, mem. Human Rights and Legal Affairs Cttee of Council of Europe Parl. Ass., Opposition Leader of Parl. 2000–01, Deputy Chair. Parl. 2001–04; cand. in presidential elections 1997, 2002; mem. Vilnius City Council April–Nov. 2000; initiator of Lithuania Forum on the Future 2002; mem. Convention on the Future of Europe and Leader of Lithuanian del. 2002–03; Minister of Health 2012–14; Commr for Health and Food Safety, European Comm. (EC), Brussels Nov. 2014–; Dir Social Econ. Research Inst. 2004–08; mem. Lithuanian Doctors' Asscn 1989–96, Lithuanian Heart Asscn 1989–, Int. Doctors' Asscn 1998–2004; Hon. mem. Lithuanian Law Univ. 2004, Europa Esperanto-Unio 2017; Orden do Merito Gra-Cruz (Portugal) 2003; Commdr's Cross of Grand Duke Gediminas 2004; Chevalier, Légion d'honneur 2015; Dr hc (State Univ. for Medicine and Pharmacy of Repub. of Moldova) 2017; 13 January 1991 Commemorative Medal 1996, 10 Year Anniversary of Lithuanian Independence Medal 2000, Baltic Ass. Medal 2002, Commemorative Medal on the occasion of Lithuania's accession to the EU 2004, Commemorative statue of Gražina on the occasion of Lithuania's accession to NATO 2004, Merit Medicine 2005, Award of Restoration of Independence 20th Anniversary Medal 2010. *Publications include:* Social Democrats in Lithuanian Parliaments 2006, The Time of Justinas Marcinkevičius 2016; more than 140 legis. proposals and amendments 1990–2004; author or co-author of the indemnities of Convention on the Future of Europe 2002–03; co-author and ed. of Lithuanian Parl. and Parl. Cttee on European Affairs publications: Parliament on the Road of Lithuania to the European Union, The Role of Parliament in the EU's Membership Conditions, Joint Interparliamentary Committee of Accession to the EU Activities: Lithuanian activities 1997–2003. *Address:* European Commission, 200 Rue de la Loi/Wetstraat 200, 1049 Brussels, Belgium (office). *Telephone:* (2) 299-11-11 (switchboard) (office). *E-mail:* cab-andriukaitis-webpage@ec.europa.eu (office). *Website:* ec.europa.eu/commission/2014-2019/andriukaitis_en (office).

ANDROSCH, Hannes, PhD; Austrian business executive and fmr politician; b. 18 April 1938, Vienna; m. Brigitte Schärf; two d.; ed Hochschule für Welthandel, Vienna; Asst Auditor Fed. Ministry of Finance 1956–66; Sec., Econ. Affairs Section, Socialist Parl. Party 1963–66, Vice-Chair. 1974–85; mem. Nationalrat (Nat. Council) 1967–85; Minister of Finance 1970–81; Vice-Chancellor 1976–81; Chair. and Gen. Man. Creditanstalt-Bankverein 1981–87; Chair. Österreichische Kontrolbank AG 1985–86; Pres. Supervisory Bd Austria Technologie & Systemtechnik AG (A.T. & S.); f. AIC Androsch Int. Man. Consulting GmbH 1989; Chair. Univ. Council of Montanuniversität Leoben 2003–13; f. Hannes Androsch Foundation at Austrian Acad. of Sciences 2004; Chief Shareholder, Salinen and Lenzing cos; Chair. Council for Research and Tech. Devt 2010; Grand Gold Medal of Honour, Great Golden Emblem of the Land of Carinthia 2013; Dr hc (Bratislava School of Law, Slovakia) 2008, (Univ. of New Orleans, USA) 2009, (Univ. of Salzburg) 2011, (Mining Univ. Leoben) 2013. *Address:* AIC Androsch International Management Consulting GmbH, Opernring 1/R/3, 1010 Vienna, Austria (office). *Telephone:* (1) 586-10-54 (office). *Fax:* (1) 586-10-54-30 (office). *E-mail:* office@aic.co.at (office). *Website:* www.androsch.com (office).

ANDSNES, Leif Ove; Norwegian pianist; b. 7 April 1970, Karmøy; m.; three c.; ed Bergen Music Conservatory, studied with Jirí Hlinka; debut, Oslo 1987; British debut with Oslo Philharmonic, Edinburgh Festival 1989; US debut with Cleveland Orchestra under Neeme Järvi 1990; recitals in London, Berlin, Vienna, Amsterdam, New York (Carnegie Hall); performed with Orchestre Nat. de France, Berlin Philharmonic, Chicago Symphony, BBC Symphony, London Symphony, LA Philharmonic, Japan Philharmonic, New York Philharmonic; soloist, Last Night of the Proms 2002; Co-Artistic Dir Risør Music Festival 1991–2010; Founding Dir Rosendal Chamber Music Festival; Music Dir Ojai Music Festival 2012; Artistic Adviser, Prof. Jirí Hlinka Piano Acad., Bergen; Commdr, Royal Norwegian Order of St Olav 2002; Dr hc (Juilliard School) 2016; First Prize, Hindemith Competition, Frankfurt am Main, Levin Prize (Bergen) 1988, Norwegian Music Critics' Prize 1988, Grieg Prize (Bergen) 1990, Dorothy B. Chandler Performing Arts Award, Los Angeles 1992, Rolf H. Gammeleng Prize 1993, Bragdprisen 1994, Gilmore Prize 1997, Lindeman Prize 1997, Anders Jahres Kulturpris 1999, Royal Philharmonic Soc. Instrumentalist Award 2000, Gramophone Award for Best Concerto Recording 2000, for Best Instrumental Recording 2002, Sibelius Prize 2005, Peer Gynt Prize 2007, inducted into Gramophone Hall of Fame 2013. *Recordings include:* Rachmaninov Piano Concertos 1 and 2 (Classical BRIT Award for Instrumentalist of the Year 2006, Gramophone Award for Best Concerto Recording 2006) 2005, Horizons (Classical BRIT Award for Instrumentalist of the Year 2007) 2006, Rachmaninov Piano Concertos 3 and 4 2010, Schumann Complete Works for Piano Trio (Gramophone Award for Best Chamber Recording 2012) 2011, The Beethoven Journey Volume 1 (Spellemannpris 2013, Prix Caecilia 2013), also works by Brahms, Chopin, Grieg, Janácek, Liszt, Schumann. *Address:* c/o Kathryn Enticott, Enticott Music Management, 18 Hearne Road, London, W4 3NJ, England (office). *Telephone:* (20) 7957-5834 (office). *E-mail:* kathryn@enticottmusicmanagement.com (office). *Website:* www.enticottmusicmanagement.com; www.andsnes.com.

ANEFAL, Sebastian L., BS; Micronesian politician; *Ambassador to Fiji;* b. 21 Jan. 1952, Guror, Gilman, State of Yap; m. Marita Phillip; two s. three d.; ed Yap High School, Sherwood High School, Ore., USA, Univ. of Guam, Eastern Oregon State Univ., Micronesian Occupational Coll., Palau, Oregon Coll. of Education, Univ. of Hawaii, Oregon State Univ., USA; radio announcer/reporter, WSZA Radio Station, Yap 1970; Asst Dorm Man., Eastern Ore. State Univ. 1972–74; Sec., Educ. for Self-Governmental Task Force 1974; Classroom Instructor in Social Studies, Dept of Educ. 1975–80, Chief of Fed. Programs 1980–82, Chief of Community Outreach Aug.–Dec. 1982, ECIA (US Govt's Educ. Consolidation and Improvement Act of 1981) Chapter I Coordinator July–Sept. 1982, Man. and Support Admin. 1982–87; Public Information Program Coordinator, Office of the Plebiscite Commr, Yap Jan.–June 1982; Convention Sec., Yap Constitutional Convention March–Aug. 1982; Dir Dept of Public Affairs, Yap 1987–88, Dept of Resources and Devt 1988–91, Office of Planning and Budget 1991–95; Special Consultant to Gov. of State of Yap 1991–95, 2007–; Chief of Gilman (Municipality), Yap 1992–2007; Sec. of Dept of Resources and Devt, FSM Nat. Govt 1995–98, Dept of Econ. Affairs 1998–2003, Dept of Foreign Affairs 2003–07; Vice-Chair. Tourist Comm. 1975; mem. Nat. Disaster Control Bd 1976; Yap SPEA Coordinator, Festival of Arts, Papua New Guinea 1980; Chair. Elementary and Secondary Educ. Act (ESEA) Title IV State Advisory Council, Trust Territory of the Pacific Islands (TTPI) 1980; mem. Old Age Program Advisory Bd 1983, COM Bd of Regents 1984–93, EPA Bd (TTPI/FSM) 1985–87; mem. Bd of Dirs Micronesia Maritime Authority 1989–95; Chair. Bd of Govs Pacific Island Devt Bank 1989–95; apptd Chair. Nat. Fisheries Corpn 1990; Vice-Chair. Bd of Dirs Yap Econ. Devt Authority 1990–95; Pres. Yap Fishing Corpn 1990–95; Vice-Pres. Yap Purse Seiners Corpn 1990–95; mem. Bd of Dirs Yap Cooperative Asscn 1990–95, Micronesia Longline Fishing Co. 1990–, FSM Devt Bank 1990–2004; Gov. of Yap 2007–15; Special Consultant to Gov. of Yap Jan.–Nov. 2015; Amb. to Fiji 2015–; American Field Service Scholarship 1969–72, Trust Territory Social Sciences Scholarship 1972, UNESCO Fellowship in Ethnic Heritage to the Gilbert Islands 1978. *Publications include:* Social Studies Curriculum Guide (ed.) 1980, Tabinaw Rodad (social studies text book) (co-ed.) 1980. *Leisure interests:* spear fishing, hunting, sailing, guitar playing, photography. *Address:* Embassy of the Republic of Fiji, 37 Loftus Street, POB 15493, Suva, Fiji (office). *Telephone:* 3304566 (office). *Fax:* 3300842 (office). *E-mail:* fsmsuva@sopacsun.sopac.org.fj (office).

ANELAY OF ST JOHNS, Baroness (Life Peer), cr. 1996, of St Johns in the County of Surrey; **Rt Hon. Joyce Anne Anelay,** DBE, OBE, PC, FRSA; British politician; *Minister of State, Foreign and Commonwealth Office;* b. (Joyce Anne Clarke), 17 July 1947; m. Richard Anelay QC; ed Enfield County School, Univ. of Bristol; secondary school teacher 1969–74; later worked as a volunteer adviser with the Citizens' Advice Bureau; JP, NW Surrey 1985–97; Opposition Whip in the House of Lords 1997–98, Opposition Spokesperson for Agric. 1997–98, for Culture, Media and Sport 1998–2002, for Home Affairs 1997–98, 2002–07, for Social Security 1997–99, for Legal Affairs 2003–04, Opposition Chief Whip 2007–10, Deputy Speaker of the House of Lords 2008–14, Deputy Chair. of Committees 2008–14, Govt Chief Whip in the House of Lords (Capt. of the Hon. Corps of Gentlemen at Arms) 2011–14, Minister of State, Foreign and Commonwealth Office 2014–; Chair. SE Area Conservative Women's Cttee 1987–90; mem. Nat. Union Exec. Cttee Conservative Party 1987–97, Vice-Chair. SE Area Exec. Cttee 1990–93; Chair. Women's Nat. Cttee 1993–96; Vice-Pres. Nat. Union 1996–97; mem. Social Security Appeal Tribunal 1983–96, Social Security Advisory Cttee for GB and NI 1989–96, Women's Nat. Comm. 1991–94, Child Support Appeal Tribunal 1993–96; Pres. World Travel Market 2003–08. *Address:* House of Lords, Westminster, London, SW1A 0PW, England (office). *Telephone:* (20) 7219-5353 (office). *Fax:* (20) 7219-6837 (office).

ANELL, Lars Evert Roland, MA, MBA; Swedish economist, international organization official and consultant; *Chairman, Swedish Research Council;* b. 23 Oct. 1941, Katrineholm, Sweden; s. of Evert Andersson and Margit Andersson; m. Kerstin Friis 1966; one s. three d.; ed Stockholm School of Econs, Univ. of Stockholm; served in Ministry of Finance 1966–70; Dir for Planning and Research, Ministry for Foreign Affairs 1970–80; Dir-Gen. Swedish Agency for Research Co-operation with Developing Countries 1980–83; Sr Adviser, Prime Minister's Office 1983–86; Perm. Rep. of Sweden to UN orgs in Geneva 1986 and EU; GATT-Uruguay Round Negotiating Group on Intellectual Property Rights 1987–92, GATT Contracting Parties 1991–92, Chair. GATT Council 1990–91; Sr Vice-Pres. AB Volvo 1992–2001, currently Sr Adviser to CEO; Freja Foundation 2001–07; Chair. Stockholm Environment Inst. –2009; Chair. Swedish Research Council 2010–; Chief Negotiator European Spallation Source (ESS) (Europe-wide scientific research facility), Lund 2011–; Chair. UN Intergovernmental Group of Experts on Science and Tech. for Devt 1980–82, UN Cttee on Science and Tech. 1985–86, Int. Org. for Immigration 1991–92, Centre for Int. Youth Exchange 1997–2002, Dag Hammarskjöld Foundation 1997–2005, Bd Univ. of Umeå 1998–2003, UNICE REX-Cttee 2001–05, Swedish Council for Working Life and Social Research 2007–09, MISTRA Research Programme on Trade and Investment 2007, Bd Jönköping Int. Business School 2008, Inst. for Media Research, (Chair. of the Council 2009–); currently Officer, Comm. on Trade and Investment Policy (fmr Chair.), Int. Chamber of Commerce; Bd mem. UN Advisory Group on Financial Flows to Africa 1987–88, UN Research Inst. for Social Devt 1990–96, Swedish Exhibition and Congress Centre 1995–2001, AB Volvo Penta 1997–98, Volvo Aero Corpn 1998–2008, Foundation for Strategic Research 1999–2003. *Publications include:* The Other Society 1969, Should Sweden be Asphalted? 1971, Recession, The Western Economies and the Changing World Order 1981, Economic Crises in Theory and Practice 1986. *Address:* Swedish Research Council, PO Box 1035, 101 38 Stockholm (office); Norr Mälarstrand 16, 112 20 Stockholm, Sweden (home). *Telephone:* (8) 546-44-000 (office); (8) 650-64-43 (home). *Fax:* (8) 546-44-180 (office). *E-mail:* lars.anell@vr.se (office); lars@anell.nu. *Website:* www.vr.se (office).

ANFIMOV, Nikolai Appolonovich, PhD; Russian scientist and academic; b. 29 March 1935, Russia; m.; one s.; ed Moscow Inst. of Physics and Tech.; Head of Group, Head of Sector, Research Inst. of Heat Processes 1958–73; Head of Div., Deputy Dir-Cen. Research Inst. of Machine Construction 1973–2000, Dir Gen. 2000–09; Chair. Council of Experts, Supreme Certification Comm. on Aviation and Rocket and Space Eng; Deputy Chair. Scientific Council of Russian Security Council; Prof., Moscow Physico-Tech. Inst.; Corresp. mem. Russian Acad. of Sciences 1984, mem. 1997, currently Bureau mem. Branch of Power Industry, Machine Building, Mechanics and Control Processes; mem. Int. Acad. of Astronautics, Russian Acad. of Space, Council on Grants of Pres. of Russia, Russian Foundation for Basic Research, American Inst. of Aeronautics and Astronautics; mem. Editorial Bd Fluid Dynamics; Ed.-in-Chief Kosmonavtika i Raketostroenie; State Prize of Russia, Allan D. Emil Memorial Award 2010, NASA Distinguished Public Service Medal. *Publications include:* Problems of Mechanics and Heat Exchange in Space Tech. 1982, Numerical Modelling in Aerohydrodynamics 1986 and numerous scientific works on heat exchange and heat protection in high-speed, high-temperature regimes, heat regimes of spaceships, radiation gas dynamics. *Leisure interest:* tennis. *Address:* Branch of Power Industry, Machine Building, Mechanics And Control Processes, Russian Academy of Sciences, 119991 Moscow, Leninskii avenue 14, Russia (office). *Telephone:* (495) 938-12-04 (office); (495) 238-40-67 (home). *Fax:* (495) 938-52-34 (office). *E-mail:* anfimov@mcc.rsa.ru (office). *Website:* www.ras.ru (office).

ANGELIDES, Savvas, LLB; Cypriot lawyer and politician; *Minister of Defence;* b. 26 Jan. 1974, Nicosia; m. Maria Charalambous Angelides; two c.; ed Univ. of Birmingham, Gray's Inn, London; joined Cypriot Army as Reserve Officer Second Lt (Infantry) 1991; obtained licence to practise law 1997; Advocate and Legal Consultant, Chrysaffinis and Polyviou/ Costas Demetriades and Assocs LLC 1997–99; Sr Partner and Gen. Man., LLPO (law firm) 1999–; Advocate and Legal Consultant, Angelides, Ioannides, Leonidou LLC 2010–; Minister of Defence 2018–; Visiting Lecturer in Criminal Law and Procedures, Frederick Univ. 2013–; mem. Cyprus Bar Asscn, Pan European Org. of Personal Injury Lawyers. *Publications:* numerous articles on legal issues. *Address:* Ministry of Defence, 4 Emmanuel Roides Avenue, 1432 Nicosia, Cyprus (office). *Telephone:* 22807500 (office). *Fax:* 22676182 (office). *E-mail:* defence@mod.gov.cy (office). *Website:* www .mod.gov.cy (office).

ANGELL, Wayne D., PhD; American economist; b. 28 June 1930, Liberal, Kan.; s. of Charlie Francis Angell and Adele Thelma Angell (née Edwards); m.; four c.; ed Univ. of Kansas; Asst Prof. Ottawa Univ. 1956–59, Prof. 1959–85, Dean 1969–72; mem. Kansas House of Reps 1961–67, Chair. Water Resources Cttee, Econ Devt Cttee; joined Fed. Reserve System as mem. Cttee of Advisors to Bd of Govs., Dir Fed. Reserve Bank, Kansas City 1979–86; mem. of Fed. Reserve Bd 1986–94; Chief Economist and Sr Man. Dir Bear Sterns & Co. Inc. 1994–2001; with Angell Econs, Arlington Va 2001–; fmr Chair. G-10 Cttee on Payment and Settlement Systems; Vice-Chair. Bd of Int. Baptist Ministries of the American Baptist Churches; Pres. Kansas Baptist Convention; mem. American Econ Asscn; Trustee, Kansas Baptist Foundation; Hon. DHumLitt (Ottawa Univ.) 1992; Outstanding Achievement Award, Ottawa Univ. Alumni Asscn 2005. *Leisure interest:* tennis. *Address:* Angell Economics, 1600 North Oak Street, Suite 1915, Arlington, VA 22209, USA (office). *E-mail:* wangell@comcast.net (office).

ANGELOPOULOS-DASKALAKI, Gianna, LLB; Greek business executive, politician and sports administrator; b. 12 Dec. 1955, Heraklion, Crete; m. Theodore Angelopoulos; two s. one d.; ed Aristotelian Univ., Thessaloniki; mem. Athens municipal council 1986–89; mem. Parl. (New Democracy Party) 1989–90 (resgnd); Vice-Chair. Dean's Council, John F. Kennedy School of Govt, Harvard Univ. 1994–; Pres. Athens 2004 Olympic Games Bid Cttee 1998–2000, Athens 2004 Olympic Cttee 2000–04; apptd Amb.-at-Large by Greek Govt 1998; mem. Athens Bar Asscn; Convening Sponsor, Clinton Global Initiative; Hellenic Public Radio Phidippides Award 1997, Archbishop Iakovos Leadership 100 Award for Excellence 2008, Aristeio Award, American Hellenic Council 2013. *Publication:* My Greek Drama: Life, Love, and One Woman's Olympic Effort to Bring Glory to Her Country 2013.

ANGELOV, Anyu, MA; Bulgarian politician and fmr army officer; *Adviser on Defence to Prime Minister;* b. 22 Dec. 1942, Haskovo; m.; two s.; ed Higher Nat. Mil. Artillery School, G.S. Rakovski Nat. Mil. Acad., Gen. Staff Acad. of the Soviet Armed Forces, Moscow; joined Bulgarian Armed Forces, apptd Lt 1966, Commdr of autonomous platoon 1966–71, Deputy Chief of Dept, Land Forces Air Defence Command 1974–80, Brigade Chief of Staff 1980–82, Brigade Commdr 1984–87, Land Forces Air Defence Chief of Staff 1987–90, Land Forces Air Defence Commdr in Chief 1990–92, Deputy Commdr in Chief of Bulgarian Land Forces 1992–94, rank of Lt-Gen. 1994, Deputy Chief of Gen. Staff of Bulgarian Armed Forces 1994, Defence Attaché, Embassy in London, UK 1997–2000, Commdr, G.S. Rakovski Nat. Mil. Acad. 2000–02, retd from Bulgarian Armed Forces 2002; Dir for Defence Planning, Ministry of Defence 2002, Pres. Centre for Nat. Security Research Foundation –2009, Deputy Minister of Defence 2009–10, Minister of Defence 2010–13; Adviser on Defence to Prime Minister Boyko Borisov 2014–; Hon. mem. NATO Defence Coll. Anciens' Asscn; several awards including Order of Merit, Commendation Medal for Meritorious Service under the Colours – First Grade. *Address:* Council of Ministers, 1594 Sofia, bul. Dondukov 1, Bulgaria (home).

ANGENOT, Marc, DPhil, DLit, FRSC; Canadian academic; *James McGill Professor Emeritus of Social Discourse Theory, McGill University;* b. 21 Dec. 1941, Brussels, Belgium; s. of Marcel Angenot and Zoé-Martha DeClercq; m. 1st Joséphine Brock 1966 (divorced 1976); one s. one d.; m. 2nd Nadia Khouri 1981; one d.; ed Univ. Libre de Bruxelles; James McGill Prof. of Social Discourse Theory, McGill Univ. 1967–2012, Prof. Emer. 2012–; Assoc. Dir Ecole des Hautes Etudes en Sciences Sociales, France 1985; Northrop Frye Prof. of Literary Theory, Univ. of Toronto 1994; Chaim Perelman Prof. of Rhetoric and Intellectual History, Université Libre de Bruxelles 2012; Vice-Pres. Acad. des Lettres et Sciences Humaines, Royal Soc. of Canada 2001; Chevalier des Palmes académiques; Prix Biguet, Acad. Française 1983, Killam Fellowship, Canada Council 1987, Prix des Sciences Humaines ACFAS (Canada) 1996, Prix Spirale Eva-Le-Grand 1996, Prix André-Laurendeau 1996, Award for High Distinction in Research, McGill Univ. 2001, Prix du Québec 'Léon Gérin' 2005. *Publications include:* Le Roman populaire 1975, Les Champions des femmes 1977, Glossaire pratique de la critique contemporaine 1979, La Parole pamphlétaire 1982, Critique de la raison sémiotique 1985, Le Cru et le faisandé 1986, Le Centenaire de la Révolution 1989, Ce que l'on dit des Juifs en 1889 1989, Mille huit cent quatre-vingt neuf 1989, L'Utopie collectiviste 1993, La Propagande socialiste 1996, Idéologies du ressentiment 1996, Colins et le socialisme rationnel 1999, La critique au service de la Révolution 2000, Religions de l'humanité et sciences de l'histoire 2000, D'où venons-nous, où allons-nous? 2001, L'Antimilitarisme, idéologie et utopie 2003, La démocratie, c'est le mal 2004, Rhétorique de l'anti-socialisme 2004, Le Marxisme dans les Grands récits 2005, Dialogues de sourds: traité de rhétorique antilogique 2008, Vivre dans l'histoire au 20e siècle 2008, Gnose et millénarisme: deux concepts pour le vingtième siècle 2008, En quoi sommes-nous encore pieux? 2009, L'immunité française envers le fascisme 2009, El discurso social 2010, Les dehors de la littérature: du roman populaire à la science-fiction 2013, L'Histoire des idées 2014, O discurso social e as retòricas da incompreensao 2015. *Address:* Arts Building, 853 Sherbrooke Street West, Montreal, PQ H3A 2T6, Canada (office). *Website:* www.marcangenot.com.

ANGJUSHEV, Kočo, MMechSci, DTechSc; Macedonian business executive and politician; *Deputy Prime Minister, responsible for Economic Affairs;* b. 20 June 1969, Titov Veles (now Veles), Socialist Repub. of Macedonia, Socialist Fed. Repub. of Yugoslavia; ed Faculty of Mechanical Eng, Skopje; postgraduate studies 1992–95; Asst, Faculty of Mechanical Eng, Skopje 1993–98; Guest Researcher, Research Faculty of Mechanical Eng, Aachen, Germany 1996; Prof., Faculty of Mechanical Eng, Skopje 1998; Visiting Eng, Faculty of Mechanical Eng, Loughborough Univ., UK 1999; Auxiliary Gen. Dir for Production and Man., Electric Power Co. of Macedonia (ESM) 2000–02; f. FEROINVEST D.o.o Export-Import, Veles 2003, acquired Brako Co. 2003, Chair. Brako 2003–, Man. Brako Weighpack Co. 2007–; f. br. office of EFT Group 2003, later f. EFT Macedonia; mem. Man. Bd and Gen. Ass. of the Union for Co-ordination of Transmission of Electricity; mem. Gen. Ass. and Exec. Cttee, Regional Group for Co-ordination of Electricity Transmission in the South-East European Interconnected System (SUDEL), Gen. Ass. of Int. Fed. for the Promotion of Machine and Mechanism Science (IFTOMM); Deputy Prime Minister, responsible for Econ. Affairs 2017–; mem. various professional asscns. *Publications:* more than 100 scientific papers at nat. and int. symposia. *Address:* Office of the Prime Minister, 1000 Skopje, Ilindenska b.b. 2, North Macedonia (office). *Telephone:* (2) 3118022 (office). *Fax:* (2)

3112561 (office). *E-mail:* primeminister@primeminister.gov.mk (office). *Website:* www.vlada.mk (office).

ANGLADA GONZALEZ, Salvador, BE, MBA; Spanish telecommunications executive; *Chief Business Officer, Etisalat;* ed Instituto de Empresa, Madrid, IESE Business School, Madrid; with Productos Organicos y Minerales and Dow Jones Markets 1990–97; Dir of Banking Sales, Dell Computer 1997, becoming Dir Preferred Accounts Div. and later Dir of Sales and Marketing for Southern Europe –2002; Dir of Sales, Telefónica de Espana 2002–03, Dir of Sales and Marketing 2003; CEO Eurotel Praha 2005–10; Exec. Dir Telefonica Europe 2005–10; mem. Bd of Dirs, Ceský Telecom 2005–10, Vice-Pres. Consumer Div. 2006–07, Chair. and CEO Telefónica O2 Czech Repub., AS (fmrly Cesky Telecom AS) 2007–10; CEO Lucrative Mobile Unit Eurotel Praha from 2005; CEO Telefonica Soluciones de Informática y Comunicaciones, Madrid 2010–13; Man. Dir Telefonica Empresas Telefonica España, Madrid 2010–13; Chair. Acens Technologies, Madrid 2011–13; Advisory Bd mem. Cionet España 2011–; Chief Business Officer Etisalat, Dubai 2013–. *Address:* Etisalat, Saeed Al Maktoum Street, PO Box 3838, Abu Dhabi, United Arab Emirates (office). *Telephone:* (2) 6283333 (office). *Fax:* (2) 6317000 (office). *E-mail:* care@etisalat.ae (office). *Website:* www.etisalat.ae (office).

ANGUE, Simeón Oyono Esono; Equatorial Guinean politician and diplomatist; *Minister of Foreign Affairs and Co-operation;* b. 18 Feb. 1967, Mongomo; fmr Amb. and Perm. Rep. to African Union, Addis Ababa; Pres. Sub-Cttee of Perm. Reps for Refugees and Displaced Persons; Minister of Foreign Affairs and Co-operation 2018–; Lecturer of Econs Nat. Univ. of Equatorial Guinea. *Address:* Ministry of Foreign Affairs and Co-operation, Malabo, Equatorial Guinea (office). *Website:* www.mfa.gov.eg (office).

ANGULA, Nahas Gideon, BEd, MA; Namibian politician; b. 22 Aug. 1943, Onyaanya; m. Katrina Tangeni Namalenga; four c.; ed Oniipa Boy's School, Engela Boy's School, Ongwediva Training Coll., Oshigambo Jr Secondary School, Nkumbi Int. Coll., Univ. of Zambia, Columbia Univ., New York, Univ. of Manchester, UK; became active in SWAPO 1967, went into exile to Zambia 1967; Sec. for Educ., SWAPO Politburo; returned from exile 1989; Head of Dept, Voter Registration, SWAPO Election Directorate, Windhoek 1989; mem. Constituent Ass. 1989, Nat. Ass. 1990–; Minister of Educ., Sport and Culture 1990–95, of Higher Educ., Training and Employment Creation 1995–2005; nominated as one of three SWAPO presidential cands 2004; Prime Minister of Namibia 2005–12; Minister of Defence 2012–15. *Publication:* The African Origin of Civilisation and the Destiny of Africa (co-ed.) 2000.

ANIL, Mohamed, LLB, LLM; Maldivian lawyer; *Attorney-General;* ed Oxford Brookes Univ., Univ. of Essex, UK; partner Nasheed Anil and Co.; mem. Maldivian Bar; advocate, Superior Courts, High Court and Supreme Court of The Maldives; Legal Officer, Attorney-Gen.'s Office 1997, Asst State Attorney 2004–06, Dir 2006–07; Commr of Legal Reform, Ministry of Legal Reform, Information and Arts 2007–08; Attorney-Gen. of The Maldives 2013–; apptd to Judicial Service Comm. 2013; taught law, Faculty of Shariah and Law of The Maldives Coll. of Higher Educ.; co-founder Democracy House. *Address:* Office of the Attorney-General, Huravee Building, 3rd Floor, Malé, Maldives (office). *Telephone:* 3323809 (office). *Fax:* 3314109 (office). *E-mail:* info@agoffice.gov.mv (office). *Website:* agoffice.gov.mv (office).

ANISTON, Jennifer Joanna; American actress, film director and producer; b. 11 Feb. 1969, Sherman Oaks, Calif.; d. of John Aniston and Nancy Dow; m. 1st Brad Pitt (q.v.) 2000 (divorced 2005); m. 2nd Justin Theroux 2015; ed New York High School of the Performing Arts. *Theatre includes:* For Dear Life, Dancing on Checker's Grave. *Films include:* Mac and Me 1988, Leprechaun 1993, Dream for an Insomniac 1996, She's the One 1996, Picture Perfect 1997, 'Til There Was You 1997, The Object of My Affection 1998, The Thin Pink Line 1998, Office Space 1999, The Iron Giant (voice) 1999, Rock Star 2001, The Good Girl 2002, Bruce Almighty 2003, Along Came Polly 2004, Derailed 2005, Rumor Has It... 2005, Friends with Money 2006, The Break-Up 2006, Management 2008, Marley & Me 2008, He's Just Not That Into You 2009, Love Happens 2009, The Bounty Hunter 2010, The Switch 2010, Just Go with It 2011, Horrible Bosses 2011, My Least Favorite Career (video short) 2011, Wanderlust 2012, Unity (documentary) (narrator) 2012, We're the Millers 2013, Life of Crime 2013, She's Funny That Way 2014, Cake (People Magazine Award for Performance of the Year, Actress) 2014, Horrible Bosses 2 2014, Mother's Day 2016. *Television includes:* Molloy (series) 1990, Camp Cucamonga (film) 1990, Ferris Bueller (series) 1990–91, Quantum Leap (series) – Nowhere to Run 1992, The Edge (series) 1992–93, Herman's Head (series) 1992–93, Burke's Law (series) – Who Killed the Beauty Queen? 1994, Muddling Through (series) 1994, Friends (series) (Emmy Award for Best Actress 2002, Golden Globe for Best TV Actress in a Comedy 2003, Screen Actors Guild Award) 1994–2004, The Larry Sanders Show (series) – Conflict of Interest 1995, Partners (series) – Follow the Clams? 1996, Hercules (series) – Hercules and the Dream Date (voice) 1998, South Park (series) – Rainforest Shmainforest (voice) 1999, Freedom: A History of Us (series documentary) – Wake Up America 2003, King of the Hill (series) – Queasy Rider (voice) 2003, Dirt (series) – Ita Missa Est 2007, 30 Rock (series) – The One with the Cast of 'Night Court' 2008, Cougar Town (series) – All Mixed Up 2010, Burning Love (series) 2012. *Address:* c/o Creative Artists Agency, 2000 Avenue of the Stars, Los Angeles, CA 90067, USA (office). *Telephone:* (424) 288-2000 (office). *Fax:* (424) 288-2900 (office). *Website:* www.caa.com (office); www.jenniferaniston.com.

ANKA, Paul, OC; Canadian/American singer, songwriter and actor; b. 30 July 1941, Ottawa, Ont.; m. Marie Ann Alison de Zogheb 1963 (divorced 2000); five d.; m. 2nd Anna Anka 2008 (divorced 2010); one s.; m. 3rd Lisa Pemberton 2016; mem. BMI; Chevalier, Ordre des Arts et des Lettres. *Films include:* Girls Town 1959, The Private Lives of Adam and Eve 1960, Look in Any Window 1961, The Longest Day 1962, Captain Ron 1992, Ordinary Magic 1993, Mad Dog Time 1996, 3000 Miles to Graceland 2001. *Television includes:* The Paul Anka Show (series host) 1982, Perry Mason: The Case of the Maligned Mobster 1991. *Compositions include:* theme for The Tonight Show 1962, theme music for films, The Longest Day, No Way Out, Atlantic City, and contrib. of songs to numerous other films; some 900 songs, including It Doesn't Matter Anymore (for Buddy Holly) 1959, My Way (for Frank Sinatra) 1969, She's A Lady (for Tom Jones) 1971, Puppy Love (for Donny Osmond); other songs performed by artists including Elvis Presley, Barbra Streisand, Linda Ronstadt, The Sex Pistols, Nina Simone, Gipsy Kings and Robbie Williams. *Recordings include:* albums: The Fabulous Paul Anka And Others 1956, Paul Anka 1958, My Heart Sings 1959, Paul Anka Sings His Big 15 1959, Vol. II 1962, Vol. III 1962, Paul Anka Swings For Young Lovers 1959, Anka At The Copa 1960, It's Christmas Everywhere 1960, Diana 1962, Young Alive & In Love! 1962, Let's Sit This One Out 1962, Our Man Around the World 1963, Three Great Guys (with Sedaka and Cooke) 1963, Songs I Wish I'd Written 1963, Paul Anka 1964, Paul Anka Italiano 1964, A Casa Nostra 1964, Strictly Nashville 1966, Goodnight My Love 1969, Sincerely 1969, Life Goes On 1969, Paul Anka 70s 1970, Jubilation 1972, My Way 1974, Anka 1974, Feelings 1975, Remember Diana 1975, She's A Lady 1975, Times Of Your Life 1976, The Painter 1977, The Music Man 1977, Listen To Your Heart 1978, Headlines 1979, Both Sides Of Love 1981, Walk A Fine Line 1983, Freedom for the World 1987, Somebody Loves You 1989, Face in the Mirror 1993, After All 1995, Amigos (with others) 1996, A Body Of Work 1998, Rock Swings 2005, Classic Songs, My Way 2007, Songs of December 2011, Duets 2013. *Publication:* My Way (autobiography) 2014. *Address:* Paul Anka Productions, 10960 Wilshire Blvd, 5th Floor, Los Angeles, CA 90024, USA (office). *Telephone:* (310) 858-0797 (office). *Fax:* (310) 553-5930 (office). *Website:* www.paulanka.com.

ANKOURAOU, Kalla; Niger politician; *Minister of Foreign Affairs, Co-operation, African Integration and Nigeriens Abroad;* Minister of Health 1995, Minister of Equipment 2011, Minister-Counsellor to the Presidency 2016–18, Minister of Foreign Affairs, Co-operation, African Integration and Nigeriens Abroad 2018–; mem. Assemblée Nationale (Parl.) 1993–95, 2004–16, Pres. PNDS—Tarayya Parl. Group; mem. Parti Nigérien pour la Démocratie et le Socialisme (PNDS—Tarayya). *Address:* Ministry of Foreign Affairs, Co-operation, African Integration and Nigeriens Abroad, BP 396, Niamey, Niger (office). *Telephone:* 20-72-29-07 (office). *Fax:* 20-73-52-31 (office).

ANKUM, Hans (Johan Albert), DJur; Dutch professor of Roman law; *Professor Emeritus of Roman Law, University of Amsterdam;* b. 23 July 1930, Amsterdam; s. of Leendert Ankum and Johanna Ankum (née Van Kuykhof); m. 1st Joke Houwink 1957 (divorced 1970); m. 2nd Pelline van Es 1971; one s. three d.; ed Zaanlands Lyceum, Zaandam, Univ. of Amsterdam, Univ. of Paris; Asst, Roman Law and Juridical Papyrology, Univ. of Amsterdam 1956–60; Lecturer in Roman Law and Legal History, Univ. of Leyden 1960–63, Prof. 1963–69; Prof. of Roman Law, Legal History and Juridical Papyrology, Univ. of Amsterdam 1965–95, Prof. Emer. 1995–; mem. Royal Netherlands Acad. of Arts and Sciences 1986–; Kt, Order of the Dutch Lion 1992; Dr hc (Aix-Marseille) 1985, (Vrije Univ., Brussels) 1986, (Ruhr Universität, Bochum) 1995, (Univ. of Belgrade) 2005, (Charles Univ., Prague) 2008, (Univ. of Murcia) 2014; Winkler Prins Award 1970. *Publications:* De geschiedenis der 'Actio Pauliana' 1962; over 320 books and articles on Roman law and legal history. *Leisure interests:* classical music, history of art, travel. *Address:* Faculty of Law, University of Amsterdam, PO Box 1030, 1000 BA, Amsterdam Oudermanhuispoort 4–6 (office); Schuttersweg 58, 1217 RA, Hilversum, Netherlands (home). *Telephone:* (20) 5253970 (office); (35) 6226333 (home).

ANKVAB, Aleksandr Zolotinska-ipa; Georgian (Abkhaz) politician; b. 26 Dec. 1952, Sukhumi, Abkhazian ASSR, Georgian SSR; ed Rostov State Univ.; worked as official of the Lenin Young Communist League (Komsomol) for many years; official in Justice Ministry of Abkhazian ASSR 1975–81; joined Exec. of Cen. Cttee of Georgian CP 1981; Deputy Interior Minister of Georgian SSR 1984–90; became mem. of Abkhazian Supreme Soviet following break-up of Soviet Union and Georgian independence 1991; apptd Interior Minister of Abkhazia's separatist govt during 1992–93 conflict with Georgian Cen. Govt; moved to Moscow and became a successful businessman 1994; returned to Abkhazian politics 2000, set up Aitaira (Revival) movt in opposition to Govt of Pres. Vladislav Ardzinba; announced intention to run for pres. 2004, disqualified on grounds that he could not speak Abkhaz and had not lived long enough in Abkhazia; supported Sergei Bagapsh instead; Prime Minister 2005–10; vice-presidential cand. 2009; Vice-Pres. 'Republic of Abkhazia' Feb. 2010–May 2011, Pres. May 2011–June 2014 (resgnd); has survived six assassination attempts since 2005.

ANN-MARGRET; American actress, singer and dancer; b. (Ann-Margret Olsson), 28 April 1941, Stockholm, Sweden; m. Roger Smith 1967; five Golden Globe Awards, three Female Star of the Year Awards. *Films include:* State Fair, Bye Bye Birdie, Once a Thief, The Cincinnati Kid, Stagecoach, Murderer's Row, CC & Co., Carnal Knowledge, RPM, The Train Robbers, Tommy, The Twist, Joseph Andrews, Last Remake of Beau Geste, Magic, Middle Age Crazy, Return of the Soldier, I Ought to Be in Pictures, Looking to Get Out, Twice in a Lifetime, 52 Pick-Up 1987, New Life 1988, Something More, Newsies 1992, Grumpy Old Men 1993, Grumpier Old Men 1995, Any Given Sunday 1999, The Last Producer 2000, A Woman's a Helluva Thing 2000, Interstate 60 2002, Taxi 2004, The Break-Up 2006, The Santa Clause 3: The Escape Clause 2006, The Loss of a Teardrop Diamond 2008, All's Faire in Love 2009, Old Dogs 2009, Lucky 2011. *Recordings include:* albums include: And Here She Is 1961, On the Way Up 1962, The Vivacious One 1962, Bachelor's Paradise 1963, Ann-Margret 1980, God is Love: The Gospel Sessions 2001, Christmas Card Selection 2004, God is Love: The Gospel Sessions 2 2011. *Television includes:* Who Will Love My Children? 1983, A Streetcar Named Desire 1984, The Two Mrs Grenvilles 1987, Our Sons 1991, Nobody's Children, 1994, Following her Heart, Seduced by Madness: The Diane Borchardt Story 1996, Blue Rodeo 1996, Pamela Hanniman 1999, Happy Face Murders 1999, Perfect Murder, Perfect Town 2000, The Tenth Kingdom 2000, A Place Called Home 2004, Ray Donovan (series) 2014. *Publication:* Ann-Margret: My Story (with Todd Gold) 1994. *Address:* PO Box 2045, Toluca Lake, CA 91610, USA. *E-mail:* mail@ann-margret.com. *Website:* www.ann-margret.com.

ANNADIF, Mahamet Saleh; Chadian politician and international organization official; *Special Representative and Head, United Nations Multidimensional Integrated Stabilization Mission in Mali (MINUSMA);* b. 25 Dec. 1956, Arada; m. twice; six c.; with Telecommunications Dept, Office Nat. de Postes et Télécommunications (ONPT) 1981–82, Head of Research 1988–89, Dir-Gen. ONPT 1995–97; Man. Soc. des Télécommunications internationales du Tchad 1990–97; in charge of information and propaganda, Front de libération nationale du Tchad (FROLINAT)/Conseil démocratique révolutionnaire (CDR) 1982–85, Second Vice-Pres. FROLINAT/CDR 1985–88; Sec. of State for Agric. 1989–90; Minister of Foreign Affairs and Co-operation 1997–2003; Dir of Civil Cabinet of

Pres. Idriss Deby 2004–06; Perm. Rep. of African Union to EU, Brussels 2006–10; Sec.-Gen. of the Presidency 2010–12; African Union Special Rep. for Somalia and Head of African Union Mission in Somalia (AMISOM) 2012–14; UN Sec.-Gen.'s Special Rep. and Head of UN Multidimensional Integrated Stabilization Mission in Mali (MINUSMA) 2016–; Commdr, Order nat. du Tchad, Chevalier, l'Ordre national de la Légion d'Honneur (France). *Leisure interests:* nature, the countryside. *Address:* United Nations Multidimensional Integrated Stabilization Mission in Mali (MINUSMA), PO Box 20182-00200, Bamako, Mali (office). *Telephone:* 4492-6003 (office). *E-mail:* annadifm@un.org (office). *Website:* www.un.org/en/peacekeeping/missions/minusma (office).

ANNADURDYEV, Merdan Ovezovich; Turkmenistani central banker; *Chairman, Türkmenistanyň Merkezi Banky (Central Bank of Turkmenistan);* served as Deputy Chair. Türkmenistanyň Merkezi Banky (Cen. Bank of Turkmenistan), and Head, Operations Dept –2015, Chair. 2015–, apptd Deputy Gov. World Bank 2012; mem. Council, Interstate Bank. *Address:* Türkmenistanyň Merkezi Banky (Central Bank of Turkmenistan), 744000 Aşgabat, Bitarap Türkmenistan köç. 36, Turkmenistan (office). *Telephone:* (12) 38-10-27 (office). *Fax:* (12) 92-08-12 (office). *E-mail:* merkezb3@online.tm (office). *Website:* www.cbt.tm (office).

ANNAUD, Jean-Jacques, LèsL; French film director and screenwriter; b. 1 Oct. 1943, Juvisy/Orge; s. of Pierre Annaud and Madeleine Tripoz; m. 1st Monique Rossignol 1970 (divorced 1980); one d.; m. 2nd Laurence Duval 1982; one d.; ed Inst. des Hautes Etudes Cinématographiques and Univ. of Paris, Sorbonne; freelance commercial film dir 1966–75; feature film dir 1975–; mem. Institut de France; Officier des Palmes académiques et du Mérite social, Commdr des Arts et Lettres; Grand Prix Nat. du Cinéma, Grand Prix de l'Acad. Française. *Films include:* Black and White in Colour 1976 (Acad. Award for Best Foreign Film), Hot Head 1979, Quest for Fire (César Award for Best Film 1982, for Best Dir 1982) 1981, The Name of the Rose (César Award 1987, David di Donatello Award for Best Dir 1987) 1986, The Bear (César Award 1988) 1988, The Lover 1992, Wings of Courage 1994, Seven Years in Tibet 1997, Enemy at the Gates 2001, Two Brothers 2004, Sa majesté Minor 2007, Day of the Falcon 2011, Le Dernier Loup 2015, Genghis Khan 2018. *Television includes:* The Truth About the Harry Quebert Affair (mini-series) 2018. *Leisure interests:* books, old cameras, world travel. *Address:* c/o Voyez Mon Agent (VMA), 20 Avenue Rapp, 75007 Paris (office); 9 rue Guénégaud, 75006 Paris, France (home). *Telephone:* 1-43-17-37-00 (office). *E-mail:* b.delabbey@vma.fr (office). *Website:* www.vma.fr (office); jjannaud.com.

ANNE, HRH The Princess (see Royal, HRH The Princess).

ANNINSKY, Lev Alexandrovich Ivanov, PhD; Russian writer and critic; b. 7 April 1934, Rostov-on-Don; s. of Alexandre Ivanov Anninsky and Anna Alexandrova; m. Alexandra Nikolayevna Ivanova Anninskaya; three d.; ed Moscow State Univ.; freelance literary critic 1956–, cinema critic 1960–, theatre critic 1962–; TV and radio broadcaster 1992–96; mem. Acad. of Russian Literature; Academician, Russian Acad. of Cinema, Russian Acad. of Theatre; jury mem. Yasnaya Polyana Award; fmr Ed. Druzhba Narodov (monthly), Rodina (monthly). *Publications include:* The Core of the Nut: Critical Reviews 1965, Married to the Idea 1971, Literary and Critical Reviews 1977, Hunting for Lev (Lev Tolstoy and Cinematography) 1980, Contacts 1982, Three Heretics: Pisemsky, Melnikov-Pechersky, Leskov 1988, Elbows and Wings: Literature of the 1980s: Hopes, Reality, Paradoxes 1989, A Ticket to Elysium: Reflections on Theatre Porches 1989, Culture's Tapestry 1991, The Sixties Generation 1991, Flying Curtain: Literary-Critical Articles on Georgia 1991, Silver and Black 1997, Bards 1999, Russians plus 2001, numerous titles in Russian, articles on literature, theatre and cinema. *Address:* 119415 Moscow, Udaltsova str. 16, Apt 19, Russia (home). *Telephone:* (495) 131-62-45 (home). *E-mail:* l_anninsky@mtu-net.ru.

ANNOU MALAM, Mamane Badamassi, MEcon, PhD, MBA; Niger economist and politician; ed Centre d'études Financières, économiques et bancaires, Paris, France, Univ. of Minnesota-St Paul, USA; Head of Accounts Centre, Ministry of Finance 1981–83, Dir of Public Debt 1983–88; Dir-Gen. Crédit du Niger 1988–90; Sec.-Gen. at the Presidency 1990–91; Minister of Finance Feb.–Aug. 1991, Minister of Economy and Finance 2010–12; Research Economist, Univ. of Arkansas-Fayetteville, USA and Univ. of Guelph, Canada 1999–2006; Prin. Economist, Prov. of Ont., Canada 2006–08; Tech. Dir UNDP Millennium Challenge Account-Niger 2008–10.

ANSARI, Anousheh, BSc, MSc; Iranian/American engineer and telecommunications industry executive; *Chairman, Prodea Systems, Inc;* b. 12 Sept. 1966, Mashhad, Iran; m. Hamid Ansari 1991; ed George Mason Univ., Fairfax, Va, George Washington Univ., Washington, DC; began career as engineer with MCI Telecommunications Corpn, Communications Satellite Corpn (COMSAT); Co-founder and CEO Telecom Technologies, Inc. 1993–2000, merged with Sonus Networks 2000, Gen. Man. and Vice-Pres. Sonus Softswitch Div.; Co-founder Prodea Systems, Inc. 2006, currently Chair.; mem. Asscn of Space Explorers, Nat. Soc. of Professional Engineers, IEEE; mem. Advisory Bd Teachers in Space; George Mason Univ. Entrepreneurial Excellence Award, George Washington Univ. Distinguished Alumni Achievement Award, Ernst & Young Entrepreneur of the Year Award for SW Region, Symons Innovator Award 2009. *Achievements include:* took part as self-funded space tourist in Soyuz TMA-9 mission, spent eight days on Int. Space Station (first Iranian in space) Sept. 2006. *Publication:* My Dream of Stars 2010. *Address:* Prodea Systems, Inc., 6101 West Plano Parkway, Plano, TX 75093, USA (office). *Telephone:* (214) 278-1850 (office). *Fax:* (214) 278-1851 (office). *E-mail:* Anousheh@anoushehansari.com (office). *Website:* www.prodeasystems.com (office); www.anoushehansari.com.

ANSARI, Shri Mohammad Hamid, BA, MA; Indian diplomatist and government official; b. 1 April 1937, Calcutta, Bengal, British India (now Kolkata); s. of Shri Mohammad Abdul Aziz Ansari and Aasiya Begum; m. Salma Ansari; two s. one d.; ed St Xavier's Coll., Kolkata, Aligarh Muslim Univ.; joined Foreign Service 1961, past positions include Amb. to Saudi Arabia and UAE 1976–79, High Commr to Australia 1985–89, Amb. to Afghanistan 1989–90, to Iran 1990–92, to Saudi Arabia 1995–99, Amb. and Perm. Rep. to UN, New York 1993–95; Vice-Chancellor, Aligarh Muslim Univ. 2000–02; Chair. Advisory Comm. for Oil Diplomacy, Ministry of Petroleum and Natural Gas 2004–05; mem. Nat. Security Advisory Bd 2004–06; Chair. Nat. Comm. for Minorities 2006–07; Vice-Pres. of India 2007–17; Chair. Rajya Sabha (Council of States) 2007–17; Pres. Indian Inst. of Public Admin; Chancellor, Panjab Univ., Chandigarh; Visiting Prof., Centre for West Asian and African Studies, Jawaharlal Nehru Univ. 1999–2000, Acad. of Third World Studies, Jamia Millia Islamia 2003–05; Distinguished Fellow, Observer Research Foundation 2002–06; Dr hc (Mohammed V Univ., Rabat, Morocco) 2016; Padma Shree 1984. *Publications include:* Iran Today: Twenty-five Years after the Islamic Revolution (ed) 2005, Travelling Through Conflict: Essays on the Politics of West Asia 2008, Teasing Questions: Exploring Disconnects in Contemporary India 2014; numerous articles on West Asian affairs. *Leisure interests:* golf, cricket.

ANSCHUTZ, Philip F., BSc; American business executive; *Chairman, Anschutz Corporation;* b. 1939, Russell, Kan.; m. Nancy Anschutz; three c.; ed Univ. of Kansas; f. Anschutz Corpn 1965, Chair. and CEO 1991–; Chair. Southern Pacific Rail Corpn, San Francisco 1988–96; f. Anschutz Entertainment with stakes in LA Kings (professional ice hockey team) 1995–, LA Galaxy (professional soccer team) 1996–, majority owner, Staples Center, LA; Chair. Southern Pacific Rail Corpn 1988–96; Founder, Qwest Communications, Chair. 1993–2006; Owner, San Francisco Examiner newspaper, The Independent (local newspaper), Grant Printing Company, San Francisco 2004–. *Address:* Anschutz Corpn, 555 17th Street, Suite 2400, Denver, CO 80202-3941, USA (office). *Telephone:* (303) 298-1000 (office). *Fax:* (303) 298-8881 (office).

ANSIP, Andrus; Estonian engineer, politician and EU official; *Commissioner for the Digital Single Market and Vice-President, European Commission;* b. 1 Oct. 1956, Tartu; m. Anu Ansip; three d.; ed Tartu Secondary School No. 5, Tartu State Univ., Univ. of York, Canada, British Council training in Brussels, Belgium, Dublin, Ireland and Edinburgh, UK; Sr Engineer, Organic Chem. Chair, Tartu State Univ. 1979–81, Sr Engineer, X-ray Contrast Substances Lab., Coronary and Cardio-surgery Div., Gen. and Molecular Pathology Inst. 1983–86; mil. service in the Baltic Fleet 1981–83; Head of Organizational Dept, Estonian CP, Tartu Dist Cttee, Instructor of Industry Dept 1986–88; Head of Regional Office, Jt Venture Estkompexim 1989–93; Chair. Radio Tartu Ltd 1994–98; Deputy Head of Tartu Dept of North Estonian Bank 1994–95; Bankruptcy Trustee, Tartu Commercial Bank 1994–98; mem. Bd of Dirs, Rahvapank (People's Bank) 1993–94, Fondijuhtide AS 1995–96, Fundmanager Ltd; Chair. Livonia Privatization IF 1995–96; CEO Fondinvesteeringu Maakler AS 1995–96, Investment Fund Broker Ltd; Mayor City of Tartu 1998–2004; Chair. Estonian Reform Party (Reformierakond) 2004–14; Minister of Econ. Affairs and Communications 2004–05; Prime Minister 2005–14; mem. Riigikogu (Parl.) 2014; mem. European Parl. and Vice-Pres. for the ALDE Group 2014; Commr for the Digital Single Market and Vice-Pres., EC Nov. 2014–(19), acting Commr for the Digital Economy and Society Jan.–July 2017; mem. Estonian voluntary home guard org. Kaitseliit (Defence League) 2009–; Officer, Nat. Order of Merit (Malta) 2001, Order of the White Star (Third Class) 2005. *Address:* European Commission, 200 Rue de la Loi/Wetstraat 200, 1049 Brussels, Belgium (office). *Telephone:* (2) 299-11-11 (switchboard) (office). *E-mail:* cab-ansip-web@ec.europa.eu (office). *Website:* ec.europa.eu/commission/2014-2019/ansip_en (office).

ANSTEY, Caroline, PhD; British banking executive; *Group Managing Director and Global Head, UBS and Society, UBS;* b. 7 Nov. 1955, London; d. of Edgar Anstey and Daphne Lilly; m. Milton W. Hudson; two s.; ed Univ. of Leeds, Univ. of California, Berkeley, USA, London School of Econs; Gwilym Gibbon Prize Research Fellow, Nuffield Coll., Oxford 1982–84; Political Asst to Prime Minister James Callaghan 1984–86; Sr Producer, BBC 1986–88, Ed. Analysis (BBC weekly current affairs programme) 1988–91; apptd Consultant in External Affairs, World Bank, Washington, DC 1995, Asst to World Bank Pres. James D. Wolfensohn 1996–99, Dir of Media Relations and Chief Spokesperson 1999–2003, Country Dir, Latin America and the Caribbean 2003–07, Chief of Staff and Vice-Pres. External Affairs 2007–11, Man. Dir World Bank Group 2011–13; consultant to Pres., Inter-American Development Bank 2013–14; Group Man. Dir and Global Head, UBS and Society, UBS, Zurich 2014–; mem. Bd of Dirs Swiss Sustainable Finance, Zurich, UBS Optimus Foundation, London; fmr Secr. mem. InterAction Council. *Publications:* contrib. to numerous journals and newspapers. *Address:* UBS, Bahnhofstrasse 45, 8001 Zurich, Switzerland (office). *Website:* www.ubs.com/global/en/about_ubs/ubs-and-society.html (office).

ANTES, Horst; German painter, sculptor and printmaker; b. 28 Oct. 1936, Heppenheim; s. of Valentin Antes and Erika Antes; m. Dorothea Grossmann 1961; one s. one d.; ed Heppenheim Coll., Akademie der Bildenden Künste, Karlsruhe; worked in Florence, then Rome; Prof., State Acad. of Fine Arts, Karlsruhe 1957–59, Berlin 1984–; teacher, Akademie der Bildenden Künste, Karlsruhe 1965, 1984–2000; Guest Prof., Staatliche Hochschule für Bildende Künste, Berlin 1974; mem. Acad. der Künste, Berlin, now living in Berlin, Karlsruhe and Tuscany, Italy; Pankofer-Preis 1959, Kulturpreis 1959, Villa Romana Prize, Florence 1962, Villa Massimo Prize, Rome 1963, UNESCO Prize, Venice Biennale 1966, Hans-Molfenter-Preis 1989, Kulturpreis (Hesse) 1991, Bienal de Sao Paulo 1991. *Address:* Hohenbergstrasse 11, 76228 Karlsruhe (Wolfartsweier), Germany. *Telephone:* (721) 491621.

ANTHONY, Kenny Davis, LLB, BSc, PhD; Saint Lucia politician; b. 8 Jan. 1951; m. Rosemarie Belle Antoine; ed Univ. of Birmingham, Univ. of the West Indies; mem. House of Ass. (Parl.) for Vieux Fort South; mem. Saint Lucia Labour Party, Leader –2016; Prime Minister of Saint Lucia, Minister of Finance, Planning, Devt, Information and the Civil Service 1997–2001, Prime Minister, Minister of Finance, Int. Financial Services, Econ. Affairs and Information 2001–06, Leader of the Opposition 2006–11, Prime Minister and Minister for Finance and Econ. Affairs 2011–16.

ANTICH VALERO, José; Spanish journalist and newspaper executive; *Editor and Director, El Nacional;* b. 23 June 1955, La Seu d'Urgell (Lérida); m.; four c.; writer for Agencia Efe, Barcelona 1977; political feature writer, El Periódico de Catalunya 1978–82; part of founding team of Catalan edn of El País, becoming political corresp. 1982–94; Chief Political Writer, La Vanguardia 1994–98, also coordinator of political affairs 1998–2000, Dir 2000–13; Ed. and Dir, El Nacional (digital newspaper) 2015–; VIII Fundación Independiente de Periodismo Camilo José Cela Prize 2004. *Publication:* El Virrey 1994. *Address:* El Nacional.cat, Grup les Notícies de Catalunya, Numància, 46, 4th floor, 08029 Barcelona, Spain (office). *Telephone:* (93) 1730099 (office). *Website:* www.elnacional.cat (office).

ANTINORI, Severino, PhD; Italian gynaecologist and embryologist; b. 6 Sept. 1945, Civitella del Tronto; m. Caterina Antinori; two d.; ed Univ. La Sapienza; Perm. Asst in Obstetrics and Gynaecology, Istituto Materno Regina Elena 1973–80, Prin. Asst 1980–82, Dir Reproductive Physiopathology Service 1985–87; at Ospedale Materno Regina Elena 1978–92; specialist in obstetrics and gynaecology, Univ. Cattolica di Roma 1978; Prof., Univ. degli Studi di Pisa 1993–94, Univ. degli Studi G. D'Annunzio, Chieti 1996–97, 1998–99, Univ. degli Studi di Roma 1998–99; Prof. of Physiopathology of Reproduction, Chair of Gynaecology and Obstetrics, Università di Modena e Reggio Emilia 2003–07; fmr Dir Centro RAPRUI (Ricercatori Associati per la Riproduzione Umana); Vice-Pres. Int. Asscn of Pvt. Assisted Reproductive Tech. Clinics and Labs; arrested on allegations of kidnapping, placed under house arrest May 2016. *Publications include:* numerous articles in medical journals. *Website:* severinoantinori.it.

ANTOINE, Frédéric, PhD; Belgian journalist and academic; *Professor, School of Communication Science, Catholic University of Louvain;* b. 27 Sept. 1955, Uccle, Brussels; s. of Paul Antoine and Suzanne Degavre; m. Christine Masuy; two s. one d.; ed Catholic Univ. of Louvain; journalist, L'Appel 1977, La Libre Belgique 1978–2008; Research Asst, Dept of Communication Science, Catholic Univ. of Louvain 1979, Prof. 1989–, Dir Research Unit on Mediatic Narrative (RECI) 1991–2000, Head of Undergraduate Programme Information and Communication 2006–; News Ed. Radio 1180, Brussels 1979–2009; Prof., Media School IAD, Louvain-la-Neuve 1981–; Ed. L'Appel 1992–; Invited Prof. Univ. of Namur 2006–; Chair. GRER (Radio Research and Studies Group), France 2010–. *Publications include:* On Nous a Changé la Télé 1987, La Télévision à Travers ses Programmes 1988, Télévision In: Le Guide des Médias 1989–97; ed. La Médiamorphose d'Alain Vanderbiest 1994; ed. Coupures de Presse 1996, Les Radios et les Télévisions de Belgique 2000, Les Multinationales des Médias 2002, Le Grand Malentendu 2003, Télé-réalité, la réalité si je mens 2008. *Address:* Ruelle de la Lanterne, Magique 14, 1348 Louvain-la-Neuve (office); Magazine L'appel, Rue du beau Mur 45, 4030 Liège (office); Rue Grande 58, 5530 Godinne, Belgium (home). *Telephone:* (1) 47-28-14 (office); (4) 341-10-04 (office); (81) 22-06-62 (home). *Fax:* (1) 47-30-44 (office); (4) 341-10-04 (office). *E-mail:* frederic.antoine@uclouvain.be (office); redacteurenchef@magazine-appel.be (office). *Website:* www.uclouvain.be/comu (office); www.magazine-appel.be (office).

ANTONAKAKIS, Dimitris; Greek architect; b. 22 Dec. 1933, Chania, Crete; m. Maria-Suzana Antonakakis (q.v.) (née Kolokytha) 1961; one s. one d.; ed School of Architecture, Nat. Tech. Univ. of Athens; partnership with Suzana Antonakakis, Athens 1959–; Asst Instructor in Architecture, Nat. Tech. Univ. of Athens 1959–64, Instructor 1964–78, mem. teaching staff 1978–92; Founder and Co-Prin. (with S. Antonakakis) Atelier 66 1965; mem. and Treas. Admin. Cttee, Greek Architectural Asscn 1962–63; Pres. Asscn of Assts and Instructors, Nat. Tech. Univ. 1975–77; Vice-Pres. Cen. Admin. Cttee, Asscn of Assts and Instructors of Greek Univs 1976–77; mem. Int. Design Seminar, Tech. Univ. Delft 1987, Split 1988; Visiting Prof., MIT, USA 1994–99, Nat. Tech. Univ. of Athens 1997–98; Art Dir Centre for Mediterranean Architecture, Crete 1997–; Corresp. mem. Acad. d'Architecture, Paris; Dr hc (Aristotle Univ. of Thessaloniki) 2007, (Democritus Univ. of Thrace) 2016; numerous awards and prizes. *Works include:* Archaeological Museum, Chios 1965–66, Hydra Beach Hotel, Hermionis 1965, vertical addition, house in Port Phaliron 1967–72, miners' housing complex, Distomo 1969, apartment bldg, Emm. Benaki 118, Athens 1973–74, Hotel Lyttos, Heraklion, Crete 1973–82, Zannas House, Philopappos Hill, Athens 1980–82, Gen. Hosp., Sitia, Crete 1982, Ionian Bank br., Rhodes 1983, Heraklion, Crete 1987, Faculty of Humanities, Rethymnon, Crete 1982, Tech. Univ. of Crete, Chania 1982, Summer Theatre, Komotini 1989, Traditional Crafts Centre, Ioannina 1990, Museum of the Acropolis, Athens 1990, Art Studio, Aegina 1990, office bldg, 342 Syngrou Ave., Athens 1990, Open-air Theatre, Thessaloniki 1995–96, Pissas House, Heraklion, Crete 1997, Rehabilitation of ancient Agora area, Athens 1997, Museum of Science and Technology, Patras 1999, Kallithea and Ano Patisia railway stations, Athens 2001–02, Kolonaki Square, Athens 2004; several pvt. houses. *Publications include:* Le Corbusier Une Petite Maison (trans.) 1998; numerous architectural articles. *Address:* Atelier 66, Emm. Benaki 118, Athens 114-73, Greece (office). *Telephone:* (210) 3300324 (office). *E-mail:* a66@otenet.gr (office). *Website:* www.a66architects.com (office).

ANTONAKAKIS-KOLOKYTHA, Maria-Suzana; Greek architect; b. 25 June 1935, Athens; m. Dimitris Antonakakis (q.v.) 1961; one s. one d.; ed School of Architecture, Nat. Tech. Univ., Athens; partnership with Dimitris Antonakakis, Athens 1959–; Founder and Co-Prin. (with Dimitris Antonakakis) Atelier 66 1965; mem. Admin. Cttee Greek Architects Asscn 1971–72; Pres. Dept of Architecture, Tech. Chamber of Greece 1982–83; mem. Int. Design Seminar, Tech. Univ. Delft 1987, Split 1988; mem. Greek Secr., Int. Union of Architects (UIA) 1985–2002; newspaper columnist 1998–2009; works include: Archaeological Museum, Chios 1965–66, Hydra Beach Hotel, Hermionis 1965, vertical additions, House in Port Phaliron 1967–72, miners' housing complex, Distomo 1969, apartment bldg, Emm. Benaki 118, Athens 1973–74, Hotel Lyttos, Heraklion, Crete 1973–82, Zannas House, Philopappos Hill, Athens 1980–82, Gen. Hosp. Sitia, Crete 1982, Ionian Bank branch, Rhodes 1983, Heraklion, Crete 1987, Summer Theatre, Komotini 1989, Art Studio, Aegina 1990, office bldg, 342 Syngrou Ave, Athens 1990, Traditional Crafts Centre, Ioannina 1990, Museum of Acropolis, Athens 1990, Open-air Theatre, Thessaloniki 1995–96, Pissas House, Heraklion, Crete 1997, rehabilitation of ancient Agora area, Athens 1997, Museum of Science and Technology, Patras 1999, Kallithea and Ano Patisia railway stations, Athens 2001–02, New Acropolis Museum, Athens 2001, Kolonaki Square, Athens 2004; several pvt. and holiday houses; Dr hc (Aristotle Univ. of Thessaloniki) 2007, (Democritus Univ. of Thrace) 2016; numerous awards and prizes. *Publications:* numerous architectural articles; trans. Entretien (Le Corbusier) 1971. *Address:* Atelier 66, Emm. Benaki 118, Athens 114-73, Greece (office). *Telephone:* (210) 3300323 (office). *E-mail:* a66@otenet.gr (office). *Website:* www.a66architects.com (office).

ANTONELLI, HE Cardinal Ennio, DPhil; Italian ecclesiastic and academic; *President Emeritus, Pontifical Council for the Family;* b. 18 Nov. 1936, Todi; ed Seminary of Todi, Pontifical Regional Seminary of Assisi, Pontifical Higher Seminary of Rome, Pontifical Lateran Univ., Rome, State Univ. of Perugia; ordained priest, Diocese of Todi 1960; Prof. of Theology, Vice-Rector, then Rector, Seminary of Perugia; Prof. of Theology, Regional Seminary of Assisi; Prof. of Art History, Superior Insts of Assisi and Deruta; Bishop of Gubbio 1982–88; Metropolitan Archbishop of Perugia-Città della Pieve 1988–95; Sec.-Gen. Italian Episcopal Conf. 1995–2001; del. to Special Ass. for Europe, World Synod of Bishops, Vatican City 1999; Archbishop of Florence 2001–08, Archbishop Emer. 2008–; cr. Cardinal (Cardinal-Priest of Sant'Andrea delle Fratte) 2003; participated in Papal Conclave 2005, 2013; Pres. Pontifical Council for the Family 2008–12, Pres. Emer. 2012–; mem. Pontifical Council for the Pastoral Care of Migrants and Itinerants 2011–, Congregation for the Causes of Saints 2012–17. *Address:* Pontifical Council for the Family, Piazza di San Calisto 16, 00153 Rome, Italy (office). *Telephone:* (06) 69887243 (office). *Fax:* (06) 69887272 (office). *E-mail:* pcf@family.va (office). *Website:* www.vatican.va/roman_curia/pontifical_councils/family/index.htm (office); www.familia.va (office).

ANTONESCU, George Crin Laurenţiu (Crin); Romanian teacher and politician; b. 21 Sept. 1959, Tulcea; m. 1st Aurelia Antonescu (died 2004); one d.; m. 2nd Adina Vălean 2009; ed Univ. of Bucharest; worked as history teacher in Soleşti, Vaslui Co. 1985; later returned to Tulcea, continuing his academic activity in Niculiţel –1989; worked as curator for Tulcea Museum of History and Archaeology 1989–90; joined Partidul Naţional Liberal (PNL—Nat. Liberal Party) 1990, elected Vice-Pres. 1995, Pres. 2009–14; mem. Chamber of Deputies 1996–2008, Leader PNL Parl. Group 2005–08; Minister of Youth and Sports 1997–2000; mem. Senate 2008–, Vice-Pres. of Senate 2008–09, Pres. 2012–14 (resgnd); unsuccessful presidential cand. 2009; Acting Pres. of Romania (following suspension of Traian Băsescu) 10 July–27 Aug. 2012. *Address:* Partidul Naţional Liberal (National Liberal Party), 011866 Bucharest, Blvd Aviatorilor 86 (office); Senatul Romaniei (The Senate), 050711 Bucharest 5, Calea 13 Septembrie 1–3, Romania (office). *Telephone:* (21) 2310795 (PNL) (office); (21) 3113532 (Senate) (office). *Fax:* (21) 2310796 (PNL) (office). *E-mail:* presedinte@pnl.ro (office). *Website:* www.pnl.ro (office); www.senat.ro (office); crinantonescu.pnl.ro.

ANTONICHEVA, Anna; Russian ballet dancer; *Principal Dancer, Bolshoi Theatre Ballet Company;* b. 1973, Baku, Azerbaijan; ed Moscow Academic School of Choreography; joined Bolshoi Theatre Ballet Co. 1991, now Prin. Dancer; coached by Marina Kondratieva and Ekaterina Maximova; Transcaucasian Competition of Ballet Artists 1988, Merited Artist of the Russian Fed. 1998, Gold Medal, Int. Ballet Competition, Jackson, Miss. 1998, Soul of Dance Prize (Up-and-Coming-Star nomination), Ballet magazine 1999, People's Artist of the Russian Fed. 2008. *Ballet:* leading and solo parts include Shirin (The Legend of Love), Odette-Odile and Swan Princess (Swan Lake), Giselle and Myrtha (Giselle), Juliet (Romeo and Juliet), Phrygia (Spartacus), Aurora and Princess Florine (Sleeping Beauty), Kitri and Dulcinea (Don Quixote), Nikiya (La Bayadere), ballet soloist (Symphony in C), Sylph (Chopiniana), Hero (Love for Love), Concert number (Carnival in Venice), Diana and Concert number (Esmeralda), Concert numbers (Listening into the Music by Mozart, Tango, Taming the Fire (S. Bobrov's version)), Esmeralda (Notre-Dame de Paris), Raymonda (Raymonda), ballet soloist (Agon). *Address:* The State Academic Bolshoi Theatre of Russia, Teatralnaya Pl. 1, Moscow, Russia (office). *E-mail:* pr@bolshoi.ru (office); support@bolshoi.net. *Website:* www.bolshoi.ru/en/theatre/ballet_troupe/soloists (office).

ANTONOV, Anatoly Ivanovich, Dr rer. pol; Russian politician and diplomatist; *Ambassador to the USA;* b. 15 May 1955, Omsk; one d.; ed Moscow State Inst. of Int. Relations; joined Ministry of Foreign Affairs 1978, becoming Amb. at Large 2002–04, Dir, Dept for Security and Disarmament 2004–11, Deputy Minister of Defence 2011–16, Deputy Minister of Foreign Affairs 2016–17; Amb. to USA 2017–; Order "For Merit to the Fatherland" (IV class), Order of Alexander Nevsky, Order of Mil. Merit, Order of Honour, Order of Friendship; Jubilee Medal (70 Years of the Armed Forces of the USSR). *Address:* Embassy of the Russian Federation, 2650 Wisconsin Avenue, NW, Washington, DC 20007, USA (office). *Telephone:* (202) 298-5700 (office). *Fax:* (202) 298-5735 (office). *E-mail:* russianembassy@mindspring.com (office). *Website:* www.russianembassy.org (office).

ANTONOVA, Irina Aleksandrovna; Russian museum researcher; b. 20 March 1922, Moscow; ed Moscow State Univ.; worked in Pushkin Museum of Fine Arts 1945–2013, Sr Researcher 1945–61, Dir 1961–2013; organizer of numerous exhbns and regular exchange with museums of Europe and America; f. together with Sviatoslav Richter Festival of Arts December Nights accompanied by art shows 1981; Vice-Pres. Int. Council of Museums 1980–92, Hon. mem. 1992, then Pres.; mem. Russian Acad. of Educ. 1989; Corresp. mem. San-Fernando Acad., Madrid; Commdr des Arts et Lettres; State Prize 1995. *Publications:* more than 60 articles on problems of museum man., art of Italian Renaissance, contemporary painting. *Leisure interests:* swimming, cars, music, ballet.

ANTONSSON, Markús Örn; Icelandic diplomatist; b. 25 May 1943; m. Steinunn Ármannsdóttir; two c.; ed Reykjavík Junior Coll., exchange student in USA; part-time journalist and photographer, Morgunbladid (daily) 1961–65; trained in broadcasting journalism and TV production in UK and Sweden; reporter, news presenter and programme producer, RUV TV 1965–70, Dir-Gen. Nat. Broadcasting Service, RUV TV and Radio 1985–91, Dir RUV Radio Div. 1995–98, Dir-Gen. RUV TV and Radio 1998–2005; mem. Broadcasting Council 1979–85, Chair. 1983–85; City Councillor, Reykjavík 1970–85, mem. Exec. Cttee Reykjavík City Council and Chair. several other cttees, Pres. City Council 1983–85, Chair. City Council Exec. Cttee and Leader of Independence Party Councillors' Group; Mayor of Reykjavík 1991–94; Amb. to Canada 2005–08; Dir Icelandic Nat. Heritage Centre, Reykjavík 2008–; mem. Bd, Atlantic Alliance Asscn of Young Political Leaders 1971–75, Man. of Eurimages, European Film Fund 1994–99, Icelandic Symphony Orchestra 1995–98, Icelandic Nat. League 1997–2003 (Pres. 1998–2003); Ed. business and travel magazines with Frjálst framtak publishing house 1972–83; mem. Rotary 1983–, Jt-Ed. Rotary Norden (regional magazine for Rotary in the five Nordic countries) 1996–; mem. Exec. Cttee and Advisory Council European Cultural Foundation, Amsterdam 1994–. *Address:* c/o Ministry for Foreign Affairs, Rauðarárstígur 25, 150 Reykjavík, Iceland. *E-mail:* postur@utn.stjr.is.

ANTONY, Arackaparambil Kurian (A. K), BA, BL; Indian politician; b. 28 Dec. 1940, Cherthala, Alappuzha Dist, Kerala; s. of Arackaparambil Kurian Pillai and Aleyamma; m. Elizabeth Antony; two s.; ed Maharajas Coll., Govt Law Coll.,

Ernakulam; Chief Minister of Kerala 1977–78, 1995–96, 2001–04; mem. Rajya Sabha (Parl.) from Kerala 1985–95, 2005–; Minister of Civil Supplies, Consumer Affairs and Public Distribution 1993–95; Leader of Opposition, Kerala Legis. Ass. 1996–2001; Minister of Defence 2006–14; Chair. Disciplinary Cttee of All India Congress Cttee. *Address:* Anjanam, Easwara Vilasam Road, Thiruvananthapuram 695 014, India (home). *E-mail:* ak.antony@sansad.nic.in.

ANUSZKIEWICZ, Richard Joseph, BS, MFA; American artist; b. 23 May 1930, Erie, Pa; s. of Adam Jacob Anuszkiewicz and Victoria Jankowski; m. Sarah Feeney 1960; one s. two d.; ed Cleveland Inst. of Art, Yale Univ., Kent State Univ.; moved to New York City 1957; Conservator, Metropolitan Museum of Art 1957–58; Silver Designer Tiffany and Co. 1958–59; teacher, Cooper Union, New York 1963–65; Artist-in-Residence, Dartmouth Coll. 1967, Univ. of Wis. 1968, Cornell Univ. 1968, Kent State Univ. 1968, Charles Foley Gallery, Columbus 1988, Newark Museum 1990, Center for Arts, Vero Beach, Fla 1993; represented in collections at Museum of Modern Art, Whitney Museum of American Art, Albright-Knox Art Gallery, Butler Art Inst., Yale Art Gallery, Chicago Art Inst., Fogg Art Museum, Corcoran Gallery of Art, Harvard Univ., Chicago Museum of Contemporary Art, Cleveland Museum of Art, Columbus Museum of Art, Denver Museum of Art, Blanton Museum of Art, Univ. of Texas, Boca Raton Museum of Art, Guggenheim Museum, New York, Hokkaido Museum of Modern Art, Metropolitan Museum of Art, Philadelphia Museum of Art, Wadsworth Atheneum, Hartford; Charles of the Ritz Oil Painting Award 1963, Silvermine Guild Award 1964, Cleveland Arts Prize 1977, Childe Hassam Fund Purchase Award 1980, 1988, New York State Art Teachers Asscn Award 1994, Emil and Dines Carlson Award 1995, New Jersey Pride Award 1996, Lee Krasner Award 2000, Lorenzo the Magnificent Award, Florence Int. Biennale of Contemporary Art 2005. *Publications include:* Anuskiewicz: OpArt 1999; several articles in learned journals. *Address:* c/o D. Wigmore Fine Art, 730 Fifth Avenue, Suite 602, New York, NY 10019, USA.

ANVELT, Andres; Estonian politician and fmr police officer; b. 30 Sept. 1969; m.; one c.; Dir Cen. Criminal Police 2001–03, Dir Police and Border Guard Coll. 2004–06; Security Adviser to Commdr of Estonian Defence Forces 2007–11; mem. Sotsiaaldemokraatlik Erakond (SDE—Estonian Social Democratic Party); mem. Tallinn City Council 2009–11, 2013; mem. Riigikogu (State Ass.—Parl.) 2011–16, Chair. Anti-Corruption Select Cttee and mem. several other cttees, Chair. Parl. faction 2015–16; Minister of Justice 2014–15, of the Interior 2016–18. *Leisure interests:* recreative sports, movies, literature. *Address:* c/o Ministry of the Interior, Pikk 61, 15065 Tallinn, Estonia (office).

ANWAR, Yaseen, BA, BSc (Econs); Pakistani banking executive and fmr central banker; *Senior Advisor, Industrial and Commercial Bank of China, (ICBC) Singapore;* b. 31 March 1951; s. of S.M. Anwar and Begum Ismat Anwar; ed Aitcheson Coll., Lahore, Grammar School, Karachi, Karachi American School, Wharton School of Business at Univ. of Pennsylvania, USA; trained at JPMorgan Chase, New York, USA 1973–75; Asst Man., Paris/London, Bank of America 1976–79, Asst Man., Cairo, Egypt 1979–81, Asst Vice Pres., New York 1982–84, Vice-Pres. and Section Head for Global Export Finance Group and Middle East 1984–91; Vice-Pres. Merrill Lynch & Co., New York/London 1992–2001; Dir (Pvt. Banking), Riggs and Co., London, UK 2001–03; Exec. Vice-Pres. Kraken Financial Group, London 2003–07; Deputy Gov. State Bank of Pakistan 2007–10, Acting Gov. June–Sept. 2010, Gov. 2011–14; currently mem. Advisory Bd, International Monetary Inst., Renmin Univ., Beijing, China; also currently Sr Advisor, Industrial and Commercial Bank of China, Singapore; mem. Bd of Dirs (non-exec.) United Nat. Bank Ltd (UK) 2001–06; Founder and Pres. Pakistan Bankers Asscn, UK 1997–99; fmr mem. Arab Bankers Asscn, UK; fmr Exec. Dir American Turkish Soc., New York; fmr Dir on US-Pakistan Econ. Council, on American Middle East Business Asscn; fmr mem. Council on Foreign Relations. *Address:* Industrial & Commercial Bank of China, (ICBC) Singapore Branch, 6 Raffles Quay, #23-01, 048580 Singapore. *Website:* www.icbc.com.sg.

ANWAR, Zainah; Malaysian writer and activist; b. Johor; d. of Tan Sri Haji Anwar bin Abdul Malik and Saodah bte Abdullah; ed MARA Inst. of Tech., Shah Alam, Fletcher School of Law and Diplomacy, Tufts Univ., Boston Univ., USA; began career as journalist, New Straits Times; Sr Analyst, Inst. of Strategic and Int. Studies (think-tank), Kuala Lumpur 1986–91; fmr Chief Programme Officer, Political Affairs Div., Commonwealth Secr., London; worked for 20 years with Sisters in Islam (non-govt org.) promoting rights of Muslim women, finishing as Exec. Dir; Founding mem. Musawah (lobby group for equality and justice in Muslim families); writes a monthly column on politics, religion and women's rights, Sharing the Nation, in the Sunday Star newspaper; fmr mem. Human Rights Comm. of Malaysia. *Publication:* Islamic Revivalism in Malaysia: Dakwah Among the Students. *Address:* The Musawah Secretariat, c/o SIS Forum (Malaysia), 4 Lorong 11/8E, 46200 Petaling Jaya, Selangor, Malaysia (office). *Telephone:* (603) 7785-6121 (office). *E-mail:* sistersinislam@pd.jaring.my (office). *Website:* www.musawah.org; www.sistersinislam.org.my (office).

ANYAOKU, Eleazar Chukwuemeka (Emeka), Ndichie Chief Adazie of Obosi, Ugwumba of Idemili, CON, BA, FRSA; Nigerian diplomatist and international organization official; b. 18 Jan. 1933, Obosi; s. of Emmanuel Chukwuemeka Anyaoku, Ononukpo of Okpuno Ire and Cecilia Adiba (née Ogbogu); m. Ebunola Olubunmi Solanke 1962; three s. one d.; ed Merchants of Light School, Oba, Univ. of Ibadan, Univ. of London, UK; Commonwealth Devt Corpn, London and Lagos 1959–62; joined Nigerian Diplomatic Service 1962, mem. Nigerian Perm. Mission to UN, New York 1963–66; seconded to Commonwealth Secr., Asst Dir Int. Affairs Div. 1966–71, Dir 1971–75, Asst Sec.-Gen. of the Commonwealth 1975–77, elected Deputy Sec.-Gen. (Political) Dec. 1977, re-elected, 1984, Sec.-Gen. 1990–2000; Minister of External Affairs, Nigeria Nov.–Dec. 1983; Sec., Review Cttee on mem. Commonwealth Intergovernmental Orgs June–Aug. 1966; Commonwealth Observer Team for Gibraltar Referendum Aug.–Sept. 1967; mem. Anguilla Comm., West Indies Jan.–Sept. 1970; Deputy Conf. Sec., meeting of Commonwealth Heads of Govt, London 1969, Singapore 1971, Conf. Sec., Ottawa 1973, Kingston, Jamaica 1975; Leader, Commonwealth Mission to Mozambique 1975; Commonwealth Observer, Zimbabwe Talks, Geneva Oct.–Dec. 1976; accompanied Commonwealth Eminent Persons Group (EPG) SA 1986; Vice-Pres. Royal Commonwealth Soc. 1975–2000, Pres. 2000–; mem. Council of Overseas Devt Inst. 1979–90, Council of the Selly Oak Colleges, Birmingham 1980–86, Council, Save the Children Fund 1984–90, Council of IISS, London 1987–93, Int. Bd of United World Colleges 1994–2000, World Comm. on Forests and Sustainable Devt 1995–98; Pres. Royal Africa Soc. 2000–; Chair. Presidential Advisory Council on Int. Relations (Nigeria) 2000–; Int. Pres. WWF (World Wide Fund for Nature) 2002–09; Freedom of City of London 1998; Hon. Fellow, Inst. of Educ., London 1994, Coll. of Preceptors 1998; Hon. mem. Club of Rome 1992; Commdr of the Order of the Niger (Nigeria) 1982; Order of the Trinity Cross (Trinidad and Tobago) 1999; Hon. GCVO 2000; Hon. DLitt (Ibadan) 1990, (Buckingham) 1994, (Zimbabwe) 1999, (UDFD Sokoto) 2001, (Rhodes, SA) 2001, (UNILORIN) 2002; Hon. DPhil (Ahmadu Bello) 1991; Hon. LLD (Nigeria) 1991, (Aberdeen) 1992, (Reading) 1992, (Bristol) 1993, (Oxford Brookes) 1993, (Birmingham) 1993, (Leeds) 1994, (South Bank, London) 1994, (New Brunswick, Canada) 1995, (North London) 1995, (Liverpool) 1997, (London) 1997, (Nottingham) 1998, (Trinity Coll. Dublin) 1999, (UNIZIK) 2001; Dr hc (Bradford) 1995; Livingston Medal, Royal Scottish Geographical Soc. 1996. *Publications:* The Missing Headlines (vol. of speeches) 1997, essays in various publs. *Leisure interests:* tennis, athletics, swimming, reading. *Address:* Orimili, Okpuno Ire, Obosi, Anambra State, Nigeria.

ANYIM, Anyim Pius, LLM; Nigerian lawyer and government official; b. 19 Feb. 1961, Ishiagu, Ebonyi State; s. of Chief Anyim Ivo Osita and Agnes Anyim; m. Chioma Blessing; two s. one d.; ed Imo State (now Abia State) Univ., Okigwe, Univ. of Jos, Jos; called to Nigerian Bar 1989; Legal Adviser, Directorate of Social Mobilisation (MAMSER) HQ, Abuja 1989–92; Head of Protection Dept Nat. Comm. for Refugees HQ, Abuja 1992–97; fmr Registrar, Refugee Appeal Bd; Senator 1999–2003, Senator for Ebonyi South 1999–2003, Speaker of the Senate 2000–03; Sec. to the Govt of the Fed. 2011–15; Fellow, Nigerian Environmental Soc., Inst. of Purchasing and Supply Man.; Grand Patron Abuja Chapter, Soc. for Int. Devt; mem. Nigerian Bar Asscn; mem. People's Democratic Party (PDP); Grand Commdr, Order of Niger, Nat. Productivity Order of Merit Award; Hon. DPA (Fed. Univ. of Agric., Umudike, Abia State), Hon. DD (Baptist Seminary and Theological Inst., Ogbomoso, Oyo State); Distinguished Service Award, Nigerian Foundation Inc., USA and other awards. *Leisure interests:* farming, swimming, reading. *Address:* Peoples Democratic Party, Plot No. 1970 Wadata Plaza, Michael Okpara Way, Wuse, Abuja (office); Legislators Quarters, Apo Mansion, Abuja, Nigeria (home). *Telephone:* (9) 5232589 (office); (9) 2310009 (home). *Fax:* (9) 3143660 (home). *E-mail:* info@peoplesdemocraticparty.org (office). *Website:* www.peoplesdemocraticparty.com.ng (office).

ANZAI, Yuichiro, BEng, MEng, PhD; Japanese engineer, academic and university administrator; b. 29 Aug. 1946; ed Keio Univ.; Instructor, Dept of Admin Eng, Faculty of Eng, Keio Univ. 1971–79, Asst Prof. 1979–85, Prof., Dept of Electrical Eng, Faculty of Science and Tech. 1988–96, Prof., Center for Computer Science, Grad. School of Science and Tech. 1989–2000, Chair. Grad. School of Science and Tech. and Dean of Faculty of Science and Tech. 1993–2001, Prof., Dept of Information and Computer Science 1996, Prof., School of Open and Environmental Systems, Grad. School of Science and Tech. 2000, Pres. Keio Univ. 2001–09, currently Prof. Emer.; Postdoctoral Research Fellow, Dept of Psychology and Computer Science, Carnegie-Mellon Univ., Pittsburgh, USA, 1976–78, Visiting Asst Prof., Dept of Psychology 1981–82; Assoc. Prof., Dept of Behavioral Science, Faculty of Letters, Hokkaido Univ. 1985–88; Visiting Prof., McGill Univ., Canada 1990; Pres. Japan Soc. for the Promotion of Science 2011–18, Japan Asscn of Pvt. Colls and Univs 2003, Fed. of Japanese Pvt. Colls and Univs Asscns 2003; Chair. Fed. of All Japan Pvt. Schools Asscns 2003; Gen. Man. 'Biosimulation' Leading Project, Ministry of Educ., Culture, Sports, Science and Tech.; Chair. Sub-div. on Cen. Council for Educ.; mem. Science Council of Japan, Admin. Council Univ. of Tsukuba, Council of Univ. Man., Tohoku Univ., Strategic Council on Intellectual Property, Cabinet Office; mem. Council for Univ. Establishment and School Corpn, Ministry of Educ., Culture, Sports, Science and Tech.; Exec. Dir Research Org. of Information and Systems, Governing Bd Japan Asscn for Philosophy of Science; Vice-Chair. Asscn of Pacific Rim Univs (Vice-Chair. Steering Cttee); Pres. Information Processing Soc. of Japan; fmr Pres. Japanese Cognitive Science Soc.; fmr mem. Council Bd Japan Soc. for Philosophy of Science, Council Bd Japan Soc. for Neuroscience; fmr Dir Soc. of Instrument and Control Engineers, Japan Soc. for Eng Educ.; mem. Bd of Dirs Daiichi Sankyo Co. Ltd, Sony Corpn 2011–12; fmr mem. Life Science Cttee Council for Science and Tech., Informatics Cttee Council for Science and Tech.; Commdr, Ordre des Palmes académiques 2005; Dr hc (Ecole Centrale de Nantes, France) 2007; Best Tech. Paper Award, Soc. for Instrumental and Control Engineers 1972, Best Paper Award, Information Processing Soc. of Japan 1988, Achievement Award, Japanese Soc. for Artificial Intelligence 2001.

AOKI, Satoshi; Japanese motor company executive; b. 19 Aug. 1946; joined Honda Motor Co. Ltd 1969, Gen. Man. Finance Div. for Business Man. Operations 1994–98, apptd Rep. Dir 1995, Chief Financial Officer and Exec. Vice-Pres. 1995–98, COO for Business Man. Operations 1998–2000, Man. Dir 1998–2000, Sr Man. Dir 2000–04, Compliance Officer 2004–05, Head of US operations 2005–07, Chair. Honda Motor Co. Ltd 2007–10; mem. Bd of Dirs and Chair. Japan Automobile Mfrs Asscn 2008.

AOUN, Gen. Michel Naim; Lebanese army officer (retd), politician and head of state; *President;* b. 18 Feb. 1935, Haret Hreik; s. of F. Naim Aoun and M. Marie Aoun; m. Nadia El Chami; three d.; attended Christian school, Beirut; enrolled in mil. school 1955; trained as artilleryman; training courses in Châlons-sur-Marne, France 1958–59, Fort Seale, USA 1966, Ecole Supérieure de Guerre, France 1978–80; became Brigade Gen. 1984; C-in-C of Army 1984; following abandoned presidential elections of Sept. 1988, outgoing Pres. Gemayel named him prime minister of interim mil. admin; evicted from Baabda Presidential Palace by Syrian forces, refuge in French Embassy 1990–91, in exile in France 1991; returned to Lebanon May 2005, elected mem. Parl. (Majlis Al-Nawab) 2005–16, Head of Change and Reform Parl. Bloc 2005; Pres. Free Patriotic Movt Party 2003–15; Pres. of Lebanon 2016–; Memorial Medal of 31 Dec. 1961, Lebanese Silver Order of Merit, War Medals (four times), Nat. Cedar Medal, Kt, Lebanese Order of Merit (Second Rank), Purple Heart Medal, Lebanese Order of Merit (First Rank), Nat. Cedar Medal, rank of Officer, Nat. Cedar Medal, rank of Grand Officer, Distinction of the Gen. C-in-C of the Army (six times), Commendations of the C-in-C of the Army (three times), Commdr, Légion d'honneur 1986, Great Sash, Nat. Order of the Cedar 1988. *Publication:* Une Certaine Vision du Liban 2007. *Address:* Presidential Palace, Baabda, Beirut, Lebanon (office). *Telephone:* (5) 900900 (office). *Fax:* (5) 900919 (office). *E-mail:* president_office@presidency.gov.lb (office). *Website:* www.presidency.gov.lb (office).

APELIAN, Diran, BS, PhD; American materials scientist and academic; *Alcoa-Howmet Professor of Mechanical Engineering, Worcester Polytechnic Institute;* b. 28 Oct. 1945, Cairo, Egypt; m. 1976; two d.; ed Drexel Univ., Massachusetts Inst. of Tech.; worked at Bethlehem Steel's Homer Research Labs; mem. Faculty, Drexel Univ. from 1976, served as Prof., Head of Dept of Materials Eng, Assoc. Dean, Coll. of Eng and Vice-Provost; apptd Provost, Worcester Polytechnic Inst. 1990, currently Alcoa-Howmet Prof. of Mechanical Eng and Dir Metal Processing Inst.; Distinguished Visiting Prof., Dept of Chemical Eng and Materials Science, Univ. of California, Davis, 2010–; serves on several tech., corp. and editorial bds; mem. NAS; Fellow, The Minerals, Metals and Materials Soc. (Pres. 2008–09), ASM International, APMI International; mem. Nat. Acad. of Eng, Armenian Acad. of Sciences; Hon. mem. North American Die Casting Asscn, Soc. Française de Métallurgie et de Matériaux (SF2M) 2000, Hon. Prof., Northwestern Polytechnic Univ., Xian, China; Dr hc (Northwestern Polytechnic Univ., Xian); numerous honours and awards, including AFS Howard Taylor Gold Medal 1987, AFS Scientific Merit Award 1990, ASM Henry Marion Howe Medal 1990, TMS Champion H. Mathewson Gold Medal 1992, TMS Bruce Chalmers Award 2006, Gordon Prize, Nat. Acad. of Eng (co-recipient) 2016. *Publications:* more than 500 papers in professional journals. *Address:* Washburn Shops 329, Metal Processing Institute, Worcester Polytechnic Institute, 100 Institute Road, Worcester, MA 01609-2280 (office); Department of Chemical Engineering and Materials Science, 3098 Bainer Hall, University of California, Davis, CA 95616, USA (office). *Telephone:* (508) 831-5992 (Worcester) (office); (530) 752-3685 (Davis) (office). *E-mail:* dapelian@wpi.edu (office). *Website:* www.wpi.edu (office); engineering .ucdavis.edu (office).

APELOIG, Yitzhak, BSc, MSc, PhD; Israeli chemist and research institute administrator; *Professor of Chemistry, Technion—Israel Institute of Technology;* b. 1 Sept. 1944, Buchara, Uzbekistan; m. Zipora Zaltzberg; two s.; ed Hebrew Univ. of Jerusalem; family emigrated to Israel 1947; Postdoctoral Research Fellow, Princeton Univ., USA 1974–76; joined Faculty of Chem., Technion—Israel Inst. of Tech. 1976, Full Prof. 1988–, Chair incumbent 1993–, Dean, Faculty of Chem. 1995–99, Pres. Technion 2001–09; Visiting DAAD (Deutscher Akademischer Austausch Dienst—German Academic Exchange Service) Fellow and Prof., Universität Erlangen-Nornberg 1979, 1985, 1992; Visiting Prof., Tel-Aviv Univ. 1983, 1986, Cornell Univ., USA 1983–84; Louis Klein Visiting Professorship in Australian Univs 1986; Visiting DAAD Prof., Technische Universität Berlin 1985, 1991; Visiting JSPS (Japan Soc. for the Promotion of Science) Prof., Kyushu Univ. 1991, Sendai Univ. 1999; Visiting Alexander von Humboldt Prof. 1994, Technische Universität Berlin and Universität Ulm 1997; Visiting Prof., Univ. of Utah, USA 2000; Co-founder and Co-Dir Lise Meitner Center for Computational Chem. 1996–; Chair. Asscn of Univ. Pres in Israel 2004; Chair. IUPAC Conf. on Physical Organic Chem., Haifa 1990, Fourth World Congress of Theoretically Oriented Chemists, Jerusalem 1996, Symposium on Frontiers in Electronic Structure Calculations, Haifa 1998; mem. International Acad. of Quantum Molecular Science 2015; mem. Acting Bd Israel Chemical Soc.; mem. Editorial Bds Journal of the Chemical Soc., Perkin Transactions II, Progress in Physical Organic Chemistry, Journal of Computational Chemistry, Theoretical Chemical Accounts, Silicon Chemistry, Molecules; Hon. Foreign mem. American Acad. of Arts and Sciences 2010; Order of Merit (Germany), Bundespräsident Christian Wulff 2011; Dr hc (Tech. Univ. of Berlin) 2006; Pres.'s Prize for Distinction in Chem. Studies, Hebrew Univ., Jerusalem, Yashinski Prize for Distinguished PhD Thesis, Hebrew Univ. 1974, Bat-Sheba de Rothschild Fellow 1977–78, Technion Award for Academic Excellence 1988, Henri Gutwirth Prize for Excellence in Research, Technion 1991, 1993, Sr Scientist Exchange Fellow (Italy) 1993, granted a Minerva Center in Computational Quantum Chem. 1996, Distinguished Teacher Award, Technion Student Asscn 1986, 1993, 1997, JSPS Sr Visiting Prof. Award 1991, 1999, Alexander von Humboldt–Lise Meitner Sr Research Award 1994–99, 2010, Coulson Lecturer, Univ. of Georgia, USA 2002, Israel Chemical Soc. Prize 2002, Wacker Silicone Award 2007, Fredric Stanely Kipping Award in Silicon Chem., ACS 2010, August Wilhelm von Hofmann Dekmünze (German Chemical Soc. 2012. *Publications include:* more than 190 publs in int. scientific journals on organosilicon chem., computational chem., mechanistic organic chem., reactive intermediates; co-ed four books (with Z. Rappoport) on Chemistry of Organic Silicon Compounds, one book (with Z. Rappoport) on Chemistry of Organic Germanium, Tin and Lead Compounds and two special journal issues dedicated to computational chem. *Address:* Department of Chemistry, Technion—Israel Institute of Technology, Technion City, Haifa 32000, Israel (office). *Telephone:* (4) 8293721 (office). *Fax:* (4) 8294601 (office). *E-mail:* apeloig@tx.technion.ac.il (office). *Website:* www.admin .technion.ac.il (office).

APICELLA, Lorenzo Franco, BA, DipArch, RIBA, AIA, FRSA; Italian architect and designer; *Partner Emeritus, Pentagram Design Ltd;* b. 4 Feb. 1957, Ravello; s. of Belfiore Carmine Apicella and Carmina Apicella (née Nolli); one d.; ed Univ. of Nottingham, Canterbury Coll. of Art, Royal Coll. of Art, UK; Asst Architect, Skidmore Owings & Merill, Houston, Tex., USA 1981; Project Architect, CZWG Architects, London 1982; Consultant Architect, Visiting Lecturer, Canterbury Coll. of Art 1983–86; Head of Architecture Interiors and Exhbn Design, Imagination, London 1986–89, f. Apicella Assocs Architecture & Design, London 1989; Partner, Pentagram Design Ltd, London and San Francisco 1998–2017, now Partner Emer.; Founder Apicella Studio 2017–; fmr External Examiner, Oxford Brookes School of Architecture, UCE Birmingham School of Design, Royal Coll. of Art, London; mem. RIBA, AIA, RSA; Design Week Annual Awards Winner 1990, 1991, Designers Minerva Award 1993, RIBA Award 1999, Aluminium Imagination Awards 1993, 1997, IDSA Award 2001, Art Directors Club 80th Annual Awards 2001. *Address:* Pentagram Design SF, 220 Montgomery Street, Suite 865, San Francisco, CA 94104, USA (office); Apicella Studio, The Flood Building, 870 Market Street, Suite #1061, San Francisco, CA 94102, USA (office). *Telephone:* (415) 398-4063 (office); (415) 373-6623 (office). *E-mail:* apicella@pentagram.com (office); info@apicellastudio.com (office). *Website:* www.pentagram.com (office); www.apicellastudio.com/studio (office).

APOSTOLAKIS, Adm. (retd) Evangelos; Greek politician and fmr naval officer; *Minister of National Defence;* b. 1957, Rethymnon, Crete; m. Despina Maggelaki; two s.; ed Hellenic Naval Acad., Underwater Disaster Man. Submarine School, Advanced Mine Warfare School, Belgium, Amphibious Warfare School, USA; commissioned as Ensign in Hellenic Navy 1980, roles include Commanding Officer, MSC HS ATALANTI, MSCHS KISSA and FFGH HS NAVARINON (warships), Adjutant to Minister of Nat. Defence, Dir of Admin, Souda Naval Base, Chief of Staff, Sr Naval Command Aegean, Deputy Chief of Staff, STRIKEFOR-NATO (NATO naval force), Commdr, Underwater Demolition Command (elite special warfare unit) 1998–2001, Dir, Hellenic Navy Gen. Staff Personnel Branch 2009, Chief of Hellenic Navy Gen. Staff 2013–15, Chief of Hellenic Nat. Defence Gen. Staff 2015–19, Hon. Chief of Staff 2019; Minister of Nat. Defence 2019–; Grand Cross, Order of the Phoenix (Greece), Commdr, Order of Honour (Greece), Commdr, Ordre nat. du Mérite (France), Grosses Verdienstkreuz mit Stern (Germany). *Address:* Ministry of National Defence, Odos Mesogeion 227–231, Holargos, 155 61 Athens, Greece (office). *Telephone:* (210) 6598100 (office). *Fax:* (210) 850060 (home). *E-mail:* minister@mod.mil.gr (office). *Website:* www.mod.mil .gr (office).

APOTHEKER, Léo, BA; German business executive; *Vice-Chairman of the Supervisory Board, Schneider Electric SA;* b. 18 Sept. 1953, Aachen; ed Hebrew Univ., Jerusalem, Israel; began career at SAP 1988, worked in a variety of positions, mem. Exec. Bd 2002–10, served as Head of North American operations, Pres. of Global Customer Solutions and Operations, Deputy CEO and Co-CEO, CEO SW Europe Region –1999, Pres. SAP EMEA (Europe, Middle East and Africa) 1999–2002, CEO and Founder SAP France and SAP Belgium, CEO SAP –2010; Founding Pres. and COO ECsoft BV (European venture capital start-up) 1992–94; mem. Bd of Dirs, Pres. and CEO Hewlett-Packard 2010–11; also held exec. positions at ABP Partners, McCormack & Dodge Europe, S.W.I.F.T. and Altex GmbH; Vice-Chair. Supervisory Bd Schneider Electric SA; Chair. KMD (Denmark) 2012–; Non-Exec. Chair. Advisory Bd Signavio GmbH 2016–; mem. Bd of Dirs GT Nexus; Ind. Dir Steria 2012–; mem. Bd PlaNet Finance (non-profit org.); Chevalier, Légion d'honneur 2007. *Address:* Schneider Electric SA, 35 rue Joseph Monier, 92500 Rueil Malmaison, France (office). *Telephone:* 1-41-29-70-00 (office). *Fax:* 1-41-29-71-00 (office). *E-mail:* info@schneider-electric.com (office). *Website:* www .schneider-electric.com (office).

APPIAH, Kwame Anthony, PhD; American (b. British) academic and writer; *Professor of Philosophy and Law, New York University;* b. (Kwame Anthony Akroma-Ampim Kusi Appiah), 8 May 1954, London, England; s. of Joe Appiah and Peggy Appiah; m. Henry David Finder; ed Ullenwood Manor School for Boys, Port Regis and Bryanston School, UK, Univ. of Cambridge, UK; raised in Ghana; taught at Univ. of Ghana; has held positions as Lecturer or Prof. of Philosophy and/or Prof. of African Studies and African-American Studies, Univ. of Cambridge, Yale Univ., Cornell Univ., Duke Univ., Harvard Univ. 1991–2002; Laurance S. Rockefeller Univ. Prof. of Philosophy and Univ. Center for Human Values, Princeton Univ. 2002–13; Prof. of Philosophy and Law, New York Univ. 2014–; Juror, Neustadt Prize, Univ. of Oklahoma 2001; delivered BBC Reith Lectures on the theme of Mistaken Identities 2016; mem. American Philosophical Soc. 2001, American Acad. of Arts and Letters 2008; Hon. DLitt (Richmond) 2000, (Colgate) 2003, (Bard Coll.) 2004, (Fairleigh Dickinson) 2006, (Swarthmore Coll.) 2006, (Dickinson Coll.) 2008, (Columbia) 2009, (The New School) 2009, Hon. LLD (Colby Coll.) 2010, (Harvard) 2012, Hon. DHumLitt (Berea Coll.) 2010, (Occidental Coll.) 2012, (Pennsylvania) 2013; invested with chieftaincy of Ashanti people of Nyaduom (family ancestral chiefdom in Ghana); Annisfield-Wolf Book Award 1993, Herskovits Award, African Studies Asscn 1993, Annual Book Award, N American Soc. for Social Philosophy 1996, Ralph J. Bunche Award, American Political Science Asscn 1997, Gustavus Myers Center Award 1997, Phi Beta Kappa Speaker, Harvard Commencement 2000, Tanner Lecturer, Univ. of California, San Diego and Univ. of Cambridge 2001, Morehouse Coll. Candle in the Dark Award in Educ. 2003, Arthur Ross Book Award, Council on Foreign Relations 2007, Joseph B. and Toby Gittler Prize 2008, Book Award, New Jersey Council of Humanities 2011, Nat. Humanities Medal 2011. *Publications include:* Assertion and Conditionals 1985, For Truth in Semantics 1986, Necessary Questions: An Introduction to Philosophy 1989, Avenging Angel (novel) 1991, In My Father's House: Africa in the Philosophy of Culture (essays) (Annisfield-Wolf Book Award 1993, African Studies Asscn Herskovits Award 1993) 1992, Nobody Likes Letitia (novel) 1994, Color Consciousness: The Political Morality of Race (with Amy Gutman) (North American Soc. for Social Philosophy Annual Book Award) 1996, The Ethics of Identity 2005, Cosmopolitanism: Ethics in a World of Strangers (Council on Foreign Relations Arthur Ross Award) 2006, Experiments in Ethics 2007, Mi Cosmopolitismo 2008, The Politics of Culture, the Politics of Identity 2008, The Honor Code: How Moral Revolutions Happen 2010, Lines of Descent 2014; ed.: Early African-American Classics 1990; co-ed. (with Henry Louis Gates, Jr): Critical Perspectives Past and Present (series) 1993–, The Dictionary of Global Culture 1996, Africana: The Encyclopedia of African and African American Experience 1999; co-ed.: (with Peggy Appiah): Bu Me Bé: The Proverbs of the Akan; co-ed. (with Martin Bunzl): Buying Freedom 2007. *Leisure interest:* gardening. *Address:* Department of Philosophy, New York University, 5 Washington Place, New York, NY 10003, USA (office). *Telephone:* (212) 998-7864 (office). *Fax:* (212) 995-4179 (office). *E-mail:* anthony.appiah@nyu.edu (office); anthony.appiah@gmail.com. *Website:* philosophy.fas.nyu.edu/page/home (office); www.appiah.net (home).

APPLEBY, Malcolm Arthur, MBE; British artist; b. 6 Jan. 1946, Beckenham, Kent; s. of James William Appleby and Marjory Stokes; m. Philippa Swann; one d.; ed Hawes Down Co. Secondary Modern School, Beckenham School of Art, Ravensbourne Coll. of Art, Cen. School of Arts and Crafts, Sir John Cass School of Art, Royal Coll. of Art; began career as an engraver 1968; Littledale Scholar 1969, Liveryman Worshipful Co. of Goldsmiths 1991; represented in collections at Birmingham City Art Gallery, Victoria and Albert Museum, London, Worshipful Co. of Goldsmiths, London, Royal Armouries, Contemporary Art Soc., London, British Museum, London, Fitzwilliam Museum, Cambridge, East Midland Arts, Aberdeen Art Gallery and Museums, Perth Art Gallery and Museum, Royal Museum, Edinburgh, Hunterian Art Gallery, Univ. of Glasgow, Nat. Maritime Museum, Finland, Aland Maritime Museum, Finland, Adelaide Maritime Museum, Australia; Founder-mem. and Chair. British Art Postage Stamp Soc.; fmr Chair. Crathes, Drumoak and Durris Community Council; mem. Hand Engravers Asscn, British Art Medal Soc., Soc. for Protection of Ancient Buildings;

Hon. mem. Strathtay and Grandtully SWRI; Hon. DLitt (Heriot-Watt Univ.) 2006; Gold Medal, Silver Award, Annual Goldsmiths Craft and Design Awards. *Leisure interests:* garden, work, family. *Address:* Hand Engravers Association, PO Box 60239, London, EC1P 1QQ, England (office); Aultbeag, Grandtully, Perthshire, PH15 2QU, Scotland (home). *Telephone:* 7500-462910 (office); (1887) 840484 (home). *Fax:* (1887) 840785 (home). *E-mail:* swapp@dircon.co.uk (home). *Website:* www.handengravers.co.uk (office).

APPY, Bernard; Brazilian economist, banking executive and consultant; ed Faculty of Econs, Univ. of São Paolo, Universidade Estadual de Campinas; fmr Prof. of Econs, Pontificia Universidade Catolica do Sao Paolo (PUC-SP), Unicamp; Partner, Luciano Coutinho & Assocs (consultancy) 1995–2002, Dir Public Policy & Taxation 2011–14; joined Ministry of Finance 1994, served as Sec. for Econ. Policies 2005–06, 2007–08, Deputy Minister of Finance 2003–05, 2006–07; Econ. Adviser to Pres. of Brazil 2008; Chair. Banco do Brasil SA –2009; Dir Strategy and Planning at BM&FBOVESPA 2009–11; Dir Tax Citizenship Center (CCiF) 2015–; fmr mem. Bd of Dirs The Brazilian Devt Bank (BNDES); Member of the Fiscal Council Vale SA 2006–. *Address:* R. Itapeva, 26 Cj.1701, 01332-000 São Paolo SP, Brazil (office). *Telephone:* (11) 2305-2630. *E-mail:* ccif@ccif.com.br. *Website:* ccif.com.br.

APTED, Michael David, CMG; British film director; b. 10 Feb. 1941, Aylesbury, Bucks.; m. 1st (divorced); two s. (one deceased); m. 2nd Dana Stevens (divorced); one s.; one d. with Tania Mellis; ed Downing Coll., Cambridge; started career as researcher, Granada TV 1963, then worked as investigative reporter for World in Action; feature film dir 1970s–; Pres. Directors Guild of America 2003–09. *Films include:* The Triple Echo 1972, Stardust 1975, The Squeeze 1977, Agatha 1979, The Coal Miner's Daughter 1980, Continental Divide 1981, Gorky Park 1983, Firstborn 1984, Critical Condition, Gorillas in the Mist 1988, Class Action 1990, Incident at Oglala, Thunderheart 1992, Blink 1993, Moving the Mountain 1993, Nell 1994, Extreme Measures 1996, Inspirations 1997, Me and Isaac Newton 1999, The World Is Not Enough 1999, Enigma 2001, Enough 2002, Lipstick 2002, Amazing Grace 2006, The Official Film of the 2006 FIFA World Cup 2006, The Chronicles of Narnia: The Voyage of the Dawn Treader 2010, Chasing Mavericks 2012, Bending the Light (documentary) 2014, Unlocked 2015. *Television includes:* (dir) episodes of Coronation Street 1963–64, Haunted 1967, There's a hole in your dustbin, Delilah 1968, The Dustbinmen 1969, Big Breadwinner Hog 1969, comedy series The Lovers 1970, Another Sunday and Sweet F.A. 1970, children's series Folly Foot 1971, Play for Today 1972–77, The Collection 1976, P'tang, Yang, Kipperbang (film) 1982, Kisses at Fifty, Poor Girl, Jack Point, New York News 1994, Up documentary series including 28 Up and 35 Up, 42: Forty-two Up 1998, Always Outnumbered 1998, Nathan Dixon 1999, Married in America 2002, Rome (series, Directors' Guild of America Best Dir of Dramatic Series) 2006, 49 Up 2005, Married in America 2 2006, 56 Up 2012, Ray Donovan (series) 2013, Masters of Sex 2013–14, Reckless (series) 2014. *Publications:* 7 Up 1999. *Address:* c/o United Agents, 12–26 Lexington Street, London, W1F 0LE, England (office). *Telephone:* (20) 3214-0800 (office). *Fax:* (20) 3214-0801 (office). *E-mail:* info@unitedagents.co.uk (office). *Website:* unitedagents.co.uk (office).

AQUINO, Benigno Simeon 'Noynoy' Cojuangco, III, AB (Econs); Philippine politician and fmr head of state; b. 8 Feb. 1960; only s. of Senator Benigno 'Ninoy' Aquino, Jr (assassinated 1983) and fmr Pres. Corazon Aquino; brother of Kris Aquino (TV host and actress); ed Ateneo de Manila Univ.; joined family in Boston, USA in exile following univ.; brief tenure as mem. of Philippine Business for Social Progress 1983; retail sales supervisor and youth promotions asst for Nike Philippines 1985–86; later an asst for advertising and promotion for Mondragon Philippines; Vice-Pres. family-owned Intra-Strata Assurance Corpn 1986; wounded by rebel soldiers led by Gregorio Honasan in failed coup attempt during his mother's presidency 28 Aug. 1987; worked for Cen. Azucarera de Tarlac sugar refinery owned by Cojuangco clan 1993; Rep. for 2nd Dist of Tarlac Prov., House of Reps 1998–2007 (re-elected 2001, 2004), mem. several parl. cttees, Deputy Speaker of House of Reps 2004–06; elected to Senate of 14th Congress under banner of Genuine Opposition (GO—coalition of several parties, including own Liberal Party) 2007–10; Sec.-Gen. Liberal Party of the Philippines 1999–2002, 2004–06, Vice-Pres. for Luzon 2002–04, apptd Vice-Chair. Liberal Party of the Philippines 2006, Chair. 2010–16; Pres. of the Philippines 2010–16. *Leisure interests:* shooting, billiards, listening to mellow, bossa nova and OPM (Original Pinoy Music).

ARABI, Nabil el-, LLB, LLM, JSD; Egyptian lawyer, diplomatist, international organization official, government official and judge; b. 15 March 1935, Cairo; m.; two s. one d.; ed Cairo Univ., New York Univ. Law School, USA; fmr Rep. of Egypt to various UN bodies, including Gen. Ass., Security Council, ECOSOC, Comm. on Human Rights, Conf. on Disarmament; Legal Adviser to Egyptian del. to UN Middle East Peace Conf., Geneva 1973–75; Dir Legal and Treaties Dept, Ministry of Foreign Affairs 1976–78, 1983–87; Amb. to India 1981–83; led Egyptian del. to Taba talks 1986–89; Deputy Perm. Rep. to UN, New York 1978–81, Perm. Rep. 1991–99; Perm. Rep., UN Office at Geneva 1987–91; apptd by ICC as Arbitrator in a dispute concerning Suez Canal 1989; Judge, Judicial Tribunal of Org. of Arab Petroleum Exporting Countries (OAPEC) 1990–; Visiting Scholar, Robert F. Wagner Grad. School of Public Service, New York Univ. 1992–93; apptd Partner, Zaki Hashem and Partners, Cairo 1998, currently Sr Partner; Commr UN Compensation Comm., Geneva 1999–2001; Pres. Ordinary Arbitration Div., Court of Arbitration for Sport; Dir Regional Cairo Centre for Int. Commercial Arbitration 2008–; Minister of Foreign Affairs March–June 2011; Sec.-Gen. League of Arab States 2011–16; mem. Governing Bd Stockholm Int. Peace Research Inst. 2000–10, Egyptian Bar Asscn; mem. Int. Law Comm. 1994–2001, Int. Court of Justice 2001–06, Perm. Court of Arbitration 2005–; Kt of Italian Repub. 1962, Order of the Repub. (Egypt) 1976. *Publications include:* several articles on UN Charter, peacekeeping and various int. issues. *Leisure interest:* tennis. *Address:* c/o League of Arab States, PO Box 11642, Arab League Building, Tahrir Square, Cairo 11211, Egypt (office).

ARAD, Ron, RA; British designer and architect; b. 24 April 1951, Tel-Aviv, Israel; ed Jerusalem Acad. of Art, Architectural Asscn, London; Founder One Off Ltd 1981–94, Ron Arad Assocs 1989–; Prof. of Product Design, Hochschule, Vienna 1994–97; Prof. of Design Product, RCA 1997–2009; Oribe Art and Design Award, Japan 2001, Giò Ponti Int. Design Award, Denver, CO 2001, Barcelona Primavera Int. Award for Design 2001, Architektur & Wohnen Designer of the Year 2004, London Design Week Medal for design excellence 2011. *Achievements:* public art works including Vortext, Seoul, Repub. of Korea, Kesher Sculpture, Tel Aviv Univ. *Leisure interests:* tennis, ping-pong. *Address:* Arad Associates, 62 Chalk Farm Road, London, NW1 8AN, England (office). *Telephone:* (20) 7284-4963 (office). *Fax:* (20) 7379-0499 (office). *E-mail:* info@ronarad.com (office). *Website:* www.ronarad.co.uk (office).

ARAGALL GARRIGA, Giacomo Jaume; Spanish singer (tenor); b. 6 June 1939, Barcelona; s. of Ramon Aragall and Paola Garriga; m. Luisa Aragall 1964; three s.; has sung in several opera productions at Verona 1965, Covent Garden 1968, Metropolitan Opera 1968, San Francisco 1973, Budapest, Venice, Genoa, Palermo, Parma, Modena, Naples, Rome and Turin; f. Concurso Internacional de Canto Jaume Aragall 1994; mem. jury, Concurso Internacional de Canto Tenor Viñas, Barcelona 2017; winner, Voci Verdian, Busseto, Peseta de Oro and Medalla de Plata for appearing at 1992 Barcelona Olympics, Medalla de Oro de Bellas Artes 1992. *Operas include:* Gerusalemme 1963, L'amico Fritz, Esclarmonde 1974, Joan Sutherland 1975, Donizetti's Caterina Cornaro, Lucia di Lammermoor, Madama Butterfly, La Favorita, La Traviata, Werther, Faust, Tosca, Manon, Don Carlo, Adriana Lecouvreur, Un Ballo in Maschera and Simon Boccanegra. *Address:* Concurso Internacional de Canto Jaume Aragall, Sra. Silvia Gasset, C/ Rocafort, 39-1st 2nd, 08015 Barcelona, Spain (office).

ARAI, Jun; Japanese business executive; *President and CEO, Showa Shell Sekiyu K.K.;* b. 28 Feb. 1959; joined Shell Sekiyu K.K. 1983 (acquired by Showa Oil Co. Ltd to form Showa Shell Sekiyu K.K. 1985), Man., Man. Information System 1999–2001, Man., Treasury 2001–02, Gen. Man., Man. Information Service 2002–04, Gen. Man., Finance and Accounting 2004–05, Exec. Officer and Gen. Man., Finance and Accounting 2005–06, Dir, Finance and Accounting 2006–07, Man. Dir 2007–08, Acting Pres. and Rep. Dir Showa Shell Sekiyu K.K. Aug.–Nov. 2008, Rep. Dir 2013–14, Group Chief Operating Officer 2013–14, currently Pres. and CEO; Outside Co. Dir Daiwa SB Investments, Ltd 2016–; Outside Co. Auditor, Kyowa Hakko Kirin Co. Ltd 2017–. *Address:* Showa Shell Sekiyu K.K., Daiba Frontier Building, 2-3-2, Daiba, Minato-ku, Tokyo 135-8074, Japan (office). *Telephone:* (3) 5531-5591 (office). *Fax:* (3) 5531-5598 (office). *E-mail:* info@showa-shell.co.jp (office). *Website:* www.showa-shell.co.jp (office).

ARAIZA ANDRADE, José Francisco; Mexican singer (tenor) and teacher; b. 4 Oct. 1950, Mexico City; s. of José Araiza and Guadalupe Andrade; m. 1st Vivian Jaffray (divorced); one s. one d.; m. 2nd Ethery Inasaridse; one s. one d.; ed Univ. of Mexico City, Nat. School of Music, Munich Acad. of Music; first engagement as lyric tenor in Karlsruhe, Germany 1974; debut as Ferrando in Così fan Tutte 1975; debut at Zurich Opera House with Almaviva 1976, perm. mem. 1978–; has performed at major opera houses in London, Paris, Munich, Berlin, Madrid, Barcelona, Milan, Parma, New York, Chicago, San Francisco, Tokyo as well as in concerts or recitals; named Kammersänger by Vienna State Opera 1988; has participated in festivals of Salzburg (debut under von Karajan 1980), Hohenems, Bayreuth, Edinburgh, Pesaro, Verona, Macerata, Aix-en-Provence, Orange, Garmisch; Prof., Staatliche Hochschule für Musik Stuttgart 2003–16, Int. Opernstudio IOS, Zurich 2005–13; Dir Int. Hugo Wolf Akad. 2007–09; Bertelsmann Neue Stimmen (Jury and Master-classes) 1998–; Artist-in-Residence, Boston Univ. Coll. of Fine Arts 2013; Dr hc (Universidad Michoacana de San Nicolás de Hildalgo) 2017 Deutscher Schallplattenpreis, Orphée d'Or, Mozart Medal, Universidad Autonoma de México (UNAM), Otello d'Oro, Goldener Merkur, Best Performer Award, Munich 1996, Dr A. Ortiz Tirado Medal (Sonora, Mexico) 2008, Gold Medal, Instituto Nacional de Bellas Artes y Literatura, Compañia Nacional de Opera Mexico City for Lifetime Achievement 2011, Grand Prix de la Culture (Vienna, Austria) 2018. *Films include:* videos: Manon, Faust, La Cenerentola (two), Falstaff, Die Entführung aus dem Serail, Don Giovanni, Die Schöpfung, Recital Tokio, Die Zauberflöte (two), Così fan tutte, Mozart Gala Verona 1 & 2, Bach Magnificat, Francisco Araiza: I am a Romantic, Fast ein Gentleman (TV film), Schumann's Dichterliebe, Schubert's Winterreise. *Television includes:* Melodien zum Muttertag 2000, Gala der Europahilfe 2000, Kein Schöner Land 2000, Zauber der Musik mit André Rieu 2002, Sternstunden der Musik 2003. *Recordings include:* The Magic Flute, Faust, Das Lied von der Erde, Die schöne Müllerin, Der Freischütz, Maria Stuarda, Don Pasquale, Die Schöpfung, Mozart Requiem, Don Giovanni, Idomeneo, Rossini's Messa di Gloria, 200 Jahre La Fenice, Die Winterreise, La Bohème, Berlioz's Requiem, Verdi, No Limits from Mozart to Wagner 2013. *Address:* c/o Opern-Agentur and Artists' Mgt, Tal 15, 80331 Munich, Germany (office). *Telephone:* (89) 29161662 (office). *Fax:* (89) 29161667 (office). *E-mail:* tschaidse@opern-agentur.com (office); faraiza@aol.com. *Website:* www.opern-agentur.de (office); www.franciscoaraiza.com.

ARAKAWA, Shoshi, BA; Japanese business executive; *Advisor, Bridgestone Corporation;* b. 8 April 1944; ed Tokyo Univ.; joined Bridgestone Tire Co. 1968, Man. Exec. Secretarial Office 1988–91, Gen. Man. F21 Planning and Promotion Project Group 1991–92, Man. Dir Bridgestone Tire Co. Thailand 1992–97, mem. Bd of Dirs 1997–, Gen. Man. China Dept 1997–2001, Dir Asia and Oceania Div. 1998–2001, CEO and Chair. Bridgestone/Firestone Europe SA 2001–06, Sr Vice-Pres. 2005–06, Chair., Pres., CEO and Rep. Dir Bridgestone Corpn 2006–12, Chair. 2012–13, Advisor 2013–, also served as Chief Risk-Management Officer; mem. Bd of Dirs Tokyo Univ. of Foreign Studies 1997–, Kirin Holdings 2015–; Commdr, Order of Leopold (Belgium) 2009. *Address:* Bridgestone Corpn, 10-1, Kyobashi 1-chome, Chuo-ku, Tokyo 104-8340, Japan (office). *Telephone:* (3) 3567-0111 (office). *Fax:* (3) 3535-2553 (office). *E-mail:* info@bridgestone.co.jp (office). *Website:* www.bridgestone.co.jp (office).

ARAKI, Minoru S. (Sam), BS, MS; American aeronautics engineer (retd); b. 12 July 1931, Saratoga, Calif.; ed Stanford Univ.; joined Lockheed Missiles & Space Co. in 1958 as Sr Scientist, held numerous positions including Asst Chief Engineer, Devt 1975–76, Dir Systems Eng 1976–78, Dir Advanced Systems, Space Systems Division (SSD) 1978–83, Vice-Pres. Space Systems Div., Vice-Pres. and Program Man. Milstar programs 1983, Vice-Pres. and Asst Gen. Man. SSD 1985–87, Pres. and Gen. Man. SSD 1987–88, also a Vice-Pres. of Lockheed Corpn, Exec. Vice-Pres. Lockheed's Missiles and Space Systems Group 1988–95, Pres. Lockheed Martin Missiles & Space Co. 1995–2007 (retd); currently Founder, CEO and Pres. ST-Infonox, Inc.; Chair. ECOPIA Farms (organic farming co.); mem. Nat. Acad. of Eng; Fellow, American Astronautical Soc.; AIAA Von Braun Award for Excellence in Space Program Man. 2004, Charles Stark Draper Prize, Nat. Acad. of

Eng (co-recipient) 2005, named a Pioneer of Nat. Reconnaissance by Nat. Reconnaissance Office, Distinguished Lifetime Achievement Award, Chinese Inst. of Engineers–USA 2007. *Address:* ECOPIA Farms, 1520 Dell Avenue, Campbell, CA 95008, USA. *Telephone:* (408) 871-9091.

ARAM I (KESHISHIAN), His Holiness, Catholicos of Cilicia, MDiv, STM, PhD; Lebanese ecclesiastic; *President, Middle East Council of Churches;* b. 8 March 1947, Beirut; ed Seminary of the Armenian Apostolic Church, Antelias, Ecumenical Inst. of Bossey, Switzerland, Near East School of Theology, Beirut, American Univ. of Beirut, Fordham Univ., New York, USA; ordained priest 1968; apptd Rep. for Ecumenical Relations, Catholicosate of the See of Cilicia of Armenian Apostolic Church 1972, Catholicos 1995–; named to WCC Faith and Order Comm. 1975; locum tenens of diocese of Lebanon 1978; Primate 1979; ordained Bishop 1980; elected to Cen. Cttee of WCC 1983, youngest person and first Orthodox to be elected Moderator of Cen. Cttee of WCC 1991–2005; Founder-mem. Middle East Council of Churches 1974, Pres. 2007–; Founder-mem. Oriental Orthodox-Eastern Orthodox Theological Dialogue, Oriental Orthodox-Reformed Theological Dialogue, Orthodox-Evangelical Dialogue; Hon. Pres. World Religions for Peace, World Religions Museum Foundation, Hon. mem. Pro-Oriente Catholic Ecumenical Foundation, Vienna, Austria; numerous decorations from states, churches and orgs. *Publications include:* Nerses the Gracious: Theologian and Ecumenist 1974, The Witness of the Armenian Church in a Diaspora Situation 1978, The True Image of the Armenian Church 1979, With the Will of Re-Building 1983, With the People 1989, Conciliar Fellowship: A Common Goal 1991, Orthodox Perspectives on Mission 1992, Towards the 1700th Anniversary of the Christianization of Armenia 1996, The Challenge to be a Church in a Changing World 1997, Jesus Christ: The Son of God – the Son of Man 1999, Church, Nation and Homeland 1999, In search of Ecumenical Vision 2000, L'eglise face aux grands défis 2000, The Armenian Church Beyond the 1700th Anniversary 2002, The Mission of Faith 2003, Justice, Paix, Réconciliation 2003, The Christian Witness at the Crossroads in the Middle East 2004, Der Zor: A National Sanctuary 2005, The Dignity of Serving 2005, For a Church Beyond Its Walls 2006, Pour un Monde Transformé 2006, To Enrich Life with Values 2010, A Journey of Faith, Hope and Vision 2011, Taking the Church to the People 2011, Issues and Perspectives 2013. *Address:* Catholicosate of Cilicia, PO Box 70317, Antelias, Lebanon (office). *Telephone:* (4) 410001 (office); (4) 410003 (office). *Fax:* (4) 419724 (office). *E-mail:* catholicos@armenianorthodoxchurch.org (office). *Website:* www.armenianorthodoxchurch.org (office).

ARAMBURUZABALA LARREGUI, María Asunción; Mexican business executive; *President and CEO, Tresalia Capital;* b. 2 May 1963, Mexico City; d. of Pablo Aramburuzabala Ocaranza; granddaughter of Felix Aramburuzabala, Co-founder of Mexican brewery Grupo Modelo; m. 1st Paulo Patricio Zapata Navarro 1982 (divorced 1997); two c.; m. 2nd Amb. Antonio O. Garza, Jr 2005 (divorced 2010); ed Instituto Tecnológico Autónomo de México (ITAM); worked as accountant at Mexican securities firm; Partner, Vice-Chair. and mem. Exec. Cttee Grupo Modelo SA de CV (brewing co.) 1996–; Vice-Chair. and mem. Exec. Cttee Grupo Televisa SA 2000–; Pres. and CEO Tresalia Capital SA de CV; Vice-Chair. DIFA; Chair. Tresalia Educación; Chair. Siemens Mexico (first woman) 2003–06; mem. Mexican Stock Exchange Bd (first woman) 2003–06; mem. Bd of Dirs Grupo Financiero Banamex-Accival, SA de CV, Banco Nacional de Mexico, SA, América Móvil, SA de CV, Empresas ICA, Aeromexico, BCBA Impulse, KIO Networks, GA&A Group; Dir (non-exec.), Anheuser-Busch InBev SA/NV 2014–; mem. New York Stock Exchange Advisory Cttee; mem. ITAM's Business School Advisory Cttee, David Rockefeller Center for Latin American Studies at Harvard Univ. Advisory Bd, Advisory Bd Ministry of Educ., Ministry of the Economy Advisory Bd for Int. Business Trade; The Leading Women Entrepreneurs of the World, Star Group 1998, Private Sector Professional Merit Award, ITAM's Alumni Asscn 2003, The Golden Plate Award, Acad. of Achievement 2004, 2000 Women of the Year, Mexican Expansion Magazine, Mont Blanc Businesswoman Award 2004, Women's Medal, Anahuac Univ. 2005. *Address:* Tresalia Capital SA de CV, Prado Sur 4th Floor, Lomas de Chapultepec, 11000 Mexico City, DF (office); Grupo Televisa SA, 2000 Avenida Vasco De Quiroga Santa Fe, 01210 Mexico City, DF, Mexico (office). *Telephone:* (55) 5261-2000 (Televisa) (office). *Fax:* (55) 5261-2494 (Televisa) (office). *Website:* www.televisa.com (office).

ARAMYAN, Vardan S.; Armenian economist and politician; b. 4 Dec. 1975, Yerevan; m.; two c.; ed Yerevan State Econ. Univ., Fletcher School, Tufts Univ., USA; served in Armenian army (rank of sergeant) 1997–98; Specialist with Monetary Div., Monetary Policy Dept, Central Bank of Repub. of Armenia 1999–2002, Specialist, Div. for Relations with State Budget 1999–2002, Sr Specialist, Real Sector Analysis and Modelling Div. 2002–03, Head, Dept for External Econ. Relations 2003–08; Deputy Minister of Finance 2008–13; First Deputy Chief of Staff, Office of the Pres. 2013–16; Minister of Finance 2016–18 (resgnd); Guest Lecturer on Int. Trade, French Univ. of Armenia 2007–11; Anania Shirakatsi Medal 2011, Medal for Services to the Fatherland (Second Class) 2015. *Publications include:* numerous articles and research papers in the fields of monetary and exchange rate policies, fiscal policy and fiscal sustainability. *Address:* c/o Ministry of Finance, 0010 Yerevan, M. Adamyan poghots 1, Armenia (office).

ARANA SEVILLA, Mario, PhD; Nicaraguan economist, government official and central banker; *CEO, Asociación de Productores y Exportadores de Nicaragua—APEN;* ed Univ. of Texas, USA; Minister of Devt, Industry and Commerce 2002–04, of Finance and Public Credit 2005–06; Pres. Central Bank of Nicaragua 2006–07, fmr Gov. for Nicaragua at IMF, World Bank, IDB, Int. Finance Corpn; Exec. Dir Nicaraguan Foundation for Econ. and Social Devt (FUNIDES), Managua 2007–11; CEO Asociación de Productores y Exportadores de Nicaragua—APEN (Asscn of Nicaraguan Exporters) 2016–; Past Fellow, Centre on Pacific Economies, Grad. School of Int. Relations and Pacific Studies; Coordinator, Presidential Comm. on Competitiveness; mem. Bd of Dirs Ram Power Corp. 2007–14, Central American Investments SA (INVERCASA) 2014–. *Address:* Asociación de Productores y Exportadores de Nicaragua—APEN (Association of Nicaraguan Exporters), Planes de Altamira No.1 Contiguo a la Alianza Francesa, Managua 14034, Nicaragua (office). *E-mail:* apen@apen.org.ni (office). *Website:* apen.org.ni (office).

ARANDA, Julieta, BFA, MFA; Mexican artist and editor; b. 1975, Mexico City; ed School of Visual Arts, Columbia Univ., USA; lives and works in Berlin and New York; with Anton Vidokle and Brian Kuan Wood, began a set of projects related to their interests, including an art collective (e-flux), a school (unitednationsplaza; Night School), an archive (e-flux video rental; Martha Rosler Library) and an activist group (The Next Documenta Should Be Curated By an Artist); co-f., with Anton Vidokle, a time bank for artists, curators, writers and others in the arts to exchange their time and skills 2008; Artist-in-Residence, Iaspis, the International Artists Studio Program in Stockholm 2007, International Residence at Recollets, Paris 2008. *Address:* e-flux, 311 East Broadway, New York, NY 10002, USA (office). *E-mail:* info@e-flux.com (office). *Website:* www.e-flux.com (office).

ARANGIO-RUIZ, Gaetano; Italian professor of law; b. 10 July 1919, Milan; s. of Vincenzo Arangio-Ruiz and Ester Mauri Arangio-Ruiz; ed Univ. of Naples; Prof. of Int. Law, Univ. of Camerino 1952–54, Univ. of Padua 1955–67, Univ. of Bologna 1968–74; Prof. of Int. Law, Univ. of Rome 1974–, now Prof. Emer.; mem. Iran-United States Claims Tribunal, The Hague 1989–; Visiting Prof., Virginia Univ. Law School 1965, European Cen., Johns Hopkins School of Advanced Int. Studies 1967–75; Lecturer, Hague Acad. of Int. Law 1962, 1972, 1977, 1984; mem. UN Int. Law Comm. 1985–96; Special Rapporteur on State Responsibility 1987–96; mem. Int. Law Inst.; Dr hc (Univ. Panthéon-Assas, Paris II, France) 1997; Giuseppe Capograssi Prize 1990, Scanno Law Prize 2001. *Publications include:* Rapporti contrattuali fra Stati e organizzazione internazionale 1950, Gli enti soggetti 1951, Sula dinamica della base sociale 1954, The Normative Role of the UN General Assembly (Hague Rec.) Vol. III 1972, Human Rights and Non-Intervention in the Helsinki Final Act (Hague Rec.) Vol. IV 1977, The UN Declaration on Friendly Relations and the System of the Sources of International Law 1979, le Domaine réservé, General Course in International Law (Hague Rec.) Vol. V 1990, Non-Appearance Before the International Court of Justice (report to the Int. Law Inst.) International Law Institute Yearbook 1991, On the Nature of the International Personality on the Holy See, Revue Belge de Droit International 1996/2, On the Security Council's 'Law-Making', Rivista di Diritto Internazionale 2000, Dualism Revisited: International Law and Interindividual Law, Rivista di Diritto Internazionale 2003, Article 39 of the ILC First-Reading Articles on State Responsibility, *ibidem*, The ICJ Statute, The Charter and Forms of Legality Review of Security Council Decisions, Liber Amicorum Cassese 2003, Customary Law, on the theory of 'spontaneous' international custom, Droit du Pouvoir, Pouvoir du Droit 2007, International Law and Interindividual Law: New Perspectives on the Divide Between National and International Law (co-eds J. Nijman and A. Nollkaemper) 2007, La Persona Internazionale dello Stato 2008. *Address:* c/o Iran-United States Claims Tribunal, Parkweg 13, 2585 JH The Hague, Netherlands (office); Corso Trieste 51, interno 4, 00198 Rome, Italy (home). *Telephone:* (70) 3520064 (office); (06) 8559720 (home); (70) 3551371 (Netherlands) (home); (0564) 819200 (Italy) (home). *Fax:* (70) 3502456 (office). *E-mail:* dameklaassen@iusct.nl (office).

ARANGO, Jerónimo; Mexican (b. Spanish) retail executive; b. 1926, Spain; f. Bodega Aurrera discount stores 1958, through Cifra Group entered into jt venture with Wal-Mart Stores in early 1990s and co. renamed Wal-Mart de México (later Walmex), fmr Chair. and CEO, also mem. Bd of Dirs Wal-Mart (now Walmart) 1997; owner of luxury resort in Acapulco, Mexico.

ARÁOZ ESPARZA, Ántero Flores; Peruvian lawyer, politician and academic; b. 28 Feb. 1942, Lima; ed Pontifical Catholic Univ. of Peru, Univ. of the Pacific, Nat. Univ. of San Marcos; Prof., Faculty of Law, Univ. of Lima, Faculty of Law, Univ. of St Martín de Porres, Inst. of Govt, Univ. of St Martín de Porres; Expository Pres. Peruvian Inst. of Humanistic Studies; Dir Estudio Flores-Aráoz & Asociados S.C. de R.L.; Vice-Pres. Sociedad de Beneficencia Pública de Lima 1980–85; Vice-Pres. and Pres. Caja de Ahorros de Lima (Savings Bank of Lima) 1980–85; Pres. Lotteries of Lima and Callao 1980–85; Metropolitan Regidor of Lima 1987–89, Dir Caja Municipal de Crédito Popular; Nat. Deputy 1990–92, mem. Constituent Congress 1993–95, Congressman of the Repub. 1995–, re-elected 2000, 2001, 2006, mem. Consultative Cttee, Constitutional Comm. of Congress 2006–07, Consultative Comm., Ministry of Justice, Pres. Congress of the Repub. 2004–05, Pres. Constitutional Comm. Regulation of the Congress of the Repub. 2005–06; Minister of Defence 2007–08 (resgnd); mem. Peruvian Del. to Socio-Econ. Advisory Cttee (CAES) of Cartagena Agreement for several years; mem. and Pres. Partido Popular Cristiano –2007; currently mem. Orden party; columnist in various media; Hon. Prof. at several univs; Gran Cruz de la Orden José Gregorio Paz Soldán, Decoration 'Hipólito Unanue', Gran Cruz del Congreso de la República, Gran Cruz de la Orden del Sol; decorations from Colombia, Chile, Russian Fed. and Morocco; decorations of Peruvian Navy, Air Force, Nat. Police; Dr hc from several univs. *Publication:* Autoritarismo o Democracia 2006.

ARÁOZ FERNÁNDEZ, Mercedes Rosalba, BEcons, MA; Peruvian economist and politician; *Second Vice-President;* b. 5 Aug. 1961, Lima; ed Universidad del Pacífico, Lima, Univ. of Miami, USA; Peruvian Co-ordinator on Competition Policies, (APEC) 1998; Exec. Co-ordinator, Andean Project for Competitiveness (jt project between Universidad del Pacífico, Harvard Univ. and Andean Devt Fund) 2000–01; Prof. of Int. Economy, Universidad del Pacífico, also mem. Universidad del Pacífico Research Center 1994–2011; Exec. Dir Nat. Council for Competitiveness 2005–06; Minister of Foreign Commerce and Tourism 2006–09, of Production July–Dec. 2009, of Economy and Finance Dec. 2009–10; Country Rep., IDB, Mexico 2012–15; mem. Congress for Lima 2016–; Second Vice-Pres. of Peru 2016–; Pres., Council of Ministers (Prime Minister) 2017–18; mem. Peruanos por el Kambio (PPK). *Address:* Office of the Vice President, Presidential Palace, Plaza Mayor, Lima (office); Partido Nacionalista Peruano, Avda Arequipa 3410, Lima 27, Peru (office).

ARAPU, Anatol; Moldovan economist, politician and fmr diplomatist; b. 27 Nov. 1962, Văsieni, Ialoveni Dist; m.; one c.; ed State Univ. of Moldova, Moscow Econ. and Statistical Inst., Russia, World Trade Org. Inst., Switzerland; Lecturer, Faculty of Econs, State Univ. of Moldova 1985–88; Deputy Dir-Gen., MOLDEX State Foreign Trade Asscn 1988–92; Deputy Minister of Foreign Econ. Relations 1992–94; Dir-Gen., Dept of Foreign Econ. Relations 1994; Adviser to Exec. Dir, World Bank, Washington, DC 1994–97; Amb. to EU and NATO, Belgium, Netherlands and Luxembourg 1997–98; Minister of Finance 1998–99, 2013–16; Chief Financial Officer, Lukoil Romania 2000–01, Deputy Dir-Gen. for Econ. and Financial Affairs 2001–13; Gov. for Moldova, World Bank, Multilateral Investment Guarantee Agency, Bank for Black Sea Trade and Devt 2013; mem. Partidul Liberal Democrat din Moldova (PLDM).

ARASKOG, Rand Vincent; American business executive; b. 30 Oct. 1931, Fergus Falls, Minn.; s. of Randolph Victor Araskog and Hilfred Mathilda Araskog; m. Jessie Marie Gustafson 1956; one s. two d.; ed US Mil. Acad., West Point and Harvard Univ.; Special Asst to Dir US Dept of Defense, Washington, DC 1954–59; Dir of Marketing, Aeronautical Div., Honeywell Inc., Minneapolis 1960–66; Vice-Pres. ITT, Group Exec. ITT Aerospace Electronics, Components and Energy Group, Nutley, NJ 1971–76, Pres. 1979–85, CEO ITT Corpn, New York 1979–80, Chair. 1980–98, also Dir, Chair., Pres. and CEO ITT Holdings Inc., New York, 1995–98, mem. Bd of Dirs ITT Industries 1980–98, ITT Educational Services Inc. 1994–2004, Chair., CEO and Pres. Starwood Hotels and Resorts Worldwide Inc. (subsidiary); Prin., RVA Investments 1998–; mem. Bd of Dirs Int. Steel Group, Inc., Arcelor Mittal USA Inc. 2004–, Cablevision Systems Corpn 2005–, CSC Holdings, LLC 2005–, Palm Beach Civic Asscn; Chair. Nat. Security Telecommunications Advisory Cttee 1982–84; Trustee, New York Zoological Soc., Salk Inst. for Biological Studies; mem. Bd of Govs Aerospace Industries Asscn, Exec. Council, Air Force Asscn; mem. Business Council, Business Roundtable, Trilateral Comm.; Officier, Légion d'honneur 1987, Grand Officer, Order of Merit (Italy), Order Gen. Bernardo O'Higgins (Chile); Hon. DHumLitt (Hofstra Univ.) 1990. *Publications include:* Dawn Raiders and White Knights: The Inside Story of a Corporation Under Siege 1989, ITT Wars 1999; numerous articles. *Address:* 320 El Vedado Road, Palm Beach, FL 33480, USA.

ARAUD, Gérard; French government official and diplomatist; *Ambassador to USA;* b. 20 Feb. 1953, Marseille; ed Ecole Polytechnique, Institut d'Etudes Politiques de Paris, Ecole Nationale de la Statistique et de l'Admin Economique, Ecole Nationale d'Admin; First Sec., Embassy in Tel-Aviv 1982–84, Policy Planning Staff, Ministry of Foreign Affairs 1984–87, Second Counsellor, Embassy in Washington, DC 1987–91, Head of Bureau for European Community Affairs (Directorate of Econ. and Financial Affairs), Ministry of Foreign Affairs 1991–93, Deputy Perm. Rep. to North Atlantic Council (NATO), Brussels 1995–2000, Diplomatic Adviser, Office of the Minister of Defence 1993–95, Dir for Strategic Affairs, Security and Disarmament, Ministry of Foreign Affairs 2000–03, Amb. to Israel 2003–06, Deputy Sec.-Gen., Ministry of Foreign and European Affairs, Dir-Gen. for Political Affairs and Security 2006–09, Amb. and Perm. Rep. to UN Security Council (Pres. Feb. 2010, May 2011, Aug. 2012, Dec. 2013) and Head of Perm. Mission to UN, New York 2009–14, Amb. to USA 2014–; Chevalier des Arts et des Lettres 2006; Officier, Légion d'honneur 2013. *Address:* Embassy of France, 4101 Reservoir Road NW, Washington, DC 20007, USA (office). *Telephone:* (202) 944-6000 (office). *Fax:* (202) 944-6166 (office). *E-mail:* info@ambafrance-us.org (office). *Website:* www.ambafrance-us.org (office); www.info-france-usa.org (office).

ARAÚJO, Ernesto Henrique Fraga, BA; Brazilian diplomat and politician; *Minister of Foreign Affairs;* b. 15 May 1967, Porto Alegre; s. of Henrique Fonseca de Araújo and Marylin Mendes Fraga Araújo; m. Maria Eduarda de Seixas Corrêa; one d., two step-c.; ed Univ. of Brasília, Rio Branco Inst.; joined diplomatic service of Ministry of Foreign Affairs (MFA) 1992, served in Mercosur Affairs Div., MFA 1992–95, posted to Brazilian Mission to European Communities in Brussels 1995–99, Head of Econ. Div., Embassy in Berlin 1999–2003, Head, Services, Investments and Financial Affairs Div., MFA 2003–05, Head, EU and Extra-Regional Negotiations Div. 2005–07, Minister-Counsellor, Embassy in Ottawa 2007–10, Deputy Head of Mission, Embassy in Washington 2010–15, Deputy Head, Office of Minister of Foreign Affairs 2015–16, Dir, Dept of US, Canada and Inter-American Affairs, MFA 2016–19, Minister of Foreign Affairs 2019–. *Publications:* Ocidente (poetry) 1985, Mercosur Hoje (with Sergio de Abreu and Lima Florêncio), Mercosur: Extra-Regional Negotiations 1996, A Porta de Mogar (fiction) 1998, Xarab Fica (fiction) 1999, Quatro 3 (fiction) 2001. *Address:* Ministry of Foreign Affairs, Esplanada dos Ministérios, Bloco H, 70170-900 Brasília, DF, Brazil (office). *Telephone:* (61) 3411-8006 (office). *Fax:* (61) 3225-8002 (home). *E-mail:* imprensa@itamaraty.gov.br (office). *Website:* www.itamaraty.gov.br (office).

ARAÚJO, María Consuelo; Colombian economist, politician and business executive; *President, Gran Colombia Gold Corporation;* b. 1971, Cesar Prov.; m.; one c.; ed Externado Univ. of Colombia, Columbia Univ., USA, Univ. of Milan, Italy, Univ. of Paris (Sorbonne), France; teaching asst, Externado Univ. of Colombia; Vice-Minister's Asst, Ministry of Law and Justice; Foreign Trade Adviser, Agricultural and Rural Devt Ministry; President's Asst, Communications Dept Chief, Housing Programme Dir, Rural and Industrial Bank; Commercial Dir Bermudez y Valenzuela Finance Co.; Botanic Garden Dir, Bogota; Recreation and Sports Inst. Dir, Bogota; Minister of Culture 2002–06, of Foreign Affairs 2006–07 (resgnd); CEO Gran Colombia Gold Corpn 2010–14, Pres. 2014–; mem. Bd of Dirs Bogota Aqueduct and Sewer Enterprise, Nat. Network of Botanical Gardens, Recreational and Sportive Local Inst., Capital Channel, Inst. for Childhood Protection; Ciudad de Bogota Civil Meritory Order. *Leisure interests:* music, film. *Address:* Gran Colombia Gold Corporation, Edificio Bogota Trade Center, Carrera 10 No. 97A-13, Torre A, Oficina 406, Bogota, DC, Colombia (office). *Telephone:* (1) 492-6910 (office). *Fax:* (1) 621-0474 (office). *Website:* grancolombiagold.com (office).

ARAÚJO, Rui Maria de, MPH; Timor-Leste physician and politician; b. 21 May 1964, Mape, Portuguese Timor; m. Teresa António Madeira Soares; two c.; ed Satya Wacana Univ., Java, Sultan Agung Univ. Medical School, Semarang, Udayana Univ., Bali, Otago Univ., New Zealand; joined RENETIL (Timor-Leste student resistance group) whilst at univ. in Bali; worked as special liaison for Commdr-in-Chief of FALINTIL (mil. wing of political party FRETILIN) in Bali 1990–92; graduated as Gen. Practitioner and Medical Doctor 1994; Gen. Practitioner and House Surgeon, Dili Provincial Hosp. 1994–98; worked for Interim Health Authority under UN Transitional Admin, as Head, Div. of Health Services 1999, Dir Interim Health Authority 2001; Minister of Health 2001–06; Deputy Prime Minister 2006–07; mem. Council of State (advisory body for Pres. of Repub.) 2007–12; Policy and Man. Adviser, Ministry of Health 2007–08; Corp. Policy Adviser, Ministry of Finance 2009–15; Prime Minister 2015–17; mem. Frente Revolucionária do Timor Leste Independente (FRETILIN, Revolutionary Front for an Independent East Timor) 2010–, mem. Cen. Cttee 2011–.

ARAÚJO PERDOMO, Fernando, DEng; Colombian politician and engineer; b. 27 June 1955, Cartagena; s. of Alberto Araújo Merlano and Judith Perdomo; m.; four s.; ed Javeriana Pontifical Univ.; Gen. Man. Empresas Públicas de Cartagena 1983–84; Dir-Gen. Inmeubles Nacional 'MOPT' 1985–86; fmr Prof. of Eng, Jorge Tadeo Lozano Univ., Univ. of Cartagena; Minister of Devt 1998–2000; captured and held hostage by Revolutionary Armed Forces of Colombia (FARC) 2000–06; Minister of Foreign Affairs 2007–08; Pres. Partido Conservador Colombiano (Colombian Conservative Party) 2009–10; unsuccessful cand. in Cartagena mayoral elections 1998; fmr Pres. Colombian Chamber of Construction (CAMACOL); fmr mem. Bd of Dirs, El Universal (magazine), Hotel Las Américas Beach Resort. *Leisure interests:* sport, reading. *Address:* c/o Ministry of Foreign Affairs, Palacio de San Carlos, Calle 10, No. 5-51, Bogotá, DC, Colombia. *E-mail:* cancilleria@cancilleria.gov.co.

ARBASINO, Alberto; Italian author, essayist and critic; b. 22 Jan. 1930, Voghera; ed Univ. of Milan; Ed. Italo Calvino 1957–59; began literary career writing reports for the weekly Il Mondo from Paris and London; also worked for newspapers Il Giorno and later Il Corriere della sera; has collaborated with la Repubblica 1975–; mem. Group 63; hosted programme Match on RAI2 1977, Che tempo che fa by Fabio Fazio 2006; Deputy, Italian Parl. (elected as ind. for Italian Republican Party) 1983–87; Cavaliere di Gran Croce Ordine al Merito della Repubblica Italiana 1995, Commdr des Arts et des Lettres 2010; Premio Chiara alla carriera 2004, Premio Scanno per la Letteratura 2012, Premio Campiello alla carriera 2013, Premio Il Vittoriale degli Italiani 2014. *Publications include:* Le piccole vacanze 1957, L'Anonimo lombardo 1959, Parigi o cara 1960, Fratelli d'Italia 1963, La narcisata – La controra 1964, Grazie per le magnifiche rose 1966, La maleducazione teatrale 1966, Off-Off 1968, Super Eliogabalo 1969, Sessanta posizioni 1971, I Turchi 1971, Il principe costante 1972, La bella di Lodi 1972, Amate Sponde (con Mario Missiroli) 1974, La narcisata 1975, Certi romanzi – La Belle Epoque per le scuole 1977, Un paese senza 1980, Matine 1983, Il meraviglioso, anzi 1985, Lettere da Londra 1997, Passeggiando tra i draghi addormentati 1997, Paesaggi italiani con zombi 1998, Le muse a Los Angeles 2000, Rap! 2001, Marescialle e libertini 2004, Dall'Ellade a Bisanzio 2006, L'Ingegnere in blu 2008, La vita bassa 2008, Romanzi e Racconti 2009, 2010, America amore 2011, Pensieri selvaggi a Buenos Aires 2012, Ritratti italiani 2014, Ritratti e immagini 2016; contrib. to L'illustrazione italiana, Officina, Il Mondo, Tempo presente, Il Verri, Espresso, il Giorno, la Repubblica. *Address:* Gruppo Editoriale L'Espresso, Div. La Repubblica, Via C. Colombo 90, 00147 Rome, Italy (office). *Telephone:* (06) 49822499 (office). *Fax:* (06) 49822651 (office). *E-mail:* segreteria_cultura@repubblica.it (office). *Website:* www.repubblica.it (office).

ARBER, Werner; Swiss microbiologist and academic; b. 3 June 1929, Gränichen, Aargau; m.; two c.; ed Aargau Gymnasium, Eidgenössische Technische Hochschule, Zürich and Univ. of Geneva; Asst at Lab. of Biophysics, Univ. of Geneva 1953–58, 1960–62, Dozent, then Extraordinary Prof. of Molecular Genetics 1962–70; Research Assoc., Dept of Microbiology, Univ. of Southern California, USA 1958–59; Visiting Investigator, Dept of Molecular Biology, Univ. of California, Berkeley 1970–71; Prof. of Microbiology, Univ. of Basel 1971–96, Rector 1986–88; Pres. Int. Council of Scientific Unions (ICSU) 1996–99; Pres. Pontifical Acad. of Sciences 2010–17; Nobel Prize for Physiology or Medicine (jtly) 1978.

ARBHABHIRAMA, Anat, PhD; Thai scientist and business executive; *Adviser to the Board of Directors, Bangkok Mass Transit System Public Company, Ltd;* b. 13 Jan. 1938, Bangkok; s. of Arun Arbhabhirama and Pathumporn Arbhabhirama; m. Mrs Benjarata 1966; three s.; ed Chulalongkorn Univ., Bangkok, Asian Inst. of Tech., Bangkok, Colorado State Univ.; Vice-Pres. for Acad. Affairs and Provost, Asian Inst. of Tech. 1979–80; Deputy Minister of Agric. and Co-operatives 1980, Minister 1980–81; Head, Regional Research and Devt Center, Asian Inst. of Tech. 1981–84; Pres. Thailand Devt Research Inst. 1984–87; Chair. Intergovernmental Council of the Int. Hydrological Programme, UNESCO 1984–88; Gov. Petroleum Authority of Thailand 1987; Chair. PTT Exploration and Production Co. Ltd 1988, The Aromatics Co. Ltd (Thailand) 1990; Ind. Dir and mem. Audit Cttee BTS Group Holdings Public Co. Ltd 1998–2009, Dir 1998–, Exec. Dir 2010–, mem. Corp. Governance Cttee 2012–, Dir BTS Asset Co. 2009–10, BTS Land Co. Ltd 2009–18; fmr Dir Bangkok Mass Transit System Public Co. Ltd 2008–13, Adviser to Bd 2015–; Dir Kampoo Property Co. Ltd 2010–12, Kamkoong Property Co. Ltd 2010–15, mem. Council of Trustees and Bd of Dirs Thailand Devt Research Inst., Petroleum Inst. of Thailand; Companion (Fourth Class) of Most Admirable Order of Direkgunabhorn 2003; Hon. DCE (Chulalongkorn Univ.), DEng (Prince of Songkla Univ.); Outstanding Researcher of the Year 1987. *Publications include:* Thailand: Natural Resources Profile 1988, numerous articles and papers on water resources and hydraulics. *Leisure interests:* golf, jogging, chess. *Address:* c/o Board of Directors, Bangkok Mass Transit System Public Company Ltd, 1000 Phahonyothin Road, Chom Phon, Chatuchak, Bangkok 10900, Thailand.

ARBIA, Silvana, LLD; Italian judge; b. 19 Nov. 1952, Senise; ed Univ. of Padua; apptd prosecutor and judge in Venice, Rome and Milan Courts of Appeal 1979, returned to Milan Court of Appeal 2013; mem. Italian Del., Diplomatic Conf. on drafting statute of Int. Criminal Court, Rome 1998; Judge, Supreme Court and Court of Cassation of Italy 1999; Sr Trial Attorney, Int. Criminal Tribunal for Rwanda 1999, becoming Acting Chief of Prosecutions and Chief of Prosecutions; Registrar, Int. Criminal Court, The Hague 2008–13; Founder and Pres. Fondazione Silvana Arbia, San Marino; mem. Advisory Bd, Forum for Int. Criminal and Humanitarian Law; Paul Harris Fellow, Rotary Int.; Chevalier, Légion d'honneur 2013; Premio Nicola Sole 2011, Peace Prize of Soroptimist International of Europe (for her work in Rwanda) 2013. *Publications include:* Mentre il Mondo, Stava a Guardare 2011; several essays and books on human rights and children's rights.

ARBOUR, Louise, CC, BA, LLL; Canadian judge (retd), international organization official and fmr UN official; *Special Representative for International Migration, United Nations;* b. 10 Feb. 1947, Montréal; one s. two d.; ed Collège Regina Assumpta, Montréal, Université de Montréal; articled to Legal Dept, City of Montréal 1970; called to Québec Bar 1971, Ont. Bar 1977; law clerk, Supreme Court of Canada 1971–72; Research Officer, Law Reform Comm. and mem. Criminal Procedure Project 1972; Lecturer in Criminal Procedure, Osgoode Hall Law School, York Univ., Toronto 1974, Asst Prof. 1975, Assoc. Prof. 1977–87,

Assoc. Dean July–Dec. 1987; called to Bar, Ont. 1977; Judge, Supreme Court of Ont. (High Court of Justice) 1987–90; Judge, Court of Appeal for Ont. 1990–96; apptd by Order-in-Council as Commr to conduct inquiry into certain events at Prisons for Women, Kingston, April 1995; Chief Prosecutor, Int. Criminal Tribunals for Fmr Yugoslavia and Rwanda, The Hague 1996–99; Puisne Judge, Supreme Court of Canada 1999–2004; UN High Commr for Human Rights 2004–08, UN Special Rep. for Int. Migration 2017–; Pres. Int. Crisis Group 2009–14; Vice-Pres. Canadian Civil Liberties Asscn –1987; Lifetime mem. l'Asscn des juristes d'expression française de l'Ontario 1992–, Int. Council, Inst. for Global Legal Studies, Washington Univ. School of Law, Saint Louis, Mo. 2001; mem. Advisory Bd International Journal of Constitutional Law 2001–; mem. Bd of Eds Journal of International Criminal Justice 2003–; Hon. Prof., Univ. of Warwick, UK 1999–2004; Hon. mem. American Soc. of Int. Law 2000, Golden Key Nat. Honour Soc. 2000; Hon. Bencher Gray's Inn, London, England 2001; Hon. Fellow, American Coll. of Trial Lawyers 2003; Grande Officière, Ordre national du Québec 2009, Order of National Merit, Grand Cross class (Columbia) 2010, Commdr, Ordre national de la Légion d'honneur 2010; Hon. LLD (York) 1995, (Law Soc. of Upper Canada, New Brunswick, Laurentian Univ., Université du Québec à Montréal) 1999, (Université Libre de Bruxelles, Univ. of Victoria, Kingston Royal Mil. Coll., Chicago-Kent Coll. of Law, Université de Montréal, McMaster Univ., Univ. of Western Ontario, Univ. of Toronto, Univ. of Glasgow, Queen's Univ., Carleton Univ.), (Mount Saint Vincent Univ., Univ. of King's Coll., Université de Moncton, Memorial Univ., St John's, Newfoundland, Windsor Univ., Concordia Univ., Univ. of British Columbia) 2001, (Lakehead Univ.) 2002, (Université de Picardie Jules Verne, St Francis Xavier Univ., Antigonish, NS) 2003; Hon. DUniv (Ottawa) 1997; Médaille de l'Université de Montréal 1995, Achievement Award, Women's Law Asscn, Toronto 1996, G. Arthur Martin Award, Criminal Lawyers' Asscn 1998, First Recipient Toronto 1999 Medal of Honour, Int. Asscn of Prosecutors 1998, Medal of Honour, Int. Asscn of Prosecutors 1999, Médaille du Mérite, Institut de recherches cliniques de Montréal 1999, Fondation Louise Weiss Prize, Paris 1999, Second Annual Service to Humanity Award, Pennsylvania Bar Foundation 2000, Franklin and Eleanor Roosevelt Four Freedoms Medal (Freedom from Fear), Roosevelt Study Centre, Middleburg, Netherlands 2000, Women of Distinction Award, Toronto Hadassah-Wizo 2000, Peace Award, World Federalists of Canada 2000, Lord Reading Law Soc.'s Human Rights Award 2000, Wolfgang Freidman Memorial Award, Columbia Law School 2000, Eid-ul-Adha Award, Asscn of Progressive Muslims of Ontario 2000, Médaille du Barreau du Québec 2001, Nat. Achievement Award, Jewish Women Int. of Canada 2001, Stefan A. Riesenfeld Symposium Award, Berkeley Journal of International Law 2002, McGill Centre for Research and Teaching on Women's Person of the Year 2002, Prix de la Fondation Justice dans le Monde de l'Union internationale des Magistrats 2002, Médaille de la Faculté de droit de l'Université de Montréal 2003, inducted into Int. Hall of Fame of International Women's Forum 2003, 125th Anniversary Medal, Faculty of Law Asscn of Law Graduates, Université de Montréal 2003, North-South Prize, Council of Europe (co-winner) 2011. *Publications:* numerous articles on criminal procedure, human rights, civil liberties and gender issues. *Address:* United Nations, New York, NY 10017, USA (office). *Telephone:* (212) 963-1234 (office). *Fax:* (212) 963-4879 (office). *Website:* www.un.org (office).

ARBUZOV, Serhiy Hennadiyovych, PhD; Ukrainian economist, central banker and government official; b. 24 March 1976, Donetsk; s. of Valentina Arbuzova; m. Iryna Arbuzova; ed Donetsk State Univ.; began career as Economist, later Head of Div. and Head of Office, Donetsk br., PrivatBank, becoming Dir Konstantyniv Br., PrivatBank; Chair. Donechchyna Bank (renamed UkrBiznesBank) 2003–04; Chair. Supervisory Bd Ukreximbank 2010; Deputy Gov. Nat. Bank of Ukraine (Natsionalny Bank Ukrainy) Sept.–Dec. 2010, Gov. Dec. 2010–12; mem. Our Ukraine 2005–10, Party of Regions 2010–; First Deputy Prime Minister 2012–14; Acting Prime Minister Jan.–Feb. 2014 (dismissed). *Address:* c/o Office of the Cabinet of Ministers, 01008 Kyiv, vul. M. Hrushevskoho 12/2, Ukraine. *E-mail:* web@kmu.gov.ua.

ARCAND, Denys, CC; Canadian film director and film producer; b. 25 June 1941, Deschambault, Québec; m. Denise Robert; ed Univ. of Montreal; worked at Office Nat. du Film 1962–65; Vice-Pres. Asscn des Réalisateurs et Réalisatrices de films du Québec; mem. Royal Canadian Acad. of Arts; Ordre national de la Légion d'honneur, Commander of L'Ordre des Arts et des Lettres. *Films include:* Seul ou avec d'autres (co-dir) 1962, Champlain (short) 1963, Les Montrealistes (short) 1964, La Route de l'Ouest (short) 1965, Montreal, un jour d'été and Parcs atlantiques (shorts) 1966, Volleyball 1967, On est au coton (documentary) 1970, Québec: Dupléssis et après 1970, La maudite galette 1971, Réjeanne Padovani 1972, Gina 1974, La lutte des travailleurs d'hôpitaux (short) 1975, Le confort et l'indifférence 1980 (Best Film Prize, Quebec Film Critics' Asscn 1982), Empire Inc. (TV) 1982, Le crime d'Ovide Plouffe 1984, Le déclin de l'empire américain (Canadian Genie Awards, Int. Critics Prize, Cannes Film Festival) 1986, Jésus de Montréal 1989 (Canadian Genie Awards, Cannes Jury Prize 1989), Love and Human Remains 1993, Poverty and Other Delights, Stardom 2001, The Barbarian Invasions (Cannes Best Screenplay, Critics' Choice Award, Best Foreign Language Film 2004, Acad. Award, Best Foreign Language Film 2004, César Awards 2004) 2003, The Age of Ignorance 2007. *Television:* Duplessis (writer) 1978, Adam & Ève (series, writer) 2012. *Plays:* Les Lettres de la religieuse portuguaise 1989.

ARCE CATACORA, Luis Alberto, MSc; Bolivian government official; b. 28 Sept. 1963, La Paz; m.; three c.; ed Universidad Mayor de San Andrés, Univ. of Warwick, UK; with Cen. Bank of Bolivia 1988–2006; fmr consultant Natsuky Co., Nacida Co., Centro de Estudios para el Desarrollo Laboral y Agrario, Sistema Contable Computarizado; Minister of Economy and Public Finance 2006–17. *Publications include:* numerous journal articles.

ARCHER, David, BS, PhD; American oceanographer and academic; *Professor, Department of the Geophysical Sciences, University of Chicago;* b. 15 Sept. 1960; ed Indiana Univ., Univ. of Washington; Asst Prof. of Geophysical Sciences, Univ. of Chicago 1993–97, Adjunct Prof. of Environmental Sciences 1996–, Assoc. Prof. of Geophysical Sciences 1997–2001, Full Prof. of Geophysical Sciences 2001–; Lamont Fellow Postdoctoral Fellowship, Lamont Doherty Earth Observatory, Columbia Univ., New York 1990–92, Postdoctoral Research Scientist 1992–93, Adjunct Prof. 1994–; Contributing Ed. realclimate.org (climate science blog). *Publications:* Global Warming: Understanding the Forecast 1992 (second edn 2011), The Long Thaw: How Humans are Changing the Next 100,000 Years of Earth's Climate 2009, The Climate Crisis: An Introductory Guide to Climate Change 2009, The Warming Papers: The Scientific Foundation for the Climate Change Forecast (co-ed.) 2010, The Global Carbon Cycle (Princeton Primers in Climate) 2010; more than 70 scientific papers in professional journals on the global carbon cycle and its relation to global climate, with special focus on ocean sedimentary processes. *Address:* HGS 449, Department of the Geophysical Sciences, 5734 South Ellis Avenue, University of Chicago, Chicago, IL 60637, USA (office). *Telephone:* (773) 702-0823 (office). *Fax:* (773) 702-9505 (office). *E-mail:* d-archer@uchicago.edu (office). *Website:* geosci.uchicago.edu/directory/david-archer (office).

ARCHER, Marco Shearer, LLB, MBA; Cayman Islands lawyer, statistician and politician; m. Tammy Archer; two d.; ed Barry Univ., USA, Univ. of Liverpool, UK, Coll. of Law, London, UK, Univ. of Miami, USA; began career with Statistics Office 1989 (merged with Econs Unit to become Econs and Statistics Office); Project Man. for govt-wide financial reform projects including Integrated Resources Information Systems (IRIS) 1998, Financial Management Initiative (FMI) 1999; held various posts within the Portfolio of Finance and Econ. Devt (PFED), becoming Sr Asst Sec. 2003, later Sr Statistician responsible for econ. and business statistics programme; called to the bar 2008; fmr attorney-at-law with Mourant Ozannes (offshore law firm); mem. Legis. Assembly for Georgetown; Minister of Finance and Econ. Devt 2013–17; Founding Dir Generation NOW (mentoring group and think-tank) 2007–13; mem. Cayman Islands Bar Asscn; mem. Peoples' Progressive Movement. *Address:* Government Administration Bldg, Elgin Avenue, George Town, Grand Cayman, Cayman Islands (office). *Telephone:* 244-2458 (office). *Fax:* 945-1746 (office). *E-mail:* tedc@gov.ky (office).

ARCHER, Dame Mary Doreen, DBE, MA, PhD, CChem, FRSC, CSci; British scientist; *Chairman, Trustees of National Science Museum Group;* b. 22 Dec. 1944, Ewell, Surrey; d. of Harold Norman Weeden and Doreen Weeden (née Cox); m. Jeffrey Howard Archer (now Baron Archer of Weston-super-Mare q.v.) 1966; two s.; ed Cheltenham Ladies' Coll., St Anne's Coll. Oxford, Imperial Coll. London; Jr Research Fellow, St Hilda's Coll. Oxford 1968–71; temporary Lecturer in Chem., Somerville Coll. Oxford 1971–72; Research Fellow, Royal Inst. of GB 1972–76; Lector in Chem., Trinity Coll. Cambridge 1976–86; Fellow and Coll. Lecturer in Chem., Newnham Coll. Cambridge 1976–86; Sr Academic Fellow, De Montfort Univ. 1990–; Visiting Prof., Dept of Biochemistry, Imperial Coll. London 1991–2000, Visiting Prof., Centre for Energy Policy and Tech. 2001–03; Visitor, Univ. of Herts. 1993–2004; Trustee Science Museum 1990–2000, Cambridge Foundation 1997–2004; Chair, Trustees of Nat. Science Museum Group 2015–; mem. Council, Royal Inst. 1984–85, 1999–2001, Cheltenham Ladies' Coll. 1991–2000, UK Stem Cell Fed. 2005–15; Chair Nat. Energy Foundation 1990–2000, Pres. 2000–; mem. Bd of Dirs Anglia TV Group 1987–95, Mid Anglia Radio 1988–94, Cambridge & Newmarket FM Radio (now Heart) 1988–97, Hydrodec Group plc 2014–; Dir, Cambridge Univ. Hosps NHS Foundation Trust 1992–, Vice-Chair. 1999–2002, Chair. 2002–12; Chair. East of England Stem Cell Network 2004–08; Convenor UK Univ. Hosps Chairs Group 2008–12; mem. Council of Lloyd's 1989–92; Pres. Guild of Church Musicians 1989–, UK Solar Energy Soc. 2001–; Hon. Patron, Prostate Action 2010, Hon. Fellow, St Anne's Coll. Oxford 2013; Hon. DSc (Hertfordshire) 1994, (Imperial) 2018; Energy Inst. Melchett Medal 2002, Inst. of Chem. of Ireland Eva Philbin Award 2007. *Publications include:* Rupert Brooke and The Old Vicarage, Grantchester 1989, Clean Energy from Photovoltaics (co-ed.) 2001, Molecular to Global Photosynthesis (co-ed.) 2004, Transformation and Change: the 1702 Chair of Chemistry at Cambridge (co-ed.) 2004, The Story of The Old Vicarage, Grantchester 2004, Solar Photon Conversion in Nanostructured and Photoelectrochemical Systems (co-ed.) 2008; contribs to chemical journals. *Leisure interests:* reading, writing, singing. *Address:* The Old Vicarage, Grantchester, Cambridge, CB3 9ND, England (home). *Telephone:* (1223) 840213 (home).

ARCHER, Robyn, AO, BA, DipEd; Australian singer, performer, writer and artistic director; b. 18 June 1948, Adelaide, S Australia; d. of Clifford Charles Smith and Mary Louisa Wohling; ed Enfield High School, Adelaide Univ.; singer 1952–; recorded ten albums including Brecht, Weill and Eisler repertoire; has toured worldwide in recital, concert and cabaret performances; has sung with Australian and Adelaide Chamber Orchestras, Adelaide, Melbourne and Tasmanian Symphony Orchestras; numerous TV appearances in Australia and UK; has written over 100 songs; writing for theatre includes Songs from Sideshow Alley, The Pack of Women (also Dir), Cut & Thrust Cabaret (also Dir), Café Fledermaus, See Ya Next Century, Ningali, A Star is Torn, Comes a Cropper; writing for TV includes The One That Got Away; also writes for radio; Artistic Counsel Belvoir Street Theatre 1986; Artistic Dir Nat. Festival of Australian Theatre 1993–95, Adelaide Festival 1998, 2000, Melbourne Int. Festival of Arts 2002–04; Artistic Adviser Australia Day, Hanover Festival EXPO 2000; Creative Consultant Melbourne Museum 1995–98; Creator and Inaugural Artistic Dir, Ten Days on the Island, Tasmania 2001–05; Artistic Dir Liverpool Capital of Culture Festival 2004; Chair. Community Cultural Devt Bd, Australia Council 1993–95; Commonwealth Appointee to Centenary of Fed. Advisory Cttee 1994; Chair. Master of Fine Arts, Nat. Inst. of Fine Arts; mem. Bd Dirs Int. Soc. of Performing Arts, Council Victorian Coll. of the Arts, Adelaide Festival Centre Trust; Trustee, Don Dunstan Foundation; Artistic Dir The Light in Winter (Federation Square, Melbourne) 2009; currently artistic adviser to Govts of S Australia and Western Australia; Patron Australian Art Orchestra, Arts Law Centre, Australian Script Centre, Brink Productions, Globalism Inst.; fmr mem. Bd Helpmann Acad.; fmr Patron Nat. Affiliation of Arts Educators; Inaugural Amb. Adelaide Festival Centre Trust; Amb. Adelaide Football Club, Int. Women's Devt Agency; Chevalier des Arts et des Lettres 2000, Fed. Medal 2001, Officer of the Crown (Belgium) 2008; Hon. DUniv (Flinders Univ.), (Univ. of Sydney), (Univ. of Canberra); Sydney Critics' Circle Award 1980, Henry Lawson Award 1980, Australian Creative Fellowship 1991–93, Australian Record Industry Award for Best Soundtrack for Pack of Women 1986, for Best Children's Album for Mrs Bottle 1989, Exec. Woman of the Year, Australian Women's Network 1998, S Australia Arts and Culture Award 1998, 2000, Int. Citation of Merit, Int. Soc. of Performing Arts, New York 2006. *Performance roles include:* Annie I in The Seven Deadly Sins 1974, 1993, Jenny in The Threepenny Opera 1976, Brecht Compilations, Never the Twain, To Those

Born Later, Sung and Unsung, Brecht & Co, Pierrot Lunaire, Out of the East, Mrs Peachum in The Threepenny Opera 1999. *One-woman shows include:* Tonight Lola Blau (Australian tour), A Star is Torn (two Australian tours, Theatre Royal, Stratford East and Wyndham's Theatre, London West End). *Theatre directed:* The Pack of Women (Australian tour), Cut and Thrust Cabaret (London), Scandals (Australian tour), On Parliament Hill (Sydney), ABC (Sydney), Akwanso Fly South (Adelaide Festival and Australian tour), Mayday (Darwin and Hobart), Labour of Love (Darwin and Hobart), Le Chat Noir (Brisbane and Canberra), The Bridge (Perth), Accidental Death of an Anarchist (Adelaide and Sydney), Boy Hamlet (Brisbane), January (Tim Finn/Dorothy Porter), Toughnut Cabaret (Pittsburgh) 2009. *Publications include:* The Robyn Archer Songbook 1980, Mrs Bottle Burps 1983, The Pack of Women 1986, A Star is Torn 1986; for theatre: Kold Komfort Kaffee 1977, The Pack of Women 1981, Cut & Thrust Cabaret 1984, Songs from Sideshow Alley 1986, Il Magnifico 1987, Akwanso Fly South 1988, Poor Johanna 1983, The Hanging of Minnie Thwaites 1983, A Star is Torn 1979, Scandals 1985, Ningali 1992, Architektin 2008; contrib. to The All Australian HaHa Book 1983, Australia Fair 1984, Mrs Bottle's Absolutely Blurtingly Beautiful World-Beating Burp 1990, Cafe Fledermaus 1990, Penguin Anthology of Contemporary Australian Women's Writing 1991, Loaves and Fishes 1991, Hope and Fear 1995, The Myth of the Mainstream 2004, Australian Greats 2008, Essentially Creative (Griffith Review) 2009, Detritus: addressing culture & the arts 2010. *Address:* c/o Rick Raftos Management, Box 445, Paddington, NSW 2021, Australia (office). *Telephone:* (2) 9281-9622 (office). *Fax:* (2) 9212-7100 (office). *Website:* www.robynarcher.com.au (home).

ARCHER OF WESTON-SUPER-MARE, Baron (Life Peer), cr. 1992, of Mark in the County of Somerset; **Jeffrey Howard Archer;** British writer and fmr politician; b. 15 April 1940, London; s. of William Archer and Lola Archer (née Cook); m. Mary Doreen Archer (q.v.) (née Weeden) 1966; two s.; ed Wellington School, Brasenose Coll., Oxford; mem. GLC for Havering 1966–70; MP for Louth (Conservative) 1969–74; Deputy Chair. Conservative Party 1985–86; mem. House of Lords 1992–; Prix Polar Int., Prix Cognac Awards 2009, Prix Relay du Roman d'Evasion 2010, Int. Recognition Award, Bord Gáis Energy Irish Book Awards 2014. *Plays include:* Beyond Reasonable Doubt 1987, Exclusive 1989, The Accused (writer and actor) 2000. *Film:* Bridget Jones's Diary (as himself) 2001. *Publications include:* Not a Penny More, Not a Penny Less 1975, Shall We Tell the President? 1977, Kane and Abel 1979, A Quiver Full of Arrows 1980, The First Miracle (with Craigie Aitchison) 1980, The Prodigal Daughter 1982, First Among Equals 1984, A Matter of Honour 1985, A Twist in the Tale (short stories) 1988, As The Crow Flies 1991, Honour Among Thieves 1993, Twelve Red Herrings (short stories) 1994, The Fourth Estate 1996, The Collected Short Stories 1997, The Eleventh Commandment 1998, To Cut a Long Story Short (short stories) 2000, Sons of Fortune 2002, A Prison Diary Vols I and II 2002, A Prison Diary Vol. III 2004, False Impression 2005, Cat o' Nine Tales (short stories) 2006, The Gospel According to Judas 2007, A Prisoner of Birth (Int. Polar Prize 2009) 2008, Paths of Glory (Prix Relay du roman d'evasion 2010) 2009, 30th Anniversary revised edn of Kane and Abel 2009, And Thereby Hangs a Tale (short stories) 2010, Only Time Will Tell 2011, The Sins of the Father 2012, Best Kept Secret 2013, Be Careful What You Wish For 2014, Mightier Than The Sword 2015, Cometh The Hour 2016, This Was a Man 2016, Tell Tale (short stories) 2017. *Leisure interests:* theatre, cricket, auctioneering. *Address:* 93 Albert Embankment, London, SE1 7TY, England (office). *E-mail:* questions@jeffreyarcher.co.uk (office). *Website:* www.jeffreyarcher.com (home).

ARDALAN, Nader, BArch, MArch; Iranian/American architect and planner; *President, Ardalan Associates LLC;* b. 9 March 1939, Tehran, Iran; s. of Abbas Gholi Ardalan and Faranguis Davar Ardalan; m. 1st Laleh Bakhtiar 1962 (divorced 1976); one s. two d.; m. 2nd Shahla Ganji 1977; one s.; ed New Rochelle High School, Carnegie-Mellon Univ., Harvard Univ. Grad. School of Design; designer, S.O.M. 1962–64; Chief Architect, Nat. Iranian Oil Co. 1964–66; Design Partner, Aziz Farmanfarmaian & Assocs 1966–72; Man. Dir Mandala Collaborative Tehran/Boston 1972–79; Prof. of Design, Tehran Univ. Faculty of Fine Arts 1972–77; Founder-Pres. Nader Ardalan Assocs LLC 1979–83; Prin. Jung/Brannen Assocs Inc., Boston 1983–94; Man. Prin. Jung/Brannen Assocs Inc., Abu Dhabi 1992; Sr Vice-Pres. and Dir of Design KEO International Consultants 1994–2006; Pres. Ardalan Associates LLC 2006–; Research Fellow, Harvard Center for Middle East Studies 2006–10; Sr Research Assoc. and Sr Ed. Gulf Encyclopedia for Sustainable Urbanism, Grad. School of Design, Harvard Univ. 2011–, Sr Advisor, Harvard Sea Level Rise Collier Co., Fla, Convener of Urbanism, Spirituality and Well Being Harvard Symposium 2013, Convener of Symposium, Environment Future Sustainable Cities of Iran 2015; Visiting Prof., Harvard Univ. Grad. School of Design 1977–78, 1981–83, Yale Univ. 1977, MIT 1980; Founding mem. Steering Cttee, Aga Khan Award 1976–80; Co-Convener, Displacement and Architecture Symposium, School of Architecture, Univ. of Miami 2018–; mem. Bd of Dirs, Architecture, Culture, Spirituality Forum 2010–; design collections exhibited at Venice Biennale; exhibitor, Smithsonian's Cooper-Hewitt Museum, New York; Perm. Collection, Avery Library, Columbia Univ.; Int. Jury Pres., Saudi Aramco Cultural Center; mem. Design Jury, Shams-i Tabrizi Memorial; King Fahd Award 1987; design awards include ADMA OPCO HQ, Information Tech. Coll., UAE Univ., Al Ain, UAE. *Radio:* interview on sustainable design, Nat. Public Radio. *Television:* interviewed by Dan Rather on Power to the People, Harvard Sea Level Rise Collier County (NBC 2). *Publications include:* Sense of Unity 1972, Masjid Al Haram Mecca 1975, Habitat Bill of Rights 1976, Pardisan, Environmental Park 1976, Blessed Jerusalem 1983, New Arab Urbanism 2010, (Persian) Gulf Sustainable Urbanism 2013; articles in leading professional journals. *Leisure interests:* study of sacred architecture, photography, swimming, hunting, drawing. *Address:* Ardalan Associates LLC, 902 Wyndemere Way, Naples, FL 34105, USA (office). *Telephone:* (239) 263-2791 (office). *E-mail:* nader.ardalan@gmail.com (office); nardalan@gsd.harvard.ac (office). *Website:* www.ardalanassociates.com (office).

ARDANT, Fanny; French actress; b. 22 March 1949, Monte Carlo; d. of Lt-Col Jean Ardant and Jacqueline Lecoq; three c.; Grand Prix Nat., Ministry of Culture. *Films include:* Les Chiens 1979, Les uns et les autres 1981, The Woman Next Door 1981, Life is a Novel, Confidentially Yours 1983, Benevenuta 1983, Desire, Swann in Love 1984, Love Unto Death, Les Enragés, L'Eté prochain 1986, Family Business 1986, Affabulazione, Melo, The Family 1987, La Paltoquet, Three Sisters, Australia 1989, Pleure pas my love, Adventure of Catherine C., Afraid of the Dark 1991, Rien que des mensonges, La Femme du déserteur, Amok, Colonel Chabert 1994, Beyond the Clouds 1995, Ridicule 1996, Pédale douce (César Award for Best Actress) 1996, Elizabeth 1998, La Débondade 1999, Le Fils du Français 1999, Le Dîner et le Libertin 2000, Callas Forever 2002, 8 Femmes 2002, Nathalie 2003, L'odore del Sangue 2004, El Año del diluvio 2004, Paris, je t'aime 2006, Roman de gare 2007, The Secrets 2007, Hello Goodbye 2008, Cendres et sang (Ashes and Blood) 2009, Visage (Face) 2009, Raspoutine 2011, Beaux Jours (Bright Days Ahead) 2013, Cadence Obstinées (Obsessive Rhythms) 2013, Chic 2015. *Theatre includes:* Polyeucte, Esther, The Mayor of Santiago, Electra, Tête d'Or. *Leisure interest:* music (piano).

ARDEBERG, Arne Lennart, PhD; Swedish astronomer and academic; *Professor Emeritus, Lund Observatory;* b. 10 Nov. 1940, Malmö; s. of Kurt Ardeberg and Elly Ardeberg; m. Margareta Vinberg 1969; one s. two d.; ed Lund Univ.; staff astronomer, Lund Observatory 1965–69, Prof. 1973–79, Dir Lund Observatory 1984–1998, 2004–07, later Prof. Emer.; apptd Prof., Lund Univ. 1980, Vice-Dean, Faculty of Science 1984–87, Dean 1987–98, Pro-Vice-Chancellor 1998–2002; staff astronomer, European Southern Observatory (ESO), La Silla, Chile 1969–73, Assoc. Astronomical Dir 1979–81, responsible for ESO VLT Site Investigation, Northern Chile 1982–87, Dir ESO 1981–84, Chair. ESO Site Evaluation Cttee 1984–89, ESO Scientific-Tech. Cttee 1987–92, ESO Site Selection Cttee 1988–91; Dir Nordic Optical Telescope Scientific Asscn 1984–95; Chair. European Telescope Consortium Euro50 2001–04; Deputy Project Man. European Extremely Large Telescope 2004–; mem. Royal Physiographical Soc. (Sweden) 1980–, Royal Swedish Acad. of Sciences 1983– (Chair. Astronomy and Space Research Bd), Royal Soc. of Sciences (Sweden) 1986–, Swedish Nat. Research Policy Working Group, Jt European ELT Exec. Cttee; Deputy Project Leader Jt European Design Study Project; Wallmark Prize, Royal Swedish Acad. of Sciences 1977. *Publications include:* 250 publs in int. journals and books on astronomy, physics and related technology. *Leisure interests:* mountaineering, forestry, literature. *Address:* Lund Observatory, Room B 256, Box 43, 221 00 Lund (office); Blåmesvägen 2, 247 35 Södra Sandby, Sweden (home). *Telephone:* (46) 222-72-90 (office); (46) 46-570-16 (home); (70) 369-70-50. *Fax:* (46) 222-46-14 (office). *E-mail:* arne.ardeberg@astro.lu.se (office). *Website:* www.astro.lu.se (office).

ARDEN, Rt Hon. Lady Mary (Howarth), DBE, PC, MA, LLM; British judge; *Justice of the Supreme Court;* b. 23 Jan. 1947; d. of Lt-Col E.C. Arden and M. M. Arden (née Smith); m. Sir Jonathan Hugh Mance 1973; one s. two d.; ed Huyton Coll., Girton Coll., Cambridge, Harvard Law School, USA; called to the Bar, Gray's Inn 1971; admitted to Lincoln's Inn 1973, Bencher 1994; QC 1986; Dept of Trade and Industry Inspector, Rotaprint PLC 1988–91; Attorney-Gen. Duchy of Lancaster 1991–93; Judge of High Court of Justice, Chancery Div. 1993–2000; Chair. Law Comm. 1996–99; Lady Justice of Appeal 2000–18; Justice of the Supreme Court 2018–; Bar mem. Law Soc.'s Standing Cttee on Company Law 1976–; mem. Financial Law Panel 1993–2000, Steering Group, Company Law Review 1998–2001; Fellow, Girton Coll. Cambridge; Hon. Fellow, Liverpool John Moores Univ. 2006; Hon. DUniv (Essex) 1997, Hon. LLD (Liverpool) 1998, (Warwick) 1999, (Royal Holloway and Bedford New Coll., London) 1999, (Nottingham) 2002; The Times Woman of Achievement Lifetime Award in 1997. *Publications include:* Buckley on The Companies Acts (Jt Gen. Ed.) 2000, Human Rights and European Law: Building New Legal Orders 2015; contrib. to numerous books, articles in legal journals. *Leisure interests:* reading, swimming. *Address:* The Supreme Court, Parliament Square, London, SW1P 3BD, England (office). *Telephone:* (20) 7960-1936 (office). *Fax:* (20) 7960-1961 (office). *E-mail:* justices@supremecourt.gsi.gov.uk (office). *Website:* www.supremecourt.gov.uk (office).

ARDITI, Pierre; French actor; b. (Pierre Marie Denis Arditi), 1 Dec. 1944, Paris; s. of Georges Arditi and Yvonne Leblicq; Pnr Évelyne Bouix 1986; Chevalier, Légion d'honneur 2002, Ordre nat. du Mérite 1994, Officier 2005. *Theatre includes:* L'aide mémoire 1993, Art 1994, En attendant Godot 1996, Le mari, la femme et l'amant 1997, Rever peut-être 1998, L'école des femmes 2001–02, Joyeuses Paques 2001–02, Mathilde 2003, Lunes de miel 2004, La danse de l'albatros 2006, Faisons un rêve 2007, 2008–09, 2010, L'idée fixe 2007, Elle est là 2008, Tailleur pour dames 2008, Les fausses confidences 2009, L'éloignement 2009, Sentiments provisoires 2009, La vérité 2011, Moi, je crois pas 2012, Comme s'il en pleuvait 2012. *Films include:* Last Leap 1970, Alyse and Chloe 1970, Le funambule 1974, Rape of Love 1978, My American Uncle 1980, Pile ou face 1980, Nestor Burma, Shock Detective 1982, Life Is a Bed of Roses 1983, Jusqu'à la nuit 1983, Swann in Love (voice) 1984, Femmes de personne 1984, Love Unto Death 1984, The Children 1985, Farewell to Fred 1985, Strictement personnel 1985, À coeur perdu (short) 1985, Follow My Gaze 1986, Mélo (César Award for Best Actor in a Supporting Role 1987) 1986, L'état de grâce 1986, Triple sec (short) 1986, Poker 1987, La petite allumeuse 1987, Agent trouble 1987, Flag 1987, De guerre lasse 1987, La passerelle 1988, Natalia 1988, Bonjour l'angoisse 1988, Vanille fraise 1989, Radio Corbeau 1989, Le pont du silence (short) (voice) 1990, The Pleasure of Love 1991, Les clés du paradis 1991, L'ombre 1992, The Little Apocalypse 1993, Smoking/No Smoking (César Award for Best Actor 1994) 1993, The Horseman on the Roof 1995, Beaumarchais (voice, uncredited) 1996, Unpredictable Nature of the River 1996, Hommes, femmes, mode d'emploi 1996, Messieurs les enfants 1997, Same Old Song 1997, Chance or Coincidence 1998, Un chat dans la gorge 1999, A Monkey's Tale (voice) 1999, La fausse suivante 2000, Actors 2000, Le dernier plan 2000, Le voeu (short) (voice) 2002, The Mystery of the Yellow Room 2003, Not on the Lips 2003, The Car Keys 2003, Why (Not) Brazil? 2004, The First Time I Turned Twenty 2004, Victoire 2004, One Stays, the Other Leaves 2005, Le courage d'aimer 2005, Le parfum de la dame en noir 2005, Nos amis les Terriens (voice) 2006, Private Fears in Public Places 2006, Le grand appartement 2006, Coup de sang 2006, The Great Alibi 2008, Tu peux garder un secret? 2008, Musée haut, musée bas 2008, Le code a changé 2009, Je vais te manquer 2009, Park Benches 2009, Bambou 2009, Together Is Too Much 2010, Je ne vous oublierai jamais 2010, Roses à crédit 2010, Streamfield, les carnets noirs 2010, Granny's Funeral 2012, You Ain't Seen Nothin' Yet 2012, La fleur de l'âge 2012, Comme un avion 2015, Capitaine Marleau 2017, The Summer House 2018; numerous TV films and series. *Address:* c/o Anna Morin, VMA, 3 rue de Turbigo, 75001 Paris, France (office). *Telephone:* 1-44-54-26-40 (office). *Fax:* 1-44-54-08-44 (office). *E-mail:* a.morin@ubbb.fr (office). *Website:* www.ubba.eu (office).

ARDITO BARLETTA, Nicolás, PhD, MS; Panamanian politician and economist; *Director-General, Centro Nacional de Competitividad;* b. 21 Aug. 1938, Aguadulce, Coclé; s. of Nicolás Ardito Barletta and Leticia de Ardito Barletta; m. María Consuelo de Ardito Barletta; two s. one d.; ed Univ. of Chicago and North Carolina State Univ., USA; Cabinet mem. and Dir Planning 1968–70; Dir Econ. Affairs OAS 1970–73; Minister of Planning 1973–78; Negotiator of econ. aspects of Panama Canal Treaties 1976–77; Vice-Pres. World Bank for Latin America and Caribbean 1978–84; Founder and first Pres. Latin American Export Bank (BLADEX) 1978; Pres. Latin American Econ. System (SELA) Constituent Ass.; Pres. of Panama 1984–85; Gen. Dir of Int. Centre for Econ. Growth 1986–95; Dir Autoridad de la Región Interoceanía 1995–2000; Chair. Asesores Estrategicos; mem. Bd of Dirs of several corpns, banks and policy insts including Superintendencia de Bancos 2006–14; currently Dir-Gen. Centro Nacional de Competitividad. *Publications:* numerous publications on econ. and social devt issues. *Leisure interests:* tennis and music. *Address:* Centro Nacional de Competitividad, Ave. Justo Arosemena y Calle 31, Edificio APEDE, piso 1, Panamá 9, Panama (office). *Telephone:* 394-4363 (office). *E-mail:* asesores@cwpanama.net. *Website:* www.cncpanama.org (home).

AREF, Mohammad Reza, BS, BEng, MS, PhD; Iranian electronics engineer, politician and academic; *Professor, Department of Electrical Engineering, Sharif University of Technology;* b. 1951, Yazd; ed Univ. of Tehran, Stanford Univ., USA; politically active as student, supporter of Ayatollah Khomeini, arrested by secret police 1963; mem. of Muslim students org. during stay in US, subsequently head of that org.; has held a number of govt posts including Minister of Posts, Telegraphs and Telecommunications, Deputy Minister of Culture and Higher Educ. in charge of Student Affairs 1981–82 and Adviser to Minister of Culture and Higher Educ., Deputy to Minister of Science, Research and Tech. 1981–84, Deputy to Minister of Science, Research and Tech. 1989–91; Deputy to Man. Dir Telecom Co. 1980–81; Faculty mem. Isfahan Univ. of Tech. 1982–95; Chancellor Univ. of Tehran 1994–97; Minister of Information, Communication and Tech. 1997–2000; First Vice-Pres. of Iran 2001–05; Prof., Electrical Engineering Dept, Sharif Univ. of Tech. 1995–; Pres. Iranian Soc. of Cryptology 2000–, Iranian Command and Intelligence Soc. 2007–, Foundation for Advancement of Science and Tech. 2007–, Bd BARAN Foundation 2005–; mem. Expediency Discernment Council of System 2003–, Supreme Cultural Revolution Council 2002–, Acad. of Sciences 2007–; cand. in 2013 presidential election (withdrew); First Prize, Nat. Math. Competition 1959, Isfahan Tech. Univ. Scholarship. *Address:* Department of Electrical Engineering, Sharif University of Technology, POB 11365-8639, Tehran, Iran (office). *Telephone:* (21) 6005419 (office); (61) 65935 (office). *Fax:* (21) 6012983 (office). *E-mail:* aref@sharif.edu (office). *Website:* ee.sharif.edu/~aref (office).

ARENAS DE MESA, Alberto, DEcon; Chilean economist, academic and politician; b. 5 Oct. 1965; ed Univ. of Chile, Univ. of Pittsburgh, USA; Economist, Research Dept, Banco Sud Americano, Santiago 1989–90; Adviser, Ministry of Finance and Budget 1990–93; Graduate Research Asst, Univ. of Pittsburgh 1993–96, Teaching Fellow, Dept of Econs 1996–97; Prof., Dept of Econs, Georgetown Univ.-ILADES, Santiago 1999–2003; Head of Research Dept, Directorate of Budget, Ministry of Finance 1997–2000, Asst, Rationalization and Public Service 2000–06, Dir of Budget 2006–10, Minister of Finance 2014–15; Asst Prof. and Researcher, Microdata Center, Dept of Econs, Univ. of Chile 2010; Dir Channel 13 (TV) 2010–; mem. (Dir) Parl. Appropriations Resolution Council 2010.

ARENDARSKI, Andrzej, PhD; Polish politician, business executive and academic; *President, National Chamber of Commerce (Poland);* b. 15 Nov. 1949, Warsaw; m. Agnieszka Łypacewicz; three s. one d.; ed Univ. of Warsaw, Inst. of Philosophy and Sociology, Polish Acad. of Sciences; teacher, East Dembowski Secondary School, Warsaw 1972–73, Inst. of Philosophy and Sociology of Polish Acad. of Sciences, Warsaw 1973–75; worked as Sr Asst and Adjunct, Inst. of History of Science, Educ. and Tech. 1977; mem. Solidarity Trade Union 1980–; Ed.-in-Chief, underground journal Zeszyty Edukacji Narodowej 1981–82; co-f. Agric.-Industrial Soc., Konin 1988; mem. Soc. for Econ. and Econ. Action, Warsaw 1988; co-f. Social Movt for Econ. Initiatives SPRING 1988; Deputy to Sejm (Parl.) 1989–93; mem. Liberal Democratic Congress (KLD) 1989–94, Deputy Chair. KLD 1989–94, mem. KLD Political Council 1991–94, then Chair.; Chair. Democratic Party 2002–06; Pres. Polish Chamber of Commerce 1990–; Minister of Foreign Econ. Co-operation 1992–93; Chair. Polish-Ukrainian Chamber of Commerce 1996; Sec.-Gen. Polish Asscn Industry, Commerce and Finance 1997; Chair. Polish-American Small Business Consultation Fund; CEO Tel-Emergo, Telephony Service Providers; Chair. Polish Quality Awards Cttee. *Publications:* contribs to underground journals 1981–89; co-author: Polska lat 80-tych: Analiza stanu obecnego i perspektywy rozwoju sytuacji politycznej w Polsce 1984, Stan środowiska przyrodniczego 1984. *Leisure interests:* travel, sailing, art of cooking. *Address:* Krajowa Izba Gospodarcza, ul. Trębacka 4, 00-074 Warsaw, Poland. *Telephone:* (22) 630-96-00 (office). *Fax:* (22) 827-46-73 (office). *E-mail:* aarendarski@kig.pl (office). *Website:* www.kig.pl (office); arendarski.blogbank.pl.

ARGENTO, Asia; Italian actress, singer, model and film director; b. (Aria Asia Anna Maria Vittoria Rossa Argento), 20 Sept. 1975, Rome; d. of Dario Argento and Daria Nicolodi; great-granddaughter of composer Alfredo Casella; one d. with Marco Castoldi; m. Michele Civetta 2008; one s.; published book of poems aged eight; began acting aged nine, playing small part in film Sogni e bisogni by Sergio Citti; also had a small part in Demons 2 (written and produced by her father) 1986 and its unofficial sequel, La chiesa (The Church) 1989; began appearing in English-language films, including B. Monkey and New Rose Hotel 1998, French-language films, including La Reine Margot 1994; made first foray into directing in short films Prospettive and A ritroso 1994; directed a documentary on her father 1996, and second on Abel Ferrara (Rome Film Festival Award) 1998; directed and wrote her first full-length film, Scarlet Diva, co-produced by her father 2000; has modelled for and endorses the brand 'Miss Sixty'; contributed a video diary 'Don't Bother To Knock' to Nick Knight's website, SHOWstudio Oct. 2006; appeared in Placebo's music video for 'This Picture'; appeared on Brian Molko (frontman of Placebo) cover version of 'Je t'aime… moi non plus'; has been part of Tiger Man's project Femina 2009; featured on the song 'Life Ain't Enough for You', released as a single along with B-side 'Il Mio Stomacco È Il Piu Violento de Tutta Italia'; mem. jury, Cannes Film Festival 2009. *Films include:* Dèmoni 2: L'incubo ritorna 1986, Palombella Rossa 1988, La chiesa (The Church) 1989, Red Lob 1989, Zoo 1990, Close Friends 1992, Condannato a nozze 1993, Trauma 1993, Perdiamoci di vista! (David di Donatello for Best Actress 1994), La Reine Margot 1994, DeGenerazione (also writer and dir) 1995, The Stendhal Syndrome 1996, Il cielo è sempre più blu 1996, Compagna di viaggio (Travelling Companion) (David di Donatello for Best Actress 1996, Grolla d'oro Award 1996) 1996, Viola bacia tutti 1998, New Rose Hotel 1998, B. Monkey 1998, The Phantom of the Opera 1998, La tua lingua sul mio cuore (short) (also writer and dir) 1999, Scarlet Diva (also writer and dir) 2000, Loredasia (short) (also writer, dir, creative producer and supervising producer) 2000, L'assenzio (also writer and dir) 2001, Love Bites 2001, La sirène rouge (The Red Siren) 2002, xXx 2002, Ginostra 2002, The Keeper 2004, The Heart Is Deceitful Above All Things (also writer and dir) 2004, Last Days 2005, Cindy: The Doll Is Mine (short) 2005, Land of the Dead 2005, Live Freaky Die Freaky (voice) 2006, Sean Lennon's Friendly Fire 2006, Marie Antoinette 2006, Transylvania 2006, Boarding Gate 2007, Go Go Tales 2007, Désengagement 2007, Une vieille maîtresse (aka The Last Mistress) 2007, Mother of Tears 2007, De la guerre (On War) 2008, Diamond 13 2009, King Shot 2010, Regular Boy 2011, Gli sfiorati 2011, Baciato dalla fortuna 2011, Do Not Disturb 2012, Cadences Obstinées (Obsessive Rhythms) 2013, Shongram 2014, Incompresa (Misunderstood) (writer, dir) 2014; as dir: Abel/Asia (documentary short) 1998, La scomparsa (short) (also producer) 2000, Lest We Forget: The Video Collection (video (s)AINT, Marilyn Manson music video) 2004. *Television includes:* Sogni e bisogni (mini-series) 1985, Turno di notte (series) 1987, Les Misérables (mini-series) 2000, Milady (film) 2004. *Recording:* Total Entropy 2013. *Publications:* I Love You Kirk (novel) 1999; several stories for magazines including Dynamo, L'Espresso, Sette and Village. *E-mail:* infoaria_23@yahoo.it (office). *Website:* www.asiargento.it (office).

ARGERICH, Martha; Argentine pianist; b. 5 June 1941, Buenos Aires; ed studied with V. Scaramuzzo, Friedrich Gulda, Nikita Magaloff, Madeleine Lipatti and Arturo Benedetti Michelangeli; debut Buenos Aires 1949; London debut 1964; soloist with leading orchestras and conductors worldwide; debut at BBC London Proms (Schumann Concerto) 2000; as chamber musician, has toured Europe, USA and Japan with Gidon Kremer and Mischa Maisky; numerous recordings including most of repertoire for four hands and for two pianos with Nelson Freire, Stephen Bishop-Kovacevich, Nicolas Economou and Alexandre Rabinovitch; performances at Lockenhaus, Munich Piano Summer, Lucerne and Salzburg Festivals; Artistic Dir, Beppu Festival, Japan 1998–; Founder and Jury Pres. Int. Martha Argerich Piano Competition 1999–; f. Progetto Martha Argerich, Lugano 2002; f. Martha Argerich Presents Project, to bring together young players and renowned artists to play rarely performed compositions and masterpieces of the repertoire; Accademica di Santa Cecilia di Roma 1997, Officier, Ordre des Arts et Lettres 1996, Commdr, Ordre des Arts et des Lettres 2004, Order of the Rising Sun, Gold Rays with Rosette (Japan) 2005; First Prize, Busoni Contest and Geneva Int. Music Competition 1957, Int. Chopin Competition, Warsaw 1965, Prix Caecilia 1991, Diapason d'Or 1992, Edison Award 1993, Tokyo Record Academy Award 1995, CD Compact Award 1997, Musical America Musician of the Year 2001, Praemium Imperiale Award (Japan) 2005, Gramophone Awards Artist of the Year, three Grammy Awards, Kennedy Center Honor 2016. *Recordings include:* works by Brahms, Rachmaninov, Ravel and Schubert (with Nelson Freire) 2009, Argerich plays Chopin 2010, Argerich Lugano Concertos 2002–2010 (four CDs) 2012, Brahms & Schumann (with Bashmet Maisky) 2012, Martha Argerich: The Complete Recordings 2015, Martha Argerich & Friends: Live from Lugano Festival 2017, Beethoven: Symphony No.1; Piano Concerto No. 1 2018. *Address:* Agence Artistique Jacques Thelen, 15 Avenue Montaigne, 75008 Paris, France (office). *Telephone:* 1-56-89-32-00 (office). *Fax:* 1-56-89-32-01 (office). *E-mail:* jthelen@wanadoo.fr (office). *Website:* jacquesthelen.com (office).

ARGUETA ANTILLÓN, José Luis (Lucho); Salvadorean economist, academic and university administrator; *Member, Administrative Council, Faculty of Economics, University of El Salvador;* b. 16 July 1932, El Salvador; s. of Tomás Antillón and Andrea Argueta; m. María Luz Márquez 1969; four s. two d.; ed Univ. of El Salvador, Univ. of Chile, Universidad del Pais Vasco; Prof., Univ. of El Salvador 1964–67, Sec., Faculty of Econ. Sciences 1967–69, Prof., Faculty of Investigative Econs 1974–78, Dir 1985–86, Asst to Acting Rector 1979–80, Dir, Inst. of Econs Research, Rector 1985–90, Sec. for Postgraduates 1993–99, Investigator, Faculty of Econs 2000–, mem. Gen. Ass., mem. Admin. Council, Faculty of Econs 2013–; Prof. and Researcher, Cen. American Univ. 1980–85; Scholar, Universidad del País Vasco 1991–92, Investigator, Faculty of Econs 2001–07, mem. Gen. Ass. 2009–13; Dr hc (Univ. of Simón Bolívar, Colombia) 1987; Economist of the Year 1985, Distinguished Economist (several times). *Publications include:* Manual de Contabilidad Nacional 1967, La Economía Salvadoreana—Algunos Elementos de Análisis 1984, La Reedición de Reforma Universitaria de Córdoba—Una Necesidad Histórica 1989, Efectos Fiscales del CAFTA, Agenda para la Integraciòn de Centroamèrica, Problemas de Población Educación y Desarrollo. *Leisure interest:* sport. *Address:* Universidad de El Salvador, Facultad de Ciencias Económicas, Ciudad Universitaria, Final Av. Héroes y Mártires del 30 de Julio, San Salvador, El Salvador (office). *Telephone:* 2225-8930 (office). *E-mail:* antillon@navegante.com.sv (office); antillon_luis@yahoo.com (home).

ARGUETA DE BARILLAS, Marisol; Salvadorean lawyer and diplomatist; *Senior Director and Head of Latin America, World Economic Forum;* b. 1968; m. Carlos R. Barillas; three d.; ed Univ. of Oxford, UK, New York Univ., USA; fmr Asst Prof. of Constitutional Law and Political Law, El Salvador; Alt. Rep. to UN, New York 1990–97, Minister Counsellor, Embassy in Washington, DC 1997–99, Gen. Dir of Foreign Policy, Ministry for Foreign Affairs –2004, Adviser to Minister of Foreign Affairs 2004–08, Minister of Foreign Affairs 2008–09; Sr Dir and Head of Latin America, World Econ. Forum 2010–; fmr Vice-Pres. OAS Nat. Authorities Meeting for the Devt of Women; Co-founder Vital Voices – El Salvador; mem. Bd of Dirs Hogares CREA-El Salvador, Salvadorean Foundation for the Elderly, Int. Inst. for Women; mem. Oxford Union Soc. *Address:* c/o World Economic Forum USA, 3 East 54th Street, 18th Floor, New York, NY 10022, USA. *Website:* www.weforum.org.

ARGUS, Donald (Don) Robert, AC; Australian banker and business executive; b. 1 Aug. 1938, Bundaberg; s. of Dudley Francis Argus and Evelyn Argus; m. Patricia Anne Argus 1961; three d.; ed Royal Melbourne Inst. of Tech., Harvard Univ.; Chief Man. Corp. Lending, Nat. Australia Bank Ltd 1983, then Gen. Man. Credit Bureau, then Gen. Man. Group Strategic Devt, then Exec. Dir and COO, Man. Dir, CEO 1990–99; Dir Broken Hill Pty Co. Ltd (BHP Ltd) 1996–2009, Chair.

1999–2009, Chair. BHP Billiton Ltd, BHP Billiton Plc 2001–09; Chair. Brambles Industries Ltd 1999–2008; Chair. Australian Bankers Asscn 1992–94; Dir Southcorp Ltd 1999–, Australian Foundation Investment Co. Ltd 1999–; mem. Bank of America/Merrill Lynch Global Advisory Council 2013–, Int. Advisory Council, Allianz AG 2000–, Int. Advisory Cttee, New York Stock Exchange Bd of Dirs 2005–; conducted review of Australian cricket team 2011. *Leisure interests:* hockey, golf, reading.

ARGYROS, George Leon; American business executive and diplomatist; *Chairman Emeritus and Treasurer, Horatio Alger Association of Distinguished Americans Inc.;* b. 1937, Detroit, Mich.; m. Julia Argyros; three c.; ed Chapman Univ.; Founder Partner, Westar Capital, Chair. 1976–2001; Co-owner AirCal 1981–87; Owner Seattle Mariners professional baseball team 1981–89; Pres. and CEO Horatio Alger Asscn of Distinguished Americans Inc. 1995–98, Chair. 1998–2000, currently Treas. and Chair. Emer.; Chair. and CEO Arnel and Affiliates CA –2001; Amb. to Spain and Andorra 2001–04; Founder-Chair. Nixon Center, Washington, DC; Chair. Beckman Foundation; fmr Chair. Richard Nixon Library and Birthplace Foundation, Orange Co. Council Boy Scouts of America; mem. Bd Fed. Home Loan Mortgage Corpn (FreddieMac) 1990–93, US Chamber of Commerce, M.D. Anderson Cancer Center, Pacific Mercantile Bank, CoreLogic, Inc. –2010, DST Systems Inc. 1998–2014, First American Financial Corpn 2005–, Pacific Mercantile BanCorp. 2010–; fmr mem. Bd of Dirs Rockwell International Corpn, Newhall Land and Farming Co., Tecstar, Doskocil Manufacturing Co., Inc., Igloo Products Corp., Harper Leather Goods Inc., Verteq Inc.; mem. Bd of Trustees, Chapman Univ. 2001–, California Inst. of Tech. (fmr Vice-Chair. Business and Finance Cttee), Center for Strategic and Int. Studies, Washington, DC, Library of Congress Open World Leadership Center; Counselor Layalina Productions Inc.; apptd Archon Mother Church of Constantinople, Greek Orthodox Church, Order of St Andrew 2005; mem. Advisory Cttee for Trade Policy and Negotiations USA Trade Rep. –1990; Hon. DHumLitt (Chapman Univ.) 2005, Hon. DIur (Pepperdine Univ.) 1997; Horatio Alger Award of Distinguished Americans 1993, Ellis Island Medal of Honor 2001. *Address:* Horatio Alger Association of Distinguished Americans Inc., 99 Canal Center Plaza, Suite 320, Alexandria, VA 22314, USA (office). *Telephone:* (703) 684-9444 (office). *Fax:* (703) 548-3822 (office). *E-mail:* info@horatioalger.org (office). *Website:* www.horatioalger.org (office).

ARHABI, Abd al-Karim Ismail al-, MA; Yemeni politician; b. 1947, Alssadah, Ibb Prov.; ed Martin Luther Univ., Germany, academic and field training in USA, Germany and UK; worked in pvt. sector 1977–79; Gen. Dir Industrial Estate Authority 1979–81; Man. Dir Yemeni Industrial Bank 1981–94; Head of Small Enterprise Devt Unit 1994; est. and was Man. Dir Social Fund for Devt 1996; Minister of Social Affairs and Labour 2001–06; Deputy Prime Minister for Econ. Affairs and Minister of Planning and Int. Cooperation 2006–12.

ARHAR, France, BA, MA, PhD; Slovenian business executive and fmr central banker; *CEO, UniCredit Banka Slovenija d.d.;* b. 24 April 1948, Ljubljana; ed Univ. of Ljubljana; joined Nat. Bank of Slovenia 1971, Head of Section 1974–76, Asst Gen. Man. Int. Div. 1976–78, Gen. Man. Int. Div. and Asst Gov. 1978–88; trainee, Linklaters & Paines Pnrs, London, UK 1979, Hessische Landensbank Frankfurt 1982; Gen. Man. Corp. Finance LHB Int. Handelsbank, Frankfurt 1988–91; Gov. Bank of Slovenia 1991–2001; Chair. Man. Bd Vzajemna (pvt. health insurer) 2001–03, Bank Austria Creditanstalt d.d. Ljubljana (now UniCredit Banka Slovenija d.d.) 2003–12, currently CEO; Asst Prof. of Int. Econ. Law, Faculty of Law, Univ. of Ljubljana 1988, Asst Prof. of Int. Finance and Int. Financial Law 2005; Chair. Supervisory Bd Nova Ljubljanska Banka d.d. –2014; Chair. Advisory Cttee, Ljubljana Stock Exchange, Cttee of the Repub. of Slovenia for Negotiations on Succession under the Vienna Treaty; Pres. Ethics Cttee of the Int. Forum for Scientific Research in Pharmaceutical Cos, Slovenian Cttee for Negotiations on Succession by the Vienna Agreement, Council of Slovene Nat. Theatre, Ljubljana; Deputy Pres. Supervisory Bd, Bank Asscn of Slovenia; Dir Bank Association of Slovenia 2012–17; mem. Man. Cttee, Univ. of Ljubljana, mem. Council of the Faculty of Econs; mem. Govt Strategic Council on the Economy, Fiscal Council of the Govt, Arbitration panel, Perm. Arbitration at the Slovenian Chamber of Commerce and Industry; mem. ILO, Geneva. *Publications include:* three books on foreign trade, int. finance and int. econ. law and over 80 articles. *Address:* UniCredit Banka Slovenija d.d., Smartinska 140, Ljubljana, 1000, Slovenia (office). *Telephone:* (1) 5876600 (office). *Website:* www.unicreditbank.si (office).

ARIARAJAH, Rev. Wesley, BSc, BD, ThM, MPhil, PhD; Swiss (b. Sri Lankan) ecclesiastic and academic; *Professor Emeritus of Ecumenical Theology, School of Theology, Drew University;* b. 2 Dec. 1941, Jaffna, Sri Lanka; s. of Ponniah David Seevaratnam and Grace Annalukshmi (née Sinnapu); m. Christine Shyamala Chinniah 1974; three d.; ed Madras Christian Coll., India, United Theological Coll., Bangalore, India, Princeton Seminary, NJ, USA, Univ. of London, UK; ordained in Methodist Church; Minister, Methodist Church of Sri Lanka, Jaffna 1966–68; Lecturer, Theological Coll. Lanka, Pilimatalawa 1969–71; Chair. North and East Dist, Methodist Church, Jaffna 1974–81; mem. staff, WCC Programme on Dialogue with People of Living Faiths, Geneva 1981–83, Dir 1983–93, Deputy Sec.-Gen. WCC 1993–97; Prof. of Ecumenical Theology, School of Theology, Drew Univ., NJ 1997–2014; Sixth Lambeth Interfaith Lecturer 1987. *Publications include:* Dialogue 1980, The Bible and People of Other Faiths 1985, Hindus and Christians: A Century of Protestant Ecumenical Thought 1991, Gospel and Culture, An Ongoing Discussion in the Ecumenical Movement 1994, Did I Betray the Gospel?: The Letters of Paul and the Place of Women 1996, Not Without My Neighbour: Issues in Interfaith Dialogue 1999, Axis of Peace: Christian Faith in Times of Violence and War 2004, We Live by His Gifts – D.T. Niles, Preacher, Teacher and Ecumenist 2009, Your God, My God, Our God – Rethinking Christian Theology for Religious Plurality 2012, Power, Politics and Plurality – An Exploration of the Impact of Interfaith Dialogue on Christian Faith and Practice 2016, Strangers or Co-Pilgrims?: The Impact of Inter faith Dialogue on Christian Faith and Practice 2017; contrib. articles to specialist journals. *Leisure interest:* reading. *Address:* 5 Chemin Taverney, 1218 Grand-Saconnex, Geneva, Switzerland (home). *Telephone:* (22) 7982638 (home). *E-mail:* wariaraj@drew.edu (office); wesley.ariarajah@hotmail.com (home). *Website:* www.drew.edu (office).

ARIAS, Ileana, BA, MA, PhD; American clinical psychologist and health official; *Principal Deputy Director, Centers for Disease Control and Prevention;* ed Barnard Coll., State Univ. of New York at Stony Brook; began career as Research Assoc., SUNY, Stony Brook; Asst Prof., later Dir of Clinical Training and Prof. of Clinical Psychology, Univ. of Georgia –2000; joined Centers for Disease Control and Prevention (CDC) and Agency for Toxic Substances and Disease Registry 2000, currently Prin. Deputy Dir CDC; Acting Dir Nat. Center for Injury Prevention and Control 2004–05, Dir 2005; mem. editorial bd Journal of Aggression, Maltreatment, and Trauma, Review of Aggression and Violent Behavior, Violence and Victims; reviewer for 11 professional journals; mem. Advisory Bd Psychiatric and Forensic Doctor of Nursing Program, Univ. of Tennessee Health Science Center Coll. of Nursing, Nat. Safety Council, Univ. of Maryland Center for Risk Communication Research, European Center for Injury Prevention; mem. Defense Task Force on Sexual Assault in the Mil. Services. *Address:* Office of the Principal Deputy Director, Centers for Disease Control and Prevention, 1600 Clifton Rd, Atlanta, GA 30329, USA (office). *E-mail:* cdcinfo@cdc.gov (office). *Website:* www.cdc.gov (office).

ARIAS, Inocencio F.; Spanish civil servant and diplomatist; b. 20 April 1940; m.; three c.; joined diplomatic service 1967, Dir of Diplomatic Information Office, Ministry of Foreign Affairs 1980–82, 1985–88, 1996–97, Under-Sec., Ministry of Foreign Affairs 1988–91; State Sec. for Int. Co-operation for Iberoamerican Affairs 1991–93; Gen. Dir Real Madrid 1993–95; Perm. Rep. to UN, New York 1998–2004; Consul-Gen., Los Angeles, Calif. –2010 (retd); fmr Prof. of Int. Relations, Univ. Complutense, Univ. Carlos III, Madrid; 30 Spanish and foreign decorations. *Publications include:* numerous papers and contribs; Confesiones de un diplomático, Tres Mitos del Real Madrid 2002, La Trastienda de la Diplomacia: De Eva Peron a Barack Obama, 25 Encuentros Que Cambiaron Nuestra Historia 2010, Yo siempre creí que los diplomáticos eran unos mamones 2016.

ARIAS, Ricardo Alberto, BS, LLB, LLM; Panamanian lawyer and fmr diplomatist; b. 11 Sept. 1939; m.; four c.; ed Edmund A. Walsh School of Foreign Service, Georgetown Univ., Univ. of Puerto Rico, Yale Univ. Law School, USA; Prof. of Fiscal Law and Admin Law, Santa Maria La Antigua Univ. 1973–78; Founding mem. and Partner, Galindo, Arias & López (law firm), practised 1998–2004; Amb. to USA 1994–96, Minister of Foreign Affairs 1996–98, Amb. and Perm. Rep. to UN, New York 2004–09; f. La Prensa newspaper; Founding Dir and fmr Pres. Panamanian Stock Exchange; mem. Panamanian Bar Asscn, Inter-american Bar Asscn, Int. Bar Asscn; mem. Bd of Dirs Banco Gen. SA, Copa Airlines (and Copa Holdings) 1985–, Empresa General de Inversiones, SA; Hon. Pres., La Prensa. *Address:* Galindo, Arias & López, Scotia Plaza, 11th floor, Federico Boyd Ave. No.18 and 51 Street, Panamá, Panama (office). *Telephone:* 303-0303 (office). *Website:* gala.com.pa (office).

ARIAS CAÑETE, Miguel, LicenDer; Spanish civil servant, politician and EU official; *Commissioner for Climate Action and Energy, European Commission;* b. 24 Feb. 1950, Madrid; m. Micaela Domecq Solís-Beaumont; three c.; ed Jesuit School, Chamartín, Universidad Complutense de Madrid; began career as a govt lawyer 1974, worked as State Attorney for Special Services, Jerez de la Frontera, later in Cádiz; Prof. of Law, Univ. of Jerez de la Frontera 1978–82; joined Alianza Popular party 1982; Rep. for Cádiz dist in Andalusian Parl. 1982–86; Senator for Prov. of Cádiz in Spanish Senate 1982–86, 2000–04; mem. European Parl. 1986–99, 2014, fmr Chair. Agricultural Cttee and Regional Politics Cttee; mem. City Council of Jerez de la Frontera 1995–2000; Minister for Agric., Fisheries and Food 2000–04; Economy Sec., Partido Popular 2004–08, Pres. Electoral Cttee 2004–08; Rep. for Cádiz dist in Spanish Congress 2004–08, for Madrid dist 2008–14; Minister of Agric., Food and Environment 2011–14; selected by Partido Popular to head its list in European Parl. elections April 2014; Commr for Climate Action and Energy, European Comm. (EC), Brussels Nov. 2014–; Grand Cross, Order of Charles III 2004; Grand Cross, Order of Civil Merit 2011. *Address:* European Commission, DG Climate Action, 1049 Brussels, Belgium (office). *Telephone:* (2) 299-11-11 (office). *Website:* ec.europa.eu/clima (office).

ARIAS CÁRDENAS, Francisco Javier, BMASc; Venezuelan academic, diplomatist and politician; b. 20 Nov. 1950, San Cristóbal, Táchira; m.; two c.; ed Javeriana Univ., Colombia, Univ. of the Andes, Venezuelan Mil. Acad.; Prof., Venezuelan Mil. Acad. 1979–81, Venezuelan Army Artillery School 1981–82; Commdr Multiple Launch Rocket Group of José Gregorio Monagas 1989–92; Pres. Foundation for Mother and Child Food Programme 1992–95; Gov. Zulia State 1995–2000, 2013–17; Pres. Colombian-Venezuelan Council for Border Govs 1997–2000; Amb. and Perm. Rep. to UN, New York 2006–10; mem. Parl. 2011–12; Pres. Union for Progress (political movt), For a Praiseworthy Venezuela (civil asscn).

ARIAS GONZÁLEZ, Fernando; Spanish diplomatist and UN official; *Director-General (Designate), Organisation for the Prohibition of Chemical Weapons (OPCW);* b. 1952, Madrid; m.; three c.; ed Universidad Complutense de Madrid; joined Foreign Service 1979, First Sec. and Cultural Counsellor, Embassy of Spain in Netherlands 1979–83, Counsellor, Embassy of Spain in Romania 1983–87, Chief Admin. Officer and Deputy Dir-Gen., Ministry of Foreign Affairs 1987–90, Minister Counsellor (Deputy Chief of Mission), Embassy of Spain in Mexico 1990–94, in Argentina 1994–98, in China 2009–12, Amb. to Mali 1998–2000, to Bulgaria 2004–09, to Netherlands 2014–, Dir-Gen. Protocol Dept of Presidency of Govt 2000–04, Perm. Rep. to UN 2012–13, Perm. Rep. to OPCW 2014–, Vice-Pres. Exec. Council 2017–18, Dir-Gen. (Desig.) 2018–; numerous Spanish and foreign decorations including Order of Civil Merit, Commdr Order of Queen Isabel la Católica, Order of Carlos III, Order of Orange Nassau (Netherlands), Order of Merit (Argentina). *Address:* Organisation for the Prohibition of Chemical Weapons (OPCW), Johan de Wittlaan 32, 2517 JR The Hague, Netherlands (office). *Telephone:* (70) 4163300 (office). *Fax:* (70) 3063535 (office). *E-mail:* public.affairs@opcw.org (office). *Website:* www.opcw.org (office).

ARIAS SÁNCHEZ, Oscar, PhD; Costa Rican politician, academic and fmr head of state; b. 13 Sept. 1940, Heredia; s. of Juan Rafael Arias Trejos and Lilliam Sánchez Cortes; m. 1st Margarita Penón (divorced); one s. one d.; m. 2nd Suzanne Fischel; ed Univ. of Costa Rica, Univ. of Essex, UK; Prof., School of Political Sciences, Univ. of Costa Rica 1969–72; Financial Adviser to Pres. of Repub. 1970–72; Minister of Nat. Planning and Econs Policy 1972–77; Int. Sec. Liberación Nacional Party 1975, Gen. Sec. 1979–83, 1983; Congressman in Legis. Ass. 1978–82; Pres. of Costa Rica 1986–90, 2006–10; f. Arias Foundation for Peace and Human Progress 1988; mem.

Bd Cen. Bank 1972–77, Vice-Pres. 1970–72; ad hoc Comm. mem. Heredia's Nat. Univ. 1972–75; mem. Bd Tech. Inst. 1974–77; mem. Rector's Nat. Council 1974–77; mem. Bd Int. Univ. Exchange Fund, Geneva 1976; mem. North–South Roundtable 1977; has participated in numerous int. meetings and socialist conventions; instrumental in formulating the Cen. American Peace Agreement 1986–87; approx. 50 hon. degrees; Nobel Peace Prize 1987, Martin Luther King Award 1987, Príncipe de Asturias Award 1988, shared Philadelphia Liberty Medal 1991, Albert Schweitzer Prize for Humanitarianism, and other awards. *Publications:* Pressure Groups in Costa Rica 1970 (Essay's Nat. Award 1971), Who Governs in Costa Rica? 1976, Latin American Democracy, Independence and Society 1977, Roads for Costa Rica's Development 1977, New Ways for Costa Rican Development 1980 and many articles in newspapers and in nat. and foreign magazines. *Address:* Arias Foundation for Peace and Human Progress, Costado suroeste de la Plaza de Democracia, sobre Avenida 2A, San José, Costa Rica. *Website:* www.arias.or.cr.

ARIAS SÁNCHEZ, Rodrigo, LLM; Costa Rican lawyer and politician; b. 1946, San Francisco de Heredia; s. of Juan Rafael Arias Trejos and Lilliam Sánchez Cortés; brother of Oscar Arias Sánchez; ed Univ. of Costa Rica, Univ. of Pennsylvania, USA; Prof. of Commercial Law, Univ. of Costa Rica 1971–73; attorney, then legal adviser, Dir and Vice-Pres. Bolsa Nacional de Valores 1971–85, Man. 1997–2003; Chair. Ingenio Taboga SA 1974–; Pres. Municipality of Heredia 1974–86; Minister of the Presidency 1986–99, 2006–10. *Website:* www .rodrigoarias.com.

ARIDJIS, Homero; Mexican author, poet and diplomatist; b. 6 April 1940, Contepec, Michoacán; m. Betty Ferber 1965, two d.; ed Autonomous Univ. of Mexico 1961; lecturer in Mexican literature at univs in USA; Cultural Attaché, Embassy in Netherlands 1972, later Amb. to Switzerland and the Netherlands; Man. Cultural Inst., Michoacán, Dir Festival Int. de Poesia 1981, 1982, 1987; f. Review Correspondencias; Chief Ed. Dialogos; Visiting Prof., Univ. of Indiana and New York Univ.; Poet-in-Residence, Columbia Univ. Translation Center, New York; co-f. Pres. Grupo de los Cien 1985 (100 internationally renowned artists and intellectuals active in environmental affairs); Nichols Chair in Humanities and Public Sphere, Univ. of Calif., Irvine; Pres. International PEN 1997–2003, Pres. Emer. 2003–09; Amb. to UNESCO 2007–10; Guggenheim Fellow 1966–67, 1979–80; Hon. DHumLitt (Indiana) 1993; Global 500 Award 1987, Novedades Novela Prize 1988, Grinzane Cavour Prize for Best Foreign Fiction 1992, Prix Roger Caillois, France 1997, Presea Generalisimo José María Morelos, City of Morelia 1998, Environmentalist of the Year Award, Latin Trade Magazine 1999, John Hay Award, Orion Soc. 2000, Forces for Nature Award, National Resources Defense Council 2001, Green Cross Millennium Award for Int. Environmental Leadership, Global Green 2002. *Publications include:* poetry: Los ojos desdoblados 1960, Antes del reino 1963, Ajedrez-Navegaciones 1969, Los espacios azules 1969 (Blue Spaces 1974), Quemar las naves 1975, Vivir para ver 1977, Construir la muerte 1982, Obra poética 1960–86 1987, Imágenes para el fin del milenio 1990, Nueva expulsión del paraíso 1990, El poeta en peligro de extinción 1992, Tiempo de ángeles 1994, Ojos de otro mirar 1998 (Eyes to See Otherwise: Selected Poems of Homero Aridjis 2002), El ojo de la ballena 2001, Los poemas solares 2005, Diario de sueños 2011, Del cielo y sus maravillas, de la tierra y sus miserias 2013, La poesía llama 2018; prose: La tumba de Filidor 1961, Mirándola dormir 1964, Perséfone 1967 (Persephone 1986), El poeta niño 1971, Noche de independencia 1978, Espectáculo del año dos mil 1981, Playa nudista y otros relatos 1982, 1492 vida y tiempos de Juan Cabezón de Castilla 1985, El último Adán 1986, Memorias del nuevo mundo 1988, Gran teatro del fin del mundo 1989, La leyenda de los soles 1993, El Señor de los últimos días: Visiones del año dos mil 1994, ¿En quién piensas cuando haces el amor? 1996, Apocalipsis con figuras 1997, La montaña de las mariposas 2000, El silencio de Orlando 2000, La zona del silencio 2002, El hombre que amaba el Sol 2005, Sicarios 2007, Ciudad de zombis 2014, Carne de Dios 2015.

ARIE, Thomas Harry David, CBE, MA, BM, DPM, FRCP, FFPH; British psychiatrist and academic; *Professor Emeritus of Health Care of the Elderly, University of Nottingham;* b. 9 Aug. 1933, Prague, Czechoslovakia; s. of Dr O. M. Arie and H. Arie; m. Eleanor Aitken 1963; one s. two d.; ed Balliol Coll., Oxford; Sr Lecturer in Social Medicine, London Hosp. Medical Coll. 1962–74; Consultant Psychiatrist for Old People, Goodmayes Hosp. 1969–77; Foundation Prof. and Head, Dept of Health Care of the Elderly, Univ. of Nottingham 1977–95, Prof. Emer. 1995–; Visiting Prof., NZ Geriatrics Soc. 1980, Univ. of the Negev, Israel 1988, UCLA, USA 1991, Univ. of Keele 1997; Consultant Psychiatrist to the Nottingham Hosps 1977–95; Vice-Pres. Royal Coll. of Psychiatrists 1984–86, Chair. Specialist Section on Old Age 1981–86, Hon. Fellow 2001; Chair. Geriatric Psychiatry Section, World Psychiatric Asscn 1989–93; mem. Standing Medical Advisory Cttee for the Nat. Health Service 1980–84, Cttee on the Review of Medicines 1981–91, Registrar Gen.'s Medical Advisory Cttee 1990–94; Gov., Centre for Policy on Ageing 1992–98; Vice-Chair. Royal Surgical Aid Soc. (AgeCare) 1995–2007, Vice-Pres. 2008; Fellow, Faculty of Public Health; Dhole-Eddlestone Memorial Prize, British Geriatrics Soc. 1996; Lifetime Award, Int. Psychogeriatric Asscn 1999, Founders' Medal, British Geriatrics Soc. 2005, Lifetime Award, Old Age Faculty, Royal Coll. of Psychiatrists 2012. *Publications include:* Health Care of the Elderly (ed.) 1981, Recent Advances in Psychogeriatrics (Vol. 1) 1985, (Vol. 2) 1992; papers on care of the aged, old age psychiatry, epidemiology and educ. *Address:* Cromwell House, West Church Street, Kenninghall, Norfolk, NR16 2EN, England (home).

ARIFFIN, Datuk Wan Zulkiflee Wan, BEng; Malaysian business executive; *President and Group CEO, Petroliam Nasional Berhad (Petronas);* ed Adelaide Univ., Australia, Sr Man. Devt Program, Institut Européen d'Admin des Affaires (INSEAD), France, Advanced Man. Program, Harvard Business School, USA; Process Engineer, Gas Processing Plant No. 1 and Export Terminal Project, Petronas Gas Sdn Berhad 1983–84, Section Head of Process Tech. of Gas Processing, Plant Kerteh, Petronas Gas Sdn Berhad 1984–87, Project Eng Man., Eng Dept, Gas Processing Plants 2 and 3, Kerteh 1988–93, Project Man., Gas Processing Plants Nos 5 & 6, Petronas Gas Berhad 1993–97, Sr Man. (Downstream Business)/Exec. Asst to Pres. 1997–2000, as Gen. Man. Int. Projects Man. Div. of OGP Tech. Services Sdn Berhad 2000–01, Gen. Man. Strategy and Business Devt Unit 2001–03, Non-Ind. Dir (non-exec.), Petronas Gas Berhad 2003–10, CEO 2003–07, Man. Dir 2003–10, Vice-Pres., Gas Business 2006–10, Chair. Petronas Gas Berhad 2008–10, Exec. Vice-Pres., Downstream Business, Petronas Dagangan Berhad 2010–15, COO and Exec. Vice-Pres., Downstream Petroliam Nasional Berhad (Petronas) –2015, Chair. Petronas Chemicals Group Berhad 2010–15, Non-Ind. Dir (non-exec.) and Chair. Petronas Dagangan Berhad 2010–15, Exec. Dir, Petronas 2012–, Pres. and Group CEO 2015–, Dir, Petronas Chemicals Group Berhad 2008–15, Star Energy Group Ltd –2012; Chair. Malaysian-Egyptian Business Council; mem. Bd of Dirs (non-exec.), MISC Berhad 2010–11; mem. Council, Project Man. Inst., Malaysian Chapter –2003, Malaysian Chemical Engineers Inst. for several years; Chair. Nat. Organizing Cttee, World Gas Conf. 2012; mem. Exec. Cttee, Int. Gas Union, Argentinian Triennium –2009; Industry Advisor, Eng Faculty, Universiti Putra Malaysia; Industrial Adviser, Gas Eng Dept, Univ. Technology Malaysia; Hon. FIChemE. *Address:* Petroliam Nasional Berhad (Petronas), Tower 1, Petronas Twin Towers, Kuala Lumpur City Centre, Kuala Lumpur 50088, Malaysia (office). *Telephone:* (3) 20515000 (office). *Fax:* (3) 20265050 (office). *E-mail:* webmaster@petronas.com.my (office). *Website:* www .petronas.com.my (office).

ARIFI, Teuta, BA, MA, PhD; Macedonian philologist and politician; *Mayor of Tetovo;* b. 19 Oct. 1969, Tetovo; m.; two c.; ed Univ. of Prishtina, Kosovo, SS. Cyril and Methodius Univ., Skopje; Fellow, Women's Leadership Inst., Santa Fe, NM, USA 1992; Fellow and Researcher, CORE Inst. on OSCE Studies, Univ. of Hamburg 1999–2001; Asst Prof. of History of Albanian Literature, Faculty of Philology, SS. Cyril and Methodius Univ. 1997–; Assoc. Prof. of Multicultural Issues, Teacher Training Faculty, SEE Univ., Tetovo 2001–, Dean of the Teacher Training Faculty 2001–06, mem. Jt Bd SEE Univ. 2001–; Vice-Pres. Democratic Union for Integration 2002–; mem. Parl. 2002–11, Head of Foreign Policy Cttee, mem. Parl. Del. in Parl. Ass. of Council of Europe, Head of Parl. Del. at North Atlantic Council, Head of Cttee on Culture 2006–11, Head of Foreign Policy Cttee; Deputy Prime Minister, responsible for European Integration 2011–13; Mayor of Tetovo 2013–; Vice-Chair. Group of Specialists of the Council of Europe on positive actions in the field of equality between women and men 1998–2000; adviser to Ministry of Foreign Affairs and Head of the Unit for OSCE and other int. orgs within the Ministry 1996–97; mem. OSCE team for monitoring of parl. elections in Albania May 1996; mem. Bd Soros Open Society Inst. in Macedonia 1995–96; Rep. of Steering Cttee of experts on equality between women and men in the Council of Europe, Strasbourg 1995–2000, mem. Bureau of the Steering Cttee on Equality 1996–2000; mem. Bd, Centre for Multiculture and Understanding, Skopje 1997–99; radio commentator, South European Dept, Radio Deutsche Welle, Cologne 1992–2002; mem. Advisory Bd, Research Team of the situation of minorities in South Europe, CEI-Budapest 1998–2000; columnist, Dnevnik (Daily) 2006–. *Publications:* Gjeografia mie (My Geography) (poetry) 1996, Feminizmi ekzistencialist (Existential Feminism) (study) 1997, Ucestvoto na zenite vo sovremenite trendovi vo Republika Makedonija (Women's Participation in Contemporary Trends in the Republic of Macedonia) (study) 1997, Shatë ditë magjike (Seven Magical Days) (novel) 1998. *Address:* Municipality of Tetovo, Dervish Cara, NN, 1200 Tetovo, North Macedonia. *Telephone:* (44) 335499. *Fax:* (44) 339420. *E-mail:* cabinet@tetova.gov.mk. *Website:* www.tetova.gov.mk.

ARIGONI, Duilio, DScTech; Swiss chemist and academic; *Professor Emeritus of Organic Chemistry, Swiss Federal Institute of Technology (ETH);* b. 6 Dec. 1928, Lugano; s. of Bernardino Arigoni and Emma Arigoni (née Bernasconi); m. Carla Diener 1958 (died 1998); two s. one d.; ed Swiss Fed. Inst. of Tech. (ETH), Zürich; Lecturer in Organic Chem., ETH Zürich 1961–62, Assoc. Prof. 1962–67, Prof. 1967–96, Prof. Emer. 1996–; Visiting Prof., Harvard Univ., USA 1969, 1983, Technion, Haifa, Israel 1970, Univ. of Cambridge 1981; Prof.-at-Large, Cornell Univ. 1980–87, Univ. of Innsbruck, Austria 2003; mem. Deutsche Akad. der Naturforscher Leopoldina 1976, Academia Europaea, London 1989, Accad. Nazionale delle Scienze, Rome 1991, European Acad. of Sciences, Brussels 2004; Foreign mem. Royal Soc., London 1991; Foreign Assoc. NAS, Washington, DC 1998, Acad. des Sciences, Paris 2005; Hon. FRSC 1978, Hon. mem. French Chem. Soc. 1976, Italian Chem. Soc. 1981, American Acad. of Arts and Sciences 1988; Dr hc (Université de Paris-Sud) 1982; Davy Medal, Royal Soc., London 1983, R.A. Welch Award, Welch Foundation, USA 1985, ACS Arthur C. Cope Award 1986, Wolf Prize, Israel 1989, Marcel Benoist Prize, Switzerland 1992 and other prizes and awards. *Publications:* over 200 publs in scientific journals. *Leisure interest:* music, especially Bach, Mozart. *Address:* Laboratorium für Organische Chemie, ETH Hönggerberg, HCI H307, Wolfgang-Pauli-Strasse 10, 8093 Zürich (office); Im Glockenacker 42, 8053 Zürich, Switzerland (home). *Telephone:* (44) 632-2891 (office); (44) 381-1383 (home). *Fax:* (44) 632-1154 (office). *E-mail:* arigoni@org .chem.ethz.ch (office); duilio.arigoni@org.chem.ethz.ch (office). *Website:* www.chab .ethz.ch/forschung/loc/index_EN (office).

ARIMA, Akito, BSc, MSc, DSc; Japanese scientist and academic; b. 13 Sept. 1930, Osaka; s. of Johji Arima and Kazuko Arima; m. Hiroko Aota 1957; one s. one d.; ed Musashi Koto Gakko Coll., Univ. of Tokyo; Research Assoc. Inst. for Nuclear Studies, Univ. of Tokyo 1956, Lecturer, Dept of Physics 1960, Assoc. Prof. 1964, Prof. of Physics, Faculty of Science 1975, Dir Computer Centre 1981–87, Councillor 1983–87, Dean, Faculty of Science 1985–87, Vice-Pres. 1987–89, Pres. 1989–93, Prof. Emer. 1993; Visiting Prof., Rutgers and Princeton Univs 1967–68, State Univ. of New York, Stony Brook 1968, USA 1971–73; Prof., Hosei Univ. April-Sept. 1993; Scientific Counsellor Ministry of Educ. 1993–98; Pres. Inst. of Physical and Chemical Research (RIKEN) 1993–98; Chair. Cen. Council for Educ. 1995–98; Minister of Educ. Science, Sports and Culture 1998–99; Minister of State for Science and Tech. Jan.-Oct. 1999; Chair. Japan Science Foundation 2000–; Dir Science Museum 2004–; Pres. and Chair. Bd of Trustees, Int. Human Frontier Science Program Org. 2009–12; Deputy Chair. Council for Relocation of Diet and other orgs 1996–98; mem. Science Council of Japan 1985–94, Admin. Reform Council 1996–98, House of Councillors 1998–2004; Hon. Prof., Univ. of Glasgow 1984, Univ. of Science and Tech., China 1992, Peking Univ., China 1998; Foreign Hon. mem., American Acad. of Arts and Sciences 1999; Grosse Verdienstkreuz (Germany) 1990, Order of Orange Nassau (Netherlands) 1991, Grand Officier, Légion d'honneur 1998, Hon. KBE 2002, Grand Cordon of the Order of the Rising Sun (Japan) 2004, Order of Culture 2010; Hon. DSc (Univ. of Glasgow) 1979; Dr hc (Drexel Univ., USA) 1992, (Chung Yuan Christian Univ., Taiwan) 1992, (State Univ. of New York, USA) 1994, (Univ. of Groningen, Netherlands) 1994, (Univ. of Birmingham, UK) 1996, (Univ. of Surrey, UK) 1999, (Weizmann Inst. of Science, Israel) 1999, (Univ. of Stellenbosch, South Africa) 1999, (Univ. of Arizona, USA) 2000; Nishina Memorial Prize 1978, Humboldt Prize 1987, Haiku Soc. Prize for a book of poetry (haikus) 1988, John Price Wetherill Medal, Franklin Inst., USA 1990, Bonner Prize, American Physical Soc. 1993, Japan Acad. Prize 1993, Person of Cultural Merit 2004. *Publications include:* Interacting Boson Model 1987, Einstein's Century: Akito Arima's Haiku 2001. *Leisure interests:* Haiku, calligraphy, reading. *Address:* International Human Frontier Science Program Organization, 12 quai Saint-Jean, BP 10034, 67000 Strasbourg Cedex, France (office); Science Museum, 2-1 Kitanomaru-koen, Chiyoda-ku, Tokyo 102-0091, Japan (office). *Telephone:* (3) 3212-8544 (office). *Fax:* (3) 3212-8443 (office). *E-mail:* akito_arima@sangiin.go.jp (office). *Website:* www.hfsp.org; www.jsf.or.jp.

ARIMURA, Haruko, PhD; Japanese politician; *Minister in charge of Women's Empowerment, of Administrative Reform and of Civil Service Reform, and Minister of State for Consumer Affairs and Food Safety, for Regulatory Reform, for Measures for Declining Birthrate and for Gender Equality;* b. 21 Sept. 1970; m.; two d.; ed Int. Christian Univ., Tokyo, School for Int. Training, Vermont, USA, Aoyama Gakuin Univ.; began career with Human Resources Div., McDonald's Japan; mem. House of Councillors (upper house of Parl.) 2001–, Chair. Environment Cttee 2008–09, mem. Cttee on Economy and Industry, Special Cttee on Reconstruction after the Great East Japan Earthquake, Research Cttee on Governing Structures; Parl. Sec. for Educ., Culture, Sports, Science and Tech. 2005–06; Minister in charge of Women's Empowerment, of Admin. Reform and of Civil Service Reform, and Minister of State for Consumer Affairs and Food Safety, for Regulatory Reform, for Measures for Declining Birthrate and for Gender Equality 2014–; mem. Liberal Democratic Party. *Address:* Cabinet Office, 1-6-1, Nagata-cho, Chiyoda-ku, Tokyo 100-8968, Japan (office). *Telephone:* (3) 5253-2111 (office). *Website:* www.cao.go.jp (office); www.arimura.tv.

ARINZE, HE Cardinal Francis A., DD, STL; Nigerian ecclesiastic; *Prefect of Congregation Emeritus for Divine Worship and the Discipline of the Sacraments;* b. 1 Nov. 1932, Eziowelle, Onitsha; s. of Joseph Arinze Nwankwu and Bernadette M. Arinze; ed Bigard Memorial Seminary, Nigeria, Urban Univ., Rome and Univ. of London; ordained priest 1958, served in Onitsha 1958, Coadjutor Bishop of Onitsha (Titular Church of Fissiana) 1965, Archbishop of Onitsha 1967–85; Pro-Prefect of the Secr. of Non-Christians 1984, Pres. 1985; cr. Cardinal 1985; Pres. Pontifical Council for Inter-Religious Dialogue 1984–2002; Prefect of Congregation for Divine Worship and the Discipline of the Sacraments 2002–08, Emer. 2009–; Hon. PhD (Univ. of Nigeria) 1986; Hon. LLD (Catholic Univ. of America) 1998; Hon. DD (Wake Forest Univ., USA) 1999, (Univ. of Our Lady of the Lake, USA) 2003; Hon. DH (Univ. of Santo Tomas, Philippines) 2001, DD hc (Christendom Coll., VA) 2004. *Publications:* Partnership in Education 1965, Sacrifice in Ibo Religion 1970, Answering God's Call 1983, Alone With God 1986, Church in Dialogue 1990, Meeting Other Believers 1997, Brücken Bauen 2000, The Holy Eucharist 2001, Religions for Peace 2002, Trust in Divine Providence 2003, God's Invisible Hand 2003. *Leisure interests:* tennis, reading. *Address:* Congregation for Divine Worship and the Discipline of the Sacraments, Palazzo delle Congregazioni, Piazza Pio XII 10, 00193 Rome, Italy (home). *Telephone:* (06) 69884316 (home). *Fax:* (06) 69883499 (home). *E-mail:* cultdiv@ccdds.va (home). *Website:* www.vatican.va/roman_curia/congregations/ccdds (home).

ARIPOV, Abdulla; Uzbekistani politician; *Prime Minister;* b. 24 May 1961, Tashkent, Uzbek SSR, USSR; m.; five d.; ed Tashkent Electro-Tech. Inst. of Communications; mem. O'zbekiston Liberal Demokratik Partiyasi (O'zlidep—Uzbekistan Liberal Democratic Party); Deputy Prime Minister 2002–12, also Head of Complex on Information and Telecommunications Technologies Issues and Dir-Gen. Communications and Information Agency of Uzbekistan 2002–09, responsible for the Social Sphere, Science, Educ., Health, Culture and for contacts with CIS-partners 2009–12; Head of Complex on Information Systems and Telecommunications 2012–16; Deputy Prime Minister Sept.–Dec. 2016, Prime Minister Dec. 2016–; Order 'Do'stlik' (Friendship), Order 'Mehnat shuhrati' (Labour Glory). *Address:* Office of the Cabinet of Ministers, 100078 Tashkent, Mustaqillik maydoni 5, Uzbekistan (office). *Telephone:* (71) 239-86-76 (office). *Fax:* (71) 239-84-63 (office). *Website:* www.gov.uz (office).

ARISMUNANDAR, Wiranto, MSc; Indonesian mechanical engineer, academic and politician; *Professor of Mechanical Engineering, Institut Teknologi Bandung;* b. 19 Nov. 1933, Semarang; s. of Raden Arismunandar and Raden Roro Sri Wuryan; m. Nyi Raden Sekarningrum Wirakusumah; three s. three d.; ed Univ. of Indonesia, Purdue and Stanford Univs, USA; Research Assoc., Dept of Mechanical Eng, Stanford Univ. 1961–62; training in rocket propulsion, Japan 1965; Vice-Chair. Indonesian Nat. Inst. of Aeronautics and Space 1978–89; Prof. of Mechanical Eng, Inst. of Tech., Bandung 1973–, Pres. 1988–97; Minister of Educ. and Culture 1998; Sr Scientist, Indonesian Agency for the Assessment and Application of Tech.; technological adviser, Indonesian Aircraft Industry 1979–; Consultant, Indonesian Nat. Atomic Energy Agency; Chair. Patent Appeal Cttee, Ministry of Justice; mem. People's Consultative Council 1992–97, Consultative Bd of Indonesian Islamic Council, Nat. Energy Cttee, World Energy Conf., Nat. Telecommunication Council, Indonesian Nat. Cttee; mem. Indonesian Nat. Research Council, AIAA, Indonesian Aeronautics and Astronautics Inst., Soc. of Automotive Engineers of Indonesia (Founding mem.) and numerous other nat. and int. eng bodies; Chief Ed. Teknology magazine; Fellow, Islamic Acad. of Sciences; Satyalancana Dwidya Sistha Medal of Merit 1968, 1983, 1989, 1992, Satyalancana Karya Satya (First Class) 1990, Satyalancana Karya Satya for 30 years' service, Bintang Jasa Utama 1998. *Publications:* 13 books and more than 100 papers. *Leisure interests:* sport, photography. *Address:* Institut Teknologi Bandung, Department of Mechanical Engineering, Faculty of Industrial Technology, Ganesa 10, Bandung 40132 (office); Bukit Dago Utara I/6, Bandung 40135, Indonesia (home). *Telephone:* (22) 2534118 (office); (22) 2503558 (home). *Fax:* (22) 2534212 (office); (22) 2503558 (home). *E-mail:* wiranto@lmbsp.ms.itb.ac.id (office). *Website:* www.itb.ac.id (office).

ARISMUNANDAR, Lt-Gen. Wismoyo; Indonesian army officer (retd); b. 10 Feb. 1940, Bondowoso, East Java; ed Mil. Acad.; brother-in-law of fmr Pres. Suharto; Danjen Kopassus 1983–85, Trikora Mil. Commdr 1983–85, Kostrad 1990–93, Commdr Jakarta Strategic Reserve Command, fmr Army Deputy Chief, Chief of Army Staff 1993–95; Chair. KONI (Nat. Sports Cttee) 1995; mem. Bd of Trustees, All Indonesian Billiards Sports Asscn, Fed. of Sports Karate-do Indonesia. *Address:* c/o Board of Trustees, All Indonesian Billiards Sports Association, Doors VII Main Stadium, Bung Karno, Senayan, Jakarta 10270, Indonesia.

ARISTIDE, Jean Bertrand, PhD; Haitian academic, fmr ecclesiastic and fmr head of state; b. 15 July 1953, Salut; m. Mildred Trouillot 1996; one d.; ed Univ. of South Africa; Roman Catholic priest; expelled from Salesian Order 1988; resgnd from priesthood Nov. 1994; Pres. of Haiti Feb.–Oct. 1991, 1993–96, 2001–04; in exile in Caracas, Venezuela Oct. 1991; returned Oct. 1993 after resignation of junta; f. La Fanmi Lavalas party 1996; fled to Africa following civil unrest Feb. 2004; Hon. Research Fellow in African Languages, Univ. of SA 2004; returned to Haiti 2011. *Publications:* In the Parish of the Poor: Writings from Haiti 1990, Aristide: An Autobiography 1993, Haiti and the New World Order 1995, Dignity 1996, Eyes of the Heart 2000.

ARITON, Ion; Romanian economist and politician; b. 15 Feb. 1956, Pitești; ed Univ. of Timisoara, Lucian Blaga Univ. of Sibiu; Commercial Dir SC Petrom SA, Sibiu 1993–2000, Dir-Gen. Sibiu Br. 2000–01; Exec. Dir SC Intermedia, Sibiu 2003–04; Financial Man. referent, CSU Sibiu, Lucian Blaga Univ. of Sibiu 2004–05; Prefect of Sibiu Co. 2005–07; Government Insp. 2007–08; mem. Senatul (Senate) 2008–12, Chair. Cttee on Budget, Finance, Banking Activity and Capital Market; Minister of the Economy, Trade and the Business Environment 2010–12; mem. Democratic Liberal Party (Partidul Democrat Liberal—PD-L), Chair. PD-L Sibiu Br. 2008; Kt, Order of the Star of Romania 2007; Prize for Excellence 2006. *E-mail:* ion.ariton@gmail.com.

ARKIN, Alan Wolf; American actor, director and author; b. 26 March 1934; s. of David Arkin and Beatrice Arkin; m. 1st Jeremy Yaffe; two s.; m. 2nd Barbara Dana; one s.; m. 3rd Suzanne Newlander; ed Los Angeles City Coll., Los Angeles State Coll., Bennington Coll.; made professional theatre debut with the Compass Players, St Louis 1959; later joined Second City group, Chicago 1960; made New York debut at Royal, in revue From the Second City 1961; played David Kolvitz in Enter Laughing 1963–64 (Tony Award 1963), appeared in revue A View Under The Bridge 1964, Harry Berline in Luv. *Films include:* Enter Laughing (New York Film Critics Theatre World Award 1964) 1964, The Russians Are Coming, The Russians Are Coming (Golden Globe Award) 1966, Women Times Seven 1967, Wait Until Dark 1967, Inspector Clouseau 1968, The Heart is a Lonely Hunter 1968, Popi 1969, Catch-22 1970, Little Murders (also Dir) 1971, Last of the Red Hot Lovers 1972, Freebie and the Bean 1974, Rafferty and the Gold Dust Twins 1975, Hearts of the West (Best Supporting Actor Award) 1975, The In-Laws 1979, The Magician of Lublin 1979, Simon 1980, Chu Chu and the Philly Flash 1981, Improper Channels (Canadian Acad. Award) 1981, The Last Unicorn 1982, Joshua Then and Now (Canadian Acad. Award) 1985, Coupe de Ville 1989, Havana 1990, Edward Scissorhands 1990, The Rocketeer 1990, Glengarry Glen Ross 1992, Indian Summer 1993, So I Married an Axe Murderer 1993, Steal Big, Steal Little 1995, Mother Night 1995, Grosse Point Blank 1997, Gattaca 1998, The Slums of Beverly Hills 1998, Jakob the Liar 1999, Arigo 2000, America's Sweethearts 2001, Thirteen Conversations About One Thing 2001, Counting Sheep 2002, Noel 2004, Eros 2004, The Novice 2004, Firewall 2006, Little Miss Sunshine (Screen Actors' Guild Award for Outstanding Performance by a Cast 2007, BAFTA Award for Best Supporting Actor 2007, Acad. Award for Best Supporting Actor 2007) 2006, The Santa Clause 3: The Escape Clause 2006, Raising Flagg 2006, Rendition 2007, Get Smart 2008, Marley & Me 2008, City Island 2009, The Private Lives of Pippa Lee 2009, Argo 2012, Stand Up Guys 2012, Grudge Match 2013, Million Dollar Arm 2014. *TV appearances include:* The Love Song of Barney Kempinski 1966, The Other Side of Hell 1978, The Defection of Simas Kudirka 1978, Captain Kangaroo, A Deadly Business 1986, Escape from Sobibor, Necessary Parties, Cooperstown, Taking the Heat, Doomsday Gun, Varian's War 2001, The Pentagon Papers 2003, And Starring Pancho Villa as Himself 2003. *Theatre includes:* dir: Eh? at the Circle in the Square 1966, Hail Scrawdyke 1966, Little Murders, 1969, White House Murder Case 1970, The Sunshine Boys, Eh? 1972, Molly 1973, Joan Lorraine 1974, Power Plays (also wrote and directed), Promenade Theatre 1998, The Sorrows of Stephen, Room Service. *Publications include:* Tony's Hard Work Day, The Lemming Condition, Halfway Through the Door, The Clearing 1986, Some Fine Grampa! 1995, One Present from Flekmans 1998, Cassie Loves Beethoven 1999, An Improvised Life: A Memoir 2011. *Telephone:* (760) 729-2000 (office). *Fax:* (866) 374-8095 (office). *E-mail:* info@celebritytalent.net (office). *Website:* www.celebritytalent.net/sampletalent/2090/alan-arkin (office).

ARLACCHI, (Giuseppe) Pino; Italian sociologist, academic, international organization official and politician; b. 21 Feb. 1951, Gioia Tauro, Reggio Calabria; m.; two c.; Assoc. Prof. of Applied Sociology, Univ. of Calabria 1982–85, Univ. of Florence 1988–94; apptd Prof. of Sociology, Univ. of Sassari 1994; elected to Chamber of Deputies 1994–95, to Senate 1995–97; Vice-Pres. Parl. Comm. on the Mafia; UN Under-Sec.-Gen. and Dir-Gen. UN, Vienna 1997–2002; Exec. Dir UN Office for Drug Control and Crime Prevention 1997–2002; Prof. of Sociology, School of Political Science, Univ. of Sassari 1998–; MEP 2009–, Vice Chair. Del. for Relations with Afghanistan, mem. Cttee on Foreign Affairs; mem. Hon. Cttee of the Foundation for Dialogue among Civilizations; Pres. Int. Asscn for the Study of Organized Crime 1984–87; Hon. Pres. Giovanni Falcone Foundation 1992–2000; Fellow, Ford Foundation; adviser to Govt of China about security for 2008 Beijing Olympic Games. *Publications:* numerous publs on int. organized crime. *Leisure interest:* sailing. *Address:* European Parliament, Bât. Altiero Spinelli, 09G309 60, rue Wiertz, 1047 Brussels, Belgium (office). *Telephone:* (2) 284-56-06 (office). *Fax:* (2) 284-96-06 (office). *E-mail:* pino.arlacchi@europarl.europa.eu (office); pino@pinoarlacchi.it. *Website:* www.pinoarlacchi.it.

ARLMAN, Paul, MA; Dutch international civil servant (retd) and trade association administrator; b. 11 July 1946, Bussum; s. of Evert Arlman and Corrie Jacobs; m. Kieke Wijs 1971; one s. one d.; ed Hilversum Grammar School, Rotterdam Econ. Univ., Peace Research Inst., Groningen, European Inst., Nice, France; served in Treasury Dept, The Hague 1970–74; Treasury Rep. Embassy in Washington, DC 1974–78; Deputy Asst Sec. Int. Affairs 1978–86; Sec.-Gen. Amsterdam Exchanges 1990–98; Sec.-Gen. Federation European Exchanges 1998–2005; Chair. Industry Advisory Cttee to European Parl. Financial Services Forum 2001–03; Chair. Plan Int. 2005–11; Pres. Transparency Int. (Dutch Chapter) 2006–15; mem. Bd of Dirs, EIB 1981–86, (Chair. Policy Cttee 1983–84); Exec. Dir, World Bank Group 1986–90, IBRD, IDA, IFC, Multilateral Agency for Investment Guarantees (Chair. Audit Cttee) 1988–90; Founding Bd mem. European Corp. Governance Inst. 2002–08, Prime Finance 2008–12; mem. Bd, European Capital Market Inst., Peters Cttee on Dutch Corp. Governance 1995,

World Legal Forum 2000–16; chair. refugee org. 2017–18; Chair. De Witte Film Soc., The Hague 2012–17; mem. Gen. Council, Hellenic Financial Stability Fund 2018–; Global Award, Plan Int. *Radio:* interviews on anti-corruption and international development policies. *Publications:* articles in various journals on financial markets. *Leisure interests:* literature, tennis, skiing, film. *Address:* Jan van Nassaustraat 33, 2596 BM The Hague (home); Vluchtelingenwerk Zuidwest, Blaak 22, Rotterdam, The Netherlands (office). *Telephone:* (70) 3244938 (The Hague) (home). *E-mail:* paul@arlman.com (home). *Website:* www.hfsf.gr (office); www.arlman.com.

ARMACOST, Michael Hayden, MA, PhD; American diplomatist, government official and academic; *Shorenstein Distinguished Fellow, Asia Pacific Research Center, Institute for International Studies, Stanford University;* b. 15 April 1937, Cleveland, Ohio; s. of George H. Armacost and Verda Gay Armacost (née Hayden); brother of Samuel Henry Armacost (q.v.); m. Roberta June Bray 1959; three s.; ed Carleton Coll., Friedrich Wilhelms Univ., Columbia Univ.; Assoc. Prof. of Govt, Pomona Coll., Claremont, Calif. 1962–70; Special Asst to Amb., Embassy in Tokyo 1972–74, mem. Policy Planning, Staff Dept, Washington, DC 1974–77, Sr Staff mem., Nat. Security Council, Washington, DC 1977–78; Deputy Asst Sec. Defense, Int. Security Affairs 1978–79, Prin. Deputy Asst Sec., E Asian and Pacific Affairs 1980–81, Amb. to Philippines 1982–84, Under-Sec. for Political Affairs 1984–89, Amb. to Japan 1989–93; Pres. Brookings Inst., Washington, DC 1995–2002; Shorenstein Distinguished Fellow, Asia Pacific Research Center, Stanford Inst. for Int. Studies 2002–; mem. Council on Foreign Relations; Visiting Prof. of Int. Relations, Int. Christian Univ., Tokyo 1968–69; Grand Cordon, Order of the Rising Sun (Japan); Dr hc (Carleton Coll., Pomona Coll., Denison Univ., Washington Coll., Univ. of Maryland, American Univ., Alaska Pacific Univ., S Dakota School of Mines, Hamyang Univ., Univ. of the City of Manila); Wig Distinguished Prof., Pomona Coll. 1966, Superior Honour Award, State Dept 1976, Distinguished Civilian Service Award, Defence Dept 1980, Presidential Distinguished Service Award, Sec. of State Distinguished Service Award. *Publications include:* The Politics of Weapons Innovation 1969, The Foreign Relations of United States 1969, Friends or Rivals 1996, America's Alliances in Northeast Asia 2004. *Leisure interests:* reading, music, golf. *Address:* Asia Pacific Research Center, Stanford University, Encina Hall, Room E301, Stanford, CA 94305-6055, USA (office). *Telephone:* (650) 724-4002 (office). *Fax:* (650) 723-6530 (office). *E-mail:* armacost@stanford.edu (office). *Website:* fsi.stanford.edu/people/michaelharmacost (office).

ARMACOST, Samuel Henry, BA, MBA; American business executive; *Chairman Emeritus, SRI International;* b. March 1939, Newport News, Va; brother of Michael Hayden Armacost (q.v.); m. Mary Jane Armacost 1962; two d.; ed Denison Univ., Granville, Ohio, Stanford Univ.; joined Bank of America as credit trainee 1961, London branch 1969–71; Advisor Office of Monetary Affairs (exec. exchange programme) 1971–72; Head Europe, Middle East and Africa Div., London 1977–79; Cashier Bank of America and Treas. of its Holding Co. BankAmerica Corpn (now Bank of America Corpn) 1979–80; Pres. and CEO Bank of America and BankAmerica Corpn 1981–86, Chair. and CEO 1986 (resgnd); Investment Banker, Merrill Lynch & Co. 1987, Man. Dir Merrill Lynch Capital Markets 1987–90; Man. Dir Weiss, Peck & Greer LLC 1990–98; Chair. SRI International (fmrly Stanford Research Inst.) 1998–2010, currently Chair. Emer.; mem. Bd of Dirs, Chevron Corpn 1982–2011, Del Monte Foods Co. 2002–, Franklin Resources 2004–, Callaway Golf Co., The James Irvine Foundation, Scios Inc., Exponent Inc., Sarnoff Corpn, Bay Area Council; mem. Exec. Bd Bay Area Science Infrastructure Consortium (BASIC); fmr mem. Advisory Council, California Acad. of Sciences. *Address:* SRI International, 333 Ravenswood Avenue, Menlo Park, CA 94025-3493, USA (office). *Telephone:* (650) 859-2000 (office). *E-mail:* info@sri.com (office). *Website:* www.sri.com (office).

ARMANI, Giorgio; Italian fashion designer and business executive; *Chairman, President and CEO, Giorgio Armani SpA;* b. 11 July 1934, Piacenza; s. of Ugo Armani and of Maria Raimondi; ed Univ. of Milan; worked in mil. hosp. –1957; window dresser, then Asst Buyer, La Rinascente, Milan 1957–64; Designer and Product Developer, Hitman (menswear co. of Cerruti Group) 1964–70; freelance designer for several firms 1970; f. Giorgio Armani SpA with Sergio Galeotti 1975, achieved particular success with unconstructed jackets of mannish cut for women, trademarks also in babywear, underwear, accessories, perfume; labels include Armani Collezioni, Emporio Armani, Armani Jeans, Armani Exchange, Armani Junior, Armani Casa, Armani Dolci, Armani Caffé, Armani Fiori, Armani Hotels, Armani Ristorante; appeared on cover of TIME magazine 1982; has designed suits for England nat. football team 2005 and a new look for the directors' suite at Chelsea Football Club 2007; designed Italian flag bearers' outfits at Opening Ceremony of Winter Olympics, Turin 2006, also designed Italy's Olympic uniforms for Summer Olympics, London 2012; Pres. Olimpia Milano basketball team; Patron Sydney Theatre Co.; Grand'Ufficiale dell'ordine al merito 1986, Gran Cavaliere 1987, Officier, Légion d'honneur 2008; Dr hc (RCA, London) 1991, (Univ. of the Arts, London) 2006, (Polytechnic Univ., Milan) 2007; Neiman-Marcus Award 1979, Cutty Sark Award 1980, 1981, 1984, 1986, 1987, (First Designer Laureate 1985), Ambrogino d'Oro, Milan 1982, Int. Designer Award, Council of Fashion Designers of America 1983, L'Occhio d'Oro 1984, 1986, 1987, 1988, L'Occhiolino d'Oro 1984, 1986, 1987, 1988, Time-Life Achievement Award 1987, Cristobal Balenciaga Award 1988, Woolmark Award, New York 1989, 1992, Senken Award, Japan 1989, Award from People for the Ethical Treatment of Animals, USA 1990, Fiorino d'Oro, Florence, for promoting Made in Italy image 1992, Hon. Nomination from Brera Acad., Milan 1993, Aguja de Oro Award, Spain, for Best Int. Designer 1993, Telva Triunfador Award, Madrid, for Best Designer of the Year 1993, Bambi 1998, 2009, inducted into the Walk of Style 2003, Gentlemen's Quarterly Man of the Year 2006. *Leisure interests:* cinema, music, books, Inter Milan football club. *Address:* Giorgio Armani SpA, Via Borgonuovo 11, 20121 Milan, Italy (office); Giorgio Armani SpA, 650 Fifth Avenue, New York, NY 10019, USA (office). *Telephone:* (02) 801481 (Italy) (office). *Fax:* (02) 46461914 (Italy) (office). *E-mail:* info@giorgioarmani.com (office). *Website:* www.armani.com (office).

ARMAŞU, Octavian, CFA; Moldovan accountant, politician and banker; *Governor, National Bank of Moldova;* b. 29 July 1969, Chişinău; m.; two c.; ed Tech. Univ. of Moldova; Consultant and Trainee in finance, accounting, marketing and man., Center for Private Business Reform (USAID project) 1996–97; worked at Agroincom SRL 1992–96; Sales Man., Glass Container Co., Moldova 1996–97; Sr Consultant, Honest Business Consulting (Dutch jt venture) 1997–99; Controller, Südzucker International GmbH 1999–2001, Head, Control Dept, Südzucker Moldova 2001–04, Financial Dir 2004–16; Minister of Finance 2016–18; Gov. Nat. Bank of Moldova 2018–. *Address:* National Bank of Moldova, 2005 Chişinău, Grigore Vieru Blvd 1, Moldova (office). *Telephone:* (22) 82-26-06 (office). *Website:* www.bnm.md (office).

ARMATRADING, Joan, MBE, BA; British singer and songwriter; b. 9 Dec. 1950, St Kitts, West Indies; d. of Amos Ezekiel Armatrading and Beryl Madge Benjamin; ed Open Univ.; moved to Birmingham, UK 1958; began professional career in collaboration with lyric-writer Pam Nestor 1972; tours worldwide; Hon. Fellow, John Moores Univ. 2000, Univ. of Northampton 2003; Hon. DLitt (Aston Univ.) 2006; Hon. DMus (Birmingham) 2002, (Royal Scottish Acad. of Music and Drama) 2008, (Open Univ.) 2013; BASCA Gold Badge Award 2011, Lifetime Achievement Award, British Folk Festival 2012. *Recordings include:* albums: Whatever's For Us 1973, Back To The Night 1975, Joan Armatrading 1976, Show Some Emotion 1977, Me Myself I 1980, Walk Under Ladders 1981, The Key 1983, Secret Secrets 1985, The Shouting Stage 1988, Hearts and Flowers 1990, The Very Best of 1991, Square the Circle 1992, What's Inside 1995, Lovers Speak 2003, Into the Blues 2007, This Charming Life 2010, Live at Royal Albert Hall 2011, Starlight 2012, Tempest Songs 2016. *Leisure interests:* British comics, vintage cars. *Address:* c/o JABA, 72 New Bond Street, London, W1S 1RR, England (office). *Website:* www.joanarmatrading.com (office).

ARMEY, Richard (Dick) Keith, BA, MA, PhD; American economist, consultant and fmr politician; b. 7 July 1940, Cando, ND; s. of Glen Armey and Marion Gutschlog; m. Susan Byrd; four s. one d.; ed Jamestown Coll., ND and Univs of N Dakota and Oklahoma; mem. Faculty of Econs, Univ. of Montana 1964–65; Asst Prof., West Texas State Univ. 1967–68, Austin Coll. 1968–72; Assoc. Prof., North Texas State Univ. 1972–77, Chair. Dept of Econs 1977–83; mem. US House of Reps from 26th Tex. Dist 1985–2002 (retd), Majority Leader 1995–2002; Sr Policy Adviser and Co-Chair. Homeland Security Task Force, DLA Piper Rudnick Gray Cary 2003–09 (resgnd); Chair. Freedom Works Inc., Washington, DC –2012 (resgnd); Republican; Hon. Patron, Univ. of Dublin Philosophical Soc. 2008. *Publications:* Price Theory 1977, The Freedom Revolution 1995, The Flat Tax 1996, Armey's Axioms 2003, Give Us Liberty: A Tea Party Manifesto (with Matt Kibbe) 2010. *Address:* c/o Freedom Works, 600 Pennsylvania Avenue NW, North Building, Suite 700, Washington, DC 20004, USA.

ARMITAGE, Richard Lee; American fmr diplomatist; *President, Armitage International LC;* b. 1945; ed US Naval Acad.; US naval officer, served in Viet Nam –1973; with US Defense Attache Office, Saigon 1973–75, consultant to Pentagon 1975, posted in Tehran, Iran –1976; worked in private sector 1976–78; Admin. Asst to Kan. Senator Robert Dole 1978–80; Sr Advisor, Interim Foreign Policy Advisory Bd 1980; Deputy Asst Sec. of Defense, E Asia and Pacific Affairs 1981–83, Asst Sec. of Defense, Int. Security Affairs 1983–89; Presidential Special Negotiator, Philippines Mil. Bases Agreement and Special Mediator for Water, Middle East 1989–92; Special Emissary to King Hussein, Jordan 1991; Coordinator, Emergency Humanitarian Assistance 1992; Dir, assistance to new independent states (NIS), fmr Soviet Union 1992–93; Pres. Armitage Associates LLC 1993–2001; Deputy Sec. of State 2001–05; Pres. Armitage Int. LC 2005–; mem. Bd of Dirs ManTech Int. Corpn 2005–, ConocoPhillips Co. 2006–, Transcutaneous Technologies Inc. (TTI) 2006–; mem. Bd of Trustees Center for Strategic and Int. Studies (CSIS); Distinguished Public Service (four times), Outstanding Public Service, State Dept Distinguished Honor Award, numerous US mil. decorations, decorations from govts of Thailand, Repub. of Korea, Bahrain, Pakistan; Dept of Defense Medal, Sec. of Defense Medal, Presidential Citizens Medal. *Address:* Armitage International LC, 2300 Clarendon Blvd, Suite 601, Arlington, VA 22201-3392, USA (office). *Telephone:* (703) 248-0344 (office). *Fax:* (703) 248-0166 (office). *Website:* www.armitageinternational.com (office).

ARMITAGE, Simon Robert, CBE, BA, MA, FRSL; British poet, writer and academic; *Professor of Poetry, University of Oxford;* b. 26 May 1963, Huddersfield, West Yorks.; ed Portsmouth Polytechnic, Univ. of Manchester; Probation Officer, Greater Manchester Probation Service 1988–93; Poetry Ed., Chatto and Windus 1993–95; Sr Lecturer, Manchester Metropolitan Univ. 1999–2011; Prof. of Poetry, Univ. of Sheffield 2011–15; Prof. of Poetry, Univ. of Oxford 2015–(19); apptd Millennium Poet 1999; Artist-in-Residence, London South Bank 2009–12; apptd Prof. of Poetry Univ. of Leeds 2017; currently Sr Lecturer, Manchester Metropolitan Univ.; Vice-Pres. Poetry Soc.; Patron Arvon Foundation, Friends of Yorkshire Sculpture Park, Wordsworth Trust; Official Patron Elmet Trust; Hon. DLitt (Portsmouth) 1996, (Huddersfield) 1996; Dr hc (Sheffield Hallam) 2009; Eric Gregory Award 1988, Sunday Times Young Writer of the Year 1993, Forward Poetry Prize 1993, Lannan Award 1994, Ivor Novello Award 2005, BAFTA Award 2005, Keats-Shelley Poetry Prize (for The Present) 2011, Hay Medal for Poetry 2012, Cholmondeley Award 2014, Hillary Lecturer, Univ. of Oxford 2015, Queen's Gold Medal for Poetry 2018. *Plays include:* Eclipse, Mister Heracles, Jerusalem, Last Days of Troy. *Radio includes:* dramatisation of The Odyssey (BBC Radio 4) (Gold Award, Spoken Word Awards 2005) 2004, Black Roses: The Killing of Sophie Lancaster 2011, regular guest, The Mark Radcliffe Show (BBC Radio 1 and BBC Radio 2), co-host Armitage and Moore's Guide to Popular Song, regular contributor The Review Show (BBC Radio 2). *Publications include:* Human Geography 1986, The Distance Between Stars 1987, The Walking Horses 1988, Zoom! 1989, Around Robinson 1991, Xanadu 1992, Kid 1992, Book of Matches 1993, The Anaesthetist 1994, The Dead Sea Poems 1995, Moon Country 1996, CloudCuckooLand 1997, All Points North (essays) 1998, Mister Heracles 2000, Little Green Man (novel) 2001, Selected Poems 2001, Travelling Songs 2002, The Universal Home Doctor 2002, The White Stuff (novel) 2004, Homer's Odyssey (trans.) 2006, Tyrannosaurus Rex Versus the Corduroy Kid 2006, Sir Gawain and the Green Knight (trans.) 2007, Gig (non-fiction) 2008, The Not Dead 2008, Seeing Stars 2010, The Death of King Arthur (trans.) 2011, Walking Home (non-fiction) 2012, Black Roses 2012, Stanza Stones 2013, Paper Aeroplane: Poems 1989–2014 2014, Walking Away (non-fiction) 2015, The Unaccompanied 2017; co-ed. Penguin Anthology of Poetry from Britain and Ireland Since 1945; contrib. to Sunday Times, TLS, Guardian, Observer, Independent. *Address:* David Godwin Associates, 55, Monmouth Street, London, WC2H 9DG, England (office); Faculty of English Language and Literature, University of Oxford, St Cross Building, Manor Road, Oxford, OX1 3UL,

England (office); Heywood House, 12 Northgate, Holmley, Huddersfield, HD9 6QL, England. *Telephone:* (20) 7240-9992 (office). *E-mail:* philippa@davidgodwinassociates.co.uk (office); english.office@ell.ox.ac.uk (office). *Website:* www.davidgodwinassociates.com (office); www.english.ox.ac.uk (office); www.simonarmitage.com.

ARMITT, Sir John Alexander, Kt, KBE, CBE, FREng, FICE; British civil engineer, transport industry executive and construction industry executive; b. 2 Feb. 1946, London; m. Mavis Sage 1969 (divorced); one s. one d.; ed Portsmouth Northern Grammar School, Portsmouth Coll. of Tech.; civil engineer, John Laing Construction Co. 1963–93, Chair. Int. and Civil Eng Divs 1987–93; CEO Union Railways 1993–97, oversaw devt of high-speed Channel Tunnel Rail Link; CEO Costain plc (eng and construction group) 1997–2001; CEO Railtrack PLC 2001–02, Network Rail 2002–07; Chair. UK Eng and Physical Sciences Research Council (EPSRC) 2007–12, Olympic Delivery Authority 2007–14, Council of the City and Guilds of London Inst. 2012–, National Express Group PLC 2013–; Dir (non-exec.), Berkeley Group Holdings PLC 2007–, currently Deputy Chair.; mem. Advisory Bd Siemens plc 2009–, PWC 2007–; mem. Airports Comm. 2012–; Dr hc (Birmingham), (Portsmouth), (Warwick), (Reading). *Address:* National Express Group PLC, National Express House, Mill Lane, Digbeth, Birmingham, B5 6DD, England (office). *Telephone:* (845) 0130130 (office). *E-mail:* info@nationalexpressgroup.com (office). *Website:* www.nationalexpressgroup.com (office).

ARMSTRONG, Billie Joe; American singer and musician (guitar); b. 17 Feb. 1972, San Pablo, Calif.; m. Adrienne Nesser 1994; two s.; Founding mem., Sweet Children, renamed Green Day 1989–; numerous tours and television appearances; side projects include Pinhead Gunpowder, Screeching Weasel, The Network and Foxboro Hot Tubs; Australian MTV Awards for Best Group 2005, for Best Rock Video (for American Idiot) 2005, MTV Award for Best Rock Video, Best Group Video (both for Boulevard of Broken Dreams), Best Group, MTV Viewer's Choice Award 2005, Kerrang! Awards for Best Band on the Planet, Best Live Act 2005, NME Award for Best Video (for American Idiot) 2005, MTV Europe Music Awards for Best Rock Act 2005, 2009, 2013, for Global Icon 2016, Billboard 200 Album Group of the Year 2005, Billboard Music Awards for Pop Group of the Year, for Hot 100 Group of the Year, for Rock Artist of the Year, for Rock Song of the Year (for Boulevard of Broken Dreams), for Modern Rock Artist of the Year 2005, Grammy Award for Record of the Year (for Boulevard of Broken Dreams) 2006, BRIT Award for Best Int. Group 2006, ASCAP Awards for Creative Voice, and for Song of the Year (for Boulevard of Broken Dreams) 2006, American Music Award for Favorite Rock Artist 2009. *Recordings include:* albums: with Green Day: 39/Smooth 1990, Kerplunk 1991, Dookie 1994, Insomniac 1994, Nimrod 1997, Warning 2000, International Superhits (compilation) 2001, Shenanigans 2002, American Idiot (Grammy Award for Best Rock Album 2005, MTV Europe Music Award for Best Album 2005, American Music Award for Favorite Pop/Rock Album 2005, BRIT Award for Best Int. Album 2006) 2004, 21st Century Breakdown (Grammy Award for Best Rock Album 2010) 2009, ¡Uno! 2012, ¡Dos! 2012, ¡Tres! 2012, Revolution Radio 2016; with The Network: Money Money 2020 2003; with Foxboro Hot Tubs: Stop Drop and Roll!!! 2008. *E-mail:* info@greenday.com (office). *Website:* www.greenday.com.

ARMSTRONG, C. Michael, BS; American business executive; *Senior Advisor, SV Investment Partners;* b. 18 Oct. 1938, Detroit, Mich.; s. of Charles H. Armstrong and Zora Jean Armstrong (née Brooks); m. Anne Gossett 1961; three d.; ed Miami Univ., Dartmouth Inst.; joined IBM Corpn 1961, Dir Systems Man. Marketing Div. 1975–76, Vice-Pres. Market Operations East 1976–78, Pres. Data Processing Div. 1978–80, Vice-Pres. Plans and Controls, Data Processing Product Group 1980–84, Asst Group Exec. 1980–83, Group Exec. 1983–92, Sr Vice-Pres. 1984–92, fmrly Pres. IBM Corpn Europe, Pres. and Dir-Gen. World Trade (Europe, Middle East, Africa) 1987–89; Chair. World Trade Corpn 1989–92; Chair., CEO Hughes Aircraft Co. 1992–93, Hughes Electronics Corpn 1993; Chair., CEO AT&T 1997–2002; Chair. Comcast Corpn 2002–04; Chair. Bd of Trustees, Johns Hopkins Medicine 2005–; Chair. Pres.'s Export Council 1994; Visiting Prof. of Practice of Man., MIT Sloan School of Man.; Chair. FCC Network Reliability and Inter-Operability Council 1999; Dir HCA Inc. 2004–10; mem. Bd of Dirs Citigroup 1989–2010, IHS, Inc. 2003–; mem. Supervisory Bd Thyssen-Bornemisza Group, Council on Foreign Relations, Nat. Security Telecommunications Advisory Cttee, Defence Policy Advisory Cttee on Trade (DPACT); Sr Advisor, SV Investment Partners (fmr Chair.), Tudor Venture Capital; mem. Bd of Trustees of Carnegie Hall, The Johns Hopkins Univ.; Hon. LLD (Pepperdine Univ.) 1997, (Loyola Marymount Univ.) 1998. *Address:* SV Investment Partners, 1700 East Putnam Avenue, Greenwich, CT 06870, USA (office). *Telephone:* (212) 735-0700 (office). *Fax:* (203) 990-0714 (office). *Website:* www.svip.com (office).

ARMSTRONG, Clay Margarave, BA, MD; American physiologist and academic; *Professor Emeritus of Physiology, School of Medicine, University of Pennsylvania;* b. 1934; m. Clara Franzini; ed Rice Univ., Houston, Tex., Washington Univ. School of Medicine, St Louis, Mo.; Intern, Univ. of Chicago Clinics 1960–61; Multiple Sclerosis Soc. Research Fellowship, Neurology Dept, Washington Univ. School of Medicine, St Louis 1961; Research Assoc. NIH 1961–64; Asst Prof. of Physiology, Duke Univ. 1966–69; Assoc. Prof., Univ. of Rochester, NY 1969–75, Prof. of Physiology, Univ. of Rochester School of Medicine 1974–75; Prof. of Physiology, Univ. of Pennsylvania School of Medicine 1976, currently Prof. Emer.; Trustee, Marine Biological Lab., Woods Hole, MA 1980–93; mem. Neurosciences Grad. Group; mem. NAS, Biophysical Soc., Soc. of Gen. Physiologists (Pres. 1985–86), Physiological Study Section, American Physiological Soc. 1975–79 (Chair. 1979), Inst. of Medicine 1996; mem. Editorial Bd Journal of General Physiology 1976–, Journal of Neurophysiology 1980–84; Hon. Research Assoc., Univ. Coll., London, UK 1964–66; Scholarship, Washington Univ. School of Medicine 1956–60, Teacher of the Year, Freshman Medical Class, Univ. of Rochester 1973, K.S. Cole Award, Biophysical Soc. 1975, Bowditch Lecturer, American Physiological Soc. 1975, Distinguished Lecturer, Soc. of Gen. Physiologists, IUPAB Meeting 1986, Distinguished Alumnus, Rice Univ. 1995, Louisa Gross Horwitz Prize 1996 (co-recipient), Albert Lasker Award for Basic Medical Research 1999, John Scott Award 2000, Gairdner Foundation Int. Award 2001, Jacob Javits Neuroscience Research Award, NIH. *Publications include:* numerous articles in scientific journals. *Address:* University of Pennsylvania, Department of Physiology, A701 Richards Building, 3700 Hamilton Walk, Philadelphia, PA 19104-6085, USA (office). *Telephone:* (215) 898-7816 (office). *Fax:* (215) 573-5851 (office). *E-mail:* carmstro@mail.med.upenn.edu (office). *Website:* www.med.upenn.edu (office).

ARMSTRONG, David John, BA; Australian journalist, media executive and academic; b. 25 Nov. 1947, Sydney; s. of Allan E. Armstrong and Mary P. Armstrong; m. Deborah Bailey 1980 (deceased); two d.; ed Marist Brothers High School, Parramatta, Univ. of New South Wales; Ed. The Bulletin 1985–86; Deputy Ed. The Daily Telegraph 1988–89; Ed. The Australian 1989–92, Ed.-in-Chief 1996–2002; Ed. The Canberra Times 1992–93; Ed. South China Morning Post, Hong Kong 1993–94, Ed.-in-Chief 1994–96; Ed.-in-Chief, South China Morning Post 2003–05, mem. Bd Dirs Post Publishing 2004–09, Pres. and COO 2005–08, mem. Exec. Cttee 2006–08, Adviser to Sr Man. 2009–11; Chair. Post Media Ltd, Phnom Penh 2010–12; Conjoint Prof., Journalism and Media Research Centre, Univ. of New South Wales 2010–13; Adjunct Prof., Macquarie Univ. 2013–; mem. Bd Dirs Deb Bailey Foundation for Motor Neurone Disease Research 2003–, Australian–Thai Chamber of Commerce 2009–10; mem. Asian Bd Int. News Media Assen 2006–; Hon. Adviser, British Chamber of Commerce, Thailand 2013–, Hon. Adviser to the Bd, Australian–Thai Chamber of Commerce 2013–; Australian Centenary Medal 2003, President's Award, Australian–Thai Chamber of Commerce 2012. *Leisure interests:* reading, golf. *Address:* Department of Media Music Communication and Cultural Studies, Building Y3A, Macquarie University, North Ryde, NSW 2109, Australia (office). *E-mail:* david.armstrong@mq.edu.au (office).

ARMSTRONG, Dido Florian Cloud de Bounevialle (see Dido).

ARMSTRONG, Fraser Andrew, BSc, PhD, FRS; British chemist and academic; *Professor of Chemistry and Fellow of St John's College, University of Oxford;* b. 1951, Cambridge; ed Univ. of Leeds; Royal Soc. Univ. Research Fellowship, Univ. of Oxford 1983–89, Prof. of Chem. and Fellow of St John's Coll. 1993–; mem. Chem. Faculty, Univ. of California, Irvine 1989–93; Pres. Soc. of Biological Inorganic Chem. 2004–06; European Medal for Biological Inorganic Chem. 1998, RSC Award for Inorganic Biochemistry 2000, Carbon Trust Academic Innovation Award (co-recipient) 2003, Max-Planck 'Frontiers in Biological Chem.' Award 2004, RSC Medal for Interdisciplinary Chem. 2006, RSC Joseph Chatt Award 2010, Davy Medal, Royal Soc. 2012, RSC Barker Award 2012. *Publications:* numerous papers in professional journals on biological redox chemistry. *Address:* Department of Chemistry, University of Oxford, South Parks Road, Oxford, OX1 3QR, England (office). *Telephone:* (1865) 272647 (office); (1865) 287182 (St John's) (office). *E-mail:* fraser.armstrong@chem.ox.ac.uk (office). *Website:* armstrong.chem.ox.ac.uk (office).

ARMSTRONG, Gillian May, AM; Australian film director; b. 18 Dec. 1950, Melbourne; d. of Raleigh Edward Armstrong and Patricia May Armstrong; m.; two d.; ed Swinburne Art Coll., Nat. Australian Film & TV School, Sydney; mem. Dirs' Guild of America, Acad. of Motion Picture Arts and Sciences; Patron Sydney Film Festival, Flickerfest Short Film Festival, Nat. Gallery of Victoria; Companion of the Australian Rotary Health Research Fund; Hon. Doctorate in Film (Swinburne Univ.) 1998, Hon. DLitt (Univ. of NSW) 2000; numerous awards including Women in Hollywood Icon Award 1988, Dorothy Arzner Directing Award, USA 1993. *Feature films include:* The Singer and The Dancer 1976, My Brilliant Career (Best Film and Best Dir, Australian Film Inst. Awards, Best First Feature British Film Critics Award) 1979, Starstruck 1982, Mrs Soffel 1984, High Tide (Best Film, Houston Film Festival, Grand Prix Festival Int. de Creteil, France) 1987, Fires Within 1990, The Last Days of Chez Nous 1991, Little Women 1995, Oscar and Lucinda 1997, Charlotte Gray 2001, Unfolding Florence 2005, Death Defying Acts 2006, Love, Lust and Lies (Australian Directors Guild Award) 2010. *Address:* c/o HLA Management, PO Box 1536, Strawberry Hills, NSW 2012, Australia (office). *Telephone:* (2) 9549-3000 (office). *Fax:* (2) 9310-4113 (office). *E-mail:* hla@hlamgt.com.au (office). *Website:* www.hlamgt.com.au (office).

ARMSTRONG, Greg L., BS, CPA; American oil executive; ed Southeastern Oklahoma State Univ.; joined Plains Resources 1981, Corp. Sec. 1981–88, Vice-Pres. and Chief Financial Officer (CFO) 1984–91, Treas. 1984–97, Sr Vice-Pres. and CFO 1991–92, Exec. Vice-Pres. and CFO June–Oct. 1992, Pres. and COO Oct.–Dec. 1992, Pres., CEO and Dir 1992–2001, Chair. and CEO Plains All American Pipeline LP 2001–18, Plains GP Holdings 2001–; mem. Bd Dirs, Petroleum Club of Houston, Varco Int. Inc. 2004–; mem. Texas SE Regional Bd Trustees, IPAA. *Address:* Plains All American Pipeline LP, 333 Clay Street, Suite 1600, Houston, TX 77002, USA (office). *Telephone:* (713) 646-4100 (office). *Fax:* (713) 646-4572 (office). *E-mail:* info@plainsallamerican.com (office). *Website:* www.plainsallamerican.com (office); ir.pagp.com/management (office).

ARMSTRONG, Lance Edward; American fmr professional cyclist; b. (Lance Edward Gunderson), 18 Sept. 1971, Plano, Tex.; s. of Eddie Charles Gunderson and Linda Gayle (née Mooneyham); adopted s. of Terry Keith Armstrong; m. Kristin Richard 1998 (divorced 2003); one s. twin d.; pnr. Anna Hansen; one s.; US Nat. Amateur Champion 1991; mem. US Olympic team 1992, 1996, 2000 (bronze medal); mem. Motorol team 1992–96, Cofidis team 1999, US Postal Service Pro Cycling Team 1998–2004, Discovery Channel 2005, Astana 2009, Team Radio-Shack 2010–11; winner of numerous races, including US Pro Championship, UCI Road World Championships 1993, Clasica San Sebastian, Tour Du Pont 1995, Tour Du Pont 1996, Tour de Luxembourg 1998, Tour de Suisse 2001, Criterium du Dauphine Libere 2002, Criterium du Dauphine Libere 2003, Tour de France 1999–2005 (first to win seven Tours); survived testicular cancer 1996; winner, Ironman 70.3 Hawaii and Fla (triathlon organized by World Triathlon Corpn) 2012; Founder and Chair. Lance Armstrong Foundation (Livestrong) 1996–2012; retd from competitive racing after completion of 2005 Tour de France; came out of retirement and joined Astana team 2008; charged by US Anti-Doping Agency (USADA) with having used illicit performance-enhancing drugs June 2012, announced lifetime ban from competition as well as the stripping of all his titles since 1 Aug. 1998 Aug. 2012, USADA findings accepted by Int. Cycling Union and confirmed the lifetime ban and the stripping of all titles Oct. 2012; Founder and Pres. WEDU Sport 2016–; Hon. DHumLitt (Tufts Univ.) 2006; Triathlon magazine's Rookie of the Year 1988, VeloNews magazine's North American Male Cyclist of the Year 1993, 1995, 1996, 1998, 1999, 2002, 2005, Union Cycliste Internationale: World Number 1 Ranked Elite Men's Cyclist 1996, US Olympic Cttee SportsMan of the Year 1999, 2001, 2002, 2003, Vélo d'Or Award, Velo magazine in France 1999, 2000, 2001, 2003, 2004, Mendrisio d'Or Award in

Switzerland 1999, Premio Coppi-Bici d'Oro Trophy, Fausto Coppi Foundation in conjunction with La Gazzetta dello Sport 1999, 2000, ESPN/Intersport's ARETE Award for Courage in Sport (Professional Div.) 1999, ABC's Wide World of Sports Athlete of the Year 1999, World's Most Outstanding Athlete Award, Mildred 'Babe' Didrikson Zaharias Courage Award, US Sports Acad. 1999, Jesse Owens International Trophy 2000, Prince of Asturias Award in Sports 2000, Laureus World Sports Award for Comeback of the Year 2000, ESPY Award for Best Comeback Athlete 2000, VeloNews magazine's International Cyclist of the Year 2000, 2001, 2003, 2004, William Hill Sports Book of the Year: It's Not About the Bike: My Journey Back to Life 2000, Associated Press Male Athlete of the Year 2002, 2003, 2004, 2005, Presidential Delegation to XIX Olympic Winter Games 2002, Sports Illustrated magazine's Sportsman of the Year 2002, Reuters Sportsman of the Year 2003, Sports Ethics Fellows, Inst. for Int. Sport 2003, Laureus World Sports Award for Sportsman of the Year 2003, BBC Sports Personality of the Year Overseas Personality Award 2003, ESPY Award for Best Male Athlete 2003, 2004, 2005, 2006, Trophee de L'Acad. des Sport (France) 2004, Marca Legend Award, Marca (Spanish sports daily in Madrid) 2004, ESPY Award for GMC Professional Grade Play Award 2005, Favorite Athlete Award, Nickelodeon Kids' Choice Awards 2006, Pace car driver for the Indianapolis 500 2006, asteroid 1994 JE9 named 12373 Lancearmstrong in his honour. *Publications:* It's Not About the Bike, The Lance Armstrong Performance Programme, Every Second Counts (with Sally Jenkins) 2003. *Address:* c/o Mark Higgins, POB 302919, Austin, TX 78703, USA (office). *Telephone:* (512) 361-7150 (office). *E-mail:* higs@wedu.team (office). *Website:* www.wedu.team (office); www.lancearmstrong .com.

ARMSTRONG, Robin Louis, BA, PhD, FRSC; Canadian physicist and academic; *Professor Emeritus of Physics, University of Toronto;* b. 14 May 1935, Galt, Ont.; s. of Robert Dockstader Armstrong and Beatrice Jenny Armstrong (née Grill); m. Karen Elisabeth Hansen 1960; two s.; ed Univ. of Toronto and Univ. of Oxford, UK; RSC Rutherford Memorial Fellowship 1961; Asst Prof. of Physics, Univ. of Toronto 1962–68, Assoc. Prof. 1968–71, Prof. 1971–90, Adjunct Prof. 1990–99, Prof. Emer. 1999–; Assoc. Chair. Physics, Univ. of Toronto 1969–74, Chair. 1974–82, Dean Faculty of Arts and Science 1982–90, Adjunct Prof. 1990–99; Visitante Distinguido, Univ. of Córdoba, Argentina 1989; Pres. and Prof. of Physics, Univ. of New Brunswick 1990–96; Adviser to Pres., Wilfrid Laurier Univ. 1997–2000; Pres. Canadian Inst. for Neutron Scattering 1986–89, Canadian Asscn of Physicists 1990–91; Dir Canadian Inst. for Advanced Research 1981–82, Huntsman Marine Lab. 1983–87; mem. Research Council of Canadian Inst. for Advanced Research 1982–2000, Natural Science and Eng Research Council of Canada (NSERC) 1991–97 (mem. Exec. 1992–97, Vice-Pres. 1994–97), Bd of Dirs Canadian Arthritis Network (Chair. 2004–), Research and Devt Advisory Panel, Atomic Energy of Canada Ltd 1999–2012 (Vice-Chair. 2004–05, Chair. 2006–07); Exec. Dir College Univ. Consortium Council 2006–08; Hon. DSc (Univ. of New Brunswick) 2001; Herzberg Medal 1973, Medal of Achievement (Canadian Asscn of Physicists) 1990, Commemorative Medal for 125th Anniversary of Canadian Confed. 1992, Preston High School Hall of Fame 2007. *Publications include:* over 180 research articles on condensed matter physics in numerous journals. *Leisure interests:* golf, gardening. *Address:* Room MP311, University of Toronto, Department of Physics, 60 St George Street, Toronto, ON M5S 1A7, Canada (home). *Telephone:* (416) 978-2940 (office). *E-mail:* r.armstrong35@gmail.com (office); robinl.armstrong@sympatico.ca (home). *Website:* www.physics.utoronto.ca (office).

ARMSTRONG, Sheila Ann, FRAM; British singer (soprano); b. 13 Aug. 1942, Ashington, Northumberland; d. of William R. Armstrong and Janet Armstrong; m. David E. Cooper 1980 (divorced 1999); ed Hirst Park Girls' School, Ashington and Royal Acad. of Music; sang Despina in Così fan tutte at Sadler's Wells 1965, Belinda in Dido and Aeneas, Glyndebourne 1966, Mozart's Pamina and Zerlina and Fiorella in Rossini's Il Turco in Italia, Glyndebourne; sang in the premiere of John McCabe's Notturni ed Alba at Three Choirs Festival 1970; New York debut with New York Philharmonic 1971; sang with Los Angeles Philharmonic under Mehta; Covent Garden debut as Marzelline in Fidelio 1973; sang Donizetti's Norina and Mozart's Donna Elvira for Scottish Nat. Opera; concert engagements included Messiah at the Concertgebouw, tour of the Far East with the Bach Choir; fmr Pres. Kathleen Ferrier Soc.; fmr Trustee, Kathleen Ferrier Award; Fellow, Hatfield Coll., Durham Univ. 1992; mem. Royal Philharmonic Soc.; Hon. MA (Newcastle); Hon. DMus (Durham) 1991; Mozart Prize 1965, Kathleen Ferrier Memorial Award 1965. *Recordings include:* Samson, Dido and Aeneas, Mozart's Requiem, Carmina Burana, Elgar's Apostles, The Pilgrim's Progress, Cantatas by Bach, Haydn's Stabat Mater, Beethoven's Ninth Symphony, Mahler's 2nd and 4th, Spring Symphony, Child of Our Time, Semele, Fauré Requiem, Rachmaninov's The Bells, Grieg's Peer Gynt Suite, Schubert's Lazarus, Holst's The Mystic Trumpeter, Messiah Highlights, Don Giovanni Highlights, Britten's Spring Symphony, Strauss' Four Last Songs with Royal Philharmonic, Elgar's Oratorios, Vaughan Williams' Sea Symphony and Hugh the Drover, Mozart Arias (with Barry Tuckwell). *Leisure interests:* collecting keys, interior decoration and design, flower-arranging, sewing, gardening and garden design, travel.

ARMSTRONG, Tim, BS; American business executive; *Chairman and CEO, AOL Inc.;* ed Lawrence Acad., Connecticut Coll.; started career by co-founding and running newspaper in Boston; joined International Data Group (IDG) Inc. to launch I-Way (consumer internet magazine); fmr Dir of Integrated Sales and Marketing, Starwave/Disney ABC/ESPN Internet Ventures; fmr Vice-Pres. of Sales and Strategic Partnerships, Snowball.com; Vice-Pres. for Advertising and Sales, Google Inc. 2000, Pres. North America 2007–08, Pres. Americas Operation and Sr Vice-Pres. Advertising Sales and Operations, Google Inc. –2009; Chair. and CEO AOL LLC (div. of Time Warner Inc.), Dulles, Va 2009, Chair. and CEO AOL Inc., New York 2009–; Dir Interactive Advertising Bureau, Advertising Council, Advertising Research Foundation. *Address:* Office of the Chairman, AOL LLC, 22000 AOL Way, Dulles, VA 20166, USA (office). *Telephone:* (703) 265-1000 (office). *Website:* corp.aol.com (office).

ARMSTRONG OF HILL TOP, Baroness (Life Peer), cr. 2010, of Crook in the County of Durham; **Hilary Jane Armstrong,** PC, BSc; British politician; b. 30 Nov. 1945, Sunderland; d. of Rt Hon Ernest Armstrong and Hannah P. Armstrong (née Lamb); m. Paul D. Corrigan 1992; ed Monkwearmouth Comprehensive School, Sunderland, West Ham Coll. of Tech., Univ. of Birmingham; mem. Labour Party 1960–; teacher with VSO, Murray Girls' High School, PO Mwatate, Kenya 1967–69; social worker, Newcastle City Social Services Dept 1970–73; community worker, Southwick Neighbourhood Action Project, Sunderland 1973–75; Lecturer in Community and Youth Work, Sunderland Polytechnic (now Univ. of Sunderland) 1975–86; Councillor, Durham City Council 1985–87; MP (Labour) for Durham NW 1987–2010; Frontbench Spokesperson on Educ. (under-fives, primary and special educ.) 1988–92, on Treasury Affairs 1994–95; Parl. Pvt. Sec. to Leader of the Opposition 1992–94; mem. Nat. Exec. Labour Party 1992–97; Minister of State Dept of Environment, Transport and the Regions 1997–2001; Parl. Sec. to HM Treasury and Govt Chief Whip 2001–06; Cabinet Office Minister, Minister for Social Exclusion and Chancellor of the Duchy of Lancaster 2006–07; fmr Vice-Pres. Nat. Children's Homes; fmr mem. British Council; fmr mem. Bd VSO; fmr mem. Manufacturing Science Finance (MSF) Union. *Leisure interests:* reading, theatre, watching football. *Address:* North House, 17 North Terrace, Crook, Co. Durham, DL15 9AZ, England (home). *Telephone:* (1388) 767065 (home). *Fax:* (1388) 767923 (home).

ARMSTRONG OF ILMINSTER, Baron (Life Peer), cr. 1988, of Ashill in the County of Somerset; **Robert Temple Armstrong,** GCB, CVO, MA; British fmr civil servant; b. 30 March 1927, Oxford; s. of Sir Thomas Armstrong and of Lady Armstrong (née Draper); m. 1st Serena Mary Benedicta Chance 1953 (divorced 1985); two d.; m. 2nd (Mary) Patricia Carlow 1985; ed Eton Coll. and Christ Church, Oxford; Asst Prin., Treasury 1950–55, Pvt. Sec. to Econ. Sec. 1953–54; Pvt. Sec. to Chancellor of the Exchequer (Rt Hon. R. A. Butler) 1954–55; Prin., Treasury 1955–64; Asst Sec., Cabinet Office 1964–66; Asst Sec., Treasury 1966–68; Prin. Pvt. Sec. to Chancellor of the Exchequer (Rt Hon. Roy Jenkins) 1968; Under-Sec., Treasury 1968–70; Prin. Pvt. Sec. to the Prime Minister 1970–75; Deputy Under-Sec. of State, Home Office 1975–77, Perm. Under-Sec. of State 1977–79; Sec. of the Cabinet 1979–87; Perm. Sec. Man. and Personnel Office 1981–87; Head, Home Civil Service 1981–87; mem. (Crossbench), House of Lords 1988–, mem. Admin and Works Cttee 2014–, Able Marine Energy Park Devt Consent Order 2014–; Chair. Biotechnology Investments Ltd 1989–2000; Chair. Forensic Investigative Assocs PLC 1997–2003; Chair. Hestercombe Gardens Trust 1995–2005, Bd of Govs Royal Northern Coll. of Music 2000–05; Sec. Radcliffe Cttee on Monetary System 1957–59; Sec. to the Dirs, Royal Opera House, Covent Garden 1968–87, Dir 1988–93; Dir Bristol and West Bldg Soc. 1988–97 (Chair. 1993–97), Bank of Ireland and other cos; Chair. of Trustees, Victoria & Albert Museum 1988–98, Sir Edward Heath Charitable Foundation –2013; mem. Rhodes Trust 1975–97; Chancellor, Univ. of Hull 1994–2006; Pres. The Literary Soc. 2004–; Trustee, Leeds Castle Foundation 1987– (Chair. 2001–), RVW Trust, Derek Hill Foundation; Fellow, Eton Coll. 1979–94; Hon. Student, Christ Church 1985; Hon. Bencher, Inner Temple 1986; Hon. LLD. *Leisure interest:* music, the arts. *Address:* House of Lords, Westminster, London, SW1A 0PW, England (office). *Telephone:* (20) 7219-4983 (office). *Fax:* (20) 7219-5979 (office). *Website:* www.parliament.uk/biographies/lords/lord-armstrong-of-ilminster/3434 (office).

ÁRNASON, Kristinn F., LLM; Icelandic diplomatist and international organization official; *Secretary-General, European Free Trade Association;* b. 5 Jan. 1954, Reykjavík; m.; three c.; ed Univ. of Iceland, Univ. of Exeter, UK, Univ. of Oslo, Norway; solicitor in pvt. attorney's office 1979–80, 1982, for Fed. of Employees 1983–85; First Sec., Ministry of Foreign Affairs (MFA) 1985–87, Deputy Perm. Rep. to Int. Orgs, Geneva 1987–92, Chief Negotiator and Spokesman on Fisheries, MFA 1992–94, Dir for External Trade 1994–98, rank of Amb. 1997, Amb. to Slovakia and Poland 1999–2002, to Norway and Czech Repub. 1999–2003, to Egypt 2000–03, Dir Defence Dept, MFA 2003–05, Amb. and Perm. Rep. to Int. Orgs, Geneva 2005–12; Sec.-Gen. EFTA, Geneva 2012–. *Address:* European Free Trade Association, 9–11 rue de Varembé, 1211 Geneva 20, Switzerland (office). *Telephone:* 22-332-26-00 (home). *Fax:* 22-332-26-77 (office). *E-mail:* kfa@efta.int (office); mail.gva@efta.int (office). *Website:* www.efta.int (office).

ARNAULT, Bernard; French business executive and art collector; *Chairman and CEO, LVMH;* b. 5 March 1949, Roubaix (Nord); s. of Jean Arnault and Marie-Jo Arnault (née Savinel); m. 1st Anne Dewavrin 1973 (divorced 1990); two c.; m. 2nd Hélène Mercier 1991; three s.; ed Ecole Polytechnique; joined Ferret-Savinel (family construction co.) 1971, Pres. 1978–84; lived in USA 1981–84; took over Boussac Saint-Frères (parent co. of Dior) 1985; CEO LVMH (luxury goods group which includes Louis Vuitton bags, Moët et Chandon champagne, Parfums Christian Dior, Hennessy and Hine cognac) 1989–, Chair. 1992–, Chair. Christian Dior SA; Pres. Bd of Dirs, Montaigne 1997–; Owner Phillips auction house 1999– (merged with Bonhams & Brooks 2001); fmr Dir Diageo; through holding co. Financière Agache owns fashion houses Dior, Lacroix and Céline and dept store Bon Marché; Commdr, Légion d'honneur 2007; Officier, Ordre nat. du Mérite. *Publication:* La Passion créative 2000. *Leisure interests:* music, tennis. *Address:* 11 rue François 1er, 75008 Paris; LVMH, 22 avenue Montaigne, 75008 Paris, France (office). *Telephone:* 1-44-13-22-22 (office). *Fax:* 1-44-13-22-23 (office). *E-mail:* info@lvmh.com (office). *Website:* www.lvmh.com (office).

ARNAULT, Jean; French United Nations official and academic; b. 1951; m.; two c.; ed Univ. of Paris I (Sorbonne), Polytechnic of Cen. London, UK; fmr Sr Political Affairs Officer in Namibia and Afghanistan, Political Adviser to Special Rep. for Western Sahara 1991, Observer, then Mediator in Guatemala peace negotiations 1994–96, Special Rep. for Guatemala 1997–2000, Rep. of UN Sec.-Gen. in Burundi 2000–01, Deputy Head of UN Assistance Mission in Afghanistan 2002–04, Special Rep. for Afghanistan and Head of UN Assistance Mission 2004–06, Sec.-Gen.'s Special Rep. for Georgia and Head of UN Observer Mission in Georgia (UNOMIG) 2006–08; UN Special Adviser to the Group of Friends of Democratic Pakistan 2008–09; mem. UN's High-Level Panel on Peace Operations 2014–15; UN Sec.-Gen.'s Del. to Sub-Commission on End of Conflict issues in Colombia Peace Talks 2015–16, Special Rep. and Head of UN Mission in Colombia 2016–18; Prof. of Practice, Paris School of Int. Affairs, Sciences Po 2011–13; Visiting Fellow, Center for Int. Studies, Princeton Univ., USA 2001; Non-resident Sr Fellow, Center on Int. Cooperation, New York Univ.; mem. Advisory Bd, Conflict Prevention and Peace Forum.

ARNETT, Emerson James, QC, BA, LLM; Canadian lawyer and business executive; b. 29 Sept. 1938, Winnipeg, Man.; s. of Emerson Lloyd Arnett and Elsie Audrey Rhind; m. Edith Alexandra Palk 1964; four c.; ed Univ. of Manitoba,

Harvard Univ.; worked in civil litigation section, Dept of Justice, Ottawa 1964–65; Assoc., Pitblado & Hoskin (law firm), Winnipeg 1965–66; Asst to Exec. Vice-Pres. Vickers & Benson Advertising, Toronto 1966–67; Assoc./Partner, Davies, Ward & Beck (law firm), Toronto 1968–73; Partner, Stikeman, Elliott (law firm), Toronto 1973–97, Resident Partner, Washington, DC 1993–96; Pres. and CEO Molson Inc. 1997–2000; Chair. Hydro One Inc. March–Dec. 2008, 2009–14; mem. Bd of Dirs, Mirabaud Asset Man. (Canada) Inc. 2002–. *Publications include:* Doing Business (co-ed.); numerous law review and newspaper articles and conf. papers. *Leisure interests:* shooting, skiing, hiking, reading. *Address:* c/o Hydro One Inc., 483 Bay Street, Toronto, ON M5G 2P5, Canada.

ARNETT, Peter Gregg, ONZM; New Zealand/American journalist and television reporter; b. 13 Nov. 1934, Riverton, New Zealand; m. Nina Nguyen 1964 (divorced 1983); two c.; ed Waitaki Coll., Oamaru, NZ; with Associated Press (AP) 1960–; war corresp. in Viet Nam, Middle East, Nicaragua, El Salvador and Afghanistan; special writer for AP, New York; worked with Cable News Network (CNN) 1981–99; served as corresp. in Moscow for two years; later nat. security reporter, Washington, DC; CNN corresp. Baghdad 1991; Chief Foreign Corresp. Foreign-TV.com, New York 1998, then reporter MSNBC, fired for making unauthorized remarks to state-run Iraqi TV 2003, then reporter in Iraq for Daily Mirror (UK newspaper); also worked for Nat. Geographic, Global Vision magazines; Visiting Prof., Cheung Kong School of Journalism and Communication, Shantou Univ., China 2007, currently Prof.; Officer of the NZ Order of Merit 2006; Pulitzer Prize 1966, George Foster Peabody Award, Golden Cable ACE Award. *Publication:* Live from the Battlefield 1994. *Leisure interests:* collector of books and oriental statuary. *Address:* Cheung Kong School of Journalism and Communication, Shantou University, 243 Daxue Road, Shantou 515063, People's Republic of China (office). *Telephone:* (54) 82902305 (office). *Fax:* (54) 82510505 (office). *Website:* www.stu.edu.cn (office).

ARNOLD, Frances Hamilton, BS, PhD; American chemical engineer and academic; *Linus Pauling Professor of Chemical Engineering, Bioengineering and Biochemistry and Director, Donna and Benjamin M. Rosen Bioengineering Center, California Institute of Technology;* b. 25 July 1956, Edgewood, Pa; d. of William Howard Arnold; m. 1st James E. Bailey, one s.; m. 2nd Andrew E. Lange, two s.; ed Princeton Univ., Univ. of California, Berkeley; Postdoctoral Researcher in Chem., Univ. of California, Berkeley 1985–86; Postdoctoral Researcher in Chem., California Inst. of Tech. 1986, fmr Dick and Barbara Dickinson Prof. of Chemical Eng, Bioengineering and Biochemistry, also Dir Donna and Benjamin M. Rosen Bioengineering Center, Linus Pauling Prof. 2017–; mem. Advisory Bd, Joint BioEnergy Inst., Packard Fellowships in Science and Eng; mem. Pres.'s Advisory Council, King Abdullah Univ. of Science and Tech.; Science Advisor Maxygen 1997–2002, Amyris Biotechnologies 2005–09, Codexis 2007–09, Mascoma, Inc. 2007–13, Arzeda 2009–12, Genomatica 2013–15; Co-Founder, Dir and Science Advisor Gevo, Inc. 2005–11, Provivi 2013–; Dir Illumina 2016–; mem. judging panel, Queen Elizabeth Prize for Eng 2013; mem. Nat. Acad. of Eng 2000, Inst. of Medicine of Nat. Acads 2004, NAS 2008, American Acad. of Arts and Sciences 2011; Fellow, American Inst. for Medical and Biological Eng 2001, American Acad. of Microbiology 2009, AAAS 2010; Int. Fellow, Royal Acad. of Eng 2018; Dr hc (Stockholm) 2013, (ETH Zurich) 2015, (Dartmouth Coll.) 2017; AIChE Professional Progress Award 2000, Sir Robert Price Lecturer, CSIRO, Melbourne 2003, ACS David Perlman Lecture Award in Biochemical Tech. 2003, Carothers Award, ACS Delaware Div. 2003, ACS Francis P. Garvan-John M. Olin Medal 2005, AIChE Food, Pharmaceuticals and Bioengineering Div. Award 2005, Excellence in Science Award, Fed. of American Socs for Experimental Biology 2007, Enzyme Eng Award 2007, Cruickshank Lecturer, Gordon Research Confs 2008, Linnaeus Lecturer, Uppsala Univ. 2008, Charles Stark Draper Prize 2011, Nat. Medal of Tech. and Innovation 2011, Emanuel Merck Lecturer in Chem. 2013, ENI Prize in Renewable and Nonconventional Energy 2013, Millennium Technology Prize 2016, Raymond and Beverly Sackler Prize in Convergence Research 2017, Nobel Prize in Chemistry (co-recipient) 2018, Bower Award & Prize for Achievement in Science 2019. *Publications:* numerous papers in professional journals. *Address:* 228228B Spalding Laboratory, Division of Chemistry and Chemical Engineering, California Institute of Technology, 1200 E California Blvd, Pasadena, CA 91125 (office). *Telephone:* (626) 395-4162 (office). *Fax:* (626) 568-8743 (office). *E-mail:* frances@cheme.caltech.edu (office). *Website:* www.che.caltech.edu (office).

ARNOLD, Hans Redlef, PhD; German writer, academic and fmr diplomatist; *Lecturer, Academy of Political Science, Munich;* b. 14 Aug. 1923, Munich; s. of Karl Arnold and Anne-Dora Volquardsen; m. Karin Baroness von Egloffstein 1954; three d.; ed Univ. of Munich; joined Foreign Service, FRG; served in Embassy in Paris 1952–55, Foreign Office, Bonn 1955–57, Embassy in Washington, DC 1957–61, Foreign Office 1961–68, sometime head of Foreign Minister Willy Brandt's office; Amb. to the Netherlands 1968–72; Head, Cultural Dept, Foreign Office 1972–77; Amb. to Italy 1977–81; Insp.-Gen. German Foreign Service 1981–82; Amb. and Perm. Rep. to UN and Int. Orgs, Geneva 1982–86; Lecturer, Acad. of Political Science, Munich; several nat. and foreign decorations. *Publications include:* Cultural Export as Policy? 1976, Foreign Cultural Policy 1980, The March (co-author) 1990, Europe on the Decline? 1993, Germany's Power 1995, Europe To Be Thought Anew: Why and How Further Unification? 1999, Security for Europe (co-ed.) 2002, How Much Unification Does Europe Need? 2004, The Magic of Film 2015; regular contribs to periodicals and newspapers. *Address:* 83083 Riedering-Heft, Germany (home). *Telephone:* (8032) 5255 (home). *E-mail:* hans.arnold@gmx.net (home).

ARNOLD, Luqman, BSc; British business executive and banker; b. April 1950, Calcutta, India; m.; one s.; ed Oundle School, Univ. of London; with Mfrs Hanover Corpn, London, Hong Kong and Singapore 1976–82; with First Nat. Bank (Dallas), Singapore and London 1972–76; with Credit Suisse First Boston, London and Tokyo 1982–92, responsible for Asia Pacific origination, Private Placements, Cen. and Eastern Europe, later Head of Investment Banking, New Business, mem. Operating Cttee; sabbatical year (research into drivers and outlook for cross-border institutional investment flows) 1992–93; Global Head of Investment Banking, Paribas Capital Markets, Banque Paribas, London 1993–95, Group Head of Business Devt, Paris 1995–96; CEO Asia Pacific UBS AG, Singapore and Tokyo 1996–98, COO, London 1998–99, Chief Financial Officer and Head of Corp. Centre, Zurich 1999–2001, Pres. and Chair., Exec. Bd, Zurich 2001; CEO Abbey National 2002–04; Chair. (also co-founder) Olivant Advisers Ltd 2006–12; Dir and Co-founder Cartesius SA 2010–, Partner, Cartesius Advisory Network AG (CAN) 2014–; Chair. Bd of Trustees Design Museum; Trustee, Architecture Foundation; Sr Advisor to Chair. of Grupo Santander; fmr Pnr Corsair Capital LLC; mem. Devt Council, Univ. of the Arts London; fmr mem. FSA Practitioner Panel, FSA Financial Capability Steering Group, British Bankers' Asscn Council, Asscn of British Insurers' Bd, European Securities Forum. *Leisure interest:* opera. *Address:* c/o Jackie Miles, Cartesius Advisory Network Limited, 4th Floor, Devonshire House, 1 Mayfair Place, London, W1J 8AJ, England (home). *Telephone:* (20) 3819-8850 (home). *E-mail:* jackie.miles@cartesius.com (home).

ARNOLD, Roseanne (see Roseanne).

ARNON, Ruth, PhD; Israeli immunologist and academic; *Paul Ehrlich Professor of Immunology, Weizmann Institute of Science;* b. 1 June 1933, Tel-Aviv; m. Uriel Arnon; one s. one d.; ed Hebrew Univ., Jerusalem, Weizmann Inst. of Science, Rehovot; Visiting Scientist, Rockefeller Inst., New York, USA 1960–62, Univ. of Washington, Seattle, USA 1968–69; Assoc. Prof., Weizmann Inst. of Science 1971, Head, Dept of Chemical Immunology 1973–74, 1975–78, Prof. 1975, now Paul Ehrlich Prof. of Immunology, Dir MacArthur Center for Parasitology 1984–89, Dean, Faculty of Biology 1985–93, Vice-Pres. 1988–93, Vice-Pres. for Int. Scientific Relations 1995–97; Visiting Scientist, UCLA 1977–78, Institut Pasteur, Paris, France 1983, 1998, Walter and Eliza Hall Inst., Melbourne, Australia 1994, Imperial Cancer Research Fund, London, UK 1995, Rockefeller Foundation's Bellagio Conf. and Study Center, Lake Como, Italy 1995; Sec.-Gen. Int. Union of Immunological Socs 1989–93; Pres. European Fed. of Immunological Socs 1983–86; mem. Steering Cttee WHO Task Force on Immunological Methods for Fertility Control 1972–77, European Molecular Biology Orgs (EMBO); mem. Israel Acad. of Sciences and Humanities 1990– (Chair. Science Div. 1995–2001), Vice-Pres. 2004–; Adviser for Science to Pres. of Israel 2001–06; Foreign mem. American Philosophical Soc. 2009–; Pres. Israel Acad. of Sciences and Humanities 2010–; Chevalier de la Légion d'honneur 1994; Dr hc (Ben-Gurion Univ., Negev) 2001, (Tel-Hai Univ.) 2008, (Israel Open Univ.) 2014, (Leuphana Univ., Luneburg) 2014; Robert Koch Prize in Medical Sciences (Germany) 1979, Jimenez Diaz Award (Spain) 1986, Fogarty Scholarship, NIH, USA 1996, 1997–98, Wolf Prize 1998, Rothschild Prize 1998, Israel Prize in Medical Research 2001. *Publications include:* more than 400 articles, chapters and books on immunology and biochemistry. *Address:* Department of Immunology, Wolfson Building, 431A, Weizmann Institute of Science, 76100 Rehovot, Israel (office). *Telephone:* (8) 934-4017 (office). *Fax:* (8) 946-9712 (office). *E-mail:* ruth.arnon@weizmann.ac.il (office). *Website:* www.weizmann.ac.il (office).

ARNOUL, Françoise; French actress; b. (Françoise Gautsch), 9 June 1931, Constantine, Algeria; d. of Gen. Arnoul Gautsch and Jeanne Gradwohl; m. Georges Cravenne (divorced); ed Lycée de Rabat, Lycée Molière, Paris and Paris Conservatoire; Chevalier de la Légion d'honneur; Officier des Arts et Lettres. *Films include:* L'Épave 1949, Nous irons à Paris 1950, La maison Bonnadieu 1951, La plus belle fille du monde 1951, Le désir et l'amour 1952, Les compagnons de la nuit 1953, Les amants du Tage 1955, French-Cancan 1955, Des gens sans importance 1955, Thérèse Etienne 1958, La chatte 1958, Asphalte 1958, La bête à l'affût 1959, Le bal des espions 1960, La chatte sort ses griffes 1960, La morte-saison des amours 1960, Les Parisiennes 1962, Le Congrès s'amuse 1966, Le Dimanche de la vie 1967, Españolas en Paris 1970, Van der Valk 1972, Dialogue d'exiles 1975, Dernière sortie avant Roissy 1977, Ronde de Nuit 1984, Nuit Docile 1987, Voir L'Éléphant 1989, Années campagne, Les 1992, Les Cent et une nuits de Simon Cinéma 1995, Temps de chien 1996, Post coïtum animal triste 1997, Photo de famille 2000, Merci pour le geste 2000; theatre debut in Les Justes (Camus), Versailles 1966. *Television includes:* La Guêpe 1965, Le Petit théâtre de Jean Renoir 1970, Van der Valk und das Mädchen 1972, La Mort d'un enfant 1974, Lockruf des Goldes (mini-series) 1975, L'Automate 1981, Les Brus 1981, Mon enfant, ma mère 1981, Vivre ma vie 1982, L' Amour s'invente 1982, Un garçon de France 1985, L'Herbe rouge 1985, La Garçonne 1988, L'Étrange histoire d'Emilie Albert 1989, Héloïse 1991, Billard à l'étage 1996, Une patronne de charme 1997, L'Alambic 1998, Duval: Un mort de trop 2001, Le voyageur de la Toussaint 2007. *Leisure interest:* dancing. *Address:* 53 rue Censier, 75005 Paris, France (home).

ARNOULT, Érik, (Érik Orsenna), DèsScEcon, PhD; French civil servant and writer; b. 22 March 1947, Paris; s. of Claude Arnoult and Janine Arnoult (née Bodé); m. 2nd Catherine Clavier; one s. one d.; m. 3rd Isabelle de Saint Aubin; ed École Saint-Jean de Béthune, Versailles, Institut d'Études Politiques, Paris, Univ. of Paris I, London School of Econs; Lecturer, Inst. d'Études Politiques, Paris 1975–80, École Normale Supérieure 1977–81; Literary Ed., Editions Ramsay 1977–81; Sr Lecturer, Université de Paris I 1978–81; Tech. Adviser to Ministry of Co-operation and Devt 1981–83, to Minister of Foreign Affairs 1990–92; Cultural Adviser to Pres. of Repub. 1983–90; Maître des Requêtes, Conseil d'État 1985–, Sr mem. 2000–; Pres. Centre Int. de la Mer 1991–, École Nat. Supérieure du Paysage 1995–; Vice-Pres. Cytale Soc. 2000–03; Chair. Prix Orange du Livre 2009–; Amb. Institut Pasteur 2016–; mem. Foundation for World Agric. and Rural Life 2006–, Acad. française 1998. *Film screenplay:* Indochine (co-writer) (Acad. Award for Best Foreign Film). *Publications include:* Loyola's blues 1974, Espace national et déséquilibre monétaire 1977, La vie comme à Lausanne 1977 (Prix Roger Nimier), Une comédie française 1980, L'Exposition coloniale (novel) (Prix Goncourt) 1988, Grand amour 1993, Histoire du monde en neuf guitares 1996, Deux étés (novel) 1996, Longtemps (novel) 1998, Portrait d'un homme heureux, André Le Nôtre 1613–1700 2000, La grammaire est une chanson douce 2001, Madame Bâ 2003, Les chevaliers du Subjonctif 2004, Portrait du Gulf Stream 2005, Voyage aux pays du coton: Petit précis de mondialisation I (Prix du livre d'économie, Second Prize, Lettre Ulysses Award) 2006, La révolte des accents 2007, L'avenir de l'eau: Petit précis de mondialisation II 2009, Et si on dansait? 2009, L'Entreprise des Indes (The Indies Enterprise) 2010, Princesse Histamine 2010, Sur la route du papier: Petit précis de mondialisation III 2012, La Fabrique des mots 2013, Mali, ô Mali 2014, La vie, la mort, la vie: Louis Pasteur 2015, L'origine de nos amours 2016, La Fontaine: une école buissonnière 2017, Géopolitique du moustique: Petit précis de mondialisation IV 2017, Désir de villes: Petit précis de mondialisation V 2018. *Leisure interest:* yachting. *Address:* Conseil d'État, 1 place du Palais Royal, 75001 Paris (office); 8 passage Sigaud, 75013 Paris, France (home). *Website:* www.erik-orsenna.com.

ARONOFSKY, Darren; American film director, producer and screenwriter; b. 12 Feb. 1969, Brooklyn, New York, NY; s. of Abraham Aronofsky and Charlotte Aronofsky; partner Rachel Weisz 2001–10; one s.; partner Brandi-Ann Milbradt 2012–; ed Harvard Univ., American Film Inst.; frequent collaborations with cinematographer Matthew Libatique, film ed. Andrew Weisblum and composer Clint Mansell; films often portray violent, bleak subject matter; f. Protozoa Pictures (production co.); Pres. of the Jury, 68th Venice Int. Film Festival 2011, 65th Berlin Int. Film Festival 2015. *Films include:* Pi (dir, writer and producer) (Sundance Film Festival Best Dir 1999) 1998, Requiem for a Dream (dir and writer) 2000, Below (producer and writer) 2002, The Fountain (dir and writer) 2006, The Wrestler (dir and producer) (Venice Film Festival Golden Lion 2007) 2008, Black Swan (dir and producer) (San Francisco Film Critics Circle Awards Best Dir 2010, Scream Award for Best Dir 2011) 2010, The Fighter (producer) 2010, Noah (dir, writer and producer) 2014, Zipper (exec. producer) 2015. *Address:* c/o Protozoa Pictures, 104 North 7th Street, Brooklyn, NY 11211-3020, USA (office). *Telephone:* (718) 388-5280 (office). *Fax:* (718) 388-5425 (office). *Website:* www.protozoa.com (office); www.darrenaronofsky.com.

ARORA, Sunil, MA; Indian government official and airline industry executive; *Chief Election Commissioner;* b. 13 April 1956; Sec. to Chief Minister, Rajasthan; Sec. (Policy and Planning) 1993–98; Dir Dept of Econ. Affairs (Banking Div.), Govt of India 1999; Jt Sec., Ministry of Civil Aviation 1999–2002; Chair. and Man. Dir Indian Airlines 2002–05; Prin. Sec. to Chief Minister, Govt, Information and Public Relations Dept, Rajasthan 2005–08; Prin. Sec. to Govt, Industries, State Enterprises and NRI 2009; Chair. Rajasthan State Industrial Devt and Investment Corpn Ltd 2008–13; Sec., Ministry of Information and Broadcasting 2015–17; Dir-Gen. and CEO Indian Inst. of Corp. Affairs 2016–18; Election Commr 2017–18, Chief Election Commr 2018–; apptd Adviser, Prasar Bharti 2016. *Address:* Election Commission of India, Nirvachan Sadan, Ashoka Road, New Delhi 110001, India (office). *Telephone:* (11) 23717391 (ECI) (office). *Fax:* (11) 23717075 (ECI) (office). *E-mail:* feedbackeci@gmail.com (office); chairman@riico.co.in (office). *Website:* eci.gov.in (office).

ARP, Fredrik, BS; Swedish business executive; *Executive Chairman, Qioptiq;* b. 1953, Köping; m. Suzanne Arp; four c.; ed Univ. of Lund; salesman Tarkett France, Swedish Match Group, later Div. Man. for Flooring; with Tyre Div., Trelleborg Group 1985, Vice-Pres. 1996; Pres. and CEO PLM (now Rexam) 1996–99; Pres. and CEO Trelleborg AB 1999–2005; Pres. and CEO Volvo Car Corpn 2005–08; Chair. and CEO Qioptiq Jan.–Aug. 2010, Exec. Chair. Sept. 2010–; Sr Adviser for Nordic region, Candover 2009–; mem. Bd of Dirs, Hilding Anders SACC–NY; fmr Chair. Thule AB, Hilding Anders; Hon. DEcon (Univ. of Lund, Sweden). *Leisure interests:* golf, skiing. *Address:* Qioptiq Photonics GmbH & Co. KG, Hans-Riedl-Str. 9, 85622 Feldkirchen (Munich), Germany (office). *Telephone:* (89) 255458-0 (office). *Fax:* (89) 255458111 (office). *E-mail:* info@qioptiq.com (office). *Website:* www.qioptiq.com (office).

ARPEY, Gerard J., BBA, MBA; American airline industry executive; *Partner, Emerald Creek Group, LLC;* b. 26 July 1958; m. Lisa Walsh 1980s; two s. one d.; ed Univ. of Texas, Austin; joined American Airlines 1982, Financial Analyst 1982–83, Sr Financial Analyst 1983–85, Man. Financial Analysis 1985–87, Dir Airline Profitability Analysis 1987–88, Man. Dir Financial Analysis 1988, Man. Dir Financial Planning 1988–89, Vice-Pres. Financial Planning and Analysis 1989–92, Sr Vice-Pres. Planning 1992–95, Sr Vice-Pres. Finance and Planning and Chief Financial Officer 1995–99, Exec. Vice-Pres., Operations 2000–02, Pres. and COO 2002–03, mem. Bd of Dirs and Pres. AMR Corpn and American Airlines Inc. 2003–10, CEO 2003–11, Chair. 2004–11; Partner, Emerald Creek Group, LLC 2011–; mem. Bd of Dirs, S. C. Johnson & Son, Inc.; Dir Dallas Museum of Art; mem. The Business Council, Advisory Council McCombs School of Business at Univ. of Texas. *Leisure interest:* private pilot (holds a FAA Multi-Engine Instrument Pilot Rating). *Address:* Emerald Creek Group, LLC, 5000 Birch Street, Suite 500, Newport Beach, CA 92660, USA (office). *Telephone:* (949) 379-7200 (office). *E-mail:* gerard.arpey@emeraldcreek.com (office). *Website:* www.emeraldcreek.com/Gerard.html (office).

ARQUETTE, Patricia; American actress; b. 8 April 1968, Chicago, Ill.; d. of Lewis Arquette and Mardi Arquette; sister of Rosanna Arquette; m. 1st Nicolas Cage 1995 (divorced 2001); m. 2nd Thomas Jane 2006 (divorced 2011); one s. (from previous relationship) one d. *Films include:* Pretty Smart 1986, A Nightmare on Elm Street 3: Dream Warriors 1987, Time Out 1988, Far North 1988, The Indian Runner 1991, Prayer of the Rollerboys 1991, Ethan Frome 1993, Trouble Bound 1993, Inside Monkey Zetterland 1993, True Romance 1993, Holy Matrimony 1994, Ed Wood 1994, Beyond Rangoon 1995, Infinity 1995, Flirting with Disaster 1996, The Secret Agent 1996, Lost Highway 1997, Nightwatch 1998, In the Boom Boom Room 1999, Goodbye Lover 1999, Stigmata 1999, Bringing out the Dead 1999, Little Nicky 2000, Human Nature 2001, Holes 2003, Tiptoes 2003, Deeper than Deep 2003, Fast Food Nation 2006, Girl in Progress 2012, A Glimpse Inside the Mind of Charles Swan III 2012, Vijay and I 2013, Boyhood (Best Supporting Actress Award, New York Film Critics Circle 2014, Golden Globe Award for Best Supporting Actress in a Motion Picture (Drama) 2015, Best Supporting Actress, Critics' Choice Movie Awards, Broadcast Film Critics Assen 2015, Supporting Actress of the Year, London Critics' Circle 2015, Outstanding Performance by a Female Actor in a Supporting Role, Screen Actors Guild 2015, BAFTA Award for Best Actress in a Supporting Role 2015, Academy Award for Best Actress in a Supporting Role 2015) 2014, Electric Slide 2014, The Wannabe 2015, Permanent 2017, Otherhood 2019. *TV includes:* Daddy 1987, Dillinger 1991, Wildflower 1991, Betrayed by Love 1994, Toby's Story 1998, The Hi-Lo Country 1998, The Badge 2002, Medium (series) (Emmy Award for Best Actress in a Drama 2005) 2005–11, Boardwalk Empire 2013–14, CSI: Cyber 2015–16, Escape at Dannemora (Golden Globe Award for Best Actress in a Limited Series or TV Movie 2019, Critics' Choice TV Awards for Best Actress in a Movie or Miniseries 2019, Screen Actors Guild Award for Outstanding Performance by a Female Actor in a Miniseries or TV Movie 2019) 2018. *Address:* c/o Gersh, 9465 Wilshire Blvd, 6th Floor, Beverly Hills, CA 90212, USA. *Telephone:* (310) 274-6611.

ARQUETTE, Rosanna; American actress; b. 10 Aug. 1959, New York; d. of Lewis Arquette and Mardi Arquette; sister of Patricia Arquette; m. 1st (divorced); m. 2nd James N. Howard (divorced); m. 3rd. John Sidel 1993; f. Flower Child Productions. *Films include:* Gorp 1980, S.O.B. 1981, Off the Wall 1983, The Aviator 1985, Desperately Seeking Susan 1985, 8 Million Ways to Die 1986, After Hours 1986, Nobody's Fool 1986, The Big Blue 1988, Life Lessons, Black Rainbow 1989, Wendy Cracked a Walnut 1989, Sweet Revenge 1990, Baby, It's You 1990, Flight of the Intruder 1990, The Linguini Incident 1992, Fathers and Sons 1992, Nowhere to Run 1993, Pulp Fiction 1994, Search and Destroy 1995, Crash 1996, Liar 1997, Gone Fishin' 1997, Buffalo '66 1997, Palmer's Pick Up 1998, I'm Losing You 1998, Homeslice 1998, Floating Away 1998, Hope Floats 1998, Fait Accompli 1998, Sugar Town 1999, Palmer's Pick Up 1999, Pigeonholed 1999, Interview with a Dead Man 1999, The Whole Nine Yards 2000, Too Much Flesh 2000, Things Behind the Sun 2001, Big Bad Love 2001, Good Advice 2001, Diary of a Sex Addict 2001, Gilded Stones 2004, Dead Cool 2004, Max and Grace 2005, Iowa 2005, Kids in America 2005, Welcome to California 2005, I-See-You.Com 2006, Ball Don't Lie 2008, Growing Op 2008, The Divide 2012, Hardflip 2012, Draft Day 2014, Asthma 2014. *TV films include:* Harvest Home, The Wall, The Long Way Home, The Executioner's Song, One Cooks, the Other Doesn't, The Parade, Survival Guide, A Family Tree, Promised a Miracle, Sweet Revenge, Separation, The Wrong Man, Nowhere to Hide, I Know What You Did, The Law and Mr. Lee 2003, Rush of Fear 2003, The L Word (series) 2004–07, What About Brian (series) 2006–07, Lipstick Jungle (series) 2008, Northern Lights (series) 2009, Rochelle (series) 2012, Ray Donovan (series) 2013–14. *Address:* c/o Abrams Artists Agency, 750 North San Vicente Blvd, East Tower, 11th Floor, Los Angeles, CA 90069, USA (office). *Telephone:* (310) 859-0625 (office). *E-mail:* contactla@abramsartistsagency.com (office). *Website:* www.abramsartists.com (office).

ARRABAL, Fernando; Spanish writer; b. 11 Aug. 1932, Melilla; s. of Fernando Arrabal and Carmen Terán González; m. Luce Moreau 1958; one s. one d; ed Univ. of Madrid; political prisoner in Spain 1967; Founder Panique Movt with Topor, Jodorowsky, others; Officier, Ordre des Arts et des Lettres 1984, Chevalier, Légion d'honneur 2005; Hon. DLitt (Aristotle Univ. of Thessaloniki, Greece) 2007; Superdotado Award 1942, Ford Foundation Award 1959, Grand Prix du Théâtre 1967, Grand Prix Humour Noir 1968, Obie Award 1976, Premio Nadal (Spain) 1983, World's Theater Prize 1984, Medalla de Oro de Bellas Artes (Spain) 1989, Prix du Théâtre (Acad. Française) 1993, Prix Int. Vladimir Nabokov 1994, Premio de Ensayo Espasa 1994, Grand Prix Soc. des Gens de Lettres 1996, Grand Prix de la Méditerranée 1996, Medal of Centre for French Civilization and Culture, New York 1997, Prix de la Francophonie 1998, Premio Mariano de Cavia 1998, Prix Alessandro Manzoni di Poesia 1999, Premio Nacional de las Letras, Premio Eninci Cine y Literatura 2000, Premio Nacional de Teatro 2001, Premio Ercilla Teatro 2001, Gold Medal of San Fando 2003, Prix Spinoza 2007, Hijo adoptivo de Ciudad Rodrigo 2008, Premier Prix Int. Théâtre du Millénaire 2010. *Publications include:* plays: numerous plays including Le cimetière des voitures, Guernica, Le grand cérémonial, L'architecte et l'Empereur d'Assyrie, Le jardin des délices, Et ils passèrent des menottes aux fleurs, Le ciel et la merde, Bella ciao, La Tour de Babel, L'extravagante réussite de Jésus-Christ, Karl Marx et William Shakespeare, Les délices de la chair, La traversée de l'empire, Luly, Cielito, Fando et Lis, Lettre d'amour; novels: Baal Babylone 1959, L'enterrement de la sardine 1962, Fêtes et rites de la confusion 1965, La tour prends garde, La reverdie, La vierge rouge, Bréviaire d'amour d'un haltérophile, L'extravagante croisade d'un castrat amoureux 1991, La tueuse du jardin d'hiver 1994, El Mono 1994, Le Funambule de Dieu 1998, Ceremonia por un teniente abandonado 1998, Porté disparu 2000, Champagne pour tous 2002, Como un paraíso de locos 2008; poetry includes: La pierre de la folie 1963, 100 sonnets 1966, Humbles paradis 1983, Liberté couleur de femme 1993, Arrabalesques 1994, Passion, Passions 1997, Le Frénétique du Spasme 1997; essays: numerous, including Le Panique, Le New York d'Arrabal, Lettre au Général Franco, Greco 1970, Lettre à Fidel Castro 1983, Goya-Dali 1992, La Dudosa Luz del Día 1994. *Films include:* directed and written: Viva la Muerte, J'irai comme un cheval fou, L'arbre de Guernica, L'odyssée de la Pacific, Le cimetière des voitures, Adieu Babylone!, J.-L. Borges (Una Vida de Poesía) 1998. *Leisure interest:* chess. *Address:* 22 rue Jouffroy d'Abbans, Paris 75017, France (home). *Fax:* 1-42-67-01-26 (home). *E-mail:* fernando.arrabal@orange.fr; arrabalf@gmail.com. *Website:* www.arrabal.org.

ARRAYED, Jawad Salim al-, BA, LLB; Bahraini politician; *Deputy Prime Minister;* b. 23 Sept. 1940; ed Cairo Univ., Leeds Univ., UK; Public Prosecution Dir 1969–71; Minister of Labour and Social Affairs 1971–73; Minister of State for Cabinet Affairs 1973–82; Minister of Health and Chair. Environmental Protection Cttee 1982–95, Minister of State 1995–99; Minister of State for Municipalities and Environmental Affairs 1999–2002; Minister of Justice 2002–05; Advisor to Prime Minister on Legal Affairs 2005–06; Deputy Prime Minister 2006–; mem. Hon. Soc. of Gray's Inn; mem. al-Wifaq party. *Address:* c/o Office of the Prime Minister, POB 2088, Government House, Government Rd, Manama, Bahrain.

ARREAZA MONSERRAT, Jorge Alberto; Venezuelan politician; *Minister of Foreign Affairs;* b. 6 June 1973; m. Rosa Virginia Chávez Colmenares (daughter of fmr Pres. of Venezuela Hugo Chávez); two c.; ed Universidad Central de Venezuela, Univ. of Cambridge, UK; fmr journalist; fmr Lecturer, Universidad Central de Venezuela; fmr presenter and interviewer on several public TV stations in Venezuela, including as host of TV series Diálogo abierto; Pres. Fundayacucho (student grant org.) 2005–10; Pres. Nat. Inst. of Training and Socialist Educ. (INCES) 2011–13; Pres. Bolivarian Agency for Space Activities (ABAE) 2012–13; Deputy Minister of Science and Tech. 2010–11, Minister of Univ. Educ., Science and Tech. 2016–17, Minister for Ecological Mining Devt Feb.–Aug. 2017; Vice-Pres. of Venezuela 2013–16, Sector Vice-Pres. for Social Devt and Revolution of the Missions 2016–17; Minister of Foreign Affairs 2017–; mem. Partido Socialista Unido de Venezuela. *Address:* Ministry of Foreign Affairs, Torre MRE, al lado del Correo de Carmelitas, Avda Urdaneta, Caracas 1010, Venezuela (office). *Telephone:* (212) 806-4400 (office). *Fax:* (212) 861-2505 (office). *E-mail:* web.master@mre.gov.ve (office). *Website:* www.mre.gov.ve (office).

ARRIOLA RAMÍREZ, Julio César; Paraguayan politician and diplomatist; *Permanent Representative to United Nations;* b. 20 July 1965, Asunción; m. Adriana Arza Spinzi; four c.; ed Catholic Univ. of Asunción, Inter-American Coll. of Continental Defense, Washington DC; Official Consulate of Paraguay, Clorinda, Argentina 1990–91, Formosa 1991–94; Int. Bureau Chief North America, Caribbean and Oceanic Dept 1994–95, Counsellor Perm. Mission of Paraguay, OAS, Washington DC 1995–99, Minister 1999–2001; Dir Int. Orgs 2001–04, Dir-Gen. Multilateral Policy, Ministry of Foreign Affairs 2004–05, 2011–12; Chargé d'affaires, Costa Rica 2005–09; Deputy Perm. Rep. to UN 2009–11, Vice-Minister Admin and Tech. Affairs 2012–15; Amb. to Canada 2015–17; Perm. Rep. to UN 2017–; Full mem. Bd of Dirs Nat. Comm. of Atomic Energy 2001–04. *Address:* Permanent Mission of Paraguay, 405 E 42nd Street, New York, NY 10017, USA (office). *Telephone:* (212) 963-1234 (office). *Fax:* (212) 963-4879 (office). *E-mail:* paraguay@un.int (office).

ARROYO, Mary T. K., BSc, PhD, FLS, FRSNZ; New Zealand biologist and academic; *Director, Institute of Ecology and Biodiversity;* b. (Mary Therese Kalin), 12 Nov. 1944, New Plymouth; d. of Alexander Meinrod Kalin and Shiela Frances Hurley; m. Manuel Patricio Arroyo; one s.; ed Univ. of Canterbury, Christchurch, New Zealand, Univ. of California, Berkeley, USA; Postdoctoral Research Fellow, with Dr Peter Raven, residing in New York Botanical Garden 1971–72; Full Prof. of Biology, Universidad de Chile, Dir Inst. of Ecology and Biodiversity; Head of Ind. Scientific Comm. of the Rio Condor Project (jt collaboration between Chilean scientific community and Chilean forestry industry); her studies led to designation of the central Chilean biodiversity hotspot and a better understanding of the conservation values of protected areas of central Chile; 68,000 hectares of the Condor River drainage basin have been protected; has worked extensively on pollination mechanisms, plant breeding systems and flower longevity in the Chilean Andes; Corresp. mem. Botanical Soc. of America 1995, NAS 1999, Chilean Acad. of Sciences 2003; mem. Third World Acad. of Sciences (now TWAS, The World Acad. of Sciences) 2004; Condecoración al Mérito 'Amanda Labarca' 1996; Percival Memorial Prize in Botany, Univ. of Canterbury 1966, Premio Cultural 'Angel Faivovich' 1982, Guggenheim Fellow 1984, Cátedra Presidencial en Ciencias, 1997–99, Medalla Rectoral, Universidad de Chile 1998, Premio Fundación BBVA a la Investigación a la Biología de la Conservación 2004, Volvo Environment Prize (Sweden) 2005, Chilean Nat. Science Prize in Natural Sciences 2010. *Publications:* numerous papers on reproductive systems of plants, studies of complete communities and conservation. *Leisure interests:* hiking, biking, reading. *Address:* Institute of Ecology and Biodiversity, University of Chile, Castilla 653, Santiago, Chile (office). *Telephone:* (2) 2715464 (office). *E-mail:* southern@uchile.cl (office). *Website:* www.ieb-chile.cl (office).

ARRUKBAN, Abdulaziz bin Mohamed; Saudi Arabian UN official and fmr transport executive; *Special Humanitarian Envoy, United Nations;* b. 1959; ed coll. in Georgia, USA; began career working in transport sector in USA, moved back to Riyadh as COO of one of Saudi Arabia's largest transportation cos; currently Chair. Middle East International (group of cos), Riyadh; Special Amb., UN World Food Programme 2005–07, UN Special Humanitarian Envoy 2007–.

ARSALA, Hedayat Amin, PhD; Afghan economist and politician; b. 12 Jan. 1942, nephew of Pir Gailani (leader of Qadiriyyah Sufi order); m.; three c.; ed high school in Kabul, George Washington Univ., USA; ethnic Pashtun descended from Jabar Khel tribe; foreign language trainer for three consecutive Peace Corps training programmes in USA; started his professional career at World Bank Youth Professional Program 1969, held various econ. and sr operational posts 1969–87; returned to Afghanistan to join Afghan resistance to Soviet occupation 1987–89, served as Sr Adviser and mem. Afghan Mujahideen Unity Council; Minister of Finance, Transitional Govt of Afghanistan 1989–92; Minister of Foreign Affairs 1993–96; Sr mem. Exec. Council of Loya Jirga (traditional council of Afghan tribal leaders) 1998–; played key role in Intra-Afghan Bonn Conf. following fall of the Taliban regime 2001; apptd Vice-Chair. and Minister of Finance of the interim admin 2001; named one of four Vice-Pres, Transitional Islamic State of Afghanistan 2001–04, Chair. Ind. Civil Services Admin Reform Comm., adviser to Cen. Statistics Office and Afghan Econ. Cooperation Cttee; mem. Afghan Nat. Security Council; Minister of Commerce and Sr Presidential Adviser 2004–06, Sr Minister in the Cabinet 2006–10, currently Sr Adviser to Pres.; apptd Chair. Govt Co-ordination Cttee 2008; Co-Chair. Jt Co-ordination and Monitoring Bd 2008; unsuccessful cand. in presidential elections 2009, 2014; Dr hc (Southern Illinois Univ., USA) 2008. *E-mail:* arsalapressoffice@gmail.com.

ARTÉS GÓMEZ, Mariano; Spanish professor of mechanics; *Professor and Director of Mechanics Department, Universidad Nacional de Educación a Distancia;* b. 5 March 1947, Murcia; s. of Mariano Artés and Elisa Gómez; m. María José Caselles 1973; three s.; ed Universidad Politécnica de Madrid, Int. Centre for Theoretical Physics, Trieste; Asst Prof. of Mechanics, Universidad Politécnica de Madrid 1971–78, Assoc. Prof. 1979–80; Prof. Universidad de Oviedo 1980–81; Prof. and Dir of Dept of Mechanics, Universidad Nacional de Educación a Distancia 1981–, Vice-Rector for Research 1986, Dean of Faculty of Industrial Eng 1987, Rector 1987–96; mem. Asocs Española de Informática y Automática, Asocs Española de Ingeniería Mecánica, Soc. for Research into Higher Educ. (UK); Premio Citema 1975, Premio Extraordinario de Doctorado 1977, Laurel de Murcia 1987. *Publications include:* El Papel Instrumental de la Informática en el Proceso Educativo 1975, Dinámica de Sistemas 1979, Mecánica 1982, numerous articles on informatics in educ. and applied mechanics. *Leisure interests:* music, reading. *Address:* Department of Mechanics, Industrial Engineering School, Universidad Nacional de Educación a Distancia, Ciudad Universitaria, Juan del Rosal 12, 28040 Madrid, Spain (office). *Telephone:* (1) 3986433 (office). *Fax:* (1) 3986536 (office). *E-mail:* martes@ind.uned.es (office); mberrocal@pas.uned.es (office). *Website:* www.uned.es (office).

ARTHUIS, Jean Raymond Francis Marcel; French politician; b. 7 Oct. 1944, Saint-Martin du Bois, Maine-et-Loire; s. of Raymond Arthuis and Marthe Cotin; m. Brigitte Lafont 1971; one s. one d.; ed Coll. Saint-Michel, Château-Gontier, Ecole Supérieure de Commerce, Nantes and Inst. d'Etudes Politiques, Paris; chartered accountant, Paris 1971–86; Mayor of Château-Gontier 1971–2001; mem. Conseil, Gen., Mayenne, Château-Gontier canton 1976–, Pres. 1992–; Senator from Mayenne (Centrist Group) 1983–86, 1988–95, 2011–; Sec. of State, Ministry of Social Affairs and Employment 1986–87, Ministry of Economy, Finance and Privatization 1987–88; Spokesman on Budget in Senate 1992–95; Minister of Econ. Devt and Planning May–Aug. 1995, of Econ. and Finance 1995–97; Vice-Pres. Force Démocrate (fmrly Centre des démocrates sociaux) 1995–; Vice-Pres. Nouvelle Union pour la Démocratie Française (UDF) 1998; Pres. Union centriste du Sénat 1998–2002, Financial Comm. in Senate 2002–11; mem. European Parl. 2014–, Chair. Budget Cttee 2014–; Chevalier du Mérite agricole, Commdr, Ordre du Mérite (Germany). *Publications:* Justice sinistrée, Démocratie en danger (co-author) 1991, Les Délocalisations et l'emploi 1993, Dans les coulisses de Bercy, Le Cinquième pouvoir 1998, Mondialisation, la France à Contre Emploi 2007, SOS Finances Publiques, osons les vraies réformes 2011, La France peut s'en sortir (co-author) 2011. *Address:* Sénat, Palais du Luxembourg, 15 rue de Vaugirard, 75006 Paris (office); Conseil général de la Mayenne, 39 rue Mazagran, BP 1429, 53014 Laval Cedex (office); 8 rue René Homo, 53200 Château-Gontier, France (home). *Website:* www.jean-arthuis.eu.

ARTHUR, James Greig, CC, PhD, FRS, FRSC; Canadian mathematician and academic; *Mossman Chair and University Professor, Department of Mathematics, University of Toronto;* b. 18 May 1944, Hamilton, Ont.; s. of John G. Arthur and Katherine Arthur (née Scott); m. Dorothy P. Helm 1972; two s.; ed Univ. of Toronto, Yale Univ.; Instructor, Princeton Univ. 1970–72; Asst Prof., Yale Univ. 1972–76; Prof., Duke Univ. 1976–79; Prof. of Math., Univ. of Toronto 1979–87, Mossman Chair and Univ. Prof. 1987–; Sloan Fellow 1975–77, Stracie Memorial Fellowship 1982–84; Vice-Pres. American Math. Soc. 1999–2001, Pres. 2005–07; Fellow, American Math. Soc. 2012; Foreign Hon. mem. American Acad. of Arts and Sciences 2003; Dr hc (Univ. of Ottawa) 2002; Synge Award in Math. 1987, CRM-Fields-PIMS Prize 1997, Henry Marshall Tory Medal 1997, Canadian Gold Medal for Science and Eng 1999, Guggenheim Fellowship 2000, Wilbur Lucius Cross Medal, Grad. School of Yale Univ. 2000, Killam Prize 2004, Wolf Prize in Math. 2015, Leroy P. Steele Prize for Lifetime Achievement 2017. *Publications:* numerous scientific papers and articles. *Leisure interests:* tennis, squash, golf. *Address:* Room BA6258 (Bahen Centre), Department of Mathematics, University of Toronto, Toronto, ON M5S 3G3 (office); 23 Woodlawn Avenue West, Toronto, ON M4V 1G6, Canada (home). *Telephone:* (416) 978-4524 (office). *E-mail:* arthur@math.toronto.edu (office). *Website:* www.math.toronto.edu/cms/arthur-james (office).

ARTHUR, Sir Michael Anthony, Kt, KCMG, BA; British diplomatist (retd) and business executive; *President, Boeing Europe;* b. 28 Aug. 1950; m. Plaxy Arthur; two s. two d.; ed St Anthony's Coll., Oxford; entered Diplomatic Service 1972; served with Mission in New York and UN Dept, FCO 1972–74; Second Sec. in Brussels 1974–76, in Kinshasa 1976–78; Desk Officer, European Integration Dept 1978–80; Pvt. Sec. to Lord Privy Seal 1980–82; Pvt. Sec., Office of Minister of State 1982–84; First Sec. in Bonn 1984–88; Head of EC Dept 1988–93; Political Counsellor and Head of Chancery in Paris 1993–97; Dir of Resources, FCO 1997–99; Minister and Deputy Head of Mission in Washington, DC 1997–99; Dir-Gen. (EU and Econ.) FCO 2001–03; High Commr to India 2003–07; Amb. to Germany 2007–10; Man. Dir Boeing U.K and Ireland 2014–; Pres. Boeing Europe 2016–. *Leisure interests:* music, travel, books. *Address:* c/o Matt Knowles, International Corporate Communications, Boeing U.K, England (office). *Telephone:* (20) 7340-1931 (Boeing U.K) (office); 7785-463-861 (mobile) (office). *E-mail:* matt.knowles@boeing.com (office). *Website:* www.boeing.co.uk (office).

ARTHUR, Michael James Paul, MB BS, MD, FRCP, FMedSci, FRSA, PFHEA; British physician, academic and university administrator; *President and Provost, University College London;* b. 3 Aug. 1954, Purley, Surrey; m. Elizabeth S. McCaughey 1979; one s. two d.; ed Burnt Mill School, Harlow, Essex, Univ. of Southampton, Univ. of California, San Francisco, USA; Fogarty Int. Travelling Fellowship, Univ. of California, San Francisco 1988–90; Research Fellow and Lecturer in Medicine, Univ. of Southampton 1982–89, Sr Lecturer 1989–92, Prof. of Medicine 1992–2004, Dir of Research 1995–98, Head of the School of Medicine 1998–2003, Dean of the Faculty of Medicine, Health and Life Sciences 2003–04; Vice-Chancellor Univ. of Leeds 2004–13; Pres. and Provost Univ. Coll. London 2013–; US/UK Fulbright Commr 2008–; mem. Council of MRC 2008–; Chair. Worldwide Univs Network, Cell and Molecular Panel of the Wellcome Trust 2003–04, Nat. Steering Group for Nat. Student Survey 2005–08, Russell Group of Univs 2009–12, Advisory Group for Nat. Specialised Services (NHS) 2010–13; mem. Higher Educ. Funding Council for England (HEFCE)'s Research Assessment Exercise panel for hospital-based medicine 2001, HEFCE's Strategic Research Cttee 2003–05, Dept of Health's Advisory Group on Hepatitis 1998–2004; Pres. British Asscn for the Study of the Liver 2001–03; Chair. Bd of Trustees, British Liver Trust 2003–06, Vice-Pres. 2007–; Council mem. Council for Industry and Higher Educ. 2012–; mem. Bd, Opera North 2006–13; fmr mem. Editorial Bd, Journal of Hepatology, Comparative Hepatology, Gut and Clinics in Gastroenterology; Prin. Fellow, Higher Educ. Acad.; American Liver Foundation Research Prize 1987, Linacre Medal, Royal Coll. of Physicians, London 1994, Fulbright Distinguished Scholar Award to conduct cell biology research at Mount Sinai School of Medicine, New York City 2002. *Publications:* numerous papers in professional journals. *Leisure interest:* sailing. *Address:* President and Provost's Office, University College London, Gower Street, London, WC1E 6BT, England (office). *Telephone:* (20) 7679-7234 (office). *Fax:* (20) 7388-5412 (office). *E-mail:* michael.arthur@ucl.ac.uk (office). *Website:* www.ucl.ac.uk/provost (office).

ARTHUR, Rt Hon. Owen Seymour, PC, BA, MSc; Barbadian economist and politician; b. 17 Oct. 1949; m. Beverley Jeanne Batchelor 1978; ed Harrison Coll., Univ. of the West Indies, Cave Hill, Barbados and Mona, Jamaica; Research Asst, Univ. of the West Indies, Jamaica 1973; Asst Econ. Planner, Chief Econ. Planner Nat. Planning Agency, Jamaica 1974–79; Dir of Econs, Jamaica Bauxite Inst. 1979–81; Chief Project Analyst, Ministry of Finance, Barbados 1981–83; Lecturer, Dept of Man., Univ. of the West Indies, Cave Hill 1986, Resident Fellow 1993; Senator 1983–84; MP for Saint Peter 1984–; Parl. Sec. Ministry of Finance 1985–86; mem. Barbados Labour Party (BLP), Chair. 1993–96, 2010–13; Prime Minister of Barbados, Minister of Defence and Security, Finance and Econ. Affairs and for the Civil Service Sept. 1994–2008; Leader of the Opposition 2010–13; Order of José Marti (Cuba). *Publications:* The Commercialisation of Technology in Jamaica 1979, Energy and Mineral Resource Development in the Jamaican Bauxite Industry 1981, The IMF and Economic Stabilisation Policies in Barbados 1984. *Leisure interests:* gardening, cooking. *Address:* Barbados Labour Party, Grantley Adams House, 111 Roebuck Street, Bridgetown, Barbados (office). *Telephone:* 429-1990 (office). *Fax:* 427-8792 (office). *E-mail:* will99@caribsurf.com (office). *Website:* www.blp.org.bb (office).

ARTHURS, Harry William, OC, OOnt, BA, LLM, FRSC, FBA; Canadian professor of law and political science; *University Professor Emeritus and President Emeritus, York University;* b. 9 May 1935, Toronto, Ont.; s. of Leon Arthurs and Ellen H. Arthurs (née Dworkin); m. Penelope Geraldine Ann Milnes 1974; two s.; ed Univ. of Toronto, Harvard Univ., USA; Asst, Assoc. then full Prof. of Law,

Osgoode Hall Law School, York Univ., Ont. 1961–95, Dean of Law School 1972–77, Pres. York Univ. 1985–92, Pres. Emer. 1992–, Univ. Prof. 1995–2005, Univ. Prof. Emer. 2005–; Assoc., Canada Inst. of Advanced Research 1995–98; mediator and arbitrator in labour disputes 1962–85; author, lecturer 1961–; Bencher, Law Soc. of Upper Canada 1979–83; mem. Econ. Council of Canada 1978–81; Chair. Consultative Group, Research and Educ. in Law 1980–84; Chair. Council of Ont. Univs 1987–89; Commr to Review Federal Labour Standards 2004–06; Chair. Ontario Expert Comm. on Pensions 2006–08, Ontario Workplace Safety and Insurance Bd, Funding Review 2010–12; Hon. LLD (Sherbrooke, McGill, Brock, Montreal, Toronto, York, Simon Fraser Univs, Law Soc. of Upper Canada), Hon. DLitt (Lethbridge), Hon. DCL (Windsor); Killam Prize for Social Sciences, Canada Council 2002, Bora Laskin Prize for contribs to Labour Law 2002, ILO Decent Work Research Prize (co-winner) 2008, Lifetime Achievement Award, Labour Law Research Network 2013. *Publications include:* Industrial Relations and Labour Law in Canada (co-author) 1984, Law and Learning (Report on Legal Research and Education in Canada) 1984, Without the Law: Administrative Justice and Legal Pluralism in Nineteenth Century England 1985, Fairness at Work (Report on Federal Labour Standards) 2006, A Fine Balance (Report on Pensions) 2008, Fair Funding (report on Workplace Insurance) 2012, Rethinking Workplace Regulation: Beyond the Standard Contract of Employment (co-author) 2013. *Address:* Osgoode Hall Law School, York University, 4700 Keele Street, North York, ON M3J 1P3 (office); 11 Hillcrest Park, Toronto, ON M4X 1E8, Canada (home). *Telephone:* (416) 736-5407 (office). *Fax:* (416) 736-5736 (office). *E-mail:* harthurs@osgoode.yorku.ca (office).

ARTHUS-BERTRAND, Yann Marie; French photographer; b. 13 March 1946, Paris; s. of Claude Arthus-Bertrand and Jeanne Arthus-Bertrand (née Schildge); m. 2nd Anne Thual 1984; three s.; early career as asst dir and actor 1963–66; worked on wildlife reserve, Allier River 1966–76; balloon pilot, Masai Mara Reserve, Kenya 1976–78; f. Altitude agency (aerial photographs) 1991, cr. Earth from Above project 1995, Six Billion Others project 2003, Good Planet 2005; Good Will Amb., UNEP 2009–; elected Académie des Beaux-Arts 2006; Officier, Légion d'Honneur; Earth Champion Prize 2009. *Publications:* more than 60 books of photographs including Lions 1981, Three Days in France 1989, La terre vue du ciel (The Earth from Above) 1999 (updated annually), 365 jours pour réfléchir sur la terre 2000 (updated annually), Etre Photographe 2003, Agenda Chevaux 2005, Bestiaux 2006. *Address:* Altitude, Domaine de Longchamp, Carrefour de Longchamp, 75116 Paris, France (office). *E-mail:* yannab@club-internet.fr (office). *Website:* www.yannarthusbertrand.com.

ARTIN, Michael, AB, MA, PhD; American mathematician and academic; *Professor Emeritus of Mathematics, Massachusetts Institute of Technology;* b. 28 June 1934, Hamburg, Germany; s. of Emil Artin and Natalia (Natascha) Naumovna Jasny; ed Princeton and Harvard Univs, USA; spent time at Institut des Hautes Études Scientifiques, France, contributing to SGA4 vols of Séminaire de géométrie algébrique in early 1960s; Benjamin Peirce Lecturer, Harvard Univ. 1960–63; joined MIT Math. Faculty 1963, apptd Prof. 1966, Norbert Wiener Prof. 1988–93, now Prof. Emer., Chair. Pure Math. 1982–83, Chair. Undergraduate Cttee 1994–97, 1997–98; mem. NAS; Foreign mem. Royal Netherlands Soc. of Sciences; Fellow, American Acad. of Arts and Sciences 1969, AAAS, Soc. for Industrial and Applied Math., American Math. Soc. (Pres. 1990–92); Hon. mem. Moscow Math. Soc.; Dr hc (Antwerp), (Hamburg); MIT Undergraduate Teaching Prize and Educational and Grad. Advising Award, Leroy P. Steele Prize for Lifetime Achievement, American Math. Soc. 2002, Harvard Grad. School of Arts & Sciences Centennial Medal 2005, Wolf Prize in Math. (co-recipient) 2013, Nat. Medal of Science for Math. and Computer Science 2013. *Publications:* numerous papers in professional journals. *Address:* Department of Mathematics, Massachusetts Institute of Technology, Room 2-274, 77 Massachusetts Avenue, Cambridge, MA 02139-4307, USA (office). *Telephone:* (617) 253-3689 (office). *E-mail:* artin@math.mit.edu (office). *Website:* math.mit.edu (office).

ARTUCIO RODRIGUEZ, Alejandro, DJur, DScS; Uruguayan diplomatist; b. 22 Aug. 1934; m.; two c.; ed Univ. of the Republic; Chief Counsel and Commr, Int. Comm. of Jurists, Geneva 1985–2005; Amb. and Perm. Rep. to UN, New York 2004–06, to UN, Geneva 2007–09; Special Rapporteur on Equatorial Guinea, UN High Comm. on Human Rights 1993–99; Chief Counsel for Human Rights, UN Verification Mission in Guatemala (MINUGUA) 1997; fmr mem. Governing Council, Inst. of Legal and Social Studies, Uruguay, Governing Council, Asscn for Prevention of Torture, Geneva, Advice Council, Int. Service for Human Rights, Geneva, Int. Consulting Council, Legal and Social Studies Centre, Argentina. *Address:* Ministry of Foreign Affairs, Edif. Nuevo Colonia 1206, Palacio Santos, Avenida 18 de Julio 1205, 11100 Montevideo, Uruguay (office). *Telephone:* (2) 9021010 (office). *Fax:* (2) 9021349 (office). *E-mail:* webmaster@mrree.gub.uy (office). *Website:* www.mrree.gub.uy (office).

ARTZT, Alice Josephine, BA; American classical guitarist, writer and teacher; b. 16 March 1943, Philadelphia, Pa; d. of Maurice Gustav Artzt and Harriett Green Artzt; m. Bruce B. Lawton, Jr; ed Columbia Univ. and studied composition with Darius Milhaud and guitar with Julian Bream, Ida Presti and Alexandre Lagoya; taught guitar at Mannes Coll. of Music, New York 1966–69, Trenton State Univ. 1977–80; worldwide tours as soloist 1969–94; f. Alice Artzt Guitar Trio (with M. Rutscho and R. Burley) 1989; toured in duo with R. Burley; fmr mem. Bd of Dirs Guitar Foundation of America (Chair. 1986–89); several Critics' Choice Awards. *Recordings include:* Baroque Recital, Guitar Music by Fernando Sor, Guitar Music by Francisco Tarrega, 20th Century Guitar Music, English Guitar Music, The Music of Manuel Ponce, The Glory of the Guitar, Virtuoso Romantic Guitar, Musical Tributes, Variations, Passacaglias and Chaconnes, American Music of the Stage and Screen, Alice Artzt Classic Guitar, Alice Artzt Plays Original Works. *Publications include:* The Art of Practicing, The International GFA Guitarists' Cookbook (ed.), Rhythmic Mastery 1997; numerous articles in guitar and music periodicals. *Leisure interests:* hi-fi, travel, Chaplin movies. *Address:* 51 Hawthorne Avenue, Princeton, NJ 08540, USA (home). *Telephone:* (609) 921-6629 (home). *E-mail:* guitartzt@aol.com. *Website:* guitartzt.com.

ARTZT, Edwin Lewis, BJ; American business executive; b. 15 April 1930, New York, NY; s. of William Artzt and Ida Artzt; m. Ruth N. Martin 1950; one s. four d.; ed Univ. of Oregon; Account Exec., Glasser Gailey Advertising Agency, Los Angeles 1952–53; joined Proctor & Gamble Co., Cincinnati 1953, Brand Man. Advertising Dept 1956–58, Assoc. Brand Promotion Man. 1958–60, Brand Promotion Man. 1960, 1962–65, Copy Man. 1960–62, Advertisement Man. Paper Products Div. 1965–68, Man. Products Food Div. 1968–69, Vice-Pres. 1969, Vice-Pres., Acting Man. Coffee Div. 1970, Vice-Pres., Group Exec. 1970–75, Dir 1972–75, 1980–95, Group Vice-Pres. Procter & Gamble Co., Europe, Belgium 1975–80, Pres. Procter & Gamble Int. 1980–89, Chair., CEO 1995–99, Vice-Chair. Procter & Gamble Co. 1980–89, Chair. 1989–95, CEO 1995–99; mem. Bd of Dirs Delta Airlines 1990–2002, American Express Co. 1991–2002, GTE (now Verizon) 1992–2002, Barilla G.E.R. SpA 1995–98, Spalding Sports and Barilla SpA, Italy, Juvenile Diabetes Foundation; Trustee, Cttee for Econ. Devt; Sr Adviser, Kohlberg, Kravis, Roberts and Co. 2001–08, Gabelli Group Capital Partners Inc. 2003–08; fmr mem. Business Council, Presidential Advisory Cttees on Trade Policy and Negotiations, Council on Foreign Relations; Martin Luther King, Jr Salute to Greatness Award 1995, Leadership Conf. on Civil Rights Pvt. Sector Leadership Award 1995. *Address:* 9495 Whitegate Lane, Cincinnati, OH 45243, USA.

ARULKUMARAN, Sir Sabaratnam, Kt, MBBS, MD, PhD, FRCS, MRCOG; British (b. Sri Lankan) obstetrician and gynaecologist and academic; *Head of Obstetrics and Gynaecology, St George's, University of London;* s. of K. Sabaratnam and Gnambikai; ed Univ. of Ceylon, Nat. Univ. of Singapore; has been in clinical practice since 1972; began career as Lecturer, rising to Prof. and Head of Dept of Obstetrics and Gynaecology, Nat. Univ. of Singapore 1982–97; Foundation Prof. at Derby as part of Univ. of Nottingham, UK 1997–2001; Dir (non-exec.) Southern Derbyshire Acute Hosp. NHS Trust 1997–2001; Prof. and Head of Obstetrics and Gynaecology, St George's Univ. of London, UK 2001–; Deputy Sec.-Gen. Asia & Oceanic Fed. 1989–97; Treas. and later Sec.-Gen. Int. Fed. of Obstetrics & Gynaecology 1997–2006, Pres. 2012–15; Vice-Pres. Royal Coll. of Obstetricians and Gynaecologists 2005–07, Pres. 2009–10; Ed.-in-Chief Best Practice & Research in Clinical Obstetrics and Gynaecology 1998–; Hon. Fellow of American, S African, Indian, Sri Lankan, Pakistan, Australia and New Zealand Colls of Obstetricians and Gynaecologists; Hon. mem. German, S African, Malaysian and Canadian Socs of Obstetrics and Gynaecology; Dr hc (Univ. of Athens). *Publications include:* 24 books as author or ed., 150 book chapters and 240 articles in professional journals. *Address:* Section of Obstetrics & Gynaecology, Division of Clinical Developmental Sciences, St George's, University of London, Cranmer Terrace, London SW17 0RE, England (office). *Telephone:* (20) 8672-9944 (office). *Fax:* (20) 8725-5958 (office). *E-mail:* sarulkum@sgul.ac.uk (office). *Website:* www.sgul.ac.uk (office).

ARUNGA, June, LLB; Kenyan journalist and film company executive; *Founder and President, Open Quest Media LLC;* b. 1981; ed Univ. of Buckingham, UK, Univ. of Nairobi; Founder and Pres. Open Quest Media LLC (film and TV production co.), New York, USA 2006–; Vice-Pres. New Liberty Films LLC; Assoc. Ed. AfricanLiberty.org; mem. Bd of Advisors Global Envision (USA), The Inter-Region Econ. Network (Kenya), Grassroot Free Markets (Hawaii), The Bastiat Soc., Charleston, SC; mem. Creative Council, Moving Pictures Inst., New York; H.B. Earhart Grad. Fellow of Law; Sr Fellow, Istituto Bruno Leoni, Milan, Italy; Fellow, IMANI Center for Policy and Educ., Int. Policy Network, London, UK. *Television:* writer/host of The Devil's Footpath (BBC TV) 2004, co-presenter/subject of Africa: Who is to Blame? (BBC World TV) 2005, writer/producer of Africa's Ultimate Resource (Victory Studios) 2005, The Cell-Phone Revolution in Kenya (BBC Newsnight mini-documentary) 2007. *Publication:* The Cell-Phone Revolution in Kenya (co-author) 2007. *Address:* Open Quest Media LLC, 119 W 72nd Street (No. 158), New York, NY 10023, USA (office). *Telephone:* (206) 719-6485 (office). *E-mail:* junearunga@openquestmedia.com (office). *Website:* www.openquestmedia.com (office).

ARVIND, B.Tech, MS, PhD; Indian computer scientist and academic; *Johnson Professor of Computer Science and Engineering, Massachusetts Institute of Technology;* b. (Arvind Mithal), 1947, Lucknow, Uttar Pradesh; m. Gita Mithal; two s.; ed Indian Inst. of Tech., Kanpur, Univ. of Minnesota, USA; Asst Prof. of Information and Computer Science, Univ. of California, Irvine, USA 1974–78; Lecturer, Indian Inst. of Tech., Kanpur, 1977–78, N. Rama Rao Chair, Dept of Computer Science and Eng 1998–99; joined MIT 1978, currently Johnson Prof. of Computer Science and Eng, also mem. Computer Science and Artificial Intelligence Lab. (CSAIL); f. Sandburst Corpn (semiconductor co.) 2002; Co-f. Bluespec Inc. 2003, currently Dir; mem. Editorial Bd several journals including Journal of Parallel and Distributed Computing, Journal of Functional Programming; Fujitsu Visiting Prof., Univ. of Tokyo 1992–93; Chief Technical Adviser, UN-sponsored Knowledge Based Computer Systems Project, India 1986–92; Gen. Chair. ICS05 (Int. Conf. on Supercomputing), Cambridge, Mass 2005; Fellow, IEEE 1994, Nat. Acad. of Eng 2008; mem. American Asscn of Arts and Sciences 2012–; IEEE Charles Babbage Outstanding Scientist Award 1994, Distinguished Alumnus Award, Indian Inst. of Tech., Kanpur 1999, Alumni Award, Univ. of Minnesota 2001, Outstanding Achievement Award, Univ. of Minnesota 2008, IEEE Harry Goode Memorial Award 2012. *Publications include:* Implicit Parallel Programming in pH (co-author) 2001, Operation-Centric Hardware Descriptions and Synthesis (co-author) 2004, Rate Guarantees and Overload Protection in Input-Queued Switches (co-author) 2004, Modular Scheduling of Guarded Atomic Actions (co-author) 2004, High-Level Synthesis: An Essential Ingredient for Designing Complex ASICs (co-author) 2004. *Address:* The Stata Center, MIT, 32 Vassar Street, 32-G866, Cambridge, MA 02139, USA (office). *Telephone:* (617) 253-6090 (office). *Fax:* (617) 253-6652 (office). *E-mail:* arvind@mit.edu (office); arvind@csail.mit.edu (office). *Website:* www.csail.mit.edu (office); csg.csail.mit.edu/Users/arvind (home).

ARYA, Satyadev Narayan, BA, LLB, MA; Indian politician; *Governor of Haryana;* b. 1 July 1939, Rajgir, Bihar; s. of Shivan Prasad and Sundari Devi; m. Sarswati Devi; three s. two d.; ed Patna Univ., Bihar; Minister of Rural Development, Bihar 1979–80, of Mines and Geology 2010–15; Pres. Scheduled Caste Cell, Bihar 1988–98; mem. Bihar Legislative Ass. for Rajgir constituency 1995–2015; Gov. of Haryana 2018–; mem. Rashtriya Swayamsevak Sangh (RSS) 1962, Arya Samaj, Bharatiya Janata Party (BJP). *Leisure interests:* reading, current affairs, football, volleyball, wrestling, kabaddi. *Address:* Haryana Raj Bhavan, Sector 6, Chandigarh, Punjab, 160019, India (office); Sarswati Bhavan, 159, Kautilya Nagar, Patna, Bihar, India (office). *Telephone:* (17) 22740581 (office);

(17) 22740583 (office). *E-mail:* governor@hry.nic.in (office). *Website:* www.haryanarajbhavan.gov.in (office).

ARYAL, Krishna Raj, MEd, MA; Nepalese politician, educationist and diplomatist; b. Dec. 1928, Kathmandu; m. Shanta Laxmi 1956; one s.; ed Durbar High School, Tri-Chandra Coll., Allahabad Univ., India, Univ. of Oregon, USA; Lecturer, Nat. Teachers' Training Centre 1954–56; Prof. Coll. of Educ., Dir Publs Govt Educ. Devt Project 1956–59; Founder, Admin. and Prin. Shri Ratna Rajya Laxmi Girls' Coll. 1961–71; Asst Minister of Educ. 1971–72, of State 1972–73, Minister 1973–75, of Foreign Affairs 1975–79; Amb. to France (also accred to Spain, Italy, Portugal and Israel) and Perm. Del. to UNESCO 1980–84; Chair. Asian Group and mem. Bureau Group 77, UNESCO 1982–83; mem. Raj Sabha 1985–90, Rastriya Panchayat (unicameral legis.) 1986–90; Chair. Brahmacharya Ashram; Ed. Education Quarterly 1956–59, Nabin Shikshya 1956–59; fmr Sec. Cricket Asscn of Nepal; Exec. mem. World Hindu Fed.; Gorakha Dakhinbahu (1st Class), Grand Cordon of Yugoslav Star, Order of the Rising Sun, 1st Class (Japan), Grand Officier, Order Nat. du Mérite (France), Order of Civil Merit, 1st Class (Spain) and other decorations. *Publications include:* Education for the Development of Nepal 1970, Monarchy in the Making of Nepal 1975, The Science of Education. *Address:* 17/93 Gaihiri Dhara, Kathmandu, Nepal.

ARZUMANYAN, Aleksander Robertovich, BS, MS; Armenian politician and diplomatist; *Ambassador to Denmark;* b. 24 Dec. 1959, Yerevan; m.; two c.; ed People's Friendship Univ., Russia, Yerevan State Univ.; engineer, Yerevan Research Inst. of Automatic Systems of City Man. 1985–88; Dir Information Cen. Armenian Nat. Movt 1989–90; Asst Chair. of Supreme Council of Armenia 1990–91; Rep. to N America 1991–92; Chargé d'affaires to USA 1992–93; Amb. and Perm. Rep. to UN, New York 1992–96; Minister of Foreign Affairs 1996–98; Chief Advisor to Pres. Armagrobank 1998–2000; Pres. Exec. Council Armenian Nat. Movt 2000–02; Founder-mem. Armenian-Turkish Reconciliation Comm. 2001–04; Head of cen. election HQ of presidential candidate Levon Ter-Petrosian 2008; Deputy to Nat. Ass. (Azgayin Zhoghov) from the Heritage party 2012–17; Amb. to Denmark 2017–; Chair. Regional Group for Eastern Europe 1992–96; participated in and headed del. to int. meetings; elected Deputy Chair. 49th Gen. UN Ass., concurrently mem. Gen. Cttee, UN, Appellation Cttee on resolutions of Admin. Court, UN 1994. *Address:* Embassy of the Republic of Armenia, Ryvangs Allé 50, 2900 Hellerup, Denmark (office). *Telephone:* 35-82-29-00 (office). *E-mail:* armembdk@mfa.am (office). *Website:* www.denmark.mfa.am/en (office).

ASAAD, Reem Mohammad, BChem, MBA; Saudi Arabian financial adviser, lecturer, writer and women's rights advocate; b. Egypt; m.; two d.; ed King Abdulaziz Univ., Jeddah, Northeastern Univ., Boston, USA; had accounting experience in family's healthcare business –2001; worked as investment analyst at Nat. Commercial Bank 2001–08; investment analyst, Saudi Fransi Capital; teaches banking and finance at Dar Al-Hekma Women's Coll. 2008–; began appearing on regional financial TV talking about financial markets and econ. affairs 2005; launched a campaign calling for better employment opportunities for women and improved consumer rights, the 'Lingerie Campaign' 2008. *Publications:* has written and published numerous econ. articles in the Saudi press. *Leisure interests:* swimming, reading, languages, discovering new talents. *Telephone:* 506646701 (mobile). *E-mail:* askreemasaad@gmail.com (office). *Website:* www.askreem.com; reemasaad.blogspot.co.uk.

ASADA, Teruo; Japanese business executive; *Chairman, Marubeni Corporation;* joined Marubeni Corpn in 1972, has held several exec. positions, including Man. Exec. Officer, Chief Information Officer, Sr Man. Exec. Dir and Dir, mem. Bd of Dirs 2005–, Pres., CEO and Rep. Dir, Marubeni Corpn 2008–13, Chair. 2013–. *Address:* Marubeni Corpn, 42 Ohtemachi 1-chome, Chiyoda-ku, Tokyo 100-8088, Japan (office). *Telephone:* (3) 3282-2111 (office). *Fax:* (3) 3282-4241 (office). *E-mail:* info@marubeni.com (office). *Website:* www.marubeni.com (office).

ÄSÄDOV, Oktay Sabir oğlu; Azerbaijani engineer and politician; *Chairman, National Assembly (Milli Mäclis);* b. 3 Jan. 1955, Şaharcik, Qafan Dist, Azerbaijan SSR, USSR; m.; two c.; ed Azerbaijan Chem. Inst.; Asst Man. then Man., Baku Air Conditioning Factory 1976–79; Sr Engineer, Azerbaijan Special Installation and Construction Co. 1979–81; Sr Engineer, Azärbaycantexqurashdirma 1981–83, Head of Dept No. 1 1983–89; CEO Santexqurashdirma Industrial Union 1989–96; Pres. Absheron Regional Jt Stock Water Co. 1996–2004; Pres. Azersu Jt Stock Co. 2004–05; mem. Yeni Azärbaycan Partiyası (YAP—New Azerbaijan Party) 1999–; Deputy, Nat. Ass. (Milli Mäclis) 2000–, Chair. 2005–; Head of Azerbaijani del. to Inter-Parl. Ass. of CIS and to Parl. Ass. of Turkic-speaking Countries (TÜRKPA); mem. Political Council of YAP; mem. Int. Water Asscn. *Address:* Office of the Chairman, Milli Mäclis (National Assembly), 1152 Baku, Parlament pr. 1, Azerbaijan (office). *Telephone:* (12) 510-87-86 (office). *Fax:* (12) 493-49-43 (office). *E-mail:* international@meclis.gov.az (office); azmm@meclis.gov.az (office). *Website:* www.meclis.gov.az (office).

ASAMOAH, Obed Y., JSD; Ghanaian politician and lawyer; b. 6 Feb. 1936, Likpe Bala, Volta Region; s. of William Asamoah and Monica Asamoah; m. Yvonne Wood 1964; two s. one d.; ed Achimota Secondary School, Woolwich Polytechnic, London, King's Coll. London and Columbia Univ., New York; called to the Bar, Middle Temple, London 1960; upon return to Ghana practised as solicitor and advocate of Supreme Court of Ghana; Lecturer, Faculty of Law, Univ. of Ghana, Legon 1965–69; fmr Chair. Bd of Dirs of Ghana Film Industry Corpn, Ghana Bauxite Co.; mem. Constituent Ass. which drafted Constitution for Second Repub. of Ghana 1969; elected to Parl. (Nat. Alliance of Liberals) 1969; mem. Constituent Ass. which drafted third Republican Constitution 1979; Gen. Sec. United Nat. Convention 1979, All People's Party 1981; Minister of Foreign Affairs 1982–97; Attorney-Gen. and Minister of Justice 1993–2001; Chair. Nat. Democratic Congress 2002–05; mem. Ghana Bar Asscn; has served on several int. and public orgs; Patron Democratic Freedom Party 2006–12; Order of the Star of Ghana 2001. *Publications include:* The Legal Significance of the Declaration of the General Assembly of the United Nations 1967, The Political History of Ghana (1950–2013): The Experience of a Non-Conformist 2014; articles in legal journals. *Leisure interests:* reading, farming. *Address:* PO Box 14581, Accra, Ghana (home). *Telephone:* (302) 335414 (home); (20) 811-99-11 (mobile). *E-mail:* obed@obedasamoah.org.

ASANKOJOEVA, Zina Mukaevna; Kyrgyzstani banker; *Governor, National Bank of the Kyrgyz Republic;* b. 1965; ed Kyrgyz State Univ.; Deputy Chief Accountant, State Bank of the USSR 1988–92, Dir of Accounting, Chief Accountant 1992–94; Head of Finance and Credit Policy for Govt Office 1994–97; Head of Financial Sector and Monetary Policy in Office of the Prime Minister 1997–2005, Head of Finance Dept 2005–07, Head of Dept responsible for examination of govt decisions 2007–10; Head, Finance and Credit Policy Dept, Presidential Admin Aug.–Dec. 2010; Deputy Gov., Nat. Bank of the Kyrgyz Repub. (central bank) Jan.–June 2011, Gov. June 2011–. *Address:* National Bank of the Kyrgyz Republic, 720040 Bishkek, Umetaliyeva 101, Kyrgyzstan (office). *Telephone:* (312) 66-90-08 (office). *Fax:* (312) 61-07-30 (office). *E-mail:* mail@nbkr.kg (office). *Website:* www.nbkr.kg (office).

ASANO, Tadanobu; Japanese actor; b. 27 Nov. 1973, Yokohama-shi, Kanagawa; m. Chara (divorced); one d. *Films include:* Bataashi kingyo 1990, Aitsu 1991, The Rocking Horsemen 1992, Nemuranai machi - Shinjuku same 1993, 119 1994, Maborosi 1995, Helpless 1996, Acri (Most Popular Performer, Japanese Acad. Awards 1997) 1996, Labyrinth of Dreams 1997, Shark Skin Man and Peach Hip Girl 1998, One Step on a Mine, It's All Over 1999, Kaza-hana 2000, Ichi the Killer 2001, Bright Future 2003, Zatoichi 2003, Last Life in the Universe (Upstream Prize for Best Actor, Venice Film Festival 2004) 2003, The Face of Jizo 2004, Eri Eri rema sabakutani 2005, Invisible Waves 2006, Mongol 2007, Kabei: Our Mother 2008, Dreaming Awake 2008, Villon's Wife 2009, Vengeance Can Wait 2010, Thor 2011, Battleship 2012, Thor: The Dark World 2013, 47 Ronin 2013, My Man (Best Actor, Moscow Int. Film Festival 2014) 2014, Kiki's Delivery Service 2014, Journey to the Shore 2015, Harmonium 2016, Shinjuku Swan II 2017. *Television:* Fried Dragon Fish (film) 1993, The Long Goodbye (mini-series) 2014, A Life: Itoshiki Hito 2017. *Address:* c/o Anore Inc., 9F Ochiai-Harajuku Building, 6-17-15 Jingumae Shibuya-ku, Tokyo, 150-0001, Japan (office). *Telephone:* (3) 5468-6606 (office). *Fax:* (3) 5468-6607 (office). *E-mail:* anore@ya2.so-net.ne.jp (office). *Website:* www.anore.co.jp/artist/actor/asano (office).

ASANTE, Nana (Chief) Samuel Kwadwo Boaten, LLB, LLM, JSD; Ghanaian lawyer, international legal consultant, international arbitrator and mediator; *Chairman, Ghana Arbitration Centre;* b. 11 May 1933, Asokore, Ashanti; s. of Daniel Y. Asante and Mary Baafi; m. Philomena Margaret Aidoo 1961; two s. three d.; ed Achimota School, Univs of Nottingham and London, UK and Yale Univ. Law School, USA; Solicitor of the Supreme Court of England (Hons); mem. Ghana Bar 1960–; State Attorney in the Ministry of Justice of Ghana 1960–61; Lecturer in Law and Acting Head of Law Dept, Univ. of Ghana 1961–65; Lecturer, Univ. of Leeds, UK 1965–66; Attorney, World Bank, Washington, DC 1966–69; Adjunct Prof. of Law, Howard Univ. Law School, Washington, DC 1967–69; Solicitor-Gen. of Ghana 1969–74; mem. Arbitration Panel, Int. Cen. for Settlement of Investment Disputes, Washington, DC 1971–90; Chair. Public Agreements Review Cttee of Ghana 1972–77; Deputy Attorney-Gen. of Ghana 1974–77; Chief Legal Adviser, UN Centre on Transnational Corpns, New York 1977–83, Dir 1983–92; Chair. Cttee of Experts on Ghana Constitution 1991; Dir UN Legal Advisory Services for Devt 1992–93; Dir Int. Third World Legal Studies Asscn, New York; installed as Paramount Chief of Asante-Asokore, Ashanti, Ghana 1995–; Chair. Ghana Public Utilities Regulatory Comm. 1997–2002, Ghana Arbitration Centre 1997–, Shawbell Consultants 2002–, Advisory Council, Ghana Inst. of Advanced Legal Studies 2012–, Nat. Working Group on the Land Bill 2015–; Pres. Inst. of Int. Negotiations 2012–; mem. Bd of Dirs, Int. Devt Law Inst., Rome 1983–95; JIC Taylor Lecturer, Lagos Univ. 1978; mem. Nat. House of Chiefs 2004–; consultant, Commonwealth Secr., African Devt Bank, UNITAR; mem. Int. Bar Asscn, Exec. Council, American Soc. of Int. Law 1979–82, Gen. Legal Council, Ghana 1969–79, Advisory Bd, Foreign Investment Law Journal-ICSID Review, Int. Court of Arbitration of ICC 1998–2012, American Arbitration Asscn, London Court of Int. Arbitration, Judicial Council of Ghana 2006–, Nat. Peace Council 2010– and of several other int. arbitral panels; Guest Fellow, Berkeley Coll., Yale Univ. 1964–65; fmr Sterling, Fulbright and Aggrey Fellow; Fellow, World Acad. of Arts and Sciences 1975, Ghana Acad. of Arts and Sciences 1976 (Pres. 2002–06); Visiting Fellow, Clare Hall, Cambridge, UK 1978–79, now Life mem.; Visiting Prof., Temple Univ. Law School, Philadelphia 1976; Patron Int. Centre for Public Law, Inst. of Advanced Legal Studies, Univ. of London; Hon. Chancellor, Graduate School of Governance and Leadership, Almond Inst., Accra 2012–, Hon. Fellow, Soc. of Advanced Legal Studies UK; Officer, Order of the Volta (Nat. Honour) 2008; Ghana Book Award 1980, Festschrift in his honour published by a group of int. scholars entitled Commitment to Law, Development and Public Policy 2016. *Publications include:* Property Law and Social Goals in Ghana 1976, Transnational Investment Law and National Development 1979, Reflections on the Constitution, Law and Development, Darquah Memorial Lectures 2002, Reflections on Governance, Law and Development 2017; numerous articles on int. investment law and various aspects of Ghana law in int. law journals. *Leisure interests:* golf, reading biographies, community work in Asokore, Ashanti. *Address:* Ghana Arbitration Centre, PO Box GP 18615, Accra, Ghana (office). *Telephone:* (30) 2240820 (office); (30) 2240924 (office); (30) 2775572 (home); 24-4319100 (mobile). *E-mail:* rskbasante46@gmail.com (office).

ASASHŌRYŪ AKINORI; Mongolian fmr sumo wrestler, business executive and politician; b. (Dolgorsuren Dagvadorj), 27 Sept. 1980, Ulan Bator; m. (divorced 2009); one s. one d.; debut in 1999; Sekitori title 2000, Makuuchi title 2001, Ozeki title 2002; first victory in Nov. 2002 in only 24th tournament (joint quickest victory in Sumo history); became 68th wrestler to reach Yokozuna level (highest rank) March 2003 (first non-Japanese or non-American to reach Yokozuna level), Yokozuna 2004–07; career record includes 25 Makuuchi titles, 1 Makushita title, 1 Sandanme title, 1 Jonidian title; retd 2010; various business interests; est. Asashoryu Foundation; mem. Democratic Party 2013–; Sansho Award, three Fighting Spirit prizes, numerous Outstanding Performance awards. *Address:* c/o Democratic Party, CPOB 578, Sükhbaatar District, Ulan Bator, Mongolia. *Telephone:* (11) 320355. *Fax:* (11) 323755. *E-mail:* info@demparty.mn. *Website:* www.demparty.mn; www.sumo.or.jp/en/sumo_data/rikishi/profile?id=100.

ASBAR, Ali Ahmad Said, (Adonis), BA, PhD; Lebanese/French (b. Syrian) poet, essayist and academic; b. 1 Jan. 1930, Al Qassabin, Latakia; m. Khalida Said (née Saleh) 1956; two d.; ed Univ. of Damascus, Univ. of St Joseph, Lebanon; Ed., cultural supplement, El-Thawra newspaper mid-1950s; imprisoned for membership in Syrian Social Nationalist Party 1955, moved to Lebanon on release 1956; Co-founder (with Yusuf al-Khal) Majallat Shi'r poetry magazine 1957–64; Founder Mawaqif literary periodical 1968; Prof. of Arabic Literature, Lebanese Univ., Beirut 1971–85; PhD Adviser, Univ. of St Joseph, Beirut 1971–85; Visiting Prof., Univ. of Damascus 1976; Prof. of Arabic, Univ. of Paris (Sorbonne) 1980–81; Visiting Lecturer, Collège de France, Paris 1983, Georgetown Univ., Washington, DC 1985; Assoc. Prof. of Arab Poetry, Univ. of Geneva 1989–95; mem. Arab Writers' Union –1995, Acad. Stéphane Mallarmé, Paris 1983, Haut Conseil de Réflexion du Collège Int. de Philosophie, Paris; Officier, Ordre des Arts et des Lettres 1993; Prix des Amis du Livre, Beirut 1968, Syria-Lebanon Award, Int. Poetry Forum 1971, Nat. Prize for Poetry, Lebanon 1974, Grand Prix des Biennales Internationales de la Poésie de Liège, Belgium 1986, Prix Jean Malrieu-Etranger, Marseille 1991, Feronia-Cita di Fiano, Rome 1993, Int. Nâzim Hikmet Poetry Award 1995, Prix Méditerranée-Etranger, France 1995, Struga Poetry Evenings Golden Wreath Laureate 1997, America Award 2003, Bjørnson Prize 2007, Goethe Prize 2011, Griffin Poetry Prize 2011, Golden Tibetan Antelope International Prize 2013, Janus Pannonius Int. Poetry Prize (jt winner) 2014, Asan Viswa Puraskaram-Kumaranasan World Prize for Poetry 2015, Erich-Maria-Remarque-Friedenspreis 2015, Stig Dagerman Prize 2016, PEN/Nabokov Award for Achievement in International Literature 2017, Highest Award of Int. Biennial Poem, Brussels. *Publications include:* Songs of Mihyar, the Damascene 1961, The Book of Changes and Migration to the Regions of Day and Night 1965, A Time Between Ashes and Roses 1970, Introduction to Arab Poetry 1971, A Tomb for New York 1971, The Blood of Adonis (Syria-Lebanon Award, International Poetry Forum) 1971, Singular in the Form of Plural 1974, Further Songs of Mihyar, the Damascene 1975, The Shock of Modernity 1978, The Book of Five Poems 1980, Manifesto of Modernity 1980, Transformations of the Lover 1982, Victims of a Map 1984, The Book of Sieges 1985, Mémoire du Vent 1991, La Prière et L'Épée 1992, Soleils Seconds 1994, The Pages of Day and Night 2001, Chants de Mihyar le Damascène 2002, If Only the Sea Could Sleep 2003, Commencement du Corps, Fin de l'Océan 2004, Histoire qui se Déchire sue le Corps d'une Femme 2008, Adonis: Selected Poems 2010; criticism and essays: An Introduction to Arab Poetics 2003. *Address:* c/o Wylie Agency, 250 West 57th Street, Suite 2114, New York, NY 10107, USA (office); 1 sq Henri Regnault, 92400 Courbevoie, France (home). *Telephone:* (212) 246-0069 (office). *Fax:* (212) 586-8953 (office). *E-mail:* mail@wylieagency.com (office). *Website:* www.wylieagency.com (office).

ÅSBRINK, Erik, BSc, BA, MBA; Swedish business executive and fmr politician; *International Adviser, Goldman Sachs & Co.;* b. 1 Feb. 1947, Stockholm; s. of Per Åsbrink; m. Anne-Marie Lindgren; three c.; ed Univ. of Stockholm, Stockholm School of Econs; worked at Inst. for Soviet and E European Econ. Affairs 1972, Nat. Inst. of Econ. Research 1972–74, Ministry of Finance 1974–76, Ministry of the Budget 1976–78; Research Sec., parl. group of Social Democratic Party (SDP) 1978–82; Under-Sec. of State, Ministry of Finance 1982–90; Deputy Minister for Fiscal and Financial Affairs, Ministry of Finance 1990–91, Minister of Finance 1996–99; Man. Dir, Vasakronan AB 1993–96; mem. of Parl. 1998–99; Chair., Comm. on Business Confidence (govt comm.); Chair., Lantbrukskredit AB 1983–85, State Housing Finance Corpn 1984–85, Governing Bd Sveriges Riksbank 1985–90, Sparbanken Första 1992, Confortia AB 1993, Swedish Bond Promotion 1993, Bd of Forsakringsbolaget SPP 2000, Budo and Martial Arts Fed. 2000–05; Chair., Exec. Bd Stockholm School; Vice-Chair., Systembolaget AB 1986–90; Dir-Gen. Building Soc. 1991; Int. Adviser, Goldman Sachs 2011–; mem. Bd, Nat. Pension Insurance Fund 1982–90, AB Vin & Sprit AB (Swedish Wine and Spirits Corpn) 1986–90, 1993–, AB Trav & Galopp 1989–90, Sparbanken Sverige AB 1991–93, ABB Investment Man. 1993–, SkandiaBanken 1994–, Swedish Concert Hall Foundation 1995–, SNS, Centre for Business and Policy Studies 1995–; AB Trav & Galopp 1989–90, Sparbanken Sverige AB 1991–93, ABB Investment Man. 1993–, SkandiaBanken 1994–, Swedish Concert Hall Foundation 1995–, SNS, Centre for Business and Policy Studies 1995–; mem. Fiscal Policy Council. *Address:* Goldman Sachs & Co., 200 West Street, New York, NY 10282, USA (office). *Website:* www.goldmansachs.com (office).

ASCHBACHER, Michael George, BS, PhD; American mathematician and academic; *Shaler Arthur Hanisch Professor of Mathematics, California Institute of Technology;* b. 8 April 1944, Little Rock, AR; ed California Inst. of Tech., Univ. of Wisconsin; joined faculty of California Inst. of Tech. 1970, Full Prof. 1976–, currently Shaler Arthur Hanisch Prof. of Math.; Fellow, American Acad. of Arts and Sciences 1992; mem. Inst. for Advanced Study, Princeton 1978–79; Cole Prize in Algebra, American Math. Soc. 1980, Royal Swedish Acad. of Sciences Rolf Schock Prize 2011, AMS Leroy P. Steele Prize for Mathematical Exposition 2012, Wolf Prize in Math. (shared with Luis Caffarelli) 2012. *Publications:* Finite Group Theory, Sporadic Groups, 3-Transposition Groups, The Finite Simple Groups and Their Classification, Overgroups of Sylow Subgroups in Sporadic Groups, The Classification of Quasithin Groups. I Structure of Strongly Quasithin K-groups, Mathematical Surveys and Monographs 111 (with Stephen D. Smith) 2004, The Classification of Quasithin Groups. II Main Theorems: The Classification of Simple QTKE-groups, Mathematical Surveys and Monographs 112 (with Stephen D. Smith) 2004; numerous papers in professional journals on finite groups, algebraic groups and combinatorics. *Address:* California Institute of Technology, Department of Mathematics 253-37, Pasadena, CA 91125, USA (office). *Telephone:* (626) 395-4364 (office). *Fax:* (626) 585-1728 (office). *E-mail:* asch@cco.caltech.edu (office). *Website:* www.math.caltech.edu/people/asch.html (office).

AŠERADENS, Arvils, MA; Latvian business executive and politician; b. 30 Dec. 1962, Rīga; m. 1st Anita Kehre (divorced); m. 2nd Evita Ašeradena; four c.; ed Rīga Secondary School No. 72, Latvian State Univ.; cameraman and Deputy Ed., Latinform information agency 1986–89; Commercial Dir, Atmoda (Revival) (Latvijas Tautas Fronte—Latvian Popular Front newspaper) 1989–90; worked at newspaper Diena 1990–2009, Chair. JSC SIA, mem. Bd, Dienas Bizness Ltd, Chair. Mukusala printing group, mem. Bd, Kauno Diena, Chair. Dienas Žurnāli; mem. Pilsoniskā Savienība (PS—Civil Union) 2010–11, Vienotība (Unity) 2011– (mem. Bd 2016–); mem. Seima (PS) 2010–11, (Vienotība) 2011–14; Parl. Sec., Ministry of Finance 2014–16; Deputy Prime Minister and Minister of the Economy 2016–19; mem. Bd, Day Foundation Future Fund, Rojas Soc. yacht club, Latvian Yachting Union Asscn; mem. Bd of Trustees, Latvian Nat. Library Foundation. *Leisure interest:* sailing. *Address:* c/o Ministry of the Economy, Brīvības iela 55, Rīga 1519, Latvia.

ASFARI, Ayman, BSc, MSc FREng; British (b. Syrian) business executive; *Group CEO, Petrofac Ltd;* b. 8 Aug. 1958; m.; four s.; ed Aleppo Coll., Syria, Villanova Univ., Univ. of Pennsylvania, USA; began career as construction site engineer in Oman, later becoming Man. Dir of civil and mechanical construction co.; acquired Petrofac 2001, est. Petrofac Int., becoming CEO –2002, Group CEO Petrofac Ltd 2002–; mem. Bd of Trustees, American Univ. of Beirut; Ernst & Young UK Entrepreneur of the Year 2010, Oil Services Exec. of the Year, World Nat. Oil Company Congress 2011, 2012. *Leisure interests:* golf, skiing. *Address:* Petrofac International, 4th Floor, 117 Jermyn Street, London, SW1Y 6HH, England (office). *Telephone:* (20) 7811-4900 (office). *Fax:* (20) 7811-4901 (office). *Website:* www.petrofac.com (office); www.aymanasfari.com.

ASGHAR, Muhammad, LLB, DPhil (Oxon.); French (b. Pakistani) physicist and academic; *Professor, Laboratoire de Physique Subatomique et de Cosmologie;* b. 7 June 1936, Pakistan; s. of Muhammad Fazal and Bibi Fazal; m.; one c.; ed Univ. of Punjab, Univ. of Oxford, UK; with Pakistan Inst. of Tech., Nilore, also worked at atomic energy research stations at Harwell, UK and Saclay, France; Assoc. Prof., Univ. of Bordeaux 1968–71; physicist, Inst. Laue-Langevin (ILL), Grenoble 1971–78, CCR Euratom, Ispra 1978–80, Centre d'Etudes Nucléaires, Grenoble 1980–81; Prof. of Physics, Houari Boumedienne Univ., Algiers 1981–94, Laboratoire de Physique Subatomique et de Cosmologie, Grenoble 1994–; field of research: low-energy nuclear physics and fundamental physics, specialist in nuclear fission and nuclear energy, has coordinated int. teams in major experiments at high flux nuclear reactor, ILL, Grenoble; Fellow, Islamic Acad. of Sciences 1998. *Publications include:* Concerto, Arpèges de la vie, Lucioles, Parfums de la Grèce, Jours ordinaires, Embruns et pincements, Reflets multiples, Tours et détours de pierres, Echos intérieurs, Paillettes des sens, Feuillettes, Les steppes de soi, Regard vagabond, Chuchotements, Plaisirs palpables, Polyphonie de rosée, Cueillettes d'ici et de là, Masques des ombres, Chemins, sentiers et voies, Eclats d'écoute, Presque rien, Colliers bavards, Voltige des instants, Shekoufeh-hayé rouzagar, Inklings, volume 1 et 2, Bruissements, Kishmakishé souz o saz, Kimonos of spring, Nashib o farazé aavaregi; more than 200 research papers. *Leisure interest:* writing poetry in English, French and Persian. *Address:* Laboratoire de Physique Subatomique et de Cosmologie, 53 avenue des Martyrs, 38026 Grenoble (office); 12 rue des Abeilles, 38240 Meylan, France (home). *Telephone:* (4) 76-28-40-00 (office); (4) 76-18-00-22 (home). *Fax:* (4) 76-28-40-04 (office). *E-mail:* masgharfr@yahoo.fr (office).

ASH, Sir Eric Albert, Kt, CBE, PhD, FRS, FCGI, FIEE, FIEEE, FInstP, FREng; British professor of physical electronics; *Consultant, TCE Ltd;* b. 31 Jan. 1928, Berlin, Germany; s. of Walter Ash and Dorothea Ash (née Schwarz); m. Clare Babb 1954; five d.; ed Univ. Coll. School and Imperial Coll., London; Research Fellow, Stanford Univ. 1952–54; Research Asst, Queen Mary Coll., London 1954–55; Research Engineer, Standard Telecommunications Labs Ltd 1955–63; Sr Lecturer, Univ. Coll. London 1963–65, Reader 1965–67, Prof. of Electrical Eng 1967–80, Pender Prof. and Head, Dept of Electronic and Electrical Eng 1980–85, Prof. of Electrical Eng 1993–97, Prof. Emer. 1997–; Rector, Imperial Coll. London 1985–93; Dir (non-exec.) British Telecom 1987–93, Student Loans Co. PLC 1994–; Consultant, TCE Ltd; Chair. BBC Science Advisory Cttee 1987–; Chair. of Council, Vice-Pres. Royal Inst. 1995– (fmr Sec., Man.); Treasurer, Royal Soc. 1997–2002; Trustee, Science Museum 1987–93, Wolfson Foundation 1988–; Foreign mem. Nat. Acad. of Eng, Russian Acad. of Sciences; Chevalier, Ordre nat. du Mérite 1990; hon. degrees from Univs of Aston, Leicester, Edinburgh, New York Polytechnic, INPG Grenoble, Westminster, Sussex, Glasgow and Surrey and Chinese Univ. of Hong Kong; Faraday Medal of the IEE 1980, Royal Medal of the Royal Soc. 1986. *Publications include:* papers on topics of physical electronics in various engineering and physics journals. *Leisure interests:* music, writing. *Address:* 11 Ripplevale Grove, London, N1 1HS, England. *Telephone:* (20) 7607-4989. *Fax:* (20) 7700-7446. *E-mail:* eric_ash99@yahoo.co.uk.

ASHANTI; American hip-hop and R&B singer, songwriter and actress; b. (Ashanti Douglas), 13 Oct. 1980, Glen Cove, New York; d. of Ken-Kaide Thomas Douglas and Tina Douglas; signed record deal when 14 years old; guest vocalist with artists, including Big Punisher, Ja Rule, J. Lo, Big Pun, Fat Joe, Notorious B.I.G.; solo artist 2002–; Music of Black Origin (MOBO) Award for Best R&B Act 2002, American Music Awards for Best New Pop/Rock Artist, Best New Hip Hop/R&B Artist 2003, Nat. Asscn for the Advancement of Colored People (NAACP) Image Award, Comet Award, Teen Choice Award, Nickelodeon's Kid Choice Award, Teen Choice Award. *Television appearances:* Diamond Life 2005, The Muppets' Wizard of Oz (TV film) 2005, Christmas in the City (TV film) 2013, Army Wives 2013. *Film appearances:* Bouge! 1997, Bride & Prejudice 2004, Coach Carter 2005, John Tucker Must Die 2006, Resident Evil: Extinction 2007, Mutant World 2014, Stuck 2015, Mothers and Daughters 2016, Stuck 2017. *Recordings include:* albums: Ashanti 2002 (Grammy Award for Best Contemporary R&B Album 2003), Foolish/Unfoolish: Reflections on Love 2002, Chapter II 2003, Ashanti's Christmas 2003, Concrete Rose 2004, The Declaration 2008, Braveheart 2014. *Website:* ashantithisisme.com.

ASHBURTON, 7th Baron, cr. 1835; **John Francis Harcourt Baring,** Kt, KG, KCVO, MA, DL, FIB; British merchant banker; b. 2 Nov. 1928, London; s. of 6th Baron Ashburton and Hon. Doris Mary Therese Harcourt; m. 1st Susan Mary Renwick 1955 (divorced 1984); two s. two d.; m. 2nd Sarah Crewe 1987; ed Eton Coll. and Trinity Coll., Oxford; Chair. Barings PLC 1985–89 (Dir (non-exec.) 1989–94), Baring Bros & Co. Ltd 1974–89 (a Man. Dir 1955–74); Dir Trafford Park Estates Ltd 1964–77; Royal Insurance Co. Ltd 1964–82 (Deputy Chair. 1975–82); Dir Outwich Investment Trust Ltd 1965–86 (Chair. 1968–86), British Petroleum Co. 1982–95 (Chair. 1992–95), Dunlop Holdings 1981–84, Bank of England 1983–91, Baring Stratton Investment Trust PLC 1986–98 (Chair. 1986–98), Jaguar PLC 1989–91; mem. British Transport Docks Bd 1966–71; Vice-Pres. British Bankers Asscn 1977–81; mem. Pres.'s Cttee CBI 1976–79, Gen. Council CBI 1976–80; Chair. Accepting Houses Cttee 1977–81, NEDC Cttee on Finance for Industry 1980–87; Pres. Overseas Bankers Club 1977–78; Rhodes Trustee 1970–79, Chair. 1987–98; Trustee, Nat. Gallery 1981–87; Trustee and Hon. Treas. Police Foundation 1989–2001; mem. Exec. Cttee Nat. Art Collections Fund 1989–99; mem. Council Baring Foundation 1971–98, Chair. 1987–98; mem. Southampton Univ. Devt Trust 1986–96 (Chair. 1989–96); mem. Winchester Cathedral Trust 1989– (Chair. 1993–2006); Lord Warden of the Stannaries, Duchy of Cornwall 1990–94, Receiver-Gen. 1974–90; apptd High Steward Winchester Cathedral 1991; apptd DL Hants. 1994; Fellow, Eton Coll. 1982–97; Hon. Fellow, Hertford Coll., Oxford 1976, Trinity Coll., Oxford 1989; Dr hc (Southampton) 2007. *Address:* Lake House, Northington, Alresford, Hants., SO24 9TG, England (office). *Telephone:* (1962) 738728 (office). *E-mail:* johnashburton@btconnect.com (office).

ASHBY, Michael Farries, MA, CBE, PhD, FRS, FREng; British professor of engineering materials; *Professor Emeritus of Materials, Engineering Design Centre, University of Cambridge;* b. 20 Nov. 1935; s. of Lord Ashby and Elizabeth Helen Farries; m. Maureen Stewart 1962; two s. one d.; ed Campbell Coll., Belfast, Queens' Coll., Cambridge; Asst, Univ. of Göttingen, FRG 1962–65; Asst Prof., Harvard Univ., USA 1965–69, Prof. of Metallurgy 1969–73; Prof. of Eng Materials, Univ. of Cambridge 1973–89, apptd Royal Soc. Research Prof., Dept of Eng 1989, now Prof. Emer. of Materials; currently Royal Acad. Visiting Prof., RCA, London; Ed. Acta Metallurgica 1974–96, Progress in Materials Science 1995–; mem. Akad. der Wissenschaften zu Göttingen 1985–, American Acad. of Arts and Sciences 1993–; Foreign mem. US Nat. Acad. of Eng 1990; Fellow Royal Swedish Acad. of Eng Sciences 1985–, Inst. of Metals, UK 1991; Hon. Life mem. Soc. Française de Matériaux 1990, Materials Research Soc. of India 1990, Materials Research Soc. of the USA 1990; Hon. MA (Harvard) 1969; Dr hc (Leuven) 1990, (Royal Inst. of Tech., Stockholm) 1995, (Tech. Univ. of Lisbon) 1996; L.B. Pfeil Medal, Metals Soc. 1975, Rosenheim Medal, Metals Soc. 1979, Mehl Medal, American Soc. for Metals 1983, Amourers and Brasiers Medal, Royal Soc. 1985, A.A. Griffiths Medal, Metals Soc. 1985, Acta Metallurgica Gold Medal 1986, Hume-Rothery Award, American Soc. for Metals 1988, Paul Bergsoe Medal, Danish Metallurgical Soc. 1989, Materials Medal, Soc. Française de Matériaux 1990, Hatfield Memorial Lecturer, Royal Soc. of Great Britain 1992, Von Hippel Award, Materials Research Soc. of the USA 1992, Gold Medal, Fed. of European Materials Socs 1993, Luigi Losana Medal, Associazione Italiana di Metallurgia 1993, Campbell Lecturer, American Soc. for Metals 1994, The Körber Prize 1996, Platinum Medal, Inst. of Materials, London 1998, Hirsch Lecturer, Univ. of Oxford 1998, A. Cemal Eringen Medal, SES, USA 1999. *Publications:* Deformation Mechanism Maps 1982, Engineering Materials (Vol. 1) 1989, (Vol. 2) 1996, Cellular Solids 1997, Materials Selection in Design (2nd edn) 1999, Materials and Design – The Art and Science of Product Design 2002, Materials and the Environment 2009. *Leisure interests:* music, design, watercolour painting. *Address:* University of Cambridge, Department of Engineering, Trumpington Street, Cambridge, CB2 1PZ (office); 51 Maids Causeway, Cambridge, CB5 8DE, England (home). *Telephone:* (1223) 748247 (office); (1223) 303015 (home). *Fax:* (1223) 332662 (home). *E-mail:* mfa2@eng.cam.ac.uk (office). *Website:* www-edc.eng.cam.ac.uk (office).

ASHCROFT, Andrew (Andy) Richard; British business executive and fmr diplomatist; *Joint Executive Director, Koolkompany Limited;* b. 28 May 1961, Almondsbury, Glos.; s. of Ivor John Ashcroft and Amy Joan Ashcroft (née Hiscock); m. Anna Danielewicz; one step-d.; ed Millfield School, Somerset; joined Diplomatic Service 1980, overseas assignments included Commercial Sec., Embassy in Muscat, Oman, various positions at Embassy in Tel-Aviv, Pvt. Sec. to Minister of State for Foreign Affairs 1992–96, First Sec., High Comm. in Harare 1996–99, Head of Caribbean Section, FCO 1999–2002, Amb. to Dominican Repub. and Haiti 2002–06; fmr Man. Dir Ambassador Communications (consultancy); fmr Bd mem. New Forest Business Partnership; Jt Partner, FAIR4DR (consultancy) 2009–14; Jt Founding Partner, Koolkompany Ltd/Koolskools Ethical School Clothing, now Jt Exec. Dir; Chair. Downton Brass Band; fmr mem. Nat. Youth Brass Band. *Leisure interests:* music (piano/singing, brass euphonium), golf. *Address:* Koolkompany Ltd, 103 The Meadows, Lyndhurst, Hants., SO43 7EJ, England (office). *Telephone:* (23) 8028-3223 (office); 7757-978898 (mobile) (home). *E-mail:* arashcroft@btinternet.com (office); andy@koolskools.co.uk (office); andy@koolkompany.com (office). *Website:* www.koolkompany.com (office); www.koolskools.co.uk (office).

ASHCROFT, Dame Frances Mary, DBE, BA, PhD, ScD, FRS, FMedSci; British physiologist and academic; *Royal Society GlaxoSmithKline Research Professor of Physiology, University of Oxford;* b. 15 Feb. 1952; d. of John Ashcroft and Kathleen Ashcroft; ed Talbot Heath School, Bournemouth, Girton Coll., Cambridge; MRC Training Fellow in Physiology, Univ. of Leicester 1978–82; Demonstrator in Physiology, Univ. of Oxford 1982–85, EPA Cephalosporin Jr Research Fellow, Linacre Coll. 1983–85, Royal Soc. Univ. Research Fellow in Physiology 1985–90, Lecturer in Physiology, Christ Church 1986–87, Trinity Coll. 1988–89 (Sr Research Fellow 1992–); Tutorial Fellow in Medicine, St Hilda's Coll. 1990–91, Univ. Lecturer in Physiology 1990–96, Prof. of Physiology 1996–2001, Royal Soc. GlaxoSmithKline Research Prof. 2001–, Dir, Oxford Centre for Gene Function; mem. European Molecular Biology Org.; Dr hc (Open Univ.) 2003, (Univ. of Leicester) 2007; Frank Smart Prize, Univ. of Cambridge 1974, Andrew Culworth Memorial Prize 1990, G.B. Morgagni Young Investigator Award 1991, G.L. Brown Prize Lecturer, Yale Univ. 1997, Peter Curran Lecturer 1999, Charter Award, Inst. of Biology 2004, Walter B. Cannon Award, American Physiological Soc. 2007, L'Oréal-UNESCO For Women in Science Award (Europe) for her discovery of an ATP-sensitive potassium channel linking glucose metabolism and insulin secretion and its role in neonatal diabetes 2012, Croonian Lecturer, The Royal Soc. 2013. *Publications include:* Insulin-Molecular Biology to Pathology (co-author) 1992, Ion Channels and Disease 2000, Life at the Extremes: The Science of Survival 2000, and numerous articles in scientific journals. *Leisure interests:* reading, walking, writing, sailing. *Address:* Department of Physiology, Anatomy and Genetics, Sherrington Building, Parks Road, Oxford, OX1 3PT, England (office). *Telephone:* (1865) 285810 (office). *Fax:* (1865) 285812 (office). *E-mail:* frances.ashcroft@dpag.ox.ac.uk (office). *Website:* www.dpag.ox.ac.uk/team/frances-ashcroft (office).

ASHCROFT, John David, JD; American lawyer, lobbyist and fmr politician; *Chairman, Ashcroft Group LLC;* b. 9 May 1942, Chicago; m. Janet Elise; two s. one d.; ed Yale Univ. and Univ. of Chicago; admitted, Missouri State Bar, Supreme Court Bar; Instructor of Business Law SW Missouri State Univ. 1967–72; legal practice, Springfield, Mo. until 1973; State Auditor, Missouri 1973–75, Asst Attorney-Gen. 1975–77, Attorney-Gen. 1976–85; Gov. of Missouri 1985–93; Senator from Missouri 1995–2001; Attorney-Gen. 2001–05 (resgnd); f. Ashcroft Group, LLC (lobbying firm) 2005; Distinguished Prof. of Law and Govt, Pat Robertson's Regent Univ.; apptd mem. of Faculty, Regent Univ. 2006; Chair. Republican Gov.'s Asscn 1989–90, Nat. Asscn of Attorneys Gen. 1991, Nat. Gov.'s Asscn 1991–92; Chair. Advisory Cttee, Pride; Chair. Bd of Advisers, Innova Holdings; mem. Federalist Soc.; mem. Advisory Bd, Russian-American Christian Univ., Ceelox, Dulles Research LLC, D2C Solutions; recordings as gospel singer. *Publications:* College Law for Business (with Janet Elise), It's the Law 1979, Never Again 2006. *Address:* The Ashcroft Group LLC, 950 North Glebe Road, Suite 2400, Arlington, VA 22203, USA (office). *Telephone:* (703) 247-5454 (office). *Fax:* (703) 247-5446 (office). *E-mail:* jashcroft@ashcroftgroupllc.com (office). *Website:* www.ashcroftgroupllc.com (office).

ASHCROFT, Baron (Life Peer), cr. 2000, of Chichester in the County of West Sussex; **Michael Anthony Ashcroft,** Kt, KCMG, PC; British/Belizean business executive, philanthropist, author and pollster; b. 4 March 1946, Chichester, West Sussex; s. of Frederic Parker Ashcroft and Mary Lavinia Long; m. 1st Wendy Mahoney 1972 (divorced 1984); two s. one d.; m. 2nd Susi Anstey 1986; ed King Edward VI Grammar School, Norwich, Royal Grammar School, High Wycombe, Mid-Essex Tech. Coll., Chelmsford; varied business interests in public and private cos in UK, USA and the Caribbean; Chair. Hawley Group, later ADT Ltd 1977–97; Chair. Impellam Group 2014–, BB Holdings, later BCB Holdings 1987–2010; Dir, Tyco International 1984–2002; Amb. from Belize to the UN 1998–2000; Party Treas., Conservative Party 1998–2001, a Deputy Chair. Conservative and Unionist Party 2005–10; mem. House of Lords 2000–15; Treas. Int. Democratic Union 2007–; Sr Ind. Adviser on Sovereign Base Areas, Cyprus 2011; Founder and Chair. Crimestoppers Trust 1988–; Chair. Ashcroft Tech. Acad. (fmrly ADT Coll.) 1991–; Chancellor, Anglia Ruskin Univ. 2001–; Pres. and Trustee, West India Cttee 2011–; Trustee, Cleveland Clinic 2004–, Imperial War and Museum Foundation 2010–18; Vice-Patron Intelligence Corps Museum 2009–; Amb. SkillForce 2012; mem. Advisory Bd for Institute for Justice Sector Devt; apptd UK Govt Special Rep. for Veterans' Transition 2012 (report, Veterans' Transition Review 2014); Fellow, Royal Canadian Geographical Soc. 2016; Kt, Grand Cross, Imperial Order of Holy Trinity (Ethiopia) 2016; Dr hc (Anglia Ruskin Univ.) 1999. *Publications include:* Smell the Coffee: A Wake Up Call to the Conservative Party 2005, Dirty Politics, Dirty Times 2005, Victoria Cross Heroes 2006 (vol. II 2016), Special Forces Heroes 2008, George Cross Heroes 2010, Minority Verdict: The Conservative Party, the Voters and the 2010 Election 2010, Heroes of the Skies 2012, Special Ops Heroes 2014, Call Me Dave 2015, Well You Did Ask: Why the UK Voted to Leave the EU 2016, Hopes and Fears: Trump, Clinton, The Voters and The Future 2017, The Lost Majority 2017, White Flag: An Examination of Britain's Modern-Day Defence Capability 2018, Half-Time!: American Public Opinion Midway Through Trump's (First?) Term—and The Race to 2020 2019. *Leisure interests:* researching the Victoria Cross, entertaining friends, trying something new, messing about in boats. *Website:* www.lordashcroft.com.

ASHER, Jane; British actress, food industry executive and writer; b. 5 April 1946, London; d. of Richard A. J. Asher and Margaret Eliot; m. Gerald Scarfe (q.v.); two s. one d.; ed North Bridge House, Miss Lambert's Parents' Nat. Educational Union; has appeared in numerous films, on TV and the London stage and has written several best-selling books; Proprietor Jane Asher Party Cakes Shop and Sugarcraft 1990–2015; designer, consultant for Sainsbury's cakes 1992–99; Pres. Nat. Autistic Soc., Arthritis Care, Parkinson's UK; spokesperson and consultant to Heinz Frozen Desserts 1999–2001; Cookware and Gift Food Designer for Debenhams 1998–2005; creator of Home Baking Mixes for Victoria Foods 1999–2012; designer, Jane Asher range of products for Poundland 2014–17; Hon. LLD. *Plays include:* Henceforward…, School for Scandal 1990, Making It Better 1992, The Shallow End 1997, Things We Do for Love 1998, House and Garden 2000, What the Butler Saw 2001, Festen 2004, The World's Biggest Diamond 2005, Bedroom Farce 2009, The Reluctant Debutante 2011, The Importance of Being Earnest 2011, Farewell to the Theatre 2011, Charley's Aunt 2012, Pride & Prejudice 2013, Moon Tiger 2014, The Gathered Leaves 2015, Great Expectations 2016, An American In Paris 2017. *Films include:* Greengage Summer, Masque of the Red Death, Alfie 1966, Deep End, Henry the Eighth and his Six Wives 1970, Success is the Best Revenge, Dreamchild, Paris By Night 1988, Tirante el Blanco 2006, Death at a Funeral 2007, I Give It A Year 2012, Burn, Burn, Burn 2014. *Television includes:* Closing Numbers 1994, The Choir 1995, Good Living 1997, Crossroads 2003, Miss Marple 2004, New Tricks 2005, Holby City 2007, The Old Guys 2009, 2010, Waterloo Road 2011, Dancing on the Edge 2012, Stella 2014, Crossing Lines 2015, Eve 2015, 2016. *Publications include:* The Moppy Stories 1987, Keep Your Baby Safe 1988, Calendar of Cakes 1989, Eats for Treats 1990, Time to Play 1993, Jane Asher's Book of Cake Decorating Ideas 1993, Cakes for Fun 2005, Beautiful Baking 2007; novels: The Longing 1996, The Question 1998, Losing It 2002. *Leisure interests:* reading, Times crossword. *Address:* c/o United Agents, 12–26 Lexington Street, London, W1F 0LE, England (office). *Telephone:* (20) 3214-0800 (office). *Fax:* (20) 3214-0801 (office). *E-mail:* info@unitedagents.co.uk (office). *Website:* www.unitedagents.co.uk (office).

ASHIDA, Akimitsu; Japanese business executive; *Chairman Executive Officer, Mitsui OSK Lines;* b. 1943; joined Mitsui OSK Lines Ltd 1967, positions held include Dir 1st Regular Line, Dir of Planning, Man. Dir, Sr Man. Dir, Sr Man. Exec. Officer, Vice-Pres., Exec. Vice-Pres., Pres. and Dir, Rep. Dir and Exec. Pres. 2005–10, Chair. Exec. Officer 2010–; mem. Bd JFE Holdings, Inc. 2015–. *Address:* Mitsui OSK Lines Ltd, 1-1 Toranomon, 2-chome, Tokyo 105-8688, Japan (office). *Telephone:* (3) 3587-6224 (office). *Fax:* (3) 3587-7734 (office). *E-mail:* info@mol.co.jp (office). *Website:* www.mol.co.jp (office).

ASHKENAZY, Vladimir Davidovich; Icelandic/Swiss (b. Russian) pianist and conductor; b. 6 July 1937, Gorky, USSR; s. of David Ashkenazy and Evstolia Ashkenazy (née Plotnova); m. Thórunn Sofia Jóhannsdóttir 1961; two s. three d.; ed Cen. Music School, Moscow and Moscow Conservatoire; Prin. Guest Conductor, Philharmonia Orchestra 1982–83, Conductor Laureate 2000–; Music Dir Royal Philharmonic Orchestra 1987–94, Deutsches Symphonie-Orchester Berlin (fmrly Berlin Radio Symphony) 1989–99; Chief Conductor Czech Philharmonic Orchestra 1998–2003; Music Dir EUYO (European Union Youth Orchestra) 2002–; Music Dir NHK Symphony, Tokyo 2004–07; Prin. Conductor and Artistic Adviser, Sydney Symphony Orchestra 2009–13; Dir Accademia Pianistica Internazionale di Imola 2013–; Conductor Laureate, Iceland Symphony Orchestra; fmr Prin. Guest Conductor, Cleveland Orchestra; apptd Artist Laureate, Royal Liverpool Philharmonic Orchestra during Liverpool's tenure as European City of Culture 2008; Hon. RAM; Order of the Falcon (Iceland); Hon. DMus (Nottingham) 1995; Second Prize,

Int. Chopin Competition, Warsaw 1955, Gold Medal, Queen Elizabeth Int. Piano Competition, Brussels 1956, Jt Winner (with John Ogdon) Int. Tchaikovsky Piano Competition, Moscow 1962, Grammy Award for Best Instrumental Soloist Performance (with orchestra) for Prokofiev's Piano Concertos Nos 2 and 3 2010, Sergei Rachmaninov Int. Award 2014. *Recordings include:* numerous recordings including Ashkenazy: 50 Years on Decca 2013. *Publication:* Beyond Frontiers (with Jasper Parrott) 1985. *Address:* Harrison Parrott, 5–6 Albion Court, London, W6 0QT, England (office). *Telephone:* (20) 7229-9166 (office). *Fax:* (20) 7221-5042 (office). *E-mail:* info@harrisonparrott.co.uk (office). *Website:* www.harrisonparrott.com/artist/profile/vladimir-ashkenazy (office); www.vladimirashkenazy.com.

ASHOK, B(alasubramanian); Indian mechanical engineer and energy industry executive; *Chairman, Indian Oil Corporation Limited (IndianOil);* ed Coll. of Eng, Univ. of Madras, Nat. Man. Programme, Man. Devt Inst., Gurgaon; worked in pvt. sector for two years before joining Indian Oil 1981, began in Lubes Tech. Services 1981–91, subsequently held numerous positions, including Training and Devt, Div. Head, Corp. Communications, Business Devt, has worked in Chennai, Kochi, Coimbatore 1997, Bangalore and at Head Office in Mumbai, Corp. Office, New Delhi and as Regional Man., SE Asia, Kuala Lumpur, Malaysia 2001–04, State Head, Kerala and State Head, Karnataka, India 2004–08, Mumbai, Chair. Indian Oil Corpn Ltd July 2014–, Exec. Dir, Retail Sales, Indian Oil Corpn Ltd (IOC) Oct. 2014–; Chair. Chennai Petroleum Corpn Ltd 2014–; mem. Bd of Dirs, Lanka IOC PLC 2012–; visiting mem. of faculty at man. insts in India. *Leisure interests:* reading, music, sports. *Address:* Indian Oil Corporation Ltd, Corporate Office, 3079/3, J.B. Tito Marg, Sadiq Nagar, 110 049 New Delhi, India (office). *Telephone:* (11) 26260000 (office). *E-mail:* amreshkapoor@indianoil.in (office). *Website:* www.iocl.com (office).

ASHRAF, Raja Pervaiz, BA; Pakistani politician; b. 26 Dec. 1950, Sanghar, Sindh; m.; two s. two d.; ed Univ. of Sindh; worked in agric. before entering politics; mem. Nat. Ass.; Fed. Minister for Water and Power 2008–11; Prime Minister 2012–13; Sr Leader Pakistan People's Party (PPP), fmr Sec.-Gen.; charged with alleged corruption Oct. 2014.

ASHRAFUL, Mohammad, (Ashraful Matin); Bangladeshi fmr professional cricketer; b. 7 July 1984, Dhaka; right-handed batsman; right-arm offbreak and leg-break bowler; plays for Dhaka Metropolis 2000–01, 2011–, Dhaka Div. 2001–11, Bangladesh 2001– (Capt. 2007–09), Mohammedan Sporting Club 2008–, Mumbai Indians 2009, Dhaka Gladiators 2012–, Asia XI; First-class debut: 2000/01; Test debut: Sri Lanka v Bangladesh, Colombo (SSC) 6–8 Sept. 2001; One-Day Int. (ODI) debut: Zimbabwe v Bangladesh, Bulawayo 11 April 2001; T20I debut: Kenya v Bangladesh, Nairobi (Gym) 1 Sept. 2007; has played in 61 Tests, taken 21 wickets and scored 2,737 runs (6 centuries, 8 half-centuries), highest score 190, average 24.00, best bowling (innings) 2/42, (match) 3/75; ODIs: 177 matches, took 18 wickets and scored 3,468 runs, highest score 109, average 22.23, best bowling (innings) 3/26, (match) 3/26; T20Is: 23 matches, took 8 wickets and scored 450 runs, highest score 65, average 19.56, best bowling (innings) 3/42; youngest player to score a test century (144 runs against Sri Lanka) in an int. match aged 17, Sept. 2001; banned by Bangladesh Cricket Bd for eight years for match-fixing 2014, ban later reduced to five years with two years suspended; Grameenphone Prothom-alo Player of the Year Award 2007. *Address:* c/o Bangladesh Cricket Board, Sher-e-Bangla National Cricket Stadium, Mirpur, Dhaka 1216, Bangladesh. *E-mail:* pd@tigercricket.com.bd. *Website:* www.tigercricket.com.bd.

ASHRAWI, Hanan Daoud Khalil, BA, MA, PhD; Palestinian politician, organization executive and academic; b. 8 Oct. 1946, Ramallah (then part of British Mandate of Palestine); d. of Daoud Mikhail (a founder of Palestinian Liberation Org.—PLO) and Wadi'a Ass'ad; m. Emile Ashrawi; two d.; ed American Univ. of Beirut, Lebanon, Univ. of Virginia, USA; joined PLO Fatah faction; Prof. of English Literature, Birzeit Univ., West Bank 1973–90, mem. Faculty 1973–95, Chair. English Dept 1973–78, 1981–84, Dean of Faculty of Arts 1986–90; activist, Palestinian Women's Movt 1974–; f. Birzeit Univ. Legal Aid Cttee/Human Rights Action Project 1974; joined Intifada Political Cttee 1988, served on its Diplomatic Cttee 1988–93; official spokeswoman for Palestinian Del. to Middle East peace process 1991–93, mem. Leadership/Guidance Cttee and Exec. Cttee of del.; mem. Advisory Cttee Palestinian Del. at Madrid Peace Conf. on Middle East; mem. Palestinian Ind. Comm. for Palestinian Repub., Head 1993–95; Founder and Commr Gen. Palestinian Ind. Comm. for Citizens' Rights 1993–95; mem. Palestinian Legis. Council 1996– (re-elected on a nat. list, The Third Way 2006); Palestinian Authority Minister of Higher Educ. and Research 1996–98 (resgnd in protest against political corruption); f. MIFTAH (Palestinian Initiative for the Promotion of Global Dialogue and Democracy) 1998; currently Human Rights Commr (semi-official ombudsman) and mem. Palestinian Legis. Council; Media Dir and Spokesperson Arab League 2001–02; mem. Exec. Cttee Palestine Liberation Org.; Trustee, Inst. for Palestine Studies; Dr hc (American Univ. of Beirut) 2008, (Earlham Coll., Smith Coll.); Olof Palme Prize 2002, Sydney Peace Prize 2003. *Publications include:* numerous poems, short stories and papers and articles on Palestinian culture, literature and politics, including Anthology of Palestinian Literature (ed., The Modern Palestinian Short Story: An Introduction to Practical Criticism, Contemporary Palestinian Literature under Occupation, Contemporary Palestinian Poetry and Fiction, Literary Translation: Theory and Practice; A Passion for Peace 1994, This Side of Peace: A Personal Account (memoirs) 1995. *Website:* www.plc.gov.ps.

ASHTON OF UPHOLLAND, Baroness (Life Peer), cr. 1999, of St Albans in the County of Hertfordshire; **Catherine Margaret Ashton,** GCMG, PC, BSc; British economist, politician and fmr EU official; b. 20 March 1956, Upholland, Lancs.; d. of Harold Ashton and Clare Ashton; m. Peter Kellner 1988; one s. one d. three step-c.; ed Upholland Grammar School, Billinge Higher End, Lancs., Wigan Mining and Tech. Coll., Wigan, Bedford Coll., London (now part of Royal Holloway, Univ. of London); Admin. Sec., Campaign for Nuclear Disarmament 1977–79; Man. Coverdale Org. 1979–81; Dir of Public Affairs, Business in the Community 1983–89; policy adviser 1989–98; Chair. Hertfordshire Health Authority 1998–2001; Parl. Under-Sec. of State and Govt Spokesperson, Dept for Educ. and Skills 2001–04, Early Years and School Standards 2001–02, Early Years and Childcare 2002, Sure Start (also Dept for Work and Pensions) 2002–04; Govt Spokesperson for Children 2003; Parl. Under-Sec. of State and Govt Spokesperson, Dept for Constitutional Affairs/Ministry of Justice 2004–07, Leader House of Lords and Lord Pres. of the Council 2007–08, on leave of absence 2010–14; Commr for Trade, EC 2008–09, High Rep. of the Union for Foreign Affairs and Security Policy, EU 2009–14, also first Vice-Pres. EC 2010–14; Grand Officer, Order of the White Double Cross (Slovakia) 2014; hon. degree from Univ. of East London 2005; House Magazine Minister of the Year 2005, Channel 4 Peer of the Year 2005, Stonewall Politician of the Year 2006, assessed by Woman's Hour on BBC Radio 4 as one of the 100 most powerful women in the UK 2013. *Address:* House of Lords, Westminster, London, SW1A 0PW, England (office).

ASHWORTH, Sir John Michael, Kt, PhD, DSc; British biologist and academic; b. 27 Nov. 1938, Luton, Beds.; s. of Jack Ashworth and Mary Ousman; m. 1st Ann Knight 1963 (died 1985); one s. three d.; m. 2nd Auriol Stevens 1988; ed Exeter Coll., Oxford, Univ. of Leicester, Brandeis Univ. and Univ. of California, San Diego, USA; Harkness Fellow, Commonwealth Fund, New York 1965–67; Lecturer, Biochemistry Dept, Univ. of Leicester 1967–71, Reader 1971–73; Prof., Biology Dept, Univ. of Essex 1973–79; Chief Scientist, Cen. Policy Review Staff, Cabinet Office 1976–81; Under-Sec. Cabinet Office 1979–81; Vice-Chancellor, Univ. of Salford 1981–89; Dir LSE and Political Science 1990–96; Chair. Bd Nat. Computer Centre 1983–91, Nat. Accreditation Council for Certification Bodies 1984–88, British Library 1996–2001; mem. Bd Granada TV 1987–89, Dir Granada Group 1990–2002; Dir J. Sainsbury 1993–96, Strategic Health Authority, NE London 2002–03; mem. Council, Inst. of Cancer Research (ICR) 1998–2007, Fellow, ICR 2007; Chair. Barts and the London Nat. Health Service (NHS) Trust 2003–07; Dir (non-exec.) Colchester Hosp. Univ. Foundation NHS Trust 2010–14; Chair. Wivenhoe Pub Co. Ltd; Hon. Fellow, Exeter Coll., Oxford 1983, LSE 1997; Hon. DSc (Salford) 1991, (City Univ.) 2005, (Essex) 2011; Hon. LLD (Leicester) 2005; Colworth Medal of Biochemical Soc. 1972. *Publications include:* ed.: Outline Studies in Biology; author: Cell Differentiation 1973, The Slime Moulds (with J. Dee) 1976; more than 100 papers on biological, biochemical and educational topics in scientific journals. *Leisure interest:* sailing. *Address:* Garden House, Wivenhoe, Essex, CO7 9BD, England (home). *Telephone:* (1206) 822256 (home). *Fax:* (1206) 822256 (home). *E-mail:* john@ashworthstevens.net (home).

ASIF, Khawaja Muhammad, LLB; Pakistani politician and fmr banker; b. 9 Aug. 1949; s. of Khawaja Muhammad Safdar; m.; one s. three d.; ed Govt Coll. Lahore, Univ. Law Coll., Lahore; worked in various banks in UAE including Bank of Credit and Commerce International –1991; mem. Senate for Punjab (Islami Jamhoori Itehad party) 1991–94; mem. Nat. Ass. (Parl.) for NA-110 Sialkot constituency 1993–99, 2002–18; Chair. Privatization Comm. of Pakistan 1997–99; Minister for Sports, also Minister for Petroleum and Natural Resources March–May 2008; Minister for Defence, also Minister for Water and Power 2013–17; Minister of Foreign Affairs Aug. 2017– April 2018 (disqualified by Islamabad High Court); mem. Pakistan Muslim League (Nawaz).

ASIM, Mohamed, BA, MA, PhD; Maldivian diplomatist and government official; b. 1960; m. Mariyam Ali Manik; one s. one d.; ed American Univ. of Beirut, Lebanon, California State Univ., Sacramento, USA, Australian Nat. Univ., Canberra, Australia; early govt career as Admin. Officer, Ministry of Educ. 1982; Personnel Services Officer, Pres.'s Office 1983, then Sr Research Officer, Int. Div.; Presidential Aide 1990–92; Dir Employment Affairs 1992–96, Dir-Gen. 1996–99; Dir-Gen. Public Service Div. of Pres.'s Office 1999–2004; High Commr to Sri Lanka 2004–07, to UK 2007–08, to Bangladesh 2015–16; Additional Sec., Ministry of Foreign Affairs 2008–14, Charge d'affaires, Maldives Mission to EU and Embassy in Belgium 2013–14, Amb.-at-Large 2014–16, Minister of Foreign Affairs 2016–18; Pres. Colombo Plan Council 2004–; mem. Maldives Dels to various Commonwealth, SAARC and Asia Pacific meetings; Grad. Asst, School of Business and Public Admin, Calif. State Univ. 1983–85; taught professional short courses in human resources man. at ANU, Canberra 1996–98; Lecturer, College of Technology, London 2010–12, Univ. of Wales TSD London Campus 2012. *Address:* c/o Ministry of Foreign Affairs, Boduthakurufaanu Magu, Malé 20-077, Maldives (office).

ASJES, Ivar Onno Odwin, MEconSc; Curaçao politician; b. 16 Sept. 1970, Rotterdam, Netherlands; ed Erasmus Univ.; mem. Island Council and Commr of Finance, Island Govt of Curaçao Sept.–Oct. 2010 (council discontinued following dissolution of Netherlands Antilles); mem. Staten (Parl.) of Curaçao 2010–13; Prime Minister 2013–15; Leader, Pueblo Soberano party 2013–15.

ASLAKHANOV, Col-Gen. Aslanbek Akhmedovich, CandJur; Chechen politician; b. 14 March 1942, Novye Atagi; m.; two c.; ed Kharkov State Pedagogical Inst., Acad. of USSR; served in Soviet Army 1962–65; teacher Moscow Mining Inst. 1965–67; served on numerous positions in USSR, Ministry of Internal Affairs 1967, investigator, then Head of Dept, then Sr Inspector, then Deputy Head, then Head of Div., Chief Inspector Organizational Dept 1981–89; head of successful operation to end hijacking of an aircraft in N Caucasus 1989; Pres. All-Russian Asscn of Security Veterans and Courts; mem. Soviet of Nationalities, USSR Supreme Soviet 1989–91; elected to State Duma (Parl.) 2000, representing Chechen Repub.; Adviser to Pres. Putin 2003–; mem. Fed. Council for Omsk region 2008–. *Leisure interests:* free-style wrestling, sport. *Address:* State Duma, 103265 Moscow, Okhotny Ryad 1, Russia. *Telephone:* (495) 292-02-04.

ASLOV, Sirodjidin; Tajikistani government official and diplomatist; *Minister of Foreign Affairs;* b. 17 Feb. 1964, Sovetskii Dist (now in Khatlon Viloyat), Tajik SSR, USSR; m.; four c.; ed Odesa Hydrometeorological Inst., Ukrainian SSR; worked in Ministry of Environment of Tajik SSR 1986–96, Deputy Chief, Hydrometeorological Service 1995–96; Perm. Rep., Exec. Cttee, Aral Sea Fund 1996–2004; Chair. Exec. Cttee, Int. Fund for Saving Aral Sea 2002–05; First Deputy Foreign Minister 2004–05; Amb. and Perm. Rep. to UN, New York 2005–13, also accred as Amb. to Cuba 2011–13; Minister of Foreign Affairs 2013–; Tajikistan Order of Glory. *Address:* Ministry of Foreign Affairs, 734001 Dushanbe, Xiyoboni Shiraz 33, Tajikistan (office). *Telephone:* (372) 21-18-08 (office). *Fax:* (372) 21-02-59 (office). *E-mail:* info@mfa.tj (office). *Website:* mfa.tj (office).

ASNER, Edward (Ed); American actor and film producer; b. 15 Nov. 1929, Kansas City; s. of Morris David Asner and Lizzie Seliger; m. 1st Nancy Sykes 1957; three c.; m. 2nd Cindy Gilmore 1998 (divorced 2015); one s. with Carol Jean Vogelman; ed Univ. of Chicago; film and TV actor 1961–; Pres. Screen Actors Guild 1981–85; f. Quince Productions, Inc. (production co.); seven Emmy Awards, five

Golden Globe Awards, Ralph Morgan Award, Screen Actors Guild 2000, Lifetime Achievement Award 2002, 2005, 2006. *Film appearances include:* Fort Apache the Bronx 1981, JFK 1991, The Golem 1995, Hard Rain 1998, The Batchelor 1999, Above Suspicion 2000, Mars and Beyond 2000, The Animal 2001, The Confidence Game (also co-producer) 2001, Academy Boyz 2001, Fair Play 2002, The Commission 2003, Missing Brendan 2003, Elf 2003, Crab Orchard 2006, All In 2005, Sleeping Dogs Lie 2005, Ways of the Flesh 2006, Hard Four 2007, Channels 2008, Gigantic 2008, So Others May Live 2008, The Raft 2009, Not Another B Movie 2010, Witness Insecurity 2011, Sheeba 2011, I Know That Voice 2013, The Games Maker 2014, Boonville Redemption 2016, The Garden Left Behind 2018; numerous TV film appearances. *Films produced:* Payback (TV) 1997, A Vision of Murder: The Story of Donielle (TV) (exec. producer) 2000. *TV series include:* The Mary Tyler Moore Show (as Lou Grant) (five Emmy Awards) 1970–77, Lou Grant (as Lou Grant) 1977–82, Witch 2006, Studio 60 on the Sunset Strip 2006–07. *Address:* Quince Production, Inc, 12400 Ventura Blvd., #371, Studio City, CA 91604.

ASO, Taro; Japanese politician; *Deputy Prime Minister, Minister of Finance and for Overcoming Deflation, and Minister of State for Financial Services;* b. 20 Sept. 1940; m. Chikako Suzuki; two c.; ed Gakushuin Univ., Stanford Univ., USA and London School of Econs, UK; joined Aso Cement Co. Ltd 1966, Pres. 1973–79; mem. House of Reps for Fukuoka Pref. 8th Dist (LDP) 1979–; Parl. Vice-Minister, Ministry of Educ., Science and Sports 1988; Chair. Standing Cttee on Foreign Affairs 1991; Minister of State for Econ. Planning 1996; mem. Judge Indictment Cttee 1998; Minister of State for Econ. and Fiscal Policy 2001–03; Minister for Public Man., Home Affairs, Posts and Telecommunications 2003–05, of Foreign Affairs 2005–07; Prime Minister 2008–09; Deputy Prime Minister 2012–, also Minister of Finance and for Overcoming Deflation, and Minister of State for Financial Services 2012–; Dir Educ. Div., LDP Policy Research Council 1990, Dir Foreign Affairs Div. 1992, Deputy Sec.-Gen. LDP 1993, Deputy Chair. Policy Research Council 1999, Dir-Gen. LDP Treasury Bureau 2000, Chair. Policy Research Council 2001, Sec.-Gen. 2007, 2008, Pres. 2008–09; mem. Japan Olympic Shooting Team, Montreal 1976; Pres. Japan Jr Chamber of Commerce 1978. *Address:* Ministry of Finance, 3-1-1, Kasumigaseki, Chiyoda-ku, Tokyo 100-8940 (office); Liberal-Democratic Party (Jiyu-Minshuto), 1-11-23, Nagata-cho, Chiyoda-ku, Tokyo 100-8910, Japan (office). *Telephone:* (3) 3581-4111 (office); (3) 3581-6211 (office). *Fax:* (3) 5251-2667 (office); (3) 3581-1910 (office). *E-mail:* info@mof.go.jp (office); koho@ldp.jimin.or.jp (office). *Website:* www.mof.go.jp (office); www.jimin.jp (office); aso-taro.jp.

ASPECT, Alain, PhD; French physicist and academic; *Augustin Fresnel Professor, Institut d'Optique;* b. 15 June 1947, Agen, Lot-et-Garonne, Aquitaine; m. Annie Aspect; two c.; ed École Normale Supérieure de Cachan, Orsay Univ.; Asst Lecturer, Orsay Univ. 1969–71; teacher, Yaoundé, Cameroon 1971–74; Lecturer, École Normale Supérieure, Cachan 1974–85; Scientist, Collège de France, Paris 1985–92; Augustin Fresnel Prof., Institut d'Optique and Prof. (part-time) École Polytechnique, Palaiseau 1992–, also CNRS Distinguished Scientist Emer. and Research Dir Emer. Laboratoire Charles Fabry and mem. Atom Optics Group; mem. Prime Minister's Higher Council for Science and Tech.; mem. Académie des Sciences 2002; Foreign Assoc. NAS 2008, Austrian Acad. of Sciences 2009; Fellow, Optical Soc. of America 2002, American Physical Soc. 2005, European Optical Soc. 2006; Chevalier, Légion d'honneur; Officier, Ordre nat. du Mérite; Commdr des Palmes académiques; Dr hc (Ecole Polytechnique, Montreal) 2006, (Univ. of Montreal) 2006, (ANU) 2008, (Heriot-Watt Univ.) 2008, (Univ. of Glasgow) 2010, (Technion Univ.) 2011; numerous awards including Académie des Sciences Prix Servan 1983, US Commonwealth Award for Science and Invention 1985, Société Française de Physique and Inst. of Physics Holweck Prize 1991, Max Born Award, Optical Soc. of America 1999, Humboldt-Gay Lussac Prize 1999, CNRS Gold Medal 2005, European Physical Soc. Quantum Electronics Prize 2009, Wolf Prize in Physics (with John F. Clauser and Anton Zeilinger) 2010, Herbert Walther Award, Optical Soc. of America and Deutsche Physikalische Gesellschaft 2011, Albert Einstein Medal, Albert Einstein Soc. 2012, Ives Medal/Quinn Prize, Optical Soc. of America 2013, Tommassoni Prize, Univ. of Rome 'La Sapienza' 2013. *Achievements include:* best known for Bell test experiments, laser cooling of atoms and experiments with Bose-Einstein Condensates. *Publications:* Lévy Statistics and Laser Cooling: How Rare Events Bring Atoms to Rest (co-author) 2002, Demain la Physique (co-author) 2004, An Introduction to Quantum Optics: From the Semi-classical Approach to Quantized Light (co-author) 2010; around 200 articles in int. journals. *Address:* Laboratoire Charles Fabry, Institut d'Optique, 2 Avenue Fresnel, 91127 Palaiseau, France (office). *Telephone:* 1-64-53-31-03 (office). *Fax:* 1-64-53-31-18 (office). *E-mail:* alain.aspect@institutoptique.fr (office). *Website:* www.lcf.institutoptique.fr (office).

ASQUITH, Hon. Sir Dominic Anthony Gerard, Kt, KCMG, CMG; British diplomatist and consultant; *High Commissioner to India;* b. 7 Feb. 1957, Zanzibar; younger s. of 2nd Earl of Oxford and Asquith by his wife Anne Palairet; great-grandson of H. H. Asquith (fmr Prime Minister); m. Louise Cotton 1988; two s. two d.; ed Ampleforth Coll., N Yorks., Balliol Coll., Univ. of Oxford; with Soviet Dept, FCO 1983–84, Southern European Dept 1984–85, Second Sec. and Head of Interests Section, Damascus 1986–87, First Sec. (Chancery), Muscat 1987–89, EC Dept (Internal), FCO 1989–90, Pvt. Sec. to Minister of State 1990–92, First Sec., Washington, DC 1992–96, Drugs and Int. Crime Dept, FCO 1996, Minister and Deputy Head of Mission, Buenos Aires 1997–2001, Deputy Head of Mission and Chargé d'affaires a.i., Riyadh 2001–04, Deputy Special Rep. for Iraq and Deputy Head of Mission, Baghdad 2004, Dir Iraq, FCO 2004–06, Amb. to Iraq 2006–07, to Egypt 2007–11, to Libya 2011–12; Dir, Asquith Consultancy 2014–; Sr Adviser to Dentons LLP 2013–15; Sr Adviser to Macro Advisory Partners 2013–15; Strategic Adviser, Group DF International 2013–15; Chairman Libyan British Business Council 2013–15; Adviser, Tatweer Research 2013–15, Libya Holdings Group; mem. Bd of Advisers, Tamweel Capital 2013–15, Bd of Trustees, Inst. of Statecraft 2013–15; High Commr to India 2016–.

ASSAD, Asma al-, BSc; Syrian state official and investment banker; *First Lady;* b. (Asma Fawaz al-Akhras), 11 Aug. 1975, Acton, London, England; d. of Dr Fawaz Akhras and Sahar Akhras; m. Bashar al-Assad 2000; two s. one d.; ed Queen's Coll. secondary school, London and King's Coll., London; economist, Hedge Fund Man., Deutsche Bank, London 1996–97; Investment Banker, Mergers and Acquisitions for Biotechnology Cos, JP Morgan, London, New York, Paris 1998–2000; First Lady of Syria 2001–, state visits to Tunisia, Spain, Morocco, France, Italy, Qatar, UK, The Vatican; represented Syria in talks with Bank of England concerning Syrian econ. reform, London 2002, with UNESCO concerning educ. and literacy, with Arab Women's Org. on the improvement of women's status in the Arab world; Founder and Chair. The Syria Trust for Devt 2001; introduced and championed rights for the disabled in Syria, including comprehensive legislation; hosted numerous int. confs, including the Women in Business Conf. (largest ever gathering of business women in Middle East) 2002; Chair. AAMAL (Syrian Org. for the Disabled) 2006–; mem. World Links Arab Region Advisory Council, Higher Council in Arab Women's Org.; Patron Syrian Comm. for Family Affairs, Damascus Arab Capital of Culture (UNESCO) 2008; Patron Transformation of Nat. Museums and Cultural Heritage Sites; Hon. Chair. Special Olympics, Syria; Hon. PhD (La Sapienza Univ., Rome) 2004; Arab First Lady of the Year 2008, Italian Presidency Gold Medal of the Year 2008. *Leisure interest:* horse riding, skiing, cycling. *Address:* Office of HE Mrs al-Assad, Rawda Square, Damascus, Syria (office). *Telephone:* (11) 2231112 (office). *Fax:* (11) 3345801 (office). *E-mail:* fares.kallas@mopa.gov.sy (office).

ASSAD, Lt-Gen. Bashar al-; Syrian ophthalmologist, army officer and head of state; *President;* b. 11 Sept. 1965, Damascus; s. of Hafiz al-Assad (Pres. of Syria 1971–2000) and Anissa Makhlouf; m. Asma al-Akhras 2001; two s. one d.; ed Al-Huria High School, Damascus, Univ. of Damascus Faculty of Medicine, also studied ophthalmology at Western Eye Hosp., London, UK, Homs Mil. Acad., Damascus; completed ophthalmology residency training in Tishreen Mil. Hosp., Damascus; recalled from studies in London to join Syrian army following death of his brother in a car accident 1994; Capt., Medical Corps 1994, fmr commdr armoured div., Syrian Armed Forces, rank of Col 1999; apptd Leader of Ba'ath Party and C-in-C of Armed Forces following death of his father 2000–; Pres. of Syria 2000–; Regional Sec. Ba'ath Party; fmr Head of Syrian Computer Soc. *Leisure interest:* surfing the internet. *Address:* Office of the President, Raouda Palace, Damascus, Syria (office). *Telephone:* (11) 2231112 (Raouda Palace); (11) 2233600 (Al-Shaeb Palace); (11) 3734535 (Teshreen Palace).

ASSAF, Ibrahim ibn Abd al-Aziz al-, PhD; Saudi Arabian economist and government official; *Minister of Foreign Affairs;* b. 28 Jan. 1949, Ayoun Al-Jawa, Qassim; m.; four c.; ed King Saud Univ. Riyadh, Univ. of Denver, Colo State Univ., USA; Teaching Asst, King Abdulaziz Mil. Acad. (KAMA) Riyadh 1971–82, Asst Prof. 1982–86, Head Dept of Admin. Sciences 1982–86; Visiting Lecturer, Staff's Acad. 1982–83; Econ. Adviser, Saudi Fund for Devt 1982–86; Alt. Exec. Dir for Saudi Arabia, IMF, Washington, DC 1986–89, Exec. Dir 1989–95; Minister of Finance and Nat. Economy 1996–2016; Minister of State and mem. Council of Ministers 2016–18, Minister of Foreign Affairs 2018–; Chair. Public Investment Fund, Pension and Retirement Fund, Saudi Fund Devt, Real Estate Devt Fund; Gov. for Saudi Arabia, Islamic Devt Bank, World Bank Group, IMF, Arab Funds and Financial Insts.; mem. Bd Supreme Econ. Council, Higher Advisory Council for Petroleum and Minerals, Saudi Arabian Oil Company (SAUDI ARAMCO), Gen. Investment Authority, Supreme Tourism Authority, Higher Council Islamic Affairs, Higher Council for Univs, Civil Service Council, Manpower Council, Mil. Service Council, Higher Council for Civil Defense, Saudi Econ. Asscn. *Address:* Ministry of Foreign Affairs, POB 55937, Riyadh 11544, Saudi Arabia (office). *Telephone:* (1) 405-5000 (office). *Fax:* (1) 403-0645 (office). *E-mail:* info@mofa.gov.sa (office). *Website:* www.mofa.gov.sa (office).

ASSANE, Abdallah-Kadre; Central African Republic statistician and politician; b. Ndélé; fmr Dir Structural Adjustment Programme Tech. Cttee (CTP/PAS); fmr holder of several ministerial posts including Minister Del. in Ministry of Finance and Budget, responsible for mobilization of financial resources, Minister Counselor in Prime Minister's office, responsible for good governance, Minister of Planning, Economy and Int. Cooperation, Minister of Post and Telecommunications, responsible for new tech., Minister of Finance and the Budget 2015–16. *Address:* c/o Ministry of Finance and the Budget, BP 696, Bangui, Central African Republic (office).

ASSANGE, Julian Paul; Australian journalist, computer programmer and activist; *Publisher, WikiLeaks;* b. 3 July 1971, Townsville, Queensland; one s.; ed Univ. of Melbourne; previously a physics and math. student, computer hacker and programmer before taking on current role as mem. Bd, Ed.-in-Chief (resgnd 2018 owing to lack of internet access) and Spokesperson for WikiLeaks (unpaid volunteer), currently Publr; represented Univ. of Melbourne at Australian Nat. Physics Competition 2005; mem. International Subversives (hacker group), pleaded guilty to 24 charges of hacking 1992; took refuge in and granted political asylum in Ecuadorean Embassy, London while awaiting extradition to Sweden to answer charges of sexual assault Aug. 2012; asylum withdrawn April 2019; sentenced to 50 weeks' imprisonment for breaching bail conditions May 2019; winner, Amnesty International Media Award (New Media) 2009 (for exposing extrajudicial assassinations in Kenya The Cry of Blood – Extra Judicial Killings and Disappearances investigation) 2009, winner, Economist Index on Censorship Award 2008, Sam Adams Award, Sam Adams Assocs for Integrity in Intelligence 2010. *Publication:* When Google Met WikiLeaks 2014. *Address:* WikiLeaks, Box 4080, Australia Post Office – University of Melbourne Branch, Melbourne, Vic. 3052, Australia (office). *E-mail:* info@wikileaks.org (office). *Website:* www.wikileaks.org (office).

ASSELBORN, Jean; Luxembourg politician; *Minister of Foreign and European Affairs and of Immigration and Asylum;* b. 27 April 1949, Steinfort; m. Sylvie Asselborn-Huber 1980; two d.; ed Athénée de Luxembourg and Univ. of Nancy; left school to work for Uniroyal Labs 1967; became involved in trade-union movt, elected to post of Youth Rep. of Fed. of Luxembourg Workers (Lëtzebuerger Aarbechterverband, precursor to current OGB-L or Ind. Fed. of Trade Unions of Luxembourg); joined civil admin of Luxembourg City 1968–69; returned to Steinfort to serve in local admin 1969; Admin. Inter-municipal Hosp., Steinfort 1976; Mayor of Steinfort 1982–2004; elected to Luxembourg Parl. 1984–, Head, Parl. Group of Luxembourg Socialist Workers' Party (LSAP) 1989, Chair. LSAP 1997–2004, Vice-Pres. Luxembourg Parl. 1999–2004, mem. Cttee of the Regions of the EU; Vice-Pres. European Socialist Party 2000–04; Deputy Prime Minister 2004–13; Minister for Foreign and European Affairs and of Immigration and Asylum 2004–. *Address:* Ministry of Foreign Affairs and and European Affairs,

Hôtel St Maximin, 5 rue Notre-Dame, 2240 Luxembourg, Luxembourg (office). *Telephone:* 247-82-301 (office). *Fax:* 22-31-44 (office). *E-mail:* officielle.boite@mae.etat.lu (office). *Website:* www.mae.lu (office).

ASSI, Lamia Mari; Syrian politician and diplomatist; *Minister of Tourism;* b. 27 Dec. 1955; m.; Vice-Minister of Finance 2002–04; Amb. to Malaysia 2004–10; Minister of Economy and Trade 2010–11 (resgnd with rest of cabinet at Pres.'s request following popular protests), Minister of Tourism 2011–. *Address:* Ministry of Tourism, BP 6642, rue Barada, Damascus, Syria (office). *Telephone:* (11) 2210122 (office). *Fax:* (11) 2242636 (office). *E-mail:* min-tourism@mail.sy (office). *Website:* www.syriatourism.org (office).

ASSOWEH, Ali Farah; Djibouti politician; b. 1965; Minister of Economy, Finance and Planning, in charge of Privatization 2005; Gov. for Djibouti IMF, World Bank, Int. Finance Corpn, Islamic Devt Bank 2005; Minister of Justice and Penal Affairs, in charge of Human Rights 2011–16.

ASTAKHOV, Pavel Alekseyevich, LLB, LLM, PhD; Russian barrister; b. 8 Sept. 1966, Moscow; m. Astakhova Svetlana; three s.; ed Higher KGB School, Univ. of Pittsburgh, USA; legal adviser, pvt. practice 1989–; has worked in Spain, France, USA, Greece, Czech Repub. –1990; Founder, Head Advocates' Group, P. Astakhov 1990–; Rep., Int. Business Centre, Moscow 1990–; currently Chair. Moscow City Bar Asscn; Presidential Commr for Children's Rights 2009–16; mem. Moscow City Collegiate of Advocates; mem. Moscow City Bar 1994–, Lawyers Bar of Moscow City 2002–, Paris Barrister Asscn 2005–; mem. Moscow Barrister Chamber; mem. Expert Advisory Council for Chair. of Accounts Chamber; mem. European (Brussels) Court of Arbitration and Mediation; mem. Arbitration Tribunal for Russian Union of Industrialists and Entrepreneurs; mem. Public Chamber Comm. for Communications, Information Policy; est. Pravo TV (production group); Prof., TGP faculty, Moscow MVD Univ.; Hon. Lawyer of Russia Medal 2001, Femida Award 2004, Person of the Year 2005. *Radio:* Barrister Defence Methods. *Television includes:* Chas Suda 2003, Defence. *Publications include:* Pravopisnye istiny ili levosudie dlja vseh 2000, Chas Suda 2003, Legal Truths or Left Judgment for Everyone, Counter Actions Against Raider Acquisitions, Your Lawyer P.Astakhov series, Raider 2007, Mayor. *Leisure interests:* travelling, hunting, writing, diving. *Website:* www.astakhov.ru.

ASTORI SARAGOSA, Danilo Ángel; Uruguayan economist and politician; *Minister of Economy and Finance;* b. 23 April 1940, Montevideo; m. Claudia Hugo; four c.; ed Univ. of the Repub., Montevideo; econs researcher in govt agric. agencies and econ. consultant to UN agencies 1961–89; consultant to Head of Frente Amplio party 1984; f. Asamblea Uruguay party 1994; elected as Senator 1995–2000, re-elected 2000–05; Minister of Economy and Finance 2005–08, 2015–; Vice-Pres. 2010–15. *Address:* Ministry of Economy and Finance, Colonia 1089, 3°, 11100 Montevideo, Uruguay (office). *Telephone:* (2) 7122910 (office). *Fax:* (2) 7122919 (office). *E-mail:* seprimef@mef.gub.uy (office). *Website:* www.mef.gub.uy (office).

ÅSTRÖM, Jan, MSc; Swedish business executive; b. 21 March 1956; m. Marana Makela; two c.; ed Royal Swedish Inst. of Tech. Stockholm; Paper Mill Man. Modo Paper, Husum Mill 1989–93; Man. Dir Svenska Cellulosa Aktiebolaget (SCA) Packaging 1993–96, Business Group Pres. SCA Fine Paper, Germany 1996–99; Pres. and CEO Modo Paper AB, Stockholm 1999–2000; Exec. Vice-Pres. and Deputy CEO SCA 2000–02, Pres. and CEO 2002–07; Owner Boxen Media; Pres. and CEO Munksjö AB 2008–18; Environmental Man. of the Year 2004.

ASYLMURATOVA, Altynai; Kazakhstani ballerina and artistic director; *Artistic Director, Astana Opera;* b. 1962, Alma-Ata (now Almaty); m. Konstantin Zaklinsky; one d.; ed Vaganova Ballet School, Leningrad (now St Petersburg); dancer with Kirov (now Mariinsky) Ballet 1980, then Prin. Dancer; numerous foreign tours including Paris 1982, USA, Canada 1987; Artistic Dir, Vaganova Ballet Acad, St. Petersburg 2000–13, Astana Opera (ballet) 2015–; Rector Kazakhstan Acad. of Choreography 2016–; Honoured Artist of Russia 1983, Baltika Prize 1998, Golden Sophit 1999, People's Artist of Russia 2001. *Roles include:* Odette/Odile in Swan Lake, Shirin in Legend of Love, Kitzi in Don Quixote, Aurora in Sleeping Beauty, Nike in Boyaderka, Giselle. *Address:* Astana Opera, 010000 Nur-Sultan, ul. Kunaev 1, Kazakhstan (office). *Telephone:* (7172) 70-96-20 (office). *E-mail:* astanaopera.doc@gmail.com (office). *Website:* www.astanaopera.kz (office).

ATABAY, Zia; American (b. Iranian) media entrepreneur; *CEO, National Iranian Television;* m. Parvin; fmr singer; first hit record aged 18; fmr exec. and Gen. Man. CBS Records, Tehran; moved to Europe 1980, lived in Sweden, Spain and UK; settled in Los Angeles, USA 1986; talk show host, cable TV late 1990s; Founder-Pres. and CEO, Nat. Iranian TV (NITV) 2000–. *Address:* National Iranian Television (NITV), 6723 Variel Avenue, Canoga Park, CA 91303, USA (office). *Telephone:* (818) 835-9800 (office). *Fax:* (818) 835-9699 (office). *E-mail:* zia@nitv.tv (office). *Website:* www.nitv.tv/index.php/zia-atabay (office).

ATAKHANOV, Shamil Yesenjanovich; Kyrgyzstani politician; b. 22 July 1948, Uzgen, Osh Oblast; ed Frunze (now Bishkek) Polytechnical Inst., USSR Ministry of Internal Affairs Acad. and Moscow State Inst. of Int. Relations (MGIMO) Int. Business School, Moscow, Russian SFSR; electrical engineer 1971–72; served in Soviet Army 1972–73; worked in Komsomol and CP posts in Kyrgyz SSR 1973–84; head of dept for combating organized crime, Ministry of Internal Affairs, Kyrgyz SSR 1986–87; head of admin in trade-financial orgs of Frunze State Municipal Enterprise 1987–88; Deputy Head, then Acting Head of Internal Affairs section, Frunze City; Gen. Dir of 'Inter-Bishkek' jt venture 1991–2005, 2005–10; First Deputy Mayor of Bishkek May–Aug. 2005; Deputy Prime Minister 2010–13 (resgnd); Acting Sec. of Defence Council 2011–13; Chair. State Cttee for Nat. Security 2011–13; mem. Social Democratic Party of Kyrgyzstan (SDPK—Kyrgyzstandyn Sotsial-Demokratiyalyk Partiyasy). *Address:* Social Democratic Party of Kyrgyzstan (Kyrgyzstandyn Sotsial-Demokratiyalyk Partiyasy), 720000 Bishkek, Shabdan Batyr 46D, Kyrgyzstan (office). *Telephone:* (312) 53-16-84 (office). *Fax:* (312) 53-16-87 (office). *E-mail:* sdpkkenesh@gmail.com (office). *Website:* www.sdpk.kg (office).

ATALLAH, Walid; Lebanese fashion designer; b. Beirut; ed Univ. of Chicago, USA; showed first collection in Dubai 1996; first US show at Couture Fashion Week, New York 2009; house now has branches in Al Ain (UAE), Qatar, Lebanon, Saudi Arabia and Libya; best known for evening and bridal designs, often incorporating diamonds, precious gems and Swarovski crystals; launched W prêt-à-porter line; mem. Advisory Bd, Dubai Fashion Week; French Asscn of Fashion Designers Excellence in Int. Design Award. *Address:* Ground Floor, Sheikh Hamdan Building, Al Maktoum Street, PO Box 22855, Deira, Dubai, United Arab Emirates (office). *Telephone:* (4) 2226172 (office). *Fax:* (4) 2226706 (office). *E-mail:* info@walid-atallah.com (office). *Website:* www.walid-atallah.com (office).

ATAMAN, Kutluğ, MFA; Turkish artist and film director; b. 16 Oct. 1961, Istanbul; ed Univ. of California, Los Angeles, USA; works held in major int. collections, including MoMA New York, Tate Modern, London, Thyssen-Bornemisza Art Contemporary, Vienna, Dimitris Daskalopoulos Collection, Athens, Carnegie Museum, Pittsburgh; art works have been shown at Venice Biennales 1999, Documenta 2002, biennials in Istanbul 1997, 2003, 2007, Berlin 2001, São Paulo 2002, 2010; f. Inst. for the Readjustment of Clocks (contemporary art production and exhibition org.); Chair. Jury, Istanbul Int. Film Festival 2009; Carnegie Prize, Carnegie Museum of Art, Pittsburgh 2004, European Cultural Fund 'Routes' Princess Margriet Award for cultural diversity 2011. *Films:* Serpent's Tale (Karanlık Sular) (Turkish Film Critics Asscn Best Film, Dir and Screenplay, Istanbul Int. Film Festival, Ankara Int. Festival Jury Prize) 1994, Lola+Bilidikid (New Festival Best Film Prize, New York, Berlin Festival Jury Special Prize) 1998, 2 Girls (Best Dir and Best Film prizes at Ankara and Antalya Film Festivals, Best Film, Asian Film Festival, India) 2005, Journey to the Moon 2009, Kuzu (also writer and screenplay) 2014. *Address:* SALT Galata, Bankalar Caddesi 11, Karaköy 34420 Istanbul (office); Institute for the Readjustment of Clocks, Gazeteci Erol Dernek Sokak, No 3/7 Beyoglu, 34433 Istanbul, Turkey. *Telephone:* (212) 334-2200 (office); (212) 259-2225. *E-mail:* salt.research@saltonline.org (office); office@witchfilms.com. *Website:* www.saltresearch.org (office); www.witchfilms.com; www.kutlugataman.com.

ATAMBAYEV, Almazbek; Kyrgyzstani engineer, politician and fmr head of state; b. 17 Sept. 1956, Alamudun, Chui Oblast, Kyrgyz SSR, USSR; m. Raisa Atambayeva; three s. three d.; ed Moscow Inst. of Man.; engineer with Kyrgyz SSR Ministry of Communications 1980–81; Sr Engineer with DU-4, Frunze (now Bishkek) 1981–83; held position in Presidium of Supreme Soviet, Kyrgyz SSR 1983–87; Deputy Chair. Exec. Cttee Pervomaisky Dist Council of People's Deputies, Frunze 1987–89; Founder and Head, Forum (business firm) 1989; Deputy in Supreme Council (Jogorku Kenesh—Parl.) 1995–2000; Gen. Dir Kyrgyzavtomash 1997–99; Chair. Kyrgyzstandyn Sotsial-Demokratiyalyk Partiyasy (Social Democratic Party of Kyrgyzstan) 1999; unsuccessful presidential cand. 2000; Minister of Industry, Trade and Tourism 2005–06 (resgnd); Co-Chair. Opposition For Reforms movt 2006; Prime Minister March–Nov. 2007, 2010–11; Acting First Deputy Chair. of Interim Govt 2010; Pres. of Kyrgyzstan 2011–17; Hero of the Kyrgyz Repub. 2017; Dank Medal 1999. *Address:* c/o Kyrgyzstandyn Sotsial-Demokratiyalyk Partiyasy, 720000 Bishkek, Shabdan Batyr 46d, Kyrgyzstan. *E-mail:* press@sdpk.kg. *Website:* www.sdpk.kg.

ATAMQULOV, Beibit B., Cand.Econ.Sci; Kazakhstani engineer, diplomatist and politician; *Minister of Foreign Affairs;* b. 19 May 1964, Almati region; m. Saparbaeva Bagila Adykhanovna; two s. one d.; ed Kazakh Polytechnic Inst., St Petersburg State Univ. of Econs and Finance; began career as smelter, Copper Smelting Factory, A. Zavenyagin Mining and Metallurgical Plant, Norilsk 1985–86; worked as smelter, shift foreman, sr foreman, leading engineer, and deputy head of dept, Chimkent Lead Plant 1986–91; Chief Specialist and Dir, Chermetexport, Republican Foreign Econ. Enterprise Kazmetallexport, later becoming First Deputy Dir Gen., Kazakhstan Sauda (foreign trade co.) 1991–95; First Deputy Dir Gen., Karaganda Metallurgical Plant, Temirtau 1995–96; engaged in private entrepreneurship 1996–2006; Counsellor and later Minister-Counsellor, Embassy in Moscow 2006–07; Minister-Counsellor, Embassy in Tehran 2007–08; Consul Gen. of Kazakhstan, Frankfurt am Main 2008–10; Amb. to Malaysia (also accred to Philippines, Indonesia and Brunei) 2010–12; Exec. Sec., Ministry of Industry and New Tech. 2012–14; Exec. Sec., Ministry for Investment and Devt 2014–15; Akim (Gov.), South Kazakhstan Oblast 2015–16; Minister of Defence and Aerospace Industry 2016–18, of Foreign Affairs 2018–; several honours including Kumet Order of Honour 2013, Parasat Order of Excellence 2018. *Address:* Ministry of Foreign Affairs, 010000 Nur-Sultan, D. Kunaev kösh. 31, Kazakhstan (office). *Telephone:* (7172) 72-05-18 (office). *Fax:* (7172) 72-05-16 (home). *E-mail:* mfa@mfa.kz (office). *Website:* www.mfa.kz (office).

ATANASIU, Teodor; Romanian politician; b. 23 Sept. 1962, Cugir, Alba Co.; m. 1st Maria Atanasiu (divorced 2005); m. 2nd Laura Maria Bisboaca; one d.; ed Faculty of Mechanics, Cluj-Napoca Polytechnic, Open Univ. Business School; engineer, U.M. Cugir 1987–95, Chief of Workshop 1995–96, Dir 1997–2001; joined Partidul Naţional Liberal (PNL—Nat. Liberal Party) 1990, Sec. Liberal Cugir 1990–92, Pres. Liberal Cugir 1992–93, Pres. Alba County PNL chapter 1993–, Vice-Pres. PNL 2006–08, mem. Perm. Cen. Bureau 2001–02, 2005–06, Exec. Cttee 2005–; briefly cand. for PNL presidency 2014; Councillor, Cugir Local Council 1992–96, Alba Co. Council 1996–2004 (Pres. of Council –2004); Parl. Expert, Chamber of Deputies 2001–04; Minister of Nat. Defence 2004–06 (resgnd); Dir APA-CTTA SA, Alba Iulia 1996–97, FPS (State Devt Fund), Bucharest 1997–2000; Head Authority for State Assets Recovery –2008; Deputy Dir-Gen., SC Cugir SA 1997–2001; Man. Palplast Sibiu SA 2001–04, B&M Direct Consulting Cugir 2003–04; mem. Chamber of Deputies, Alba County 2008–09; cand. for Pres. of Alba Co. Council 2012. *Address:* National Liberal Party (Partidul Naţional Liberal), 011866 Bucharest 1, Bd Aviatorilor 86, Romania (office). *Telephone:* (21) 2310795 (office). *Fax:* (21) 2310796 (office). *E-mail:* dre@pnl.ro (office). *Website:* www.pnl.ro (office).

ATANASOF, Alfredo Nestor; Argentine politician; b. 24 Nov. 1949, La Plata; official, Gen. Confed. of Labour; Minister of Labour, Employment and Social Affairs; Chief Cabinet of Ministers 2002–03; Nat. Deputy for Buenos Aires 2009–13, Pres. Comm. for Foreign Affairs, Chamber of Deputies; mem. Gremios Solidarios Group. *E-mail:* info@alfredoatanasof.com.ar. *Website:* alfredoatanasof.com.ar.

ATANGANA MEBARA, Jean-Marie; Cameroonian politician; b. 27 March 1954; Minister of Higher Educ. 1997–2002; Pres. Int. Inst. of Admin. Sciences 2001–04; Minister of State and Sec.-Gen. Presidency of Cameroon 2002–06; Minister of State and Minister of External Relations 2006–07; arrested for embezzlement of public funds 2008, acquitted of those charges and new charges issued against him May 2012.

ATAYEVA, Aksoltan Toreevna; Turkmenistani physician, politician and diplomatist; *Permanent Representative, United Nations;* b. 6 Nov. 1944, Ashgabat; m. Tchary Pirmoukhamedov 1969; one s. one d.; ed Turkmenistan State Medical Inst., Ashgabat; doctor, Hosp. Number 1, Ashgabat 1968–79, Asst to Chief Doctor 1979–80; Vice-Dir Regional Health Dept, Ashgabat 1980–85; Vice-Minister of Health 1985–90, Minister 1990–94; Minister of Social Security 1994–95; Amb. and Perm. Rep. to UN, New York 1995– (also accred as Amb. to Cuba 2008–, Brazil 2011–, Bolivia 2013–); mem. Democratic Party 1992–, Khalk Maslakhaty (Supreme People's Council of Turkmenistan) 1993–; Pres. Trade Unions of Turkmenistan 1994–95; Hon. Assoc. of Int. Acad. of Computer Sciences and Systems, Kiev, Ukraine 1993; Neutrality Order, Gairat Medal 1992, Medal for Love of Motherland 1996, Order of Gurbansoltan Eje 1997, Order of Bitaraplyk 1999, Order for the Great of Independent Turkmenistan; Hon. DrMed (Russian Scientific Research Inst. for Social Hygiene and Health Care Man.). *Publications include:* 108 publs and two monographs on health and maternity care. *Leisure interests:* books, arts, sports. *Address:* Permanent Mission of Turkmenistan to the United Nations, 866 United Nations Plaza, Suite 424, New York, NY 10017, USA (office). *Telephone:* (212) 486-8908 (office). *Fax:* (212) 486-2521 (office). *E-mail:* turkmenistan@un.int (office). *Website:* www.turkmenistanun.org (office).

ATHEL, Saleh Abdul Rahman al-, BSc, MSc, PhD; Saudi Arabian professor of mechanical engineering and fmr university president; b. 1940, Al-Rus; m.; several c.; ed Stanford Univ., Univ. of Texas, USA; joined teaching staff of King Saud Univ., Vice-Dean, Coll. of Eng 1974–75, Dean 1975–76, Vice-Pres. for Grad. Studies and Research 1976–84; Pres. King Abdulaziz City for Science and Tech., Riyadh 1984–2004; mem. American Soc. of Mechanical Engineers, UN World Comm. on Environment and Devt, UN Advisory Cttee on Science and Tech. for Devt; mem. Saudi Working Cttee for Educ. Policy, Scientific Cttee Pio Manza Int. Research Centre; fmr mem. Exec. Cttee Org. for Islamic Co-operation Ministerial Cttee of Scientific and Tech. Co-operation; mem. ASME; Fellow, Islamic World Acad. of Sciences (Vice-Pres. 1986–90). *Publications:* a book on eng structures, trans of three books, more than 60 articles. *Address:* Islamic World Academy of Sciences, 17 Djibouti Street, Sixth Circle, PO Box 830036, Amman 11183, Jordan (office). *Telephone:* (6) 5522104 (office). *Fax:* (6) 5511803 (office). *E-mail:* ias@go.com.jo (office). *Website:* www.iasworld.org/prof-saleh-al-athel (office).

ATHERTON, David, OBE, MA, LRAM, LTCL, LGSM; British conductor; *Conductor Laureate, Hong Kong Philharmonic Orchestra;* b. 3 Jan. 1944, Blackpool, Lancs.; s. of Robert Atherton and Lavinia Atherton; m. 1st Ann Gianetta Drake 1970; one s. two d.; m. 2nd Eleanor Ann Roth 2012; ed Univ. of Cambridge; Répétiteur, Royal Opera House 1967–68, Resident Conductor 1968–79; Co-founder and Artistic Dir London Sinfonietta 1968–73, 1989–91; conductor at Royal Opera House and Henry Wood Promenade Concerts, London 1968; debut, Royal Festival Hall, London 1969, La Scala, Milan 1976, San Francisco Opera 1978, Metropolitan Opera, New York 1984; has conducted performances in Europe, Middle East, Far East, Australasia, N America; Artistic Dir and Conductor, London Stravinsky Festival 1979–82, Ravel/Varèse Festival 1983–84; Prin. Conductor and Artistic Adviser, Royal Liverpool Philharmonic Orchestra 1980–83, Prin. Guest Conductor 1983–86; Music Dir and Prin. Conductor, San Diego Symphony Orchestra 1980–87; Prin. Guest Conductor, BBC Symphony Orchestra 1985–89; Music Dir and Prin. Conductor, Hong Kong Philharmonic Orchestra 1989–2000, Conductor Laureate 2000–; Founder and Artistic Dir Mainly Mozart Festival 1989–2013; Prin. Guest Conductor, BBC Nat. Orchestra of Wales 1994–97; Co-founder, Pres. and Artistic Dir Global Music Network 1998–2002; Conductor of the Year Award, Composers' Guild of GB 1971, Edison Award 1973, Grand Prix du Disque 1977, Koussevitzky Award 1981, Int. Record Critics' Award 1982, Prix Caecilia 1982. *Publications include:* The Complete Instrumental and Chamber Music of Arnold Schoenberg and Roberto Gerhard (ed.) 1973, Pandora and Don Quixote Suites by Roberto Gerhard (ed.) 1973; contrib. to The Musical Companion 1978, The New Grove Dictionary 1981. *Leisure interests:* travel, films, theatre, computers. *E-mail:* hugh@kaylormanagement.com (office).

ATHERTON, Michael Andrew, OBE; British broadcaster, journalist, author and fmr professional cricketer; *Cricket Correspondent, The Times;* b. 23 March 1968, Newton Heath, Manchester, Lancs.; s. of Alan Atherton and Wendy Atherton; ed Manchester Grammar School and Downing Coll., Cambridge; right-hand opening batsman; leg spin bowler; played for Cambridge Univ. 1987–89 (Capt. 1988–89), Lancs. 1987–2001, MCC 1987–90; England Test debut against Australia 1989; toured Australia 1990–91, 1994–95 (Capt.); ODI debut against India 1990, 54 ints (43 as Capt.) to 20 Aug. 1998; toured SA 1995–96, Zimbabwe and NZ 1996–97, West Indies 1998; mem. team touring Australia 1998–99, SA 1999–2000, Pakistan and Sri Lanka 2000–01 (retd); played in 115 Tests, took 2 wickets and scored 7,728 runs (16 centuries), highest score 185 not out, average 37.69, best bowling (innings) 1/20, (match) 1/20; ODIs: 54 matches, scored 1,791 runs, average 35.11, highest score 127; First-class: 336 matches 21,929 runs, average 40.83, highest score 268 not out, best bowling (innings) 6/78; fmr journalist, Sunday Telegraph; Cricket Corresp., The Times 2008–; cricket commentator for Channel 4 TV 2002–05; worked as a commentator for BBC Radio and Talksport on test matches outside England 2002–05; mem. Sky Sports commentary team 2005–; Jack Hobbs Memorial Award as the Outstanding Schoolboy Cricketer at under-15 level 1983, Wisden Cricketer of the Year 1991, Cornhill Player of the Year 1994, Sports Journalist of the Year, British Press Awards 2010, Sports Writer of the Year, Sports Journalists Asscn 2011. *Publications:* A Test of Cricket 1995, Opening Up (autobiography) 2002, Gambling: A Story of Triumph and Disaster 2006, Atherton's Ashes 2009. *Leisure interests:* decent novels, good movies, food, wine, travel, most sports, music. *Address:* The Times, 1 Virginia Street, London, E98 1XY, England (office); c/o Sky Sports, British Sky Broadcasting Ltd, Grant Way, Isleworth, TW7 5QD, England (office). *Telephone:* (20) 7782-5000 (The Times) (office). *E-mail:* contact@mikeatherton.co.uk. *Website:* www.timesonline.co.uk/tol/sport/cricket (office); www.mikeatherton.co.uk.

ATHY, Simeon Malachi, BEcons; Ni-Vanuatu economist, banking executive and central banker; *Governor, Reserve Bank of Vanuatu;* ed Univ. of Papua New Guinea; held various positions at Reserve Bank of Vanuatu 1991–2003, including Dir Research and Statistics Dept; Dir-Gen., Ministry of Finance and Econ. Man. 2003–08, Dir-Gen. Prime Minister's Office 2008–13; Gov. Reserve Bank of Vanuatu 2013–, also mem. Bd of Dirs and mem. Bd of Govs IMF; apptd Chair., Millennium Steering Cttee 2000, Financial Services Advisory Group 2006; fmr Chair. Air Vanuatu; fmr Bd mem. Vanuatu Financial Services Comm. *Publications include:* 20 Years of Central Banking (co-ed); numerous articles in professional publs. *Address:* Reserve Bank of Vanuatu, PMB 9062, Port Vila, Vanuatu (office). *Telephone:* 23333 (office). *Fax:* 24231 (office). *E-mail:* rbvinfo@rbv.gov.vu (office). *Website:* www.rbv.gov.vu (office).

ATILIO BENÍTEZ PARADA, Gen. José; Salvadorean army officer, government official and diplomatist; *Ambassador to Germany;* fmr Insp.-Gen. of Armed Forces, also Commdr, Logistics Support Command of the Armed Forces and Commdr, Artillery Brigade; veteran of missions to Iraq including as Commdr, Cuscatlan Bn, Ninth Contingent in Iraq; Deputy Minister of Nat. Defence –2011, Minister 2011–14; Amb. to Spain 2013–15, to Germany 2015–. *Address:* Embassy of El Salvador, Joachim-Karnatz-Allee 47, 10557 Berlin, Germany (office). *Telephone:* (30) 2064660 (office). *Fax:* (30) 20646629 (office). *E-mail:* embasalvarfa@googlemail.com (office). *Website:* www.botschaft-elsalvador.de (office).

ATKINS, Dame Eileen June, DBE, CBE; British actress; b. 16 June 1934; d. of Arthur Thomas Atkins and of Annie Ellen Elkins; m. Bill Shepherd (died 2016); ed Latymer Grammar School, Edmonton and Guildhall School of Music and Drama; Hon. DLitt; Evening Standard Award for best film script 1999; OFFIE Award for Best Actress 2013; numerous other awards in the USA. *Stage appearances include:* Twelfth Night, Richard III, The Tempest 1962, The Killing of Sister George (Best Actress, Evening Standard Awards) 1965, The Cocktail Party 1968, Vivat! Vivat Regina! (Variety Award) 1970, Suzanne Andler, As You Like It 1973, St Joan 1977, Passion Play 1981, Medea 1986, The Winter's Tale, Cymbeline (Laurence Olivier Award for Best Actress) 1988, Mountain Language 1988, A Room of One's Own (New York Drama Critics Circle Special Citation) 1989, Exclusive 1989, The Night of the Iguana 1992, Vita and Virginia 1993, Indiscretions 1995, John Gabriel Borkman 1996, A Delicate Balance (Evening Standard Award for Best Actress 1997) 1997, The Unexpected Man (Laurence Olivier Award for Best Actress) 1998, 2000–01, Honor (Laurence Olivier Award) 2003, The Retreat from Moscow 2003–04, There Came a Gypsy Riding 2007, The Sea 2008, The Female of the Species 2008, All That Fall 2013. *Films include:* Equus 1974, The Dresser 1984, Let Him Have It 1990, Wolf 1994, Cold Comfort Farm 1995, Jack and Sarah 1995, The Avengers 1998, Women Talking Dirty 1999, Gosford Park 2002, The Hours 2003, Cold Mountain 2003, Vanity Fair 2004, Ask the Dust 2006, Scenes of a Sexual Nature 2006, Evening 2007, Wild Target 2008, Last Chance Harvey 2008, Robin Hood 2010, The Scapegoat 2012, Beautiful Creatures 2013, Magic in the Moonlight 2014, ChickLit 2016, Simon Amstell: Carnage 2017. *Radio work includes:* adaptation of To the Lighthouse 2000, Restless 2009. *TV appearances include:* The Duchess of Malfi, Sons and Lovers, Smiley's People, Nelly's Version, The Burston Rebellion, Breaking Up, The Vision, Mrs Pankhurst in In My Defence (series) 1990, A Room of One's Own 1990, The Lost Language of Cranes 1993, The Maitlands 1993, Talking Heads 2 1998, Madame Bovary 2000, The Sleeper 2000, Wit 2001, Bertie and Elizabeth 2001, The Lives of Animals 2002, Cranford (BAFTA for Best Actress, Emmy Award for Best Supporting Actress) 2007, Waking the Dead 2007, Ballet Shoes 2007, Psychoville (series) 2009–11, Upstairs Downstairs (series) 2010, Poirot: Murder on the Orient Express 2010, Doc Martin (series) 2011–15, Vicious (series) 2016, The Crown (series) 2016. *Play:* as writer: Vita and Virginia. *Co-creator:* Upstairs Downstairs, The House of Eliott TV series. *Adaptation:* Mrs Dalloway (Evening Standard Film Award) 1999. *Leisure interests:* books, cats. *Address:* c/o Paul Lyon Maris, ICM, Oxford House, 76 Oxford Street, London, W1D 1BS, England (office); 2 The Moorings, Strand on the Green, Chiswick, London, W4 3PG, England. *Telephone:* (20) 7636-6565 (office); (20) 8994-6577. *Fax:* (20) 7323-0101 (office).

ATKINSON, Conrad, NDD, ATD, ADF, Cert RAS (Hons); American (b. British) artist and academic; *Professor Emeritus of Art, University of California, Davis;* b. 15 June 1940, Cleator Moor, Cumbria, England; m. Margaret Harrison 1967; two d.; ed Whitehaven Grammar School, Carlisle and Liverpool Coll. of Art and Royal Acad. Schools, London; Granada Fellow in Fine Art 1967–68; Churchill Fellow in Fine Art 1972; Fellow in Fine Art, Northern Arts 1974–76; Lecturer, Slade School of Fine Art 1976–79; Visual Art Adviser to GLC 1982–86; Power Lecturer, Univ. of Sydney, Australia 1983; Artist-in-Residence, London Borough of Lewisham 1984–86, Univ. of Edinburgh 1986–87; Adviser, Visual Arts Policy, Labour Party 1985–86; Adviser, California Arts Council; Distinguished Visiting Prof., Courtauld Inst., London; Prof. Emer. of Art, Univ. of California, Davis; Artist in Residence, Villeroy and Boch, Stockholm, Sweden 2000; Churchill Fellow; Hon. Fellow, Univ. of Cumbria 2006. *Leisure interest:* rock and roll music. *Address:* c/o Ronald Feldman Gallery, 31 Mercer Street, New York, NY 10013, USA (home); The Cottage, Boustead Hill, Carlisle, Cumbria, CA5 6AA, England (home). *Telephone:* (1228) 576463 (home). *E-mail:* cratkinson@ucdavis.edu (office). *Website:* www.conradatkinson.com.

ATKINSON, Kate, MBE, BA; British writer and playwright; b. 1951, York; m. (divorced); two d.; ed Univ. of Dundee; fmrly home help, teacher and short story writer for women's magazines; writer 1988–; Woman's Own Short Story Competition 1986, Ian St James Award 1993, E.M. Forster Award, American Acad. of Arts and Letters 1997, Waterstones UK Author of the Year 2013. *Plays include:* Nice 1996, Abandonment 2000. *Publications include:* Behind the Scenes at the Museum (novel) (Whitbread First Novel Award and Book of the Year 1995, Boeker Prize, SA, Livre Book of the Year, France) 1995, Human Croquet (novel) 1997, Abandonment (book and play) 2000, Emotionally Weird (novel) 2001, Not the End of the World (short stories) 2002, Case Histories (novel) 2004, One Good Turn (novel) 2006, When Will There be Good News? (British Book Award for Best Read of the Year 2009) 2008, Started Early, Took My Dog 2010, Life After Life (Costa Novel Award 2013, South Bank Sky Arts Literature Prize 2014, Independent Booksellers Book of the Year Winner (UK) 2014, Indies Choice Book of the Year Winner—ABA (USA) 2014) 2013, A God in Ruins (Costa Novel Award 2015) 2015, Transcription 2018; contrib. of short stories to Daily Telegraph, BBC 2, BBC Radio 4, Daily Express, Daily Mail, Scotsman. *Address:* c/o Transworld Publishers Ltd,

20 Vauxhall Bridge Road, London, SW1V 2SA, England. *Website:* www.booksattransworld.co.uk; www.kateatkinson.co.uk.

ATKINSON, Roger, BA, PhD; British/American environmental scientist and academic; *Professor Emeritus of Atmospheric Chemistry, University of California, Riverside;* ed Univ. of Cambridge; Post-doctoral Researcher, Nat. Research Council of Canada, Ottawa 1969–71, York Univ. Centre for Research in Experimental Space Science, Downsview, Ont. 1971–72; Asst Research Chemist, Statewide Air Pollution Research Center, Univ. of California, Riverside 1972–76, Assoc. Research Chemist 1976–78, 1980–81, Research Chemist 1981, Prof. of Environmental Science and Chem. 1990, Assoc. Dir Dept of Environmental Sciences 1990–92, Interim Dir 1993–96, Dir 1996–2005, now Prof. Emer. of Atmospheric Chem.; Sr Scientist, Shell Research Ltd, Thornton Research Centre, Chester 1978–79; Sr Scientific Adviser, Environmental Research and Technology Inc., Westlake Village, Calif. 1979–80; mem. ACS, American Geophysical Union, AAAS. *Publications:* numerous specialist publs on atmospheric chem. *Address:* Air Pollution Research Center, University of California, Riverside, Fawcett Laboratory 123, Riverside, CA 92521-0312, USA (office). *E-mail:* roger.atkinson@ucr.edu (office). *Website:* www.chem.ucr.edu (office).

ATKINSON, Rowan Sebastian, CBE, MSc; British actor and writer; b. 6 Jan. 1955, Consett, Co. Durham; s. of Eric Atkinson and Ella Atkinson; m. Sunetra Sastry 1990; one s. one d.; ed Durham Cathedral Choristers' School, St Bees School and Univs of Newcastle and Oxford; Stage appearances include: Beyond a Joke, Hampstead 1978, Oxford Univ. revues at Edinburgh Fringe, one-man show, London 1981, The Nerd 1985, The New Revue 1986, The Sneeze 1988, Oliver! 2008–09, Quartermaine's Terms 2013. *Films:* Never Say Never Again 1983, The Tall Guy 1989, The Appointments of Dennis Jennings 1989, The Witches 1990, Four Weddings and a Funeral 1994, Hot Shots – Part Deux 1994, Bean: The Ultimate Disaster Movie 1997, Blackadder – Back and Forth 2000, Maybe Baby 2000, Rat Race 2002, Scooby Doo 2002, Johnny English 2003, Love Actually 2003, Mickey's PhilharMagic (voice) 2003, Keeping Mum 2005, Mr. Bean's Holiday 2007, Johnny English Reborn 2011. *Television includes:* Not the Nine O'Clock News 1979–82, Blackadder 1983, Blackadder II 1985, Blackadder the Third 1987, Blackadder Goes Forth 1989, Mr Bean (13 episodes) 1990–96, Rowan Atkinson on Location in Boston 1993, Full Throttle 1994, The Thin Blue Line 1995–96, Bean 1997, The Jubilee Girl 2002, Maigret 2016–. *Leisure interests:* motor cars, motor sport. *Address:* c/o PBJ Management Ltd, 22 Rathbone Street, London, W1T 1LA, England (office). *Telephone:* (20) 7054-5950 (office). *Fax:* (20) 7287-1191 (office). *E-mail:* general@pbjmgt.co.uk (office).

ATMAR, Mohammad Hanif, BA, MA; Afghan politician; b. 1968, Laghman Prov.; s. of Mohammad Asef Atmar; ed Univ. of York, UK; adviser to aid agencies in Afghanistan and Pakistan 1992–94; Program Man. Norwegian Cttee for Afghanistan 1994–2000; Deputy Dir-Gen. Int. Rescue Cttee 2000–02; Minister of Rural Rehabilitation and Devt 2002–06, of Educ. 2006–08, of Interior Affairs 2008–10; high-level adviser to int. orgs in Afghanistan 2010; mem. Hizb-i Haq wa Edalat (Right and Justice Party) 2011–; Nat. Security Adviser to Head of State 2014–18. *Publications include:* Development of Non-Governmental Organizations in Developing Countries, From Rhetoric to Reality, Humanitarian Aid, War and Peace in Afghanistan: What to Learn?, Politics and Humanitarian Aid in Afghanistan and Its Aftermath for the People of Afghanistan, Afghanistan or a Stray War in Afghanistan. *Address:* c/o Hizb-i Haq wa Edalat (Right and Justice Party), District 10, Kabul, Afghanistan. *Telephone:* 79-8333111 (mobile).

ATNAFU, Teklewold, BSc, MSc; Ethiopian politician and central banker; began career with Building Construction Authority; fmr Prof., Addis Ababa Univ.; joined Nat. Bank of Ethiopia (central bank) 1998, Gov. 2006–18; mem. House of People's Reps (Parl.) for Boloso Sore constituency 2005–06; mem. Southern Ethiopian Peoples' Democratic Movt.

ATRASH, Muhammad al-, PhD; Syrian banker, politician and international organization official; b. 13 Nov. 1934, Tartous; s. of Hassan Sayed al-Atrash and Aziza Sayed al-Atrash; m. Felicia al-Atrash 1958; two s. one d.; ed American Univ., Beirut, Lebanon, American Univ., USA, London School of Econs, UK; joined Cen. Bank of Syria 1963, Research Dept 1963, Head of Credit Dept 1966–70; Alt. Exec. Dir IMF 1970–73; Deputy Gov. Cen. Bank of Syria 1974; Exec. Dir IBRD 1974–76, IMF 1976–78; Del. to Second Cttee of UN Gen. Ass., to UNCTAD and other int. econ. confs 1963–70; part-time Lecturer, Univ. of Damascus 1963–70; mem. Deputies of IMF Interim Cttee of the Bd of Govs on Reform of Int. Monetary System 1972–74; Assoc. mem. IMF Interim Cttee 1974–76, ex officio mem. 1976–78; Minister of Economy and Foreign Trade 1980–82; Minister of Finance 2001–03. *Publications include:* articles in Al-Abhath (Quarterly of the American Univ. of Beirut) 1963, 1964, 1966; several articles on int. political economy, regional econs, Arab–Israeli conflict etc. *Leisure interests:* swimming, walking, reading books on history and literature.

ATTAF, Ahmed; Algerian diplomatist and politician; b. 10 July 1953, Ain Defla; ed Ecole Nationale d'Administration, Algiers; fmr Amb. to India and to Yugoslavia; Minister of Foreign Affairs 1996–99; Amb. to UK 2001–05; Co-founder Rassemblement National Démocratique (RND). *Address:* Rassemblement National Démocratique, BP 10, Cité des Asphodèles, Ben Aknoun, Algiers, Algeria. *Telephone:* (21) 91-64-10. *Fax:* (21) 91-47-40. *E-mail:* contact@rnd-dz.com. *Website:* www.rnd-dz.com.

ATTALI, Bernard; French business executive; *Senior Adviser, TPG Capital;* b. 1 Nov. 1943, Algiers; s. of Simon Attali and Fernande Abecassis; twin brother of Jacques Attali (q.v.); m. Hélène Scebat 1974; one d.; ed Lycée Gauthier, Algiers, Lycée Janson-de-Sailly, Paris, Faculté de Droit, Paris, Inst. d'Etudes Politiques, Paris and Ecole Nat. d'Admin; auditeur, Cour des Comptes 1968, adviser 1974; on secondment to Commissariat Général du Plan d'Equipement et de la Productivité 1972–74; Délégation à l'Aménagement du Térritoire et à l'Action Regionale (Datar) 1974–80, 1981–84; Finance Dir Soc. Club Mediterranée 1980–81; Pres. Regional Cttee of EEC 1981–84; Pres. Groupe des Assurances Nationales 1984–86; Pres. Banque pour l'Industrie Française 1984–86; Adviser on European Affairs, Commercial Union Assurance 1986–88, Chair. Air France 1988–93; Pres. Supervisory Council, Sociétés Epargne de France 1986–88, Commercial Union Lard 1986–88; Pres. Euroberlin 1988, Union de Transports Aériens 1990, Asscn des Transporteurs Aériens Européens 1991; Vice-Pres. Supervisory Bd BIGT 1995; Admin. Aérospatiale 1989, Air Inter 1990; Chief Adviser, Revenue Court 1991–93; Chair. Supervisory Bd Banque Arjil (part of Lagadère) 1993–96; Chair. Bankers Trust Co. France 1996–99; Vice-Pres. Investment Banking in Europe Div., Deutsche Bank 1999–2000; currently Sr Adviser, TPG Capital; mem. European Bd Orrick Rambaud Martel, Bd Air Canada, Bd Baccarat; Commdr, Légion d'honneur; Commdr, Ordre nat. du Mérite. *Publication:* Les Guerres du Ciel 1994. *Address:* TPG, 6, rue Christophe Colomb, 75008 Paris (office). *E-mail:* contact@bernardattali.com; battali@tpg.com (office). *Website:* www.bernardattali.com; www.tpg.com (office).

ATTALI, Jacques, PhD; French international bank official and writer; *President, Attali et Associés;* b. 1 Nov. 1943, Algiers; s. of Simon Attali and Fernande Abecassis; twin brother of Bernard Attali (q.v.); m. Elisabeth Allain 1981; one s. one d.; ed Ecole Polytechnique, Inst. d'Etudes Politiques de Paris, Ecoles des Mines de Paris, Ecole Nat. d'Admin; started career as mining engineer, then Lecturer in Econs, Ecole Polytechnique; Auditeur, Council of State; Adviser to Pres. François Mitterrand 1981–91; State Councillor 1989–91; Pres. EBRD, London 1991–93; Pres. Attali et Associés (ACA) 1994–; mem. Council of State 1981–90, 1993–; Admin. KeeBoo 2000–; Pres. Attali Comm. (est. to evaluate means of liberalising econ. growth in France) 2007–; columnist, L'Express magazine; mem. Supervisory Bd, Kepler Capital Markets, Geneva 2012; Dr hc (Univ. of Kent, Univ. of Haifa). *Publications include:* Analyse économique de la vie politique 1972, Modèles politiques 1973, Anti-économique (with Marc Guillaume) 1974, La parole et l'outil 1975, Bruits, Essai sur l'économie politique de la musique 1976, La nouvelle économie française 1977, L'ordre cannibale 1979, Les trois mondes 1981, Histoires du temps 1982, La figure de Fraser 1984, Un homme d'influence 1985, Au propre et au Figuré 1988, La vie éternelle (novel) 1989, Millennium: Winners and Losers in the Coming World Order 1991, 1492 1991, Verbatim (Tome I) 1993, Europe(s) 1994, Verbatim (Tome II) 1995, Economie de l'Apocalypse 1995, Tome III 1996, Chemins de Sagesse 1996, Au delà de nulle part 1997, Dictionnaire du XXIe siècle 1998, Les portes du ciel 1999, La femme du menteur 1999 (novel), Fraternités 1999, Blaise Pascal ou le génie français 2000, Bruits 2001, Nouv'Elles 2002 (novel), L'homme nomade 2003, La Confrérie des Eveillés 2004 (novel), Karl Marx ou l'esprit du Monde 2004, Une brève histoire de l'avenir 2007, La crise, et après? 2008, The Economic History of the Jewish People 2010. *Address:* Attali et Associés 5 Avenue de Messine, 75008 Paris, France (office). *Telephone:* 1-53-57-38-38 (office). *E-mail:* sec@attali.com. *Website:* www.attali.com/en (office).

ATTALIDES, Michalis A., BSc (Econ.), PhD; Cypriot sociologist, academic, university administrator and diplomatist; *Rector Emeritus, University of Nicosia;* b. 1941; m.; two c.; ed London School of Econs, UK and Princeton Univ., USA; Lecturer in Sociology, Univ. of Leicester 1966–68; sociologist, Cyprus Town and Country Planning Project 1968–70; counterpart of UNESCO expert, Social Research Centre, Cyprus 1971, 1973–74; mil. service 1972; Guest Lecturer Otto Suhr Inst., Free Univ. of Berlin 1974–75; journalist 1975–76; worked in Int. Relations Service, House of Reps of Cyprus 1977–89, Dir 1979–89; Amb. and Dir of Political Affairs Division B (Cyprus question), Ministry of Foreign Affairs 1989–91; Amb. of Cyprus to France (also accred to Morocco, Portugal and Spain) 1991–95, Amb. to Belgium (also accred to Luxembourg) and Perm. Del. of Cyprus to EU 1995–98, High Commr to UK 1998–2000; Perm. Sec., Ministry of Foreign Affairs 2000–01; Rep. of Govt of Cyprus to European Convention 2002–03; Dean, School of Humanities, Social Sciences and Law, InterCollege, Nicosia 2003–06, Rector 2006–07; Rector, Univ. of Nicosia 2007–16, then Rector Emer., Jean Monnet Chair. ad Personam in Diplomacy and Politics of European Integration 2011–14, Chair. Jean Monnet Centre of Excellence 2015–18; Chair. Cyprus Rectors Conf. 2011–13; Grand Officier, Ordre nat. du Mérite. *Publications include:* Social Change and Urbanization in Cyprus: A Study of Nicosia 1971, Cyprus: Nationalism and International Politics 1980, Cyprus: State, Society and International Environment (in Greek) 2009; articles on Cyprus, Greece, Turkey and EU. *Address:* PO Box 24005, 1700 Nicosia (office); 8 Sachtouris Street, 1080 Nicosia, Cyprus (home). *Telephone:* (22) 841572 (office); (22) 680808 (home). *Website:* www.unic-jean-monnet.eu (office).

ATALLAH, Béatrice Jeanine; Malagasy lawyer and politician; ed Centre d'études diplomatiques et stratégiques, Antananarivo; served three years as magistrate, Antananarivo Court of Appeal; fmr Office Man., Ministry of Finances and Budget; mem. Nat. Electoral Council (CNE, Conseil Nat. Electoral) 2002–09, (abolished and its duties transferred to CENIT 2010), Pres. Comm. Electorale Nat. Indépendante pour la Transition (CENIT) 2012–15; Minister of Foreign Affairs 2015–17.

ATTALLAH, Naim Ibrahim, CBE, FRSA; British publisher and financial adviser; *Chairman, Namara Group;* b. 1 May 1931, Haifa, Palestine; s. of Ibrahim Attallah and Genevieve Attallah; m. Maria Nykolyn 1957; one s.; ed Coll. des Frères, Haifa and Battersea Polytechnic, London; Propr Quartet Books 1976–, Women's Press 1977–, Robin Clark 1980–, Pipeline Books 1978–2000, The Literary Review 1981–2001, The Wire 1984–2000, Acad. Club 1989–96, The Oldie 1991–2001; Group Chief Exec. Asprey PLC 1992–96, Deputy Chair. Asprey (Bond Street) 1992–98; Man. Dir Mappin and Webb 1990–95; Exec. Dir Garrard 1990–95; Chair. Namara Group of cos 1973–, launched Parfums Namara 1985, Avant L'Amour and Après L'Amour 1985, Naïdor 1987, L'Amour de Namara 1990; Hon. MA (Surrey) 1993; Retail Personality of the Year, UK Jewellery Awards 1993. *Films produced:* The Slipper and the Rose (with David Frost) 1975, Brimstone and Treacle (Exec. Producer) 1982 and several TV documentaries. *Theatre:* Happy End (Co-Presenter) 1975, The Beastly Beatitudes of Balthazar B. (Presenter and Producer) 1981, Trafford Tanzi (Co-Producer) 1982. *Publications:* Women 1987, Singular Encounters 1990, Of a Certain Age 1992, More of a Certain Age 1993, Speaking for the Oldie 1994, A Timeless Passion 1995, Tara and Claire (novel) 1996, Asking Questions 1996, A Woman a Week 1998, In Conversation with Naim Attallah 1998, Insights 1999, Dialogues 2001, The Old Ladies of Nazareth 2004, The Boy in England (memoir) 2005, In Touch with His Roots: a Second Memoir 2006, Fulfilment & Betrayal 2007. *Leisure interests:* classical music, opera, theatre, cinema, photography and fine arts. *Address:* 25 Shepherd Market, London, W1J 7PP, England (home). *Telephone:* (20) 7499-2901 (home). *Fax:* (20) 7499-2914 (home). *E-mail:* nattallah@aol.com (office).

ATTANASIO, Paul; American screenwriter; m. Katie Jacobs; one d.; ed Harvard Univ., Harvard Law School; began career as a journalist; film critic for Washington

Post 1984–87. *Films include:* Quiz Show 1994, Disclosure 1994, Donnie Brasco 1997, Sphere 1998, The Sum of All Fears 2002, The Good German 2006. *TV includes:* Doctor, Doctor 1989, Homicide: Life on the Street 1993, Gideon's Crossing (also producer) 2000, R.U.S.H. (also producer) 2002, House (exec. producer) 2004–12. *Address:* c/o CAA, 2000 Avenue of the Stars, Los Angeles, CA 90067, USA.

ATTAR, Najah al-, PhD; Syrian academic, politician and writer; *Second Vice-President, responsible for Cultural Policy;* b. 12 Dec. 1933, Damascus; sister of Issam al-Attar (leader of Damascus Faction of Syrian Muslim Brotherhood who has lived in exile in Aachen, Germany since 1970s); m. Dr Majed Al-Azmeh; one s. one d.; ed Damascus Univ., Univ. of Edinburgh, UK; school teacher in Damascus 1960–62; Dir of Composition and Literature Translation, Ministry of Culture 1962, Minister of Culture and Nat. Guidance (first woman minister) 1976–2000, served as spokeswoman for Syrian Govt early 1980s, co-f. Nat. Symphonic Orchestra 1995, initiated construction of Syrian Opera House; Dir Centre for the Dialogue of Civilisations 2002–06; mem. Bd Kalamoun Univ., Dayr Atiya 2003–; Pres. Bd of Trustees, Syrian Virtual Univ. 2003–; Second Vice-Pres. of Syria (first woman and first non-Baath Party mem.), responsible for Cultural Policy 2006–; Friendship Among People's Order (USSR), Polish Culture Order, Grand Officier, Ordre nat. du Mérite 1983, Commdr, Légion d'honneur 1992, Order of Great Lady, Malta Kts, Order of Holy Cross (Poland) 1999, Order of Holy Treasure of Grand Sash (Japan) 2002, Medallion of Honour (Chile) 2004, Order of Katrina the Great, Acad. of Security, Defence and Law (Russian Fed.) 2007. *Publications include:* For Us To Be or Not To Be (two vols), The Literature of War, Who Remembers Those Days?, A Diary, Life's Questions, Coloured Words, The Revolutionary Fabric Between March and November, Spain, Hemingway and the Bulls; weekly newspaper and magazine columns; numerous articles. *Address:* c/o Office of the President, Damascus, Syria (office). *Telephone:* (11) 3323023 (office). *Fax:* (11) 3341404 (office). *E-mail:* center-cs@mail.sy (office).

ATTENBOROUGH, Sir David Frederick, Kt, OM, CH, CVO, CBE, MA, FRS; British broadcaster, naturalist and writer; b. 8 May 1926, London; s. of Frederick Attenborough and Mary Attenborough; brother of Lord Attenborough; m. Jane Elizabeth Ebsworth Oriel 1950 (died 1997); one s. one d.; ed Wyggeston Grammar School, Leicester and Clare Coll., Cambridge; served with RN 1947–49; editorial asst in publishing house 1949–52; with BBC TV 1952–73, Producer of zoological, archaeological, travel, political and other programmes 1952–64, Controller BBC 2 1964–68, Dir of Programmes, TV 1969–73; Huw Wheldon Memorial Lecturer, RTS 1987; Pres. BAAS 1990–91, Royal Soc. for Nature Conservation 1991–96; mem. Nature Conservancy Council 1975–82; Fellow, Soc. of Film and TV Arts 1980; Int. Trustee, World Wild Life Fund 1979–86; Trustee, British Museum 1980–2000, Science Museum 1984–87, Royal Botanical Gardens, Kew 1986–92; Hon. Fellow, Clare Coll., Cambridge 1980, UMIST 1980, Inst. of Biology, Hon. mem., Moscow Soc. of Naturalists 2017; Order of Merit; Hon. DLitt (Leicester, London, Birmingham, City), Hon. DSc (Liverpool, Ulster, Sussex, Bath, Durham, Keele, Heriot-Watt, Bradford, Nottingham), Hon. LLD (Bristol, Glasgow) 1977, Hon. DUniv (Open Univ.) 1980, (Essex) 1987, Antwerp 1993, Dr hc (Edin.) 1994; Special Award, Guild of TV Producers 1961, Silver Medal, Royal TV Soc. 1966, Silver Medal, Zoological Soc. of London 1966, Desmond Davis Award, Soc. of Film and TV Arts 1970, UNESCO Kalinga Prize 1982, Medallist, Acad. of Natural Sciences, Philadelphia 1982, Founders Gold Medal, Royal Geographical Soc. 1985, Int. Emmy Award 1985, Encyclopedia Britannica Award 1987, Kew Award 1996, Edin. Medal, Edin. Science Festival 1998, BP Natural World Book Prize 1998, Faraday Prize, Royal Soc. 2003, Int. Documentary Asscn Career Achievement Award 2003, Raffles Medal, Zoological Soc. of London 2004, Caird Medal, Nat. Maritime Museum 2004, British Book Awards Lifetime Achievement Award 2004, Prince of Asturias Award 2009, Fonseca Prize 2010, Britain–Australia Soc. Award for outstanding contribution to strengthening British/Australian bilateral understanding and relations 2017, Gold Medal, Royal Canadian Geographical Soc. 2017, several newly discovered species, fossils and research vessel named in his honour. *Television includes:* writer, presenter BBC series: Tribal Eye 1976, Wildlife on One 1977–2004, Life on Earth 1979, The Living Planet 1984, The First Eden 1987, Lost World, Vanished Lives 1989, The Trials of Life 1990, Life in the Freezer 1993, The Private Life of Plants 1995, The Life of Birds 1998, State of the Planet 2000, The Blue Planet (narrator) 2001, The Life of Mammals 2002, Life in Cold Blood 2008, Charles Darwin and the Tree of Life 2009, First Life 2010, Frozen Planet 2011, Kingdom of Plants 3D 2012, Galapagos 3D 2013, Africa 2013, Life Story 2014, Attenborough's Paradise Birds 2015, The Hunt 2015, Great Barrier Reef with David Attenborough 2016, The Blue Planet II (narrator) (Emmy Award for Outstanding Narrator 2018) 2017. *Publications include:* Zoo Quest to Guiana 1956, Zoo Quest for a Dragon 1957, Zoo Quest in Paraguay 1959, Quest in Paradise 1960, Zoo Quest to Madagascar 1961, Quest under Capricorn 1963, The Tribal Eye 1976, Life on Earth 1979, The Zoo Quest Expeditions 1982, The Living Planet 1984, The First Eden, The Mediterranean World and Man 1987, The Trials of Life 1990, The Private Life of Plants 1994, The Life of Birds (BP Natural World Book Prize) 1998, The Life of Mammals 2002, Life on Air (memoirs) 2002, Life in the Undergrowth 2005, Life in Cold Blood 2008, Life Stories 2009, Drawn from Paradise 2012, Adventures of a Young Naturalist: The Zoo Quest Expeditions 2017. *Leisure interests:* music, tribal art, natural history. *Address:* 5 Park Road, Richmond, Surrey, TW10 6NS, England. *Website:* www.davidattenborough.co.uk.

ATTENBOROUGH, Hon. Michael John, CBE, BA (Hons); British theatre director; b. 13 Feb. 1950, London, England; s. of Richard Attenborough (Baron Attenborough of Richmond) and Sheila Sim; m. 1st Jane Seymour 1971 (divorced); m. 2nd Karen Lewis 1984; two s.; ed Westminster School, Univ. of Sussex; Assoc. Dir, Mercury Theatre, Colchester 1972–74, Leeds Playhouse 1974–79, Young Vic Theatre 1979; Artistic Dir, Palace Theatre, Watford 1980–84, Hampstead Theatre 1984–89; Exec. Producer/Prin. Assoc. Dir, RSC 1990–2002; Artistic Dir, Almeida Theatre 2002–13; freelance dir 2013–; mem. Council, Royal Acad. of Dramatic Art for 17 years, now Dir Emer.; Trustee, Belarus Free Theatre; Patron, Attenborough Arts Centre, Leicester, Attenborough Centre for the Creative Arts, Univ. of Sussex, Harts Theatre Co.; Hon. Prof. of English and Drama, Univ. of Sussex, Hon. Distinguished Fellow, Univ. of Leicester 2017; Hon. DLitt (Sussex) 2005, (Leicester) 2009; Award for Excellence, Int. Theatre Inst. 2012. *Productions include:* freelance: Nat. Theatre, Royal Court, Tricycle, West End, Broadway; RSC: The Herbal Bed, Romeo and Juliet, Othello, Pentecost, After Easter, Henry IV Parts 1 and 2, Antony and Cleopatra; Almeida Theatre: Measure For Measure, The Knot of the Heart, Reasons To Be Pretty, Filumena, King Lear, Enemies, Big White Fog, The Late Henry Moss, The Mercy Seat, When The Rain Stops Falling, In a Dark, Dark House, Awake and Sing, There Came a Gypsy Riding, Through a Glass Darkly, Macbeth (Aus), As You Like It (Washington), Dangerous Corner (No. 1 tour), Someone Who'll Watch Over Me (Chichester), Godchild, Luna Gale, Reasons To Be Happy (Hampstead Theatre). *Radio:* The H File by Timberlake Wertenbaker. *Television:* The Importance of Being Earnest 1983, King Lear (digital theatre) 2012. *Leisure interests:* music, football, literature, family. *Address:* c/o Rose Cobbe, United Agents, 12–26 Lexington Street, London, W1F 0LE, England (office). *Telephone:* (20) 3214-0800 (office). *E-mail:* rcobbe@unitedagents.co.uk (office). *Website:* www.unitedagents.co.uk (office).

ATTERSEE, Christian Ludwig; Austrian artist; b. 28 Aug. 1940, Pressburg; s. of Christian Ludwig and Susanne Ludwig; m. Ingried Brugger; ed Akad. für Angewandte Kunst, Vienna; has worked as an artist since 1963; more than 400 solo exhbns in USA, Germany, France, Netherlands, Italy, Austria, Switzerland, including Venice Biennale 1984; Prof., Universität für angewandte Kunst, Vienna 1990–; Austrian Cross of Honour for Science and Art 1st Class 2005; Grand Austrian State Prize 1997, Lovis Corinth Prize of the Künstlergilde Esslingen, Germany 2004. *Publications include:* Attersee Werksquer 1962–82, Attersee, Biennale Venedig 1984. *Leisure interest:* sailing. *Address:* Atelier/Archiv Attersee, Tuchlauben 17/4/7, 1010 Vienna, Austria. *E-mail:* attersee@utanet.at. *Website:* www.attersee-christian-ludwig.com.

ATTIYA, Abdul Rahman bin Hamad Al-, BA; Qatari diplomatist and international organization official; b. 15 April 1950, Doha; m.; two s. four d.; ed Univ. of Miami, USA; joined Ministry of Foreign Affairs 1972, Consul-Gen. in Geneva, Switzerland 1974–81, Perm. Rep. to UN and other Int. Orgs, Geneva 1975–81, Perm. Rep. to FAO, Rome 1975–81, Amb. to Saudi Arabia (also accred to Yemen and Djibouti) 1981–84, Amb. to OIC 1981–84, Perm. Rep. to UNESCO 1984–90, Amb. to France (also accred to Italy and Greece) 1984–92; Alt. Gov. IFAD 1985–92, Deputy Minister, Ministry Foreign Affairs 1988–2002; Sec.-Gen. of the Cooperation Council for the Arab States of the Gulf 2002–11; Legion of Merit (Italy) 1992, Chevalier, Légion d'honneur 1993; Independence Medal 2005, Unity Medal 2006, Diamond Medal 2010. *Leisure interests:* reading, exercising. *E-mail:* Alattiyah50@hotmail.com.

ATTIYA, Khalid bin Muhammad al-, LLB, PhD; Qatari politician and fmr lawyer; *Minister of State for Defence Affairs;* b. 9 March 1967; m.; ed King Faisal Air Acad., Saudi Arabia, Arab Univ. of Beirut, Lebanon, Cairo Univ., Egypt; fighter pilot, Qatar Emiri Air Force 1987–95; f. own law firm 1995, pvt. legal practice 1995–2008; Minister of State for Int. Cooperation 2008–11, Acting Minister of Business and Trade 2009, Minister of State for Foreign Affairs and mem. Council of Ministers 2011–13, Minister of Foreign Affairs 2013–16, Minister of State for Defence Affairs 2016–; Chair. Nat. Cttee for Human Rights 2003–08; Chair. Qatar Exchange 2009; Chair. Exec. Cttee Qatari Diar (property investment co.) 2009; Deputy Chair. Supreme Council for Information and Communication Tech. 2009, Qatar Financial Centre 2009; mem. Bd of Trustees Arab Democracy Foundation 2007–. *Address:* Ministry of Defence, Qatar Armed Forces, POB 37, Doha, Qatar (office). *Telephone:* 44614111 (office).

ATTIYAH, Abdullah bin Hamad al-, BA; Qatari government official; *Chairman, Abdullah Bin Hamad Al-Attiyah International Foundation for Energy and Sustainable Development;* b. 1952, Qatar; m.; six c.; ed Univ. of Alexandria, Egypt; joined Ministry of Finance and Petroleum 1972, Head Dept of Int. and Public Affairs 1973–86, Dir Office of Minister 1986–89; Chair. Gulf Helicopters 1975–; Dir Office of Minister of Interior and Acting Minister of Finance and Petroleum 1989–92; Minister of Energy and Industry 1992–99, 2001–11, of Energy, Industry, Electricity and Water 1999–2000, Second Deputy Premier 2003–07, Deputy Premier 2007–11, Chair. Emiri Diwan 2011; Chair. Qatar Amateur Radio Asscn 1992–, State Planning Council 1998, Qatar Gen. Electricity and Water Corpn 1999, UN Comm. on Sustainable Devt 2006; Deputy Chair. Q-Tel 1987–95; Man. Dir and Chair. of Bd Qatar Petrol Co. 1992; currently Chair. Abdullah Bin Hamad Al-Attiyah Int. Foundation for Energy and Sustainable Devt; fmr Pres. Qatar Admin. Control and Transparency Authority; fmr Head Al-Sadd Sports Club; mem. Bd of Dirs Gulf Airways Corpn 1986–2002. *Leisure interests:* reading, fishing, amateur radio, football, travelling. *Address:* Abdullah Bin Hamad Al-Attiyah International Foundation for Energy and Sustainable Development, 4th Floor, Barzan Tower,West Bay, Doha, Qatar (office). *Telephone:* 40428000 (office). *E-mail:* info@abhafoundation.org (office). *Website:* www.abhafoundation.org (office).

ATTRIDGE, Harold W., PhD; American academic; *Sterling Professor of Divinity, Yale Divinity School;* b. Nov. 1946; m. Janis Ann Farren; one s. one d.; ed Boston Coll., Cambridge Univ., UK, Hebrew Univ. of Jerusalem, Israel, Harvard Univ.; Asst Prof. of New Testament, Perkins School of Theology, Southern Methodist Univ. 1977–82, Assoc. Prof. of New Testament 1982–85; Assoc. Prof., Dept of Theology, Univ. of Notre Dame 1985–87, Prof., Dept of Theology 1988–97, Dean, Coll. of Arts and Letters 1991–97; Lillian Claus Prof. of New Testament, Yale Univ. Divinity School 1997–2012, Dean 2002–12, Sterling Prof. of Divinity 2012–; mem. Soc. of Biblical Literature 1969–, Chair. SW Region Progam 1980–81, mem. Annual Meeting Program Cttee 1985–88, Cttee on Research and Publs 1990–93, Devt Cttee 1995–2002 (Vice-Pres. 2000), Finance Cttee 2001– (Pres. 2001); mem. Catholic Biblical Asscn 1974– (Pres. 2011–12), Int. Asscn for Coptic Studies 1975–, American Philosophical Asscn 1976–, Soc. for New Testament Studies 1981–; mem. Editorial Bd Catholic Biblical Quarterly 1983–90, Journal of Biblical Literature 1982–87, 1996–2001, Hermeneia Commentary Series 1984–; Editorial Consultant, Harvard Theological Review 1978–90; Ed., Soc. of Biblical Literature, Texts and Trans: Pseudepgrapha Series 1979–85, Early Christian Literature Series 1990–95; Fellow American Acad. of Arts and Sciences 2015; Nat. Endowment for the Humanities Summer Research Stipend 1982; John Simon Guggenheim Fellowship 1983–84. *Publications:* The Testament of Job 1974, The Syrian Goddess 1976, The Interpretation of Biblical History in the Antiquitates Judaicae of Flavius Josephus 1976, First-Century Cynicism in the Epistles of Heraclitus 1976, Philo of Byblos, The Phoenician History 1981, Nag Hammdi Codex I (The Jung Codex) 1985, Hebrews: A Commentary on the Epistle to the Hebrews 1989, The Acts of Thomas 2010; numerous articles; ed. of twelve books.

Address: Yale Divinity School, 409 Prospect Street, New Haven, CT 06511, USA (office). *Telephone:* (203) 432-5372 (office). *E-mail:* harold.attridge@yale.edu (office). *Website:* www.yale.edu/divinity (office).

ATUKORALE, Thalatha; Sri Lankan politician and attorney; *Minister of Justice and Prison Reforms;* b. 30 May 1963, Panawenna Watta, Kahawatta; m.; joined United Nat. Party 2004, elected mem. Parl. for Ratnapura 2004–; Minister of Foreign Employment Promotion and Welfare 2015–18, Minister of Justice 2017–, of Prison Reforms 2018–; Career Women Award for Woman of the Year 2017. *Address:* Ministry of Justice and Prison Reforms, Superior Courts Complex, Adhikarana Mawatha, Colombo, 1201000, Sri Lanka (office). *Telephone:* (11) 2324681 (office). *Fax:* (11) 2435294 (office). *E-mail:* secretary@moj.gov.lk (office); thalatha.unp@gmail.com; atukorale_t@parliament.lk (office). *Website:* www.moj.gov.lk (office).

ATWAN, Abdel Bari, MA; British (b. Palestinian) journalist and editor; *Editor-in-Chief, Rai al-Youm;* b. 17 Feb. 1950, Deir al-Balah, Gaza; s. of Muhammad Atwan and Zilfa Atwan; m. 1984; three c.; ed Cairo Univ., Egypt, School of Oriental and African Studies, London, UK; began career as journalist in Libya 1974; later worked for newspapers al-Madina and Asharq al-Awsat in Saudi Arabia; Founding Ed.-in-Chief and Chair. Al Quds Al Arabi (pan-Arabian daily newspaper), London 1989–2013; Ed.-in-Chief Rai al-Youm 2013–; frequent appearances in TV debates on CNN, Al Jazeera English, Channel 4 News; also regular lecturer world-wide and contrib. to int. confs. *Publications:* The Secret History of Al Qaeda 2006, A Country of Words: The Life of Abdel Bari Atwan: A Palestinian Journey from the Refugee Camp to the Front Page (memoir) 2008, After Bin Laden: Al Qaeda, Thle Next Generation 2013. *Address:* Rai al-Youm, One Lyric Square, Hammersmith, London, W6 0NB, England (office). *Telephone:* (20) 3542-7936 (office). *E-mail:* info@raialyoum.com (office); abatwan@googlemail.com (office). *Website:* www.raialyoum.com (office); www.abdelbariatwan.com (office); www.bariatwan.com (office).

ATWOOD, Margaret Eleanor, CC, AM, FRSC; Canadian writer; b. 18 Nov. 1939, Ottawa, Ont.; m. Graeme Gibson; one d.; ed Victoria Coll., Univ. of Toronto, Radcliffe Coll. and Harvard Univ., USA; Lecturer in English, Univ. of British Columbia, Vancouver 1964–65; Instructor in English, Sir George Williams Univ., Montreal 1967–68, Univ. of Alberta 1969–70; Asst Prof. of English, York Univ., Toronto 1971; Writer-in-Residence, Univ. of Toronto 1972–73, Maquarie Univ., Australia 1987, Trinity Univ., San Antonio, Tex. 1989; Berg Chair, New York Univ. 1986; Pres. Writers' Union of Canada 1981–82, International PEN (Canadian Centre—English Speaking) 1984–86; MFA Hon. Chair, Univ. of Alabama, Tuscaloosa 1985, Foreign Hon. mem. American Acad. of Arts and Sciences 1988; Order of Ont. 1990, 125th Anniversary of Canadian Confederation Commemorative Medal 1992, Chevalier, Ordre des Arts et des Lettres 1994, Order of Literary Merit (Norway) 1996, Markets Initiative Order of the Forest 2006; Hon. DLitt (Trent) 1973, (Concordia) 1980, (Smith Coll., Mass) 1982, (Toronto) 1983, (Mount Holyoke) 1985, (Waterloo) 1985, (Guelph) 1985, (Oxford) 1998, (Ontario Coll. of Art and Design) 2009, Hon. LLD (Queen's Univ.) 1974, Dr hc (Victoria Coll.) 1987, (Université de Montréal) 1991, (Leeds) 1994, (McMaster) 1996, (Lakehead) 1998, (Oxford) 1998, (Cambridge) 2001, (Algoma) 2001, (Harvard) 2004, (Sorbonne Nouvelle) 2005, (Literary and Historical Soc., Univ. Coll. Dublin) 2005, (Ontario Coll. of Art and Design) 2009, (Nat. Univ. of Ireland) 2011, (Ryerson Univ.) 2012, (Royal Mil. Coll.) 2012, (Univ. of Athens) 2013, (Univ. of Edinburgh) 2013; E.J. Pratt Medal 1961, Pres.'s Medal, Univ. of Western Ontario 1965, First Prize, Centennial Comm. Poetry Competition 1967, Union Poetry Prize, Chicago 1969, Bess Hoskins Prize for Poetry, Chicago 1974, City of Toronto Book Award 1977, Canadian Bookseller's Asscn Award 1977, Periodical Distributors of Canada Short Fiction Award 1977, St Lawrence Award for Fiction 1978, Radcliffe Grad. Medal 1980, Molson Award 1981, Guggenheim Fellowship 1981, Welsh Arts Council Int. Writer's Prize 1982, Ida Nudel Humanitarian Award 1986, Toronto Arts Award 1986, Los Angeles Times Fiction Award 1986, Arthur C. Clarke Award for Best Science Fiction 1987, Commonwealth Literary Prize (regional winner) 1987, 1994, Silver Medal for Best Article of the Year, Council for Advancement and Support of Educ. 1987, Humanist of the Year Award 1987, YWCA Women of Distinction Award 1988, First Prize, Nat. Magazine Award for Environmental Journalism 1988, Canadian Booksellers Asscn Author of the Year 1989, 1996, Harvard Univ. Centennial Medal 1990, John Hughes Prize, Welsh Devt Bd 1992, Commemorative Medal for the 125th Anniversary of Canadian Confed. 1992, Best Local Author, NOW Magazine Readers' Poll 1995, 1997, 1998, 1999, 2000, 2003, 2004, Nat. Arts Club Medal of Honor for Literature 1997, London Literature Award 1999, Int. Crime Writers' Asscn Dashiell Hammett Award 2001, Canadian Booksellers Asscn People's Choice Award 2001, Radcliffe Medal 2003, Harold Washington Literary Award 2003, Edinburgh Int. Book Festival Enlightenment Award 2005, Chicago Tribune Literary Prize 2005, Premio Príncipe de Asturias, Spain 2008, Dan David Prize 2010, Crystal Award, World Econ. Forum 2010, Sun Life Financial Arts & Communications Award: Canada's Most Powerful Women Top 100 2011, Canadian Booksellers' Lifetime Achievement Award 2012, Nashville Public Library Foundation Literary Award 2012, Sun Life Financial Arts and Communications Award, Gov.-Gen. of Canada's Golden Jubilee Medal 2012, Nashville Public Library Foundation Literary Award 2012, Companion, Royal Soc. of Literature 2012, L.A. Times Innovator's Award 2013, Heart and Vision Award, Toronto United Church Council 2013, President's Medal (with Graeme Gibson), BirdLife Int. 2013, 2014, Harvard Arts Medal 2014, Orion Book Award for MaddAddam (fiction) 2014, Toronto Botanical Gardens Aster Award 2014, Inst. for Arts & Humanities Medal, Pennyslvania State Univ., Barnes & Noble Writers for Writers Award 2014, Gold Medal, Royal Canadian Geographical Soc. 2015, Golden Wreath of Struga Poetry Evenings 2016, PEN Pinter Prize 2016, Peace Prize of German Book Trade 2017, Lifetime Achievement Award, PEN Center USA Literary Awards Festival 2017, St Louis Literary Award 2017, Franz Kafka Prize 2017, Adrienne Clarkson Prize for Global Citizenship 2018. *Play:* The Penelopiad – The Play 2007. *Radio script:* The Trumpets of Summer (CBC Radio) 1964. *Television screenplays include:* The Servant Girl (CBC) 1974, Snowbird 1981, Heaven on Earth (with Peter Pearson) 1986. *Recordings include:* The Poetry and Voice of Margaret Atwood 1977, Margaret Atwood Reads From A Handmaid's Tale, Margaret Atwood Reads Unearthing Suite 1985, audio edns of her novels. *Publications include:* fiction: The Edible Woman 1969, Surfacing 1972, Lady Oracle 1976, Dancing Girls (short stories) 1977, Life Before Man 1979, Bodily Harm 1981, Encounters with the Element Man 1982, Murder in the Dark (short stories) 1983, Bluebeard's Egg (short stories) (Periodical Distributors of Canada/Foundation for The Advancement of Canadian Letters Book of the Year Award) 1983, Unearthing Suite 1983, The Handmaid's Tale (Gov.-Gen.'s Award 1986) 1985, Cat's Eye (Torgi Talking Book—CNIB 1989, City of Toronto Book Award 1989, Coles Book of the Year 1989, Foundation for the Advancement of Canadian Letters/Periodical Marketers of Canada Book of the Year 1989) 1988, Wilderness Tips (short stories) (Govt of Ont. Trillium Award (with Jane Urquhart) for Excellence in Ontario Writing 1992, Periodical Marketers of Canada Book of the Year Award 1992) 1991, Good Bones (short stories) 1992, The Robber Bride (Canadian Authors' Asscn Novel of the Year 1993, Trillium Award for Excellence in Ontario Writing 1994, Commonwealth Writers' Prize for the Canadian and Caribbean Region 1994, Sunday Times Award for Literary Excellence 1994, Swedish Humour Asscn's Int. Humorous Writer Award 1995) 1993, Bones and Murder 1995, The Labrador Fiasco 1996, Alias Grace (Giller Prize 1996, Premio Mondello 1997, Salon Magazine Best Fiction of the Year 1997) 1996, The Blind Assassin (Booker Prize 2000) 2000, Oryx and Crake 2003, Telling Tales (contrib. to charity anthology) 2004, Bottle 2004, The Penelopiad 2005, The Tent (short stories) 2006, Moral Disorder (short stories) 2006, The Year of the Flood 2009, MaddAddam: A Novel 2013, Stone Mattress (short stories) 2014, The Heart Goes Last 2015, Hag Seed 2016; poetry: Double Persephone 1961, The Circle Game (Gov.-Gen.'s Award 1966) 1964, Kaleidoscopes Baroque 1965, Talismans for Children 1965, Speeches for Doctor Frankenstein 1966, The Animals in That Country 1968, The Journals of Susanna Moodie 1970, Procedures for Underground 1970, Power Politics 1971, You Are Happy 1974, Marsh, Hawk 1977, Two-Headed Poems 1978, True Stories 1981, Notes Towards a Poem That Can Never Be Written 1981, Snake Poems 1983, Interlunar 1984, Selected Poems II: Poems Selected and New 1976–1986 1986, Selected Poems 1966–1984 1990, Margaret Atwood Poems 1965–1975 1991, Morning in the Burned House (Trillium Award for Excellence in Ontario Writing) 1995, The Door 2007; sjuvenile: Up in the Tree 1978, 2006, Anna's Pet 1980, For the Birds 1990, Princess Prunella and the Purple Peanut 1995, Rude Ramsay and the Roaring Radishes 2003, Bashful Bob and Doleful Dorinda 2004, Wandering Wenda 2011; non-fiction: Survival: A Thematic Guide to Canadian Literature 1972, Days of the Rebels 1815–1840 1977, Second Words: Selected Critical Prose 1982, Strange Things: The Malevolent North in Canadian Literature 1995, Negotiating with the Dead: A Writer on Writing 2002, Moving Targets: Writing With Intent 1982–2004 2004, Curious Pursuits: Occasional Writing 2005, Writing with Intent: Essays, Reviews, Personal Prose 1983–2005 2005, Payback: Debt and the Shadow Side of Wealth (Libris Award for Best Non-Fiction Book 2009) 2008, In Other Worlds: SF and the Human Imagination 2011; editor: The New Oxford Book of Canadian Verse in English (ed.) 1982, The Oxford Book of Canadian Short Stories in English (with Robert Weaver) 1986, The Canlit Foodbook 1987, The Best American Short Stories (with Shannon Ravenel) 1989, The New Oxford Book of Canadian Short Stories in English (with Robert Weaver) 1995; reviews and critical articles have appeared in Canadian Literature, Maclean's, Saturday Night, This Magazine, New York Times Book Review, Globe and Mail, National Post, The Nation, Books In Canada, Washington Post, Harvard Educational Review, and many others; works have been translated into many languages, including French, German, Italian, Urdu, Estonian, Romanian, Serbo-Croat, Catalan, Turkish, Russian, Finnish, Dutch, Danish, Norwegian, Swedish, Portuguese, Greek, Polish, Japanese, Icelandic, Spanish, Hebrew. *Address:* c/o McClelland & Stewart Ltd, 1 Toronto Street, Suite 300, Toronto, ON M5C 2V6, Canada (office). *Telephone:* (416) 364-4449 (office). *Fax:* (416) 957-1587 (office). *E-mail:* suzanna_owtoad@hotmail.com (office). *Website:* www.mcclelland.com (office); www.margaretatwood.ca.

ATZMON, Moshe; Israeli conductor; b. (Miklos Groszberger), 30 July 1931, Budapest, Hungary; m. 1954; two d.; ed Tel-Aviv Acad. of Music, Jerusalem Acad. of Music, Guildhall School of Music, UK; left Hungary for Israel 1944; played the horn professionally in various orchestras for several years; has conducted in Israel, England, Australia, Germany, Sweden, Norway, Switzerland, Spain, Finland, Italy, Austria, Turkey and USA; Chief Conductor, Sydney Symphony Orchestra 1969–71; Chief Conductor, North German Radio Symphony Orchestra 1972–74; Musical Dir Basel Symphony Orchestra 1972–86; Chief Conductor, Tokyo Metropolitan Orchestra 1979–83; Chief Conductor, Nagoya Philharmonic Orchestra 1987–92, Conductor Laureate 1992–; Musical Dir Dortmund Opera House and Philharmonic Orchestra 1991–93; Second Prize, Dimitri Mitropoulos Competition for Conductors, New York 1963, Leonard Bernstein Prize 1963, First Prize, Int. Conductors Competition, Liverpool, England 1964. *Leisure interests:* reading, travelling. *Address:* Artists Management Company srl unipersonale, Piazza R. Simoni, 1E, 37122 Verona, Italy (office); Patrick Garvey Management, 40 North Parade, York, YO30 7AB, England (office). *E-mail:* panozzo@amcmusic.com (office); patrick@patrickgarvey.com (office). *Website:* www.amcmusic.com/en/artists/biography/moshe-atzmon (office); www.patrickgarvey.com (office).

AUBERGER, Bernard, Ing Civil, Gen. Insp. of Finances; French banker; b. 5 Dec. 1937, Gennevilliers; s. of Paul Auberger and Jeanne Auberger (née Geny); m. Christine Baraduc 1963; three s. one d.; ed Ecole des Mines, Paris, Inst. d'Etudes Politiques, Paris, Ecole Nat. d'Admin, Paris; Investigating Officer, French Ministry of Finance 1966–70; Adviser to Gen. Man. Crédit Nat., Paris 1970–72; Financial Attaché, Embassy in New York 1972–74; Dir of Cabinet for Under-Sec. for Finance 1974; attached to Industrial Relations Cttee 1974–75; Dir Production and Trade, Ministry of Agric. 1975–80; Cen. Man. Société Générale 1983–86; Gen. Man. Caisse Nat. de Crédit Agricole 1986–88; Insp.-Gen. of Finances 1988; Advisor to Pres. of Paluel-Marmont 1990; Pres. Cortal Bank 1991–98, Banque Directe 1994–2001; Vice-Pres., Dir-Gen. Crédit du Nord 1993–94, Chair., CEO 1994–95; Pres. Asscn Opéra Comique-Salle Favart 1994–2001; Dir Compagnie Bancaire 1991–98, Banque Paribas 1994–97; Judge, Tribunal de Commerce de Paris 1998–2012; mem. Econ. and Social Council 1982–84; Officier, Ordre nat. du Mérite, Chevalier du Mérite agricole, Officier, Légion d'honneur. *Leisure interest:* opera. *Address:* 193 Boulevard St Germain, 75007 Paris, France (home). *Telephone:* 1-45-48-94-11 (home).

AUBERT, Guy, PhD; French scientist and academic; *Scientific Advisor, Commissariat à l'Energie Atomique;* b. 9 May 1938, Les Costes, Hautes-Alpes; s. of Gontran Aubert and Marguerite Vincent; m. 1st 1962; two d.; m. 2nd 1998; ed Ecole normale supérieure de Saint-Cloud; Research Assoc. Lab. d'Electrostatique et de Physique du Metal, CNRS, Grenoble; Titular Prof. Univ., Scientifique et Médicale de Grenoble 1970, Vice-Pres. in Charge of Research 1981–84; Scientific Del. of CNRS for Rhône-Alpes region 1981–83; Dir Ecole Normale Supérieure de Lyon 1985–94; Dir-Gen. CNRS 1994–97; Extraordinary mem. Conseil d'Etat 1997–2000; Dir-Gen. CNED 2000–03; Scientific Advisor to Commissariat à l'Energie Atomique 2003–; mem. French Physics Soc.; Officier, Légion d'honneur, Ordre nat. du Mérite; Commdr des Palmes académiques; Chevalier du Mérite agricole. *Publications:* papers in scientific journals and several patents. *Leisure interests:* skiing, tennis. *Address:* Université de Poitiers, Présidence, 15 rue de l'Hôtel Dieu, TSA 71117, 86073 Poitiers Cedex 9 (office); 34T, rue des Feuillants, 86000 Poitiers, France (home). *Telephone:* (5) 49-45-43-39 (office). *Fax:* (5) 49-36-62-34 (office). *E-mail:* guy.aubert@ext.univ-poitiers.fr (office).

AUBOUIN, Jean Armand, DèsSc; French academic; b. 5 May 1928, Evreux; s. of Jean Aubouin and Yvonne Joubin; m. Françoise Delpouget 1953; two d.; ed Lycées Buffon and St-Louis, Ecole Normale Supérieure (St-Cloud) and Univ. of Paris; Lecturer, Univ. of Paris 1952–61, Prof. 1961–90 (Univ. Pierre et Marie Curie from 1969), now Prof. Emer.; mem. Acad. of Sciences, Inst. of France 1981–, Vice-Pres. 1986–88, Pres. 1989–90; mem. Univ. Consultative Cttee 1967–73, Nat. Cttee CNRS 1976–84; Pres. Soc. Géologique de France 1976, Cttee de Télédétection du CNES (Centre National d'Etudes spatiales) 1974–78, 23rd Int. Geological Congress 1980, Cttee Geological Map of the World 1984–92, Scientific Advisory Bds of GPF (Géologie profonde de la France) program 1982–86, Bureau de Recherches Géologiques et Minières 1982–91, Inst. Français de Recherche pour l'Exploitation de la Mer 1985–90; mem. Scientific Advisory Bds Planning Cttee Int. Programme of Ocean Drilling 1980–84, Fondation de France 1984–87, Inst. Français du Pétrole 1985–91; mem. Bd of Dirs Office de Recherche Scientifique d'Outre-mer 1984–88, Bureau de Recherche Géologique et Minières 1989–92, Inst. Océanographique, Paris and Monaco 1994– (Pres. Comité Perfectionnement 1992–); mem. Conseil Supérieur Recherche et Technologie 1983–87; Pres. French Cttee of Int. Decade for the Reduction of Natural Disasters 1990–93; mem. Advisory Bd Parc Naturel du Verdun 1996–2000; Founder and mem. Acad. des Technologies 2000–; Admin. Chancellery Acad. de Nice 1996–, Acad. de Paris 2000–04; Foreign mem. Accad. dei Lincei, Italy 1974–, USSR (now Russia) Acad. of Sciences 1976–, Acad. of Athens, Greece 1980–, Academia Europaea 1988–, Acad. of Zagreb, Croatia 1990–, Acad. Royale Sciences, Arts et Lettres de Belgique 1994–, Deutsche Akad. der Naturforscher Leopoldina 1995–, Acad. de la Latinité 2000–; Hon. mem. Geological Soc. of London 1976–, Soc. Physique Histoire Naturelle (Geneva) 1990–, Geological Soc. of Greece 2001–; Hon. Fellow, Geological Soc. of America 1980–; Chevalier, Ordre des Palmes académiques 1965, Ordre Nat. du Mérite 1981, Légion d'honneur 1989; Dr hc (Athens) 1992; CNRS Medal 1959, Prix Viquesnel de la Soc. Géologique de France 1962, Prix Charles Jacob Acad. des Sciences 1976, Museo de la Plata Medal 1977, Argentina, Dumont Medal, Soc. Géologique de Belgique 1977, Ville de Paris Medal 1980, Gaudry Prize, Soc. Géologique de France 1990, Gold Medal, Acad. Royale des Sciences de Belgique 1990. *Publications:* Géologie de la Grèce septentrionale 1959, Geosynclines 1965, Manuel de Cartographie (co-ed.) 1970, Précis de Géologie (co-ed., four vols) 1968–79, approx. 400 scientific articles. *Leisure interests:* reading, mountain walking and swimming at sea. *Address:* c/o Académie des technologies, Grand Palais des Champs Elysées, Porte C, Avenue Franklin D. Roosevelt, 75008 Paris, France (office). *E-mail:* jean.aubouin@academie-technologies.fr (office).

AUBRY, Martine Louise Marie; French politician; *Mayor of Lille;* b. (Martine Delors), 8 Aug. 1950, Paris; d. of Jacques Delors (q.v.) and Marie Lephaille; m. 1st Xavier Aubry; one d.; m. 2nd Jean Louis Brochon 2004; ed Lycée Paul-Valéry, Panthéon-Assas Paris II Univ., Univ. of Paris 1 Panthéon-Sorbonne, Institut Saint-Pierre-Fourier, Faculté de Droit, Paris, Institut des Sciences Sociales du Travail, Institut d'Etudes Politiques, Paris and Ecole Nat. d'Admin, Strasbourg; Ministry of Labour 1975–79; Instructor, Ecole Nat. d'Admin 1978; Dir of preparations for econ. competition for admin. of Univ. Paris-Dauphiné 1978; civil admin., Conseil d'Etat 1980–81; Deputy Dir Pvt. Office of Minister of Labour 1981; special assignment for Minister of Social Affairs and Nat. Solidarity 1983–84; Dir of Labour Relations, Ministry of Labour 1984–87; Maître des Requêtes, Conseil d'Etat 1987; Deputy Dir-Gen. Pechiney 1989–91; Minister of Labour, Employment and Professional Training 1991–93; Pres. FACE 1993–97; First Asst Mayor of Lille 1995–2001, Mayor 2001–; Vice-Pres., Lille Urban Council 1995–2008, Pres. 2008–14; mem. Nat. Ass. for Nord region (Socialist Party) 1997–2002; Minister of Employment and Social Affairs 1997–2000; Nat. Sec. Socialist Party (Parti socialiste—PS) 2000–05, First Sec. 2008–12, joined Reformer (think-tank) 2000; launched Renaissance (think tank) 2013; presidential candidate 2012; special representative to China, Ministry of Foreign Affairs 2013; mem. club Le Siècle; Int. Press Prize, Le Trombinoscope 1999. *Publications include:* Pratique de la fonction personnel: le management des ressources humaines (co-author) 1982, Le Choix d'Agir 1994, Carnet de route d'un maire de banlieue: entre innovations et tempêtes 1995, Petit dictionnaire pour lutter contre l'extrême droite (co-author) 1995, Il est grand temps 1997, C'est quoi la solidarité? 2002, Muscler sa conscience du bonheur en trente jours 2004, Quel projet pour la gauche? 2004, Une vision pour espérer, une volonté pour transformer 2004, Agir contre les discriminations 2006, Et si on se retrouvait... 2008. *Leisure interests:* tennis, skiing. *Address:* Parti socialiste, 10 rue de Solférino, 75333 Paris Cedex 07 (office); Mairie, BP 667, 59033 Lille Cedex, France. *Telephone:* 1-45-56-77-00 (office). *Fax:* 1-47-05-15-78 (office). *E-mail:* infosp@parti-socialiste.fr (office). *Website:* www.parti-socialiste.fr/l-equipe/martine-aubry (office).

AUCOIN, Louis M., BA, JD; American lawyer and UN official; b. 26 Jan. 1950; ed Coll. of Holy Cross, Worcester, Boston Coll. Law School; numerous academic positions including Fulbright Lecturer, Sorbonne Law Dept, Assoc. Prof., Inst. of Comparative Law, Lecturer in Comparative Law, Int. Human Rights and Trial Advocacy, Boston Univ. School of Law 1984–2000; adviser on drafting new constitutions in Cambodia 1993, E Timor 2001–02, Rwanda 2001–03, Kosovo 2007–08; Legal Adviser to Haiti's Minister for Justice 1997–98; Acting Head of Judicial Affairs, UN Transitional Authority in E Timor (UNTAET) 2000; Program Officer in Rule of Law Program, US Inst. of Peace 2000–03; US Supreme Court Fellow 2001–02; Prin. Foreign Adviser to Haitian Parl. on reform of Criminal Code and Code of Criminal Procedure 2003–06; Academic Dir Master of Law Programme in Int. Law, Fletcher School of Law, Tufts Univ., Medford, Mass –2011; Deputy Special Rep. of Sec.-Gen. for Operations and Rule of Law, UN Mission in Liberia (UNMIL) 2011–12. *Publications include:* The French Constitution 2003, Constitution-Making, Peace-Building and National Reconciliation 2004, The Role of Informal Justice Systems in Fostering the Rule of Law in Post Conflict Countries 2005, Improving Transitional Justice: an Assessment of Progress in the Former Yugoslav States (co-author) 2006.

AUDIBET, Marc; French fashion designer; b. 1955, Boulogne-sur-Seine; celebrated in fashion world for his research into stretch fabrics and their use in garments without hooks, eyes, buttons or zippers, expertise acquired while working as an assistant to Emanuel Ungaro in 1972, and then as designer for Pierre Balmain, Madame Gres and Nino Cerruti; presented first collection in 1975; took over design at house of Christian Aujard 1977–81; designed for Basile and Laure Biagiotti 1981–84; continued with own label until 1988 when he designed for Parallel; collaborated with Azzedine Alaia to work closely with Du Pont on project to mix Lycra with fabrics such as satin and silk 1984, became textile adviser to Du Pont and helped create and launch single and two-way stretch fabrics made from Du Pont's Lycra; has continued to design and create seamless garments made from Lycra mixed with a wide range of other fabrics such as cotton, silk, linen and wool; also designed for Hermes 1990s; designed nine collections for Prada 1990–96; worked as consultant for Italian house of Trussardi; designer for Salvatore Ferragamo 2000–02, Cesare Paciotti (shoes maker) 2002–06; Artistic Adviser to Vionnet 2007–08; design consultant for Max Mara and Krizia and industrial clothing cos in Japan and Italy; exhbn 'Histoire idéale de la mode contemporaine Vol. 1 1970–1980', Musée des Arts Décoratifs, Paris 2010; Dr hc (China Acad. of Art) 2009. *E-mail:* info@marcaudibet.com. *Website:* www.marcaudibet.com.

AUDRAIN, Paul André Marie; French business executive; b. 17 May 1945, Chambéry, Savoie; s. of Jean Audrain and Margueritte Gubian; m. Danièle Pons 1967; two s.; ed Lycée d'Etat de Chambéry, Lycée du Parc Lyon, Ecole Supérieure des Sciences Economiques et Commerciales, Paris; Engineer, IBM France 1969–70; Financial and Admin. Dir Aiglon, Angers 1970–74; Financial Dir Christian Dior 1974–79, then Sec.-Gen., Financial and Admin. Dir 1979–84, Chair. and CEO 1984–85, Pres. 1985–86; Int. Dir Financière Agache 1986–87; Chair. and CEO Christian Lacroix 1987–88, Pierre Balmain 1988–89; CEO Société Crillon 1990–93, Int. Consulting & Licensing; Chevalier, Ordre nat. du Mérite 1985. *Address:* 27 rue du Phare, Port Navalo, 56640 Arzon (home); 20 boulevard du Montparnasse, 75015 Paris, France (home). *Telephone:* (6) 87-78-46-15 (office); (2) 97-53-85-45 (home). *E-mail:* paulaudrain@wanadoo.fr (home).

AUDRAN, Stéphane (see Dacheville, Colette).

AUERBACH, Frank Helmuth; British (b. German) artist; b. 29 April 1931, Berlin, Germany; s. of Max Auerbach and Charlotte Auerbach; m. Julia Wolstenholme 1958; one s.; ed St Martin's School of Art, London, Royal Coll. of Art; works in public collections in UK, Australia, Brazil, USA, Mexico, Israel, SA, Canada; Silver Medal for Painting, Royal Coll. of Art. *Address:* c/o Marlborough Fine Art, 6 Albemarle Street, London, W1S 4BY, England.

AUF, Lt-Gen. Ahmed Awad ibn; Sudanese politician, fmr army officer and diplomatist; b. 1954; several years in army, becoming Head of Mil. Intelligence during Darfur conflict, also Chair. of Jt Chiefs of Staff –2010; fmr Amb. to Oman; Minister of Defence 2015–19, also First Vice-Pres. Feb.–April 2019; Chair. Transitional Military Council 11–12 April 2019. *Address:* c/o Ministry of Defence, POB 371, Khartoum, Sudan (office).

AUGUST, Bille; Danish film director; b. 9 Nov. 1948; m. 1st Pernilla August 1991 (divorced 1997); m. 2nd Masja Dessau; m. 3rd Annie Munksgaard; m. 4th Sara-Marie Maltha; eight c.; ed Christer Stroholm School of Photography, Stockholm, Danish Film School; worked as cameraman on Homewards at Night, Manrape, The Grass is Singing, Love, before making first feature film 1978; Hans Christian Andersen Prize 2003. *Television includes:* The World is So Big, So Big, May, Three Days with Magnus, Buster's World (series), episode of The Young Indiana Jones, Detaljer. *Feature films:* In My Life 1978, Zappa 1983, Twist and Shout 1986, Pelle the Conqueror (Oscar for Best Foreign Film, Palme d'Or, Cannes Film Festival, Golden Ram, Stockholm, Golden Globe, LA) 1989, The Best Intentions (Palme d'Or 1992) 1991, The House of the Spirits, Smilla's Feeling for Snow, A Song for Martin 2001, Return to Sender 2004, Goodbye Bafana 2007, Night Train to Lisbon 2013, Silent Heart 2014.

AUGUSTINE, Norman Ralph, BSc, MSc, FIEEE; American aerospace industry executive; b. 27 July 1935, Denver, Colo; s. of Ralph Harvey Augustine and Freda Irene Augustine (née Immenga); m. Margareta Engman 1962; two c.; ed Princeton Univ.; Research Asst, Princeton Univ. 1957–58; Program Man., Chief Engineer Douglas Aircraft Co. Inc., Santa Monica, Calif. 1958–65; Asst Dir of Defense Research and Eng, Office of US Sec. for Defense, Washington, DC 1965–70; Vice-Pres. Advanced Systems, Missiles and Space Co., LTV Aerospace Corpn, Dallas 1970–73; Asst Sec. of the Army, The Pentagon, Washington, DC 1965–70, Under-Sec. 1973–75; Vice-Pres. Operations, Martin Marietta Aerospace Corpn, Bethesda, Md 1977–82, Pres. Martin Marietta Denver Aerospace Co. 1982–85, Sr Vice-Pres. Information Systems 1985, Pres. COO 1986–87, Vice-Chair. and CEO 1987–88, Chair. and CEO 1988–95; Pres. Lockheed Martin 1995–96, Pres. CEO 1996–97, Chair. –1997, Chair. Exec. Cttee, Bd of Dirs 1997–98; Chair. NASA Space Systems and Tech. Advisory Bd 1985–89, American Red Cross 1992–2001, Review of US Human Space Flight Plans Cttee 2009, US Antarctic Program Blue Ribbon Panel 2011–12; fmr Chair. Nat. Acad. of Eng (NAE) Council, now Chair. Nat. Acads Philanthropy Council; mem. NATO Group of Experts on Air Defence 1966–70, NASA Research and Tech. Advisory Council 1973–75; mem. Bd of Dirs Phillips Petroleum Co. (now ConocoPhillips), Procter & Gamble Co., Black and Decker Corpn; fmr mem. Bd of Dirs Riggs Nat. Bank Corpn; Prof., Princeton Univ. 1997–99; Fellow, AIAA, IEEE, American Acad. of Arts and Sciences, Royal Aeronautical Soc., American Astronautical Soc.; mem. United States Energy Security Council, Int. Acad. of Astronautics, New York Acad. of Sciences, Nat. Acad. of Eng; fmr Pres. Boy Scouts of America; 18 hon. degrees including Hon. DEng (Princeton) 2007; Distinguished Service Medal, Dept of Defense five times, Goddard Medal, AIAA 1988, Nat. Eng Award, American Asscn of Eng Socs 1991, Nat. Medal of Tech. 1997, AAAS Philip Hauge Abelson Prize 2005, Public Welfare Medal, Nat. Acad. of Sciences 2006, Harold W. McGraw, Jr. Prize in Educ. 2006, Bower Award for Business Leadership 2007. *Publications:* Augustine's Laws, The Defense Revolution (co-author) 1990, Augustine's Travels 1997, Shakespeare in

Charge: The Bard's Guide to Leading and Succeeding on the Business Stage (with K. Adelman) 2001.

AUGUSTO, Manuel Domingos; Angolan journalist, diplomatist and politician; *Minister of External Relations;* b. 2 Sept. 1957, Luanda; ed Univ. of Luanda; Head of Human Resources, Jumbo-Pão de Açúcar (retail chain) 1974–76; Journalist, Televisão Pública de Angola 1976–80; Journalist, Jornal de Angola (daily newspaper) 1980–81; Head of Western Countries Dept, Secr. of State for Cooperation 1981–85, with Western Countries Dept, Ministry of Foreign Trade 1985–88, First Sec., Angolan Embassy in Abuja, Nigeria 1988–92, Head of First Mission to South Africa 1992–94, Amb. to Zambia 1995–99; Deputy Minister of Social Communication 1999–2005; Amb. to Ethiopia and also Perm. Rep. to African Union and ECA 2005–10, Sec. of State for Foreign Affairs (Political Affairs) 2010–12, Sec. of State for Foreign Affairs 2012–17, Minister of External Relations 2017–; del. to several SADC summits; del. to 4th Comm. of UN Gen. Ass. 2003, 2004. *Address:* Ministry of External Relations, Rua Major Kanhangulo, Luanda, Angola (office). *Telephone:* 222394827 (office). *Fax:* 222393246 (office). *E-mail:* geral@mirex.gov.ao (office). *Website:* www.mirex.gov.ao (office).

AUKIN, David, BA, FRSA; British theatre, film and television producer; b. 12 Feb. 1942, Harrow; s. of Charles Aukin and Regina Aukin; m. Nancy Meckler 1969; two s.; ed St Paul's School, London and St Edmund Hall, Oxford; Co-founder Foco Novo and Jt Stock Theatre cos and admin. producer for various fringe theatre groups 1970–75; Admin. Dir Hampstead Theatre 1975–79, Dir 1979–84; Dir Leicester Haymarket Theatre 1984–86; Exec. Dir Royal Nat. Theatre of Great Britain 1986–90; Pres. Soc. of West End Theatres 1988–90; Head of Drama, Channel 4 TV 1990–97, Head of Film 1997–98; Jt Chief Exec. HAL Films 1998–2000; Producer and Man. Dir David Aukin Productions Ltd 2001–. *Television:* as producer: The Hamburg Cell 2004, The Government Inspector 2005, The Trial of Tony Blair 2007, The Promise 2011, The Politician's Husband 2013, Sirens 2014, Churchill's Secret 2016. *Films produced include:* Maya 1993, Mansfield Park 1998, Elephant Juice 1999, About Adam 2000, Mrs. Henderson Presents 2005, Endgame 2009, Hyde Park on Hudson 2012. *Address:* c/o Act Productions Ltd, 20–22 Stukeley Street, London WC2B 5LR, England (office). *E-mail:* info@actproductions.co.uk (office). *Website:* actproductions.co.uk (office).

AULETTA ARMENISE, Giampiero, BEcons; Italian banking executive; b. 1957, Rome; s. of Giovanni Auletta Armenise; m.; three c.; ed Univ. of Rome, La Sapienza; with Bonifiche Siele Finanziaria Group 1978–98; Head of Analyses, Planning and Investments Dept, then Head of Financial Control and Risk Monitoring Dept, Banco Ambrosiano Veneto 1995–98, Man. Planning, Investments and Financial Control Sector, Banca Intesa 1998–2002; CEO Banca Popolare Commercio e Industria 2002–03, Banche Popolari Unite Group 2003–07, Unione di Banche Italiane SpA 2007–08; Chair. Rothschild Italia SpA 2009–17, Mistralfin SpA 2017–; Chair. Giovanni Armenise Harvard Foundation 2013–; mem. Bd of Dirs Banca Popolare di Bergamo SpA, Banca Popolare Commercio e Industria SpA, Banca Popolare di Ancona SpA, Banca Carime SpA, Centrobanca SpA, Banco di Brescia SpA. *Address:* Giovanni Armenise Harvard Foundation, 180 Longwood Avenue, Suite 110-C, Boston, MA 02115, USA. *Telephone:* (617) 432-6256. *E-mail:* armeniseharvardfdnpress@hms.harvard.edu. *Website:* www.armeniseharvard.org.

AUMANN, Robert John, BS, SM, PhD; Israeli/American mathematician, economist and academic; *Professor Emeritus, The Hebrew University of Jerusalem;* b. 8 June 1930, Frankfurt am Main, Germany; s. of Siegmund Aumann and Miriam Aumann (née Landau); m.; five c.; ed City Coll. of New York, Massachusetts Inst. of Tech., USA; Instructor, Dept of Math., Hebrew Univ. of Jerusalem 1956–58, Lecturer 1958–61, Sr Lecturer 1961–64, Assoc. Prof. 1964–68, Prof. 1968–2000, Prof. Emer. 2000–, Fellow, Inst. for Advanced Studies 1979–80, mem. Center for the Study of Rationality 1991–; Research Assoc., Princeton Univ. 1960–61; Visiting Prof., Yale Univ. 1964–65, Univ. of California, Berkeley 1971, 1985–86, Univ. Catholique de Louvain, Belgium 1972, 1978, 1984, Stanford Univ. 1975–76, 1980–81, New York Univ. 1997; External Prof. (part-time), Tel-Aviv Univ. 1969–93; Prof. (part-time), Center for Game Theory in Econs, Stony Brook Univ. 1986–89, 1991–2013; Visiting Scholar, Cowles Foundation for Research in Econs, Yale Univ. 1989; Nemmers Prof. of Econs, Northwestern Univ. 1999–2000; Assoc. Ed. Journal of Economic Theory 1974–79, Econometrica 1975–78, Journal of the European Mathematical Soc. 2000–15; mem. Editorial Bd International Journal of Game Theory 1971–, Journal of Mathematical Economics 1974–, SIAM Journal on Applied Mathematics 1976–80, Games and Economic Behavior 1989–; Pres. Israel Math. Union 1990–92, Game Theory Soc. 1998–2003; mem. Inst. for Math., Univ. of Minn. 1984, Math. Sciences Research Inst., Berkeley 1985–86, Fellow, Econometric Soc. 1966–, mem. Council 1977–82, Exec. Cttee 1982–85; mem. NAS 1985, Israel Acad. of Sciences and Humanities 1989; Corresp. FBA 1995; Corresp. mem. Royal Acad. of Financial Science and Econs (Spain) 2011; Foreign Hon. mem. American Acad. of Arts and Sciences 1974, Hon. mem. American Econ. Assen 1993–; Dr hc (Univ. of Bonn) 1988, (Univ. Catholique de Louvain) 1989, (Univ. of Chicago) 1992, (CUNY) 2006, (Bar Ilan Univ.) 2006, (Ben Gurion Univ.) 2015; Harvey Prize in Science and Technology 1983, Israel Prize in Econs 1994, Lanchester Prize in Operations Research 1995, Erwin Plein Nemmers Prize in Econs, Northwestern Univ. 1998, EMET Prize in Econs, Prime Minister of Israel 2002, Von Neumann Prize in Operations Research 2005, Nobel Memorial Prize in Econs 2005. *Publications:* Values of Non-atomic Games (with L. S. Shapley) 1974, Lectures on Game Theory 1989, Repeated Games with Incomplete Information (with M. Maschler) 1995, Collected Papers 2000, Handbook of Game Theory with Economic Applications (co-ed) 1992, 1994, 2002; numerous articles in professional journals and conf. papers on game theory, econ. theory and theory of choice. *Leisure interests:* skiing, hiking, cooking, Talmud study. *Address:* Center for the Study of Rationality, The Hebrew University, 91904 Jerusalem, Israel (office). *Telephone:* (2) 6586254 (office). *Fax:* (2) 6513681 (office). *E-mail:* nobel@huji.ac.il (office). *Website:* www.ma.huji.ac.il/raumann (office); www.ratio.huji.ac.il (office).

AUMONT, Jacques; French author and professor of film aesthetics; b. 25 Feb. 1942, Avignon; m. Lyang Kim; two c.; ed École polytechnique, École nationale supérieure des télécommunications; began career as engineer, ORTF (nat. broadcasting co.) 1965–70; film reviewer, Les Cahiers du cinéma 1967–74; Dir Editions de l'Etoile 1970–74; Lecturer in Cinema, Univ. of Paris III 1970–76, later Prof. of Film Aesthetics; apptd Dir of Studies, École des hautes études en sciences socials (EHESS) 1995; mem. of various film festival juries and selection cttees; visiting lecturer at numerous foreign establishments, including Berkeley, Madison, Iowa City, Nijmegen, Lisbon; Chevalier des Palmes académiques. *Publications include:* Montage Eisenstein 1979, Esthétique du film (co-author) 1983, L'analyse des films (co-author) 1988, L'oeil interminable 1989, L'image 1990, Du visage au cinéma 1992, A quoi pensent les films 1997, De l'ésthetique au présent 1998, Dictionnaire critique et théorique du cinéma (co-author) 2001, Ingmar Bergman 2003, Matière d'images 2005, Le Cinéma et la mise en scène 2006, Moderne? Comment le cinéma est devenu le plus singulier des arts 2007; over 200 reviews in periodicals. *Leisure interests:* piano/chamber music. *Address:* c/o Université Paris-3, 13 rue Santeuil, 75005 Paris, France (office).

AUN, Porn Moniroth, PhD; Cambodian politician and government official; *Minister of Economy and Finance;* b. 1 Oct. 1969, Phnom Penh; m.; four c.; ed Moscow State Univ., Moscow School of Business, Russian Econ. Acad.; Asst to Prime Minister 1993–94, Economic Adviser to Prime Minister 1998–2013; Adviser to Sr Minister-in-charge, Ministry of Rehabilitation and Devt 1994–96; Advisor to Minister, Ministry of Economy and Finance 1994–96, Sec.-Gen. (with the rank of Sec. of State) 1999–2003, Sec. of State 2003–13, Minister of Economy and Finance 2013–; Dir of Cabinet, Council for Devt of Cambodia 1996–99; Chair. Supreme National Econ. Council 2002–, Public Financial Management Reform Steering Cttee, Securities and Exchange Comm. of Cambodia; Perm. Vice-Chair. Econ. and Financial Policy Cttee; Gov., Cambodia's Council Govs. of World Bank and Asian Devt Bank, Cambodia's Council Govs. of Multilateral Investment Guarantee Agency; Grand Officer, Royal Order of Cambodia 2003, Royal Order of Sowathara 2008, Grand Cross, Royal Order of Sowathara 2008, Order of H.M The Queen Preah Kossomak Nearyreath 2010, Medal of Nat. Merit 2010. *Address:* Ministry of Economy and Finance, 60 rue 92, Sangkat Wat Phnom, Khan Duan Penh, Phnom Penh, Cambodia (office). *Telephone:* (23) 428960 (office). *Fax:* (23) 427798 (office). *E-mail:* efi@camnet.com.kh (office). *Website:* www.mef.gov.kh.

AUNG SAN SUU KYI, BA; Myanma politician; *State Counsellor, Minister of Foreign Affairs and of the President's Office;* b. 19 June 1945, Rangoon; d. of Gen. Aung San and of Khin Kyi; m. Michael Aris 1972 (died 1999); two s.; ed St Francis Convent, Methodist English High School, Lady Shri Ram Coll., Delhi Univ., St Hugh's Coll., Oxford; Asst Sec. Advisory Cttee on Admin. and Budgetary Questions UN Secr., New York 1969–71; Resident Officer, Ministry of Foreign Affairs, Bhutan 1972; Visiting Scholar Centre for SE Asian Studies, Kyoto Univ., Japan 1985–86; Fellow, Indian Inst. of Advanced Studies 1987; Co-founder and Gen. Sec. Nat. League for Democracy 1988 (expelled from party), reinstated as Gen. Sec. 1995, Chair. 2013–; returned from UK 1988, under house arrest 1989–95, house arrest lifted July 1995, placed under de facto house arrest Sept. 2000, released unconditionally May 2002, arrested following Depayin massacre 30 May 2003, held in secret detention for over three months before being returned to house arrest, house arrest extended by one year 25 May 2007, mil. junta extended her house arrest another year 27 May 2008, release date set by court ruling Aug. 2009, released from house arrest 13 Nov. 2010; elected to Parl. 2012; Minister of Foreign Affairs and of the Pres.'s Office March 2016–, of Educ. and of Electric Power and Energy March–April 2016, State Counsellor April 2016–; Freeman, City of Dublin, Ireland 1999 (withdrawn 2017), Hon. mem. Bd Council Int. Inst. for Democracy and Electoral Assistance 2003, Hon. Canadian citizenship 2007 (revoked 2018), Hon. Pres. LSE Students' Union 2007, Freeman, City of Glasgow, Scotland 2009 (withdrawn 2017); Hon. AC 1996; numerous hon. degrees, including Hon. LLD (Memorial Univ. of Newfoundland) 2004, (Colgate Univ.) 2008, (Univ. of Ulster) 2009, Hon. Dr (Seoul Nat. Univ.) 2013, (Bologna) 2013, (Monash Univ., Australian Nat. Univ., Univ. of Sydney and Univ. of Tech., Sydney) 2013; Thorolf Rafto Memorial Prize 1990, Sakharov Prize 1990, European Parl. Human Rights Prize 1991, Nobel Peace Prize 1991, Simón Bolívar Int. Prize 1992, Liberal Int. Prize for Freedom 1995, Jawaharlal Nehru Award for Int. Understanding 1995, Freedom Award of Int. Rescue Cttee 1995, Presidential Medal of Freedom 2000, UNESCO Madanjeet Singh Prize for the Promotion of Tolerance and Non-Violence 2002, Free Spirit Prize, Freedom Forum USA 2003, Gwangju Prize for Human Rights 2004, Olof Palme Prize 2005, Freedom from Fear Award 2006, US Congressional Gold Medal 2008, Premi Internacional Catalunya 2008, Mahatma Gandhi Int. Award for Peace and Reconciliation 2009, Amb. of Conscience Award, Amnesty International 2009 (withdrawn 2018), Int. Bhagwan Mahavir World Peace Award 2012. *Publications:* Tibetan Studies in Honour of Hugh Richardson (co-ed.) 1979, Aung San 1984, Burma (Let's Visit Series) 1985, Nepal (Let's Visit Series) 1985, Bhutan (Let's Visit Series) 1986, Burma and India: Some Aspects of Intellectual Life Under Colonialism 1990, Aung San (Leaders of Asia Series) 1990, Aung San of Burma: A Biographical Portrait by His Daughter 1991, Freedom from Fear 1991, Towards a True Refuge 1993, Burma's Revolution of the Spirit: The Struggle for Democratic Freedom and Dignity (co-author) 1994, Freedom from Fear and Other Writings (co-author) 1995, Letter to Daniel: Despatches from the Heart by Fergal Keane (foreword by Aung San Suu Kyi) 1996, The Voice of Hope (with Alan Clements) 1998 (revised edn 2008), Letters from Burma (with Fergal Keane) 1998, Der Weg zur Freiheit (with U Kyi Maung and U Tin O) 1999. *Address:* President's Office, Bldg 18, Nay Pyi Taw (office); National League for Democracy, 97B West Shwegondine Road, Bahan Township, Yangon, Myanmar (office). *Website:* www.president-office.gov.mm (office); www.dassk.com (office).

AUPETIT, Most Reverend Michel Christian Alain, MD; French ecclesiastic and fmr physician; *Archbishop of Paris;* b. 23 March 1951, Versailles; ed Univ. Paris-Est Créteil Val de Marne; trained as doctor and began career in gen. practice in Colombes 1979–90; lecturer in medical ethics, Centre hospitalier universitaire Henri-Mondor, Créteil 1997–2006; ordained as priest for Archdiocese of Paris 1995; Vicar, Church of Saint-Louis-en-l'Île 1995–98, Saint-Paul-Saint-Louis 1998–2001; assigned to parish of Église Notre-Dame-de-l'Arche-d'Alliance 2001–06; Deacon, Pasteur-Vaugirard 2004–06; Vicar Gen., Archdiocese of Paris 2006–13; Auxiliary Bishop of Paris 2013–14; Titular Bishop of Maxita 2013–14; Bishop of Nanterre 2014–17; Archbishop of Paris 2018–; apptd Ordinary of Catholics of the Eastern Churches residing in France 2018; apptd mem. Congregation for Bishops 2018; Chevalier, Légion d'honneur 2018. *Publications include:* Contraception: la réponse de l'Église 1999, La mort, et après?: un prêtre médecin témoigne et répond aux interrogations 2009, L'homme, le sexe et Dieu: pour une sexualité plus humaine 2011, Construisons-nous une société humaine ou inhumaine? 2016. *Address:* Archdiocese of Paris, 10 rue du Cloître Notre-Dame, 75004 Paris, France (office). *Telephone:* 1-78-91-91-91 (office). *Fax:* 1-78-91-92-73 (office). *E-mail:* communication@diocese-paris.net (office). *Website:* paris .catholique.fr (office).

AURAKZAI, Lt-Gen. (retd) Ali Mohammad Jan; Pakistani army officer (retd) and government administrator; b. 1 Dec. 1947; s. of Haji Khial Din and Naze Gul Aurakzai; m. Mujahida Khanum; three s. one d.; ed Peshawar Univ., Balochistan Univ.; fmr Commdr 11th Corps, Peshawar; fmr Adjutant-Gen. of Gen. HQ; Gov. of North-West Frontier Prov. 2006–08 (resgnd); Sitara-e-Basalat 1999, Hilal-e-Imtiaz (Mil.) 2000, Hilal-e-Imtiaz (Civil) 2004. *Publication:* Beyond Tora Bora: The Aurakzai Memoirs 2017. *Leisure interests:* music, hunting. *Address:* House #2, Street 2, Sector 2, DHA Phase 1, Morgah, Islamabad, Pakistan (home). *Telephone:* (51) 5788298 (home). *E-mail:* ali.aurakzai@hotmail.com (office).

AURESCU, Bogdan Lucian, PhD; Romanian lawyer, diplomatist and politician; b. 9 Sept. 1973, Bucharest; ed Univ. of Bucharest, Institut Franco-Roumain du Droit des Affaires et Cooperation Internationale, Bucharest, The Hague Acad. of Int. Law, Nat. Defence Coll. of Romania; Attaché, Int. Law and Treaties Dept, Ministry of Foreign Affairs 1996–98, Counsellor, Office of the Minister 1998–99, Deputy Dir Int. Law and Treaties Dept 1999, Dir 2000–01, Dir Office of the Minister 1999, Dir-Gen. Dept for Legal Affairs 2001, Under-Sec. of State for Legal Affairs 2003–04, Sec. of State for European Affairs 2004–05, for Strategic Affairs 2009–14, Minister of Foreign Affairs 2014–15; Univ. Asst 2002, Lecturer in Law 2004; Rep. of Romanian Govt at European Court of Human Rights 2003–04; Visiting Prof., Faculty of Law, Univ. of Hamburg, Germany 2006; Ed.-in-Chief, Romanian Journal of International Law; mem. Romanian Asscn for Int. Law and Int. Relations 1996–; Kt, Ordinul Național Serviciul Credincios 2002, Ordinul Meritul Diplomatic 2007. *Publications include:* Contemporary International Law (co-author) 2000, The New Sovereignty: Between Legal Reality and Political Necessity in the Contemporary International System 2003, The System of International Jurisdictions 2005.

AUSAF, Ashtar, BA, LLB, MCL; Pakistani lawyer and govt official; b. 19 June 1956, Lahore; ed Forman Christian Coll., Punjab Univ., George Washington Univ., USA; Adjunct Lecturer of Int. Law, Punjab Univ. 1984–88; Founding Partner, Ashtar Ali & Co. (law firm), Lahore 1985–; admitted to Supreme Court Bar 1995, Advocate Gen. of Punjab 1998–99, 2012–13, Prosecutor Gen. 2011–12; Adviser to the Prime Minister on Human Rights 1997–99, Special Asst to the Prime Minister on Law, Justice and Human Rights, with the charge of Minister of State 2015–16; Attorney-Gen. 2016–18; mem. Lahore Bar Asscn 1986–, American Arbitration Asscn. *Address:* Ashtar Ali & Co., Flat No. 16 M-U, Ganga Ram Mansion, 53 Lahore 44000, Pakistan (office). *Telephone:* (42) 37112486 (office). *Fax:* (42) 37112487 (office). *E-mail:* info@ashtarali.com. *Website:* www.ashtarali.com.

AUSHEV, Lt-Gen. Ruslan Sultanovich; Russian/Ingush politician; b. 29 Oct. 1954, Volodarskoye, Kokchetav Region, USSR (now Kazakhstan); s. of Sultan Aushev and Tamara Aushev; m. Aza Bamatgirovna Ausheva 1983; two s. two d.; ed Ordzhonikidze Gen. Troops School, M. Frunze Mil. Acad.; Commdr motorized infantry co., then platoon 1975–80; Chief of HQ, then Commdr motorized Bn in Afghanistan 1980–82; Chief of Regt HQ in Afghanistan 1985–87; Commdr motorized infantry regt, then Deputy Commdr motorized infantry div. Far East Command 1987–91; at Council of Heads of Govts of CIS countries 1991–92; USSR People's Deputy 1989–91; Chair., Cttee on Affairs of Soldiers-Internationalists, USSR Aug.–Dec. 1991, CIS Council of Heads of Govt 1992–; Head of Admin in newly formed Ingush Repub. Nov.–Dec. 1992; Pres. Repub. of Ingushetiya 1993–2001 (resgnd); mem. CPSU 1977–91; mem. Fed. Council of Russia 1993–2000 (also mem. of Cttee on Defence and Security), Rep. of Ingushetiya to Fed. Council 2002–03; fmr Chair. Political Council, Rossiiskaya Partiya Mira (Russian Party of Peace); Order of Lenin 1982, Orders of Red Star (twice) 1980, 1987, Order of Honor 2007, Order for Service to Motherland (2nd and 3rd degrees) 2007, 2014, Order of Friendship (2nd degree) 2011, 2014, Order of Merit 2012, Order of Glory (twice), Order for Service to Homeland in Armed Forces of USSR (3rd class); Hero of Soviet Union (Gold Star) 1982, medal for Certificate of Honor of President of Russian Federation 2013, 1st class medal, "For Distinction in Military Service". *Leisure interest:* football.

AUST, Stefan; German journalist and writer; b. 1 July 1946, Stade; Ed. Concrete magazine 1966–69; staff mem. NDR TV 1970–72; journalist, Panorama (political magazine) 1972–86; Chief Ed. Der Spiegel TV 1988–94, Ed.-in-Chief Der Spiegel 1994–2008; Man. Dir Der Spiegel TV GmbH 1994–2008; fmr TV host with talk show Talk in the Tower, currently Host Spiegel-TV; Publisher Die WeltN24 2014–, Ed.-in-Chief Jan.–Sept. 2016; Goldenen Kamera 2005, Ernst Dieter Lueg-Preis 2016. *Publications include:* Kennwort 100 Blumen – Verwicklung des Verfassungsschutzes in den Mordfall Ulrich Schmücker 1980, Brokdorf: Symbol Einer Politischen Wende 1981, Der Baader Meinhof Komplex 1985, Stammheim (film script) 1986, Werner Mauss – Ein Deutscher Agent 1988, Der Pirat: Die Drogenkarriere des Jan C. 1990, Die Flucht: Über die Vertreibung der Deutschen aus dem Osten 2002, Der Lockvogel. 2002, Irak: Geschichte eines modernen Krieges 2003, Die Gegenwart der Vergangenheit: Der lange Schatten des Dritten Reichs 2004, Wettlauf um die Welt: Die Globalisierung und wir 2007, Deutschland, Deutschland: Expedition durch die Wendezeit 2011, Heimatschutz (with Dirk Laabs) 2014, Hitlers erster Feind: Der Kampf des Konrad Heiden 2016.

AUSTEN, K(arl) Frank, MD; American professor of medicine; *Astra Zeneca Professor of Respiratory and Inflammatory Diseases, Department of Medicine, Brigham and Women's Hospital;* b. 14 March 1928, Akron, Ohio; s. of Karl Arnstein and Bertle J. Arnstein; m. Jocelyn Chapman 1959; two s. two d.; ed Amherst Coll. and Harvard Medical School; Intern in Medicine, Mass. Gen. Hosp. 1954–55, Asst Resident 1955–56, Sr Resident 1958–59, Chief Resident 1961–62, Asst in Medicine 1962–63, Asst Physician 1963–66; Capt., US Army Medical Corps, Walter Reed Army Inst. of Research 1956–58; U.S.P.H.S. Postdoctoral Research Fellow, Nat. Inst. for Medical Research, Mill Hill, London, UK 1959–61; Physician-in-Chief, Robert B. Brigham Hosp. Boston 1966–80; Physician, Peter Bent Brigham Hosp. Boston 1966–80; Chair. Dept Rheumatology and Immunology, Brigham and Women's Hosp., Boston 1980–95, Dir Inflammation and Allergic Diseases Research Section, Div. of Rheumatology and Immunology 1995, now Astra Zeneca Professor of Respiratory and Inflammatory Diseases; Asst in Medicine, Harvard Medical School 1961, Instr. 1962, Assoc. 1962–64, Asst Prof. 1965–66, Assoc. Prof. 1966–68, Prof. 1969–72, Theodore Bevier Bayles Prof. of Medicine 1972–; Pres. Int. Soc. of Immunopharmacology 1994; mem. numerous professional orgs; recipient of numerous prizes and awards. *Publications:* numerous publications on immunology, etc. *Leisure interests:* skiing, jogging, gardening. *Address:* Department of Medicine, Brigham and Women's Hospital, Smith Building, Room 638, One Jimmy Fund Way, Boston, MA 02115, USA (office). *Telephone:* (617) 525-1300 (office). *Fax:* (617) 525-1310 (office). *Website:* dms.hms .harvard.edu/immunology (office).

AUSTER, Paul Benjamin, MA; American writer, poet and film director; b. 3 Feb. 1947, Newark, New Jersey; s. of Sam Auster and Queenie Auster; m. 1st Lydia Davis 1974 (divorced 1982); one s.; m. 2nd Siri Hustvedt 1982; one d.; ed Columbia High School, New Jersey, Columbia Coll., Columbia Univ.; worked as census taker; oil tanker utility man. on Esso Florence; moved to Paris, France 1971, returned to USA 1974; worked as translator; Lecturer in Creative Writing and Translation, Princeton Univ. 1986–90; juror, Cannes Film Festival 1997; Fellow, American Acad. of Arts and Sciences 2003; mem. PEN America (mem. Bd of Trustees 2004–09 (Vice-Pres. 2005–07)), American Acad. of Arts and Letters 2006; Commdr, Ordre des Arts et des Lettres 2007; Nat. Endowment for the Arts fellowships 1979, 1985; Prix France Culture de Littérature Étrangère (for The New York Trilogy) 1989, Prince of Asturias Prize for Literature 2006, Premio Leteo 2009, Médaille Grand Vermeil de Paris 2010, Premio di Napoli 2011, NYC Literary Honors for fiction 2012. *Films include:* screenplays: Smoke 1995, Blue in the Face (co-dir) 1995, Lulu on the Bridge (also dir) 1998, The Inner Life of Martin Frost (also dir) 2007. *Publications include:* fiction: The New York Trilogy: City of Glass 1985, Ghosts 1986, The Locked Room 1986; In the Country of Last Things 1987, Moon Palace 1989, The Music of Chance 1990, Leviathan (Prix Médicis Étranger 1993) 1992, Mr Vertigo 1994, Timbuktu 1999, The Book of Illusions 2002, Oracle Night 2003, The Brooklyn Follies 2005, Travels in the Scriptorium 2006, Man in the Dark 2008, Invisible 2009, Sunset Park 2010, Day/Night 2013, 4 3 2 1 2017; non-fiction: White Spaces 1980, The Invention of Solitude 1982, The Art of Hunger 1982, Hand to Mouth (memoir) 1989, The Red Notebook 1995, Why Write? 1996, Translations 1996, Collected Prose 2003, Winter Journal 2012, Here and Now: Letters 2008–2011 2013, Report from the Interior 2013, A Life in Words: In Conversation with I. B. Siegumfeldt 2017; poetry: Unearth 1974, Wall Writing 1976, Fragments From Cold 1977, Facing the Music 1980, Disappearances: Selected Poems 1988, Collected Poems 2003; ed.: The Random House Book of Twentieth-Century French Poetry 1982, True Tales of American Life 2001, Samuel Beckett: The Grove Centenary Edn 2006. *Address:* c/o Carol Mann Agency, 55 Fifth Avenue, New York, NY 10003, USA (office). *Website:* paul-auster.com.

AUSTRIAN, Neil R.; American business executive; b. 1940; fmr CEO Doyle, Dane, Bernbach (advertising co.); Chair. and CEO Showtime/The Movie Channel –1987; Man. Dir Dillon, Read & Co. 1987–91; Pres. and COO Nat. Football League (NFL) 1991–99; mem. Bd of Dirs Office Depot Inc. 1998–2013, CEO and Interim Chair. 2004–05, CEO 2011–13; mem. Bd of Dirs DirecTV Group 2003, Viking Office Products 1988–98; mem. Advisory Bd Mid-Ocean Pnrs.

AUTEUIL, Daniel; French actor; b. 24 Oct. 1950, Algeria; s. of Henri Auteuil and Yvonne Auteuil; m. Aude Ambroggi 2006; two d. (one with Emmanuelle Béart q.v.); worked in musical comedies in Paris; screen debut in L'Agression 1974; stage appearances include Le Garçon d'Appartement 1980; Chevalier des Arts et des Lettres. *Films include:* Attention les yeux 1975, La nuit Saint-Germain des Prés 1976, L'Amour violé 1976, Monsieur Papa 1977, Les héros n'ont pas froid aux oreilles 1978, A nous deux 1979, Bête mais discipliné 1979, Les Sous-Doués 1980, Clara et les chics types 1980, Les hommes préfèrent les grosses 1981, Les Sous-Doués en vacances 1981, T'empêches tout le monde de dormir 1981, Pour cent briques t'as plus rien 1981, Que les gros salaires lèvent le doigt 1982, P'tit Con 1983, Les fauves 1983, Palace 1983, L'Arbalete 1984, L'Amour en douce 1984, Manon des sources (César for Best Actor 1986, Best Actor Award, Cannes Film Festival) 1985, Jean de Florette (César for Best Actor 1987, BAFTA Award for Best Actor in a Supporting Role 1987) 1986, Le paltoquet 1986, Quelques jours avec moi 1988, Romuald and Juliette 1989, Lacenaire 1989, Ma vie est un enfer 1991, Un coeur en hiver (European Film Award for Best Actor 1993) 1992, Ma saison préférée 1993, L'Elegant criminel, tout ça pour ça 1993, La séparation 1994, La Reine Margot 1994, The Eighth Day 1996, Les voleurs 1998, La fille sur le pont (César for Best Actor 2000) 1999, The Lost Son 1999, La veuve de Saint Pierre 2000, Sade (Lumière Award for Best Actor 2001) 2000, Le placard 2001, L'Adversaire 2002, Après vous 2003, Pourquoi (pas) le Brésil 2004, 36 Quai des Orfèvres 2004, L'Un reste, l'autre part 2005, Caché (European Film Award for Best Actor) 2005, Peindre ou faire l'amour 2005, La Doublure 2006, L'Entente cordiale 2006, Mon meilleur ami 2006, N (Io e Napoleone) 2006, Dialogue avec mon jardinier 2007, La personne aux deux personnes 2008, Je l'aimais 2009, Donnant, donnant 2010, La fille du puisatier (also director) (The Well Digger's Daughter) 2011, The Lookout 2012, Jappeloup 2013, Marius 2013, Fanny 2013, Before the Winter Chill 2013, Nos femmes 2015, Entre amis 2015, Kalinka 2015. *Address:* c/o Claire Blondel, Artmédia, 20 avenue Rapp, 75007 Paris, France (office). *Telephone:* 1-43-17-33-00 (office). *Fax:* 1-44-18-34-60 (office). *E-mail:* c.blondel@artmedia.fr (office). *Website:* www.artmedia.fr (office).

AVAKOV, Arsen Borysovych; Ukrainian engineer and politician; *Minister of Internal Affairs;* b. 2 Jan. 1964, Kirov settlement, Kirov Dist (now Binäqädi Dist), Baku, Azerbaijan SSR, USSR; m.; one s.; ed Kharkiv Polytechnic Inst.; lab. asst, Chair for Automated Control Systems, Kharkiv Polytechnic Inst. 1981–82; engineer, All-Union Scientific-Research Inst. on Water Protection (Kharkiv) 1987–90; Founder and Head of Supervisory Bd, Investor JSC 1990–2005, Basis Commercial Bank 1992–2005; elected mem. Exec. Cttee, Kharkiv City Council 2002; apptd Head of Kharkiv Oblast State Admin 2005; Deputy of Kharkiv Oblast Council 2006–10, mem. Standing Cttee on Budgetary Issues 2006–10, Deputy of Kharkiv Oblast Council 2010–12, mem. Standing Cttee on Science, Educ., Culture, Historical Heritage, Intellectual Wealth and Nat. Minorities 2010; withdrew from Nasha Ukraina (Our Ukraine) party 2010; mem. Batkivshchyna Obyednana Opozytsiya (Fatherland United Opposition) 2010–, accepted offer from Yuliya Tymoshenko to become Chair. of regional org. of Blok Yuliya Tymoshenko (Yuliya Tymoshenko Bloc); charged with illegally transferring land Jan. 2012, put on Interpol int. wanted list March 2012, detained in Frosinone, Italy late March 2012, placed under house arrest by Italian court as a preventive measure April 2012; mem. Verkhovna Rada (Parl.) Oct. 2012–; restriction measures and arrest warrant cancelled by a court ruling Dec. 2012; Minister of Internal Affairs 2014–; arrested in absentia by a Moscow Dist court July 2014; Founding mem. Narodny Front (People's Front) party Sept. 2014; Pres. Supervisory Bd, Renaissance Charity Foundation, Kharkiv Oblast Charitable Org.; Head of Kharkiv Oblast Div. of Nat. Olympic Cttee 2005–10; Co-founder Marianna Avakova Fund; Co-Chair. Star Bridge Int. Science Fiction Festival Organizing Cttee; Founder Producing Foundation of Arsen Avakov. *Publications:* Strategy of Social and Economic Development of Kharkiv Oblast For the Period till 2015 (monograph) 2008; 12 scientific papers and several essays on political and social issues. *Address:* Ministry of Internal Affairs, 10124 Kyiv, vul. Ak. Bohomoltsya 10, Ukraine (office). *Telephone:* (44) 256-03-33 (office). *Fax:* (44) 254-96-34 (office). *E-mail:* zmi@mvsinfo.gov.ua (office). *Website:* mvs.gov.ua (office).

AVARENA MORI, Alejandro Gastón; Chilean architect; *Executive Director, Elemental SA;* b. 22 June 1967, Santiago; ed Univ. Católica de Chile; f. Alejandro Aravena Architects 1994; Exec. Dir Elemental SA (architectural practice) 2006–; first project was new Math. Faculty for Univ. Católica de Chile 1998, work includes schools, institutional, corp. and public buildings, museums and housing; extensive portfolio of private, public and educational projects in Chile, USA, Mexico, People's Repub. of China, Germany, Russia, Italy and Switzerland; Visiting Prof., Harvard Grad. School of Design 2000–05; Elemental-Copec Prof., Univ. Católica de Chile 2006–; Dir, Architecture Section of Venice Biennale 2015–; mem. jury, Pritzker Architecture Prize 2009–15; Int. Fellow, RIBA; Erich Schelling Architecture Medal 2006, Global Award for Sustainable Architecture 2008, Venice Architecture Biennale Silver Lion Award 2008, INDEX: Design to Improve Life Award 2011, Pritzker Architecture Prize 2016. *Projects include:* Casa para una Escultora (House for a Sculptor), Santiago 1997, Montessori School, Santiago 2001, Medical School, Univ. Católica de Chile 2001–04, Siamese Towers (School of Architecture), Univ. Católica de Chile 2003–06, social housing, Iquique, Chile 2004, House on the Lake, Pirehueico, Chile 2004, dormitory for St Edward's Univ., Austin, Texas 2008, art workshops, Weil am Rhein, Germany 2008, Ordos Villa, Inner Mongolia, People's Repub. of China 2008, Prefabricated House Prototype, Milan, Italy 2008, social housing, Monterrey, Mexico 2010, Etlin House, São Paulo, Brazil 2010, Las Cruces, Jalisco, Mexico 2010, Bicentennial Garden, Santiago 2012, Teheran Stock Exchange 2012, Ekaterinburg TV Tower, Russia 2013, Anacleto Angelini Research and Innovation Centre, Santiago 2014, House of Writing, Montricher, Switzerland 2014, Constitución Civic Centre, Santiago 2014, Ayelén School, Rancagua, Chile 2015, Novartis Building, Shanghai, People's Repub. of China 2015. *Publications:* Los Hechos de la Arquitectura 1999, El Lugar de la Arquitectura 2002, Elemental (monograph) 2010. *Address:* Elemental SA, Av. Los Conquistadores 1700, Piso 25A, 7520282 Providencia, Santiago, Chile (office). *Telephone:* (2) 2963-7500 (office). *E-mail:* info@elementalchile.cl (office). *Website:* alejandroaravena.com (office).

AVDEYEV, Aleksander Alekseyevich; Russian politician and diplomatist; *Ambassador to the Holy See (Vatican City);* b. 8 Sept. 1946, Kremenchug, Poltava Region, Ukrainian SSR, USSR; m.; one s.; ed Moscow State Inst. of Int. Relations; entered Diplomatic Service of USSR Ministry of Foreign Affairs 1968, Second, then First Sec., USSR Embassy in Paris 1977–85, Head of Sector, First European Dept, USSR Ministry of Foreign Affairs 1985–87, USSR Amb. to Luxembourg 1987–90, First Deputy Head, First European Dept, Ministry of Foreign Affairs 1990–91, USSR Deputy Minister of Foreign Affairs 1991–92, Amb. at Large, Russian Ministry of Foreign Affairs 1992, Amb. to Bulgaria 1992–96, Deputy Minister of Foreign Affairs 1996–98, First Deputy Minister 1998–2002, Amb. to France 2002–08 (also accred to Monaco 2007–08); Minister of Culture 2008–12; Amb. to the Holy See (Vatican City) 2012–; Order of Honour, Order of Friendship. *Address:* Embassy of the Russian Federation, Via della Conciliazione 10, 00193 Rome, Italy (office). *Telephone:* (06) 6877078 (office). *Fax:* (06) 6877168 (office). *E-mail:* russsede@libero.it (office).

AVEN, Petr Olegovich, PhD; Russian economist; *Chairman, Alfa Banking Group;* b. 16 March 1955, Moscow; s. of Oleg I. Aven; m.; two c.; ed Moscow State Univ.; researcher, All-Union Inst. for Systems Studies, USSR (now Russian) Acad. of Sciences 1981–88; Int. Inst. of Applied System Analysis, Laxenburg, Austria 1989–91, First Deputy Minister of Foreign Affairs, Chair. Cttee of Foreign Econ. Relations 1991–92; Russian Minister of Foreign Econ. Relations Feb.–Dec. 1992; mem. State Duma 1993–94; Pres. and Deputy Chair. Alfa Bank 1994–2011, Chair. Alfastrakhovaniye (Alfa Insurance) 2007–; Chair. STS Television 1998, Golden Telecom Inc. 2001–; Co-Chair. CTC Media; mem. Bd Competitiveness and Entrepreneurship Council, Bolshoi Theatre; Trustee Russian Econ. School, Nat. Asscn for Nat. Financial Reporting Standards; lectures internationally on econ. devts in Russia; several int. awards, named Russia's Most Admired Exec. in the Financial Services by Institutional Investor magazine 2004. *Publications include:* The International Economy 2003; numerous books, scientific papers and articles on econ. and trade issues and reform of the rural economy. *Leisure interests:* the arts, theatre, collecting early 20th century Russian art. *Telephone:* (495) 620-91-91 (office). *Fax:* (495) 974-25-15 (office). *E-mail:* mail@alfabank.ru (office). *Website:* www.alfabank.ru (office).

AVERCHENKO, Vladimir Alexandrovich, CandEcon; Russian engineer, politician, business executive and academic; *Chairman, Business Centre Investment Group;* b. 23 July 1950, Belaya Kalitva, Rostov Region; m.; three c.; ed Novocherkassk Polytechnical Inst., New York Univ., USA; army service 1969–71; on staff, Belokalitvinsky City CPSU Cttee 1975–80; constructor, major industrial sites, Rostov Region; Head of Itominstroi, then Promstroi Rostov Region 1980–89; Deputy Chair. Novocherkassk City Exec. Cttee 1989–91; First Vice-Maj. Novocherkassk 1991–98; Deputy Gov., Minister of Econ., Int. and Foreign Relations, Rostov Region 1998–99; concurrently Head of Econ. Council, Asscn of Social-Econ. Devt, N Caucasus; Deputy, State Duma, People's Deputies Group 1999; Head of Del. of Fed. Ass. in Parl. Ass. of Black Sea Econ. Co-operation (PACHES); Deputy Chair. State Duma 2000–03; Dir Fed. Agency for Construction and Housing Utilities 2004–05; currently Chair. Business Centre Investment Group; Chair. Council of the Acad. of Modern Building; Prof. of Financial Strategy, Moscow School of Econs (Lomonosov Moscow State Univ.; Hon. Builder of the Russian Fed.; Hon. Worker in Housing and Public Utilities in the Russian Fed.; hon. mem. of several acads; state awards and int. award for contrib. to devt of free market relations between Russia and CIS countries 1994. *Publications:* 16 books on management, investment policy and ecology and numerous articles. *Leisure interests:* chess, basketball, collecting figurines of lions, collecting coins. *Address:* Business Centre Investment Group, 115114 Moscow, 6 Bld. 4, Shlyuzovaya emb., Russian Federation (office). *Telephone:* (495) 662-94-38 (office). *Fax:* (499) 702-30-89 (office). *E-mail:* office@applenewz.ru (office). *Website:* applenewz.ru (office).

AVICE, Edwige, LèsL; French consultant and fmr politician; b. 13 April 1945, Nevers; d. of Edmond Bertrant and Hélène Guyot; m. Etienne Avice 1970; ed Cours Fénelon, Nevers, Lycée Pothier, Orléans, Univ. of Paris; worked for Nat. Cttee for Housing Improvement 1970; Int. Dept, Crédit Lyonnais 1970–73; on staff of Dir-Gen. of Paris Hosps 1973–78; Pres. Asscn Démocratique des Français de l'Etranger 1991–93; mem. Parti Socialiste (PS) 1972, mem. Exec. Bureau 1977, Nat. Secr. 1987–94, PS Nat. Del. for Nat. Service; mem. Nat. Ass. 1978–81, 1986–88; Minister-Del. for Free Time, Youth and Sports 1981–84; Sec. of State attached to the Minister of Defence 1984–86; Minister-Del. attached to the Minister for Foreign Affairs 1988–91; Minister of Co-operation and Devt 1991–93; Conseillère de Paris 1983–88; Pres. and Dir-Gen. Financière de Brienne 1993–2005, Chair Brienne Council and Finance 1993–2005; currently Assoc. Dir BIPE (econ. consultancy); Pres. Int. Defence Council 1999–2003. *Publication:* Terre d'élection 1993. *Leisure interests:* travelling, music, swimming, walking, fencing. *Address:* BIPE, 43–47 avenue Grande Armée, 750116 Paris, France (office). *Telephone:* 1-58-36-04-30 (office). *E-mail:* information@bipe.com (office). *Website:* lebipe.com (office).

ÁVILA, Rodrigo, BEng, BA; Salvadorean police officer and politician; b. 25 June 1965, San Salvador; s. of Roberto Ávila Moreira and Thelma Avilez; m. Celina Denys de Ávila; three d.; ed North Carolina State Univ., Gainesville Coll., Ga, FBI Nat. Acad., and Texas A&M Univ., USA; interim Dir, then Dir Policía Nacional Civil 1993–99; rose through ranks of police force to serve as Deputy Chief of Police Operations Feb.–June 1994, Chief of Police 1994–99, 2006–08; Deputy Head of Alianza Republicana Nacionalista (ARENA) Bench in Congress 2000–03; cand. in mayoral elections for Santa Tecla 2003; Deputy Minister for Security 2003–06; Vice Minister of Public Security 2004–09; ARENA party, cand. for Pres. of El Salvador 2008. *Address:* Alianza Republicana Nacionalista (ARENA), Prolongación Calle Arce 2423, entre 45 y 47 Avda Norte, San Salvador, El Salvador (office). *Telephone:* 2260-4400 (office); 2281-9437. *Website:* arena.org.sv (office); www.rodrigoavila.org. *E-mail:* comunicacionesra@icloud.com.

ÁVILA CORDEIRO DE MELO, Artur, PhD; Brazilian/French mathematician; *Director of Research, Centre national de la recherche scientifique (CNRS);* b. 29 June 1979, Rio de Janeiro; s. of Raimundo Ávila and Lenir Ávila; m. Susan Schommer; ed Instituto Nacional de Matemática Pura e Aplicada, Collège de France; Assoc. Lecturer, Coll. de France 2001–03; Researcher, CNRS 2003–08, Dir of Research, Institut de Mathématiques de Jussieu–Paris Rive Gauche, Univ. Paris Diderot 2008–; Research Fellow, Clay Mathematics Inst., Rhode Island 2006–09; currently also Researcher, Instituto Nacional de Matemática Pura e Aplicada, Rio de Janeiro; numerous awards including Salem Prize 2006, European Math. Soc. Prize 2008, French Acad. of Sciences Herbrand Prize 2009, Michael Brin Prize 2011, Prêmio da Sociedade Brasileira de Matemática 2013, World Acad. of Sciences Prize 2013, Fields Medal 2014. *Achievements include:* awarded gold medal at Int. Mathematical Olympiad 1995; research focuses on dynamical systems and spectral theory, chaos theory. *Address:* Université Paris Diderot, UFR Mathématiques, Bâtiment Sophie Germain, Case 7012, 5 rue Thomas Mann, 75205 Paris Cedex 13, France (office). *Telephone:* 1-44-27-53-37 (office). *E-mail:* artur.avila@imj-prg.fr (office). *Website:* www.institut.math.jussieu.fr (office).

ÁVILA VILLEGAS, Eruviel, LLB, LLM; Mexican lawyer and politician; b. 1 May 1969, Ecatepec de Morelos; m. (divorced); four c.; ed Universidad Tecnológica de México, Nat. Autonomous Univ. of Mexico; fmr teacher, Universidad Tecnológica de México; Sec., Ecatepec de Morelos City Council 1994–96; mem. Congreso de la Unión (Parl.) 1997–2000, 2006–09; Mayor of Ecatepec de Morelos 2003–06, 2009–11; Gov. State of Mexico 2011–17; Pres. Federación Nacional de Municipios de México (Nat. Fed. of Municipalities of Mexico); mem. Partido Revolucionario Institucional (PRI), Pres. PRI Edomex 2006. *Publications:* La Creación de la Corte Constitucional del Estado de México 2003. *Address:* Partido Revolucionario Institucional (PRI), Insurgentes Norte 59, Col. Buenavista, Delegation Cuauhtémoc, 06359 México City, Mexico (office). *Telephone:* (55) 5729-9600 (office). *Website:* pri.org.mx (office).

AVINERI, Shlomo; Israeli political scientist and academic; *Professor Emeritus of Political Science, Hebrew University of Jerusalem;* b. 20 Aug. 1933, Bielsko, Poland; s. of Michael Avineri and Erna Groner; m. Dvora Nadler 1957; one d.; ed Shalva Secondary School, Tel-Aviv, Hebrew Univ., Jerusalem, London School of Econs, UK; has lived in Israel since 1939; Prof. of Political Science, Hebrew Univ. Jerusalem 1971–, now Emer., Dir Eshkol Research Inst. 1971–74, Dean of Faculty of Social Sciences 1974–76; Dir-Gen. Ministry of Foreign Affairs 1976–77; Dir Inst. for European Studies, Hebrew Univ. 1997–; visiting appointments at Yale Univ. 1966–67, Wesleyan Univ., Middletown, Conn. 1971–72, Research School of Social Sciences, ANU 1972, Cornell Univ. 1973, Univ. of California 1979, Queen's Coll., New York 1989, Univ. of Oxford 1989; mem. Int. Inst. of Philosophy 1980–; Fellow, Woodrow Wilson Center, Washington, DC 1983–84; Visiting Prof., Cardozo School of Law, New York 1996–97, 2000–01, Brookings Inst., Washington, DC 1991, Cen. European Univ., Budapest 1994, Northwestern Univ. 1997, Carnegie Endowment for Int. Peace, Washington, DC 2000–01; mem. Israel Acad. of Sciences and Humanities, Polish Acad. of Arts and Sciences; Fellow, Collegium Budapest 2002; Commdr, Star of Italian Order of Solidarity 2009; Dr hc (Univ. of Cluj-Napoca, Romania) 1994, (Weizmann Inst. of Science) 2010; British Council Scholarship 1961, Rubin Prize in the Social Sciences 1968, Naphtali Prize for Study of Hegel 1977, Present Tense Award for Study of Zionism 1982, Carlyle Lecturer, Univ. of Oxford 1989, Israel Prize 1996, Life Award, Israel Political Science Asscn 2005, Freedom Medal, Senate of the Czech Repub. 2008, EMET Prize in Political Science 2014. *Publications include:* The Social and Political Thought of Karl Marx 1968, Karl Marx on Colonialism and Modernization 1968, Israel and the Palestinians 1971, Marx's Socialism 1972, Hegel's Theory of the Modern State 1973, Varieties of Marxism 1977, The Making of Modern Zionism 1981, Moses Hess – Prophet of Communism and Zionism 1985, Arlosoroff: A Political Biography 1989, Communitarianism and Individualism (co-author) 1992, Herzl's Diaries 1998, Identity and Integration 1999, The Law of Religious Identity (co-author) 1999, Identities in Transformation 2002, Herzl: Theodor Herzl and the Foundation of the Jewish State 2013. *Address:* Faculty of Social Sciences, Hebrew University of Jerusalem, Mount Scopus, Jerusalem 91905 (office); 10 Hagedud Ha-ivri Street, Jerusalem 92345, Israel (home). *Telephone:* (2) 588-3009 (office); (2) 566-0862 (office). *Fax:* (2) 588-1333 (office). *E-mail:* shlomo.avineri@huji.ac.il (office). *Website:* politics.huji.ac.il (office).

AVNET, Jonathan (Jon) Michael, BA; American film industry executive and film director; b. 17 Nov. 1949, Brooklyn, New York; m. Barbara Brody; one s. two d.; ed Sarah Lawrence Coll., Univ. of Pennsylvania, Conservatory for Advanced Film Studies; Reader, United Artists, LA 1974; Dir of Creative Affairs, Sequoia Pictures, LA 1975–77; Pres. Tisch/Avnet Productions, LA 1977–85; Chair. Avnet/Kerner Co., LA 1985–; Pres. Allied Communications Inc.; Trustee LA Co. Opera; Fellow, American Film Inst.; mem. Dirs Guild of America, Writers Guild of America, Acad. of Motion Pictures Arts and Sciences. *Films:* Dir and Producer: Fried Green Tomatoes at the Whistle Stop Cafe (three Golden Globes), The War, Up Close and Personal, George of the Jungle, 88 Minutes 2007, Righteous Kill 2008; Producer: Coast to Coast 1980, Risky Business 1983, Less than Zero 1987, Men Don't Leave 1990, When a Man Loves a Woman, Mighty Ducks 1994, Deal of the Century, Miami Rhapsody 1995, Three Musketeers 1993, Three Christs (Dir) 2017; Exec. Producer: The Burning Bed, Silence of the Heart, Heatwave (four Cable Ace Awards, including Best Picture), Do You Know the Muffin Man, No Other Love, Steal This Movie. *Television includes:* films: No Other Love 1979, Homeward Bound 1980, Prime Suspect 1982, Calendar Girl Murders 1984, Between Two Women 1986, In Love and War 1987, Side by Side 1988, Breaking Point 1989, Heat Wave 1990, Backfield in Motion 1991, The Nightman 1992, The Switch 1993, Naomi & Wynonna: Love Can Build a Bridge 1995, My Last Love 1999, A House Divided 2000, Uprising 2001, Bunker Hill 2009, Pleading Guilty 2010, Have a Little Faith 2011; series: Call to Glory 1984–85, Boomtown 2002–03, Conviction 2005, Jan 2013, Justified 2010–13, Blue 2012–14, Ro 2012, Kendra 2012, Ruth & Erica 2012, Lauren 2013, Susanna 2013, Paloma 2013–14; others: The Starter Wife (mini-series) 2007. *Leisure interests:* basketball, skiing, biking.

AVOKA, Apul Cletus, LLB, BL; Ghanaian lawyer and politician; b. 30 Nov. 1951, Teshie, nr Zebilla, Upper East Region; m.; four c.; ed Univ. of Ghana; Chair. Public Tribunal for Northern Ghana 1983–84; mem. Parl. (Nat. Democratic Congress) for Bawku W 1992–2005, for Zebilla 2009–, Majority Leader 2009–13, mem. Cttee of Selection, Cttee for Defence and the Interior, Cttee for Mines and Energy, Subsidiary Legislation Cttee; Minister of State 1995–97, Minister of Lands and Forestry 1997, of Environment, Science and Tech. 1998, of the Interior 2009–10; Sr Partner, Malsim Chambers, Accra 2005–09. *Address:* Office of Parliament, Parliament House, Accra, Ghana (office). *Telephone:* (302) 664530 (office). *Website:* www.parliament.gh/parliamentarians/22 (office).

AVRAMOPOULOS, Dimitris, LLB; Greek politician, fmr diplomatist and EU official; *Commissioner for Migration, Home Affairs and Citizenship, European Commission;* b. 6 June 1953, Athens; s. of Lambros Avramopoulos and Helene Avramopoulos; m. Vivian Avramopoulos; two s.; ed Univ. of Athens, Boston Univ., USA, Univ. Libre de Bruxelles, Belgium, Diplomatic Acad. of Ministry of Foreign Affairs; served in diplomatic service 1981–93, postings included Consul in Liège, Belgium 1983–88, Consul-Gen., Geneva 1992, Dir of Diplomatic Office of Prime Minister Konstantinos Mitsotakis 1993; mem. Vouli (Parl.) (New Democracy) for Athens A Electoral Dist 1993–94, 2004–11; Mayor of Athens 1995–2002; Minister of Tourism Devt 2004–06, of Health and Social Solidarity 2006, 2007–09, of Nat. Defence 2011–12, 2013–14, of Foreign Affairs 2012–13; Commr for Migration, Home Affairs and Citizenship, European Comm. (EC), Brussels Nov. 2014–; mem. New Democracy party 1993–95, 2004–, mem. Cen. Cttee 1993–95, Vice-Pres. 2010–; Visiting Fellow, Kennedy School of Govt, Harvard Univ., USA 2003; Hon. Prof., Moscow State Acad. of Technological Sciences 2002, Peking Univ., Beijing 2002; numerous awards and decorations from several countries; Dr hc (Adelphi Univ., New York) 1995, (Deree Coll., Athens) 1997, (Drexel Univ., Philadelphia) 2000, (Kingston Univ.) 2000. *Address:* European Commission, 200 Rue de la Loi/Wetstraat 200, 1049 Brussels, Belgium (office). *Telephone:* (2) 299-11-11 (switchboard) (office). *E-mail:* dimitris.avramopoulos@ec.europa.eu (office). *Website:* ec.europa.eu/commission/2014-2019/avramopoulos_en (office).

AVRANAS, Alexandros; Greek film director; b. 1977, Larissa; ed Athens School of Fine Arts, Universität der Kunste, Berlin, Germany. *Films include:* Without (also writer) (seven awards at Festival of Thesaloniki) 2008, Miss Violence (also producer and writer) (Silver Lion for Best Dir, Venice Film Festival, Critics' Prize for Best European-Mediterranean film, Fed. of Film Critics of Europe and the Mediterranean, Arca CinemaGiovani, several awards at Stockholm film Festival) 2013. *Television includes:* Ektos ton teihon (series documentary) 2011. *Address:* Anthony Mestriner, Casarotto Ramsay & Associates Ltd, Waverley House, 7–12 Noel Street, London, W1F 8GQ, England (office). *Telephone:* (20) 7287-4450 (office). *Fax:* (20) 7287-9128 (office). *E-mail:* anthony@casarotto.co.uk (office). *Website:* www.casarotto.co.uk (office).

AVRIL, Pierre; French professor of constitutional law; *Professor Emeritus, University of Paris;* b. 18 Nov. 1930, Pau; s. of Stanislas Avril and Geneviève Camion; m. Marie-Louise Hillion 1959; one s.; Asst, Pierre Mendès France 1955–62, Ed.-in-Chief Cahiers de la République 1960–62; Sub-Ed., Soc. Gen. de Presse 1962–69; Prof., Faculté de Droit de Poitiers 1972–79, Univ. de Paris X 1979–88, Inst. d'études politiques 1982–97, Univ. de Paris II 1988–99; mem. Conseil supérieur de la magistrature 1998–2002; Pres. Comm. de réflexion sur le statut pénal du Président de la République 2002; mem. Comité scientifique de la Comm. Nat. des archives constitutionnelles 2002–12; Hon. Pres. Asscn française de droit constitutionnel 2005. *Publications:* Le Régime politique de la Ve République 1964, Un président pour quoi faire? 1965, Lexique de droit constitutionnel (co-author) 1986 (new edn 2009), Droit parlementaire (with others) 1988 (fourth edn 2010), Essais sur les partis politiques 1990, La Ve République: histoire politique et constitutionnelle 1994, Les conventions de la Constitution 1997. *Address:* 48 rue Gay-Lussac, 75005 Paris, France. *Telephone:* 1-43-26-36-43.

AVRIL, Brig.-Gen. Prosper; Haitian politician and army officer; b. 12 Dec. 1937; ed Mil. Acad., Haiti and Univ. of Haiti Law School; fmr adviser to deposed Pres. Jean-Claude Duvalier; adviser to mil.-civilian junta headed by Gen. Namphy and mem. Nat. Governing Council 1986; Commdr Presidential Guard 1988; major participant in June 1988 coup which overthrew civilian Govt of Leslie Manigat; leader of coup which deposed regime of Gen. Namphy Sept. 1988; Pres. of Haiti 1988–90; arrested for allegedly plotting against the state 2001, freed 2004. *Publication:* An Appeal to History: The Truth about a Singular Lawsuit 1999.

AWAD, Ahmed Isse, MA; Somali-Canadian diplomatist and politician; *Minister of Foreign Affairs and International Co-operation;* b. 20 March 1955, Garowe; m. Sarah Ashraf; one d.; ed Inst. for Peace and Security Studies, Addis Ababa Univ.; left Somalia during civil war 1991; settled in Canada and became a citizen there; returned to Somalia 2001; Chief of Staff to Prime Minister 2001–04; worked at UN peacekeeping missions in Sudan (Abyei, Kadugi and Darfur) for 10 years; Amb. to USA 2015–18; Minister of Foreign Affairs and Int. Co-operation 2018–. *Address:* Ministry of Foreign Affairs, 1 Villa Somalia, 2525 Mogadishu, Somalia (office). *Telephone:* (5) 424640 (office). *Website:* www.mfa.somaligov.net (office).

AWAD, Nihad; Palestinian/American organization official; *Executive Director, Council on American-Islamic Relations;* b. Amman New Camp, Amman, Jordan; ed Univ. of Minnesota; began career at Univ. of Minnesota Medical Center; fmr Public Relations Dir Islamic Asscn for Palestine; Co-founder and Exec. Dir Council on American-Islamic Relations, Washington, DC 1994–; mem. Vice-Pres. Al Gore's Civil Rights Advisory Panel, White House Comm. on Aviation Safety and Security 1997, American Muslim Political Co-ordinating Cttee 2000. *Address:* Council on American-Islamic Relations, 453 New Jersey Avenue SE, Washington, DC 20003, USA (office). *Telephone:* (202) 488-8787 (office). *Fax:* (202) 488-0833 (office). *E-mail:* info@cair.com (office). *Website:* www.cair.com (office); nihadawad.blogspot.com.

AWADALLAH, Bassem I, PhD; Jordanian business executive and fmr government official; b. 1964; ed Georgetown Univ., USA, London School of Econs, UK; worked in investment banking in UK 1986–91; Econ. Sec. to Prime Minister of Jordan 1992–96, Econ. Adviser 1996–99; Dir Econ. Dept, Royal Hashemite Court 1999–2001; Minister of Planning and Int. Co-operation 2001–Feb. 2005; Minister of Finance April–June 2005; Dir Office of His Majesty King Abdullah II of Jordan 2006–07, Chief of the Royal Hashemite Court 2007–08 (resgnd); Founder and CEO Tomoh Advisory (consultancy), Dubai; fmr Vice-Chair. Bd of Trustees King Abdullah II Fund for Devt; apptd Sec.-Gen. Islamic Chamber of Commerce and Industry 2010; mem. Bd of Dirs Al Baraka Banking Group; Trustee Dubai School of Govt; mem. Bd of Trustees Al Quds Univ.; mem. Advisory Bd LSE, Standard Chartered Bank for the MENA region; Lee Kuan Yew Fellow 2005; Al Kawkab and Al Istiqlal Decorations of the First Order of the Hashemite Kingdom of Jordan; Al Hussein Medal for Distinguished Service, Royal Hashemite Award for Distinguished Service 1995, named Young Global Leader by World Econ. Forum 2009.

AWORI, Arthur Moody; Kenyan politician and business executive; b. 5 Dec. 1927, Butere; s. of Jeremiah Awori and Maria Awori; m. Rose Awari; two s. three d.; ed Mang'u High School, Kakamega School, Makerere Univ., Uganda, Chartered Inst. of Secs; MP for Funyula constituency 1983–; numerous posts as Asst Minister under Pres. Daniel arap Moi, including Asst Minister for Educ.; left Kanu Party late 2002 to join new Nat. Rainbow Coalition; Minister of Home Affairs 2002–05; Vice-Pres. of Kenya 2003–08; fmr Chair. Western Province Kanu MPs Parl. Group; Chair. Francis Da Gama Rose Group 1981–; Dir East Africa Building Soc., Akiba Bank Ltd, Mercantile Life and General Insurance Co. Ltd, Macmillan Publrs Kenya Ltd, Securicor Security Services Ltd; Founding Chair. Asscn for the Physically Disabled of Kenya; Propr of Gulumwoyo Ltd, Western Sunrise Properties Ltd, Mocian Ltd, Rose Mareba Ltd, Mareba Enterprises Ltd; Sec. to the Bd of East African Industries (EAI); Elder of the Burning Spear, Elder of the Golden Heart; Hon. LLD (Southern New Hampshire Univ., USA) 2004. *Leisure interests:* tennis, swimming. *Address:* National Office, Association for the Physically Disabled of Kenya, PO Box 46747, Nairobi 00100, Kenya (office). *E-mail:* nat@apdk.org (office).

AXEL, Richard, MD; American biochemist and academic; *Professor of Biochemistry and Molecular Biophysics, Columbia University;* b. 2 July 1946; ed Columbia Coll., Johns Hopkins Univ. School of Medicine; began academic career as Fellow, Columbia Univ. Inst. of Cancer and Nat. Inst. of Health; currently Prof. of Biochemistry and Molecular Biophysics, Columbia Univ. and Prof. of Pathology, Columbia Univ. Coll. of Physicians and Surgeons 1978–, Univ. Prof. 1999–; Investigator, Howard Hughes Medical Inst. (HHMI) 1984–; mem. NAS, American Philosophical Soc., American Acad. of Arts and Sciences; Hon. DS (Bar Ilan Univ.) 2005, (Montclair State Univ.) 2010, (Rockefeller Univ.) 2011; Eli Lilly Award in biological chemistry, Richard Lounsberry Award, NAS, Bristol-Myers Squibb Award for distinguished achievement in neuroscience research, Gairdner Foundation Int. Award, Nobel Prize in Physiology or Medicine (jtly with Linda B. Buck, q.v.) 2004, Louise T. Blouin Foundation Inaugural Award for Science and Creativity 2005, Mike Hogg Award, M.D. Anderson Cancer Center 2006, Lifetime Achievement Award, YIVO Inst. for Jewish Research 2006, Double Helix Medal 2007, Charles Butcher Award in Genomics and Biotechnology 2014. *Address:* Columbia University Medical Center, Room 1014, 701 West 168 Street, New York, NY 10032 (office); Howard Hughes Medical Institute, 4000 Jones Bridge Road, Chevy Chase, MD 20815-6789, USA (office). *Telephone:* (212) 305-6915 (office); (301) 215-8500 (office). *Fax:* (212) 923-7249 (office). *E-mail:* ra27@columbia.edu (office). *Website:* cpmcnet.columbia.edu/dept/gsas/biochem/faculty/axel.html (office); cpmcnet.columbia.edu/dept/neurobeh/axel (office); www.hhmi.org (office).

AXELROD, David M., AB; American political consultant and fmr government official; b. 22 Feb. 1953, New York City; m. Susan Landau 1979; ed Univ. of Chicago; reporter and columnist, Chicago Tribune newspaper 1977–84; Communications Man. then Co-Dir Paul Simon's US Senate campaign in Illinois 1984; Founding Pnr, Axelrod & Assocs (political consultancy firm, now AKP&D Message and Media) 1985–; worked on mayoral campaigns of Harold Washington, Dennis Archer, Michael R. White, Anthony A. Williams, Lee P. Brown and John F. Street; worked with John Edwards' Presidential campaign team and Barack Obama's Senate campaign 2004; consultant for gubernatorial campaigns of Eliot Spitzer in New York and Deval Patrick in Massachusetts 2006; chief political advisor to Rahm Emanuel in US House of Reps election 2006; chief strategist and media advisor for Barack Obama's presidential campaign 2007–08; Sr Advisor to Pres. of

USA, The White House 2009–11, Sr Strategist for Pres. Barack Obama's re-election campaign 2011–12; Dir Inst. of Politics, Univ. of Chicago 2012–; apptd Sr Political Analyst, NBC News and MSNBC 2013; Sr Strategic Adviser, Labour Party, UK 2014–. *Publication:* Believer: My Forty Years in Politics 2015. *Address:* University of Chicago Institute of Politics, 5707 South Woodlawn, Chicago, IL 60637, USA. *Website:* politics.uchicago.edu.

AXFORD, David Norman, MA, MSc, PhD, CEng, FIEE, FRMetS; British meteorologist (retd); b. 14 June 1934, London; s. of Norman Axford and Joy A. Axford (née Williams); m. 1st Elizabeth A. Stiles 1962 (divorced 1980); one s. two d.; m. 2nd Diana R. J. Bufton 1980; three step-s. one step-d.; ed Merchant Taylors School, Plymouth Coll., St John's Coll., Cambridge, Univ. of Southampton, Kellogg Coll., Oxford (Diploma and Advanced Diploma in English Local History, Dept of Continuing Educ., Univ. of Oxford); Scientific Officer, Kew Observatory 1960–62; Sr Scientific Officer, various RAF stations 1962–68; Prin. Scientific Officer, Meteorological Research Flight, Royal Aircraft Establishment, Farnborough 1968–76; Asst Dir (SPSO) Operation Instrumentation Branch 1976–80, Asst Dir (SPSO), Telecommunications 1980–82; Deputy Dir Observational Services 1982–84; Dir of Services and Deputy to Dir-Gen. Meteorological Office 1984–89; Pres. N Atlantic Ocean Station Bd 1982–85; Chair. Cttee of Operational World Weather Watch System Evaluations –N Atlantic (CONA) 1985–89; Deputy Sec.-Gen. World Meteorological Org., Geneva 1989–95, Special Exec. Adviser to Sec.-Gen. Jan.–May 1995; Consultant Meteorologist 1995–; Consultant to Earthwatch Europe, Oxford 1996–2000; Chair. of Trustees, Stanford-in-the-Vale Public Purposes Charity 2000–02, Clerk/Corresp. 2002–; Hon. Sec., Royal Meteorological Soc. 1983–88, Vice-Pres. 1989–91, Chair. Accreditation Bd 1999–2004, Sec., Special Group on Observations and Instruments 1999–2001; Trustee, Thames Valley Hospice, Windsor 1996–98; mem. Exec. Cttee British Asscn of Former UN Civil Servants 1996–2004, Vice-Chair. 1998, Chair. 1999–2004, 2009–10, Vice-Pres. 2004–; Chartered Meteorologist of Royal Meteorological Soc. 1994–2012; Vice-Pres. and Treas. European Meteorological Soc. 2002–05; Chair. Stanford-in-the-Vale Public Purposes Charity 2000-2002; Clerk/Corresp., SitV PPC 2002–18; Chair. Stanford-in-the-Vale Local History Soc. 2004–11; Trustee, Friends of the Ridgeway 2008–15, Stanford-in-the-Vale Village Hall Man. Cttee 2010–15; Groves Award 1972. *Publications include:* articles in meteorological professional journals and local history magazine The Stanfordian. *Leisure interests:* home and garden, food and wine, Tibetan terrier, 12 grandchildren, two great-grandsons, one great-granddaughter, local and family history. *Address:* 3. Penstones Court, Marlborough Lane, Stanford-in-the-Vale, Oxon., SN7 8SW, England (home). *Telephone:* (1367) 718480 (home).

AXMEDBAYEV, Lt-Gen. Adxam Akramovich; Uzbekistani army officer and government official; b. 14 Feb. 1966, Tashkent, Uzbek SSR, USSR; ed Tashkent State Univ., Acad. of Ministry of Internal Affairs; worked in Dept of Internal Affairs of Tashkent Viloyat 1990–2000; Deputy Head, State Dept of Internal Affairs, Tashkent City 2000–04; worked in Apparatus of Pres. of Uzbekistan 2004–06; Deputy Minister of Internal Affairs, responsible for Finance 2006–11, First Deputy Minister of Internal Affairs 2001–13, Minister of Internal Affairs 2013–17; Head of Co-ordination of Law Enforcement Activities and Regulatory Agencies and State Advisor to the Pres. 2017–; Chair. Uzbekistani Centre of Martial Arts 2014–. *Address:* Office of the President, 100163 Tashkent, O'zbekiston shoh ko'ch. 43, Uzbekistan (office). *Telephone:* (71) 239-54-04 (office). *Fax:* (71) 239-53-25 (office). *E-mail:* presidents_office@press-service.uz (office). *Website:* www.press-service.uz (office).

AXMETOV, Serik Nigmetulı, DEcon; Kazakhstani metallurgist and politician; b. 25 June 1958, Qarağandi Oblast; m.; two c.; ed Technical Univ. of Qarağandi, Russian Acad. of Man.; started career at Qarağandi Metallurgical Plant, becoming Head, Foreign Econ. Relations Dept; worked in Komsomol (Communist Party youth movt) and CP bodies, becoming First Sec., Qarağandi regional Komsomol Cttee 1983–90; engaged in business 1993–95; Pres. Ken Dala (Cen. Kazakhstan commodity exchange) 1995–2001; Akim (Gov.) Temirtaw city 2001–03; fmr First Deputy Akim of Astana; Head, State Inspection for Admin. Supervision and Personnel Policies, Kazakhstan Presidential Admin 1998–2001; Chair. Atameken (Nat. Union of Entrepreneurs and Employers) 2005; Minister of Transport and Communications 2006–09; Deputy Prime Minister 2009; Akim of Qarağandi Oblast 2009–12; First Deputy Prime Minister Jan.–Sept. 2012, Prime Minister Sept. 2012–14 (resgnd); Minister of Defence April–Oct. 2014; mem. Light of the Fatherland People's Democratic Party ('Nur Otan'—Khalyktyk Demokratiyalyk Partiyasy); Order of Parasat (Nobility), Kurmet Medal of Honour 2005, 10 years of Astana Medal 2008. *Address:* 'Nur Otan' Khalyktyk Demokratiyalyk Partiyasy, 010000 Nur-Sultan, Kunaev kosh. 12/1, Kazakhstan (office). *Telephone:* (7172) 55-55-62 (office). *Fax:* (7172) 279-40-66 (office). *E-mail:* partyotan@nursat.kz (office). *Website:* nurotan.kz (office).

AX:SON JOHNSON, Antonia, BA, MA; Swedish business executive; *Chairman, Axel Johnson Group;* b. 6 Sept. 1943, New York City, USA; d. of Axel Ax:son Johnson, Jr and Antonia de Souza; m. Göran Ennerfelt; four c.; ed Radcliffe Coll., USA, Univ. of Stockholm; succeeded father as Chair. of family-owned A. Johnson & Co. (now Axel Johnson Group) 1982–, group has interests in energy, telecommunications and real estate, holds 45% share of Axfood AB (one of largest food operations in Scandinavia), mem. Bd of Dirs AxFast AB, Axfood AB, Mekonomen AB, Nordstjernan AB, NCC AB, Axel and Margaret Ax:son Johnson Foundation, and others; mem. City Council Täby Municipality; mem. Liberal Party; Chair. Dressage Cttee, Swedish Equestrian Fed. 2001–08; mem. numerous Swedish charities, including World Childhood Foundation; Hon. DCL (Bishop's Univ., Canada), Hon. DHumLitt (Middlebury Coll. of Vermont). *Leisure interest:* horseriding. *Address:* Axel Johnson AB, Villagatan 6, PO Box 26008, 100 41 Stockholm, Sweden (office). *Telephone:* (8) 7016100 (office). *Fax:* (8) 213026 (office). *Website:* www.axeljohnson.se (office); www.axeljohnson.com (office).

AXTON, David (see KOONTZ, Dean Ray).

AXWORTHY, Hon. Lloyd, BA, MA, PhD, PC, OM, OC; Canadian academic administrator and fmr politician; *President, World Federalist Movement-Institute for Global Policy;* b. 21 Dec. 1939, North Battleford, Saskatchewan; s. of Norman Joseph Axworthy and Gwen Jane Axworthy; m. Denise Ommaney 1984; two s. one d.; ed United Coll. (now Univ. of Winnipeg), Princeton Univ., USA; Asst Prof. of Political Science, Univ. of Winnipeg 1964–79, Dir Inst. of Urban Studies 1970–79, Pres. and Vice-Chancellor 2004–14; mem. Man. Legis. 1973–79; mem. House of Commons 1979–2000; MP for Winnipeg Fort-Garry 1979–88, for Winnipeg South-Centre 1988–2000; Minister of Employment and Immigration 1980–83, Minister responsible for Status of Women 1980–81; Minister of Transport 1983–84; Minister of Human Resources Devt and Minister of Western Econ. Diversification 1993–96, of Foreign Affairs 1996–2000; UN Special Envoy to Ethiopia and Eritrea 2004; Dir and CEO Liu Centre for the Study of Global Issues, Univ. of British Columbia 2001–04; Pres. World Federalist Movt–Inst. for Global Policy 2004–; Chair. World Refugee Council 2017–, Human Security Centre for UN Univ. for Peace, State of the World Forum, Comm. on Globalization; mem. Cttee High Level Comm. for the Empowerment of the Poor, UNDP 2005–08; Head, OAS Electoral Observation Mission to Peru 2006; mem. Int. Advisory Bd, Inc. 2006–, Tilray, Inc. 2018–; mem. Bd Univ. of Winnipeg Foundation, MacArthur Foundation, Human Rights Watch (Chair. Advisory Bd For Americas Watch), Lester B. Pearson Coll., Univ. of the Arctic, Pacific Council on Int. Policy, Churchill Gateway Devt Corpn; mem. Advisory Bd Port of Churchill, Ethical Globalization Initiative; mem. Liberal Party; Hon. Fellow, American Acad. of Arts and Sciences, Hon. Chair. Canadian Landmine Foundation, hon. mem. Sagkeeng First Nation, Manitoba 2010; Dr hc (Queen's, Lakehead, Victoria, Denver, Niagara, Winnipeg, Dalhousie, Guelph, Waterloo) 2014; Peace Award, North-South Inst., Senator Patrick J. Leahy Award, Vietnam Veterans of America Foundation, Madison Medal, Princeton Univ., CARE Int. Humanitarian Award, Pearson Peace Medal. *Publication:* The Axworthy Legacy 2001, Navigating a New World: Canada's Global Future 2003, Liberals at the Border 2004, Boulevard of Broken Dreams: A 40 Year Journey through Portage Avenue 2014. *Leisure interest:* golf. *Address:* President's Office, World Federalist Movement-Institute for Global Policy, 708 Third Avenue, Suite 1715, New York, NY 10017, USA (office). *Telephone:* (212) 599-1320 (office). *Fax:* (212) 599-1332 (office). *Website:* www.wfm-igp.org (office).

AXWORTHY, Thomas Sidney, OC, BA (Hons), MA, PhD; Canadian civil servant, political scientist, writer, philanthropist and academic; *President and CEO, Walter & Duncan Gordon Foundation;* b. 23 May 1947, Winnipeg, Man.; m.; two c.; ed Univ. of Winnipeg, Queen's Univ., Kingston, Ont.; began career in public policy as a research asst to Task Force on Structure of the Canadian Economy 1967; served as asst to Minister of Housing and Urban Affairs, then Minister of Nat. Revenue, before joining Prime Minister's office as Sr Policy Adviser; Prin. Sec. to Prime Minister Pierre Trudeau 1981–84, key strategist on repatriation of the Constitution and the Charter of Rights and Freedoms; Chair. Arctic Advisory Steering Group, Walter & Duncan Gordon Foundation 1989–96 (worked on creation of the Arctic Council), Renewal Comm. of the Liberal Party of Canada 2006, Advisory Panel on the Creation of a Canadian Democracy Promotion Agency 2009; taught at Inst. of Politics, Kennedy School of Govt, Harvard Univ. 1984–85, Visiting Mackenzie King Chair of Canadian Studies 1985–86, subsequently taught for many years at the Kennedy School; Chair. Centre for the Study of Democracy, School of Policy Studies, Queen's Univ. 2003–09, currently Distinguished Sr Fellow, Munk School of Global Affairs; Sr Fellow, Massey Coll.; career in philanthropy began with appointment to the CRB Foundation 1986, initiated Heritage Minutes and Nat. Heritage Fairs Programs; worked at Historica Foundation of Canada 1999–2005; mem. Bd, then Chair. Asia Pacific Foundation of Canada 2001–06; Pres. and CEO Walter & Duncan Gordon Foundation 2009–; has worked extensively with the InterAction Council of Fmr Heads of State and Govt, co-drafted, with theologian Hans Kung, A Universal Declaration of Human Responsibility 1997, Sec.-Gen. InterAction Council 2011; frequent commentator on public and nat. issues; Hon. LLD (Wilfrid Laurier Univ.) 2003; Public Affairs Asscn Award of Distinction, Public Affairs Asscn of Canada 2008, Diamond Jubilee Medal 2012. *Publications include:* Politics of Innovation 1972, Our American Cousins (ed.) 1987, Marching to a Different Drummer: An Essay on the Liberals & Conservatives in Convention (with Martin Goldfarb) 1988, Towards a Just Society: The Trudeau Years (co-ed.) 1990, Searching for the New Liberalism: Perspectives, Policies, Prospects (co-ed.) 2003, Bridging the Divide: Religious Dialogue and Universal Ethics (co-ed.) 2008; contrib. of specialist articles to various academic journals, magazines and newspapers, especially the opinion pages of the Toronto Star, Globe and Mail and the National Post. *Address:* The Gordon Foundation, Suite 400, 11 Church Street, Toronto, ON M5E 1W1, Canada (office). *Telephone:* (416) 601-4116 (office). *E-mail:* taxworthy@gordonfn.org (office); interact@vega.ocn.ne.jp (office). *Website:* www.interactioncouncil.org (office); gordonfoundation.ca (office).

AYAD, Jelloul, MEconSc; Tunisian economist and politician; b. 6 Feb. 1951, Khniss; m.; three c.; ed Univ. of Tunis, Univ. of Maryland, USA; joined Citibank 1980 as Man., Tunisian operations, becoming Vice-Pres. Citicorp 1987, Dir Gen., Corp. Bank Div., UAE 1988, Man. Dir Citibank Maghreb, Casablanca and Citicorp/Citibank Country Corp. Officer for Morocco 1990–95, Sr Banker, Europe, Africa and Middle East Finance Div., Citicorp International Ltd, London 1996–98; joined Banque marocaine du commerce extérieur (BMCE), in charge of corp. and business banking 1998, Chair. Gen. Man. Cttee, BMCE 2002, Gen. Man., Corp. and Investment Div. and Deputy Dir-Gen. 2004, Vice-Pres. London br. 2010; Minister of Finance Jan.–Dec. 2011; fmr Vice-Pres. Supervisory Council, RMA Watanya (insurance co.), Morocco; Pres. American Chamber of Commerce, Casablanca 1993–95, now Hon. Pres.; fmr Vice-Pres. Euromed Forum; mem. Morocco–American Council for Trade and Investment. *Musical compositions:* composer of classical symphonies, which have been performed in Tunisia and Morocco; symphonies include Magador, Hannibal Barca, Parfum de Jasmin.

AYALA, Francisco Jose, BS, MA, PhD; American (naturalized) biologist, geneticist and academic; *Donald Bren Professor of Biological Sciences and University Professor, University of California, Irvine;* b. 12 March 1934, Madrid, Spain; s. of Francisco Ayala and Soledad Ayala (née Pereda); m. Hana Lostakova 1985; two s. (by previous m.); ed Univ. of Madrid, Columbia Univ., New York; Research Assoc. Rockefeller Univ., New York 1964–65, Asst Prof. 1967–71; Asst Prof., Providence Coll., RI 1965–67; Assoc. Prof., later Prof. of Genetics, Univ. of California, Davis 1971–87, Dir Inst. of Ecology 1977–81, Assoc. Dean of Environmental Studies 1977–81; Distinguished Prof. of Biology, Univ. of California, Irvine 1987–89, Donald Bren Prof. of Biological Sciences 1989–, Univ. Prof. 2003–; Pres. AAAS 1994–95; Pres.-Elect Sigma Xi, The Scientific Research Soc. 2003–04, Pres. 2004–05; mem. NAS, American Acad. of Arts and Sciences, American Philosophical Soc. (Pres. Cttee of Advisers on Science and Tech. 1994–2001); Dr hc (León, Spain) 1982, (Madrid) 1986, (Barcelona) 1986, (Athens) 1991, (Vigo, Spain) 1996, (Valencia) 1999, (Bologna) 2000, (Vladivostok) 2002, (Masaryk, Czech Repub.) 2003, (Las Islas Baleares) 2006, (Padua) 2006, (Nacional de La Plata) 2007, (Salamanca) 2009, (Warsaw) 2009, (Buenos Aires) 2009, (Pais Vasco) 2010, (South Bohemia, Czech Repub.) 2010, (Ohio State) 2010, (Nacional de Chile) 2010, (Macao) 2011, (Int. Univ. of Menéndez Pelayo, Spain) 2013, (Changshu Inst. of Tech., China) 2014, (Universidad Autónoma de Barcelona, Spain) 2015, (Universidad de Comillas, Madrid, Spain) 2016; US Nat. Medal of Science 2001, Templeton Prize 2010. *Publications:* Studies in the Philosophy of Biology 1974, Molecular Evolution 1976, Evolution 1977, Evolving: The Theory and Processes of Organic Evolution 1979, Population and Evolutionary Genetics 1982, Modern Genetics 1984, Darwin and Intelligent Design 2006, Darwin's Gift to Science and Religion 2007, Human Evolution: Trails from the Past 2007, Contemporary Debates in Philosophy of Biology 2010, Am I a Monkey? The Big Questions: Evolution 2012, Essential Readings in Evolutionary Biology 2014, Evolution, Explanation, Ethics, and Aesthetics 2016, and more than 1,100 scientific articles. *Leisure interests:* travel, reading, collecting fine art. *Address:* Department of Ecology and Evolutionary Biology, University of California, Irvine, CA 92697 (office); 2 Locke Court, Irvine, CA 92617, USA (home). *Telephone:* (949) 824-8293 (office). *Fax:* (949) 824-2474 (office). *E-mail:* fjayala@uci.edu (office). *Website:* www.faculty.uci.edu/profile.cfm?faculty_id=2134 (office).

AYALA-LASSO, José; Ecuadorean lawyer and diplomatist (retd) and international civil servant; b. 29 Jan. 1932, Quito; m.; four c.; ed Pontificia Universidad Católica del Ecuador, Universidad Cen. del Ecuador, Université Catholique de Louvain, Belgium; several foreign service postings including at embassies in Tokyo, Seoul, Beijing, Rome, Minister of Foreign Affairs 1977, 1997–99, fmr Amb. to Belgium, Luxembourg, Peru, EEC; Lecturer, Int. Law Inst., Universidad Cen. del Ecuador; Deputy Legal Sec., Perm Comm. for the South Pacific, Amb. and Perm. Rep. to UN, New York 1989–94, Rep. of Ecuador on UN Security Council 1991–92, Chair. Security Council Cttee concerning Fmr Yugoslavia 1991, 1992, Chair. working group to establish post of High Commr for Human Rights 1993, UN High Commr for Human Rights 1994–97, Amb. to Holy See 1999–2002; columnist, El Comercio; Grand Cross, Nat. Order of Merit (Ecuador), decorations from Japan, Belgium, Brazil, others. *Website:* www.elcomercio.com/column/jose-ayala-lasso.

AYALDE, Liliana, BA; American diplomatist; b. 1956, Baltimore, Md; m.; two d.; ed American Univ., Tulane Univ.; joined int. devt intern programme, USAID with Office of Health, Population and Nutrition, Dhaka 1982, worked with USAID in Guatemala 1985, then posted to Nicaragua 1990s, Deputy Dir, Office of Cen. American Affairs, Bureau for Latin America, Caribbean, Dept of State 1993–95, Dir 1995–97, Deputy Mission Dir USAID, Nicaragua 1997–99, Mission Dir USAID, Bolivia 1999–2005, in Colombia 2005–08, Amb. to Paraguay 2008–11, Sr Deputy Asst Admin. for Latin America and the Caribbean, USAID 2011–13, Amb. to Brazil 2013–16; seven Performance Awards, Presidential Performance Award 2003. *Address:* Department of State, 2201 C Street, NW, Washington, DC 20520, USA. *Website:* www.state.gov.

AYALON, Adm. (retd) Amihai (Ami), MA, MPA, MSL; Israeli naval officer (retd) and politician; *Senior Fellow, The Israel Democracy Institute;* b. 27 June 1945, Tiberias; m.; three c.; ed Bar-Ilan Univ., Naval War Coll., Newport, RI and John F. Kennedy School of Govt, Harvard Univ., USA; grew up in Kibbutz Ma'agan; drafted into Flotilla 13 elite commando unit, Israeli Navy 1963, commissioned officer, participated in hundreds of secret missions, served with distinction in Six Day and Yom Kippur wars, Lebanon War 1982, South Lebanon conflict, First Intifada, Commdr Israeli Navy 1992–96 (retd); Dir Shin-Bet (Israeli internal security service) 1996–2000; Co-founding Dir The People's Voice (with Sari Nusseibeh—civil org. advocating two states for Israel and Palestine secured through non-violent means) 2003–; mem. Labour Party 2004–08; mem. Knesset (Parl.) 2006–09, Chair. State Control Cttee; came second in Labor Party leadership election 2007; apptd Minister without Portfolio 2007, later became mem. of the Security Cabinet; Sr Fellow, The Israel Democracy Inst. 2012–; Ribbon of Valour, Medal of Supreme Bravery, Kt of Quality Govt Award. *Film:* featured in a documentary, The Gatekeepers directed by Dror Moreh 2012. *Address:* The Israel Democracy Institute, 4 Pinsker Street, PO Box 4702, Jerusalem 9104602, Israel (office). *Telephone:* 2-5300888 (office). *Fax:* 2-5300837 (office). *E-mail:* info@idi.org.il (office). *Website:* en.idi.org.il/about-idi/idi-staff/senior-fellows/amichay-ami-ayalon (office); www.thepeoplesvoice.org/TPV3.

AYALON, Daniel (Danny), BA, MBA; Israeli fmr diplomatist; b. 17 Dec. 1955, Tel-Aviv; m. Anne Ayalon; two d.; ed Tel-Aviv Univ., Bowling Green State Univ., USA; fmr Capt. Armored Corps, Israel Defense Forces; sr finance exec. before joining Foreign Service; Deputy Chief of Mission, Panama 1991–92, Dir Bureau of Israel's Amb. to UN, New York 1993–97, Deputy Foreign Policy Adviser to fmr Prime Ministers Ehud Barak and Benjamin Netanyahu 1997–2001, Chief Foreign Policy Adviser to Prime Minister Ariel Sharon 2002, Amb. to USA 2002–06; mem. Yisrael Beiteinu 2008–12; apptd mem. Knesset (representing Yisrael Beiteinu party) 2009; Deputy Foreign Minister 2009–13; Deputy to Deputy Prime Minister 2009–; Co-Chair. Nefesh B'Nefesh, Jerusalem 2006–08; Brandeis Award 2005, Builder of Jerusalem Award 2008. *Telephone:* 50-6203900 (mobile); (9) 7406133 (office). *E-mail:* dannyayalon@gmail.com (office). *Website:* www.dannyayalon.com.

AYARI, Chédli, LenD, DèsSc (Econ), PhD; Tunisian economist, diplomatist, politician and central bank governor; b. 24 Aug. 1933, Tunis; s. of Sadok Chedly and Fatouma Chedly; m. Elaine Vatteau 1959; three c.; ed Collège Sadiki and Inst. de Hautes Etudes, Sorbonne, Paris; with Société Tunisienne de Banque 1958; Asst, Faculté de Droit et des Sciences Economiques et Politiques, Tunis 1959; Econ. Counsellor, Perm. Mission to UN, New York 1960–64; Exec. Dir IBRD (World Bank) 1964–65; Dean, Faculté de Droit, Tunis 1965–67; Dir CERES 1967–69; Sec. of State in charge of Planning 1969–70; Minister of Nat. Educ., Youth and Sport 1970–71; Amb. to Belgium Feb.–March 1972; Minister of Nat. Economy 1972–74, of Planning 1974–75; Chair. and Gen. Man. Arab Bank for Econ. Devt in Africa 1975; Gov. Banque Centrale de Tunisie 2012–18; Prof. of Economics, Agrégé de Sciences Economiques, Tunis, now Prof. Emer.; Assoc. Prof., Univ. of Aix-Marseilles 1989–; mem. UN Cttee of Planning for Devt; currently Vice-Pres., Nat. Consultative Counsel on Scientific Research and Tech.; Sr Assoc., Econ. Research Forum, Cairo; Hon. Pres., Int. Asscn of French-Speaking Sociologists; Grand Officier, Légion d'honneur, Grand Cordon, Ordre de la République; Dr hc (Aix-Marseilles) 1972. *Publications include:* Les Enjeux méditerranéens 1992, La Méditerranée economique 1992, Mélanges en l'honneur de Habib Ayadi 2000, Le système de développement tunisien: vue rétrospective Les années 1962–1986 2003; books and articles on econ. and monetary problems. *Leisure interest:* music. *Address:* c/o Banque Centrale de Tunisie, 25 rue Hédi Nouira, BP 777, 1080 Tunis; Rue Tanit, Gammarth, La Marsa, Tunis, Tunisia (home).

AYASSOR, Adji Othèth, LLD, LLM; Togolese lawyer and politician; b. 1952; m.; four c.; ed Univ. of Bordeaux, France, Univ. of Wisconsin, Harvard Univ., USA; fmr Prof. of Law, Lomé Univ.; fmr Prof., École nationale d'administration (ENA), Lomé; int. consultant and expert on educ.; mem. Nat. Assembly (Parl.) for Doufelgou Pref. 2007–; Dir-Gen. Ministry of Educ. 1990–2006; Sec.-Gen. Cabinet Office 2006–07; Minister of the Economy and Finance 2007–16; mem. Union pour la République (UNIR).

AYAZ, Qibla, PhD; Pakistani academic; *Chairman, Council of Islamic Ideology;* ed Univ. of Edinburgh; Ad Hoc Lecturer, Dept of Islamic Studies, Univ. of Peshawar 1976–77, Lecturer 1977–85, Asst Prof. 1985–93, Assoc. Prof. 1993–95, Warden, Sheikh Zayed Islamic Centre 1988–90, f. Dept of Seerat Studies/Prophetology/Prophet Studies 1995, Prof. 1995–2017, Chair. 1995–2009, Dean, Faculty of Islamic & Oriental Studies 2002–07, 2012–13 (retd), Dir Inst. of Islamic and Arabic Studies 2009–12, Acting Vice-Chancellor 2012–13, Ed. Peshawar Islamicus, Al-Idah-Journal of the Sheikh Zayed Islamic Centre; apptd Vice-Chancellor, Islamia Coll. 2014; Chair. Council of Islamic Ideology, Govt of Pakistan 2017–; Pres. Pakistan Students Asscn, Univ. of Edinburgh; Ed. The Review of Faith and Int. Affairs, Arlington, USA; f. Pakistan Council of World Religions 2004, Al-Farabi Council for Citizen Diplomacy, Academia for Knowledge and Review; Presidential Award 1975, US Gold Star Alumni 2011. *Publications:* Islam aur Tahaffuz Mahaul 2002, Barudi Surangen aur Islami Talimat 2005, Mazahibi aalam men Asasiyyati ama (ed.) 2006, TB ka Insadad aur Islami Talimat 2006, Themes for Research in Islamic Studies and Arabic 2009, Reconstruction of the National Narratives and Counter-Violent Extremism Model for Pakistan 2016, Role of Post-Noon Engagements of Madrassa Students in Radical Orientation 2017. *Address:* Council of Islamic Ideology, Plot No. 46, Ataturk Avenue, Sector G5/2, Islamabad, Pakistan (office). *Telephone:* (51) 9205652 (office). *Fax:* (51) 9217381 (office). *E-mail:* contact@cii.gov.pk (office). *Website:* cii.gov.pk.

AYCKBOURN, Sir Alan, Kt, CBE, FRSA; British playwright and theatre director; b. 12 April 1939, London; s. of Horace Ayckbourn and Irene Maud Ayckbourn (née Worley); m. 1st Christine Helen Roland 1959 (divorced 1997); two s.; m. 2nd Heather Elizabeth Stoney 1997; ed Haileybury; on leaving school went straight into the theatre as stage man. and actor with various repertory cos in England; Founder-mem. Victoria Theatre Co., Stoke on Trent 1962–64; Drama Producer, BBC Radio 1964–70; Artistic Dir Stephen Joseph Theatre, Scarborough 1972–2009; Prof. of Contemporary Theatre, Univ. of Oxford 1992; Hon. Fellow, Bretton Hall Coll. 1982, Cardiff Univ. 1995; Hon. Prof., Univ. of Hull 2007; Hon. Fellowship, Oxford Literary Festival 2016; Hon. DLitt (Hull) 1981, (Keele, Leeds) 1987, (Bradford) 1994, (York St John) 2011, (Coventry) 2018, Hon. DUniv (York) 1992, (Open Univ.) 1998, (Manchester) 2003; Variety Club of GB Playwright of the Year 1974, Lifetime Achievement Award, Writers' Guild of GB 1993, John Ederyn Hughes Rural Wales Award for Literature 1993, Birmingham Press Club Personality of the Year Award 1993, Yorkshire Man of the Year 1994, Montblanc de la Culture Award for Europe 1994, Sunday Times Award for Literary Excellence 2001, Variety Club of GB Lifetime Achievement Award 2004, Yorkshire Arts and Entertainment Personality Award, Yorkshire Awards 2005, Soc. of West End Theatre's Special Award (Olivier) 2009, inducted into Hall of Fame for Achievements in American Theatre 2009, Laurence Olivier Awards Special Award 2009, Critics' Circle Award for Services to the Arts 2010, Special Tony Award for Lifetime Achievement in the Theatre 2010, Old Drama King Of The Year, The Oldie Of The Year Awards 2018. *Plays include:* Mr Whatnot 1963, Relatively Speaking 1965, How the Other Half Loves 1969, Ernie's Incredible Illucinations 1969, Family Circles 1970, Time and Time Again 1971, Absurd Person Singular (Evening Standard Award for Best New Comedy 1973) 1972, The Norman Conquests (Evening Standard Award for Best New Play 1974, Plays and Players Award for Best New Play 1974, New York Drama Critics' Circle Special Citation 2009, Outer Critics' Circle Award for Outstanding Revival 2009, Drama Desk Award for Outstanding Revival 2009, Tony Award for Best Revival of a Play 2010) 1973, Jeeves (book and lyrics for Andrew Lloyd Webber musical) 1975 (rewritten as By Jeeves – TMA Regional Theatre Awards for Best Musical 1996), Absent Friends 1974, Confusions 1974, Bedroom Farce 1975, Just Between Ourselves (Evening Standard Award for Best New Play 1977) 1976, Ten Times Table 1977, Joking Apart (Co-winner Plays and Players Award for Best New Comedy 1979) 1978, Family Circles 1978, Sisterly Feelings 1979, Taking Steps 1979, Suburban Strains (musical play with music by Paul Todd) 1980, Season's Greetings 1980, Me, Myself & I (with Paul Todd) 1981, Way Upstream 1981, Intimate Exchanges 1982, It Could Be Any One Of Us 1983, A Chorus of Disapproval (London Evening Standard Award, Olivier Award and DRAMA Award for Best Comedy 1985) 1984 (film 1988), Woman in Mind 1985, A Small Family Business (London Evening Standard Award for Best New Play 1987) 1987, Henceforward (London Evening Standard Award for Best Comedy 1989) 1987, A View from the Bridge (Plays and Players Director of the Year Award) 1987, Man of the Moment (Evening Standard Best Comedy Award 1990) 1988, Mr A's Amazing Maze Plays (TMA/Martini Regional Theatre Award for Best Show for Children and Young People 1993) 1988, The Revengers' Comedies 1989, Invisible Friends 1989, Body Language 1990, This Is Where We Came In 1990, Callisto 5 1990 (rewritten as Callisto 7 1999), Wildest Dreams 1991, My Very Own Story 1991, Henceforward... (Drama-Logue Critic Award) 1991, Time of My Life 1992, Dreams From a Summer House (with music by John Pattison) 1992, Communicating Doors (Writers' Guild of GB Award for Best West End Play 1996, Molière Award for Best Comedy 1997) 1994, Haunting Julia 1994, A Word from Our Sponsor (with music by John Pattison) 1995, The Champion of Paribanou 1996, Things We Do For Love (Lloyds Pvt. Banking Playwright of the Year Award 1997, Moliere for Best Comedy 2003) 1997, Comic Potential 1998, The Boy Who Fell into a Book 1998, House & Garden 1999, Whenever (with music by Denis King) 2000, Damsels in Distress (trilogy: GamePlan, FlatSpin, RolePlay) 2001, Snake in the Grass 2002, The Jollies 2002, Sugar Daddies 2003, Orvin – Champion of Champions (with music by Denis King)

2003, My Sister Sadie 2003, Drowning on Dry Land 2004, Private Fears in Public Places 2004, Miss Yesterday 2004, Improbable Fiction 2005, The Girl Who Lost Her Voice 2005, If I Were You 2006, Life and Beth 2008, Awaking Beauty 2008, My Wonderful Day 2009, Life of Riley 2010, Dear Uncle (adaptation of Chekhov's Uncle Vanya) 2011, Neighbourhood Watch 2011, Surprises 2012, Arrivals & Departures 2013, Farcicals (pair of one-act plays) 2013, Roundelay 2014, Hero's Welcome 2015, Consuming Passions 2016, No Knowing 2016, A Brief History of Women 2017, Better Off Dead 2018, Birthdays Past, Birthdays Present 2019; as Dir: A View from the Bridge (Plays and Players Director of the Year Award) 1987; has directed over 300 plays written by himself and others. *Publications include:* fiction: majority of plays have been published; non-fiction: Conversations with Ayckbourn (with I. Watson) 1981, The Crafty Art of Playmaking 2002. *Leisure interests:* music, watching cricket. *Address:* c/o Casarotto Ramsay & Associates Ltd, Waverley House, 7–12 Noel Street, London, W1F 8GQ, England (office). *Telephone:* (20) 7287-4450 (office). *Fax:* (20) 7287-9128 (office). *E-mail:* info@casarotto.uk.com (office). *Website:* www.casarotto.uk.com (office); www.alanayckbourn.net.

AYEBARE, Adonia, MA, PhD; Ugandan journalist and diplomatist; *Permanent Representative to United Nations;* b. 18 Oct. 1966; m.; five c.; ed Makerere Univ., Kampala, Long Island Univ., Fletcher School of Law and Diplomacy, Tufts Univ., Indiana Univ., Rutgers Univ.; Staff Reporter Eastern African Business Week, Kampala 1996–98; Information Officer Integrated Regional Information Network (IRIN) 1998–2000; Prin. Adviser and Special Envoy to Burundi Peace Process 2001–08; Amb. and Head of Mission to Rwanda and Burundi 2002–05; Deputy Perm. Rep. and Chargé d'affaires to UN, New York 2005–08, 2010–12; Sr Adviser on Peace and Security, African Union's Perm. Observer Mission to UN, New York 2013–17; Perm. Rep. to UN 2017–; Dir Africa Program Int. Peace Inst., New York 2009–11. *Address:* Permanent Mission of Uganda, 336 E 45th Street, New York, NY 10017, USA (office). *Telephone:* (212) 949-0110 (office). *Fax:* (212) 687-4517 (office). *E-mail:* admin@ugandaunny.com (office). *Website:* newyork.mofa.go.ug (office).

AYER, Ramani, BS, DEng, PhD; American (b. Indian) insurance industry executive; b. 27 May 1947, Kerala; m. Louise D. Ayer; two; ed Indian Inst. of Tech., Drexel Univ.; joined The Hartford Financial Services Group Inc. 1973, Asst Sec. and Staff Asst to Chair. 1979, Vice-Pres. HartRe (subsidiary) 1983, Pres. Hartford Specialty Co. 1986, Sr Vice-Pres. The Hartford 1989, Exec. Vice-Pres. 1990, apptd mem. Bd of Dirs 1991, COO 1991–97, Chair., Pres. and CEO 1997–2007, Chair. and CEO 2007–09, also Chair. Hartford Life; Chair. Hartford Healthcare; Vice-Chair. Connecticut Council of Educ. Reform; f. Ramani and Louise D Ayer Family (independent foundation) mem. Bd of Dirs XL Group plc, David Lynch Foundation; mem. Bd of Trustees Maharishi Univ. of Man. *Leisure interest:* meditating. *Address:* Ramani and Louise D Ayer Family Foundation, 75 Isham Road, Suite 400, West Hartford, CT 06107, USA. *Telephone:* (860) 313-4930.

AYÉVA, Zarifou; Togolese politician; *President, Parti pour la démocratie et le renouveau;* b. 22 April 1942, Sokode; m.; ed Collège Moderne de Sokodé, Lycée Classique de COCODI, Abidjan, Univ. of Mons, Belgium; Financial Dir, SGGG, Lomé 1969–73, Head of Sales Dept 1973–85; Lecturer, Univ. of Lomé 1975–77; Asst Gen. Dir Soc. Nlle de Sidérurgie 1977–79, Gen. Dir 1979–82; Minister of Commerce and Transport 1978, of Information 1979; Dir CODIS 1983–, STOP-FEU-TOGO 1986–; Minister of State, Minister of Foreign Affairs and African Integration 2005–07; Pres. Parti pour la démocratie et le renouveau (PDR) 1991–. *Address:* Parti pour la démocratie et le renouveau (PDR), Lomé, Togo (office).

AYISSI, Henri, PhD; Cameroonian politician and civil servant (retd); b. (Henri Eyebe Ayissi), 24 Sept. 1955, Obala-Cameroun; s. of Valère Ayissi and Françoise Aboudi; m. Odile Metso; four s.; three d.; ed Nat. Advanced School of Admin and Magistracy of Yaoundé, Yaoundé Univ., Cameroon; Minister of Housing and Urban Affairs 1990–92; Inspector of Gen. Affairs, Ministry of Higher Educ. 1998–2004; fmr mem. Nat. Census Comm. and Inspector-Gen. of elections 2004; State Minister for External Relations 2007–11; Minister-Del. at the Presidency of the Repub. in charge of Supreme State Audit Office 2011–. *Leisure interests:* music, associative and spiritual activities. *Address:* c/o Office of the President, Palais de l'Unité, Yaoundé, Cameroon (office). *Telephone:* 2222-3657 (office); 2222-5334 (office). *Fax:* 2223-4403 (office). *E-mail:* secretariat_crri@crefiaf.org (office); e_ayissi_h@yahoo.fr (office).

AYKROYD, Daniel (Dan) Edward, CM; American (b. Canadian) actor; b. 1 July 1952, Ottawa, Ont., Canada; s. of Peter Hugh Aykroyd and Lorraine Gougeon Aykroyd; m. 1st Maureen Lewis 1974 (divorced); three s.; m. 2nd Donna Dixon 1984; two d.; ed Carleton Univ., Ottawa; started as a stand-up comedian; worked on Saturday Night Live ensemble TV show (NBC) 1975–79, guest appearances 1988–2013; cr. and performed as The Blues Brothers (with the late John Belushi); Mem. Order of Canada 1998; Hon. DLitt (Carleton Univ.) 1994; Emmy Award 1976–77, inducted into Canada's Walk of Fame. *Films include:* 1941 1979, Mr. Mike's Mondo Video 1979, The Blues Brothers (also screenwriter) 1980, Neighbors 1981, Doctor Detroit 1983, Trading Places 1983, Twilight Zone 1983, Ghostbusters 1984, Nothing Lasts Forever 1984, Into the Night 1985, Spies Like Us (also screenwriter) 1985, Dragnet (co-screenwriter) 1987, Caddyshack II 1988, The Great Outdoors 1988, My Stepmother is an Alien 1988, Ghostbusters II 1989, Driving Miss Daisy 1990, My Girl, Loose Canons, Valkemania, Nothing But Trouble 1991, Coneheads 1993, My Girl II 1994, North, Casper (also co-screenwriter) 1995, Sergeant Bilko (also co-screenwriter) 1996, Grosse Pointe Blank (also co-screenwriter) 1997, Blues Brothers 2000 1997, The Arrow 1997, Susan's Plan 1998 (also dir and screenwriter), Antz (voice) 1999, Diamonds (also dir and screenwriter) 1999, The House of Mirth 2000, Stardom 2000, The Loser 2000, The Devil and Daniel Webster 2001, Pearl Harbor 2001, Evolution 2001, Crossroads 2002, The Curse of the Jade Scorpion 2002, Unconditional Love 2002, Bright Young Things 2003, 50 First Dates 2004, Intern Academy 2004, Christmas with the Kranks 2004, I Now Pronounce You Chuck and Larry 2007, The Campaign 2012, The Ultimate Sacrifice (narrator) 2012, Legends of Oz: Dorothy's Return (voice) 2014, Tammy 2014, Get On Up 2014. *Television includes:* The Gift of Winter (voice) 1974, Coming Up Rosie 1975, Saturday Night Live 1975–79, The Beach Boys: It's OK (also writer) 1976, All You Need Is Cash 1978, The Real Ghostbusters (creator) 1986–91, The Dave Thomas Comedy Show 1990, It's Garry Shandling's Show 1990, The Earth Day Special 1990, Tales from the Crypt 1991, The Nanny 1994, Kelsey Grammer Salutes Jack Benny 1995, Psi Factor: Chronicles of the Paranormal 1996–2000, The Arrow (also creative consultant) 1997, Home Improvement 1997, Soul Man 1997, Earth vs. the Spider 2001, History's Mysteries 2001, According to Jim 2002, Family Guy 2009, X-Play 2009, The Defenders 2011, Behind the Candelabra 2013, The Tonight Show Starring Jimmy Fallon 2014. *Albums include:* Briefcase Full of Blues, Made in America, The Blues Brothers, Best of the Blues Brothers. *Address:* c/o Fred Specktor, Creative Artists Agency, 2000 Avenue of the Stars, Los Angeles, CA 90067 (office); 9200 Sunset Boulevard, #428, Los Angeles, CA 90069, USA (office). *Telephone:* (424) 288-2000 (office). *Fax:* (424) 288-2900 (office). *Website:* www.caa.com (office).

AYKUT, İmren; Turkish organization official and fmr politician; *President, ÇESAV—Çevre Eğitim Sağlık ve Sosyal Yardımlaşma Vakfı;* b. 1941, Adana; d. of Şevket Şadi and Rahime Aykut; ed Istanbul Univ., Univ. of Oxford, UK; fmr man. of trades unions; industrial relations expert in Turkish glass industries; fmr Sec.-Gen. Paper Industry Employers' Union; mem. Constitutional Ass. 1981; Deputy, Nat. Ass. 1983–; Minister of Labour and Social Security 1987–91; Govt Spokesperson 1991; Vice-Chair. Inter-Parl. Union Turkish Group 1994–95; State Minister by Premier Minister (Women and Family Affairs) 1996; Minister of Environment 1997–99; Pres. Turkish Inter-Parl. Group 1991; currently Pres. ÇESAV—Çevre Eğitim Sağlık ve Sosyal Yardımlaşma Vakfı (Environment, Educ., Health and Social Solidarity Foundation); mem. Anavatan Partisi (Motherland Party); Order of Isabella Catolica of Spain 1993, Order Grand Cruz Medallion (Chile) 1996; Economist of the Year 1988, chosen one of 100 Most Successful Women of the Century, World Assocn of Women's Clubs 1994. *Publications:* numerous articles and research papers. *Leisure interests:* hand-made carpets, antiquities. *Address:* ÇESAV, Meşrutiyet Caddesi, Bayındır 2, Sokak No 59/6, 06620 Kızılay, Ankara, Turkey (office). *Telephone:* (312) 4174925 (office). *Fax:* (312) 4252432 (office). *E-mail:* cesav@cesav.org.tr (office). *Website:* www.cesav.org.tr (office).

AYLING, Robert (Bob) John, CBE; British business executive; b. 3 Aug. 1946; m. Julia Crallan 1972; two s. one d.; ed King's Coll. School, Wimbledon; joined Elborne, Mitchell & Co. 1968; legal adviser on British accession to the EEC 1973–75, Head of Dept of Trade Aviation Law br. 1978 (responsible for parl. bill that led to privatization of British Airways), Under-Sec. for EC, int. trade, competition issues 1981; with British Shipbuilders 1975; joined British Airways (legal and govt affairs) 1985, Co. Sec. 1987, organized legal arrangements concerning BA's privatization 1987 and BA's acquisition of British Caledonian 1988, Dir Human Resources 1988, Dir Marketing and Operations 1991, Group Man. Dir 1993–95, CEO 1996–2000; Dir (non-exec.) Holidaybreak 2003, Chair. 2003–09; Dir (non-exec.) Royal & SunAlliance Insurance Group PLC 1993–2004; Dir (non-exec.) Welsh Water (Dwr Cymru Cyfyngedig) 2008–17, Chair. 2010–17; Chair. Dyson Ltd 2010–12; Chair. HM Courts and Tribunals Service 2011–18; Gov. King's Coll. School 1996; Hon. FRIBA 2001; Hon. LLD (Brunel) 1996.

AYNSLEY-GREEN, Sir Albert, Kt, MA, MBBS, DPhil, MRCS, FRCP, FRCPE, FRCPCH, FMedSci, FRSA; British paediatrician and writer; *Director, Aynsley-Green Consulting;* b. 30 May 1943; m. Rosemary Boucher 1967; two d.; ed Glyn Grammar School, Epsom and Univs of London and Oxford; House Officer, Guy's Hosp. London, St Luke's Hosp. Guildford, Radcliffe Infirmary, Oxford and Royal Postgraduate Medical School, Hammersmith 1967–70; Wellcome Research Fellow, Radcliffe Infirmary 1970–72, Clinical Lecturer in Internal Medicine 1972–73, Sr House Officer and Registrar in Paediatrics (also John Radcliffe Hosp.) 1973–74; European Science Exchange Fellowship, Univ. Children's Hosp. Zürich 1974–75; Clinical Lecturer in Paediatrics, Univ. of Oxford 1975–78, Univ. Lecturer 1978–83; Prof. of Child Health and Head of Dept, Univ. of Newcastle-upon-Tyne 1984–93; Nuffield Prof. of Child Health, Univ. of London 1993–; Dir of Clinical Research and Devt, Great Ormond St Hosp. and Inst. of Child Health, London 1993–2003, now Prof. Emer.; Chair. Nat. Children's Taskforce and Nat. Clinical Dir for Children, Dept of Health 2001–05; Children's Commr for England 2005–10; Founder and Dir Aynsley-Green Consulting 2010–; Pres. BMA 2015–16; Canon Emer. Salisbury Cathedral; hon. fellow UNICEF (UK), Oriel Coll., Univ. of Oxford, hon. mem. Faculty of Public Health and of the Paediatric Societies of Finland, Sweden, South Africa and Hungary; six hon. doctorates; numerous nat. and int. esteem indicators. *Publications:* papers on child health, childhood and government policy for children. *Leisure interests:* family, walking, music, photography. *Address:* Old Parsonage, Harnham, Salisbury, Hants., SP2 8LE, England. *Telephone:* 7500-338353 (mobile). *E-mail:* al@aynsley-green.com (office). *Website:* www.aynsley-green.com.

AYONG, Most Rev. James Simon, BTheol; Papua New Guinea ecclesiastic; b. 3 Sept. 1944, Kumbun, West New Britain Prov.; s. of Julius Ayong and Margaret Ayong; m. Gawali Ayong 1967; two d. (one deceased); ed Newton Theological Coll., Chichester Theological Coll., UK; Local Govt Officer 1964–70, 1974–76; Purchasing Officer and Radio Operator for the Anglican Diocesan Office in Lae 1976–80; Asst Priest, Lae 1982–87; Lecturer in Old Testament Studies and Theology, Newton Theological Coll. 1987–89, Prin. 1989–93; Parish Priest of Gerehu 1994–95; Archbishop of Papua New Guinea and Bishop of Diocese of Aipo Rongo 1995–2009 (retd); Primate of Anglican Prov. of Papua New Guinea 1996–2009; Grand Companion of the Order of Logohu (Chief) 2012. *Leisure interest:* watching football. *Address:* Kumbun Village, PO Box 806, Kimbe, West New Britain, Papua New Guinea.

AYOTTE, Kelly A., BA, JD; American lawyer and politician; *Senator from New Hampshire;* b. 27 June 1968, Nashua, NH; m. Joseph Daley; one s. one d.; ed Nashua High School, Pennsylvania State Univ., Villanova Univ. School of Law; admitted to the Bar of NH and Me; Ed. Environmental Law Journal, Villanova Univ. School of Law; clerked for Hon. Sherman D. Horton, Assoc. Justice of NH Supreme Court 1993–94; Assoc., McLane, Graf, Raulerson & Middleton (law firm) 1994–98; Asst Attorney-Gen., Homicide Unit, NH 1998–2000, Sr Asst Attorney-Gen. and Chief, Homicide Unit 2000–02, Deputy Attorney-Gen. of NH 2003–04, Attorney-Gen. 2004–09; Legal Counsel to Gov. Craig Benson 2003; Senator from NH 2011–17, mem. Select Cttee on Aging, Commerce, Science and Transportation Cttee, Small Business and Entrepreneurship Cttee, Armed Services Cttee, Homeland Security and Governmental Affairs Cttee, Budget Cttee; mem. New Hampshire Bar Assn, Maine Bar Assn; Republican; Kirby Award, New Hampshire Bar Foundation 2004, named Citizen of the Year, New Hampshire

Union Leader 2008. *Address:* c/o 144 Russell Senate Office Building, Washington, DC 20510, USA (office). *Telephone:* (202) 224-3324 (office). *Fax:* (202) 224-4952 (office). *Website:* www.ayotte.senate.gov (office).

AYOUB, Gen. Ali Abdullah; Syrian army officer and government official; *Deputy Prime Minister and Minister of Defence;* b. 28 April 1952, Latakia; m.; three c.; ed Homs Mil. Acad., Frunze Mil. Acad., Moscow; joined Syrian Arab Army 1972, roles include Commdr, several armoured brigades of Syrian Land Forces and Syrian Republican Guard, Commdr, Fourth Armoured Div., Commdr, First Army Corps, Chief of Gen. Staff of Syrian Arab Army 2012–17; Deputy Prime Minister and Minister of Defence 2018–, also Deputy Commdr in Chief 2018–; 6th Oct. Medal, Syrian Order of Merit, Long Service Medal. *Address:* Ministry of Defence, Umayyad Square, Damascus, Syria (office). *Telephone:* (11) 2131702 (office). *Fax:* (11) 2125280 (office). *E-mail:* info@mod.gov.sy (office). *Website:* www.mod.gov.sy (office).

AYRAULT, Jean-Marc; French politician; b. 25 Jan. 1950, Maulévrier (Maine-et-Loire); s. of Joseph Ayrault and Georgette Uzenot; m. Brigitte Terrien; two c.; ed Lycée Colbert, Cholet, Univ. of Nantes, spent a term in Würzburg, Germany, graduate teaching diploma; probationary teaching year at Rezé, Nantes; worked as a German language teacher in Saint-Herblain 1973–86; youth mem. of a movement of young Christians in rural areas; joined Parti socialiste (PS—Socialist Party) after Epinay Congress 1971, affiliated to Jean Poperen's faction, mem. PS Nat. Cttee 1979–81, Exec. 1981–; mem. Gen. Council of Loire-Atlantique département 1976–82, Mayor of Saint-Herblain (suburb of Nantes) 1977–89 (youngest mayor of a French city of more than 30,000 inhabitants), Mayor of Nantes 1989–2012; Deputy for Loire Atlantique in Nat. Ass. 1986–, Pres. Socialist Parl. group 1997–; Pres. Urban Community of Nantes Métropole 2002; Prime Minister of France 2012–14; Minister of Foreign Affairs and Int. Devt 2016–17. *Address:* Parti Socialiste, 10 rue de Solférino, 75333 Paris Cedex 07 (office); 47 place de Preux, BP 50351, 44800 Saint-Herblain, France. *Telephone:* 1-45-56-77-00 (office). *Fax:* 1-47-05-15-78 (office). *E-mail:* interps@parti-socialiste.fr (office). *Website:* www.parti-socialiste.fr (office); jmayrault.fr.

AYRE, Richard James, BA; British journalist; b. 1 Aug. 1949, Newcastle upon Tyne; s. of Thomas Henry Ayre and Beth Carson; m. Guy Douglas Burch; ed Univ. Coll., Durham; Pres. Durham Univ. Students' Union 1969–70; producer and reporter, BBC NI 1973–76, Home News Ed., TV News 1979–84, Head of BBC Westminster 1989–92, Controller of Editorial Policy 1993–96, Deputy Chief Exec., BBC News 1996–2000; Chair. Asian and Afro-Carribean Reporters' Trust 1997–2000; mem. Bd Food Standards Agency 2000–07; Freedom of Information Adjudicator, Law Soc. 2001–15; Chair. Article 19 2002–05; Civil Service Commr 2005–06; Bd mem. for England, Ofcom Content Bd 2006–10; Chair. Dairy Partnership 2008–10; mem. Bd BBC Trust 2010–17; Benton Fellow, Univ. of Chicago, USA 1984–85. *E-mail:* Richard@thatsmymail.com (office).

AYUSHEYEV, Pandito Hambo Lama Damba Badmayevich; Russian Buddhist leader; b. 1963, Russia; abbot in Buddhist monastery Baldan Braybun 1995; elected Head of Buddhists of Russia (Khambo Lama) at conf. of Buddhist clergy, Ulan-Ude 1995–; Shiretuy Buddhist datsan Baldan-Braybun; mem. Presidium of the Interreligious Council of Russia 1998, Presidium of the Interreligious Council of the CIS 2004, Council for Co-operation with Religious Union Under the Pres. of the Russian Fed.; Vice-Pres. Asian Buddhist Conf. for Peace. *Address:* c/o Buddist Centre, Petrovsky blvd., 17/1, Suite 35, 103051 Moscow, Russia (office). *Telephone:* (495) 925-16-81 (office).

AYUSO GARCÍA, Joaquín, BEng; Spanish business executive; b. 1955, Madrid; ed Univ. Politécnica de Madrid; joined Ferrovial as Site Engineer 1982, becoming Project Supervisor, Group Man., Area Man. and Regional Man., CEO Ferrovial Agromán 1999–2002, CEO Grupo Ferrovial (now Ferrovial SA) and Ferrovial Infraestructuras 2002–09, Second Vice-Chair. and Exec. Mem. of Bd of Dirs; fmr First Vice-Chair. Cintra Concesiones de Infraestructuras de Transporte SA; Dir BAA PLC 2006–07; Lead Dir Bankia 2016; fmr Dir Budimex SA, Poland; Madrid Inst. of Civil Engineers Medal of Honour 2006. *Website:* www.informes.bankia.com (office).

AZA, Alberto; Spanish diplomatist; b. 22 May 1937, Tetuán, Morocco; s. of Alberto Aza and Marcela Arias; m. María Eulalia Custodio Martí 1963; two s. four d.; ed Univ. of Oviedo and Madrid; joined Diplomatic Service 1965, served in Libreville, Algiers, Rome, Madrid; Dir Cabt. of Prime Minister of Spain 1977–83; Chief Dir OAS, Latin America Dept, Ministry of Foreign Affairs 1983; Minister Counsellor, Lisbon 1983–85; Amb. to OAS, Washington, DC 1985–89 (also accred to Belize); Amb. to Mexico 1990–92, to UK 1992–99; Gen. Dir O.I.D. 2000–02; Head of the Spanish Royal Household 2002–12; Perm. Advisor of State and Pres., Council of State 2012–; Gran Cruz del Mérito Civil 1979; Gran Cruz de la Order del Mérito Naval 1996; Hon. DLitt (Portsmouth) 1997. *Leisure interests:* golf, fishing, walking. *Address:* Council of State, Mayor 79, 28013 Madrid, Spain (office). *Telephone:* (91) 5166262 (office). *Fax:* (91) 5166244 (office). *E-mail:* tramitaciones@consejo-estado.es (office). *Website:* www.consejo-estado.es (office).

AZAD, Ghulam Nabi, MSc; Indian politician; *AICC General Secretary in-charge for Haryana, Indian National Congress;* b. 7 March 1949, Soti village, Bhadarwah, Doda Dist, Jammu and Kashmir; s. of Rahamatullah and Basa Begum; m. Shrimati Shameem Dev Azad 1980; one s. one d.; ed Kashmir Univ.; began political career in 1973; mem. Lok Sabha (lower house of Parl.) for Washim constituency 1980–89, mem. Rajya Sabha (upper house of Parl.) for Jammu and Kashmir 1990–; Union Deputy Minister of Law, Justice and Co. Affairs 1982–83, of Information and Broadcasting 1983–84, Union Minister of State of Parl. Affairs 1984–86, of Home Affairs 1986, Union Minister of State, Ministry of Food and Civil Supplies 1986–87; Union Minister of Parl. Affairs 1991–93, of Civil Aviation and Tourism 1993–96, of Parl. Affairs, Civil Aviation and Tourism 1995–96, of Parl. Affairs and Minister of Urban Devt 2004–05; Chief Minister of Jammu and Kashmir 2005–08; Minister of Health and Family Welfare 2009–14; Chair. Youth Services Cttee IX Asian Games 1982, also mem. Special Organizing Cttee; Chair. Rajghat Samadhi Cttee 2004–05; Block Sec., Congress Cttee, Blessa 1973–75; Pres. Congress Cttee, Doda Dist 1977; Pres. All India Muslim Youth Conf. 1978–81; Pres. Jammu and Kashmir Pradesh Congress Cttee; Gen. Sec. All India Congress Cttee (AICC) 1987 (re-elected as Gen. Sec. nine times), AICC Gen. Sec. in-charge for Haryana 2018–; mem. Cttee on Public Undertakings 1980–82. *Leisure interests:* gardening, meeting people and cultural activities, secularism and national integration. *Address:* Haryana Pradesh Congress, Plot no.140, Sec-9B, Chandigarh, Haryana (office); House No. 58, New Rehari, Jammu Jogi Gate, Gujjar Nagar, Jammu (home); 5, South Avenue Lane, New Delhi, India (home). *Telephone:* (172) 2743666 (office); (11) 23792052 (New Delhi) (home); (11) 23792944 (New Delhi) (home). *Fax:* (172) 2741426 (office). *E-mail:* azadg@sansad.nic.in (office); connect@haryanapcc.com (office). *Website:* www.haryanacongress.com.

AZALI, Col. Assoumani; Comoran politician and head of state; *President;* b. 1 Jan. 1959; Chief of Staff, Comoran Armed Forces –1999; seized power in coup d'état April 1999; Head of State of the Comoros and C-in-C of the Armed Forces 1999–2002, Fed. Pres. of the Union of the Comoros 2002–06; Pres. 2016–. *Address:* Office of the Head of State, Palais de Beit Salam, BP 521, Moroni, Comoros (office). *Telephone:* 7744808 (office). *Fax:* 7744829 (office). *E-mail:* presidence@comorestelecom.km (office). *Website:* www.beit-salam.km (office).

AZANNAÏ, Candide Armand-Marie, MPh; Benin politician; b. 14 June 1959, Porto Novo; m.; two s. two d.; Founder-mem. and fmr Exec. Sec., Parti Renaissance de Benin, Deputy Sec.-Gen. 1994; mem. Ass. Nat. (Parl.) (Union fait la Nation) for 16th Constituency; Minister of Industry and Govt Spokesman –2011; Minister-Del. in Pres.'s office in charge of Defence 2016–17; fmr mem. Conference des Presidents de l'Ass. Nat.; Founding Pres., Restaurer l'Espoir; mem. Force Cauris pour un Bénin émergent (FCBE).

AZAR, Alex M., AB, JD; American lawyer, pharmaceuticals executive and government official; *Secretary of Health and Human Services;* b. 17 June 1967, Johnstown, Pa; s. of Alex Azar and Lynda Azar (née Zarisky); m.; two c.; ed Dartmouth Coll., Yale Univ.; law clerk for Judge J. Michael Luttig, US Court of Appeals for the Fourth Circuit 1991–92; law clerk, Assoc. Justice Antonin Scalia, US Supreme Court 1992–93; Assoc. Ind. Counsel for Kenneth W. Starr, US Office of the Ind. Counsel 1994–96; worked for Wiley Rein (law firm), later becoming partner, Washington DC 1996–2001; Gen. Counsel, US Dept of Health and Human Services 2001–05, Deputy Sec. 2006–07, Sec. of Health and Human Services 2018–; Sr Vice Pres. for corp. affairs and communications, Eli Lilly and Co. 2007–09, Vice Pres., Managed Healthcare Services and Puerto Rico, Lilly USA LLC 2009–11, Pres. Lilly USA LLC 2012–17; Founder and Chair. Seraphim Strategies LLC Feb.–Dec. 2017; mem. Bd of Dirs Biotechnology Innovation Organization 2013–17, HMS (hosp. and healthcare) 2016–17; Republican. *Address:* Department of Health and Human Services, Hubert H. Humphrey Bldg, 200 Independence Ave, SW, Washington, DC 20201, USA (office). *Telephone:* (202) 690-6162 (office). *Fax:* (202) 690-8715 (office). *E-mail:* secretary@hhs.gov (office). *Website:* www.hhs.gov (office).

AZARENKA, Victoria (Vika); Belarusian professional tennis player; b. (Viktoriya Fiodorovna Azarenka), 31 July 1989, Minsk, Byelorussian SSR, USSR; plays right-handed (two-handed backhand); turned professional 2003; jr highlights include Grand Slam singles titles at Australian Open 2005, US Open 2005, Grand Slam doubles titles at Wimbledon (with Govortsova) 2004, (with Szavay) 2005, French Open (with Szavay) 2005; winner, ITF/Petange, Luxembourg 2005, Miami 2009, Memphis 2009, Brisbane 2009, Stanford 2010, Moscow 2010, Miami 2011, Marbella 2011, Qatar Total Open, Doha 2013, Miami 2016; winner, Women's Doubles, ITF/Ramat Hasharon, Israel (with Govortsova) 2003, ITF/Tucson (with Poutchek) 2005, Tashkent (with Poutchek) 2006, ITF/Las Vegas (with Poutchek) 2007, Indian Wells (with Zvonareva) 2009, Memphis (with Wozniacki) 2009, Cincinnati (with Kirilenko) 2010, Madrid (with Kirlenko) 2011; gold medal, Mixed Doubles (with Max Mirnyi), Olympic Games, London 2012, bronze medal, Women's Singles 2012; Grand Slam Singles results: fourth round, US Open 2007, quarterfinalist, French Open 2009, 2011, Australian Open 2010, semifinalist, Wimbledon 2011, 2012, French Open 2013, finalist, US Open 2012, 2013, winner, Australian Open 2012, 2013; Grand Slam Doubles results: finalist, Australian Open 2008, 2011, quarterfinalist, Wimbledon 2008, finalist, French Open 2009; Grand Slam Mixed Doubles results: winner US Open (with Mirnyi) 2007, Roland Garros (with Bob Bryan) 2008, finalist, Australian 2007, winner Brisbane International 2016; mem. Federation Cup Team for Belarus 2005, 2007, 2009, Belarusian Olympic Team 2008; ITF Jr Girls World Champion 2005. *Address:* Lagardère Unlimited, 16-18 rue du Dôme, Boulogne-Billancourt, 92100 Paris, France (office). *Telephone:* 1-74-31-72-08 (office). *E-mail:* jtobias@lagardere-unlimited.com (office). *Website:* www.lagardere-unlimited.com (office); www.vikaazarenkatennis.com.

AZARNOFF, Daniel Lester, MS, MD; American physician, academic and business executive; *President, D.L. Azarnoff Associates;* b. 4 Aug. 1926, Brooklyn, New York; s. of Samuel J. Azarnoff and Kate Azarnoff; m. Joanne Stokes 1951; two s. one d.; ed Rutgers Univ., Univ. of Kansas School of Medicine; Instructor in Anatomy, Univ. of Kansas 1949–50, Research Fellow 1950–52, Intern 1955–56, Nat. Heart Inst. Resident Research Fellow 1956–58, Asst Prof. of Medicine 1962–64, Assoc. Prof. 1964–68, Dir Clinical Pharmacology Study Unit 1964–68, Assoc. Prof. of Pharmacology 1965–68, Prof. of Medicine and Pharmacology 1968, Dir Clinical Pharmacology-Toxicology Center 1967–68, Distinguished Prof. 1973–78, Clinical Prof. of Medicine 1982–; Asst Prof. of Medicine, St Louis Univ. 1960–62; Visiting Scientist, Fulbright Scholar, Karolinska Inst., Stockholm, Sweden 1968; Clinical Prof. of Pathology and Prof. of Pharmacology, Northwestern Univ. 1978–85; Prof. of Medicine, Univ. of Kansas Coll. of Health Sciences 1984, Stanford Univ. School of Medicine 1998–2002; Sr Vice-Pres. Clinical Regulatory Affairs, Cellegy Pharmaceuticals 1999–2006; Sr Vice-Pres. Worldwide Research and Devt, G. D. Searle & Co., Chicago 1978, Pres. Searle Research and Devt, Skokie, Ill. 1979–85; Pres. D.L. Azarnoff Assocs, Inc. 1987–; mem. Bd of Dirs De Novo Inc. 1994–95, Oread Inc. 1994–98 (Chair. 1998–), Entropin Inc. 1997–2000; mem. Editorial Bd Drug Investigation 1989–2002; Chair. Cttee on Problems of Drug Safety, NAS 1972–76; consultant to numerous govt agencies; mem. Nat. Comm. on Orphan Diseases, Dept of Health and Human Services; mem. Bd of Dirs Oread Laboratories Inc. 1993; Ed. Review of Drug Interactions 1974–77, Yearbook of Drug Therapy 1977–79; Series Ed. Monographs in Clinical Pharmacology 1977–84; Fellow, American Coll. of Physicians, New York Acad. of Scientists; mem. American Soc. of Clinical Nutrition, American Nutrition Inst., American Fed. of Clinical Research, British Pharmacological Soc., Royal Soc. for the Promotion of Health, Inst. of Medicine (NAS), insts of medicine of nat. acads; Distinguished Prof. of Medicine and Pharmacology, Univ. Kansas Medical Center; Burroughs

Wellcome Scholar 1964, Markle Scholar 1963–68, Ciba Award for gerontological research 1958, Rector's Medal, Univ. of Helsinki 1968, Oscar B. Hunter Award, American Soc. for Clinical Pharmacology and Therapeutics, Distinguished Alumni Award, Univ. of Kansas School Medicine, Nathanial T. Kwit Memorial Service Award, American Coll. of Clinical Pharmacology. *Publications:* more than 175 publs in scientific and medical journals. *Address:* 610 Edgewood Drive, Rio Vista, CA 94571, USA (office). *Telephone:* (707) 374-2715 (office). *Fax:* (765) 374-2716 (office). *E-mail:* dan@azarnoffassociates.com (office). *Website:* www.azarnoffassociates.com (office).

AZAROV, Mykola Yanovych, PhD; Ukrainian geologist, economist and politician; b. (Nikolai Yanovich Pakhlo), 17 Dec. 1947, Kaluga, Russian SFSR, USSR; s. of Yan Robertovich Pakhlo and Yekaterina Kvasnikova; m. Lyudmyla Azarova; one s.; ed M. Lomonosov Moscow State Univ.; Lab. Man. and Head of Dept, Moscow Research Design Coal Inst. 1976–84; Deputy Dir Ukrainian State Research and Design Inst. of Mining Geology, Geomechanics and Mine Survey, Coal Ministry 1984–95; Chief of State Tax Admin 1996–2002; First Deputy Prime Minister and Minister of Finance 2002–05, 2006–07; mem. Partiya Rehioniv (Party of the Regions) 2001–14, apptd Chair. Political Council 2003; Acting Prime Minister 7–28 Dec. 2004, 5–24 Jan. 2005; Prime Minister 2010–14 (resgnd following riots and Euromaidan protests); fled to Austria then to Russia, on int. wanted list for alleged abuse of power July 2014, arrest warrant issued by Kiev Dist Court as a preventative measure to allow for extradition from Russian Fed. Jan. 2015; mem. Nat. Acad. of Sciences of Ukraine 1997; Honoured Economist of Ukraine 1997. *Publications:* numerous books and articles on geology and taxation. *Leisure interests:* reading, painting. *Address:* c/o Partiya Rehioniv (Party of the Regions), 01021 Kyiv, vul. Lypska 10, Ukraine.

AZCUNA, Adolfo S., AB, LLB; Philippine lawyer; *Chancellor, Philippine Judicial Academy;* b. 16 Feb. 1939, Katipunan, Zamboanga del Norte; s. of Felipe Azcuna and Carmen Sevilla; m. Maria Asuncion Aunario 1968; one s. three d.; ed Ateneo de Manila and Univ. of Salzburg, Austria; elected Del. 1971 Constitutional Convention 1971–73; mem. Constitutional Comm. 1986–87; Press Sec. 1989; Presidential Legal Counsel 1987–90, Presidential Spokesman 1989–90; Pres. Manila Hotel 1997–98; Partner, Azcuna, Yorac, Sarmiento, Arroyo & Chua Law Offices 1992–2002; Corazon Aquino Fellowship, Harvard Univ. 1990 (deferred); Assoc. Justice, Supreme Court of the Philippines 2002–09, Chancellor Philippine Judicial Acad. 2009–; holder of the Chief Justice Artemio V. Panganiban Professorial Chair on Liberty and Prosperity. *Publications include:* Doing Business in the Philippines, Foreign Judgment Enforcement in the Philippines, Asian Conflict of Law, The Philippine Writ of Amparo, The Aquino Presidency: Destiny with Valor and Grace, International Humanitarian Law: A Field Guide to the Basics, The Writ of Amparo – A New Constitutional Remedy in the Philippines. *Leisure interests:* reading, biking, photography. *Address:* Philippine Judicial Academy, Supreme Court, 3rd Floor Centennial Building, Padre Faura Street, Ermita, Manila 1000 (office); 140 CRM Avenue, Las Pinas, Metro Manila, Philippines (home). *Telephone:* (2) 552-9637 (office); 801-1685 (home). *Fax:* (2) 552-9621 (office). *E-mail:* philja@sc.judiciary.gov.ph (office). *Website:* philja.judiciary.gov.ph (office).

AZÉMA, Jean, BEng; French agricultural engineer and insurance executive; *Vice-Chairman, La Banque Postale Assurances IARD;* b. 1953; ed Ecole Supérieure d'Agriculture de Purpan, Centre Nat. d'Etudes Supérieures de Sécurité; various positions within Groupe Groupama, including Man. Caisse Régionale des Pyrénées Orientales 1975–78, Caisse Régionale de l'Allier 1979–86, Finance Dir Groupama Cie 1987–95, later Dir of Investment, Consolidation and Insurance, Groupama, Man. Dir Groupama Sud-Ouest 1996–98, Groupama Sud 1998–2000, CEO Caisse Centrale Groupama 2000–03, CEO Groupama SA, Féd. Nat. Groupama, Groupama Holding 2003–11; Chair. Féd. Française des Soc. d'Assurance Mutuelles 2001–11; currently Vice-Chair. La Banque Postale Assurances IARD; Admin. Mediobanca; Dir Mediobanca, Véolia Environnement, Société Générale, Bolloré. *Address:* La Banque Postale, 11 rue Bourseul, 75900 Paris Cedex 15, France (office). *Website:* www.labanquepostale.fr (office).

AZEREDO LOPES, José Alberto, PhD; Portuguese lawyer and politician; b. 1961, Porto; ed Universidade Católica Portuguesa, Institut Européen des Hautes Études Internationales, The Hague Acad. of Int. Law; Prof., Faculty of Law, Universidade Católica Portuguesa, Porto, also Dir, Int. Studies Office 1993–2004, Dir, School of Law 2005–06; Adviser, UN Mission in East Timor 1999, coordinated team of int. observers to East Timor independence referendum 1999; apptd mem. working group for public service TV 2002; Pres., Media Regulatory Authority 2006–11; Chef de Cabinet to Mayor of Porto 2013–15; Minister of Nat. Defence 2015–18; fmr Guest Prof., Blanquerna-Universitat Ramon Llul, Barcelona; fmr Lecturer, Instituto Superior Naval de Guerra, Instituto de Defesa Nacional; commentator on int. relations, Rádio e Televisão de Portugal; contrib., Jornal de Notícias (daily newspaper). *Address:* c/o Ministry of National Defence, Av. Ilha da Madeira 1, 1400-204 Lisbon, Portugal (office).

AZESKI, Branko; Macedonian business executive; *President, Managing Board, Economic Chamber of Macedonia;* b. 31 Jan. 1962, Ohrid; Gen. Man. Alexandar Palace Hotel 1998–2003; Founder and Owner, Hit Plus DOOEL, Skopje 1998–2003; Pres. Man. Bd Econ. Chamber of Macedonia 2005–; Pres. Asscn of Balkan Chambers 2005; Rep. Nat. European Integration Council, Parl. of Macedonia 2005–13; mem. Supervisory Bd Sparkasse Banka AD; Hon. Consul of Montenegro to Macedonia 2016. *Address:* Economic Chamber of Macedonia, Str. Dimitrie Cupovski 13, 1000 Skopje, North Macedonia (office). *Telephone:* (2) 3244000 (office). *Fax:* (2) 3244088 (office). *E-mail:* ic@ic.mchamber.org.mk (office). *Website:* www.mchamber.org.mk (office).

AZEVEDO E SILVA, Gen. Fernando; Brazilian politician and fmr army officer; *Minister of Defence;* b. 4 Feb. 1954, Rio de Janeiro; ed Academia Militar das Agulhas Negras; served in Brazilian army 1973–2018, including as Instructor, Academia Militar das Agulhas Negras 1989, Commdr, 2nd Light Infantry Bn, São Vicente (São Paulo) 1999, many years with Parachute Infantry Brigade, becoming Commdr 2007–09, Chief of Operations, UN Peacekeeping Mission in Haiti, Commdr, Eastern Mil. Region, Head of Parl. Advisory Council in Office of Army Commdr, Chief of Gen. Staff of the Army 2016–18; retd from army with rank of Gen. 2018; Pres. Olympic Public Authority 2013–15; Special Advisor to Supreme Federal Court Judge José Dias Toffoli 2018; Minister of Defence 2019–; Grand Cross, Order of Merit of Defence, Grand Cross, Order of Mil. Merit. *Address:* Ministry of Defence, Esplanada dos Ministérios, Bloco Q, 70049-900 Brasília, DF, Brazil (office). *Telephone:* (61) 3312-4000 (office). *Fax:* (61) 3225-4151 (home). *E-mail:* faleconosco@defesa.gov.br (office). *Website:* www.defesa.gov.br (office).

AZHARI, Yasmina, BA; Syrian business executive; *Owner and General Manager, Mira Trading LLC;* b. 19 June 1961, Lattakia; one s. one d.; ed Tishreen Univ.; Partner and Vice-Pres. Trade Coordination Office (shipping agency representing Maersk Line in Syria) 1979–; Rep. of Dutch org. PUM 1999; Head of Lattakia Business Women Cttee 2002–; mem. British Syrian Soc. 2002–, local rep. in Lattakia and Tartous; Founder Mawred (non-governmental org. (NGO) for modernizing and activating women's role in econ. devt) 2003, elected rep. of Mawred in the western region, Pres. Mawred 2006–; est. environmental non-governmental cttee for protecting Slounfeh and Kassab forests 2006; Pres. Bashaer Al Nour NGO for care of children affected by autism and Down syndrome 2006–; Head of Bd, Al Dalfin housing society, Lattakia 2008; Founder Mira Trading LLC 2010, Al Yam LLC (import and export) 2011; mem. Bd of Admin, Lattakia Chamber of Commerce and Industry (first woman) 2005–; mem. Arab Business Women Council representing Syria 2006; mem. Bd Syrian Business Council 2007, Bd UN Global Compact Advisory Council in Syria 2008; mem. Advisory Bd, Bank Audi, Syria 2005; mem. Bd Tartous Port Co. (first woman) 2009; mem. Admin. Bd, Syrian Dutch Business Council 2010, Syrian Chinese Business Council 2010, OECD 2010, Syrian Indian Business Council 2010, Al Aman Holding 2018; Hon. Consul of the Netherlands, Lattakia & Tartous 1999–; Kt, Order of the Netherlands Lion 2009; Ernst & Young World Entrepreneur of the Year Winner for Syria 2011. *Address:* Trade Coordination Office, Al-Mutanabi Street, Lattakia (office); Mira Trading llc, Qudssya Main Square, Damascus, Syria (office). *Telephone:* (41) 235183 (Lattakia) (office); (41) 235184 (Lattakia) (office). *Fax:* (41) 235189 (Lattakia) (office); (41) 235190 (Lattakia) (office). *E-mail:* yasmina.azhari@gmail.com (office). *Website:* www.maerskline.com (office); www.mirallc.com (office).

AZIMI, Abdul Salam, PhD; Afghan judge, politician and academic; b. 1937, Now Bahar, Farah Prov.; ed Kabul Univ., Al-Azhar Univ., Egypt, George Washington Univ., USA; Head of Scientific and Research Centre, Univ. of Neb. in Afghanistan 1986–99; Minister of Educ. 2001–03; mem. Constitutional Comm. to draft a new Afghan Constitution (primary drafter) 2002–03, Vice-Chair. Constitutional Review Comm. 2003, 2006; legal adviser to Pres. Hamid Karzai and Dir of Legal and Judicial Bd of Office of the Pres. 2004–06; Chief Justice of the Supreme Court (Stera Mahkama) 2006–14 (resgnd).

AZIMI, Capt. Jahed; Afghan airline industry executive; fmr pilot, Ariana Afghan Airlines, Pres. 2002–05; fmr CEO Kam Airlines; apptd CEO East Horizon Airlines 2011; fmr Deputy Minister in charge of Admin, Ministry of Transport. *E-mail:* info@flyeasthorizon.com. *Website:* flyeasthorizon.com.

AZIMOV, Rustam Sodiqovich, PhD; Uzbekistani economist and politician; b. 20 Sept. 1958, Tashkent, Uzbek SSR, USSR; s. of Azimov Sodiq Azimovich; ed Tashkent State Univ., Tashkent Inst. of Agricultural Engineers; Economist, Yulius Fuchik collective farm; Chief Economist of agricultural amalgamation in Jizzax; Chair. Ipak July Uzbek Bank for Innovation –1991, Nat. Bank for Foreign Econ. Activity 1991–98; mem. Oly Majlis (Supreme Ass.) 1994–; Minister of Finance 1998–2000, 2005–16; Deputy Prime Minister and Minister of Macroeconomics and Statistics 2000–02; Deputy Prime Minister and Economy Minister 2002–05; Minister of Foreign Econ. Relations July–Nov. 2005; Deputy Prime Minister, responsible for the Econ. Sector and Foreign Econ. Relations 2005–10, First Deputy Prime Minister, responsible for Macroeconomic Devt, Structural Econ. Transformation, the Attraction of Foreign Investment and Integrated Regional Devt 2010–16, Deputy Prime Minister, responsible for Macroeconomic Devt, Structural Econ. Transformation and the Attraction of Foreign Investment 2016–17; Uzbekistan Del. to Asian Devt Bank; fmr Lecturer in Econs, Tashkent State Univ.; Gov., EBRD, London. *Publications include:* numerous articles on econs.

AZINGER, Paul William; American professional golfer; b. 6 Jan. 1960, Holyoke, Mass.; m. Toni Azinger; two d.; ed Brevard Jr Coll. and Florida State Univ.; started playing golf aged five; turned professional 1981; won Phoenix Open 1987, Herz Bay Hill Classic 1988, Canon Greater Hartford Open 1989, MONY Tournament of Champions 1990, AT&T Pebble Beach Nat. Pro-Am 1991, TOUR Championship 1992, BMW Int. Open 1990, 1992, Memorial Tournament, New England Classic, PGA Championship, Inverness 1993; GWAA Ben Hogan Trophy 1995; mem. US Ryder Cup Team 1989, 1991, 1993, 2002, Capt. 2008; mem. Pres.'s Cup 1994, 2000; broadcasting debut as reporter for NBC, 1995 Ryder Cup; golf analyst, American Broadcasting Corpn (ABC) Sports 2005–15; lead golf analyst ESPN 2006–15; head golf analyst Fox Sports 2016–; PGA Tour Player of the Year 1987, Ben Hogan Award 1995. *Publications:* Zinger 1995, Cracking the Code: The Winning Ryder Cup Strategy: Make it Work for You 2010. *Leisure interest:* fishing. *Website:* www.paulazinger.com.

AZIZ, Tan Sri Paduka Rafidah, MEcons; Malaysian academic and fmr politician; b. 4 Nov. 1943, Selama Perak; m. Mohammed Basir bin Ahmad; three c.; ed Univ. of Malaya; held several positions at Univ. of Malaya 1966–76, including tutor, Asst Lecturer, Lecturer and Chair. Rural Devt Div., Faculty of Econs; apptd Senator 1974; apptd Parl. Sec. 1976; mem. Parl. 1986–2013; Deputy Minister of Finance 1977–80; Minister of Public Enterprise 1980–88, of Int. Trade and Industry 1987–2008; mem. UMNO, mem. Supreme Council 1975–2013, Chair. Women's Wing 1999–2009; Ind. non-Exec. Chair. AirAsia X Berhad 2011– (AirAsia X 2013–), Supermax Corpn Berhad 2015–18; Ahli Mangku Negara, Datuk Paduka Mahkota Selangor. *Leisure interests:* reading, decoration, music, squash. *Address:* United Malays National Organization (Pertubuhan Kebangsaan Melayu Bersatu), Menara Dato' Onn, 38th Floor, Jalan Tun Ismail, 50480 Kuala Lumpur, Malaysia. *Telephone:* (3) 40429511. *Fax:* (3) 40412358. *E-mail:* email@umno.net.my. *Website:* www.umno-online.com.

AZIZ, Sartaj; Pakistani economist, politician and fmr international organization official; *Deputy Chairman, Planning Commission;* b. 7 Feb. 1929; ed Punjab Univ., Harvard Univ., USA; joined Ministry of Finance as civil servant 1952, becoming Jt Sec., Plan Coordination, Planning Comm. 1967–71, Deputy Chair. 2017–; Dir of

Commodities and Trade Div., FAO, Rome 1971–74, Deputy Sec.-Gen. World Food Conf. 1974, Deputy Exec. Dir World Food Council 1975–77, Asst Pres. Policy and Planning, IFAD 1977–84; Minister of State for Food and Agric. 1984–88, Minister of Finance 1990–93, 1997–98, of Foreign Affairs 1998–99, Adviser to the Prime Minister on Nat. Security and Foreign Affairs 2013–17; mem. Senate 1985–89; Vice-Chancellor, Beaconhouse Nat. Univ., Lahore 2004–13; Sitara-e-Khidmat 1967. *Publications include:* Rural Development: Learning from China 1978, Between Dreams and Realities: Some Milestones in Pakistan's History 2009. *Address:* Planning Commission, 'P' block Pakistan Secretariat, Islamabad, Pakistan (office). *Telephone:* (51) 9209442 (office). *Fax:* (51) 9201777 (office). *E-mail:* webmanager@pc.gov.pk. *Website:* pc.gov.pk; www.mofa.gov.pk (office).

AZIZ, Shaukat, BSc, MBA; Pakistani banker and politician; b. 6 March 1949, Karachi; m.; three c.; ed Gordon Coll., Rawalpindi, Pakistani Business School Inst. of Business Admin, Karachi, Univ. of Karachi; various posts with Citibank including Head of Corp. and Investment Banking, Asia Pacific Region, Head of Corp. and Investment Banking for Cen. and Eastern Europe, Middle East and Africa, Corp. Planning Officer, Citicorp, Man. Dir, Saudi American Bank, Global Head, Pvt. Banking, Vice-Pres. 1969–99; Minister of Finance and Revenue, Econ. Affairs and Statistics and of Planning and Econ. Devt 1999–2004; mem. Senate 2002–04; Prime Minister of Pakistan and Minister of Finance and Revenue, Econ. Affairs and Statistics 2004–07; Bd mem. Millennium and Copthorne Hotels PLC, Blackstone Group; apptd Financial Adviser to Indian businessman Lakshmi Mittal 2010; included by a special court among "the abettors" of fmr ruler Gen. (retd) Pervez Musharraf, contested the verdict Dec. 2014. *Leisure interests:* golf, music, art.

AZIZ, Ungku Abdul, DEcons; Malaysian academic and university administrator; b. 28 Jan. 1922, London, UK; m. Sharifah Azah Aziz; one d.; ed Raffles Coll. and Univ. of Malaya in Singapore, Waseda Univ., Tokyo, Johore State Civil Service; Lecturer in Econs, Univ. of Malaya in Singapore –1952; Head, Dept of Econs, Univ. of Malaya, Kuala Lumpur 1952–61, Dean of Faculty 1961–65, Vice-Chancellor 1968–88, Royal Prof. of Econs 1978; Pres. Nat. Co-operative Movement (ANGKASA) 1971, Asscn of SE Asian Institutions of Higher Learning (ASAIHL) 1973–75; Chair. Asscn of Commonwealth Univs 1974–75, Malaysian Nat. Council for ASAIHL, Malaysian Examinations Council 1980; mem. UN Univ. Council; Corresp. mem. of Advisory Bd, Modern Asian Studies 1973–75; mem. Econ. Asscn of Malaysia, Int. Asscn of Agricultural Economists, Jt Advisory Cttee of FAO, UNESCO and ILO; mem. Nat. Consultative Council and Nat. Unity Advisory Council, Govt of Malaysia; mem. numerous cttees and orgs; Fellow, World Acad. of Arts and Sciences 1965–; Ordre des Arts et Lettres (France) 1965; Hon. DHumLitt (Univ. of Pittsburgh); Hon. EdD (Chulalongkorn Univ., Thailand) 1977; Hon. DJur (Waseda Univ., Japan) 1982; Hon. DLitt (Univ. of Warwick) 1982; Hon. DIur (Univ. of Strathclyde) 1986, (Utara Univ., Malaysia) 1988; Hon. DEcon (Kebangsaan Univ., Malaysia) 1986; Hon. LLD (Buckingham) 1987; Tun Abdul Razak Foundation Award 1978, Japan Foundation Award 1981; Special Award, Muslim Pilgrim Savings Fund Bd 1988; Grand Cordon of the Order of the Sacred Treasure, Emperor of Japan 1989; ASEAN Achievement Award (Educ.) 1992, Int. Academic Prize (City of Fukoka) 1993, Tokoh Ekonomi Melayu 2005, Anugerah Melayu Terbilang 2005, National Academic Award 2006. *Leisure interests:* jogging, reading and photography.

AZIZOV, Lt-Gen. Abdusalom; Uzbekistani civil servant, government official and business executive; *Chairman, State Security Service;* b. 14 Feb. 1966; m.; two s. one d.; fmr officer, Tashkent City Dept of Internal Affairs, Head of Dept 2005–06; Chair. Uzneftmahsulot Joint Stock Co. 2006–08; First Deputy Minister of Internal Affairs 2008–09; Head of Interior Dept of Jizzax Viloyat 2009–17; Minister of Internal Affairs 2017, of Defence 2017–19; Chair. State Security Service (Davlat Xavfsizlik Xizmati) 2019–; apptd mem. Bd of Dirs, Uzbekneftegaz Nat. Holding Co. 2006; apptd Vice-Pres. Football Fed. of Uzbekistan 2008. *Address:* Davlat Xavfsizlik Xizmati, Tashkent, Matbuotchilar ko'ch. 9, Uzbekistan (office).

AZMAT, Ali; Pakistani musician; b. 20 April 1970, Lahore; ed Ashfield Business School, Sydney, Australia; began musical career in band Jupiters, Lahore 1990; Founder-mem. Junoon (with Salman Ahmad and Brian O'Connell) 1990–, banned by Pakistani authorities for criticism of govt corruption early 1990s; upon invitation of UN Sec.-Gen., Kofi Annan, performed at UN Gen. Ass. (first band to play at Gen. Ass.) 2001; tours throughout Asia, N America, Middle East and Europe; Jazbe-e-Junoon selected as official song of cricket world cup, hosted by Pakistan 1996; simultaneous solo career 2002–; Channel V Music Award for International Group 1998, UNESCO Award for Outstanding Achievement in Music and Peace 1999, BBC Asia Award 1999, Indus Music Award for Best Rock Band 2004. *Film music:* Paap (directed by Pooja Bhatt), Jism-2 2012. *Recordings include:* albums: with Junoon: Junoon 1990, Talaash 1993, Inquilaab 1995, Khashmakash 1996, Azaadi 1997, Parvaaz 1999, The Millennium Edition (compilation) 2000, Andaz 2001, Daur-e-Junoon 2002, Dewaar 2003; solo: Social Circus 2005, Klashinfolk 2008, Josh-E-Junoon 2010, Bum Phatta 2011, Chalta Mein Jaaon 2011, Josh 2012, Waar 2013, Babu Bhai 2014, Sawal 2014; singles: with Junoon: Jazbe-e-Junoon 1996, Saeein, Ehtesaab 1996, Sayonee 1997, Taara jala. *Address:* Samina Ahmad, Junoon Inc., 210 Old Tappan Road, Tappan, NY 10983, USA (office). *E-mail:* saminadr@gmail.com (office). *Website:* aliazmat.com.

AZMI, Khaled; Egyptian diplomatist; *Ambassador to Israel;* fmr Dir, Counter-terrorism Unit, Ministry of Foreign Affairs and Deputy Head of Mission, Embassy in London; Amb. to Israel 2018–. *Address:* Embassy of Egypt, 54 Basel Street, Tel-Aviv 62744, Israel (office). *Telephone:* 3-5464151 (office). *Fax:* 3-5441615 (office). *E-mail:* egyptelaviv@hotmail.com (office).

AZMI, Shabana, BA; Indian actress, politician and human rights activist; b. 18 Sept. 1951, Hyderabad; d. of Kaifi Azmi and Shaukat Kaifi; m. Javed Akhtar 1984; ed St Xavier's Coll. Mumbai, Film and TV Inst., Pune; mem. Rajya Sabha (Upper House of Parl.) 1997–2003; speaker on women's rights and communication in USA; campaigner on social justice issues; Chair. Nivara Hakk Suraksha Samiti (campaigning org. for upgrading of slum dwellings); Chair. Children's Film Soc. 1992–94; Goodwill Amb. UN Population Fund (UNFPA) 1998–; Chair. of Jury Montréal and Cairo Int. Film Festivals; Pres. Mijwan Welfare Soc.; mem. Nat. Integration Council, Advisory Council Endowment Campaign for Chair. in Indian Studies, Columbia Univ.; Visiting Prof., Univ. of Michigan, USA; Dr hc (Leeds Metropolitan Univ., UK) 2007, (Jamia Millia Univ.) 2008, (Simon Fraser Univ.) 2013, (TERI Univ.) 2014, (Viswva Bharati Univ.); Soviet Land Nehru Award 1985, Padma Shri Award 1988, Rajiv Gandhi Award for Excellence in Secularism 1994, Yash Bhartiya Award for promoting women's issues, Govt of Uttar Pradesh 1988, King Chevaz Award, Univ. of Michigan, Martin Luther King Professorship Award, Univ. of Michigan 2002, Gandhi Foundation Int. Peace Award 2006, Crystal Award, World Econ. Forum 2006, Lifetime Achievement Award, Filmfare 2006, Pres.'s Memorial Award for Nat. Integration 2007, Global Leadership Award, Int. Indian Film Acad., Macao 2009. *Plays include:* Nora (Singapore Repertory Theatre), The Waiting Room (Nat. Theatre, London), Sufaid Kundali, Tumhari Amrita, Emma in Betrayal (Singapore Repertory Theatre), Shaukat Kaifi in Kaifi Aur Main, Manjula and Malini Sharma in Broken Images. *Films include:* nearly 150 films including Ankur (Nat. Award for Best Actress) 1974, Nishant 1976, Swami (Filmfare Award) 1977, Shatranj Ke Khiladi 1977, Junoon 1978, Amardeep 1979, Sparsh 1980, Masoom 1983, Arth (Nat. Award) 1983, Mandi 1983, Doosri Dulhan 1983, Khandhar (Nat. Award) 1984, Paar (Nat. Award) 1985, Libaas (Int. Best Actress Award, N Korea 1993) 1988, Bhavna (Filmfare Award) 1984, Madame Sousatzka 1988, Bengali Night 1988, City of Joy 1992, The Journey, Son of the Pink Panther 1993, Patang (Best Actress Award, Taormina Art Festival Italy) 1994, Fire (Silver Hugo Award for Best Actress, Chicago Int. Film Festival, Outstanding Actress in a Feature Film, LA Outfest) 1996, Saaz 1997, Godmother (Nat. Award, Bengal Film Journalists' Asscn Awards) 1999, Hari-Bhari: Fertility 2000, Makdee 2002, Tehzeeb (Zee Cine Award) 2003, Lakshya 2004, Morning Raga 2004 (Star Screen Award) 2005, 15 Park Avenue 2005, Waterborne 2005, Umrao Jaan 2006, Honeymoon Travels Pvt. Ltd 2007, Loins of Punjab Presents 2007, Sorry Bhai! 2008, It's a Wonderful Afterlife 2010, Kalpvriksh 2011, A Decent Arrangement 2011, Matru Ki Bijlee Ka Mandola 2012, The Reluctant Fundamentalist 2013, A Decent Arrangement 2014, Kalpvriksh 2015, Jazbaa 2015, Chalk n Duster 2016, Neerja 2016, The Black Prince 2017. *Television:* Anupama (Hindi serial). *Leisure interests:* reading, singing. *Address:* 702 Sagar Samrat, Green Fields, Juhu, Mumbai 400 049, India (home). *Telephone:* (22) 26200066 (home). *Fax:* (22) 26202602 (office). *E-mail:* azmishabana@gmail.com (office).

AZNAN, Syed Jaafar bin Syed, MBA, PhD; Malaysian civil servant and banker; b. 1947, Parit Buntar; m.; three c.; ed Univ. of Malaya, Wharton School, USA, Henley Man. Coll./Brunel Univ., UK; civil servant in Malaysia holding several sr positions in various ministries 1970–97; Vice-Pres. Trade and Policy, Islamic Devt Bank, Jeddah, Saudia Arabia 1997–2009; apptd Ind. Dir (non-exec.), Bank Pembangunan Malaysia Berhad 2010; Chair. Perbadanan Kemajuan Ekonomi Islam Negeri Perak; mem. Council Majlis Agama Islam dan Adat Melayu Perak. *Address:* c/o Bank Pembangunan Malaysia Berhad (16562-K), Menara Bank Pembangunan Bandar Wawasan, No. 1016, Jalan Sultan Ismail, 50250 Kuala Lumpur, Malaysia. *Website:* sjaznan.wordpress.com.

AZNAR LÓPEZ, José María; Spanish politician and academic; *President, Fundación para el Análisis y los Estudios Sociales;* b. 1953, Madrid; s. of Manuel Aznar Acedo; m. Ana Botella; two s. one d.; ed Universidad Complutense; fmr tax inspector; fmr Chief Exec. Castile-Leon region; joined Rioja br. Alianza Popular 1978, Sec.-Gen. 1982–87, apptd Vice-Pres. 1989, Pres. 1991; elected mem. Cortes (Parl.) 1982; Premier Castilla y León Autonomous Region 1987–89; Leader of Opposition 1989–96; Pres. Partido Popular (PP, fmrly Alianza Popular) 1990–2004, Hon. Chair. –2016; Prime Minister of Spain and Pres. of the Council 1996–2004; mem. Council of State 2005–06; currently Pres. Fundación para el Análisis y los Estudios Sociales (FAES), Madrid; Distinguished Scholar in the Practice of Global Leadership, Georgetown Univ., Washington, DC 2004–; Vice-Pres. European Democratic Union; Pres. Int. Democratic Centre 2001; Chair. Friends of Israel Initiative; mem. Bd of Dirs News Corpn 2006–; Distinguished Fellow, School of Advanced Int. Studies, Johns Hopkins Univ. (Chair. Atlantic Basin Initiative); mem. Int. Advisory Bd Atlantic Council (Co-Chair. Transatlantic Task Force on Latin America), Centaurus Capital 2007–; mem. Int. Advisory Bd Barrick Gold Corpn; Sr Advisor to Global Bd, DLA Piper; mem. Club de Madrid, Leadership Council for Concordia 2013–; Hon. Prof., Universidad de Ciencias Aplicadas, Perú 2006; Dr hc (Sophia Univ., Tokyo) 1997, (Florida International Univ.) 1998, (Bar-Ilan Univ., Israel) 2005, (Universidad Andrés Bello, Chile) 2006, (Universidad Francisco Marroquín, Guatemala) 2006, (Università Cattolica Sacro Cuore, Milán) 2007, (Universidad Cardenal Herrera CEU) 2009, (Universidad San Ignacio de Loyola, Perú) 2009, (Ilia Chavchavadze Univ., Georgia) 2009, (Universidad San Antonio) 2010, (Universidad de las Américas, Ecuador) 2011; Pres.'s Medal, Georgetown Univ. 2004. *Publication:* Libertad y solidaridad 1991, La España en que yo creo 1995, España: la segunda transición 1995, Ocho años de gobierno: una visión personal de España 2004, Retratos y perfiles: de Fraga a Bush 2005, Cartas a un joven español 2007, España puede salir de la crisis 2009, Memorias I 2012. *Address:* Fundación para el Análisis y los Estudios Sociales, Ruiz de Alarcón Street 13, 2, 28014 Madrid, Spain (office); Mortara Center for International Studies, Edmund A. Walsh School of Foreign Service, Georgetown University, ICC, Suite 304, 37th and O Streets, NW, Washington, DC 20057, USA (office). *Telephone:* (91) 5766857 (office). *Fax:* (91) 5754695 (office). *E-mail:* presidencia@fundacionfaes.org (office); atencion@pp.es (office). *Website:* www.fundacionfaes.org (office); www.georgetown.edu/sfs/mortara (office); www.pp.es (office).

AZOULAY, Audrey, MBA; French politician, civil servant and UN official; *Director-General, United Nations Educational, Scientific and Cultural Organization (UNESCO);* b. 4 Aug. 1972, La Celle-Saint-Cloud; d. of André Azoulay; m.; two c.; ed Ecole nationale d'administration, Paris Inst. of Political Studies, Lancaster Univ., UK; started as Head of Public Broadcasting Sector Office, Media Devt Directorate; worked as Rapporteur for Court of Auditors and Legislation Expert for EC 2000–03; apptd Deputy Dir for Multimedia Affairs, Chief Financial and Legal Officer, Deputy Dir-Gen., Nat. Centre of Cinematography and Moving Image 2006; Culture Adviser to Pres. 2014–16; Minister of Culture and Communication 2016–17; Dir-Gen. UNESCO 2017–; mem. Parti Socialiste; Commandeur de l'Ordre des Arts et des Lettres. *Achievements:* presented Draft Resolution 2347 on protection of cultural heritage in armed conflicts to UN Security Council 2017. *Address:* UNESCO, 7 place de Fontenoy, 75007 Paris 07 SP, France (office). *Telephone:* 1-45-68-10-00 (office). *Fax:* 1-45-67-16-90 (office). *E-mail:* bpi@unesco.org (office). *Website:* www.unesco.org (office).

AZOUR, Jihad, MS, PhD; Lebanese economist, government official and business executive; *Managing Partner, Inventis Partners;* b. 4 May 1964, Sir Denniye; m. Roula Rizk; ed Assad Univ., Univ. of Paris, IEP Paris, France, Harvard Univ., USA; with McKinsey and Co., Paris 1989–93; Program Man. and Adviser to Dir Gen., Asscn d'Economie Financière 1993–94; Man. Partner, AM&F Consulting 1996–98; consultant to IMF and Booz Allen Hamilton 2005; Prof., American Univ. of Beirut 1998–2000; Dir UNDP/World Bank project 1999–2005; Adviser to Ministry of Finance 1999–2004; Minister of Finance 2005–08; mem. Middle East Regional Advisory Group, IMF 2009–; Vice-Pres. and Sr Exec. Adviser (Middle East), Booz & Company 2009–12; Man. Partner, Inventis Partners, Lebanon 2013–; mem. Bd of Dirs CMA CGM 2012–, Lebanon Renaissance Foundation; mem. Jury Cttee, WOW Award, New Arab Woman Forum 2014; Chevalier, Legion d'honneur.

AŽUBALIS, Audronius; Lithuanian journalist and politician; b. 17 Jan. 1958, Vilnius; m. Loreta Ažubalienė; two d.; ed Antanas Vienuolis Secondary School, Vilnius, Vilnius State Univ., World Press Inst., Macalester Coll., USA; various positions in journalism and publishing 1979–88, including Lithuanian State Cttee of Publishing Houses, Polygraph Enterprises and Book Trade, Scientific Methodological Culture Centre of Lithuania, State Cttee for TV and Radio Broadcasting, Lithuanian Cinema Rental Bureau; corresp., Atgimimas (weekly newspaper) 1989–90; Spokesman for Chair. of Supreme Council (Reconstituent Seimas) 1990–92, Head of Seimas Information and Analysis Centre 1991–93; f. Lithuania's first public relations consultancy 1993, Chair. 1993–96; mem. Seimas (Parl.) 1996–2000, 2008–10, apptd Chair. Cttee on Foreign Affairs 2004, Deputy Chair. Cttee on European Affairs; Dir-Gen. Translation, Documentation and Information Centre, Govt Chancellery 2001–04; Minister of Foreign Affairs 2010–12; Pres. Lithuania–GB Chamber of Commerce 1998–2000; mem. Homeland Union—Lithuanian Conservatives (now Homeland Union—Lithuanian Christian Democrats) 1998–; Pres. Nat. Magazine Publrs Asscn 2001–03; Third Degree, Order of Merit (Ukraine) 2007; 13th Jan. Commemorative Medal 1999, Commemorative Badge of Lithuania's admission to NATO 2003. *Leisure interests:* reading historical themes, homestead farm work, fishing. *Address:* Homeland Union—Lithuanian Christian Democrats, L. Stuokos-Gucevičiaus g. 11, Vilnius 01122, Lithuania (office). *Telephone:* (5) 212-1657 (office). *Fax:* (5) 278-4722 (office). *E-mail:* sekretoriatas@tsajunga.lt (office). *Website:* www.tsajunga.lt (office).

AZUMI, Jun; Japanese lawyer and politician; *Deputy Secretary-General, Democratic Party of Japan;* b. 17 Jan. 1962, Oshika Dist, Miyagi Pref.; m.; two s.; ed Waseda Univ.; began career as political reporter for NHK (Japan Broadcasting Corpn) 1985–93; mem. House of Reps for Miyagi No. 5 Dist 1993–; apptd Chair. Security Cttee, Democratic Party of Japan 2009, Parl. Affairs Cttee 2011, Deputy Sec.-Gen. 2012–; Sr Vice-Minister of Defence 2010, Minister of Finance 2011–12. *Address:* Democratic Party of Japan, 1-11-1, Nagata-cho, Chiyoda-ku, Tokyo 100-0014, Japan (office). *Telephone:* (3) 3595-9988 (office). *Fax:* (3) 3595-9988 (office). *E-mail:* dpjenews@dpj.or.jp (office). *Website:* www.dpj.or.jp (office).

B

BÂ, Amadou; Senegalese politician; *Minister of Foreign Affairs and Senegalese Nationals Abroad;* b. 17 May 1961, Dakar; m.; three c.; ed École nat. d'admin et de magistrature (Enam), Univ. Cheikh Anta Diop (UCAD); has held numerous positions in Ministry of the Economy and Finance, including Controller of Insurance, Dept of Insurance 1992–94, Head of Training, Centre Ouest Africain de Formation et d'Etudes Bancaires (part of Banque centrale des Etats de l'Afrique de l'Ouest) 1995–2000, Auditor, Audit and Verification Dept 2000–02, Dir of Taxes 2004–06, Dir-Gen. of Taxation 2006–13, Minister of the Economy and Finance 2013–19, of Foreign Affairs and Senegalese Nationals Abroad 2019–. *Address:* Ministry of Foreign Affairs, place de l'Indépendance, BP 4044, Dakar, Senegal (office). *Telephone:* (33) 889-1300 (office). *Fax:* (33) 823-5496 (office). *E-mail:* maeuase@senegal.diplomatie.sn (office). *Website:* www.diplomatie.gouv.sn (office).

BA, Amadou Lamine, BSc, MSc, PhD; Senegalese development consultant and diplomatist; m. Oulimata Ba; two c.; ed Ecole des Cadres Ruraux, Ohio State Univ., USA; Dir Regional Educ. Centre, Crop Protection Directorate (Direction de la Protection des Végétaux/DPV), Dakar 1980–82; consultant in int. devt, USAID-Washington, in The Gambia 1981, in Guinea-Bissau 1981, in Niamey 1983; Research Asst, Coll. of Agric., Ohio State Univ., Columbus 1988–93, Researcher and Asst Prof. 1997–99; Consultant and Visiting Scholar, Dept of Int. Studies, Univ. of Vermont 1993; consultant in int. devt 1993–97; Jt Leader, Human Rights, Democracy and New Leadership in Africa (HDNA) 1995–97; mem. Exec. Bd US-Africa Inst. 1997–99; Prof. of Science, Bunker Hill Coll., Boston, Mass 1999–; Amb. to USA 2002–10; mem. Forum des Citoyens pour l'Alternance, Asscn des Professeurs de Sciences, Int. Soc. of Quality Assurance; Key to City of Baton Rouge, La 2006. *Publications:* Integrated Pest Management and International Agriculture Development Policies: A Case Study of the United States and Africa 1993, Global Issues in Pesticides Regulation 1999. *Address:* c/o Ministry of Foreign Affairs, place de l'Indépendance, BP 4044, Dakar, Senegal (office).

BA, Ousmane, BA; Mauritanian diplomatist and politician; *Permanent Representative to United Nations;* ed Univ. of Nouakchott; Expert Admin and Man. on UN Project, Assaba Region 1997–2003; Coordinator IFAD 2003–07; Sec.-Gen. Ministry of Commerce and Industry 2007, for Govt of Mauritania 2008–13; Minister for Primary Educ. Sept. 2013–Feb. 2014, for Nat. Educ. 2014–16; Amb. to Gambia July 2016–Jan. 2017; Perm. Rep. to UN 2017–. *Address:* Permanent Mission of Mauritania, 116 E 38th Street, New York, NY 10016, USA (office). *Telephone:* (212) 252-0113 (office). *Fax:* (212) 252-0175 (office). *E-mail:* mauritaniamission@gmail.com (office). *Website:* www.un.int/mauritania (office).

BAALBAKI, Ayman, DEA; Lebanese artist; b. 1975, Odeissé; ed Inst. des Beaux Arts, Lebanese Univ., Beirut, Univ. Paris VIII, Ecole nat. supérieure des Arts Décoratifs, Paris; works include oil paintings and installations; chosen to take part in The Future of a Promise (first pan-Arab exhbn of contemporary art), 2011 Venice Biennale; mem. Asscn des Artistes libanais; Silver Medal (painting), Jeux de la Francophonie, Niger 2005. *Address:* c/o Agial Art Gallery, 63 Abdul Aziz Street, Hamra District, Beirut, Lebanon (office). *Telephone:* (1) 1345213 (office). *Website:* www.radisnoir.com/ayman (office).

BABA AMMI, Hadji; Algerian economist and politician; b. 3 Feb. 1944, Béni-Isguen; m.; four c.; ed Ecole Nat. Polytechnique, Algiers; Dir of Planning, Industrial Devt and Services, Ministry of Planning 1984–88; Dir of Research and Forecasting, Ministry of Finance 1989–90, Dir-Gen. of Research and Forecasting 1995–2005, Dir-Gen., Treasury Dept 2005–13, Deputy Minister of Finance, in charge of Budget and Forecasting 2014–16, Minister of Finance 2016–17; fmr Chair. Insurance Supervisory Comm.; Central Dir, Banque d'Algérie 1991–92; mem. Bd of Dirs Banque africaine pour le développement 2013; fmr mem. Bd of Dirs Sonatrach SpA, Air Algérie.

BABACAN, Ali, BSc, MBA; Turkish politician; b. 1967, Ankara; m.; three c.; ed Middle East Tech. Univ., Kellogg School of Management, Northwestern Univ., USA; worked at QRM, Inc., Chicago, Ill. 1992–94; chief adviser to Mayor of Ankara 1994; ran family-owned textile co. 1994–2002; mem. Grand Nat. Ass., representing Ankara 2002–; Minister of State for Economy 2002–07, also Chief Negotiator in accession talks with EU 2005; Minister of Foreign Affairs 2007–09; Deputy Prime Minister and Minister of State in charge of coordination of the Economy 2009–15, also mem. Nat. Security Council; Co-founder and Bd mem. AKP (Adalet ve Kalkinma Partisi/Justice and Devt Party). *Address:* c/o Adalet ve Kalkınma Partisi (Justice and Development Party), Söğütözü Cad. 6, Çankaya, Ankara, Turkey. *Website:* www.akparti.org.tr.

BABAEV, Agadzhan Geldyevich, DrGeogSc; Turkmenistani geographer and academic; b. 10 May 1929, Mary; s. of Geldy Babaev and Ogulbek Babaevai; m. Dunyagozel Palvanova 1951; two s. six d.; ed State Pedagogical Inst., Ashkhabad (now Ashgabat), Turkmenistan State Univ.; Head, Geography Dept, Turkmenistan State Univ. 1952–59; Deputy Dir Desert Research Inst., Turkmenistan Acad. of Sciences 1959–60, Dir 1960–99; apptd Chair. Scientific Council for Desert Problems 1967; Ed.-in-Chief Problems of Desert Devt 1967; Dir Turkmenistan Research and Training Centre on Desertification Control for ESCAP; Deputy to USSR Supreme Soviet 1979–89; Chair. Turkmenistan Soc. for Chinese-Soviet Friendship; mem. Turkmenistan Acad. of Sciences, Pres. 1975–86, 1989–93; Corresp. mem. USSR (now Russian) Acad. of Sciences 1976; Academician, Islamic Acad. of Sciences 1996; Vice-Pres. Turkmens of the World Humanitarian Asscn; Deputy, Turkmenistan Parl.; Order of the Badge of Honour; USSR State Prize 1981, Academician Karpinskii Medal 1990, Jerald Piel Medal 1992. *Publications:* 12 monographs, 329 articles for professional journals. *Address:* 113 Kosaev Street, Ashgabat 744020, Turkmenistan (home). *Telephone:* (12) 34-26-24 (home).

BABANGIDA, Maj.-Gen. Ibrahim Badamasi, CFR; Nigerian army officer (retd) and fmr head of state; b. 17 Aug. 1941, Minna; m. Maryam King 1969 (died 2009); two s. two d.; ed Niger provincial secondary school, Bida, Kaduna Mil. Training Coll. and Indian Mil. Acad.; commissioned 1963, Lt 1966; training with RAC, UK 1966; CO during Biafran Civil War; Co Commdr and Instructor, Nigerian Defence Acad. 1970–72; rank of Maj. then Lt-Col Armoured Corps 1974; trained at US Army Armoury School 1974; promoted to Maj.-Gen., Dir of Army Duties and Plans 1983; took part in overthrow of Pres. Shehu Shagari 1983; mem. Supreme Mil. Council and Chief Army Staff 1983–85; Pres. of Nigeria following coup overthrowing Maj.-Gen. Muhammadu Buhari 1985–93; Pres. Police Council 1989; Minister of Defence Dec. 1989–90; Defence Service Medal, Nat. Service Medal, Royal Service Medal, Forces Services Star, General Service Medal Hon. GCB 1989. *Publications:* Civil and Military Relationship, The Nigerian Experience 1979, Defence Policy within the Framework of National Planning 1985.

BABANOV, Omurbek; Kyrgyzstani politician and business executive; *Co-Chairman, Respublika-Ata Jurt Sayasiy Partiyasy (Republic-Homeland Political Party);* b. 20 May 1970, Kara-Buura Dist, Talas Oblast, Kyrgyz SSR, USSR; m., four c.; ed Timiryazev Moscow Agricultural Acad., Acad. of Nat. Economy at Govt of the Russian Fed., Higher Coll. of Financial Man., Moscow, Kyrgyz State Judicial Acad. at Govt of the Kyrgyz Repub.; served in Soviet Army in GDR 1988–89; rep. of Shımkentnefteosintez (Shimkent Oil Refinery) Co. in Kyrgyz Repub. –1999; Dir, Arlan LLP, Taras, Kazakhstan 1995–98; Deputy Gen. Dir Munai Co., Bishkek 1999–2000; Pres. Kyrgyzkhlopok (Kyrgyz Cotton) Co., Jalal-Abad 2000–04; Chief Rep., Petro Kazakhstan Oil Products in Kyrgyz Repub., Bishkek 2002–05; mem. Bd of Dirs, Munai Myrza Invest Co. 2004–05, Chair. 2008, 2009–10; Adviser to Chair. of Kommerchiskii Bank-Kyrgyzstan Jan.–Oct. 2010; Deputy in Jogorku Kenesh (Parl.) 2005–07, 2010–12, 2015–, Rep. of Karabuurinsky Electoral Dist No. 56 2005–07, mem. Parl. Cttee for Int. Affairs and Interparliamentary Communications, Social and Religious Orgs, mem. El Birimdigi factions of deputies, Head of Deputy Group for Friendship of the Supreme Council (Jogorku Kenesh) with Parl. of the Russian Fed., Turkey and Kazakhstan; First Deputy Prime Minister (expelled from Kyrgyzstandyn Sotsial-Demokratiyalyk Partiyasy—Social Democratic Party of Kyrgyzstan in consequence) Jan.–Oct. 2009; participant and Co-Chair. Ak-niet Movt April–June 2010; Founder and Chair. Respublika Sayasiy Partiyasy (Respublika) (Repub. Political Party) 2010–, Co-Chair. Respublika-Ata Jurt Sayasiy Partiyasy (R-AJ—Republic-Homeland Political Party) 2014–; First Deputy Prime Minister Dec. 2010–Sept. 2011 (suspended from office at own request April–May 2011), Acting Prime Minister Sept.–Nov., 1–23 Dec. 2011, Prime Minister 23 Dec. 2011–1 Sept. 2012 (resgnd); cand. in presidential election 2017; Businessman of the Year in Kyrgyzstan 2004. *Address:* Respublika-Ata Jurt Sayasiy Partiyasy (Republic-Homeland Political Party), 720000 Bishkek, Gorkogo 1/2 (office); Jogorku Kenesh (Supreme Council), 720053 Bishkek, Abdymomunov 207, Kyrgyzstan (office). *Telephone:* (312) 98-68-15 (R-AJ) (office); (312) 63-87-39 (Parl.) (office). *Fax:* (312) 62-50-12 (Parl.) (office). *E-mail:* office@respublika-atajurt.kg (office); zs@kenesh.gov.org (office). *Website:* www.respublika-atajurt.kg (office); www.kenesh.kg (office).

BABAR, Alamgir Khan, BA, LLB; Pakistani diplomatist; b. 4 Jan. 1954; joined Foreign Service 1980, Section Officer 1982, Third, then Second Sec., Embassy in Madrid 1983–87, Section Officer, Ministry of Foreign Affairs 1987–90, First Sec., Perm. Mission to the UN, New York 1990–94, First Sec./Counsellor in New Delhi, 1994–97, Dir Ministry of Foreign Affairs 1997–99, Deputy Perm. Rep., Perm. Mission to the UN, New York 1999–2001, on deputation with UN Peace Keeping Mission in Bosnia and Kosovo 2001–03, later Acting Perm. Rep. to UN, New York, Dir-Gen. (Americas), Ministry of Foreign Affairs 2004–05, High Commr to Bangladesh 2005–10, Amb. to Brazil 2010–11, Special Sec. 2011–13, Amb. to Russia 2013–14.

BABBAR, Raj; Indian politician, actor and filmmaker; b. 23 June 1952, Agra Dist, Uttar Pradesh; s. of Kaushal Kumar and Shobha Rani; m. 1st Nadira Babbar 1975; m. 2nd Smita Patil (died 1986); two s. one d.; ed Nat. School of Drama, New Delhi; mem. Janata Dal 1989; mem. Samajwadi Party (suspended 2006); mem. Indian National Congress 2008–; mem. Rajya Sabha 1994–99, 2016– (for Uttarakhand), mem. Home Affairs Cttee, Rules Cttee, Consultative Cttee, Ministry of Civil Aviation; elected to Lok Sabha 1999, 2004, 2009, mem. Defence Cttee, Environment Cttee, Transport, Tourism and Culture Cttee 1999–2000, 2004, Petitions Cttee; mem. Personnel, Public Grievances, Law & Justice 2007; Pres. Uttar Pradesh Congress Cttee 2016–18; Yash Bharti Award, Uttar Pradesh Govt, Punjabi Male Actor of the Millennium, Punjabi American Festival 2000. *Films include:* Shaheed Uddham Singh 2000, LoC Kargil 2003, Kyaa Dil Ne Kahaa 2002, The Legend of Bhagat Singh 2002, Talaash 2003, Sheen 2004, Police Force: An Inside Story 2004, Shikaar 2004, Yaaran Naal Baharaan 2005, Bunty Aur Babli 2005, Ek Dhun Banaras Kee 2006, Corporate 2006, UNNS: Love Forever 2006, Ek Jind Ek Jaan 2006, Sirf Romance: Love by Chance 2007, Aap Kaa Surroor: The Moviee 2007, Fashion 2008. *Address:* Uttar Pradesh Congress Committee, Nehru Bhawan, 10, Mall Avenue, Lucknow, Uttar Pradesh (office); House No. 94, Ellora Enclave, Dayal Bagh, New Agra 282005, Uttar Pradesh (home); Nepathay 20, Gulmohar Road, J.V.P.D. Scheme, Mumbai 400 049, India (home). *Telephone:* (522) 2238858 (Lucknow) (office); (22) 26282819 (Mumbai) (home). *Fax:* (22) 26248868 (Mumbai) (home); (522) 2239825 (Lucknow) (office). *E-mail:* upcclko@hotmail.com (office); rajbabbars@yahoo.in. *Website:* loksabha.nic.in (office); www.uttarpradeshcongress.com (office).

BABBITT, Bruce Edward, MSc, JD, LLB; American lawyer, business executive and fmr politician; b. 27 July 1938, Flagstaff, AZ; m. Hattie Coons; two c.; ed Univ. of Notre Dame, Univ. of Newcastle, UK, Harvard Univ. Law School; Attorney-Gen. AZ 1975–78; Gov. of AZ 1978–87; Pnr, Steptoe & Johnson, Phoenix; US Sec. of Interior 1993–2001; Sec. of Counsel, Environmental Dept, Latham & Watkins LLP (law firm) 2001; Pres. Raintree Ventures (investment firm), Washington, DC; Chair. World Wildlife Fund 2006, now Dir Emer.; Chair. Nat. Groundwater Policy Forum 1984; Pres. League of Conservation Voters 1993–2001; Marshall Scholar 1960–62; mem. Bd of Dirs Amazon Conservation Asscn; Democrat; Thomas Jefferson Award, Nat. Wildlife Fed. 1981, Special Conservation Award 1983. *Publications:* Color and Light: The Southwest Canvases of Louis Akin 1973, Grand Canyon: An Anthology 1978, Cities in the Wilderness: A New Look at Land Use in America 2005. *Address:* Raintree Ventures, 5169 Watson Street, NW, Washington, DC 20016, USA (office).

BABESHKO, Vladimir A., DSc; Russian physicist and university official; b. 30 May 1941; m.; two d.; ed Rostov State Univ.; with Rostov Univ. 1966–82, fmr Asst,

Prof., Deputy Dir; Rector, Kuban State Univ. 1982–2008; Chair. Russian S Branch, Int. Acad. of Higher Educ. Sciences; apptd mem. Council for Sciences, Tech. and Educ. under Pres. of Russian Fed. 2004; mem. Russian Acad. of Sciences 1997; Hon. Senator, Berlin Univ. of Applied Sciences 2006; Order of People's Friendship 1986; Lenin Komsomol Prize 1977, Vavilov Medal 1990, State Award of Russian Fed. in the Field of Science and Eng 2001, Hero of Labour of Kuban Medal 2003, Rector of the Year Hon. Breastplate 2004, 2005, Distinguished Citizen of Krasnodar. *Publications:* author or co-author of more than 300 scientific publs, including five monographs.

BABICH, Mikhail Viktorovich; Russian politician and diplomatist; *Ambassador to Belarus;* b. 28 May 1969; m.; two c.; ed Ryazan Higher Mil. School of Communications, Moscow Inst. of Econ. Man. and Law, State Acad. of Man.; sr officer in airborne troops 1990–94, retd with rank of Capt. 1995; worked in pvt. sector 1995–99; Deputy Dir-Gen. Fed. Agency for Food Market Regulation, Ministry of Agric. 1999–2000; Deputy Gov. Moscow Region 2000, forced to resign following accusations of misappropriating US humanitarian aid; First Deputy Gov. Ivanovskaya Region 2001–02; Chair. Republican Govt (Prime Minister) of Chechnya Nov. 2002–Jan. 2003 (resgnd); mem. State Duma 2003–11, Deputy Chair. Defence Cttee; Asst to Minister of Econ. Devt 2003–; Presidential Rep. to Volga Fed. Okrug 2011–18; Amb. to Belarus 2018–; Chair. State Comm. on Chemical Disarmament 2011–; State Adviser of the Russian Fed., First Class 2012–; Dir of election staff, Vladimir Oblast regional br., United Russia (Yedinaya Rossiya) party; Order of Friendship 2006, Order 'For Merit' (Fourth Degree) 2011, Order of Holy Prince Daniel of Moscow (Third Degree) 2014; Certificate of Merit of the Pres. of the Russian Fed. 2010. *Address:* Embassy of the Russian Federation, 220053 Minsk, vul. Novovilenskaya 1A, Belarus (office). *Telephone:* (17) 233-35-90 (office). *Fax:* (17) 233-35-97 (office). *E-mail:* rusemb-minsk@yandex.ru (office). *Website:* www.belarus.mid.ru (office).

BABIŠ, Andrej; Czech business executive and politician; *Prime Minister;* b. 2 Sept. 1954, Bratislava, Czechoslovak Repub. (now Slovakia); s. of Štefan Babiš and Andriana Babišová; m. (divorced); two c.; partner Monika Babišová; two c.; ed gymnasium in Bratislava, Univ. of Economics; worked as employee of Slovak Communist-controlled int. trade co. Petrimex in Morocco; returned to Czechoslovakia after Velvet Revolution and resided in Czech Repub. following dissolution of Czechoslovakia; Owner and CEO Agrofert from 1993; Founder and Leader, Akce Nespokojených Občanů (Action of Dissatisfied Citizens) 2011– (renamed Ano—Yes 2012); First Deputy Prime Minister, responsible for the Economy, and Minister of Finance 2014–17; Prime Minister 2017–. *Address:* Office of the Government, náb. Edvarda Beneše 4, 118 01 Prague 1 (office); 9. května 21, 682 01 Vyškov, Czech Republic (home). *Telephone:* (2) 24002111 (office). *Fax:* (2) 57531283 (office). *E-mail:* posta@vlada.cz (office). *Website:* www.vlada.cz (office).

BABIUC, Victor, PhD; Romanian politician and lawyer; b. 3 April 1938, Răchiţi Commune, Botoşani Co.; s. of Victor Babiuc and Olga Babiuc; m. Lucia Babiuc 1978; one d.; ed Law School of Bucharest, Romanian Acad. for Econ. Studies, Univ. of Bucharest; juridical counsellor, judge in Braşov; Chief Juridical Counsel Ministry of Foreign Trade, Sr Researcher at the World Economy Inst. 1977–90; mem. House of Deputies 1992–2000; Minister of Justice 1990–91, Minister of the Interior 1991–92, Minister of Nat. Defence 1996–98, Minister of State, Minister of Nat. Defence 1998–2000; mem. Chamber of Deputies for Brasov Ward 2000–04; mem. Democratic Party (PD) 1992–2000, Vice Pres. 1995–2000; mem. Nat. Liberal Party 2000–02; Chair. Commercial Arbitration Court, Chamber of Commerce and Industry of Romania (CCIR) 1993–2008, Pres. CCIR 2005–07; apptd Prof. of Int. Trade Law, Acad. of Econ. Studies of Bucharest 1992; Chair. Cttee for Investigation into Corruption and Cases of Abuse and for Petitions of the Chamber of Deputies 1992–96; mem. Panel of Arbitrators of American Arbitration Asscn, Moscow, Sofia, Abu Dhabi, Warsaw, New Delhi, Cairo 1991–; mem. Cen. European Acad. of Science and Art 2004; sentenced to two years' imprisonment for bribery and abuse of office May 2013 (released Feb. 2014). *Publications:* over 200 publications mainly in the field of econ. legislation and int. trade law. *Leisure interests:* theatre, walking, reading books on politics, history, memoirs. *Address:* Individual Office Attorney, Bd. Hristo Botev, MR 3, Apartment, Sector 3, Bucharest (office); Bd Libertatii No. 20, Sector 5, Bucharest, Romania (home). *Telephone:* (4021) 3147722 (office); (4021) 3147788 (office); (4021) 3143732 (home). *Fax:* (4021) 3147799 (office). *Website:* babiuc.victor@yahoo.com (office).

BABLOYAN, Ara Saeni, MD; Armenian paediatrician and politician; *Chairman, National Assembly;* b. 5 May 1947; m.; two c.; ed M. Heratsi State Medical Univ., Yerevan; Asst physician, later physician, Urology Div., Outpatient Clinic No. 8 1970–71, Paediatric surgeon and urologist 1971–72; Paediatric surgeon and urologist, Children's Clinical Hosp. No. 1 1972–82; Head of Urology Dept, Yerevan Children's Clinical Hosp. No. 3 1982–90; Founder, Specialist Urology Nephrology and Paediatric Surgery Centre 1990; Sr Lecturer and Prof., Faculty of Paediatric Surgery, Yerevan State Medical Univ. 1977–97, Chair. of Paediatric Surgery 1997; Minister of Health 1991–97; Gen. Dir, Arabkir Children's Clinical Centre 1997–2002, Chair., Bd of Man., Arabkir Jt Inst. and Medical Centre of Child and Adolescent Health 2003–07, Gen. Dir and Scientific Dir 2007–; mem. Azgayin Zhoghov (Nat. Ass., parl.) (Hayastani Hanrapetakan Kutsaktsutyun—HHK—Republican Party of Armeniaparty list) 2007–, Chair. (Speaker) 2017–; Chair. Armenian Asscn of Paediatricians 2007–15; mem. WHO Exec. Cttee 2008–12; mem. European Soc. of Paediatric Urology, Swiss Soc. of Nephrology, Belgian Royal Acad. of Medicine; mem. HHK; Officier, Ordre Nat. du Mérite (France) 2005, Order of Services to Motherland (second rank) 2016; Mkhitar Heratsi Medal 2007, Armed Forces of the Repub. of Armenia Jubilee Medal 2012, Nagorno-Karabakh Repub. Gratitude Medal 2013, St Sahak/St Mesrop Medal of Honour 2014, Award of the Pres. of the Repub. of Armenia Award for scientific achievements in the field of medicine 2015. *Publications:* over 215 scientific publications. *Address:* Azgayin Zhoghov, 0095 Yerevan, Marshal Baghramyan poghota 19, Armenia (office). *Telephone:* (10) 52-05-15 (office). *Fax:* (10) 52-96-95 (office). *E-mail:* abrahamyan@parliament.am (office). *Website:* www.parliament.am (office).

BABO SOARES, Dionísio, PhD; Timor-Leste professor of law and politician; *Minister of Foreign Affairs and Co-operation;* b. 16 Aug. 1966, Ermera; ed Udayana Univ. Denpasar, Indonesia, Massey Univ., NZ; Prof., Faculty of Social and Political Sciences, Nat. Univ. of Timor-Timur (UNTIM) 1992–99; Lecturer, Faculty of Law, Univ. Dili 2003–04; Lecturer, Law School, Univ. of Peace (UNPAZ), Dili 2003–12; mem. Higher Council for Defence and Security of Timor-Leste 2004–05, 2012–17; Co-Chair. Truth and Friendship Comm. (CTF) 2005–08; Sr Legal Adviser to Deputy Prime Minister 2008–12; mem. Nat. Parl. 2012–18, mem. Comm. for Constitutional Affairs, Justice, Public Admin, Local Jurisprudence and Anti-Corruption 2017–18; Minister of Justice 2012–15, Minister of State, Coordinator of Admin. Affairs and Minister of State Admin 2015–17, Minister of Foreign Affairs and Co-operation 2018–; mem. Congresso Nacional da Reconstrução Timorense (CNRT, Nat. Congress for the Reconstruction of Timor-Leste), Sec.-Gen. 2007–11. *Publications:* Elections and Constitution Making in East Timor 2003, Branching from the Trunk: East Timorese Perceptions of Nationalism in Transition 2003, Out of the Ashes: Destruction and Reconstruction of East Timor (co-ed with James J. Fox) 2003, Tetum Language Manual for East Timor (co-author) 2005. *Address:* Ministry of Foreign Affairs and Co-operation, Edif. 1, Av. Presidente Nicolau Lobato, POB 6, Dili, Timor-Leste (office). *Telephone:* 3339600 (office). *Fax:* 3339025 (office). *Website:* www.mnec.gov.tl (office).

BABURIN, Sergei Nikolaevich, LLD, JSD; Russian politician, academic and university administrator; b. 31 Jan. 1959, Semipalatinsk; s. of Nikolay Baburin and Valentina Baburina; m. Tatiana Nikolaevna Baburina; four s.; ed Omsk State Univ., Leningrad State Univ.; mem. CPSU 1981–91; mil. service in Afghanistan 1982–83; worked as lawyer; lecturer, Dean of Law Faculty, Omsk Univ. 1988–90, apptd Professor of Law 1999; People's Deputy of RSFSR (now Russia); mem. Supreme Soviet 1990–93; mem. Constitutional Comm. 1991; Co-Chair. Exec. Bd of All Russian Peoples' Union 1991; Co-Chair. Nat. Salvation Front 1992–; mem. State Duma (Parl.) 1995–99, Deputy Chair. 1996–99, 2003–07; Rector, Russian State Trade and Economics Univ. 2002–04, 2007–12; Chair. All Russian People's Union 1994–2001; Deputy Chair. Parl. Ass. Union of Russia and Belarus 1996–2000; Pres. Inst. of Nat. Reform Strategy 2000; Deputy Dir for Research, Russian Acad. of Sciences (Inst. of Social and Political Research) 2001; Chair. Bd Inter-regional Collegium of Advocates of Businessmen and Citizens' Interactions 2001–02; Leader People's Will—Party of National Rebirth (Narodnaya volya—Partiya natsionalnogo vozrozhdeniya) 2001; Co-Chair. Exec. Council, Motherland–National-Patriotic Union electoral block (Rodina–Narodno-patrioticheskii soyuz); Rector, Int. Slavic Acad. 2015–. *Publications:* Russian Way: Selected Speeches and Essays 1990–95 1995, Russian Way: Losses and Acquisitions 1997, Territory of State: Law and Geopolitical Problems 1997.

BACA DE LA COLINA, Susana; Peruvian singer; b. Chortillos, Lima; m. Ricardo Pereira; formed experimental group combining poetry and song; took part in int. Agua Dulce Festival in Lima; with husband f. Instituto Negrocontinuo 1992; first US performance in Brooklyn 1995; one US and six European tours; Minister of Culture July–Dec. 2011; Pres. OAS Comm. of Culture 2011–13; Ordre des Arts et Lettres, Order of Merit (Peru). *Albums include:* Susana Baca 1997, Del Fuego y del Agua 1999, Eco de Sombras 2000, Lamento Negro (early Cuban recordings, Latin Grammy Award for Best Folk Album) 2001, Espiritu Vivo 2002, Travesias 2006, Cantos de Adoración 2010, Afrodiaspora 2011. *Publication:* The Cultural Importance of Black Peruvians (co-author with Richard Pereira) 1992. *Address:* c/o Iris Musique, 5 Passage St-Sebastien, 75011 Paris, France. *Telephone:* (1) 4769933 (office). *Website:* www.susanabaca.com.

BACALE NCOGO, Col Alejandro; Equatorial Guinean army officer and government official; *Minister of National Defence;* long career in army, roles include Mil. Attaché, Embassy in Morocco 2012, Gen. Inspector of Armed Forces (Continental Region) –2018; Minister of Nat. Defence 2018–. *Address:* Ministry of National Defence, Malabo, Equatorial Guinea (office). *Telephone:* 333092794 (office).

BACCOUCHE, Taïeb, DES; Tunisian politician; b. 1944, Jemmal; ed Univ. of Paris (Sorbonne), France; teacher and researcher, Univ. of Tunis 1969; Gen. Sec., trade union Union Générale Tunisienne du Travail (UGTT) 1981–84, Dir of Echaâb (UGTT newspaper) 1981–85; Minister of Educ. and Govt Spokesman Jan.–Dec. 2011; Minister of Foreign Affairs 2015–16; Pres. Tunisian Linguistics Asscn 1995–2002; Pres. Inst. arabe des droits de l'homme 1998–2011; fmr Gen. Sec. Mediterranean Linguistics Meetings; mem. Nidaa Tunis (Call for Tunisia), Sec.-Gen. 2012–15. *Address:* c/o Ministry of Foreign Affairs, ave de la Ligue des états arabes, 1030 Tunis, Tunisia (office).

BACH, Christian Friis, MSc, PhD; Danish politician, journalist and UN official; b. 29 April 1966, Rødovre; m. Karin Friis Bach; three c.; ed Royal Danish Agricultural Univ.; Vice-Chair., U-landsimporten 1991–92, Bd mem. 1999–2000; Asst Prof. in Devt Econs, Inst. of Econs, Univ. of Copenhagen 1996–99, Hon. Prof. 2009–14; Assoc. Prof. in Int. Econs and Devt Econs, Royal Veterinary and Agricultural Univ. 1999–2005; Chair. Danish Asscn for Int. Cooperation 1997–2001; journalist, Danish Broadcasting Corpn 2002; consultant for several orgs including World Bank, Royal Danish Ministry of Foreign Affairs, EU, UNDP and others; mem. Folketinget (Parl.) (Social Liberal Party) 2006–14, Deputy SLP Parl. group leader and party spokesperson on foreign affairs; Minister for Devt Cooperation 2011–13; UN Under-Sec.-Gen. and Exec. Sec., UN Econ. Comm. for Europe (UNECE) 2014–17; Special Adviser to EC for UN Global Sustainability Panel 2010–11; mem. numerous Danish dels to int. bodies including GATT Uruguay Round 1994, UNCTAD 1996, High-Level Meeting on Integrated Initiatives for Least Developed Countries' Trade Devt, Geneva 1997, WTO 1999, COP-13 Climate Summit, Bali 2007; Int. Dir, DanChurchAid 2005–10; mem. Scientific Cttee, WWF Denmark 2003–. *Address:* c/o UN Economic Commission for Europe, Palais des Nations, 1211 Geneva 10, Switzerland (office).

BACH, Thomas, DJur; German lawyer, business executive, sports administrator and international organization official; *President, International Olympic Committee;* b. 29 Dec. 1953, Wurzburg, Franconia; ed Univ. of Würzburg; fmr fencer, won gold medal in team foil fencing event at Summer Olympics, Montreal 1976, World Champion, Buenos Aires 1977; mem. IOC 1991, Chair. Legal Comm. and Head of Anti-Doping investigations, mem. Exec. Bd 1996–2000, Vice-Pres. 2000–04, 2006–13, Pres. IOC 2013–; Pres. Deutscher Olympischer Sportbund 2006–13; Pres. German Olympic Cttee; mem. Supervisory Bd FIFA 2006 World Cup Organizing Cttee; Chair. Bd of Trustees, FIFA Women's World Cup, Germany 2011 Organizing Cttee; Head of Munich's bid for the 2018 Winter Olympics; Head Michael Weinig AG Co. (Chair., Supervisory Bd –2008). *Address:* International Olympic Committee, Château de Vidy, 1007 Lausanne, Switzerland (office).

Telephone: 216216111 (office). *Fax:* 216216216 (office). *Website:* www.olympic.org (office).

BACH NUÑEZ, Jaume, PhD; Spanish architect; *Founder, Bach Arquitectes;* b. 4 April 1943, Sabadell; s. of Miquel Bach and Josefa Nuñez; m. Carmen Triadó Tur 1978; two s.; ed Tech. Superior Univ. of Architecture, Barcelona (ETSAB); architect, ETSAB 1969, apptd tutor 1972, later PhD Prof.; in partnership with Gabriel Mora Gramunt (q.v.), Bach/Mora Architects 1976–98; f. Bach Arquitectes (with son Eugeni) 1998–; Tutor, Int. Lab. of Architecture and Urban Design, Urbino, Italy 1978; Visiting Prof., Univ. of Dublin 1993, Univ. of Hanover 1994; has lectured and shown work in Spain, Germany, Austria, France, Netherlands, Italy, Slovenia, UK, Ireland, Finland, Portugal, Romania, USA, Argentina, Mexico, Venezuela, Chile and Japan; Hon. Mem. Caracas Contemporary Art Museum Foundation; Hon. PhD (Polytechnic Univ. of Barcelona) 1991; various professional awards including eight FAD Prizes and four Brunel Commendations; two ASCER Ceramics Prizes, Bonaplata Award. *Works include:* UAB Bellaterra Station 1984, Urban Design Superblock, Olympic Village 1986, Auditorium Reina Sofia, Madrid 1987, Cellar Raventós i Blanc 1988, Health Clinic Corachán 1990, Palau Macaya (la Caixa) 1991, Telephone Exchange, Olympic Village, Barcelona 1992, Operating Railway Center FGC 1995, Multicomplex Fleming, Barcelona 1999, social housing, Gavà 2000, Tarragona sea front 2000, Landscape Office bldg, Sant Cugat del Vallés 2003, Casa 4C, Barcelona 2003, Tibet House, Barcelona 2004, Liturgical adaptation for Parma Cathedral, Italy (First Prize, Int. Invited Competition 2005) 2005, Landscape Office bldg, Barcelona, Sant Cugat del Valles, Barcelona 2005, Apartment block Casp 74, Barcelona 2009, HQ of Banc Sabadell, Sant Cugat del Valles 2012. *Publications include:* Junge Architekten in Europa (co-author) 1983, Young Spanish Architecture (co-author) 1985, Bach/Mora, Contemporary Architectural Catalogues 1987, Bach – Mora, Architects 1996, Architecture Guide Spain 1920–2000 1998, Twentieth-Century Architecture Spain 2000, Landscape Office Building 2003; numerous magazine articles. *Address:* Calle Hercegovina 24–27, 08006 Barcelona, Spain (office). *Telephone:* (93) 200-29-11 (office). *Fax:* (93) 200-29-98 (office). *E-mail:* j.bach@coac.es (office). *Website:* www.bacharquitectes.com (office).

BACHA, Edmar Lisboa, PhD; Brazilian economist; *Director, Institute of Political and Economic Studies, Casa das Garças;* b. 14 Feb. 1942, Lambari, Minas Gerais; s. of Felicio Bacha and Maria de Jesus Lisboa Bacha; m. Maria Laura Cavalcanti; ed Fed. Univ. of Minas Gerais, Yale Univ., USA; Research Assoc., MIT, Cambridge, Mass, USA 1968–69; Prof. of Econs, Vargas Foundation, Rio de Janeiro 1970–71, Univ. of Brasília 1972–78, Catholic Univ. of Rio de Janeiro 1979–93, Fed. Univ. of Rio de Janeiro 1993–97; Pres. Statistical Office of Brazil, Rio de Janeiro 1985–86; Econ. Adviser to Brazilian Govt 1993; Pres. Nat. Devt Bank, Rio de Janeiro 1995; Sr Consultant, Banco Itaú BBA 1996–2010; Visiting Prof., Harvard Univ. 1975, Columbia Univ. 1983, Yale Univ. 1984, Univ. of California, Berkeley 1988, Univ. of Stanford 1989; Founder and Dir Inst. of Political and Econ. Studies, Casa das Garças 2003–; Pres. Nat. Asscn of Investment Banks (ANDIB) 2000–03; mem. Exec. Cttee, Int. Econ. Asscn, Paris 1987–92, Cttee for Devt Planning, UN, New York 1987–94, Int. Consultative Cttee Yale Univ. 1999–, Consultative Cttee, Brazil Foundation, Rio de Janeiro 2001–, Consultative Cttee Faculdade Pitágoras, Belo Horizonte 2001–, Admin. Cttee Companhia Siderúrgica Nacional (CSN) 2001–03, Admin. Cttee, Banco Itaú BBA 2003–09, Comitê de Datação de Ciclos Econômicos (CODACE) 2011–, Instituto Brasileiro de Economia da Fundação Getúlio Vargas, Rio de Janeiro 2011–; mem. Academia Brasileira de Ciências 2010; Hon. mem. Latin American and Caribbean Econ. Asscn (LACEA) 1998; Grand Officer, Ordem do Cruzeiro do Sul 1995, Ordem do Mérito Legislativo do Estado de Minas Gerais 2011, Medalha de Honra ao Mérito, Ordem dos Economistas do Brasil, São Paulo 2012; Prêmio Diaz Alejandro 1998, Medalha de Mérito Pedro Ernesto, Câmara Municipal do Rio de Janeiro 2007. *Publications:* numerous books and articles, including Mitos de uma Decada 1976, Models of Growth and Distribution for Brazil 1980, El Milagro y la Crisis 1986, Social Change in Brazil 1986, Recessão ou Crescimento 1987, Savings and Investment for Growth Resumption in Latin America 1993, Economics in a Changing World: Development, Trade and the Environment 1994, Poverty, Prosperity and the World Economy: Essays in Memory of Sidney Dell 1995, Mercado de Capitais e Crescimento Econômico: Lições Internacionais, Desafios Brasileiro 2005, Mercado de Capitais e Dívida Pública: Tributação, Indexação e Alongamento 2006, Como Reagir à Crise? Políticas Econômicas para o Brasil 2009, Novos Dilemas da Política Econômica: Ensaios em Homenagem a Dionisio Dias Carneiro 2011, Brasil: A Nova Agenda Social 2011, Belíndia 2.0: Fábulas e Ensaios sobre o País dos Contrastes 2012, O Futuro da Indústria no Brasil: A Desindustrialização em Debate 2013. *Address:* Instituto de Estudos de Política Econômica/Casa das Garças, Avenida Padre Leonel Franca 135, Casa das Garças, Gávea, Rio de Janeiro 22451-000, Brazil (office). *Telephone:* (21) 2512-6166 (office). *E-mail:* iepecdg@iepecdg.com (office). *Website:* www.iepecdg.com (office).

BACHARACH, Burt; American composer, arranger, conductor and musician (piano); b. 12 May 1928, Kansas City, MO; m. 1st Paula Stewart 1953 (divorced 1958); m. 2nd Angie Dickinson 1965 (divorced 1980); one d. (deceased); m. 3rd Carole Bayer Sager 1982 (divorced 1990); one s.; m. 4th Jane Hansen 1993; two c.; ed McGill Univ., Montréal, Music Acad. West, Santa Barbara; jazz musician 1940s; accompanist, arranger, conductor for various artists, including Vic Damone, Marlene Dietrich, Joel Grey, Steve Lawrence; writer of songs, film music and stage musicals; regular collaborations with Hal David 1962–70, Carole Bayer Sager from 1981; Cue Magazine Entertainer of the Year (with Hal David) 1969, three Acad. Awards, four Grammy Awards, two Emmy Awards, one Tony Award, Royal Swedish Acad. of Music Polar Music Prize 2001, Gershwin Prize for Popular Song (with Hal David), US Library of Congress 2012. *Film appearance:* Magic of Marlene (TV) 1965. *Film scores:* What's New, Pussycat? 1965, After the Fox 1966, On the Flipside 1966, Casino Royale 1967, Butch Cassidy and the Sundance Kid 1969, Lost Horizon 1973, Arthur 1981, Night Shift 1982, Arthur 2 On the Rocks 1988, Grace of My Heart 1996, My Best Friend's Wedding 1997. *Compositions include:* Promises, Promises (musical) 1969; with Hal David: The Story of My Life, Magic Moments, Tower of Strength, Wives and Lovers, 24 Hours From Tulsa, What The World Needs Now Is Love, Walk On By, Trains and Boats and Planes, Do You Know The Way To San Jose?, Alfie, Anyone Who Had A Heart, There's Always Something There To Remind Me, Make It Easy On Yourself, What's New Pussycat?, This Guy's In Love With You, Raindrops Keep Fallin' On My Head, Close To You; with Carole Bayer Sager: Making Love, Heartlight, That's What Friends Are For, On My Own; with Carole Bayer Sager, Peter Allen and Christopher Cross: Arthur's Theme. *Recordings include:* albums: Searching Wind 1958, Brigitte Bardot 1961, Move It On The Backbeat (with The Backbeats) 1961, Saturday Sunshine 1963, Don't Go Breaking My Heart 1965, Hit Maker! 1965, The Man 1965, Nikki 1966, Alfie 1967, Reach Out 1967, The Bell That Couldn't Jingle 1968, I'll Never Fall In Love Again 1969, Make It Easy On Yourself 1969, All Kinds of People 1971, Burt Bacharach 1971, Portrait In Music 1971, Living Together 1973, Saturday Sunshine 1973, Futures 1977, Painted from Memory 1998, One Amazing Night 1998, Isley Meets Bacharach – Here I Am (with Ronald Isley) 2003, At This Time (Grammy Award for Best Pop Instrumental Album 2006) 2005. *Publications:* Anyone Who Had a Heart (autobiography) 2013. *Address:* c/o Tina Brausam, 8033 Sunset Boulevard #996, Los Angeles, CA 90046, USA (office); c/o Sony BMG, 550 Madison Avenue, New York, NY 10022, USA.

BACHCHAN, Amitabh, BSc; Indian actor, singer and television presenter; b. 11 Oct. 1942, Allahabad, Uttar Pradesh; s. of Harivansh Rai and Teji Bachchan; m. Jaya Bachchan; one s. one d.; ed Sherwood Coll. Nainital, Delhi Univ.; mem. Lok Sabha (Parl.) 1984–87; re-launched film co. AB Corpn 2003; Goodwill Amb. for UNICEF 2003–, WHO for Hepatitis, SE Asia Region 2017–; Hon. Citizen, Deauville, France 2003–; Chevalier, Ordre nat. de la Légion d'honneur 2006; Dr hc (Jhansi Univ.) 2004, (Delhi Univ.) 2006, (De Montfort Univ., UK) 2006, (Leeds Metropolitan Univ.) 2007, (Queensland Univ. of Tech., Australia) 2009; Padma Shri 1984, Greatest Star of the Millennium (result of BBC online poll) 1999, Special Hon. Award, Int. Indian Film Acad. Awards 2000, Star of the Century Award, Alexandria Int. Film Festival 2001, Padma Bhushan 2001, Living Legend Award, Fed. of Indian Chambers of Commerce and Industry 2004, Shyam Sunder Dyay Kishan Munshi Lifetime Achievement Award 2004, Deenanath Mangeshkar Award 2005, Special Award, Mumbai Acad. of Moving Image Int. Film 2007, Visit London Special Award for Outstanding Achievement 2007, Crystal Award, World Econ. Forum 2009, Asian Film Cultural Award 2009, Padma Vibhushan 2015 and numerous other nat. and int. awards. *Films include:* Saat Hindustani (Nat. Award 1970) 1969, Anand (Filmfare Award) 1971, Parwaana 1971, Bombay to Goa 1972, Zanjeer 1973, Namak Haraam (Filmfare Award) 1973, Abhimaan 1973, Majboor 1974, Deewar 1975, Sholay 1975, Chupke Chupke 1975, Kabhi Kabhie 1976, Imaan Dharam 1977, Amar Akbar Anthony (Filmfare Award) 1977, Don (Filmfare Award) 1978, Kasme Vaade 1978, Mr. Natwarlal 1979, Jurmana 1979, Ram Balram 1980, Shaan 1980, Barsaat Ki Ek Raat 1980, Manzil 1981, Lawaaris 1981, Silsila 1981, Nammak Halal 1982, Shakti 1982, Coolie 1983, Mahaan 1983, Sharaabi 1984, Mard 1985, Aakhree Raasta 1986, Kaun Jeeta Kaun Hara 1987, Shahenshah 1988, Jadugar 1989, Agneepath (Nat. Award 1991) 1990, Hum (Filmfare Award) 1991, Ajooba 1991, Khuda Gawah 1992, Insaniyat 1994, Bade Miyan Chote Miyan 1998, Tumhare Liye 1999, Sooryavansham 1999, Mohabbatein (IIFA 2001, Filmfare Award) 2000, Aks (Filmfare Award) 2001, Kabhi Khushi Kabhi Gham 2001, Kaante 2002, Baghban 2003, Khakee 2004, Veer-Zaara 2004, Ab Tumhare Hawale Watan Saathiyo 2004, Waqt 2005, Sarkar 2005, Black 2005 (Nat. Award, Filmfare Award) 2006, Kabhi Alvida Naa Kehna (Never Say Goodbye) 2006, Eklavya: The Royal Guard 2007, Nishabd 2007, Zamaanat 2007, Cheeni Kum 2007, The Last Lear (Stardust Award) 2008, Paa 2009, Rann 2009, Teen Patti 2010, The Great Gatsby 2013, Piku (National Award 2016) 2015. *Television includes:* presenter, Kaun Banega Crorepati? (Who Wants To Be A Millionaire?). *Address:* Pratiksha, 10th Road, JVPD Scheme, Mumbai, 400 049, India (home). *Telephone:* (22) 6207579 (home); (22) 6206162 (home).

BACHELET JERIA, (Verónica) Michelle, MD; Chilean physician, politician, UN official and fmr head of state; *United Nations High Commissioner for Human Rights;* b. 29 Sept. 1951, Santiago; d. of Gen. Aire Alberto Bachelet (died 1974) and Ángela Jeria; m. Jorge Leopoldo Dávalos Cartes; three c.; ed Universidad de Chile, Inter-American Coll. of Defense, Washington, DC, USA; placed in Villa Grimaldi and Cuatro Alamos detention centres for father's resistance to Pinochet regime 1975; lived in Australia, then Germany 1975–80; trained as medical surgeon and epidemiologist, Universidad de Chile; Head of Medical Dept, PIDEE (NGO assisting the children of victims of the military regime); consultant to Panamerican Health Org. and WHO 1990; mem. Cen. Cttee Socialist Party 1995–, Political Cttee 1998–; Adviser to Under-Sec. of Health 1994–97, to Ministry of Defence 1998–99; Minister of Health 2000–02, of Nat. Defence (first woman in position) 2002–04; Pres. of Chile (first woman) 2006–10, 2014–18; Under-Sec.-Gen. for Gender Equality and the Empowerment of Women, UN and Exec. Dir UN Women 2010–13, mem. Sec.-Gen.'s High-Level Advisory Bd on Mediation, UN 2017–, UN High Commr for Human Rights 2018–; f. think-tank Fundación Dialoga 2010; Chair. Bd The Partnership for Maternal, Newborn and Child Health 2018–, also Co-Chair. High-Level Steering Group for Every Woman Every Child; mem. Club of Madrid; Knight Grand Cross of the Order of Merit (Italy) 2007, Order of Vytautas the Great with Golden Chain (Lithuania) 2008, Companion of the Order of Australia 2012; Dr hc (Univ. of Brasilia) 2006, (Universidad de San Carlos de Guatemala) 2007, (Univ. of Essex) 2008, (Pompeu Fabra Univ.) 2010, (Nat. Univ. of Córdoba) 2010, (Catholic Univ. of Córdoba) 2010, (Universidad Internacional Menéndez Pelay) 2010, (Universidad Autónoma de Santo Domingo) 2010, (Univ. of Paris III: Sorbonne Nouvelle) 2010, (Columbia Univ.) 2012; World Jewish Congress Shalom Award 2008, Washington Office on Latin America Human Rights Award 2010, Eisenhower Medal for Leadership and Service 2012. *Address:* Office of the United Nations High Commissioner for Human Rights, Palais des Nations, 1211 Geneva, Switzerland (office); c/o Socialist Party of Chile, Paris 873, Santiago, Chile (office). *Telephone:* (2) 5499900 (office). *E-mail:* contacto@pschile.cl (office). *Website:* web.pschile.cl (office); michellebachelet.cl.

BACHELIER, Bernard; French agronomist; b. 27 July 1950, Levallois-Perret; s. of Pierre Bachelier and Claire Pardon; ed Inst. Nat. Agronomique, Paris-Grignon; worked in Africa for several years; Del. for Africa and Indian Ocean, Centre de Coopération Internationale en Recherche Agronomique pour de Développement (Cirad), Paris 1988–90; Pres. Cirad Centre, Montpellier 1993; Head of Devt Research, Ministry of Educ. and Research 1993–96; Dir-Gen. Cirad 1996–2002; Chair., Council of Admin., Centre Nat. d'Etudes Agronomiques des Régions Chaudes (CNEARC) 1998–2003; adviser to minister in charge of Research and New Tech. 2002–04, to Minister for Research and Higher Educ. 2005; Dir Fondation pour l'agriculture et la ruralité dans le monde (FARM) 2006, now mem. Bd of Dirs; mem. Council for European and Int. Prospective Analysis of Agric. and

Food (COPEIAA); Chevalier, Ordre nat. du Mérite, Ordre du Mérite agricole. *Address:* 9 rue Thérèse, 75001 Paris, France (home). *Website:* www.fondation-farm.org (office).

BACHELOT-NARQUIN, Roselyne, PharmD; French pharmacist and politician; b. 24 Dec. 1946, Nevers (Nièvre); d. of Jean Narquin and Yvette Narquin (née Le Dû); m. Jacques Bachelot (divorced); one c.; Gen. Councillor, Maine-et-Loire 1982–88; mem. Regional Council, Pays de la Loire 1982–88, 2004–07, Vice-Pres. 2001–04; elected Deputy for Maine-et-Loire 1988–2002, 2007; mem. RPR, Sec.-Gen. 1989–92, 2001–02, Del.-Gen. for the Status of Women 1992–93, for Labour and Social Exclusion 1995–97, Sec.-Gen. for Labour 1998–2001; mem. Political Bureau Union pour un mouvement populaire 2002–, Asst Sec.-Gen. 2006–08; Reporter-Gen. Observatoire de la parité 1995–98; Pres. Nat. Council on Handicapped Persons 1995–98; mem. European Parl. 2004–07; Minister of Ecology and Sustainable Devt 2002–04, of Health, Youth and Sports 2007–10, for Solidarity and Social Cohesion 2010–12; quit politics 2012; TV political commentator 2012–; Chevalier de la Légion d'honneur 2013. *Publications include:* Le PACS entre haine et amour 2000, Les Maires: fête ou défaite? 2001, À feu et à sang: Carnets secrets d'une présidentielle de tous les dangers 2012, Verdi amoureux 2013. *Address:* c/o Union pour un Mouvement Populaire (UMP), 238 rue de Vaugirard, 75015 Paris, France (office). *Telephone:* 1-40-76-60-00 (office). *Website:* www.u-m-p.org (office).

BACHER, Aron ('Ali'), MB BCh; South African sports administrator and fmr cricketer; *Chairman, Community Trust;* b. 24 May 1942, Johannesburg, Gauteng; s. of Kopel Bacher and Rose Bacher; m. Shira Ruth Teeger 1965; one s. two d.; ed King Edward VII High School and Univ. of the Witwatersrand, Johannesburg; right-hand batsman; played for Transvaal 1959–74 (Capt. 1963–74); 12 tests for S Africa 1965–70, four (all won) as Capt. against Australia 1970; scored 7,894 First-Class runs (18 centuries); toured England 1965; intern, Baragwanath and Natalspruit Hosps; pvt. practice, Rosebank, Johannesburg 1970–79; Man. Dir Delta Distributors (Pty) Ltd 1979–81; Man. Dir The Transvaal Cricket Council 1981–86; Man. Dir The South African Cricket Union 1986–91, United Cricket Bd of South Africa 1991–2000; mem. Exec. Bd, Int. Cricket Council (ICC) 1997–2000, Exec. Dir 2003 ICC Cricket World Cup 2001–03; South African Sports Award Admin. 1991; Pres. Sports Award Admin. (Cricket) 1997; Exec. Dir Wits Foundation 2003–06; Chair. Seniors' Finance 2007, Right to Care 2008–, Alexander Forbes Community Trust 2012–, Community Trust; Dr hc (Rhodes Univ.) 1998, Hon. Legum Doctoris (Witwatersrand) 2001; South African Sports Merit Award 1972, 1991, Paul Harris Fellow Award 1989, Jack Cheetham Memorial Award 1990, Int. Jewish Sports Hall of Fame 1991, Da Vinci Laureate Award for Social Architecture 2013. *Leisure interest:* jogging. *Address:* PO Box 55041, Northlands 2116, South Africa (office). *Telephone:* (11) 276-8850 (office); (11) 783-1263 (home); 83-2128008 (mobile) (home). *E-mail:* ali.bacher@righttocare.org (office). *Website:* www.righttocare.org (office).

BACHIRI, Mohamed, MBA; Moroccan administrator, engineer and business executive; b. 14 July 1948, Berkane; s. of Mimoun Bachiri and Aïcha Ouadi; m. Badia Khelfaoui 1972; three c.; ed Ecole Mohammedie d'Ingénieurs, Rabat, Ecole Nationale des Ponts et Chaussées, Paris, France; qualified civil engineer; responsible for public works, Berkane and Nador Provs. 1969; Asst Dir Moroccan Ports 1978; Regional Dir of Public Works, Marrakesh 1983; Dir Nat. Vocational Training 1984; Insp.-Gen. Council of Public Works 1991–95; CEO Drapor Port Dredging Co. 1995–2008; apptd CEO HP Construction Co. 2009; Founder and Chair. Investment GID Group 1991; Founding Pres. Public Works Foundation; Founder and Dir Al Handassa Lwatania Eng journal 1981; mem. Bd of Dirs Cen. Dredging Asscn (CEDA), Chair. CEDA–African Section; Royal Decoration of Chevalier for Merit and Knighthood 1998; trophée d'Ingénieur Créateur. *Publications:* Drainage and Environment (ed.), Reference Dredging and Environment; articles and editorials in Al Handassa Lwatania, contrib. to other professional journals. *Leisure interest:* golf. *Address:* 3 Avenue Ma Al Aynine, Agdal, Rabat, Morocco (home). *Telephone:* (37) 77-46-24 (home). *Fax:* (37) 68-14-94 (home). *E-mail:* bachiri@iam.net.ma (home).

BACHMAN, Richard (see KING, Stephen Edwin).

BACHMANN, John William, AB, MBA; American business executive; *Senior Partner, Edward D. Jones & Co., LP;* b. 16 Nov. 1938, Centralia, Ill.; s. of George Adam Bachmann and Helen Bachmann (née Johnston); m. Katharine I. Butler; one s. one d.; ed Wabash Coll., Crawfordsville, Ind., Northwestern Univ.; broker, Edward Jones, St Louis 1962–63, investment rep. 1963–70, Gen. Pnr 1970–80, Man. Pnr 1980–2003, Sr Pnr 2004–; mem. Bd of Dirs Trans World Airlines 1996–2001, American Airlines Inc., Monsanto Co.; Trustee Wabash Coll. 1980–, Washington Univ., now Trustee Emer.; apptd mem. Bd of Dirs US Chamber of Commerce, Washington, DC 1995, Chair. 2004–05, Chair. Exec. Cttee 2005–06; Campaign Chair. United Way of Greater St. Louis 2002; Chair. St Louis Regional Chamber and Growth Association 2000–02; Chair. Bd of Visitors Drucker Center, Claremont (Calif.) Grad. School 1987; fmr Chair. Arts and Educ. Council of Greater St Louis, St Louis Symphony Orchestra; fmr Commr St Louis Art Museum; mem. Nat. Asscn of Securities Dealers (fmr district Chair.), Securities Industry Asscn (Chair. 1976–79), Securities Industry Foundation for Econ. Educ. (Chair. of Trustees 1988–92), Trustee Emer., Wabash Coll.; Hon. Life mem., Univ. of S Carolina Alumni Asscn 2013; Hon. LLD (Wabash Coll.) 1990, (Univ. of Missouri, St Louis) 2003, (Westminster Coll.) 2005; Winston Churchill Medal for Leadership 2005, Touchstone Award 2015. *Address:* Edward D. Jones & Co., LP, 12555 Manchester Road, St Louis, MO 63131, USA (office). *Telephone:* (314) 515-2626 (office). *Fax:* (314) 515-2622 (office). *E-mail:* john.bachmann@edwardjones.com (office). *Website:* www.edwardjones.com (office).

BACHMANN, Michele Marie, BA, LLM, JD; American lawyer and politician; b. 6 April 1956, Waterloo, Ia; d. of David John Amble and Jean Amble (née Johnson); m. Dr Marcus Bachmann 1978; two s. three d.; ed Anoka High School, Winona State Univ., O.W. Coburn School of Law at Oral Roberts Univ., Coll. of William and Mary Law School; following graduation, spent time working on a kibbutz in Israel 1974; worked as research asst on John Eidsmoe's 1987 book, Christianity and the Constitution; tax attorney, Internal Revenue Service 1988–93; mem. Minnesota State Senate from 56th Dist 2001–03, from 52nd Dist 2003–07, Asst Minority Leader in charge of Policy for Senate Republican Caucus 2004–05; mem. US House of Reps for 6th Congressional Dist of Minn. (first Republican woman to represent the state in Congress) 2007–15, founder of House Tea Party Caucus 2010; cand. for Republican 2012 presidential nomination June 2011, withdrew Jan. 2012; owns (with her husband) Bachmann & Assocs (counselling practice); Republican. *Publication:* Core of Conviction (autobiog.) 2011. *Address:* 2417 Rayburn HOB, Washington, DC 20515, USA (office). *Telephone:* (202) 225-2331 (office). *Fax:* (202) 225-6475 (office). *Website:* bachmann.house.gov (office); www.michelebachmann.com.

BACHVAROVA, Rumiana; Bulgarian politician; b. 13 March 1959, Shipka; ed St Clement of Ohrid Univ. of Sofia; Head of Program Analysis Dept, Bulgarian Nat. Radio 1985–95; Dir of Research, Market Test AD 1995–2001; CEO Market Links polling agency 2001–09; Head of Political Office of the Prime Minister and Sec. of Council for Devt to Council of Ministers 2009–13; project consultant, ML Consult 2014; mem. Grazhdani za Evropeysko Razvitie na Balgariya (GERB—Citizens for European Devt of Bulgaria); mem. Narodno Sobraniye (Nat. Ass.) 2014–; Deputy Prime Minister for Coalition Policy and State Admin 2014–17, Minister of the Interior 2015–17; Chief of Prime Minister's Political Cabinet 2017–. *Address:* Office of the Council of Ministers, 1594 Sofia, Blvd Dondukov 1, Bulgaria (office). *Telephone:* (2) 940-30-08 (office). *E-mail:* r.dilova@government.bg (office).

BAČKIS, HE Cardinal Audrys Juozas, BPhil, LTh, DCL; Lithuanian ecclesiastic; *Archbishop Emeritus of Vilnius;* b. 1 Feb. 1937, Kaunas; ed Inst. Catholique, Paris, Pontifical Gregorian Univ., Rome, Pontifical Lateran Univ., Rome; ordained priest 1961; served in Holy See diplomatic corps in The Philippines 1964–65, Costa Rica 1966–68, Turkey 1969–70, Nigeria 1971–73; with Vatican Secr. of State 1974–88; Titular Archbishop of Meta and Apostolic Pro-Nuncio to Netherlands 1988–91; Archbishop of Vilnius 1991–2013, Archbishop Emer. 2013–; cr. Cardinal (Cardinal-Priest of Natività di Nostro Signore Gesù Cristo a Via Gallia) 2001; participated in Papal Conclave 2005, 2013; decorations include Grande Oficial da Ordem Militar de Cristo (Portugal) 1981, Grand Officier, Order of the Phoenix (Greece) 1982, Officier, Légion d'honneur 1984, Grande Ufficiale, Ordine al Merito della Repubblica Italiana 1985, Commdr, Ordre Gran-Ducal de la Couronne de Chêne (Luxembourg) 1988, Commendator cum nomismate (Ordo equester S. Sepulcri Hierosolymitani) 1990, Groot Kruis in de Orde van Oranje-Nassau (Netherlands) 1992, Commdr, Royal Norwegian Order of Merit 1998, Order of Grand Duke Gediminas (Second Degree) 2000, Order of Vytautas the Great Grand Cross 2003; Dr hc (Vilnius Pedagogical Univ.) 1997, (Krakow Pontifical Theological Acad.) 2003. *Address:* Vilnius Archdiocesan Curia, Šventaragio 4, 01122 Vilnius, Lithuania (office). *Telephone:* (5) 2123653 (office); (5) 2123413 (home). *Fax:* (5) 2122807 (office). *E-mail:* curia@vilnensis.lt (office). *Website:* www.vilnius.lcn.lt (office).

BACKLEY, Steve, OBE; British consultant and fmr professional athlete; b. 12 Feb. 1969, Sidcup, Kent; s. of John Backley and Pauline Hogg; javelin thrower; coached by John Trower; Commonwealth record-holder 1992 (91.46m); Gold Medal European Jr Championships 1987; Silver Medal World Jr Championships 1988; Gold Medal European Cup 1989, 1997, Bronze Medal 1995; Gold Medal World Student Games 1989, 1991; Gold Medal World Cup 1989, 1994, 1998; Gold Medal Commonwealth Games 1990, 1994, 2002, Silver Medal 1998; Gold Medal European Championships 1990, 1994, 1998, 2002; Bronze Medal Olympic Games 1992, Silver Medal 1996, 2000; Silver Medal World Championships 1995, 1997; retd 2004; Prin. Javelin Business Strategies 2006; Partner, BackleyBlack (consultancy); Athlete of the Year, UK Athletics 2000. *Publication:* The Winning Mind. *E-mail:* info@BackleyBlack.com. *Website:* www.stevebackley.com; www.backleyblack.com.

BÄCKSTRÖM, Urban, BSc; Swedish banker and business executive; b. 25 May 1954, Sollefteå; s. of Sven-Ake Bäckström and Maj-Britt Filipsson; m. Ewa Hintze 1978; one s. one d.; ed Stockholm Univ. and Stockholm School of Econs; Research Asst Inst. for Int. Econ. Studies, Stockholm 1978–80; First Sec. Int. Dept Ministry of Foreign Affairs 1980–82; Chief Economist, Moderate Party 1982–83, 1986–89; Under-Sec. of State, Ministry of Finance 1991–93; Gov. Sveriges Riksbank (Swedish Cen. Bank) 1994–2002; Bd mem. BIS 1994–2002, Chair. and Pres. 1999–2002; CEO Skandia Liv 2002–05; CEO Svenskt Naringsliv (Confed. of Swedish Enterprise) 2005–14; Chair. Rederi AB Gotland and of a subsidiary 2014–18; Dir, Danske Bank 2012–18; mem. Bd, Stiftelsen Fritt Näringsliv/Timbro; mem. Royal Swedish Acad. of Eng Sciences 2003.

BACKUS, George Edward, SM, PhD, FRAS, FRSA, FAGU; American theoretical geophysicist and academic; *Research Professor Emeritus of Geophysics, University of California, San Diego;* b. 24 May 1930, Chicago, Ill.; s. of Milo Morlan Backus and Dora Backus (née Mendenhall); m. 1st Elizabeth E. Allen 1961; two s. one d.; m. 2nd Marianne McDonald 1971; m. 3rd Varda Peller 1977; ed Thornton Township High School, Harvey, Ill. and Univ. of Chicago; Asst Examiner, Univ. of Chicago 1949–50; Jr Mathematician, Inst. for Air Weapons Research, Univ. of Chicago 1950–54; Physicist, Project Matterhorn, Princeton Univ. 1957–58; Asst Prof. of Math., MIT 1958–60; Assoc. Prof. of Geophysics, Univ. of California, La Jolla 1960–62, Prof. 1962–94, Research Prof. 1994–99, Prof. Emer. 1999–; mem. Scientific Advisory Cttee to NASA on Jt NASA/CNES Magnetic Satellites; Co.-Chair. Int. Working Group on Magnetic Field Satellites 1983–92; mem. Visiting Cttee, Inst. de Physique du Globe de Paris (IPGP) 1987; Guggenheim Fellowship 1963, 1971; mem. NAS; Foreign mem. Acad. des Sciences de l'Institut de France; Fellow, American Geophysical Union; Dr hc (IPGP) 1995; Gold Medal, Royal Astronomical Soc. 1986, John Adam Fleming Medal, American Geophysical Union 1986. *Publications:* numerous scientific works 1958–. *Leisure interests:* hiking, swimming, history, reading, skiing. *Address:* Munk Lab 331, Institute of Geophysics and Planetary Physics, Scripps Institution of Oceanography, University of California San Diego, La Jolla, CA 92093-0225 (office); 9362 La Jolla Farms Road, La Jolla, CA 92037, USA (home). *Telephone:* (858) 534-2468 (office); (858) 455-8972 (home). *Fax:* (858) 534-8090 (office). *Website:* www.igpp.ucsd.edu (office); www-mpl.ucsd.edu/cg/people/gbackus.html (office).

BACON, Kevin Norwood; American actor and musician; b. 8 July 1958, Philadelphia, Pa; m. Kyra Sedgwick 1988; one s. one d.; ed Manning Street Actor's Theatre; mem. Bacon Brothers band, has released six albums; has appeared in major advertising campaign for EE mobile network, UK 2012–; commercial spokesperson for US egg industry 2015–. *Stage appearances include:* Getting On 1978, Glad Tidings 1979–80, Mary Barnes 1980, Album 1980, Forty-Deuce 1981,

Flux 1982, Poor Little Lambs 1982, Slab Boys 1983, Men Without Dates 1985, Loot 1986, Road, Spike Heels, 8 (Wilshire Ebell Theatre) 2012. *Films include:* National Lampoon's Animal House 1978, Starting Over 1979, Hero at Large 1980, Friday the 13th 1980, Only When I Laugh 1981, Diner 1982, Footloose 1984, Quicksilver 1985, White Water Summer 1987, Planes, Trains and Automobiles 1987, End of the Line 1988, She's Having a Baby 1988, Criminal Law 1989, The Big Picture 1989, Tremors 1990, Flatliners 1990, Queens Logic 1991, He Said/She Said 1991, Pyrates 1991, JFK 1992, A Few Good Men 1992, The Air Up There 1994, The River Wild 1994, Murder in the First (Broadcast Film Critics Asscn Award for Best Actor 1996) 1995, Apollo (Outstanding Performance by a Cast in a Motion Picture, Screen Actors Guild Award 1996) 1995, Sleepers 1996, Telling Lies in America 1997, Picture Perfect 1997, Digging to China 1997, Wild Things 1998, My Dog Skip 1999, The Hollow Man 1999, Stir of Echoes 1999, Novocaine 2000, We Married Margo 2000, 24 Hours 2001, Trapped 2002, In the Cut 2003, Mystic River (Boston Soc. of Film Critics Award for Best Cast) 2003, The Woodsman 2004, Cavedweller 2004, Loverboy 2005, Beauty Shop 2005, Where the Truth Lies 2005, The Air I Breathe 2007, Death Sentence 2007, Rails and Ties 2007, Saving Angelo 2007, Frost/Nixon 2008, My One and Only 2009, Beyond All Boundaries (voice) 2009, X-Men First Class 2011, Crazy, Stupid, Love 2011, Jayne Mansfield's Car 2012, 8 (video) 2012, R.I.P.D. 2013, Cop Car 2015, 6 Miranda Drive 2015, Black Mass 2015. *Television includes:* The Gift 1979, Enormous Changes at the Last Minute 1982, The Demon Murder Case 1983, The Tender Age, Lemon Sky, Frasier (voice), Happy Birthday Elizabeth: A Celebration of Life 1997, Taking Chance (Golden Globe for Best Performance by an Actor in a Mini-series or Motion Picture made for Television 2010, Outstanding Performance by a Male Actor in a Miniseries or Television Movie, Screen Actors Guild Awards 2010) 2009, Robot Chicken (series) 2011, The Presidents' Gatekeepers (film) 2013, The Following (series) (Saturn Award for Best Actor on Television) 2013–. *Address:* c/o Frank Frattaroli, WME Entertainment, 9601 Wilshire Boulevard, Beverly Hills, CA 90210-5213, USA (office). *Telephone:* (310) 285-9000 (office). *Fax:* (310) 285-9010 (office). *Website:* www.wma.com (office); baconbros.com.

BACONSCHI, Teodor, PhD; Romanian diplomatist and politician; b. 14 Feb. 1963, Bucharest; m.; two c.; ed Bucharest Theological Univ. Inst., New Europe Coll., Bucharest, Université de Paris IV-Sorbonne, France; post-doctoral studies as Fellow of New Europe Coll. of Bucharest 1996; began career as Dir, Anastasia Publr, Bucharest; fmr Ed.-in-Chief Spiritual Life (TV series); fmr adviser with Ministry of Culture; fmr Ed. Biblical and Mission Inst. Publishing Office, Romanian Orthodox Church; joined diplomatic service, becoming Amb. to The Holy See 1999–2001, Dir-Gen. Ministry of Foreign Affairs 2001, Amb. to Portugal 2002–04, State Sec. for Global Affairs, Ministry of Foreign Affairs 2005–06; Adviser to Pres. on political affairs 2006–07; Amb. to France 2007–09, Minister of Foreign Affairs 2009–12 (dismissed); mem. Partidul Mişcarea Populară (PMP—People's Movt Party) 2014–; Affiliate mem. Int. Asscn of Patristic Studies (AIEP), Paris; Founding mem. Reflection Group for the Renewal of the Church, Bucharest; mem. New Europe Coll., Bucharest, Social Dialogue Group, Bucharest. *Publications:* more than ten books in French and Romanian, including Jacob and the Angel: 45 Hypostases of the Religious Dimension 1996, The Temptation of Goodness: Essays on the Urban Dimension of Faith 1999, The Power of Schism: A Portrait of European Christianity 2001. *Address:* c/o Partidul Mişcarea Populară (People's Movement Party), 010432 Bucharest, str. Iorga 11, Romania. *Telephone:* (754) 200390. *E-mail:* secretariat@pmponline.ro.

BADA, Hajime, MSc; Japanese business executive; b. Oct. 1948; ed Tokyo Univ.; joined Kawasaki Steel Corpn 1973, held positions as Man. Chiba Works Steelmaking Shop No. 1, Man. Mizushima Works Steelmaking Shop No. 2, Steel Business Planning Man., Gen. Man. Steel Business Planning Dept and Gen. Man. Corpn Planning Dept, mem. Bd of Dirs JFE Holdings, Inc. and JFE Steel Corpn (subsidiary), Dir California Steel Industries Inc. 1998–, Sr Vice-Pres. JFE Steel Corpn –2005, Pres., CEO and Rep. Dir 2005–10, Pres. and CEO JFE Holdings, Inc. 2010–15, Adviser 2015–; Chair. World Steel Asscn 2010–11; Dir Mitsui Chemicals, Inc. *Address:* Mitsui Chemicals Inc., Shiodome City Center, 5-2, Higashi-Shimbashi 1-chome, Minato-ku, Tokyo 105-7122, Japan (office).

BADAL, Parkash Singh, BA; Indian agriculturist and politician; b. 8 Dec. 1927, Abulkhurana, Punjab; s. of Raghuraj Singh and Sundri Kaur; m. Surinder Kaur 1959 (died 2011); one s. one d.; ed Forman Christian Coll., Lahore; entered politics 1947, fmr Sarpanch and Chair. Block Samiti Lambi, first elected to Punjab Vidhan Sabha (Legis. Ass.) 1957, re-elected 1969; mem. Shiromani Akali Dal party (SAD), Pres. 1996–2008; fmr mem. Shiromani Gurdwara Prabandhak Cttee; elected to Ass. 1957, re-elected 1969–2012 (exception in 1992, SAD boycotted state elections); Minister for Community Devt Panchayati Raj, Animal Husbandry, Dairying and Fisheries 1969–70; Chief Minister of Punjab 1970–71, 1977–80, 1997–2002, 2007–17; imprisoned during State of Emergency 1975–77; elected to Lok Sabha (Parl.) 1977; Minister for Agric. 1977; elected Leader of Opposition, Punjab Vidhan Sabha (Legis. Ass.) 1972, 1980, 2002; Chair. Punjab Arts Council; mem. Nankana Sahib Educational Trust, Ludhiana; Panth Rattan Award 2011, Gadaar-e-Quam Award 2015, Padma Vibhushan 2015. *Leisure interest:* social service. *Address:* Room No.1, Floor 2, Punjab Civil Secr., Chandigarh, India (office). *Telephone:* (172) 740737 (home). *Website:* punjabgovt.nic.in (office).

BADAWI, Tun Abdullah Bin Haji Ahmad, BA; Malaysian politician and poet; b. 26 Nov. 1939, Pulau Pinang; m. 1st Datin Endon bint Datuk Mahmud (died 2005); m. 2nd Jeanne Abdullah 2007; ed Univ. of Malaya; Asst Sec., Public Service Dept 1964; Asst Sec., MAGERAN 1969; Asst Sec., Nat. Security Council 1971; Dir (Youth), Ministry of Sport, Youth and Culture 1971–74, Deputy Sec.-Gen. 1974–78; MP for Kepala Batas 1978–2013; Minister without Portfolio, Prime Minister's Dept 1982; Minister of Educ. 1984–86, of Defence 1986–87; mem. UMNO Supreme Council 1982–, Vice-Pres. 1999–2003, Pres. 2003–09; Minister of Foreign Affairs 1991–99; Deputy Prime Minister and Minister of Home Affairs 1999–2004, Prime Minister and Minister of Finance 2003–08 (resgnd); Minister of Defence 2008–09; Sec.-Gen. Non-Aligned Movt 2003–06; Ahli Mangku Negara 1971, Kesatria Mangku Negara 1974, Darjah Johan Negeri 1979, Darjah Yang Mulia Pangkuan Negeri 1981, The Kwangha Medal (South Korea) 1983, Grand Cordon, Order of the Sacred Treasure (Japan) 1991, Grand Cross, Order of Merit (Chile) 1994, Most Exalted Order of the White Elephant (First Class) (Thailand) 1994, Darjah Gemilang Pangkuan Negeri 1997, Order of Friendship (First Class) (North Korea) 1997, Seri Panglima Darjah Kinabalu 1999, Darjah Kebesaran Sultan Ahmad Shah Pahang Yang Amat DiMulia 1999, Darjah Kebesaran Seri Paduka Mahkota Selangor 2000, Darjah Seri Paduka Negeri Sembilan 2000, Darjah Setia Tuanku Syed Sirajuddin Jamallulail 2001, Darjah Seri Paduka Sultan Azlan Shah 2003, Datuk Patinggi Bintang Kenyalang 2003, Darjah Kerabat Johor Yang Amat Dihormati Pangkat Pertama 2004, Darjah Utama Negeri Melaka 2004, Order of José Marti (Cuba) 2004, Darjah Seri Utama Sultan Mizan Zainal Abidin 2005, Bintang Republik Indonesia Adipradana (Indonesia) 2007, Seri Maharaja Mangku Negara 2009, Seri Utama Mahkota Wilayah 2010. *Publication:* his poem I Seek Eternal Peace translated into more than 80 languages and published as a book Ku Cari Damai Abadi (I Seek Eternal Peace) 2008. *Address:* c/o United Malays National Organization (Pertubuhan Kebangsaan Melayu Bersatu), Menara Dato' Onn, 38th Floor, Jalan Tun Ismail, 50480 Kuala Lumpur, Malaysia. *Website:* www.umno-online.com.

BADAWI, Zeinab Mohammed-Khair, MA; British (b. Sudanese) journalist and broadcaster; b. 3 Oct. 1959; d. of Mohammed-Khair El Badawi and Asia Malik; m. David Antony Crook 1991; two s. two d.; ed Hornsey School for Girls, St Hilda's Coll. Oxford and Univ. of London; presenter and journalist, current affairs and documentaries on Yorkshire TV 1982–86; current affairs reporter, BBC TV 1987–88; newscaster and journalist, ITN Channel Four News 1988, co-presenter Channel Four News with Jon Snow 1989–98; joined BBC 1998, worked in radio presenting The World Tonight (Radio 4), Newshour and Rendezvous 2012 (BBC World Service), The World 2005–07 and World News Today 2007– (BBC Four), and HardTalk 2009– (BBC World News); Vice-Pres. UN Int. Asscn; Chair. Article 19 Int. Org. for Freedom of Speech; Chair. Africa Medical Partnership Fund, Royal African Soc.; Advisor Foreign Policy Centre; mem. Bd British Council; Trustee, BBC World Service Trust, Nat. Portrait Gallery, British Council, Centre for Contemporary British History; mem. jury for Diageo Africa Business Reporting Award; Hon. DLit (SOAS) 2011; TV Personality of the Year, Asscn of Int. Broadcasters 2009. *Publications include:* numerous articles. *Leisure interests:* languages, opera, family, reading. *Website:* www.bbc.co.uk/bbcfour.

BADHAM, John Macdonald, BA, MFA; American (b. British) film director; b. 25 Aug. 1939, Luton; s. of Henry Lee Badham and Mary Iola Hewitt; m. Julia Laughlin 1992; one d.; ed Yale Univ., Yale Drama School; joined Universal Studio as mailroom employee, then tour guide, subsequently Casting Dir and Assoc. Producer; Pres. Great American Picture Show; Chair. Bd JMB Films Inc.; Founder and Pres. Badham Co., Calif. 1975–; currently Prof. and Head of Directing Program, Graduate Conservatory of Motion Pictures, Chapman Univ., Orange, Calif.; George Pal Award. *Films include:* The Bingo Long Travelling All-Stars and Motor Kings, Saturday Night Fever 1977, Dracula (Best Horror Film Award, Acad. of Science Fiction, Fantasy and Horror Films) 1979, Whose Life Is It Anyway? (San Rafael Grand Prize) 1981, War Games (Best Dir, Science Fiction/Fantasy Acad.) 1983, Stakeout (also exec. producer) 1987, Disorganized Crime (exec. producer only), Bird on a Wire 1989, The Hard Way 1990, Point of No Return 1993, Another Stakeout (also exec. producer) 1993, Drop Zone (also exec. producer) 1994, Nick of Time (also producer) 1995, Incognito 1997, Brother's Keeper 2002. *Television includes:* The Impatient Heart (Christopher Award 1971), Isn't It Shocking? 1973, The Law, The Gun (Southern Calif. Motion Picture Council Award 1974), Reflections of Murder 1973, The Godchild 1974, The Keegans, Sorrow Floats 1998, Floating Away 1998, The Jack Bull 1999, Footsteps 2003, Evel Knievel 2004; several series episodes. *Publication:* I'll Be In My Trailer: The Creative Wars Between Directors and Actors 2006. *Address:* MKS 352, Dodge College of Film and Media Arts, Chapman University, One University Drive, Orange, CA 92866, USA. *Website:* www.johnbadham.com (office).

BADIE, Mohammed, MVD; Egyptian professor of veterinary medicine, religious leader and politician; b. 7 Aug. 1943, El-Mahalla el-Koubra; m. Samia Alshenawy; four c. (one deceased); ed Cairo Univ.; Lecturer, Faculty of Veterinary Medicine, Assiut Univ. 1965; imprisoned 1965–74; Asst Teacher, Univ. of Zagazig 1977–79, Teacher 1979–83, Asst Prof. 1983; Expert, Veterinary Inst., Sana'a, Yemen 1982–86; Prof. of Veterinary Medicine, Beni Suef Univ. 1987, also Chair., Dept of Pathology, Faculty of Veterinary Medicine 1990; mem. Muslim Brotherhood (Al-Ikhwan al-Muslimun), mem. Admin. Office, El-Mahalla el-Koubra 1975, mem. Admin. Office, Beni Suef 1986, Admin. Official, Beni Suef 1990, Educ. Official 1994, mem. Exec. Guidance Bureau 1996, mem. Int. Guidance Bureau 2007, Supreme Guide (leader) Muslim Brotherhood 2010–13; arrested 2013 on charges of killing protesters, sentenced to death (later commuted to life imprisonment). *Website:* www.ikhwanonline.com (office).

BADIBANGA NTITA, Samy; Democratic Republic of Congo mining industry executive and politician; b. 12 Sept. 1962, Kinshasa; ed Univ. of Kinshasa, Geneva Higher Inst. of Human Sciences, Switzerland, Inst. Int. de Gemmologie, Belgium; began career as Deputy Admin., SOCODAM sprl (freight agency) 1986; Diamond Valuer and Buyer, Arslanian & Frères, Antwerp 1991–95, Consultant 1998–2005; Admin. and Dir-Gen. SAMEX TRADING sprl 1995; Consultant to BHP Billiton (mining co.) 2003–09; Rep. in Congo, Infrastructure Partnerships for African Devt (iPAD) 2006–09; Conf. Organizer (mining sector confs and exhbns) 2006–10; apptd Pres. Fédération des explorateurs et extracteurs de Congo (mining trade asscn) 2006; Man. Dir Lubilanji Mining sprl (jt venture with BHP Billiton) 2007–10; Consultant, Minco Mining 2009–10; Special Adviser to Étienne Tshisekedi (cand. in presidential election) 2009–11; mem. Nat. Ass. 2012–, Pres. UDPS Parl. Group, mem. Natural Resources Cttee; Prime Minister 2016–17; mem. Technical Cttee, Extractive Industries Transparency Initiative (EITI) 2005–07; mem. Union pour la démocratie et le progrès social (UDPS); Founding mem. Initiative panafricaine pour la défense de la démocratie (IPDD).

BADINTER, Élisabeth; French author, historian, academic and business executive; *Non-Executive Chairperson, Publicis Omnicom Group;* b. 5 March 1944, Boulogne-Billancourt (Hauts-de-Seine); d. of Marcel Bleustein-Blanchet (founder of Publicis Groupe) and Sophie Vaillant; m. Robert Badinter 1966; two s. one d.; Prof. of Philosophy, École Polytechnique, Paris; Chair. (non-exec.) Publicis Omnicom Group 2014–; Commdr, Order of Arts and Letters (France) 2007, Order of Cultural Merit (Monaco) 2011; Dr hc (Univ. of Liège) 2004. *Publications include:* L'Amour en plus: histoire de l'amour maternel (XVIIe–XXe siècle) 1981, Les Goncourt: Romanciers et historiens des femmes, La Femme au XVIIe siècle d'Edmond et Jules de Goncourt (foreword) 1981, Émilie, Émilie, L'ambition féminine au XVIIIe siècle 1983, Les Remontrances de Malesherbes (1771–1775) 1985, L'Un est l'autre 1986, Condorcet. Un intellectuel en politique 1988, Correspondance inédite de Condorcet et Madame Suard (1771–1791) 1988, Condorcet, Prudhomme, Guyomar: Paroles d'hommes (1790–1793) 1989, XY, de l'identité masculine 1992, Les Passions intellectuelles, Vol. 1: Désirs de gloire (1735–1751) 1999, Vol. 2: L'exigence de dignité (1751–1762) 2002, Vol. 3: Volonté Pouvoir (1762–1778) 2007, Simone de Beauvoir, Marguerite Yourcenar, Nathalie Sarraute (co-author) 2002, Fausse route 2003, Dead End Feminism 2006 (translated from Fausse route by Julia Borossa), Madame du Châtelet, Madame d'Épinay: Ou l'Ambition féminine au XVIIIe siècle 2006, Le conflit, la femme et la mère 2010, Le Pouvoir au féminin 2016. *Address:* Publicis Omnicom Group, 133 avenue des Champs Elysées, 75008 Paris, France (office). *Telephone:* 1-44-43-70-00 (office). *Fax:* 1-44-43-75-25 (office). *E-mail:* contact@publicisgroupe.com (office). *Website:* www.publicisgroupe.com (office).

BADINTER, Robert, AM, LLD; French lawyer and professor of law; b. 30 March 1928, Paris; s. of Simon Badinter and Charlotte Rosenberg; m. 1st Anne Vernon 1957; m. 2nd Elisabeth Bleustein-Blanchet 1966; two s. one d.; ed Univ. of Paris, Columbia Univ., New York; Lawyer, Paris Court of Appeal 1951; Prof. of Law, Paris I (Sorbonne) 1974–81; Minister of Justice and Keeper of the Seals 1981–86; Pres. Constitutional Council 1986–95; Pres. Court of Conciliation and Arbitration, OSCE 1995–2013; Senator (Hauts de Seine) 1995–2011; Foreign hon. mem., American Acad. of Arts and Sciences 2006, Hon. Chair. World Justice Project. *Play:* C.3.3., Paris 1995. *Publications:* L'exécution 1973, Liberté, libertés 1976, Condorcet (with Elisabeth Badinter) 1988, Libres et égaux: L'émancipation des juifs sous la révolution française 1989, La prison républicaine 1992, C.3.3. 1995, Un antisémitisme ordinaire: Vichy et les avocats juifs 1940–44 1997, L'abolition 2000, Une Constitution européenne 2002, Le plus grand bien 2004, Contre la peine de mort 2006, Les épines et les roses 2011. *Address:* 38 rue Guynemer, 75006 Paris, France (home). *Telephone:* 1-45-49-04-59 (home). *Fax:* 1-45-44-87-47 (home).

BADNORE, V. P. Singh, BA; Indian agriculturalist and politician; *Governor of Punjab;* b. 12 May 1948, Bhilwara Dist, Rajasthan; s. of Lt-Col Th. Gopal Singh Badnore; m. Alka Singh; one s. one d.; ed Mayo Coll., Ajmer, Admin. Staff Coll. of India, Hyderabad; mem. Rajasthan Legis. Ass. 1977–80, 1985–90, 1993–98, 1998–99; mem. BJP, Vice-Pres. BJP, Rajasthan 1989–90, 2001–10; Cabinet Minister for Irrigation, Govt of Rajasthan 1998–99; mem. Lok Sabha (lower house of parl.) 1999–2004, 2004–09, 2010–16, mem. Energy and Defence Cttee 1999–2000, Jt Parl. Cttee on Stock Market Scam 2001–03, Convenor Sub-Cttee on Electricity Bill 2001, Sub-Cttee on Nuclear Energy 2001; mem. Rajya Sabha (upper house of parl.) 2010–16, Chair. Select Cttee on the Payment and Settlement Systems (Amendment) Bill 2014–15, mem. House Cttee, Consultative Cttee for Ministry of Environment and Forests 2010, Cttee on Petitions 2010–11, 2012–14, Cttee on Energy 2012–14, Jt Parl. Cttee on Security 2014, Consultative Cttee for the Ministry of Defence 2014–15, Gen. Purpose Cttee 2014–, Ministry of External Affairs Consultative Cttee, Nat. Advisory Cttee; Gov. of Punjab 2016–, also Admin. of Chandigarh; mem. Indian dels to Commonwealth Parl. Asscn, Canada 1994, 2004, to South Asia Free Media Asscn, Pakistan; Chair. Tiger Task Force, Sariska (Rajasthan) 2005–09, Empowered Cttee of Forests & Wild Life Man. in Rajasthan; Co-Chair. Indo-US Parl. Forum; Founder mem. and Exec. mem. Indo-British Parl. Forum. *Address:* Office of the Governor, Raj Bhavan, Vigyan Path, Chandigarh 760 001, Punjab, India (office). *Telephone:* (172) 2740740 (office). *Fax:* (172) 2741058 (office). *E-mail:* governor@punjabmail.gov.in (office).

BADRAN, Adnan, PhD; Jordanian politician, university administrator and international organization official; b. 15 Dec. 1935, Jerash, Amman; m. Maha Badran; six c.; ed Oklahoma State Univ., Michigan State Univ., USA; Research Asst, Michigan State Univ. 1960–63; Sr Research Plant Physiologist and Biochemist, United Fruit Research Laboratories 1963–66; Asst then Assoc. Prof., Faculty of Science, Univ. of Jordan 1966–71, Dean Faculty of Science 1971–76; Founding Pres. Yarmouk Univ. 1976–86; Sec. Gen. Higher Council for Science and Technology, Jordan 1986–87; Minister of Agric. and Minister of Educ. 1989; Asst Dir Gen. for Science, UNESCO, Paris 1990–94, Deputy Dir Gen. 1994–98; Pres. Philadelphia Univ., Jordan 1998–2005; Prime Minister and Minister of Defence April–Nov. 2005 (resgnd); Senator and Chair. Senate Cttee on Educ. Science, Culture and Media 2006–10; Pres. Univ. of Petra 2007–14; Chair. Nat. Center for Human Rights, Jordan 2008–11; Sec.-Gen. and Fellow, Third World Acad. of Sciences 1991–98; mem. Bd of Trustees University of Jordan for Women 1992–, Arab Thought Forum 2008–, Jordanian Renewable Energy Soc. 2012–; mem. AAAS 1993–; Fellow, Islamic Acad. of Sciences, mem. Council and Treas. 1999–; Dr hc (Sung Kyuakwan Univ., Seoul); Al-Nahda Medal (Jordan), Al-Yarmouk Medal (Jordan), Istilal Medal (Jordan) 1995, Alfonso X Medal (Spain). *Publications include:* author and ed. of over 18 books and 90 research papers in the fields of botany, economic devt, educ. and int. co-operation. *Address:* PO Box 117, Amman 11822, Jordan (home). *E-mail:* abadran12@gmail.com (home).

BADRAN, Ibrahim, BSc, PhD; Jordanian government official, foundation director and academic; *Adviser to the President for International Relations and Scientific Centres, Philadelphia University;* b. 19 July 1939, Nablus, Palestine; m.; four c.; ed Univs. of Cairo and London; Lecturer in Electrical Eng, Univ. of Libya, Tripoli 1970–74; Chief Engineer and Head, Electricity Section, Consultancy and Architecture, Ministry of Planning, Baghdad 1974–76; Dir of Planning and Dir of Standards and Specifications, Jordan Electricity Authority 1978–80; Dir of Energy, Ministry of Trade and Industry 1980–84; Sec.-Gen. (Under-Sec.) Ministry of Industry and Trade 1984–85; Sec.-Gen. Ministry of Energy and Natural Resources 1985–90; Adviser to Prime Minister 1991–94; Co-ordinator-Gen. of Peace Process, Ministry of Foreign Affairs 1994–95; Exec. Dir Noor Al-Hussein Foundation 1995–97; Supervisor, Human Rights Unit, Prime Minister's Office; Asst Pres. Philadelphia Univ. 1999–, Dean of Faculty of Eng 2000–07, currently Adviser to Pres. for Int. Relations and Scientific Centres; Minister of Education 2009–10; mem. Arab Language Acad.; Chair. Bd of Dirs Jordan Glass Co. 1985–87, Commercial Centers Cooperation-Jordan 1984–85, 1990–91; mem. Bd of Dirs Jordan Atomic Energy; mem. Bd Consultance Albayan Magazine; fmr Dir Jordanian Petroleum Refinery, Jordanian Phosphate Co., Jordan Valley Authority, Jordan Water Authority, Jordan Electricity Authority, Jordan Natural Resources Authority, Industrial Bank of Jordan etc.; mem. Royal Advisory for Educ.; mem. Higher Council for Family Affairs; Gov. for Jordan, IAEA 1982–90; writes weekly column in Aldustou (daily newspaper); Al Istiqlal Decoration of the 1st Order 1990; Hussein Gold Medal for Scientific Distinctions, State Appreciation Award for Human Sciences and Arab Thoughts 2000. *Publications:* Study on the Arab Mind, On Progress and History in the Arab World, Science and Technology in the Arab World, Culture Decline, National Strategy for Societal Culture 2004, Renaissance and Survival 2005, Engineering and Engineers 2007, Entrepreneurship 2012, and other books on aspects of science, tech., nuclear energy, natural resources and devt in the Arab world; two theoretical plays. *Leisure interests:* farming, reading, writing, travelling. *Address:* Office of the President, Philadelphia University, PO Box 1, Amman 19392 (office); 29 Ali Thyabat Street, Tla'a Al Ali, Amman, Jordan (home). *Telephone:* (2) 6374444 (office); (2) 5347777 (home). *Fax:* (2) 6374370 (office); (2) 5344448 (home). *E-mail:* ibadran@philadelphia.edu.jo (office); ebrbadran2@gmail.com (home). *Website:* www.philadelphia.edu.jo (office).

BADRÉ, Bertrand, MA; French business executive and international organization official; *Managing Director and Chief Financial Officer, World Bank Group;* b. 10 May 1968; s. of Denis Badré; m. Vanessa du Merle 1995; four c.; ed Hautes études commerciales de Paris, Institut d'Etudes Politiques de Paris, Université Paris Sorbonne (Paris IV), Ecole nationale d'Administration; Asst Group Controller, BFI-Ibexsa 1989–91; Inspecteur des Finances 1995–99; seconded to World Bank, Togo 1997, Asst Dir Lazard 1999–2000, Vice-Pres. 2000–02, Man. Dir 2004–07, Man. Dir and Chief Financial Officer, World Bank Group, Washington, DC 2013–; Chief Financial Officer, Crédit Agricole 2007–11; Group Chief Financial Officer Société Générale 2012–13; Deputy Personal Rep. of Pres. Chirac for Africa for the G8 2003; fmr mem. Bd of Dirs Haulotte Group, Sofiouest; mem. global panel on 'Financing Water for All' 2002, Supervisory Bd Eurazeo 2010–12, Fin Stability Bd (FSB) 2013. *Address:* World Bank Group, 1818 H Street, NW, Washington, DC 20433, USA (office). *Telephone:* (202) 473-1000 (office). *Fax:* (202) 473-1000 (office). *Website:* www.worldbank.org (office).

BADRI, Abdalla Salem el-, BS; Libyan oil industry executive and international organization official; b. 25 May 1940, Ghemmines; m.; five c.; ed Univ. of Southern Florida, USA; began career at Esso-Libya 1965, Asst Accountant and Co-ordinator, Man. Information Systems, then Asst Controller; Chair. Waha Oil Co. 1980–83; Chair. Nat. Oil Corpn 1983–90, 2000, 2004–06, Sec.-Gen. People's Cttee of Petroleum 1990–92, Sec.-Gen. People's Cttee of Energy 1993–2000, Deputy Sec.-Gen. People's Cttee for Services 2000–02, Deputy Sec.-Gen. People's Cttee 2002–04; Sec.-Gen. OPEC 1994, 2007–Aug. 2016; Pres. OPEC Conf. 1994, 1996–97; Pres. OAPEC 1998; Chair. Bd of Dirs Arab Petroleum Services Co. 1987–90; mem. Bd Libya Oil Invest (Tamoil), Chair. 2005–06; mem. Bd of Dirs Umm Al-Jawabi Oil Co. 1977–80. *Address:* c/o Organization of the Petroleum Exporting Countries (OPEC), Helferstorferstrasse 17, 1010 Vienna, Austria.

BADRISING, Niermala Hindori; Suriname diplomatist and politician; *Ambassador to USA;* b. 4 July 1962, Paramaribo; ed Int. Inst. of Social Studies, The Hague, Tufts Univ.; has held several positions with Ministry of Foreign Affairs, becoming Political Adviser to Pres. for Int. Orgs., Perm. Rep. to OAS 2011–15, Minister of Foreign Affairs 2015–17, Amb. to USA 2017–. *Address:* Embassy of the Republic of Suriname, 4201 Connecticut Ave. NW, Suite 400, Washington, DC 20008, USA (office). *Telephone:* (202) 629-4302 (office). *Fax:* (202) 629-4769 (office). *E-mail:* amb.vs@foreignaffairs.gov.sr (office). *Website:* www.surinameembassy.org (office).

BAE, Jung Choong; South Korean insurance industry executive (retd); ed Korea Univ.; joined Dongbang Life (now Samsung Life Insurance) 1969, with Samsung Fire and Marine Insurance 1995–98, returned to Samsung Life Insurance 1999 as Exec. Vice-Pres. and Rep. Dir, Pres. and CEO 2000–06, also mem. restructuring cttee of Samsung Group and non-standing Dir Hana Bank and Samsung Investment Trust and Securities Co.; honoured by Korea Man. Asscn three times for leadership in customer service. *Address:* c/o Samsung Life Insurance, Samsung Life Insurance Building, 150 Taepyong-ro 2-ga, Chung-gu, Seoul 100-716, Republic of Korea.

BAEZ, Joan Chandos; American folk singer; b. 9 Jan. 1941, Staten Island, NY; d. of Albert V. Baez and Joan Baez (née Bridge); m. David Harris 1968 (divorced 1973); one s.; ed School of Fine and Applied Arts, Boston Univ.; began career as singer in coffee houses, appeared at Ballad Room, Club 47 1958–68, Gate of Horn, Chicago 1958, Newport, RI, Folk Festival 1959–69, Town Hall and Carnegie Hall, New York 1962, 1967, 1968; gave concerts in black colls in southern USA 1963; toured Europe and USA 1960s–90s, Democratic Repub. of Viet Nam 1972, Australia 1985; recordings with Vanguard Records 1960–72, A & M Record Co. 1972–76, Portrait Records 1977–80, Gold Castle Records 1987–89, Virgin Records 1990–93, Guardian Records 1995–, Grapevine Label Records 1995–; began refusing payment of war taxes 1964; detained for civil disobedience opposing conscription 1967; speaking tour of USA and Canada for draft resistance 1967–68; Founder and Vice-Pres. Inst. for Study of Non-Violence (now called Resource Center for Non-Violence) 1965–; Founder Humanitas Int. Human Rights Comm. 1979–92; Chevalier, Légion d'honneur, Orden de las Artes y las Letras de España (Spain) 2010; awarded eight gold albums, one gold single; Gandhi Memorial Int. Foundation Award 1988, Lifetime Achievement Award, Nat. Acad. of Recording Arts and Sciences 2007, Spirit of Americana Free Speech Award, Americana Music Asscn 2008, Humanitarian Award, Children's Health Fund 2010, Lifetime Achievement Award, Folk Alliance International 2011, inducted into Grammy Hall of Fame 2011, ASCAP Centennial Award 2014, Amnesty International Amb. of Conscience Award 2015, inducted into Rock and Roll Hall of Fame 2016. *Recordings include:* albums: Joan Baez 1960, Joan Baez, Vol. 2 1961, In Concert, part 2 1963, 5 1964, Farewell Angelina 1965, Noel 1966, Joan 1967, Baptism 1968, Any Day Now 1968, David's Album 1969, One Day At A Time 1969, First Ten Years 1970, Carry It On (soundtrack) 1971, Ballad Book 1972, Come From The Shadows 1972, Where Are You Now My Son? 1973, Hits, Greatest and Others 1973, Gracias A La Vida 1974, Contemporary Ballad Book 1974, Diamonds and Rust 1975, From Every Stage 1976, Gulf Winds 1976, Blowin' Away 1977, Best Of 1977, Honest Lullaby 1979, Very Early Joan 1982, Recently 1987, Diamonds and Rust In The Bullring 1989, Speaking Of Dreams 1989, Play Me Backwards 1992, Rare Live and Classic 1993, Ring Them Bells 1995, Gone from Danger 1997, Dreams 1997, Best Of... 1997, 20th Century Masters: The Millennium 1999, Dark Chords on a Big Guitar 2003, Bowery Songs 2005, Day After Tomorrow 2008, How Sweet the Sound 2009, Whistle Down The Wind 2018. *Publications include:* Joan Baez Songbook

1964, Daybreak 1968, Coming Out (with David Harris) 1971, And Then I Wrote… (songbook) 1979, And a Voice to Sing With 1987. *Address:* Diamonds and Rust Productions, PO Box 1026, Menlo Park, CA 94026-1026, USA (office). *Telephone:* (650) 328-0266 (office). *Fax:* (650) 917-1020 (office). *E-mail:* jbwebpages@aol.com (office). *Website:* www.joanbaez.com.

BAGABANDI, Natsagiin, PhD, ScD; Mongolian politician and fmr head of state; b. 22 April 1950, Zavkhan Prov.; s. of Mendiin Natsag and Rashjamtsiin Dogoo; m. Azadsurengiin Oyunbileg 1971; one s. one d.; ed Refrigeration Jr Coll., Leningrad (now St Petersburg), USSR, Food Tech. Inst. of USSR, Odessa, Acad. of Social Science, Moscow, USSR; machine operator, mechanic and engineer, Ulan Bator City Brewery and Distillery 1972–75; Chief of Dept Mongolian People's Revolutionary Party's (MPRP) Cttee of Tuv Aimag 1980–84; Chief of Div., Div. Adviser Cen. Cttee of MPRP 1987–90; Sec., Deputy Chair. Cen. Cttee of MPRP 1990–92, Chair. Feb.–June 1997; mem. of State Great Hural, Chair. 1992–96; Pres. of Mongolia and C-in-C of the Armed Forces 1997–2005; Dir Oyu Tolgoi LLC; Hon. Prof., Mongolian Socio-Econ. Inst. 'Explorer XXI'; 70th Anniversary Order of the People's Revolution 1991, 'Golden Star' Olympic Order 1997, Academician Title 'Bilguun Nomch', Mongolian Nomadic Civilization Acad. and 'Ikh-Zasag' Univ. 2000, 'Peace' Order of Russian Fed. 2000, Order of Chinggis Khaan 2000; Dr hc (Nat. Food Tech. Acad. of Odessa, Ukraine) 1995, (Seng-Shui Univ., Japan) 1998, (Ankara Univ., Turkey) 1998, (Alma-Ata Univ., Kazakhstan) 1998, (Mongolian Admin Acad.) 1999, (Mongolian 'Otgontenger' Univ.) 2001, (Mongolian Defense Univ.) 2001, (Sougan Univ., S Korea) 2001, (Mongolian Science and Tech. Univ.) 2002, (Soka Univ., Japan), (Tokyo Univ. of Agric.), (Indiana Univ., USA) 2005, (Hokuriku Univ., Japan) 2007; Sukhbaatar Fund Prize 1996, Peter the Great Int. Prize 2001. *Publications include:* Mongolian Behaviour 1992, The President: Thought and Recommendation Before the New Century 1998, The President: Policy and Objectives Before the New Century 1998, Policy and Mind of the President 2000, Significance of Restoration and Tradition to the Development 2000, Mongolian Intelligence 2001, Policy and Diligence of the President 2001, Thought and Ideas of the President 2001, XXI Century Will Test You 2001, New Era and New Objectives of Mongolian Buddhist Religion 2001, Let Us Respect and Admire Elders 2001, Children, Youths and the President 2001, Multi-Sided National Security 2001, New Century: Adore Consent and Friendship, Develop the Country 2003, New Century: Meaning of Self-reliance upon Globalization, and Globalization upon Self-reliance 2004, New Century: Meaning of Cherishing the Democracy 2005, Policy and Activity of President of Mongolia N. Bagabandi 2005. *Leisure interests:* reading, fishing.

BAGÃO FÉLIX, António; Portuguese politician and economist; b. 9 April 1948, Ílhavo; s. of João Bagão Félix and Marília Nunes de Castro; ed Inst. of Econ. and Financial Sciences, Institut Européen d'Admin des Affaires (INSEAD), France; Financial Dir, Companhia de Seguros Mundial 1973–76; Dir Bank of Commerce and Industry 1985–87; Sec. of State for Work and Professional Training 1987, for Social Security 1987–91; Dir, Bank of Portugal 1992–93, Vice-Gov. 1993–94; Dir-Gen. Portuguese Commercial Bank 1994–2002; Minister of Social Security and Employment 2002–04, of Finance 2004–05; Chair. Conselho Directivo do Centro de Informação, Mediação, Provedoria e Arbitragem de Seguros 2010–; currently Visiting Prof., Lusíada Univ. of Lisbon 2006–; Chair. Supervisory Bd, Bank Against Hunger 1997–2002; consultant to Portuguese Episcopal Conf. for Social Affairs and Ethics 2001–; Chair. Supervisory Council, Cerebral Palsy Asscn of Lisbon 2006–11, Asscn of Friends of the Botanical Garden Help 2010–; Pres. Gen. Ass. of the Carers Network 2008–, Bd of Hon. Mems of Portuguese Association of Missing Children 2009–, Gen. Ass. of the Brotherhood of Mercy and San Roque 2011–; mem. Bd, Special Olympics 2009–12; mem. Bd of Dirs, Asscn for Econ. and Social Devt; mem. Council of State 2011–; mem. Gen. Council, Univ. of Évora 2013–14, Superior Council, Portuguese Catholic Univ. *Publications include:* several books and articles for numerous journals, newspapers and magazines. *Address:* Av. Almirante Gago Coutinho 92, 1700-031 Lisbon, Portugal.

BAGAYEV, Sergei Nikolayevich; Russian physicist and research institute director; *Scientific Director, Institute of Laser Physics, Russian Academy of Sciences (Siberia);* b. 9 Sept. 1941; m.; one s.; ed Novosibirsk State Univ.; Jr, Sr Researcher, Head of Lab., Inst. of Semiconductor Physics, Siberian Br., USSR Acad. of Sciences 1965–78, Head of Lab., Head of Div., Deputy Dir Inst. of Thermophysics, Siberian Br., USSR Acad. of Sciences 1978–91, Deputy Dir Inst. of Laser Physics, Siberian Br., Russian Acad. of Sciences 1991–92, Dir 1992–2016, Scientific Dir 2016–; Corresp. mem. USSR (now Russian) Acad. of Sciences 1990, Academician 1993–; research in non-linear laser spectroscopy of superhigh resolution, laser frequency standards, physics and their applications in precision physical experiments; Order of Friendship 1999, Chevalier, Légion d'honneur 2004, Medal of the Order 'For Services to the Motherland' 2006; State Prize of Russian Fed. 1998, V. A. Koptyug Prize, SBRAS/Belarus Nat. Acad. of Sciences 1999. *Publications include:* Laser Frequency Standards 1986, Single-frequency Intracavity Doubled Yb:YAG Ring Laser 2005, Investigation of Transcapillary Exchange by the Laser Method 2005, and numerous articles. *Address:* Institute of Laser Physics, Siberian Branch of Russian Academy of Sciences, Prosp. Lavrentyev 13/3, 630090 Novosibirsk, Russia (office). *Telephone:* (383) 333-24-89 (office). *Fax:* (383) 333-20-67 (office). *E-mail:* bagayev@laser.nsc.ru (office). *Website:* www.laser.nsc.ru (office).

BAGEL-TRAH, Simone, Dr rer. nat; German microbiologist and business executive; *Chairwoman of the Supervisory Board and Shareholders' Committee, Henkel KGaA;* b. 10 Jan. 1969, Düsseldorf; m. Christoph Trah; two c.; ed Univ. of Bonn; consultant, Project Man. for Verein für angewandte Mikrobiologie (Asscn of Applied Microbiology) 1998–2000, Co-ordination of industrial projects for Pharmaceutical Microbiology Dept, Bonn Univ. 1998–2000; Pnr and Dir Antiinfectives Intelligence Gesellschaft für klinisch mikrobiologische Forschung und Kommunikation mbH (Clinical Microbiological Research & Communication) 2000–; mem. Supervisory Board of Henkel KGaA 2001–05, mem. Shareholders' Cttee 2005–08, mem. Supervisory Bd and Vice-Chair. Shareholders' Cttee Henkel AG & Co. KGaA 2008–09, Chair. 2009–, Vice-Chair. Supervisory Bd Henkel Management AG 2008–09, Chair. 2009–; mem. Advisory Bd HSBC Trinkaus & Burkhardt AG, Supervisory Bd Bayer AG, Central Advisory Bd Commerzbank AG, Supervisory Bd Heraeus Holding GmbH; mem. Rotary Düsseldorf, Bd of Trustees Düsseldorf Business School, Bd of Trustees Stiftung Schloss und Park Benrath (Benrath Castle and Park Foundation), Bd of Trustees Dr Konrad Henkel Foundation, Bd of Trustees Jost Henkel Foundation, Bd of Heinrich Heine Univ., Düsseldorf, Bd Fritz Henkel Foundation. *Address:* Henkel AG & Co. KGaA, Henkelstrasse 67, Düsseldorf 40191, Germany (office). *Telephone:* (211) 797-0 (office). *Fax:* (211) 7982484 (office). *E-mail:* info@henkel.com (office). *Website:* www.henkel.com (office).

BAGGE, Sverre Hakon, PhD; Norwegian historian and academic; b. 7 Aug. 1942, Bergen; s. of Sverre Olsen and Gunvor Bagge; m. Guro Mette Skrove; two s. one d.; Lecturer, Univ. of Bergen 1973, apptd Sr Lecturer 1974, Prof. 1991–, Dir Centre for Medieval Studies 2002–13; Visiting Fellow, Clare Hall, Cambridge, UK 1979-80; Directeur d'études associé at Maison des Sciences de l'Homme, Paris 1992; Visiting Scholar, Stanford Univ., USA 1995; Visiting Prof., Aarhus Univ., Denmark 1996; Brage Prize, Clara Lachmann's Prize, Jarl Gallén Prize for Medieval Studies, Univ. of Helsinki 2004, Møbius Prize from Norwegian Research Council 2008. *Publications:* The Political Thought of the King's Mirror 1987, Society and Politics in Snorri Sturluson's Heimskringla 1991, From Gang Leader to the Lord's Anointed 1996, Kings, Politics, and the Right Order of the World in German Historiography c. 950–1150, From Viking Stronghold to Christian Kingdom, State Formation in Norway c. 900-1350 2010. *Address:* University of Bergen, Øysteinsgate 3, 5020 Bergen (office); Moldbakken 13, 5035 Bergen, Norway (home). *Telephone:* 55-58-23-25 (office). *Fax:* 55-58-80-90 (office). *E-mail:* sverre.bagge@.uib.no (office). *Website:* www.uib.no/en/ahkr (office).

BAGGIO, Roberto; Italian fmr professional footballer; b. 18 Feb. 1967, Caldogno, Veneto; s. of Fiorindo Baggio and Matilde Baggio; m. Andreina Fabbri; two d.; second striker; with Vicenza 1982–85, Fiorentina 1985–90, Juventus 1990–95, Milan 1995–97, Bologna 1997–98, Inter Milan 1998–2000, Brescia 2000–04, 488 appearances, 318 career goals; played for Italian Nat. Team in 1990 (third place), 1994 (second place) and 1998 World Cups; only Italian player ever to score in three World Cups (nine goals); made 56 appearances and scored 27 goals for Italy; apptd Goodwill Amb. for FAO 2002; U-23 European Footballer of the Year 1990, UEFA Cup Winners' Cup Top Scorer 1990–91, FIFA World Player of the Year 1993, European Footballer of the Year 1993, Platinum Football Award, TV Sorrisi and Canzoni 1992, Onze D'Or by French Magazine Onze Mondial 1993, Bravo Award with Fiorentina 1990, Golden Guerin with Vicenza 1985, Golden Guerin with AC Milan 1996, Golden Guerin with Brescia 2001, Azzuri Team of the Century 2000, FIFA Dream Team of All Time 2002, Giuseppe Prisco Award 2004, The Champions Promenade – Golden Foot 2003, Peace Summit Award 2010. *Publication:* Una porta nel cielo (autobiography) 2001. *Leisure interests:* hunting, music. *Address:* Via Bazoli 10, 25127 Brescia, Italy (office). *Telephone:* (30) 241075 (office). *Fax:* (30) 2410787 (office). *E-mail:* info@bresciacalcio.it (office). *Website:* www.bresciacalcio.it (office); www.robertobaggio.com (home).

BAGHDADI, Abu Bakr al-, PhD; Iraqi guerrilla leader; *Leader, Islamic State of Iraq and the Levant (ISIL);* b. (Ibrahim Awwad Ibrahim Ali Muhammad al-Badri al-Samarrai), 28 July 1971, Samarra; ed Islamic Univ. of Baghdad; co-f. militant group Jamaat Jaysh Ahl al-Sunnah wa-l-Jamaah (JJASJ) following US invasion of Iraq 2003, becoming Head of Sharia Cttee; imprisoned by US forces Feb.–Dec. 2004; joined Mujahideen Shura Council (MSC) 2006, becoming mem. Sharia Cttee (MSC renamed Islamic State of Iraq, ISI 2006); Gen. Supervisor, ISI Sharia Cttee and mem. Sr Consultative Council, Leader ISI 2006–13, Islamic State of Iraq and the Levant (ISIL) 2013–.

BAGHDASARIAN, Artur, DJur; Armenian politician; b. 8 Nov. 1968, Yerevan; m.; two c.; ed Yerevan State Univ.; army service 1988–89; Corresp., Head of Dept Avangard newspaper 1989–93; mem. Nat. Ass. 1995–, Chair. 2003–06; Chair. Council on State and Legal Affairs 1998–; Leader Orinats Yerkir Kusaktsutyun (Law-Governed Country Party of Armenia—OYeK) 1998–; Chair. French Univ. of Armenia 2000–; Chair. European Regional Acad. in the Caucasus 2002–; Sec. Nat. Security Council 2008–14. *Publications:* several scientific monographs and articles. *Address:* Orinats Yerkir Kusaktsutyun, 0009 Yerevan, Abovyan poghots 43, Armenia (office). *Telephone:* (10) 56-65-05 (office). *Fax:* (10) 56-99-69 (office). *E-mail:* info@oek.am (office).

BAGIS, Egemen, MPA, BBA; Turkish politician; b. 23 April 1970, Bingol; m. Beyhan N. Bagis; two c.; ed Baruch Coll., City Univ. of New York, USA; elected to Nat. Ass. for Istanbul 2002–, Foreign Policy Adviser to Prime Minister 2002–09, Minister for EU Affairs and Chief Negotiator 2009–13; mem. AK Party (Justice and Devt Party), serves as Deputy Chair. for Foreign Affairs; Chair. NATO Parl. Ass. on Transatlantic Relations; Chair. Turkey–USA Inter-Parl. Friendship Caucus; Chair. Advisory Cttee, Istanbul 2010 European Capital of Culture Initiative; Founding Patron, Istanbul Modern Museum, Santral Museum of Art and Industry; fmr Pres. Fed. of Turkish-American Asscns; Hon. mem. Bd of Dirs Siirt Solidarity Foundation. *Address:* Turkish Grand National Assembly, A Blok, Alt Zemin, 3 Banko, No. 3, Bakanliklar, 06543 Ankara, Turkey (office). *Telephone:* (312) 4205908 (office). *Fax:* (312) 4206947 (office). *E-mail:* egemen@egemenbagis.com (office). *Website:* www.egemenbagis.com (office).

BAGLAY, Marat Viktorovich, DJur, DHist; Russian lawyer; b. 13 March 1931, Baku, Azerbaijan; m.; three d.; ed Rostov State Univ., Inst. of State and Law; Researcher, Inst. of State and Law 1957–62; Prof., Moscow Inst. of Int. Relations 1962–95; Head of Dept, Inst. of Int. Workers' Movt Acad. of Sciences 1967–77; Pro-Rector and Prof., Acad. of Labour and Social Relations 1977–95; judge, Constitutional Court of Russian Fed. 1996–2003, Chair. 1997–2003; Corresp. mem. Russian Acad. of Sciences 1997–; mem. Bureau, European Comm. for Democracy Through Law 2005; Hon. LLD (Baku Univ., Rostov-on-Don Univ., Odessa Nat. Acad. of Law); Merited Scientist of Russia. *Publications include:* Way to Freedom, Constitutional Law of Russian Federation, numerous books and articles.

BAGNASCO, HE Cardinal Angelo; Italian ecclesiastic; *Archbishop of Genoa;* b. 14 Jan. 1943, Pontevico; ed Univ. of Genoa; ordained priest, Genoa 1966; served as Prof. of Metaphysics and Atheism, Theological Faculty of Northern Italy, also led archdiocesan liturgical and catechesis offices; fmr diocesan rep. to FUCI (Italian Catholic Fed. of Univ. Students); Bishop of Pesaro 1998–2000, Archbishop of Pesaro 2000–03; Archbishop of the Mil. Ordinariate of Italy 2003–06; Archbishop of Genoa 2006–; cr. Cardinal (Cardinal-Priest of Gran Madre di Dio) 2007; participated in Papal Conclave 2013; has held several posts within Italian Episcopal Conf. (CEI) 2001–, including Pres. Admin. Bd of newspaper Avvenire and Sec. for Schools and Univs 2001–, Pres. CEI 2007–; Vice-Pres. Consiglio delle conferenze episcopali europee 2011–16, Pres. 2016–. *Address:* Arcivescovado, Piazza Matteotti 4, 16123 Genoa, Italy (office). *Telephone:* (010) 27-001 (office). *Fax:* (010) 27-00-220 (office). *E-mail:* info@diocesi.genova.it (office). *Website:* www.diocesi.genova.it (office).

BAGRATIAN, Hrant Araratovich, PhD; Armenian economist and politician; *Deputy Chairman, National Assembly;* b. 18 Oct. 1958, Yerevan; m.; two c.; ed Yerevan Inst. of Nat. Econ., Inst. of Economy of Armenian Acad. of Sciences; Jr researcher, then Sr researcher, Inst. of Econs, Armenian Acad. of Sciences 1982–90; First Deputy Chair. Council of Ministers of Armenian SSR, Chair. State Cttee on Econs 1990; Vice-Prime Minister and Minister of Econs Repub. of Armenia 1991–93; Prime Minister of Armenia 1993–96; Adviser to IMF 1996–97; Deputy Head and Dir Human Resources, Yerevan Brandy Factory 1998–2006; Lecturer, Russian-Armenian (Slavonic) Univ. 2007–, Kiev Univ. of Int. Relations 2008–10, Kiev Univ. of Banking 2010–12; Deputy Chair. Nat. Ass. of Armenia 2012–; Founder and Leader, Liberty (Azatutiun) Party; cand. in presidential election Feb. 2013. *Publications include:* more than 52 scientific articles and 7 books including The Society and the State 2000. *Address:* National Assembly, 0095 Yerevan, Marshal Baghramyan poghota 19, Armenia (office). *Telephone:* (10) 52-05-15 (office). *Fax:* (10) 52-96-95 (office). *E-mail:* abrahamyan@parliament.am (office). *Website:* www.parliament.am (office).

BAGSHAWE, Kenneth Dawson, CBE, MD, FRCP, FRCR, FRCOG, FRS; British physician and medical oncologist; *Professor Emeritus of Medical Oncology, Charing Cross Hospital Medical School;* b. 17 Aug. 1925, Marple, Cheshire; s. of Harry Bagshawe and Gladys Bagshawe; m. 1st Ann A. Kelly 1946 (divorced 1976, died 2000); one s. one d.; m. 2nd Sylvia D. Lawler (née Corben) 1977 (died 1996); m. 3rd Surinder Kanta Sharma 1998; ed Harrow Co. School, London School of Econs and St Mary's Hosp. Medical School, Univ. of London; served in RN 1943–46; Research Fellow, Johns Hopkins Hosp., USA 1955–56; Sr Registrar, St Mary's Hosp. 1956–60; Sr Lecturer in Medicine, Charing Cross Hosp. Medical School 1961–63; Consultant Physician and Dir Dept of Medical Oncology 1961–90, Prof. of Medical Oncology 1974–90, Prof. Emer. 1990–; Chair. Enzacta Scientific Co. Ltd 1998–2000; Chair. Council Cancer Research Campaign 1988–90; Pres. Asscn of Cancer Physicians 1986–93, British Asscn for Cancer Research 1990–94; Fellow, Royal Coll. of Radiologists; Hamilton Fairley Lectureship 1989; Hon. DSc (Bradford) 1990; Krug Award for Excellence in Medicine 1980; Edgar Gentilli Prize, Royal Coll. of Obstetricians and Gynaeocologists 1980, Galen Medal, London Soc. of Apothecaries 1993. *Achievements include:* invented cytotoxic drug therapy. *Publications:* Choriocarcinoma 1969, Medical Oncology 1976, Germ Cell Tumours 1983, Antibody Directed Prodrug Therapy 1987 and articles in professional journals. *Leisure interests:* travel, walking, photography, music, art. *Address:* 115 George Street, London, W1H 7HF, England (home). *Telephone:* (20) 7262-6033 (home).

BAHADIAN, Adhemar Gabriel; Brazilian diplomatist and company director; b. 22 Oct. 1940, Rio de Janeiro; s. of Aziz Bahadian and Gracinda Gabriel Bahadian; ed Università Gama Filho, Istituto Rio Branco; joined Ministry of Foreign Affairs 1967, Head Int. Commerce Div. 1987, Chief of Cabinet, Secr.-Gen. for Foreign Affairs 1994, Asst Sec.-Gen. 1995, First Sec., Perm. Mission to UN, Geneva 1976, Counsellor 1980, Minister Counsellor 1990, Alt. Perm. Rep. 2000, Consul-Gen. in Buenos Aires 2002, Amb. to Italy 2005–09; fmr Chief Free Trade Area of the Americas negotiator; Ind. Dir, TIM Participacoes SA 2010–; Gran Croce, Ordine del Rio Branco 1994, Grande Ufficiale, Ordine al Merito Navale 1994, Grande Ufficiale, Ordine al Merito Militare 1995, Grande Ufficiale, Ordine al Merito dell'Aeronautica 1996, Commdr, Légion d'honneur 1996, Ordine Francisco de Miranda (Venezuela) 1997, Cavalieri di Gran Croce (Italy) 1997, Gran Croce, Ordine di Bernardo O'Higgins (Chile) 1998, and other decorations from Germany, Finland, Portugal. *Address:* c/o Board of Directors, TIM Participacoes SA, Avenida das Américas Rio de Janeiro, Rio de Janeiro 22640-102, Brazil.

BAHAH, Khalid Abdullah Mahfouz; Yemeni diplomatist and politician; b. 1965; ed Pune Univ., India; supported protests leading to removal of Pres. Ali Abdullah Saleh 2012; Minister of Oil and Mineral Resources –2014; Amb. to Canada 2014, Amb. and Perm. Rep. to UN, New York Aug.–Oct. 2014; Prime Minister of Yemen 2014–16; Vice-Pres. 2015–16.

BAHAR, Shaikha Khalid al-, BA, MBA; Kuwaiti banking executive; *Deputy Group CEO, National Bank of Kuwait;* ed Kuwait Univ., Harvard Business School, Stanford Univ., Duke Univ., USA; fmr Chair. Al Watany Bank of Egypt; Group Gen. Man., Corp. Banking, Nat. Bank of Kuwait 2003–08, Deputy CEO Nat. Bank of Kuwait 2008–10, CEO 2012–13, Deputy Group CEO 2013–; Chair. Nat. Bank of Kuwait (Lebanon) 2005–; mem. Bd of Dirs International Bank of Qatar, Zain Group 2005–. *Address:* National Bank of Kuwait, PO Box 95 Safat, Abdullah Al Ahmad Street, 13001 Kuwait City, Kuwait (office). *Telephone:* 22422011 (office). *Fax:* 22462469 (office). *E-mail:* info@nbk.com (office). *Website:* www.nbk.com (office).

BAHARNA, Husain Mohammad al-, PhD; Bahraini lawyer and politician; b. 5 Dec. 1932, Manama; s. of Mohammad Makki Al-Baharna and Zahra Sayed Mahmood; m.; three s. two d.; ed Baghdad Law Coll., Iraq, London Univ. and Cambridge Univ., UK; mem. English Bar (Lincoln's Inn) and Bahraini Bar; Legal Adviser, Ministry of Foreign Affairs, Kuwait 1962–64; Legal Adviser and Analyst Arab Gulf Affairs, Arabian-American Oil Co., Saudi Arabia 1965–68; Legal Adviser, Dept of Foreign Affairs, Bahrain 1969–70; Legal Adviser to the State and mem. Council of State, Pres. Legal Cttee 1970–71; Minister of State for Legal Affairs 1971; mem. Del. of Bahrain to Sixth (Legal) Cttee UN Gen. Ass. 1986, UN Int. Law Comm., Geneva 1987, Del. of Bahrain to Summit of Heads of State of Gulf Co-operation Council 1991; fmr legal adviser and del. to numerous int. confs and summit meetings; Chair. Del. of Bahrain to UN Preparatory Comm. for Int. Sea Bed Authority and Int. Tribunal for Law of the Sea 1983; mem. Cttee of Experts on Control of Transnational and Int. Criminality and for the establishment of the Int. Criminal Court, Siracusa, Italy 1990; Council mem. Centre for Islamic and Middle East Law, SOAS, London Univ., Editorial Bd Arab Law Quarterly; Hon. mem. Euro-Arab Forum for Arbitration and Business Law, Paris; mem. British Inst. of Int. and Comparative Law, American Soc. of Int. Law, Int. Law Asscn, Egyptian Soc. of Int. Law; Assoc. mem. Int. Comm. of Jurists, Int. Law Comm., UN; Arab Historian Medal (Union of Arab Historians) 1986, State of Bahrain Medal of First Grade 1996, Shaikh Isa Bin Salman Medal of First Grade 2001. *Publications:* The Legal Status of the Arab Gulf States 1968, Legal and Constitutional Systems of the Arabian Gulf States (in Arabic) 1975, The Arabian Gulf States – Their Legal and Political Status and their International Problems 1975, British Extra Territorial Jurisdiction in the Gulf 1913–1971 1998, Bahrain Between Two Constitutions (in Arabic) 2005, The Bahrain Nationality Law and the State's Open-door Policy Regarding Naturalization of Foreigners (in Arabic) 2007, A Legal Study and Analysis of the Constitutional State of the Kingdom of Bahrain (in Arabic) 2008, Iran's Claim to Sovereignty over Bahrain and the Resolution of the Anglo-Iranian Dispute over Bahrain (in Arabic and English) 2008; articles in learned journals. *Leisure interest:* reading. *Address:* Dr Husain M. al-Baharna & Associates, PO Box 10407, Manama, Bahrain (office). *Telephone:* 17533773 (office). *Fax:* 17535242 (office). *E-mail:* hbaharna@batelco.com.bh (office).

BAHÇELI, Devlet, DEcon; Turkish politician and academic; *Chairman, Milliyetçi Hareket Partisi;* b. 1948, Osmaniye; ed Ankara Econ. and Commercial Sciences Acad., Gazi Univ. Social Sciences Inst.; Sec.-Gen. Turkish Nat. Students Fed. 1970–71; instructor, Ankara Econ. and Commercial Sciences Acad., mem. Faculty of Econ. and Admin. Sciences, Gazi Univ. 1972–87; mem. Parl. 2007–; Sec.-Gen. Milliyetçi Hareket Partisi (Nationalist Action Party—MHP) 1987, Chair. 1997–; Deputy Prime Minister and State Minister 1999–2002; Founder mem. and Pres. Financiers and Economists Asscn. *Address:* Milliyetçi Hareket Partisi (Nationalist Action Party), Ceyhun Atif Kansu Cad. 128, Balgat, Ankara, Turkey (office). *Telephone:* (312) 4725555 (office). *Fax:* (312) 4731544 (office). *E-mail:* bilgi@mhp.org.tr (office). *Website:* www.mhp.org.tr (office).

BAHDON, Ali Hassan; Djibouti politician; *Minister of Defence, in charge of Relations with Parliament;* b. 17 April 1967, Ethiopia; m.; two c.; fmr Dir-Gen., Agence Nationale de la Promotion des Investissements (ANPI); fmr mem. Bd of Dirs, Autorité des Ports et des Zones Franches; apptd Minister of Equipment and Transportation 2008, Minister of Labour 2011, Minister of Communications, in charge of Post and Telecommunications 2013, Minister of Defence, in charge of Relations with Parl. 2016–; fmr Alt. Dir, Banque Africaine de Développement. *Address:* Ministry of Defence, BP 42, Djibouti (office). *Telephone:* 21352034 (office). *E-mail:* contact@defense.gouv.dj (office).

BAHIDDHA-NUKARA, Parnpree, LLB, MPA, PhD; Thai politician, government official and company chairman; ed Chulalongkorn Univ., Univ. of Southern California and Claremont Graduate Univ., USA, certifications from Thailand Energy Acad. and Judicial Training Inst. at King Prajadhipok's Inst.; mem. Pheu Thai Party, Deputy Leader 2008–10; served as Thailand Trade Rep. 2005, Vice-Minister for Commerce, Vice-Minister for Industry, Adviser to Prime Minister, Adviser to Deputy Prime Minister, Thailand's Chief Negotiator for Thailand-India Free Trade Agreement (FTA), Thailand-BIMST-EC FTA, Chair. Cttee on Investment and Trade Promotion under FTA, Chair. Public Warehouse Org., Chair. Bangkok Fashion City; Ind. Dir and Chair. PTT Public Co. Ltd 2013–14 (resgnd).

BAHK, Jae-wan, BA, MPP, PhD; South Korean politician; ed Seoul Nat. Univ., Harvard Univ., USA; Asst Dir, Bd of Audit and Inspection, Seoul 1983–92; Deputy Dir, Ministry of Finance 1992–94; Asst Chief Sec. to Pres. for Policy Planning, Office of the Pres. 1994–96; Prof., Graduate School of Governance, Sungkyunkwan Univ. 2004–; mem. Nat. Ass. (Grand Nat. Party) 2004–08; Head, Task Force for Govt Restructuring & Regulatory Reform, Presidential Transition Cttee 2007–08; Sr Sec. to Pres. for Political Affairs Feb.–June 2008, for State Affairs Planning 2008–10; Minister of Employment and Labour 2010–11, of Strategy and Finance 2011–13; Chair. Policy Coordination Cttee, Citizens' Coalition for Econ. Justice; mem. Grand Nat. Party (renamed Saenuri Party, New Frontier Party 2012). *Address:* c/o Ministry of Strategy and Finance, Govt Complex II, 88, Gwanmunro, Gwacheon City 427-725, Gyeonggi Province, Republic of Korea (office).

BAHMANI, Mahmoud, PhD; Iranian economist, academic, politician and fmr central banker; b. 2 Jan. 1947, Karaj, Alborz Prov.; 17 years as Lecturer, Islamic Azad Univ. and Inst. of Banking and Man.; various sr man. roles with Bank Melli Iran, including Vice-Pres. of Finance; Gov. Central Bank of Iran 2008–13; mem. Parl. 2016–. *Address:* Islamic Parliament of Iran, Baharestan Square, Tehran 11575-177, Iran (office). *Telephone:* (21) 39931 (office). *Fax:* (21) 33440309 (office). *E-mail:* en@parliran.ir (office). *Website:* en.parliran.ir/eng/en/home (office).

BAHRAMI, Maj.-Gen. Tariq Shah; Afghan army officer and politician; *Minister of Defence;* b. 1967, Qarghayee Dist, Laghman Prov.; ed Mil. Coll., Loyal Command and Gen. Staff Coll., United Kingdom; joined army as Deputy Co. Commdr 1986, later promoted to Commdr, Deputy Commdr of Bn 1988, Commdr of the Bn 1989, Office-in-Charge, 201st Corps Commdr 2003–08, Commdr for 444 Commando Forces Unit in Helmand Prov. 2009–12; apptd Senior Adviser, Documentation and Planning Dept, Ministry of Defence 1990, Gen. Man., Planning and Operations Directorate for Special Forces Units, Ministry of Interior Affairs 2012, Head of Nat. Coordination Centre (TAWHED centre) (with the rank of Brig.-Gen.), Office of the Nat. Security Council (ONSC) 2015, also Dir, Communication and Information Coordination Centre (with rank of Maj.-Gen.), Asst, Office of Nat. Security Council for Commdr and Chief of Armed Forces 2016, Deputy Chief Minister of Interior Affairs 2016, Acting Minister of Defence 2017, Minister of Defence 2017–. *Address:* Ministry of Defence, Shash Darak, Kabul, Afghanistan (office). *Telephone:* (20) 2100451 (office). *Fax:* (20) 2104172 (office). *Website:* mod.gov.af (office).

BAHUGUNA, Vijay, BA, LLB; Indian politician and lawyer; b. 28 Feb. 1947, Allahabad, UP; s. of Hemwati Nandan Bahuguna and Kamla Bahuguna; m. Sudha Bahuguna 1969; two s. one d.; ed Univ. of Allahabad; started career as Advocate, Allahabad High Court, later Judge; Judge, Bombay (now Mumbai) High Court –1998; Vice-Chair. Planning Comm., Uttarakhand 2002–07; mem. Lok Sabha (lower house of Parl.) (mem. Indian Nat. Congress) 2007–12, mem. Consultative Cttee, Ministry of Power, Standing Cttee on Defence, Cttee on Public Accounts, Cttee on Health and Family Welfare, Cttee on Ethics, Cttee on Offices of Profit; Chief Minister of Uttarakhand 2012–14 (resgnd); worked at Perm. Mission, UN Gen. Ass., New York in support of perm. seat for India in Security Council 2008; joined Bharatiya Janata Party (Indian People's Party—BJP) 2016. *Leisure interests:* reading, travelling, golf. *Address:* D 13, Sector 1, Defence Colony, Dehradun, 248 001, India (home). *Telephone:* (135) 2666660 (home).

BAI, Chunli, MS, PhD, FRSC; Chinese chemist, academic and nanoscientist; *President, Chinese Academy of Sciences;* b. 26 Sept. 1953, Liaoning; s. of Bai Fuxin and Li Fengyun; m. Li Chunfang 1981; one s.; ed Peking Univ., Inst. of Chem., Chinese Acad. of Sciences; Research Asst, Changchun Inst. of Applied Chem., Chinese Acad. of Sciences (CAS) 1978, Research Assoc., Inst. of Chem. 1981–85; Visiting Research Assoc., Calif. Inst. of Tech., USA 1985–87; Assoc. Prof. and Dir Study Group on Scanning Tunnelling Microscopy (STM), Inst. of Chem., CAS 1987–89, Prof. 1989–, Deputy Dir 1992–96, Vice-Pres. CAS 1996–2004, Exec. Vice-Pres. 2004–11, Pres. 2011–, Academician 1997–, Pres. Presidium of the Academic Divisions, Graduate Univ. 2001–; Dir Nat. Centre of Nanoscience 2003–08; Visiting Prof., Inst. for Materials Research, Tohoku Univ., Japan 1991–92; apptd Vice-Pres. China Material Research Soc. 2000, China Asscn for Science and Tech. 2001–11; Sec.-Gen. and mem. Exec. Council Chinese Chemical Soc. 1994–98, Pres. 1999–2010; Vice-Pres. All-China Youth Fed. 1995–2000; Pres. China Young Scientists' Asscn 1996–2006; Vice-Chair. Nat. Science and Tech. Award Cttee of China 2002–; mem. Editorial Advisory Bd Journal of the American Chemical Society, Angewandte Chemie, Advances in Materials; mem. 8th CPPCC Nat. Cttee 1993–98; Alt. mem. 15th CCP Cen. Cttee 1997–2002, 16th CCP Cen. Cttee 2002–07, 17th CCP Cen. Cttee 2007–12, mem. 18th CCP Cen. Cttee 2012; Fellow, Third World Acad. of Sciences 1997; Foreign mem. Mongolian Acad. of Sciences 2005–, NAS (USA) 2006–, Russian Acad. of Sciences 2008, Royal Danish Acad. of Sciences and Letters 2012, Academia Europaea 2016–; Hon. Prof., Hong Kong Univ. 2001–, Univ. of Queensland, Australia 2006; Hon. FRSC 2007; Hon. Fellow, Indian Acad. of Sciences 2008, Chemical Research Soc. of India 2009; Dr hc (LTH/Lund) 2007, (Aarhus) 2007, (York) 2008, (Nottingham) 2009, (Minnesota) 2011, (Queensland) 2010, (Griffith) 2012; Hon. DSc (Univ. Coll. London); Outstanding Young Scholar, Hong Kong Qiu Shi Science and Tech. Foundation 1995, Ho Leung Ho Lee Prize; numerous prizes and awards. *Publications:* 10 books and more than 350 papers in scientific journals. *Address:* Chinese Academy of Sciences, 52 San Li He Road, Beijing 100864, People's Republic of China (office). *Telephone:* (10) 68597606 (office). *Fax:* (10) 68512458 (office). *E-mail:* clbai@cashq.ac.cn (office).

BAI, Donglu, PhD; Chinese professor of medicinal chemistry; b. 8 Feb. 1936, Dinghai Co., Zhejiang Prov.; s. of Bai Daxi and Zhang Yunxiao; m. Ni Zhifang 1969; one d.; ed Shanghai First Medical Coll., Czechoslovak Acad. of Sciences, Prague; fmr Prof. and Dir, Shanghai Inst. of Materia Medica, Chinese Acad. of Sciences; Science and Tech. Progress Award, Nat. Natural Science Prize of China 2000. *Publications include:* three monographs and more than 160 papers in scientific journals. *Leisure interest:* stamp collecting. *Address:* c/o Shanghai Institute of Materia Medica, 555 Zuchongzhi Road, Zhangjiang 201203, People's Republic of China (office).

BAI, Enpei; Chinese fmr politician; b. 8 Sept. 1946, Qingjian Co., Shaanxi Prov.; ed Northwest Tech. Univ. 1965; sent to do manual labour (Ind. Div. Farm, Shaanxi Prov. Mil. Command) 1970–73; joined CCP 1973; Deputy Dir and Dir Yan'an Diesel Engine Plant, Shaanxi Prov. 1974–83, Deputy Sec. CCP Party Cttee 1974–83; Vice-Sec. CCP Yan'an Prefectural Cttee 1983–90; Sec. CCP Yan'an Prefectural Cttee 1985; Alt. mem. 13th CCP Cen. Cttee 1987–92, 14th CCP Cen. Cttee 1992–97, mem. 15th CCP Cen. Cttee 1997–2002, mem. 16th CCP Cen. Cttee 2002–07, mem. 17th CCP Cen. Cttee 2007–12; Head CCP Inner Mongolia Autonomous Regional Cttee, Org. Dept 1990–93, mem. CCP Inner Mongolia Autonomous Regional Cttee Standing Committee 1990–93, Deputy Sec. Inner Mongolia Autonomous Regional Cttee 1993–97; Vice-Sec. CCP Qinghai Prov. Cttee 1997–99, Sec. 1999–2001; Acting Gov. Qinghai Prov. 1997–1998, Gov. 1998–99; Chair. Qinghai Prov. People's Congress 2000–01; Sec. CCP Yunnan Prov. Cttee 2001–11, mem. Standing Cttee 2001–11; dismissed from CCP on charges of corruption 2015; sentenced to death (suspended for two years) 2016.

BAI, Keming; Chinese journalist and party official; b. Oct. 1943, Jingbian, Shaanxi Prov.; s. of Bai Jian; ed Harbin Mil. Eng Inst.; joined CCP 1975; worker, Metallurgy and Geology Bureau, Harbin City, Heilongjiang Prov. 1968–70; Teacher Harbin Shipbuilding Inst. 1970–73, National Defence Industry Cttee, Shaanxi Prov. 1973–78; Deputy Div. Chief, Gen. Office, Ministry of Educ. 1978–86, Vice Div. Chief then Deputy Dir 1986–89; Head Educ. Science, Culture and Public Health Group, Research Office of the State Council 1989–93; Sec.-Gen. Propaganda Dept of CCP Cen. Cttee 1993, Deputy Head 1993–2000; Del. 15th CCP Nat. Congress 1997–2002; Deputy Dir CCP Cen. Cttee Gen. Office 2000–01; Pres. CCP Cen. Cttee People's Daily (newspaper) 2000–01; Sec. CCP Hainan Prov. Cttee and Chair. Hainan People's Congress 2001–02; Sec. CCP Prov. Cttee, Hebei Prov. 2002–07; mem. 16th CCP Cen. Cttee 2002–07; Vice-Chair. Cttee for Educ., Science, Culture and Public Health, Nat. People's Congress 2007–08, Chair. 2008–13. *Address:* c/o National People's Congress, Beijing, People's Republic of China (office). *Website:* npc.people.com.cn (office).

BAI, Lichen; Chinese politician; b. Jan. 1941, Lingyuan, Liaoning Prov.; ed Shenyang Agricultural Coll.; technician, Yingkou Agricultural Coll., Agricultural Machinery Inst., Yingkou, Liaoning Prov. 1964–68; joined CCP 1971; clerk, CCP City Cttee Org. Dept, Yingkou 1972–80, Deputy Section Chief Personnel Supervision Bureau 1972–80, Deputy Sec. then Sec. CCP City Cttee, Yingkou 1980–83, Mayor of Yingkou 1983–84; Sec. CCP City Cttee, Panjin City, Liaoning Prov. 1984–85; mem. Standing Cttee CCP Liaoning Prov. Cttee 1985–87; Asst to Gov. Liaoning Prov. 1984–85, Vice-Gov. 1985–86; mem. 13th Cen. Cttee CCP 1987–92, 14th Cen. Cttee CCP 1992–97, 15th Cen. Cttee 1997–2002, 16th Cen. Cttee 2002–07, 17th Cen. Cttee 2007–12; Vice-Chair., Acting Chair. and Chair. Ningxia Hui Autonomous Regional People's Govt 1987–97; Deputy Sec. CCP Regional Cttee 1988–97; Sec. CCP Leading Party Group, All-China Fed. of Supply and Marketing Co-operatives 1997–99, Pres. Second Council 1999–2002; Vice-Chair. 9th Nat. Cttee of CPPCC 1998–2003, 10th Nat. Cttee of CPPCC 2003–08, 11th Nat. Cttee of CPPCC 2008–13. *Address:* c/o National Committee of the Chinese People's Political Consultative Conference, 23 Taiping Qiao Street, Beijing, People's Republic of China.

BAI, Shuxian; Chinese ballerina; *Honorary Chairperson, Chinese Dancers Association;* b. 1939; ed Beijing Coll. of Dancing; Prin. Dancer, Cen. Ballet Co. 1958, Dir 1984–90; mem. 5th Nat. Cttee CPPCC 1978–82, 6th Nat. Cttee 1983–87, 7th Nat. Cttee 1988–92, 8th Nat. Cttee 1993–97; Vice-Dir Beijing Ballet 1980–; Performing Artist, Longjiang Opera; Perm. mem. Chinese Dancers Asscn, Chair. 1992–, now Hon. Chair.; Vice-Chair. China Fed. of Literary and Art Circles 1996–; Deputy Chair. China Dramatists' Asscn; First Grade Dancer of the Nation, Chinese Opera Plum Blossom Award, Shanghai Theatrical Festival White Magnolia Prize. *Films:* Absurd Baoyu (Grand Wenhua Prize), The Legend of Hua Mulan (Grand Wenhua Prize, Huabiao Prize, Expert's Golden Rooster Prize) 1994, Saga of Mulan 2004. *Performances include:* Swan Lake, Giselle, The Fountain of Bakhchisarai, The Emerald, Sylvia, Red Women Army, Song of Yimeng, Song of Jiaoyang, The Trilogy, Shuangsuo Mountain. *Address:* Longjiang Opera, No 114, Ashihe Street, Nangong, 150001 Harbin, Heilongjiang Province, People's Republic of China.

BAIBOLOV, Lt-Gen. Kubatbek; Kyrgyzstani politician; b. 2 Jan. 1952, Chong-Aryk Alamedin; m.; two s. six d.; fmr Col, KGB and Head of Intelligence Dept 1991–92; Deputy, Parl. 1995–2007, Speaker 2004–05; Chair. constituent ass. responsible for drafting new Kyrgyz constitution 2006; lived in self-exile in USA 2008–10; First Deputy Chair. Kyrgyz State Cttee for Nat. Security –2010; apptd Commdt, Jalal-Abad Oblast after ethnic clashes 2010; Minister of Internal Affairs June–Sept. 2010; Prosecutor-Gen. 2010–11; Founder and Co-Chair. Union of Democratic Forces 2005; Leader, Kyrgyz Parliamentarians Against Corruption 2005; joined For Reforms! (opposition movt) 2006.

BAIDYA, Mohan, (Kiran); Nepalese politician; *Chairman, Communist Party of Nepal (Maoist);* b. Pyuthan; m. Susma Baidya; three d.; fmr Nepali language teacher in high school in Pyuthan dist; joined Nepal Communist Party 1964; fmr Gen. Sec., Communist Party of Nepal (Masaal), then mem. Unified Communist Party of Nepal (Maoist) (UCPN—M); mem. First Constituent Ass., resgnd 2008; left UCPN—M and co-f. Communist Party of Nepal (Maoist) 2012, now Chair. *Address:* Communist Party of Nepal (Maoist), Kathmandu, Nepal (office).

BAIGUTTIYEV, Zhenishbek S.; Kyrgyzstani politician; b. 9 May 1966, Bishkek; ed Kyrgyz State Univ.; served in Soviet Army Service 1985–87; Chair. Tolubay Bank 1996; Minister of Econ. Regulation 2009. *Address:* c/o Ministry of Economic Regulation, 720003 Bishkek, Kyrgyzstan. *E-mail:* mail@mineconom.kg.

BAIJAL, Anil, MA; Indian public servant and politician; *Lieutenant-Governor of Delhi;* ed Univ. of Allahabad, Univ. of East Anglia; joined Indian Admin. Services (IAS) 1969, various roles including Vice-Chair., Delhi Devt Authority, Chief Sec. of Andaman & Nicobar Islands, Additional Sec., Ministry of Information and Broadcasting, Union Home Sec. Feb.–May 2004, Jt Sec., Ministry of Civil Aviation 2004, Chair. and Man. Dir Indian Airlines, CEO Prasar Bharati (public broadcasting agency), Devt Commr of Goa, Commr (Sales Tax and Excise) of Delhi, Counsellor in charge of Indian Aid Programme in Nepal, Embassy of India, Kathmandu; Sec., Urban Devt Ministry 2006; Chair., Ministry of Corp. Affairs High Level Cttee on Corp. Social Responsibility 2016; Lt-Gov. of Delhi 2016–; fmr mem. Exec. Council Vivekananda Int. Foundation (think tank); Non-Exec. Dir ITC Ltd 2007–09, Ind. Non-Exec. Dir 2010–16; Ind. Dir MMTC Ltd 2009–12; Ind. Non-Exec. Dir International Travel House Ltd 2009–16; Dir Agre Developers Ltd 2010–12 (Chair. –2012). *Address:* Lieutenant Governor's Secretariat, Raj Niwas, Delhi 6, Raj Niwas Marg, New Delhi 110 054, India (office). *Telephone:* (11) 23975022 (office). *Fax:* (11) 23937099 (office). *Website:* lgdelhi.nic.in (office).

BAILEY, Andrew John, BA, PhD; British economist and fmr banking executive; *Chief Executive Officer, Financial Conduct Authority;* b. 30 March 1959; m. Cheryl Schonhardt-Bailey; one s. one d.; ed Queens' Coll., Cambridge; began career as research officer, London School of Econs; joined Bank of England 1985, becoming Private Sec. to Gov. and Head of Int. Econ. Analysis, later Exec. Dir of Banking and Chief Cashier 2004–11, Deputy Gov. for Prudential Regulation 2013–16, CEO, Bank of England Prudential Regulation Authority 2013–16; Deputy Head of Prudential Business Unit and Dir of UK Banks and Building Societies, Financial Services Authority 2011–13 (FSA replaced by Financial Conduct Authority 2013); mem. Bd of Dirs, Financial Conduct Authority 2013–, CEO 2016–. *Address:* Financial Conduct Authority, 25 The North Colonnade, London, E14 5HS, England (office). *Telephone:* (20) 7066-1000 (office). *Website:* www.fca.org.uk (office).

BAILEY, Christopher, MBE, MA; British fashion designer and business executive; b. 1971, Halifax, West Yorks.; m. Simon Woods 2012; two d.; ed Royal Coll. of Art, London; Womenswear Designer, Donna Karan, New York 1994–96; Sr Designer of Womenswear, Gucci, Milan 1996–2001; Design Dir, Burberry 2001–04, Creative Dir 2004–09, Chief Creative Officer 2009–18, CEO 2014–17, Pres. 2017–18, co-f., with Angela Ahrendts, Burberry Foundation 2008; mentor to emerging creative talent from UK insts including RCA and Univ. of Huddersfield; Hon. Fellow, RCA 2003, Arts Univ. Bournemouth 2016; Hon. Patron Univ. Philosophical Soc., Trinity Coll., Dublin 2009; Dr hc (Westminster) 2006, (Huddersfield) 2007, (Sheffield Hallam) 2011, (RCA) 2013; Designer of the Year, British Fashion Awards 2005, Menswear Designer of the Year, British Fashion Awards 2007, 2008, 2013, Designer of the Year, British Fashion Awards 2009, Int. Award Council of Fashion Designers of America 2010, Menswear Designer of the Year, British Fashion Awards 2013.

BAILEY, David, CBE, FRPS, FSIAD, FCSD; British photographer and film director; b. 2 Jan. 1938, London; s. of Herbert William Bailey and Gladys Agnes Bailey; m. 1st Rosemary Bramble 1960; m. 2nd Catherine Deneuve 1965 (divorced 1972); m. 3rd Marie Helvin 1975 (divorced 1985); m. 4th Catherine Dyer 1986; two s. one d.; self-taught; photographer for Vogue, UK, USA, France, Italy and advertising photography 1959–; Dir Commercials 1966–, TV documentaries 1968–; photographer for Harpers and Queen 1999; directed and produced TV film Who Dealt? 1993; documentary: Models Close Up 1998; Dir feature film The Intruder 1999; Dr hc (Bradford) 2001; V&A Award for Outstanding Achievement in Fashion, British Fashion Awards 2004. *Publications:* Box of Pinups 1964, Goodbye Baby and Amen 1969, Warhol 1974, Beady Minces 1974, Mixed Moments 1976, Trouble and Strife 1980, NW1 1982, Black and White Memories 1983, Nudes 1981–84 1984, Imagine 1985, The Naked Eye: Great Photographs of the Nude (with Martin Harrison) 1988, If We Shadows 1992, The Lady is a Tramp 1995, Rock & Roll Heroes 1997, Archive One 1999, Chasing Rainbows 2001, Bailey's Democracy 2005, Pictures that Mark Can Do 2007, Fotographie Portfolio Stern 2007, Is That So Kid 2008, 8 Minutes 2009, EYE 2009, Flowers, Skulls and Contacts 2010, British Heroes in Afghanistan 2010, Delhi Dilemma 2012. *Leisure interests:* photography, aviculture, travel, painting. *E-mail:* studio@camera-eye.co.uk (office).

BAILEY, Donovan; Canadian marketing consultant and fmr athlete; b. 16 Dec. 1967, Manchester, Jamaica; s. of George Donovan and Icilda Donovan; one d. by Michelle Mullin; ed Sheridan Coll.; grew up in Jamaica and emigrated to Canada 1981; mem. Canada's winning 4×100m team, Commonwealth Games 1994, Olympic Games 1996; world indoor record-holder for 50m 1996; Canadian 100m record-holder 1995, 1996; world, Commonwealth and Olympic 100m record-holder 1996; retd from athletics 2001; Pres. and CEO DBX Sport Management; f. Donovan Bailey Fund to assist Canadian amateur athletes; Founder and Chair. Tranz4M 2003; Amb. of Goodwill for Canadian Fed. Govt; mem. Bd of Dirs Big Brothers and Sisters of Canada, ParticipAction Canada, Circle of Champions, Merge Inc.; Sprinter of the Decade, Track and Field News 1998, inducted into Canada's Sports Hall of Fame 2004. *Website:* www.donovanbailey.com.

BAILEY, Jerry D.; American professional jockey (retd) and television analyst; b. 29 Aug. 1957, Dallas, Tex.; s. of James Bailey; m. Suzee; one s.; thoroughbred racing jockey 1974–2006, began career with win at Sunland Park, New Mexico 1974 (Fetch); moved to New York 1982; winner Gulfstream Park Handicap 1990, 1995 (Cigar), 1996, 1997, 1998; 14 Breeders' Cup titles, including Breeders' Cup Classic 1991 (Black Tie Affair), 1993 (Arcangues), 1994 (Concern), (Cigar) 1995, (Saint Liam) 2005, Breeders' Cup Mile (Six Perfections) 2003; winner Belmont 1991 (Hansel); winner Preakness Stakes 1991 (Hansel), 2000 (Red Bullet); winner Hollywood Gold Cup Handicap 1992, 1995 (Cigar), 1998, 1999; winner Woodward Stakes 1992, 1995 (Cigar), 1996 (Cigar), 1998; winner Kentucky Derby 1993 (Sea Hero), 1996 (Grindstone); winner Travers Stakes 1993 (Sea Hero); winner Oaklawn Park Handicap, Pimlico Special, Jockey Club Gold Cup, Don Handicap 1995 (Cigar); winner Massachussets Handicap 1995 (Cigar), 1996 (Cigar), 1998 (Skip Away); winner Dubai World Cup 1996 (Cigar), 1997 (Singspiel), 2001 (Captain Steve); Saratoga riding title 1994, 1995, 1996, 1997, 2000; 16 straight victories on Cigar 1995–96; seven winners on one card, Florida Derby Day 1995; North America's leading money-winning rider 1995–97 and 2001, 2002; first rider to win more than US $20 million in one season (2001); retd with 5,892 career wins 2006; currently TV analyst for ABC and ESPN; Nat. Pres. Jockeys' Guild 1989–96; George Woolf Memorial Jockey Award 1992, Mike Venezia Award (New York Racing Asscn) 1993, Eclipse Award for Outstanding Jockey 1995, 1996, 1997, 2000, 2001, 2002, 2003, elected to racing's Hall of Fame 1995, Broward Co. Sports Hall of Fame 2006. *Publication:* Against the Odds: Riding for My Life (with Tom Pedulla) 2005. *E-mail:* info@jerrybailey.com.

BAILEY, Michael (Mike) J.; British business executive; *Chairman, Elior North America;* s. of Sidney William Bailey and Joyce Mary Bailey; m. Michelle Bailey; one s. three d.; ed Southend Culinary School, Westminster Coll., London; Food Service Man., Gardner Merchant 1961, later becoming Man. Dir, Pres., US subsidiary 1985–91; Exec. Vice-Pres. Nutrition Man. Services 1991–93; joined Compass Group PLC 1993, Group Devt Dir 1993–94, CEO N American Div. 1994–99, Group CEO 1999–2006; Co-founder, Chair. and CEO TrustHouse Services Group 2008–15; Fellow, Hotel and Catering Int. Man. Asscn. *Address:* Elior North America, 300 South Tryon Street, Suite 400, Charlotte, NC 28202, USA (office). *Telephone:* (704) 424-1071 (office). *Fax:* (704) 424-1074 (office). *Website:* elior-na.com (office).

BAILEY, Norman A., PhD; American economist, academic and government official; ed Oberlin Coll. and Columbia Univ.; fmr economist, Mobil Oil Co.; f. Overseas Equity Inc. (later Bailey, Tondu, Warwick & Co., Inc.), Pres. 1980–84; fmr Prof. of Econs, CUNY, now Prof. Emer.; Prof., Center for Strategic and Int. Studies 1980–81; Dir Cttee for Monetary Research and Educ. 1980–81; Sr Dir of Econ. Affairs, Nat. Security Council 1981–83; Special Asst to Pres. Ronald Reagan 1983–89; Pres. Norman A. Bailey Inc. 1984–; Sr Fellow, Potomac Foundation, Inc. 2003–06; Adjunct Prof., Inst. of World Politics, Washington, DC 2003–06, currently Consultant Economist; Mission Man. for Cuba and Venezuela, Office of the Dir of Nat. Intelligence 2006–07; Adviser, Inst. for Global Economic Growth and Vice-Chair. The Americas Forum; Sr Researcher, Center for Nat. Security Studies, Univ. of Haifa; columnist, WorldTribune.com; Kt Royal Order of Our Lady of the Conception of Vila Vicosa (Portugal); Nat. Security Award, Cold War Commemorative Medal, Medal of the Pan American Soc. *Publications:* The Strategic Plan that Won the Cold War 1999; numerous articles in professional journals. *Address:* Institute for Global Economic Growth, 2944 Hunter Mill Road, Suite 204, Oakton, VA 22124, USA (office). *Telephone:* (703) 553-3700 (office). *Website:* www.igeg.org (office).

BAILEY, Paul, FRSL; British writer; b. (Peter Harry Bailey), 16 Feb. 1937; s. of Arthur Oswald Bailey and Helen Maud Burgess; ed Sir Walter St John's School, London; actor 1956–64, appearing in The Sport of My Mad Mother 1958 and Epitaph for George Dillon 1958; Literary Fellow at Univs of Newcastle and Durham 1972–74; Bicentennial Fellowship 1976; Visiting Lecturer in English Literature, North Dakota State Univ. 1977–79; Somerset Maugham Award 1968, E.M. Forster Award 1978, George Orwell Memorial Prize 1978. *Publications include:* At the Jerusalem (Author's Club First Novel Award, Somerset Maugham Award 1968) 1967, Trespasses 1970, A Distant Likeness 1973, Peter Smart's Confessions 1977, Old Soldiers 1980, An English Madam 1982, Gabriel's Lament 1986, An Immaculate Mistake (autobiography) 1990, Hearth and Home 1990, Sugar Cane 1993, The Oxford Book of London (ed.) 1995, First Love (ed.) 1997, Kitty and Virgil 1998, The Stately Homo: A Celebration of the Life of Quentin Crisp (ed.) 2000, Three Queer Lives: An Alternative Biography of Naomi Jacob, Fred Barnes and Arthur Marshall 2001, Uncle Rudolf (novel) 2002, A Dog's Life 2003, Chapman's Odyssey 2011, The Prince's Boy 2014; numerous newspaper articles. *Leisure interests:* visiting churches, opera, watching tennis. *Address:* Rogers, Coleridge and White Ltd., 20 Powis Mews, London W11 1JN, England (office); 2/79 Davisville Road, London, W12 9SH, England (home). *Telephone:* (20) 7221-3717 (office); (20) 8248-2127 (home). *Fax:* (20) 7229-9084 (office). *E-mail:* info@rcwlitagency.com (office). *Website:* www.rcwlitagency.com (office).

BAILEY, Sly; British publishing and media executive; b. (Sylvia Grice), 24 Jan. 1962, London; d. of Thomas Lewis and Sylvia Grice (née Bantick); m. Peter Bailey 1998; ed St Saviours and St Olaves Grammar School for Girls; telephone sales exec. at The Guardian 1984–87; Advertisement Sales Man., The Independent 1987–89; moved to IPC Magazines 1989, Advertising Sales Exec. 1994, mem. Bd of Dirs 1994–2003, Man. Dir TX 1997, CEO 1999–2003; mem. Bd of Dirs and CEO Trinity Mirror PLC 2003–12; Dir (non-exec.) Littlewoods PLC April–Sept. 2002, EMI 2004–07 (Sr Ind. Dir 2007), Ladbrokes 2009–, Greencore 2013–; mem. Ind. Panel on BBC Charter Review 2004; Dir The Press Asscn –2012; Pres. NewstrAid Benevolent Soc. –2014; Gov. English National Ballet School; Dr hc (Univ. of East London) 2005; Periodical Publrs Asscn Marcus Morris Award for Outstanding Contrib. to Publishing Industry 2002. *Leisure interest:* family. *Address:* c/o Board of Directors, Ladbrokes plc, Imperial House, Imperial Drive, Rayners Lane, Harrow, HA2 7JW, England.

BAILIE, Robert Ernest (Roy), OBE; British business executive; *Chairman, The Baird Group;* b. 2 June 1943; s. of Robert Bailie and Rosetta Bailie; ed Harvard Business School, USA; joined W&G Baird (later The Baird Group) 1965, Man. Dir 1972, Dir 1977–, Chair. 1982–; Chair. CBI, Northern Ireland 1992–94, Northern Ireland Tourist Bd 1996–2002, 105.8 FM 2005–; Vice-Pres. British Printing Industries Fed. 1997–99, Pres. 1999–2001; Dir Graphic Plates Ltd 1977–, MSO Ltd 1984–2013; Dir (non-exec.) Blackstaff Press Ltd 1995–, UTV 1997–2013, Court, Bank of England 1998–2003, Court, Bank of Ireland 1999–2005, Corporate Document Services Ltd 2000–; Chair. Northern Ireland Opera 2010–, National Trust (Northern Ireland) 2010–16. *Leisure interests:* golf, sailing, walking. *Address:* Baird Group, Greystone Press, Greystone Road, Antrim, BT41 2RS, Northern Ireland (office). *Telephone:* (28) 9446-6107 (office). *Fax:* (28) 9446-6266 (office). *E-mail:* roy.bailie@thebairdgroup.co.uk (office). *Website:* www.thebairdgroup.co.uk (office).

BAILLIE, A. Charles, Jr, OC, BA, MBA, DJur; Canadian fmr banker; b. 20 Dec. 1939, Orillia, Ont.; s. of Charles Baillie and Jean G. Baillie; m. Marilyn J. Michener 1965; three s. one d.; ed Trinity Coll., Univ. of Toronto, Harvard Business School, USA, Queen's Univ.; joined The Toronto Dominion Bank 1964, Vice-Pres. and Gen. Man., USA Div. 1979, Sr Vice-Pres. 1981, Exec. Vice-Pres., Corp. and Investment Banking Group 1984, Vice-Chair. 1992, Pres. The Toronto Dominion Bank 1995, CEO 1997–2002, Chair. 1998–2003 (retd); Chancellor, Queen's Univ. 2002–08, Chancellor Emer. 2008–; fmr Pres. Art Gallery of Ont.; mem. Bd of Dirs Telus Corpn 2003–15, Canadian Nat. Railway Co. 2003–15, Dana Corpn, Ballard Power Systems, George Weston Ltd; Chair. Campaign 2000, United Way of Greater Toronto; Chair. Capital Campaign, Shaw Festival; Campaign Co-Chair. Nature Conservancy; Campaign Hon. Chair. Sir Sam Steele Art Gallery; Vice-Chair. Exec. Cttee Business Council on Nat. Issues; mem. Corpn and Hon. Cabinet, Trinity Coll.; Fellow, Inst. of Canadian Bankers 1967; Hon. LLD (Queen's Univ.) 2000. *Leisure interests:* birdwatching, travelling, collecting antiquarian books.

BAILLY, Jean-Paul, MSc; French engineer and business executive; b. 29 Nov. 1946, Hénin-Beaumont (Pas-de-Calais); s. of Jean Bailly and Hélène Bailly (née Viénot); m. Michèle Moulard 1972; two s.; ed Lycées d'Oujda, Morocco, Louis-le-Grand and Ecole polytechnique, Paris, Massachusetts Inst. of Tech., USA; engineer, Regie Autonome des Transports Parisiens (RATP) 1970, Chief Consultant SOFRETU for Mexico City Metro 1978–81, Sr Engineer 1981–88, Personnel Dir 1989, Jt Dir-Gen. 1990–94, Pres. and Dir-Gen. 1994–97; Pres. Int. Union of Public Transport (UITP) 1997–2001; Chair., Pres. and CEO La Poste 2002–13, Chair. Supervisory Bd La Banque Postale 2006–13; Pres. French Section, Centre européen des entreprises à participation publique (CEEP) 1998–2001, Int. Post Corpn 2006–; mem. Supervisory Bd La Banque Postale Asset Management, Sogeposte; mem. Bd of Dirs CNP Assurances SA 2007–, GDF Suez 2008–12, Accor SA 2009–, Edenred 2010–, Gaz de France SA, SF2 and Systar SA, Sofipost, Geopost, Xelian, SF 12, Efipost, Poste Immo, Sopassure, The Jean-Jacques Laffont-Toulouse School of Econs Foundation, Fondation du Collège de France, Groupement des Commerçants du Grand Var intercompany partnership; mem. Conseil Economique, Social et Environnemental (Econ., Social and Environmental Advisory Cttee) 1995–; Officier, Légion d'honneur, Ordre nat. du Mérite; Dr hc (Univ. of Montreal); Pitney Bowes Industry Leadership Award, World Mail Awards, London 2007. *Publications:* Tomorrow is already there: prospective, debate, public decision 1999, The challenges of public transport in European cities 2000, Reform! Through dialogue and trust 2016. *Leisure interest:* tennis.

BAILY, Martin Neil, PhD; American economist and fmr government official; *Senior Fellow, Brookings Institution;* b. 13 Jan. 1945, Exeter, England; s. of Theodore Baily and Joyce Baily; m. Vickie Lyn Baily (née Hyde) 1986; two s. two d.; ed King Edward's School, Birmingham, Christ's Coll., Cambridge, Massachusetts Inst. of Tech.; teaching positions at MIT and Yale Univ. 1972–79; Sr Fellow, Brookings Inst. 1979–94, 1996–99, 2007–, also Bernard L. Schwartz Chair in Econ. Policy Devt and Dir Business and Public Policy Initiative; Prof. of Econs, Univ. of Maryland 1989–94; mem. Council of Econ. Advisers 1994–96 during Clinton administration, Chair. and mem. of the Cabinet 1999–2001; Prin. McKinsey and Co. 1996–99, Sr Advisor 2002–; Sr Fellow, Peterson Inst., Washington, DC 2001–07; Sr Dir Albright Stonebridge Group; Co-Chair. Bipartisan Policy Center Financial Reform Initiative; mem. Bd of Dirs The Phoenix Companies; mem. Squam Lake Group (financial economists); Prizewinner in Econs, Christ's Coll., Cambridge 1967. *Publications:* Macroeconomics, Financial Markets and the International Sector 1994, Efficiency in Manufacturing (Brookings Papers) 1995, Economic Report of the President: 2000, Transforming the European Economy (co-author) 2004. *Leisure interests:* squash, music, travel. *Address:* Brookings Institution, 1775 Massachusetts Avenue, NW, Washington, DC 20036, USA (office). *Website:* www.brookings.edu (office).

BAILYN, Bernard, PhD; American historian, author and academic; *Professor Emeritus of History, Harvard University;* b. 10 Sept. 1922, Hartford, Conn.; s. of Charles Manuel Bailyn and Esther Schloss; m. Lotte Bailyn (née Lazarsfeld) 1952; two s.; ed Williams Coll. and Harvard Univ.; joined Faculty, Harvard Univ. 1953, Prof. of History 1961–66, Winthrop Prof. of History 1966–81, Adams Univ. Prof. 1981–93, Prof. Emer. 1993–, James Duncan Phillips Prof. in Early American History 1991–93, Prof. Emer. 1993–; Dir Charles Warren Center for Studies in American History 1983–94; Pitt Prof. of American History, Univ. of Cambridge, UK 1986–87; Dir Int. Seminar on History of Atlantic World 1995–; Ed.-in-Chief John Harvard Library 1962–70; Co-Ed. Perspectives in American History (journal) 1967–77, 1984–86; mem. American Historical Asscn (Pres. 1981), American Acad. of Arts and Sciences, Nat. Acad. of Educ., American Philosophical Soc.; Foreign mem. Russian Acad. of Sciences, Academia Europaea, Mexican Acad. of History and Geography; Sr Fellow, Soc. of Fellows; Hon. Fellow Christ's Coll., Cambridge Univ.; Corresp. Fellow, British Acad. 1989, Royal Historial Soc.; Trustee, Inst. of

Advanced Study, Princeton 1989–94; Trevelyan Lecturer, Cambridge Univ. 1971; Jefferson Lecturer, Nat. Endowment for the Humanities 1998; 15 hon. degrees; Robert H. Lord Award, Emmanuel Coll. 1967, Pulitzer Prize for History 1968, 1987, Thomas Jefferson Medal 1993, Henry Allen Moe Prize, American Philosophical Soc. 1994, Foreign Policy Assen Medal 1998; Catton Prize, Soc. American Historians 2000, Nat. Humanities Medal 2010, Samuel Eliot Morison Award 2011. *Publications include:* The New England Merchants in the 17th Century 1955, Massachusetts Shipping 1697–1714: A Statistical Study (jtly) 1959, Education in the Forming of American Society 1960, Pamphlets of the American Revolution 1750–1776, Vol. I (ed.) (Faculty Prize, Harvard Univ. Press) 1965, The Apologia of Robert Keayne (ed.) 1965, The Ideological Origins of the American Revolution (Pulitzer and Bancroft Prizes 1968) 1967, The Origins of American Politics 1968, The Intellectual Migration 1930–1960 (co-ed.) 1969, Law in American History (co-ed.) 1972, The Ordeal of Thomas Hutchinson (Nat. Book Award 1975) 1974, The Great Republic (co-author) 1977, The Press and the American Revolution (co-ed.) 1980, The Peopling of British North America 1986, Voyagers to the West (Pulitzer Prize 1986) 1986, Faces of Revolution 1990, Strangers Within the Realm (co-ed.) 1991, The Debate on the Constitution (two vols, ed.) 1993, On the Teaching and Writing of History 1994, To Begin the World Anew: The Genius and Ambiguities of the American Founders 2003, Atlantic History 2005, The Barbarous Years 2012. *Address:* Atlantic History Seminar, Emerson Hall, 4th Floor, Harvard University, Cambridge, MA 02138 (office); 170 Clifton Street, Belmont, MA 02478-2604, USA (home). *E-mail:* bailyn@fas.harvard.edu. *Website:* www.fas.harvard.edu/~atlantic.

BAINDURASHVILI, Kakha, MA; Georgian business executive and fmr government official; *President, Chamber of Commerce and Industry of Georgia;* b. 26 Sept. 1978, Tbilisi; ed Tbilisi State Univ., Williams Coll., USA; Ed. Prime-News news agency, Tbilisi 1999–2000; Chief Specialist, Ministry of Finance 2000–01; consultant, UNDP 2002–04; 2004–2005 Deputy Chair. of Supervisory Council, state-owned Georgian Railways Ltd 2004–05; adviser to the Prime Minister 2005–06; Chair. Tax Dept, Ministry of Finance 2006–07, First Deputy Minister of Finance 2007–09, Minister of Finance 2009–11; fmr Gov. for Georgia and Vice-Chair. Bd of Govs Asian Devt Bank; Chair. Supervisory Bd state-owned Georgian Post 2011–12; Chair. Exec. Bd Georgian Lottery Co. 2011–12; Pres. Chamber of Commerce and Industry of Georgia 2011–; Dir-Gen. TV-3 2013–14; mem. Council, GLG – Gerson Lehrman Group 2011–. *Address:* Georgian Chamber of Commerce and Industry, 150, D. Agmashenebeli Avenue, 0112 Tbilisi, Georgia (office). *Website:* www.gcci.ge (office).

BAINIMARAMA, Rear Adm. (retd) Josaia Voreqe, (Frank Bainimarama), CF, MSD, OStJ; Fijian fmr naval officer and politician; *Prime Minister and Minister for iTaukei Affairs, Sugar Industry and Foreign Affairs;* b. 27 April 1954, Kiuva, Tailevu Prov.; m. Maria Makitalena; six c.; ed Maris Brothers High School, numerous mil. courses and insts; enlisted in Fiji Navy as Ordinary Seaman 1975, commissioned as Ensign 1977, Navigation Officer Aug. 1978, Sub-Lt Nov. 1978, Exec. Officer HMFS Kiro 1979, Commdr HMFS Kikau 1982–84, HMFS Kula 1984–86, Lt Commdr 1986, served with Multinational Force and Observers in Sinai 1986–87, CO and Commdr Fiji Navy 1988, promoted to Capt. 1994, Chief of Staff 1997–99, Cdre and Commdr of Armed Forces 1999–2014; promoted to Rear Adm. March 2014; Head, Interim Mil. Govt of Fiji May–July 2000; Acting Pres. of Fiji (after mil. overthrow of govt of Prime Minister Laisenia Qarase) Dec. 2006–07, Prime Minister Jan. 2007– (formally sworn in Sept. 2014), also Minister of Home Affairs, Immigration and Information 2007, Minister of Finance 2008, Minister for iTaukei Affairs and Sugar Industry 2014–, also Minister for Foreign Affairs 2016–, acting Minister for Education, Heritage, Arts and Nat. Archives 2017; fmr Chair. Fiji Rugby Union; Companion of the Order of Fiji, Meritorious Service Decoration; Most Venerable Order of the Hosp. of Saint John of Jerusalem; Peacekeeping Medal, General Service Medal, Fiji Republic Medal, 25th Anniversary Medal. *Address:* Office of the Prime Minister, PO Box 2353, New Government Buildings, Suva, Fiji (office). *Telephone:* 3211201 (office). *Fax:* 3306034 (office). *E-mail:* pmsoffice@connect.com.fj (office). *Website:* www.pmoffice.gov.fj (office).

BAINS, Navdeep Singh, PC, MP, MBA; Canadian accountant and politician; *Minister of Innovation, Science and Economic Development;* b. 16 June 1977, Toronto; s. of Balwinder Bains and Harminder Bains; m. Brahamjot Bains; two d.; ed York Univ., Univ. of Windsor; certified management accountant; Financial Processing Analyst, Nike Canada 2000–01; Accounting and Financial Analyst, Ford Motor Co. of Canada 2000–04; mem., House of Commons (Parl.) for Mississauga–Brampton South 2004–11, for Mississauga-Malton 2015–; Parl. Sec. to Prime Minister Paul Martin 2005–06; Minister of Innovation, Science and Econ. Devt 2015–; fmr Adjunct Lecturer, Univ. of Waterloo; Distinguished Visiting Prof., Ryerson Univ. Ted Rogers School of Man. 2013–15; Dir Municipal Property Assessment Corpn 2012–15; mem. Bd of Dirs Mississauga Food Bank, Ont. Heart and Stroke Foundation; worked with Juvenile Diabetes Research Foundation and Guru Gobind Singh Children's Foundation; mem. Liberal Party of Canada. *Address:* Industry Canada, C. D. Howe Bldg, 11th Floor, East Tower, 235 Queen Street, Ottawa, ON K1A 0H5, Canada (office). *Telephone:* (613) 954-5031 (office). *Fax:* (613) 954-2340 (office). *E-mail:* info@ic.gc.ca (office). *Website:* www.ic.gc.ca (office); navdeepbains.liberal.ca.

BAINWOL, Mitch, BA, MBA; American business executive; *President and CEO, Alliance of Automobile Manufacturers;* b. 2 March 1959, Munich, Germany; m. Susan Bainwol; three c.; ed Georgetown Univ., Rice Univ.; fmr Budget Analyst, Pres. Ronald Reagan's Office of Management and Budget, Chief of Staff Senator Connie Mack (R-FL); Leadership Staff Dir Senate 1993–97; Chief of Staff Republican Nat. Cttee 1998; lobbyist Clark & Weinstock 1999; Leader The Bainwol Group 2002–; Chair. and CEO Recording Industry Assen of America (RIAA) 2003–11; Pres. and CEO Alliance of Automobile Manufacturers 2011–; mem. Bd of Dirs Nat. Fatherhood Initiative, Bryce Harlow Foundation, Leadership Music Foundation. *Address:* Alliance of Automobile Manufacturers, 1401 Eye Street, NW, Suite 900, Washington, DC 20005, USA (office). *Telephone:* (202) 326-5500 (office). *Website:* www.autoalliance.org (office).

BAÏPO TÉMON, Sylvie, BEcons; Central African Republic economist and politician; *Minister of Foreign Affairs and Central Africans Abroad;* ed Paris X Nanterre Univ., Univ. of Poitiers, Univ. of Orléans; Researcher, Foreign Trade Dept, BRED Banque Populaire, Paris 1998–2000; Consultant, Deloitte France, Neuilly sur Seine 2000–03; Accounting and Financial Analyst, BNP Paribas Group 2003–08, Head, Accounting Standards, Credit and Savings Sector 2008–13, Man., Accounting Standards Office 2013–18; spokesperson for Central African Repub. diaspora group 2014–15; Minister of Foreign Affairs and Central Africans Abroad 2018–. *Address:* Ministry of Foreign Affairs and Central Africans Abroad, Bangui, Central African Republic (office).

BAIR, Sheila Colleen, BA, JD; American academic, college administrator, author and fmr banking official; *President, Washington College;* b. 3 April 1954, Wilchita, Kan.; d. of Albert Bair and Clara Bair (née Brenneman); m. Scott P. Cooper; one s. one d.; ed Univ. of Kansas, Univ. of Kansas School of Law; called to the Bar, Kan. 1979; Teaching Fellow, Univ. of Arkansas School of Law 1978–79; Advisor, Kan. State Dept of Health 1979–81; Research Dir, Deputy Counsel and Counsel to Senate Majority Leader Robert Dole 1981–88; Of Counsel, Kutak, Rock & Campbell (law firm) 1986–87; Legis. Counsel, New York Stock Exchange, Washington, DC 1988–91, Sr Vice-Pres. for Govt Relations 1995–2000; Commr US Commodity Futures Trading Comm. 1991–95, Acting Chair. 1993; Asst Sec. for Financial Insts, US Dept of the Treasury 2001–02; Dean's Prof. of Financial Regulatory Policy, Isenberg School of Man., Univ. of Massachusetts-Amherst 2002–06; Chair. Fed. Deposit Insurance Corpn 2006–11; Sr Advisor, Pew Charitable Trusts 2011–15; Pres. Washington Coll. 2015–; mem. Insurance Marketplace Standards Asscn, Women in Housing and Finance, Center for Responsible Lending, NASD Ahead-of-the-Curve Advisory Cttee, Mass Savings Makes Cents, ABA, Exchequer Club, Soc. of Children's Book Writers and Illustrators; mem. Bd of Dirs, Thomson Reuters Corpn 2014–, Industrial and Commercial Bank of China Ltd 2017–; The Treasury Medal 2002, Distinguished Achievement Award, Asscn of Educ. Publrs 2005, Personal Service Feature of the Year, Author of the Month Award, Highlights Magazine for Children 2002, 2003, 2004, Philip Hart Public Service Award, Consumer Fed. of America 2009, Admin. of the Year, Romney Inst. of Public Man. 2012. *Publications:* Rock, Brock, and the Savings Shock 2006, Isabel's Car Wash 2008, Bull by the horns: fighting to save Main Street from Wall Street and Wall Street from itself 2012, The Bullies of Wall Street: This Is How Greed Messed Up Our Economy 2016. *Address:* Washington College, 300 Washington Avenue, Charlestown, MD 21620, USA (office). *Telephone:* (410) 778-2800 (office). *Fax:* (800) 422-1782 (office). *E-mail:* sbair2@washcoll.edu (office). *Website:* www.washcoll.edu (office).

BAIRAMOV, Maj. Dovrangeldy; Turkmenistani government official; Deputy Minister of Nat. Security –2011; apptd Head of State Migration Agency 2011; Head of State Customs Service –2016; Minister of Nat. Security 2016–18.

BAIRD, Hon. John Russell (Rusty), PC, BA; Canadian politician; b. 26 May 1969, Ottawa, Ont.; ed Queen's Univ., Kingston, Ont.; Pres. youth wing of Ont. Progressive Conservative Party late 1980s; worked on political staff of Perrin Beatty, Fed. Minister of Nat. Defence, and through subsequent cabinet shifts early 1990s; worked as a lobbyist in Ottawa 1993–95; MPP (Conservative Party of Canada) for Nepean, Legis. Ass. of Ont. 1995–99, for Nepean—Carleton 1999–2005, Parl. Asst to Minister of Labour 1995–97, Parl. Asst to Chair. Man. Bd of Cabinet April–Nov. 1997, Parl. Asst to Minister of Finance Nov. 1997–99, Minister of Community and Social Services and Minister responsible for Francophone Affairs 1999–2002, Minister responsible for Children 2001–02, Chief Govt Whip and Assoc. Minister for Francophone Affairs April–Aug. 2002, Minister for Energy Aug. 2002–03, Leader of Govt in Ont. Legislature 2003, Official Opposition Critic for Finance, Culture, Francophone Affairs, Intergovernmental Affairs and Health 2003–05; Co-Chair. Ont. Conservative Party for fed. elections 2004; left prov. politics to campaign for Fed. House of Commons 2005; MP for Ottawa West-Nepean 2006–, Leader of the Govt in House of Commons 2010–11; Pres. Treasury Bd 2006–07, also held ministerial responsibilities for Harbourfront Centre and Toronto Waterfront Revitalization Corpn; Minister of the Environment 2007–08, of Transport, Infrastructure and Communities 2008–10, of the Environment 2010–11, of Foreign Affairs 2011–15; mem. Royal Canadian Legion (Bell's Corners Br.); Life mem. Asscn for Community Living; Hon. mem. Nepean Kiwanis. *Address:* c/o Foreign Affairs and International Trade Canada, Lester B. Pearson Bldg, 125 Sussex Drive, Ottawa, ON K1A 0G2, Canada (office). *E-mail:* bairdj@parl.gc.ca (office). *Website:* www.johnbaird.com.

BAIRD, Nicholas (Nick) Graham Faraday, CMG, CVO; British diplomatist and business executive; *Group Corporate Affairs Director, Centrica plc;* b. 15 May 1962; m. Caroline; one s. two d.; Third, later Second Sec. (Chancery), Kuwait 1986–89, First Sec. (Econ./Finance), UK Representation to EU, Brussels 1989–93, Pvt. Sec. to Parl. Under-Sec. of State, FCO 1993–95, Head of Amsterdam IGC Unit, EU Dept (Internal) 1995–97, Deputy Head of Mission, Muscat 1997–98, Counsellor (Justice and Home Affairs), UK Representation to EU, Brussels 1998–2002, Head of EU Dept (Internal) 2002–03, on secondment to Immigration and Nationality Directorate at Home Office as Dir of Int. Delivery 2003–04, as Sr Policy Dir 2004–06, Amb. to Turkey 2006–09, Dir-Gen. for Europe and Globalization, FCO 2009–11, Chief Exec. UK Trade & Investment 2011–13; Group Corp. Affairs Dir, Centrica plc 2014–. *Address:* Centrica plc, Millstream, Maidenhead Road, Windsor, Berks., SL4 5GD, England (office). *Telephone:* (1753) 494000 (office). *Fax:* (1753) 494001 (office). *E-mail:* info@centrica.com (office). *Website:* www.centrica.com (office).

BAIS, Ramesh; Indian agriculturalist and politician; b. 2 Aug. 1947, Raipur, Chhattisgarh; s. of Khomlal Bais and Kejabai Bais; m. Rambai Bais; one s. two d.; ed B.S.E., Bhopal, Madhya Pradesh; Councillor, Raipur Municipal Corpn 1978–83; mem. Madhya Pradesh Legis. Ass. 1980–84, mem. Estimates Cttee 1980–82, Library Cttee 1982–84; elected mem. Lok Sabha (Parl.) 1989, re-elected 1996, 1998, 2004, 2009, Chair. Standing Cttee on Social Justice & Empowerment; Union Minister of State for Steel and Mines 1998–99, for Information and Broadcasting 2000–03, for Ministry of Mines 2003–04, for Environment and Forests Jan.–May 2004; mem. Pradesh Mantri Bharatiya Janata Party (BJP), Madhya Pradesh 1982–88, Vice-Pres. 1989–90, 1994–96, mem. BJP Nat. Exec. 1993–; Chair. Seed and Agricultural Devt Corpn of Madhya Pradesh 1992–93; Pres. Chhattisgarh Archery Olympic Asscn. *Leisure interests:* woodcrafting, painting, interior decoration, gardening. *Address:* 85, Lodhi Estate, New Delhi 110 003 (home); 9 Ravi Nagar, Raipur 492 001 India (home). *Telephone:* (11) 24634315 (home); (11) 24692730 (home); (0771) 2423000 (Raipur) (home). *Fax:* (11) 24692731 (home); (0771) 2423000 (Raipur) (home). *E-mail:* rameshbais47@gmail.com (home). *Website:* www.bjp.org; www.india.gov.in (office); loksabha.nic.in (office).

BAJAJ, Rahul, BA, LLB, MBA; Indian automobile industry executive; *Chairman, Bajaj Group;* b. 10 June 1938, Bengal Presidency, British India (now Kolkata); s. of Kamalnayan Bajaj and Savitri Bajaj; m. Rupa Bajaj 1961; two s. one d.; ed St Stephen's Coll., Delhi, Govt Law Coll., Bombay (now Mumbai), Harvard Univ., USA; Dir Bajaj Group 1956–60, CEO 1968, Chair. and Man. Dir 1972–2008, Chair. 2008–; Chair. Devt Council for Automobiles and Allied Industries 1975–77, Maharashtra Scooters Ltd 1975–2006, Indian Airlines 1986–89, Tech. Devt Advisory Group 1991; Pres. Asscn of Indian Automobile Mfrs 1976–78, Mahratta Chamber of Commerce and Industries 1983–85, Confed. of Indian Industry 1979–80, 1999–2000; Vice-Chair., Chair. and Dir Mukand Group 1994–2007; apptd Chair. Bd of Govs, Indian Inst. of Tech., Mumbai 2003; elected to Rajya Sabha (Parl.) 2006; fmr Co-Chair. Commonwealth Business Council; mem. Exec. Cttee Confed. of Eng Industry 1978 (Pres. 1979–80), Governing Council, Automotive Research Asscn of India 1972, Devt Council for Automobiles and Allied Industries 1987, World Econ. Forum Advisory Council 1984, Prince of Wales Int. Business Leaders Forum 1992, Indo-German Consultative Group 1992, Soc. of Indian Automobile Mfrs; mem. Global Advisory Bd, Indian School of Business, Harvard Business School, Int. Advisory Cttee, NYSE Euronext, Int. Advisory Council, Brookings Inst.; Dr hc (Indian Inst. of Tech., Roorkee) 2005, (Rani Durgavati Vishwa Vidyalaya) 2005; Man of the Year Award, Nat. Inst. of Quality Assurance 1975, Business Man of the Year Award, Business India Magazine 1985, Bombay Man. Asscn Award 1990, Rashtrabhushan Award 1996, Lokmanya Tilak Award 2000, Padma Bhushan 2001, Jeevan Sadhana Gaurav Puraskar, Pune Univ. 2002, Economic Times Life Time Achievement Award 2004, Ernst & Young Life Time Achievement Award 2004, Alumni Achievement Award, Harvard Business School 2005, Marathwada Mitra Puraskar, Marathwada Lok Vikas Manch 2006, JRD Tata Corp. Leadership Award, All India Man. Asscn 2007. *Address:* Bajaj Auto Ltd, Akurdi, Pune 411 035 (office); 4 Meena Bagh, New Delhi 110 002, India (home). *Telephone:* (20) 27472851 (office); (20) 27476151 (office); (11) 23795255 (home). *Fax:* (11) 23795055 (home). *E-mail:* rahulbajaj@bajajauto.co.in (office); rahul.bajaj@sansad.nic.in (office). *Website:* www.bajajauto.com (office).

BAJNAI, (György) Gordon; Hungarian economist, business executive and politician; *Group Chief Operating Officer, Meridiam;* b. 5 March 1968, Szeged; m. (separated); two c. and two c. with current partner; ed Budapest Univ. of Econ. Sciences; with Creditum (financial consulting co.) 1991–93; consultant, EUROCORP Int. Finance plc 1993–94; Dir Corp. Finance and Equity Capital Market Div., CA IB Securities plc 1995–2000; CEO Wallis PLC 2000–05, mem. Bd of Dirs 2000–06, Vice-Pres. 2006; Pres. Budapest Airport Inc. 2005; Chair. Budapest Airport PLC 2006; Govt Commr for Devt Policy 2006–07; Minister of Local Govt and Regional Devt 2007–08, of Nat. Devt and Economy 2008–09; Prime Minister 2009–10; f. Patriotism and Progress Public Policy Foundation (Haza és Haladás Közpolitikai Alapítvány) 2011; Leader of Together 2014 (Együtt 2014, officially Together—Party for a New Era (Együtt—A Korszakváltók Pártja)) 2012–14, Head of party's Nat. Bd 2014–; Group COO Meridiam investment fund, Paris 2014–; Adjunct Prof. of Int. and Public Affairs, Columbia Univ., New York, USA 2011; mem. Bd of Dirs Danubius Radio 1998–99, Graboplast PLC 2001–04, Rába PLC 2003–05; mem. Investment Cttee Equinox Pvt. Equity Fund 1999; mem. Supervisory Bd Zwack Inc. 2003–06; mem. Econ. Council, Budapest Univ. of Econ. Sciences 2006; Officer's Cross, Order of Merit 2006; Pro Universitate 1994, voted one of the 30 most promising Cen.–Eastern European business execs by Central European Business Review 1999, Young Manager of the Year, Nat. Asscn of Managers 2003. *Leisure interests:* football (plays as goalkeeper for Építők SK football club, Footballer of the Year 2001). *Address:* Meridiam, 4 place de l'Opéra, 75002 Paris, France (office); Együtt 2014 (Together 2014), 1122 Budapest, Városmajor u. 48/b, Hungary. *Telephone:* 1-53-34-96-96 (office); (1) 919-1414. *Fax:* 1-53-34-96-99 (office). *E-mail:* meridiam@meridiam.com (office). *Website:* www.meridiam.com (office).

BAJO, Lamin Kaba, MA; Gambian politician, diplomatist and sports administrator; *President, Gambia Football Federation;* b. 10 Nov. 1964, Brikama; m. Mariama Jarju-Bajo; several c.; ed Muslim High School, Univ. of Leicester, UK; joined gendarmerie 1984, rose to position of commdr in mil. police 1989, subsequently Deputy Commdr Mobile Gendarmerie; served as Presidential Guard at State House before coup of 22 July 1994; apptd Commr Western Div. 1994; mem. Armed Forces Provisional Ruling Council 1995; Minister for Interior and Religious Affairs 1995–98, served in Ministry of Youth and Sports 1997 and Ministry for Local Govt and Lands 1998; Amb. to Saudi Arabia 2002–05, Perm. Rep. to OIC; Sec. of State for Foreign Affairs 2005–06; Amb. to Iran 2007–09, to Qatar 2009; Minister of Fisheries, Water Resources and Religious Affairs 2010–11, of Fisheries, Water Resources and Nat. Ass. Matters 2011–12, of the Interior 2012; Amb. to Morocco 2012; Pres. KGI Football Club, Gambia Football Fed. 2014–; Gen. Service Medal, Long Service and Good Conduct Medal, Order of the Repub. of The Gambia, Al Noot (Libya). *Leisure interests:* jogging, watching and listening to world and current affairs, watching sports, farming, reading. *Website:* www.fifa.com/associations/association=gam.

BAJWA, Gen. Qamar Javed; Pakistani army officer; *Chief of Army Staff;* b. 11 Nov. 1960, Karachi; s. of Muhammad Iqbal Bajwa; ed Pakistan Mil. Acad., Canadian Army Command and Staff Coll., Nat. Defence Univ., Pakistan; commissioned into 16 Baloch Regt, Pakistan Army Oct. 1980, command roles have included Force Commdr of Gilgit-Baltistan, commanded brigade with UN peacekeeping mission in Congo 2007, fmr Instructor, School of Infantry and Tactics, Quetta, Command and Staff Coll., Quetta and Nat. Defence Univ., Pakistan, Commdr, X Corps, Rawalpindi 2013–15, Col Commdt, Baloch Regt 2014, Inspector Gen. of Training and Evaluation 2015–16, Chief of Army Staff 2016–; attained rank of Maj.-Gen. 2009, Lt-Gen. 2013, Four Star Gen. 2016; Hilal-i-Imtiaz (Mil.) 2011. *Address:* Pakistan Army General Headquarters, Peshawar Road, Rawalpindi, Pakistan (office). *Telephone:* (51) 9271600 (office). *Website:* www.pakistanarmy.gov.pk (office).

BAJWA, Tariq, MPA; Pakistani government official and central banker; *Governor, State Bank of Pakistan;* ed Kennedy School of Govt, Harvard Univ., Nat. School of Public Policy Lahore, Nat. Inst. of Public Admin; past positions held include Asst Commr and Deputy Commr both in the Fed. and Prov. Secr.; fmr Dir-Gen. Planning and Finance, Earthquake Reconstruction & Rehabilitation Authority (ERRA) UNDP; Gen. Man., Pakistan Int. Airlines 1992–96; Head, Pakistan Trade Mission, Los Angeles 1999–2004; Sec. of Finance, Punjab 2010–13; Dir Board of Bank of Punjab 2010–13; Chair. Fed. Bd of Revenue 2013–15; Sec. Economic Affairs Div. and then Sec. of Finance 2015–17; Gov. State Bank of Pakistan 2017–. *Address:* I.I. Chundrigar Road, Karachi, Pakistan (office). *Telephone:* 111-727-111 (office). *E-mail:* info@sbp.org.pk (office). *Website:* www.sbp.org.pk.

BAKA, András B., JSD, PhD; Hungarian judge and professor of law; b. 11 Dec. 1952, Budapest; ed St Stephen's High School, Budapest and Eötvös Loránd Univ., Budapest; Research Fellow, Comparative Law Dept, Inst. for Legal and Admin. Sciences of Hungarian Acad. of Sciences 1978–82, Sr Research Fellow, Constitutional and Admin. Dept 1982–90; Prof. of Constitutional Law, Budapest School of Public Admin. 1990–; Dir-Gen. and Pres. Bd Budapest School of Public Admin. 1990–; mem. Parl. and Sec., Human Rights Comm. of Hungarian Parl. 1990–91; Judge, European Court of Human Rights 1991–2008, Section Vice-Pres. 2000–08; Chief Justice, Supreme Court 2009–11; Pres. Network of the Presidents of the Supreme Judicial Courts of the EU –2011, Hon. Pres. 2011–; Visiting Prof., Brown Univ. 1986, Univ. of Virginia 1987, Univ. of Calif., Berkeley 1987, Columbia Univ. 1987; Prof., Santa Clara Univ. School of Law, Inst. of Int. and Comparative Law, Santa Clara, Calif. 1991; Hon. Pres. Scientist Award, Hungarian Acad. of Sciences 1988. *Publications:* several publs on minority rights. *Address:* c/o Network of the Presidents of the Supreme Courts of the European Union, 5 quai de l'Horloge, 75001 Paris, France.

BAKANI, Loi Martin, BEcons, MEconSc; Papua New Guinea economist and central banker; *Governor, Bank of Papua New Guinea;* b. 12 Aug. 1963, Kulungi village, Talasea; m.; three c.; ed Univ. of Papua New Guinea, Univ. of Wollongong, Australia; joined Bank of Papua New Guinea as Research Officer, Monetary and Banking Div. of Econs Dept 1985, Head of Econs Dept and Chief Econ. Adviser for the Bank 1998–2005, Deputy Gov. 2005–09, Gov. 2009–; mem. Papua New Guinea Inst. of Dirs, Australian Econ. Soc., Papua New Guinea Econ. Soc. *Leisure interests:* rugby, sightseeing, travel. *Address:* Office of the Governor, Bank of Papua New Guinea, PO Box 121, Port Moresby 121, Papua New Guinea (office). *Telephone:* 3227200 (office); 3227253 (office). *Fax:* 3211617 (office). *E-mail:* info@bankpng.gov.pg (office). *Website:* www.bankpng.gov.pg (office).

BAKATIN, Vadim Viktorovich; Russian politician (retd) and company director; b. 6 Nov. 1937, Kiselevsk, Kemerovo Oblast; s. of Victor Aleksandrovich Bakatin and Nina Afanasievna Bakatina; m. Ludmila Antonovna Bakatina; two s.; ed Novosibirsk Construction Eng Inst., Acad. of Social Sciences; supervisor, chief engineer, Dir of construction works 1960–71; mem. CPSU 1964–91; chief engineer of housing construction combine, Kemerovo 1971–73; Second Sec., Kemerovo City Cttee 1973–75; Sec., Kemerovo Dist Cttee 1977–83; Insp., CPSU Cen. Cttee 1985; First Sec. Kirov Dist Cttee 1985–87; mem. CPSU Cen. Cttee 1986–90; First Sec., Kemerovo Dist Cttee 1987–88; USSR Minister of Internal Affairs 1988–90; mem. Presidential Council Jan.–Nov. 1990; Head of KGB Aug.–Dec. 1991, Inter-republican Security Service 1991–92; Vice-Pres. and Dir Dept of Political and Int. Relations, Reforma Fund 1992–98; fmr Dir, Vostok Capital, mem. Advisory Cttee, Baring Vostok Capital Partners. *Publication:* The Deliverance from the KGB 1992. *Leisure interests:* painting, reading, tennis. *Address:* c/o Baring Vostok Capital Partners, 125047 Moscow, 9 Lesnaya Street, White Gardens Business Centre, Building B, 6th Floor, Russian Federation. *E-mail:* info@bvcp.ru.

BAKAYOKO, Hamed; Côte d'Ivoirian journalist and politician; *Minister of State, Minister of Defence;* b. 8 March 1965, Abidjan; s. of Anliou Bakayoko and Mayama Bakayoko; m. Yolande Tanoh Bakayoko; four c.; ed Collège Notre Dame of Africa, Univ. of Ouagadougou; Ed. in Chief, Journal du Collège Moderne d'Adjamé 1978; Founding Dir Le Patriote (daily newspaper) 1990–93 (newspaper suspended by the authorities 1994); spent several months in prison for contempt 1994; Dir Radio Nostalgie (first private radio station in Côte d'Ivoire) 1993, CEO Nostalgie Afrique 2000; Minister of New Technologies, Information and Communication 2003–10; mem. presidential campaign team of Alassane Dramane Ouattara 2011; Minister of the Interior 2011–17; Minister of State, Minister of Defence 2017–; Mayor of Abobo 2018–; Pres. Nat. Council of Press Patrons of Côte d'Ivoire 2001; mem. Rassemblement des républicains (RDR); Ordine della Stella della Solidarietà Italiana 2016. *Address:* Ministry of State, Ministry of Defence, BP 12243, Abidjan, Côte d'Ivoire (office). *Telephone:* 20-21-07-84 (office). *Website:* info@defense.gouv.ci (office); www.defense.gouv.ci (office); www.hamedbakayoko.com (office).

BAKAYOKO, Youssouf; Côte d'Ivoirian politician and diplomatist; *President, Electoral Commission;* b. 9 April 1943, Bouaké; ed Univ. of Paris X, France, Institut Universitaire de Hautes Études Internationales, Switzerland; began diplomatic career 1973, Counsellor, Perm. Mission to EU and Int. Orgs in Geneva 1973–76, worked at Embassy in Berne 1977–79, in Bonn 1979–83, in Paris 1983–90; Mayor of Séguéla 1990–95; Chair. Société ivoirienne de (SIPF), Abidjan 1996–97; Deputy to Nat. Ass. 1995–2005; Minister of Foreign Affairs 2006–10; Pres. Electoral Comm. 2010–; Commander of the National Order. *Address:* Commission électorale indépendant, 08 BP 2648, Abidjan, Côte d'Ivoire (office). *Telephone:* 21-30-58-01 (office). *Website:* www.cei-ci.org (office).

BAKER, Akbar al-, BEcons; Qatari airline industry executive; *CEO, Qatar Airways;* b. 1960, Doha; ed studied in India; worked at Civil Aviation Directorate –1997; joined Qatar Airways 1997, CEO 1997–, also CEO Qatar Airways Holidays, Qatar Aviation Services, Qatar Duty Free Co., Doha Int. Airport, Qatar Distribution Co., Qatar Aircraft Catering Co.; Chair. Qatar Tourism Authority 2004, Arab Air Carriers Organization; mem. Bd Govs IATA; mem. Bd of Dirs Cargolux Airlines Int. SA 2011–, Heathrow Airport Ltd 2013–; mem. Supervisory Bd Volkswagen AG 2015–16; Légion d'honneur 2015. *Address:* Qatar Airways, PO Box 22550, Qatar Airways Tower, Airport Road, Doha, Qatar (office). *Telephone:* 4496666 (office). *Fax:* 4621792 (office). *E-mail:* infodesk@qatarairways.com (office). *Website:* www.qatarairways.com (office).

BAKER, Charles (Charlie) Duane, Jr, BA, MBA; American business executive and politician; *Governor of Massachusetts;* b. 13 Nov. 1956; m. Lauren Baker; three c.; ed Harvard Coll., Northwestern Univ.; Co-founder, The Pioneer Inst. for Public Policy Research 1988–91; Under-Sec. for Health and Human Services, State of Mass 1991–92, Sec. for Health and Human Services 1991–94, Sec. of Admin and Finance 1994–98; Pres. and CEO Harvard Vanguard Medical Associates 1998; Pres. and CEO, Harvard Pilgrim Health Care 1999–2009; unsuccessful Republican cand. for Gov. of Mass 2010; Gov. of Mass 2015–; Entrepreneur-in-Residence, General Catalyst Partners, Cambridge, Mass 2011; mem. Mass Asscn of Health Plans (fmr Chair.); Republican; Nat. Gov.'s Asscn Distinguished Service Award 1998. *Address:* Office of the Governor, State House, Room 280, Boston, MA 02133, USA (office). *Telephone:* (617) 725-4005 (office). *Fax:* (617) 727-9725 (office). *Website:* www.mass.gov/governor (office).

BAKER, James Addison, III, LLB; American lawyer and fmr government official; *Senior Partner, Baker Botts LLP;* b. 28 April 1930, Texas; s. of James A. Baker, Jr and Bonner Means; m. Susan Garrett 1973; eight c.; ed Princeton Univ. and Univ. of Texas Law School; served in US Marine Corps 1952–54; with law firm Andrews, Kurth, Campbell and Jones, Houston, Tex. 1957–75; Under-Sec. of Commerce under Pres. Ford 1975; Nat. Chair. Ford's presidential campaign 1976; Campaign Dir for George Bush in primary campaign 1980, later joined Reagan campaign; White House Chief of Staff and on Nat. Security Council 1981–85; Trustee, Woodrow Wilson Int. Center for Scholars, Smithsonian Inst. 1977–; Sec. of the Treasury 1985–88, Sec. of State 1989–92; White House Chief of Staff and Sr Counsellor 1992–93; Gov. Rice Univ. 1993; Sr Pnr, Baker Botts LLP 1993–; also currently Sr Counselor, The Carlyle Group; Personal Envoy of UN Sec.-Gen., UN Mission for the Referendum in Western Sahara (MINURSO) 1997–2004 (resgnd); apptd special envoy on Middle East debt by US Pres. George W. Bush 2003; mem. Bd of Dirs Howard Hughes Medical Inst.; Hon. Chair. James A. Baker III Inst. for Public Policy, Univ.; Co-Chair. Iraq Study Group, US Inst. of Peace 2006–07; currently Co-Chair. Nat. War Powers Comm. *Publications:* The Politics of Diplomacy 1995, Work Hard, Study . . . and Keep Out of Politics! Adventures and Lessons from an Unexpected Public Life 2006. *Leisure interests:* jogging, tennis, hunting. *Address:* Baker Botts LLP, One Shell Plaza, 910 Louisiana Street, Houston, TX 77002-4995, USA (office). *Telephone:* (713) 229-1234 (office). *Fax:* (713) 229-1522 (office). *E-mail:* james.baker@bakerbotts.com (office). *Website:* www.bakerbotts.com (office).

BAKER, Dame Janet Abbott, CH, DBE, CBE, FRSA; British singer (mezzo-soprano); b. 21 Aug. 1933, Hatfield, Yorks.; d. of Robert Abbott Baker and May Baker (née Pollard); m. James Keith Shelley 1957; ed York Coll. for Girls and Wintringham School, Grimsby; Pres. London Sinfonia 1986–; Chancellor Univ. of York 1991–2004; Trustee, Foundation for Sport and the Arts (foundation closed 2012); mem. Munster Trust; Hon. Fellow, St Anne's Coll., Oxford 1975, Downing Coll., Cambridge 1985; Hon. DMus (Birmingham) 1968, (Leicester) 1974, (London) 1974, (Hull) 1975, (Oxford) 1975, (Leeds) 1980, (Lancaster) 1983, (York) 1984, (Cambridge) 1984, Hon. LLD (Aberdeen) 1980, Hon. DLitt (Bradford) 1983; Commdr des Arts et des Lettres; Daily Mail Kathleen Ferrier Memorial Prize 1956, Queen's Prize, Royal Coll. of Music 1959, Hamburg Shakespeare Prize, Hamburg 1971, Grand Prix, French Nat. Acad. of Lyric Recordings 1975, Léonie Sonning Prize (Denmark) 1979, Gold Medal of Royal Philharmonic Soc. 1990, Inc. Soc. of Musicians' Distinguished Music Award 2008, Gramophone Award for Lifetime Achievement 2011. *Publication:* Full Circle (autobiography) 1982. *Leisure interests:* walking, reading.

BAKER, Sir John Hamilton, Kt, QC, PhD, LLD, FBA, FRHistS; British legal historian; *Emeritus Downing Professor of the Laws of England, University of Cambridge;* b. 10 April 1944, Sheffield; s. of Kenneth Lee Vincent Baker and Marjorie Bagshaw; m. 1st Veronica Margaret Lloyd 1968 (divorced 1997); two d.; m. 2nd Fiona Rosalind Holdsworth (née Cantlay) 2002 (died 2005); m. 3rd Elisabeth Maria Cornelia Faber (née van Houts) 2010; ed King Edward VI Grammar School, Chelmsford and Univ. Coll. London; Asst Lecturer in Law, Univ. Coll. London 1965–67, Lecturer 1967–70; Barrister Inner Temple, London 1966; Librarian, Squire Law Library, Cambridge 1971–73; Lecturer in Law, Univ. of Cambridge 1973–83, Reader in English Legal History 1983–88, Prof. 1988–98, Downing Prof. of the Laws of England 1998–2011, currently Emer. Downing Prof., Fellow of St Catharine's Coll. 1971– (Pres. 2004–07), Hon. Fellow 2012–; Visiting Prof., New York Univ. School of Law 1988–2010; Corresp. Fellow, American Soc. for Legal History 1992; Visiting Fellow, All Souls Coll. Oxford 1995; Jt Literary Dir Selden Soc. 1981–90, Literary Dir 1991–2011; Fellow of Univ. Coll. London 1991; Hon. Bencher, Inner Temple, London 1988, Gray's Inn 2013; Hon. Fellow, Soc. for Advanced Legal Studies 1998; Hon. Foreign mem. American Acad. of Arts and Sciences 2001; Hon. LLD (Chicago) 1991; Yorke Prize (Cambridge) 1975, Ames Prize (Harvard Law School) 1985. *Publications:* An Introduction to English Legal History 1971, The Reports of Sir John Spelman 1977, Manual of Law French 1979, The Order of Serjeants at Law 1984, English Legal MSS in the USA (Part I) 1985, The Legal Profession and the Common Law 1986, Sources of English Legal History (with S.F.C. Milsom) 1986, The Notebook of Sir John Port 1987, Readings and Moots at the Inns of Court 1990, English Legal MSS in the USA (Part II) 1990, Cases from the Lost Notebooks of Sir James Dyer 1994, Catalogue of English Legal MSS in Cambridge University Library 1996, Spelman's Reading on Quo Warranto 1997, Monuments of Endless Labours 1998, Caryll's Reports 1999, The Common Law Tradition 2000, The Law's Two Bodies 2001, Readers and Readings 2001, Oxford History of the Laws of England (Vol. VI) 2003, Reports from the Time of Henry VIII 2003–04, An Inner Temple Miscellany 2004, The Men of Court 2012, Collected Papers on English Legal History 2013, Readings and Commentaries on Magna Carta 1400-1604 2015. *Address:* St Catharine's College, Cambridge, CB2 1RL, England.

BAKER, Baron (Life Peer), cr. 1997, of Dorking in the County of Surrey; **Kenneth Wilfred Baker,** CH, PC, BA; British politician and writer; b. 3 Nov. 1934, Newport, Wales; s. of W. M. Baker; m. Mary Elizabeth Gray-Muir 1963; one s. two d.; ed St Paul's School and Magdalen Coll., Oxford; nat. service 1953–55; served Twickenham Borough Council 1960–62; as Conservative cand. contested Poplar 1964, Acton 1966; Conservative MP for Acton 1968–70, St Marylebone 1970–83, Mole Valley 1983–97; Parl. Sec. Civil Service Dept 1972–74, Parl. Pvt. Sec. to Leader of Opposition 1974–75; Minister of State and Minister for Information Tech., Dept of Trade and Industry 1981–84; Sec. of State for the Environment 1985–86, for Educ. and Science 1986–89; Chancellor of the Duchy of Lancaster and Chair. Conservative Party 1989–90; Sec. of State for the Home Dept 1990–92; mem. Public Accounts Cttee 1969–70; mem. Exec. 1922 Cttee 1978–81; Chair. Hansard Soc. 1978–81, MTT PLC 1996–97, Business Serve PLC, Northern Edge Ltd, Museum of British History, Belmont Press (London) Ltd, Trilantic Capital Partners' European Merchant Banking Advisory Council; Deputy Chair. Genting UK plc; Pres. Royal London Soc. for the Blind; Sec.-Gen. UN Conf. of Parliamentarians on World Population and Devt 1978; Dir and Trustee, Booker Prize Foundation; Trustee, Cartoon Art Trust, Career Colleges Trust; Companion of Honour 1997. *Publications include:* I Have No Gun But I Can Spit 1980, London Lines (ed.) 1982, The Faber Book of English History in Verse (ed.) 1988, The Faber Book of English Parodies (ed.) 1990, Unauthorized Versions (ed.) 1990, The Faber Book of Conservatism (ed.) 1993, The Turbulent Years: My Life in Politics 1993, The Prime Ministers: An Irreverent Political History in Cartoons 1995, The Kings and Queens: An Irreverent Cartoon History of the British Monarchy 1995, The Faber Book of War Poetry (ed.) 1996, Children's English History in Verse (ed.) 2000, The Faber Book of Landscape Poetry (ed.) 2000, George III: A Life in Caricature 2007, 14–18: A New Vision for Secondary Education 2013. *Leisure interests:* collecting books, political cartoons. *Address:* House of Lords, Westminster, London, SW1A 0PW, England (office). *Telephone:* (20) 7219-5353 (office). *Fax:* (20) 7219-5979 (office). *E-mail:* contactholmember@parliament.uk (office).

BAKER, Meredith Attwell, BA, LLB; American lawyer, business executive and fmr government official; *President and CEO, CTIA;* b. 5 July 1968, Houston, TX; d. of Kirby Attwell; m. James Addison (Jamie) Baker IV 2006; four step-d.; ed Washington & Lee Univ., Lexington, VA, Univ. of Houston; worked in Legis. Affairs Office of US Dept of State, Washington, DC 1990–92; worked at US Court of Appeals Fifth Circuit in Houston and with DeLange and Hudspeth, LLP (law firm); Dir of Congressional Affairs, Cellular Telecommunications Industry Asscn 1998–2000; Sr Counsel, Covad Communications 2000–02; participated in the George W. Bush presidential campaign 2000; served briefly as Vice-Pres. Williams Mullen Strategies (lobbying firm) 2004; political appointee as Sr Advisor to Nat. Telecommunications and Information Admin 2004, named a Deputy Asst Sec. of Commerce by Pres. George W. Bush 2007, Acting Asst Sec. of Commerce for Communications and Information and Acting Admin. Nat. Telecommunications and Information Admin 2007–09; also served as Acting Assoc. Admin. for Office of Int. Affairs and on detail to Office of Science and Tech. Policy, The White House; apptd by Pres. Barack Obama as mem. Fed. Communications Comm. 2009–11; Sr Vice-Pres. of Govt Affairs, NBCUniversal (following merger with Comcast), Washington, DC 2011–14; Pres. and CEO CTIA—The Wireless Association 2014–; mem. Texas State Bar. *Address:* CTIA, 1400 16th Street, NW Suite 600, Washington, DC 20036, USA (office). *Telephone:* (202) 736-3200 (office). *Website:* www.ctia.org (office).

BAKER, Raymond, CBE, PhD, FRS; British research scientist and academic (retd); b. 1 Nov. 1936, Ilkeston, Derbyshire; s. of Alfred Baker and May Golds; m. Marian Slater 1960; one s. two d.; ed Ilkeston Grammar School, Univ. of Leicester, Univ. of California, Los Angeles, USA; Postdoctoral Fellow, UCLA 1962–64; Lecturer in Organic Chem., Univ. of Southampton 1964–72, Sr Lecturer 1972–74, Reader 1974–77, Prof. 1977–84; Dir Wolfson Unit of Chemical Entomology 1976–84; Dir of Medicinal Chem., Merck Sharp Dohme Research Labs 1984–89, Exec. Dir 1989–96; Chief Exec. Biotechnology and Biological Sciences Research Council 1996–2001; Visiting Prof., Univ. of Edinburgh 1988–96, Univ. of Leicester 1990–93; Hon. DSc (Nottingham Trent) 1990, (Aston) 1997, (Leicester) 1998, (St Andrews) 1998, (Southampton) 1999; RSC Prize for Medicinal Chem. 1991, Hugo Muller Medal for Chem. associated with Biology 1992. *Publications include:* Mechanism in Organic Chemistry 1971; over 300 articles in professional journals. *Leisure interests:* golf, gardening, travel. *Address:* 2 Thirlestaine Place, Thirlestaine Road, Cheltenham, Glos., GL53 7ED, England (home).

BAKER, Richard, MA; British retail executive; *Chairman, Whitbread PLC;* b. 6 Aug. 1962; m.; two c.; ed Univ. of Cambridge, Harvard Business School; began career at MG Rover Group; various positions with Mars Inc. in UK, including roles in Nat. Account Man., Marketing and Head of Sales for UK Multiples 1986–1995; COO and Marketing Officer Asda Group Ltd 1995–2003; CEO Boots Group PLC 2003–06, CEO Alliance Boots PLC (after merger with Alliance Unichem) 2006–07; Operating Partner, Advent Int. 2009–, Chair. DFS group 2010–; apptd Chair. (non-exec.) Virgin Active 2007, European Div., Groupe Aeroplan; mem. Bd of Dirs Whitbread PLC 2009–, Chair. 2014–. *Leisure interests:* hockey, tennis, golf, sailing, playing drums. *Address:* Whitbread Court, Houghton Hall Business Park, Porz Avenue, Dunstable, LU5 5XE, England (office). *Telephone:* (58) 2424-200 (office). *Website:* www.whitbread.co.uk (office); www.adventinternational.com (office); www.aeroplan.com (office).

BAKER, (Winifred) Mitchell, AB, JD; American software development executive; *Chairperson, Mozilla Foundation;* b. 7 June 1957, Berkeley, Calif.; d. of Theodore Baker and Anne Baker; m. Casey Dunn; one s.; ed Univ. of California, Berkeley, Boalt Hall School of Law; Corp. and Intellectual Property Assoc., Fenwick & West LLP 1990–93; Assoc. Gen. Counsel, Sun Microsystems 1993–94; Assoc. Gen. Counsel, Netscape Communications Corpn 1994–99; joined Mozilla.org 1998, Gen. Man. (officially known as Chief Lizard Wrangler) Mozilla project 1999–, involved in open-source software devt, creators of Mozilla Firefox and Mozilla Thunderbird, Pres. Mozilla Foundation 2003–05, CEO Mozilla Corpn 2005–08, Chair. 2008–; mem. Bd of Dirs Open Source Applications Foundation 2002–; Anita Borg Inst. Women of Vision Award 2009, Aenne Burda Award for Creative Leadership 2010, Growth, Innovation and Leadership Award, Frost & Sullivan 2010. *Address:* Mozilla Foundation, 1981 Landings Drive, Building K, Mountain View, CA 94043-0801, USA (office). *Telephone:* (650) 903-0800 (office). *Fax:* (650) 903-0875 (office). *E-mail:* mitchell@mozilla.org (office). *Website:* www.mozilla.org/foundation (office); www.mozilla.com (office).

BAKEWELL, Baroness (Life Peer), cr. 2011, of Stockport in the County of Greater Manchester; **Joan Dawson Bakewell,** DBE, MA; British broadcaster and author; b. 16 April 1933, Stockport, Cheshire (now Greater Manchester), England; d. of John Rowlands and Rose Bland; m. 1st Michael Bakewell 1955 (divorced 1972); one s. one d.; m. 2nd Jack Emery 1975 (divorced 2001); ed Stockport High School for Girls and Newnham Coll., Cambridge; TV Critic, The Times 1978–81, columnist, Sunday Times 1988–90; columnist ('Just Seventy'), The Guardian 2003; began fortnightly column in Times2 section of The Times 2008; currently writes weekly column in The Independent; Assoc. Newnham Coll., Cambridge 1980–91, Assoc. Fellow 1984–87; Council mem. Aldeburgh Foundation 1985–99; Gov. BFI 1994–99, Chair. 2000–02; Pres. Birkbeck, Univ. of London 2013–; Govt-apptd Voice of Older People 2008–10; Chair. and Trustee, Shared Experience theatre co.; mem. (Labour) House of Lords 2011–; Dr hc (Royal Holloway London, Queen

Margaret's Edinburgh, Chester, Lancaster, Univ. of the Arts London, Essex, Stafford, Open Univ.); Dimbleby Award, BAFTA 1995, Journalist of the Year, Stonewall Awards 2009. *Radio includes:* Artist of the Week 1998–99, The Brains Trust 1999–, Belief (BBC Radio 3) 2000–, Saturday Live (BBC Radio 4), Inside the Ethics Committee (BBC Radio 4). *Television includes:* Sunday Break 1962, Home at 4.30 (writer and producer) 1964, Meeting Point, The Second Sex 1964, Late Night Line Up 1965–72, 2008, The Youthful Eye 1968, Moviemakers at the National Film Theatre 1971, Film 72, Film 73, Holiday 74, 75, 76, 77, 78 (series), Reports Action (series) 1976–78, Arts UK: OK? 1980, Heart of the Matter (BBC 1) 1988–2000, My Generation 2000, One Foot in the Past 2000, Taboo (series) 2001, Daily Politics (BBC 1), Permissive Night (BBC Parliament) 2008, GMTV's Sunday programme, Panorama (BBC 1) 2010, 2012. *Publications:* The New Priesthood: British Television Today (co-author) 1970, A Fine and Private Place (co-author) 1977, The Complete Traveller 1977, The Heart of the Heart of the Matter 1996, The Centre of the Bed: An Autobiography 2004, selection of her interviews for radio series Belief published 2005, The View from Here: Life at 70 2007, All the Nice Girls (novel) 2009, She's Leaving Home (novel) 2011, Stop the Clocks: Thoughts on What I Leave Behind 2016; contribs to journals. *Leisure interests:* theatre, travel, cinema. *Address:* c/o Knight Ayton Management, 35 Great James Street, London, WC1N 3HB, England (office); House of Lords, Westminster, London, SW1A 0PW, England. *Telephone:* (20) 7831-4400 (office); (20) 7219-5353 (House of Lords). *Fax:* (20) 7831-4455 (office). *E-mail:* info@knightayton.co.uk (office). *Website:* knightayton.co.uk (office).

BAKHIT, Maj.-Gen. (retd) Marouf Suleiman al-, PhD; Jordanian government official and army officer (retd); b. 1947; ed Univ. of Jordan, Univ. of Southern California, USA, Univ. of London, UK, Royal Jordanian Mil. Coll.; served with Jordan Armed Forces 1964–99, positions included Dir of Studies, Devt, and Procurement and Personnel Affairs, retd with rank of Maj.-Gen. 1999; fmr Prof. of Political Science and Vice-Pres. for Mil. Affairs, Muta Univ.; fmr Amb. to Turkey, Israel; fmr Nat. Security Chief; Prime Minister and Minister of Defence 2005–07, Feb.–Oct. 2011 (resgnd); apptd Senator 2009, currently Chair. Senate Foreign Affairs Cttee; mem. Jordanian Del. for Israel–Jordan peace treaty; Lecturer in Political Science, Mutah Univ. 1997–99; 14 Jordanian medals. *Address:* Majlis al-Aayan (Assembly of Senators), House of Parliament, Amman 11118, Jordan (office). *E-mail:* info@senate.jo (office). *Website:* www.senate.jo (office).

BAKHREṢA, Said Salim Awadh; Tanzanian business executive; *Chairman, Bakhresa Group of Companies;* b. 1949, Zanzibar; m.; two c.; opened shoe repair shop in Dar es Salaam 1968, restaurant 1973, bakery and ice cream parlour 1975; est. Bakhresa Group of Cos 1983, currently Chair. *Address:* Bakhresa Group of Companies, PO Box 2517, Dar Es Salaam, Tanzania (office). *Telephone:* (22) 2861116 (office). *Fax:* (22) 2861140 (office). *E-mail:* azam@raha.com (office). *Website:* www.bakhresa.com (office).

BAKHTADZE, Mamuka, BEng, MBA; Georgian politician; *Prime Minister;* b. 9 June 1982, Tbilisi, Georgian SSR, USSR; ed Tbilisi State Univ., Georgian Tech. Univ., Lomonosov Moscow State Univ., INSEAD Business School; Project Man., Georgian Railways (Sakartvelos Rkinigza) 2005–06, CEO 2013–17; mem. Supervisory Bd Rcheuli (hotel chain) 2007–08; Dir-Gen. Georgian Int. Energy Corpn 2010–12; Minister of Finance 2017–18; Prime Minister 2018–. *Address:* Chancellery of the Government, 0114 Tbilisi, P. Ingorovka 7, Georgia (office). *Telephone:* (32) 299-09-00 (office). *Website:* gov.ge (office).

BAKIYEV, Kurmanbek Saliyevich; Kyrgyzstani politician, engineer and fmr head of state; b. 1 Aug. 1949, Masadan (now Teyyit), Suzdak Dist, Jalal-Abad, Kyrgyz SSR, USSR; s. of Sali Bakiyev; m. Tatyana Vasilyevna Bakiyeva; two s.; ed Kuibyshev (now Samara) Polytechnic Inst., Russian SFSR; trained as electrical engineer 1972; served in Soviet Armed Forces 1974–86; electrical engineer, Maslennikov Plant, Kuibyshev (now Samara, Russia) 1976–79; Sr Engineer, Head of VTs, then Deputy Chief Engineer, Jalal-Abad Electrical Factory 1979–85; Dir Profil Plant, Kok-Yangak 1985–90; First Sec. CP Kok-Yangak City Council 1990; Deputy Chair. Jalal-Abad Council of People's Deputies 1991–92; Head of Toguz-Torou Regional Admin 1992–94; Deputy Chair. State Property Fund 1994–95; First Deputy Head, then Head Jalal-Abad State Admin and Gov. of Jalal-Abad Oblast 1995–97; Gov. of Chui Oblast 1997–2000; Prime Minister of Kyrgyzstan 2000–02, Acting Prime Minister March–June 2005; mem. Supreme Council (Jogorku Kenesh—Parl.) 2003–05; Acting Pres. of Kyrgyzstan March–Aug. 2005, Pres. Aug. 2005–April 2010 (forced to flee the capital during a popular uprising; went into exile in Belarus still insisting he was legitimate head of state); Leader, Bright Road People's Party (Ak Jol) 2007, 2009– (in exile 2010–); reported by news agency that he was granted citizenship of Belarus in 2010 Feb. 2012; sentenced by a Kyrgyz court in absentia to 24 years' imprisonment for abuse of power Feb. 2013, and in absentia to life imprisonment for ordering troops to fire on unarmed protesters July 2014.

BAKKE-JENSEN, Frank; Norwegian politician; *Minister of Defence;* b. 8 March 1965, Finnmark; ed Finnmark Univ. Coll.; worked as ship's electrician 1984–89; mil. service with UN Interim Force in Lebanon (Unifil) 1990–91; Teacher, Båtsfjord school 1991–95; Man., Båtsfjord Reiseservice AS 1995–99, Man. and Owner 1999–; mem. Båtsfjord Municipal Council 1999–2007, Mayor of Båtsfjord 2007–09; mem. Finnmark County Council 2007–09; Deputy Leader, Finnmark Høyre 2008–09; mem. Storting (parl.) for Finnmark 2009–; Minister of EEA and EU 2016–17; Minister of Defence 2017–; mem. Høyre (Conservative). *Address:* Ministry of Defence, Glacisgt. 1, POB 8126 Dep., 0032 Oslo, Norway (office). *Telephone:* 23-09-80-00 (office). *E-mail:* postmottak@fd.dep.no (office). *Website:* www.regjeringen.no/no/dep/fd (office).

BAKKER, M. Peter, BA, MA; Dutch business executive and international organization official; *President, World Business Council for Sustainable Development;* b. 1961; ed Erasmus Univ., Rotterdam, HTS Alkmaar; began career with TS Seeds Holding BV 1984–91; joined PTT Post (later TPG Post) 1991, Finance Dir Parcels Business Unit 1993–95, Dir of Marketing and Sales, PTT Post Logistics 1995–96, Financial Control Dir, TPG Post 1996, mem. Bd of Man. 1997–98, Chief Financial Officer and mem. Bd of Man., TPG NV (cr. following demerger of PTT Post from Royal PTT Nederland NV) 1998–2001, Chair. Man. Bd and CEO TNT NV 2001–11 (led demerger of TNT into TNT Express NV and PostNL NV); Pres. World Business Council for Sustainable Devt 2011–; Chair. War Child Netherlands; Co-Chair. Redefining the Role of Business for Sustainable Devt, UN Sustainable Devt Solutions Network; Vice-Chair. Int. Integrated Reporting Council; fmr Chair. Dutch Cttee on Labour Market Participation; mem. Advisory Bd, World Press Photo, Advisory Council, Royal Bank of Scotland NV, Moving the World Foundation; fmr mem. Dutch Cttee Kapitaalmarkt; Amb. Against Hunger, UN WFP 2011; Industry Leadership Award 2009, Clinton Global Citizen Award 2009, SAM Sustainability Leadership Award 2010. *Address:* World Business Council for Sustainable Development, Maison de la Paix, Chemin Eugène-Rigot 2, Case Postale 246, 1211 Geneva 21, Switzerland (office). *Telephone:* (22) 8393100 (office). *Fax:* (22) 8393131 (office). *E-mail:* info@wbcsd.org (office). *Website:* www.wbcsd.org (office); president.wbcsd.org/about-peter-bakker.html (office).

BAKO ARIFARI, Nassirou, PhD; Benin social scientist and politician; b. 30 Oct. 1962, Karimama; m.; six c.; ed Univ. of Bayreuth, Univ. of Cologne, Germany, Institut des Hautes Etudes en Sciences Sociales, France; Assoc., Institut für Ethnologie und Afrikastudien, Mainz, Germany in 1990s; fmr Dean of Sociology, Univ. d'Abomey-Calavi, Cotonou; Founder and Dir Laboratoire d'Etudes et de Recherches sur les Dynamiques Sociales et le Développement Local (LASDEL) (research inst.) –2009; mem. Assemblée Nationale 2007–, mem. cttees on Culture, Educ., Social Affairs and Employment, Gen. Supervisor, Commission politique de supervision 2010–11, Pres. Defence and External Relations Commission 2015–; Minister of Foreign Affairs, African Integration, Francophone Affairs and Beninois Abroad 2011–15; mem. Union pour la Relève; Coordinator G13 (political alliance); mem. Cttee on the Human Rights of Parliamentarians, Inter-Parliamentary Union. *Publications:* author of several academic publications. *E-mail:* nassirou.bakoarifari@assemblee-nationale.bj (office). *Website:* www.assemblee-nationale.bj/index.php/depute/menu-liste-des-deputes/liste-des-deputes/nassirou-bako-arifari (office).

BAKOYANNIS, Dora; Greek politician; b. (Theodora Mitsotaki), 6 May 1954, Athens; d. of Constantine Mitsotakis (fmr Prime Minister) and Marika Yannoukou; m. 1st Pavlos Bakoyannis 1974 (assassinated 1989); one s. one d.; m. 2nd Isidoros Kouvelos 1998; ed German School of Athens and Paris, France, Univ. of Munich, Germany, Univ. of Athens; family fled to Paris to escape mil. dictatorship that ruled Greece 1967–74; worked at Ministry of Econ. Co-ordination and later Ministry of Foreign Affairs 1974–84; Chief of Staff, New Democracy Party 1984–1990; elected Deputy for Evrytania 1990, re-elected three times and later moved candidacy to central Athens; served as Under-Sec. of State 1990, later as Minister of Culture 1992–93; apptd shadow Foreign and Defence Minister 2000; Mayor of Athens (first woman) 2003–06; Minister of Foreign Affairs (first woman) 2006–09; Chair.-in-Office OSCE Jan.–Oct. 2009; expelled from New Democracy Party 2010; founder and leader, liberal party Democratic Alliance 2010–12, formed alliance with New Democracy Party May 2012 (Democratic Alliance suspended its operation June 2012), re-elected to Parl. 2012, mem. Parl. Cttees on Economic Affairs, National Defence and Foreign Affairs, and Cttee for Obligations and Commitments to Council of Europe; Head nat. del. to Parl. Ass. of Council of Europe (PACE) 2012–, apptd co-rapporteur for Russia by the PACE Monitoring Cttee 2013–, elected Vice-Pres. European People's Party/Christian Democratic Group in Council of Europe 2013, Chair. Political Affairs and Democracy Cttee 2014–; Foreign Assoc. Acad. Française des Sciences Morales et Politiques 2009; Grand Commdr Order of Makarios III (Cyprus) 2003, Commdr of Merit (Poland) 2004, Commdr Order of Merit (Hungary) 2005, Grand Cross Royal Order (Denmark) 2006, Grand Cross Jerusalem Patriarchate 2007, Grosses Goldenes Ehrenzeichen am Bande (Austria) 2007, Grand Cross Order of the Phoenix (Greece) 2008, Cavaliere di Gran Croce, Ordine al Merito (Italy) 2009, Chevalier de la Legion d'honneur 2010; Hon. Emer. Prof. (European Polytechnic Univ., Bulgaria) 2013; Int. Leadership Award, Women's Int. Center 1992, Fontana di Roma Award, 14th Int. Symposium 1993, World Mayor Award 2005, Emperor Maximilian Award-European Award for Regional Policy and Local Govt, Prov. of Tyrol and the City of Innsbruck 2008, OSCE medal 2013, Venizelos Award, Pancretan Assn of America 2013. *Address:* D. Aeropagitou 3, 117 42 Athens, Greece. *Telephone:* (210) 9249487. *E-mail:* politikografeio@dorabak.gr. *Website:* www.dorabak.gr.

BAKRADZE, David, PhD, MPA; Georgian physicist and politician; *Chairman, Modzraoba Tavisuplebistvis—Evropuli Saqartvelo (Movement for Liberty—European Georgia);* b. 1 July 1972, Tbilisi, Georgian SSR, USSR; m. Maka Metreveli; two d.; ed Georgian Tech. Univ., Georgian-American Inst. of Public Admin, Swiss Int. Relations Univ. Seminars (SIRUS), Geneva, G. Marshall European Center for Security Studies, Garmisch-Partenkirchen, Germany, NATO Defense Coll., Rome, Italy, Japanese Inst. of Political Sciences, Tokyo, Galilee Coll., Tivon, Israel, Nat. Defence Coll., Stockholm, Sweden, Int. Law Enforcement Acad., Budapest, Hungary; First Class State Counsellor; holds diplomatic rank of Chief Minister Counsellor; Deputy Head of Disarmament and Arms Control Div., Politico-Mil. Dept, Ministry of Foreign Affairs 1996–98, Head of Disarmament and Arms Control Div. 1998–2000, Deputy Dir Politico-Mil. Dept 2000–02, Head, Service for Security Issues, Nat. Security Council of Georgia 2002–03, Dir Dept for Int. Security and Conflict Man. 2003–04, Dir Dept for Political Security 2004; mem. Parl. 2004–, Chair. Cttee on European Integration 2004–07, Chair. Parl. 2008–12, Parl. Minority Leader 2012–, Chair. Standing Del. to European Parl., Co-Chair. EU-Georgia Parl. Co-operation Cttee, mem. numerous dels; State Minister on Conflict Resolution Issues 2007–08; Minister of Foreign Affairs Feb.–May 2008; mem. Ertiani natsionaluri modzraoba (ENM—United Nat. Movt) Party 2002–17, named as ENM cand. for Oct. 2013 presidential election July 2013, placed second Oct. 2013; cand. in presidential election Oct. 2018; Chair. Modzraoba Tavisuplebistvis—Evropuli Saqartvelo (MT—ES—Movement for Liberty—European Georgia) 2017–; Commdr's Cross, Order of Merit (Poland) 2010; St George's Cross 2013; numerous awards, including Special Prize of Pres. of Georgia for Academic Excellence to the Best Student of Inst. of Public Admin 1996, NATO/EAPC Research Fellowship 1998, Swiss Leadership Award in Int. Relations, Special Award of Grad. Inst. of Int. Studies, Geneva 2005. *Address:* Modzraoba Tavisuplebistvis—Evropuli Saqartvelo, Tbilisi, Gulia 1 (office); Sakartvelos Parlamenti, 4600 Kutaisi, Abashidze 26, Room C-508, Georgia (office). *Telephone:* (32) 228-91-56 (Parl.) (office); (32) 2281139 (MT—ES) (office). *Fax:* (32) 299-93-86 (office). *E-mail:* info@europeangeorgia.ge (office); dbakradze@parliament.ge (office). *Website:* www.parliament.ge (office); europeangeorgia.ge (office).

BAKRADZE, David; Georgian diplomatist and politician; *Ambassador to USA;* b. 30 Dec. 1975, Tbilisi, Georgian SSR, USSR; ed Tbilisi State Univ.; worked for Nat. Security Council 1997–2002; joined Diplomatic Service 2002, served at embassies in Bern and Helsinki 2005–12, Amb. to Greece 2012–14; State Minister of European and Euro-Atlantic Integration 2014–16; Amb. to USA 2016–. *Address:* Embassy of Georgia, 1824 R Street NW, Washington, DC 20009, USA (office). *Telephone:* (202) 387-2390 (office). *Fax:* (202) 387-0864 (office). *E-mail:* embgeo .usa@mfa.gov.ge (office). *Website:* usa.mfa.gov.ge (office).

BAKRIE, Aburizal, BEng; Indonesian business executive and politician; b. 15 Nov. 1946, Lampung; m.; three c.; ed Bandung Inst. of Tech.; Chair. Grup Bakrie & Bros; Pres. ASEAN Business Forum 1991–95; Chair. Indonesian Chamber of Commerce and Industry (Kadin) 1994–2004, now adviser; major shareholder in Bank Nusa, May Bank Nusa International, PT Daya Sarana Pratama and other cos; f. Indonesian Young Entrepreneurs Org. 1972; adviser, Indonesia-Australia Business Council, Jakarta; Co-ordinating Minister for the Economy, Finance and Industry 2004–05, Co-ordinating Minister for the People's Welfare 2005–09; Pres. and Chair. Partai Golongan Karya (Golkar) 2009–14. *Address:* c/o Partai Golongan Karya (Golkar), Jalan Anggrek Nellimurni, Jakarta 11480, Indonesia (office).

BALA-GAYE, Mousa G., BA; Gambian politician; b. 13 Aug. 1946; ed Legon Univ., Univ. of Manchester, UK, IMF Inst.; Asst Sec., Ministry of Works and Communications 1971–73; Sec., Public Service Comm. 1973; Asst Sec., Ministry of Local Govt and Lands 1973; Sr Asst, Ministry of Finance and Trade 1976–79, Under-Sec. 1979–80, Deputy Perm. Sec. 1980–82, Perm. Sec. 1982–86; Exec. Dir African Devt Bank, Abidjan, Côte D'Ivoire 1986–89; Perm. Sec., Office of the Pres. 1989–90; Man. Dir Heron Ltd 1990; Chair. and Man. Dir Afri-Swiss Travel Ltd 1993; Vice-Chair. First Int. Bank Ltd 1999, Acting Chair. 2002; Alt. Dir Senegambia Beach Hotel 2000; Vice-Chair. Int. Trust Insurance Co. Ltd 2000; Sec. of State for Finance and Econ. Affairs 2003–05, for Foreign Affairs March–Oct. 2005, for Trade, Industry and Employment Oct.–Nov. 2005, for Finance and Econ. Affairs Nov. 2005–09; fmr mem. Bd Dirs Cen. Bank of The Gambia, Gambia Produce Marketing Bd, Social Security and Housing Finance Corpn, Gambia Nat. Insurance Corpn; del. to numerous int. and multilateral confs and meetings of IMF, World Bank, OPEC Fund, the Commonwealth; Alt. Gov. African Devt Bank, Islamic Devt Bank, World Bank; Order of the Republic of The Gambia 2006.

BALAKRISHNAN, Arun, BE; Indian chemical engineer and oil industry executive; ed Govt Coll. of Eng, Indian Inst. of Man.; spent five years as Dir of Planning with Oil Coordination Cttee; several positions in Marketing, Corp. and Human Resources, Hindustan Petroleum Corpn Ltd, Dir Human Resources –2007, Chair. and Man. Dir 2007–10 (retd); Chair. Scientific Advisory Cttee for Hydrocarbons, Centre for High Technology, Ministry of Petroleum and Natural Gas 2010–14; mem. Bd of Dirs HPCL-Mittal Energy Ltd 2007–, Shipping Corpn of India Ltd 2014–; Fellow, All India Man. Asscn; Scroll of Honour, Inst. of Engineers (India). *Address:* C – 122, 12th Floor, Trinity Tower, DLF Phase – V, Gurgaon 122 002, India.

BALAKRISHNAN, K(onakuppakatil) G(opinathan), BSc, LLB, LLM; Indian lawyer and judge; b. 12 May 1945, Thalayolaparambu, Kottayam, Kerala; s. of Gopinathan Balakrishnan; m. Nirmala Balakrishnan; one s. two d.; ed Maharaja Coll., Ernakulam, Maharaja Law Coll., Ernakulam; enrolled as advocate of Kerala Bar Council 1968; practised civil and criminal law in Ernakulam; apptd a Munsif in Kerala Judicial Service 1973, later resgnd and resumed practice as advocate in Kerala High Court; judge, Kerala High Court 1985–97, Gujarat High Court 1997–98; Chief Justice of High Court of Gujarat 1998–99, of High Court of Judicature, Madras 1999; Judge, Supreme Court 2000–07, Chief Justice of India 2007–10; Chair. National Human Rights Comm. 2010–15; mem. Lincoln's Inn, England; several hon. degrees, including Dr hc (Kurukshetra Univ.), (Univ. of Gulbarga), (Univ. of Kerala), (Univ. of Bangalore), (Mahatma Gandhi Univ.), (Kottayam, Kerala), (Andhra Pradesh Univ.); Sri V K Krishna Menon Award.

BALAKRISHNAN, Dr Vivian, FRCS; Singaporean ophthalmologist and politician; *Minister for Foreign Affairs;* b. 25 Jan. 1961; m. Joy Balakrishnan; four c.; ed Nat. Univ. of Singapore; Specialist Sr Registrar, Moorfields Eye Hosp., London 1993–95; fmr Consultant ophthalmologist, Singapore Nat. Eye Centre (SNEC), becoming Deputy Dir 1997–99, Medical Dir 1999; fmr Consultant ophthalmologist, Nat. Univ. Hosp., also Assoc. Prof., Nat. Univ. of Singapore; CEO, Singapore Gen. Hosp. 2000; mem. Parl. for Holland-Bukit Panjang GRC 2001–06, for Holland-Bukit Timah GRC 2006–; fmr Second Minister for Trade and Industry, Minister responsible for Entrepreneurship, Second Minister for Information, Communications and the Arts, Minister of State for Nat. Devt; Minister for Community Devt, Youth and Sports 2004–11, Minister for the Environment and Water Resources 2011–15, Minister for Foreign Affairs 2015–, also Minister-in-charge of Smart Nation Initiative, Acting Minister for Transport 2019; fmr Chair. Remaking Singapore Cttee; fmr Chair. Nat. Youth Council; mem. People's Action Party (PAP). *Address:* Ministry of Foreign Affairs, MFA Bldg, Tanglin, off Napier Road, Singapore City 248163, Singapore (office). *Telephone:* 63798000 (office). *Fax:* 64747885 (office). *E-mail:* mfa@sgmfa.gov.sg (office). *Website:* www.mfa.gov.sg (office).

BĂLAN, Gheorghe; Moldovan politician and government official; b. 25 Aug. 1975, Chişinău, Moldovan SSR, USSR; ed Mihai Eminescu Romanian-French Lyceum, Chişinău, Alexandru Ioan Cuza Univ., Iaşi, Romania, Nat. School of Political Science and Public Admin, Bucharest, Romania, European Inst. of Political Studies, IMF Inst., Vienna, Austria, George C. Marshall European Center for Security Studies, Germany, int. programme of studies for leaders in USA, Alexandru cel Bun Mil. Acad.; expert in Regional Policy and European Integration, UNDP Project 'Development Strategy', Centre for Strategic Studies and Reforms, Chişinău 1998–2002; local expert and Rep. of Swedish Inst. for Public Admin in Cahul and Bender (Tighina) 1999–2002; Lecturer, Acad. of Public Admin, Chişinău 1999–2009; Minister for Reintegration and Sr Consultant 2003; Head of Information and Analysis, Ministry of Reintegration, State Chancellery of Moldova 2008–09, Head of Information and Analysis Bureau for Reintegration 2009–10, Head of Bureau for Reintegration 2010–16; Expert, Perm. Del. of Moldova to Jt Co-operation Cttee 2012; Chair. Cttee for selecting projects under the programme of reintegration activities 2014; Deputy Prime Minister, responsible for Reintegration 2016–17.

BALANCY, Marc France Eddy, LLB, MA; Mauritian judge; *Chief Justice;* b. 6 May 1953; m.; two c.; ed Royal Coll., Port Louis, King's Coll., Univ. of London, UK, Brunel Univ., UK; worked as journalist, also fmr teacher of English and French, Darwin Coll., Flacq; apptd Judge, Supreme Court 1994, then Sr Puisne Judge 2014–19, Chief Justice 2019–. *Publications:* law books: The Information, The Law of Conspiracy in Mauritius, Basic Criminal Procedure and Evidence for Prosecutors. *Address:* Supreme Court, Pope Henessy Street, Port Louis, Mauritius (office). *Telephone:* 212-5330 (office). *Website:* www.supremecourt.govmu.org (office).

BALANKIN, Alexander Sergeevich, MSc, PhD, DSc; Mexican/Russian scientist and academic; *Professor, National Polytechnic Institute of Mexico;* b. 3 March 1958, Moscow, Russia; m.; one d.; ed Moscow Eng Physics Inst.; served as mem. Council of the Union (fmr USSR) for the Physics of Materials Resistance and Fracture (Russia) 1991–92; Full Prof., Monterrey Inst. of Tech. and Higher Educ., Mexico City 1992–97; joined Dept of Electromechanical Eng, Nat. Polytechnic Inst. (IPN) 1997, cr. Lab. of Fracture Mechanics; apptd mem. Advisory Council in Science and Tech. to the Presidency of Mexico 2003; fmr Counsellor of Membership Cttee of Nat. Researcher System; Adviser, Mexican Petroleum Inst., Mexican Transport Inst.; consultant, Mexican Nat. Petroleum Co. (PEMEX); f. Nat. Interdisciplinary Research Group Fractal Mechanics (jt venture between industry and academia) 1998; cr. Inter-university Lab. Fractal Analysis of Complex Systems; mem. Mexican Acad. of Sciences 1998; Fellow, Nat. Researcher System 1998; State Prize of Russian Ministry of Defence 1990, Prize of Acad. of Sciences of USSR 1991, Pleiades Publishing Inc. Prize 1996, First Place Romulo Garza Prize for Research and Technological Devt in Mexico 1996, Nat. Prize of Arts and Sciences in Tech. and Design 2002, Nat. Prize in Financial Research 2004, Lazaro Cardenas' Gold Medal (highest award for Science and Tech. achievements), Pres. of Mexican Repub. 2005, UNESCO Science Prize 2005, Amalia Solórzano de Cárdenas Silver Medal 2006, Juchimán de Plata Award 2009. *Publications:* six books and more than 120 scientific papers in professional journals on fractal solid mechanics, probabilistic fracture mechanics, fluid flow through porous media mechanics and their eng applications. *Address:* Instituto Politécnico Nacional, CP 07738, Mexico City, DF, Mexico (office). *Telephone:* (55) 5729-6000 (office). *E-mail:* info@ipn.mx (office). *Website:* www.ipn.mx (office).

BALARAM, Padmanabhan, MSc, PhD; Indian research institute director and molecular biophysicist; *Director, Indian Institute of Science;* b. 1949; ed Fergusson Coll., Pune Univ., Indian Inst. of Tech., Carnegie-Mellon Univ., USA; postdoctoral researcher, Dept of Chem., Harvard Univ., USA; Lecturer, Indian Inst. of Science 1973–77, Asst Prof. 1977–82, Assoc. Prof. 1982–85, Prof. 1986–, Astra Prof. of Biological Sciences 1997–2000, Chair. Molecular Biophysics Unit 1995–2000, Chair. Div. of Biological Sciences 2000–05, Dir Indian Inst. of Science 2005–; Assoc. Ed. Indian Journal of Chemical Educ. 1977–82; mem. Editorial Bd Proceedings of the Indian Academy of Sciences, Chemical Sciences 1980–83, Proceedings of the Indian Nat. Science Acad., Section B 1985–90, Indian Journal of Biochemistry and Biophysics 1989–91, Indian Journal of Chemistry Section B 1985–91, Int. Journal of Peptide and Protein Research 1984–97, Journal of Peptide Research 1997, Protein Eng, Design and Selection 2004, Biopolymers (Peptide Science) 2004; mem. Editorial Cttee Current Science 1991–94, Ed. Current Science 1995–2013; mem. Editorial Advisory Bd Chem Biochem: A European Journal of Chemical Biology 2000–13; Fellow, Indian Acad. of Sciences, Indian Nat. Science Acad., Third World Acad. of Sciences; Young Scientist Medal, Indian Nat. Science Acad. 1977, Shanti Swaroop Bhatnagar Award, Indian Science Congress Asscn 1986, G D Birla Award 1994, Distinguished Alumnus Award, Indian Inst. of Tech., Kanpur 2000, Padma Shri 2002, Third World Acad. of Sciences Award in Chem., Padma Bhushan 2014. *Publications include:* ed one book and has written more than 400 publs on structural biology, protein eng and design. *Address:* Indian Institute of Science, Bangalore 560 012, India (office). *Telephone:* (80) 23600690 (office); (80) 22932222 (office). *Fax:* (80) 23600936 (office). *E-mail:* diroff@admin .iisc.ernet.in (office); pb@mbu.iisc.ernet.in (office). *Website:* www.iisc.ernet.in (office).

BALAYAN, Roman Gurgenovich; Armenian film director; b. 15 April 1941, Nagorno-Karabak Autonomous Region; m. Natalia Balayan; two s.; ed Yerevan Inst. of Theatrical Arts, Kiev Theatre Inst., USSR; State Prize 1987. *Films include:* The Romashkin Effect, 1973, Kashtanka 1976, Biryuk (Morose) 1977, The Kiss 1983, Dream and Waking Flights 1983, Keep Me Safe, My Talisman (Tulip Award, Int. Istanbul Film Festival 1987) 1985, Police Spy 1988, Lady Macbeth of Mtcensk 1989, Two Moons, Three Suns 1998 (dir and writer), Letniy Dozhd 2002 (producer), The Night is Bright 2004, Birds of Paradise 2008. *TV:* Who's Afraid of Virginia Woolf 1992, The Tale of the First Love 1995. *Address:* 125212 Moscow, Leningradsky Prosp. 33, Apt. 70, Russia. *Telephone:* (495) 159-99-74.

BALAZS, Artur Krzysztof, MEng; Polish politician, trade union official and farmer; b. 3 Jan. 1952, Ełk; s. of Adam Balazs and Irena Balazs; m. Jolanta Balazs 1973; three d.; ed Agricultural Acad., Szczecin; worked in agric. service of Communal Office, Kołczewo 1974–76; own farm in Łuskowo 1976–; mem. Polish United Workers' Party (PZPR) 1975–81; active in Agric. Solidarity Independent Self-governing Trade Union 1980–81, participant 1st Nat. Congress of Solidarity of Pvt. Farmers Trade Union, Warsaw 1980; participant agric. strikes and co-signatory agreements in Ustrzyki, Rzeszów and Bydgoszcz 1981; mem. All-Poland Founding Cttee of Solidarity of Private Farmers Trade Union, mem. Comm. for Realization of Rzeszów-Ustrzyki Agreements; interned 1981–82; mem. Presidium of Solidarity Provisional Nat. Council of Farmers 1987; mem. Inter-factory Strike Cttee Szczecin 1988; mem. Civic Cttee attached to Lech Wałęsa, Chair. of Solidarity Trade Union 1988–91; participant Round Table debates, mem. group for union pluralism and team for agric. matters Feb.–April 1989; apptd mem. Episcopate Comm. for the Pastoral Care of Farmers 1989; Deputy to Sejm (Parl.) 1989–93, 1997; apptd mem. Solidarity Election Action Parl. Club 1997; Chair. Sejm Cttee for Admin. and Internal Affairs 1992–93; Vice-Chair. Christian Peasant Party 1990–94, 1995–97, Chair. 1994–95; mem. Nat. Bd Conservative Peasant Party (SKL) 1997–, Vice-Chair. 1998–99, Chair. 2000–02, Chair. Conservative Party–New Poland Movt (SKL–RNP) 2002–03, 2007–09; Chair. European Fund for the Devt of Polish Villages 1990–; Minister, mem. Council of Ministers 1989–90, Minister without Portfolio 1991–92; mem. Senate 1995–97; mem. Cttee for Agric.; Minister of Agric. and Rural Devt 1999–2002; Officer's Cross of Order of the Rebirth of Poland 2006, Cross of Freedom and Solidarity 2012. *Leisure interests:* press, politics.

BALÁZS, Péter, PhD, Dr (Habil), DrSci; Hungarian economist, diplomatist, politician and academic; b. 5 Dec. 1941, Kecskemét; ed Budapest School of Econs, Hungarian Acad. of Sciences; early position as economist, Elektroimpex (trading co.) 1963–68; Desk Officer, later Dir Ministry of Foreign Trade 1969–82; Counsellor, Embassy in Brussels 1982–87; served in Prime Minister's Office 1987–88, responsible for int. econ. orgs; Dir-Gen. Ministry of Int. Econ. Relations 1988–92; Perm. State Sec., Ministry of Industry and Trade 1992–93; Amb. to Denmark 1994–96, to Germany 1997–2000; Prof., Budapest Univ. of Econs and Public Admin 2000–02, Corvinus Univ. 2005–, Cen. European Univ. 2005–, Prof. Dept of Int. Relations and European Studies 2010–; State Sec. for Integration and External Econ. Relations, Ministry of Foreign Affairs 2002–03; Perm. Rep. to EU 2003–04, EU Commr (without Portfolio) May–Nov. 2004; Minister of Foreign Affairs 2009–10; Ed. Európa Fórum Budapest; Founding mem. ECSA Hungary, Hungarian Foreign Affairs Soc., European Movt Hungary; mem. Union of Hungarian Economists; Dr hc (Hungarian Acad. of Sciences); Dr Jean Mayer Global Citizenship Award, Tufts Univ. 2016. *Publications include:* Legal and Theoretical Questions of the Implementation of the Europe Agreement (co-ed.) 1995, Preparations of Hungary for EU membership (co-ed.) 1996, The External Relations of the EU and Hungary 1996, European Unification and Modernisation 2001, Foreign Policy of the European Union and the Development of Relations Between Hungary and the EU 2002, The EU budget: challenges and reform plans (co-ed.) 2007, Hungary and Europe 2011. *Address:* Nador u. 11, Room 604, Central European University, 1051 Budapest, Hungary (office). *Telephone:* (1) 327-3000 (office). *E-mail:* balazsp@ceu.hu (office). *Website:* www.ceu.hu (office).

BALBINOT, Sergio, MBA; Italian business executive; *Vice-Chairman of the Supervisory Board, Allianz SpA;* b. 8 Sept. 1958, Tarvisio (Udine); m.; one s. one d.; began career with business scholarship, EC, Brussels; joined Assicurazioni Generali as graduate trainee, Munich 1983, positions in Trieste, later Zurich 1989, Paris 1992, returned to HQ, Trieste 1995, Gen. Man., Generali Group 2000, Man. Dir 2002–12, CEO for Insurance 2010–14, Chief Insurance Officer 2012–14, mem. Supervisory Bd, Generali Investments SpA; Vice-Chair. and Dir of several Austrian, Chinese, French, Israeli, Dutch, Spanish, US and German cos, including Generali España Holding Entidades de Seguros SA, Generali Holding Vienna AG, Generali France SA, Generali China Life Insurance Co. Ltd, Graafschap Holland Participatie Maatschappij NV, Generali Deutschland Holding AG, Generali España -SA de Seguros y Reaseguros, Future Generali India Insurance Co. Ltd and Future Generali India Life Insurance Co. Ltd; mem. Supervisory Bd Commerzbank AG; Chair. Generali PPF Holding BV; mem. Man. Bd, Allianz SE 2015–, Vice-Chair. Supervisory Bd, Allianz SpA 2015–; Pres. Insurance Europe (European insurance and reinsurance federation) 2011–; mem. Bd Geneva Asscn; mem. European Financial Services Round Table, Pan European Insurance Forum. *Address:* Allianz SpA, Largo Ugo Irneri 1, 34132 Trieste TS, Italy (office). *Telephone:* (040) 7781111 (office). *Fax:* (040) 7781311 (office). *E-mail:* info@allianz.it (office). *Website:* www.allianz.it (office).

BALBUS, Steven A., BS, PhD, FRS; American astronomer, astrophysicist and academic; *Savilian Professor of Astronomy, University of Oxford;* b. 23 Nov. 1953, Philadelphia, Pa; s. of Theodore G. and Rita F. Balbus; m. Caroline Terquem; four c.; ed William Penn Charter School, Massachusetts Inst. of Tech., Univ. of California, Berkeley; held postdoctoral appointments at Princeton Univ., MIT and Univ. of Virginia 1985; Professeur des Universités, Physics Dept, École Normale Supérieure de Paris 2004–12; Savilian Prof. of Astronomy, Univ. of Oxford and Professorial Fellow, New Coll., Oxford 2012–; Bohdan Paczynski Visitor and Spitzer Lecturer, Princeton Univ. 2011; Visiting Miller Prof., Univ. of California at Berkeley 2012; mem. NAS; Fellow, Royal Soc.; Wolfson Research Merit Award, awarded a Chaire d'excellence by French Ministry of Higher Educ. 2004, Shaw Prize in Astronomy (co-recipient) 2013. *Publications include:* numerous papers in professional journals on astrophysical fluid dynamics, especially the behaviour of magnetized gases. *Address:* Denys Wilkinson Building, Keble Road, Oxford, OX1 3RH, England (office). *Telephone:* (1865) 273639 (office). *E-mail:* steven.balbus@physics.ox.ac.uk (office). *Website:* www2.physics.ox.ac.uk (office).

BALCEROWICZ, Leszek, MBA, DEconSc; Polish politician, economist, academic and fmr central banker; *Head, Department of Comparative International Studies, Warsaw School of Economics;* b. 19 Jan. 1947, Lipno; s. of Wacław Balcerowicz and Barbara Balcerowicz; m. Ewa Balcerowicz 1977; two s. one d.; ed Cen. School of Planning and Statistics, Warsaw, St John's Univ., New York; on staff, Cen. School of Planning and Statistics (now Warsaw School of Econs), Warsaw 1970–, Inst. of Int. Econ. Relations 1970–80; Head, Research Team attached to Econ. Devt Inst. 1978–81, Scientific Sec. Econ. Devt Inst. 1980–; Prof. and Head, Dept of Comparative Int. Studies, Warsaw School of Econs 1992–; mem. Polish United Workers' Party (PZPR) 1969–81; consultant, Network of Solidarity Ind. Self-governing Trade Union 1981–84; Deputy Prime Minister and Minister of Finance 1989–91, 1997–2000; Leader, Freedom Union (UW) 1995–2000; Pres. Nat. Bank of Poland 2001–07; Deputy to Sejm (Parl.) 1997–2000; fmr mem. Council of Econ. Advisers to Pres. Wałesa; Head of Inst. for Comparative Int. Studies, Warsaw School of Econs 1993–; Chair. Council of Centre for Social and Econ. Research, Warsaw 1992–2000, Bruegel, Brussels (think tank) 2008–12; apptd mem. Polish Econ. Soc. 1970, Vice-Chair. Gen. Bd 1981–82; apptd mem. Polish Sociological Soc. 1983, Warsaw Civic Cttee Solidarity 1989, Group of Thirty Consultative Group on Int. Econ. and Monetary Affairs, Inc., Washington, DC, Distinguished Assocs of the Int. Atlantic Econ. Soc. 2006, Group of Trustees, Inst. of Int. Finance 2006, Bd Peterson Inst., Washington, DC; Corresp. mem. History and Philosophy Class of Polish Acad. of Arts and Sciences 2006; Grand Cross of the Order of Merit 2000, Kt of the Order of the White Eagle 2005, Order Cross Earth Marian (Class II) 2014; numerous hon. degrees including Dr hc (Univ. of Aix-en-Provence, France) 1993, (Univ. of Sussex, UK) 1994, (De Paul Univ. of Chicago, USA) 1996, (Univ. of Szczecin, Poland) 1998, (Staffordshire Univ., UK) 1998, (Nikolaj Kopernik Univ. of Toruń, Poland) 1998, (Univ. of Dundee, UK) 1998, (Univ. of Econs, Bratislava, Slovakia) 1999, (Viadrina European Univ., Frankfurt (Oder), Germany) 2001, (Univ. of the Pacific, Lima, Peru, 'Alexandru Ioan Cuza' Univ., Iasi, Romania) 2002, (Gerhard Mercator Univ., Duisburg, Germany) 2004, (Karol Adamiecki Univ. of Econs, Katowice) 2006, (Poznań Univ. of Econs) 2006, (Wroclaw Univ. of Econs) 2006, (Univ. of Gdańsk) 2006, (Warsaw School of Econs) 2007, (Univ. of Warsaw) 2008, (Univ. of New South Wales, Australia) 2008, (Babeş-Bolyai Univ., Romania) 2009, (Acad. of Economic Studies of Moldova) 2010, (Burgas Prof. Assen Zlatarov Univ., Bulgaria) 2010, (Russian Presidential Acad. of Nat. Economy and Public Admin) 2011, (Higher School of Economics, Russia) 2011, (Central Connecticut State Univ., USA) 2011, (Universidad Francisco Marroquín, Guatemala) 2015; Awards of Minister of Science, Higher Educ. and Tech. 1978, 1980, 1981, Ludwig Erhard Prize, Ludwig Erhard Foundation (Germany) 1992, Euromoney Finance Minister of the Year 1998, Transatlantic Leadership Award, European Inst. of Washington 1999, Cen. European Award for Finance Minister of the Year 1999, Friedrich von Hayek Prize (Germany) 2001, Carl Bertelsman Prize 2001, Fasel Foundation Prize for Merits for the Social Market Economy 2002, European Cen. Banker of the Year, The Banker magazine 2004, Emerging Markets Award for Emerging Europe's Cen. Bank Gov. of the Year 2004, St George Medal 2009, Jana Nowaka-Jeziorański Award 2010. *Publications include:* Socialism, Capitalism, Transformation 1995, Freedom and Development: The Economics of the Free Market (in Polish) 1995, Post-communist Transition: Some Lessons 2002, Toward a Limited State 2003; numerous scientific works on int. econ. relations and problems of econ. systems. *Leisure interests:* basketball, detective stories. *Address:* Warsaw School of Economics, Aleja Niepodległości 162, 02-554 Warsaw, Poland (office). *Telephone:* (22) 5649345 (office). *Fax:* (22) 5649833 (office). *E-mail:* kmsp@sgh.waw.pl (office). *Website:* www.sgh.waw.pl (office); www.balcerowicz.pl.

BALČYTIS, Zigmantas; Lithuanian economist and politician; b. 16 Nov. 1953, Žemaičių Naumiestis, Šilutė Dist Municipality; m. Severina Balčytienė; one s. one d.; ed Faculty of Finance and Accounting, Vilnius Univ.; Engineer, Planning and Design Bureau, Ministry of Food Industry 1976–78; Young Communist League 1978–84; Deputy Dir Lithuanian Nat. Philharmonic 1984–89; Man. of Trade Union Affairs and Dir of Training Centre 1989–91; Dir Vilnius Asphalt and Concrete Factory 1992–94; mem. Vilnius City Council 1994, Deputy Gov. Vilnius Co. 1994–96; First Deputy Dir of Lithuanian-Hungarian Jt Venture Lithun 1996–2000; Minister of Transport and Communications 2001–05; mem. Siemas 2004–09; Minister of Finance and Gov. of EIB for Lithuania 2005–07 (resgnd); Acting Prime Minister June–July 2006; second-placed cand. in presidential election 2014; mem. Social Democratic Party; mem. Parl. Ass. of Council of Europe 2008–09; mem. European Parl. 2009–; f. Padėkime kitiems (Let's Help Others) Foundation 2003; Order of the Cross of the Gunner (Lithuania), Order of the Great Cross (Spain), (Portugal), Order of Merit (Lithuania); Medal of Afanasij Nikitin, Commemorative Medal of 750th Anniversary of King Mindaugas' Coronation. *Leisure interests:* hunting, tennis. *Address:* European Parliament, Bât. Altiero Spinelli, 13G146 60, rue Wiertz, Brussels, Belgium (office); Ž. Liauksmino g. 3/8, Vilnius 01101, Lithuania (office). *E-mail:* info@balcytis.lt (office). *Website:* www.balcytis.lt (office).

BALDACCI, John Elias, BA; American politician; b. 30 Jan. 1955, Bangor, Me; m. Karen Weston; one s.; ed Bangor High School, Univ. of Maine; worked in family restaurant Momma Baldacci's, Bangor; mem. Bangor City Council 1978–81; mem. Maine State Senate 1982–94; mem. US House of Reps from Second Dist of Maine, Washington, DC 1995–2003; Gov. of Maine 2003–11; hired by Under-Sec. of Defense Clifford L. Stanley to study mil. health care 2011–12; Democrat; Nat. Energy Assistance Dirs Asscn Award 1997, Small Business Assistance Award, NASA, Big M Award, Maine State Soc., Washington, DC 2000. *Leisure interest:* holds technician class amateur radio licence with call sign KB1NXP. *Address:* c/o Office of the Governor, 1 State House Station, Augusta, ME 04333, USA.

BALDAUF, Sari Maritta, MSc, DSc; Finnish business executive; b. 10 Aug. 1955, Kotka; ed Helsinki School of Econs and Business Admin; Researcher, Finland Int. Business Operations project, Helsinki School of Econs and Business Admin 1977–78; Training Officer, Finnish Inst. of Exports 1979–80; Market Man. Falcon Communications, Abu Dhabi 1981–82; Planning Man. Nokia Corpn 1983–85, Vice-Pres. Corp. Planning, Nokia Electronics 1985–86, Asst Vice-Pres. Business Devt and Venture Capital, Nokia, New York 1986–87, Vice-Pres. Business Devt, Telenokia 1987–88, Pres. Cellular Systems, Nokia Telecommunications 1988–96, mem. Group Exec. Bd Nokia Corpn 1994, Exec. Vice-Pres. Nokia APAC 1997–98, Pres. Nokia Networks 1998–2003, Exec. Vice-Pres. and Gen. Man. of Networks 2004–05; mem. Bd of Dirs Fortum 2009–, Chair. Nomination and Remuneration Cttee 2016–; apptd mem. Bd of Dirs F-Secure Corpn 2006, YIT Corpn 2006, Int. Youth Foundation 2000, Foundation for Econ. Educ. 2002, SanomaWSOY 2003, Hewlett-Packard Co. 2006, CapMan 2007, Finland-China Trade Asscn 1997–99, Tech. Research Centre of Finland 1998–2001, currently Deutsche Telekom AG, Akzo Nobel NV, Daimler AG, Muuvit Health & Learning Oy, Tukikummit Foundation, Connected Day Ltd; Chair. Savonlinna Opera Festival; mem. Nat. Cttee for the Information Soc. Issues 1996–2003, Finnish Acad. of Tech., Consultative Cttee of Sibelius Acad. Support Foundation 2003–; mem. Int. Advisory Bd Instituto de Empresa (business school) 2007–; Knight, 1st Class of the Order of the White Rose of Finland 1996; Hon. DTech (Helsinki Univ. of Tech.). *Leisure interests:* classical music, hiking, skiing, spending time with family and friends.

BALDESCHWIELER, John Dickson, PhD; American chemist and academic; *J. Stanley Johnson Professor and Professor Emeritus of Chemistry, California Institute of Technology;* b. 14 Nov. 1933, Elizabeth, NJ; s. of Emile L. Baldeschwieler and Isobel M. Dickson; m. Marlene Konnar 1991; two s. one d. from previous m.; ed Cornell Univ. and Univ. of California, Berkeley; Asst Prof., Harvard Univ. 1962–65; Assoc. Prof., Stanford Univ. 1965–67, Prof. of Chem. 1967–73; Deputy Dir Office of Science and Tech., The White House, Washington, DC 1971–73; Prof. of Chem., Calif. Inst. of Tech. 1973, then J. Stanley Johnson Prof., now Prof. Emer., Chair., Div. of Chem. and Chem. Eng 1973–78; mem. Bd of Trustees Keck Graduate Inst.; Founder and Chair. Vestar Research Inc. 1981–; Founder and fmr Dir Combion Inc.; fmr Chair. Acad. Cttee on Commercial Aviation Security; fmr advisor to US Fed. Aviation Admin; Alfred P. Sloan Foundation Fellow 1962–65; Fellow, NAS, American Acad. of Arts 1972, American Philosophical Soc.; ACS Award in Pure Chem. 1967, William H. Nichols Award 1990, Nat. Medal of Science 2000, ACS Award for Creative Invention 2001, Othmer Gold Medal, Chemical Heritage Foundation 2003. *Publications:* numerous articles in professional journals. *Leisure interests:* hiking, skiing, photography, music, travel. *Address:* Division of Chemistry and Chemical Engineering, 232 Noyes, Mail Code 127-72, California Institute of Technology, Pasadena, CA 91125 (office); PO Box 50065, Pasadena, CA 91115-0065, USA (home). *Telephone:* (626) 395-6088 (office). *Fax:* (626) 568-0402 (office). *E-mail:* jb@caltech.edu (office). *Website:* www.cce.caltech.edu (office).

BALDESSARI, John, MA; American artist and academic; b. 17 June 1931, National City, Calif.; ed San Diego State Univ., Univ. of California, Berkeley, Univ. of California, Los Angeles, Otis Art Inst., Los Angeles, Chouinard Art Inst., Los Angeles; teacher, Calif. Inst. of the Arts, Valencia 1970–88; Prof. of Art, UCLA 1996–2007; Los Angeles Inst. for the Humanities Fellow, Univ. of Southern Calif. 2002; Guggenheim Fellowship 1988; Hon. DFA (Otis Art Inst. of Parsons School of Design of the New School of Social Research) 2000, (San Diego State Univ.) 2003, (Calif. State Univ.) 2003; Oscar Kokoschka Prize (Austria) 1996, Gov. of Calif.'s Award for Lifetime Achievement in the Visual Arts 1997, Spectrum-International Award for Photography, Foundation of Lower Saxony, Germany 1999, Coll. Art Asscns' Lifetime Achievement Award 1999, Artist Space, New York 2000, Best Web-Based Original Art, AICA USA Best Show Awards 2002, 2nd Place, Best Show Commercial Gallery National for exhibit at Margo Leavin Gallery, US Art Critics Asscn 2003, Americans for the Arts Lifetime Achievement Award, New York 2005, honoured by Rolex Mentor and Protégé Arts Initiative, New York 2005, BACA Int. 2008, Golden Lion for Lifetime Achievement, La Biennale di Venezia 2009. *Publications:* Throwing a Ball to Get Three Melodies and Fifteen Chords 1975, Close-Cropped Tales 1981, The Life and Opinions of Tristam Shandy (39 photo-collage illustrations for the novel by Laurence Sterne) 1988, The Telephone Book (With Pearls) 1988, Lamb (co-author) 1989, Zorro (Two Gestures and One Mark) 1998, The Metaphor Problem Again (co-author) 1999, Brown and Green and Other Parables 2001; numerous articles and reviews. *Address:* c/o John Baldessari, 626½ Vernon Avenue, Venice, CA 90291, USA. *E-mail:* john@baldessari.org (office). *Website:* www.baldessari.org.

BALDING, Clare Victoria, OBE; British television presenter, writer, broadcaster and amateur jockey (retd); b. 29 Jan. 1971, Kingsclere, Hants.; d. of Ian Balding and Emma Balding (née Hastings-Bass); civil partner Alice Arnold 2006– (m. 2015); ed Downe House, Berks., Newnham Coll., Cambridge; amateur flat jockey 1988–93, Champion Lady Rider 1990; Pres. Cambridge Union Soc. 1992; trainee with BBC Nat. Radio 1994, worked on 5 Live, Radio 1, Radio 2 and Radio 4; debut as TV presenter introducing highlights of Royal Ascot 1995, became BBC's lead horse racing presenter 1997, covered Grand National 1998–2012, for Channel 4 2013–, anchored coverage of Cheltenham Festival March 2013; has worked on five Summer Olympic Games, four Paralympic Games, four Winter Olympic Games and three Commonwealth Games; continues to present horse racing for Channel 4; has also presented a wide range of sporting and other events; host, Ramblings (BBC Radio 4) 1999–; worked on Britain's Hidden Heritage and Countryfile 2011–12; presented Sport and the British for BBC Radio 4 2012; regular presenter, Good Morning Sunday (BBC Radio 2) 2012–; presenter, Britain's Brightest on BBC TV 2013; host, Clare Balding Show (BT Sport and BBC 2) 2013–; has written regular columns for The Observer, Evening Standard, The Sporting Life; Patron British Thyroid Foundation 2010–; mem. of several BAFTA Award-winning programmes, Best Sports Presenter, Royal Television Soc. (RTS) Television Sport Awards 2003, Racing Journalist of the Year Award 2003, RTS Presenter of the Year Award for her coverage of the London 2012 Olympic and Paralympic Games, Sports Presenter of the Year, TRIC Awards, Special Achievement Award, Women in Film and Television Awards for her work on the Olympics and Paralympics, also honoured with awards from Attitude Magazine, Red Magazine, Tatler and the Horserace Writers' Asscn, British Sports Journalism Award for Sports Broadcaster of the Year (BBC and Channel 4), Sports Journalists' Asscn 2012, Award for Sports Presenter, Television and Radio Industries Club Awards 2013, Special BAFTA Award 2013. *Publication:* My Animals and Other Family (autobiog.) (Biography/Autobiography of the Year, Nat. Book Awards) 2012. *Address:* c/o David Phillips, James Grant Group Ltd, 94 Strand on the Green, Chiswick, London, W4 3NN, England (office). *E-mail:* david@jamesgrant.co.uk (office). *Website:* www.clarebalding.co.uk.

BALDINI, Stefano; Italian long distance runner; b. 25 May 1971, Castelnovo di Sotto; m. Virna De Angeli; one d.; competed in 5,000m, 10,000m and marathon events; held nat. record for marathon; winner World Half Marathon 1996; Gold Medal Marathon, European Championships 1998, 2006, Athens Olympics 2004; works for Fox Sports TV Commentator 2; Consultant and Spokesperson, Asics cos 2000–, Born2Run 2009–, Enervit 2013–, Garmin 2015–; Tutor of the Youth Federazione Italiana Di Atletica Leggera 2010–12, Tech. Collaborator 2011–12, Technical Dir of the Youth 2012–, Coach 2013–, Tech. Specialist ASA 2016–; Commendatore, Ordine al Merito della Repubblica Italiana 2004. *Publications:* Con le ali ai piedi 2005, Quelli che corrono 2007, Maratona per tutti 2009. *Website:* www.stefanobaldini.net (home).

BALDISSERI, HE Cardinal Lorenzo; Italian ecclesiastic and diplomatist; *Secretary-General of the Synod of Bishops;* b. 29 Sept. 1940, Barga; ed Pontifical Lateran Univ., Univ. of Perugia; ordained priest, Archdiocese of Pisa 1963; assigned to Guatemala as part of the Diplomatic Service of the Holy See 1973, also worked in many other areas of the world; consecrated Titular Archbishop of Diocletiana 1992; Apostolic Nuncio to Haiti 1992–95, to Paraguay 1995–99, to India (also accred to Nepal) 1999–2002, to Brazil 2002–12; Sec. of the Congregation for Bishops 2012–13; Sec. of the Coll. of Cardinals 2012–14; Sec.-Gen. of the Synod of Bishops 2013–; Sec. of the Papal Conclave 2013; cr. Cardinal (Cardinal-Deacon of Sant'Anselmo all'Aventino) 2014–. *Address:* Synod of Bishops, Palazzo del Bramante, Via della Conciliazione 34, 00193 Rome, Italy (office). *Telephone:* (06) 69884821 (office). *Fax:* (06) 69883392 (office). *Website:* www.vatican.va (office).

BALDWIN, Alexander (Alec) Rae, III; American actor; b. 3 April 1958, Massapequa, NY; s. of Alexander Rae Baldwin, Jr and Carol Baldwin (née Martineau); m. Kim Basinger (q.v.) 1993 (divorced 2002); one d.; ed George Washington and New York Univs, Lee Strasberg Theater Inst.; also studied with Mira Rostova and Elaine Aiken; mem. Screen Actors' Guild, American Fed. of TV and Radio Artists, Actors Equity Asscn; mem. Bd of Dirs People for the American Way, New York Philharmonic 2011–; Hon. DFA (New York Univ) 2010. *Stage appearances include:* Loot (Theatre World Award 1986) 1986, Serious Money 1988, Prelude to a Kiss 1990, A Streetcar Named Desire 1992. *Film appearances include:* Forever Lulu 1987, She's Having a Baby 1987, Beetlejuice 1988, Married to the Mob 1988, Talk Radio 1988, Working Girl 1988, Great Balls of Fire 1989, The Hunt for Red October 1990, Miami Blues 1990, Alice 1990, The Marrying Man 1991, Prelude to a Kiss 1992, Glengarry Glen Ross 1992, Malice 1993, The Getaway 1994, The Shadow 1994, Heaven's Prisoners 1995, Looking for Richard 1996, The Juror 1996, Ghosts of Mississippi 1996, Bookworm 1997, The Edge 1997, Thick as Thieves 1998, Outside Providence 1998, Mercury Rising 1998 (also producer), The Confession 1999, Notting Hill 1999, Thomas and the Magic Railroad 2000, State and Main 2000, Pearl Harbor 2001, Cats and Dogs (voice) 2001, Final Fantasy: The Spirits Within 2001, The Royal Tenenbaums (voice) 2001, The Devil and Daniel Webster 2001, Path to War 2002, Dr Seuss' The Cat in the Hat 2003, The Cooler 2003, Along Came Polly 2004, The Last Shot 2004, The Aviator 2004, Elizabethtown 2005, Fun with Dick and Jane 2005, Mini's First Time 2006, The Departed 2006, Running with Scissors 2006, The Good Shepherd 2006, Suburban Girl 2007, Brooklyn Rules 2007, Lymelife 2008, My Best Friend's Girl 2008, Madagascar: Escape 2 Africa (voice) 2008, My Sister's Keeper 2009, It's Complicated 2009, AmeriQua 2011, Rock of Ages 2012, Rise of the Guardians 2012, Blue Jasmine 2013, Torrente 5: Operación Eurovegas 2014, Still Alice 2014, Mission: Impossible–Rogue Nation 2015, Concussion 2015, Paris Can Wait 2016, Rules Don't Apply 2016. *TV appearances include:* The Doctors 1980–82, Cutter to Houston 1982, Knots Landing 1984–85, Love on the Run 1985, A Dress Gray 1986, The Alamo: 13 Days to Glory 1986, Sweet Revenge 1990, Nuremberg 2000, Path to War 2002, Second Nature 2002, Dreams and Giants 2003, Thomas and Friends: The Best of Gordon 2004, 30 Rock (series) (Golden Globe Award for Best Actor in a Musical or Comedy TV Series 2007, 2009, Screen Actors' Guild Award for Outstanding Performance by a Male Actor in a Comedy Series 2007, 2008, Emmy Award for Outstanding Lead Actor in a Comedy Series 2009, Golden Globe Award for Best Actor in a Musical or Comedy TV Series 2010) 2006–13, The Marriage Ref 2010, Saturday Night Live (Emmy Award for Outstanding Supporting Actor in a Comedy Series 2017) 2007–. *Publication:* A Promise to Ourselves: A Journey through Fatherhood and Divorce (with Mark Tabb) 2008. *Website:* www.alecbaldwin.com.

BALDWIN, Sir Jack Edward, Kt, BSc, PhD, FRS; British chemist and academic; *Professor, Chemistry Research Laboratory, University of Oxford;* b. 8 Aug. 1938, London; s. of Frederick C. Baldwin and Olive F. Headland; m. Christine L. Franchi 1977; ed Lewes County Grammar School and Imperial Coll., London; Asst Lecturer in Chem., Imperial Coll. London 1963–66, Lecturer 1966–67; Asst Prof. of Chem., Pennsylvania State Univ. 1967–69, Assoc. Prof. 1969–70; Assoc. Prof. of Chem., MIT, USA 1970–71, Prof. 1971–78; Daniell Prof. of Chem., King's Coll., London 1972; Waynflete Prof. of Chem., Univ. of Oxford 1978–2005, now Prof., Chemistry Research Lab., Head, Dyson Perrins Lab. 1978–2003, Dir Oxford Centre for Molecular Sciences, Fellow, Magdalen Coll. 1978–; mem. Biotechnology and Biological Sciences Research Council 1994–; Corresp. mem. Academia Scientiarum Gottingensis, Göttingen 1988; Foreign Hon. mem. American Acad. of Arts and Sciences 1994; Hon. DSc (Warwick) 1988, (Strathclyde) 1989; Corday Morgan Medal and Prize, Chemical Soc. 1975, RSC Medal and Prize for Synthetic Organic Chem. 1980, Paul Karrer Medal and Prize, Univ. of Zurich 1984, RSC Medal and Prize for Natural Product Chem. 1984, RSC Hugo Muller Medal 1987, Max Tischler Award, Harvard Univ. 1987, Dr Paul Janssen Prize for Creativity in Organic Synthesis (Belgium) 1988, Davy Medal, Royal Soc. 1994, Leverhulme Medal, Royal Soc. 1999, Kitasako Medal 2000. *Publications:* papers on organic and bio-organic chem. in Journal of the American Chemical Society, Journal of the Chemical Society and Nature. *Leisure interests:* British motorbikes, gardening. *Address:* Chemistry Research Laboratory, University of Oxford, Mansfield Road, Oxford, OX1 3TA, England (office). *Telephone:* (1865) 275670 (office). *E-mail:* jack.baldwin@chem.ox.ac.uk (office). *Website:* research.chem.ox.ac.uk/jack-baldwin.aspx (office).

BALDWIN, Mark Phillip, OBE, BFA; British choreographer and ballet company director; *Artistic Director, Rambert;* b. Fiji; ed Univ. of Auckland, NZ; raised and educated in NZ; danced with Royal New Zealand Ballet before joining Ballet Rambert (now known as Rambert) 1983–93, Artistic Dir 2002–; Resident Choreographer, Sadler's Wells 1993, est. Mark Baldwin Dance Co. 1993–2001, cr. more than 40 works for major dance cos, including Royal Ballet, Royal New Zealand Ballet, Berlin State Opera House, Phoenix Dance Theatre, Scottish Ballet, London City Ballet, Ballet Rambert; Bonnie Bird Choreographic Award 1992, Time Out Award for Dance 1995, South Bank Show Award for The Bird Sings With Its Fingers 2001, French Grand Prix Award for Film for Echo (collaboration with Anish Kapoor and Brian Elias) 1996, Dance Artist Fellowship for Outstanding Contrib. to Dance 2002, TMA Theatre Award for Achievement in Dance 2005, Olivier Award 2010, Hon. Amber Faun, Sergei Diaghilev Int. Asscn for the Promotion of Choreographic Art 2012. *Address:* Rambert, 99 Upper Ground, London, SE1 9PP, England (office). *Telephone:* (20) 8630-0600 (office). *E-mail:* info@rambert.org.uk (office). *Website:* www.rambert.org.uk (office).

BALDWIN, Peter Jeremy, BEE, BA; Australian fmr politician; b. 12 April 1951, Aldershot, UK; ed Univ. of Sydney, Macquarie Univ.; fmr engineer and computer programmer; mem. NSW State Parl. (Upper House) 1976–82; mem. House of Reps (Labor Party) for Sydney 1983–98, mem. Parl. Cttee on Foreign Affairs, Defence and Trade 1987–90, House of Reps Standing Cttee on Industry, Science and Tech. 1987–90; Minister for Higher Educ. and Employment Services and Minister Assisting Treasurer 1990–93; Minister for Social Security 1993–96; apptd Shadow Minister for Finance 1997; Co-founder DebateGraph (web-based collaborative tool) 2008. *Address:* Level 3, 10 Mallet Street, Camperdown, NSW 2050, Australia. *Website:* debategraph.org.

BALDWIN, Tammy Suzanne Green, BA, JD; American lawyer and politician; *Senator from Wisconsin;* b. 11 Feb. 1962, Madison, Wis.; d. of Joseph Edward Baldwin and Pamela Baldwin (née Green); partner Lauren Azar 1995–2010; ed Madison West High School, Smith Coll., Univ. of Wisconsin, Madison; practised law 1989–92; elected to Dane Co. Bd of Supervisors 1986–94; mem. Wisconsin State Ass. from 78th Dist 1993–99, Chair. Educ. Cttee, mem. Criminal Justice Cttee; mem. US House of Reps for the 2nd Congressional Dist of Wis. 1999–2013, mem. Cttee on Energy and Commerce; Senator from Wisconsin 2013–, mem. Cttees on Health, Education, Labor and Pensions, Budget, Homeland Security and

Governmental Affairs, Energy and Natural Resources and Special Cttee on Aging; Democrat. *Address:* 717 Hart Senate Office Building, Washington, DC 20510, USA (office). *Telephone:* (202) 224-3121 (office). *Website:* www.baldwin.senate.gov (office); www.tammybaldwin.com.

BALE, Christian; British actor; b. 30 Jan. 1974, Haverfordwest, Pembrokeshire, Wales; s. of David Bale and Jenny James; m. Sandra Blažić 2000; one s. one d. *Films include:* Mio min Mio (aka The Land of Faraway) 1987, Empire of the Sun (Nat. Bd of Review Award for Outstanding Juvenile Performance 1987) 1987, Henry V 1989, Newsies 1992, Swing Kids 1993, Prince of Jutland 1994, Little Women 1994, Pocahontas 1995, The Portrait of a Lady 1996, The Secret Agent 1996, Metroland 1997, Velvet Goldmine 1998, All the Little Animals 1998, A Midsummer Night's Dream 1999, American Psycho 2000, Shaft 2000, Captain Corelli's Mandolin 2001, Laurel Canyon 2002, Reign of Fire 2002, Equilibrium 2002, The Machinist 2004, Hauru no ugoku shiro (aka Howl's Moving Castle; voice: English version) 2004, Batman Begins 2005, The New World 2005, Rescue Dawn 2006, Harsh Times 2006, The Prestige 2006, I'm Not There 2007, 3:10 to Yuma 2007, The Dark Knight 2008, Terminator Salvation 2009, Public Enemies 2009, The Fighter (Nat. Bd of Review Award for Best Supporting Actor 2010, Golden Globe Award for Best Supporting Actor 2011, Acad. Award for Actor in a Supporting Role 2011, New York Film Critics Online Best Supporting Actor, Washington, DC Area Film Critics Asscn Award for Best Supporting Actor) 2010, The Flowers of War 2011, The Dark Knight Rises 2012, American Hustle 2013, Exodus: Gods and Kings 2014, Knight of Cups 2015, The Big Short 2015, The Promise 2016, Hostiles 2017, Mowgli: Legend of the Jungle (voice) 2018, Vice (Golden Globe Award for Best Actor in a Motion Picture - Musical or Comedy 2019) 2018, Ford v. Ferrari (2019). *Television includes:* Anastasia: The Mystery of Anna 1986, Heart of the Country (mini-series) 1987, Treasure Island 1990, A Murder of Quality 1991, Mary, Mother of Jesus 1999, Nyhetsmorgon (episode) 2009. *Address:* c/o WME Entertainment, 9601 Wilshire Blvd, Beverly Hills, CA 90210, USA (office). *Telephone:* (310) 285-9000 (office). *Website:* www.wma.com (office).

BALE, Gareth Frank; Welsh professional football player; b. 16 July 1989, Cardiff, Wales; s. of Frank Bale and Debbie Bale; partner Emma Rhys-Jones; one s. two d.; ed Whitchurch High School, Cardiff; winger; youth career at Southampton, playing at left back 2005–06 (won Premier Academy League 2005–06); has played for Southampton 2006–07 (45 appearances, 5 goals), Tottenham Hotspur 2007–13 (203 appearances, 55 goals) (runner-up, League Cup 2009), Real Madrid 2013– (winners, Copa del Rey 2013–14, UEFA Champions League 2013–14, 2015-16, 2016-17, 2017-18, UEFA Super Cup 2014, 2017, FIFA Club World Cup 2014, 2017, 2018, La Liga 2016/17); played for Wales U17 2005–06 (7 appearances, 1 goal), Wales U19 2006 (1 appearance, 1 goal), Wales U21 2006–08 (4 appearances, 2 goals), Wales 2006– (75 appearances, 31 goals to March 2019); Wales Player of the Year Award 2010, 2011, 2013, 2014, 2015, 2016, BBC Wales Sports Personality of the Year 2010, Premier League Player of the Season 2012–13, Footballer of the Year, Football Writers' Asscn 2012–13. *Address:* c/o FC Real Madrid, Estadio Santiago Bernabéu, Paseo de la Castellana 104, Madrid, Spain. *E-mail:* info@realmadrid.com. *Website:* www.realmadrid.com.

BALESTRINI, Nanni; Italian poet, author and artist; b. 2 July 1935, Milan; mem. group of poets called Novissimi and Co-founder of Gruppo 63 in Palermo 1963; one of prin. eds of literary magazine Il Verri; co-editor (with Alfredo Giuliani) Quindici magazine 1966–68; has organized numerous confs and exhbns; also a figurative artist, exhibiting in many galleries in Italy and abroad, and at Venice Biennale in 1993; co-owner Alfabeta2. *Publications include:* poetry: Come si agisce 1963, Ma noi facciamone un'altra 1966, Le ballate della signorina Richmond 1977, Blackout 1980, Ipocalisse 1986, Il ritorno della signorina 1987, Osservazioni sul volo degli uccelli, poesie 1954–56 1988, The Unseen 1989, Il pubblico del labirinto 1992, Estremi rimedi 1995, Le avventure complete della signorina 1999, Elettra, operapoesia 2001, Sfinimondo 2003, Sconnessioni 2008, Blackout e altro 2009, Lo sventramento della storia 2009, Caosmogonia 2010, Una poesia totale 2014; novels: Tristano 1964, Vogliamo tutto 1971, La violenza illustrata 1976, Gli invisibili 1987, L'editore 1989, I furiosi 1994, Una mattina ci siam svegliati 1995, La Grande Rivolta (comprising Vogliamo tutto, Gli invisibili, L'editore) 1999, Sandokan, storia di camorra 2004, Liberamilano seguito da Una mattina ci siam svegliati 2011; other works: Gruppo 63. Il romanzo sperimentale 1965, L'Opera di Pechino (with Letizia Paolozzi) 1966, L'orda d'oro (with Primo Moroni) 1988, Paladino 2002, Parma 1922 (radio drama) 2002, Con gli occhi del linguaggio 2006, Les yeux invisibles 2008, Qualcosaper tutti 2010, Tristanoil 2012, I maestri del colore 2012; contrib. to many periodicals and journals. *E-mail:* info@nannibalestrini.it (office). *Website:* www.nannibalestrini.info; www.nannibalestrini.it (office).

BALIBAR, Jeanne; French actress; b. 13 April 1968, Paris; d. of Etienne Balibar and Françoise Balibar; pnr, Mathieu Amalric; two s.; ed Univ. de Paris I. *Plays:* Dom Juan (Avignon) 1993, Le Square, Les Bonnes, La Glycine, Clitandre (Comédie Française), Macbeth 1997, Penthesilea 1997, Uncle Vanya (Paris) 2003, Le cadavre vivant (Paris) 2003, Le Soulier de Satin (Paris) 2003. *Films:* La Sentinelle 1992, Un dimanche à Paris 1994, Comment je me suis disputé ... (ma vie sexuelle) 1996, J'ai horreur d'amour 1997, Trois ponts sur la rivière 1999, Sade 2000, Comédie d'innocence 2000, Va savoir 2001, Avec tout mon amour 2001, Intimisto 2001, Une affaire privée 2002, Saltimbank 2003, Code 46 2003, Toutes ces belles promesses 2003, Clean 2004, Mademoiselle Y 2006, Call Me Agostino 2006, J'aurais voulu être un danseur 2007, Ne touchez pas la hache 2007, Sagan 2008, The Ball of the Actresses 2009, A Town Called Panic 2009, Ne Change Rien 2009, Layla Fourie 2013, Grace of Monaco 2014, Summer Nights 2014, Deadweight 2016, Never Ever 2016. *Television:* A Cursed Monarchy (mini-series) 2005, To Die of Love 2009, Clara's End 2012, The Tunnel (series) 2013, La Tueuse Caméléon 2015. *Recordings include:* Paramour 2003. *Address:* Zelig, 57 rue de Turbigo, 75003 Paris, France (office).

BALKENENDE, Jan Peter, MA, LLM, PhD, DIur; Dutch politician and academic; *Professor of Governance, Institutions and Internationalisation, Erasmus University;* b. 7 May 1956, Kapelle; m. Dr Bianca Hoogendijk; one d.; ed Free Univ. of Amsterdam; Legal Affairs Policy Officer, Netherlands Univs Council 1982–84; mem. Amstelveen Municipal Council 1982–98, Leader, Council Christen-Democratisch Appèl (CDA) Group 1994–98; Prof. of Econs, Free Univ. of Amsterdam 1993–2002; mem. staff, Policy Inst. of the CDA 1984–98; mem. Parl. 1998–2002, Parl. Leader CDA 2001, Party Leader –2010 (resgnd); Prime Minister of the Netherlands 2002–10, also Minister of Gen. Affairs 2002–10; Prof. of Governance, Insts and Internationalisation, Erasmus Univ., Rotterdam 2010–; Partner, Corp. Responsibility, Ernst and Young (EY) 2011–16, External Sr Advisor 2016–; Grand Crosses from Netherlands, Luxembourg, Jordan, Germany, Brazil, Ghana, Sweden, Chile; Dr hc (Károli Gáspár Reformed Univ., Budapest) 2005, (Keio Univ., Tokyo) 2009, (Yonsei Univ., Seoul) 2010, (Hope Coll., Michigan) 2012; Abraham Kuyper Prize, Princeton, 2004, Foreign Policy Asscn Award, New York 2008, Benelux-Europa Prize 2008, Nordrhein-Westfalen Staatspreis 2009, Rus Prix 2010. *Publications include:* numerous articles on liberal individualism and communitarianism in Dutch society. *Address:* Erasmus School of Economics, Erasmus Univ., PO Box 1738, 3000 DR, Rotterdam, Netherlands (office). *Telephone:* (10) 884078832 (office). *E-mail:* sieglinde.van.veen@nl.ey.com (office). *Website:* www.ese.eur.nl (office); www.ey.com (office).

BALKHEYOUR, Khalid Ahmed; Saudi Arabian engineer and international organization executive; *President and CEO, Arab Satellite Communications Organization (ARABSAT);* ed California State Polytechnic Univ.; fmr Vice-Pres. Operations and Maintenance, Saudi Telecommunications Co., also fmr Dir of Int. Relations; Exec. Vice-Pres. Lucent Technologies (Saudi Arabia) 1999–2003; Pres. and CEO Arab Satellite Communications Org. (ARABSAT) 2003–; Vice-Chair. Thuraya Telecommunications Co. 2012–; currently Chair. Hellas Sat Consortium Ltd. *Address:* Arab Satellite Communications Organization (ARABSAT), Diplomatic Quarter, Alfazari Square, Abdulla Bin Huthafa Al Sahmy Street, Public Pension Agency Complex, Riyadh 11431, Saudi Arabia (office). *Telephone:* (1) 4820000 (office). *Fax:* (1) 4887999 (office). *E-mail:* khalid@arabsat.com (office). *Website:* www.arabsat.com (office).

BALL, Anthony (Tony), MBA; British media industry executive; b. 18 Dec. 1955; m. 2nd Gabriella Ball; ed Kingston Univ.; with Thames TV 1976–88; fmr sports broadcaster for Trans World Int.; with BSB Sport 1988–91; with Int. Man. Group 1991–93; with BSkyB 1993–95; with Fox/Liberty Network 1995–99; fmr Pres and COO Fox Sports International; Exec. Dir British Sky Broadcasting (BSkyB) 1999–2004; mem. Bd of Dirs Kabel Deutschland 2005–13, Chair. Supervisory Bd 2010–13; Dir (non-exec.) Marks & Spencer PLC 2000–02, Grupo Corporativo ONO 2006–, BT Plc 2009–, Portland Communications; mem. Supervisory Bd ProSiebenSat.1 Media 2004–; Chair. Ingenious Media Active Capital 2006–08; Sr Advisor, Providence Equity Partners 2012–; Fellow, Royal Television Soc.; Dr hc (Kingston Univ.), (Middlesex Univ.).

BALL, Sir Christopher John Elinger, (John Elinger), Kt, MA, FRSA; British academic (retd); b. 22 April 1935, London; s. of Laurence Elinger Ball and Christine Florence Mary (née Howe) Ball; m. Wendy Ruth Colyer 1958; three s. three d.; ed St George's School, Harpenden, Merton Coll., Oxford; Second Lt in Parachute Regt 1955–56; Lecturer in English Language, Merton Coll., Oxford 1960–61; Lecturer in Comparative Linguistics, SOAS, Univ. of London 1961–64; Fellow and Tutor in English Language, Lincoln Coll., Oxford 1964–69, Bursar 1972–79, Warden, Keble Coll., Oxford 1980–88; Jt Founding Ed. Toronto Dictionary of Old English 1970; mem. General Bd of the Faculties 1979–82, Hebdomadal Council 1985–89, Council and Exec., Templeton Coll., Oxford 1981–92, Editorial Bd, Oxford Review of Educ. 1984–96, CNAA 1982–88; Chair. Bd of Nat. Advisory Body for Public Sector Higher Educ. in England 1982–88, Univ. of Oxford English Bd 1977–79, Jt Standing Cttee for Linguistics 1979–83, Conf. of Colls. Fees Cttee 1979–85, Higher Educ. Information Services Trust 1987–90; Sec., Linguistics Asscn GB 1964–67; Publications Sec., Philological Soc. 1969–75; Gov. St George's School, Harpenden 1985–89, Centre for Medieval Studies, Oxford 1987, Brathay Hall Trust 1988–91, Manchester Polytechnic 1989–91; Founding Fellow in Kellogg Forum for Continuing Education, Univ. of Oxford 1988–89, RSA Fellow in Continuing Educ. 1990–92, Dir of Learning 1992–97; Founding Chair. Nat. Advisory Council for Careers and Educational Guidance (NACCEG); Pres. Nat. Campaign for Learning 1995–97, Patron 1998–; Chancellor Univ. of Derby 1995–2003; Founding Chair. The Talent Foundation 1999–2004; Chair. Global Univ. Alliance 2000–05; Millennium Fellow, Auckland Univ. of Tech., NZ 2000; Vice-Pres. Autistica 2010–15; Chair. DownsEd Int. 2010–15; Hon. Fellow, Lincoln Coll., Oxford 1981, Merton Coll., Oxford 1987, Keble Coll., Oxford 1989, Manchester Polytechnic 1988, Polytechnic of Cen. London 1991, Auckland Univ. of Tech., NZ 1992, North East Wales Inst. 1996, Oxford Brookes Univ. 2007; Hon. DLitt (CNAA) 1989; Hon. DUniv (Univ. of N London) 1993, (Open Univ.) 2002, (Univ. of Derby) 2003; Hon. DEd (Greenwich Univ.) 1994. *Publications:* Fitness for Purpose 1985, Aim Higher 1989, Higher Education into the 1990s (co-ed.) 1989, More Means Different 1990, Learning Pays 1991, Sharks and Splashes!: The Future of Education and Employment 1991, Profitable Learning 1992, Start Right 1994; poetry (as John Elinger): Still Life 2008, Operatic Interludes 2008, That Sweet City (with Katherine Shock) 2013, That Mightin Heart (with Katherine Shock) 2014; various contribs to philological, linguistic and educ. journals. *Address:* 45 Richmond Road, Oxford, OX1 2JJ, England (home). *Telephone:* (1865) 310800 (home).

BALL, Dwight William, MHA; Canadian pharmacist, business executive and politician; *Premier of Newfoundland and Labrador;* b. Deer Lake, Newfoundland and Labrador; m. Sharon Ball; one d.; began career as community pharmacist, Deer Lake and Springdale; owner of several residential care homes; also involved in real estate devt and venture capital investments; mem. Newfoundland and Labrador (NL) House of Ass. for Humber-Gros Morne Feb.–Oct. 2007, 2011–15, Leader of the Opposition 2012–13, 2013–15; Premier of Newfoundland and Labrador 2015–; mem. Liberal Party of Newfoundland and Labrador, Leader 2013–; fmr Pres. Canadian Pharmacists Asscn, Deer Lake Chamber of Commerce; fmr mem. Bd of Dirs Deer Lake Airport Authority, Western Regional Hosp. Foundation, Deer Lake and Area Food Bank; fmr West Coast Dir for Senior Hockey in NL. *Leisure interests:* salmon fishing, hockey, snowshoeing. *Address:* Office of the Premier, Confederation Building, East Block, POB 8700, St John's, NL A1B 4J6, Canada (office). *Telephone:* (709) 729-3570 (office). *Fax:* (709) 729-5875 (office). *E-mail:* premier@gov.nl.ca (office). *Website:* www.premier.gov.nl.ca/premier (office).

BALL, Sir John Macleod, Kt, BA (Hons), DPhil, FRS, FRSE; British mathematician and academic; *Sedleian Professor of Natural Philosophy and Director of the Oxford Centre for Nonlinear Partial Differential Equations, University of Oxford;*

b. 19 May 1948, Farnham, Surrey; m.; three c.; ed Mill Hill School, London, St John's Coll., Cambridge, Univ. of Sussex; SRC Postdoctoral Fellow, Heriot-Watt Univ. 1972–74, on leave to Lefschetz Center for Dynamical Systems, Brown Univ., USA 1972–74, Lecturer in Math., Heriot-Watt Univ. 1974–78, Reader in Mathematics 1978–82, Science and Eng Research Council Sr Fellow 1980–85, Prof. of Applied Analysis 1982–96, Hon. Prof. 1998–; Sedleian Prof. of Natural Philosophy and Dir Oxford Centre for Nonlinear Partial Differential Equations, Univ. of Oxford 1996–, Fellow, The Queen's Coll.; Visiting Prof., Univ. of California, Berkeley 1979–80, Inst. for Advanced Study, Princeton 1993–94 (mem. 2002–03), Tata Inst. of Fundamental Research, Bangalore 2001, Univ. of Montpellier II 2003, Univ. of Chile, Santiago 2004, Université Pierre et Marie Curie, Paris 2009; mem. Exec. Bd, Int. Council for Science; Chair. Isaac Newton Inst. Scientific Steering Cttee; mem. Conseil Scientifique du CNRS, Conseil Scientifique d'Electricité de France; Council mem. Eng and Physical Sciences Research Council 1994–99; Pres. Edinburgh Math. Soc. 1989–90, London Math. Soc. 1996–98; fmr Pres. Int. Math. Union; Chief Ed. (with R. D. James) Archive for Rational Mechanics and Analysis; Ed. Oxford Mathematical Monographs, Oxford Lecture Series in Mathematics and its Applications; Consulting Ed. World Scientific Series in Applied Analysis; mem. Editorial Bd, Annali di Matematica Pura ed Applicata, Applicable Analysis, Calculus of Variations and Partial Differential Equations, Control, Optimization and Calculus of Variations, Dynamics and Differential Equations, Mathematics in Action, Journal de Mathématiques Pures et Appliquées, Mathematical Methods and Models in Applied Science, Tbilisi Mathematical, Unione Matematica Italiana Lecture Notes Series Journal; mem. Academia Europaea 2008; Associé Etranger, Acad. des Sciences 2000; Foreign mem. Istituto Lombardo 2005, Norwegian Acad. of Science and Letters 2007; Fellow, Inst. of Math. and its Applications 2003; Hon. mem. Edinburgh Math. Soc. 2008, Hon. Fellow, St John Coll., Cambridge 2005, King Faisal Prize for Science 2018; Dr hc (École Polytechnique Fédérale de Lausanne); Hon. DSc (Heriot-Watt) 1998, (Sussex) 2000, (Univ. of Montpellier II) 2003, (Edinburgh) 2005; Whittaker Prize, Edinburgh Math. Soc. 1981, Keith Prize, Royal Soc. of Edinburgh 1990, Naylor Prize in Applied Math., London Math. Soc. 1995, Theodore Von Karman Prize, Soc. of Industrial and Applied Math. 1999, David Crighton Medal, Inst. of Math. and its Applications and London Math. Soc. 2003, Royal Medal, Royal Soc. of Edinburgh 2006, Sylvester Medal, Royal Soc. 2009. *Publications:* numerous papers in professional journals. *Address:* Room S1.17, Mathematical Institute, University of Oxford, Andrew Wiles Building, Radcliffe Observatory Quarter, Woodstock Road, Oxford, OX2 6GG, England (office). *Telephone:* (1865) 615110 (office). *E-mail:* john.ball@maths.ox.ac.uk (office). *Website:* www.maths.ox.ac.uk (office).

BALL, Michael Ashley, OBE; British actor, singer and broadcaster; b. 27 June 1962, Bromsgrove, Worcs.; s. of Anthony George Ball and Ruth Parry Ball (née Davies); partner Cathy McGowan; ed Plymouth Coll., Farnham Sixth Form Coll., Guildford School of Acting; numerous nat. and int. concert tours; co-founder and patron Research into Ovarian Cancer; Dr hc (Plymouth); Variety Club of Great Britain Most Promising Artiste Award 1989, The Variety Club Best Recording Artiste 1998, Theatregoers Club of Great Britain Most Popular Musical Actor 1999, Olivier Award for Best Actor in a Musical 2008, 2012, Classic BRIT Awards Group of the Year (with Alfie Boe) 2018. *Theatre includes:* Judas/John the Baptist in Godspell (debut), Aberystwyth 1984, Frederick in The Pirates of Penzance, Manchester Opera House 1984, Marius in Les Misérables, London 1985–86, Raoul in The Phantom of the Opera, London 1987–88, Alex in Aspects of Love, London 1989–90, New York (debut) 1990, Giorgio in Passion, London 1996, Alone Together (part of Divas Season), London 2001, Caractacus Potts in Chitty Chitty Bang Bang, London 2002–04, The Woman in White 2005, Hairspray (Olivier Award for Best Actor in a Musical) 2008, Sweeney Todd: The Demon Barber of Fleet Street (Olivier Award for Best Actor in a Musical) 2012. *Film:* England My England 1995. *Radio:* The Michael Ball Show (BBC Radio 2). *Television:* represented UK in Eurovision Song Contest 1992, own TV series 'Michael Ball' 1993, 1994, Royal Variety performances, Michael Ball in Concert (video) 1997, An Evening with Michael Ball 1998, Lord Lloyd Webber's 50th Birthday 1998, Michael Ball at Christmas 1999, Ball & Boe: One Night Only 2016, Ball & Boe: Back Together 2017. *Recordings include:* albums: Rage of the Heart 1987, Michael Ball 1992, Always 1993, One Careful Owner 1994, The Best of Michael Ball 1994, First Love 1996, Michael Ball – The Musicals 1996, Michael Ball – The Movies 1998, Christmas 1999, Live at the Royal Albert Hall 1999, This Time It's Personal 2000, Centre Stage 2001, Music 2005, One Voice 2006, Back to Bacharach 2007, Past and Present 2009, Songs of Love 2009, Encore 2010, Heroes 2011, Both Sides Now 2013, If Everyone Was Listening 2014, Together (with Alfie Boe) 2016, Together Again (with Alfie Boe) 2017; stage show cast recordings include Les Miserables 1986, Aspects of Love 1989, West Side Story 1993, Passion 1996, Chitty Chitty Bang Bang 2002, Sweeney Todd: The Demon Barber of Fleet Street 2012. *Leisure interests:* collecting graphic novels and single malt whiskies, country walking, music, theatre, cooking. *Address:* c/o Phil Bowdery, Live Nation (Music) UK Ltd, Regent Arcade House, 19–25 Argyll Street, London, W1F 7TS, England (office). *Telephone:* (20) 7009-3333 (office). *Fax:* (20) 7009-3211 (office). *E-mail:* sarah .donovan@livenation.co.uk (office). *Website:* www.livenation.co.uk (office); ww .mbfanclub.co.uk (office); www.michaelball.co.uk.

BALL, Sir (Robert) James, Kt, MA, PhD, CBIM, FIAM; British economist and academic; *Professor Emeritus of Economics, London Business School;* b. 15 July 1933, Saffron Walden; s. of Arnold James Hector Ball; m. 1st Patricia Mary Hart Davies 1954 (divorced 1970); one s. (deceased) three d. (one d. deceased); m. 2nd Lindsay Jackson (née Wonnacott) 1970; one step-s.; ed St Marylebone Grammar School, Queen's Coll., Oxford, Univ. of Pennsylvania, USA; RAF 1952–54; Research Officer, Univ. of Oxford Inst. of Statistics 1957–58; IBM Fellow, Univ. of Pennsylvania 1958–60; Lecturer, Univ. of Manchester 1960–63, Sr Lecturer 1963–65; Prof. of Econs, London Business School 1984–98, Prof. Emer. 1998–, Deputy Prin. 1971–72, Prin. 1972–84; Dir Barclays Bank Trust Co. Ltd 1973–86, Tube Investments 1974–84, IBM UK Holdings Ltd 1979–95, IBM UK Pensions Trust 1994; Chair. Legal and General Group PLC 1980–94, Royal Bank of Canada Holdings (UK) Ltd 1995–98; Dir LASMO 1988–94, Royal Bank of Canada 1990–98; Vice-Pres. Chartered Inst. of Marketing 1991–94; mem. Council British-N American Cttee 1985–98, Research Asscn 1985–, Marshall Aid Commemoration Comm. 1987–94; Econ. Adviser, Touche Ross & Co. 1984–95; Trustee Foulkes Foundation 1984–, Civic Trust 1986–91, The Economist 1987–99, ReAction Trust 1991–93; mem. Advisory Bd IBM UK Ltd 1995–98; Freeman of City of London 1987; Hon. DSc (Aston) 1987; Hon. DSocSc (Manchester) 1988. *Publications:* An Economic Model of the United Kingdom 1961, Inflation and the Theory of Money 1964, Inflation (ed.) 1969, The International Linkage of National Economic Models (ed.) 1972, Money and Employment 1982, The Economics of Wealth Creation (ed.) 1992, The British Economy at the Crossroads 1998, articles in professional journals. *Leisure interests:* chess, fishing, gardening. *Address:* London Business School, Sussex Place, Regent's Park, London, NW1 4SA, England (office). *Telephone:* (20) 7000-8419 (office). *Fax:* (20) 7000-7001 (office). *E-mail:* jball@ london.edu (office). *Website:* www.london.edu/economics (office).

BALLANTYNE, Sir Frederick Nathaniel, Kt, GCMG, MD, DrSci; Saint Vincent and the Grenadines cardiologist and government official; *Governor-General;* b. 5 July 1936, Layou; m. Sally Ann Ballantyne; ed Howard Univ. and Syracuse Univ. School of Medicine, USA; fmr Chief of Medicine, Kingstown General Hosp.; fmr Chief Medical Officer for Saint Vincent; Gov.-Gen. St Vincent and the Grenadines 2002–. *Address:* Office of the Governor-General, Government House, Old Montrose, Kingstown, Saint Vincent and the Grenadines (office). *Telephone:* 456-1401 (office). *Fax:* 457-9710 (office). *E-mail:* govthouse@vincysurf .com (office).

BALLARD, Mark, MA; British consultant and fmr politician; *Assistant Director for Policy, Barnardo's Scotland;* b. 27 June 1971, Leeds; m. Heather Stacey; one s.; ed Univ. of Edinburgh; with European Youth Forest Action 1994–98; Ed. Reforesting Scotland (journal) 1998–2001; MSP (Green Party) for Lothians 2003–07, mem. Parl. Finance Cttee; fmr consultant for several charities and social enterprises on business devt, promotion and lobbying; Rector Univ. of Edinburgh 2006–09, Life mem. Edinburgh Univ. Union; Communications Man. Scottish Council for Voluntary Orgs 2007; currently Asst Dir of Policy, Barnardo's Scotland; Ed.-in-Chief Bright Green (website); mem. Editorial Bd Scottish Left Review; mem. Friends of the Earth, Sustrans, Campaign for Nuclear Disarmament, Democratic Left Scotland, Reforesting Scotland, Water of Leith Conservation Trust. *Address:* Barnardo's Scotland, 111 Oxgangs Road, North Edinburgh, EH14 1ED, Scotland (office). *Telephone:* (131) 314-6611 (office). *Website:* www .barnardos.org.uk (office); www.brightgreenscotland.org.

BALLARD, Robert Duane, PhD; American fmr naval officer and oceanographer; *President, Institute for Exploration;* b. 30 June 1942, Wichita, Kan.; Barbara Earle Ballard; two s. one d.; ed Univs of California, Southern California, Hawaii and Rhode Island; Second Lt, US Army Intelligence 1965–67, later transferred to USN 1967–70; served with USN during Vietnam War, Consultant, Deputy Chief of Naval Operations for Submarine Warfare 1984–90, Consultant, Nat. Research Council, Marine Bd Comm. 1984–87, Commdr USNR 1987–2001; Research Assoc., Woods Hole Oceanographic Inst., Cape Cod, Mass 1969–74, Asst Scientist 1974–76, Assoc. Scientist 1976–83, Sr Scientist 1983–, Founder Deep Submergence Lab. 1983–, Dir Center for Marine Exploration 1989–95, Dir Emer. 1997–; Visiting Scholar, Stanford Univ., Calif. 1979–80, Consulting Prof. 1980–81; Founder and Chair. Jason Foundation for Educ. 1989–; Founder Inst. for Exploration, Mystic, Conn. 1995–, Pres. 1997–; Founder and Pres. Immersion Inst. 2001–; Prof. of Oceanography, URI 2002–; has led or participated in over 100 deep-sea expeditions, including discoveries of German battleship Bismarck, RMS Titanic 1985, warships from lost fleet of Guadalcanal, the Lusitania, Roman ships off coast of Tunisia 1997, USS Yorktown 1998 and John F. Kennedy's PT-109; expeditions included first manned exploration of Mid-ocean Ridge, discovery of warm water springs and their fauna in Galapagos Rift, first discovery of polymetallic sulphides; has participated in numerous educ. programmes with major TV networks in Europe, Japan and USA, hosted Nat. Geographic Explorer show 1989–91; Founder Inst. for Archaeological Oceanography, Graduate School of Oceanography, Univ. of Rhode Island 2003; Hon. Dir Explorers Club 1988–; Hon. Dir Sigma Pi Sigma, Physics Soc. 1996–; Dr hc (Clark Univ.) 1986, (Univ. of Rhode Island) 1986, (Southeastern Massachusetts Univ.) 1986, (Long Island Univ.) 1987, (Univ. of Bath, UK) 1988, (Tufts Univ.) 1990, (Lenoir-Rhyne Coll.) 1991, (Skidmore Coll.) 1992, (Worcester Polytechnic Inst.) 1992, (Bridgewater State Coll.) 1993, (Lehigh Univ.) 1993, (Maine Maritime Acad.) 1994, (Massachusetts Maritime Acad.) 1994, (Univ. of Wisconsin) 2000, (Univ. of Hartford) 2001, (Univ. of Delaware) 2001; Distinguished Mil. Grad., US Army 1967, Newcomb-Cleveland Award, American Asscn for the Advancement of Science 1981, Nat. Geographic Soc. Centennial Award 1988, American Geological Inst. Award 1990, USN Robert Dexter Conrad Award 1992, The Kilby Award 1994, Explorers Medal, Explorers Club 1995, Nat. Geographic Soc. Hubbard Medal 1996, USN Memorial Foundation Lone Sailor Award 1996, NII Award for Best Internet Site for Education 1996, American Geophysical Union 'Excellence in Geophysical Education' Award 1997, Commonwealth Award 2000, Lindbergh Award 2001, The Navy League Award Robert M. Thompson Award for Outstanding Leadership 2001, Caird Medal, Nat. Maritime Museum 2002, Nat. Humanities Medal 2003; numerous other awards and prizes. *Films:* Secrets of the Titanic (Int. Film Festival Award) 1987, Search for Battleship Bismarck (Emmy Award for Best Documentary) 1990, Last Voyage of the Lusitania (Emmy Award for Best Documentary) 1994. *Publications:* Photographic Atlas of the Mid-Atlantic Ridge 1977, The Discovery of the Titanic (with Rick Archbold) (New York Times and The Times No. 1 Best Seller 1987) 1987, The Discovery of the Bismarck (New York Times and The Times No. 1 Best Seller 1990) 1990, Bright Shark (novel) 1992, The Lost Ships of Guadalcanal (with Rick Archbold) 1993, Explorations (autobiography) 1995, Exploring the Lusitania (with Spencer Dunmore) 1995, Lost Liners (with Rick Archbold) 1997, Return to Midway 1999, The Water's Edge 1999, Eternal Darkness: A Personal History of Deep-Sea Exploration (with Will Hively) 2000, Graveyards of the Pacific 2001, Adventures in Ocean Exploration 2001; non-fiction for children: Exploring the Titanic (Virginia State Reading Asscn Young Readers Award 1993) 1988, The Lost Wreck of the Isis 1990, Exploring the Bismarck 1991, Explorer 1992, Ghost Liners 1998; Deep Sea Explorer (CD-ROM) 1999; has also published more than 57 articles in scientific journals and numerous popular articles. *Leisure interest:* family. *Address:* Mystic Aquarium & Institute for Exploration, 55 Coogan Boulevard, Mystic, CT 06355-1997, USA (office). *Telephone:* (860) 572-5955 (ext. 602) (office). *Fax:* (860) 572-5969 (office). *E-mail:* info@mysticaquarium.org (office). *Website:* www.mysticaquarium.org (office).

BALLARD, Shari L.; American business executive; b. MI; joined Best Buy 1993, has held several positions including Asst Store Man., Gen. Store Man., Vice-Pres. and Sr Vice-Pres., Exec. Vice-Pres., Human Resources and Legal 2004–07, Exec. Vice-Pres., Retail Channel Man. 2007–10, Exec. Vice-Pres. and Pres., Americas 2010–12, Enterprise Exec. Vice-Pres. and Pres., International 2012–18, Pres. US Retail 2014–18; mem. Bd Ecolab Inc.; mem. Bd of Trustees, Univ. of Minnesota Foundation, mem. Exec. Cttee, Human Resources Cttee. *Address:* c/o Best Buy Company Inc., 7601 Penn Avenue South, Richfield, MN 55423, USA (office). *Telephone:* (612) 291-1000 (office). *Fax:* (612) 292-4001 (office). *E-mail:* info@bestbuy.com (office). *Website:* www.bestbuy.com (office).

BALLE, Francis, DèsSc, PhD; French academic; *Professor, Université de Paris II—Panthéon-Assas;* b. 15 June 1939, Fourmies; s. of Marcel Balle and Madeleine (née Leprohon) Balle; m. Marie Derieux 1972; three d.; ed Inst. d'Etudes Politiques, Univ. de Paris-Sorbonne; philosophy teacher, Ecole Normale d'Oran 1963–65; Asst Lecturer, Faculté des Lettres, Ecole de Journalisme, Algiers 1965–67, Univ. de Paris-Sorbonne 1967–70, Univ. René Descartes, Univ. Paris VI 1970–72; Lecturer, Univ. de Paris II—Panthéon-Assass 1972, Prof. 1978–; Vice-Chancellor Universités de Paris 1986–89; Visiting Prof., Stanford Univ. 1981–83; apptd Pres. statistical Cttee for TV action outside France 1997; Dir Inst. Français de Presse 1976–86, Inst. de Recherche et d'Etudes sur la Communication 1986–; mem. Conseil Supérieur de l'Audiovisuel 1989–93; Dir Information and New Technologies at Ministry of Nat. Educ. 1993–95, of Scientific Information, Tech. and of Libraries 1995; Dir French Media Inst. 1997; apptd mem. Conseil d'administration de Radio France 2004, mem. Fulbright Comm.; Founding Ed. Le Revue Européenne des Médias; Chevalier, Légion d'honneur 1998, Commandeur 2007, Officier, Palmes académiques; Prize of Acad. des Sciences Morales et Politiques 1995;. *Publications:* Médias et Sociétés 1980, 2013, The Media Revolution in America and Western Europe 1984, Les nouveaux médias (with Gerard Eymery) 1987, Et si la Presse n'existait pas 1987, La Télévision 1987, Le Mandarin et le marchand 1995, Dictionnaire des médias 1998, Les Médias 2000, Dictionnaire du Web 2002, Les médias, PUF, Que sais-je? 2012, Lexique d'information communication 2006. *Leisure interests:* music, painting. *Address:* Université Panthéon-Assas (Paris II), I.R.E.C., 92 rue d'Assas, 75006 Paris (office); 18 rue Greuze, 75116 Paris, France (home). *Telephone:* 1-43-26-15-66 (office); 1-47-27-78-31 (also fax) (home). *Fax:* 1-43-26-15-78. *E-mail:* balle@u-paris2.fr (office); francisballe@gmail.com (home). *Website:* www.u-paris2.fr (office).

BALLESTRAZZI, Mireille; French police officer and fmr international organization official; b. 1954; ed Nat. Higher Police Acad.; Head of Organized Crime Div., Regional Dept of Judicial Police, Bordeaux 1978–79, Head of Judicial Police Unit, Creil 1979–82, Head of Judicial Police Unit, Argenteuil 1982–87, Head of Cen. Office for Suppression of Art Theft, Cen. Directorate of Judicial Police, Paris 1987–93, Dir of Regional Dept of Judicial Police, Ajaccio, Corsica 1993–96, Dir of Regional Dept of Judicial Police, Montpellier 1996–98, Asst Dir of Econ. and Financial Matters, Cen. Directorate of Judicial Police, Paris 1998–2002, Asst Dir of Resources, Evaluation and Strategy 2005–10, Deputy Cen. Dir of Judicial Police 2010–14, Cen. Dir of Judicial Police 2014–; mem. Exec. Cttee INTERPOL 2002–05, mem. Comm. for the Control of INTERPOL Files 2009–10, Vice-Pres. for Europe, INTERPOL Exec. Cttee 2010–12, Pres. of INTERPOL 2012–16; Chevalier des Arts et des Lettres 1992; Chevalier, Ordre nat. du Mérite 1994, Grand Officier 2016; Chevalier, Légion d'honneur 1997, Commdr 2013; Medal of Honour of the Nat. Police 1996. *Address:* Ministry of the Interior, place Beauvau, 75008 Paris, France (office). *Website:* www.interieur.gouv.fr (office).

BALLIN, Ernst Hirsch (see Hirsch Ballin, Ernst).

BALLMER, Steven (Steve) Anthony, BA; American software industry executive; b. 24 March 1956, Detroit, MI; m. Connie Ballmer; three c.; ed Detroit Country Day School, Harvard Univ., Stanford Univ. Grad. School of Business; while a student, managed football team, worked on Harvard Crimson newspaper and univ. literary magazine; fmr accountant; Asst Product Man. Procter & Gamble, Vice-Pres. Marketing; Sr Vice-Pres. Systems Software, Microsoft Corpn, Redmond, WA 1980–92, Exec. Vice-Pres. Sales and Support, Pres. 1998, CEO 2000–14, Dir –2014; Owner, Los Angeles Clippers professional basketball team 2014–; teacher, Marshall School of Business, Univ. of Southern California 2014–; Gen. Partner, Accenture SCA 2001, mem. Bd of Dirs 2001–06; mem. Bd of Dirs Detroit Country Day School; Chevalier, Légion d'honneur. *Leisure interests:* exercise, basketball. *Address:* Los Angeles Clippers, Staples Center, 1111 South Figueroa Street, Suite 1100, Los Angeles, CA 90015, USA. *Website:* www.nba.com/clippers.

BALLS, Edward (Ed) Michael; British economist and politician; b. 25 Feb. 1967, Norwich, Norfolk, England; s. of Prof. Michael Balls and Carolyn J. Balls; m. Yvette Cooper 1998; one s. two d.; ed Nottingham High School, Keble Coll., Oxford, John F. Kennedy School of Govt, Harvard Univ., USA; Teaching Fellow, Dept of Econs, Harvard Univ. 1989–90; fmr Research Asst, Nat. Bureau of Econ. Research, USA; econs leader writer, Financial Times 1990–94; econs columnist, The Guardian 1994–97; Econ. Adviser to Gordon Brown 1994–97; Chief Econ. Adviser to HM Treasury 1999–2004; Research Fellow, Smith Inst. 2004–05; Labour MP for Normanton 2005–10, for Morley and Outwood 2010–15; Econ. Sec. to the Treasury 2006–07; Sec. of State for Children, Schools and Family 2007–10; Shadow Educ. Sec. May–Oct. 2010; Shadow Home Sec. 2010–11; unsuccessful cand. in Labour Party leadership election Sept. 2010; Shadow Chancellor of the Exchequer 2011–15; Sr Fellow, Kennedy School of Govt, Harvard Univ., USA 2015–; Visiting Prof., King's Coll. London 2015–; Chair. Norwich City Football Club 2015–; Ed. European Economic Policy 1994–97; mem. Transport and Gen. Workers' Union, Unison, Co-operative Party; Hon. LLD (Nottingham) 2003; Young Financial Journalist of the Year, Wincott Foundation 1992. *Television includes:* contestant on BBC reality show Strictly Come Dancing 2016. *Publications include:* Reforming Britain's Economic and Financial Policy (co-ed.) 2001, Microeconomic Reform in Britain: Delivering Opportunities for All (co-ed.) 2004, Speaking Out: Lessons in Life and Politics (memoir) 2016. *Leisure interest:* Norwich City Football Club. *Address:* 5 King Street, Covent Garden, London, WC2E 8SD, England. *E-mail:* ed@edballs.com. *Website:* www.edballs.co.uk.

BALMER, Jean-François; Swiss actor; b. 18 April 1946, Valangin; ed Conservatoire d'Art Dramatique de Paris; has worked extensively in French cinema, TV and stage productions since early 1970s; played Pres. George Pompidou in the TV film Death of a President 2011. *Theatre includes:* Henri IV, Le Bien-Aimé, Théâtre des Mathurins 2010. *Films include:* Nothing to Report 1973, Le mouton enragé 1974, The Mouth Agape (scenes deleted) 1974, The Night Caller 1975, Le petit Marcel 1976, The Castaways of Turtle Island 1976, La menace 1977, Mountain Pass 1978, L'adolescente 1979, Les égouts du paradis 1979, Ils sont grands, ces petits 1979, Cop or Hood 1979, Rien ne va plus 1979, Neige 1981, Strange Affair 1981, Bluff (short) 1982, The Good Soldier 1982, Le quart d'heure américain 1982, L'africain 1983, Swann in Love 1984, Polar 1984, Les fauves 1984, Le sang des autres 1984, Folie suisse 1985, Urgence 1985, Le transfuge 1985, L'amour ou presque 1985, Golden Eighties 1986, La dernière image 1986, La révolution française 1989, Bal perdu 1990, Madame Bovary 1991, La fenêtre 1992, Diên Biên Phú 1992, Sam suffit 1992, Desencuentros 1992, Vent d'est 1993, Mauvais garçon 1993, Rocking Poponguine 1994, La lumière des étoiles mortes 1994, Le livre de cristal 1994, Ma soeur chinoise 1994, Lou n'a pas dit non (voice) 1994, XY, drôle de conception 1996, Beaumarchais 1996, Rien ne va plus 1997, Time Regained 1999, La dilettante 1999, T'aime 2000, The King's Daughters 2000, Charming Fellow 2001, Belphégor: Le fantôme du Louvre 2001, That Day 2003, Ripoux 3 2003, L'ivresse du pouvoir 2006, A Winter in Paris 2006, Elephant Tales (voice) 2006, Le grand appartement 2006, Lucifer et moi 2008, Tokyo! 2008, The Valley 2009, Lucky Luke 2009, Mumu 2010, Celles qui aimaient Richard Wagner 2011, Equinox 2011, Dead Europe 2012, In the House 2012, Cosmos 2015. *Television includes:* films: Bonheur, impair et passe 1977, Le chandelier 1977, La vie séparée 1979, Une page d'amour 1980, Les amours du mal-aimé 1980, Le mariage de Figaro 1981, Concierto barroco 1982, Par ordre du Roy (segment 'Madame Tiquet') 1983, Le roi de la Chine 1984, Le scénario défendu 1984, Visa pour nulle part 1985, En attendant Godot 1989, L'enveloppe 1991, Spender: The French Collection 1993, Le misanthrope 1994, Le héron (also dir) 1995, La pitié du diable 1996, Le propre de l'homme 1996, Le dernier chant 1996, Parfum de famille 1997, Le censeur du lycée d'Epinal 1997, La vérité est un vilain défaut 1997, Aventurier malgré lui 1997, Meurtres sans risque 1998, Deutschlandspiel 2000, Bien agités! 2004, Pierre et Jean 2004, Novecento 2006, Henry Dunant: Red on the Cross 2006, La française doit voter 2007, L'affaire Sacha Guitry 2007, Clémentine 2008, Beauregard 2009, Chateaubriand 2010, Colère 2010, La joie de vivre 2011, Mort d'un président 2011, Territoire de mensonges (film) 2011, L'infiltré 2011, La joie de vivre 2012; series: Gil Blas de Santillane 1974, Le petit théâtre d'Antenne 2 1980–81, Les poneys sauvages (mini-series) 1983, Cinéma 16 1983, Espionne et tais-toi (seven episodes) 1988, Médecins des hommes 1988, L'or du diable (mini-series) 1989, Antoine Rives, juge du terrorisme 1993, Spender 1993, Christmas Special – The French Collection 1993, Arithmétique appliquée et impertinente 1995, Louise et les marchés (mini-series) 1998, Boulevard du Palais 1999–. *Address:* c/o Rosalie Cimino, UBBA, 6 rue de Braque, 75003 Paris, France (office). *Telephone:* 1-44-54-26-40 (office). *Fax:* 1-44-54-08-44 (office). *E-mail:* info@ubba.eu (office). *Website:* www.ubba.eu (office).

BALOCH, Abdul Malik, MB BS; Pakistani ophthalmologist and politician; b. Sigenisar village, Turbat Dist, Balochistan; s. of Haji Abdul Salam Hoth; ed Ata Shad Degree Coll., Turbat, Bolan Medical Coll., Quetta; began political career with Baloch Student Org.; est. Balochistan Nat. Movt 1988; won Balochistan Nat. Ass. (BNM) seat 1988; Prov. Health Minister in Nawab Akbar Khan Bugti's cabinet; Prov. Educ. Minister 1993–94; merged with political followers of Mir Ghaus Bakhsh Bizenjo in BNM and became the National Party 2004; Senator 2006–12, Chair. Functional Cttee on Problems of Less Developed Areas, mem. Standing Cttee on Minorities Affairs, Standing Cttee on Ports and Shipping, Standing Cttee on Food and Agric.; Pres. National Party 2008–; Chief Minister of Balochistan (first non-tribal leader) 2013–15.

BALOHA, Viktor Ivanovich; Ukrainian politician; b. 15 June 1963, Zavydovo, Mukachev dist, Transcarpathian Oblast; ed Lviv Trade and Econ. Inst.; fmr commodities researcher; Chair. Admin Transcarpathian Oblast 1999–2001, Feb.–Sept. 2005; mem. Our Ukraine party; mem. Verkhovna Rada (Parl.) 2002–05, 2012–; Mayor of Mukachevo 2004–06; Minister of Emergency Situations 2005–06, 2010–12; Chief of the Presidential Secr. 2006–09; Order of St Sylvester Pope and Martyr 2012, Order of the Saint Equal-to-the-Apostles Great Prince Vladimir, 1st and 2nd degree. *Address:* Verkhovna Rada, 01008 Kyiv, vul. M. Hrushevskoho 5, Ukraine (office). *Telephone:* (44) 255-21-15 (office). *Fax:* (44) 253-32-17 (office). *E-mail:* umz@rada.gov.ua (office). *Website:* www.rada.gov.ua (office).

BALÓI, Oldemiro Júlio Marques; Mozambican economist, business executive and politician; b. 9 April 1955, Lourenço Marques (Maputo); m.; two c.; ed Universidade Eduardo Mondlane, Univ. of London, UK; Dir in ministries of trade and industry 1986–89; Deputy Minister of Co-operation 1990–94; Minister of Industry and Trade and Tourism 1995–2000; active in pvt. business, notably as mem. Bd of Dirs and of Exec. Bd Millennium-BIM (Int. Bank of Mozambique); Minister of Foreign Affairs and Co-operation 2008–17. *Address:* c/o Ministry of Foreign Affairs and Co-operation, Av. Julius Nyerere 4, CP 2787, Maputo, Mozambique (office).

BALSAI, István, DIur; Hungarian politician and judge; *Member, Constitutional Court;* b. 5 April 1947, Miskolc; s. of József Balsai and Mária Szalontai; m. Ilona Schmidt; two s.; chemical lab. asst 1966; on staff, Faculty of Political and Legal Sciences, Eötvös Loránd Univ., Budapest 1967–72; worked as attorney, Budapest; mem. Hungarian Democratic Forum 1988; mem. Parl. 1990–2011, Pres. Cttee for Employment and Labour, mem. Cttee on Constitution and Justice, Second Vice-Pres. Hungarian Nat. Group of IPU; Minister of Justice 1990–94; Leader of Legal Cabinet of Magyar Demokrata Fórum (Hungarian Democratic Forum)—MDF Parl. Group, 1994–98, Group Leader of MDF 1998–2002; mem. European Parl. (Group of the European People's Party (Christian Democrats) and European Democrats) May–July 2004, mem. Cttee on Constitutional Affairs, Cttee on Petitions; mem. Constitutional Court of Hungary 2011–; Founding mem. Asscn of Christian Intellectuals 1989–. *Leisure interest:* folk architecture. *Address:* Constitutional Court (Alkotmánybíróság), 1015 Budapest, Donáti u. 35–45, Hungary (office). *Telephone:* (1) 488-3100 (office). *Fax:* (1) 488-3187 (office). *E-mail:* balsai@mkab.hu (office). *Website:* www.mkab.hu (office).

BALSEMÃO, Francisco Pinto (see Pinto Balsemão).

BALSHAW, Maria Jane, CBE, BA, MA, DPhil; British arts administrator; *Director, Tate Art Museums and Galleries;* b. 24 Jan. 1970, Birmingham; m. 1st

Liam Kennedy; one s. one d.; m. 2nd Nick Merriman; ed Univ. of Liverpool, Univ. of Sussex; Lecturer in Cultural Studies, Univ. Coll. Northampton 1994–97; Research Fellow and Lecturer in Visual Culture, Univ. of Birmingham 1997–2002; Dir, Creative Partnerships, Arts Council England, Birmingham 2002–05; Dir, Whitworth Art Gallery 2006–17, also Dir Manchester City Galleries 2011–17; Dir of Culture, Manchester City Council 2013–17; Dir, Chief Exec. and Accounting Officer (first female), Tate Art Museums and Galleries 2017–; mem. Nat. Council, Arts Council England; mem. Strategic Advisory Bd, Clore Leadership Programme; Dir Rothesay Pavilion Charity, Hallé Orchestra; Hon. Prof., Hong Kong Univ. 2014; Hon. DArt (Manchester Metropolitan Univ.) 2016; Paul Hamlyn Breakthrough Award 2010, Apollo Magazine Personality of the Year 2015. *Publications include:* Urban Space and Representation 2000, Looking for Harlem: Urban Aesthetics in African American Cultur 2000. *Address:* Tate Art Museums and Galleries, Bankside, London, SE1 9TG, England (office). *Telephone:* (20) 7887-8888 (office). *Website:* www.tate.org.uk (office).

BALSILLIE, James Laurence (Jim), CA, BCom, MBA, PhD; Canadian electronics industry executive; *Chairman, Sustainable Development Technology Canada;* b. 3 Feb. 1961, Seaforth, Ont.; m. Heidi Balsillie; ed Peterborough Collegiate and Vocational School, Trinity Coll. at Univ. of Toronto, Harvard Grad. Business School, USA, Wilfrid Laurier Univ.; trained as accountant and held various positions at Ernst & Young, Toronto, including Sr Assoc., Strategy Consulting Group and Sr Accountant, Entrepreneurial Services Group; Exec. Vice-Pres. and mem. Bd of Dirs Sutherland-Schultz Ltd, Kitchener, Ont. –1992; mem. Bd of Dirs and Chair. Research In Motion Ltd (name changed to BlackBerry 2013) (designer and mfr of wireless products including BlackBerry email device), Waterloo, Ont. 1992–2007, Co-Chair. and Co-CEO 1992–2012 (resgnd); f. Centre for Int. Governance Innovation (research inst.) 2002, currently Chair.; f. Balsillie School of Int. Affairs 2008; apptd to UN Sec.-Gen.'s High-level Panel on Global Sustainability 2010; Chair., Canadian Int. Council 2007, Sustainable Devt Tech. Canada 2013; Dir Ont. Mfg Council 2008; Fellow, Ont. Inst. of Chartered Accountants 2003; numerous hon. doctorate degrees; inducted into Business Hall of Fame 2009. *Leisure interest:* triathlete. *Address:* Sustainable Development Technology Canada, 144–4 Avenue SW, Suite 1600, Calgary, Alberta T2P 3N4, Canada (office). *Telephone:* (403) 290-1186 (office). *Website:* www.sdtc.ca (office).

BALTIMORE, David, PhD; American biologist and university administrator; *Robert A. Millikan Professor of Biology, California Institute of Technology;* b. 7 March 1938, New York, NY; s. of Richard Baltimore and Gertrude Lipschitz; m. Alice Huang 1968; one d.; ed Swarthmore Coll., Rockefeller Univ.; Postdoctoral Fellow, MIT 1963–64, Albert Einstein Coll. of Medicine, New York 1964–65; Research Assoc., Salk Inst., La Jolla, Calif. 1965–68; Assoc. Prof., MIT 1968–72, Prof. of Microbiology 1972–95, Ivan R. Cottrell Prof. of Molecular Biology and Immunology 1994–97, Inst. Prof. 1995–97; American Cancer Soc. Prof. of Microbiology 1973–83, 1994–97; Dir Whitehead Inst. for Biomedical Research 1982–90; Pres. Rockefeller Univ. 1990–91, Prof. 1990–94; Pres. Calif. Inst. of Tech. 1997–2006, Pres. Emer. 2006–, currently Robert A. Millikan Prof. of Biology; Fellow, AAAS (Pres. 2007); mem. NIH Advisory Council on AIDS Research, Chair. Vaccine Cttee 1997–2002, NAS, Inst. of Medicine; Foreign mem. The Royal Soc.; Eli Lilly Award in Microbiology and Immunology 1971, US Steel Foundation Award in Molecular Biology 1974, Nobel Prize in Physiology or Medicine (jt recipient) 1975, Nat. Medal of Science 1999, Warren Alpert Foundation Prize 2000, American Medical Asscn Scientific Achievement Award 2002. *Publications:* more than 700 scientific articles. *Leisure interests:* fly fishing, skiing. *Address:* California Institute of Technology, MC 147-75, 1200 East California Boulevard, Pasadena, CA 91125-3100, USA (office). *Telephone:* (626) 395-3581 (office). *Fax:* (626) 585-9495 (office). *E-mail:* baltimo@caltech.edu (office). *Website:* biology.caltech.edu/Members/Baltimore (office).

BALUYEVSKII, Col-Gen. Yurii Nikolayevich; Russian army officer and government official; b. 9 Jan. 1947, Trubavets, Drohobych Raion, Lviv Oblast, Ukrainian SSR; ed Leningrad (now St Petersburg) Higher Mil. Command School of Gen. Army, M. Frunze Mil. Acad., Mil. Acad. of Gen. Staff; infantry officer 1970–82; Sr Officer, Operator, and Head of Group Chief Operation Dept of Gen. Staff; First Deputy Commdr of Group, Russian Forces in Caucasus; Deputy Head, Chief Operation Dept of Gen. Staff 1982–2001, First Deputy Chief of Gen. Staff 2001–04, Chief and First Deputy Minister of Defence 2004–08; apptd to Security Council of Russian Fed. 2004, Deputy Sec. 2008–12; Order for Service to Motherland in Armed Forces, Order of Audacity; nine medals. *Address:* c/o Security Council of Russian Federation, Moscow, Ipatyevsky per. 4/10, entr. 6, Russia (office).

BALZA, Lt-Gen. (retd) Martín Antonio; Argentine army officer (retd) and diplomatist; b. 13 June 1934, Salto, Buenos Aires; joined Nat. Mil. Coll. 1952, Instructor 1962–66, Instructor, Artillery School 1968–70, Head of Dept of Educ., Artillery School 1978, Asst Dir Nat. Mil. Coll. 1984–86; Head of artillery battalion 1979–82; Commdr 3rd Artillery Group during Falklands War 1982; Prof., Army War Coll. 1979–82; Inspector of Artillery 1987; Commdr Sixth Mountain Brigade 1987–88; Dir Mil. Insts 1989; Deputy Chief of Jt Staff of the Armed Forces 1989, Deputy Chief of Gen. Staff of the Army 1990–91, Chief of Staff of the Army 1992–99; Amb. to Colombia 2003–11; Order of Mil. Merit (Paraguay) 1993, Ordre National de la Légion d'honneur 1994, Order of Mil. Merit (Brazil) 1994, Order of Merit, Star of Carabobo (Venezuela) 1995, Ancient Order of Saint Barbara (USA) 1995, Mil. Order to Merit (Uruguay) 1997, Nat. Ordem Do Cruzeiro Do Sul (Brazil) 1998, Sovereign Mil. Order of Malta 1998; UN Medal 1970, Medal Santa Barbara 1973, Diploma of Honor, Nat. Acad. of Geography 1973, Great Prize of Honor 1983, Diploma of Honor, Armed Conflict with Great Britain and NI 1984, Medal to Mil. Merit 1984, Medal, Congress of Nation 1990, Medal of Gen. Liberator Bernardo O'Higgins (Chile) 1992, Medal of Merit, First Cross (Honduras) 1992, Hood Dell Ordine to the Merit Della Italian Repubblica (Italy) 1992, Great Mil. Service Cross (Spain) 1992, Cross of Mil. Merit 1993, Prócer of Freedom Maj.-Gen. Jose Miguel Lance (Bolivia) 1993, Great Cross of Political Mil. (Chile) 1993, Hon. Medal of Commando of Artillery (Paraguay) 1993, Hon. Medal of Army (Paraguay) 1994, Meritorious Mil. Service Order Jose Maria Cordoba (Colombia) 1994, Legion of Merit (USA) 1994, Great Cross, John F. Kennedy Univ. 1995, Star of Armed Forces (Ecuador) 1996, Marshal Andres of Santa Cruz (Bolivia) 1998, Cross of Earth Forces (Guatemala) 1998, Great Cross (Venezuela) 1999, Belgraniana Cross, Belgraniano Inst.

BALZANI, Vincenzo, Laurea in Chimica cum laude; Italian chemist and academic; *Professor Emeritus of Chemistry, University of Bologna;* b. 15 Nov. 1936, Forlimpopoli; m. Carla Balzani; six c.; ed Univ. of Bologna; Asst Prof., Univ. of Bologna 1963–68, Assoc. Prof. 1969–73, Prof. of Chem. 1973–2010, Prof. Emer. 2010–, Chair. Doctorate in Chem. Science 2002–, also Dir Center for the Photochemical Conversion of Solar Energy 1981–; Asst Prof., Univ. of Ferrara 1968–89; Dir Italian Nat. Research Council /Photochemistry and Radiation Chem. Inst. (FRAE) 1977–88; Visiting Prof., Hebrew Univ. of Jerusalem Energy Research Center, Israel 1979; Visiting Prof., Univ. of Strasbourg, France 1990; Dir NATO Science Forum, Taormina 1991; Visiting Prof., Univ. of Leuven, Belgium 1991; Dir ICS School of Photochemistry, Trieste 1993; Visiting Prof., Univ. of Bordeaux, France 1994; mem. Editorial Bd several journals including Nanotechnology 1994–2000, Chemistry European Journal 1995–, Chemical Society Reviews 1997–98, ChemPhysChem 2000–, Tetrahedron 2003–, Comptes Rendus Chimie 2004–, Topics in Current Chemistry 2005–, Small 2005–, ChemSusChem 2008–; mem. Academia Europaea, European Photochemical Asscn, Societa Chimica Italiana; Fellow, AAAS, Royal Soc. of Chem., Accademia Nazionale delle Scienze del XL, Accademia Nazionale dei Lincei; Grande Ufficiale dell'Ordine al Merito della Repubblica Italiana 2006; Dr hc (Univ. of Fribourg) 1989; Univ. of Bologna Miriam Borsari Medal 1960, Italian Chemical Soc. Cannizzaro Gold Medal 1988, Accademia Nazionale dei Lincei Chem. Award 1992, Porter Medal 2000, French Chem. Soc. Prix Franco-Italien 2002, Premio al Merito, Camera di Commercio, Industria e Agricoltura della Provincia di Forlì-Cesena 2003, Quilico Gold Medal, Italian Chemical Soc. 2006, Blaise Pascal Medal 2009, Leonardo da Vinci Award 2017, European Acad. of Sciences, Rotary Club Int. Galileo Prize for scientific research 2011, Nature Award for Mentoring in Science 2013, Archiginnasio d'oro Città di Bologna 2016, Grand Prix de la Maison de la Chimie 2016, Premio Genus Romandiolae per la Scienza e la Comunicazione 2017, Premio Guglielmo Marconi per la Creatività 2017, Nicholas J. Turro Award, Inter-American Photochemical Soc. 2017. *Publications:* Photochemistry of Coordination Compounds 1970, Supramolecular Photochemistry 1991, Molecular Devices and Machines: A Journey in the Nano World 2003, Molecular Devices and Machines: Concepts and Perspectives for the Nano World 2008, Energy for a Sustainable World 2011, Photochemistry and Photophysics: Concepts, Research, Applications 2014. *Address:* Dipartimento di Chimica, Università di Bologna, Via Selmi 2, 40126 Bologna, Italy (office). *E-mail:* vincenzo.balzani@unibo.it (office). *Website:* www.ciam.unibo.it/photochem/balzani.html (office).

BAMBANG YUDHOYONO, Lt-Gen. Susilo, MA; Indonesian politician and fmr head of state; b. 1949, East Java; m. Ani Herrawati; two s.; ed Indonesian Mil. Acad. and Webster Univ., USA; participated in Operation Seroja (invasion of Timor Leste) and commanded Dili-based Battalion 744 1970s; spent much of mil. career with Kostrad airborne units; mil. training in USA and Europe 1980s–90s; lectured at Army Staff Command Coll. (Seskoad) 1980s; worked in territorial commands in Jakarta and S. Sumatra (Pangdam II/Sriwijaya) mid 1990s; Chief Mil. Observer in Bosnia 1995–96; Chief of the Armed Forces Social and Political Affairs Staff (Kassospol Abri) (renamed Chief of Territorial Affairs (Kaster) Nov. 1998) 1997–2000; retd from active mil. service 2000; Minister of Mines 1999–2000; Co-ordinating Minister for Political Affairs, Security and Social Welfare 2000–04 (resgnd); Chair. Partai Demokrat 2013–; Pres. of Indonesia 2004–14; Pres. and Council Chair. Global Green Growth Inst. 2014–16; UNPKF Medal; Mil. Service medals include Bintang Dharma, Bintang Mahaputera Adipurna, Bintang Republik Indonesia Adipurna. *Address:* Partai Demokrat, Jalan Kramat Raya 146, Jakarta Pusat 10450, Indonesia (office). *Telephone:* (21) 31907999 (office). *Fax:* (21) 31908999 (office). *Website:* www.demokrat.or.id (office).

BAMBAWALE, Gautam, MA; Indian diplomatist; *Ambassador to China;* b. 1958, Pune, Maharashtra; s. of Hemant Bambawale and Usha Bambawale; m. Asmita Bambawale; two s.; ed Gokhale Inst. of Politics and Econs; joined Indian Foreign Service 1984, served in Hong Kong and Beijing 1985–91, apptd Desk Officer for China, Ministry of External Affairs (MEA) 1991, Dir America's Div. (responsible for relations with US and Canada), MEA 1993–94, Dir Indian Cultural Centre, Berlin 1994–98, Deputy Chief of Mission, Embassy of India, China 1998–2001, Staff Officer to Foreign Sec., MEA 2001–02, Deputy Chief, Div. of Nat. Security Affairs, Defence and Int. Policy 2002–04, Minister (Political) and Head of Political Wing, Embassy of India, Washington 2004–07, Consul-Gen. of India, Guangzhou 2007–09, Jt Sec. (East Asia), Ministry of External Affairs (responsible for ties with China, Japan, South Korea, Mongolia and North Korea) 2009–14, Amb. to Bhutan 2014–15, to China 2017–, High Commr to Pakistan 2015–17. *Address:* Embassy of India, 5 Liang Ma Qiao Bei Jie, Chaoyang Qu, Beijing 100600, People's Republic of China (office). *Telephone:* (10) 65321908 (office). *Fax:* (10) 65324684 (office). *E-mail:* hoc@indianembassy.org.cn (office). *Website:* www.indianembassy.org.cn (office).

BAMERT, Matthias; Swiss conductor and composer; b. 5 July 1942, Ersigen; m. Susan Exline 1969; one s. one d.; ed studied in Bern and Paris, studied composition with Jean Rivier and Pierre Boulez; asst conductor to Leopold Stokowski 1970–71; Resident Conductor, Cleveland Orchestra 1971–78; Music Dir Swiss Radio Orchestra, Basel 1977–83; Prin. Guest Conductor, Scottish Nat. Orchestra 1985–90; Dir Musica Nova Festival, Glasgow 1985–90, Lucerne Festival 1992–98; Music Dir London Mozart Players 1993–2000; has appeared with Orchestre de Paris, Rotterdam Philharmonic, Cleveland Orchestra, Pittsburgh Symphony, Montreal Symphony, Royal Philharmonic Orchestra, London, London Philharmonic Orchestra, BBC Philharmonic, City of Birmingham Symphony Orchestra and at BBC Promenade Concerts, London; Prin. Conductor and Artistic Adviser, Malaysian Philharmonic Orchestra 2005–08; Prin. Guest Conductor, Daejeon Philharmonic Orchestra 2017–; Chief Conductor Sapporo Symphony Orchestra 2018–; George Szell Memorial Award 1971. *Compositions include:* Concertino for English horn, string orchestra and piano 1966, Septuria Lunaris for orchestra 1970, Rheology for string orchestra 1970, Mantrajana for orchestra 1971, Once Upon an Orchestra for narrator, 12 dancers and orchestra 1975, Ol-Okun for string orchestra 1976, Keepsake for orchestra 1979, Circus Parade for narrator and orchestra 1979. *Address:* c/o Aya Yoshigoe, Sarperi Artists Management, Breitingerstrasse 17, 8002 Zurich, Switzerland (office). *E-mail:* info@

sarperiartists.com (office). *Website:* www.sarperiartists.com (office); www.matthias-bamert.com.

BAMFORD, Baron (Life Peer), cr. 2013, of Daylesford in the County of Gloucestershire and of Wootton in the County of Staffordshire; **Anthony Paul Bamford;** British business executive; *Chairman, J C Bamford Excavators Limited (JCB);* b. 23 Oct. 1945; s. of Joseph Cyril Bamford and of Marjorie Griffin; m. Carole Gray Whitt 1974; two s. one d.; ed Ampleforth Coll., Grenoble Univ., France; joined JCB 1962, Chair. and Man. Dir 1975–; Dir Tarmac 1987–94; Pres. Midlands Industrial Council, Staffs. Agricultural Soc. 1987–88, Burton-upon-Trent Conservative Asscn 1987–90; Pres.'s Cttee CBI 1986–88; mem. Design Council 1987–89; mem. (Conservative), House of Lords 2013–; DL Staffs., High Sheriff of Staffs. 1985–86; Trustee, Bamford Charitable Foundation, Sir Anthony Bamford Charitable Foundation, Daylesford Foundation; Chevalier, Ordre nat. du Mérite 1989, Commendatore della Repubblica Italiana 1995; Hon. MEng (Birmingham) 1987; DUniv (Keele) 1988; Hon. DSc (Cranfield) 1994; Hon. DBA (Robert Gordon Univ., Aberdeen) 1996; Hon. DTech (Staffordshire) 1998, (Loughborough) 2002; Young Exporter of the Year (UK) 1972, Young Businessman of the Year (UK) 1979, Top Exporter of the Year (UK) 1995, IAgrE Award of Merit 2008. *Leisure interests:* farming, gardening, collecting vintage Ferraris. *Address:* JCB World Headquarters, Rocester, Uttoxeter, Staffs., ST14 5JP (office); House of Lords, Westminster, London, SW1A 0PW, England. *E-mail:* contactholmember@parliament.uk. *Website:* www.jcb.co.uk (office); www.parliament.uk/biographies/lords/lord-bamford/4305.

BAMFORD-ADDO, Rt Hon. Joyce Adeline; Ghanaian lawyer, judge and politician; b. 26 March 1937, Accra; five c.; called to English Bar 1961, Ghana Bar 1963; practised law 1961–63; Asst State Attorney 1963–65, State Attorney 1965–70, Sr State Attorney 1970–73, Prin. Attorney 1973–76, Chief State Attorney 1976–86, Dir of Public Prosecutions 1986–91; Justice, Supreme Court 1991–2004 (retd); Speaker of Parl. (first woman) 2009–13; Ghana Rep. to UN Comm. on the Status of Women 1990, 1991; fmr mem. Ghana Law Reform Comm., Legal Aid Bd, Gen. Legal Council.

BAN, Ki-moon, BA, MPA; South Korean politician, diplomatist and UN official; *Chairman, Board of Directors, Boao Forum for Asia;* b. 13 June 1944, Eumseong, North Chungcheong; m. Yoo Soon-taek; one s. two d.; ed Seoul Nat. Univ., Kennedy School of Govt, Harvard Univ., USA; early assignments at Embassy in New Delhi, two terms at Embassy in Washington, DC, First Sec., Perm. Observer Mission to UN, New York; fmr Dir UN Div.; Amb. to Austria, also Chair. Preparatory Comm. for the Comprehensive Nuclear Test Ban Treaty Org. (CTBTO) 1999; Dir-Gen. of American Affairs 1990–92; Vice-Chair. South-North Jt Nuclear Control Comm. 1992; Deputy Minister for Policy Planning 1995–96; Nat. Security Adviser to the Pres. 1996–2000; Chef-de-Cabinet to Pres. of UN Gen. Ass. 2001; Vice-Minister 2000, then Foreign Policy Adviser to the Pres.; Minister of Foreign Affairs and Trade 2004–06; Sec.-Gen. UN 2007–16; Chair. Bd of Dirs, Boao Forum for Asia 2018–; Order of Service Merit 1975, 1986, 2006, Grand Decoration of Honour (Austria) 2001, Grand Cross of Rio Blanco (Brazil) 2002, Gran Cruz del Sol (Peru) 2006, Grand'Croix, Ordre Nat. (Burkina Faso) 2008, Ordre national de la Légion d'honneur 2016, Grand Officier, Ordre Nat. (Côte d'Ivoire); Dr hc (Seoul Nat. Univ.) 2008, Hon. LLD (Univ. of the Philippines Coll. of Law) 2008; James A. Van Fleet Award, Korea Soc., New York 2005. *Address:* Boao Forum Asia, Room 2210, China World Tower A, No. 1 Jianguomenwai Avenue, Beijing 100004, People's Republic of China (office). *Telephone:* (10) 65057377 (office). *Fax:* (10) 65051833 (office). *E-mail:* bfa@boaoforum.org (office). *Website:* english.boaoforum.org.

BAN, Shigeru, BArch; Japanese architect and academic; *Director, Shigeru Ban Architects;* b. 5 Aug. 1957, Tokyo; m. Masako Ban; ed Southern Calif. Inst. of Architecture and Cooper Union, New York, USA; worked for Arata Isozaki, Tokyo 1982–83; est. Shigeru Ban Architects, Tokyo 1985; Consultant, UNHCR 1995; est. Voluntary Architects Network 1995; Adjunct Prof. of Architecture, Tokohama Nat. Univ. 1995–99, Nihon Univ. 1996–2000; Visiting Prof., Columbia Univ., New York 2000; Prof. of Architecture, Keio Univ. 2001–08, Guest Prof., Faculty of Environment and Information Studies 2015–; Visiting Prof., Harvard Univ. Grad. School of Design 2010–; mem. jury for Pritzker Architecture Prize 2006–09; Hon. Fellow, Royal Architectural Inst. of Canada 2005, Hon. mem., Japan Inst. of Architects 2014, Hon. Citizen of Tainan City, Taiwan 2018; Ordre nat. de la Légion d'honneur 2009, Ordre des Arts et des Lettres 2010; Dr hc (Tech. Univ. of Munich) 2009; Third Kansai Architect Grand Prize, Japan Inst. of Architecture 1996, Japan Inst. of Architecture Best Young Architect of the Year 1997, 18th Tohoku Architecture Prize, Architectural Inst. of Japan 1998, Interior Magazine Best Designer of the Year 2000, World Architecture Awards Best Architecture of the Year in Europe 2001, Matsui Gengo Award 2001, World Architectural Awards Best House of the Year 2002, Grande Medaille d'Or, Academie d' Architecture 2004, Thomas Jefferson Medal in Architecture, Univ. of Virginia 2005, Arnold W. Brunner Memorial Prize in Architecture 2005, Grand Prize of AIJ 2009, Pritzker Architecture Prize 2014, Asahi Prize 2015 Crystal Award, World Econ. Forum 2015, Medal with Purple Ribbon 2017. *Architectural works include:* Paper Arbor 1989, House of Double Roof 1993, MDS Gallery 1994, Curtain Wall House 1995, Furniture House 1995, Paper Church 1995, Paper Loghouse 1995, Tazawako Station 1997, Wall-less House 1997, 9 Square Grid House 1997, Hanegi Forest 1997, Paper Dome 1998, Ivy Structure House 1998, Japan Pavilion for Expo 2000 Hanover 2000, A Paper Arch, Museum of Modern Art Courtyard, New York 2000, GC Osaka Bldg 2000, Naked House 2000, Day-Care Center 2001, Gymnasium 2001, Paper Art Museum 2002, Paper Theater 2003, Paper Dome 2003, Paris Temporary Structure 2004, Paper House 2005, Singapore Bienale Pavilion 2006, Paper Bridge 2007, Paper Tea House 2008, Paper Dome Taiwan 2008, Paper Tower 2009, Quinta Botanica 2009. *Publications include:* Shigeru Ban 1997, Ban Shigeru 1998, Paper Tube Architecture from Kobe to Rwanda 1998, Shigeru Ban—Projects in Progress 1999, Shigeru Ban 2001, Shigeru Ban 2003, Shigeru Ban 2008, Shigeru Ban 2012, How to make Houses, Shigeru Ban 2013, Shigeru Ban – Material, Structure and Space 2017. *Address:* Shigeru Ban Architects, 5-2-4 Matsubara Ban Building, First Floor, Setagaya, Tokyo 156-0043, Japan (office). *Telephone:* (3) 3324-6760 (office). *Fax:* (3) 3324-6789 (office). *E-mail:* tokyo@shigerubanarchitects.com (office). *Website:* www.shigerubanarchitects.com (office).

BANDA, Joyce, BA; Malawi politician, business executive and fmr head of state; b. 1952, Malemia, Zomba; m. 1st Roy Kachale, three c.; m. 2nd Richard Banda, two c.; early career working as sec.; mem. Parl. for Zomba-Malosa constituency –2009; Minister of Foreign Affairs and Int. Co-operation 2006–09; Vice-Pres. of Malawi 2009–12, Pres. 2012–14; fmr mem. United Democratic Front; mem. Democratic Progressive Party (DPP) 2004–10; Founder-mem. and Pres. People's Party 2011–; Chair. Malawi Housing Corpn; mem. Bd Malawi Entrepreneurs Devt Inst., Malawi Polytechnic; Founder and Chair. Nat. Asscn of Business Women 1989, now Exec. Dir; f. Hunger Project, Young Emerging Leader's Network, Joyce Banda Foundation; numerous awards, including Africa Prize for Leadership 1997, 100 Heroines Award 1998. *Address:* c/o Office of the President and Cabinet, Private Bag 301, Capital City, Lilongwe 3, Malawi (office).

BANDA, Rupia Bwezani; Zambian diplomatist, politician, business executive and fmr head of state; b. 13 Feb. 1937, Gwenda, Southern Rhodesia (now Zimbabwe); m. 1st Hope Mwansa Makulu 1966 (died 2000); five s.; m. 2nd Thandiwe Banda; two s.; ed Munali Secondary School, Univ. of Ethiopia, Univ. of Lund, Sweden, Wolfson Coll., Cambridge, UK; UNIP rep. in Europe 1960–64; Amb. to UAR 1965–67, to USA 1967–70; Exec. Chair. Rural Devt Corpn and Gen. Man. Nat. Marketing Bd of Zambia 1970–74; Perm. Rep. to UN, New York 1974–75, Chair. UN Council on Namibia; Minister of Foreign Affairs 1975–76; fmr MP for Munali for many years; Vice-Pres. of Zambia 2006–08, Pres. 2008–11; fmr Chair. Chipoza Holdings, Robert Hudson Ltd, Allenwest and Chiparamba Enterprise.

BANDARANAYAKE, Shirani, LLB, PhD; Sri Lankan lawyer, academic and judge; b. April 1958, Kurunagala; d. of Wilson Bandaranayake and Flora Bandaranayake; m. Pradeepa Kariyawasam; one s.; ed Univ. of Colombo, Univ. of London, England; Visiting Lecturer, Faculty of Law, Univ. of Colombo 1981, Head 1987–92, Dean 1992, Assoc. Prof. of Law 1993; Attorney-at-Law, Supreme Court 1983, apptd Judge 1996, Chief Justice 2011–13; Founder and Co-ordinator Kotalawala Defence Acad. (now Gen. Sir John Kotelawala Defence Univ.); mem. Faculty of Humanities and Social Sciences, Open Univ. of Sri Lanka; mem. Postgraduate Inst. of Man., Univ. of Sri Jayawardenapura; mem. Judges Inst., Judicial Service Comm., Human Rights Task Force, Council of Legal Educ., Law Comm. of Sri Lanka, Nat. Task Force on Forestry Legislation, Working Cttee for Law and Computers, Expert Working Cttee on Banking and Law, Nat. Task Force on Environmental Law; mem. Bd of Govs International Jurists Org., India; Commonwealth Open Scholarship 1983, Chevening Scholarship 1989, British Council Award 1990, British Council Assert Award 1993, 1994, Fulbright-Hays Fellowship 1996, Woman of Achievement Award 1998, District 306 C, International Lions Club 2004, Int. Women's Day Award 2007.

BANDE, Tijjani Muhammad, MA, PhD; Nigerian academic and diplomatist; *Permanent Representative to United Nations;* b. 7 Dec. 1957, Zagga (now Kebbi State); m.; four c.; ed Boston Univ., Univ. of Toronto; Dir-Gen., African Training and Research Centre in Admin for Devt, Morocco 2000–04, Nat. Inst. for Policy and Strategic Studies, Nigeria 2010–16; Vice-Chancellor Usmanu Danfodiyo Univ. 2004–09; Perm. Rep. to UN 2017–; Officer of the Order of the Fed. Repub. 2005. *Address:* Permanent Mission of Nigeria, 828 Second Avenue, New York, NY 10017, USA (office). *Telephone:* (212) 953-9130 (office). *Fax:* (212) 697-1970 (office). *E-mail:* permny@nigeriaunmission.org (office). *Website:* nigeriaunmission.org (office).

BANDERAS, Antonio; Spanish film actor, director and producer; b. (José Antonio Domínguez Banderas), 10 Aug. 1960, Málaga, Andalucia; s. of José Domínguez and Anna Banderas; m. 1st Anna Leza 1987 (divorced 1996); one d.; m. 2nd Melanie Griffith 1996 (divorced 2014); ed School of Dramatic Art; began acting aged 14; performed with Nat. Theatre, Madrid for six years; Dr hc (Univ. of Málaga) 2010. *Films include:* Labyrinth of Passion 1982, El Señor Galíndez 1984, El Caso Almería 1984, The Stilts, 27 Hours, Matador 1986, Law of Desire 1987, Women on the Verge of a Nervous Breakdown 1988, Tie Me Up! Tie Me Down! 1989, The House of Spirits, Interview with the Vampire, The Mambo Kings 1992, Philadelphia 1993, Love and Shadow, Miami Rhapsody, Young Mussolini, Return of Mariaolu, Assassins, Desperado 1995, Evita 1996, The Mask of Zorro 1997, Never Talk to Strangers; Crazy in Alabama (dir), The 13th Warrior, White River Kid (producer) 1999, Dancing in the Dark 2000, Malaga Burning (dir) 2000, The Body 2000, Forever Lulu (producer) 2000, Spy Kids 2001, Femme Fatale 2002, Frida 2003, Once Upon a Time in Mexico 2003, Imagining Argentina 2003, Shrek II 2004, The Legend of Zorro 2005, Take the Lead 2006, El Camino de los Ingleses (Summer Rain, Dir) 2006, Bordertown 2007, Shrek the Third (voice) 2007, Missing Lynx (producer) 2008, My Mom's New Boyfriend 2008, The Other Man 2008, Thick as Thieves 2009, The Big Bang 2010, Shrek Forever After (voice) 2010, You Will Meet A Tall Dark Stranger 2010, La piel que habito (The Skin I Live In) 2011, Puss in Boots (voice) 2011, Black Gold 2011, Haywire 2011, Ruby Sparks 2012, I'm So Excited! 2013, Justin and the Knights of Valour 2013, Machete Kills 2013, The Expendables 3 2014, Autómata 2014, The SpongeBob Movie: Sponge Out of Water 2015, Knight of Cups 2015, Altamira 2015, The 33 2015. *Television:* And Starring Pancho Villa as Himself 2003. *Address:* c/o Creative Artists Agency, 2000 Avenue of the Stars, Los Angeles, CA 90067, USA (office); c/o Agents Associés, 201 rue du Faubourg Saint-Honoré, 75008 Paris, France (office). *Telephone:* (424) 288-2000 (office). *Fax:* (424) 288-2900 (office). *Website:* www.caa.com (office).

BANDIĆ, Milan; Croatian politician; *Mayor of Zagreb;* b. 22 Nov. 1955, Bandića Brig, Cerov Dolac, nr Grude, Socialist Repub. of Bosnia and Herzegovina, Socialist Fed. Repub. of Yugoslavia; s. of Jozo Bandić and Blagiça Bandić (née Tomić); m. Vesna Bandić (divorced 1996); one d.; ed Antun Branko Šimić High School, Grude, Univ. of Zagreb; worked for Ledo Co. 1980–83; worked in Municipality of Peščenica 1989–90; joined Savez Komunista Hrvatske (League of Communists of Croatia) (later reformed as Socijaldemokratska Partija Hrvatske—SDP—Social Democratic Party of Croatia) 1990; mem. Zagreb City Council 1995–, Leader of Zagreb SDP 1997, Mayor of Zagreb 2000–02, 2005–; Rep. in House of Reps of Croatian Parl. 2000–, Vice-Pres. Parl. Cttee for Internal Policy and Nat. Security; mem. SDP 2000–09, unsuccessful cand. for party pres. 2007, expelled from party Nov. 2009; unsuccessful presidential cand. Jan. 2010; arrested, along with 19 other officials, on charges of corruption, bribery and organized crime Oct. 2014, released on bail of two million euros awaiting an appeal and forbidden to return to work as Mayor Nov. 2014; released from custody and resumed duties as Mayor April 2015; f. Milan Bandić 365—Stranka Rada i Solidarnost (Milan Bandić 365—Party of

Labour and Solidarity), Pres. 2015–; Citizen of Honour of Srebrenica 2009. *Leisure interest:* distance running. *Address:* Office of the Mayor, Zagreb City Council, 10000 Zagreb, trg Stjepana Radića (office); Milan Bandić 365—Stranka Rada i Solidarnosti, 10000 Zagreb, Praška 2, Croatia (office). *Telephone:* (1) 6101111 (Office of the Mayor) (office); (1) 6460694 (Party) (office). *Fax:* (1) 6101313 (Office of the Mayor) (office); (1) 6458005 (Party) (office). *E-mail:* uprava@zagreb.hr (office); info@365ris.hr (office). *Website:* www.zagreb.hr (office); www.365ris.hr (office).

BANDIER, Martin N., BA, LLD; American lawyer and entertainment business executive; *Chairman and CEO, Sony/ATV Music Publishing;* b. 21 July 1941, New York; m. Dorothy Bandier; three c.; ed Syracuse Univ., Brooklyn Law School; began career with law firm in Manhattan; joined legal dept at LeFrank Organisation, becoming Sr Vice-Pres.; Co-f. Entertainment Co. 1975, Entertainment Music Co. 1985, SBK Entertainment World 1987; Vice-Chair. Thorn EMI 1989–91, CEO EMI Music Publishing 1991–2007, Chair. 1992–2007, mem. Bd of Dirs EMI Group plc 1998–2006; Chair. and CEO, Sony/ATV Music Publishing LLC 2007–; mem. Bd of Dirs United Jewish Appeal, City of Hope, Songwriter's Hall of Fame, Nat. Music Publrs' Asscn, Rock and Roll Hall of Fame; Trustee, T.J. Martell Foundation, Syracuse Univ.; mem. Metropolitan New York Advisory Bd, Nat. Acad. of Recording Arts and Sciences; f. music and entertainment industry degree programme at Syracuse Univ. named The Bandier Program for Music and Entertainment Industries 2006; Abe Olman Publisher Award 1990, Arents Award 1994, Patron of the Arts inductee, Songwriters Hall of Fame 2003. *Leisure interests:* playing the piano, golf. *Address:* Sony/ATV Music Publishing LLC, 550 Madison Avenue, Fifth Floor, New York, NY 10022, USA (office). *Telephone:* (212) 833-8000 (office). *Fax:* (212) 833-5552 (office). *E-mail:* info@sonyatv.com (office). *Website:* www.sonyatv.com (office).

BANDLER, John William, OC, PhD, DSc (Eng), FIEEE, FIET, FEIC, FCAE, FRSC; Canadian professor of electrical and computer engineering; *Professor Emeritus, McMaster University;* b. 9 Nov. 1941, Jerusalem; m. 3rd Beth Budd 1990; two d.; ed Imperial Coll. London; Mullard Research Labs, Redhill, Surrey 1966; Univ. of Manitoba 1967–69; McMaster Univ. 1969, Prof. 1974, Prof. Emer. 2000–; Chair. Dept of Electrical Eng, McMaster Univ. 1978–79, Dean of Faculty 1979–81, Dir of Research, Simulation Optimization Systems Research Lab. 1983–; Pres. Optimization Systems Assocs Inc. 1983–97, Bandler Corpn 1997–; ARFTG Automated Measurements Career Award for Automated Microwave Techniques 1994, IEEE Microwave Theory and Techniques Soc. Microwave Application Award 2004, IEEE Canada A. G. L. McNaughton Gold Medal 2012, Queen Elizabeth II Diamond Jubilee Medal 2012, IEEE Microwave Theory and Techniques Soc. Microwave Career Award 2013, McMaster Univ. Faculty of Engineering Research Achievement Award 2014, McMaster Univ. Pres.'s Lifetime Achievement Award 2018, OPEA Gold Medal 2018. *Plays:* nine stage plays (four performed, one self-directed). *Publications:* more than 500 papers in journals and books and book chapters. *Address:* Department of Electrical and Computer Engineering, McMaster University, Hamilton, Ont., L8S 4K1, Canada (office). *Telephone:* (905) 525-9140 (office). *Website:* www.sos.mcmaster.ca (office); www.bandler.com (home).

BANDUCCI, Brad, BL, BCom, MBA; Australian (b. South African) business executive; *Managing Director and CEO, Woolworths Limited;* m.; two c.; ed Univ. of KwaZulu-Natal, South Africa, Australian Grad. School of Man.; fmr Vice-Pres. and Dir with The Boston Consulting Group, core mem. of their retail practice for 15 years; Chief Financial Officer, Tyro Payments –2007; CEO Cellarmasters 2007–11, joined Woolworths following acquisition of Cellarmasters Group 2011, Dir of Liquor 2012–15, Man. Dir Woolworths Food Group 2015–16, mem. Bd of Dirs, Man. Dir and CEO Woolworths Ltd 2016–. *Address:* Woolworths Ltd, PO Box 8000, Baulkham Hills, NSW 2153 (office); Woolworths Ltd, 1 Woolworths Way, Bella Vista, NSW 2153, Australia (office). *Telephone:* (2) 8885-0000 (office). *E-mail:* info@woolworthslimited.com.au (office). *Website:* www.woolworthslimited.com.au (office).

BANDURA, Albert, OC, PhD; Canadian psychologist and academic; *David Starr Jordan Professor Emeritus of Social Science in Psychology, Stanford University;* b. 4 Dec. 1925, Mundare, Alberta; m. Ginny Bandura; two d.; ed University of British Columbia, Univ. of Iowa, USA; Instructor then Prof. of Psychology, Stanford Univ., USA 1953, then David Starr Jordan Prof. of Social Science in Psychology, now Prof. Emer.; Chair. Dept of Psychology 1976–77; Fellow, Center for Advanced Study in the Behavioral Sciences 1969–70; Sir Walter Scott Distinguished Visiting Prof., Univ. of New South Wales, Australia 1988; mem. Bd of Scientific Affairs, American Psychological Asscn 1968–70, mem. Credentials Cttee (Div. 7) 1970, mem. Bd of Convention Affairs 1973, Pres. and Chair. Bd of Dirs 1974, Chair. Council of Reps 1974, Chair. Cttee on Constitutional Issues 1975, Chair. Election Cttee 1975, mem. Comm. on Org. 1978–82; mem. Inst. of Medicine, NAS 1989; Trustee, American Psychological Foundation 1975–82; mem. Western Psychological Asscn 1979–82, Chair. Bd of Dirs 1980, Pres. 1980; mem. US Nat. Cttee for the Int. Union of Psychological Sciences 1985–93, Cttee on Int. Affairs of Soc. for Research in Child Devt 1991–95; Series Ed. on Social Learning Theory 1970–; mem. Editorial Bd Journal of Personality and Social Psychology 1963–77, Journal of Experimental Social Psychology 1967–77, Journal of Experimental Child Psychology 1967–82, Behaviour Research and Therapy 1963–, Journal of Applied Behavior Analysis 1968–72, 1975–78, 1980–81, Behavior Therapy 1970–73, 1989–91, 1992–, Personality: An International Journal 1970–72, Journal of Behavior Therapy and Experimental Psychiatry 1970–, Child Development 1971–77, Journal of Abnormal Psychology 1973, Aggression: An International Interdisciplinary Journal 1974–82, Cognitive Therapy and Research 1977–79, 1982–, Journal of Mental Imagery 1978–, Clinical Behavior Therapy Review 1979–81, Gestalt Therapy: An International Multidisciplinary Journal 1979–, Review of Personality and Social Psychology 1979–85, 1999–2002, Humboldt Journal of Social Relations 1979–, Psychological Review 1980–82, 1999–2004, Journal of Cognitive Psychotherapy 1986–, Behaviour Change 1985–95, Journal of Anxiety Disorders 1986–91, British Journal of Clinical Psychology 1987–, Annual Review of Psychology 1987–91, Anxiety Stress and Coping 1988–, Psychological Inquiry 1989–2002, Applied and Preventive Psychology: Current Scientific Perspectives 1991–, Medienpsychologie 1990–2000, Applied Psychology: An International Review 1993–, Social Behavior and Personality: An International Journal 1992–, Media Psychology 1998–, Journal of Social and Clinical Psychology 2002–, International Journal of Clinical and Health Psychology 2005–; Special Research Fellowship, Nat. Inst. of Mental Health 1969; Guggenheim Fellow 1972; Fellow, American Acad. of Arts and Sciences 1980, Japan Soc. for the Promotion of Science 1982; Hon. Pres. Canadian Psychological Asscn 1999, Hon. Fellow, World Innovation Foundation 2004; Dr hc (Univ. of British Columbia) 1979, (Univ. of Lethbridge) 1983, (Univ. of New Brunswick) 1985, (State Univ. of New York) 1987, (Univ. of Waterloo) 1990, (Freie Universität Berlin) 1990, (Univ. of Salamanca) 1992, (Indiana Univ.) 1993, (Univ. of Rome) 1994, (Leiden Univ.) 1995, (Alfred Univ.) 1995, (Pennsylvania State Univ.) 1999, (Grad. School and Univ. Center, City Univ. of New York) 2002, (Universitat Jaume I) 2002, (Univ. of Athens) 2003, (Univ. of Catania) 2004; Distinguished Scientist Award (Div. 12), American Psychological Asscn 1972, Distinguished Scientific Achievement Award, Calif. Psychological Asscn, 1973, Distinguished Contrib. Award, Int. Soc. for Research on Aggression 1980, Distinguished Scientific Contribs Award, American Psychological Asscn 1980, Distinguished Scientist Award, Soc. of Behavioral Medicine, William James Award, American Psychological Soc. 1989, Distinguished Lifetime Contribs Award, Calif. Psychological Asscn 1998, Thorndike Award for Distinguished Contribs of Psychology to Educ., American Psychological Asscn 1999, Lifetime Achievement Award, Asscn for the Advancement of Behavior Therapy 2001, Healthtrac Award for Distinguished Contributions to Health Promotion 2002, Lifetime Achievement Award, Western Psychological Asscn 2003, McGovern Medal for Distinguished Contribution to Health Promotion Science 2004, James McKeen Cattell Award, American Psychological Soc. 2004, Outstanding Lifetime Contribution to Psychology, American Psychological Asscn 2004, Distinguished Achievement Alumni Award, Univ. of Iowa 2005, Distinguished Lifetime Achievement Award, American Acad. of Health Behavior 2006, Gold Medal Award for Distinguished Lifetime Contribs to the Advancement of Psychology, American Psychological Foundation 2006, Everett M. Rogers Award 2007, Grawemeyer Award 2008. *Publications:* Adolescent Aggression (co-author) 1959, Social Learning and Personality Development (co-author) 1963, Principles of Behavior Modification 1969, Psychological Modeling: Conflicting Theories (ed.) 1971, Aggression: Social Learning Analysis 1973, Social Learning Theory 1977, Social Foundations of Thought and Action: A Social Cognitive Theory 1986, Self-efficacy in Changing Societies (ed.) 1995, Self-efficacy: The Exercise of Control 1997; numerous articles in scientific journals. *Address:* Department of Psychology, Jordan Hall, Bldg 420, 450 Serra Mall, Stanford University, Stanford, CA 94305-2130, USA (office). *Telephone:* (650) 725-2409 (office). *Fax:* (650) 725-5699 (office). *E-mail:* bandura@psych.stanford.edu (office). *Website:* www-psych.stanford.edu (office).

BANERJEE, Mamata, BEd, LLB, MA; Indian politician; *Chief Minister of West Bengal;* b. 5 Jan. 1955, Hazra, Calcutta (now Kolkata); d. of Shri Promileswar and Gayetri Banerjee; ed Sikshayatan Coll., Jogesh Chandra Choudhury Coll. of Law, Univ. of Calcutta; Gen. Sec. Mahila Congress (I), W Bengal 1970–80; Sec. Dist Congress Cttee, Calcutta S 1978–81; mem. Lok Sabha (House of the People, Parl.) 1984, 1991–, mem. Consultative Cttee, Ministry of Human Resource Devt 1987–93, of Home Affairs 1987–88, 1993–96, 1996–97, 1998–99, 2006–07, of Industries 2001–03, mem. Gen. Purposes Cttee 1998–99, 2001–, Chair. Cttee on Railways 1998–99, Cttee on Personnel, Public Grievances, Law & Justice 2004; Union Minister of State, Human Resource Devt, Dept of Youth Affairs and Sports, and Women and Child Devt 1991–93, of Railways 1999–2001, 2009–11, Minister without Portfolio 2003–04, of Coal and Mines 2004; Leader, All India Trinamool Congress Parl. Party 1999–; Chief Minister of W Bengal 2011–; Gen. Sec. and mem. Nat. Council, All India Youth Congress (I) Cttee 1985–87, Pres. Youth Congress (W Bengal) 1990; mem. Exec. Cttee Congress Parl. Party 1988–, Pradesh Congress Cttee 1989–; Sec. W Bengal TUC 1981–87. *Publications include:* Upalabdhi, Janatar Darbare, Maa, Pallabi, Manabik, Struggle for Existence, Motherland, Crocodile Island, Trinamool, Sishu Sathi, Anubhuti, Abishasya, Janmaini, Ekantee, Ashubho Shanket, Jago Banglaa, Ganotantre Lazza, Anoson Keno, Andolaner Katha, Soroni, Langoli, Maa-Mati-Manush, Ajab Chora, Ek Guchho Bhavana, Struggle for Existence, Smile, Dark Horizon, Slaughter of Democracy, Nandi Ma. *Leisure interests:* music, writing, painting. *Address:* Ministry of Railways, Rail Bhavan, Raisina Road, New Delhi 110 001 (office); All India Trinamool Congress, 125-D, Parliament House, New Delhi 110 001 (office); 5, Ashoka Road, New Delhi 110 001 (home); 30B Harish Chatterjee St, Kolkata 700 026, India (home); C-4, M. S. Flats, B. K. S. Marg, New Delhi 110 001 (home). *Telephone:* (11) 23386645 (Ministry) (office); (11) 24540881 (Parl.) (office); (33) 24753000 (Kolkata) (home); (11) 23722975 (home). *Fax:* (11) 23387333 (Ministry) (office); (33) 24540880 (Kolkata) (home). *E-mail:* secyrb@rb.railnet.gov.in (office); mamata.sansad@sansad.nic.in (home). *Website:* www.indianrailways.gov.in (office); www.trinamoolcongress.com (office).

BANFIELD, Jillian (Jill) Fiona, BSc, MSc, PhD, FRS, FAA; Australian scientist and academic; *Professor of Earth and Planetary Science, University of California, Berkeley;* b. 18 Aug. 1959, Armidale, NSW; d. of James E. Banfield and Eve Banfield; m. Perry Smith; two s. one d.; ed Australian Nat. Univ., Johns Hopkins Univ., USA; exploration geologist, Western Mining Corpn 1982–83; Asst Prof., Dept of Geology and Geophysics, Univ. of Wisconsin 1990–95, Assoc. Prof. 1995–99, Prof. 1999–2001, Dept of Chem. 1998–2001; Prof. Dept of Earth and Planetary Science, Univ. of California, Berkeley 2001–, Prof. Dept of Environmental Science, Policy and Man. 2001–, Researcher and mem. geochemistry group, Lawrence Berkeley Nat. Lab.; Assoc. Prof., Mineralogical Inst., Univ. of Tokyo 1996–97, Prof. 1998; John D. and Catherine T. MacArthur Foundation Fellow 1999–2004; John Simon Guggenheim Foundation Fellowship 2000; Distinguished Lecturer, Mineralogical Soc. of America 1994–95, Fellow 1997–; Paul W. Gast Lecturer, Geochemical Soc. 2000, NSF Earth Science Week Lecturer (Inaugural) 2000, Rosenqvist Lecturer, Norway 2005, Pioneer Lecturer, Clay Minerals Soc. 2005; mem. NAS Bd on Earth Sciences and Resources 2002–05; mem. Mineralogical Soc. of America, Councilor 1997–99, Chair. Roebling Award Cttee 1998, Chair. Mid Career Award Cttee 1998–99, Assoc. Ed. American Mineralogist, Journal of the Mineralogical Society of America 1997–2000; mem. US Dept of Energy, Basic Energy Sciences Geoscience Advisory Cttee; mem. American Soc. for Microbiology; mem. Clay Minerals Soc., Councilor, Student Awards Cttee, Bailey Award Cttee 2000; Dr hc (Ben-Gurion Univ.) 2015 Geological Soc. of Australia Prize 1978, Award for Outstanding Research, US Dept of Energy 1995, Mineralogical Soc. of America Award 1997, D.A. Brown Medal, ANU 1999, Dana Medal, Mineralogical Soc. of America 2010, Benjamin Franklin Medal in Earth and

Environmental Science, Franklin Inst. 2011, L'Oréal-UNESCO Women in Science Award (North America) 2011, V.M. Goldschmidt Award 2017, and several other prizes and awards. *Publications:* numerous scientific papers. *Address:* Department of Environmental Science, Policy and Management, 130 Mulford Hall #3114, University of California, Berkeley, CA 94720, USA (office). *Telephone:* (510) 643-2155 (office); (510) 642-3804 (Lab.) (office); (510) 642-5438 (home). *Fax:* (510) 643-9980 (office). *E-mail:* jbanfield@berkeley.edu (office); jill@nature.berkeley.edu (office). *Website:* ourenvironment.berkeley.edu/people_profiles/jill-banfield (office); geomicrobiology.berkeley.edu (office).

BANGA, Manvinder (Vindi) Singh, BSc, MBA; Indian business executive; *Operating Partner, Clayton, Dubilier & Rice, LLC;* b. 31 Oct. 1954, Shimla; s. of Jaswant Banga and Harbhajan Singh Banga; m. Kamini Banga; two s.; ed Indian Inst. of Tech., Delhi, Indian Inst. of Man., Ahmedabad; joined Hindustan Lever Ltd 1977, served in various sales and marketing roles including Head of Personal Products, Chair. and Exec. Dir Soaps and Detergents Div. 1995–98, Sr Vice-Pres. Hair and Oral Care Divs 1998–2000, Chair. and Man. Dir Hindustan Unilever Ltd (fmrly Hindustan Lever Ltd) 2000–04, Business Group Pres. Home and Personal Care Asia, Unilever PLC and Chair. Hindustan Unilever 2004–05, Pres. Foods, Unilever PLC 2005–08, Pres. Foods, Home and Personal Care, Unilever PLC 2008–10; Operating Partner, Clayton, Dubilier & Rice, LLC 2010–; apptd mem. Bd of Dirs, Maruti Suzuki India Ltd 2003, Marks & Spencer Group plc, Thomson Reuters; mem. Bd of Govs, Indian Inst. of Man., Ahmedabad, Indian School of Business, Hyderabad, Prime Minister of India's Council of Trade and Industry, Wharton Asia and Int. Bd, World Pres Org.; Charter Mem. Indus Entrepreneur; Gold Medal, Indian Inst. of Tech. Delhi, Indian Inst. of Man. Ahmedabad; Padma Bhushan 2010. *Leisure interest:* golf. *Address:* CD&R LLP, Cleveland House, 33 King Street, London, SW1Y 6RJ, England (office). *Telephone:* (20) 7747-3800 (office). *Fax:* (20) 7747-3801 (office). *Website:* www.cdr-inc.com (office).

BANGA-BOTHY, Léonie Mbazoa, LLM; Central African Republic lawyer and politician; Dir Legal Affairs and Litigation Dept, Ministry of Foreign Affairs 2011; Minister of Foreign Affairs, African Integration, Francophony and Central Africans Abroad 2013–14; Pres. Central African Repub. Br., Avocats sans Frontières. *Address:* c/o Ministry of Foreign Affairs, African Integration, Francophony and Central Africans Abroad, Bangui, Central African Republic (office).

BANGEMANN, Martin, DJur; German lawyer, telecommunications industry executive and fmr politician; b. 15 Nov. 1934, Wanzleben; s. of Martin Bangemann and Lotte Telge; m. Renate Bauer 1962; three s. two d.; ed secondary school, Emden and Univs of Tübingen and Munich; mem. Freie Demokratische Partei (FDP) 1963–, Deputy 1969, mem. Regional Exec. Baden-Württemberg FDP 1973–78 (resgnd), mem. Nat. Exec. 1969– (resgnd as Gen. Sec. 1975), Chair. FDP 1985–88; mem. Bundestag 1972–80, 1987–88, European Parl. 1979–84; Minister of Finance 1984–88; EEC (now EU) Commr for Internal Market, Industry, Relations with European Parl. 1989–92, for Industrial Affairs and Tech. 1993–95, for Industrial Affairs, Information and Telecommunications Technologies 1995–99, a Vice-Pres. 1993–95; Dir Telefonica, Madrid 1999, mem. Advisory Bd 2000–05; mem. Bd of Trustees, Friedrich-Naumann-Stiftung 1974–98, Deputy Chair. of Bd 1975–76; Bundesverdienstkreuz (Great Cross), Great Golden Medal with ribbon for services to Repub. of Austria 1988, Grand Cross of the Order of Infante Dom Henrique 1989, Thomas Dehler Prize 1989, Reinhold Maier medal of the Reinhold-Maier-Stiftung 1999. *Leisure interests:* philosophy, horticulture.

BANGURA, Zainab Hawa, BA; Sierra Leonean human rights activist, politician and UN official; b. (Zainab Sesay), 18 Dec. 1959, Yonibana Chiefdom, Tonkolili Dist, Northern Prov.; ed Fourah Bay Coll.; apptd Asst Reinsurance Man. Nat. Insurance Co. 1983; f. Women Organized for a Morally Enlightened Nation (WOMEN) 1995, Nat. Accountability Group 2001; co-f. Campaign for Good Governance 1996, Movt for Progress (political party promoting good governance and empowerment of women, youth and the disabled) 2002, nominated Chair.; contested presidential elections (only female cand.) 2002; Chief Civil Affairs Officer to UN Mission in Liberia; Minister of Foreign Affairs and Int. Co-operation 2007–10, of Health and Sanitation 2010–12; Special Rep. of the Sec.-Gen. on Sexual Violence in Conflict, UN 2012–17; Assoc. and Fellow, Chartered Insurance Inst. (UK) 1991–; fmr Reagan-Fascell Democracy Fellow, The Nat. Endowment for Democracy; mem. Steering Cttee World Movt for Democracy; African Int. Award of Merit for Leadership 1999, New York Lawyers Cttee for Human Rights Human Rights Award 2000, A. Philip Randolph Inst. Bayard Rustin Humanitarian Award 2002, Nat. Endowment for Democracy Award, Washington, DC 2006, an award from Project 1808 Inc. 2013.

BANHAM, Sir John Michael Middlecott, Kt, MA, LLD, DL; British business executive; b. 22 Aug. 1940, Torquay, Devon; s. of Terence Middlecott Banham and Belinda Joan Banham CBE; m. Frances Favell 1965; one s. two d.; ed Charterhouse, Queens' Coll., Cambridge; with HM Foreign Service 1962–64; Dir of Marketing, Wallcoverings Div., Reed Int. 1965–69; with McKinsey & Co. Inc. 1969, Assoc. 1969–75, Prin. 1975–80, Dir 1980–83; Controller Audit Comm. for Local Authorities in England and Wales 1983–87; Dir-Gen. CBI March 1987–92; Chair. WestCountry TV Ltd 1992–95, John Labatt Ltd (now Interbrew Ltd) 1992–95, ECI Ventures LLP 1992–2005, Local Govt Comm. for England 1992–95, Tarmac PLC 1992–2000, Kingfisher 1996–2000, Whitbread PLC 2000–06, Geest PLC 2002–06, Johnson Matthey PLC 2006–11, Sultan Scientific Ltd 2008–; Sr Non-executive Dir Invesco Ltd; Dir Cyclacel Ltd, Nat. Westminster Bank 1992–98, Nat. Power PLC 1992–98, Amvescap PLC; Man. Trustee Nuffield Foundation 1988–97, ShelterBox 2011–12 (resgnd); Hon. Treas. Cancer Research Campaign 1991–2002; DL Cornwall 1999; Hon. LLD (Bath) 1987; Hon. DSc (Loughborough) 1989, (Exeter) 1993, (Strathclyde) 1995. *Publications:* Future of the British Car Industry 1975, Realising the Promise of a National Health Service 1977, The Anatomy of Change 1994 and numerous reports for Audit Comm. on educ., social services, housing, etc. 1984–87 and on the economy, skill training, infrastructure and urban regeneration for the CBI 1987–. *Leisure interests:* gardening, walking, music. *Address:* Penberth, St Buryan, nr Penzance, Cornwall, England. *Fax:* (1736) 810-722 (home). *E-mail:* frances@peaver.plus.com (home).

BANI, Father John Bennett; Ni-Vanuatu politician and fmr head of state; b. 4 July 1941, Pentecost; Dir of Rural Devt, Youth and Sport Vanua'aku Parti 1979–80; Pres. of Vanuatu March 1999–2004; fmr mem. Union of Moderate Parties.

BANISADR, Abolhassan; Iranian economist and politician; b. 22 March 1933, Hamadan; s. of the Ayatollah Seyed Nasrollah Banisadr; m. Ozra Banisadr; one s. two d.; ed Univ. of Paris (Sorbonne), France, Univ. of Tehran; supporter of Mossadeq (Prime Minister of Iran 1951–53); joined underground anti-Shah movt 1953; imprisoned after riots over Shah's land reforms 1963; in exile in Paris 1963–79; taught at the Sorbonne; close assoc. of the Ayatollah Ruhollah Khomeini and returned to Iran after overthrow of Shah; Minister of Econ. and Financial Affairs 1979–80; Acting Foreign Minister 1979 (resgnd); Pres. of Iran and C-in-C of the Armed Forces 1980–81; mem. Supervisory Bd of Cen. Bank of Iran 1979; mem. Revolutionary Council 1979–81 (Pres. 1980–81); overthrown in 'creeping coup' June 1981, fled to France 1981, subsequently formed Nat. Council of Resistance to oppose the Govt (in alliance with Massoud Rajavi, Leader of Mujaheddin Kalq and Abdel-Rahman Ghassemlov, Leader of Democratic Party of Kurdistan, Nat. Democratic Front and other resistance groups), Chair. 1981–84; opposed decision of Rajavi about collaborating with Saddam Hussein which consequently ended his alliance with Council of Nat. Resistance. *Publications include:* Oil and Violence (with Paul Vielle) 1974, The Economy of Tawhid 1975, Cult of Personality 1978, Women in Shahnameh 1979, Equilibriums 1979, Relationship Between Spirituality and Materialism 1979, Principles and Precepts of Islamic Government 1981, L'espérance trahie 1982, My Turn to Speak: Iran, the Revolution, and Secret Deals with the U.S. 1991, Human Rights in Islam and the Guiding Principles of Islamic Law 2003, Free Intellect 2005, Social Justice 2009, A Critique of Contrast and Contradiction in Syllogistic Logic 2010, Totalitarianism, The Foundations of Democracy, Leadership in Democracy, Social Justice, The Progress, Dignity in the 21st Century, Hoghoogh Panjganeh; numerous articles and pamphlets on philosophy, theology, economics and politics. *Address:* 5 rue General Pershing, 78000 Versailles, France (home). *Telephone:* 1-39-54-01-48 (home); 1-39-54-01-47 (home). *E-mail:* ab_banisadr@yahoo.de (home). *Website:* www.banisadr.com.fr (home).

BANJADE, Yagyamurti; Nepalese lawyer and government official; Attorney-Gen. of Nepal 2006–08; mem. Nepal Law Soc. *E-mail:* ybanjade@ntc.net.np.

BANJO, Ladipo Ayodeji, CON, PhD; Nigerian linguist, academic and university administrator; b. 2 May 1934, Ijebu-Igbo, Ogun State; s. of Ven Banjo and S. A. Banjo; m. Alice Mbamali; two s. two d.; ed Nigerian Coll. of Arts, Science and Tech., Univs of Glasgow and Leeds, UK, Univ. of California, Los Angeles, USA, Univ. of Ibadan; Educ. Officer W Nigeria 1960–64 (Sr Educ. Officer Jan.–Oct. 1966); Lecturer, Dept of English, Univ. of Ibadan 1966–71, Sr Lecturer 1971–73, Reader and Acting Head 1973–75, Prof. 1975–97, Prof. Emer. 1997–, Dean Faculty of Arts 1977–79, Chair. Cttee of Deans 1978–79, Deputy Vice-Chancellor 1981–84, Vice-Chancellor 1984–91; fmr Pro-Chancellor, Univ. of Port Harcourt; Pro-Chancellor, Univ. of Ilorin; Pro Chancellor Ajayi Crowther Univ., Oyo 2005–14; Dir Reading Centre 1970–72 (Co-Dir 1966–70); Chair. Int. Panel on English Language, West African Examination Council 1979–85, Advisory Cttee Nat. Language Centre 1980–85; Pres. West African Modern Languages Asscn 1981–; Vice-Pres. Int. Fed. of Languages and Literatures 1985–89, Yoruba Studies Asscn 1979–82; J. P. Oyo State 1986–; Dir Spectrum Books 1997, Blackwell Safari 1997; Pres. and Fellow, Nigerian Acad. of Letters 2000–; Chair. Cttee of Vice-Chancellors 1989–90, Chair. Cttee of Pro-Chancellors of Nigerian Univs 2000–04; Commander of the Order of the Niger 2001. *Publications:* Oral English 1971, Letter Writing 1973, Effective Use of English 1976, Developmental English 1985, New Englishes: A West African Perspective (ed. with A. Bamgbose and A. Thomas) 1995, Making a Virtue of Necessity: An Overview of the English Language in Nigeria 1996, In the Saddle: A Vice-Chancellor's Story 1997. *Leisure interests:* music, photography, reading.

BANKS, Charles A., BA; American business executive; b. Greensboro, NC; m.; three c.; ed San Bernardino High School, Calif., Hempstead High School, NY, Brown Univ.; served in USN 1962–64, attained rank of Lt, served in US Naval Reserve 1964–69; joined Peebles Supply Div., Ferguson Enterprises 1967, becoming Gen. Man., Ferguson Herndon and later Regional Man., Southeast Region, Sr Exec. Vice-Pres. Ferguson Enterprises 1987–89, Pres. 1992–2001; mem. Bd of Dirs Wolseley PLC 1992, Group CEO 2001–06 (retd); Partner, Clayton, Dubilier & Rice (pvt. equity investment firm) 2006–10 (retd); fmr Exec. Advisor, Gryphon Investors; Chair. VWR Int.; mem. Bd of Dirs William and Mary Business School Foundation 1989 (Chair. 1992–2001), mem. Bd of Visitors 2006–, currently Vice Rector of the Coll. and Vice-Chair. Exec. Cttee; mem. Bd of Dirs TowneBank/Peninsula; mem. Bd of Regents, Harris Manchester Coll., Univ. of Oxford, UK; Hon. DrSc (Christopher Newport Univ.); T.C. and Elizabeth Clarke Medallion, William and Mary Business School Foundation 2006. *Leisure interests:* travelling with family, golf, wines.

BANKS, Jeff, CBE, DArts, FRSA; Welsh fashion designer; b. (Jeffrey Tatham-Banks), 17 March 1943, Ebbw Vale, Gwent, S Wales; m. 1st Sandie Shaw 1967 (divorced 1978); one d.; m. 2nd Sue Mann; ed Brockley County Grammar School, Camberwell School of Art, Cen. St Martin's Coll. of Art and Design, Parsons The New School for Design, New York, USA; studied interior design and textiles; opened Clobber boutique in London 1964, launched own fashion label 1969, opened first stand-alone Jeff Banks shop in London, as well as retail outlets in 22 dept stores, including Harrods and Harvey Nichols 1975; co-launched fashion chain Warehouse late 1970s, taken over by retail chain Sears; continued to work as freelance designer of both men's and women's clothing, jewellery and home furnishings; started fashion design studio in partnership with Richard Carnill, HQ Design 1989; cr. homewear range Ports Of Call 1994; cr. own corp. clothing co., Incorporatewear 1996, produces clothing for Barclays Bank plc, My Travel, Nationwide Building Society, BAA, Abbey National, Swinton Building Society, Bradford & Bingley Building Society, Thompson Holidays, Local Authority Dinner Ladies, Stagecoach, Boots, Butlins, J Sainsbury plc (Jeff & Co shops 2000–04, Jeff & Co brand now part of Matalan portfolio), Guide Asscn, England football team, London's 2012 Olympics bid; launched first of stand-alone Jeff Banks retail concept 2006, nine shops by 2008; Visiting Lecturer, Cen. St Martin's, Harrow School of Art, Univ. of Middlesex, Univ. of Northumbria, Univ. of Kingston, Croydon Art School, Bournemouth School of Art, London Coll. of Fashion, Swire

School of Fashion, Hong Kong, La Salle School of Fashion, Shanghai; External Examiner, John Moores Univ., Liverpool, Brighton Univ., Univ. of Cen. Lancashire, Cen. St Martin's, Harrow School of Art (now Westminster Univ.), Univ. of Northumbria, RCA, Surrey Inst.; mem. Council CNAA 1978; formed charity Graduate Fashion Week 1990; Chair. Royal Soc. Fashion Medal Awards Scheme 1992–2002; Pres. Chartered Soc. of Designers 2002; co-hosted with Mary Quant The Clothes Show Expo, Hong Kong 1996; cr. Chartered Soc. of Designers Awards Medal for Fashion, DR Ind. Retailer of the Year Awards 1988, Prima Retailer of the Year Awards (in conjunction with National Magazines) 1991 (also Chair. judging panel and host of event); Fellow, Chartered Soc. of Designers 1978; hon. degrees from Univs of Lancaster, East London, Newcastle & Northumbria, Westminster, Univ. Coll. for the Creative Arts; British Designer of the Year 1980, 1982, British Coat Designer of the Year 1981, British Retailer of the Year 1984, Drapers Lifetime Achievement Award 2007. *Television includes:* presenter, with Selina Scott and Caryn Franklin, The Clothes Show (BBC TV) 1986–95; cr. Clothes Show Live (BBC TV) 1988; cr. and presented more than 120 episodes of The Style Challenge (BBC TV) 1997–98. *Address:* Incorporatewear, Edison Road, Hams Hall, National Distribution Park, Coleshill, B46 1DA, England (office). *Telephone:* (1675) 432-235 (office). *Fax:* (1675) 432-200 (office). *E-mail:* enquiries@icwuk.com (office). *Website:* www.jeffbanks.co.uk (office); www.incorporatewear.co.uk (office).

BANKS, Russell, BA; American writer; b. 28 March 1940, Barnstead, NH; s. of Earl Banks and Florence Banks; m. 1st Darlene Bennett (divorced 1962); one d.; m. 2nd Mary Gunst 1963 (divorced 1977); three d.; m. 3rd Kathy Walton (divorced 1988); m. 4th Chase Twichell 1989; ed Colgate Univ. and Univ. of North Carolina; fmr teacher of creative writing at Emerson Coll., Boston, Univ. of NH, Univ. of Ala, New England Coll.; teacher of creative writing, Princeton Univ. 1982–97; fmr Pres. Parl. Int. des Écrivains; Best American Short Stories Awards 1971, 1985, Fels Award for Fiction 1974, O. Henry Awards 1975, St Lawrence Award for Fiction 1976, Guggenheim Fellowship 1976, Nat. Endowment for the Arts Fellowships 1977, 1983, John Dos Passos Award 1985, American Acad. of Arts and Letters Award 1985. *Publications include:* poetry: Waiting to Freeze 1967, 30/6 1969, Snow: Meditations of a Cautious Man in Winter 1974; novels: Family Life 1975, Hamilton Stark 1978, The Book of Jamaica 1980, The Relation of My Imprisonment 1984, Continental Drift 1985, Affliction 1989, The Sweet Hereafter 1991, Rule of the Bone 1995, Cloudsplitter 1998, The Angel on the Roof 2000, The Darling 2004, The Reserve 2008, Outer Banks 2008, Lost Memory of Skin 2011, A Permanent Member of the Family 2013; collected short stories: Searching for Survivors 1975, The New World 1978, Trailerpark 1981, Success Stories 1986; contrib. short stories to magazines and periodicals, including New York Times Book Review, Washington Post, American Review, Vanity Fair, Antaeus, Partisan Review, New England Review, Fiction International, Boston Globe Magazine; non-fiction: Invisible Stranger 1998, Dreaming Up America 2008, Voyager 2016. *Address:* Steven Barclay Agency, 12 Western Avenue, Petaluma, CA 94952, USA (office); 1000 Park Avenue, New York, NY 10028, USA. *Telephone:* (707) 773-0654 (office). *Fax:* (707) 778-1868 (office). *Website:* www.barclayagency.com (office).

BANKS, Tyra; American television presenter and fmr model; b. 4 Dec. 1973; d. of Carolyn London; ed Immaculate Heart High School, Los Angeles, Harvard Business School; has modelled since 1991 for Karl Lagerfeld, Yves St Laurent, Oscar De La Renta, Chanel, Victoria's Secret, etc.; featured on covers of Elle, GQ, Sports Illustrated, German Cosmopolitan, Spanish Vogue, Scene, Arena; retd from modelling 2005; TV presenter, producer, talk show host; conceived reality programme America's Next Top Model; f. TYInc. *Video appearances include:* Too Funky by George Michael, Black or White by Michael Jackson, Love Thing by Tina Turner. *Film appearances include:* Black or White 1991, Higher Learning 1995, A Woman Like That 1997, Love Stinks 1999, Love & Basketball 2000, Coyote Ugly 2000, Halloween: Resurrection 2002, Eight Crazy Nights (voice) 2002. *Television appearances include:* Inferno 1992, The Apartment Complex 1999, Life-Size 2000, Felicity 2000; exec. producer America's Next Top Model 2003–, Stylista 2008–; exec. producer and host The Tyra Banks Show (talk show) 2005–10. *Publications:* Tyra's Beauty Inside and Out 1998. *Address:* c/o IMG Models, 304 Park Avenue South, 12th Floor, New York, NY 10010, USA. *Telephone:* (212) 253-8884. *Fax:* (212) 253-8883. *Website:* tyrashow.warnerbros.com.

BANKS, Victor Franklin, MA; Anguillan politician; *Chief Minister;* b. 8 Nov. 1947, The Valley; m. Cerise Banks; three c.; ed The Valley Secondary School, Coll. of the Virgin Islands, St Thomas and New School, New York, USA; teacher, The Valley Secondary School 1964–68; Man. Shipping Dept, SARAND, Inc., New York 1974–80; Gov. Liaison Officer, Anguilla 1980–81; Deputy to House of Ass. (Anguilla People's Party) for Valley North 1981–84, Deputy (Anguilla Democratic Party) for Valley South 1985–; Minister of Social Services 1981–84; Leader Anguilla Democratic Party 1985–2000, Anguilla United Front (AUF) 2000–; Minister of Finance, Econ. Devt, Investment and Commerce 2002–10; Chief Minister 2015–; Pres. Banx Professional Services Ltd 1981–. *Leisure interests:* community work, counselling, political educ., volleyball, squash, handball, duck shooting. *Address:* Office of the Chief Minister, The Secretariat, POB 60, The Valley, Anguilla (office). *Telephone:* 497-2518 (office). *Fax:* 497-3389 (office). *E-mail:* chief-minister@gov.ai (office).

BANKSY; British artist; anonymous graffiti artist 1990–; painted numerous murals in public places usually depicting anti-war, anti-capitalist or anti-establishment messages. *Exhibitions and works include:* 33 1/3 collective, Los Angeles 2002, Balloon Girl 2002, Turf War, warehouse in East London 2003, Show Me the Money 2005, Bristol City Museum and Art Gallery 2009, Exit Through the Gift Shop (film) 2010, Dismaland, Weston-super-Mare 2015, The Walled Off Hotel, Bethlehem, Palestinian Territories 2017. *E-mail:* faq@banksy.co.uk. *Website:* www.banksy.co.uk.

BANNISTER, (Richard) Matthew, LLB; British radio presenter and fmr broadcasting executive; b. 16 March 1957, Sheffield, Yorks., England; s. of Richard Neville Bannister and of Olga Margaret Bannister; m. 1st Amanda Gerrard Walker 1984 (died 1988); one d.; m. 2nd Shelagh Margaret Macleod 1989 (died 2005); one s.; m. 3rd Katherine Jane Hood 2007; ed King Edward VII School, Sheffield, Univ. of Nottingham; Presenter, BBC Radio Nottingham 1978–81; Reporter/Presenter Capital Radio, London 1981–83, Deputy Head News and Talks 1985–87, Head 1987–88; with Newsbeat, BBC Radio 1 1983–85; Man. Ed. BBC Greater London Radio 1988–91, Project Co-ordinator, BBC Charter Renewal 1991–93, Controller BBC Radio 1 1993–98, Dir BBC Radio 1996–98, Chief Exec. of Production BBC 1999–2000; Dir Marketing and Communications, BBC 2000; Chair. Trust the DJ 2001; fmr Presenter BBC Radio 5 Live, currently Presenter of Outlook on BBC World Service and Last Word on BBC Radio 4; mem. Bd Chichester Festival Theatre 1999–2005; Fellow, Radio Acad.; Hon. DLitt (Nottingham) 2011. *Publications:* articles in The Times. *Leisure interests:* rock music, theatre, collecting P.G. Wodehouse first edns. *Address:* c/o Knight Ayton Management, 35 Great James Street, London, WC1N 3HB, England (office). *Telephone:* (20) 7831-4400 (office). *E-mail:* info@knightayton.co.uk (office). *Website:* knightayton.co.uk/male-presenters/matthew-bannister (office).

BANNON, Steven (Steve) Kevin, BA, MA, MBA; American media executive, film producer and fmr government official; b. 27 Nov. 1953, Norfolk, Va; s. of Martin Bannon and Doris Bannon (née Herr); m. 1st Cathleen Suzanne Houff (divorced), one d.; m. 2nd Mary Louise Piccard (divorced), two d.; m. 3rd Diane Clohesy (divorced); ed Virginia Polytechnic Inst., Georgetown Univ., Harvard Univ.; served in USN 1976–83; investment banker, Goldman Sachs 1984–90; CEO Bannon & Co. (investment bank) 1990–98; Chair. First Look Media Inc. 1993–96, Vice-Chair. 1996–2000; Acting Dir Biosphere 2 (science research project) 1993–95; exec. producer in film and media industry 1995–; Head, Strategic Advisory Services, The Firm, Inc. (film and TV man. co.) 2002–03; Exec. Chair. and Co-Founder Government Accountability Inst.; CEO and Chair. Affinity Media 2007–11; Founding mem. Bd of Dirs Breitbart News LLC, Exec. Chair. 2012–16, Aug. 2017–Jan. 2018; CEO Donald Trump's presidential campaign 2016; White House Chief Strategist Jan.–Aug. 2017; Trustee American Acad. of Dramatic Arts. *Films include:* as producer: The Indian Runner 1991, Titus 1999, In the Face of Evil: Reagan's War in Word and Deed 2004, Cochise County USA: Cries from the Border 2005, Border War: The Battle Over Illegal Immigration 2006, The Chaos Experiment 2009, Generation Zero 2010, Battle for America 2010, Fire from the Heartland: The Awakening of the Conservative Woman 2010, Still Point in a Turning World: Ronald Reagan and His Ranch 2011, The Undefeated 2011, Occupy Unmasked 2012, The Hope & The Change 2012, District of Corruption 2012, Sweetwater 2013, Rickover: The Birth of Nuclear Power 2014, The Last 600 Meters 2015.

BANNY, Charles Konan; Côte d'Ivoirian fmr central banker and economist; b. 11 Nov. 1942, Divo; m.; four c.; ed Ecole Supérieure des Sciences Economiques et Commerciales, Paris; served as Chargé de Mission, Stabilisation and Support Fund of Agric. Product Prices; Deputy Sec.-Gen. Inter-African Coffee Org., Paris 1970, Sec.-Gen. 1971; Dir of Admin. and Social Affairs, Cen. Bank of West African States (BCEAO) 1976, later Cen. Dir of Securities, Investment, Borrowing and Lending, then Cen. Dir of Research, apptd Nat. Dir BCEAO for Côte d'Ivoire 1983, Gov. BCEAO 1994–2007; interim Prime Minister of Côte d'Ivoire 2005–07; cand. for presidency of Parti Démocratique de la Côte d'Ivoire—Rassemblement Démocratique Africain (PDCI—RDA) 2014. *Address:* c/o Parti Démocratique de la Côte d'Ivoire—Rassemblement Démocratique Africain, 05 BP 36, Abidjan 05, Côte d'Ivoire. *E-mail:* sg@pdcirda.org. *Website:* www.pdcirda.org.

BANSAL, Binny, B.Tech.; Indian business executive; b. 1982, Chandigarh; m. Trisha Vasudeva; two c.; ed Indian Inst. of Tech., Delhi; software engineer Sarnoff 2005–07; software engineer Amazon Jan.–Sept. 2007; co-founder (with Sachin Bansal) and COO Flipkart 2007–16, CEO 2016–17, Group CEO 2017–18; Asian of the Year Award 2016. *Leisure interests:* reading, playing basketball, football. *Address:* c/o Flipkart Internet Pvt Ltd, Vaishnavi Summit, Ground Floor, 7th Main, 80 Feet Road, 3rd Block, Bengaluru 560034, India (office).

BANSAL, Brij Mohan, BTech, DIIT; Indian oil industry executive; ed Indian Inst. of Tech., Delhi; mem. Bd of Dirs Indian Oil Corpn Ltd (IndianOil) 2005–11, briefly headed IndianOil's Research and Devt function, Dir of Planning and Business Devt 2005–11, Dir of Human Resources –2010, Chair. Indian Oil Corpn Ltd 2010–11, also Chair. of IndianOil's subsidiaries: Chennai Petroleum Corpn Ltd (CPCL), IndianOil Mauritius Ltd (IOML), IOT Infrastructure & Energy Services Ltd (Jt Venture of IndianOil and Oiltanking GmbH); fmr mem. Bd Bongaigaon Refinery & Petrochemicals Ltd (now merged with IndianOil), Petronet LNG Ltd, Engineers India Ltd, Lubrizol India Pvt. Ltd; fmr Chair. IndianOil Technologies Ltd (subsidiary of IndianOil), Green Gas Ltd (Jt Venture of IndianOil and GAIL (India) Ltd), IndianOil Petronas Pvt. Ltd (Jt Venture of IndianOil and Petroliam Nasional Berhad (Petronas), Malaysia); first Chair. India Chapter of Int. DME (Di-Methyl Ether) Asscn (IDA), USA; Chair. Emer. Bio-Diesel Asscn of India. *Address:* c/o Indian Oil Corpn Ltd, Corporate Office, 3079/3, J. B. Tito Marg, Sadiq Nagar, New Delhi 110 049, India.

BANSAL, Pawan Kumar, BSc, LLB; Indian lawyer and politician; b. 16 July 1948, Sunam, Sangrur Dist, Punjab; s. of Piara Lal Aggarwal (Tapa Wale) and Rukmani Devi; m. Madhu Bansal; two s.; ed Yadavindra Public School, Patiala, Govt Coll., Chandigarh, Punjab Univ., Chandigarh; Gen. Sec. Chandigarh Territorial Youth Congress 1976–78, Pres. 1982; Gen. Sec. Punjab Pradesh Youth Congress 1978–82, Pres. 1982–83; elected to Rajya Sabha (upper house of Parl.) 1984–90, mem. Rajya Sabha Panel of Vice-Chairmen 1985–87, Whip, Congress (I) Parl. Party, Rajya Sabha 1989–90; elected to 10th Lok Sabha (lower house of Parl.) for Chandigarh constituency 1991, Whip, Congress (I) Parl. Party, Lok Sabha 1992–96, re-elected to 13th Lok Sabha 1999–2004, 14th Lok Sabha 2004–09, 15th Lok Sabha 2009–; Pres. Chandigarh Territorial Congress Cttee 1997–98; Sec. All India Congress Cttee 1999; Treas. Indian Parl. Group 2004–09; Minister of State for Expenditure, Banking and Insurance, Ministry of Finance 2006–09, Minister of State for Parl. Affairs 2008–09, Union Cabinet Minister for Parl. Affairs 2009–12, for Water Resources 2009–11, for Science and Tech. and Earth Sciences Jan.–July 2011, for Parl. Affairs and Water Resources 2011–12, Minister of Railways 2012–13; mem. Indian Nat. Congress, Indian parl. dels to numerous countries. *Address:* Lok Sabha, Parliament House Annexe, New Delhi 110 011 (office); c/o Indian National Congress, 24 Akbar Road, New Delhi 110 011, India (office). *Telephone:* (11) 23017465 (Lok Sabha) (office); (11) 23019080 (office). *Fax:* (11) 23792107 (Lok Sabha) (office); (11) 23017047 (office). *E-mail:* vnathan@sansad.nic.in (office); connect@inc.in (office). *Website:* loksabha.nic.in (office); www.inc.in (office).

BANVILLE, John; Irish writer; b. 8 Dec. 1945, Wexford; m. Janet Dunham; two s.; partner Patricia Quinn; two d.; ed St Peter's Coll., Wexford; fmrly night copy ed.,

The Irish Times, Literary Ed. 1988–99, Chief Literary Critic and Assoc. Literary Ed. 1999–2002; elected to Aosdána (Irish arts asscn) 1984; Foreign Honorary Member, American Acad. of Arts and Sciences 2007; Cavaliere of the Ordine della Stella d'Italia 2017; Franz Kafka Prize 2011, Irish PEN Award for Outstanding Achievement in Irish Literature 2013, Austrian State Prize for European Literature 2013, Bob Hughes Lifetime Achievement Award, Irish Book Awards 2013, Prince of Asturias Award for Literature 2014, RBA Prize for Crime Writing 2017. *Film scripts include:* The Last September 1998, Albert Nobbs 2011, The Sea 2013. *Plays include:* The Broken Jug (after Kleist) 1994, God's Gift (after Kleist's 'Amphitryon') 2000. *Publications include:* novels: Nightspawn 1971, Birchwood 1973, Dr Copernicus 1976, Kepler 1983, The Newton Letter 1985, Mefisto 1987, The Book of Evidence (Guinness Peat Aviation Prize 1989) 1989, Ghosts 1993, Athena 1995, The Untouchable (Lannan Literary Award for Fiction 1997) 1996, Eclipse 2000, Shroud 2003, The Sea (Man Booker Prize 2005, Irish Novel of the Year 2005) 2005, The Infinities 2009, Ancient Light 2012, The Blue Guitar 2015, Mrs Osmond 2017; as Benjamin Black: Quirke series: Christine Falls 2006, The Silver Swan 2007, Elegy for April 2010, A Death in Summer 2011, Vengeance 2012, Holy Orders 2013, Even the Dead 2015; The Lemur 2008, The Black-Eyed Blonde, Prague Nights 2017; short stories: Imagined Lives: Portraits of Unknown People 2011; non-fiction: Prague Pictures: Portraits of a City 2003, Time Pieces: A Dublin Memoir 2016; contribs to New York Review of Books, Irish Times, Guardian, New Republic. *Address:* c/o United Agents, 12–26 Lexington Street, London, W1F 0LE, England (office). *Telephone:* (20) 3214-0800 (office). *Fax:* (20) 3214-0802 (office). *E-mail:* glegrice@unitedagents.co.uk (office). *Website:* www.unitedagents.co.uk (office).

BAO, Xuding; Chinese government official and business executive; *President, China International Engineering Consulting Corporation;* b. Feb. 1939, Wuxi City, Jiangsu Prov.; ed Shenyang School of Machine Industry, CCP Cen. Party School; joined CCP 1961; Deputy Dir then Dir City Machine Building Industry Bureau, Sichuan Prov. 1986–88; Dir Sichuan Prov. Econ. Planning Comm. 1988–90; Vice-Minister of Machine Building and Electronics Industries 1990–93; Vice-Minister of Machine Building Industry 1993–96, Minister 1996–98; Vice-Minister State Devt and Reform Comm. 1998–99; mem. CCP Municipal Cttee, Chongqing 1999– (Deputy Sec. 1999–2000, 2002–); Deputy Mayor of Chongqing 1999–2000, Mayor 2000–02; Pres. China Int. Engineering Consulting Corpn 2002–; mem. 15th CCP Cen. Cttee 1997–2002; mem. 10th CPPCC Nat. Cttee 2003–08. *Address:* China International Engineering Consulting Corporation, 32 Che Gong Zhuang West Road, Haidian District, 100044 Beijing, People's Republic of China. *E-mail:* ciecc@ciecc.com.cn. *Website:* www.ciecc.com.cn.

BAPTISTA NETO, Clovis José; Brazilian engineer and international organization executive; *Executive Secretary, Inter-American Telecommunication Commission (Comisión Interamericana de Telecomunicaciones—CITEL);* ed Pontifical Catholic University of Rio de Janeiro; held several sr positions with EMBRATEL (telecommunications operator) 1974–95; held several key positions with Ministry of Communications; fmr Head of Int. Affairs, Brazilian Telecommunications Regulatory Agency, ANATEL; currently Exec. Sec. Inter-American Telecommunication Comm. (Comisión Interamericana de Telecomunicaciones—CITEL), Washington, DC 2000–; participant in confs and int. meetings of ITU, CITEL and WTO, among others; represents OAS at Hemispheric Advisory Bd Inst. for Connectivity in the Americas (Govt-supported Canadian org.). *Address:* Inter-American Telecommunication Commission (CITEL), 1889 F Street NW 6th Floor, Washington, DC 20006, USA (office). *Telephone:* (202) 370-4713 (office). *E-mail:* citel@oas.org (office). *Website:* www.citel.oas.org (office).

BAPTISTE, Alva Romanus, MSc; Saint Lucia politician and fmr transport official; ed Cranfield Univ., UK; Air Traffic Control Asst 1985–86, Air Traffic Control Officer 1988–97, Asst Airport Man., Hewanorra Int. Airport 2001–02, with St Lucia Air and Sea Ports Authority 1985–2002, Civil Aviation Officer, Ministry of Civil Aviation 2003–05; mem. House of Ass. for Laborie constituency 2006–; Minister for Foreign Affairs, Int. Trade and Civil Aviation 2011–16; mem. St Lucia Labour Party. *Address:* c/o Ministry of Foreign Affairs, International Trade and Civil Aviation, Conway Business Centre, 7th Floor, Waterfront, Castries, St Lucia (office).

BAQUET, Dean Paul; American journalist and editor; *Executive Editor, New York Times;* b. 21 Sept. 1956, New Orleans; s. of Edward Joseph Baquet and Myrtle Baquet (née Romano); m. Dylan Landis 1986; one s.; ed Columbia Univ., New York; investigative reporter, New Orleans 1978–84; investigative reporter, Chicago Tribune 1984–87, Chief Investigative Reporter 1987–90; investigative reporter, New York Times 1990–92, Projects Ed. 1992–95, Deputy Metropolitan Ed. 1995, Nat. Ed. 1995–2000, Asst Man. Ed., then Man. Ed. and Washington Bureau Chief 2007–11, Exec. Ed. 2014–; Man. Ed. Los Angeles Times 2000–05, Ed. 2005–06; mem. Bd of Dirs Cttee to Protect Journalists; Pulitzer Prize for Investigative Reporting 1988, Fourth Estate Award, Nat. Press Club 2018. *Address:* New York Times, 620 Eighth Avenue, New York, NY 10018, USA (office). *Website:* www.nytimes.com (office).

BAR-ON, Ronnie; Israeli lawyer and politician; b. 2 June 1948, Tel-Aviv; m.; three c.; ed Hebrew Univ., Jerusalem; completed mil. service with rank of Lt-Col, served as judge, Mil. Court of Appeals in Judea, Samaria, Gaza; mem. Cen. Cttee of Israel Bar 1995–2003, also served as mem. Jerusalem Regional Cttee of Israel Bar, Council for Admin. Courts, Advisory Comm. to Govt Cos Authority, Public Defenders Comm.; mem. Knesset (Likud and Kadima) 2003–11, Chair. House Cttee, mem. Constitution, Law and Justice and State Control Cttee, Parl. Inquiry Cttee on Violence in Sports and of the Environmental Lobby, substitute mem. Foreign Affairs and Defence Cttee; Minister of Nat. Infrastructures and Minister of Science and Tech., January–May 2006, of the Interior 2006–07, of Finance 2007–09; Ind. Dir Gazit Globe Ltd 2013–, Delek Drilling Management (1993) Ltd 2016–; mem. Bd of Dirs Alrov (Israel) Ltd 2013–, IDB Development Corp. Ltd, Migdal Makefet Pension and Provident Funds Ltd.

BARADEI, Mohammad Mostafa el-, BL, DEA, PhD; Egyptian lawyer, diplomatist, international organization official and politician; b. 17 June 1942, Cairo; s. of Mostafa el-Baradei; m. Aida el-Kachef; one s. one d.; ed Univ. of Cairo, Grad. Inst. of Int. Studies, Geneva, Switzerland, New York Univ., USA; with Egyptian Ministry of Foreign Affairs, Dept of Int. Orgs 1964–67; mem. Perm. Mission to UN, New York 1967–71; Sr Fellow, Center for Int. Studies, New York Univ. 1973–74; Special Asst to Foreign Minister, Ministry of Foreign Affairs 1974–78; mem. Perm. Mission to UN, Geneva and Alt. Rep. Cttee on Disarmament 1978–80; Sr Fellow and Dir Int. Law and Orgs Programme, UN Inst. for Training and Research, New York 1980–84; Adjunct Prof. of Int. Law, New York Univ. 1981–87; Rep. of Dir-Gen. of IAEA to UN, New York 1984–87, Legal Adviser, then Dir Legal Div., IAEA, Vienna 1987–91, Dir of External Relations 1991–93, Asst Dir-Gen. for External Relations 1993–97, Dir-Gen. IAEA 1997–2009 (three terms); f. Nat. Asscn for Change (political reform movt) 2010–; co-f. Dustour (Constitution) Party 2012; Acting Vice-Pres. of Egypt July–Aug. 2013 (resgnd); mem. Int. Law Asscn, American Soc., of Int. Law, Nuclear Law Asscn; Hon. Patron Trinity's Univ. Philosophical Soc. 2006; Greatest Nile Collar (highest Egyptian civilian decoration), Order of Francisc Skorina (Belarus), Order of Friendship of Peoples (Belarus), Decoration for Services to the Repub. of Austria (Grand Decoration in Gold with Sash) 2009, Order of Merit of the FRG (Grand Cross with Star and Sash) 2010; Dr hc (New York Univ., Univ. of Maryland, American Univ., Cairo, Free Mediterranean Univ. (LUM), Bari, Italy, Soka Univ. of Japan, Tsinghua Univ., Beijing, Polytechnic Univ., Bucharest, Universidad Politecnica de Madrid, Konkuk Univ., Seoul, Univ. of Florence, Univ. of Buenos Aires, Nat. Univ. of Cuyo, Argentina, Amherst Coll., Cairo Univ.); Nobel Peace Prize (jt winner with IAEA) 2005, Franklin D. Roosevelt Four Freedoms Award 2006, James Park Morton Interfaith Award, Golden Plate Award, American Acad. of Achievement, Jit Trainor Award, Georgetown Univ., Human Security Award, Muslim Public Affairs Council, Prix de la Fondation, Crans Montana Forum, El Athir Award (Algeria's highest nat. distinction), Golden Dove of Peace Prize, Pres. of Italy, Award for Distinguished Contrib. to the Peaceful Worldwide Use of Nuclear Tech., World Nuclear Asscn 2007, Mostar Int. Peace Award, Mostar Center for Peace and Multiethnic Cooperation 2007, Peacebuilding Award, EastWest Inst. 2008, Int. Seville NODO Prize for Peace, Security and Inter-Cultural Dialogue 2008, Indira Gandhi Prize for Peace, Disarmament and Devt 2009, Delta Prize for Global Understanding, sponsored by Univ. of Georgia and Delta Airlines 2009. *Publications:* The International Law Commission: The Need for a New Direction 1981, Model Rules for Disaster Relief Operations 1982, The Role of International Atomic Energy Agency Safeguards in the Evolution of the Non-Proliferation Regime 1991, The International Law of Nuclear Energy 1993, On Compliance with Nuclear Non-Proliferation Obligations (Security Dialogue) 1996, The Age of Deception: Nuclear Diplomacy in Treacherous Times 2011; articles in int. law journals. *Website:* www.iaea.org/about/dg/elbaradei/biography.

BARAK, Lt-Gen. Ehud; Israeli politician, fmr army officer and business executive; b. 12 Feb. 1942; s. of Israel Brog and Esther Brog; m. Nava Cohen; three d.; ed Hebrew Univ. Jerusalem and Stanford Univ. Calif.; enlisted in Israeli Defence Force (IDF) 1959; grad. Infantry Officers' course 1962; commando course, France 1963; Armoured Corps Co. Commdrs' course 1968; various command roles; also served in operations br. of Gen. Staff; active service in Six Day War 1967 and Yom Kippur War 1973; Commdr Tank Commdrs' course 1974; Head, Gen. Staff Planning Dept 1982–83; Dir IDF Mil. Intelligence 1983–86; Commdr Cen. Command 1986–87; Deputy Chief of Gen. Staff Israeli Defence Force 1987–91, Chief of Gen. Staff 1991–94; Minister of Interior July–Nov. 1995, of Foreign Affairs 1995–96; Chair. Israel Labour Party 1997–2001, 2007–11; f. breakaway party Ha'atzmaut (Independence) Jan. 2011–; Prime Minister of Israel 1999–2001; Deputy Prime Minister and Minister of Defence 2007–13; mem. Knesset (Parl.) and of Parl. Security and Foreign Affairs Cttee 1996; Chair. Barak & Assocs LLC; most decorated soldier in history of IDF. *Leisure interest:* playing the piano. *Address:* c/o Ministry of Defence, Kaplan Street, Hakirya, Tel-Aviv 67659, Israel.

BARAKA, Nizar, PhD; Moroccan economist and government official; *President, Economic and Environmental Council;* b. 6 Feb. 1964, Rabat; m. Radia el-Fassi; one c.; ed Univ. of Aix-Marseille, France; held sr teaching positions at Faculty of Law, Econs and Social Sciences, Univ. Mohammed V, Rabat; joined Ministry of Finance 1996, Head, Econ. Watch Service, Financial Research and Forecasts Unit 1998, Div. Head, Econ. Policy and Macro-Economic Analysis 2006, Deputy Dir, Financial Research and Forecasts Unit, Ministry of Finance and Privatization, Minister-del. to Prime Minister in charge of Econ. and Gen. Affairs 2010–12, Minister of Economy and Finance 2012–13; Pres. Social, Econ. & Environmental Council (CESE) 2013–; mem. Parti de l'Istiqlal. *Address:* Economic and Environmental Council, 1, Angle rues Al Michmich & Addalbout, Secteur 10, Groupe 5, Hay Riad, 10100 Rabat, Morocco (office). *Telephone:* (5) 38010300 (office). *Fax:* (5) 38010350 (office). *Website:* www.ces.ma (office).

BARAKAUSKAS, Dailis Alfonsas; Lithuanian politician; b. 29 June 1952, Geručiai, Pakruojis Dist; m.; two c.; ed Žeimelis Secondary School, Pakruojis Dist, Kaunas Polytechnic Inst. (now the Kaunas Univ. of Tech.), Vilnius Univ., Harvard Inst. for Int. Devt, USA, study programmes in Sweden, Germany, the Netherlands, UK, Denmark and Canada; Head of Shift, Head of Programming Bureau, Deputy Chief Engineer, Head of Foreign Relations and Marketing Service, Šiauliai Machine Tools Enterprise 1975–92; Dir Šiauliai Regional Chamber of Commerce and Industry 1992–96, Dir-Gen. Šiauliai Chamber of Commerce, Industry and Crafts 1996–2000; elected to Šiauliai City Council 1997, 2000, mem. Bd and Chair. Investment and Zokniai Devt Cttee; mem. Seimas (Parl.) 2000–04, 2006–12, mem. Cttee on Econs 2000–02, later Cttee on Legal Affairs, Chair. Group for Interparliamentary Relations with UK 2000–04, Deputy Chair. Petitions Comm. 2000–04, mem. Cttee of Foreign Affairs 2006–12, mem./Deputy Chair. Cttee of European Affairs 2006–12, Chair. Group for Interparliamentary Relations with Sri Lanka 2008–12; Minister of Communications 2001; Dir Econ.-Social Research and Training Centre 2005–06; Minister of the Interior 2012–14 (resgnd); mem. and mem. Bd Liberal Union of Lithuania 1992–2000, Deputy Chair. 1996–99; mem. and Deputy Chair. Liberal Democratic Party (Party Order and Justice) 2002–, Adviser to the Chair. of Party Order and Justice 2004–08, Deputy Chair. Party Order and Justice 2012–; participated in re-establishment of Rotary International in Lithuania; First Pres. Šiauliai Rotary Club 1992; mem. Bd of Experts, Baltic-American Partnership Fund 1998–2000; Hon. Consul of Sri Lanka in Lithuania Feb.–Nov. 2008; Commemorative Badge to mark Lithuania's invitation to NATO 2003. *Publications:* Nuomonių sankryžos (Crossroads of Opinions) 2008; more than 150 articles on economic, social and political topics. *Leisure interests:* gardening, fishing, history of Lithuanian art. *Address:* c/o Ministry of the Interior, Šventaragio 2, Vilnius 01510; Pergalės g. 8-201, Vilnius, Lithuania.

BARAMIDZE, Giorgi; Georgian politician and engineer; *Deputy Chairman, Sakartvelos Parlamenti (Georgian Parliament);* b. 5 Jan. 1968, Tbilisi; m. Eka Jafaridze; one d.; ed Polytechnic Inst. of Georgia, George C. Marshall Center for European Security Studies, Germany; Founding mem. Green Party of Georgia 1990; commanded state centre responsible for the search for the missing and for freeing prisoners during war in Abkhazia 1992–93; Chair. Comm. for the Protection of Human Rights and Nat. Minorities 1992–94; mem. Sakartvelos Parlamenti (Georgian Parl.) 1992–, Chair. Anti-Corruption Comm. 1996–98, Defence and Security Cttee 2000–03, a Deputy Chair. of the Parl. 2012–; Founding mem. Citizens' Union of Georgia 1995, Chair. Parl. Group 1996–98; Research Assoc., Georgetown Univ., Washington, DC, USA 1998–99; Minister of Internal Affairs 2003–04, of Defence June–Dec. 2004; State Minister, responsible for European and Euro-Atlantic Integration 2004–12, also Deputy Prime Minister 2006–12; Cross of Commdr, Order for Merits to Lithuania 2006. *Address:* Parliament of Georgia, 4600 Kutaisi, Abashidze 26, Georgia (office). *Telephone:* (32) 228-90-53 (office). *E-mail:* contact@parliament.ge (office). *Website:* www.parliament.ge (office).

BARBA, Eugenio, MA; Italian theatre director; *Director, International School of Theatre Anthropology;* b. 29 Oct. 1936, Brindisi; s. of Emanuele Barba and Vera Gaeta; m. Judith Patricia Howard Jones 1965; two s.; ed Univ. of Oslo, Theatre School, Warsaw and Jerzy Grotowski's Theatre Lab. Opole; Founder and Dir Odin Teatret (Interscandinavian Theatre Lab.) 1964–; more than 72 productions 1965–; Founder and Dir Int. School of Theatre Anthropology 1979–; mem. Bd of Advisers, Int. Cttee Théâtre des Nations 1975–80; mem. Bd of Advisers, Int. Asscn of Performing Arts Semiotics 1981–85; adviser, Danish Ministry of Culture 1981–82; UNESCO adviser, Centro de Estudios Teatrales, Museo de Arte Moderno, Bogotá 1983; adviser, Centre of Theatre Exchanges, Rio de Janeiro 1987–; mem. Bd of Advisers, Int. Comparative Literature Asscn 1998; lectures regularly at univs, theatre schools, etc.; Order of the Dannebrog (Denmark); Dr hc (Århus) 1988, (Ayacucho) 1998, (Bologna) 1998, (Havana) 2002, (Warsaw) 2003, (Plymouth) 2005, (Hong Kong) 2006, (Buenos Aires) 2008, (Tallinn) 2009, (Cluj-Napoca) 2012; Danish Acad. Award 1980, Mexican Theatre Critics' Prize 1984, Diego Fabbri Prize 1986, Pirandello Int. Prize 1996, Reconnaissance de Mérite Scientifique (Montreal) 1999, Sonning Prize 2000, Gold Gloria Artis Medal 2009, Atahualpa del Cioppo (Uruguay) 2013. *Publications include:* In Search of a Lost Theatre 1965, The Floating Islands 1978, Il Brecht dell' Odin 1981, La Corsa dei Contrari 1981, Beyond the Floating Islands 1985, The Dilated Body 1985, Anatomie de l'Acteur (with N. Savarese) 1988, Brechts Aske, Oxyrhincus Evangeliet (two plays) 1986, The Secret Art of the Performer 1990, The Paper Canoe 1992, Theatre – Solitude, Craft, Revolt 1996, Land of Ashes and Diamonds 1999, Arar el cielo 2002, Burning the House 2009, La conquista della differenza 2012; numerous articles, essays etc. *Address:* International School of Theatre Anthropology, Odin Teatret, Box 1283, 7500 Holstebro, Denmark (office). *Telephone:* 97-42-47-77 (office). *Fax:* 97-41-04-82 (office). *E-mail:* odin@odinteatret.dk (office). *Website:* www.odinteatret.dk (office).

BARBARAS, Renaud; French philosopher and academic; b. 1955; ed École normale supérieure de Saint-Cloud; Prof. of Contemporary Philosophy, Université Paris 1 Panthéon-Sorbonne; Grand Prix de philosophie de l'Académie Française 2014. *Publications include:* De l'être du phénomène. Sur l'ontologie de Merleau-Ponty 1991 (translated by Ted Toadvine and Leonard Lawlor as The Being of the Phenomenon: Merleau-Ponty's Ontology 2004), La Perception. Essai sur le sensible 1994, Merleau-Ponty 1997, Le tournant de l'expérience. Recherches sur la philosophie de Merleau-Ponty 1998, Le désir et la distance. Introduction à une phénoménologie de la perception 1999 (translated by Paul B. Milan as Desire and Distance: Introduction to a Phenomenology of Perception 2005), Vie et intentionnalité. Recherches phénoménologiques 2003, Introduction à la philosophie de Husserl 2004, The Being of the Phenomenon: Merleau-Ponty's Ontology (Studies in Continental Thought) (co-author) 2004, Desire and Distance: Introduction to a Phenomenology of Perception (Cultural Memory in the Present) (co-author) 2005, Le mouvement de l'existence. Études sur la phénoménologie de Jan Patočka 2007, Introduction à une phénoménologie de la vie 2008, L'ouverture du monde: Lecture de Jan Patočka 2011, La vie lacunaire 2011, Dynamique de la manifestation 2013, Métaphysique du sentiment 2016; numerous papers in professional journals. *Address:* Centre d'histoire des systèmes de pensée moderne, Université Paris 1 Panthéon-Sorbonne, UFR de Philosophie, 17 rue de la Sorbonne, 75231 Paris Cedex 05, France (office). *Telephone:* 1-40-46-27-93 (office). *Fax:* 1-40-46-31-57 (office). *E-mail:* renaud.barbaras@univ-paris1.fr (office). *Website:* www.univ-paris1.fr (office).

BARBARIN, HE Cardinal Philippe Xavier Ignace, MA, PhD; French ecclesiastic; *Archbishop of Lyon;* b. 17 Oct. 1950, Rabat, Morocco; ed Sorbonne, Paris and Institut Catholique, Paris; ordained priest of Créteil 1977; priest in parishes of Notre-Dame d'Alfortville and Notre-Dame de Vincennes 1977–85, St Hilaire de la Varenne 1985–90; asst, Parish of St François de Sales, d'Adamville, St-Maur; Chaplain of St-Maur secondary school 1985–90; Pastor of St Léger Parish, Boissy St Léger 1991–94; Fidei donum priest and Prof. of Theology, Sr Seminary of Vohitsoa, Fianarantsoa, Madagascar 1994–98; Pastor, Bry-sur-Marne, Créteil; Bishop of Moulins 1998; Archbishop of Metropolitan See of Lyon and Primate of Gaul 2002–; cr. Cardinal (Cardinal-Priest of Santissima Trinità al Monte Pincio) 2003; participated in Papal Conclave 2005, 2013; mem. Congregation for Divine Worship and Discipline of Sacraments, Congregation for Insts. of Consecrated Life and Societies of Apostolic Life 2003, Doctrinal Comm. 2005–11; Chancellor Catholic Univ. of Lyon; Chevalier, Légion d'honneur 2002, Officier 2012, Officier, Ordre nat. du Mérite 2007, Knight Grand Cross, Order of Holy Sepulchre 2010. *Address:* Archdiocese of Lyon, 1 Place de Fourviere, 69321 Lyon, Cedex 05, France (office). *Telephone:* (4) 72-38-80-90 (office). *Fax:* (4) 78-36-06-00 (office). *E-mail:* archeveche.de.lyon@wanadoo.fr (office). *Website:* catholique-lyon.cef.fr (office).

BARBENEL, Joseph Cyril, BDS, BSc, MSc, PhD, FInstP, FSBiol, FRSE, FIPEM, FEAMBES; British bioengineer and academic; *Professor Emeritus, University of Strathclyde;* b. 2 Jan. 1937, London; s. of Tobias Barbenel and Sarah Barbenel; m. Lesley Mary Hyde Jowett 1964; two s. one d.; ed Hackney Downs Grammar School, London, London Hosp. Dental School, Univ. of London, Queen's Coll., Univ. of St Andrews, Univ. of Strathclyde, Glasgow; Dental House Surgeon, London Hosp. 1960; Royal Army Dental Corps 1960–62; gen. dental practice, London 1963; Lecturer, Dental Prosthetics, Univ. of Dundee 1967–69; Lecturer, Univ. of Strathclyde 1970, Sr Lecturer, Bioengineering Unit 1970–82, Reader 1982–85, Prof. 1985–2001, Head Dept 1992–98, Vice-Dean (Research) Faculty of Eng 1997–2001, Prof. Emer. 2001–; Consulting Prof., Chongqing Univ., China 1986–; Co-Chair. Constitution and Bylaws Cttee, Int. Fed. of Medical and Biological Eng; mem. Eng Advisory Bd, Inst. of, Physics and Eng in Medicine; Founding Fellow and mem. Exec. Bd, European Alliance for Medical and Biological Eng Sciences; Nuffield Foundation Award 1963–66, Pres.'s Medal, Soc. of Cosmetic Scientists 1994, European Pressure Ulcer Advisory Panel Lifetime Achievement Award 2002. *Publications include:* Clinical Aspects of Blood Rheology (with Lowe and Forbes) 1981, Pressure Sores (with Lowe and Forbes) 1983, Blood Flow in Artificial Organs and Cardiovascular Prostheses (co-ed.) 1988, Blood Flow in the Brain (co-ed.) 1988; 115 papers in professional journals. *Leisure interests:* music, theatre, reading. *Address:* Royal College Building, University of Strathclyde, Glasgow, G1 1XW (office); 151 Maxwell Drive, Glasgow, G41 5AE, Scotland (home). *Telephone:* (141) 427-0765 (home). *E-mail:* jcbarbenel@btinternet.com; j.c.barbenel@strath.ac.uk (office).

BARBER, Sir Brendan Paul, Kt, BA (Hons); British trade union official; *Chairman, Advisory, Conciliation and Arbitration Service;* b. 3 April 1951, Southport, Lancs.; m Mary Gray; two d.; ed St Mary's Coll., Sefton, City Univ., London; taught in Ghana with VSO; Pres. Students' Union, City Univ., London; worked for Ceramics, Glass and Mineral Products Industrial Training Bd; joined Org. and Industrial Relations Dept, TUC 1975, Head Dept 1987–93, Head Press and Information Dept 1979–87, Deputy Gen. Sec. TUC 1993–2003, Gen. Sec. 2003–12; mem. Council of Advisory, Conciliation and Arbitration Service (ACAS) 1995–2004, Chair. 2014–; mem. Court of Bank of England 2003–12, Bd of Transport for London 2013–, Banking Standards Board 2015–, Council of City Univ. 2013–, Bd of Mountview Acad. of Theatre Arts 2014–, Bd of Britain Stronger in Europe 2015–; Visiting Fellow, Nuffield Coll., Oxford 2013–, Said Business School, Oxford 2013–; Hon. DSc (City Univ., London) 2007. *Leisure interests:* Everton Football Club, golf. *Address:* ACAS National, Euston Tower, 286 Euston Road, London, NW1 3JJ, England (office). *E-mail:* info@acas.org.uk (office). *Website:* www.acas.org.uk/index.aspx?articleid=1499 (office).

BARBER, Eunice; French athlete; b. 17 Nov. 1974, Freetown, Sierra Leone; d. of Margaret Barber; heptathlete/long jumper; personal best: heptathlon 6,889 points (Arles, June 2005), long jump 7.05m (Monaco, June 2003); African record holder heptathlon 6,416 points 1996; Sierra Leone record holder at 100m, high jump, long jump, shot put, javelin, heptathlon; became French citizen 1999; winner, African Championships long jump 1995, European Cup heptathlon 1999, Meeting International d'Arles 1999, 2003, Decastar Talence heptathlon 1999, IAAF World Combined Events Challenge 1999, runner up 2005, World Championships heptathlon 1999, 1995 (fourth place), 2003 (runner-up), 2005 (runner-up), Hypo-Meeting Götzis heptathlon 2000, 2001, European Cup long jump 2003, World Championships long jump 2003, 2005 (third place); fifth place, Olympic Games heptathlon 2000; sixth place, World Indoor Championships pentathlon 1997; coach Bob Kersee. *Leisure interests:* fashion, cinema, music, singing, travelling. *Address:* c/o Fédération Française d'Athlétisme, 33 avenue Pierre de Coubertin, 75013 Paris, France. *Telephone:* 1-53-80-74-91. *Fax:* 1-53-80-74-97. *E-mail:* contact_barber@athleteline.com (office). *Website:* www.barber-eunice.com.

BARBER, Lionel, BA; British journalist; *Editor, Financial Times;* b. 1955, London; m. Victoria Greenwood; two c.; ed Univ. of Oxford; journalist, The Scotsman 1978–81; Business Corresp., The Times (London) 1981–85; Washington Corresp. and US Ed. Financial Times 1986–92, Brussels bureau chief 1992–98, News Ed. 1998–2000, Ed. Continental European Edn 2000–02, US Man. Ed. 2002–05, Ed. Financial Times 2005–; Visiting Fellow, European Univ. Inst., Florence, Italy 1996; mem. Bd of Dirs Int. Center for Journalists; mem. Bd of Trustees Tate Gallery; Woodrow Wilson Foundation Fellow 1991, Eliot-Winant Fellow, British-American-Canadian Foundation 1994; Laurence Stern Fellowship, Washington Post 1985; Trustee, The Tate 2011–; Ordre National de la Légion d'Honneur 2016. *Publications include:* Price of Truth: Story of the Reuters Millions (with John Lawrenson) 1984, Not With Honour: Inside the Westland Scandal (co-author) 1986, Britain and the New European Agenda 1998. *Leisure interests:* watching rugby, cycling, reading American presidential biographies, listening to opera. *Address:* Financial Times, One Southwark Bridge, London, SE1 9HL, England (office). *Telephone:* (20) 7873-4222 (office). *Fax:* (20) 7873-3924 (office). *Website:* www.ft.com (office).

BARBERIS, Alessandro; Italian business executive; *President, Turin Chamber of Commerce;* b. 28 Aug. 1937, Turin; m.; three c.; ed Polytechnic Univ. of Turin; trained as engineer; joined Fiat SpA 1964, Dir 1972, Dir Fmb (Fiat Group in Latin America), Brazil 1976–78, Head of Metalworks 1978–82, Dir-Gen. Magneti Marelli 1982–93, Dir of Industrial Co-ordination Fiat Auto 1993–96, COO 2002, CEO Dec. 2002, then Vice-Chair. Feb.–May 2003; Dir-Gen. Isituto Bancario San Paulo di Torino 1996–97; Pres. Piaggio & C. SpA 1997–2002, Unione Industriale di Pisa 1998–2001, ANCMA (construction asscn) 1999–2001, Confindustria Toscana 1999–2003, Chamber of Commerce of Industry Crafts and Agric. of Torino 2004–, EuroChambres (asscn of European chambers of commerce), Brussels 2010–; Pres. Infocamere 2008–, Chair. 2010–; Chair. CDC Point SpA 2001; Vice-Pres. Unioncamere Italiana 2006–09, Piemonte Agency for Investments, Export and Tourism 2007–, Int. Chamber of Commerce 2008–; mem. Gen. Council World Fed. of Chambers of Commerce 2011–; mem. Bd of Dirs Polytechnic of Turin 2013–.

BARBIZET, Patricia Marie Marguerite; French business executive; b. 17 April 1955, Paris; d. of Philippe Dussart and Monique Cartier; m. Jean Barbizet 1979; one d.; ed Ecole Supérieure de Commerce de Paris; Man. Asst Renault Véhicules Industriels 1977–79, Int. Treas. 1979–82, Group Treas. 1977–84; Financial Dir Renault Crédit Int. 1984–89; Financial Dir Groupe Pinault 1988–90, Deputy Dir-Gen. in charge of Finance and Communication 1990–92, Dir-Gen. Financière Pinault 1992, Chair. Pinault-Printemps-Redoute (owner of Gucci) and Pres. PPR (new name from 2005) Group Supervisory Bd 2002, later Vice-Chair. Bd of Dirs Kering (fmrly PPR); Admin., Dir-Gen. and CEO Artémis Group 1992–2018; Chair. and CEO Christie's Int. PLC Dec. 2014–16, Temaris & Associés 2018, Zoé SAS; Chair. of the Supervisory Bd, Investissements d'Avenir 2018–; Chair. Société Nouvelle du Théâtre Marigny; Chair. of Bd of Dirs, Cité de la Musique; Dir TF1 (also Chair. Audit Cttee), Fnac SA; Pres. French Asscn for Co. Treasurers (AFTE)

1989–92, now Hon. Pres.; mem. Supervisory Bd Gucci Group NV (Netherlands), Yves Saint Laurent Couture; Perm. Rep. of Artémis on Bd of Dirs of Agefi, Bouygues, Sebdo le Point; mem. Man. Bd Château Latour; mem. Bd of Dirs Total SA 2008–, PSA Peugeot Citroën; Lead Ind. Dir Pernod Ricard 2019–; apptd to head Investment Cttee of Strategic Investment Fund (subsidiary of Caisse des Dépôts et Consignations) 2008–13; Officier, Légion d'honneur; Commdr, Ordre nat. du Mérite 2002. *Leisure interests:* literature, music. *Address:* 10 rue du Dragon, 75006 Paris, France (home).

BARBOSA, Marcia C. B., PhD; Brazilian physicist and academic; *Professor, Institute of Physics, Federal University of Rio Grande do Sul;* b. Rio de Janeiro; ed Colégio Marechal Rondon, Canoas, Rio Grande do Sul, Universidade Federal do Rio Grande do Sul (UFRGS), Porto Alegre; Postdoctoral Researcher, Univ. of Maryland, USA for two years; Prof. of Physics, UFRGS 1991–, Dir Instituto de Física 2008–, Full Prof. 2012–; fmr Chair. IUPAP Working Group on Women in Physics; Vice-Pres. Union of Pure and Applied Physics 2008; mem. Brazilian Acad. of Sciences 2014–; Nicholson Medal, American Physical Soc. 2009, Laureate for Latin America, L'Oréal-UNESCO Awards for Women in Science 2013. *Publications:* numerous papers in professional journals. *Address:* Instituto de Física, Federal University of Rio Grande do Sul, CP15051, 91501-970 Porto Alegre, Brazil (office). *Telephone:* (51) 33086516 (office). *Fax:* (51) 33087286 (office). *E-mail:* marcia.barbosa@ufrgs.br (office). *Website:* www.if.ufrgs.br/~barbosa (office).

BARBOSA, Rubens Antonio, MA; Brazilian diplomatist and business consultant; *President, Rubens Barbosa & Associados;* b. 13 June 1938, São Paulo; m. Maria Ignez Correa da Costa 1969; one s. one d.; ed Univ. of São Paulo, Brazilian Foreign Service Acad. and London School of Econs, UK; Exec. Sec. Brazilian Trade Comm. with socialist countries of Eastern Europe 1976–84; Chief of Staff, Ministry of Foreign Affairs 1985–87; Under-Sec.-Gen. for Multilateral and Special Political Affairs 1986; Sec. for Int. Affairs, Ministry of the Economy 1987–88; Amb. and Perm. Rep. to Latin American Integration Asscn (ALADI) 1988–91; Pres. Cttee of Reps ALADI 1991–92; Under-Sec.-Gen. for Trade, Regional Integration and Econ. Affairs, Ministry of Foreign Affairs 1991–93; Co-ordinator, Brazilian section of Mercosul (Southern Cone Common Market) 1991–93; Amb. to Court of Saint James, London 1994–99, to USA 1999–2004; currently Head of Council on Foreign Trade of Fed. of Industries of the State of São Paulo (FIESP); Pres. Rubens Barbosa & Associados (consultancy); Sr Dir Albright Stonebridge Group; Publisher, Interesse Nacional (politics and econs journal); Hon. LVO, Hon. GCVO, Grand Cross, Order of Rio Branco, Commdr, Légion d'honneur, decorations from Argentina, Mexico and Italy. *Publications include:* Integração Econômica da América Latina: da retórica à realidade, Panorama Visto de Londres, The Mercosur Codes, Mercosul Quinze Anos, National Interest and Vision of the Future 2012, Washington Dissensus 2014; essays and articles in newspapers and magazines. *Leisure interests:* classical music, tennis. *Address:* Avenida Brigadeiro Faria Lima 2413, Sobreloja-Conj. B, CEP 01452-000 São Paulo, Brazil (office). *Telephone:* (11) 3039-6330 (office). *Fax:* (11) 3039-6334 (office). *E-mail:* rubarbosa@terra.com.br. *Website:* www.rbarbosaconsult.com.br (office).

BARBOSA FILHO, Nelson Henrique, BEcons, MEcons, PhD; Brazilian economist, academic, government official and banking executive; *Professor, Fundação Getúlio Vargas-Escola de Administração de Empresas de São Paulo;* b. 17 Nov. 1969, Rio de Janeiro; s. Nelson Henrique Barbosa and Neuza Mattos Barbosa; ed Fed. Univ. of Rio de Janeiro, The New School for Social Research (later New School Univ., now The New School), New York, USA; Substitute Prof., Fluminense Fed. Univ. 1993–94; Asst Prof., Candido Mendes Univ. 1997; Adjunct Prof., Grad. Faculty, New School Univ. 1999–2002, Researcher, Center for Econ. Policy Analysis 1998–2001, Asst Dir 2001–02; Asst Prof., Saint Francis Coll., New York 2000–01; Adjunct Prof., Inst. of Econs, Fed. Univ. of Rio de Janeiro 2002–17, Prof. of Macroeconomics and Public Finance; Analyst, Cen. Bank of Brazil, Rio de Janeiro Police Force 1994–97; Deputy Chief Econ. Advisor, Ministry of Planning, Budget and Man. 2003; Special Adviser to Pres. of Banco Nacional de Desenvolvimento Economico e Social (BNDES—Brazilian Devt Bank) 2005–06; Asst Sec. for Macroeconomic Policy and Analysis Survey, Ministry of Finance 2006–07, Sec. of Econ. Monitoring 2007–08, Sec. for Economic Policy and Analysis Survey 2008–11, Exec. Sec., Ministry of Finance 2011–14, Minister of Finance 2015–16; Chair. Banco do Brasil SA 2009–14; Adjunct Prof. of Econs Univ. of Brasília 2017–; currently Prof. Fundação Getúlio Vargas-Escola de Administração de Empresas de São Paulo (FGV-EAESP); mem. Bd of Dirs EPE-Empresa de Pesquisa Energetica 2007–09, Brasilcap 2010–11, Brasil Veículos 2011, Vale SA 2011–13; mem. Bd, Regional Bank of Brasília 2013–14, Devt Bank of Minas Gerais 2017–. *Address:* Fundação Getúlio Vargas, Avenida L2 Norte SGAN Quadra 602, 70830-051 Brasília, DF, Brazil (office). *Telephone:* (61) 3799-8055. *E-mail:* nelson.barbosa@fgv.br.

BARBOSA GOMES, Joaquim Benedito, LLB, DJur; Brazilian judge; b. 7 Oct. 1954, Paracatu; one c.; ed Univ. of Brasilia, Univ. of Paris II, France; began career as janitor at electoral tribunal, Brasilia; fmr worker at congressional printing press; served in Chancellery, Embassy in Helsinki 1976–79; Counsel, Fed. Service of Data Processing, Serpro 1979–84; Chief Legal Counsel, Ministry of Health 1985–88; Dist Attorney, Rio de Janeiro 1988–2003; Judge, Supreme Fed. Tribunal 2003–12, Vice-Pres. April–Nov. 2012, Pres. 2012–14; Visiting Scholar, Human Rights Inst., Columbia Univ. School of Law, New York 1999–2000; Visiting Scholar, UCLA School of Law 2002–03; Fellow, Conselho Nacional de Desenvolvimento Científico e Tecnológico (CNPq) 1988–92, Ford Foundation 1999–2000, Fulbright Foundation 2002–03. *Publications include:* La Cour Suprême dans le Système Politique Brésilien 1994, Bibliothèque et de Science Politique constitutionnelle 2001, Affirmative Action and Constitutional Principle Equality 2001, Law as an Instrument of Social Transformation 2001, The US Experience 2001.

BARBOSA PEQUENO, Ovídio Manuel; São Tomé and Príncipe journalist, politician and diplomatist; b. 5 Nov. 1954; m.; ed Pacific Western Univ., Inst. of Tech. of New York, USA; joined diplomatic service, overseas assignments included First Sec., Perm. Mission to UN, New York 1983–90; Sr Ed. Voice of America, Washington, DC 1990–99, headed Angola Bureau 1998–99; returned to diplomatic service and served as Amb. to Taiwan 1999–2004, Minister of Foreign Affairs and Co-operation 2004–06 (resgnd) 2007–08, Perm. Rep. to UN, New York and Amb. to USA (also accred to Canada and Brazil) 2006–07, 2009–12. *Address:* c/o Ministry of Foreign Affairs, Co-operation and Communities, Avda 12 de Julho, CP 111, São Tomé, São Tomé e Príncipe.

BARBOT, Ivan, BA, LèsL; French police commissioner and government official; b. 5 Jan. 1937, Ploeuc; s. of Pierre Barbot and Anne Barbot (née Le Calvez); m. Roselyne de Lestrange 1971; three c.; ed Lycée de Saint-Brieuc, Univ. of Paris; Prin. Pvt. Sec. to Chief Commr, Tarn-et-Garonne 1961; Prin. Pvt. Sec., later Dir of Staff to Chief Commr, Haute-Savoie 1962; Dir of Staff, Paris Region Pref. 1967; Deputy Chief Commr, Etampes 1969; Deputy Chief Commr without portfolio, Official Rep. to the Cabinet 1974; Tech. Adviser to Minister of the Interior 1974–77; Sec.-Gen. Seine-Saint-Denis 1977–82; Chief Commr and Supt, Dept de la Charente 1982–85, du Var 1985–87; Dir-Gen. Police Nat. 1987–89; Pres. Interpol 1988–92; Prefect Poitou-Charentes 1989, Vienne 1989–91; with Prime Minister's office, responsible for security 1991–92; Pres. Admin. Council of French concessionary co. for the construction and exploitation of the road tunnel under Mont-Blanc 1992–94; Chair. and CEO OFEMA (French Office of Aeronautics Equipment) 1993–97, Chair. and CEO SOFEMA (formed after merger with SOFMA) 1997–2004; currently consultant; Commdr, Légion d'honneur, du Mérite agricole, Ordre nat. du Mérite; Chevalier des Palmes académiques, des Arts et des Lettres. *Address:* 10 place de Séoul, 75014 Paris, France. *E-mail:* ibarbotconseil@wanadoo.fr (office).

BARBOUR, Haley Reeves, JD; American state official; b. 22 Oct. 1947, Yazoo City, Miss.; s. of Jeptha F. Barbour Jr and LeFlore Johnson; m. Marsha Dickson 1971; two s.; ed Univ. of Mississippi Law School; field rep., Miss. Republican Party 1968, Deputy Exec. Dir 1972–73, Exec. Dir 1973–76; Regional Technician, Bureau of Census 1969–70; Exec. Dir Southern Asscn of Republican State Chairmen 1973–76; Southeastern Campaign Dir Pres. Ford Cttee 1976; Chair. 3rd Congressional Dist Cttee Miss. 1976–84; Republican nominee for US Senator from Miss. 1982; Municipal Judge, Yazoo City 1980–81, City Attorney 1981–85; Co-founder, Chair. and CEO Barbour Griffith & Rogers LLC (lobbying firm), Washington, DC 1991–99; Founder Nat. Policy Forum 1993; Chair. Republican Nat. Cttee 1993–97; Gov. of Miss. 2004–12; Chair. Republican Govs Asscn 2009; formed, with his nephew Henry Barbour, a Super PAC (Political Action Cttee) named Mississippi Conservatives which supported re-election campaign of Senator Thad Cochran 2014; fmr mem. Bd of Dirs Deposit Guarantee Corpn, Amtrak, Mobil Telecommunications Technologies Inc.; Deacon, First Presbyterian Church of Yazoo City; Hon. Patron, Univ. Philosophical Soc., Trinity Coll., Dublin 2009; Gulf Guardian Award, US Environmental Protection Agency. *Publication:* Agenda for America 1996. *Address:* c/o Office of the Governor, PO Box 139, Jackson, MS 39205, USA.

BARBUT, Monique, MA (Econs), MPhil (Econs); French international organization official; b. 22 Aug. 1956; m.; three c.; ed Univ. of Paris I, Grad. Inst. of Int. Studies, IHE, Paris II; Program Man. Saint-Denis La Réunion, Caisse Centrale de Cooperation Economique 1981–84, Head of Dept of sector-based policies and retrospective evaluation 1984–89, in charge of all public credit and housing cos in French Overseas Depts 1990, at Ministry of Cooperation and Devt 1990–93, in charge of Secr. of French Global Environment Fund (inter-ministerial field) 1994–96; Deputy Dir French Overseas Depts and Territories and Dir Div. in charge of Devt inside same Dept, Agence Française de Développement (AFD) 1996–2000, Exec. Dir at AFD, in charge of all activities in French Overseas Depts and Territories, and responsible for all programmes for Pacific, Indian, Caribbean Ocean Islands 2000–02, Special Adviser to the CEO 2012–13; Exec. Sec. UN Convention to Combat Desertification (UNCCD) 2013–19; Dir Div. of Tech., Industry and Econs, UNEP 2003–06; Chair. and CEO Global Environment Facility 2006–12; currently Councillor, World Future Council; mem. French Govt Del., Earth Summit, Rio de Janeiro, Brazil 1992; mem. Bd WWF, France; Officier, L'ordre national de la légion d'honneur Dr. hc (Teri Univ., India). *Address:* c/o United Nations Convention to Combat Desertification, UNCCD Secretariat, PO Box 260129, 53153 Bonn, Germany.

BARBUY, Beatriz Leonor Silveira, PhD; Brazilian astrophysicist and academic; *Professor, Institute of Astronomy, Geophysics and Atmospheric Sciences, University of São Paulo;* b. 16 Feb. 1950; ed Univ. of Paris, France; currently Prof. at Inst. of Astronomy, Geophysics and Atmospheric Sciences, Univ. of São Paulo; Pres. Sociedade Astronômica Brasileira 1992–94; Brazilian Rep. for NSF's Gemini Project through Asscn of Univs for Research in Astronomy 1998–2002; Vice-Pres. Int. Astronomical Union (IAU), Co-Chair. triennial Gen. Ass. of IAU, Rio de Janeiro 2009, mem. Finance Cttee of IAU 2009–12; Vice-Co-ordinator Instituto Nacional de Ciência e Tecnologia de Astrofísica, Ministry of Science and Tech. 2009–12; mem. Haut Comité Scientifique de l'Observatoire de Paris 2010–14, Aura Cttee for Gemini AOC-G 2011–14, Council of the Int. Inst. of Physics, MCTI/Universidade de Natal; mem. Academia Brasileira de Ciência 2001, TWAS, The World Acad. of Sciences 2007, Acad. of Developing Countries 2009–; Foreign Assoc., Acad. des sciences (France) 2005–; Hon. FRAS 2010; Comendador, Ordem Nacional do Mérito Científico 2005, Grã-Cruz 2010; Officier, Ordre nat. du Mérite 2011; Trieste Science Prize in Earth, Space, Ocean and Atmospheric Sciences (co-recipient) 2008, L'ORÉAL-UNESCO Award for Women in Science (Latin America) 2009, Prêmio Scopus, Elsevier-Capes 2010. *Publications:* 12 books edited; more than 210 papers in scientific journals on the evolution of the chemical composition of the stars. *Address:* Instituto de Astronomia, Geofísica e Ciências Atmosféricas, Universidade de São Paulo, Rua de Matão 1226, Cidade Universitária, São Paulo 05508-090, Brazil (office). *Telephone:* (11) 3091-2810 (office). *Fax:* (11) 3091-2860 (office). *E-mail:* b.barbuy@iag.usp.br (office). *Website:* www.astro.iag.usp.br/~barbuy (office).

BARCELÓ ARTIGUES, Miquel; Spanish painter; b. 8 Jan. 1957, Felanitx, Majorca; ed Escuela de Artes y Oficios, Palma de Majorca, Escuela Superior de Bellas Artes de San Jorge, Barcelona; known as one of the youngest artists to showcase his work in a museum; travelled extensively in the 1980s and set up studios in Paris and Segou, Mali; Dr hc (Universitat de les Illes Balears) 2001, (Universitat Pompeu Fabra) 2012, (Univ. of Salamanca); Premio Icaro de Artes Plásticas 1984, Premio Nacional de Artes Plásticas de España 1986, Premi Nacional d'Arts Plàstiques, Generalitat de Catalunya 1999, Premio Diario de Mallorca 1999, Premio Princesa de Asturias de las Artes 2003, Gran Premio AECA for the best int. artist alive 2003, Premio Alzina, El GOB, Grup Ornitològic Balear, Palma de Mallorca 2003, 2008, Gran Premio AECA 2003, Premio FAD Sebastià

Gasch d'arts parateatrals 2006, Premio Sorolla, Hispanic Society of America 2007 2012. *E-mail:* info@miquelbarcelo.org. *Website:* www.miquelbarcelo.org.

BÁRCENA IBARRA, Alicia, BSc, MSc, MPA; Mexican biologist and UN official; *Executive Secretary, United Nations Economic Commission for Latin America and the Caribbean;* b. 5 March 1952; ed Universidad Nacional Autónoma de Mexico (UNAM), Harvard Univ., USA, Instituto Miguel Angel, Mexico; Research Asst, UNAM 1975–76, Assoc. Prof. of Botany, UNAM (Universidad Autónoma Metropolitana) 1976–78; Researcher on Ethnobotany, Instituto Nacional sobre Recursos Bióticos 1978–80; Regional Exec. Dir/Research Coordinator Instituto Nacional de Investigaciones sobre Recursos 1980–82; Under-Sec. of Ecology (Vice-Minister), Secretaría de Desarrollo Urbano y Ecología—SEDUE), Ministry of Urban Devt and Ecology 1982–86; consultant, IDB Aug.–Nov. 1987; Pres. Cultura Ecológica, Civil Soc. Org. in Mexico 1987–88; Dir-Gen. Nat. Inst. of Fisheries, SEPESCA (Secretaría de Pesca) 1988–90; Prin. Officer, Programme Unit II, UN Conf. on Environment and Devt, Geneva, Switzerland 1990–92; Exec. Dir Earth Council Foundation, San Jose, Costa Rica 1992–95; Programme Coordinator Global Environmental Citizenship Programme, UNEP 1996–97; Chief Tech. Adviser on Environment and Devt, seconded by UNEP, Regional Bureau for Latin America and the Caribbean, UNDP 1998–99; Chief, Div. of Sustainable Devt and Human Settlements, ECLAC 1999–2003, Deputy Exec. Sec. 2003–06; Deputy Chef de Cabinet, UN, New York Feb.–March 2006, Acting Chef de Cabinet March 2006–07, Under-Sec.-Gen. for Man. 2007–08; Exec. Sec. ECLAC 2008–. *Publications:* The Millenium Development Goals: A Latin American and Caribbean Perspective 2005; numerous articles in professional journals. *Address:* Economic Commission for Latin America and the Caribbean, Casilla de Correo 179-D, Av. Dag Hammarskjöld, 3477 Vitacura, Santiago, Chile (office). *Telephone:* (2) 471-2000 (office). *Fax:* (2) 208-0252 (office). *E-mail:* secretaria.se@cepal.org (office). *Website:* www.eclac.org (office).

BARCHI, Robert, BSc, MS, PhD, MD; American neurologist, biochemist, biophysicist, academic and university administrator; *President, Rutgers, The State University of New Jersey;* ed Georgetown Univ., Univ. of Pennsylvania; Fellow, Medical Scientist Training Program, NIH 1969–72; Resident in Neurology, Hosp. of the Univ. of Pennsylvania 1973–75, Asst Prof., Dept of Biochemistry and Biophysics 1974–75, Asst Prof. of Neurology and of Biochemistry and Biophysics 1975–78, Assoc. Prof. of Neurology and of Biochemistry and Biophysics 1978–81, Prof. of Neurology and of Biochemistry and Biophysics 1981–85, David Mahoney Prof. of Neurological Sciences 1985–2002, Fairhill Prof. of Medicine 2002–04, Fairhill Prof. Emer. of Medicine 2004–, Chair. Grad. Group in Neuroscience 1983–89, Dir Dana Fellowship Program in Neuroscience 1986–92, Vice-Dean for Research, School of Medicine 1989–90, Dir Clinical Neuroscience Track 1993–95, Dir Mahoney Inst. of Neurological Sciences 1983–96, Pres. Penn NeuroCare 1995–99, Chair. Dept of Neuroscience, School of Medicine 1992–99, Chair. Dept of Neurology, School of Medicine 1995–99, Provost and Chief Academic Officer, Univ. of Pennsylvania 1999–2004; Prof. of Neurology and Pres., Thomas Jefferson Univ. 2004–12; Univ. Prof., Prof. II and Pres. Rutgers, The State Univ. of NJ 2012–; mem. Bd NIH Physiology Study Section 1984–87; mem. Bd of Dirs, Covance, Inc., VWR International, PA BioAdvance (Vice-Chair.) 2002–07, Ben Franklin Technology Partnership (SE PA) 2002–07, The International House, Philadelphia, Pa 1999–2004, ICEAD, Kitakyushu, Japan 2000–04; mem. Bd of Overseers, The Wistar Inst., Philadelphia 2000–05; mem. Scientific Advisory Bd, Philadelphia Ventures, Inc. 1992–97, TransMolecular, Inc. 1997–2003; mem. Bd of Trustees, Thomas Jefferson Univ. Hosp. 2004–12, Ursinus Coll. 2005–12, Jefferson Health System 2004–10; mem. Editorial Bd, Journal of Neurochemistry 1981–90, Muscle and Nerve 1981–92, 1995–2004 (Assoc. Ed. 1997–2000), Journal of Neuroscience (Assoc. Ed.) 1988–91, Current Concepts in Neurology and Neurosurgery 1992–2002, The Neuroscientist 1993–2002, Neurobiology of Disease 1994–2002, inScight 1998–2000; mem. NAS 1993, Soc. of Medical Admins, American Neurological Asscn, American Soc. for Clinical Investigation, Asscn of American Physicians, Inst. of Medicine; Fellow, AAAS, Coll. of Physicians, American Acad. of Neurology; Sr Investigator Achievement Award, American Heart Asscn, NIH Research Career Devt Award, Lindback Award – Outstanding Teacher, Penn Medical School, Javits Neuroscience Investigator Award, Distinguished Grad. Award, Univ. of Pennsylvania School of Medicine 2000, Rev. Clarence E. Shaffrey SJ Award 2009. *Publications:* numerous papers in professional journals. *Address:* Rutgers, The State University of New Jersey, 83 Somerset Street, New Brunswick, NJ 08901, USA (office). *Telephone:* (848) 932-7454 (office). *Fax:* (732) 932-0308 (office). *E-mail:* president@rutgers.edu (office). *Website:* president.rutgers.edu (office).

BARCLAY, H(ugh) Douglas, BA, JD; American attorney, business executive and fmr diplomatist; *Of Counsel, Hiscock & Barclay, LLP;* b. 5 July 1932, Pulaski, NY; m. Sara J. 'Dee Dee' Seiter; two s. three d.; ed Yale Univ. and Syracuse Univ.; Pnr, Hiscock & Barclay, NY 1961–2003; various positions, NY State Senate 1965–84, including Chair. Codes Cttee, Select Task Force on Court Reorganization, Senate Republican (Majority) Conf.; several sr advisory positions at KeyCorp 1971–89; fmr Chair. Panthus Corpn, QMP Enterprises Inc., Eagle Media Inc.; Amb. to El Salvador 2003–06; Of Counsel, Hiscock & Barclay, LLP 2007–; fmr mem. Bd of Dirs Overseas Private Investment Corpn, Mohawk Airlines, Syracuse China, Giant Portland & Masonry Cement Co., Coradian Corpn, Empire Airlines Inc., Excelsior Insurance Co.; fmr mem. New York State Econ. Devt Power Allocation Bd; fmr Overseer, Nelson A. Rockefeller Inst. of Govt, State Univ. of New York; Trustee, Syracuse Univ. 1979–2003, Chair. Bd of Trustees 1992–98; fmr Trustee, New York Racing Asscn, Clarkson Univ.; Noble Amigo de El Salvador (El Salvadorian Nat. Congress) 2006, Orden Nacional Jose Matias Delgado en el Grado de Gran Cruze de Plata (El Salvador) 2007; several hon. doctorates; law library at Syracuse Univ. Coll. of Law is named in his honour; numerous prestigious academic awards. *Address:* Hiscock & Barclay, LLP, One Park Place, 300 South State Street, Syracuse, NY 13202, USA (office). *Telephone:* (315) 425-2738 (office). *Fax:* (315) 425-8550 (office). *E-mail:* dbarclay@hblaw.com (office). *Website:* www.hblaw.com (office).

BARD, Allen J., BS, MA, PhD; American chemist and academic; *Norman Hackerman-Welch Regents Chair in Chemistry, University of Texas;* b. 18 Dec. 1933, New York; m. Frances Segal 1957 (deceased); one s. one d.; ed City Coll. of New York and Harvard Univ.; Thayer Scholarship 1955–56; NSF Postdoctoral Fellowship 1956–58; joined staff of Univ. of Texas, Austin 1958, Prof. of Chem. 1967–, Jack S. Josey Prof. 1980–82, Norman Hackerman Prof. 1982–85, Norman Hackerman-Welch Regents Chair in Chem. 1985–; consultant to several labs including E.I. duPont, Texas Instruments and several govt agencies; Vice-Chair. Nat. Research Council; Ed.-in-Chief Journal of American Chemical Society 1982–2001; Chair. NAS Chemical Section 1996–; mem. editorial bd of numerous journals; Gov. Weizmann Inst. 1995–; mem. NAS 1982, ACS, Electrochemical Soc.; Dr hc (Paris) 1986, (Weizmann Inst.); Award Medal in Chem. 1955, ACS Harrison Howe Award 1980, Electrochemical Soc. Carl Wagner Memorial Award 1981, Royal Australian Chem. Inst. Bruno Breyer Memorial Medal 1984, ACS Fisher Award in Analytical Chem. 1984, Soc. of Electroanalytical Chem. Charles N. Reilley Award 1984, New York Acad. of Sciences Award in Math. and Physical Sciences 1986, ACS Willard Gibbs Award 1987, Electrochemical Soc. Olin-Palladium Award 1987, Univ. of Cincinnati Oesper Award 1989, NAS Chemistry Award 1998, Linus Pauling Award 1998, Pittsburgh Analytical Chem. Award 2001, ACS Priestley Medal 2002, Welch Award 2004, Wolf Prize in Chem. 2008, SURA Distinguished Scientist Award 2009. *Publications include:* Chemical Equilibrium 1966, Electrochemical Methods (with L. R. Faulkner) 1980, Integrated Chemical Systems: A Chemical Approach to Nanotechnology 1994, approx. 850 papers and book chapters; Ed. Electroanalytical Chemistry (23 vols) 1966–, The Encyclopedia of the Electrochemistry of the Elements, 16 vols 1973–83, Encyclopedia of Electrochemistry (11 vols) 2002–07. *Address:* Chemistry and Biochemistry Department, University of Texas at Austin, 1 University Station A5300, Austin, TX 78712-0165, USA (office). *Telephone:* (512) 471-3761 (office). *Fax:* (512) 471-0088 (office). *E-mail:* ajbard@cm.utexas.edu (office). *Website:* www.cm.utexas.edu/allen_bard (office); bard.cm.utexas.edu (office).

BARDACH, Hannes, PhD; Austrian engineer, business executive and fmr academic; *CEO, Frequentis AG;* b. 24 March 1952, Vienna; ed Vienna Univ. of Tech., Vienna Univ. of Econs and Business Admin, SMP Man. Programme at St Gallen, Switzerland, Man. of Corp. Growth Exec. Program at Stanford Univ., USA; fmr Asst Prof., Inst. for Computer Sciences, Vienna and Univ. Lecturer on microprocessor technologies; began professional career as tech. consultant for system eng in the field of microprocessors, worked for several high-tech cos in Austria and Germany; f. own eng and tech. consulting office in Vienna 1979; Man. Dir Frequentis 1983, Owner 1986, retained ownership following change to legal form of a public co. 2007, currently CEO of co. designs and manufactures integrated voice- and data-switching systems and other products for air traffic control, air defence, C3I and public safety markets; mem. Supervisory Bd Austrian Research Promotion Agency 2004–; Goldene Ehrenzeichen für Verdienste um die Republik Österreich 1997; Hon. DrTech. (Tech. Univ. of Vienna) 2006; First Prize for EU Export Award 1995, Chair.'s Citation of Merit, US Air Traffic Control Asscn 1999, Wilhelm Exner Medal, Austrian Asscn for SME (Oesterreichischer Gewerbeverein—OGV) (jtly) 2006, chosen as part of the 'Austria 10' in the business category for Austrians of the Year 2010. *Publications:* several papers in professional journals on computer science; European and US technology patents for 'Method of and Apparatus for Transmission of Data'. *Address:* Frequentis AG, Innovationsstraße 1, 1100 Vienna, Austria (office). *Telephone:* (1) 81150-0 (office). *Fax:* (1) 81150-5009 (office). *E-mail:* info@frequentis.com (office). *Website:* www.frequentis.com (office).

BARDEM, Javier; Spanish actor; b. 1 March 1969, Las Palmas, Gran Canaria; s. of José Carlos Encinas Doussinague and Pilar Bardem; m. Penélope Cruz 2010; one s.; Star on the Walk of Fame 2012. *Films include:* Jamón, Jamón 1992, Huidos 1992, El Amante bilingüe 1993, Huevos de oro 1993, Días contados 1994, El Detective y la muerte 1994, La Teta y la luna 1995, Boca a boca 1995, La Madre 1995, Más que amor, frenesí 1996, El Amor perjudica seriamente la salud 1997, Airbag 1997, Carne trémula 1997, Perdita Durango 1997, Los Lobos de Washington 1999, Segunda piel 2000, Before Night Falls 2000 (Best Actor Prize, Venice Film Festival 2000), The Dancer Upstairs 2002, Los Lunes al Sol 2002, Collateral 2004, The Three Ages of the Crime 2004, Mar Adentro (The Sea Inside) (ADIRCAE Award for Best Actor 2003, Best Actor, Goya Awards 2005) 2004, Goya's Ghosts 2006, No Country for Old Men (BAFTA Film Award for Best Supporting Actor 2007, Golden Globe for Best Supporting Actor 2008, Outstanding Performance by a Male Actor in a Supporting Role, Screen Actors Guild 2008, Acad. Award for Best Supporting Actor 2008, Saturn Award, Acad. of Science Fiction, Fantasy & Horror Films 2008) 2007, Love in the Time of Cholera 2007, Vicky Cristina Barcelona 2008, Biutiful (Best Actor, Cannes Film Festival 2010) 2010, Eat Pray Love 2010, Skyfall 2012, To the Wonder 2012, The Counselor 2013, Alacrán enamorado (Scorpion in Love) 2013, Autómata (voice) 2014, The Gunman 2015, The Last Face 2016, Pirates of the Caribbean: Dead Men Tell No Tales 2017, Mother! 2017, Loving Pablo 2017, Everybody Knows 2018. *Address:* c/o WME, 9601 Wilshire Blvd, 10th Floor, Beverly Hills, CA 90210, USA (office). *Telephone:* (310) 285-9000 (office). *Website:* wmeentertainment.com (office).

BARDIN, Garry Yakovlevich; Russian actor, producer, film director and screenwriter; *President and Artistic Director, Animated Film Studio Stayer;* b. 11 Sept. 1941, Orenburg; m.; one s.; ed Studio-School of Moscow Art Theatre; actor, Moscow Gogol Drama Theatre; Stage Dir Moscow Puppet Theatre; animation film dir in studio Soyuzmultfilm 1975–90; also scriptwriter; Founder, Pres. and Artistic Dir Animated Film Studio Stayer 1991–; Diplomas, Moscow Int. Film Festival, Bilbao Int. Film Festival, Spain, Tampere Int. Film Festival, Finland, Hon. Diploma Krakow Int. Film Festival, Poland, TV Prize, Rennes Int. Film Festival, France, Jury Prizes, Los Angeles Film Festival, USA, Hiroshima Int. Film Festival, Japan, Grand Prix Ruan Int. Film Festival, Annecy Int. Film Festival, France, Golden Dove Prize, Leipzig Int. Film Festival, Germany, Golden Palm Branch Prize, Cannes Film Festival, France, Nika Prize of Russian Acad. of Cinematic Arts (three times), State Prize of Russian Fed. 1999, Golden Prize, New York Int. Film Festival, USA. *Films include:* Dostat do neba (Reach the Sky) 1975, Veselaya karusel (Happy Carousel) (TV) 1976, Letuchiy korabl (Flying Ship) 1979, Pif-paf, oy-oy-oy! 1980, Prezhde my byli ptitsami (We Were Birds Before) 1982, Konflikt (Conflict) 1983, Break! 1985, Banket 1986, Vykrutasy 1988, Seryi volk & Krasnaya Shapochka (Grey Wolf and Little Red Riding Hood) 1990, The Coiling Prankster 1990, Chucha (Choo Choo) 1997, Adagio 2000, Chucha 2 (Choo Choo 2) 2002, Chucha 3 (Choo Choo 3) 2005, Gadkiy Utienok (Ugly Duckling) 2010, Try melodii (Three melodies) 2013, Slushaia Bethovena (Listening to Beethoven) 2015. *Address:* Animated Film Studio Stayer Ltd, 107143 Moscow, Otkrytoye shosse 28, korp. 6A (office); 119021 Moscow, Lev Tolstoy str. 3, Apt 11, Russian Federation (home). *Telephone:* (499) 167-01-54 (office); (499) 246-45-86 (home). *Fax:* (499) 167-01-54 (office). *E-mail:* garry@bardin.ru (office). *Website:* www.bardin.ru.

BARDOT, Brigitte; French actress; b. 28 Sept. 1934, Paris; d. of Louis Bardot and Anne-Marie (Mücel); m. 1st Roger Vadim 1952 (divorced 1957, died 2000); m. 2nd Jacques Charrier 1959 (divorced 1962); one s.; m. 3rd Gunther Sachs 1966 (divorced 1969, died 2011); m. 4th Bernard d'Ormale 1992; ed Paris Conservatoire; stage and film career 1952–; Founder and Pres. Fondation Brigitte Bardot; Chevalier, Légion d'honneur 1985; Étoile de Cristal from Acad. of Cinema 1966. *Recordings include:* Behind Brigitte Bardot 1960; albums include: Brigitte Bardot Sings 1963, Special Bardot 1968. *Films include:* Manina: la fille sans voile 1952, Le trou normand 1952, Le portrait de son père 1953, Un acte d'amour 1953, Tradita 1954, Le fils de Caroline chérie 1955, Futures vedettes 1955, Doctor at Sea 1955, Les grandes manoeuvres 1955, La lumière d'en face 1955, Mi figlio Nerone 1956, Cette sacrée gamine 1956, La mariée est trop belle 1956, Helen of Troy 1956, Et Dieu… créa la femme 1956, En effeuillant la marguerite 1956, Une parisienne 1957, Les bijoutiers du clair de lune 1958, En cas de malheur 1958, La femme et le pantin 1959, Babette s'en va-t-en guerre 1959, Voulez-vous danser avec moi? 1959, Le testament d'Orphée, La bride sur le cou 1961, Amours célèbres 1961, Vie privée 1962, Le repos du guerrier 1962, Le mépris 1963, Une ravissante idiote 1964, Viva Maria! 1965, Masculin, A coeur joie 1967, Histoires extraordinaires 1968, Shalako 1968, L'ours et la poupée 1969, Les femmes 1969, Les novices 1970, Boulevard du rhum 1971, Les pétroleuses 1971, Don Juan ou Si Don Juan était une femme… 1973, L'Histoire très bonne et très joyeuse de Colinot trousse-chemise 1973. *Television:* Étoiles et toiles: L'érotisme au cinéma (episode) 1983. *Publications include:* Initiales BB 1996 (Prix Paul Léautaud 1996) 1996, Le Carré de Pluton 1999, Un Cri Dans Le Silence 2003, Pourquoi? 2006. *Address:* Fondation Brigitte Bardot, 28 rue Vineuse, 75116 Paris, France (home). *Telephone:* 1-45-05-14-60. *Fax:* 1-45-05-14-80. *E-mail:* fbb@fondationbrigittebardot.fr (office). *Website:* www.fondationbrigittebardot.fr (office).

BAREIRO SPAINI, Gen. (retd) Luis Nicanor; Paraguayan military officer and politician; ed Mariscal Francisco Solano López Mil. Coll.; fmr Commdr Cadets Corps, Mil. Acad., Commdr Army Artillery Corps, Commdr Army Mil. Inst.; fmr Dir Inst. of High Strategic Studies, Ministry of Defence; fmr Dir Inspectorate Gen., Armed Forces; Commdr Paraguayan Army –2005; Minister of Defence 2008–12; currently Pres. Centre for Nat. and Int. Studies (CENI); prof. of his areas of expertise in various univs. *Address:* c/o Ministry of National Defence, esq. Vicepresidente Sánchez y 22 de Septiembre, Asunción, Paraguay.

BAREKOV, Nikolay Tihomirov; Bulgarian journalist, business executive and politician; *Leader, Balgariya bez tsenzura (Bulgaria Without Censorship);* b. 16 Oct. 1972, Banya, Karlovo Municipality, Plovdiv Oblast; began career as a radio journalist 1992, joined Kanal Kom radio, Plovdiv; presented morning segment on BTV channel 2003–10; subsequently hosted several shows on TV7; Founder and Leader, Balgariya bez tsenzura (Bulgaria Without Censorship) 2014–, participated in European elections as part of a coalition bloc with nationalist IMRO and other smaller parties 2014, gained two seats in European Parl., mems European Conservatives and Reformists. *Address:* Balgariya bez tsenzura (Bulgaria Without Censorship), 1421 Sofia, Hemus Business Centre, 1st Floor, bul. Cherni vrah 25A, Bulgaria (office). *Telephone:* 87-9876174 (mobile). *E-mail:* info@bulgariabezcenzura.bg (office); info@barekov.com. *Website:* bulgariabezcenzura.bg (office); barekov.com.

BAREKZAI, Shukria, (Dawi); Afghan journalist, editor and politician; *Editor-in-Chief, Aina-e Zan;* b. 1972, Kabul; m.; three d.; ed Univ. of Kabul; organized and funded secret women's schools during Taliban regime; mem. Afghanistan's Constitutional Reviewing Comm. 2001; Founder and Ed.-in-Chief Aina-e Zan (Women's Mirror) weekly newspaper 2002–; f. Asia Women Org. 2002; mem. Parl. 2005–; Int. Ed. of the Year Award, Worldpress.org 2005. *Address:* Aina-e Zan (Women's Mirror), House 26, Muslim Wat, Shahr-i-Nau, District 10, Kabul, Afghanistan (office). *Telephone:* (70) 281864. *E-mail:* womensmirror@hotmail.com; women.mirror@gmail.com; shukriabarakzai@yahoo.com. *Website:* shukriabarakzai.net.

BARENBOIM, Daniel, FRCM; Israeli/Palestinian pianist and conductor; *Music Director, Teatro alla Scala, Milan;* b. 16 Nov. 1942, Buenos Aires, Argentina; s. of Enrique Barenboim and Aida Barenboim (née Schuster); m. 1st Jacqueline du Pré 1967 (died 1987); m. 2nd Elena Bashkirova 1988; two s.; studied piano with his father and other musical subjects with Nadia Boulanger, Edwin Fischer and Igor Markevitch; debut in Buenos Aires aged seven; played Bach D Minor Concerto with orchestra at Salzburg Mozarteum aged nine; has played in Europe regularly 1954–; yearly tours of USA 1957–; has toured Japan, Australia and S America; has played with or conducted London Philharmonic, Philharmonia Orchestra, London Symphony Orchestra, Royal Philharmonic, Chicago Symphony Orchestra, New York Philharmonic, Philadelphia Orchestra, Israel Philharmonic, Vienna Philharmonic, Berlin Philharmonic; frequently tours with English Chamber Orchestra and with them records for EMI (projects include complete Mozart Piano Concertos and late Symphonies); other recording projects include complete Beethoven Sonatas and Beethoven Concertos (with New Philharmonia Orchestra conducted by Klemperer); has appeared in a series of masterclasses on BBC TV; presented Festival of Summer Music on South Bank, London 1968, 1969; leading role in Brighton Festival 1967–69; appears regularly at Edinburgh Festival; conductor, Edinburgh Festival Opera 1973; Music Dir Orchestre de Paris 1975–89, Chicago Symphony Orchestra 1991–2006, Hon. Conductor for Life 2006–; Gen. Music Dir Deutsche Staatsoper, Berlin 1992– (Chief Conductor for Life Staatskapelle Berlin 2000–); projects with Edward Said, the West-Eastern Divan Workshop (Orchestra) 1999–; Music Dir and mem. Bd of Trustees, Barenboim-Said Foundation (promotes music and co-operation through projects targeted at young Arabs and Israelis); Charles Eliot Norton Prof., Harvard Univ. 2006; Maestro Scaligero, La Scala, Milan 2006–11, Music Dir 2011–; debut with Metropolitan Opera 2008; Hon. KBE 2011; Commdr, Légion d'honneur 2007, Grand Officer 2011, Bundesverdienstkreuz (Germany) 2013; Hon. DMus (Manchester) 1997, (Oxford) 2007, (Weizmann Inst. of Science) 2013; Beethoven Medal 1958, Paderewski Medal 1963, Beethoven Soc. Medal 1982, Prix de la Tolérance, Protestant Acad. of Tutzing 2002, Premio Príncipe de Asturias 2002, Grammy Award (for recording of Wagner's Tannhäuser) 2003, Wilhelm Furtwängler Prize (with Staatskapelle Berlin) 2003, Wolf Foundation Prize in Arts 2004, chosen to deliver Reith Lectures 2006, Zwickau Robert Schumann Prize 2006, Conductor of the Year, ECHO Klassik Awards 2006, Ernst von Siemens Prize 2006, Hessischer Peace Prize 2006, Goethe Medal 2007, Praemium Imperiale 2007, Royal Philharmonic Soc. Gold Medal 2008, Otto Hahn Peace Medal 2010, Edison Award for Lifetime Achievement 2011, Willy-Brandt-Prize 2011, ECHO Klassik Award for Lifetime Achievement 2012, inducted into Gramophone Hall of Fame 2012, Marion Dönhoff Prize 2013, Freedom Award, Freie Universität Berlin 2013, BBC Music Magazine Award for Recording of the Year (for Elgar & Carter Concerti 2012) 2014. *Publications include:* A Life in Music (jtly) 1991, Parallels and Paradoxes (with Edward W. Said) 2003, La Musica Sveglia il Tempo 2007, Everything is Connected 2008. *Address:* Opus 3 Artists, 470 Park Avenue South, 9th Floor North, New York, NY 10016, USA (office); Teatro alla Scala, Via Filodrammatici 2, 20121 Milan, Italy (office). *Telephone:* (212) 584-7500 (office); (02) 88791 (office). *Fax:* (646) 300-8200 (office). *E-mail:* info@opus3artists.com (office); danielbarenboim@hotmail.com. *Website:* www.opus3artists.com (office); www.teatroallascala.org (office); www.danielbarenboim.com.

BARFIELD, Julia, MBE, RIBA, FRSA; British architect; *Director, Marks Barfield Architects;* b. 15 Nov. 1952; d. of Arnold Robert Barfield and Iolanthe Mary Barfield; m. David Joseph Marks 1981; one s. two d.; ed Godolphin and Latymer School, London, Architectural Asscn School of Architecture, London; spent year out designing for Barriadas, Lima, Peru 1975; Co-founder Tetra Ltd 1978–79, Richard Rogers Partnership 1979–81, Foster Assocs 1981–88; co-f. Marks Barfield Architects with David Marks 1989–, London Eye Co. (formerly Millennium Wheel Co.) to realize London Eye project 1994–2005; lectures include RA 2000, 2001, RIBA 2000, The Prince's Foundation Urban Villages Forum 2000, Royal Inst. 2001, Cooper-Hewitt Nat. Design Museum, New York 2001, Univ. of Virginia 2006, 'G-Maggiube Summit', Beijing 2011; Civic Trust/RIBA Awards Assessor; Vice-Pres. Architectural Asscn School of Architecture; mem. Lambeth Democracy Comm. 2000–01, Nat. Design Review Cttee, Comm. for Architecture and the Built Environment (CABE) 2001–06, Architectural Asscn Council 2000–06, Council of Guys and St Thomas' Hosp. for five years; Gov. Godolphin & Latymer School; RIBA Awards for Architecture 2000, 2004, 2006, 2007, 2008, 2009, 2010, London First Millennium Award 2000, Royal Inst. of Chartered Surveyors Award 2000, AIA Design Award 2000, Prince Philip Designers Prize 2000, Pride of Britain Award for Innovation 2001, Design Week Special Award 2001, D&AD Awards, Silver and Gold 2001, 2004, Blueprint Award 2001, Architectural Practice of the Year 2001, Civic Trust Award 2002, 2006, 2008, 2009, Queen's Award for Enterprise (for Innovation) 2003, Coolbrands 2003–05, BDI Excellence in Architecture Award 2005, People's Choice Award 2008, Arts Fund Prize 2008, Structural Steel Design Award 2009, BD Architect of the Year Award 2009. *Publications:* Eye: The Story Behind the London Eye, Gentle Landmarks. *Leisure interests:* family, travel, art, film, current affairs, social responsibility. *Address:* Marks Barfield Architects, 50 Bromells Road, London, SW4 0BG, England (office). *Telephone:* (20) 7501-0180 (office). *Fax:* (20) 7498-7103 (office). *E-mail:* jbarfield@marksbarfield.com (office). *Website:* www.marksbarfield.com (office).

BARFOOT, Joan Louise, BA; Canadian novelist and journalist; b. 17 May 1946, Owen Sound, Ont.; d. of Robert Barfoot and Helen MacKinnon; ed Univ. of Western Ontario; reporter, Religion Ed. Windsor Star 1967–69; feature and news writer, Mirror Publications, Toronto 1969–73, Toronto Sunday Sun 1973–75; with London Free Press 1976–79, 1980–94; taught both journalism and creative writing at Univ. of Western Ontario and creative writing through Humber Coll.; juror, Books in Canada First Novel Award 1987, Gov.-Gen.'s Award; mem. Writers' Union of Canada, PEN Canada; Dr hc (Univ. of Western Ontario) 2012; Women of Distinction Award 1986, Marian Engel Award 1992, Medal of Distinction, Huron Univ. Coll. 2005. *Publications include:* Abra (Books in Canada First Novel Award 1978) 1978, Dancing in the Dark 1982, Duet for Three 1985, Family News 1989, Plain Jane 1992, Charlotte and Claudia Keeping in Touch 1994, Some Things About Flying 1997, Getting Over Edgar 1999, Critical Injuries 2001, Luck 2005, Exit Lines 2008. *E-mail:* jbarfoot@sympatico.ca (home). *Website:* www.joanbarfoot.ca.

BARGHATHI, Col Mahdi al-; Libyan military commander and politician; fmr army commdr, Eastern Libya, including commdr, tank Bn, fmr head, 204 Tank Brigade; joined Khalifa Haftar's Operation Dignity 2014; Minister of Defence, Govt of Nat. Accord (recognized by UN as legitimate governing authority for Libya) 2016–May 2017 (suspended), dismissed July 2018.

BARGHOUTHI, Mustafa, MD, MSc; Palestinian politician, human rights activist and physician; *Member, Palestinian Legislative Council;* b. 15 Jan. 1954, Jerusalem; ed trained as medical doctor in fmr Soviet Union, post-graduate training in Jerusalem and Stanford Univ., Calif., USA; lectured at Harvard, Johns Hopkins and Stanford Univs, also at IISS and Chatham House, London, UK, Brookings Inst., USA, Sydney Inst., Australia; est. Palestinian Medical Relief Soc. 1979, currently Pres.; Co-founder Health, Devt, Information and Policy Inst., Ramallah, Grassroots Int. Protection for the Palestinian People; del. to Madrid Peace negotiations 1991; fmr mem. steering cttee of tech. cttee that prepared establishment of various Palestinian ministries; Co-founder and Sec. Palestinian Nat. Initiative (Mubadara); twice arrested for speaking out against Israeli blockade of Occupied Territories Jan. 2002; presidential cand. (ind.) in Palestinian Authority elections Jan. 2005; mem. Palestinian Legis. Council 2006–; Ordine Della Stella della Solidaritá Italiana 2007, Chevalier, Légion d'honneur 2010. *Publications:* author or co-author of books and research on health development; numerous articles on civil society, democracy issues and the political situation in Palestine; Our Story (DVD). *Address:* PO Box 51483, Jerusalem, Israel (office). *Telephone:* 59-9201528 (mobile) (office). *Fax:* 2-2969993 (office). *E-mail:* mustafa@hdip.org (home).

BARGHOUTI, Marwan Haseeb, MA; Palestinian resistance leader; b. 6 June 1959, Kobar, Ramallah; m. Fadwa Bargouthi; three s. one d.; ed Bir Zeit Univ.; joined Fatah Movt aged 15; imprisoned for involvement in an intifada (uprising) 1976; placed under admin. detention without charges for six months 1985; deported to Jordan by Israeli authorities for allegedly inciting struggle against occupation 1987; returned to W Bank, Pres. student body, Bir Zeit Univ.; served in PLO in Tunis, cen. liaison officer between PLO and Fatah; helped organize political aspects of the first Intifada 1987; mem. Revolutionary Council of Fatah 1989, Sec.-Gen. in W Bank; returned to Ramallah under Oslo Accords 1994; mem. Palestinian Legis. Council (PLC) 1996–, mem. Legal Cttee, Political Cttee, Chair. Parl. Cttee with French Parl.; participated in outbreak of second Intifada in W Bank and Gaza 2000; sponsor of Tanzim (Fatah's operation dept); arrested by Israeli armed forces during incursion into Ramallah April 2002, accused of being the leader of the al-Aqsa Martyrs Brigade, indicted on terrorism charges Aug. 2002; found guilty of organizing suicide attacks May 2004, given five consecutive life sentences June 2004; Founder and Head, Al-Mustaqbal (electoral list) 2005; leader Fatah Conference in Bethlehem 2009; has remained politically active in jail.

BARGMANN, Cornelia (Cori) Isabella, BS, PhD; American geneticist, neuroscientist and academic; *Torsten N. Wiesel Professor and Director, Lulu and Anthony Wang Laboratory of Neural Circuits and Behavior, The Rockefeller University;* b. 1961, Athens, Ga; d. of Rolf Bargman; m. 1st Michael J. Finney; m. 2nd Richard Axel; ed Univ. of Georgia, Massachusetts Inst. of Tech.; Postdoctoral Fellow, MIT –1991; mem. Faculty, Univ. of California, San Francisco 1991–2004; Torsten N. Wiesel Prof., The Rockefeller Univ., New York 2004–, Dir Lulu and Anthony Wang Lab. of Neural Circuits and Behavior, Co-Dir Shelby White and Leon Levy Center for Mind, Brain and Behavior; Investigator, Howard Hughes Medical Inst. 1995–; mem. NAS 2003, American Philosophical Soc.; Fellow, American Acad. of Arts and Sciences 2002; Lucille P. Markey Award 1990–95, Searle Scholar Award 1992–95, Taskago Prize, W. Alden Spencer Award, Charles Judson Herick Award, Dargut and Milena Kemali Int. Prize for Research in Basic and Clinical Neurosciences 2004, Richard Lounsbery Award, NAS and Acad. des sciences 2009, Biotechnology Achievement Award, Dart/New York Univ. 2012, Kavli Prize in Neuroscience 2012, Breakthrough Prize in Life Sciences (co-recipient) 2013. *Publications:* numerous papers in professional journals. *Address:* The Rockefeller University, 1230 York Avenue, New York, NY 10065, USA (office). *Telephone:* (212) 327-8000 (office). *Fax:* (212) 327-7974 (office). *E-mail:* cori.bargmann@rockefeller.edu (office). *Website:* www.rockefeller.edu/research/faculty/labheads/CoriBargmann (office).

BARI, Air Marshal (retd) Muhammad Enamul; Bangladeshi business executive and air force officer (retd); *Chairman, Biman Bangladesh Airlines Ltd;* b. 1960, Dhaka; m. Mary Enam; one s. two d.; ed Flying Instructor Course, UK, Jt Air War Course, India, Defence Services Command and Staff Coll., Command and Staff Coll., Indonesia, Air Force Command Coll., China, Nat. Defense Univ., USA; joined Bangladesh Air Force (BAF) as a flight cadet 1978, commissioned in Gen. Duties (Pilot) Br. 1981, joined operational fighter squadron of BAF and served in almost all fighter squadrons in various appointments, has flown FUJI-200, AA-5A, PT-6, T-37B, FOUGA, FT-5, FT-6, F-6 and A-5IIIA fighter aircraft, also a Qualified Flying Instructor and carried out extensive instructional flying in various fixed-wing trainers and fighter aircraft, logged more than 2,000 flying hours, commanded the Trendsetters (25 Squadron, BAF), also commanded the Avengers (21 Squadron), subsequently commanded two BAF bases at Chittagong and Jessore, also served as a Directing Staff in Defence Services Command and Staff Coll., Mirpur and Deputy Commdt of BAF Acad., staff assignments have included Dir of Air Operations and Dir of Air Training at Air HQ and Dir of Training at Armed Forces Div., served in two Prin. Staff Officer positions at Air HQ level as Asst Chief of Air Staff for five years, Asst Chief of Air Staff (Operations and Training) followed by Asst Chief of Air Staff (Admin) 2009–12, Chief of Air Staff 2012–15 (retd); Chair. Biman Bangladesh Airlines Ltd 2016–; Fellow, Nat. Defence Coll., Mirpur; Maj.-Gen. Theodore Antonelli Award for Industry Study Excellence, Nat. Defense Univ. (USA) 2006. *Address:* Biman Bangladesh Airlines Ltd, Head Office, Balaka Kurmitola, Dhaka, 1229, Bangladesh (office). *Telephone:* (2) 8901600 (office). *Fax:* (2) 8901558 (office). *E-mail:* ibebiman@bdbiman.com (office). *Website:* www.biman-airlines.com (office).

BARIANI, Didier, DèsSc; French politician; *Vice-President, Conseil régional d'Île-de-France;* b. 16 Oct. 1943, Bellerive sur Allier; m. Chantal Maufroy (divorced); two c.; ed Inst. d'Etudes Politiques de Paris; Chargé de Mission, then Dept Head, Conseil Nat. du Patronat Français 1969–74; Dir, later Chair. Bd of Dirs, Centre de Perfectionnement et de Recherche des Relations Publiques 1974–79; Prin. Pvt. Sec. to Sec. of State for Environment, Ministry of Quality of Life June–Oct. 1974, to Sec. of State in charge of Public Admin, Prime Minister's Office 1974–76; Lecturer, Inst. d'Etudes Politiques de Paris 1975–79; Pres. Paris Fed. of Parti Radical Socialiste (PRS) 1973–78; Sec.-Gen. of Party 1977–79, UDF Deputy for Paris 20th Arrondissement 1978–81, Vice-Pres. UDF Group in Nat. Ass. 1978–81, Exec. Vice-Pres. 1994–97, Nat. Vice-Pres. UDF 1979–83, 1995–97, Pres. UDF, Paris 1999–2002; Pres. PRS 1979–83; mem. Steering Cttee, Exec. Cttee PRS 1971; mem. UDF Nat. Council 1978; Paris Councillor 1983, mem. Perm. Comm., Conseil de Paris; Pres. and Dir-Gen. Saemar Saint-Blaise 1983–2001; Mayor 20th Arrondissement, Paris 1983–95, Deputy Mayor of Paris 1983–2001; Sec. of State, Ministry of Foreign Affairs 1986–88; Pres. Parti Radical 1979–83; Nat. Del. of UDF (relations with int. orgs) 1988–92; Man. Soc. INFORG (Information, Communication et Organisation) 1977; Pres. Parti Radical Fédération Régionale de l'Ile de France 1979–81; Exec. Vice-Pres. (in Nat. Ass.) UDF 1994–97, 1999–, Pres. UDF, Paris Council 1999–; Jt Sec.-Gen. responsible for UDF's relations with int. insts 1992–96; mem. Nat. Ass. 1993–97, Vice-Pres. 1995–97; Vice-Pres. (Interregional Cooperation), Conseil régional d'Île-de-France 2015–; mem. Comm. for Foreign Affairs 1993–97; Titular Judge High Court of Justice 1995–97; Pres. France-Israel Friendship Group 1993–97; Adviser to Mayor of Paris 1995–2001; Co-Producer UDF/RPR Project 'Gouverner ensemble' 1986, 'Projet UDF/RPR pour la France' 1993; Hon. Pres. Parti Radical, Paris Football Club; Chevalier Légion d'honneur, Officier Ordre nat. du Mérite. *Publication:* Les immigrés: pour ou contre la France? 1985, Manifeste des Radicaux (jtly) 1995, Manifestement Radical (jtly) 1996. *Leisure interests:* football, skiing, tennis. *Address:* Conseil régional d'Île-de-France, 2 rue Simone Veil, 93400 Saint-Ouen, France. *Telephone:* 1-53-85-53-85 (office). *E-mail:* contactformationpro@iledefrance.fr (office). *Website:* www.iledefrance.fr (office).

BARICCO, Alessandro; Italian writer and playwright; b. 25 Jan. 1958, Turin; two s.; music critic, La Repubblica; cultural correspondent, La Stampa; Co-founder La Scuola Holden (narrative skills workshop) 1994; collaboration with French band, Air, to produce backing music for City 2003; Assoc., Fandango Libri Publishing House 2005–; several literary prizes. *Television includes:* L'amore è un dardo 1993, Pickwick, del leggere e dello scrivere 1994, Totem. Letture, suoni, lezioni 1998–2001. *Plays:* Novecento 1994, Davila Roa 1996, Partita Spagnola 2003. *Film:* Lezione 21 2008, Jun 2012, La Guerra 2015. *Publications include:* novels: Castelli di rabbia (trans. as Lands of Glass) (Premio Selezione Campiello, Prix Médicis étranger) 1991, Oceano Mare (trans. as Ocean Sea) (Premio Viareggio) 1993, Novecento. Un Monologo 1994, Seta (trans. as Silk) 1996, City 1999, Senza sangue (trans. as Without Blood) 2002, Omero, Iliade 2004, Questa Storia 2005, Emmaus 2009, Mr Gwyn 2011, Tre volte all'alba 2012, Smith & Wesson 2014, La Sposa giovane 2015; non-fiction: Il Genio in fuga 1988, L'anima di Hegel e le mucche del Wisconsin 1992, Barnum (collection of articles) 1995, Barnum 2 (collection of articles) 1998, Next 2002, I Barbari 2006. *Address:* Fandango Libri, viale Gorizia 19, 00198, Rome, Italy (office).

BARING, Hon. Sir John Francis Harcourt (see Ashburton, Baron).

BARISH, Barry Clark, BA, PhD; American physicist; *Ronald and Maxine Linde Professor of Physics, Emeritus California Institute of Technology;* b. 27 Jan. 1936, Omaha, Neb.; s. of Harold Barish and Lee Barish; m. Samoan Barish; one s. one d.; ed Univ. of California, Berkeley; Research Fellow, Univ. of California, Berkeley 1962–63; Research Fellow, Calif. Inst. of Tech. 1963–66, Asst Prof. 1966–69, Assoc. Prof. 1969–72, Prof. 1972–91, Ronald and Maxine Linde Prof. of Physics 1991–2005, Prof. Emer. 2005–; Principal Investigator Laser Interferometer Gravitational-wave Observatory (LIGO) 1994–2005, Dir 1997-2005, Researcher 2006–, mem., LIGO Scientific Collaboration Executive Cttee 2013–; mem. National Science Board 2003–09 (also, Consultant 2010–11), AAAS 2005, NAS; Fellow, AAAS, American Physical Soc. 2009–; hon. doctor (Univ. of Bologna) 2006, (Southern Methodist Univ.) 2018, Hon. DrSc (Univ. of Florida) 2007, (Univ. of Glasgow) 2013; Klopsteg Award, American Asscn of Physics Teachers 2002, Enrico Fermi Prize 2016, American Ingenuity Award, Smithsonian magazine 2016, Henry Draper Medal, NAS 2017, Giuseppe and Vanna Cocconi Prize, European Physical Society 2017, Princess of Asturias Award (with Rainer Weiss and Kip Thorne) 2017, Fudan-Zhongzhi Science Award 2017, Nobel Prize in Physics (with Rainer Weiss and Kip Thorne) 2017. *Publications include:* Joining Minds: Science Diplomacy and International Politics (with Anne-Marie Brady and Eligar Sadeh) 2013. *Address:* California Institute of Technology, LIGO MS 100-36, 1200 East Calif. Blvd, Pasadena, CA 91125, USA (office). *Telephone:* (626) 395-3853 (office). *Fax:* (626) 395-2973 (office). *E-mail:* barish@ligo.caltech.edu (office). *Website:* labcit.ligo.caltech.edu (office).

BARKAT, Nir, BSc; Israeli business executive and politician; *Mayor of Jerusalem;* b. 19 Oct. 1959, Jerusalem; m. Beverly Barkat; three d.; ed Hebrew Univ.; served as paratrooper in Israel Defence Forces 1977–83; Co-founder BRM Group (antivirus software co.) 1988, BRM Capital 2000; Co-founder Snunit (nonprofit org. for promotion of use of computer software in elementary educ.); Founding mem. New Spirit; Co-founder Israel Venture Network 2001; Founder Jerusalem Will Succeed party 2003; unsuccessful candidate for Mayor of Jerusalem 2003; mem. Jerusalem City Council 2003–08; Mayor of Jerusalem 2008–; fmr Chair. BackWeb and Checkpoint. *Address:* Jerusalem Municipality, Information Unit, 1 Safra Square, Jerusalem 91007, Israel (office). *Telephone:* 2-6296910 (office). *Website:* www.jerusalem.muni.il (office).

BARKER, Graeme William Walter, CBE PhD, FBA, FSA; British archaeologist and academic; *Senior Fellow, McDonald Institute for Archaeological Research, University of Cambridge;* b. 23 Oct. 1946, Orpington; s. of Reginald Walter Barker and Kathleen Walton; Pnr Genevieve Protiere Lebrun; one d.; ed St John's Coll., Cambridge; Lecturer in Prehistoric Archaeology, Univ. of Sheffield 1972–84; Dir British School at Rome 1984–88; Prof. of Archaeology and Head, School of Archaeology and Ancient History, Univ. of Leicester 1988–2004, Founding Grad. Dean 2000–03, Pro-Vice-Chancellors 2003–04; Disney Prof. of Archaeology and Dir McDonald Inst. for Archaeological Research, Univ. of Cambridge 2004–14, Sr Fellow, McDonald Inst. for Archaeological Research 2014–, Professorial Fellow, St John's Coll., Cambridge 2004–; has conducted archaeological fieldwork in Borneo, Iraq, Italy, Libya, Jordan and Mozambique; mem. British Acad.'s Review Cttee of the British Schools and Insts Abroad 1990–95, British Acad.'s Bd for Acad.-Sponsored Insts and Socs 1996–2005 (Chair. 2004–05); mem. RAE archaeology sub-panel 2001 (Chair. 2008), archaeology/geography sub-panel 2014; UK mem. AHRB Bd, AHRC Council 2003–08; mem. Soc. for Libyan Studies Council 2004–10 (also Hon. Vice-Pres. 2017–), British School at Rome Council 2009–15, British Acad. Archaeology Section H7 2012–15 (Chair. 2015–18), European Research Council SH6 panel for Starter and Consolidator Awards 2012–13 (Chair. 2014–15), Mediterranean Archaeology Trust 2014–, REF Panel C 2021; mem. Radiocarbon Facility Coordinating Cttee, Natural Environment Research Council 2008–11 (Chair. 2011–15); Trustee, Asscn for Southeast Asianists UK 2014–, Antiquity journal 2016–, Council for British Research in the Levant 2018–; Trustee Governing Council, Bishops Stortford Coll. 2019–; mem. several editorial panels, including Cambridge University Press 'Manuals in Archaeology', Journal of Mediterranean Archaeology, Journal of Quaternary Science; Pres. Prehistoric Soc. 2001–05; Sr Research Fellow, Netherlands Inst. for Advanced Study in the Humanities and Social Sciences 1999; Mem. Academia Europaea 2013; Hon. DLitt (Univ. of Sheffield) 2014, (Univ. of Leicester) 2019; James R. Wiseman Book Award, Archaeological Inst. of America 2000, Dan David Prize (co-recipient) 2005, Field Discovery Award, Shanghai Archaeology Forum 2017. *Publications:* more than 20 books, including Prehistoric Farming in Europe 1985, Beyond Domestication in Prehistoric Europe (co-ed.) 1985, Roman Landscapes: Archaeological Survey in the Mediterranean Region (co-ed.) 1991, A Mediterranean Valley: Landscape Archaeology as Annales History in the Biferno Valley 1995 (Italian trans. 2001), The Biferno Valley Survey: The Archaeological and Geomorphological Record 1995, Farming the Desert: The UNESCO Libyan Valleys Archaeological Survey (two vols) 1996, The Etruscans 1998, Companion Encyclopedia of Archaeology 1999, The Archaeology of the Mediterranean Landscape (co-ed.) (five vols) 2000, The Archaeology of Drylands: Living on the Margin (co-ed.) 2000, The Human Use of Caves in Peninsular and Island Southeast Asia (co-ed.) 2005, The Agricultural Revolution in Prehistory: Why Did Foragers Become Farmers? 2006, Archaeology and Desertification: The Wadi Faynan Landscape Survey, Southern Jordan 2007, (Archaeology and Desertification: The Wadi Faynan Landscape Survey (co-author) 2008, Why Cultivate? Anthropological and Archaeological Approaches to Foraging-Farming Transitions in Southeast Asia (co-ed.) 2011,

Rainforest Foraging and Farming in Island Southeast Asia: The Archaeology of the Niah Caves, Sarawak 2013, A World With Agriculture (co-ed.) 2015, Archaeological Investigations in the Niah Caves, Sarawak (co-ed.) 2016; more than 250 papers on subsistence archaeology, forager-farmer transitions, Mediterranean landscape history, desertification, rainforest foraging and farming, the dispersal of modern humans and Neanderthal behaviour. *Leisure interests:* walking, sailing, skiing, cinema. *Address:* Department of Archaeology, University of Cambridge, Downing Street, Cambridge, CB2 3DZ, England (office). *Telephone:* (1223) 339284 (office). *Fax:* (1223) 333536 (office); (1223) 339285 (office). *E-mail:* gb314@cam.ac.uk (office). *Website:* www.arch.cam.ac.uk/directory/gb314 (office); www.mcdonald.cam.ac.uk (office).

BARKER, Patricia (Pat) Margaret, CBE, BSc (Econ), FRSL; British author; b. 8 May 1943, Thornaby-on-Tees; d. of Moyra Drake; m. David Barker 1978 (died 2009); one s. one d.; ed London School of Econs; taught in colls of further educ. 1965–70; Patron New Writing North; mem. Soc. of Authors, PEN; Hon. Fellow, LSE 1998; Hon. MLitt (Teesside) 1993; Hon. DLitt (Napier) 1996, (Durham) 1998, (Hertfordshire) 1998, (London) 2002; Dr hc (Open Univ.) 1997; Northern Electric Special Arts Award 1994. *Publications include:* novels: Union Street (Fawcett Prize 1983) 1982, Blow Your House Down 1984, The Century's Daughter 1986 (retitled Liza's England 1996), The Man Who Wasn't There 1989; trilogy of First World War novels: Regeneration 1991, The Eye in the Door (Guardian Prize for Fiction 1993) 1993, The Ghost Road (Booker Prize 1995) 1995; Another World 1998, Border Crossing 2001, Double Vision 2003, Life Class 2007, Toby's Room 2012, Noonday 2015, The Silence of the Girls 2018. *Address:* 10 The Avenue, Durham, DH1 4ED, England (home); c/o Aitken Alexander Associates Ltd, 291 Gray's Inn Road, London, WCIX 8QJ, England. *Telephone:* (20) 7373-8672. *E-mail:* reception@aitkenalexander.co.uk. *Website:* www.aitkenalexander.co.uk.

BARKER, The Hon. Richard (Rick); New Zealand politician; b. 27 Oct. 1951, Greymouth; m.; three c.; ed Greymouth High School, Otago Univ.; various jobs including shop assistant, bartender, storeworker, farmhand, driver, factory worker, quarrier; Nat. Sec. Service Workers' Union; Exec. mem. Council of Trade Unions; Labour Party MP for Hastings 1993–2011, Asst Speaker 2008–11; Minister of Customs 2002–05, for the Community and Voluntary Sector 2004–05, for Courts 2003–08, of Internal Affairs, of Civil Defence, of Veterans' Affairs 2005–08; Trustee, Nga Tukimata O Kahungunu; Chair. Hawke's Bay Work Trust; Patron SPELD (Specific Learning Disabilities Federation), Deerstalkers Asscn, Schizophrenics Soc.; elected member for Hastings Constituency, Hawke's Bay Regional Council 2013–. *Address:* Hawke's Bay Regional Council, Private Bag 6006, Napier 4142, New Zealand (office). *Telephone:* (6) 835-9200 (office). *Fax:* (6) 835-3601 (office). *E-mail:* info@hbrc.govt.nz (office). *Website:* www.hbrc.govt.nz (office).

BARKIN, Ellen; American actress; b. 16 April 1955, New York; m. 1st Gabriel Byrne 1988 (divorced 1999); two c.; m. 2nd Ronald Perelman 2000 (divorced 2006); ed City Univ. of New York and Hunter Coll. Ind. *Films:* Diner 1982, Daniel 1983, Tender Mercies 1983, Eddie and the Cruisers 1983, The Adventures of Buckaroo Banzai 1984, Harry and Son 1984, Enormous Changes at the Last Minute 1985, Down by Law 1986, The Big Easy 1987, Siesta 1987, Sea of Love 1989, Johnny Handsome, Switch, Man Trouble 1992, Mac 1993, This Boy's Life 1993, Into the West 1993, Bad Company 1995, Wild Bill 1995, Mad Dog Time 1996, The Fan 1996, Fear and Loathing in Las Vegas, Popcorn, Drop Dead Gorgeous, The White River Kid 1999, Crime and Punishment in Suburbia 2000, Mercy 2000, Someone Like You 2001, Palindromes 2005, Trust the Man 2005, Ocean's Thirteen 2007, Brooklyn's Finest 2009, Happy Tears 2009, Twelve 2010, The Chameleon 2010, Shit Year 2010, Rogues Gallery 2010, Another Happy Day 2011, Very Good Girls 2013, The Cobbler 2014, Hands Of Stone 2016. *Stage appearances include:* Shout Across the River 1980, Killings on the Last Line 1980, Extremities 1982, Eden Court, The Normal Heart (Tony Award for Best Featured Actress in a Play 2011) 2011, Happyish 2015, Kingdom 2016–. *TV appearances include:* Search for Tomorrow, Kent State 1981, We're Fighting Back 1981, Terrible Joe Moran 1984, Before Women Had Wings 1998 (Emmy Award), A Mann's World (film) 2011, The New Normal (series) 2012–13. *Address:* c/o CAA, 9830 Wilshire Boulevard, Beverly Hills, CA 90212, USA (office).

BARKINDO, Mohammed Sanusi, BSc, MBA; Nigerian petroleum industry executive and international organization official; *Secretary-General, Organization of the Petroleum Exporting Countries;* b. 1959, Yola; ed Ahmadu Bello Univ., Coll. of Petroleum Studies, Univ. of Oxford, UK, South Eastern Univ., USA; 23-year career with Nigerian Nat. Petroleum Corpn (NNPC), including as Deputy Man. Dir and CEO, Nigeria Liquefied Natural Gas, Man. Dir/CEO, HYSON/CALSON (int. trading arm of NNPC), fmr Gen. Man., NNPC London Office and Head, Int. Trade, NNPC London Office, Group Man. Dir, NNPC 2009–10; 15 years as Nigeria's Nat. Rep. to OPEC Econ. Comm. Bd (including as fmr Chair.), fmr Chair. OPEC Strategic Production Quota Cttee, Acting Sec.-Gen., OPEC 2006, apptd Sec.-Gen., OPEC 2016–. *Address:* Organization of the Petroleum Exporting Countries, Helferstorferstrasse 17, 1010 Vienna, Austria (office). *Telephone:* (1) 211-12-3303 (office). *Fax:* (1) 216-43-20 (office). *E-mail:* prid@opec.org (office). *Website:* www.opec.org (office).

BARLEY, Katarina; German-British lawyer and politician; *Federal Minister of Justice and Consumer Protection;* b. 19 Nov. 1968, Cologne; (divorced); two s.; ed Philipps-Univ. Marburg, Univ. Paris-Sud, Univ. of Münster; called to the bar 1998; worked as lawyer with Wessing & Berenberg-Gossler, Hamburg 1998–99; legal adviser for state govt of Rhineland-Palatinate 1999–2001; Asst to constitutional judge Renate Jaeger, Karlsruhe 2001; German rep. to Maison de la Grande Région/Haus der Großregion (regional body) 2005–06; Judge, Trier Dist Court 2007–08; Adviser on bioethics to Rhineland-Palatinate State Ministry of Justice and Consumer Protection 2008–13; mem. Bundestag (lower house of parl.) for Trier and Trier-Saarburg (SPD) 2013–; Fed. Minister of Family Affairs, Senior Citizens, Women and Youth 2017–18, Acting Fed. Minister of Labour and Social Affairs 2017–18, Fed. Minister of Justice and Consumer Protection 2018–; mem. Social Democratic Party (SPD) 1994–, Sec.-Gen. 2015–17. *Address:* Federal Ministry of Justice and Consumer Protection, Mohrenstr. 37, 10117 Berlin, Germany (office). *Telephone:* (30) 185800 (office). *Fax:* (30) 185809525 (office). *E-mail:* postelle@bmjv.bund.de (office). *Website:* www.bmjv.de (office); katarina-barley.de.

BARLOW, Sir Frank, Kt, CBE; British business executive; b. 25 March 1930; s. of John Barlow and Isabella Barlow; m. Constance Patricia Ginns 1950 (died 2000); one s. two d.; ed Barrow Grammar School, Cumbria; with Nigerian Electricity Supply Corpn 1952–59; worked for Daily Times, Nigeria 1960–62; Man. Dir Ghana Graphic 1962–63, Barbados Advocate 1963, Trinidad Mirror Newspapers 1963–64, Daily Mirror 1964–67, King & Hutchings 1967–75; Dir and Gen. Man. Westminster Press 1975–83, CEO Westminster Press Group 1985–90; Dir Economist 1983–99; CEO Financial Times Group 1983–99 (Chair. 1993–96); Man. Dir Pearson PLC 1990–96; Chair. BSkyB 1991–95, Logica PLC 1995–2002; Pres. Les Echos, Paris 1988–90; Dir Elsevier UK 1991–94; Chair. Lottery Products Ltd 1997–; Dir Press Asscn 1985–93; fmr Chair. Printers' Charitable Corpn; Dir Royal Philharmonic Orchestra 1988–93; mem. Bd of Dirs, Soc. Européene des Satellites SA 2000–. *Leisure interests:* golf, fell walking, angling.

BARLOW, Miriam, BS, MS, PhD; American microbiologist and academic; *Associate Professor, University of California, Merced;* d. of Mark O. Barlow and Carroll K. Barlow; ed Univ. of Utah, Univ. of Rochester; Postdoctoral Researcher, Experimental Evolution, Epidemiology, Antibiotic Resistance, Clinical Microbiology, Emory Univ. 2004–05; Assoc. Prof., Univ. of California, Merced 2005–, Assoc. Dir, Network Experimental Research Evolution 2007–; mem. American Soc. for Microbiology; Siemens Medical Diagnostics Young Investigator Award, World Tech. Award (Health and Medicine) (co-recipient) 2015. *Publications:* numerous papers in professional journals; several patents for method for identifying potential resistance genes and for rapidly identifying and characterizing infectious bacteria. *Address:* Room 310, S&E 1 Building, University of California, 5200 North Lake Road, Merced, CA 95343, USA (office). *Telephone:* (209) 228-4174 (office). *E-mail:* mbarlow@ucmerced.edu (office). *Website:* mcb.ucmerced.edu (office); faculty1.ucmerced.edu/mbarlow (office).

BARLOW, Phyllida, CBE, RA; British artist (sculptor); b. 4 April 1944, Newcastle upon Tyne; d. of Erasmus Darwin Barlow and Biddy Barlow; m. Fabian Peake; five c.; ed Chelsea Coll. of Art, Slade School of Fine Art; work 'Table' included in first group exhbn Young Contemporaries, Inst. of Contemporary Art, London 1965; part-time teacher, Chelsea Coll. of Arts 1967–78, part-time visiting lecturer in sculpture 1991, 1992; teaching position in sculpture, Fine Art Dept, Brighton Polytechnic 1984–86; part-time teaching position, Camberwell School of Art 1986–88; Acting Head of Sculpture, Slade School of Fine Art 1992, Reader in Fine Art and Head of Undergraduate Studies 1997–2009, Prof. of Fine Art and Dir of Undergraduate Studies 2004–09, Jt Acting Head of School 2006–09, Prof. Emer. 2009–; McDermott Visiting Artist, Univ. of Texas, Dallas 2003; Townsend Lecture, Slade School of Fine Art 2014; known for her large sculptures and installations (three-dimensional collages); work held in numerous perm. collections; chosen to represent Britain at 2017 Venice Biennale; Royal Academician 2011; Elephant Trust Award, Museum of Installation, London 1995, Dean's Award, Univ. Coll. London 1996, 2003, Henry Moore Foundation Award for Black Dog Publishing monograph 2003, Dupree Family Award to a Woman Artist, Royal Acad. of Art 2006, Aachen Art Prize 2012. *Address:* Hauser & Wirth, 23 Savile Row, London, W1S 2ET, England (office). *Telephone:* (20) 7287-2300 (office). *Fax:* (20) 7287-6600 (office). *Website:* www.hauserwirth.com/artists/50/phyllida-barlow/biography (office).

BÄRLUND, Kaj-Ole Johannes, MSc(Econ); Finnish politician and international organization official; b. 9 Nov. 1945, Porvoo; s. of Elis Bärlund and Meri Bärlund; m. Eeva-Kaisa Oksama 1972; one s. one d.; journalist, Finnish Broadcasting Co. 1967–71; Public Relations Officer, Cen. Org. of Finnish Trade Unions 1971–72; Legis. Sec. Ministry of Justice 1972–79; mem. Parl. 1979–91; Chair. Porvoo City Bd 1979–87, 2009–12, Nat. Cttee on Natural Resources 1979–83; Chair. Swedish Labour Union of Finland 1983–90; mem. Nordic Council, Vice-Chair. Nordic Council Social and Environment Cttee 1983–87; mem. Exec. Bd Finnish Broadcasting Co. 1982–83, Neste Oy 1983–90; Chair. Bureau of the Montreal Protocol 1989–90; Chair. UN/ECE Cttee on Environmental Policy 1991–95; Minister of the Environment and Housing 1987–91; Dir-Gen. Nat. Bd of Waters and the Environment 1990–95; Dir-Gen. Finnish Environment Inst. 1995–2001; Dir Environment and Human Settlements Div. (later Environment, Housing and Land Man. Div.) UN ECE 1995–2008; Chair. Consumers' Union of Finland 1983–90, Peoples of Finland and Russia Friendship Soc. 1991–95, Union of the Pulmonary Disabled in Finland 1993–95; mem. Party Exec., Finnish Social Democratic Party 1984–91, Chair. Environmental Working Group 1981–87; Hon. Minister 2014; State Publicity Prize (Finland) 1972. *Publications include:* Miksi Ei EEC 1971, Palkat Paketissa 1972. *Leisure interests:* tennis, cross-country skiing, literature. *Address:* Sorsatie 4, 06100 Porvoo, Finland (home). *Telephone:* 405284844 (mobile) (home). *E-mail:* kaj.barlund@pp.inet.fi (office).

BARMAK, Wais Ahmad, MSc; Afghan politician and international organization official; b. 1972, Kabul; ed Kabul Univ., School of Oriental and African Studies (SOAS), Univ. of London; started working with Médecins Sans Frontières and ICRC 1993; Sr Programme Officer, Agency Coordinating Body for Afghan Relief and Devt 1996–98, apptd Programme Officer, Programme, Policy, and Planning Unit, UN Assistance Mission in Afghanistan (UNAMA) 2002, later Programme Officer and Deputy Regional Coordination Officer, UN Coordinator's Office, also Officer-in-Charge and Area Security Coordinator for all UN agencies, fmr Special Envoy for HE Pres. Mohammad Ashraf Ghani on good governance and security, followed by engagement with IFAD; joined Ministry of Rural Rehabilitation and Devt as Sr Adviser on Capacity Devt and Programmes 2004, Senior Adviser and Chief Coordinator Nat. Rural Access Programme –2006, fmr Exec. Dir Nat. Solidarity Programme, then Deputy Minister of Rural Rehabilitation and Devt, later Minister of Rural Rehabilitation and Devt; State Minister for Disaster Man. and Humanitarian Affairs and head of the Afghanistan Nat. Disaster Man. Authority 2015–17; Minister of Interior Affairs 2017–18; Deputy Head of the Disaster Man. Comm.; Coordinator, Agriculture and Rural Devt Cluster; mem. Bd Microfinance Investment Support Facility for Afghanistan. *Address:* c/o Ministry of Interior Affairs, Shar-i-Nau, Kabul, Afghanistan (office).

BARMANBEK, İmre, BSc; Turkish business executive; *Deputy Chairperson, Doğan Holding;* b. 1942; ed Ankara Univ.; began career as asst tax auditor, Bd of Accountancy Specialists, Ministry of Finance, later Chief Accountant Specialist –1977; fmr State Planning Specialist, State Planning Org.; mem. Tax Appeals Comm. –1977; Chief Financial Officer, jt venture co. formed between Koç and

Doğus Akü Industry Inc., later Gen. Man.; Chief Financial Officer, Doğan Group of Companies Holding Inc., mem. Exec. Bd 1999–, CEO 1999–2003, Deputy Chair. 2003–; mem. Turkish Industrialists and Businessmen's Asscn (TÜSİAD); Best Woman Manager of the Year (Turkey) 1999. *Address:* Office of the Deputy Chairperson, Doğan Şirketler Grubu Holding A.Ş., Oymacı Sok., 51 Altunizade, Üsküdar, 34662 İstanbul, Turkey (office). *Telephone:* (216) 556-9000 (office). *Fax:* (216) 556-9398 (office). *Website:* www.doganholding.com.tr (office).

BARNABY, Charles Frank, BSc, MSc, PhD; British physicist; b. 27 Sept. 1927, Andover, Hants.; s. of Charles H. Barnaby and Lilian Sainsbury; m. Wendy Elizabeth Field 1972; one s. one d.; ed Andover Grammar School and Univ. of London; Physicist, UK Atomic Energy Authority 1950–57; mem. Sr Scientific Staff, MRC, Univ. Coll. Medical School 1957–68; Exec. Sec. Pugwash Confs on Science and World Affairs 1968–70; Dir Stockholm Int. Peace Research Inst. (SIPRI) 1971–81; Prof. of Peace Studies, Free Univ., Amsterdam 1981–85; Dir and Scientific Adviser, World Disarmament Campaign (UK) 1982–; fmr Consultant, Oxford Research Group, now Consultant Emer.; Ed. Int. Journal of Human Rights; Hon. DSc (Frei Univ., Amsterdam) 1982, (Southampton) 1996, (Bradford) 2007. *Publications:* Man and the Atom 1971, Preventing the Spread of Nuclear Weapons (ed.) 1971, Anti-ballistic Missile Systems (co-ed.) 1971, Disarmament and Arms Control 1973, Nuclear Energy 1975, The Nuclear Age 1976, Prospects for Peace 1980, Future Warfare (co-author and ed.) 1983, Space Weapons 1984, Star Wars Brought Down to Earth 1986, The Automated Battlefield 1986, The Invisible Bomb 1989, The Gaia Peace Atlas 1989, The Role and Control of Weapons in the 1990s 1992, How Nuclear Weapons Spread 1993, Instruments of Terror 1997, How to Build a Nuclear Bomb and Other Weapons of Mass Destruction 2003, The Future of Terror 2007; articles in scientific journals. *Leisure interest:* natural history. *Address:* Brandreth, Station Road, Chilbolton, Stockbridge, Hants., SO20 6AW, England (home). *Telephone:* (1264) 860423 (home). *Fax:* (1264) 860868 (home). *E-mail:* frank.barnaby@btinternet.com (home).

BARNARD, Lukas Daniël (Niel), MA, DPhil; South African intelligence officer and academic; b. 14 June 1949, Otjiwarongo; s. of Nicolaas Evehardus Barnard and Magdalena Catharina Beukes; m. Engela Brand 1971; three s.; ed Otjiwarongo High School, Univ. of Orange Free State; Sr Lecturer, Univ. of OFS 1976, Prof. and Head, Dept of Political Science 1978; Dir-Gen. Nat. Intelligence Service (fmrly Dept of Nat. Security) 1980–91, Head of Constitutional Devt Service 1992; Dir-Gen. Prov. Admin of Prov. of the Western Cape 2001; S African Police Star for Outstanding Service 1985, Order of the Star of S Africa (Class 1), Gold 1987, Nat. Intelligence Service Decoration for Outstanding Leadership, Gold Nat. Intelligence Service Medal for Distinguished Service, Senior Service Award, Gold (CDS) 1992. *Publications include:* Die magsfaktor in internasionale verhoudinge 1975, Secret Revolution: Memoirs of a Spy Boss 2015; numerous articles in popular and technical scientific journals. *Leisure interest:* tennis.

BARNDORFF-NIELSEN, Ole Eiler, mag.scient., ScD; Danish mathematician, statistician and academic; *Professor Emeritus, Department of Mathematics, Århus University;* b. (Ole Eiler Nielsen), 18 March 1935, Copenhagen; s. of Niels Eiler Nielsen and Edith Barndorff; m. Bente Jensen-Storch 1956; two s. one d.; ed Univ. of Copenhagen, Århus Univ.; Prof. of Math. Statistics, Inst. of Math., Århus Univ. 1973, now Prof. Emer., Scientific Dir Math. Centre 1995–97, MaPhySto (Centre for Math. Physics and Stochastics) 1998–2003; invited visitor to univs in Europe, Australia, Brazil, Japan, Mexico, USA; Pres. Bernoulli Soc. for Math. Statistics and Probability 1993–95; Chair. European Research Centres on Math. (ERCOM), European Math. Soc. 1997–2002; Ed. Int. Statistical Review 1981–87; Ed.-in-Chief Bernoulli 1994–2000; Co-Ed. Journal of the European Mathematical Society 1998–2011; mem. Royal Danish Acad. of Sciences and Letters 1980, Academia Europaea 1990; Assoc., Inst. of Advanced Studies, Tech. Univ. of Munich; Fellow, World Innovation Foundation 2004; Corresp. Fellow, Royal Soc. of Edinburgh; Hon. Fellow, Royal Statistical Soc., Hon. mem. Danish Soc. for Theoretical Statistics, Int. Statistical Inst.; Dr hc (Univ. Paul Sabatier, Toulouse) 1993, (Katholieke Univ. Leuven) 1999; Humboldt Research Award 2001, Faculty of Science Prize, Århus Univ. 2010, Rigmor og Carl Holst-Knudsens Videnskabspris 2014. *Film:* Blown Sands. *Publications include:* six monographs, nine edited collected works, approx. 275 scientific papers. *Leisure interests:* biographies, opera. *Address:* Department of Mathematics, Århus University, Ny Munkegade 118, 8000 Århus (office); Dalvangen 48, 8270 Højbjerg, Denmark (home). *Telephone:* 23-28-68-99 (home). *E-mail:* oebn@math.au.dk (office); oebn@imf.au.dk (office). *Website:* math.au.dk/en (office).

BARNER, Andreas, PhD, MD; German business executive; *Chairman of the Board of Managing Directors, Boehringer Ingelheim GmbH;* ed Univ. of Freiburg, Swiss Fed. Inst. of Tech.; began career at Ciba-Geigy AG (Novartis), Basle, Switzerland in Cen. Function of Research and Medical Dept, later Head of Devt Indication Area for Inflammatory, Bone and Allergy Diseases within Research and Devt Dept –1992; joined Boehringer Ingelheim GmbH 1992, later Head of Corp. Medical Dept, later Corp. Medical Dir responsible for global clinical research, drug regulatory affairs, information and biometry, and drug safety, mem. and Spokesperson of the Bd of Man. Dirs 2009–12, Chair. 2012–, responsible for Corp. Bd Div., Human Resources, Research and Devt and Medicine; Chair. German Asscn of Research-based Pharmaceutical Cos (VFA); Deputy Chair. Nat. Genome Research Network Steering Cttee; mem. Advisory Bd NGN Capital, EFPIA R&D Dirs Group, Advisory Bd to Univ. of Mainz, Bd of Trustees German Chemical Industry Fund. *Address:* Boehringer Ingelheim GmbH, Binger Strasse 173, 55216 Ingelheim, Germany (office). *Telephone:* (6132) 77-0 (office). *Fax:* (6132) 72-92300 (office). *E-mail:* info@boehringer-ingelheim.com (office). *Website:* www .boehringer-ingelheim.com (office).

BARNES, Christopher Richard, CM, BSc, PhD, DSc, FRSC, PGeol; Canadian (b. British) geologist and academic; *Professor Emeritus, University of Victoria;* b. 20 April 1940, Nottingham, England; m. Susan M. Miller 1961; three d.; ed Univ. of Birmingham, UK, Univ. of Ottawa; NATO Research Fellow, Univ. of Wales, Swansea 1964–65; Asst Prof., Earth Sciences Dept, Univ. of Waterloo 1965–70, Assoc. Prof. 1970–76, Prof. and Chair. 1976–81, Biology Dept 1973–81, Sr Research Fellow, Univ. of Southampton, UK 1971–72; Univ. of Cambridge 1980–81; Prof. and Head, Memorial Univ. of Newfoundland 1981–87; Acting Dir Centre for Earth Resources Research 1984–87; Dir-Gen. Sedimentary and Marine Geosciences, Geological Survey of Canada 1987–89; Dir Centre for Earth and Ocean Research, Univ. of Victoria 1989–2000, Dir School of Earth and Ocean Sciences 1991–2002, Dir Neptune Canada 2001–11, Prof. Emer. 2012–; Pres. Canadian Geoscience Council 1979, Geological Asscn of Canada 1983–84, Acad. of Sciences, RSC 1990–93; Commr American Comm. of Stratigraphic Nomenclature 1973–75; Chair. Council of Chairs of Canadian Earth Science Departments 1983–85, 1995–97, 1997–99; mem. Earth Science Grants Selection Cttee, Natural Sciences and Eng Research Council of Canada 1977–80, Chair. 1979–80, Group Chair. Earth Sciences 1987–90, Group Chair. Interdisciplinary 1988–90; mem. Canadian Nat. Cttee and Int. Exec. Cttee, Int. Ocean Drilling Program 1987–89; mem. Bd of Dirs, Canadian Geological Foundation 1991–96; mem. Science Council of BC 1991–95, Atomic Energy Control Bd 1996–2000, Canadian Nuclear Safety Comm. 1996–2010; Chair. ITU/WMO/UNESCO-IOC Jt Task Force on SMART submarine telecommunications cables for ocean and climate monitoring and disaster warning 2012–16; mem. Acad. of Sciences, Cordoba, Argentina 2003; Order of Canada 1996; Hon. DSc (Waterloo) 2007, (Memorial Univ. of Newfoundland) 2016; Past-Pres.'s Medal, Geological Asscn of Canada 1977, Geological Asscn of Canada Nat. Lecturer 1978, Bancroft Award, Royal Soc. of Canada 1982, J. Willis Ambrose Medal, Geological Asscn of Canada 1991, Queen's Golden Jubilee Medal 2002, Elkanah Billings Medal, Geological Asscn of Canada 2005, Pander Soc. Medal 2009, Logan Medal, Geological Asscn of Canada 2010, Brady Medal, The Micropalaeontology Soc. 2010, Queen's Diamond Jubilee Medal 2012. *Publications:* more than 155 refereed publs in scientific journals; 50 other scientific publs and 280 published conf. abstracts. *Address:* School of Earth and Ocean Sciences, University of Victoria, PO Box 1700, Victoria, BC V8W 2Y2, Canada (office). *Telephone:* (250) 721-8847 (office). *Fax:* (250) 721-6200 (office). *E-mail:* crbarnes@uvic.ca (office). *Website:* web.uvic.ca/~crbarnes (office).

BARNES, Jonathan, FBA, FAAS; British academic (retd); b. 26 Dec. 1942, Much Wenlock, Salop.; s. of A. L. Barnes and K. M. Barnes; m. Jennifer Mary Postgate 1964; two d.; ed City of London School, Balliol Coll., Oxford; Lecturer in Philosophy, Exeter Coll., Oxford 1967–68, Fellow, Oriel Coll., Oxford 1968–78, Balliol Coll., Oxford 1978–94; Prof. of Ancient Philosophy, Univ. of Oxford 1989–94, Univ. of Geneva 1994–2002, Univ. of Paris IV-Sorbonne 2003–06; visiting posts at Univ. of Chicago 1966–67, Inst. for Advanced Study, Princeton 1972, Univ. of Mass 1973, Univ. of Tex. 1981, Wissenschaftskolleg zu Berlin 1985, Univ. of Alberta 1986, Univ. of Zurich 1987, Istituto Italiano per la Storia della Filosofia 1989, 1994, 1999, Ecole Normale Supérieure, Paris 1996, Scuola Normale di Pisa 2002; mem. L'Acad. scientifique, Geneva, Aristotelian Soc., Mind Asscn; Hon. Fellow, Oriel Coll., Oxford 2008–, Hon. Citizen of Velia 2010; Dr hc (Université de Genève) 2010, (Humboldt Univ. of Berlin) 2012; Condorcet Medal 1996, John Locke Lecturer, Univ. of Oxford 2004. *Publications include:* The Ontological Argument 1972, Aristotle's Posterior Analytics 1975, The Presocratic Philosophers 1979, Doubt and Dogmatism (with M. F. Burnyeat and M. Schofield) 1980, Aristotle 1982, Science and Speculation (with J. Brunschwig and M. F. Burnyeat) 1982, The Complete Works of Aristotle 1984, The Modes of Scepticism (with J. Annas) 1985, Early Greek Philosophy 1987, Matter and Metaphysics (with M. Mignucci) 1988, Philosophia Togata (with M. Griffin) Vol. I 1989, Vol. II 1997, The Toils of Scepticism 1991, Sextus Empiricus: Outlines of Scepticism (with J. Annas) 1994, The Cambridge Companion to Aristotle 1995, Logic and the Imperial Stoa 1997, The Cambridge History of Hellenistic Philosophy (with K. Algra, J. Mansfield and M. Schofield) 1999, Porphyry: Introduction 2003, Coffee with Aristotle 2008, Zenone e l'infinito 2009, Method and Metaphysics 2011, Logical Matters 2012, Proof, Knowledge and Scepticism 2014, Mantissa 2014. *Address:* Les Charmilles, l'Auvergne, 36200, Ceaulmont (home); 12 boulevard Arago, 75013 Paris, France (home). *E-mail:* jonathanbarnes@wanadoo.fr.

BARNES, Julian Patrick, (Dan Kavanagh, Basil Seal), BA; British writer; b. 19 Jan. 1946, Leicester; m. Pat Kavanagh (died 2008); ed City of London School, Magdalen Coll., Oxford; lexicographer, Oxford English Dictionary Supplement 1969–72; Asst Literary Ed. New Statesman 1977–79, reviewer 1977–81, TV critic 1979–82; Contributing Ed. New Review, London 1977–78; Deputy Literary Ed. Sunday Times, London 1979–81; TV Critic, The Observer 1982–86; Hon. Fellow, Magdalen Coll., Oxford 1996–, Hon. Foreign Mem. American Acad. of Arts and Letters 2016; Chevalier, Ordre des Arts et des Lettres 1988, Officier 1995, Commdr 2004, Officier, Ordre National de la Légion d'Honneur 2017; E. M. Forster Award, US Acad. of Arts and Letters 1986, Gutenberg Prize 1987, Grinzane Cavour Prize, Italy 1988, Shakespeare Prize, Germany 1993, Austrian State Prize for European Literature 2004, David Cohen Prize for Literature 2011, Siegfried Lenz Prize 2016. *Publications include:* Metroland (Somerset Maugham Award 1981) 1980, Before She Met Me 1982, Flaubert's Parrot (Geoffrey Faber Memorial Prize, Prix Médicis 1986) 1984, Staring at the Sun 1986, A History of the World in $10\frac{1}{2}$ Chapters 1989, Talking it Over (Prix Femina Etranger 1992) 1991, The Porcupine 1992, Cross Channel (short stories) 1996, England, England 1998, Love, etc. 2000, In the Land of Pain, by Alphonse Daudet (ed. and trans.) 2002, The Lemon Table (short stories) 2004, Arthur & George 2005, Pulse 2011, The Sense of an Ending (Man Booker Prize 2011) 2011, The Noise of Time 2016, The Only Story 2018; non-fiction: Letters from London 1990–95 1995, Something to Declare (essays) 2002, The Pedant in the Kitchen 2003, Nothing to Be Frightened Of 2008, Through the Window 2012, A Life with Books 2012, Levels of Life 2013, Keeping an Eye Open: Essays on Art 2015; as Dan Kavanagh: Duffy 1980, Fiddle City 1981, Putting the Boot In 1985, Going to the Dogs 1987. *Address:* c/o Sarah Ballard, United Agents, 12–26 Lexington Street, London, W1F 0LE, England (office). *Telephone:* (20) 3214-0775 (office). *Fax:* (20) 3214-0801 (office). *E-mail:* ekeren@unitedagents.co.uk (office). *Website:* unitedagents.co.uk (office); www.julianbarnes.com.

BARNES, Peter John, MA, DM, DSc, FRS, FRCP, FMedSci; British medical scientist and academic; *Professor Thoracic Medicine, National Heart and Lung Institute, Imperial College London;* b. 29 Oct. 1946, Birmingham; s. of John Barnes and Eileen Barnes; m. Olivia Harvard-Watts 1976; three s.; ed Leamington Coll., Univ. of Cambridge, Urniv. of Oxford Clinical School; medical positions at Oxford, Brompton Hosp., Nat. Hosp., Univ. Coll. Hosp. 1972–78; Sr Registrar, Hammersmith Hosp. 1979–82; Sr Lecturer, Consultant Physician, Royal Postgrad. Medical School 1982–85 (MRC Research Fellow 1978–79); Prof. of Clinical Pharmacology, Cardiothoracic Inst., Imperial Coll. London 1985–87, of Thoracic Medicine, Nat. Heart and Lung Inst. 1987–, Head of Respiratory Medicine 1987–2017; Hon. Consultant Physician, Royal Brompton Hosp. 1987–; MRC Travelling Fellow, Cardiovascular Research Inst., San Francisco 1981–82; Pres. European Respiratory Soc.; hon. medical degrees from Univs of Ferrara, Athens, Tampere, Leuven and Maastricht; numerous awards. *Publications:* Asthma: Basic Mechanics and Clinical Management, The Lung: Scientific Foundations 1991, Pharmacology of the Respiratory Tract 1993, Conquering Asthma 1994, Molecular Biology of Lung Disease 1994, Asthma (two vols) 1997, Airway Disease 2003, An Atlas of COPD 2004, New Drugs and Targets for Asthma and COPD 2010. *Leisure interests:* ethnic art, foreign travel, gardening. *Address:* Airway Disease Section, National Heart and Lung Institute (Imperial College), Dovehouse Street, London, SW3 6LY (office); 44 Woodsome Road, London, NW5 1RZ, England (home). *Telephone:* (20) 7351-8174 (office); (20) 7485-6582 (home). *Fax:* (20) 7351-5675 (office). *E-mail:* p.j.barnes@imperial.ac.uk (office). *Website:* www.imperial.ac.uk/people/p.j.barnes (office).

BARNETT, Correlli Douglas, CBE, MA, FRHistS, FRSL, FRSA; British historian; b. 28 June 1927, Norbury, Surrey; s. of Douglas A. Barnett and Kathleen M. Barnett; m. Ruth Murby 1950; two d.; ed Trinity School, Croydon and Exeter Coll. Oxford; Intelligence Corps 1945–48; North Thames Gas Bd 1952–57; public relations 1957–63; Keeper of Archives, Churchill Coll. Cambridge 1977–95; Defence Lecturer, Univ. of Cambridge 1980–83; Fellow, Churchill Coll., Cambridge 1977–2001; mem. Council, Royal United Services Inst. for Defence Studies 1973–85; mem. Cttee London Library 1977–79, 1982–84; Winston Churchill Memorial Lecturer, Switzerland 1982; Hon. Fellow, City and Guilds of London Inst. 2003; Hon. DSc (Cranfield Univ.) 1993; Screenwriters' Guild Award for Best British TV Documentary (The Great War) 1964, FRSL Award for Britain and Her Army 1971, Chesney Gold Medal Royal United Services Inst. for Defence Studies 1991. *Television includes:* The Great War (BBC TV) 1964, The Lost Peace (BBC TV) 1966, The Commanders (BBC TV) 1972. *Publications include:* The Hump Organisation 1957, The Channel Tunnel (with Humphrey Slater) 1958, The Desert Generals 1960, The Swordbearers 1963, Britain and Her Army 1970, The Collapse of British Power 1972, Marlborough 1974, Bonaparte 1978, The Great War 1979, The Audit of War 1986, Hitler's Generals 1989, Engage the Enemy More Closely 1991 (Yorkshire Post Book of the Year Award 1991), The Lost Victory: British Dreams, British Realities 1945–1950 1995, The Verdict of Peace: Britain Between Her Yesterday and the Future 2001, Post-conquest Civil Affairs: Comparing War's End in Iraq and in Germany 2005, Supreme Leadership in War from Lincoln to Churchill 2012. *Leisure interests:* gardening, interior decorating, eating, idling, mole-hunting. *Address:* Catbridge House, East Carleton, Norwich, Norfolk, NR14 8JX, England (home). *Telephone:* (1508) 570410 (home). *Fax:* (1508) 570410 (home).

BARNETT, Mickey D., BBA, JD; American lawyer, politician and government official; m. Janet Barnett; one s. one d.; ed Eastern New Mexico Univ., George Washington Univ. Nat. Law Center; mem. Bar Asscn of State of NM, US Court of Appeals 10th Circuit, US Supreme Court; currently Man. Partner, Barnett Law Firm, Albuquerque, NM; Legis. Asst to Senator Pete Domenici 1972–76; NM State Senator 1980–84; mem. Appellate Nominating Comm. for NM Supreme Court and Court of Appeals 1995–2002; apptd Gov. of US Postal Service (USPS) by Pres. George W. Bush 2006–, Vice-Chair. Bd of Govs 2011–12, Chair. 2012–14, mem. Audit and Finance Cttee; mem. Federalist Soc. *Address:* c/o United States Postal Service, 475 L'Enfant Plaza SW, Washington, DC 20260-0010, USA. *E-mail:* pmgceo@usps.gov.

BARNETT, Peter Leonard, AM; Australian journalist, broadcaster and administrator; b. 21 July 1930, Albany, Western Australia; s. of Leonard Stewart and Ruby Barnett; m. Siti Nuraini Jatim 1970; one s.; ed Guildford Grammar School, Western Australia, Univ. of Western Australia; Canberra Rep. and Columnist, The Western Australian 1953–57; SE Asia Corresp., Australian Broadcasting Comm. 1961, 1963, 1964, Jakarta Rep. 1962, New York and UN Corresp. 1964–67, Washington Corresp. 1967–70; News Ed. Radio Australia, Melbourne 1971–72, Washington Corresp. 1972–80, Controller, Melbourne 1980–84, Dir 1984–89; Exec. Dir Australian Broadcasting Corpn 1984–89; fmrly Exec. Dir Media Centre, Islamic Council of Victoria; fmr Co. Chair., Light Technologies Pty Ltd; convenor, Melbourne City Circle; mem. editorial Bd Dialogue/Asia Pacific; Australia Award 1988. *Publication:* Foreign Correspondence 2001. *Leisure interests:* swimming, literature, musical composition. *Address:* 66/46 Lansell Road, Toorak, Vic. 3142, Australia (home). *Telephone:* (3) 9827-5979 (home). *E-mail:* plsnb@netspace.net.au (home).

BARNEVIK, Percy Nils, MBA; Swedish business executive; *Honorary Chairman, Hand in Hand International;* b. 13 Feb. 1941, Simrishamn; s. of Einar Barnevik and Anna Barnevik; m. Aina Orvarsson 1963; two s. one d.; ed Gothenburg School of Econs, Stanford Univ., USA; Man. Corp. Devt, Group Controller, Sandvik AB 1969–74, Pres. US subsidiary 1975–79, Exec. Vice-Pres. parent co. 1979–80, Chair. Sandvik AB 1983; Pres. and Chief Exec. ASEA AB, Västerås 1980–87; Pres. and CEO ABB Ltd 1988–96, Chair. 1996–2001; Dir Skanska 1986–92, Chair. 1992–97; Chair. Investor AB 1997–2002, AstraZeneca PLC 1999–2005; mem. Bd of Dirs, General Motors Corpn 1996–2009, Du Pont Co. 1991–98; Adviser, Hand in Hand India (charity) 2000–, Co-founder and Chair. Hand in Hand International, now Hon. Chair.; mem. of numerous professional orgs; Hon. Fellow, Royal Acad. of Eng 1998; Foreign Hon. mem. American Acad. of Arts and Sciences 1999; Manager of the Year Award in Europe, European Business and Financial Press Asscn 1991, Int. Exec. of the Year Award, Fellows of the Acad. of Int. Business 1992, Emerging Markets CEO of the Year Award from a worldwide survey of 1,000 CEOs, Washington, DC 1995, European Leadership Award, Stanford University 1997, Global Exec. of the Decade 1998, Change-maker of the Year Award 2008, The Empowerer of Women of the Year Award, Swedish American Chamber of Commerce 2009, G.D. Birla Int. Award for Rural Upliftment in India 2010. *Address:* Hand in Hand International, 20 York Street, London, W1U 6PU, England. *Telephone:* (20) 7514-5091. *E-mail:* percy.barnevik@hihinternational.org. *Website:* www.hihinternational.org.

BARNEY, Matthew, BA; American film director, actor, artist and sculptor; b. 25 March 1967, San Francisco, Calif.; s. of Marsha Gibney; m. Mary Farley (divorced); pnr Björk; one d.; ed Capital High School, Yale Univ.; Europa 2000 Prize, 45th Venice Biennale 1996, Guggenheim Museum Hugo Boss Award 1996, James D. Phelan Art Award in Video, Bay Area Video Coalition, San Francisco Foundation 1999, Glen Dimplex Award, Irish Museum of Modern Art, Dublin 2001, Kaiser Ring Award 2007. *Films include:* Cremaster 4 1995, Cremaster 1 1996, Cremaster 5 1997, March of the Anal Sadistic Warrior 1998, Cremaster 2 1999, Cremaster 3 2002, De Lama Lamina 2005, Drawing Restraint 9 2005, Destricted 2006, Matthew Barney: No Restraint (documentary) 2007, River of Fundament 2014. *Address:* c/o Regen Projects, 633 North Almont Drive, Los Angeles, CA 90069, USA. *Website:* www.cremaster.net.

BARNIER, Michel; French politician and EU official; *Chief Negotiator for Brexit Talks with the UK, European Union;* b. 9 Jan. 1951, l'Isère; m.; three c.; ed Ecole Supérieure de Commerce, Paris; Pvt. Office of the Ministers for the Environment, Youth and Sport and for Trade and Craft Industries 1973–78; Departmental Councillor for Savoie 1973; mem. Nat. Ass. for Savoie 1978–93; Chair. Departmental Council of Savoie 1982; Co-Pres. Organizing Cttee for XVIth Olympic Games, Albertville and Savoie 1987–92; Minister of the Environment 1993–95; Minister of State for European Affairs 1995–97; Senator for Savoie 1997; Chair. French Asscn of Council of European Municipalities and Regions 1997; Pres. Senate Del. for the EU 1998; EU Commr for Regional Policy and Institutional Reform 1999–2004, Special Adviser to EU Pres. Barroso 2006–07, Commr for Internal Market and Services, EC 2010–14; Minister of Foreign Affairs 2004–05, for Agric. and Fisheries 2007–10; EU Chief Negotiator for Brexit Talks with the UK 2016–; Chevalier, Légion d'honneur. *Publications:* Vive la politique 1985, Le défi écologique, chacun pour tous 1990, L'Atlas des risques majeurs 1992, Vers une mer inconnue 1994. *Leisure interest:* skiing. *Address:* European Commission, 200 Rue de la Loi, 1049, 1049 Brussels, Belgium (office). *Telephone:* (2) 299-11-11 (office). *Fax:* (2) 295-01-38 (office). *Website:* www.ec.europa.eu (office).

BARNSLEY, Victoria, OBE, BA, MA; British publisher; b. 4 March 1954; d. of Thomas E. Barnsley and Margaret Gwyneth Barnsley (née Llewellin); m. Nicholas Howard 1992; one d. one step-s.; ed Loughborough High School, Beech Lawn Tutorial Coll., Univ. of Edinburgh, Univ. Coll. London, Univ. of York; with Junction Books 1980–83; Founder, Chair. and CEO Fourth Estate 1984–2000; CEO HarperCollins UK 2000–13, also for Australia, New Zealand, India and South Africa 2008–13, CEO HarperCollins UK and International 2008–13; Trustee, Tate Gallery 1998–; Dir Tate Enterprises Ltd 1998–; council mem. Publishers Asscn 2001–, Vice-Pres. 2009–10, Pres. 2010–11.

BAROIN, François, MA; French lawyer and politician; *Mayor of Troyes;* b. 21 June 1965, Paris; m. 1st Valérie Broquisse 1991 (divorced 2006); m. 2nd Michèle Laroque Baroin; three c.; ed Pantheon-Assas Paris II Univ., Inst. of Higher Man. Studies (ISG), Paris; town councillor for Nogent-sur-Seine, Aube 1989; Deputy for Aube (Union for a Popular Movement—UMP), Assemblée Nationale 1993–95, 1997–2005, 2007–10; Mayor of Troyes 1995–; Sec. of State and Govt Spokesperson 1995–97; Pres. Town Community Council (Mayor) of Troyes 2001–; barrister in pvt. law firm, Paris 2001–; Vice-Pres. Nat. Ass. 2002–05; Spokesperson for UMP 2003; Minister of Overseas Territories 2005–07, Minister of the Interior, Internal Security and Local Freedoms March–May 2007, Minister of the Budget, Public Accounts and State Reform 2010–11, also Govt Spokesperson 2010–12, Minister of the Economy, Finance and Industry 2011–12; mem. Dawn 1993–95, 1997–2005, 2007–10. *Leisure interests:* hunting, fishing, reading, chess, sports. *Address:* Hôtel de ville, Place Alexandre Israël, BP 767, 10026 Troyes Cedex, France (office). *Telephone:* (3) 25-42-33-33 (office). *Fax:* (3) 25-73-47-43 (office). *E-mail:* francoisbaroin3@aol.com. *Website:* www.ville-troyes.fr (office).

BARON, Martin, BA, MBA; American journalist and publishing executive; *Executive Editor, The Washington Post;* b. 24 Oct. 1954, Tampa, Fla; ed Lehigh Univ.; state reporter, business writer The Miami Herald 1976–79; joined Los Angeles Times 1979, apptd Business Ed. 1983, Asst . Man. Ed. for 'Column One' 1991, Ed. Orange Co. Edn 1993; joined The New York Times 1996, Assoc. Man. Ed. responsible for night-time news operations 1997–99; Exec. Ed. The Miami Herald 1999–2001; Ed. The Boston Globe 2001–12; Exec. Ed. The Washington Post 2012–; Pulitzer Prize 2001, 2013, 2014, 2015, 2016, Ed. of the Year, Editor & Publisher Magazine 2002, Hitchens Prize 2016, Al Neuharth Award for Excellence in Media 2017, Ellen M. Zane Award for Visionary Leadership 2017, Al Neuharth Award for Excellence in the Media 2017, Benton Medal for Distinguished Public Service 2018, Fourth Estate Award, Nat. Press Club 2018. *Address:* The Washington Post, 1301 K Street, NW, Washington, DC 20071, USA (office). *Telephone:* (202) 334-6000 (office). *Website:* www.washingtonpost.com (office).

BARON COHEN, Sacha; British actor and screenwriter; b. 13 Oct. 1971, London; m. Isla Fisher 2010; two c.; ed Christ's Coll., Cambridge; f. Four By Two Films (production co.) 2009. *Films include:* Punch 1996, The Jolly Boys' Last Stand 2000, Ali G Indahouse 2002, Spyz 2003, Madagascar (voice) 2005, Talladega Nights: The Ballad of Ricky Bobby 2006, Borat: Cultural Learnings of America for Make Benefit Glorious Nation of Kazakhstan (Best Actor, Los Angeles Film Critics Asscn, Toronto Film Critics Asscn 2006, London Evening Standard Peter Sellers Award for Best Comedy 2007) 2006, Sweeney Todd: The Demon Barber of Fleet Street 2007, Madagascar: Escape 2 Africa (voice) 2008, Brüno 2009, Hugo 2011, The Dictator 2012, Les Misérables 2012, Anchorman 2: The Legend Continues 2013, Grimsby 2015. *Television includes:* Jack and Jeremy's Police 4 1995, Live from the Lighthouse 1998, Comedy Nation 1998, The 11 O'Clock Show 1998–99, Ali G's Alternative Christmas Message 1999, Da Ali G Show (series) 2000–04, Curb Your Enthusiasm (episode) 2005, Night of Too Many Stars: An Overbooked Event for Autism Education 2006, Friday Night with Jonathan Ross (episode as Borat Sagdiyev) 2006, Saturday Night Live (episode as Borat Sagdiyev) 2006, Late Show with David Letterman (episode as Borat Sagdiyev) 2006, Reel Comedy: Borat Moviefilms Special Preview 2006, The Daily Show (episode as Borat Sagdiyev) 2006, The Tonight Show with Jay Leno (episode as Borat Sagdiyev) 2006, Howard Stern on Demand (episode as Borat Sagdiyev) 2006, Jensen! (episode,) 2006, Comic Relief 2007: The Big One 2007, El hormiguero (episode) 2009. *Publication:* Borat: Touristic Guidings to Glorious Nation of Kazakhstan (as Borat Sagdiyev) 2007. *Address:* Four By Two Films, 9100 Wilshire Blvd, Suite 1000 West, Beverly Hills, CA 90212 (office); c/o Jimmy Miller, 10th Floor, 9200 Sunset Blvd, Los Angeles, CA 90069 (office); c/o WME Entertainment, 9601 Wilshire Blvd, 10th Floor, Beverly Hills, CA 90212, USA (office). *Telephone:* (310) 248-2000 (WME Entertainment) (office). *Fax:* (310) 248-2020 (WME Entertainment) (office).

BARÓN CRESPO, Enrique; Spanish lawyer and politician; b. 27 March 1944, Madrid; m.; one s.; ed Calasancio de las Escuelas Pías Coll., Instituto Católico de Dirección de Empresas, Ecole Supérieure des Sciences Economiques et Commerciales, Paris; fmr Prof. of Agrarian Econs, INEA, Valladolid, Prof. of Econ. Structures, Universidad Complutense of Madrid 1966–70; practised as human rights lawyer before Tribunal of Public Order 1970–74; ran legal and econ. consultancy with Agapito Ramos; mem. Convergencia Socialista and Federación de Partidos Socialistas (FPS); negotiated electoral coalition of FPS with the Partido Socialista Obrero Español (PSOE); mem. Congress of Deputies 1977–87, PSOE Spokesman for Econ. Affairs, Public Finance and the Budget 1977–82; Minister of Transport and Tourism 1982–85; mem. European Parl. 1986–2009, Pres. 1989–92, Party of European Socialists Group Chair. 1999–2004, Cttee on Foreign Affairs 1992–95; fmr Pres. International Yehudi Menuhin Foundation, then Pres. of Honour; mem. Bd of Dirs Dali Foundation, Istituto per l'Opera e la Poesía di Verona. *Publications:* Population and Hunger in the World, Europa 92, Europe at the Dawn of the Millennium. *Leisure interests:* jazz, painting, walking, skiing.

BAROUD, Ziad S.; Lebanese lawyer, civil servant and politician; b. 29 April 1970, Jeita, Keserwan; s. of Salim Baroud and Antoinette Baroud; m. Linda Karam; one s. two d; ed St Joseph Univ., Beirut; admitted to Bar 1993; Lecturer on Public Law, Labour Law and Educational Law, St Joseph Univ., Beirut 1995–, also mem. Bd, Law Faculty; Lecturer on Institutional Law, Finance Inst. 2000–, Univ. St Esprit, Kaslik 2001–; Founding mem. Democratic Renewal Movt 2001; Founding Pnr, HBDT (law firm) 2003–; Research Assoc., Lebanese Centre for Policy Studies; Minister of the Interior and Municipalities 2008–11 (resgnd); Sec.-Gen. Lebanese Asscn for Democratic Elections 2004–05; mem. Nat. Council for a New Electoral Law; Legal Consultant to UNDP, UNESCO, UNEP; mem. Beirut Bar Asscn 1993–, Bd of Trustees, Notre Dame Univ.; Commdr, Order nat. du Mérite 2009; Chevalier, Légion d'honneur 2011; Commdr, Orden del Mérito Civil (Spain) 2011; named Young Global Leader by the World Econ. Forum 2007, named 2010 Man of the Year by Capital Issues newspaper and Data & Investment Consult-Lebanon 2009, Charles T. Manatt Democracy Award, Int. Foundation for Electoral Systems 2010. *Address:* c/o Ministry of the Interior and Municipalities, Grand Sérail, place Riad es-Solh, Beirut, Lebanon. *Website:* www.ziyadbaroud.com.

BARQUÍN DURÁN, Edgar Baltazar; Guatemalan accountant and fmr central banker; ed Universidad San Carlos de Guatemala, Centro de Estudios Monetarios Latinoamericanos (CEMLA), Mexico, Univ. of Hartford, USA; Head, Credit Dept, Banco de Occidente SA 1979–82; Head, Investment Dept, Credomatic Latinoamericana 1982–83; Insp., later Supervisor and Dir, Superintendencia de Bancos (regulatory body) 1985–2005; Man. Grupo Financiero de Occidente (financial risk group) 2005; fmr Dir of Tech. Co-ordination, Banco de Guatemala (central bank), Pres. 2010–14. *Address:* c/o Banco de Guatemala, 7A Avenida 22-01, Zona 1, Apdo 365, Guatemala City, Guatemala. *E-mail:* info@banguat.gob.gt.

BARR, Roseanne (see Roseanne).

BARR, William Pelham, MA, JD; American lawyer, business executive and government official; *Attorney-General;* b. 23 May 1950, New York, NY; s. of Donald Barr and Mary Ahern; m. Christine Moynihan 1973; three d.; ed Columbia Univ., George Washington Univ.; staff officer in CIA, Washington, DC 1973–77; barrister 1977–78; law clerk to US Circuit Judge 1977–78, Assoc., Shaw, Pittman, Potts & Trowbridge (law firm), Washington, DC 1978–82, 1983–84, Partner 1985–89, 1993–; Deputy Asst Dir Domestic Staff Policy, The White House, Washington, DC 1982–83; Asst Attorney-Gen., Office of Legal Counsel, US Dept of Justice, Washington, DC 1989–91, Attorney-Gen. of USA 1991–93, 2019–; Exec. Vice-Pres. and Gen. Counsel, GTE Corpn (now Verizon Communications Inc.), Washington, DC 1994–2008 (retd); Counsel, Kirkland & Ellis LLP Jan.–July 2009; Ind. Dir, Time Warner Inc. 2009–18, Dominion Resources, Inc., Selected Funds, Holcim US; mem. Virginia State Bar Asscn, DC Bar Asscn; mem. Bd of Visitors, Coll. of William & Mary 1997–2005; Republican. *Leisure interests:* music, playing the bagpipes. *Address:* Office of the Attorney-General, US Department of Justice, 950 Pennsylvania Avenue, Washington, DC 20530-0001, USA (office). *Telephone:* (202) 514-2000 (office). *Website:* www.justice.gov (office).

BARRA, Mary T., BS (ElecEng), MBA; American automotive industry executive; *Chairman and CEO, General Motors Company;* b. 24 Dec. 1961, Royal Oak, Mich.; m.; two c.; ed Kettering Univ., Stanford Grad. School of Business (GM fellowship); began career with General Motors Co. (GM), Detroit, as a General Motors Inst. (Kettering Univ.) co-op student at Pontiac Motor Div. 1980, held numerous senior positions in manufacturing, including Exec. Dir, Vehicle Manufacturing Eng 2004–08, Vice-Pres., Global Manufacturing Eng, 2008–09, Vice-Pres., Global Human Resources 2009–11, mem. Bd of Dirs 2011–, Sr Vice-Pres., Global Product Devt 2011–13, CEO 2014–, Chair. 2016–; mem. Bd of Dirs, General Dynamics, Inforum Center For Leadership; mem. Pres.'s Strategic and Policy Forum Jan.–Aug. 2017; mem. Bd of Trustees, Kettering Univ.; Key Exec. for Stanford Univ. *Address:* General Motors Company, PO Box 33170, Detroit, MI 48232-5170, USA (office). *Telephone:* (313) 556-5000 (office). *E-mail:* info@gm.com (office). *Website:* www.gm.com (office).

BARRA, Ornella; Italian business executive and pharmacist; *Chief Executive, Pharmaceutical Wholesale Division, Alliance Boots;* b. nr Genoa; ed Univ. of Genoa; started as pharmacist, first managing and then establishing own pharmacy; f. pharmaceutical wholesaler Di Pharma 1984, taken over by Alleanza Salute Italia 1986, apptd Man. Dir 1986, mem. Bd of Dirs Alliance Santé France 1990–, Chair. Alleanza Salute Italia (now Alliance Healthcare Italia) 1994, Exec. Dir Alliance UniChem Bd following merger of Alliance Santé with UniChem to form Alliance UniChem Group 1997, mem. Bd of Dirs Safa Galenica (Spain) 1998, Chair. Alliance UniChem Farmaceutica (Portugal) 1999–2005, Chair. Safa Galenica (now Alliance Healthcare Espana) and mem. Bd Alliance UniChem Farmaceutica (now Alliance Healthcare Portugal) 2005–06, Alliance Boots formed following merger of Alliance UniChem Plc with Boots Group Plc 2006, mem. Bd of Dirs following acquisition of the Group by Stefano Pessina and Kohlberg Kravis Roberts (AB Acquisitions) 2007–, Chief Exec. Pharmaceutical Wholesale Div., Alliance Boots 2009–, Chair. Alliance Boots Social Responsibilities Cttee 2009–, also responsible for Boots International; following merger of Walgreens and Alliance Boots, Exec. Vice-Pres. Walgreens Boots Alliance 2014–, Pres. and Chief Exec. Global Wholesale and International Retail; f. European Pharmacists Forum 1999; mem. Bd, AmerisourceBergen 2015–16; Int. Amb. Business in the Community 2015; Hon. Prof., School of Pharmacy, Univ. of Nottingham, UK; Hon. DSc (Nottingham) 2012; William L. Ford Prize, Int. Fed. of Pharmaceutical Wholesalers 2002, Int. Pericles Prize or outstanding achievement in science and social causes 2012. *Address:* Alliance Boots GmbH, Baarerstrasse 94, 6300 Zug, Switzerland (office). *Telephone:* (41) 727-7575 (office). *E-mail:* enquiries@allianceboots.com (office). *Website:* www.allianceboots.com (office); www.ornellabarra.com.

BARRAK, Saad Hamad al-, BSc, MSc, PhD; Kuwaiti engineer and business executive; *Chairman, ILA Group;* ed Ohio and Harvard Univs, USA, Univ. of London, UK; fmr Chair. IT Soft, Cairo, Arab Telecom; Dir (non-exec.), Arab Man. Asscn, Cairo; Man. Dir International Turnkey Systems –2002; Deputy Chair. and Man. Dir (CEO) MTC (renamed Zain 2007) 2002–10, mem. Exec. Bd Celtel International; Chair. ILA Group (consultancy firm) 2012–, est. ILA Advanced Technology SAE in Cairo; fmr Vice-Chair. Social Devt Office, Amiri Diwan, Kuwait; E-businessman of the Year Award 2003, Middle East CEO of the Year Award in the Information Communication Tech. sector 2005, Lifetime Achievement Award, Comms MEA 2007, Arab Ad Man of the Year, Arab Ad 2008, Int. Investor Award, Africa Investor 2008, Telecom CEO of the Year, CEO Middle East 2008, Visionary Award, Bespoke 2008, Editor's Award for Individual Contribution to the Telecoms Industry, Global Telecoms Business 2009, Outstanding Contribution to Business Award, CEO Middle East Awards 2012. *Publication:* A Passion for Adventure: Turning Zain into a Telecom Giant 2012. *Address:* ILA Group, Seef District, Building 2491, Road 2832, Block 428, Manama, Bahrain (office). *Telephone:* 3602-9999 (office). *E-mail:* info@ila-group.com (office). *Website:* www.ila-group.com (office); saadalbarrak.com.

BARRANGOU, Rodolphe, BS, MS, PhD, MBA; American medical researcher and academic; *Todd R. Klaenhammer Distinguished Scholar in Probiotics Research, North Carolina State University;* m. Lisa Barrangou; three c.; ed Univ. René Descartes, Univ. of Tech., Compiègne, North Carolina State Univ. and Univ. of Wisconsin, USA; Scientist, Cultures Devt, Danisco USA, a subsidiary of E. I. du Pont de Nemours and Company (DuPont), Wis. 2005–06, Sr Scientist 2006–07, Group Man., Genomics DuPont 2007–11, Research and Devt Dir, Genomics, DuPont 2011–13; Adjunct Prof. of Food Science, Pennsylvania State Univ. 2010–; Assoc. Prof. of Food Science, North Carolina State Univ. 2013–, Todd R. Klaenhammer Distinguished Scholar in Probiotics Research 2016–, Assoc. mem. Microbiology graduate program, Biotechnology graduate program, Functional Genomics graduate program, Center for Integrative Medicine; Founding Investor, Locus Biosciences; Co-Founder and mem. Scientific Advisory Bd, Intellia Therapeutics 2014–; Chair. Caribou BioSciences 2013–; Ed.-in-Chief, CRISPR journal 2017–; mem. American Soc. for Microbiology 2013–, Inst. of Food Technologists 2013–; mem. Editorial Bd Applied and Environmental Microbiology 2015–; Warren Alpert Foundation Prize 2016, Canada Gairdner Int. Award 2016, NAS award in Molecular Biology 2017, NAS prize in Food and Agriculture Sciences. *Achievements include:* established and characterized CRISPR-Cas bacterial immune defence system. *Address:* Department of Food, Bioprocessing and Nutrition Sciences, North Carolina State University, Raleigh, NC 27695-7624, USA (office). *Telephone:* (919) 513-1644 (office). *E-mail:* rbarran@ncsu.edu (office). *Website:* www.ncsu.edu (office).

BARRASSO, John Anthony, III, BS, MD; American orthopaedic surgeon and politician; *Senator from Wyoming;* b. 21 July 1952, Reading, Pa; m. 1st Linda Nix (divorced); m. 2nd Bobbi Brown; three c.; ed Georgetown Univ.; orthopaedic surgeon in pvt. practice, Casper, Wyo.; ran unsuccessfully for Republican nomination for Senator 1996, elected to Wyo. State Senate 2002, re-elected 2006, served as Chair. Transportation, Highways and Mil. Affairs Cttee, mem. Labor, Health and Social Services Cttee, Select Cttee on Legis. Tech., Dept of Health Advisory Council; apptd Senator from Wyo. (upon death of Senator Craig Thomas) 2007–, won a special election to fill the remaining four years of Thomas's term 2008, Chair. Senate Republican Policy Cttee 2013–, Senate Western Caucus, mem. Energy and Natural Resources Cttee, Environment and Public Works Cttee, Indian Affairs Cttee (Chair. 2015–), Senate Foreign Relations Cttee; Chief of Staff Wyo. Medical Center; State Pres. Wyo. Medical Soc.; Pres. Nat. Asscn of Physician Broadcasters; mem. American Medical Asscn Council of Ethics and Judicial Affairs; physician for Professional Rodeo Cowboys' Asscn; mem. Bd of Dirs Presidential Classroom; mem. Casper Chamber of Commerce, Casper Rotary Club; Republican; Wyo. Physician of the Year, Wyo. Nat. Guard Medal of Excellence, Veterans of Foreign Wars Legislative Service Award. *Publications:* Keeping Wyoming Healthy, Caring for Wyoming's Seniors newspaper columns. *Address:* 307 Dirksen Senate Office Building, Washington, DC 20510 (office); 100 East B Street, Suite 2201, PO Box 22201, Casper, WY 82602, USA (office). *Telephone:* (202) 224-6441 (DC) (office); (307) 261-6413 (Casper) (office). *Fax:* (202) 224-1724 (office). *Website:* www.barrasso.senate.gov/public (office).

BARRAULT, Marie-Christine; French actress; b. 21 March 1944, Paris; d. of Max-Henri Barrault and Marthe Valmier; m. 1st Daniel Toscan de Plantier (divorced); one s. one d.; m. 2nd Roger Vadim 1990 (died 2000); ed Conservatoire national d'art dramatique; Officier, ordre des Arts et des Lettres, Officier, Legion d'honneur. *Theatre includes:* Andorra, Othon, Un couple pour l'hiver, Travail à domicile, Conversation chez les Stein sur Monsieur de Goethe absent, Dylan, cet animal étrange, Partage du midi, L'Etrange intermède, Même heure l'année prochaine, Enfin seuls!, La Cerisaie, Le bonheur des autres, Qui a peur de Virginia Woolf?, La mènagerie de verre, Barrage contre le pacifique. *Films include:* Ma nuit chez Maude 1966, Le distrait 1970, Cousin, cousine 1975 (Prix Louis Delluc), Du côté des tennis 1976, L'état sauvage 1978, Femme entre chien et loup 1978, Ma chérie 1979, Stardust Memories 1980, L'amour trop fort 1981, Un amour en Allemagne 1983, Les mots pour le dire 1983, Un amour de Swann 1984, Pianoforte 1985, Le jupon rouge 1987, Adieu je t'aime 1988, Sanguines 1988, Prisonnières 1988, Un été d'orage 1989, Dames galantes 1990, L'amour nécessaire 1991, Bonsoir 1994, C'est la tangente que je préfère 1997, La dilettante 1999, Azzurro 2000, Berlin Niagara 2000, Les amants de Mogador 2002, L'empreinte de l'ange 2004. *Musical:* L'homme rêvé 2000. *Television includes:* Marie Curie (series; Nymphe d'argent, Monte Carlo TV Festival 1991, 7 d'Or for best comedienne 1991), Le vieil ours et l'enfant 2001, Garonne (mini-series) 2002, Le don fait à Catchaires 2003, La deuxième vérité 2003, Rêves en France 2003, Droit d'asile 2003, Saint-Germain ou La négociation 2003, L'empreinte de l'ange 2004, Parlez-moi d'amour

2005, Ange de feu (mini-series) 2006. *Publication:* Le Cheval dans la pierre 1999. *Address:* c/o Babette Pouget, 10 avenue George V, 75008 Paris, France.

BARRÉ-SINOUSSI, Françoise Claire, DèsSc; French scientist; *Director, Retroviral Infections Unit, Institut Pasteur;* b. 30 July 1947, Paris; d. of Roger Sinoussi and Jeanine Fau; m. Jean-Claude Barré 1978; ed Lycée Bergson, Faculty of Science, Paris VII and Paris VI; Research Asst, Inst. nat. de la Santé et de la recherche médicale (Inserm) 1975–80, Researcher 1980–86, Dir of Research 1986–; Head of Lab., Biology of Retroviruses Unit, Inst. Pasteur 1988–92, Dir Retroviral Infections Unit 1993–; Co-Chair. UN Panel on AIDS Prevention; Pres. Int. AIDS Soc. 2012– (mem. Governing Council 2006–); Chevalier, Ordre nat. du Mérite; Officer, Légion d'honneur 2006, Grand Officer 2013; Hon. DSc (Tulane Univ.) 2009; Prize of Fondation Körber pour la promotion de la Science européenne 1986, Prize of Acad. de médecine 1988, King Faisal Int. Prize for Medicine 1993, Prix du Rayonnement Français 2003, Nobel Prize in Physiology or Medicine (jtly) 2008; inducted into Women in Tech. Int. Hall of Fame 2006, Georgia Research Alliance Pioneer Award 2011. *Publications include:* more than 200 scientific publs including co-author of publ. in Science that first reported discovery of a retrovirus later named HIV 1983. *Leisure interests:* theatre, reading. *Address:* Régulation des Infections Rétrovirales, Institut Pasteur, 25–28 rue du Docteur Roux, 75724 Paris Cedex 15, France (office). *Telephone:* 1-45-68-87-33 (office). *Fax:* 1-45-68-89-57 (office). *E-mail:* francoise.barre-sinoussi@pasteur.fr (office). *Website:* www.pasteur.fr (office).

BARREIRO, Magdalena, PhD; Ecuadorean academic and government official; b. 1954; ed Escuela Politécnica del Ejército, Massachusetts Inst. of Tech. Sloan School of Man., Illinois Inst. of Tech.; Financial Sector Coordinator, Cen. Bank of Ecuador 1992–96; Econ. and Financial Adviser, Nat. Council for State Modernization and Privatization 1997–98; Prof. and Dean of Finance, Universidad San Francisco de Quito 2000–05, 2006–; apptd Deputy Minister for Economy and Finance 2005, Minister of Economy and Finance Aug.–Dec. 2005; currently local partner (Ecuador), GlobalSource Partners, also ind. consultant. *Address:* GlobalSource Partners, 708 Third Avenue, 18th Floor Suite 1801, New York, NY 10017, USA (office). *Telephone:* (212) 317-8015 (office). *Fax:* (212) 317-8318 (office). *E-mail:* info@globalsourcepartners.com (office). *Website:* www.globalsourcepartners.com (office).

BARRERA, Marco Antonio; Mexican boxer; b. 17 Jan. 1974, Iztacalco; m.; one s.; professional flyweight boxing debut age 15; winner Super Flyweight Title, Mexico 1992, 1993, NABF Super Flyweight Title 1993, WBO Super Bantamweight Title 1995–96, 1998–2001; Ring Featherweight Title, WBC Super Featherweight Title 2004–07, IBF Super Featherweight Title 2005–06; 74 fights, 66 wins, seven losses, 43 knockouts; commentator ESPN Deportes' weekly boxing show Golpe a Golpe 2009–; inducted into Int. Boxing Hall of Fame, Canastota, New York 2011. *Website:* www.marcobarrera.com.

BARRETO OTAZÚ, César Amado, MA; Paraguayan economist and politician; ed Universidad Nacional de Asunción, Pontificia Universidad Católica de Chile; with Entidad Binacional Itaipú 1988–94; Econ. Adviser, Nat. Econ. Equipment, Ministry of Finance 1997–98; Product Man., Cash Man. and Trade, Citibank NA, Paraguay Br. 1998–2000; Founding Partner, Macroanálisis Consultora 1999; Project Man., Hutchison Telecom Paraguay SA Jan.–Oct. 2001, Gen. Man. 2001–02, Exec. Dir 2002–05; Exec. Dir Devt in Democracy 2004–05; Pres. Directory and Gen. Man. Agencia Financiera de Desarrollo 2005–07; Minister of Finance 2007–08; Dir, Banco Familiar; fmr Prof. of Int. Economy and Master's Programme in Economy and Finances, Universidad Católica de Asunción. *Address:* c/o Banco Familiar, Asunción, Paraguay.

BARRETT, Colleen C.; American airline industry executive; *President Emeritus, Southwest Airlines Co.;* b. 14 Sept. 1944, Bellows Falls, Vt; m. (divorced); one s.; ed Becker Jr Coll., Worcester, Mass; Exec. Asst to Herb Kelleher (Southwest Airlines founder) at his law firm –1978; joined Southwest Airlines Co. 1978, Corp. Sec. 1978–2008, Vice-Pres. Admin 1986–90, Exec. Vice-Pres. Customer Services 1990–2001, Pres. 2001–08, now Emer.; mem. Bd of Dirs Better Business Bureau of Metropolitan Dallas Inc. 2002–, JCPenney Co. Inc. 2004–; mem. Advisory Bd Ken Blanchard Coll. of Business 2006–; Trustee, Becker Coll. 2006–; mem. Int. Women's Forum 1985–, Dallas Forum 1990–; mem. Hon. Bd of Advisors, Nat. Soc. of High School Scholars 2003–; numerous awards and honours including The Most Powerful Woman in Travel, Travel Agent Magazine, Top Women Execs, Women's Enterprise 1999, Tex. Business Woman of the Year, Tex. Women's Chamber of Commerce 2001, America's Most Powerful Business Women, Fortune Magazine 2001, Kupfer Distinguished Exec. Award 2002, Women's Leadership Exchange Compass Award 2002, Best Managers, BusinessWeek 2002, Distinguished Women's Award, Northwood Univ. 2003, Horatio Alger Award 2005. *Address:* c/o Southwest Airlines, PO Box 36647-ICR, Dallas, TX 75235-1647, USA (office).

BARRETT, Craig R., BS, MS, PhD; American computer industry executive; b. 29 Aug. 1939, San Francisco, Calif.; m. Barbara Barrett; one s. one d.; ed Stanford Univ.; Assoc. Prof., Dept of Materials Science and Eng, Stanford Univ. 1964–74; NATO Postdoctoral Fellowship, Nat. Physical Lab., England 1964–65; Fulbright Fellowship, Tech. Univ. of Denmark 1972; joined Intel Corpn as a Tech. devt man. 1974, Vice-Pres. 1984–87, Sr Vice-Pres. 1987–90, Exec. Vice-Pres. 1990–92, mem. Bd Dirs 1992–, COO 1993–97, Pres. 1997–2005, CEO 1998–2005, Chair. 2005–09; Chair. UN Global Alliance for Information and Communication Technologies and Devt –2009; Co-Chair. Business Coalition for Student Achievement, Nat. Innovation Initiative Leadership Council, Achieve, Inc.; Pres. and Chair. BASIS School, Inc.; apptd to Pres.'s Advisory Cttee for Trade Policy and Negotiations and to American Health Information Community; apptd by Pres. Obama as one of pvt. sector leaders for a nat. educ. science, tech., eng and math. (STEM) initiative now known as Change The Equation 2010; apptd by Pres. of Russian Fed. as Int. Co-Chair. to lead the Bd of the Fund for Devt of the Center for Elaboration and Commercialization of New Technologies; fmr mem. Nat. Govs' Asscn Task Force on Innovation America, Nat. Infrastructure Advisory Council, Cttee on Scientific Communication and Nat. Security, US-Brazil CEO Forum; mem. Bd Dirs Society for Science and the Public, Dossia, Nat. Forest Foundation (Vice-Chair.), Science Foundation Arizona; fmr mem. Bd Dirs US Semiconductor Industry Asscn, Nat. Action Council for Minorities in Eng, TechNet; mem. Bd of Trustees US Council for Int. Business, Advisory Bd Clinton Global Initiative Educ., Advisory Bd Peter G. Peterson Foundation, Arizona Commerce Authority Bd, faculty of Thunderbird School of Global Man.; mem. and fmr Chair. Nat. Acad. of Eng; Hon. Chair. Irish Tech. Leadership Group; Hardy Gold Medal, American Inst. of Mining and Metallurgical Engineers. *Publications:* Principles of Engineering Materials; more than 40 tech. papers on the influence of the microstructure of materials. *Leisure interests:* hiking, skiing, horse riding, cycling, fly-fishing. *Address:* c/o Intel Corporation, 2200 Mission College Boulevard, Santa Clara, CA 95052-1537, USA. *E-mail:* info@intel.com.

BARRETT, George S., BA, MBA; American business executive; *Chairman and CEO, Cardinal Health Inc.;* ed Brown Univ., New York Univ.; served in various positions with NMC Laboratories 1981–91, served as Pres. from 1988 through its acquisition by Alpharma Inc., Pres. Barre National (subsidiary of Alpharma Inc.) 1991–94, Pres. Alpharma's US pharmaceutical group 1994–97; Pres. and CEO Diad Research (tech. start-up based at Johns Hopkins School of Medicine) 1997–98; Pres. Teva USA 1998–2005, Pres. and CEO Teva North America and Group Vice-Pres. (North America) 2005–06, Pres. and CEO Teva North America and Exec. Vice-Pres. (Global Pharmaceutical Markets) and mem. Office of the CEO of Teva Pharmaceutical Industries Ltd 2006–08; Vice-Chair. Cardinal Health Inc. and CEO Healthcare Supply Chain Services Jan.–Aug. 2009, Chair. and CEO Cardinal Health Inc. Aug. 2009–; mem. Bd of Dirs IVAX Corpn 2006–; mem. Business Advisory Bd Cera Products, Inc.; mem. Bd and fmr Chair. Generic Pharmaceutical Industry Asscn; mem. Bd American Foundation for Pharmaceutical Educ., Univ. of Maryland School of Pharmacy; Distinguished Alumni Award of Excellence in Global Business, New York Univ. Stern School of Business, Ellis Island Medal of Honor. *Address:* Cardinal Health Inc., 7000 Cardinal Place, Dublin, OH 43017, USA (office). *Telephone:* (614) 757-5000 (office). *Fax:* (614) 757-8871 (office). *E-mail:* info@cardinal.com (office). *Website:* www.cardinal.com (office).

BARRETT, Matthew W., OC, LLD; Irish/Canadian banker; b. 20 Sept. 1944, Co. Kerry, Ireland; m. 1st Irene Korsak 1967 (divorced 1995); four c.; m. 2nd Anne-Marie Sten 1997 (divorced); ed Harvard Business School; joined Bank of Montreal, London, UK 1962; moved to Canada 1967; Vice-Pres. Man. Services, Bank of Montreal 1978, Vice-Pres. BC Div. 1979, Sr Vice-Pres. Eastern and Northern Ont. 1980, Sr Vice-Pres. and Deputy Gen. Man. Int. Banking Group 1981, Sr Vice-Pres. and Deputy Group Exec. Treasury Group 1984, Exec. Vice-Pres. and Group Exec. Personal Banking 1985, Pres. and COO 1987, CEO 1989–99, Chair. 1990–99; Group CEO Barclays plc 1999–2004, Chair. 2004–06; mem. Bd of Dirs Harry Winston Diamond Corpn 2008–13, Goldman Sachs Bank USA 2009–, Samuel, Son & Co. Ltd 2009–, Samuel Manu-Tech Inc. 2009–, Joseph E. Seagram & Sons, Inc.; Trustee, First Canadian Mortgage Fund; fmr Gov. London Business School; mem. Int. Advisory Bd Nat. Bank of Kuwait; Hon. Dir Bank of Montreal; Hon. LLD (St Mary's Univ., Halifax, NS, York Univ., Ont., Concordia Univ., Univ. of Waterloo, Acadia Univ.); Hon. DCL (Bishop's Univ.) 1993; Canadian Catalyst Prize, Canada's Outstanding CEO of the Year 1995, Harvard Business School Alumni Achievement Award 1997, Communicator of the Year Award, British Asscn of Communicators in Business 2001. *Leisure interests:* fly-fishing, tennis, reading.

BARRIE, George Napier, BA, LLD; South African professor of law and advocate; *Special Professor, Faculty of Law and Researcher, Centre for the Study of International Law in Africa, University of Johannesburg;* b. 10 Sept. 1940, Pietersburg; m. Marie Howell 1970; two s. one d.; ed Pretoria Univ., Univ. of South Africa and Univ. Coll., London, UK; State Advocate, Supreme Court 1964–69; Sr Law Adviser, Dept of Foreign Affairs 1970–80; Prof. of Int. and Constitutional Law, Rand Afrikaans Univ. 1981–, Dean Faculty of Law 2001–04; Visiting Prof., Free Univ. of Brussels 1992; Leader of S African del. to numerous int. confs; mem. S African del. to Int. Bar Asscn Conf. 1984, Nat. Council on Correctional Services 1996–; Special Prof., Faculty of Law and Researcher, Centre for Study of Int. Law in Africa, Univ. of Johannesburg 2005–. *Publications include:* Topical International Law 1979, Self-Determination in Modern International Law 1995 and numerous works and articles on int. and constitutional law; co-author: Nuclear Non-Proliferation: The Why and the Wherefore 1985, Constitutions of Southern Africa 1985, Law of South Africa 1986, Law of the Sea 1987, Bill of Rights Compendium 1996, Managing African Conflicts 2000. *Leisure interests:* long distance running, long distance cycling. *Address:* Faculty of Law, University of Johannesburg, PO Box 524, Auckland Park, Johannesburg 2006, South Africa (office). *Telephone:* (11) 7044376 (home). *Fax:* (11) 5592027 (office); (11) 7044376 (home). *E-mail:* barriegm@telkomsa.net. *Website:* www.uj.ac.za (office).

BARRINGTON, Edward John, BA, MA; Irish civil servant and diplomatist; b. 26 July 1949, Dublin; m. Clare O'Brien 1972; one s.; ed Univ. Coll. Dublin; Third Sec. Dept of Foreign Affairs, EC Div. 1971–73, First Sec. 1973–75, First Sec. EC Perm. Rep. Office, Brussels 1975–80, First Sec. Press Section, HQ Aug.–Dec. 1980, Counsellor Political Div., HQ 1980–85, Asst Sec.-Gen. Admin. Div., HQ 1985–89, Asst Sec.-Gen. EC Div., HQ 1989–91, Asst Sec.-Gen. Political Div. and Political Dir, HQ 1991–95, Deputy Sec. 1995; Amb. to UK 1995–2001; currently Hon. Prof., Research Inst. for Irish and Scottish Studies, Univ. of Aberdeen, UK; Visiting Research Fellow, Inst. for British-Irish Studies, Univ. Coll. Dublin; Hon. DUniv (Univ. of North London) 2001. *Leisure interests:* cinema, hiking, jazz, theatre. *Address:* Sun Villa, Mauritius Town, Rosslare Strand, Co. Wexford, Ireland (home). *Telephone:* (53) 32880 (home).

BARRINGTON, Sir Nicholas John, KCMG, CVO, MA, FRSA; British diplomatist; b. 23 July 1934; s. of Eric A. Barrington and Mildred Bill; ed Repton School and Clare Coll., Cambridge; joined HM Diplomatic Service 1957, served in Kabul 1959, UK Del. to European Communities, Brussels 1963, Rawalpindi 1965, Tokyo 1972–75, Cairo 1978–81, Minister and Head, British Interests Section, Tehran 1981–83, Extra Amb. to UN, New York 1983; Coordinator for G7 London Summit 1984; Asst Under-Sec. of State, FCO 1984–87, Amb. to Pakistan 1987–89, High Commr 1989–94, also Amb. (non-resident) to Afghanistan 1994; Trustee, Ancient India and Iran Trust, Cambridge 1992–; served on various bodies linking Britain with Asia and Christianity with Islam; Hon. Fellow, Clare Coll. Cambridge 1992; Order of the Sacred Treasure, Japan 1975. *Publications:* A Passage to Nuristan 2005; memoirs: Envoy 2013, Nicholas Meets Barrington 2013. *Leisure interests:* theatre, drawing, prosopography, Persian poetry. *Address:* 2 Banhams Close, Cambridge, CB4 1HX, England (home). *Telephone:* (1223) 360802 (home).

BARRINGTON-WARD, Rt Rev. Simon, KCMG, BA, MA; British ecclesiastic; *Honorary Assistant Bishop of Ely;* b. 27 May 1930, London; s. of Robert McGowan Barrington-Ward and Margaret A. Radice; m. Dr Jean Caverill Taylor 1963; two d.; ed Eton Coll., Magdalene Coll. Cambridge and Westcott House, Cambridge; ordained, diocese of Ely 1956; Chaplain, Magdalene Coll. Cambridge 1956–60; Lecturer, Ibadan Univ. Nigeria 1960–63; Fellow and Dean of Chapel, Magdalene Coll. Cambridge 1963–69, Hon. Fellow 1991–, Hon. Asst Chaplain 1999–; Prin., Church Missionary Soc. Coll., Selly Oak, Birmingham 1969–74; Gen. Sec. Church Missionary Soc. 1974–85; Canon, Derby Cathedral 1975–85; Chaplain to HM The Queen 1983–85; Bishop of Coventry 1985–97; Chair. Int. and Devt Affairs Cttee, Gen. Synod of Church of England 1986–96; Prelate to the Most Distinguished Order of St Michael and St George 1989–2005; apptd Asst Bishop of Ely 1997, now Hon. Asst Bishop; Hon. Fellow in Residence, Magdalene Coll., Cambridge 1977, Hon. Asst Chaplain 1999; Hon. DD (Wycliffe Coll. Toronto) 1983, Hon. DLitt (Warwick Univ.) 1988, Dr hc (Anglia-Ruskin Univ., Cambridge) 2008. *Publications:* Love Will Out 1988, Christianity Today 1988, The Weight of Glory 1991, Why God? 1993, The Jesus Prayer 1996, Praying the Jesus Prayer Together 2001, revised edn 2008; articles and book chapters. *Leisure interests:* hill walking, music, cycling, calligraphy. *Address:* 4 Searle Street, Cambridge, CB4 3DB, England. *Telephone:* (1223) 740460. *E-mail:* sb292@cam.ac.uk.

BARRIOS DE CHAMORRO, Violeta; Nicaraguan politician, publisher and fmr head of state; *President, Fundación Violeta Chamorro;* b. 18 Oct. 1929, Rivas; m. Pedro Joaquín Chamorro (died 1978) 1950; two s. two d.; ed Our Lady of the Lake Catholic School, San Antonio and Blackstone Coll., USA; mem. and Dir Sociedad Interamericana de Prensa 1978–89, Prensa Freedom Comm. 1978–89; Pres. and Dir-Gen. La Prensa (daily newspaper) 1978–89; Nat. Opposition Union cand. for Pres. 1989–90; Pres. of Nicaragua 1990–97, also Minister of Nat. Defence 1990; Founder and Pres. Fundación Violeta Chamorro; Grand Cross of the Order of Isabel la Católica (Spain) 1991, Grand Collar of the Order of the Aztec Eagle (Mexico) 1993, Grand Cross of the Order of Merit (Germany) 1996; six hon. degrees including Hon. LLD (American Univ., Washington, DC) 1997; Hon. DH (Catholic Univ. of Nicaragua Redemptores Mater) 1995; Dr hc (American Univ., Managua) 1998, (Univ. for Peace, Costa Rica) 1999; numerous nat. and int. awards including Louis Lyon Prize, Harvard Univ. 1986, American Soc. Gold Ensign Award 1990, Int. Rescue Cttee Freedom Award 1990, Int. Peace Asscn Woman for Peace Award 1990, Pan-American Devt Foundation Inter-american Leadership Award 1991, Lutheran Univ. of Calif. Thomas Wade Landry Award 1991, The Path to Peace Foundation Award 1997. *Publication:* Dreams of the Heart (autobiog.) 1996. *Address:* Fundación Violeta Chamorro, Plaza España, Edificio Málaga, Módulo B-9, Managua, Nicaragua (office). *Telephone:* (2) 68-6500 (office). *Fax:* (2) 68-6502 (office). *E-mail:* violetabch@ibw.com.ni (office). *Website:* www.violetachamorro.org.ni (office).

BARRO, Robert Joseph, PhD; American economist and academic; *Paul M. Warburg Professor of Economics, Harvard University;* b. 28 Sept. 1944, New York; m. Rachel McCleary; four c.; ed Harvard Univ., California Inst. of Tech.; Asst Prof., Brown Univ. 1968–72, Assoc. Prof. of Econs 1972–73; Visiting Assoc. Prof., Univ. of Chicago 1972–73, Assoc. Prof. 1973–75, Prof. of Econs 1982–84; Prof., Univ. of Rochester 1975–78, John Munro Prof. of Econs 1978–82, Distinguished Prof. of Arts and Sciences 1984–87; Prof. of Econs, Harvard Univ. 1987–95, Robert C. Waggoner Prof. 1995–2004, Paul M. Warburg Prof. of Economics 2004–; Research Assoc., Nat. Bureau of Economic Research 1978–; Fellow, Hoover Inst., Stanford Univ. 1977–78, 1989–90, 1993–94, Sr Fellow 1995–; Visiting Prof., UCLA 1986; Viewpoint Columnist, Business Week magazine 1998–2006; Co-Ed. Quarterly Journal of Economics 2004–; Academic Advisor, New York Fed. Reserve Bank 2006–; Pres. Western Econ. Asscn 2002–05; Vice-Pres. American Econ. Asscn 1998; mem. Mont Pelerin Soc. 1990–; Hoover Inst. Nat. Fellowship 1977–78; John Simon Guggenheim Memorial Fellowship 1982–83; Fellow, Econometric Soc. 1980–; mem. American Acad. of Arts and Sciences 1988–; Houblon-Norman Fellow, Bank of England 1994–95; Hon. Prof., Wuhan Univ. 2003, Seoul National Univ. 2003, Tsinghua Univ. 2005; Hon. Dean, China Econs and Man. Acad., Cen. Univ. of Beijing 2006; Dr hc (Universidad Francisco Marroquin); Frank Paish Lecturer, Meeting of Royal Econ. Soc., Oxford, 1985; Henry Thornton Lecturer, City Univ. Business School, London 1987; Horowitz Lecturer, Israel 1988; Lionel Robbins Lecturer, LSE 1996, ranked by the Research Papers in Economics project as the third most influential economist in the world 2013. *Publications include:* Money, Employment and Inflation (co-author) 1976, The Impact of Social Security on Private Savings: Evidence from the US Time Series 1978, Money, Expectations, and Business Cycles 1981, Macroeconomics 1984, Macroeconomic Policy 1990, European Macroeconomics (co-author) 1994, Canadian Macroeconomics (co-author) 1994, Economic Growth (co-author) 1995, Getting it Right: Markets and Choice in a Free Society 1996, Determinants of Economic Growth: A Cross-Country Empirical Study 1997, Currency Unions (co-ed.) 2001, Nothing Is Sacred: Economic Ideas for the New Millennium 2002, Macroeconomics: A Modern Approach 2008; numerous articles in journals. *Address:* Littauer Center 218, 1805 Cambridge Street, Harvard University, Cambridge, MA 02138 (office); 183 Kings Grant Road, Weston, MA 02493, USA (home). *Telephone:* (617) 495-3203 (office); (781) 894-8184 (home). *Fax:* (617) 496-8629 (office); (781) 894-4521 (home). *E-mail:* rbarro@harvard.edu (office). *Website:* scholar.harvard.edu/barro (office); rbarro.com.

BARRON, Eric J., BS, MS, PhD; American geologist, oceanographer, academic and university administrator; *President, Pennsylvania State University;* b. 26 Oct. 1951, Lafayette, Ind.; m. Molly Barron; two c.; ed Florida State Univ., Univ. of Miami; Cray Supercomputing Fellowship, Nat. Center for Atmospheric Research, Boulder, Colo 1976, Postdoctoral Research Fellow 1980, Scientist, Climate Section 1981–85, Dir 2008–10; Assoc. Prof., Univ. of Miami 1985–86; Dir Earth System Science Center and Assoc. Prof. of Geosciences, Pennsylvania State Univ. 1986–89, Prof. of Geosciences 1989–2006, Dir Earth and Mineral Sciences Environment Inst. 1998–2003, Distinguished Prof. of Geosciences 1999–2006, Dean, Coll. of Earth and Mineral Sciences 2002–06, Trustee, Univ. Corpn for Atmospheric Research 2002–06; Jackson Chair in Earth System Science and Dean, Jackson School of Geosciences, Univ. of Texas at Austin 2006–08; Dir National Center for Atmospheric Research, Boulder, Colo 2008–10; Pres. Florida State Univ. 2010–14, Pennsylvania State Univ. 2014–; mem. Bd of Govs Jt Oceanographic Insts, Inc. 2003–; Ed.-in-Chief Palaeogeography, Palaeoclimatology, Palaeoecology 1985–91, Earth Interactions (electronic journal) 1995–99; Ed. Global and Planetary Change 1988–96; Assoc. Ed. Journal of Climate 1989–95; mem. Editorial Bd Geology 1982–89, Palaeogeography, Palaeoclimatology, Palaeoecology 1984–85, 1992–, Geotimes 1994–96, Consequences 1994–2000, Global Change Encyclopedia 1998; Chair. Nat. Research Council (NRC) Climate Research Cttee 1990–96, Co-Chair. Bd on Atmospheric Sciences 1997–99, Chair. 1999; mem. NRC Cttee on Global Change Research, Assessment of NASA Post-2000 Plans, Climate Change Science, Human Dimensions of Global Change, Panel on Grand Environmental Challenges, Cttee on Tools for Tracking Chemical, Biological, and Nuclear Releases in the Atmosphere: Implications for Homeland Security; fmr Chair. Science Exec. Cttee for NASA's Earth Observing System and NASA's Earth Science and Applications Advisory Cttee, US Global Change Research Program Forum on Climate Modeling, Allocation Panel for the Interagency Climate Simulation Lab., US Nat. Cttee for PAGES, NSF Earth System History Panel; mem. American Geophysical Union (Chair. Selection Cttee, Ed. Paleoceanography, Biogeochemical Cycles 1995, 1997) 1991; Fellow, American Geophysical Union, American Meteorological Soc. 1995, AAAS 2004, Geological Soc. of America; Fellow, Nat. Inst. for Environmental Science, Univ. of Cambridge, UK 2002; Texaco Fellow 1975–77, Outstanding Student Award, Miami Geological Soc. 1977–78, Koczy Fellowship (most outstanding student in last year of study) 1979–80, Smith Prize (most creative dissertation) 1980, Excellence of Presentation Award, Soc. of Econ. Paleontologists and Mineralogists 1988, Hon. Mention for Excellence of Presentation Award, Soc. of Econ. Paleontologists and Mineralogists 1989, Wilson Research Award, Coll. of Earth and Mineral Sciences, Pennsylvania State Univ. 1992, Provost Award for Collaborative Instruction and Curricular Innovations 1992, 1993, Excellence of Presentation Award, Soc. of Sedimentary Geology (SEPM) 1993, American Geophysical Union Fellow 1993, Hon. Mention for Excellence of Presentation (Poster), American Asscn of Petroleum Geologists 1993, Distinguished Lecturer, American Asscn of Petroleum Geologist 1997, Wilson Teaching Award, Coll. of Earth and Mineral Sciences 1999, NASA Outstanding Earth Science Educ. Product (Discover Earth: Earth-as-a-System) 1999, NASA Group Achievement Award for Research Strategy for the Earth Science Enterprise 2001, Frontiers in Geophysics Lecturer, American Geophysical Union 2002, NASA Distinguished Public Service Medal 2003. *Publications:* numerous scientific papers in professional journals on climatology, numerical modelling and Earth history. *Address:* Office of the President, Pennsylvania State University, 201 Old Main University Park, PA 16802, USA (office). *Telephone:* (814) 865-7611 (office). *Fax:* (814) 863-8583 (office). *E-mail:* president@psu.edu (office). *Website:* president.psu.edu (office).

BARROS, Rui Duarte; Guinea-Bissau economist and politician; b. 1964; Minister of Employment and Civil Service 2001, of Economy and Finance 2002; Commr responsible for Dept of Admin. and Financial Affairs, Econ. Community of West African States (ECOWAS) 2006–08, for Dept of Social and Cultural Devt 2008–09, Acting Pres. of ECOWAS 2009; Prime Minister (in interim govt following coup) 2012–14; Conselho Africano e Malgaxe para o Ensino Superior (CAMES) Ordem Internacional das Palmas Académicas. *Address:* c/o Office of the Prime Minister, Av. dos Combatentes da Liberdade da Pátria, CP 137, Bissau, Guinea-Bissau (office).

BARROSO, José Manuel Durão, MPolSci; Portuguese academic, politician and fmr EU official; b. 23 March 1956, Lisbon; s. of Luís António Saraiva Barroso and Maria Elisabete de Freitas Durão; m. Maria Margarida Pinto Ribeiro de Sousa Uva; three s.; ed Univs of Lisbon and Geneva; mem. Maoist party after revolution in Portugal 1974; Lecturer, Faculty of Law, Univ. of Lisbon, Dept of Political Science, Univ. of Geneva; mem. Parl. 1985–; fmr Sec. of State for Home Affairs and for Foreign Affairs and Co-operation; Minister of Foreign Affairs 1992–95; mem. Nat. Council Social Democratic Party (PSD), apptd Leader 1999; Prime Minister of Portugal 2002–04 (resgnd); Chair. Comm. for Foreign Affairs 1995–96; Pres. European Comm. 2004–14, Vice-Pres. (ex officio) European People's Party (EPP) 2004–14; Head, Dept of Int. Relations, Univ. Lusíada 1995–99; Visiting Scholar, Georgetown Univ., Washington, DC, Visiting Prof. 1996–98; Hon. Citizen of Rio de Janeiro 2006; Hon. Citizen of Delphi and Golden Medal of the 'Amfiktyons', Delphi, Greece 2007; Hon. Medal and Hon. Diploma of the City of Nicosia, Cyprus 2008; Hon. mem. Academia Portuguesa da História, Lisbon 2008; Chave de Honra da Cidade de Lisboa 2008; Ciudadino Andino Honorifico, Lima, Peru 2008; Grand Cross, Order of Christ 1996; Grand Cross, Order of Vytautas the Great (Lithuania) 2007; State Medal 'Stara Planina' First Degree (Bulgaria) 2008; Order of the Cross of Terra Mariana, First Class (Estonia) 2009; Grand Cross, Order of the Netherlands Lion; Collar of the Order pro merito Melitensi (Civilian Class), Order of Malta, Rome 2010, Great Collar of the Order of Timor-Leste, Brussels 2010; Hon. DUniv (Roger Williams Univ., RI) 2005; Hon. DH (Georgetown Univ.) 2006; Hon. Dr rer. pol (Univ. of Genoa) 2006; Hon. DIur (Kobe Univ.) 2006; Hon. HEC diploma, Paris 2006; Hon. Doctorate in Social and Human Sciences (Candido Mendes Univ., Rio de Janeiro) 2006; Hon. DSc (Univ. of Edinburgh) 2006; Hon. Degree, Economics Faculty of 'La Sapienza' Univ. of Rome) 2007; Hon. LLD (Univ. of Liverpool) 2008; Hon. Dr of Public and Int. Affairs (Univ. of Pittsburgh) 2009; Dr hc (Warsaw School of Econs) 2007, (Pontifical Catholic Univ. of São Paulo) 2008, (Université Nice Sophia Antipolis) 2008, (Tomas Bata Univ., Zlin, Czech Repub.) 2009, (Chemnitz Univ. of Tech.) 2009, (Univ. Estácio de Sá, Rio de Janeiro) 2010, (Łódź Univ., Poland) 2010, (Univ. of Geneva) 2010, (Univ. of Bucharest) 2010, (Baku State Univ., Azerbaijan) 2011, (Luiss Guido Carli Univ., Rome) 2011, (Ghent Univ.) 2011; Casa da Imprensa Prize 1992, named Global Leader for Tomorrow by World Econ. Forum 1993, chosen as Personality of the Year by Foreign Press Asscn in Portugal 1991, 2004, Medalla de la Universidad de Alcala de Henares and Medalla de Oro de la Ciudad de Zamora (Spain) 2005, Golden Medal: The Bell Celebration—Message to the United Europe, Ferdinand Martinengo Co., Slovakia 2006, EFR-Business Week Award, Erasmus Univ. Rotterdam 2006, European of the Year Award, European Voice newspaper 2006, Special Prize, Business Centre Club, Poland 2007, Gold Medal of the City of Lamego, Portugal 2007, Transatlantic Leadership Prize, European Inst., Washington, DC 2007, Conde de Barcelona Int. Prize, Conde de Barcelona Foundation 2007, Prémio Rotary da Paz, Rotary International Distrito 1960, Portugal 2008, Confraria Queijo S. Jorge, Acores 2008, Transatlantic Business Award, American Chamber of Commerce to the EU, Brussels 2008, Prémio Política e Responsabilidade Social, Fundação Luso-Brasileira, Lisbon 2008, Gold Medal,

Royal Inst. of European Studies, Madrid 2009, Gold Medal of the Hellenic Parliament, Athens 2009, Medal of Honour and Benefaction of the City of Athens 2009, European Excellence Award, Govt Council of the Community of Madrid 2009, European of the Year, The European Movt in Denmark 2009, Quadriga Prize 2009, Medal of Merit, Federação das Associações Portuguesas e Luso-brasileiras, Brazil 2010, Man of the Year 2009 of Central and Eastern Europe, Krynica 2010, Golden Victoria European of the Year 2010 Award, Union of German Magazine Publrs VDZ, Berlin 2010, Collar of the European Merit Foundation, Luxembourg 2010, Steiger Award, Bochum, Germany 2011, Gold Medal for Outstanding contrib. to Public Discourse, Coll. Historical Soc. of Trinity Coll., Dublin 2011. *Publications include:* Governmental System and Party System (co-author) 1980, Le Système Politique Portugais face à l'Intégration Européenne 1983, Política de Cooperação 1990, A Política Externa Portuguesa 1992–93, A Política Externa Portuguesa 1994–95, Uma Certa Ideia de Europa 1999, Uma Ideia para Portugal 2000; several studies on political science and constitutional law in collective works, encyclopaedias and int. journals. *Address:* c/o Social Democratic Party, Rua de São Caetano 9, 1249-087 Lisbon Codex, Portugal.

BARROW, Adama; Gambian politician, business executive and head of state; *President;* b. 16 Feb. 1965, Mankamang Kunda, Fulladu East Dist; two wives, Fatou Barrow and Sarjo Barrow; five c.; fmr Sales Man., Alhaji Musa Njie (import co.); spent three and a half years working as security guard at Argos department store, London early 2000s; returned to The Gambia and f. Majum Real Estate 2006; Pres. of The Gambia 19 Jan. 2017–; mem. United Democratic Party (UDP), fmr Treasurer; Dr hc (Univ. of The Gambia) 2018. *Address:* Office of the President, PMB, State House, Banjul, The Gambia (office). *Telephone:* 4223811 (office). *E-mail:* info@statehouse.gm (office). *Website:* www.statehouse.gm (office).

BARROW, Dean Oliver, MA, LLM; Belizean politician; *Prime Minister and Minister of Finance;* b. 2 March 1951, Belize City; m. 1st Lois Young (divorced); three c.; m. 2nd Kim Simplis; one d.; ed Univ. of West Indies and Center for Advanced Int. Studies, Univ. of Miami, USA; elected to Belize City Council 1983; elected to Nat. Ass. (United Democratic Party—UDP) for Queen's Square 1984, Leader of the Opposition 1998–2008; Minister of Foreign Affairs and Econ. Devt 1984–89; Attorney-Gen. 1986–89; Deputy Prime Minister and Minister of Foreign Affairs and Nat. Security and Attorney-Gen. 1993–98, also Minister of Nat. Security, Immigration and Nationality Matters 1995; Prime Minister 2008–, also Minister of Finance 2008–, of Econ. Devt 2012, of Public Service, Energy and Public Utilities –2016, also apptd Minister of Home Affairs 2016; Deputy Leader UDP 1990, currently Leader; Partner, Barrow and Williams (law firm). *Address:* Office of the Prime Minister, Sir Edney Cain Building, 3rd Floor, Left Wing, Belmopan (office); United Democratic Party, South End Bel-China Bridge, POB 1898, Belize City, Belize (office). *Telephone:* 822-2346 (office); 227-2576 (UDP) (office). *Fax:* 822-0898 (office); 227-6441 (UDP) (office). *E-mail:* secretarypm@opm.gov.bz (office); info@udp.org.bz (office). *Website:* www.belize.gov.bz (office); www.udp.org.bz (office).

BARROW, John David, BSc, DPhil, FRS, FRAS, CPhys, FInstP; British astrophysicist and academic; *Professor of Mathematical Sciences and Dean of Clare Hall, University of Cambridge;* b. 29 Nov. 1952, London; s. of Walter Henry Barrow and Lois Miriam Barrow (née Tucker); m. Elizabeth Mary East 1975; two s. one d.; ed Van Mildert Coll., Durham Univ., Magdalen Coll., Oxford; Lindemann Fellow, Astronomy Dept, Univ. of California, Berkeley 1977–78, Miller Fellow, Physics Dept 1980–81; Jr Research Lecturer, Christ Church Coll. and Astrophysics Dept, Univ. of Oxford 1977–80; Lecturer, Astronomy Centre, Univ. of Sussex 1981, later Sr Lecturer, Prof. 1989–99, Dir Astronomy Centre 1995–99; Prof. of Math. Sciences, Univ. of Cambridge 1999–, Fellow, Clare Hall 1999–, Vice-Pres. 2004–07, Dean 2017–, Gresham Prof. of Astronomy 2003–07, Gresham Prof. Emer. of Astronomy, Gresham Coll. 2007–08, Gresham Prof. of Geometry 2008–12, Fellow, Gresham Coll. 2012–18; Gordon Godfrey Visiting Prof., Univ. of New South Wales 2000, 2003; First Eastern Visiting Cambridge Prof. (China and Hong Kong) 2005; Li Ka Shing Foundation Visiting Scholar (China and Hong Kong) 2006; Dir Millennium Math. Project 1999–; Pres. British Science Asscn (Physics and Astronomy Section) 2008–09, (Math. Section) 2011–12; mem. Int. Soc. for Science and Religion 2002, Academia Europea 2009; Titular mem. L'Acad. Internationale de Philosophie des Sciences 2009; Nuffield Fellow 1986–87, Leverhulme Royal Soc. Fellow 1992–93, PPARC Sr Fellow 1994–99; Hon. Prof., Nanjing Univ. 2005–; Hon. Citizen, Louisville, Ky 2006; Hon. Fellow, Van Mildert Coll., Durham 2015, Gresham Coll.; Hon. DSc (Hertfordshire) 1999, (Szczecin) 2007, (Durham) 2008, (Sussex) 2010, (South Wales) 2014; numerous awards, including Gifford Lecturer, Univ. of Glasgow 1988, Samuel Locker Prize 1989, Collingwood Lecture, Durham 1990, Spinoza Lecturer, Amsterdam 1993, George Darwin Lecturer, Royal Astronomical Soc. 1993, Elizabeth Spreadbury Lecturer, Univ. Coll. London 1993, Templeton Award 1995, Robert Boyle Memorial Lecturer, Oxford 1996, RSA Lecturer 1999, Kelvin Medal 1999, Tyndall Lecturer, Bristol 2001, Darwin Lecturer, Cambridge 2001, Whitrow Lecturer, Royal Astronomical Soc. 2002, Brasher Lecturer, Kingston 2002, Italgas Prize 2003, Hubert James Lecturer, Purdue 2004, Von Weizsäcker Lecturer, Hamburg 2004, McCrea Centenary Lecturer, Sussex 2004, Wood Memorial Lecturer, Newcastle 2005, Lacchini Prize 2005, Hamilton Lecturer, Dublin 2005, Queen's Anniversary Prize 2005, Templeton Prize 2006, Knight Lecturer, Bath 2006, Boyle Lecturer, St Mary-le-Bow 2007, Roscoe Lecturer, Liverpool 2007, Kallen Lecturer, Lund 2007, John D. Barrow Drama Room named in his honour at Cranbrook School, Kent 2007, Phillips Lecturer, Cardiff 2008, Si-Wei Lecturer, Nat. Chengchi Univ. 2008, Sciama Lecturer, Oxford and Trieste 2008, Faraday Medal, Royal Soc., London 2008, Faraday Prize Lecturer, Royal Soc., London 2009, Kelvin Medal and Prize, Inst. of Physics, London 2009, Gresham Prize, Gresham Coll., London 2009, Premio Oriente Science Prize, Colletti Foundation 2010, Merck-Serono Prize for Science and Literature, Merck-Serono 2011, Christopher Zeeman Medal, London Math. Soc. and IMA 2011, Antico Pignolo Prize 2012, Presidential Lecture, BSA Mathematics Section, Aberdeen 2012, McCrea Astronomy Lecture, Royal Irish Acad., Cork 2013, Annual Correspondents Day Lecture, Newton Inst., Cambridge 2014, IMO Lecture, Int. Mathematics Olympiad, Cape Town 2014, Enriques Lecture, Milan 2014, Dirac Gold Medal, Inst. of Physics 2015, Gold Medal of the Royal Astronomical Soc. 2016. *Play:* Infinities (Italian Theatre Prize, Premi Ubu 2002, Italgas Prize 2003) 2002, 2003, 2008, Valencia 2002. *Publications include:* The Left Hand of Creation 1983, L'Homme et le Cosmos 1984, The Anthropic Cosmological Principle 1986, The World Within the World 1988, Theories of Everything 1991, Perche il Mondo è Matematico? 1992, Pi in the Sky 1992, The Origin of the Universe 1994, The Artful Universe 1995, Impossibility 1998, Between Inner Space and Outer Space 1999, The Universe That Discovered Itself 2000, The Book of Nothing 2000, The Constants of Nature 2002, Science and Ultimate Reality (ed.) 2003, The Infinite Book 2005, The Artful Universe Expanded 2005, New Theories of Everything 2007, Cosmic Imagery 2008, 100 Essential Things You Didn't Know You Didn't Know 2008, The Book of Universes 2011, One Hundred Essential Things You Didn't Know You Didn't Know About Sport 2012, Mathletics 2013, One Hundred Essential Things You Didn't Know You Didn't Know About Maths and the Arts 2014. *Leisure interests:* athletics, books, theatre, writing. *Address:* Centre for Mathematical Sciences, University of Cambridge, Wilberforce Road, Cambridge, CB3 0WA, England (office). *Telephone:* (1223) 766696 (office). *E-mail:* j.d.barrow@damtp.cam.ac.uk (office). *Website:* www.damtp.cam.ac.uk/user/jdb34 (office); www.clarehall.cam.ac.uk/our-people/professor-john-d-barrow (office).

BARRY, Alpha, BA, MA; Burkinabè journalist and politician; *Minister of Foreign Affairs, Co-operation and Burkinabè Abroad;* b. 1 Jan. 1970, Niakara; m.; ed Univ. of Ouagadougou; journalist, Horizon FM 1992–94, Journal du Soir 1994–2000, Reuters Television 2002–04; journalist corresp., Jeune Afrique 2000–02, France 24 2009–12; Corresp., Radio France internationale (RFI), Burkina Faso, Niger, Ivory Coast, Nigeria 1997–2012; CEO Radio Omega (pvt. radio station), Ouagadougou 2008–; Special Adviser on communications to Pres. of Guinea Alpha Condé 2011–; Minister of Foreign Affairs, Co-operation and Burkinabè Abroad 2016–. *Address:* Ministry of Foreign Affairs and Regional Co-operation, rue 988, blvd du Faso, 03 BP 7038, Ouagadougou 03, Burkina Faso (office). *Telephone:* 50-31-80-17 (office). *Fax:* 50-30-87-92 (office). *E-mail:* mae@diplomatie.gov.bf (office). *Website:* www.mae.gov.bf (office).

BARRY, Nancy Marie, BA, MBA; American banking executive; *President, NBA Enterprise Solutions to Poverty;* b. 1949; ed Stanford Univ., Harvard Business School; joined World Bank 1975, various sr positions including Head of Global Industry Devt Div., Chair. Donor's Cttee on Small and Medium Enterprises, Founding mem. CGAP Policy Advisory Group; Pres. Women's World Banking 1990–2006, mem. Bd of Trustees 1981–; Social Entrepreneur in Residence, Harvard Business School 2006, advisor to Social Cos and Poverty initiative; f. Nancy Barry Assocs (NBA) 2006–, Founder and Pres. NBA Enterprise Solutions to Poverty 2006–; Chair. Donald A. Strauss Foundation; mem. Council on Foreign Relations; Founding mem. Advisory Bd Harvard Business School Social Enterprise Initiative; mem. Asia Soc. Asian Social Issues Cttee; Outstanding Women in Finance and Consulting, HBS Women's Student Asscn 2001, Forbes Exec. Women's Summit Trailblazer Award 2002, Kellogg-McKinsey Award for Distinguished Leadership 2004. *Address:* c/o Advisory Board, Social Enterprise Initiative, Loeb House, 3rd Floor, Soldiers Field, Boston, MA 02163, USA (office). *Telephone:* (617) 495-6421 (office). *Fax:* (617) 496-7416 (office). *Website:* www.hbs.edu/socialenterprise (office).

BARRYMORE, Drew; American film actress and producer; b. 22 Feb. 1975, Los Angeles, Calif.; d. of John Barrymore, Jr and Jaid Barrymore; m. 1st Jeremy Thomas 1994 (divorced 1995); m. 2nd Tom Green 2001 (divorced 2002); 3rd Will Kopelman 2012 (divorced 2016); appeared in dog food commercial 1976; film debut in TV movie Suddenly Love 1978; f. Flower Films (production co.); apptd Amb. for Hunger, WFP 2007. *Films include:* Altered States 1980, E.T.: The Extra-Terrestrial 1982, Irreconcilable Differences 1984, Firestarter 1984, Cat's Eye 1985, See You In The Morning 1988, Far From Home 1989, Motorama 1991, Guncrazy 1992, Poison Ivy 1992, Beyond Control: The Amy Fisher Story 1992, No Place to Hide 1993, Doppelganger 1993, Wayne's World 2 1993, Bad Girls 1994, Inside the Goldmine 1994, Boys On The Side 1995, Batman Forever 1995, Mad Love 1995, Scream 1996, Everyone Says I Love You 1996, All She Wanted 1997, Best Men 1997, Never Been Kissed (also producer) 1998, Home Fries 1998, The Wedding Singer 1998, Ever After 1998, Titan A.E. (voice) 2000, Charlie's Angels (also producer) 2000, Donnie Darko (also producer) 2001, Riding in Cars With Boys 2001, Confessions of a Dangerous Mind 2002, Duplex (also producer), So Love Returns (also producer), Charlie's Angels: Full Throttle (also producer) 2003, Fifty First Dates 2004, Fever Pitch (also producer) 2005, The Perfect Catch 2005, Music and Lyrics 2006, Lucky You 2007, He's Just Not That Into You (also exec. producer) 2009, Whip It (also dir) 2009, Everybody's Fine 2009, Going the Distance 2010, Big Miracle 2012, Blended 2014, Animal (exec. producer) 2014, Happy Camp (exec. producer) 2014, Miss You Already 2015. *Television includes:* Family Guy (voice) 2006–13, Tough Love (exec. producer) (series) 2009–13, Grey Gardens (Golden Globe for Best Performance by an Actress in a Mini-series or Motion Picture made for TV 2010, Screen Actors Guild Award) 2009, Charlie's Angels (exec. producer) (series) 2011, The Essentials (co-host) 2012–14, Knife Fight (exec. producer) (series) 2013–15, Santa Clarita Diet (also exec. producer) (series) 2017. *Address:* c/o Creative Artists Agency, 2000 Avenue of the Stars, Los Angeles, CA 90067, USA.

BARSALOU, Yves; French banking executive and wine producer; *Chairman, Crédit Foncier de Monaco;* b. 18 Sept. 1932, Bizanet; s. of Marcell Barsalou and Marie-Louise Salvan; m. Claire-Marie Vié 1955; two s.; ed Ecoles de Carcassonne et Narbonne; mem. Dept Centre of Young Farmers 1957–67; Pres. Caisse Locale de Crédit Agricole de Narbonne 1974–; mem. Cen. Cttee, then Vice-Pres. Caisse nat. du Crédit agricole (CNCA) 1981–88, Pres. 1988–2000, Chair. CNCA 1989, Vice-Pres. Fed. Nationale du Crédit Agricole (FNCA) 1992–2000, mem. Plenary Comm., Fed. nat. du Crédit agricole 1975–77, Dir 1977–81, Pres. 1982–92; Vice-Pres., Pres. Fed. Int. du Crédit Agricole (CiCa) 1993–2001, Vice-Pres. Bd Crédit Agricole Indosuez 1996–2001, Chair. Crédit Foncier de Monaco (owned by Crédit Agricole Group) 1999–; Chair. Domaines Listel SAS, theh Pres. Listel SA, Sète (wine producer) 2013–; mem. Bd of Dirs Elf Aquitaine Group 1994–, TotalFinaElf 2000–03; fmr mem. Bd of Dirs Total SA, Banco Espirito Santo SA; Hon. Chair. Credit Agricole; Commdr, Légion d'honneur, Mérite agricole. *Address:* Domaines Barsalou, 14, rue Jean-Jacques Rousseau, 11200 Bizanet, France; Crédit Foncier de Monaco, 11 Boulevard Albert 1er 98012 Monaco (office). *Telephone:* 93-10-20-00 (office). *Fax:* 93-10-23-50 (office). *Website:* www.cfm.mc (office); domainesbarsalou.com; www.listel.com (office).

BARSHCHEVSKY, Mikhail Yuryevich, LLD; Russian lawyer and government official; *Representative of the Government of the Russian Federation to the Constitutional Court, the Supreme Court and the Higher Arbitration Court;* b. 27 Dec. 1955, Moscow; m. Olga Barkalova; one d.; ed Moscow State Law Acad., All-Union Inst. of Law; legal consultant in Moscow butter factory 1973–79; Sr Legal Consultant, Dept of Trade, Reutov Town 1979–80; Founder, Head Moscow Lawyers 1991–, (Barschevsky and Partners Co. 1993–), defended Obshchaya Gazeta newspaper 1993, Oblik TV Co. 1997; TV arbiter, What? Where? When? 1997–; Prof., State Acad. of Law, Moscow State Jurists' Acad.; Govt Rep., Constitutional Court, Supreme Court, Higher Arbitration Court 2001–; Acting State Counsellor of the Russian Federation, Class 1 2002; Prof., Moscow State Academy of Law 2000, Chair. Advokatura and Notariate, Moscow Inst. of Econs, Politics and Law; joined Civilian Power Party 2006, Chair. High Council 2007–08; Pres. Moscow Int. Business Asscn 2012–; mem. Moscow City Bar 1980–; mem. Bd All Russian Co-ordination Council for Public-Political Union, Moscow Region 1999–; mem. Russian Acad. of Natural Sciences 1997, Russian Acad. of Lawyers, Moscow Collegiate of Advocates 1980–2001; Hon. Lawyer of the Russian Federation 2007; Advocate of Honour, Plevako Gold Medal 2000. *Publications:* seven books and over 100 legal publs. *Leisure interests:* theatre, chess, travelling. *Address:* Krasnopresnenskaya emb. 2, 103274 Moscow, Russia (office). *Telephone:* (495) 205-40-51 (office); (495) 605-53-29 (office). *Fax:* (495) 205-65-25 (office); (495) 605-52-43 (office). *E-mail:* duty_press@aprf.gov.ru (office). *Website:* www.government.ru (office).

BARSHEFSKY, Charlene, BA, JD; American lawyer and fmr government official; *Senior International Partner, Wilmer Cutler Pickering LLP;* b. 11 Aug. 1950, Chicago, IL; m.; two d.; ed Univ. of Wisconsin; Partner, Steptoe & Johnson (law firm), Washington, DC 1975–93; Deputy US Trade Rep. 1993–96, Acting US Trade Rep. April–Nov. 1996, US Trade Rep. 1997–2001; Sr Int. Partner, Wilmer Cutler Pickering LLP (law firm) 2001–; mem. Bd of Dirs American Express 2001–, Estée Lauder Cos 2001–, Idenix Pharmaceuticals Inc. 2002–, Starwood Hotels & Resorts Worldwide Inc. 2001–, Intel Corpn 2004–; mem. Bd America China Soc. of Indiana (ACSI); numerous hon. degrees; Lifetime Achievement Award, Chambers & Partners 2007. *Address:* Wilmer Cutler Pickering LLP, 1875 Pennsylvania Avenue, NW, Washington, DC 20006, USA (office). *Telephone:* (202) 663-6130 (office). *E-mail:* charlene.barshefsky@wilmerhale.com (office). *Website:* www.wilmerhale.com (office).

BARSKIY, Maxim, MSc (Econs); Russian business executive; *CEO, Matra Petroleum;* b. 1974; ed Leningrad State Univ., State University of St Petersburg, Univ. of California, Berkeley, USA; held series of trading and investment banking positions at Troika Dialog (investment co.) during late 1990s; performed duties of Corp. Devt Dir at Cityline, Man. Dir at Salford Continental Inc. (investment fund) and Sr Investment Dir at Finartis 2000–04; mem. Bd of Dirs West Siberian Resources Ltd 2004, Man. Dir 2004–08, worked as Gen. Dir for WSR Invest –2008; Investment Dir at rep. office of Alltech Investments Ltd 2009; Exec. Vice-Pres., Strategy and New Business Devt, TNK-BP May–Dec. 2009, Deputy CEO TNK-BP 2009–11; CEO and Man. Dir Matra USA 2013–, mem. Bd of Dirs and Man. Dir Matra Petroleum AB 2017–; CEO Receiptless Software Inc. (app Devt co.). *Address:* Matra Petroleum AB, Eriksbergsgatan, 10, 103 90 Stockholm, Sweden (office). *Telephone:* (8) 611-49-95 (office). *E-mail:* ir@matrapetroleum.com (office). *Website:* matrapetroleumab.se (office).

BARSTOW, Dame Josephine Clare, DBE, CBE, BA; British singer; b. 27 Sept. 1940, Sheffield, Yorks., England; d. of Harold Barstow and Clara Barstow; m. 1st Terry Hands 1964 (divorced 1968); m. 2nd Ande Anderson 1969 (died 1996); ed Univ. of Birmingham; taught English in London area for two years; debut in operatic profession with Opera for All 1964; for short time company mem. Welsh Nat. Opera, then ENO; now freelance singer in all nat. opera houses in UK and in Paris, Vienna, Salzburg, Zürich, Geneva, Turin, Florence, Cologne, Munich, Berlin, USSR, Chicago, San Francisco, New York, Houston and many other American opera houses; Co-founder (with Ande Anderson) Malthouse Arabians (horse breeding operation); Hon. DMus (Birmingham, Kingston, Sheffield, Sheffield Hallam, Leeds, Hull); Fidelio Medal. *Chief roles:* Violetta in La Traviata, Leonora in Forza del Destino, Elisabeth in Don Carlos, Lady Macbeth, Amelia in Ballo in Maschera, Attila, Leonore in Fidelio, Sieglinde, Senta, Arabella, Salome, Octavian, The Marschallin, Chrysothemis, Amelia, Tosca, Mimi, Minnie, Musetta, Manon Lescaut, Emilia Marty, Jenůfa, Katya Kabanova, Medea, Renata in The Fiery Angel, Katerina Ismailova, Kostelnicka in Jenůfa, Marie in Wozzeck, Gloriana, Lady Billows in Albert Herring; world premieres of Tippett, Henze and Penderecki. *Television films:* Macbeth 1972, Idomeneo 1974, Un ballo in maschera 1989, Gloriana 2000, Owen Wingrave 2001. *Recordings include:* Verdi Recital Record with ENO Orchestra and Mark Elder, Amelia with Herbert von Karajan, Anna Maurant in Street Scene, Kate in Kiss Me Kate, Four Finales, Gloriana, Albert Herring, Wozzeck, Carmelites. *Leisure interests:* farming (cattle), breeding Arabian horses, gardening. *Address:* c/o Musichall Ltd, Oast House, Crouch's Farm, Hollow Lane, East Hoathly, BN8 6QX, England (office). *E-mail:* info@musichall.uk.com (office). *Website:* www.musichall.uk.com (office); www.malthousearabians.com.

BART, Hon. Delano Frank, QC, LLB; Saint Kitts and Nevis lawyer, politician, international organization official and diplomatist; b. 28 Oct. 1952; ed Basseterre Sr School, Matthew Bolton Tech. Coll., Birmingham and Queen Mary Coll. and Inns of Court School, London, UK; teacher, Molineux All Age School 1970–72; mem. Lincoln's Inn, London 1976; part-time Lecturer in Law, Coll. of Distributive Justice, London 1977–79; admitted to Bar of England and Wales 1977, of Anguilla 1984, of Saint Kitts and Nevis 1984, of Antigua and Barbuda 1989; in pvt. practice from Chambers, The Temple, London 1977–95, appeared in variety of criminal and civil rights cases; Asst Counsel to Comm. of Inquiry, Bahamas 1993–94; Legal Rep. of Govt 1995–2001; mem. Legal Affairs Cttee Org. of Eastern Caribbean States 1995–; various positions with Caribbean Community and Common Market (CARICOM) 1995–, including mem. Legal Affairs Cttee, Attorney-Gen. to Caribbean Asscn of Regulators of Int. Business (CARIB), mem. Del. to Heads of Govt Meetings, Barbados, Bahamas, Canada; Head Del. to Defence Ministerial of the Americas Meetings 1995, 1996, 1998, 2000; head numerous other govt dels including Commonwealth Law Ministers Conf., Malaysia; Attorney-Gen. and Minister of Justice and Legal Affairs 2001–04, Minister of Justice 2006; Amb. and Perm. Rep. to UN, New York 2006–2015; owner of Delano Bart & Co.; Del. to Talks on Drafting Saint Kitts and Nevis Constitution 1982; fmr Exec. mem. Soc. of Black Lawyers in England and Wales. *Leisure interests:* music, art, reading, swimming. *Address:* #45 Horizon Villa, Frigate Bay, Basseterre, Saint Kitts and Nevis (home). *Telephone:* (869) 465-3581 (home).

BARTÁK, Martin, MD; Czech neurosurgeon and politician; b. 14 Feb. 1967, Prague; m.; ed High School Voděradská, Prague, Charles Univ., Prague, postgraduate studies at Harvard Univ., USA, Univ. of Oxford, UK, Hanover Univ., Germany; neurosurgeon, 'Na Homolce' Hosp., Prague 1992–96, 1996–2006, Radcliffe Infirmary, Oxford, UK 1996; Adviser to Vice-Chair. of Civic Democratic Party (ODS) Petr Nečas, for security and defence issues 2000–06; Adviser to Chair. of Defence and Security Cttee, Chamber of Deputies (Parl.) 2002–06; First Deputy Minister of Defence 2006–09; Deputy Prime Minister and Minister of Defence 2009–10; Deputy Minister of Finance 2010–11; on trial for corruption, Prague Municipal Court, Jan. 2014. *Leisure interests:* sports, literature, music.

BARTELS, Gen. Knud; Danish military officer; b. 8 April 1952, Copenhagen; m. Inge Vansteenkiste; ed Royal Danish Army Acad., Ecole Supérieure de Guerre, Paris, US Army War Coll.; promoted to First Lt 1977, Capt. 1982, Major 1987, Lt-Col 1992, Col 1996, Brig. 2001, Maj.-Gen. 2001, Lt-Gen. 2006, Gen. 2009; regimental service 1977–80, UN Forces Cyprus 1980–81; Jr Army and Jt Staff Course 1981–82; Instructor in tactics, Army Combat School 1982–84, Instructor in tactics/operations, Royal Danish Defence Coll. 1986–87, 1988–90, Dir Army Command and Gen. Staff Course 1994–96; Co. Commdr, 2nd Armoured Bn Zealand Life Regt 1987–88, Staff Officer Danish Defence Command 1990–92, Commdg Officer 1st Bn Slesvig Foot Regt 1992–93, Commdr 3rd Jutland Brigade 1996–97, ACOS Plans Danish Defence Command 1997–99, Gen. Officer Commdg Danish Div. 2004–06; Sr Nat. Rep. KFOR/MNB (North) 1999, Dir for Operations, NATO Int. Mil. Staff 2000–04, Deputy Mil. Rep., NATO 2001, Gen. Officer Commanding Div. 2004–06, Mil. Rep., NATO, EU 2006–09; Chief of Defence 2009–12; Chair. NATO Mil. Cttee 2012–15; Grand Cross of the Order of Dannebrog, Commdr with Star of the Royal Norwegian Order of Merit (Norway), Commdr of the French Order of the Legion of Honour (France), Commdr of the Legion of Merit (USA), Greek Commendation Medal Star of Merit of Honour (Greece), Knight 1st Class of the French National Order of Merit, France; 25 Years Good Service Medal, The Home Guard Good Service Medal, UN Peacekeeping Force in Cyprus Medal, NATO KFOR Medal. *Address:* NATO, Boulevard Leopold III, 1110 Brussels, Belgium (office). *Website:* www.nato.int (office).

BARTENSCHLAGER, Ralf F. W., PhD (Habil.); German virologist and academic; *Professor and Head of Molecular Virology, Department of Infectious Diseases, University of Heidelberg;* b. 29 May 1958, Mannheim; ed Univ. of Heidelberg; Postdoctoral Researcher and Leader of HCV programme, Central Research Unit, Hoffmann-LaRoche AG, Basel, Switzerland 1991–93; Ind. Group Leader, Inst. for Virology, Univ. of Mainz 1994–99, Assoc. Prof. 1999–2000, Full Prof. for Molecular Virology 2000–02; Full Prof. of Molecular Virology, Univ. of Heidelberg 2002–; mem. Scientific Advisory Bd, Soc. for Virology 2005–, Hepatitis Network (HepNet) 2007–; Co-ordinator, project 'Infektionsstrategien humanpathogener Viren', Landesstiftung Baden-Württemberg 2005–08; mem. Steering Cttee Excellence Cluster 'CellNetworks' 2008–; elected Major Reviewer, German Research Council ('Fachkollegium' der DFG) 2008–; Co-ordinator, DFG-funded research unit FOR 1202 'Mechanisms of Persistence of Hepatropic Viruses' 2009–; mem. Steering Cttee SFB/TRR 77 'Liver Cancer' 2010–; Jt Co-ordinator, TTU Hepatitis, German Centre for Infection Research 2010–; mem. American Soc. for Biochemistry and Molecular Biology 2008, American Soc. of Microbiology 2008, Int. Soc. for Antiviral Research 2008, European Asscn for the Study of the Liver 2010; Award for the best PhD thesis, Soc. for Molecular Biological Research, Heidelberg 1991, Robert-Koch-Förderpreis, Bergstadt Clausthal-Zellerfeld 2000, Löffler Frosch Prize, Soc. for Virology 2001, William Prusoff Young Investigator Award, Int. Soc. for Antiviral Research 2002, Aschoff Medal, Medical Soc., Freiburg 2006, Behring Lecturer 2008, Lasker~DeBakey Clinical Medical Research Award, Lasker Foundation (co-recipient) 2016. *Publications:* numerous papers in professional journals. *Address:* Molecular Virology, Department of Infectious Diseases, University of Heidelberg, Im Neuenheimer Feld 345, 69120 Heidelberg, Germany (office). *Telephone:* (6221) 564225 (office); (6221) 564569 (office). *Fax:* (6221) 564570 (office). *E-mail:* ralf_bartenschlager@med.uni-heidelberg.de (office). *Website:* www.klinikum.uni-heidelberg.de/Molecular-Virology.104862.0.html (office).

BARTENSTEIN, Martin, PhD; Austrian politician and business executive; *CEO, Gerot Lannach Holding GmbH;* b. 3 June 1953, Graz; m. Ilse Bartenstein 1983; four s. one d.; ed Akademisches Gymnasium, Miami Univ., OH, USA, Karl Franzens Univ., Graz; joined Lannacher Heilmittel GmbH (family-owned pharmaceutical co.) 1978, Man. Dir 1980–86; Chief Exec. Genericon Pharma GmbH 1986–90; mem. Bd of Dirs, Pharmavit AG, Budapest 1990; Chair. Asscn of Young Austrian Industrialists 1988; mem. Österreichische Volkspartei (ÖVP—Austrian People's Party), Party Spokesman on Industry 1991; Deputy Regional Chair. Styrian People's Party 1991; mem. Nationalrat (ÖVP) 1991–; State Sec., Fed. Ministry for Public Economy and Transport 1994; Minister for the Environment 1995, for Environment, Youth and Family Affairs 1996, for Econ. Affairs and Labour 2000–08; Chair. Cancer Relief Fund for the Children of Styria 1988–92, Austrian Cancer Relief Fund for Children 1993–; Pres. Österreichischen Basketballbundesliga 2002–; CEO Gerot Lannach Holding GmbH 2009–; Hon. Pres. Austrian Children's Cancer Aid Soc. 2009. *Address:* Parlamentsklub der ÖVP, Dr-Karl-Renner-Ring 3, 1017 Vienna, Austria (office). *Telephone:* (1) 401-10-0 (office). *E-mail:* martin.bartenstein@parlament.gv.at (office). *Website:* www.parlament.gv.at (office); gl-pharma.at (office).

BARTH, John M.; American business executive; b. 1946; ed Carnegie-Mellon Univ., Gannon Univ., Northwestern Univ. Inst. for Man.; joined Johnson Controls Inc. 1969, various man. positions including Dir Johnson Controls Automotive Systems Group 1990, mem. Bd of Dirs 1997–2007, Pres. and COO 1998, CEO 2002, Chair. 2004–07; Chair. Nat. Minority Supplier Devt Council 2003–05; mem. Bd of Dirs, Handleman Co. 1995–2003, Covisint Corpn; mem. The Business Roundtable, Greater Milwaukee Cttee; Dir, Metropolitan Milwaukee Asscn of Commerce; Leadership Award, Nat. Minority Supplier Devt Council 2006, three times named one of America's best CEOs by Institutional Investor. *Address:* c/o Johnson

Controls Inc., 5757 North Green Bay Avenue, PO Box 591, Milwaukee, WI 53201, USA.

BARTH, John Simmons, MA; American novelist and academic; *Professor Emeritus in the Writing Seminars, Johns Hopkins University;* b. 27 May 1930, Cambridge, Md; s. of John J. Barth and Georgia Simmons; m. 1st Harriette Anne Strickland 1950 (divorced 1969); two s. one d.; m. 2nd Shelly Rosenberg 1970; ed Johns Hopkins Univ.; Instructor, Pennsylvania State Univ. 1953, Assoc. Prof. until 1965; Prof. of English, State Univ. of New York at Buffalo 1965–73, Johns Hopkins Univ. 1973–91, Prof. Emer. in the Writing Seminars 1991–; Rockefeller Foundation Grant; mem., American Acad. of Arts and Letters 1974–; Fellow, American Acad. of Arts and Sciences 1974; Hon. LittD (Univ. of Maryland) 1969, (Salisbury Univ.) 1975, Hon. DHL (Pennsylvania State Univ.) 1996, (Western Maryland Coll.) 1973, (Towson Univ.) 1981, (Univ. of Colorado) 2009, Laurea hc in Letters (Univ. Macerata, Italy) 1990, Hon. LittD (Colby Coll.) 2007; Brandeis Univ. Citation in Literature, Nat. Acad. of Arts and Letters Award, Nat. Book Award 1973, F. Scott Fitzgerald Award 1997, President's Medal, Johns Hopkins Univ. 1997, PEN/Malamud Award 1998, Lifetime Achievement Award, Lannan Foundation 1998, Lifetime Achievement in Letters Award, Enoch Pratt Soc. 1999, Roozi Rozegari (Iranian literature prize) 2008. *Publications include:* The Floating Opera 1956, The End of the Road 1958, The Sot-Weed Factor 1960, Giles Goat-Boy 1966; Lost in the Funhouse (stories) 1968, Chimera 1972, Letters 1979, Sabbatical 1982, The Friday Book (essays) 1984, The Tidewater Tales: A Novel 1987, The Last Voyage of Somebody the Sailor 1991, Once Upon a Time 1994, On With the Story (stories) 1996, The Book of Ten Nights and a Night (stories) 2004, Three Roads Meet (novella) 2005, The Development (stories) 2008, Every Third Thought: A Novel in Five Seasons 2011. *Address:* The Writing Seminars, 135 Gilman Hall, Johns Hopkins University, 3400 North Charles Street, Baltimore, MD 21218, USA (office). *Telephone:* (410) 516-7563 (office). *Website:* www.jhu.edu/writsem (office).

BARTHOLOMEOS I, DCnL; Turkish ecclesiastic; *Archbishop of Constantinople (New Rome) and Ecumenical Patriarch;* b. (Dimitrios Arhondonis), 29 Feb. 1940, Hagioi Theodoroi, Island of Imvros; s. of Christos Archondonis and Merope Archondonis; ed Theological School of Halki, Pontifical Oriental Inst., Rome, Ecumenical Inst. Bossey, Switzerland and Univ. of Munich; mil. service 1961–63; ordained deacon 1961, priest 1969; Asst Dean, Theological School of Halki 1968; elevated to rank of Archimandrite 1970; Admin. Pvt. Patriarchal Office of Ecumenical Patriarch Dimitrios 1972–90; Metropolitan, See of Philadelphia, Asia Minor 1973; mem. Holy and Sacred Synod 1974; Metropolitan of Chalcedon 1990–91; Archbishop of Constantinople (New Rome) and Ecumenical Patriarch 1991–; Founding mem. and Vice-Pres. Soc. of Canon Law of the Oriental Churches; mem. Exec. and Cen. Cttees, WCC 1991–; Fellow, Orthodox Acad. of Crete, Greece; Hon. mem. Pro-Oriente Foundation, Vienna; Dr hc (Athens), (Holy Cross Orthodox School of Theology, Brookline, Mass) and from numerous other univs; US Congressional Gold Medal 1997, Sophie Foundation Award 2002, Binding Foundation Award 2002. *Address:* Chief Secretariat of the Holy and Sacred Synod of the Ecumenical Patriarchate, Greek Orthodox Church, Rum Ortodoks Patrikhanesi, 34220 Fener-Haliç, Istanbul, Turkey (office). *Telephone:* (212) 5319671 (office). *Fax:* (212) 5316533 (office). *E-mail:* patriarchate@ec-patr.org (office). *Website:* www.patriarchate.org (office).

BARTKUS, Gintautas; Lithuanian lawyer, academic and fmr government official; *Managing Partner, Baltic Legal Solutions Lithuania;* b. 30 June 1966, m.; two c.; ed Vilnius State Univ., Helsinki Univ., Jean Moulin Univ., Lyon, France; Adviser to Dir Dept of Nat. Lithuanian Govt 1990–92; Visiting Prof., John Marshall Law School, Chicago, USA 1993–96; Founder and Pnr, Law Co. Lideika, Petrauskas, Valiunas and Pnrs 1990–2000; Minister of Justice 2000–01; Managing Partner, Advocate, Baltic Legal Solutions Lithuania; mem. Working Group for Drafting the Civil Code of Lithuania 1992–2000; Asst Prof., Vilnius Univ. 1989–; mem. EC Advisory Group on Corp. Governance and Co. Law 2005–; Arbitrator, Vilnius Court of Commercial Arbitration; mem. Lithuanian Bar Asscn. *Address:* Baltic Legal Solutions Lithuania, Subačiaus 7, 01302 Vilnius, Lithuania (office). *Telephone:* (5) 274-24-10 (office). *E-mail:* Gintautas.Bartkus@lt.blslawfirm.com (office). *Website:* www.blslawfirm.com (office).

BARTLETT, Jennifer, BA, BFA, MFA; American artist; b. 14 March 1941, Long Beach, Calif.; m. 1st Ed Bartlett in 1964 (divorced 1972); m. 2nd Mathieu Carrière 1983 (divorced); one d.; ed Mills Coll., Oakland, Calif., Yale Univ. School of Art and Architecture; taught art at Univ. of Connecticut 1964–72, School of Visual Arts, New York 1972–77; first New York exhbn, Alan Saret's SoHo gallery 1970; numerous public commissions; Harris Prize, Art Inst. of Chicago 1976, Award of American Acad. and Inst. of Arts and Letters 1983, American Inst. of Architects Award 1987. *Address:* 134 Charles Street, New York, NY 10014, USA (office). *Website:* www.richardgraygallery.com.

BARTLETT, John Vernon, CBE, MA, FICE; British fmr consulting engineer; b. 18 June 1927, London; s. of Vernon F. Bartlett and Olga Bartlett (née Testrup); m. Gillian Hoffman 1951; four s.; ed Stowe School, Trinity Coll., Cambridge; engineer, John Mowlem & Co., Ltd 1951–57; joined Mott Hay & Anderson (now Mott MacDonald Group) 1957, Pnr 1966, Chair. 1973–88, Consultant 1988–95; Chair. British Tunnelling Soc. 1977–79; Pres. Inst. of Civil Engineers 1982–83; mem. Governing Body Imperial Coll. London 1991–95; Master Worshipful Co. of Engineers 1992–93; Founder, Bartlett Library, Nat. Maritime Museum Cornwall 2002; Fellow, Royal Acad. of Engineering; Telford Gold Medals 1971, 1973, S.G. Brown Medal, Royal Soc. 1973. *Publications include:* Tunnels: Planning, Design and Construction (co-author) 1981, Ships of North Cornwall 1996; various professional papers. *Leisure interests:* sailing, maritime history. *Address:* 6 Cottenham Park Road, Wimbledon, London, SW20 0RZ, England. *Telephone:* (20) 8946-9576.

BARTOLI, Cecilia; Italian singer (coloratura mezzo-soprano) and recitalist; b. 4 June 1966, Rome; d. of Pietro Angelo Bartoli and Silvana Bazzoni; ed Accademia di Santa Cecilia; professional career began with TV appearance aged 19; US debut in recital at Mostly Mozart Festival, New York 1990; Paris debut as Cherubino in The Marriage of Figaro, Opéra de Paris Bastille 1990–91; debut, La Scala, Milan in Rossini's Le Comte Ory 1990–91 season; appeared as Dorabella in Così fan tutte, Maggio Musicale, Florence 1991; debut with Montreal Symphony Orchestra and Philadelphia Orchestra 1990–91 season; recitals in collaboration with pianist András Schiff since 1990; appeared in Marriage of Figaro and Così fan tutte conducted by Daniel Barenboim in Chicago Feb. 1992; debut at Salzburg Festival 1992; appeared in recital at Rossini bicentenary celebration at Lincoln Center, New York 1992; has appeared with many leading conductors including Herbert von Karajan, Claudio Abbado, Riccardo Chailly, Myung-Whun Chung, William Christie, Charles Dutoit, Adam Fischer, Nikolaus Harnoncourt, Christopher Hogwood, James Levine, Sir Neville Marriner, Zubin Mehta, Riccardo Muti, Giuseppe Sinopoli and Sir George Solti; particularly associated with the operas of Mozart and Rossini; Artistic Dir, Salzburg Whitsun Festival 2012–; European concert tour with Rolando Villazón 2015; Hon. mem. RAM 2005, Royal Swedish Acad. of Music; Hon. mem. Advisory Bd Halle Handel House Foundation 2009; Chevalier, Ordre des Arts et des Lettres, Officier, Légion d'Honneur, Ordre du Mérite, Chevalier, Ordre du Mérite Culturel (Monaco) 2012; two Grammy Awards for Best Classical Vocal Album 1994, Deutsche Schallplatten Preis, La Stella d'Oro, Italy, Caecilia Award, Belgium, Diapason d'Or, France, Best Opera Recording of the Year for La Cenerentola, Japan, Classical BRIT Award for Female Artist of the Year 2004, Echo Klassik Award for Female Singer of the Year 2008, Sonning Music Prize 2010, Halle Handel Prize 2010, Herbert von Karajan Prize 2012, Swiss Award for Culture 2012, Bellini d'Oro, Medalla de Oro al Mérito en las Bellas Artes (Spain), Médaille Grand Vermeil de la Ville de Paris, Polar Music Prize 2016. *Recordings include:* albums: Rossini Arias, Rossini Songs, Mozart Arias, Rossini Heroines, Chants d'amour, If You Love Me 1992, Mozart Portraits 1995, An Italian Songbook 1997, Cecilia Bartoli – Live Vivaldi Album 1999, Cecilia & Bryn, Il Turco in Italia, Mitridate, Rinaldo, Armida in Italy, The Salieri Album, The Vivaldi Album, Gluck Italian Arias, Opera proibito 2005, Maria (Gramophone Award for Best Recital 2008) 2007, Sacrificium (Grammy Award for Best Classical Vocal Performance 2011) 2009, St Petersburg 2014, Giulio Cesare (as Cleopatra, DVD) 2016, Dolce Duello (with Sol Gabetta) 2017. *Website:* www.ceciliabartolionline.com.

BARTOLONE, Claude, BS; French politician; *President of National Assembly;* b. 29 July 1951, Tunis, Tunisia; m. 2nd Véronique Bartolone (née Ragusa) 2006; started career as an exec. in the pharmaceutical industry; Councillor Le Pré-Saint-Gervais 1977–83, 1995–2008, Les Lilas 1983–89; Deputy Mayor Le Pré-Saint-Gervais 1977–83, June–Oct. 1995, 2001–08, Mayor 1995–98; Councillor Seine-Saint-Denis department 1979–92, Vice-Pres. 1985–92, Pres. 2008–12; Regional Councillor Ile-de-France 1998–2002; Minister for the City 1998–2002; mem. Nat. Assembly 1981–, Vice-Pres. 1992–93, Pres. 2012–; Chair. Cttee on Cultural, Family and Social Affairs 1997–98; Chair. Parl. Comm. on borrowing and risk products 2011; Grand Cross of the Order of Merit of the Italian Republic 2012. *Address:* National Assembly, 126 Rue de l'Université, 75355 Paris 07 SP (office); 45 Avenue of General Leclerc, 93500 Pantin, France (office). *Telephone:* (1) 49-15-38-54 (office). *Fax:* (1) 49-15-73-01 (office). *E-mail:* cbartolone@assemblee-nationale.fr (office). *Website:* www2.assemblee-nationale.fr (office).

BARTON, Dominic, BA; Canadian management consultant; *Global Managing Partner, McKinsey & Co.;* b. 1962, Kampala, Uganda; s. of John Barton and Barbara Barton; m. Sheila Labatt (separated); one s. one d.; ed Univ. of British Columbia, Brasenose Coll., Oxford; began career as currency analyst, Rothschild & Co., London; joined McKinsey & Co. 1986, worked in Toronto office 1986–97, becoming Man. Partner, McKinsey Korea, Seoul 2000–04, Asia Chair., McKinsey & Co. 2004–09, Sr Partner, McKinsey & Co. 1986–, Global Man. Partner 2009–; Chair. Canadian Minister of Finance's Advisory Council on Econ. Growth; Chair. Seoul Int. Business Advisory Council; Adjunct Prof. Tsinghua Univ., Beijing; mem. Bd, Univ. of Oxford Said Business School; Trustee, Rhodes Trust, Brookings Inst.; Hon. DTech (British Columbia Inst. of Tech.) 2016; Hon. Fellow, Brasenose Coll., Oxford 2010. *Publications:* Dangerous Markets: Managing in Financial Crises (co-author) 2002, China Vignettes: An Inside Look at China (co-author) 2007. *Address:* McKinsey & Co, 1 Jermyn Street, St James's, London, SW1Y 4UH, England (office). *Telephone:* (20) 7839-8040 (office). *Website:* www.mckinsey.com (office).

BARTON, Jacqueline K., AB, PhD; American chemist and academic; *Professor of Chemistry, California Institute of Technology;* b. 7 May 1952, New York, NY; d. of William Kapelman and Claudine Kapelman (née Gutchen); m. Prof. Peter Brendan Dervan 1990; one d.; ed Barnard Coll. and Columbia Univ., New York; Visiting Research Assoc., Dept of Biophysics, Bell Labs 1979; Postdoctoral Fellow, Bell Labs and Yale Univ. 1980; Asst Prof. of Chem. and Biochemistry, Hunter Coll., CUNY 1980–82; returned to Columbia Univ. 1983, Assoc. Prof. of Chem. and Biological Sciences 1985–86, Prof. 1986–89; Prof., California Inst. of Tech. 1989–, Arthur and Marian Hanisch Memorial Prof. of Chem. 1997–2016, apptd Chair. Div. of Chem. and Chemical Eng 2009, currently John G. Kirkwood and Arthur A. Noyes Prof. of Chemistry and Norman Davidson Leadership Chair Div. of Chem. and Chemical Eng; co-f. GeneOhm Sciences 2001 (became part of Becton, Dickinson and Co. 2006); mem. NSF Chem. Advisory Cttee 1985–88, NIH Metallobiochemistry Study Section 1986–90 (Chair. 1988–90); mem. Bd of Dirs Dow Chemical Co. 1993–, currently Chair. Environment, Health and Safety Cttee and mem. Governance and Compensation Cttees; Fellow, American Acad. of Arts and Sciences 1991, American Philosophical Soc. 2000, NAS 2002; fmr Fellow, Sloan Foundation; fmr NSF Presidential Young Investigator; Hon. FRSC 2014; many hon. degrees, including Hon. DSc (Knox Coll.) 1991, (Williams Coll.) 1992, (New Jersey Inst. of Tech.) 1993, (Kenyon Coll.) 1994, (Lawrence Univ.) 1994, (Skidmore Coll.) 1997, (Yale Univ.) 2005, (Columbia Univ.) 2010; NSF Predoctoral Fellow 1975–78, NIH Postdoctoral Fellow 1979–80, Harold Lamport Award, New York Acad. of Sciences 1984, NSF Alan T. Waterman Award 1985, Camille and Henry Dreyfus Teacher-Scholar 1986–91, ACS Award in Pure Chem. 1988, ACS Eli Lilly Award in Biological Chem. 1987, ACS Baekeland Medal 1991, Fresenius Award 1986, Univ. Medal, Barnard Coll. 1990 and Columbia Univ. 1992, MacArthur Foundation Fellowship 1991, ACS Garvan Medal 1992, ACS Tolman Medal 1994, Mayor of New York's Award in Science and Tech. 1988, Havinga Medal 1995, Paul Karrer Medal 1996, ACS Nichols Medal 1997, Weizmann Women and Science Award 1998, ACS Ronald Breslow Award in Biomimetic Chem. 2003, named an Outstanding Dir by ODX 2006, Willard Gibbs Award, Chicago Section of ACS 2006, ACS Cotton Medal 2007, ACS Pauling Medal 2007, Nat. Medal of Science 2010, Gold Medal, American Inst. of Chemists 2015, ACS Priestley Medal 2015, NAS Award in Chemical Sciences 2019. *Publications:* more than 250 publs in scientific journals on the application of transition metal complexes as tools to probe recognition and reactions of double helical DNA.

Address: 233 Noyes Laboratory, Department of Chemistry, M/C 127-72, California Institute of Technology, 1200 East California Blvd, Pasadena, CA 91125-7200, USA (office). *Telephone:* (626) 395-6075 (office). *E-mail:* jkbarton@caltech.edu (office). *Website:* www.its.caltech.edu/~jkbgrp (office).

BARTON, Rev. John, MA, DPhil, DLitt, FBA; British academic; *Professor Emeritus, University of Oxford;* b. 17 June 1948, London; s. of Bernard A. Barton and Gwendolyn H. Barton; m. Mary Burn 1973; one d.; ed Latymer Upper School, London and Keble Coll. Oxford; Jr Research Fellow, Merton Coll. Oxford 1973–74; Univ. Lecturer in Theology, Univ. of Oxford 1974–89, Reader in Biblical Studies 1989–91, currently Prof. Emer.; Oriel and Laing Prof. of the Interpretation of Holy Scripture and Fellow, Oriel Coll. Oxford 1991–2014; Canon Theologian of Winchester Cathedral 1991–2003; mem. Norwegian Acad. of Arts and Sciences 2008; Senior Research Fellow, Campion Hall, Oxford 2014–; Fellow, St Cross Coll. Oxford 1974–91; Hon. DrTheol (Bonn) 1998. *Publications include:* Amos's Oracles Against the Nations 1980, Reading the Old Testament 1984, Oracles of God 1986, People of the Book? 1988, Love Unknown 1990, What is the Bible? 1991, Isaiah 1–39 1995, The Spirit and the Letter 1997, Making the Christian Bible 1997, Ethics and the Old Testament 1998, The Cambridge Companion to Biblical Interpretation 1998, Oxford Bible Commentary 2001, Joel and Obadiah 2001, The Biblical World 2003, Understanding Old Testament Ethics 2003, The Original Story (with J. Bowden) 2004, Living Belief 2005, The Nature of Biblical Criticism 2007, The Old Testament: Canon, Literature, Theology 2007, The Theology of the Book of Amos 2012, Ethics in Ancient Israel 2014. *Telephone:* (1865) 286119 (office). *E-mail:* john.barton@oriel.ox.ac.uk (office). *Website:* www.oriel.ox.ac.uk (office).

BARTON, Nicholas Hamilton (Nick), PhD, FRS, FRSE; British biologist and academic; *Professor, Institute of Science and Technology Austria;* b. 30 Aug. 1955, London; ed Univ. of East Anglia; Demonstrator, Dept of Genetics, Univ. of Cambridge 1980–82; Lecturer, Dept of Genetics and Biometry, Univ. Coll. London 1982–90; mem. staff, Univ. of Edinburgh 1990, Prof. of Evolutionary Biology 1994–2008, currently Visiting Prof., Inst. of Evolutionary Biology; Prof., Inst. of Science and Tech. Austria (IST Austria), Klosterneuburg, Austria 2008–, Dean Grad. School; Handling Ed. Evolution (text book) 2008–11; mem. Editorial Bd Public Library of Science 2003; Bicentennial Medal, Linnean Soc. 1985, Zoological Soc. Scientific Medal 1992, David Starr Jordan Prize 1994, Pres.'s Award, American Soc. of Naturalists 1998, Wolfson Merit Award 2005, Darwin Medal, Royal Soc. 2006, Darwin-Wallace Medal and Award (co-recipient), Linnean Soc. 2009, Mendel Medal, German Nat. Acad. of Sciences Leopoldina 2013, Erwin Schrödinger Prize, Austria Acad. of Sciences 2013. *Publications:* numerous scientific papers in professional journals on hybrid zones, speciation and multi-locus evolution, and on understanding the evolution of traits which depend on interactions between large numbers of genes. *Address:* Institute of Science and Technology Austria (IST Austria), Am Campus 1, 3400 Klosterneuburg, Austria (office); Room 126, Ashworth Labs, School of Biological Sciences, University of Edinburgh, Michael Swann Building, King's Buildings, Mayfield Road, Edinburgh, EH9 3JR, Scotland. *Telephone:* (43) 9000-3001 (office). *E-mail:* nick.barton@ist.ac.at (office); n.barton@ed.ac.uk. *Website:* ist.ac.at/research-groups-pages/barton-group (office).

BARTOŠ, Ivan, PhD; Czech computer scientist and politician; *Leader, Česká Pirátská Strana (Czech Pirate Party);* b. 20 March 1980, Jablonec nad Nisou, Czech Socialist Repub., Czechoslovak Socialist Repub.; m. Lydie Franka Bartošová; ed Charles Univ., Prague; Consultant, State Tech. Library, Prague 2001–03; Database Admin. and Designer, Newton Media a.s. 2003–05; Sr Database Engineer, Monster Technologies 2005–10; Sr Marketing Information System Consultant, Mobilkom a.s. 2009–10; Functional Systems Architect, T-Mobile Czech Repub. 2010–14; Marketing Dir, AirJobs CZ 2015–16; Business Intelligence Consultant, Physter Technology a.s. 2016–; mem. Chamber of Deputies (parl.) for Central Bohemia (Česká Pirátská Strana) 2017–; mem. Česká Pirátská Strana (Czech Pirate Party), Leader 2009–. *Address:* Česká Pirátská Strana, Řehořova 943/19, 130 00 Prague, Czech Republic (office). *E-mail:* info@pirati.cz (office). *Website:* www.pirati.cz (office).

BARTOV, Omer, DPhil; Israeli/American historian and academic; *John P. Birkelund Distinguished Professor of European History and Professor of History and Professor of German Studies, Brown University;* ed Univ. of Oxford, UK; fmrly at Rutgers Univ.; John P. Birkelund Distinguished Prof. of European History and Prof. of History and Prof. of German Studies, Brown Univ. 2000–, Chair. Dept of History 2009–12; Visiting Fellow, Davis Center, Princeton Univ.; Jr Fellow, Soc. of Fellows, Harvard Univ.; Distinguished Visiting Prof., Dept of History, Nat. Taiwan Univ. 2011; J.B. and Maurice C. Shapiro Sr Scholar-in-Residence, Center for Advanced Holocaust Studies, US Holocaust Memorial Museum 2012–13; mem. American Acad. of Arts and Sciences; Fellow, Nat. Endowment for the Humanities (NEH), Alexander von Humboldt Foundation, Radcliffe Inst. for Advanced Study, Harvard Univ. 2002–03, American Acad., Berlin 2007; NEH Fellowship 2008–09; Fellow, American Acad. of Arts and Sciences 2005; Guggenheim Fellow 2003–04, Berlin Prize Fellowship, American Acad. in Berlin 2007, Center for Advanced Holocaust Studies at US Holocaust Memorial Museum Fellowship 2012–13. *Publications include:* The Eastern Front, 1941–45: German Troops and the Barbarisation of Warfare 1985, Hitler's Army 1991, Murder in Our Midst (Fraenkel Prize in Contemporary History) 1996, Mirrors of Destruction: War, Genocide and Modern Identity 2000; Ed.: The Holocaust: Origins, Implementation, Aftermath 2000; co-ed.: In God's Name: Genocide and Religion in the Twentieth Century 2001, The Crimes of War: Guilt and Denial in the Twentieth Century 2002, Germany's War and the Holocaust 2003, The "Jew" in Cinema 2005, Erased: Vanishing Traces of Jewish Galicia in Present-Day Ukraine 2007; numerous book chapters, articles and reviews in several languages. *Address:* Department of History, Brown University, Peter Green House, 79 Brown Street, Box N, Providence, RI 02912, USA (office). *Telephone:* (401) 863-1375 (office). *Fax:* (401) 863-1040 (office). *E-mail:* omer_bartov@brown.edu (office). *Website:* vivo.brown.edu/display/obartov (office).

BARTSITS, Beslan; Georgian lawyer and politician; b. 22 July 1978, Gagra, Abkhaz ASSR, Georgian SSR, USSR; m., two s.; ed Abkhazian State Univ., Rostov State Univ., Russian Fed.; Asst to Raul Khajimba, Vice-Pres. of Abkhazia 2007–09; Deputy of Gagra Dist Ass. for Constituency No. 5 2011–12, later Deputy Chair.; elected mem. People's Ass. of Abkhazia for Constituency No. 11 (Gagra) 2012, Deputy Chair. Cttee for Legal Policy, State Building and Human Rights; Acting Head of Gagra Dist 2014–15, Head of Gagra Dist 2015–16; Head of Presidential Admin May–Aug. 2016; Prime Minister of the 'Republic of Abkhazia' 2016–18; Ind. *Address:* c/o Office of the Cabinet of Ministers of the 'Republic of Abkhazia', 384900 Sukhumi, nab. Makhajirov 32, Georgia (office).

BARTUMEU CASSANY, Jaume; Andorran lawyer and politician; b. 10 Nov. 1954, Andorra la Vella; m. Carme Garcia Puy; two s.; ed Univ. of Barcelona, Spain, Univ. of Toulouse, France; legal practice, Andorra la Vella 1982–; Minister of Finance, Commerce and Industry 1990–92; mem. Andorran Del. to European Council 1995–2001, 2004–08, Vice-Pres. Human Rights Sub-Comm. 2004, Pres. Sub-Comm. on Crime Problems and the Fight against Terrorism 2005–; Founding mem. Partit Socialdemòcrata (Social Democratic Party) 2000, First Sec. 2000–04; Leader of the Opposition, Consell Gen. 2005–09, Cap del Govern (Head of Govt) 2009–11; mem. Andorran Bar Council 1986–89; mem. Exec. Cttee Int. Asscn of Young Lawyers 1987–90. *Website:* www.jaumebartumeu.com.

BARTZ, Carol Ann, BA; American business executive; b. 29 Aug. 1948; m. Bill Marr; two s. one d.; ed Univ. of Wisconsin; fmr Man. Product Line and Sales, Digital Equipment Corpn and 3M Corpn; various roles with Sun Microsystems rising to Exec. Officer 1983–92; mem. Bd of Dirs and Chair., Pres. and CEO Autodesk, Inc. 1992–2006, Exec. Chair. 2006–09; mem. Bd of Dirs and CEO Yahoo! Inc. 2009–11, Pres. 2009–11; mem. Bd of Dirs BEA Systems, Cisco Systems, Network Appliance, TechNet, Foundation for the Nat. Medals of Science and Tech., New York Stock Exchange; mem. Pres. Bush's Council of Advisors on Science and Tech.; Hon. DHumLitt (New Jersey Inst. of Tech.), Hon. DSc (Worcester Polytechnic Inst.), Hon. DLitt (Williams Woods Univ.); numerous awards including Soc. of Manufacturing Engineers Donald C. Burnham Manufacturing Man. Award 1994, Women in Tech. Int. Hall of Fame 1997, Ernst & Young's Northern Calif. Master Entrepreneur of the Year Award 2001, Ada Lovelace Award, Asscn for Women in Computing 2003, Avatar Award for Women of Excellence, Nat. Asscn of Female Execs 2003. *Leisure interests:* golf, tennis, gardening. *Address:* c/o Yahoo! Inc., 701 1st Avenue, Sunnyvale, CA 94089, USA.

BARYSHNIKOV, Mikhail (Misha); Latvian/American ballet dancer; *Artistic Director, Baryshnikov Arts Center;* b. 28 Jan. 1948, Riga, Latvia; s. of Nikolay Baryshnikov and Aleksandra (née Kisselov) Baryshnikova; one d.; ed Riga Ballet School and Kirov Ballet School, Leningrad; mem. Kirov Ballet Co. 1969–74; guest artist with many leading ballet cos including American Ballet Theater, Nat. Ballet of Canada, Royal Ballet, Hamburg Ballet, FRG, Ballet Victoria, Australia, Stuttgart Ballet, FRG, Alvin Ailey Co., USA 1974–; joined New York City Ballet Co. 1978, resgnd 1979; Artistic Dir, American Ballet Theater 1980–89; Co-Founder (with Mark Morris) and Dir White Oak Dance Project 1990–2002; Founder and Artistic Dir, Baryshnikov Arts Center, New York 2005–; granted Latvian Citizenship 2017; Fellow, American Acad. of Arts and Sciences 1999; Officer, nat. Légion d'honneur 2010; Dr hc (Northwestern Univ.) 2013; Gold Medal, Varna Competition, Bulgaria 1966, First Int. Ballet Competition, Moscow, USSR 1968, Nijinsky Prize, First Int. Ballet Competition, Paris Acad. de Danse 1968, Kennedy Center Honors, Nat. Medal of Honor 2000, Jerome Robbins Award 2005, Commonwealth Award, Vilcek Prize in Dance 2012. *Ballets (world premières):* Vestris 1969, Medea 1975, Push Comes to Shove 1976, Hamlet Connotations 1976, Other Dances 1976, Pas de Duke 1976, La Dame De Pique 1978, L'Après-midi d'un Faune 1978, Santa Fe Saga 1978, Opus 19 1979, Rhapsody 1980. *Films:* The Turning Point 1977, White Nights 1985, Giselle 1987, Dancers 1987, Dinosaurs 1991. *Television:* appeared in episodes of Sex and the City 2003–04. *Choreography:* Nutcracker 1976, Don Quixote 1978, Cinderella 1984. *Publications:* Baryshnikov at Work 1977, Moments in Time 2005. *Address:* Baryshnikov Arts Center, 450 West 37th Street, Suite 501, New York, NY 10018, USA (office). *Telephone:* (646) 731-3200 (office). *Fax:* (646) 731-3207 (office). *E-mail:* info@bacnyc.org (office). *Website:* www.bacnyc.org (office).

BARZANI, Masoud; Iraqi (Kurdish) politician; *President, Kurdistan Democratic Party;* b. 16 Aug. 1946, Mahabad, Iran; s. of Mustafa Barzani, founder of Kurdistan Democratic Party (KDP); m.; five s. three d.; ed Tehran Univ.; father forced to flee to USSR 1946, returned to Iraq following overthrow of Iraqi monarchy in 1958; reunited with his father, family returned to their home village of Barzan; Kurdistan Democratic Party (KDP) launched armed struggle to defend Kurdish people 1961, joined Peshmerga forces 1962; participated in del. that signed autonomy agreement with Govt in Baghdad March 1970; engaged in renewed Kurdish armed struggle 1970s; succeeded his father as Pres. of KDP 1979–; led KDP in establishing a govt in Iraqi Kurdistan with PUK; mem. Iraqi Governing Council following invasion of Iraq 2003, Pres. Council April 2004; Pres. Kurdistan Region in Iraq 2005–17; Italian Atlantic Cttee Atlantic Award 2011. *Publication:* Mustafa Barzani and the Kurdish Liberation Movement (with Ahmed Ferhani) (three vols in Arabic; first vol. also in English and Turkish). *Leisure interests:* reading and football. *Address:* Kurdistan Democratic Party, European Office, 10749 Berlin, POB 301516, Germany (office). *Telephone:* (30) 79743741 (office). *Fax:* (30) 79743746 (office). *E-mail:* party@kdp.se (office). *Website:* www.kdp.se (office).

BARZANI, Nechirvan Idris; Iraqi (Kurdish) politician; *Prime Minister, Kurdistan Regional Government;* b. 21 Sept. 1966, Barzan, southern Kurdistan; grandson of Mustafa Barzani, founder of Kurdistan Democratic Party (KDP), nephew of Masoud Barzani, Pres. of Kurdistan Region; m. Nabila Barzani; three s. two d.; ed Tehran Univ.; family forced to flee to Iran 1975; often accompanied his father and sr Kurdistan Democratic Party (KDP) mem. Idris Barzani on his missions abroad; political science studies in Tehran cut short due to sudden death of his father 1987; took up active role in Kurdish politics, working in KDP youth orgs, rose rapidly through ranks of KDP; first elected to leadership of KDP in 1989, re-elected 1999; participated in negotiations with Iraqi Govt following Gulf War 1991; Deputy Prime Minister of KDP's controlled region in Iraqi Kurdistan 1996–99, Prime Minister 1999–2006, first Prime Minister of unified Govt of Kurdistan Region 2006–09, Prime Minister 2012–14, re-elected 2014–. *Leisure interest:* Kurdish and Persian poetry. *Address:* Office of the Prime Minister, Council of Ministers Building, Kurdistan Regional Government, Erbil, Iraq (office). *Website:* www.krg.org (office).

BARZEL, Amnon, MSc; Israeli art writer, critic, consultant and museum director; b. 5 July 1935, Tel-Aviv; m. Shafrira Glikson 1956; one s. one d.; ed Hebrew Univ., Jerusalem, Sorbonne, Paris; Lecturer, Avni Inst., Univ. of Haifa; Founding Ed. Painting and Sculpture 1971; Art Consultant for City of Tel-Aviv 1975–76; Curator, Biennale of Venice, Italy 1976–78, 1980, Two Environments, Forte Belvedere, Florence and Castle of Prato, Italy 1978, São Paulo Biennale, Brazil 1985; Founding Curator Contemporary Art Meetings, Tel Hai, Israel 1980–83, Villa Celle Art Spaces Collection, Giuliano Gori, Prato, Italy 1981–82; Founding Dir Centre of Contemporary Art Luigi Pecci, Prato, Italy 1986, Dir School for Curators 1991; Artistic Dir European Sculpture City (UNESCO), Turku, Finland 1992–95, Premio Mercedes Benz for Contemporary Art, Monte Firidolfi 1997, Artostrada 1998, Int. Project of Environmental Sculpture, Israel 1997–98; Dir Berlin Jewish Museum 1994–97; Consultant, Leube Foundation, Gartenau, Salzburg 1985; Consultant for creation of Museum of Contemporary Art, Florence 1989; fmr Consultant, Phoenix Int. Art Collection; mem. Curatorial Cttee for Int. Sculpture Center, Washington, DC 1990. *Publications include:* Isaac Frenel 1973, Dani Karavan 1978, Art in Israel 1986, Europe Now 1988, Julian Schnabel 1989, Enzo Cucchi 1989, Contemporary Russian Artists (co-ed.) 1990, Der Wettbewerb für das 'Denkmal für die ermordeten Juden Europas': Eine Streitschrift (co-author) 1995, Hermann Pedit: Arbeiten 1954–1997 (co-author) 1997, Leben Im Wartesaal: Exil in Shanghai, 1938–1947 (co-author) 1997, Massimo Lippi: L'albero Della Vita (co-author) 2001, Light Art: Targetti Light Art Collection 2006, Hans Hartung: In the Beginning There Was Lightning/In Principio Era Il Fulmine (co-author) 2007, Arte Ambientale 2008. *Leisure interests:* poetry, holy contemporary philosophy.

BARZUN, Matthew Winthrop, AB; American diplomatist and business executive; b. 23 Oct. 1970, New York, NY; m. Brooke Brown 1999; three c.; ed St Paul's School, Harvard Coll.; joined CNET Networks 1993, Vice-Pres., Software Services 1995, Sr Vice-Pres. 1998, Chief Strategy Officer 2000, then Exec. Vice-Pres. CNET Networks' Business Tech. group; Founder-Pres. BrickPath LLC 2004; f. Med-TrackAlert 2006; Amb. to Sweden 2009–11; Nat. Finance Chair for Barack Obama presidential campaign 2012 2011–12; Amb. to UK 2013–17; mem. Bd Louisville Free Public Library Foundation, Louisville Public Media, and Teach Kentucky, Kentucky Long Term Policy Research Centre, The Greater Louisville Project, Centre for Interfaith Relations.

BAS, Philippe Paul André; French politician; b. 20 July 1958, Paris; ed Inst. of Political Studies, Nat. School of Man., Paris; mem. Council of State 1987–92; Advisor to Minister of Social Affairs, Health and Towns and to Minister of State for Health 1993–94; Asst Dir, Cabinet of Minister of Social Affairs, Health and Towns 1994–95; Dir, Cabinet of Minister of Employment and Social Affairs 1995–97; Social Affairs Advisor to Pres. of France 1997–2000; Asst Sec.-Gen., Cabinet of Pres. 2000–02, Sec.-Gen. 2002–07; Minister of Health and Social Protection March–May 2007; Chair. French Office for Immigration and Integration, Ministry of Immigration, Integration, Nat. Identity and Shared Devt 2007–11; Vice-Pres. Gen. Council of La Manche 2008–; Senator of La Manche 2011–; Chevalier, Légion d'honneur 2009. *Film appearance:* The Assault 2010. *Publications:* L'Afrique Australe dans la Tourmente (with Denis Tersen) 1988. *Address:* Sénat, Casier de la Poste, 15 rue de Vaugirard, 75291 Paris Cedex 06, France (office). *Telephone:* 1-42-34-30-65 (office); 6-20-46-82-21 (mobile). *Fax:* 1-42-34-30-65 (office). *E-mail:* p.bas@senat.fr (office). *Website:* www.senat.fr/senateur/bas_philippe05008e.html (office); www.philippe-bas.fr.

BASANT ROI, Rameswurlall, GCSK, MA (Econs); Mauritian central banker; b. 17 Aug. 1946; m.; two c.; ed Delhi School of Econs, Univ. of Delhi, India; joined Bank of Mauritius 1976, Research Officer 1976–84, Asst Dir Dept of Research 1984–87, Dir 1987–98, Gov. 1998–2006, 2014–17, also Chair. Monetary Policy Cttee; Chair. Asscn of African Central Banks; mem. Council, Islamic Financial Services Bd; mem. Governing Bd Int. Islamic Liquidity Man. Corpn; Grand Commdr, Order of the Star and Key of the Indian Ocean 2004. *Publications include:* several papers on econs, including Monetary Policy Making in Mauritius (co-author with Maxwell Fry) 1995. *Address:* c/o Bank of Mauritius, Sir William Newton Street, PO Box 29, Port Louis (office); 15 Couvent de Lorette, Vacoas, Mauritius (home). *Telephone:* 202-3800 (office). *Fax:* 208-9204 (office). *E-mail:* governor.office@bom.mu. *Website:* www.bom.mu (office).

BAŞÇI, Erdem, BSc, MBA, MA, PhD; Turkish economist, diplomatist and fmr central banker; *Permanent Representative, Organisation for Economic Co-operation and Development (OECD);* b. 9 Aug. 1966, Ankara; m.; three c.; ed TED Ankara Coll., Middle East Tech. Univ., Bilkent Univ., Johns Hopkins Univ., USA; Teaching Asst, Dept of Man., Bilkent Univ. 1988–89, Research Asst, Dept of Econs 1989–95, Asst Prof. 1996, promoted to Assoc. Prof. 1999; Deputy Gov. Türkiye Cumhuriyet Merkez Bankası AŞ (Central Bank of the Repub. of Turkey) 2008–11, Gov. 2011–16; Perm. Rep. to OECD, Paris 2016–; mem. Econometric Soc., Royal Econ. Soc.; Hon. Visiting Fellow, Univ. of York, UK 1999. *Address:* Permanent Mission of Turkey to the OECD, 9 rue Alfred Dehodencq, 75116 Paris, France (office). *Telephone:* (1) 42-88-50-02 (office). *Fax:* (1) 45-27-28-24 (office). *E-mail:* tr-delegation.oecd@mfa.gov.tr (office). *Website:* www.oecd.dt.mfa.gov.tr (office).

BASELITZ, Georg; German artist; b. (Hans-Georg Bruno Kern), 23 Jan. 1938, Deutschbaselitz, Saxony; m. Elke Kretzschmar 1962; two s.; ed Gymnasium, Kamenz, Kunstakad. E. Berlin and Akad. der Künste, W. Berlin; Instructor, Staatliche Akad. der Bildenden Kunste, Karlsruhe 1977–78, Prof. 1978–83; Prof. Hochschule der Kunste, Berlin 1983–2003; mem. Acad. of the Arts, Berlin 1984–92, Bavarian Acad. of Fine Arts 2009–; works in numerous public collections; Hon. mem., Royal Acad. of Art (UK) 1999, Hon. Citizen, town of Imperia, Italy 2006; Commdr, Ordre des Arts et des Lettres 2002; Hon. Prof. (Acad. of Fine Art, Krakow) 2000, (Accademia di Belle Arti, Florence) 2004; Kaiserring Prize, Goslar 1986, Rhenus Art Prize, Mönchen-Gladbach 1999, Julio González Prize, Valencia 2001, Niedersächsischer Staaspreis 2003, Praemium Imperial, Japan 2004, Decoration for Science and Art, Vienna, Austria 2005, B.Z. Culture Prize 2008, Cologne Fine Art Award of the Asscn of German Galleries and Editions 2009. *Publications:* books, pamphlets, manifestos and articles. *Address:* Schloss Derneburg, 31188 Holle, Germany (office). *Website:* www.georgbaselitz.com.

BĂSESCU, Traian; Romanian politician, fmr head of state and fmr naval officer; b. 4 Nov. 1951, Basarabi, Constanţa Co.; s. of Dumitru Băsescu and Elena Băsescu; m. Maria Băsescu; two d.; ed Inst. of Civil Marine Mircea cel Bătrân and Norwegian Acad.; Officer Grades III, II and I, Romanian Navy 1976–81, Capt., Merchant Navy 1981–87; Head of Navrom Agency, Antwerp, Belgium 1987–89; Gen. Dir State Inspectorate of Civil Navigation, Ministry of Transportation 1989–90, Under-Sec. of State and Head of Naval Transportation Dept 1990–91, Minister of Transport 1991–92, 1996–2000; mem. Partidul Democrat (DP—Democratic Party), Pres. 2001–04; mem. Chamber of Deputies 1992–96, 1996–2000; Vice-Pres. Chamber of Deputies Comm. for Industry and Services 1992–96; investigated for corruption and fraud 1996; Dir electoral campaign for Petre Roman (pres. cand.) 1996; Co-Pres. Alianţa Dreptate şi Adevăr (DA—Yes-Justice and Truth Alliance) 2003–; Mayor of Bucharest 2000–04; Pres. of Romania 2004–14 (suspended from post 20 April–23 May 2007, 6 July–27 Aug. 2012); mem. Partidul Mişcarea Populară (PMP—People's Movt Party) 2015–, Pres. 2015–18, Hon. Pres. 2018–; Collar of the Order of the Cross of Terra Mariana (Estonia), First Class with Chain of the Order of the Three Stars (Latvia), Order of the Republic (Moldova), Order of the White Eagle (Poland), Grand Cross, Order of Saint-Charles (Monaco) 2009. *Address:* Partidul Mişcarea Populară (People's Movement Party), 010432 Bucharest, Str. Iorga 11, Romania (office). *Telephone:* (31) 4381266 (office). *E-mail:* secretariat@pmponline.ro (office). *Website:* www.pmponline.ro (office).

BASHA, Lulzim Xhelal, LLM; Albanian lawyer and politician; *Chairman, Partia Demokratike e Shqipërisë (Democratic Party of Albania);* b. 12 June 1974, Tirana; m. Aurela Isufi; one d.; ed Utrecht Univ., Netherlands; worked for Int. Criminal Tribunal for the fmr Yugoslavia and was mem. war crimes investigation team of Serbian forces in Kosovo 1998–99; Legal Adviser, Justice Dept, UN Mission in Kosovo (UNMIK) 2000–01, Deputy Chief of Cabinet of Dir of Justice Dept 2001–02, Special Adviser for Transition, Justice Dept 2002–05; mem. Partia Demokratike e Shqipërisë (PDSh—Democratic Party of Albania) 2005–, Co-ordinator Cttee for Policy Orientation 2005–, Nat. Council 2005–, mem. Presidency 2005–, Chair. 2013–, Spokesman of Gen. Election Campaign May–July 2005; mem. Parl. 2005–, Minister of Public Works, Transport and Telecommunications 2005–07, of Foreign Affairs 2007–09, of the Interior 2009–11; Mayor of Tirana 2011–15; Freedom of the City of London 2013. *Address:* Partia Demokratike e Shqipërisë, Rruga Punëtorët e Rilindjes 1, 1001 Tirana, Albania (office). *Telephone:* (4) 2228091 (office). *Fax:* (4) 2223525 (office). *E-mail:* denonco@pd.al (office). *Website:* www.pd.al (office); www.facebook.com/lulzimbasha.al.

BASHAH MOHD HANIPAH, Datuk Seri Ahmad; Malaysian politician; b. 10 Oct. 1950, Alor Setar, Kedah; m. Hizam Awang Ahmad; mem. Kota Setar Municipal Council 1988–94; mem. Kedah State Legis. Ass. for Alor Merah 1995–2004, for Bakar Bata 2004–18; mem. Dewan Negara (Senate) 2013–16; Deputy Minister of Domestic Trade, Co-operatives and Consumerism 2013–16; Menteri Besar (Chief Minister) of Kedah 2016–18; mem. Bd of Dirs Muda Agricultural Devt Authority 1991–95; Deputy Pres. Kedah Football Asscn; mem. United Malays Nat. Org. (UNMO), Treas. UNMO Kedah 1994–97; Officer, Order of the Defender of the Realm 1997, Companion, Illustrious Order of Loyalty to the Royal House of Kedah 1996; Meritorious Service Medal 1985, Pingat Pangkuan Negara Medal 1986, Public Service Star 1990, Ahli Mahkota Kedah Medal 1994.

BASHIR, Maria; Afghan lawyer and government official; b. 1970; m.; one s. one d.; ed Kabul Univ.; criminal investigator in prosecutor's office 1994–95, 2001–; Chief Prosecutor Gen. Herat Prov. (first woman) 2006–14 (removed from office by Pres. Ahmadzai); Int. Women of Courage Award, US State Dept 2011. *Address:* c/o Attorney-General's Office, Herat, Afghanistan (office). *Website:* www.ago.gov.af (office).

BASHIR, The Hon. Dame Marie Roslyn, AD, CVO, DStJ, MBS; Australian fmr state governor and professor of psychiatry; b. Narrandera; d. of M. Bashir; m. Sir Nicholas Shehadie 1957; three c.; ed Sydney Girls High School, Univ. of Sydney; elected to Women's Coll. Council, Univ. of Sydney 1959, Hon. Sec. 1960, Chair. 1982–90, life mem. Coll. Union 1969–; fmr teacher Univs of Sydney and New South Wales; Foundation Dir, Rivendell Child Adolescent and Family Service 1972–87; Dir Community Health Services, Cen. Sydney 1987–93; Clinical Prof. of Psychiatry, Univ. of Sydney 1993–2001; Consultant to NSW Juvenile Justice Facilities 1993–2000; Area Dir of Mental Health Services, Cen. Sydney 1994–2001; Sr Consultant to Aboriginal Medical Service, Redfern and Kempsey 1996–2001; Gov. of NSW 2001–14; Chancellor Univ. of Sydney 2007–12; Co-Chair. NSW Mental Health Strategy for Aboriginal People; Fellow, Royal Australian and New Zealand Coll. of Psychiatrists 1971–; mem. Amnesty International, Nat. Trust, NSW Camellia Research Soc., Tandanya Nat. Aboriginal Cultural Centre; Patron Sydney Symphony and Opera Australia; Patron New South Wales Branch, Order of Australia Asscn; mem. numerous univ. cttees, medical research bodies, mental health bds; involved in establishment of postgraduate medical training in psychiatry in Viet Nam and other medical educ. visits to Laos and Cambodia; Officier de la Légion d'honneur, Grand Cordon, Order of the Cedar (Lebanon); named Mother of the Year NSW 1971. *Publications include:* research papers and publs on child, adolescent, refugee and Aboriginal mental health issues. *Leisure interests:* int. affairs, Australian history, early Australian antique furniture, classical music, opera, Aboriginal art, growing camellias. *Address:* c/o Office of the Governor, Macquarie Street, Sydney, NSW 2000 (office); Order of Australia Association, Old Parliament House, King George Terrace, Parkes, ACT 2600, Australia (office). *Telephone:* (2) 6273-0322 (Parkes) (office). *E-mail:* oaasecretariat@ozemail.com.au (office). *Website:* www.parliament.nsw.gov.au (office); www.theorderofaustralia.asn.au (office).

BASHIR, Lt-Gen. Omar Hassan Ahmad al-; Sudanese army officer and head of state; b. 1 Jan. 1944, Hoshe Bannaga, Anglo-Egyptian Sudan; ed Sudan Mil. Acad., Egyptian Mil. Acad., Cairo; fought in Egyptian army during 1973 war with Israel; career army officer rising to rank of Brig., then Lt-Gen.; overthrew Govt of Sadiq al-Mahdi in coup 30 June 1989; Chair. Revolutionary Command Council for Nat. Salvation 1989–; Minister of Defence 1989–93; Pres. and Prime Minister of Sudan 1993–2019 (ousted in military coup and detained); Pres. National Congress Party; Chair. Ass. Intergovernmental Authority on Devt 2000–01; charged with genocide by Int. Criminal Court (ICC) 14 July 2008, warrant issued for his arrest on two counts of war crimes and five counts of crimes against humanity in Darfur (first ICC warrant for a serving head of state) 4 March 2009.

BASHIR, Salaheddin al-, MA, PhD; Jordanian lawyer, academic and politician; b. 1966; ed Univ. of Jordan, Harvard Law School, USA, McGill Univ., Canada; Adjunct Prof. of Law, Univ. of Jordan 1996–, Dir Centre for Strategic Studies 1999; Minister of Industry and Trade 2001–03, Minister of State for Cabinet Affairs and Minister of Justice 2003–05, Minister of Foreign Affairs 2007–09; Senator –2011; Founder and Sr Man. Pnr, International Business Legal Assocs (law firm), Amman; fmr Man. Pnr, Abu Ghazaleh Legal Services; Co-Chair. Jordanian–American Comm. for Educational Exchange; mem. Jordan Bar Asscn, International Bar Asscn, Jordanian Intellectual Property Asscn, Licensing Exec. Soc.—Arab Countries (Vice-Pres.), Arab Soc. for the Protection of Intellectual Property; named Young Global Leader by World Economic Forum. *Address:* International Business Legal Associates, PO Box 9028, Amman 11191, Jordan (office). *E-mail:* sbashir@iblaw.com.jo (office). *Website:* www.iblaw.com.jo (office).

BASHIR, Salman, MA, LLB; Pakistani diplomatist; b. 4 March 1952, Haripur; m.; two s. one d.; ed Univ. of Peshawar; joined Foreign Service 1976, Section Officer, Ministry of Foreign Affairs 1976–80, assignments abroad at Mission to UN, Geneva 1980–84, Section Officer, Ministry of Foreign Affairs 1984, Dir, UN 1985–87, OIC Secr., Jeddah 1988–99, Dir Gen., UN 1995–99, Amb. to Denmark 1999–2003, Additional Sec., Asia-Pacific, Ministry of Foreign Affairs 2003–05, Amb. to People's Repub. of China 2005–08, Foreign Sec. 2008–12, High Commr to India 2012–14 (retd). *Leisure interests:* reading, music, cricket.

BASHMACHNIKOV, Vladimir Fedorovich, DEcon; Russian politician; b. 27 March 1937; m.; three d.; ed Urals State Univ.; worker, deputy chair. kolkhoz, Sverdlovsk Region 1959–62; teacher, docent, Prof., Urals State Univ. 1962–65; Founder All-Russian Inst. of Labour (now All-Russian Inst. of Econ. and Man. in Agric.) 1964–72, Deputy Dir 1972–84; consultant, Econ. Dept, Cen. Cttee CPSU 1984–89; mem. Cttee on Land Reform Cen. Cttee CPSU 1989–91; active participant in movt for privatization of land; mem. State Duma; mem. faction Our Home Russia; mem. Cttee on Agrarian Problems 1995–; Pres. Asscn of Farmers' and Agric. Co-operatives of Russia 1991–2005; Chair. Union of Land-Owners of Russia 1994; mem. Co-ordination Council, Round Table Business of Russia. *Publications:* over 150 books and articles on org. of labour in agric. *Address:* c/o Association of Farmers' and Agricultural Co-operatives of Russia, 107139 Moscow, Orlikov per 3, Suite 405, Russia.

BASHMET, Yuri Abramovich; Russian violist and conductor; *Artistic Director and Principal Conductor, Symphony Orchestra of New Russia (Novaya Rossiya State Symphony Orchestra);* b. 24 Jan. 1953, Rostov-on-Don; m. Natalia Bashmet; one d.; ed Moscow State Conservatory; concerts since 1975; gave recitals and played with maj. orchestras of Europe, America and Asia; played in chamber ensembles with Sviatoslav Richter, Vladimir Spivakov, Victor Tretyakov and others; restored chamber repertoire for viola, commissioned and was first performer of music by contemporary composers, including concertos by Alfred Schnittke, Giya Kancheli, Aleksander Tchaikovsky; first viola player to give solo recitals at leading concert halls including Tchaikovsky Hall, Moscow, Concertgebouw, Amsterdam, La Scala, Milan, Suntory Hall, Tokyo; Founder and Artistic Dir Chamber Orchestra Soloists of Moscow 1989–; Founder and Artistic Dir Moscow Soloists 1992–; Artistic Dir and Prin. Conductor Symphony Orchestra of New Russia (Novaya Rossiya State Symphony Orchestra) 2002–; f. Yuri Bashmet Int. Competition for Young Viola Players 1994; Artistic Dir December Nights Festival, Moscow 1998–, Moscow Soloists; Founder and Artistic Dir Elba Music Festival 1998–; f. Yuri Bashmet Viola Competition, Moscow 1999–; f. Int. Foundation to award annual Shostakovich Prize; prize winner of int. competitions in Budapest 1975, Munich 1976, People's Artist of Russia 1986, State Prize of Russia 1993, Sonning Prize (Denmark) 1995, Russian Biographic Soc. Man of the Year 2000, Olympus Nat. Award 2003. *Address:* International Classical Artists, Dunstan House, 14a St Cross Street, London, EC1N 8XA, England (office); 103009 Moscow, Briyusov per. 7, Apt. 16, Russia (home). *E-mail:* info@icartists.co.uk (office). *Telephone:* (495) 561-66-96 (office); (495) 229-73-25 (home). *Website:* www.nros.ru/nros/ru.

BASHUA, Abiodun Oluremi, BSc; Nigerian diplomatist and UN official; b. 1951, Ibadan; ed Univ. of Ibadan, Univ. of Besançon, France; spent more than 35 years in Nigerian Foreign Service, 18 months as Sec. to Conf. of Parties of UN Framework Convention on Climate Change, Bonn, Germany; Dir Political Affairs Div., UN Mission in Sudan (UNMIS) 2006–07, Dir Political Affairs Div., African Union-UN Hybrid Operation in Darfur (UNAMID) 2009–11, Dir and Head of Office of Jt Support and Coordination Mechanism of UNAMID to African Union Comm., Addis Ababa 2011–14, Deputy Jt Special Rep., also Acting Jt Special Rep., for AU-UN Hybrid Operation in Darfur (UNAMID) 2014–15; apptd by UN Sec.-Gen. as Head, Special Investigation into Malakal Incident in South Sudan 2016–; has worked with several UN peacekeeping operations in Africa, including in Côte d'Ivoire, Liberia, Sierra Leone and Sudan. *Publications:* numerous papers on int. affairs, peacekeeping and peacebuilding. *Address:* Office of the Secretary-General, United Nations, New York, NY 10017, USA (office). *Telephone:* (212) 963-1234 (office). *Fax:* (212) 963-4879 (office). *Website:* www.un.org (office).

BASILASHVILI, Oleg Valeriyanovich; Russian actor; b. 26 Sept. 1934, Moscow; m. Galina Mshanskaya; two d.; ed Moscow Art Theatre; debut at Leningrad Theatre of Lenin's Komsomol 1956–59; leading actor, Leningrad (now St Petersburg) Bolshoi Drama Theatre of Tovstonogov 1959–; several leading roles, including Gayev (The Cherry Orchard), Voynitsky (Uncle Vanya), Khlestakov (The Government Inspector); active participant of democratic movt since end of 1980s, People's Deputy of Russia 1990–93; Hon. mem. Russian Acad. of Arts; Order of Friendship 1994, Order Merit to Fatherland Fourth Degree 2004, Order of Radiance (Georgia) 2010, Order of Honour 2014; People's Actor of Russia 1977, State Prize of Russia 1978, USSR People's Actor 1984, Laureat Golden Soffit 1997. *Films include:* Alive Corpse 1969, Take Aim 1974, A Slave of Love 1976, Business Love Affair 1977, Autumn Marathon 1979, Say a Word for the Poor Hussar 1981, Station for Two 1982, Railway Station for Two 1983, Confrontation 1985, Courier 1986, Zerograd 1988, The Promised Heaven 1991, The Prophecy 1992, Prediction 1993, The Ticket in the Red Theatre 1994, Heads and Tails 1995, The Romanovs: An Imperial Family 2000, Poisons or the World History of Poisoning 2001, Idiot (TV) 2003; Dorogaya Masha Berezina 2004, The Master and Margarita (TV) 2005, Sonka: Zolotaya Ruchka (Sonka: Golden Pen) 2006; numerous TV productions. *Address:* Borodinskaya str. 13, Apt 58, 196180 St Petersburg, Russia (home). *Telephone:* 113-55-56 (home).

BASIN, Yefim Vladimirovich, DEcon; Russian engineer, business executive and fmr politician; b. 3 Jan. 1940, Khislovichi, Tambov Region; m.; one s. one d.; ed Belarus Inst. of Transport Eng, Acad. of Nat. Econs; Master, Chief Engineer, Head, Yaroslavl Construction Dept 1962–69; Deputy Man., Chief Engineer, Gortransstroi, Gorky (now Nizhny Novgorod) 1969–72; Head Construction Dept, Pechorstroi 1972–78; First Deputy Head Glavbamstroi 1980–86; USSR Deputy Minister of Transport Construction; Head, Glavbamstroi and Bamtransstroi production cos 1986–90; Deputy, State Duma of RSFSR; mem. Supreme Soviet; Chair. Cttee on Construction, Architecture and Housing 1990–92; Chair. State Cttee on Problems of Architecture and Construction 1992–94; Minister of Construction 1994–97; Chair. State Cttee on Construction Policy 1997–98; First Deputy Head, Complex of Perspective Construction, then Head, Dept of Construction Devt, Moscow Govt May–Oct. 1998; Chair. State Cttee on Construction, Architecture and Housing Policy 1998–99; First Vice-Pres. Inzhtransstroi Corpn 1999, fmr CEO; apptd Pres. Nostroi (Nat. Asscn of Builders) 2009; Pres. Self-Regulating Org., Interregional Union of Builders; Vice-Pres. Russian Union of Builders; mem. Int. Real Estate Business Forum, Bd of Dirs World Trade Centre, Moscow; mem. La Spinetta One Liter Club; Hero of Socialist Labour 1990, Merited Constructor of Russian Fed. 1998, State Prize of Russian Fed. 1998. *Leisure interests:* hunting, tennis, tourism. *Address:* c/o Inzhtransstroi Corporation, 107217 Moscow, Sadovaya-Spasskaya str. 21/1, Russia. *Telephone:* (495) 777-79-04 (office). *Fax:* (495) 777-73-78 (office). *E-mail:* nzm@transstroy.ru (office).

BASINDWA, Muhammad Salem; Yemeni politician; b. Jan. 1935, Aden; Founder-mem. People's Socialist Party 1962; fmr political adviser to leadership council; Minister of Social Affairs, Labour and Youth 1974, of Devt and Chair. Cen. Planning Org. 1976, Minister of Information and Culture 1978, of Foreign Affairs (first govt following reunification of N and S Yemen) 1993–94, of Information and political adviser to Pres. Saleh 1994–95, Prime Minister of Yemen 2011–14; mem. Shura (consultative council) 1988; fmr mem. Gen. People's Congress; Chair. Nat. Opposition Council. *Address:* c/o Office of the Prime Minister, San'a, Yemen.

BASINGER, Kim; American actress; b. 8 Dec. 1953, Athens, Ga; d. of Don Basinger; m. 1st Ron Britton 1980 (divorced 1990); m. 2nd Alec Baldwin (q.v.) 1993 (divorced 2002); one d.; model 1971–76; first TV role 1976; f. Skyfish Productions (film production co.). *Films include:* Hard Country 1981, Mother Lode 1982, Never Say Never Again 1982, The Man Who Loved Women 1983, The Natural 1984, 9½ Weeks 1985, Fool for Love 1985, No Mercy 1986, Batman 1989, The Marrying Man 1990, Too Hot to Handle 1991, Final Analysis 1992, Cool World 1992, The Real McCoy 1993, Getaway 1994, Wayne's World II 1994, Pret-a-Porter 1994, LA Confidential (Acad. Award and Golden Globe for Best Supporting Actress 1998) 1997, Bless the Child 2000, I Dreamed of Africa 2000, People I Know 2002, 8 Mile 2003, Elvis Has Left the Building 2004, Cellular 2004, The Door in the Floor 2004, The Sentinel 2006, Even Money 2006, The Burning Plain 2008, While She Was Out 2008, The Informers 2009, Charlie St. Cloud 2010, Black November 2012, Grudge Match 2013, Third Person 2013, 4 Minute Mile 2014, I Am Here 2014. *Address:* CAA, 9830 Wilshire Boulevard, Beverly Hills, CA 90212; c/o Judy Hofflund, Hofflund Polone, 9465 Wilshire Boulevard, Suite 820, Beverly Hills, CA 90212; Skyfish Productions, 725 Arizona Avenue, Suite 100, Santa Monica, CA 90401, USA.

BAŠKA, Jaroslav; Slovak politician; *Chairman, Trenčín Self-Governing Region;* b. 5 April 1975, Považská Bystrica; m.; three c.; ed Univ. of Žilina; Project Man. for information systems, Matador Púchov 1998–2000, Asst Dir for Econs 2001–02; mem. Parl. (Smer-Sociálna demokracia) 2002–06, 2010–12, 2012–, mem. Perm. Del. to Parl. Ass. of Council of Europe 2002–06; Mayor of Dohňany 2003–06; State Sec., Ministry of Defence 2006–08, Minister of Defence 2008–10; Chair. Trenčín Self-Governing Region 2013–. *Leisure interests:* informatics, music, cycling, skiing, squash, fitness. *Address:* Trenčín Self-Governing Regional Administration, K dolnej stanici 7282/20A, 911 01 Trenčín, Slovakia (office). *Telephone:* (32) 6555-811 (office). *Fax:* (32) 6555-909 (office). *E-mail:* info@tsk.sk (office). *Website:* www.tsk.sk (office).

BAŞOĞLU, Hasan, MA; Turkish-Cypriot politician; b. 1962, Gaziveren; ed Boğaziçi Univ.; worked as sr man. in numerous banks, Istanbul –1994; Gen. Man. Deniz Bank Ltd 1995–96; Finance Dir, Cyprus Turkish Electricity Authority (KIB-TEK) 2008–10, 2013–15 (resgnd); Minister of Finance July–Oct. 2015. *Website:* www.kktcmaliye.com.

BASRI, Muhammad Chatib, PhD; Indonesian economist and politician; b. 22 Aug. 1965, Jakarta; ed Univ. of Indonesia, Australian Nat. Univ.; Chair. Inst. for Econ. and Social Research 2005–09; mem. Advisory Team to Indonesian Nat. Team on Trade Negotiation 2005–12; Deputy Minister of Finance for G-20 2006–09; Special Adviser to Minister of Finance 2006–10; 'Sherpa' to Pres. of Indonesia for G-20 meeting, Washington, DC Nov. 2008; Co-founder and Sr Partner, CReco Research Inst. (econ. consulting firm), Jakarta 2010–12; Vice-Chair. Nat. Econ. Cttee of Pres. of Indonesia 2010–12; Chair. Indonesian Investment Coordinating Bd 2012–13; Minister of Finance 2013–14; Sr Lecturer, Dept of Econs, Univ. of Indonesia 1992–; ind. mem. IMF Asia Pacific Regional Advisory Group; mem. Davos High Level Trade Experts Group 2010–11; ind. Dir (non-exec.) Axiata Group Bhd 2010–12; fmr mem. Regional Advisory Bd, Toyota Motor Asia Pacific; fmr consultant for World Bank, Asian Development Bank, USAID, AUSAID, OECD and UNCTAD. *Publications:* author of numerous papers in int. journals; contributor to various leading nat. newspapers and magazines. *Address:* c/o Ministry of Finance, Jalan Lapangan Banteng Timur 2–4, Jakarta 10710, Indonesia. *Website:* chatibbasri.net.

BASS, John R., BA; American diplomatist; *Ambassador to Turkey;* b. New York; ed Syracuse Univ.; worked as newspaper ed. and political campaign consultant; joined Foreign Service 1988, Special Asst for Europe and Eurasia 1998–2000, Chief of Staff to Deputy Sec. of State Strobe Talbott 2000–01, served at Embassy in Rome 2002–04, Special Advisor to Vice-Pres. Richard Cheney 2004–05, Dir Operations Center, Dept of State 2005–08, led Baghdad Prov. Reconstruction Team 2008–09, Amb. to Georgia 2009–12, to Turkey 2014–. *Address:* US Embassy, 110 Atatürk Bul., Kavaklıdere, 06100 Ankara, Turkey (office). *Telephone:* (312) 4555555 (office). *Fax:* (312) 4670019 (office). *E-mail:* webmasterankara@state.gov (office). *Website:* turkey.usembassy.gov (office).

BASS, Ronald (Ron); American songwriter and screenwriter; b. 26 March 1942, Los Angeles, Calif.; ed Yale Univ., Harvard Law School; began career as entertainment lawyer. *Films include:* screenplays: Code Name: Emerald, Black Widow, Gardens of Stone, Rain Man (Acad. Award for Best Original Screenplay) 1988, Sleeping with the Enemy, The Joy Luck Club, When a Man Loves a Woman 1994, Dangerous Minds 1995, Waiting to Exhale, My Best Friend's Wedding 1997, What Dreams May Come 1998, Stepmom 1998, Entrapment 1999, Snow Falling on Cedars 1999, Passion of Mind 1999, The Lazarus Child (exec. producer) 2004, Mozart and the Whale 2005, Just Like Heaven 2005, Amelia 2009, Snow Flower and the Secret Fan 2011, Before We Go 2014, The King's Daughter 2016. *Television includes:* Dangerous Minds (series), Moloney. *Publications include:* novels: The Perfect Thief 1978, Lime's Crisis 1982, The Emerald Illusion 1984.

BASSET, Lytta, DTheol; Swiss theologian, writer and academic; *Professor Emeritus of Theology, University of Neuchâtel;* b. 1950, French Polynesia; m.; three c. (one deceased); ed Univs of Strasbourg and Geneva; missionary work in India, Iran, Djibouti, French Polynesia and USA 1970–; fmr Lecturer in Philosophy and Theology, Faculty of Theology, Univ. of Lausanne; fmrly Prof. (now Emer.) and Vice-Dean, Faculty of Theology, Univ. of Neuchâtel; Editorial Dir, La Chair et le Souffle magazine. *Publications include:* Le pardon original 1995, La joie imprenable 1998, Moi, je ne juge personne 1998, Guérir du malheur 1999, Le pouvoir de pardonner 1999, Culpabilité, paralysie du cœur 2000, La fermeture à l'amour 2000, Histoire et Herméneutique 2002, Sainte colère 2002, Ce lien qui ne meurt jamais 2007, Aimer sans dévorer 2010, Oser la bienveillance 2014; numerous articles and essays on Protestant theology. *Address:* c/o University of Neuchâtel, Faculty of Theology, Faubourg de l'Hôpital 41, 2000 Neuchâtel, Switzerland (office). *Telephone:* 327181907 (office). *E-mail:* lytta.basset@unine.ch (office). *Website:* www2.unine.ch/theol (office).

BASSETT, Angela, MFA; American actress; b. 16 Aug. 1958, New York; d. of Daniel Benjamin Bassett and Betty Jane; m. Courtney B. Vance; one s. one d.; ed Yale School of Drama; Amb. UNICEF; Dr hc (Yale Univ.) 2018. *Theatre includes:* Colored People's Time 1982, Antigone, Black Girl, The Mystery Plays 1984–85, The Painful Adventures of Pericles, Prince of Tyre 1986–87, Joe Turner's Come and Gone 1986–87, Ma Rainey's Black Bottom, King Henry IV (Part I) 1987. *Films include:* F/X 1986, Kindergarten Cop 1990, Boyz 'N the Hood 1991, City of Hope 1991, Critters 4, Innocent Blood 1992, Malcolm X 1992, Passion Fish 1992, What's Love Got to Do with It 1993 (Golden Globe Award Best Actress 1994), Strange Days 1995, Panther 1995, Waiting to Exhale 1995, A Vampire in Brooklyn 1995, Contact 1997, How Stella Got Her Groove Back 1998, Music of the Heart 1999, Supernova 2000, Boesman and Lena 2000, The Score 2001, Sunshine State 2002, Masked and Anonymous 2003, The Lazarus Child 2004, Mr 3000 2004, Akeelah and the Bee 2005, Time Bomb 2006, Meet the Robinsons (voice) 2007, Olympus Has Fallen 2013, White Bird in a Blizzard 2014, Survivor 2015, Curious George 3: Back to the Jungle 2015, London Has Fallen 2016, Black Panther 2018. *TV films include:* Line of Fire: The Morris Dees Story 1991, The Jacksons: An American Dream 1992, A Century of Women 1994, Ruby's Bucket of Blood (Black Reel Award for Outstanding Television Actress 2002, NAACP Image Award for Outstanding Actress in a Television Movie, Mini-Series or Dramatic Special 2002) 2001, The Rosa Parks Story (Black Reel Award for Outstanding Television Actress 2003, NAACP Image Award for Outstanding Actress in a Television Movie, Mini-Series or Dramatic Special 2003) 2002, Alias (Series) 2005, Time Bomb 2006, ER (Series) 2008–09, Identity 2011, Rogue 2012, Betty and Coretta 2013, American Horror Story (Series) 2013–18, BoJack Horseman (Series) 2015–18, The Snowy Day 2016, Close to the Enemy (Mini Series) 2016, 9-1-1 (Series) 2018–. *Website:* www.entertainmentbookingagency.com/artists/angela-bassett/. *E-mail:* bvmedia@bassettvance.com.

BASSETTI, HE Cardinal Gualtiero; Italian ecclesiastic; *Archbishop of Perugia-Città della Pieve;* b. 7 April 1942, Popolano di Marradi; ordained priest, Archdiocese of Florence 1966; consecrated Bishop of Massa Marittima-Piombino 1994–98; Bishop of Arezzo-Cortona-Sansepolcro 1998–2009; Archbishop of Perugia-Città della Pieve 2009–; cr. Cardinal (Cardinal-Priest of Santa Cecilia) 2014–; Head of Catholic Bishops Conf. of Umbria 2012–; Deputy Pres. Italian Episcopal Conf. *Address:* Piazza IV Novembre 6, 06123 Perugia, Italy (office). *Telephone:* (075) 5731685 (office). *Fax:* (075) 5732672 (office). *E-mail:* info@diocesi.perugia.it (office). *Website:* www.diocesi.perugia.it (office).

BASSEY, Dame Shirley Veronica, DBE; British singer; b. 8 Jan. 1937, Tiger Bay, Cardiff, Wales; d. of Henry Bassey and Eliza Bassey (née Mendi); one d.; m. 1st Kenneth Hume 1961 (divorced 1965; deceased); m. 2nd Sergio Novak 1971 (divorced 1981); one d. (deceased) one adopted s.; sang at Astor Club, London; signed up for Such is Life by impresario Jack Hylton 1955; started making records 1956; appeared in cabaret in New York 1961; Artist for Peace, UNESCO 2000; Int. Amb., Variety Club 2001; Chevalier, Légion d'honneur 2010; numerous awards, including 20 Gold Discs and 14 Silver Discs for sales in UK, Netherlands, France, Sweden and other countries; Best Female Singer (TV Times) 1972, 1973, (Music Week) 1974, Best Female Entertainer (American Guild of Variety Artists) 1976, Britannia Award for Best Female Singer 1977. *Film:* La Passione 1996. *Albums include:* Born to Sing the Blues 1958, And I Love You So 1972, Magic is You 1978, I Am What I Am 1984, Sassy Bassey 1985, New York, New York 1991, Great Shirley Bassey 1999, Thank You For the Years 2003, Get the Party Started 2007, The Performance 2009, Hello Like Before 2014. *Singles include:* Banana Boat Song, As I Love You, Kiss Me Honey Honey Kiss Me, As Long As He Needs Me, theme song for James Bond films Goldfinger 1964, Diamonds Are Forever 1971, Moonraker 1979. *Address:* 31 Avenue Princesse Grace, 98000 MC, Monaco (office). *E-mail:* burnmycandle@monaco.mc (office). *Website:* shirleybassey.wordpress.com.

BASSIL, Gebran, BE, MSc; Lebanese politician; *Minister of Foreign Affairs and Emigrants;* b. 21 June 1970, Batroun; m. Chantale Michel Aoun; three c.; ed American Univ. of Beirut; began career by founding co. that built residential projects and renovated old houses; Minister of Telecommunications 2008–09, of Energy and Water 2011–14, of Foreign Affairs and Emigrants 2014–; Leader and mem., Free Patriotic Movt 2015–; mem. Parliament 2018–; mem. Lebanese Red Cross, Rotary Club, Lebanon Green. *Address:* Ministry of Foreign Affairs and Emigrants, al-Sultana Bldg, al-Jnah, Sultan Ibrahim, Beirut, Lebanon (office). *Telephone:* (1) 840767 (office). *Fax:* (1) 840924 (office). *E-mail:* director@emigrants.gov.lb (office). *Website:* www.mfa.gov.lb (office); www.gebranbassil.com.

BASSLER, Bonnie Lynn, BS, PhD; American biochemist, molecular biologist and academic; *Squibb Professor in Molecular Biology, Endowed Chair, Princeton University;* b. 1962, Chicago, Ill.; ed Univ. of California, Davis, Johns Hopkins Univ.; raised in Danville, Calif.; Prof., Princeton Univ. 1994–, Squibb Prof. in Molecular Biology, Endowed Chair 2007–, Director, Council on Science and Tech.; mem. NAS 2006, USA Science & Eng Festival's Nifty Fifty (group of the most influential scientists and engineers in USA dedicated to re-invigorating the interest of young people in science and eng); Fellow, American Acad. of Microbiology 2002, AAAS 2004, American Acad. of Arts and Sciences 2007; Dr hc (Swarthmore Coll.) 2010; MacArthur Fellowship 2002, Theobald Smith Soc. Waksman Award 2003, Thomas Edison Patent Award, Medical Technology, New Jersey R and D Council 2004, Inventor of the Year, New York Intellectual Property Lawyers Asscn 2004, Eli Lilly & Co. Research Award, American Soc. for Microbiology 2006, Pres.'s Distinguished Teaching Award, Princeton Univ. 2008, World Cultural Council Award for Scientific Merit 2008, Wiley Prize in Biomedical Sciences 2009, NAS Richard Lounsbery Award 2011, L'Oréal-UNESCO For Women in Science Award (N America) (for discovering the chemical signals and mechanisms bacteria use to communicate and coordinate group behaviours) 2012, Shaw Prize in Life Science and Medicine (co-recipient) 2015, Ernst Schering Prize 2018. *Publications:* numerous papers in professional journals. *Address:* Department of Molecular Biology, Princeton University, 119 Lewis Thomas Laboratory, Washington Road, Princeton, NJ 08544-1014, USA (office). *Telephone:* (609) 258-2857 (office); (609) 258-2864 (Lab.) (office). *Fax:* (609) 258-3980 (office). *E-mail:* bbassler@princeton.edu (office). *Website:* molbio.princeton.edu/faculty/molbio-faculty/31-bassler (office).

BASSOLÉ, Djibril Yipènè; Burkinabè government official and UN official; b. 30 Nov. 1957, Nouna; ed Collège Charles Luanga de Nouna, Prytanée Militaire de Kadiogo, Université de Ouagadougou, Acad. Royale Militaire de Meknès, Ecole Nationale de la Gendarmerie, Abidjan, Côte d'Ivoire, Ecole Supérieure de la Gendarmerie, Maisons Alfort, France; served as Commdt, Gendarmerie Nationale (nat. police force) 1983–95, served in various sr positions including Chef d'Etat-Major (head of police force) 1997–99; Minister-Del. for Security 1999–2000, Minister for Security 2000–07, Minister of Foreign Affairs and Regional Co-operation 2007–08, 2011–14 (govt dissolved by Pres. Blaise Compaoré); Jt UN-African Union Chief Mediator for Darfur 2008–11; Officier et Commdr de l'Ordre Nat. de Burkina Faso, Médaille d'honneur Militaire, Médaille d'honneur de la Police, Officier de l'Ordre Nat. du Lion (Senegal), Commdr de l'Ordre du Mérite du Niger, Commdr de l'Ordre du Mérite du Gabon, Officier de l'Ordre Nat. du Mérite. *Address:* c/o Ministry of Foreign Affairs and Regional Co-operation, rue 988, blvd du Faso, 03 BP 7038, Ouagadougou 03, Burkina Faso (office).

BASTARRECHE SAGÜES, Carlos, LLB; Spanish diplomatist; *Ambassador to UK;* b. 27 Jan. 1950, Madrid; m. Rosalía Gómez-Pineda Goizueta; four c.; entered diplomatic corps 1976, served at Embassy in Bucharest 1976–79, Sec., Conf. for Spanish Accession to EU, Perm. Mission of Spain to EU, Brussels 1979–84, Adviser to Sec. of State for EU Affairs, Madrid 1984–85, Asst Dir-Gen. for EU Co-ordination, Secr. of State for EU Affairs 1986–90, Dir-Gen. of Legal and Institutional Co-ordination 1990–91, Asst Perm. Rep. to EU 1991–96, Sec.-Gen. of Foreign Political and EU Affairs 1996–2000, Sec.-Gen. of European Affairs 2000–02, Amb. and Perm. Rep. to EU 2002–10, Amb. to France 2010–14, to UK 2017–; Prof. of Community Affairs, Escuela Diplomatica. *Address:* Embassy of Spain, 39 Chesham Place, London, SW1X 8SB, England (office). *Telephone:* (20) 7235-5555 (office). *Fax:* (20) 7259-5392 (office). *E-mail:* emb.londres@maec.es (office). *Website:* www.maec.es/embajadas/londres (office).

BASTIAN, Edward H., BBA, CPA; American business executive; *CEO, Delta Air Lines, Inc.;* b. 1957; m. Anna Bastian; four c.; ed St Bonaventure Univ., New York; fmr Partner, Price Waterhouse, New York, then Strategic Planning Partner; fmr Vice-Pres. Finance and Controller Frito-Lay International, then Vice-Pres. of Business Processes Re-engineering, later Vice-Pres. of Finance, PepsiCo International (parent co.); Vice-Pres. of Finance and Controller, Delta Air Lines, Inc. 1998–2000, Sr Vice-Pres. 2000–05, Chief Financial Officer 2005–09, Chief Restructuring Officer 2005–07, Pres. 2007–16, CEO 2016–, Pres. and CEO NWA (wholly owned subsidiary) 2008–09; Sr Vice-Pres. and Chief Financial Officer Acuity Brands June–July 2005; mem. Int. Bd of Dirs, Habitat for Humanity, Woodruff Arts Center, Atlanta. *Address:* Delta Air Lines Inc., PO Box 20706, 1030 Delta Blvd, Atlanta, GA 30320-6001, USA (office). *Telephone:* (404) 715-2600 (office). *Fax:* (404) 715-5042 (office). *E-mail:* info@delta.com (office). *Website:* www.delta.com (office).

BASTID-BRUGUIÈRE, Marianne, PhD; French sinologist and academic; *Research Director Emeritus, Centre national de la recherche scientifique (CNRS);* b. 13 Nov. 1940; ed Ecole Nationale des Langues et Civilisations Orientales, Peking Univ., China; taught at Peking Univ. 1964–65; worked for CNRS from 1966, successively Researcher 1966–69, in charge of Research 1969–73, Master of Research 1973–80, Dir of Research 1981–88, from 1993, now Research Dir Emer.; Deputy Dir Ecole Normale Supérieure 1988–93; Guest Prof., Institut d'études politiques de Strasbourg, École des hautes études en sciences sociales, Paris Diderot Univ., Harvard Univ., Seikei Univ., Univ. of London, Univ. of Kyoto; Advisory Prof., Univ. of Eastern China 2002–, Central China 2003–; mem. Comité nat. de la recherche scientifique 1971–80, 1987–92, 1997–2000, Scientific Council, French School in Rome 2007–, Scientific Council, École des Chartes 2010–; Municipal Councillor, Mage (Orne) 1995–2008; reader for The China Quarterly; Pres. Asscn Européenne d'Etudes Chinoises 1992–96, Asscn philotechnique 2009–; Vice-Pres. Asscn des Anciens Élèves de l'ENS 2002–06, Pres. 2006–07; mem. Acad. des sciences morales et politiques 2001 (Pres. 2012), Soc. for Asian Studies, Academia Europaea 2002; Hon. mem. Institut d'histoire moderne de l'Acad. des sciences sociales de Chine 2000; Grand Officier, Légion d'honneur 2010, Grand Croix 2014; Hon. PhD Russian Acad. of Sciences, Univ. of Aberdeen). *Publications:* La Chine 1: Des Guerres de l'Opium à la Guerre Franco-Chinoise, 1840–1885 (with J. Chesneaux) 1965, Aspects de la Réforme de l'Enseignement en Chine au Début du XXe siècle 1971, La Chine 2: De la Guerre Franco-Chinoise à la Fondation du Parti Communiste Chinois, 1885–1921 (with J. Chesneau and M.-C. Bergère)

1972, L'Evolution de la Société Chinoise à la Fin de la Dynastie des Qing, 1873–1911 1979, The Cambridge History of China (co-author) 1980, The Scope of State Power in China (co-author) 1985, China's Education and the Industrialized world: Studies in Cultural Transfer (with R. Hayhoe) 1987, Educational Reform in Early Twentieth-Century China (translated by P. J. Bailey) 1988; numerous papers in professional journals. *Address:* Centre national de la recherche scientifique, 3 rue Michel-Ange, 75794 Paris Cedex 16, France (office). *Telephone:* 1-44-96-40-00 (office). *Fax:* 1-44-96-53-90 (office). *E-mail:* info@cnrs.fr (office). *Website:* www.cnrs.fr (office).

BASTIEN, Yves Romain; Haitian engineer and politician; m. Carline Choute (divorced); Coordinator, Public Enterprise Modernization Council (privatization agency) –2016; Minister of the Economy and Finance 2016–17.

BAT-ERDENE, Badmaanyambuu; Mongolian politician and fmr professional wrestler; b. 7 June 1964, Khentii Prov.; won 11 nat. level wrestling tournaments at Naadam State Festival 1988–99; retd from wrestling 2006; Chef de mission, Mongolian nat. team, Asian Games 2014; Dir, Avarga (Champion) Physical Culture Inst. 1999–2004; mem. State Great Khural (Parl.) 2004–, Chair., Standing Cttee on Justice 2009–10; Minister of Defence 2016–17; cand. in presidential election 2013; mem. Exec. Bd Mongolian Judo Asscn; mem. Mongolian People's Party; Honoured Athlete of Mongolia 1989, Great Mongolian 800th Anniversary Honorary Medal 2006, Sukhbaatar Medal 2012. *Address:* State Great Khural, Sukhbaatar Square, 14201 Ulaanbaatar, Mongolia (office). *Telephone:* (51) 267016 (office). *Fax:* (11) 327016 (office). *E-mail:* baterdeneb@parliament.mn. *Website:* baterdeneb.parliament.mn.

BAT-ÜÜL, Erdeniin; Mongolian politician; *Mayor of Ulaanbaatar;* b. 1 July 1957, Ulan Bator; m. B. Delgertuja 1977; two s. one d.; teacher, First Constructing Tech. Training School, Ulaanbaatar 1981–82, secondary school, Höbsögöl Prov. 1982–85; scientist, Observatory of Acad. of Sciences 1985–89; Founder-mem. Mongolian Democratic Union, mem. Gen. Co-ordinating Council 1989–, Gen. Co-ordinator Political Consultative Centre 1990–; elected Deputy to Great People's Hural 1990, 1996, 2004, 2008; mem. Political Consultative Centre of Mongolian Democratic Party 1992–; mem. Gen. Council and Dir Political Policy Inst. of Mongolian Nat. Democratic Party 1992, Regional Sec. 1993, Gen. Sec. and Presidium of Co-ordinating Council of Mongolian Democratic Union 1993–96; Mayor of Ulaanbaatar 2012–; Insignia of Red Banner of Labour Merit, Hero of Mongolia. *Address:* Mongolian National Democratic Party, Ulaanbaatar (office); Suchbaatar District 1-40,000, 62-1-4 Ulaanbaatar, Mongolia (home). *Telephone:* 321105 (home). *Website:* www.ulaanbaatar.mn/en.

BATALOV, Andrei Yevgenyevich; Russian ballet dancer; *Founder and Art Director, Saint Petersburg Classical Ballet of Andrey Batalov;* b. 22 April 1974, Izhevsk, Udmurt Repub., Russia; ed Vaganova Acad. of Russian Ballet; Prin. Dancer, Maly Theatre of Opera and Ballet 1992–94; joined Mariinsky Theatre 1994, Prin. Dancer 1996–; Prin. Dancer, Danish Royal Theatre of Opera and Ballet (Danish Royal Ballet) 2000–02; Choreographer, Mihailovski Theatre 2010–; currently Prin. Artist and Ballet Master, Moscow Ballet; Founder and Art Dir St Petersburg Classical Ballet of Andrey Batalov; collaborations including Altynay Asylmuratova, Diana Vishneva, Ulyana Lopatkina, Nadezhda Pavlova; Int. Ballet Competition, Nagoya, Japan, First Prize and Gold Medal 1996, Int. Ballet Competition, Budapest, Second Prize and Silver Medal 1996, Int. Ballet Competition, Perm, First Prize and Gold Medal, The Mikhail Baryshnikov Prize 1996, Int. Ballet Competition, Paris, First Prize and Gold Medal 1996, VIII Int. Ballet Competition, Moscow, Grand Prix 1997, Honoured Artist of Russia 2010. *Roles in ballets include:* James (La Sylphide), Blue Bird (Sleeping Beauty), Prince (Nutcracker), Peasants' Pas de Deux (Giselle), Clown (Legend of Love), Bozhok and Solor (La Bayadère), Basil (Don Quixote), Ali (Le Corsaire), Golden Slave (Sheherazada), Lescaut (Manon Lescaut), Ondine (Matteo), The Prodigal Son (Prodigal Son), Pas de Deux (Diana and Acteon), Le Jeune Homme et la mort, Études, Duet of the Autumn Colours, Flames of Paris (pas de deux), Duet of Autumn Colours. *Telephone:* (921) 848-83-48. *E-mail:* andreybatalov@mail.ru. *Website:* www.batalov-ballet.ru.

BATBAYAR, Bat-Erdeniin, BSc; Mongolian scientist, publisher and fmr politician; *General Director, Nepko Publishing Co.;* b. 1955, Arkhangai Prov.; ed Mongolian State Univ., Imperial Coll., Univ. of London, UK; Researcher, Microbiological Research and Production Centre 1981–91; teacher at secondary school, Hentii Prov. 1982–84; scientist, Inst. of Microbiology 1984–; Founding mem. Democratic Socialist Movt; Founding mem. Mongolian Social Democratic Party, Chair. 1990–94 (resgnd); mem. State Great Hural 1996–2000; Minister of Finance 1998–99 (resgnd); Foreign Policy Adviser to Prime Minister 2004–05; Founder and Gen. Dir Nepko Publishing Co. 2006–; mem. Advisory Bd World Growth Mongolia. *Publications include:* Don't Forget. Otherwise, We'll Be Doomed 1989, History of Mongolia (State Award 2009) 1996. *E-mail:* info@nepko.mn (office). *Website:* www.nepko.mn (office).

BATBOLD, Sükhbaataryn; Mongolian business executive and politician; *Chairman, Mongolian People's Party;* b. 1963, Ulaanbaatar; ed Univ. of Moscow, Russia, Diplomacy Acad. of Moscow, London School of Business, England; Adviser, Ministry of Econ. Foreign Relations 1986–88, Head, Mongol Impex Cooperative (export co.) 1988–92; Dir-Gen., Altai Trading LLC 1992–2000; mem. Parl. 2004–; Vice-Minister of Foreign Affairs 2000–04, Minister of Trade and Industry 2004–06, of External Affairs 2008–09, Prime Minister 2009–12; Chair. Mongolian People's Party 2010–; fmr Chair. Mongolian Devt Strategy Inst. *Address:* Mongolian People's Party, Independence Palace, Ulaanbaatar, Mongolia (office). *Telephone:* (77) 444167 (office). *E-mail:* contact@mpp.mn (office). *Website:* www.mpp.mn (office).

BATCHELOR, Paul John; Australian financial services executive; *Principal and Co-Founder, Yorkway Partners;* b. 22 Sept. 1950, Sydney; s. of John Eastley Batchelor and Patricia Fay Batchelor (née Smith); m. Therese Batchelor 1974; three s.; Pnr, Touche Ross & Co. 1981–85; Financial Dir Nat. Mutual Royal Bank 1985–87; Exec. Dir of Operations Westmax 1987–89; Dir Retail Asia Man. 1993–96; Group Chief Financial Officer and Group Exec. Australasia Fiji Colonial Mutual Assurance Soc. Ltd 1995–97; Chief Financial Officer AMP Ltd Group 1997–99, Man. Dir and CEO 1999–2002; fmr CEO Home Credit & Finance Bank, Russia; Prin. and Co-Founder Yorkway Partners 2009–; Pnr, DB Capital Partners Ltd; mem. Bd of Dirs Jardine CMG Life Holdings Ltd 1994–, Colonial Mutual Funds 1993–, Colonial Mutual Funds Man. Ltd 1993–, Colonial Investment Man. Ltd 1993–, Colonial State Bank 1995–, Jacques Martin Pty Ltd 1993–; fmr Chair. Henderson Asset Management PLC, GIO Insurance Ltd; mem. Business Council of Australia, Financial Sector Advisory Council, Investment Advisory Cttee, Australian Olympic Foundation; Fellow, Inst. of Charted Accountants. *Address:* Yorkway Partners, Buildings 2-3, 1110 Middle Head Road, Mosman, NSW 2088, Australia (office). *Telephone:* (2) 9969-5086 (Australia) (office). *Website:* www.yorkwaypartners.com.

BATE, Sir (Andrew) Jonathan, Kt, CBE, PhD, FBA, FRSL; British college principal, academic, biographer and critic, broadcaster, novelist and playwright; *Provost, Worcester College, Oxford;* b. 26 June 1958, Sevenoaks, Kent; s. of Ronald Montagu Bate and Sylvia Helen Bate; m. 1st Hilary Gaskin 1984 (divorced 1995); m. 2nd Paula Jayne Byrne 1996; two s. one d.; ed Sevenoaks School, St Catharine's Coll., Cambridge; Harkness Fellow, Harvard Univ. 1980–81; Research Fellow, St Catharine's Coll., Cambridge 1983–85, Hon. Fellow 2000–, Fellow, Trinity Hall, Cambridge, Lecturer 1985–90; King Alfred Prof. of English Literature, Univ. of Liverpool 1991–2003; Research Reader, British Acad. 1994–96; Leverhulme Personal Research Prof. 1999–2004; Prof. of Shakespeare and Renaissance Literature, Univ. of Warwick 2003–11; Prof. of English Literature, Univ. of Oxford and Provost, Worcester Coll., Oxford 2011–; Vice-Pres. for Humanities, British Acad.; consultant curator for the British Museum round reading room exhbn for the Cultural Olympiad, Shakespeare: Staging the World 2012; Gov. and mem. Bd, RSC, Ed. Shakespeare Edition; mem. Council of the Arts and Humanities Research Council 2007–11, European Advisory Bd, Princeton University Press; Hon. Fellow, St Catharine's Coll., Cambridge; Calvin & Rose Hoffman Prize 1996, NAMI NY Book Award 2003. *Plays include:* Shakespeare: The Man from Stratford 2010. *Radio:* features and reviews for BBC Radio 3 and Radio 4 (subjects have included The Elizabethan Discovery of England, Faking the Classics and The Poetry of History). *Television:* South Bank Show and other arts programmes. *Publications:* Shakespeare and the English Romantic Imagination 1986, Charles Lamb: Essays of Elia (ed.) 1987, Shakespearean Constitutions: Politics, Theatre, Criticism 1730–1830 1989, Romantic Ecology: Wordsworth and the Environmental Tradition 1991, The Romantics on Shakespeare (ed.) 1992, Shakespeare and Ovid 1993, The Arden Shakespeare: Titus Andronicus (ed.) 1995, Shakespeare: An Illustrated Stage History (ed.) 1996, The Genius of Shakespeare 1997, The Cure for Love (novel) 1998, The Song of the Earth 2000, John Clare: A Biography (Hawthornden Prize 2003, James Tait Black Memorial Prize 2003) 2003, I Am: The Selected Poetry of John Clare (ed.) 2003, Andrew Marvell: Complete Poems (ed.) 2005, The RSC Shakespeare: Complete Works (ed.) 2007, The RSC Shakespeare: Individual Works, 34 vols (ed.) 2008–12, Soul of the Age: The Life, Mind and World of William Shakespeare 2008, English Literature: A Very Short Introduction 2010, The Public Value of the Humanities (ed.) 2011, Shakespeare Staging the World (co-author) 2012, The RSC Shakespeare: Collaborative Plays by Shakespeare and Others (co-ed.) 2013, Ted Hughes: The Unauthorised Life 2015, How the Classics Made Shakespeare 2019; contrib. to the Guardian, Times, TLS and Sunday Telegraph. *Leisure interests:* gardening, tennis, walking, opera, home. *Address:* c/o Wylie Agency Ltd, 17 Bedford Square, London, WC1B 3JA, England (office); Provost's Office, Worcester College, Oxford, OX1 2HB, England (office). *Telephone:* (1865) 278362 (office). *Fax:* (1865) 278303 (office). *E-mail:* provost@worc.ox.ac.uk (office). *Website:* www.english.ox.ac.uk/about-faculty/faculty-members/permanent-post-holders/bate-professor-sir-jonathan (office); www.worc.ox.ac.uk/about/provost (office).

BATE, Jennifer Lucy, OBE, BA, FRCO, FRSA, LRAM, ARCM; British organist; b. 11 Nov. 1944, London; d. of Horace Alfred Bate and Dorothy Marjorie Bate; ed Univ. of Bristol; Shaw Librarian, LSE 1966–69; full-time concert career 1969–; has performed world-wide; has organised several teaching programmes; collaboration with Olivier Messiaen 1975–92; designed portable pipe organ with N.P. Mander Ltd 1984 and a prototype computer organ 1987; gives masterclasses world-wide and lectures on a wide range of musical subjects; mem. Inc. Soc. of Musicians, British Music Soc. (Vice-Pres.), Royal Philharmonic Soc., Royal Soc. of Arts; North London Festival (Vice-Pres.); hon. Italian citizenship for services to music 1996; Officier, Ordre des Arts et des Lettres 2011; Chevalier, Légion d'honneur 2012; Hon. DMus (Bristol) 2007; F.J. Read Prize, Royal Coll. of Organists, Young Musician 1972, voted Personnalité de l'Année, France 1989, one of the Women of the Year, UK 1990–97, Grand Prix du Disque (Messiaen), Diapason d'Or, Prix de Répertoire, France, Preis der deutschen Schallplattenkritik, Germany and MRA Award for 18th-century series From Stanley to Wesley. *Compositions include:* Toccata on a Theme of Martin Shaw, Introduction and Variations on an Old French Carol, Four Reflections, Homage to 1685: Four Studies, The Spinning Wheel, Lament, An English Canon, Variations on a Gregorian Theme, Suite on 'Veni Creator Spiritus'. *Recordings include:* Complete Works of Messiaen, Complete Works of Franck, An English Choice, Virtuoso French Organ Music, Panufnik: Metasinfonia, Vivaldi Double and Triple Concertos, Jennifer Bate and Friends, Jennifer Bate Plays Vierne, From Stanley to Wesley on period instruments, Reflections: The Organ Music of Jennifer Bate, Samuel Wesley Organ Music, The Wesleys and their Contemporaries, Complete Works of Felix Mendelssohn, Complete Organ Works of Peter Dickinson. *Television:* South Bank Show on Messiaen (ITV), Messiaen's La Nativité du Seigneur (Channel 4), Messiaen's Livre du Saint Sacrement (Channel 4), A Ladies' Knight (Channel 4), live recital from Pisa Cathedral (Italian TV2). *Publications include:* articles in Grove's Dictionary of Music and Musicians, Organist's Review. *Leisure interests:* cooking, theatre, philately, gardening. *Address:* c/o Andrew Roberts, 28 Oakenbrow, Sway, Lymington, Hants., SO41 6DY, England (office); 35 Collingwood Avenue, Muswell Hill, London, N10 3EH, England (office). *Telephone:* (1590) 682060 (office); (20) 8883-3811 (office). *E-mail:* andrewlroberts@btinternet.com (office); jenniferbate@classical-artists.com (office). *Fax:* (20) 8444-3695 (office). *Website:* www.classical-artists.com/jbate.

BÄTE, Oliver, BA, MBA; German business executive; *Chairman of the Board of Management (CEO), Allianz SE;* b. 1 March 1965, Bensberg; ed Univ. of Cologne, Leonard Stern School of Business, New York Univ., USA; apprenticeship at Westdeutsche Landesbank, Cologne 1984–88; mil. service with German Air Force, Sardinia, Italy 1987–88; with McKinsey & Co., New York 1993–94, McKinsey & Co., Germany 1995–98, Prin. and Leader of German Insurance Practice

1998–2003, Dir and Leader of European Insurance and Asset Man. Sector 2003–07; mem. Bd of Man., Allianz SE 2008–, COO 2008–09, Chief Financial Officer 2009–12, responsible for insurance business in France, Benelux, Italy, Greece, Turkey, and for Centre of Competence 'Global Property & Casualty' 2013–14, Chair. Bd of Man. (CEO) Allianz SE 2015–, mem. Allianz Deutschland AG (Group mandate), Allianz France SA (Group mandate, Vice-Chair.), Allianz SpA (Group mandate); Chair. Pan European Insurance Forum; teaching position at Univ. of Cologne. *Address:* Allianz SE, Königinstrasse 28, 80802 Munich, Germany (office). *Telephone:* (89) 3800-5592 (office). *Fax:* (89) 3800-5593 (office). *E-mail:* info@allianz.com (office). *Website:* www.allianz.com (office).

BATEMAN, Barry Richard James, BA, MA; British investment services industry executive; *Chief Investment Officer, Fidelity International Investment Advisors (UK) Ltd;* b. 21 June 1945; m. Christine Bateman; one s.; ed Univ. of Exeter; investment analyst, Hoare Govett 1967–72, Research Dir 1972–75; Marketing Dir Datastream 1975–81; Sr Marketing Dir Fidelity Int. Man. Ltd 1981–86, Man. Dir Fidelity Investment Ltd 1986–97, Pres. Fidelity Int. Ltd 1991–2001, apptd Vice-Chair. Fidelity International Investment Advisors (UK) Ltd 2001, Chief Investment Officer 2012–; Chair. Unit Trust Asscn 1991–93; mem. Bd of Dirs Colt Group 1996–2006, Chair. (non-exec.) 2003–07; mem. Bd of Dirs Investment Management Asscn 2001–06, 72 Eaton Square Ltd 2008–15; mem. Advisory Bd Univ. of Exeter. *Address:* Fidelity International Ltd, Oakhill House, 130 Tonbridge Road, Hildenborough, Tonbridge, Kent, TN11 9DZ, England (home). *Fax:* (1732) 838886 (office). *Website:* www.fidelity.co.uk (office).

BATEMAN, Robert McLellan, OC, BA (Hons), RCA, DSc, DLitt, LLD, DFA; Canadian artist; b. 24 May 1930, Toronto; s. of Joseph W. Bateman and Anne Bateman (née McLellan); m. 1st Suzanne Bowerman 1961; two s. one d.; m. 2nd Birgit Freybe 1975; two s.; ed Forest Hill Collegiate Inst., Univ. of Toronto, Ontario Coll. of Educ.; high school art teacher for 20 years; began full-time painting 1976, numerous museum exhbns since 1959, including the Smithsonian Inst. 1987, Nat. Museum of Wildlife Art, Jackson, Wyo. 1997, Everard Read Gallery, Johannesburg 2000, Retrospective Tours, 2002–03, 2008–09, Gerald Peters Gallery, Santa Fe 2004, Robert Bateman in Russia 2009–10; permanent collection at The Robert Bateman Centre, Victoria, BC 2012–; Hon. Dir Kenya Wildlife Fund, EcoJustice Canada, Hon. Chair. Harmony Foundation, Bateman Foundation, Hon. Fellow, Royal Canadian Geographical Soc., Hon. Life mem. Audubon Soc., Canadian Wildlife Fed., Sierra Club, Fed. of Canadian Artists 1983–, Royal Canadian Acad. of Arts; Order of British Columbia 2001; Hon. DFA, Hon. DLitt, Hon. DSc, Hon. LLD; Queen Elizabeth II Silver Jubilee Medal 1977, Soc. of Animal Artists Award of Excellence 1979, 1980, 1981, 1986, 1990, Master Artist, Leigh Yawkey Woodson Art Museum 1982, Member of Honour Award, World Wildlife Fund 1985, Lescarbot Award, Canadian Govt 1992, Rachel Carson Award 1996, Golden Plate Award, American Acad. of Achievement 1998, One of 20th Century's 100 Champions of Conservation, US Nat. Audubon Soc. 1998, Rungius Medal 2001, Pres.'s Medal, Sir Edmund Hillary Foundation of Canada 2005, Human Rights Defender Award, Amnesty International 2007, Royal Canadian Geographical Soc. Gold Medal 2013, World Ecology Award, Univ. of Missouri-St Louis 2015, Int. Brandwein Medal, Brandwein Inst. 2017, Jay N. Ding Darling Memorial Award, The Wildlife Soc. 2017 and numerous other awards. *Publications include:* with Ramsay Derry: The Art of Robert Bateman 1981, The World of Robert Bateman 1984; with Rick Archbold: Robert Bateman: An Artist in Nature 1990, Robert Bateman: Natural Worlds 1996, Safari 1998, Thinking Like a Mountain 2000; with Kathryn Dean: Birds 2002; with Ian Coutts: Backyard Birds 2005; with Nancy Kovacs: Birds of Prey 2007, Polar Worlds 2008, Vanishing Habitats 2010, New Works 2010, Hope & Wild Apples 2012, Sight Unseen 2014, Life Sketches: a memoir 2015, Robert Bateman's Canada 2017. *Address:* PO Box 115, Fulford Harbour, Salt Spring Island, BC V8K 2P2, Canada (office). *Telephone:* (250) 653-4647 (office). *Fax:* (250) 653-9211 (office). *E-mail:* boshkung@saltspring.com (office); rb@gulfislands.com (office). *Website:* www.robertbateman.ca (office); www.batemancentre.org (office).

BATENIN, Vyacheslav Mikhailovich, DrPhys-MathSc; Russian physicist and academic; b. 12 March 1939; m.; one s.; ed Moscow Energy Inst.; Engineer, then Sr Engineer, Jt Inst. of High Temperatures, USSR (now Russian) Acad. of Sciences 1962, Dir 1986–2006, apptd Deputy Dir 2007; Ed.-in-Chief High Temperature 1986–2002; Corresp. mem. Russian Acad. of Sciences 1987–. *Publications include:* works on physics of gas explosion and low-temperature plasma, problems of applied superconductivity and magnetic hydrodynamics, unconventional energy sources. *Leisure interests:* tennis, travelling. *Address:* c/o Joint Institute for High Temperatures RAS (IVTAN), 125412 Moscow, Izhorskaya str. 13/19, Russia (office). *Telephone:* (495)485-23-11 (office); (495) 331-32-52 (home). *Fax:* (495) 485-99-22 (office).

BATES, Kathy, BFA; American actress; b. 28 June 1948, Memphis, Tenn.; d. of Langdon Doyle Bates and Bertye Kathleen Talbert; m. Tony Campisi 1991; ed White Station High School, Southern Methodist Univ.; singing waitress Catskill mountains, cashier Museum of Modern Art, Manhattan; Dr hc (Southern Methodist Univ.) 2002; Mary Pickford Award, Int. Press Acad. 2007. *Theatre work includes:* Varieties 1976, Crimes of the Heart 1979 (won Pulitzer Prize 1981), The Art of Dining 1979, Goodbye Fidel 1980, Chocolate Cake 1980, Extremities 1980, The Fifth of July 1981, Come Back to the 5 & Dime Jimmy Dean, Jimmy Dean 1982, 'night, Mother 1983 (Outer Critics Circle Award), Days and Nights Within 1985, Rain of Terror 1985, Deadfall 1985, Curse of the Starving Class 1985, Frankie and Johnny in the Clair de Lune 1987 (Obie Award), The Road to Mecca 1988. *Films include:* Taking Off 1971, Straight Time 1978, Summer Heat 1987, Arthur 2 on the Rocks 1988, High Stakes 1989, Dick Tracy 1990, White Palace 1990, Men Don't Leave 1990, Misery 1990 (Acad. Award for Best Actress 1991, Golden Globe Award from Hollywood Foreign Press Asscn), Prelude to a Kiss 1991, At Play in the Fields of the Lord 1991, The Road to Mecca 1991, Fried Green Tomatoes at the Whistle Stop Café 1991, Used People 1992, A Home of Our Own 1993, North 1994, Curse of the Starving Class 1994, Diabolique 1996, The War at Home 1996, Primary Colors 1998, Swept from the Sea 1998, Titanic 1998, A Civil Action 1999, Dash and Lilly 1999, My Life as a Dog 1999, Bruno 2000, Rat Race 2001, American Outlaws 2001, About Schmidt 2002, Love Liza 2002, Evelyn 2003, The Tulse Luper Suitcases: The Moab Story 2003, The Ingrate 2004, Little Black Book 2004, Around the World in 80 Days 2004, The Bridge of San Luis Rey 2004, Rumor Has It 2005, Charlotte's Web (voice) 2006, Bee Movie (voice) 2007, Fred Claus 2007, Christmas Is Here Again (voice) 2007, P.S., I Love You 2007, The Golden Compass 2007, The Family That Preys 2008, The Day the Earth Stood Still 2008, Revolutionary Road 2008, Chéri 2009, Personal Effects 2009, Valentine's Day 2010, A Little Bit of Heaven 2011, You May Not Kiss the Bride 2011, Midnight in Paris 2011, Cadaver (short) 2012, Tammy 2014, The Great Gilly Hopkins 2014, Boychoir 2014. *TV films include:* Johnny Bull, Uncommon Knowledge, No Place like Home, One for Sorrow—Two for Joy, Signs of Life, Murder Ordained, Straight Time, Hostages, The West Side Waltz 1995, The Late Shift (Golden Globe 1997) 1996, Annie 1999, My Sister's Keeper 2002. *Television includes:* Alice (mini-series) 2009, The Office (series) 2010–11, Harry's Law (series) 2011–12, Two and a Half Men (series) (Emmy Award for Best Guest Actress in a Comedy) 2012, Mike & Molly (series) 2014, American Horror Story: Coven (series) (Primetime Emmy Award for Outstanding Supporting Actress in a Miniseries or a Movie 2014) 2013–14, Freak Show (series) 2015–16, Roanoke (series) 2016. *Address:* c/o The Harry Walker Agency Inc., 355 Lexington Avenue, 21st Floor, New York, NY 10017, USA (office). *Telephone:* (646) 227-4900 (office). *E-mail:* info@harrywalker.com (office). *Website:* www.harrywalker.com (office); www.mskathybates.com.

BATES, Mason; American composer, producer and DJ; *Composer-in-Residence, Kennedy Center for the Performing Arts;* b. 23 Jan. 1977, Philadelphia, Pa; ed Juilliard School, Univ. of California, Berkeley, studied with Edmund Campion; apptd Margaret Lee Crofts Fellow in Composition, Tanglewood Music Festival aged 20; Composer-in-Residence, Young Concert Artists, Inc. 2000–02; Composer-in-Residence, Mobile Symphony 2005–06, Young American Composer-in-Residence, California Symphony 2007–10; Mead Composer-in-Residence, Chicago Symphony Orchestra 2010–15; Composer-in-Residence, Kennedy Center for the Performing Arts, Washington, DC 2015–, performances with Nat. Symphony, appearances with Jason Moran on Kennedy Center Jazz; works have been championed by Riccardo Muti, Michael Tilson Thomas and Leonard Slatkin; featured in San Francisco Symphony's Beethoven & Bates Festival; sessions as DJ in clubs and art spaces in San Francisco; Charles Ives Fellowship 2002, Guggenheim Fellowship 2008; Rome Prize, American Acad. in Rome, American Acad. in Berlin Prize, American Acad. of Arts and Letters Award in Music 2007, Van Cliburn American Composers Invitational (for White Lies for Lomax) 2009, Heinz Medal for the Humanities 2012, Composer of the Year, Pittsburgh Symphony Orchestra 2012–13, Musical America Composer of the Year 2018. *Music for film:* The Sea of Trees. *Compositions include:* numerous compositions, including Alternative Energy (premiered by Chicago Symphony 2011), Liquid Interface 2006–07, The B-Sides, Auditorium (premiered by San Francisco Symphony 2015), Anthology of Fantastic Zoology, acoustic work for orchestra 2015, Auditorium, for orchestra 2016, Drum-Taps, for choir 2017, The (R)evolution of Steve Jobs (opera) 2017. *Recordings include:* solo: Mothership 2015; other: Digital Loom 2009, Stereo is King 2014, Riccardo Muti Conducts Mason Bates and Anna Clyne–Alternative Energy 2014, American Masters–Violin Concerto 2015. *Address:* c/o Opus 3 Artists, 5670 Wilshire Boulevard, Suite 1790, Los Angeles, CA 90036, USA (office); John F. Kennedy Center for the Performing Arts, 2700 F Street, NW, Washington, DC 20566, USA (office). *Telephone:* (323) 954-1776 (office). *E-mail:* info@opus3artists.com (office). *Website:* www.opus3artists.com (office); www.kennedy-center.org (office); www.masonbates.com.

BATES, Suzannah (Suzie) Wilson; New Zealand cricketer; b. 16 Sept. 1987, Dunedin; right-handed batswoman; right-arm medium pace bowler; plays for Otago Sparks 2002–, White Ferns 2006–, Southern Vipers 2015–; ODI debut: New Zealand vs India, Lincoln 4 March 2006; T20I debut: New Zealand vs South Africa, Taunton 10 Aug. 2007; played 115 ODIs (to March 2019), scored 4,245 runs (average 43.76) with 10 centuries and 24 fifties, best score of 168; played 108 T20Is (to Feb. 2019), scored 3,007 runs (average 30.68) with one century and 20 fifties, best score of 124; Captain New Zealand national team (ODI and T20I 2011–); ICC Women's ODI Cricketer of the Year 2013, 2015, named Wisden Leading Woman Cricketer in the World 2015, ICC Women's T20I Cricketer of the Year 2015. *Address:* c/o White Ferns, New Zealand Cricket, POB 8353, Level 4, 8 Nugent Street, Grafton, Auckland 1023, New Zealand. *Telephone:* (9) 972-0605. *Fax:* (9) 972-0606. *E-mail:* info@nzcricket.org.nz. *Website:* www.nzc.nz/international/white-ferns.

BATHIA, Diallo Mamadou; Mauritanian lawyer and politician; ed Ecole Nat. d'Admin (ENA), Nouakchott, Université d'Orléans, France; Prof., ENA Nouakchott 1984–2014; Adviser to the Minister, Ministry of the Interior and Inspector of Territorial Admin 1984–86, Head of Mission and Dir of Local Communities 1986–89; Adviser on Matters of Sovereignty, Office of the Prime Minister 1992–97; Sr Adviser to Pres., with rank of Minister 2008–09; Adviser on Admin Affairs, Office of the Prime Minister 2009–14; Sec.-Gen. of the Govt (rank of Minister) Feb.–Aug. 2014, Minister of Nat. Defence 2014–18. *Address:* c/o Ministry of National Defence, Nouakchott, Mauritania (office).

BATHILY, Abdoulaye, PhD; Senegalese politician, academic and UN official; *Special Representative of Secretary-General for Central Africa and Head, Regional Office for Central Africa (UNOCA), United Nations;* b. 1947, Tuabou; m.; four c.; ed Univ. of Birmingham, UK, Université Cheikh Anta Diop; taught at Université Cheikh Anta Diop, Dakar for more than thirty years; elected Democratic League Sec.-Gen. 1984; elected to Nat. Ass. 1993, 1998, Deputy Speaker 2001–06; Minister for the Environment and the Protection of Nature 1993–98, for Energy and Hydraulics 2000–01, Sr Minister in charge of African Affairs 2012–13, Minister of State to Pres. of Senegal 2012–13; Deputy Special Rep., UN Multidimensional Integrated Stabilization Mission in Mali (MINUSMA) 2013–14, Special Rep. of Sec.-Gen. for Central Africa and Head, UN Regional Office for Central Africa (UNOCA) 2014–; mem. Bd of Dirs, Coalition for Dialogue on Africa; fmr mem. Parl. of Econ. Community of West African States, African Union Contact Group on the crisis in Madagascar; Dr hc (Université Cheikh Anta Diop). *Publication:* The Military and Militarism in Africa (with Eboe Hutchful) 1997. *Address:* United Nations Regional Office for Central Africa (UNOCA), BP 23773, Cité de la Démocratie, Villas 55–57, Libreville, Gabon (office). *Telephone:* 01-74-14-01 (office). *Fax:* 01-74-14-02 (office). *Website:* www.unoca.unmissions.org (office).

BATISTA, Eike Fuhrken; Brazilian entrepreneur and philanthropist; *CEO, EBX Group;* b. 3 Nov. 1956, Governador Valadares, Minas Gerais; s. of Eliezer Batista da Silva, fmr head of mining co. Vale (Companhia Vale do Rio Doce); m.

Luma de Oliveira 1991 (divorced 2004); three s.; ed Univ. of Aachen, Germany; childhood in Brazil, lived in Geneva, Switzerland, Düsseldorf, Germany, and Brussels, Belgium with his family during early teens; moved back to Brazil to begin a gold and trading co. in the Amazon 1980; worked as intermediary between producers in Amazonia and buyers in Brazil and Europe; set up first mechanized alluvial gold plant in Amazonia 1980s; then joined Canadian mining firm TVX Gold Inc., served as Chair., Pres. and CEO, sold stake in co. for $1 billion 2000; reinvested in several businesses, including mining; large portion of wealth made from OGX (oil and gas exploration co.) founded 2007 (renamed Oleo e Gas Participacoes following bankruptcy 2013), Chair. and CEO, also CEO EBX Group, Chair. MMX (mining), MPX (energy); Chair. EBX Investimentos Group, Rio de Janeiro since 1980s; other cos founded include LLX (logistics), OSX, Mr Lam (Chinese restaurant), Porto de Peruíbe 2004–08. *Achievements include:* completed 220 nautical miles between Santos and Rio de Janeiro in three hours, 1 minute and 47 seconds in his powerboat 'Spirit of Brazil', breaking record for the crossing 2006. *Leisure interests:* running, swimming, speed boats. *Address:* EBX Group, Praia do Flamengo 154, 10° Andar, Flamengo, Rio de Janeiro 22210-030, Brazil (office). *Telephone:* (21) 21636100 (office). *E-mail:* faleconosco@osx.com.br (office). *Website:* www.osx.com.br (office).

BÁTIZ CAMPBELL, Enrique; Mexican conductor; *Director, Orquesta Sinfónica del Estado de México;* b. 4 May 1942, Mexico City; s. of José Luis Bátiz and María Elena Campbell; m. 1st Eva María Zuk 1965 (divorced 1983); one s. one d.; m. 2nd Elena Campbell Lombardo; ed Centro Universitario México, Southern Methodist Univ. and Juilliard School, USA, Warsaw Conservatoire, Poland; Founder and Prin. Conductor, Orquesta Sinfónica del Estado de México 1971–83, now Dir; Artistic Dir Orquesta Filarmónica de la Ciudad de México 1983–90; Prin. Guest Conductor, Royal Philharmonic Orchestra, London 1984–; Chief Conductor, Symphonic Orchestra of Guanajuato 2005–; Guest Conductor with numerous orchestras; Order of Rio Branco (Brazil) 1986; Distinguished Artist of the Year, Mexican Union of Theatrical and Musical Broadcasters 1971, 1981, 1983, 1996, Mozart Medal, Domecq Cultural Inst. 1991, Sor Juana Ines de la Cruz Award for Arts and Letters 1994, State of Mexico Prize 1995. *Leisure interest:* swimming. *Website:* www.edomexico.gob.mx.

BATKHUYAG, Jamyandorjiin, MA, PhD; Mongolian economist and politician; b. 1964; ed Univ. of Colorado at Denver, USA; fmr Lecturer, Mongolian Nat. Univ. and Higher Polytechnic; fmr Sr Adviser on Econ. Policy to Prime Minister; fmr Learned Sec. and Dir Inst. of Finance and Econs; mem. Great Khural (Parl.) from 2004; Minister of Defence 2007–08; mem. Nat. New Party.

BATTEN, Alan Henry, PhD, DSc, FRSC; Canadian (b. British) astronomer; b. 21 Jan. 1933, Whitstable, Kent, England; s. of George Cuthbert Batten and Gladys Batten (née Greenwood); m. 1st Lois Eleanor Dewis 1960 (died 2010); one s. one d.; m. 2nd Erica Frances Dodd 2011; ed Wolverhampton Grammar School, Univ. of St Andrews, Univ. of Manchester; Research Asst, Univ. of Manchester and Jr Tutor, St Anselm Hall of Residence 1958–59; Post-doctoral Fellow, Dominion Astrophysical Observatory, Victoria, BC, Canada 1959–61, staff mem. 1961–91, Sr Research Officer 1976–91, Guest Worker 1991–2011; Visiting Erskine Fellow, Univ. of Canterbury, New Zealand 1995; Vice-Pres. Astronomical Soc. of Pacific 1966–68; Pres. Canadian Astronomical Soc. 1974–76, Royal Astronomical Soc. of Canada 1976–78 (Hon. Pres. 1994–98, elected to Fellowship 2016), Comm. 30 of Int. Astronomical Union 1976–79, Comm. 42 1982–85; Vice-Pres. Int. Astronomical Union 1985–91; mem. Advisory Council, Centre for Studies in Religion and Society, Univ. of Victoria 1993–2002 (Chair. 1997–2000), 2006–12, mem. Editorial Bd, Journal of Astronomical History and Heritage 1998–, Sessional Lecturer in History 2003–04; mem. Craigdarroch Research Awards Cttee, Univ. of Victoria 2004–06; Queen's Silver Jubilee Medal 1977, Donald Osterbrock Prize of History of Astronomy Division of American Astronomical Soc. 2017. *Publications include:* The Determination of Radial Velocities and their Applications (co-ed.) 1967, Extended Atmospheres and Circumstellar Matter in Close Binary Systems (ed.) 1973, Binary and Multiple Systems of Stars 1973, Resolute and Undertaking Characters: The Lives of Wilhelm and Otto Struve 1988, Algols (ed.) 1989, Astronomy for Developing Countries (ed.) 2001, Our Enigmatic Universe: One Astronomer's Reflections on the Human Condition 2011; over 200 scientific papers. *Leisure interest:* campanology. *Address:* 2594 Sinclair Road, Victoria, BC V8N 1B9, Canada (home).

BATTISTON, Giuseppe; Italian actor; b. 22 July 1968, Udine. *Films include:* Italia–Germania 4–3 (Italy–Germany 4–3) 1990, Un'Anima divisa in due (A Soul Split in Two) 1993, Le acrobate (The Acrobat) 1997, Il più lungo giorno 1998, Pane e tulipani (Bread and Tulips) (David di Donatello Award for Best Supporting Actor 2000, Ciak d'Oro for Best Supporting Actor 2000) 2000, Guarda il cielo: Stella, Sonia, Silvia (Watch the Sky: Stella, Sonia, Silvia) 2000, Chiedimi se sono felice (Ask Me If I'm Happy) 2000, La forza del passato (The Power of the Past) 2002, Nemmeno in un sogno 2002, Un aldo qualunque 2002, Agata e la tempesta (Agata and the Storm) 2004, L'Uomo perfetto 2005, La bestia nel cuore (The Beast in the Heart; aka Don't Tell (UK)) 2005, La tigre e la neve (The Tiger and the Snow) 2005, Apnea 2005, Non prendere impegni stasera 2006, Uno su due (One Out of Two) 2006, A casa nostra (Our Country) 2006, La fine del mare 2007, Non pensarci (Don't Think About It) 2007, Giorni e nuvole (Days and Clouds) 2007, La giusta distanza (The Right Distance) 2007, Le pere di Adamo (voice) 2007, Amore, bugie e calcetto 2008, We Can Do That 2008, The Hush 2009, Come Undone 2010, The Passion 2010, Notizie degli scavi 2010, Unlikely Revolutionaries 2010, Make a Fake 2011, Shun Li and the Poet 2011, Bar Sport 2011, The Commander and the Stork 2012, Il comandante e la cicogna (Garibaldi's Lovers) 2012, La variabile umana (The Human Factor) 2013, Zoran, il mio nipote scemo (Zoran, My Nephew the Idiot) 2013, First Snowfall (La prima neve) 2013, La sedia della felicità 2013, Pitza e datteri 2015, La felicità è un sistema complesso (The Complexity of Happiness) 2015, Perfetti sconosciuti (Perfect Strangers) 2016, Dopo la guerra (After the War) 2017, L'ordine delle cose (The Order of Things) 2017, (Finché c'è Prosecco c'è speranza) The Last Prosecco 2017, Io c'è 2018, Tu mi nascondi qualcosa 2018, (Troppa grazia) Lucia's Grace 2018, Hotel Gagarin 2018. *Television includes:* L'Avvocato (episode La prova del fuoco) 2003, Al di là delle frontiere (mini-series) 2004, Una famiglia in giallo (mini-series) 2005, La notte breve 2006, A Mother's Ray of Hope 2008, The Collegno Amnesiac 2009, Non pensarci, la serie (series) 2009, Tutti pazzi per amore (series) 2010, The Swing Girls (film) 2010, I fantasmi di Portopalo (mini-series) 2017, Trust (series) 2018.

BATTLE, Kathleen Deanna, MMus; American singer (soprano); b. 13 Aug. 1948, Portsmouth, Ohio; d. of Ollie Layne Battle and Grady Battle; ed Coll. Conservatory of Music, Univ. of Cincinnati; professional debut in Brahms Requiem, Cincinnati May Festival, then Spoleto Festival, Italy 1972; debut with Metropolitan Opera, New York as shepherd in Wagner's Tannhäuser 1977; regular guest with orchestras of New York, Chicago, Boston, Philadelphia, Cleveland, LA, San Francisco, Vienna, Paris and Berlin, at Salzburg, Tanglewood and other festivals and at major opera houses including Metropolitan, New York, Covent Garden, London, Paris and Vienna; returned to Metropolitan Opera in recital Kathleen Battle: Underground Railroad—A Spiritual Journey 2016; Dr hc (Univ. of Cincinnati), (Westminster Choir Coll.), (Ohio Univ.), (Xavier Univ., Cincinnati), (Amherst Coll.), (Seton Hall Univ.), (Wilberforce Univ.), (Manhattanville Coll.), (Shawnee State Univ.); five Grammy Awards, Emmy Award for Outstanding Individual Achievement in a Classical Program on Television 1991, inducted into NAACP Image Award Hall of Fame and Hollywood Bowl Hall of Fame, Ray Charles Award, Wilberforce Univ. *Recordings include:* Brahms Requiem and Songs, Mozart Requiem, Don Giovanni, Seraglio and concert arias, Verdi's Un Ballo in Maschera and Berg's Lulu Suite, New Year's Eve Gala, Vienna, Best of Kathleen Battle 2004. *Leisure interests:* gardening, cooking, sewing, piano, dance. *Address:* Columbia Artists Management Inc., 1790 Broadway, New York, NY 10019-1412, USA (office). *Telephone:* (212) 841-9500 (office). *Fax:* (212) 841-9744 (office). *E-mail:* info@cami.com (office). *Website:* www.cami.com (office).

BATTS, Warren Leighton, BS, MBA; American business executive and academic; b. 4 Sept. 1932, Norfolk, Va; s. of John Leighton Batts and Allie Belle Batts (née Johnson); m. Eloise Pitts 1957; one d.; ed Georgia Inst. of Tech., Harvard Business School; with Kendall Co. 1963–64; Exec. Vice-Pres. Fashion Devt Co. 1964–66; Vice-Pres., Douglas Williams Assocs 1966–67; Founder, Triangle Corpn 1967, Pres. and Chief Exec. Officer 1967–71; Vice-Pres. Mead Corpn 1971–73, Pres. 1973–80, CEO 1978–80; Pres. Dart Industries 1980–81, Pres. Dart & Kraft 1981–86; Chair. Premark Int. Inc. 1986–97, CEO 1986–96; Chair., CEO Tupperware Corpn 1996–97; Adjunct Prof. of Strategic Man., Booth School of Business, Univ. of Chicago; Chair. Cook County Health & Hospital System; Life Trustee Northwestern Univ.; fmr Chair. now Life Dir Children's Memorial Hospital, Chicago; Dir of the Year Award, Nat. Asscn of Corp. Dirs 2006.

BATTULGA, Khaltmaa; Mongolian business executive, politician, head of state and fmr wrestler; *President;* b. 3 March 1963, Ulaanbaatar; s. of Khaltmaa Battulga and Doljinsuren Battulga; m. 2nd Anjelica Davaín; two c.; ed Fine Arts Coll., Ulaanbaatar; fmr professional wrestler; mem. Mongolian Nat. sambo (wrestling) team 1979–90; won two Gold Medals, two Silver Medals and two Bronze Medals from world championship competitions, including Gold Medal, World Sambo Championships 1983, Silver Medal, World Sambo Championships 1990; worked as painter with Mongolian Artists' Union Cttee 1982; started his business career producing jeans and children's clothing and exporting it to Hungary, and importing audio and recording equipment from Singapore to Mongolia; Gen. Dir Genko LLC 1992–97; Exec. Dir Bayangol Hotel Co. 1997–2004, Makh Impex Co. 1999–2004; mem. State Great Khural (Parl.) from Bayankhongor Prov. 2004–16; Minister of Roads, Transportation, Construction and Urban Devt 2008–12; Pres. of Mongolia 2017–; Pres. Mongolian Judo Asscn 2006–; mem. Democratic Party; Honoured Athlete of Mongolia 1995, Int. Fed. of Bodybuilding and Fitness Diamond Cup 2017, Int. Judo Fed. Golden Star 2017. *Address:* Office of the President, State Palace, Chingisiin Talbai 1, Ulaanbaatar, Mongolia (office). *Website:* www.president.mn (office).

BATUMUBWIRA, Antoinette, MA; Burundian corporate communications executive and government official; *Head of External Relations and Communication Unit, African Development Bank Group;* m. Jean-Marie Ngendahayo; two d.; ed Univ. of Bordeaux III, France; emigrated to Finland as refugee 2003; journalist, La voix de la Révolution du Burundi 1979–81; Information Officer, UN Information Center, Bujumbura, Burundi 1981–95; Head of Public Relations and Communications, ICO Global Communications 1997–99; Head of Communications, Office of Resident Coordinator, UN, Comoros 1999–2000; consultant responsible for organization of African Regional Conference on the Information Society, UN, Comoros 2002; Head, Centre for Planning, Employment and Economic Development for Southern Finland, Helsinki 2003–04; Minister of External Relations and Int. Co-operation 2005–09; Head of External Relations and Communication Unit, African Development Bank Group 2009–. *Publications:* The Route Towards Integration: The Share of Everyone 2004. *Address:* External Relations and Communication Unit, African Development Bank Group, 15 Avenue du Ghana, PO Box 323-1002, Tunis-Belvedère, Tunisia (office). *E-mail:* afdb@afdb.org (office). *Website:* www.afdb.org (office).

BATURIN, Yuri Mikhailovich, DJur; Russian politician, cosmonaut, lawyer and journalist; *Director, S.I. Vavilov Institute of the History of Science and Technology, Russian Academy of Sciences;* b. 12 June 1949, Moscow; m.; one d.; ed Moscow Inst. of Physics and Tech., All-Union Inst. of Law, Moscow State Univ. School of Journalism, Mil. Acad. of Gen. Staff; worked in research production union Energia 1973–80; Inst. of State and Law USSR (now Russian) Acad. of Sciences 1980–91; Research Scholar, Kennan Inst. for Advanced Russian Studies, The Woodrow Wilson Center, Washington, DC, USA 1991; on staff of Pres. Mikhail Gorbachev Admin 1991; mem. Pres.'s Council 1993, Asst to Pres. on legal problems 1993–94, on Nat. Security Problems 1994–96, mem. Council on Personnel Policy of Pres. 1994–97; Sec., Defence Council of Russian Fed. 1996–97; Asst to Pres., Chair. Cttee for Mil. Ranks and Posts 1995–97; currently Dir S.I. Vavilov Inst. of the History of Science and Tech., Russian Acad. of Sciences; columnist, Novaya Gazeta newspaper 1997–; cosmonaut and test pilot of the Cosmonaut Corps 1998–2009, Deputy Commr 2000–09, participated in space flight to Mir Station EP-4 1998, second space flight to Int. Space Station EP-1 2001; Prof. of Computer Law, Moscow Inst. of Eng and Physics; Prof., Moscow Inst. of Physics and Tech.; Prof., School of Journalism, Moscow Univ., Pres. of the School, Media Law and Policy Centre; Chair. Centre for Anti-Corruption Research and Initiative Transparency Int. 2000–; Union of Journalists Prize 1990, Award for Outstanding Contribution to Mass-Media Law 1997, Themis Award 1998. *Films:* documentaries: We barely made it with one nozzle left 1997, Stairway to the sky 2000. *Publications:* drafts of the laws on the freedom of the press of the USSR 1989 and of Russia 1991, Problems of Computer Law 1991. *Address:* Institute for the History of Science and Technology, 109012 Moscow, Staropansky per. 1/5, Russian Federation (office). *Telephone:* (495) 988-22-80 (office). *Fax:* (495) 988-22-80 (office). *E-mail:* postmaster@ihst.ru (office). *Website:* www.ihst.ru (office).

BAUCHARD, Denis M(ichel) B(ertrand), MA; French diplomatist; *Senior Fellow, Institut français des relations internationales;* b. 20 Sept. 1936, Paris; s. of Charles Bauchard and Marguerite Duhamel; m. Geneviève Lanoë 1961; two s. two d.; ed Sciences Po, Paris, Ecole nat. d'admin; Civil Admin., Ministry of Finance 1964–66, 1968–74; Financial Attaché, Near and Middle East, Embassy in Beirut 1966–68; Asst to Minister 1974–76; Financial Counsellor, Perm. Mission to UN, New York 1977–81, Deputy Asst Sec., Ministry of Foreign Affairs 1981–85, Asst Sec. 1986–89, Amb. to Jordan 1989–93, Asst Sec., Ministry of Foreign Affairs (N Africa and Middle East) 1993–96, Chief of Staff to Minister of Foreign Affairs 1996–97, Amb. to Canada 1998–2001; Pres. Institut du Monde Arabe 2002–04; Consultant and Sr Fellow, Institut français de relations internationales 2004–; Officier, Légion d'honneur, Ordre nat. du Mérite. *Publications:* Le jeu mondial des pétroliers 1970, Economie financière des collectivités locales 1972, La démocratie est-elle soluble dans l'islam? 2007, Le nouveau monde arabe 2012; many articles and policy papers on the Middle East. *Address:* Institut français des relations internationales, 27 rue de la Procession, 75015 Paris (office); 91 rue de Rennes, 75006 Paris, France (home). *Telephone:* 1-40-61-60-00 (office); 1-45-44-18-05 (home); 6-19-35-44-46 (home). *E-mail:* bauchard@ifri.org (office); denis.bauchard@wanadoo.fr (home). *Website:* www.ifri.org (office).

BAUCHEREL, Jean-Luc; French farmer and insurance industry executive; joined Groupama SA 1975, Dir Morbihan Mutual 1975–78, mem. Exec. Bd 1978–2012, mem. Bd of Dirs, Groupama Bretagne 1992–2012, Vice-Chair. 1996–2000, Chair. 2000–05, Chair. Groupama Loire-Bretagne 2002–12, Chair. Fédération Nationale Groupama and Groupama SA 2004–12, also Dir Groupama Holding, mem. Supervisory Bd Groupama SA –2003 (Vice-Chair. –2003, Vice-Chair. Bd of Dirs –2004), Supervisory Bd Groupama Assurances et Services –2003, Bd of Dirs Groupama Plus Ultra –2004, Supervisory Bd Groupama International –2003 (Dir –2006), Supervisory Bd Groupama Banque –2005; Chair. Supervisory Bd Groupama Vie –2003, Chair. Bd of Dirs –2004; Chair. Supervisory Bd Gan Prévoyance –2003; mem. Supervisory Bd Gan Assurances Vie –2003; Dir, Gan Patrimoine –2004, Minster Insurance Co. Ltd –2004. *Address:* c/o Groupama SA, 8–10 rue d'Astorg, 75383 Paris Cedex 08, France. *E-mail:* relations.exterieures@groupama.com.

BAUCUS, Max Sieben, LLB; American lawyer, politician and diplomatist; *Ambassador to China;* b. 11 Dec. 1941, Helena, Mont.; m. 1st Ann Geracimos (divorced 1982); one s.; m. 2nd Wanda Minge 1983; ed Helena High School, Stanford Univ. and Stanford Law School; staff attorney, Civil Aeronautics Bd, Washington, DC 1967–69; legal staff, SEC, Washington, DC 1969–71, Legal Asst to SEC Chair. 1970–71; in pvt. law practice in Missoula, Mont. 1971; Attorney, George and Baucus (law firm) 1971; Acting Exec. Dir and Cttee Coordinator, Mont. Constitutional Convention; elected to Montana State Legislature 1972; served two terms for Mont. Western Dist in US House of Reps, Washington, DC, mem. House Appropriations Cttee and Deputy Whip; Senator from Montana 1979–2014, Chair. Senate Int. Trade Sub-cttee of Finance, Senate Environment and Public Works Cttee, Senate Agric. and Intelligence Cttee, Finance Cttee 2001; Amb. to People's Repub. of China 2014–. *Leisure interests:* hunting, fishing, hiking. *Address:* US Embassy, 55 An Jia Lou Lu, Beijing 100600, People's Republic of China (office). *Telephone:* (10) 85313000 (office). *Fax:* (10) 85314200 (office). *E-mail:* ircacee@state.gov (office). *Website:* beijing.usembassy-china.org.cn (office).

BAUDOUIN, Jean-Louis, OC, BA, BCL, PhD; Canadian lawyer, professor of law and fmr judge; *Partner, Fasken Martineau DuMoulin LLP;* b. 8 Aug. 1938, Boulogne, France; s. of Louis Baudouin and Marguerite Guerin; m. Christianne Dubreuil; four d.; ed Univ. of Paris, McGill Univ., Montreal; admitted to Bar of Québec 1959; Prof. of Law, Univ. of Montreal 1962–89, Assoc. Prof. of Law 1989–; Commr, Law Reform Comm. of Canada 1976–78, Vice-Chair. 1978–80; Judge, Court of Appeal, Québec 1989–2009; currently Partner, Fasken Martineau DuMoulin LLP (law firm), Montreal; Ed. Civil Law Quarterly Review 1968–89, Supreme Court Law Review 1982–89, Canadian Bar Review 1983–89; Pres. Asscn Henri Capitant (Québec chapter) 1973–; Pres. Asscn of Law Teachers of Quebec 1974–75; mem. RSC 1979; Grand officier Ordre du Québec; Dr hc (Sherbrooke) 1990, (Paris) 1994, (Namur) 1998, (Ottawa) 2001, (McGill) 2007, (Université de Lyon III) 2009; Henri Capitant Medal 1973, 1986, 2004, Médaille du Bureau du Lieutenant-Gouverneur de Québec 1988, Award of Excellence, Quebec Bar 1988, Yves Pélicier Award, Int. Acad. of Law and Mental Health 2001, Canadian Bar Asscn Ramon John Hnatyshyn Award 2004. *Publications include:* Les Obligations 1970–2014, La Responsabilité Civile 1973–2014, Le Secret Professionnel 1964, Produire l'Homme: de quel Droit? 1987, Ethique de la Mort, Droit à la Mort 1992. *Leisure interests:* skiing, fishing, wine-tasting. *Address:* Fasken Martineau DuMoulin LLP, The Stock Exchange Tower, PO Box 242, Suite 3700, 800 Victoria Square, Montreal, PQ H4Z 1E9 (office); 875 rue Antonine Maillet, Montreal, PQ H2V 2Y6, Canada (home). *Telephone:* (514) 270-1884 (home); (514) 397-5299 (office). *Fax:* (514) 397-7600 (office). *E-mail:* jbaudouin@fasken.com (office). *Website:* www.fasken.com (office).

BAUGH, Hon. Kenneth Leigh O'Neill, MD; Jamaican politician and physician; b. Montego Bay, St James; m. Vilma Baugh; two s. one d.; ed Univ. of West Indies, Royal Coll. of Surgeons; MP for NW St James 1980–89, currently for St Catherine West Central; fmr Deputy Leader of the Opposition; fmr Minister of Health; Shadow Minister for Health and Environment –2007; Deputy Prime Minister and Minister of Foreign Affairs and Foreign Trade 2007–12; mem. Jamaica Labour Party (currently Chair.). *Leisure interests:* art, drawing, swimming. *Address:* c/o Office of the Deputy Prime Minister, 1 Devon Road, Kingston 10, Jamaica.

BAULCOMBE, Sir David Charles, Kt, BSc, PhD, FRS, FMedSci; British botanist and academic; *Regius Professor of Botany, Royal Society Research Professor and Head of Department of Plant Sciences, University of Cambridge;* b. 7 April 1952; m.; four c.; ed Univs of Leeds and Edinburgh; Postdoctoral Fellow, McGill Univ., Montreal, Canada 1977–78, Univ. of Georgia, Athens, USA 1978–80; Higher Scientific Officer, Plant Breeding Inst., Cambridge 1980–86, Prin. Scientific Officer 1986–88; joined The Sainsbury Lab., Norwich 1988, Sr Research Scientist and Head of Lab. 1990–93, 1999–2003; Prof., Univ. of East Anglia 2002–07; Regius Prof. of Botany, Royal Soc. Research Prof., Univ. of Cambridge 2007–22, Fellow, Trinity Coll., Cambridge 2009–; mem. European Molecular Biology Org. 1997, Academia Europaea 2002; Foreign Assoc. mem. NAS 2005; Hon. Prof., Univ. of East Anglia 1998–2002; Dr hc (Wageningen Univ.) 2008; numerous awards including Prix des Céréaliers de France for work on hormonally regulated genes of cereals 1990, Kumho Science Int. Award in Plant Molecular Biology and Biotechnology, Kumho Cultural Foundation (S Korea) 2002, Ruth Allen Award, American Phytopathology Soc. 2002, Wiley Prize in Biomedical Science, Wiley Foundation, Rockefeller Univ. (co-recipient) 2003, M.W. Beijerinck Virology Prize, Royal Netherlands Acad. of Arts and Sciences 2004, Royal Medal, Royal Soc. 2006, Benjamin Franklin Medal in Life Science (co-recipient) 2008, Albert Lasker Basic Medical Research Award (co-recipient) 2008, Harvey Prize in Science and Tech. 2009, Wolf Prize in Agric. 2010, Gruber Genetics Prize (co-recipient) 2014. *Publications:* numerous scientific papers in professional journals. *Leisure interests:* music, sailing, hill walking. *Address:* Department of Plant Sciences, University of Cambridge, Downing Street, Cambridge, CB2 3EA, England (office). *Telephone:* (1223) 339386 (office). *Fax:* (1223) 333953 (office). *E-mail:* dcb40@cam.ac.uk (office). *Website:* www.plantsci.cam.ac.uk/research/davidbaulcombe (office).

BAULIEU, Etienne-Emile, DenM, DèsSc; French physician, biochemist and academic; *Chairman, Institut Professor Baulieu;* b. 12 Dec. 1926, Strasbourg; s. of Léon Blum and Thérèse Lion; m. Yolande Compagnon 1947; one s. two d.; ed Lycée Pasteur, Neuilly-sur-Seine, Faculté de Médecine and Faculté des Sciences, Paris; Intern, Paris Hosps. 1951–55; Chef de Clinique, Faculté de Médecine, Paris 1955–57, Assoc. Prof. of Biochemistry 1958; Visiting Scientist, Dept of Obstetrics, Gynaecology and Biochemistry, Columbia Univ. New York 1961–62; Dir Research Inst. 33, Hormones Lab., Inst. Nat. de la Santé et de la Recherche Médicale (INSERM) 1963–97; Prof. of Biochemistry, Faculté de Médecine de Bicêtre, Univ. Paris-Sud 1970; Prof. at Collège de France 1993, a chair. 1994, now Hon. Prof.; Consultant, Roussel Uclaf; Founder and Chair. Institut Professor Baulieu 2008–; mem. Editorial Bds several French and int. journals; mem. and Past Pres. INSERM, Fondation pour la Recherche Médicale Française; Pres. Société Française d'Endocrinologie 1975; Vice-Pres. Acad. of Sciences 2000–02, Pres. 2003–; mem. Organizing Cttee Karolinska Symposia on Reproductive Endocrinology, NCI-INSERM Cancer and Hormones Programme (Past French Scientific Chair.), fmr mem. Scientific Advisory Bd WHO Special Programme in Human Reproduction; mem. Endocrine Soc., USA 1966–, Royal Soc. of Medicine, London 1972–, Inst. de France (Acad. des Sciences) 1982– (Vice-Pres. 2000–02, Pres. 2003–04), New York Acad. of Sciences 1985–; Foreign Assoc. mem. NAS 1990–; mem. Nat. Consultative Ethics Cttee for Life Sciences and Health 1996–; mem. Expert Advisory Panel, Int. Fed. of Gynaecology and Obstetrics (FIGO) 1997–; Mem. Emer. Academia Europaea 1997–; developed RU486 abortion pill and anti-ageing pill from human hormone, DeHydroEpiAndrosterone (more commonly known as DHEA); Hon. mem. American Physiological Soc. 1993, Acad. Nationale de Médecine 2002; Chevalier Ordre nat. du Mérite 1967; Officier Ordre du Mérite du Gabon 1979; Commdr Légion d'honneur 1990, Grand Officier de la Légion d'honneur 2003; Dr hc (Ghent) 1991, (Tufts) 1991, (Karolinska Inst.) 1994, (Worcs. Foundation, Shrewsbury) 1994; Reichstein Award, Int. Soc. of Endocrinology 1972, Grand Prix Scientifique 1989 de la Ville de Paris 1974, First European Medallist of Soc. of Endocrinology (GB) 1985, Albert & Mary Lasker Clinical Research Award 1989, American Acad. of Achievement Golden Plate Award 1990, Premio Minerva, Rome 1990, Christopher Columbus Discovery Award in Biomedical Research (Genoa and NIH) 1992, Nat. Award, American Asscn for Clinical Chem. 1992, Grand Prix Scientifique, Fondation pour la Recherche Médicale, Paris 1994, Ken Myer Medal (Australia) 2000, Int. Acad. of Humanism Laureat 2002, Charles H. Sawyer Distinguished Lecture 2003 and numerous other prizes and awards. *Publications:* The Antiprogestin Steroid Ru 486 and Human Fertility Control 1985, Génération pilule 1989, Hormones 1990, The Abortion Pill: Ru-486: A Woman's Choice 1991, Contraception: Constraint or Freedom?; numerous specialist papers. *Address:* Institute Professor Baulieu, Pincus Building, 80 rue du Général Leclerc, Le Kremlin Bicêtre, 94276 Paris Cedex, France (office). *Website:* www.institut-baulieu.org (office).

BAUM, Bernard René, MSc, PhD, FRSC; Canadian agricultural research scientist; b. 14 Feb. 1937, Paris, France; s. of Kurt Baum and Marta Berl; m. Danielle Habib 1961; one d.; ed Hebrew Univ., Jerusalem; Research Scientist, Plant Research Inst., Dept of Agric., Ottawa, Canada 1966–74; Sr Research Scientist, Biosystematics Research Inst., Agriculture and Agri-Food Canada, Ottawa 1974–80, Prin. Research Scientist, Biosystematics Research Centre 1980–90, Prin. Research Scientist, Centre for Land and Biological Resources Research 1990–95, Eastern Cereal and Oilseed Research Centre 1996; Section Chief, Cultivated Crops Section 1973–77, Section Head, Vascular Plants Section 1982–87, Acting Dir, Geostrategy Div., Devt Policy Directorate 1981–82; mem. Acad. of Sciences (RSC) 1981, Botanical Soc. of America, Soc. Botanique de France, Int. Asscn for Plant Taxonomy and other socs; Founder-mem. Hennig Soc.; George Lawson Medal, Canadian Botanical Asscn 1979. *Publications:* Material of an International Oat Register 1973, Oats: Wild and Cultivated. A Monograph of the Genus Avena 1977, The Genus Tamarix 1978, Barley Register 1985, Triticale Register; more than 330 scientific publs. *Leisure interests:* swimming long distance, running 10k, pilates, classical music.

BAUMAN, Robert Patten, BA, MBA; American business executive; b. 27 March 1931, Cleveland, OH; s. of John Nevan Bauman, Jr and Lucille Miller Patten; m. Patricia Hughes Jones 1961; one s. one d.; ed Ohio Wesleyan Univ., Harvard Business School; fmr officer in USAF; joined Gen. Foods Corpn 1958, Corp. Vice-Pres. 1968, Group Vice-Pres. 1970, Exec. Vice-Pres. and Corp. Dir 1972–81; Dir Avco Corpn 1980, Chair. and CEO 1981–85; Vice-Chair. and Dir Textron Inc. 1985–86; Chair. and Chief Exec. Beecham Group 1986–89, CEO SmithKline Beecham 1989–94; Chair. British Aerospace PLC 1994–98, BTR PLC, London 1998–99; mem. Bd of Dirs Russell Reynolds Assocs, Bolero International Ltd; fmr mem. Bd of Dirs BTR plc, CIGNA Corpn, Hathaway Holdings, Inc., Morgan Stanley Dean Witter, Union Pacific Corpn, Cap Cities/ABC Inc., Bolero.net, Reuters; Trustee, Ohio Wesleyan Univ.; Hon. Fellow, London Business School. *Publication:* Plants as Pets 1982, From Promise to Performance 1997. *Leisure* *interests:* growing orchids, paddle tennis, jogging, tennis, photography, golf, sailing.

BAUMANN, Herbert Karl Wilhelm; German composer and conductor; b. 31 July 1925, Berlin; s. of Wilhelm Baumann and Elfriede Baumann (née Bade); m. Marianne Brose 1951; two s.; ed Berlin Classical High School, Schillergymnasium and Int. Music Inst.; Conductor, Tchaikovsky Symphony Orchestra 1947; Composer and Conductor, Deutsches Theater, Berlin 1947–53, Staatliche Berliner Bühnen: Schillertheater and Schloss-parktheater 1953–70, Bayerisches Staatsschauspiel: Residenztheater, Munich 1971–79; freelance composer 1979–; mem. GEMA for 50 years; Mem. of Honour, BDZ 1990; Bundesverdienstkreuz 1998; Diploma of Honour Salsomaggiore (Italy) 1981; Silbernes Ehrenzeichen GDBA 1979. *Works include:* stage music for more than 500 plays, 40 TV plays and the ballets Alice in Wonderland and Rumpelstiltskin, music for radio, cinema and TV, orchestral, chamber and choir works, several suites for plucked instruments, music for strings, music for wind instruments, three concertos and works for organ. *Films include:* Das Jahrhundert des Kindes, Die Stadt von Morgen, Menschen in der Stadt, König Fußball, Timpi Tox und Ali Bum, Berlin Sketchbook. *Leisure interests:* reading, especially books on fine arts. *Address:* Weitlstrasse 66, Apt 2049, 80935 Munich, Germany (home). *Telephone:* (89) 38582049 (home). *Fax:* (89) 38582049 (home). *E-mail:* hkwbau@augustinum.net. *Website:* www.komponisten.net/baumann.

BAUMANN, Karl-Hermann, Dipl.-Kfm, Dr.rer.oec; German business executive; b. 22 July 1935, Dortmund; Asst, Dept of Business Admin, Univ. of Saarland, Saarbrücken 1964–70; joined Siemens AG 1970, various positions in Corp. Finance Div. 1970–78, Sr Vice-Pres. Siemens Capital Corpn, NY and Siemens Corpn, Iselin, NJ, USA 1978–83, Head of Corp. Financial Accounting Div., Munich 1983–84, Vice-Pres. Siemens AG 1984–88, apptd to Bd of Man. 1987, apptd mem. Exec. Cttee 1988, Head of Corp. Finance 1988–98, Chair. Supervisory Bd Siemens AG 1998–2005; mem. Supervisory Bds Allianz AG 1998–2001, Bayer Schering Pharma AG (fmrly Schering AG) 1994–2009, Deutsche Bank AG 1989–2005, E.ON AG 1998–2008, Linde AG 1998–2008, MG Technologies AG 1998–2003, Thyssen Krupp AG 1998–2005.

BAUMANN, Werner; German business executive; *Chairman of the Board of Management, Bayer AG;* b. 6 Oct. 1962, Krefeld; m.; four c.; ed RWTH Aachen Univ., Univ. of Cologne; joined Bayer 1988, worked in Corp. Finance Dept, Leverkusen, transferred to Bayer Hispania Comercial, Barcelona, Spain as Controller 1991–95, became Asst to the Man. Dir 1995–96, moved to Bayer Corpn, Tarrytown, NY, USA as Head of Global Business Planning and Admin Org. of Diagnostics Business Group 1996–2002, returned to Germany to become mem. Exec. Cttee and Head of Cen. Admin and Org., Bayer HealthCare 2002–03, mem. Bd of Man. and Labour Dir of newly formed subgroup Bayer HealthCare AG 2003–06, mem. Bd of Man. and Labour Dir, Bayer Schering Pharma AG, Berlin 2006–09, Chief Financial Officer, Bayer AG 2010–14, Chief Strategy and Portfolio Officer and also responsible for Europe, Middle East and Africa Region 2014–16, Chair. Bd of Man. (CEO), Bayer HealthCare AG April–Dec. 2015, Chair. Bd of Man. (CEO), Bayer AG 2016–. *Address:* Bayer AG, Building W11, Kaiser-Wilhelm-Allee, 51368 Leverkusen, Germany (office). *Telephone:* (214) 301 (office). *Fax:* (214) 3066328 (office). *E-mail:* info@bayer.com (office). *Website:* www.bayer.com (office).

BAUMEISTER, Wolfgang, Dr rer. nat (Habil.); German biochemist and academic; *Professor and Head of Department of Structural Biology, Max Planck Institute of Biochemistry;* b. 1946 Nov. 1946, Wesseling; ed Univs of Münster, Bonn and Düsseldorf; worked at Cavendish Lab., Cambridge, UK 1970s, Lecturer in Biophysics 1978–83; Prof., Univs of Düsseldorf and Munich; Group Leader, Max Planck Inst. of Biochemistry, Martinsried 1983–88, Dir and Head of Dept of Structural Biology 1988–; mem. Bavarian Acad. of Sciences 2000, Acad. of German Scientists Leopoldina 2001, American Acad. of Arts and Sciences 2003, Nat. Acad. of Sciences 2010; Hon. Prof. of Physics, Tech. Univ. of Munich 2000; Otto Warburg Medal, Schleiden Medal, Louis-Jeantet Prize for Medicine, Stein and Moore Award, Harvey Prize in Science and Tech., Technion—Israel Inst. of Tech. 2005, Ernst Schering Prize 2006, Ernst-Jung Medal for Medicine in Gold 2018. *Publications:* numerous scientific papers in professional journals on cellular protein quality control. *Address:* Department of Molecular Structural Biology, Max Planck Institute of Biochemistry, Am Klopferspitz 18, 82152 Martinsried, Germany (office). *Telephone:* (89) 8578-2642 (office); (89) 8578-2387 (office). *Fax:* (89) 8578-2641 (office); (89) 8578-3557 (office). *E-mail:* baumeist@biochem.mpg.de (office). *Website:* www.biochem.mpg.de/baumeister (office).

BAUTISTA FLORES, Manuel de Jesús, MA, PhD; Honduran economist and central banker; *President, Banco Central de Honduras;* ed Autonomous Nat. Univ. of Honduras, Univ. of Colorado, USA; joined Banco Central de Honduras as Asst Economist, Econ. Research Dept 1974, apptd Deputy Man., Tech. Area 2006, Dir 2011–14, Vice-Pres. 2014–16, Pres. Banco Central de Honduras 2016–; fmr Pres. Colegio Hondureño de Economistas (Honduran Coll. of Economists); apptd Alternate Gov. Inter-American Investment Corpn 1985; mem. Consejo Monetario Centroamericano. *Address:* Banco Central de Honduras, Avda Juan Ramón Molina, 7a Avda y 1a Calle, Apdo 3165, Tegucigalpa, Honduras (office). *Telephone:* 2222-3422 (office). *Fax:* 2237-4502 (office). *E-mail:* manuel.bautista@bch.hn (office). *Website:* www.bch.hn (office).

BAVIN, Rt Rev. Dom Timothy John, MA; British monk; *Oblate Master, Alton Abbey;* b. 17 Sept. 1935, Northwood; s. of Edward Bavin and Marjorie Bavin; ed St George School, Windsor, Brighton Coll., Worcester Coll., Univ. of Oxford, Cuddesdon Coll.; Asst Priest, St Alban's Cathedral, Pretoria 1961–64, Chaplain 1964–69; Asst Priest, Uckfield, Sussex 1969–71; Vicar, Church of the Good Shepherd, Brighton 1971–73; Dean of Johannesburg 1973–74, Bishop 1974–84; Bishop of Portsmouth, England 1985–95, Hon. Asst Bishop 2012–; Hon. Asst Bishop, Diocese of Winchester 2013–; Monk, Order of St Benedict, Alton Abbey 1996–, Oblate Master 2011–; mem. Oratory of the Good Shepherd 1987–95; Hon. Fellow, Royal School of Church Music 1991. *Publications:* Deacons in the Ministry of the Church 1986, In Tune with Heaven (ed.) 1992. *Leisure interests:* music, walking, gardening. *Address:* Alton Abbey, Alton, Hants., GU34 4AP, England.

BAXTER, Glen; British artist; b. 4 March 1944, Leeds, Yorks.; s. of Charles Baxter and Florence Baxter; m. Carole Agis; one s. one d.; ed Cockburn Grammar School, Leeds and Leeds Coll. of Art; has exhibited drawings in New York, San Francisco, Venice, Amsterdam, Lille, Munich, Tokyo and Paris and rep. UK at Sydney Biennale 1986, Adelaide Festival 1992, Hôtel Furkablick (Switzerland) 1993; major retrospectives at Musée de l'Abbaye Sainte-Croix, Les Sables d'Olonne, France 1987, 'Une Ame en Tourment', Centre nat. de l'art imprimé Chatou, Paris; illustrated Charlie Malarkey and the Belly Button Machine 1986; tapestry commissioned by French Govt to commemorate 8th centenary of death of Richard the Lion-Heart; Chevalier des Arts et des Lettres, Chevalier dans l'ordre des Arts et Lettres. *Television:* South Bank Show 1983. *Publications include:* Atlas 1979, The Impending Gleam 1981, His Life: The Years of Struggle 1983, Jodhpurs in the Quantocks 1986, Welcome to the Weird World of Glen Baxter 1989, The Billiard Table Murders, A Gladys Babbington Morton Mystery 1990, Glen Baxter Returns to Normal 1992, The Collected Blurtings of Baxter 1993, The Further Blurtings of Baxter 1994, The Wonder Book of Sex 1995, Glen Baxter's Gourmet Guide 1997, Blizzards of Tweed 1999, Podium 2000, The Unhinged World of Glen Baxter 2002, Trundling Grunts 2002, Loomings Over the Suet 2004, Le Monde de Glen Baxter 2009, Ominous Stains 2009, Colonel Baxter's Dutch Safari 2012. *Leisure interests:* marquetry, snood retrieval. *E-mail:* glenbaxter@mac.com (home). *Website:* www.glenbaxter.com (home).

BAXTER, Rodney James, ScD, GradDip (Theol), FRS, FAA; Australian (b. British) mathematical physicist and academic; *Professor Emeritus, Australian National University;* b. 8 Feb. 1940, London, England; s. of Thomas J. Baxter and Florence Baxter; m. Elizabeth A. Phillips 1968; one s. one d.; ed Bancroft's School, Essex, Trinity Coll., Cambridge and Australian Nat. Univ.; Reservoir Engineer, Iraq Petroleum Co. 1964–65; Research Fellow, ANU 1965–68, Fellow 1971–81, Prof., Dept of Theoretical Physics, Research School of Physical Sciences 1981–, jtly with School of Math. Sciences 1989–, now Emer. and Visiting Fellow; Asst Prof., MIT, USA 1968–70; Royal Soc. Research Prof., Univ. of Cambridge 1992; Pawsey Medal, Australian Acad. of Science 1975, IUPAP Boltzmann Medal 1980, Thomas Ranken Lyle Medal, Australian Acad. of Science 1983, Dannie Heineman Prize, American Physical Soc. 1987, Harrie Massey Medal and Prize, Australian Inst. of Physics/Inst. of Physics (UK) 1994, Centenary Medal, Australian Govt 2003, Onsager Prize, American Physical Soc. 2006, Lars Onsager Lecture and Medal, Norwegian Univ. of Science and Tech. 2006, Royal Medal, Royal Soc. 2013. *Publication:* Exactly Solved Models in Statistical Mechanics 1982, contrib. to professional journals. *Leisure interest:* theatre. *Address:* Centre for Mathematics and Its Applications, Mathematical Sciences Institute, Building 27, Australian National University, Canberra, ACT 0200, Australia. *Telephone:* (2) 6125-3511. *Fax:* (2) 6125-5549.

BAY, Michael Benjamin; American film director and producer; b. 17 Feb. 1965, Los Angeles, Calif.; adopted s. of Jim Bay and Harriet Bay; ed Crossroads School, Santa Monica, Wesleyan Univ., Art Center Coll. of Design, Pasadena; interned with George Lucas aged 15; began working at Propaganda Films, directing commercials for Nike, Reebok, Coca-Cola, Budweiser and Miller Lite and cr. music videos for Tina Turner, Meat Loaf, Lionel Richie, Wilson Phillips, Donny Osmond and The Divinyls; directed Goodby, Silverstein & Partners Got Milk? advertisement campaign for the California Milk Processors Bd 1993, campaign now resides in perm. collection of Museum of Modern Art, New York; gained attention of producers Jerry Bruckheimer and Don Simpson, and as a result directed his first feature-length film, Bad Boys 1995; Co-founder The Institute, aka The Inst. for the Devt of Enhanced Perceptual Awareness; Co-Chair. and part Owner of Digital Domain digital effects house; Co-owner Platinum Dunes production house; Clio Award for first nat. commercial for the Red Cross 1992, Grand Prix Clio for Commercial of the Year for his Got Milk/Aaron Burr commercial, Gold Lion for The Best Beer campaign for Miller Lite, as well as the Silver for Got Milk, Cannes Film Festival, Commercial Dir of the Year, Dirs Guild of America 1995, Action Movie Director Award, World Stunt Awards 2002, Filmmaker's Award 2008, ShoWest Vanguard Award for Excellence in Filmmaking 2009. *Films directed:* Play That Funky Music (video short) (segment 'I Love You') 1990, Playboy: Kerri Kendall – September 1990 Video Centerfold (video documentary) 1990, Great White: My... My... My... the Video Collection (video 'Call It Rock 'N' Roll') 1991, Shadows and Light: From a Different View (video documentary short) 1992, Meat Loaf: Bat Out of Hell II—Picture Show (music videos) 1994, Bad Boys 1995, The Rock (Best Action Scene, MTV Movie Awards) 1996, Armageddon (Saturn Award for Best Director 1999) 1998, Pearl Harbor (Best Action Scene, MTV Movie Awards) 2001, Bad Boys II (also actor) (Best Action Scene, MTV Movie Awards) 2003, The Lionel Richie Collection (video documentary) ('Do It to Me') 2003, The Island 2005, Transformers (also exec. producer) (MTV Movie Awards: Best Movie and Best Summer Movie You Haven't Seen Yet) 2007, Transformers: Revenge of the Fallen (also exec. producer) 2009, Transformers: Dark of the Moon (also exec. producer) 2011, Pain and Gain (also producer) 2013, Transformers: Age of Extinction (also exec. producer) 2014, Transformers: The Last Knight (also exec. producer) 2017. *Film roles in:* Mystery Men 1999, Coyote Ugly 2000, Zigs 2001. *Films produced:* The Texas Chainsaw Massacre 2003, The Amityville Horror 2005, The Island 2005, Pissed 2005, The Texas Chainsaw Massacre: The Beginning, 2006, The Hitcher 2007, Their War (video documentary) (exec. producer) 2007, Our World (video documentary) (exec. producer) 2007, From Script, to Sand: The Skorponok Desert Attack (video documentary short) (exec. producer) 2007, Horsemen 2009, The Unborn 2009, Friday the 13th 2009, A Nightmare on Elm Street 2010, I Am Number Four 2011, Uncharted Territory: NASA's Future Then and Now (video documentary short) (exec. producer) 2012, Above and Beyond: Exploring Dark of the Moon (video documentary) (exec. producer) 2012, Vigilandia 2013, 13 Hours 2016. *Television includes:* Miami Vice (series) 1986, Vengeance: The Story of Tony Cimo (film) 1986, Black Sails (series) 2014–17, The Last Ship (series) 2014–18, Jack Ryan (series) 2018–, The Purge (series) 2018–. *Address:* c/o William Morris Endeavor, One William Morris Place, Beverly Hills, CA 90212, USA (office); Bay Films, 2110 Broadway, Santa Monica, CA 90404 (office); The Institute, 448 S Hill Street, Suite 506, Los Angeles, CA 90013, USA (office). *Telephone:* (310) 859-4000 (office); (310) 859-4131 (office). *Fax:* (310) 859-4462 (office); (310) 859-4262 (office). *Website:* www.wma.com (office); www.theinstitute.tv (office); www.michaelbay .com. *E-mail:* info@theinstitute.tv (office).

BAYAR, Sanjaagiin (Sanjiin); Mongolian politician, diplomatist and journalist; b. 1956, Ulaanbaatar; ed Moscow State Univ., USSR; fmr officer, Ulaanbaatar City Ass. and Nairamdal Dist Office 1978–79; officer, Gen. HQ Nat. Defence Army 1979–83; journalist and ed., Novosti Mongolii newspaper, Chief Ed. and Gen. Ed.

Montsame news agency 1983–88; Deputy Head of Admin Agency, Mongolian Radio TV 1988–90; mem. Nat. Congress 1990–92; Head, Strategy and Research Centre, Ministry of Defence 1992–97; Chief of Staff, Office of the Pres. 1997–2001; Amb. to Russian Fed. 2001–05; Gen. Sec. Mongolian People's Revolutionary Party 2005–07, Chair. 2007–; Prime Minister of Mongolia 2007–09 (resgnd). *Address:* Mongolian People's Revolutionary Party, Sukhbaatar District, UB-14191, Ulaanbaatar, Mongolia (office). *Telephone:* 50067805 (office). *Fax:* 50067805 (office). *E-mail:* contact@mprp.mn (office). *Website:* www.mprp.mn (office).

BAYARDI, José, MD; Uruguayan physician and politician; *Minister of National Defence;* b. 30 June 1955, Montevideo; Deputy (Vertiente Artiguista) Cámara de Representantes (Parl.) 1990–; Deputy Minister of Nat. Defence 2005–08, Minister of Nat. Defence 2008–09, 2019–; Chair. Vertiente Artiguista 1994–2001. *Address:* Ministry of National Defence, Edif. General Artigas, Avda 8 de Octubre 2628, Montevideo, Uruguay (office). *Telephone:* 2487 2828 (office). *Fax:* 2481 4833 (office). *E-mail:* rrpp.secretaria@mdn.gub.uy (office). *Website:* www.mdn.gub.uy.

BAYARTSAIKHAN, Nadmidyn; Mongolian academic, politician and central banker; *President, Bank of Mongolia;* b. 27 Jan. 1971, Ulaanbaatar; m.; two c.; ed State People's Econs Inst. and State Man. Acad. of Moscow, Russia; Teacher, Mongolian People's Revolutionary Party Central Cttee Inst. 1982–89; mem. State Great Hural (Parl.) 1992–2008, Chair. Standing Cttee on Food 1993–95, on Budget 2000–04; Minister of Finance 2006–07; Pres. Nat. Agricultural Cooperative Fed. 2002–14, Chair. 2014–16; Pres. Bank of Mongolia 2016–; mem. Mongolian People's Party (MPP). *Address:* Office of the President, Bank of Mongolia, Baga toiruu 3, Sükhbaatar District, Ulaanbaatar, Mongolia (office). *Telephone:* (11) 320413 (office). *Fax:* (11) 311471 (office). *E-mail:* info@mongolbank.mn (office). *Website:* www.mongolbank.mn (office).

BAYÉ, Jules, MSc; Niger government official; b. 1 Sept. 1945, Barra; ed Univ. Paris–Dauphine, Ecole Nat. des Douanes, Neuilly, France; Head of Audit and Verification, Customs Directorate-Gen. Jan.–May 1974, Deputy Dir-Gen. of Customs 1974–86; Dir-Gen. of Taxation 1986–88, 1993–96, 1999–2000; with Ministry of Finance, in charge of relations with Communauté Économique de l'Afrique de l'Ouest (CEAO)/Communauté Économique des États de l'Afrique de l'Ouest (CEDEAO)/Conseil de Coopération Douanière (CCD) 1988–89, Financial Controller, CEDEAO, Lagos 1989–93, Technical Adviser, Ministry of Finance 1996–99; with West African Econ. and Monetary Union 2000–01; Minister of the Economy and Finance 2012; mem. numerous cttees including nat. CEAO/CEDEAO cttees; fmr Chair. Société Nationale des Transports Nigériens.

BAYE, Nathalie; French actress; b. 6 July 1948, Mainneville; d. of Claude Baye and Denise Coustet; one d. by Johnny Hallyday; ed Conservatoire nat. d'art dramatique de Paris; Chevalier, Légion d'honneur 2019; Femme en or—Trophée Whirlpool 2000, Margritte Award 2012. *Stage appearances include:* Galapages 1972, Liola 1973, Les trois soeurs 1978, Adriana Monti 1986, Les fausses confidences 1993, La parisienne 1995. *Television:* Marie-Octobre (film) 2008, Le grand restaurant (film) 2010, La collection - Écrire pour (series) 2011, Les hommes de l'ombre (series) 2012, Nox (mini-series) 2018. *Films include:* Two People 1972, La nuit américaine 1973, La gueule ouverte 1974, La Gifle 1974, Un jour la fête 1974, Le voyage de noces 1975, Le plein de super 1976, Mado 1976, L'homme qui aimait les femmes 1977, Monsieur Papa 1977, La communion solenelle 1977, La chambre verte 1978, Mon premier amour 1978, La mémoire courte 1978, Sauve qui peut 1979, Je vais craquer 1979, Une semaine de vacances 1980, Provinciale 1980, Beau-père, Une étrange affaire, L'ombre rouge 1981, Le retour de Martin Guerre 1981, La balance (César for Best Actress 1983) 1982, J'ai épousé une ombre 1982, Notre histoire 1983, Rive droite, rive gauche 1984, Détective 1984, Le neveu de Beethoven 1985, Lune de Miel 1985, De guerre lasse 1987, En toute innocence 1988, La Baule-les-Pins 1990, Un week-end sur deux 1990, The Man Inside 1990, L'Affaire Wallraff 1991, La Voix 1992, Mensonges 1993, La machine 1994, Les soldats de l'espérance 1994, Enfants da salud 1996, Si je t'aime… prends garde à toi 1998, Food of Love 1998, Paparazzi 1998, Vénus beauté 1999, Une liaison pornographique (Volpi Cup, Venice Int. Film Festival, European Film Award for Best Actress) 1999, Ça ira mieux demain 2000, Selon Matthieu, Barnie et ses petites contrariétés 2001, Absolument fabuleux 2001, Catch Me If You Can 2002, La Fleur du mal 2003, Les Sentiments 2003, France Boutique 2003, Une vie à t'attendre 2004, L'un reste, l'autre part 2005, Le Petit Lieutenant (César Award for Best Actress 2006) 2005, Ne le dis à personne 2006, Mon fils à moi 2006, Le prix à payer 2007, Passe-passe 2008, Visage 2009, HH, Hitler à Hollywood 2010, Je n'ai rien oublié 2010, Lou! Journal infime 2014, Préjudice 2015, Les gardiennes 2017. *Address:* c/o Artmédia, 20 avenue Rapp, 75007 Paris, France (office).

BAYER, Oswald; German ecclesiastic and professor of theology; *Professor Emeritus of Systematic Theology, Evangelical Theological Faculty, Eberhard Karls University of Tübingen;* b. 30 Sept. 1939, Nagold; s. of Emil Bayer and Hermine Bayer; m. Eva Bayer 1966 (deceased 1993); ed Tübingen, Bonn and Rome, Italy; Vicar, Evangelische Landeskirche, Württemberg 1964; Asst Univ. of Tübingen 1965–68; Evangelical Stift, Tübingen 1968–71; Pastor, Tübingen 1972–74; Prof. of Systematic Theology, Univ. of Bochum 1974–79, Evangelical Theological Faculty, Univ. of Tübingen 1979–2005 (now Emer.), Dir Inst. of Christian Ethics 1979–95; Ed. Zeitschrift für Systematische Theologie und Religionsphilosophie 1986–2006. *Publications:* Worship and Ethics: Lutherans and Anglicans in Dialogue (co-author) 1995, Living by Faith: Justification and Sanctification (trans.) 2003, Martin Luther's Theology: A Contemporary Interpretation (trans.) 2003, Theology the Lutheran Way (trans.) 2007; numerous essays on theological and philosophical topics. *Address:* Kurhausstr. 138, 53773 Tübingen. *Telephone:* (2242) 918951. *E-mail:* bayer@unitybox.de.

BAYH, Birch Evans (Evan), III, BS, JD; American lawyer, politician and broadcaster; *Partner, McGuireWoods LLP;* b. 26 Dec. 1955, Shirkieville, Ind.; s. of Birch Evans Bayh Jr and Marvella Hern; m. Susan Bayh; twin s.; ed Indiana Univ., Univ. of Virginia; Sec. of State of Ind. 1987–89; Gov. of Ind. 1989–97; Partner, Baker & Daniel Assocs (law firm), Indianapolis 1997; Lecturer, Indiana Univ. Kelley School of Business 1997–98; Senator from Ind. 1999–2011 (retd); Partner, McGuireWoods LLP law firm, Washington, DC 2011–; Chair. Democratic Leadership Council 2001–05; f. Moderate Dems Working Group; mem. Bd of Dirs Nat. Endowment for Democracy; Sr Advisor, Apollo Global Management, New York; contrib., Fox News 2011–; Democrat; Dr hc (Golden Gate Univ. School of Law). *Publications include:* From Father to Son: A Private Life in the Public Eye 2003. *Address:* McGuireWoods LLP, 2001 K Street NW, Suite 400, Washington, DC 20006-1040 (office); 10 West Market Street, Suite 1650, Indianapolis, IN 46204-2934, USA. *Telephone:* (202) 828-2825 (office). *Fax:* (202) 828-3331 (office). *E-mail:* ebayh@mcguirewoods.com (office). *Website:* www.mcguirewoods.com (office).

BAYI, Filbert, BSc (Educ.); Tanzanian sports administrator and fmr athlete; *Secretary-General, National Olympic Committee;* b. (Habiye), 22 June 1953, Karatu, Arusha Region; s. of Sanka Bayi and Magdalena Qwaray; m. Anna Lyimo 1977; two s. two d.; ed Univ. of Texas at El Paso, USA; joined Air Transport Battalion (TPDF), Dar es Salaam; middle distance runner; beat Tanzanian Nat. Champion over 1,500m, Dar es Salaam 1972; 1,500m Gold Medal Nat. Championships, Dar es Salaam 1972, All African Games, Lagos, Nigeria (record time) 1973; first competed Europe June 1973; 1,500m Gold Medal (and world record), Commonwealth Games, Christchurch, New Zealand 1974; 1,500m Gold Medal, All African Games, Algiers, Algeria 1978; 1,500m Silver Medal Commonwealth Games, Edmonton, Canada 1978; 3,000m Steeplechase Silver Medal, Olympic Games, Moscow, USSR 1980; Athletic Nat. Coach; Army Chief Coach ATHL; Sec. TAAA Tech. Cttee, Tanzania Olympic Cttee; mem. TAAA Exec. Cttee, IAAF Tech. Cttee; IAAF Athletic Coaching Lecturer; Nat. Chief Instructor and Athletic Coach; IOC Nat. Course Dir; Exec. mem. Nat. Olympic Cttee, Sec.-Gen. Nat. Olympic Cttee 2002–; Gen. Chair. Bd of Dirs Filbert Bayi Nursery, Primary and Secondary School, Filbert Bayi Foundation; United Repub. of Tanzania Medal 1995. *Leisure interests:* reading, sports, watching TV, talking to children. *Address:* Filbert Bayi Nursery and Primary School—Kimara, Morogoro Road, PO Box 60240, Dar es Salaam, Tanzania. *Telephone:* (22) 2420635 (office); (22) 2420634 (home). *Fax:* (22) 2420178 (office); (22) 2420178 (home). *E-mail:* filbertbayischools@yahoo.com (office); fsbayi@yahoo.com (home). *Website:* www.filbertbayischools.org.

BAYKAM, Bedri; Turkish painter, writer and politician; b. 26 April 1957, Ankara; s. of Suphi Baykam and Mutahhar Baykam; m. Sibel Yağci; one s.; ed French Lycée, Istanbul, Univ. of Paris I (Panthéon-Sorbonne), France, California Coll. of Arts and Crafts, USA; numerous solo exhbns Paris, Brussels, Rome, New York, Istanbul, Munich, Stockholm, Helsinki, London 1963–99; mem. Cen. Bd CHP (Republican Party of the People) 1995–98; Pres. Int. Asscn of Art; f. Piramid Publishing 1998; Founder, The Patriotic Movement 2005; Painter of the Year, Nokta magazine 1987, 1989, 1990, 1996–97, Best Artist and Best Performance, Art Jonction, Cannes 1994. *Major art works include:* The Prostitute's Room 1981, The Painting 1985, This Has Been Done Before 1987, Livart 1994, The Years of 68 1997, Curatorial Schizophrenia 2005. *Publications include:* The Brain of Paint (Boyanin Beyni) 1990, Monkey's Right to Paint 1994, Mustafa Kemal's on Duty Now 1994, Secular Turkey Without Concession 1995, Fleeting Moments, Enduring Delights 1996, His Eyes Always Rest on Us 1997, The Color of the Era 1997, The Years of 68 (Vols 1 and 2) 1998–99, I'm Nothing but I'm Everything 1999, The Last Condottiere of the Millennium, Che 2000, The Bone 2000 (English trans. 2005), The Millennium Crack 2002, End of the Empire of Fear 2004. *Leisure interests:* tennis, football, music, pool. *Address:* Piramid Publishing, Feridiye Cad 23–25 Taksim, Istanbul (office); Palanga Cad 33/23, Ortaköy, Istanbul 80840, Turkey (home). *Telephone:* (212) 2973120 (office); (212) 2580809 (home). *E-mail:* bedri.baykam@gmail.com. *Website:* www.bedribaykam.com; www.piramidsanat.com (office).

BAYLEY, Stephen Paul, MA; British design consultant, writer, exhibition organizer and museum administrator; b. 13 Oct. 1951, Cardiff, Wales; s. of Donald Bayley and Anne Bayley; m. Flo Fothergill 1981; one s. one d.; ed Quarry Bank School, Liverpool, Univ. of Manchester, Univ. of Liverpool School of Architecture; Lecturer in History of Art, Open Univ. 1974–76, Univ. of Kent 1976–80; Dir Conran Foundation 1981–89; Dir Boilerhouse Project, Victoria & Albert Museum, London 1982–86; Founding Dir then Chief Exec. Design Museum 1986–89; Creative Dir New Millennium Experience Co. 1997–98 (resgnd); lectured throughout the UK and abroad; Hon. Fellow, Univ. of Wales Inst., Cardiff 2007; Hon. FRIBA 2008; Chevalier des Arts et des Lettres 1990; Periodical Publrs Asscn Magazine Columnist of the Year 1995. *Publications include:* In Good Shape 1979, The Albert Memorial 1981, Harley Earl and the Dream Machine 1983, Conran Directory of Design 1985, Sex, Drink and Fast Cars 1986, Commerce and Culture 1989, Taste 1991, Labour Camp 1998, Moving Objects (ed.) 1999, General Knowledge 2000, Sex: An Intimate History (ed.) 2001, Dictionary of Idiocy 2003, Life's a Pitch 2007, Design: Intelligence Made Visible 2007, Cars 2008, Woman as Design 2009, La Dolce Vita 2011, Ugly: The Aesthetics of Everything 2012. *Leisure interests:* travel-related services, solitary sports, books. *Address:* 23 Ganton Street, London, W1F 9BW, England (office). *Telephone:* (20) 7287-5888 (office). *E-mail:* guru@stephenbayley.com (home).

BAYLY LETTS, Jaime; Peruvian journalist, writer and broadcaster; b. 19 Feb. 1965, Lima; s. of Jaime Bayly Llona and Doris Letts; m. Sandra Masías; two d.; ed Inmaculado Corazón, Markham Coll., Lima, Colegio San Agustín de Lima, Pontificia Universidad Católica del Perú; began career as columnist for La Prensa (newspaper) 1980; anchor, 24-hour news network CBS Telenoticias 1996–2000; fmr political corresp., TV series Pulso, Canal 5; fmr presenter 1,990 en America; presenter, El Francotirador (TV show) 2006–10; presenter, Bayly (chat show), Mega TV, Miami, Nuestra Tele Noticias (NTN) 24; columnist, The Miami Herald, Peru 21; GLAAD Visibility Award, USA 2007. *Publications include:* novels: No se lo digas a nadie (Don't Tell Anyone) 1994, Yo amo a mi mami (I Love my Mummy) 2000, Y de Repente, Un Angel (Suddenly, an Angel) 2005, El Cojo y el Loco (The Crippled and the Crazy) 2009, Morirás mañana: El Escritor Sale a Matar (You Will Die Tomorrow: The Writer Goes On to Kill) 2010, Morirás mañana 2: El misterio de Alma Rossi 2011, Morirás mañana 3: Escupirán sobre mi tumba 2012.

BAYM, Gordon Alan, AM, PhD, FAAS; American physicist and academic; *Professor of Physics, University of Illinois;* b. 1 July 1935, New York, NY; s. of Louis Baym and Lillian Baym; two s. two d.; ed Brooklyn Technical High School, Cornell Univ., Harvard Univ.; Fellow, Universitetets Institut for Teoretisk Fysik, Copenhagen 1960–62; Lecturer, Univ. of Calif., Berkeley 1962–63; Prof. of Physics, Univ. of Ill., Urbana 1963–; Visiting Prof., Univs of Tokyo and Kyoto 1968, Nordita, Copenhagen 1970, 1976, Niels Bohr Inst. 1976–, Univ. of Nagoya 1979; Visiting Scientist, Academia Sinica, Beijing 1979; mem. Advisory Bd Inst. of Theoretical Physics, Santa Barbara, Calif. 1978–83; mem. Sub-cttee on Theoretical Physics,

NSF 1980–81, Physics Advisory Cttee 1982–85; mem. Nuclear Science Advisory Cttee, Dept of Energy/NSF 1982–86; mem. Editorial Bd Procs. NAS 1986–92; Fellow, American Acad. of Arts and Sciences, American Physical Soc.; Research Fellow, Alfred P. Sloan Foundation 1965–68; NSF Postdoctoral Fellow 1960–62; Trustee, Assoc. Univs Inc. 1986–90; Assoc. Ed. Nuclear Physics; mem. American Astronomical Soc., Int. Astronomical Union, NAS (fmr Chair. Physics Section), American Philosophical Soc.; Sr US Scientist Award, Alexander von Humboldt Foundation 1983, Hans A. Bethe Prize, American Physical Soc. 2002, Lars Onsager Prize (co-recipient), American Physical Soc. 2008, Eugene Feenberg Memorial Medal 2011. *Publications:* Quantum Statistical Mechanics (co-author) 1962, Lectures on Quantum Mechanics 1969, Neutron Stars 1970, Neutron Stars and the Properties of Matter at High Density 1977, Landau Fermi-Liquid Theory (co-author) 1991. *Leisure interests:* photography, mountains. *Address:* 337C Loomis Laboratory, University of Illinois, 1110 West Green Street, Urbana, IL 61801, USA (office). *Telephone:* (217) 333-4363 (office). *Fax:* (217) 244-7559 (office); (217) 333-9819 (office). *E-mail:* gbaym@illinois.edu (office). *Website:* physics .illinois.edu/people/profile.asp?gbaym (office).

BAYMENOV, Alixan Mukhamedyevich; Kazakhstani politician; b. 25 March 1959, Qarağandi; held numerous govt posts, including Head of Presidential Admin 1998–99; Minister of Labour and Social Security 2000–01; Co-founder Democratic Choice of Kazakhstan party 2001; Co-founder and Chair. Kazakstannyn Ak Jol Demokratiyalyk Partiyasy (Ak Jol) (Bright Road Democratic Party of Kazakhstan) 2002–12; unsuccessful presidential cand. 2005. *Address:* Kazakstannyn Ak Jol Demokratiyalyk Partiyasy (Ak Jol) (Bright Road Democratic Party of Kazakhstan), 010000 Nur-Sultan, Saraishyk kosh. 11, Kazakhstan (office). *Telephone:* (7172) 50-70-01 (office). *Fax:* (7172) 50-70-20 (office). *E-mail:* akzholpress@mail.ru (office). *Website:* www.akzhol.kz (office).

BAYNE, Sir Nicholas Peter, KCMG, MA, DPhil; British diplomatist (retd); *Fellow, International Trade Policy Unit, London School of Economics;* b. 15 Feb. 1937, London; s. of late Capt. Ronald Bayne, RN and Elizabeth Bayne (née Ashcroft); m. Diana Wilde 1961; three s. (one deceased); ed Eton Coll. and Christ Church, Oxford; joined HM Diplomatic Service 1961; served in Manila 1963–66, Bonn 1969–72; seconded to HM Treasury 1974–75; Financial Counsellor, Paris 1975–79; Head of Econ. Relations Dept, FCO 1979–82; Royal Inst. of Int. Affairs 1982–83; Amb. to Zaïre (also accred to Congo, Rwanda, Burundi) 1983–84; Amb. and Perm. Rep. to OECD, Paris 1985–88; Deputy Under-Sec. of State, FCO 1988–92; High Commr in Canada 1992–96; Fellow, Int. Trade Policy Unit, LSE 1997–. *Publications:* Hanging Together: The Seven-Power Summits (with R. Putnam) 1984, Hanging In There: The G7 and G8 Summit in Maturity and Renewal 2000, The Grey Wares of North-West Anatolia and their Relations to the Early Greek Settlements 2000, The New Economic Diplomacy (with S. Woolcock) 2003, Staying Together: The G8 Summit Confronts the 21st Century 2005, Economic Diplomat 2010. *Leisure interests:* reading, sightseeing. *Address:* 2 Chetwynd House, Hampton Court, Surrey, KT8 9BS, England.

BAYONA, Juan Antonio; Spanish film director; b. 9 May 1975, Barcelona; ed Cinema and Audiovisual School of Catalonia (ESCAC); began career directing commercials and pop videos for Spanish musical groups, including OBK, Hevia, Ella Baila Sola and Camela. *Films include:* Mis vacaciones (short) (also writer) 1999, Diminutos del calvario (short) (segment 'Muerte') 2001, El hombre Esponja (short) (also writer and exec. producer) 2002, Sonorama (video) (as J. A. Bayona) 2004, 10 años con Camela (video) 2004, Lo echamos a suertes (video short) (segment 'Cómo repartimos los amigos') 2005, Tierra de Hevia (music video) 2005, The Orphanage (as J. A. Bayona) 2007, The Impossible 2012, A Monster Calls (Goya Awards' Best Director 2016) 2016, Jurassic World: Fallen Kingdom 2018; actor (as J. A. Bayona): Spanish Movie 2009, The Queen of Spain 2016. *Address:* c/o Creative Artists Agency, 2000 Avenue of the Stars, Los Angeles, CA 90067, USA (office). *Telephone:* (424) 288-2000 (office). *Fax:* (424) 288-2900 (office). *Website:* www.caa.com (office).

BAYROU, François; French politician; b. 25 May 1951, Bordères, Basses-Pyrénées; s. of Calixte Bayrou and Emma Sarthou; m. Elisabeth Perlant; three s. three d.; ed Lycée de Nay-Bourdettes, Lycée Montaigne, Bordeaux and Univ. of Bordeaux III; fmr school teacher; Prof., Pau 1974–79; special attachment to Office of Minister of Agric. 1979; Ed.-in-Chief, Démocratie Moderne (weekly) 1980–91; Nat. Sec. Centre des Démocrates Sociaux (now Force démocrate) 1980–86, Deputy Sec.-Gen. 1986–94, Pres. 1994–97 (then merged into Nouvelle UDF then into Union pour la Démocratie Française (UDF), Gen. Del. (UDF) 1989–91, Sec.-Gen. 1991–94, Pres. 1998–2007; Pres. Mouvement démocrate 2007–; Conseiller Gen. Pau 1982–93, 2008–; Pres. Conseil Gen. des Pyrénées-Atlantiques 1992–2001; Conseiller Régional, Aquitaine 1982–86; Town Councillor, Pau 1988–92; Adviser to Pierre Pflimlin (Pres. of Ass. of EC) 1984–86; Deputy to Nat. Ass. 1986–93, 1997–99, 2002–12; Minister of Nat. Educ. 1993–95, also of Higher Educ., Research and Professional Training 1995–97, of Justice May–June 2017; mem. European Parl. 1999–2002; presidential cand. 2002, 2007, 2012. *Publications include:* La Décennie des mal-appris 1990, Henri IV, le roi libre 1994, le Droit au sens 1996, Saint-louis 1997, Henri IV 1998, L'Edit de Nantes 1998, Hors des sentiers battus 1999, Relève 2001, Oui: Plaidoyer pour la Constitution européenne 2005, Au nom du Tier-Etat 2006. *Leisure interests:* raising horses, literature. *Address:* Mouvement Démocrate, 133 Bis Rue de l'Université, 75007 Paris (office); 27 rue Duboué, 64000 Pau, France (home). *Telephone:* 1-53-59-20-00 (office). *E-mail:* fbayrou@ assemblee-nationale.fr (office). *Website:* www.bayrou.fr.

BAZALGETTE, Sir Peter Lytton (Baz), Kt, FRTS; British television industry executive; *Chairman, ITV plc;* b. 22 May 1953, Romney Marsh, Kent; great-great-grandson of Victorian civil engineer Sir Joseph Bazalgette; m. Hilary Newiss; two c.; ed Dulwich Coll., London, Fitzwilliam Coll., Cambridge; joined BBC News graduate news training scheme, subsequently chosen by Esther Rantzen as researcher on That's Life! from 1977; reporter for BBC for Man Alive; joined Epic video production co.; responsible for producing the Food and Drink programme; formed own co. Bazal Productions 1987, Man. Dir 1987–89, co. acquired by Broadcast Communications 1990, latter acquired by Endemol, Chair. Endemol UK 2002–07, Creative Dir of Endemol Group world-wide 2005–07, adviser 2007; Chair. ITV plc 2016–; Chair. Arts Council England 2013–16; fmr Pres. Royal Television Soc.; Dir (non-exec.), Dept of Culture Media & Sport 2011–13; Chair. MirriAd; Deputy Chair. ENO (Trustee 2004–), Crossness Engines Trust, Nat. Film & Television School; Vice-Chair. British Acad. of Gastronomes 1993–; Dir (non-exec.) Base79, Nutopia, Victoria Real, Zeppotron, Channel 4 2001–04, YouGov.com 2005–; mem. Advisory Bd BBH; Trustee, Debate Mate; Ind. Producer of the Year, Broadcast Production Awards 1997, McTaggart Lecturer, Edinburgh Int. TV Festival 1998, Hat Trick Pioneer Award Indies 1998, Indie-vidual Award for Outstanding Personal Contrib. to the Ind. Sector 2000, Weldon Lecturer, Royal Television Soc. (RTS) 2001, RTS Judges' Award 2003, BAFTA Fellowship 2000. *Television includes:* cr. Ready Steady Cook (BBC 2), Can't Cook Won't Cook (BBC 1), Changing Rooms (BBC 2), Ground Force (BBC 1), formats sold to 30 countries; Food and Drink (series documentary) (producer) 1988, Southern Italian Feast (series documentary) (exec. producer) 1998, Big Brother and Beyond: The Royal Television Society Huw Wheldon Memorial Lecture 2001, Tabloid Tales (series documentary) 2003, Faking It (series) (judge) 2003, Happy Birthday BBC Two (documentary) 2004, Who Killed Saturday Night TV? (documentary) 2004, HARDtalk Extra (series) 2005, The 50 Greatest Documentaries (documentary) 2005, This Week (series) 2006–07, Channel 4 at 25 (documentary) 2007, TV Is Dead? (mini-series documentary) 2007, How TV Changed Britain (series documentary) 2008, The Money Programme (series documentary) 2009, The TV Show (series documentary) 2009, The Noughties... Was That It? (documentary) 2009, History of Now: The Story of the Noughties (series documentary) 2010, The Review Show (series) – British TV Special 2011. *Publications include:* B.B.C. Food Check: Your Practical Guide to Safe Food (with D. Edwards) 1989, The Food Revolution (with Tom Sanders) 1991, You Don't Have to Diet (with T. A. B. Sanders) 1994, Entertaining with Food and Drink (with Michael Barry and Jilly Goolden) 1995, Billion Dollar Game: How 3 Men Risked it All and Changed the Face of TV 2005. *Leisure interests:* gluttony, cricket. *Address:* ITV plc, 200 Gray's Inn Road, London, WC1X 8HF, England (office). *Website:* www.itvplc.com (office).

BAŽANT, Zdeněk Pavel, CE, PhD, Docent (habil.); American (b. Czech) engineer, physicist and academic; *McCormick Institute Professor and Walter P. Murphy Professor of Civil and Environmental Engineering, Mechanical Engineering and Material Science and Engineering, Robert R. McCormick School of Engineering and Applied Science, Northwestern University;* b. 10 Dec. 1937, Prague, Czechoslovakia; ed Czech Tech. Univ. (ČVUT), Czechoslovak (now Czech) Acad. of Sciences, Charles Univ., Prague; worked as bridge engineer for state consulting firm Dopravoprojekt, Prague; Visiting Researcher, Centre Experimental de Recherches et d'Études du Bâtiment et des Travaux Publics, France 1966; appointments at Univ. of Toronto, Canada and Univ. of California, Berkeley, USA; remained in USA following Russian invasion of Czechoslovakia 1968; Assoc. Prof. of Civil Eng, Northwestern Univ. 1969–73, Prof. 1973–, Dir, Center for Geomaterials 1981–87, currently McCormick Inst. Prof. and Walter P. Murphy Prof. of Civil and Environmental Eng, Mechanical Eng and Material Science and Eng; mem. Nat. Acad. of Eng 1996, NAS 2002; Fellow, American Acad. of Arts and Sciences 2008; Founding Pres. IA-FraMCoS, IA-ConCreep; Past Pres. Soc. of Eng Science; Hon. mem. ASCE, ASME, ACI, IA-FRAMCOS; Dr hc (ČVUT) 1991, (Karlsruhe Inst. of Tech.) 1997, (Univ. of Colorado, Boulder) 2000, (Politecnico di Milano) 2001, (INSA de Lyon) 2004, (Vienna Univ. of Tech.) 2005, (Ohio State Univ.) 2011; winner Czechoslovak Math. Olympics 1955, ASME Timoshenko, Nadai and Warner Medals, ASCE von Karman, Newmark, Biot and Croes Medals and Life Achievement Award, SES Prager Medal, RILEM L'Hermite Medal, Wilhelm Exner Medal, Austrian Asscn for SME (Oesterreichischer Gewerbeverein—OGV) (jtly) 2008, Torroja Medal, Madrid, American Ceramic Soc. Roy Award, Solin Medal, Bazant Medal (Prague), Stodola Medal (Slovakia), IACMAG Outstanding Contrib. Award, ICOSSAR Lecture Award, SEAOI Meritorious Paper Award, Best Eng Book of the Year (SAP). *Achievements include:* developed a new method to analyse fracturing and cracking in concrete structures. *Publications:* Creep of Concrete in Structural Analysis (monograph, in Czech) 1966, Stability of Structures: Elastic, Inelastic, Fracture and Damage Theories (with L. Cedolin) 1991, Concrete at High Temperatures: Material Properties and Mathematical Models (with M. F. Kaplan) 1996, Fracture and Size Effect in Concrete and Other Quasibrittle Materials (with J. Planas) 1998, Inelastic Analysis of Structures (with M. Jirásek) 2002, Scaling of Structural Strength 2002; several book chapters and more than 550 research papers in peer-reviewed journals. *Leisure interests:* music, skiing, tennis, history. *Address:* Department of Civil and Environmental Engineering, Robert R. McCormick School of Engineering and Applied Science, Northwestern University, 2145 Sheridan Road, #A135, Evanston, IL 60208-3109, USA (office). *Telephone:* (847) 491-4025 (office). *Fax:* (847) 491-4011 (office). *E-mail:* z-bazant@northwestern.edu (office). *Website:* www.mccormick .northwestern.edu (office); www.civil.northwestern.edu (office).

BAZER, Fuller W., BS, MS, PhD; American biologist and academic; *Regents Fellow, O.D. Butler Chair in Animal Science, Associate Vice-President for Research and Associate Dean for Agricultural and Life Sciences, Texas A&M University;* b. 1938, Shreveport, La; ed Centenary Coll. of Louisiana, Louisiana State Univ., North Carolina State Univ.; Grad. Research Prof. in Animal Science, NC State Univ., then Research Prof. in Paediatrics, Univ. of Florida 1968–92; joined Faculty of Biosciences, Texas A&M Univ. 1992, currently holds several positions including Regents Fellow, Prof. and O.D. Butler Chair in Animal Science, Assoc. Vice-Pres. for Research and Exec. Assoc. Dean for Agricultural and Life Sciences and Dir Centre for Animal Biotechnology, Inst. of Biosciences and Tech. (Dir IBT 1994–2001); fmr Pres. and Ed.-in-Chief, Biology of Reproduction Journal, Soc. for the Study of Reproduction (SSR); Assoc. Dir Tex. Agricultural Experimental Station 2001–04; co-f. Gordon Research Conf. on Reproductive Tract Biology 1972; Fellow, AAAS; mem. Bd of Dirs Texas Soc. for Biomedical Research 2005–; mem. Texas Dept of Agric.-Texas Israel Exchange/Binational Agricultural Research and Devt Program Jt Advisory Cttee 2004–; Dr hc (Univ. of Guelph) 2004; L.E. Casida Award for Grad. Educ., American Soc. of Animal Science Physiology and Endocrinology, distinguished service awards from Soc. for the Study of Reproduction Research, Biotechnology 94, Distinguished Achievement in Agric. Award, Gamma Sigma Delta 1996, Alexander von Humboldt Research Award in Agric. 2000, Tex. A&M Vice-Chancellor for Agric. Award in Excellence for Research 2000, inducted into Byrd Alumni Hall of Fame 2002, Wolf Prize for Agric. 2003, SSR Research Award, SSR Distinguished Award, SSR Carl G. Hartman Award 2004, Distinguished Professor Award, Texas A&M Univ. 2004, Vice-Chancellor for Agric. Award for Team Research in Uterine Biology and Pregnancy 2006, Soc. for Research and Fertility Distinguished Research Award 2007, SSR Trainee

Mentoring Award 2009. *Publications:* Endocrinology of Pregnancy (ed.) 1998; numerous articles in professional journals. *Address:* Department of Animal Science, Room 442 D Kleberg, Mail Stop 2471, Texas A&M University, College Station, TX 77843-2471, USA (office). *Telephone:* (979) 862-2659 (office). *Fax:* (979) 862-2662 (office). *E-mail:* fbazer@cvm.tamu.edu (office). *Website:* animalscience .tamu.edu/people/bazer-fuller (office); www.ibt.tamhsc.edu.

BAZHANOV, Evgeny Petrovich, CSc, MA, PhD, DHist; Russian diplomatist, political scientist, historian and writer; *Rector, Diplomatic Academy of the Ministry of Foreign Affairs;* b. 6 Nov. 1946, Lvov, Ukraine; s. of Petr Bazhanov and Anna Bazhanova; m. Natalia Bazhanova 1968; ed Nanyang Univ., Singapore, Moscow Inst. of Int. Relations, Inst. of the Far East, Diplomatic Acad., Inst. of Oriental Studies; Political Officer, Ministry of Foreign Affairs, USSR 1970–72; Vice-Consul, USSR Gen. Consulate, San Francisco 1973–79; Political Counsellor, USSR Embassy in Beijing 1981–85; Adviser on foreign policy to USSR Pres. Mikhail Gorbachev 1985–91; Dir Inst. for Contemporary Int. Studies, Moscow 1991–2006; Vice-Rector for Research and Int. Affairs, Diplomatic Acad. of the Ministry of Foreign Affairs 1991–2011, Rector 2011–; Chair. Dissertation Council, Diplomatic Acad., Moscow 1992–, Chair. Editorial Bd 1992; Chair. Advisory Bd Ministry of Educ. 1994–, Examination Cttee, Friendship Univ., Moscow 2000–; mem. Exec. Cttee Asscn for Dialogue and Co-operation in Asian-Pacific Region 1991–, Nat. Cttee on Security 1996–, Council on Foreign Policy 2001–; mem. Int. Ecological Acad., Acad. of Humanitarian Research, American Acad. of Political Sciences, Asscn of Russian Sinologists 1986–, Russian Acad. of Humanities, World Ecological Acad., Political Science Asscn, Asscn of Asian Studies; Hon. Prof., People's Univ. of China; Dr hc (Bishkek Univ.) 2009; Best Journalist Award, New Times Magazine 1987, Distinguished Scholar of the Russian Fed. 1997. *Publications:* 40 books and over 1,000 articles and book chapters on world affairs, internal and foreign policy of Russia, China, USA, North Korea, Europe, Middle East and Southeast Asia. *Address:* Diplomatic Academy of the Ministry of Foreign Affairs, Moscow 119992, Ostozhenka 53/2 (office); 121165 Moscow, 30 Kutuzovsky Av. #462, Russia (home). *Telephone:* (499) 940-13-55 (office); (495) 249-15-60 (home). *Fax:* (499) 244-18-78 (office). *E-mail:* info.rector@dipacademy.ru (office). *Website:* www.dipacademy.ru (office).

BAZIN, Henry; Haitian economist, academic and fmr government official; ed State Univ. of Haiti, Univ. of Paris, France; taught econs at Ecole Nationale d'Administration, Mali 1962–68; held various positions at UN Econ. Comm. for Africa, Addis Ababa, Ethiopia, including Dir Div. of Int. Trade and Finance and Dir of Econ. Cooperation 1974–85; Sr Econ. Adviser and Dir UNDP Regional Programme for Africa, New York 1986–91; Technical Adviser to Prime Minister Marc Bazin 1992; Minister of Finance, Minister of Economy and Finance 2004–06; Prof. of Econs, Quisqueya Univ. 2006–. *Address:* Université Quisqueya, 218 Avenue Jean-Paul II, Haut de Turgeau, Port-au-Prince, Haiti (office). *Website:* www.uniq.edu (office).

BAZOLI, Giovanni; Italian lawyer, academic and banking executive; *Chairman of the Supervisory Board, Intesa Sanpaolo SpA;* b. 18 Dec. 1932, Brescia; Prof. of Law, Faculty of Econs, Univ. Cattolica di Milano –2001, Prof. of Admin. Law and Insts of Public Law –2003; Chair. Banca Intesa SpA 1982–2006, Chair. Supervisory Bd Sanpaolo IMI (following merger between Banca Intesa and Sanpaolo) 2007–, Chair. Supervisory Bd Intesa Sanpaolo SpA 2010–; apptd Dir Fondazione Giorgio Cini 1987, Chair. 1999–; Chair. Fondazione Giorgio Cini, Mittel SpA; fmr Chair. Istituto Studi Direzionale SpA; Deputy Chair. Banca Lombarda, Editrice La Scuola SpA; mem. Bd of Dirs Banco di Brescia, ABI Associazione Bancaria Italiana (mem. Exec. Cttee), Alleanza Assicurazione SpA, FAI Fondo per l'Ambiente Italiano, Ente Bresciano Istruzione Superiore; mem. Supervisory Bd UBI Banca SpA; mem. Gen. Advisory Bd Assonime, Exec. Cttee Istituto Paolo VI, Congregazione dei Conservatori di Biblioteca Ambrosiana; Cavaliere del Lavoro 2000, Cavaliere di Gran Croce 2002, Officier, Légion d'honneur 2002; Dr hc (Università degli Studi di Macerata) 1997, (Università degli Studi di Udine) 2001. *Address:* Intesa Sanpaolo SpA, Piazza San Carlo 156, 10121 Turin, Italy (office). *Telephone:* (011) 5551 (office). *E-mail:* info@sanpaoloimi.comt (office). *Website:* www.intestasanpaolo.com (office).

BAZZAZ, Saad al-, MA; Iraqi journalist and broadcaster; *Editor-in-Chief, Al-Zaman (Time);* b. 18 April 1952, Mosul; ed Univ. of Baghdad, Arab League Inst. for Research and Studies, Univ. of Exeter, UK; Dir Iraqi TV Second Channel 1974–79; Dir Iraqi Cultural Centre, London 1979–84; Gen. Man. Nat. House for Printing and Distribution, Baghdad 1984–86; Gen. Man. Iraq News Agency 1986–88; Gen. Dir Iraqi TV and Radio 1988–90; Ed.-in-Chief, Al-Jammhoria 1990–92; left Iraq Oct. 1992; Founder and Ed.-in-Chief, Al-Zaman (Time), London 1997–2003, Baghdad 2003–; Owner Al Sharqiya satellite channel 2004–. *Publications include:* Alhijrat (Migrations) 1972, Searching for the Sea Birds 1976, Future of the Boy and the Girl 1980, Future of Radio Broadcasts 1980, The Secret War 1987, The Scorpion 1987, At 6:30 Hours: Secrets of FAO Battle 1988, A War Gives Birth to Another 1992, Ashes of War 1995, The Generals are the Last to Know 1996, Kurds in Iraqi Question 1996. *Address:* Al-Zaman (Time), Baghdad, Iraq. *Telephone:* (1) 717-7587. *E-mail:* postmaster@azzaman.com. *Website:* www.azzaman.com; www .alsharqiya.com.

BEACH, David Hugh, PhD, FRS, FMedSci; British molecular biologist and academic; *Professor of Stem Cell Biology, Blizard Institute, Barts and The London School of Medicine and Dentistry, University of London;* b. 18 May 1954, London; s. of Gen. Sir Hugh Beach and Estelle Beach; ed Winchester Coll., Peterhouse, Cambridge, Univ. of Miami, USA; Postdoctoral Fellow, Univ. of Sussex 1978–82; Postdoctoral Fellow, Cold Spring Harbor Lab., NY 1982–83, Jr then Sr Staff Investigator 1984–89, Tenured Scientist 1992– (Sr Staff Scientist 1989–97, Adjunct Investigator 1997–2000); Investigator, Howard Hughes Medical Inst. 1990–97; Adjunct Assoc. Prof., State Univ. of NY at Stony Brook 1990–97; f. Mitotix Inc. 1992; Founder and Pres. Genetica Inc. 1996–; fmr Hugh and Catherine Stevenson Prof. of Cancer Biology, Univ. Coll. London; currently Prof. of Stem Cell Biology, Blizard Inst., Barts and The London School of Medicine and Dentistry, Univ. of London; elected Fellow, Acad. of Medical Sciences 2008; Eli Lilly Research Award 1994, Bristol-Myers Squibb Award 2000, Raymond Bourgine Award 2001. *Publications:* numerous papers in scientific journals. *Address:* Blizard Institute, Barts and The London School of Medicine and Dentistry, Turner Street, London, E1 2AD (office); 15 Springalls Wharf, 25 Bermondsey Wall West, London, SE16 4TL, England (home). *Telephone:* (77) 9962-0947 (office). *E-mail:* dhbeach@btinternet.com (home). *Website:* www.qmul.ac.uk (office).

BEAGLE, Jan, MA; New Zealand diplomatist and UN official; *Under-Secretary-General of Management, United Nations;* m.; three d.; ed University of Auckland; joined New Zealand diplomatic service, worked as a del. to UN, chaired various UN inter-agency bodies including Human Resources Network, High-level Cttee on Man., UN Devt Group, Political Affairs Officer, UN 1979–89, then Sr Political Affairs Officer, Sr Officer, Office of Under-Sec.-Gen. for Man. and Special Asst to Controller 1989–90, Special Asst to Assoc. Admin., UNDP 1990–92, Prin. Officer, Exec. Office of Sec.-Gen. 1992–96, Dir of Div. for Organizational Devt, Office of Human Resources Man. 1996–2005, Asst Sec.-Gen. Human Resources Man. 2005–07, Deputy Dir-Gen. UN, Geneva 2009–09, Deputy Exec.-Dir Man. and Governance, Jt UN Programme on HIV/AIDS (UNAIDS) 2009–17, Under-Sec.-Gen. Man. 2017–. *Address:* Department of Management, United Nations, 405 E 42nd Street, New York, NY 10017, USA (office). *Telephone:* (212) 963-1234 (office). *Fax:* (212) 963-4879 (office). *Website:* www.un.org (office).

BEALE, Graham John, CBE; British chartered accountant and business executive; *Chief Executive, Nationwide Building Society;* m.; one s. one d.; ed Univ. of Leicester; training as an accountant at Thomson McLintock (now part of KPMG); joined Anglia Building Society 1985, merged with Nationwide Building Society 1987, held several sr and gen. man. positions, including Man. Dir of a wholly owned property co. and Divisional Dir of Commercial Lending 1997, Div. Dir, Commercial 2002–03, mem. Bd of Dirs and Group Finance Dir 2003–07, Chief Exec. 2007–; Dir (non-exec.), Visa Europe Ltd, Visa Europe Services; mem. FCA Practitioner Panel (representing Building Socs) 2011–, Chair. 2013–. *Leisure interests:* wildlife photography, renovating his Georgian townhouse in Bath, travel, walking the dog. *Address:* Nationwide Building Society, Pipers Way, Swindon, Wilts., SN38 1NW, England (office). *Telephone:* (1793) 656789 (office). *Fax:* (1793) 455341 (office). *E-mail:* info@nationwide.co.uk (office). *Website:* www .nationwide.co.uk (office).

BEALES, Derek Edward Dawson, BA, PhD, LittD, FBA; British historian and academic; *Professor Emeritus of Modern History, Sidney Sussex College, Cambridge;* b. 12 June 1931, Felixstowe, Suffolk; s. of Edward Beales and Dorothy K. Dawson; m. Sara J. Ledbury 1964; one s. one d.; ed Bishop's Stortford Coll. and Sidney Sussex Coll., Cambridge; Research Fellow, Sidney Sussex Coll., Cambridge 1955–58, Fellow 1955–, Asst Lecturer in History, Univ. of Cambridge 1962–65, Lecturer 1965–80, Prof. of Modern History 1980–97, Prof. Emer. 1997–; Stenton Lecturer, Univ. of Reading 1992, Birkbeck Lecturer, Trinity Coll., Cambridge 1993; Recurring Visiting Prof., Cen. European Univ., Budapest 1995–; Ed. Historical Journal 1971–75; mem. Standing Cttee for Humanities, European Science Foundation 1994–99; Leverhulme 2000, Emer., Fellowship 2001–03; Prince Consort Prize, Univ. of Cambridge 1960, Henry Paolucci/Walter Bagehot Prize, Intercollegiate Studies Inst., Wilmington, Del. 2004. *Publications:* England and Italy 1859–60 1961, From Castlereagh to Gladstone 1969, History and Biography 1981, History, Society and the Churches (with G. Best) 1985, Joseph II, Vol. I: In the Shadow of Maria Theresa 1987, Mozart and the Habsburgs 1993, Sidney Sussex Quatercentenary Essays (with H. B. Nisbet) 1996, The Risorgimento and the Unification of Italy (second edn with E. Biagini) 2002, Prosperity and Plunder: European Catholic Monasteries in the Age of Revolution 2003, Enlightenment and Reform in the 18th Century 2005, Joseph II, Vol. II: Against the World 2009, Pietro Leopoldo d'Asburgo Lorena, Relazione sullo Stato della Monarchia (1784) (co-ed with Renato Pasta) 2013, Edizioni di Storia e Letteratura 2013. *Leisure interests:* music, walking, bridge. *Address:* K1, Sidney Sussex College, Cambridge, CB2 3HU, England (office). *Telephone:* (1223) 338833 (office). *E-mail:* deb1000@cam.ac.uk (office); derek@beales.ws.

BEALL, Donald Ray, BS, MBA; American business executive; *Partner, Dartbrook Partners LLC;* b. 29 Nov. 1938, Beaumont, Calif.; s. of Ray C. Beall and Margaret Beall (née Murray); m. Joan Frances Lange 1961; two s.; ed San Jose State Coll. and Univ. of Pittsburgh; various financial and management positions, Ford Motor Co., Newport Beach, Calif., Philadelphia and Palo Alto, Calif. 1961–68; Exec. Dir Corporate Financial Planning, Rockwell Int., El Segundo, Calif. 1968–69, Exec. Vice-Pres. Electronics Group 1969–71; Exec. Vice-Pres. Collins Radio Co., Dallas 1971–74; Pres. Collins Radio Group, Dallas, Rockwell Int. 1974–76, Pres. Electronics Operations 1976–77, Exec. Vice-Pres. 1977–79; Pres. Rockwell Int. (now Rockwell Collins) 1979–88, COO 1979–88, Chair. and CEO 1988–98 (CEO 1988–97), Chair. Exec. Cttee 1998, mem. Bd Dirs 2001, Chair. 2001–02, Chair. Emer. 2002–; mem. Pres.'s Export Council 1981–85; Chair. Beall Family Foundation; Pnr, Dartbrook Partners LLC (family investment partnership); mem. Foundation Bd of Trustees Univ. of Calif., Irvine 1988–; mem. Bd of Dirs Conexant Systems, Proctor & Gamble, Skyworks Solutions 2002–05, Mindspeed Technologies, Inc. 2003–07; Overseer, Hoover Inst.; Trustee, Calif. Inst. of Tech., Naval Postgraduate School Foundation; mem. Business Council; Founding mem. New Majority, Orange Co.; Fellow, American Inst. of Aeronautics and Astronautics; Sword of Life Award, American Cancer Soc. 1989, Horatio Alger Award 1998. *Leisure interests:* tennis, boating. *Address:* Dartbrook Partners, 5 Civic Plaza, #320, Newport Beach, CA 92660, USA (office). *E-mail:* beallfoundation@gmail.com. *Website:* www.beallfoundation.com.

BEAN, Sir Charles (Charlie) Richard, Kt, PhD; British economist and banker; *Professor, London School of Economics;* b. 16 Sept. 1953, Basildon, Essex; s. of Charles Ernest Bean and Mary Bean; m. Elizabeth Nan Callender-Bean; ed Brentwood School, Emmanuel Coll., Cambridge, Massachusetts Inst. of Tech., USA; Econ. Asst, Short-Term Forecasting Div., HM Treasury 1975–79, Econ. Adviser, Monetary Policy Div. 1981–82; Lecturer in Econs, LSE 1982–86, Reader 1986–90, Prof. 1990–2000, 2014–, Deputy Dir Centre for Econ. Performance 1990–94, Head of Econs Dept 1999–2000; Visiting Prof., Stanford Univ., USA 1990, Reserve Bank of Australia 1999; mem. Monetary Policy Cttee, Bank of England 2000–14, Exec. Dir and Chief Economist 2000–08, Deputy Gov., Monetary Policy 2008–14, mem. Financial Policy Cttee 2011–14; Pres. Royal Econ. Soc. 2013–15. *Address:* Department of Economics, London School of Economics, Houghton Street, London, WC2A 2AE, England (office).

BEAN, Sean; British actor; b. (Shaun Mark Bean), 17 April 1959, Sheffield, Yorks.; m. 1st Debra James 1981 (divorced 1988); m. 2nd Melanie Hill 1990 (divorced 1997); two d.; m. 3rd Abigail Cruttenden 1997 (divorced 2000); one d.; m. 4th Georgina Sutcliffe 2008 (divorced 2010); ed Royal Acad. of Dramatic Art, London; professional debut as Tybalt in Romeo and Juliet, Watermill Theatre, Newbury; Dr hc (Sheffield Hallam) 1997; Hon. DLitt (Sheffield) 2007; selected as an inaugural mem. Sheffield Legends (Sheffield equivalent of Hollywood Walk of Fame) and a plaque in his honour placed before Sheffield Town Hall. *Stage appearances include:* The Last Days of Mankind and Der Rosenkavalier at Citizens' Theatre, Glasgow, Lederer in Deathwatch, Young Vic Studio, Who Knew Mackenzie? and Gone, Theatre Upstairs, Royal Court, Starvling in Midsummer Night's Dream and Romeo in Romeo and Juliet, RSC, Stratford-upon-Avon 1986, Captain Spencer in The Fair Maid of the West, RSC, London, Macbeth in Macbeth, Albery Theatre, London 2002. *Films include:* Winter Flight 1984, Samson and Delilah 1985, Caravaggio 1986, Stormy Monday 1988, War Requiem 1989, How to Get Ahead in Advertising 1989, Windprints 1990, The Field 1990, In the Border Country 1991, Prince 1991, Patriot Games 1992, Shopping 1994, Black Beauty 1994, Goldeneye 1995, When Saturday Comes 1996, Anna Karenina 1997, Airborne 1998, Ronin 1998, Bravo Two Zero 1999, Essex Boys 2000, Don't Say a Word 2001, The Lord of the Rings: The Fellowship of the Ring 2001, Tom and Thomas 2002, The Lord of the Rings: The Two Towers 2002, Equilibrium 2002, The Big Empty 2003, The Lord of the Rings: The Return of the King 2003, Troy 2004, National Treasure 2004, North Country 2005, The Dark 2005, The Island 2005, Flightplan 2005, Silent Hill 2006, The Hitcher 2007, Outlaw 2007, Far North 2007, Drumhead (short) (voice) 2009, Percy Jackson & the Lightning Thief 2010, Ca$h 2010, Black Death 2010, Death Race 2 (video) 2010, Age of Heroes 2011, Mirror Mirror: The Untold Adventures of Snow White 2012, Cleanskin 2012, Soldiers of Fortune 2012, Silent Hill: Revelation 3D 2012, Wicked Blood 2014, The Snow Queen: Magic of the Ice Mirror 2015, Any Day 2015, Jupiter Ascending 2015, Pixels 2015, Enemy of Man 2015, The Martian 2015, The Young Messiah 2016. *Radio work:* A Kind of Loving, The True Story of Martin Guerre, Saturday Night and Sunday Morning. *Television includes:* Lorna Doone 1990, Small Zones 1990, Wedded 1990, My Kingdom for a Horse (series) 1991, Clarissa 1991, Tell Me That You Love Me 1991, Fool's Gold: The Story of the Brink's-Mat Robbery 1992, Sharpe's Rifles 1993 (also several Sharpe episodes in subsequent years), Lady Chatterley 1993, A Woman's Guide to Adultery 1993, Scarlett (mini-series) 1994, Jacob 1994, Extremely Dangerous 1999, Henry VIII 2003, Pride (voice) 2004, Faceless (film) 2006, Sharpe's Challenge (film) 2006, Sharpe's Peril (film) 2008, Crusoe (series) 2008–10, Red Riding: In the Year of Our Lord 1974 (mini series) 2009, Red Riding: In the Year of Our Lord 1983 (mini-series) 2009, The Lost Future (film) 2010, Game of Thrones (series) 2011, Missing (series) 2012, Accused (series) (Best Actor, Royal Television Soc. 2013, Int. Emmy Award 2013) 2012, Family Guy (voice) 2013, Robot Chicken (voice) 2014, Legends (series) 2014–, The Frankenstein Chronicles (series) 2015, The Untamed (2016). *Leisure interest:* Sheffield United Football Club. *Address:* c/o ICM, 3rd Floor, Marlborough House, 10 Earlham Street, London, WC2H 9LN, England (office). *Telephone:* (20) 7836-8564 (office). *Website:* www.icmtalent.com (office).

BEARPARK, Andrew, CBE, BSc; British fmr security industry executive and fmr international organization official; ed Univ. of London; with UK Overseas Devt Admin. (ODA) responsible for Devt programmes in Asia and Africa 1973–86, Head of Information and Emergency Aid Dept, responsible for programmes in Bosnia, Rwanda, N Iraq and Somalia 1991–97, Press Sec. to ODA Minister Baroness Chalker 1991–95; Pvt. Sec. to Prime Minister Margaret Thatcher 1986–89, responsible for Home Affairs, then Parl. Affairs, Chief of Staff to Lady Thatcher 1990–91; UN Deputy High Rep. for Reconstruction and Return Task Force, Sarajevo 1998–2000; Deputy Special Rep. for Reconstruction and Econ. Devt, UN Interim Admin. Mission in Kosovo 2000–03; fmr Dir of Reconstruction, Coalition Provisional Authority, Baghdad; fmr Vice-Pres. Special Projects, Olive Group LLC (pvt. security firm); f. Punchline (public relations consultancy) 1989; Founder and Dir Post Conflict People (consultancy); Dir-Gen. then Hon. Dir-Gen. British Asscn of Private Security Cos; Trustee, CARE International (UK); retd in 2013; currently practising as a Yogi in New Zealand.

BÉART, Emmanuelle; French actress; b. 14 Aug. 1965, Gassin; d. of Guy Béart and Geneviève Galéa; one d. with Daniel Auteuil (q.v.); began acting career with appearance as a child in Demain les Momes 1978. *Films:* Un Amour Interdit, L'Enfant Trouvé 1983, L'Amour en Douce 1984, Manon des Sources 1985, Date with an Angel 1987, A Gauche en Sortant de l'Ascenseur 1988, Les Enfants du Désordre 1989, Capitaine Fracasse 1990, La Belle Noiseuse 1991, J'Embrasse Pas 1991, Un Coeur en Hiver 1991, Ruptures 1992, L'Enfer 1993, Mission Impossible 1995, Nelly and M. Arnaud 1995, Time Regained 1999, Les Destinées Sentimentales 2000, La Repetition 2001, 8 Femmes 2002, Strayed 2003, Histoire de Marie et Julien 2003, Nathalie 2003, À boire 2004, D'Artagnan et les trois mousquetaires 2005, Un fil à la patte 2005, L'Enfer 2005, A Crime 2006, Le Héros de la famille 2006, Les Témoins 2007, Mes Stars et moi 2008, Nous trois 2010, Ça commence par la fin 2010, Bye Bye Blondie 2011, Pirate TV 2012, Par exemple, Electre 2013.

BEARY, Maj.-Gen. Michael, BSc, MBS, MSc; Irish army officer and UN official; *Chief of Mission and Force Commander, United Nations Interim Force in Lebanon (UNIFIL);* b. 1956; m.; three c.; ed Nat. Univ. of Ireland, Michael Smurfit Graduate Business School, Univ. Coll. Dublin, Irish Defence Forces Command and Staff School, Nat. War Coll., Nat. Defense Univ.; Officer, Irish Army Infantry Corps 1975, Commanding Officer Eastern Brigade Training Centre, Defence Forces Headquarters (DFHQ), Sr Instructor Command and Staff School, Military Coll., Defence Forces Training Centre (DFTC), promoted to Col 2009, apptd Dir Defence Forces Training 2009, promoted to Brig.-Gen. 2013, Gen. CO 2nd Brigade 2013–; deployed to Southern Lebanon with UN Interim Force in Lebanon (UNIFIL) 1982, 1989, 1994, Chief of Mission and Force Commdr UNIFIL 2016–; apptd Liasion Team Leader Int. Security Assistance Force (ISAF), Afghanistan (led by NATO) 2004; served with EU Military Staff Intelligence Div., Gen. Secr. of Council, EU 2004–07, commanded EU Training Mission Somalia 2011–13; numerous medals and awards. *Address:* Department of Peacekeeping Operations, Room S-3727B, United Nations, New York, NY 10017, USA (office). *Telephone:* (212) 963-8077 (office). *Fax:* (212) 963-9222 (office). *Website:* peacekeeping.un.org (office); unifil .unmissions.org/mission-leadership (office).

BEASLEY, David Muldrow, JD; American consultant and fmr politician; *Executive Director of World Food Programme, United Nations;* b. 26 Feb. 1957, Lamar, SC; s. of Richard L. Beasley and Jacqueline A. Blackwell; m. Mary Wood Payne; two s. two d.; ed Clemson Univ. and Univ. of South Carolina; practising attorney Beasley, Ervin & Warr; Rep. for SC State, Dist 56 1979–92; Majority Leader, SC House of Reps 1987; Gov. of S. Carolina 1995–99; Fellow, Inst. of Politics, Kennedy School of Govt, Harvard Univ. 1999; Prin. Bingham Consulting Group 1999–2001; mem. Bd of Trustees, Francis Marion Coll. 1988-91, Univ. of South Carolina 1990–91; unsuccessful campaign for US Senate 2004; fmr Chair. Nat. Advisory Cttee on Rural Health and Human Services, US Dept of Health and Human Services; Exec. Dir UN World Food Programme 2017–; currently Chair. Center for Global Strategies, Columbia, SC; mem. Bd of Trustees, Francis Marion Coll. 1988–91, Univ. of South Carolina 1990–91, Bd, Peace Research Endowment 2011–; Republican; Dr hc (Univ. of South Carolina, The Citadel, Charleston Southern Univ., Regent Univ., Medical Univ. of South Carolina, Coll. of Charleston, Bob Jones Univ., Newberry Coll.); American Swiss Foundation Friendship Award 1996, John F. Kennedy Profile in Courage Award 2003. *Address:* World Food Programme, Via Cesare Giulio Viola 68, Parco dei Medici, 00148 Rome, Italy (office). *Telephone:* (06) 65131 (office). *Fax:* (06) 6590632 (office). *Website:* www.wfp.org (office).

BEATH, John Arnott, OBE, MA, MPhil, FRSE, FRSA; British economist and academic; *Vice-President, Royal Economic Society;* b. 15 June 1944, Thurso, Caithness, Scotland; s. of James Beath and Marion McKendrick Beath (née Spence); m. Monika Schröder 1980; ed Hillhead High School, Univs of St Andrews, London, Pa and Cambridge; Thouron Scholar, Univ. of Pennsylvania 1968–71, Fels Fellow 1971–72; Research Officer, Univ. of Cambridge 1972–79, Fellow, Downing Coll. 1978–79; Lecturer, then Sr Lecturer, Univ. of Bristol 1979–91; Prof. of Econs, Univ. of St Andrews 1991–2009, currently Prof. Emer., also Head, School of Social Sciences 1997–2003; Chair. Econ. Research Inst. of Northern Ireland 2003–09; mem. Doctors' and Dentists' Review Body 2003–09; Sec.-Gen. Royal Economic Soc. 2008–15, Vice-Pres. 2015–; Chair. Training and Skills Cttee 2009–14, mem. Council 2009–14; mem. Prison Service Pay Review Body 2010–16, Competition Appeal Tribunal 2011–; Fellow, Acad. of Social Sciences; Thouron Scholar. *Publications include:* Economic Theory of Product Differentiation. *Leisure interests:* gardening, golf, walking. *Address:* School of Economics and Finance, University of St Andrews, St Andrews, Fife, KY16 9AL, Scotland (office). *Telephone:* (1334) 462420 (office). *Fax:* (1334) 462444 (office). *E-mail:* jab@st-and .ac.uk (office). *Website:* www.st-andrews.ac.uk/economics (office).

BEATRIX WILHELMINA ARMGARD, HRH Princess, Princess of the Netherlands, Princess of Orange-Nassau, Princess of Lippe-Biesterfeld, Mevrouw van Amsberg; b. 31 Jan. 1938, Baarn; d. of Queen Juliana (died 2004) and Bernhard, Prince of the Netherlands (died 2004); m. Claus George Willem Otto Frederik Geert Jonkheer von Amsberg 10 March 1966 (died 2002); children: Willem-Alexander Claus George Ferdinand, King of The Netherlands, b. 27 April 1967; Prince Johan Friso Bernhard Christiaan David, b. 25 Sept. 1968 (died 12 Aug. 2013); Prince Constantijn Christof Frederik Aschwin, b. 11 Oct. 1969; ed Baarn Grammar School, Leiden State Univ.; succeeded to the throne on abdication of her mother 30 April 1980; Queen of The Netherlands 1980–2013, abdicated in favour of her eldest son 30 April 2013; Hon. KG. *Leisure interests:* sculpting, riding, sailing. *Address:* Noordeinde Palace, Postbus 30412, 2500 The Hague, Netherlands. *Website:* www.koninklijkhuis.nl/english.

BEATSON, Sir Jack, Kt, QC, DCL, LLD, FBA; British arbitrator and judge; *Judge, Astana International Financial Centre Court;* b. 3 Nov. 1948, Haifa, Israel; s. of John James Beatson and Miriam White; m. Charlotte H. Christie-Miller 1973; one s. (deceased) one d.; ed Whittingehame Coll. Brighton and Brasenose Coll., Oxford; Lecturer in Law, Univ. of Bristol 1972–73; Fellow and Tutor in Law, Merton Coll. Oxford 1973–93, Hon. Fellow 1994–, Hon. Fellow, Brasenose Coll. 2009–; Rouse Ball Prof. of Law, Univ. of Cambridge 1993–2003, Chair. Faculty of Law 2001–03, Fellow, St John's Coll., Cambridge 1994–2003, Hon. Fellow 2005–; Dir Centre for Public Law, Cambridge 1997–2001; QC 1998; Deputy High Court Judge 2000–03, Justice of the High Court, Queen's Bench Div. 2003–13; Judge of the Court of Appeal 2013–18; currently Judge, Cayman Islands Court of Appeal, Astana Int. Financial Centre Court; Visiting Prof., Osgoode Hall Law School, Toronto, Canada 1979, Univ. of Virginia Law School, USA 1980, 1983, 2016, 2019, Oxford Univ. 2018–; Distinguished Visiting Prof., Univ. of Toronto 2000; Sr Visiting Fellow, Nat. Univ. of Singapore 1987; Visiting Fellow, Univ. of Western Australia 1988; Law Commr for England and Wales 1989–94; Recorder of Crown Court 1994–2003; Pres. British Acad. of Forensic Science 2007–09; Fellow, British Acad. of Humanities; mem. Competition Comm. 1995–2001; Bencher, Inner Temple; Professorial Fellow, Univ. of Melbourne 2018–. *Publications include:* Administrative Law: Cases and Materials (second edn with M. Matthews 1989), The Use and Abuse of Restitution 1991, Good Faith and Fault in Contract Law 1995, European Public Law (co-ed.) 1998, Chitty on Contracts (co-ed., 28th edn) 1999, Human Rights: The 1998 Act and the European Convention (with S. Grosz and P. Duffy), Unjustified Enrichment: Cases, Materials and Texts (co-ed.) 2003, Jurists Uprooted: German Speaking Émigré Lawyers in Twentieth Century Britain (co-ed.) 2004, Rights: Judicial Protection in the UK (co-author) 2009, Anson's Law of Contract (30th edn) 2016. *Leisure interest:* attempting to relax. *Address:* Essex Court Chambers, 24 Lincoln's Inn Fields, London, WC2A 3EG, England (office). *E-mail:* JBeatson@essexcourt.com (office).

BEATTIE, Ann, BA, MA; American writer and academic; *Edgar Allan Poe Professor Emerita of Literature and Creative Writing, University of Virginia;* b. 8 Sept. 1947, Washington, DC; d. of James Beattie and Charlotte Crosby; m. Lincoln Perry; ed American Univ., Univ. of Connecticut; Visiting Asst Prof., Univ. of Virginia, Charlottesville 1976–77, Visiting Writer 1980, Edgar Allan Poe Prof. of Literature and Creative Writing, now Prof. Emer.; Briggs Copeland Lecturer in English, Harvard Univ. 1977; Guggenheim Fellow 1977; mem. American Acad. of Arts and Letters 1993–, (Vice-Pres. for Literature 1998–99); mem. American Acad. of Arts and Sciences, PEN, Authors Guild; Contrib. The New Yorker; Hon. LHD (American Univ.); Award in Literature, American Acad. of Arts and Letters 1980, PEN/Bernard Malamud Award (co-recipient) 2000, Rea Award for the Short Story 2005. *Publications include:* Chilly Scenes of Winter 1976, Distortions 1976, Secrets and Surprises 1979, Falling in Place 1980, Jacklighting 1981, The Burning House 1982, Love Always 1985, Where You'll Find Me 1986, Alex Katz (art criticism) 1987, Picturing Will 1990, What Was Mine (story collection) 1991, My Life

Starring Dara Falcon 1997, Park City: New and Selected Stories 1998, Perfect Recall 2001, The Doctor's House 2002, Follies 2005, Walks with Men 2010, The New Yorker Stories 2010, Mrs. Nixon: A Novelist Imagines a Life 2011, The State We're In: Maine Stories 2015; articles in numerous magazines and journals, including Life, The New Yorker, Harper's, Esquire. *Address:* Department of English, University of Virginia, 219 Bryan Hall, PO Box 400121, Charlottesville, VA 22904-4121, USA (office). *Website:* www.engl.virginia.edu (office); www.newyorker.com/contributors/ann-beattie; authors.simonandschuster.co.uk/Ann-Beattie/1926455.

BEATTY, (Henry) Warren; American actor and director; b. 30 March 1937, Richmond, Virginia; s. of Ira Beatty and Kathlyn Maclean; brother of Shirley Maclaine (q.v.); m. Annette Bening (q.v.) 1992; two s. two d.; ed Stella Adler Theatre School; Fellow, BAFTA 2002; Hon. Chair. Stella Adler School of Acting 2004; Commdr Ordre des Arts et des Lettres; Irving Thalberg Special Acad. Award 2000, recipient of Kennedy Center Honors 2004, Golden Globe Cecil B DeMille Award 2007, American Film Inst. Life Achievement Award 2008. *Film appearances include:* Splendor in the Grass 1961, The Roman Spring of Mrs. Stone 1961, All Fall Down 1962, Lilith, 1965, Mickey One 1965, Promise Her Anything 1966, Kaleidoscope 1966, Bonnie and Clyde 1967, The Only Game in Town 1969, McCabe and Mrs. Miller 1971, Dollars 1972, The Parallax View 1974, Shampoo (producer and co-screenwriter) 1975, The Fortune 1976, Heaven Can Wait (producer, co-dir and co-screenwriter) 1978, Reds (producer, dir, Acad. Award for Best Dir 1981) 1981, Ishtar 1987, Dick Tracy 1989, Bugsy 1991, Love Affair 1994, Bulworth (also dir) 1998, Town and Country 2001, Dean Tavoularis: The Magician of Hollywood (documentary) 2003, One Bright Shining Moment (documentary) 2005. *Theatre roles include:* A Loss of Roses 1960. *TV includes:* Studio One and Playhouse 90, A Salute to Dustin Hoffman 1999. *Address:* c/o Risa Gertner, CAA, 9830 Wilshire Boulevard, Beverly Hills, CA 90212-1825, USA (office). *Telephone:* (310) 288-4545 (office). *Fax:* (310) 288-4800 (office). *Website:* www.caa.com (office).

BEATTY, Hon. Perrin, BA; Canadian business executive and fmr politician; *President and CEO, Canadian Chamber of Commerce;* b. 1 June 1950, Toronto; s. of George Ernest Beatty and Martha Beatty (née Perrin); m. Julia Kenny 1974; two s. (one deceased); ed Upper Canada Coll., Univ. of Western Ont.; Special Asst to Minister of Health, Prov. of Ont.; mem. House of Commons 1972–93; Minister of State for Treasury Bd 1979; Minister of Nat. Revenue 1984–85; Solicitor-Gen. for Canada 1985–86, Acting Solicitor-Gen. 1989; Minister of Defence 1986–89, of Nat. Health and Welfare 1989–91, of Communications 1991–93, of External Affairs 1993; Pres. and CEO CBC 1995–2000, Canadian Mfrs & Exporters 1999–2007, Canadian Chamber of Commerce 2007–; Chancellor, Univ. of Ontario Inst. of Tech. 2008–; mem. Special Jt Cttee on Constitution 1978, Chair. Progressive Conservative Caucus Cttee on Supply and Services, Spokesperson on Communications; Co-Chair. of Standing Jt Cttee on Regulations and Other Statutory Instruments; Caucus spokesperson on Revenue Canada; Chair. of Caucus Cttee on Fed. Prov. Relations and of Progressive Conservative Task Force on Revenue Canada 1983; Hon. DJur (Western Univ.) 2013, Dr hc (Univ. of Ontario Inst. of Tech. 2016. *Leisure interests:* music, travel, technology and reading. *Address:* Canadian Chamber of Commerce, 360 Albert Street, Suite 420, Ottawa, ON K1R 7X7, Canada (office). *Telephone:* (613) 238-4000 (office). *Fax:* (613) 238-7643 (office). *E-mail:* info@chamber.ca (office). *Website:* www.chamber.ca (office).

BEAUCE, Thierry Martin de, LenD; French government official; b. 14 Feb. 1943, Lyon; s. of Bertrand Martin de Beauce and Simone de Beauce (née de la Verpillere); m. Diana Segard (divorced); two d.; ed Univ. of Paris and Ecole Nat. d'Admin; Civil Admin., Ministry of Cultural Affairs 1968–69; seconded to Office of Prime Minister 1969–73; Tech. Adviser, Pvt. Office of Pres. of Nat. Ass. 1974; seconded to Econ. Affairs Directorate, Ministry of Foreign Affairs 1974–76; Cultural Counsellor, Japan 1976–78; Second Counsellor, Morocco 1978–80; Vice-Pres. for Int. Affairs Société Elf Aquitaine 1981–86; Dir-Gen. of Cultural, Scientific and Tech. Relations, Ministry of Foreign Affairs 1986–87; State Sec. attached to Minister of Foreign Affairs 1988–91; Adviser to the Pres. for African Affairs 1991–94; Vice-Pres. of Conf. for Yugoslavia 1992; Amb. to Indonesia 1995–97; Special Adviser to Chair. and CEO for Int. Affairs, Vivendi Universal (became Vivendi 2006) 1997–2000, fmr Sr Exec. Vice-Pres. for Int. Affairs, Vivendi Environnement; apptd Pres. MEDEF Int. for Middle East 1998; apptd Deputy Pres. Asscn of Democrats 1989; Chevalier, Légion d'honneur. *Publications:* Les raisons dangereuses (essay) 1975, Un homme ordinaire (novel) 1978, L'Ile absolue (essay) 1979, Le désir de guerre 1980, La chute de Tanger (novel) (Prix Contrepoint 1985) 1984, Nouveau discours sur l'universalité de la langue française 1988, Le livre d'Esther 1989, La République de France 1991, La nonchalence de Dieu 1995, L'archipel des épices 1998, L'absent de Marrakech 2006. *Address:* 45 rue de Richelieu, 75001 Paris, France (home).

BEAUDET, Alain, MD, PhD, FRSC; Canadian physician, neuroscientist and research administrator; b. 21 Sept. 1947, Montréal, Québec; m. Nathalie Beaudet; one s.; ed Univ. of Montreal; Postdoctoral Research, Centre d'études nucléaires, Saclay, France 1977–79, Univ. of Zürich Brain Research Inst., Switzerland 1979–80; Researcher, Montréal Neurological Inst. 1980, becoming Assoc. Dir of Research 1985–92; Head of Neurobiology Group, McGill Univ., Montréal 1988–96, becoming Prof. of Neurosciences; Pres. Canadian Asscn for Neuroscience 1995–97, Canadian Insts of Health Research 2008–17; Pres. and CEO Fonds de la recherche en santé du Québec 2004–08; Fellow, Canadian Acad. of Health Sciences 2007; Officier, Ordre des Palmes académiques 2007; Chevalier, Ordre nat. du Québec 2011; Dr hc (Univ. Pierre et Marie Curie, France) 2007, (Univ. of Sherbrooke) 2013; Prix Adrien-Pouliot, Asscn francophone pour le savoir 2004, Lifetime Achievement Award, Montreal Neurological Inst. 2005, Genesis Prize, BioQuebec 2008. *Publications:* more than 200 publs in professional journals.

BEAUDOIN, Laurent Robert, CC, CMG, BA, MComm, CA, FCA; Canadian financial executive; *Chairman Emeritus, Bombardier Inc.;* b. 13 May 1938, Laurier Station, PQ; son-in-law of Joseph Armand Bombardier; m.; one s.; ed St-Anne Coll., NS, Univ. of Sherbrooke, PQ; began career with Beaudoin, Morin, Dufresne & Assocs Chartered Accountants 1961–63; Comptroller, Bombardier Ltd 1963–64, Gen. Man. 1964–66, Pres. 1966–79, Chair. and CEO 1979–99, Chair. Bd and Exec. Cttee Bombardier Inc. 1999–, CEO 2004–08, Chair. Bombardier Recreational Products Inc. 2003–2015, Chairman Emeritus 2015–; Chair. Regroupement Économie et Constitution 1991; mem. Advisory Bd Lazard Canada 2000–, Carlyle Group (Canada) 2001–; mem. Bd of Dirs Championnat des Amériques 2003; Fellow, Ordre des comptables agréés du Québec 1989; Officier, Ordre Nat. du Québec 1990, Golden Emblem of Merit, Prov. Govt of Upper Austria 1999, Grosse silberne Ehrenzeichen mit Stern (Austria) 2009; Hon. PhD (Montreal), (York); Hon. DBA (Sherbrooke); Hon. DEcon (St-Anne); Hon. DCL (Bishop's Univ.); Hon. DJur (Toronto), (McGill); Hon. DEng (Carleton); numerous awards including mem. Canadian Business Hall of Fame, Canadian Business Leader Award, Univ. of Alberta 1991, CEO of the Year, The Financial Post 1991, Laureate Award in Aeronautics/Propulsion, Aviation Week & Space Tech. Magazine 1993, CD Home Award, Canadian Aeronautics and Space Inst. 1995, Canadian Business Leadership Award, Harvard Business Club of Toronto 1996, Prix de Carrière, Conseil du Patronat du Québec 1997, Canadian Business Hall of Fame Award 1997, Int. Distinguished Entrepreneur Award, Univ. of Man. 1998, Lifetime Achievement Award, Ernst and Young Entrepreneur of the Year Program in Québec 2000, Golden Honorary Medal, City of Vienna 2001, Aguila Azteca Award from Pres. of Mexico 2005, Canadian Youth Business Foundation Lifetime Achievement Award 2006, Woodrow Wilson Award for Corp. Citizenship, Canada Inst. of the Woodrow Wilson Int. Center for Scholars, Washington, DC 2007, Int. Michael Smurfit Business Achievement Award, The Ireland Chamber (USA) 2008, Best Global Business Award, Canada China Business Council, Beijing 2008, Prix Hommage de l'Ordre des comptables agréés du Québec 2010. *Address:* Bombardier Inc., 800 René-Lévesque Boulevard West, Montréal, PQ H3B 1YB, Canada (office). *Telephone:* (514) 861-9481 (office). *Fax:* (514) 861-7053 (office). *E-mail:* piero.scaramuzzi@defence.bombardier.com (office). *Website:* www.bombardier.com (office).

BEAUDOIN, Pierre; Canadian business executive; *President and CEO, Bombardier Inc.;* s. of Laurent Robert Beaudoin; ed Brébeuf Coll., McGill Univ.; worked as Canadian Customer Service Man. for BIC Sport Inc.; helped organize Marine Products Div. of Bombardier 1985, Vice-Pres. Product Devt for Sea-Doo/Ski-Doo (following fusion of marine products and snowmobile divs Oct. 1990) 1990–92, Exec. Vice-Pres. Sea-Doo/Ski-Doo Div., Bombardier Inc. 1992–94, Pres. 1994–96, Pres. and COO Bombardier Recreational Products 1996–2001, also responsible for Bombardier-Rotax, Pres. Bombardier Aerospace, Business Aircraft Feb.–Oct. 2001, Pres. Bombardier Aerospace, Inc. 2001–08, Pres. and COO Oct. 2001–04, Exec. Vice-Pres. Bombardier Inc. 2004–08, Pres. and CEO 2008–, Exec. Chair. 2015–; mem. Bd of Dirs Power Corporation of Canada. *Address:* Bombardier Inc., 800 René-Lévesque Boulevard West, Montréal, PQ H3B 1YB, Canada (office). *Telephone:* (514) 861-9481 (office). *Fax:* (514) 861-7053 (office). *E-mail:* piero.scaramuzzi@defence.bombardier.com (office). *Website:* www.bombardier.com (office).

BEAUMONT, Lady Mary Rose, BA (Hons); British art historian, academic, teacher and writer; b. (Mary Rose Wauchope), 6 June 1932, Petersfield, Hants.; d. of Charles Edward Wauchope and Elaine Margaret Armstrong-Jones; m. Lord Beaumont of Whitley, The Rev. Timothy Wentworth Beaumont 1955 (died 2008); two s. (one deceased) two d.; ed Prior's Field School, Godalming, Surrey, Courtauld Inst. of Fine Art, Univ. of London; f. Centre for the Study of Modern Art, Inst. of Contemporary Arts (ICA) 1972; art critic for Art Review 1978–96; Lecturer in Modern Art for Christies' Educ. 1978–2001; Exhbn curator for British Council in E Europe and Far East 1983–87; Exhbn Curator The Human Touch, Fischer Fine Art Gallery 1986, The Dark Side of the Moon, Rhodes Gallery 1990, Three Scottish Artists, Pamela Auchincloss Gallery, New York 1990; Picker Fellow, Kingston Polytechnic 1986–87; Lecturer in Humanities, Dept City & Guilds School of Art 1996–2008; mem. Exec. Cttee of Contemporary Art Soc. 1979–89, Advisory Cttee Govt Art Collection 1994–2001; retd; Hon. Fellow, Royal Soc. of British Sculptors. *Publications include:* An American Passion: The Susan Kasen Summer and Robert D. Summer Collection of Contemporary British Painting (contrib. artists' profiles) 1995, Open Studio: Derek Healey 1997, Jean MacAlpine: Intervals in Light 1998, Carole Hodgson 1999, George Kyriacou 1999, Jock McFadyen: A Book About a Painter (contrib.) 2000, New European Artists Vol. I (contrib.) 2000, Albert Irvin: The Complete Prints 2010. *Leisure interests:* reading novels, listening to opera, audio books. *Address:* 40 Elms Road, London, SW4 9EX, England (home). *Telephone:* (20) 7498-8664 (home). *Website:* www.cityandguildsartschool.ac.uk (office).

BEAZLEY, Hon. Kim Christian, AC, BA, MA, MPhil; Australian politician and diplomatist; *Governor of Western Australia;* b. 14 Dec. 1948, Perth, WA; s. of Kim Edward Beazley and Betty Judge; m. 1st Mary Beazley 1974 (divorced 1989); two d.; m. 2nd Susie Annus 1990; one d.; ed Hollywood Sr High School, Perth, Univ. of WA, Balliol Coll., Oxford, UK; fmr Lecturer in Social and Political Theory, Murdoch Univ. Perth; MP for Swan 1980–96, for Brand 1996–2007; Minister for Aviation 1983–84, for Defence 1984–90, for Transport and Communications 1990–91, of Finance 1991, 1993–96, of Employment, Education and Training 1991–93; Deputy Prime Minister 1995–96; Special Minister of State 1983–84; Leader of the House 1988–96; Leader of Australian Labor Party 1996–2001, 2005–06; apptd Winthrop Prof., Dept of Politics and Int. Relations, Univ. of WA 2007; Chancellor, ANU 2008–09; Amb. to USA 2010–16; Pres. Australian Inst. for Int. Affairs 2016–17; Co-Chair. Australian American Education Leadership Foundation 2016–, mem. Bd of Dirs Australian American Leadership Dialogue; Gov. of WA 2018–; Distinguished Fellow, Australian Strategic Policy Inst.; Sr Fellow, Perth USAsia Centre, currently mem. Bd of Dirs; mem. Bd of Dirs Lockheed Martin Australia; mem. Council of Advisors, US Studies Centre, Univ. of Sydney; mem. Bd Ramsay Centre for Western Civilisation; Hon. LLD (Notre Dame Univ., Australia) 2014, Dr hc (Murdoch Univ.) 2016; Rhodes Scholarship, Univ. of WA 1973. *Publications include:* The Politics of Intrusion: the Super-Powers in the Indian Ocean (with I. Clark) 1979. *Leisure interests:* reading, swimming, watching cricket. *Address:* Government House, St Georges Terrace, Perth, WA 6000; Australian American Leadership Dialogue, PO Box 1387, Hawksburn, VIC. 3142, Australia (office). *Telephone:* (3) 9510-6111 (office); (8) 9429-9199 (Government House) (office). *Fax:* (3) 9510-6222 (office); (8) 9325-4476 (Government House) (office). *E-mail:* mail@govhouse.wa.gov.au (office). *Website:* www.aald.org (office); www.govhouse.wa.gov.au (office).

BEBA, Ümran, BEng MBA; Turkish business executive; *Senior Vice-President and Chief Human Resources Officer, Asia Middle East and Africa, PepsiCo;* ed Bosphorus Univ.; pursued marketing career at Colgate-Palmolive; began career with PepsiCo when joining Frito-Lay 1994, served in various roles including human resources, sales and marketing, Gen. Man. PepsiCo South East Europe Region 2001–10, Pres. PepsiCo Asia Pacific 2010, currently Sr Vice-Pres. and Chief Human Resources Officer, PepsiCo Asia Middle East and Africa; Pres. Food Industry Asia (industry asscn) 2013; mem. Bd Calbee Group, Japan; mem. Advisory Council Women International Network, Switzerland, Hong Kong Univ. of Science and Technology Business School, Mentorship for Women for Board Seats initiative, Turkey. *Address:* PepsiCo Asia Pacific, 20th Floor, Caroline Center, 28 Yun Ping Road, Causeway Bay, Hong Kong Special Administrative Region, People's Repub. of China (office). *Telephone:* 2839-0288 (office). *E-mail:* huw.gilbert@pepsico.com (office). *Website:* www.pepsico.com (office); www.pepsiworld.com (office).

BÉBÉAR, Claude; French business executive; *Honorary Chairman, AXA;* b. 29 July 1935, Issac; s. of André Bébéar and Simone Bébéar (née Veyssière); m. Catherine Dessagne 1957; one s. two d.; ed Lycées of Périgueux and St Louis, Paris, Ecole Polytechnique, Paris; joined Ancienne Mutuelle (renamed Mutuelles Unies 1978) 1958, CEO 1975–82; Chair. and CEO AXA 1982–2000, Chair. Supervisory Bd 2000–08, Hon. Chair. AXA 2008–; mem. Bd of Dirs, Schneider Electric SA 1986–2013, BNP Paribas 2012–, Vivendi 2012– (mem. Supervisory Bd 2005–); Founder and Chair. Institut Montaigne 2001–15, Hon. Chair. 2015–; Hon. Pres. Inst. des Actuaires Français 1989–; Hon. Chair. IMS-entreprendre pour la Cité; Grand Officier, Légion d'honneur; Officier, Ordre nat. du Mérite. *Publications include:* Le courage de réformer 2002, Ils vont tuer le capitalisme 2003, Réformer par temps de crise 2012. *Address:* AXA, 25 avenue Matignon, 75008 Paris, France (office). *Telephone:* 1-40-75-58-00 (office). *Fax:* 1-40-75-57-50 (office). *Website:* www.axa.com (office).

BEBIĆ, Luka; Croatian agricultural engineer and politician; b. 21 Aug. 1937, Desne-Kula Norinska; m. Gerda Bebić; two c.; ed Faculty of Agric., Sarajevo; mem. Croatian Democratic Union (Hrvatska demokratska zajednica—HDZ) 1989–; mem. Sabor (Parl.) since Croatia's independence 1990–, Deputy Speaker, Parl., mem. and Vice-Chair. Cttee for Consideration and Political System, Chair. Club of Reps of HDZ 2003–08, Pres. (Speaker) of Sabor 2008–11; Minister of Defence July–Sept. 1991. *Leisure interests:* reading, olives and clementines, fishing. *Address:* Sabor, 10000 Zagreb, trg sv. Marka 6–7, Croatia (office). *Telephone:* (1) 4569444 (office); (1) 6303544 (office). *Fax:* (1) 1 6303010 (office). *E-mail:* marija.dujic@sabor.hr (office); sabor@sabor.hr (office). *Website:* www.sabor.hr/Default.aspx?sec=2562 (office).

BEBLAWI, Hazem Abdel Aziz al-, LLB, PhD; Egyptian economist, academic and politician; b. 17 Oct. 1936, Cairo; m.; ed Cairo Univ., Univ. of Grenoble, France, Univ. of Paris 1 Pantheon-Sorbonne; Asst Prof., Assoc. Prof., then Prof., Univ. of Alexandria 1965–80, now Prof. Emer. of Econs; Sr Economist, Arab Fund for Econ. and Social Devt 1974–79; Man., Econs Dept, Industrial Bank of Kuwait 1980–83; Chair. and CEO Export Devt Bank of Egypt 1983–95; Under-Sec.-Gen. and Exec. Sec., UN Econ. and Social Comm. for Western Asia (ESCWA) 1995–2000; Adviser, Arab Monetary Fund, Abu Dhabi 2001–11; Founding mem. Egyptian Social Democratic Party following Egyptian revolution Jan.–Feb. 2011; Deputy Prime Minister for Econ. Affairs and Minister of Finance July–Dec. 2011; Acting Prime Minister of Egypt 2013–14; columnist, Al-Ahram newspaper; Chevalier, Légion d'honneur 1992, Commdr, Order of Leopold II (Belgium) 1992, Grand Officier, Nat. Order of the Cedar (Lebanon) 2000. *Publications include:* L'Interdependance Agriculture – Industrie et le Développement Economique: le cas de l'Egypte, 1968, The Arab Gulf Economy in a Turbulent Age 1984, The Rentier State (co-author) 1987, Arba Shohour Fi Qafas Al Hokouma (Four Months in the Government's Cage) 2012; numerous articles on money and banking, int. trade, finance, and devt. *Address:* Egyptian Social Democratic Party, Mahmoud Bassiouni Street 16, second round Abdel Moneim Riad Square Downtown, Cairo, Egypt (office). *Telephone:* (2) 25772515 (office). *Fax:* (2) 25772512 (office). *E-mail:* info@egysdp.com (office); feedback@hazembeblawi.com. *Website:* www.egysdp.com (office); hazembeblawi.com.

BECH NIELSEN, Brian, PhD; Danish physicist, academic and university administrator; *Rector, Aarhus University;* b. Holstebro, West Jutland; Prof. of Experimental Solid State Physics and Head of Dept of Physics and Astronomy, Aarhus Univ. 2007–, co-operated with iNANO (univ.'s centre for nanotechnology research), Dean of Faculty of Science and Tech. –2013, Rector Aarhus Univ. 2013–; served on several bds of dirs; mem. Royal Danish Acad. of Sciences and Letters. *Publications:* numerous papers in professional journals on semiconductor materials. *Address:* Rector's Office, Aarhus University, Room 224, Building 1430, Nordre Ringgade 1, 8000 Aarhus C, Denmark (office). *Telephone:* 87-15-20-25 (office); 23-38-23-49 (mobile). *E-mail:* rector@au.dk (office). *Website:* pure.au.dk/portal/en/rektor@au.dk (office).

BECHTEL, Marie-Françoise; French jurist and politician; b. 19 March 1946, Coarraze, Basses Pyrénées; d. of Gaston Cassiau and Marie Cassiau (née Sahores); one s. one d.; ed Univ. of Paris (Sorbonne), Ecole Nat. d'Admin.; secondary school teacher 1972–75; civil servant at Ecole Nat. d'Admin. 1978–80; Officer, Council of State 1980–84, Counsel 1984–85, Sr mem. 1996–2012; Adviser to Minister of Justice 1992–93, to Minister of the Interior 1999–2000; Dir Ecole Nat. Admin. 2000–02; Tech. Adviser to Minister of Nat. Educ. 1984–86; Sr Lecturer, Inst. d'Etudes Politiques 1983–87; mem. UN Cttee of Experts on Admin. Reforms 2002–08, Vice-Pres. 2006–08; Vice-Pres. Fondation Res Publica 2008–; mem. Int. Civil Service Comm., UN Gen. Ass. 2010–; Deputy (Socialist Party) for Aisne, Nat. Ass. 2012–. *Publications include:* contribs to Revue Française d'administration publique on institutions, organization, justice, civil rights etc. 1983–99, to "Ofer dire non", Fayard, Pais 2005; Rapport général du Comité pour la révision de la Constitution 1993. *Leisure interest:* modern art. *Address:* 1 avenue du Général de Gaulle, 02200 Soissons (office); 29 boulevard Edgard Quinet, 75014 Paris, France (home). *Telephone:* (3) 23-59-60-69 (office). *Fax:* 1-43-20-59-53 (home). *E-mail:* permanence@bechtelpourlaisne.fr (office). *Website:* www.bechtelpourlaisne.fr (office).

BECK, Aaron T., MD; American psychotherapist and academic; *Professor Emeritus of Psychiatry, University of Pennsylvania;* b. 18 July 1921, Providence, RI; m.; four c.; ed Brown Univ., Yale Univ. Medical School; fmr Assoc. Ed. Brown Daily Herald; Resident in Pathology, RI Hosp. 1946; Resident in Neurology, Cushing Veterans Admin Hosp., Framingham, Mass; Fellow, Austin Riggs Center, Stockbridge; Asst Chief of Neuropsychiatry, Valley Forge Army Hosp.; joined Dept of Psychiatry, Univ. of Pennsylvania 1954, currently Prof. Emer. of Psychiatry; developed field of cognitive behaviour therapy research; funded research investigations of psychopathology of depression, suicide, anxiety disorders, alcoholism, drug addiction and personality disorders 1959–; f. Beck Inst. for Cognitive Therapy and Research; fmr Visiting Scientist, Medical Research Council, Oxford, Visiting Fellow, Wolfson Coll., Visiting Prof., Harvard, Yale and Columbia Univs; mem. Inst. of Medicine, NAS; consultant or mem. several review panels, Nat. Inst. of Mental Health; served on editorial bds of several professional journals; Hon. DMedSc (Brown Univ.), Hon. DHumLitt (Assumption Coll.); Brown Univ.: Francis Wayland Scholarship, Bennet Essay Award, Gaston Prize for Oratory; MERIT Award, Nat. Inst. of Mental Health, American Psychiatric Asscn Research Award, Sarnat Award, Inst. of Medicine, Albert Lasker Clinical Medical Research Award 2006, Bell of Hope Award 2010, Sigmund Freud Award 2010, Scholarship and Research Award 2010, Edward J. Sachar Award 2011, Prince Mahidol Award in Medicine 2011, Kennedy Community Mental Health Award 2013. *Publications:* author or co-author of 23 books; more than 550 articles. *Address:* Aaron T. Beck Psychopathology Research Center, Room 2032, 3535 Market Street, Philadelphia, PA 19104-3309, USA (office). *Fax:* (215) 573-3717 (office). *E-mail:* abeck@mail.med.upenn.edu (office). *Website:* www.med.upenn.edu/suicide/beck (office); www.beckinstitute.org (office).

BECK, Rev. Brian Edgar, MA, DD; British ecclesiastic; b. 27 Sept. 1933, London; s. of A. G. Beck and C. A. Beck; m. Margaret Ludlow 1958; three d.; ed City of London School, Corpus Christi Coll., Cambridge and Wesley House, Cambridge; Asst Tutor, Handsworth Coll. 1957–59; ordained Methodist Minister 1960; Circuit Minister, Suffolk 1959–62; St Paul's United Theological Coll., Limuru, Kenya 1962–68; Tutor Wesley House, Cambridge 1968–80, Prin. 1980–84; Sec. Methodist Conf. of GB 1984–98, Pres. 1993–94; Co.-Chair. Oxford Inst. of Methodist Theological Studies 1976–2002; Sec. E African Church Union Consultation Worship and Liturgy Cttee 1963–68; mem. World Methodist Council 1966–71, 1981–98; Visiting Prof., Wesley Theological Seminary, Washington, DC 1999. *Publications:* Reading the New Testament Today 1977, Christian Character in the Gospel of Luke 1989, Gospel Insights 1998; Exploring Methodism's Heritage 2004; (contrib. to) Christian Belief, A Catholic-Methodist Statement 1970, Unity the Next Step? 1972, Suffering and Martyrdom in the New Testament 1981, Community-Unity-Communion 1998, Rethinking Wesley's Theology 1998, Managing the Church? 2000, Apostolicity and Unity 2002, Reflections on Ministry 2004, Unmasking Methodist Theology 2004, A Thankful Heart and a Discerning Mind 2010, The Ashgate Research Companion to World Methodism 2013, and articles in theological journals. *Leisure interests:* walking, cross-stitch, DIY. *Address:* 26 Hurrell Road, Cambridge, CB4 3RH, England (home). *Telephone:* (1223) 312260 (home).

BECK, Sir (Edgar) Philip, Kt, MA; British business executive; b. 9 Aug. 1934; s. of Sir Edgar Charles Beck and Mary Agnes Sorapure; m. 1st Thomasina Joanna Jeal 1957 (divorced); two s.; m. 2nd Bridget Alexandra Heathcoat Amory 1991; ed Jesus Coll., Cambridge; Chair. John Mowlem and Co. PLC 1979–95 (Dir 1963–95), Railtrack 1999–2001; fmr Dir numerous assoc. cos; Chair. Fed. of Civil Eng. Contractors 1982–83; Dir (non-exec.) Invensys PLC 1991– (Interim Chair. 1998, Deputy Chair. 1998–99), Delta PLC 1994–2004, Yorks. Electricity Group PLC 1995–97, Railtrack Group 1999–2001 (non-exec. Dir 1995–99). *Leisure interest:* sailing. *Address:* Lower Park House, Westholme, Pilton, Somerset, BA4 4EN, England. *Telephone:* (1749) 899491. *E-mail:* philipbeck98@aol.com.

BECK, Kurt; German politician; b. 5 Feb. 1949, Bad Bergzabern; m. Roswitha Beck 1968; one s.; apprenticeship as mechanic, specializing in electronics; mem. ÖTV (Public Employees' Union) 1969; mem. SPD 1972–; mem. Rhineland-Palatinate State Ass. 1979–, Whip of SPD Parl. Group 1985–91, Chair. 1991–94; Chair. Rhineland-Palatinate SPD 1993–, Deputy Chair. SPD Party (Germany) 2003–06, Chair. 2006–08; Minister-Pres. of Rhineland-Palatinate 1994–2013; Chair. Bundesrat 2000–01; Mayor of Steinfeld 1989–94; Chair. Broadcasting Comm. of Fed. States' Minister-Pres.'s 1994–13; responsible for cultural matters under German-French co-operation agreement 1999–2002; Chair. Bd Dirs Zweites Deutsches Fernsehen (ZDF) 1999–2017; Hon. Citizen, Burgundy 2012; Grand Cross of the Star of Romania 2001, Order of Merit of the Federal Republic of Germany 2004, Order of Merit, Grand Officier, Légion d'Honneur; Dr hc (Francis Marion Univ.); SME Award of the Union of Medium-sized Enterprises 2005, Leibniz Medal, Acad. of Sciences and Literature, Mainz 2013.

BECKE, Axel Dieter, PhD, FRSC, FRS; Canadian (b. German) chemist and academic; *Canada Council Killam Research Fellow and Chair in Computational Science, Dalhousie University;* b. 6 Oct. 1953, Esslingen; ed Queen's Univ., McMaster Univ., Canada; moved to Canada with family at age of three; NSERC Postdoctoral Fellow, Dalhousie Univ., Halifax, NS 1981–83, E.B. Eastburn Postdoctoral Fellow 1983–84, Canada Council Killam Research Fellow and Chair in Computational Science 2006–; NSERC Univ. Research Fellow, Queen's Univ., Kingston, Ont. 1984–94, Prof. of Chem. 1994–2006; mem. Int. Acad. of Quantum Molecular Science; Fellow, Chemical Inst. of Canada, World Asscn of Theoretically Oriented Chemists; Medal of Int. Acad. of Quantum Molecular Science 1991, Noranda Lecture Award, Canadian Soc. for Chem. 1994, Prize for Excellence in Research, Queen's Univ. 1999, Schroedinger Medal, World Asscn of Theoretically Oriented Chemists 2000, American Chemical Soc. Award in Theoretical Chemistry 2014, Gerhard Herzberg Canada Gold Medal for Science and Eng 2015. *Publications:* more than 50 articles in scientific journals. *Address:* Department of Chemistry, Dalhousie University, 6274 Coburg Road, PO Box 15000, Halifax, NS B3H 4R2, Canada (office). *Telephone:* (902) 494-2986 (office). *Fax:* (902) 494-1310 (office). *E-mail:* axel.becke@dal.ca (office). *Website:* chemistry.dal.ca (office).

BECKENBAUER, Franz Anton; German sports administrator and professional football manager; b. 11 Sept. 1945, Munich; s. of Franz Beckenbauer Sr and Antonia Beckenbauer; m. three times, including to Brigitte Wittmann; five c.; ed Northern Coll. of Insurance Studies; sweeper; played for Bayern Munich 1959–64 (youth team), 1964–77 (sr team), New York Cosmos 1977–80, 1983, Hamburg 1980–82 football clubs, West Germany B 1965, West Germany 1965–77 (Capt. 1972–77, 103 appearances, 14 goals); won West German Cup (with Bayern Munich) 1966, 1967, 1969, 1971, West German Championship 1972, 1974,

European Cup Winners 1967, European Cup 1974–76, World Club Championship 1976; won European Nations Cup (with West German Nat. Team) 1972, World Cup (only man to have won the World Cup both as Capt. and man.) 1974; won North American Championship (with New York Cosmos) 1977, 1978–80; retd 1984; Man. West German Nat. Team 1984–90; briefly coach for Marseilles; Pres. FC Bayern Munich 1994–2002, Chair. Advisory Bd 2002–; apptd Vice-Pres. Deutscher Fussball-Bund 1998, currently Rep. for Int. Tasks; Pres. 2006 World Cup Organizing Cttee; f. Franz Beckenbauer Foundation 1982; Adviser, Mitsubishi Mrawa Football Club 1992–; mem. Exec. Cttee, FIFA 2007–; Bundesverdienstkreuz, Bayerischer Verdienstorden 1982; West German Footballer of the Year 1966, 1968, 1974, 1976, FIFA World Cup Young Player of the Tournament 1966, FIFA World Cup Team of the Tournament 1966, 1970, 1974, European Football Championships Team of the Tournament 1972, 1976, European Footballer of the Year 1972, 1976, Winner, World Soccer Magazine of the Year 1972, 1976, Order of FIFA 1984, one of FIFA World Cup Winning Managers 1990, UEFA Cup Winning Coach 1995–96, IFFHS The Universal Genius of World Football 2007, Marca Leyenda 2012, FIFA Presidential Award 2012, UEFA Pres.'s Award 2013. *Publication:* Einer wie ich (Someone like Me) 1975, Franz Beckenbauer's Soccer Power 1978. *Address:* Deutscher Fußball-Bund e.V. (DFB), Hermann-Neuberger-Haus, Otto-Fleck-Schneise 6, 60528 Frankfurt am Main, Germany (office); Fédération Internationale de Football Association, FIFA-Strasse 20, PO Box 8044 Zurich, Switzerland (office). *Telephone:* (69) 67-88-0 (Frankfurt) (office); (43) 222-77-77 (Zurich) (office). *Fax:* (69) 67-88-266 (Frankfurt) (office); (43) 222-78-78 (Zurich) (office). *E-mail:* info@dfb.de (office); info@fifa.com (office). *Website:* www.dfb.de (office); www.fifa.com (office).

BECKER, Boris; German tennis coach and fmr professional tennis player; b. 22 Nov. 1967, Leimen, nr Heidelberg; s. of Karl-Heinz Becker and Elvira Becker; m. 1st Barbara Feltus (divorced 2001); two s. one d.; m. 2nd Sharlely Becker 2009; one s.; started playing tennis aged three, later joined Blau-Weiss Club, Leimen; won West German Jr Championship 1983; subsequently runner-up US Jr Championship; turned professional and coached by Ion Tiriac from 1984; quarter-finalist, Australian Championship, Winner Young Masters Tournament, Birmingham, England 1985, Grand Prix Tournament, Queen's 1985; won Men's Singles Championship, Wimbledon 1985 (youngest ever winner and finalist; beat Kevin Curren), also won 1986, 1989, finalist 1988, 1990, 1991, 1995; finalist, Benson and Hedges Championship, Wembley, London 1985; Masters Champion 1988, finalist 1989; US Open Champion 1989; Semi-finalist French Open 1989; Winner Davis Cup for Germany 1989, Australian Open Championships 1991, 1996, IBM/ATP Tour Championship 1992, 1995, Grand Slam Cup 1996; named World Champion 1991, 64 career titles (49 singles, 15 doubles); Gold Medal (with Michael Stich), Olympic Games, Barcelona 1992; retd from professional tennis 1999; mem. Bd Bayern Munich Football Club 2001–; Co-founder Boris Becker & Co., Völkl GmbH; Partner, DaimlerChrysler; owner of three car dealerships; Chair. Laureus Sports for Good Foundation 2002–, Tennis Masters Hamburg Rothenbaum; commentator for BBC TV –2013, Premiere channel (Germany); Head Coach, Novak Djokovic 2014; columnist, The Times, Handelsblatt (Germany), Blick (Switzerland); Founder Cleven-Becker-Stiftung; Amb. for German AIDS Foundation, for Youwin.com (online betting co.); mem. Bd Elton John AIDS Foundation; convicted of tax evasion, given a two-year suspended sentence Oct. 2002; Hon. Citizen of Leimen 1986; Sportsman of the Year 1985. *Publication:* The Player (autobiog.) 2004. *Leisure interests:* football, basketball, chess, backgammon. *Address:* Boris Becker & Co., Grafenauweg 4, 6300 Zug, Switzerland (office). *Telephone:* (41) 724-65-11 (office). *Fax:* (41) 724-65-05 (office). *Website:* borisbeckertennis.com.

BECKER, Gert O.; German business executive; b. 21 Aug. 1933, Kronberg; s. of Otto Becker and Henriette Becker (née Syring); m. Margrit Bruns 1960; one s. one d.; ed Akad. für Welthandel, Frankfurt; with Sales Dept, Degussa, Frankfurt 1956, with rep. office in Tehran, Iran 1960, with subsidiary in São Paulo, Brazil 1963, Div. Man., Frankfurt 1966, Dir 1971, Man. Dir Degussa, Frankfurt 1977–96, Chair. Supervisory Bd 1996–2001; fmr Pres. and CEO; Pres. Asscn of Chemical Industries 1994–95; fmr Chair. Supervisory Bd Bilfinger Berger Industrial Services AG, now Hon. Chair. *Leisure interests:* literature, book collecting, golf. *Address:* Bilfinger SE, Oskar-Meixner-Straße 1, 68163 Mannheim, Germany. *Telephone:* (49) 6214590. *Fax:* (49) 6214592366. *E-mail:* info@bilfinger.com. *Website:* www.bilfinger.com.

BECKER, Thomas; American business executive and consultant; Man. American Express Co. 1998–2000, Dir 2000–01; Vice-Pres. & Sr Strategy Man. Treasury Services New Business Devt Group, J.P. Morgan 2005–07; CEO Thom Browne (fashion co.), New York 2007–09; Founding Prin. BSI-NYC 2009–; Prin. Becker Harris and Co. (man. consultancy), New York 2010–. *Address:* Becker Harris & Co., 154 Grand Street, New York, NY 10013, USA (office). *Telephone:* (917) 727-1242 (office). *E-mail:* hello@beckerharris.com (office). *Website:* www.beckerharris.com (office).

BECKERS, Pierre-Olivier, MA, MBA; Belgian retail executive; *Chairman of Audit Committee, International Olympic Committee;* b. 3 May 1960; m.; three c.; ed IAG Louvain-La-Neuve, Harvard Business School, USA; began working in food retail industry as store manager for bakery chain in Belgium 1982; joined Delhaize Group 1983, positions include store man., buyer, Dir of Purchasing, mem. Exec. Cttee 1990–98, later Exec. Vice-Pres. responsible for int. activities, Dir Delhaize Group 1995–2015, Pres. and CEO 1999–2013, Chair. Delhaize America 2002–; Co-Chair. Consumer Good Forum –2010; Dir Food Marketing Inst., CIES – The Food Business Forum (Chair. 2002–04); Pres. Belgian Olympic Interfederal Cttee 2004–13; mem. IOC 2012–, Chair. Audit Cttee 2014–; mem. Bd Guberna 2006–, The Corporate Governance Cttee, Belgian Comm. on Corp. Governance –2010, D'Ieteren Group 2014–, ARAMARK Inc. 2015–, Bata Shoe Co. 2015–; Commander of the Order of Leopold 2013; Manager of the Year, Trends/Tendances magazine 2000, Best CEO for investor relations for Belgium – Thomson Extel 2010. *Website:* www.olympic.org.

BECKETT, Rt Hon. Dame Margaret Mary, DBE, PC; British politician; b. 15 Jan. 1943, Ashton-under-Lyne, Lancs.; d. of Cyril Jackson and Winifred Jackson; m. Leo Beckett 1979; two step-s.; ed Notre Dame High School, Manchester and Norwich, Manchester Coll. of Science and Tech., John Dalton Polytechnic; eng apprentice (metallurgy), Associated Electrical Industries Ltd, Manchester, subsequently Experimental Officer, Univ. of Manchester; Sec. Trades Council and Labour Party 1968–70; researcher (Industrial Policy), Labour Party HQ 1970–74; Political Adviser to Minister of Overseas Devt Feb.–Oct. 1974; MP (Labour) for Lincoln 1974–79, for Derby S 1983–; Parl. Pvt. Sec., Minister for Overseas Devt 1974–75; Asst Govt Whip 1975–76; Minister, Dept of Educ. 1976–79; Prin. Researcher, Granada TV 1979–83; Opposition Spokeswoman with responsibility for Social Security 1984–89; Shadow Chief Sec. 1989–92; Shadow Leader of House, Campaigns Co-ordinator, Deputy Leader of Opposition 1992–94, Leader of Opposition May–July 1994; Shadow Sec. of State for Health 1994–95; Shadow Pres. Bd of Trade 1995–97, Pres. Bd of Trade and Sec. of State for Trade and Industry 1997–98; Pres. of Council and Leader House of Commons 1998–2001; Sec. of State for Environment, Food and Rural Affairs 2001–06, for Foreign and Commonwealth Affairs 2006–07; Chair. Intelligence and Security Cttee 2008; Minister of State for Housing and Planning, Dept for Communities and Local Govt 2008–09; ministerial visits and trade missions to USA, Japan, Mexico, The Netherlands, Australia, Paris, Brussels, Singapore, China, Hong Kong and Pakistan, India 1997–2001; mem. Labour Party 1963–, Nat. Exec. Cttee 1980–81, 1985–86, 1988–97, Transport & General Workers Union 1964–, T&GWU Parl. Labour Party Group; mem. Nat. Union of Journalists, BECTU, Fabian Soc., Anti-Apartheid Movt, Tribune Group, Socialist Educ. Cttee, Labour Women's Action Cttee, Derby Co-op Party, Socialist Environment & Resources Asscn, Amnesty International, Council of St George's Coll., Windsor 1976–82; PC 1993–; Hon. Pres. Labour Friends of India. *Publications:* Vision for Growth – A New Industrial Strategy for Britain 1996, Renewing the NHS 1995, relevant sections of Labour's Programme 1972, 1973, The Nationalisation of Shipbuilding, Ship Repair and Marine Engineering, The National Enterprise Board, The Need for Consumer Protection. *Leisure interests:* cooking, reading, caravanning. *Address:* House of Commons, Westminster, London, SW1A 2NE, England (office). *Telephone:* (20) 7219-3000 (office); (1332) 345636 (constituency office) (office). *Fax:* (20) 7944-4101 (office); www.parliament.uk/biographies/commons/margaret-beckett/328 (office).

BECKHAM, David Robert Joseph, OBE; British professional footballer (retd); b. 2 May 1975, Leytonstone, London; m. Victoria Beckham (née Adams) (q.v.) 1999; three s. one d.; youth played with Brimsdown Rovers, Tottenham Hotspur 1987–91, Manchester United 1991–93; sr career with Manchester United 1993–2003 (team debut 1992), on loan to Preston North End 1995, League debut 1995, 386 appearances for Manchester United, 80 goals; player with Real Madrid 2003–07, with Los Angeles Galaxy (Major League Soccer, USA) (Capt. 2007–08) 2007–12, on loan to AC Milan 2009, 2010, with Paris Saint-Germain 2013 (retd); nine caps for England Under-21s 1994–96, rep. England 1996–2009 (115 caps, 17 goals), Capt. 2000–06; Football Asscn Youth Cup medal, six Premiership medals, two Football Asscn Cup medals, European Cup medal, Intercontinental Cup medal, four Community Shield winner medals; Supercopa de España medal 2003, La Liga medal (both with Real Madrid) 2006–07; Western Conference medal (with LA Galaxy) 2009, helped LA Galaxy to a 1–0 win over Houston Dynamo in MLS Cup final 2011, helped them retain championship with 3–1 win over Houston Dynamo 2012; only English player, and 21st player regardless of nationality, to score in three World Cups, and only fifth player in World Cup history to score twice from a direct free kick; first England player ever to collect two red cards and first England capt. to be sent off; UNICEF Goodwill Amb. 2005–; involved in promoting London's successful bid for the 2012 Olympic Games and in Opening Ceremony of the Olympic Games in Stratford, East London 27 July 2012; announced retirement from professional football 16 May 2013; f. David Beckham Acad. football school, London and Los Angeles, Calif.; Bobby Charlton Skills Award 1987, Sir Matt Busby Player of the Year 1996–97, Professional Football Asscn Young Player of the Year 1996–97, Sky Football Personality of the Year 1997, FIFA World Cup Team of the Tournament 1998, UEFA Club Player of the Year 1999, Premier League 10 Seasons Awards 1992/93–2001/02: Overall Team of the Decade, Goal of the Decade (17 Aug. 1996), BBC Sports Personality of the Year 2001, FIFA 100, England Player of the Year 2003, ESPY Award—Best Male Soccer Player 2004, ESPY Award—Best MLS Player 2008, English Football Hall of Fame 2008, Britain's Greatest Ambassador, 100 Greatest Britons Awards, Time 100 2008, BBC Sports Personality of the Year Lifetime Achievement Award 2010, MLS Comeback Player of the Year Award 2011, Major League Soccer Best XI 2011, ESPY Award for Best MLS Player 2011, Do Something Athlete Award 2011. *Films:* cameo appearance with Zinedine Zidane and Raúl in Goal!: The Dream Begins 2005, appears in sequels Goal! 2: Living the Dream..., Goal! 3: Taking on the World (DVD) 2009. *Publications:* David Beckham: My Side 2002, David Beckham: My World (with Dean Freeman) 2001, Beckham: Both Feet on the Ground (with Tom Watt) 2003. *Address:* c/o Simon Fuller, 19 Entertainment, Unit 33 Ransome's Dock Business Centre, 35–37 Parkgate Road, London, SW11 4NP, England (office). *Website:* www.davidbeckham.com.

BECKHAM, Victoria Caroline, OBE; British singer, model, actress, fashion designer and business executive; b. 17 April 1974, Harlow, Essex; d. of Tony Adams and Jackie Adams; m. David Beckham (q.v.) 1999; three s. one d.; ed St Mary's High School, Cheshunt, Herts., Jason Theatre School, Laine Arts Theatre Coll.; mem. Touch, later renamed The Spice Girls 1993–2001, as 'Posh Spice,' then solo artist, reunion tour 2007–08; launched dvb Denim collection in New York 2007, also new eye-wear range, launched Intimately Beckham perfume 2007, debut cosmetics line V-Sculpt launched in Tokyo 2008; the face of Marc Jacobs for his Spring collection 2008; own fashion collection debuted during New York Fashion Week at the Waldorf Hotel 2008; appeared on covers of British Vogue April 2008, Indian Vogue Nov. 2008, Russian Vogue Feb. 2009; launched secondary line, Victoria by Victoria Beckham 2011; guest judge, Project Runway 2008, Germany's Next Topmodel 2009, American Idol 2010; spokesperson for the Ban Bossy campaign advocating leadership roles for girls 2014–; two Ivor Novello songwriting awards 1997, Smash Hits Award for Best Band 1997, BRIT Awards for Best Single (for Wannabe) 1997, for Best Video (for Say You'll Be There) 1997, for Best Performance of the last 30 years 2010, three American Music Awards 1998, Special BRIT Award for Int. Sales 1998, Glamour Magazine Awards for Woman of the Year and for Entrepreneur of the Year 2007, Walpole Award 2011, named by Management Today magazine as Britain's most successful entrepreneur of 2014. *Films:* Spiceworld: The Movie 1997, Ugly Betty (episode, A Nice Day for a Posh Wedding) 2007, Spongebob Squarepants (voice of Queen Amphitrite) 2010. *Television:* documentaries: Victoria's Secrets 2000, Being Victoria Beckham

2002, The Real Beckhams 2003, Full Length & Fabulous, Victoria Beckham: Coming to America 2007, Giving You Everything 2007. *Recordings include:* albums: with The Spice Girls: Spice 1996, Spiceworld 1997, Forever 2000, Greatest Hits 2007; solo: Victoria Beckham 2001, Not Such An Innocent Girl 2004. *Publications:* Learning to Fly (autobiog.) 2001, That Extra Half an Inch 2006. *Leisure interest:* shopping. *Address:* 19 Entertainment, Unit 5B, The Albion Riverside, London, SW11 4AX, England (office). *E-mail:* info@xixentertainment.com (office). *Website:* www.xixentertainment.com (office); www.victoriabeckham.com.

BECKINSALE, Kate; British actress; b. 26 July 1973; d. of Richard Beckinsale and Judy Loe; one d. (with Michael Sheen); m. Len Wiseman 2004; ed Godolphin and Latymer School, London and New Coll., Oxford. *Films include:* Much Ado About Nothing 1993, Prince of Jutland 1994, Uncovered 1994, Haunted 1995, Marie-Louise ou la permission 1995, Shooting Fish 1997, The Last Days of Disco (London Critics Circle Supporting Actress Award 1999) 1998, Brokedown Palace 1999, The Golden Bowl 2000, Pearl Harbor 2001, Serendipity 2001, Laurel Canyon 2002, Underworld 2003, Tiptoes 2003, Van Helsing 2004, The Aviator 2004, Underworld Evolution 2005, Click 2006, Snow Angels 2007, Vacancy 2007, Winged Creatures 2008, Nothing But the Truth 2008, Underworld: Rise of the Lycans 2009, Whiteout 2009, Everybody's Fine 2009, Contraband 2012, Underworld: Awakening 2012, Total Recall 2012, Happy Holidays, Katherine Sloane 2012, The Trials of Cate McCall 2014, Stonehearst Asylum 2014. *Play:* The Seagull 1995. *Television:* Devices and Desires (series) 1991, One Against the Wind 1991, Rachel's Dream 1992, Cold Comfort Farm 1994, Emma 1996, Alice Through the Looking Glass 1998. *Address:* c/o Tracy Brennan, Creative Artists Agency, 2000 Avenue of The Stars, Los Angeles, CA 90067, USA (office). *Website:* www.caa.com (office).

BECKLES, Pennelope Althea; Trinidad and Tobago attorney, politician and diplomatist; *Permanent Representative to United Nations;* b. 12 Sept. 1961, Borde Narve Village; d. of Lionel Beckles; m. Noel Robinson; four step-c.; ed Univ. of the West Indies, Barbados; worked as Attorney, Chambers of Theodore R Guerra and Assocs; mem. People's Nat. Movt 1995, Vice-Chair. 2012–13; Opposition Senator of Parl. (People's Nat. Movt) 1995–98, Deputy Speaker 2007–10, Leader of Opposition Business in Senate 2010–13; mem. House of Reps (Arima Constituency) 2000–10; Minister of Social Devt Dec. 2001–Oct. 2002, of Culture and Tourism Oct. 2002–03, of Public Utilities and Environment 2003–07; Perm. Rep. to UN 2016–, Co-Chair. Open-ended Informal Consultative Process on Oceans and the Law of the Sea, Div. of Ocean Affairs and Law of Sea 2019. *Address:* Permanent Mission of Trinidad and Tobago, 633 Third Avenue, 12th Floor, New York, NY 10017, USA. *Telephone:* (212) 697-7620. *Fax:* (212) 682-3580. *E-mail:* tto@un.int. *Website:* www.foreign.gov.tt/missions-consuls/tt-missions-abroad/diplomatic-missions/permanent-mission-un-new-york-us (office).

BECKMANN, David; American economist and pastor; *President, Bread for the World;* ed Yale Univ., Christ Seminary, London School of Econs, UK; worked at World Bank 1976–91; Pres. Bread for the World 1991–, Bread for the World Inst.; Founder and Pres. Alliance to End Hunger; Co-Chair. Modernizing Foreign Assistance Network; fmr mem. Bd InterAction, Partnership to Cut Hunger and Poverty in Africa, ONE Campaign, Nat. Anti-Hunger Orgs, UN Millennium Hunger Task Force; serves as Lutheran pastor; seven hon. doctorates; World Food Prize (co-recipient) 2010, Extraordinary Commitment of Service to the Community, Rumi Forum Peace and Dialogue Awards 2014, Int. Peace Award, Community of Christ 2014, Anti-Poverty Champion Award, National Latino Evangelical Coalition 2015. *Publications include:* Transforming the Politics of Hunger and Grace at the Table: Ending Hunger in God's World, Exodus from Hunger: We Are Called to Change the Politics of Hunger; numerous articles. *Address:* Bread for the World, 425 3rd Street, SW, Suite 1200, Washington, DC 20024, USA (office). *Telephone:* (202) 639-9400 (office). *Fax:* (202) 639-9401 (office). *E-mail:* bread@bread.org (office); institute@bread.org (office). *Website:* www.bread.org (office).

BECKSTROM, Rod Allen, BA, MBA; American business executive and international organization official; *President, Rod Beckstrom Group;* ed Stanford Univ.; Analyst, Morgan Stanley International 1984–85; mem. and Leader, YPO 1995–2011; Chair. Privada Inc. 1999–2001; Co-founder CATS Software Inc. (later sold to Misys PLC); Chair. and Chief Catalyst Twiki.net 2007–08; Dir Nat. Cybersecurity Center, Dept of Homeland Security 2008–09 (resgnd); Pres. Rod Beckstrom Group 2001–; Pres. and CEO Internet Corpn for Assigned Names and Numbers (ICANN) 2009–12; mem. World Econ. Forum Partnering for Cyber Resilience Initiative 2011–, Vice-Chair. Global Agenda Council on the Future of the Internet 2012–13, Chair. 2013–14; Advisor, Uniloc 2010–11; Chief Security Advisor, Samsung Electronics SSIC 2013–14; Chair. Global Peace Networks 2001–07; Investor and Advisor, American Legal Net 2001–07; Co-founder Mergent Systems; Chair. Council of Pres. of Associated Students, Stanford Univ.; Fulbright Scholar, Univ. of St Gallen, Switzerland; Trustee, Environmental Defense Fund 1994–2013, Advisory Trustee 2013–; Advisor, Jamii Bora Trust (African Micro-lending Inst.) 2002–10. *Publication:* The Starfish and the Spider: The Unstoppable Power of Leaderless Organizations (co-author) 2008. *Address:* Rod Beckstrom Group, Palo Alto, CA, USA (office). *Website:* www.beckstrom.com (office).

BECTON, Henry P., Jr; American broadcast executive; *Vice Chairman, WGBH Educational Foundation;* b. 16 Oct. 1943; s. of Maxwell Becton; ed Yale Univ., Harvard Univ.; joined WGBH as producer 1970, Program Manager for Cultural Affairs 1974–78, Vice-Pres. and Gen. Man. 1978–99, Pres. WGBH Educational Foundation 1984–2007, Vice-Chair. 2007–; Founding Dir American Documentary, Inc.; mem. Bd of Dirs Public Broadcasting Service (PBS) 1987–93, 1995–2001, Belo Corpn 2008–13, Becton, Dickinson & Co., Deutsche Investment Management Americas Inc., American Public Television; mem. Bd of Overseers New England Aquarium; Trustee, Boston Museum of Science. *Address:* WGBH Educational Foundation, 1 Guest Street, Boston, MA 02135, USA.

BEDDALL, David Peter; Australian (b. British) business executive and fmr politician; *Chairman, Industrea Limited;* b. 27 Nov. 1948, Manchester, England; s. of G. A. Beddall; m. Helen Beddall; one d.; two s. from previous m.; mem. staff, Commonwealth Banking Corpn 1967–78; Loans Officer, Australian Guarantee Corpn Ltd 1978–83; commercial finance consultant 1979–83; mem. House of Reps for Fadden, Queensland 1983, for Rankin 1984–98 (retd); Minister for Small Business and Customs 1990–93, for Communications 1993, for Resources 1993–96; Chair. Jt Standing Cttee on Foreign Affairs and Defence 1984–87, House of Reps Standing Cttee on Industry, Science and Tech. 1987–93; Chair. GPS Online Ltd (later GPS Online Solutions, now Industrea Ltd) 1999–; Pres. Australian Franchisees Asscn Inc. *Address:* Industrea Ltd, PO Box 567, Sumner Park, Brisbane, Qld 4074 (office); Industrea Ltd, Centenary Technology Park, 532 Seventeen Mile Rocks Road, Sinnamon Park, Brisbane, Qld 4073 (office); Inala Plaza, Corsair Avenue, Inala, Qld 4077, Australia; David Beddall & Associates Pty Ltd, 22 Redgum Place, Calamvale, Qld 4116. *Telephone:* (7) 3725-5400 (office). *Fax:* (7) 3376-6702 (office). *E-mail:* info@industrea.com.au (office). *Website:* www.industrea.com.au (office).

BEDFORD, Steuart John Rudolf, OBE, BA, FRCO, FRAM; British conductor; b. 31 July 1939, London, England; s. of L. H. Bedford and Lesley Bedford (née Duff); m. 1st Norma Burrowes 1969 (divorced 1980); m. 2nd Celia Harding 1980; two d.; ed Lancing Coll., Sussex, Univ. of Oxford, Royal Acad. of Music; operatic training as repetiteur, Asst Conductor, Glyndebourne Festival 1965–67; English Opera Group (later English Music Theatre), Aldeburgh and London 1967–73; Co-Artistic Dir, English Musical Theatre 1976–80, Artistic Dir English Sinfonia 1981–90, Artistic Dir (also Exec. Artistic Dir) Aldeburgh Festival 1987–98; freelance conductor, numerous performances with ENO, Welsh Nat. Opera, Metropolitan Opera, New York (operas include Death in Venice, The Marriage of Figaro), Royal Danish Opera; also at Royal Opera House, Covent Garden (operas include Owen Wingrave, Death in Venice, Così fan tutte) Santa Fe Opera, Teatro Colón, Buenos Aires, Opéra de Lyon, Garsington Opera, Opéra de Toulon, San Diego Opera, Boston Lyric Opera, Opera Theatre of St Louis etc.; conductor for Orchestre Philharmonique de Montpellier, Mahler Chamber Orchestra, Southern Sinfonia; Medal of the Worshipful Co. of Musicians. *Recordings include:* Death in Venice, Phaedra, Beggar's Opera, Collins Britten series, Britten: Peter Grimes (BBC Music Magazine Opera Award 2014). *Film:* Peter Grimes. *Leisure interests:* golf, skiing. *Address:* c/o Harrison Parrott, 5–6 Albion Court, London, W6 0QT, England (office). *Telephone:* (20) 3725-9120 (office). *E-mail:* linda.marks@harrisonparrott.co.uk (office); katie.cardell-oliver@harrisonparrott.co.uk (office). *Website:* www.harrisonparrott.com (office).

BEDI, Bishan Singh, BA; Indian fmr professional cricketer; b. 25 Sept. 1946, Amritsar; s. of Gyan Singh Bedi and Rajinder Kaur Bedi; m. 1st Glenith Jill Bedi 1969; one s. one d.; m. 2nd Inderjit Bedi 1980; ed Punjab Univ.; fmr employee, Steel Authority of India, New Delhi; slow left-arm bowler; played for Northern Punjab 1961–62 to 1966–67, Delhi 1968–69 to 1980–81, Northants. 1972–77; played in 67 Tests for India (1967/68–79), 22 as Capt. 1975–79, taking 266 wickets (average 28.71) and scored 656 runs (highest score 50 not out); took 1,560 first-class wickets; toured England 1971, 1974, 1976 and 1975 (World Cup); coach, Indian cricket team 1990–; fmr nat. selector; Hon. Life mem. MCC 1981; Padma Shri Award 1969, Arjuna Award 1971. *Leisure interests:* reading, photography, swimming, letter writing. *Address:* Ispat Bhawan, Lodhi Road, New Delhi 110 003, India.

BEDI, Kiran; Indian police professional (retd) and government official; *Lieutenant-Governor of Puducherry;* b. 9 June 1949, Amritsar; d. of Prakash Peshawaria and Prem Peshawaria; m. Brij Bedi; one d.; ed Sacred Heart School, Amritsar, Govt Coll. for Women, Amritsar, Punjab Univ., Chandigarh, Delhi Univ., Indian Inst. of Tech., Delhi; Lecturer, Khalsa Coll. for Women, Amritsar 1970–72; joined Indian Police Service 1972, held various assignments including Dist Police, Delhi Traffic Police, Special Traffic, Goa, Narcotics Control Bureau; fmr Deputy Insp.-Gen., Mizoram; fmr Insp.-Gen. of Prisons, of Tihar Jails, Delhi; fmr Special Sec. to Lt Gov. of Delhi; fmr Jt Commr, Delhi Police; fmr Insp.-Gen. of Police, Chandigarh; fmr Jt Commr of Police (Training), Delhi; UN Civilian Police Adviser 2003; fmr Dir-Gen. Bureau of Police Research and Devt, Ministry of Home Affairs; Lt-Gov. of Puducherry 2016–; f. website www.saferindia.com 2007; Founder and Gen. Sec. Navjyoti (residential community-based therapeutic treatment centre) 1987; Founder and Chair. India Vision Foundation 1994–; Host and presiding judge on TV series Aap Ki Kachehri; Jawaharlal Nehru Fellowship; Dr hc (Guru Nanak Dev Univ.), Hon. LLD CUNY School of Law 2005; Pres.'s Gallantry Award 1979, Women of the Year Award 1980, Asia Region Award for Drug Prevention and Control 1991, Int. Org. of Good Templars Asia-Region Award, Ramon Magsaysay Peace Award for Gov Service 1994, Father Machismo Humanitarian Award 1995, Lion of the Year Award 1995, Joseph Beuys Foundation Award for Holistic and Innovative Man. Award 1997, Asscns of Christian Colls and Univs Int. Award 1998, Pride of India Award, American Fed. of Muslims from India 1999, Serge Sotiroff Memorial Award (for Navjyoti Centre) 1999, State Award (for Navjyoti Centre), Indian Inst. of Tech. Alumni Asscn Award 2000, Western Soc. of Criminology USA Tom Gitchoff Award 2001, Blue Drop Group Man. Cultural and Artistic Asscn (Italy) Woman of the Year Award 2002, Chinmoy Award for Welfare Policing 2003, FICCI Award 2005, Mother Teresa Award for Social Justice 2005, Transformative Leadership in Indian Police Service 2006, Public Service Excellence Award 2007, Amity Woman Achiever for Social Justice 2007, Suryadatta Nat. Award 2007, Lifetime Achievement Award, Bank of Baroda 2008, Indian Soc. of Criminology Award 2008, Pride of Punjab Award 2008, Indo-American Award 2009, Certificate of Recognition, City of LA 2009, Women Excellence Award Aaj Tak 2009, Kalpana Chawla Excellence Award 2010. *Film:* Real Salute 2001. *Achievements include:* fmr Nat. Jr, Sr and Asian tennis champion. *Publications include:* It's Always Possible (autobiography) 1998; Government@net (jtly with Sandeep Srivastava); writes a fortnightly column 'What Went Wrong' in The Times of India and Navbharat Times (compilation of 37 of these articles published in book form, also Hindi trans. Galti Kiski). *Leisure interest:* community work. *Address:* Officer of the Lieutenant Governor, Raj Nivas (Government House), Puducherry 605 001, India (office). *Telephone:* (413) 2334051 (office). *Fax:* (413) 2334025 (office). *E-mail:* lg.pon@nic.in (office); kiranbedioffice@gmail.com. *Website:* www.py.gov.in (office); www.kiranbedi.com.

BÉDIÉ, Henri Konan, LenD; Côte d'Ivoirian politician and diplomatist; *President, Parti démocratique de la Côte d'Ivoire—Rassemblement démocratique africain (PDCI—RDA);* b. 5 May 1934, Dadiékro, French West Africa; m. Henriette Koinzan Bomo 1958; two s. two d.; ed Univ. of Poitiers; Asst Dir Caisse de Sécurité de la Côte d'Ivoire 1959–60; Counsellor, Embassy in Washington, DC March–Aug. 1960, mem. Perm. Mission to UN, New York 1960, Chargé d'affaires a.i., Embassy in Washington, DC Aug.–Dec. 1960, Amb. to USA 1960–66; Minister-Del. for Econ. and Financial Affairs 1966–68; Minister of Economy and Finance 1968–75; Special

Adviser, IFC 1976–80; re-elected Deputy, Nat. Ass. 1980; Pres. Nat. Ass. 1980, re-elected 1985, 1986; mem. Political Bureau, Parti démocratique de la Côte d'Ivoire—Rassemblement démocratique africain (PDCI—RDA), Pres. 1994, 2002–; Pres. Office Africain et Malgache de la Propriété Industrielle; Acting Pres. of Côte d'Ivoire 1993–95, Pres. 1995–99 (overthrown in coup d'état), in exile in France, returned to Côte d'Ivoire 2005. *Address:* Parti démocratique de la Côte d'Ivoire—Rassemblement démocratique africain (PDCI—RDA), 05 BP 36, Abidjan 05, Côte d'Ivoire (office). *E-mail:* sg@pdcirda.org (office). *Website:* www.pdcirda.org (office).

BEDJAOUI, Mohammed; Algerian judge and diplomatist; b. 21 Sept. 1929, Sidi-Bel-Abbès; s. of Benali Bedjaoui and Fatima Oukili; m. Leila Francis 1962; two d.; ed Univ. of Grenoble and Institut d'Etudes Politiques, Grenoble; Lawyer, Court of Appeal, Grenoble 1951; research worker at CNRS, Paris 1955; Legal Counsellor of the Arab League in Geneva 1959–62; Legal Counsellor Provisional Republican Govt of Algeria in Exile 1958–61; Dir Office of the Pres. of Nat. Constituent Ass. 1962; mem. Del. to UN 1957, 1962, 1977, 1978–82; Sec.-Gen. Council of Ministers, Algiers 1962–63; Pres. Soc. Nat. des Chemins de Fer Algériens (SNCFA) 1964; Dean of the Faculty of Law, Algiers Univ. 1964; Minister of Justice and Keeper of the Seals 1964–70; mem., special reporter, Int. Law Comm. 1965–82; Amb. to France 1970–79; Perm. Rep. to UNESCO 1971–79, to UN, New York 1979–82; Vice-Pres. UN Council on Namibia 1979–82; mem. UN Comm. of Inquiry (Iran) 1980; Pres. Group of 77 1981–82; Judge Int. Court of Justice 1982–2001 (Pres. 1994–97); Pres. Algerian Constitutional Council 2002–05; Minister of State for Foreign Affairs 2005–07; fmr Pres. African Soc. of Int. and Comparative Law; Head of Algerian Del. to UN Conf. on Law of the Sea 1976–80; mem. Int. Inst. of Law; Commr Int. Comm. Against the Death Penalty; Ordre du Mérite Alaouite (Morocco), Order of the Repub. (Egypt), Commdr Légion d'honneur, Ordre de la Résistance (Algeria). *Publications:* International Civil Service 1956, Fonction publique internationale et influences nationales 1958, La révolution algérienne et le droit 1961, Succession d'états 1970, Terra nullius, droits historiques et autodétermination 1975, Non-alignment et droit international 1976, Pour un nouvel ordre économique international 1979, Droit international: bilan et perspectives 1992. *Address:* 39 rue des Pins, Hydra, Algiers, Algeria.

BEDNARSKI, Krzysztof, PhD; Polish sculptor, performer and graphic designer; *Professor of Sculpture, Academy of Fine Arts, Warsaw;* b. 25 July 1953, Kraków; m. Marina Fabbri; two s.; ed Acad. of Fine Arts, Warsaw; worked for Laboratorium Theatre of Jerzy Grotowski, Wrocław 1976–82; Artist-in-Residence, OMI Foundation, New York 1995; Guest Teacher, studio of Prof. Grzegorz Kowalski, Sculpture Dept, Acad. of Fine Arts, Warsaw 1996–97, currently Prof. of Sculpture; Artist-in-Residence, Art Foundation by Daniel Spoerri 'The Garden', Tuscany, Italy 1998–99; contrib. to European project 'Global Village Garden' (Germany) 2002–03; has participated in more than 300 exhbns worldwide; Golden Gloria Artis (Govt of Poland); Grant from Leube Foundation, Salzburg, Austria 2003, K. Kobro Award, Łódź 2004, 'Exit-New Art in Poland' Award 2004. *Works include:* created series of posters for productions including Vigil 1976–77, Project Mountain 1977, Project Earth 1977–79, Human Tree 1979, and others; installations such as Total Portrait of Karl Marx 1978 (realised in many versions up to 1999, such as The Collected Works of Karl Marx 1988), In Memory of Jan Szeliga 1980, sculptures such as Victoria Victoria 1983, Moby Dick (Best Polish Sculpture 1987) 1987, The Xram Lrak Burial Mound 1988, Moby Dick – Mask 1989, La Rivoluzione siamo Noi 1989, Finite Column 1991, Unsichtbar 1993, Missing Lenin's Hand 1995; monument of Federico Fellini, Rimini designed 1994, tomb of Krzysztof Kieślowski, Warsaw 1997, Vision & Prayer 1998–; artwork in Light Art Collection, Targetti Group, Florence, Italy 2005; works in numerous collections in Poland, Italy and elsewhere. *Publications include:* Linda Nochlin, The Body in Pieces, The Fragment as a Metaphor of Modernity 1994, Moby Dick Museum of Art 1994, Dictionary of Contemporary Artists 2001, Achille Bonito-Oliva, Oggetti di turno. Dall'arte alla critica 1997, Stownik Sztuki xx wieku 1998, L'arte come forma di difesa 2010. *Address:* Via Dei Banchi Vecchi 134, 00-186 Rome, Italy (home); ul. Nowowiejska 28/55, 010–02 Warsaw, Poland (home). *Telephone:* 3486529476 (Italy; mobile) (office); 504653975 (Poland; mobile) (office); (06) 6896068 (home). *E-mail:* kmbednarski@gmail.com. *Website:* www.bednarski.art.pl (office).

BEDNORZ, Georg, PhD; German physicist; b. 16 May 1950, North-Rhine Westphalia; s. of Anton Bednorz and Elisabeth Bednorz; ed Univ. of Münster, Swiss Federal Inst. of Tech.; with IBM Research Lab., Rüschlikon, Zürich 1982–; Fellow, IBM 1987; apptd Foreign Assoc. Nat. Acad. of Sciences 2018; Marcel Benoist Prize (jtly) 1986, Nobel Prize in Physics (jtly) 1987, Fritz London Memorial Award (jtly) 1987, Dannie Heineman Prize (jtly) 1987, Robert Wichard Pohl Prize (jtly) 1987, Otto Klung Prize 1987, Viktor Mortiz Goldschmidt Prize 1987, Hewlett-Packard Europhysics Prize 1988, APS Int. Prize for Materials Research (jtly) 1988, Minnie Rosen Award 1988. *Address:* IBM Zürich Research Laboratory, Säumerstrasse 4, 8803 Rüschlikon, Zürich, Switzerland (office). *Telephone:* 447248111 (office). *Fax:* 447248911 (office). *E-mail:* iho@zurich.ibm.com (office). *Website:* www .zurich.ibm.com (office).

BEDOUI, Noureddine; Algerian politician; *Prime Minister;* b. 22 Dec. 1959, Aïn Taya; ed École nat. d'admin, Algiers; fmr Magistrate, Court of Accounts; fmr Deputy Dir of regulations, Algiers wilaya (dept); fmr Dir of Admin, Tizi Ouzou and Annaba cities; fmr Dist Head, Bologhine (Algiers) and Ain Touila (Khenchla); fmr Sec.-Gen., Oran wilaya; Head, Sidi-Bel-Abbes wilaya, Bordj Bouarreridj wilaya 2004, Setif wilaya 2004–10, Constantine wilaya 2010–13; Minister of Vocational Training and Educ. 2013–15, Minister of the Interior and Local Authorities 2015–19; Prime Minister 2019–; independent. *Address:* Office of the Prime Minister, rue Docteur Saâdane, Palais du Gouvernement, Algiers, Algeria (office). *Telephone:* (21) 73-12-00 (office). *Fax:* (21) 71-07-83 (office). *Website:* www.cg.gov.dz (office).

BEEBE, Michael Dale (Mike), BA, LLB; American lawyer, politician and fmr state governor; b. 28 Dec. 1946, Amagon, Jackson Co., Ark.; m. Ginger Beebe; three c.; ed Newport High School, Arkansas State Univ., Univ. of Arkansas at Fayetteville; family lived in Detroit, St Louis, Chicago, Houston and Alamagordo, NM before moving back to Ark.; served in US Army Reserve; practised law in Searcy, Ark. for 10 years after graduating from law school; Ark. State Senator 1983–2002; Ark. Attorney-Gen. 2003–06; Gov. of Arkansas 2007–Jan. 2015; Democrat. *Address:* c/o Office of the Governor, Room 250, State Capitol, Little Rock, AR 72201, USA. *Website:* mikebeebe.com.

BEEBEEJAUN, Ahmed Rashid, FRCP; Mauritian politician; b. 22 Dec. 1934; m.; ed Univ. of Birmingham, UK; Child Health Consultant 1971–93; mem. Mouvement Militant Mauricien (MMM) 1993–97; mem. Mauritius Labour Party 2000–, Deputy Leader -2004; mem. Nat. Ass. 2005, 2010–14; Deputy Prime Minister 2005–08, 2010–14, Minister of Public Infrastructure, Land Transport and Shipping 2005–08, of Energy and Public Utilities 2008–14; Hon. DUniv (Univ. Birmingham) 2011. *Leisure interests:* music, theatre. *Address:* Victor Hugo Street, Beau Bassin, Mauritius (home). *Telephone:* 201-2664 (home). *Fax:* 213-1840 (home). *E-mail:* premin@intnet.mu (office).

BEEBY, Thomas Hall; American architect and academic; *Chairman Emeritus, Hammond Beeby Rupert Ainge;* b. 12 Oct. 1941, Oak Park, Ill.; m. 1st Marcia D. Greenlease 1960 (divorced 1973); one s. one d.; m. 2nd Kirsten Peltzer 1975; two s.; ed Lower Merion High School, Ardmore, Pa, Gresham's School, Holt (UK), Cornell and Yale Univs; Assoc., C.F. Murphy Associates, Chicago 1965–71; Pnr, Hammond Beeby & Associates, Chicago 1971–76; Pnr and Dir of Design, Hammond Beeby & Babka (now Hammond Beeby Rupert Ainge—HBRA), Chicago 1976, now Chair. Emer.; Assoc. Prof., Dept of Architecture, Illinois Inst. of Tech., Chicago 1973–80; Dir School of Architecture, Univ. of Ill. at Chicago 1980–85; Dean and Prof., School of Architecture, Yale Univ. 1985–91, Adjunct Prof. 1992–; mem. Advisory Bd Dept of Architecture, Illinois Inst. of Tech. 1993–, Trustee 1997–; contributor to numerous exhbns of architecture and design in USA and Europe including Venice Biennale 1980; Distinguished Building Award, American Inst. of Architects, Chicago Chapter (numerous times); Nat. Design Award 1984, 1987, 1989, 1991, 1993, Driehaus Award, Univ. of Notre Dame 2013. *Publications:* articles in professional journals. *Address:* Hammond Beeby Rupert Ainge Inc., 372 West Ontario Street, 2nd Floor, Chicago, IL 60654, USA (office). *Telephone:* (312) 527-3200 (office). *Fax:* (312) 527-1256 (office). *E-mail:* info@hbra-arch.com (office). *Website:* www.hbra-arch.com (office).

BEERING, Steven Claus, BS, MD; American physician, academic and university administrator; *President Emeritus, Purdue University;* b. 20 Aug. 1932, Berlin, Germany; s. of Steven Beering and Alice Friedrichs Beering; m. Jane Pickering 1956 (died 2015); three s.; ed Univ. of Pittsburgh; Prof. of Medicine, Indiana Univ. School of Medicine 1969, Asst Dean 1969–70, Assoc. Dean 1970–74, Dean 1974–83, Dir Indiana Univ. Medical Center 1974–83; Pres. Purdue Univ. and Purdue Univ. Research Foundation 1983–2000, Pres. Emer. 2000–; Chair. Nat. Science Bd 2010; Hon. ScD (Indiana) 1988; Hon. LLD; numerous awards and prizes. *Publications:* numerous articles in professional journals. *Leisure interests:* music, photography, reading, travel. *Address:* Purdue University, Purdue Memorial Union, Room 218, West Lafayette, IN 47906-3584 (office); 10487 Windemere Drive, Carmel, IN 46032, USA (home). *Telephone:* (765) 496-7555 (office); (317) 581-1414 (home). *Fax:* (765) 496-7561 (office). *E-mail:* scb@purdue.edu (office); sbeering@indy.rr.com (home). *Website:* www.purdue.edu (office).

BEEVOR, Sir Antony, Kt, FRSL, FRHistS; British historian and writer; b. 14 Dec. 1946, London; s. of John Grosvenor Beevor and Carinthia Jane Beevor (née Waterfield); m. Artemis Cooper 1986; one s. one d.; ed Winchester Coll., Grenoble Univ., Royal Mil. Acad. Sandhurst; Exec. Council French Theatre Season 1997; Lees-Knowles Lecturer, Univ. of Cambridge 2002–03; Visiting Prof., Birkbeck Coll., London 2002–, Univ. of Kent 2010–; Boeing Visiting Fellow, Australian War Memorial 2012; Cttee mem. Soc. of Authors 2001–05 (Chair. 2003–05), mem. of Council 2005–; mem. Steering Cttee Samuel Johnson Prize 2004–, Cttee Waterloo 200 conference 2012–, mem. Academic Advisory Cttee, European Centre for Tolerance and Reconciliation 2018–; judge, British Acad. Book Prize 2004, David Cohen Prize 2004; mem. Anglo Hellenic League, Friends of the British Libraries, London Library; Hon. Fellow, King's Coll. London; Chevalier des Arts et des Lettres 1997, Order of Cross of Terra Mariana (Estonia) 2008; Hon. DLitt (Kent) 2004, (Bath) 2010, (East Anglia) 2014, (York) 2015; Pritzker Literature Award for Lifetime Achievement in Military Writing 2014, Norton Medlicott Medal 2016. *Publications include:* The Spanish Civil War 1982, The Enchantment of Christina Von Retzen (novel) 1988, Inside the British Army 1990, Crete: The Battle and the Resistance (Runciman Award 1992) 1991, Paris After the Liberation 1944–49 (with Aretmis Cooper) 1994, Stalingrad (Samuel Johnson Prize for Non-Fiction 1999, Wolfson Prize for History 1999, Hawthornden Prize 1999) 1998, Berlin: The Downfall 1945 (Longman-History Today Trustees Award 2003) 2002, The Mystery of Olga Chekhova 2004, A Writer at War: Vasily Grossman with the Red Army 1941–1945 (co-ed.) 2005, The Battle for Spain: The Spanish Civil War 1936–39 (Premio Vanguardia 2005) 2005, D-Day: The Battle for Normandy (Prix Henry Malherbe, Duke of Westminster Medal for Military Literature, Royal United Services Inst. 2010) 2009, The Second World War 2012, Ardennes 1944 2015, Arnhem: The Battle for the Bridges, 1944 2018; contribs to New York Review of Books, New York Times, Washington Post, TLS, Times, Telegraph, Independent, Spectator, Guardian. *Address:* c/o Andrew Nurnberg Associates, 20–23 Greville Street, London, EC1N 8SS, England (office). *Telephone:* (20) 3327-0400 (office). *Fax:* (20) 7430-0801 (office). *E-mail:* contact@andrewnurnberg.com (office). *Website:* www.antonybeevor.com.

BEFFA, Jean-Louis Guy Henri; French business executive; *Honorary Chairman, Compagnie de Saint-Gobain;* b. 11 Aug. 1941, Nice; s. of Edmond Beffa and Marguerite Feursinger; m. Marie-Madeleine Brunel-Grasset 1967; two s. one d.; ed Lycée Masséna, Nice, École Nat. Supérieure des Mines and Inst. d'Études Politiques, Paris; mining engineer, Clermont-Ferrand 1967, motor fuel man. 1967–74, head of refinery service 1970–73, Asst to Dir 1973–74, Chief Mining Eng 1974; Dir of Planning, Pont-à-Mousson (subsidiary of Saint-Gobain Group) 1975–77, Dir-Gen. 1978, Pres. Dir-Gen. 1979–82, Deputy Dir (Pipelines) Saint-Gobain-Pont-à-Mousson 1978, Dir 1979–82, Dir-Gen. Compagnie de Saint-Gobain 1982–86, CEO 1982, Chair. and CEO 1986–2007, Chair. 2007–10, Hon. Chair. 2010–, apptd Chair. Saint-Gobain Centre for Econ. Research 2000, currently Co-Chair. Centre Cournot pour la Recherche en Économie; Pres. Inst. de L'Histoire de L'Industrie (Idni) 1992–98; Pres. Supervisory Bd Poliet 1996–; Vice-Pres. Compagnie Générale des Eaux 1998–; Vice-Pres. Admin. Bd BNP Paribas 2000–10; mem. Int. Consultative Cttee, Chase Manhattan Bank 1986–, AT&T 1987; mem. Admin. Council Ecole Polytechnique 1993–; Admin. Banque Nat. de Paris, Cie Gen. des Eaux, Cie de Suez et de Petrofina; Sr Advisor, Lazard, Chair.

Lazard Asia Investment Banking; mem. Bd of Dirs Groupe Bruxelles Lambert 2001–13, GDF-Suez 2008–15, Le Monde SA (Chair. Supervisory Bd); mem. Supervisory Bd Siemens AG 2008–13; Chair. Asscn pour le Rayonnement de l'Opéra nat. de Paris; Grand Officier, Légion d'honneur; Officier, Ordre nat. du Mérite, des Arts et des Lettres; Commdr du Mérite (FRG); CBE (UK) (Foreign mem.). *Leisure interests:* swimming, golf. *Address:* Compagnie de Saint-Gobain, Les Miroirs, 18 avenue d'Alsace, 92096 Paris la Défense Cedex, France (office). *Telephone:* 1-47-62-30-00 (office). *E-mail:* info@saint-gobain.com (office). *Website:* www.saint-gobain.com (office).

BEG, Gen. (retd) Mirza Aslam, BA, MSc; Pakistani army officer (retd) and politician; b. 2 Aug. 1931, Azamgarh, Uttar Pradesh, British India; s. of Mirza Murtuza Beg; m.; one s. two d.; ed Shibli Coll., Azamgarh, Aligarh Univ., India, Command and Staff Coll., Quetta and Nat. Defence Coll., Quaid-Azam Univ., Rawalpindi; commissioned 1952; served in Baluch (Infantry) Regt; joined Special Service Group (Commandos) 1961; Brig.-Maj. of an Infantry Brigade during India–Pakistan war 1965; Lt-Col 1969; in command, Infantry Bn, India–Pakistan war 1971; Brig. in command of Infantry Brigade 1974; Maj.-Gen. in command of Infantry Div. 1978; Chief of Gen. Staff 1980–85; Lt-Gen. 1984; Corps Commdr 1985; Gen. and Vice-Chief of Army Staff 1987; Chief of Army Staff 1988–92; Chair. Friends Foundation, Pakistan; Founder, Pres. and Chair. Awami Qiyadat Party; Tamgha-e-Jamhuriat, Sitara-e-Basalat 1981, Hilal-e-Imtiaz (Mil.) 1982, Nishan-e-Imtiaz (Mil.) 1988, Tongil (First Class) Medal (S Korea) 1988, US Legion of Merit 1989, Bintang Yudha Dharm (Indonesia) 1990, Kt Grand Cross (First Class) (Thailand) 1991. *Publications include:* Development and Security: Thoughts and Reflections 1994, National Security: Diplomacy and Defence 1999; articles in journals and nat. and int. newspapers. *Address:* No. 1, National Park Road, Rawalpindi, Pakistan (home). *Telephone:* (51) 5567637 (home). *Fax:* (51) 5521219 (home).

BEGG, David, MPhil, PhD, FRSE; British economist and academic; *Professor Emeritus of Economics, Imperial College London;* b. 1951; ed Univs of Cambridge and Oxford, Massachusetts Inst. of Tech., USA; Fellow and Lecturer, Worcester Coll., Oxford 1976–86; Research Fellow, Centre for Econ. Policy Research 1983–; Prof. of Econs, Birkbeck Coll., London 1986–2003; Prof. of Econs, Imperial Coll., London 2003–11, Prof. Emer. 2011–, Prin. of Business School 2003–11; Econ. Policy Adviser to Bank of England 1986–, also Adviser on monetary policy to IMF, HM Treasury; commissioned to provide econs training to Govt of Czechoslavakia 1991, to Nat. Bank of Hungary 1998–99; Chair. Begg Comm. 1999–2005; fmr Research Dir, Centre for Econ. Forecasting, London Business School; mem. Bellagio Group 1999–, Keynes Seminar (convened quarterly by UK Chancellor of the Exchequer) 1999–; mem. HM Treasury Academic Panel 1981–96; mem. Research Awards Advisory Cttee, Leverhulme Trust 1986–93; Founding Man. Ed. Economic Policy 1984–2000. *Publications include:* The Rational Expectations Revolution in Macroeconomics, Economics 2000, Foundations of Economics 2002, The Making of Monetary Union 2005, Emu: Getting The Endgame Right 2005. *Address:* Business School, 396 Tanaka Building, Imperial College, South Kensington Campus, London, SW7 2AZ, England (office). *Telephone:* (20) 7594-2516 (office). *E-mail:* d.begg@imperial.ac.uk (office). *Website:* www.imperial.ac.uk/people/d.begg (office).

BEGGS, Jean Duthie, CBE, PhD, FRS, FRSE; British molecular biologist and academic; *Professor of Molecular Biology, University of Edinburgh;* b. 16 April 1950, Glasgow, Scotland; d. of William Renfrew Lancaster and Jean Crawford Lancaster (née Duthie); m. Ian Beggs 1972; two s.; ed Univ. of Glasgow; Postdoctoral Fellow, Dept of Molecular Biology, Univ. of Edinburgh 1974–77; Plant Breeding Inst., Cambridge 1977–79; Beit Memorial Fellow for Medical Research 1976–79; Lecturer in Biochemistry, Imperial Coll., London 1979–85; Univ. Research Fellow, Dept of Molecular Biology, Univ. of Edinburgh 1985–89, Professorial Research Fellow 1994–99, Prof. of Molecular Biology 1999–, Royal Soc. Darwin Trust Research Prof. 2005–16; Vice-Pres. Royal Soc. of Edinburgh 2009–12; Hon. DSc (St Andrews); Chancellor's Award, Univ. of Edinburgh, Royal Soc. Gabor Medal 2003, UK Biochemical Soc. Novartis Medal 2004, RNA Soc. Lifetime Achievement Award 2018. *Leisure interests:* walking, dogs, scuba diving. *Address:* Wellcome Centre for Cell Biology, University of Edinburgh, King's Buildings, Mayfield Road, Edinburgh, EH9 3BF, Scotland (office). *Telephone:* (131) 650-5351 (office). *E-mail:* j.beggs@ed.ac.uk (office). *Website:* www.wcb.ed.ac.uk/beggs (office); beggs.bio.ed.ac.uk (office).

BEGICH, Mark Peter; American politician; b. 30 March 1962, Anchorage, Alaska; s. of Nick Begich and Margaret Jean (Pegge) Begich (née Jendro); m. Deborah Bonito 1990; one s.; ed Steller Secondary School; mem. Anchorage Ass. 1988–98, Chair. 1996–98; Mayor of Anchorage 2003–09; Senator from Alaska 2009–15, Chair. Commerce Cttee's Subcommittee on Oceans, Atmosphere, Fisheries and Coast Guard, Senate Democratic Steering and Outreach Cttee 2011–15; Owner, Carson Hot Springs Resort, Carson City, Nev., also owner of vending machine and property rental cos in Anchorage; mem. Bd of Dirs Boys and Girls Club, Spirit of Youth Foundation, Family Resource Center; mem. Air Force Asscn, Nat. Rifle Asscn; fmr Chair. Alaska Student Loan Corpn; f. Making a Difference Program for first time juvenile offenders; Democrat; named Friend of Educ. by Anchorage Educ. Asscn, voted Alaska's top state official by municipal officials 1997, 2004. *Leisure interests:* spending time with family, reading, travelling. *Address:* c/o 111 Russell Senate Office Building, Washington, DC 20510, USA.

BEGLEY, Charlene T., BS; American business executive; m.; three d.; ed Univ. of Vermont; began her career at General Electric (GE) 1988, held a variety of leadership roles including Vice-Pres. Operations, GE Capital Mortgage Services, Quality Leader, GE Transportation Systems 1995, Chief Financial Officer 1997, Dir of Finance, GE Plastics-Europe 1998–99, Vice-Pres. Corp. Audit Staff 1999, Pres. and CEO GE Fanuc Automation North America, Inc. 2001–03, Pres. and CEO Transportation Systems (fmrly known as GE Transportation Rail) of GEFS (Suisse) AG (div. of General Electric Co.) 2003–05, Pres. and CEO SABIC Innovative Plastics (fmrly GE Plastics Inc.) of General Electric Co. 2005–07 (first woman Sr Vice-Pres. in GE history), Pres. and CEO GE Enterprise Solutions 2007–10, Pres. and CEO GE Home & Business Solutions 2010–13, also Sr Vice-Pres. and Chief Information Officer, GE; spent a year as Acting CEO Casablanca Fan Co.; mem. Bd of Dirs, Nat. Asscn of Mfrs, WPP plc 2013–17; serves on World Econ. Forum's Young Global Leaders, Business Advisory Council of Univ. of Vermont.

BEGLITIS, Panagiotis (Panos); Greek diplomatist and politician; b. 1957, Velo, Corinthia; m. Maria Gargali; one s. one d.; ed Nat. Kapodistrian Univ. of Athens, Univ. of Paris (Sorbonne), France; joined diplomatic service 1987, with Hellenic Perm. Del. to EU, Brussels 1992–96, Dir of Information Service and Spokesman, Ministry of Foreign Affairs 1999–2004; MEP (Panhellenic Socialist Movt, PASOK) 2004–07, Vice-Chair., Del. to EU–Turkey Jt Parl. Cttee, mem. European Parl. Foreign Affairs Cttee, Euro-Mediterranean Parl. Ass.; mem. Vouli (Parl.) for Corinthia 2007–; Alt. Minister of Nat. Defence 2009–11, Minister of Nat. Defence 2011. *Address:* Politburo Of Corinth, Cyprus 82, mezzanine, 20100, Corinth, Greece (office). *E-mail:* panos.beglitis@gmail.com. *Website:* www.beglitis.gr.

BEGLOV, Alexander Dmitryevich; Russian politician; *Acting Governor of Saint Petersburg;* b. 19 May 1956, Baku; m. Natalia Beglova; three d.; ed St Petersburg State Univ. of Architecture and Civil Engineering, North-West Acad. of Public Admin; worked in engineering and man. positions 1979–85; Head of Dept of Construction and Building Materials, Lensovet Exec. Cttee 1985–88; Head of Social and Econ. Dept of the Leningrad Regional Cttee 1989–90; Deputy Head of Capital Construction Dept of Exec. Cttee of Leningrad Council 1990–91; Chief Engineer and Co-owner, Melazel 1991–97; Sr Researcher, Dept of Theoretical Mechanics, St Petersburg State Univ. of Architecture and Civil Engineering 1997–99; Head of Admin, K Kurortny Administrative District of St Petersburg 1999–2002; Vice-Gov. of St Petersburg, Acting Gov. 2018–; mem., United Russia Party 2003–, Sec., political council of the St Petersburg Branch 2003–04; Deputy Head of Presidential Admin 2008–12; Chair., Bd of Dirs Almaz-Antey 2008; Hon. Citizen of Sestroretsk 2010; Order For Merit For The Fatherland 2006, Order of St Prince Daniel of Moscow, (First Degree) 2011. *Address:* Office of the Governor, 191060 St Petersburg, Smolnyi Russian Federation (office). *Telephone:* (812) 576-45-01 (office). *Fax:* (812) 576-78-27 (office). *E-mail:* gubernator@gov.spb.ru (office). *Website:* gov.spb.ru (office).

BEHBEHANI, Kazem, PhD, FRCPath, OBE; Kuwaiti international organization official; ed Univs of Liverpool and London, UK; fmr Deputy Dir-Gen. Kuwait Inst. for Scientific Research; Prof. Kuwait Medical Faculty; Vice-Rector for Research, Kuwait Univ.; Programme Man., Special Programme for Research and Training, Tropical Diseases, WHO 1991–94, Dir of Tropical Diseases 1994–99, Dir Eastern Mediterranean Liaison Office and in charge of Resource Mobilization for the Eastern Mediterranean Region 1999–2003, Asst Dir-Gen. WHO 2003–05, then Envoy; Dir-Gen. Dasman Diabetes Inst., Kuwait 2009–16, now Chair. Bd of Trustees; Visiting Prof./Scholar, Harvard Medical School, USA, currently Co-Chair. Scientific Advisory Bd for the Environment and Public Health; mem. British Soc. of Parasitology, American Soc. for Tropical Medicine and Hygiene, Electron Microscopy Soc. of America and European Acad. of Arts, Science and the Humanities; Fellow, Islamic Acad. of Sciences; Award for Research in Medicine, Kuwait Foundation for the Advancement of Sciences. *Publications:* a book on science and tech. and more than 100 scientific papers. *Address:* Dasman Diabetes Institute, PO Box 1180, Dasman 15462, Kuwait (office). *Website:* www.dasmaninstitute.org; www.kazembehbehani.com.

BEHNISCH, Stefan, Dipl.Ing; German architect; *Principal Partner, Behnisch Architekten;* b. 1 June 1957, Stuttgart; s. of Günter Behnisch; m. Petra Behnisch; two s.; with Behnisch & Pnr 1987–; f. Buero Innenstadt 1989, Prin. 1990–, co. became ind. 1991, later renamed Behnisch Architekten; teaches at various univs; also Visiting Prof. at several American univs and External Examiner at several European univs; frequent lecturer at architectural symposia in Germany and abroad; Hon. FAIA 2008; awards include several RIBA awards, Architectural Record/Business Week Awards, Trophée Sommet de la terre et bâtiment (France) 2002, Environmental Champion Award (USA) 2004, Global Award for Sustainable Architecture 2007, Chicago Athenaeum Good Design Award (People Category) 2009. *Projects include:* numerous residential buildings in Germany, USA and several other countries, as well as office buildings, museums, laboratories, healthcare buildings, etc including Swimming Pool Complex Grünauer Welle, Leipzig, Oceaneum–German Oceanographic Museum, Stralsund, WIPO HQ, Geneva, Marco Polo Tower, Hamburg, Genzyme Center, Cambridge, Mass 2004, Harvard Univ. Allston Science Complex, Allston/Boston 2010, Brooklyn Arts Tower 2010, John and Frances Angelos Law Center, Univ. of Baltimore (Green Good Design Award 2014) 2013, office building for Comune di Ravenna, Italy, Riverparc City District, Pittsburgh, Pa 2014–16. *Address:* Behnisch Architekten, Rotebühlstraße 163, 70197 Stuttgart (office); Blumenstraße 17, 80331, Munich, Germany (office); 125 Kingston Street, Boston, MA 02111, USA (office). *Telephone:* (711) 607720 (Stuttgart) (office); (89) 85630980 (Munich) (office); (617) 375-9380 (Boston) (office). *Fax:* (711) 6077299 (Stuttgart) (office); (617) 348-2114 (Boston) (office). *E-mail:* buero@behnisch.com (office); bamuc@behnisch.com (office); bueroboston@behnisch.com (office). *Website:* www.behnisch.com (office).

BEHRMAN, Richard Elliot, MD, JD; American professor of pediatrics and consultant; *Executive Director, Non-Profit Healthcare and Educational Consultants to Medical Institutions;* b. 13 Dec. 1931, Philadelphia, Pa; s. of Robert Behrman and Vivian Keegan; m. Ann Nelson 1954; one s. three d.; ed Amherst Coll., Harvard Univ., Univ. of Rochester and Johns Hopkins Univ.; Oregon Regional Primate Research Center and Univ. of Oregon Medical School 1965–68; Prof. of Pediatrics and Dir Neonatal Intensive Care Unit and Nurseries, Univ. of Illinois Coll. of Medicine 1968–71; Prof. and Chair. Dept of Pediatrics and Dir Babies Hosp., Columbia Univ. Coll. of Physicians and Surgeons 1971–76; Prof. and Chair. Dept of Pediatrics and Dir Dept of Pediatrics, Rainbow Babies and Children's Hosp., Case Western Reserve Univ. School of Medicine 1976–82, Dean, School of Medicine 1980–89, Vice-Pres. Medical Affairs 1987–89; Dir Center for Future of Children, David and Lucile Packard Foundation 1989–99; Clinical Prof. of Pediatrics, Stanford Univ. and Univ. of California, San Francisco (UCSF) 1989; Chair. Lucile Packard Foundation for Children 1997–99, Sr Vice-Pres. Medical Affairs 1999–2002; Exec. Chair. Fed. of Pediatric Orgs 2002; currently Exec. Dir Non-Profit Healthcare and Educational Consultants to Medical Insts, Santa Barbara, Calif.; Ed.-in-Chief Nelson Textbook of Pediatrics 1980–2006; mem. Bd of Dirs, UCSF Stanford Health Care 1997, Children's Hospices and Palliative Care Coalition, Teddy Bear Cancer Foundation 2007–; mem. Inst. Medicine, NAS; mem. Medical Advisory Bd iMetrikus, Inc.; Fellow, American Acad. of Pediatrics; Hon.

DSc (Medical Coll., Wis.) 2000. *Publications:* The Future of Children (ed.) 1990–, Essentials of Paediatrics (ed.) 2002, Nelson Textbook of Paediatrics (ed.) 2003. *Leisure interests:* running, hiking, reading. *Address:* Non-Profit Healthcare and Educational Consultants to Medical Institutions, PO Box 4446, Santa Barbara, CA 93140, USA. *Telephone:* (805) 729-1266 (mobile).

BEHURIA, Sarthak, BA, MBA; Indian oil industry executive; *President and Chairman, Corporate Executive Committee, K. K. Modi Group;* b. 2 March 1952, Chatrapur, Orissa; s. of Nrusingha Behuria and Suvarnalata Behuria; one s. one d.; ed St Stephen's Coll., Delhi, Indian Inst. of Man., Ahmedabad; trainee with Burmah-Shell (later renamed Bharat Petroleum Corpn Ltd) 1973, held various positions including Dir of Operations, Oil Co-ordination Cttee, Exec. Dir of Sales 1995–98, Dir of Marketing 1998–2002, Chair. and Man. Dir 2002–05; Chair. Indian Oil Corpn (IOC) Ltd 2005–10, also fmr Chair. (part-time) group cos Chennai Petroleum Corpn Ltd, Bongaigaon Refinery & Petrochemicals Ltd; fmr Head of Indian Oiltanking Ltd (jt venture); Chair. Petroleum Fed. of India (PetroFed) 2003, currently Hon. Chair.; Chair. Lanka IOC Ltd –2007; Pres. and Chair. Corporate Exec. Cttee, K.K. Modi Group 2011–; Chair. Standing Conf. of Public Enterprises (SCOPE) 2006–, Council of Indian Employers, Governing Council at Petroleum Fed. of India; First Vice-Pres. (representing Asia) World LPGas Asscn 2006–08, Pres. 2008–; mem. Bd of Dirs SPML Ltd 2010–, SKIL Infrastructure Ltd 2010–11, IBP Co Ltd 2005–, LimitedInfraGandhar Oil Refinery (India) Ltd 2012–, Petronet India Ltd, RSB Transmissions (I) Ltd, Larsen and Toubro Hydrocarbon Engineering Ltd, GSPC LNG Ltd, Adani Petroleum Terminal Pvt. Ltd, Dhamra LNG Terminal Pvt. Ltd, Adani Dhamra LPG Terminal Pvt. Ltd, Mundra LPG Terminal Pvt. Ltd, PC Jeweller Ltd, Bharat Oman Refineries Ltd, Kochi Refineries Ltd; Dir (non-Exec.) Adani Ports and Special Economic Zone Ltd 2015–16; Hon. Fellow, Energy Inst. (UK); named by Upstream journal amongst the 10 Most Influential Oilmen in India, Udyog Ratna Award, Progress, Harmony and Devt Chamber of Commerce and Industry 2006, SCOPE Award for Excellence and Outstanding Contrib. to Public Sector Man. (Individual Category) 2006–07, Odisha Living Legend Award 2013. *Address:* K. K. Modi Group, 49, Community Centre, Friends Colony, New Delhi 110 025, India. *Telephone:* (11) 26832155 (home). *Fax:* (11) 26840775 (home). *E-mail:* info@modi.com. *Website:* www.modi.com.

BEHZAD, Mohamed Ben Yousef, BBA, MS (Econ); Qatari economist and international organization executive; b. 30 June 1954, Doha; ed Cairo Univ., Egypt, California State Polytechnic Univ., Pomona, USA; Econs Researcher, Econs Dept, Qatar Petroleum 1979–88, Economist and Planning Engineer, Tech. Dept 1988–89, Planning Dept 1989–91; Planning Economist, Industrial Studies Dept, Gulf Org. for Industrial Consulting, Qatar 1992–93; Sr Economist and Head of Econ. Planning Dept, Supreme Council for Planning Doha Jan.–Oct. 1994; Financial Economist, OPEC, Vienna, Austria 1998–2006; Dir-Gen. Arab Industrial Devt and Mining Org. 2006–14.

BEILHARZ, Manfred; German director and producer; b. 13 July 1938, Böblingen; ed Univ. of Tübingen, Univ. of Munich, Paris, London; f. Studiobühne, Munich; Asst Dir Münchner Kammerspiele; Dir and head of literary dept, Westfälisches Landestheater 1968; Artistic Dir, Tübingen Landestheater 1970–75, City Theatre of Freiburg 1976–83, City Theatre of Kassel 1983–91, Schauspiel, Bonn 1991–92; Genralintendant, Municipal Theatre of Bonn 1997–2002; Dir Hessisches Staatstheater Wiesbaden 2002–14, now Hon. Mem.; mem. Acad. of Performing Arts, Frankfurt, European Theatre Convention, Brussels and Paris; Vice-Pres. Hessischen Theaterakademie, Frankfurt; Pres. Int. Theatre Inst. 2002–08; Chair. Dramaturgische Gesellschaft, Berlin –2007; Federal Cross of Merit 2007. *Plays and opera directed:* Marat Sade, The Mother, Threepenny Opera, Rise and Fall of the City of Mahagonny, A Romantic Woman, A Midsummer Night's Dream, Fidelio, The Hot Oven, L'enfant et les sortilèges, Love of Three Oranges, Falstaff, Spring Awakening, Schauspiel Bonn 1997, Wozzeck, Opera Bonn, Der Zerbrochne Krug. *Address:* c/o Hessisches Staatstheater Wiesbaden, Christian-Zais-Str. 3, 65189 Wiesbaden, Germany.

BEILIN, Yossi, PhD; Israeli politician; b. 1948, Israel; m.; two c.; ed Tel-Aviv Univ.; fmr journalist and mem. Editorial Bd of Davar; Spokesman for Labour Party 1977–84; Cabinet Sec. 1984–86; Dir-Gen. for Political Affairs of Foreign Ministry 1986–88; mem. Knesset 1988–99, 2004–08, mem. Foreign Affairs and Defence, Immigration and Absorption and Constitution, Law and Justice Cttees 1990–92, Foreign Affairs and Defence, Constitution, Law and Justice, Advancement of the Status of Women Cttees 1996–99; Deputy Minister of Finance 1988–90; Deputy Minister of Foreign Affairs 1992–95; Minister of Econs and Planning July–Nov. 1995; Minister without Portfolio 1995–96; Minister of Justice 1999–2001; Minister of Religious Affairs 2000–01; Founder and Leader Meretz-Yahad (Social Democratic) Party 2002–04, Chair. 2004–08; founded 'Beilink', a business consultancy company; Chevalier, Légion d'honneur 2009; Dr hc (Univ. of Paris 13); Int. Activist Award, The Gleitsman Foundation 1999, Seligmann Prize 2004. *Publications:* Sons in the Shadow of their Fathers, The Price of Unity, Industry in Israel, Touching Peace, His Brother's Keeper, Israel, A Concise Political History, Touching Peace 1997, The Manual for Leaving Lebanon 1998, From Socialism to Social Liberalism 1999, His Brother's Keeper 2000, Manual for a Wounded Dove 2001, The Path to Geneva: The Quest for a Permanent Agreement. *Telephone:* (2) 747786 (office). *E-mail:* beilin@myparty.org.il (office); beilin@beilink.com.

BEILINSON, Alexander (Sasha), PhD; Russian mathematician; *David and Mary Winton Green University Professor, University of Chicago;* b. 13 June 1957, Moscow; s. of Alexander Alekseevich Beilinson; ed Moscow State Univ.; Scientist, Landau Inst. for Theoretical Physics, Chernogolovka 1989–98; Visiting Lecturer, MIT (fall semesters) 1989–98; Lecturer, Inst. for Advanced Study, Princeton, New Jersey 1994, 1996–98; David and Mary Winton Green Univ. Prof., Dept of Math., Univ. of Chicago 1998–; mem. American Acad. of Arts and Sciences 2008, NAS 2017; Foreign mem. Academia Europaea 2000; Ostrowski Prize (jt recipient) 1999, Wolf Prize in Math. 2018. *Address:* Department of Mathematics, University of Chicago, 5734 S University Ave, Chicago, IL 60637, USA (office). *Telephone:* (773) 702-7100 (office). *E-mail:* sasha@math.uchicago.edu (office). *Website:* math.uchicago.edu (office).

BEINEIX, Jean-Jacques; French film director and producer; b. 8 Oct. 1946, Paris; several films as Asst Dir 1970–77; Founder Cargo Films; a main exponent of the style known as 'cinéma du look' of the 1980s; numerous prizes and awards at film festivals. *Films include:* Le chien de Monsieur Michel (Mr. Michel's Dog) (short) 1977, Diva 1981, La lune dans le caniveau (The Moon in the Gutter) 1983, 37.2° le matin (Betty Blue) 1986, Roselyne and the Lions 1989, IP5: L'île aux pachydermes 1992, Otaku (documentary) 1994, Mortal Transfer 2001, 2 infinities (L2i) (corp. CNRS film) 2008. *Television includes:* Locked-in Syndrome (short documentary) 1997, Loft Paradoxe (film documentary) 2002, Le mystère des momies coptes d'Antinoé (documentary) (producer) 2012, Les Gaulois au-delà du mythe (film documentary) (also producer) 2013. *Publications:* Diva 1991, L'île aux pachydermes 1992, Les Chantiers de la gloire (autobiog.) 2006. *Address:* Cargo Films, 12–16 Villa Saint-Michel, 75018 Paris, France (office). *Telephone:* 1-53-34-13-80 (office). *Fax:* 1-53-34-13-81 (office). *E-mail:* cargo@cargofilms.com (office). *Website:* www.cargofilms.com (office).

BEIT-ARIÉ, Malachi, MA, MLS, PhD; Israeli palaeographer and codicologist; *Ludwig Jesselson Professor Emeritus of Codicology and Palaeography, Hebrew University of Jerusalem;* b. 20 May 1937, Petah-Tiqva; s. of Meir Beit-Arié and Esther Beit-Arié (née Elpiner); one s. two d.; ed Hebrew Univ., Jerusalem; Dir Hebrew Palaeography Project, Israel Acad. of Sciences and Humanities 1965, Inst. of Microfilmed Hebrew Manuscripts 1970–78; Sr Lecturer in Codicology and Palaeography, Hebrew Univ. of Jerusalem 1975–78, Assoc. Prof. 1979–83, Prof. 1984, then Ludwig Jesselson Professor of Codicology and Palaeography, Prof. Emer. 2005–; Dir Nat. and Univ. Library 1979–90; Chair. Int. Advisory Council Jewish Nat. Library 1991; Founding Doctor, Academia Ambrosiana, Milano 2009; mem. Israel Acad. of Sciences and Humanities 2003, Steering Cttee and Codicology Team, European Science Foundation's Comparative Oriental Manuscripts Study 2010–14; Visiting Researcher, IRHT (CNRS) Paris 1991; Visiting Scholar, Harvard Univ. 1992; Visiting Fellow, Wolfson Coll., Oxford 1984–85; Fellow, Center for Advanced Judaic Studies, Univ. of Pennsylvania 1996, 1999–2000, 2006; Visiting Research Fellow, Christ Church, Oxford 2003; Visiting Fellow, Oxford Centre for Hebrew and Jewish Studies 2007–11; Hon. Fellow of Oxford Centre for Hebrew and Jewish Studies 2012; Dr hc (Bologna Univ.) 2002; Anne Frank Award for poetry 1961, Landau Prize for Scientific Research. *Publications include:* These Streets, Those Mountains (lyrics) 1963, The Hills of Jerusalem and All the Pain (poems) 1967, Manuscrits médiévaux en caractères hébraiques (with C. Sirat), Parts I–III 1972–86, Hebrew Codicology 1977, The Only Dated Medieval MS Written in England 1985, Medieval Specimens of Hebrew Scripts 1987–2015, The Makings of the Medieval Hebrew Book 1993, Hebrew Manuscripts of East and West: Towards Comparative Codicology 1993, Catalogue of the Hebrew MSS in the Bodleian Library (Supplement) 1994, Codices hebraicis litteris exarati quo tempore scripti fuerint exhibentes I–IV (with C. Sirat and M. Glalzer) 1997–99, Hebrew Manuscripts in the Biblioteca Palatina in Parma (with B. Richler) 2001, Hebrew Codicology: Historical and Comparative Typology of Hebrew Medieval Codices Based on the Documentation of the Extant Dated Manuscripts in Quantitative Approach 2014. *Leisure interest:* classical music. *Address:* The Hebrew University, Mt Scopus, Jerusalem 91905 (office); PO Box 34165, Jerusalem 91341 (office); 11C Alkalai Street, Jerusalem 92223, Israel (home). *Telephone:* 2-5619270 (office); 2-5633940 (home). *E-mail:* beitarie@vms.huji.ac.il (office). *Website:* www.huji.ac.il (office).

BEJO, Bérénice; Argentine/French actress; b. 7 July 1976, Buenos Aires, Argentina; d. of Miguel Bejo and Silvia Bejo; m. Michel Hazanavicius; two c.; moved from Argentina to France aged three; est. film and TV career in France mid-1990s; US film debut 2001. *Plays:* L'Opéra de Quat' Sous 1999, Tout Ce Que Vous Voulez 2016 Trois Sacres 2017. *Films include:* Les soeurs Hamlet 1996, Meilleur espoir feminin 2000, Passionnément 2000 A Knight's Tale 2001, 24 Hours in the Life of a Woman 2002, Like an Airplane 2002, Sem Ela 2003, The Great Role 2003, Cavalcade 2005, OSS 117: Cairo, Nest of Spies 2006, 13 m^2 2007, The House 2007, Modern Love 2008, Bouquet final 2008, L'Enfer d'Henri-Georges Clouzot 2009, Prey (La Traque) 2010, The Artist (César Award for Best Actress 2011, Capri Actress Award 2011, Hollywood Film Festival Spotlight Award 2011, Best Actress Lumiere Award 2011, Romy Schneider Award 2012, Best Supporting Actress Award, Phoenix Film Critics Soc. 2012, Best Supporting Actress Award, St Louis Gateway Film Critics Asscn 2012) 2011, Brave (voice) 2012, Populaire 2012, The Scapegoat (Au Bonheur des Ogres) 2013, Le Passé (Award for Best Actress, Cannes Film Festival 2013) 2013, The Last Diamond 2014, The Search 2014, L'Enfance d'un chef 2015, Eternity 2015, Fais De Beaux Rves 2015, L'Economie Du Couple 2015, Three Peaks 2016, Tout La Haut 2016, Le Redoutable 2016, The Extraordinary Journey Of The Fakir 2017, Le Jeu 2017. *Television includes:* Le juge est une femme 1997, Un et un font six 1997–99, Alliés 1998, La Famille Sapajou (film) 1999, Sauvetage 2000, Koan 2001 Dissonnances 2002, Nuages (film) 2006, Sa raison d'être (film) 2008, Frères d'armes 2014–15. *Address:* c/o Adéquat Talent Agency, 108 rue Réaumur, 75002 Paris (office); c/o MIAM Communication Agency, 39 rue de Rome, 75008 Paris, France (office). *Telephone:* 1-42-80-00-42 (office). *Fax:* 1-42-80-00-43 (office). *E-mail:* agence@agence-adequat.com (office); n.iund@miamcom.com (office). *Website:* www.agence-adequat.com (office); www.miamcom.com/berenicebejo (office).

BEKELE, Kenenisa; Ethiopian athlete; b. 13 June 1982, Bekoji; ran first competitive race aged 15; set world jr record for 3,000m 2001; won long and short races at World Cross Country Championships 2002, became first to repeat in consecutive years 2003, won both events again 2004; primarily competes in 5,000m and 10,000m events; won Golden League 5,000m in Oslo 2003; gold medal 10,000m, bronze medal 10,000m World Championships 2003; gold medal 10,000m, silver medal 5,000m Olympic Games, Athens 2004; gold medal 10,000m, gold medal 5,000m Olympic Games, Beijing 2008; gold medal 10,000m World Championships 2009; holds world records at 5,000m (set in Hengelo, Netherlands 2004) and 10,000m (set in Ostrava, Czech Repub. 2004); winner Berlin marathon (in 2:03:03, world second fastest to date) 2016; Goodwill Amb. for UNICEF 2004; Int. Asscn of Athletics Feds World Athlete of the Year 2004. *Address:* PO Box 3241, Addis Ababa, Ethiopia. *Website:* www.ethiosports.com.

BEKKER, Koos, LLB, MBA; South African business executive; *Chairman, Naspers Ltd;* b. 14 Dec. 1952, Potchefstroom; m. Karen Roos; two c.; ed Stellenbosch Univ., Univ. of Witwatersrand, Columbia Univ., USA; CEO M-Net

Ltd 1985–90; CEO Myriad International Holdings (MIH) Group, Netherlands 1991–97, mem. Bd of Dirs 1998–; Founder-Dir MTN Group Ltd 1992–98; Group CEO 1997–2014, Man. Dir 2008–, Chair. Naspers Ltd 2015–; Commr Global Information Infrastructure Comm. 1990–97; Dir Local Organising Cttee 2010 FIFA World Cup 2004–10; Dir OpenTV Corp.; mem. Bd of Dirs MultiChoice Africa (Pty) Ltd 1984–, NetHold 1995–97, Media24 1997–, Tencent Holdings Ltd 2012–, MIH B.V., MIH (Mauritius) Ltd, MultiChoice South Africa Holdings, Nasboek, SuperSport International; Dr hc (Univ. of Stellenbosch); Best Entrepreneur (South Africa) Award, Ernst & Young 2006, Lifetime Achievement Award, Business Times. *Address:* Naspers Ltd, 40 Heerengracht, Cape Town 8001, South Africa (office). *Telephone:* (21) 4062121 (office). *Website:* www.naspers.com (office).

BEKRI, Tahar, PhD; Tunisian poet; *Lecturer, University of Paris X-Nanterre;* b. 7 July 1951, Gabès; m. Annick Le Thoër 1987; ed Univ. of Tunisia, Univ. of Paris (Sorbonne), France; Lecturer, Univ. of Paris X-Nanterre; mem. Soc. des Gens de Lettres de France, Maison des Ecrivains; Officier, Mérite Culturel, Tunisia 1993; Prix Tunisie-France 2006. *Recordings:* album: Si la musique doit mourir 2011. *Publications include:* Poèmes bilingues 1978, Exils 1979, Le laboureur du soleil 1983, Les lignes sont des arbres 1984, Le chant du roi errant 1985, Malek Haddad 1986, Le coeur rompu aux océans 1988, Poèmes à Selma 1989, La sève des jours 1991, Les chapelets d'attache 1993, Littératures de Tunisie et du Maghreb 1994, Les songes impatients 1997, Journal de neige et de feu 1997, Le pêcheur de lunes 1998, Inconnues saisons (translated as Unknown Seasons) 1999, De la littérature tunisienne et maghrébine 1999, Marcher sur l'oubli 2000, L'horizon incendié 2002, La brûlante rumeur de la mer 2004, Le vent sans abri 2005, Dernières nouvelles de l'été 2005, Si la musique doit mourir 2006, Le livre du souvenir 2007, Les Dits du fleuve 2009, Salam Gaza 2010, Je te nomme Tunisie 2011, Au souvenir de Yunus Emre 2012, Poésie de Palestine 2013, La nostalgie des rosiers sauvages 2014; contrib. to various publs. *Address:* 32 rue Pierre Nicole, 75005 Paris, France (home). *Telephone:* 1-43-29-33-39 (home). *Fax:* 1-43-29-33-39 (home); 1-40-97-71-51 (office). *E-mail:* taharbekri@wanadoo.fr (home); tahar.bekri@u_paris10.fr (office). *Website:* tahar.bekri.free.fr.

BEL, Jean-Pierre, MA; French lawyer and fmr politician; b. 30 Dec. 1951, Lavaur (Tarn); m. 1st 1985 (divorced 2001); two d.; m. 2nd 2009; one d.; ed Lycée Berthelot and Univ. of Social Sciences, Toulouse (diplôme d'études approfondies de droit public); head of a resort at Font-Romeu and dir of a tourist office 1977–82; active in Ligue communiste révolutionnaire until 1978, then moved to Mijanès; Mayor of Mijanès 1983–95; joined the Parti Socialiste 1983; Regional Councillor, Midi-Pyrenees 1992; technical adviser to Minister of Relations with Parl. 1997–98; elected to Gen. Council of Ariège in neighbouring canton of Lavelanet 1998–2001; Mayor of Lavelanet 2001–08; elected Senator (Parti Socialiste) from Ariège (Midi-Pyrénées) 1998–2014, Sec. of the Senate 2001–04, Pres. of Socialist Group in Senate 2004–11, Socialist cand. for post of Pres. of the Senate 2008, Pres. of the Senate (first Socialist) 2011–14, Chair. France-Spain Group; mem. Conseil nat. de la montagne 1998–2001; joined Nat. Council of Parti Socialiste 1993, served in nat. office –2003, Nat. Sec. of Fed. 1994–97, Nat. Sec. of Elections –1998, Nat. Sec. to First Sec. 1997–2007; Chair. Asscn of Mayors and Elected Officials of Ariège 2001; mem. Office of the Asscn of Mayors of France 2001–06; Chevalier, Légion d'honneur 2015. *Address:* c/o Sénat, Palais du Luxembourg, 75291 Paris Cedex 06, France. *E-mail:* anciens-senateurs@senat.fr; bel1.jean-pierre@wanadoo.fr (office).

BELAFONTE, Harry; American singer, composer and actor; b. (Harold George Belafonte Jr.), 1 March 1927, New York; s. of Harold George Belafonte Sr and Malvene Love Wright; m. 1st Marguerite Byrd 1948 (divorced); two c.; m. 2nd Julie Robinson 1957 (divorced); one s. three d.; m. 3rd Pamela Frank; ed George Washington High School, New York; in Jamaica 1935–39; service with US Navy 1943–45; student, American Negro Theater, then at Manhattan New School for Social Research Dramatic Workshop 1946–48; first engagement at the Vanguard, Greenwich Village; European tours 1958, 1976, 1981, 1983, 1988; Pres. Belafonte Enterprises Inc.; Goodwill Amb. for UNICEF 1987; Host of Nelson Mandela Birthday Concert, Wembley, UK 1988; concerts in USA, Europe 1989, Canada 1990, USA and Canada 1991, N America, Europe and Far East 1996; mem. Bd New York State Martin Luther King Jr Inst. for Nonviolence 1989–; mem. Bd of Trustees, Inst. for Policy Studies; Hon. DHumLitt (Park Coll., Mo.) 1968, Hon. Dr Arts, New School of Social Research, New York 1968, Hon. DCL (Newcastle) 1997, numerous other hon. doctorates; Grammy Award 1985, Kennedy Center Honors 1989, Golden Acord Award, Bronx Community Coll. 1989, Mandela Courage Award 1990, Nat. Medal of the Arts 1994, New York Arts and Business Council Award 1997, Award of Excellence, Ronald McDonald House Charities 2000, Grammy Lifetime Achievement Award 2000, Distinguished American Award, John F. Kennedy Library, Boston 2002, BET Humanitarian Award 2006, Andrew Goodman Foundation Lifetime Achievement Award 2011, Humanitarian Oscar 2014. *Achievements include:* RCA album Calypso made him the first artist in industry history to sell over one million LPs. *Recordings include:* Calypso 1956, An Evening with Belafonte 1957, Belafonte at Carnegie Hall 1959, Belafonte Returns to Carnegie Hall 1960, Jump Up Calypso 1961, To Wish You a Merry Christmas 1962, The Midnight Special 1962, The Many Moods of Belafonte 1962, An Evening with Belafonte/Mouskouri 1966, Belafonte and Miriam Makeba 2003. *Films include:* Bright Road 1953, Carmen Jones 1954, Island in the Sun 1957, The World, the Flesh and the Devil 1959, Odds Against Tomorrow 1959, The Angel Levine 1970, Buck and the Preacher 1972, Uptown Saturday Night 1974, White Man's Burden 1995, Kansas City 1996, Bobby 2006, Motherland 2009, Sing Your Song 2011. *Publication:* My Song: A Memoir 2011. *Leisure interests:* photography, water skiing, recording. *Address:* c/o The Agency Group Ltd, 1880 Century Park East, Suite 711, Los Angeles, CA 90067, USA. *Telephone:* (310) 385-2800. *Fax:* (310) 385-1220. *Website:* www.theagencygroup.com.

BÉLAÏZ, Tayeb, LenD; Algerian politician and fmr judge; *President, Conseil Constitutionnel;* b. 21 Aug. 1948, Maghnia; ed Univ. of Oran; early positions at Ministry of the Interior; fmr judge and Pres. of the Chamber, Court of Oran, also fmr Pres. Court of Saida, Court of Sidi-Bel-Abbès and adviser to Supreme Court Judge; Minister of Labour and Social Security 2002–03, Minister of Justice and Attorney-Gen. 2003–12, Minister of State and Minister of the Interior 2013–15; Pres. Conseil Constitutionnel 2019–; mem. Nat. Comm. for Judicial Reform 1999. *Address:* Conseil Constitutionnel, Blvd du 11 Décembre 1960, El-Biar, Algiers, Algeria (office). *Telephone:* (21) 92-27-70 (office). *Fax:* (23) 25-38-13 (office). *E-mail:* info@conseil-constitutionnel.dz (office). *Website:* www.conseil-constitutionnel.dz (office).

BÉLANGER, Gérard, MA, MSocSc, RSC; Canadian economist and academic; b. 23 Oct. 1940, St Hyacinthe, Quebec; s. of Georges Bélanger and Cécile Girard; one d.; ed Princeton Univ., USA, Université Laval; Prof., Dept of Econs, Université Laval 1967–2016; Research Co-ordinator, Howe Inst., Montreal 1977–79; mem. Task Force on Urbanization, Govt of Québec 1974–76; Sec. Acad. of Letters and Social Sciences, RSC 1985–88; Woodrow Wilson Fellow; Doug Purvis Memorial Prize 2008. *Publications include:* The Price of Health 1972, Le financement municipal au Québec 1976, Taxes and Expenditures in Québec and Ontario 1978, Le prix du transport au Québec 1978, L'économique du secteur public 1981, Croissance du Secteur Public et Fédéralisme 1988, L'Économique de la santé et l'État providence 2005. *Address:* Department of Economics, Pavillon J.-A.-DeSève, local 2256, Université Laval, Québec, PQ G1V 0A6, Canada (office). *Telephone:* (418) 656-5363 (office); (418) 681-3075 (home). *Fax:* (418) 656-2707 (office). *E-mail:* gebe@ecn.ulaval.ca (office); gerard.belanger.2@ulaval.ca (office). *Website:* www.ulaval.ca/Al/bienvenueanglais.html (office).

BÉLAVAL, Philippe Marie, LLM; French public servant; *President, Centre des monuments nationaux;* b. 21 Aug. 1955, Toulouse; s. of Jacques Bélaval and Marie-Thérèse Bélaval (née Chazarenc); ed Faculté des Sciences Sociales de Toulouse, Inst. d'études politiques de Toulouse, École nationale d'admin.; mem. Council of State 1979–, with litigation and finance div. 1979–93; Adviser to Sec. of State for Budget and Consumption 1984–86; Chief of Staff to Minister of State in charge of Civil Service and Admin. Reforms 1988–90; Dir-Gen., Théâtre nationale de l'Opéra de Paris 1990–92; Dir-Gen., Bibliothèque nationale de France 1994–98; Dir-Gen., Archives de France 1998–2000; Pres., Cour administrative d'appel, Bordeaux 2001–04, Cour administrative d'appel, Versailles 2004–08; Chair. Nat. Heritage Inst. 2008; Chief of Heritage, Ministry of Culture and Communication 2010–12; Pres., Centre des monuments nationaux 2012–; mem. European Heritage Heads Forum –2012; mem. Admin. Council, École Nat. des Chartes; Sr Lecturer, Inst. d'études politiques de Paris; mem. Bd of Trustees Fondation Napoléon; Chevalier Légion d'honneur, Chevalier Ordre nat. du Mérite, Commdr des Arts et des Lettres. *Address:* Centre des monuments nationaux, 62 Rue Saint-Antoine, 75186 Paris, France (office). *Telephone:* 1-44-61-20-00 (office). *Website:* www.monuments-nationaux.fr (office).

BELCHIOR, Miriam, MA; Brazilian academic and politician; *President, Caixa Econômica Federal;* b. 5 Feb. 1958, Santo André; m. Celso Daniel (deceased); ed Fundação Getúlio Vargas, São Paulo, Universidade Estadual de Campinas; Sec. of Admin and Modernization, municipality of Santo André (São Paulo) 1997–2000, Sec. for Social Inclusion and Housing 2001–02; Prof., Univ. São Marcos 1999–2002; Prof., Foundation for Research and Devt 2001–08; joined transition staff of Pres. Lula da Silva 2002, Special Adviser to Pres. Lula 2003–04; General Co-ordinator, Growth Acceleration Programme 2010; Minister of Planning, Budget and Admin 2011–14; Pres. state-owned bank Caixa Econômica Federal 2015–; mem. Bd, Eletrobras, Petrobras 2011–15; mem. Partido dos Trabalhadores. *Address:* Caixa Econômica Federal, SBS Quadra 4, Lotes 3/4, Ed. Sede, Asa Sul, 21° Andar, Brasília, Brazil (office). *Website:* www.caixa.gov.br (office).

BELDA, Alain J. P., BBA; French business executive; b. 23 June 1943; ed Universidade Mackenzie, Brazil; joined Aluminum Co. of America 1969, Pres. Alcoa Aluminio SA, Brazil 1979–94, Vice-Pres. Alcoa (Latin America) 1982–91, Pres. 1991–94, Exec. Vice-Pres., Alcoa Inc. 1994–95, Vice-Chair. 1995–97, Exec. Dir 1998, Pres. and COO 1997–99, Pres. and CEO 1999–2001, Chair. and CEO 2001–08, Chair. 2008–09; joined Warburg Pincus LLC 2009, fmrly–Man. Dir, currently Special Ltd Partner; Dir Banco Indusval & Partners, International Business Machines, Omega Energia Renovavel SA, Renault SA 2009–; Co-Chair. Brazil Project Advisory Bd at The Woodrow Wilson Int. Center for Scholars; mem. The Business Council, Business Roundtable, Cttee to Encourage Corp. Philanthropy, World Business Council for Sustainable Devt, World Econ. Forum, Int. Business Council; Trustee, Ford Foundation, The Conference Bd, Brown Univ. Corpn. *Address:* Warburg Pincus do Brasil Ltda., Av. Brig. Faria Lima 2277 - 9° andar, Jd.Paulistano, 01451-001 São Paulo SP, Brazil (office). *Telephone:* (11) 3096-3500 (office). *Fax:* (11) 3096-3509 (office). *E-mail:* info@warburgpincus.com (office). *Website:* www.warburgpincus.com (office).

BELEFFI, Damiano; San Marino diplomatist; *Permanent Representative to United Nations;* m.; two d.; ed Univ. of Genoa, Italy; Head Finance Dept, Ministry of Finance and Budget 1998–2001; Deputy Perm. Rep. to Council of Europe, Strasbourg 2001–08; Amb. to Germany 2007–12, Deputy Perm. Rep. to UN 2008, Chargé d'affaires May–Aug. 2016, Perm. Rep. 2016–, also Amb. to USA 2017–. *Address:* Permanent Mission of San Marino, 327 E 50th Street, New York, NY 10022, USA (office). *Telephone:* (212) 751-1234 (office). *Fax:* (212) 751-1436 (office). *E-mail:* sanmarinoun@gmail.com (office).

BELÉN ELGOYHEN, Ana, PhD; Argentine geneticist and academic; *Adjunct Professor, Department of Pharmacology, Faculty of Medicine, University of Buenos Aires;* b. 13 Dec. 1959; Asst Researcher, Inst. of Pharmacological Research, Consejo Nacional de Investigaciones Científicas y Técnicas (CONICET) 1990–96, Research Asst, Inst. for Research on Genetic Engineering and Molecular Biology 1997, Research Assoc. 1998, Ind. Investigator 2003–07, Prin. Investigator 2008–; Adjunct Prof., Dept of Pharmacology, Faculty of Medicine, Univ. of Buenos Aires 2001–; Adjunct Prof., Dept of Otolaryngology-Head and Neck Surgery, Johns Hopkins Univ. School of Medicine 2009–; PEW Fellow 1991–94; John Simon Guggenheim Memorial Foundation Fellow 2003–04; Howard Hughes Medical Inst. Int. Scholar 1997–2001, 2002–06, 2007–11; Vice-Pres. Soc. for Neuroscience Argentina 2011–13; Assoc. Ed. Journal of the Association for Research in Otolaryngology 2012–; Strauss Award in Auditory Science 1995, Penny and Bob Fox Award in Auditory Science 1997, Prize Bernardo Houssay, Argentina Soc. of Biology 2000, Joan and Marc Millar Auditory Award in Science 2003, HF Lenfest in Auditory Science Award 2005, Laureate for Latin America, L'Oréal-UNESCO Awards for Women in Science 2008, TWAS Prize in Biology 2011, KONEX Basic Biomedical Sciences Award 2013. *Publications:* numerous papers in professional journals. *Address:* Av Cordoba 1233, 5th Floor, C1055AAC, Buenos Aires, Argentina (office). *Telephone:* (11) 4816-0500 (office). *Fax:* (11) 4816-0500 (office). *E-mail:* elgoyhen@dna.uba.ar (office). *Website:* www.ingebi-conicet.gov.ar (office).

BELENKOV, Yuri N., DrMed; Russian neurophysiologist and university administrator; *Vice-Rector, Lomonosov Moscow State University;* b. 9 Feb. 1948, Leningrad (now St Petersburg); s. of Nikita Yu. Belenkov and Marina T. Koval; m. Natalia V. Belenkova; one s.; ed Leningrad State Univ.; held several posts at Myasnikov Inst. of Cardiology 1975–91, including Jr Researcher, Sr Researcher, Head of Lab., Deputy Dir, Dir 1991–2008; Head of Fed. Agency for Health and Social Devt 2006–08; currently Vice-Rector, Lomonosov Moscow State Univ.; fmr Chief Cardiologist of Russian Ministry of Public Health; Founder and Pres. Russian Asscn for Heart Failure Research; mem. Presidium, Russian Soc. of Cardiologists, CIS Asscn of Cardiologists; Ed.-in-Chief Kardiologya; mem. Editorial Bd International Journal of Medical Practice, Circulation, European Journal of Heart Failure; Corresp. mem. Russian Acad. of Medical Sciences 1993 (Full mem. 1999), Russian Acad. of Sciences 2000; Hon. mem. Acad. of Medicine of Colombia 1989; Order of Friendship of People 1988, Order of Honour 1998, Order for Service to the Fatherland (third degee); Lenin Komsomol Prize 1978, USSR State Prize 1980, 1989, RF Government Prize 2003. *Achievements include:* first to introduce to USSR echocardiography 1973 and cardiovascular MRI 1983. *Publications include:* more than 600 scientific papers on ultrasonic diagnostics, magnetic resonance tomography and cardiology; 18 monographs, including Ultrasound Diagnostics in cardiology 1981, Practical Echocardiography 1982, Clinical Application of Magnetic Resonance Tomography 1996, Magnetic Resonance Tomography of Heart and Vessels 1997, Primary Lung Hypertension 1999, Principles of Rational Treatment of Cardiac Insufficiency 2000. *Leisure interests:* driving, classical music, jazz, sports. *Address:* Lomonosov Moscow State University, 119991 Moscow, GSP-1, Leninskie Gory, Russia (office). *Telephone:* (495) 939-10-00 (office). *Fax:* (495) 939-01-26 (office). *E-mail:* info@rector.msu.ru (office). *Website:* www.msu.ru (office).

BELICHICK, William (Bill) Stephen, BEcons; American football coach; *Head Coach, New England Patriots;* b. 16 April 1952, Nashville, Tenn.; s. of Steve Belichick; m. Debby Clarke (divorced 2006); two s. one d.; ed Annapolis High School, Phillips Acad., Andover, Mass, Wesleyan Univ., Middletown, Conn.; raised in Annapolis, Md; Special Asst to Head Coach Ted Marchibroda, Baltimore Colts 1975–76; Asst Special Teams Coach, Tight Ends and Receivers Coach, Detroit Lions 1976–78; Asst Special Teams Coach and Asst to Defensive Coordinator Joe Collier, Denver Broncos 1978–79; Defensive Asst and Special Teams Coach, New York Giants 1979–86, Defensive Coordinator 1986–90; Head Coach, Cleveland Browns 1991–95; Asst Head Coach and Defensive Asst, New England Patriots 1996, Head Coach 2000– (winning 16 divisional titles and six Super Bowls to 2018); Asst Head Coach and Defensive Backs Coach, New York Jets 1997–99; only head coach in league history to win three Super Bowl championships in a four-year span 2001, 2003, 2004; inducted into Annapolis High School Hall of Fame, AP Nat. Football League Coach of the Year 2003, 2007, 2010. *Address:* New England Patriots, 1 Patriot Place, Foxborough, MA 02035-1388, USA (office). *Telephone:* (508) 543-8200 (office). *Fax:* (508) 543-0285 (office). *Website:* www.patriots.com (office).

BELINGA-EBOUTOU, Martin; Cameroonian diplomatist, government official and international organization official; b. 17 Feb. 1940, Nkilzok; m.; six c.; ed Catholic Univ., Lavanium-Kinshasa, Univ. of Paris; joined Ministry of Foreign Affairs 1968, Chargé d'Affaires, Congo 1970–74, Chief, Regional Orgs Unit 1974–85, Head Econ. Mission of Cameroon, Paris, Rome, Tunis, Rabat 1985–89; Dir then Chief of State Protocol, Office of Pres. 1989–97, Dir Civil Cabinet 1996–97, 2009–18; Perm. Rep. to UN, New York and Geneva and Amb. to Jamaica 1998–2007; Pres. ECOSOC 2001, Pres. UN Security Council Oct. 2002, Chair. Third Cttee of Gen. Ass. (Social, Humanitarian and Cultural Cttee) 2003, also Perm. Rep. to UN, Geneva and Amb. to Jamaica; Special Adviser to Pres. of Cameroon 2007–09; Assoc. Prof., Inst. of Int. Relations 1974–76. *Address:* c/o Office of the President, Palais de l'Unité, Yaoundé, Cameroon (office).

BELIZ, Gustavo, LLD; Argentine politician and academic; *Director, Institute for the Integration of Latin America and the Caribbean, Inter-American Development Bank (IDB);* b. 7 Jan. 1962, Buenos Aires; m. Mary Florence Meritello; three s. one d.; ed Univ. of Buenos Aires, London School of Econs, UK; sports journalist, El Gráfico magazine 1979–85; political journalist and head of editorial dept, La Razón 1985–89; sec. of public functions to the presidency and speechwriter for Pres. Carlos Menem 1989–93; Minister of the Interior 1992–93; consultant and researcher, ECLAC 1994–95; Deputy, Buenos Aires Legis. Ass. 1996–2003, Senator and Head of City Govt 1999–2003; Research Assoc., Inst. of Higher Business Studies, Universidad Austral 2000–01, Prof., Faculty of Information Sciences 1995–2001; Minister of Justice, Human Rights and Internal Security 2003–04 (resgnd); mem. Perm. Staff, Inter-American Devt Bank, Washington 2005–13, Dir, Inst. for Integration of Latin America and Caribbean, Buenos Aires 2014–; fmr Pres. Nat. Inst. of Public Admin; fmr mem. Bd of Dirs Latin American Council for Devt Research; chosen as one of 10 outstanding young talents in Argentina, Cámara Junior de Buenos Aires 1992. *Publications include:* Argentina hacia el año 2000 1986, CGT, el otro poder 1988, La Argentina ausente 1990, Vale la pena. Adiós a la vieja política. 1993, Política social, la cuenta pendiente 1995, Buenos Aires vale la pena 1996, No Robarás ¿Es posible ganarle a la corrupción? 1997, Proyecto Ciudad 1999, La cultura profesional del periodismo argentino 1999, El otro modelo 2000. *Address:* Inter-American Development Bank, Esmeralda 130, Floor 16, Buenos Aires, Argentina (office). *Telephone:* (11) 4323-2365 (office). *E-mail:* intal@iadb.org (office). *Website:* www.iadb.org (office).

BELKA, Marek Marian, MA, PhD; Polish politician, economist, academic, UN official and fmr central banker; b. 9 Jan. 1952, Łódź; m.; two c.; ed Łódź Univ., Univ. of Chicago, USA, London School of Econs, UK; Master of Econs and Sociology Faculty, Łódź Univ. 1972, Asst Prof., then Prof. of Econs 1973–96; Visiting Scholar, Columbia Univ. (Fulbright Foundation), USA 1978–79; American Council of Scholarly Socs, Univ. of Chicago 1985–86; LSE 1990; Asst Prof., Inst. of Econs, Polish Acad. of Sciences (PAN) 1986–97, Dir 1993–97; adviser and consultant Finance Ministry, Privatisation Ministry and Cen. Planning Office 1990–96; Deputy Chair. Govt Council of Socio-Econ. Strategy 1994–96; Econ. Adviser to the Pres. of Poland 1996–97, 1997–2001; consultant to World Bank 1990–96; adviser to JP Morgan Chase; Deputy Prime Minister and Minister of Finance 1997, 2001–02; Head Coalition Council for Int. Co-ordination in Iraq 2003; Dir in charge of econ. policy, Coalition Provisional Authority 2003–04; Prime Minister of Poland 2004–05; Exec. Sec. UN ECE 2005–08; Dir European Dept, IMF 2008–10; Pres. Narodowy Bank Polski (NBP—Nat. Bank of Poland) (cen. bank) 2010–16; Hon. mem. Int. Raoul Wallenberg Foundation; elected to Polish Economy Hall of Fame 2013. *Publications include:* about a dozen books and more than 100 articles in Polish and foreign press on anti-inflation policy in developed countries, the Milton Friedman socio-economic doctrine and macro-economic policy in transition periods. *Leisure interests:* travelling, basketball, music.

BELKEZIZ, Abdelouahed, DrIur; Moroccan international organization official, lawyer, diplomatist and university administrator; b. 5 July 1939, Marrakesh; ed Sidi Mohammed Coll., Marrakesh, Faculty of Law, Rabat, Univ. of Rennes, France; Dean Faculty of Juridical, Econ. and Social Sciences, Moroccan Univ., Rabat 1966, Hassan II Univ., Casablanca 1985, Univ. of Ibn Tofail, Kenitra 1992, Univ. Muhammad V, Rabat 1997–2000; Pres. High Studies Reform Comm. 1969; mem. Perm. Royal Comm. for Judicial Reforms, Trade Codification, Penal and Civil Procedures 1971; Juridical Adviser, Moroccan Del. to UN 1976–77; Amb. to Iraq 1977–79; Minister of Information 1979–81, of Information, Youth and Sports 1981–83, of Foreign Affairs 1983–85; Pres. Exec. Cttee of Islamic World Univs Fed., Council of Maghreb Univs 1997–2000; Chair. Nat. Conf. of Moroccan Univ. Deans 1997–2000; Sec.-Gen. OIC 2001–04; fmr Pres. Univ. of Mohammed V Agdal; mem. Moroccan Award Comm. for Social Sciences 1968–74, Nat. Council for Youth and Future 1985; mem. American Asscn of Comparative Law 1970; King Abdulaziz Decoration of the Second Rank 1979, Great Spanish Civil Merit Cordon 1979, Commdr of the Civil Div., Order of the British Empire 1980, Great Officer of the Merit Order, Senegal 1981, Grand Officier, Ordre nat. du Mérite 1983, Great Cross of the Order of Rio Branco, Brazil 1984, Commdr of the Throne Order 1994.

BELKHADEM, Abdelaziz; Algerian politician; b. 8 Nov. 1945, Aflou; Deputy Dir of Int. Relations, Office of the Pres. 1972–77; Rapporteur, Planning and Finance Comm. 1978–87; mem. Front de Libération Nationale (FLN) 1977–, mem. Bureau Politique 1991–97, Sec.-Gen. 2005–13; Deputy for Sougueur to Assemblée Populaire Nationale (APN) 1977–92, Vice-Pres. 1988–90, Pres. 1990–91, Pres. Educ., Training and Scientific Research Comm. 1987; Minister of State for Foreign Affairs 2000–05; Minister of State and Special Rep. of the Pres. 2005–06; Prime Minister 2006–08; Minister of State and Personal Rep. to Head of State 2008–13. *Address:* Front de libération nationale (FLN), 7 rue du Stade, 16405, Hydra, Algiers, Algeria (office). *Telephone:* (21) 69-42-81 (office). *Fax:* (21) 69-47-07 (office). *E-mail:* contact@pfln.dz (office). *Website:* www.pfln.dz (office).

BELL, Edward (Eddie); British publisher and literary agent; *Partner, Bell Lomax Moreton Agency;* b. 2 Aug. 1949; s. of Eddie Bell and Jean Bell; m. Junette Bannatyne 1969; one s. two d.; ed Airdrie High School; with Hodder & Stoughton 1970–85; Man. Dir Collins Gen. Div. 1985–89; launched Harper Paperbacks in USA 1989; Deputy Chief Exec., HarperCollins UK 1990–91, Chief Exec. 1991–92, Chair. 1992–2000; Chair. HarperCollins India 1994–2000; Dir (non-exec.) Haynes Publishing 2001–09, Sr Ind. non-exec. Dir 2009–; Dir (non-exec.) Be Cogent Ltd, Management Diagnostics Ltd; Chair. (non-exec.) OAG Worldwide Ltd 2001; Pnr, Bell Lomax Moreton Agency 2002–. *Leisure interests:* golf, supporting Arsenal, collecting old books. *Address:* The Bell Lomax Moreton Agency, Suite C, 131 Queensway, Petts Wood, Kent, BR5 1DG, England (office). *E-mail:* eddie@bell-lomax.co.uk. *Website:* belllomaxmoreton.co.uk.

BELL, Geoffrey Lakin, BSc (Econ); British international banker; *President, Geoffrey Bell & Company Ltd;* b. 8 Nov. 1939, Grimsby, Lincs.; s. of Walter Lakin Bell and Anne Bell; m. Joan Rosine Abel 1973; one d.; ed Grimsby Tech. High School, London School of Econs; HM Treasury 1961–63; Visiting Scholar, Fed. Reserve System, Fed. Reserve Bank of St Louis 1963–64; HM Treasury and Lecturer, LSE 1964–66; adviser, British Embassy, Washington, DC 1966–69; joined J. Henry Schroder Wagg and Co. Ltd 1969, Asst to Chair. 1969–72; Dir and Exec. Vice-Pres. Schroder Int. Ltd; Dir Schroder Bermuda Ltd; Founder, Exec. Sec. and mem. Bd of Dirs Group of Thirty Consultative Group on Int. Econ. and Monetary Affairs, Inc., Washington, DC 1978–; Pres. Geoffrey Bell & Co. Ltd 1982–; Chair. Guinness Mahon Holdings 1987–93; mem. Court of Govs LSE 1994–; fmr financial adviser to Cen. Bank of Venezuela, currently financial adviser to Govt of Barbados and Govt of Jamaica; Companion of Honour of Barbados. *Publications include:* The Euro-Dollar Market and the International Financial System 1973 (translated into French and Japanese); contrib. The Times, International Herald Tribune and numerous academic and other publs. *Address:* 780 Third Avenue, 7th Floor, New York, NY 10017-2024, USA (office). *Telephone:* (212) 888-3700 (office). *E-mail:* geoffrey.bell@verizon.net. *Website:* www.group30.org.

BELL, Graeme I., PhD; Canadian biologist and academic; *Louis Block Distinguished Service Professor, Departments of Medicine and Human Genetics, University of Chicago;* b. Victoria, BC; ed Univ. of Calgary, Alberta, Univ. of California, San Francisco, USA; Postgraduate Research Biochemist, Dept of Biochemistry and Biophysics, Univ. of California, San Francisco 1977–78, Asst Research Biochemist 1978–81, Asst Adjunct Prof. 1981–84, Asst Adjunct Prof., Metabolic Research Unit 1984–86; also worked as Sr Scientist, Chiron Corpn 1981–86; Assoc. Prof., Dept of Biochemistry and Molecular Biology, Univ. of Chicago 1986–90, Assoc. Prof., Dept of Medicine 1987–90, Prof., Depts of Biochemistry and Molecular Biology, and Medicine 1990–94, Louis Block Prof., Depts of Biochemistry and Molecular Biology, and Medicine 1994–98, Louis Block Distinguished Service Prof., Depts of Medicine and Human Genetics 1998–; Assoc. Investigator, Howard Hughes Medical Inst., Chevy Chase, Md 1986–90, Investigator 1990–; mem. NAS 1998, Inst. of Medicine 1998; Fellow, American Acad. of Arts and Sciences 2008; Hon. Foreign mem. La Sociedad Artina de Diabetes 2000; Elliot P. Joslin Research and Devt Award, American Diabetes Asscn (ADA) 1980–82, Rolf Luft Award, Swedish Medical Soc. 1989, Mary Jane Kugel Award, Juvenile Diabetes Foundation Int. (JDFI) 1989, Outstanding Scientific Achievement Award by an Investigator (Lilly Award), ADA 1990, William C. Stadie Award, Greater Philadelphia Affiliate of ADA 1990, Distinguished Alumni Award, Univ. of Calgary 1991, Gerold and Kayla Grodsky Basic Research Scientist Award, JDFI 1995, Naomi Berrie Award for Outstanding Achievement in Diabetes Research, Columbia Univ., New York 2000, Benjamin F. Stapleton, Jr Lecturer, Univ. of Colorado Health Science Center 2002, J. Allyn Taylor Int. Prize in Medicine for Diabetes 2002. *Address:* University of Chicago, 5841 South Maryland Avenue AMB N237, MC1027, Chicago, IL 60637-1027, USA (office). *Telephone:* (773) 702-9116 (office). *Fax:* (773) 702-9237 (office). *E-mail:* g-bell@uchicago.edu (office). *Website:* genes.uchicago.edu/contents/faculty/bell-graeme.html (office); drtc.bsd.uchicago.edu (office); gbell.bsd.uchicago.edu (office).

BELL, John Anthony, OBE, AO; Australian theatre director and actor; *Artistic Director, The Bell Shakespeare Company;* b. 1 Nov. 1940, Newcastle, NSW; s. of Albert Bell and Joyce Feeney; m. Anna Volska 1965; two d.; ed Maitland Marist Brothers High School, NSW and Univ. of Sydney; actor with Old Tote Theatre Co. 1963–64, with RSC, UK 1964–69; Co-founder Nimrod Theatre Co. 1970–85; Founder and Artistic Dir Bell Shakespeare Co. 1990–; roles include King Lear, Macbeth, Shylock, Malvolio and Richard III, Prospero; Hon. DLitt (Newcastle) 1994, (Sydney) 1996, (NSW) 2006; Australia Nat. Living Treasure, Nat. Trust of Australia 1997, Dame Elisabeth Murdoch Cultural Leadership Award, Australian Business Arts Foundation 2003. *Publications include:* The Time of My Life (autobiog.) 2002, On Shakespeare 2011. *Leisure interests:* reading, music, painting. *Address:* The Bell Shakespeare Company, PO Box 10, Millers Point, Sydney NSW 2000, Australia (office). *Telephone:* (2) 8298-9000 (office). *Fax:* (2) 9241-4643 (office). *E-mail:* mail@bellshakespeare.com.au (office). *Website:* www.bellshakespeare.com.au (office).

BELL, Sir John Irving, Kt, GBE, DM, FRS, FRCP, FMedSci; Canadian medical scientist and academic; *Regius Professor of Medicine, University of Oxford;* b. 1 July 1952, Edmonton, Alberta; s. of Robert Edward Bell and Mary Agnes Bell (née Wholey); m. Prof. Jenny Bell; two s. one d.; ed Ridley Coll., Univ. of Alberta, Magdalen Coll., Oxford, UK, Stanford Univ., USA; Clinical Fellow, Dept of Medicine, Stanford Univ., Calif., USA 1982–87; Wellcome Sr Clinical Fellow and Hon. Consultant, Radcliffe Hosp., Oxford 1987–89, Lecturer, Nuffield Dept of Clinical Medicine, Univ. of Oxford 1989–92, Nuffield Prof. of Clinical Medicine 1992–2002, Regius Prof. of Medicine 2002–, Emer. Fellow, Magdalen Coll.; f. Wellcome Trust Centre for Human Genetics 1993; Chair. Office for the Strategic Co-ordination of Health Research (OSCHR) 2006–, Oxford Health Alliance, GMEC Management Co. Ltd, Human Genome Strategy Group; one of two Life Sciences Champions for the UK, reporting to the Prime Minister 2011–; Chair. Genomics England Science Advisory Bd 2014–; mem. Bd of Dirs, Roche AG 2001–, Genentech 2009–, Oxford Biomedical Research Centre 2009–, Gray Laboratory Cancer Research Trust, Edward Jenner Inst. for Vaccine Research, Isis Innovation Ltd, Oxagen Ltd, Genomics England 2014–; Chair. Bill and Melinda Gates Foundation Scientific Advisory Cttee, Scientific Advisory Bd AstraZeneca 1997–2000, Scientific Advisory Bd Roche Palo Alto 1998–2002; Trustee, Rhodes Trust 2002–15; fmr mem. Oxford Univ. Council, MRC Council; Founder Fellow, Acad. of Medical Sciences 1998 (Pres. 2006–11); Hon. Fellow, Royal Acad. of Eng 2009; Hon. DSc (Univ. of Alberta) 2003; Dr hc (Univs of York, Warwick, Glasgow, Dundee, Toronto and Imperial Coll. London) 2014. *Publications:* numerous scientific papers in professional journals on immunology and genetics. *Address:* The Offices of the Regius Professor, Level 4, Academic Centre, John Radcliffe Hospital, Headley Way, Headington, Oxford, OX3 9DU, England (office). *Telephone:* (1865) 289782 (office). *Fax:* (1865) 220993 (office). *E-mail:* regius@medsci.ox.ac.uk (office). *Website:* www.medsci.ox.ac.uk/support-services/regius (office).

BELL, Joshua; American violinist and music director; *Music Director, Academy of St Martin in the Fields;* b. 9 Dec. 1967, Indiana; ed Indiana Univ.; European tour with St Louis Symphony 1985; German tour with Indianapolis Symphony 1987; European tour with Dallas Symphony 1997; European tours with Nat. Symphony Orchestra 2002, Minnesota Orchestra 2003; guest soloist with numerous orchestras in USA, Canada, Europe; has also appeared in USA and Europe as a recitalist; played premiere of violin concerto by Nicholas Maw, written for him, with Philharmonia Orchestra 1993; Music Dir, Acad. of St Martin in the Fields 2011–; Artistic Partner, St Paul Chamber Orchestra; currently Sr Lecturer, Jacobs School of Music, Indiana Univ.; Visiting Prof., RAM, London; mem. Artist Cttee, Kennedy Center Honors; mem. Bd of Dirs New York Philharmonic; collaborated with Chick Corea, Wynton Marsalis, Chris Botti, Anoushka Shankar, Frankie Moreno, Josh Groban, Sting; Gramophone Award for Best Concerto Recording 1998 (for Barber Concerto), Mercury Music Award 2000, Acad. Award for Best Soundtrack (for Red Violin), Grammy Award 2001, Avery Fisher Prize 2007, named Young Global Leader by World Econ. Forum 2007, Musical America Award for Instrumentalist of the Year 2010, Paul Newman Award, Arts Horizons 2011, Huberman Award, Moment Magazine 2011, Nat. YoungArts Foundation Award 2013, Helpmann Award for Best Individual Classical Performance 2013, Glashütte Original Music Festival Award 2019. *Recordings include:* Mendelssohn and Bruch concertos with the Academy of St Martin in the Fields and Sir Neville Marriner, Tchaikovsky and Wieniawski concertos with the Cleveland Orchestra and Vladimir Ashkenazy, recital album of Brahms, Paganini, Sarasate and Wieniawski with Samuel Sanders, Lalo Symphonie Espagnole and Saint-Saëns Concerto with Montreal Symphony Orchestra and Charles Dutoit, Franck, Fauré and Debussy, Chausson Concerto for violin, piano and string quartet with Thibaudet and Isserlis, Poème with Royal Philharmonic Orchestra and Andrew Litton, Mozart Concertos Nos 3 and 5 with the English Chamber Orchestra and Peter Maag, Prokofiev violin concertos with Montréal Symphony Orchestra and Charles Dutoit, Barber and Walton concertos and Bloch Baal Shem with Baltimore Symphony Orchestra and David Zinman, recital disc with Olli Mustonen, Gershwin Fantasy with London Symphony Orchestra and John Williams, Short Trip Home with Edgar Meyer, The Red Violin film soundtrack with Philharmonia Orchestra, Sibelius Goldmark Concertos with Los Angeles Philharmonic Orchestra and Esa-Pekka Salonen, Maw Concerto for violin with London Philharmonic Orchestra and Roger Norrington, Bernstein Serenade and West Side Story Suite with Philharmonia Orchestra and David Zinman, Beethoven and Mendelssohn concertos with Camerata Salzburg and Sir Roger Norrington, Irish film soundtrack, Romance of the Violin 2003, Tchaikovsky Violin Concerto 2005, Voice of the Violin 2006, The Red Violin Concerto 2007, Vivaldi: The Four Seasons 2008, At Home with my Friends 2009, French Impressions with Jeremy Denk (ECHO Klassik Award for Chamber Music Recording of the Year/Strings—19th Century, Diapason D'or award) 2012, Bach 2014. *Leisure interests:* chess, computers, golf. *Address:* c/o Cindy Liu, Park Avenue Artists, 129 W 22nd Street #12B, New York, NY 10035 (office); Jane Covner, JAG Entertainment, 4265 Hazeltine Avenue, Sherman Oaks, CA 91423, USA (office); Academy of St Martin in the Fields, The Griffin Building, 83 Clerkenwell Road, London, EC1R 5AR, England (office). *E-mail:* cindy.liu@parkavenueartists.com (office); jcovner@jagpr.com (office); info@asmf.org (office); heidi@joshuabell.com; jb@joshuabell.com. *Website:* www.joshuabell.com (office); www.asmf.org/joshua-bell (office); www.joshuabell.com. *Telephone:* (20) 7702-1377 (office).

BELL, Marian, CBE, MA, MSc; British economist; *Director, Alpha Economics;* b. 28 Oct. 1957, London; d. of Joseph Denis Milburn Bell and Wilhelmenia Maxwell Bell (née Miller); m. Richard Adkin; two d.; ed Hertford Coll., Oxford, Birkbeck Coll. London; Econ. Adviser, HM Treasury 1989–91; Sr Treasury Economist, Head of Research, Treasury and Capital Markets, Royal Bank of Scotland 1991–2000; Dir, Alpha Economics 2000–02, 2005–; External Mem. Monetary Policy Cttee, Bank of England 2002–05; Dir (non-exec.), Emerging Health Threats Forum 2006–12; mem. European Advisory Council, Zurich Insurance Group 2007–14, Fiscal Policy Panel, States of Jersey 2007–14; Gov. Contemporary Dance Trust, The Place 2005–14, Vice-Chair. 2008–14; Gov. National Inst. of Economic and Social Research 2014–. *Leisure interests:* contemporary dance, art. *E-mail:* Assist.bell@btinternet.com (office).

BELL, Martin, OBE, MA; British broadcaster and politician; *Humanitarian Ambassador, United Nations International Children's Emergency Fund (UNICEF);* b. 31 Aug. 1938; s. of Adrian Bell and Marjorie Bell (née Gibson); m. 1st Nelly Gourdon 1971 (divorced); two d.; m. 2nd Rebecca Sobel 1985 (divorced 1993); m. 3rd Fiona Goddard 1998; ed The Leys School, Cambridge, King's Coll., Cambridge; joined BBC 1962, news Asst, Norwich 1962–64, gen. reporter, London and overseas 1964–76, Diplomatic Corresp. 1976–77, Chief N American Corresp. 1977–89, Berlin Corresp. BBC TV News 1989–93, Vienna Corresp. 1993–94, Foreign Affairs Corresp. 1994–96, Special Corresp., Nine O'Clock News 1997; has reported from over 70 countries and has covered wars in Viet Nam, Middle East 1967, 1973, Angola, Rhodesia, Biafra, El Salvador, Gulf 1991, Nicaragua, Croatia, Bosnia; MP (Ind.) for Tatton 1997–2001; Humanitarian Amb. for UNICEF 2001–; Dr hc (Derby) 1996; Hon. MA (E Anglia) 1997, (Aberdeen) 1998; Royal TV Soc. Reporter of the Year 1976, 1992, TV and Radio Industries Club Newscaster of the Year 1995, Inst. of Public Relations Pres.'s Medal 1996. *Publications:* In Harm's Way 1995, An Accidental MP 2000, Through Gates of Fire 2003, The Truth That Sticks: New Labour's Breach of Trust 2007, For Whom the Bell Tolls 2011. *Address:* 71 Denman Drive, London, NW11 6RA, England (home).

BELL, Baron (Life Peer), cr. 1998, of Belgravia in the City of Westminster; **Timothy John Leigh Bell,** FIPA; British public relations executive; *Chairman, Sans Frontières Associates;* b. 18 Oct. 1941; s. of Arthur Leigh Bell and Greta Mary Bell (née Findlay); m. Virginia Wallis Hornbrook 1988; one s. one d.; ed Queen Elizabeth's Grammar School, Barnet, Herts.; with ABC Television 1959–61, Colman Prentis & Varley 1961–63, Hobson Bates 1963–66, Geers Gross 1966–70; Man. Dir Saatchi & Saatchi 1970–75, Chair. and Man. Dir Saatchi & Saatchi Compton 1975–85; Group Chief Exec. Lowe Howard-Spink Campbell Ewald 1985–87, Deputy Chair. Lowe Howard-Spink & Bell PLC 1987–89; Chair. Lowe-Bell Communications 1987–89, Chime Communications 1994–12; f. Lowe-Bell Govt Relations 1993–; arranged man. buy-out of Lowe-Bell Communications 1989; Special Adviser to Chair. Nat. Coal Bd 1984–86; Chair. Bell Pottinger Private –2016; currently Chair. Sans Frontières Assocs.; Chair. Charity Projects 1984–93, apptd Pres. 1993; Dir Centre for Policy Studies; mem. Industry Cttee SCF, Public Relations Cttee Greater London Fund for the Blind 1979–86, Council Royal Opera House 1982–85, Public Affairs Cttee, Worldwide Fund for Nature 1985–88, South Bank Bd 1985–86; Creative Leaders' Network Gov. British Film Inst. 1983–86. *Leisure interests:* golf, politics. *Address:* House of Lords, London, SW1A 0PW (office); Sans Frontières Associates, 78 Pall Mall, London, SW1Y 5ES, England. *Telephone:* (20) 7219-5353 (House of Lords) (office); (20) 3170-7465 (Sans Frontières Associates) (office). *Fax:* (20) 7219-5979 (House of Lords) (office). *E-mail:* contactholmember@parliament.uk (office). *Website:* www.parliament.uk (office); www.sansfrontieresassociates.com (office).

BELL BURNELL, Dame S(usan) Jocelyn, DBE, CBE, PhD, FRS, FRSE, MRIA; British astrophysicist, academic and univ. administrator; *Visiting Professor, University of Oxford;* b. 15 July 1943, Belfast, Northern Ireland; d. of (George) Philip Bell and (Margaret) Allison Bell (née Kennedy); m. (divorced); one s.; ed Univs of Glasgow and Cambridge; Lecturer, Univ. of Southampton 1968–73; part-time with Mullard Space Lab., Univ. Coll. London 1974–82; part-time with Royal Observatory, Edin. 1982–91; Chair. Physics Dept, Open Univ. 1991–99; Dean of Science, Univ. of Bath 2001–04; Visiting Prof. for Distinguished Teaching, Princeton Univ., USA 1999–2000; Visiting Prof. of Astrophysics, Univ. of Oxford 2004–; Pres. Royal Astronomical Soc. 2002–04; Pres. Inst. of Physics 2008–10; Pro-Chancellor, Trinity Coll. Dublin 2013–18; Pres. Royal Soc. of Edinburgh 2015–18; Foreign Assoc., NAS 2005; mem. American Philosophical Soc. 2016–; frequent speaker and radio and TV broadcaster on science, on being a woman in science, on astronomy and poetry and on science and religion; Hon. Fellow, New Hall, Cambridge 1996, British Science Asscn 2006, Singapore Inst. of Physics 2008, European Physical Soc. 2010, Science Museum London 2010, Glyndwr Univ. 2011, Inst. of Physics 2012, Distinguished Fellow, Inst. of Advance Studies, Ewha Univ. 2006, Hon. Prin., No 35 School, Beijing 2012, Hon. mem. Royal Irish Acad. 2012, American Astronomical Soc. 2015, Bilim Akademisi (Science Acad.), Istanbul 2016, Hon. Prof., Xinjiang Astronomical Observatory 2013; 36 hon. doctorates, including Univs of Cambridge, London, Michigan, McGill Univ., Harvard Univ.; Joseph Black Medal and Cowie Book Prize, Univ. of Glasgow 1962, Michelson Medal, Franklin Inst., USA 1973, J. Robert Oppenheimer Memorial Prize, Center for Theoretical Studies, Fla 1978, Beatrice M. Tinsley Prize, American Astronomical Soc. (first recipient) 1987, Herschel Medal, Royal Astronomical Soc., London 1989, Edinburgh Medal 1999, Magellanic Premium, American Philosophical Soc. 2000, Joseph Priestly Award, Dickinson Coll., Pa 2002, Robinson Medal, Armagh Observatory 2004, Kelvin Medal 2007, Royal Soc. Faraday Award 2010, Grote Reber Medal 2011, Sven Berggren Prize, Royal Physiographic Soc. (Sweden) 2012, Royal Medal, Royal Soc. 2015, Inst. of Physics President's Medal 2017, French Acad. of Sciences Grande Médaille 2018, Special Breakthrough Prize in Fundamental Physics 2018. *Achievements include:* discovered the first four pulsars. *Radio:* Scientific Life 2011. *Television:* Beautiful Minds 2010. *Publications include:* three books, including Broken for Life 1989, Dark Matter: Poems of Space (co-ed.) 2008; three book chapters, approx. 70 scientific papers and 35 Quaker publs. *Leisure interests:* popularizing astronomy, walking, Quaker activities, listening to choral music, gardening. *Address:* University of Oxford, Astrophysics, Denys

Wilkinson Building, Keble Road, Oxford, OX1 3RH, England (office). *Telephone:* (1865) 273306 (office). *Fax:* (1865) 273390 (office).

BELL LEMUS, Gustavo Adolfo; Colombian lawyer, economist, historian and academic, journalist, diplomatist and fmr politician; *Ambassador to Cuba;* b. 1 Feb. 1957, Barranquilla; m. Maria Mercedes de la Espriella; one d.; ed Javeriana Univ. of Bogotá, Andes Univ. and Univ. of Oxford, UK; fmr Prof., Univ. del Norte e del Atlantico; fmr Man. Nat. Industrial Asscn (Andi), Barranquilla; fmr Gov. of Atlantico; Vice-Pres. of Colombia 1998–2002, also High Commr for Human Rights; Minister of Nat. Defence 2001–02; fmr Dir El Heraldo (newspaper), Barranquilla, Atlantico; Amb. to Cuba 2011–. *Address:* Embassy of Colombia, Calle 14, No 515, entre 5 y 7, Miramar, Havana, Cuba (office). *Telephone:* (7) 204-1248 (office). *Fax:* (7) 204-0464 (office). *E-mail:* ecuba@cancilleria.gov.co (office). *Website:* cuba.embajada.gov.co (office).

BELLAMY, Carol, JD; American lawyer and international organization official; *Chairman, International Baccalaureate;* b. 1942, Plainfield, NJ; ed Gettysburg Coll., New York Univ.; Peace Corps Volunteer, Guatemala 1963–65; Assoc., Cravath, Swaine & Moore, New York 1968–71; spent 13 years as elected public official including term as mem. New York State Senate 1973–77; Pres. New York City Council (first woman) 1978–85; Prin., Morgan Stanley and Co. 1986–90; Man. Dir Bear Stearns & Co. 1990–93; Prin. Morgan Stanley & Co. New York; Dir Peace Corps, Washington, DC 1993–95; Exec. Dir UNICEF 1995–2005; Pres. School for Int. Training and CEO World Learning 2005–09; Chair. Bd of Dirs Fair Labor Foundation 2007; Chair. Global Partnership for Education 2009–13; Chair. Bd of Govs Int. Baccalaureate 2009–; Chair. Alliance for Ethical Int. Recruitment Practices; mem. Advisory Bd Innovative Finance Foundation 2012–; fmr Fellow, Inst. of Politics, Kennedy School of Govt, Harvard Univ.; Hon. mem. Phi Alpha Alpha, the US Nat. Honor Soc. for Accomplishment and Scholarship in Public Affairs and Admin; Chevalier, Légion d'Honneur 2009; Hon. LHD (Bates Coll.) 2003. *Address:* International Baccalaureate, Route des Morillons 15, Grand-Saconnex, Geneva 1218, Switzerland (office). *E-mail:* ibhq@ibo.org (office). *Website:* www.ibo.org (office).

BELLAMY, Sir Christopher (William), Kt, MA, QC; British barrister and consultant; *Senior Consultant, Linklaters;* b. 25 April 1946, Waddesdon, Bucks.; s. of William Albert Bellamy and Vyvienne Hilda Bellamy (née Meyrick); m. Deirdre Patricia Turner; one s. two d.; ed Tonbridge School, Brasenose Coll., Oxford; called to the Bar, Middle Temple 1968 (Bencher 1994), in full-time practice 1970–92, QC 1986, Asst Recorder 1989–92; Judge of Court of First Instance of the EC 1992–99; Pres. of Appeal Tribunals, Competition Comm. (now Competition Appeal Tribunal) 1999–2007; Deputy High Court Judge 2000–15; Judge of Employment Appeal Tribunal 2000–07; mem. Council, British Inst. of Int. and Comparative Law 2000–06, Advisory Bd 2007–; Recorder, Crown Court 2001–07; Sr Consultant, Linklaters, London (law firm) 2007–, Chair. Global Competition Practice 2011–; Gov. Ravensbourne Coll. of Design and Communication 1988–92. *Publication:* European Community Law of Competition (6th edn) (ed. P. Roth and V. Rose) 2007. *Leisure interests:* family life, walking, history. *Address:* Linklaters, 1 Silk Street, London, EC2Y 8HA, England (office). *Telephone:* (20) 7456-3457 (office). *E-mail:* christopher.bellamy@linklaters.com (office). *Website:* www.linklaters.com (office).

BELLAMY, David James, OBE, PhD, CBiol, FIBiol; British botanist, writer, broadcaster and environmental organization administrator; b. 18 Jan. 1933, London; s. of Thomas Bellamy and Winifred Green; m. Rosemary Froy 1959; two s. three d.; ed Sutton County Grammar School, Chelsea Coll. of Science and Tech., Bedford Coll., Univ. of London; Lecturer, then Sr Lecturer, Dept of Botany, Univ. of Durham 1960–80, Hon. Prof. of Adult and Continuing Educ. 1980–82; Visiting Prof., Massey Univ., NZ 1988–89; Special Prof. of Botany, Univ. of Nottingham 1987–; TV and radio presenter and scriptwriter; Founder Dir Conservation Foundation; Pres. WATCH 1982, Youth Hostels Asscn 1983, Population Concern 1988–, Nat. Asscn of Environmental Educ. 1989–, Plantlife 1990–2005, Wildlife Trust's Partnership 1996–2005, British Inst. of Cleaning Science 1997–, Council Zoological Soc. of London 1991–94, BH&HPA 2000–, Camping and Caravanning Club 2002–; Vice-Pres. BTCV, Fauna and Flora International, Marine Conservation Soc., Australian Marine Conservation Soc.; Chair. Int. Cttee for the Tourism for Tomorrow Awards; Dir David Bellamy Assocs (environmental consultants) 1988–97, Bellamy & Nevard Environmental Consultants 2003–; Trustee, Living Landscape Trust, World Land Trust 1992–2002; Patron Project AWARE Foundation, The Space Theatre, Dundee, Te Pua O Whirinaki Regeneration Trust, NZ; Hon. Fellow, Chartered Inst. of Water and Environmental Man.; Hon. FLS; Hon. Prof., Central Queensland Univ.; Hon. mem. BSES Expeditions; Dutch Order of the Golden Ark 1989; Hon. DSc (Bournemouth); Hon. DUniv; Dr hc (CNAA) 1990; UNEP Global 500 Award 1990, Busk Medal, Royal Geographical Soc., Duke of Edinburgh's Award for Underwater Research, BAFTA Richard Dimbleby Award, BSAC Diver of the Year Award. *Television series include:* Life in Our Sea 1970, Bellamy on Botany 1973, Bellamy's Britain 1975, Bellamy's Europe 1977, Botanic Man 1978, Up a Gum Tree 1980, Backyard Safari 1981, The Great Seasons 1982, Bellamy's New World 1983, End of the Rainbow Show 1986, S.W.A.L.L.O.W. 1986, Turning the Tide 1986, Bellamy's Bugle 1986, 1987, 1988, Bellamy on Top of the World 1987, Bellamy's Journey to the Centre of the World 1987, Bellamy's Bird's Eye View 1989, Wheat Today What Tomorrow? 1989, Moa's Ark 1990, Bellamy Rides Again 1992, Blooming Bellamy 1993, 1994, Routes of Wisdom 1993, The Peak 1994, Bellamy's Border Raids 1996, Westwatch 1997, A Welsh Herbal 1998, Salt Solutions 1999, The Challenge 1999. *Publications include:* more than 45 books, including Bellamy on Botany 1972, Peatlands 1974, Bellamy's Britain 1974, Life Giving Sea 1975, Green Worlds 1975, The World of Plants 1975, Bellamy's Europe 1976, Botanic Action 1978, Botanic Man 1978, Half of Paradise 1979, Forces of Life 1979, Bellamy's Backyard Safari 1981, The Great Seasons (with Sheila Mackie, illustrator) 1981, Il Libro Verde 1981, Discovering the Countryside with David Bellamy (Vols I, II) 1982, (Vols III, IV) 1983, The Mouse Book 1983, Bellamy's New World 1983, The Queen's Hidden Garden 1984, Bellamy's Bugle 1986, Bellamy's Ireland 1986, Turning the Tide 1986, Bellamy's Changing Countryside (four vols) 1987, England's Last Wilderness 1989, England's Lost Wilderness 1990, Wetlands 1990, Wilderness Britain 1990, How Green Are You? 1991, Tomorrow's Earth 1992, World Medicine: Plants, Patients and People 1992, Blooming Bellamy 1993, Trees of the World 1993, Poo, You and the Poteroo's Loo 1997, Bellamy's Changing Countryside 1998, The Glorious Trees of Great Britain 2002, Jolly Green Giant (autobiog.) 2002, A Natural Life (autobiog.) 2002, The Bellamy Herbal 2003, Conflicts in the Countryside: The New Battle for Britain 2005, and books connected with TV series; Consultant Ed. and contrib. for series published by Hamlyn in conjunction with Royal Soc. for Nature Conservation: Coastal Walks 1982, Woodland Walks 1982, Waterside Walks 1983, Grassland Walks 1983. *Leisure interests:* children and ballet. *Address:* The Mill House, Bedburn, Bishop Auckland, Co. Durham, DL13 3NN, England (home).

BELLERIVE, Jean-Max; Haitian economist and politician; b. 1958, Port-au-Prince; electoral co-ordinator for municipal and presidential elections, Ouest Dept 1999–2000; has held positions in govt under six different prime ministers 1990–; Chief of Staff to Prime Minister Jean-Marie Chérestal 2001–02; mem. staff of Prime Minister Yvon Neptune 2002–04; Minister of Planning and External Co-operation –2009; Prime Minister 2009–11 (resgnd).

BELLINI, Mario; Italian architect, designer and academic; *CEO, Mario Bellini Architects S.r.l.;* b. 1 Feb. 1935, Milan; ed Politecnico di Milano; Dir of Design, La Rinascente 1961–63; Prof., Istituto Superiore del Disegno Industriale 1962–65; Chief Design Consultant, Olivetti 1963–91; Prof., Domus Acad. 1986–91; fmr Visiting Prof., Royal Coll. of Art, London; Ed. Domus 1986–91; CEO Mario Bellini Architects S.r.l. 1980–; has designed projects including Tokyo Design Centre, Sakurada Dori Dist, Exhbn Centre in Villa Erba on Lake Como, Natuzzi America HQ, Trade Fair in Essen, Germany, Nat. Gallery of Victoria, Melbourne, HQ of Deutsche Bank, Frankfurt, Verona Forum complex, Museum of the History of Bologna, Museum of Islamic Art, The Louvre, Paris, Milan Convention Centre, Milan Trade Fair (Portello); current projects include Cultural Centre, Turin, renovation and restyling of Pinacoteca di Brera, Milan, Science and Tech. Park, Genoa; numerous exhbns in Italy and abroad; works in perm. collections, including 25 works at Museum of Modern Art, New York; numerous talks worldwide; Medaglia d'Oro, Pres. of Italy 2004, Ambrogino d'oro, Municipality of Milan 2011; Compasso d'Oro 1962, 1964, 1970, 1979, 1981, 1984, 2001, Kasumigaseki Prize 1991, Award of Japanese Soc. of Commercial Space Designers 1992, Pinnacle Award 1998, Tre numberone Award 2010, Dama d'Argento Award 2006, PIDA Ischia Architecture Award for Lifetime Achievement 2013, Red Dot Germany Award for High Design Quality 2016, Master of Architecture Award, Associazione Italiana di Architettura e Critica 2017. *Address:* Mario Bellini Architects S.r.l., Piazza Arcole 4, 20143 Milan, Italy (office). *Telephone:* (2) 5815191 (office). *Fax:* (2) 58113466 (office). *E-mail:* info@mariobellini.com (office). *Website:* www.mariobellini.com (office).

BELLO, Col (retd) Sani; Nigerian business executive, diplomatist and fmr army officer; *Chairman, Amni International Petroleum Development Company Limited;* b. 27 Nov. 1942, Kontagora, Niger State; m.; three c.; ed Bida Govt Coll., Royal Mil. Acad., Sandhurst, UK; joined Army as Cadet 1962, held various posts including Co. Commdr, Asst Quarter Master-Gen. 3rd Marine Commando Div., ADC to Supreme Commdr, Deputy Adjutant-Gen. of the Army, 1st Nigerian Principal Staff Officer, Armed Forces Command and Staff Coll.; Mil. Gov. old Kano State 1975–78, retd 1979; High Commr to Zimbabwe 1984–86; Founder-Chair. Amni International Petroleum Devt Co. Ltd; currently also Chair. MH Healthcare Ltd, Sani Bello Foundation, Dantata and Sawoe Construction Company Ltd; Vice-Chair. MTN Nigeria Communications Ltd 1999–; fmr Chair. Niger State Green Revolution, Niger State Nat. Youth Service Corps, Niger State Polytechnic School Bd, Niger State Science and Technical School Bd, Nigerian Table Tennis Fed., Continental Merchant Bank Plc, Globe Re-Insurance Plc, Law, Union and Rock Insurance Plc, Broadbank Nigeria Ltd; mem. Bd of Dirs Dantata and Sawoe Construction Co. Ltd 1991–, Equatel Communication Ltd 2006–; fmr Pres. Nat. Asscn of Indigenous Petroleum Explorers in Nigeria. *Address:* Amni International Petroleum Development Company Limited, Plot 1377, Tiamiyu Savage Street, Victoria Island, Lagos, Nigeria (office). *Telephone:* (1) 7404679 (office). *Fax:* (1) 4613904 (office). *Website:* www.amnipetroleum.com (office).

BELLOCH JULBE, Juan Alberto, LLB; Spanish politician; b. 3 Feb. 1950, Mora de Rubielos (Teruel); m. Mari Cruz Soriano; one s.; ed Univ. of Barcelona; mem. Democratic Justice; Founder Asscn of Judges for Democracy, Asscn des Magistrats Européens pour la démocratie et les libertés; Founder and Pres. Asscn for the Human Rights of the Basque Country; Judge, La Gomera, Berga Vic y Alcoy from 1975; Magistrate and Pres. Court of Justice of Biscay 1981–90; mem. Gen. Council of Judiciary 1990–93; Minister of Justice 1993–96, of the Interior 1994–96; Senator 1999–2003; Mayor of Zaragoza 2003–15; Pres. European Forum for Urban Security 2007–10; Chair. Asscn of Cities and Regions Hosting an Int. Exposition (AVE).

BELLOCHIO, Marco; Italian director, actor, writer and producer; b. 9 Nov. 1939, Piacenza, Emilia-Romagna; retrospective at Locarno Int. Film Festival 1998; mem. Jury, Venice Film Festival 1999, Cannes Film Festival 2007; Bronze Leopard for his complete works, Locarno Int. Film Festival 1976, Jury Distinction for his artistic contrib. to the art of cinema, Montréal World Film Festival 1988, Silver St George for Contrib. to World Cinema, Moscow Int. Film Festival 1999, Career Award (Cinema), Flaiano Int. Prizes 2002, Pietro Bianchi Award, Venice Film Festival 2006, Sergei Parajanov Lifetime Achievement Award, Yerevan Int. Film Festival 2006. *Film roles in:* Francesco d'Assisi (Francis of Assisi) 1966, Sbatti il mostro in prima pagina (Slap the Monster on Page One) 1972, Pianeta Venere (Planet Venus) 1974, Salò o le 120 giornate di Sodoma (Salo, or the 120 Days of Sodom) (voice; uncredited) 1975, Vacanze in Val Trebbia (Vacation in Val Tribbia) 1980, L'ora di religione (Il sorriso di mia madre) (The Religion Hour (My Mother's Smile)) 2002, Buongiorno, notte (Good Morning, Night) (uncredited) 2003. *Films directed:* Ginepro fatto uomo 1962, La colpa e la pena 1965, I pugni in tasca (Fists in the Pocket) (Silver Sail, Locarno Int. Film Festival 1965, Silver Ribbon for Best Original Story, Italian Nat. Syndicate of Film Journalists 1966) 1965, La Cina è vicina (China is Near) (FIPRESCI Prize and Special Jury Prize, Venice Film Festival 1967, Silver Ribbon for Best Original Story, Italian Nat. Syndicate of Film Journalists 1968) 1967, Amore e rabbia (Love and Anger; segment 'Discutiamo, discutiamo') 1969, Nel nome del padre (In the Name of the Father) 1972, Sbatti il mostro in prima pagina (Slap the Monster on Page One) 1972, Matti da slegare (Fit to be Untied) (OCIC Award and FIPRESCI Prize – Recommendation, Berlin Int. Film Festival 1975) 1975, Marcia trionfale (Victory March) 1976, Vacanze in Val Trebbia (Vacation in Val Tribbia) 1980, Salto nel vuoto (Leap into the Void) (David di Donatello Award for Best Dir 1980) 1980, Gli occhi, la bocca (Those Eyes, That Mouth) 1982, Enrico IV (Henry IV) 1984, Il diavolo in corpo (Devil in the Flesh) 1986, La visione del Sabba 1988, La condanna (The Conviction) (Silver Berlin Bear, Berlin Int. Film Festival 1991) 1991, Il sogno della farfalla (The Butterfly's Dream) 1994, Sogni infranti (Broken Dreams) 1995, Elena 1997, Il Principe di Homburg (The Prince of Homburg) 1997, La religione della storia 1998, La balia (The Nanny) 1999, L'Affresco 2000, Un altro mondo è possibile (Another World is Possible) 2001, L'ora di religione (Il sorriso di mia madre) (The Religion Hour (My Mother's Smile)) (also producer) (Prize of the Ecumenical Jury – Special Mention, Cannes Film Festival 2002, Best Film, Flaiano Film Festival 2002, Silver Ribbon for Best Dir, Italian Nat. Syndicate of Film Journalists 2002) 2002, Buongiorno, notte (Good Morning, Night) (also producer) (FIPRESCI Prize, European Film Awards 2003, CinemAvvenire Award for Best Film, Little Golden Lion Award and Outstanding Individual Contrib. Award, Venice Film Festival 2003) 2003, Il regista di matrimoni (The Wedding Director) (also producer) 2006, Sorelle 2006, Vincere 2009, Sorelle Mai 2010, Dormant Beauty 2012, Blood of My Blood 2015, Sweet Dreams 2016. *Television:* Il gabbiano 1977, La macchina cinema (The Cinema Machine, USA) (FIPRESCI Prize, Berlin Int. Film Festival 1979) 1979, L'uomo dal fiore in bocca 1992, . . .Addio del passato. . . (also producer) 2002.

BELLON, Pierre; French business executive; *Chairman Emer., Sodexo SA;* b. 24 Jan. 1930, Marseille; m.; four c.; ed École des Hautes Études Commerciales; began career with family's ship chandlery business, Marseille 1950s; Asst Man. Soc. d'Exploitations Hôtelières, Aériennes et Terrestres 1958, later Man. Dir, Chair. and CEO; f. Sodexho SA, food and management services co., Marseille 1966 (renamed Sodexho Alliance SA 1997, renamed Sodexo SA 2008), CEO 1966–2005, Chair. 1974–2016, Chair. Emer. 2016–; Chair. and CEO Bellon SA (family holding co. that controls Sodexo) 1988–, Chair. Man. Bd 1996–2002, Chair. Supervisory Bd 2002–; joined Bureau Francis Lefebvre law firm 1991, Chair. Man. Bd –2004; mem. Bd Lafarge Ciments –2010; mem. Supervisory Bd ELS (Éditions Lefebvre Sarrut) –2010; Nat. Pres. Nat. Centre for Young Business Leaders (fmrly the Centre for Young Employers) 1968–70; Pres. Nat. Fed. of Hotel and Restaurant Chains 1972–75; mem. Exec. Council of CNPF (French employers' fed.) 1976–, Vice-Chair. CNPF (now known as MEDEF) 1980–2005; Founder Asscn Progrès du Man. 1986; currently Chair. and CEO ANSA (French Nat. Asscn of Jt Stock Cos); mem. Econ. and Social Council 1969–79, Conseil des Prélèvements Obligatoires (French Tax and Social Charges Bd); Commdr, Légion d'honneur, Ordre nat. du Mérite, Chevalier, Ordre du Mérite Agricole, Commdr, Order of Rio Branco (Brazil); French Inst. Alliance Française (FIAF) Pilier d'Or 2007. *Publication:* I Have Had a Lot of Fun (The Sodexo Story). *Address:* Sodexo SA, 255 quai de la Bataille de Stalingrad, 92130 Issy-les-Moulineaux, France (office). *Telephone:* 1-57-75-82-03 (office). *Fax:* 1-57-75-80-01 (office). *E-mail:* noelle.robillard@sodexo.com (office). *Website:* www.sodexo.com (office).

BELLUCCI, Monica; Italian fashion model and actress; b. 30 Sept. 1964, Città di Castello, Perugia; d. of Pasquale Bellucci and Brunella Briganti; m. 1st Claudio Carlos Basso 1990 (divorced 1994); m. 2nd Vincent Cassel 1999 (divorced 2013); two d.; ed Univ. of Perugia; model Elite Model Man., Milan 1988–90, appeared in advertising campaigns for Dolce & Gabbana; began taking acting lessons 1989; debut in TV film Vita Coi Figli (Life With the Sons) 1990; European Golden Globe 2005, Donostia Lifetime Achievement Award, San Sebastián Int. Film Festival 2017. *Films include:* Briganti 1990, La riffa 1991, Bram Stoker's Dracula 1992, Ostinato destino 1992, I mitici 1994, Palla di neve 1995, Il cielo è sempre più blu 1995, L'appartement 1996, Come mi vuoi 1996, Dobermann 1997, Mauvais genre 1997, L'ultimo capodanno dell'umanità (Best Actress, Globo d'Oro) 1998, A los que aman 1998, Méditerranées 1998, Comme un poisson hors de l'eau 1999, Under Suspicion 2000, Franck Spadone 2000, Malèna 2000, Il patto dei lupi 2000, Astérix et Obélix: Mission Cléopâtre 2001, Le pacte des loups 2001, Irreversible 2002, Ricordati di me (Silver Ribbon for Best Supporting Actress, Italian Nat. Syndicate of Film Journalists 2003) 2002, The Matrix Reloaded 2003, Tears of the Sun 2003, She Hate Me 2004, The Passion of the Christ 2004, The Brothers Grimm 2005, Combien tu m'aimes? 2005, Sheitan 2006, N (Io e Napoleone) 2006, Le Concile de pierre 2006, Manuale d'amore 2 (Capitoli successivi) 2007, Shoot 'Em Up 2007, Le Deuxième Souffle 2007, Sanguepazzo 2008, L'Uomo che ama 2008, The Private Lives of Pippa Lee 2009, The Whistleblower 2010, The Ages of Love 2011, Un été brûlant 2011, Rhino Season 2012, Des gens qui s'embrassent 2013, The Wonders 2014, Na Quebrada 2014, Ville-Marie 2015, Spectre 2015, On the Milky Road (European Nastro D'Argento, Italian Nat. Syndicate of Film Journalists 2017) 2016, Nekrotronic 2018. *Television:* Vita coi figli (film) 1990, Dolce & Gabbana Parfums (short film) 1994, Rose, c'est Paris (film) 2010, Platane (series) 2011, Mozart in the Jungle (series) 2016. *Address:* c/o Laurent Grégoire, Adéquat, 21 rue D'uzès, 75002 Paris, France (office). *Telephone:* 1-42-80-00-42 (Paris) (office). *Fax:* 1-42-80-00-43 (Paris) (office). *E-mail:* agence@agence-adequat.com (office). *Website:* www.agence-adequat.com (office); monicabellucci.net.

BELLUZZI, Andrea; San Marino lawyer and politician; b. 23 March 1968; m.; one s.; semi-professional racing driver since 1990, Ferrari Challenge World Champion 2001, 2006 and 2011, runner up 2000 and 2003; driving instructor and training inspector, BMW Italy 1990–2001; consultant to numerous professional motor racing and motorcycle teams; pvt. legal practice 1998–; Dir, Township Council of San Marino City 1999–2001; mem. Consiglio Grande e Generale (Parl.) 2012–, mem. Foreign Affairs, Emigration and Immigration, Security, Public Order and Information Cttees; Co-Captain Regent (jt head of state) April–Oct. 2015; fmr Legal Adviser, Banca del Titano, GE.FIN. SA; mem. Bd of Auditors, Savings Bank of San Marino SpA 1997–2001, Dir 2002–08; mem. Bd of Auditors, Central Bank of the Repub. of San Marino 2001–02, Fineuro SA 2005–08; Dir Hera Rimini Srl 2006–08; mem. Supervisory Bd Bank Kovanica Varazdin (Croatia) 2007–08; Dir Automobile Club San Marino 1997–, Vice-Chair. 2001–04; mem. Panathlon International Club of San Marino 1998–; mem. Board of Dirs San Marino Motoring Fed. 2005–08, Sec.-Gen. 2009–12; mem. San Marino del. to Inter-Parliamentary Union; mem. Partito dei Socialisti e dei Democratici 2007–. *Address:* Studio Legale E Notarile Belluzzi Avv. Andrea, P. Tini, 12, 47890, San Marino (office). *E-mail:* andrea@studiobelluzzi.com (office).

BELMONDO, Jean-Paul; French actor; b. 9 April 1933, Neuilly-sur-Seine; s. of Paul Belmondo and Madeline Rainaud-Richard; m. 1st Elodie Constantin 1953 (divorced 1967); m. 2nd Natty Belmondo 2002 (divorced 2008); one s. two d. (one deceased); ed Ecole Alsacienne, Paris, Cours Pascal and Conservatoire nat. d'art dramatique; started career on the stage; mainly film actor since 1957; Pres. French Union of Actors 1963–66; Pres. Annabel Productions 1981–; Dir Théâtre des Variétés 1991; Officier Légion d'honneur, Chevalier, Ordre nat. du Mérite 1986, des Arts et des Lettres; Prix Citron 1972, Career Achievement Award, Los Angeles Film Critics Asscn 2010. *Plays include:* L'hôtel du libre-échange, Oscar, Trésor-Party, Médée, La mégère apprivoisée, Kean 1987, Cyrano de Bergerac 1990, Tailleur pour Dames 1993, La Puce à l'oreille 1996, Frédérick ou le boulevard du crime 1998. *Films include:* Sois belle et tais-toi, A pied, à cheval et en voiture, les Tricheurs, Charlotte et son Jules, Drôle de dimanche 1958, Les Copains du dimanche, Mademoiselle Ange, A double tour, Classe tous risques, À bout de souffle, L'Amour, La Novice, La Ciociara, Moderato Cantabile, Léon Morin Prêtre, Le Doulos 1962, Dragées au poivre, L'Aîné des Ferchaux, Peau de banane, 100,000 dollars au soleil 1963, Two Women, The Man From Rio, Echappement libre 1964, Les tribulations d'un Chinois en Chine, Pierrot le Fou 1965, Paris, brûle-t-il? 1966, Le Voleur 1966, Casino Royale 1967, The Brain 1969, La Sirène du Mississippi 1969, Un Homme qui me plaît 1970, Borsalino 1970, The Burglars 1972, La Scoumoune 1972, L'Héritier 1972, Le Magnifique 1973, Stavisky 1974, Peur sur la ville 1975, L'Incorrigible 1975, L'Alpageur, Le corps de mon ennemi 1976, L'Animal 1977, Flic ou Voyou 1979, L'As de as (also produced) 1982, Le Marginal 1983, Joyeuses Pâques, Les Morfalous 1984, Hold-up 1985, Le Solitaire 1987, Itinéraire d'un enfant gâté (César for Best Actor 1988), L'Inconnu dans la Maison 1992, Les Cent et une Nuits 1995, Les Misérables 1995, Désiré 1996, Une chance sur deux 1998, Peut-être 1999, Les Acteurs 2000, Amazone 2000, L'Aîné des Ferchaux (TV) 2001, Down in the Boondocks 2008, A Man and His Dog 2009. *Publication:* 30 Ans et 25 Films (autobiog.) 1963. *Leisure interests:* boxing, football. *Address:* Artmédia, 20 avenue Rapp, 75007 Paris, France (office).

BELNAP, Nuel, PhD; American philosopher and academic; *Alan Ross Anderson Distinguished Professor of Philosophy Emeritus, University of Pittsburgh;* b. 1 May 1930, Evanston, Ill.; s. of Nuel Dinsmore and Elizabeth Belnap (née Dafter); m. 1st Joan Gohde 1953; m. 2nd Gillian Hirth 1982; four c.; m. 3rd Birgit Herbeck 1997; ed Univ. of Illinois, Yale Univ.; instructor in Philosophy, then Asst Prof., Yale Univ. 1958–63; Assoc. Prof. of Philosophy, Univ. of Pittsburgh 1963–66, Prof. 1966–2011, Alan Ross Anderson Distinguished Prof. of Philosophy 1984–2011, then Emer., Prof. of Sociology 1967–80, of History and Philosophy of Science 1971, of Intelligent Systems 1988–93, Fellow, Center for Philosophy of Science; Visiting Prof. of Philosophy, Univ. of Calif., Irvine 1973; Visiting Fellow, ANU 1976; Visiting Oscar R. Ewing Prof. of Philosophy, Indiana Univ. 1977, 1978, 1979; Visiting Leibniz-Prof., Zentrum für Höhere Studien 1996; mem. several editorial bds; Sterling Jr Fellow 1955–56; Fulbright Fellow 1957–58; Morse Research Fellow 1962–63; Guggenheim Fellow 1975–76; Fellow, Center for Advanced Studies in Behavioral Science 1982–83; Hon. DPhil (Leipzig) 2000. *Publications:* Computer Programs Bindex Tester 1976; The Logic of Questions and Answers (co-author) 1976, Entailment: The Logic of Relevance and Necessity (co-author) (Vol. I) 1975, (Vol. II) 1992, The Revision Theory of Truth (co-author) 1993, Facing the Future: Agents and Choices in Our Indeterministic World (co-author) 2001. *Address:* Department of Philosophy, University of Pittsburgh, Fifth Avenue, Pittsburgh, PA 15260 (office); 401 Shady Avenue, Pittsburgh, PA 15206, USA (home). *Telephone:* (412) 624-5777 (office); (412) 665-0406 (home). *Fax:* (412) 624-5377 (office). *E-mail:* belnap@pitt.edu (office). *Website:* www.pitt.edu/~belnap (office).

BELO-OSAGIE, Hakeem, MA, MBA; Nigerian petroleum economist, lawyer and business executive; *Chairman, First Securities Discount House;* b. 1955; s. of Tiamiyu Bello-Osagie; m.; ed King's Coll., Oxford, King's Coll., Cambridge, UK, Harvard Business School, USA; worked as Special Asst to Nigerian Minister of Petroleum and Energy; also worked in Petrochemicals Div., Nigerian Nat. Petroleum Corpn –1986 (resgnd); est. CTIC (energy consultancy firm) 1986; f. First Securities Discounts House Ltd 1992; Chair. Emerging Markets Telecommunication Services Ltd (Etisalat Nigeria) –2017; also Chair. United Bank for Africa Plc –2004, Abuja Investment Co. –2012, Chocolate City Group 2012–; Founder and Chair. First Securities Discount House; mem. Bd of Dirs Metis Capital Partners Ltd, Timbuktu Media; mem. Global Advisory Council, African Leadership Acad.; Leadership Excellence Award, Africa Business Club of Harvard Business School 2012. *Website:* www.fsdhgroup.com (office).

BĚLOBRÁDEK, Pavel, MVDr, MPA, PhD; Czech veterinary physician and politician; *Deputy Prime Minister and Minister of Science, Research and Innovation;* b. 25 Dec. 1976, Náchod; m.; two c.; ed Veterinary and Pharmaceutical Univ., Brno, CEVRO Inst., Liberal Conservative Acad.; obtained 1st level attestation at Czech State Veterinary Admin 2003; veterinary inspector, Regional Veterinary Service for Hradec Králové 2001–09; mem. Christian and Democratic Union–Czechoslovak People's Party (KDU-ČSL) 2004–, mem. Local Org. Cttee, Náchod 2004, mem. Regional Cttee, Hradec Králové region 2005, Vice-Chair. Dist Cttee, Náchod 2007–09, Chair. 2008–09, Pres. Dist Cttee 2009, mem. KV PKV KDU-ČSL, Pardubice Region 2009–10, mem. Bureau of KV KDU-ČSL, Hradec Králové region 2010, Chair. KDU-ČSL 2010–; mem. Young Christian Democrats (MKD) 2005–, Vice-Pres. 2008–09; Rep. of City of Náchod 2010; mem. Parl. for the Hradec Králové region 2012–; Deputy Prime Minister for Science, Research and Innovation 2014–, Chair. Research, and Innovation Council. *Leisure interests:* home and garden, nature, history, literature, art. *Address:* Office of the Government, náb. E. Beneše 4, 118 01 Prague 1 (office); Palác Charitas, Karlovo nám. 5, 128 01 Prague 2, Czech Republic (home). *Telephone:* (2) 24002111 (office); (2) 26205111; 73-1603880 (mobile) (home). *Fax:* (2) 57531283 (office). *E-mail:* posta@vlada.cz (office); predseda@kdu.cz (office). *Website:* www.vlada.cz (office).

BELOUSOV, Andrei, DEcon; Russian economist, government official and business executive; *Chairman, Rosneft;* b. 17 March 1959, Moscow; ed Lomonosov Moscow State Univ.; Probationer-Researcher, then Jr Researcher, Simulation Lab. of Human-Machine Systems, Cen. Econ. Math. Inst. 1981–86; Head of Lab., Inst. of Econ. Forecasting, Russian Acad. of Science 1991–2006; External Adviser to Prime Minister 2000–06; Deputy Minister of Econ. Devt and Trade 2006–08; Dir Econs and Finance Dept, Prime Minister's Office 2008–12; Minister of Econ. Devt 2012–13; Asst in Econ. Affairs to Pres. of Russian Fed. 2013–; mem. Bd of Dirs and Chair. Rosneft Oil Co. 2015–. *Address:* Rosneft, 117997 Moscow, Sofiiskaya nab.

26/1, Russian Federation (office). *Telephone:* (499) 517-88-99 (office). *Fax:* (499) 517-72-35 (office). *E-mail:* postman@rosneft.ru (office). *Website:* www.rosneft.com (office).

BELY, Mikhail Mikhailovich; Russian diplomatist; m.; two d.; ed Moscow State Inst. of Int. Relations, Nanyang Univ., Singapore; fmr Dir First Dept of Asia-Pacific Region, Ministry of Foreign Affairs, served as Attaché, Embassy in Singapore, First Sec. Embassy in Beijing 1994–99, Counsellor, Perm. Mission to UN, New York 1999–2004, Amb. to Indonesia 2004–07, to Japan 2007–12. *Address:* Ministry of Foreign Affairs, 119200 Moscow, Smolenskaya-Sennaya pl. 32/34, Russia (office). *Telephone:* (495) 244-16-06 (office). *Fax:* (495) 230-21-30 (office). *E-mail:* ministry@mid.ru (office). *Website:* www.mid.ru (office).

BEM, Pavel, MD; Czech physician and politician; b. 18 July 1963; m. Radmila Bem; two s.; ed Faculty of Medicine, Charles Univ., Prague and post-grad. studies in psychiatry, Johns Hopkins Univ., Baltimore, Florida State Univ. and Univ. of California, San Diego, USA, Mediterranean Inst. for Research and Training in Physiotherapy and Psychiatry, Italy; specialized in psychiatry working with drug addicts; House Officer, Psychiatric Clinic Kosmonosy, Mlada Boleslav 1987; House Officer, Detoxification Ward, Psychiatric Clinic, Charles Univ. 1988–90, Chief Psychiatrist, Outpatient Treatment Centre for Drug Addicts, Faculty Hosp. 1990–91; Man. Dir Filia Foundation for the Support of Mentally Disabled and Drug Dependent Persons 1992–94; Dir and Chief Psychiatrist (Outreach Programme), Contact Centre, Prague 1994; Sec.-Gen. (Anti-Drug Policy Implementation), Nat. Drug Comm., Office of Govt of Czech Repub. 1994–95, Exec. Sec. (Coordination of entire Drug Policy), Nat. Drug Comm., Cabinet of Prime Minister 1997–98; Adviser on Law Enforcement Aspects and Legislation to Minister of the Interior 1996; mem. Civic Democratic Party (ODS) 1998–, Deputy Leader 2006–08, Chair. 2008–10; Mayor of Municipal Dist of Prague 6 1998–2002, Mayor of Prague 2002–10; mem. Parl. 2010–; mem. Exec. Bd Soc. of Addictive Disorders of Czech Medical Asscn; mem. Advisory Bd to Ministry of Health on Drug Matters 1993–95; mem. Soc. for Psychotherapy and Family Therapy of Czech Medical Asscn, Chamber of Physicians of Czech Repub., Int. Council on Alcohol and Addiction, Euro—Methwork. *Publications:* Risks of HIV Transmission among IVDUs in the Czech Republic, Minimum Standards and Criteria of Effective Primary Prevention, Methodological Guidelines for School Based Primary Prevention – Manual, Teaching the Teachers Didactics, Risk Behaviour Among Drug Users in Prague, Extent of Substance Abuse in the Czech Republic, Drugs and AIDS – Parents' Guide, Methodological Guide for Community Based Prevention, Organization and Management of Drug Problems at Local Level, The Minimum Criteria for Workers in the Prevention and Treatment of Drug Addiction, Methodology for Primary Prevention in Primary and Secondary Schools (co-author), Rapid Assessment of the Extent of Drug Abuse in the Republic (co-author). *Leisure interests:* hiking, cycling, tennis, diving, classical music, rock, jazz, travel. *Address:* Chamber of Deputies (Poslanecká sněmovna), Sněmovní 4, 118 26 Prague 1, Czech Republic (office). *Telephone:* 257172017 (office). *E-mail:* bemp@psp.cz (office). *Website:* www.pavelbem.cz (office).

BEMBAMBA, Lucien Marie-Noël; Burkinabè economist and politician; b. 8 Jan. 1957; m.; three c.; Finance Admin., Central Bank of West African States 1982–93; Gen. Dir Treasury and Public Accounting Dept, Ministry of Economy and Finance 1993–2007, Del. in Charge of the Budget 2007–08, Minister of Economy and Finance 2008–14 (govt dissolved by Pres. Blaise Compaoré); Alt. Gov. IMF 2006; Chair. Nat. Public Debt Cttee 2006. *Address:* c/o Ministry of the Economy and Finance, 03 BP 7050, Ouagadougou, Burkina Faso (office).

BEMENT, Arden L., Jr, DrIng; American organization official, engineer and academic; *David A. Ross Distinguished Professor of Nuclear Engineering Emeritus, Purdue University;* b. 22 May 1932, Pittsburgh, Pa; s. of Arden Lee Bement and Edith Ardella Bement; m. 1st Mary Ann Bement (née Baroch) (deceased); three c.; m. 2nd Louise Bement (née Capistrain); eight c.; ed Colorado School of Mines, Univ. of Idaho, Univ. of Michigan; Sr Research Assoc., Gen. Electric é Co. 1954–65; Man. of Fuels and Materials Dept and Metallurgy Research Dept, Battelle Northwest Labs 1965–70; Prof. of Nuclear Materials, MIT 1970–76; Dir Office of Materials Science, Defense Advanced Research Projects Agency (DARPA) 1976–79; Deputy Under-Sec. of Defense for Research and Eng, Dept of Defense 1979–80; Vice-Pres. of Tech. Resources and of Science and Tech., TRW Inc. 1980–92; Presidential appointment: Nat. Science Bd 1989–95; Dir Midwest Superconductivity Consortium and Basil S. Turner Distinguished Prof. of Eng, Purdue Univ. 1993–98, Head of School of Engineering and David A. Ross Distinguished Prof. of Nuclear Eng 1998–2001, 2010–13, Founding Dir Global Policy Research Inst. 2010–13, Chief Global Affairs Officer 2010–13, currently Prof. Emer.; Dir Nat. Inst. of Standards and Tech. (NIST) Dept of Commerce 2001–04; Acting Dir NSF 2004, Dir 2004–10; mem. US Nat. Science Board 1989–95, Head NIST's Advanced Tech. Program Advisory Cttee 1999, with US Nat. Comm. for UNESCO, and Vice-Coordinator of Natural Sciences and Eng Cttee 2004, with G-8 Heads of Research Councils 2004–10; has given over 100 invited lectures and presentations; Lt Col (retd) Corps of Engineers US Army Reserve; mem. Nat. Acad. of Eng, European Acad. of Sciences 1999, Pan American Acad. of Eng 2012, Indiana Acad. of Science 2011 (President 2014–15); Trustee, Radian Research Corp.; Fellow, AAAS, American Inst. of Chemists, American Nuclear Soc., ASM Int., American Acad. of Arts and Sciences; Trustee, Skolkovo Inst. of Science and Tech.; Hon. Prof., Chinese Acad. of Sciences Graduate School 2011; Order of the Rising Sun, Gold and Silver Star (Japan) 2009, Chevalier, Ordre nat. de la Légion d'honneur 2011; Hon. PhD (Cleveland State Univ.) 1989, (Case Western Reserve Univ.) 2000, (Colorado School of Mines) 2004, (Korean Advanced Inst. of Science and Tech.) 2010, (Univ. of Macau, China) 2012, (Michigan Technological Univ.) 2012; Distinguished Civilian Service Medal of the Dept of Defense 1980, White House Distinguished Federal Executive Award 1980, American Nuclear Soc. Outstanding Achievement Award 2004, Washington Acad. of Science Award for Distinguished Career in Science 2006, American Chemical Soc. Public Service Award 2006, Navigator Award, Potomac Inst. for Policy Study 2010, State of Indiana Sagamore of the Wabash Award 2012. *Publications:* materials sciences and engineering courses; books and monographs on chemistry, engineering, and metals and alloys; reports of the Atomic Energy Comm.; research articles in prof. journals; science policy articles in trade journals. *Leisure interests:* philately, history, biography.

BEN ACHOUR, Mohamed al Aziz, DHist; Tunisian historian and international organization official; b. 5 Jan. 1951, La Marsa; ed Univ. of Tunis, Univ. of Paris (Sorbonne); fmr Dir-Gen. Institut supérieur d'histoire du mouvement nat., Univ. of Tunis; Councillor, Tunis Municipal Council 1995–2000; Vice-Mayor of Tunis and City Man. of the Medina (UNESCO World Heritage Site) 2000–05; Minister of Culture and Nat. Heritage 2004–08; Dir-Gen. Arab League Educational, Cultural and Scientific Org. 2009–13; Keeper, Sidi Bou Saïd historical site; Head Researcher, Museum of Tunisian Contemporary and Modern History Ksar Said Castle project; Conservator, Centre for Arts and Popular Culture, Nat. Heritage Inst.; Grand Officier, Ordre de la République de Tunisie, Commdr, Ordre du 7 Novembre (Tunisia), Ordre des Arts et des Lettres, Chevalier, Ordre Nat. du Mérite de la République française, Officier, Ordre des Palmes académiques; Aga Khan Award for Architecture, Lahore 1980, Prize of the Foundation, Crans Montana Forum, Baku 2012. *Publications include:* La mosquée-université de la Zitouna 1992, Les décorations tunisiennes d'époque husseïnite 1994, Le Bardo, palais des beys de Tunis 2000, La cour du bey de Tunis 2003, Zaouïas et confréries 2004.

BEN-DAVID, Zadok; British-Israeli sculptor; b. 1949, Bayhan, Yemen; s. of Moshe Ben-David and Hana Ben-David; ed Bezalel Acad. of Art and Design, Jerusalem, Univ. of Reading, St Martin's School of Art, London; emigrated to Israel 1949; Sculpture Teacher, St Martin's School of Art 1977–82, Ravensbourne Coll. of Art and Design, Bromley 1982–85; first solo show at Air Gallery, London 1980; represented Israel at Venice Biennale 1988, London at Kunst Im Schloss (KISS) Untergroningen 2007; commissioned to make a sculpture for the Beijing Olympics 2008; works featured in collections of major public and pvt. insts in Europe, East Asia, USA, Israel and Australia; Tel-Aviv Museum Prize for Sculpture 2005, Grande Prémio, XIV Biennial Internacional de Arte de Vila Nova de Cerveira, Portugal 2007. *Publications include:* (catalogues) Zadok Ben-David 1987, The Israeli Pavilion: The Venice Biennale 1988, De Circasia et al. 2007. *Address:* 65 Warwick Avenue, London, W9 2PP, England (home). *Telephone:* (20) 7266-0536 (home); (20) 7328-6857 (office). *Fax:* (20) 7266-3892 (home); (20) 7328-6857 (office). *E-mail:* zadokbd@yahoo.com; zadokstudio@gmail.com (office). *Website:* www.zadokbendavid.com.

BEN HAMMOUDA, Hakim, DEcon; Tunisian economist and government official; b. 7 Aug. 1961; ed Univ. de Grenoble, France; Consultant, UNDP 1997–2000; Dept Dir, Council for Devt of Social Research in Africa, Dakar 1997–2000; Dir, ECA office in Central Africa, Yaoundé 2001–03, Dir, Trade and Regional Integration Div., Addis Ababa 2003–06, Chief Economist and Dir, Trade, Finance and Econ. Devt Div. 2006–08; Dir Inst. for Training and Technical Cooperation, WTO 2008–11; Special Adviser to Pres. of ADB 2011–14; Minister of Economy and Finance 2014–15; regular lecturer on int. econs and devt econs at several univs including Institut d'Etudes et de Recherches Economiques et Sociales, Paris 1988–90, Univ. de Grenoble 1987–90, 1993–95. *Publications:* more than 25 books on econs and more than 40 articles in int. journals. *Address:* c/o Ministry of Finance, place du Gouvernement, La Kasbah, 1008 Tunis, Tunisia.

BEN JELLOUN, Tahar; Moroccan writer and poet; b. 1 Dec. 1944, Fès; m. Aicha Ben Jelloun 1986; two s. two d.; ed Lycée Regnault de Tanger, Faculté de Lettres, Mohammed-V Univ., Univ. of Paris, France; worked as prof. in Morocco, teaching philosophy first in Tetouan and then in Casablanca; emigrated to France 1971; columnist, Le Monde 1973–, La Repubblica (Italy) and La Vanguardia (Spain); mem. Conseil supérieur de la langue française; UN Goodwill Amb. for Human Rights; Dr hc (Montréal) 2008, (Louvain); Chevalier des Arts et des Lettres 1983, Chevalier, Légion d'honneur 1988, Grand Croix 2008; Prix de l'Amitié Franco-Arabe 1976, Médaille du Mérite Nat. (Morocco), Prix Goncourt 1987, Prix des Hemisphere 1991, UN Global Tolerance Award 1998, Prix Ulysse 2005, Special Prize for "peace and friendship between people" at Lazio between Europe and the Mediterranean Festival 2006, Prix de la ville Catania 2009, Argana Int. Poetry Award 2010, Erich Maria Remarque Peace Prize 2011, Prix de la Fondation Crans Montana 2011, Prix de Poésie de la ville d'Aquilla 2012, Prix de poésie Padula 2013. *Publications include:* fiction: Harrouda 1973, La Réclusion solitaire 1976 (trans. as Solitaire 1988), Moha le fou, Moha le sage 1978, La Prière de l'absent 1980, Muha al-ma'twah, Muha al-hakim 1982, L'Ecrivain public 1983, L'Enfant de sable 1985 (trans. as The Sand Child 1987), La Nuit sacrée 1987 (trans. as The Sacred Night 1989), Jour de silence à Tanger 1990 (trans. as Silent Day in Tangier 1991), Les Yeux baissés 1991, L'Ange aveugle 1992, L'Homme rompu 1994, Corruption 1995, Le Premier amour est toujours le dernier 1995, Les Raisins de la galère 1995, La Soudure fraternelle 1995, La Nuit de l'erreur 1997, L'Auberge des pauvres 1999, Labyrinthe des Sentiments 1999, Cette aveuglante absence de lumière (trans. as This Blinding Absence of Light) (Int. IMPAC Dublin Literary Award 2004) 2001, Amours sorcières 2003, La Belle au bois dormant 2004, Le Dernier Ami (trans. as The Last Friend) 2004, Partir 2005, L'ecole perdue 2006, Yemma 2007, Sur ma mère 2008, Au pays 2009, Leaving Tangier 2009, A Palace in the Old Village 2010, Le bonheur conjugal 2012, La Prière de l'absent, L'Enfant de sable, La Nuit sacrée, Les Yeux baissés, La Nuit de l'erreur 2013, L'Ablation 2014, Le mariage du plaisir 2016; poetry: Hommes sous linceul de silence 1970, Cicatrice du soleil 1972, Le Discours du chameau 1974, La Mémoire future: Anthologie de la nouvelle poésie du Maroc 1976, Les Amandiers sont morts de leurs blessures 1976, A l'insu du souvenir 1980, Sahara 1987, La Remontée des cendres 1991, Poésie Complète (1966–95) 1995, The Rising of the Ashes 2010; plays: Chronique d'une solitude 1976, Entretien avec Monsieur Said Hammadi, ouvrier algérien 1982, La Fiancée de l'eau 1984; non-fiction: La Plus haute des solitudes: Misère sexuelle d'émigrés nord-africains 1977, Haut Atlas: L'Exil de pierres 1982, Hospitalité française: Racisme et immigration maghrebine 1984, Marseille, comme un matin d'insomnie 1986, Giacometti 1991, Le Racisme expliqué à ma fille 1998, L'islam expliqué aux enfants 2002. *Address:* c/o Éditions Gallimard, 5 rue Sébastien-Bottin, 75328 Paris Cedex 07, France. *E-mail:* tbjweb@gmail.com (office). *Website:* www.taharbenjelloun.org.

BEN YAHIA, Habib; Tunisian politician and international organization official; *Secretary-General, Arab Maghreb Union;* b. 30 July 1938, Tunis; m. Naget Ben Yahia; one s. one d.; ed Univ. of Tunis, Columbia Univ., USA; fmr Dir African Div., Ministry of Foreign Affairs, then Dir Econ. Co-operation with US Div., fmr Econ. Counsellor, Embassies in Paris and Washington, DC, fmr Chief of Staff, Ministry of Foreign Affairs, apptd Amb. to UAE 1976, to Japan 1977, to Belgium, Amb. to

USA 1981–88, Sec. of State, Ministry of Foreign Affairs 1988–91, Minister of Foreign Affairs 1991–97, of Defence and Foreign Affairs 1999–2004, Diplomatic Councillor to Pres. of Tunisia 2005; Sec.-Gen. Arab Maghreb Union 2006–; Grand cordon des insignes of the Tunisian Republic, Grand cordon des insignes of 7 November. *Address:* Union du Maghreb Arabe, 14 Rue Zalagh Agdal, Rabat, Morocco (office). *Telephone:* (3) 7671274 (office); (3) 7671280 (office). *Fax:* (3) 7671253 (office). *E-mail:* sg.uma@maghrebarabe.org (office). *Website:* www.maghrebarabe.org (office).

BENABID, Alim-Louis, MD, PhD; French neurosurgeon and academic; *Professor Emeritus, Joseph Fourier University;* b. 2 May 1942, Grenoble; ed Joseph Fourier Univ., Grenoble; staff neurosurgeon, Joseph Fourier Univ. 1972–78, Prof. of Experimental Medicine 1978–83, Prof. of Biophysics 1983–2007, Prof. Emer. 2007–; Fellow in Preclinical Neuropharmacology, Salk Inst., La Jolla, Calif., USA 1979–80; Dir of Preclinical Neurosciences Unit, Institut nat. de la santé et de la recherche médicale (INSERM) 1988–2007; Head of Neurosurgery Dept, Univ. Hosp. of Grenoble 1989–2007; co-ordinated Claudio Munari Centre for Surgery of Epilepsy and Movement Disorders, Hosp. Niguarda, Milan, Italy 1998–2007; staff consultant, Cleveland Clinic Foundation, Ohio, USA 2000–03; joined French Commissariat d'Energie Atomique as a scientific adviser during the time a campus for public-private innovation was being created (Grenoble Innovation for Advanced New Technologies (Giant) campus) 2007; Chair. Edmond J. Safra Biomedical Research Centre, Clinatec 2009; mem. Acad. des sciences, Institut Universitaire de France 1999, Royal Acad. of Medicine of Belgium 2002, French Nat. Acad. of Medicine; Hon. mem. Belgian Soc. of Neurology; Chevalier, Légion d'honneur, Ordre des Palmes académiques; Dr hc (Nat. Univ. of Ireland, Galway) 2005, (Univ. of London and McGill Univ., Canada); Dehomag Prize for Robotics 1993, Prix Électricité-Santé de l'EDF 1994, Medicine and Biology Prize, Comité du rayonnement français 1997, Biomedical PCL Research Prize, Acad. des sciences 1998, Scientific Prize, Nat. Foundation for Health Promotion and Research Devt (Algeria) 1999, Jean Valade Prize, Foundation of France 1999, Klaus Joachim Zülch Prize, Gertrud Reemtsma Foundation, Cologne 2000, Scientific Award 2000, Int. Neurobionics Foundation, Hanover 2000, Cotzias Award, Spanish Soc. of Neurology, Barcelona 2000, Sherrington Medal, Royal Soc. of Medicine, London 2002, Research and Health Prize, Institut des sciences et de la santé 2002, Betty and David Koetser Foundation Prize, Zurich 2002, Dingebauer Prize, German Neurological Soc. 2002, Spiegel and Wycis Medal 2005, Matmut Prize for Medical Innovation, Foundation of the Future 2006, James Parkinson Award 2007, Victor Horsley Award 2007, Movement Disorders Research Award, American Acad. of Neurology 2008, INSERM Honour Award 2008, Victory of Medicine under the Jubilee Hosp. (co-recipient) 2008, Jay van Andel Award for Outstanding Achievement in Parkinson's Disease Research 2013, Robert A. Pritzker Prize for Leadership in Parkinson's Research, Michael J. Fox Foundation 2013, Lasker–DeBakey Clinical Medical Research Award (co-recipient) 2014, Breakthrough Prize in Life Sciences (co-recipient) 2015. *Publications:* more than 520 papers in professional journals. *Address:* Université Joseph Fourier, BP 53, 38041 Grenoble Cedex 9, France (office). *Telephone:* (4) 76-51-46-00 (office). *E-mail:* info@ujf-grenoble.fr (office). *Website:* www.ujf-grenoble.fr (office).

BENAÏSSA, Muhammad, BA; Moroccan politician; b. 3 Jan. 1937, Asilah; m. Laila Hajoun-Benaïssa; five c.; ed Univ. of Minnesota, Columbia Univ., USA; Press Attaché, Perm. Mission of Morocco to UN, New York 1964–65; Information Officer, UN Dept of Information, 1965–67; Regional Information Adviser, FAO, Rome 1967–71, Head of Devt Support Communication 1971–73, Asst to Dir of Information 1973–74, Dir of Information Div. 1974–76; Asst Sec.-Gen. of UN, World Food Conf. 1975; elected to City Council of Asilah 1976–83, elected Mayor 1992, then Pres. City Council of Asilah; Founder and Chair. Asilah Forum Foundation; Co-Founder Moussem Cultural International Asikah (arts festival) 1978; mem. Moroccan Parl. 1977–83; Co-Founder and Exec. mem. Moroccan Social Democratic Party (Rassemblement Nat. des Independents) 1978; consultant, UNDP, IFAD, UNFPA 1978–85; Chief Ed. Al-Mithak Al-Watani and Al-Maghrab publs 1980–85; Amb. to USA 1993–99; Minister of Foreign Affairs and Co-operation 1999–2007; Dr hc (Univ. of Minnesota) 2007. *Publications include:* Grains de Peau 1974. *Address:* Asilah Forum Foundation, Hassan II Centre, Asilah, Morocco (office). *Website:* www.assilah.net (office).

BÉNASSY, Jean-Pascal, PhD; French economist and researcher; *Director Emeritus of Research, Centre National de la Recherche Scientifique (CNRS);* b. 30 Dec. 1948, Paris; s. of Jean Bénassy and Jeannine Bénassy; ed Ecole Normale Supérieure, Paris, Univ. of California, Berkeley, USA; Research Assoc., CEPREMAP 1973–, Dir Emer. of Research, CNRS 1981–; Dir Laboratoire d'Economie Politique, Ecole Normale Supérieure 1984–88; Dept of Econs Ecole Polytechnique 1987–2002; Fellow, Econometric Soc. 1981, mem. Council 1990–92; Guido Zerilli Marimo Prize, Acad. des Sciences Morales et Politiques 1990. *Publications include:* The Economics of Market Disequilibrium 1982, Macroéconomie et théorie du déséquilibre 1984, Macroeconomics: An Introduction to the Non-Walrasian Approach 1986, Macroeconomics and Imperfect Competition 1995, The Macroeconomics of Imperfect Competition and Nonclearing Markets: A Dynamic General Equilibrium Approach 2002, Imperfect Competition, Nonclearing Markets and Business Cycles 2006, Money, Interest and Policy 2007, Macroeconomic Theory 2011; numerous articles in specialized journals. *Address:* CEPREMAP-ENS, 48 boulevard Jourdan, Bâtiment E, 75014 Paris, France (office). *Telephone:* 33-1-43-13-63-38 (office). *E-mail:* benassy@pse.ens.fr (office).

BENATAR, Pat; American singer; b. (Pat Andrejewski), 1953, Brooklyn, New York; m. Neil Giraldo; one c.; Grammy Awards for Best Female Rock Vocal Performance 1981, 1982, 1983, 1984, three American Music Awards; inducted into Long Island Hall of Fame 2008. *Recordings include:* albums: In the Heat of the Night 1979, Crimes of Passion 1980, Precious Time 1981, Get Nervous 1982, Live From Earth 1983, Tropico 1984, Seven the Hard Way 1985, Wide Awake in Dreamland 1988, Best Shots 1989, True Love 1991, Gravity's Rainbow 1993, All Fired Up: The Very Best of Pat Benatar 1994, Best of Pat Benatar Vols 1 and 2 2001, Christmas In America 2001, Go 2003, 35th Anniversary Tour (Live) 2015. *Publication:* Between a Heart and a Rock Place 2010. *Website:* benatargiraldo.com.

BENAVIDES FERREYROS, Ismael Alberto, MBA; Peruvian politician and fmr banker; b. 10 May 1945, Lima; s. of Ismael Benavides de la Quintana; ed Univ. of California, Berkeley, USA; Minister of Fisheries 1984–85; mem. Congreso for Ica constituency 1990–92 (parl. dissolved); Dir and Gen. Man. Banco Internacional del Perú (Interbank) 1994–2007; spent time with family business producing traditional Huamaní pisco (brandy) mid-1990s; Minister of Agric. 2007–08, of Economy and Finance 2010–11; fmr adviser to World Bank; fmr Pres. Asociación de Bancos, Cámara de Comercio Peruano-Chilena. *Address:* c/o Ministry of Economy and Finance, Jirón Junín 319, 4°, Circado de Lima, Lima 1, Peru. *E-mail:* postmaster@mef.gob.pe.

BENAVIDES GANOZA, Roque, BS, MBA; Peruvian business executive; *Chairman, Compañía de Minas Buenaventura SAA;* b. 20 Aug. 1954; s. of Alberto Benavides de la Quintana; ed Pontificia Universidad Catolica del Peru, Henley Business School, Harvard Business School, USA, Univ. of Oxford, UK; served in various exec. positions at Compañía de Minas Buenaventura SAA 1978–85, Chief Financial Officer 1985–2000, Pres. and CEO 2000–11, mem. Bd of Dirs 2004–, Chair. 2011–; Chair. Nat. Asscn of Minerals, Petroleum and Energy 1993–95; Pres. Nat. Confed. of Pvt. Business Insts (Confiep) 1999–2001, 2017–; Vice-Chair. World Gold Council 2001, Silver Inst. 2007; mem. Bd of Dirs Banco de Crédito, Cementos Lima. *Address:* Compañía de Minas Buenaventura SAA, Avenida Carlos Villarán 790, Santa Catalina, La Victoria, Lima 13, Peru (office). *Telephone:* (1) 4192500 (office). *Fax:* (1) 4716522 (office). *E-mail:* recursos@buenaventura.com.pe (office). *Website:* www.buenaventura.com.pe (office).

BENBITOUR, Ahmed, MBA, PhD; Algerian economist, academic and fmr politician; b. 20 June 1946, Ghardaia; m.; four c.; ed Univ. of Algiers, Univ. of Montreal, Canada; fmr CEO National Co. of Studies and Processing, National Co. of Juice and Tinned Fruits of Algeria; Prof., National Inst. of Productivity and Industrial Devt (INPED) 1975–79; fmr mem. Parl., Chair. Econ. and Finance Comm. at Council of the Nation (Senate); fmr consultant at World Bank and IMF; fmr Minister of Finance, of Energy, of Treasury; Prime Minister of Algeria 1999–2000; Lecturer (external), African Inst. for Econ. Devt and Planning, Dakar, Senegal 2003–06; announced then withdrew candidacy for Pres. of Algeria 2014. *Publications:* several publs on econ. reforms and finance.

BENCHAABOUN, Mohamed; Moroccan politician and fmr banker; *Minister of the Economy and Finance;* b. 12 Nov. 1961, Casablanca; m.; two c.; ed Ecole Nat. Supérieure des Télécommunications, Paris; several sr positions in the private sector, including as Dir, Industrial Div., Alcatel Alsthom Group, Morocco; Dir, Admin of Customs and Indirect Taxes 1996–99; Deputy CEO, in charge of common services and later Devt Div., Banque Centrale Populaire (BCP) 1999–2003, CEO 2008–18; Dir-Gen. Nat. Telecommunications Regulatory Agency (ANRT) 2003–08; Pres. Réseau francophone de la régulation des télécommunications (FRATEL) 2005–06; Pres. Int. Confed. of Banques Populaires 2012–15; Minister of the Economy and Finance 2018–; mem. Econ., Social and Environmental Council; mem. Bd of Dirs British Arab Commercial Bank Ltd 2010–12; mem. Bd of Dirs Mohammed V Foundation for Solidarity, Mohammed VI Foundation for the Protection of the Environment; Chevalier, Order of Ouissam Al-Arch 2010. *Address:* Ministry of the Economy and Finance, blvd Muhammad V, Quartier Administratif, Chellah, Rabat, Morocco (office). *Telephone:* (53) 7677501 (office). *Fax:* (53) 7677526 (office). *E-mail:* internet@finances.gov.ma (office). *Website:* www.finances.gov.ma (office).

BENDER, Sir Brian Geoffrey, Kt, KCB, PhD; British civil servant (retd); *Chairman, London Metal Exchange;* b. 25 Feb. 1949, Sheffield; s. of Prof. Arnold Eric Bender; m. Penelope Clark 1974; one s. one d.; ed Imperial Coll., London; joined Dept of Trade and Industry 1973; Pvt. Sec. to Sec. of State for Trade 1976–77; First Sec., Office of Perm. Rep. to EC 1977–82; Prin., Dept of Trade and Industry 1982–84; Counsellor, Office of Perm. Rep. to EC 1985–89; UnderSec. and Deputy Head of European Secr., Cabinet Office 1990–93; Head of Regulation Devt Div., Dept of Trade and Industry 1993–94; Deputy Sec. and Head of European Secr., Cabinet Office 1994–98; Head of Public Service Delivery, Cabinet Office 1998–99; Perm. Sec. Cabinet Office 1999–2000, Ministry of Agric., Fisheries and Food 2000–01, Dept for Environment, Food and Rural Affairs 2001–05, Dept of Trade and Industry 2005–07, Perm. Sec., Dept for Business, Enterprise and Regulatory Reform 2007–09 (retd); Chair. London Metal Exchange 2010–; Chair. Honda European Communication and Consultation Group; Dir (non-exec.) Financial Reporting Council 2014–; Dir (non-exec.) Pool Re-insurance 2014–; Bd Mentor, Criticaleye; Sr Adviser, MHP Communications; Trustee Lloyds Register Foundation 2013–; Gov. Dulwich Coll. *Address:* London Metal Exchange, 56 Leadenhall Street, London, EC3A 2DX, England (office). *Telephone:* (20) 7264-5555 (office). *Website:* www.lme.com (office).

BENDINE, Aldemir, BA, MBA; Brazilian banker and business executive; fmr Br. Man., Banco do Brasil SA, then Exec. Man. Directory of Retail, then Exec. Sec. Bd of Officers, then Vice-Pres. of Retail and Distribution, mem. Exec. Bd 2006–, Vice-Pres. of Credit and Debit Cards and New Business on Retail Services –2009, Vice-Chair. and Pres. (CEO) Banco do Brasil SA 2009–15; CEO Petróleo Brasileiro SA (Petrobras) 2015–16 (resgnd); Exec. Dir Federacão de Bancos Brasileiros (Febraban); mem. Bd of Dirs and CEO Brazilian Asscn of Business Cards and Services (ABECS); Chair. Visa Vale—CBSS; CEO BB Administradora de Cartoes, BB Administradora de Consorcios. *Address:* c/o Office of the CEO, Petrobras, Av. República do Chile, nº 65 - Centro, Rio de Janeiro 20031-912, Brazil.

BENDTSEN, Bendt; Danish politician; b. 25 March 1954, Odense; m. Kirsten Bendtsen; three c.; ed agricultural school, Danish Police Acad.; farm hand 1971–75; Police Inspector, Odense 1980–84, Detective Inspector 1984–99, Vice-Chair. Odense Criminal Police Asscn 1986–94; mem. Odense City Council 1990–99; parl. cand. (Conservative People's Party) 1990, 1992, 2001; substitute mem. Parl. April 1994, mem. Parl. Sept. 1994–2008, Deputy Prime Minister 2001–08; Leader, Conservative Party and Conservative Group in Danish Parl. 1999–2008 (resgnd); Minister for Econ. and Business Affairs 2001–08 (resgnd), Minister for Nordic Cooperation 2001–02; mem. Internal Market Council 2001–08 (Chair. 2002), Vice-Chair. Globalisation Council 2005–06; mem. European Parl. (European People's Party) 2009–; Commdr, Order of the Dannebrog 2002, Commdr 1st Degree, Order of the Dannebrog 2008, Grand Cross of the Order of the Crown (Belgium) 2002, Grand Cross of the Order of Merit (Germany) 2002, Commdr Grand Cross of the Royal Swedish Order of the Northern Star 2007, Grand Cross (Brazil) 2007, Order of the Aztec Eagle (Mexico) 2009; Schuman Medal from European Parliament's PPE-DE Group 2003. *Leisure interests:* hunting, playing golf, driving a motorcycle. *Address:* European Parliament, Bât. Altiero Spinelli 10E116, 60, rue Wiertz, 1047 Brussels, Belgium (office). *Telephone:* (2) 284-51-25 (office). *E-mail:* bendt.bendtsen@europarl.europa.eu (office). *Website:* www.konservative.dk/Personer/B/Bendt-Bendtsen (office).

BENEDICT XVI, His Holiness Pope (Joseph Alois Ratzinger); German ecclesiastic; b. 16 April 1927, Marktl am Inn, Bavaria; s. of Joseph Ratzinger and Maria Peintner; ed Univ. of Munich; ordained Chaplain 1951; Prof. of Theology, Freising 1958, Bonn 1959–63, Münster 1963–66, Tübingen 1966–69, Regensburg 1969; co-f. Communio (theological journal) 1972; apptd Archbishop of Munich-Freising 1977–82; cr. Cardinal of Munich by Pope Paul VI 1977; Cardinal Bishop of the Episcopal See of Velletri-Segni 1993; fmr Chair. Bavarian Bishops' Conf.; Prefect, Sacred Congregation for the Doctrine of the Faith 1981–2005; Vice-Dean Coll. of Cardinals 1998–2002, Dean 2002–05; Titular Bishop of Ostia 2002; presided over funeral of Pope John Paul II and the Conclave which elected him April 2005; elected Pope and Bishop of Rome 2005–13 (resgnd), Pope Emer. 2013–; Pres. Int. Theological Comm., Pontifical Biblical Comm.; mem. of the Congregations for the Oriental Churches, for the Divine Worship and the Discipline of the Sacrament, for the Bishops, for the Evangelization of Reapers, for Catholic Educ.; mem. Pontifical Council for the Promotion of Christian Unity; Dr hc (Navarra) 1998, numerous other hon. doctorates. *Publications:* books and articles on theological matters including Without Roots (with Marcello Pera) 2006. *Address:* c/o Palazzo Apostolico Vaticano, 00120 Città del Vaticano, Rome, Italy. *Website:* www.vatican.va.

BENEDIKTSSON, Bjarni, LLM; Icelandic lawyer and politician; *Minister of Finance and Economic Affairs;* b. 26 Jan. 1970; m. Þóra Margrét Baldvinsdóttir; four c.; ed Univ. of Iceland, Univ. of Miami, USA; Deputy Dist Commr, Keflavik 1995; private legal practice with own law firm 1999–2003; Chair. BNT hf (bank) and N1 (retail and service co.) 2005–08; mem. Althingi (parl.) for SW Constituency 2003–, mem. Budget Cttee 2003–07, Foreign Affairs Cttee 2005–13 (Chair. 2007–09), mem. Icelandic del. to WEU Assembly 2003–05 (Chair. 2003–05), to EFTA and EEA Parl. Cttees 2005–09 (Vice-Chair. 2007–09), to Nordic Council 2009–12, mem. EU–Iceland Jt Parl. Cttee 2010–13; Minister of Finance and Econ. Affairs 2013–Jan. 2017, Nov. 2017–; Prime Minister Jan.–Nov. 2017 (resgnd); mem. Independence Party (IP), Chair. 2009–. *Leisure interests:* football, fishing. *Address:* Ministry of Finance and Economic Affairs, Arnarhvoli við Lindargötu, 101 Reykjavík, Iceland (office). *Telephone:* 5459200 (office). *Fax:* 5459299 (office). *E-mail:* postur@fjr.is (office). *Website:* www.fjarmalaraduneyti.is (office).

BENEGAL, Shyam, MA; Indian film director and screenwriter; b. 14 Dec. 1934, Aliwal, Hyderabad; m. Neera Benegal; ed Osmania Univ., Film and TV Inst. of India Pune; advertising copywriter and dir of more than 620 advertising shorts for Lintas Agency, Bombay 1960–66; Dir Indian Nat. Film Devt Corpn 1980; Chair. Film and TV Inst. of India during 1980–83, 1989–92; mem. Nat. Integration Council 1986–89, Nat. Council of Arts; Chair. Academic Council Whistling Woods Int.; Advisor, Partners for Urban Knowledge, Action and Research; Trustee India Foundation for the Arts; Homi Bhabha Fellowship 1970; Dr hc (Calcutta) 2012; Padma Shri 1976, Sovietland Nehru Award 1989, Padma Bhushan 1991, Indira Gandhi Award 2004, Dadasaheb Phalke Award 2006, V Shantaram Lifetime Achievement Award 2018. *Films:* Dir: Gher Betha Ganga 1962, Close to Nature 1967, A Child of the Streets 1967, Indian Youth: An Exploration 1968, Flower Garden 1969, Quest for a Nation 1970, The Pulsating Giant 1971, Raga and Melody 1972, Power to the People 1972, Suhani Sadak 1973, Violence: What Price? Who Pays? 1974, The Quiet Revolution 1974, Bal Sansar 1974, Hero 1975, Charandas Chor 1975, Nishaant (Nat. Film Award 1976) 1975, Bhumika (Nat. Film Award 1978) 1976, Manthan (Nat. Film Award 1977) 1976, Kondura 1978, Pashu Palan 1979, Jawaharlal Nehru (Nat. Film Award 1984) 1982, Satyajit Ray (Nat. Film Award 1985) 1982, Arohan (Nat. Film Award 1982) 1982, Mandi 1983, Vardan 1985, Festival of India 1985, Nature Symphony 1990, Antarnaad 1991, Suraj Ka Satvan Ghoda (Nat. Film Award 1993) 1993, Mammo (Nat. Film Award 1995) 1994, Sardari Begum (Nat. Film Award 1997) 1996, The Making of the Mahatma (Nat. Film Award 1996) 1996, Hari-Bhari 2000, Zubeidaa (Nat. Film Award 2001) 2001, Bose: The Forgotten Hero (Nat. Film Award 2005) 2004, Welcome to Sajjanpur 2008, Well Done Abba 2009; Writer: Ankur (Nat. Film Award 1975) 1974, Manthan 1976, Bhumika 1976, Junoon (Nat. Film Award 1979) 1978, Anugraham 1978, Kalyug (Golden Prize 1981, Filmfare Award 1982) 1980, Mandi 1983, Trikal 1985; Producer: Susman 1987, Powaqqatsi 1988, Sardari Begum 1996, Welcome to Sajjanpur 2008, Well Done Abba 2009. *Television:* Yatra 1986, Katha Saagar 1986, Bharat Ek Khoj (mini-series) 1988, Amravati ki Kahaniyan. *Address:* India Foundation for the Arts, 'Apurva' Ground Floor, No 259, 4th Cross, Raj Mahal Vilas IInd Stage, IInd Block, Bangalore 560 094, India. *Telephone:* (80) 23414681; 9820290888 (home). *Fax:* (80) 23412683. *E-mail:* contactus@indiaifa.org (office). *Website:* www.indiaifa.org (office).

BENETTON, Alessandro, BS, MBA; Italian business executive; *Chairman, Benetton Group;* b. 2 March 1964, Treviso; s. of Luciano Benetton (q.v.) and Maria Teresa Benetton; m. Deborah Compagnoni; three c.; ed Boston Univ., Harvard Business School, USA; early position as Analyst, Global Finance Dept, Goldman Sachs, London; Chair. Benetton Formula Ltd 1988–98; Founder, Chair. and Man. Dir. 21 Investimenti SpA (investment bank) 1992–; mem. Bd of Dirs Benetton Group 2004–, Exec. Deputy Chair. 2007–12, Chair. 2012–; mem. Bd of Dirs Edizione Holding SpA, Autogrill SpA, Permasteelisa SpA, Industrie Zignago Santa Margherita SpA, Sirti SpA; Chair. 21 Pnrs S.G.R. SpA, 21 Investimenti Pnrs SpA; Vice Chair. Nordest Marchant SpA; Sole Dir. Saibot S.r.l.; mem. Supervisory Bd 21 Centrale Pnrs SA; mem. Advisory Cttee Robert Bosch Internationale Beteiligungen; mem. Council, Confindustria; Entrepreneur of the Year, Ernst & Young 2011. *Address:* Benetton Group Headquarters, Villa Minelli, 31050 Ponzano, Treviso (office); 21 Investimenti SpA, Via G. Felissent, 90, 31100 Treviso, Italy (office). *Telephone:* (0422) 316611 (office). *Fax:* (0422) 316600 (office). *E-mail:* info@21investimenti.it (office). *Website:* www.benettongroup.com (office); www.21investimenti.it (office); www.alessandrobenetton.com.

BENETTON, Luciano; Italian business executive; b. 13 May 1935, Treviso; s. of Leone Benetton and Rosa Benetton; m. Maria-Teresa Benetton (separated); four c.; Co-founder (with three brothers) Benetton 1965, Chair. Benetton Group SpA 1965–2012; mem. Bd of Dirs Edizione Holding (family-owned financial holding co.), Atlantia SpA, Autogrill SpA; mem. Italian Senate 1992–94; Hon. MBA (Instituto de Empresa, Madrid) 1992, Hon. JD (Boston Univ.) 1994, Hon. Laurea in Economia Aziendale (Università ca' Foscari di Venezia) 1995; Civiltà Veneta 1986, Premio Creatività 1992. *Address:* c/o Benetton Group SpA, Via Minelli, 31050 Ponzano (Treviso), Italy. *Website:* www.benettongroup.com.

BENGOA ALBIZU, Vicente, BSc; Dominican Republic economist and government official; ed Univ. of Chile; Prof. of Econs and Public Finance, Univ. of Santo Domingo 1973–94, Dir Econs Dept, Technological Inst. 1978–82; Superintendent of Banking 1997–2000; Founder Dominican Liberation Party (PLD), Deputy in Nat. Ass. 1982–90; Sec. of State for Finance 2004–10, fmr Gov. IDB, Central American Bank for Economic Integration; Dir-Gen. Reserve Bank of Dominican Republic (BanReservas) 2011–13; hon. financial adviser to the Pres. 2013–.

BENGSTON, Billy Al, (Moon Doggie, Moondoggy, Moontang, Two Moons); American artist and designer; b. 7 June 1934, Dodge City, Kan.; m. Wendy Al; one d.; ed Los Angeles City Coll., California Coll. of Arts and Crafts, Oakland and Otis Art Inst.; instructor, Chouinard Art Inst. Los Angeles 1961; Lecturer, UCLA 1962–63; Guest Artist, Univ. of Oklahoma 1967; Guest Prof., Univ. of Colorado 1969; Guest Lecturer, Univ. of California, Irvine 1973; Dir Pelican Club Productions Los Angeles 1981–84; Exec. Dir Westfall Arts 1995–98; numerous solo and group exhbns; works in numerous public collections, including American Fed. of Arts, Centre Georges Pompidou, Paris, Art Inst. of Chicago, Contemporary Arts Museum, Houston, Tex., Honolulu Academy of Arts, Laguna Art Museum, Calif., La Jolla Museum of Contemporary Art, Calif., Los Angeles County Museum of Art, Museum of Contemporary Art, Los Angeles, Museum of Fine Arts, Houston, Museum of Modern Art, New York, Norton Simon Museum, Pasadena, Calif., Oakland Museum, Calif., Orange County Museum of Art, Newport Beach, Calif., Philadelphia Museum of Art, Portland Museum of Art, Ore., San Diego Museum of Art, Calif., San Francisco Museum of Art, Seattle Art Museum, Wash., Solomon R. Guggenheim Museum, New York, The Contemporary Museum, Honolulu, Corcoran Gallery of Art, Washington, DC, The Frederick R. Weisman Foundation of Art, Los Angeles, Palm Springs Desert Museum, Calif., Santa Barbara Museum of Art, Calif., Whitney Museum of American Art, New York, Yale Univ. Art Museum; Judge, Orange Co. Business Cttee for the Arts 1999; Nat. Foundation for the Arts Grant 1967, Tamarind Fellow 1968, 1982, 1987, Guggenheim Fellowship 1975, California Arts Council, Art in Public Buildings Program Comm. (Long Beach State Bldg) 1981, California Arts Council, Maestro/Apprentice Program 1982–83, California Arts Council Comm. for the Los Angeles (Ronald Reagan) State Bldg 1990, Brandeis Univ. Nat. Women's Cttee, Art Venture Los Angeles Chapter 1994, Art in Embassies Program, US Dept of State for Ambassadorial Residences. *Publications:* contribs to Art in America, Art Forum, Paris Review. *Address:* 110 Mildred Avenue, Venice, CA 90291, USA (office). *Telephone:* (310) 822-2201 (office). *E-mail:* lab@billyal.com (office); artiststudio@billyalbengston.com (office). *Website:* www.billyalbengston.com (office).

BENGU, Sibusiso Mandlenkosi Emmanuel, PhD; South African politician, diplomatist and academic; b. 8 May 1934, Kranskop, Natal; s. of Rev. Jackonia Bengu and Augusta Bengu; m. Ethel Funeka 1961; one s. four d.; ed Univ. of Geneva; Founder and Prin. Dlangezwa High School 1968–76; Publicity Sec., Natal African Teachers' Asscn 1969–71; Dir Students' Advisory Services, Univ. of Zululand 1977–78; Exec. Sec. for Research and Social Action, Lutheran World Fed., Geneva 1978–91; Rector and Vice-Chancellor Univ. of Fort Hare 1991–94, Head of History Writing Project 2004; Minister of Educ. Govt of Nat. Unity 1994–99; Pres. Intergovernmental Cttee, Ministers of Educ. of Africa (MINEDAF) 1998–99; Amb. to Germany 2000–04; First Gen. Sec. Inkatha Freedom Party, now mem. ANC; Trustee, African Centre for Constructive Resolution of Disputes; Hon. Fellowship of the Coll. of Perceptors (Manchester Univ.) 1997; Hon. DD (Wartburg Theological Seminary, Dubuque Univ.) 1986, Hon. LLD (California State Univ.) 1996, Hon. PhD in Political Science (Univ. of Fort Hare) 2001, Dr hc (Univ. of Kwazulu-Natal) 2009; Gamaliel Chair for Peace and Justice, Lutheran Campus Ministry, Univ. of Wisconsin in Milwaukee 1985; Distinguished Int. Educator Award, American Council of Education 1998. *Publications:* African Cultural Identity and International Relations 1975, Chasing Gods Not our Own 1975, Mirror or Model. *Leisure interests:* listening to music, watching sports, reading, research.

BENHABIB, Seyla, MA, PhD; American political scientist, philosopher and academic; *Eugene Meyer Professor of Political Science and Professor of Philosophy, Yale University;* b. 9 Sept. 1950, Istanbul, Turkey; of Sephardic Jewish parentage; m. James A. Sleeper; one d.; ed American Coll. for Girls, Istanbul, Brandeis and Yale Univs, USA; Prof. of Philosophy and Political Science, New School for Social Research 1991–93; Prof., Dept of Govt and Sr Research Fellow, Center for European Studies, Harvard Univ. 1993–2000, Chair., Program in Social Studies 1996–2000; Ed.-in-Chief Constellations: An International Journal of Critical and Democratic Theory 1993–97; Visiting Sr Fellow, Institut für Wissenschaft vom Menschen, Vienna, Austria 1996; Eugene Meyer Prof. of Political Science and Prof. of Philosophy, Yale Univ. 2000–, Dir, Program in Ethics, Politics and Econs 2002–08; Baruch de Spinoza Distinguished Professorship, Univ. of Amsterdam 2000; Pres. American Philosophical Asscn 2007; Visiting Prof., European Univ Inst., Florence 2015; Diane Middlebrook and Carl Djerassi Visiting Prof., Center for Gender Studies, Univ of Cambridge, UK 2017; Scholar-in-Residence, Columbia Law School (also James S. Carpentier Visiting Prof. of Law 2019) and Sr Assoc., Center for Contemporary Critical Thought, Columbia Univ 2016–18; Russell Sage Foundation Fellow 2000–01; Sr Research Fellow, Wissenschaftskolleg, Berlin 2009, Strauss Inst. for Advanced Legal Studies 2012; Fellow, Advanced Study Inst. in Human Sciences 2010; Chair., Scientific Cttee, RESET.doc 2013; Sr Fellow, Transatlantic Acad., German Marshall Fund 2013, Inaugural Fellow, Center for Humanities and Social Change, Humboldt Univ 2018; Hon. Corresponding Fellow, British Acad. of Humanities and Social Sciences 2018; Dr hc (Univ. of Utrecht) 2004, (Univ. of Valencia) 2010, (Bogazici Univ.) 2012, (Georgetown Univ.) 2014, (Univ. of Geneva) 2018; Seeley Lecturer, Cambridge 2002, Tanner Lecturer, Berkeley 2004, Ernst Bloch Prize 2009, Guggenheim Fellow 2012, New York Univ. Law School Spring 2012, Leopold Lucas Prize 2012, Meister Eckhart Prize Spring 2014. *Publications include:* Critique, Norm and Utopia: A Study of the Foundations of Critical Theory 1986, Situating the Self: Gender, Community and Postmodernism in Contemporary Ethics (American Educational Studies Asscn Critics' Choice Award 1993) 1992, The Reluctant Modernism of Hannah Arendt

1996, Feminist Contentions: A Philosophical Exchange 1996; (as ed.): Feminism as Critique: Essays on the Politics of Gender in Late-Capitalist Societies 1987, The Communicative Ethics Controversy (co-ed. with Fred Dallmayr) 1990, On Max Horkheimer (co-ed. with Wolfgang Bonss and John McCole) 1993, The Philosophical Discourses of Modernity (ed. with M. Passerin d'Entreves) 1996, Democracy and Difference: Changing Boundaries of the Political 1996, Transformation of Citizenship: Dilemmas of the Nation-State in the Era of Globalization 2000, The Claims of Culture: Equality and Diversity in the Global Era 2002, The Rights of Others: The John Seeley Lectures (Ralph Bunche Award, American Political Science Asscn 2005, North American Soc. for Social Philosophy Best Book Award 2005) 2004, Another Cosmopolitanism, with Responses by Jeremy Waldron, Bonnie Honig and Will Kymlicka, Mobility and Immobility: Gender, Borders and Citizenship (ed. with Judith Resnik) 2010, Dignity in Adversity. Human Rights in Troubled Times 2011, The Democratic Disconnect. Citizenship and Accountability in the Transatlantic Era 2013, Toward New Democratic Imaginaries: Istanbul Dialogues on Islam, Culture and Politics (ed. with Volker Kaul) 2016, Exile, Statelessness and Migration: Playing Chess with History from Hannah Arendt to Isaiah Berlin 2018; (trans.): Hegel's Ontology and the Theory of Historicity by Herbert Marcuse 1987; more than 165 articles on social and political thought, feminist theory, legal theory and the history of modern political theory. *Address:* Room 225, Department of Political Science, Yale University, PO Box 208301, 115 Rosenkranz Hall, New Haven, CT 06520-8301, USA (office). *Telephone:* (203) 432-5246 (office). *Fax:* (203) 432-6196 (office). *E-mail:* seyla.benhabib@yale.edu (office). *Website:* www.yale.edu/polisci/people/sbenhabib.html (office).

BENHAMOUDA, Boualem, DIur; Algerian politician and lexicographer; b. 8 March 1933, Cherchell; m.; two s. one d.; ed Algiers Univ.; served with Army of Nat. Liberation 1956–62; mem. Parl. 1962–65; Minister of Ex-Combatants 1965–70, of Justice 1970–77, of Public Works 1977–80, of the Interior 1980–82, of Finance 1982–86; responsible for Inst. of Global Studies of Strategy 1986–90; mem. Political Bureau of Nat. Liberation Front (FLN) 1979–, Chair. FLN Cttee on Educ. Training and Culture 1979–80, Gen. Sec. FLN 1995–2001, currently mem. Cen. Cttee; Medal of Liberation. *Publications:* The Keys of Arabic Language 1991, The Arabic Origin of Some Spanish Words 1991, The Democratic Practice of Power (Between Theory and Reality) 1992, Spanish-Arabic Pocket Dictionary 1993, The Arabic Origin of About 1000 French Words, General French-Arabic Dictionary 1996, General Arabic-French Dictionary 2000, 2001, Citizenship and Power 2006, Read and Understand The Koran 2006. *Leisure interests:* reading, studying, cultural travel, philosophy, science, languages. *Address:* Siege du Parti du FLN, Rue du Stade, Hydra, Algiers (office); 5 Rue de Frère Zennouch, El-Biar, Algiers, Algeria (home). *Telephone:* (21) 694701 (office). *Fax:* (21) 923538 (home).

BÉNICHOU, Alain; French engineer and business executive; *President, IBM France;* b. 9 July 1959, Oran, Algeria; m. Claire-Isabelle Albu 1986; two s. one d.; ed Lycée J. Audiberti, Antibes, École supérieure d'électricité (Supelec), Gif-sur-Yvette; family moved to Antibes 1962; mil. service as Engineer in the Directorate Gen. of Armaments –1984; joined IBM as Client, Univ. 1984, has held several man. positions in Europe and USA, including as Dir French Gen. Business Div. and Dir Operations, Global SMB, Vice-Pres. IBM Global Services 2001, Vice-Pres. Distribution Sector, Europe Middle East and Africa 2002, Vice-Pres. Gen. Business, Northeast Europe 2005–07, Gen. Man. Global Distribution Sector, IBM Corpn 2007–10, Pres. IBM France 2010–; mem. Bd French-American Foundation; Chevalier, Légion d'honneur 2014. *Address:* IBM France, Centre Relations Clients, 110 boulevard de la Salle, 45760 Boigny-sur-Bionne, France (office). *Telephone:* (2) 38-55-77-77 (office). *Fax:* (2) 38-86-17-27 (office). *E-mail:* frmail@uk.ibm.com (office). *Website:* www.ibm.com/fr/fr (office); www-05.ibm.com/fr/biographie/bio_general_manager_fr.html (office); www.ibm.com/planetwide/fr (office).

BENIGNI, Roberto Remigio; Italian actor, director and writer; b. 27 Oct. 1952, Misericordia, Tuscany; s. of Remigio Benigni and Isolina Papini; m. Nicoletta Braschi 1991; ed Instituto Tecnico Commerciale Datini di Prato; Cavaliere di Gran Croce OMRI; Dr hc (Ben-Gurion Univ.) 1999, (Univ. of Bologna) 2002, (Univ. Vita-Salute San Raffaele) 2003, (Univ. of Malta) 2008. *Films include:* Belingua ti voglio bene (actor, writer) 1977, Down by Law (actor) 1986, Tutto Benigni (actor, writer) 1986, Johnny Stecchino (dir, actor, writer), Night on Earth (actor) 1992, Son of the Pink Panther (acted) 1993, Mostro (dir, actor, writer), Life is Beautiful (dir, actor, writer, Acad. Award for Best Actor and Best Foreign Film) 1998, Asterix and Obelix vs Caesar 1999, Pinocchio 2002, Coffee and Cigarettes 2003, The Tiger and the Snow (dir, actor) 2006, To Rome with Love (actor) 2012. *Publications include:* E l'alluce fu monologhi e gags 1996.

BENING, Annette; American actress; b. 29 May 1958, Topeka, Kan.; m. 1st Steven White (divorced); m. 2nd Warren Beatty (q.v.) 1992; four c.; ed San Francisco State Univ.; stage appearances in works by Ibsen, Chekhov and Shakespeare in San Diego and San Francisco; other stage roles in Coastal Disturbances, The Great Outdoors; European Achievement in World Cinema Award 2000. *Films:* The Great Outdoors 1988, Valmont 1989, Postcards from the Edge 1990, The Grifters 1990, Guilty by Suspicion 1991, Regarding Henry 1991, Bugsy 1991, Love Affair 1994, Richard III 1995, The American President 1995, Mars Attacks! 1996, The Siege 1998, In Dreams 1999, American Beauty 1999, What Planet Are You From? 2000, Open Range 2003, Being Julia (Best Actress Award, Nat. Bd of Review, Best Actress in a Musical or Comedy, Golden Globe Awards 2005) 2004, Running with Scissors 2006, The Women 2008, Mother and Child 2009, The Kids Are All Right (Hollywood Award for Best Actress 2010, Golden Globe Award for Best Actress in a Comedy or Musical 2011) 2010, Ruby Sparks 2012, Ginger & Rosa 2012, Girl Most Likely 2012, The Face of Love 2013, The Search 2014, Danny Collins 2015. *Television includes:* Mrs Harris (film) 2005. *Address:* c/o Kevin Huvane, CAA, 2000 Avenue of the Stars, Los Angeles, CA 90067, USA (office). *Telephone:* (424) 288-2000 (office). *Fax:* (424) 288-2900 (office). *Website:* www.caa.com (office).

BENÍTEZ, Mario Abdo; Paraguayan business executive, politician, fmr army officer and head of state; *President;* b. 10 Nov. 1971, Asunción; s. of Mario Abdo Sr and Ruth Perrier; m. 1st Fátima Díaz Benza (divorced); two s.; m. 2nd Silvana López Moreira; ed Teikyo Post Univ. in Waterbury; joined Paraguayan Armed Forces 1989, promoted to Second Lt; Chair. Asfaltos SA 1997–2012; Man. Partner Aldia SRL Asphalt Emulsions Factory 1998–2012; mem. Republican Nat. Reconstruction Movt 2005; Vice-Pres. Colorado Party (Colorado Añetete) 2008–11; elected to Senate 2013–18, Pres. 2015–16; Pres. of Paraguay 2018–. *Address:* Office of the President, Palacio Gobierno, El Paraguayo Independiente, entre O'Leary y Ayolas, Asunción, Paraguay (office). *Telephone:* (21) 414-0200 (office). *Website:* www.presidencia.gov.py (office).

BENIZRI, Shlomo; Israeli politician; b. 7 Feb. 1961, Haifa; m.; seven c.; army service; ordained as a rabbi at Or Hachaim Talmudic Coll., Jerusalem; fmr Head of Talmudic Coll.; mem. (Shas Party) Knesset 1992–2008, mem. Finance and Anti-Drug Abuse Cttees 1992–96, fmr Head of Shas Knesset Faction; Deputy Minister of Health 1996–99, Minister of Health 1999–2001; Minister of Labour and Social Welfare 2001–02, 2002–03; convicted of accepting bribes and breaching the public trust April 2008, sentenced to four years' imprisonment June 2009, released early March 2012. *Publication:* The Sky is Talking (astrology). *Leisure interests:* sports, computers, nature.

BENJAMIN, David (see SLAVITT, David Rytman).

BENJAMIN, Sir George William John, CBE; British composer, conductor, pianist and teacher; b. 31 Jan. 1960, London; s. of William Benjamin and Susan Benjamin (née Bendon); civil partner Michael Waldman; ed Westminster School, Paris Conservatoire, King's Coll., Cambridge, Institut de recherche et coordination acoustique/musique, France; first London orchestral performance, BBC Proms 1980; Prince Consort Prof. of Composition, Royal Coll. of Music, London 1984–2001; Henry Purcell Prof. of Composition, King's Coll. London 2001–; has conducted widely in GB, Europe, USA, Australia and Far East; Prin. Guest Artist, Hallé Orchestra 1993–96; operatic conducting debut: Pelléas et Mélisande, La Monnaie, Brussels 1999; Carte Blanche at Opéra Bastille, Paris 1992; Founding Artistic Dir Wet Ink Festival, San Francisco Symphony Orchestra 1992, Meltdown Festival, South Bank 1993; Featured Composer, 75th Salzburg Festival 1995, Tanglewood Festival 1999, 2000, 2003, Deutsches Symphonie Orchester 2004–05, Strasbourg Musica Festival 2005, Spanish Nat. Orchestra 2005, Festival d'Automne, Paris 2006, Lucerne Festival 2008, Project San Francisco 2010; London Symphony Orchestra Retrospective 'By George', Barbican, London 2002–03; Artistic Consultant, BBC Sounding the Century 1996–99; Music Dir Ojai Music Festival, Calif. 2010; mem. Bavarian Acad. of Fine Arts 2000; Hon. RAM, Hon. RCM, Hon. GSMD, Hon. mem. Royal Philharmonic Soc.; Chevalier, Ordre des Arts et des Lettres 1996; Lili Boulanger Award, USA 1985, Koussevitzky Int. Record Award 1987, Grand Prix du Disque de l'Académie Charles Cros 1987, Gramophone Contemporary Award 1990, Edison Award 1998, Schönberg Prize, Deutsche Sinfonie Berlin 2002, Royal Philharmonic Soc. Award 2003, 2004, Gramophone Contemporary Award 2017. *Compositions include:* orchestral works: Ringed by the Flat Horizon 1980, A Mind of Winter 1981, At First Light 1982, Jubilation 1985, Antara 1987, Sudden Time 1993, Three Inventions for chamber orchestra 1995, Sometime Voices 1996, Palimpsests 2002, Dance Figures 2004, Duet for piano and orchestra 2008; chamber music: Piano Sonata 1978, Octet 1978, Flight 1979, Sortilèges 1981, Three Studies for piano 1985, Upon Silence 1990, Viola, Viola 1997, Shadowlines for solo piano 2001, Three Miniatures for violin 2001, Olicantus 2002, Piano Figures 2004; stage works: Into the Little Hill (Royal Philharmonic Soc. Award for Best Large-Scale Composition 2009) 2006, Written on Skin 2012, Lessons in Love and Violence 2018. *Website:* www.askonasholt.co.uk/artists/conductors/george-benjamin (office); www.fabermusic.com (office). *Address:* c/o Faber Music, 74–77 Great Russell Street, London, WC1B 3DA, England (office). *Telephone:* (20) 7908-5310 (office). *Fax:* (20) 7908-5339 (office). *E-mail:* information@fabermusic.com (office).

BENJAMIN, John Oponjo, BSc; Sierra Leonean economist and politician; b. 29 Nov. 1952, Segbwema, Kailahun dist; ed University of Sierra Leone; worked as head of IT Dept, Sierra Leone Commercial Bank, General Manager 1986–92; Chief Sec. of State, Nat. Provisional Ruling Council (NPRC) 1992; Sec.-Gen. NPRC Govt 1993; Interim Chair. Nat. Unity Party 1997; Councillor, elected Chair. 2004, Kailahun Dist Council; Minister of Finance 2005–07; Nat. Chair. and Leader, Sierra Leone People's Party (SLPP) 2009–13; Exec. Dir African Information Tech. Holdings. *Address:* Sierra Leone People's Party, 15 Wallace Johnson St, Freetown, Sierra Leone (office). *Telephone:* (22) 2256341 (office). *E-mail:* info@slpp.ws (office). *Website:* www.slpp.ws (office).

BENJAMIN, Raymond; French civil aviation official; responsible for negotiating bilateral air transport agreements on behalf of French Civil Aviation Authority 1976–77; Air Transport Officer, European Civil Aviation Conf. 1977–82, Deputy Sec. 1982–83, Exec. Sec. 1983–89; Chief of Aviation Security Br., ICAO 1994–2007, also served as Sec. Aviation Security Panel and Group of Experts for the Detection of Plastic Explosives 1989–94, Sec.-Gen. ICAO 2009–15; Special Adviser to Jt Aviation Authorities Training Org. (JAA/TO) and to European Aviation Security Training Inst. 2007–. *Address:* c/o International Civil Aviation Organization, 999 University Street, Montréal, PQ H3C 5H7, Canada (office). *E-mail:* ray.benjamin@hotmail.com (home).

BENJAMIN, Regina Marcia, BS, MD, MBA; American physician; b. 26 Oct. 1956, Mobile, Ala; ed Morehouse School of Medicine, Xavier Univ., New Orleans, Univ. of Alabama, Birmingham, Tulane Univ., New Orleans; intern and resident in family practice at Medical Center of Cen. Georgia; Founder and CEO Bayou La Batre Rural Health Clinic, Ala 1990–; Surgeon-Gen. of USA 2009–13; fmr Assoc. Dean for Rural Health, Coll. of Medicine, Univ. of South Alabama, Mobile; Pres. Medical Asscn of the State of Alabama 2002–03; mem. Bd of Trustees, American Medical Asscn (first physician under age 40 and first African-American woman) 1995; Diplomate of American Bd of Family Practice; apptd to Clinical Lab. Improvement Act Cttee and to Council of Grad. Medical Educ., US Dept of Health and Human Services; mem. numerous bds and cttees, including Kaiser Comm. on Medicaid and the Uninsured, Catholic Health East, Medical Asscn of the State of Alabama, Alabama Bd of Medical Examiners, Alabama State Cttee of Public Health, Mobile Co. Medical Soc., Alabama Rural Health Asscn, Leadership Alabama, Mobile Area Red Cross, Mercy Medical, Mobile Chamber of Commerce, United Way of Mobile, and Deep South Girl Scout Council; mem. Step 3 Cttee; has served as Vice-Pres. of Gov.'s Comm. on Aging; fmr mem. Gov.'s Health Care Reform Task Force, Gov.'s Task Force on Children's Health; Fellow, American Acad. of Family Physicians; fmr Kellogg Nat. Fellow; fmr Rockefeller Next Generation Leader; US recipient of Nelson Mandela Award for Health and Human

Rights 1998, chosen by CBS This Morning as "Woman of the Year" 1998, chosen by People Magazine as "Woman of the Year" 1998, Nat. Caring Award 2000, awarded Papal Cross Pro Ecclesia et Pontifice by Pope Benedict XVI 2006, named by U.S. News & World Report as one of "America's Best Leaders" 2008, one of 25 recipients of the $500,000 Genius Awards, John D. and Catherine T. MacArthur Foundation 2008, Vanderbilt Univ. Nichols-Chancellor's Medal 2014. *Address:* Bayou Clinic, 13833 Tapia Lane, Bayou La Batre, AL 36509, USA (office). *Telephone:* (251) 824-4985 (office). *Fax:* (251) 626-2200 (office). *E-mail:* info@bayouclinic.org (office). *Website:* www.bayouclinic.org (office).

BENJELLOUN, Othman; Moroccan business executive; *Chairman and CEO, BMCE Bank;* b. 1931, Casablanca; s. of Haj Abbas Benjelloun; m. Leila Meziane; one s. one d.; ed Ecole Polytechnique de Lausanne; acquired Royale Marocaine d'Assurances (RMA) 1988, est. RMA Watanya; Chair. and CEO BMCE Bank 1995–; acquired Al Wataniya (insurance co.) 1998; Chair. Meditelecom 2005–; Pres. Finance.com Groupe, Professional Asscn of Banks in Morocco, Union of Maghreb Banks; Founder-mem. World Union of Arab Bankers, currently also Deputy Chair. for Overseas Region; Chair. Moroccan Bankers' Asscn; fmr Chair. US Moroccan Trade Investment Council; Dir Espirito Santo Financial Group SA 2002, Banque Marocaine Du Comm Exter; mem. Arab Thought Foundation, Global Philanthropist Circle, Synergos Inst., New York, USA; Chancellor, Al Akhawayn Univ., Ifrane 1998–2004; Adviser, Centre for Strategic International Studies, USA, mem. Int. Councillors; Officier de l'Ordre de Trône du Royame du Maroc, Commdr, Royal Order of the Polar Star (Sweden), Nat. Order of the Lion (Senegal); Arab Banker of the Year 2007. *Address:* BMCE Bank, Avenue Hassan Ii 140, Casablanca, Morocco (office). *Telephone:* (52) 2200325 (office). *Website:* www.bmcebank.ma (office).

BENKHELFA, Abderrahmane; Algerian economist and politician; b. 2 July 1959, Tiaret; ed Algiers Univ., Grenoble Univ., France, Univ. of Warsaw, Poland; Tech. Adviser, Institut nat. de la productivité et du développement industriel (Inped) 1977–80; Sr Man., hydraulics sector 1981–93; Sr Dir in charge of Restructuring, Ministry of Fisheries and Marine Resources 1993–94; Man. Dir Asscn of Banks and Financial Establishments of Algeria 1994–2014; mem. Treasury and Credit Council, Banque d'Algérie 1994–2014; Sec.-Gen., Union des banques maghrébines 2005; Minister of Finance 2015–16; Chair. OPEC Fund for Int. Devt 2015–16. *Address:* c/o Ministry of Finance, Immeuble Ahmed Francis, Ben Aknoun, Algiers, Algeria.

BENKIRANE, Abdelilah, BSc; Moroccan politician; b. 4 April 1954, Rabat; m.; six c.; ed Univ. Mohammed V-Agdal; began career as teacher, Ecole normale supérieure de l'enseignement technique, Rabat; mem. Chabiba Islamiya (Islamist group) 1976; f. Al Jamaa Al Islamiya 1981 (renamed Réforme et Renouveau 1992); mem. Parl. for Salé constituency 1997–; Leader of the Opposition 2008–11; Prime Minister 2011–17; mem. Mouvement populaire démocratique constitutionnel, renamed Parti de la justice et du développement (PJD) 1998, PJD Sec.-Gen. 2008–.

BENKÖ, Col-Gen. Tibor; Hungarian army officer and government official; *Minister of Defence;* b. 16 Oct. 1955, Nyíregyháza; m.; two d.; ed Kossuth Lajos Mil. Coll., US Army War Coll., Carlisle, Pa, Szent István Univ.; long career with Hungarian Defence Forces (MH), including Section Commdr and Deputy Commdr, 36th Armoured Div., Kiskunhalas 1979–81, Regimental Operations Officer 1981–85, Chief Officer, Fifth Army Div., Székesfehérvár 1988–90, Deputy Commdr-in-Chief, 36th Armoured Artillery Div., Kiskunhalas 1990–93, Brig.-Gen. 1993–95, Regt Commdr 1995–2000, Brig.-Gen., Fifth István Bocskai Infantry Brigade, Debrecen 2001–05, First Deputy Commdr, MH Land Command, Székesfehérvár 2005–06, Commdr-in-Chief 2006, Deputy Commdr, MH Command HQ 2007–09, Commdr in Chief, MH Command 2009–10, Chief of Defence Forces 2010–18, Minister of Defence 2018–; , Commdr, US Legion of Merit, Officer, Order of Merit of the Repub. of Hungary (mil. section), Service Cross (First Class); St George Merit Award, Hunyadi János Prize. *Address:* Ministry of Defence, 1055 Budapest, Balaton u. 7–11, Hungary (office). *Telephone:* (1) 236-5111 (office). *Fax:* (1) 474-1335 (office). *E-mail:* hmugyfelszolgalat@hm.gov.hu (office). *Website:* www.kormany.hu/hu/honvedelmi-miniszterium (office).

BENKOVIC, Stephen James, BS, PhD, FRSC; American chemist and academic; *Evan Pugh Professor and Eberly Chair in Chemistry, Pennsylvania State University;* b. 20 April 1938, Orange, NJ; ed Lehigh Univ., Cornell Univ., Univ. of California, Santa Barbara; Post-Doctoral Research Assoc., Univ. of Calif., Santa Barbara 1964–65; joined Dept of Chem., Pennsylvania State Univ. 1965, Prof. of Chem. 1970, Evan Pugh Prof. 1977–, Eberly Chair in Chem. 1986–; Scientific Partner, RhO Ventures; co-founder Anacor Pharmaceuticals, mem. Bd of Dirs 2000–; Visiting Prof. Vallee Foundation 2012; Head of Scientific Advisory Bd, Glaxo SmithKline; Fellow Coll. of Physicians of Philadelphia 2018; mem. NAS 1985, Inst. of Medicine 1994, American Philosophical Soc. 2002; Fellow, American Acad. of Arts and Sciences 1984, Nat. Acad. of Inventors 2015; Hon. DSc (Lehigh Univ.) 1995; Guggenheim Fellowship, Alfred P. Sloan Fellowship, NIH Career Devt Award, Pfizer Award 1977, Gowland Hopkins Award 1986, Arthur C. Scope Scolar Award 1988, Repligen Award 1989, Alfred Bader Award 1995, Chemical Pioneer Award, American Inst. of Chemists, Christian B. Afinsen Award 2000, Nakanishi Prize 2005, Benjamin Franklin Medal 2009, Ralph F. Hirschmann Award 2010, Nat. Medal of Science 2010, NAS Award in Chemical Sciences 2011. *Address:* 414 Wartik Laboratory, Department of Chemistry, Pennsylvania State University, University Park, PA 16802, USA (office). *Telephone:* (814) 865-2882 (office). *Fax:* (814) 865-2973 (office). *E-mail:* sjb1@psu.edu (office). *Website:* chem.psu.edu/directory/sjb1 (office); sites.psu.edu/benkoviclab (office).

BENMAKHLOUF, Alexandre; French lawyer; b. 9 Sept. 1939, Oran, Algeria; s. of Tahar Benmakhlouf and Sylviane Jan; m. Gabrielle Steinmann 1965; one s. one d.; ed Institut d'Etudes Politiques; Deputy Public Prosecutor, Meaux 1970, Versailles 1972; seconded to Chancellery 1974–84; Pres. Nanterre Magistrates' Court 1984–86; Deputy Sec.-Gen. Professional Asscn of Magistrates 1984–86; Adviser to Prime Minister Jacques Chirac 1986–89; Legal Adviser to Jacques Chirac, Mayor of Paris 1989–91; Pres. Court of Appeal, Versailles 1991–93; Dir of Civil Affairs and Dir of Cabinet of Guardian of the Seal, Ministry of Justice 1993–96; Attorney-Gen., Court of Appeal 1996–97, Solicitor-Gen. 1997–2000, First Counsel for the Prosecution 2001–07, apptd Hon. First Counsel 2007; Chevalier Légion d'honneur, Ordre des Palmes académiques. *Leisure interests:* reading, travelling, cinema. *Address:* c/o Cour de Cassation, 5 quai de l'Horloge, 75055 Paris RP, France (office).

BENN, Rt Hon. Hilary James Wedgwood, BA; British politician; b. 26 Nov. 1953, Hammersmith, London, England; s. of Tony Benn and Caroline Benn; m. 1st Rosalind Retey (died 1979); m. 2nd Sally Christina Clark 1982; three s. one d.; ed Holland Park School, London, Univ. of Sussex, Brighton; Research Officer, ASTMS, rose to become Head of Policy for Manufacturing, Science and Finance (MSF, trade union); Council Deputy Leader and Chair of Educ. in Ealing, W London 1986–90; Labour cand. for Ealing N in Gen. Elections 1983, 1987; Special Adviser to David Blunkett MP, Sec. of State for Educ. and Employment 1997–99; MP (Labour) for Leeds Cen. 1999–, fmr mem. Environment, Transport and Regions Select Cttee, mem. House of Commons Comm. 2010–, Chair. Exiting the EU Cttee 2016–; with Dept for Int. Devt 2001–02; Home Office Minister 2002–03; unsuccessful cand. for Deputy Leadership of Labour Party June 2007; Sec. of State for Int. Devt 2003–07, for Environment, Food and Rural Affairs 2007–10; Shadow Sec. of State for Environment, Food and Rural Affairs May–Oct. 2010; Shadow Leader of the House of Commons Oct. 2010–11; Shadow Sec. of State for Communities and Local Govt 2011–15; Shadow Foreign Sec. 2015–16; Patron, Holbeck Elderly Aid, Leeds, Faith Together, Leeds, Caring Together, Woodhouse and Little London. *Leisure interests:* gardening, watching sport. *Address:* House of Commons, Westminster, London, SW1A 0AA (office); Leeds Central Parliamentary Office, 2 Blenheim Terrace, Leeds, W Yorks., LS2 9JG, England (office). *Telephone:* (20) 7219-5770 (London) (office); (113) 244-1097 (Leeds) (office). *E-mail:* hilary.benn.mp@parliament.uk (office); boxj@parliament.uk (office). *Website:* www.parliament.uk/biographies/commons/hilary-benn/413 (office); www.hilarybenn.org.

BENNACK, Frank Anthony, Jr; American publishing executive; *Executive Vice-Chairman, Hearst Corporation;* b. 12 Feb. 1933, San Antonio, Tex.; s. of Frank Bennack and Lula Connally; m. Luella Smith 1951; five d.; ed Univ. of Maryland and St Mary's Univ.; advertising account exec., San Antonio Light 1950–53, 1956–58, Advertising Man. 1961–65, Asst Publr 1965–67, Publr 1967–74; Gen. Man. (newspapers), Hearst Corpn New York 1974–76, Exec. Vice-Pres. and COO 1975–78, Pres. and CEO 1978–2002, Vice-Chair. Bd 2002–, Chair. Exec. Cttee 2002–08, Chair. Hearst-Argyle Television 2008–, CEO 2008–; Chair. Museum of TV and Radio, NY City 1991–; Pres. Tex. Daily Newspaper Asscn 1973–; mem. Bd of Dirs J.P. Morgan Chase & Co., Wyeth, Polo Ralph Lauren Corpn, Metropolitan Opera of New York; Dir, Vice-Chair. Lincoln Center for the Performing Arts; Dir Newspaper Asscn of American (fmrly American Newspaper Publrs Asscn), Chair. 1992–93; Gov., Vice-Chair. New York Presbyterian Hosp.; mem. Bd of Dirs Mfrs Hanover Trust Co., New York; mem. American Acad. of Arts and Sciences 2007–. *Address:* Hearst Corporation, Hearst Tower, 12th Floor, 300 West 57th Street, New York, NY 10019, USA (office). *Telephone:* (212) 649-4190 (office). *Fax:* (212) 649-2108 (office). *E-mail:* hearstnewspapers@hearst.com (office). *Website:* www.hearstcorp.com (office).

BENNET, Michael Farrand, BA, JD; American lawyer, politician, college administrator and media executive; *Senator from Colorado;* b. 28 Nov. 1964, New Delhi, India; s. of Douglas J. Bennet and Susanne Christine Bennet (née Klejman); m. Susan Diane Daggett 1997; three d.; ed Wesleyan Univ., Yale Law School; worked for Ohio Gov. Richard Celeste 1988–90; Ed.-in-Chief The Yale Law Journal; worked as law clerk 4th Circuit Court of Appeals; later Counsel to US Deputy Attorney Gen. during Clinton Admin; Man. Dir Anschutz Investment Co. 1997–2003; Chief of Staff to Mayor of Denver, John Hickenlooper 2003–05; Supt of Denver Public Schools 2005–09; apptd to US Senate 2009, Senator from Colorado 2010–, Sr Senator 2014–, mem. Cttee on Agric., Nutrition and Forestry, Cttee on Health, Educ., Labor and Pensions, Cttee on Banking, Housing and Urban Affairs, Special Cttee on Aging, Chair. Democratic Senatorial Campaign Cttee for the 2014 elections; Democrat. *Address:* 261 Russell Senate Office Building, Washington, DC 20510, USA (office). *Telephone:* (202) 224-5852 (office). *Fax:* (202) 228-5097 (office). *Website:* www.bennet.senate.gov (office).

BENNETT, Alan, BA; British playwright and actor; b. 9 May 1934, Leeds; s. of Walter Bennett and Lilian Mary Peel; ed Leeds Modern School, Exeter Coll., Oxford; Jr Lecturer, Modern History, Magdalen Coll., Oxford 1960–62; co-author and actor Beyond the Fringe, Edin. 1960, London 1961, New York 1962; Trustee Nat. Gallery 1993–98; Hon. Fellow, Royal Acad. 2000, Hon. Fellow, Exeter Coll., Oxford, Freeman of Leeds 2004; Hon. DLitt (Leeds); Evening Standard Award 1961, 1969, Hawthornden Prize 1988, two Olivier Awards 1993, Evening Standard Film Award 1996, Lifetime Achievement Award, British Book Awards 2003, Evening Standard Best Play Award 2004, Olivier Award for outstanding contrib. to British theatre 2005, British Book Awards Reader's Digest Author of the Year 2006, Bodley Medal 2008. *Plays include:* On the Margin (TV series, author and actor) 1966, Forty Years On (author and actor) 1968, Getting On 1971, Habeas Corpus 1973, The Old Country 1977, Enjoy 1980, Kafka's Dick 1986, Single Spies 1988, The Wind in the Willows (adapted for Nat. Theatre) 1990, The Madness of George III 1991, The Lady in the Van 1999, The History Boys (Royal Nat. Theatre, London) (Evening Standard Award for Best Play 2004, Critics Circle Theatre Award for Best New Play 2005, Olivier Award for Best New Play 2005, New York Drama Critics' Circle Play of the Year 2006, Drama Desk Award for Best Play 2006, Tony Award for Best Play 2006) 2004, The Habit of Art 2009, People 2012, Untold Stories 2012. *Radio:* The Last of the Sun 2004, Denmark Hill 2013. *Television scripts:* A Day Out (film) 1972, Sunset Across the Bay (TV film) 1975, A Little Outing 1975, A Visit from Miss Prothero (plays) 1977, Doris and Doreen 1978, Me! I'm Afraid of Virginia Woolf 1978, The Old Crowd 1979, All Day on the Sands 1979, Afternoon Off 1979, One Fine Day 1979, Intensive Care 1982, Our Winnie 1982, A Woman of No Importance 1982, Rolling Home 1982, Marks 1982, Say Something Happened 1982, An Englishman Abroad 1983, The Insurance Man 1986, Talking Heads (Olivier Award) 1988, 102 Boulevard Haussmann 1991, A Question of Attribution 1991, Talking Heads 2 1998. *Films:* A Private Function 1984, Prick Up Your Ears 1987, The Madness of King George 1994, The History Boys 2006, The Lady in the Van 2015. *Television documentaries:* Dinner at Noon 1988, Poetry in Motion 1990, Portrait or Bust 1994, The Abbey 1995, Telling Tales 1999. *Publications include:* Beyond the Fringe (with Peter Cook, Jonathan Miller and Dudley Moore) 1962, Forty Years On 1969, Getting On 1972, Habeas Corpus 1973, The Old Country 1978, Enjoy 1980, Office Suite 1981, Objects of Affection

1982, The Writer in Disguise 1985, Two Kafka Plays 1987, Talking Heads 1988, Single Spies 1989, Poetry in Motion 1990, The Lady in the Van 1991, The Wind in the Willows (adaptation) 1991, The Madness of George III 1992, Writing Home (autobiography) 1994, Diaries 1997, The Clothes They Stood Up In 1998, Talking Heads 2 1998, The Complete Talking Heads 1998, A Box of Alan Bennett 2000, Father, Father! Burning Bright 2000, The Laying on of Hands 2001, The History Boys 2004, Untold Stories 2005, The Uncommon Reader 2007, Smut (short stories) 2011, Keep On Keeping On 2016; regular contrib. to London Review of Books. *Address:* c/o Chatto & Linnit, World's End Studios, 132–134 Lots Road, London, SW10 0RJ, England (office). *Telephone:* (20) 7349-7722 (office).

BENNETT, Amanda; American news editor and writer; *Director, Voice of America;* m. 1st Terence Foley; two c.; m. 2nd Donald Graham 2012; ed Harvard Univ.; worked 23 years with Wall Street Journal, positions included Auto Industry Reporter, Detroit 1970s–1980s, Pentagon and State Dept Reporter, Beijing Corresp., Man. Ed./Reporter, Nat. Econs Corresp., Atlanta Bureau Chief 1994–98; Man. Ed./Projects The Oregonian, Portland 2001; Ed. The Lexington Herald-Leader, Ky 2001–03; Ed. and Exec. Vice-Pres. The Philadelphia Enquirer 2003–06; Exec. Ed. of Enterprise Stories, Bloomberg News 2007, then Exec. Ed., Projects and Investigations, resgnd 2013; Dir Voice of America 2016–; fmr Pulitzer Prize juror, mem. Pulitzer Prize Bd 2002–08, Co-Chair. 2010; fmr Nat. Headliners' Judge; mem. Bd of Dirs Temple Univ. Press, Rosenbach Museum; Bd mem. American Soc. of News Editors, Loeb Awards; mem. Pennsylvania Women's Forum, Nat. Asscn of Black Journalists; contributing columnist, The Washington Post; Co-founder (with husband) TheDream.US nat. scholarship fund; Pulitzer Prize for Nat. Reporting (co-recipient) 1997, Pulitzer Prize for Public Service (co-recipient) 2000. *Publications include:* Death of the Organization Man 1991, The Man Who Stayed Behind (co-author) 1993, Your Child's Symptoms (with John Garwood, M.D) 1995, In Memoriam (co-author) 1998, The Cost of Hope 2012. *Address:* Voice of America, 330 Independence Avenue, SW, Washington, DC 20237, USA (office). *Website:* www.voanews.com (office); www.thedream.us.

BENNETT, Brian Maurice, BA; British fmr diplomatist; *Co-Chairman, Anglo-Belarusian Society;* b. 1 April 1948, Portsmouth, Hants.; s. of Valentine Bennett and Dorothy Bennett; m.; three s.; ed Univ. of Sheffield; joined FCO 1971, Desk Officer, Western Orgs Dept 1971–73, Desk Officer, Personnel Policy Dept 1979–83, Desk Officer, Man. Review 1992–94, Desk Officer, Cen. European Dept 1994–97, Deputy Head, Personnel Services Dept 2001–02; Third Sec., Information, Prague, Czechoslovakia 1973–76; Third Sec., Chancery, Helskinki, Finland 1977–79; Second Sec., Commercial, Bridgetown, Barbados 1983–86; Second, later First, Sec., UK Del. to Mutual and Balanced Force Reductions Talks, Vienna, Austria 1986–88; First Sec., The Hague, Netherlands 1988–92; Deputy Head of Mission, Tunis, Tunisia 1997–2000; Amb. to Belarus 2003–07; Admin., Humphrey Richardson Taylor Charitable Trust 2008–18; Co-Chair. Anglo-Belarusian Soc. 2014–. *Publication:* The Last Dictatorship in Europe: Belarus under Lukashenko 2011. *Leisure interests:* walking, singing. *E-mail:* mail@absociety.org.uk (office). *Website:* www.anglobelarus.org.uk (office).

BENNETT, Carolyn Ann, PC, MD; Canadian politician and fmr physician; *Minister of Crown-Indigenous Relations and Northern Affairs;* b. 20 Dec. 1950; m. Peter O'Brian; two s.; ed Univ. of Toronto; family physician, Wellesley Hospital and Women's Coll. Hospital, Toronto 1977–97; Founding Pnr, Bedford Medical Assocs., Toronto; fmr Pres. Medical Staff Asscn, Women's Coll. Hospital; fmr Asst Prof., Dept of Family and Community Medicine, Univ. of Toronto; MP (Liberal) for St Paul's 1997–2015, for Toronto-St Paul's 2015–; fmr Opposition Critic for Aboriginal Affairs; Minister of State for Public Health 2003–06, Minister of Indigenous and Northern Affairs 2015–17, Minister of Crown-Indigenous Relations and Northern Affairs 2017–; Chair. Liberal Women's Caucus; mem. Bd of Dirs Havergal Coll., Women's Coll. Hospital, Ont. Medical Asscn, Medico-Legal Soc. of Toronto; Hon. Fellow, Soc. of Obstetricians and Gynaecologists of Canada; Royal Life Saving Soc. Service Cross 1986, EVE Award 2002, Canadian Alliance on Mental Health and Mental Illness (CAMIMH) Mental Health Champion Award 2003, May Cohen Leadership Award 2006, Nat. Award of Excellence for Outstanding Leadership and Dedication to Injury Prevention and Safety Promotion in Canada, Coll. of Family Physicians of Canada W. Victor Johnston Award 2009. *Publication:* Kill or Cure?: How Canadians Can Remake their Health Care System 2000. *Address:* Indigenous and Northern Affairs Canada, Terrasses de la Chaudière, 10 rue Wellington, Tour Nord, Gatineau, PQ K1A 0H4, Canada (office). *Telephone:* (819) 953-1160 (office). *Fax:* (866) 817-3977 (office). *E-mail:* InfoPubs@aadnc-aandc.gc.ca (office). *Website:* www.aadnc-aandc.gc.ca (office); carolynbennett.liberal.ca (home).

BENNETT, Charles Henry, BS, PhD; American physicist and computer scientist; *IBM Fellow, Thomas J. Watson Research Center, International Business Machines;* b. 1943, New York, NY; s. of Boyd Bennett and Anne Bennett (née Wolfe); m. Theodora M. Bennett; three c.; ed Croton-Harmon High School, Brandeis and Harvard Univs; Researcher, Argonne Nat. Lab. 1971–73; joined IBM Research 1972, currently an IBM Fellow, Thomas J. Watson Research Center; Visiting Prof. of Computer Science, Boston Univ. 1983–85; mem. NAS; Fellow, American Physical Soc.; Rank Prize in opto-electronics 2006, Technion, Israel Harvey Prize (co-recipient) 2008, ICTP Dirac Medal 2017, Wolf Prize for Physics 2018. *Achievements include:* co-discovered 'quantum teleportation' 1993, helped found the quantitative theory of entanglement and introduced several techniques for faithful transmission of classical and quantum information through noisy channels 1995–97. *Publications:* numerous papers in professional journals; six US patents. *Leisure interests:* photography, music. *Address:* Thomas J. Watson Research Center, 1101 Kitchawan Road, Yorktown Heights, NY 10598, USA (office). *Telephone:* (914) 945-3118 (office). *Fax:* (914) 945-2141 (office). *E-mail:* bennetcatus@ibm.com (office). *Website:* www.watson.ibm.com (office).

BENNETT, Charles L., BS, PhD; American astronomer and academic; *Alumni Centennial Professor of Physics and Astronomy and Gilman Scholar, Johns Hopkins University;* b. Nov. 1956; ed Univ. of Maryland, Carnegie Inst. of Washington, Massachusetts Inst. of Tech.; astrophysicist, NASA Goddard Space Flight Center (GSFC) 1984–2004, Acting Head, Infrared Astrophysics Br. April–Aug. 1993, April–Aug. 1994, Head 1994–2000, Sr Scientist for Experimental Cosmology 2004; Prof., Johns Hopkins Univ. 2005–, Alumni Centennial Prof. of Physics and Astronomy and Gilman Scholar 2011–; fmr Deputy Prin. Investigator, Differential Microwave Radiometers (DMR) instrument and mem. Science Team of Cosmic Background Explorer (COBE) mission; Leader and Prin. Investigator, Wilkinson Microwave Anisotropy Probe mission; mem. American Acad. of Arts and Sciences 2004, NAS 2005, American Astronomical Soc., American Inst. of Physics, Int. Astronomical Union; Fellow, American Physical Soc. 1999, AAAS 2004; numerous awards including NASA Outstanding Performance 1985, 1994, NASA Exceptional Scientific Achievement Medal for COBE 1992, GSFC Group Award for MAP Proposal 1996, NASA/GSFC Performance Award 1996, 1998, 2002, Popular Science 'Best of What's New' Award in Aviation and Space for WMAP 2001, ISI Highly Cited Researchers 2002, Sr Scientist for Experimental Cosmology 2002, NASA/GSFC Center of Excellence Group Achievement Award for MAP 2002, NASA/GSFC Group Achievement Award for MAP 2002, Distinguished Alumnus of the Year, Univ. of Maryland 2003, John C. Lindsay Memorial Award for Space Science 2003, NASA Outstanding Leadership Medal 2003, NASA Performance Award 2003, Science Magazine Breakthrough of the Year for WMAP/Sloan proof of Dark Energy 2003, NASA Group Achievement Award to WMAP Science Team 2004, Rotary Nat. Award for Space Achievement Mid-Career Stellar Award 2005, NAS Henry Draper Medal 2005, Gruber Foundation Cosmology Prize (as mem. COBE Team) 2006, Harvey Prize, Technion—Israel Inst. of Tech. 2006, NAS Comstock Prize in Physics 2009, Shaw Prize (co-recipient) 2010, Gruber Cosmology Prize (co-recipient with WMAP team) 2012, Karl G. Jansky Prize Lecturer 2013, Breakthrough Prize in Fundamental Physics 2018. *Publications:* After The First Three Minutes, AIP Conference Procedings 222 (co-author) 1991, Dark Matter, AIP Conference Procedings 336 (co-author) 1995; more than 150 scientific papers in professional journals. *Address:* Bloomberg 209, Department of Physics and Astronomy, The Johns Hopkins University, 3400 North Charles Street, Baltimore, MD 21218-2686, USA (office). *Telephone:* (410) 516-6177 (office). *Fax:* (410) 516-7239 (office). *E-mail:* cbennett@jhu.edu (office). *Website:* physics-astronomy.jhu.edu/directory/charles-l-bennett (office); cosmos.pha.jhu.edu/bennett (office).

BENNETT, Jana Eve, OBE, BA, MSc, FRTS; British broadcasting executive; *President, FYI and LMN, A+E Networks;* b. 6 Nov. 1955, Cooperstown, New York, USA; d. of Gordon Willard Bennett and Elizabeth Bennett (née Cushing); m. Richard Clemmow 1996; one s. one d.; ed Bognor Comprehensive School, St Anne's Coll., Oxford, London School of Econs; news trainee, BBC 1979, fmrly Asst Producer, The Money Programme, Producer, Newsnight, Producer/Dir, Panorama, Series Producer, Antenna, Ed. Horizon, Head of BBC Science; Dir of Production and Deputy Chief Exec. BBC 1997–99, Dir of TV 2002–06, mem. Exec. Bd BBC 2004, mem. Bd BBC Worldwide 2006–09, Comic Relief (Trustee), Dir BBC Vision (in charge of BBC TV, BBC Films and BBC Productions) 2006–11, apptd Pres. BBC Worldwide Networks and Global iPlayer 2011; Pres. FYI and LMN, A+E Networks 2013–; Exec. Vice-Pres. Learning Channel, US Discovery Communications Inc. 1999–2002; mem. Bd UKTV 2006–; mem. Exec. Cttee, Int. Acad. of Television Arts and Sciences 2010–; mem. BAFTA, Advisory Cttee Natural History Museum, Univ. of Oxford; Gov. RSC; Golden Nymph Award (Panorama), BAFTA, Emmy, Prix Italia (Horizon). *Publication:* The Disappeared: Argentina's Dirty War 1986 (co-author). *Leisure interests:* skiing, family, world music, travel, mountains, guitar. *Address:* A&E Television Networks, LLC, 235 East 45th Street, New York, NY 10017, USA (office). *Website:* www.aenetworks.com/about/executive/jana-bennett-0 (office).

BENNETT, Martin Arthur, PhD, DSc, FRS, FAA, FRSC; British/Australian chemist and academic; *Professor Emeritus, Australian National University;* b. 11 Aug. 1935, Harrow, Middx, England; s. of Arthur Edward Charles Bennett and Dorothy Ivy Bennett; m. Rae Elizabeth Mathews 1964; two s.; ed Haberdashers' Aske's Hampstead School, Imperial Coll. of Science and Tech., London; Postdoctoral Fellow, Univ. of Southern California 1960–61; Turner and Newall Fellow, Univ. Coll. London 1961–63, Lecturer 1963–67; Fellow, Research School of Chemistry, ANU 1967–70, Sr Fellow 1970–79, Professorial Fellow 1979–91, Prof. 1991–2000, Prof. Emer. 2001–; Adjunct Prof., Royal Melbourne Inst. of Tech. Univ. 2000–; various professorial and visiting fellowships in Canada, Germany, USA, NZ and Japan; mem. Int. Advisory Bd for Dictionary of Organometallic Compounds 1984 and Dictionary of Inorganic Compounds 1988; Corresp. mem. Bavarian Acad. of Sciences 2005; H.G. Smith Medal, Royal Australian Chem. Inst. 1977, RSC Award 1981, G.J. Burrows Award, Royal Australian Chem. Inst. 1987, Nyholm Medal, RSC 1991, Max Planck Soc. Research Award 1994. *Publications:* chapters on ruthenium in Comprehensive Organometallic Chemistry; over 280 papers in journals. *Leisure interests:* golf, reading, foreign languages. *Address:* Research School of Chemistry, Australian National University, Canberra, ACT 0200 (office); 21 Black Street, Yarralumla, ACT 2600, Australia (home). *Telephone:* (2) 6125-3639 (office); (2) 6282-4154 (home). *Fax:* (2) 6125-3216 (office). *E-mail:* bennett@rsc.anu.edu.au (office). *Website:* rsc.anu.edu.au/index.php (office).

BENNETT, Maxwell Richard, AO, BEng, DSc, FAA; Australian physiologist and academic; *Professor of Neuroscience, Sydney Medical School, University of Sydney;* b. 19 Feb. 1939, Melbourne; s. of Herman Adler Bennett (Bercovici) and Ivy G. Arthur; m. Gillian R. Bennett 1965; one s. one d.; ed Christian Brothers Coll., St Kilda, Melbourne and Univ. of Melbourne; John & Alan Gilmour Research Fellow, Univ. of Melbourne 1965; Lecturer in Physiology, Univ. of Sydney 1969, Reader 1973, Prof. of Physiology 1982–2000, Dir Neurobiology Research Centre 1982–90, Prof. of Neuroscience, Sydney Medical School 2000–, also Head, Neurobiology Laboratory, Founder and Dir Brain and Mind Research Inst. 2003–; Convener, Sydney Inst. of Biomedical Research 1995; Founder Fed. Australian Scientific and Tech. Socs 1985; Co-Founder Australian Neural Networks Soc. 1990; Pres. Australian Neuroscience Soc. 1989–92; Pres. Int. Soc. for Autonomic Neuroscience 2001–03; First Univ. Chair., Univ. of Sydney 2000; Fellow, Australian Acad. of Science 1981–; Dir Neuroscience Australia 2002, Brain Foundation 2004, Brain and Mind Research Foundation 2004; mem. Bd of Dirs Australian Brain Foundation 2004; Sr Adviser, Templeton Foundation 2009; Ed. Journal of the Autonomic Nervous System 1997–, Neuroscience News 1997–, Progress in Neurobiology 1997–, NeuroReport 2001–04, Purinergic Mechanisms 2005–; mem. Council of Mental Health Research Inst. 2003, Mental Health Council of Australia; mem. Council Int. Brain Research Org. 1989–91; Hon. Fellow, Australian Neuroscience Soc. 2010; Opening Plenary Lecture, World Congress of Neuroscience 1995, Goddard Research Prize Nat. Heart Foundation 1996, Ramaciotti Medal for Excellence in Biomedical Research 1996, Renenessin

Research Prize Nat. Heart Foundation 1998, Almigren Research Prize, Nat. Heart Foundation 1999, Burnet Medal and Lecture Australian Acad. of Science 1999, Neuroscience Distinguished Achievement Medallion 2001, Plenary Lecture, Research Soc. for Alcoholism 2001, Ophthalmologica Internationalis Award 2002, Tall Poppy for Excellence in Science Prize 2002, Centenary Medal 2003, American Philosophical Asscn 2005, Int. Congress of Neuropsychiatry 2006, World Congress in Medical Informatics 2008, World Congress of Mental Health Nurses 2009, Franke Lectures 2013. *Publications:* Autonomic Neuromuscular Transmission 1972, Development of Neuromuscular Synapses 1983, Optimising Research and Development 1985, The Idea of Consciousness 1997, History of the Synapse 2001, Philosophical Foundations of Neuroscience 2003, Neuroscience and Philosophy: Brain, Mind, and Language (co-author) 2006, History of Cognitive Neuroscience (co-author) 2008, Virginia Woolf and Neuropsychiatry 2013; 350 papers on neuroscience. *Leisure interests:* history and philosophy of science, science policy. *Address:* Department of Physiology, Anderson Stuart Building F13, University of Sydney, Sydney, NSW 2006, Australia (office). *Telephone:* (2) 9351-0872 (office). *E-mail:* info.centre@sydney.edu.au (office). *Website:* www.physiol.usyd.edu.au/research/labs/nrc (office).

BENNETT, Michael Vander Laan, BS, DPhil; American neuroscientist and academic; *Sylvia and Robert S. Olnick Chair in Neuroscience and Distinguished Professor, Dominick P. Purpura Department of Neuroscience, Albert Einstein College of Medicine;* b. 7 Jan. 1931, Madison, Wis.; s. of Martin Toscan Bennett and Cornelia Vander Laan Bennett; m. 1st Ruth Berman 1963 (divorced 1993); one s. one d.; m. 2nd Ruth Suzanne Zukin 1998; ed Yale Univ., Univ. of Oxford, UK; research worker, Dept of Neurology, Coll. of Physicians and Surgeons, Columbia Univ. 1957–58, Research Assoc. 1958–59; Asst Prof. of Neurology, Columbia Univ. 1959–61, Assoc. Prof. 1961–66; Prof. of Anatomy, Albert Einstein Coll. of Medicine, Yeshiva Univ., NY 1967–74, Co-Dir Neurobiology Course, Marine Biological Lab. 1970–74, Prof. of Neuroscience 1974–, Dir Div. of Cellular Neurobiology 1974–, Chair. Dept of Neuroscience 1982–96, Sylvia and Robert S. Olnick Prof. Chair in Neuroscience 1986–, also Distinguished Prof., Dominick P. Purpura Dept of Neuroscience; mem. Editorial Bds Brain Research 1975–, Journal of Cell Biology 1983–85, Journal of Neurobiology 1969–95 (Assoc. Ed. 1979–93), Journal of Neurocytology 1980–82, Journal of Neuroscience (Section Ed. 1981–85); mem. NAS 1982, American Asscn of Anatomists, American Physiological Soc., American Soc. for Cell Biology, American Soc. of Zoologists, Biophysical Soc., Soc. for Neuroscience, Soc. of Gen. Physiologists; Fellow, Nat. Neurological Research Foundation 1958–60, New York Acad. of Sciences, AAAS; Rhodes Scholar 1952, Sr Research Fellowship, NIH 1960–62. *Publications:* more than 300 papers in scholarly books and journals. *Leisure interests:* running, hiking, skiing and scuba. *Address:* Albert Einstein College of Medicine, 1300 Morris Park Avenue, Bronx, NY 10461, USA (office). *Telephone:* (718) 430-2536 (office). *Fax:* (718) 430-8932 (office). *E-mail:* michael.bennett@einstein.yu.edu (office). *Website:* www.einstein.yu.edu/faculty/8219/michael-bennett (office).

BENNETT, Naftali; Israeli business executive and politician; *Minister of Education and Minister for Diaspora Affairs;* b. 25 March 1972, Haifa; s. of Jim Bennett and Myrna Bennett; m. Gilat Bennett; four c.; ed Hebrew Univ. of Jerusalem; Co-founder and CEO Cyota (anti-fraud software co.), New York 1999–2005; served as bureau head to Leader of Opposition Benjamin Netanyahu 2006–08; fmr CEO Soluto (computing service); Dir-Gen., Yesha Council (regional council for West Bank settlements) 2010–12; co-f. My Israel (extra-parl. movt) 2011; mem. Knesset 2013–; Minister of Economy 2013–15, Minister of Religious Services 2013–15, Minister for Jerusalem and Diaspora Affairs 2013–15, Minister of Educ. and for Diaspora Affairs 2015–; mem. Jewish Home Party (HaBayit HaYehudi), Leader 2012–. *Address:* Ministry of Education, POB 292, 34 Shivtei Israel Street, Jerusalem 91911, Israel (office). *Telephone:* 2-5602222 (office). *Fax:* 2-5602223 (office). *E-mail:* info@education.gov.il (office). *Website:* www.education.gov.il (office).

BENNETT, Natalie Louise, BAgricSci (Hons), BA (Hons), MA; British (b. Australian) politician; b. 10 Feb. 1966, Sydney, NSW, Australia; ed MLC School, Burwood, NSW, Univ. of Sydney, Univ. of New England (Australia), Univ. of Leicester; began career in journalism at Eastern Riverina Observer, Henty, NSW, then worked for Cootamundra Herald and Northern Daily Leader, Tamworth; spent two years as Australian Volunteer Abroad working in Office of the Nat. Comm. of Women's Affairs; worked as Chief Foreign Sub-Ed. for Bangkok Post newspaper; began writing for Guardian newpaper's 'Comment is Free' section 2006, Deputy Ed. The Guardian Weekly –2007, Ed. 2007–12; mem. Green Party of England and Wales 2006–, Internal Communications Coordinator on Nat. Exec. 2006–10, Leader 2012–16; cand. in Camden Council election for Regent's Park Ward 2006, for Somerstown Ward 2010; selected to stand for parl. seat of Holborn and St Pancras 2010, 2015, Sheffield Central 2017; cand. in London Ass. elections on London-wide list for Green Party 2012; Chair. Camden Green Party 2011–; Founding Chair. Green Party Women 2008–12; Founder Carnival of Feminists; Editorial Bd Convenor, Green World 2010–12; books ed. on Blogcritics.org; Trustee, Fawcett Soc., Green European Foundation. *Publications include:* Thailand Country Study: Best Practice Guide on Sustainable Action Against Child Labour (ed.) 1998, Women's Health and Development, Country Profile Thailand (ed.); contrib. to The Independent, The Times. *Address:* The Biscuit Factory, Unit 201 A Block, 100 Clements Road, London, SE16 4DG, England (office). *Telephone:* (20) 3691 9401 (office). *E-mail:* natalie.bennett@greenparty.org.uk (office). *Website:* natalie4sheffield.org (office); nataliebennett.co.uk.

BENNETT, Tony, MusD; American singer and entertainer; b. (Anthony Dominick Benedetto), 3 Aug. 1926, Astoria, New York; s. of John Benedetto and Anna Suraci; m. 1st Patricia Beech 1952 (divorced 1971); two c.; m. 2nd Sandra Grant 1971 (divorced 1984); two d.; m. 3rd Susan Crow 2007; ed American Theatre Wing, NY and Univ. of Berkeley; frequent appearances on TV and in concert; owner and recording artist with Improv Records; paintings exhibited at Butler Inst. of American Art, Youngstown, Ohio 1994; f. Frank Sinatra School of the Arts 2001; Grammy Award for Best Traditional Pop Vocal Performer 1998, Kennedy Center Honor 2005, Billboard Century Award 2006, Nat. Endowment for the Arts Jazz Masters Award 2006, Grammy Award for Best Pop Collaboration with Vocals (with Stevie Wonder) 2007, Ronnie Scott Lifetime Achievement Award 2007, inducted into New Jersey Hall of Fame 2011, Gershwin Prize for Popular Song 2017. *Recordings include:* The Art of Excellence 1986, Bennett/Berlin 1988, Astoria: Portrait of the Artist 1990, Perfectly Frank (Grammy Award for Best Traditional Vocal Performance) 1992, Steppin' Out (Grammy Award for Best Traditional Pop Vocal) 1993, The Essence of Tony Bennett 1993, MTV Unplugged (Grammy Award for Album of the Year, Best Traditional Pop Vocal) 1994, Here's to the Ladies 1995, The Playground 1998, Cool (Grammy Award) 1999, The Ultimate Tony 2000, A Wonderful World (with k.d. lang) (Grammy Award for Best Traditional Pop Vocal Album 2004) 2003, The Art of Romance (Grammy Award for Best Traditional Pop Vocal Album 2006) 2005, Duets: An American Classic (Grammy Award for Best Traditional Pop Vocal Album 2007) 2006, Tony Bennett Sings the Ultimate American Songbook, Vol. 1 2007, A Swingin' Christmas 2008, Body and Soul (Grammy Award for Pop Duo/Group Performance with the late Amy Winehouse 2012) 2011, Duets II (Grammy Award for Traditional Pop Vocal Album 2012) 2011, Viva Duets 2012, Cheek to Cheek (with Lady Gaga) (Grammy Award for Best Traditional Pop Vocal Album 2015) 2014, The Silver Lining: the Songs of Jerome Kern (with Bill Charlap) (Grammy Award for Best Traditional Pop Vocal Album) 2016, Tony Bennett Celebrates 90 (Grammy Award for Best Traditional Pop Vocal Album 2018) 2016. *Publications:* The Good Life: The Autobiography of Tony Bennett 1998, Life is a Gift: The Zen of Bennett 2012. *Address:* 130 West 57th Street, Apartment 9D, New York, NY 10019, USA. *Website:* www.tonybennett.com.

BENNOUNA, Mohamed, DIntLaw; Moroccan diplomatist, academic, lawyer and international judge; *Judge, International Court of Justice;* b. 29 April 1943, Marrakech; m.; three c.; ed Univ. of Nancy, Sorbonne Univ., Paris, France and The Hague Acad. of Int. Law, Netherlands; Prof. of Public Law and Political Science, Univ. of the Sorbonne, Paris 1972–75; Prof., Faculty of Law, Mohammed V Univ. of Rabat and Casablanca 1975–79, Dean 1979–85; Dir-Gen. Arab World Inst. 1991–98; Judge, Int. Criminal Tribunal for the fmr Yugoslavia 1998–2001; Perm. Rep. of Morocco to UN, New York 1985–89, 2001–05; Judge, Int. Court of Justice, The Hague 2006–, Judge ad hoc for dispute between Benin and Niger 2002; Chair. UN Compensation Comm., Geneva 1992–95, Group of 77 and China, UN 2003; mem. UNESCO Int. Panel on Democracy and Devt 1997–, UNESCO World Comm. on Ethics of Scientific Knowledge and Tech. (COMEST) 2002–, UNESCO Int. Bioethics Cttee 1992–98, UN Int. Law Comm., Geneva 1992–95; Chevalier, Légion d'honneur, France Commander of the Order of the Throne, Morocco; Nat. Prize for Culture, Morocco, Medal for Culture, Yemen. *Publications:* numerous books, essays and articles on int. law. *Address:* International Court of Justice, Peace Palace, Carnegieplein 2, 2517 KJ The Hague, The Netherlands (office). *Telephone:* (70) 302-23-23 (office). *Fax:* (70) 302-24-09 (office). *E-mail:* info@icj-cij.org (office). *Website:* www.icj-cij.org (office).

BENOIST, Gilles, LenD; French insurance industry executive; b. 12 Dec. 1946; ed Institut d'Etudes Politiques, Ecole Nat. d'Admin; began his career with French Interior Ministry, first as Dir Office of the Prefect of Oise Dept 1974–76, then Sec.-Gen. Ariège Dept 1976–78; Prin. Pvt. Sec. to Dir-Gen. of Local Authorities at Ministry of the Interior 1978–81, Prin. Pvt. Sec. to Minister of the Economy, Finance and Budget 1981–83; Public Auditor, Cour des Comptes (Court of State Auditors) 1983, served successively as rapporteur on Budget and Finance Disciplinary Court and rapporteur to MODAC governmental org. project, seconded to Caisse des Dépôts et Consignations as adviser to Deputy CEO 1987, mem. Exec. Bd and Corp. Sec. Crédit Local de France, promoted to Sr Public Auditor at Cour des Comptes 1989–91, Dir of Cen. Services, Caisse des Dépôts et Consignations 1991–95, mem. Exec. Cttee 1993–98, Group Corp. Sec. and Dir of Human Resources, Caisse des Dépôts Group 1995–96, Chief Advisor, Cour des Comptes 1996–98; Pres. Exec. Bd and CEO CNP Assurances 1998–2012, mem. Bd of Dirs 2007–12; mem. Bd of Dirs, Dexia, ISODEV, Suez Environnement 2008–; mem. Supervisory Bd, Compagnie Internationale André Trigano, Louis Dreyfus Holding BV (Netherlands); Pres. Fédération française des sociétés anonymes d'assurance; Officier, Légion d'honneur.

BENOMAR, Jamal, MA, PhD; Moroccan diplomatist and UN official; *Under-Secretary-General and Special Adviser to Secretary-General, United Nations;* b. April 1957; m.; four c.; ed Univ. of Rabat, Univ. of Paris (Sorbonne), Univ. of London, UK; imprisoned in Morocco after opposing govt 1976–83; Lecturer and Assoc. Researcher, Univ. of Paris VII 1983–86; Africa Research Specialist, Int. Secr., Amnesty International, London 1987–91; Dir of Human Rights Program, Center, Emory Univ., USA 1991–94; Head of Technical Cooperation Branch, UN Office of High Commr for Human Rights; worked in UNDP in various capacities 1994, including as Head of Technical Cooperation Branch, Office of High Commr for Human Rights, as Sr Adviser on Governance and Rule of Law in Conflict and Post-Conflict Countries, as Head, Conflict Prevention and Peacebuilding Unit, as Special Adviser –2006; Envoy of UN Sec.-Gen. in Afghanistan and Iraq, to facilitate Nat. Dialogue Conf. 2004; Dir Office of UN Sec.-Gen., establishing Peacebuilding Comm. and Peacebuilding Support Office 2006; Dir Rule of Law Unit, Office of UN Sec.-Gen. 2008–11; Special Adviser to UN Sec.-Gen. on Yemen 2011–15 (resgnd); Under-Sec.-Gen. and Special Adviser to UN Sec.-Gen. 2015–. *Address:* United Nations Headquarters, 405 E 42nd Street, New York, NY 10017, USA (office). *Telephone:* (212) 963-1234 (office). *Fax:* (212) 963-4879 (office). *Website:* www.un.org (office).

BENSCHOP, Brig.-Gen. Ronni; Suriname military commander and government official; *Minister of Defence;* b. 19 Nov. 1955, Paramaribo; m. Lalita Sewnath; ed Defence Resources Man. Inst., Naval Postgraduate School, USA, Inst. of Defense Training, Netherlands, Escola Superior de Guerra, War Coll., Brazil; numerous positions in Surinamese Armed Forces, including as Deputy Army Chief 2013–14, Commdr of Armed Forces (Mil. Chief) 2014–15; apptd Head of Military Affairs, Ministry of Defence 1998, then Head of Defence Strategic Planning and Training 2001, Advisor to Minister of Defence 2002–11, Minister of Defence 2015–; attained rank of Brig.-Gen. 2014 (highest mil. rank in Suriname, first person ever to attain this level). *Address:* Ministry of Defence, Kwattaweg 29, Paramaribo, Suriname (office). *Telephone:* 471511 (office). *Fax:* 420055 (office). *E-mail:* defensie@sr.net (office). *Website:* www.gov.sr/ministerie-van-defensie (office).

BENSON, Bruce D., BSc; American business executive and university administrator; *President, University of Colorado;* b. 4 Aug. 1938, Chicago; m. Marcy Benson; three c.; ed Univ. of Colorado; f. Benson Mineral Group 1965; Chair. Colo Comm. on Higher Educ. 1986–89; Chair. Colo Republican Party 1987–93, 2002–03;

Chair. Gov.'s Blue Ribbon Panel for Higher Educ. for 21st Century 2001–03; Chair. Metropolitan State Coll. Bd of Trustees 2002–07; Pres. Univ. of Colorado 2008–, also Exec. in Residence and Prof. Attendant, Univ. of Colorado Business School; fmr mem. Bd of Dirs US Exploration Inc., American Land Lease Corpn, Asset Investors Corpn; mem. Smith Coll. Bd of Trustees 1990–95; Hon. DHumLitt (Colo) 2004 Univ. of Colorado Medal 1999, Ira C. Rothgerber Award 2003. *Address:* Office of the President, University of Colorado, 1800 Grant Street, Suite 800, Denver, CO 80203, USA. *Telephone:* (303) 860-5600 (office). *Fax:* (303) 860-5610 (office). *E-mail:* bdbenson2000@yahoo.com; OfficeofthePresident@cu.edu (office). *Website:* www.cu.edu (office).

BENSON, Sir Christopher John, Kt, FRICS, JP, DL; British business executive and chartered surveyor; b. 20 July 1933, Wheaton Aston; s. of Charles Woodburn Benson and Catherine Clara Bishton; m. Margaret Josephine Bundy 1960; two s.; ed Worcester Cathedral King's School, Thames Nautical Training Coll. HMS Worcester; Midshipman RNR 1949–52; Sub-Lt RNVR 1952–53; worked as chartered surveyor and agricultural auctioneer 1953–64; Dir Arndale Devts Ltd 1965–69; Chair. Dolphin Devts Ltd 1969–71, Dolphin Farms Ltd 1969–, Dolphin Property (Man.) Ltd 1969–; Asst Man. Dir The Law Land Co. Ltd 1972–74; Dir Sun Alliance and London Insurance Group 1978–84, Chair. Sun Alliance Insurance Group PLC 1993–96 (Dir 1988, Vice-Chair. 1991, Deputy Chair. 1992), Chair. Royal and Sun Alliance Insurance Group PLC 1996–97; Adviser to British Petroleum Pension Fund 1979–84, Cathedral PLC; Underwriting Mem. of Lloyd's 1979–97; mem. Council CBI 1979–97; Pres. British Property Fed. 1981–83; Dir House of Fraser PLC 1982–86; Chair. London Docklands Devt Corpn 1984–88; Chair. Reedpack Ltd 1989–90; Man. Dir MEPC PLC 1976–88, Chair. 1988–93; Chair. Housing Corpn; Chair. Boots Co. PLC 1990–94 (Dir 1989); Chair. Costain Group PLC 1993–96; Chair. Funding Agency for Schools 1994–97; Deputy Chair. Thorn Lighting Group PLC 1994–98; Chair. Albright and Wilson PLC 1995–; Chair. Devt Bd Macmillan Cancer Relief 1995–2001, Cross London Rail Links 2001–05, Stratford (East London) Renaissance Partnerships 2009–13, Salisbury Vision 2009–13; Gov. Inns of Court School of Law 1996–2000, Prin. 2000–02; Pres. London Chamber of Commerce and Industry 2000–02, Nat. Deaf Children's Soc. 1995–; Vice-Pres. RSA 1992–97; High Sheriff of Wilts. 2002–03; mem. Advisory Bd Hawkpoint Partners Ltd 1999–2001; Master Co. of Watermen and Lightermen of the River Thames 2004–05; Chair. and Trustee Coram Family 2005–12; Liveryman of Hon. Co. of Air Pilots; Lay Canon, Salisbury Cathedral; Chair. Britain-Australia Soc. Educ. Trust 2012–; Trustee, Magna Carta Trust, Salisbury Cathedral, Marine Soc. and Sea Cadets 2002– (Hon. Vice-Pres.); Patron Changing Faces; Friend, Royal Coll. of Physicians; numerous other public and charitable interests; Hon. Vice-Pres. Nat. Fed. of Housing Asscns 1994–; Hon. Fellow, Wolfson Coll. Cambridge 1990, Chartered Inst. of Bldg 1992–, Royal Coll. of Pathologists 1992–, Southampton Univ.; Hon. Bencher Hon. Soc. of Middle Temple 1984–; Hon. DSc (City), (Bradford). *Leisure interests:* opera, ballet, farming in Wiltshire, flying, swimming. *Address:* Pauls Dene House, Castle Road, Salisbury, SP1 3RY (home); Flat 2, 50 South Audley Street, London, W1K 2QE, England (home). *Telephone:* (20) 7629-2398 (office). *Fax:* (1722) 336980 (home). *E-mail:* sircjbenson@me.com (office).

BENSON, George; American musician (guitar) and singer; b. 22 March 1943, Pittsburgh, Pa; session musician in Pittsburgh; guitarist with Brother Jack McDuff; session work with Herbie Hancock, Wes Montgomery 1966; solo artist 1966–; regular world-wide tours, concerts and festivals; Grammy Awards for Best R&B Instrumental 1976, 1980, Record of the Year 1976, Best Pop Instrumental 1976, 1984, Best R&B Male Vocal Performance 1978, 1980, Best Jazz Vocal Performance 1980, Best Jazz Instrumental Performance 1991, Grammy Award for Best Pop Instrumental Performance (for Mornin') 2007, for Best Traditional R&B Vocal Performance (for God Bless the Child) 2007. *Recordings include:* albums: It's Uptown 1966, Benson Burner 1966, Giblet Gravy 1967, Tell It Like It Is 1969, The Other Side Of Abbey Road 1970, Beyond The Blue Horizon 1972, Good King Bad 1973, Bad Benson 1974, Supership 1975, Breezin' 1976, Benson And Farrell (with Joe Farrell) 1976, George Benson In Concert: Carnegie Hall 1977, In Flight 1977, Weekend In LA 1978, Livin' Inside Your Love 1979, Give Me The Night 1981, George Benson Collection 1981, In Your Eyes 1983, 20/20 1985, The Love Songs 1985, While The City Sleeps 1986, Collaboration 1987, Twice The Love 1988, Tenderly 1989, Big Boss Band 1990, Midnight Moods: The Love Collection 1991, Love Remembers 1993, The Most Exciting New Guitarist On The Jazz 1994, Take Five 1995, Live and Smokin' 1995, California Dreamin' 1996, That's Right 1996, Lil' Darlin' 1996, Talkin' Verve 1997, Essentials 1998, Standing Together 1998, Masquerade 1998, Masquerade Is Over 1999, Love And Jazz 1999, Live At Casa Caribe 2000, Absolute Benson 2000, All Blues 2001, Irreplaceable 2004, Givin' It Up 2006, Songs and Stories 2009, Guitar Man 2011, Inspiration: A Tribute to Nat King Cole 2013. *Address:* c/o Stephanie Gonzalez, Apropos Management & Marketing, 365 Avenida de los Arboles, Suite 220, Thousand Oaks, CA 91360, USA (office). *E-mail:* stephanie@aproposmanagement.com (office). *Website:* www.georgebenson.com.

BENSOUDA, Fatou B., LLM; Gambian lawyer and fmr government official; *Chief Prosecutor, International Criminal Court;* b. 31 Jan. 1961, Banjul; m.; two c.; ed Univ. of Ife, Nigeria, Nigeria Law School, Int. Maritime Law Inst., Malta; various roles with state prosecution service, including Public Prosecutor, Sr State Counsel and Prin. State Counsel 1987–93, Deputy Dir of Public Prosecutions 1993–97, Solicitor-Gen. and Legal Sec. 1997–98, Attorney-Gen. and Sec. of State (Minister of Justice) 1998–2000; served in pvt legal practice, Ya Sadi, Bensouda and Co. Chambers, Banjul 2000–02; Gen. Man. Int. Bank for Commerce (Gambia) Ltd Jan.–May 2002; Legal Adviser and Trial Attorney, Int. Criminal Tribunal for Rwanda, becoming Sr Legal Adviser and Head of Legal Advisory Unit, Tanzania 2002–04; Deputy Prosecutor in charge of Prosecutions Div., Int. Criminal Court (ICC) 2004–12, Chief Prosecutor 2012–; Visiting Lecturer, Univ. of Turin, Italy, Kennesaw State Univ., USA; mem. Int. Asscn of Prosecutors, Gambian Bar Asscn, Nigerian Bar Asscn; mem. Int. Advisory Council, Int. Bd of Maritime Healthcare 2000–, Professional Women's Advisory Bd 2000–, Advisory Bd African Centre For Democracy and Human Rights Studies 1998–2000; mem. Bd of Govs The Gambia High School 1992–95; Int. Jurists Award, Int. Comm. of Jurists 2009, World Peace Through Law Award, Whitney Harris World Law Inst., Washington Univ. in St Louis, USA 2011. *Achievements include:* first int. maritime law expert in The Gambia. *Address:* International Criminal Court, Maanweg 174, 2516 AB, The Hague, Netherlands (office). *Telephone:* (70) 5158515 (office). *Fax:* (70) 5158555 (office). *Website:* www.icc-cpi.int (office).

BENTALL, Richard, BSc, MClinPsychol, MA, PhD, FBA; British psychologist and academic; *Professor of Clinical Psychology, University of Liverpool;* b. 30 Sept. 1956, Sheffield, Yorks.; m. Aisling O'Kane; one s. one d.; ed Uppingham School, Rutland, High Storrs School, Sheffield, Univ. Coll. of North Wales, Bangor, Univ. of Liverpool and Univ. Coll., Swansea; worked as forensic clinical psychologist in Nat. Health Service 1986; Lecturer, Univ. of Liverpool 1986–94, Prof. of Clinical Psychology 1994–99; Prof. of Experimental Clinical Psychology, Univ. of Manchester 1999, later held Chair in Experimental Psychology; Prof. of Clinical Psychology, School of Psychology, Bangor Univ. 2006–10; Prof. of Clinical Psychology, Univ. of Liverpool 2011–, Univ. of Sheffield; Fellow, British Psychological Soc.; May Davidson Award, British Psychological Soc. 1989, British Psychological Society Book Award 2005. *Publications:* Sensory Deception: A Scientific Analysis of Hallucination (co-author) 1988, Reconstructing Schizophrenia (co-author) 1992, Madness Explained: Psychosis and Human Nature 2003, Doctoring the Mind: Is Our Current Treatment of Mental Illness Really Any Good? 2009; numerous book chapters and articles in scientific journals on psychiatric classification and methodology in psychopathology, cognitive-behavioural therapy, subjective appraisal of neuroleptic drugs and the treatment of chronic fatigue syndrome. *Address:* Institute of Psychology, Health and Society, University of Liverpool, Waterhouse Building, Block B, 2nd Floor, Brownlow Street, Liverpool, L69 3BX, England (office). *Telephone:* (15) 1794-8041 (office). *E-mail:* Richard.Bentall@liverpool.ac.uk (office). *Website:* www.liverpool.ac.uk/psychology-health-and-society (office).

BENTÉGEAT, Gen. Henri; French army officer and diplomatist; b. 27 May 1946, Talence; m.; four c.; ed Mil. Acad. of St Cyr, Institut d'Études Politiques de Paris; jr officer in French Armed Forces, serving in Germany, Senegal, France and Djibouti 1968–73; as field grade officer, served in Army Public Information Service, Chief Operations of 9th Marine Div., Commdr Marine Infantry and Armoured Bn 1988–90; Asst Defence Attaché, Embassy in Washington, DC 1990–92; Asst to Chief of Mil. Staff of Pres. of Repub. 1993–96; Commdr French Forces in West Indies 1996–98; Asst to Dir for Strategic Affairs, Ministry of Defence 1998–99; Chief of Mil. Staff of Pres. of Repub. 1999–2002; Chief of Defence Staff 2002–06; Chair. EU Mil. Cttee 2006–09; apptd Maj.-Gen. 1998, Lt-Gen. 1999, Gen. 2001; Commandeur, Ordre nat. du Mérite, Grand Officier, Légion d'honneur 2006; numerous foreign decorations; Prix de l'Institut français de la mer 2006. *Leisure interest:* reading. *Address:* c/o EU Military Committee, rue de la loi 175, 1048 Brussels, Belgium (office).

BENTHAM, Richard Walker, BA, LLB, FRSA; British professor of law and barrister; *Professor Emeritus, University of Dundee;* b. 26 June 1930; s. of Richard H. Bentham and Ellen W. Fisher; m. Stella W. Matthews 1955; one d.; ed Trinity Coll., Dublin and Middle Temple, London; called to Bar 1955; Lecturer in Law, Univ. of Tasmania 1955–57, Univ. of Sydney 1957–61; Legal Dept British Petroleum Co. PLC 1961–83, Deputy Legal Adviser 1979–83; Prof. of Petroleum and Mineral Law and Dir Centre for Petroleum and Mineral Law Studies, Univ. of Dundee 1983–90, Prof. Emer. 1991–; Russian Petroleum Legislation Project (Univ. of Houston, World Bank, ODA) 1991–96; mem. Council ICC Inst. of Int. Business Law and Practice 1988–95; British nominated mem. panel arbitrators IEA Dispute Settlement Centre; mem. Bd Scottish Council for Int. Arbitration 1988–98; mem. Int. Law Asscn, Int. Bar Asscn; Julian Prize, Trinity Coll. Dublin 1952. *Publications:* publications in learned journals in the UK and overseas. *Leisure interests:* cricket, military history. *Address:* University of Dundee, Nethergate, Dundee, DD1 4HN, Scotland (office). *Telephone:* (1382) 384300 (office). *E-mail:* cepmlp@dundee.ac.uk (office). *Website:* www.dundee.ac.uk/cepmlp.

BENTLEY, Robert Julian, BS, MD; American dermatologist, business executive, politician and state governor; b. 3 Feb. 1943, Columbiana, Shelby Co., Ala; s. of David Harford Bentley and Mattie Boyd Bentley (née Vick); m. Martha 'Dianne' Jones 1965; four s.; ed Shelby Co. High School, Univ. of Alabama, Tuscaloosa, Univ. of Alabama School of Medicine; internship, Carraway Methodist Hosp., Birmingham 1968–69; joined USAF as Capt. 1969–75, served as gen. medical officer at Pope Air Force Base, Fayetteville, NC; residency in dermatology, Univ. of Alabama 1974; dermatology practice in Tuscaloosa 1974–98; mem. (Republican) Alabama House of Reps for 63rd Dist 2002–10; Gov. of Alabama 2011–17; f. several small businesses, including Alabama Dermatology Assocs (currently Pres.); Chair. Nat. Govs Asscn (NGA)'s Econ. Devt and Commerce Comm., Appalachian Regional Comm.; Co-Chair. Gov.'s Task Force on Prescription Drug Abuse through the NGA; fmr mem. State Advisory Bd for Sexually Transmitted Diseases; Founder and fmr Pres. Alabama Dermatology Soc.; mem. American Acad. of Dermatology, Medical Asscn of Ala, American Legion, Veterans of Foreign Wars (Life); mem. Bd of Trustees, Judson Coll., Marion, Ala, Alabama Medical Educ. Consortium (co-founder); Deacon and Sunday School Teacher, First Baptist Church, Tuscaloosa, Chair. Bd of Deacons four times, mem. Youth for Christ Advisory Bd, Family Counseling Advisory Bd; Republican; named to Best Doctors in America, Statesmanship Award, Christian Coalition of Alabama 2009. *Address:* c/o Office of the Governor, State Capitol, 600 Dexter Avenue, Suite N104, Montgomery, AL 36130-2751, USA (office).

BENTON, Fletcher Chapman, II, BFA; American artist, painter, sculptor and academic; b. 25 Feb. 1931, Jackson, Ohio; m. Roberta Lee 1964; one s. one d.; ed Miami Univ.; mem. Faculty, Calif. Coll. of Arts and Crafts 1959, San Francisco Art Inst. 1964–67; Prof. of Art, Calif. State Univ., San Jose 1967–86; Hon. DFA (Miami Univ.) 1993, (Columbus Univ. of Rio Grande, Rio Grande, Ohio) 1994; American Acad. of Arts and Letters Award for Distinguished Service to the Arts 1979, President's Scholar Award, Calif. State Univ. San José 1980, San Francisco Arts Comm. Award of Honor for Outstanding Achievement in Sculpture 1982; Lifetime Achievement Award in Contemporary Sculpture, Int. Sculpture Center 2008, Distinguished Artist Alumni Award, School of Fine Arts and Dept of Art, Miami Univ. 2012. *Address:* Fletcher Benton Studio, 250 Dore Street, San Francisco, CA 94103, USA (office). *E-mail:* bstudio@penn.com (office). *Website:* www.fletcherbenton.com (office).

BENTON, Peter Faulkner, MA, CCMI; British science and economic consultant (retd); b. 6 Oct. 1934, London; s. of S. Faulkner Benton and Hilda Benton; m. Ruth

S. Cobb 1959; two s. three d.; ed Oundle School, Queens' Coll. Cambridge; jr man. positions in Unilever, Shell Chemicals and Berger, Jenson and Nicholson 1959–64; consultant, McKinsey & Co., London and Chicago 1964–71; Dir Gallaher Ltd 1971–77, also Chair. subsidiaries; Man. Dir Post Office Telecommunications 1978–81; Deputy Chair. British Telecom 1981–83; Special Adviser to EEC 1983–84; Chair. European Practice, Nolan, Norton & Co. 1984–87, Enfield Dist Health Authority 1986–92; Vice-Pres. European Council of Man. 1989–92; Dir Singer & Friedlander Ltd 1983–89, Tandata Holdings PLC 1983–89, Turing Inst. 1985–95, Woodside Communications Ltd 1995–96; Dir-Gen. British Inst. of Man. 1987–92; Chair. Enterprise Support Group 1993–96; Chair. Visiting Group Inst. for Systems, Eng and Informatics, Italy 1993–94, Visiting Group Inst. for Systems, Informatics and Safety, Italy 1996–99; Adviser to Arthur Andersen 1992–98; mem. Int. Advisory Bd for Science and Tech. to Govt of Portugal 1996–2002, Industrial Devt Advisory Bd (DTI) 1988–94; Adviser to Stern Stewart Inc. 1995–2001; gave lectures at Univ. of Pennsylvania 2002–05; mem. Exec. Cttee Athenaeum 1997–2002; Chair. Ditchley Conf. on Information Tech. 1980, North London Hospice 1985–89, World Bank Confs on Catastrophe 1988, 1989, Chair. Delhi Conf. on Indian Infrastructure 1998; Adam Smith Lecturer 1991; Pres. Highgate Literary and Scientific Inst. 1981–88; Treas. Harington Scheme, London 1983–93; Gov. Molecule Theatre, London 1985–91; Ind. mem. British Library Advisory Council 1988–93; IEE Award 1994. *Achievements include:* led reorganization of UK gas industry 1966–71. *Publication:* Riding the Whirlwind 1990. *Leisure interests:* reading, conversation, sailing, early music. *Address:* Northgate House, Highgate Hill, London, N6 5HD (home); Dolphins, Polruan-by-Fowey, Cornwall, PL23 1PP, England (home). *Telephone:* (20) 8341-1122 (London) (home).

BENYAN, Yousef Abdullah al-, BEcons, MA; Saudi Arabian business executive; *Vice-Chairman and CEO, Saudi Basic Industries Corporation;* has held several sr posts at Saudi Basic Industries Corpn (SABIC) since 1987, including Man. of Exhbns 1990–94, Gen. Man. Fiber Intermediates, SABIC HQ, Gen. Man. SABIC Asia Pacific 2002–05, Gen. Man. SABIC Americas, Inc., Houston, USA 2005–07, later Exec. Vice-Pres., Corp. Human Resources 2008–, Exec. Vice-Pres., Chemicals –2014, Chief Financial Officer SABIC 2014–15, Vice-Chair. and CEO 2015–; Chair. Yanbu Nat. Petrochemical Co. 2015–; Chair. Gulf Petrochemicals and Chemicals Asscn 2016–, Saudi Arabian Fertilizer Co. *Address:* Saudi Basic Industries Corporation, PO Box 5101, Riyadh 11422, Saudi Arabia (office). *Telephone:* (1) 2259655 (office). *Fax:* (1) 2259660 (office). *E-mail:* info@sabic.com (office). *Website:* www.sabic.com (office).

BENYON, Margaret, MBE, PhD, BFA; British/Australian artist; b. 29 April 1940, Birmingham; m. William Rodwell 1974; one s. one d.; ed Kenya High School, Slade School of Fine Art, Univ. Coll. London, Royal Coll. of Art, London; Visiting Tutor, Coventry Coll. of Art 1966–68, Trent Polytechnic, Nottingham 1968–71, Holography Unit, RCA 1985–89; Fellow in Fine Art, Univ. of Nottingham 1968–71; pioneered holography as an art medium 1968; Leverhulme Sr Art Fellow, Univ. of Strathclyde 1971–73; Co-ordinator Graphic Investigation, Canberra School of Art, Australia 1977–80; Creative Arts Fellow ANU, Canberra 1978; Artist-in-Residence, Museum of Holography, New York 1981, Center for Holographic Arts, New York 1999; moved to Sydney, Australia 2005; Hon. Professorial Visiting Fellow, Coll. of Fine Arts, Univ. of NSW, Australia 2006–09; works in public collections including Australian Nat. Gallery, Nat. Gallery of Vic., Australia, MIT Museum Boston, USA, Calouste Gulbenkian Foundation, Portugal, Victoria and Albert Museum, London; over 100 exhbns to date, including USA, Canada, Portugal, Italy, Australia, France, Germany, Japan, UK, Austria, Spain and China; Hon. FRPS 2001; Audrey Mellon Prize 1964, Carnegie Trust Award 1972, Kodak Photographic Bursary 1982, Calouste Gulbenkian Holography Award 1982, Agfa 'Best of Exhibition' Award (USA) 1985, Shearwater Foundation Holography Award (USA) 1987, Lifetime Achievement Award, Art in Holography International Symposium (UK) 1996, Shearwater Foundation Holography Purchase Award (USA) 2002. *Publications:* articles in more than 100 publs. *Address:* 18 Burra Close, Mount Colah, NSW 2079, Australia (office). *E-mail:* mbenyon@optusnet.com.au (office).

BENZ, Edward J., Jr, MD, MA; American professor of medicine, paediatrics and pathology, physician and hospital administrator; *President and CEO, Dana-Farber Cancer Institute, Harvard University;* b. 22 May 1946, Pittsburgh; m. Margaret A. Vettese; one s. one d.; ed Allentown Cen. Catholic High School, Princeton Univ., Harvard Medical School, Yale Univ.; research fellowships at Princeton and Boston Univs 1967–71; Jr Asst Health Services Officer, US Public Health Service, NJH, NHLBI 1972–73, Sr Asst Surgeon 1973–75; intern, Peter Bent Brigham Hosp., Boston 1973–74, Asst Resident Physician 1974–75; Clinical Fellow, Harvard Medical School 1973–75; Fellow in Medicine (Hematology), Children's Hosp. Medical Center, Boston 1974–75; Research Assoc., Molecular Hematology Br. NHLBI, NIH, Bethesda, Md 1975–78; Fellow in Hematology, Yale Univ. School of Medicine 1978–80, Asst Prof. of Medicine, Hematology Section, Dept of Internal Medicine, Yale Univ. School of Medicine 1979–82, Assoc. Prof. of Medicine 1982–84, Assoc. Prof. of Human Genetics (Jt) 1983–87, Assoc. Prof. of Internal Medicine 1984–87, Prof. of Internal Medicine and Genetics 1987–93, Chief of Hematology Section, Dept of Internal Medicine 1987–93, Assoc. Chair. for Academic Affairs 1988–90, Vice-Chair. 1990–93, Assoc. Attending in Medicine Yale-New Haven Hosp. 1979–81, Attending Physician 1981–93; Jack D. Myers Prof. and Chair. Dept of Medicine, Univ. of Pittsburgh School of Medicine 1993–95, Prof. of Molecular Genetics and Biochemistry (Jt) 1993–95; Adjunct Prof. of Biological Sciences, Carnegie Mellon Univ., Pittsburgh 1993–95; Chief of Medicine Service, Univ. of Pittsburgh Medical Center 1993–95; Sir William Osler Prof. and Dir Dept of Medicine, Johns Hopkins Univ. School of Medicine 1995–2000, Prof. of Molecular Biology and Genetics 1995–2000, Physician-in-Chief Johns Hopkins Hosp. 1995–2000; Richard and Susan Smith Prof. of Medicine, Prof. of Pediatrics, Prof. of Pathology, Faculty Dean for Oncology, Harvard Medical School 2000–, Pres. and CEO Dana-Farber Cancer Inst., Harvard Univ. 2000–, CEO Dana-Farber/Partners Cancer Care 2000–, Dir Dana-Farber/Harvard Cancer Center, mem. Governing Bd Dana-Farber/Children's Center; Chair. Red Cells and Hemoglobin Sub-cttee, American Soc. of Hematology 1983, 1989, Molecular Genetics Educ. Panel 1984–87, Hematology I Study Section, NIH Research 1993–95; Pres. American Soc. of Clinical Investigation 1992, Scientific Affairs Cttee 1992, Educ. Program 1994; mem. Exec. Cttee American Soc. of Hematology 1994–, (Vice-Pres. 1998, Pres. 2000); mem. Scientific Advisory Bd Inst. of Molecular Medicine, Univ. of Oxford 1998, Cardiokine, Inc.; Chair. NIH Dir's Blue Ribbon Panel on the Future of Intramural Clinical Research 2003; mem. Editorial Bd American Journal of Hematology 1985–, International Journal of Hematology, Tokyo 1990–99, American Journal of Medicine 1994–; Adviser in Medicine, Oxford University Press 1994–; Consulting Ed. Journal of Clinical Investigation 1998–; Assoc. Ed. New England Journal of Medicine 2001–; mem. AAAS, American Acad. of Arts and Sciences, American Soc. for Clinical Investigation, Asscn of American Physicians, Inst. of Medicine; Fellow, American Asscn of Physicians 1992; Basil O'Connor Award, March of Dimes, Nat. Foundation 1980, NIH Research Career Devt Award 1982, Scientific Research Award, American Asscn of Blood Banks 1986, Inst. of Medicine Award, American Soc. of Hematology Mentoring Award in Basic Science 2007, Margaret L. Kripke Legend Award 2011 and other awards. *Publications:* Molecular Genetics (Methods in Hematology series) (ed.) 1989, Hematology: Principles and Practice (co-ed.) 1990, Oxford Textbook of Medicine (co-ed.) (Royal Soc. of Medicine Book Award 2003) 1997; more than 200 articles in professional journals. *Leisure interests:* tennis, reading, travel, hiking. *Address:* Office of the President, Dana-Farber Cancer Institute, 450 Brookline Avenue, Boston, Mailstop: Dana 1626A, MA 02215 (office); 28 Chestnut Hill Terrace, Chestnut Hill, MA 02467, USA (home). *Telephone:* (617) 632-4266 (office); (617) 916-5345 (home). *Fax:* (617) 632-2161 (office); (617) 916-5681 (home). *E-mail:* edward_benz@dfci.harvard.edu (office); ebenz@comcast.net (home). *Website:* www.dfhcc.harvard.edu/membership/profile/member/240/0 (office); www.dana-farber.org/About-Us/Our-Leadership-Team.aspx (office).

BÉRARD, Jean-Luc; French business executive; *Executive Vice-President for Human Resources, Safran;* b. 4 Dec. 1958; m.; two c.; began career as lawyer, Groupement des Industries Métallurgiques d'Île de France 1983–86; Dir, Groupe Esys-Montenay (Compagnie Générale des Eaux) 1986–92; Human Resources Dir, Union Nationale pour l'Emploi dans l'Industrie et le Commerce (UNEDIC) (nat. unemployment insurance scheme) 1992–99, Dir-Gen. 2007–10; Human Resources Dir, Compagnie Air Liberté 1999–2000; Human Resources Dir, CEGETEL, Groupe Vivendi 2000–01; Human Resources Dir, Groupe AOM Air Liberté 2001; Labour Relations Dir, Snecma Moteurs 2002–07; Vice-Pres., Human Resources, Safran 2010, currently Exec. Vice-Pres. *Address:* Safran, 2, bd du Général Martial Valin, 75724 Paris Cedex 15, France (office). *Telephone:* 1-40-60-80-80 (office). *Fax:* 1-40-60-85-01 (office). *Website:* www.safran-group.com (office).

BERARDI, Antonio, BA; British fashion designer; b. 21 Dec. 1968, Grantham; ed Cen. St Martin's School of Art and Design; career launched when graduation collection was purchased by Liberty and A la Mode; first Spring/Summer own label collection also bought by Liberty and A la Mode 1995; designs featured in New Generation catwalk promotion sponsored by Marks and Spencer 1996; joined Italian Mfrs Givuesse 1996; launched Autumn/Winter label 1997; apptd design consultant Ruffo leather and suede mfrs 1997; has showcased collection at London, Paris, Milan Fashion Weeks; Best New Designer, VHI Awards (USA) 1997, Dress of the Year, Harper's Bazaar magazine 2009. *Telephone:* (20) 7938-5007 (London) (office); (02) 5748061 (Milan) (office). *E-mail:* annika@tcs-uk.net (office); info@antonioberardi.com (office). *Address:* c/o Show-Room Gibo-Co SpA, via Orobia 34, 20139 Milan, Italy (office); c/o The Communication Store, 2 Kensington Square, London, W8 5EP, England. *Fax:* (20) 7938-1010 (London) (office).

BERARDI, Fabio, BSc; San Marino geologist and politician; b. 26 May 1959, Borgo Maggiore; m. Emanuele Bollini; two s.; ed Liceo Classico, Univ. of Bologna; began career with Sotecsa SA (Studio di Geologia Tecnica), San Marino 1984–86; mem. Council Borgo Maggiore 1984–89, 1995–98; Consultant, Studio Geotecnico Italiano, Milan 1986–89; pvt. practice as geologist 1989–95; Co-ordinator Dept of Territory, Environment and Agric. 1995–98; Pres. Admin. Council Azienda Autonoma di Stato per i Servizi Pubblici 1997–98; mem. Consiglio Grande Generale (Parl.) 1998–, Co-Capt.-Regent of San Marino April–Oct. 2001, Oct. 2016–April 2017, Sec. of State for Territory, Environment and Agric. 2001–03, for Foreign and Political Affairs and Econ. Planning 2003–06, for Tourism and Relations with the Azienda Autonoma di Stato per i Servizi Pubblici (AASS) 2008–13; mem. Partito Socialista Sammarinese (PSS) –2008, mem. PSS Secr. 1999–2005; fmr Pres. Order of San Marino Geologists. *Address:* Palazzo Arcipretura, Piazza della Libertà, 47890 San Marino, San Marino (office). *Website:* www.sanmarino.sm (office).

BERCA, Gabriel; Romanian politician; b. 6 Dec. 1968; m.; one c.; ed Polytechnic Univ. of Bucharest, Nat. Inst. of Admin (INA), Ecole Nat. d'Admin, Paris, France, Univ. 'Gheorghe Asachi', Iaşi; Design Engineer, Industrial Valves SA SC 1995–2000; Dir of Marketing, Monitor Bacău 2000–01; Dir of Sales, SC Prod Cressus SA 2001–04; Adviser to Gen. Dir of SC CET SA Oct.–Nov. 2004; Dir Public Social Services, Municipality of Bacău June–Sept. 2004; Prefect, Pref., Bacău Co. 2005–08; Sec.-Gen. of Govt March–Sept. 2008; Sec. of State, SGG Sept. 2008–11; Minister of Admin and the Interior Feb.–April 2012; Vice-Pres. Bacău Br., Red Cross 2007–; mem. Bd responsible for the North-East, Asscn of Prefects and Deputy Prefects of Romania 2007–; mem. competition for recruitment of sr civil servants 2008–; resigned from Liberal Party 2010; apptd Interim Pres. Partidul Democrat Liberal, Bacău; Hon. mem. academic community 'George Bacovia' 2005, Senate's 'George Bacovia' 2005. *Address:* c/o Ministry of Internal Affairs, 010086 Bucharest 1, Piaţa Revoluţiei 1A, Romania. *E-mail:* petitii@mai.gov.ro. *Website:* ro-ro.facebook.com/pages/Gabriel-Berca/139473409478657.

BERCAW, John E., BS, PhD; American chemist and academic; *Centennial Professor of Chemistry, California Institute of Technology;* b. 3 Dec. 1944, Cincinnati, Ohio; ed North Carolina State Univ., Univ. of Michigan; postdoctoral research at Univ. of Chicago 1971–72; Arthur Amos Noyes Research Fellow, California Inst. of Tech. 1972–74, Asst Prof. of Chem. 1974–77, Assoc. Prof. of Chem. 1977–79, Prof. of Chem. 1979–93, Shell Distinguished Prof. 1985–90, Centennial Prof. of Chem. 1993–, Exec. Officer for Chem. 1999–2002; mem. NAS 1990; Fellow, American Acad. of Arts and Sciences 1991; ACS Award in Pure Chem. 1980, ACS Award in Organometallic Chem. 1990, ACS Award for Distinguished Service in the Advancement of Inorganic Chem. 1997, ACS George A. Olah Award in Hydrocarbon or Petroleum Chem. 1999, American Inst. of Chemists Chemical Pioneer Award 1999, ACS Arthur C. Cope Scholar Award 2000, Basolo Medal, Chem. Dept, Northwestern Univ. 2005, Closs Lecturer, Chem. Dept, Univ. of Chicago 2008, ACS Tolman Medal, Southern California Section 2013, ACS Willard Gibbs Medal Award, Chicago Local Section 2014. *Publications:*

numerous papers in professional journals on synthetic, structural and mechanistic organotransition metal chemistry. *Address:* Room 328A Noyes, MC 127-72, California Institute of Technology, Pasadena, CA 91125, USA (office). *Telephone:* (626) 395-6577 (office). *Fax:* (626) 795-1547 (office). *E-mail:* bercaw@caltech.edu (office). *Website:* chemistry.caltech.edu (office).

BERCOW, John, PC; British politician; *Speaker of House of Commons;* b. 19 Jan. 1963; m. Sally Bercow (née Illman) 2002; three c.; ed Univ. of Essex; mem. Conservative Party; councillor London Borough of Lambeth 1986–90, Deputy Leader opposition group 1987–89; Special Adviser to the Chief Sec. to the Treasury 1995, later Special Adviser to the Sec. of State for National Heritage; MP for Buckingham 1997–, Shadow Minister for Educ. 1999–2000, Shadow Spokesperson for Home Affairs 2000–01, Shadow Chief Sec. to the Treasury 2001–02, Shadow Spokesperson for Works and Pensions July–Nov. 2002, Shadow Sec. of State for Int. Devt 2003–04; mem. Int. Devt Select Cttee 2004–09; Speaker of the House of Commons 2009–; mem. Privy Council 2009–; mem. Speaker's Cttee for the Ind. Parl. Standards Authority 2009–, Speakers' Cttee on the Electoral Comm. 2009–; Chancellor Univ. of Bedfordshire 2014–, Univ. of Essex 2017–; fmrly co-Chair. All Party Parl. Group on Burma, fmrly Vice-Chair. All Party Group on the Prevention of Genocide, Africa and Sudan, Sec. All Party Group on Human Rights; Channel 4/Hansard Soc. Political Award for Opposition MP Parl. of the Year 2005. *Publications:* Incoming Assets: why Tories should change policy on immigration and asylum 2005, Promote Freedom or Protect Oppressors: the choice at the UN Review Summit 2005. *Leisure interests:* tennis, squash, swimming, reading, music. *Address:* Speaker's Office, House of Commons, London, SW1A 0AA, England (office). *Telephone:* (20) 7219-4272 (office); (20) 7219-6346 (office). *Fax:* (20) 7219-6901 (office). *E-mail:* speakersoffice@parliament.uk (office); john.bercow.mp@parliament.uk (office). *Website:* www.parliament.uk (office); www.johnbercow.co.uk.

BERDIYEV, Col-Gen. Qobul Raimovich; Uzbekistani army officer and government official; *Chief, Civil Protection Institute, Ministry of Emergency Situations;* b. 5 April 1955, Akkurgan, Uzbek SSR; ed Frunze Mil. Acad.; joined the Armed forces 1998, Deputy Chief of Staff 1998–2000, Deputy Chief of Joint Staff 2000–03; Head Tashkent Higher Mil. Command School 2003–06; Minister of Emergency Situations 2006–08; Deputy Minister of Defence and Commdr, SW Special Mil. Dist Sept. 2008, Minister of Defence 2008–17; Rector Acad. of the Armed Forces of Uzbekistan Sept. 2017–Jan. 2018; Chief, Civil Protection Inst., Ministry of Emergency Situations 2018–. *Address:* Ministry of Emergency Situations, 100084 Tashkent, Small Ring Road, 4th floor, Uzbekistan (office). *Telephone:* (71) 239-16-85 (office). *Fax:* (71) 150-62-99 (office). *E-mail:* info@fvv.uz (office). *Website:* fvv.uz (office).

BERDYMUHAMEDOV, Gurbanguly, PhD; Turkmenistani politician, head of state and fmr dentist; *President and Chairman of the Government;* b. 29 June 1957, Babarab, Ahal Velayat, Turkmen SSR, USSR; m.; one s. three d.; ed Turkmen State Medical Inst.; mem. Dentistry Faculty, Turkmen State Medical Inst. 1979–97, Assoc. Prof. and Dean 1995–97; Head of Dentistry Centre, Ministry of Health 1995–97; Minister of Health 1997–2001; Deputy Prime Minister 2001–07; Acting Pres. (following death of Saparmyrat Niyazov) 2006–07, Pres. of Turkmenistan and Chair. of the Govt 2007–; Chair. Nat. Olympic Cttee 2007–; Chair. Türkmenistanyň Demokratik Partiýasi (Democratic Party of Turkmenistan) 2006–13 (Acting Chair. 2006–07); Ind. 2013–; Star of President Order 1994; Order of Zayed (UAE) 2007; Order of Distinguished Service (Uzbekistan) 2007; Medal of the Tenth Anniversary of the Capital City of Aştana (Kazakhstan) 2008; Order Ismoili Samoni (Tajikistan) 2010; Order of Sheikh Isa bin Salman al-Khalifa (Bahrain) 2011; Order of the State of Repub. of Turkey (First Class) 2012; Order of the Repub. of Serbia 2013. *Address:* Office of the President and the Council of Ministers, 744000 Aşgabat, Galkynyş köç. 20, Turkmenistan (office). *Telephone:* (12) 35-45-34 (office). *Fax:* (12) 35-51-12 (office). *E-mail:* nt@online.tm (office). *Website:* www.turkmenistan.gov.tm (office).

BERDYYEV, Lt-Gen. Yilym; Turkmenistani politician; *Minister of National Security;* b. 1972, Baharly Dist, Ahal Velayat, Turkmen SSR, USSR; ed Turkmenistani Agricultural Univ.; worked in Man. Cttee of Nat. Security in Ahal Velayat 1995–2003; Sr Insp. in State Service for Registration of Foreign Citizens, Deputy Head of Dept in Aşgabat City, then Deputy Head of State Service for Registration of Foreign Citizens 2003–06, Chair. State Service for Registration of Foreign Citizens and Head of Analytical Dept of Law Enforcement and Mil. Organs of the Presidential Apparatus 2006–08; Head of State Migration Service May–June 2008, of State Customs Service 2008–09; Minister of Defence and Sec. of State Security Council 2009–11, Minister of Nat. Security 2011–15, 2018–, of Defence 2015–18; 20 Years of Independence of Turkmenistan Medal. *Address:* Ministry of National Security, 744000 Aşgabat, Magtymguly Şaýoly 93, Turkmenistan (office). *Telephone:* (12) 39-71-58 (office).

BEREJIKLIAN, Gladys, BA, MCom; Australian government official and fmr banker; *Premier of New South Wales;* b. 22 Sept. 1970, Sydney; d. of Krikor Berejiklian and Arsha Berejiklian; ed Univ. of Sydney, Univ. of New South Wales; mem. Exec., Commonwealth Bank of Australia 1998–2003; mem. NSW Legis. Ass. for Willoughby 2003–, Shadow Minister Assisting the Leader on Ethnic Affairs 2005–06, Shadow Minister for Cancer and Medical Research, also for Mental Health and for Youth Affairs 2005–06, for Waterways 2006–07, for Citizenship 2007–08, for Transport 2006–11, Minister of Transport 2011–15, Treas. 2015–17, also Minister for Industrial Relations 2015–17; Premier of NSW 2017–; mem. Liberal Party 1991–, Pres. NSW Young Liberals 1996–97, Leader, NSW Liberal Party 2017–. *Address:* Office of the Premier, GPOB 5341, Sydney, NSW 2001, Australia (office). *Telephone:* (2) 9228-5239 (office). *Fax:* (2) 9228-3935 (office). *E-mail:* office@premier.nsw.gov.au (office). *Website:* www.premier.nsw.gov.au (office); www.gladys.com.au.

BEREND, Ivan T., PhD, DEcon; American (b. Hungarian) economic historian and academic; *Distinguished Professor of History, University of California, Los Angeles;* b. 11 Dec. 1930, Budapest, Hungary; s. of Mihály Berend and Elvira Gellei; two d.; ed Univ. of Economics and Eötvös Loránd Univ. of Sciences, Faculty of Philosophy, Hungary; Asst Lecturer, Karl Marx Univ. of Economics 1953, Sr Lecturer 1960, Prof. of Econ. History 1964–, Head of Dept 1967–85, Rector 1973–79; Distinguished Prof. of History, UCLA 1990–, Dir Center for European and Eurasian Studies 1993–2005, Chair. European Studies Interdepartmental Program 2008–10; Gen. Sec. Hungarian Historical Soc. 1966–72, Pres. 1975–79; Corresp. mem. Hungarian Acad. of Sciences 1973–79, mem. 1979–, Pres. 1985–90; Fellowship, Ford Foundation, New York 1966–67; Visiting Fellow, St Antony's Coll. Oxford, UK 1972–73, All Souls Coll. Oxford 1980; Visiting Prof., Univ. of California, Berkeley 1978; Fellow, Woodrow Wilson Int. Center for Scholars, Washington, DC 1982–83; Co-Chair. Inst. for East-West Security Studies 1986; mem. Exec. Cttee of Int. Econ. History Soc. 1982–86, Vice-Pres. 1986–94; First Vice-Pres. Int. Cttee of Historical Sciences 1990–95, Pres. 1995–2000; Corresp. mem. Royal Historical Soc. 1981, Academia Europaea 1987, Bulgarian Acad. of Sciences 1988, British Acad. 1989, Austrian Acad. of Sciences 1989, Czechoslovak Acad. of Sciences 1988; Hon. mem. Portuguese Asscn of Int. Relations 1996; Hon. DLitt (St John's Univ., New York) 1986, (Glasgow) 1990, (Janus Pannonius Univ., Pécs) 1994; Kossuth Prize 1961, State Prize 1985, Konstantin Jireček Gold Medal, Suedosteuropa Gesellschaft 2005. *Publications:* (with György Ránki): Magyarország gyáripara 1900–1914 1955, Magyarország gyáripara a II. világháboru elött és a háboru idöszakában 1933–1944 1958, Magyarország a fasiszta Németország "életterében" 1960, Magyarország gazdasága az I. világháboru után 1919–1929 1966, Economic Development in East-Central Europe in the 19th and 20th Centuries 1974, Hungary—A Century of Economic Development, Underdevelopment and Economic Growth, The European Periphery and Industrialization 1780–1914 1982, The Hungarian Economy in the Twentieth Century 1985, The European Economy in the Nineteenth Century 1987; (as sole author): Ujjáépités és a nagytöke elleni harc Magyarországon 1945–1948 1962, Gazdaságpolitika az elsö ötéves terv meginditásakor 1948–1950 1964, Öt elöadás gazdaságról és oktatásról 1978, Napjaink a történelemben 1980, Válságos évtizedek 1982, Gazdasági utkeresés 1983, The Crisis Zone of Europe 1986, Szocializmus és reform 1986, The Hungarian Economic Reforms 1990, Central and Eastern Europe 1944–93 – Detour from the Periphery to the Periphery 1996, Decades of Crisis: Central and Eastern Europe Before World War II 1998, History Derailed: Central and Eastern Europe in the 'Long' 19th Century 2003, An Economic History of 20th Century Europe 2006, From the Soviet Bloc to the European Union: The Economic and Social Transformation of Central and Eastern Europe since 1973 2009, History in My Life – A Memoir in Three Eras 2009, Europe Since 1980 2010. *Leisure interests:* walking, swimming. *Address:* Department of History, UCLA, 6343 Bunche Hall, Box 951473, Los Angeles, CA 90095-1473, USA (office). *Telephone:* (310) 825-1178 (office). *Fax:* (310) 206-3556 (office); (310) 247-9844 (home). *E-mail:* iberend@history.ucla.edu (office). *Website:* www.history.ucla.edu/berend (office).

BERENDT, John, BA; American writer and journalist; b. (John Lawrence Berendt), 5 Dec. 1939, Syracuse, NY; s. of Ralph Berendt and Carol Berendt (née Deschere); ed Nottingham High School, Syracuse, NY and Harvard Univ.; Assoc. Ed. Esquire 1961–69, columnist 1982–94; Ed. New York magazine 1977–79; freelance writer 1979–; mem. PEN, The Century Asscn. *Publications include:* Midnight in the Garden of Good and Evil (Southern Book Award for Non-fiction) 1994, The City of Falling Angels 2005. *Address:* c/o Suzanne Gluck, William Morris Endeavor, 11 Madison Avenue, New York, NY 10010, USA (office). *Telephone:* (121) 586-5100 (office). *E-mail:* SGluck@WMEentertainment.com (office).

BÉRENGER, Paul Raymond, BA; Mauritian politician; b. 26 March 1945, Quatre Bornes; m. Arline Perrier 1971; one s. one d.; ed Collège du Saint Esprit, Univ. of Wales, UK, Univ. of Paris (Sorbonne), France; Co-Founder, Mouvement Militant Mauricien 1969, Gen. Sec. 1969–82, Leader 1983–2016; MP 1976–87, 1991–; Minister of Finance 1982–83, of Foreign Affairs 1991–93; Deputy Prime Minister and Minister of Foreign Affairs and Int. and Regional Co-operation 1995; Deputy Prime Minister and Minister of Finance Sept. 2000–03; Prime Minister, Minister of Defence and Home Affairs and of External Communications Sept. 2003–05; Special Adviser to the Prime Minister for Disarmament Affairs 1990; Gov. IMF, African Devt Bank/African Devt Fund. *Leisure interests:* reading, swimming. *Address:* 27 River Walk, Vacoas (home); Parliament House, Place D'Armes, Port Louis, Mauritius (office). *Telephone:* 201-1414 (office). *Fax:* 212-8364 (office). *E-mail:* pberenger@govmu.org (office); clerk@govmu.org (office). *Website:* www.govmu.org/English/Pages/default.aspx (office).

BERENGER, Tom; American actor; b. (Thomas Michael Moore), 31 May 1950, Chicago, Ill.; m. 1st Barbara Wilson 1976 (divorced 1984); m. 2nd Lisa Williams 1986 (divorced 1997); m. 3rd Patricia Alvaran 1998; one s. five d.; ed Univ. of Missouri; stage appearances in regional theatre and off-Broadway including The Rose Tattoo, Electra, A Streetcar Named Desire, End as a Man. *Films include:* Beyond the Door 1975, Sentinel, Looking for Mr Goodbar, In Praise of Older Women, Butch and Sundance: The Early Days, The Dogs of War, The Big Chill, Eddie and the Cruisers, Fear City, Firstborn, Rustler's Rhapsody, Platoon, Someone to Watch Over Me, Shoot to Kill, Betrayed, Last Rites, Major League, Love at Large, The Field, Shattered, Chasers, Sniper 1993, Sliver 1993, Major League 2 1994, Last of the Dogmen 1994, Gettysburg 1994, The Substitute 1996, An Occasional Hell 1996, The Gingerbread Man 1997, Takedown 2000, One Man's Hero (also producer) 1999, Diplomatic Siege 1999, A Murder of Crows 1999, The Hollywood Sign 2000, Fear of Flying 2000, Training Day 2001, Watchtower 2001, Eye See You 2001, D-Tox 2002, Sniper 2 2002, Sniper 3 2004, The Christmas Miracle of Jonathan Toomey 2007, Stiletto 2008, Charlie Valentine 2009, Breaking Point 2009, Silent Venom (video) 2009, Smokin' Aces 2: Assassins' Ball (video) 2010, Sinners & Saints 2010, Last Will 2010, Firedog 2010, Inception 2010, Faster 2010, War Flowers 2011, Last Will 2012, Quad 2013. *Television includes:* One Life to Live (series), Johnny We Hardly Knew Ye, Flesh and Blood, If Tomorrow Comes, Johnson County War 2002, Junction Boys 2002, Sniper 2 2002, Peacemakers 2003, Capital City 2004, The Detective 2005, Into the West (mini-series) 2005, Amy Coyne 2006, Nightmares and Dreamscapes: From the Stories of Stephen King (mini-series) 2006, October Road (series) 2006–07, Desperate Hours: An Amber Alert (film) 2008, XIII: The Series (series) 2011, Hatfields & McCoys (mini-series) (Emmy Award for Supporting Actor in a Miniseries or Movie 2012) 2012. *Address:* c/o ICM, 10250 Constellation Boulevard, Los Angeles, CA 90067, USA.

BERENGO GARDIN, Gianni; Italian photographer; b. 10 Oct. 1930, Santa Margherita Ligure; s. of Alberto Berengo Gardin and Carmen Maffei Berengo Gardin; m. Caterina Stiffoni 1957; one s. one d.; began working as photographer 1954; has lived and worked in Switzerland, Rome, Venice; living in Milan 1965–; photographs originally published by Il Mondo magazine, now published by major magazines in Italy and world-wide; photographs in perm. collections of Museum of Modern Art, New York, Bibliothèque Nationale Paris, Eastman House, Rochester, NY, Musée de l'Elysée, Lausanne, Museum of Aesthetic Art, Beijing, Maison Européene de la Photographie, Paris; Dr hc (Univ. of Milan); Mois de la Photo Brassaï Award, Paris 1990, Leica Oskar Barnack Award, Arles 1995, Oscar Goldoni Award 1998, Werner Biscof Award 2006, Award for Lifetime Achievement, Lucie Awards 2008, Leica Hall of Fame Award 2017. *Publications:* over 210 photographic books. *Leisure interests:* photography, farming, his little dog Nina. *Address:* Via S. Michele del Carso 21, 20144 Milan, Italy (home). *Telephone:* (02) 4692877. *Fax:* (02) 4692877.

BERESFORD, Bruce; Australian film and opera director; b. 16 Aug. 1940, Sydney, NSW; s. of Leslie Beresford and Lona Beresford; m. 1st Rhoisin Beresford 1965; two s. one d.; m. 2nd Virginia Duigan 1989; one d.; ed Univ. of Sydney; worked in advertising; worked for Australian Broadcasting Comm.; went to UK 1961; worked in odd jobs, including teaching; film ed. in Nigeria 1964–66; Sec. to British Film Inst.'s Production Bd 1966–71; has also directed several operas and theatre productions. *Play directed:* Moonlight and Magnolias by Ron Hutchinson (Melbourne Theatre Company) 2009. *Opera and theatre productions:* Girl of the Golden West (Spoletto Festival) 1986, Elektra (Richard Strauss) (State Opera of South Australia) 1991, Sweeney Todd (Sondheim) (Portland Opera) 1996, The Crucible (Robert Ward) (Washington Opera) 1998, Rigoletto (Los Angeles Opera) 2000, Cold Sassy Tree (Carlisle Floyd) (Houston Grand Opera) 2000, re-staged for San Diego Opera 2001, A Streetcar Named Desire (Opera Australia) 2007, Of Mice and Men (Carlisle Floyd) (Opera Australia) 2011, Die tote Stadt (Erich Wolfgang Korngold) (Opera Australia) 2012, Albert Herring (Griffith Conservatorium, Brisbane) 2016. *Films directed:* The Adventures of Barry Mackenzie 1972, Barry Mackenzie Holds His Own 1974, Side by Side 1975, Don's Party (Australian Film Inst. Award 1976) 1976, The Getting of Wisdom 1977, Money Movers 1979, Breaker Morant (Australian Film Inst. Award 1980) 1980, Puberty Blues 1981, The Club 1981, Tender Mercies 1983, King David 1984, Crimes of the Heart 1986, Fringe Dwellers 1986, Aria (segment) 1987, Her Alibi 1988, Driving Miss Daisy 1989 (Acad. Award Best Film 1990), Mr. Johnson 1990, Black Robe (Canadian Film Acad. Awards 1990) 1990, Rich in Love 1993, A Good Man in Africa 1993, Silent Fall 1994, The Last Dance 1995, Paradise Road 1996, Double Jeopardy 1998, Rigoletto (opera) 2000, Bride of the Wind 2001, Evelyn 2002, The Contract 2006, Mao's Last Dancer 2009, Peace, Love and Misunderstanding 2011, Mr Church 2015. *Television includes:* And Starring Pancho Villa as Himself 2003, Bonnie and Clyde (mini-series) 2013, Roots (episode 4) 2016. *Publications include:* Josh Hartnett Definitely Wants to Do This: True Stories from a Life in the Screen Trade 2007, There's a Fax from Bruce 2016. *Address:* c/o David Gersh (Los Angeles) (office); c/o Steve Kenis (London) (office); c/o Geoffrey Radford (Sydney) (office). *Telephone:* (310) 205-5812 (Los Angeles) (office); (20) 7434-9055 (London) (office); (2) 9699-9604 (Sydney) (office); (2) 9818-5742 (Sydney). *E-mail:* dgersh@gershla.com (office); sk@sknco.com (office); bruce@ozdrongo.com (office); awagency@iprimus.com.au (office). *Website:* bruceberesford.org (office).

BEREZOVSKY, Boris Vadimovich; Russian pianist; *Artistic Director, Festival Pianoscope;* b. 4 Jan. 1969, Moscow; three c.; ed Moscow Conservatoire; London début Wigmore Hall 1988; appeared with Soviet Festival Orchestra, London 1990; recitals in New York, Washington, London, Amsterdam, Salzburg, Moscow, Leningrad, Tokyo, Osaka, etc.; appearances with orchestras including Philharmonia, New York Philharmonic, Philadelphia Orchestra, NDR Hamburg and Danish Nat. Radio Symphony Orchestra; Artistic Dir Festival Pianoscope, Beauvais 2013–; winner, Prize of Hope competition, City of Ufa 1985, Gold Medal, Int. Tchaikovsky Piano Competition, Moscow 1990. *Recordings:* numerous recordings including Chopin Godowsky Etudes 2005, Saint-Saëns's Carnaval des Animaux (Choc de la Musique of the Year 2010) 2010. *Address:* Festival Pianoscope, Direction des Affaires Culturelles, Rue de Gesvres, 60000 Beauvais, France (office). *Website:* pianoscope.beauvais.fr (office).

BERG, Christian, DPhil; Danish mathematician and academic; *Professor Emeritus of Mathematics, University of Copenhagen;* b. 2 June 1944, Haarslev; m. Margrete Vergmann 1967; one s. one d.; ed Univ. of Copenhagen; Assoc. Prof., Univ. of Copenhagen 1972, apptd Prof. of Math. 1978, Chair. Math. Dept 1996–97, Dir Inst. for Math. Sciences 1997–2002, currently Prof. Emer.; Pres. Danish Mathematical Soc. 1994–98; mem. Danish Natural Sciences Research Council 1985–92, Royal Danish Acad. of Sciences and Letters 1982– (Vice-Pres. 1999–2005); Univ. of Copenhagen Gold Medal 1970. *Publications include:* research monographs: Potential Theory on Locally Compact Abelian Groups (with Forst) 1975, Harmonic Analysis on Semigroups (with Christensen and Ressel) 1984; more than 100 research papers on potential theory and mathematical analysis. *Telephone:* 35-32-07-77 (office). *Fax:* 35-32-95-55 (office). *E-mail:* berg@math.ku.dk (office). *Website:* www.math.ku.dk/~berg (office).

BERG, Jeffrey (Jeff) Spencer, MA; American arts management agent; b. 26 May 1947, Los Angeles, Calif.; m. Denise Lura 1981; ed Univ. of California, Berkeley, Univ. of Southern California; fmrly Head of Literature Div., Creative Management Assocs, fmrly Vice-Pres.; Vice-Pres. Motion Picture Dept, International Creative Man. (ICM) Inc. 1975–80, Pres. 1980–85, Chair. and CEO ICM Partners 1985–2012; Founder and Chair. Resolution (literary and talent agency), Century City, Los Angeles 2013–14; fmr Co-Chair. California's Council on Information Tech.; mem. Bd of Dirs, Oracle Corpn 1997–, Leapfrog Enterprises, Inc., Josephson International Inc., Marshall McLuhan Center of Global Communication; Pres. Letters and Science Exec. Bd, Univ. of California, Berkeley; Trustee, UCLA Anderson School of Man. *Address:* Resolution Talent and Literary Agency, 1801 Century Park East, 23rd Floor, Los Angeles, CA 90067, USA (office). *Telephone:* (424) 274-4200 (office). *Website:* www.resolution-ent.com (office).

BERG, Paul, PhD, FAAS; American biochemist and academic; *Professor Emeritus, Department of Biochemistry, Stanford University;* b. 30 June 1926, New York; s. of Harry Berg and Sarah Brodsky; m. Mildred Levy 1947; one s.; ed Pennsylvania State Univ., Case Western Reserve Univ.; Postdoctoral Fellow, Copenhagen Univ., Denmark 1952–53; Postdoctoral Fellow, Wash. Univ., St Louis, Mo. 1953–54, Scholar in Cancer Research 1954–57, Asst to Assoc. Prof. of Microbiology 1955–59; Prof. of Biochemistry, Stanford Univ. School of Medicine 1959, Willson Prof. of Biochemistry 1970–94, Chair. of Dept 1969–74, Dir Beckman Center for Molecular and Genetic Medicine 1985–2001, Robert W.and Vivian K. Cahill Prof. of Cancer Research 1994–2000, Prof. Emer., Dept of Biochemistry 2000–; Dir Nat. Biomedical Research Foundation 1994–; Pres. American Soc. of Biological Chemists 1974–75; Chair. Nat. Advisory Cttee Human Genome Project 1990–92; Chair. Scientific Advisory Bd Beckman Foundation; currently Chair. Bd of Advisory Scientists, Whitehead Inst., MIT; Sr Post-Doctoral Fellow, NSF 1961–68; Non-resident Fellow, Salk Inst. 1973–83; Foreign mem. Académie des Sciences, France 1981, Royal Soc., London 1992; mem. Inst. of Medicine, NAS; Hon. mem. Alpha Omega Alpha Honor Medical Soc. 1992; Dr hc (Washington Univ.) 1986, (Pennsylvania State Univ.) 1995; Eli Lilly Prize in Biochemistry 1959, Calif. Scientist of the Year 1963, V. D. Mattia Award 1972, Nobel Prize for Chem. (jtly) 1980, Nat. Medal of Science 1983 and other awards and prizes. *Publications:* Genes and Genomes 1991, Dealing with Genes. The Language of Heredity 1992, Exploring Genetic Mechanisms 1997. *Leisure interests:* travel, art and sports. *Address:* c/o Stanford University School of Medicine, Department of Biochemistry, MC: 5307, Beckman Center, B400, 279 West Campus Drive, Stanford, CA 94305, USA (office). *Website:* berg-emeritusprofessor.stanford.edu (office).

BERGANT, Boris; Slovenian journalist and broadcasting executive; *Senior Consultant, European Broadcasting Union;* b. 19 April 1948, Maribor; s. of Evgen Bergant and Marija Bergant; m. Verena Bergant 1969; one s.; ed Univ. of Ljubljana, Kenyon Coll., USA; Co-founder of broadcasting project, Alpe Adria 1983; est. first pan-European TV co-production, Minorities – The Wealth of Europe 1983–86 (14 participating countries); est. regional centre for professional assistance and humanitarian help in Ljubljana 1991–95; fmrly Ed. Foreign Affairs, Ed.-in-Chief of News TV Slovenia; fmr radio journalist; fmr Deputy Dir-Gen., Int. Relations and Programme Co-operation, RTV Slovenija, Deputy Dir-Gen. RTV Slovenija 1992–2006, Adviser to Dir-Gen. for Int. Relations and Projects 2006; mem. Asscn of Journalists of Slovenia (Pres. 1987–91), CIRCOM Regional (Pres. 1990–92, Sec.-Gen. 1993–); mem. Admin. Council, European Broadcasting Union (EBU) 1990–92, 1996–, Vice-Chair. TV Programme Cttee 1993–98, mem. Radio Cttee 1993, Vice-Pres. EBU 1999–2009, Sr Consultant 2012–; Pres. South East Europe Media Org. (SEEMO), Vienna 2009–12; mem. European Inst. for the Media; Tomšičeva Nagrada Prize for Best Journalistic Achievement in Slovenia, Awards at Monte Carlo, New York and Leipzig TV festivals, Dr Erhard Busek SEEMO Award for Better Understanding 2009. *Leisure interests:* tennis. *Address:* BorBER Media Activities, Abramova ulica 8, 1000 Ljubljana (office); Abramova Ulica 8, 1000 Ljubljana, Slovenia (home). *Telephone:* 41-641877 (mobile) (office); (1) 256-15-58 (home). *Fax:* (1) 256-15-59 (home). *E-mail:* boris.bergant@borber.si (office); bergantb@siol.net (home).

BERGANZA, Teresa; Spanish singer (mezzo-soprano); b. 16 March 1933, Madrid; d. of Guillermo Berganza and Ascensión Berganza; m. 1st Felix Lavilla 1957; one s. two d.; m. 2nd José Rifa 1986; debut in Aix-en-Provence 1957, in UK at Glyndebourne 1958; has sung at La Scala, Milan, Opera Rome, Metropolitan, New York, Chicago Opera House, San Francisco Opera, Covent Garden, etc.; has appeared at festivals in Edinburgh, the Netherlands, Glyndebourne; concerts in France, Belgium, the Netherlands, Italy, Germany, Spain, Austria, Portugal, Scandinavia, Israel, Mexico, Buenos Aires, USA, Canada; sung Carmen, at opening ceremony of Expo 92, Seville, also at opening ceremonies of Barcelona Olympics 1992; mem. Real Academia de Bellas Artes de San Fernando, Spanish Royal Acad. of Arts 1994; Grande Cruz, Isabel la Católica, Commdr, Ordre des Arts et des Lettres; Premio Lucrezia Arana, Premio Extraordinario del Conservatorio de Madrid, Harriet Cohen Award, Int. Critic Award 1988, Grand Prix du Disque (six times), Grand Prix Rossini, Lifetime Achievement Award, Int. Opera Awards 2018. *Films include:* The Barber of Seville 1972, Don Giovanni 1979, Werther 1980, Carmen 1980. *Publication:* Flor de Soledad y Silencio 1984. *Leisure interests:* art, music, reading. *Address:* c/o Javier Lavilla, Avenida Juan de Borbón y Battenberg, 16, 28200 San Lorenzo del Escorial, Madrid, Spain (office). *Telephone:* (67) 0237485 (office). *E-mail:* info@teresaberganza.com (office). *Website:* www.teresaberganza.com.

BERGARA DUQUE, Mario Esteban, MEconSc, PhD; Uruguayan economist, accountant and central banker; *President, Banco Central del Uruguay;* b. 4 May 1965, Montevideo; ed Univ. de la República Oriental del Uruguay, Univ. of California, Berkeley, USA; began career with Banco de la República Oriental del Uruguay; Head, Dept of Econ. Studies, Banco Central del Uruguay 1998–2001, Pres. 2008–13, 2015–18; Vice-Minister of Economy and Finance 2005–08, Minister of Economy and Finance 2013–15; mem. Bd Communication Services Regulatory Agency 2001–05; fmr Prof., Univ. of the Repub. and Univ. ORT Uruguay; fmr mem. Partido Comunista de Uruguay.

BERGARECHE BUSQUET, Santiago, LicenDer; Spanish business executive; *Chairman, Vocento;* ed Univ. of Deusto, Bilbao; held several man. positions until becoming Gen. Man. and mem. Exec. Man. Cttee BBVA, apptd Chair. Metrovacesa; Chair. Agromán (following acquisition by Ferrovial Group), later Chair. Ferrovial, subsequently CEO, currently Ind. Vice-Chair. Ferrovial Group, Chair. (non-exec.) Dinamia Ferrovial Group; Chair. (non-exec.) Compañía Española de Petróleos SA (CEPSA) 2008–11, Dir 2008–14; Dir, Uralita SA 1994–, Gamesa Corporación Tecnológica SA 2007–11, Vocento 2013– (currently Chair.), Maxam Corp. Holding, SL, Deusto Business School; mem. Advisory Bd, Willis Iberia. *Address:* Vocento, Pintor Losada 7, 48004 Bilbao, Bizkaia, Spain (office). *Telephone:* (902) 090155 (office). *E-mail:* prensa@vocento.com (office). *Website:* www.vocento.com (office).

BERGEN, André, MEconSc; Belgian banking executive; *Chairman, Confinimmo NV;* b. 1950, Sint-Truiden; ed Univ. of Louvain; joined Econs Research Dept, Kredietbank NV 1977, Foreign Exchange and Treasury Dept, Kredietbank, NY 1979; with Foreign Exchange Advisory Service, Chemical Bank, NY 1980–82; joined Generale Bank, Belgium 1982, mem. Exec. Cttee, Generale (Fortis) Bank 1993–2000; Vice-Pres., Chief Financial and Admin. Officer, Agfa-Gevaert NV, Belgium 2000–01, Deputy Chair. Man. Bd 2001–03; CEO KBC Bank 2003–09, Deputy CEO KBC Group 2003–05, Man. Dir and Deputy CEO 2005–06, Pres. Exec. Cttee, Exec. Dir and Group CEO KBC Group 2006–09, mem. Agenda Cttee, Nomination Cttee, mem. Bd Dirs, KBC Bank, KBC Insurance; Chair. Cofinimmo NV; mem. Supervisory Bd, NYSE Euronext NV, NIBC, Sapient Investment Management, Delta Lloyd NV 2014–; mem. Bd of Dirs, Recticel NV; Adviser, Verstraete NV; International NV, UFG-LFP; mem. Flemish Architecture Inst. *Address:* Cofinimmo SA/NV, Boulevard de la Woluwe 58 Woluwedal, 1200

Brussels, Belgium (office); NYSE Euronext NV, Beursplein 5, 1000 GD, Amsterdam, The Netherlands. *Telephone:* (2) 373-00-00 (Brussels) (office); (20) 550-4444 (Amsterdam). *Fax:* (2) 373-00-10 (Brussels) (office); (20) 550-4900 (Amsterdam). *E-mail:* info@cofinimmo.be (office). *Website:* www.cofinimmo.com (office); www.nyse.com.

BERGEN, Candice Patricia; American actress and photojournalist; b. 9 May 1946, Beverly Hills; d. of Edgar Bergen and Frances Bergen (née Westerman); m. 1st Louis Malle 1980 (died 1995); one d.; m. 2nd Marshall Rose 2000; ed Westlake School for Girls, Univ. of Pennsylvania; photo-journalist work has appeared in Vogue, Cosmopolitan, Life and Esquire. *Films include:* The Group 1966, The Sand Pebbles 1966, The Day the Fish Came Out 1967, Vivre Pour Vivre 1967, The Magus 1968, Getting Straight 1970, Soldier Blue 1970, The Adventurers 1970, Carnal Knowledge 1971, The Hunting Party 1971, T. R. Baskin 1972, 11 Harrowhouse 1974, Bite the Bullet 1975, The Wind and the Lion 1976, The Domino Principle 1977, A Night Full of Rain 1977, Oliver's Story, 1978, Starting Over 1979, Rich and Famous 1981, Gandhi 1982, Stick 1985, Au Revoir les Enfants (Co-Dir) 1987, Miss Congeniality 2000, Sweet Home Alabama 2002, View from the Top 2003, The In-Laws 2003, Sex and the City 2008, The Women 2008, Bride Wars 2009, The Romantics 2010. *Television appearances include:* Murphy Brown (series) (Emmy Award 1989, 1990) 1988–98, Mary and Tim 1996, Footsteps 2003, Boston Legal (series) 2005–08, House (series) 2011, Beautiful and Twisted (film) 2015. *Publications:* The Freezer (in Best Short Plays of 1968), Knock Wood (autobiog.) 1984, A Fine Romance 2015. *Address:* c/o WME, 9601 Wilshire Blvd, Beverly Hills, CA 90210, USA.

BERGER, Albert, LLB; German lawyer and university administrator; *Chancellor, Technische Universität München (TUM);* b. 1962, Munich; ed Ludwig-Maximilians-Universität, Munich; civil servant, Legal Div., Munich Regional High Court 1989–92; Lecturer, Deutsche Privat Finanzakademie AG 1991–92; Prof. of Public Law, Inst. of Law, Armed Forces Univ., Munich 1992–93; lawyer in Personnel and Org. Div., Technische Universität München (TUM) 1994–95, Head of Personnel Div. 1995–98, Admin Dir Weihenstephan Life and Food Sciences Centre 1998–2003, Chancellor TUM 2006–; Chancellor Rosenheim Univ. of Applied Science 2003–06; Deputy Nat. Spokesman, Kanzlerinnen und Kanzler der Universitäten Deutschlands 2009–12, Nat. Spokesman 2012–. *Address:* Office of the Chancellor, Technische Universität München, Arcisstrasse 21, 80333 Munich, Germany (office). *Telephone:* (89) 289-01 (office). *Fax:* (89) 289-22000 (office). *E-mail:* eckenweber@zv.tum.de (office). *Website:* portal.mytum.de (office).

BERGER, Geneviève, PhD, MD; French physician, medical researcher and academic; *Chief Research and Development Officer, Unilever PLC;* b. 1955, Moselle; ed Ecole Normale Supérieure, Cachan, Univ. of Paris VI-Pierre et Marie Curie, Univ. of Paris V-René Descartes; mem. Scientific Bd Dept of Eng, CNRS 1991–98, Scientific Sec., Treatment and Drugs, Design and Resources Section, CNRS Nat. Cttee Scientific Research 1991–95, Chair. 1995–98, Founder and Researcher Parametric Imaging Lab. 1991–, Dir 1991–2000; Dir-Gen. CNRS 2000–03; Prof. and Hosp. MD, Univ. of Paris VI-Pierre et Marie Curie 1996–2008; Head, Dept Biophysics and Nuclear Medicine, Hôtel-Dieu Hosp. 1997–2000; Dir Dept of Bio-Eng, Drugs and Agri-Food, Ministry of Educ., Research and Tech. 1998–2000; Pres. Consultative Cttee Tech. Devt 1999–2000; Pres. Bd of Dirs CNRS Diffusion Soc. 2000–03, INIST-Diffusion Soc. 2000–03, FIST Soc. 2000–03; Prof. and Hosp. Practitioner, La Pitié-Salpétrière Teaching Hosp. 2003–08; Chair. Health Advisory Group, EC 2006–08; Non-exec. mem. Bd of Dirs Unilever PLC 2007–08, Chief Research and Devt Officer 2008–; Dir (non-exec.) Smith & Nephew 2010–12, AstraZeneca 2012– (mem. Science Cttee); mem. Tech. Programme Cttee IEEE 1990–2008, Conseil de l'ordre des Palmes académiques 2000, French Research Inst. for Sea Expolitation 2000; Govt Commr Office of Geological and Mining Research 2000; Chair. Health Advisory Bd for Commr of Research, EU 2006–08; mem. Bd of Dirs Commissariat à l'Energie Atomique 2000, French Research Inst. for Sea Exploitation 2000, Ecole Normale Supérieure, Cachan 2000–03; Hon. Fellow, American Inst. of Ultrasound in Medicine 2006; Chevalier, Légion d'honneur 1988, Commdr des Palmes académiques 2000; Gold Medal, Univ. of Paris V-René Descartes 1985, CNRS Silver Medal 1994, Yves Rocard Prize, French Physics Soc. 1997, Pan-European Grand Prix for Innovation Award 2001. *Address:* Unilever PLC, Unilever House, 100 Victoria Embankment, London, EC4Y 0DY, England (office). *Telephone:* (20) 7822-5252 (office). *Fax:* (20) 7822-5951 (office). *Website:* www.unilever.com (office).

BERGER, Helmut; Austrian actor; b. 29 May 1944, Bad Ischl; pnr Luchino Visconti 1964–76; m. Francesca Guidato 1994; ed Feldkirk Coll., Univ. of Perugia, Italy; first film role in Luchino Visconti's Le Streghe 1966; Berlin Int. Film Festival Teddy Award 2007, Prix Lumière 2010, Kristián Award 2011. *Films include:* The Young Tigers 1968, The Damned 1069, Do You Know What Stalin Did To Women?, The Garden of the Finzi-Continis 1970, The Picture of Dorian Gray, A Butterfly with Bloody Wings 1971, The Greedy Ones, The Strange Love Affair, Ludwig (David di Donatello for Best Actor 1973) 1972, Ash Wednesday 1973, Conversation Piece 1974, The Romantic Englishwoman 1975, Orders to Kill 1975, Madame Kitty 1976, Merry-Go-Round, Code Name: Emerald 1985, The Glass Heaven, Faceless 1988, The Betrothed, The Godfather Part III 1990, Once Arizona, Still Waters, Unter den Palmen 1999, Die Haupter Meiner, Honey Baby 2004, Damals warst du still 2005, Blutsfreundschaft 2008, Iron Cross 2010, Mörderschwestern 2011, The Devil's Violinist 2013, Saint Laurent 2014, Timeless 2016. *Publication:* Ich (autobiog.) 1998. *Address:* c/o e-Talenta, Passauerstr. 35, 81369 Munich, Germany (office). *Telephone:* (89) 235193970 (office). *E-mail:* info@e-talenta.eu (office). *Website:* www.e-talenta.eu (office).

BERGER PERDOMO, Oscar José Rafael, LLD; Guatemalan business executive, lawyer, politician and fmr head of state; b. 11 Aug. 1946, Guatemala City; m. Wendy Widmann 1967; three s. two d.; ed Liceo Javier, Univ. Rafael Landívar; Founder-mem. Partido de Avanzada Nacional (PAN) 1984; Councillor, Guatemala City 1984–89, Mayor 1990–99; fmr Pres. Federación de Municipios de Centroamérica y Panamá, Pres. Asociación Nacional de Municipalidades 1991–93, Pres. Federación de Municipios del Istmo Centroamericano 1996–97; defeated in presidential elections 1999; left PAN 1999, rejoined 2002, selected as PAN presidential cand. Nov. 2002, won primary elections at head of Gran Alianza Nacional (Gana) Nov. 2003, President 2003–08; Order of Leopold II (Belgium) 1992, Légion d'honneur 2000.

BERGGREN, Bo Erik Gunnar; Swedish business executive; b. 11 Aug. 1936, Falun; s. of Tage Berggren and Elsa Höglund; m. Gunbritt Haglund 1962; two s. two d.; ed Royal Inst. of Tech.; metallurgical research and Devt, STORA Kopparbergs Bergslags AB (now STORA), Domnarvet 1962–68, Mill Man., Söderfors 1968–74, Exec. Vice-Pres., Falun 1975–78, Pres. 1984–92, CEO 1984–94, apptd Chair. Bd 1992, Chair. Bd STORA Stockholm 1995–98; Pres. Incentive AB, Stockholm 1978–84; mem. Prime Minister's Special Industry Advisory Cttee 1994–; Chair. Astra; fmr Chair. SAS (Sweden), SAS (Sverige) AB; Vice-Chair. Investor, Fed. of Swedish Industries, Skandinaviska Enskilda Banken; mem. Bd Telefonaktiebolaget L. M. Ericsson, Danisco A/S, Royal Inst. of Tech.; fmr mem. Bd of Dirs Marcus Wallenberg Prize; mem. Int. Council J. P. Morgan & Co. Inc., Robert Bosch Internationale Beteiligungen Advisory Cttee, Royal Swedish Acad. of Eng Sciences, of Forestry and Agric.; Dr hc (Royal Inst. of Tech., Stockholm) (Dalhousie Univ.) 1996; King's Medal 12th Dimension with Ribbon of Order of the Seraphim 1987. *Leisure interests:* the arts, family, music. *Address:* Granvägen 14, 791 37, Falun, Sweden.

BERGGREN, Thommy; Swedish actor; b. 12 Aug. 1937, Mölndal; ed The Pickwick Club (pvt. dramatic school), Atelierteatern, Stockholm and Gothenburg Theatre; with Gothenburg Theatre 1959–63, Royal Dramatic Theatre, Stockholm 1963. *Plays include:* Gengangaren (Ibsen) 1962, Romeo and Juliet 1962, Chembalo 1962, Who's Afraid of Virginia Woolf? 1964. *Films include:* Pärlemor 1961, Barnvagnen (The Pram) 1962, Kvarteret Korpen (Ravens End) 1963, En söndag i september (A Sunday in September) 1963, Karlek 65 (Love 65) 1965, Elvira Madigan 1967, The Black Palm Trees 1969, The Ballad of Joe Hill 1971, Kristoffers hus 1979, Brusten himmel 1982, Berget på månens baksida (A Hill on the Dark Side of the Moon) 1983, La Sposa americana (The American Bride) 1986, Söndagsbarn 1992, Stora och små män 1995, Glasblåsarns barn 1998, Kontorstid 2003, Godheten 2013. *Publication:* Tommy (memoir) 2017.

BERGKAMP, Dennis Nicolaas Maria; Dutch football manager and coach and fmr professional footballer; b. 10 May 1969, Amsterdam; m. Henrita Ruizendaal; one s. one d.; second striker; played for Ajax Amsterdam youth team 1981–86, sr team 1986–93, Inter Milan 1993–95, Arsenal, London, UK 1995–2006, Premiership winner 1998, 2002, 2004, Football Asscn (FA) Cup winner 1998, 2002, 2003, 2005, Community Shield winner 1998, 1999, 2002, 2004; player for Holland 1990–2000, made 79 appearances and scored 37 goals, fmr all-time leading scorer; fourth place, FIFA World Cup 1998; undertook trainee role at Ajax, Asst Coach 2008–; signed contract with Koninklijke Nederlandse Voetbal Bond as Team Man. for newly formed Netherlands B team 2008; Dutch Talent of the Year 1990, Eredivisie Top Scorer 1991, 1992, 1993, UEFA Euro 1992 Team of the Tournament, UEFA Euro 1992 Top Scorer, Dutch Player of the Year 1992, 1993, UEFA Cup Top Scorer 1994, European Footballer of the Year: third place 1992, second place 1993, English PFA Players' Player of the Year 1998, English Football Writers' Player of the Year 1998, English PFA Team of the Year 1998, FIFA World Cup All-Star Team 1998, English Goal of the Season 1997–98, 2001–02, Arsenal FC Player of the Year 1998, FIFA Player of the Year: third place 1993, 1997, FA Premier League Player of the Month Aug. 1997, Sept. 1997, March 2002, Feb. 2004, inducted into English Football Hall of Fame (first and currently only Dutch player to receive this honour) 2007, FIFA 100, Unitar Dean's List Award 2008–09, selected by Pelé as one of the FIFA 125 greatest living players. *Leisure interests:* snooker, golf, reading, films, basketball. *Address:* AFC Ajax, Arena Boulevard 29, 1101 AX Amsterdam Zuidoost, The Netherlands. *Telephone:* (548) 377666. *E-mail:* ajax@oad.nl. *Website:* www.ajax.nl.

BERGKAMP, Ger, MA, PhD; Dutch environmental scientist, hydrologist and international organization official; *President and CEO, ARCOWA;* ed Univ. of Amsterdam; has worked in environmental sciences, hydrology, irrigation and drainage, and soil and water conservation throughout Latin America, the Mediterranean, Africa and S and SE Asia and at int. level since late 1980s; Freshwater Man. Adviser, Wetlands and Water Resources Programme, Int. Union for Conservation of Nature (IUCN—The World Conservation Union) 1997–2008; Gen. Dir World Water Council 2008–13; Exec. Dir International Water Asscn 2012–17; Pres. and CEO ARCOWA 2017–. *Address:* ARCOWA, Rue de College 18, 1260 Nyon, Switzerland (office). *E-mail:* admin@arcowa.com (office). *Website:* arcowa.com (office).

BERGMAN, Robert George, BS, PhD; American chemist and academic; *Gerald E. K. Branch Distinguished Professor, University of California, Berkeley;* b. 23 May 1942, Chicago, Ill.; ed Carleton Coll., Univ. of Wisconsin; NATO Fellow, Columbia Univ. 1966–67; Noyes Research Instructor, California Inst. of Tech. 1967–69, Asst Prof. 1969–71, Assoc. Prof. 1971–73, Prof. 1973–77; Prof. of Chem., Univ. of California, Berkeley 1977–, Gerald E. K. Branch Distinguished Prof. 2002–, Vice-Chair. Dept of Chem. 1985–87, Asst Dean, Coll. of Chem. 1987–91, 1996, 2004–06; mem. Chemical Sciences Div., Lawrence Berkeley Nat. Lab.; mem. Editorial Bd Journal of Organic Chemistry 1980–83, 1996–98, Organometallics 1981–84, 1992–95, Chemical Reviews 1981–84, International Journal of Chemical Kinetics 1986–89, Journal of the American Chemical Society 1990–95, Organic Letters 1999–; mem. NAS 1984, American Acad. of Arts and Sciences 1984; NIH Predoctoral Fellowship, Alfred P. Sloan Fellowship 1969, Camille and Henry Dreyfus Foundation Teacher-Scholar Award 1970, California Inst. of Tech. Student Government Award for Excellence in Teaching 1978, ACS Award in Organometallic Chem. 1986, ACS Arthur C. Cope Scholar Award 1987, E.O. Lawrence Award in Chem., US Dept of Energy 1994, ACS Arthur C. Cope Award 1996, Edward Leete Award for Teaching and Research in Organic Chem. 2001, Dept of Chem. Teaching Award, Univ. of California, Berkeley 2002, ACS James Flack Norris Award in Physical Organic Chem. 2003, Award for Excellence in Tech. Transfer, Lawrence Berkeley Nat. Lab. 2005, NAS Award in Chemical Sciences 2007, T.W. Richards Medal, Northeastern Section of ACS 2008, RSC Sir Edward Frankland Prize Lectureship 2008, Chancellor's Award for Public Service, Univ. of California, Berkeley 2008–09, 2011–12, Willard Gibbs Award, ACS Chicago Section 2011, Welch Award in Chem. 2014. *Publications:* numerous research papers in professional journals. *Address:* Department of Chemistry, University of California, Berkeley, 419 Latimer Hall, Berkeley, CA 94720-1460, USA (office). *Telephone:* (510) 642-2156 (office). *Fax:* (510) 642-7714 (office). *E-mail:* rbergman@berkeley.edu (office). *Website:* www.cchem.berkeley.edu/rgbgrp (office).

BERGMANIS, Raimonds; Latvian politician and fmr weightlifter; b. 25 July 1966, Pļaviņas; ed Latvian Acad. of Sports Educ., Rīga Tech. Univ.; mem. Latvian Olympic Weightlifting team 1992 (carried Latvian flag at Opening Ceremony), 1996, 2000, set 21 Latvian records; Sports Dept Instructor, Ministry of Educ. 1992–94; Instructor, Latvian Sports Admin 1995–99; Trainer, Latvian Nat. Sports School 1999–2001; worked in Latvian TV and presented several programmes, including Happy Family and The Royal Jokes Tournament, commentator for Latvian Strongman Championships; Training Instructor, Nat. Armed Forces, Security Service for Saeima (Parl.) and State Pres. 2001–04, Sr Training Instructor 2004–08; Adviser to State Sec., Ministry of Defence March–Dec. 2008, Sr Desk Officer, Mil. Educ. Div., Ministry of Defence 2008–09; Recruitment Div. Specialist, Recruitment and Youth Guard Centre 2010–14; mem. Security and Defence Comm., NATO Parl. Ass. 2014–15; Head, Latvian Del. to Baltic Ass. 2014–15; mem. Saeima 2014–15; Minister of Defence 2014–19; mem. Zaļo un Zemnieku Savienība (Greens' and Farmers' Union); fmr Pres. Latvian Olympic Club; Vice-Pres. Latvian Olympic Cttee 2013–. *Achievements:* won World Muscle Power Championships 1997, also competed in Arnold's Strongest Man Contest, finishing third in 2003, reached finals of World's Strongest Man competition several times, finishing 3rd in 2002 and 4th in 2003 and 2004. *Address:* c/o Ministry of Defence, K. Valdemāra iela 10–12, Rīga 1473, Latvia (office).

BERGMANN, Thaisa Storchi, PhD; Brazilian astrophysicist and academic; *Professor of Physics and Astronomy, Federal University of Rio Grande do Sul;* b. 19 Dec. 1955; ed Fed. Univ. of Rio Grande do Sul, Porto Alegre; Postdoctoral Researcher, Space Telescope Science Inst., Fed. Univ. of Rio Grande do Sul, currently Prof. of Physics and Astronomy and Head of Astrophysics Research Group; Pres. Nat. Time Allocation Cttee, Brazilian Rep. on Int. Time Allocation Cttee; mem. Working Group on Gemini Wide Field Multi-Object Spectrograph (GWFMOS); mem. Brazilian Acad. of Sciences 2009; Laureate, L'Oréal-UNESCO Awards for Women in Science (Latin America) 2015. *Publications include:* A Spectral Atlas of 99 Nearby Quiescent, Starburst and Active Galaxies (co-author), The Interplay Among Black Holes, Stars and ISM in Galactic Nuclei (Proceedings of part of 226th Symposium of the Int. Astronomical Union) (ed.) 2005; more than 100 papers in professional journals. *Address:* Room 102, Building 43173 (N), Departamento de Astronomia, Instituto de Física, Universidade Federal do Rio Grande do Sul, Campus do Vale, Avenida Bento Goncalves 9500, Caixa Postal 15051, CEP 91501-970, Porto Alegre, RS, Brazil (office). *Telephone:* (51) 3308-6443 (office). *Fax:* (51) 3308-7286 (office). *E-mail:* thaisa@ufrgs.br (office). *Website:* www.if.ufrgs.br/~thaisa (office).

BERGNER, Christoph, DrAgrar; German politician; b. 24 Nov. 1948, Zwickau; m.; three c.; ed Univs of Jena and Halle; mem. CDU without office in fmr GDR 1971; Research Asst Inst. of Biochemistry of Plants, Univ. of Halle 1974–90; mem. Landtag (State Parl.) of Saxony-Anhalt 1990–2002; Vice-Chair. Saxony-Anhalt CDU Asscn 1991–94; Chair. CDU Parl. Party in Landtag 1991–93, 1994–2001; Minister-Pres. of Saxony-Anhalt 1993–94; mem. Bundestag (Fed. Ass.) 2002–17, fmr mem. Foreign Affairs Cttee, Cttee on European Union Affairs; Parl. Under-Sec. of State, Fed. Ministry of the Interior 2005–13; Fed. Commr for Matters Related to Repatriates and Nat. Minorities 2006–13; Pres. Sports Association Hall; mem. Inst. for Economic Research; Officer, Nat. Order Star of Romania 2013, Central Cross of the Hungarian Order of Merit 2013; Medal Cordi Poloniae, Konvents der Polnischen Organisationen in Deutschland 2011, Kazakh Jubilee Medal 2012. *Address:* c/o Deutscher Bundestag, Platz der Republik, 11011 Berlin, Germany (office). *Telephone:* (30) 22773775 (office). *E-mail:* christoph.bergner@bundestag.de (office). *Website:* www.bergner.de.

BERGSTEN, C. Fred, MA, PhD; American economist and research institute director; *Senior Fellow and Director Emeritus, Peterson Institute for International Economics;* b. 23 April 1941, New York, NY; s. of Dr Carl Bergsten and Halkaline Bergsten; m. Virginia W. Bergsten; one s.; ed Cen. Methodist Univ., Fletcher School of Law and Diplomacy, Tufts Univ.; Asst for Int. Econ. Affairs, US Nat. Security Council 1969–71; Asst Sec. for Int. Affairs, US Treasury, Washington, DC 1977–81; Dir Inst. for Int. Econs (now Peterson Inst. for Int. Econs) 1981–2012, Sr Fellow and Dir Emer. 2012–; Chair. Competitiveness Policy Council 1991–95, Asia-Pacific Econ. Co-operation Eminent Persons Group 1993–95; mem. President's Advisory Cttee on Trade Policy and Negotiations; Global Advisor to Pres. of Repub. of Korea 2009; Co-Chair. Private Sector Advisory Group to United States–India Trade Policy Forum; Sr Fellow, Council on Foreign Relations 1967–68, Brookings Inst. 1972–76, Carnegie Endowment for Int. Peace 1981; Hon. Fellow, Chinese Acad. of Social Sciences 1997; Chevalier Légion d'honneur 1985, Order of the Polar Star (Sweden) 2013, Nat. Foreign Trade Council World Trade Award 2013, Order of Merit (Germany) 2014, Gwanghwa Medal (1st class) (Korea) 2017; Dept of State Meritorious Honor Award 1965, Dept of Treasury Exceptional Service Award 1981, Distinguished Alumnus Award, Fletcher School of Law and Diplomacy, Tufts Univ. 2010, Swedish American of the Year 2014. *Publications include:* America in the World Economy: A Strategy for the 1990s 1988, Pacific Dynamism and the International Economic System (with M. Noland) 1993, Reconcilable Differences? United States-Japan Economic Conflict (with M. Noland) 1993, The Dilemmas of the Dollar (second edn) 1996, Global Economic Leadership and the Group of Seven 1996, Whither APEC? The Progress to Date and Agenda for the Future 1997, No More Bashing: Building a New Japan-United States Economic Relationship 2001, The Korean Diaspora in the World Economy 2003, Dollar Overvaluation and the World Economy 2003, Dollar Adjustment: How Far? Against What? 2004, The United States and the World Economy (ed.) 2005, China: The Balance Sheet 2006, The Long-Term International Economic Position of the United States 2009, Bridging the Pacific: Toward Free Trade and Investment between China and the United States 2014, International Monetary Cooperation: Lessons from the Plaza Accord After Thirty Years 2016, Currency Conflict and Trade Policy: A New Strategy for the United States 2017, A Path Forward for NAFTA 2017; numerous other books and journal articles. *Leisure interests:* photography, basketball, snorkelling. *Address:* Peterson Institute for International Economics, 1750 Massachusetts Avenue NW, Washington, DC 20036-1903 (office); 4106 Sleepy Hollow Road, Annandale, VA 22003, USA (home). *Telephone:* (202) 328-9000 (office); (703) 256-3802 (home). *Fax:* (202) 659-3225 (office). *E-mail:* fbergsten@piie.com (office). *Website:* www.piie.com (office).

BERGSTRÖM, Lars, PhD; Swedish academic; *Professor Emeritus of Practical Philosophy, Stockholm University;* b. 17 July 1935, Stockholm; m. Ulla von Heland 1960; one s.; ed Stockholm Univ.; Assoc. Prof., Lecturer in Philosophy, Stockholm Univ. 1967–74; Prof. of Practical Philosophy, Uppsala Univ. 1974–87; Prof. of Practical Philosophy, Stockholm Univ. 1987–2001, Prof. Emer. 2001–; mem. Royal Swedish Acad. of Sciences 1998–. *Publications include:* Imperatives and Ethics 1962, The Alternatives and Consequences of Actions 1966, Objektivitet 1972, Frågor om livets mening (Questions about the Meaning of Life) 1979, Grundbok i Värdeteori (Foundations of Value Theory) 1990, Ubåtsfrågan: en kritisk granskning av den svenska nutidshistoriens viktigaste säkerhetspolitisk dilemma (The Question of Submarines: A Critical Investigation of the Main Foreign Policy Dilemma in Contemporary Sweden) (co-ed.) 1999, Filosofin genom tiderna: Efter 1950, 2:a upplagan (Edition of Philosophical Texts After 1950) 2000, Döden, Livet och Verkligheten 2004, Tankegångar. Sexton kapitel om kunskap, moral och metafysik. (Reasonings. Sixteen Chapters on Knowledge, Morals, and Metaphysics) 2011. *Leisure interests:* music, tennis. *Address:* Department of Philosophy, Stockholm University, 106 91 Stockholm (office); Telegrafgränd 1B, 111 30 Stockholm, Sweden (home). *Telephone:* (8) 6698899 (home). *E-mail:* lars.bergstrom@philosophy.su.se (office). *Website:* www.philosophy.su.se/english/research/our-researchers/emeriti/lars-bergström-1.232033 (office).

BERISHA, Kolë; Kosovo politician; b. 26 Oct. 1947, Dobërdol; m.; two c.; ed Univ. of Priština; fmr high school teacher in Klina; fmrly Sec., Democratic League of Kosovo (LDK), Vice-Pres. 1998–; Pres., Ass. of Kosovo 2006–07; mem. Parl. Group of LDK, Cttee for Rules of Procedure of Ass.

BERISHA, Rrustem; Kosovo politician and former army officer; *Minister of the Kosovo Security Force;* b. 2 March 1965, Dobërdol, Pejë/Peć, Socialist Autonomous Province of Kosovo, Socialist Repub. of Serbia, Socialist Fed. Repub. of Yugoslavia; m.; four c.; ed Kosovo Security Forces Mil. Acad.; began army career as non-commissioned officer, Karlovac 1984–85; Diplomacy Officer with army of fmr Yugoslavia, Sarajevo 1985–88; Co. Commdr, Yugoslav People's Army Barracks, Delnice, Croatia 1988–91; fought in Croatian War of Independence 1991–92; served in Coastal Mountain Prefecture, Croatia 1992–98; Commdr, Agim Ramadani Brigade 131, Ushtria Çlirimtare e Kosovës (Kosovo Liberation Army), Koshare/Košare 1998–99; Chief of Staff, Second Kosovo Protection Corps Protection Zone 1999–2002; Commdr, Hamëz Jashari Defence Acad. 2002–09; Deputy Commdr, Kosovo Security Force Rapid Reaction Force 2009–12; mem. Kosovo Ass. (parl.) 2014–17; Minister of the Kosovo Security Force 2017–; mem. Aleanca për Ardhmërinë e Kosovës (AAK—Alliance for the Future of Kosovo), mem. Steering Council 2013, mem. AAK Presidency 2013. *Address:* Ministry of the Kosovo Security Force, 10000 Prishtina, Kazerma Adem Jashari, Kosovo (office). *Telephone:* (38) 551437 (office). *E-mail:* labinot.canolli@rks-gov.net (office). *Website:* mksf-ks.org (office).

BERISHA, Sali, PhD; Albanian cardiologist, academic and politician; b. 15 Oct. 1944, Viçidol, Tropojë Dist, Kukës Co.; m. Liri Ramaj; one s. one d.; ed Univ. of Tirana and studies in Paris, France; worked as cardiologist in Tirana Cardiology Clinic; taught at Univ. of Tirana 1980–90; fmr mem. Partia e Punës e Shqipërisë (Party of Labour of Albania); co-f. Partia Demokratike e Shqipërisë (Democratic Party of Albania), Leader 1991–92, 1997–2013; mem. Kuvendi Popullor (People's Ass.) 1991–; Pres. of Albania 1992–97 (re-elected Feb. 1997, resgnd July 1997); Prime Minister of Albania 2005–13; mem. Nat. Medical Research Cttee, European Cttee on Medical Scientific Research 1968–; Hon. mem. Int. Raoul Wallenberg Foundation. *Publications:* has published several textbooks and scientific articles on cardiology; numerous political articles in newspapers and magazines. *Address:* Partia Demokratike e Shqipërisë (Democratic Party of Albania), Rruga Punëtorët e Rilindjes 1, 1001 Tirana, Albania. *Telephone:* (4) 2228091. *Fax:* (4) 2223525. *E-mail:* denonco@pd.al. *Website:* www.pd.al.

BERIZIKY, Omer; Malagasy politician and fmr diplomatist; b. 9 Sept. 1950, Vohemar; fmr Prof. of History, Univ. of Madagascar, Ambohitsaina; Amb. to Belgium and Perm. Rep. to EU, Brussels 1995–2006; Prime Minister 2011–14, also Acting Minister of Environment and Forests; mem. Libéralisme économique et action démocratique pour la reconstruction nationale (LEADER/Fanilo). *Address:* c/o Office of the Prime Minister, BP 248, Palais dEtat Mahazoarivo, 101 Antananarivo, Madagascar.

BERKELEY OF KNIGHTON, Baron (Life Peer), cr. 2013, of Knighton in the County of Powys; **Michael Fitzhardinge Berkeley,** CBE, FRAM, FRWCMD; British composer and broadcaster; b. 29 May 1948, London; s. of Sir Lennox Berkeley and Elizabeth Freda Berkeley (née Bernstein); m. 1st Deborah Jane Coltman-Rogers 1979 (died 2014); one d.; m. 2nd Elizabeth West 2016; ed Westminster Cathedral Choir School, The Oratory School, Royal Acad. of Music; writer on music and arts for the Observer, Vogue and The Listener 1970–75; presenter, music programmes (including Proms) for BBC TV 1975–; BBC Radio 3 announcer 1974–79; apptd Assoc. Composer, Scottish Chamber Orchestra 1979; Dir Britten-Pears Foundation 1996–; mem. Exec. Cttee Asscn of Professional Composers 1982–84, Cen. Music Advisory Cttee, BBC 1986–90; Music Panel Adviser to Arts Council 1986–90; Visiting Prof. Huddersfield Univ. (fmrly Polytechnic) 1991–94; Artistic Dir Cheltenham Int. Festival 1995–2004; Co-Dir Spitalfields Festival 1994–97; Dir Royal Opera House, Covent Garden 1996–2000 (mem. 1994–98, Chair. Opera Bd 1998); Chair. Bd of Govs Royal Ballet 2003–; Composer-in-Asscn, BBC Nat. Orchestra of Wales 2000–09; Visiting Prof. in Composition, Royal Welsh Coll. of Music and Drama (RWCMD) 2002–; has also composed music for film, TV and radio; mem. (Crossbench), House of Lords 2013–; Trustee, Benjamin Britten Will Trust, Cambrian Music Trust; Guinness Prize for Composition 1977, Silver Medal, Worshipful Co. of Musicians 2003. *Major works include:* Meditations for Strings, Oboe Concerto 1977, Fantasia Concertante, Gregorian Variations (orchestra), For The Savage Messiah (piano quintet), Or Shall We Die? (oratorio to text by Ian McEwan) 1982, 4 String Quartets, Piano Trio, Songs of Awakening Love, Entertaining Master Punch, Clarinet Concerto, Speaking Silence, Viola Concerto, Catch Me If You Can (chamber), Dark Sleep (keyboard), Tristessa (orchestra), Magnetic Field (string quartet), Winter Fragments, Odd Man Out, Abstract Mirror (string quartet), Gabriel's Lament for orchestra, Piano Quintet, Gethsemane (for tenor and ensemble) 1990, Twenty-One 1991, Baa Baa Black Sheep (opera, libretto by David Malouf based on the childhood of Rudyard Kipling) 1993, Secret Garden (orchestra) 1997, The Garden of Earthly Delights (orchestra) 1998, Jane Eyre (opera, libretto by David Malouf) 2000, For You (chamber opera, libretto by Ian McEwan) 2009, Collision (electro-acoustic and visual installation, collaboration with artist Kevin Laycock) 2009, Three Rilke Sonnets (written for the Nash Ensemble and soprano Claire Booth) 2011, Hollow Fires (song cycle for baritone and piano setting texts by Housman and Hardy) 2011, Atonement (opera, libretto by Craig Raine) 2013, Tango! 2015, The Tale of Andrew 2015. *Radio:* presenter, Private Passions (BBC Radio 3). *Publications:* The Music Pack 1994; numerous articles in newspapers and magazines. *Leisure interests:* walking, farming, reading, contemporary painting. *Address:* c/o Oxford University Press, Repertoire Promotion Department, Great Clarendon Street, Oxford, OX2 6DP, England (office). *E-mail:* repertoire .promotion.uk@oup.com (office). *Website:* ukcatalogue.oup.com/category/music/ composers/berkeley.do (office); www.michaelberkeley.co.uk.

BERKMAN, Lisa, BA, MS, PhD; American epidemiologist and academic; *Thomas D. Cabot Professor of Public Policy and of Epidemiology and Director, Harvard Center for Population and Development Studies, Harvard University;* ed Northwestern Univ., Evanston, Ill., Univ. of California, Berkeley; Lecturer, Dept of Epidemiology and Int. Health, School of Medicine, Univ. of California, San Francisco 1977–78; Research Specialist in Epidemiology, Human Population Lab., Calif. State Dept of Health, Berkeley 1977–78; Asst Prof., Dept of Epidemiology and Public Health and Inst. for Social and Policy Studies, Yale School of Medicine 1979–83, Assoc. Prof. 1983–85, Assoc. Prof. with tenure 1986–92, Prof. 1992–95, Head of Div. of Health Policy and Resources 1988–91, Head of Div. of Chronic Disease/Epidemiology 1991–95; Florence Sprague Norman and Laura Smart Norman Prof., Health and Social Behavior and Epidemiology, Harvard School of Public Health 1995–2001, Chair. Health and Social Behavior 1995–2003, Dir Center for Society and Health, Harvard Univ. 1997–99, Chair. 1999–, Thomas D. Cabot Prof. of Public Policy 2001–, Chair. Society, Human Devt and Health, Harvard School of Public Health 2003–08, Dir Harvard Center for Population and Devt Studies 2007–; Researcher, Unit 136, Institut Nat. de la Santé et de la Recherche Médicale (INSERM), Paris, France 1993–94, Visiting Prof., Unit 88 1994–; Hon. Sr Lecturer, Dept of Community Medicine, Univ. Coll. London and Middlesex Hosp., London, UK; Pres. Soc. for Epidemiological Research 2002; Chair. Bd of Scientific Counselors, Nat. Inst. of Aging 2005–08; mem. American Epidemiological Soc. 1991, Inst. of Medicine 2001, US Health and Retirement Study Advisory Bd, SHARE Advisory Bd, ELSA Advisory Bd, Macarthur Foundation Aging Soc. Network; Foreign mem. Academia Europaea; Regents of Univ. of California Fellowship, Univ. of California, Berkeley 1974–75, NIMH Mental Health Epidemiology Training Grant, Univ. of California, Berkeley 1975–77, Grossman Endowment for Doctoral Research, Univ. of California, Berkeley 1975–77, Sr Fulbright Scholar, London 1985–86, Alumna of the Year Award School of Public Health, Univ. of California, Berkeley 1997. *Publications:* Health and Ways of Living (with L. Breslow) 1983, Social Epidemiology (co-ed. with I. Kawachi) 2000, Neighborhoods and Health (co-ed. with I. Kawachi) 2003; numerous book chapters and more than 200 papers in peer-reviewed journals. *Address:* Department of Society, Human Development and Health, Harvard School of Public Health, 9 Bow Street, Cambridge, MA 02138, USA (office). *Telephone:* (617) 495-8498 (office). *E-mail:* lberkman@hsph.harvard.edu (office). *Website:* www.hsph.harvard.edu (office).

BERKOFF, Steven; British actor, writer and director; b. 3 Aug. 1937, Stepney, London; s. of Alfred Berkoff and Pauline Berkoff; m. 1st Alison Minto 1970; m. 2nd Shelley Lee 1976 (divorced); ed Hackney Downs Grammar School, Webber-Douglas School of Drama; Hon. DLit (Brunel). *Films include:* Octopussy, First Blood 2, Beverly Hills Cop, Absolute Beginners, War and Remembrance (TV) 1988, The Krays 1990, Decadence 1994, Rancid Aluminium 2000, Head in the Clouds 2004, Brides 2004, Forest of the Gods 2005. *Plays/Productions include:* Agamemnon (London) 1973, The House of Usher 1974, The Trial 1976, East 1978, Hamlet 1980, 2001, Greek 1980, Decadence 1981, Agamemnon (USA) 1984, Harry's Xmas 1985, Kvetch 1986, 1991 (Evening Standard Award for Comedy of the Year 1991, Herald Angel, Edinburgh Fringe Firsts), Sink the Belgrano 1987, Coriolanus 1988, Metamorphosis 1988, Salome 1989, The Trial 1991, Brighton Beach Scumbags 1994; Dir West (London) 1983, Acapulco (LA) 1990, One Man (London) 1993, Coriolanus 1996, Mermaid 1996, Massage (LA and Edinburgh) 1997, Shakespeare's Villains 1998, Messiah 2000 (London 2003), Dir Sit and Shiver (Los Angeles) 2004, (London) 2006, Dir Richard II (Ludlow Festival) 2005, Biblical Tales (London) 2010. *Publications include:* America 1988, I am Hamlet 1989, A Prisoner in Rio 1989, The Theatre of Steven Berkoff (photographic) 1992, Coriolanus in Deutschland 1992, Overview (collected essays) 1994, Free Association (autobiog.) 1996, Graft: Tales of an Actor 1998, Shopping in the Santa Monica Mall, Ritual in Blood, Messiah 2000 (Glasgow Herald Golden Angel Award, Edinburgh Festival Fringe First), Oedipus 2000, The Secret Love Life of Ophelia 2001 (Glasgow Herald Golden Angel Award), Tough Acts 2003, My Life in Food 2008. *Leisure interests:* photography, travelling, table tennis, eating. *Address:* East Productions, 1 Keepier Wharf, 12 Narrow Street, London, E14 8DH, England (office). *Telephone:* (20) 7790-6313 (office). *Fax:* (20) 7790-1752 (office). *E-mail:* eastproductions@stevenberkoff.com (office). *Website:* www.stevenberkoff.com.

BERKOWITZ, Richard Lee, MD; American physician, endocrinologist, geneticist, obstetrician and gynaecologist and academic; *Professor of Obstetrics and Gynecology, Columbia Medical Center, Columbia University;* ed New York Univ. School of Medicine, Yale Univ. School of Medicine; Internship, Kings County Medical Center; Residency, Cornell Medical Center, New York Hosp. 1971; served for 18 years as Chair. Dept of Obstetrics and Gynecology, Mount Sinai School of Medicine and Dir Div. of Maternal-Fetal Medicine; currently Prof. of Obstetrics and Gynecology, Columbia Medical School, Columbia Univ., New York; affiliated with New York-Presbyterian Hosp./Columbia Univ., apptd Dir of Resident Educ. 2005, currently Dir of Quality Assurance; King Faisal Int. Prize for Medicine (co-recipient) 2012. *Publications:* author or editor of more than 35 books and book chapters; more than 200 papers in peer-reviewed journals. *Address:* Columbia Ob/ Gyn Midtown, 51 West 51st Street, Suite 320, New York, NY 10019, USA (office). *Telephone:* (212) 326-8951 (office). *Fax:* (212) 326-5610 (office). *E-mail:* info@www .columbiaobgyn.org (office). *Website:* www.columbiaobgyn.org (office).

BERLIJN, Gen. (retd) Dick L.; Dutch fmr military officer; *Senior Board Advisor, Deloitte Nederland;* b. 18 March 1950, Amsterdam; m. Elly M. A. Hermelink; two s.; ed Royal Mil. Acad., Breda, Air Force Staff Coll.; served as Operations Officer, later Commdr, Transition and Conversion Div., Leeuwarden Air Base 1983–85; Supervisor, Fighter Weapon Instruction Training, Denmark 1987; Head, Fighter Weapons Br., Tactical Air Command 1988; Head of Operations and Training, Royal Netherlands Air Force Staff 1991–92, Head, Fighter Operations Div. 1994, Deputy Chief (Operations) and Air Commodore 1995; Chief of Flying Operations, Twenthe Air Base 1992; Commdr first F-16 detachment to Italy 1993; apptd Commdr Tactical Air Force, rank of Maj.-Gen. 1998, later Gen.; C-in-C Royal Netherlands Air Force 2000–04; Chief of the Defence Staff 2004–08; mem. Supervisory Bd, Thales Nederland 2008–, fonds slachtofferhulp 2008–; mem. Foundation Bd, Foundation naNOcancer 2010–; Sr Bd Advisor, Deloitte Nederland 2008–, also mem. Bd of Dirs; mem. Int. Advisory Bd Royal Ten Cate 2010–; mem. Bd of Advisors Subsolar Energy 2011–; Legion of Merit (USA), Légion d'honneur; Long Service Medal, NATO Medal, Multinational Peace Operations Medal. *Address:* Deloitte Nederland, Schenkkade 47, PO Box 90721, 2509 LS The Hague, The Netherlands (office). *E-mail:* dberlijn@deloitte.nl (office). *Website:* www.deloitte.com/view/nl_NL/nl/index.htm (office).

BERLUSCONI, Marina Elvira; Italian business executive; *Chairman, Fininvest SpA;* b. (Maria Elvira Berlusconi), 10 Aug. 1966, Milan; d. of Silvio Berlusconi and Carla Elvira Lucia Dall'Oglio; m. 2nd Maurizio Vanadia; two s. (one from previous m.); worked in London boutique aged 18; Deputy Chair. Fininvest SpA 1996–2005, Chair. 2005–; Chair. Arnoldo Mondadori SpA (Italy's largest publishing co.) 2003–; mem. Bd Dirs Mediaset SpA 1995–, Medusa Film 1995–2007 (Pres. 2001–02), 21 Investimenti SpA 2000–07, Mediobanca SpA 2008–12. *Address:* Fininvest SpA, Via Paleocapa 3, 20121 Milan, Italy (office). *Telephone:* (02) 85411 (office). *Website:* www.fininvest.it (office); www.mondadori.it (office).

BERLUSCONI, Silvio; Italian politician and business executive; b. 29 Sept. 1936, Milan; s. of Luigi Berlusconi and Rosa Bossi; m. 1st; one d. one s.; m. 2nd Veronica Lari; three c.; ed Univ. of Milan; started building and property devt business aged 26; f. Elinord construction co. 1962; built up Fininvest, major conglomerate with interests in commercial TV, printed media, publishing, advertising, insurance and financial services, retailing and football; worked on Milan 2 Housing project 1969; Canale 5 network began broadcasting 1980; bought Italia 1 TV network 1983, Rete 4 TV network 1984; took stake in La Cinq commercial TV network 1985, Chain, Cinema 5 (largest in Italy); bought Estudios Roma 1986; Milan AC Football Club 1986; La Standa (Italy's largest Dept store chain) 1988; Chair. Arnoldo Mondadori Editore SpA Jan.–July 1990, (half-share) 1991; Founder and Pres. Forza Italia political movt 1993, began full-time political career 1994, declaring he had stepped down from exec. posts in Fininvest, owned 51% of Mediaset (Italy's largest pvt. TV network operator) through Fininvest, reduced stake by one-third 2005; led Forza Italia to win general elections in alliance with Lega Nord and Alleanza Nazionale parties 1994; Prime Minister of Italy April–Dec. 1994, 2001–06, 2008–11 (resgnd), also Minister of Foreign Affairs 2002; Founder and Pres. Casa delle Libertà (House of Freedoms) 2002–07, replaced by Popolo della Libertà 2007–13, relaunched Forza Italia 2013, current leader; Pres. EU Council July–Sept. 2003; mem. European Parl. 1999; convicted of fraud by an Italian court for tax evasion and sentenced to four years in prison, shortened to one year Oct. 2012, sentence confirmed by Court of Appeals May 2013, by Court of Cassation Aug. 2013, ordered by Tribunale di sorveglianza in Milan to serve sentence through part-time community service in a home for elderly people April 2014; convicted of paying for sex with an underage prostitute and of abusing his office June 2013, sentenced to seven years in prison and banned from public office for life, conviction and sentence overturned July 2014; mem. Senate March–Nov. 2013 (expelled); convicted of bribing a Senator, sentenced to three years' imprisonment (not served owing to expiry of statute of limitations) 2015; Ordine al Merito del Lavoro 1977, Kt Grand Cross, Order of the Star of Romania 2002, Kt Grand Cross, Order of Merit of the Repub. of Poland 2002, Hon. Companion of Honour of the Nat. Order of Merit (Malta) 2004, Grand Officer, Order of the Three Stars (Latvia) 2005, Al-Fateh Medal (Libya) 2009, Mem. (First Class), Order of Abdulaziz al Saud (Saudi Arabia) 2009, Kt Grand Cross, Sacred Mil. Constantinian Order of St George. *Recording:* Meglio'ne Canzone (album) 2003. *Website:* www.forzasilvio.it.

BERMAN, Gail, BA; American media executive; *President, Producers Guild of America;* b. 17 Aug. 1956, Long Island, NY; m. Bill Masters; two c.; ed Univ. of Maryland Coll. of Arts and Humanities; co-produced with Susan Rose first US production of Andrew Lloyd Webber's Joseph and the Amazing Technicolour Dreamcoat, Broadway, New York 1982–83; Supervisor Original Production, HBO's Comedy Channel (precursor of Comedy Central) late 1980s; Head of Sandollar Television, Southern Calif. early 1990s; Founder-Pres. and Partner, Regency Television Inc. 1998–2000; Pres. of Entertainment, Fox Broadcasting Co. 2000–05; Pres. Paramount Pictures Corpn 2005–07; Co-owner and Co-founder BermanBraun LLC 2007–; mem. National Bd of Directors, Producers Guild of America, mem. Producers Council Bd of Delegates 2016–, Pres. 2018–; mem. Bd of Trustees, Univ. of Maryland 2010; mem. Advisory Bd, Carsey-Wolf Center; Women in Film Lucy Award 2003, Brandon Tartikoff Legacy Award, Nat. Asscn of Television Production Execs, Exec. of the Year, Caucus for Television Producers, Writers and Directors 2005, 2006, She Made It honoree, Paley Center for Media. *Plays produced:* Almost an Eagle 1982, Hurlyburly 1984, Blood Knot (co-producer) 1985–86, The Nerd 1987–88. *Television:* co-producer: Joseph and the Amazing Technicolor Dreamcoat, Hurlyburly by David Rabe 1984, Athol Fugard's Blood Knot 1985, The Nerd 1987; exec. producer: Someone Like Me 1994, All-American Girl 1994, Social Studies 1997, Buffy the Vampire Slayer 1997, Angel 1999, Firefly 2002, HBO Presents Hazelle, American Idol, 24, That 70s Show, House, Arrested Development, Bones, Family Guy. *Address:* Producers Guild of America, 8530 Wilshire Blvd, Suite 400, Beverly Hills, CA 90211, USA (office); . *Telephone:* (310) 358-9020 (Producers Guild of America) (office); (310) 255-7272 (BermanBraun LLC) (office). *Fax:* (310) 255-7058 (BermanBraun LLC) (office). *E-mail:* info@ producersguild.org (office); info@bermanbraun.com (office). *Website:* www .producersguild.org (office); www.bermanbraun.com (office).

BERMAN, Jason (Jay); American music industry executive; fmr rep. for Warner Music, Recording Industry Asscn of America (RIAA) Bd –1987, Pres. RIAA 1987–92, Chair. 1992–98; Chair. and CEO Int. Federation for the Phonographic Industry (IFPI) 1998–2004, Chair. Emer. 2005–; US Special Counsel for Trade to

President Clinton 1998; est. anti-piracy consultancy, Berman Rosen Global Strategies 2006–09; mem. Bd of Dirs Loudeye Corpn 2005–, Wurld Media 2005–, Musicloads 2005–.

BERMANN, Sylvie-Agnès; French diplomatist; *Ambassador to Russia;* b. 19 Oct. 1953; ed Univ. of Paris-Sorbonne, Inst. of Political Studies, Nat. Inst. for Oriental Languages and Civilizations, Beijing Language Inst.; Vice-Consul, Consulate-Gen., Hong Kong 1979–80, Second Sec., Embassy in Beijing 1980–82, Head of China, Hong Kong and Taiwan Affairs, Asia and Oceania Dept, Ministry of Foreign Affairs 1982–86, Second Counsellor, Embassy in Moscow 1986–89, Deputy Dir SE Asia and Oceania Dept, Ministry of Foreign Affairs 1989–92, Second Counsellor, Perm. Mission to UN, New York 1992–96, Head, Common Foreign and Security Policy Dept, Directorate-Gen. of Political Affairs and Security 1996–2002, Amb. and Perm. Rep. to WEU and EU Political and Security Cttee, Brussels 2002–05, Dir UN, Int. Orgs, Human Rights and Francophony Dept, Ministry of Foreign Affairs 2005–11, Amb. to People's Repub. of China 2011–14, to UK 2014–17, to Russia 2017–; Chevalier, Ordre nat. du Mérite 1996, Officier 2008; Chevalier, Légion d'honneur 2003, Officier 2012. *Address:* Embassy of France, 115127 Moscow, ul. B. Yakimanka 45, Russia (office). *Telephone:* (495) 937-15-00 (office). *Fax:* (495) 937-14-30 (office). *E-mail:* amba@ambafrance.ru (office). *Website:* www.ambafrance-ru.org (office).

BERMÚDEZ AMADO, Brig. Gen. Francisco; Guatemalan military officer, government official and diplomatist; fmr Brig.-Gen., Guatemalan Armed Forces; Minister of Nat. Defence 2005–06; Amb. to Taiwan 2007. *Address:* c/o Ministry of National Defence, Antiguas Instalaciones de la Escuela Politécnica, Avda La Reforma 1-45, Zona 10, Guatemala City, Guatemala. *E-mail:* dip@mindef.mil.gt.

BERMÚDEZ MERIZALDE, Jaime, PhD; Colombian lawyer, politician and diplomatist; *President, MBA Lazard Colombia;* b. 1966, Bogotá; m.; two c.; ed Univ. de los Andes, Univ. of Oxford, UK; with Human Rights Advisory Office 1991–93; Adviser to Minister of Foreign Affairs 1993–94, also coordinator Neighborhood Commissions; pvt. communications consultant -2002; Dir Asociación Primero Colombia (political asscn) 2002–06; communications adviser during presidential election campaign of Alvaro Uribe 2002, Presidential Adviser in Communications 2002–06; Amb. to Argentina 2006–07; Minister of Foreign Affairs 2008–10; Pres. MBA Lazard Colombia 2010–; served as UN observer during South African presidential elections 1994. *Address:* MBA Lazard Colombia, Carrera 7 N° 71 – 21 Torre B Of. 908, Bogotá, DC Colombia (office).

BERNABÈ, Franco; Italian business executive; b. 18 Sept. 1948, Vipiteno/Sterzing (Bozen); s. of Bruno Bernabè and Clara Frigerio; m. Maria Grazia Curtetto; one s. one d.; ed Univ. of Turin; postgraduate fellow, Einaudi Foundation and Prof. of Econs, Univ. of Turin 1973; Sr Economist, Dept of Econs and Statistics, OECD, Paris 1976–78; Chief Economist, FIAT, Turin 1978–83; Asst to Chair. ENI SpA 1983–86, Head of Corp. Planning, Financial Control and Corp. Devt 1986–92, CEO ENI SpA 1992–98; fmr Chair. Telecom Italia SpA, apptd CEO 2007, Pres. Telecom Italia Foundation 2012; f. FB Group (investment co.) 1999, Vice-Chair. Rothschild Europe (following merger of financial advisory activities of FB Group with Rothschild Group) 2004–; Ind. Dir (non-exec.) PetroChina 2000–; Chair. GSMA (int. org. of mobile operators); apptd by Prime Minister as special rep. of Italian Govt for the reconstruction of Kosovo 1999; Chair. La Biennale di Venezia 2001–03, Mart (Italian museum of modern art) 2004–; mem. European Roundtable; Co-Pres. Italy-Brazil Business Council; Vice-Pres. Rome Industrialist and Enterprises Asscn with special responsibility for innovation and broadband; fmr mem. Bd of Dirs Fiat, TPG-TNT; apptd Pres. Palaexpo 2015; mem. Advisory Bd of Observatoire Méditérranéen de l'Energie; fmr mem. Advisory Bd Council on Foreign Relations, Bd Peres Center for Peace; Cavaliere del Lavoro 2011. *Publications include:* Financial Structure and Economic Policy in Italy 1975, Labour Market and Unemployment (with A. Boltho) 1982, Industrial Policies and Industrialization: The Case of the Automobile Industry 1982.

BERNANKE, Ben Shalom, BA, PhD; American economist, academic, fmr central banker and fmr government official; *Distinguished Fellow in Residence, Hutchins Center on Fiscal and Monetary Policy, Brookings Institution;* b. 13 Dec. 1953, Augusta, Ga; s. of Philip Bernanke and Edna Bernanke; m. Anna Bernanke; two c.; ed J.V. Martin Junior High, Dillon High School (class valedictorian), Harvard Univ., Massachusetts Inst. of Tech.; Asst Prof., Stanford Univ. Graduate School of Business 1979–83, Assoc. Prof. 1983–85; Prof. of Econs and Public Affairs, Princeton Univ. 1985–96, Howard Harrison and Gabrielle Snyder Beck Prof. of Econs and Public Affairs and Chair. Econs Dept 1996–2002, Dir Bendheim Center for Finance 1997–98; Dir Monetary Econs Program, Nat. Bureau of Econ. Research (NBER) 2000–02, fmr mem. Business Cycling Dating Cttee; mem. Bd of Govs, Fed. Reserve System 2002–05; Chair. Pres.'s Council of Econ. Advisors, The White House 2005–06; Chair. Bd of Govs, Fed. Reserve System 2006–14; Distinguished Fellow in Residence, Hutchins Center on Fiscal and Monetary Policy, Brookings Inst., Washington, DC 2014–; Sr Advisor, PIMCO 2015–, Citadel 2015–; Vice-Pres. American Economic Asscn 2015–; Ed., American Economic Review 2001–03; Co-ed. NBER Macroeconomics Annual, 1994–2001; Hoover Inst. Nat. Fellow 1982–83; Alfred P. Sloan Research Fellow 1983–84; Guggenheim Fellowship 1999–2000; Fellow, Econometric Soc. 1997–, American Acad. of Arts and Sciences 2001–; fmr mem. Montgomery Township Bd of Educ.; Guggenheim Fellowship, Sloan Fellowship; Distinguished Leadership in Govt Award, Columbia Business School 2008, TIME magazine Person of the Year 2009. *Publications include:* Principles of Microeconomics (co-author), Principles of Economics (co-author), Macroeconomics (co-author) 2001, Essays on the Great Depression 2005, Inflation Targeting: Lessons from the International Experience (co-author) 2005, Principles of Macro Economics (co-author) 2007, The Federal Reserve and the Financial Crisis (lectures) 2013, The Courage to Act: A Memoir of a Crisis and its Aftermath 2015; numerous articles. *Address:* The Brookings Institution, 1775 Massachusetts Avenue, NW, Washington, DC 20036-2103, USA (office). *Telephone:* (202) 797-6125 (office). *E-mail:* bbernanke@brookings.edu (office). *Website:* www.brookings.edu/experts/bernankeb (office).

BERNARD, Claire Marie Anne; French violinist; b. 31 March 1947, Rouen; d. of Yvan Bernard and Marie Chouquet; ed Conservatoire Régional de Musique, Rouen and Conservatoire Nat. Supérieur de Musique (CNSM); began professional career as solo violinist 1965; mem. jury, Tchaikovsky Int. Competition, Moscow 1974; Prof. of Violin at state-run conservatoires and music schools in France; Asst at Conservatoire nat. supérieur de musique, Lyon 1990–; mem. contemporary music ensemble Les Temps Modernes 1993–; Prof., CNR, Conservatoire Nat. Supérieur de Musique (CNSM); recordings include works by Khatchaturian, Prokofiev, Barber, Milhaud, Mozart, Haydn, Sarasate, Leclair, Gaviniès, Telemann and Vivaldi; Chevalier, Ordre nat. du Mérite; Carl Flesch Acad. Medal, Baden-Baden, First Prize, Conservatoire de Paris 1959, First Prize, George Enesco Int. Competition 1964 and other awards and prizes. *Leisure interests:* painting, gymnastics, swimming. *Address:* 53 rue Rabelais, 69003 Lyon, France (home). *Telephone:* 6-69-45-53-07 (mobile). *E-mail:* bernard-claire16@bbox.fr (home).

BERNARD, Daniel; French business executive; *Honorary President, HEC Foundation;* b. 18 Feb. 1946; s. of Paul Bernard and Simone Bernard (née Doise); m. Chantal Leduc 1968; one s. two d.; ed Lycée Camille Desmoulins, Cateau, Lycee Faidherbe, Lille, École des Hautes Etudes Commerciales (HEC), Univ. of Paris; worked with Delcev Industries 1969–71, Socam Miniprix 1971–75, Ruche Picarde 1975–80; Dir Mammouth and Delta hypermarket chains 1976–81; Man. Dir Metro France 1981–89, mem. Bd of Dirs Metro International (Switzerland) 1989–92; CEO Carrefour SA 1992–98, Chair. and CEO 1998–2005; Deputy Chair. Kingfisher plc 2006–09, Chair. 2009–17; Founder and Pres. Provestis (investment co.); mem. Bd of Dirs Alcatel-Lucent (fmrly Alcatel) 1997–, Cap Gemini 2005–; Sr Advisor, Towerbrook Capital Partners 2010–; Pres. HEC Foundation 2008–14, currently Hon. Pres.; Chevalier, Légion d'honneur; Officier, Ordre nat. du Mérite; Commdr, l'ordre de Rio Branco; Grande Croix de l'Ordre du Congrès; Best Global Retailer, Nat. Retail Fed. 2000. *Leisure interests:* mountains, skiing, opera. *Address:* HEC Foundation, 1 rue de la Libération, 78351 Paris, France (office). *Telephone:* (01) 3967-7000 (office). *Fax:* (01) 3967-7400 (office). *E-mail:* dircom@hec.fr (office). *Website:* www.hec.edu (office).

BERNARD, Desiree Patricia, LLB; Guyanese attorney-at-law and judge; *Judge, Court of Appeal, Bermuda;* b. 2 March 1939, Georgetown; d. of William Bernard and Maude Bernard; one d.; ed Bishops' High School, Georgetown, Univ. of London, UK; solicitor 1963–79; Commr of Oaths and Notary Public 1976; admitted to English Roll of Solicitors 1977; magistrate 1979–80; Judge (first woman), High Court of Guyana 1980–92; Justice of Appeal 1992–96; Chief Justice (first woman) 1996–2001; Chancellor of the Judiciary (first woman) 2001–05; Judge of the Caribbean Court of Justice (first woman) 2005–14; Judge of the Court of Appeal, Bermuda 2015–; Founding Pres. Guyana Asscn of Women Lawyers; Founding mem. Conf. on the Affairs and Status of Women in Guyana; Sec. Caribbean Women's Asscn (CARIWA) 1970–74; Pres. Org. of Commonwealth Bar Asscn 1976; mem. and Chair. Caribbean Steering Cttee for Women's Affairs 1978; Rapporteur UN Cttee for Convention on Elimination of All Forms of Discrimination Against Women (CEDAW) 1982–84, Chair. 1985–89, mem. 1982–98; Chair. Georgetown Legal Aid Clinic 1994, Family Matters and Maintenance Cttee 1996–97; Chancellor of Anglican Diocese 1994; mem. Commonwealth Magistrates and Judges Asscn, Int. Asscn of Women Judges, Commonwealth Lawyers Asscn; involved in writing laws on equal rights of women and children, property rights of women, discrimination and domestic violence; Cacique Crown of Honour 1985, Order of Roraima 2002; Hon. LLD (Univ. of the West Indies) 2007; Univ. of Guyana Award for Achievements in Law 1989, Caribbean Women's Asscn Award 1991, Guild of Grads of Univ. of the West Indies Award, New York Chapter 1992, Bishops' High School Alumni Achievement Award 1999, Caribbean Bar Asscn Award 2001, CARICOM Triennial Award for Women 2005. *Leisure interests:* travel, cricket, promoting women's rights. *Address:* c/o Court of Appeal, 113 Front Street, Hamilton HM 12, Bermuda (office); 9 Barbados Road, Federation Park, Port-of-Spain, Trinidad & Tobago (home). *Telephone:* 292-1350 (office); 622-3588 (home). *Fax:* 292-2268 (office).

BERNARDIĆ, Davor, PhD; Croatian physicist and politician; *Chairman, Socijaldemokratska Partija Hrvatske (SDP—Social Democratic Party of Croatia);* b. 5 Jan. 1980, Zagreb, Socialist Repub. of Croatia, Socialist Fed. Repub. of Yugoslavia; s. of Damir Bernardić and Dragica Bernardić (née Tešo); m. Irena Coljak 2011; ed Nikola Tesla Tech. Vocational High School and Zagreb Faculty of Science; competed in Int. Physics Olympiad 1996, came second in nat. competition 1997, winner 1998; Research Fellow, postgraduate doctoral studies in physics, Zagreb Faculty of Science 2009; joined Socijaldemokratska Partija Hrvatske (SDP—Social Democratic Party of Croatia) 1998, Pres. Youth Forum Br. 2005–07, mem. Exec. Bd 2005–09, Pres. SDP Youth Forum 2008–10, mem. SDP Main Bd 2008–12, Leader of Zagreb Br. of SDP 2010–16, Chair. SDP and Leader of the Opposition 2016–; mem. Zagreb City Ass. 2007–09, Pres. SDP's Councillor Club; mem. Ass. (Sabor—Parl.) 2008–. *Address:* Socijaldemokratska Partija Hrvatske (Social Democratic Party of Croatia), 10000 Zagreb, Iblerov trg 9, Croatia (office). *Telephone:* (1) 4552055 (office). *Fax:* (1) 4552842 (office). *E-mail:* info@sdp.hr (office). *Website:* www.sdp.hr (office).

BERNAUER, David W., BPharm; American pharmaceutical industry executive (retd); b. 1944; m. Mary Bernauer; three c.; ed North Dakota State Univ.; joined Walgreen Co. in 1966, Dist Man. 1979–87, Regional Vice-Pres. 1987–90, Vice-Pres. and Treas. 1990–92, Vice-Pres. of Purchasing 1992–95, Vice-Pres. 1995, Sr Vice-Pres. 1996–99, Pres. and COO 1999–2002, CEO 2002–06, Chair. 2003–07; mem. Bd of Dirs Nat., Asscn of Chain Drug Stores (now Vice-Chair.), Office Depot 2004–11, Students in Free Enterprise, Lowe's Companies, Inc. 2007– (Lead Ind. Dir 2010–), Alphabet Holding Co., Inc. 2011–, NBTY, Inc. 2011–; mem. Bd of Trustees, Field Museum, Chicago; Co-Chair. North Dakota State Univ. Coll. of Pharmacy Devt Fund; Hon. DPharm (North Dakota State Univ.) 2000; North Dakota State Univ. Distinguished Alumni Award 1999. *Address:* c/o Board of Directors, Lowe's Companies, Inc., 1000 Lowes Blvd, Mooresville, NC 28117, USA (office). *Telephone:* (704) 758-1000 (office); (704) 758-2917 (office). *E-mail:* publicrelations@lowes.com (office). *Website:* www.lowes.com (office).

BERNERD, Elliott; British property developer; *Executive Chairman, Chelsfield Group Limited;* b. 23 May 1945, London, England; s. of Geoffrey Bernerd and Trudie Malawer (née Melzack); m. 1st Susan Elizabeth Lynton 1968 (divorced 1989); two d.; m. 2nd Sonia Ramsay (née Ramalho) 1992; Co-founder and Exec. Chair. Chelsfield PLC (now Chelsfield Group Ltd) 1987–, Chair. Duelguide PLC (after taking Chelsfied PLC pvt.) 2004–; Chair. and CEO Michael Laurie & Partners; Co-founder Stockley PLC; Chair. London Philharmonic Trust 1987–94, Wentworth Group Holdings Ltd 1990–, South Bank Foundation 1996–2002, South

Bank Bd Ltd 1998–2002, CancerBACUP Benefactor's Scheme 2003–; Chair. of Trustees, Facial Surgery Research Foundation; mem. Bd of Dirs, Investment Property Databank 2005–; Hon. FRIBA. *Leisure interests:* tennis, skiing. *Address:* Chelsfield Group Ltd, 50 Hans Crescent, London, SW1X 0NA, England (office). *Telephone:* (20) 7290-2388 (office). *E-mail:* ebernerd@chelsfield.com (office). *Website:* www.chelsfield.com (office).

BERNERS-LEE, Sir Timothy John, Kt, OM, KBE, OBE, BA, FRS, FREng; British computer scientist and academic; *Senior Research Scientist and Director of World Wide Web Consortium, Laboratory for Computer Science and Artificial Intelligence, Massachusetts Institute of Technology;* b. 8 June 1955, London; s. of Conway Berners-Lee and Mary Lee Woods; ed Emanuel School, London, Queen's Coll., Oxford; with Plessey Telecommunications Ltd 1976–78; software engineer, D.G. Nash Ltd 1978; consultant software engineer CERN June–Dec. 1980, fellowship to work on distributed real-time systems for scientific data acquisition and system control 1984; with Image Computer Systems Ltd, responsible for tech. design 1981–84; began work on global hypertext project (now known as World Wide Web) 1989, launched within CERN 1990, on Internet 1991; joined Lab. for Computer Science (now Lab. for Computer Science and Artificial Intelligence), MIT 1994–, currently Sr Research Scientist and Dir World Wide Web Consortium; 3Com Founders Chair 1999–; Dir World Wide Web Foundation 2009–; Pres. Open Data Inst. 2012–; helped launch the Alliance for Affordable Internet (A4AI) 2013; mem. NAS 2009; Fellow, IEEE 2008; Distinguished Fellow, British Computer Soc.; Hon. FIEE; Sultan Qaboos Order for Culture, Science and Arts (First Class) (Oman) 2012; Hon. DFA (Parsons School of Design, New York) 1996; Hon. DSc (Southampton) 1996, (Oxford) 2001, (Port Elizabeth) 2002, (Lancaster) 2004, (Harvard) 2011, (St Andrews) 2013; Hon. DUniv (Essex) 1998, (Southern Cross) 1998; Dr hc (Universidad Politécnica de Madrid) 2009, (Vriji Universiteit Amsterdam) 2009; one of only six members of the World Wide Web Hall of Fame 1994, Young Innovator of the Year, Kilby Foundation 1995, Software Systems Award, Asscn for Computing Machinery (ACM) (co-recipient) 1995, ACM Kobayashi Award 1996, IEEE Computer Soc. Wallace McDowell Award 1996, Computers and Communication Award (co-recipient) 1996, Duddell Medal, Inst. of Physics 1997, Charles Babbage Award 1998, Mountbatten Medal, Nat. Electronics Council 1998, Royal Soc. Royal C Medal 2000, Greatest Briton Award 2004, Millennium Tech. Prize 2004, Charles Stark Draper Prize 2007, Lovelace Medal, British Computer Soc. 2007, D&AD Pres.'s Award 2007, BITC Award for Excellence 2008, Pathfinder Award, Kennedy School of Govt, Harvard Univ. 2008, IEEE/RSE Wolfson James Clerk Maxwell Award 2008, Lifetime Achievement Award, Webby Awards 2009, one of first three recipients of the Mikhail Gorbachev Award for "The Man Who Changed the World" 2011, inducted into IEEE Intelligent Systems' AI's Hall of Fame 2011, inducted into Internet Hall of Fame by the Internet Soc. 2012, honoured as the "Inventor of the World Wide Web" during the Summer Olympic Games opening ceremony, London 2012, Queen Elizabeth Prize for Eng (co-recipient) 2013 and numerous other awards. *Publications:* Weaving the Web: The Original Design and Ultimate Destiny of the World Wide Web by its Inventor 1999; several articles in professional journals. *Address:* Laboratory for Computer Science and Artificial Intelligence, Massachusetts Institute of Technology, Stata Center, Building 32, 32 Vassar Street, Cambridge, MA 02139, USA (office). *Telephone:* (617) 253-5702 (office). *Fax:* (617) 258-5999 (office). *E-mail:* timbl@w3.org (office). *Website:* www.w3.org (office).

BERNES, Thomas Anthony, BA; Canadian international organization official; *Distinguished Fellow, Centre for International Governance Innovation;* b. 21 March 1946, Winnipeg; m. Ann Boyd 1974 (divorced 1997); one s. one d.; ed Univ. of Manitoba; Dir-Gen. Trade Policy, Dept of Industry, Trade and Commerce 1981–82, Economic Policy Planning Secr. 1982–83; Head Gen. Trade Policy Div., OECD 1983–85; Dir GATT Affairs, Dept of Foreign Affairs and Int. Trade, Govt of Canada 1985–87; Dir Internal Econ. Relations, Dept of Finance 1987–88, Gen. Dir Int. Trade and Finance Br. 1988–91, Exec. Dir Coordinating Secr. on Canadian Unity, Office of the Deputy Minister 1991–92, Asst Deputy Minister, Int. Trade and Finance Br. 1992–95; G7 Finance Deputy 1995–96; Alt. Gov. for Canada, IMF, Asia Devt Bank, African Devt Bank and IDB 1996; Dir Canadian Export Devt Corpn 1996; Exec. Dir IMF 1996–2001; Exec. Sec., Devt Cttee of Int. Bank for Reconstruction and Devt (World Bank) and IMF 2001–05, Dir Ind. Evaluation Office, IMF 2005–09; Exec. Dir Centre for Int. Governance Innovation 2009–12, Distinguished Fellow 2012–; mem. Governing Bd INET 2011–13; Bd mem. New Rules For Global Finance 2013–. *Address:* Centre for International Governance Innovation, 67 Erb Street West, Waterloo, ON N2L 6C2, Canada (office). *Telephone:* (202) 250-3426 (office). *E-mail:* tbernes@cigionline.org (office). *Website:* www.cigionline.org (office).

BERNHARD, Sandra; American actress, comedienne, singer and author; b. 6 June 1955, Flint, Mich.; d. of Jerome Bernhard and Jeanette Bernhard; partner Sara Switzer; one d.; stand-up comedienne in nightclubs in Beverly Hills 1974–78; Dir HGOCo initiative, Houston Grand Opera 2007–; Davidson/Valentini Award, GLAAD Media Awards 2002, Artistic Achievement Award, Philadelphia QFest Awards 2006. *Films include:* Cheech and Chong's Nice Dreams 1981, The King of Comedy 1983 (Nat. Soc. Film Critics Award), The House of God 1984, Sesame Street Presents: Follow That Bird 1985, Track 29 1988, Hudson Hawk 1991, Truth or Dare 1991, Inside Monkey Zetterland 1992, Dallas Doll 1994, Museum of Love 1996, The Apocalypse 1997, Plump Fiction 1997, Lover Girl 1997, Exposé 1998, An Alan Smithee Film: Burn Hollywood Burn 1998, Somewhere in the City 1998, Wrongfully Accused 1998, I Woke Up Early the Day I Died 1998, Hercules: Zero to Hero (voice) 1999, Dinner Rush 2000, Playing Mona Lisa 2000, Zoolander 2001, The Third Date 2003, The Easter Egg Adventure (voice) 2004, Twenty Dollar Drinks 2006, Dare 2009, See You in September 2010. *Stage appearances (solo):* Without You I'm Nothing 1988, Giving Till It Hurts 1992, I'm Still Here...Damn It! 1998, Everything Bad and Beautiful 2006. *TV appearances:* Without You I'm Nothing 1990, Roseanne (series) 1991–97, Sandra Bernhard: I'm Still Here... Damn It! 1999, The Sandra Bernhard Experience 2001, Silver Lake 2004, The L Word (series) 2005, The Queer Edge 2005–06, 2 Broke Girls 2015. *Radio includes:* Sandyland 2015–. *Recordings include:* albums: I'm Your Woman (co-author 8 songs) 1985, Without You I'm Nothing 1989, Excuses For Bad Behavior (Part One) 1991, (Part Two) 2004, I'm Still Here... Damn It! 1988, The Love Machine 2001, Hero Worship 2003, Everything Bad & Beautiful 2006. *Publications include:* Confessions of a Pretty Lady 1988, Love Love and Love 1993, May I Kiss You on the Lips, Miss Sandra? 1998. *Address:* c/o Jeremy Katz, The Katz Company, Inc., 1560 Broadway, 12th Floor, New York, NY 10036, USA (office). *Telephone:* (212) 767-0189 (office). *E-mail:* jk@thekatzcompany.com (office). *Website:* www.sandrabernhard.com (office).

BERNHARD, Wolfgang, MSc, MBA, PhD; German automobile industry executive; b. (Wolfgang Ayerle), 3 Sept. 1960, Böhen, Landkreis Unterallgäu; ed Maristenkolleg, Mindelheim, Tech. Univ. of Darmstadt, Columbia Univ., USA, Johann Wolfgang Goethe Univ.; Man. Consultant, Mercedes-Benz AG 1990–92, Project Man. 1992–94, Man. for S-Class Ass., Sindelfingen Plant 1994–99, CEO Mercedes-AMG GmbH 1999–2000; Deputy mem. Bd of Man. Daimler-Chrysler AG 2000–02, mem. 2002–04, COO Chrysler Group 2000–04, mem. Bd of Man. Daimler AG (Daimler Trucks) 2010–18; mem. Bd of Man. and Chair. Volkswagen AG 2005–07; adviser, Cerberus Capital Management LP 2007; mem. Supervisory Bd OeIAG, Austria.

BERNIER, The Hon. Maxime, BCom; Canadian politician and lawyer; b. 18 Jan. 1963, Beauce; s. of Gilles Bernier and Doris Bernier; divorced; ed Univ. of Québec, Univ. of Ottawa; called to Québec Bar 1990; fmr Legis. Asst Office of the Deputy Premier of Quebec; Vice-Pres. Standard Life of Canada 2003–05; Man. Corp. and Int. Relations, Comm. des valeurs mobilières du Québec 2003–05; MP 2006–, Minister of Industry 2006–07, of Foreign Affairs 2007–08 (resgnd); Minister of State for Small Business and Tourism 2011–15, Minister of State for Agric. 2013–15; mem. Conservative Party of Canada; fmr mem. Bd of Dirs Montreal Econ. Inst. *Address:* Conservative Party of Canada, 130 Albert Street, Suite 1204, Ottawa, ON K1P 5G4, Canada (office). *Telephone:* (613) 755-2000 (office). *Fax:* (613) 755-2001 (office). *Website:* www.conservative.ca (office).

BERNIK, France, PhD; Slovenian academic; b. 13 May 1927, Ljubljana; s. of Franc Bernik and Cecilija Bernik (née Smole); m. Marija Kanc 1956 (died 1998); one d.; ed Univ. of Ljubljana; teaching asst in Slovene literature, Univ. of Ljubljana 1951–57; Ed., Sec. Slovenska Matica, Ljubljana 1961–72; affiliated with Slovenian Acad. of Sciences and Arts Research Centre 1972–99; Scientific Adviser Inst. for Slovene Literature and Literary Sciences 1977–99, Assoc. mem. 1983, mem. 1987, Pres. Slovenian Acad. of Sciences and Arts 1992–2002; mem. Senator Academia Scientiarum et Artium Europaea, Salzburg 1993; mem. Croatian Acad. of Sciences and Arts 1994, Int. Acad. of Energy 1997, Sankt Peterburg 1995, L'Accad. del Mediterraneo, Napoli 1999; mem. Akademie der Wissenschaften zu Göttingen 2003, Liebniz Sozietät der Wissenschaften zu Berlin 2003; Hon. mem. Slovenian Acad. of Sciences and Arts 2003, Hon. Citizen (Ljubljana) 2005, Hon. Senator, European Acad. of Sciences and Arts, Salzburg 2010; Eques commendator Ordinis sancti Gregorii Magni, Vatican 1996, Golden Hon. Decoration of Freedom of Repub. of Slovenia 1997, Maréchal Ordre de Saint Fortunat 2001; Dr hc (Maribor) 2002; Int. Cultural Diploma of Honour, Raleigh, USA 1996, Zois Award of Repub. of Slovenia 1999, Grand Award of Excellence and Mastery 2005, Austrian Medal for Sciences and Arts I 2011. *Publications include:* The Lyrics of Simon Jenko 1962, Fran Levec (1846–1916) 1965, Cankar's Early Prose 1976, Simon Jenko 1979, Problems of Slovenian Literature 1980, Typology of Cankar's Prose 1983, Ivan Cankar: A Monograph Study 1987, Slovenian War Prose 1941–80 (with Marjan Dolgan) 1988, Studies on Slovenian Poetry 1993, Slowenische Literatur im europäischen Kontext 1993, Ivan Cankar: Ein slowenischer Schriftsteller des europäischen Symbolismus 1997, Horizons of Slovenian Literature 1999, Spektrum creativity 2004, Simon Jenko 2004, Slovenian Academy of Arts and Sciences: From 1992 to 2002 2005, Ivan Cankar 2006, Chronicle of My Life (I–II) 2012; Ed.-in-Chief Collected Works of Slovene Poets and Writers 1981–2010. *Address:* Zidovska 1, 1000 Ljubljana, Slovenia (home). *Telephone:* (1) 4706151 (office); (1) 4250365 (home). *Fax:* (1) 4253423 (office). *E-mail:* ana.batic@sazu.si (office).

BERNINI, Giorgio, LLM, SJD; Italian lawyer, politician and university lecturer; b. 9 Nov. 1928, Bologna; ed Univ. of Bologna, Univ. of Michigan Law School, USA; Prof., Univ. of Ferrara 1964–66, Univ. of Padua 1966–70; Pres. Int. Council for Commercial Arbitration 1986–94, Hon. Pres. and mem. Advisory Bd 1986–98; fmr Prof. in Commercial Law, Univ. of Bologna; fmr adviser to EC (now EU) and Italian Govt on questions of int. commercial law, customs tariffs and tech. transfer; mem. Camera dei deputati (Forza Italia) 1994–96; Minister for Foreign Trade 1994–95; Sr Pnr, Studio Bernini e Associati; Pres. Asscn for the Teaching and Study of Arbitration and Int. Trade Law; mem. Exec. Cttee Italian Arbitration Asscn; Cavalier, Grand'croix; Dean's Medal, New York Law School. *Publications:* articles in specialized journals and in daily newspapers.

BERNSTEIN, Carl, LLD; American journalist and author; b. 14 Feb. 1944, Washington, DC; s. of Alfred Bernstein and Sylvia Walker; m. 2nd Nora Ephron 1976 (divorced); two s.; m. 3rd Christine Bernstein; ed Univ. of Maryland and Boston Univ.; copyboy, reporter, Washington Star 1960–65; reporter, Elizabeth (NJ) Journal 1965–66, Washington Post 1966–77; Washington bureau chief, ABC 1979–81; corresp., ABC News, New York 1981–84; Corresp. and contrib. Time Magazine 1990–91; Visiting Prof., New York Univ. 1992–93; Exec. Vice-Pres. and Exec. Dir Voter.com –2001; contributing ed. Vanity Fair 1997–; frequent political commentator on network TV; fmr rock and music critic for Washington Post; Drew Pearson Prize for investigative reporting of Watergate 1972, George Polk Memorial Award and other awards for journalism. *Publications include:* All the President's Men (with Bob Woodward) (Pulitzer Prize 1977) 1974, The Final Days (with Bob Woodward) 1976, Loyalties: A Son's Memoir 1989, His Holiness: John Paul II and the Hidden History of Our Time (with Marco Politi) 1996, A Woman in Charge: the Life of Hillary Rodham Clinton 2007; numerous articles in The New Republic, Rolling Stone, The New York Times, Newsweek and Der Spiegel. *Address:* c/o Knopf Publishing/Author Mail, 1745 Broadway, New York, NY 10019, USA (office). *Website:* www.carlbernstein.com.

BERNSTEIN, Nils, MSc; Danish government official (retd) and fmr central banker; b. 4 Jan. 1943; m. Ulla Agenfeld 1964; ed Univ. of Copenhagen; Sec., Ministry of Finance 1970–75; First Sec., Financial Affairs, Embassy in Washington, DC 1975–77; Private Sec. to Minister of Finance 1978–79, Head, Dept of Budget, Ministry of Finance 1980–83, Perm. Sec., Dept of Man. 1984–86; Perm. Sec., Ministry of Agric. 1986–94, Ministry of Agric. and Fisheries 1994–96, Perm. Sec., Prime Minister's Office 1996–2005; Sec. of The Queen in Council 1996–2005; Gov. by Royal Appointment and Chair. Bd of Govs, Danmarks Nationalbank (central bank) 2005–13; mem. Gen. Council, European Central Bank 2005–; Chair.

Kongeriget Danmarks Fiskeribank (Danish Fisheries' Bank) 1995–96, Dansk-Færøsk Kulturfond (Danish-Faroese Cultural Foundation) and Dansk-Grønlandsk Kulturfond (Danish-Greenlandic Cultural Foundation) 1996–2005; mem. Bd of Dirs Landbrugslotteriet (lottery) 1988–2005, GiroBank A/S 1995–96, Den Kgl. Grønlandsfond (Royal Greenland Foundation) 1996–2005, North Atlantic House Foundation 2002–05, Dansk Ekspeditionsfond (Danish Expedition Foundation) 2004–05. *Address:* c/o Danmarks Nationalbank, Havnegade 5, 1093 Copenhagen K, Denmark.

BERNSTEIN, Robert Louis; American publisher and human rights activist; b. 5 Jan. 1923, New York; s. of Alfred Bernstein and Sylvia Bernstein; m. Helen Walter 1950; three s.; ed Harvard Univ.; served with US Army Air Force 1943–46; with Simon & Schuster (book publrs) 1946–57, Gen. Sales Man. 1950–57; Random House Inc. 1958–61, Vice-Pres. (Sales) 1961–63, First Vice-Pres. 1963–65, Pres. and CEO 1966–89, Chair. 1975–89; Publr at Large, Adviser John Wiley & Sons Inc. 1991–98; Vice-Chair. Asscn of American Publrs 1970–72, Chair. 1972–73; Chair. Asscn of American Publrs Cttee on Soviet-American Publishing Relations 1973–74, on Int. Freedom to Publish 1975; Chair. US Helsinki Watch Cttee, New York, 1979–92, Founding Chair. 1992; Chair. Fund for Free Expression 1975–90, Founding Chair. 1990; Founding Chair. Human Rights Watch 1975–98, now Emer. Bd Mem.; apptd Co-Chair. Human Rights in China 1999, now Chair. Emer.; Founder and Chair. Advancing Human Rights 2011–; fmr mem. Council on Foreign Relations, Nat. Advisory Cttee Amnesty Int.; mem. Americas Watch, Asia Watch, Middle East Watch, Africa Watch, Advisory Cttee Carter-Menil Human Rights Foundation, Advisory Bd Robert F. Kennedy Foundation Human Rights Award, Int. Liberal Education Bd Bard Coll.; Vice-Pres. Bd of Dirs Aaron Diamond Foundation, The Century Asscn; Hon. LLD (New School for Social Research) 1991, (Swarthmore Coll.) 1997; Hon. DHumLitt (Bard Coll.) 1998, (Hofstra) 1998, (Tougaloo Coll.) 2000, (Bates Coll.) 2000, (Yale) 2003; Human Rights Award (Lawyers' Cttee for Human Rights) 1987, Spirit of Liberty Award for the American Way 1989, Barnard Medal of Distinction, Barnard Coll. 1990, Liberty Award, Brandeis Univ. 1994, Eleanor Roosevelt Human Rights Award 1998, and other awards. *Publication:* Speaking Freely: My Life in Publishing and Human Rights 2016. *Leisure interests:* skiing, tennis, swimming. *Address:* Advancing Human Rights, 333 Seventh Avenue, 14th Floor, New York, NY 10001 (office); 277 Park Avenue, 49th Floor, New York, NY 10172-0003, USA (office). *E-mail:* info@advancinghumanrights.org (office). *Website:* www.advancinghumanrights.org (office).

BERNTSEN, Thorbjørn; Norwegian trade union official and politician; b. 13 April 1935, Aker municipality (now in Oslo); s. of Hans Bertrand Berntsen and Anna Mathilde Halvorsen; m. Adda Berntsen; ed Tech. Coll., Officers' Training School; with Nylands Shipyard 1951–66; Information Sec., Norwegian Union of Iron and Metalworkers, Leader 1965–66; Leader, Akers mek. Verksted AS 1962–64; Chair., later Deputy Chair. Oslo Municipal Consultative Cttee for Trade and Industry 1969–83; Deputy Chair. Labour Party 1989; Minister of the Environment 1990–97; mem. Cttee of Reps, Oslo Labour Party 1962 (Chair. 1976–82); mem. Storting (Parl.) 1977–97, mem. Standing Cttee on Local Govt and the Environment 1973–86 (Chair. 1989–90); Polar statuette, Tromsø 1999, Norwegian Air Award 2004, Bypatrioten Award, Oslo Byes Vel 2006. *Publications:* several books on politics, nature conservation and environmental issues; series of lectures and notes distributed at major confs and seminars.

BERRESFORD, Susan Vail; American foundation executive; b. 1943, New York, NY; ed The Brearley School, Vassar Coll., Radcliffe Coll.; Program Officer, Neighborhood Youth Corps 1965–67; Manpower Career Devt Agency 1967–68; Project Asst Div. of Nat. Affairs, Ford Foundation 1970–72, Program Officer 1972–80, Officer in charge of Women's Programs 1980–81, Vice-Pres. US and Int. Affairs Programs 1981, Vice-Pres. Program Div. in charge of Worldwide Programming, then Exec. Vice-Pres. and COO, Pres. and mem. Bd of Trustees 1996–2007; Visiting Philanthropist, New York Community Trust 2008–; fmr mem. Bd of Dirs Council on Foundations, Chase Manhattan Bank, Chase Manhattan Corpn, Hermine and Robert Popper Foundation; mem. American Acad. Arts and Sciences, Council on Foreign Relations, N American Cttee Trilateral Comm.; Leadership for Equity and Diversity (LEAD) Award 1997, Work Life Legacy Award 2005. *Address:* New York Community Trust, 909 Third Avenue, 22nd Floor, New York, NY 10022, USA (office). *Telephone:* (212) 686-0010 (office). *Website:* www.nycommunitytrust.org (office).

BERRI, Nabih, BA, LLM; Lebanese lawyer and politician; *President, Majlis al-Nuab;* b. 28 Jan. 1938, Freetown, Sierra Leone; s. of Mustaha Berri; m. 1st; six c.; m. 2nd; ed Ecole de la Sagesse, Beirut, Lebanese Univ., Faculté de Droit, Sorbonne, Paris, France; Pres. Nat. Fed. of Lebanese Students (UNUL), Sorbonne, Paris 1963; lawyer, Court of Appeals, Beirut 1963; joined resistance movt of Imam Moussa Al-Sadr against Israeli occupation of S Lebanon 1975; Head of Amal Movt (militia) 1984–; Minister of Justice 1984–88; Minister of Hydraulic & Electric Resources and of Housing & Cooperatives 1989–90; Minister of State May–Oct. 1992; Pres. Majlis al-Nuab (Nat. Ass.) 1992–. *Address:* Majlis al-Nuab, Place de l'Etoile, Beirut, Lebanon (office). *Telephone:* (1) 982047 (office). *Fax:* (1) 982059 (office). *E-mail:* nberri@lp.gov.lb (office). *Website:* www.lp.gov.lb (office).

BERRIDGE, Baroness (Life Peer), cr. 2011, of the Vale of Catmose in the County of Rutland; **Elizabeth Berridge,** MA (Cantab.); British barrister; b. Oakham, Rutland; ed Vale of Catmose Coll., Oakham Rutland Sixth Form Coll., Emmanuel Coll., Cambridge, Inns of Court, School of Law, London; fmr personal injury barrister in King's Chambers, Manchester; Parl. cand. for Stockport in Gen. Election 2005; mem. House of Lords 2011–, mem. Jt Cttee on Human Rights 2011–, Chair. All Party Parliamentary Group on International Religious Freedom 2012–; mem. Advisory Council, Foundation for Relief and Reconciliation in the Middle East (charity); Dir and Trustee, Kainos (prisons charity), More than Gold (charity), British Future (think-tank); Dir, Conservative Christian Fellowship (allied with British Conservative Party) 2005–11, Patron 2011–; Hon. LLB. *Leisure interests:* swimming, Ghana, Church. *Address:* House of Lords, Westminster, London, SW1A 0PW, England (office). *Telephone:* (20) 7219-8943 (office). *Fax:* (20) 7219-5979 (office). *E-mail:* walls@parliament.uk (office). *Website:* www.baronessberridge.com.

BERRIDGE, Sir Michael (John), Kt, PhD, FRS; British biologist and academic; *Emeritus Fellow, Babraham Institute;* b. 22 Oct. 1938, Gatooma, Rhodesia (now Zimbabwe); s. of George Kirton Berridge and Stella Elaine Hards; m. Susan Graham Winter 1965; one s. one d.; ed Univ. Coll. of Rhodesia and Nyasaland, Univ. of Cambridge, UK; Post-doctoral Fellow, Univ. of Virginia, USA 1965–66; Postdoctoral Fellow, Case Western Reserve Univ., USA 1966–67, Research Assoc. 1967–69; Sr Scientific Officer, Unit of Invertebrate Chem. and Physiology, Univ. of Cambridge 1969–72, Prin. Scientific Officer 1972–78, Sr Prin. Scientific Officer, Unit of Insect Neurophysiology and Pharmacology 1978–90, Hon. Prof. of Cell Signalling 1994–, Fellow, Trinity Coll. 1972–; Deputy Chief Scientific Officer, Lab. of Molecular Signalling, Babraham Inst., Cambridge 1990–94, Head of Signalling Programme 1996–2003, Emer. Fellow 2003–; mem. numerous editorial bds, including Biochemical Journal 1987–, Journal of Endocrinology 1989–, Molecular Biology of the Cell 1989–, Advances in Second Messenger and Phosphoprotein Research 1990–, Journal of Basic and Clinical Physiology and Pharmacology 1990–, Journal of Experimental Biology 1993–; Advisory Ed. BioEssays 1994–; mem. Scientific Advisory Bd Venetian Inst. for Molecular Medicine 2013–; Gov. Strangeways Research Lab. 1987–98; Trustee, Isaac Newton Trust 1991–2000; Foreign Corresp., Acad. Royale de Médecine de Belgique 1994–; mem. Soc. of Gen. Physiologists, Academia Europaea 1989, European Molecular Biology Org. 1991, Acad. of Medical Sciences 1998, NAS 1999, American Philosophical Soc. 2007; Hon. mem. American Physiological Soc. 1992, Biochemical Soc. 2004, European Calcium Soc. 2006, Japanese Biochemical Soc.; Hon. Life mem. Soc. for Experimental Biology 1995; Foreign Hon. mem. American Acad. of Arts and Science 1999; Hon. Fellow, Gonville and Caius Coll. Cambridge 1998, Inst. of Biology 2000; Dr hc (Limburgs Universitaire Centrum, Belgium) 1993, (Univ. of Liverpool) 2007; numerous prizes, awards and medals including Feldberg Prize 1984, King Faisal Int. Prize in Science 1986, Louis Jeantet Prize in Medicine 1986, William Bate Hardy Prize, Cambridge Philosophical Soc. 1987, Gairdner Foundation Int. Award 1988, Baly Medal, Royal Coll. of Physicians 1989, Albert Lasker Basic Medical Research Award 1989, Dale Medal, Soc. for Endocrinology 1990, Royal Medal, Royal Soc. 1991, Dr H. P. Heineken Prize for Biochemistry and Biophysics 1994, Wolf Foundation Prize in Medicine, (Israel, jtly) 1995, Massry Prize 1996, Ernst Schering Prize 1999, Shaw Prize in Life Science and Medicine 2005. *Publications:* more than 100 scientific papers. *Leisure interests:* gardening, golf. *Address:* The Babraham Institute, Babraham Research Campus, Cambridge, CB22 3AT, England (office). *Telephone:* (1223) 496621 (office). *E-mail:* michael.berridge@babraham.ac.uk (office). *Website:* www.babraham.ac.uk (home).

BERROU, Claude, MEng; French electrical engineer and academic; *Professor, Electronics Department, Télécom Bretagne;* b. 23 Sept. 1951, Penmarc'h; two c.; ed Institut Nat. Polytechnique de Grenoble; joined École Nationale Supérieure des Télécommunications de Bretagne (now Télécom Bretagne) 1978, currently Prof., Electronics Dept; mem. Acad. des sciences 2007; Fellow, IEEE 2008; Chevalier, Légion d'honneur; Officier des Palmes académiques; SEE Médaille Ampère 1997, IEEE (Information Theory) Golden Jubilee Award for Technological Innovation 1998, IEEE Richard W. Hamming Medal 2003, Grand Prix France Télécom de l'Acad. des sciences 2005, Marconi Prize, Marconi Foundation 2005. *Achievements include:* inventor in 1991 of groundbreaking quasi-optimal error-correcting coding scheme called Turbo codes (French patent EP 0511141 B1) and co-author of the publ. on Turbo codes 1993 (with Alain Glavieux and Punya Thitimajshima). *Publications include:* Codage de canal: des bases théoriques aux turbocodes (Channel encoding: from theoretical grounds to turbocodes; co-author) 2005, Codes et turbocodes (Codes and turbocodes; co-author) 2007; several book chapters and more than 100 scientific papers in professional journals on algorithm/silicon interaction, electronics and digital communications at large, error correction codes, turbo codes and iterative processing, soft-in/soft-out (probabilistic) decoders, informational neuroscience; author or co-author of 12 registered patents. *Address:* Télécom Bretagne, CS 83818, 29238 Brest Cedex 3, France (office). *Telephone:* (2) 29-00-13-06 (office). *Fax:* (2) 29-00-11-84 (office). *E-mail:* claude.berrou@telecom-bretagne.eu (office). *Website:* www.telecom-bretagne.eu (office); perso.enst-bretagne.fr/claudeberrou (office).

BERRUGA FILLOY, Enrique, BA, MA; Mexican diplomatist, business executive and writer; *Vice-President of Corporate Affairs and Communication, Grupo Modelo;* ed El Colegio de México, Johns Hopkins Univ., USA, Instituto Tecnológico Autónomo de México; began career in Foreign Service 1984, Press Attaché, Embassy in Washington, DC 1986–89, Sec., Political Affairs, Embassy in London 1989–90, Chargé d'affaires ad hoc, Embassy in Dublin 1991, Sec. Gen., Mexican Comm. UNESCO 1993, Chief of Staff to Minister of Foreign Affairs 1993–97; Dir-Gen. Int. Affairs Div., Ministry of Educ. 1994; Personal Rep. of Pres. of Mexico for Reform of UN 1995–97; Amb. to Costa Rica 1997–99; Exec. Dir Mexican Inst. Int. Cooperation 1999–2000; Undersecretary of Foreign Affairs 2000–03; Perm. Rep. to UN, New York 2003–07; Vice-Pres. of Corp. Affairs and Communication, Grupo Modelo 2007–; Prof. Instituto Tecnológico Autónomo de México; columnist, El Universal (daily newspaper). *Publications include:* novels: Destino los Pinos 1982, El Martes del Silencio 1995, Propiedad Ajena 2000 (translated as Foreign Property 2003); numerous articles and papers. *Address:* Grupo Modelo, Campos Elíseos #400, 8th Floor, Colonia Lomas de Chapultepec 11000 México DF, Mexico (office). *Telephone:* (55) 5283-3600 (office). *Fax:* (55) 5280-6718 (office). *Website:* www.gmodelo.com.mx (office).

BERRUIEN, Nuri A., BA, PhD; Libyan oil industry executive; b. 1946; ed Texas A&M Univ., USA; Gen. Man. of Production, Eng and Operation, Arabian Gulf Oil Co. (Agoco), Benghazi 1983–90, also mem. Bd 1983–90; Sr Eng Adviser and mem. Bd, Teknica Ltd, London, UK 1990–93; Chair. state-owned Nat. Oil Corpn, Tripoli 2011–14. *Address:* c/o National Oil Corporation, Assekka Road, Tripoli, Libya.

BERRUTI, Azucena; Uruguayan lawyer, human rights advocate and politician; b. 1929; Sec.-Gen. City Admin of Montevideo 1980s; mem. Partido del Sol (PS); Minister of Nat. Defence 2005–08; Dir SODRE (Servicio Oficial de Radio, TV y Espectaculos) 2009.

BERRY, Brian Joe Lobley, BSc, MA, PhD, FRGS, FBA, FAICP; American/British geographer, academic, political economist and policy analyst; *Lloyd Viel Berkner Regental Professor and Professor of Political Economy, University of Texas at Dallas;* b. 16 Feb. 1934, Sedgley, Staffs., England; s. of Joe Berry and Gwendoline Alice Berry (née Lobley); m. Janet E. Shapley 1958; one s. two d.; ed

Univ. Coll., London and Univ. of Washington; Asst Prof., then Prof., Univ. of Chicago 1958–76; Faculty mem. Brookings Inst. 1966–76; Prof., Harvard Univ. 1976–81; Prof. and Dean, School of Urban and Public Affairs, Carnegie Mellon Univ. 1981–86; Prof., Univ. of Tex. at Dallas 1986–, Lloyd Viel Berkner Regental Prof. and Prof. of Political Economy 1991–, Dean of the School of Econ., Political and Policy Sciences 2005–10; mem. NAS (mem. Council 1999–2002), Asscn of American Geographers (Pres. 1978–79), American Inst. of Certified Planners, Regional Science Asscn Int.; Founding mem. Acad. of Medicine, Eng and Science of Texas; Fellow, American Inst. of Certified Planners, NAS, Univ. Coll. London 1983, American Acad. of Arts and Sciences, AAAS, Texas Acad. of Medicine, Eng and Science, Weimar School of Land Econs, Inst. of British Geographers; Hon. AM (Harvard) 1976; Anderson Medal, Asscn of American Geographers 1987, Victoria Medal, Royal Geographical Soc. 1988, Rockefeller Prize 1991, Lauréat, Prix Int. de Géographie Vautrin Lud 2005, and others. *Publications include:* several books and more than 500 articles and other professional publs. *Leisure interests:* family history, genealogy, travel, pseudonymous novelist. *Address:* School of Economic, Political and Policy Sciences, 800 W Campbell Road, GR31, University of Texas-Dallas, PO Box 83-0688, Richardson, TX 75080 (office); 2404 Forest Court, McKinney, TX 75070, USA (home). *Telephone:* (972) 569-7173 (office); (972) 562-1058 (home). *Fax:* (972) 883-6297 (office); (972) 562-1058 (home). *E-mail:* brian.berry@utdallas.edu (office). *Website:* brianjlberry.com (office).

BERRY, Halle; American actress and model; b. 14 Aug. 1966, Cleveland, Ohio; d. of Jerome Berry and Judith Berry (née Hawkins); m. 1st David Justice 1993 (divorced 1996); m. 2nd Eric Benet 2001 (divorced 2005); partner Gabriel Aubry 2005–10; m. 3rd Olivier Martinez 2013; one s. one d.; ed Cuyahoga Community Coll.; began competing in formal beauty contests 1980s, won title Miss Ohio 1986; mem. Nat. Breast Cancer Coalition; Harvard Foundation for Intercultural and Race Relations Award. *Films include:* Strictly Business 1991, Jungle Fever 1991, The Last Boy Scout 1991, Boomerang 1992, Father Hood 1993, Alex Haley's Queen 1993, The Program 1993, The Flintstones 1994, Losing Isaiah 1995, The Rich Man's Wife 1996, Executive Decision 1996, Race the Sun 1996, Girl 6 1996, B.A.P.S. 1997, Why Do Fools Fall in Love 1998, The Wedding 1998, Bulworth 1998, Victims of Fashion 1999, Ringside 1999, Introducing Dorothy Dandridge (also producer) (Golden Globe for Best Actress, Screen Actors' Guild Award) 1999, X-Men 2000, Swordfish 2001, Monster's Ball (Acad. Award for Best Actress 2002) 2001, James Bond: Die Another Day (Nat. Asscn for the Advancement of Colored People–NAACP Award for Best Supporting Actress 2003) 2002, X-Men 2 2003, Gothika 2003, Catwoman 2004 (BET Award for Best Actress 2004), Robots (voice) 2005, X-Men: The Last Stand 2006 (People's Choice Award for Favorite Female Action Hero 2007), Perfect Stranger 2007, Things We Lost in the Fire 2007, Frankie and Alice 2010 (Nat. Asscn for the Advancement of Colored People–NAACP Award for Outstanding Actress in Motion Picture 2011), Dark Tide 2011, New Year's Eve 2011, Cloud Atlas 2012, The Call 2013 (Teen Choice Award for Movie Actress: Drama 2013). *Television:* TV debut with sitcom Living Dolls 1989, Knots Landing 1991–92, Their Eyes Were Watching God 2005. *Address:* c/o Vincent Cirrincione Associates, 8721 Sunset Blvd, Suite 205, Los Angeles, CA 90069 (office); c/o ICM, 8942 Wilshire Blvd, Beverly Hills, CA 90211, USA (office). *E-mail:* info@vincentcirrincione.com (office).

BERRY, John; American government official and diplomatist; b. Maryland; m. Curtis Yee 2013; ed Univ. of Maryland, Maxwell School of Public Admin, Syracuse Univ.; began govt career as man. intern in Montgomery Co., Md 1982, served as legis. aide in Maryland Gen. Ass.; Legis. Dir for US Rep. Steny Hoyer (Democrat-Md) 1985–94; Deputy Asst Sec. and Acting Asst Sec. for Law Enforcement, US Treasury Dept 1994–95; Dir Govt Relations and Sr Policy Advisor, Smithsonian Inst. 1995–97; Asst Sec. for Policy, Man. and Budget (Chief Financial Officer and COO), Dept of the Interior 1997–2000; Dir Nat. Fish and Wildlife Foundation 2000–05; Dir Nat. Zoo 2005–09; Dir US Office of Personnel Man. 2009–13; Amb. to Australia 2013–16.

BERRY, L(eonard) Michael, BA; Canadian fmr diplomatist; b. 28 Sept. 1937, Bolton, Greater Manchester, UK; s. of Leonard Berry and Margaret Berry (née Wynne); m. 1st Linda Kathleen Randal 1963 (deceased); one s. two d.; m. 2nd Anna Sumanti Gill 2002; ed McGill Univ.; joined Dept of External Affairs 1964, served in Berlin 1966–68 and London 1971–75, High Commr to Singapore 1979–82, Amb. to OECD 1988–91, High Commr to Australia 1991–95, Canadian Special Co-ordinator for the Reconstruction of Fmr Yugoslavia 1995–97, Diplomat-in-Residence, Vancouver Island Univ., BC 1997–99; Int. Adviser, Berry Assocs 1999–; mem. Bd of Dirs, British Columbia Centre for Int. Educ. 2001–03, Port of Nanaimo Authority 2002–05, Pacific Pilotage Authority 2005–13. *Leisure interests:* skiing, golf, cricket, music, investment. *E-mail:* lmichaelberry@hotmail.com (office).

BERRY, Mary Frances, PhD; American lawyer, historian and academic; *Geraldine R. Segal Professor of American Social Thought and Professor of History, University of Pennsylvania;* b. 17 Feb. 1938, Nashville, Tenn.; d. of George Ford and Frances Southall; ed Howard Univ., Univ. of Michigan; Asst Prof. of History, Cen. Mich. Univ. 1966–68; Asst Prof. Eastern Mich. Univ. 1968–69, Assoc. Prof. 1969–70; Acting Dir Afro-American Studies, Univ. of Md 1970–72, Dir 1972–74, Acting Chair. Div. of Behavioural and Social Sciences 1973–74, Provost 1973–76; Prof. of Law, Univ. of Colo 1976–80, Chancellor 1976–77; Asst Sec. for Educ. US Dept of Health, Educ. and Welfare 1977–80; Prof. of History and Law, Howard Univ., Washington 1980–; Geraldine R. Segal Prof. of American Social Thought and Prof. of History, Univ. of Pa 1987–; Vice-Chair. US Comm. on Civil Rights 1980–82, Chair. 1982–2004; mem. Advisory Bd Feminist Press 1980–, Inst. for Higher Educ. Law and Governance, Univ. of Houston; Fellow, Soc. of American Historians, Nat. Acad. of Public Admin; mem. Council UN Univ. 1986–; numerous awards and hon. degrees. *Publications:* Black Resistance/White Law 1971, Military Necessity and Civil Rights Policy 1977, Stability, Security and Continuity, Mr Justice Burton and Decision-Making in the Supreme Court 1945–58 1978, Long Memory: The Black Experience in America 1982 (jtly), The Pig Farmer's Daughter and Other Tales of American Justice: Episodes of Racism and Sexism in the Courts from 1865 to the Present 1999, And Justice for All: The United States Commission on Civil Rights and the Continuing Struggle for Freedom in America 2009, Power in Words: The Stories Behind Barack Obama's Speeches, from the State House to the White House (with Josh Gottheimer) 2010. *Address:* Department of History, University of Pennsylvania, 208 College Hall, Philadelphia, PA 19104-6379, USA (office). *Telephone:* (215) 898-9587 (office). *E-mail:* mfberry@sas.upenn.edu (office); mfb@maryfrancesberry.com. *Website:* www.maryfrancesberry.com.

BERRY, Sir Michael Victor, Kt, BSc, PhD, FRS, FRSA, FRSE; British physicist and academic; *Melville Wills Professor Emeritus of Physics, University of Bristol;* b. 14 March 1941, Surrey, England; ed Univs of Exeter and St Andrews; Dept of Scientific and Industrial Research Fellow, Dept of Physics, Univ. of Bristol 1965–67, Lecturer 1967–74, Reader in Physics 1974–79, Prof. of Physics 1979–88, Royal Soc. Research Prof. 1988–, Melville Wills Prof. of Physics, now Prof. Emer.; visiting lecturer at numerous int. univs; mem. Council, BAAS 2002–; mem. Bd of Govs, Weizmann Inst., Israel 2000–; Ed. Proceedings of the Royal Society 2006–; mem. Editorial Bd of several journals, including Journal of Physics A 1994–; mem. Royal Soc. of Sciences, Uppsala 1986, European Acad. 1989, Indian Acad. of Sciences 1990, London Mathematical Soc. 1995; Foreign mem. NAS 1995, Royal Netherlands Acad. of Arts and Sciences 2000; Fellow, Royal Inst. 1983; Hon. Prof., Wuhan Univ. 1994; Hon. FInstP 1999; Hon. DSc (Trinity Coll. Dublin) 1996, (Open Univ.) 1997, (St Andrews) 1998, (Warwick) 1998, (Univ. of Ulm) 2001, (Weizmann Inst.) 2003, (Glasgow) 2007, (Russian-Armenian (Slavonic) Univ., Yerevan) 2012; Maxwell Medal, Inst. of Physics 1978, Julius Edgar Lilienfeld Prize, American Physical Soc. 1990, Paul Dirac Medal, Inst. of Physics 1990, Royal Medal, Royal Soc. 1990, Naylor Prize, London Math. Soc. 1993, 'Science for Art' Prize, Louis-Vuitton Moët-Hennessey 1994, Hewlett-Packard Europhysics Prize 1995, Dirac Medal, Int. Centre for Theoretical Physics, Trieste 1996, Kapitsa Medal, Russian Acad. of Sciences 1997, Wolf Prize in Physics 1998, Ig Nobel Prize in Physics 2000, Onsager Medal, Norwegian Tech. Univ., Trondheim 2001, Novartis/Daily Telegraph Visions of Science Prize 2002, Polya Prize, London Math. Soc. 2005, Chancellor's Medal, Univ. of Bristol 2005, Lorentz Medal, Royal Netherlands Acad. of Arts and Sciences 2014. *Publications:* Diffraction of Light by Ultrasound 1966, Principles of Cosmology and Gravitation 1976; more than 400 research papers. *Address:* H.H. Wills Physics Laboratory, Royal Fort, Tyndall Avenue, Bristol BS8 1TL, England (office). *Telephone:* (117) 928-8778 (office). *Fax:* (117) 925-5624 (office). *E-mail:* asymptotico@bristol.ac.uk (office). *Website:* michaelberryphysics.wordpress.com (office).

BERRY, Richard Stephen, AM, PhD, FAAS, FRSC; American chemist and academic; *James Franck Distinguished Service Professor Emeritus of Chemistry, University of Chicago;* b. 9 April 1931, Denver, Colo; s. of Morris Berry and Ethel (Alpert) Berry; m. Carla Lamport Friedman 1955; one s. two d.; ed Harvard Univ.; Instructor, Univ. of Mich. 1957–60; Asst Prof. Yale Univ. 1960–64; Assoc. Prof. Univ. of Chicago 1964–67, Prof. Dept of Chem., James Franck Inst. 1967–89, James Franck Distinguished Service Prof. 1989–, now Prof. Emer.; Gaest Prof. Univ. of Copenhagen 1967, 1979; consultant, Los Alamos Science Lab. 1973–2003, Argonne Nat. Lab. 1976–2006; Visiting Prof., Univ. de Paris-Sud 1979–80; Hinshelwood Lecturer, Oxford 1980; Chair., Numerical Data Advisory Bd, National Research Council 1978–84; Newton Abraham Prof., Oxford Univ., England 1986–87; mem. Visiting Comm. of Applied Physics, Harvard Univ. 1977–81; mem. NAS (Home Sec. 1999–2003); mem. numerous cttees and orgs; Foreign mem. Royal Danish Acad. of Sciences; Fellow, American Acad. of Arts and Sciences (Vice-Pres. 1995–98), American Philosophical Soc. 2011; Dr hc (Romanian Medical Soc.) 2009; MacArthur Prize Fellow 1983, Alexander von Humboldt Preistraeger 1993, J. Heyrosky Medal 1997, inducted into East High School Alumni Heritage Hall, Denver, Colo 2010. *Publications:* (with L. Gaines and T. V. Long II) TOSCA: The Social Costs of Coal and Nuclear Power 1979, (with S. A. Rice and J. Ross) Physical Chemistry 1980, Understanding Energy: Energy, Entropy and Thermodynamics for Everyman 1991, (with others) Optimization Methods in Finite Time Thermodynamics 1999, Phase Changes in Simple Systems (with B. M. Smirnov) 2008; approx. 540 scientific papers in specialist journals. *Leisure interests:* music, skiing, hiking and climbing, photography, fly-fishing. *Address:* Department of Chemistry, GCIS E 129, University of Chicago, 57th Street, Chicago, IL 60637 (office); 5317 South University Avenue, Chicago, IL 60615, USA (home). *Telephone:* (773) 702-7021 (office). *Fax:* (773) 702-0805 (office). *E-mail:* berry@uchicago.edu (office). *Website:* berrygroup.uchicago.edu (office); chemistry.uchicago.edu/faculty/faculty/person/member/r-stephen-berry.html (office).

BERSANI, Pier Luigi; Italian politician; *President, Articolo Uno—Movimento Democratico e Progressista;* b. 29 Sept. 1951, Bettola, Emilia-Romagna; s. of Giuseppe Bersani; m. Daniela Ferrari; two d.; ed Univ. of Bologna; began career as teacher; Pres. of Emilia-Romagna Region 1994–96; Minister of Industry, Commerce and Craftsmanship 1996–99, of Transport and Navigation 1999–2001, of Econ. Devt 2006–08; mem. Chamber of Deputies (Camera dei Deputati) for Emilia-Romagna 2001–04, 2006–; mem. European Parl. (Socialist Group) 2004–06; mem. Partito Democratico 2007–17, Nat. Sec. 2009–13; Pres. Articolo Uno—Movimento Democratico e Progressista 2017–; Chair. Nuova Romea Soc. 2002–07; Légion d'honneur. *Publication:* Per una buona ragione 2011. *Address:* Articolo Uno, Via Zanardelli 34, 00186 Rome, Italy (office). *E-mail:* info@articolo1mdp.it.

BERSELLINI, Anita, PhD; French physicist, academic and university administrator; *Full Professor, Exceptional Class, Université Paris-Sud XI;* b. 10 Jan. 1943, Nice; d. of Sosthène Bersellini and Anna Migliore; m. Henri Marchal; one d.; ed Université Paris-Sud XI; researcher, Laboratoire d'Infrarouge, Université Paris-Sud XI 1965–76, Lecturer 1966–76, Asst Prof. 1976–87, Full Prof. 2nd Class 1987–91, Head, NFI Optronics Eng Degree 1991–2000, Full Prof. 1st Class 1992–99, Full Prof., Exceptional Class 1999–, Vice-Pres. 1998–2004, Pres. 2004–09; Researcher, Laboratoire de Photophysique Moléculaire, CNRS 1977–2008; Sec. of State responsible for the Paris region 2009–10; Chevalier, Légion d'honneur 2008. *Publications include:* over 55 journal contribs. *Leisure interests:* African art, modern art, music. *Address:* Université Paris Sud XI, Campus d'Orsay, Bât. 300, 91405 Orsay, France (office). *Telephone:* 6-07060762 (mobile); 6-46014753 (mobile). *E-mail:* anita.bersellini@u-psud.fr (office). *Website:* www.u-psud.fr (office).

BERSET, Alain, Dr.oec; Swiss politician; *Head, Federal Department of Home Affairs;* b. 9 April 1972, Fribourg; m. Muriel Zeender; three c.; ed Univ. of Neuchâtel; Asst Lecturer and Researcher, Research Inst. for Regional Econ. Devt, Univ. of Neuchâtel 1996–2000; Visiting Researcher, Inst. for Econ. Research, Hamburg 2000–01; Strategic Adviser, Canton of Neuchâtel Dept of Econ. Affairs

2001–04; pvt. practice as strategy and communications consultant 2006–11; mem. Ständerat/Conseil des Etats (Council of States) for Fribourg 2003–11, Pres. 2008–09, Vice-Pres. Socialist Group 2005–11, mem. Finance Cttee, Econ. Affairs and Taxation Cttee, Law Cttee; mem. Fed. Council 2012–, Head, Fed. Dept of Home Affairs (Health, Social and Retirement Insurances, Educ., Research and Culture Affairs) 2012–, Vice-Pres. Fed. Council Jan.–Dec. 2017, Pres. Jan.–Dec. 2018; Pres. Les Buissonnets (foundation for children and adults with disabilities), Fribourg 2004–11, Swiss Asscn for the Promotion of AOC/IGP, Bern 2005–11, Swiss Tenants' Asscn– Western Switzerland Section, Lausanne 2005–11. *Publications:* several books and some 30 articles on econ. devt, migration and regional devt. *Address:* Federal Department of Home Affairs, Inselgasse 1, 3003 Bern, Switzerland (office). *Telephone:* (31) 584628041 (office). *Fax:* (31) 58462790 (office). *E-mail:* info@gs-edi.admin.ch (office). *Website:* www.edi.admin.ch (office).

BERTARELLI, Ernesto, BA, MBA; Swiss entrepreneur; b. 22 Sept. 1965, Rome, Italy; m. Kirsty Roper; three c.; ed Babson Coll., Boston, Harvard Business School, USA; began career with Serono SA (family-owned biotechnology co.) 1985, several positions in Sales and Marketing 1985–90, Deputy CEO 1990–95, Vice-Chair. Bd of Dirs 1991–2006, CEO and Chair. Exec. Cttee 1996–2006 (Serono acquired by Merck 2006); Chair. Waypoint Group; f. Ares Life Sciences (investment co.) 2008, Northill Capital 2010; mem. Bd of Dirs UBS 2002–09; mem. Strategic Advisory Bd, École Polytéchnique Fédérale de Lausanne (EPFL); Pres. Fondation Bertarelli; collaborating with Univ. of Geneva and EPFL to create Campus Biotech SA biotech centre, Geneva 2012–; f. Team Alinghi (yachting syndicate) 2000; Légion d'Honneur, Cavaliere di Gran Croce; Hon. Dr of Marine Science (Plymouth Univ.) 2013; five times winner Bol d'Or (Lake Geneva) 1997, 2000, 2001, 2002, 2003, winner 12-Metre and Farr 40 Championships 2001, winner America's Cup with Alinghi 2003, 2007; Paolo Venanzangeli Sailing Award 2008. *Leisure interest:* yachting. *E-mail:* enquiries@waypointcapital.net. *Website:* www.waypointcapital .net; www.bertarelli.com/en.

BERTELLO, HE Cardinal Giuseppe, DCL; Italian ecclesiastic and diplomatist; *President, Governorate of Vatican City State;* b. 1 Oct. 1942, Foglizzo; ed Pontifical Ecclesiastical Acad., Rome; ordained priest 1966; entered diplomatic service of the Holy See 1971, served in Apostolic Nunciatures of Sudan, Turkey and Venezuela; apptd Titular Archbishop of Urbs Salvia 1987; Apostolic Pro-Nuncio to Benin (also accred to Ghana and Togo) 1987–91; Apostolic Nuncio to Rwanda 1991–95, to Perm. Mission of the Holy See at UN Office, Geneva 1995–97, Perm. Observer of Holy See to UN Office, Geneva and to WTO 1997–2000, Apostolic Nuncio to Mexico 2000–07, to Italy (also accred to San Marino) 2007–11; Pres. Governorate of Vatican City State 2011–; Pres. Pontifical Comm. for Vatican City State 2011–; cr. Cardinal (Cardinal-Deacon of Santi Vito, Modesto e Crescenzia) 2012; participated in Papal Conclave 2013. *Address:* Governorate of Vatican City State, Palazzo Apostolico Vaticano, 00120 Città del Vaticano, Rome, Italy (office). *E-mail:* info@ vatican.va (office). *Website:* www.vatican.va/vatican_city_state (office).

BERTHELOT, Yves M.; French statistician, economist and international organization official; *President, World Organisation Against Torture;* b. 15 Sept. 1937, Paris; m. Dosithée Yeatman 1961; three s. one d.; ed Ecole Polytechnique and Ecole Nationale de la Statistique et de l'Admin Economique; Dir of Studies in the Ministry of Planning, Côte d'Ivoire 1965–68; Chief of the Study of Enterprises Div., then Chief of Service of Programmes of Institut Nat. de la Statistique et des Etudes Economiques 1971–75; Chief, Service des Etudes et Questions Int., Ministry of Co-operation 1976–78; Dir of Research, Devt Centre of OECD, Paris 1978–81; Dir CEPII (Prospective Studies and Int. Information Centre) 1981–85; Deputy Sec.-Gen. of UNCTAD 1985–93; Exec. Sec. UN Econ. Comm. for Europe 1993–2000; Vice-Pres. Fondation Européenne pour le Développement durable des Régions 1996–; Pres. Comité Français de Solidarité Internationale 2002–, Développement et Civilisations—Lebret-Irfed 2005, World Org. Against Torture; Officier, Ordre nat. du Mérite, Ordre Nat. (Côte d'Ivoire), Chevalier, Légion d'honneur. *Publications:* numerous articles on economics. *Leisure interests:* sailing, skiing. *Address:* World Organisation Against Torture, PO Box 21, 8 rue du Vieux-Billard, Geneva 8, Switzerland (office); Développement et Civilisations—Lebret-Irfed, 49 rue de la Glaciére, 75013 Paris (office); 3 rue Auguste Comte, 75006 Paris, France (home); Comité Français de Solidarité Internationale, 32 rue Le Peletier, 75009 Paris (office). *E-mail:* berthelotyd@wanadoo.fr (home). *Website:* www.lebret-irfed.org (office).

BERTHOIN, Georges Paul, LenD, LèsL; French civil servant; b. 17 May 1925, Nérac; s. of Jean Berthoin and Germaine Mourgnot; m. 1st Anne W. Whittlesey (deceased); m. 2nd Pamela Jenkins 1965 (deceased); two s. four d.; ed Univ. of Grenoble, Ecole des Sciences Politiques, Univ. of Paris, Harvard Univ., USA and McGill Univ., Canada; Pvt. Sec. to Minister of Finance 1948–50; Head of Staff, Prefecture of Alsace-Lorraine-Champagne 1950–52; Prin. Pvt. Sec. M. Jean Monnet, Pres. of ECSC 1952–55; Counsellor for Information, ECSC 1955–56; Deputy Chief Rep. of ECSC in UK 1956; Acting Chief Rep. of Comm. of EEC 1967–68, Deputy Chief Rep. 1968–71, Chief Rep. 1971–73; Exec. mem. Trilateral Comm. 1973–75, European Chair. 1975–92, Hon. Chair. 1993–; Int. Chair of European Movement 1978–81; Dir Int. Peace Acad., New York; Bd mem. Aspen-Berlin Inst.; mem. Int. Advisory Bd Johns Hopkins Univ., Bologna, Nine Wise Men Group on Africa; Aspen Inst. Distinguished Fellow; Hon. Chair. Jean Monnet Asscn; Officier, Légion d'honneur 2006, Médaille Militaire, Croix de Guerre, Médaille de la Résistance. *Leisure interests:* art, theatre, walking, collecting objects. *Address:* 67 avenue Niel, 75017 Paris, France (home).

BERTI, Gian Nicola; San Marino lawyer, politician and fmr sportsman; b. 9 Aug. 1960; s. of Gian Luigi Berti (fmr Captain Regent) and María Luisa Berti; m.; two c.; ed Univ. degli Studi, Urbino; practise as lawyer 1988–; mem. Consiglio Grande e Generale (parl.) 2008–; Co-Capt.-Regent (jt head of state) April–Oct. 2016; positions within Exec. Council of Order of Lawyers and Notaries of Repub. of San Marino, Sammarinese Shooting Fed. and San Marino Fed. of Hunting; fmr Pres. Equestrian Fed. of San Marino; Pres. Comm. of Appeal, San Marino Football Fed.; fmr Vice-Pres. Murata Sports Club; mem. Noi Sammarinesi (We Sammarinese). *Achievements include:* fmr mem. San Marino nat. shooting team (Gold Medals at Games of Small States of Europe 1985, 1987, Silver Medal at Mediterranean Games 1987, represented San Marino at Seoul Olympics 1988. *Address:* Noi Sammarinesi, Via XXVIII Luglio 160, 47893 Borgo Maggiore, San Marino (office). *Telephone:* 0549 907101 (office). *E-mail:* info@noisammarinesi.com (office). *Website:* www.noisammarinesi.com (office).

BERTINI, Hon. Catherine Ann, BA; American government official, UN official and academic; *Professor of Practice, Public Administration and International Affairs, Maxwell School of Citizenship and Public Affairs, Syracuse University;* b. 30 March 1950, Syracuse, New York; d. of Fulvio Bertini and Ann Vino Bertini; ed Cortland High School, NY, State Univ. of New York at Albany; Youth Dir, New York Republican State Cttee 1971–74, Republican Nat. Cttee 1975–76; Man., Public Policy, Container Corpn of America 1977–87; Dir Office of Family Assistance, US Dept of Health and Human Services 1987–89; Acting Asst Sec., US Dept of Health and Human Services 1989, Asst Sec. US Dept of Agric. 1989–92; Exec. Dir WFP, Rome 1992–2002, mem. UN Sec.-Gen.'s Panel of High-Level Personalities on African Devt 1992–95, UN Sec.-Gen.'s Special Envoy on Drought in the Horn of Africa 2000–01, UN Sec.-Gen.'s Personal Humanitarian Envoy to Middle East 2002, Chair. UN System Standing Cttee on Nutrition 2002–06, UN Under-Sec.-Gen. for Man. 2002–05; Prof. of Practice, Public Admin and Int. Affairs, Maxwell School of Citizenship and Public Affairs, Syracuse Univ. 2005–; Fellow, Inst. of Politics, Harvard Univ. 1986; Commr Ill. State Scholarship Comm. 1979–84, Ill. Human Rights Comm. 1985–87; Towsley Foundation Policy Maker in Residence, Gerald R. Ford School of Public Policy, Univ. of Michigan 2002; Sr Fellow, The Chicago Council on Global Affairs, Bill & Melinda Gates Foundation 2007–08; mem. Accountability Review Board on Benghazi 2012; Order of Merit (Italy) 2002; Hon. DSc (McGill Univ., Montreal) 1997, (Pine Major Coll.) 2000; Hon. DHL (State Univ. of New York, Cortland) 1999, (American Univ., Rome) 2001, (Loyola Univ., Chicago) 2002, (Dakota Wesleyan Univ., Mitchell, SDak) 2003, (Univ. of S Carolina, Spartanburg) 2003, (Colgate Univ.) 2004; Dr hc (Slovak Agricultural Univ., Nitra) 1999, Hon. DPS (John Cabot Univ., Rome) 2001; Leadership in Human Services Award, American Public Welfare Asscn 1990, Excellence in Public Service Award, American Acad. of Pediatrics 1991, Leadership Award, Nat. Asscn of WIC Dirs 1992, Quality of Life Award, Auburn School of Human Sciences 1996, Building World Citizenship Award, World Asscn of Girl Guides/Scouts 2001, Prize of Excellence, Asscn of African Journalists 2002, World Food Prize Laureate 2003, Univ. of Albany Medallion 2002, Leadership Award, Chicago Council on Foreign Relations 2004, Life Time Achievement in Child Nutrition Award, School Nutrition Asscn 2007. *Leisure interest:* music, including playing clarinet. *Address:* 351 Eggers Hall, The Maxwell School of Syracuse University, Syracuse, NY 13244, USA (office). *Telephone:* (315) 443-1341 (office). *Fax:* (315) 443-9085 (office). *E-mail:* cbertini@maxwell.syr.edu (office). *Website:* faculty.maxwell.syr.edu/cbertini (office); www.maxwell.syr.edu (office).

BERTINOTTI, Fausto; Italian politician; b. 22 March 1940, Milan; joined Gen. Confed. of Italian Labour 1964, Regional Sec. in Piedmont 1975–85; joined Italian Communist Party (PCI) 1972, left to join Partito della Rifondazione Comunista (PRC) (Party of Communist Refoundation), Nat. Sec. 1994–2006; mem. Camera dei Deputati 1994–2004, Pres. Camera dei Deputati 2006–08; Dir Rivista Binestrale Alternative il Socialism; mem. European Parl. 1999–2006. *Publications:* La camera dei lavori 1987, Verso la democrazia autoritaria 1991, Tutti i colori del rosso 1995, Le due sinistre (co-author) 1997, Pensare il '68 (co-author) 1998, Le idee che non muoiono (co–author) 2000, Per una pace infinita (co-author) 2002, Analisi collettiva (co–author) 2004, Non violenza – Le ragioni del pacifismo 2004, Il ragazzo con la maglietta a strisee 2005, La città degli uomini: Cinque riflessioni in un mondo che cambia 2007, Devi augurarti che la strada sia lunga 2009, L'Europa delle passioni forti (co-author), Io ci provo (co-author). *Address:* Alternative per il socialismo, Via della Consulta, 1, 00184 Rome, Italy (office). *E-mail:* posta@ alternativeperilsocialismo.it (office). *Website:* www.alternativeperilsocialismo.it (office).

BERTMAN, Dmitry Aleksandrovich; Russian theatre director; *Artistic Director, Helikon Opera Theatre;* b. 17 Oct. 1967, Moscow; s. of Alexander Bertman and Ludmila Zhumaeva; ed Lunacharsky State Inst. of Theatre Arts, Russian Acad. of Theatre Arts; started career as dir in theatres in Moscow, Tver, Odessa, Syktyvkar; music theatre dir, Elizabet Buhne Theatre, Salzburg, Austria 1990; Founder and Artistic Dir Helikon Opera Theatre, Moscow 1990–; has also directed productions abroad, including in Vienna and Klagenfurt, Austria; Prof., Russian Acad. of Theatre Arts 1996–; teaches masterclasses on acting, Bern Opera Studio 1994–; mem. Council of Culture 2012–; Maltese Cross (Malta) 2003, Count of Sovereign Military and Hospitaller Order of St John of Jerusalem (Rhodes) 2003, Officier des Palmes Academiques 2003, Order of Santa Maria Land (Estonia) 2008, Order of Friendship; Honored Art Worker of Russia 1997, People's Artist of Russia 2005, Golden Mask Nat. Prize 1998, 1999, 2001. *Stage productions include:* Iolanta 1985, Kashchey The Immortal 1986, Turtle's Day 1987, The Golden Cockerel 1988, 1999, About You I Sing 1989, Mavra 1990, Maddalena 1991, Le fils prodigue 1991, Ugly Duckling 1992, Appolo et Hyacinthus 1992, Pagliacci 1993, Undine 1994, La Voix Humaine 1994, La Traviata 1995, The Queen of Spades 1995, Carmen (Nat. Golden Mask award for best opera dir 1998) 1996, Die Fledermaus 1996, Eugene Onegin 1997, The Tsar's Bride (Nat. Golden Mask award for best opera dir 1999) 1997, Mazeppa 1999, Lady Macbeth of Mtsensk (Nat. Golden Mask award for best opera dir 2001) 2000, The Rake's Progress 2000, Falstaff 2002, Lulu 2002, Pierre le Grand 2003, The Makropulos Affair 2003, Gershwin Gala 2004, Tosca 2004, Vampuka The African Bride 2005, Falling from the Sky 2005, Siberia 2006, Boris Godunov 2006, Russalka 2007, The Barber of Seville 2007, Il Re Nudo 2009, Rusalka 2009, The Love for Three Oranges 2010, Andrea Chenier 2010, Othello 2011. *Address:* Helikon Opera, 125009 Moscow, Bolshaya Nikitskaya str. 19/16, Russia (office). *Telephone:* (495) 690-09-71 (office). *Fax:* (495) 291-13-23 (office). *E-mail:* pr@helikon.ru (office). *Website:* www.helikon.ru (office); www.bertman.ru.

BERTOLINI, Mark T., BS, MBA; American business executive; *Chairman and CEO, Aetna Inc.;* b. 1957; ed Wayne State Univ., Cornell Univ.; COO, later CEO SelectCare Inc. 1992–95; fmr Exec. Vice-Pres. NYLCare Health Plans; Exec. Vice-Pres. Cigna HealthCare 2000–02, Sr Vice-Pres., Regional & Middle Market 2002–03; joined Aetna Inc. 2003, Head of Specialty Products 2003–05, Sr Vice-Pres. Specialty Group 2005, Sr Vice-Pres. Regional Business 2005–06, Exec. Vice-Pres. Regional Business 2006–07, Exec. Vice-Pres. and Head of Business Operations 2007, Pres. Aetna Inc. 2007–14, CEO 2010–, Chair. 2011–; Chair. Operations Cttee, Asscn of Health Insurance Plans; mem. Bd Dirs US-China Business Council, Hole in the Wall Gang Camp, FIDELCO, Univ. of Connecticut

Health Center; elected the first straight ally Bd mem. Nat. Gay and Lesbian Chamber of Commerce 2009–; mem. Advisory Bd, Cornell Univ. School of Human Ecology; Nat. Gay and Lesbian Chamber of Commerce Healthcare Leadership Award 2007, honoured for his leadership by Nat. Italian American Foundation, Outward Bound, Nat. Kidney Registry, Out & Equal Workplace Advocates, Quinnipiac Univ. Business School, Wayne State Univ. School of Business, among others. *Address:* Aetna Inc., 151 Farmington Avenue, Hartford, CT 06156, USA (office). *Telephone:* (860) 273-0123 (office). *Fax:* (860) 273-3971 (office). *E-mail:* info@aetna.com (office). *Website:* www.aetna.com (office).

BERTONCELJ, Andrej, DEcon; Slovenian academic and politician; *Minister of Finance;* b. 28 July 1957; Prof. of Man., Univ. of Primorska 2009–18; Minister of Finance 2018–; Pres., Lek Consulting; Asst to Dir-Gen., Lek d. d.; Adviser to the Pres. of Man. Bd for Corporate Governance, Kemofarmacija d. d.; mem. Man. Bd, Slovenian Sovereign Holding Co. *Publications include:* 10 books; contrib. to more than 40 scientific papers. *Address:* Ministry of Finance, 1000 Ljubljana, Župančičeva 3, Slovenia (office). *Telephone:* (1) 3696600 (office). *Fax:* (1) 3696659 (office). *E-mail:* andrej.bertoncelj@mf-rs.si (office). *Website:* www.mf.gov.si (office).

BERTONE, HE Cardinal Tarcisio Pietro Evasio, DCnL, SDB; Italian ecclesiastic and professor of canon law; *Secretary Emeritus of State, Roman Curia;* b. 2 Dec. 1934, Romano Canavese; ed Oratorio di Valdocco, Turin, Salesian novitiate of Monte Oliveto, Pinerolo, Pontifical Salesian Athenaeum (now Univ.), Rome; entered Soc. of St Francis and St John (Salesian Order); made religious profession 1950; ordained priest by Albino Mensa, Bishop of Ivrea 1960; Prof. of Special Moral Theology, Pontifical Salesian Univ. 1967, Dir of Theologians 1974–76, Prof. of Canon Law 1976–91, Dean Faculty of Canon Law 1979–85, Vice-Rector 1987–89, apptd Rector 1989; Guest Prof. of Public Ecclesiastical Law, Pontifical Lateran Univ. 1978; collaborated in drafting revision of Code of Canon Law; Archbishop of Vercelli 1991–95; Sec. of Congregation of Doctrine of Faith 1995–2002; entrusted with publ. of third secret of Fatima by Pope John Paul II 2000; Archbishop of Genoa 2002–06; cr. Cardinal (Cardinal Priest of Santa Maria Auxiliatrice in via Tuscolana) 2003, Cardinal-Bishop of Frascati 2008; participated in Papal Conclave 2005, 2013; Sec. of State, Roman Curia 2006–13, Sec. Emer. of State 2013–; Camerlengo of the Holy Roman Church 2007–14; consultant to several dicasteries of Roman Curia; served temporarily as Admin. of Holy See and Acting head of state of Vatican City state from resignation of Benedict XVI in Feb. 2013 until election of Pope Francis in March 2013; Hon. PhD (Catholic Univ. of Salta, Argentina) 2005.

BERTOZZI, Carolyn R., AB, PhD; American chemist and academic; *T.Z. and Irmgard Chu Distinguished Professor of Chemistry and Professor of Molecular and Cell Biology, University of California, Berkeley;* b. 10 Oct. 1966, Boston, Mass; d. of William Bertozzi; ed Harvard Univ., Univ. of California, Berkeley; postdoctoral work in cellular immunology at Univ. of California, San Francisco 1993–96; mem. Faculty, Univ. of California, Berkeley 1996–, currently T.Z. and Irmgard Chu Distinguished Prof. of Chem. and Prof. of Molecular and Cell Biology; Investigator, Howard Hughes Medical Inst.; Sr Faculty Scientist, Lawrence Berkeley Nat. Lab.; mem. NAS 2005, American Acad. of Arts and Sciences 2003, German Acad. of Sciences Leopoldina 2008, Inst. of Medicine 2011; Fellow, AAAS 2002; Danforth Teaching Award 1987, New England American Inst. of Chemists Award 1988, Thomas T. Hoopes Undergraduate Thesis Prize 1988, Outstanding Grad. Student Instructor Awards 1989, 1990, Camille and Henry Dreyfus New Faculty Award 1995, Bruce Mahan Teaching Award 1992, Exxon Educ. Fund Young Investigator Award 1996, Pew Scholars Award in the Biomedical Sciences 1996, Burroughs Wellcome New Investigator Award in Pharmacology 1997, Alfred P. Sloan Research Fellow 1997, ACS Horace S. Isbell Award in Carbohydrate Chem. 1997, Office of Naval Research Young Investigator Award 1998, Research Corpn Research Innovation Award 1998, Glaxo Wellcome Scholar 1998, Prytanean Faculty Award 1998, Beckman Young Investigator Award 1998, Joel H. Hildebrand Chair in Chem. 1998–2000, ACS Arthur C. Cope Scholar Award 1999, Camille Dreyfus Teacher-Scholar Award 1999, MacArthur Foundation Award 1999, Presidential Early Career Award in Science and Eng 2000, Dept of Chem. Teaching Award, Univ. of California, Berkeley 2000, Merck Academic Devt Program Award 2000, ACS Award in Pure Chem. 2001, Distinguished Teaching Award, Univ. of California, Berkeley 2001, Donald Sterling Noyce Prize for Excellence in Undergraduate Teaching 2001, Irving Sigal Young Investigator Award of Protein Soc. 2002, Iota Sigma Pi Agnes Fay Morgan Research Award 2004, Havinga Medal, Univ. of Leiden 2005, Ernst Schering Prize 2007, GLBT Scientist of the Year Award, Nat. Org. of Gay and Lesbian Scientists and Tech. Professionals 2007, Li Ka Shing Women in Science Award 2008, Roy L. Whistler Int. Award in Carbohydrate Chem. 2008, Willard Gibbs Medal, ACS Chicago Local Section 2008, W.H. Nichols Award 2009, Harrison Howe Award 2009, Albert Hofmann Medal, Univ. of Zurich 2009, Lemelson-MIT Prize 2010, Bio-organic Chem. Award, RSC Organic Div. 2010, Tetrahedron Young Investigator Award for Bio-organic and Medicinal Chem. 2011, Emanuel Merck Lectureship 2011, Heinrich Wieland Prize 2012. *Publications:* Glycochemistry: Principles, Synthesis and Applications (co-ed.) 2001, Essentials of Glycobiology (second edn, co-ed.) 2009; more than 290 papers in scientific journals. *Address:* 820 Latimer Hall, Department of Chemistry, B84 Hildebrand Hall #1460, University of California, Berkeley, CA 94720-1460, USA (office). *Telephone:* (510) 643-1682 (office). *Fax:* (510) 643-2628 (office). *E-mail:* crb@berkeley.edu (office). *Website:* chem.berkeley.edu (office); www.cchem.berkeley.edu/crbgrp/bio.htm (office).

BERTRAND, Xavier, PhD; French politician; *Mayor of Saint-Quentin;* b. 21 March 1965, Châlons-sur-Marne (now Châlons-en-Champagne) (Marne); s. of Jean-Pierre Bertrand and Madeleine Bedin; m. Emmanuelle Gontier; three c.; ed Univ. of Reims; began career as an insurance agent; volunteered for RPR and entered politics aged 16; mem. Union pour un Mouvement Populaire, Sec.-Gen. March–Dec. 2008, 2009–10; Deputy Mayor of Saint-Quentin, Aisne 1995–2010, Mayor 2010–; Deputy in Nat. Ass. for Aisne 2002–04, 2007, 2009–10; Sec. of State for Health Insurance, Ministry of Health and Social Welfare 2004–05; Minister of Health and Social Protection 2005–07 (resgnd), for Labour, Labour Relations and Solidarity 2007–09, of Labour, Employment and Health 2010–12; Spokesman for Nicolas Sarkozy's presidential campaign 2007; mem. Grand Orient of France 1995–. *Address:* Hôtel de ville, BP 345, 02107 Saint-Quentin, Aisne, France (office). *Telephone:* (3) 23-06-90-00 (office). *E-mail:* mairie@ville-saint-quentin.fr (office). *Website:* www.ville-saintquentin.fr (office).

BERTRANOU, Armando Victorio, PhD; Argentine academic; b. 14 May 1942, Mendoza; s. of Pablo Luis Bertranou and Susana Angélica Saligari; m. Clara Alicia Jalif 1965; two s. two d.; ed Universidad Nacional de Cuyo, Univ. of California, Davis; Titular Prof., Faculty of Agricultural Sciences, Universidad Nacional de Cuyo, fmr Rector; fmr Dir-Gen. Fund for Scientific and Technological Research, Nat. Scientific and Technological Promotion; fmr Chair. Nat. Council of Scientific and Technical Research; fmr Chair. Nat. Inst. of Science and Tech. Basins, Ministry of Natural Resources and Sustainable Devt; apptd Pres. Nat. Agency for Promotion of Science and Tech. 2009; mem. Bd of Dirs Nat. Water Inst., Center for Econs, Law and Water Man., Nat. Parks Admin. *Publications:* numerous articles and papers on irrigation and water man. *Leisure interests:* aerobics, rugby, rowing.

BERUCHASHVILI, Tamar, PhD; Georgian politician and diplomatist; *Ambassador to UK;* b. 9 April 1961, Tbilisi, Georgian SSR, USSR; m.; two c.; ed Patrice Lumumba People's Friendship Univ., Moscow, Russian SFSR, Indiana Univ., USA, Javakhishvili Tbilisi State Univ.; Research Officer, Kutateladze Inst. of Pharmacochemistry, Georgian Acad. of Sciences 1986–90; Chief Specialist, Int. Co-operation Dept, Ministry of Science and Tech. 1990–92; Administrator, TACIS Coordination Bureau, State Foreign Econ. Relations Cttee 1992–94; Deputy Exec. Dir, TACIS Coordination Bureau, Ministry of Science and Tech. 1994–96; Minister of Trade and Foreign Econ. Relations 1998–2000; Deputy Minister of Foreign Affairs 2000–03; Deputy Minister of State, State Chancellery 2003–04; First Deputy Minister of State for Integration with European and Euro-Atlantic Structures 2004–11; Chief Adviser to Vice-Premier and Minister of State for European and Euro-Atlantic Integration 2011–13; Deputy Minister of Foreign Affairs 2013–14, Minister of Foreign Affairs 2014–15; Amb. to UK 2016–. *Address:* Embassy of Georgia, 4 Russell Gardens, London, W14 8EZ, England (office). *Telephone:* (20) 7348-1941 (office). *Fax:* (20) 7603-6682 (office). *E-mail:* london.emb@mfa.gov.ge (office). *Website:* uk.mfa.gov.ge (office).

BĒRZIŅŠ, Andris; Latvian politician, business executive and fmr head of state; b. 10 Dec. 1944, Nītaure; m. 2nd Dace Seisuma 2011; ed First Middle School of Sigulda, Rīga Polytechnical Inst., Latvian State Univ.; became a radio engineer at 'Elektrons' factory, worked his way up to Dir; apptd Deputy Minister of Municipal Services of Latvian SSR 1988; elected to Valmiera Dist Council (Soviet) of People's Deputies 1989–93, apptd Chair. Exec. Comm.; elected to Supreme Council of Latvian SSR representing Valmiera 1990; joined Latvian Popular Front faction in Supreme Council; Chair. Privatization Fund of Bank of Latvia 1993; Pres. Latvijas Unibanka (jt-stock co.) 1993–2004; also owned numerous real-estate properties; worked as adviser to Pres. of SEB; mem. Bd several jt-stock cos, including Valmiera stikla šķiedra (Valmiera Fibreglass) and Lode; returned to politics when he ran unsuccessfully for Mayor of Rīga as Leader of Zaļo un Zemnieku Savienība (ZZS—Union of Greens and Farmers) party list 2005; Pres. Latvian Chamber of Industry and Commerce 2006–10; Chair. Latvenergo –2009; elected Deputy of the Saeima (ZZS) 2010; Pres. of Latvia 2011–15; Patron European Acad. of Science and Art 2013–; Hon. mem. Rīga Tech. Univ. 2012, Univ. of Latvia 2012; Commemorative badge for participants in the 1991 barricades 1996, Commdr, Order of the Three Stars 2000, Cross of Recognition (First Class) 2011, Order of Viesturs (First Class) 2011, Order of the Three Stars (First Class) with Chain 2011. *Address:* c/o Chancery of the President, Pils lauk. 3, Rīga 1900, Latvia.

BĒRZIŅŠ, Andris; Latvian historian and politician; b. 4 Aug. 1951, Rīga; m.; two c.; ed Latvian State Univ.; teacher and admin. in several schools 1975–82; Head, Div. of Personnel Training Cttee for Vocational and Tech. Training 1982–86; Head, Div. State Cttee for Labour and Social Affairs 1986–90; Head, Div., Deputy Dir Welfare Dept Ministry of Econs 1990–92; Deputy Minister, concurrently Head, Labour Dept Ministry of Welfare 1992–93; State Minister of Labour 1993–94; Deputy Prime Minister, Minister of Welfare 1994–95; Minister of Labour 1995–97; Chair. Riga City Council 1997–2000; Prime Minister of Latvia 2000–02; Chair. Latvian Way (Latvijas ceļš) 2000–03; strategic consultant for UNDP, Latvia 2003–04; currently mem. (Union of Greens and Farmers) Saeima (Parl.), Chair. Public Expenditure and Audit Cttee 2014–; Consultant, Owner ABkonsultants 2003–06; mem. Bd, Parex Banka 2003–06, mem. EU Econ. and Social Cttee, employers' rep.; Hon. mem. The Int. Raoul Wallenberg Foundation. *Address:* Saeima (Parliament), Jekaba iela 11, Rīga 1811, Latvia (office). *Telephone:* 6708-7111 (office). *Fax:* 6708-7100 (office). *E-mail:* andris.berzins@saeima.lv (office). *Website:* www.saeima.lv (office).

BĒRZIŅŠ, Gaidis; Latvian politician, lawyer and university lecturer; *Co-Chairman, National Alliance;* b. 20 Oct. 1970, Rīga; Minister for Justice 2006–09; elected as one of two For Fatherland and Freedom Union/Latvian Nat. Conservative Party reps on joint Nat. Alliance list the party shared with All For Latvia! 2010, Co-Chair. (with Raivis Dzintars), when Nat. Alliance became a unitary party 2010–, party formed a centre-right coalition with Zatlers' Reform Party, and Unity; Minister for Justice 2011–12. *Address:* Nacionālā apvienība (National Alliance), Kaļķu iela 11, Rīga 1050, Latvia (office). *Telephone:* 2775-5997 (office). *E-mail:* info@nacionalaapvieniba.lv (office). *Website:* www.nacionalaapvieniba.lv (office).

BESANCENOT, Bertrand; French diplomatist; b. 6 April 1952; m.; four c.; joined Ministry of Foreign Affairs 1977, with African and Malagasy Affairs Dept 1978, Third Sec., Embassy in Doha 1978–79, Second Sec. 1979–81, with Strategic Affairs and Disarmament Dept, Ministry of Foreign Affairs 1981–85, Deputy Consul in New York 1985–88, Second Counsellor, Perm. Mission to North Atlantic Council, Brussels 1988–90, Deputy Rep. to Conf. on Disarmament, Geneva 1991–95, Deputy Dir of Strategic Affairs, Strategic Affairs, Security and Disarmament Dept, Ministry of Foreign Affairs 1995–98, Amb. to Qatar 1998–2002, Diplomatic Adviser to Minister of Defence 2002–07, Amb. to Saudi Arabia 2007–16; diplomatic counsellor to French Govt 2017–; Chevalier, ordre nat. du Mérite, Légion d'honneur; Grand officier, Ordre du Mérite de l'Etat du Qatar; Insignes de Grand Croix, Ordre de Saint-Grégoire le Grand. *Address:* c/o Ministry for Europe and Foreign Affairs, 37 quai d'Orsay, 75351 Paris Cedex 07, France (office). *Telephone:* 1-43-17-53-53 (office). *Fax:* 1-43-17-47-53 (office). *Website:* www.diplomatie.gouv.fr (office).

BESCH, Werner Walter, DPhil; German professor of German; *Professor Emeritus, University of Bonn;* b. 4 May 1928, Erdmannsweiler, Black Forest; s. of Matthias Besch and Elisabeth Besch (née Fuss); m. Katharina Müller 1957; one s. two d.; Prof. of German Language and Early German Literature, Ruhr Univ., Bochum 1965–70, Univ. of Bonn 1970–93, Prof. Emer. 1993–, Rector, Univ. of Bonn 1981–83, Pro-Rector 1983–85; mem. Scientific Bd, Inst. für Deutsche Sprache, Mannheim 1976–93; mem. Nordrhein-Westfälische Akad. der Wissenschaften; mem. Publishing Cttee on writings of Martin Bucers, Heidelberg Akademie 1968–2008; mem. Rat für Deutsche Rechtschreibung 2004–10; Corresp. mem. Heidelberg Akad. der Wissenschaften, Inst. of Germanic Studies, Univ. of London; Hon. mem. Gesellschaft Ungarischer Germanisten 2005; Wolfgang Paul Medaille, Univ. of Bonn, Hon. mem Internationalen Gesellschaft für Dialektologie des Deutschen 2003. *Publications include:* Lautgeographie und Lautgeschichte im obersten Neckar-u. Donaugebiet 1961, Sprachlandschaften und Sprachausgleich im 15. Jahrhundert 1967, Dialekt/Hochsprache-Kontrastiv 1977, Handbuch Dialektologie 1983, 1984 (co-ed.), Handbuch Sprachgeschichte 1985, (2nd edn) (co-ed.) 1998–2004, Duzen, Siezen, Titulieren. Zur Anrede im Deutschen heute und gestern (2nd edn) 1998, Zur Rolle Luthers in der deutschen Sprachgeschichte 1999, Grundlagen der Germanistik (co-ed.) 1989–2007, Deutsche Sprache im Wandel 2003, Deutscher Bibelwortschatz in der frühen Neuzeit, Auswahl-Abwahl-Veralten 2008, Geschichte der deutschen Sprache: Längsschnitte, Zeitstufen, linguistische Studien 2009, Luther und die deutsche Sprache 2014; various essays and articles. *Address:* Römerstrasse 118, Apt 2512, 53117 Bonn, Germany (home).

BESHEAR, Steven (Steve) Lynn; American lawyer, politician, business executive and state governor; b. 21 Sept. 1944, Dawson Springs, Hopkins Co., Ky; s. of Orlando Russell Beshear and Mary Elizabeth Beshear (née Joiner); m. Jane Beshear; two s.; ed Dawson Springs High School, Univ. of Kentucky; served in US Army Reserve 1969–75, intelligence analyst, also carried out certain Judge Advocate Gen. duties; elected to Kentucky House of Reps for 76th Dist 1974–79; Attorney Gen. of Kentucky 1980–84, Lt Gov. 1983–87, cr. and headed Kentucky Tomorrow Comm.; cand. in election for Gov. of Kentucky 1987; practised law in Lexington, Kentucky, sr exec. of multi-state law firm; was the Democratic nominee for US Senate 1996; Gov. of Kentucky 2007–15; mem. Commerce Lexington, Inc., Kentucky Horse Park Foundation, God's Pantry Food Bank, Bluegrass Tomorrow, Kentucky World Trade Center, Univ. of Kentucky Coll. of Law Visiting Cttee; Democrat. *Address:* c/o 700 Capital Avenue, Suite 100, Frankfort, KY 40601, USA (office). *E-mail:* info@stevebeshear.com (office). *Website:* www.stevebeshear.com (office).

BESIMI, Fatmir, PhD; Macedonian politician; b. 18 Nov. 1975, Tetovo; m. Albertina Besimi; one d.; ed Kiril Pejčinovik Gymnasium, Tetovo, Faculty of Econs, SS Cyril and Methodius Univ., Skopje, Staffordshire Univ., Stoke-on-Trent, UK, postgraduate studies at Univ. of South-Eastern Europe, Tetovo; foreign exchange work, br. office of Stopanska Banka AD, Tetovo Jan.–July 2000; researcher and analyst, Nat. Bank of the Repub. of Macedonia 2001–02, Vice-Gov. 2003–04; Man., PE for Airport Services-Makedonija 2002–03; Minister of the Economy 2004–06, 2008–11; Economist, World Bank, Prishtina, Kosovo 2007–08; Minister of Defence 2011–13; Deputy Prime Minister, responsible for European Affairs 2013–16; Lecturer, State Univ., Tetovo 1999–2008, Univ. Riinvest, Prishtina 2007; part-time mem. of staff, Doctoral Programme, Staffordshire Univ., UK 2010–; Guest Lecturer, Harvard Univ., Georgetown Univ., Johns Hopkins Univ. and Univ. of Vermont, USA. *Publications:* two books in English and several professional and academic articles in the fields of economics and politics published in English, Albanian and Macedonian in journals in Macedonia and abroad. *Address:* c/o Office of the Prime Minister, 1000 Skopje, Ilindenska bb 2, North Macedonia (office).

BESSER, Gordon Michael, MB, MD, DSc, FRCP, FMedSci; British physician, endocrinologist and professor of medicine (retd); b. 22 Jan. 1936, London, England; ed Medical Coll. of St Bartholomew's Hosp., Univ. of London; Sr Lecturer in Medicine, St Bartholomew's Hosp. Medical Coll. 1970–74, Head of Endocrinology and Hon. Consultant Physician 1970–95, Prof. of Endocrinology 1974–92, Prof. of Medicine 1992–2001, Prof. of Medicine and Head of Endocrinology, St Bartholomew's and Royal London School of Medicine and Dentistry 1995–2001, Prof. Emer. 2001–; Civilian Consultant in Endocrinology, RN 1989–97, to the Triservice Medical Service 1997–2004; Visiting Consultant Endocrinologist to Govt of Malta 1989–2002; Chief Exec. Barts NHS Trust 1992–94; Consultant Endocrinologist, The London Clinic Centre for Endocrinology from 2001; Fellow, Queen Mary Univ. of London 2005; Lecturer to Royal Coll. of Physicians: Goulstonian 1974, Lumlean 1993, Simms 1999, Soc. for Endocrinology; Hon. Fellow, Royal Soc. of Medicine 2007; Hon. MD (Turin) 1985; Jubilee Medalist and Lecturer 2002, William Julius Mickle Fellowship for the Advancement of Medical Science, Univ. of London 1976, Medal of Soc. for Endocrinology 1978, Clinical Endocrinology Prize 1986, Medal of European Neuroendocrinology Asscn 1999. *Publications:* Clinical Endocrinology 1984, DeGroot's Endocrinology (section ed.) 1985, 26 textbooks in gen. medicine and endocrinology and over 500 articles in journals of basic and clinical endocrinology and medicine. *Leisure interests:* early Chinese ceramics, modern European art, physical fitness, opera, ballet. *Address:* Department of Endocrinology, St Bartholomew's Hospital, West Smithfield, London, EC1A 7BE, England (office). *Telephone:* (20) 7601-8343 (office). *Fax:* (20) 7601-8505 (office).

BESSHO, Koro; Japanese diplomatist; *Permanent Representative, United Nations;* b. 5 Feb. 1953; ed Univ. of Tokyo Faculty of Law; joined Ministry of Foreign Affairs 1975, First Sec., Embassy in Washington, DC 1990–92, Counsellor 1992–93, Dir First Int. Orgs Div., Econ. Affairs Bureau 1993–95, Dir Northeast Asia Div., Asian Affairs Bureau 1995–97, Counsellor, Embassy in London 1997–98, Counsellor, then Minister, Perm. Del. to OECD 1998–2000, Dir Policy Coordination Div., Foreign Policy Bureau 2000–01, Exec. Asst to the Prime Minister 2001–06, Dir-Gen. Int. Cooperation Bureau 2006–08, Deputy Vice-Minister for Foreign Policy/Dir-Gen., Foreign Policy Bureau 2008–10, Deputy Minister for Foreign Affairs 2010–12, Amb. to South Korea 2012–16, Amb. and Perm. Rep., UN, New York 2016–. *Address:* Permanent Mission of Japan to the United Nations, 866 United Nations Plaza, Suite 230, 2nd Floor, New York, NY 10017, USA (office). *Telephone:* (212) 223-4300 (office). *Fax:* (212) 751-1966 (office). *E-mail:* p-m-j@dn.mofa.go.jp (office).

BESSHO, Yoshiki; Japanese business executive; *Chairman and Executive Officer, Suzuken Company Limited;* began career at Bank of Tokyo-Mitsubishi UFJ Ltd; joined Suzuken Co. Ltd 1970, served successively as Man. Dir, Sr Man. Dir, Pres. (from 1983), Exec. Pres. and Dir, Rep. Dir, CEO 2004–07, Chair. and Exec. Officer, Suzuken Co. Ltd 2007–. *Address:* Suzuken Co. Ltd, 8 Higashi Kataha-machi, Higashi-ku, Nagoya, Aichi 461-8701, Japan (office). *Telephone:* (52) 961-2331 (office). *Fax:* (52) 961-4071 (office). *E-mail:* info@suzuken.co.jp (office). *Website:* www.suzuken.co.jp (office).

BESSMERTNYKH, Alexander Alexandrovich, CandJurSc; Russian politician and diplomatist; *President, International Foreign Policy Association;* b. 10 Nov. 1933, Biisk; s. of Alexander Bessmertnykh and Maria Bessmertnykh; m.; one s. one d.; ed Moscow State Inst. of Int. Relations; joined Diplomatic Service 1957, served at Embassy in Washington, DC 1970–83, fmr arms control negotiator, First Deputy Foreign Minister (with special responsibility for N America and the Middle East) 1987–90, Deputy 1986, Amb. to USA 1990–91, Minister of Foreign Affairs Jan.–Aug. 1991; mem. CP Cen. Cttee 1990–91; Head of Policy Analysis Centre Soviet (now Russian) Foreign Policy Asscn 1991–92; Pres. Int. Foreign Policy Asscn 1992–, Chair. World Council of Fmr Foreign Ministers 1993–; Dir-Gen. Ass. for Int. Business and Political Connections 2011–; Chair. Supervisory Bd Advanced Tech. Research Programs Foundation; Prof. Moscow Univ.; mem. Acad. of Social Sciences of Russian Fed.; Corresp. mem. Chilean Acad. of Social and Political Sciences; Order of Friendship of Peoples, Order of Peter the Great, Order of Lomonosov; Badge of Honour, various medals. *Publications include:* numerous articles on foreign policy, diplomacy and military strategy. *Leisure interests:* literature, classical music, tennis. *Address:* International Foreign Policy Association, 105064 Moscow, Yakovo-apostolsky per. 10, Russia (office). *Telephone:* (495) 917-25-14 (office); (495) 917-15-85 (office). *Fax:* (495) 917-19-13 (office). *E-mail:* fpa@forpolicy.ru (office). *Website:* www.fpamoscow.org (office).

BESSON, Luc; French film director, producer and screenwriter; b. 18 March 1959, Paris; s. of Claude Besson and Danièle Plane; m. 1st Anne Parillaud 1986 (divorced 1991); one d.; m. 2nd Maïwenn Le Besco 1992 (divorced 1997); one d.; m. 3rd Milla Jovovich 1997 (divorced 1999); m. 4th Virginie Silla 2004; three d.; worked as asst on films in Paris and Hollywood; First Asst for several advertising films; two features (Homme libre and Les Bidasses aux grandes manoeuvres) and four shorts; f. Les Films du Loup (now Leeloo Productions) 1982; Co-founder and Chair. EuropaCorp 1999–; main figure in 'Cinéma du look' movement 1980s–90s. *Films include:* L'Avant dernier 1981, Le Dernier Combat 1983, Subway 1985, The Big Blue 1988, Nikita (Italian Nat. Syndicate of Film Journalists Silver Ribbon for Best Dir, Foreign Film 1990) 1990, Atlantis 1991, Leon 1994, The Fifth Element (Cesar Award for Best Dir 1997) 1997, The Messenger: The Story of Joan of Arc 1999, Angel-A 2006, Arthur and the Invisibles 2006, Taken 2008, District 13: Ultimatum 2009, Arthur and the Great Adventure 2009, From Paris with Love 2010, Les aventures extraordinaires d'Adèle Blanc-Sec 2010, Arthur 3: The War of the Two Worlds 2010, The Lady 2011, Colombiana (screenplay) 2011, Taken 2 2012, The Family 2013, Lucy 2014, 3 Days to Kill (producer) 2014, Taken 3 (producer) 2014, The Transporter Refueled (producer) 2015. *Television includes:* Confession (film; assoc. producer) 2006, Valérian & Laureline (series; producer) 2007, Transporter: The Series (series; exec. producer) 2012–13, No Limit (series; producer) 2012–13. *Publications:* Arthur and the Minimoys (juvenile) 2005, Arthur and the War of the Two Worlds. *Address:* Leeloo Productions, 53 rue Boissée, 91540 Mennecy (office); c/o CBC, 11 rue de la Croix Boissée, 91540 Mennecy, France. *Telephone:* 1-44-71-94-94 (Europacorp) (office). *E-mail:* lucbesson@luc-besson.com (office); contact@europacorp.com (office). *Website:* luc-besson.com (office); www.europacorp-corporate.com (office).

BETANCOURT DE GARCÍA, Edmeé; Venezuelan politician and fmr central banker; ed Univ. of Carabobo, Univ. Simón Bolívar; Administrative Vice Chancellor, Univ. of Carabobo 1988–92; Vice-Minister of Labour 2000–02; Minister of Light Industry and Trade 2005–07; Rep. to Comm. of Comunidad Andina 2005; Vice-Chancellor of Social Affairs, Univ. Nacional Experimental Politécnica de la Fuerza Armada (Unefa) 2006–09; Pres. Banco de Desarrollo Económico y Social de Venezuela (Bandes) 2010; Minister of Commerce 2011; Rep. of Venezuela to FAO 2011; Pres. and Chair. Banco Central de Venezuela 2013. *Address:* c/o Banco Central de Venezuela, Avda Urdaneta, esq. de Carmelitas, Caracas 1010, Venezuela.

BÉTEILLE, André Marie, MSc, PhD; Indian sociologist and academic; *Professor Emeritus, Delhi School of Economics;* b. 30 Sept. 1934, Chandannagore; s. of Maurice Béteille and Renuka Béteille (née Mukherjee); m. Esha Ghoshal; two d.; ed Univs of Calcutta and Delhi; Research Assoc. Indian Statistical Inst. 1958–59; Lecturer in Sociology, Delhi School of Econs 1959–64, Reader 1964–72, Prof. 1972–99, Prof. Emer. 1999–; fmr teacher, Univ. of Oxford, Univ. of Cambridge, Univ. of Chicago, LSE; mem. Nat. Knowledge Comm. 2005–06 (resgnd); Nat. Research Prof. 2007–; fmr Chair. Indian Council of Social Science Research (ICSSR); Chancellor, North-Eastern Hill Univ., Shillong, Ashoka Univ. 2014–; Chair. Centre for Studies in Social Sciences, Kolkata; Corresp. Fellow, British Acad. 1992; Trustee Sameeksha Trust, Nat. Foundation for India, New India Foundation; Hon. Fellow, Royal Anthropological Inst. 2002; Hon. DSc (Vidyasagar Univ.) 2004, Hon. DLitt (Kolkata) 2006; Padma Bhushan Award 2005. *Publications:* Caste, Class and Power: Changing Patterns of Stratification in a Tanjore Village 1965, Castes: Old and New, Essays in Social Structure and Social Stratification 1969, Studies in Agrarian Social Structure 1974, Six Essays in Comparative Sociology 1974, Inequality Among Men 1977, The Idea of Natural Inequality and Other Essays 1983, Society and Politics in India: Essays in a Comparative Perspective 1991, Antinomies of Society: Essays on Ideologies and Institutions 2000, Chronicles of Our Time 2000, Sociology: Essays on Approach and Method 2002, Equality and Universality: Essays in Social and Political Theory 2003, Anti-Utopia: Essential Writings of André Béteille (ed. by Dipankar Gupta) 2005, Ideology and Social Science 2006, Marxism and Class Analysis 2007; numerous articles in professional journals. *Address:* 69 Jor Bagh, New Delhi 110 003, India (home). *Telephone:* (11) 24645172 (home).

BETHENOD, Martin; French museum director; *CEO and Director, Palazzo Grassi and Punta della Dogana, Venice;* b. 1966; began career as special adviser to Jean-Jacques Aillagon, Dir Vidéothèque de Paris; Chief of Staff to Jean-Jacques Aillagon 1996–98; Dir Culture Ville de Paris 1993–96; Pres. Centre Georges Pompidou 1996–98, Dir of Publs 1998–2001; fmr Journalist, Connaissance des Arts, Vogue; Head of Visual Arts, Ministry of Culture and Communication

2003–04; Commr Gen. Foire Internationale d'Art Contemporain (FIAC—Int. Contemporary Art Fair), Paris 2004–10; CEO and Dir Palazzo Grassi and Punta della Dogana owned by François Pinault in Venice, Italy 2010–; Deputy CEO Bourse de Commerce—Collection Pinault-Paris 2016–; Chevalier, Ordre nat. du Mérite 2007. *Address:* Palazzo Grassi, Campo San Samuele 3231, 30124 Venice, Italy (office). *Telephone:* (041) 2401353 (office). *Fax:* (041) 2401338 (office). *E-mail:* suzel.berneron@palazzograssi.it (office). *Website:* www.palazzograssi.it (office).

BETHKE, Siegfried, PhD; German physicist and academic; *Director, Max-Planck-Institute for Physics;* b. 15 April 1954, Ludwigshafen; ed Univ. of Heidelberg; Asst, Univ. of Heidelberg 1983–86; Feodor-Lynen Fellow, Univ. of Calif., Berkeley Lab., USA 1988–89; Prof. of Physics, Rheinisch-Westfälische Technische Hochschule, Aachen 1993–96; Dir Max-Planck-Inst. for Physics, Munich 1999–, Man. Dir 2000–06; Heisenberg Fellow, CERN, Geneva 1989–93; Co-Ed. European Physical Journal C 1994–; mem. numerous specialist cttees including High Energy Physics Referee Bd, Ministry of Science, Research, Tech. and Educ. 1995–2002; mem. Editorial Bd, Journal of Physics G 1997–2002; Chair. CERN LHC (Large Hadron Collider) Computing Review 2000–01; Chair. ATLAS Collaboration Bd 2004–05, Deputy Chair. 2003–06; Man. Dir MPG Semiconductor Laboratory (HLL) 2013–; mem. German Physical Soc.; Scientific mem. Max-Planck Soc. 1999–; mem. Deutsches Elektronen Synchrotron (German Synchrotron Research Centre, DESY) Scientific Council, Hamburg 2000–, Chair. 2002–05; Hon. Prof., Technische Universität München; Gottfried Wilhelm Leibniz Prize 1995. *Publications:* numerous specialist publs. *Address:* Max-Planck-Institute for Physics, Foehringer Ring 6, Room 219, 80805 Munich, Germany (office). *Telephone:* (89) 32354-381 (office). *Fax:* (89) 32354-305 (office). *E-mail:* bethke@mppmu.mpg.de (office). *Website:* www.mpg.de (office); www.mppmu.mpg.de/common/members/bethke.html (office).

BETI ASSOMO, Joseph; Cameroonian politician; *Minister-delegate at the Presidency, in charge of Defence;* b. 17 Aug. 1959, Ayos, Nyong-et-Mfoumou Dept; m.; six c.; ed Yaoundé Univ., Ecole nationale d'admin et de magistrature (ENAM); Chef du Cabinet to Gov. of South Prov. 1983–90; Sub-Prefect of Ma'an, Ntem Dept 1990, later Sub-Prefect, Yaoundé Third Dist and Dja-et-Lobo Dept 1998–2005; Prefect, Mfoundi Dept 2005; Gov., North Prov. 2010–12, Littoral Prov. 2012–15; Minister-del. at the Presidency, in charge of Defence 2015–; Chevalier and officier, Ordre du mérite camerounais, Ordre de la valeur. *Address:* Ministry of Defence, Quartier Général, Yaoundé, Cameroon (office). *Telephone:* 222-23-40-55 (office).

BETORI, HE Cardinal Giuseppe, LicTheol, DSacredScript; Italian ecclesiastic and academic; *Archbishop of Florence;* b. 25 Feb. 1947, Foligno; ed Pontifical Gregorian Univ. and a doctorate in Sacred Scripture at the Pontifical Biblical Inst.; ordained priest, Diocese of Foligno 1970; fmr Prof. of Anthropology and Biblical Exegesis; Dean of the Theological Inst. of Assisi; Dir Nat. Catechetical Office; apptd Titular Bishop of Falerone 2001; Sec.-Gen. Italian Episcopal Conf. 2001–08; Archbishop of Florence 2008–; elected Pres. Tuscan Episcopal Conf. 2009; cr. Cardinal (Cardinal-Priest of San Marcello) 2012; mem. Pontifical Council for Culture 2011–; participated in Papal Conclave 2013. *Address:* Arcivescovado, Piazza S. Giovanni 3, 50129 Florence, Italy (office). *Telephone:* (055) 271071 (office). *Fax:* (055) 2710741 (office). *E-mail:* info@diocesifirenze.it (office). *Website:* www.diocesifirenze.it (office).

BETRIAN, Stanley Mario; Curaçao politician; b. 1 Nov. 1951; ed HTS Eindhoven, Netherlands, Catholic Univ. of Nijmegen; Exec. Vice-Pres. Central Bank of the Netherlands Antilles 1983–92; Lt-Gov. of Curaçao (whilst still part of Netherlands Antilles) 1992–94; Chair. Curaçao Social and Econ. Council (SER) –2012; Prime Minister of Curaçao and Minister of Gen. Affairs, of Justice, and of Traffic, Transport and Spatial Planning and Energy Sept.–Dec. 2012; fmr Chair. Foundation for Privatization Implementation (StIP), Antillean Co-Financing Org.

BETT, Sir Michael, Kt, CBE, MA; British fmr business executive; b. 18 Jan. 1935, Liverpool; s. of Arthur Bett OBE and Nina Daniells; m. Christine Angela Reid 1959; one s. two d.; ed Aldenham School, Pembroke Coll., Cambridge; Dir Industrial Relations, Engineering Employers Fed. 1970–72; Personnel Dir General Electric Co. Ltd 1972–77; Personnel Dir BBC 1977–81; Bd mem. for Personnel British Telecom (BT) 1981–84, Corp. Dir, Personnel and Corp. Services 1984–85, Man. Dir Local Communications Services 1985–87, Man. Dir UK Communications 1987–88, Man. Dir BT UK 1988–91, Exec. Deputy Chair. 1991–94, Dir (non-exec.) 1994–96; Pres. Chartered Inst. of Personnel and Devt 1992–98; Chair. Nurses' Pay Review Body 1990–95, Cellnet Group 1991–99, Save the Children Fund 1992–97, Social Security Advisory Cttee 1993–95, Review of Armed Forces' Manpower and Pay 1994–95, Chair. Inspectorate of the Security Industry 1994–2000, One World Broadcasting Trust, 1996–2002, English Shakespeare Company International 1997–2000, Nat. Security Inspectorate 2000–07; Pro-Chancellor, Aston Univ. 1993–2003, Chancellor 2004–11; First Commr for the Civil Service 1995–2000, Pensions Protection Investment Accreditation Bd 2000–06, Pace Micro Technology PLC 2000–06, J2C PLC 2000–02; mem. Bd of Dirs English Shakespeare Co. 1988–95; mem. Advisory Bd Tribold 2005–06; fmr mem. Campaign Bd, New Marlowe Theatre, Canterbury; Hon. Fellow, Pembroke Coll., Cambridge 2004; Hon. DSc (Aston) 1996, Hon. DUniv (Kent) 2013, Hon. DBA (Liverpool John Moores) 2013; Hon. DBA (IMCB). *Leisure interests:* theatre, music, gardening, cooking.

BETTEL, Xavier, DEA; Luxembourg lawyer and politician; *Prime Minister;* b. 3 March 1973, Luxembourg-Ville; s. of Claude Bettel and Aniela Bettel; ed Univ. Nancy 2, France, Aristotle Univ., Greece; several years' practice as lawyer; four years as host, Sonndes em 8 (weekly talk show), T.TV TV network early 2000s; elected to Luxembourg-Ville communal council 1999, Municipal Councillor, Luxembourg 2000–05, Alderman 2005–11, Mayor of Luxembourg-Ville 2011–13; elected to Chamber of Deputies (Parl.) 1999, 2004, 2009, 2013, Vice-Chair. Legal Affairs Cttee 2004–13, Chair. Demokratesch Partei Parliamentary Group 2009–11; Cttee Enquiry into the State Intelligence Service 2012–13; Prime Minister, and Minister of State of Communications and Media and of Religious Affairs 2013–, of Digitization 2018–, of Admin. Reform 2018–; mem. Demokratesch Partei 1989–, Chair. 2013–15; Orden del Mérito Civil 2007, Grand Officer, Order of Orange-Nassau 2012, Kt Grand Cross, Order of the Oak Crown 2014, Grand Cross, Order of Crown 2017, Order of Prince Henry 2017. *Address:* Office of the Prime Minister, 4 rue de la Congrégation, 1352 Luxembourg, Luxembourg (office). *Telephone:* 247-82101 (office). *Fax:* 46-17-20 (office). *E-mail:* ministere.etat@me.etat.lu (office). *Website:* www.gouvernement.lu (office).

BETTENCOURT SANTOS, Humberto, (Humbertona); Cabo Verde business executive and fmr diplomatist; *Chairman, Cabo Verde Telecom SA;* b. 17 Feb. 1940, Santo Antão Island; s. of Severino Santos and Inacia Bettencourt; m.; two c.; ed Catholic Univ. of Louvain, Belgium, Licencié en Sciences Économiques Appliquées; mem. del. in negotiations on colonial dispute with Portugal 1975; elected Deputy to Nat. Ass. 1975, re-elected 1980; Dir-Gen. Fisheries 1975–82; Amb. to EC and to Nordic and Benelux countries 1982–87, Amb. and Perm. Rep. to UN, New York 1987–91; mem. Nat. Comm. on the Law of the Sea 1979–82; int. consultant; dir of pvt. computer training centre; pvt. consultant in econ. and fisheries for FAO and UNDP 1991; Dist Gov. Rotary International 2006–07; currently Chair. Cabo Verde Telecom SA; Hon. Consul of the Netherlands for the Cape Verde Islands; Hon. Consul of Belgium; Chevalier, Order of Orange Nassau (Netherlands) 2010. *Recordings:* six LPs and CDs under Humbertona label. *Leisure interests:* music (guitar), tennis, golf. *Address:* Rua Cabo Verde Telecom, Várzea, CP 220, Praia, Santiago, Cabo Verde (office). *Telephone:* (260) 9200 (office). *Fax:* (261) 9935 (office). *E-mail:* humbertona@hotmail.com (office); humberto.bettencourt@cvt.cv. *Website:* www.cvtelecom.cv (office).

BETTINI, Paolo; Italian fmr road cyclist; b. 1 April 1974, Cecina; m. Monica Orlandini 2000; one d.; Tuscany Prov. Champion 1994; professional debut 1997; mem. Nat. Team, World Championships, Valkenburg 1998; winner Liège-Bastogne-Liège 2000, 2002, Championship of Zürich 2001, 2005, Milan-San Remo 2003, Züri-Metzgete 2001, 2005, Union Cycliste Internationale (UCI) World Cup 2002–04, HEW Cyclassics 2003, Clásica de San Sebastián 2003, Tirreno–Adriatico 2004, Tour of Lombardy 2005, 2006; Silver Medal World Championships, Lisbon 2001; first in UCI Ranking 2003, second 2004; winner, Il Lombardia 2005, 2006; winner World Road Race Championships 2006, 2007; fmrly with Mapei-Quick Step Cycling Team (now Quick Step-Innergetic Cycling Team); coach of Italian national cycling team 2010–14; Sports commentator La Gazzetta dello Sport.

BETZIG, Eric, BS, MS, PhD; American microscopist, researcher and entrepreneur; *Group Leader, Janelia Farm Research Campus, Howard Hughes Medical Institute;* b. 13 Jan. 1960; ed California Inst. of Tech., Cornell Univ.; undergraduate research asst, Grad. Aeronautical Labs, California Inst. of Tech. summer 1979, 1980; Grad. Research Asst, Dept of Applied and Eng Physics, Cornell Univ. 1983–88; mem. tech. staff, Semiconductor Physics Research Dept, AT&T Bell Labs, Murray Hill, NJ 1988–94; Owner, NSOM Enterprises, Berkeley Heights, NJ 1994–96; Vice-Pres. of R&D, Ann Arbor Machine Co., Chelsea, Mich. 1996–2002; Owner, New Millennium Research, Okemos, Mich. 2002–05; Group Leader, Janelia Farm Research Campus, Howard Hughes Medical Inst. 2005–; William L. McMillan Award, NAS Award for Initiatives in Research, Nobel Prize in Chem. (co-recipient with Stefan Hell and William Moerner for the development of super-resolved fluorescence microscopy) 2014. *Publications:* numerous papers in professional journals; 22 US patents. *Address:* Janelia Farm Research Campus, Howard Hughes Medical Institute, 19700 Helix Drive, 2C.185, Ashburn, VA 20147, USA (office). *Telephone:* (571) 209-4143 (office). *E-mail:* betzige@janelia.hhmi.org (office). *Website:* www.hhmi.org/scientists/eric-betzig (office); www.janelia.org/lab/betzig-lab (office).

BEUTLER, Bruce Alan, MD; American geneticist and academic; *Regental Professor and Director, Center for the Genetics of Host Defense, University of Texas Southwestern Medical Center;* b. 29 Dec. 1957, Chicago, Ill.; s. of Ernest Beutler and Brondelle May Fleisher; m. Barbara Lanzl 1979 (divorced 1988); three s.; ed Pritzker School of Medicine, Univ. of Texas Southwestern Medical Center, Rockefeller Univ.; Postdoctoral Fellow, The Rockefeller Univ. 1983–85, Asst Prof. 1985, Assoc. Physician, The Rockefeller Univ. Hosp. 1984–86; Asst Prof., Dept of Internal Medicine, Univ. of Texas Southwestern Medical Center, Dallas 1986, Dir Center for the Genetics of Host Defense and Regental Prof. 2011–, also Raymond and Ellen Willie Distinguished Chair in Cancer Research; Asst Investigator, Howard Hughes Medical Inst., Md 1986–90, Assoc. Prof. and Assoc. Investigator 1990–96, Prof. 1996; Prof., Dept of Immunology, Scripps Research Inst., La Jolla, Calif. 2000–11, Chair. Dept of Genetics 2007–11; mem. NAS, Nat. Acad. of Medicine, Leopoldina, Asscn of American Physicians, American Soc. for Clinical Investigation; Assoc. mem. European Molecular Biology Org.; MD hc (Technical Univ. of Munich) 2007; Robert Koch Foundation Robert Koch Prize (with Jules Hoffmann and Shizuo Akira) 2004, US Cancer Research Inst. William B. Coley Award (with Shizuo Akira) 2006, Balzan Prize for Innate Immunity (with Jules Hoffmann) 2007, Will Rogers Inst. Annual Prize for Research 2009, Albany Medical Center Prize (with Charles Dinarello and Ralph Steinman) 2009, Shaw Prize (with Jules Hoffmann and Ruslan Medzhitov) 2011, Nobel Prize in Physiology or Medicine (with Jules Hoffmann and Ralph Steinman) 2011. *Publications include:* more than 300 papers and reviews. *Leisure interests:* hiking, listening to music. *Address:* Beutler Lab, UT Southwestern Medical Center, 5323 Harry Hines Blvd, Dallas, TX 75390-8505, USA (office). *Telephone:* (214) 648-5838 (office). *E-mail:* bruce.beutler@utsouthwestern.edu (office). *Website:* www.utsouthwestern.edu/labs/beutler (office).

BEVAN, Sir James David, Kt, KCMG, CMG; British diplomatist and government official; *Chief Executive, Environment Agency;* m. Janet Purdie; three d.; ed Univ. of Sussex; joined FCO 1982, Western European Dept 1982–83, Near East and North Africa Dept 1983–84, Second Sec., Embassy in Kinshasa 1984–86, First Sec., UK Del. to NATO, Brussels 1986–90, EU Dept (External), FCO 1991–92, First Sec., Embassy in Paris 1992–93, First Sec., Embassy in Washington, DC 1994–98, Head of Africa Dept (Equatorial), FCO 1998–2000, Head of EU Dept 2000–01, Dir for the Balkans 2002–03, Dir for Africa 2003–06; Visiting Fellow, Centre for Int. Affairs, Harvard Univ., USA 2006–07; COO and Dir-Gen. for Corp. Affairs, FCO 2007–11, High Commr to India 2011–15; Chief Exec. Environment Agency 2016–. *Address:* Environment Agency, National Customer Contact Centre, PO Box 544, Rotherham, S60 1BY, England (office). *Telephone:* (370) 8506506 (office). *Website:* www.gov.uk/government/organisations/environment-agency (office).

BEVAN, Tim, CBE; British film producer; *Co-Chairman, Working Title Films;* b. 1958, Queenstown, New Zealand; m. 1st Joely Richardson (q.v.) 1992; one d.; m. 2nd Amy Gadney; one s. one d.; began career as a runner for John Cleese's Video Arts; f. Aldabra (music video production co.) with Sarah Radclyffe; formed Working Title Films (film production co.) with Eric Fellner (q.v.) 1984, now Co-Chair.; Chair. UK Film Council 2009–; Dr hc (Univ. of York) 2013; Empire Film Award for outstanding contrib. to British cinema (jtly) 2005, six Acad. Awards, six BAFTA Awards, Michael Balcon Award for Outstanding contrib. to British Cinema, Alexander Walker Award for Film, Tribute Award, Gotham Ind. Film Awards. *Films include:* My Beautiful Laundrette 1985, Personal Services 1987, Wish You Were Here, Caravaggio, Pascali's Island, The Tall Guy 1989, The Rachel Papers, Hidden Agenda, Dakota Road, Map of the Human Heart 1993, Bob Roberts, Posse 1993, Romeo is Bleeding 1993, The Hudsucker Proxy 1994, Four Weddings and a Funeral 1994, Dead Man Walking 1995, Elizabeth 1998, Notting Hill 1999, High Fidelity 2000, Fargo, O Brother, Where Art Thou? 2000, Captain Corelli's Mandolin 2001, The Big Lebowski, Plunkett & Macleane 1999, The Man Who Cried 2000, Bridget Jones' Diary 2001, Man Who Wasn't There, Long Time Dead 2002, 40 Days and 40 Nights 2002, Ali G. Indahouse 2002, About a Boy 2002, The Guru 2002, My Little Eye 2002, Thirteen 2003, Shape of Things, Ned Kelly 2003, Johnny English 2003, The Italian Job 2003, Gettin' Square 2003, Love Actually 2003, Shaun of the Dead 2004, The Calcium Kid 2004, Thunderbirds 2004, Wimbledon 2004, Bridget Jones: The Edge of Reason 2004, Mickybo and Me, United 93 (Best British Producer, London Film Critics' Circle Awards 2007) 2006, Hot Fuzz 2007, Wild Child 2008, Burn After Reading 2008, Frost/Nixon 2008, The Boat that Rocked 2009, The Soloist 2009, State of Play 2009, A Serious Man 2009, Nanny McPhee and the Big Bang 2010, Green Zone 2010, The Secrets 2014, The Theory of Everything (BAFTA Award for Outstanding British film 2015) 2014. *TV includes:* Tales of the City, The Borrowers, High Fidelity. *Address:* Working Title Films, 26 Aybrook Street, London, W1U 4AN, England (office). *Telephone:* (20) 7307-3000 (office). *Fax:* (20) 7307-3001 (office). *Website:* www.workingtitlefilms .com (office).

BEVANDA, Vjekoslav; Bosnia and Herzegovina politician; *Deputy Chairman of the Council of Ministers and Minister of Finance and the Treasury;* b. 13 May 1956, Mostar; m. Ljiljana; two d.; ed Univ. of Mostar; worked in SOKO aeroplane factory, Mostar 1979–89; with APRO bank, Mostar 1990–93; fmrly with Eurosped Group Zagreb (mem. EG Man.); Dir, Nord Adria Trieste, Italy, Nord Adria Wien, Austria 1993–99; with Euro Center, Split 2000–01; Dir Commerce Bank, Sarajevo 2001–07; mem. Hrvatska Demokratska Zajednica BiH (Croatian Democratic Union of Bosnia and Herzegovina); Deputy Prime Minister and Minister of Finance, Bosnia and Herzegovina 2007–11, Minister of Finance and the Treasury 2015–; Chair. Council of Ministers (Prime Minister) 2012–15, Deputy Chair. 2015–. *Address:* Ministry of Finance and the Treasury, 71000 Sarajevo, trg Bosne i Hercegovine 1, Bosnia and Herzegovina (office). *Telephone:* (33) 205345 (office); (33) 219923 (office). *Fax:* (33) 202930 (office). *E-mail:* trezorbih@mft.gov.ba (office). *Website:* www.mft.gov.ba (office); www.vijeceministara.gov.ba (office).

BEVIN, Matthew (Matt) Griswold, BA; American business executive and politician; *Governor of Kentucky;* b. 9 Jan. 1967, Denver, Colo; s. of Avery Bevin and Louise Bevin; m. Glenna Bevin 1996; six c.; ed Washington and Lee Univ.; Captain, US Army 1989–93; fmr Financial Consultant, SEI Investments Co., Pennsylvania and Boston; with Nat. Asset Management 1999–2003; Co-founder, Integrity Asset Management 2003–11; took over management, Bevin Brothers Manufacturing Co. (family firm) 2008, Pres. 2011–; Partner, Waycross Partners, Kentucky; Gov. of Kentucky 2015–; Republican. *Address:* Office of the Governor, 700 Capitol Avenue, Suite 100, Frankfort, KY 40601, USA (office). *Telephone:* (502) 564-2611 (office). *Fax:* (502) 564-0437 (office). *Website:* governor.ky.gov (office).

BEWKES, Jeffrey (Jeff) L., BA, MBA; American broadcasting executive; b. 25 May 1952, Paterson, NJ; s. of Eugene Garrett Bewkes, Jr; m. Margaret (Peggy) Brim; one c.; ed Yale Univ., Stanford Univ. Grad. School of Business; early career as Operations Dir Sonoma Vineyards, Calif.; Accountant Officer, Citibank, New York 1984–86; Exec. Vice-Pres. and Chief Financial Officer Home Box Office Inc. 1986–91, Pres. and COO 1991–95, Chair. and CEO 1995–2002; Chair. Entertainment and Network Group, AOL Time Warner Inc. (now Time Warner Inc.) 2002–05, Pres. Time Warner Inc. 2005–08, also COO 2005–07, mem. Bd of Dirs 2007–14, CEO 2008–18, Chair. 2009–18, then Sr Advisor; mem. Bd of Dirs Nixon Center; mem. Advisory Bd Stanford Univ. Grad. School of Business, American Museum of Natural History, Museum of Television and Radio, The Creative Coalition, Paley Center for Media; Trustee, Yale Univ., Museum of the Moving Image; mem. Council on Foreign Relations. *Address:* c/o Time Warner Inc., 1 Time Warner Center, New York, NY 10019, USA (office).

BEWLEY, Thomas Henry, MA, MD, FRCP, FRCPI; Irish consultant psychiatrist; *Consultant Emeritus, St Thomas' Hospital;* b. 8 July 1926, Dublin; s. of Geoffrey Bewley and Victoria Jane Wilson; m. Beulah Knox 1955; one s. four d.; ed St Columba's Coll., Dublin, Trinity Coll., Dublin; trained at St Patrick's Hosp., Dublin, Maudsley Hosp., London and Univ. of Cincinnati, USA; Consultant Psychiatrist, Tooting Bec and St Thomas' Hosps, London 1961–88, now Consultant Emer., St Thomas' Hosp.; mem. Standing Advisory Cttee on Drug Dependence 1966–71, Advisory Council on Misuse of Drugs 1972–84; Consultant Adviser on Drug Dependence to Dept of Health and Social Security 1972–81; Consultant WHO 1969–78; Hon. Sr Lecturer, St George's Hosp. Medical School, Univ. of London 1974–96; Pres. Royal Coll. of Psychiatrists 1984–87 (Dean 1977–82); Jt Founder and mem. Council, Inst. for the Study of Drug Dependence 1967–96; Hon. CBE. *Publications include:* Handbook for Inceptors and Trainees in Psychiatry 1976, Madness to Mental Illness 2008; papers on drug dependence, medical manpower and side effects of drugs. *Address:* 4 Grosvenor Gardens Mews North, London, SW1W 0JP, England. *Telephone:* (20) 7730-9592. *E-mail:* thomasbewley@ waitrose.com.

BEXELL, Göran Bertil David, PhD; Swedish academic and fmr university administrator; *Senior Professor of Ethics, Lund University;* b. 24 Dec. 1943, Högsby; m. Ingrid Bexell; one s. one d.; Sr Prof. of Ethics, Dept of Theology, Lund Univ. 1990–, Dean, Theology Faculty 1995–99, Dean, Faculty of Humanities and Theology 2000–03, Vice-Chancellor Lund Univ. 2003–08; Ed. Svensk Teologisk Kvartalskrift 1990–97; fmr Pres. Asscn of Swedish Higher Educ. *Publications:* Teologisk etik: en introduktion (co-author), Universal Ethics: Perspectives and Proposals from Scandinavian Scholars (co-ed.) 2002, Academic Values Show the Way 2011. *Address:* The Pufendorf Institute, Lund University, PO Box 117, 221 00 Lund, Sweden (office). *Telephone:* (46) 222-71-79 (office). *Fax:* (46) 222-47-20 (office). *E-mail:* goran.bexell@rektor.lu.se (office). *Website:* www.lu.se (office).

BEYENE, Tekie, BA; Eritrean fmr central banker; b. 15 June 1941, Asmara; m. Maaza Haile; ed Univ. of Asmara; fmr Gov. Bank of Eritrea; mem. Bd of Govs, IMF 2007. *Publications:* contribs to magazine Hewyet (Recovery). *Leisure interest:* writing. *Address:* Tiro Alvolo Street 702, No. 14–16, Asmara, Eritrea (home). *Telephone:* (1) 184351 (home).

BEYLE, Abdirahman Duale, PhD; Somali economist and politician; *Minister of Finance;* b. Awdal region; ed Univ. of Wisconsin, USA; taught econs, statistics and finance at King Saud Univ., Saudi Arabia and Tennessee State Univ., USA; fmr Finance Officer with African Devt Bank, Tunisia, becoming Head, Dept of Agric. and Agro-Industry; Minister of Foreign Affairs and Int. Co-operation 2014–15, Minister of Finance 2017–; Chair. Nat. Ind. Election Comm. 2017; mem. Bd of Trustees, African Fertilizer and Agribusiness Partnership. *Address:* Ministry of Finance, Corso Somalia Street, Shangaani District, Mogadishu, Somalia (office). *Telephone:* (7) 747363 (office). *E-mail:* info@mof.gov.so (office). *Website:* mof.gov.so (office).

BEYNON, John David Emrys, PhD; British professor of electronics and college principal; b. 11 March 1939, Risca, Gwent, Wales; s. of John Emrys Beynon and Elvira Beynon; m. Hazel Janet Hurley 1964; two s. one d.; ed Univ. of Wales and Univ. of Southampton; Scientific Officer, Radio Research Station, Slough 1962–64; Lecturer, Sr Lecturer, then Reader, Univ. of Southampton 1964–67; Prof. of Electronics, Univ. of Wales Inst. of Science and Tech., Cardiff 1977–79; Head of Dept of Electronic and Electrical Eng, Univ. of Surrey 1979–83, Pro Vice-Chancellor 1983–87, Sr Pro Vice-Chancellor 1987–90; Prin., King's Coll., London 1990–92, Fellow 1990; Fellow, Royal Acad. of Engineering; Hon. Fellow, Univ. Coll. of Swansea 1990; mem. British Library Advisory Council 1994–99, Ind. TV Comm. 1995–2000; Chair. Westminster Christian Council 1999–2000; Sec., Bloomsbury Central Baptist Church, London 2000–14. *Publications include:* Charge-coupled Devices and Their Applications (with D. R. Lamb) 1980; papers on plasma physics, semi-conductor devices and integrated circuits and eng educ. *Leisure interests:* music, photography, travel. *Address:* Chalkdene, 13 Great Quarry, Guildford, GU1 3XN, England (home). *Telephone:* (1483) 503458 (home).

BEYONCÉ; American singer, songwriter, actress and producer; b. (Beyoncé Giselle Knowles), 4 Sept. 1981, Houston, Tex.; d. of Mathew Knowles and Tina Knowles; m. Jay-Z (Shawn Carter) 2008; one s. two d.; Founding mem. GirlsTyme (with Kelly Rowland, later joined by LaTavia Roberson and LeToya Luckett), group renamed Something Fresh, then The Dolls before settling on Destiny's Child 1989–2005; numerous live performances, tours; solo artist 2001–; numerous collaborations including The Carters (with Jay-Z); est. clothing label Touch of Couture; Amb. for World Humanitarian Day campaign 2012; with Destiny's Child: Billboard Award for Artist of the Year, Group of the Year, Hot 100 Singles Artist of the Year, Hot 100 Group of the Year 2000, NAACP Image Award for Outstanding Duo or Group (for Say My Name) 2001, MTV Video Award for Best R&B Video (for Say My Name) 2001, American Music Award for Favorite Soul/R&B Group 2001, Soul Train Sammy Davis Jr Award for Entertainer of the Year 2001, American Music Award for Favorite Pop/Rock Band, Duo or Group 2002, BRIT Award for Best Int. Group 2002, MOBO Award for Best Gospel Act 2002, World Music Award for World's Best Pop Group 2005, Lady of Soul Award for Best Group Single (for Soldier) 2005, American Music Award for Favorite Soul/R & B Band, Duo or Group 2005; solo: Billboard Awards for New Female Artist of the Year, New R&B Artist, Hot 200 Female Artist 2003, Female R&B/Hip Hop Artist of the Year 2006, Female Artist of the Decade 2009, Radio Artist of the Decade 2009, Millennium Award 2011, BRIT Awards for Best Int. Female Solo Artist 2004, 2017, Billboard R&B/Hip Hop Awards for Top Female Artist, New Artist 2004, Grammy Awards for Best R&B Song, Best R&B Performance by a Duo or Group with Vocal (for Say My Name) 2001, for Best R&B Performance by a Duo or Group with Vocals (for Survivor) 2002, for Best R&B Song, Best Rap/Sung Collaboration (for Crazy in Love, with Jay-Z) 2004, for best R&B performance by a duo or group (for The Closer I Get To You, with Luther Vandross) 2004, for Best Female R&B Vocal Performance (for Dangerously In Love) 2004, (for Single Ladies) 2010, for Best R&B Performance by a Duo or Group with Vocals (for So Amazing, with Stevie Wonder) 2006, for Song of the Year (for Single Ladies) 2010, for Best Female Pop Vocal Performance (for Halo) 2010, for Best Traditional R&B Vocal Performance (for At Last) 2010, for Best R&B Song (for Single Ladies) 2010, for Best Traditional R&B Performance (for Love on Top) 2013, for Best R&B Performance, for Best R&B Song (both for Drunk in Love, with Jay-Z) 2015, BET Award for Best Female R&B/Pop Artist 2016, Billboard Music Awards for R&B/Hip-Hop Group of the Year 2005, for Top Female Artist 2017, for Top Touring Artist 2017, for Top R&B Artist 2017, MOBO Awards for Best Song and Best Video (both for Deja Vu), for Best Int. Female 2006, Soul Train Award for Best Single by a Female (for Irreplaceable) 2007, for Best Dance Performance (for Run the World (Girls)) 2011, BET Award for Best R&B Female 2007, for Video of the Year (for Irreplaceable) 2007, MTV Video Music Award for Best Collaboration (for Beautiful Liar with Shakira) 2007, MTV Europe Music Awards for Best Female 2009, for Best Song (for Halo) 2009, for Best Live Act 2013, for Best Song with a Social Message 2014, American Music Awards for Favorite Female Soul/Rhythm and Blues Artist 2009, 2011, 2012, 2014, 2017, for Tour of the Year 2016, Writing Award, New York Asscn of Black Journalists 2012, MTV Video Music Award for Best Collaboration (for Drunk in Love featuring Jay Z) 2014, for Best Video with a Social Message (for Pretty Hurts) 2014, MTV Video Music Award for Video of the Year, for Best Direction, for Best Cinematography, for Best Editing, for Best Pop Video (for Formation) 2016, for Best Female Video (for Hold Up) 2016, BET Award for Best Female R&B/Pop Artist Award 2018, GLAAD Vanguard Award (co-recipient) 2019. *Recordings include:* albums: with Destiny's Child: Destiny's Child 1998, The Writing's On The Wall 1999, Survivor (American Music Award for Favorite Pop/Rock Album 2002) 2001, Eight Days Of Christmas 2001, Destiny Fulfilled (Lady of Soul Award for Best Group Album 2005, American Music Award for Favorite Soul/R&B Album 2005) 2004; solo: Soul Survivors 2002, Dangerously in Love (Grammy Award for Best Contemporary R&B Album 2004) 2003, Live At Wembley 2004, B-Day (Grammy Award for Best Contemporary R&B Album 2007) 2006, I Am... Sasha Fierce

(Grammy Award for Best Contemporary R&B Album 2010) 2008, 4 2011, Beyoncé (American Music Award for Favorite Soul/R&B Album 2014) 2013, Lemonade (MTV Video Music Award for Best Long Form Video, Grammy Award for Best Urban Contemporary Album 2017, BET Award for Album of the Year 2017, Billboard Music Award for Top R&B Album 2017) 2016; with The Carters: Everything is Love 2018. *Films include:* Austin Powers in Goldmember 2002, The Fighting Temptations 2003, The Pink Panther 2006, Dreamgirls 2006, Cadillac Records (also exec. producer) 2008, Obsessed (also exec. producer) 2009, Epic (voice) 2013, The Lion King (voice) 2019. *Television includes:* Carmen: A Hip Hopera (film) 2001, Wow! Wow! Wubbzy! (series) 2009, Robins (series) 2010. *Address:* c/o Music World Entertainment, 5120 Woodway Drive, Houston, TX 77056, USA (office). *Telephone:* (713) 772-5175 (office). *Website:* musicworldent .com (office); www.beyonceonline.com; www.destinyschild.com.

BEYRER, Markus J.; Austrian diplomatist and business executive; *Director General, BusinessEurope;* b. 19 Aug. 1965, St Pölten; m. Petra Beyrer; one s. one d.; ed Univ. of Vienna, Vienna Univ. of Econs and Business Admin, postgraduate studies of European Law at Danube Univ., Krems Stanford Exec. Program, Grad. School of Business, Stanford Univ.; mem. EU Expert Team (EU Cadet), Dept for European Integration and Trade Policy, Austrian Fed. Econ. Chamber 1992–94; Stage in European EC, Directorate Gen. XI (Environment) Spring 1994; Attaché for Industrial and Commercial Affairs, Perm. Rep. of Austria to EU 1994–96; Expert for European and Int. Affairs, Dept for Environmental Policy, Austrian Fed. Econ. Chamber 1996–99; Sr Econ. Adviser to Fed. Vice-Chancellor and Fed. Minister for Foreign Affairs, then to Austrian Fed. Chancellor 1999–2002; Dir for Econ. Affairs, Austrian Fed. Econ. Chamber 2002–04; Dir-Gen. Fed. of Austrian Industries (IV) 2004–11; CEO Österreichische Industrieholding AG (ÖIAG) 2011–12; Chair. Supervisory Bd OMV Group 2011–12, Österreichische Post AG 2011–12, Telekom Austria AG 2011–12, APK Pensionskasse AG 2011–12; Dir (non-exec.) Austrian Cen. Bank (Österreichische Nationalbank) 2008–; Vice-Chair. Supervisory Bd Raiffeisen Holding Niederösterreich, Vienna (financial expert in Audit Cttee) 2006–11; mem. Exec. Cttee BusinessEurope 2004–11, Dir Gen. 2012–; mem. Supervisory Bd G4S Security Services AG 2007–11, Siemens AG Österreich 2010–11. *Address:* BusinessEurope a.i.s.b.l., Avenue de Cortenbergh 168, 1000 Brussels, Belgium (office). *Telephone:* (2) 237-65-11 (office). *Fax:* (2) 231-14-45 (office). *E-mail:* main@businesseurope.eu (office). *Website:* www .businesseurope.eu (office).

BEZHUASHVILI, Gela, LLM, LLM, MPA; Georgian politician, diplomatist and lawyer; b. 1 March 1967, Tetritskaro Region; m.; two s. one d.; ed Kiev State Univ., Ukraine, Southern Methodist Univ. Law School and John F. Kennedy School of Govt, Harvard Univ., USA; positions at Ministry of Foreign Affairs including Second Sec. of Int. Law Problems Div., Deputy Head of Dept then Deputy Head of Int. Law Bd 1991–93; Envoy, Embassy in Kazakhstan 1993–96; Dir Int. Law Dept 1997–2000; Deputy Minister of Defence 2000–04, Minister of Defence 2004; Asst to Pres. of Georgia on Nat. Security Issues and Sec. Nat. Security Council 2004–05; Minister of Foreign Affairs 2005–08; Head of Special Service, Intelligence Service 2008–13; mem. Cttee on Int. Law, Cttee Against Corruption and Sub-Cttee on Protection of Nat. Minorities, European Council; Rep. of Georgia, Baku-Tbilisi-Ceyhan Law Documentation Package 1999–2000; Order of Merit, First Class (Ukraine) 2006, Order of Maarjamaa Rist III Class 2007; winner Edmund Muskie Fellowship Program (USA) 1995. *Publications include:* International Law Aspects of the Foreign Policy of Georgia 2003; articles in professional journals of int. law, nat. minorities and self-determination.

BEZOS, Jeffrey (Jeff) Preston, BS; American online retail executive; *Chairman, President and CEO, Amazon.com, Inc.;* b. 12 Jan. 1964, Albuquerque, NM; m. Mackenzie Bezos; two s.; ed Miami Palmetto Senior High School, Princeton Univ.; worked on Wall Street in computer science field; later worked on building a network for int. trade for Fitel; with Bankers Trust Co. 1988–90; joined D. E. Shaw & Co. 1990, Sr Vice-Pres. 1992–94; f. Amazon.com Inc., Seattle, Wash. 1994, Chair., Pres. and CEO 1995–; f. Blue Origin LLC (human spaceflight startup co.) 2000; f. Bezos Expeditions (investment co.); acquired Washington Post newspaper 2013; Dr hc in Science and Tech. (Carnegie Mellon Univ.) 2008; Silver Knight Award 1982, TIME magazine Person of the Year 1999, selected by US News & World Report as one of America's Best Leaders 2008. *Address:* Amazon.com Inc., 410 Terry Avenue North, Seattle, WA 98109-5210, USA (office). *Telephone:* (206) 266-1000 (office). *Fax:* (206) 266-1821 (office). *Website:* www.amazon.com (office); www.blueorigin.com (office).

BGANBA, Valeri Ramshukhovich; Georgian agronomist and politician; *Prime Minister, 'Republic of Abkhazia';* b. 26 Aug. 1953, Bzyb, Gagra Dist; m.; two s. one d.; ed Kuban State Agrarian Univ., Krasnodar; began career as agronomist, Gardalinsky state farm, Argun 1976–78; agronomist, Dept of Agric., Gagra City Exec. Cttee 1978–79; Second Sec., Gagra City Komsomol (All-Union Leninist Young Communist League) Cttee 1979–82; Dir Tobacco Plant, Tandripsh 1989; Chair. Gagra Agroindustrial Asscn 1989; mem. Abkhazia Supreme Soviet 1991; Chair. Gagra Dist Ass. 1998; Gov., Gagra Dist 2002–06; mem. Nat. Ass. of Abkhazia 2007–, Speaker 2012–17; Acting Pres., 'Repub. of Abkhazia' June–Sept. 2014; Prime Minister, 'Repub. of Abkhazia' 2018–. *Address:* Office of the Cabinet of Ministers, 384900 Sukhumi, nab. Makhajirov 32, 'Republic of Abkhazia', Georgia (office). *Telephone:* (840) 226-12-22 (office). *Fax:* (840) 226-46-32 (office). *E-mail:* sukhum-krma@yandex.ru (office). *Website:* km-ra.org (office).

BHABHA, Homi K., MA, DPhil; Indian writer and academic; *Anne F. Rothenberg Professor of the Humanities, Harvard University;* b. 1949; ed Univ. of Bombay (now Mumbai), Christ Church Coll., Oxford, UK; Tutor, Wadham Coll., St Anne's Coll., Oxford, 1976–78; Lecturer in Creative Writing, Warwick Univ. 1977–78; Reader in English Literature, Sussex Univ. 1978–94; Visiting Scholar, Brown Univ. 1987, SUNY Stonybrook 1990, Univs of Pennsylvania and Queensland, Australia 1991, Princeton Univ. 1992, Dartmouth Coll. 1993; Distinguished Prof., Univ. of Edmonton, Canada 1992; Mellon Prof., Tulane Univ., New Orleans 1994; Prof. of English Literature, Univ. of Chicago 1994, Chester D. Tripp Distinguished Prof. in the Humanities 1996–2000; Chair. Program in History and Literature, Harvard Univ. 2001–04, Anne F. Rothenberg Prof. of English and American Literature and Language, Harvard Univ. 2001–06, Anne F. Rothenberg Prof. of the Humanities 2006–, Dir Humanities Center 2005–; Distinguished Visiting Prof., Univ. Coll. London 2004–; Faculty Advisor, World Econ. Forum, Davos; Fellow, Wissenschaftskolleg zu Berlin 2001–02; British Council Scholarship 1976, Violet Vaughan-Morgan Grad. Fellowship Univ. of Oxford; Asian American Inst. Milestone Award 2000. *Publications include:* Nation and Narration (ed.) 1990, The Location of Culture 1993, Die Bhagavadgita 1997, Anish Kapoor (co-author) 1998, Die Verortung der Kultur 2000, Cosmopolitanism (ed.) 2002, Habitations of Modernity: Essays in the Wake of Subaltern Studies 2002, Edward Said: Continuing the Conversation (ed.) 2005, Without Boundary (co-author) 2006, The Urgency of Theory 2008, Beyond Photography 2011, Our Neighbours, Ourselves 2011; numerous essays and articles in professional journals. *Address:* Humanities Center, Harvard University, 12 Quincy Street, Barker Center 134, Cambridge, MA 02138, USA (office). *Telephone:* (617) 495-0739 (office). *Fax:* (617) 495-0730 (office). *E-mail:* hbhabha@fas.harvard.edu (office). *Website:* www.aaas .fas.harvard.edu (office).

BHADESHIA, Sir Harshad (Harry) Kumar Dharamshi Hansraj, Kt, BSc, PhD, FRS, FREng, FInstP, FIM, CEng, CPhys; British metallurgist and academic; *Tata Steel Professor of Metallurgy, University of Cambridge;* b. 27 Nov. 1953, Nairobi, Kenya; s. of Dharamshi Hansraj Bhadeshia and Narmda Dharamshi Bhadeshia; m. 1978 (divorced 1992); two d.; ed City of London Polytechnic, Univ. of Cambridge; Science Research Council Research Fellow, Univ. of Cambridge 1979–81, Demonstrator 1981–85, Lecturer 1985–94, Reader in Physical Metallurgy 1994–99, Prof. of Physical Metallurgy 1999, Tata Steel Prof. of Metallurgy 2008–; Prof. of Computational Metallurgy, Grad. Inst. of Ferrous Tech., Pohang Univ. of Science and Tech., South Korea; Vice-Pres. Industrial Trust; Dir SKF Univ. Tech. Centre 2009–; Founding Ed. Science and Technology of Welding and Joining 1996–; mem. Editorial Bd, Australasian Journal of Welding 2000–, Material Transactions of JIM 2000–, Science and Technology of Advanced Materials 2001–, Materials Science and Technology 2002–, Current Opinion: Solid-State and Materials Science 2002–; mem. European Acad. of Sciences; Fellow, Darwin Coll., Cambridge 1985–, Inst. of Materials 1998–; Foreign Fellow, Indian Nat. Acad. of Eng 2004–; Royal Charter Prize 1976, Pfeil Medal and Prize 1979, 1991, Larke Medal 1992, Hume-Rothery Prize 1992, Rosenhain Medal and Prize 1994, CBMM Charles-Hatchett Medal and Award, Brazil, 1996, Royal Soc. Armourers and Brasiers' Co. Award 1997, Medal and Rose Bowl 2000, Reaumur Medal 2001, 5th Tendolkar Memorial Lecture India 2002, 37th John Player Memorial Lecture 2002, Brooker Medal 2003, Sawamura Award 2003, Comfort A. Adams Award Lecture 2004, 52nd Hatfield Lecture 2004, 17th Hume-Rothery Lecture 2005. *Publications include:* Geometry of Crystals 1987, Bainite in Steels 1992, Steels (co-author) 1995; numerous scientific papers in professional journals. *Leisure interests:* television, squash. *Address:* Department of Materials Science and Metallurgy, Phase Transformations and Complex Properties Research Group, University of Cambridge, Pembroke Street, Cambridge, CB2 3QZ (office); 57 Barrons Way, Comberton, Cambridge, CB3 7EQ, England (home). *Telephone:* (1223) 334301 (office). *Fax:* (1223) 334567 (office). *E-mail:* hkdb@cam.ac.uk (office); hkdb@postech.ac.kr (office). *Website:* www.msm.cam.ac.uk/phase-trans/ Bhadeshia.html (office).

BHAGWAT, Mohan Madhukar, BSc; Indian veterinarian and politician; *Sarsanghachalak (Supreme Chief), Rashtriya Swayamsevak Sangh;* b. 11 Sept. 1950, Chandrapur, Maharashtra; s. of Madhukar Rao Bhagwat and Malatibai Bhagwat; ed Janata Coll., Punjabrao Agriculture Univ. (Punjabrao Krishi Vidyapeeth); worked as veterinary officer at Animal Husbandry Dept, Chandrapur and then transferred to Chamorshi; joined Rashtriya Swayamsevak Sangh—RSS (Hindu nationalist org.) as Pracharak (worker), Akola 1977, then Pracharak of Nagpur and Vidarbha region, Akhil Bharatiya Sharirik Pramukh (all-India chief of physical training) 1991–99, Gen. Sec. 2000–09, Sarsanghachalak (Supreme Chief) 2009–. *Address:* Rashtriya Swayamsevak Sangh, 9, Dr Hedgewar Bhavan CY Chintamani Road, George Town, Allahabad, Uttar Pradesh, India (office). *E-mail:* contactus@rss.org (office); mohanbhagwat59@gmail.com. *Website:* rss.org (office).

BHAI, Aziz Mohammad; Bangladeshi business executive; *Chairman, Ambee Pharmaceuticals Limited;* b. Kanpur, India; Founding Chair. Ambee Pharmaceuticals Ltd 1976–; fmr Pres. Dhaka Chamber of Commerce and Industry, Aga Khan Supreme Council for Bangladesh; mem. Rotary Club. *Address:* Ambee Pharmaceuticals Ltd, 184/1, Tejgaon Industrial Area, Dhaka 1208, Bangladesh (office). *Telephone:* (2) 8870897 (office). *Fax:* (2) 8870799 (office). *E-mail:* info@ ambeepharma.com (office). *Website:* www.ambeepharma.com (office).

BHALLA, Bhupinder S.; Indian civil servant and government official; *Chairman, Chandigarh Housing Board;* ed Univ. of Georgia, USA, Indian Inst. of Man.; Admin. Service Officer, posted to Goa 1992–94, Daman and Diu, Dadra and Nagar Haveli 1994–97, Jt Sec. (L&B), Delhi Govt 1997–2000, Sec. (IT) and Chief Electoral Officer, Govt of Goa 2002–04, Dir of Econ. Affairs (Banking Div.) 2004–08, Counsellor (Econ.) Econ. Wing, Embassy in Washington, DC 2008–11, Sec. (Health, Revenue, Educ., IT), Andaman and Nicobar Islands 2011–12, Admin. of Dadra and Nagar Haveli (DNH) Aug. 2012–14 and of Daman and Diu (DD) Sept. 2012–14; Chair. Chandigarh Housing Bd 2014–. *Address:* Chandigarh Housing Board, 8 Jan Marg, Sector 9, Chandigarh 160 017, India (office). *Telephone:* (17) 24601822 (office). *E-mail:* chb_chd@yahoo.com (office). *Website:* www.chandigarh .gov.in/chb_ppl.htm (office).

BHANDARE, Murlidhar Chandrakant, BSc, LLB; Indian lawyer and politician; b. 10 Dec. 1928, Bombay (now Mumbai); s. of Chandrakant Laxmikant Bhandare and Sunanda Bhandare; m.; one s. one d.; Sr Advocate in Supreme Court of India, Pres. Supreme Court Bar Asscn 1986–88; mem. Rajya Sabha 1980–94; Gov. of Orissa 2007–13; Chair. UN Sub-Comm. for Prevention of Discrimination and Protection of Minorities 1984–89, UNESCO's Appeals Body 1990–2003, Indira Gandhi Nat. Integration Award Cttee; active in supporting empowerment of women and protection of rights of children and physically handicapped. *Publications include:* The World of Gender Justice (ed.); articles on law, human rights, population control, gender parity and justice published in leading magazines and journals.

BHANDARI, Bidhya Devi; Nepalese politician and head of state; *President;* b. June 1961, Ambote, Bhojpur dist; d. of Ram Bahadur Pandey; m. Madan Bhandari 1982 (died 1993); ed Bhojpur Campus, Mahendra Morang Campus, Biratnagar; mem. All Nepal National Free Student Union during student years; elected to

House of Reps 1993, 1994, 1999; Minister for Population and Environment 1997; mem. All Nepalese Women's Asscn (ANWA) 1980–, fmr Pres. Biratnagar chapter, Morang dist and Koshi zone, then Chair. ANWA 1998; detained and held in custody following public protests against monarchy 2005, released 2006; mem. Interim Parl. formed after Jana Andolan II 2006; Minister of Defence 2009–11; Pres. of Nepal 2015–; mem. Central Cttee, Communist Party of Nepal (Unified Marxist-Leninist) 1998–, Vice-Chair. 2009–; Patron Madan Bhandari Study and Research Centre. *Address:* Office of the President, Kathmandu, Nepal (office); Communist Party of Nepal (Unified Marxist-Leninist), Madan Nagar, Balkhu, POB 5471, Kathmandu, Nepal (office). *Telephone:* (1) 4278081 (office). *Fax:* (1) 4278084 (office). *E-mail:* uml@ntc.net.np (office). *Website:* www.cpnuml.org (office).

BHANDARI, Sarat Singh; Nepalese politician; *Chairman, Rastriya Madhes Samajbadi Party;* b. Mahottari Dist; fmr Minister for Health, for Culture and for Tourism and Civil Aviation; Minister of Defence 2011; fmr mem. Nepali Congress Party; fmr mem. Madhesi Jana Adhikar Forum Nepal (Madhesi People's Rights Forum Nepal); Co-founder and Chair. Rastriya Madhes Samajbadi Party 2012–. *Address:* Rashtriya Madhesh Samajwadi Party, Gwarko, Lalitpur, Nepal.

BHANSALI, Sanjay Leela; Indian director, producer and screenwriter; b. 24 Feb. 1963, Mumbai, Maharashtra; s. of Navin Bhansali and Leela Bhansali; ed Film and Television Inst. of India; Padma Shri Award 2015. *Films:* 1942: A Love Story (writer) 1994, Khamoshi: The Musical (dir, writer) (Filmfare Award for Critics' Best Film 1997) 1996, Hum Dil De Chuke Sanam (dir, producer, wirter) (Filmfare Award for Best Dir and Best Film 2000, IIFA Award for Best Dir, Best Movie, Best Screenplay and Best Story 2000) 1999, Devdas (dir) (Nat. Film Award for Best Popular Film 2002, Filmfare Award for Best Dir and Best Film 2003, IIFA Award for Best Dir 2003) 2002, Black (dir, producer) (Nat. Film Award for Best Feature Film in Hindi 2005, Filmfare Award for Best Dir, Best Film and Critics' Best Film 2006, IIFA Award for Best Dir and Best Movie 2006) 2005, Saawariya (dir, producer, ed.) 2007, Guzaarish (dir, producer, writer, music dir) 2010, My Friend Pinto (producer) 2011, Rowdy Rathore (producer) 2012, Shirin Farhad Ki Toh Nikal Padi (producer, writer) 2012, Goliyon Ki Raasleela Ram-Leela (dir, producer, writer, ed., music dir) 2013, Mary Kom (producer) (Nat. Film Award for Best Popular Film 2014) 2014, Gabbar Is Back (producer) 2015, Bajirao Mastani (dir, producer, music dir) (Nat. Film Award for Best Direction 2015, Filmfare Award for Best Dir and Best Film 2016, IIFA Award for Best Dir 2016) 2015, Padmaavat (dir, producer, writer, ed., music dir) (Filmfare Award for Best Music Dir 2019) 2018. *Television:* Saraswatichandra (producer) 2013.

BHARDWAJ, Hans Raj, LLB, MA; Indian politician and lawyer; b. 17 May 1937, Haryana; s. of Jagan Nath Prasad Sharma and Sarti Devi; m. Prafulata Bhardwaj 1960; one s. two d.; ed B.M. Coll., Shimla, Agra Univ. and Panjab Univ., Chandigarh; mem. Nat. Exec., Indian Youth Congress 1957; Public Prosecutor, Delhi High Court 1972–77; Sr Standing Counsel for UP, Supreme Court of India 1980–82; mem. Rajya Sabha (Parl.) for Haryana 1982–2006, Leader Parl. Del. to Repub. of Korea 1989; mem. Cttee of Privileges, Rajya Sabha (Parl.) 1996–2004, of Home Affairs Cttee 1998–2004, Advisory Council, Delhi Devt Cttee 2000–04, Business Advisory Cttee 2002–04; Minister of State for Law and Justice 1984–89, 1992–96; Sr Vice-Pres. Inst. of Constitutional and Parl. Studies, New Delhi 1988–90; Minister of State for Planning and Programme Implementation 1991–92; Minister of Law and Justice 2004–09; Gov. of Karnataka 2009–14, additional charge of Kerala 2012–13; mem. Bar Asscn of India, Legal Affairs Cttee for Asian Games 1982, Indo-US Sub-Comm. for Educ. and Culture 1982–84, Law Asia, Int. Law Asscn, United Int. Advocates; Hon. Chair. Int. Centre for Alternative Dispute Resolution; Dr hc (Kurukshetra Univ.). *Publications include:* Law, Lawyers and Judges, Soul of India, Crime, Criminal Justice and Human Rights. *Leisure interests:* gardening and farming. *Address:* E-7/19, Charimili, Bhopal, Madhya Pradesh, India (home).

BHARGAVA, Manjul, AB, PhD; Canadian mathematician and academic; *Professor of Mathematics, Princeton University;* b. 1974, Hamilton, Ont.; ed Harvard Univ., Princeton Univ.; grew up in Long Island, New York; with Nat. Security Agency, summer 1994; Duluth Summer Research Program, summer 1995; Center for Communications Research, Princeton, summer 1996; AT&T Labs Research, Florham Park, New Jersey, summer 1997; Clay Research Fellowship (first recipient), Clay Math. Inst., Cambridge, Mass 2000–05; Visiting Mathematician, Princeton Univ. 2001–02; Visiting Asst Prof., Harvard Univ., spring 2003; Prof. of Math., Princeton Univ. (hired at rank of full prof. with tenure just two years after finishing grad. school) 2003–; fmr Co-Pres. Harvard Math Club; Winner, New York State Science Talent Search 1992, Detur Prize for Outstanding Academic Achievement, Harvard Univ. 1993, Derek Bok Award for Excellence in Teaching, Harvard Univ. 1993, 1994, 1995, Hoopes Prize for Excellence in Scholarly Work and Research, Harvard Univ. 1996, Hertz Foundation Grad. Fellowship in Math. 1996–2000, AMS-MAA-SIAM Frank and Brennie Morgan Prize 1997, named one of Popular Science Magazine's "Brilliant 10" 2002, Hasse Prize for Exposition, Math. Asscn of America 2003, Packard Foundation Fellowship in Science and Eng 2004, Leonard M. and Eleanor B. Blumenthal Award for the Advancement of Research in Pure Math. 2005, Clay Research Award, Clay Math. Inst. (co-recipient) 2005, SASTRA Ramanujan Prize (co-recipient) 2005, MS Frank Nelson Cole Prize in Number Theory, American Math. Soc. 2008, Fermat Prize 2011, Simons Investigator Award 2012, Infosys Prize 2012, Fields Medal 2014. *Achievements include:* 13 new Gauss composition laws, including quartic and quintic degree cases; proof of 15 theorem, including extension of theorem to other number sets such as prime numbers; proof of 290 theorem; novel generalization of factorial function, resolving decades-old conjecture by George Pólya. *Publications:* several papers in professional journals on algebraic number theory, combinatorics and representation theory. *Leisure interests:* tabla player (studied under Zakir Hussain), linguistics and its various connections to math. and music. *Address:* 1206 Fine Hall, Department of Mathematics, Princeton University, Princeton, NJ 08544, USA (office). *Telephone:* (609) 258-4192 (office). *Fax:* (609) 258-1367 (office). *E-mail:* bhargava@math.princeton.edu (office). *Website:* www.math.princeton.edu (office).

BHARTI, Uma; Indian politician and writer; *Minister of Water Resources, River Development and Ganga Rejuvenation;* b. 3 May 1959, Tikamgarh Dist, Madhya Pradesh; apptd Vice-Pres. Bhartiya Janata Party (BJP), Madhya Pradesh 1988, Sec.-Gen. BJP –2004; elected to Lok Sabha for Khajurao, Chhatarour Dist 1989, 1991, 1996, 1998, for Bhopal 1999; Union Minister of State (ind. charge) for Human Resource Devt, for Tourism 1999–2000, for Youth Affairs and Sports 2000–02, for Coal and Mines 2002–03; Chief Minister of Madhya Pradesh 2003–04; Minister of Water Resources, River Devt and Ganga Rejuvenation 2014–; f. Bharatiya Janashakti Party 2005; mem. Consultative Cttee Ministry of Agric., Public Consultative Cttee Mata Betibai Charitable Trust and Manav Jagriti Sangh. *Publications include:* Swami Vivekanand 1972, Peace of Mind 1978, Maanav Ek Bhakti Ka Naata 1983. *Leisure interests:* protecting the environment and wildlife, discussing religion and culture, writing poetry, reading, watching movies, travelling, driving. *Address:* Ministry of Water Resources, Shram Shakti Bhawan, Rafi Marg, New Delhi 110 001, India (office). *E-mail:* egov-mowr@nic.in (office). *Website:* mowr.gov.in (office).

BHARTIA, Shobhana; Indian newspaper executive; *Chairperson and Editorial Director, HT Media;* b. 4 Jan. 1957, Calcutta (now Kolkata); d. of Dr Krishna Kumar Birla and Manorama Devi; m. Shyam Sunder Bhartia 1974; two s.; ed Loreto House, Calcutta; Exec. Dir The Hindustan Times Ltd 1986, Chair. and Editorial Dir 2008–; Chair. HT Vision Ltd 1990–, currently also Chair. HT Media; nominated mem. Rajya Sabha (upper house of Parl.) 2006–12, Pres. FICCI (women's org.); Chair. and Treas. Bd of Govs Delhi Coll. of Arts and Commerce 1988–90; Chair. Bd of Govs Shyama Prasad Mukherjee Coll. (for Women) 1992; mem. Bd of Dirs Press Trust of India Ltd 1987– (Chair.), Indian Airlines Ltd, New Delhi 1988–90, Air Travel Bureau Pvt. Ltd 1989, Shri Mata Vaishno Devi Shrine, Katra 1991, Hero Honda Ltd; Chair. Endeavor India; Deputy Chair. Exec. Cttee, Audit Bureau of Circulations; Pro-Chancellor, Birla Inst. of Tech. and Science, Pilani; Leader of dels to Australia, NZ, the Philippines and to World Congress of Women Conf. (Moscow, fmr USSR) 1987–88; mem. Bd North Regional Bd of Reserve Bank of India; mem. Exec. Cttee Indian Newspaper Soc. and Commonwealth Press Union, London; mem. Apex Cttee of Commonwealth Games 2010, Governing Council, India Habitat Centre, Alliance of Civilizations Bd of Govs., Nat. Inst. of Fashion Tech., Indian Public School Society (The Doon School); Trustee, Indira Gandhi Memorial Trust, Bhartiya Vidya Bhavan; Int. Cultural Devt Org. Award 1989, Mahila Shiromani Award 1990, Lok Shri Award, Inst. of Econ. Studies 1990, Vijaya Shri Award, Int. Friendship Soc. of India 1991, Nat. Press India Award 1992, Nat. Unity Award 1993, Global Leader for Tomorrow, World Econ. Forum 1996, Outstanding Businesswoman Award, PHD Chamber of Commerce & Industry, Punjab, Haryana, Delhi Chamber of Commerce and Industry 2001, Padma Shri 2005, Ernst and Young Entrepreneur of the Year Award 2005, Business Woman Award, The Economic Times Awards for Corp. Excellence 2007. *Leisure interests:* reading, music. *Address:* Hindustan Times House, 18–20 Kasturba Gandhi Marg, New Delhi, 110 001 (office); HT Media Ltd, Park Centra Building, 7th Floor, Sector-30, Delhi–Jaipur Highway, Gurgaon 122 001, India (office). *Telephone:* (11) 23361234 (office); (124) 3954700 (office); (11) 6830260 (home). *Fax:* (11) 66561270 (office). *E-mail:* feedback@hindustantimes.com (office). *Website:* www.hindustantimes.com (office); www.htmedia.in (office).

BHATIA, Mick, BSc, PhD; Canadian biologist and academic; *Director and Senior Scientist, Stem Cell and Cancer Research Institute, McMaster University;* b. 1970; ed McMaster Univ., Univ. of Guelph; worked for Dept of Human Biology, Univ. of Guelph; Postdoctoral Fellow, Hosp. for Sick Children, Univ. of Toronto; Canadian Research Chair and Dir Krembil Centre for Stem Cell Biology, Robarts Research Inst., Univ. of Western Ont., London 2003–05; currently Prof. of Biochemistry and Biomedical Sciences, Assoc. Mem. Dept of Pathology and Molecular Medicine, McMaster Univ., Hamilton, Dir and Sr Scientist, McMaster Stem Cell and Cancer Research Inst., also Dir and Sr Scientist, DeGroote Chair in Stem Cell and Cancer Biology 2006–; Postdoctoral Fellowship, Nat. Cancer Inst. of Canada 1995–97; Canada Research Chair in Stem Cell Biology and Regenerative Medicine (Tier 2) 2002–05, Canada Research Chair in Human Stem Cell Biology (Tier 1) 2006–11; Krembil Foundation Research Chair in Stem Cell Biology and Regenerative Medicine 2003–05; mem. Medical Review Panel, Gairdner Foundation; Annual Trainee Award, American Soc. of Dermatology 1997, Young Scientist Scholarship Award, Medical Research Council 1999–2002, Premiers' Research Excellence Award, Ministry of Energy, Science and Tech. 2000–05, Univ. of Guelph Alumni Medal of Achivement 2008, Molecular and Cellular Biology Award, Canadian Soc. for Biochemistry 2009, McMaster University Innovator of the Year 2011, Queen's Diamond Jubilee Medal 2012, CBMTG 2013 Till and McCulloch Award 2013. *Publications:* numerous articles in professional journals. *Address:* Michael G. DeGroote Centre for Learning and Discovery, 1280 Main Street West, Hamilton, ON L8S 4K1, Canada (office). *Telephone:* (905) 525-9140 (office). *Fax:* (905) 522-7772 (office). *E-mail:* mbhatia@mcmaster.ca (office). *Website:* sccri.mcmaster.ca/bhatia_mick.html (office); sccri.mcmaster.ca/bhatia_lab.html.

BHATIA, Raghunanthanlal, LLB; Indian politician; b. 3 July 1921, Amritsar, Punjab; s. of Arooramal Bhatia and Lal Devi Bhatia; m. Sarala Bhatia; one s. one d.; ed Univ. of the Punjab; fmr Pres. Students' Union; mem. Lok Sabha for Amritsar Constituency 1972, 1980–99, mem. Select Cttee for Amendment of the Constitution 1992, several consultative parl. cttees, including Ministry of Home Affairs, Educ., Railways, Information and Broadcasting, Law and Justice and Company Affairs, leader or mem. del. of AICC to People's Repub. of China, USSR, Poland, Bulgaria, Czechoslovakia, USA, Cambodia, Viet Nam, Afghanistan, Japan, UK; Pres. Punjab Pradesh Congress Cttee 1982–84; Union Minister of State for External Affairs July 1992; Gov. of Kerala 2004–08, of Bihar 2008–09; mem. Exec. Cttee Congress Parl. Party 1975–77, India Council for Cultural Relations 1983–84; Gen. Sec. All India Congress Cttee 1991; Chair. Cttee on Petitions 1983, India Bulgaria Friendship Soc., India GDR Friendship Asscn 1983–90; Co-Chair. All India Peace and Solidarity Org. 1981–83; Vice-Pres. Friends of the Soviet Union 1983–84; mem. Local Body of Amritsar for nine years; represented India as a del. to UN, del. to 7th NAM Summit, Delhi 1983, Commonwealth Heads of Govt Meeting, New Delhi 1983, 6th SAARC Summit, Colombo 1991, 5th Meeting of Coordinating Countries of the Action Programme for Econ. Cooperation of Non-aligned Countries, Delhi 1986. *Leisure interests:* reading, gardening. *Address:* 44 Kamalpushpa, Congress Nagar, Amravati 444 601, India (office). *Telephone:* (612) 2226207 (office).

BHATIA, Sabeer, BSc, MS; Indian/American internet services industry executive and entrepreneur; *Chairman, Arzoo.com;* b. 30 Dec. 1968, Chandigarh,

Punjab, India; s. of Baldev Bhatia and Daman Bhatia; m. Tania Sharma 2008 (divorced 2013); ed Birla Inst. of Tech. and Science, Pilani, California Inst. of Tech. and Stanford Univ., USA; Systems Integrator, Apple Computers; joined Firepower Systems Inc. 1994, co-f. Hotmail Corpn 1995, launched pioneering web-based email service Hotmail (with Jack Smith), sold to Microsoft 1997; worked for Microsoft 1998–99; Cofounder and Chair. Arzoo.com 1999, relaunched as travel portal 2006; launched Blogeverywhere.com. *Address:* Arzoo.com, Samruddhi Venture Park, 5th Floor, MIDC Central Road, Andhei East, Mumbai 400 093, India (office). *Telephone:* (22) 67134444 (office). *Fax:* (22) 28316680 (office). *Website:* www.arzoo.com (office).

BHATT, Om Prakash, BSc, MA; Indian fmr central banker; b. 7 March 1951; joined State Bank of India (SBI) as probationary officer 1972, held several positions, including Scheme Co-ordinator of br. computerization at Cen. Office of SBI, Regional Man. with Jaipur Zone, Gen. Man. with Lucknow Zone and Chief Gen. Man. with North Zone, Man. Dir State Bank of Travancore, Man. Dir and Group Exec. SBI April–Oct. 2006, Chair. 2006–11; Chair. Banking and Financial Insts Cttee, Fed. of Indian Chambers of Commerce and Industry, Indian Banks' Asscn 2010–11; Ind. Dir (non-exec.), Natural Gas Corpn, Tata Consultancy Services, Tata Steel Ltd, Hindustan Unilever Ltd 2011–, Standard Chartered PLC 2013–; mem. Bd of Dirs, EXIM Bank and GIC, Indian Council for Research on Int. Econ. Relations; mem. Xavier Labour Relations Inst. of Banking Personnel Selection, Inst. for Devt and Research in Banking Tech., Khadi and Village Industries Comm., Nat. Co-operative Devt Corpn; mem. Bd of Govs, Center for Creative Leadership (USA); Banker of the Year, Business Standard 2006–07, CNN-IBN Businessman of the Year 2007, Transformational Leader Award 2007, Best Executive Award 2008. *Address:* c/o Board of Directors, Hindustan Unilever Ltd, Unilever House, B. D. Sawant Marg, Chakala, Andheri East, Mumbai 400 099, India; c/o Board of Directors, Standard Chartered Bank, 1 Basinghall Avenue, London, EC2V 5DD, England.

BHATTACHARYA, Arundhati; Indian banker; *Chairman, SWIFT India Domestic Services Private Limited;* b. 18 March 1956, Calcutta (now Kolkata), West Bengal; d. of Pradyuman Kumar and Kalyani Mukherjee; m. Pritimoy Bhattacharya; one d.; ed St Xavier's School, Bokaro, Lady Brabourne Coll., Jadavpur Univ.; joined State Bank of India (SBI) as Probationary Officer 1977, subsequent positions held include Chief Gen. Man. (Bangalore Circle), Chief Gen. Man. of New Businesses for Corp. Centre, Gen. Man. (Network-II, Lucknow), Chief Devt Officer, Corp. Devt Officer, Deputy Managing Dir, Head of External Audit and Corresp. Relations, New York, Managing Dir and Chief Financial Officer Aug.–Oct. 2013, Chair. (first woman) 2013–17, involved in setting up several new cos and initiatives including SBI Gen. Insurance, SBI Macquarie Infrastructure Fund and SBI SG Global Securities Services, launch of IT platforms such as mobile banking; Chair. SWIFT India Domestic Services Pvt. Ltd 2018–; mem. Bd of Dirs, Reliance Industries Ltd 2018–, Wipro Ltd 2018–. *Address:* SWIFT India Domestic Services Private Limited, Unit No.1303, 13th Floor The Capital, Plot No. C-70, G Block, Bandra-Kurla Complex, Bandra (East) 400 051, India (office). *Telephone:* (2) 6196 6900 (office). *Fax:* (2) 6615 6974 (office). *E-mail:* contactus@swiftindia.org.in. *Website:* www.swiftindia.org.in.

BHATTACHARYA, Buddhadev, BA; Indian politician; b. 1 March 1944, Calcutta (now Kolkata); s. of Nepal Chandra Bhattacharya; m. Meera Bhattacharya; one d.; ed Sailendra Sarkar Vidyalaya and Presidency Coll., Kolkata; mem. Communist Party of India—Marxist Secr., Cen. Cttee, mem. of Politburo –2008; Minister-in-Charge, W Bengal Information and Public Relations Dept 1977–82, Dept of Information and Cultural Affairs 1987–99, Dept of Local Govt, Dept of Urban Devt and Metropolitan Devt 1987–91, Dept of Information and Cultural Affairs 1991–93, 1994, 1996, Dept of Urban Devt and Municipal Affairs 1991–93, Dept of Home Affairs and Dept of Information Tech. 1996–99; MLA for Jadavpur constituency 1987–2011; Deputy Chief Minister of West Bengal 1999–2000, Chief Minister 2000–11. *Publication:* collection of poems and plays. *Leisure interests:* cricket, travelling. *Address:* West Bengal State Committee, 31, Alimuddin Street Muzaffar Ahmad Bhawan, Kolkata 700 016, India (office). *Telephone:* (33) 22176633 (office). *Fax:* (33) 22640721 (office). *E-mail:* wbcpim@gmail.com (office). *Website:* www.cpimwb.org.in (office).

BHATTACHARYA, Tara Shankar, MSc; Indian banking executive; ed Jadavpur Univ., Kolkata, Saha Inst. of Nuclear Physics, Jamnalal Bajaj Inst. of Man., Mumbai; fmr Man. Dir State Bank of India, Mumbai, held various positions, including Head Retail Banking, Marketing and Product Devt Dept and Gen. Man., Chandigarh, Deputy Man. Dir State Bank of India 2004–05, Man. Dir 2005–08, Acting Chair. and Group Exec. for Corp. Banking 2006–08; Advisor, Ernst & Young Pvt. Ltd, Mumbai; Dir, Infrastructure Leasing & Financial Services Ltd, Sayaji Hotels Ltd, Nuclear Power Corpn of India Limited 2008–13, Jagson Airlines Ltd from 2010; Ind. Dir, JSL Stainless Ltd 2009–, Abhijeet Power Ltd 2010–; Ind. Dir (non-exec.), Surya Roshni Ltd 2011–; Additional Dir, AGS Transact Technologies Ltd 2010–11; Certified Assoc. Indian Inst. of Bankers. *Address:* JSL Stainless Ltd, Jindal Centre, 12 Bhikaji Cama Place, New Delhi 110 066, India (office). *Telephone:* (11) 26188345 (office). *Fax:* (11) 26170691 (office). *E-mail:* info@jindalsteel.com (office). *Website:* www.jindalsteel.com (office).

BHATTACHARYYA, Sanjay K.; Indian banking executive; ed St Stephen's Coll.; joined State Bank of India (SBI) 1972; positions include Man. Dir SBI Int. (Mauritius) Ltd, Chief Gen. Man. Hyderabad Circle, Deputy Gen. Man. (Vigilance), Chennai Circle; Man. Dir State Bank of Bikaner & Jaipur –2007, Man. Dir and Chief Credit and Risk Officer, SBI 2007–10; Dir, Dabur India Ltd. *Address:* Dabur India Ltd, Kaushambi, Ghaziabad 201 010, Uttar Pradesh, India (office). *Telephone:* (120) 3982000 (office). *E-mail:* info@dabur.com (office). *Website:* www.dabur.com (office).

BHATTARAI, Baburam, BArch (Hons), PhD; Nepalese politician, academic and fmr guerrilla leader; b. 26 May 1954, Belbas, Khoplang VDC of Gorkha Dist; ed Amar Jyoti Janata Secondary School, Luintel, Gorkha (also known as Luintel School), Tribhuvan Univ., Chandigarh Coll. of Architecture, Jawaharlal Nehru Univ., New Delhi, India; became politically active during student days in India; f. All India Nepalese Students Asscn 1977; became active in CP of Nepal (Masal), Spokesperson of United Nat. People's Movt during uprising 1990, broke away with others from CPN (Masal) 1991; joined CP of Nepal (Unity Centre) 1991, became head of Samyukta Janamorcha Nepal (United People's Front Nepal, political front of CP of Nepal (Unity Centre) in Parl.), sided with hardline section, which later took name CPN(M) when CPN (UC) split in 1994, became leader of parallel SJM led by Maoists; became known throughout Nepal after start of Nepalese People's War; fmr commdr of rebel army; Head of Int. Dept of the party for a time and Convener of United Revolutionary People's Council, Nepal; Sr mem. Standing Cttee of Politburo, Unified Communist Party of Nepal (Maoist); elected to Constituent Ass. from Gorkha 2008; Minister of Finance 2008–09; Prime Minister 2011–13. *Publications include:* Nepal: A Marxist View 1996, Politico-Economic Rationale of People's War in Nepal 1998, The Nature of Underdevelopment and Regional Structure of Nepal: A Marxist Analysis 2003, Nepal! krantika adharharu (in Nepali) 2004, Monarchy vs. Democracy: The Epic Fight in Nepal 2005; numerous articles in nat. and int. journals and newspapers. *Telephone:* (1) 4211096. *E-mail:* press@baburambhattarai.com. *Website:* baburambhattarai.com.

BHATTARAI, Bijaya Nath, BCom, MCom, MA (Econs); Nepalese fmr central banker; b. 9 Nov. 1949; m.; two c.; ed Tribhuvan Univ., Vanderbilt Univ., USA; Asst Research Officer, Research Dept, Nepal Rastra Bank (Cen. Bank) 1972–81, Research Officer 1981–92, Econ. Advisor 1992–95, Chief Controller, Foreign Exchange Dept 1995–98, Chief Accountant, Accounts and Expenditure Dept 1998–2000, Deputy Gov. and mem. Bd of Dirs 2000–05, Gov. and Chair. 2005–07 (suspended on charges of corruption, won protracted legal battle and was subsequently reinstated) 2009–10; Chair. Asian Clearing Union 2005–; fmr Chair. Rural Self-Reliance Fund; fmr mem. Bd of Dirs Environment Protection Fund, Nepal Inter-modal Transport Devt Bd, Poverty Alleviation Fund, Nepal Bangladesh Bank 1993–97, Agricultural Devt Bank 1998–2000. *Publications:* articles and contribs to various bank publs. *Address:* Kha-1, 964 Kalimati, Kathmandu 4, Nepal (home). *Telephone:* (1) 4271148 (home); (1) 4271829 (home).

BHAVE, Chandrasekhar Bhaskar, BE; Indian economist and government official; b. Nagpur; started career in Admin. Service 1975; Additional Industries Commr for Maharasthra 1989–92; fmr Under-Sec., Ministry of Finance; Deputy Sec., Ministry of Petroleum 1984–89; Sr Exec. Dir Securities and Exchange Bd of India 1992–96, Chair. 2008–11; fmr Chair. and Man. Dir Nat. Securities Depository Ltd; mem. Bd of Dirs, CMC (now part of Tata Group), Avaya Global Connect; mem. Public Interest Oversight Bd 2011–. *Address:* PIOB Secretariat, C/ Oquendo 12, 28006 Madrid, Spain (office). *Telephone:* (91) 7820528 (office). *Fax:* (91) 7824887 (office). *E-mail:* info@ipiob.org (office). *Website:* www.ipiob.org (office).

BHAVSAR, Natvar, BA, AM, MFA; American (b. Indian) artist; b. 7 April 1934, Gothava, Gujarat; s. of Prahladji Bhavsar and Babuben Bhavsar; m. Janet Brosious Bhavsar; three c.; ed Gujarat Univ., Univ. of Pennyslvania School of Design, USA; art instructor, Seth School of Fine Arts, Ahmedabad, Gujarat 1957–62; Prof., Univ. of Rhode Island, USA 1967–69; work in public collections including: Australian Nat. Gallery, Boston Museum of Fine Arts, Solomon R. Guggenheim Museum, Metropolitan Museum of Art, MIT, Philadelphia Museum of Art; work in numerous pvt. collections; John D. Rockefeller 3rd Fund Fellowship 1965–66, John Simon Guggenheim Fellowship 1975–76, Aspen Inst. Fellowship 1980, 1983; Vishva Gurjari, Gujarat, India 1987, Cultural Reader, World Econ. Forum 2000, 2002. *Publication:* Monogram 1998. *Leisure interests:* travel, reading, music, dance. *Address:* 131 Greene Street, New York, NY 10012, USA. *Telephone:* (212) 674-1293. *E-mail:* info@NatvarBhavsar.com. *Website:* www.natvarbhavsar.com.

BHEENICK, Rundheersing, MA; Mauritian economist, fmr politician and fmr central banker; b. 1944, Bon Accueil; ed Merton Coll., Oxford, UK; Lecturer in Devt Econs, Univ. of Mauritius 1968–69; Economist, Prime Minister's Office 1969–70; Industrial Devt Officer, UNIDO, Vienna 1970–74; with Ministry of Econ. Planning and Devt 1974–95, becoming Sec. for Aid Coordination, Deputy Dir and Dir-Gen.; mem. Nat. Assembly (Parl.) 1995–2000; Minister of Finance 1995–96, of Econ. Devt, Productivity and Regional Cooperation 1997–2000; Prin. Consultant, Development Associates 2001–07; Gov. Bank of Mauritius (central bank) 2007–14, also Chair. Monetary Policy Cttee; Chair., Council of Ministers, Indian Ocean Rim Asscn for Regional Co-operation 1997–99, COMESA 2000, ADB/EU/IMF/World Bank-sponsored Cross-Border Initiative (subsequently Regional Integration Facilitation Forum) 1997–2000, Commonwealth Partnership Tech. Man. Finance Working Group 2001–06; arrested for money laundering and receiving stolen goods 2015, cleared of charges 2016; Hon. Prof. of Political Economy, Univ. of Mauritius 1989.

BHOSLE, Asha; Indian singer, composer and restaurateur; b. 8 Sept. 1933, Sangli, Maharashtra; d. of Dinanath Mangeshkar; m. 1st Ganpatrao Bhosle (divorced); m. 2nd Rahul Dev Burman 1980 (died 1994); two s. one d.; Indian film playback singer; has recorded over 12,000 songs in 18 languages; first film Chunaria 1948; first solo in Raat Ki Rani 1949; sang in styles influenced by Latin American and American Big Band Jazz; worked extensively with Kishore Kumar 1970s; owns restaurants in several cities world-wide; Dr hc (Univ. of Amravati), (Univ. of Jalgaon), DLitt (Jodhpur Nat. Univ.); Filmfare Award 1967, 1968, 1971, 1972, 1973, 1974, 1977, 1996, Nat. Award 1981, 1986, Nightingale of Asia 1987, Lata Mangeshkar Award, Madhya Pradesh Govt 1989, Maharashtra Govt 1999, Filmfare Special Award, Rangeela Re 1996, Screen Videocon Award 1997, MTV Contribution to Music Award 1997, five Channel V Awards, Singer of the Millennium, Dubai 2000, Kolhapuri Bhushan Award 2000, Sangli Bhushan Award 2000, Omega Excellence Lifetime Achievement Award 2000, Filmfare Lifetime Achievement Award 2001, Dada Saheb Phalke Award 2001, Dayawati Modi Award 2001, BBC Mega Mela Lifetime Achievement Award 2002, Swaralaya Yesudas Award 2003, Living Legend Award, Fed. of Indian Chamber of Commerce and Industry 2004, MTV Immies 2005, Padma Vibhushan 2008, Yash Chopra Memorial Award 2018. *Recordings include:* albums (soundtracks): Dus Lakh 1967, Shikhar 1968, Hare Rama Hare Krishna 1972, Naina 1973, Pran Jaye Par Vachan Na Jaye 1974, Don 1977, Umrao Jaan 1981, Ijazat 1986, Dilwale Dulhania Le Jayeng 1995, Rangeela 1996; solo: Songs of My Soul – Rare and Classic Vols 1 and 2 2001, You've Stolen My Heart (with the Kronos Quartet) 2005, 75 Years of Asha 2008. *Film:* Mai (as actress) 2013. *Leisure interest:* cooking. *Address:* 1st Floor, Prabhu Kunj Apartment, Pedder Road, Mumbai 400 026, India (home). *Telephone:* (22) 64938070. *E-mail:* info@ashasrestaurants.com. *Website:* www.ashasrestaurants.com.

BHOWMIK, Neem Chandra; Bangladeshi diplomatist, physicist and academic; fmr Prof. and Chair. Dept of Applied Physics, Electronics and Communication Eng, Dhaka Univ., Dir Renewable Energy Research Centre; has worked in India, UK, Germany, Italy and Thailand –2009; Amb. to Nepal 2009–12; Pres. Bangladesh Muktijodha Foundation, Bangladesh Puja Udjapan Parishad; Gen. Sec. Bangladesh Hindu Bouddha Christian Oikya Parishad (protects the rights of minority groups in Bangladesh); participated in World Renewable Energy Congress; UNESCO Young Scientist Award 1988.

BHUIYAN, Lt-Gen. Iqbal Karim; Bangladeshi military officer; b. 2 June 1957, Comilla; m. Tahmina Yasmin; one s. two d.; ed Bangladesh Mil. Acad., Defence Services Command and Staff Coll., Command and Gen. Staff Coll., USA; commissioned into Bangladeshi Army 1976, later attained rank of Lt Gen., held numerous positions including UN Force Commdr during deployment of Bangladeshi peacekeepers, Commdr, Ghatail Div. and Chittagong Div., GOC, 9th Infantry Div., Savar, Chief of Gen. Staff of Army, Quartermaster Gen. of the Army –2012, Chief of Army Staff 2012–15, also served as Platoon Commdr, Bangladesh Mil. Acad., Directing Staff, Defence Services Command and Staff Coll., Commdt, School of Infantry and Tactics, Defence Services Command and Staff Coll.; fmr Commdr, Sector-4, UN Mission in Sierra Leone; Liberation of Kuwait Medal.

BHUPATHI, Mahesh Shrinivas; Indian tennis player; b. 7 June 1974, Chennai; s. of C.G. Krishna Bhupathi and Mira Bhupathi; m. 1st Shvetha Jaishankar 2002 (divorced 2009); m. 2nd Lara Dutta 2011; one d.; ed Univ. of Mississippi, USA; NCAA doubles championship in 1995, French Open (mixed doubles) 1997, (men's doubles) 1999, 2001, US Open (mixed doubles) 1999, 2005, (men's doubles) 2002, Wimbledon 1999, (mixed doubles) 2002, 2005, Asian Games (men's doubles), Doha 2006, Australian Open (mixed doubles) 2006, 2009, Canada Masters (men's doubles) 2007, Commonwealth Games (silver medal), Delhi 2010, French Open (mixed doubles) 2012, Paris Masters (men's doubles) 2012; Founder-Man. Dir Globosport; Founder Int. Premier Tennis League, Mahesh Bhupathi Tennis Acad.; mem. Indian Davis Cup team 1995–, apptd non-playing Captain 2016; Arjuna Award 1995, Padma Shri 2001. *Address:* Globosport, Anand – 105, 5th Floor, Ambedkar Road, Bandra West, Mumbai 400 050, India (office). *Telephone:* (22) 26065101 (office). *Fax:* (22) 26065199 (office). *E-mail:* connect@globosportworld.com (office); work@globosportworld.com (office). *Website:* www.globosportworld.com (office).

BHUTTO, Fatima Murtaza, BA, MA; Pakistani writer; b. 29 May 1982, Kabul, Afghanistan; d. of Murtaza Bhutto and Fauzia Fasihudin Bhutto; grand-d. of Zulfikar Ali Bhutto (fmr Prime Minister of Pakistan); niece of Benazir Bhutto (fmr Prime Minister of Pakistan); ed Columbia Univ., USA, SOAS, Univ. of London, UK; fmr columnist, Jang (Urdu daily newspaper), The News (sister publ.); currently writes columns for The Daily Beast, The New Statesman, The Guardian, The Caravan Magazine. *Publications include:* Whispers in the Desert (poetry) 1997, 8.50 a.m. 8 October 2005 2006, Songs of Blood and Sword: A Daughter's Memoir 2010, The Shadow of the Crescent Moon 2013. *Address:* 70 Clifton Road, Old Clifton, Karachi, Pakistan. *Website:* www.fatimabhutto.com.pk.

BHUTTO ZARDARI, Bilawal; Pakistani politician; *Chairman, Pakistan People's Party;* b. 21 Sept. 1988, Karachi; s. of Asif Ali Zardari and Benazir Bhutto (fmr Prime Minister); grandson of fmr Prime Minister Zulfikar Ali Bhutto; ed Karachi Grammar School, Froebels Int. School, Islamabad, Rashid School for Boys, Dubai, Christ Church, Oxford, UK; spent most of early life outside Pakistan, travelling with his mother who went into self-imposed exile in 1999, moving between London and Dubai; fmr Vice-Pres. Student Council, Rashid School for Boys, Dubai; Co-Chair. (with his father) Pakistan People's Party following assassination of his mother Benazir Bhutto Dec. 2007–13, apptd Patron-in-Chief 2013, Chair. 2017–; Tumandar (Chief) of Baloch Zardari tribe 2011–; mem. National Assembly (for Larkana-I) 2018–. *Leisure interests:* cricket, shooting, horse riding, black belt in Taekwondo. *Address:* Pakistan People's Party, House No. 8, Street 19, F-8/2, Islamabad, Pakistan (office). *Telephone:* (51) 2255264 (office). *Fax:* (51) 2282741 (office). *E-mail:* ppp@comsats.net.pk (office). *Website:* www.ppp.org.pk (office).

BIALYSTOK, Ellen, PhD, FRSC; Canadian psychologist and academic; *Distinguished Research Professor of Psychology, York University;* ed Univ. of Toronto; currently Distinguished Research Prof. of Psychology, York Univ.; Assoc. Scientist, Rotman Research Inst. of the Baycrest Centre for Geriatric Care; Killam Research Fellowship, Walter Gordon Research Fellowship, Dean's Award for Outstanding Research, Language Learning Distinguished Scholar in Residence, York Univ., Killam Prize in Social Sciences, Canada Council for the Arts 2010, Hebb Award, Canadian Soc. for Brain Behaviour and Cognitive Science 2011. *Publications:* Spatial Cognition: The Structure and Development of the Mental Representation of Spatial Relations (with D. R. Olson) 1983, Communication Strategies: A Psychological Analysis of Second-Language Use 1990, Language Processing in Bilingual Children (ed.) 1991, In Other Words: The Psychology and Science of Second Language Acquisition (with K. Hakuta) 1994, Bilingualism in Development: Language, Literacy, and Cognition 2001, Lifespan Cognition: Mechanisms of Change (co-ed.) 2006, Language Acquisition and Bilingualism: Special Issue of Applied Psycholinguistics (co-ed.) 2007; more than 100 scientific papers in journals and books. *Address:* Department of Psychology, Faculty of Health, Behavioural Sciences Building, 234 York University, 4700 Keele Street, Toronto, ON M3J 1P3, Canada (office). *Telephone:* (416) 736-2100 (ext. 66109) (office). *E-mail:* ellenb@yorku.ca (office). *Website:* www.yorku.ca/coglab (office).

BIANCHERI, Franck; Monegasque government official and business executive; *CEO, Monaco QD International Hotels and Resorts;* m.; two c.; ed Ecole Supérieure de Commerce de Paris; Diplôme d'Expertise Comptable Supérieure (chartered accountancy qualification); Franco-German and British Chambers of Commerce Diplomas; Man. Boulogne-Billancourt Group, Credit Lyonnais 1983–90, responsible for product line for small- and medium-sized firms, Marcel Sembat Agency 1983–90, Channel Man. for product line for cos, Boulogne-Billancourt 1985–88; Dir Aeronautic Dept, Faugère & Jutheau/Groupe Marsh & McLennan 1990–95; Dir-Gen. Dept of Finance and the Economy, Principality of Monaco 1995–2000, Rep. Dept of Finance and the Economy within Asscns Sportel and Festival de Télévision de Monte-Carlo 1995–2000; Govt Counsellor for Finance and the Economy 2000–05; Official Rep. to Cabinet of HSH the Prince while retaining the functions of Govt Counsellor for Finance and the Economy 2003–05; Govt Counsellor for External Relations and Int. Econ. and Financial Dossiers 2008–10; CEO Monaco QD Hotels and Resorts Management 2010–; Dir Cube Infrastructure Fund at Natixis Environnement and Infrastructures, VisuRay Plc.

BIANCHI, Andrés, MA, PhD; Chilean diplomatist and banking executive; b. 12 Sept. 1935, Valdivia; m. Lily Urdinola; two s. one d.; ed Univ. of Chile, Yale Univ., USA; Dir Int. Labour Office, Regional Employment Program of Latin America and the Caribbean 1971–73; Visiting Research Assoc., Woodrow Wilson School of Public and Int. Affairs, Princeton Univ. 1973–75; Visiting Prof., Center for Latin American Devt Studies, Boston Univ. 1978; Dir Econ. Devt Div., UN Econ. Comm. for Latin America and the Caribbean 1981–88, Deputy Exec. Sec. 1988–89; Gov. Cen. Bank of Chile 1989–91; Chair. Credit Lyonnais Chile 1992–96, Dresdner Banque Nationale de Paris, Chile 1996–2000; mem. External Advisory Group, Latin America and Caribbean Regional Office, World Bank 1994–2000; mem. Pres. of Chile's Nat. Savings Comm. 1997–98; Amb. to USA 2000–06; fmr adviser to cen. banks of Bolivia, Colombia, Mexico and Venezuela. *Leisure interests:* tennis, travel, classical music.

BIANCHI, Tancredi; Italian banker and professor of banking economics; b. 1928, Caravaggio; ed Bocconi Univ.; Lecturer, 'Ca Foscari', Venice 1959–64; Full Prof., Univ. of Rome 'La Sapienza' 1964–68; Prof. of Banking Econs, Bocconi Univ., Milan 1979, now Prof. Emer.; Exec. Vice-Chair., CEO then Chair. Credito Bergamasco 1981–89; Chair. Italian Private Banking Asscn 1982–2003; Chair. Italian Banking Asscn 1991–98, now Hon. Chair.; fmr Chair. Centrobanca, Fondo Immobiliare Polis.

BIANCO, Jean-Louis; French civil servant and politician; *President, Observatoire de la laïcité;* b. 12 Jan. 1943, Neuilly-sur-Seine; s. of Louis Bianco and Gabrielle Bianco (née Vandries); m. Martine Letoublon 1971; three s.; ed Lycée Janson-de-Sailly and Inst. d'études politiques, Paris; auditor, Conseil d'Etat 1971; Official Rep. Groupe central des villes nouvelles 1973–74; attached to Ministry of Health 1976–79; Counsel, Conseil d'Etat 1976; Official Rep. Syndicat intercommunal de Devt Durance-Bléone 1979–81; Official Rep. to the advisers of the Pres. 1981; Sec.-Gen. to the Pres. 1982–91; Minister of Social Affairs and Integration 1991–92, of Equipment, Transport and Housing 1992–93; mem. Regional Council of Alpes-de-Haute-Provence 1992–2012, Pres. 1998–2012; Mayor of Digne-les-Bains (Alpes de Haute Provence) 1995–2001; Deputy from Alpes de Haute-Provence (Socialist) June 1997–2012; Pres. François Mitterrand Inst. 1999–2002; Pres. High Council for Int. Co-operation 1999–2002; campaign dir for Ségolène Royal during Presidential elections 2007; Pres. Observatoire de la laïcité 2013–; Chevalier, ordre nat. de la Légion d'honneur 2001. *Address:* Observatoire de la laïcité, 101 rue de Grenelle, 75007 Paris, France (office). *Telephone:* 1-42-75-76-46 (office). *E-mail:* secretariat.laicite@pm.gouv.fr. *Website:* www.gouvernement.fr/gouvernement/observatoire-de-la-laicite.

BIBEAU, Marie-Claude, PC, MP, BSc; Canadian business executive and politician; *Minister of Agriculture;* b. Sherbrooke; m. Bernard Sévigny; ed Univ. de Sherbrooke; started career with Canadian Int. Devt Agency, working in Ottawa-Gatineau, Montréal, Morocco and Benin; Asst Dir, Sherbrooke, Cité des rivières (city devt plan) 1999–2004; Co-owner Camping de Compton (tourism business) 2000–; Exec. Dir, Sherbrooke Museum of Nature and Science 2008–15; mem. House of Commons (Parl.) for Compton-Stanstead 2015–; Minister of Int. Devt 2015–19, responsible for La francophonie 2015–18, of Agriculture 2019–; fmr Dir of Accreditation, Sherbrooke 2013 Canada Summer Games; Founder and Coordinator, Regroupement des institutions muséales des Cantons-de-l'Est (museum asscn); fmr mem. Bd of Dirs, Commerce Sherbrooke, Destination Sherbrooke, Animation Centre-ville, Société des musées québécois; fmr Chair. Governing Bd, École Louis-St-Laurent, Compton; mem. Liberal Party of Canada. *Address:* Agriculture and Agri-Food Canada, 1341 Baseline Rd, Ottawa, ON K1A 0C5, Canada (office). *Telephone:* (613) 773-1000 (office). *Fax:* (613) 773-1081 (office). *E-mail:* info@agr.gc.ca (office). *Website:* www.agr.gc.ca (office).

BIBILOV, Maj.-Gen. Anatolii Ilyich; Russian politician and fmr army officer; *President, 'Republic of South Ossetia';* b. 6 Feb. 1970, Tskhinvali, South Ossetian Autonomous Oblast, Georgian SSR, USSR; m.; three s. two d.; ed Higher Airborne Command School, Ryazan, State Fire Acad. of Emergency Situations Committee of the Russian Federation; served in Soviet Army 1988–91, Russian Army 1991–94, 1998–2008, South Ossetia Army 1994–96; pvt. business in Kyiv, Ukraine 1996–98; Co. Commdr, later Deputy Bn Commdr, peacekeeping troops, Tskhinvali 1998–2008; took active part in South Ossetian (Russo-Georgian) war 2008; South Ossetia Minister of Emergency Situations 2008–14; Chair. (speaker) Parl. of the 'Republic of South Ossetia' 2014–17; Yuzhno-Osetinskaya Respublikanskaya Politicheskaya Partiya 'Yedinstvo' (Unity South Ossetian Republican Political Party) cand. in (subsequently invalidated) South Ossetian presidential election 2011; Pres. 'Republic of South Ossetia' 2017–; mem. Respublikanskaya Politicheskaya Partiya 'Yedinaya Osetiya' (United Ossetia Republican Political Party); Order of Uatsamonga 2008, Russian Order of Friendship 2011. *Address:* Office of the President of the 'Republic of South Ossetia', 100001 Tskhinvali, Government House, ul. Stalina 18, South Ossetia, Georgia (office). *Telephone:* (9974) 45-25-37 (office). *Fax:* (9974) 45-25-37 (office). *E-mail:* ospress@mail.ru (office). *Website:* presidentruo.org (office).

BICHARD, Baron (Life Peer), cr. 2010, of Nailsworth in the County of Gloucestershire; **Michael (George) Bichard,** KCB, LLB, MScS, FIPD, CCMI, FRSA; British civil servant; b. 31 Jan. 1947, Southampton; s. of George Bichard and Nora Reeves; m. Gillian Bichard; ed Univ. of Manchester, Univ. of Birmingham; articled clerk, solicitor, Sr Solicitor Reading Borough Council 1969–73; Co. Liaison Officer, Berks. Co. Council 1973–77; Head of Chief Exec.'s Office, Lambeth Borough Council 1977–80; Chief Exec. Brent Borough Council 1980–86, Glos. Co. Council 1986–90, Social Security Benefits Agency 1990–95; Jt Perm. Sec. Dept for Educ. and Employment July–Dec. 1995, Perm. Sec. 1996–2002; Rector, The London Inst. (now Univ. of the Arts London) 2001; Chair. Social Care Inst. For Excellence, Mentora Trust, Rathbone Training Ltd 2001–08, RSe Consulting 2003–08, ARTIS, 2003–08, Legal Services Comm. 2005–08; mem. Econ. and Social Research Council 1989–92, Prince's Trust Volunteers Nat. Bd 1992–97; mem. ESRC 1989–92; Fellow, Chartered Inst. of Personnel and Devt, Birmingham Inst. of Local Govt Studies; mem. NESTA Creative Pioneer

Programme Cttee; Gov. Henley Man. Coll. 2002; mem. Bd of Companions, Inst. of Man.; mem. Guild of Educators; apptd by UK Home Office to chair Soham/Bichard Inquiry Jan. 2004; Ed. Solace Foundation, Chair. Film Club 2006–, The Design Council 2008–; Exec. Dir Inst. for Govt 2008–10; Vice-Pres. Local Govt Asscn; Adviser, Cronin Management Consultants, Ten Lifestyle Management Ltd; Trustee Globe Theatre, River and Rowing Museum; Hon. Fellow, Inst. of Local Govt Studies (Birmingham Univ.); Hon. DUniv (Leeds Metropolitan) 1992, (Middlesex) 2001; Hon. LLD (Birmingham) 1999; Dr hc (Bradford) 2004, (Solent). *Address:* House of Lords, London, SW1A 0PW, England (office). *Telephone:* (20) 7219-5353 (office). *Fax:* (20) 7219-5979 (office).

BICHIR, Demián; Mexican/American actor; b. (Demián Bichir Nájera), 1 Aug. 1963, Torreon, Mexico; s. of Alejandro Bichir and Maricruz Nájera; m. Lisset Gutiérrez 2001 (divorced 2003); one d. from another relationship. *Films include:* Choices of the Heart 1983, Viaje al paraiso 1985, Astucia 1986, Hotel Colonial 1987, The Penitent 1988, Rojo amanecer 1989, Marea suave 1992, Miroslava 1993, La vida conyugal 1993, Hasta morir (Silver Ariel Award for Best Actor 1995) 1994, Ya la hicimos 1994, Pruebas de amor 1994, Nadie hablará de nosotras cuando hayamos muerto 1995, Salón México 1996, Solo 1996, Perdita Durango 1997, Luces de la noche 1998, Cilantro y perejil 1998, Santitos 1999, Sexo, pudor y lágrimas 1999, Ave Maria 1999, Cerebro 2000, Todo el poder 2000, La toma de la embajada 2000, Sin noticias de Dios 2001, Dark Cities 2002, Heartbreak Hospital 2002, Bendito infierno (MTV Movie Awards-Mexico Special Award for Best Bichir in a Movie 2003) 2003, Hipnos 2004, Zapata: Amor en rebeldia 2004, American Visa 2007, Fuera del cielo 2007, Enemigos intimos 2008, Che: Parts One and Two 2008, The Runway 2010, Hidalgo – La historia jamás contada (also co-producer) 2010, A Better Life 2011, Foreverland 2011, El sueño de Iván 2011, Savages 2012, El Santos vs. La Tetona Mendoza (voice) 2012, The Heat 2013, Machete Kills 2013, Dom Hemingway 2013, Death in Buenos Aires 2014, Words with Gods 2014, Good Kids 2015, The Hateful Eight 2015, Refugio (also writer, dir and producer) 2015. *Television includes:* Rina 1977, Vivir enamorada 1982, Cuando los hijos se van 1983, Los años felices 1984, Guadalupe 1984, El rincón de los prodigios 1988, Lazos de amor 1996, Nada personal 1996, Demasiado corazón 1998, In the Time of the Butterflies 2001, La otra mitad del sol 2005, Sombreros 2005, Capadocia 2008, Weeds 2008–10, The Bridge (series) 2013–. *Address:* c/o Carlos Carreras, APA Talent and Literary Agency, 405 South Beverly Drive, Beverly Hills, CA 90212, USA (office).

BIČKAUSKAS, Egidijus; Lithuanian politician and lawyer; b. 29 May 1955, Prienai; m. Jurate Bičkauskienė; ed Vilnius Univ.; investigator, special cases investigator, Procurator Gen.'s Office 1978–89; joined People's Front Movt Sajudis 1988; Deputy of USSR Supreme Soviet 1989–90; elected to Parl. Restoration Seimas of Repub. of Lithuania 1990–92, signatory of the Lithuanian Repub. Independence Restoration Act 1990; Head Lithuanian diplomatic mission to Moscow 1990–96; mem. Parl. (Seimas) of Repub. of Lithuania, Deputy Chair. 1992–96, head of faction of Centre Party in Seimas of Lithuania 1996–2000; Vice-Chair. Presidium of Baltic Ass. *Address:* Laurų 35, 2046 Vilnius, Lithuania (home). *Telephone:* (3702) 225493 (home); (8698) 88761 (home). *E-mail:* info@bickauskas.lt (home). *Website:* www.bickauskas.lt (home).

BIDAYA, Thanong, MA, PhD; Thai business executive, academic and fmr government official; b. 28 July 1947, Supanburi Prov.; ed Yokohama Nat. Univ., Japan, Northwestern Univ., USA; Pres. Thai Military Bank Public Co. 1988–99, currently Chair. Advisory Bd, TMB Asset Management; fmr positions include Commercial Union Insurance (Thailand) Co., N.C.C. Man. and Devt Co.; fmr Dean Assumption Univ., Business Admin Dept, Nat. Inst. of Devt Admin, fmr Dean Grad School Business MBA Program, also Distinguished Prof.; Chair. Thai Airways Int. Public Co. 2002–05; Minister of Finance 1997, 2005–06, Chair. Nat. Econ. and Social Devt Bd 2001–05, Vice-Chair. Council of Econ. Advisers to Prime Minister 2001–05; Thai Trade Rep. 2001–02; Minister of Commerce 2005; Visiting Prof., Int. Grad. School of Social Sciences, Yokohama Nat. Univ. 2007; Chair. Thai Tap Water Supply PLC 2009–, MSIG Insurance; mem. Bd of Counsellors, Asia Mezzanine Capital Advisers Ltd, Hong Kong; Hon. mem. Suphanburi Chamber of Commerce, Hon. Chair. TMB Asset Management Co. Ltd, Hon. Chair. Charoensin Group of Co.; Commdr (Third Class) of the Most Noble Order of the Crown of Thailand 1991, Kt Grand Cross (First Class) of the Most Exalted Order of the White Elephant 1997, Kt Grand Cordon (First Class) of the Most Noble Order of the Crown of Thailand 2003, Grand Cordon of the Order of the Rising Sun (Japan) 2005, Kt Grand Cordon (Special Class) of the Most Exalted Order of the White Elephant 2005, Officier, Ordre national du Mérite 2005; Dr hc (Yokohama Nat. Univ.) 2004. *Address:* c/o Board of Counsellors, Asia Mezzanine Capital Advisers Ltd, 3205 Alexandra House, 16–20 Chater Road, Hong Kong Special Administrative Region, People's Republic of China.

BIDDISS, Michael Denis, MA, PhD, FRHistS, FHA; British academic and writer; *Professor Emeritus of History, University of Reading;* b. 15 April 1942, Farnborough, Kent; s. of Daniel Biddiss and Eileen Biddiss (née Jones); m. Ruth Margaret Cartwright 1967; four d.; ed Queens' Coll., Cambridge, Centre des Hautes Etudes Européennes, Univ. of Strasbourg, France; Fellow in History, Downing Coll., Cambridge and Dir of Studies in History, Social and Political Sciences 1966–73; Lecturer, then Reader in History, Univ. of Leicester 1973–79; Prof. of History, Univ. of Reading 1979–2004, Prof. Emer. 2004–, Dean, Faculty of Letters and Social Sciences 1982–85; Visiting Prof., Univ. of Victoria, Canada 1973, Univ. of Cape Town, South Africa 1976, 1978, Univ. of Cairo, Egypt 1985, Monash Univ., Australia 1989, Univ. of Nanjing, China 1997; Chair. History at the Univs Defence Group 1984–87; mem. Council, The Historical Asscn 1985– (Pres. 1991–94), Vice-Pres. Royal Historical Soc. 1995–99 (mem. Council 1988–92); Lister Lecturer, BAAS 1975; Hon. Fellow, Faculty of the History of Medicine (Pres. 1994–98), Soc. of Apothecaries 1986–; several awards from Soc. of Apothecaries of London including Osler Medal 1989, Locke Medal 1996, Thomas Sydenham Medal 2000, Master's Medal 2009. *Publications include:* Father of Racist Ideology 1970, Gobineau: Selected Political Writings (ed.) 1970, Disease and History (co-author) 1972, The Age of the Masses 1977, Images of Race (ed.) 1979, Thatcherism (co-ed.) 1987, The Nuremberg Trial and the Third Reich (co-author) 1992, The Uses and Abuses of Antiquity (co-ed.) 1999, The Humanities in the New Millennium (co-ed.) 2000, Themes in Modern European History 1890–1945 (co-ed.) 2008, The Wiley-Blackwell Dictionary of Modern European History since 1789 (co-author) 2010. *Leisure interests:* cricket, music and opera, mountain walking, art, travel. *E-mail:* m.d.biddiss@reading.ac.uk (office).

BIDDLE, Martin, CBE, OBE, MA, FBA, FSA; British archaeologist and academic; *Professor Emeritus of Medieval Archaeology, University of Oxford;* b. 4 June 1937, North Harrow, Middx; s. of Reginald Samuel Biddle and Gwladys Florence Biddle (née Baker); m. 1st Hannelore Becker; two d.; m. 2nd Birthe Kjølbye 1966 (died 2010); two d.; ed Merchant Taylors' School and Pembroke Coll., Cambridge; 2nd Lt, Lt 4th Royal Tank Regt, 1st Ind. Squadron, RTR, Berlin, 1956–57; Asst Insp. of Ancient Monuments, Ministry of Public Building and Works 1961–63; Lecturer in Medieval Archaeology, Univ. of Exeter 1963–67; Visiting Fellow, All Souls Coll., Oxford 1967–68; Dir Winchester Research Unit 1968–; Dir Univ. Museum and Prof. of Anthropology and History of Art, Univ. of Pennsylvania 1977–81; Lecturer of The House, Christ Church, Oxford 1983–86; Astor Sr Research Fellow in Medieval Archaeology, Hertford Coll. Oxford 1989–2002; Prof. of Medieval Archaeology, Univ. of Oxford 1997–2002, Prof. Emer. 2002–, Emer. Fellow, Hertford Coll. 2002–; Dir excavations and investigations at Nonsuch Palace 1959–60, Winchester 1961–71, Repton 1974–88, 1993, St Alban's Abbey 1978, 1982–84, 1991, 1994–95, Holy Sepulchre, Jerusalem 1989–90, 1992, 1993, 1998, Qasr Ibrim, Egypt 1990, 1992, 1995, 2000; archaeological consultant to Canterbury Cathedral 1987–2016, St Alban's Abbey, Eurotunnel, etc.; mem. Royal Comm. on Historical Monuments for England 1984–95; Trevelyan Lecturer, Univ. of Cambridge 1991; Pres. Soc. for Medieval Archaeology 1995–98; Chair. Historic Towns Trust 1994–2013; Hon. Fellow, Pembroke Coll., Cambridge 2006–; Hon. Freeman of Winchester 2010; Frend Medal, Soc. of Antiquaries (with Birthe Kjølbye-Biddle) 1986. *Publications:* The Future of London's Past (with C. Heighway) 1973, Winchester in the Early Middle Ages (with others) 1976, The History of the King's Works, Vol. IV, Part 2 (with others) 1982, King Arthur's Round Table 2000, Object and Economy in Medieval Winchester 1990, The Tomb of Christ 1999, King Arthur's Round Table 2000, The Church of the Holy Sepulchre 2000, Nonsuch Palace: The Material Culture of a Noble Restoration Household 2005, Winchester Historic Town Atlas 2017; papers in learned journals. *Leisure interests:* travel, especially Hellenic travel, architecture, Renaissance art. *Address:* Hertford College, Oxford, OX1 3BW (office); 19 Hamilton Road, Oxford, OX2 7PY, England (home); c/o Knight Ayton Management, 114 St Martin's Lane, London, WC2N 4BE, England (office). *Telephone:* (1865) 559017 (office); (1865) 513056 (home). *E-mail:* martin.biddle@hertford.ox.ac.uk (office). *Website:* winchesterstudies.org.uk/martin-biddle-obe (office).

BIDDLE, Michael (Mike), BS, PhD, MBA; American chemical engineer and business executive; *CEO, Material Solutions;* ed Jeffersontown High School, Ky, Univ. of Louisville, Case Western Reserve Univ., Stanford Univ. (Sloan Fellow); Product Devt Engineer, GE Plastics 1978–81; Corp. Plastics Engineer, Cummins Engine Co. 1981–87; Research Man., Dow Chemical Co. 1987–92; Founder and Prin., Michael Biddle & Assocs 1992–95; Founder and Dir, MBA Polymers, Inc. 1994–; CEO iAQ Systems 2015–; Founder and CEO Material Solutions 2015–; numerous CleanTech Awards, Earthkeeper Hero Award, Ascent Award for Entrepreneurship, Thomas Alva Edison Award for Innovation 2002, Tech Museum Tech Laureate Award 2006, World Econ. Forum Tech Pioneer 2006, Economist Innovation Award for Energy and Environment 2010, Gothenburg Award for Sustainable Devt 2012, World Tech. Award, World Tech. Network (Environment) 2014. *Address:* iAQ Systems, 12 Reinman Road, Warren, NJ 07059-5122, USA (office). *E-mail:* mike@mikebiddle.com; marketing@iaqsys.com (office). *Website:* www.materialsolutions.net (office); www.iaqsys.com (office).

BIDEN, Joseph (Joe) Robinette, Jr, JD; American lawyer, politician and academic; *Benjamin Franklin Presidential Practice Professor, University of Pennsylvania;* b. 20 Nov. 1942, Scranton, Pa; s. of Joseph R. Biden and Jean F. Biden; m. 1st Neilia Hunter (deceased); two s. one d. (deceased); m. 2nd Jill Tracy Jacobs 1977; one d.; ed Univ. of Delaware, Syracuse Univ. Coll. of Law; Trial Attorney in the Public Defender's Office, Del. 1968; Founder Biden & Walsh Law Firm, Wilmington 1968–72; mem. New Castle Co. Council 1970–72; Senator from Delaware 1972–2008, mem. Foreign Relations Cttee (fmr Chair.), Judiciary Cttee (Chair. 1987–95), Chair. Senate Caucus on Int. Narcotics Control, Co-Chair. Senate NATO Observer Group, Senate Nat. Security Working Group, Congressional Fireman's Caucus, Congressional Int. Anti-Piracy Caucus, mem. Democratic Steering and Coordinating Cttee, Nat. Guard Caucus, Senate Auto Caucus, Senate Biotechnology Caucus, Congressional Port Security Caucus, Congressional Air Force Caucus; fmr Vice-Chair. NATO Parl. Ass.; unsuccessful cand. for Democratic nomination for US Pres. 2007; Vice-Pres. of the USA 2009–17; Benjamin Franklin Presidential Practice Prof., Univ. of Pennsylvania (jt appointments in Annenberg School for Communication and School of Arts and Sciences, with secondary affiliation in Wharton School) 2017–, also Dir Penn Biden Center for Diplomacy and Global Engagement, Washington, DC; Founding Chair. Biden Inst., Univ. of Delaware 2017–; apptd Adjunct Prof., Widener Univ. School of Law 1991; mem. Del. Bar Asscn, ABA, American Trial Lawyers Asscn; Democrat; numerous awards, including Presidential Medal of Freedom (with Distinction) 2017. *Leisure interests:* sports, history, public speaking, American architecture. *Address:* University of Pennsylvania, Philadelphia, PA 19104, USA (office). *Telephone:* (215) 898-5000 (office). *Website:* www.upenn.edu (office).

BIEBER, Justin; Canadian singer; b. (Justin Drew Bieber), 1 March 1994, London, Ont.; s. of Jeremy Bieber and Pattie Mallette; m. Hailey Baldwin 2018; discovered by Scooter Braun after posting videos of his performances on YouTube 2008, came to the attention of Usher who signed him to a recording contract; professional solo artist 2009–; tours: Urban Behavior Tour 2009, My World Tour 2010–11, Believe Tour 2012–13, Purpose World Tour 2016–17; Queen Elizabeth II Diamond Jubilee Medal 2012; numerous awards including: TRL Award for Best Int. Act 2010, Teen Choice Awards for Best Male Artist, for Best Breakout Male Artist 2010, MTV Video Music Awards for Best New Artist 2010, for Best Male Video (U Smile) 2011, MTV Europe Music Awards for Best Male 2010, 2011, 2012, 2013, 2014, 2015, for Best Push Act 2010, for Best Pop Act 2011, 2012, for Best World Stage Performance 2012, for Best North America Act 2015, for Biggest Fans 2015, 2016, for Best Look 2015, for Best Collaboration (for Where Are Ü Now?, with Skrillex and Diplo) 2015, for Best Song (for Sorry) 2016, Young Hollywood Awards Newcomer of the Year 2010, American Music Awards for Artist of the Year 2010, 2012, for Favorite Pop/Rock Male Artist 2010, 2012, for T-Mobile Breakthrough

Artist 2010, for Collaboration of the Year (for Where Are Ü Now?) 2015, BRIT Award for Best Int. Breakthrough Act 2011, Juno Fan Choice Awards 2011, 2012, Billboard Music Awards for Top New Artist 2011, for Top Social Artist 2011, 2012, 2016, for Top Streaming Artist 2011, for Top Digital Media Artist 2011, Billboard Music Awards for Top Male Artist 2013, 2016, for Top Social Artist 2013, 2014, 2015, 2016, Much Music Award for Favorite Artist 2014, Grammy Award for Best Dance Recording (for Where Are Ü Now?) 2016, BRIT Award for Int. Male Solo Artist 2016. *Recordings include:* albums: My World 2.0 (Teen Choice Award for Best Pop Album 2010, American Music Award for Favorite Pop/Rock Album 2010, Billboard Music Award for Top Pop Album 2011, Juno Award for Pop Album of the Year 2011) 2009, Under the Mistletoe 2011, Believe (American Music Award for Favorite Pop/Rock Album 2012) 2012, Complete My Journals 2013, Purpose 2015; singles: Where Are Ü Now 2015, What Do You Mean? 2015, Sorry 2016, Despacito (Collaboration Of The Year, Favorite Song, American Music Awards 2017) (co-recipient with Luis Fonsi and Daddy Yankee) 2017, I'm The One (with Lil Wayne) (American Music Awards for Favorite Song 2017), Friends (with BloodPop) 2017. *Address:* c/o Scott Braun, SB Projects, 1755 Broadway, New York, NY 10019, USA (office). *E-mail:* info@scooterbraun.com (office). *Website:* scooterbraun.com (office); www.justinbiebermusic.com.

BIEDENKOPF, Kurt Hans, DJur; German politician and lawyer; b. 28 Jan. 1930, Ludwigshafen; s. of Wilhelm Biedenkopf and Agathe Biedenkopf (née Schmidt); m. Ingrid Ries 1979; ed Davidson Coll., USA, Georgetown Univ.; Prof. of Law, Ruhr Univ., Bochum 1964–70, Rector 1967–69; Chair. Govt Comm. on Co-determination 1968–70; Gen. Sec. Christian Democratic Party (CDU) 1973–77, Vice-Pres. 1977–83, Pres. CDU Regional Asscn, North Rhine-Westphalia 1980–84; mem. Bundestag 1976–80, 1987–90; Prime Minister of Saxony 1990–2002; Pres. Dresden International Univ. 2003–05, Hon. Pres. 2006–; apptd Chair. Comm. on Reform of Enterprise 2005; Chair. Kuratorium Trust of Devt and Peace; Research Prof., Wissenschaftszentrum Berlin für Sozialforschung 2011–; Chair. Bd of Trustees, Global School of Governance, Hertie Stiftung 2003–10, Hon. Chair. 2010–; mem. Bd Inst. for Econ. and Social Policy, Bonn 1977; mem. Bd German Nat. Trust; mem. Landtag of North Rhine-Westphalia 1980–88; mem. Senate Max Planck Gesellschaft; Hon. Citizen, City of Gröditz 2011; Great Golden Medal with Riband for Services to the Repub. of Austria 1991, Grand Federal Cross of Merit 1993, Norwegian Order of Merit 1994, Order of Merit of the Free State of Saxony 1997, Grand Cross of the Federal Cross of Merit 1999, Constitutional Medal of the Free State of Saxony 2002, St George's award, Semper Opera Ball, Dresden 2010, Order of Merit of North Rhine-Westphalia 2017; Hon. DrJur (Davidson Coll.) 1974, (Georgetown) 1978, (New School for Social Research) 1993, (Katholic Univ., Brussels) 1994; Hans Böckler Prize 1993, Moses Mendelssohn Medal 1998, Alexander Rüstow plaque 2001, International Bridge Prize 2003, Erich Kästner Prize 2010, Steiger Award 2013. *Publications:* Vertragliche Wettbewerbsbeschränkung und Wirtschaftsverfassung 1958, Grenzen der Tarifautonomie 1964, Fortschritt in Freiheit 1974, Die programmierte Krise–Alternativen zur staatlichen Schuldenpolitik 1979, Die neue Sicht der Dinge 1985, Zeitsignale–Parteienlandschaft im Umbruch 1989, Einheit und Erneuerung 1994, Ordnungspolitik in einer Zeit des Umbruchs 1998, Ein deutsches Tagebuch 1989–90 2000. *Leisure interests:* skiing, sailing. *Address:* Biedenkopf Rechtsanwälte, Ferdinandplatz 1, 01069 Dresden, Germany. *Website:* www.biedenkopf-kurt.de.

BIELECKI, Jan Krzysztof, MSc; Polish politician and economist; b. 3 May 1951, Bydgoszcz; s. of Anastazy Bielecki and Janina Bielecka; m. Barbara Bielecka 1976; one s. one d.; ed Economics Coll., Sopot, Gdańsk Univ.; Asst Lecturer, Gdańsk Univ. 1973–81 (lost his job for his alleged anti-Communist political activities); Head of Research Unit, Centre for Training Managerial Staff, Ministry of Trade and Ministry of Machine Industry 1972–82; trade union and workers' rights activist, expert for econ. affairs, Solidarity Trade Union 1980–81; continued union activity under martial law as assoc. of underground regional and nat. authorities; lorry driver 1982–85; CEO Doradca consulting co-operative, Sopot 1985–90; Deputy to Sejm (Parl.) 1989–93, mem. Civic Parl. Caucus 1989–91, Leader Parl. Liberal-Democratic Congress Caucus; Prime Minister of Poland Jan.–Dec. 1991; Minister for Poland–EU Relations 1992–93; mem. Liberal-Democratic Congress (mem. Provisional Bd Presidium) 1989–94; apptd by Polish Govt to Bd of Dirs EBRD, London 1993–2003; Pres. and CEO Bank Pekao SA 2003–10; Sr Econ. Adviser to Prime Minister Donald Tusk; Chair. Council of the Polish Inst. of Int. Affairs. *Publications include:* Histoire de l'Europe 1997; numerous articles in nat. and int. specialist newspapers and magazines. *Leisure interests:* horse riding, tennis, football. *Address:* Economic Council, Chancellery of the Prime Minister, 1/3 Ujazdowskie Avenue, 00-583 Warsaw, Poland (office). *Telephone:* (22) 6947292 (office). *Fax:* (22) 6946155 (office). *E-mail:* economic.council@kprm.gov.pl (office). *Website:* www.premier.gov.pl (office).

BIELENBERG, David, BS (AgricEng); American business executive; *Chairman, CHS Inc.;* ed Oregon State Univ., Texas A&M Univ. Exec. Program for Agricultural Producers, Nat. Asscn of Corp. Dirs Director Professionalism course (Certificate of Dir Educ.); fmr mem. Bd of Dirs and Pres. Wilco Farmers Co-operative, Mt Angel, Ore., Chair. East Valley Water Dist; mem. Bd of Dirs CHS Inc. 2002–06, 2009– (also Asst Sec.-Treas. 2012), Chair. 2012–, Chair. Exec. Cttee; operates a diverse agricultural business near Silverton, Ore. *Address:* CHS, 5500 Cenex Drive, Inver Grove Heights, MN 55077, USA (office). *Telephone:* (651) 355-6000 (office). *E-mail:* info@chsinc.com (office). *Website:* www.chsinc.com (office).

BIELSA, Rafael; Argentine politician and business executive; *Executive Chairman, Aeropuertos Argentina 2000 SA;* b. 15 Feb. 1953, Rosario, Santa Fe; m. Andrea D'Arza; two c. from previous m.; ed Univ. de Rosario; Asst Fed. Tribunals of Rosario 1974–78; various positions at Ministry of Justice, Ministry of Educ. and Office of the Presidency; Minister of Foreign Affairs, International Trade and Worship 2003–05; mem. Chamber of Deputies for Buenos Aires 2005–07; Sec., Secretaria de Programación para la Prevención de la Drogadicción y la Lucha Contra el Narcotráfico (SEDRONAR) 2011–13; Exec. Chair. Aeropuertos Argentina 2000 SA 2013–; mem. Partido Justicialista. *Address:* Aeropuertos Argentina 2000 SA, Honduras 5663, Buenos Aires C1414BNE, Argentina (office). *Telephone:* (11) 4779-6900 (office). *Website:* www.aa2000.com.ar (office).

BIENEN, Henry Samuel, BA, MA, PhD; American political scientist and fmr university administrator; *President Emeritus, Northwestern University;* b. 5 May 1939; m. Leigh Bienen; three d.; ed Cornell Univ. and Univ. of Chicago; Asst Prof., Princeton Univ. 1966–69, Assoc. Prof. of Politics and Int. Affairs 1969–72, Prof. of Politics and Int. Affairs 1972–81, William Stewart Tod Prof. of Politics and Int. Affairs 1981–85, James S. McDonnell Distinguished Univ. Prof. and Dean of the Woodrow Wilson School of Public and Int. Affairs 1985–94; Pres. Northwestern Univ. 1995–2009, Pres. Emer. 2009–; Visiting Prof., Makerere Coll., Kampala, Uganda 1963–65, Univ. Coll., Nairobi, Kenya 1968–69, Columbia Univ. 1971–72, Univ. of Ibadan, Nigeria 1972–73; Fellow, Center for Advanced Studies in Behavioral Sciences, Stanford Univ. 1976–77; Polsky Fellow, Aspen Inst. 1982–83; mem. Inst. for Advanced Studies, Princeton 1984–85; consultant to US Dept of State 1972–88, Nat. Security Council 1978–79, Agency for Int. Devt 1980–81, CIA 1982–88 (mem. Sr Review Panel in late 1980s), World Bank 1981–89, Hambrecht and Quist Investment Co., Boeing Corpn, Carnegie Corpn, Ford Foundation, Rockefeller Foundation, John D. and Catherine T. MacArthur Foundation; Chair. United Football League; Vice-Chair. Rasmussen Coll. 2009–; mem. Bd of Dirs The Bear Stearns Cos Inc., Deltak Inc., Council on Foreign Relations (Chair. Nominating and Governance Cttee and mem. Exec. Cttee), Chicago Council on Foreign Relations (mem. Exec. Cttee); mem. Bd Govs Argonne Nat. Lab. (mem. Exec. and Nominating Cttees); mem. Exec. Cttee Asscn of American Univs; mem. Cttee on Roles of Academic Health Centers in the 21st Century, Nat. Acads Inst. of Medicine; mem. Bd Univ. Corpn for Advanced Internet Devt (Internet 2) 1998–2002; mem. American Political Science Asscn; Hon. DHumLitt (Northwestern Univ.) 2009; Univ. of Chicago Professional Achievement Alumni Award 2000, Niagara Peace & Dialogue Award, Niagara Foundation 2008, Carnegie Corpn Academic Leadership Award for innovative leadership in higher educ. *Address:* Office of the President Emeritus, Arthur Rubloff Building, 375 East Chicago Avenue, Room 11-410, Chicago, IL 60611, USA (office). *Telephone:* (312) 503-7460 (office). *Fax:* (312) 503-5388 (office). *E-mail:* hsbienen@northwestern.edu (office). *Website:* www.northwestern.edu/Bienen (office).

BIEŃKOWSKA, Elżbieta, MA, MBA; Polish politician and EU official; *Commissioner for Internal Market, Industry, Entrepreneurship and SMEs, European Union;* b. 4 Feb. 1964, Katowice, Silesia; ed Jagiellonian Univ., Polish Nat. School of Public Admin, Warsaw School of Econs; began admin. career working in Business Dept of Śląskie Voivodship, involved in local application of EU's Phare programme; mem. Platforma Obywatelska (Civic Platform); Minister of Regional Devt 2007–13; Deputy Prime Minister and Minister of Infrastructure and Devt 2013–14; Commr for Internal Market, Industry, Entrepreneurship and SMEs, EC, Brussels Nov. 2014–. *Address:* European Commission, 200 Rue de la Loi/Wetstraat 200, 1049 Brussels, Belgium (office). *Telephone:* (2) 299-11-11 (switchboard) (office). *Website:* ec.europa.eu/commission/2014-2019/bienkowska_en (office).

BIESENBACH, Klaus; German gallery curator; *Director, Museum of Contemporary Art, Los Angeles;* b. 1967, Bergisch Gladbach, North Rhine-Westphalia; Founding Dir Kunst-Werke Inst. for Contemporary Art, Berlin 1991–, Berlin Biennale 1996–; joined Museum of Modern Art (MoMA) PS1 (fmrly P.S.1 Contemporary Art Center), New York as a curator 1996, apptd a curator in MoMA Dept of Film and Media 2004, Chief Curator Dept of Media 2006 (subsequently Dept of Media and Performance Art 2009), presented major retrospective of work of Marina Abramović 2010, Dir MoMA PS1 and Chief Curator at Large, MoMA –2018; adviser to Christine Macel and Hans Ulrich Obrist for Based in Berlin (six-week exhbn); co-staged, with Hans Ulrich Obrist, 11 Rooms, an installation of durational performance works by Marina Abramović, Tino Sehgal, Simon Fujiwara, amongst others, at Manchester Int. Festival 2011; restaged Abramovic's The Artist Is Ever-Present at Dasha Zhukova's Garage, Moscow 2011; Dir Museum of Contemporary Art, Los Angeles 2018–; mem. Bd of Trustees American Acad. in Berlin; Verdienstkreuz, FRG 2016; City of New York Proclamation of Honor 2018. *Address:* The Museum of Contemporary Art, 250 South Grand Avenue, Los Angeles, CA 90012, USA (office). *Telephone:* (213) 626-6222 (office). *E-mail:* msirisoma@moca.org (office); info@moca.org (office). *Website:* www.moca.org (office).

BIÉTRY, Charles-Pierre; French sports reporter and television executive; *Director, Al Jazeera Sport France;* b. 5 Nov. 1943, Rennes; ed Centre de formation des journalistes, Paris; reporter, Agence-France Presse 1966–84; Dir of Sports, Canal+ 1984–98; Dir of Sports and adviser to Chair., France Télévision 1999–2001; Producer and consultant, Onzeo (TV satellite channel of town of AS Saint-Etienne and RC Lens) 2006–; Editorial Dir L'Équipe TV –2011; Dir Al Jazeera Sport France 2011–; Man. Dir beIN Sports TV channel 2012–14; Pres. PSG omnisports 1992–98, Paris Saint-Germain July–Dec. 1998; Vice-Pres. Créteil June–July 2001; mem. Admin. Council, FC Lorient 2004–05, 2005–06; Recruiter for Stade Rennes 2007–13; Hon. Pres. Brittany Football Asscn 1997–. *Address:* Al Jazeera Sport France, PO Box 23123, Doha, Qatar (office). *Telephone:* 489-7446 (office). *Fax:* 489-7472 (office). *E-mail:* press.int@aljazeera.net (office). *Website:* www.ar.beinsports .net (office).

BIG BOI; American rap artist; b. (Antoine André Patton), 1 Feb. 1975, Savannah, Ga; ed Tri-City High School, Atlanta; mem. Outkast (with Andre 3000, aka Dré) 1992–, signed to LaFace Records; designed Outkast Clothing line; also solo artist; numerous collaborations including Mary J. Blige, Cutty, Missy Elliott, Fantasia, Janelle Monáe, Raekwon, Kelly Rowland, Trick Daddy; Source Award for Best New Rap Group of the Year 1995, American Music Awards for Best Hip Hop/R&B Group 2003, 2004, Grammy Award for best urban/alternative performance 2004, World Music Awards for Best Group, Best Pop Group, Best Rap/Hip-Hop Artist 2004, MTV Europe Best Group Award 2004, Best Song Award, Best Video Award (both for Hey Ya) 2004. *Recordings include:* albums: with Outkast: Southernplayalisticadillacmuzik 1994, ATLiens 1996, Aquemini 1998, Stankonia 2000, Big Boi And Dre Present. . . 2002, Speakerboxxx/The Love Below (Grammy Awards for Album of the Year, Best Rap Album 2004, American Music Award for Best Rap/Hip-Hop Album 2004) 2003, My Life In Idlewild 2005, Idlewild 2006; solo: Sir Lucious Left Foot: The Son of Chico Dusty 2010, Vicious Lies and Dangerous Rumors 2012. *Address:* c/o Career Artist Management, 9350 North Civic Center Drive, Beverly Hills, CA 90210, USA (office). *Telephone:* (310) 776-7640 (office). *Fax:* (424) 230-7839 (office). *Website:* camanagement.com (office); www.outkast .com; www.bigboi.com.

BIGELOW, Kathryn Ann; American film director, producer and screenwriter; b. 27 Nov. 1951, San Carlos, Calif.; d. of Ronald Elliot Bigelow and Gertude Kathryn Bigelow (née Larson); m. James Cameron (q.v.) 1989 (divorced 1991); ed San

Francisco Art Inst. and Columbia Univ., New York; worked with Art and Language performance group, UK; awarded scholarship to Ind. Study Program, Whitney Museum, New York. *Films include:* The Set Up (short), The Loveless 1982, Near Dark 1987, Blue Steel 1990, Point Break 1991, Strange Days (Saturn Award for Best Dir 1995) 1995, The Weight of Water 2000, K-19: The Widowmaker 2002, Mission Zero 2007, The Hurt Locker (numerous awards, including BAFTA Award for Best Dir 2010, Academy Awards for Best Dir (first woman) and Best Movie 2010, Directors Guild of America Award for Outstanding Directing, Critics' Choice Award for Best Dir, Nat. Soc. of Film Critics Award for Best Dir, Hollywood Film Festival Dir of the Year) 2009, Zero Dark Thirty (New York Film Critics' Circle Award for Best Dir, amongst others) 2012, Detroit 2017. *Television includes:* Wild Palms (mini-series, episode 3) 1993, Homicide: Life on the Street (three episodes) 1998–99, Karen Sisco (one episode) 2004, The Miraculous Year 2011. *Address:* c/o Ken Stovitz, Creative Artists Agency, 2000 Avenue of the Stars, Los Angeles, CA 90067, USA (office). *Telephone:* (424) 288-2000 (office). *Fax:* (424) 288-2900 (office). *Website:* www.caa.com (office).

BIGGAM, Sir Robin Adair, Kt; British business executive and chartered accountant; b. 8 July 1938, Carluke; s. of Thomas Biggam and Eileen Biggam; m. Elizabeth McArthur Biggam (née McDougall) 1962; one s. two d.; ed Lanark Grammar School; CA, Peat Marwick Mitchell 1960–63, ICI 1964–81; ICL Finance Dir 1981–84; Exec. Dir Dunlop 1984–85; Chair. Cadcentre Ltd 1983–86; Man. Dir BICC PLC 1986–87, CEO 1987–91, Deputy Chair. 1991–, Chair. 1992–96; Dir Fairey Group PLC 1995– (Chair. 1996–2001); Chair. Ind. TV Comm. 1997–2003; Chair. Macquarie European Infrastructure 2000–05; Dir (non-exec.) Chloride Group PLC 1985–87, Lloyds Abbey Life PLC (fmrly Abbey Life Group) 1985–90, Redland Group PLC 1991–97, British Aerospace PLC 1994–2003, British Energy 1996–2002 (Deputy Chair. 2001–02); Pres. German-British Chamber of Industry and Commerce 1996–98; Chancellor, Univ. of Luton (now Univ. of Bedfordshire) 2001–09; mem. Inst. of Chartered Accountants of Scotland. *Leisure interests:* golf, gardening, swimming, watching TV, fishing. *Address:* c/o Institute of Charted Accountants of Scotland, CA House, 21 Haymarket Yards, Edinburgh, EH12 5BH, Scotland (office).

BIGGS, Peter Martin, CBE, DSc, FRS, FRCVS, FRCPath, CBiol, FRSB, FMedSci; British veterinary scientist and academic (retd); b. 13 Aug. 1926, Petersfield, Hants.; s. of Ronald Biggs and Cecile Biggs (née Player); m. Alison Janet Molteno 1950; two s. one d.; ed Bedales School, Petersfield, Cambridge School, Mass., Royal Veterinary Coll., London, Univ. of Bristol; with RAF 1944–48; with Royal Veterinary Coll., London 1948–53; Research Asst, Dept of Veterinary Anatomy, Univ. of Bristol 1953–55; Lecturer in Veterinary Clinical Pathology, Dept of Veterinary Medicine 1955–59; Prin. Scientific Officer, Houghton Poultry Research Station 1959–66, Sr Prin. Scientific Officer 1966–71, Deputy Dir 1971–74, Dir 1974–86; Dir Inst. for Animal Health 1986–88; Chief Scientific Officer 1981–88; Visiting Prof. of Veterinary Microbiology, Royal Veterinary Coll. London 1982–2008, Hon. Prof. of Veterinary Microbiology 2009–, Vice-Chair. of Council 2002–08; Andrew D. White Prof.-at-Large, Cornell Univ., USA 1988–94; Vice-Pres. British Veterinary Asscn 1996–98; Fellow, Inst. of Biology 1973, Pres. 1990–92; Fellow, Royal Coll. of Pathologists 1978, Royal Coll. of Veterinary Surgeons 1979, Royal Veterinary Coll. 1983, Acad. Of Medical Sciences 1998; Hon. Fellow, Royal Agricultural Soc. of England 1986; Hon. Dr of Veterinary Medicine (Ludwig-Maximilians Univ., Munich); Dr hc (Univ. of Liège) and numerous others; Wolf Foundation Prize in Agric. 1989; Dalrymple-Champneys Cup and Medal of the British Veterinary Asscn 1973, Chiron Award, British Veterinary Asscn 1999. *Publications include:* more than 100 scientific papers. *Leisure interests:* music making, natural history. *Address:* 'Willows', London Road, St Ives, PE27 5ES, England (home). *Telephone:* (1480) 463471 (home). *E-mail:* petermartinbiggs@btinternet.com (home).

BIGOT, Charles André Marie; French aviation engineer and business executive; b. 29 July 1932, Angers; s. of Charles Bigot and Marcelle Pousset; m. Marie-Odile Lambert 1959; one s. three d.; ed Ecole Sainte-Geneviève, Versailles, Ecole Nat. Supérieure de l'Aéronautique, Ecole Polytechnique and Cranfield Coll. of Aeronautics, Centre de Perfectionnement Affaires; aeronautical engineer 1957–61; Tech. Dir of Aeronautical Services, Ministry of Aeronautics, CNRS 1961–63; Dir of launch vehicle div., Centre Nat. des Etudes Spatiales (CNES) 1963–70; Deputy Dir Centre Spatial de Brétigny 1970–71; Dir of Devt Air Inter 1971–75; Soc. d'Etudes et de Réalisations Industrielles (Seri-Renault Eng), Dir-Gen. 1975–80; Commercial Dir Soc. Nat. Industrielle Aérospatiale (Snias) 1980–82; Dir-Gen. Arianespace 1982–90, Pres.-Dir-Gen. 1990–98, Hon. Chair. 1998–; mem. Bd of Dirs, Ellipso, Inc. (Ellipsat, Inc.), Washington, DC 1998–; mem. Int. Acad. of Astronautics, Acad. Nat. de l'Air et de l'Espace; Chevalier, Légion d'honneur; Commdr, Ordre nat. du Mérite; Médaille de Vermeil, CNES. *Address:* c/o Board of Directors, Ellipso, Inc., 1133 21st Street NW, Floor 8, Washington, DC 20036-3390, USA. *Telephone:* (202) 466-4488. *E-mail:* info@ellipsat.com. *Website:* www.ellipso.com.

BIGUM, Jens, MSc; Danish business executive and fmr university administrator; b. 28 July 1938, Gislum; ed Royal Veterinary and Agricultural Univ., Copenhagen; Admin. Officer, Oxexport 1965–70; Financial Man. Mejeriselskabet Danmark amba 1970–72, Financial Dir 1972; Dir MD Foods amba 1987–92, Man. Dir 1992–2000 (renamed Arla Foods), Man. Dir Arla Foods amba 2000–04, also Dir and Deputy Chair. Arla Foods UK PLC 2003; Chair. Chr. Hansen Holding A/S 2005–06; Chair. Aarhus Univ. 2004–2011; Dir Carlsberg Breweries A/S 1997–09, Chair. 2002–09, Deputy Chair. Carlsberg A/S 2002–09; Kt of the Dannebrog 1993.

BIHI ABDI, Musa; Somali politician and fmr military officer; *President, 'Republic of Somaliland';* ed Gagarin Air Force Acad., USSR, US Mil. Acad., West Point, Univ. of Hargeisa; served as pilot in Somali Air Force 1970s; Mil. Attaché, Embassy of Somalia in Washington, DC mid 1980s; joined Somali Nat. Movt in armed struggle against Siad Barre regime; Minister of Interior and Nat. Security 1993; Pres. of self-proclaimed ' Repub. of Somaliland' (NW Somalia) 2017–; mem. Kulmiye (Peace, Unity and Devt Party), Chair. 2010–. *Address:* Office of the President, Hargeisa, Somaliland (office). *Website:* www.somalilandgov.com (office).

BIJLEVELD, Anna (Ank) Theodora Bernardina, MA; Dutch politician; *Minister of Defence;* b. 17 March 1962, IJsselmuiden; m. Riekele Bijleveld; two d.; ed Univ. of Twente; Policy Officer, municipality of Hengelo 1986; mem. Enschede city council (CDA) 1986–89; mem. States Gen. Second Chamber (lower house of parl.) 1989–2001, 2010–11; Mayor of Hof van Twente 2001–07; Sec. of State for Interior and Kingdom Relations 2007–10; King's Commr (Head), Overijssel Prov. 2011–17; Minister of Defence 2017–; mem. Christen Democratisch Appèl (CDA) (Christian Democratic Appeal); Kt, Order of Orange-Nassau 2001. *Address:* Ministry of Defence, Plein 4, POB 20701, 2500 ES The Hague, Netherlands (office). *Telephone:* (70) 3188188 (office). *Fax:* (70) 3187888 (office). *E-mail:* defensievoorlichting@mindef.nl (office). *Website:* www.rijksoverheid.nl/ministeries/def (office).

BÍLÁ, Lucie; Czech singer; b. (Hana Zaňáková), 7 April 1966, Otvovice; d. of Josef Zaňák; fmr partner Petr Kratochvíl; one s.; fmr partner Vaclav Noid Barta; co-owner Theatre Ta Fantastika, Prague; has toured throughout Western Europe; has performed in charity concerts in Czech Repub.; numerous awards including Czech Grammy Prize 1992–96, Most Popular Singer (Czech Repub.) 1994–2007, Czech Musical Acad. Prize 1997, Czech Nightingale Trophy 1996–2004, 2007–17. *Theatre includes:* Les Misérables 1992, Dracula 1995, Rat-Catcher 1996, Joan of Arc (Thalia Prize) 2000, Love is Love 2004, Elixir Zivota 2006, Nemcova 2007, Carmen 2008, Aida 2012, The Addams Family 2014, Sister in Act 2017. *Films include:* Horká kaše 1988, Divoká srdce 1989, Volná noha 1989, Prazákům, těm je hej 1990, Zkoušové období 1990, Fontána pro Zuzanu 2 1993, Princezna ze miejna 1994, King Král Ubu 1996, Čas dluhů 1998, V peřině, Babovřesky. *Recordings include:* albums: Missariel 1993, Lucie Bílá 1994, Hvezdy jako hvezdy (Stars as Stars) 1998, Uplne naha (Totally naked) 1999, Jampadampa 2003, Koncert (Concert) 2006, Woman 2007, Bang Bang! 2009, Bíle Vánoce 2010, Modi 2012, Recital 2013, Hana 2016, Bile Vanoce Lucie Bile II 2017. *Publications include:* Ted uz to vim (Now I Know It Already) 1999, Jen kratka navsteva potesi (Just short visit delights) 2007. *Leisure interest:* family. *Address:* Agentura 44, s.r.o. Karlova 8, 110 01 Prague 1, Czech Republic (office). *Telephone:* 603-548530 (mobile) (office). *E-mail:* produkce@luciebila.com (office). *Website:* www.luciebila.com.

BILALI, Mohamed Gharib, MA; Tanzanian nuclear scientist and politician; *Vice-President;* b. 6 Feb. 1945; ed Howard Univ., Univ. of California, Berkeley, USA; joined Univ. of Dar es salaam as Lecturer in Physics 1976, Head of Dept of Physics and in charge of Nuclear Physics Unit 1983, Head of Faculty of Science 1988–90; Fellow, Univ. of Singapore under IAEA 1984–85; apptd Prin. Sec. to Ministry of Science, Tech. and Higher Educ. 1990; Chief Minister, Supreme Revolutionary Council of Zanzibar 1995–2000; Vice-Pres. of Tanzania 2010–; Chair. Dodoma Univ. Council 2007–; mem. CCM (Party for Democracy and Progress). *Address:* Office of the Vice-President, Luthuri Street, PO Box 5380, Dar es Salaam, Tanzania (office). *Telephone:* (22) 2113857 (office). *Fax:* (22) 2113856 (office). *E-mail:* ps@vpo.go.tz (office). *Website:* vpo.go.tz (office).

BILBRAY, James Hubert, BA, JD; American lawyer, politician and government official; *Chairman of the Board of Governors, United States Postal Service;* b. 19 May 1938, Las Vegas, Nev.; m.; several c.; ed Las Vegas High School, Univ. of Nevada, Las Vegas (UNLV), American Univ. and its Law School; student body pres., UNLV, Co-founder and first pres. UNLV's Alumni Asscn; served in Nevada Army Nat. Guard 1955–56, Nevada Army Reserves 1957–63; mem. State Bar of Nev. 1965–; attorney with Kaempfer Crowell Renshaw Gronauer & Fiorentino, Las Vegas; Deputy Dist Attorney, Clark Co., Nev. 1960s, served as Chief Counsel for Clark Co. Juvenile Dept 1967–68; Alt. Las Vegas Municipal Judge 1978–80; mem. California-Nevada High Speed Train Comm. 2007–09; elected to Nev. State Senate 1981–87; mem. US House of Reps from Nev. 1987–95; mem. 2005 Base Closing and Realignment Comm.; Gov., US Postal Service 2006–, apptd Vice-Chair. 2012, Chair. 2015–, mem. Audit and Finance Cttee, Compensation and Man. Resources Cttee; mem. Advisory Council, Safefreight Technology Ltd; mem. Bd of Regents, Univ. of Nevada system 1968–72; mem. Bd of Visitors US Mil. Acad. 1996–2000; Democrat; Hon. LLD (Univ. of Nevada) 2001; James H. Bilbray Elementary School, Las Vegas named in his honour. *Address:* US Postal Service, 475 L'Enfant Plaza SW, Washington, DC 20260, USA (office). *Telephone:* (202) 268-3118 (office). *E-mail:* info@usps.com (office). *Website:* www.usps.com (office).

BILDT, Carl; Swedish politician and diplomatist; b. 15 July 1949, Halmstad; m. 3rd Anna Maria Corazza 1998; one s.; one s. one d. from previous m.; ed Univ. of Stockholm; Chair. Confed. of Liberal and Conservative Students 1973–74, European Democrat Students 1974–76; mem. Stockholm Co. Council 1974–77; Political Advisor on Policy Co-ordination Ministry of Econ. Affairs 1976–78; Under-Sec. of State for Co-ordination and Planning at the Cabinet Office 1979–81; mem. Parl. 1979–2001; mem. Exec. Cttee Moderate Party 1981, Leader 1986–99; mem. Advisory Council on Foreign Affairs 1982–99; mem. Submarine Defence Comm. 1982–83; mem. 1984 Defence Policy Comm. 1984–87; Prime Minister of Sweden 1991–94; EU Peace Envoy in Fmr Yugoslavia 1995; High Rep. of the Int. Community in Bosnia and Herzegovina 1995–97; Vice-Chair. Int. Democrat Union 1989–92, Chair. 1992–99; Special Envoy of Sec.-Gen. of the UN to the Balkans 1999–2001; Chair. At-Large-Membership Study Cttee Internet Corpn for Assigned Names and Numbers (ICANN) 2001–02; currently Chair. Bd of Dirs Kreab Group (public affairs and strategic communication cos), Nordic Venture Network, Teleoptimering AB; Minister of Foreign Affairs 2006–14; mem. Bd of Dirs Centre for European Reform, Vostok Nafta, Lundin Petroleum, HiQ, Öhmans; Trustee RAND Corpn; Fellow, Inst. for the Study of Terrorism and Political Violence, Univ. of St Andrews, Scotland; mem. IISS, London. *Publications:* Landet som steg ut i kylan (The Country that Stepped Out into the Cold) 1972, Framtid i frihet (A Future in Freedom) 1976, Hallanning, svensk, europe (A Citizen of Holland, Sweden and Europe) 1991, Peace Journey 1997. *Address:* c/o Ministry for Foreign Affairs, Gustav Adolfs torg 1, 103 39 Stockholm, Sweden (office). *E-mail:* carl@bildt.net. *Website:* www.bildt.net.

BILE, Pastor Micha Ondo, MSc; Equatorial Guinean mining engineer, diplomatist and politician; b. 2 Dec. 1952, Nsinik-Esawong; m.; six c.; ed Inst. of Mining, Krivoi-Rog Univ.; engineer, Mines and Quarries Section, Dept of Mines and Hydrocarbons, Ministry of Mines and Energy 1982, Chief of Section 1983–84, Dir-Gen. Dept 1984–94, Sec.-Gen. Ministry 1994–95; Amb. and Perm. Rep. to UN, New York and Amb. to USA 1995–2000, Amb. to Spain 2000–03, also Amb. to Italy 2001–03; Minister of External Relations, Int. Co-operation and Francophone Affairs 2003–12; Kt (Second Class), Order of Independence.

BILGIÇ, Abdurrahman; Turkish diplomatist; *Ambassador to UK;* b. 1963; m.; two c.; ed Ankara Univ.; joined Ministry of Foreign Affairs 1986, overseas posts in Tripoli and Canberra and in Consulate in Deventer; Dir-Gen., Directorate Gen. for Press and Information of the Prime Ministry 2003–; Consul Gen., Consulate Gen., Munich 2005–07, various posts in Ministry of Foreign Affairs, Amb. to Japan 2011; Deputy Undersecretary, MIT (Nat. Intelligence Org.) 2011–14, Amb. to UK 2014–. *Address:* Embassy of Turkey, 43 Belgrave Square, London, SW1X 8PA, England (office). *Telephone:* (20) 7393-0202 (office). *Fax:* (20) 7393-0066 (office); (20) 7393-9213 (office). *E-mail:* embassy.london@mfa.gov.tr (office). *Website:* londra.be.mfa.gov.tr (office).

BILI, Laurent; French diplomatist and government official; *President, Conseil d'Administration, Agence pour l'enseignement français à l'étranger;* b. 12 Aug. 1961; ed Lycée Michelet, Vanves, Univ. of Paris I-Sorbonne, Institut d'études politiques de Paris, École nat. d'admin, Institut du Roi Prachadiphok, Thailand; with Foreign Service 1982–88, Dept of Strategic Affairs and of Disarmament 1991–93, Diplomatic Counsellor, attached to Minister of Defence 1993–99, First Sec. then Second Counsellor, Embassy in Ankara 1995–98, First Sec. and Perm. Rep., Perm. Mission to WEU, Brussels 1998–2000, Counsellor to Political Cttee and to Temporary Security of the EU 2000–02, delegated to the functions of Deputy Dir of Strategic Affairs, Ministry of Foreign Affairs Jan.–April 2002, Dir of the Cabinet, then Counsellor to Minister Del. for European Affairs May–Oct. 2002, Tech. Counsellor, Diplomatic Cell of the Presidency of the Repub. 2002–07; Amb. to Thailand 2007–09; Dir Civil and Mil. Cabinet, Ministry of Defence 2009–10; Amb. to Turkey 2011–15, to Brazil 2015–17; Pres. Conseil d'Administration, Agence pour l'enseignement français à l'étranger, also Dir-Gen. Globalization, Culture, Educ. and Int. Devt; Chevalier, Légion d'honneur, Médaille d'honneur des Affaires étrangères (Silver), Grand Cross of the Most Exalted Order of the White Elephant (Thailand); Dr hc (Univ. of Kasetsat, Bangkok). *Address:* Agence poue l'enseignement français à l'étranger, 23, place de Catalogne, 75014 Paris, France (office). *Telephone:* (1) 53-69-30-90 (office). *Website:* www.aefe.fr (office).

BILLAUD, Bernard; French fmr civil servant; *Conseiller maître honoraire de la Cour des comptes;* b. 3 Sept. 1942, Béziers; s. of Bernard Billaud and Raymonde Mazet; m. Claude Devitry 1967; two s. one d.; ed Inst. d'études politiques de Paris and Ecole nat. d'admin, Faculté de droit de Paris; obtained Diplôme de Inst. d'études politiques de Paris and Diplôme d'études supérieures de droit public; auditor 1968, Public Auditor Cour des Comptes 1976, Conseiller maître 1989, now hon.; Adviser to French Embassy, Holy See 1974–76; Official Rep. to the Prime Minister 1976; Sr Lecturer Inst. d'études politiques de Paris 1977–92; Dir of Staff, Mayor of Paris 1979–83; mem. comm. Vieux Paris 1983–; Pres. comm. on historical works of Ville de Paris 1983–2009; Dir-Gen. Int. Relations, Paris 1983–84; Gen. Commr of the French Language 1987–89; Prime Minister's Rep. of Admin. Council of AFP 1993–98, France 3 1995–98; Vice-Pres. organizing Cttee for 'de la Gaule à la France' 1996; Pres. du conseil d'admin de l'Ecole nationale des chartes 2004–07; currently Conseiller maître honoraire de la Cour des comptes; Commdr, Légion d'honneur, Officier, Ordre nat. du Mérite, Grand Croix Ordre de Saint-Grégoire-le-Grand, Grand Medaille de Vermeil, Ville de Paris 2010. *Publications include:* Jean Guitton vu par ses contemporains 1963, L'aide de l'Etat à l'enseignement privé 1966, Georges Bidault – Les éditoriaux de L'Aube (1938–1940) 2001, D'un Chirac l'autre 2005. *Leisure interest:* history. *Address:* 12 rue des Jardins Saint Paul, 75004 Paris, France (home). *Telephone:* 1-48-87-91-68 (home).

BIN LADEN, Bakr Mohammed; Saudi Arabian business executive; *Chairman, Saudi Binladin Group;* b. 1947; s. of Mohammad Awad bin Laden; half-brother of Osama bin Laden; ed Univ. of Miami, Fla, USA; Chair. Saudi Binladin Group (took over leadership of construction co. from his brother the late Salem M. Bin Laden). *Address:* Saudi Binladin Group Bldg, Prince Mohd Bin Abdul Aziz Street, Al Rawdah District, Jeddah 21492, Saudi Arabia (office). *Telephone:* (2) 664-3033 (office). *Fax:* (2) 664-3261 (office). *E-mail:* info@sbg.com.sa (office). *Website:* www.sbg.com.sa (office).

BINAY, Jejomar (Jojo) C.; Philippine lawyer and politician; b. 11 Nov. 1942, Makati; s. of Diego Binay and Lourdes Cabauatan; m. Elenita Sombillo; five c.; ed Philippine Normal Coll., Univ. of the Philippines; taught law, political science and public admin at Philippine Coll. of Commerce, Philippine Women's Univ. and St Scholastica's Coll.; Mayor of Makati 1986–98, 2001–10; Vice-Pres. of the Philippines 2010–16; Chair. Metropolitan Manila Devt Authority 1990–92, 1998–2001; fmr Vice-Chair. Pasig River Rehabilitation Comm.; fmr Traffic Czar for Metro Manila; Pres. PDP-Laban Party.

BINDING, Günther, DrIng, DPhil; German professor of art and architecture; *Emeritus Professor, University of Cologne;* b. 6 March 1936, Koblenz; s. of Kurt Binding and Margot Binding (née Masur); m. Elisabeth Dietz 1969; one s. two d.; ed gymnasium in Arnsberg and Cologne, Technische Hochschule, Aachen and Univs of Cologne and Bonn; Dir Lower Rhine section, Rheinisches Landesmuseum, Bonn 1964–70; Prof., Univ. of Cologne 1970–2000, Rector 1981–83, Pro-Rector 1983–85, now Prof. Emer.; Vice-Pres. W German Rectors' Conf. 1982–84; mem. Sächsische Akad. der Wissenschaften 1999–, Wissenschaftliche Gesellschaft an der Universität Frankfurt 2002–06; Ruhrpreis für Kunst und Wissenschaft 1966, Josef-Humar-Preis 1986, Rheinland-Taler 1987. *Publications include:* 40 books and 320 articles about European architecture and history of art. *Address:* University of Cologne, Albertus-Magnus-Platz, 50923 Cologne (office); Wingertsheide 65, 51427 Berg.-Gladbach, Germany (home). *Telephone:* (221) 470-4440 (office); (2204) 64956 (home). *E-mail:* guenther.binding@uni-koeln.de. *Website:* www.guentherbinding.de (office).

BINDOUMI, Joseph; Central African Republic politician; *President, Central African League of Human Rights;* fmr magistrate; Pres. Central African League of Human Rights 1991–2015, 2016–, Monitoring Cttee of Bangui Forum; Minister of Nat. Defence, Restructuring of the Armed Forces, Fmr Combatants and War Victims 2015–16. *Address:* Central African League of Human Rights, BP 994, Bangui, Central African Republic (office). *Telephone:* 72-28-54-58 (office). *E-mail:* tiangaye@hotmail.com.

BINDRA, Abhinav, BBA; Indian fmr air rifle shooter; b. 28 Sept. 1982, Dehradun; s. of Apjit Singh Bindra and Babli Bindra; ed Univ. of Colorado, USA; Nat. Champion 1999–2003, 2005, Jr World Record Holder, Air Rifle, Munich 2001, European Circuit Champion (seven gold, four silver, one bronze) 2002, Commonwealth Games, Manchester (gold and silver medals) 2002, Asian Shooting Championship (silver medals) 2003, World Cup, Munich (bronze medal) 2003, All American Shooting Championship, Colorado Springs (gold medal) 2004, Commonwealth Games Record Holder 2004, Asian Shooting Championship, Bangkok (gold medal) 2005, Commonwealth Games, Melbourne (gold, silver, bronze medals) 2006, World Champion, Air Rifle World Championship, Zagreb 2006, Air Rifle Asian Shooting Championship (gold medal) 2007, Air Rifle Australian Cup, Sydney (gold medal) 2007, Beijing Olympic (gold medal) 2008, Commonwealth Games, Delhi (gold and silver medals) 2010, INTERSHOOT Netherlands (gold and silver medals) 2010, Asian Games, Guangzhou (silver medal) 2010, Commonwealth Games, Glasgow (gold medal) 2014, Asian Games, Incheon (bronze medals, team and individual) 2014; Dir Abhinav Futuristics Ltd, Abhinav Hotels and Inns Pvt. Ltd; mem. Cen. Selection Cttee, Nat. Youth Awards 2008–09; Hon. Lt Col, Indian Territorial Army 2011; Dr hc (SRM Univ., Chennai) 2008; Arjuna Award 2000, Rajiv Gandhi Khel Ratna 2001, Maharaja Ranjit Singh Award 2001, K.K. Birla Award 2002, UT Government Most Elite Sportsman Award 2002, Uttaranchal Praman Patra Award 2003, Punjab Praman Patra Award 2006, NDTV - India Sportsman of the Year 2008, Madhya Pradesh Khel Ratna 2008, Padma Bhushan 2009, Padma Bhushan 2009, Rajiv Gandhi Award 2009, Bharat Shiromani Award 2009, India Youth Sports Icon 2009, The Sportsman of the Year, SAHARA Indian Sports Awards. *Publications:* Ways of Rifle (with Heinz Reinkemier), A Shot at History: My Obsessive Journey to Olympic Gold (autobiog.; with Rohit Brijnath) 2011. *Address:* Abhinav Futuristics Ltd, SCO 62-63, Sector 34-A, Chandigarh, India (office). *Telephone:* (172) 2645978 (office); (172) 5074620 (office). *Fax:* (172) 2647940. *E-mail:* info@abhinavfuturistics.com (office). *Website:* www.abhinavbindra.com.

BINGAMAN, Jesse Francis (Jeff), Jr, BA, JD; American politician and lawyer; b. 3 Oct. 1943, El Paso, Tex.; s. of Jesse Francis Bingaman and Frances Bethia (née Ball); m. Anne Kovacovich 1968; one s.; ed Silver High School, Harvard and Stanford Univs; grew up in Silver City, NM; admitted to the NM Bar 1968; served in US Army Reserve 1968–74; Pnr, Campbell, Bingaman & Black, Santa Fe 1972–78; Attorney-Gen. of NM 1979–82; Senator from New Mexico 1983–2013 (retd), Chair. Energy and Natural Resources Cttee 2001–03, 2007–13, Chair. Cttee Outreach for the Senate Democratic Caucus; Distinguished Fellow, Steyer-Taylor Center for Energy Policy and Finance, Stanford Law School 2013–14; Trustee, Santa Fe Inst.; Democrat; Hon. DHumLitt (New Mexico State Univ.) 2008; Distinguished Eagle Scout Award, Boy Scouts of America. *Address:* Santa Fe Institute, 1399 Hyde Park Road, Santa Fe, NM 87501, USA. *Telephone:* (505) 984-8800. *Fax:* (505) 982-0565. *E-mail:* jeff.bingaman@gmail.com. *Website:* www.santafe.edu/about/people/profile/Senator%20Jeff%20Bingaman.

BINGHAM, H. Raymond, BS, MBA; American business executive; b. 1947; ed Weber State Univ., Harvard Business School, USA; held sr man. positions at Marriott Corpn, Red Lion Hotels and Inns, Agrico Overseas Investment Co. and N-ReN Int.; Exec. Vice-Pres. and Chief Financial Officer Cadence Design Systems, Inc. 1993–99, mem. Bd of Dirs 1997–2004, Pres. and CEO 1999–2004, Exec. Chair. 2004–05; Man. Dir General Atlantic LLC (pvt. equity firm) 2006–10, also Co-head of Palo Alto, Calif. office; apptd Chair. Flextronics Int. Ltd 2008 (mem. Bd of Dirs 2005); mem. Bd of Dirs Oracle Corpn –2017, Cypress Semiconductor Corpn (CY.O) –2017, Freescale Semiconductor, Inc., KLA Tencor Corpn, STMicroelectronics NV; Co-founder and Dir Silicon Valley Educ. Foundation; mem. Bd of Dirs Nat. Parks Conservation Asscn; named an Outstanding Director by the Outstanding Director Exchange (div. of the Financial Times) 2009; Hon. DH (Weber State Univ.).

BINGHAM, John, CBE, FRS; British scientist, plant breeder and farmer; b. 19 June 1930; s. of Thomas Frederick Bingham and Emma Maud Lusher; m. Jadwiga Anna Siedlecka 1983; one s.; ed Univ. of East Anglia; mem. staff, Plant Breeding Inst. of Cambridge (subsequently Plant Breeding Int. Cambridge Ltd) 1954–86, Deputy Chief Scientific Officer 1981–91; research in plant breeding, culminating in production of improved winter wheat varieties for British agric.; Pres. Royal Norfolk Agric. Asscn 1991; Hon. Fellow, Royal Agric. Soc. of England 1983, Nat. Inst. of Agric. Botany; Hon. DSc (East Anglia); Mullard Medal, Royal Soc. 1975, Royal Agric. Soc. of England Research Medal 1975, Massey Ferguson Nat. Award for Services to UK Agric. 1984. *Leisure interests:* farming and wildlife conservation (one floral meadow discovered now classified as Site of Special Scientific Interest). *Address:* Hereward Barn, Church Lane, Mattishall Burgh, Dereham, Norfolk, NR20 3QZ, England (home). *Telephone:* (1362) 858354 (home). *E-mail:* johnbingham@btinternet.com (home).

BINMORE, Kenneth (Ken) George, CBE, PhD, FBA; British mathematician, economist and academic; *Research Fellow in Economics, Finance and Management, University of Bristol;* b. 27 Sept. 1940, London; s. of Ernest Binmore and Maud Binmore (née Holland); m. Josephine Ann Lee 1972; two s. two d.; ed Imperial Coll., London; Prof. of Math., LSE 1974–88; Prof. of Econs, Univ. of Michigan, USA 1988–93; Prof. of Econs, Univ. Coll. London 1991–2003, Prof. Emer. and Research Fellow 2003–; currently Visiting Prof. Emer. of Econs and Research Fellow in Econs, Finance and Man., Univ. of Bristol; Dir Centre for Econ. Learning and Social Evolution 1994–2003; Fellow, Econometric Soc., American Acad. of Arts and Sciences; a founder of the modern economic theory of bargaining (along with Nash and Rubinstein). *Publications:* Mathematical Analysis 1977, Foundations of Analysis: Book 1: Logic, Sets and Numbers 1980, Foundations of Analysis: Book 2: Topological Ideas 1980, Economic Organizations as Games (co-ed.) 1986, The Economics of Bargaining (co-ed.) 1987, Essays on the Foundations of Game Theory 1990, Fun and Games: A Text on Game Theory 1991, Playing Fair: Game Theory and the Social Contract I 1994, Just Playing: Game Theory and the Social Contract II 1998, Calculus (co-author) 2002, Natural Justice 2005, Playing for Real – A Text on Game Theory 2007, Does Game Theory Work? The Bargaining Challenge 2007, Game Theory: A Very Short Introduction 2008, Rational Decisions 2009; 125 published papers. *Leisure interest:* philosophy, watercolours. *Address:* 3B3, The Priory Road Complex, Priory Road, Clifton, Bristol, BS8 1TU, England (office); Newmills, Whitebrook, Monmouth, Gwent, NP25 4TY, Wales (home). *Telephone:* (117) 928-8432 (office); (1600) 860691 (home). *Fax:* (1600) 860691 (home). *E-mail:* k.binmore@bristol.ac.uk (office). *Website:* www.bristol.ac.uk/efm/people/kenneth-g-binmore (office).

BINNIG, Gerd; German physicist and business executive; *Chief Technology Officer and Member of the Executive Board, Definiens AG;* b. 20 July 1947,

Frankfurt; s. of Karl Franz Binnig and Ruth Bracke Binnig; m. 1st Lore Wagler 1969; one s. one d.; m. 2nd Renate Binnig 2003; ed Johann Wolfgang Goethe Univ., Univ. of Frankfurt; mem. Physics Group, IBM Zurich Research Lab., Rüschlikon 1978–2005, Group Leader 1984–2005; Assignment to IBM Almaden Research Centre, San José, Calif., collaboration with Stanford Univ. 1985–86, 1987; IBM Fellow 1986; Visiting Prof., Stanford Univ. 1986–88; Foreign Assoc. mem. NAS, Washington, DC 1987; mem. IBM Acad. 1989, Bd Mercedes Automobil Holding AG 1989–93, Bd Daimler Benz Holding 1990–; Founder, Chief Tech. Officer and mem. Exec. Bd, Definiens AG 1994–; Hon. Prof., Univ. of Munich 1986–; Hon. Fellow, Royal Microscopical Soc. 1988; OM (FRG) 1987; Physics Prize, German Physical Soc. 1982, Otto-Klung-Weberbank Prize 1983, EPS Europhysics Prize 1984, King Faisal Int. Prize for Physics (co-recipient) 1984, Hewlett Packard Europhysics Prize (co-recipient) 1984, Nobel Prize for Physics (with E. Ruska and H. Rohrer) 1986, Eliot Cresson Medal, Franklin Inst., Phila 1987, Distinguished Service Medal, Minnie Rosen Award, Ross Univ. 1988, Bayerischer Verdienstorden 1992, named to Nat. Inventors Hall of Fame 1994. *Publications include:* Aus dem Nichts 1989. *Leisure interests:* music, reading, swimming, golf. *Address:* Definiens AG, Bernhard-Wicki-Straße 5, 80636 Munich, Germany (office). *Telephone:* (89) 231180-0 (office). *Fax:* (89) 231180-90 (office). *E-mail:* gclark@ricochetpr.com (office). *Website:* www.definiens.com (office).

BINNING, Paviter (Pavi) Singh; American business executive; b. 1961; held several Sr Corp. and Operational Finance positions at Diageo PLC from 1986, as Corp. Finance Dir, Group Financial Controller, Chief Financial Officer (CFO) of Europe and CFO of Americas; CFO Telent PLC (fmrly Marconi Corpn PLC) 2003–06; Finance Dir Hanson plc 2006–07, apptd Exec. Dir 2007, Exec. Dir Hanson Ltd 2009; fmr Prin. Accounting Officer, Nortel Networks Corpn, Exec. Vice-Pres. and CFO Nortel Networks Corpn 2007–10, Chief Restructuring Officer 2009–10; CFO George Weston Ltd 2010–12, Pres. 2011–17; Special Advisor, Wittington Investments, Ltd 2017–; currently Faculty mem. Rotman School of Man., Univ. of Toronto; fmr Dir Solex PLC, Electrolux Ltd, Loblaw Cos Ltd; Fellow, Chartered Inst. of Man. Accountants (UK). *Address:* Wittington Investments, Limited, 22 St Clair Avenue E, Toronto, ON M4T 2S3, Canada (office). *Telephone:* (416) 967-7990 (office). *Website:* www.wittington-investments.co.uk (office).

BINNS, Malcolm, ARCM; British pianist; b. 29 Jan. 1936, Nottingham; s. of Douglas Priestley Binns and May Walker; ed Bradford Grammar School, Royal Coll. of Music; soloist with numerous leading orchestras and conductors around the world, including Boulez, Boult, Dorati, Haitink and Rattle, 1960–; toured with Scottish Nat. Orchestra and Limbourg Orchestra 1987–88; regular performer at Wigmore Hall 1958–, the Promenade Concerts 1962–; concerts at Aldeburgh, Leeds, Three Choirs and Canterbury Festivals; solo and concerto performances broadcast regularly on BBC; Chappell Medal 1956, Medal of Worshipful Co. of Musicians 1956. *Recordings:* more than 30 recordings, including piano sonatas by Bax, Ireland and Bridge for the British Music Soc. 2007, Balakirev Piano Concerti 1 and 2, Rimsky-Korsakov Piano Concerto (English Northern Philharmonia) 1992. *Leisure interests:* gardening, collecting antique gramophone records. *Address:* c/o Michael Harrold Artist Management, 13 Clinton Road, Leatherhead, Surrey, KT22 8NU, England (office); 233 Court Road, Orpington, Kent, BR6 9BY, England (home). *Telephone:* (1372) 375728 (office); (1689) 831056 (home). *E-mail:* management@angelus.co.uk (office). *Website:* www.angelus.co.uk (office).

BINNS, Hon. Patrick (Pat) George, MA; Canadian politician and diplomatist; *Consul-General to New England;* b. 8 Oct. 1948, Sask.; s. of Stan Binns and Phyllis Binns; m. Carol Binns; three s. one d.; ed Univ. of Alberta; worked with PEI Rural Devt Council 1972–78; mem. Legis. Ass. representing 4th Kings Dist 1978–88, fmr Minister of Industry, Municipal Affairs, Fisheries, Environment, Labour, Housing, responsibilities for Econ. Devt; mem. House of Commons representing Cardigan, Ottawa 1984–88; Pres. Island Bean Ltd and Pat Binns & Assocs 1988–96; Leader, Progressive Conservative Party of PEI 1996–2007, MLA for Dist 5, Murray River-Gaspereaux 1996–2007, Premier, Pres. of Exec. Council, Minister Responsible for Intergovernmental Affairs 1996–2007, Minister of Agric., Fisheries and Aquaculture 2006–07; Amb. to Ireland 2007–10, Consul-Gen. to New England, Boston, Mass, USA 2010–. *Address:* Canadian Consulate-General, Three Copley Place, Suite 400, Boston, MA 02116, USA (office). *Telephone:* (617) 247-5100 (office). *Fax:* (617) 247-5190 (office). *E-mail:* bostn@international.gc.ca (office).

BINOCHE, Juliette; French actress; b. 9 March 1964, Paris; d. of Jean-Marie Binoche and Monique Stalens; one s. by André Halle, one d. by Benoît Magimel; ed Nat. Conservatory of Drama and private theatrical studies. *Films include:* Les nanas 1985, La vie de famille 1985, Rouge Baiser, Rendez-Vous 1985, Mon beau-frère a tué ma soeur 1986, Mauvais Sang 1986, Un tour de manège 1989, The Unbearable Lightness of Being 1988, Les amants du Pont-Neuf 1991, Wuthering Heights 1992, Damage 1992, Trois Couleurs: Bleu 1993, Le Hussard sur le Toit 1995, The English Patient (Acad. Award for Best Supporting Actress 1996, Berlin Film Festival Award 1996, BAFTA Award 1997) 1996, Alice et Martin 1999, Les Enfants du Siècle (Children of the Century) 1999, La Veuve de Saint-Pierre 2000, Chocolat (European Film Award for Best Actress) 2001, Code Unknown 2001, Décalage horaire (Jet Lag) 2002, Caché 2005, Country of My Skull 2004, Bee Season 2005, Mary 2005, Paris, je t'aime 2006, A Few Days in September 2006, Breaking and Entering 2006, Le Voyage du ballon rouge 2007, Désengagement 2007, Dan in Real Life 2007, Paris 2007, Summer Hours 2008, Certified Copy (Cannes Film Festival Award for Best Actress) 2010, The Son of No One 2011, Sponsoring 2011, Elles 2011, Cosmopolis 2012, An Open Heart 2012, Camille Claudet 2013, Godzilla 2014, Clouds of Sils Maria 2013. *Theatre includes:* The Seagull (Odéon, Paris) 1988, Naked (Almeida, London) 1998, Betrayal (Broadway) 2000, in-i (Nat. Theatre, London and world tour) 2008, Antigone (Barbican, London) 2015. *Address:* c/o UTA, 9560 Wilshire Boulevard, Floor 5, Beverly Hills, CA 90212, USA.

BIO-TCHANÉ, Abdoulaye, MA; Benin economist, banker and international organization official; *Minister of State in charge of Planning and Development;* b. 25 Oct. 1952, Parakou; s. of Hadj Moussa Bio-Tchané and Lamissi Bio-Tchané; divorced; three c.; ed Univ. of Dijon, France, Centre Ouest-Africain de Formation et d'Etudes, Senegal; economist, Central Bank for West African Countries (BCEAO), Dakar, Asst to Gov. 1992–96, Dir Econ. and Monetary Survey Dept 1996–98; Minister of Economy and Finance 1998–2002; Dir African Dept, IMF 2002–08; Pres. West African Development Bank 2008–11; Chair. African Guarantee Fund 2013–16; cand. in presidential elections March 2011, March 2016; Minister of State in charge of Planning and Devt 2016–. *Address:* Ministry of Planning and Development, Route de l'Aéroport, 08 BP 755, Cotonou, Benin (office). *Telephone:* 21-30-00-30 (office). *Fax:* 21-30-49-05 (office). *E-mail:* contact@developpement.bj (office). *Website:* plan.gouv.bj (office).

BIONDI, Frank J., Jr, BA, MBA; American business executive; b. 9 Jan. 1945, New York; s. of Frank Biondi and Virginia Willis; m. Carol Oughton 1974; two d.; ed Princeton and Harvard Univs; Assoc., Corp. Finance, Prudential Securities, New York 1969, Shearson-Lehman Inc. New York 1970–71; Prin. Frank Biondi & Assocs, New York 1972; Dir Business Analysis, Teleprompter Corpn New York 1972–73; Asst Treas., Assoc. Dir Business Affairs, Children's TV Workshop, New York 1974–78; Dir Entertainment Planning, HBO, New York 1978, Vice-Pres. Programming Operations 1979–82, Exec. Vice-Pres. Planning and Admin. 1982–83, Pres. and CEO 1983, Chair. and CEO 1984; Exec. Vice-Pres. Entertainment Business Sector, The Coca-Cola Co. 1985; Chair. and CEO Coca-Cola TV 1986; Pres., CEO and Dir Viacom Int. Inc. New York 1987–96, Pres., CEO and Dir Viacom Inc. 1987–96; Chair., CEO Universal Studios Inc. 1996–98; mem. Bd of Dirs Amgen 2002–17, Hasbro 2002–15, Cablevision Systems 2005–16, Seagate Technology 2005–17, Yahoo Inc. 2008–10, RealD Inc. 2010–16, ViaSat, Inc. 2015–; Pres. Biondi Reiss Capital Man., New York 1998; fmr Sr Man. Dir Waterview Advisors LLC (private equity fund); Trustee, Claremont Graduate Univ.; Founding mem. Board of Councilors, School of Cinema-Television, Univ. of Southern California. *Address:* c/o ViaSat, Inc., 6155 El Camino Real, Carlsbad, CA 92009-1699 (office); 110 North Rockingham Avenue, Los Angeles, CA 90049, USA. *Telephone:* (760) 476-2200 (office). *Fax:* (760) 929-3941 (office). *E-mail:* viasatlistens@viasat.com (office). *Website:* www.viasat.com (office).

BIONDI, Matt, MA; American teacher and fmr swimmer; b. 8 Oct. 1965, Moraga, Calif.; m. Kirsten Biondi 1995; two s. one d.; ed Univ. of California, Berkeley, Lewis & Clarke Coll.; mem. USA Water Polo Team, then became freestyle swimmer; career highlights include Olympic Games: 50m freestyle 1st (1988), 2nd (1992); 100m freestyle 1st (1988); 200m freestyle 3rd (1988); 100m butterfly 2nd (1988); 4x100m freestyle 1st (1984, 1988, 1992); 4x200m freestyle 1st (1988); 400m medley 1st (1988, 1992); World Championships: 100m freestyle 1st (1986, 1991); world records: 50m freestyle 22.14 (Seoul 1988), 100m freestyle 48.42 (Austin 1988), 400m medley 3:34.84 (Atlanta 1996), 4x100m freestyle 3:16.53 (Seoul 1988); spokesman Olympic Movt; mem. Int. Hall of Fame Selection Cttee; mem. US Olympic Hall of Fame; math. teacher at Parker School (secondary school), Kamuela, Hawaii 2001–, launched school swim team 2004; Int. Swimming Hall of Fame 1997, World Swimmer of the Year 1998. *Address:* c/o Parker School, 65–1224 Lindsey Road, Kamuela, HI 96743, USA.

BIOT, Jacques; French engineer, academic and university administrator; b. 6 Dec. 1952; ed École Polytechnique; engineer from Corps des Mines; dedicated first years of professional career to industrial recovery and innovation funding within Ministry of Industry and Research; then served as adviser, in charge of Industry and Technology, in the Prime Minister's office –1985; subsequently held exec. positions in French biopharmaceutical cos, Roussel Uclaf, then Pasteur Mérieux Serums and Vaccines (both later integrated into the Sanofi Group); Founder and Pres. JNBD (strategic consulting firm) 1992–2012; also served as an Ind. Dir and Deputy Chair. Guerbet Laboratories; investor in French start-ups in the healthcare field; mem. Scientific and Tech. Comm. of the Corps des Mines 2003–; participated, as Chair. École des Mines d'Alès, in working parties in charge of designing strategy of Écoles des Mines and in formation of Mines Telecom Inst.; Chair. Admin. Council and Pres. École Polytechnique 2013–18.

BIRCH, Bryan John, PhD, FRS; British mathematician and academic; *Professor Emeritus of Mathematics, University of Oxford;* b. 25 Sept. 1931, Burton-on-Trent, Staffs.; s. of Arthur Jack Birch and Mary Edith Birch; m. Gina Margaret Christ 1961; two s. one d.; ed Shrewsbury School, Trinity Coll., Cambridge; Research Fellow, Trinity Coll. 1956–60; Harkness Fellow, Princeton Univ. 1957–58; Fellow, Churchill Coll., Cambridge 1960–62; Sr Lecturer, later Reader, Univ. of Manchester 1962–65; Reader in Math., Univ. of Oxford 1966–85, Prof. of Arithmetic 1985–98, Prof. Emer. 1998–, Fellow, Brasenose Coll. 1966–98, Emer. Fellow 1998–; Del. of Oxford University Press 1988–98; Ed. Proceedings of the London Mathematical Society 2001–03; Fellow, American Math. Soc. 2012; Hon. Fellow, Trinity Coll. Cambridge 2016; Sr Whitehead Prize 1993, De Morgan Medal 2007. *Publications:* Computers in Number Theory (ed.) 1973, Modular Functions of One Variable IV (co-ed.) 1975, The Collected Works of Harold Davenport (ed.) 1977; scholarly articles, particularly on number theory. *Leisure interests:* theoretical gardening, opera, watching marmots and, of course, mathematics. *Address:* Mathematical Institute, University of Oxford, Andrew Wiles Building, Radcliffe Observatory Quarter, Woodstock Road, Oxford, OX2 6GG (office); Green Cottage, Boars Hill, Oxford, OX1 5DQ, England (home). *Telephone:* (1865) 735367 (home). *E-mail:* birch@maths.ox.ac.uk (office). *Website:* www.maths.ox.ac.uk (office).

BIRCH, Peter Gibbs, CBE; British business executive; b. 4 Dec. 1937; m. Gillian Benge 1962; three s. one d.; ed Allhallows School, Devon; served Royal West Kent Regt 1957–58; with Nestlé Co. 1958–65; Sales Man. Gillette 1965–69, Gen. Sales Man. Gillette Australia 1969–71, Man. Dir Gillette NZ 1971–73, Gen. Man. Gillette South East Asia 1973–75, Group Gen. Man. Gillette, Africa, Middle East, Eastern Europe 1975–81, Man. Dir Gillette UK 1981; mem. Bd of Dirs Abbey Nat. (fmrly Abbey Nat. Bldg Soc.) 1984–98, Chief Exec. 1984–88, Chief Exec. Abbey Nat. PLC 1988–98; mem. Bd of Dirs Land Securities PLC 1997–2007 (Chair. 1998–2007); Chair. Trinity PLC 1998–99, Legal Services Comm. 2000–03, Kensington Group PLC 2000–07, UCTX Ltd 2001; Chair. Council of Mortgage Lenders 1991–92, Clubs for Young People 2010–; Deputy Chair. Lamprell PLC 2007–08 (Chair. Feb.–Dec. 2008); fmr Pres. Middx Asscn of Boys' Clubs; Sr Dir (non-exec.) Trinity Mirror PLC 1999–2007; mem. Bd of Dirs, Hoskyns Group 1988–93, Argos 1990–98, Scottish Mutual 1992–98, Dalgety 1993–98, N.M. Rothschild and Sons 1998–2007, Travelex 1999–2001, Sainsbury's Bank PLC 2002–, Dah Sing Bank Ltd 2006–, Banco Finantia SA 2007–08. *Leisure interests:* active holidays, swimming, cycling, skiing.

BIRCHALL, Ana, LLB, JSD; Romanian lawyer and politician; *Deputy Prime Minister, responsible for implementing strategic partnerships of Romania;* b. 30 Aug. 1973, Mizil; m. Martyn Birchall 1998; one s.; ed Nicolae Titulescu Univ., Univ. of Bucharest, Yale Law School; Head of Legal Office, SC Omniasig SA 1996–98; Attorney, White & Case LLP, New York City 2002–03, Of Counsel, White & Case LLP Bucharest 2008–10; Adviser to Minister of Foreign Affairs 2003–04; Lecturer, Dimitrie Cantemir Univ., Bucharest 2005–; Adviser, Foreign Policy Cttee, Senate (upper house of parl.) 2005–06; Head of Practice Group (financial restructuring and insolvency), Biris Goran, Bucharest 2010–11; Of Counsel, Musat si Asociatii-Restructuring & Insolvency, Bucharest 2011–12; mem. Chamber of Deputies (lower house of parl.) (Partidul Social Democrat—PSD—Social Democratic Party) for Vaslui County 2012–, Chair. European Affairs Cttee 2015–16; Adviser to the Prime Minister 2012–14; High Rep. of the Prime Minister for European Affairs and partnership with the USA 2014–15; Minister-del. for European Affairs Jan.–June 2017; Deputy Prime Minister, responsible for implementing strategic partnerships of Romania 2018–; Head of Romanian Parl. Del. to OSCE Parl. Ass. 2017–18; mem. Bucharest Bar; mem. Exec. Cttee, Yale Law School Asscn 2014–; mem. Global Advisory Council, WeConnect International 2013–; mem. PSD; Goldman Scholarship, Yale Law School. *Publications:* Banking Insolvency in Post-Socialist Economies 2006; legal articles. *Leisure interests:* travelling, golf, dancing. *Address:* Office of the Prime Minister, 011791 Bucharest 1, Piața Victoriei 1, Romania (office). *Telephone:* (21) 3191515 (office). *E-mail:* parteneriatestrategice@gov.ro (office); deputatzorleni@gmail.com (office); ana.birchall@cdep.ro (office). *Website:* www.gov.ro (office); www.anabirchall.ro.

BIRD, Sir Adrian Peter, Kt, CBE, PhD, FRS, FRSE, FMedSci; British geneticist and academic; *Buchanan Professor of Genetics, University of Edinburgh;* b. 3 July 1947; s. of Kenneth George Bird and Aileen Mary Bird; m. 1st 1976; one s. one d.; m. 2nd Catherine Mary Abbott 1993; one s. one d.; ed Univs of Sussex and Edinburgh; Damon Runyon Fellow, Yale Univ., USA 1972–73; Postdoctoral Fellowship, Univ. of Zurich, Switzerland 1974–87, MRC, Edin.; mem. scientific staff, Mammalian Genome Unit; Sr Scientist, Inst. for Molecular Pathology, Vienna 1988–90; Buchanan Prof. of Genetics, Univ. of Edinburgh 1990–, Dir Wellcome Trust Centre for Cell Biology 1999–2011, Gov. Wellcome Trust 2000–10; fmr Chair. Scientific Advisory Bd Rett Syndrome Research Foundation, Breakthrough Breast Cancer UK, now Trustee and Scientific Advisor; mem. Bd of Eds, Molecular and Cellular Biology, Molecular Cell; Trustee, Cancer Research UK, Kirkhouse Trust; Foreign Assoc. NAS 2016; Hon. DrSc (Sussex) 2010; Louis Jeantet Prize for Medical Research 1999, Gabor Medal, Royal Soc. 1999, Gairdner Foundation Prize 2011, GlaxoSmithKline Prize 2012, Shaw Prize in Life Science and Medicine (co-recipient) 2016. *Publications include:* numerous papers in scientific journals. *Address:* Wellcome Trust Centre for Cell Biology, University of Edinburgh, Michael Swann Building, King's Buildings, Mayfield Road, Edinburgh, EH9 3JR, Scotland (office). *Telephone:* (131) 650-5668 (office). *Fax:* (131) 650-5379 (office). *E-mail:* a.bird@ed.ac.uk (office). *Website:* www.wcb.ed.ac.uk/research/bird (office); birdlab.bio.ed.ac.uk (office).

BIRD, Harold Dennis (Dickie), OBE; British fmr international umpire and fmr cricketer; *President, Yorkshire County Cricket Club;* b. 19 April 1933, Barnsley, Yorks.; s. of James Harold Bird and Ethel Bird (née Smith); ed Raley Secondary Modern School, Barnsley; right-hand batsman and right-arm medium-fast bowler; played for Yorks. Co. Cricket Club 1956–59, Leicestershire Co. Cricket Club 1960–64; played in 93 First-class matches, scored 3,314 runs (average 20.71, highest score 181 not out 1959) with two hundreds; First-class Umpire 1970–98; umpired 68 Test matches (world record 1973–96), 69 limited-overs ints (1973–95), including 1975, 1979, 1983 and 1987–88 World Cups (officiating in the first three finals), 92 one-day int. matches and seven Sharjah (UAE) tournaments; only person to umpire both men's and women's World Cup Finals; served on Int. Umpires Panel 1994–96; MCC Advanced Cricket Coach; f. Dickie Bird Foundation (for less privileged children) 2004; Pres., Yorkshire Co. Cricket Club 2014–16; Hon. Life mem. MCC, Yorks. Co. Cricket Club, Leics. Co. Cricket Club, Barnsley Football Club; Freeman Borough of Barnsley 2000; Hon. DUniv (Sheffield Hallam) 1996; Hon. LLD (Leeds) 1997; Hon. DCL (Huddersfield) 2008; Yorks. Personality of the Year 1977, Rose Bowl, Barnsley Council 1988, Variety Club of GB Yorkshire Award 1988, Carlsberg-Tetley Yorkshireman of the Year 1996, People of the Year Award 1996, Radar Abbey Nat. 1996, Special Sporting Award, Variety Club of GB 1997, Lifelong Achievement Award 1998, Professional Cricketers Asscn Special Merit Award 1998, Yorkshire Co. Cricket Club 50 Years Service Award 1998, The Barnsley Millennium Award of Merit for outstanding services to the community and to cricket and in particular for the promotion of the image and civic pride of the Borough 2000, England and Wales Cricket Bd 30 Years of Service Award, Anglo-American Sporting Club Award for services to cricket, BBC TV Sports Awards, Yorkshire Hall of Fame 2006; statue erected in his honour, Barnsley 2008. *Radio:* Down Your Way with Brian Johnston 1975, Harry Carpenter Show (BBC) 1975, Desert Island Discs with Sue Lawley 1996. *Television appearances include:* The Terry Wogan Show (BBC) 1988, This is Your Life (ITV) 1992, BBC Grandstand 1996, Document of the Year (BBC 2) 1996, Newsnight (BBC 2) 1996, A Question of Sport (six times) 1999, The Clive Anderson Show 1998, Through the Keyhole (three times), Breakfast with Frost and Songs of Praise (BBC), The Gloria Hunniford Show (ITV, four times), Ready Steady Cook (BBC 2), They Think It's All Over (BBC 1), The Young Ones (BBC 1) 2010. *Publications:* Not Out 1978, That's Out 1985, From the Pavilion End 1988, Dickie Bird – My Autobiography 1997, White Cap and Bails 1999, Dickie Bird's Britain 2002, Eighty Not Out 2013. *Leisure interest:* watching football. *Address:* White Rose Cottage, 40 Paddock Road, Staincross, Barnsley, Yorks., S75 6LE, England (home). *Telephone:* (1226) 384491 (home).

BIRD, Lester Bryant, BA; Antigua and Barbuda lawyer and politician; b. 21 Feb. 1938; m.; one s. four d.; ed Antigua Grammar School, Univ. of Michigan, USA, Gray's Inn, UK; lawyer in pvt. practice 1969–76; Leader, Antigua Labour Party (ALP) 1971–2012; Senator, Upper House of Parl. and Leader of Opposition in Senate 1971–76; mem. Parl. 1976–; Deputy Premier and Minister of Econ. Devt, Tourism and Energy 1976–81; Deputy Prime Minister and Minister of Foreign Affairs, Econ. Devt, Tourism and Energy 1981–91; Minister of External Affairs, Planning and Trade 1991–94; Prime Minister of Antigua and Barbuda 1994–2004, Minister of External Affairs, Planning, Social Services and Information 1994, of Communications, Civil Aviation and Int. Transport 1996–98, of Foreign Affairs, Social Services, Civil Aviation and Int. Transport and Information 1998–99, of Foreign Affairs, Caribbean Community Affairs, Defence and Security and Merchant Shipping 1999–2001, of Justice and Legal Affairs 2001–04; del. to numerous Caribbean and int. confs. *Address:* Antigua Labour Party (ALP), S46 North Street, POB 948, St John's, Antigua, West Indies (office). *Telephone:* 462-2235 (office). *E-mail:* alp@antigualabourparty.net (office). *Website:* www.antigualabourparty.net (office).

BIRD, Phillip Bradley (Brad); American director, writer, actor and producer; b. 11 Sept. 1957, Kalispell, Mont.; m. Elizabeth Canney 1988; three c.; ed Corvallis High School, Ore.; trained as Disney animator; first person to receive a solo writing credit on feature-length film (The Incredibles) from Pixar Animation Studios; provided voices of Don Carlo in Doctor of Doom 1979, Edna Mode in The Incredibles 2004 and Ambrister Minion in Ratatouille 2007. *Films directed:* Amazing Stories: Book Two (segment 'Family Dog'; also writer) 1992, The Iron Giant 1999, The Incredibles (also writer) 2004, Jack-Jack Attack (also writer) 2005, One-Man Band (producer) 2005, Ratatouille (also screenplay) 2007, Mission: Impossible – Ghost Protocol 2011. *Animator:* Animalympics 1980, The Plague Dogs 1982. *Address:* c/o Jake Bloom, Bloom Hergott Diemer Rosenthal LaViolette & Feldman, LLP, 150 South Rodeo Drive, Third Floor, Beverly Hills, CA 90212, USA.

BIREN SINGH, Nongthombam; Indian politician and fmr journalist; *Chief Minister of Manipur;* b. 1 Jan. 1961, Imphal East, Manipur; s. of N. Gouro Singh; m. Hiyainu Devi; two s. one d; ed Manipur Univ.; served in Border Security Force (BSF) 1979–93, played in BSF Jhalluder football team 1979–82; Ed., Naharolgi Thoudang (daily newspaper) 1992–2001; mem. Manipur Legis. Ass. from Heingang constituency (Democratic Revolutionary People's Party) 2002–03, (Indian Nat. Congress) 2003–16, (BJP) 2017–; Manipur Minister of State for Vigilance 2003, Minister of Irrigation & Flood Control and Youth Affairs & Sports 2007; Chief Minister of Manipur 2017–; Pres., All Manipur Working Journalist Union 2001; Founder mem. and Pres., Heingang Kendra Sporting Union; mem. Democratic Revolutionary People's Party 2002–03; mem. Indian Nat. Congress 2003–16, Vice Pres., Manipur Pradesh Congress Cttee –2016; mem. Bharatiya Janata Party (BJP) 2016–, Leader, BJP Parl. Party in Manipur 2017–. *Address:* Government of Manipur, 4th floor, Western Block New Secretariat, Imphal 795001, Manipur, India (office). *Telephone:* (385) 2450137 (office). *Fax:* (385) 2451398 (office). *Website:* manipur.gov.in (office).

BIRGENEAU, Robert J., PhD, FRS, FInstP, FAAS, FRSC; Canadian physicist, academic and university administrator; b. 25 March 1942, Toronto; m. Mary Catherine Birgeneau; ed Univ. of Toronto and Yale Univ., USA; instructor, Yale Univ. 1966–67; Nat. Research Council of Canada Postdoctoral Fellow, Univ. of Oxford, UK 1967–68; mem. tech. staff, Bell Labs 1968–74, Research Head, Scattering and Low Energy Physics 1975; Prof. of Physics, MIT 1975–82, Cecil and Ida Green Prof. of Physics 1982–2000, Assoc. Dir, Research Lab. of Electronics 1983–86, Head, Condensed Matter, Atomic and Plasma Physics 1987–88, Head, Dept of Physics 1988–91; Dean of Science, Univ. of Toronto 1991–2000, Pres. Univ. of Toronto 2000–04; Chancellor and Prof. of Physics, also Prof. of Materials Science and Eng, Univ. of California, Berkeley 2004–13 (retd); mem. Advisory Bd World Premier Research Center, Tohoku Univ., Japan 2007; Fellow, American Physical Soc., American Acad. of Arts and Sciences 1987, American Philosophical Soc. 2006, AAAS; Foreign Assoc. NAS 2004; Fellow, Neutron Scattering Soc. of America 2008; Morris Loeb Lecturer, Harvard Univ. 1986, H.L. Welsh Lecturer, Univ. of Toronto 1994, A.W. Scott Lecturer, Cambridge Univ. 2000, Tercentennial Lecturer, Yale Univ. 2001; Dr hc (Tsinghua Univ.) 2007, Hon. DEng (Colo School of Mines) 2007; numerous awards including Yale Science and Eng Alumni Achievement Award 1981, Wilbur Lucius Cross Medal, Yale Univ. 1986, Oliver E. Buckley Prize for Condensed Matter Physics, APS 1987, Bertram Eugene Warren Award, ACA 1988, DOE Materials Science Outstanding Accomplishment Award 1988, IUPAP Magnetism Award 1997, J.E. Lilienfeld Award, APS 2000, American Acad. of Arts and Sciences Founders Award 2006, Level Playing Field Inst. Lux Award 2007, Carnegie Corpn Academic Leadership Award 2008, Karl T. Compton Medal for Leadership in Physics, American Inst. of Physics 2012. *Address:* c/o Office of the Chancellor, 200 California Hall, #1500, Berkeley, CA 94720-1500, USA.

BIRKAR, Caucher, PhD; Iranian (Kurdish) mathematician; *Professor of Mathematics, Cambridge University;* b. (Fereydoun Derakhshani), 1978, Marivan County, Kurdistan Prov., Iran; s. of Majid and Sakina Derakhshani; m.; ed Univ. of Tehran, Univ. of Nottingham; sought political asylum in UK 2000; currently Prof. of Math., Dept of Pure Math. and Mathematical Statistics, Cambridge Univ.; Leverhulme Prize 2010, Fondation Sciences Mathématiques de Paris Prize 2010, American Math. Soc. Moore Prize 2016, Int. Math. Union Fields Medal 2018. *Address:* DPMMS, Centre for Mathematical Sciences, University of Cambridge, Wilberforce Road, Cambridge, CB3 0WB, England (office). *E-mail:* c.birkar@dpmms.cam.ac.uk (office). *Website:* www.dpmms.cam.ac.uk/~cb496/ (office).

BIRKAVS, Valdis, PhD, DrIur; Latvian politician and lawyer; *Honorary President, Partnership of Latvian Construction Entrepreneurs;* b. 28 July 1942, Rīga; s. of Voldemars Birkavs and Veronika Birkavs (née Zihelmane); one s.; ed Rīga Industrial Polytech. School, Univ. of Latvia; expert, Sr Researcher, Head of Div., Latvian Research Lab. of Forensic Medicine and Criminology 1969–86; Lecturer, Univ. of Latvia 1969–86, Deputy Dean Law Faculty 1986–89; Founder and Pres. Latvian Bar Asscn 1988–; Deputy to Supreme Council of Latvian Repub. from Popular Front of Latvia 1990–93, Deputy Chair. Legis. Cttee, Deputy Chair. Supreme Council of Latvian Repub. 1992–93; Prime Minister of Latvian Repub. 1993–94; Minister of Foreign Affairs 1994–99; Minister of Justice 1999–2000; currently Chair. Latvian Cttee, Business Software Alliance; fmr Chair. Partnership of Latvian Construction Entrepreneurs, currently Hon. Pres.; mem. Club of Madrid, Wise Man Group for Nordic-Baltic Co-operation; Royal Order of the Polar Star (Sweden) 1995, Dannebrog Order (Denmark) 1997, Norwegian Royal Order 1998, Légion d'honneur 1997, Grand Master Three Star Order of Latvia 1999, Medal of the Order of Malta 2002, Order of Lithuania 2003, Medal of Baltic Ass. *Publications:* contrib. of more than 200 articles. *Leisure interests:* golf, yachting, reading, downhill skiing. *Address:* Partnership of Latvian Construction Entrepreneurs, Rīga 1010, Latvia (office). *Telephone:* (2) 949-8195 (office). *Fax:* (2) 6745-1099 (office). *E-mail:* valdis.birkavs@gmail.com (office). *Website:* www.basp.lv (office).

BIRKE, Adolf Matthias, PhD, FRHistS; German historian and academic; b. 12 Oct. 1939, Wellingholzhausen; s. of Matthias Birke and Maria Birke (née Enewoldsen); m. 1st Linde D. Birn 1968; m. 2nd Sabine Volk 1988; one s. two d.; ed Univ. of Berlin; Prof. of Modern History, Free Univ. of Berlin 1979; Visiting Prof. of German and European Studies, Trinity Coll., Univ. of Toronto, Canada 1980–81; Asst St Antony's Coll., Oxford, also Assoc. Fellow 1985; Prof. of Modern History, Univ. of Bayreuth 1982–85; Prof. of Modern History, Univ. of Munich 1995–2000, now Prof. Emer.; Dir German Historical Inst., London 1985–94; Chair. Prince Albert Soc. 1983–95; Heisenberg Fellow 1979; mem. Advisory Bd Komm. f. Parlamentarismus 1987, Museum of the Allies 1993, Inst. für. Zeitgesch 1994; mem. Royal Historical Soc.; Corresp. mem. Berliner Wissenschaftlichen Gesellschaft; Fed. Cross of Merit 1996; Cusanuswerk Grant 1962. *Publications:* Bischof Ketteler und der deutsche Liberalismus 1971, Pluralismus und Gewerkschaftsautonomie 1978, Britain and Germany 1987, Nation ohne Haus. Deutschland 1945–1961 1989, (4th edn) 1998, Prince Albert Studies (ed.) Vols I–XIII 1983–95, Die Herausforderung des europäischen Staatensystems 1989, Princes, Patronage and the Nobility (ed with R. Asch) 1991, The Quest for Stability (ed. with R. Ahmann and M. Howard) 1992, Control Commission for Germany (British Element) (11 vols) Inventory (with H. Booms and O. Merker) 1993, Die Bundesrepublik Deutschland. Verfassung: Parlament und Parteien 1997, Deutschland und Grossbritannien 1999, An Anglo-German Dialogue (co-ed. with Magnus Brechtken and Alaric Searle) 2000; numerous articles on 19th- and 20th-century German and English history. *Leisure interests:* music, walking. *Address:* Friedenstr. 16, 06114 Halle, Germany (home).

BIRKIN, Jane, OBE; French (b. British) actress and singer; b. 14 Dec. 1946, London; d. of David Birkin and Judy Campbell; m. John Barry (divorced); one d.; one d. with the late Serge Gainsbourg (Charlotte Gainsbourg); one s. with Jacques Doillon; Chevalier des Arts et des Lettres; Gold Leaf Award Canada 1968, Triomphe du cinéma 1969, 1973, Victoire de la musique (for best female singer) 1992. *Theatre includes:* Carving a Statue 1964, Passion Flower Hotel 1965, La Fausse suivante 1985, L'Aide-Mémoire 1993, Créatrice et Interprète de Oh! pardon tu dormais 1999, Electra by Sophocles. *Films include:* The Knack 1965, Blow Up 1966, Les Chemins de Katmandou 1969, Je t'aime moi non plus 1976, Mort sur le Nil 1978, Jane B par Agnès V 1988, Oh pardon! Tu dormais 1992, Noir comme le souvenir 1995, La fille d'un soldat ne pleure jamais 1999, The Last September 2000, Ceci est mon corps 2001, Reines d'un jour 2001, Merci Docteur Rey 2002, Mariées mais pas trop 2003, Boxes (actor and dir) 2007, 36 Views from the Pic Saint-Loup 2009, Thelma, Louise et Chantal 2010, Twice Born 2012, Quai d'Orsay 2013. *Recordings include:* albums: Je t'aime (Beautiful Love) 1970, Lolita Go Home 1975, Ex Fan des Sixties 1978, Baby Alone in Babylone 1983, Lost Song 1987, Au Bataclan 1987, Je Suis Venue Te Dire Que Je M'en Vais 1992, Jane B., Vol. 1 1993, Concert Integral à l'Olympia 1997, Je t'aime moi non plus 1998, Quoi Générique TV 1998, Jane Birkin Coffret 1998, Ballade de Johnny 1998, A la Légère 1998, Jane en Concert au Japan 2001, Jane Birkin et Serge Gainsbourg 2001, Arabesque 2003, Rendez-Vous 2004, Fictions 2006, Enfants d'Hiver 2008; singles: (songs by Serge Gainsbourg) C'est la vie qui veut ça, La Baigneuse de Brighton, Je t'aime moi non plus (Le Métier trophy 1970), Di doo dah, Le Canari est sur le balcon, Baby Song, Si ça peut te consoler, Tu n'es pas le premier garçon, Lolita Go Home, Love for Sale, La Ballade, Ex-fan des sixties, Baby Alone in Babylone (Grand Prix du disque, Acad. Charles-Cros). *Publication:* Oh pardon! Tu dormais 1999. *Address:* c/o Olivier Gluzman, Les Visiteurs du Soir, 40 rue de la Folie Regnault, 75011 Paris, France (office). *Telephone:* (1) 44-93-02-02 (office). *Fax:* (1) 44-93-04-40 (office). *E-mail:* ogluzman@visiteurdusoir.com (office). *Website:* www.visiteursdusoir.com/en/portfolio-type/jane-birkin-2 (office); www.janebirkin.net/uk.

BIRKIN, Sir (John) Derek, Kt, TD, CBIM; British business executive; b. 30 Sept. 1929; s. of Noah Birkin and Rebecca Birkin (née Stranks); m. Sadie Smith 1952; one s. one d.; ed Hemsworth Grammar School; Man. Dir Velmar Ltd 1966–67, Nairn Williamson Ltd 1967–70; Deputy Chair. and Man. Dir Tunnel Holdings Ltd 1970–75, Chair. and Man. Dir 1975–82; Dir Rio Tinto-Zinc (then RTZ) Corpn 1982–96, Deputy Chief Exec. 1983–85, Chief Exec. and Deputy Chair. 1985–91, Chair. 1991–96; Chair. Watmoughs (Holdings) PLC 1996–98; Dir Smiths Industries Ltd 1977–84, British Gas Corpn 1982–85, George Wimpey PLC 1984–92, CRA Ltd (Australia) 1985–94, Rio Algom Ltd (Canada) 1985–92, The Merchants Trust PLC 1986–99, British Steel PLC (formerly British Steel Corpn) 1986–92, Barclays Bank PLC and Barclays PLC 1990–95, Merck & Co. Inc. (USA) 1992–2000, Carlton Communications PLC 1992–2001, Unilever PLC 1993–2000; mem. Council, Industrial Soc. 1985–97, UK Top Salaries Review Body 1986–89; Trustee, Royal Opera House 1990–93, Dir 1993–97; Hon. LLD (Bath) 1998. *Leisure interests:* opera, rugby, cricket.

BIRLA, Basant Kumar; Indian business executive; *Chairman, Century Textiles and Industries Limited;* b. 16 Feb. 1921, Calcutta (now Kolkata); s. of Ghanshyam Das Birla and Mahadevi; m. Sarala Birla 1942; one s. two d.; Chair. Century Textiles and Industries Ltd, BK Birla Group, Century Enka Ltd, Jay Shree Tea and Industries Ltd, Kesoram Industries and Cotton Mills Ltd, Bharat Commerce and Industries Ltd; Gov. Birla Inst. of Tech., Krishnarpan Charity Trust, BK Birla Inst. of Eng and Tech., Pilani; Order of Menelik II (Ethiopia); Officer, Order of Orange-Nassau (Netherlands), Order of the Crown (Belgium). *Publications:* Svantah Sukhaya (autobiog.) and numerous others. *Leisure interests:* music, art, literature, photography, sports. *Address:* Century Textiles and Industries Ltd, Century Bhavan, Dr Annie Besant Road, Worli, Mumbai, 400 030, India (office). *Telephone:* (22) 24957000 (office). *Fax:* (22) 24309491 (office). *E-mail:* info@birlacentury.com (office). *Website:* www.birlacentury.com (office); www.bkbiet.ac.in.

BIRLA, Kumar Mangalam, BCom, MBA; Indian business executive; *Chairman, Aditya Birla Group;* b. 14 June 1967, Jeddah, Saudi Arabia; s. of Aditya Vikram Birla; m. Neerja Birla; one s. two d.; ed London Business School, UK; Chair. Aditya Birla Group 1997–, Hindalco Industries Ltd (aluminium manufacturing subsidiary); apptd mem. Governing Bd Securities and Exchange Bd of India 1998, also served as Chair. Cttees on Corp. Governance and Insider Trading; mem. Cen. Bd of Dirs Reserve Bank of India; mem. Bd Tata Iron and Steel Co., Larsen & Toubro, Maruti Udyog Ltd; mem. Bd of Dirs G.D. Birla Medical Research and Educ. Foundation; mem. Bd of Govs Birla Inst. of Tech. and Science, Indian Inst. of Man.; mem. London Business School's Asia Pacific Advisory Bd; has served on various professional and regulatory bds including Prime Minister's Advisory Council on Trade and Industry, Nat. Council of Confed. of Indian Industry, Apex Advisory Council of Associated Chambers of Commerce and Industry of India, Govt of UP's High Powered Investment Task Force; Hon. Fellow, London Business School, All India Man. Asscn; Hon. DLitt (Banaras Hindu Univ.); Dr hc (G. D. Pant Univ. of Agriculture & Technology) 2008, (SRM Univ.) 2008, (Visvesvaraya Technological Univ., Karnataka) 2012; Man. Man of the Year, Bombay Man. Asscn 2000, Golden Peacock Nat. Award for Business Leadership, Inst. of Dirs 2001, Mumbai Pradesh Youth Congress's Rajiv Gandhi Award for Business Excellence and Contribution to the Country 2001, Outstanding Business Man of the Year, Nat. HRD Network, Pune 2001, Qimpro Platinum Standard Award, Qimpro Foundation 2002, Business Leader of the Year, Economic Times Awards 2003, 2013, Lakshya–Business Visionary Award, Nat. Inst. of Industrial Eng 2003, Young Achiever Award, Indo-American Soc. 2003, Ernst & Young Indian Entrepreneur of the Year 2005, Udyog Ratna, PHD Chamber of Commerce and Industry 2005, Global Indian Leader of the Year, NDTV Profit 2007, AIMA–JRD Tata Corp. Leadership Award 2008, Business Leader of the Year, All India Man. Asscn 2010, GQ Business Leader of the Year Award, Condé Nast India Pvt. Ltd 2011, Entrepreneur of the Year, Flagship Award, Forbes India Leadership Awards 2012, NASSCOM's Global Business Leader Award 2012. *Address:* Aditya Birla Centre, 1st Floor, S. K. Ahire Marg, Worli, Mumbai 400 030, India (office). *Telephone:* (22) 66525000 (office). *Fax:* (22) 66525741 (office). *E-mail:* pragnya.ram@adityabirla.com (office). *Website:* www.adityabirla.com (office).

BIRLA, Sudarshan Kumar; Indian fmr business executive; *Chairman Emeritus, S K Birla Group;* fmr Chair. Mysore Cement Ltd, Birla Eastern Ltd, Birla Metals Ltd, Digjam Ltd; fmr Chair. SK Birla Group, currently Chair. Emer.; Chair. HeidelbergCement India Ltd 2007; fmr Dir Century Textiles and Industries Ltd –2006, Birla Brothers Pvt. Ltd; fmr Pres. Fed. of Indian Chambers of Commerce, Indian Nat. Cttee of ICC, Indian Chamber of Commerce, Chamber of Commerce of G-77 countries of UN, New York; fmr mem. various Govt of India bodies, including the Prime Minister's Nat. Integration Council, official del. to UNCTAD'72 and CAFEA '66; associated with several educ. and philanthropic insts.

BIRLE, James Robb, BS; American insurance industry executive (retd); b. 25 Jan. 1936, Philadelphia, Pa; ed Villanova Univ.; numerous positions at General Electric Co. 1958–88, including Sr Vice-Pres. and Group Exec.; Gen. Pnr, Blackstone Group 1988–94, CEO Collins & Aikman Group 1988–94; Founder and Chair. Resolute Pnrs LLC (pvt. investment firm) 1994–; mem. Bd of Dirs Mass Mutual Life Insurance Co. 1992, Chair. 2005–07, Lead Dir 2007–08; mem. Bd of Dirs IKON Office Solutions, Conn. Health and Educ. Facilities Authority, Transparency Int.; Trustee, Villanova Univ. 1993–; Hon. DEng (Villanova Univ.) 1992; J. Stanley Morehouse Memorial Award, Villanova Univ. 1988. *Address:* 2 Pine Lane East, Village of Golf, FL 33436, USA (office).

BIRNBAUM, Daniel, PhD; Swedish author, art critic, philosopher, teacher and curator; *Director, Moderna Museet;* b. 10 July 1963, Stockholm; ed Stockholm Univ., Free Univ., Berlin, Columbia Univ., New York; spent childhood and youth in Geneva, Vienna, Boston and Stockholm; art critic at Expressen and Dagens Nyheter daily newspapers, Stockholm 1988; Lecturer in Philosophy, Stockholm Univ. 1990–95; Lecturer in Art Theory, Univ. Coll. of Art, Craft and Design, Stockholm 1995–97; Founding mem. Artnode Stockholm (internet site for art and theory and venue for art and tech.) 1996; Dir IASPIS (Int. Artists Studio Programme in Sweden) 1997–2000; Contributing Ed., Artforum, New York 1999; Rector Städelschule Art Acad., Frankfurt am Main, Germany 2001–10; Dir Kunsthalle Portikus, Frankfurt am Main 2001–10; Dir Moderna Museet, Stockholm 2010–; Int. Bd mem. Yokohama Triennial of Contemporary Art 2001–, Manifesta Foundation, Amsterdam 2002–; mem. Jury, Turner Prize 2008. *Publications:* Teaching Art: Staedelschule Frankfurt am Main 2007, Under Pressure 2008, Defining Contemporary Art: 25 Years in 200 Pivotal Artworks 2011; articles in int. art magazines including Artforum and frieze; series of academic texts and translations on Novalis, Edmund Husserl, Martin Heidegger, Gottlob Frege, Ludwig Wittgenstein, Jacques Derrida and Thomas Bernhard. *Address:* Moderna Museet, Box 16382, 103 27 Stockholm, Sweden (office). *Telephone:* (8) 5202-3500 (office). *E-mail:* info@modernamuseet.se (office). *Website:* www.modernamuseet.se (office).

BIROL, Fatih, BSc, MSc, PhD; Turkish economist and international organization official; *Executive Director, International Energy Agency;* b. 22 March 1958, Ankara; ed Tech. Univ. of Istanbul, Tech. Univ. of Vienna, Austria; economist with OPEC, Vienna 1989–95; joined IEA 1995, Chief Economist 2006–, Exec. Dir 2015–, also Dir of Global Energy Econs and Founder and Chair., IEA Energy Business Council; Chair. Energy Advisory Bd, World Econ. Forum; mem. UN Sec.-Gen.'s High-level Group on Sustainable Energy for All; Hon. Life Mem. Galatasaray Football Club 2013–; Ordre des Palmes Académiques 2006, Decoration of Honour for Services to Repub. of Austria 2007, First Class Order of Merit, (Germany) 2009, Officer, Order of Merit (Italy) 2012, First Class Order of the Polar Star (Sweden) 2013, Order of the Rising Sun (Japan) 2013; Hon. DSc (Imperial Coll. London) 2013; Award of Russian Acad. of Sciences 2002, US Dept of Energy Award 2004, Int. Asscn of Energy Econs Award for Outstanding Contribution to the Profession 2005, Medal for Outstanding Service of Ministry of Foreign Affairs of Turkey 2005, Eurelectric Award 2013, Carnot Prize, Kleinman Center for Energy Policy 2016. *Address:* International Energy Agency, 9 rue de la Fédération, 75739 Paris Cedex 15, France (office). *Telephone:* (1) 40-57-65-00 (office). *Fax:* (1) 40-57-65-09 (office). *E-mail:* info@iea.org (office). *Website:* www.iea.org (office).

BIRT, Baron (Life Peer) cr. 2000, of Liverpool in the County of Merseyside; **John Birt,** Kt, MA, FRTS; British business executive; *Chairman, JLA Group;* b. 10 Dec. 1944, Liverpool, England; s. of Leo Vincent and Ida Birt; m. 1st Jane Frances Lake 1965 (divorced 2006); one s. one d.; m. 2nd Eithne Victoria Wallis CB 2006; ed St Mary's Coll., Liverpool, St Catherine's Coll., Oxford; Television Producer of Nice Time 1968–69, Jt Ed. World in Action 1969–70, Producer The Frost Programme 1971–72, Exec. Producer Weekend World 1972–74, Head of Current Affairs, London Weekend Television (LWT) 1974–77, Co-Producer The Nixon Interviews 1977, Controller of Features and Current Affairs, LWT 1977–81, Dir of Programmes 1982–87; Deputy Dir-Gen. BBC 1987–92, Dir-Gen. 1992–2000; Vice-Pres. Royal TV Soc. 1994–2000 (Fellow 1989); mem. Media Law Group 1983–94,

Working Party on New Technologies 1981–83, Broadcasting Research Unit, Exec. Cttee 1983–87, Int. Museum of TV and Radio, New York 1994–2000, Opportunity 2000 Target Team, Business in the Community 1991–98; Adviser to Prime Minister on criminal justice 2000–01, Strategy Adviser 2001–05; Adviser to McKinsey and Co. Inc. 2000–05; Adviser, Terra Firma (pvt. equity firm) 2005–, Capgemini UK plc 2006–10; Chair. Lynx Capital Ventures 2000–04, WRG Holdings 2006, Infinis Ltd 2006–07 (after sale of WRG waste disposal business), Maltby Capital Ltd 2007–10; Dir (non-exec.) PayPal (Europe) Ltd 2004–14 (Chair. 2010–14), Eutelsat 2006– (Vice-Chair. 2012–); Chair. CPA Global 2015–18 JLA Group 2018–; Visiting Fellow, Nuffield Coll., Oxford 1991–99; Hon. Fellow, Univ. of Wales, Cardiff 1997, St Catherine's Coll., Oxford 1992; Hon. DLitt (Liverpool John Moores) 1992, (City) 1998, (Bradford) 1999, (Westminster) 2010; Emmy Award, US Nat. Acad. of Television, Arts and Sciences. *Publication:* The Harder Path: The Autobiography. *Leisure interests:* walking, football, cinema. *Address:* House of Lords, London, SW1A 0PW, England (home). *Telephone:* (20) 7219-8723 (home). *E-mail:* birtj@parliament.uk (home).

BIRTWISTLE, Sir Harrison, Kt, CH; British composer; b. 15 July 1934, Accrington, Lancs.; m. Sheila Birtwistle 1958; three s.; ed Royal Manchester Coll. of Music and Royal Acad. of Music; Dir of Music, Cranborne Chase School 1962–65; Visiting Fellow, Princeton Univ. (Harkness Int. Fellowship) 1966; Cornell Visiting Prof. of Music, Swarthmore Coll. 1973–74; Slee Visiting Prof., State Univ. of New York, Buffalo 1975; Assoc. Dir Nat. Theatre 1975–88; Composer-in-Residence, London Philharmonic Orchestra 1993–98; Henry Purcell Prof. of Composition, King's Coll., London 1994–2001; Visiting Prof., Univ. of Alabama at Tuscaloosa 2001–02; Dir of Contemporary Music, RAM 1996–2001; works have been widely performed at major festivals in Europe including Venice Biennale, Int. Soc. of Contemporary Music Festivals in Vienna and Copenhagen, Warsaw Autumn Festival and at Aldeburgh, Cheltenham and Edinburgh; co-f. (with Sir Peter Maxwell Davies) The Pierrot Players; Hon. FRNCM 1990; Chevalier, Ordre des Arts et des Lettres; Siemens Prize 1995, Grawemeyer Award, Univ. of Louisville 1987, Ivor Novello Award for Classical Music 2006. *Operatic and dramatic works:* The Mark of the Goat (cantata) 1965, Punch and Judy (one-act opera) 1966, The Visions of Francesco Petrarca (sonnets for baritone and orchestra) 1966, Monodrama for soprano, speaker, ensemble 1967, Down by the Greenwood Side (dramatic pastoral) 1969, The Mask of Orpheus 1973, Ballet, Frames, Pulses and Interruptions 1977, Bow Down 1977, Yan Tan Tethera 1983, Gawain 1988, The Second Mrs Kong 1992, The Last Supper 1999. *Orchestral works:* Chorales for Orchestra 1962, Three Movements with Fanfares 1964, Nomos 1968, The Triumph of Time 1970, An Imaginary Landscape 1971, Grimethorpe Aria for Brass Band 1973, Melencolia I 1976, Silbury Air for small orchestra 1977, Still Movement for 13 solo strings 1984, Earth Dances 1985, Endless Parade for trumpet, vibraphone, strings 1987, Ritual Fragment 1990, Antiphonies for piano and orchestra 1992, The Cry of Anubis for tuba and orchestra 1994, Panic 1995, Night's Black Bird (British Composer Award, British Acad. of Composers and Songwriters 2005), Concerto for Violin and Orchestra (British Composer Award, British Acad. of Composers and Songwriters 2012) 2011. *Choral works and narration:* Monody for Corpus Christi for soprano and ensemble 1959, A Description of the Passing Year for chorus 1963, Entr'actes and Sappho Fragments for soprano and ensemble 1964, Carmen Paschale for chorus and organ 1965, Ring a Dumb Clarion for soprano, clarinet, percussion 1965, Cantata for soprano and ensemble 1969, Nenia on the Death of Orpheus for soprano and ensemble 1970, Meridian for mezzo, chorus, ensemble 1970, The Fields of Sorrow for two sopranos, chorus, ensemble 1971, Epilogue: Full Fathom Five for baritone and ensemble 1972, arrangement for 16 solo voices and three instruments 1979, On the Sheer Threshold of the Night for four solo voices and 12-part chorus 1980, White and Light for soprano and ensemble 1989, Four Poems by Jaan Kaplinski for soprano and ensemble 1991, The Woman and the Hare, for soprano, reciter and ensemble 1999, Ring Dance of the Nazarene (British Composer Award, British Acad. of Composers and Songwriters 2005). *Instrumental works:* Refrains and Choruses for wind quintet 1957, The World is Discovered for ensemble 1960, Tragoedia for ensemble 1965, Three Lessons in a Frame 1967, Chorales from a Toyshop 1967, Verses for Ensembles 1969, Ut heremita solus, arrangement of Ockeghem 1969, Hoquetus David, arr of Machaut 1969, Medusa for ensemble 1970, Chronometer for 8-track tape 1971, For O For O the Hobby Horse is Forgot for six percussion 1976, Carmen Arcadiae Mechanicae Perpetuum for ensemble 1977, Pulse Sampler 1980, Clarinet Quintet 1980, Secret Theatre 1984, Words Overheard 1985, Fanfare for Will 1987, Salford Toccata for brass band and bass drum 1988, Nine Movements for string quartet 1991, An Uninterrupted Endless Melody for oboe and piano 1991, Five Distances for five instruments 1992, Tenebrae for soprano and ensemble 1992, Night for soprano and ensemble 1992, Movement for string quartet 1992, Slow Frieze for piano and 13 instruments 1996, Pulse, Shadows 1997, Harrison's Clocks for piano 1998, The Silk House Tattoo for two trumpets and percussion 1998, Three Niedecker Verses for soprano and cello 1998, Exody 1998, The Axe Manual 2000, The Shadow of Night 2001, Theseus Game 2002, The Io Passion 2004, Night's Black Bird 2004, Orpheus Elegies 2004, The Tree of Strings (Royal Philharmonic Soc. Award for Best Chamber-Scale Composition 2009) 2007, The Minotaur 2008, Tree of Strings 2008, The Corridor 2009, Angel Fighter 2010, Piano Trio 2011, Oboe Quartet 2011, Concerto for Violin and Orchestra 2011, The Moth Requiem 2012, Responses: Sweet Disorder and the Carefully Careless 2014, The Cure 2015, The Silk House Sequences 2015, Deep Time (British Composer Award—Orchestral 2018) 2016. *Theatre:* music for Hamlet, Nat. Theatre 1975, The Oresteia, Nat. Theatre 1986, The Bacchae, Nat. Theatre 2002. *Address:* Rayfield Allied, Southbank House, Black Prince Road, London, SE1 7SJ, England (office). *E-mail:* info@rayfieldallied.com (office). *Website:* www.rayfieldallied.com (office).

BIRULÉS Y BERTRÁN, Ana Maria, PhD; Spanish politician and fmr business executive; b. 28 June 1954, Gerona; ed Univ. of Barcelona, Univ. of California, Berkeley; worked for regional Govt of Catalonia; with Banco Sabadell 1990–97, negotiated acquisition of Banco NatWest 1996; Man. Dir Retevisión 1997–2000; Minister of Science and Tech. 2000–04; Bd mem. Circulo de Economia de Barcelona. *Address:* c/o Ministry of Science and Technology, Paseo de la Castellana 160, 28071 Madrid, Spain.

BISARIA, Ajay, BEcons, MBA, MPP; Indian civil servant and diplomatist; *High Commissioner to Pakistan;* b. 22 June 1962; m. Bharati Chaturvedi; ed St Stephen's Coll., Delhi Univ., Indian Inst. of Man., Kolkata, Princeton Univ., Foreign Service Inst., New Delhi; joined Indian Foreign Service 1987, Third Sec., later Second Sec., Embassy in Moscow 1988–91, Under-Sec. (Eastern Europe), Ministry of External Affairs 1991–92, First Sec., Embassy in Berlin 1995–99, Jt Sec. (Eurasia), Ministry of External Affairs 2009–14, Amb. to Poland (also accred to Lithuania) 2015–17, High Commr to Pakistan 2017–; Under-Sec., Ministry of Commerce 1992–95; Private Sec. to Prime Minister 1999–2004; Advisor to Exec. Dir for South Asia, World Bank, Washington, DC 2004–08. *Address:* Indian High Commission, G-5, Diplomatic Enclave, Islamabad, Pakistan (office). *Telephone:* (51) 2206950 (office). *Fax:* (51) 2823102 (office). *E-mail:* info2.islamabad@mea.gov.in (office). *Website:* www.india.org.pk (office).

BISCHOFF, Manfred, Dr rer. pol; German business executive; *Chairman of the Supervisory Board, Daimler AG;* b. 22 April 1942, Calw; ed Univs of Tübingen and Heidelberg; Asst Prof. of Econ. Politics and Int. Trade, Alfred-Weber-Inst., Univ. of Heidelberg 1968–76; joined Daimler-Benz AG 1976, Project Co-ordinator for Mercedes Benz Cross Country Cars, Corp. Subsidiaries, M&A Dept 1976–81, Int. Products, M&A, Finance Dept 1981–88 (Vice-Pres. Finance Cos and Corp. Subsidiaries), mem. Bd of Man. and Chief Financial Officer Mercedes do Brazil, São Paulo 1988–89, Deutsche Aerospace AG (later Daimler-Benz Aerospace AG) 1989–95, mem. Bd of Man. Daimler-Benz AG (later DaimlerChrysler AG then Daimler AG) 1995–2003, Chair. Supervisory Bd 2007–, also Chair. Presidential Cttee; mem. Bd of Man., Pres. and CEO DASA (now European Aeronautic Defence and Space Co.—EADS) 1995–2000, Chair. EADS 2000–09; mem. Bd of Man. Mitsubishi Motors Corpn 2000–03; Chair. Supervisory Bd MTU Aero Engines, Munich 2000–03; mem. several supervisory bds, including Royal KPN NV, SMS GmbH (Chair.), Unicredit SpA, Voith AG (Chair.); Pres. European Asscn of Aerospace Industries 1995–96, Fed. of German Aerospace Industries 1996–2000; Verdienstkreuz (First Class) der Bundesrepublik Deutschland 2011, Bayerischer Verdienstorden. *Address:* Willy-Messerschmitt-Str. 1, 82014 Taufkirchen, Germany (office). *E-mail:* dialog@daimler.com (office). *Website:* www.daimler.com (office).

BISCHOFF, Sir Winfried Franz Wilhelm (Win), Kt, BCom; British/German investment banker; *Chairman, Financial Reporting Council;* b. 10 May 1941, Aachen, Germany; s. of Paul Helmut Bischoff and Hildegard Bischoff (née Kühne); m. Rosemary Elizabeth Leathers 1972; two s.; ed Marist Brothers, Johannesburg and Univ. of the Witwatersrand; with Int. Dept, Chase Manhattan Bank 1962–63; joined Company Finance Div., J. Henry Schroder & Co. Ltd, London 1966, Man. Dir Schroders Asia Ltd, Hong Kong 1971–82, Dir J. Henry Schroder & Co. Ltd 1978–94 (Chair. 1983–94), Dir Schroders PLC 1983 (Group Chief Exec. 1984–95), Chair. Schroders PLC 1995–2000, then Citigroup Europe (after acquisition of Schroders by Citigroup) 2000–07, interim CEO Citigroup Nov.–Dec. 2007, Chair. Citigroup 2007–09; Chair. Lloyds Banking Group 2009–14; Chair. Financial Reporting Council 2014–; mem. Nat. Advisory Bd of UK Career Acad. Foundation (Chair. –2010), Akbank International Advisory Bd; current Chair. of Advisory Council, The CityUK; Dir (non-exec.) Cable and Wireless PLC 1991– (Deputy Chair. 1995–2003), The McGraw Hill Cos 1999–, Land Securities PLC 1999–2008, Eli Lilly and Co., Indianapolis 2000–, IFIL, Finanziaria di Partecipazioni SpA, Italy 2001–04, Siemens Holdings PLC 2001–03, AkBank, Turkey 2007–08; Johnson Hon. Fellow, St Anne's Coll. Oxford 2001; Dr hc (City Univ.) 2000. *Leisure interests:* opera, music, golf. *Address:* Financial Reporting Council, Fifth Floor, Aldwych House, 71–91 Aldwych, London, WC2B 4HN, England (office). *Telephone:* (20) 7492-2300 (office); (20) 7492-2301 (office). *E-mail:* enquiries@frc.org.uk (office). *Website:* www.frc.org.uk (office).

BISH-JONES, Trevor Charles, BSc (Pharm); British business executive; *Chairman and CEO, Consumer Durables and Projects Division, Al Faisaliah;* b. 23 April 1960; m. Amanda Bish-Jones 1991; two d.; ed Varndean Grammar School, Portsmouth School of Pharmacy; research chemist, The Tosco Corpn, Colo 1980–81; Store Man. Boots PLC 1981, rising to Sr Man. position –1994; various man. positions with Dixons Group 1994–2002, including Commercial Dir PC World 1994–95, Marketing Dir Dixons PLC 1995, Man. Dir The Link, Man. Dir Dixons, Dir Currys 2000–02; CEO Woolworths Group PLC 2002–08, mypeoplebiz.com 2008–10; moved to Middle East 2010; COO United Electronics Co. (also known as eXtra) 2010–14; Chair. and CEO Consumer Durables and Projects Div., Al Faisaliah 2014–; part Owner and Creator of Mypeoplebiz.com (online recruitment platform); has held non-exec. roles at Royal London (Financial Services) 2006–10, ConcertLive (Media) 2009–; Gov. Ashridge Business School; mem. Bd of Dirs and Bd of Trustees, Ashridge; Dir (non-exec.), Royal London Mutual Insurance Soc. Ltd 2005–10. *Leisure interests:* horse riding, motorbikes. *Address:* Al Faisaliah Group, POB 16460, Business Gate, Building 19, Qurtubah District, Riyadh 11464, Saudi Arabia (office). *Telephone:* (11) 243-9878 (office). *Fax:* (11) 243-9952 (office). *E-mail:* info@alfaisaliah.com (office). *Website:* www.alfaisaliah.com (office).

BISHARA, Shukri, BEcons, MEconSc; Palestinian banker and politician; *Minister of Finance and of Planning;* ed American Univ. of Beirut, Univ. Coll. London, UK; fmr Chair. AIMS (financial advisory co.), Damascus; fmr Vice-Chair. Palestine Electric Co.; fmr CEO Housing Bank for Trade and Finance; numerous high-level positions within the Arab Bank, including Chief Banking Officer, Sr Exec. Vice-Pres. and country head for Palestine and France, also Regional Man., Europe-Arab Bank; fmr Asst Group Head for Middle East and N Africa, Fidelity Bank, USA; fmr Chair. Palestine Investment Fund; Minister of Finance and of Planning 2013–. *Address:* Ministry of Finance, POB 795, Sateh Marhaba, al-Birah, Ramallah, Palestinian Territories (office). *Telephone:* (2) 2825255 (office). *Fax:* (2) 2848900 (office). *E-mail:* mof@mof.ps (office). *Website:* www.mof.gov.ps (office).

BISHOP, Bronwyn Kathleen; Australian solicitor and politician; b. (Bronwyn Kathleen Setright), 19 Oct. 1942, Sydney; d. of Kathleen Congreve; m. Alan Bishop (divorced); two d.; ed Univ. of Sydney; early acting role in TV drama series Divorce Court 1960s; practising solicitor 1967–; writer and producer Law for Mr and Mrs Everyman (radio series) during early 1970s; mem. Senate for New South Wales 1987–94 (resgnd); mem. House of Reps (Parl.) for Mackellar, NSW 1994–2016, Speaker 2013–15 (resgnd); Minister for Defence Industry, Science and Personnel 1996–98, for Aged Care 1998–2001; Patron Opera Australia; mem. Liberal Party of Australia, Pres. Balmoral Br. 1973–79, NSW Br. 1985–87. *Television:* Political Contrib., Sky News Live 2016.

BISHOP, John Michael, MD; American scientist, academic and university administrator; b. 22 Feb. 1936; m. 1959; two c.; ed Gettysburg Coll. and Harvard Univ.; intern in internal medicine Mass. Gen. Hosp., Boston 1962–63, Resident 1963–64; Research Assoc. in Virology, NIH, Washington, DC 1964–66, Sr Investigator 1966–68, Asst Prof. to Assoc. Prof. 1968–72; Prof. of Microbiology and Immunology, Univ. of Calif. Medical Center, San Francisco 1972–, Prof. of Biochemistry and Biophysics 1982–, Univ. Prof. 1994–2000, Chancellor 1998–2009 (now Chancellor Emer.), Dir G. W. Hooper Research Foundation 1981–; Gairdner Foundation Int. Award 1984, Medal of Honor, American Cancer Soc. 1984, Nobel Prize for Physiology or Medicine 1989, and many other awards and distinctions. *Address:* UCSF School of Medicine, Department Microbiology and Immunology, 513 Parnassus Avenue, San Francisco, CA 94143-0402, USA (office). *Telephone:* (415) 476-5158 (office). *E-mail:* bishop@cgl.ucsf.edu (office). *Website:* hooper.ucsf.edu/hooper/bishop_lab.html (office).

BISHOP-KOVACEVICH, Stephen (see Kovacevich, Stephen).

BISIGNANI, Giovanni, LLM; Italian airline industry executive; b. 10 Dec. 1946, Rome; s. of Renato Bisignani and Vincenza Carpano; m. Elena Pasanisi; one d.; ed Sapienza Law School, Univ. of Rome and Harvard Business School, USA; Sr Asst Prof. in Public Law, Univ. of Rome 1969; with First Nat. City Bank, New York 1970; research and econ. planning, EFIM, Rome 1973–76; Asst to Pres. ENI, Rome 1976–79; Chief of Staff, IRI, Rome 1979–89, Corp. Sr Vice-Pres. (Foreign Affairs) 1981–83, Corp. Exec. Vice-Pres. and Head of Foreign Affairs 1983–89, IRI Rep. on Bd of Finsider, Italstat, SME, Fincantieri 1979–89; Man. Dir and CEO Alitalia 1989–94, mem. Bd of Dirs 2014–; Pres. Tirrenia di Navigazione SpA 1994–98; Man. Dir and CEO SM Logistics–Gruppo Serra Merzario SpA 1998–2000; CEO Opodo (European airline-owned online travel agency) 2001–02; Founding mem. Exec. Cttee Int. Air Transport Asscn 1989–94, Dir-Gen. and CEO 2002–11, now Dir-Gen. Emer.; Chair. Asscn of European Airlines 1992, Chair. Galileo International (global computer reservation system group) 1993–94; mem. Advisory Bd United Technologies 1998–2001; mem. Bd of Dirs Assolombarda, Milan 1998–2000, NATS Ltd 2002–11, SaFran Group, Paris 2011–17, Air Castle, ILVA (IRI steel co.), Italo-German Chamber of Commerce, Inst. for Int. Affairs; Visiting Prof. School of Engineering, Cranfield Univ., UK 2011–; Hon. DSc (Cranfield Univ.) 2011; L. Welch Pogue Award for Lifetime Achievement in Aviation 2011, ATW Airline Industry – Decade of Excellence Award 2012, Public Service Star (Singapore) 2012. *Publications:* Shaking the Skies (memoir) 2013; articles on law, economic and financial subjects in professional publs. *Leisure interests:* golf, tennis, riding. *Address:* 12–14 De Vere Gardens, London, W8 5AE, England (office). *Telephone:* (20) 7937-2895. *E-mail:* bisignanig@gmail.com (home).

BIŠKUPIĆ, Božo, LLB, MA; Croatian lawyer and politician; b. 26 April 1938, Mala Mlaka; m.; one d.; ed Univ. of Zagreb; f. Biškupić Collection 1964; worked as lawyer in Zagreb 1974–80; collated and ed monographs in the Graphics Inst. in Zagreb and fine art in the Nat. and Univ. Library; f. Vukovar Museum in Exile and project on contemporary Croatian art for the Museum of Croatian Art, Mostar; mem. Croatian Democratic Union (HDZ) 1990–; Dir Republican Fund for Culture, Ministry of Culture 1990–92; Asst Minister of Culture and Educ. 1992–95; Deputy Mayor of Zagreb 1993–95; Minister of Culture 1995–2000, 2003–10; mem. Parl. 2000–10; Vladimir Nazor Award 1993. *Leisure interests:* music, chess. *Address:* c/o Ministry of Culture, 10000 Zagreb, Runjaninova 2, Croatia. *E-mail:* kabinet@min-kulture.hr.

BISSET, Jacqueline; British actress; b. (Winnifred Jacqueline Fraser-Bisset), 13 Sept. 1944, Weybridge, Surrey; ed French Lycée, London; Chevalier, Légion d'honneur 2010. *Films include:* The Knack 1965, Two for the Road 1967, Casino Royale 1967, The Sweet Ride 1968, The Detective 1968, Bullitt 1968, The First Time 1969, Airport 1970, The Grasshopper 1970, The Mephisto Waltz 1971, Believe in Me 1971, The Life and Times of Judge Roy Bean 1972, Stand Up and Be Counted 1972, The Thief Who Came to Dinner 1973, Day for Night 1973, Murder on the Orient Express 1974, The Spiral Staircase 1974, End of the Game 1974, St Ives 1975, The Deep 1976, Le Magnifique 1977, Sunday Woman 1977, The Greek Tycoon 1978, Secrets 1978, Too Many Chefs 1978, I Love You, I Love You Not 1979, When Time Ran Out 1980, Rich and Famous 1981, Inchon 1981, Class 1982, Under the Volcano 1983, Forbidden 1986, Choices 1986, High Season 1988, Scenes from the Class Struggle in Beverly Hills 1989, Wild Orchid 1989, La Cérémonie 1995, The Maid, A Judgement in Stone, Once You Meet a Stranger 1996, The Honest Courtesan 1996, Let the Devil Wear Black 1998, Dangerous Beauty 1998, Joan of Arc 1999, In the Beginning 2000, Jesus 2000, Britannic 2000, The Sleepy Time Gal 2001, Sundance Holiday Gift Pack 2003, Latter Days 2003, Swing 2004, Fascination 2004, Domino 2005, Save the Last Dance 2 2006, Death in Love 2008, Two Jacks 2012. *Television includes:* Nip/Tuck (series) 2006, Carolina Moon (film) 2007, An Old Fashioned Thanksgiving (film) 2008, The Eastmans (film) 2009, An Old Fashioned Christmas (film) 2010, Rizzoli & Isles (series) 2011, Dancing on the Edge (series) (Golden Globe Award for Best Supporting Actress in a Series, Mini-series, or TV Movie 2014) 2013. *Address:* c/o Annabel Karouby, Agence Cinéart, 28 rue de Mogador, 75009 Paris, France (office). *E-mail:* a.karouby@cineart.fr (office). *Website:* www.cineart.fr (office).

BISSON, Thomas Noel, PhD; American historian and academic; *Henry Charles Lea Professor Emeritus of Medieval History, Harvard University;* b. 30 March 1931, New York; s. of Thomas A. Bisson and Faith W. Bisson; m. Margaretta C. Webb 1962; two d.; ed Port Washington High School, New York, Haverford Coll., Univ. of California, Berkeley, Princeton Univ.; Instructor in History, Amherst Coll. 1957–60; Asst Prof., Brown Univ. 1960–65; Assoc. Prof., Swarthmore Coll. 1965–67; Assoc. Prof., Univ. of California, Berkeley 1967–69, Prof. 1969–87; Prof., Harvard Univ. 1986–88, Henry Charles Lea Prof. of Medieval History 1988–2005, Prof. Emer. 2005–, Assoc. of Lowell House, Chair. Dept of History 1991–95; mem. American Philosophical Soc., American Acad. of Arts and Sciences; Fellow, Medieval Acad. of America (Pres. 1994–95), Royal Historical Soc., British Acad., Institut d'Estudis Catalans, others; Creu de Sant Jordi (Generalitat of Catalonia) 2001; Dr hc (Barcelona) 1991; Guggenheim Fellow 1964–65. *Publications include:* Assemblies and Representation in Languedoc in the Thirteenth Century 1964, Medieval Representative Institutions: Their Origins and Nature 1973, Conservation of Coinage: Monetary Exploitation and its Restraint in France, Catalonia and Aragon (c. AD 1000–c. AD 1225) 1979, Fiscal Accounts of Catalonia under the Early Count-Kings 1151–1213 (two vols) 1985, The Medieval Crown of Aragon: A Short History 1986, Medieval France and Her Pyrenean Neighbors 1989, Tormented Voices: Power, Crisis and Humanity in Rural Catalonia 1140–1200 1998, The Crisis of the Twelfth Century 2009; numerous articles in professional journals. *Leisure interests:* classical music, English literature. *Address:* 21 Hammond Street, Cambridge, MA 02138, USA (home). *Telephone:* (617) 354-0178 (home). *E-mail:* tnbisson@fas.harvard.edu (office). *Website:* history.fas.harvard.edu (office).

BISWAL, Nisha Desai; American (b. Indian) politician; *President U.S.–India Business Council;* b. 1969, Gujarat, India; d. of Kanu and Lata Desai; m. Subrat Biswal; two d.; ed Univ. of Virginia; Account Exec. The Kamber Group 1989–93; Int. Del. American Red Cross 1993–95; Desk Officer, Office of US Foreign Disaster Assistance, USAID 1995–97, Chief of Staff for Man. and Special Asst to Admin. 1997–99, Asst Admin. for Asia 2010–13; Sr Professional Staff Cttee on Foreign Affairs, US House of Reps 1999–2002; Sec. Bd, US Global Leadership Coalition 2002–05; Dir of Public Policy and Advocacy InterAction 2002–05; Staff Dir Subcommittee on State/Foreign Operations, House Cttee on Appropriations 2005–10; Exec. Br. Commr, Congresional-Exec. Comm. on China 2011–13; Asst Sec. for South and Central Asian Affiairs Dept of State 2013–17; Pres. US–India Business Council 2017–; Sr Advisor Albright Stonebridge Group 2017–; Ind. Business Consultant Biswal Strategy Group 2017–; mem. Int. Advisory Council, US Inst. for Peace 2017–; mem. Bd of Dirs, Inst. for Sustainable Communities 2017–; Samman Award by Pres. of India 2017. *Address:* US–India Business Council, 1615 H Street NW, Washington, DC 20062, USA (office). *Telephone:* (202) 463-5679 (office). *Fax:* (202) 463-3173 (office). *E-mail:* press@uschamber.com. *Website:* www.usibc.com (office).

BITI, Tendai Laxton; Zimbabwean lawyer and politician; b. 6 Aug. 1966, Dzivarasekwa, Harare; m. Charity Maguwah-Biti; one c.; ed Goromonzi High School, Univ. of Zimbabwe Law School; joined Honey and Blackenberg (law firm), Partner 1992; co-f. Movt for Democratic Change 1999, Sec.-Gen. 2000–05, mem. Movt for Democratic Change—Tsvangirai 2005–15, People's Democratic Party 2015–; MP for Harare E 2000–14, mem. Cttee on Budget, Finance and Econ. Devt, fmr mem. Parl. Portfolio Cttee on Lands, Agric., Water Devt, Rural Resources and Resettlement, Cttee on Defence and Home Affairs; Minister of Finance 2009–13.

BITSCH, Hans-Ullrich; German architect, industrial designer and academic; *Professor, Peter Behrens School of Architecture, University of Düsseldorf;* b. 13 June 1946, Essen; s. of Prof. Heinz W. Bitsch and Lore L. Bitsch (née Falldorf); m. Evelyn R. Koch 1981; two s.; ed Saarbrücken, State Coll. of Art, Saarbrücken and Illinois Inst. of Tech.; architect, Univ. of Saarbrücken 1968; Instructor, Int. Inst. of Design, Washington, DC, USA 1969; Visiting Lecturer, Harrington Inst., Chicago, Ill. 1970–71; Prof., Dept of Architecture, Univ. of Düsseldorf 1972–; Pres. German Inst. of Interior Architects 1977–82; Visiting Prof., Univ. of Texas 1981; Prof., Univ. of Naples 1997–; Pres. Professor Bitsch & Assocs (design and architectural office), Düsseldorf; Pres. World Congress of Int. Fed. of Internal Designers, Hamburg 1983; several awards for architecture and design. *Publications:* Menschengerechte Gestaltung des Kassenarbeitsplatzes 1978, Farbe und Industrie-Design 1982, Design und Formentwicklung von Stuhlen 1988, Visuelle Wahrnehmung in Architektur und Design 1989, Projekt Hotel 1992, Architectural Visions for Europe 1994, Stilströmungen 1998, Studien aus dem Architekturbüro 1999. *Leisure interests:* skiing, sailing, photography. *Address:* Peter Behrens School of Architecture, Room A1.41, Department of Applied Sciences, University of Düsseldorf, Georg-Glock-Strasse 15, 40474 Düsseldorf (office); Kaiser-Wilhelm-Ring 23, Rive Gauche, 40545 Düsseldorf, Germany. *Telephone:* (211) 4351122 (office); (211) 95449000. *Fax:* (211) 553814 (office). *E-mail:* hans-ulrich.bitsch@fh-duesseldorf.de (office); prof.bitsch@web.de. *Website:* arc.fh-duesseldorf.de (office).

BITTERLICH, Joachim; German/French business executive, consultant and diplomatist (retd) and academic; *Adjunct Professor, Economics, Law and Social Sciences, ESCP Europe, Paris;* b. 10 July 1948, Saarbrücken-Dudweiler; m. 1969; two s. one d.; ed Univ. of Saarbrücken, Ecole Nat. d'Admin; entered Foreign Office 1976; posted to Algiers 1978–81; Perm. Rep. to EC, Brussels 1981–85; Adviser, Pvt. Office of the Minister of Foreign Affairs 1985–87; Head of European Policy Dept, Fed. Chancellor's Office 1987–93; Dir of Foreign Policy, Econ. Co-operation and External Security, Fed. Chancellor's Office and Foreign and Security Policy Adviser to Fed. Chancellor 1993–98; Amb. and Perm. Rep. to N Atlantic Council, Brussels 1998–99; Amb. to Spain and Andorra 1999–2003; Exec. Vice-Pres. for Int. Affairs, Veolia Environnement, Paris 2003–12, Chair. Veolia Environment Germany 2009–12, mem. Bd of Admin, Veolia Propreté –2012, Veolia Transport –2012, ENA; Adjunct Prof., Econs, Law and Social Sciences, ESCP Europe, Paris 2008–; Pres. Franco-German Business Circle Berlin; Sr Adviser, BGA, Berlin, EUTOP Brussels, Cranemere Frankfurt/New York –2017; mem. Supervisory Bd DEKRA eV, Stuttgart –2014; Founding mem. CogitoPraxis, Paris; mem. Bd of Trustees, Friends of Europe, Notre Europe; mem. Deutsche Gesellschaft für Auswärtige Politik; mem. Independent Historical Comm., Ministry of Food and Agriculture; Assoc. mem. IISS, London, Euro 50 Group, Atlantik-Brücke, Berlin and others; Hon. CBE 1992; numerous decorations including Grosses Silbernes Ehrenzeichen mit Stern (Austria) 1994, Grande Oficial do Ordem de Rio Branco (Brazil) 1995, Officier, Légion d'honneur 1996, Grande Ufficiale dell Ordine al Merito (Italy) 1997, Orden do Infante Dom Enrique (Portugal) 1998, Gran Cruz de la Orden del Mérito Civil (Spain) 1998, Commdr des Palmes académiques 2016. *Publications include:* Commentaire du traité de l'Union Européenne 1999, (new edn 2006), L'Europe du futur 2004, France-Allemagne: mission impossible? Comment relancer la construction européenne 2005, Le Futur de la politique énergétique de l'Union européenne: avons-nous besoin d'une Haute Autorité Européenne pour l'énergie 2006, (new edn 2009), EU-Treaties: A Legal Commentary (co-author) 2012; numerous articles in newspapers and journals. *Address:* 4 rue Charles Dickens, 75016 Paris, France (home); Reinhardtstrasse 23, 10117 Berlin, Germany (office). *Telephone:* 1-42-15-16-80 (home); (30) 30882703 (office). *E-mail:* jbitterlich@escpeurope.eu (office); joachim@bitterlich.fr (office). *Website:* www.escpeurope.eu (office).

BIYA, Paul, LenD; Cameroonian politician and head of state; *President;* b. 13 Feb. 1933, Mvomeka'a; m. 1st Jeanne (née Atyam) Biya (deceased); one c.; m. 2nd Chantal Biya 1994; ed Ndem Mission School, Edea and Akono Seminaries, Lycée Leclerc, Yaoundé, Univ. of Paris, Inst. d'Etudes Politiques, Inst. des Hautes Etudes d'Outre-Mer, Paris; Head of Dept of Foreign Devt Aid 1962–63; Dir of

Cabinet in Ministry of Nat. Educ., Youth and Culture 1964–65; on goodwill mission to Ghana and Nigeria 1965; Sec.-Gen. in Ministry of Educ., Youth and Culture 1965–67; Dir of Civil Cabinet of Head of State 1967–68; Minister of State, Sec.-Gen. to Pres. 1968–75; Prime Minister 1975–82; Pres. of Cameroon 1982–; Second Vice-Pres., Central Cttee, mem. Union Nationale Camerounaise (UNC), Pres. 1983–85; Pres. Rassemblement Démocratique du Peuple Camerounais (RDPC) 1985–; mem. Politbureau; Hon. Prof. (Univ. of Beijing); Commdr de l'Ordre de la Valeur Camerounaise, Commdr of Nat. Order of FRG and of Tunisia, Great Commdr of the Medal of St George UK, Great Commdr of Order of Nigeria, Grand Cross of Nat. Order of Merit of Senegal, Grand Officier, Légion d'honneur, Grand Collier of the Ordre of Ouissam Mohammadi, Morocco; Dr hc (Univ. of Maryland); Peace Laureate, Centre European Peace Studies 1988. *Publication:* Communal Liberalism 1987. *Address:* Office of the President, Palais de l'Unité, Yaoundé, Cameroon (office). *Telephone:* 2223-4025 (office). *Website:* www.camnet.cm/celcom/homepr.htm (office).

BIYANI, Kishore, BCom, PGD; Indian business executive; *Founder and Group CEO, The Future Group;* b. 9 Aug. 1961, Bombay (now Mumbai); m. Sangita Biyani; two d.; ed HR Coll. of Commerce; Founder, Pantaloon Retail (India) Ltd 1997, Chair. and Man. Dir 2005–; Founder, Big Bazaar 2001; Founder and Group CEO, The Future Group 2006–; Man. Partner and Chair., Indivision Capital Fund 2006–; Man. Dir and Exec. Dir Future Ventures India Ltd 2007–; Non-Exec. Chair., Future Capital Holdings 2006–; Dir Jagran Prakashan Ltd 2005–, Ambit Investment Advisory Co. Ltd 2005–, Fame India Ltd 2010–, Embassy Property Developments Ltd 2010–, Galaxy Entertainment Corpn Ltd –2011; mem. Bd National Innovation Foundation in India, New York Fashion Bd; Ernst & Young Entrepreneur of the Year Award (Services Sector) 2006, Lakshmipat Singhania – IIM Lucknow Young Business Leader Award 2006, CNBC First Generation Entrepreneur of the Year Award 2006. *Publication:* It Happened in India: The Story of Pantaloons, Big Bazaar, Central and the Great Indian Consumer 2007. *Address:* The Future Group, Future Media (India) Ltd, Future Retail Home Office, Tower C, 7th Floor, 247 Park, LBS Marg, Vikhroli West, Mumbai, Maharashtra, 400 083 (office); Knowledge House, Shyam Nagar, Mumbai, Maharashtra, 200 060, India (office). *Telephone:* (22) 61190000 (office); (22) 30841300 (office). *Fax:* (22) 66442201 (office). *Website:* www.futuregroup.in (office).

BIZENJO, Mir Abdul Quddus, MA; Pakistani politician; *Speaker, Provincial Assembly of Balochistan;* b. 1 Jan. 1974, Awaran Dist, Balochistan; s. of Mir Abdull Majeed Bizenjo; m.; ed Univ. of Balochistan; mem. Prov. Ass. of Balochistan (Pakistan Muslim League–Q) 2002–18, (Balochistan Awami Party) 2018–, Deputy Speaker 2013–15, Speaker 2018–; Balochistan Prov. Minister for Livestock and Dairy Devt 2008–13; Chief Minister of Balochistan Jan.–June 2018. *Address:* Provincial Assembly of Balochistan, Zarghoon Road, Quetta, Pakistan (office). *Telephone:* (81) 9203074 (office). *Website:* www.pabalochistan.gov.pk (office).

BJARNASON, Björn, cand. jur.; Icelandic journalist and politician; *Chairman, Varðberg;* b. 14 Nov. 1944, Reykjavik; s. of Bjarni Benediktsson and Sigríður Björnsdóttir; m. Rut Ingólfsdóttir; two c.; ed Univ. of Iceland; Ed. Almenna bókafélagið (book publr) 1971–74; Foreign News Ed. Vísir 1974; Div. Chief, Prime Minister's Office 1974, Deputy Sec.-Gen. 1975–79; journalist, Morgunblaðið 1979–84, Asst Ed. 1984–91; mem. Parl. (Independence Party) for Reykjavik 1991–2009; Minister of Educ., Science and Culture 1995–2002, of Justice and Ecclesiastical Affairs 2003–09 (resgnd); currently Chair. Varðberg (Atlantic council of Iceland); mem. Reykjavik City Council 2002–06; Ed./Publr Evropuvaktin 2010–13, www.vardberg.is 2015–, TV talk show at INN 2010–17. *Publications include:* The Security of Iceland, Five Roads to Nordic Security 1973, Strategic Factors in the North Atlantic 1977, No Other Option in Security Affairs: The Resurgence of Liberalism 1979, Iceland and Nuclear Weapons, Nuclear Weapons Policy in the North, Copenhagen 1982, From the Prime Ministry to Morgunbladid 1983, Iceland's Security Policy: Vulnerability and Responsibility 1985, I hita kalda stríðsins (In the Heat of the Cold War) 2001, Hvað er Íslandi fyrir bestu? (What is Best for Iceland?) 2009, Rosabaugur yfir Íslandi (Threatening Baugur over Iceland) 2011; numerous articles. *Leisure interests:* swimming, hiking, books, films, farming. *Address:* Háahlíð 14, 105 Reykjavík, Iceland (home). *Telephone:* 5512261 (home). *E-mail:* bjorn@bjorn.is. *Website:* www.bjorn.is; www.vardberg.is.

BJARNASON, Gudmundur; Icelandic administrator and fmr politician; b. 9 Oct. 1944, Húsavík; s. of Bjarni Stéfánsson and Jakobina Jónsdóttir; m. Vigdís Gunnarsdóttir; three d.; ed Húsavík Secondary School and Co-operative Coll.; with Co-operative Soc., Húsavík 1963–67; Húsavík Br. Co-operative Bank of Iceland 1967–77, Br. Dir 1977–80; elected mem. Húsavík Town Council 1970, Chair. 1974; mem. Althing 1979–99; Minister of Health and Social Security 1987–91, of Environment and Agric. 1995–99; mem. Althing Appropriation Cttee 1979–87, 1991–95, Vice-Chair. 1983–87; Chair. Cttee on Housing Affairs; Chair. Icelandic Asscn of Heart Patients 2007–; mem. Jt Cttee on public projects; Gen. Man. Housing Financing Fund (ind. govt inst. that grants house mortgages) 1999–2010; Bd Research Council; mem. Icelandic del. to Parl. Ass. of Council of Europe 1991–95. *Address:* Kirkjusandur 5, 105 Reykjavik, Iceland (home). *Telephone:* 553-9898 (home).

BJERREGAARD, Ritt; Danish fmr politician; b. 19 May 1941, Copenhagen; d. of Gudmund Bjerregaard and Rita Bjerregaard; m. Søren Mørch 1966; mem. Parl. 1971–95, 2001–05; Minister of Educ. 1973, 1975–78, for Social Affairs 1979–81; Chair. Parl. Group, Social Democratic Party (SDP) 1981–92, 1987–92, Deputy Chair. 1982–87; Chair. Parl. Cttee on Public Accounts 1990–95; mem. Parl. Ass. of Council of Europe 1990–95; Pres. Danish European Movt 1992–94; Vice-Pres. Parl. Ass. of CSCE 1992–95; Vice-Pres. Socialist Int. Women 1992–94; EU Commr for Environment 1995–99; Minister of Food, Agric. and Fisheries 2000–01; Lord Mayor of Copenhagen 2006–09; trade amb. to China; mem. Trilateral Comm., Centre for European Policy Studies. *Publications:* several books on politics in general and the role of women in politics. *Leisure interests:* her apple farm, organic farming, the environment. *Address:* Jens Juels Gade 4, 2100 Copenhagen Ø, Denmark (home). *Telephone:* 35430897 (home). *Website:* www.ritt.dk.

BJØERNDALEN, Ole Einar; Norwegian professional biathlete; b. 27 Jan. 1974, Drammen; m. Nathalie Santer 2006; ed Norwegian Ski Gymnas; gold medals (Individual, Sprint), Junior/Youth World Championships, Ruhpolding 1993; winner of eight Olympic gold medals: gold medal (Sprint) in Nagano, Japan 1998, four gold medals (Sprint, Pursuit, Individual, Relay) in Salt Lake City, USA 2002 (became third Olympian to win four gold medals at a single Winter Games), gold medal (Relay) in Vancouver 2010, two gold medals (Sprint and Mixed Relay) in Sochi, Russia 2014; World Championships: gold medals (Team), Pokljuka 1998, (Sprint, Mass Start), Khanty-Mansiysk 2003, (Sprint, Pursuit, Mass Start, Relay), Hochfilzen 2005, (Sprint, Pursuit), Antholz 2007, (Pursuit), Östersund 2008, (Individual, Sprint, Pursuit, Relay), Pyeongchang 2009, (Relay, Mixed Relay), Khanty-Mansiysk 2011, (Relay, Mixed Relay), Ruhpolding 2012, (Relay), Nové Město 2013; World Cup (Overall) titles 1997–98, 2002–03, 2004–05, 2005–06, 2007–08, 2008–09; winner FIS Cross-Country World Cup, Sweden 2006; winner four gold medals Biathlon World Championships, South Korea 2009; most medalled Olympian in the history of the Winter Games, with 13 medals; Norwegian Sportsperson of the Year 2002, Egebergs Ærespris 2002. *Leisure interests:* motorbikes, climbing, off-road, cycling. *Address:* Skavelandsvei 12E, Trondheim 7022, Norway (office). *Website:* www.oleeinarbjoerndalen.com.

BJÖRCK, Anders Per-Arne; Swedish politician; b. 19 Sept. 1944, Nässjö, Jönköping Co.; m. Py-Lotte Björck; one d.; Nat. Pres. Swedish Young Moderates 1966–71; mem. Parl. 1968–2009; mem. Parl. Ass. Council of Europe 1976–91, Pres. (Speaker) 1989–91; Minister of Defence 1991–94; First Deputy Speaker of Swedish Parl. 1994–2009; Gov. Uppsala Co. 2003–09; mem. Bd, Swedish Broadcasting Co. 1978–91, Swedish TV Co. 1979–91; mem. numerous govt comms dealing with constitutional matters, the mass media, environmental protection. *Publications:* various articles on defence, foreign policy and constitutional issues.

BJÖRK; Icelandic singer, songwriter, musician, record producer and actress; b. (Björk Guðmundsdóttir), 21 Nov. 1965, Reykjavík; m. Thór Eldon (divorced); one s. one d.; first solo release aged 11; fmr singer for various Icelandic groups, including Exodus, Tappi Tikarras; singer, Kukl, later renamed The Sugarcubes 1986–92; solo artist 1992–; BRIT Award for Best Int. Newcomer 1994, MTV European Music Award for Best Int. Female Artist 1994, 1996, 1997, Q Inspiration Award 2005, MOJO Inspiration Award 2007, Polar Music Prize 2010, BRIT Award for Int. Female Solo Artist 2016. *Films:* Dancer in the Dark (Cannes Film Festival Best Actress Award 2000) 2000, Drawing Restraint 9 2005, Anna and the Moods (voice) 2007. *Recordings include:* albums: with The Sugarcubes: Life's Too Good 1988, Here Today, Tomorrow Next Week 1989, Stick Around For Joy 1992, It's It 1992; solo: Björk 1977, Debut 1993, Post 1995, Telegram 1996, Homogenic 1997, Selmasongs 2000, Vespertine 2001, Dancer in the Dark 2001, Greatest Hits 2002, Family Tree 2002, Medúlla 2004, Army of Me: Remixes and Covers (charity album) 2005, Drawing Restraint 9 (OST) 2005, Volta 2007, Voltaic 2009, Biophilia 2011, Vulnicura 2015, Utopia 2017. *Address:* Quest Management, 36 Warple Way, Unit 1D, London, W3 0RG, England (office); c/o Nonesuch Records, Warner Music Group, 75 Rockefeller Plaza, New York, NY 10019, USA (office). *Telephone:* (20) 8749-0088 (office); (212) 275-2000 (office). *Fax:* (20) 8749-0080 (office). *E-mail:* info@quest-management.com (office); info@nonesuch.com (office). *Website:* www.quest-management.com (office); www.nonesuch.com (office); www.bjork.com.

BJÖRK, Claes; Swedish business executive; b. 9 June 1948; joined Skanska AB 1967, moved to USA 1971, responsible for Skanska's construction operations in USA 1983, Pres. Skanska (USA) Inc. 1987, Sr Vice-Pres. Skanska AB, Head of Skanska USA Operations –1997, mem. Group Man. Skanska AB 1995, Pres. and Group CEO 1997–2002 (retd), Chair. Scancem Cement Co. 1998–2000; Chair. Swedish-American Chamber of Commerce 1992–95, currently mem. Bd of Dirs; mem. Bd of Dirs Banister Foundation 1990–, Granite Construction Inc. 2006– (also Chair. 2018–), Qliktech Inc. –2009, Consolidated Management Group; mem. Bd of Trustees American Scandinavian Foundation; Lucia Trade Award, Swedish-American Chamber of Commerce. *Address:* Granite Construction Inc., 585 West Beach Street, Watsonville, CA 95076, USA (office). *Telephone:* (831) 724-1011 (office). *Website:* www.graniteconstruction.com (office).

BJORKEN, James Daniel, BS, PhD; American physicist and academic; *Professor Emeritus, Stanford Linear Accelerator Center, Stanford University;* b. 22 June 1934, Chicago, Ill.; ed Massachusetts Inst. of Tech., Stanford Univ.; Research Assoc., then Asst Prof., Stanford Univ. 1959–62, Assoc. Prof., then Prof., Stanford Linear Accelerator Center 1962–79, Theoretical Physicist 1989–98, Prof. Emer. 1998–; Theoretical Physicist and Assoc. Dir for Physics, Fermi Lab. 1979–89; Eastman Prof., Univ. of Oxford, UK 1995–96; mem. NAS, American Acad. of Arts and Sciences; Foreign mem. Swedish Acad. of Sciences; Hon. PhD (Univ. of Turin, Italy); Putnam Fellow 1954, Dannie Heinemann Prize in Math. Physics, American Physical Soc., Ernest Orlando Lawrence Medal, Dept for Energy, Dirac Medal, Abdus Salam Int. Centre for Theoretical Physics 2004, Wolf Prize in Physics (co-recipient) 2015, High Energy and Particle Physics Prize, European Physical Soc. 2015. *Publications include:* Relativistic Quantum Mechanics (co-author) 1964, Relativistic Quantum Fields (co-author) 1965. *Address:* Stanford Linear Accelerator Center, 2575 Sand Hill Road, Menlo Park, CA 94025, USA (office). *Telephone:* (650) 926-3900 (office). *Fax:* (650) 926-2525 (office). *E-mail:* bjorken@slac.stanford.edu (office). *Website:* www.slac.stanford.edu (office).

BJÖRKLUND, Leni, BA; Swedish politician; b. 5 July 1944, Örebro; ed Uppsala Univ.; Research Asst, Dept of Pedagogical Studies, Stockholm Inst. of Educ. 1969–71; Educ. Consultant, Nat. Bd of Educ. 1971–74; Expert, Dept for Cultural Affairs, Ministry of Educ. and Science 1974–76; Municipal Commr Municipality of Järfälla 1977–79; Co. Council Commr Stockholm Co. Council 1980–98; Man. Dir of Planning and Rationalisation, Inst. for Health and Social Services 1989–99; Sec.-Gen. Church of Sweden 1999–2002; Minister of Defence 2002–06; apptd First Vice-Chair. Civilförsvarsförbundet (Civil Defense League) 2007; mem. SDP, held numerous party positions including Vice-Chair. Exec. Cttee Stockholm Co. SDP; fmr Chair. Expert Group on Public Finance (ESO); mem. Nat. Heritage Bd, Mid-Sweden Univ.; fmr Chair. Swedish Medical Research Council; fmr Vice-Chair. Stockholm Co. Admin Bd; fmr mem. Foundation of Strategic Research; Hon. DrMed (Karolinska Institutet). *Address:* Civilförsvarsförbundet, Box 2034, 169 02 Solna, Sweden. *Telephone:* (8) 629-63-70. *E-mail:* info@civil.se. *Website:* www.civil.se.

BJÖRKMAN, Olle Erik, MS, PhD, DSc, FAAS; American (b. Swedish) professor of plant biology; *Member of Faculty, Department of Plant Biology, Carnegie Institution of Washington;* b. 29 July 1933, Jönköping, Sweden; s. of Erik Gustaf Björkman and Dagmar Kristina Björkman (née Svensson); m. Monika Birgit

Waldinger 1955; two s.; ed Univs of Stockholm and Uppsala; Research Fellow, Swedish Natural Science Research Council, Univ. of Uppsala 1961–63; Post-doctoral Fellow, Carnegie Inst. of Washington Dept of Plant Biology, Stanford, Calif. 1964–65, Faculty mem. 1966–, Prof. of Biology by courtesy, Stanford Univ. 1977–; mem. Cttee on Carbon Dioxide Effects, US Dept of Energy 1977–82, Cttee on Bioscience Research in Agric. 1984–85; Scientific Adviser, Desert Research Inst., Nevada 1980–81; mem. Editorial Bd Planta 1993–96; mem. NAS; Fellow, American Acad. of Arts and Sciences; Corresp. (Foreign) mem. Australian Acad. of Sciences; Foreign mem. Royal Swedish Acad. of Sciences; Linnaeus Prize, Royal Swedish Physiographic Soc. 1977, The Stephen Hale's Award, American Soc. of Plant Physiologists 1986, The Selby Award, Australian Acad. of Sciences 1987, The Barnes Life Membership Award, American Soc. of Plant Biologists 2001. *Publications:* Experimental Studies on the Nature of Species V (co-author) 1971, Physiological Processes in Plant Ecology 1980, more than 170 articles in scientific journals. *Leisure interest:* opera. *Address:* Carnegie Institution of Washington Department of Plant Biology, 260 Panama Street, Stanford, CA 94305 (office); 3040 Greer Road, Palo Alto, CA 94303-4007, USA (home). *Telephone:* (650) 858-0880 (home). *E-mail:* olle_bjorkman@msn.com (home). *Website:* dpb.carnegiescience .edu (office).

BJORKMAN, Pamela J., BA, PhD; American biologist and academic; *Max Delbrück Professor of Biology and Investigator, Howard Hughes Medical Institute, California Institute of Technology;* b. Portland, Ore.; m. Kai Zinn; two c.; ed Univ. of Oregon and Harvard Univ.; Post-doctoral Researcher, Harvard Univ. 1984–87, Stanford Univ. 1987–88; Asst Prof., California Inst. of Tech. 1988–95, Assoc. Prof. 1995–98, Prof. 1998–2004, Max Delbrück Prof. of Biology 2004–, Asst Investigator, Howard Hughes Medical Inst. Div. of Biology 1989–95, Assoc. Investigator 1995–98, Investigator 1988–99, 2005–, Full Investigator 2000–05, Exec. Officer for Biology 2000–; currently also Adjunct Prof. of Biochemistry, School of Medicine, Univ. of Southern California, Los Angeles; fmr Pew Scholar in the Biomedical Sciences; fmr American Cancer Soc. Post-doctoral Fellow; fmr American Soc. of Histocompatibility and Immunogenetics Young Investigator; mem. NAS 2001–, American Acad. of Arts and Sciences (Fellow), American Philosophical Soc., American Crystallographic Asscn, American Soc. for Cell Biology, American Asscn of Immunologists; William B. Coley Award for Distinguished Research in Fundamental Immunology 1993, Gairdner Foundation Int. Award (co-author) 1994, AAI-PharMingen Investigator Award 1996, Paul Ehrlich and Ludwig Darmstaedter Award, L'Oréal-UNESCO Women in Science Award 2006, Max Planck Research Award, James R. Klinenberg Science Award, Arthritis Foundation. *Publications:* numerous papers in scientific journals on the structures of proteins mediating the immune response and on protein crystallography. *Address:* Howard Hughes Medical Institute, Division of Biology, Office 361 Broad, MC 114-96, California Institute of Technology, 1200 E California Blvd, Pasadena, CA 91125, USA (office). *Telephone:* (626) 395-8350 (office). *Fax:* (626) 792-3683 (office). *Website:* www.its.caltech.edu/~bjorker (office).

BJØRNEBOE, Gunn-Elin Aasprong, Cand. med. (MD), MA, PhD; Norwegian physician, academic and university administrator; b. 6 April 1956; ed Univ. of Oslo; fmr Adjunct Prof., Dept of Community Medicine, Univ. of Tromsø; has extensive man. experience and completed the Solstrand Leadership Devt Programme; fmr Admin. Man. and fmr Dir Nat. Nutrition Council; Deputy Dir-Prof., Dept of Nutrition, Univ. of Oslo, Dir Univ. of Oslo 2007–19; Chair. Cancer Soc.; Deputy Dir Norwegian Non-fiction Writers and Translators Asscn 1998–2002; Deputy mem. Norwegian FAO Cttee 1994–98; mem. WHO Multicentre Growth Reference Study 1998–2007; mem. Bd Student Welfare Org. of Oslo and Arkeshus. *Publications:* several book chapters as well as scientific papers in professional journals. *Address:* University Director's Office, University of Oslo, Administration Building, 9th Floor, Problemveien 7, 0313 Oslo, Norway (office). *Telephone:* 22-85-63-01 (office). *Fax:* 22-85-44-42 (office). *E-mail:* universitetsdirektor@uio.no (office). *Website:* www.uio.no.

BJØRNHOLM, Sven, DPhil; Danish physicist; b. 8 Sept. 1927, Tønder; s. of Lt-Col H. L. Bjørnholm and Inger Hillerup; m. Iran Park 1957; two s. one d.; ed Tech. Univ. of Denmark, Sorbonne, Paris and Univ. of Copenhagen; Research Asst, Niels Bohr Inst., Copenhagen 1955–68; Assoc. Prof., Univ. of Copenhagen 1968–96; visiting scientist at research insts in France, USSR, USA, Germany and Brazil 1951–97; mem. Bd Int. Fed. of Insts of Advanced Study 1972–77, Danish Natural Science Research Council 1973–79, Danish Energy Policy Council 1976–86, IUPAP Comm. on Nuclear Physics 1978–84, EC Comm. on Research and Devt 1980–82; Pres. Danish Physical Soc. 1978–80; mem. Royal Danish Acad., Danish Acad. of Tech. Sciences, Royal Physiographical Soc. of Lund, Sweden, Danish Pugwash Cttee; Officier, Ordre des Palmes académiques 1989; Ole Rømer Award 1965, Ulrich Brinch Award 1973. *Publications:* Energy in Denmark 1990–2005 1976; and articles on the structure and reactions of atomic nuclei and metal clusters, including fission, in professional journals. *Address:* The Niels Bohr Institute, Blegdamsvej 17, 2100 Copenhagen Ø (office); Fuglevangsvej 6B, 1962 Frederiksberg C, Denmark (home). *Telephone:* 33-22-48-85 (home).

BJURSTRØM, Hanne Inger; Norwegian lawyer, politician and fmr academic; b. 1960; m.; two c.; ed Inst. for Foreign Students, Univ. of Florence, Italy, Univ. of Oslo, Univ. of London and London School of Econs, UK; legal consultant (women's rights), Univ. of Oslo 1981–82, Scientific Asst (maritime law) 1984–85, part-time teacher and External Examiner (Admin. Law) 1987–2006; Visiting Researcher, Inst. for Social Research 1992; Sr Exec. Officer/Adviser, Legislation Dept, Ministry of Justice 1987–94; Political Sec. to Commr for Finance and Planning, Rune Bjerke, Oslo City Govt 1994–95; Corp. Counsellor, Aker Oil and Gas Technology PLC 1995–97; barrister training for lawyers (mandatory) 1996; Agent, Attorney Gen. of Civil Affairs 1997–2000; Vice-Pres. and Judge, The Labour Court 2000–03; Sr Adviser with responsibility for devt of Norway's cap and trade system (climate change), Ministry of Environment 2003–07, Norway's Chief Negotiator under UN climate change negotiations 2007–09; Minister of Labour Affairs 2009–12 (resigned); mem. Cttee overseeing official policy review (pricing of public information) 1993; Norwegian Adviser to Council of Europe (Civil Law) 1993–96; mem. Nat. Cttee for Research Ethics (Social Sciences, Law, Humanities) 1997–2003, complaints bd relating to decisions made by Data Inspectorate (protection of personal privacy) 2001–08; Deputy Bd mem. European Surveillance Authority Coll. 2001–04; Leader of UN ECE Convention on Access to Information, Public Participation in Decision-making and Access to Justice in Environmental Matters 2005–08; leader of dispute cttee (workplace environment) 2006–08; Deputy mem. Oslo City Govt 1980–83, Oslo School Bd 1980–83, Oslo Price Bd 1980–83, Norwegian Children and Youth Council 1982–83; mem. Oslo Municipal Youth Cttee 1981–83; Bd mem. Norwegian Student Soc. 1982, Chateu Neuf 1982, Ullevål Hosp. 1996–99.

BLACK, Dame Carol M., DBE, CBE, MD, FRCP, FMedSci, FACP; British physician and academic; *Chairman, British Library;* b. 26 Dec. 1939; m. Christopher Morely; ed Dixie Grammar School, Market Bosworth, Univ. of Bristol, Royal Coll. of Physicians; Consultant Rheumatologist, West Middlesex Univ. Hospital 1981–89; Consultant Rheumatologist, Royal Free and Univ. Coll. Medical School, Univ. of London 1989–94, Prof. of Rheumatology 1994–2006, Prof. Emer. 2006–; Medical Dir Royal Free Hospital, London 2000–02; Chair. Nuffield Trust for Research and Policy Studies in Health Services 2006–16; Nat. Dir for Health and Work 2006–11; Expert Adviser on Work and Health, Dept of Health; Pro-Chancellor, Univ. of Bristol 2007–10; Public Appointments Amb., Govt Equalities Office, Cabinet Office 2009–; Chair. of Research Cttee and Vice-Chair. of Bd, Imperial Coll. Healthcare Charity 2008–; Chair. Skills for Health, Widening Participation Strategy Group, Dept of Health 2009–; Chair., Governance Bd, Centre for Workforce Intelligence 2010–; elected to Royal Coll. of Physicians 1996, Clinical Vice-Pres. 1999–2002, Pres. 2002–06; Dir (non-exec.), NHS Inst. for Innovation and Improvement 2006–; Chair. British Library 2018–; mem. Nat. Inst. for Health and Clinical Excellence (NICE) Appraisal Cttee 1999–2002, Partners Council 2002–06; mem. Nat. Specialist Commissioning Advisory Group 2000–04; mem. Imperial Cancer Research Fund Council 2002–04; mem. Council of Acad. of Medical Sciences 2002–06; mem. Postgraduate Medical Educ. and Training Bd 2003–07; mem., CBRC Scientific Advisory Bd, Guy's and St. Thomas's Medical School 2007–; mem. Advisory Bd, Business in the Community, Nat. Campaign Business Action on Health 2008–; Founding mem. Cttee, Queen's Awards for Voluntary Services 2009–; mem. Wellbeing Through Work Expert Reference Group, NHS Wales 2009–, Advisory Bd, Centre for Organisational Health and Well-Being, Univ. of Lancaster 2009–, Employee Engagement Task Force, Dept of Business Innovation and Skills 2011–, Life Sciences Skills Strategy Bd, Cogent 2011–, Int. Advisory Bd, US Preventive Medicine 2011–; Foreign Assoc., Inst. of Medicine, Washington, DC 2006; Fellowship of Univ. Coll. London 2004; Trustee, Nat. Portrait Gallery 2010–; Master, American Coll. of Physicians 2005; Companion, Chartered Man. Inst. 2004; mem. Bd of Govs. The Health Foundation 2004–07; Hon. Pres. Scleroderma Soc. 2006–, Raynaud's and Scleroderma Asscn 2007–, British Lung Foundation 2007–; Hon. Patron, Treat Trust, Wales 2009–; Hon. Physician, Royal Soc. of Musicians of Great Britain 2008–; Hon. Fellow, Lucy Cavendish Coll., Univ. of Cambridge 2004, Univ. Coll. London 2004; Hon. MD (Nottingham); Hon. DrSc (Bristol, Leicester, Sheffield, Hertfordshire, Exeter, Glasgow, Southampton). *Leisure interests:* hill-walking, running, opera, reading, travel. *Website:* www.bl.uk (office).

BLACK, Cathleen (Cathie) Prunty; American publishing executive; b. 26 April 1944, Chicago, Ill.; d. of James Hamilton Black and Margaret Black (née Harrington); m. Thomas E. Harvey 1982; two c.; ed Trinity Coll., Washington, DC; sold advertising for magazines such as Holiday and Travel & Leisure; joined New York magazine in 1970, Publr 1979; helped launch Ms. magazine 1972, Assoc. Publr; Pres. and Publr USA Today 1983–91, mem. Bd Dirs and Exec. Vice-Pres. Marketing, Gannett Co. Inc. (parent-co.) 1985–91; Pres. and CEO Newspaper Asscn of America 1991–95; Pres. Hearst Magazines, New York 1996–2010, Chair. 2010, mem. Bd of Dirs Hearst Corpn 1996–; Chancellor, New York City Dept of Educ. Jan.–April 2011; mem. Bd of Dirs Coca-Cola Co. 1990–91, 1993–, International Business Machines Corpn (IBM) 1995–, Women.com Networks Inc. 1999–, Advertising Council; Chair. Magazine Publrs of America 1999–2001; Trustee, Univ. of Notre Dame; mem. Council on Foreign Relations; hon. degrees from St Mary's Coll., South Bend, Ind., Capitol Coll., Laurel, Md, Ithaca Coll., NY, Lehigh Univ., Bethlehem, Pa, Simmons Coll., Boston, Mass, Trinity Washington Univ., Washington, DC, Trinity Coll., Hartford, Conn., Marymount Coll., Tarrytown, NY, Loyola Univ., New Orleans, La, Hamilton Coll., Clinton, NY; Woman of the Year Award Financial Women's Asscn 1986–87, Advertising Age Publishing Executive of the Year 2000, Lifetime Achievement Award, Magazine Publrs of America 2005, named Corp. Publr of the Year, The Delaney Report 2006, Prism Award, New York Univ. 2007. *Publication:* Basic Black: The Essential Guide for Getting Ahead at Work (and in Life) 2007. *Address:* c/o New York City Department of Education, Tweed Courthouse, 52 Chambers Street, New York, NY 10007, USA; c/o Crown Publishing Group Publicity Department, Random House Inc., 1745 Broadway, New York, NY 10019, USA. *E-mail:* crownpublicity@randomhouse .com. *Website:* www.randomhouse.com/author/79886/cathie-black.

BLACK, Robert Lincoln, MD, FAAP; American paediatrician and academic; *Voluntary Clinical Professor of Pediatrics, Stanford University;* b. 25 Aug. 1930, Los Angeles; s. of Harold Black and Kathryn Stone; m. Jean Wilmott McGuire 1953; two s. one d.; ed Stanford Univ., Kings County Hosp., Brooklyn, Stanford Univ. Hosp.; Capt. in USAF Medical Corps 1956–58; Asst Clinical Prof., Stanford Univ., Clinical Prof. 1962–, Assoc. Prof. 1968–79, Prof. of Pediatrics 1980, currently Voluntary Clinical Prof. of Pediatrics; mem. Bd of Dirs Lyceum of Monterey Peninsula 1973–; mem. Bd Mid Coast Health System Agency 1975–81; mem. various cttees of American Acad. of Pediatrics 1962–, Alt. Chapter Chair. 1984–87; Consultant, State of Calif. Dept of Health Service 1962– and of Office of Statewide Health Planning 1975–81; mem. State Maternal, Child, Adolescent Health Care Bd 1984–93; mem. Inst. of Medicine, NAS, Calif. State Maternal, Child, Adolescent Health Bd; Fellow, American Acad. of Pediatrics (FAAP); mem. Bd of Educ. Monterey Peninsula Unified School Dist 1965–73; Martin Gershman Award for Child Advocacy, American Acad. of Pediatrics 1996, Physician of the Year, Monterey County Medical Soc. 2001, Child Advocacy Award, American Acad. of Pediatrics 2003. *Publications:* California Health Plan for Children, California's Use of Health Statistics in Child Health Planning. *Leisure interests:* music, hiking, travel, photography. *Address:* 920 Cass Street, Monterey, CA 93940, USA (office). *Telephone:* (831) 372-5841 (office). *Fax:* (831) 372-4820 (office). *E-mail:* rblack@ chomp.org (office).

BLACK OF BRENTWOOD, Baron (Life Peer), cr. 2010, of Brentwood in the County of Essex; **Guy Vaughan Black,** MA, FRSA, FCIPR; British newspaper executive; *Deputy Chairman, Telegraph Media Group;* b. 6 Aug. 1964, Chelmsford, Essex; s. of Thomas Black and Monica Black; m. Mark Bolland 2015; ed Brentwood School, Essex, Peterhouse, Cambridge; Grad. Trainee, Corp. Banking Div., BZW 1985–86; Desk Officer, Conservative Party Research Dept 1986–89; Special Adviser to Sec. of State for Energy 1989–92; Account Dir, Westminster Strategy 1992–94; Assoc. Dir, Lowe Bell Good Relations 1994–96; Dir Press Complaints Comm. 1996–2003; Dir of Communications, Conservative Party 2004–05; Exec. Dir, Telegraph Media Group 2005–18, Deputy Chair. 2018–; Dir Advertising Standards Bd of Finance 2005–, Press Standards Bd of Finance 2007–14 (Chair. 2009–14); Conservative mem. Brentwood Dist Council 1988–92; Trustee, Sir Edward Heath Charitable Foundation 2006–10, Imperial War Museum 2007–15, Imperial War Museum Foundation 2010–; Chair. Commonwealth Press Union Media Trust 2009–; Chair. Royal Coll. of Music 2017–; mem. Council, The Guild of St Bride's, Fleet Street 2010–; Patron, Rory Peck Trust 2015–, Int. Cat Care 2016–, Terrence Higgins Trust 2017–; Hon. mem. London Press Club, Inc. Soc. of Musicians; Sir Herbert Butterfield Prize for History, Univ. of Cambridge 1985. *Leisure interests:* reading, music, playing the piano, cats. *Address:* Telegraph Media Group, 111 Buckingham Palace Road, London SW1A 0DT, England (office). *Telephone:* (20) 7931-3806 (office). *E-mail:* guy.black@telegraph.co.uk (office); blackgv@parliament.uk. *Website:* www.telegraph.co.uk (office); www.parliament.uk/biographies/lords/lord-black-of-brentwood/4171.

BLACK OF CROSSHARBOUR, Baron (Life Peer), cr. 2001, of Crossharbour in the London Borough of Tower Hamlets; **Conrad Moffat Black,** Kt, BA, LLL, MA, LittD; British (b. Canadian) publisher, business executive, author, columnist and investor; *Chairman, Conrad Black Capital Corporation;* b. 25 Aug. 1944, Montreal, Quebec; s. of George Montegu and Jean Elizabeth Black (née Riley); m. 1st Joanna Catherine Louise Black 1978 (divorced 1992); two s. one d.; m. 2nd Barbara Amiel 1992; ed Carleton, Laval, McGill Univs; Chair. and CEO Ravelston Corpn Ltd; Chair. Hollinger Int. 1985–2004, acquired Daily Telegraph newspaper group 1985, Chair. Telegraph Group –2004; CEO Chair. Argus Corpn 1978–2005; Chair. Conrad Black Capital Corpn; mem. Advisory Bd, The Nat. Interest, Washington, DC; Patron, The Malcolm Muggeridge Foundation; charged with 17 counts of criminal offences by US Dept of Justice, which sought life imprisonment and fine of US $140 million 2005, four counts dropped, nine led to acquittals, remaining four vacated unanimously by US Supreme Court after spending 29 months in a low security fed. prison, two counts revived by a lower court but US Supreme Court refused to grant leave to appeal these May 2011, resentenced to a reduced term of 42 months and a fine of $125,000, returned to prison to serve remaining 13 months of his sentence June 2011, released from prison and deported to Canada May 2012, granted a one-year temporary resident's permit to re-enter Canada as he had renounced his Canadian citizenship in 2001; television presenter, author, columnist for Nat. Post, Nat. Review (USA) and American Greatness (USA); fined $4.1 million and barred from becoming dir of a US co. 2013; Kt Commdr, Order of St Gregory the Great; Hon. LLD (St Francis Xavier) 1979, (McMaster) 1979, (Windsor) 1979, (Carleton) 1992. *Publications include:* Duplessis 1977, A Life in Progress (autobiography) 1994, Franklin D. Roosevelt: Champion of Freedom 2003, Richard Milhous Nixon: The Invincible Quest 2007, A Matter of Principle 2011, Flight of The Eagle: A Strategic History of the U.S. 2013, Rise to Greatness: The History of Canada from the Vikings to the Present 2014, Backward Glances 2016, Donald J. Trump: A President Like No Other 2018, The Canadian Manifesto 2019. *E-mail:* dconnors@blackam.net (office).

BLACK OF DERWENT, Rt Hon Dame Jill Margaret, DBE, PC, BA (Law); British judge; *Justice of the Supreme Court;* b. 1 June 1954; d. of Dr James Irvine Currie and Margaret Yvonne Currie; m. 1st David Charles Black 1978 (divorced 2013); one s. one d.; m. 2nd Sir Richard McCombe; ed Penrhos Coll., Colwyn Bay and Univ. of Durham; called to the Bar, Inner Temple 1976, QC 1994, Recorder 1998, Justice of the High Court, Family Div. 1999–2010; Lady Justice of Appeal 2010–17; Justice, The Supreme Court 2017–. *Publications:* The Working Mother's Survival Guide (jtly) 1988, Divorce: The Things You Thought You'd Never Need to Know (5th edn) 2004, The Family Court Practice (contrib.) 2012, A Practical Approach to Family Law (jtly, 9th edn) 2012. *Address:* The Supreme Court, Parliament Square, London, SW1P 3BD, England (office). *Telephone:* (20) 7960-1936 (office). *Fax:* (20) 7960-1961 (office). *E-mail:* justices@supremecourt.gsi.gov.uk (office). *Website:* www.supremecourt.gov.uk (office).

BLACKADDER, Dame Elizabeth Violet, DBE, MA, RA, RSA; British artist; b. 24 Sept. 1931, Falkirk, Scotland; m. John Houston 1956 (died 2008); ed Falkirk High School, Edinburgh Coll. of Art and Univ. of Edinburgh; teacher of art, St Thomas of Aquinas School, Edin. 1958–59; Librarian, Fine Art Dept, Univ. of Edin. 1959–61; teacher, Edin. Coll. of Art 1962–86; Scottish Arts Council retrospective Exhbn Edin., Sheffield, Aberdeen, Liverpool, Cardiff 1981–82; participant in numerous group shows in UK, USA, Canada etc. British Painting 1952–77; Royal Acad., London 1977; HM Painter and Limner in Scotland 2000–; work includes drawings and watercolours (especially botanical), prints, lithographs, portraits, tapestries and stained glass (window commissioned by Nat. Library of Scotland 1987); Hon. FRSE; Hon. DLitt (Heriot-Watt) 1989, (Strathclyde) 1998; Dr hc (Edin.) 1990, (Stirling, St Andrews, London); Hon. LLD (Aberdeen) 1997, (Glasgow) 2001; Jt Winner, Watercolour Foundation Award, RA Summer Exhbn 1988. *Publication:* Favourite Flowers (with Deborah Kellaway) 1994. *Address:* 57 Fountainhall Road, Edinburgh, EH9 2LH, Scotland. *Telephone:* (131) 667-3687 (home).

BLACKBOURN, David Gordon, BA, PhD, FBA, FRHistS; British historian and academic; *Cornelius Vanderbilt Distinguished Chair and Professor of History, Vanderbilt University;* b. 1 Nov. 1949, Spilsby, Lincs.; s. of Harry Blackbourn and Pamela Jean Blackbourn; m. 1st Deborah Frances Langton (divorced); one s. one d.; m. 2nd Celia Stewart Applegate; ed Leeds Modern Grammar School, Christ's Coll., Cambridge; Research Fellow, Jesus Coll., Cambridge 1973–76; Lecturer in History, Queen Mary Coll., Univ. of London 1976–79, Birkbeck Coll. 1979–85, Reader in Modern History 1985–89, Prof. of Modern European History 1989–92; Coolidge Prof. of History, Harvard Univ., USA 1992–2012, Dir Minda de Gunzburg Center for European Studies 2007–12; Cornelius Vanderbilt Distinguished Chair and Prof. of History, Vanderbilt Univ. 2012–; lectures and contribs to confs in UK, Ireland, Germany, France, Italy, fmr Yugoslavia, USA and Canada 1973–; Fellow, Inst. for European History, Mainz, FRG 1974–75; Research Fellow, Alexander von Humboldt Foundation, Bonn-Bad Godesberg, FRG 1984–85, 1994–95; Visiting Kratter Prof. of German History, Stanford Univ., Calif., USA 1989–90; Fellow, Guggenheim Foundation, New York 1994–95; Sec. German History Soc. 1978–81, mem. Cttee 1981–86; mem. Academic Advisory Bd, German Historical Inst., London 1983–92; mem. Editorial Bd Past and Present 1988–2018; mem. European Sub-cttee of Labour Party Nat. Exec. Cttee 1978–80, Academic Advisory Bd, Inst. for European History, Mainz, Germany 1995–2005, Cttee on Hon. Foreign mems, American Historical Asscn 2000–02; Pres. Conf. Group on Cen. European History, American Historical Asscn 2003–04; mem. Advisory Bd, Edmund Spevack Memorial Foundation 2003–06, mem. Bd, Friends of the German Historical Inst., Washington, DC 2004, Chair. Bd 2007–; mem. Academic Advisory Bd Lichtenberg Coll. Univ. of Goettingen 2007–13; mem. Inst. for Advanced Study, Princeton Univ. 2017–18; mem. Editorial Bd, Central European History 2014–19, German Politics and Society 2017–18; Ed. Penguin Custom Editions: The Western World Database 2000–; consultant to SMASH/The History Channel, USA; Fellow, American Acad. of Arts and Sciences 2007; Visiting Fellow, Center for Advanced Study, Munich Univ. 2012; mem. Bd of Trustees, Nat. Humanities Center 2016–; gave Annual Lecture of German Historical Inst., London 1998, Malcolm Wynn Lecture, Stetson Univ., Fla. 2002, George C. Windell Memorial Lecture, Univ. of New Orleans 2006, Crayenborgh Lecture, Leiden Univ., Netherlands 2007, Jakob and Wilhelm Grimm Lecture, Univ. of Waterloo, Canada 2010; American Historical Asscn Book Prize 1996, Walter Channing Cabot Fellow, Harvard Univ. 2003–04, George L. Mosse Prize, American Historical Asscn 2007, Charles A. Weyerhaeuser Prize, Forest History Soc. 2007. *Publications include:* Class, Religion and Local Politics in Wilhelmine Germany 1980, The Peculiarities of German History (with Geoff Eley) 1984, Populists and Patricians: Essays in Modern German History 1987, Volksfrömmigkeit und Fortschrittsglaube im Kulturkampf 1988, The German Bourgeoisie (co-ed. with Richard J. Evans) 1991, Marpingen: Apparitions of the Virgin Mary in Bismarckian Germany 1993, The Fontana History of Germany: The Long Nineteenth Century 1780–1918 1997, The Conquest of Nature: Water, Landscape and the Making of Modern Germany 2006, Landschaften der deutschen Geschichte 2016; scholarly articles in English, German, French, Serbo-Croat, Japanese and Italian; contribs to several magazines and the BBC. *Leisure interests:* family, reading, music, sport, politics. *Address:* Department of History, Vanderbilt University, PMB 351802, 2301 Vanderbilt Place, Nashville, TN 37235, USA (office). *Telephone:* (615) 343-7196 (office). *E-mail:* david.blackbourn@vanderbilt.edu (office).

BLACKBURN, Elizabeth Helen, AC, BSc, MSc, PhD, FRS; Australian/American biochemist and academic; *Morris Herzstein Professor of Biology, Department of Biochemistry and Biophysics, University of California, San Francisco;* b. 26 Nov. 1948, Hobart, Tasmania, Australia; d. of Harold Stewart Blackburn and Marcia Constance Jack; m. John Sedat 1975; one s.; ed Univ. of Melbourne, Australia and Univ. of Cambridge, UK; Researcher, Molecular Biology Lab., Univ. of Cambridge 1971–74; Post grad. Researcher, Yale Univ., USA 1975–77; mem. Faculty Univ. of California, Berkeley 1978–90; Prof., Dept of Microbiology and Immunology, Univ. of California, San Francisco 1990, Dept Chair. 1993–99, currently Morris Herzstein Prof. of Biology and Physiology, Dept of Biochemistry and Biophysics; Steven and Michele Kirsch Foundation Investigator Fellowship 2000; Non-Resident Fellow, Salk Inst.; Memorial Sloan-Kettering Cancer Center Katharine Berkan Judd Award Lectureship 2001; Pres. American Soc. for Cell Biology 1998, American Asscn for Cancer Research 2010; mem. Bd Genetics Soc. of America 2000–02; mem. Pres.'s Council on Bioethics 2001–04; mem. American Acad. of Excellence 2000, Inst. of Medicine 2000; Foreign Assoc. NAS 1993; Fellow, American Acad. of Arts and Sciences 1991, American Acad. of Microbiology 1993, AAAS 2000, Royal Soc. of NSW 2010; Hon. DSc (Yale) 1991; Australian Soc. for Microbiology Prize 1967, Travelling Gowrie Research Scholar 1971–73, Anna Fuller Fund Fellowship 1975–77, Eli Lilly Research Award for Microbiology and Immunology 1988, NAS Award in Molecular Biology 1990, Gairdner Foundation Award 1998, Australia Prize 1998, California Scientist of the Year 1999, Novartis-Drew Award for Biomedical Science 1999, Feodor Lynen Award 2000, Dickson Prize in Medicine 2000, American Cancer Soc. Medal of Honor 2000, American Asscn for Cancer Research-Pezcoller Foundation Int. Award for Cancer Research 2001, General Motors Cancer Research Foundation Alfred P. Sloan Award 2001, Bristol-Meyers Squibb Award for Distinguished Achievement in Cancer Research 2003, Dr A. H. Heineken Prize for Medicine 2004, American Soc. for Cell Biology Public Service Award 2004, Benjamin Franklin Medal in Life Science 2005, Albert Lasker Award for Basic Medical Research (with Carol W. Greider and Jack W. Szostak) 2006, Genetics Prize, Peter Gruber Foundation 2006, Vanderbilt Prize in Biomedical Science 2007, named to the TIME 100 2007, L'Oréal-UNESCO Award for Women in Science 2008, Nobel Prize in Physiology or Medicine (with Carol W. Greider and Jack W. Szostak) 2009, inducted into California Hall of Fame 2011, Gold Medal, American Inst. of Chemists 2012, Royal Medal, Royal Soc. 2015. *Publications include:* numerous articles in scientific journals. *Leisure interest:* music. *Address:* Department of Biochemistry and Biophysics, University of California, 600 16th Street, GH-S312F, Box 2200, San Francisco, CA 94158-2517, USA (office). *Telephone:* (415) 476-2824 (office); (415) 476-7284 (Lab.) (office). *Fax:* (415) 514-2913 (office). *E-mail:* telomer@itsa.ucsf.edu (office); elizabeth.blackburn@ucsf.edu (office). *Website:* biochemistry2.ucsf.edu/labs/blackburn (office).

BLACKBURN, Hon. Jean-Pierre, PC, BBA, MA; Canadian politician, business executive and diplomatist; b. 6 July 1948, Jonquière, Quebec; m. Ginette Laforest; ed Université du Québec, Chicoutimi; MP (Jonquière—Alma) 1984–93, 2006–11; fmr Parl. Sec. to Minister of Nat. Defence; fmr Pres. Blackburn Communication Inc.; Minister of Labour and Minister of the Econ. Devt Agency of Canada for the Regions of Quebec 2006–08, of Nat. Revenue and Minister of State (Agric.) 2008–10, of Veterans Affairs 2010–11; Amb. and Perm. Del. to UNESCO, Paris 2012–14. *Address:* Foreign Affairs, Trade and Development Canada, Lester B. Pearson Building, 125 Sussex Drive, Ottawa, ON K1A 0G2, Canada (office). *Telephone:* (613) 944-4000 (office). *Fax:* (613) 996-9709 (office). *E-mail:* enqserv@international.gc.ca (office). *Website:* www.international.gc.ca (office).

BLACKBURN, Jeffrey Michael, BA, MBA, FCIB, FRSA, CVO; British business executive; *Senior Vice-President, Business Development, Amazon.com Inc.;* b. 16 Dec. 1941, Manchester; s. of Jeffrey Blackburn and Renee Blackburn; m. 2nd Louise Clair Jouny 1987; two s.; one s. one d. from previous m.; ed Northgate

Grammar School, Ipswich, Dartmouth Coll., Grad. School of Business, Stanford Univ., USA; Chief Man. Business Advisory Service, Lloyds Bank 1979–83; Dir and CEO Jt Credit Card Co. Ltd (Access) 1983–87, Leeds Permanent Building Society 1987–93; CEO Halifax Building Society (now Halifax PLC) 1993–98; Asst Vice-Pres. Deutsche Morgan Grenfell 1998; joined Amazon.com Inc. 1998, Vice-Pres. Operations Integration 2002–03, Vice-Pres. European Customer Service 2003–04, Vice-Pres. Business Devt 2004–06, Sr Vice-Pres. Business Devt 2006–; Pres. Chartered Inst. of Bankers 1998–99; mem. Bd of Dirs DFS Furniture PLC 1999–, George Wimpey PLC 1999–, Town Centre Securities PLC 1999–2003; mem. court, Univ. of Leeds 1989–2000; Companion, Chartered Man. Inst.; Gov. Nat. Youth Orchestra 1999–; Trustee, Duke of Edin.'s Award 1998–; Hon. DUniv (Leeds Metropolitan) 1998; Hon. DLitt (Huddersfield) 1998. *Leisure interest:* the arts. *Address:* Amazon.com Inc., PO Box 81226, Seattle, WA 98108-1226, USA (office). *Telephone:* (206) 266-2477 (office). *Fax:* (206) 266-1355 (office). *Website:* www.amazon.com (office).

BLACKBURN, Marsha, BS; American business executive and politician; *Senator from Tennessee;* b. 6 June 1952, Laurel, Miss.; d. of Hilman Wedgeworth and Mary Jo Wedgeworth (née Morgan); m. Chuck Blackburn; one s. one d.; ed Mississippi State Univ.; Man. Southwestern Co. 1971–73, Sales Man. 1973–75; Pres. Caster Knott Co. 1975–78; Exec. Dir, Tenn. Film, Entertainment, and Music Comm. 1995–97; currently founder and owner, Marketing Strategies; Senator, State of Tenn. 1998–2002; mem. US House of Reps 2002–19, Asst Minority Whip 2002–06; Senator from Tennessee 2019–; mem. Cttees on Commerce, Science & Transportation, Judiciary, Veterans' Affairs and Armed Services; mem. Advisory Bd, Smithsonian Libraries; mem. Brentwood Chamber of Commerce, Rotary Club; Republican; Hon. DLit (King Univ.); Conservative Leadership Award 2007, Woman of the Year 2016, Clare Boothe Luce Policy Inst., Congressional Grammy, Recording Acad. 2007, White Hat Award, Nashville Songwriters Asscn 2007, Platinum Award, Recording Industry Asscn of America 2008, Innovation Award, Health IT Now 2012, Woman of Valor, Independent Women's Forum 2014, Visionary Award, Cecil Scaife Foundation, Distinguished Leader Award and Jawed Angel Award for Excellence in Public Service, Family Research Council, Spirit of Enterprise Award, US Chamber of Commerce, Best and Brightest Award, American Conservative Union. *Address:* United States Senate, B40B Dirksen Senate Office Building, Washington, DC 20510, USA (office). *Telephone:* (202) 224-3344 (office). *Fax:* (202) 228-0566 (office). *Website:* www.blackburn.senate.gov (office); www.marshablackburn.com.

BLACKBURN, Simon W., PhD, DPhil, FBA; British philosopher and academic; *Distinguished Research Professor, University of North Carolina, Chapel Hill;* b. 12 July 1944, Bristol; s. of Cuthbert Blackburn and Edna Blackburn; m. Angela Bowles 1968; one s. one d.; ed Clifton Coll., Bristol and Trinity Coll., Cambridge; Research Fellow, Churchill Coll. Cambridge 1967–69; Fellow and Tutor in Philosophy, Pembroke Coll. Oxford 1969–90; Ed. Mind 1984–90; Edna J. Koury Distinguished Prof. of Philosophy, Univ. of North Carolina, Chapel Hill, USA 1990–2000, part-time Distinguished Research Prof. 2008–; Adjunct Prof., ANU 1993–; Prof. of Philosophy, Univ. of Cambridge 2001–11, Fellow, Trinity Coll. 2001–; Prof., New Coll. of the Humanities; Pres. Aristotelian Soc. 2009–10; Vice-Pres. British Humanist Asscn; Hon. Foreign mem. American Acad. of Arts and Sciences 2007, Australian Acad. of the Humanities 2015; Hon. LLD (Sunderland); Hon. DLitt (Glasgow). *Publications:* Reason and Prediction 1970, Spreading the Word 1984, Essays in Quasi-Realism 1993, The Oxford Dictionary of Philosophy 1994, Ruling Passions 1998, Truth (co-ed.) 1999, Think: A Compelling Introduction to Philosophy 1999, Being Good 2001, Lust 2004, Truth: A Guide for the Perplexed 2005, Plato's Republic: A Biography 2006, How to Read Hume 2008, Practical Tortoise Raising 2010, Mirror, Mirror: The Uses and Abuses of Self-Love 2014. *Leisure interests:* reading, travel, sailing. *Address:* Trinity College, Cambridge, CB2 1TQ (office); 141 Thornton Road, Cambridge, CB3 0NE, England (home). *Telephone:* (1223) 528278 (office). *E-mail:* swb24@cam.ac.uk (office). *Website:* www.phil.cam.ac.uk/~swb24 (office).

BLACKER, Coit D., AB, MS, PhD; American political scientist, academic, research institute director and international relations consultant; *Senior Fellow, Freeman Spogli Institute for International Studies and Olivier Nomellini Professor in International Studies, School of Humanities and Sciences, Stanford University;* ed Occidental Coll., Fletcher School of Law and Diplomacy, Tufts Univ.; Professor, Stanford Univ. 1978–, and succession of other positions at Stanford, including Dir of Studies, Center for Int. Security and Arms Control, Co-Chair. Int. Relations and Int. Policy Studies Programs, Olivier Nomellini Prof. in Int. Studies, School of Humanities and Sciences, Deputy Dir, Freeman Spogli Inst. for Int. Studies, now Dir and Sr Fellow; Assoc. Prof., School of Int. Relations, Univ. of Southern Calif., Dir ad interim Peace and Conflict Studies Program; Special Asst for Nat. Security Affairs to US Senator Gary Hart, then to Pres. Clinton during first admin; Sr Dir Russian, Ukrainian and Eurasian Affairs, Nat. Security Council; Co-Dir Aspen Inst. US-Russia Dialogue 1998–2003; mem. study group US Comm. on Nat. Security in the 21st Century; mem. Council on Foreign Relations; mem. Bd of Dirs Int. Research and Exchanges Bd, Washington, DC; Chair. Exec. Cttee of the Int. Initiative 2005–; mem. Stanford Bd of Trustees Cttee on Devt 2004–07; Dr hc (Russian Acad. of Sciences Inst. of Far Eastern Studies) 1993; Laurance and Naomi Carpenter Hoagland Prize for Undergraduate Teaching 2001. *Publications include:* International Arms Control: Issues and Agreements (co-Ed.) 1984, Reluctant Warriors: the United States, The Soviet Union and Arms Control 1987, Hostage to Revolution: Gorbachev and Soviet Security Policy, 1985–91 1993, NATO After Madrid: Looking to the Future (Vol I) (co-Ed.) 1999, Belarus and the Flight from Sovereignty 2001, Arms Control 2002. *Address:* Freeman Spogli Institute for International Studies, Stanford University, Encina Hall, C137, Stanford, CA 94305-6055, USA (office). *Telephone:* (650) 725-5368 (office). *Fax:* (650) 725-3435 (office). *E-mail:* cblacker@stanford.edu (office). *Website:* www.iis-db.stanford.edu (office).

BLACKMAN, Honor; British actress; b. 22 Aug. 1926, London. *Films include:* Fame is the Spur 1947, Green Grow the Rushes 1951, Come Die My Love 1952, The Rainbow Jacket 1953, The Glass Cage 1954, Dead Man's Evidence 1955, A Matter of Who 1961, Goldfinger 1964, Life at the Top 1965, Twist of Sand 1967, The Virgin and the Gipsy 1970, To the Devil a Daughter 1975, Summer Rain 1976, The Cat and the Canary 1977, Talos—The Mummy, To Walk With Lions, Bridget Jones's Diary 2001, Jack Brown and the Curse of the Crown 2001, Colour Me Kubrick: A Trueish Story 2005, Summer Solstice 2005, Reuniting the Rubins 2010, Cockneys vs Zombies 2011, I, Anna 2012. *Plays include:* Mademoiselle Colombe 2000, Cabaret 2007. *TV appearances include:* Four Just Men 1959, Man of Honour 1960, Ghost Squad 1961, Top Secret 1962, The Avengers 1962–64, The Explorer 1968, Visit from a Stranger 1970, Out Damned Spot 1972, Wind of Change 1977, Robin's Nest 1982, Never the Twain 1982, The Secret Adversary 1983, Lace 1985, The First Modern Olympics 1986, Minder on the Orient Express 1986, Dr. Who 1986, William Tell 1986, The Upper Hand (series) 1990–96, Jack and the Beanstalk: The Real Story 2001, Revolver (series) 2001–04, Midsomer Murders 2003, The Royal 2003, Coronation Street 2004, New Tricks (series) 2004, Summer Solstice (film) 2005, Sound (film) 2007, Hotel Babylon (series) 2009. *Website:* www.honorblackman.co.uk.

BLACKMOORE, Rayburn, BA; Dominican politician; *Minister of Justice, Immigration and National Security;* b. Mahaut; ed Humber Coll., York Univ., Canada; served as police officer for seventeen years, attaining rank of Sergeant –2000; MP (Dominica Labour Party—DLP) for Mahaut 2005–; fmr Parl. Sec., later Minister of State in Prime Minister's Office with responsibility for Security; Minister of Nat. Security, Immigration and Labour 2007–10, of Public Works, Energy and Ports 2010–14, Minister of Justice, Immigration and Nat. Security 2014–; Chair. Nat. Symposium on Crime 2003; Chair. Regional Security System –2008. *Address:* Ministry of Justice, Immigration and National Security, Government Headquarters, Kennedy Avenue, Roseau, Dominica (office). *Telephone:* 4482401 (office). *Fax:* 4488960 (office). *E-mail:* burnray@hotmail.com (office).

BLACKSTONE, Baroness (Life Peer), cr. 1987, of Stoke Newington in Greater London; **Rt Hon. Tessa Ann Vosper Blackstone,** PC, BSc, PhD; British politician and university vice-chancellor; b. 27 Sept. 1942, London; d. of Geoffrey Vaughan Blackstone, CBE, GM and Joanna Blackstone; m. Tom Evans 1963 (divorced, died 1985); one s. one d.; ed Ware Grammar School, London School of Econs, Univ. of London; Assoc. Lecturer, Enfield Coll. 1965–66; Asst Lecturer, then Lecturer, Dept of Social Admin., LSE 1966–75; Fellow, Centre for Studies in Social Policy 1972–74; Adviser, Cen. Policy Review Staff, Cabinet Office 1975–78; Prof. of Educational Admin., Univ. of London Inst. of Educ. 1978–83; Deputy Educ. Officer (Resources), then Clerk and Dir of Educ., Inner London Educ. Authority 1983–87; Master, Birkbeck Coll., Univ. of London 1987–97; mem. (Labour), House of Lords 1987–, Opposition Spokesperson on Educ. and Science, House of Lords 1990–92, on Foreign Affairs 1992–97; Minister of State in Dept of Educ. and Employment 1997–2001; Minister of State for the Arts, Dept for Culture, Media and Sport 2001–03; Dir, Royal Opera House 1987–97, Trustee 2010–; Chair. General Advisory Council BBC 1987–91, RIBA Trust 2003–10, Great Ormond Street Hosp. Trust 2009–; Chair. Bd of Trustees, Inst. for Public Policy Research 1988–97; Chair. British Library Bd 2011–18, Orbit Group Bd 2013–, Bar Standards Bd 2018–, British Lung Foundation 2018–; Co-Chair. Franco-British Council 2013–; mem. Bd of Dirs Thames TV 1991–92, Rover Learning Business Bd 1991–97, Granada Learning 2003–07, VT Group 2004–, Teachers TV 2004–09, Mott MacDonald 2005–08; Visiting Prof., LSE 2003–05; Vice-Chancellor, Univ. of Greenwich 2004–11; Trustee, British Museum (Natural History) 1992–97; Hon. Fellow, LSE 1995, Birkbeck Coll. 1998, Canterbury Christchurch Univ. 2010; Hon. DLitt (Bradford) 1990, (Bristol Polytechnic) 1991; Hon. DUniv (Middlesex) 1993, (Strathclyde) 1996, (Leeds Metropolitan) 1996; Hon. LLD (Aberdeen) 1994, (St Andrews) 1995; Dr hc (Dauphine, Sorbonne, Paris) 1998, (Univ. of Rome Roma 3) 2005, (Queen's, Belfast) 2007, (Kent) 2011, (Greenwich) 2012, Hon. DSc (Univ. of London) 2016. *Publications:* A Fair Start 1971, Education and Day Care for Young Children in Need 1973, Social Policy and Administration in Britain 1975; co-author: Students in Conflict 1970, The Academic Labour Market 1974, Disadvantage and Education 1982, Education Policy and Educational Inequality 1982, Response to Adversity 1983, Testing Children 1983, Inside the Think Tank: Advising the Cabinet 1971–83, 1988, Prisons and Penal Reform 1990, Race Relations in Britain 1997. *Leisure interests:* tennis, walking, ballet, opera, bridge. *Address:* House of Lords, Westminster, London, SW1A 0PW, England (office). *Telephone:* (20) 7219-5409 (office). *E-mail:* blackstonet@parliament.uk (office).

BLACKWELL, Kimberly L., MD; American oncologist and academic; *Assistant Professor in Radiation Oncology, School of Medicine, Duke University;* b. 1969; two s.; ed Duke Univ., Mayo Medical School; currently Prof. of Medicine and Asst Prof. of Radiation Oncology, Duke Univ. Medical Center, also Dir Breast Cancer Program, Duke Cancer Inst., Durham, NC; prin. investigator or co-prin. investigator in over 50 clinical trials in breast cancer. *Publications:* author or co-author of over 60 articles or book chapters in journals including Clinical Cancer Research, The Journal of Clinical Oncology, Cancer, Radiation Research, Molecular Cancer Therapeutics. *Address:* Duke University Medical Center 3893, Durham, NC 27710, USA (office). *Telephone:* (919) 668-1748 (office). *Fax:* (919) 681-0874 (office). *Website:* medicine.duke.edu (office).

BLACKWELL, Baron (Life Peer), cr. 1997, of Woodcote in the County of Surrey; **Norman Roy Blackwell,** MA, PhD, MBA; British business executive and fmr civil servant; *Non-Executive Chairman, Lloyds Banking Group Plc;* b. 29 July 1952, London; s. of Albert Edward Blackwell and Frances Evelyn Blackwell (née Lutman); m. Brenda Clucas 1974; three s. two d.; ed Latymer Upper School, Trinity Coll., Cambridge, Wharton Business School, Univ. of Pennsylvania (Thouron Scholar); Jr Exhibitioner, RAM 1963–69; Chair. Cambridge Univ. Conservative Asscn 1973; with Strategic Planning Unit, Plessey Co. 1976–78, McKinsey & Co. 1978–86, 1988–95 (Partner 1984), Prime Minister's Policy Unit 1986–88, Head 1995–97; Dir of Group Devt NatWest Group 1997–2000; Chair. Smartstream Technologies Group 2001–05, Interserve plc 2006–, Scottish Widows Group 2012–; Dir (non-exec.), Dixons Group 2000–03, Corp. Services Group 2000–06, SEGRO Plc 2001–10, Standard Life 2003–12, Halma Plc 2010–; Chair. (non-exec.), Lloyds Banking Group Plc 2012–; Special Adviser, KPMG Corp. Finance 2000–09; Chair. Centre for Policy Studies 2000–09; mem. Bd, Office of Fair Trading 2003–10, Ofcom 2009–; mem. (Conservative), House of Lords 1997–, mem. Delegated Powers and Regulatory Reform Cttee 2008–13, Secondary Legislation Scrutiny Cttee (fmrly Merits Cttee) 2013–14; Gov., The Yehudi Menuhin School 2016–. *Leisure interests:* classical music, walking. *Address:* Lloyds Banking Group Plc, 25 Gresham Street, London, EC2V 7HN (office); House of Lords, Westminster, London, SW1A 0PW, England. *Telephone:* (20) 7626-1500 (office); (20) 7219-5353. *Fax:* (20) 7356-2049 (office). *E-mail:* blackwelln@parliament.uk; info@lloydsbankinggroup.com (office). *Website:* www.lloydsbankinggroup.com (office); www.parliament.uk/biographies/lords/lord-blackwell/3550.

BLAGA, Vasile; Romanian politician; b. 26 July 1956, Petrileni, Bihor Co.; m.; two c.; ed Nat. Defence Coll., Timişoara Polytechnic Univ.; work team head, SC Hiperion SA, Bihor, then workshop head, plant section deputy head, plant section coordinating head, manager, 1981–90; Deputy of Bihor for Frontul Salvării Naţionale (Nat. Salvation Front) party 1990–91; Prefect of Bihor 1991–93; Gen. Dir, Oradea Customs Regional Authority 1993–96; Senator of Bihor 1996–2000, of Bucharest 2004–; Minister of Admin and Interior Affairs 2004–07, interim Minister of the Interior Oct. 2009, Minister of Devt and Tourism Nov. 2009, of the Interior and Admin. Reform Dec. 2009–10 (resgnd); cand. for Mayor of Bucharest 2008; Pres. Senate 2011–12; Founding mem. Partidul Democrat (PD—Democratic Party, later renamed Partidul Democrat Liberal—PD-L—Democratic Liberal Party), Pres. of Bihor Co. PD Org. 1991–97, Sec.-Gen. PD 1997–2001, 2005–08, Sec.-Gen. PD-L 2008–11, Pres. PD Bucharest, party Vice-Pres. 2001–04, Pres. PD-L 2012–14, Co-Pres. Partidul Naţional Liberal (PNL—Nat. Liberal Party) 2014–16; mem. Alianţa Dreptare şi Adevăr (Justice and Truth Alliance) 2003–04. *Address:* c/o Partidul Naţional Liberal (National Liberal Party), 011866 Bucharest 1, Bd Aviatorilor 86, Romania (office). *Telephone:* (21) 2310795 (office). *Fax:* (21) 2310796 (office). *E-mail:* dre@pnl.ro (office). *Website:* www.pnl.ro (office).

BLAGOJEVICH, Rod R., BA, JD; American fmr politician; b. 10 Dec. 1956, Chicago, Ill.; s. of Rade Blagojevich and Millie Blagojevich (née Govedarica); m. Patricia Blagojevich; two d.; ed Northwestern Univ., Pepperdine Univ.; est. pvt. law practice, Chicago 1983; Asst State Attorney, Cook Co. 1983–92; mem. Ill. Gen. Ass. 1992–96; mem. US House of Reps, Washington, DC 1997–2003; Gov. of Ill. 2003–09, impeached and removed from office, convicted of 17 public corruption charges, sentenced to 14 years in prison 2011, pending appeal with US Court of Appeals for the Seventh Circuit Dec. 2013, sentence upheld April 2017; Democrat; Library Man of the Year, American Library Assen, Friends of Libraries USA, Whitehouse Conf. on Libraries. *Publication:* The Governor 2009.

BLAHNIK, Manolo, CBE; Spanish couturier; b. 28 Nov. 1942, Santa Cruz, Canary Islands; ed Univ. of Geneva; studied architecture and literature but left univ. and travelled to Paris 1968; moved to London and worked briefly as photographer for Sunday Times 1970; cr. first shoe collection 1972; Founder and Dir Manolo Blahnik International Ltd; opened shop in Chelsea, London 1973, USA 1981, Hong Kong 1991; biannual collections in London and New York; Hon. Royal Designer for Industry, Royal Soc. of Arts (GB) 2001; La Medalla de Oro en Merito en las Bellas Artes 2002; Hon. CBE 2007; Dr hc (RCA) 2001, (Bath Spa Univ.) 2012; Council of Fashion Designers of America Awards 1987, 1990, 1998, American Leather New York Award 1991, British Fashion Award 1992, Neiman Marcus Award 1993, 2000, Accessory Designer of the Year, British Fashion Council 1990, 1999, 2003, Footwear News Designer of the Year Award 1998, 2003, Lifetime Achievement Award 2011, Silver Slipper Award, Houston Museum of Fine Art 1999, La Aguja de Oro (Spain) 2001, La Medalla de Oro de Canarias 2003, Accessory Designer of the Year Award, British Style Awards 2003, Pinnacle in Art & Design Award, Pratt Inst., New York (USA) 2005, Lifetime Achievement Award, Telva Magazine 2005, Prix de la Mode: Outstanding Achievement Award, Marie Claire (Spain) 2008, André Leon Talley Lifetime Achievement Award, Savannah Coll. of Art & Design (USA) 2011. *Publications:* Manolo Blahnik Drawings 2003, Manolo's New Shoes 2010, The Tale of the Elves and the Shoemaker (illustrator) 2011; various int. publs on fashion. *Leisure interests:* painting, reading, watching old films. *Address:* 30 Welbeck Street, London, W1G 8ER, England (office). *Telephone:* (20) 7352-8622 (office). *Fax:* (20) 7351-7314 (office). *E-mail:* info@manoloblahnik.com (office). *Website:* www.manoloblahnik.com (office).

BLAINEY, Geoffrey Norman, AC; Australian historian and author; b. 11 March 1930, Melbourne, Vic.; s. of Rev. Samuel C. Blainey and Hilda Blainey; m. Ann Heriot 1957; one d.; ed Ballarat High School, Wesley Coll., Univ. of Melbourne; freelance historian 1951–61; Reader in Econ. History, Univ. of Melbourne 1963–68, Prof. 1968–76, Ernest Scott Prof. of History 1977–88, Dean of Faculty of Arts 1982–87, now Emer. Prof.; Prof. of Australian Studies, Harvard Univ., USA 1982–83; columnist in daily newspapers 1974–2012; Deputy Chair. Nat. Inquiry into Museums 1974–75; Commr, Australian Heritage Comm. 1976–77; Chair. Australia Council 1977–81, Chair. Fed. Govt's Australia-China Council 1979–84, Chair. Commonwealth Literary Fund 1971–73; Pres. Council, Queen's Coll., Univ. of Melbourne 1971–89; Chair. Australian Selection Cttee Commonwealth Fund (Harkness) Fellowships 1983–90; Chancellor Univ. of Ballarat 1994–98; Dir Royal Humane Soc. 1996–2004; Gov. Ian Potter Foundation 1991–2015; Councillor, Nat. Council for the Centenary of Fed. 1997–2002 (Chair. 2001–02), Bd Australian War Memorial 1997–2004; Del. to Australian Constitutional Convention 1998; Trustee, Deafness Foundation 1992–; Hon. LLD (Melbourne, Ballarat) 2002; Gold Medal, Australian Literature Soc. 1963, Capt. Cook Bicentenary Literary Award 1970, Britannica Award for dissemination of learning, New York 1988, Dublin Prize 1986, Australian Authors' Soc. Book of the Year 2000, Centenary Medal 2003, Prime Minister's Prize for Australian History 2015, John Douglas Kerr Medal of Distinction 2017. *Television includes:* The Blainey View (10-part series for ABC) 1982–83. *Publications include:* The Peaks of Lyell 1954, Gold and Paper: A History of the National Bank 1958, Mines in the Spinifex 1960, The Rush That Never Ended 1963, A History of Camberwell 1965, If I Remember Rightly: The Memoirs of W. S. Robinson 1966, The Tyranny of Distance 1966, Wesley College: The First Hundred Years (co-author and ed.) 1967, Across a Red World 1968, The Rise of Broken Hill 1968, The Steel Master 1971, The Causes of War 1973, Triumph of the Nomads: A History of Ancient Australia 1975, A Land Half Won 1980, The Blainey View 1982, Our Side of the Country 1984, All for Australia 1984, The Great Seesaw 1988, A Game of Our Own 1990, Eye on Australia 1991, Odd Fellows 1992, The Golden Mile 1993, Jumping over the Wheel 1993, A Shorter History of Australia 1994, White Gold 1997, In Our Time 1999, A Short History of the World 2000, This Land is All Horizons 2001, Black Kettle and Full Moon: Daily Life in a Vanished Australia 2003, A Very Short History of the World 2004, A Short History of the Twentieth Century 2005, A History of Victoria 2006, Sea of Dangers: Captain Cook and His Rivals 2009, A Short History of Christianity 2011, A History of Australia's People Vol. 1 2015, Vol. 2 2016. *Leisure interests:* travel, wood chopping, Australian football. *Address:* PO Box 257, East Melbourne, VIC 8002, Australia (home). *Telephone:* (3) 9417-7782 (home).

BLAIR, Rt Hon. Anthony (Tony) Charles Lynton, PC, BA; British barrister, consultant and fmr politician; b. 6 May 1953, Edinburgh, Scotland; s. of Leo Blair and Hazel Blair; m. Cherie Booth (q.v.) 1980; three s. one d.; ed Fettes Coll., Edinburgh, St John's Coll., Oxford; barrister, specializing in trade union and employment law; MP for Sedgefield 1983–2007; Shadow Spokesman on the Treasury 1984–87, on Trade and Industry 1987–88, on Energy 1988–89, on Employment 1989–92, on Home Affairs 1992–94; Leader of the Labour Party 1994–2007; Prime Minister, First Lord of the Treasury and Minister for the Civil Service 1997–2007 (re-elected 2001, 2005); Special Envoy to Middle East on behalf of Quartet (USA, Russia, EU and UN) 2007–15 (resgnd); Chair. European Council on Tolerance and Reconciliation 2015–; mem. Bd of Dirs World Econ. Forum Foundation Bd 2007–; f. Tony Blair Sports Foundation 2007, Tony Blair Faith Foundation; Founder and Patron, Africa Governance Initiative; Founder and Exec. Chair. Tony Blair Institute for Global Change 2016–; Sr Adviser, JP Morgan Chase & Co. 2008–; Adviser, Zurich Financial Services working on int. politics and climate change 2008–, Khosla Ventures working on investment in environmentally friendly technologies 2010–, Albanian Govt in joining EU 2013; Howland Distinguished Fellow, Yale Univ. 2008–09; Hon. Bencher, Lincoln's Inn 1994; Hon. LLD (Northumbria) 1995; numerous awards including Charlemagne Prize 1999, Ellis Island Medal of Honor for Int. Leadership 2003, US Congressional Gold Medal of Honor 2003, Thomas J. Dodd Prize in Int. Justice and Human Rights (jtly) 2003, Polio Eradication Champion, Rotary International 2006, US Presidential Medal of Freedom 2009, Dan David Prize for present leadership 2009, Philadelphia Liberty Medal 2010, Global Legacy Award, Save the Children 2014, Philanthropist of the Year, GQ magazine 2014, Lincoln Leadership Prize, Abraham Lincoln Presidential Library Foundation 2018. *Publications:* New Britain: My Vision of a Young Country 1996, The Third Way 1998, A Journey 2010. *Address:* The Office of Tony Blair, PO Box 60519, London, W2 7JU, England (office). *E-mail:* info@institute.global (office). *Website:* institute.global (office); ectr.eu.

BLAIR, Cherie (see BOOTH, Cherie).

BLAIR, Dennis Cutler, BA; American naval officer (retd) and government official; b. 4 Feb. 1947, Kittery, Me; s. of Capt. Carvel Hall Blair and Abbie Dora Blair (née Ansel); m. Diane Blair; one s. one d.; ed US Naval Acad., Univ. of Oxford, UK; commissioned as ensign in USN, attained rank of Vice-Adm., Commdr USS Cochrane 1984–86, mem. Naval Staff, Pearl Harbor 1988–89, Kittyhawk Battlegroup 1993–95; Assoc. Dir Mil. Support, CIA 1995–96, also mem. Nat. Security Council; Dir Jt Staff 1996–99; C-in-C US Pacific Command, HI 1999–2002 (retd); Sr Fellow, Inst. for Defence Analyses 2002–03, Pres. 2003–07, then consultant; US Dir of Nat. Intelligence, Washington, DC 2009–10 (resgnd); held John M. Shalikashvili Chair in Nat. Security Studies, Nat. Bureau of Asian Research and Gen. of the Army Omar N. Bradley Chair of Strategic Leadership, Dickinson Coll. and US Army War Coll.; served as Deputy Exec. Dir Project on Nat. Security Reform; mem. IISS Council, Energy Security Leadership Council of Securing America's Future Energy, Aspen Homeland Security Council; mem. Bd of Dirs Nat. Bureau of Asian Research, Nat. Cttee on US-China Relations; mem. Bd of Trustees Freedom House; Defense Distinguished Service Medal with three oak leaf clusters, Defense Superior Service Medal, Legion of Merit, Meritorious Service Medal, Navy and Marine Corps Commendation Medal, Navy and Marine Corps Achievement Medal, Nat. Intelligence Distinguished Service Medal with star. *Publication:* Military Engagement: Influencing Armed Forces Worldwide to Support Democratic Transitions 2013.

BLAIS, Marie-Claire, CC; Canadian writer; b. 5 Oct. 1939, Québec City; d. of Fernando Blais and Véronique Nolin; ed studied in Québec, Paris, France and USA; Guggenheim Foundation Fellowship, New York 1963, 1964; mem. Royal Soc. of Canada, Acad. Royale de Belgique, Acad. des Lettres françaises; Hon. mem. Boivin Center of French Language and Culture, Univ. of Massachusetts, USA, Hon. Prof., Univ. of Calgary 1978; Chevalier, Légion d'honneur; Dr hc (York Univ.) 1975, (Lyon) 2003, (Ottawa) 2004, (Lyon) 2005; Prix de la langue française 1961, Prix France-Québec 1964, Prix Médicis 1966, Prix de l'Acad. Française 1983, Prix Athanase-David (Québec) 1983, Prix Nessim Habif (Acad. Royale de Belgique) 1991, Prix de la Fondation Prince Pierre de Monaco, Prix du Gouverneur Général (Canada) (three times), Prix Gilles Corbeil 2005, Matt Cohen Award 2006, and others. *Publications include:* La belle bête 1959, Tête blanche 1960, Le jour est noir 1962, Existences (poems), Pays voilés (poems) 1964, Une saison dans la vie d'Emmanuel 1965, L'insoumise 1966, Les voyageurs sacrés 1966, David Sterne 1967, L'océan 1967, L'exécution 1968, Manuscrits de Pauline Archange 1968, Vivre, vivre 1969, Les apparences 1970, Le loup 1972, Un Joualonais sa Joualonie 1973, Théâtre radiophonique 1974, Fièvre 1974, Une liaison parisienne 1976, La nef des sorcières 1976, Les nuits de l'underground 1978, Le sourd dans la ville 1980, Visions d'Anna 1982, Pierre 1984, Sommeil d'hiver 1985, Fière 1985, L'île 1988 (plays), L'ange de la solitude (novel) 1989, Un jardin dans la tempête (play) 1990, Parcours d'un Ecrivain: Notes Américaines (essay) 1993, L'Exile (short stories) 1993, Soifs (novel) 1995, Théâtre (Ed.), Des Rencontres Humaines 2002, Dans la foudre et la lumière (novel) 2002, Noces à midi au-dessus de l'abîme (play) 2004, Augustino et le choeur de la destruction (novel) 2007, Naissance de Rebecca à l'ère des Tourments (Gov. Gen's Award for Fiction) 2008, Mal au Bal des Prédateurs 2010, Le jeune homme sans avenir 2012, Aux jardins des acacias 2014, Le festin au crépuscule 2015, Des chants pour Angel 2017, Une réunion près de la mer 2018. *Leisure interests:* painting and drawing, cycling, handwriting analysis, travel. *Address:* c/o Patrick Leimgruber, Agence Goodwin, 839 Sherbrooke Street, Suite 2, Montréal, H26 1K6, Canada (office); 717 Windsor Lane, Key West, FL 33040, USA (home). *Telephone:* (514) 598-5252 (office); (305) 292-9450 (home). *Fax:* (514) 598-1878 (office). *E-mail:* pleimgruber@agencegoodwin.com (office).

BLAIS, Hon. Pierre, PC, BA, LLL; Canadian lawyer, fmr judge, politician and academic; *Chairman and CEO, Canadian Security Intelligence Review Committee;* b. 30 Dec. 1948, Berthier-sur-Mer, Québec; m. Chantal Fournier; two s. two d.; ed Sainte-Anne-de-la-Pocatière Coll., Laval Univ.; mem. House of Commons 1984–93; Parl. Sec. to Minister of Agric. 1984–86, to Deputy Prime Minister 1986–87; Solicitor-Gen. of Canada 1989–90; Minister of State (Agric.) 1990; Minister of Consumer and Corp. Affairs 1990–93; Minister of Justice, Attorney-Gen. and Pres.

Privy Council 1993; Partner, Langlois Gaudreau law practice, Québec 1993–98; Judge, Fed. Court of Canada, Trial Division and ex officio mem. Court of Appeal and Judge, Court Martial Appeal Court of Canada 1998; mem. Competition Tribunal 2002–08; Pres. Public Servants Disclosure Protection Tribunal 2007–08; Judge, Fed. Court of Appeal 2008–14, Chief Justice 2009–14; Chair. and CEO Canadian Security Intelligence Review Cttee 2015–(20), Quebec Judges Remuneration Review Cttee 2016–18; Fellow, Inst. of Advanced Legal Studies, Univ. of London, UK 2008. *Leisure interests:* skiing, reading, swimming, tennis. *E-mail:* blaipie@outlook.com (home).

BLAKE, Francis (Frank) S., BA, JD; American lawyer and business executive; *Chairman and CEO, The Home Depot Inc.;* b. 30 Aug. 1949, Boston, Mass; s. of George Baty Blake and Rosemary Blake (née Shaw); m. Anne McChristian 1977; one s. one d.; ed Harvard Coll., Columbia Univ. School of Law; Legis. Aide, Jt Cttee on Social Welfare, Mass Legislature, Boston 1971–73; law clerk, US Court of Appeals, NY 1976–77, to Justice Stevens, US Supreme Court, Washington, DC 1976–78; Assoc., Leva, Hawes, Symington, Martin & Oppenheimer 1978–81; Deputy Counsel to Vice-Pres. George Bush, The White House 1981–83; Partner, Swidler Berlin & Strelw 1983–85; Gen. Counsel, US Environmental Protection Agency 1985–88; Vice-Pres. and Gen. Counsel, GE Power Systems 1991–95, Vice-Pres. Business Devt & Alliances 1995–98, Pres. Business Devt 1998–2000, Sr Vice-Pres. Corp. Business Devt and Gen. Counsel 2000–01; Deputy Sec. US Dept of Energy 2001–02; Exec. Vice-Pres. Business Devt and Corp. Operations, The Home Depot Inc. 2002–07, Vice-Chair. and Exec. Vice-Pres. 2006–07, Chair. and CEO 2007–; mem. Bd of Dirs Southern Co., Atlanta 2004–, Hudson Inst., Washington, DC, Georgia Aquarium. *Address:* The Home Depot Inc., 2455 Paces Ferry Road, NW, Atlanta, GA 30339-4024, USA (office). *Telephone:* (770) 433-821 (office). *Fax:* (770) 384-2356 (office). *E-mail:* info@homedepot.com (office). *Website:* www.homedepot.com (office).

BLAKE, John Clemens, MA, RCA; American artist; b. 11 Jan. 1945, Providence, RI; s. of John Holland Blake and Elizabeth Clemens (now Romano); ed Carnegie Inst. of Tech. (now Carnegie-Mellon Univ.), Yale Univ., Royal Coll. of Art, London; freelance visual artist in various media including drawing, installations, photographic constructions, film and time-based works, etc.; teaching positions include Hull Polytechnic 1975–76, London Coll. of Printing 1978–82, S Glamorgan Inst. of Higher Educ., S Wales 1983–84, W. de Kooning Academie, Rotterdam 1988–2009; residencies include Hokkaido Fellowship, Japan 1984, Banff Centre for the Arts, Canada 1992, Bemis Center for the Arts, Omaha, Neb., USA 2000; Nat. Endowment (USA) 1977; has lived and worked in London and Amsterdam/Woerden 1967–; Fulbright Fellow 1967–69, Nat. Endowment for the Arts 1977, Arts Council Award (UK) 1979, Hokkaido Foundation Award (Japan) 1984. *Works in public collections:* Stedelijk Museum, Amsterdam, Museum Fodor, Amsterdam, Rijksmuseum Kroller-Muller, Otterlo, British Council, London, Eastern Arts Asscn, Cambridge, Musée de Toulon, France, Nat. Gallery of Australia, Melbourne, Stadhuis Middelburg, Netherlands, Tate Gallery, London, Museum Sztucki, Łódź, Arts Council of GB, London, Frans Hals Museum, Haarlem, Victoria & Albert Museum, London, Haagsgemeentemuseum, The Hague, Rijksdienst Collectie, Netherlands, Museum Pavillions, Almere, Netherlands, Muzeum Narodowe, Warsaw, Van Reekum Museum, Apeldoorn, Netherlands, New Museum of Contemporary Art, Warsaw, Museum of Contemporary Art, Krakow, Poland. *Commissioned works and works in public spaces include:* photo-construction installation (outdoor) for Entrepotdok (residential and business complex), Amsterdam 1987, Verpleeghuis 'De Vijf Havens' (jtly), Zevenkamp 1989, Light Trap (jtly) for St Jacobus Ziekenhuis, Zwijndrecht 1990, Veurs Coll., Leideschedam, Netherlands 1991, Haags Montessori Lyceum, The Hague 1991, photo-construction for 'De Cascade', Prov. Archive Offices, Groningen 1998, Dukaat/De Aker (residential and business complex, in collaboration with Tangram Architekten), Osdorp, Amsterdam 2000, outdoor installation incorporating two tram shelters and related object for Kunsthalte With de Withstraat – 'De hals', Museum Quarter/Westersingel, Rotterdam 2000. *Films:* Tongue Film, Arrest 1970, Rose, Focus A/B, Untitled (Juggler) 1972, Five Glass Panes Broken/Not Broken 1973, Bridge Film 1974. *Publications:* catalogue of ICA, London 1980, De Vleeshal in De Vleeshal: Their Eves/Hun Ogen (two catalogues) (co-author) 1983, 600 Eyes for Krzysztofory (text and photos) 1987, River: A Work in Almere (text and photos) 1991, Guard 1991, River 1991, John Blake on Aleph 1993, On the Ideal Place 1994, Remember Wtedy i Teraz: Teraz i Wtedy: John Blake's Works in Poland 1980–1994 1995, John Blake: Bunker—München 1996, De Hals: Kunsthalte witte de Withstraat 2000, S-P-I-N-E (with Peter Mason) 2002. *Address:* c/o J. P. Blonk, Gedempte Binnengracht 19A, 3441 AE Woerden, The Netherlands (office). *Telephone:* (348) 481850 (office). *Fax:* (348) 482554 (office). *E-mail:* jb@studiojohnblake.com. *Website:* www.studiojohnblake.com.

BLAKE, Sir Peter Thomas, Kt, CBE, RA, ARCA, RDI; British artist; b. 25 June 1932, Dartford, Kent, England; s. of Kenneth William Blake; m. 1st Jann Haworth 1963 (divorced 1982); two d.; m. 2nd Chrissy Wilson 1987; one d.; ed Gravesend Tech. Coll., Gravesend School of Art, Royal Coll. of Art; third assoc. artist of Nat. Gallery, London 1994–96; works exhibited in Inst. of Contemporary Art 1958, 1960, Guggenheim Competition 1958, Cambridge 1959, Royal Acad. 1960, Musée d'Art Moderne, Paris 1963; works in perm. collections, Trinity Coll., Cambridge, Carlisle City Gallery, Tate Gallery, Arts Council of GB, Museum of Modern Art, New York, Victoria and Albert Museum, other major galleries; designed cover of Beatles' album Sgt. Pepper's Lonely Hearts Club Band 1967, posters for Live Aid 1985, Live 8 2005; Hon. Academician, Royal West of England Acad., Bristol 2014; Dr hc (RCA), (Brunel) 2010, (Roehampton) 2010; Hon. DMus (Leeds) 2011; Hon. Dr of Art (Nottingham Trent) 2011. *Publications:* illustrations for Oxford Illustrated Old Testament 1968, Venice Fantasies, several Arden Shakespeares, Alice Through the Looking Glass, Peter Blake's ABC, Peter Blake Alphabets, Peter Blake Design, Paris Escapades 2011, and in various periodicals and magazines. *Leisure interests:* sculpture, wining and dining, going to rock and roll concerts, Chelsea Football Club. *Address:* c/o Waddington Galleries Ltd, 11 Cork Street, London, W1X 2LT, England.

BLAKE, Sir Quentin Saxby, Kt, CBE, OBE, RDI, MA, FCSD, KBE; British artist, writer, illustrator and teacher; b. 16 Dec. 1932, Sidcup, Kent; s. of William Blake and Evelyn Blake; ed Downing Coll., Cambridge, London Inst. of Educ., Chelsea School of Art; freelance illustrator 1957–; Tutor, RCA 1965–86, Head of Illustration Dept 1978–86, Sr Fellow RCA 1988, Visiting Prof. 1989–; first British Children's Laureate 1999–2001; Hon. Fellow, Univ. of Brighton 1996, Downing Coll. Cambridge 2000, Cardiff Univ. 2006, Hon. RA, Hon. Freeman, City of London 2015; Officier and Chevalier, Ordre des Arts et des Lettres 2002, Chevalier, Légion d'honneur 2014; Dr hc (London Inst.) 2000, (Northumbria) 2001, (RCA) 2001, (Open Univ.) 2006, (Loughborough) 2007, (Anglia Ruskin Univ.); Hon. DLitt (Cambridge) 2004. *Publications include:* Patrick 1968, Angelo 1970, Mister Magnolia 1980, Quentin Blake's Nursery Rhyme Book 1983, The Story of the Dancing Frog 1984, Mrs Armitage on Wheels 1987, Mrs Armitage Queen of the Road, Quentin Blake's ABC 1989, All Join In 1992, Cockatoos 1992, Simpkin 1993, La Vie de la Page 1995, The Puffin Book of Nonsense Verse 1996, Mrs Armitage and the Big Wave 1997, The Green Ship 1998, Clown 1998, Drawing for the Artistically Undiscovered (with John Cassidy) 1999, Fantastic Daisy Artichoke 1999, Words and Pictures 2000, The Laureate's Party 2000, Zagazoo 2000, Tell Me a Picture 2001, Loveykins 2002, A Sailing Boat in the Sky 2002, Laureate's Progress 2002, Angel Pavement 2004, The Life of Birds 2005, You're Only Young Twice 2008, Daddy Lost his Head 2009, Quentin Blake: Beyond the Page 2012; illustrations for over 250 works for children and adults, including collaborations with Roald Dahl, Russell Hoban, Joan Aiken, Michael Rosen, John Yeoman, Michael Morpurgo, David Walliams. *Address:* c/o AP Watt at United Agents LLP, 12–26 Lexington Street, London, W1F 0LE, England (office). *Telephone:* (20) 3214-0800 (office). *Fax:* (20) 3214-0801 (office). *E-mail:* info@unitedagents.co.uk (office). *Website:* www.quentinblake.com.

BLAKE, Robert O., Jr, MA; American diplomatist (retd); *Senior Director, McLarty Associates;* b. 1957; s. of Robert O. Blake and Sylvia Whitehouse; m. Sofia Blake; three d.; ed Harvard Coll., Johns Hopkins School of Advanced Int. Studies; career mem. Sr Foreign Service since 1985, has served at Embassies in Tunis, Algiers, Abuja and Cairo, has also held several positions at Dept of State, Washington, DC, Deputy Chief of Mission, New Delhi 2003–06, Amb. to Sri Lanka (also accred to the Maldives) 2006–09, Asst Sec., Bureau of South and Cen. Asian Affairs 2009–13, Amb. to Indonesia 2013–16; Man. Dir Washington Office, American Inst. in Taiwan 2014–; Sr Dir India & South Asia Practice, McLarty Assocs 2016–; mem. Bd, US-Indonesia Soc.; Distinguished Service Award, US State Department. *Address:* McLarty Associates, 900 Seventeenth Street, NW Suite 800, Washington, DC 20006, USA (office). *Telephone:* (202) 419-1420 (office). *E-mail:* info@maglobal.com (office). *Website:* maglobal.com (office).

BLAKE, Yohan; Jamaican track and field athlete; b. 26 Dec. 1989, St James; s. of Shirley Blake and Veda Blake; ed St Jago High School; gold medal, 100m, 200m, Caribbean Free Trade Asscn (CARIFTA) Games (Youth), Bacolet 2005, gold medal, 200m, 4×100m relay, CARIFTA Games (Junior), Les Abymes 2006; gold medal, 100m, 200m, 4×100m relay, Central American and Caribbean (CAC) Junior Championships (U20), Port of Spain 2006; gold medal, 4×100m relay, bronze medal, 100m, World Junior Championships, Beijing 2006; gold medal, 100m, 4×100m relay, CARIFTA Games (Junior), Providenciales 2007; silver medal, 100m, bronze medal, 4×400m relay, Pan American Junior Championships, São Paulo 2007; gold medal, 100m, CARIFTA Games (Junior), Basseterre 2008; silver medal, 4×100m relay, World Junior Championships, Bydgoszcz 2008; gold medal, 100m (9.92 seconds, became youngest 100m world champion ever), 4×100m relay, World Championships, Daegu 2011; won 100m, Diamond League, Zurich 2011, 200m, Brussels 2011; gold medal, 100m, Int. Asscn of Athletics Feds (IAAF) World Challenge, Berlin 2011, gold medal, 100m, Kingston 2011, silver medal, 200m, Ostrava 2011, gold medal, 200m, Kingston 2012; gold medal, 4×100m relay, silver medal, 100m, 200m, Olympic Games, London 2012; gold medal, 4×100m relays, 4×200m relays, IAAF World Relays 2014; gold medal, 4×100m Olympic Games, Rio 2016; est. YB Afraid Foundation 2011; holds nat. (junior) record for 100m, is the youngest sprinter to have broken 10-second barrier (at 19 years, 196 days); coached by Glen Mills; Austin Sealy Trophy for Most Outstanding Athlete, CARIFTA Games 2007. *Leisure interest:* cricket. *Address:* c/o Racers Track Club, 3 Port of Spain Drive, University of the West Indies, Mona, Kingston, Jamaica. *Telephone:* 970-4854 (home). *E-mail:* admin@racerstrackclub.com; contact@ybafraidfoundation.org (office). *Website:* www.racerstrackclub.com; www.ybafraid.com (office).

BLAKELY, Sara, BA; American business executive; *Founder, Spanx Inc.;* b. 21 Feb. 1971, Clearwater, Fla; m. Jesse Itzler 2008; one s.; ed Florida State Univ.; began career as sales rep. with Danka Business Systems (fax and photocopier co.), Tampa; f. Spanx Inc. (based on own prototype design for shapewear lingerie) 2000; f. Sara Blakely Foundation (charitable foundation) 2006; TV appearances include The Rebel Billionaire (Fox TV) 2004, judge on American Inventor (ABC) 2007; named by Forbes Magazine as world's youngest self-made female billionaire 2012. *Address:* Spanx Inc., 3344 Peachtree Road NE, #1700, Atlanta, GA 30305, USA (office). *Telephone:* (404) 321-1608 (office). *Website:* www.spanx.com (office).

BLAKEMORE, Sir Colin (Brian), Kt, PhD, ScD, DSc, FRS, FMedSci, CBiol; British neuroscientist and academic; *Director, Centre for the Study of the Senses and Professor of Neuroscience and Philosophy, School of Advanced Study, University of London;* b. 1 June 1944, Stratford-upon-Avon, Warwicks.; s. of Cedric Norman and Beryl Ann Blakemore; m. Andrée Elizabeth Washbourne 1965; three d.; ed King Henry VIII School, Coventry, Corpus Christi Coll., Cambridge, Univ. of California, Berkeley, USA; Harkness Fellowship, Univ. of California, Berkeley 1965–67; Univ. Demonstrator, Physiological Lab., Univ. of Cambridge 1968–72, Lecturer in Physiology 1972–79, Fellow and Dir of Medical Studies, Downing Coll. Cambridge 1971–79; Visiting Prof., New York Univ. 1970, MIT 1971, Univ. of Toronto 1984, McMaster Univ. 1992, Univ. of California, Davis 1980, 1995–97; Visiting Scientist, Salk Inst., San Diego 1982–83, 1992; Locke Research Fellow, Royal Soc. 1976–79; Waynflete Prof. of Physiology, Univ. of Oxford 1979–2007, Prof. of Neuroscience 2007–12, Prof. Emer. 2012–; Prof. of Physiology, Univ. of Warwick; Prof. of Neuroscience and Philosophy, School of Advanced Study, Univ. of London 2012–, Dir Centre for the Study of the Senses; Professorial Fellow, Magdalen Coll. Oxford 1979–; Vice-Chair. European Dana Alliance for the Brain 1996–; CEO MRC 2003–07; Vice-Pres. BAAS 1990–97, 1998–2001, Pres. 1997–98, Chair. 2001–03; Pres. British Neuroscience Asscn 1997–2000, Physiological Soc. 2001–03, Biosciences Fed. 2002–04; Dir McDonnell-Pew Centre for Cognitive Neuroscience, Oxford 1990–2003, MRC Interdisciplinary Research Centre for Cognitive Neuroscience, Oxford 1996–2003; Assoc. Dir MRC

Research Centre in Brain and Behaviour, Oxford 1990–96; Commr UK Drug Policy Comm. 2006–; mem. Advisory Council Asscn of the British Pharmaceutical Industry 2007–; Chair. Gen. Advisory Cttee on Science, Food Standards Agency 2007–, A*STAR – Duke-NUS Grad. Medical School Partnership in Neuroscience, Singapore 2007–; Dir (non-exec.) Harkness Fellows Asscn and Transatlantic Trust 2001–, Physiological Soc. 2001–, SANE 2001–, Biosciences Fed. 2002–, Coalition for Medical Progress, British Technology Group plc 2007–; Assoc. Ed. NeuroReport 1989–2003; Ed.-in-Chief IBRO News 1986–2000; mem. Editorial Bd Perception 1971, Behavioral and Brain Sciences 1977, Journal of Developmental Physiology 1978–86, Experimental Brain Research 1979–89, Language and Communication 1979, Reviews in the Neurosciences 1984–, News in Physiological Sciences 1985, Clinical Vision Sciences 1986, Chinese Journal of Physiological Sciences 1988, Advances in Neuroscience 1989–, Vision Research 1993–, Int. Review of Neurobiology 1996–, EuroBrain 1998, American Journal of Bioethics 2006–; Leverhulme Fellowship 1974–75; Lethaby Prof., RCA, London 1978; Storer Lecturer, Univ. of California, Davis 1980, Regents' Prof. 1995–96; Macallum Lecturer, Univ. of Toronto 1984; Fellow, World Econ. Forum 1994–98; Founder Fellow, Acad. of Medical Sciences 1998–; Foreign mem. Royal Netherlands Acad. of Arts and Sciences 1993; mem. Experimental Psychology Soc. 1968–, Research Defence Soc. (Chair. of Council 2007–) 1969–, European Brain and Behaviour Soc. 1972–, Int. Brain Research Org. 1973–, Cambridge Philosophical Soc. 1975–, Soc. foe Neuroscience 1981–, Oxford Medical Soc. 1986–, Child Vision Research Soc. 1986–, British Asscn for the Advancement of Science (Pres. 1997–98, Chair. 2001–03) 1989–, Int. Soc. for Myochemistry 1989–, European Biomedical Research Asscn (founder mem.) 1994–, Inst. of Biology 1996–, Worshipful Co. of Spectacle Makers (mem. Livery 1998–) 1997–, Fed. of European Neuroscience Socs 2000–; Patron and mem. Professional Advisory Panel Headway (Nat. Head Injuries Asscn) 1997–; Patron Asscn for Art, Science, Eng and Tech. (ASCENT) 1997–; Freeman of the City of London 1997; Hon. Pres. World Cultural Council 1983–; Hon. Prof., Peking Union Medical Coll. 2005; Hon. Fellow, Corpus Christi Coll. Cambridge 1994, Cardiff, Univ. of Wales 1998, Downing Coll. Cambridge 1999; Hon. FRCP 2004; Hon. Fellow, BAAS 2001, Inst. of Biology 2004, Indian Acad. of Neurosciences 2007, British Pharmacological Soc. 2007; Hon. mem. Chelsea Arts Club 1992, Alpha Omega Alpha Honor Medical Soc. 1996, Physiological Soc. 1998, Maverick Club 1999, Motor Neurone Disease Asscn; Hon. Assoc. Rationalist Press Asscn 1986, Rationalist Int. 2000, Cambridge Union Soc. 2003; Hon. DSc (Aston) 1992, (Salford) 1994, (Manchester) 2005, (Aberdeen) 2005, (King's Coll. London) 2007; Hon. DM (Nottingham) 2008; Robert Bing Prize, Swiss Acad. of Medical Sciences 1975, Man of the Year, Royal Soc. for Disability and Rehabilitation 1978, John Locke Medal, Worshipful Soc. of Apothecaries 1983, Netter Prize, Acad. Nat. de Médecine, Paris 1984, Bertram Louis Abrahams Lecture, Royal Coll. of Physicians 1986, Cairns Memorial Lecture and Medal, Soc. of British Neurological Surgeons 1986, Norman McAllister Gregg Lecture and Medal, Royal Australian Coll. of Ophthalmologists 1988, Royal Soc. Michael Faraday Medal 1989, Robert Doyne Medal, Oxford Ophthalmology Congress 1989, John P. McGovern Science and Soc. Lecture and Medal 1990, Montgomery Medal 1991, Sir Douglas Robb Lectures, Univ. of Auckland 1991, Osler Medal, Royal Coll. of Physicians 1993, Ellison-Cliffe Medal, Royal Soc. of Medicine 1993, Charles F. Prentice Award, American Acad. of Optometry 1994, Annual Review Prize Lecture, Physiological Soc. 1995, Centenary Lecture, Univ. of Salford 1996, Alcon Prize 1996, Newton Lecture 1997, Cockcroft Lecture, UMIST 1997, Memorial Medal, Charles Univ., Prague 1998, Alfred Meyer Award, British Neuropathological Soc. 2001, Inst. of Biology Charter Award and Medal 2001, Baly Medal, Royal Coll. of Physicians (Dyster Trust) 2001, British Neuroscience Asscn Outstanding Contrib. to Neuroscience 2001, Menzies Medal, Menzies Foundation, Melbourne 2001, Bioindustry Asscn Award for Outstanding Personal Contrib. to Bioscience 2004, Lord Crook Gold Medal, Worshipful Co. of Spectacle Makers 2004, Edinburgh Medal, City of Edinburgh 2005, Science Educator Award, Soc. for Neuroscience 2005, Kenneth Myer Medal, Howard Florey Inst., Univ. of Melbourne 2006, Harveian Oration, Royal Coll. of Physicians, Ferrier Award, Royal Soc., Friendship Award (China), Ralph W. Gerard Award, Soc. for Neuroscience. *Films:* several educational films on neuroscience (Silver Award, BMA Film Competition 1972, Silver Award, Padua Int. Film Festival 1973, BMA Certificate of Educational Commendation 1974). *Radio:* The Reith Lectures (BBC Radio 4) 1976, Machines with Minds (five-part series) 1983. *Television:* Royal Inst. Christmas Lectures 1983, The Mind Machine (13-part series) 1988. *Publications:* Handbook of Psychobiology (ed.) 1975, Mechanics of the Mind 1977, Mindwaves (ed.) 1987, The Mind Machine 1988, Images and Understanding (ed.) 1990, Vision: Coding and Efficiency 1990, Sex and Society 1999, Oxford Companion to the Body 2001, The Physiology of Cognitive Processes (co-ed.) 2003, The Roots of Visual Awareness (co-ed.) 2003; contribs to Constraints on Learning 1973, Illusion in Art and Nature 1973, The Neurosciences Third Study Program 1974 and to professional journals and to nat. newspapers and magazines. *Leisure interests:* running and the arts. *Address:* Centre for the Study of the Senses, University of London, Senate House, Malet Street, London, WC1E 7HU, England (office). *Telephone:* (20) 7862-8682 (office). *Fax:* (20) 7862-8639 (office). *E-mail:* colin.blakemore@sas.ac.uk (office). *Website:* philosophy.sas.ac.uk/centres/censes (office).

BLAKEMORE, Michael Howell, AO, OBE; Australian theatre and film director; b. 18 June 1928, Sydney; s. of Conrad Blakemore and Una Mary Blakemore (née Litchfield); m. 1st Shirley Bush 1960; one s.; m. 2nd Tanya McCallin 1986; two d.; ed The King's School, NSW, Sydney Univ., Royal Acad. of Dramatic Art, UK; actor with Birmingham Repertory Theatre, Shakespeare Memorial Theatre etc. 1952–66; Co-Dir Glasgow Citizens' Theatre 1966–68 (first production The Investigation); Assoc. Artistic Dir Nat. Theatre, London 1971–76; Dir Players, New York, USA 1978; Resident Dir Lyric Theatre, Hammersmith, London 1980; Scottish Television Theatre Award (Arturo Ui) 1969, Variety Poll of London Critics Award (Forget-Me-Not Lane) 1971, Plays & Players Award (The Front Page) 1972, Evening Standard Award (A Personal History of the Australian Surf) 1982, Drama Desk Awards, New York (Noises Off) 1983, (Copenhagen) 2000, (Kiss Me Kate) 2000, Hollywood Drama League Award (Noises Off) 1984, Evening Standard Awards for Best Musical Theatre (City of Angels) 1993, (Kiss Me Kate) 2001, Film Critics Circle of Australia Award (Country Life) 1994, Molière Award, France (Copenhagen) 1999, Tony Awards (Copenhagen, Kiss Me Kate) 2000, Critics Circle Award (Kiss Me Kate) 2001, Helpmann Award, Australia (Copenhagen) 2003; inducted into American Theater Hall of Fame 2010. *Films include:* A Personal History of the Australian Surf (writer and dir) 1981, Privates on Parade (dir) 1983, Country Life (writer and dir) 1994. *Productions include:* UK: A Day in the Death of Joe Egg 1967, Arturo Ui 1969, Forget-Me-Not Lane 1971, Design for Living 1973, Separate Tables 1976, Privates on Parade 1977, Candida 1977, Make and Break 1980, Travelling North 1980, The Wild Duck 1980, All My Sons 1981, Noises Off 1982, Benefactors 1984, Lettice and Lovage 1987, Uncle Vanya 1988, Tosca (Welsh Nat. Opera) 1992, City of Angels 1993, Kiss Me Kate 2001, The Three Sisters 2003; at National Theatre, London: The National Health 1969, Long Day's Journey into Night 1971, The Cherry Orchard 1973, Plunder 1976, After the Fall 1990, The Front Page 1992, Macbeth 1992, Copenhagen 1998 (also in France 1999, Australia 2003 and USA 1999), Democracy 2004; USA: A Day in the Death of Joe Egg 1968, Noises Off 1983, Benefactors 1986, City of Angels 1989, Lettice & Lovage 1990, Death Defying Acts 1995, The Life 1997, Kiss Me Kate 1999, Copenhagen 1999, Deuce 2007, Is He Dead 2007, Blithe Spirit 2009. *Television productions include:* Long Day's Journey into Night 1972, Hay Fever (Denmark) 1978, Tales from the Hollywood Hills (USA) 1988. *Publications include:* Next Season (novel) 1969, Australia Fair? (anthology) 1985, Arguments with England (autobiography) 2004, Stage Blood (autobiography) 2013. *Leisure interest:* surfing. *Address:* 47 Ridgmount Gardens, London, WC1E 7AT, England (home). *Telephone:* (20) 7209-0608 (home). *Fax:* (20) 7209-0141 (home).

BLAKENHAM, 2nd Viscount (cr. 1963), of Little Blakenham; **Michael John Hare;** British business executive; b. 25 Jan. 1938, London; s. of 1st Viscount Blakenham and Hon. Beryl Nancy Pearson; m. Marcia P. Hare 1965; one s. two d.; ed Eton Coll. and Harvard Coll., USA; nat. service 1956–57; with English Electric Co. 1958; with Lazard Brothers 1961–63; with Standard Industrial Group 1963–71; with Royal Doulton 1972–77; Chief Exec. Pearson PLC 1978–90, Chair. 1983–97; Chair. Financial Times 1983–93; Partner, Lazard Partners 1984–97 (Dir Lazard Brothers 1975–97); Dir MEPC PLC 1990–98 (Chair. 1993–98); Chair. Royal Soc. for Protection of Birds 1981–86; Chair. Suffolk Together; fmr Chair. Comm. on the Governance of the Nat. Trust, UK; mem. Bd of Dirs Sotheby's Holdings Inc. 1987–2013, Lafarge SA 1997–2008; Pres. Sussex Wildlife Trust 1983–2003, British Trust for Ornithology 2001–05; mem. Int. Advisory Bd Lafarge 1979–97; mem. Int. Advisory Group Toshiba 1997–2002; mem. House of Lords Select Cttee on Science and Tech. 1984–88, Nature Conservancy Council 1986–90; Trustee, The Royal Botanic Gardens, Kew 1991–2003 (Chair. 1997–2003); Order of the Rising Sun (Japan) 2002. *Address:* Cottage Farm, Little Blakenham, Ipswich, Co. Suffolk, IP8 4LZ, England (home).

BLAKERS, Andrew, PhD; Australian scientist and academic; *Foundation Director, Centre for Sustainable Energy Systems, Australian National University;* currently Foundation Dir Centre for Sustainable Energy Systems and Dir Australian Research Council (ARC) Centre for Solar Energy Systems, ANU; fmr Humboldt Fellow; has held ARC QEII and Sr Research Fellowships; Fellow, Acad. of Technological Sciences and Eng, Inst. of Energy, Inst. of Physics; Banksia Award, Environmental Leadership in Infrastructure & Services 2005, Aichi World Expo Global Eco-Tech 100 Award 2005, Australian Inst. of Energy Innovation in Energy Science & Eng Award 2005, Australian Inst. of Physics Alan Walsh Medal for services to industry 2006, ACT Sustainable Cities Environmental Innovation Award 2006, ACT Sustainable Cities Overall Award 2006, Engineers Australia Australian Eng Excellence Award 2007, Int. Solar Energy Soc. Weeks Award 2007, Engineers Australia (ACT Div.) Eng Excellence Award 2007, Chairman's Award, duPont Innovation Awards 2008. *Achievements include:* co-invented, with Dr Klaus Weber, sliver cell photovoltaic tech. which uses one-tenth of the silicon used in conventional solar panels, with similar power, performance and efficiency. *Publications:* more than 200 scientific papers in professional journals on photovoltaic and solar energy systems, particularly advanced thin film silicon solar cell tech. and solar concentrator cells, components and systems; 12 patents. *Address:* Room E224, College of Engineering and Computer Science (Bldg 32), Australian National University, Canberra, ACT 0200, Australia (office). *Telephone:* (2) 6125-5905 (office). *E-mail:* andrew.blakers@anu.edu.au (office). *Website:* solar.anu.edu.au (office).

BLANC, Christian; French business executive and politician; b. 17 May 1942, Talence (Gironde); s. of Marcel Blanc and Emcarma Miranda; m. Asa Hagglund 1973; two d.; ed Ecole Montgolfier, Bordeaux, Lycée Montesquieu, Bordeaux and Inst. d'Etudes Politiques, Bordeaux; Asst Dir Sopexa-Scandinavie 1969; Société centrale d'équipement du territoire 1970–74; Chef du bureau, State Secr. for Youth and Sport 1974–76; Asst Del.-Gen. Agence technique interministérielle pour les loisirs et le plein air 1976–80; Dir du Cabinet to Edgard Pisani, mem. of Comm. of EC, Brussels 1981–83; Prefect, Commr, République des Hautes-Pyrénées 1983–84; special Govt assignment, New Caledonia 1985; Prefect for Seine-et-Marne 1985–89; Special Prefect 1989; Chair. and CEO RATP 1989–93; Chair. and CEO Air France (Admin. Council) 1993–97; Dir Middle East Airlines 1998–99, Marceau Investissements 1998–; Chair. Merrill Lynch France SA 2000–02; presidential cand. 2002; Dir Action contre la Faim 1998–, Chancellery Univs of Paris 1991–2001; Pres. Karaval 2001–; f. L'Ami Public; mem. Assemblée Nationale for Yvelines 2002–08, 2010–12; Sec. of State of Région Capitale (Great Paris) 2008–10 (resgnd); Founder and Chair. Énergies démocrates 2002–; CEO Syphax Airlines 2014; Chevalier, Légion d'honneur; Officier, Ordre nat. du Mérite. *Publication:* Le Lièvre et La Tortue (co-author) 1994, La Croissance ou le chaos 2006. *E-mail:* cblanc@christian-blanc.net.

BLANC, Georges; French chef, author and business executive; *CEO, Georges Blanc Parc & Spa;* b. 2 Jan. 1943, Bourg-en-Bresse; s. of Jean Blanc and Paule Blanc (née Tisserand); m. Jacqueline Masson 1966; two s. one d.; ed Ecole Hôtelière de Thonon-les-Bains; worked at Réserve de Beaulieu and Grand Hôtel de Divonne; mil. service as chef to Adm. Vedel on the Foch and the Clémenceau; returned to work in family business 1965, became head of firm 1968; Man. Dir Georges Blanc SA, CEO Georges Blanc Parc & Spa; Maître Cuisinier de France 1975; finalist in Meilleur Ouvrier de France competition 1976; has organized numerous events abroad to promote French cuisine; Founder mem., Second Vice-Pres. Chambre Syndicale de la Haute Cuisine Française 1986; Muncipal Councillor, Vonnas 1989; Officier, Ordre nat. du Mérite 1993, Chevalier, des Palmes Académiques 2002, Commdr, du Mérite agricole 1993, des Arts et des Lettres 2004, Commdr, Légion d'honneur 2008. *Publications:* Mes recettes 1981, La cuisine de Bourgogne (co-author), La nature dans l'assiette 1987, Le livre blanc des quatre saisons 1988, Les Blanc (jtly) 1989, Le Grand Livre de la Volaille (jtly) 1991, De la vigne à l'assiette 1995, la Cuisine de nos mères 2000, Cuisine de la vigne à la Carte 2000, Plat du jour 2003, Fêtes des Saveurs 2004, La Vie en Blanc 2008, Le plus simple du Meilleur 2009. *Leisure interests:* skiing, tennis. *Address:* Relais & Châteaux Georges Blanc Parc & Spa, 01540 Vonnas (Ain), France (home). *Telephone:* (4) 74-50-90-90 (home). *E-mail:* gblanc@georgesblanc.com (home). *Website:* www.georgesblanc.com (home).

BLANC, Pierre-Louis, MenD, MèsL; French diplomatist; b. 18 Jan. 1926; s. of Lucien Blanc and Renée Blanc; m. 1st (wife deceased); one s. two d.; m. 2nd Jutta Freifrau von Cramm 1988; ed Univ. of Paris, Paris Inst. of Political Studies and Ecole Nat. d'Admin; served in French embassies in Rabat 1956, Tokyo 1962, Madrid 1965; served in Office of Pres. of Repub. 1967–69; pvt. staff of Gen. de Gaulle 1969–70; Acting Deputy Dir for Asia/Oceania, Govt of France 1969–71; Cultural Counsellor, London 1971–75; Deputy Dir for Personnel and Gen. Admin., Ministry of Foreign Affairs 1975; Dir Ecole Nat. d'Admin 1975–82; Amb. to Sweden 1982–85, to Greece 1985–87; Perm. Rep. to UN, New York 1987–91; apptd Pres. Council of Francophone Affairs 1992; Vice-Pres. Soc. des Amis des Archives de France 1994–2000; Commdr, Légion d'honneur 1992, Grand Croix de l'Etoile Polaire. *Publications:* De Gaulle au soir de sa vie 1990, Valise Diplomatique 2004, Retour à Colombey 2012, Arille, Compagnon de Napoléon 2013. *Leisure interest:* writing. *Address:* 549 Chemin de Gergouven, 84560 Ménerbes, France. *Telephone:* 4-90-72-26-52 (home).

BLANC, Raymond René Alfred; French chef; b. 19 Nov. 1949, Besançon; s. of Maurice Blanc and Anne-Marie Blanc; two s.; ed Besançon Tech. Coll.; various positions 1968–76, mil. service 1970–71; Man. and Chef de cuisine, Bleu, Blanc, Rouge, Oxford 1976–77; opened Les Quat'Saisons, Oxford as Chef Proprietor 1977; opened Maison Blanc, patisserie and boulangerie 1978, Dir and Chair. 1978–88; opened Le Manoir aux Quat'Saisons 1984; Le Petit Blanc launched, Oxford 1996, relaunched as Brasserie Blanc 2006 and extended to numerous new locations including Manchester, Leeds, Bristol and several in London; Consultant to Maison Blanc 2009; weekly recipe column in the Observer newspaper 1988–90; Pres. Sustainable Restaurant Asscn 2012–; mem. Acad. Culinaire de France, British Gastronomic Acad., Restaurateurs' Asscn of GB; rep. GB at Grand Final of Wedgwood World Master of Culinary Arts, Paris 2002; Hon. OBE; Hon. DBA (Oxford Brookes Univ.) 1999; European Chef of the Year 1989, Personalité de l'Année 1990, Craft Guild of Chefs Special Award 2002, AA Restaurant Guide Chef of the Year 2004, Lifetime Achievement Award 2009, Chef of the Year Award 2009, many awards for both the restaurant and hotel. *Television:* Blanc Mange (series) 1994, Passion for Perfection (series, Carlton TV) 2002, The Restaurant (series, BBC2) 2007–, Kitchen Secrets 2010, 2011, The Very Hungry Frenchman 2012, Raymond Blanc: How to Cook Well 2013. *Publications:* Recipes from Le Manoir aux Quat'Saisons 1988, Cooking for Friends 1991, Blanc Mange 1994, A Blanc Christmas 1996; contrib. to Take Six Cooks 1986, Taste of Health 1987, Restaurants of Great Britain 1989, Gourmet Garden 1990, European Chefs 1990, Masterchefs of Europe 1998, Blanc Vite 1998, Foolproof French Cooking 2002, A Taste of My Life 2008. *Leisure interests:* classical music, opera, swimming, tennis, sailing. *Address:* Le Manoir aux Quat'Saisons, Church Road, Great Milton, Oxford, OX44 7PD, England (home). *Telephone:* (1844) 278881 (office). *Fax:* (1844) 278847 (home); (1844) 277212 (office). *E-mail:* raymond.blanc@blanc.co.uk (office). *Website:* www.raymondblanc.com; www.manoir.com.

BLANCHARD, James J., BA, MBA, JD; American lawyer, diplomatist and fmr politician; *Partner, DLA Piper US LLP;* b. 8 Aug. 1942, Detroit, Mich.; m. 2nd Janet Eifert; one s.; ed Michigan State Univ. and Univ. of Minnesota; admitted to Mich. Bar 1968; Legal Aid, elections bureau, Office of the Sec. of State, Mich. 1968–69; Asst Attorney-Gen., State of Mich. 1969–74, Admin. Asst to Attorney-Gen. 1970–71, Asst Deputy Attorney-Gen. 1971–72; mem. House of Reps 1975–83; Gov. of Mich. 1983–91; Pnr, Verner, Liipfert, Bernhard, McPherson and Hand 1991–93; Amb. to Canada 1993–96; Partner, DLA Piper US LLP, Washington, DC 1996–, Chair. Emer. Government Affairs Practice Group; Chair. Bd of Trustees, Meridian International Center; Co-Chair. Canada-US Law Inst., Ambassadors Circle for the Nat. Democratic Inst.; Vice-Pres. Foundation for the National Archives; Dir Enbridge, Inc; fmr mem. Pres.'s Comm. on Holocaust; several honorary degrees; Foreign Affairs Award for Public Service 1996, Henry T. King, Jr Award, Canada–USA Law Inst., numerous other awards. *Publication:* Behind the Embassy Door 1998. *Address:* DLA Piper US LLP, 500 8th Street, NW, Washington, DC 20004, USA (office). *Telephone:* (202) 799-4303 (office). *Fax:* (202) 799-5303 (office). *E-mail:* james.blanchard@dlapiper.com (office). *Website:* www.dlapiper.com (office).

BLANCHARD, Marc-André, LLB, LLM, MPA; Canadian lawyer and diplomatist; *Permanent Representative, United Nations;* b. 10 Nov. 1965, Salaberry-de-Valleyfield, Québec; m. Monique Ryan; two s.; ed Univ. de Montréal, Columbia Univ. School of Int. and Public Affairs, USA; intern, Robert F. Kennedy Human Rights 1990–92; Lawyer, Woods LLP 1992–97; Lawyer, McCarthy Tetrault 1997–2003, Regional Managing Pnr (Québec), McCarthy Tetrault 2003–09, Chair. and CEO, McCarthy Tétrault LLP 2010–16; Perm. Rep. of Canada to UN 2016–; mem. Bd of Dirs Canadian Heart & Stroke Foundation, Conf. Bd of Canada, Inst. for Research in Immunology and Cancer, WoodGreen Foundation; fmr mem. Advisory Bd Glendon Coll.; mem. campaign cabinet, Univ. de Montréal, United Way Toronto; mem. Young Presidents Org.; mem. Liberal Party of Canada, Pres. Québec Liberal Party 2000–08. *Address:* Permanent Mission of Canada to the United Nations, 885 Second Avenue, 14th Floor, New York, NY 10017, USA (office). *Telephone:* (212) 848-1100 (office). *Fax:* (212) 848-1195 (office). *E-mail:* canada.un@international.gc.ca (office). *Website:* www.canadainternational.gc.ca (office).

BLANCHARD, Olivier Jean, PhD; French economist and academic; *Economic Counsellor and Director of Research Department, International Monetary Fund;* b. 27 Dec. 1948, Amiens; m. Noelle Golinelli 1973; three d.; ed Univ. of Paris and Massachusetts Inst. of Tech.; Asst Prof., Harvard Univ., USA 1977–81, Assoc. Prof. 1981–83; Assoc. Prof., MIT, Cambridge, Mass, USA 1983–85, Prof. of Econs 1985–, Class of 1941 Prof. 1994–, Chair. Econs Dept 1998–2003; Econ. Counsellor and Dir Dept of Research, IMF 2008–; Vice-Pres. American Econ. Asscn 1995–96; Fellow, Econometric Soc.; mem. American Acad. of Arts and Sciences. *Publications:* Lectures on Macroeconomics (with S. Fischer) 1989, Reform in Eastern Europe 1991, Pour l'Emploi et Cohésion Sociale 1994, Spanish Unemployment: Is There a Solution? 1994, The Economics of Transition 1996, Macroeconomics 1997. *Leisure interest:* tennis. *Address:* International Monetary Fund, 700 19th Street NW, Washington, DC 20431; Department of Economics, E52-357, Massachusetts Institute of Technology, Cambridge, MA 02139, USA (office). *Telephone:* (202) 623-7000 (DC) (office); (617) 253-8891 (office). *Fax:* (202) 623-4661 (DC) (office); (617) 258-8112 (office). *E-mail:* publicaffairs@imf.org (office); blanchar@mit.edu (office). *Website:* www.imf.org (office); econ-www.mit.edu (office).

BLANCHETT, Cate; Australian actress; b. 14 May 1969, Melbourne, Vic.; m. Andrew Upton 1997; three s.; ed Univ. of Melbourne, Nat. Inst. of Dramatic Art; Co-Artistic Dir Sydney Theatre Co. 2008–; BAFTA Award for Best Actress 1999, Best Actress, Nat. Bd of Review 2001, Golden Camera Award 2001, Career Achievement Award, Palm Springs Int. Film Festival 2007. *Plays include:* Top Girls 1992–93, Kafka Dances (1993 Newcomer Award), Oleanna (Rosemont Best Actress Award) 1993, Hamlet 1994, Sweet Phoebe 1995, The Tempest 1995, The Blind Giant is Dancing 1995, Plenty 1999, Hedda Gabler 2004, A Streetcar Named Desire 2009, Uncle Vanya 2010. *Films include:* Police Rescue 1994, Parklands 1996, Paradise Road 1997, Thank God He Met Lizzie 1997, Oscar and Lucinda 1997, Elizabeth 1998 (Golden Globe Award), Dreamtime Alice (also co-producer), Bangers 1999, The Talented Mr Ripley 1999, An Ideal Husband 1999, Pushing Tin 1999, Bandit 2000, The Man Who Cried 2000, The Gift 2000, Bandits 2000, The Lord of the Rings: The Fellowship of the Ring 2001, Charlotte Gray 2001, The Shipping News 2002, The Lord of the Rings: The Two Towers 2002, Heaven 2002, Veronica Guerin 2003, The Lord of the Rings: The Return of the King 2003, Coffee and Cigarettes 2003, The Aviator (Best Supporting Actress, Screen Actors Guild Awards 2005, Best Actress in a Supporting Role, BAFTA Awards 2005, Best Supporting Actress, Acad. Awards 2005) 2004, The Life Aquatic 2004, Stories of Lost Souls 2005, Little Fish 2005, Babel 2006, The Good German 2006, Notes on a Scandal (Best Supporting Actress, Toronto Film Critics Asscn) 2006, I'm Not There (Best Actress, Venice Film Festival 2007, Golden Globe for Best Supporting Actress 2008) 2007, Elizabeth: The Golden Age 2007, Indiana Jones and the Kingdom of the Crystal Skull 2008, Ponyo (English version, voice) 2008, The Curious Case of Benjamin Button 2008, Robin Hood 2010, The Last Time I Saw Michael Gregg 2011, Hanna 2011, The Hobbit: An Unexpected Journey 2012, A Cautionary Tail (short) 2012, Blue Jasmine (Best Actress, Nat. Soc. of Film Critics, Golden Globe Award for Best Actress in a Motion Picture, Drama, Screen Actors Guild Award for Outstanding Performance by a Female Actor in a Leading Role, BAFTA Award for Best Actress in a Leading Role, Academy Award for Best Actress in a Leading Role 2014) 2013, The Turning 2013, The Hobbit: The Desolation of Smaug 2013, The Monuments Men 2014, How to Train Your Dragon 2 (voice) 2014, The Hobbit: The Battle of the Five Armies 2014, Carol (Desert Palm Achievement Award, Palm Springs Int. Film Festival 2016) 2015, Knight of Cups 2015, Cinderella 2015, Truth 2015. *Television includes:* Police Rescue (series) 1994, Heartland (mini-series) 1994, G.P. (series) 1994, Bordertown (mini-series) 1995, Family Guy (series) 2012. *Address:* c/o Hylda Queally, Creative Artists Agency, 2000 Avenue of the Stars, Los Angeles, CA 90067, USA (office); c/o Robyn Gardiner, PO Box 128, Surry Hills, 2010 NSW, Australia. *Telephone:* (424) 288-2000 (office). *Fax:* (424) 288-2900 (office). *Website:* www.caa.com (office).

BLANCHFLOWER, David G., CBE, BA, MSc, PhD; American/British economist and academic; *Bruce V. Rauner 1978 Professor of Economics, Dartmouth College;* b. 2 March 1952; m. Carol Blanchflower; one s. two d.; ed Univ. of Leicester, UK, Univ. of Wales, Univ. of London (Queen Mary Coll.); Teacher Northicote High School 1975–76; Lecturer Kilburn Polytechnic 1976–77, Farnborough Coll. of Tech. 1977–79; Research Officer, Inst. for Employment Research, Univ. of Warwick 1984–86; Lecturer, Dept of Econs, Univ. of Surrey 1986–89; Assoc. Prof., Dept of Econs, Dartmouth Coll. 1989–93, Prof. 1993–, Bruce V. Rauner 1978 Prof. of Econs 2002–, Dept Chair. 1998–2000, Assoc. Dean of Faculty of Social Sciences 2000–01; Prof., Dept of Econs, Management School, Univ. of Stirling 2006–; Bloomberg columnist 2010–, Contributing Ed., Bloomberg TV 2011–15; Visiting Scholar, Federal Reserve Bank of Boston 2011–13; Sr Visiting Fellow, Peterson Inst. 2013–14; Econs Columnist, New Statesman 2009–12, The Independent 2012–15; Research Assoc., Nat. Bureau of Econ. Research (NBER); Research Fellow, CESifo, Center for Econ. Studies, Univ. of Munich, Germany; Research Fellow, Inst. for the Study of Labor (IZA), Univ. of Bonn; mem. Monetary Policy Cttee, Bank of England 2006–09; mem. Editorial Bd Industrial and Labor Relations Review 1996–99, Scottish Journal of Political Economy 2000–05, Small Business Econs 2000–05; mem. Int. Advisory Bd, Nat. Inst. of Econ. and Social Research 2014–; Hon. Fellow, Cardiff Univ. 2014; Hon. MA (Dartmouth Coll.) 1996, Hon. DLitt (Univ. of Leicester) 2007, (Univ. of Sussex) 2011, Hon. DrSc DSc (Univ. of London) 2009; Richard A. Lester Prize, Princeton Univ. 1994, Business Person of the Year, Daily Telegraph 2008. *Publications:* numerous articles in professional journals. *Address:* Department of Economics, Dartmouth College, 6106 Rockefeller Hall, Hanover, NH 03755, USA (office). *Telephone:* (603) 646-2536 (office). *Fax:* (603) 646-2122 (office). *E-mail:* david.g.blanchflower@dartmouth.edu (office); blanchflower@dartmouth.edu (office). *Website:* www.dartmouth.edu/~blnchflr (office).

BLANDFORD, Roger David, BA, MA, PhD, FRS, FRAS; British astrophysicist and academic; *Professor of Physics and Luke Blossom Professor in the School of Humanities and Sciences, Stanford University;* b. 28 Aug. 1949, Grantham, Lincs.; s. of Jack George Blandford and Janet Margaret Blandford (née Evans); m. Elizabeth Kellett 1972; two s.; ed Magdalene Coll., Cambridge; Research Fellow, St John's Coll., Cambridge 1973–76; Asst Prof., California Inst. of Tech. 1976–79, Prof. 1979–89, Richard Chace Tolman Prof. of Theoretical Astrophysics 1989–2003, Exec. Officer for Astronomy 1992–95; Pehong and Adele Chen Dir, Kavli Inst. of Particle Astrophysics and Cosmology, Stanford Univ., Calif. 2003–13, Prof. at the Stanford Linear Accelerator Center 2003–, Prof. of Physics and Luke Blossom Prof., School of Humanities and Sciences, Stanford Univ. 2003–; mem. Inst. for Advanced Study, Princeton, NJ 1974–75, 1998; Blaauw Prof., Groningen, The Netherlands 2012; Miller Prof., Univ. of California, Berkeley 2013–14; Kingsley Visitor, California Inst. of Tech. (Caltech) 2014; Chair. Astro2010; mem. American Astronomical Soc. (AAS), NAS 2005; Fellow, American Acad. of Arts and Sciences 1993; W.B.R. King Scholar 1967–70, Charles Kingsley Bye Fellow 1972–73, Alfred P. Sloan Fellow 1980–84, AAS Helen B. Warner Prize 1982,

Guggenheim Fellow 1988–90, AAS Dannie Heineman Prize 1998, Eddington Medal, Royal Astronomical Soc. (RAS) 1999, Humboldt Research Award, Humboldt Foundation 2011, Simons Fellowship 2013–14, RAS Gold Medal 2013 Greenstein Lecturer, Caltech 2013, Physics Memorial Lecturer, Univ. of California, San Diego 2014, Crafoord Prize (Astronomy), Royal Swedish Acad. of Sciences (co-recipient) 2016. *Publications include:* numerous papers in professional journals on cosmology, black hole astrophysics, gravitational lensing, galaxies, cosmic rays, neutron stars and white dwarfs. *Address:* KIPAC, 452 Lomita Mall, Stanford, CA 94305-4085, USA (office). *Telephone:* (650) 723-4233 (office). *Fax:* (650) 725-4096 (office). *E-mail:* rdb3@stanford.edu (office). *Website:* physics.stanford.edu (office); stanford.edu/~rdb3 (office); kipac-web.stanford.edu (office).

BLANK, Sir (Maurice) Victor, Kt, MA; British business executive; *Chairman, Wellbeing of Women;* b. 9 Nov. 1942; s. of Joseph Blank and Ruth Blank (née Levey); m. Sylvia Helen Richford 1977; two s. one d.; ed Stockport Grammar School, St Catherine's Coll., Oxford; solicitor, Supreme Court; joined Clifford-Turner as articled clerk 1964, Solicitor 1966, Partner 1969; Dir and Head Corp. Finance Charterhouse Bank 1981, Chief Exec. 1985–96, Chair. 1985–97, Chief Exec. Charterhouse PLC 1985–96, Chair. 1991–97, Dir Charterhouse Europe Holding 1993–, Chair. 1993–97; Chair. Wellbeing of Women 1989–; Deputy Chair. Great Universal Stores (renamed GUS PLC) 1996–2000, Chair. 2000–06 (Dir 1993–2006); Founding Chair. Trinity Mirror 1999–2006; Chair. Lloyds TSB Group plc (renamed Lloyds Banking Group plc following acquisition of HBOS plc Jan. 2009) 2006–09; Dir (non-exec.) Coats Ltd (fmrly Coats Viyella PLC), Chubb PLC (fmrly Williams PLC); Chair. Industrial Devt Advisory Bd; mem. Financial Reporting Council 2002–07; mem. Council, adviser to Environmental Change Unit and Chair. Devt Programme Advisory Bd, Univ. of Oxford 2000–07; Sr Adviser, Texas Pacific Group; Chair. UJS Hillel, Council of Univ. Coll. School, Royal Coll. of Obstetricians and Gynaecologists' health research charity; mem. CBI Boardroom Issues Group, Jewish Leadership Council (also Vice Pres.), Orchestra of the Age of Enlightenment; Patron, Royal Coll. of Obstetricians and Gynaecologists; apptd UK Business Amb. 2010; Hon. Fellow, St Catherine's Coll. Oxford; Hon. FRCOG. *Publication:* Weinberg and Blank on Take-overs and Mergers (co-author) 1971. *Leisure interests:* cricket, family, tennis, theatre. *Address:* Wellbeing of Women, First Floor, Fairgate House, 78 New Oxford Street, London, WC1A 1HB, England. *Telephone:* (20) 3697-7000. *E-mail:* hello@wellbeingofwomen.org.uk. *Website:* www.wellbeingofwomen.org.uk; www.sirvictorblank.co.uk.

BLANK, Rebecca M., BS, PhD; American economist, academic and government official; *Chancellor, University of Wisconsin-Madison;* b. 19 Sept. 1955, Mo.; m. Hanns Kuttner; one d.; ed Univ. of Minnesota, Massachusetts Inst. of Tech.; Consultant and Educational Coordinator, Data Resources, Chicago Office 1976–79; Asst Prof. of Econs and Public Affairs, Dept of Econs and Woodrow Wilson School of Public and Int. Affairs, Princeton Univ. 1983–89; Sr Staff Economist, Council of Econ. Advisers, Washington, DC 1989–90, mem.-nominee 1997–98, mem. 1998–99; Visiting Asst Prof. of Econs, MIT 1988–89; Assoc. Prof. of Econs, Northwestern Univ. 1989–94, Prof. of Econs 1994–99, Research Faculty, Center for Urban Affairs and Policy Research 1989–99, Assoc. Prof., School of Educ. and Social Policy 1989–93, Dir Jt Center for Poverty Research 1996–97; Joan and Sanford Weill Dean of Public Policy, Gerald R. Ford School of Public Policy, Univ. of Michigan 1999–2007, Henry Carter Adams Collegiate Prof. of Public Policy, Gerald R. Ford School of Public Policy Prof. of Econs, Dept of Econs, Co-Dir Nat. Poverty Center 2002–08; Robert S. Kerr Visiting Fellow, Econ. Studies, Brookings Inst. 2007–08, Robert S. Kerr Sr Fellow, Econ. Studies 2008–09; Under-Sec. for Econ. Affairs 2009–12, Acting Deputy Sec. of Commerce 2010–12, Deputy Sec. of Commerce 2012–13, Acting Sec. of Commerce 2012–13; Chancellor Univ. of Wisconsin-Madison 2013–; Faculty Research Fellow, Nat. Bureau of Econ. Research 1985–90, Faculty Research Assoc. 1990–2009; Faculty Assoc. NAS 2004–; Co-Ed. Journal of Human Resources 1995–97, Labour Economics 2004–07 (Assoc. Ed. 2007–); mem. Bd of Eds, American Economic Review, 1993–97, American Economic Journal: Economic Policy 2007–09; mem. Advisory Bd, Journal of Public Economics 1993–97, Journal of Economic Education 1992–97, 2002–09, Feminist Economics 1994–97; mem. Bd of Dirs MRDC (fmrly Manpower Demonstration Research Corpn) 1993–97, Center for Budget and Policy Priorities 1994–97, 2000–09, Economic Policy Inst. 2008–09; mem. Bd of Trustees, Urban Inst. 2007–09; mem. Advisory Council, Spotlight on Poverty and Opportunity 2007–09; mem. Scientific Advisory Cttee, DIW (research/policy think tank), Berlin, Germany 2001–04; mem. Hon. Advisory Council, DIW-DC 2008–09; mem. Advisory Cttee, New Hope Project (job training and employment programme), Milwaukee, Wis. 1992–97, Advisory Cttee on Poverty Research, Russell Sage Foundation 1994–97, Research Advisory Cttee, W.E. Upjohn Inst. for Employment Research 1995–96, 2000; mem. Visiting Cttee, Kennedy School of Govt, Harvard Univ. 2004–09; mem. NAS, mem. Div. Cttee for the Behavioral and Social Sciences and Educ. (DBASSE), Nat. Research Council 2003–08, DBASSE Exec. Cttee mem. 2005–08, Chair. Workshop to Reconsider the Fed. Poverty Measure, Cttee on Nat. Statistics 2004–05, Panel on Methods for Assessing Discrimination, Cttee on Nat. Statistics 2001–04; Pres. Asscn for Public Policy Analysis and Man. 2007, Exec. Cttee mem. 2006–08, Policy Council mem. 2001–04; mem. American Econ. Asscn (mem. Exec. Cttee 1995–97, Vice-Pres. American Econ. Asscn 2007), Nat. Acad. of Social Insurance; Lifetime Nat. Assoc., Nat. Acads of Sciences 2004; Fellow, American Acad. of Arts of Sciences 2005, Soc. of Labor Economists 2006; Hon. PhD (Univ. of Maryland) 2012; Outstanding Alumni Achievement Award, Univ. of Minnesota 2008, Winter Commencement Speaker, Coll. of Liberal Arts, Univ. of Minnesota 2008, Eleanor Roosevelt Fellow, American Acad. of Political and Social Science 2010, numerous named lectures. *Publications include:* Do Justice: Linking Christian Faith and Modern Economic Life 1992, Social Protection vs. Economic Flexibility: Is There a Tradeoff? (ed. and author of two articles) 1994, It Takes A Nation: A New Agenda for Fighting Poverty 1997, Finding Jobs: Work and Welfare Reform (co-ed. with David Card and co-author of two articles) 2000, The New World of Welfare (co-ed. with Ron Haskins and co-author of two articles) 2001, Is the Market Moral? A Dialogue on Religion, Economics, and Justice (with William McGurn) 2004, Measuring Racial Discrimination (with Marilyn Dabady and Connie Citro) 2004, Working and Poor: How Economic and Policy Changes are Affecting Low Wage Workers (co-ed. with Sheldon Danziger and Robert Schoeni and co-author of two articles) 2006, Insufficient Funds: Savings, Assets, Credit and Banking Among Low-Income Households (co-ed. with Michael S. Barr and co-author of one article) 2009, Changing Inequality 2011; several book chapters and book reviews and numerous articles in professional journals. *Address:* Office of the Chancellor, 161 Bascom Hall, 500 Lincoln Drive, Madison, WI 53706, USA (office). *Telephone:* (608) 262-9946 (office). *E-mail:* chancellor@news.wisc.edu (office). *Website:* www.chancellor.wisc.edu (office).

BLANKFEIN, Lloyd Craig, BA, JD; American lawyer and business executive; *Chairman and CEO, Goldman Sachs;* b. 1954, New York; m. Laura Susan Jacobs 1983; three c.; ed Harvard Univ. and Harvard Univ. Law School; corp. tax lawyer, Donovan, Leisure, Newton & Irvine 1978–81; joined J. Aron div. of Goldman Sachs as a gold bar and coin salesman 1981, Head or Co-head Currency and Commodities Div. 1994–97, Co-head Fixed Income, Currency and Commodities Division (FICC) 1997–2002, Vice-Chair. Goldman Sachs, with man. responsibility for FICC and Equities Div. 2002–04, mem. Bd of Dirs Goldman Sachs 2003–, Pres. and COO 2004–06, Chair. and CEO 2006–; mem. Dean's Advisory Bd of Harvard Law School, Dean's Council, Harvard Univ., Advisory Bd of Tsinghua Univ. School of Econs and Man.; mem. Bd of Overseers, Weill Medical Coll. of Cornell Univ.; mem. Bd of Dirs Partnership for New York City. *Address:* The Goldman Sachs Group, 85 Broad Street, 17th Floor, New York, NY 10004, USA (office). *Telephone:* (212) 902-1000 (office). *Fax:* (212) 902-3000 (office). *E-mail:* info@gs.com (office). *Website:* www.goldmansachs.com (office).

BLANNING, Timothy Charles William, LittD, FBA; British academic; *Fellow in History, Sidney Sussex College, Cambridge;* b. 21 April 1942, Wells, Somerset; s. of Thomas Walter Blanning and Gwendolen Marchant-Jones; m. Nicky Susan Jones 1988; one s. one d.; ed King's School, Bruton, Somerset, Sidney Sussex Coll., Cambridge; Research Fellow, Sidney Sussex Coll., Cambridge 1965–68, Fellow 1968–, Asst Lecturer in History, Univ. of Cambridge 1972–76, Lecturer 1976–87, Reader in Modern European History 1987–92, Prof. of Modern European History 1992–2009; British Acad. Medal 2017. *Publications include:* Joseph II and Enlightened Despotism 1970, Reform and Revolution in Mainz 1743–1803 1974, The French Revolution in Germany 1983, The Origins of the French Revolutionary Wars 1986, The French Revolution: Aristocrats versus Bourgeois? 1987, Joseph II 1994, The French Revolutionary Wars 1787–1802 1996, The French Revolution: Class War or Culture Clash? 1998, The Culture of Power and the Power of Culture 2002, The Pursuit of Glory: Europe 1648–1815 2007; Ed.: The Oxford Illustrated History of Modern Europe 1996, The Rise and Fall of the French Revolution 1996, History and Biography: Essays in Honour of Derek Beales (with Peter Wende), Reform in Great Britain and Germany 1750–1850 1999, The Short Oxford History of Europe: The Eighteenth Century 2000, The Short Oxford History of Europe: The Nineteenth Century 2000, Unity and Diversity in European Culture *c.* 1800 2006, The Triumph of Music 2008, The Romantic Revolution 2010, Frederick the Great, King of Prussia 2015, George I 2017. *Leisure interest:* music. *Address:* Sidney Sussex College, Cambridge, CB2 3HU, England (office). *E-mail:* tcb1000@cam.ac.uk (office).

BLASHFORD-SNELL, Col John Nicholas, CBE, MBE, OBE, FRSGS; British explorer, writer and broadcaster; *President, Scientific Exploration Society;* b. 22 Oct. 1936, Hereford, Herefords.; s. of Rev. Prebendary Leland John Blashford-Snell and Gwendolen Ives Blashford-Snell (née Sadler); m. Judith Frances Sherman 1960; two d.; ed Victoria Coll., Jersey, Royal Mil. Acad., Sandhurst; commissioned in Royal Engineers 1957; Commdr Operation Aphrodite (Expedition), Cyprus 1959–61; Instructor, Jr Leaders Regt Royal Engineers 1962–63; Instructor, RMA, Sandhurst 1963–66; Adjt, 3rd Div. Engineers 1966–67; Commdr The Great Abbai Expedition (Blue Nile) 1968; attended Staff Coll., Camberley 1969; Chair. Scientific Exploration Soc. 1969–2009, currently Pres.; Commdr Dahlak Quest Expedition 1969–70, British Trans-Americas Expedition (Darien Gap) 1971–72; Officer Commdg 48th Field Squadron, Royal Engineers 1972–74; Commdr, Zaïre River Expedition 1974–75; CO, Jr Leaders Regt, Royal Engineers 1976–78; Dir of Operations, Operation Drake 1978–81; Staff Officer, Ministry of Defence 1978–91, Consultant 1992–; Commdr, Fort George Volunteers 1982; Operations Dir, Operation Raleigh 1982–88, Dir-Gen. 1989–91; Dir SES Tibet Expedition 1987; Leader, Kalahari Quest Expedition 1990, Karnali Quest Expedition 1991, Karnali Gorges Expedition 1992, numerous exploration projects thereafter; Trustee, Operation New World 1995–; Chair. Just a Drop Charity 2001–04, Pres. 2004–, The Liverpool Construction-Crafts Guild 2003–05; Pres. The British Travel Health Asscn 2006–; Patron, The Gorilla Org. 2019; Hon. Pres. The Vole Club 1996–, Hon. Life Pres. The Centre for Fortean Zoology 2003–, Hon. Fellow, Liverpool John Moores Univ. 2010, Hon. Keeper of Quaich 2013, Freeman of the City of Hereford; Hon. DSc (Durham), Hon. DEng (Bournemouth) 1997; The Livingstone Medal, The Darien Medal (Colombia) 1972, The Segrave Trophy, Paul Harris Fellow, Rotary International, Royal Geographical Soc. Patrons' Medal 1993, Gold Medal, Inst. of Royal Engineers 1994, La Paz Medal (Bolivia) 2000. *Publications include:* Weapons and Tactics (with T. Wintringham) 1970, The Expedition Organiser's Guide (with Richard Snailham) 1970, Where the Trails Run Out 1974, In the Steps of Stanley 1975, Expeditions the Experts' Way (with A. Ballantine) 1977, A Taste for Adventure 1978, Operation Drake (with M. Cable) 1981, In the Wake of Drake (with M. Cable) 1982, Mysteries: Encounters with the Unexplained 1983, Operation Raleigh, The Start of an Adventure 1987, Operation Raleigh, Adventure Challenge (with Ann Tweedy) 1988, Operation Raleigh, Adventure Unlimited (with Ann Tweedy) 1990, Something Lost Behind the Ranges 1994 (revised edn 2015), Mammoth Hunt (with Rula Lenska) 1996, Kota Mama: Retracing the Lost Trade Routes of Ancient South American Peoples (with Richard Snailham) 2000, East to the Amazon (with Richard Snailham) 2002. *Leisure interests:* shooting, food, photography, cryptozoology. *Address:* Scientific Exploration Society, Expedition Base, Motcombe, nr Shaftesbury, Dorset, SP7 9PB, England (office). *Telephone:* (1747) 854456 (office). *E-mail:* jbs@ses-explore.org (office). *Website:* www.johnblashfordsnell.org.uk.

BŁASZCZAK, Mariusz; Polish historian, politician and local government official; *Minister of National Defence;* b. 19 Sept. 1969, Legionowo, Mazowieckie Voivodship; ed Nat. School of Public Admin, Warsaw and Acad. of Entrepreneurship and Man. (now Kozminski Univ.), Warsaw; served an internship in Ireland; fmr mem. and adviser, Ind. Students' Asscn, Catholic Academic Youth Asscn, Centre Alliance Party; mem. Porozumienie Centrum (Centre Agreement) party –2001,

Prawo i Sprawiedliwość (PiS—Law and Justice) 2001–; Deputy Mayor of Wola Dist, Warsaw 2002–04; Mayor of Śródmieście Dist, Warsa 2004–05; Chief of Staff, Chancellery of Prime Minister 2005–07; mem. Mazowieckie Voivodship Ass. 2006–07; Minister without Portfolio March–Nov. 2007; mem. Sejm (Parl.) 2007–11, 2011–15, 2015–; mem. PiS party bd in Mazowieckie Voivodship br., Political Council of PiS, Head of Parl. Group of PiS 2010–15; Minister of the Interior and Admin 2015–18, of Nat. Defence 2018–. *Address:* Ministry of National Defence, 00-909 Warsaw, ul. Klonowa 1, Poland (office). *Telephone:* (261) 871201 (office). *Fax:* (261) 870950 (office). *E-mail:* dyrsekmon@mon.gov.pl (office). *Website:* www.mon.gov.pl (office); mariuszblaszczak.pl.

BLATHERWICK, Sir David (Elliott Spiby), KCMG, OBE, MA; British diplomatist (retd); *Chairman, Egyptian-British Chamber of Commerce;* b. 13 July 1941, Lincoln, Lincs.; s. of Edward S. Blatherwick; m. (Margaret) Clare Crompton 1964; one s. one d.; ed Lincoln School, Wadham Coll., Oxford; Foreign Office 1964; Second Sec., Embassy in Kuwait 1968–70; First Sec., Embassy in Dublin 1970–73; FCO 1973–77; Head of Chancery, Cairo 1977–80; NI Office, Belfast 1981–83; FCO 1983–85; sabbatical, Stanford Univ., USA 1985–86; Head of Chancery, Perm. Mission to UN, New York 1986–89; Prin. Finance Officer and Chief Insp., FCO 1989–91; Amb. to Ireland 1991–95, to Egypt 1995–99; Chair. Egyptian-British Chamber of Commerce 1999–; Jt Chair. Anglo-Irish Encounter 2003–08; Trustee, British Univ. in Egypt 2005–; Patron The British Humanist Asscn. *Publication:* The Politics of International Telecommunications 1987. *Leisure interests:* walking, sailing, music. *Address:* Egyptian-British Chamber of Commerce, PO Box 4EG, 299 Oxford Street, London, W1A 4EG, England (office). *Telephone:* (20) 7499-3100 (office). *Fax:* (20) 7499-1070 (office). *E-mail:* info@theebcc.com (office). *Website:* www.theebcc.com (office).

BLATTER, Johann W. (Gianni), PhD; Swiss physicist and academic; *Professor of Theoretical Physics, Institute of Theoretical Physics, ETH Zürich;* b. 10 Nov. 1955; ed Eidgenössische Technische Hochschule Zürich (ETH Zürich); Researcher, Brown Boveri Co. (later Asea Brown Boveri), Baden, Switzerland 1983, 1987–93; fmr Post-Doctoral Researcher, Cornell Univ., Ithaca, NY, USA; Assoc. Prof., Inst. of Theoretical Physics, ETH Zürich 1993–96, Prof. of Theoretical Physics 1996–, Head of Dept 2007–; Fellow, American Physical Soc. *Address:* Institute of Theoretical Physics, HPZ G 10, Schafmattstr. 32, Hönggerberg, 8093 Zürich, Switzerland (office). *Telephone:* (44) 633-2568 (office). *Fax:* (44) 633-1115 (office). *E-mail:* johann.blatter@itp.phys.ethz.ch (office). *Website:* www.itp.phys.ethz.ch (office).

BLATTER, (Joseph) Sepp, BBA; Swiss international organization official and sports administrator; b. 10 March 1936, Visp, Viège; one d.; ed Sion and St Maurice Colls, Univ. de Lausanne; footballer (played for Swiss amateur league in top div.) 1948–71; mem. Bd Xamax Neuchâtel Football Club 1970–75; fmr Sec. Tourist Office, Valais; Sec.-Gen. Swiss Fed. of Ice Hockey 1964; pursued journalistic and public relations activities in the fields of sport and pvt. industry; fmr Dir of Sports Timing and Public Relations, Longines SA; Tech. Dir of Devt Programmes, FIFA 1975–81, Gen. Sec. 1981–90, CEO 1990–98, elected Pres. 1998, announced he would step down as Pres. in Dec. 2015, suspended for 90 days from all FIFA activities pending investigation into alleged corruption Oct. 2015, suspended for eight years from all football-related activities Dec. 2015, reduced to six years 2016; mem. IOC 1999–2015; mem. Swiss Asscn of Sportswriters, Panathlon Club; Hon. mem. Swiss Football Asscn, German Football Asscn, Swiss Olympic Asscn, Real Madrid CF; Hon. Citizen of Timor Leste 2011, City of Visp 2006, City of Bangkok 2006, Guatemala City and Managua 2011; Olympic Order, knighthood (with title of Dato') from Sultanate of Pahang, Order of Good Hope (South Africa), Order of Independence (First Class) (Jordan), Grand Cordon du Wissam Alaouite (Morocco), Medalla al Mérito Deportivo (Bolivia), Grand Cordon de l'Ordre de la République Tunisienne, Rank of Grand Officer of Wissam Al Arch (Morocco), Order of Merit in Diamond, Union of European Football Asscns (UEFA), Award of Merit (Yemen), Chevalier de la Légion d'honneur, Order of the Two Niles (Sudan), Commdr de l'Ordre Nat. du 27 Juin 1977 (Djibouti), Supreme Companion of Tambo (SA), Ordre de la Médaille de la Reconnaissance (Commdr Grade) (Cen. African Repub.), Commdr's Cross with Star of the Order of Merit (Hungary) 2006, Commdr de l'Ordre Nat. du Lion (Senegal) 2006, 1st Grau da Ordem do Dragoeiro (Cape Verde) 2006, Grosse Verdienstkreuz (Germany) 2006, Collar Estrella del Centenario de la Asociación de Fútbol (Paraguay) 2006, Order of Prince Yaroslav the Wise, Grade V (Ukraine) 2007, Order of Nat. Friendship (Uzbekistan) 2007, Order of Danaker (Kyrgyzstan) 2007, Crown of Peace (India) 2007, Order of Francisco de Miranda, First Class (Venezuela) 2007, Grand Cordon, Order of the Rising Sun (Japan) 2009, Order of Friendship (Kazakhstan) 2009, Order of Merit for Sports (South Korea) 2010, Order of the Companions of O. R. Tambo (SA) 2010, Dato' Sri, First Class, Grand Commdr of the Most Distinguished Order of the Sri Sultan Ahmad Shah Pahang (Malaysia) 2011; Hon. DArts (De Montfort Univ.) 2005; Hon. PhD (Nelson Mandela Metropolitan Univ., SA) 2006; Dr hc (Azerbaijan State Acad. of Physical Training and Sport, Baku), (Int. Univ., Geneva) 2007, (Univ. of Benin, Nigeria) 2011; Hon. Diploma from Pres. Aliyev of Azerbaijan; 'Int. Humanitarian of the Year' and 'Golden Charter of Peace and Humanitarianism', American Global Award for Peace, Int. Humanitarian League for Peace and Tolerance, UEFA Order of Merit in Diamond 2004, Diamond of Asia Award, Asian Football Conf. 2006, Necklace of Honour, Ecuadorian Football Fed. 2010, numerous awards from clubs, nat. asscns and confeds.

BLATTMANN, René, LicIurU; Bolivian judge; b. 28 Jan. 1948, La Paz; m. Marianne Blattmann; one s. two d.; ed Bolivian Univ., La Paz, Univ. of Basle, Switzerland, Acad. of American and Int. Law, USA, Int. Faculty of Comparative Law, France and Italy; Prof. of Criminal Law, San Andrés State Univ., La Paz 1973–80, Bolivian Catholic Univ., La Paz 1990–94; Attorney at Law 1975–93; Minister of Justice and Human Rights 1994–97; Chief of Human Rights and Justice Area, UN Human Rights Verification Mission in Guatemala 1998–2000; Dir Andrean Jurists Comm. (CAJ) 1997–2002; Judge, Trial Div., Int. Criminal Court 2003–09, Second Vice-Pres. 2006–09, assigned to Trial Chamber I for the Courts First Trial (Prosecutor vs. Thomas Lubanga in the situation of the Democratic Republic of Congo) 2007; mem. La Paz Bar Asscn, Bolivian Bar Asscn, Andrean Jurists Comm.; Hon. Life mem. Wilshire Bar Asscn, LA, USA 1977; Hon. mem. Experts Asscn on Criminal Law of Bogota and Cundinamarca, Colombia 1995; Bundesverdienstkreuz 2005; Dr hc (Univ. of Basle) 1998, (Humboldt Univ., Berlin) 2010; Robert J. Storey Int. Award of Leadership, Southwestern Legal Foundation, Univ. of Texas at Dallas 1995, Diosa Temis Medal, Nat. Foundation Fora and Interdisciplinary Studies of Colombia 1995, Monseñor Leonidas Proaño Latin American Prize of Human Rights, Latin American Asscn of Human Rights (ALDHU) 1995, Carl Bertelsmann Int. Prize 2001; distinctions from Bolivian Nat. Police 1995, Journalists Asscn of La Paz 1996, Superior Court of Justice of Santa Cruz 1997, Superior Court of Justice of Tarija 1997, Nat. Chamber of Commerce 1997, City Council of La Paz 2000. *Address:* c/o International Criminal Court, Maanweg 174, 2516 AB The Hague, Netherlands. *Telephone:* (70) 515-85-15. *E-mail:* pio@icc-cpi.int.

BLAVATNIK, Kt Sir Leonard (Len), MS, MBA, PhD; American/British (b. Ukrainian) business executive and philanthropist; *Chairman and President, Access Industries, Inc.;* b. (Leonid Valentinovich Blavatnik), 14 June 1957, Odessa, Ukraine; m. Emily Blavatnik; ed Moscow Inst. of Transport Eng, Columbia Univ. and Harvard Business School, USA; emigrated with his family from Russia to USA 1978; served in various man. positions at Arthur Andersen & Co., Macy's Dept Stores and General Atlantic Partners; f. Access Industries industrial group, New York 1986, Chair. and Pres. 1986–; fmr Man. Dir Access Technology Capital; co-f. Russian-American investment group Renova 1990; Partner, Faena Group; Chair. Supervisory Bd LyondellBasell Industries 2007–10; Vice-Chair. Kennan Council of the Woodrow Wilson Center, Washington, DC; Dir of numerous cos in the Access portfolio (including Basell Holdings BV), Wmg Acquisition Corpn 2004–, TNK-BP International Ltd, Svenska Bredbandsbolaget AB and other cos, United Company RUSAL (UC RUSAL) 2009–, Public Jt Stock Co. TNK-BP Holding 2009–10; fmr Dir Tyumen Oil Co., OAO SUAL Holding of Sual Group; fmr mem. Advisory Bd Eurasia Group Ltd; serves on academic boards at Univ. of Cambridge, Harvard Business School and Tel-Aviv Univ.; Dir, The White Nights Foundation of America, 92nd Street Y, The Center for Jewish History, New York; mem. Global Advisory Bd Center for Int. Business and Man., Univ. of Cambridge; mem. Bd of Dean's Advisors, Harvard Business School; Dir, Warner Music Group Corpn 2004–08; mem. Bd Govs New York Acad. of Sciences. *Address:* Access Industries Inc., 730 5th Avenue, 20th Floor, New York, NY 10019-4105, USA (office). *Telephone:* (212) 247-6400 (office). *E-mail:* info@accessindustries.com (office). *Website:* www.accessindustries.com (office).

BLAY-AMIHERE, Kabral; Ghanaian diplomatist and journalist; fmr Ed. The Independent newspaper, Ghana, arrested for publishing criticism of mil. regime 2000; fmr Pres. West African Journalists' Asscn; High Commr to Sierra Leone 2001–05, Amb. to Côte d'Ivoire 2006–09; fmrly Chair. Nat. Media Comm. of Ghana; Chair. McOttley Capital; fmr Dir Ghana Inst. of Journalism; mem. editorial team of ADEA-COMED working group on a toolkit for communication for educ.; Dr hc (Univ. of Sierra Leone) 2007. *Publications include:* Tears for a Continent: An American Diary 1994, Fighting for Freedom: The Autobiography of an African Journalist 2001, Between the Lion and the Elephant: Memoirs of an African Diplomat 2010.

BLÁZQUEZ PÉREZ, HE Cardinal Ricardo, DTheol; Spanish ecclesiastic, theologian and academic; *Archbishop of Valladolid;* b. 13 April 1942, Villanueva del Campillo, Ávila; ed Minor Seminary of Ávila, Arenas de San Pedro, Seminary of Ávila, Pontifical Gregorian Univ., Rome; ordained priest 1967; Sec., Abulense Theological Inst. 1972–76; Prof., Faculty of Theology, Pontifical Univ. of Salamanca 1974–88, Dean of Faculty 1978–81, Chancellor of Univ. 2000–05; Auxiliary Bishop of Santiago de Compostela 1988–92, consecrated Titular Bishop of Germa in Galatia 1988–92; Bishop of Palencia 1992–95; Bishop of Bilbao 1995–2010; Archbishop of Valladolid 2010–; Pres. Episcopal Comm. for Doctrine of Faith, Spanish Episcopal Conf. 1993–2002, Interfaith Relations 2002–05, Pres. Spanish Episcopal Conf. 2005–08, 2014–, Vice-Pres. 2008–14, represented Episcopal Conf. at XIIIth Ordinary Gen. Ass. of Synod of Bishops 2012; apptd by Holy See as Man. of Apostolic Visitation of Regnum Christi Movt 2010; mem. Congregation for Insts of Consecrated Life and Socs of Apostolic Life 2014–; cr. Cardinal (Cardinal-Priest of Santa Maria in Vallicella) 2015. *Publications include:* La resurrección en la cristología de Wolfhart Pannenberg 1976, Jesús sí, la Iglesia también 1983, Jesús, el Evangelio de Dios 1985, Las comunidades neocatecumenales. Discernimiento teológico 1988, La Iglesia del Concilio Vaticano II 1989, Tradición y esperanza 1989, Iniciación cristiana y nueva evangelización 1992, Transmitir el Evangelio de la verdad 1997, En el umbral del tercer milenio 1999, La esperanza en Dios no defrauda: consideraciones teológico-pastorales de un obispo 2004, Iglesia, ¿qué dices de Dios? 2007, Iglesia y Palabra de Dios 2011, Del Vaticano II a la Nueva Evangelización 2013, Un obispo comenta el Credo 2013; numerous documents of the Spanish Episcopal Conf. *Address:* Arzobispado, San Juan de Dios 5, 47003 Valladolid, Spain (office). *Telephone:* (983) 217929 (office). *Fax:* (983) 217930 (office). *E-mail:* informatica@archivalladolid.org (office). *Website:* www.archivalladolid.org (office).

BLAZWICK, Iwona, OBE; British art critic and curator; *Director, Whitechapel Art Gallery, London;* b. 1955, London; ed Exeter Univ.; Dir AIR Gallery, London 1984–86; Curator, Inst. of Contemporary Arts (ICA), becoming Dir of Exhbns 1987–93; Commissioning Ed. Phaidon Press during 1990s; ind. curator for museums and public arts projects in Europe and Japan 1993–97; Head of Exhbns, Tate Modern 1997–2001; Dir Whitechapel Art Gallery, London 2001–; Visiting Tutor at several art colls and acads in Europe and Canada; Series Ed. Documents of Contemporary Art; mem. several cultural juries including Turner Prize 1993, Jerwood Painting Prize 1997, Wexner Prize 2002, Vincent Prize, Max Mara Art Prize for Women, Golden Lion Award, Venice Biennale; mem. London Cultural Strategy Group; Fellow, RCA; hon. degrees from London Metropolitan Univ., Univ. of Plymouth. *Publications include:* numerous exhbn catalogues; An Endless Adventure, An Endless Passion, An Endless Banquet 1989, Alan Charlton: Paintings 1991, Katharina Fritsch 2002, Lawrence Weiner, Ilya Kabakov, Tate Modern: the Handbook (ed.), Century City (ed.), Fresh Cream (ed.) 2000. *Address:* Whitechapel Gallery, 77–82 Whitechapel High Street, London, E1 7QX, England (office). *Telephone:* (20) 7522-7888 (office). *Fax:* (20) 7377-1635 (office). *E-mail:* info@whitechapelgallery.org (office). *Website:* www.whitechapelgallery.org (office).

BLEARS, Hazel Anne, BA; British politician; b. 14 May 1956, Salford, Greater Manchester; d. of Arthur Blears and Dorothy Blears; m. Michael Halsall 1989; ed Wardley Grammar School, Trent Polytechnic; trainee solicitor, Salford Council 1978–80; in pvt. practice 1980–81; solicitor, Rossendale Council 1981–83, Wigan

Council 1983–85; Councillor, Salford City Council 1984–92; Prin. Solicitor, Manchester City Council 1985–97; contested Tatton 1987 and Bury South 1992 general elections; MP (Labour) for Salford 1997–2010, for Salford and Eccles 2010–15; Parl. Pvt. Sec. to Alan Milburn: as Minister of State, Dept of Health 1998, as Chief Sec., HM Treasury 1999; Parl. Under-Sec. of State, Dept of Health 2001–03; Minister of State, Home Office 2003–06; Minister without Portfolio 2006–07; Sec. of State for Communities and Local Govt 2007–09 (resgnd); mem. Intelligence and Security Cttee 2010–; mem. North West Exec., Labour Party 1997–99, Nat. Policy Forum 1997–2001, Leadership Campaign Team 1997–98, Labour Party Devt Co-ordinator and Deputy to Ian McCartney 1998–2001, Leader, Parl. Campaign Team 2003–, Labour Party Nat. Exec. Cttee 2004–, Chair. Labour Party 2006–07; Chair. Social Action Forum 2010–12. *Publications:* Communities in Control 2003, The Politics of Decency 2004. *Leisure interests:* dance, motorcycling.

BLEASDALE, Alan; British playwright and novelist; b. 23 March 1946, Liverpool; s. of George Bleasdale and Margaret Bleasdale; m. Julia Moses 1970; two s. one d.; ed Wade Deacon Grammar School, Widnes, Padgate Teachers Training Coll.; schoolteacher 1967–75; playwright, Liverpool Playhouse 1975, Contact Theatre 1976; Hon. DLitt (Liverpool Polytechnic) 1991; BAFTA Writers Award 1982, Royal TV Soc. Writer of the Year 1982, Pye Television Award 1983, Toronto Film Festival Critics' Award 1984, Broadcasting Press Guild Award 1991. *Publications include:* Scully 1975, Who's Been Sleeping in My Bed? 1977, No More Sitting on the Old School Bench 1979, Boys from the Blackstuff 1982, Are You Lonesome Tonight? (Best Musical, Evening Standard Drama Awards 1985) 1985, No Surrender (film script) 1986, Having a Ball 1986, It's a Madhouse 1986, The Monocled Mutineer (televised 1986) 1986, GBH (TV series) 1991, On the Ledge 1993, Jake's Progress (TV, Best Writer, Monte Carlo Int. TV Festival 1996) 1995, Oliver Twist (Best Drama Series, TV and Radio Industries Club 2000) 1999, The Sinking of the Laconia (TV script) 2011. *Leisure interest:* rowing. *Address:* c/o Stephen Durbridge, The Agency, 24 Pottery Lane, Holland Park, London, W11 4LZ, England (office). *Telephone:* (20) 7727-1346 (office). *E-mail:* sd-office@theagency.co.uk (office); info@theagency.co.uk (office). *Website:* www.theagency.co.uk (office).

BLECHA, Karl; Austrian fmr politician; *President, Austrian Union of Pensioners;* b. 16 April 1933, Vienna; s. of Karl Matthias Blecha and Rosa Blecha; m. 1st Ilse Steinhauser 1965; two d.; m. 2nd Burgunde Teuber 1982; m. 3rd Radostina Belcheva 1999; one d.; ed Univ. of Vienna; vocational adviser in Vienna Employment Exchange and later reader in publishing firm; Founder and Dir Inst. for Empirical Social Research 1963–75; mem. Lower Austrian SPÖ (Austrian Socialist Party) Exec. 1964–90; mem. Nationalrat 1970–89; Gen. Sec. SPÖ HQ 1976–81, Vice-Chair. SPÖ 1981–89; Federal Minister of the Interior 1983–89; Founder and Man. Dir Mitropa Inst. for Econ. and Social Research, Vienna 1989–; fmr Chair. Socialist Student Movt, Socialist Young Generation, Austrian Asscn for Cultural Affairs; Pres. Austrian Soc. for Promotion of Research 1994–; Pres. Austrian Union of Pensioners 1999–, Council of Sr in Austria 1999–, Society for Austro-Arab Relations, Social Democratic Party Retirees Asscn; mem. Nat. Council 1970–83, Feb.–April 1989; mem. Advisory Bd Mediamixx Group. *Publications include:* numerous essays on sociology and various articles and brochures on political principles. *Address:* Society for Austro-Arab Relations, Anschützgasse 1, 1150 Vienna (office); Mitropa Institute for Economic and Social Research, Stubenring 14, 1010 Vienna, Austria (office). *Telephone:* (1) 31372-0 (office); (664) 340-42-86 (office). *Fax:* (1) 31372-12 (office). *E-mail:* office@mitropa-institut.at (office). *Website:* www.saar.at (office); mitropa-institute.eu (office).

BLECHARCZYK, Nathan, BSc; American software engineer and business executive; *Co-Founder and Chief Technology Officer, Airbnb, Inc.;* b. 1984; s. of Paul Blecharczyk and Sheila Blecharczyk (née Underwood); m. Elizabeth Morey; one d.; ed Harvard Univ.; Teaching Fellow, Harvard Univ. Feb.–June 2005; Software Engineer, OPNET Technologies, Inc. 2005–06; Chief Developer, Batiq 2007–08; Owner, Consult Mavens, LLC 2006–08; Co-Founder and Chief Tech. Officer, Airbnb, Inc. 2008–. *Address:* Airbnb Inc., 888 Brannan Street, Suite 400, San Francisco, CA 94103-4932, USA (office). *Website:* www.airbnb.com (office).

BLENCATHRA, Baron (Life Peer), cr. 2011, of Penrith in the County of Cumbria; **Rt Hon. David John,** PC; British politician; b. 16 May 1953, Cromarty, Ross and Cromarty, Scotland; ed Fortrose Acad., Univ. of Aberdeen; elected to House of Commons in by-election as MP (Conservative) for Penrith and The Border 1983–2010; Asst Govt Whip 1987–88, Govt Whip 1988–89; Parl. Sec. to Ministry of Agric., Fisheries and Food 1989–92; Minister of State at Dept of the Environment 1992–93, at Home Office 1993–97; returned to back benches 1997–2001; Opposition Chief Whip 2001–03, 2003–05; returned to back benches 2005–10; mem. House of Commons Comm. 2006; Chair. Jt Cttee on Statutory Instruments 2006, mem. Liaison 2006. *Address:* House of Lords, Westminster, London, SW1A 0PW, England (office). *Telephone:* (20) 7219-3000 (office).

BLENDON, Robert J., ScD, MPH, MBA; American academic; *Senior Associate Dean for Policy Translation and Leadership Development, Harvard University;* b. 19 Dec. 1942, Philadelphia, Pa; s. of Edward G. Blendon and Theresa M. Blendon; m. Marie C. McCormick 1977; ed Marietta Coll., Univ. of Chicago and Johns Hopkins Univ., Baltimore, Md; Instructor, Johns Hopkins Univ. School of Hygiene and Public Health 1969, Asst to Assoc. Dean (Health Care Programs) 1969–70, Asst Prof. 1970–71, Asst Dir for Planning and Devt, Office of Health Care Programs 1970–71; Special Asst for Health Affairs to Deputy Under-Sec. for Policy Co-ordination, Dept of Health Educ. and Welfare 1971–72, Special Asst for Policy Devt to Asst Sec. for Health and Scientific Affairs 1971–72; Visiting Lecturer, Princeton Univ. 1972–80, Co-ordinator, Medicine in Modern America Course 1980–; Sr Vice-Pres. The Robert Wood Johnson Foundation 1980–87; Prof., Dept of Health Policy and Political Analysis, Harvard Univ. School of Public Health 1987–, Chair. 1987–96, Sr Assoc. Dean for Policy Translation and Leadership Devt 2010–, Richard L. Menschel Prof. of Public Health and Prof. of Health Policy and Political Analysis; Prof., Kennedy School of Govt 1987–; numerous other professional appointments; Distinguished Investigator Award, AHSR 2000, Warren G. Mitofsky Award. *Publications:* numerous articles in professional journals. *Address:* Harvard University School of Public Health, Kresge Building, Room 402, 677 Huntington Avenue, Boston, MA 02115 (office); 478 Quinobequin Road, Waban, MA 02468-2127, USA (home). *Telephone:* (617) 432-4502 (office); (617) 965-8279 (home). *E-mail:* rblendon@hsph.harvard.edu (office). *Website:* www.hsph.harvard.edu/faculty/robert-blendon (office).

BLESSED, Brian, OBE; British actor and writer; b. 9 Oct. 1936, Mexborough, S Yorks.; s. of William Blessed and Hilda Wall; m. Hildegard Neil 1978; one d.; ed Bolton-on-Dearne Secondary Modern School, Bristol Old Vic Theatre School; began acting career in repertory cos, mainly Nottingham and later Birmingham Repertory Co.; appeared with RSC as Claudius in Hamlet, Hastings in Richard III, Exeter in Henry V; one-man show An Evening with Brian Blessed; Pres. Council for Nat. Parks; Hon. DLitt (Bradford), (Sheffield). *Theatre includes:* Cats, Metropolis, Lion In Winter, Chitty Chitty Bang Bang, London Palladium, State of Revolution, The Relapse, Royal Nat. Theatre, King Lear, The Hollow (Dir), Spider's Web (Dir). *Films include:* The Christmas Tree 1966, Asterix the Gaul (voice) 1967, Till Death Us Do Part 1969, The Same Skin 1970, The Last Valley 1971, The Trojan Women 1971, Henry VIII and His Six Wives 1972, Man of La Mancha 1972, King Arthur, the Young Warlord 1975, Flash Gordon 1980, High Road to China 1983, Asterix and the Big Fight (voice: English version) 1989, Henry V 1989, Waiting for Godot 1991, Robin Hood: Prince of Thieves 1991, Back in the U.S.S.R. 1992, Freddie as F.R.O.7. (voice) 1992, Agincourt 1415: The Triumph of the Longbow (video) (narrator) 1993, Much Ado About Nothing 1993, Chasing the Deer 1994, The Bruce 1996, Hamlet 1996, King Lear: A Critical Guide (video documentary short) 1997, Macbeth 1997, King Lear (also dir) 1999, Star Wars: Episode I – The Phantom Menace 1999, Tarzan 1999, Day Return (short) 2000, The Mumbo Jumbo 2000, Olympiad 448 BC: Olympiad of Ancient Hellas (narrator) 2004, Alexander 2004, Midsummer Dream 2005, Day of Wrath 2006, The Conclave 2006, As You Like It 2006, Back in Business 2007, Agent Crush 2008, Mr. Bojagi (short) 2009, Re-Evolution 2011, The Pirates! In an Adventure with Scientists! 2012, Legends of Oz: Dorothy's Return (voice) 2013, Shed of the Dead (narrator) 2017, Robin Hood - The Rebellion 2018. *Television includes:* role of Fancy Smith in Z Cars 1963–78, Ghost Squad (series) 1963, The Three Musketeers (mini-series) 1966–67, The Further Adventures of the Musketeers (series) 1967, The Troubleshooters (series) 1968, Cold Comfort Farm (mini-series) 1968, The Avengers (series) 1967–69, Barrister at Law (film) 1969, Randall and Hopkirk (Deceased) (series) 1969, The Wednesday Play – Son of Man 1969, The Wednesday Play – Wine of India 1970, Whom God Hath Joined (film) 1970, Jackanory (series) (storyteller) 1971, The Expert (series) 1971, Shirley's World (series) 1971, The Venturers (film) 1972, Public Eye (series) 1973, Justice (series) 1973, Love Story (series) 1973, ITV Sunday Night Theatre – Lorna and Ted 1973, Hadleigh (series) 1973, Arthur of the Britons (series) 1972–73, BBC Play of the Month – The Recruiting Officer 1973, Boy Dominic (series) 1974, Notorious Woman (mini-series) 1974, The Great Alfred (film) 1975, The Sweeney (series) 1975, Churchill's People (series) 1975, Thriller (series) 1975, NBC Special Treat (series) 1975, The Story of David (film) 1976, The Day After Tomorrow (film) 1976, Space: 1999 (series) 1975–76, I, Claudius (mini-series) 1976, Survivors (series) 1977, A Christmas Carol (film) 1977, Blakes 7 (series) 1978, ITV Playhouse – Double Agent 1969, The Aphrodite Inheritance (mini-series) 1979, Tales of the Unexpected (series) 1979, ITV Playhouse – Saint Vitus' Dance 1979, Leap in the Dark (series) 1980, The Little World of Don Camillo (series) 1981, Cosmic Princess (film) 1982, Black Adder (series) 1983, The Hound of the Baskervilles (film) 1983, The Master of Ballantrae (film) 1984, The Last Days of Pompeii (mini-series) 1984, Return to Treasure Island (series) 1986, Doctor Who (series) 1986, The Kenny Everett Television Show (series) 1986, William Tell (series) 1987, My Family and Other Animals (series) 1987, David Macaulay: Pyramid (film) 1988, Once in a Life Time (film) 1988, Boon (series) 1989, Minder (series) 1989, War and Remembrance (mini-series) 1988–89, Blood Royal: William the Conqueror (film) 1990, The Castle of Adventure (series) 1990, Galahad of Everest 1991, Lovejoy (series) 1991, Prisoner of Honor (film) 1991, Blood and Dust (film) 1992, Exam Conditions (film) 1992, Lady Chatterley (series) 1993, MacGyver: Lost Treasure of Atlantis (film) 1994, Johnny and the Dead (series) 1995, Kidnapped (film) 1995, Catherine the Great (film) 1996, The History of Tom Jones, a Foundling (mini-series) 1997, Dennis the Menace (series) 1998, Adam's Family Tree (series) 1999, The Big Knights (series) 1999, The Greatest Store in the World (film) 1999, The Nearly Complete and Utter History of Everything (film) 1999, Devil's Harvest 2003, Winter Solstice (film) 2003, Let's Write a Story (series documentary) 2004, The Legend of the Tamworth Two (film) 2004, Alexander the Great (video documentary) (narrator) 2006, Mist: The Tale of a Sheepdog Puppy (film) 2006, Peppa Pig (series) 2006–10, Doctors (series) 2007–11, Kika & Bob (mini-series) 2008, The Wrong Door (series) 2008, Family Guy (series) 2008, The Royal (series) 2008, Henry 8.0 (series) 2009, Fee Fi Fo Yum (series) 2010, Little Princess (series) 2010, The Legend of Dick and Dom (series) 2010–11, Lego Star Wars: The Empire Strikes Out (film) 2012, Wizards vs. Aliens (series) 2012–13, Let's Dance for Sport Relief (series) (voice) 2013, Henry Hugglemonster (series) 2013–15, Sooty (series) 2013, The Amazing World of Gumball (series) 2013, Danger Mouse (series) 2015, Toast of London (series) 2015, The Lodge 2017. *Publications:* The Turquoise Mountain, The Dynamite Kid, Nothing's Impossible, Blessed Everest, Quest to the Lost World, Absolute Pandemonium, Panther In My Kitchen 2017. *Leisure interests:* mountaineering, judo (black belt), animal welfare. *Address:* c/o Stephen Gittins, Associated International Management LLP, Studio 405, The Print Rooms, 164–180 Union Street, London, SE1 0LH, England (office). *Telephone:* (20) 7831-9709 (office). *E-mail:* info@aimagents.com (office). *Website:* aimagents.com/actors/brian-blessed (office).

BLESSING, Martin, MBA; German banker; *Chairman, Board of Managing Directors, Commerzbank AG;* b. 6 July 1963, Bremen; m.; three d.; ed Univ. of Frankfurt, Univ. of St Gallen, Switzerland, Univ. of Chicago, USA; apprenticeship at Dresdner Bank AG, Frankfurt 1983–84, Jt Man. Pvt. Customers 1997–2000; univ. studies 1984–88; Frankfurt and New York consultant, McKinsey 1989–96, Pnr 1994; Chair. Advance Bank AG, Munich 2000–01; mem. Bd of Man. Dirs Commerzbank AG, Frankfurt 2001– (responsible for retail banking div. 2001–04, for Information Tech. and Transaction Banking and for Mittelstand Banking Depts of Corp. Banking and Financial Insts 2004–07), Chair. 2008–; mem. Supervisory Bd AMB Generali, Heidelberger Druckmaschinen, ThyssenKrupp Services. *Leisure interests:* jogging, skiing, running the marathon. *Address:* Commerzbank AG, 60261 Frankfurt, Germany (office). *Telephone:* (69) 13620 (office). *Fax:* (69) 285389 (office). *E-mail:* info@commerzbank.com (office). *Website:* www.commerzbank.com (office).

BLETHYN, Brenda Anne, OBE; British actress; b. 20 Feb. 1946, Ramsgate, Kent; d. of William Charles Bottle and Louisa Kathleen Bottle; m. Michael Mayhew 2010; ed St Augustine's RC School, Ramsgate, Thanet Tech. Coll., Guildford School of Acting; with Nat. Theatre (now Royal Nat. Theatre) 1975–90; mem. Poetry Soc. 1976–; Hon. DLitt (Kent) 1999, (Surrey) 2006; numerous awards including Boston Film Critics' Award 1997, LA Film Critics' Award 1997, Golden Globe 1997, London Film Critics' Award 1997, BAFTA 1997. *Theatre appearances include:* for Royal Nat. Theatre: A Midsummer Night's Dream, Troilus and Cressida, Bedroom Farce, Tales From the Vienna Woods, The Guardsman, Fruits of Enlightenment, Madras House, The Provoked Wife, Strife, Force of Habit, Tamburlaine, Plunder (also Old Vic), Camilla Ringbinder Show, Bloody Neighbours (at ICA), The Mysteries 1979, The Double Dealer 1982, Dalliance 1987, The Beaux Stratagem 1989; for Comedy Theatre, London: Steaming (Theatre Critics' Best Supporting Actress Award) 1981; for Vaudeville Theatre, London: Benefactors 1984; for Royal Exchange Theatre, Manchester: A Doll's House 1987, Born Yesterday 1988, An Ideal Husband 1992; for RSC: Wildest Dreams 1993; for Bush Theatre, London: Crimes of the Heart; for Almeida Theatre, London: The Bed Before Yesterday 1994; for Donmar Theatre, London, Habeas Corpus 1996; for Nuffield Theatre, Southampton: The Dramatic Attitudes of Miss Fanny Kemble; for Manhattan Theater Club, New York: Absent Friends (Theatre World Award for Outstanding New Talent 1996) 1996; Mrs Warren's Profession (West End, London) 2002–03, Haunted (Manchester, Sydney, New York) 2014. *Films:* Witches, A River Runs Through It 1992, Secrets and Lies (Golden Globe Best Actress 1996, Best Actress Award, Cannes Film Festival 1996, London Film Critics' Circle Best Actress of the Year Award 1996, Boston Critics' Circle Best Actress Award 1996, LA Critics' Circle Best Actress Award 1996, British Acad. Award: Best Actress 1997, Premier Magazine Best Actress Award 1997) 1996, Remember Me 1996, Music From Another Room 1997, Girls' Night 1997, Little Voice (Dallas Fort Worth Critics' Asscn Best Supporting Actress 1999) 1999, Saving Grace (Sundance Film Festival Audience Award 2000, Variety Club of Great Britain Best Screen Actress Award 2001) 1999, On the Nose, In the Winter Dark, Night Train 1999, Daddy and Them 1999, RKO 281 1999, The Sleeping Dictionary 2000, Yellow Bird, Pumpkin 2000, Anne Frank – The Whole Story 2001, Lovely and Amazing 2001, Plots with a View 2002, Sonny 2002, Blizzard 2002, Beyond the Sea 2004, A Way of Life 2004, On a Clear Day 2005, Pride and Prejudice 2006, Atonement 2007, Clubland 2007, Dead Man Running 2009, My Angel 2011, Two Men in Town 2014. *Television includes:* Mona, All Good Things, Grown Ups, The Imitation Game, That Uncertain Feeling, Floating Off, Claws, Sheppey, Yes Minister, Alas Smith and Jones, The Shawl, Rumpole, Maigret, Bedroom Farce, The Double Dealer, Death of an Expert Witness, The Storyteller, The Richest Woman in the World, The RNT Mysteries, Henry VI (Part I) 1981, King Lear 1983, Chance in a Million 1983–85, The Labours of Erica 1987, The Bullion Boys 1993, The Buddha of Suburbia 1993, Sleeping with Mickey 1993, Outside Edge (Television's Best Comedy Actress Award) 1994–96, First Signs of Madness 1996, Between the Sheets 2003, Belonging 2004, Mysterious Creatures 2006, War and Peace 2007, Law & Order: Special Victims Unit 2008, The New Adventures of Old Christine (series) 2008, Vera (series) 2011–, King of the Teds (film) 2012, Mary and Martha (TV Movie) 2013. *Publication:* Mixed Fancies (memoir) 2006. *Leisure interests:* reading, swimming, cryptic crosswords, running. *Address:* c/o Independent Talent Group Limited, Oxford House, 76 Oxford Street, London, W1D 1BS, England. *Telephone:* (20) 7636-6565. *Fax:* (20) 7323-0101. *E-mail:* info@independenttalent.com. *Website:* www.independenttalent.com.

BLEWETT, Neal, AC, MA, DPhil, FRHistS, FASSA; Australian politician; b. 24 Oct. 1933, Sydney; s. of James Blewett and Phyllis Blewett (née Kerrison); m. Jill Myford 1962 (died 1988); one s. one d.; ed Launceston High School, Tasmania, Univ. of Tasmania, Univ. of Oxford, UK; Lecturer, Univ. of Oxford 1959–64; Prof., Dept of Political Theory and Insts, Flinders Univ. 1974–77; MP for Bonython, South Australia 1977–94; Minister for Health 1983–87, for Community Services and Health 1987–90, for Trade and Overseas Devt 1990–91, Minister for Social Security 1991–93; High Commr in UK 1994–98; Pres. Australian Inst. of Int. Affairs 1998–2006; Pres. Alcohol and Other Drugs Council of Australia 2002–; mem. Exec. Bd WHO 1995–98; Visiting Prof., Faculty of Medicine, Univ. of Sydney 1999–; Hon. Fellow, Jesus Coll. (Oxford); Hon. DLit (Hull), Hon. LLD (Tasmania, ANU) 2003; Dr hc (Univ. of Technology, Sydney) 2010. *Publications:* Playford to Dunstan: The Politics of Transition (with Dean Jaensch) 1971, The Peers, the Parties and the People 1972, A Cabinet Diary 1999. *Leisure interests:* reading, bush walking, cinema. *Address:* 32 Fitzroy Street, Leura, NSW 2780, Australia. *Telephone:* (2) 4784-3478 (home). *Fax:* (2) 4784-3478 (home).

BLIER, Bertrand; French film director and screenwriter; b. 14 March 1939, Paris; s. of Bernard Blier and Gisèle Brunet; m. Catherine Florin 1973; one d.; also one s. by Anouk Grinberg; ed Lycée Claude Bernard, Paris; Grand Prix Nat. du Cinema 1989. *Films include:* Hitler, connais pas 1963, Si j'étais un espion (Breakdown) 1967, Les valseuses (Making It) 1974, Calmos 1975, Préparez vos mouchoirs (Oscar for Best Foreign Film) 1977, Buffet froid (three Césars) 1979, Beau-père 1981, La femme de mon pote (My Best Friend's Girl) 1983, Notre histoire (Separate Rooms) 1984, Tenue de soirée 1986, Trop belle pour toi (Cannes Special Jury Prize 1989) 1988, Merci la vie 1991, Tango 1992, Un deux trois – soleil 1993, Mon homme 1996, Les acteurs 2000, Les côtelettes 2003, Combien tu m'aimes? 2005, Le Bruit des glaçons 2010. *Publications:* several novels and film scripts. *Address:* c/o Artmédia, 10 avenue Georges V, 75008 Paris (office); 11 rue Margueritte, 75017 Paris, France (home).

BLIGE, Mary J.; American singer and songwriter; b. 11 Jan. 1971, Bronx, New York; m. Kendu Isaacs 2003; solo artist; numerous tours and live appearances; has collaborated with numerous musicians, including the late George Michael, Lauryn Hill; Co-founder Foundation for the Advancement of Women Now; American Music Award for Favorite Female Hip-Hop/R&B Artist 2003, for Favorite Female Soul/R&B Artist 2006, Grammy Award for Best Pop Collaboration with Vocals (jtly) 2004, BET Award for Best Female R&B Artist 2006, nine Billboard Awards 2006, Grammy Award for Best Female R&B Vocal Performance (for Be Without You) 2007. *Films:* I Can Do Bad All By Myself 2009, Mudbound 2017. *Recordings include:* albums: What's The 411? 1992, My Life 1994, Mary Jane 1995, Share My World 1997, The Tour 1998, Mary 1999, No More Drama 2001, Ballads 2001, Love & Life 2003, The Breakthrough (American Music Award for Favorite Soul/R&B Album 2006, Grammy Award for Best R&B Album 2007, Best R&B/Soul Album by a Female Artist, Soul Train Awards 2007) 2005, Growing Pains (Grammy Award for Best Contemporary R&B Album 2009) 2007, Stronger with Each Tear 2009, My Life II: The Journey Continues 2011, Think Like a Man Too 2014, The London Sessions 2014, Strength of a Woman (BET Her Award 2018) 2017. *Address:* Steve Lucas Associates, 156 West 56th Street, New York, NY 10019, USA (office). *Website:* www.maryjblige.com.

BLIKLE, Andrzej, PhD; Polish mathematician and academic; *Professor Emeritus, Institute of Computer Science, Polish Academy of Sciences;* b. 24 Sept. 1939, Warsaw; s. of Jerzy Blikle and Aniela Blikle; m.; one s.; ed Warsaw Univ.; master of confectioner's trade 1975; scientific worker, Inst. of Math., Polish Acad. of Sciences 1963–71, Computational Centre, Polish Acad. of Sciences 1971–77, Prof., Inst. of Computer Science, Polish Acad. of Sciences 1977–2004, Prof. Emer. 2004–; Pres. and CEO A. Blikle Ltd 1991–2010, Chair. Bd 2008–10, Chair. Supervisory Bd 2010–12, Vice-Chair. 2013–; Pres. Family Business Initiative 2008–; Vice-Pres., then Pres. Polish Fed. of Food Industries 1998–2005; mem. Polish Math. Soc. 1962–, Polish Information Processing Soc. 1981– (Pres. 1987–93), Asscn for Theoretical Computer Science 1982–, Academia Europaea 1993, Asscn of Association of Mathematics and Informatics with Disabilities; mem. European Acad. of Sciences; Hon. mem. Polish Information Processing Soc.; Hon. Amb. of Warsaw 2009; Golden Cross of Merit 1987, Cross of Merit 2005, Tadeusz Kotarbinski Medal, Polish Acad. of Sciences 2008; Young Mathematician Award, Polish Math. Asscn 1967, Golden Award, Polish Tech. and Scientific Publisher 1989, Jan Kilinski Silver Medal of Merit, Bd of Polish Craft Asscn 2001, Warsaw Medal of Merit 2001, Tadeusz Kotarbinski Medal, Polish Acad. of Sciences 2008. *Publication:* MetaSoft Primer – Towards a Metalanguage for Applied Denotational Semantics Series: Lecture Notes in Computer Science (Vol. 288) (co-ed.) 1987. *Leisure interests:* skiing, windsurfing, films, history. *Address:* ul. Czarnieckiego 82, 01-541 Warsaw, Poland (home). *Telephone:* (22) 8396365 (home). *Fax:* (22) 8396365 (office). *E-mail:* andrzej.blikle@blikle.pl (office). *Website:* www.moznainaczej.com.pl (office).

BLINDER, Alan Stuart, AB, MSc, PhD; American economist and academic; *Gordon S. Rentschler Memorial Professor of Economics and Public Affairs, Princeton University;* b. 14 Oct. 1945, New York; s. of Morris Blinder and Shirley Blinder; m. Madeline Schwartz 1967; two s.; ed Princeton Univ., London School of Econs, UK, Massachusetts Inst. of Tech.; Deputy Asst Dir US Congressional Budget Office 1975; Gordon S. Rentschler Memorial Prof. of Econs, Princeton Univ. 1982–2007, of Econs and Public Affairs 2007–, Dir Center for Econ. Policy Studies 1989–93, Co.-Dir 1996–2011; mem. Council of Econ. Advisors to Pres. Clinton 1993–94; Vice-Chair. Bd of Govs, Fed. Reserve System 1994–96; Vice-Chair. G7 Group 1997–; Pnr, Promotory Financial Group 2000–; mem. American Philosophical Soc. 1996–; Fellow, American Acad. of Arts and Sciences 1991–. *Publications include:* Growing Together: An Alternative Economic Strategy for the 1990s 1991, Central Banking in Theory and Practice 1998, Asking About Prices: A New Approach to Understanding Price Stickiness (jtly) 1998, Economics, Principles and Policy (jtly) 2000, The Fabulous Decade: Macroeconomic Lessons from the 1990s (jtly) 2001, The Quiet Revolution: Central Banking Goes Modern 2004, Offshoring of American Jobs: What Response from U.S. Economic Policy? (jtly) 2009, After the Music Stopped 2013. *Address:* Department of Economics, Princeton University, 105 Fisher Hall, Princeton, NJ 08544, USA (office). *Telephone:* (609) 258-4023 (office). *Fax:* (609) 258-5398 (office). *E-mail:* blinder@princeton.edu (office). *Website:* www.princeton.edu/blinder (office).

BLISS, Timothy Vivian Pelham, PhD, FRS, FMedSci; British neuroscientist and academic; *Visiting Worker, Division of Neurophysiology, National Institute for Medical Research;* b. 27 July 1940, Weymouth; s. of Pelham Marryat Bliss and Elizabeth Bliss (née Sproule); m. 1st Virginia Catherine Morton-Evans 1975; one step-s. two step-d.; m. 2nd Isabel Frances Vasseur; two step-s.; one d. by Katherine Clough; ed McGill Univ., Montreal, Hatfield Polytechnic (Univ. of Hertfordshire); mem. of scientific staff, MRC at Nat. Inst. for Medical Research 1967–, Head, Div. of Neurophysiology 1988–2006, Visiting Worker 2006–, Head, Neurosciences Group 1996–2006; Visiting Prof., Dept of Physiology, Univ. Coll. London 1993–; Researcher, Francis Crick Inst.; Trustee, Sir John Soane's Museum 2003–08; Dr hc (Dalhousie Univ.) 2013, (Univ. of Hertfordshire) 2014; Bristol Myers Squibb Prize for Neuroscience 1991, Feldberg Prize 1994, British Neuroscience Asscn Award for Outstanding Contribution to British Neuroscience 2003, Royal Society Croonian Lecture 2012, Fondation Ipsen Prize for Neuronal Plasticity (jt winner) 2013, Brain Prize (jt winner) 2016. *Publications include:* more than 100 papers in scientific journals relating to the neural basis of learning and memory. *Leisure interests:* architecture, food, wine, naval history, travelling. *Address:* 18 Market Place, Aylsham, Norfolk, NR11 6EH, England (home). *Telephone:* (1263) 734216 (home). *E-mail:* tbliss@nimr.mrc.ac.uk (office).

BLIX, Hans Martin, LLD, PhD; Swedish lawyer and international official (retd); b. 28 June 1928, Uppsala; s. of Gunnar Blix and Hertha Blix (née Wiberg); m. Eva Kettis 1962; two s.; ed Uppsala Univ., Univ. of Cambridge, UK, Columbia Univ., New York, USA, Univ. of Stockholm; Asst Prof. of Int. Law, Univ. of Stockholm 1960–63; Legal Consultant on Int. Law, Foreign Ministry 1963–76; Under-Sec. of State for Int. Devt Co-operation, Foreign Ministry 1976–78, 1979–81; Minister for Foreign Affairs 1978–79; Dir-Gen. IAEA, Vienna 1981–97; mem. Swedish del. to UN Gen. Ass. 1961–81; mem. del. to Conf. on Disarmament, Geneva 1962–78; Exec. Chair. UN Monitoring, Verification and Inspection Comm. for Iraq 2000–03; Hon. Chair. World Nuclear Asscn; Commdr, Légion d'honneur 2004; Dr hc (Moscow State Univ.) 1987, (Cambridge) 2007, and several other univs; Henry de Wolf Smyth Award 1988, Gold Medal, Uranium Inst. (now World Nuclear Asscn) 1997, Olof Palme Prize 2003, Fulbright Prize 2014. *Publications include:* Treaty-Making Power (dissertation), Statsmyndigheternas Internationella Förbindelser (monograph) 1964, Sovereignty, Aggression and Neutrality 1970, The Treaty-Maker's Handbook 1973, Disarming Iraq: The Search for Weapons of Mass Destruction 2004, Why Nuclear Disarmament Matters 2008; numerous articles in scientific journals. *Leisure interests:* Oriental rugs, art.

BLIZNAKOV, Veselin Vitanov; Bulgarian scientist and politician; b. 18 June 1944, Straldga, Yambol Dist; m.; ed Vassil Kkaragyizov High School, Yambol, Medical Acad., Sofia; began career in general practice, Bourgas Dist 1972–75; Researcher Assoc. and Head of Lab., Nat. Centre for Radio-Biology and Radiation Protection, Sofia 1976–86, Head, Radiation Protection Dept 1986–99; Chair.

Bulgarian Nuclear Soc. 1999–2001; fmr mem. Civil Cttee for Protection of Nuclear Power Plant Kozloduy; co-owner Dr. Atanas Shterev's Clinic; mem. Nat. Ass. for Vratsa 2001–05, for Haskovo 2005–09, Chair. Energy Cttee 2001–05, mem. Foreign Policy, Defence and Security Cttees 2001–05; Deputy Chair. Parl. Group of Simeon II Nat. Movt 2001–03; mem. Del. to Jt Bulgarian-EU Parl. Cttee 2001; Minister of Defence 2005–08; mem. Governing Council, European Nuclear Soc. 1999–2001.

BLIZNASHKI, Georgi Petkov, PhD; Bulgarian professor of law and politician; *Professor of Constitutional Law, St Clement of Ohrid University of Sofia;* b. 4 Oct. 1956, Skravena, Sofia; ed St Clement of Ohrid Univ. of Sofia; Asst Prof., Dept of Constitutional and Legal Studies, St Clement of Ohrid Univ. of Sofia 1983–87, Chief Asst Prof. 1987–90, Asst Prof. of Constitutional Law 1990–2004, Prof. of Constitutional Law 2009–, mem. Faculty Council, Law Faculty 2011–; fmr Lecturer at South-West Univ. Neofit Rilski, Blagoevgrad, Varna Free Univ., New Bulgarian Univ.; mem. Nat. Ass. 1992–94, 2005–09; Observer at European Parl. 2005–06, mem. European Parl. (Socialist Group) Jan.–June 2007; Prime Minister (in caretaker govt) Aug.–Nov. 2014; mem. Balgarska Sotsialisticheska Partiya (Bulgarian Socialist Party) –2014 (expelled). *Publications:* author of more than 70 scientific papers on constitutional and legal topics. *Address:* Faculty of Law, St Clement of Ohrid University of Sofia, 1504 Sofia, bul. Tsar Osvoboditel 15, Bulgaria (office). *Telephone:* (2) 9308577 (office). *Fax:* (2) 9443293 (office). *E-mail:* g.bliznashki@law.uni-sofia.bg (office). *Website:* www.uni-sofia.bg (office).

BLOCH, Immanuel, Dr rer. nat; German physicist and academic; *Professor and Vice-Dean, Faculty of Physics, Ludwig Maximilian University, Munich;* b. 16 Nov. 1972, Fulda, Hesse; m.; ed Univ. of Bonn; Research Visitor, Stanford Univ., USA 1997–98; Sr Scientist, Max Planck Inst. of Quantum Optics, Garching 2000–02, Scientific Dir 2008–, Man. Dir 2012–14; Sr Scientist, Ludwig Maximilian Univ. (LMU), Munich 2002–03, Full Prof. (W3) 2009–, Vice-Dean of Faculty of Physics 2012–; Full Prof. (C4), Johannes Gutenberg Univ., Mainz 2003–09; mem. Int. Editorial Bd, Annalen der Physik 2013–, Physical Review B, American Physical Society 2013–; mem. Int. Scientific Advisory Bd, KITP Santa Barbara 2014–, Bd, Hector Fellow Acad. 2014–, Advisory Bd, Int. Conf. on Atomic Physics 2014–; mem. Canadian Inst. for Advanced Research 2008, German Nat. Acad. of Sciences Leopoldina 2011, Deutsche Physikalische Gesellschaft, European Physical Soc. (EPS), American Physical Soc.; Scientific mem. Max Planck Soc.; Bundesverdienstorden 2005; Philip Morris Research Prize (co-recipient) 2000, Research Prize, Physics Faculty of LMU, Munich 2000, PhD Prize, LMU, Munich 2001, Otto-Hahn Medal, Max Planck Soc. 2002, Rudolf Kaiser Prize 2003, EU Marie Curie Excellence Grant 2004, Gottfried Wilhelm Leibniz Prize, German Science Foundation 2004, Arkadi Aronov Memorial Lecturer, Weizmann Inst. of Science, Israel 2004, Int. Comm. for Optics Prize 2005, Philip Morris Research Prize 2007, Distinguished Lecturer, Technion, Israel 2008, Kavli Colloquium Lecturer, Delft Univ. of Tech. 2010, EPS Sr Prize for Fundamental Aspects of Quantum Electronics and Optics 2011, Distinguished Lecturer – MPI for the Science of Light 2012, Dr Alexander M. Cruickshank Lecturer, Gordon Research Conf. Program 2013, Hector Science Prize and Hector Fellow 2013, ERC Synergy Grant 'UQUAM' (co-recipient) 2013, Körber European Science Prize 2013, Int. BEC Award 2013, Einstein Colloquium, Weizmann Inst. of Science 2014, Harvey Prize, Technion, Israel 2015. *Publications:* more than 120 papers in professional journals. *Address:* Room B1.22, Max Planck Institute for Quantum Optics, Hans Kopfermann Str. 1, 85748 Garching (office); Faculty of Physics, Ludwig Maximilian University, Schellingstrasse 4/1 & 2 Stock, 80799 Munich, Germany (office). *Telephone:* (89) 32905138 (Inst.) (office); (89) 21806130 (Univ.) (office). *Fax:* (89) 32905313 (Inst.) (office). *E-mail:* immanuel.bloch@mpq.mpg.de (office); immanuel.bloch@physik.uni-muenchen.de (office). *Website:* www.quantum-munich.de (office).

BLOCHER, Christoph, DEA, DrIur; Swiss politician and business executive; *Vice-President, Swiss People's Party;* b. 11 Oct. 1940, Laufen am Rheinfall; m. Sylvia Kaiser; one s. three d.; ed Univ. of Zurich, Univs of Montpellier and Paris, France; joined Legal Dept, Ems-Chemie AG 1969, acquired co. 1983, Pres. and Rep. to the Bd, Ems-Chemie Holding AG 1984–; mem. Meilen Dist Council 1974–78; mem. Zurich Canton Council 1975–80; Pres. Swiss People's Party (Schweizerische Volkspartei—SV), Zurich Canton 1977–, a Vice-Pres. Swiss People's Party 2008–; mem. Nat. Ass. 1979–2003, 2011–14; Founder and Pres. Aktion für eine unabhängige und neutrale Schweiz (AUNS) 1986–; mem. Swiss Fed. Council 2004–07, Minister of Justice and Police Affairs 2004–07; Chair. Robinvest AG 2008–; Air-Force Regt Commdr and Col (retd). *Address:* Robinvest AG, Kugelgasse 22, 8708 Männedorf (office); Schweizerische Volkspartei, Brückfelderstr. 18, 3000 Bern, Switzerland (office). *Telephone:* (31) 3005858 (SV) (office). *Fax:* (31) 3005859 (SV) (office). *E-mail:* christoph@blocher.ch (office). *Website:* www.svp.ch (office); www.blocher.ch.

BLOCK, Gene D., AB, MA, PhD; American biologist, academic and university administrator; *Chancellor, University of California, Los Angeles;* b. 1948, Monticello, NY; m. Carol Block; two c.; ed Stanford Univ., Univ. of Oregon; postdoctoral work, Stanford Univ. 1975–78; joined Faculty at Univ. of Virginia 1978, Vice-Provost for Research 1993–98, Vice-Pres. for Research and Public Service 1998–2001, Vice-Pres. and Provost 2001–07; Chancellor Univ. of California, Los Angeles (UCLA) 2007–; Fellow, American Acad. of Arts and Sciences, AAAS; Commonwealth of Va Outstanding Public Service Award 1998. *Achievements:* inventor of several devices, holds a patent for a non-contact respiratory monitor for the prevention of Sudden Infant Death Syndrome. *Leisure interest:* avid collector of vacuum-tube radios. *Address:* Office of the Chancellor, University of California, Los Angeles, Box 951405, 2147 Murphy Hall, Los Angeles, CA 90095-1405, USA (office). *Telephone:* (310) 825-2151 (office). *Fax:* (310) 206-6030 (office). *E-mail:* chancellor@ucla.edu (office). *Website:* www.chancellor.ucla.edu (office).

BLOCK, Ned Joel, PhD; American academic; *Silver Professor, Departments of Philosophy, Psychology and Center for Neural Science, New York University;* b. 21 Aug. 1942, Chesterton, Ind.; s. of William Block and Beatrice Rabinowitz; m. Susan Carey 1970; one d.; ed Massachusetts Inst. of Tech., St John's Coll., Oxford, UK, Harvard Univ.; Asst Prof., MIT 1971–77, Assoc. Prof. 1977–83, Prof. of Philosophy, Dept of Linguistics and Philosophy 1983–96, Chair. of Philosophy 1989–95; Prof. of Philosophy, New York Univ. 1996–, Silver Prof., Depts of Philosophy, Psychology and Center for Neural Science 2005–; Visiting Prof., Harvard Univ. 2002–03; Distinguished Visiting Prof., Univ. of Hong Kong 2008–09; Townsend Visitor, Univ. of California, Berkeley 2008–09; Pres. Soc. for Philosophy and Psychology 1978–79, Asscn for the Scientific Study of Consciousness; Chair. MIT Press Cognitive Science Bd 1992–95; NSF Fellow 1985–86, 1988–89; Robert A. Muh Alumni Award in the Humanities, Arts and Social Sciences, MIT 2005; Nat. Endowment for the Humanities Fellow 2006–07; Fellow, American Council of Learned Socs, Center for Study of Language and Information, American Acad. of Arts and Sciences 2004–, Cognitive Science Soc., Jose Gaos Lecturer, Instituto de Investigaciones Filosóficas, Nat. Autonomous Univ. of Mexico 2015; Guggenheim Fellow, Petrus Hispanus Lecturer, Univ. of Lisbon, Jack Burstyn Memorial Lecturer, Manhattan Marymount, Francis W. Gramlich Lecturer, Dartmouth, Burman Lecturer, Univ. of Umea, Sweden 2004–05, Lone Star Tourist 2004–05, Jack Smart Lecturer, ANU 2008–09, Lansdowne Lecturer, Univ. of Victoria 2009–10, Josiah Royce Lecturer, Brown Univ. 2009–10, Royal Inst. of Philosophy Annual Lecturer 2009–10, Thalheimer Lecturer, Johns Hopkins Univ. 2010–11, William James Lecturer, Harvard Univ. 2011–12, Immanuel Kant Lecturer, Stanford Univ. 2011–12, John Locke Lecturer, Univ. of Oxford 2012–13, Jean Nicod Lecturer and Jean Nicod Prize, Paris Univ. 2014, Marc Jeannerod Lecturer 2014–15, Sanders Lecturer, American Philosophical Asscn 2016. *Publications include:* The IQ Controversy (with G. Dworkin) 1976, Readings in Philosophy of Psychology (Vol. 1) 1980, (Vol. 2) 1981, Imagery 1981, The Nature of Consciousness (with O. Flanagan and G. Güzeldere), Functionalism, Consciousness and Representation: Collected Papers (Vol. 1) 2007; articles chosen for The Philosophers' Annual 1983, 1990, 1995, 2002. *Address:* Department of Philosophy, New York University, Room 405, 5 Washington Place, New York, NY 10003 (office); 37 Washington Square West, New York, NY 10011, USA (home). *Telephone:* (212) 998-8322 (office). *Fax:* (212) 995-4179 (office). *E-mail:* ned.block@nyu.edu (office). *Website:* www.nyu.edu/gsas/dept/philo/faculty/block (office).

BLOK, Stephanus (Stef) Abraham, BBA, MBA; Dutch politician and fmr banker; *Minister of Foreign Affairs;* b. 10 Dec. 1964, Emmeloord; m.; one c.; ed Groningen Univ.; Trainee, Société Générale, Paris 1987–88; Man. Trainee, ABN-Amro Bank NV 1988–89, Dir, ABN-Amro office, Nieuwkoop 1989–91, Sr Policy Officer for Credits, ABN-Amro 1992, Credit Analyst Sec., Policy Group Risk Cttee, Vice Pres., Corp. Banking, ABN-Amro 1996–98; mem. Nieuwkoop City Council (VVD) 1994–98; mem. Tweede Kammer (Second Chamber, Parl.) (VVD) 1998–2002, 2002–12; Minister for Housing and Civil Service 2012–17, Minister of Security and Justice 10–20 March 2015, Jan.–Oct. 2017, Minister of Foreign Affairs 2018–; mem. Volkspartij voor Vrijheid en Democratie (VVD) 1988–; mem. Supervisory Bd Rivierduinen Inst. for Mental Health Care; mem. Bd Zuid-Hollands Landschap. *Address:* Ministry of Foreign Affairs, Bezuidenhoutseweg 67, POB 20061, 2500 EB The Hague, The Netherlands (office). *Telephone:* (70) 2140214 (office). *Website:* www.rijksoverheid.nl/ministeries/bz (office).

BLOKHIN, Oleg Vladimirovich; Ukrainian football coach, politician and fmr footballer; b. 5 Nov. 1952, Kiev, Ukrainian SSR, Soviet Union; s. of Volodimir Ivanovich Blokhin and Katerina Zakharivna Adamenko (fmr sprint hurdler); m. Irina Ivomovna Deryugina (divorced early 1990s); one d.; ed Kiev Physical Culture Inst. and Kiev Univ.; forward; played for Dynamo Kiev youth team 1962–69, sr team 1969–88, Vorwärts Steyr 1988–89, Aris Limassol 1989–90; played 432 matches in USSR Championships, 112 matches for USSR team (record) 1972–88; scored over 200 career goals; fmr coach, Greek clubs Olympiacos 1990–93 (won Greek Cup 1990, 1992, Greek Super Cup 1992), PAOK Saloniki 1993–94, 1997–98, Ionikos 1994–97, 1999–2002, AEK Athens 1998–99; coach Ukraine nat. football team 2003–07, 2011–12, FC Moscow 2007–08, Chornomorets Odesa (Sportive Dir) 2009–11; Man. FC Dynamo Kiev 2012–14; Chair. Oleg Blokhin Int. Fund 1994–; elected to Verkhovna Rada (Parl.) 1998, 2002, mem. Cttee on Problems of Youth Policy and Sport; mem. Batkishchina faction 1999–, CP faction 2002–; mem. United Social Democratic Party of Ukraine 2002–; Soviet Top League Top Scorer 1972, 1973, 1974, 1975, 1977, Soviet Top League All-Time Goals and Appearances Leader, Ukrainian Footballer of the Year 1972, 1973, 1974, 1975, 1976, 1977, 1978, 1980, 1981, Soviet Footballer of the Year 1973, 1974, 1975, Golden Boot Award 1975, European Footballer of the Year (first Ukrainian player) 1975, Best Footballer of USSR 1973–75, seven times Champion USSR, five times winner USSR Cup, winner Cup Winners' Cup 1975, winner Supercup 1975, UEFA Cup Winners' Cup Top Scorer 1985–86, USSR nat. football team All-Time Goals and Caps Leader, Ukraine's Golden Player Rep., UEFA Jubilee Awards 2004. *Address:* c/o FC Dynamo Kiev, vul. Hrushevskoho 3, 1001 Kiev, Ukraine. *Website:* www.fcdynamo.kiev.ua/en.

BLOMSTEDT, Herbert Thorsson; Swedish conductor; *Conductor Laureate, San Francisco Symphony Orchestra;* b. 11 July 1927, Springfield, Mass, USA; s. of Adolphe Blomstedt and Alida Armintha Thorson; m. Waltraud Regina Peterson 1955 (died 2003); four d.; ed Royal Acad. of Music, Stockholm, Uppsala Univ., Mozarteum, Austria, Schola Cantorum, Switzerland, Juilliard School and Tanglewood, USA; Music Dir, Norrköping Symphony Orchestra 1954–61; Prof. of Conducting, Swedish Royal Acad. of Music 1961–70; Perm. Conductor, Oslo Philharmonic 1962–68; Music Dir Danish Radio Symphony Orchestra 1967–77, Dresden Staatskapelle Orchestra 1975–85, Swedish Radio Symphony Orchestra 1977–82; Music Dir and Conductor, San Francisco Symphony Orchestra 1985–95, Conductor Laureate 1995–; Music Dir NDR Symphony Orchestra, Hamburg 1996–98, Leipzig Gewandhaus Orchestra 1998–2005; mem. Royal Acad. of Music, Stockholm 1965; Hon. Conductor, NHK Symphony, Tokyo 1985, Bamberg Symphony Orchestra 2006, Danish Nat. Symphony Orchestra 2006, Swedish Radio Symphony Orchestra 2006, Gewandhausorchester, Leipzig; Kt, Royal Order of the North Star, Kt, Royal Order of Dannebrog (Denmark), Grosses Verdienstkreuz der Bundesrepublik Deutschland 2003, Order of the Rising Sun (Japan) 2018; Hon. DMus (Andrews); Dr hc (Gothenburg) 1999, (Southwestern-Adventist Univ., Tex.) 1993; Jenny Lind Scholarship, Swedish Royal Acad. of Music, Litteris et Artibus, Gold Medal (Sweden), Deutscher Schallplattenpreis 1978, Golden Reward Prize, Tokyo 1984, Grand Prix du Disque 1989, Gramophone Award, London 1990, Record Acad. of Japan Award 1991, Ditson Award for Distinguished Services to American Music, Columbia Univ., New York 1992, Grammy Awards 1993, 1996, Schallplattenpreis der Deutschen Musikkritik 1994, Ehrenpräsident der Stiftung Musikforschung Zentralschweiz 2001, Anton-Bruckner-Preis der Betil-Östbo-Bruckner-Stiftung, Linz 2001, Julio Kilenyi Medal of Honor, Bruckner Soc. of

America 2012, Haederpris, Carl Nielsen Soc., Denmark 2002, Léonie Sonning Music Prize 2016, Int. Classical Music Award for Best Collection (Bruckner Symphonies 1–9) 2013, (Beethoven Symphonies 1–9) 2018. *Publications:* Till Kennedomen om Johann Christian Bachs Symfonies 1951, Lars-Erik Larsson och Lars Convertinor (co-author) 1957, Berwald: Sinfonie Singulière 1965. *Leisure interests:* hiking, history, philosophy, literature, art. *Address:* Künstler-Sekretariat am Gasteig, Rosenheimer Strasse 52, 81669 Munich, Germany (office). *Telephone:* (89) 444-8879-0 (office). *Fax:* (89) 444-9522 (office).

BLÖNDAL, Halldór; Icelandic politician; b. 24 Aug. 1938, Reykjavík; m. Kristrún Eymundsdóttir; ed Akureyri High School; teacher and journalist, Morgunbladid 1959–80; mem. staff Authorised Public Accountant office, Akureyri 1976–78; Chief Surveyor of the State Account 1976–87; mem. Bd Dirs Regional Devt Inst. 1983–91, Agric. Bank of Iceland 1985–91; mem. Independence Party, Vice-Chair. Parl. Group 1983–91, Chair. Asscn of Sr Independents 2009–; mem. Parl. for Northeastern Dist 1979–2007, Speaker of the Althingi (Parl.) 1999–2005, Chair. Cttee on Foreign Affairs 2005–07, Chair. Icelandic Del. to West Nordic Council 2005–07; Minister of Transport and Communications 1991–99, of Communications and Agric. 1991–95; Rep. to UN Gen. Ass. 1983; mem. Icelandic Del. to Council of Europe 1984–86. *Address:* Sjálfstæðisflokkurinn (Independence Party), Háaleitisbraut 1, 105 Reykjavík, Iceland. *Telephone:* 5151700. *Fax:* 5151717. *E-mail:* halldorblondal@simnet.isxd@xd.is. *Website:* www.xd.is.

BLOOM, Barry R., BS, DrSc, MA, PhD; American immunologist, academic and university administrator; *Distinguished Service Professor, Department of Immunology and Infectious Diseases and Joan L. and Julius H. Jacobson Professor of Public Health, School of Public Health, Harvard University;* b. 1937; ed Amherst Coll., Harvard Univ., Rockefeller Univ.; consultant to White House on Int. Health Policy 1977–78; joined faculty Albert Einstein Coll. of Medicine 1964, Prof. 1973–90, Chair. Dept of Microbiology and Immunology, 1978–90; Dean of Faculty, Harvard School of Public Health 1998–, Joan L. and Julius H. Jacobson Prof. of Public Health 1998–, also Distinguished Service Prof., Dept of Immunology and Infectious Diseases; Investigator, Howard Hughes Medical Inst. 1990–98; Chair. Tech. and Research Advisory Cttee to Global Programme on Malaria, WHO; Founding Chair., Bd of Trustees, Int. Vaccine Inst., South Korea; fmr Chair. Advisory Cttee on Health Research, Leprosy Research and Tuberculosis Research Cttees, WHO, Scientific and Tech. Advisory Cttees, UNDP/World Bank/WHO Special Programme for Research and Training, Vaccine Advisory Cttee on UNAIDS; mem. Ellison Medical Foundation Scientific Advisory Bd; mem. Wellcome Trust Pathogens, Immunology and Population Health Strategy Cttee; mem. Nat. Advisory Bd, Howard Hughes Medical Inst. 1990–98; mem. Scientific Advisory Bd Earth Inst., Columbia Univ.; mem. Advisory Council, Paul G. Rogers Soc. for Global Health Research; fmr Pres. Fed. of American Socs for Experimental Biology; fmr mem. US AIDS Research Cttee, Nat. Advisory Council, Nat. Inst. for Allergy and Infectious Diseases; fmr mem. Scientific Advisory Bd Nat. Center for Infectious Diseases for Disease Control and Prevention; fmr mem. Nat. Advisory Bd Fogarty Int. Center, NIH; fmr mem. Governing Bd Inst. of Medicine; Fellow, American Acad. of Arts and Sciences; mem. NAS, Inst. of Medicine, AAAS, American Asscn of Immunologists (Pres. 1984), American Philosophical Soc.; Hon. DSc (Amherst Coll.); Bristol-Myers Squib Award for Distinguished Research in Infectious Diseases, Novartis Award in Immunology (jtly) 1998; Robert Koch Gold Medal 1999. *Address:* Harvard School of Public Health, Building 1, Room 805, Boston, MA 02115, USA (office). *Telephone:* (617) 432-7684 (office). *E-mail:* bbloom@hsph.harvard.edu (office). *Website:* www.hsph.harvard.edu (office).

BLOOM, Claire, CBE; British actress; b. (Patricia Claire Blume), 15 Feb. 1931, Finchley, London, England; d. of Edward Blume and Elizabeth Grew; m. 1st Rod Steiger 1959 (divorced 1969, died 2002); m. 2nd Philip Roth 1990 (divorced 1995); ed Badminton School, Bristol, Fern Hill Manor, New Milton, Guildhall School of Music and Drama, London under Eileen Thorndike, Central School of Speech and Drama, London and in New York; Oxford Repertory Theatre 1946, Stratford-on-Avon 1948; first major stage appearances in The Lady's Not For Burning 1949, Ring Around the Moon 1950; at Old Vic 1951–53; Fellow, Guildhall School of Music and Drama 1975. *Other stage performances include:* Duel of Angels 1956, 1967, Andromache in The Trojan Women 1964, Sascha in Ivanov, London 1966, Nora in A Doll's House, New York 1971, London 1973, Hedda Gabler in Hedda Gabler, New York 1971, Mary Queen of Scots in Vivat, Vivat Regina!, New York 1972, A Streetcar Named Desire, London (Evening Standard Drama Award for Best Actress) 1974, The Innocents, USA 1976, Rosmersholm, London 1977, The Cherry Orchard, Chichester Festival 1981, When We Dead Awaken 1990, The Cherry Orchard, USA 1994, Long Day's Journey into Night, USA 1996, Electra, New York 1998, Conversations after a Burial, London 2000, A Little Night Music 2003, Whispering Psyche 2004, Six Dance Lessons in Six Weeks 2006–07. *Films include:* The Blind Goddess 1948, The Shepherdess and the Chimneysweep (voice: English version) 1952, Limelight (BAFTA Award for Most Promising Newcomer to Leading Film Roles 1953) 1952, Innocents in Paris 1953, The Man Between 1953, Richard III 1955, Alexander the Great 1956, The Brothers Karamazov 1958, The Buccaneer 1958, Look Back in Anger 1959, Three Moves to Freedom 1960, The Wonderful World of the Brothers Grimm 1962, The Chapman Report 1962, The Haunting 1963, 80,000 Suspects 1963, The Teacher from Vigevano 1963, Alta infedeltà 1964, The Outrage 1964, The Spy Who Came in from the Cold 1965, Charly 1968, The Illustrated Man 1969, Three into Two Won't Go 1969, A Severed Head 1970, Red Sky at Morning 1971, A Doll's House (Taormina Arte Award for Best Actress 1973) 1973, Islands in the Stream 1977, Beauty and the Beast (short) 1981, Clash of the Titans 1981, Always 1984, Déjà Vu 1985, Sammy and Rosie Get Laid 1987, Brothers 1988, Crimes and Misdemeanours 1989, Pas de deux (short) 1990, The Princess and the Goblin (voice) 1991, The Age of Innocence (uncredited) 1993, Mad Dogs and Englishmen 1995, Mighty Aphrodite 1995, Daylight 1996, Shakespeare's Women and Claire Bloom, Wrestling with Alligators 1998, The Book of Eve 2002, The Republic of Love 2003, Imagining Argentina 2003, Daniel and the Superdogs 2004, Kalamazoo? 2006, The King's Speech 2010, While We Were Here 2012, Max Rose 2016, Miss Dalí 2018. *Television appearances:* The Marvellous History of St. Bernard (film) 1952, BBC Sunday-Night Theatre – Martine 1952, Producers' Showcase (series) 1955–57, Robert Montgomery Presents – Victoria Regina 1957, Shirley Temple's Storybook – Beauty and the Beast 1958, Playhouse 90 – Misalliance 1959, Checkmate 1961, Anna Karenina (film) 1961, Wuthering Heights (film) 1962, Camera Three – Claire Bloom Reads Poetry 1964, ITV Play of the Week – Ivanov 1966, Theatre of Stars – A Time to Love 1967, Soldier in Love (film) 1967, The Bell Telephone Hour – The Many Faces of Romeo and Juliet 1967, Late Night Horror – The Triumph of Death 1968, The Going Up of David Lev (film) 1973, Wessex Tales – An Imaginative Woman 1973, Great Mysteries – Ice Storm 1974, Aquarius (series) 1974, A Legacy (series) 1975, Backstairs at the White House (mini-series) 1979, The Oresteia (mini-series) 1979, The Famous History of the Life of King Henry the Eight (film) 1979, Hamlet, Prince of Denmark (film) 1980, CBS Library – Misunderstood Monsters 1981, Brideshead Revisited (mini-series) 1981, Cymbeline (film) 1982, Separate Tables (film) 1983, American Playhouse – The Ghost Writer 1984, Ellis Island (mini-series) 1984, King John (film) 1984, Time and the Conways (film) 1985, Ann and Debbie (film) 1985, Florence Nightingale (film) 1985, Shadowlands (film) (BAFTA Award for Best Actress) 1985, Promises to Keep 1985, Oedipus the King 1985, This Lightning Always Strikes Twice (film) 1985, Liberty (film) 1986, The Theban Plays by Sophocles (series) 1986, Hold the Dream (film) 1986, Anastasia: The Mystery of Anna (film) 1986, Queenie (film) 1987, The Belle of Amherst 1986, Intimate Contact (film) 1987, Beryl Markham: A Shadow on the Sun (film) 1988, The Lady and the Highwayman (film) 1989, The Camomile Lawn (mini-series) 1991, The Mirror Crack'd from Side to Side 1992; The Poetry Hall of Fame (film) 1993, It's Nothing Personal (film) 1993, Remember (film) 1993, As the World Turns (series) 1993–95, American Masters (series documentary) 1994, A Village Affair (film) 1995, Family Money (series) 1997, What the Deaf Man Heard (film) 1997, Imogen's Face (series) 1998, The Lady in Question (film) 1999, Tales from the Madhouse (mini-series) 2000, Love and Murder (film) 2000, Yesterday's Children (film) 2000, Law & Order: Criminal Intent (series) 2004, Jericho (series) 2005, Doc Martin (series) 2005, Marple: By the Pricking of My Thumbs (film) 2006, Trial & Retribution (series) 2006, The Chatterley Affair (film) 2006, The Ten Commandments (film) 2006, New Tricks (series) 2008, Fiona's Story (film) 2008, Doctor Who (series) 2009–10, The Bill (series) 2010, Midsomer Murders 2015; also performs her one-woman shows Enter the Actress and These are Women, A Portrait of Shakespeare's Heroines, throughout the USA. *Publications:* Limelight and After 1982, Leaving a Doll's House 1996. *Leisure interests:* walking, music. *Address:* c/o Jeremy Conway, 18–21 Jermyn Street, London, SW1Y 6HB, England. *Telephone:* (20) 7287-0077. *Fax:* (20) 7287-1940.

BLOOM, Floyd Elliott, AB, MD, DSc, FAAS; American physician, research scientist and academic; *Professor Emeritus, Department of Business Administration, The Scripps Research Institute;* b. 8 Oct. 1936, Minneapolis, Minn.; m. 1st D'Nell Bingham 1956 (died 1973); two c.; m. 2nd Jody Patricia Corey 1980; ed Southern Methodist Univ., Washington Univ., Hahnemann Univ., Univ. of Rochester, Mount Sinai Univ. Medical School, Thomas Jefferson Univ.; intern, Barnes Hosp., St Louis 1960–61, resident internal medicine 1961–62; Research Assoc., Nat. Inst. of Mental Health (NIMH), Washington, DC 1962–64; Fellow, Depts of Pharmacology, Psychiatry and Anatomy, Yale Univ. School of Medicine 1964–66, Asst Prof. 1966–67, Assoc. Prof. 1968; Chief of Lab. of Neuropharmacology, NIMH 1968–75, Acting Dir Div. of Special Mental Health 1973–75; Commissioned Officer, Public Health Service 1974–75; Prof., Salk Inst., La Jolla, Calif. 1975–83; Founder and mem. Bd of Dirs, Alkermes Inc. 1987–; Dir Div. of Preclinical Neuroscience and Endocrinology, The Scripps Research Inst., La Jolla 1983–89, Chair. Dept of Neuropharmacology 1989–2005, now Prof. Emer., Dept of Business Admin; Founding CEO, Chief Scientific Officer and Chair. Neurome, Inc. 2000–06; Chair. Nat. Medical Council 2000–; mem. Nat. Advisory Mental Health Council 1976–80, Comm. on Alcoholism 1980–81; mem. Scientific Advisory Bd Neurocrine Inc. 1993–2000, Neurobiological Tech. Inc. 1994–98, Healthcare Ventures Inc. 1998–2000, Advancis Pharmaceuticals 1999–, SafeMed 2003–, Saegis Pharmaceuticals 2004–; Ed.-in-Chief Science Magazine 1995–2000; Trustee, Washington Univ., St Louis 1998–; mem. AAAS (Pres. 2002–03), NAS 1977, Inst. of Medicine, American Philosophical Soc., American Acad. of Arts and Sciences, Swedish Acad. of Sciences; Hon. DSc (Southern Methodist Univ.) 1983, (Hahnemann Univ., Philadelphia), (Univ. of Rochester, NY), (Mount Sinai School of Medicine, NY), (Thomas Jefferson Univ., Philadelphia), (Washington Univ.) 1998; A. Cressy Morrison Award, New York Acad. of Sciences 1971, Mathilde Solowey Award 1973, McAlpin Research Achievement Award, Mental Health Asscn 1980, Steven Beering Medal 1985, Janssen Award, World Psychiatry Asscn 1989, Herman von Helmholtz Award 1991, Meritorious Achievement Award, Council of Biology Eds 1999, Distinguished Service Award, American Psychiatric Asscn 2000, Walsh McDermott Award, Inst. of Medicine 2004, Bernard and Rhoda Sarnat Award for Mental Health Research, Inst. of Medicine 2005. *Publications include:* Biochemical Basis of Neuropharmacology (co-author) 1971, Brain, Mind and Behavior (co-author) 1984, Brain Browser (co-author) 1989; Ed. Peptides: Integrators of Cell and Tissue Function 1980, Neuro-Psychopharmacology: The Fourth Generation of Progress 1994, Handbook of Chemical Neuroanatomy 1997, The Primate Nervous System 1997, Funding Health Sciences Research (co-author) 1990. *Leisure interests:* cruise travel, fine food and wine, abstract art. *Address:* Scripps Research Institute, 10550 North Torrey Pines Road, La Jolla, CA 92037-1000 (office); 628 Pacific View Drive, San Diego, CA 92109, USA (home). *Telephone:* (858) 784-9730 (office). *Fax:* (858) 784-8851 (office). *E-mail:* fbloom@scripps.edu (office). *Website:* www.scripps.edu/research/faculty/bloom (office).

BLOOM, Harold, PhD; American academic and writer; *Sterling Professor of Humanities and English, Yale University;* b. 11 July 1930, New York; s. of William Bloom and Paula Lev; m. Jeanne Gould 1958; two s.; ed Cornell and Yale Univs, Pembroke Coll., UK; mem. Faculty, Yale Univ. 1955–, Prof. of English 1965–77, DeVane Prof. of Humanities 1974–77, Prof. of Humanities 1977–, Sterling Prof. of Humanities and English 1983–; Visiting Prof., Hebrew Univ. Jerusalem 1959, Breadloaf Summer School 1965–66, Soc. for Humanities, Cornell Univ. 1968–69; Visiting Univ. Prof., New School of Social Research, New York 1982–84; Charles Eliot Norton Prof. of Poetry, Harvard Univ. 1987–88; Berg Visiting Prof. of English, New York Univ. 1988–2004; mem. American Acad. and Inst. of Arts and Letters, American Philosophical Soc.; Fulbright Fellow 1955, Guggenheim Fellow 1962; Dr hc (St Michael's Coll., Univ. of Rome, Univ. of Bologna, Univ. of Coimbra, Boston Coll., Yeshiva Univ., Univ. of Mass. at Dartmouth, Univ. of Buenos Aires); Newton Arvin Award 1967, Melville Cane Award, Poetry Soc. of America 1970, Zabel Prize, American Inst. of Arts and Letters 1982, MacArthur Foundation Fellowship 1985, Christian Gauss Prize 1989, Gold Medal for Criticism, American Acad. of Arts and Letters 1999, Int. Prize of Catalonia 2002, Alfonso Reyes Prize

(Mexico) 2003, Hans Christian Anderson Bicentennial Prize (Denmark) 2005. *Publications include:* Shelley's Mythmaking 1959, The Visionary Company 1961, Blake's Apocalypse 1963, Commentary to Blake 1965, Yeats 1970, The Ringers in the Tower 1971, The Anxiety of Influence 1973, Wallace Stevens: The Poems of Our Climate 1977, A Map of Misreading 1975, Kabbalah and Criticism 1975, Poetry and Repression 1976, Figures of Capable Imagination 1976, The Flight to Lucifer: A Gnostic Fantasy 1979, Agon: Towards a Theory of Revisionism 1981, The Breaking of the Vessels 1981, The Strong Light of the Canonical 1987, Freud: Transference and Authority 1988, Poetics of Influence: New and Selected Criticism 1988, Ruin the Sacred Truths 1989, The Book of J 1990, The American Religion 1991, The Western Canon 1994, Omens of Millennium 1996, Shakespeare: The Invention of the Human 1998, How to Read and Why 2000, Stories and Poems for Extremely Intelligent Children of All Ages 2000, Genius: A Mosaic of One Hundred Exemplary Creative Minds 2002, Hamlet: Poem Unlimited 2003, Best Poems of the English Language: Chaucer to Hart Crane 2003, Where Shall Wisdom be Found? 2004, The Names Divine: Jesus and Yahweh 2005, Yetziat: Fallen Angels, Demons and Devils 2006, Till I End My Song: A Gathering of Last Poems 2010, The Anatomy of Influence: Literature as a Way of Life 2011, The King James Bible: A Literary Appreciation 2011, The Daemon Knows: Literary Greatness and the American Sublime 2015, Falstaff: Give Me Life 2017, Cleopatra: I Am Fire and Air 2017, Lear: The Great Image of Authority 2018, Iago: The Strategies of Evil 2018, Macbeth: A Dagger of the Mind 2019. *Leisure interest:* reading. *Address:* Department of English, WHC 202, Yale University, 63 High Street, POB 208302, New Haven, CT 06520-8302, USA (office). *Telephone:* (203) 432-0029 (office). *E-mail:* harold.bloom@yale.edu (office). *Website:* www.yale.edu/english (office).

BLOOM, Orlando Jonathan Blanchard; British actor; b. 13 Jan. 1977, Canterbury, Kent, England; m. Miranda Kerr 2010; one s.; ed The King's School Canterbury, St Edmund's School, Canterbury, Guildhall School of Music and Drama, London, Hampstead Fine Arts Coll., London; early acting experience with Nat. Youth Theatre; cinema debut in Wilde 1997; UNICEF Goodwill Amb. 2009–; hon. degree (Kent at Canterbury) 2010; received a star on Hollywood Walk of Fame 2014. *Theatre includes:* In Celebration (Duke of York's Theatre, London) 2007, Broadway stage debut as Romeo in Romeo and Juliet (Richard Rodgers Theatre) 2013. *Films include:* Wilde 1997, The Lord of the Rings: The Fellowship of the Ring (Empire Award for Best Debut 2002) 2001, Black Hawk Down 2001, The Lord of the Rings: The Two Towers 2002, Ned Kelly 2003, Pirates of the Caribbean: The Curse of the Black Pearl 2003, The Lord of the Rings: The Return of the King 2003, The Calcium Kid 2004, Troy 2004, Haven 2004, Kingdom of Heaven 2005, Elizabethtown 2005, Pirates of the Caribbean: Dead Man's Chest 2006, Love and Other Disasters 2006, The Armenian Genocide (documentary) 2006, Pirates of the Caribbean: At World's End 2007, Everest: A Climb for Peace (documentary) 2007, New York, I Love You 2009, Sympathy for Delicious 2010, Main Street 2010, The Good Doctor 2011, Fight for Your Right Revisited (short) 2011, The Three Muskateers 2011, The Hobbit: An Unexpected Journey 2012, Zulu 2013, The Bling Ring 2013, The Hobbit: The Desolation of Smaug 2013, Romeo and Juliet 2014, The Hobbit: The Battle of the Five Armies 2014, Digging for Fire 2015, Unlocked 2015. *Television includes:* Casualty 1994–96, Midsomer Murders 2000, Extras 2006, LA Phil Live 2011. *Address:* c/o Creative Artists Agency, 2000 Avenue of the Stars, Los Angeles, CA 90067, USA (office). *Telephone:* (424) 288-2000 (office). *Fax:* (424) 288-2900 (office). *Website:* www.caa.com (office).

BLOOM, Sir Stephen Robert, Kt, MA, MD, DSc, FRS, FRCP, FRCPath, FMedSci, FRSB; British physician, academic and biomedical researcher; *Head of Division of Investigative Science, Imperial College London;* b. 24 Oct. 1942, Maidstone, Kent; s. of Arnold Bloom and Edith Nancy Bloom (née Fox); m. Margaret Janet Sturrock 1965; two s. two d.; ed Univ. of Cambridge; Medical Unit Registrar, Middx Hosp., London 1970–72; MRC Clinical Research Fellow 1972–74; Sr Lecturer, Royal Postgraduate Medical School, Hammersmith Hosp. 1974–78, Reader in Medicine 1978–82, Prof. of Endocrinology 1982–, Head Dept of Endocrinology and Metabolic Medicine, Dir of Pathology and Therapy Services, Hammersmith Hosps NHS Trust 1996–; Prof. of Medicine, Imperial Coll. School of Medicine (ICSM) (fmrly Royal Postgraduate Medical School) 1982–, Dir of Metabolic Medicine and Chief of Service for Chemical Pathology 1994–; Chair. Div. of Diabetes, Endocrinology and Metabolism, ICSM 1997–; Vice-Pres. (Sr Censor) Royal Coll. of Physicians 1999–2001; Sec. Soc. for Endocrinology 1999–2001, Chair. 2001–; Fellow, Royal Soc. of Biology; Hon. DSc (Univ. of Warwick) 2017. *Publications include:* Gut Hormones (ed.) 1978, Endocrine Tumours 1985, Surgical Endocrinology 1992. *Leisure interests:* jogging, classical music, computing. *Address:* Department of Metabolic Medicine, Division of Investigative Science, Imperial College London at Hammersmith Hospital, 6th Floor, Commonwealth Building, Du Cane Road, London, W12 0NN, England (office). *Telephone:* (20) 8383-3242 (office). *Fax:* (20) 8383-3142 (office). *E-mail:* s.bloom@imperial.ac.uk (office). *Website:* www.imperial.ac.uk (office).

BLOOMBERG, Michael Rubens, MBA; American business executive, politician and UN official; *Special Envoy of the Secretary-General for Cities and Climate Change, United Nations;* b. 14 Feb. 1942, Medford, Mass; m. (divorced); two c.; ed Johns Hopkins Univ., Harvard Univ.; with Salomon Brothers (investment bank) 1966–81, made Partner 1972; Founder, Chief Exec., Chair. Bloomberg Financial Markets 1981, Founder-Pres. and CEO Bloomberg LP 1982–2002, 2014–, also Publr Bloomberg Business News, Bloomberg Magazine, Bloomberg Personal Magazine, Gen. Man. Bloomberg Television, Bloomberg Radio WBBR-AM 1130; Mayor of New York 2001–13; Special Envoy of the Sec.-Gen. for Cities and Climate Change, UN 2014–; Chair. Bd of Trustees, Johns Hopkins Univ. –2002; mem. Bd Lincoln Center for Performing Arts, Jewish Museum, New York, Police & Fire Widows' and Children's Fund, Metropolitan Museum of Art and numerous other bodies; Trustee, Big Apple Circus; Hon. KBE 2014. *Publication:* Bloomberg by Bloomberg (autobiog.) 1998. *Address:* Office of the Secretary-General, United Nations, New York, NY 10017 (office); Bloomberg LP, 731 Lexington Avenue, New York, NY 10022, USA (office). *Telephone:* (212) 963-1234 (UN) (office); (212) 318-2000 (Bloomberg) (office). *Fax:* (212) 963-4879 (UN) (office). *Website:* www.bloomberg.com (office); www.mikebloomberg.com; unenvoy.mikebloomberg.com.

BLOOMER, Jonathan, BSc, ARCS, FCA, CIMgt; British insurance industry executive; *Executive Chairman, Jardine Lloyd Thompson Employee Benefit Solutions Ltd;* b. 23 March 1954; m. Judy Bloomer (née May); one s. two d.; ed Imperial Coll., London; joined Arthur Andersen 1974, Man. Pnr of European Insurance Practice –1994; Group Finance Dir Prudential PLC 1995–2000, Group CEO 2000–05, also mem. Bd of Dirs; Pnr, Cerberus European Capital Advisors LLP 2006–12, Exec. Chair. Lucida plc 2006–12; Exec. Chair. Jardine Lloyd Thompson Employee Benefit Solutions Ltd 2013–, Arrow Global Group plc 2013–; fmr Chair. Scottish RE Group Ltd; Deputy Chair. Financial Services Practitioner Panel 2001–03, Chair. 2003–05; mem. Bd of Dirs Railtrack PLC 1999–2002, Asscn of British Insurers 2001–05, Geneva Asscn 2001–05, Hargreaves Lansdown PLC 2006–; Trustee and Treasurer Nat. Soc. for the Prevention of Cruelty to Children; mem. Urgent Issues Task Force of Accounting Standards Bd 1995–99. *Leisure interests:* rugby, boats.

BLOOMFIELD, Sir Kenneth Percy, KCB, MA, MRIA; British public servant; b. 15 April 1931, Belfast, NI; s. of Harry Percy Bloomfield and Doris Bloomfield; m. Mary E. Ramsey 1960; one s. one d.; ed Royal Belfast Academical Inst. and St Peter's Coll., Oxford; joined NI Civil Service 1952; Private Sec. to Minister of Finance 1956–60; Deputy Dir British Industrial Devt Office, New York 1960–63; Asst later Deputy Sec. to Cabinet, NI 1963–72; Under-Sec. NI Office 1972–74; Perm. Sec., Office of Exec. of NI 1974–75; Perm. Sec., Dept of Environment, NI 1975–81, Dept of Econ. Devt 1981–84; Head of NI Civil Service and Second Perm. Under-Sec. of State, NI Office 1984–91; Nat. Gov., Chair. Broadcasting Council for NI, BBC 1991–99; Chair. Children in Need Trust 1992–98, NI Higher Educ. Council 1993–2001, NI Victims Commr 1997–98, Bangor and Holywood Town Centre Man. Ltd 2001, BBC Audit Cttee, NI Chief Execs Forum, Higher Educ. Council for NI; fmr Chair. NI Legal Services Comm.; Pres. Ulster People's Coll. 1996–; mem. NI Advisory Bd Bank of Ireland 1991–2001, Green Park Trust 1996–2001; Hon. Fellow, St Peter's Coll. Oxford; Hon. LLD (Belfast), Hon. DUniv (Open Univ.) 2000, Hon. DLitt (Univ. of Ulster) 2002; NI Chamber of Commerce Award for Personal or Corp. Excellence 1990. *Publications include:* Stormont in Crisis (a memoir) 1994, We Will Remember Them 1998, A Tragedy of Errors 2007, A New Life 2008, The BBC at the Watershed: An Insider's Account from Hussey to the Hutton Enquiry 2009. *Leisure interests:* reading history and biographies, writing, swimming. *Address:* 16 Larch Hill, Holywood, Co. Down, BT18 0JN, Northern Ireland (home). *Telephone:* (28) 9042-8340 (home). *Fax:* (28) 9042-8340 (home). *E-mail:* kenbloomfield@tiscali.co.uk (home).

BLUM, Brad, BA, MBA; American business executive; *CEO, Blum Enterprises LLC;* b. 1954; m.; two step-s.; ed Denison Univ., Granville, OH, Northwestern Univ. J. L. Kellogg Business School, Evanston, Ill.; joined General Mills as Asst Product Man. Big G (Cereal) Div. 1978, served 16 years in marketing, Gen. Man., becoming Vice-Pres. of Marketing, Cereal Partners Worldwide, Morges, Switzerland 1990–94; Sr Vice-Pres. of Marketing, Olive Garden Div., Darden Restaurants June–Dec. 1994, Pres. Dec. 1994–1997, Exec. Vice-Pres. and Dir Darden Restaurants 1997–2002, Vice-Chair. March–Dec. 2002; Chief Exec. Burger King Corpn 2003–2004 (resgnd); Founder and CEO Blum Enterprises LLC (restaurant industry consultancy) 2005–; CEO Romano's Macaroni Grill 2008–10; adviser, Starboard Value LP 2014–; Chair. Econ. Devt Bd, City of Winter Park, Fla; mem. Bd of Trustees Atlantic Center for the Arts; mem. Advisory Bd Sun Trust Bank; Multi-unit Foodservice Operators Operator of the Year 2000, Menu Master's Innovator of the Year, Nation's Restaurant News 2010. *Leisure interests:* tennis, skiing, motor racing. *Address:* Blum Enterprises LLC, 250 S Park Avenue 510, Winter Park FL 32789-4388 (office); Starboard Value LP, 777 3rd Avenue, New York, NY 10017, USA. *Telephone:* (407) 622-5700 (Winter Park) (office); (212) 845-7977 (New York). *E-mail:* info@starboardvalue.com. *Website:* www.starboardvalue.com.

BLÜM, Norbert, DPhil; German politician; b. 21 July 1935, Rüsselsheim; s. of Christian Blüm and Margarete Blüm (née Beck); m. Marita Binger 1964; one s. two d.; ed Volksschule; apprentice, Opel AG, Rüsselsheim, 1949–53, toolmaker 1953–57; worked in building trade and as lorry driver while studying evenings 1957–61; univ. student in Cologne and Bonn 1961–67; Ed. Soziale Ordnung 1966–68; Chief Man. Social Comm. of Christian Democrat employees' Asscn 1968–75, Regional Chair. Rhineland-Palatinate 1974–77, Fed. Chair. 1977–87; mem. Fed. Exec. CDU 1969–; mem. Bundestag 1969–81, 1983–2002; Deputy Chair. CDU 1981–2000; Senator for Fed. Affairs for Berlin 1981; Minister of Labour and Social Affairs 1982–98; Regional Chair. CDU North Rhine-Westphalia 1987–98; mem. IG Metall; fmr Chair. Kindernothilfe Stiftung (Children in Need Foundation); Karl-Valentin-Orden 1987, Heinrich-Brauns Preis 1990, Leipzig Human Rights Award 2001 and numerous other awards and prizes. *Publications include:* Reform oder Reaktion–Wohin geht die CDU 1972, Gewerkschaften zwischen Allmacht und Ohnmacht 1979, Werkstücke 1980, Die Arbeit geht weiter–zur Krise der Erwerbsgesellschaft 1983, 40 Jahre Socialstaat Bundesrepublik Deutschland 1989, Politikals Balanceakt 1993, Dann Willichs mal probieren–Geschichten vom Lachen und Weinen 1994, Sommerfrische-Regentage inclusive 1995, Die Glücksmargerite–Geschichten zum Vorlesen 1997, Diesseits und Jenseits der Politik 1998. *Leisure interests:* reading, walking. *Address:* c/o Kindernothilfe Stiftung, Düsseldorfer Landstraße 180, 47249 Duisburg, Germany.

BLUM, Timothy (Tim); American gallery owner and art dealer; *Co-Owner, Blum & Poe;* b. 5 Aug. 1965; m. Maria Blum 1993; moved to Tokyo to work as an art dealer 1990; returned to Los Angeles 1994 and with Jeff Poe opened small exhbn space in art gallery complex in Santa Monica 1994; introduced Japanese artists Takashi Murakami and Yoshito Nara in USA; Co-Owner Blum & Poe gallery, expanded to larger spaces in 2003 and 2009; regularly exhibits local and internationally recognized artists, including Chiho Aoshima, J. B. Blunk, Slater Bradley, Chuck Close, Nigel Cooke, Carroll Dunham, Sam Durant, Kōji Enokura, Anya Gallaccio, Mark Grotjahn, Tim Hawkinson, Drew Heitzler, Julian Hoeber, Zhang Huan, Zhu Jinshi, Matt Johnson, Susumu Koshimizu, Friedrich Kunath, Shio Kusaka, Linder, Sharon Lockhart, Florian Maier-Aichen, Victor Man, Dave Muller, Takashi Murakami, Yoshitomo Nara, Matt Saunders, Hugh Scott-Douglas, Nobuo Sekine, Jim Shaw, Dirk Skreber, Kishio Suga, Henry Taylor, Keith Tyson, Lee Ufan, Chris Vasell and Michael Wilkinson, Theodora Allen, Darren Bader, Tomoo Gokita, Mark Grotjahn, Julian Hoeber, Zhu Jinshi, Kwon Young-woo, Mimi Lauter, J.B. Blunk, Pia Camil. *Address:* Blum & Poe, 2727 S La Cienega Blvd, Los Angeles, CA 90034, USA (office). *Telephone:* (310) 836-2062 (office). *Fax:* (310) 836-2104 (office). *E-mail:* info@blumandpoe.com (office). *Website:* www.blumandpoe.com (office).

BLUM, Yehuda Z., PhD; Israeli diplomatist, lawyer and academic; *Hersch Lauterpacht Professor of International Law, Hebrew University of Jerusalem;* b. 2 Oct. 1931, Bratislava, Czechoslovakia (now Slovakia); s. of Joseph Blum and Selda Blum (née Dux); m. Moriah Rabinovitz-Teomim; two s. one d.; ed Hebrew Univ., Univ. of London, England; detained in Nazi concentration camp of Bergen-Belsen 1944; Asst to Judge Advocate-Gen. of Israel Defence Forces 1956–59; Sr Asst to Legal Adviser, Ministry for Foreign Affairs 1962–65; UNESCO Fellow, Univ. of Sydney July–Aug. 1968; Office of UN Legal Counsel Sept.–Dec. 1968; Sr Research Scholar, Univ. of Michigan Law School 1969; Visiting Prof., School of Law, Univ. of Texas 1971, New York Univ. 1975–76, Univ. of Michigan Law School 1985, Cardozo School of Law, New York 1991, 2000, Univ. of Southern California 1991–92, Tulane Univ., New Orleans 1994, 2003, Univ. of Miami 1999, Univ. of California, Berkeley 2002; Dir Harry Sacher Inst. for Legis. Research and Comparative Law, Hebrew Univ. of Jerusalem 1977–78, Hersch Lauterpacht Prof. of International Law 1991–; mem. Israeli del., Third UN Conf. on Law of the Sea 1973, 31st Session of UN Gen. Ass. 1976; Perm. Rep. to UN 1978–84; Law Ed. Encyclopedia Hebraica 1973–78; Hon. DrJur (Yeshiva Univ.) 1981; Jabotinsky Prize 1984. *Publications include:* Historic Titles in International Law 1965, Secure Boundaries and Middle East Peace 1971, For Zion's Sake 1987, Eroding the United Nations Charter 1993; more than 40 articles in Hebrew, English and German, on various int. law topics. *Address:* Faculty of Law, Hebrew University, Mount Scopus, Jerusalem 91905, Israel (office). *Telephone:* (2) 5882562 (office). *Fax:* (2) 5823042 (office). *E-mail:* msblumy@mscc.huji.ac.il (office). *Website:* law.huji.ac.il/eng (office).

BLUME, Judy, BS; American writer; b. 12 Feb. 1938, Elizabeth, NJ; d. of Rudolph Sussman and Esther Sussman (née Rosenfeld); m. 1st John M. Blume 1959 (divorced 1975); one s. one d.; m. 2nd George Cooper 1987; one step-d.; ed New York Univ.; Founder and Trustee The Kids Fund 1981; mem. PEN Club, Authors' Guild, Nat. Coalition Against Censorship, Soc. of Children's Book Writers and Illustrators, Key West Literary Seminar, Nat. Coalition Against Censorship; Hon. LHD (Kean Coll.) 1987; Chicago Public Library Carl Sandburg Freedom to Read Award 1984, Civil Liberties Award, American Civil Liberties Union of Atlanta 1986, American Library Asscn Margaret A. Edwards Award for Lifetime Achievement 1996, Library of Congress Living Legends Award, Medal for distinguished contrib. to American Letters, Nat. Book Foundation 2004, E.B. White Award 2017; Nat. Book Foundation Medal for Distinguished Contribution to American Letters 2004. *Publications include:* juvenile fiction: The One in the Middle Is the Green Kangaroo 1969, Iggie's House 1970, Are You There God? It's Me, Margaret (Outstanding Book of the Year Award 1970, Nene Award 1975, Young Hoosier Award 1976, North Dakota Children's Choice Book Award 1979, Great Stone Face Award 1980) 1970, Then Again, Maybe I Won't 1971, Freckle Juice (Michigan Young Reader's Award 1980) 1971, It's Not the End of the World 1972, Tales of a Fourth Grade Nothing 1972, Otherwise Known as Sheila the Great (South Carolina Children's Book Award 1982) 1972, Deenie 1973, Blubber (Outstanding Book of the Year Award 1974, North Dakota Children's Choice Award 1983) 1974, Forever 1975, Starring Sally J. Freedman as Herself 1977, Superfudge (Golden Sower Award 1983, Iowa Children's Choice Award 1983, Arizona Young Readers' Award, Georgia Children's Book Award, California Young Reader Medal Reader's Choice Award 1984, Great Stone Face Award 1985, 1986) 1980, Tiger Eyes (Buckeye Children's Book Award 1983, Iowa Teen Award 1985, Colorado Blue Spruce Young Adult Book Award 1985) 1981, Fudge-a-mania (California Young Reader Medal, Iowa Children's Choice Award, Nene Award, Nevada Young Reader's Award, Sunshine State Young Reader's Award, Pennsylvania Young Reader's Choice Award, Michigan Readers' Choice Award) 1983, The Pain and the Great One (Young Readers' Choice Award 1989) 1984, Just As Long As We're Together 1987, Here's to You, Rachel Robinson (Parents' Choice Award) 1993, Places I Never Meant To Be (ed) 1999, Double Fudge 2002, The Pain and the Great One: Soupy Saturdays 2008, The Pain and the Great One: Cool Zone 2008, The Pain and the Great One: Going, Going, Gone! 2009, The Pain and the Great One: Friend or Fiend? 2009; adult fiction: Wifey 1978, Smart Women 1983, Summer Sisters 1998, In the Unlikely Event 2015; non-fiction: Letters to Judy: What Kids Wish They Could Tell You 1986, The Judy Blume Memory Book 1988. *Address:* c/o William Morris Endeavor, 1325 Avenue of the Americas, New York, NY 10022, USA (office). *E-mail:* JudyB@judyblume.com. *Website:* www.judyblume.com.

BLUMENTHAL, Richard M., BA, JD; American lawyer and politician; *Senator from Connecticut;* b. 13 Feb. 1946, Brooklyn, NY; s. of Martin A. Blumenthal and Jane Blumenthal (née Rosenstock); m. Cynthia Allison Markle; three s. one d.; ed Harvard Coll., Univ. of Cambridge, UK (Fiske Fellowship), Yale Univ. Law School; Editorial Chair. The Harvard Crimson; summer intern reporter for Washington Post, London Bureau, UK; Ed.-in-Chief Yale Law Journal; served in US Marine Corps Reserve, honourably discharged with rank of Sergeant; served as aide to Daniel P. Moynihan (later Senator Moynihan) when Asst to Pres. Richard Nixon, and as law clerk to Hon. Jon O. Newman, US Dist Court, Conn. 1973–74, and to Supreme Court Justice Harry A. Blackmun 1974–75; Admin. Asst to Senator Abraham A. Ribicoff 1975–76; US Attorney for the Dist of Conn. 1977–81, and Chief Fed. Prosecutor of Conn.; volunteer counsel for Nat. Asscn for the Advancement of Colored People (NAACP) Legal Defense Fund 1981–86; Partner, Cummings & Lockwood law firm 1981–84, Silver Golub & Teitell LLP, Stamford, Conn. 1984–90; Founder and Chair. Citizens Crime Comm. of Conn. 1982; mem. Conn. House of Reps for 145th Dist 1984–87; won special election to fill vacancy in 27th Dist of Conn. Senate 1987–90; Attorney Gen. of Conn. 1991–2011; Senator from Conn. 2011–, mem. Special Cttee on Aging 2011–, Judiciary Cttee 2011–, Armed Services Cttee 2011–, Health, Educ. Labor and Pensions Cttee 2011–; Democrat; Raymond E. Baldwin Award for Public Service, Quinnipiac Univ. School of Law 2002. *Address:* 706 Hart Senate Office Building, Washington, DC 20510 (office); 90 State House Square, 10th Floor, Hartford, CT 06103, USA (office). *Telephone:* (202) 224-2823 (DC) (office); (860) 258-6940 (Hartford) (office). *Fax:* (202) 224-9673 (DC) (office); (860) 258-6958 (Hartford) (office). *Website:* www.blumenthal.senate.gov (office).

BLUMENTHAL, W(erner) Michael, PhD; American business executive; b. 3 Jan. 1926, Oranienburg, Germany; s. of Ewald Blumenthal and Rose Valerie (Markt) Blumenthal; ed Univ. of California, Berkeley, Princeton Univ.; went to US 1947, naturalized 1952; Research Assoc., Princeton Univ. 1954–57; Vice-Pres., Dir Crown Cork Int. Corpn 1957–61; Deputy Asst Sec. of State for Econ. Affairs, Dept of State 1961–63; also served as USA Rep. to UN Comm. on Int. Commodity Trade; President's Deputy Special Rep. for Trade Negotiations (with rank of Amb.) 1963–67; Chair. US Del. to Kennedy Round tariff talks in Geneva; Pres. Bendix Int. 1967–70; Dir Bendix Corpn 1967–77, Vice-Chair. June–Dec. 1970, Pres. and Chief Operating Officer 1971–72, Chair. and CEO 1972–77; Sec. of the Treasury 1977–79; Dir Burroughs Corpn (now Unisys) 1979–90, Vice-Chair. 1980, CEO 1981–90, Chair. 1990; Sr Advisor, Lazard Frères & Co. 1990–96; Dir, Jewish Museum Berlin 1997–; mem. Council on Foreign Relations; Charter Trustee Emer., Princeton Univ.; Große Verdienstkreuz. *Publications:* The Invisible Wall 1998, From Exile to Washington: A Memoir of Leadership in the Twentieth Century 2013. *Leisure interests:* tennis, skiing. *Address:* 227 Ridgeview Road, Princeton, NJ 08540, USA (office). *Telephone:* (609) 497-7676 (office). *Fax:* (609) 497-1888 (office).

BLUMGART, Leslie Harold, BDS, MSc, FACS, FRCS (Glas.), FRCSE, FRCPS; British academic and surgeon; *Enid A. Haupt Professor of Surgery, Memorial Sloan-Kettering Cancer Center;* b. 7 Dec. 1931, South Africa; s. of Harold Herman Blumgart and Hilda Blumgart; m. 1st Pearl Navias 1955 (deceased); m. 2nd Sarah Raybould Bowen 1968; two s. two d.; ed Jeppe High School, Johannesburg, Univ. of Witwatersrand, Univ. of Sheffield, UK; Sr Lecturer and Deputy Dir, Dept of Surgery, Welsh Nat. School of Medicine, Cardiff 1970–72; St Mungo Prof. of Surgery, Univ. of Glasgow, Hon. Consultant Surgeon, Glasgow Royal Infirmary 1972–79; Prof. of Surgery and Dir Dept of Surgery, Royal Postgraduate Medical School, Univ. of London and Hon. Consultant, Hammersmith Hosp., London 1979–86; Prof. of Visceral and Transplantion Surgery, Univ. of Bern and Inselspital Bern, Switzerland 1986–91; Enid A. Haupt Prof. of Surgery, Memorial Sloan-Kettering Cancer Center, New York 1991–, Chief of Section of Hepato-Biliary Surgery and Dir Hepato-Biliary Program 1995–2007; Prof. of Surgery, Cornell Univ. Medical Coll. 1993, American Surgery Soc.; Moynihan Fellowship, Asscn of Surgeons of GB and Ireland 1972; mem. Hong Kong Surgical Soc., Hellenic Surgical Soc., LA Surgical Soc.; Pres. Int. Biliary Asscn 1986; Hon. Fellow, Royal Coll. of Surgeons in Ireland; Hon. mem. Soc. for Surgery of the Alimentary Tract, USA, Danish Surgical Soc. 1988, Asscn Française de Chirurgie, Yugoslav Soc. of Surgery, Soc. Italiana di Chirurgia 2002, Austrian Soc. of Surgery 2007, French Acad. of Surgery 2008; Order of Prasidda Prabala Gorkha-Dakshin Bahu (Nepal) 1984; Hon. DSc (Sheffield) 1998. *Publications include:* Essentials of Medicine and Surgery for Dental Students (with A. C. Kennedy), 4th Edn 1982, The Biliary Tract, in Clinical Surgery Int., Vol. 5 1982, Liver Surgery, in Clinical Surgery Int., Vol. 12 (with S. Bengmark) 1986, Difficult Problems in General Surgery 1989, Surgery of the Liver and Biliary Tract, Vols 1 and 2 (3rd edn) 2000, Surgery of the Liver, Biliary Tract and Pancreas, Vols 1 and 2 (4th edn); numerous publs concerned with medical educ., gastrointestinal surgery and aspects of oncology with particular interest in surgery of the liver, pancreas and biliary tract. *Leisure interests:* watercolour painting, wood carving, sculpture. *Address:* Memorial Sloan-Kettering Cancer Center, 1275 York Avenue, New York, NY 10065 (office); 447 East 57th Street, 3E, New York, NY 10022, USA (home). *Telephone:* (212) 639-5526 (office); (212) 755-0836 (home). *Fax:* (212) 794-5852 (office). *E-mail:* blumgarl@mskcc.org (office); lesblumgart@aol.com (office). *Website:* www.mskcc.org (office).

BLUNDELL, Sir Tom Leon, Kt, DPhil, FRS, FMedSci; British biochemist, academic, entrepreneur and administrator; *Professor Emeritus and Director of Research, Department of Biochemistry, University of Cambridge;* b. 7 July 1942, Brighton, Sussex; s. of Horace Leon Blundell and Marjorie Blundell; m. Bancinyane Lynn Sibanda 1987; one s. two d.; ed Steyning Grammar School, Brasenose Coll., Oxford; Jr Research Fellow in Molecular Physics, Linacre Coll., Oxford 1968–70; Lecturer, Hertford Coll., Oxford 1970–72; Lecturer in Biological Sciences, Univ. of Sussex 1973–76; Prof. of Crystallography, Birkbeck Coll., London 1976–90, Fellow 1997; Dir-Gen. Agricultural and Food Research Council (AFRC) 1991–94; Chief Exec. Biotechnology and Biological Sciences Research Council (BBSRC) 1994–96, Chair. 2009–15; Sir William Dunn Prof. of Biochemistry, Univ. of Cambridge 1995–2009, Fellow, Sidney Sussex Coll. 1995–, Head, Dept of Biochemistry 1996–2009, Chair. School of Biological Sciences 2003–09, Prof. Emer. 2009–, currently Dir of Research, also Dir Int. School of Crystallography 1982–; Chair. Scientific Advisory Bd Bioprocessing Ltd 1996–99; Dir (non-exec.) Celltech 1997–2004 (Chair. Scientific Advisory Bd 1998–2004); Scientific Adviser, Oxford Molecular Ltd 1996–99; mem. R&D Bd SmithKline Beecham 1997–99, Bd Babraham Inst., Cambridge 1996–2003, Astex Technology Limited 2014–; Hon. Dir Imperial Cancer Research Fund Unit of Structural Molecular Biology 1989–96; Chair. Biological Sciences, Science and Eng Research Council (SERC) Council 1983–87, SERC Council 1989–90, AFRC Council 1985–90, Advisory Council on Science and Tech. 1988–90, Royal Comm. on Environmental Pollution 1998–2005, Science Advisory Bd 2000–11; Co-founder and Dir (non-exec.) Astex Technology 1999–2011, Chair. Scientific Advisory Bd, Astex Pharmaceuticals 2011–13; consultant, Pfizer 1983–90; Pres. UK Biochemical Soc. 2009–12; Deputy Chair. Inst. of Cancer Research, London 2009–; mem. Bd Parl. Office of Science and Tech. 1998–2005; Trustee, Daphne Jackson Trust 1996–2011, Lawes Trust 1996–2007; mem. Academia Europaea 1993, Council, Royal Soc. 1997–99; Foreign Assoc. Acad. of Sciences for the Developing World 2008–; Corresp. mem. Chilean Acad. of Science 2011, Pres. Science Council 2011–16; Fellow, EMBO 1985–; Foreign Fellow, Indian Nat. Science Acad. 1994; Hon. Fellow, Royal Agricultural Soc. of England 1993, Brasenose Coll., Oxford 1989–, Linacre Coll., Oxford 1991–; Dr hc (Stirling) 2000, (Sussex) 2001, (Pavia) 2002; Hon. DSc (London) 2003 and numerous other hon. degrees; Gold Medal, Inst. of Biotechnologies 1987, Sir Hans Krebs Medal 1987, CIBA Medal 1988, Feldberg Prize 1988, Medal of Soc. for Chemical Industry 1995, Nat. Equal Opportunities Award 1996, Pfizer European Prize for Innovation 1998, Biochemical Society Award 2013, Hon. Fellows Prize, Cambridge Philosophical Soc. 2013. *Publications include:* Protein Crystallography 1976, Progress in Biophysics and Molecular Biology (ed.) 1980–; various publs in Nature, Journal of Molecular Biology. *Leisure interests:* opera, playing jazz, foreign travel, walking. *Address:* Department of Biochemistry, 80 Tennis Court Road, University of Cambridge, Cambridge, CB2

1GA, England (office). *Telephone:* (1223) 333628 (office). *E-mail:* tlb20@cam.ac.uk. *Website:* www.bioc.cam.ac.uk/people/uto/blundell (office).

BLUNKETT, Baron (Life Peer), cr. 2015, of Brightside and Hillsborough in the City of Sheffield; **Rt Hon. David Blunkett,** PC, BA; British politician; b. 6 June 1947; m. 1st (divorced); four s.; m. 2nd Dr Margaret Williams 2009; ed Univ. of Sheffield; worked for E Midlands Gas Bd before entering univ.; subsequently taught industrial relations and politics at Barnsley Coll. of Tech.; joined Labour Party 1963; mem. Sheffield City Council 1970–87, Leader 1980–87; mem. S. Yorks. Co. Council 1973–77; MP for Sheffield Brightside 1987–2015; elected to Nat. Exec. Cttee (NEC) of Labour Party 1983, Chair. NEC Local Govt Cttee 1984; Local Govt Front Bench Spokesman in Opposition's Environment Team 1988–92; Shadow Sec. of State for Health 1992–94, for Educ. 1994–95, for Educ. and Employment 1995–97; Sec. of State for Educ. and Employment 1997–2001, for the Home Dept 2001–04 (resgnd); Sec. of State for Work and Pensions 2005 (resgnd); Vice-Chair. Labour Party 1992–93, Chair. 1993–94; mem. (Labour), House of Lords 2015–; Academician, Acad. of Social Sciences 2012. *Publications:* On a Clear Day (autobiog.) 1995; co-author: Local Enterprise and Workers' Plans 1981, Building from the Bottom: the Sheffield Experience 1983, Democracy in Crisis: the Town Halls Respond 1987, Politics and Progress 2001, The Blunkett Tapes: My Life In The Bearpit (autobiog.) 2006. *Leisure interests:* walking, sailing, poetry. *Address:* House of Lords, Westminster, London, SW1A 0PW, England (office). *Telephone:* (20) 7219-5353 (office). *E-mail:* contactholmember@parliament.uk (office). *Website:* www.parliament.uk/biographies/lords/lord-blunkett/395 (office).

BLUNT, Charles William, BEcons, CPA; Australian politician and business executive; b. 19 Jan. 1951, Sydney, NSW; s. of R. S. G. Blunt; mem. House of Reps (for Richmond, NSW) 1984–90, Shadow Minister for Community Service 1987; Exec. Dir Nat. Party 1980–84, Leader 1989–90; CEO American Chamber of Commerce in Australia 1990–2013; Chair. Maxis Ltd, Permo-Drive Technologies Ltd, Pacific Star Resorts Ltd, Capital Policy and Trade Pty Ltd, Palamedia Ltd; Man. Dir American Business Services Pty Ltd. *Leisure interests:* tennis, squash, golf, motor racing, travel, trekking. *Address:* Suite 4, Gloucester Walk, 88 Cumberland Street, Sydney, NSW 2000, Australia.

BLUNT, Matt Roy, BA; American consultant and fmr politician; *President, American Automotive Policy Council;* b. 20 Nov. 1970, Greene Co., Mo.; s. of Roy Blunt; m. Melanie Blunt 1997; two s.; ed Jefferson City's public high school, US Naval Acad., Annapolis, Md; spent five years on active duty with USN as Eng Officer aboard USS Jack Williams (FFG-24) and then as Navigator and Admin. Officer aboard USS Peterson (DD-969), currently Lt-Commdr, USNR; mem. Mo. State House of Reps for 139th Legis. Dist 1998–2000; Sec. of State for Mo. 2001–05; served in support of Operation Enduring Freedom 2001–02; Gov. of Mo. 2005–09; Sr Advisor, Ashcroft Group 2009–, Solamere Capital; Pres. American Automotive Policy Council 2011–; Dir Copart; Republican; four USN and Marine Corps Achievement Medals and Humanitarian Service Medal. *Address:* American Automotive Policy Council, 1030 15th Street, NW Suite 560W, Washington, DC 20005-1503, USA (office). *Telephone:* (202) 789-0030 (office). *Fax:* (202) 789-0054 (office). *E-mail:* mblunt@americanautocouncil.org (office). *Website:* www.americanautocouncil.org (office).

BLUNT, Roy Dean, BA, MA; American politician and fmr college administrator; *Senator from Missouri;* b. 10 Jan. 1950, Niangua, Mo.; s. of Leroy O. Blunt and Neva Dora Blunt (née Letterman); m. 1st Roseann Ray 1967 (divorced 2002); two s. one d.; m. 2nd Abigail Perlman 2003; one s. (adopted); ed Southwest Baptist Univ., Missouri State Univ. (then Southwest Missouri State Univ.); teacher, Marshfield High School, Mo. 1970–73; instructor, Drury Coll., Springfield 1973–82; Co. Clerk and Chief Election Official of Greene Co. 1973–85; Republican nominee for Lt Gov. of Mo. 1980; Sec. of State of Mo. (first Republican in 50 years) 1985–93; unsuccessful cand. for Gov. of Mo. 1992; Pres. Southwest Baptist Univ. 1993–96; mem. US House of Reps for 7th Congressional Dist of Mo. 1997–2011, Chief Deputy Majority Whip 1999–2002, Asst Majority Leader (Majority Whip) 2002–07, Interim Majority Leader 2005–06, Asst Minority Leader (Minority Whip) 2007–09; Senator from Mo. 2011–, Chair. Senate Rules Cttee 2015–, Joint Library Cttee 2015–; del., Atlantic Treaty Asscn Conf. 1987; mem. Bd of Dirs Center for Democracy; mem. Missouri Mental Health Advocacy Council 1998–99, Exec. Bd American Council of Young Political Leaders 1998–99; Chair. Missouri Housing Devt Comm., Kansas City 1981, Republican State Convention, Springfield 1980; Chair. Gov.'s Advisory Council on Literacy; Co-Chair. Missouri Opportunity 2000 Comm. 1985–87; active in local American Red Cross, Muscular Dystrophy Asscn, and others; mem. Nat. Asscn of Secs of State (Chair. Voter Registration and Educ. Cttee, Sec., Vice-Pres. 1990), American Council of Young Political Leaders, Kiwanis, Masons, Smithsonian Council for American Art; Trustee, State Historical Soc. of Missouri; Republican; named one of The 10 Outstanding Young Americans, US Jaycees 1986, Springfield's Outstanding Young Man, Jaycees 1980, Missouri's Outstanding Young Civic Leader 1981, Missouri Republican of the Year 2002, Distinguished Member of Congress Award, American Wire Producers Asscn 2002, Health Leadership Award, American Asscn of Nurse Anesthetists 2003, Arthur T. Marix Congressional Leadership Award, Mil. Officers Asscn of America 2004, Community Health Defender Award, Nat. Asscn of Community Health Centers Inc. 2005. *Publications:* Missouri Election Procedures: A Layman's Guide 1977, Jobs Without People: The Coming Crisis for Missouri's Workforce 1989. *Address:* 260 Russell Senate Office Building, Washington, DC 20510, USA (office). *Telephone:* (202) 224-5721 (office). *Fax:* (202) 224-8149 (office). *Website:* www.blunt.senate.gov (office).

BLY, Robert Elwood, MA; American writer and poet; b. 23 Dec. 1926, Madison, Minn.; s. of Jacob Thomas Bly and Alice Bly (née Aws); m. 1st Carolyn McLean 1955 (divorced 1979); m. 2nd Ruth Counsell 1980; five c.; ed Harvard Univ. and Univ. of Iowa; served in USN 1944–46; Founder and Ed. The Fifties 1958, later The Sixties and Seventies Press; f. American Writers Against the Vietnam War 1966; Fulbright Award 1956–57, Amy Lowell Fellow 1964–65, Guggenheim Fellow 1965–66, Rockefeller Foundation Fellow 1967, Nat. Book Award in Poetry 1968, Distinguished Artist Award, McKnight Foundation 2002, Maurice English Poetry 2002, Robert Frost Medal, Poetry Soc. of America 2013. *Publications include:* poems: Silence in the Snowy Fields 1962, The Light Around the Body 1967, Chrysanthemums 1967, Ducks 1968, The Morning Glory: Another Thing That Will Never Be My Friend 1969, The Teeth Mother Naked at Last 1971, Poems for Tennessee (with William Stafford and William Matthews) 1971, Christmas Eve Service at Midnight at St Michael's 1972, Water Under the Earth 1972, The Dead Seal Near McClure's Beach 1973, Sleepers Joining Hands 1973, Jumping out of Bed 1973, The Hockey Poem 1974, Point Reyes Poems 1974, Old Man Rubbing his Eyes 1975, The Loon 1977, Visiting Emily Dickinson's Grave and Other Poems 1979, This Tree Will Be Here for a Thousand Years 1979, Finding An Old Ant Mansion 1981, The Man in the Black Coat Turns 1982, Four Ramages 1983, The Whole Moisty Night 1983, Out of the Rollling Ocean 1984, Mirabai Versions 1984, In the Month of May 1985, A Love of Minute Particulars 1985, Loving a Woman in Two Worlds 1985, Selected Poems (ed.) 1986, The Moon on the Fencepost 1988, The Apple Found in the Plowing 1989, What Have I Ever Lost By Dying?: Collected Prose Poems 1993, Gratitude to Old Teachers 1993, Meditations on the Insatiable Soul 1994, Morning Poems 1997, Eating the Honey of Words: New and Selected Poems 1999, The Best American Poetry (ed.) 1999, The Night Abraham Called to the Stars 2001, My Sentence was a Thousand Years of Joy 2005, The Urge to Travel Long Distances 2005, Talking into the Ear of a Donkey 2011, Stealing Sugar from the Castle: Selected and New Poems, 1950–2013: Selected Poems, 1950–2011 2013, The Lion's Tail and Eyes: Poems Written Out of Laziness and Silence 2015, Like the New Moon I Will Live My Life 2015; prose poems: The Morning Glory 1973, This Body is Made of Camphor and Gopherwood 1977, This Body is Made of Eating the Honey of Words: New and Selected Poems 1999, The Best American Poetry (ed.) 1999; prose: Iron John 1990, More Than True: The Wisdom of Fairy Tales 2018; criticism: A Poetry Reading Against the Vietnam War 1966, The Sea and the Honeycomb 1966, Forty Poems Touching on Recent American History (ed.) 1967, Leaping Poetry 1975, The Soul is Here for its Own Joy 1995; trans. of vols of poetry from Swedish, Norwegian, German, Spanish and Hindi. *Address:* 1904 Girard Avenue South, Minneapolis, MN 55403, USA (home). *Website:* www.robertbly.com (home).

BLYTH OF ROWINGTON, Baron (Life Peer), cr. 1995, of Rowington in the County of Warwickshire; **James Blyth,** MA, FRSA; British business executive; b. 8 May 1940; s. of Daniel Blyth and Jane Power Carlton; m. Pamela Anne Campbell Dixon 1967; one d. (one s. deceased); ed Spiers School, Univ. of Glasgow; with Mobil Oil Co. 1963–69, Gen. Foods Ltd 1969–71, Mars Ltd 1971–74; Dir and Gen. Man. Lucas Batteries Ltd 1974–77, Lucas Aerospace Ltd 1977–81; Dir Joseph Lucas Ltd 1977–81; Head of Defence Sales, Ministry of Defence 1981–85; Man. Dir Plessey Electronic Systems 1985–86; CEO Plessey Co. PLC 1986–87; CEO Boots Co. PLC 1987–98, Deputy Chair. 1994–98, Chair. 1998–2000; Dir (non-exec.) Imperial Group PLC 1984–86, Cadbury-Schweppes PLC 1986–90, British Aerospace 1990–94, Anixter Int. Inc. 1995–, NatWest Group 1998–2000; Dir Diageo PLC 1998–2008 (Chair. 2000–08); fmr Vice-Chair. Greenhill & Co., now Sr Adviser; mem. Council, Soc. of British Aerospace Cos 1977–81; Gov. London Business School 1987–96 (Hon. Fellow 1997); Pres. ME Asscn 1988–93; Chair. Advisory Panel on Citizen's Charter 1991–97; Patron Combined Services Winter Sports Asscn 1997–2002; Liveryman, Coachmakers'and Coach Harness Makers' Co.; Hon. LLD (Nottingham) 1992. *Leisure interests:* skiing, tennis, paintings, theatre. *Address:* House of Lords, Westminster, London, SW1A 0PW, England. *Telephone:* (20) 7219-5353.

BO, HE Cardinal Charles Maung, SDB; Myanma ecclesiastic; *Archbishop of Yangon;* b. 29 Oct. 1948, Monhla Village, Shwebo Dist, Mandalay Div., Burma; s. of John Aye Tin and Juliana Aye Tin; ed Nazareth Aspirantate, Anisakan village, nr Maymyo (now Pyin Oo Lwin); ordained priest of Salesians of Don Bosco (SDB) 1976; Prefect of Lashio 1986–90; consecrated Bishop of Lashio 1990–96; Bishop of Pathein 1996–2003; Archbishop of Yangon 2003–; cr. Cardinal (Cardinal-Priest of Sant'Ireneo a Centocelle) 2015. *Address:* Archbishop's House, 289 Theinbyu Street, Botataung PO 11161, Yangon, Myanmar (office). *Telephone:* (1) 245467 (office); (1) 392517 (office); (1) 392667 (office). *Fax:* (1) 379059 (office). *E-mail:* contact@yangondiocese.org (office). *Website:* www.yangonarchdiocese.org (office).

BO, Xilai, MA; Chinese politician; b. 3 July 1949, Dingxiang, Shanxi Prov.; s. of Bo Yibo (one of the Eight Elders of the CCP); m. 1st Li Danyu; one s.; m. 2nd Gu Kailai 1986; one s.; ed Peking Univ., Graduate School, Chinese Acad. of Social Sciences; worked in hardware factory, No. 2 Light Industry Bureau, Beijing 1968; joined CCP 1980; fmrly cadre, Research Dept of Secr. of CCP Cen. Cttee and Gen. Office of CCP Cen. Cttee; Vice-Sec. then Sec. CCP Cttee of Dalian Econ. and Technological Devt Zone; Sec. CCP Jinzhou Dist Cttee; Deputy Mayor (also Acting Mayor) of Dalian, Liaoning Prov. 1992–93, Mayor 1993–2000; Deputy Sec. CCP Dalian City Cttee 1995–99, Sec. 1999–2000; mem. CCP Prov. Cttee Standing Cttee, Liaoning Prov. 1999, Deputy Sec. CCP Prov. Cttee 2001–04; Vice-Gov. Gov. Liaoning Prov. 2001 (also Acting Gov.), Gov. 2001–04; mem. 16th CCP Cen. Cttee 2002–07; Minister of Commerce 2004–07; Sec., CCP Chongqing Municipal Cttee 2007–12 (removed from office); suspended from the Politburo April 2012; mem. 17th CCP Cen. Cttee 2007–12, mem. Politburo 2007–12; expelled from CCP Nov. 2012; on trial Aug. 2013 accused of accepting bribes and abuse of power, found guilty and sentenced to life imprisonment.

BOADEN, Helen, BA; British broadcasting executive; *Chairman of Funding Panel, Audio Content Fund;* b. 1 March 1956, Colchester, Essex; d. of William John Boaden and Barbara Mary Boaden; m. Stephen Burley 1994; ed Univ. of Sussex; Care Asst, Hackney Social Services, London 1978; Reporter, Radio WBAI, NY, USA 1979, Radio Tees and Radio Aire 1980–83; Producer, BBC Radio Leeds 1983–85; Reporter, File on 4, Radio 4 1985–91, Brass Tacks, BBC 2 1985–91; Presenter, Woman's Hour, Radio 4 1985–91, Verdict, Channel 4 1991–; Ed., File on 4, Radio 4 1991–94; Head of Network Current Affairs, BBC Manchester (first woman in position) 1994–97; Head of Business Programmes, BBC News 1997, Head of Current Affairs and Business Programmes 1998–2000; Controller, BBC Radio 4 2000–04, BBC 7 2002–04; Dir BBC News 2004–11, Dir BBC News Group, with additional responsibility for the Global News div., and mem. Exec. Bd 2011–13, Dir BBC Radio 2013–16; Chair. of Funding Panel, Audio Content Fund 2019–; Fellow, Radio Acad., Chair. 2003–; Hon. Fellow, Univ. of the Arts, London; Dr hc (East Anglia, Sussex, York, Open Univ.); Sony Gold Award (File on 4 investigation into AIDS in Africa in 1987), Sony Gold Award (File on 4 investigation into bullying in Feltham Young Offenders Inst. 1993), Radio Station of the Year 2003, 2004. *Leisure interests:* walking, food, travel. *E-mail:* info@audiocontentfund.org.uk. *Website:* www.audiocontentfund.org.uk (office).

BOAGIU, Anca-Daniela; Romanian engineer and politician; b. 30 Nov. 1968, Constanta; one adopted s.; ed Ovidius Univ., Constanta; Asst to Dir Gen., S.E.Co.L SpA 1994–95, Construction Site Man. 1995–96; Dir Dept of External Financing Programmes, Nat. Admin of Roads 1996–97; Dir Dept for External Financial Relations, Ministry of Transport 1997–99; Dir Programme for Industrial Restructuring and Professional Conversion (RICOP) 1999–2000; Admin. of External Financing Projects, Programme for the Restructuring the Pvt. Sector 1999–2000; Minister of Transport June–Dec. 2000; Deputy of Romanian Parl. 2000–08, Senator, Senatul 2008– (Vice-Pres. 2010–); Vice-Pres. of Parl. Cttee for European Integration 2004–05; Minister of European Integration 2005–07; Minister of Transport and Infrastructure 2010–12 (resgnd); mem. friendship parl. groups with Italy, Tunisia and Germany; mem. Romania-EU Jt Parl. Cttee; mem. European Parl. Network; Rep. Democratic Liberal Party (PD-L) within the working group of mems of European Parl.; mem. and Exec. Sec., PD-L; Chevalier, Légion d'honneur 2010. *Address:* Calea Moşilor 199, Sector 2, Bucharest, Romania. *E-mail:* anca .boagiu@gmail.com. *Website:* www.ancaboagiu.ro.

BOARDMAN, Christopher (Chris) Miles, MBE, MSc; British fmr professional cyclist; b. 26 Aug. 1968; s. of Keith Boardman and Carole Boardman; m. Sally-Anne Edwards 1988; six c.; ed Hilbre Secondary School and Withens Coll.; competed in nine world championships; holder of various nat. records and 20 nat. titles; bronze medal, Commonwealth Games, Edinburgh 1986; two bronze medals, Commonwealth Games, Auckland 1990; gold medal, 4,000m individual pursuit, Olympic Games, Barcelona 1992, Double World Champion (pursuit and time trial) 1994; winner Tour de France Prologue and holder Yellow Jersey 1994, 1997, 1998; World Record for distance cycled in one hour 1993 and 1996; won World 4,000m cycling championships, broke his own world record Sept. 1996; retd Oct. 2001; Co-founder Boardman Bikes; mem. English Sports Council (now Sport England) 1996; mem. Bd Nat. Cycling Strategy; expert adviser to British cycling team 2004 Olympic Games; Co-Founder, Boardman Bikes, Ltd 2007; took part in London marathon 2009; equipment and technical manager to TeamGB cyclists during 2008 Olympic Games; apptd first ever Commr of Greater Manchester for walking and cycling 2017; writes for various publications, including Diver magazine, Pro Cycling, commentator for ITV (resgnd 2018) and BBC covering major cycling events; Hon. DSc (Brighton) 1997; Hon. MSc (Liverpool); Pat Besford Award, Sports Journalists' Asscn, Bidlake Memorial Prize 1992, Man of Year Award, Cheshire Life magazine 1997, inducted into the British Cycling Hall of Fame 2010. *Publication:* Chris Boardman's Complete Book of Cycling. *Leisure interests:* carpentry, swimming, scuba diving, writing, archery, family. *E-mail:* media@ chrisboardman.com (office). *Website:* www.chrisboardman.com (office).

BOARDMAN, Sir John, Kt, MA, FSA, FBA; British archaeologist and academic; *Professor Emeritus of Classical Archaeology and Art, University of Oxford;* b. 20 Aug. 1927; s. of Frederick Boardman and Clare Wells; m. Sheila Stanford 1952; one s. one d.; ed Chigwell School and Magdalene Coll., Cambridge; Asst Dir British School, Athens 1952–55; Asst Keeper, Ashmolean Museum, Oxford 1955–59; Reader in Classical Archaeology, Univ. of Oxford 1959–78, Lincoln Prof. of Classical Archaeology and Art 1978–94, Hon. Fellow 1995, now Prof. Emer.; Fellow, Merton Coll., Oxford 1973–78, Hon. Fellow 1978–, Sub-Warden 1975–78; Prof. of Ancient History, Royal Acad. of Arts 1989–; conducted excavations on Chios 1953–55, Crete 1964–65, in Tocra, Libya 1964–65; Visiting Prof., Columbia Univ. 1965; Geddes-Harrower Prof., Univ. of Aberdeen 1974; Fellow, Inst. of Etruscan Studies, Florence 1983, Austrian and German Archaeological Insts; Foreign mem. Royal Danish Acad.; Assoc. mem. Acad. des Inscriptions et des Belles Lettres, Institut de France; Corresp. mem. Bavarian Acad. of Sciences; Foreign mem. American Philosophical Soc., Accad. dei Lincei, Rome, Russian Acad. of Sciences; Hon. RA; Hon. MRIA; Dr hc (Athens) 1991, (Sorbonne) 1994; Kenyon Medal (British Acad.) 1995, Onassis Prize for Humanities 2009. *Publications include:* Cretan Collection in Oxford 1961, Island Gems 1963, Archaic Greek Gems 1968, Athenian Black Figure Vases 1974, Escarabeos de Piedra de Ibiza 1984, The Oxford History of the Classical World (with others) 1986, Athenian Red Figure Vases: Classical Period 1989, Oxford History of Classical Art 1993, The Diffusion of Classical Art in Antiquity 1994, Greek Sculpture, Later Classical 1995, Runciman Prioxe 1995, Early Greek Vase Painting 1997, Persia and the West 2000, The History of Greek Vases 2001, Greek Gems and Finger Rings 2001, The Archaeology of Nostalgia 2002, Classical Phoenician Scarabs 2003, The World of Ancient Art 2006, The Marlborough Gems 2009, The Triumph of Dionysos 2014; articles in learned journals. *Address:* 11 Park Street, Woodstock, Oxford, OX20 1SJ (home); Beazley Archive, Classics Centre, Oxford, OX1 3LU, England. *Telephone:* (1993) 811259 (home); (1865) 278084. *Fax:* (1865) 610237 (office). *E-mail:* john.boardman@ashmus.ox.ac.uk (office).

BOARDMAN, Norman Keith, AO, PhD, ScD, FAA, FRS, FTSE; Australian biochemist and academic; b. 16 Aug. 1926, Geelong, Vic.; s. of William R. Boardman and Margaret Boardman; m. Mary C. Shepherd 1952; two s. five d.; ed Melbourne Univ., St John's Coll., Cambridge, UK; Research Officer, Wool Research Section, CSIRO 1949–51; Sr Research Scientist, Div. of Plant Industry, CSIRO 1956–61, Prin. Research Scientist 1961–64; Fulbright Scholar, UCLA, USA 1964–65; Sr Prin. Research Scientist, Div. of Plant Industry, CSIRO 1966–68, Chief Research Scientist 1968–77, mem. of Exec., CSIRO 1977–85, Chair. and Chief Exec. 1985–86, CEO 1986–90, post-retirement Fellow 1990–97; Pres. Australian Biochemical Soc. 1976–78; fmr Chair. Nat. Science and Industry Forum; Treas. Australian Acad. of Science 1978–81; Dir Sirotech Ltd 1986–90, Landcare Australia Ltd 1990–98; Sec. for Science Policy, Australian Acad. of Science 1993–97; mem. Australian Research Grants Cttee 1971–75, ANU Council 1979–89, 1990–91, Australian Centre for Int. Agric. Research 1982–88, CRA Scientific Advisory Bd 1983–98, Prime Minister's Scientific Council 1989–90; Foreign mem. Korean Acad. of Science and Tech.; Hon. DSc (Newcastle Univ.); David Syme Research Prize, Melbourne Univ. 1967, Centenary Medal, Lemberg Medal, Australian Biochemical Soc. 1969. *Publications include:* scientific papers on plant biochemistry, particularly photosynthesis and structure, function and biogenesis of chloroplasts. *Leisure interests:* listening to music, reading, walking. *Address:* 6 Somers Crescent, Forrest, ACT 2603, Australia (home). *Telephone:* (2) 6295-1746 (home). *E-mail:* keithboardman@bigpond.com (home).

BOASE, Martin, MA; British advertising executive; b. 14 July 1932, Sheffield; s. of Alan Boase and Elizabeth Grizelle Boase (née Forster); m. 1st Terry Ann Moir 1960 (divorced 1971); one s. one d.; m. 2nd Pauline Valerie Brownrigg 1974; one s. one d.; ed Rendcomb Coll., New Coll., Oxford; with Pritchard Wood and Partners 1961–68; Pnr, The Boase Massimi Pollitt Partnership (subsequently Boase Massimi Pollitt PLC, now part of Omnicom UK PLC), Chair. 1977–89, Chair. Omnicom UK PLC 1989–95; Chair. Predator Three PLC 1990–97; Chair. Advertising Asscn 1987–92, Kiss 100 FM 1993–2000, Maiden Outdoor 1993–2006, British TV Advertising Awards Ltd 1993–2000, Herald Investment Trust 1994–2009, Investment Trust of Investment Trusts 1995–2005, Heal's 1997–2002, Jupiter Dividend and Growth Investment Trust PLC, 1999–2008, Global Professional Media PLC 1999–2005, New Star Investment Trust 2000–06, New Media Industries PLC 2001–05; Dir Omnicom Group Inc. 1989–93, EMAP PLC 1991–2000, Taunton Cider PLC 1993–97, Matthew Clark PLC 1995–98; mem. Inst. of Practitioners in Advertising. *Leisure interest:* the Turf.

BOATENG, Ozwald, OBE; British fashion designer; b. 28 Feb. 1967, London; m. 1st Pascale Boateng (divorced); m. 2nd Gyunel Boateng (divorced 2009); two c. (with Gyunel Boateng); has designed for Pierce Brosnan, Mick Jagger, Will Smith, Stephen Baldwin, Laurence Fishburne, Billy Zane and others; signed exclusive licensing deal with Marchpole Holdings to produce new formal and casual wear ranges 2002–08; Creative Dir of Menswear, Givenchy 2003–07; opened flagship store in London 2007; Hon. MA (Univ. for the Creative Arts) 2011; Dr hc (Univ. of the Arts London) 2013; Trophée de la Mode for Best Menswear Designer 1996, British Menswear Designer of the Year Award 2001, named Young Global Leader by World Econ. Forum 2007, Veritas Award, Harvard Univ. 2014. *Address:* 30 Savile Row, London, W1S 3PT, England (office). *Telephone:* (20) 7437-2030 (office). *E-mail:* pr@ozwaldboateng.co.uk (office). *Website:* ozwaldboateng.co.uk (office).

BOATENG, Baron (Life Peer), cr. 2010, of Akyem in the Republic of Ghana and of Wembley in the London Borough of Brent; **Rt Hon. Paul (Yaw) Boateng,** PC, LLB; British diplomatist, politician, lawyer and broadcaster; b. 14 June 1951, Hackney, London; s. of Kwaku Boateng and Eleanor Boateng; m. Janet Alleyne 1980; two s. three d.; ed Ghana Int. School, Accra Acad., Apsley Grammar School and Univ. of Bristol; solicitor, Paddington Law Centre 1976–79; solicitor and Pnr, B. M. Birnberg & Co. 1979–87; called to the Bar, Gray's Inn 1989; Legal Adviser, Scrap Sus Campaign 1977–81; mem. GLC (Labour) for Walthamstow 1981–86, Chair. Police Cttee 1981–86, Vice-Chair. Ethnic Minorities Cttee 1981–86; MP (Labour) for Brent S 1987–2005; Home Office mem. House of Commons Environment Cttee 1987–89; Opposition Frontbench Spokesman on Treasury and Econ. Affairs 1989–92, on Legal Affairs, Lord Chancellor's Dept 1992–97; Parl. Under-Sec. of State, Dept of Health 1997–98; Minister of State 1998–2001, Deputy Home Sec. 1999–2001; Minister for Young People 2000–01; Financial Sec. to HM Treasury 2001–02, Chief Sec. 2002–05; High Commr to S Africa 2005–09; Chair. Afro-Caribbean Educ. Resource Project 1978–86, Westminster CRC 1979–81; Gov. Police Staff Coll., Bramshill 1981–84; mem. Home Sec.'s Advisory Council on Race Relations 1981–86, WCC Comm. on Programme to Combat Racism 1984–91, Police Training Council 1981–85; Exec. Nat. Council for Civil Liberties 1980–86; mem. Court of Univ. of Bristol 1994–97; Dir, ENO 1984–97; Dir (non-exec.) Aegis Defence Services Ltd 2009–, Ghana International Bank plc; mem. Bd of Govs, LSE 2011; Founder and Chair. Akyem Law and Advisory Services Ltd 2012–; Gov., English Speaking Union; mem. Unified Bd, Food for the Hungry; Trustee, Museum of London 2009–; Patron, Barbara Kwateng Lupus Trust, MTN-Ghana Foundation; Hon. LLD (Lincoln Univ., USA, Univ. of fBristol). *Radio:* Looking Forward to the Past 1990. *Television work includes:* Behind the Hardlines (BBC), Nothing but the Truth (Channel 4). *Publications include:* Reclaiming the Ground (contrib.) 1993, Introduction to Sense and Sensibility, The Complete Jane Austen 1993. *Leisure interests:* opera, swimming, art history. *Address:* House of Lords, Westminster, London, SW1A 0PW, England (office). *Telephone:* (20) 7219-5353 (office). *Fax:* (20) 7219-5979 (office). *E-mail:* contactholmember@parliament.uk (office). *Website:* www.parliament.uk/biographies/lords/lord-boateng/147 (office).

BOATSWAIN, Anthony; Grenadian economist and politician; ed Long Island Univ., USA, Univ. of Toronto, Canada; early career as teacher at McDonald Coll. St John's Christian Secondary School; held several positions in Public Service including Perm. Sec., Deputy Dir-Gen. and Chief Econ. Planner, Ministry of Finance; fmr Gen. Man. Grenada Industrial Devt Corpn; fmr Chair. Marketing and Nat. Importing Bd, Grenada Ports Authority, Land Devt Control Authority; fmr mem. Bd of Dirs Grenada Bd of Tourism, Grenada Banana Cooperative Soc., Grenada Bureau of Standards, Grenada Chamber of Industry and Commerce, Grenada Devt Bank; elected MP for St Patrick W 1999, re-elected 2003; Minister of Finance and Planning 2003–07, of Econ. Devt and Planning 2007; apptd Senator 2010; Minister of Educ. and Human Resource Devt 2013–17; Minister of Youth, Sports and Religious Affairs 2017–18; mem. New Nat. Party. *Address:* c/o Ministry of Youth, Sports and Religious Affairs, Ministerial Complex, 3rd Floor, Botanical Gardens, Tanteen, Saint George's, Grenada (office).

BOBBITT, Philip Chase, AB, JD, PhD; American academic and government official; *Herbert Wechsler Professor of Jurisprudence, Columbia University;* b. 22 July 1948, Temple, Tex.; s. of Oscar Price Bobbitt and Rebekah Johnson Bobbitt; m. Maya Ondalikoglu Bobbitt; one s. three d.; ed Princeton Univ., Yale Univ., Univ. of Oxford, UK; Asst Prof. of Law, Univ. of Texas School of Law 1976–79, Prof. 1979, A. W. Walker Centennial Chair 1996–2007, now Distinguished Sr Lecturer and Sr Fellow, Robert S. Strauss Center for Int. Security and Law; Jr Research Fellow, Nuffield Coll., Oxford 1982–84, Research Fellow 1984–85, Anderson Sr Research Fellow 1985–91, mem. Modern History Faculty 1984–91; Sr Research Fellow, War Studies Dept, Kings Coll. London, UK 1994–97; Assoc. Counsel to Pres. of USA for Intelligence and Int. Security 1980–81; Legal Counsel to US Senate Intra-Contra Cttee 1987–88; Counsellor on Int. Law, US State Dept 1990–93; Dir for Intelligence, Nat. Security Council 1997–98, Sr Dir of Critical Infrastructure 1998–99, Sr Dir for Strategic Planning 1999; Herbert Wechsler Prof. of Jurisprudence, Columbia Univ. 2007–; fmr mem. Editorial Bd Biosecurity and Bioterrorism; Fellow, American Acad. of Arts and Sciences, Club of Madrid; Life Mem. American Law Inst.; mem. Council on Foreign Relations, Pacific Council on Int. Policy, Int. Inst. for Strategic Studies, Exec. Council of American Soc. of Int. Law; fmr Trustee, Princeton Univ. *Publications include:* Tragic Choices (co-author) 1978, Constitutional Fate 1982, Democracy and Deterrence 1987, US Nuclear Strategy (co-author) 1989, Constitutional Interpretation 1991, The Shield of Achilles: War, Peace and the Course of History 2002, Terror and Consent: The

Wars for the Twenty-First Century 2008, The Garments of Court and Palace: Machiavelli and the World That He Made 2013, The Ages of American Law (co-author) 2014, Impeachment: A Handbook (co-author) 2018. *Address:* Oakwell, 1505 Windsor Road, Austin, TX 78703, USA (office). *E-mail:* pbobbitt@law.utexas.edu (office); bobbitt@law.columbia.edu (office). *Website:* www.law.columbia.edu (office); www.utexas.edu/law (office); philipbobbitt.com.

BOBINAC, Franjo, BEcons, MSc, MBA; Slovenian business executive; *President and CEO, Gorenje Group;* b. 16 Oct. 1958, Celje; m. Polonca Bobinac; one s. one d.; ed Univ. of Ljubljana, Ecole Supérieure de Commerce, Paris, France; began career with Emo Celje 1983–86; Asst to Dir of Export, Gorenje gospodinjski aparati d.d. (Gorenje Household Appliances) 1986–91, Export Dir 1990, Marketing Dir 1991–93, Gen. Dir Gorenje Sidex France 1993–98, mem. Man. Bd, Gorenje d.d. 1998–, Pres. Man. Bd 2003–, currently also CEO; fmr Pres. BIO 19 Organizing Cttee; Pres. Slovenian Handball Fed.; mem. Supervisory Bd ETI Izlake; mem. Man. Cttee, Chamber of Commerce and Industry of Slovenia, Council, Bled School of Man., Steering Cttee, Int. Asscn Conseil Européen de la Construction d'appareils Domestiques 2010–, Jozef Stefan Inst.; Chevalier, Ordre nat. du Mérite 2009; Award by the Chamber of Commerce and Industry of Slovenia for exceptional results, Janez Vajkard Valvasor Medal, Int. Asscn of Business Communicators Merit Excel Award (Excellence in Communication Leadership), Slovenian Asscn for Public Relations Primus Award for Best Slovenian Manager. *Address:* Gorenje gospodinjski aparati d.d., Partizanska 12, 3503 Velenje, Slovenia (office). *Telephone:* (3) 8991000 (office). *Fax:* (3) 8991460 (office). *E-mail:* franjo.bobinac@gorenje.si (office). *Website:* www.gorenje.com (office).

BOBOJONOV, Po'lat; Uzbekistani politician; *Minister of Internal Affairs;* b. 1 Jan. 1961, Bog'ot Dist, Xorazm Viloyat, Uzbek SSR, USSR; ed Tashkent State Univ.; Asst to Prosecutor, Gurlan Dist 1982–83; Public Prosecutor, Office of Prosecutor Gen., Xorazm Viloyat 1983–85, Head of Gen. Supervision Dept 1985–91; Prosecutor, Gurlan Dist, Xorazm Viloyat 1991–92; First Deputy Mayor of Bog'ot Dist, Xorazm Viloyat 1992–96; Deputy Hokim (Gov.), Xorazm Viloyat 1996–99, also Head of Inspection Dept 1996–99; Advisor on personnel policy, Office of the Pres. 1999–2000; Acting Inspector of State Personnel Services 2000; Deputy Prosecutor Gen., Repub. of Uzbekistan 2000–05; Head, Dept for Combating Tax and Currency Crimes, Prosecutor Gen.'s Office 2005–06; Prosecutor, Jizzax Viloyat 2006–11, Buxoro Viloyat 2011; First Deputy Hokim (Gov.), Xorazm Viloyat 2011–12, Hokim 2012–17; Minister of Internal Affairs 2017–. *Address:* Ministry of Internal Affairs, 100029 Tashkent, Yu. Rajaby ko'ch. 1, Uzbekistan (office). *Telephone:* (71) 233-39-39 (office). *Fax:* (71) 233-38-82 (office). *E-mail:* info@mvd.uz (office). *Website:* www.mvd.uz (office).

BOBONAZAROVA, Oinihol; Tajikistani lawyer and politician; b. 10 June 1948, Java dist; m.; one s. one d.; ed Faculty of Law, Tajik State Univ.; has taught at Faculty of Law, Tajik State Univ. since 1976, Dean of Faculty 1989–; human rights lawyer known for advocacy of human rights with non-governmental org. Perspective-Plus, has also worked with Western insts including OSCE and Open Society Foundations, chaired Bd of Open Society Inst. Assistance Foundation – Tajikistan (under auspices of Soros Foundations Network); convicted for being mem. of an opposition party, but later pardoned early 1990s; Adviser on Human Rights to Tajikstan Rep. of OSCE 1996–2004; mem. Islamic Rebirth Party of Tajikistan (IRPT); apptd to represent United Reformist Forces (merger of IRPT, Social Democratic Party and several non-governmental groups and others in opposition) Sept. 2013; opposition cand. in presidential election 6 Nov. 2013. *Address:* Islamic Rebirth Party of Tajikistan, 734000 Dushanbe, pos. Kalinina, Kuchai Tukhagul 55, Tajikistan (office). *Telephone:* (372) 27-25-30 (office). *Fax:* (372) 27-53-93 (office).

BOBROW, Martin, CBE, DScMed, FRS, FRCP, FRCPath, FMedSci; British medical scientist, geneticist and academic; b. 6 Feb. 1938, Johannesburg, South Africa; s. of Joe Bobrow and Bessie Bobrow; m. Lynda Strauss; three d.; ed Univ. of the Witwatersrand, S Africa; Prof. of Human Genetics, Univ. of Amsterdam 1981–82; Prince Philip Prof. of Paediatric Research, United Medical and Dental Schools of Guy's and St Thomas' Hosps, London, 1982–95; Prof. and Head, Dept of Medical Genetics, Univ. of Cambridge 1995–2005, Emer. Fellow, Wolfson Coll., Dir (non-exec.), Cambridge Univ. Hosps NHS Foundation Trust 2004–13; mem. Black Advisory Group on possible increased incidence of cancer in W Cumbria 1983–84, Cttee to examine ethical implications of gene therapy 1989–93, NHS Cen. R&D Cttee, Dept of Health 1991–97, Gene Therapy Advisory Cttee 1993–94, Lewisham NHS Trust Bd 1994–95, Nuffield Council on Bioethics 1996–2003 (fmr Deputy Chair.), Human Genetics Advisory Comm. 1997–99; fmr mem. MRC; Gov. Wellcome Trust 1996–2007, Deputy Chair. 2004–07; Chair. Muscular Dystrophy Campaign 1995–2010; fmr Chair. ULTRA (Unrelated Living Transplant Regulating Authority), COMARE (Dept of Health Advisory Cttee on Radiation in the Environment); Founding Fellow, Acad. of Medical Sciences 1998. *Publications:* papers in science books and journals 1967–. *Address:* Wolfson College, Barton Road, Cambridge, CB3 9BB, England (office). *Telephone:* (1223) 335900 (office). *Fax:* (1223) 335908 (office). *E-mail:* lms28@cam.ac.uk (office). *Website:* www.wolfson.cam.ac.uk/people/professor-martin-bobrow (office).

BOBUŢAC, Valeriu; Moldovan politician and diplomatist; b. 13 March 1945, Khankaun; m. Maria Bobutac; two c.; ed Lvov Trade-Econ. Inst., Ukraine, Higher CP School, Kiev, Ukraine; worked in Comsomol, First-Sec. Cen. Cttee then Sec. Cen. Cttee Moldovan CP; Deputy Minister of Econs and Reforms; Amb. to Russia 1997–99, 2001; Prime Minister of Moldova 1999–2000; at Ministry of Foreign Affairs 2002–05; Amb. to Hungary 2005–09, also Rep. to Danube Comm. 2005–09.

BOC, Emil, DPhil; Romanian politician and academic; *Mayor of Cluj-Napoca;* b. 6 Sept. 1966, Răchiţele; s. of Ioan Boc and Ana Boc; m. Oana Boc 1994; two d.; Sr Law Lecturer; Deputy, Romanian Parl. 2000–04, Vice-Chair. of Legal, Discipline, and Immunity Cttee 2000–04, Vice-Chair. Cttee for Elaboration of Bills Concerning the Revision of Romania's Constitution 2001–04; mem. parl. friendship groups with UK, South Africa, Repub. of Korea 2000–04; Mayor of Cluj-Napoca 2004–08, 2012–; joined Democratic Liberal Party (PD-L) 2003, Exec.-Pres., then Pres. 2008–12; Prime Minister 2008–09, 2009–12 (resgnd), Acting Prime Minister Oct.–Dec. 2009; Acting Minister of Educ., Research and Innovation Oct.–Dec. 2009; apptd Acting Minister of Labour, Family and Social Protection 2011. *Publication:* Separation of Powers in the State 2000. *Address:* Cluj-Napoca City Hall (Primăria Cluj-Napoca), 400001 Cluj-Napoca, Motilor 1-3, Romania (office). *Telephone:* (264) 592301 (office); (264) 596030 (office). *E-mail:* boc@yahoo.com (home); cabinet@primariaclujnapoca.ro (office). *Website:* primariaclujnapoca.ro (office).

BOCCARDO, Archbishop Renato; Italian ecclesiastic; *Archbishop of Spoleto-Norcia;* b. 21 Dec. 1952, Sant'Ambrogio; ordained priest 1977; apptd Titular Bishop of Aquipendium 2004; Sec. Pontifical Council for Social Communications 2003–; Sec. Governorate of the Vatican City State 2005–09; Archbishop of Spoleto-Norcia 2009–; mem. Congregazione per le Cause dei Santi 2012–; mem. Conferenza Episcopale Italiana 2015–17; Pres. Conferenza Episcopale Umbria 2017–. *Address:* Arcivescovado, Via Aurelio Saffi 13, 06049 Spoleto, Italy (office). *Telephone:* (07) 4323101 (office). *Website:* www.arcidiocesidispoleto-norcia.it.

BOCELLI, Andrea; Italian singer (tenor); b. 22 Sept. 1958, Lajatico, Pisa; s. of Alessandro Bocelli and Edi Bocelli; m. 1st Enrica Cenzatti 1992; two s.; m. 2nd Veronica Berti 2014; one d.; ed Univ. of Pisa; began piano lessons aged six, later learned to play the flute, saxophone, trumpet, trombone, harp, guitar and drums; became blind following a football accident aged 12; won first song competition, Margherita d'Oro in Viareggio with O sole mio aged 14; earned money performing in piano bars; completed law school and spent one year as a court-appointed lawyer; won Newcomers section of Sanremo Music Festival 1994; recordings include 13 solo studio albums, of both pop and classical music, two greatest hits albums and nine complete operas; biggest-selling solo artist in history of classical music; duet with Celine Dion, The Prayer, for animated film The Quest for Camelot, won Golden Globe for Best Original Song 1999; Grande Ufficiale, Ordine al merito della Repubblica Italiana 2006, Grand Officer, Orden al Mérito de Duarte, Sánchez y Mella (Dominican Repub.) 2009; named one of People Magazine's 50 Most Beautiful People 1998, honoured with a star on Hollywood Walk of Fame 2010, World Music Award for World's Best-selling Classical Artist 2010, America Award, Italy-USA Foundation 2012, Classic BRIT Award for Int. Artist of the Year in association with Raymond Weil 2012, ECHO Klassik Ohne Grenzen Prize 2016, Classic BRITs Icon 2018. *Recordings include:* albums: Bocelli 1995, Viaggio Italiano 1995, Romanza 1997, Aria 1998, Sacred Arias 1999, Sogno 1999, Verdi 2000, La Bohème 2000, Verdi Requiem 2001, Cieli di Toscana 2001, Sentimento (Classical BRIT Award for Best Album 2003) 2002, Tosca 2003, Aria: The Opera Album 2005, MW 2006, Vivere 2007, Incanto 2008, My Christmas 2009, Andrea Chénier 2010, Carmen: Duets & Arias 2010, Concerto: One Night in Central Park 2011, Notte Illuminata 2011, Opera 2012, Roméo et Juliette 2012, Passione 2013, Manon Lescaut 2014, Turandot 2015, Cinema 2015. *Publications:* The Music of Silence: A Memoir (La musica del silenzio) (autobiog.) 2000 (reworked 2010). *Address:* Almud Edizioni Musicali srl, Andrea Bocelli Business Management, via Padre da Carrara 1, 55042 Forte dei Marmi (office); c/o Michele Torpedine, MT Opera and Blues Production and Management, via Mario Musolesi, 40138 Bologna, Italy (office). *Telephone:* (51) 251117 (office). *Fax:* (51) 251123 (office). *E-mail:* mtorped@tin.it (office). *Website:* www.almudmusic.com (office); www.mt-operaandblues.it (office); www.andreabocelli.com.

BOCEVSKI, Ivica, BPolSci, MPIA; Macedonian politician, teacher and diplomatist; *Ambassador to Brazil;* b. 15 June 1977, Skopje; s. of Angel Bocevski and Spasenija Jovanovikj; m. Valentina Popovska; one d.; ed Nikola Karev High School, SS Cyril and Methodius Univ., Skopje, Univ. of Pittsburgh, USA; fmr columnist, Utrinski Vesnik; Co-founder and fmr Exec. Dir Inst. for Democracy, Skopje; Chief of Staff, Office of the Deputy Prime Minister for Econ. Affairs 2004–06; Analyst, Ministry of Foreign Affairs 2006–07; Govt Spokesman 2007–08; Deputy Prime Minister, responsible for European Integration 2008–09; Special Adviser to the Pres. for Foreign Affairs 2015; Social Sciences Teacher, NOVA Int. Schools 2010; Amb. to Brazil 2016–. *Publications:* several expert articles in domestic and foreign journals. *Address:* Embassy of North Macedonia, SHIS, QL 26 Conjunto 05, Casa 15, Lago Sul, 71665-155 Brasilia, DF, Brazil (office). *Telephone:* (61) 3256-2939 (office). *E-mail:* brasilia@mfa.gov.mk (office). *Website:* www.mfa.gov.mk/brasilia (office).

BOCHEŃSKI, Jacek; Polish writer and essayist; b. 29 July 1926, Lvov; m.; one d.; ed State Coll. of Theatrical Arts, Warsaw; Co-founder and Ed. Zapis (first Polish underground periodical) 1977–81; Pres. Polish PEN Club 1996–99; currently Pres. Authors & Composers Asscn's Council; Solidarity Prize 1987, Polish PEN Club Parandowski Prize 2006, Gloria Artis Golden Medal 2009. *Radio:* Post-Breakdown, Naso Poet, The Elderely Man's Fantasies 1998–2002. *Television and stage plays:* Taboo, Post-Breakdown. *Publications include:* fiction: Farewell to Miss Syngilu 1960, Roman Trilogy: Divine Julius 1961, Taboo 1965, Naso Poet 1969, Post-Breakdown 1987, The Elderly Man's Fantasies 2004, Tiberius Caesar 2009; non-fiction: Bloody Italian Rarities 1982, Thirteen European Exercises 2005, Antiquity after Antiquity 2010; several essays and contribs to magazines on politics and culture. *Address:* ul. Sonaty 6 m. 801, 02-744 Warsaw, Poland (home). *E-mail:* jacek.bochenski@gazeta.pl. *Website:* www.jacekbochenski.blox.pl.

BOCHNIARZ, Henryka Teodora, PhD; Polish economist and politician; *President, Polish Confederation of Private Employers;* b. 29 Oct. 1947, Świebodzin; m. Zbigniew Bochniarz 1969; one s. one d.; ed Warsaw School of Econs and Foreign Trade Research Inst.; Asst, Deputy Head Agric. Div., Foreign Trade Research Inst., Warsaw 1976–80, Asst Prof., Lecturer 1980–84, Dir Agric. Div. and Negotiator 1984–90; Research Asst, Int. Inst. of Socialist Econ. Systems, Moscow, USSR (now Russian Fed.) 1978; Visiting Asst Prof., Vienna Inst. for Comparative Econ. Systems 1983–84; Sr Fulbright Scholar and Visiting Prof., Dept of Agric. and Applied Econs, Univ. of Minn., USA 1985–87; Dir Proexim Ltd 1988–90; Pres. Nicom Consulting Ltd, Warsaw 1990–91, 1992–, Asscn of Econ. Consultants in Poland 1991–; Minister of Industry and Trade 1991–92; Pres. Polish Business Roundtable 1996–99, Polish Confed. of Pvt. Employers 1999–; Co-Chair. (with Leszek Balcerowicz q.v.) Cttee on Deregulation of the Polish Economy 1998–; currently Exec. Pres. Polish Business Council; mem. Bd Dirs TVN SA, Computerland SA, ITI SA; mem. Polish Del. to UN Cttee on Agric., Econ. Comm. for Europe, Geneva, Switzerland 1976–85; Visiting Prof., Dept of Agricultural and Applied Econs, Univ. of Minnesota, USA 1985–87; mem. Negotiating Group on Agric., Uruguay Round GATT talks 1987; Order of the Rebirth of Poland, Japanese Order of the Rising Sun. *Publications include:* Polish Agricultural Trade (annual reports) 1975–90, Poland: The Impact of Foreign Trade Policy on Self-Sufficiency in Agriculture 1987; numerous papers and contribs to professional journals. *Leisure* *interests:* skiing, volleyball, theatre. *Address:* Polskej Konfederacji Pracodawców Prywatnych Lewiatan (Polish Confederation of Private Employers), ul. Klonowa 6, 00-591 Warsaw (office); c/o Nicom Consulting Ltd, 10 Inwalidów Square, 01-552 Warsaw, Poland. *Telephone:* (22) 845-95-50 (office). *Fax:* (22) 845-95-51 (office). *E-mail:* pkpp@prywatni.pl (office). *Website:* www.prywatni.pl (office); www.nicom.pl; www.bochniarz.pl.

BOCK, Kurt, PhD; German business executive; b. 1958, Rahden, Eastern Westphalia; m.; three c.; ed Univs of Münster and Cologne, Pennsylvania State Univ., USA, Univ. of Bonn; joined Finance Div., BASF AG 1985, mem. of staff to BASF's Chief Financial Officer (CFO) 1987–91, Dir of Tech., Planning and Controlling, Eng Plastics, BASF AG 1991–94, Sr Vice-Pres. Finance 1992–94, Sr Vice-Pres. Finance and Accounting, Robert Bosch GmbH, Stuttgart, Germany 1994–96, Man. Dir Robert Bosch Ltda, Campinas, Brazil 1996, CFO BASF Corpn, NJ, USA 1998–2000, Pres. Logistics & Information Services, BASF AG 2000–03, mem. Bd of Exec. Dirs and CFO BASF AG (renamed BASF SE 2008) 2003–11, Chair. and CEO BASF Corpn, USA 2007–, Chair. Bd of Exec. Dirs BASF SE 2011–18; Pres. Verband der Chemischen Industrie eV 2016–18. *Address:* c/o BASF SE, Carl-Bosch Strasse 38, 67056 Ludwigshafen, Germany (office). *Telephone:* (621) 60-0 (office); (621) 60-20916 (Corporate Media Relations) (office). *Fax:* (621) 60-92693 (office); (621) 60-42525 (office). *E-mail:* presse.kontakt@basf.com (office); info@basf.de (office). *Website:* www.basf.com (office); www.basf.de (office).

BOCKERIA, Leo Antonovich, DrMedSci; Russian cardiovascular surgeon and academic; *Chairman and Head, A. Bakulev Scientific Centre for Cardiovascular Surgery, Russian Academy of Medical Sciences;* b. 22 Dec. 1939, s. of F. Anton Bockeria and Olga M. Bockeria; m.; two d.; ed I. M. Sechenov First Moscow Medical Inst. (now Sechenov First State Medical Univ.); with A. Bakulev Scientific Centre for Cardiovascular Surgery (SCCVS) 1968–, Chair. and Head 1994–, Dir, SCCVS Prof. Burakovsky Research Inst. of Cardiosurgery 1993–; mem. Russian Acad. of Medical Sciences 1994–, Russian Acad. of Sciences 2011–; main research in cardiovascular surgery, hyperbaric oxygenation, treatment of cardiopulse violation problems; apptd mem. Public Chamber of the Russian Fed. 2005, Chair. Comm. for the Formation of a Healthy Lifestyle 2006–; Order of Peter the Great 2006; Order of Honour, Sovereign Award with Hon. Title Outstanding Surgeon of the Present 2008; Order of St Daniel 2008; Kadyrov's Order 2009; Lenin Prize 1976, USSR State Prize 1986, Russian Fed. State Prize 2002, Russian Govt Prize 2003, Russian Acad. Prize 2004, Moscow City Prize 2009. *Publications:* numerous articles on cardiovascular surgery. *Leisure interests:* painting, collecting encyclopaedias and dictionaries. *Address:* Bakulev Scientific Centre for Cardiovascular Surgery, 121552 Moscow, Roublyevskoe Shosse 135, Russia (office). *Telephone:* (495) 414-75-71 (office). *Fax:* (495) 414-78-67 (office). *E-mail:* leoan@heart-house.ru (office). *Website:* www.bakulev.ru (office).

BOCLET, Franck; French fashion designer; fmr Textile Engineer; Collection Man. Kenzo 1984–85; Product Man. Arrow 1985–89; Licensing Man. Courreges 1989–90; Artistic Dir for Francesco Smalto 1990–2007, 2017–; Chief Men's Designer for Emanuel Ungaro 2007–10; Founder and CEO Franck Boclet Parfums 2010–; consultant, FBN Consulting 2012–. *Address:* Franck Boclet Parfums, AG Ludovic Perrin, Parc de la Radio, Bâtiment F1 La Chaufferie, 28100 Dreux, France (office). *Telephone:* 2-46-83-03-69 (office). *E-mail:* info@fragrancesfranckboclet.com (office). *Website:* www.fragrancesfranckboclet.com (office).

BOD, Péter Ákos, PhD; Hungarian economist, politician and academic; *Professor, Economic Policy Department, Corvinus University of Budapest;* b. 28 July 1951, Szigetvár; s. of Andor Bod and Rózsa Nagy; m.; two s. one d.; ed high school, Miskolc, Univ. of Economics, Budapest; worked as researcher, Dept Head, Inst. for Econ. Planning 1975–90; UNDP adviser in Ghana 1986–87; mem. of Parl. (Hungarian Democratic Forum) 1990–91; Minister of Industry and Trade 1990–91; Pres. Nat. Bank of Hungary 1991–94; mem. Bd EBRD, London 1995–97; Prof., Econ. Policy Dept, Corvinus Univ. of Budapest, fmr Chair. and Dir Inst. of Econs; Personal Econ. Adviser to Pres. of the Repub. 2001–05; Vice-Pres. Hungarian Econ. Soc. 2009–; Medal of Merit, Pres. of the Repub. 2005, Commdr's Cross (Hungarian Repub.) 2011; Dr hc (Hungarian Acad. of Sciences); Popovics Award, Hungarian Nat. Bank 2002, Pro Universitate, Corvinus Univ. of Budapest 2016. *Publications include:* The Entrepreneurial State in the Contemporary Market Economy 1987, Foundations of Economic Theory and Policy 1999, The World of Money: The Money of the World 2001, Economic Policy 2002, Introduction into Finance and Financial Policy 2008, Foundation of Finance 2012, Non-Conventional Economic Policies 2014 (all in Hungarian); regular column in Hungarian Review, Vilaggazdasag, Heti Valasz (Budapest). *Leisure interests:* tennis, music, history. *Address:* Corvinus University of Budapest, 1093 Budapest, Fövam tér 8, Hungary (office). *Telephone:* (1) 482-5510 (office). *Fax:* (1) 482-5034 (office). *E-mail:* petera.bod@uni-corvinus.hu (office). *Website:* www.corvinus.hu (office).

BODDE, Peter William, BA; American diplomatist; *Ambassador to Libya;* b. 1954; son of William Bodde and Ingrid Bodde; m. Tanya Lee Will Bodde; one s. one d.; ed Univ. of Maryland; upon graduation worked as commodity industry analyst with US Int. Trade Comm., Washington, DC; joined Foreign Service 1981, has served in various posts, including Consular Officer, Embassy in Georgetown, Guyana, Embassy in Kathmandu (Attaché 1982–84, Deputy Chief of Mission 1994–97), Consulate in Hamburg, Germany, Admin. Officer, Embassy in Sofia 1988–90, Admin. Officer, Embassy in Copenhagen 1990–94, Minister Counselor for Admin. Affairs, Embassy in New Delhi, fmr Dir Office of Man. Policy, Office of Man. Policy, Rightsizing and Innovation, Consul-Gen. in Frankfurt, Germany 2002–06, Deputy Chief of Mission, Embassy in Islamabad 2006–08, Amb. to Malawi 2008–10, Asst Chief of Mission for Assistance Transition in Iraq and Coordinator for Minority Issues, Embassy in Baghdad 2010–11, Amb. to Nepal 2012–15, Amb. to Libya 2015–; numerous Department of State performance awards. *Address:* US Embassy, Sidi Slim Area, Sharia Wali al-Ahed, Tripoli, Libya (office). *Telephone:* (91) 2203239 (office). *E-mail:* tripolipao@state.gov (office). *Website:* libya.usembassy.gov (office).

BODE, Lucian Nicolae; Romanian politician; b. 27 Oct. 1974, Valcau de Jos, Salaj; m.; one c.; ed Faculty of Electrotechnics and Informatics, Univ. in Oradea, Advance Training Program in Int. Relations, Romanian Diplomatic Inst., Ministry of Foreign Affairs, Nat. Coll. of Defence 'Carol I', Nat. Univ. of Defence, Faculty of History and Philosophy, Babes-Bolyai Univ., Cluj-Napoca; Service Engineer, Br. of Electricity Distribution in Zalau, S.C. Electrica SA 2001–08, also spokesperson, head of service and trade union pres.; Sec., Biroul Permanent Judetean (BPJ), Partidul Democrat (PD), Salaj 2001–02, Vice-Pres. 2002–05, Sec.-Gen. 2005–07, Sec.-Gen. BPJ Partidul Democrat Liberal (PD-L), Salaj 2007–08, Pres. BPJ PD-L Salaj 2008–, Exec. Sec. Northwest Region 2013–; mem. Parl. 2008–12; Minister of Economy, Trade and Business Environment 2011–12; Pres. Electrica Zalau Trade Union 2003–08; Councillor, Local Council of Valcau de Jos 2000–04, Co. Councillor in Salaj 2004–08; Founding mem. Prodemos Zalau Asscn. *Address:* Şimleu-Silvaniei, str., 1 Decembrie 1918 nr. 1, Romania. *Website:* www.lucianbode.ro.

BODE, Thilo, PhD; German business executive and consultant; *Executive Director, Foodwatch International;* b. 14 Jan. 1947, nr Munich; ed Univ. of Munich, Univ. of Regensburg; int. consultant, Lahmeyer Int., Frankfurt; Project Man. German Bank for Reconstruction and Devt 1978–81; ind. consultant for int. orgs, govts and businesses 1981; Special Asst to Chief Exec. of int. pvt. corpn 1986; Exec. Dir Greenpeace Germany 1989–95, Greenpeace Int. 1995–2001; Founder Foodwatch 2002–, also Exec. Dir 2002–17, Exec. Dir Foodwatch Int. 2017–; Verdienstkreuz, FRG 2001. *Publications:* Die Demokratie verrät ihre Kinder 2003. *Address:* Foodwatch, Brunnenstrasse 181, 10119 Berlin, Germany (office). *Telephone:* (30) 2404760 (office). *Fax:* (30) 240476-26 (office). *E-mail:* bode@foodwatch.de (office). *Website:* www.foodwatch.de (office).

BODEK, Arie, BS, PhD; American physicist and academic; *George E. Pake Professor of Physics, University of Rochester;* b. 1947, Tel-Aviv, Israel; ed Massachusetts Inst. of Tech.; Research Assoc., Lab. for Nuclear Science, MIT 1972–74; Milkan Fellow, Calif. Inst. of Tech. 1974–76; Asst Prof. of Physics, Univ. of Rochester, New York 1977–80, Assoc. Prof. 1980–87, Prof. 1987–, George E. Pake Prof. of Physics 2005–, Assoc. Chair. Dept of Physics and Astronomy 1995–98, Chair. 1998–2007; mem. Editorial Bd several journals including European Physics Journal 1992–; Fellow, American Physical Soc. 1985, Japan Soc. for the Promotion of Science 1986–87; Alfred P. Sloan Fellow, Univ. of Rochester 1978, Panofsky Prize in Experimental Particle Physics, American Physical Soc. 2004, Grad. Teaching Award, Univ. of Rochester 2004. *Publications:* more than 700 articles in scientific journals. *Address:* Department of Physics and Astronomy, University of Rochester, Bausch & Lomb 354, Rochester, NY 14627, USA (office). *Telephone:* (585) 275-5445 (office). *Fax:* (585) 273-3237 (office). *E-mail:* bodek@pas.rochester.edu (office). *Website:* www.pas.rochester.edu/urpas/faculty_page/bodek_arie (office).

BODEN, Margaret Ann, OBE, ScD, PhD, FBA; British cognitive scientist and professor of cognitive science; *Research Professor of Cognitive Science, Centre for Research in Cognitive Science, University of Sussex;* b. 26 Nov. 1936, London; d. of Leonard F. Boden and Violet Dorothy Boden (née Dawson); m. John R. Spiers 1967 (divorced 1981); one s. one d.; ed Newnham Coll., Cambridge (Major Scholar) and Harvard Grad. School (Harkness Fellow), USA; Lecturer in Philosophy, Univ. of Birmingham 1959–65; Lecturer, then Reader in Philosophy and Psychology, Univ. of Sussex 1965–80, Prof. 1980–, Founding Dean School of Cognitive and Computing Sciences 1987, Research Prof. of Cognitive Science, Centre for Research in Cognitive Science 2002–; Curator Univ. of London Inst. for Advanced Study 1995–; Co-founder, Harvester Press Ltd 1970, Dir 1970–85; Vice-Pres. British Acad. 1989–91, Royal Inst. of GB 1993–95, Chair. of Council 1993–95, mem. of Council 1992–95; mem. Advisory Bd for the Research Councils 1989–90, Academia Europaea 1993–, Animal Procedures Cttee 1995–99; Fellow, American Asscn for Artificial Intelligence 1993–, European Coordinating Cttee for Artificial Intelligence 1999–; Hon. DSc (Sussex) 2001, (Bristol) 2002, Hon. DUniv (Open) 2004. *Publications include:* Purposive Explanation in Psychology 1972, Artificial Intelligence and Natural Man 1977, Piaget 1979, Minds and Mechanisms 1981, Computer Models of Mind 1988, Artificial Intelligence in Psychology 1989, The Philosophy of Artificial Intelligence (ed.) 1990, Dimensions of Creativity (ed.) 1994, Artificial Intelligence and the Mind (co-ed.) 1994, The Philosophy of Artificial Life (ed.) 1996, Artificial Intelligence (ed.) 1996, The Creative Mind (2nd edn) 2004, Mind as Machine 2006, Creativity and Art 2010. *Leisure interests:* dressmaking, travelling, passion for India and Polynesia. *Address:* Centre for Research in Cognitive Science, University of Sussex, Falmer, Brighton, BN1 9QJ, England (office). *Telephone:* (1273) 678386 (office). *Fax:* (1273) 671320 (office). *E-mail:* maggieb@cogs.susx.ac.uk (office). *Website:* www.cogs.susx.ac.uk (office).

BODEWIG, Kurt; German politician; b. 26 April 1955, Rheinberg; m.; two s.; ed commercial coll.; joined SPD 1973, mem. Nat. Exec. Cttee 2000–05; held various party posts 1982–98; mem. Bundestag 1998–2009; Minister of Transport, Building and Housing 2000–02; Maritime Amb. of EU 2006–; Chair. Baltic Sea Forum e.V., Bd Trustees German-Lithuanian-Forum; Deputy Chair. Cttee on the Affairs of the EU; Pres. Deutsche Verkehrswacht e.V.; mem. European Council and Parl. Ass., Baltic Sea Parl. Conf.; Deputy mem. NATO Parl. Ass. *Address:* Deutsche Verkehrswacht e.V., Budapester Straße 31, 10787, Berlin, Germany (office). *Telephone:* (30) 516510544 (office). *Fax:* (30) 516510569 (office). *E-mail:* mail@kurt-bodewig.de. *Website:* www.kurt-bodewig.de.

BODEWITZ, Hendrik Wilhelm, PhD; Dutch professor of Sanskrit (retd); b. 13 Oct. 1939, Gramsbergen; s. of Johan Adriaan Bodewitz and Jennigjen Lenters; m. Janneke van Uchelen 1964; one s. one d.; ed Lyceum Coevorden, Univ. of Utrecht; Lecturer in Sanskrit, Utrecht Univ. 1966–68, Prof. 1976–92, Dean of Faculty 1980–82, 1984–86; Sr Lecturer, Leiden Univ. 1969–76, Prof. 1992–2002; mem. Netherlands Royal Acad.; Founding mem. Academia Europaea. *Publications:* Jaiminīya Brāhmaṇa I, 1-65, with a study of the Agnihotra and the Prāṇāgnihotra 1973, The daily evening and morning offering according to the Brāhmaṇas 1976, The Jyotiṣṭoma Ritual: Jaiminīya Brāhmaṇa I, 66-364 1990, Kauṣitaki Upaniṣad 2002; articles: Vedic agham: evil or sin, distress or death? 2007, The Vedic Concepts āgas and enas 2007, Sins and Vices, their Enumerations and Specifications in the Veda 2008, The Special Meanings of śrama and other derivations of the root śram in the Veda 2008, The refrain kasmai devaya havisa vidhema 2009, On the Interpretation of Bhagavad Gita (Vol. I–VI) 2009, The Dialogue of Yama and Yami 2009, The Legend of Urvas'ī and Pururavas and Their Dialogue 2011, The Chronology of the Upaniṣads and Their Basic Ideas 2011, Vedic Terms Denoting Virtues and Merits 2013. *Address:* Stolberglaan 29, 3583 XL Utrecht, Netherlands (home). *Telephone:* (30) 2510047 (home).

BODHA, Nandcoomar (Nando), BA, MA, LLB, PhD; Mauritian politician; *Minister of Foreign Affairs;* b. 3 Feb. 1954, Long Mountain; ed Royal Coll., Port Louis, Université de Rennes, France; Prof. Lycée La Bourdonnais 1981; Journalist, Mauritius Broadcasting Corpn 1982–85; Man. Dir MBC 1991–95; Sec.-Gen. Mouvement Socialiste Militant 1996–; mem. of Parliament, Vacoas & Floreal 2000–, Leader of the Opposition 2006–07; Minister of Tourism and Leisure 2000–03, 2010–11, of Agric. 2003–05, of Public Infrastructure and Land Transport 2014–17, of Foreign Affairs, Regional Integration and Int. Trade 2019–; Chair. Broadcasting Cttee. *Address:* Ministry of Foreign Affairs, Newton Tower, 9th–11th Floors, Sir William Newton Street, Port Louis, Mauritius (office). *Telephone:* 405-2500 (office). *Fax:* 208-8087 (office). *E-mail:* mfa@govmu.org (office). *Website:* www.foreign.govmu.org (office).

BODIN, Manfred; German banker; b. 14 Nov. 1939, Münster; m.; ed German Savings Banks Acad.; Stadtsparkasse, Münster 1960–64; Stadtsparkasse, Witten 1964–70; mem. Man. Bd Kreissparkasse Recklinghausen 1970–75, Chair. 1976–83; Chair. Man. Bd Sparkasse Essen 1984–91, Norddeutsche Landesbank Girozentrale NORD/LB 1991–2004; Chair. Lower Saxony Bd of Trustees, German Econ. Research; fmr Chair. Man. Bd, Landeskuratoriums Niedersachsen; Vice-Pres. German Savings Banks Asscn, Chamber of Trade and Commerce, Hanover-Hildesheim, Lower Saxony Foundation; mem. Fed. Asscn of Public Sector Banks, Lower Saxony Savings Banks Asscn; mem. Advisory Bd Deutsche Bundesbank; mem. Bd Carolo-Wilhelmina Technical Univ., Braunschweig.; Hon. Registrar Lower Saxon Inst. for Economic Research, Hon. Consul Kingdom of Denmark; Knight's Cross of the Order of Dannebrog (Denmark); Dr hc (Tech. Univ. Braunschweig) 1996; Lower Saxony Land Medal. *Leisure interests:* art, sailing.

BODINE, Barbara K., BA MA; American fmr diplomatist, academic and university administrator; *Director, Institute for Study of Diplomacy, Georgetown University;* b. 28 Aug. 1948, St Louis, Mo.; ed Univ. of California, Santa Barbara, Fletcher School of Law and Diplomacy, Chinese Univ. of Hong Kong; career mem. Foreign Service, initial tours Hong Kong and Bangkok; Country Officer then Political-Mil. Officer, Bureau of Nr East Affairs, Office of Arabian Peninsula Affairs, later Deputy Office Dir; Congressional Fellow, Office of US Senator Robert Dole; Deputy Prin. Officer in Baghdad, US State Dept. 1980s, Deputy Chief of Mission in Kuwait (held captive by Iraqi invading forces for 137 days) 1990, Assoc. Co-ordinator for Operations early 1990s, Acting Co-ordinator for Counterterrorism 1990s; Dean of Professional Studies, Foreign Service Inst., US State Dept, later Dir of East African Affairs, Amb. to Yemen (arranged release of captured Americans) 1999–2001, US Co-ordinator for Cen. Iraq April–May 2003, Sr Advisor Bureau of Political-Mil. Affairs 2003; Treasurer, Alumni Asscns, Univ. Calif., Santa Barbara; Diplomat-in-Residence, Global and Int. Studies Program, Univ. Calif., Santa Barbara 2001–02; Regent-desig. Univ. of Calif. 2002–03, ex-officio Regent 2003–04, Vice-Pres. Alumni Asscns of the Univ. of Calif. 2004, later Regent Emerita; currently Distinguished Prof. in Practice of Diplomacy and Dir, Inst. for Study of Diplomacy, Georgetown Univ.; fmr Sr Research Fellow and Dir of the Governance Initiative in the Middle East, Kennedy School, Harvard Univ., also fmr Fellow at Center for Public Leadership and Inst. of Politics; fmr Robert Wilhelm Fellow, MIT Center for Int. Studies; fmr Diplomat In Residence and Lecturer of Public Affairs, Woodrow Wilson School of Public and Int. Affairs, Princeton Univ.; US Sec. of State Award for Valor (for work in occupied Kuwait) 1990, Univ. Calif., Santa Barbara Distinguished Alumni Award 1991, US Dept of State Distinguished Honor Award (for work in Yemen) 2001. *Address:* Institute for Study of Diplomacy, Georgetown University, 1316 36th Street, NW, Washington, DC 20007, USA (office). *Telephone:* (202) 965-5206 (office). *E-mail:* bb842@georgetown.edu (office). *Website:* www.isd.georgetown.edu (office).

BODKIN, Teresina; Montserratian statistician and government official; fmr secondary school teacher; Dir Dept of Statistics, Govt of Montserrat 1995–2010; Speaker Legis. Council (first woman) 2010–14. *Address:* Office of the Speaker, Legislative Council, Brades, Montserrat (office).

BODMER, Sir Walter Fred, Kt, PhD, FRS, FRCPath, FMedSci; British research scientist, academic and university administrator; *Head, Cancer and Immunogenetics Laboratory, Weatherall Institute of Molecular Medicine, University of Oxford;* b. 10 Jan. 1936, Frankfurt am Main, Germany; s. of Ernest Julius Bodmer and Sylvia Emily Bodmer; m. Julia Gwynaeth Pilkington 1956 (died 2001); two s. one d.; partner Ann Ganesan; ed Manchester Grammar School, Clare Coll., Cambridge; Research Fellow, Clare Coll., Cambridge 1958–60, Fellow 1961, Hon. Fellow 1989; Demonstrator, Dept of Genetics, Univ. of Cambridge 1960–61; Fellow, Visiting Asst Prof., Dept of Genetics, Stanford Univ. 1961–62, Asst Prof. 1962–66, Assoc. Prof. 1966–68, Prof. 1968–70; Prof. of Genetics, Univ. of Oxford 1970–79, Prin. Hertford Coll., Oxford 1995–2005, currently Head of Cancer and Immunogenetics Lab., Weatherall Inst. of Molecular Medicine; Vice-Pres. Royal Inst. 1981–82; Pres. Royal Statistical Soc. 1984–85; Pres. British Asscn for Advancement of Science 1987–88, Chair. of Council 1996–2003; mem. Advisory Bd for the Research Councils 1983–88; Chair. BBC Science Consultative Group 1981–87; mem. BBC Gen. Advisory Council; Chair. Bd of Trustees, British Museum (Natural History) 1989–93; Pres. Human Genome Org. 1990–92; Dir-Gen. Imperial Cancer Research Fund 1991–96 (Dir of Research 1979–91); Chancellor Univ. of Salford 1995–2005; Chair. Cttee on the Public Understanding of Science (COPUS) 1990–94; Pres. Int. Fed. of Asscns for the Advancement of Science and Tech. 1992–94; Dir (non-exec.) Fisons PLC 1990–96; Chair. UK Nat. Radiological Protection Bd 1998–2003, Leukaemia Research Fund Medical and Scientific Panel 2003–09; Pres. British Assoc. for Cancer Research 1998–2002; Foreign Assoc. NAS; Hon. Vice-Pres. Research Defence Soc. 1990–; Hon. Fellow, Green Coll., Oxford, Keble Coll., Oxford, Hertford Coll., Oxford, Clare Coll., Cambridge, Royal Soc. of Medicine; Hon. FRCP; Hon. FRCS; Hon. FRSE; Foreign Hon. mem. American Acad. of Arts and Sciences, American Asscn of Immunologists, Companion of Trinity Laban 2008; Hon. MD (Bologna, Birmingham); Hon. DSc (Bath, Oxford, Hull, Edin.) 1990, (Aberdeen, Lancaster) 1994, (London, Plymouth, Salford) 1996, (UMIST) 1997; Hon. DUniv (Surrey) 1990; William Allan Memorial Award, American Soc. of Human Genetics 1980, Conway Evans Prize, Royal Coll. of Physicians/Royal Soc. 1982, Rabbi Shai Shacknai Memorial Prize Lectureship in Immunology and Cancer Research 1983, John Alexander Memorial Prize and Lectureship, Univ. of Pennsylvania Medical School 1984, Royal Inst. Christmas Lecturer 1984, Rose Payne Distinguished Scientist Lectureship 1985, Ellison Cliffe Lecture and Medal 1987, Neil Hamilton-Fairley Medal, Royal Coll. of Physicians 1990, Faraday Award, Royal Soc. 1994, Dalton Medal, Manchester Literary and Philosophical Soc. 2002, D.K. Ludwig Award 2002, Seroussi Research Award 2003, Royal Medal, Royal Soc. 2013. *Publications include:* co-author: The Genetics of Human Populations 1971, Our Future Inheritance – Choice or Chance? 1974, Genetics, Evolution and Man 1976, The Book of Man 1994; more than 700 papers in scientific and medical journals. *Leisure interests:* playing piano, riding, swimming, scuba diving. *Address:* Weatherall Institute of Molecular Medicine, University of Oxford, John Radcliffe Hospital, Oxford OX3 9DS, England (office). *Telephone:* (1865) 222356 (office). *Fax:* (1865) 222431 (office). *E-mail:* walter.bodmer@hertford.ox.ac.uk (office). *Website:* www.imm.ox.ac.uk (office).

BODROV, Sergey Vladimirovich; Russian screenwriter and film director; b. 28 June 1948, Khabarovsk; m. Carolyn Cavallaro; one s. (died 2002); ed Inst. of Energetics, All-Union Inst. of Cinematography. *Films include:* Golosa voyny 1974, Balamut (writer) 1978, Lyubimaya zhenshchina mekhanika Gavrilova (writer) 1981, Molodye lyudi (writer) 1983, Sladkiy sok vnutri travy (also writer) 1984, Yurka: syn komandira (writer) 1984, Ochen vazhnaya persona (writer) 1984, Neprofessionaly (also writer) 1985, Ne khodite, devki, zamuzh (writer) 1985, Ya tebya nenavizhu (also writer) (TV) 1986, Moy dom na zelyonykh kholmakh (writer) 1986, Na pomoshch, brattsy! (writer) 1988, Frantsuz (writer) 1988, S.E.R.—Svoboda eto rai (also writer) 1989, Krejzi 1989, Katala (also writer) 1989, ...I vsya lyubov (writer) 1989, Nash chelovek v San-Remo (writer) 1990, Ya khotela uvidet angelov (also writer) 1992, Belyy korol, krasnaya koroleva (Russkie) (also writer) 1992, Somebody to Love (writer) 1994, Kavkazskiy plennik (also writer) (Nika Award) 1996, Est–Ouest (writer) 1999, Running Free 1999, Syostry (story) 2001, The Quickie (also writer) 2001, Bear's Kiss (also writer) 2002, Shiza (writer) 2004, Nomad 2004, Mongol: Part One (also writer) (Nika Award) 2007, A Yakuza's Daughter Never Cries (also writer) 2010, In the Same Garden 2016. *Address:* 117513 Moscow, Leninsky prosp. 129, korp. 3, Apt 20, Russia. *Telephone:* (495) 438-38-04.

BOECKMANN, Alan Lee, BEng; American construction industry executive; ed Univ. of Arizona; joined Fluor Corpn as engineer 1974, various man. positions in Calif., Tex., SC, S Africa and Venezuela, becoming Vice-Pres., DuPont Alliance and Head of Eng Div., also Pres. and CEO Fluor Daniel, mem. Bd of Dirs, Pres. and CEO Fluor Corpn 2001–02, Chair. and CEO 2002–11, Chair. (non-exec.) 2011–12; Chair. Eng and Construction Govs, World Econ. Forum; mem. Bd of Dirs, Burlington Northern Santa Fe, LLC 2001–, Burlington Northern Santa Fe, Nat. Petroleum Council 2001–, BHP Billiton 2008–11, Sempra Energy 2011–, Archer Daniels Midland Co. 2004–08, 2012–, American Petroleum Inst., Boys and Girls Clubs of America, Southern Methodist Univ.'s Cox School of Business; Ind. Dir (non-exec.), BP plc 2014–; mem. Business Roundtable, World Econ. Forum, Univ. of Arizona's Coll. of Eng's Industry Advisory Council; was instrumental in formation of World Econ. Forum's Partnering Against Corruption Initiative 2004. *Address:* c/o Fluor Corpn, 6700 Las Colinas Blvd, Irving, TX 75039, USA. *E-mail:* info@fluor.com.

BOEDIONO, MEcons, PhD; Indonesian academic, fmr central banker and fmr government official; b. 25 Feb. 1943, Blitar, Jawa Timur; m. Herawati 1969; four c.; ed Univ. of Western Australia, Monash Univ., Melbourne, Australia, Wharton School, Univ. of Pennsylvania, USA; fmr Prof., Faculty of Econs, Gajah Mada Univ., Togyakarta; Deputy Gov. Bank Indonesia in charge of fiscal monetary policy 1997–98, Gov. Bank Indonesia 2008–09; State Minister for Nat. Planning and Devt 1998–99; Minister of Finance and State Enterprises Devt 2001–04; Co-ordinating Minister for the Economy 2005–08; Vice-Pres. of Indonesia 2009–14; Mahaputra Star Adipradana 1999; Distinguished Int. Alumnus Award, Univ. of Western Australia 2007. *Publications include:* Ekonomi Indonesia, mau ke mana? Kumpulan esai ekonomi (The Economy of Indonesia, Where To? A Collection of Economic Essays) 2009. *Address:* c/o Office of the Vice-President, Istana Wakil Presiden, Jalan Medan Merdeka Selatan 14, Jakarta 10110, Indonesia. *Website:* boedionomendengar.com.

BOEDORO, Philip; Ni-Vanuatu politician; b. 21 May 1958, Maewo; ed Voreas High School; fmr police officer; fmrly self-employed in own security business; MP for Maewo Constituency 2002–16, fmr Minister for Econ. Reforms, Chair. Parl. Institutional Cttee, Speaker of Parl. 2013–15; Acting Pres. of Vanuatu 2–22 Sept. 2014; mem. Vanuaaku Pati (VP).

BOEHM, Gottfried Karl, DPhil; German art historian and academic; *Emeritus Professor of Art History, University of Basel;* b. 19 Sept. 1942, Braunau, Bohemia; s. of Karl Boehm and Olga Boehm; m. Margaret Hunold 1980; one d.; ed Univs of Cologne, Vienna and Heidelberg; Lecturer in History of Art, Ruhr Univ. Bochum 1975–79, Prof. 1977; Prof. of History of Art, Justus Liebig Univ., Giessen 1979–86; apptd Prof. of Art History, Univ. of Basel 1986, now Emer. Prof.; Dir Nat. Centre of Competence in Research; Perm. Fellow, Inst. für die Wissenschaften vom Menschen, Vienna 1981–; Fellow, Wissenschaftskolleg, Berlin 2001–02; Corresp. mem. Heidelberger Acad. of Sciences 2006–; Johannes Gutenberg Endowed Professorship 2011; Ehrenkreuz für Wissenschaft und Kunst (First Class) (Austria). *Publications:* Studien zur Perspektivität, Philosophie und Kunst in der frühen Neuzeit 1969, Zur Dialektik der ästhetischen Grenze 1973, Philosophische Hermeneutik 1976, Die Hermeneutik und die Wissenschaften 1978, Bildnis und Individuum, Über den Ursprung der Porträtmalerei in der italienischen Renaissance 1985, Paul Cézanne, Montagne Sainte-Victoire 1988, Konrad Fiedler, Schriften zur Kunst 1991, Was ist ein Bild? 1994, Beschreibungskunst-Kunstbeschreibung. Ekphrasis von der Antike bis zut Gegenwart 1995, Canto d'amore. Klassizistische Moderne in Musik und bildender Kunst 1996, Paul Cézanne und die Moderne 1999, Der Maler Max Weiler. Das Geistige in der Natur 2001, Homo Pictor 2001, Zwischen-Räume. Malerei, Relief und Skulptur im Werk von Ellsworth Kelly 2002, Der Topos des Lebendigen: Bildgeschichte und ästhetische Erfahrung (in Dimensionen ästhetische Erfahrung) 2003, Mit durchdringendem Blick 2003, Die Härte der Grossen Dinge: Arp und Schwitters in ihren frühen Jahren 2004, Jenseits der Sprache? Anmerkungen zur Logik der Bilder (in Iconic Turn: Die Neue Macht der Bilder) 2004, Ausdruck und Dekoration: Henri Matisse auf dem Weg zu sich selbst 2005, Zeit-Räume. Zum Begriff des plastischen Raumes. Im Schatten von Lessings 'Laokoon' 2006, Das Ende als Anfang – Eine Reflexionsfigur der modernen Kunst, in: End of Art – Endings in Art / La fin de l'art – Les fins dans les arts / Ende der Kunst – Enden in der Kunst 2006, Unbestimmtheit. Zur Logik des Bildes, in: Bild und Einbildungskraft 2006, Wie Bilder Sinn erzeugen 2007. *Address:* Kunstgeschichtliches Seminar, St Alban-Graben-8, 4051 Basel (office); Sevogelplatz 1, 4051 Basel, Switzerland (home). *Telephone:* (61) 2066292 (office); (61) 3116241 (home). *Fax:* (61) 2066297 (office). *E-mail:* gottfried.boehm@unibas.ch (office). *Website:* kunstgeschichte.philhist.unibas.ch (home).

BOEHM, Peter M., BA, MA, PhD; Canadian diplomatist; *Senator for Ontario;* b. Kitchener, Ont.; ed Wilfrid Laurier Univ., Waterloo, Ont., Norman Paterson School of Int. Affairs, Carleton Univ., Ottawa, Ont., Univ. of Edinburgh, UK; joined Canadian Foreign Service 1981, held several positions at Dept of Foreign Affairs and Int. Trade, including Dir of Econ. Summit Div. in Policy Staff of Dept, and Co-ordinator of Halifax G7 Econ. Summit 1995, apptd Minister (Political and Public Affairs), Embassy in Washington, DC 1997, Amb. and Perm. Rep. to OAS, Washington, DC 1997–2005; Asst Deputy Minister, N America, Dept of Foreign Affairs and Int. Trade 2005–08; Amb. to Germany 2008–12; Assoc. Deputy Minister of Foreign Affairs 2012–16, Deputy Minister of Int. Devt, Global Affairs Canada 2016–17, Deputy Minister for G7 Summit and Personal Rep. (Sherpa) of the Prime Minister 2017–18, mem. Senate for Ontario 2018–; Commonwealth Scholarship to Univ. of Edinburgh 1978, Canadian Foreign Service Officer Award for contrib. to establishment of peace in Cen. America 1993, Public Service of Canada's Outstanding Achievement Award. *Address:* Senate of Canada, Ottawa, ON K1A 0A4, Canada (office). *Telephone:* (613) 992-4416 (office). *E-mail:* sencom@sen.parl.gc.ca (office). *Website:* sen.parl.gc.ca (office).

BOEHM, Thomas, Dr rer. nat; German immunobiologist, geneticist and academic; *Director, Max Planck Institute of Immunobiology and Epigenetics;* b. 21 July 1956, Gelnhausen; ed Johann Wolfgang Goethe Univ., Frankfurt; study visits to Columbia Univ., USA and Royal Marsden Hosp., UK; qualified as univ. lecturer 1988; MRC Lab. of Molecular Biology, Cambridge, UK 1988–91; Prof., Univ. of Freiburg 1991–94; Full Prof., Heidelberg Univ. and German Cancer Research Centre 1994–97; Dir Max-Planck Inst. of Immunobiology and Epigenetics, Freiburg, and Scientific Mem. Max-Planck Soc. 1998–; Gottfried-Wilhelm-Leibniz Award, German Science Council 1997, Ernst Jung Prize for Medicine 2014. *Publications:* numerous papers in professional journals. *Leisure interests:* music, manual work, especially carpentry. *Address:* Max-Planck Institute of Immunobiology and Epigenetics, Stübeweg 51, 79108 Freiburg, Baden-Württemberg, Germany (office). *Telephone:* (761) 5108328 (office). *Fax:* (761) 5108220 (office). *E-mail:* boehm@ie-freiburg.mpg.de (office). *Website:* www.ie-freiburg.mpg.de/boehm (office).

BOEHNER, John Andrew, BA; American fmr politician; b. 17 Nov. 1949, Cincinnati, Ohio; s. of Earl Henry Boehner and Mary Anne Boehner; m. Debbie Boehner 1973; two d.; ed Xavier Univ., Cincinnati; early career as Sale Rep. then Pres. Nucite Sales; Trustee, Union Township, Ohio 1982–84; mem. Ohio State Legislature 1984–90; mem. US House of Reps, Washington, DC 1990–2015 (resgnd), Chair. House Cttee on Educ. and the Workforce 2001–06, House Majority Leader 2006–07, House Minority Leader 2007–11, Speaker of the House 2011–15. *Leisure interests:* golf, wine. *Address:* The Tampico, 930 Cape Marco Drive, Marco Island, FL 34145, USA (home).

BOEKHOUDT, (Juan) Alfonso; Aruban government official; *Governor of Aruba;* b. 27 Jan. 1975; Passenger Officer, ALM Antillean Airlines 1982–84; volunteer, Faith Revival Foundation (Christian foundation) 1984–98; mem. Exec. Cabinet of Minister Plenipotentiary of Aruba 1991–94; Financial Officer, Tabacal Freezone NV 1999–2004; CFO Universal Brands NV 2001–04; CEO Manrique Capriles & Sons 2004–05; Dir Aruba Ports Authority, Oranjestad 2005–13; Minister Plenipotentiary of Aruba 2013–16, Gov. of Aruba Jan. 2017–; fmr Pres. Red Cross Aruba; mem. Arubaanse Volkspartij (AVP). *Address:* Office of the Governor, Plaza Henny Eman 3, POB 53, Oranjestad, Aruba (office). *Telephone:* 5834445 (office). *Fax:* 582073 (office). *E-mail:* consulair@kabga.aw (office). *Website:* www.kabga.aw (office).

BOER, Dick; Dutch business executive; b. 31 Aug. 1957; spent more than 17 years in various retail positions for SHV Holdings in the Netherlands and abroad, and for Unigro NV; joined Ahold as CEO Ahold Czech Repub. 1998, Pres. and CEO Albert Heijn 2000–03, Pres. and CEO Ahold's Dutch operating cos 2003–06, COO Ahold Europe 2006–11, mem. Corp. Exec. Bd 2007, Chair. Man. Bd, Pres. and CEO Royal Ahold NV 2011–18 (Ahold Delhaize 2016–18), Adviser, Ahold Delhaize 2018–; Pres. European Retail Round Table; mem. Exec. Bd, The Confederation of Netherlands Industry and Employers (VNO-NCW); mem. Advisory Bd, G-star, Red Cross Hosp. Beverwijk; mem. Supervisory Bd, AMS Sourcing BV. *Address:* Ahold Delhaize Provincialeweg 11, 1506 MA Zaandam, The Netherlands (office). *Telephone:* (88) 6599111 (office). *Website:* www.aholddelhaize.com (office).

BOESAK, Rev. Allan; South African clergyman and politician; b. 23 Feb. 1946, Kakamas; s. of Andreas Boesak and Sarah Helena Boesak; m. 1st Dorothy Rose Martin 1969; one s. three d.; m. 2nd Elna Botha 1991; two d.; ed Univ. of Western Cape, Theological Univ., Kampen, Netherlands, Union Theological Seminary; prominent anti-apartheid campaigner; Pres. World Alliance of Reformed Churches, Ottawa 1982–89; co-f. United Democratic Front 1983; Pres. Asscn of Christian Students in SA 1984–90; Vice-Pres. South African Council of Churches 1984–87; fmr mem. Dutch Reformed Mission Church; mem., African Nat. Congress (ANC) 1991–2008, Leader in Western Cape 1991–98; Dir Foundation for Peace and Justice 1991; faced 32 theft and corruption charges 1997; on trial for fraud Aug. 1998; sentenced to six years' imprisonment March 1999, sentence halved on appeal May 2000; conviction for misuse of aid money set aside, conviction for theft upheld 2000; released on parole June 2001; granted presidential pardon 2005; mem. Congress of the People 2008–09; fmr Moderator, Cape Synod, Uniting Reformed Church in Southern Africa; Desmond Tutu Chair for Peace, Global Justice, and Reconciliation Studies, Christian Theological Seminary and Butler Univ. 2013–17; Hon. DD (Victoria) 1983, (Yale) 1984, (Interdenominational Theological Center, Atlanta) 1985; Hon. DIur (Warwick) 1989; Third World Prize 1989. *Publications:* Farewell to Innocence 1976, Black and Reformed 1984, Walking on Thorns 1984, A Call for an End to Unjust Rule 1986, If This is Treason, I am Guilty (Speeches) 1988, Comfort and Protest 1988, Shadows of the Light 1996, Tot Sterwens Toe (poems) 2001, Running with Horses: Reflections of an Accidental Politician 2009, Radical Reconciliation: Beyond Political Pietism and Christian Quietism 2012, Dare We Speak of Hope: Searching for a Language of Life in Faith and Politics 2014, Kairos, Crisis, and Global Apartheid: The Challenge to Prophetic Witness 2015. *Leisure interests:* reading, walking, sports, music. *Address:* 16 Villa Bellini, Constantia Street, Strand 7140, South Africa (home). *Telephone:* (21) 854-4937 (home). *E-mail:* boesak@mweb.co.za (home).

BOFF, Leonardo Genezio Darci, DPhil, DTheol; Brazilian academic, writer and editor; b. 14 Dec. 1938, Concórdia, Santa Catarina; s. of Mansueto Boff and Regina Fontana Boff; ed Inst. Teológico Franciscano, Petrópolis, Univ. of Munich, Germany; Prof. of Systematic Theology and of Franciscan Spirituality, Inst. Teológico Franciscano, Petrópolis, Rio de Janeiro 1971–92, also Prof. of Theology of Liberation; Adviser to Latin American Conf. of Religions (CLAR) 1971–80, to Nat. Conf. of Brazilian Bishops (CNBB) 1971–80; mem. Editorial Bd of Revista Eclesiástica Brasileira 1971–92; mem. Bd of Dirs Vozes publishing house 1971–92; Pres. Bd of Eds, Theology and Liberation collection 1985; mem. Editorial Bd Concilium; ordered by Roman Curia to period of 'obedient silence' 1985–86; Dr hc (Turin, Lund); Paz y Justicia Award, Barcelona, Menschenrechte in der Kirche Award, Herbert Haag Foundation, FRG and Switzerland, Right Livelihood Award, Stockholm 2001. *Publications include:* over 60 books including Jesus Christ Liberator 1971, Die Kirche als Sakrament im Horizont der Welterfahrung 1972, Theology of Captivity and Liberation 1972, Ecclesiogenesis 1977, The Maternal Face of God 1979, Church: Charisma and Power 1980, Theology Listening to People 1981, St Francis: A Model for Human Liberation 1984, Trinity and Society 1988, The Gospel of the Cosmic Christ 1989, The New Evangelization: The Perspective of the Oppressed 1990, Ecology and Spirituality 1991, Mística e Espiritualidade 1994, Nova Era: a Consciência Planetária 1994, Igreja: entre Norte e Sul 1995, Ecology: Cry of the Earth, Cry of the Poor 1995, Casamento entre o céu e a terra 2001, Princípio de compaixão e cuidado 2001, Fundamentalismo. A globalização e o futuro da humanidade 2002, Liberating Grace 2005, Fundamentalism, Terrorism and the Future of Humanity 2007, Church, Charism and Power 2011. *Leisure interests:* gardening, social work at the 'favelas', child minding. *E-mail:* contato@leonardoboff.com (office). *Website:* leonardoboff.com.

BOFFO, Dino; Italian journalist and editor; b. 19 Aug. 1952, Asolo; Ed.-in-Chief and Man. Dir Avvenire (daily newspaper) and News Ed. SAT 2000 satellite TV network 1994–2009; Ed.-in-Chief TV2000 (TV network) 2010–14; Sec.-Gen. Azione Cattolica Italiana; taught course on communications and citizenship at Catholic Univ. of the Sacred Heart, Milan 2002–03; Premio Ambrogino d'oro 2010, San Francesco di Sales Penna d'oro 2012, Santa Chiara TV Award 2012, Arturo Esposito Penisola Sorrentina Prize 2014. *Address:* c/o TV2000, Via Aurelia, 796 00165 Rome, Italy. *E-mail:* dir.rete@tv2000.it.

BOFILL, Ricardo; Spanish architect; b. 5 Dec. 1939, Barcelona; s. of Emilio Bofill and Maria Levi; two s.; ed Ecole Française, Barcelona, architectural studies in Geneva; Founder-mem. and leader, Taller de Arquitectura, Paris, Barcelona; Dr hc (Univ. of Hamburg, Germany) 1968, (Metz Univ., France) 1995; Hon. Fellow, FAIA 1985, Bund Deutscher Architekter (BDA) Bonn, Germany 1996; Associació de Disseny Industrial del Foment de les Arts Decoratives (ADI-FAD) Award in Architecture for building on calle Nicaragua 99, Barcelona, Spain 1963, American Soc. of Interior Designers Int. Prize, New York, 1978, Architecte Agrée Degree Ordre National des Architectes, Paris, France 1979, Ciudad de Barcelona Prize of Architecture 1980, Architect in Belgium, Ordre des Architectes Conseil du Brabant, Brussels 1989, Chicago Architecture Award, Ill. Council/American Inst. of Architects/Architectural Record, Chicago 1989, Académie Internationale de Philosophie de l'Art, Bern, Switzerland 1989, Lifetime Achievement Award, Israeli Building Center 2009; Officier de l'Ordre des Arts et des Lettres Degree, Ministry of Culture, Paris, France 1984. *Works include:* headquarters for Cartier, Christian Dior, Axa Insurance, BNP Paribas, JP Morgan, Shiseido; also Shangri-la Hotel, Beijing, Corso Karlin and Corso II, Prague, Donnelley Building, Chicago, Metz Theatre, Barcelona Theatre, Rothschild wine cellars, Palacio de Congresos, Madrid, Shepherd School of Music, Houston, Tex., USA. *Publications:* Memory Future 1993, L'Architecture des villes (co-author) 1995, Spazi di una vita (co-author) 1996. *Leisure interests:* travelling, sea, desert. *Address:* Taller de Arquitectura, 14 Avenida Industria, 08960 Saint Just Desvern, Barcelona, Spain (office). *Telephone:* (3) 4999900 (office). *Fax:* (3) 4999950 (office). *E-mail:* rbofill@bofill.com (office). *Website:* www.bofill.com (office).

BOFINGER, Helge; German architect and academic; *Professor of Design and Building Theory, Faculty of Architecture, University of Dortmund;* b. 30 March 1940, Stettin/Pommern; s. of Christa Bofinger and Hans Ullrich Bofinger; m. Margret Schreib Schmitz-Mathies 1965; ed Ratsgymnasium Goslar, Tech. Univ. of Brunswick; Scientific Asst, Tech. Univ. of Brunswick 1968–69; est. Bofinger & Partner (with wife), Brunswick 1969–81, Berlin 1974–, Wiesbaden 1978–; Visiting Prof., Univ. of Dortmund 1979–81, Prof. of Design and Building Theory, Faculty of Architecture 1986–; Visiting Prof. and Lecturer, Venice, Amsterdam, Rotterdam, Buenos Aires, São Paulo, Brasília, Curitiba, Shanghai 1984–91; Hon. Prof., Univ. of Buenos Aires, Argentina 1985; Hon. Prof. (Tbilisi) 1995; Deubau Special Prize 1979, German Architectural Prize 1983, Hon. Prize, Transcaucasian Biennale, Tbilisi 1988, German Civil Engineering Prize 1992, Renault Traffic Award 2002. *Publications:* Architecture in Germany 1979, Young Architects in Europe 1983, Helmut Jacoby – Master of Architectural Drawing (ed.); numerous contribs to German and int. architectural magazines. *Address:* Bofinger & Partner Architekten Architects, Biebricher Allee 49, 65187 Wiesbaden, Germany (office). *Telephone:* (611) 87094 (office). *Fax:* (611) 87095 (office). *E-mail:* bofinger@bofinger-partner.de (office). *Website:* www.bofinger-partner.de (office).

BOGAN, Sir Nagora Y., MBE, KBE, LLB; Papua New Guinea diplomatist and business executive; b. Sept. 1956, Lae; m. Lady Nohoranie; two c.; ed Univ. of Papau New Guinea; fmr Sr Civil Servant, Internal Revenue Service; Oceania Del. to Commonwealth Asscn of Tax Admin 1988–91; Chair. Policy Working Group on Tax and Customs, Govt of Papua New Guinea 1988–91, Chair. Man. Cttee 1991–95, First Commr Gen. Internal Revenue Comm. 1992–95; Amb. to USA 1995–2003; Chair. Bd of Dirs Public Officers Superannuation Fund (public sector pension fund) 2002; Chair. Nambawan Super Ltd 2009–15; Pres. Indigenous Business Council; Chancellor, Papua New Guinea Univ. of Technology (Unitech) 2012–16; mem. Bd of Dirs Mapai Transport Ltd.

BOGATIKOV, Oleg A., PhD; Russian geologist and academic; *Head, Zavaritski Laboratory of General Petrography, Institute of Geology of Ore Deposits, Petrography, Mineralogy and Geochemistry, Russian Academy of Sciences;* b. 15 Dec. 1934; m.; two d.; ed Moscow Inst. of Geological Survey; Jr, then Sr Researcher, Scientific Sec., Lead Researcher, Inst. of Geology of Ore Deposits, Petrography, Mineralogy and Geochemistry 1957–, Head of Zavaritski Lab. of Gen. Petrography 1975–, also currently Chair. Interdisciplinary Petrographic Cttee; mem. Russian Acad. of Sciences (Sec. 2002); Ed.-in-Chief Petrologiya; A. E. Fersman Prize 1985, State Prize of the Russian Fed. 1997, Prize of the Govt of the Russian Fed. 1999. *Publications include:* numerous scientific articles and monographs. *Leisure interest:* travelling. *Address:* Institute of Geology of Ore Deposits, Petrography, Mineralogy and Geochemistry, Russian Academy of Sciences, 119017 Moscow, Staromonetny Per., 35, Russia (office). *Telephone:* (495) 951-72-70 (office). *Fax:* (495) 951-15-87 (office). *E-mail:* oleg@igem.ru (office). *Website:* www.igem.ru (office).

BOGDANCHIKOV, Sergey Mikhailovich, DSc; Russian petroleum industry executive; *President, RN-Yuganskneftegaz, OOO;* b. 10 Aug. 1957, Severny Dist, Orenburg Oblast, USSR; ed Buguruslansky Oil Tech. School, Ufa Petroleum Inst.; began career in oil and gas industry, Sakhalin Island 1981; joined Sakhalinmorneftegaz 1988, Gen. Dir 1993–97; mem. Bd of Dirs, Rosneft Oil Co. 1995–2011, Vice-Pres. 1997–98, Chair. Man. Bd and Pres. 1998–2010, mem. Bd of Dirs, OJSC Rosneftegaz; currently Pres. RN-Yuganskneftegaz, OOO; mem. Union of Oil and Gas Producers of Russia; Pres. Union of All-Russian Public Asscns 'All-Russian Asscn of Summer Olympic Sports'; mem. Int. Acad. of Fuel and Energy; Hon. Oil Worker and Hon. Oil and Gas Industry Worker of the Russian Fed.; Medal of Honour 1995, Honoured Oil and Gas Industry of the Russian Fed. 1998, Order of Merit for the Fatherland (Fourth Class) 2002, (Third Class) 2007, Order of St Seraphim of Sarov (Second Class), Russian Orthodox Church 2010; Prize of the Russian Federation in Science and Tech. 2005. *Publications:* several scientific publs and academic works. *Address:* RN-Yuganskneftegaz, OOO, Nefteyugansk 628309, 26 Lenin str., Tyumenskaya Oblast, Russian Federation (office). *Telephone:* (346) 323-5204 (office). *Fax:* (346) 323-5200 (office). *E-mail:* rn-yng@yungjsc.com (office). *Website:* www.yungjsc.com (office).

BOGDANOR, Vernon, CBE, MA, FRSA, FBA; British academic; *Research Professor, Institute of Contemporary History, King's College London;* b. 16 July 1943, London, England; s. of Harry Bogdanor and Rosa Weinger; m. Judith Beckett 1972 (divorced 2000); two s.; m. 2nd Sonia Robertson 2009; ed Queen's Coll. and Nuffield Coll., Oxford; Fellow, Brasenose Coll., Oxford 1966–2010, Sr Tutor 1979–85, 1996–97; mem. Council of Hansard Soc. for Parl. Govt 1981–97; Special Adviser, House of Lords Select Cttee on European Communities 1982–83; adviser to Govts of Czech Repub., Slovakia, Hungary and Israel on constitutional and electoral matters 1988–; Reader in Govt, Univ. of Oxford 1989–96, Prof. of Govt 1996–2010, Prof. Emer. 2010–; Gresham Prof. of Law, Gresham Coll., London 2004–07; Research Prof., Inst. of Contemporary History, King's Coll., London 2010–; mem. UK del. to CSCE Conf., Oslo 1991; Special Adviser, House of Commons Public Service Cttee 1996; mem. Int. Advisory Council, The Israel Democracy Inst. 2010–; Fellow, Acad. of Social Sciences 2009; Hon. Fellow, Soc. for Advanced Legal Studies 1997, Queen's Coll., Oxford 2009, Hon. Bencher, Middle Temple 2010; Chevalier, Légion d'honneur 2009; Hon. DLitt (Kent) 2010; Mishcon Lecturer 1994, Magna Carta Lecturer 2006, Sir Isaiah Berlin Prize for Lifetime Contribution to Political Studies. *Publications include:* Devolution 1979, The People and the Party System 1981, Multi-party Politics and the Constitution 1983, What is Proportional Representation? 1984, The Blackwell Encyclopaedia of Political Institutions (ed.) 1987, Comparing Constitutions (co-author) 1995, The Monarchy and the Constitution 1995, Politics and the Constitution 1996, Power and the People 1997, Devolution in the United Kingdom 1999, The British Constitution in the Twentieth Century (ed.) 2003, Joined-Up Government (ed.) 2005, The New British Constitution 2009, From New Jerusalem to New Labour: British Prime Ministers from Attlee to Blair (ed.) 2010, The Coalition and the Constitution 2011. *Leisure interests:* music, walking, talking. *Address:* Institute for Contemporary History, Strand Building, King's College, Strand, London, WC2R 2LS (office); 21 Edmunds Walk, East Finchley, London, N2 0HU, England (home).

BOGDANOV, Vladimir Leonidovich, DEcon; Russian energy industry executive; *Director-General, OJSC Surgutneftegas;* b. 28 May 1951, Suyerka, Tyumen Oblast; m.; one d.; ed Tiumen Industrial Inst., Acad. of Nat. Economy; worked for Nizhnevartovsk Drilling Admin as Driller Asst, Driller, Sr Engineer, Chief Deputy Technological Dept, Chief of Shift 1973–76; Chief, Sr Technologist, Sr Engineer Surgut Drilling Works Administration No. 2, Industrial Asscn (Surgutneftegas) 1976–78; Chief Deputy Drilling Dept, Deputy CEO, Deputy, Head of Drilling Dept Industrial Asscn (Uganskneftegas) 1978–80; Deputy CEO for Northern regions and Head of Drilling Dept Surgutneftegas 1980–83; Deputy Drilling Chief Glavtyumenneftegas 1983–84; CEO Surgutneftegas (now OJSC Surgutneftegas) 1984–, Chair. and CEO 1990, Dir-Gen. 1993–1997, 2018–, Deputy Chair. 2018–; Delegate Tyumen Regional Council from Surgut 1985–90; Chair. Zao Surgutneftegas Bank –2012; apptd mem. Bd of Dirs Kirishinefteproduct 1994, Lennefteproduct 1994, Bulk Plant (Ruchi) 1994, Red Oiler (Krasnyi Neftyanik) 1994, Onegoneft 1994, Mosbusinessbank 1996, ONEXIM Bank 1996, Nafta Moscow 1997, AKB Rosbank 2002; mem. Khanty-Mansi legislature 1996–, mem. Issuer Council, Fed. Comm. on Securities Market 1999–, Industrial Council 2000–, Steering Cttee, Delovaya Rossiya 2001–; mem. Bd of Dirs, Rosneft OJSC 2009–12, Arkhangelskgeoldobycha 2011–, mem. Acad. of Mining Sciences, Acad. of Natural Sciences, Nat. Council on Corp. Governance; Corresp. mem. Acad. of Technological Sciences; Trustee, Global Energy Int. Prize; Fellow of the Tech. Acad. of the Russian Fed., Acad. of Mining Sciences of the Russian Fed.; Hon. Citizen of Leningradskaya Oblast, Khanty-Mansiysky Autonomous Okrug-Yugra, Surgut and Surgutsky Dist; Order of the Badge of Honour, Order of the Red Banner of Labour, Order of Merit for the Fatherland (IV Degree, III Degree, II Degree), Order of Honour; Entrepreneur of the Year, Russian Union of Industrialists and Entrepreneurs 2000, Medal for Exploitation of Mineral Resources and Devt of the West-Siberian Petroleum Complex, The Honoured Worker of the Russian Oil and Gas Industry 1993; awards granted by the Repub. of Sakha (Yakutia): Badge of Civil Merit, Order of the Polar Star, Medal of Honour (Belarus) 2001, Hero of Labour of the Russian Federation 2016. *Address:* OJSC Surgutneftegas, ul. Kukuyevitskogo 1, Surgut 628415, Tyumen, Russia (office). *Telephone:* (3462) 42-61-33 (office). *Fax:* (3462) 33-32-35 (office). *E-mail:* secret_b@surgutneftegas.ru (office). *Website:* www.surgutneftegas.ru (office).

BOGDANOV, Vsevolod Leonidovich; Russian journalist; *Chairman, Russian Union of Journalists;* b. 6 Feb. 1944, Arkhangelsk Region; m.; three d.; ed Leningrad State Univ.; corresp., ed. in newspapers, radio and TV Magadan 1961–76; Head of Dept of Periodicals, State Cttee of Publs 1976–89; Dir-Gen. TV programmes State Radio and TV Cttee 1989–92; Chair. Russian Union of Journalists 1992–; Prof., Leningrad State Univ.; Pres. Nat. Journalist Trade Union 1999–; Pres. Int. Confed. of Journalists' Unions 1999–. *Leisure interests:* book rarities, fishing, hunting, Russian cuisine, music. *Address:* Russian Union of Journalists, Zubovsky blvd 4, 1199911 Moscow, Russia (office). *Telephone:* (495) 637-51-01 (office). *Fax:* (495) 637-44-55 (office). *E-mail:* inter@ruj.ru (office). *Website:* www.ruj.ru (office).

BOGDANOVICH, Peter; American film director, writer, producer and actor; b. 30 July 1939, Kingston, NY; s. of Borislav Bogdanovich and Herma Bogdanovich (née Robinson); m. 1st Polly Platt 1962 (divorced 1970); two d.; m. 2nd Louise Straten 1988 (divorced 2001); actor, American Shakespeare Festival, Stratford, Conn. 1956, NY Shakespeare Festival 1958; Dir and Producer of off-Broadway plays The Big Knife 1959, Camino Real, Ten Little Indians, Rocket to the Moon 1961, Once in a Lifetime 1964; film feature writer for Esquire, New York Times, Village Voice, Cahiers du Cinéma, Los Angeles Times, New York Magazine, Vogue, Variety etc. 1961–; Owner The Holly Moon Co. Inc. 1992; mem. Dirs Guild of America, Writers' Guild of America, Acad. of Motion Picture Arts and Sciences; NY Film Critics' Award 1971 and BAFTA Award for Best Screenplay (The Last Picture Show) 1971, Writers' Guild of America Award for Best Screenplay (What's Up, Doc?) 1972, Pasinetti Award, Critics' Prize, Venice Festival (Saint Jack) 1979 and other awards and prizes. *Films include:* The Wild Angels (2nd unit dir, co-writer, actor) 1966, Targets (dir, co-writer, producer, actor) 1968, The Last Picture Show (dir, co-writer) 1971, Directed by John Ford (dir, writer) 1971, What's Up Doc? (dir, co-writer, producer) 1972, Paper Moon (dir, producer) 1973, Daisy Miller (dir, producer) 1974, At Long Last Love (dir, writer, producer) 1975, Nickelodeon (dir, co-writer) 1976, Saint Jack (dir, co-writer, actor) 1979, They All Laughed (dir, writer) 1981, Mask (dir) 1985, Illegally Yours (dir, producer) 1988, Texasville (dir, producer, writer) 1990, Noises Off (dir, exec. producer) 1992, The Thing Called Love (dir) 1993, Who The Devil Made It (dir) 1997, Mr Jealousy (actor) 1997, Highball (actor) 1997, Coming Soon (actor) 1999, Rated X (actor) 2000, The Independent (actor) 2000, The Cat's Meow (dir) 2003, Scene Stealers (actor) 2003, Infamous (actor) 2006, The Doorman (actor) 2007, Broken English (actor) 2007, Dedication (actor) 2007, The Dukes (actor) 2007, The Fifth Patient (actor) 2007, Humboldt County (actor) 2008, The Doorman (actor) 2008, Queen of the Lot (actor) 2010, Abandoned (actor) 2010, Don't Let Me Go (actor) 2013, While We're Young (actor) 2014, Pearly Gates (actor) 2015, Durant's Never Closes (actor) 2016, Willie and Me (actor) 2017, Los Angeles Overnight (actor) 2018, The Other Side of the Wind (actor) 2018. *Television:* The Great Professional: Howard Hawks (film) (co-dir, writer), BBC 1967; dir: Saintly Switch (film) 1999, Hustle (film) 2004, The Mystery of Natalie Wood (film) 2004; regular commentator for CBS This Morning 1987–89; actor: Northern Exposure, CBS 1993, Fallen Angels (series) 1995, Painted Word 1995, To Sir With Love II (film) 1996, Naked City: A Killer Christmas (film) 1998, Rated X (film) 2000, The Sopranos (series) (also dir 2004) 2000–07, Out of Order (mini-series) 2003. *Publications include:* The Cinema of Orson Welles 1961, The Cinema of Howard Hawks 1962, The Cinema of Alfred Hitchcock 1963, John Ford 1968, Fritz Lang in America 1969, Allan Dwan, the Last Pioneer 1971, Pieces of Time, Peter Bogdanovich on the Movies 1961–85, The Killing of the Unicorn: Dorothy Stratten (1960–80) 1984, A Year and a Day Calendar (ed.) 1991, This is Orson Welles (with Orson Welles) 1992, Who the Devil Made It 1997, Who the Hell's In It? 2004. *Address:* c/o William Pfeiffer, 30 Lane of Acres, Haddonfield, NJ 08033.

BOGLE, Ellen Gray; Jamaican diplomatist and government official (retd); b. 9 Oct. 1941, St Andrew; d. of Victor Gray Williams and Eileen Averil (née Rampie); one s. one d.; ed St Andrew High School for Girls, Univ. of the West Indies; Dir Foreign Trade Div., Ministry of Foreign Affairs, with responsibility for formulation of Jamaica's Foreign Trade policy 1978–81; fmr Dir Jamaica Nat. Export Corpn; High Commr in Trinidad & Tobago 1981–89; High Commr in UK 1989–94; fmr Amb., Ministry of Foreign Affairs and Foreign Trade; Amb. and Special Envoy to the Asscn of Caribbean States and CARICOM 1997; fmr Under-Sec. Bilateral and Regional Affairs, Ministry of Foreign Affairs and Foreign Trade; represented Jamaica at numerous int. confs; Int. Trade Consultant, Lascelles DeMercado Co. Ltd 2002–09; Commdr Order of Distinction 1987. *Leisure interests:* gardening, reading, cooking, listening to music. *Telephone:* (876) 879-8297 (office). *E-mail:* boglee@hotmail.com (office).

BOGNER, Willy, Jr.; German business executive, film director and fashion designer; *Chairman and Managing Director, Willy Bogner GmbH & Co. KGaA;* b. 23 Jan. 1942, Munich; s. of Willy Bogner Sr and Maria Bogner; m. Sonia Ribeiro 1973; ed Altes Realgymnasium, Munich and business and technical studies in Munich and Hohenstein; Chair. and Man. Dir Willy Bogner GmbH & Co. KGaA (sportswear co. f. in 1932 by Willy Bogner Sr); Founder and Man. Willy Bogner Film GmbH, Munich 1968–; mem. German Nat. Olympic Cttee; dir of documentary, advertising, sports (especially skiing) films; Bundesverdienstkreuz Medal 1996, Goldene Seidenschleif 1999. *Films include:* Skivision 1974, 1975, 1979, Skifaszination, Ski Fantasie 1981, Crystal Dreams 1982, Feuer und Eis 1986, Feuer, Eis und Dynamit 1990, White Magic 1994, Mountain Magic 1999, Ski to the Max 2001, Skimagination 2009, Magic in Motion 2010; directed ski scene sequences in On Her Majesty's Secret Service 1969, Snow Job 1972, The Spy Who Loved Me 1977, For Your Eyes Only 1981, A View to a Kill 1985. *Achievements include:* several times German ski champion and participated in Winter Olympics, Squaw Valley 1960, Innsbruck 1964 and World Ski Championships, Chamonix 1962, Portillo (Chile) 1966. *Leisure interests:* sport (tennis, skiing, golf), sailing, flying, filming and photography. *Address:* Willy Bogner GmbH & Co. KGaA, Sankt-Veit-Strasse 4, 81673 Munich, Germany (office). *Telephone:* (89) 436060 (office). *Fax:* (89) 43606429 (office). *E-mail:* communication@bogner.com (office). *Website:* www.bogner.com (office).

BOGOLLAGAMA, Rohitha; Sri Lankan lawyer and politician; *Governor of Eastern Province;* b. 5 Aug. 1954, Nikaweratiya; m.; two c.; ed Ananda Coll. and Sri Lanka Law Coll.; apptd attorney 1976; fmr Chair. Sri Lanka Cement Corpn, Sathosa Printers; fmr Dir Foreign Employment Bureau; Legal and Political Adviser to Voice of America project in Sri Lanka 1991–99; Chair. and Dir-Gen. Bd of Investment of Sri Lanka 1993–2000; mem. Parl. (United National Party—UNP) 2000–10, served on Parl. Consultative Cttees on Finance, Foreign Affairs, Defence, Industrial Devt and Investment Promotion and Power and Energy 2000–05, Chair. Cttee on Public Enterprises 2005–07, Minister of Industrial Devt 2001–04, of Enterprise Devt and Investment Promotion 2004–07, of Foreign Affairs 2007–10; Gov. of Eastern Prov. 2017–. *Address:* Office of Governor, Lower Road, Orr's Hill, Trincomalee, Sri Lanka (office). *Telephone:* (26) 2222102 (office). *Fax:* (26) 2222320 (office). *E-mail:* governor@ep.gov.lk (office). *Website:* www.ep.gov.lk (office).

BOGOLYUBOV, Gennadiy; Ukrainian business executive and philanthropist; b. 20 Jan. 1962; m.; four c.; Co-owner of Privat business group; first made his fortune in 1990 trading in computer parts, then est. one of Ukraine's first privately owned banks, PrivatBank (nationalized in 2016); Pres. Dnipropetrovsk Jewish Philanthropic Fund; f. Bogolyubov Foundation (charity); The Yad Vashem Soc. in Ukraine Award in recognition of his activity on behalf of Yad Vashem 2005. *Leisure interest:* enjoys sports. *Website:* www.bogolyubovfoundation.com.

BOGOSIAN, Eric, BA; American actor and writer; b. 24 April 1953, Woburn, Mass; s. of Henry Bogosian and Edwina Bogosian; m. Jo Anne Bonney 1990; two c.; ed Univ. of Chicago and Oberlin Coll.; Obie Award 1986, 1990, 1994, Drama Critics' Circle Award, Berlin Film Festival Silver Bear Award 1988. *Films include:* Born in Flames 1983, Special Effects 1984, Chasing the Dragon 1987, Arena Brains 1988, Talk Radio 1988, Suffering Bastards 1989, Dolores Claiborne 1995, Under Siege 2: Dark Territory 1995, The Substance of Fire 1996, Beavis and Butt-Head Do America (voice) 1996, Deconstructing Harry 1997, In the Weeds 2000, Wake Up and Smell the Coffee 2001, Ararat 2002, Igby Goes Down 2002, Charlie's Angels: Full Throttle 2003, Wonderland 2003, King of the Corner 2004, Heights 2004, Blade: Trinity 2004, Heights 2005, Cadillac Records 2008, Don't Go in the Woods 2010, Listen Up Philip (voice) 2014, Rebel in the Rye 2017. *Television includes:* The Caine Mutiny Court-Martial 1988, Last Flight Out 1990, Witch Hunt 1994, High Incident 1995, A Bright Shining Lie 1998, Blonde 2001, Shot in the Heart 2001, Love Monkey (series) 2006, Law & Order: Criminal Intent (series) 2006–10, The Get Down 2016–17, Succession 2018. *Plays include:* The New World, Men Inside, The Ricky Paul Show, Funhouse, Talk Radio, subUrbia, Griller, Drinking in America, Pounding Nails in the Floor with My Forehead, Sex, Drugs, Rock & Roll, Wake Up and Smell the Coffee, Red Angel, Humpty Dumpty, This is Now!, 100 (Monologues) 2013, Mall 2014. *Publications:* Mall 2000, Wasted Beauty 2005, Perforated Heart 2009. *Address:* c/o Emily Gerson-Saines, Brookside Artist Management, 250 West 57th Street, Suite 2303, New York, NY 10107, USA (office).

BOGOV, Dimitar, MSc, MBA; Macedonian economist and fmr central banker; *Regional Lead Economist, European Bank for Reconstruction and Development;* b. 24 Dec. 1967; ed Univ. of St Cyril and Metodius, Skopje, City Univ. Thessaloniki, Greece, Sheffield Univ., UK; Adviser for Nat. Accounts and Head of Div., State Statistical Office 1993–98, Adviser for Macroeconomics to Gen. Man. 1999–2001; Assoc. Account Man., Macedonian Business Resource Centre 1998–99; Head of Macroeconomics Dept, Ministry of Finance 2001–02; Co-founder and mem. Center for Econ. Analysis, Skopje 2003–07; mem. Supervisory Bd Zito Luks AD Skopje (food mfr) 2005–07; Chief Economist, Stopanska Banka AD 2002–07; Vice-Gov. Nat. Bank of Repub. of Macedonia (central bank) 2007–11, Gov. 2011–18; Regional Lead Economist, EBRD 2018–; mem. Cttee of Govs, Vienna Econ. Forum. *Address:* European Bank for Reconstruction and Development, 46–46A Antonovycha Str., 03150 Kiev Ukraine (office). *Telephone:* (44) 354-40-84 (office). *E-mail:* kiev@kev.ebrd.com (office). *Website:* www.ebrd.com (office).

BOHAN, Marc; French couturier; b. 22 Aug. 1926, Paris; s. of Alfred Bohan and Geneviève Baudoux; m. Huguette Rinjonneau (deceased); one d.; ed Lycée Lakanal, Sceaux; Asst with Piguet 1945, later with Molyneux and Patou; Dior org. London 1958, later Paris, Artistic Dir Soc. Christian Dior 1960–89; Artistic Dir Hartnell, London 1990–92; designed costumes for numerous films 1961–89, for Athens Opera 1992–96; Chevalier, Légion d'honneur, Ordre de Saint-Charles (Monaco); Médaille de la Ville de Paris. *Leisure interests:* classical music, theatre, reading, antiques. *Address:* 35 rue du Bourg à Mont, 21400 Châtillon-sur-Seine, France (home).

BOHATYROVA, Raisa Vasylivna, DMedSc; Ukrainian gynaecologist and politician; b. 6 Jan. 1953, Bakal, Chelyabinsk Oblast, Russian SFSR, USSR; m. Ihor Oleksandrovych Bohatyrov; two s.; ed Kharkiv Medical Inst., T.H. Shevchenko Nat. Univ., Kyiv; Machinist, Kramatorg Clothing Factory 1970–71; Intern Physician, Therapy Centre No. 2, Horlivka 1977–79; Obstetric Gynaecologist, later Head of Professional Cttee and Deputy Head Physician, Kramatorg Cen. Town Therapy Centre 1979–91; People's Deputy of Ukraine 1990–94, 2000–08; Deputy, later First Deputy, then Minister of Health 1994–2000; Academic Consultant to Pres. of Ukraine 2000–; mem. Partiya Rehioniv (Party of Regions) –2008, Leader Parl. faction in Verkhovna Rada (Parl.) 2002–08; mem. Parl. Ass., Council of Europe 2006–08; Chair. Nat. Security and Defence Council 2007–12; Deputy Prime Minister 2012–14; Minister of Health 2012–14 (dismissed); declared a suspect by Prosecutor-Gen. in embezzlement of six million Ukrainian hryvnia in budget funds Oct. 2014; int. Red Notice issued by Interpol against her as wanted for corruption and charges of "misappropriation, embezzlement or conversion of property by malversation" Jan. 2015; assets frozen by EU; Sec., Supervisory Council, 'Ukraina–Dityam' Nat. Social Protection Fund for Mothers and Children 1997–2003; Hon. Pres. Chamber of Tendering of Ukraine 2006–07; Hon. Citizen of Donetsk Oblast 2007; Order of St Stanislaus 1999, Honoured Physician of Ukraine 2001, Order of Princess Olha (Third Degree) 2002; State Prize of Ukraine in Science and Tech. 1999. *Address:* c/o Ministry of Health, 01021 Kyiv, vul. M. Hrushevskoho 7, Ukraine. *E-mail:* moz@moz.gov.ua.

BOHIGAS GUARDIOLA, Oriol, DArch; Spanish architect; b. 20 Dec. 1925, Barcelona; s. of Pere Bohigas and María Guardiola; m. Isabel Arnau 1957; five c.; ed Escuela Técnica Superior de Arquitectura, Barcelona; partnership with Josep Martorell 1951–, with David Mackay 1962–, with Oriol Capdevila and Francesc Gual 2000–, forming MBM Arquitectes; Chair. of Composition, Escuela Técnica Superior de Arquitectura, Barcelona (ETSAB) 1971–, Head of ETSAB 1977–80; Head of Urban Planning Dept, Barcelona City Council 1980–84; Councillor of Culture 1991–94; Pres. Joan Miró Foundation 1981–88, Barcelona Athenaeum 2003–11; mem. Accademia Nazionale di San Luca, Rome 1981, Royal Swedish Acad. of Engineering Sciences 1991, Académie d'Architecture de Paris 1991, Real Académia de Bellas Artes de San Fernando 2011; Hon. mem. Sociedad Colombiana de Arquitectos 1982, Asscn of Architects of Bulgaria 1987, Bund Deutscher Architecten 1990, Hon. FAIA 1993, Hon. FRIBA 1996; Ordem dos Arquitetos Lisboa (Portugal) 2010; Dr hc (Darmstadt) 1992, (Menéndez y Pelayo) 1995, Hon. Chair. Universitat Politécnica de Catalunya 1995; numerous awards including Gold Medal for Artistic Merits, City of Barcelona 1986, Medal of Urbanism, Acad. d'Architecture de Paris 1988, Sikkens Award, Rotterdam 1989, Gold Medal for Architecture, Consejo Superior de Arquitectos de España, Madrid 1990, Creu de Sant Jordi, Generalitat de Catalunya 1991, Volker Stevin Innovatieprijs Award, Rotterdam 1992, RIBA Royal Gold Medal to City of Barcelona (with others) 1999, Gold Medal, Artistic Circle of St Lluc, Barcelona 2004, ArpaFIL Architecture Prize, Mexico 2004, Pres. Macia Medal, Barcelona 2006, Gold Medal, COAC, Barcelona 2007, Nat. Award of Architecture, Madrid 2006, Culture's Nat. Award for his Professional and Artistic Path, Barcelona 2011, Gold Medal, Generalitat de Catalunya 2013; firm awarded First Prize in many architectural competitions including Foment de les Arts Decoratives for best bldg in Barcelona 1959, 1962, 1966, 1976, 1979, 1984, 1991, Delta de Plata (industrial design) 1966, 1976, First Prize, Internationale Bauhausstellung Berlin 1981, Un Progetto per Siena, Italy 1990, FAD Award for the Olympic Port 1991, Gold Medal, Barcelona 92 1992, Cardiff Bay, Wales 1993, Eric Lyons Housing Award for bldg in Olympic Village, Barcelona 1994, 'Mission Perrache-Confluent', Lyon, France 1997, 'London's Arc of Opportunity', UK 1999, 'Programma di riqualificazione urbana dell'area De-Cecco', Pescara, Italy 2000, Prize of City of Barcelona for the Pompeu Fabra Univ. bldg 2001, Barcelona Design Museum competition (DHUB), Barcelona 2001, International railway station of Canfranc (Huesca) competition 2001, Award Década for the Olympic Port, Barcelona 2001, competition Groot Zieken Gasthuisterrein in 's-Hertogenbosch competition, The Netherlands 2003, Silver Jubilee Cup for the Vision for Plymouth Plan, UK 2006, Urbanistica Award for new railway station in Parma, Italy 2009, urban planning of Via Trento, Parma, Italy 2010, urban planning of Hyères city centre, France 2010, Trophée ARCHIZINC 2012 for La Casa dels Xuklis 2012, Teula de Plata Award, Collegi d'Arquitectes de Catalunya 2012, Gold Medal, Generalitat de Catalunya 2013. *Publications include:* Barcelona entre el plà Cerdà i el barraquisme 1963, Arquitectura modernista 1968, Contra una arquitectura adjetivada 1969, La arquitectura española de la Segunda República 1970, Polemica d'arquitectura catalana 1970, Reseña y catálogo de la arquitectura modernista 1972, Proceso y erótica del diseño 1972, Once arquitectos 1976, Reconstrucció de Barcelona 1985, Combat d'incerteses. Dietari de records 1989, Dit o fet. Dietari de records II 1992, Gràcies i desgràcies de Barcelona 1993, el Present des del Futur. Epistolari Públic 1994–1995 1996, Del dubte a la Revolució. Epistolari públic 1995–1997 1998, Modernidad en la arquitectura de la España Republicana 1998, Oriol Bohigas. Realismo, urbanidad y fracasos 1999, Tra Strada del Dubbio e Piazza della Revoluzione. Epistolario sulle arti, l'architettura e l'urbanistica 2003, Cartes de la Baralla. Epistolari públic sobre cultura i política 2003, Modernité en l'architecture dans l'Espagne républicaine 2004, Contra la incontinencia urbana. Reconsideración moral de la arquitectura y la ciudad 2004, Contra la incontinència urbana. Reconsideració moral de l'arquitectura i la ciutat 2004, Epistolario 1951–1994 2005, Contro l'incontinenza urbana. Riconsiderazione morale sull'architettura e la città 2008, Passar Comptes Dietari de records III 2012, Refer la memòria, Dietàris complets, RBA La Magrana, Barcelona 2014. *Telephone:* (93) 3170061 (office); (93) 4124771 (home). *Fax:* (93) 3177266 (office). *E-mail:* obohigas@mbmarquitectes.cat (office). *Website:* www.mbmarquitectes.cat (office).

BOHL, Friedrich; German lawyer and politician; b. 5 March 1945, Rosdorf, Göttingen; s. of Heinrich Bohl and Gerda Heyden; m. Elisabeth Bocking; two s. two d.; ed Univ. of Marburg; lawyer 1972–, notary 1976–; mem. CDU and Jungen Union (JU) 1963–; local Chair. JU Marburg-Biedenkopf 1964–70; Dist Chair. JU Mittelhessen 1969–73; mem. Prov. Parl. Hessen 1970–80, Chair. Legal Cttee 1974–78; Acting Chair. CDU Landtagsfraktion 1978–80; Chair. CDU Kreistagsfraktion Marburg-Biedenkopf 1974–90; mem. Fed. German Parl. 1980–, Parl. Man. CDU/CSU Bundestagsfraktion 1984–91; Fed. Minister for Special Tasks and Head of Fed. Chancellery 1991–98; Head of Press and Information, Fed. Govt 1998; mem. Exec. Bd Deutsche Vermögensberatung AG 1991–2009, Chair. Supervisory Bd 2009–; Pres. von Behring-Röntgen Foundation 2011–; Chair. Bd of Trustees Max Planck Inst. for Heart and Lung Research 2013–; Bundesverdienstkreuz (1st Class) 1987. *Address:* c/o Von Behring-Röntgen-Stiftung, Schloss 1, 35037 Marburg; Finkenstrasse 11, 35043 Marburg Cappel, Germany (home). *Telephone:* 41333 (home).

BOHRER, Karl Heinz, PhD, Dr. habil.; German academic; *Professor Emeritus of Modern Literature, University of Bielefeld;* b. 26 Sept. 1932, Cologne; m. 1st Barbara Schwarze 1959 (divorced 1989); one s. one d.; m. 2nd Undine Gruenter 1991 (divorced 2002); m. 3rd Angela Bielenberg 2003; ed Univ. of Göttingen, Univ. of Heidelberg; Prof. of History of Modern Literature, Univ. of Bielefeld 1982–97, Prof. Emer. 1997–; Visiting Prof. of Comparative Literature, Stanford Univ. 2003–; Ed. Merkur 1984–2011; J.H. Merck Prize 1978, Lessing Prize 2000, Gadamer Prize 2001, Prize of the Bavarian Acad. of Arts 2005, Prize of the Berlin Acad. of Arts 2007. *Publications:* Die gefährdete Phantasie oder Surrealismus und Terror 1970, Der Lauf des Freitag – Die lädierte Utopie und der Dichter 1973, Die Ästhetik des Schreckens 1978, Plötzlichkeit. Der Augenblick des ästhetischen Scheins 1981, Mythos und Moderne 1983, Der romantische Brief, Die Entstehung aesthetischer Subjektivität 1987, Nach der Natur, Über Politik und Ästhetik 1988, Die Kritik der Romantik 1989, Das absolute Präsens. Die Semantik ästhetischer Zeit 1994, Der Abschied. Theorie der Trauer 1996, Die Grenzen des Aesthetischen 1998, Ästhetische Negativität 2002, Ekstasen der Zeit: Augenblick, Gegenwart, Erinnerung 2003, Imaginationen des Bösen 2004, Großer Stil 2007, Das Tragische: Erscheinung, Pathos, Klage 2009, Selbstdenker und Systemdenker 2011, Der Granatsplitter: Erzählung einer Jugend 2012. *Address:* 110 Lansdowne Way, London, SW8 2EP, England (home); Universität Bielefeld, Fakultät für Linguistik und Literaturwissenschaft, 33501 Bielefeld (office); Franziskastr. 9, Cologne, Germany. *Telephone:* (20) 7622-3861 (home). *Fax:* (20) 7501-0067 (home).

BOISCLAIR, André, MPA; Canadian fmr politician; *President, Institut de Développement Urbain du Québec;* b. 14 April 1966, Montréal; s. of Marc-André Boisclair; ed Jean-de-Brébeuf Coll., Univ. of Laval, John F. Kennedy School of Govt, Harvard Univ., USA; elected to Quebec Nat. Ass. representing Gouin riding 1989 (youngest mem. ever elected), Govt House Leader 2001–04 (resgnd); Minister of Immigration and Citizens 1996–98, Minister of Social Solidarity 1998–2001, Minister of the Environment and Water 2001–03; Leader, Parti Québécois 2005–07 (resgnd); Adjunct Prof., Strategic Communication, Concordia Univ. 2008–12; Pres. Bd Regroupement des événements majeurs internationaux 2010–11; Advisor to Bd Questerre Energy 2011–12; Del.-Gen. of Quebec in New York 2012–13; Pres. Environmental and Social Impact Review Cttee, COMEX 2014–16; Special Advisor on Climate Matters to Minister of Environment 2014–16; CEO Institut de Développement Urbain du Québec 2016–. *Address:* Institut de Développement Urbain du Québec, 1010 Rue de la Gauchetière O, Montreal, QC H3B 2N2, Canada (office). *Telephone:* (514) 866-3625 (office). *E-mail:* info@iduquebec.com (office). *Website:* iduquebec.com (office).

BOISSET, Yves; French author and film director; b. 14 March 1939, Paris; s. of Raymond Boisset and Germaine Bonnet; m. Micheline Paintault 1964; two s.; ed Lycée Louis-le-Grand, Faculté des Lettres, Paris and Inst. des Hautes Etudes Cinématographiques; journalist on Cinéma, Paris-Jour etc. 1958–63; Asst Dir to Yves Ciampi 1959, to Jean-Pierre Melville 1962, Claude Sautet and Antoine Bourseiller 1964, Vittorio de Sica and René Clemént 1965, Ricardo Freda 1966; TV and film dir 1967–; Chevalier des Arts et des Lettres. *Films include:* Coplan sauve sa peau 1968, Cran d'arrêt 1969, Un condé 1970, Le Saut de l'ange 1971, L'Attentat (Grand Prix, Moscow Film Festival 1972) 1972, R.A.S. 1973, Dupont Lajoie (Silver Bear, Berlin Film Festival 1974) 1974, Folle à tuer 1975, Le Juge Fayard dit le Sheriff (Prix Louis Delluc 1977) 1976, Un taxi mauve 1977, La Clé sur la porte 1978, La Femme flic (Award for Best Dir, Karlov Vivary Festival 1979) 1979, Allons z'enfants 1981, Espion lève-toi 1982, Le Prix du danger 1983, Canicule 1984, Bleu comme l'Enfer 1986, La Travestie 1988, Radio Corbeau 1989, La Tribu 1991. *Television includes:* La Fée carabine 1987, Le Suspect 1989, Double Identity 1990, Les Carnassiers 1991, Morlock 1993, L'Affaire Seznec (Best Film, Best Screenplay, Best Dir, seven D'Or Awards 1993) 1993, L'Affaire Dreyfus (Silver Prize, Monte Carlo TV Festival 1995) 1995, Morlock: Le tunnel 1996, Les Amants de rivière rouge (mini-series) 1996, La Fine équipe 1997, Une leçon particulière 1997, Le Pantalon (Best Film, Best Dir 1997) 1997, Sam 1999, Dormir avec le diable 2001, Cazas 2001, Jean Moulin 2002, Le Blues des Medias 2003, Ils Veulent Cloner le Christ 2004, Les Mystères Sanglants de l'OTS 2005, La Bataille D'Alger 2006, L'Affaire Salengro 2008, Douze balles dans la peau pour Pierre Laval 2009. *Publications:* 20 ans de cinéma américain 1962, La vie est un choix 2011. *Leisure interests:* athletics, basketball, tennis. *Address:* 61 boulevard Inkerman, 92200 Neuilly-sur-Seine (office); 88 boulevard Victor Hugo, 92200 Neuilly-sur-Seine, France (home). *Telephone:* 1-47-47-52-05 (home). *E-mail:* yves.boisset@yahoo.fr (home).

BOISSIER, Patrick Marie René; French business executive; *Chairman, GICAN (Groupement des industries de construction et activités navales);* b. 18 Feb. 1950, Versailles; s. of Pierre Boissier and Françoise Boissier (née Hennebicque); m. Isabelle Joly 1972; two s. one d.; ed Ecole Polytechnique, Harvard Business School, USA; engineer, Cegedur Rhenalu 1973–75, Forges de Crans 1976–79, Asst Factory Man. Cegedur 1980–83, Man. Pipes Div. 1984–87, Gen. Man. 1987–90; Deputy Chair. and CEO Tréfimétaux 1990–93; Dept Head Péchiney 1994; Gen. Man. Heating and Air-Conditioning Div., Elfi 1994–97; Chair. and CEO Technibel 1994–97; Gen. Man., then Chair. and CEO Chantiers d'Atlantique 1997–2006; CEO GEC Alsthom Leroux Naval (later Alstom Leroux Naval) 1997–2006; Chair. Alstom Marine 1998–2006; mem. Supervisory Bd Vallourec 2000–, Vice-Pres. 2005–; CEO Cegelec electrical engineering group 2007–; Chair. and CEO DCNS (fmrly Direction Technique des Constructions Navales and Direction des Constructions Navales) shipbuilders 2009–14; Chair. GICAN (Groupement des industries de construction et activités navales) 2014–; mem. Advisory Bd Steria; mem. Bd of Dirs Sperian; Chair. European Shipbuilders Asscn Cttee 2004–; mem. Acad. des Technologies; Chevalier, Ordre nat. du Mérite, Légion d'honneur. *Leisure interest:* sailing. *Address:* GICAN (Groupement des industries de construction et activités navales), 60 rue de Monceau, 75008 Paris, France (office). *Telephone:* 1-56-59-15-15 (office). *Fax:* 1-45-63-59-37 (office). *E-mail:* contact@gican.asso.fr (office); boissier@academie-technologies.fr (office). *Website:* www.gican.asso.fr (office).

BOISSON, Jacques-Louis, PhD, LLD; Monegasque diplomatist and government official; *Secretary of State, Principality of Monaco;* b. 8 Jan. 1940, Monaco; s. of Robert Boisson and Léonie-Jeanne Gastaud; m. Carmen Gómez Parejo; one s.; ed Institut d'Etudes Politiques, Institut des Relations Int., Paris, Faculté de Droit et de Sciences Economiques, Aix-en-Provence, Acad. of Int. Law, Netherlands; int. civil servant (responsible for training, research and protection of human rights) UNESCO 1968–83; Amb. to France 1984–93, 2006–08, to Spain 2003–04, to Andorra 2007–08; Amb. and Perm. Rep. to UN, New York 1993–2003; Del. to Council of Europe 2004–06; Amb. to Int. Org. of Francophony 2006–08; Perm. Del. to UNESCO 2007–08; Sec. of State (Head of Govt) 2008–; mem. Advisory Council, AMADE 2010–; Commdr, Ordre de St Charles (Monaco) 2004; Grand Officier, Ordre de Grimaldi (Monaco) 2011; Chevalier, Ordre des Palmes académiques, Légion d'honneur. *Publications:* Le Particularisme Institutionnel de la Principalité de Monaco 1966, Le Droit de la Nationalité Monégasque 1968, La Protection Internationale des Minorités, Vers un Enseignement Universel des Droits de l'Homme, L'Autorité internationale des Fonds Marins 2001; numerous articles on the protection and promotion of int. human rights 1971–99. *Leisure interests:* baroque music, opera, philosophy, poetry. *Address:* Palais Princier, 98000 (office); 31 boulevard Charles III, 98000, Monaco (home). *Telephone:* 93-25-18-31 (office); 93-25-59-64 (home). *Fax:* 93-30-26-26 (office). *E-mail:* jboisson@palais.mc (office); carfac.boisson@monaco.mc.

BOJANIĆ, Mladen; Montenegrin economist and politician; b. 14 Oct. 1962, Titograd (now Podgorica), People's Repub. of Montenegro, Fed. People's Repub. of Yugoslavia; m.; two c.; ed Veljko Vlahović Univ., Univ. of Montenegro; worked as stockbroker with Montenegroexpress, Budva 1987–90, Titex, Podgorica 1990–93, DD MAP Industriaimport, Podgorica 1993–95, Aktiva Integra AD, Podgorica 2007–12; worked for Montenegro Stock Exchange AD 1995–96, 2001–06; Founder and Chair. Holder Broker AD 1996–2001; Deputy Chair., Union of Economists of Montenegro 2011–; mem. Ass. of Montenegro (Parl.) 2012–14; Founding mem. Positive Montenegro 2012–14, fmr Sec. Gen.; ind. 2014–; ind. cand. in presidential election 2018. *Address:* Bulevar Ivana Crnojevica 107, Podgorica, Montenegro (office). *Telephone:* (67) 209-555 (office). *E-mail:* info@mladenbojanic.me (office). *Website:* www.mladenbojanic.me (office).

BØJER, Jørgen R. H.; Danish diplomatist (retd); b. 5 March 1940, Hjørring; s. of Svend Rud Hansen Bøjer and Ingeborg Bøjer (née Frederiksen); m. Lone Heilskov 1964; two d.; ed Univ. of Århus, Institut d'Etudes Politiques, Paris; became Foreign Service Officer 1967, Sec., Embassy in Prague 1971; Head of Section, Ministry of Foreign Affairs, Copenhagen 1973, Dir 1982, Deputy Under-Sec. 1992; Visiting Fellow, Stanford Univ. 1978; Counsellor, Embassy in Washington, DC 1979; Amb. to Egypt, then to Austria, Slovenia, Bosnia and Herzegovina; Perm. Rep. to Int. Orgs, Vienna 1993; Perm. Rep. to UN, New York 1997–2001, Co-Chair. UN Int. Conf. on Financing for Devt 2001; Amb. to Czech Repub. 2001–07; Chair. Danish Centre for Int. Studies and Human Rights 2006.

BOJINOV, Bojidar; Bulgarian lawyer and legal adviser; b. 30 Jan. 1939, Pleven City; s. of Boris Bojinov and Nina Bojinova; m. Fani Vladimorova; one s. two d.; ed Charles Univ., Prague; lawyer, Pleven 1967–72; Legal Adviser to Bulgarian Chamber of Commerce and Industry (BCCI), Sofia 1972–77, Dir Patent and Trade Marks Div. 1977–85, Vice-Pres. BCCI 1985–93, Pres. 1993–2009; Arbitrator at BCCI Court of Arbitration 1975–2004; currently Pnr, Bojinov & Bojinov Ltd (law firm); mem. Advisory Council to Pres. of Repub. on Foreign Investments, Nat. Council for Tripartite Cooperation, Council of Econ. Growth 2002–; fmr Pres. Asscn of Black Sea Zone Chambers of Commerce and Industry, Asscn of Balkan Chambers, Bulgarian Nat. Group of AIPP. *Leisure interests:* music, art, skiing, tennis. *Address:* Patents and Trademarks Bureau, Bojinov & Bojinov Ltd, 38 Alabin Street, PO Box 728, 1000 Sofia (office). *Telephone:* (2) 9862974 (office). *Fax:* (2) 9873209 (office); (2) 9863508 (office). *E-mail:* office@ptmbojinov.com (office).

BOK, Derek, MA, JD; American lawyer, university administrator and academic; *300th Anniversary University President Emeritus, Harvard University;* b. 22 March 1930, Bryn Mawr, Pa; s. of Curtis Bok and Margaret Plummer; m. Sissela Ann Myrdal Bok (d. of Karl Gunnar and Alva Myrdal) 1955; one s. two d.; ed Stanford Univ., Harvard Univ., George Washington Univ., Inst. of Political Science, Univ. of Paris, France; served in US Army 1956–58; Asst Prof. of Law, Harvard Univ. 1958–61, Prof. 1961, Dean 1968–71, 300th Anniversary Univ. Prof. 1991, now Prof. Emer.; Pres. Harvard Univ. 1971–91, now Pres. Emer., Interim Pres. 2006–07; Dir, Nat. Chair. Common Cause 1999–; Chair. Spencer Foundation 2002–; apptd Faculty Chair. Hauser Center for Non-Profit Orgs 2002. *Publications include:* The First Three Years of the Schuman Plan, Cases and Materials on Labor Law (with Archibald Cox), Labor and the American Community (with John Dunlop), The Federal Government and the University, Beyond the Ivory Tower: Social Responsibilities of the Modern University 1982, Higher Learning 1986, Universities and the Future of America 1990, The Cost of Talent 1993, The State of the Nation 1997, The Shape of the River (jtly) 1998, The Trouble with Government 2001, Universities in the Marketplace 2004, book, Our Underachieving Colleges: A Candid Look at How Much Students Learn and Why They Should Be Learning More 2007, The Politics of Happiness: What Government Can Learn from the New Research on Well-Being 2010, The Politics of Happiness: What Government can Learn from the New Research on Well-Being 2010, Higher Education in America 2013, The Struggle to Reform Our Colleges 2017. *Leisure interests:* gardening, tennis, swimming. *Address:* Hauser Center for Nonprofit Organizations, 5 Bennett Street, Cambridge, MA 02138 (office); John F. Kennedy School of Government, Harvard University, 79 John F. Kennedy Street, Cambridge, MA 02138, USA (office). *Telephone:* (617) 495-1199 (office). *Fax:* (617) 496-6886 (office). *E-mail:* derek_bok@harvard.edu (office). *Website:* www.ksg.harvard.edu/hauser (office).

BOKOVA, Irina Georgieva, MBA; Bulgarian diplomatist, politician and UN official; b. 12 July 1952; d. of Georgi Bokov; m.; two c.; ed First English Language School, Sofia, Moscow State Inst. of Int. Relations, Russia, Univ. of Maryland, John F. Kennedy School of Govt, Harvard Univ., USA; Attaché and Third Sec., Ministry of Foreign Affairs, Sofia 1977–82, Third Sec., Perm. Mission to UN, New York 1982–84, Third, later Second Sec., UN Dept, Ministry of Foreign Affairs 1984–86, Adviser to Minister of Foreign Affairs (rank of First Sec.) 1986–90, First Sec., European Security Dept 1991–92, State Sec. on European Integration 1995–97, Minister of Foreign Affairs 1996–97, Adviser to Minister of Foreign Affairs (rank of Amb.) Feb.–Sept. 1997, Amb. to France 2005–09; mem. Constituent Nat. Ass. 1990–91; elected mem. Narodno Sobranie (Parl.) for Bulgarian Socialist Party 2001; Dir-Gen. UNESCO, Paris 2009–17; NATO Fellow, Program for Cen. and Eastern Europe on democratic insts focusing on the nat. and legal mechanism for the protection of minorities 1992–94; Order of Stara Planina (1st class) 2014, Magtymguly Pyragy Medal 2014; Dr hc (Univ. Cattolica del Sacro Cuore) 2010, (Philippine Normal Univ.) 2011. *Publications:* numerous articles on foreign policy and European integration issues.

BOKROS, Lajos, PhD; Hungarian economist, banker, academic and politician; b. 26 June 1954, Budapest; s. of Lajos Bokros and Irén Szarka; m. Maria Gyetuai; one s. one d.; ed Univ. of Econs, Budapest, Univ. of Panama; Research Fellow, Financial Research Inst., Hungarian Ministry of Finance, Budapest 1980–86, Chief of Public Finance Div. 1986–87; Deputy Gen. Man. Econ. Dept, Nat. Bank of Hungary 1987–89, Man. Dir 1989–91, Dir Capital Market Dept 1989–91; Dir State Property Agency 1990–91; Chair. Budapest Stock Exchange 1990–95; Chair. and CEO Budapest Bank 1991–95; Chair. Budapest Stock Exchange in early 1990s; Minister of Finance 1995–96; Sr Adviser, Financial Sector Devt, IBRD 1996–97, Dir Pvt. and Financial Sector Devt, ECA 1997–99, Dir Financial Advisory Services, Europe and Cen. Asia 1999–2004; Prof. of Econs and Public Policy, Cen. European Univ. 2004–, also Sr Vice-Pres. for Research and Int. Projects and COO; Chief Econ. Adviser to Prime Minister of Croatia 2002–, to Deputy Prime Minister of Poland 2001–; MEP 2009–, mem. Cttee on Budgets, Del. for relations with Albania, Bosnia and Herzegovina, Serbia, Montenegro and Kosovo; f. Modern Magyarország Mozgalom (Modern Hungary Movement) political party 2013; mem. Bd of Dirs State Property Agency 1990–91. *Publications:* Development Commodity Production, Market Economy 1984, Market and Money in the Modern Economy

1985, Public Finance Reform during Transition – The Experience of Hungary (co-author) 1998, Visegrad Twins' Diverging Path to Relative Prosperity 2000, Financial Transition in Europe and Central Asia – The World Bank (co-author) 2001, Competition and Solidarity – Comparative Economic Studies 2004. *Address:* European Parliament, 60, rue Wiertz, 1047 Brussels, Belgium (office). *Telephone:* (2) 284-57-07 (office). *Fax:* (2) 284-97-07 (office). *E-mail:* lajos.bokros@europarl.europa.eu (office). *Website:* www.europarl.europa.eu (office).

BOKSENBERG, Alexander, CBE, PhD, FRS, FInstP, FRAS; British astronomer and academic; b. 18 March 1936; s. of Julius Boksenberg and Ernestina Steinberg; m. Adella Coren 1960; one s. one d.; ed Stationers' Co.'s School, Univ. of London, Univ. of Cambridge; SRC Research Asst, Dept of Physics and Astronomy, Univ. Coll. London 1960–65, Lecturer in Physics 1965–75, Head of Optical and Ultraviolet Astronomy Research Group 1969–81, Reader in Physics 1975–78, SRC Sr Fellow 1976–81, Prof. of Physics and Astronomy 1978–81; Sherman Fairchild Distinguished Scholar, Calif. Inst. of Tech. 1981–82; Dir Royal Greenwich Observatory 1981–93, Royal Observatories (Royal Greenwich Observatory, Royal Observatory, Edin., Isaac Newton Group of Optical Telescopes, Canary Islands, Jt Astronomy Centre, Hawaii) 1993–96; apptd Hon. Prof. of Experimental Astronomy, Univ. of Cambridge 1991; Research Prof. Inst. of Astronomy Univ. of Cambridge and PPARC Sr Research Fellow, Univs of Cambridge and London 1996–99; Extraordinary Fellow, Churchill Coll., Cambridge 1996, mem. Council 1998–2003; Visiting Prof., Dept of Physics and Astronomy, Univ. Coll. London 1981–, Astronomy Centre, Univ. of Sussex 1981–89; Exec. Ed. Experimental Astronomy 1995–; Hon. Pres. Astronomical Soc. of Glasgow 1995; Chair. New Industrial Concepts Ltd 1969–81; Pres. West London Astronomical Soc. 1978–; Chair. SRC Astronomy Cttee 1980–81; mem. ESA Hubble Space Telescope Instrument Definition Team 1973–95, S African Astronomical Observatory Advisory Cttee 1978–85, British Council Science Advisory Cttee 1987–91, Anglo-Australian Telescope Bd 1989–91 (Deputy Chair. 1991–92), Max Planck Institut für Astronomie Advisory Cttee 1991–95, European Southern Observatory Vis. Cttee 1993–95, Council and Trustee Royal Soc. 1995–97 (Technical Steering Group 1997–98, Chair. Int. Exchanges Far East Panel 2000), Int. Astronomical Union Finance Cttee 1997–2000, UK-Japan N+N Bd on Cooperation in Astronomy 1997, PPARC VISTA Review Bd 1999–2000, Foundation Cttee UK Nat. Comm. for UNESCO (Chair. Science Cttee 2000–03, mem. Council 2000–03, Chair. Steering Cttee UK Nat. Comm. for UNESCO Campaign Group 2003–04; Fellow, Royal Soc. 1978–, Univ. Coll. London 1991–; Asteroid (3205) named Boksenberg 1988; 37th Herstmonceux Conf. The Hubble Space Telescope and the High Redshift Universe in honour of Alec Boksenberg 1996; lecture tours: Royal Soc./Russian Acad. of Sciences 1989, Royal Soc./Chinese Acad. of Sciences 1995, British Council India 1999 and Royal Soc./Japan Acad. 1999; Freeman Clockmakers Co. 1984; Liveryman 1989; Dr hc (l'Observatoire de Paris) 1982; Hon. DSc (Sussex) 1991; Hannah Jackson Medal and Gift 1998, Royal Soc. Hughes Medal 1999, Glazebrook Medal and Prize 2000. *Publications:* Modern Technology and its Influence on Astronomy 1990 (ed.); 220 contribs to learned journals. *Leisure interest:* skiing. *Address:* c/o University of Cambridge, Institute of Astronomy, The Observatories, Madingley Road, Cambridge, CB3 0HA, England (office). *Telephone:* (1223) 339909 (office). *Fax:* (1223) 339910 (office). *E-mail:* boksy@ast.cam.ac.uk (office). *Website:* www.ast.cam.ac.uk/IoA (office).

BOLAÑOS GEYER, Enrique; Nicaraguan business executive and fmr head of state; b. 13 May 1928, Masaya, nr Managua; s. of Nicolás Bolaños Cortés and Amanda Geyer; m. Lila T. Abaunza 1949 (deceased); four s. (three deceased) one d.; ed Colegio Centro-América, Granada, St Louis Univ., USA, Instituto Centroamericano de Administración de Empresas; worked as farmer 1952–59; Gen. Man. Fábrica de Calzados Lorena SA, Masaya 1956–59; Spanish teacher, Berlitz School of Languages, St Louis, Mo., USA 1960–62; Gen. Man. Cía. Leonesa de Productos Lácteos SA, León 1962–64; Chair. Bd Impresora Serigráfica SA, Managua 1967–73; Founder and Chair. numerous cos in Grupo Bolaños-SAIMSA; Head of COSEP (pvt. business asscn) 1979–90; Vice-Pres. of Nicaragua 1997–2000; Pres. of Nicaragua 2002–06; f. Fundación Enrique Bolaños; fmr Pres. Asoc. de Algodoneros de Oriente; fmr Dir Unión de Productores Agropecuarios de Nicaragua, Cámara de Industrias de Nicaragua; fmr mem. Partido Liberal Constitucionalista (PLC); mem. Alianza por la República 2004–; Hon. mem. Int. Raoul Wallenberg Foundation; Rubén Darío Medal, Cardinal Mindszenty Foundation Freedom Award, Democracy Service Medal, Nat. Endowment for Democracy 2003. *E-mail:* info@enriquebolanos.org. *Website:* www.enriquebolanos.org.

BOLAÑOS WEISS, Meisi, LLB; Cuban politician; *Minister of Finance and Prices;* b. 1971; ed Univ. of Havana; Legal Dir, Ministry of Finance and Prices 2005–07, Deputy Minister of Finance and Prices 2007–19, Minister of Finance and Prices 2019–. *Address:* Ministry of Finance and Prices, Calle Empredrado 302, esq. Aguiar, Habana Vieja, Havana, Cuba (office). *Telephone:* (7) 867-1800 (office). *Website:* www.mfp.gob.cu (office).

BOLAÑOS ZAMORA, Rodrigo Alberto, MA, PhD; Costa Rican economist and central banker; b. 29 Dec. 1950; m.; ed Instituto Tecnologico Autonomo de México, Univ. of Chicago, USA; Sec., Ministry of Finance 1984–85, Minister of Finance 1989–90; various man. roles at Banco Central de Costa Rica 1985–86, Gov. 1995–98, 2010–14; Pres. Bolsa Nacional de Valores (stock exchange) 1986–89, 1990–95; Exec. Pres. Fondo Latinoamericano de Reservas 2008–10; sr positions with IDB and Inter-American Investment Co. (Corporación Interamericana de Inversiones); Partner, Ecoanálisis (consultancy); fmr consultant for several int. orgs including USAID, World Bank, IDB and UN.

BOLD, Luvsanvandangiin; Mongolian economist and politician; b. 1961, Ulaanbaatar; ed Trade Union Univ. Bernau, Berlin; Instructor, Central Council of Mongolian Trade Unions 1983–89; Vice-Chair. and Sec.-Gen. Mongolian Students' Asscn 1989–90; mem. and Deputy of the People's Great Hural of Mongolia State Baga Hural (Parl.) 1990–92; Chair. Centre of Youth and Students of Mongol Origin 1992–93; Pres. Bodi International Group 1993–96; mem. Parl. 1996–2000, 2008–; Chair. Mongolia-Germany Business Council 1997–2010, Mineral Resources and Petroleum Authority of Mongolia 2004–08, Golomt Bank 2000–04; Minister of Defence 2008–11, of External Relations 2012–14; Pres. Asscn of Mongolian Banks 2000–05; mem. Mongolian Social-Democratic Party; Pres. Mongolian Athletes Fed. 2005–; Polar Star Order 2005, Bundesverdienstkreuz 2006, Order of the Red Banner of Labour 2009, Order of Mil. Merit 2011; Resolution of Recognition, Missouri House of Reps (USA) 2007. *Address:* c/o Ministry of Foreign Affairs, Enkhtaivny Örgön Chölöö 7A, Sükhbaatar District, Ulaanbaatar, Mongolia. *E-mail:* info@mfa.gov.mn.

BOLDON, Ato; Trinidad and Tobago athlete (retd) and politician; b. 30 Dec. 1973, Port of Spain; m. Cassandra Mills 1998 (divorced 2005); two d.; ed Univ. of California, Los Angeles; resident in USA since 1988; coached by John Smith; Cen. American and Caribbean record-holder at 60m indoors (6.49 seconds), 100m (9.86 seconds) and 200m (19.77 seconds); gold medal World Jr Championships 100m and 200m 1992; fourth Commonwealth Games 100m 1994; bronze medal World Championships 100m 1995; gold medal NCAA Championships 100m 1996; bronze medals Olympic Games 100m and 200m 1996; 100m World Champion 1997, 1999; gold medal World Championships 200m 1997; gold medal Goodwill Games, New York 200m 1998; gold medal Commonwealth Games 100m 1998; silver medal Olympic Games 100m 2000, bronze medal 200m; youngest sprinter ever to run under 10 seconds in the 100m and under 20 seconds in the 200m; Sprint Analyst NCAA Championships, CBS Sports 2005–2009; mem. Senate, Trinidad and Tobago 2006–07; global ambassador, IAAF 2013–; coach to Khalifa St Fort 2015–. *Television:* Once in a Lifetime: Boldon in Bahrain (writer, producer, director) 2006. *Website:* www.atoboldon.com (office).

BOLDRINI, Laura; Italian broadcast journalist, international organization official and politician; *President of the Chamber of Deputies;* b. 28 April 1961, Macerata, Marche; one d.; ed Univ. 'La Sapienza'; worked at RAI (Italian public service broadcasting corpn) for both TV and radio 1985–89; with UN Agencies 1989–93, Spokesman for Italy, FAO and WFP 1993–98, Spokesperson for UN High Commr for Refugees for Southern Europe, mainly dealing with migratory flows in the Mediterranean 1998–2013; mem. (ind. cand. in Left Ecology Freedom party list), Camera dei Deputati (Parl.) for Second Electoral Dist of Sicily Feb. 2013–, Pres. March 2013–; Kt, Order of Merit 2004; Primadonna, Montecassiano 2008; Official Medal, Nat. Comm. for equality and equal opportunities between men and women 1999, Premio Consorte, Pres. of the Repub. 2006, Journalism Prize for Lifetime Achievement of the Year, Addetto Stampa dell'Anno del Consiglio Nazionale Ordine Giornalisti 2009, named by Famiglia Cristiana weekly as Italian of the Year 2009, Renato Benedetto Fabrizi Award, Associazione Nazionale Partigiani d'Italia 2011. *Publications include:* Tutti indietro: storie di uomini e donne in fuga e di un'Italia tra paura e solidarietà nel racconto della portavoce dell'Alto Commissariato Onu per i Rifugiati 2010, Solo le montagne non si incontrano mai. Storia di Murayo e dei suoi due padri 2013; has written articles for several magazines and blogs on websites of La Repubblica newspaper and The Huffington Post Italy. *Address:* Office of the President, Camera dei Deputati, Palazzo di Montecitorio, Piazza Montecitorio, 00186 Rome, Italy (office). *Telephone:* (06) 67601 (office). *E-mail:* dlwebmast@camera.it (office). *Website:* presidente.camera.it (office); www.lauraboldrini.it.

BOLDUC, Kim, MA; Canadian UN official; *Deputy Special Representative for United Nations Stabilization Mission in Democratic Republic of Congo;* b. 1952, Viet Nam; m.; one s.; ed Univ. of Ottawa, Univ. of Geneva, Switzerland; early career with Canadian International Development Agency; joined UN 1987, has held various field appointments with UN Office for Emergency Operations in Africa, delegate for Office of UN Disaster Relief Coordinator in Mozambique; served in Ecuador 1992–97 and as UN Devt Programme (UNDP) Resident Coordinator and Resident Rep. in Peru 1997–2002, Special Adviser to UN Humanitarian Coordinator for Iraq, as well as Area Humanitarian Coordinator for Southern Iraq 2003; UNDP Resident Coordinator and Resident Rep. in Honduras 2004–06, in Brazil 2006–09, in Panama 2010–14, Deputy Special Rep. of Sec.-Gen. and Humanitarian Coordinator, UN Stabilization Mission Haiti (MINUSTAH) 2009–10, Special Rep. for Western Sahara and Head of UN Mission for Referendum in Western Sahara (MINURSO) 2014–17, Deputy Special Rep. for UN Stabilization Mission in Democratic Repub. of Congo (MONUSCO) 2017–, concurrently Resident Coordinator, Humanitarian Coordinator and Resident Rep., UNDP. *Address:* Department of Peacekeeping Operations, MONUSCO, Room S-3727B, United Nations, New York, NY 10017, USA (office). *Telephone:* (212) 963-8077 (office). *Fax:* (212) 963-9222 (office). *Website:* www.un.org/en/peacekeeping (office); monusco.unmissions.org (office).

BOLDYREV, Yuri Yuryevich; Russian politician; b. 29 May 1960, Leningrad; m. 1990; one s.; ed Leningrad Electrotech. Inst., Leningrad Inst. of Finance and Econs; worked as engineer at Cen. Research Inst. of Vessel Electronics and Tech. 1983–89; mem. CPSU 1987–90; USSR People's Deputy 1989–91; mem. del. of 28 CPSU Congress; left CPSU 1990; mem. Council of Reps, then of Co-ordination Council of Democratic Russia Movt 1990–91; mem. Higher Advisory Council to Chair. of Russian Supreme Soviet (later to Pres. of Russian Fed.) 1990–92; consultant, Russian Govt Feb.–March 1992; Chief State Inspector of Russian Fed., Chief Control Man. of Admin. of Presidency 1992–93; mem. Centre of Econ. and Political Research (Epicentre) 1993–94; mem. Duma (Parl.) 1993–95; Founder-mem. and Deputy Chair. Yabloko Movt 1993–95, left Party Sept. 1995; Deputy Chair. Accountant Chamber of Russian Fed. 1995–2001; Head of St Petersburg electoral cands, Spravedlivaya Rossiya party (Fair Russia) 2007; mem. Organising Cttee Moscow Econ. Forum 2013–; Bunin Literary Prize 2016. *Publications:* The Russian Miracle: The Secrets of Economic Backwardness 2003, The Chronicle of a Turbid Time (series) 2009–12; contrib. to various newspapers. *Website:* yuriboldyrev.ru.

BOLGER, Dermot; Irish writer, dramatist and poet; b. 6 Feb. 1959, Finglas, Dublin; s. of Roger Bolger and Bridie Flanagan; m. Bernadette Clifton 1988 (died 2010); two s.; ed St Canice's BNS, Finglas and Benevin Coll., Finglas; worked as factory hand, library asst and professional author; Founder and Ed. Raven Arts Press 1979–92; Founder and Exec. Ed. New Island Books, Dublin 1992–; mem. Arts Council of Ireland 1989–93; elected mem. Aosdána 1991–; Playwright in Asscn, The Abbey (Nat.) Theatre 1997; Writer Fellow, Trinity Coll., Dublin 2003; Writer-in-Residence, Farmleigh House, Dublin 2008, Nat. Museum of Ireland, Collins Barracks 2016; A.E. Memorial Prize 1986, Macauley Fellowship 1987, A.Z. Whitehead Prize 1987, Samuel Beckett Award 1991, Edinburgh Fringe First Awards 1991, 1995, Stewart Parker BBC Award 1991, The Hennessy Irish Literature Hall of Fame Award 2003, Irish Times/EBS Prize for Best New Irish Play of 2004, Worldplay Int. Radio Prize for Best Script 2005, Irish Newspapers Commentator of the Year 2012. *Plays include:* The Lament for Arthur Cleary 1989,

Blinded by the Light 1990, In High Germany 1990, The Holy Ground 1990, One Last White Horse 1991, A Dublin Bloom 1994, April Bright 1995, The Passion of Jerome 1999, Consenting Adults 2000, From These Green Heights 2004, The Townlands of Brazil 2006, Walking the Road 2007, The Consequences of Lightning 2008, The Parting Glass 2010, Tea Chests & Dreams 2012, Ulysses—A Stage Version of Joyce's Novel 2012, Bang Bang and Other Dublin Monologues 2017, Last Orders at the Dockside 2019. *Radio:* The Woman's Daughter 2005, Hunger Again 2006, The Fortunestown Kid 2006, The Night Manager 2007, The Kerlogue 2007, Moving In Day 2008, Accident & Emergency 2010, Outline Permission 2012, The Venice Suite 2013, Walking the Road 2014. *Television screenplay:* Edward No Hands 1996. *Publications include:* novels: Night Shift 1985, The Woman's Daughter 1987, The Journey Home 1990, Emily's Shoes 1992, A Second Life 1994, Father's Music 1997, Finbar's Hotel (co-author) 1997, Ladies Night at Finbar's Hotel (co-author) 1999, Temptation 2000, The Valparaiso Voyage 2001, The Family on Paradise Pier 2005, A Second Life: A Renewed Novel 2010, New Town Soul 2010, The Fall of Ireland 2012, Tanglewood 2015, The Lonely Sea and Sky 2016, An Ark of Light 2018; poetry: The Habit of Flesh 1979, Finglas Lilies 1980, No Waiting America 1981, Internal Exile 1986, Leinster Street Ghosts 1989, Taking My Letters Back, New and Selected Poems 1998, The Chosen Moment 2004, External Affairs 2008, The Venice Suite – A Voyage through Loss 2012, That Which is Suddenly Precious: New & Selected Poems 2015; Ed.: The Dolmen Book of Irish Christmas Stories 1986, The Bright Wave: Poetry in Irish Now 1986, 16 on 16: Irish Writers on the Easter Rising 1988, Invisible Cities: The New Dubliners: A Journey through Unofficial Dublin 1988, Invisible Dublin: A Journey through its Writers 1992, The Picador Book of Contemporary Irish Fiction 1993, 12 Bar Blues (with Aidan Murphy) 1993, The New Picador Book of Contemporary Irish Fiction 2000, Druids, Dudes and Beauty Queens: The Changing Face of Irish Theatre 2001, The Hennessy Book of Irish Fiction (with Ciaran Carty) 2005, The New Hennessy Book of Irish Fiction (with Ciaran Carty) 2005, The Hennessy Book of Irish Fiction (with Ciaran Carty) 2005–15, Ledwidge Treasury 2007, Night & Day: 24 Hours in the Life of Dublin 2008, Selected Poems of Francis Ledwidge 2017 (Ed.). *Leisure interests:* soccer, golf. *Address:* New Island Books, 6 Priory Office Park, Stillorgan, Dublin, Ireland (office). *Telephone:* (1) 2784225 (office). *E-mail:* info@newisland.ie (office). *Website:* www.newisland.ie (office); www.dermotbolger.com (office).

BOLGER, James Brendan, PC, ONZ; New Zealand politician, diplomatist and business executive; b. 31 May 1935, Taranaki; s. of Daniel Bolger and Cecilia Bolger (née Doyle); m. Joan Maureen Riddell 1963; six s. three d.; ed Opunake High School; farmer of sheep and beef cattle, Te Kuiti 1965–72; mem. Parl. 1972–98; Parl. Under-Sec. to Minister of Agric. and Fisheries, Minister of Maori Affairs, Minister in Charge of Rural Banking and Finance Corpn 1975–77, Minister of Fisheries and Assoc. Minister of Agric. 1977–78, Minister of Labour 1978–84, of Immigration 1978–81, Prime Minister of New Zealand and Minister in Charge of Security Intelligence Service 1990–97; Leader Nat. Party 1986–98; Leader of the Opposition 1986–90; Amb. to USA 1998–2002; Pres. ILO 1983, New Zealand/US Council; Chair. Kiwibank 2001–10, New Zealand Post Ltd 2002–10, Ian Axford Foundation 2002–, Gas Industry Company and Trustees Executors Ltd 2004–, Mount Cook Alpine Salmon Ltd; Chair. Advisory Bd World Agricultural Forum 2002–; Chancellor, Waikato Univ. 2007–; mem. Bd of Dirs New Zealand Trade Liberalisation Network Inc.; mem. Collegium Int.; Trustee, Rutherford Trust; Patron Inst. of Rural Health 2004–; Founding Patron New Zealand United World Coll. Trust 2007–, NZ Business Excellence; Distinguished Fellow, New Zealand Inst. of Dirs 2011; Hon. DSc (Khon Kaen Univ., Thailand) 1994; Hon. DLitt (Massey Univ.) 2002; Queen's Silver Jubilee Medal 1977, NZ Commemoration Medal 1990, NZ Suffrage Centennial Medal 1993. *Publication:* A View from the Top (political autobiog.). *Leisure interests:* hiking, reading, politics. *Address:* Sommeville Road, PO Box 406, Te Kuiti, New Zealand (home). *Telephone:* (7) 8786-213 (home). *Fax:* (7) 8786-215 (home).

BOLKESTEIN, Frederik (Frits), MPh, LLM; Dutch fmr politician; b. 1933; m.; three c.; ed Oregon State Univ., Gemeentelijke Univ. Amsterdam, Univ. of London, UK, Univ. of Leiden; with Shell Group 1960–76; Dir Shell Chimie, Paris 1973–76; mem. of Parl. for VVD (Liberals) 1978–82, 1986–88, 1989–99; Minister for Foreign Trade 1982–86; Chair. Atlantic Comm., Netherlands 1986–88; Minister of Defence 1988–89; Chair. VVD Parl. Group 1990–98; Pres. Liberal Internationale 1996–99; EU Commr for Internal Market, Financial Services, Customs and Taxation 1999–2004; apptd Pres. TeldersStichting (Telders Foundation) (VVD think-tank) 2004; mem. Supervisory Bd Central Bank of The Netherlands; mem. Bd of Dirs Air France-KLM; mem. Royal Inst. of Int. Affairs. *Play:* Floris Count of Holland. *Publications include:* Floris, Count of Holland 1976, Modern Liberalism 1982, De Engel en het Beest 1990, Woorden hebben hun betekenis 1992, Islam en Democratie 1994, Het Heft in Handen 1995, Moslim in de Polder 1997, Boren in hard Hout 1998, De Grenzen van Europa 2004, Grensverkenningen 2005, De twee lampen van de staatsman 2006, Overmoed en onverstand 2008, De politiek der dingen 2009, De Goede Vreemdeling 2011, Cassandra tegen wil en dank 2013. *Leisure interest:* tennis. *Address:* TeldersStichting, Koninginnegracht 55a, 2514 AE The Hague, Netherlands (office). *E-mail:* info@teldersstichting.nl (office). *Website:* www.teldersstichting.nl (office); www.fritsbolkestein.com.

BOLKIAH, HRH Crown Prince, Haji al-Muhtadee Billah; Brunei; b. 17 Feb. 1974, Istana Darul Hana, Bandar Seri Begawan; s. of HM Sultan Haji Hassanal Bolkiah Mu'izuddin Waddaulah and HM Raja Isteri Pengiran Anak Hajah Saleha; m. HRH Pengiran Anak Isteri Pengiran Anak Sarah binti Pengiran Salleh Ab Rahaman 2004; two s. one d.; ed Univ. of Brunei Darussalam, Oxford Centre for Islamic Studies, England; proclaimed Crown Prince 10 Aug. 1998; attachments to various govt ministries and depts, and to private cos; Gen., Royal Brunei Armed Forces; Deputy Inspector Gen., Royal Brunei Police Force; Sr Minister at the Prime Minister's Office; Chair. Autoriti Monetari Brunei Darussalam (AMBD—Monetary Authority of Brunei Darussalam); Hon. GCVO 1998. *Address:* Autoriti Monetari Brunei Darussalam, Ministry of Finance Building, Tingkat 14, Commonwealth Drive, Bandar Seri Begawan, BB 3910, Brunei (office). *Telephone:* 2384626 (office). *Fax:* 2383787 (office). *E-mail:* info@ambd.gov.bn. *Website:* www.ambd.gov.bn; www.crownprince.bn.

BOLKIAH, HRH Prince Haji Mohamed; Brunei politician; b. 27 Aug. 1947; s. of Sultan Haji Omar Ali Saifuddien Sa'adul Khairi Waddien (28th Sultan of Brunei) and Suri Seri Begawan Raja Isteri Pengiran Anak Damit; brother of Sultan Haji Hassanal Bolkiah Mu'izuddin Waddaulah of Brunei; m. Pengiran Anak Isteri Pengiran Anak Hajah Zariah; 10 c.; ed Royal Mil. Acad., Sandhurst, UK; Minister of Foreign Affairs 1984–2015; Chief Vizier (Perdana Wazir) in the Royal Court. *Address:* Hijau Baiduri, Bukit Kayangan, Jalan Tutong, Bandar Seri Begawan BD 2710, Brunei (home).

BOLKIAH, HRH Prince Haji Jefri; Brunei politician; b. 6 Nov. 1954; s. of Sultan Haji Omar Ali Saifuddien Saadul Khairi Waddien and HM Raja Isteri Pengiran Anak Damit; brother of Sultan Haji Hassanal Bolkiah Mu'izuddin Waddaulah of Brunei; m.; 18 c.; fmrly Minister of Culture, Youth and Sports, Deputy Minister of Finance; Minister of Finance 1988–97; fmr Chair. Royal Brunei Airlines, Brunei Investment Agency; fmr Propr Asprey & Garrad.

BOLKIAH MU'IZUDDIN WADDAULAH, HM Sultan and Yang di-Pertuan of Brunei Darussalam, Haji Hassanal, DK, PSPNB, PSLI, SPBM, PANB; head of state; *Head of State, Prime Minister, Minister of Defence, Minister of Finance and Minister of Foreign Affairs;* b. 15 July 1946, Brunei Town (now called Bandar Seri Begawan); s. of Sultan Haji Omar 'Ali Saifuddien Sa'adul Khairi Waddien, KCMG AND PENGIRAN RAJA ISTERI PENGIRAN ANAK DAMIT; m. HM Raja Isteri Pengiran Anak Hajah Saleha 1965; two s. (including HRH Prince Haji al-Muhtadee Billah) four d.; also m. Mariam Abd Aziz 1981 (divorced 2003); two s. two d.; also m. HRH Pengiran Isteri Azrinaz Mazhar Hakim 2005 (divorced 2010); one s. one d.; ed privately and Victoria Inst., Kuala Lumpur, Malaysia and Royal Mil. Acad., Sandhurst, UK; appointed Crown Prince and Heir Apparent 1961; Ruler of State of Brunei Oct. 1967–; Prime Minister of Brunei Jan. 1984–, Minister of Finance and Home Affairs 1984–86, also of Finance 1984–, of Defence 1986–, of Foreign Affairs 2015–; Sovereign and Chief of Royal Orders instituted by Sultans of Brunei; Head of Dept of Islamic Religious Faith and Royal Custom and Tradition; est. the Sultan Haji Hassanal Bolkiah Foundation; Hon. Gen. of the British Army 1984; Hon. Air Marshal, RAF 1992; Hon. Patron World Org. of the Scout Movt 1993; Hon. Adm. of the RN 2001; Hon. Col, Special Service Group (Pakistan) 2004; Hon. mem. Indonesian Satgas Atbara Special Operations Unit 2008; Royal Family Order of the Crown of Brunei; Order of the Crown of the Realm (Malaysia) 1980; Hon. CMG 1968, Hon. GCMG 1972, Hon. GCB 1992; Collar of the Order of the Nile (Egypt) 1984, Adipurna (or First Class) of the Star of the Repub. of Indonesia 1984, Collar of the Supreme Order of the Chrysanthemum (Japan) 1984, Order of al-Hussein bin Ali (Jordan) 1984, The Civil Order of Oman, First Class (Oman) 1984, Grand Order of Mugunghwa (South Korea) 1984, Order of Khalifa (Bahrain) 1988, Collar of the Order of Muhammad (Morocco) 1988, Raja of the Order of Sikatuna (Philippines) 1988, Order of Rajamitrabhorn (Thailand) 1988, First Class of the Order of Temasek (Singapore) 1990, Mil. Distinguished Service Order (Singapore) 1990, Order of the Netherlands Lion, Nishan-e-Pakistan 1992, Grand Croix, Légion d'honneur 1996, Grand Cross, Special Class of the Order of Merit of the FRG 1998, Punong Komandante (Chief Commdr) of the Philippine Legion of Honour 1998, Collar of the Order of Badr Chain (Saudi Arabia) 1999, Kt, Royal Order of the Seraphim (Sweden) 2004, Phoxay Lane Xang (Laos) 2004, Order of Prince Yaroslav the Wise, 1st Class (Ukraine) 2004 and Cross of Honour 2007, Order of the Netherlands Lion 2013, Collar of the Order of Mubarak the Great (Kuwait) 2015; Hon. DLitt (Univ. of Brunei Darussalam) 1989; Hon. LLD (Univ. of Malaya) 1992, (Univ. of Aberdeen) 1995, (Univ. of Queensland) 2001, (Univ. of the Philippines) 2003, (Nat. Univ. of Singapore) 2005; Hon. DCL by Diploma (Univ. of Oxford) 1992; Hon. PhD (Nat. Univ. of Malaysia) 1997; Hon. Dr of Political Science (Int. Islamic Univ., Malaysia) 2001, (Chulalongkorn Univ., Thailand) 2002; Hon. Dr of Int. Relations (Beijing Foreign Studies Univ.) 2001; Hon. Dr of Humanities and Culture (Gadjah Mada Univ., Indonesia) 2003; Dr hc (Kyiv Polytechnic Inst.) 2004, (Moscow State Inst. of Int. Relations) 2005; Hon. Dr of Philosophy and Humanities (Universitas Indonesia) 2011; Peace Award, Foundation for Peace Together (Italy) 1989, Pres.'s Gold Medal Award, Royal Coll. of Surgeons of Edinburgh 2000, first Companion of the Coll., Royal Coll. of Gen. Practitioners (UK) (cr. in his honour) 2013. *Leisure interests:* collecting automobiles, playing polo, golf and badminton, race car driving, piloting helicopters and aircraft. *Address:* Istana Nurul Iman, Bandar Seri Begawan, BA 1000, Brunei (office). *Telephone:* (2) 229988 (office). *Fax:* (2) 241717 (office). *E-mail:* info@jpm.gov.bn (office). *Website:* www.pmo.gov.bn (office).

BOLLAÍN, Icíar; Spanish actress and screenwriter; b. (María Icíar Bollaín Pérez-Mínguez), 12 June 1967, Madrid; two c.; film debut in El Sur (The South) 1983; Pnr, La Iguana (film production co.) 1991–; writer and dir of feature film Hola, ¿estás sola? (Best New Dir Award and Audience Award, Valladolid Int. Film Festival) 1995; Founding mem. Asscn of Women of Audiovisual, CIMA. *Film appearances include:* El Sur 1983, Al acecho 1987, Malaventura 1988, Sublet 1991, Un Paraguas para tres 1992, Entretiempo 1992, Dime una mentira 1993, Jardines colgantes 1993, Land and Freedom 1995, El techo del mundo (Silver Precolumbian Circle, Bogota Film Festival 1999, Golden Wave for Best Screenplay, Bordeaux Int. Festival of Women in Cinema 1999, Mercedes-Benz Award, Cannes Film Festival 1999) 1995, Subjudice 1998, Leo 2000, La balsa de piedra (The Stone Raft) 2002, Nos miran 2002, La Noche del hermano 2005. *Films written include:* Los amigos del muerto 1993, Hola, ¿estás sola? 1995, Flores de otro mundo (co-written with Julio Llamazares, Best Film in Int. Critics' Week, Cannes Film Festival) 1999, Amores que matan 2000, Poniente 2000, Te doy mis ojos (Best Dir, ADIRCAE Award 2004, Cinema Writers Circle Award for Best Screenplay, Original 2004, Grand Prix, Audience Award for Best Feature Film, Créteil Int. Women's Film Festival 2004) 2003. *Films directed include:* Baja corazón 1992, Los amigos del muerto 1993, Hola, ¿estás sola? 1995, Flores de otro mundo (co-written with Julio Llamazares, Best Film in Int. Critics' Week, Cannes Film Festival) 1999, Amores que matan 2000, Te doy mis ojos 2003, Hay motivo 2004, Mataharis (also screenwriter) 2007, Even the Rain (Cinema Writers Circle Award for Best Film 2011, Best Latin-American Film, Ariel Awards 2011, Panorama Audience Award for Fiction Film 2011) 2010, Katmandú, un espejo en el cielo (also screenwriter) 2011, The Olive Tree 2016, Yuli 2018. *Publication:* Ken Loach, un observador solitario 1996. *Address:* Producciones La Iguana S.L., Jardín de San Federico, 15–1D, 28009 Madrid, Spain (office). *Telephone:* (91) 4010254 (office). *Fax:* (91) 3095008 (office). *E-mail:* iguana@la-iguana.com (office).

BOLLAND, Marc; Dutch retail executive; *Senior Operating Partner, Portfolio Operations, Blackstone;* b. 28 March 1959, Apeldoorn, Amsterdam; ed Hotelschool,

The Hague, Univ. of Groningen, London Business School, Institut Européen d'Admin des Affaires (INSEAD), France; began at Heineken International NV 1987, worked in numerous int. man. positions across Africa and Cen. Europe before joining the Heineken Bd 2001, COO 2005–06; CEO William Morrison Supermarkets PLC 2006–09; CEO Marks and Spencer Group plc 2009–16; Sr Operating Partner, Portfolio Operations, Blackstone 2016–; mem. Bd of Dirs Coca-Cola Company 2015–, Quilmes, Argentina 2001–03, Hotel de l'Europe, Amsterdam 2003–06, Manpower Inc. 2004–15, Consumer Goods Forum; apptd UK Trade and Investment Business Amb. 2014; mem. Dutch Centre for Trade Devt, American Chamber of Commerce, The Netherlands; Hon. Vice-Pres. UNICEF UK; Dr hc (York St John Univ.) 2011; The Times Businessman of the Year 2008, named as the "most admired business leader" in the UK, Management Today magazine awards 2011. *Address:* The Blackstone Group, 40 Berkeley Square, Mayfair, London, W1J 5AL, England (office). *Telephone:* (20) 7451-4000 (office). *Website:* www.blackstone .com (office).

BOLLARD, Alan, PhD; New Zealand fmr central banker and international organization official; *Executive Director, Asia-Pacific Economic Cooperation Secretariat;* b. 1951, Auckland; s. of Edward (Ted) Bollard; m. Jenny Morel; two s.; ed Univ. of Auckland; Dir New Zealand Inst. of Econ. Research 1987–94; Chair. New Zealand Commerce Comm. 1994–2008; Sec. to the Treasury 1998–2002; Gov. Reserve Bank of New Zealand 2002–12; Exec. Dir APEC Secr. 2013–; served as Alternate Gov. to Asian Development Bank, World Bank Group, IMF; Companion, New Zealand Order of Merit 2013; Dr hc (Univ. of Auckland) 2007, (Massey Univ.) 2012. *Publications include:* Crisis: One Central Bank Governor & the Global Financial Collapse (with Sarah Gaitanos) 2010, The Rough Mechanical 2012, Small Business in New Zealand, The Structure and Dynamics of New Zealand Industries, A Few Hares to Chase: The Economic Life and Times of Bill Phillips 2016. *Address:* APEC Secretariat, 35 Heng Mui Keng Terrace, Singapore 119616, Singapore (office). *Telephone:* 68919600 (office). *Fax:* 68919690 (office). *E-mail:* info@apec.org (office). *Website:* www.apec.org (office).

BOLLIGER, Herbert, Lic. Oec., MBA; Swiss business executive; b. 23 Nov. 1953; m. Beatrice Bolliger; two c.; ed Univ. of Zurich; with Bayer AG, Zurich 1980–83; joined Fed. of Migros Cooperatives 1983, Controller 1983–86, Head of Finance/IT Migros, Berne and mem. Bd of Dirs 1987–94, Head of IT Migros Group 1994–97, Man. Dir Migros Aare 1997–2005, CEO Migros 2005–18, also Chair. Migrosbank AG; Chair. Hotelplan AG; mem. Supervisory Bd METRO AG 2018–; mem. Bd of Dirs BNP Paribas SA 2018–, Magazine zum Globus AG, Migros Beteiligungen AG, Denner AG, Interio AG, Gurten–Park im Grüene, 'Im Grüene' Foundation Rüschlikon; Del. to Nat. Climate Forum, Thun Sept. 2007. *Address:* c/o METRO AG, Metro-Strasse 1, 40235 Düsseldorf, Germany (office). *Website:* www.metroag .de (office).

BOLLING, Claude; French jazz pianist, composer and band leader; b. 10 April 1930, Cannes; s. of Harry Bolling and Geneviève Brannens; m. Irène Dervize-Sadyker 1959; two s.; ed Nice Conservatory, studied with pvt. music teachers, including Bob Colin, Earl Hines, Maurice Duruflé, Willie 'The Lion' Smith, André Hodeir; worked with Dizzy Gillespie, Stéphane Grappelli, Rex Stewart, Roy Eldridge, Sidney Bechet, Albert Nicholas, Lionel Hampton, The Ellingtonians, Carmen McRae, Jo Williams; formed groups Les Parisiennes, Claude Bolling Big Band; Hon. Citizen of Los Angeles; Commdr, Ordre des Arts et des Lettres 2006, Chevalier, Ordre nat. du Mérite, Officier Légion d'honneur 2010; Médaille d'or Maurice Ravel, SACEM Gold Medal and Grand Prix 1984. *Compositions include:* piano solos, duos, trios and all instrumental combinations, including jazz, big band and symphony orchestra; written and recorded with Jean-Pierre Rampal (Suite for Flute), Alexandre Lagoya (Guitar Concerto), Maurice André (Toot Suite), Pinchas Zukerman (Suite for Violin), Yo-Yo Ma (Suite for Cello). *Compositions for film:* more than 100 film soundtrack scores, including Le Jour et l'Heure 1963, Borsalino 1970, Le Magnifique 1973, Flic Story 1975, California Suite 1978, L'Homme en Colère 1979, The Awakening 1980, Willie and Phil 1980, La Mandarine, Le Mur de l'Atlantique, On ne meurt que deux fois 1985, Netchaiev est de retour 1991, Hasards ou coïncidences 1998. *Compositions for television include:* Jazz Memories, Les Brigades du Tigre (series) 1974–83, Chantecler 1977, Claudine à l'école 1978, L'étrange monsieur Duvallier (series) 1979, Georges Dandin 1980, Le calvaire d'un jeune homme impeccable 1981, Panurge 1982, Les Dalton en cavale 1983, Lucky Luke (series) 1984, La garçonne 1988, Renseignements généraux (series) 1989–90, L'amant de ma soeur 1991, Ce que savait Maisie 1995, Antoine 1996, Maintenant ou jamais 1997, Letter from an Unknown Woman 2001. *Leisure interests:* ecology, model railroading. *Address:* CAID Music, 20 avenue de Lorraine, 92380 Garches, France (office). *Telephone:* (1) 47-41-41-84 (office). *Fax:* (1) 47-01-03-63 (office). *E-mail:* bollingclaude@yahoo.fr. *Website:* www.claude-bolling.com (home).

BOLLINGER, Lee Carroll, DJur; American lawyer, academic and university administrator; *President, Columbia University;* b. 30 April 1946, Santa Rosa, Calif.; s. of Lee Bollinger and Patricia Bollinger; m. Jean Magnano Bollinger; one s. one d.; ed Univ. of Oregon, Columbia Univ. Law School; began career as law clerk, US Court of Appeals 1971–72, then US Supreme Court, Washington, DC 1972–73; Faculty mem. Univ. of Michigan Law School 1973–94, Dean 1987–94; Provost and Prof. of Govt, Dartmouth Coll. 1994–96; Pres. Univ. of Michigan 1996–2002; Pres. Columbia Univ. 2002–; Dir Fed. Reserve Bank of New York 2007–12, Chair. 2010–12; mem. Bd of Dirs Washington Post Co. 2007–; mem. Bd Gerald R. Ford Foundation, RSC, Pulitzer Prize; Trustee, Kresge Foundation, Inst. of Int. Educ.; Fellow, American Acad. of Arts and Sciences, American Philosophical Soc.; Clark Kerr Award for Distinguished Leadership in Higher Educ. 2005, Nat. Humanitarian Award, Nat. Equal Justice Award. *Publications include:* The Tolerant Society: Freedom of Speech and Extremist Speech in America 1986, Images of a Free Press 1991, Eternally Vigilant: Free Speech in the Modern Era 2002, Uninhibited, Robust, and Wide Open: A Press for a New Century 2010; numerous books, articles and essays in scholarly journals. *Address:* Office of the President, Columbia University, 535 West 116th Street, 202 Low Library, New York, NY 10027, USA (office). *Telephone:* (212) 854-9970 (office). *Fax:* (212) 854-9973 (office). *E-mail:* officeofthepresident@columbia.edu (office). *Website:* www.columbia.edu/ content/office-president-1.html (office).

BOLLORÉ, Vincent Marie, LLM; French financial investor and industrialist; *Chairman and CEO, Groupe Bolloré;* b. 1 April 1952, Boulogne-Billancourt (Hauts-de-Seine); s. of Michel Bolloré and Monique Bolloré (née Follot); m. Sophie Fossorier 1977; three s. one d.; ed Lycée Janson-de-Sailly, Université Paris X Nanterre; with EIB 1970–75; Deputy Man. Cie financière Rothschild 1976–81; Chair. and CEO Groupe Bolloré and Bolloré Papermills 1981–, Bolloré, Inc., USA 1981–, Banque Rivaud 1996–; mem. Bd of Dirs Banque de France 1988–; mem. Supervisory Bd Vallourec 2004–07; mem. Bd Dirs then Chair. Havas 2005–; mem. Bd of Dirs Natexis Banques Populaires (now Natixis) 2006–, Médiamétrie 2007–, Mediobanca, Financière Moncey, Plantations des Terres Rouges 2008–; mem. Exec. Cttee Conseil nat. du patronat français (CNPF) 1987–96; Chair. Cen. Cttee Armateurs de France 1993–95, Fondation de la deuxième chance 1998; f. Direct8 (TV channel) 2005 (transferred to Groupe Canal+ 2011), DirectSoir (first free evening newspaper in France) 2006; launched Autolib' electric car service in Paris (modelled on Vélib' bike-sharing scheme) 2011, inaugurated BlueIndy in Indianapolis, USA 2014; Chevalier, Légion d'honneur, Grand Officier, Ordre du Lion (Senegal), Légion d'honneur (Côte d'Ivoire); Entrepreneur de l'année 1986, Man. de l'année 1987. *Address:* Groupe Bolloré, Tour Bolloré, 31–32 quai Dion Bouton, 92811 Puteaux (office); Havas, 2 alle de Longchamp, 92281 Suresnes Cedex, France (office). *Telephone:* 1-58-47-90-00 (office). *Fax:* 1-58-47-99-99 (office). *Website:* www.bollore.com (office); www.havas.com (office).

BOLLOYEV, Taimuraz Kazbekovich; Russian/Ossetian business executive; b. 28 Feb. 1953, North Ossetia; m.; one s.; ed Moscow Inst. of Food Industry; mechanic, then Head of Beer Production, Stepan Razin factory, Leningrad 1981–84, becoming Chief Technologist 1987–91; Dir Vsevolzhsk Industrial Plant, Leningrad Region 1984–87; Dir-Gen. Baltika (brewery) 1991–2004, Pres. 1998–2004; Business adviser to Russian Govt 2000–; acquired St Petersburg Clothing Factory and Trud Factory (uniform manufacturer) 2005; est. Real Estate Investment Trust Baltika 2005; Chair. Bd of Dirs, ZAO BTK Group and ZAO Clothes Factory, St Petersburg 2005–; Vice-Pres. Olympstroi Corpn (designer and builder of facilities for 2014 Winter Olympic facilities in Sochi) –2009, Pres. 2009–11 (resgnd); Vice-Chair. Union of Russian Beer and Non-Alcoholic Beverages Producers; mem. Bd, Foundation Centre for Strategic North-West Research; Hon. Consul of Brazil in St Petersburg 2002; Order of Merit for Country (2nd and 4th class) 1995, 2000, Order of Honour 1997, Order of St Sergey Radonezhsky 1998, Kt, Légion d'Honneur (France) 2003; Prize of Govt of Russian Fed. 1997. *Leisure interests:* classical music, football, Russian baths, wrestling, fishing, cooking.

BOLOR, Bayarbaatar; Mongolian politician; b. Chuluut, Arhangay Prov.; m. Bayansan Enkhtsetseg; ed European Union Business School; Foreign Relations Officer, NIK Co. 1997–2000; Gen. Dir, Gardi Tour Co. Ltd 2001–06; Project Coordinator, Tiara Mongolia (tourist resort) 2006–08; Vice-Minister for Foreign Affairs and Trade 2008–12; Pres. Democratic Youth Asscn 2010; mem. State Great Hural (Parl.) of Mongolia 2012–; Minister of Finance 2015–16; mem. Democratic Party. *Address:* c/o Ministry of Finance, Negdsen Ündestnii Gudamj 5/1, Chingeltei District, Ulaanbaatar, Mongolia (office).

BOLSHOV, Leonid Aleksandrovich, DS; Russian physicist; *Scientific Leader, Institute of Nuclear Safety (IBRAE), Russian Academy of Sciences;* b. 23 July 1946, Moscow; m.; three c.; ed Moscow State Univ., Kurchatov Inst.; engineer, Jr then Sr Researcher, later Head of Lab., Moscow Kurchatov Inst. of Atomic Energy (Troisk Br.) 1970–91; Dir Inst. of Nuclear Safety (IBRAE), Russian Acad. of Sciences 1991–2017, Scientific Leader 2017–; participated in mitigation of consequences of Chernobyl nuclear accident 1986; mem. Scientific Council, Ministry of Emergency Affairs; Head of Science and Tech. Council on Safety, Rosatom (State Atomic Energy Corpn); mem. nuclear safety group, Eurobank; mem. Russian Acad. of Sciences 1997, full mem. 2016–; mem. Editorial Bd, Atomnaya Energiya journal; Order of Courage 1997, Order of Honour 2006, Order of Friendship 2013; USSR State Prize 1988, Russian Govt Prize 2014. *Publications include:* over 300 scientific publs and monographs on physics of solid surfaces, non-linear optics, physics of laser thermonuclear synthesis and problems of nuclear power safety. *Address:* Institute of Nuclear Safety (IBRAE), Russian Academy of Sciences, 115191 Moscow, Bolshaya Tulskaya str. 52, Russia (office). *Telephone:* (495) 952-24-21 (office). *Fax:* (495) 958-00-40 (office). *E-mail:* bolshov@ibrae.ac.ru (office). *Website:* www.ibrae.ac.ru (office).

BOLSONARO, Jair Messias; Brazilian politician, fmr military officer and head of state; *President;* b. 21 March 1955, Glicério, São Paulo; s. of Percy Geraldo Bolsonaro and Olinda Bonturi Bolsonaro; m. 1st Rogéria Nantes Braga (divorced), three s.; m. 2nd Ana Cristina Valle (divorced), one s.; m. 3rd Michelle Reinaldo 2007, one d.; ed Agulhas Negras Mil. Acad.; served in army 1973–88; mem. City Council, Rio de Janeiro 1989–91; mem. Chamber of Deputies (lower house of parl.) for Rio de Janeiro 1991–2019; Pres. of Brazil 2019–; mem. Partido Trabalhista Brasileiro (PTB) 2003–05, Partido Progressista (PP) 2005–16, Partido Social Cristão (PSC) 2016–18, Partido Social Liberal (PSL) 2018–; Grand Master, Order of the Southern Cross 2019, Grand Master and Grand Cross, Order of Rio Branco 2019. *Address:* Office of the President, Palácio do Planalto, 3° andar, Praça dos Três Poderes, 70150-900 Brasília, DF, Brazil (office). *Telephone:* (61) 3411-1221 (office). *Fax:* (61) 3411-2222 (home). *E-mail:* protocolo@planalto.gov.br (office). *Website:* www2.planalto.gov.br (office).

BOLT, Usain St Leo, OJ, CD; Jamaican athlete (retd); b. 21 Aug. 1986, Sherwood Content, Trelawny; s. of Wellesley Bolt and Jennifer Bolt; ed William Knibb Memorial High School; holds world records for 100m at 9.58 seconds and 200m at 19.19 seconds, both set at World Championships, Berlin 2009; holds Olympic records for 200m at 19.30 seconds (set at Olympic Games, Beijing 2008), 100m at 9.63 seconds, and as mem. Jamaican team, 4×100m relay at 36.84 seconds (set at Olympic Games, London 2012); first man to win all three events at a single Olympics since Carl Lewis in 1984, and first man in history to set world records in all three at a single Olympics); made first appearance on world stage at Int. Asscn of Athletics Feds (IAAF) World Youth Championships, Debrecen, Hungary 2001 (set new personal best of 21.73 seconds in 200m); moved to Kingston to train with Jamaica Amateur Athletic Asscn at Univ. of Tech.; gold medal, 200m, World Jr Championships (youngest-ever gold medallist), Kingston 2002, 200m, World Youth Championships, Sherbrooke 2003; silver medal, 4×100m and 4×400m relays, World Jr Championships, Kingston 2002; first jr sprinter to run 200m in under 20 seconds with time of 19.93 seconds at CARIFTA Games 2004; turned professional 2004; missed most of his first two seasons due to injuries; eliminated in first round of 200m heats at Athens Olympics 2004; gold medal, Int. Asscn of Athletics Feds (IAAF) World Cup, Athens 2006; beat Don Quarrie's 200m

Jamaican nat. record with time of 19.75 seconds in 2007; set his first 100m world record with time of 9.72 seconds at Reebok Grand Prix, New York City, May 2007; gold medal, 100m and 200m, Olympic Games, Beijing 2008; gold medal, 100m, 200m and 4×100m relay, World Championships, Berlin 2009, Olympic Games, London 2012, World Championships, Moscow 2013, World Championships, Beijing 2015, Olympic Games, Rio de Janeiro 2016; gold medal, World Athletics Final, Thessaloniki 2009; gold medal, 200m and 4×100m relay (set world record time of 37.04 seconds), World Championships, Daegu 2011; silver medal, 200m, World Championships, Osaka 2007; won 100m race in Diamond League in 9.79 seconds 2012; gold medal, 4×100m relay, Commonwealth Games, Glasgow 2014; coached by Glen Mills 2004–; retd 2017; Dr hc (Univ. of the West Indies); IAAF Rising Star Award 2002, 2003, IAAF World Athlete of the Year 2008, 2009, 2011, 2012, 2013, 2016, Track & Field Athlete of the Year 2008, 2009, BBC Overseas Sports Personality of the Year 2008, 2009, 2012, L'Équipe Champion of Champions 2008, 2009, 2012, Jamaica Sportsman of the Year 2008, 2009, 2011, 2012, 2013, Laureus World Sportsman of the Year 2009, 2010, 2013, Marca Leyenda 2009, UNESCO Champion for Sport 2012, ESPY Award 2013. *Publications include:* Usain Bolt; My Story: 9.58 2010. *Leisure interests:* music, dancing, sports, especially cricket and football (fan of Manchester United and Real Madrid). *Website:* www.usainbolt.com.

BOLTANSKI, Christian; French artist; b. 6 Sept. 1944, Paris; s. of Etienne Boltanski and Marie-Elise Ilari-Guérin; m. Annette Messager; participant in numerous group exhbns in Europe, USA, Canada and Australia; Prof. Ecole Nationale Supérieure des Beaux Arts 1986; Grand Prix nat. de la Sculpture 1990, Roland-Preis 1997, Kunstpreis 2001, Goslau Kaiserring Prize, Monchhausmuseum Goslar 2001, Laureate of the Praemium Imperiale, Japan Art Asscn 2006, Créateurs sans frontières Award, Cultures France 2007. *Publications:* L'Album de la Famille B. 1971, Les Compositions Photographiques 1976, Murales 1977. *Address:* 146 boulevard Carmélina, 92240 Malakoff, France. *Telephone:* 1-46-57-63-71. *Website:* www.christian-boltanski.com.

BOLTEN, Joshua (Josh) Brewster, BA, JD; American lawyer, business executive and fmr government official; *President and CEO, Business Roundtable;* b. 16 Aug. 1954, Washington, DC; m. Ann Kelly Bolten 2015; ed Princeton Univ., Stanford Univ. Law School; fmr Ed. Stanford Law Review; law clerk, US Dist Court, San Francisco 1980; Int. Trade Counsel to US Finance Cttee 1985–89, fmr Gen. Counsel to US Trade Rep.; Exec. Dir for Legal and Govt Affairs, Goldman Sachs Int., London 1994–99; Policy Dir Bush-Cheney presidential campaign 1999–2000; Asst to Pres., Deputy Chief of Staff for Policy, The White House 2001–03, Dir Office of Man. and Budget (OMB) 2003–06; White House Chief of Staff 2006–09; Visiting Prof., Woodrow Wilson School of Public and Int. Affairs, Princeton Univ. 2009–11; Co-founder Rock Creek Global Advisors LLC 2011–, Man. Dir 2011–17; Pres. and CEO Business Roundtable 2017–; mem. Bd of Dirs US Holocaust Memorial Museum (Vice-Chair.), ONE Campaign. *Address:* Business Roundtable, 300 New Jersey Avenue, NW Suite 800, Washington, DC 20001, USA (office). *Telephone:* (202) 872-1260 (office). *E-mail:* info@brt.org (office). *Website:* www.businessroundtable.org (office).

BOLTON, John Robert, BA, JD; American lawyer, academic, government official and fmr diplomatist; *National Security Advisor;* b. 20 Nov. 1948, Baltimore, Md; s. of Edward Jackson Bolton and Virginia Bolton (née Godfrey); m. 2nd Gretchen Brainerd 1986; one d.; ed Yale Univ.; Assoc., Covington & Burling (law firm), Washington, DC 1974–81, Pnr 1983–85; Gen. Counsel, USAID 1981–82, Asst Admin. for Program and Policy Coordination 1982–83; Asst Attorney-Gen. for Legis. Affairs, US Dept of Justice 1985–88, Asst Attorney-Gen., Civil Div. 1988–89; Asst Sec. for Int. Org. Affairs, US State Dept 1989–93; Pnr, Lerner, Reed, Bolton & McManus LLP (law firm), Washington, DC 1993–99; Of Counsel, Kutak Rock 1999–2001; Sr Vice-Pres. American Enterprise Inst. for Public Policy Research, Washington, DC 1999–2001, Sr Fellow 2007–; Under-Sec. of State for Arms Control and Int. Security, US State Dept 2001–05; Perm. Rep. to UN, New York (recess appointment) 2005–06; Of Counsel, Kirkland & Ellis (law firm) 2008–; Nat. Security Advisor 2018–; Sr Fellow, Manhattan Inst. 1993; Adjunct Prof., George Mason Univ. Law School 1994–2001; Pres. Nat. Policy Forum 1995–96; mem. US Comm. on Int. Religious Freedom 1999–2001. *Publications:* Surrender is Not an Option: Defending America at the United Nations and Abroad 2008, How Barack Obama is Endangering our National Sovereignty 2010. *Address:* The White House, 1600 Pennsylvania Avenue, NW, Washington, DC 20500, USA (office). *Telephone:* (202) 456-1414 (office). *Fax:* (202) 456-2461 (office). *E-mail:* vice_president@whitehouse.gov (office). *Website:* www.whitehouse.gov (office).

BOLY, Yéro; Burkinabè politician and diplomatist; b. 1954, Komki-Ipala; m.; ed Ecole Nat. d'Admin; subprefect, Dori region 1978–80, Oudalan region 1980; civil servant, Ministry of the Interior 1983; Sec.-Gen. Namentenga Prov. and Prefect, Boulsa region 1983–84; High Commr, Gnagna Prov. 1984–86; Amb. to Côte d'Ivoire 1986–88, to Libya (also accred to Iran 1990–92), 1988–95, Minister for Regional Affairs and Security 1995–2000; Head of Presidential Staff 2000–04; Minister of Defence and War Veterans 2004–11; Amb. to Morocco 2011–15; Grand Officier, Ordre Nat. de Côte d'Ivoire 1988, Officier, Ordre du Mérite 2004, Commdr, Ordre Nat. du Burkina Faso 2004; Médaille d'Honneur des Sapeurs Pompiers 2000, Médaille d'Honneur de la Police Nationale 2005.

BOMBIERI, Enrico, PhD; American (b. Italian) mathematician and academic; *IBM von Neumann Professor Emeritus of Mathematics, Institute for Advanced Study, Princeton University;* b. 26 Nov. 1940, Milan; ed Univ. of Milan, Trinity Coll., Cambridge, UK; Prof. of Math., Univ. of Pisa 1966–73; Prof. of Math., Scuola Normale Superiore, Pisa 1974–; Visiting mem. Inst. for Advanced Study, Princeton, NJ, USA 1977, IBM von Neumann Prof. of Math. 1984–2011, Prof. Emer. 2011–; mem. Exec. Cttee Int. Math. Union 1979–82; mem. Accad. Nazionale dei Quaranta, Rome, Accad. Nazionale dei Lincei, European Acad. of Sciences, Arts and Humanities; Foreign mem. Acad. des Sciences, Paris 1984, Royal Swedish Acad., Academia Europaea, Accad. Nazionale dei XL, Rome; Fellow, NAS, American Acad. of Arts and Sciences; Cavaliere di Gran Croce al Merito della Repubblica 2002; Fields Medal, Int. Congress of Mathematicians, Vancouver 1974, Balzan Int. Prize 1980, Premio Internazionale Pitagora 2006, Joseph Doob Prize, American Math. Soc. 2008, Feltrinelli Prize, King Faisal Int. Prize for Science (with Terence Tao) 2010. *Publications:* Geometric Measure Theory and Minimal Surfaces 1973, Le Grand Crible dans la théorie analytique des nombres (The Large Sieve in Analytic Number Theory) 1974, Seminar on Minimal Submanifolds 1983, An Introduction to Minimal Currents and Parametric Variational Problems 1985, Number Theory, Trace Formulas, and Discrete Groups 1989. *Address:* Simonyi Hall 213, School of Mathematics, Institute for Advanced Study, Einstein Drive, Princeton, NJ 08540, USA (office). *Telephone:* (609) 734-8397 (office). *Fax:* (609) 924-8399 (office). *E-mail:* eb@math.ias.edu (home); gustafss@ias.edu (home). *Website:* www.ias.edu/people/faculty-and-emeriti/bombieri (office).

BON, Michel; French business executive; *Chairman of Supervisory Bd, Devoteam SA;* b. 5 July 1943, Grenoble; s. of Emmanuel Bon and Mathilde Bon (née Aussedat); m. Catherine Brunet de Sairigné; four c.; ed Ecole Supérieure Sciences Economiques et Commerciales, Paris Inst. of Political Studies, Ecole Nationale d'Admin., Stanford Business School; auditor, Ministry of Finance 1971–75; banker, Crédit Nat. 1975–78; joined Crédit Agricole 1978, Head of Commitments, later Deputy CEO 1981–85; Deputy CEO, later CEO and Chair., Carrefour 1985–92; Head Nat. Job Placement Agency 1993–95; Chair. France Télécom 1995–2002; Chair. (non-exec.) Orange (after merger with France Télécom) 2001–02; Chair. Supervisory Bd Editions du Cerf 1997–, Devoteam SA 2006–; Chair. Supervisory Council Ecole Supérieure Sciences Economiques et Commerciales, Inst. Pasteur 2003–05, Institut de l'Entreprise 2001–04; Sr Adviser Roland Berger Strategy Consultants, Vermeer Capital; fmr mem. Advisory Bd Banque de France; Officier, Légion d'honneur; Chevalier du Mérite agricole; Officier, Ordre nat. du Mérite; Man. of the Year 1991, 1992, 1998. *Address:* Devoteam SA, 73 rue Anatole France, 92300, Levallois-Perret (office); 4 avenue de Camoëns, 75116 Paris, France (home). *Telephone:* 1-41-49-48-48 (office); 1-42-88-84-90 (home). *E-mail:* communication@devoteam.com (office); michel.bon@wanadoo.fr. *Website:* www.devoteam.com (office).

BON JOVI, Jon; American singer, songwriter, musician (guitar), record producer and actor; b. (John Francis Bongiovi, Jr), 2 March 1962, Perth Amboy, NJ; m. Dorothea Hurley 1989; three s. one d.; singer in local bands Raze, Atlantic City Expressway; Founder-mem. and lead singer in rock group Bon Jovi 1983–88, 1992–; solo artist 1988–; numerous tours, radio, TV and live appearances worldwide; soundtrack for numerous films; Owner man. co. BJM; Owner record label Jambco; Founder and primary Owner Philadelphia Soul of the Arena Football League 2004–; American Music Awards for Favorite Pop/Rock Band 1988, for Favorite Pop/Rock Single 1991, Nordoff-Robbins Music Therapy Silver Clef 1990, Golden Globe Award for Best Original Song from a Motion Picture (for Blaze of Glory) 1991, BRIT Award for Best Int. Group (with band) 1995, VH-1 Award for Favorite Video (for It's My Life) 2000, Grammy Award for Best Country Collaboration with Vocals (with Jennifer Nettles) 2007, Billboard Music Award for Top Touring Artist 2014. *Films include:* Young Guns II: Blaze of Glory (uncredited) 1990, Moonlight and Valentino (Motion Picture Club Premier Performance Award) 1995, The Leading Man 1996, Little City 1997, Destination Anywhere (video) 1997, No Looking Back 1998, Homegrown 1998, Row Your Boat 1998, U-571 2000, Pay It Forward 2000, Ally McBeal 2001–02, Vampires: Los Muertos 2002, Cry Wolf 2005, Pucked 2006, New Year's Eve 2011. *Television includes:* Unsolved Mysteries 1988, Sex and the City (series) 1999, Ally McBeal (series) 2002. *Recordings include:* albums: with Bon Jovi: Bon Jovi 1984, 7800° Fahrenheit 1985, Slippery When Wet 1986, Bon Jovi Live 1987, New Jersey 1988, Keep The Faith 1991, Cross Road (compilation) 1994, These Days 1995, Crush 2000, One Wild Night 1985–2001 (live) 2001, Tokyo Road: Best of Bon Jovi (compilation) 2001, Bounce 2002, Distance 2003, This Left Feels Right (compilation) 2003, Have a Nice Day 2005, Lost Highway 2007, The Circle 2009, Greatest Hits (compilation) 2010, What About Now 2013, Burning Bridges 2015, This House Is Not For Sale 2016; solo: Young Guns II: Blaze of Glory 1990, Destination Anywhere 1997; box set: 100,000,000 Bon Jovi Fans Can't Be Wrong 2004. *Address:* c/o Bon Jovi Management, PO Box 237040, New York, NY 10023, USA (office). *Telephone:* (212) 336-9413 (office). *Fax:* (212) 336-5385 (office). *Website:* www.bonjovi.com.

BONASSAR, Lawrence, BS, MS, PhD; American biomedical engineer and academic; *Associate Professor and Associate Chairman, Department of Biomedical Engineering, Cornell University;* ed Johns Hopkins Univ., Massachusetts Inst. of Tech.; postdoctoral fellowships in Orthopaedic Research Lab., Massachusetts Gen. Hosp., Center for Biomedical Eng, MIT; mem. Faculty, Center for Tissue Eng, Univ. of Massachusetts Medical School 1998–2003; joined Cornell Univ. 2003, currently Assoc. Prof. and Assoc. Chair., Dept of Biomedical Eng, Dir Search Cttee, Sibley School of Mechanical and Aerospace Eng Strategic Planning Cttee; mem. Editorial Bd, Tissue Engineering; Fellow, American Inst. of Medical and Biological Engineers 2009; Fiona Ip '78 and Donald Li '75 Excellence in Teaching Award, Coll. of Eng, Cornell Univ. 2009, Hansjörg Wyss Research Focus Award, AO Spine International, World Forum for Spine Research 2010, World Technology Award (Health and Medicine) (co-recipient) 2013. *Publications:* numerous papers in professional journals on the regeneration and analysis of musculoskeletal tissues, including bone and cartilage. *Address:* 149 Weill Hall, Department of Biomedical Engineering, Cornell University, Ithaca, NY postcode, USA (office). *Telephone:* (607) 255-9381 (office). *Fax:* (607) 255-9606 (office). *E-mail:* LB244@cornell.edu (office). *Website:* www.engineering.cornell.edu (office).

BOND, Alan Maxwell, PhD, DSc, FAA, FRACI, FRSC; Australian chemist and academic; *Emeritus Professor of Chemistry, Monash University;* b. 17 Aug. 1946, Cobden, Vic.; s. of Ian T. Bond and Joyce M. Bond; m. Tunde-Maria Bond 1969; two s.; ed Univ. of Melbourne; Sr Demonstrator, Dept of Inorganic Chem., Univ. of Melbourne 1970–73, Research Fellow 1973–78; Foundation Prof. of Chem., Deakin Univ. 1978–90; Prof. of Chem., La Trobe Univ. 1990–95; Prof. of Chem., Monash Univ. 1995–, Deputy Head Dept of Chem. 1996–97, 1999, Head, School of Chem. 2000–02, R.L. Martin Distinguished Prof. of Chem., Fed. Fellow 2004–, now Emer. Prof.; 150th Anniversary Royal Soc. of Chem., Robert Boyle Fellow in Analytical Chem., Univ. of Oxford 1991, Hinshelwood Lecturer 1998, Vallee Visiting Prof. 2004–; mem. numerous editorial bds, including Reviews in Analytical Chemistry 1971–, Bulletin of Electrochemistry 1987–, Inorganica Chimica Acta 1988–, Journal of Electroanalytical Chemistry 1997–, Green Chemistry 1999, Encyclopedia of Analytical Science (second edn) 2001–; mem. Chem. Panel, Australian Research Council 1993–95, Council, Australian Acad. of Science 1993–96 (Vice-Pres. 1995–96), ACS, USA Electrochemical Soc.; Fulbright Fellow 1972; Fellow, Japan Soc. for Promotion of Science 1990, IUPAC, Royal Australian Chemical Inst.; Erskine Fellowship 1993; Christensen Fellowship, St Catherine's Coll.,

Oxford 1998; Fed. of Asian Chemical Socs Foundation Lectureship 1993; Rennie Medal 1975, David Syme Prize 1978, Australian Analytical Chem. Medal 1989, Stokes Medal 1992, Liversidge Award, Australian and NZ AAS 1992, Australian Research Council Special Investigator Award 1997–99, Royal Soc. of Chem. (London) Electrochemistry Group Medal 1997, Royal Australian Chemical Inst. H.G. Smith Medal 1998, Royal Soc. of Vic. Medal 1999, Burrows Medal 2000, Faraday Medal, Royal Soc. of Chem. 2000, Gov.-Gen.'s Centenary Medal for Service to Australian Soc. and Science in Electrochemistry 2003, Craig Medal, Australian Acad. of Science 2004, Reilley Award 2005, Int. Soc. of Electrochemistry Electrochimica Acta Gold Medal 2014. *Publications include:* Modern Polarographic Methods in Analytical Chemistry 1981, Broadening Electrochemical Horizons 2002; more than 500 publs on different aspects of electrochemistry. *Leisure interest:* cricket. *Address:* School of Chemistry, Monash University, Clayton, Vic. 3800, Australia (office). *Telephone:* (3) 9905-1338 (office). *Fax:* (3) 9905-4597 (office). *E-mail:* alan.bond@monash.edu (office). *Website:* www.monash.edu/science/schools/chemistry/our-people/staff/bond (office).

BOND, Christopher Samuel (Kit), BA, LLB; American lawyer and fmr politician; *Partner, Public Finance and Public Law Practice Group, Thompson Coburn LLP;* b. 6 March 1939, St Louis, Mo.; s. of Arthur Doerr Bond and Elizabeth Green Bond; m. 1st Carolyn Reid 1967 (divorced 1995); m. 2nd Linda Bond 2002; one s.; ed Deerfield Acad., Mass, Woodrow Wilson School of Public and Int. Affairs, Princeton Univ., Univ. of Virginia; clerk, Fifth Circuit, US Court of Appeals 1963–64; with Covington & Burling (law firm), Washington, DC 1964–67; in pvt. practice 1968; Asst Attorney-Gen., Chief Counsel of Consumer Protection Div. 1969–70; State Auditor, Mo. 1970–72; Gov. of Mo. 1973–77, 1981–84; Chair. Republican Govs Asscn 1974–75, Midwestern Govs Conf. 1976; mem. Exec. Cttee Nat. Govs Conf. 1974–75; Chair. NGA Cttee on Econ. Devt 1981–82; Pres. Great Plains Legal Foundation, Kansas City, Mo. 1977–81; Partner, Gage & Tucker (law firm), Kansas City and St Louis 1981–87, Thompson Coburn LLP, Washington, DC and St Louis 2011–; Senator from Mo. 1987–2011 (retd); launched own firm, Kit Bond Strategies 2011, Chair. Senate Small Business Cttee 1995–2001; Republican; Hon. LLD (Westminster and William Jewell Colls, Mo.) 1973; Hon. DLitt (Drury Coll., Springfield, Mo.) 1976. *Publications include:* The Next Front: Southeast Asia and the Road to Global Peace with Islam (co-author) 2009. *Address:* Thompson Coburn LLP, 1909 K Street NW, Suite 600, Washington, DC 20006-1167 (office); Thompson Coburn LLP, One US Bank Plaza, St Louis, MO 63101-1693 (office); 14 South Jefferson Road, Mexico, MO 65265, USA (home). *Telephone:* (202) 585-6946 (Washington, DC) (office); (314) 552-6546 (St Louis) (office). *Fax:* (202) 508-1033 (Washington, DC) (office); (314) 552-7546 (St Louis) (office). *E-mail:* kbond@thompsoncoburn.com (office). *Website:* www.thompsoncoburn.com (office); www.kitbondstrategies.com (office).

BOND, Edward; British playwright, director and poet; b. 18 July 1934, London; m. Elisabeth Pablé 1971; Northern Arts Literary Fellowship 1977–79; resident theatre writer, Univ. of Essex 1982–83; City of Lyon Medal 2007; Hon. DLitt (Yale) 1977, (Newman Univ., Birmingham) 2013; George Devine Award 1968, John Whiting Award 1968, Obie Award 1976. *Publications include:* plays: The Pope's Wedding 1962, Saved 1965, Narrow Road to the Deep North 1968, Early Morning 1968, Passion 1971, Black Mass 1971, Lear 1972, The Sea 1973, Bingo 1974, The Fool 1976, A-A-America! (Grandma Faust and The Swing) 1976, Stone 1976, The Bundle 1978, The Woman 1979, The Worlds 1980, The Activist Papers 1980, Restoration 1981, Summer: A Play for Europe 1982, Derek 1983, Human Cannon 1985, The War Plays (Red Black and Ignorant, The Tin Can People, Great Peace) 1985, Jackets 1989, In the Company of Men 1990, September 1990, Olly's Prison 1993, Tuesday 1993, Coffee: A Tragedy 1994, At the Inland Sea (A Play for Young People) 1996, Eleven Vests (A Play for Young People) 1997, The Crime of the Twenty-first Century 1999, The Children (A Play for Two Adults and Sixteen Children) 2000, Chair 2000, Have I None 2000, Existence 2002, Born 2004, The Balancing Act 2004, The Short Electra 2004, My Day (Song Cycle for Children) 2005, The Under Room 2006, Arcade 2006, Tune 2007, People 2007, A Window 2009, There Will Be More 2010, Collected Plays (nine vols) 1977–2011 2011, Innocence 2011, The Hungry Bowl 2011, The Edge 2012, The Chair Trilogy 2012, The Angry Roads 2014, The Price of One 2016, Dea 2016; short stories: Fables 1982; opera librettos of music by Hans Werner Henze: We Come to the River 1977, The English Cat 1983; ballet libretto of music by Henze: Orpheus 1982; translations: Chekhov's The Three Sisters 1967, Wedekind's Spring Awakening 1974, Wedekind's Lulu: A Monster Tragedy (with Elisabeth Bond-Pablé) 1992; other: Theatre Poems and Songs 1978, Collected Poems 1978–1985 1987, Notes on Post-Modernism 1990, Letters (five vols) 1994–2001, Notes on Imagination 1995, Selected Notebooks Vol. 1 2000, Vol. 2 2001, The Hidden Plot: Notes on Theatre and the State 2000. *Address:* Casarotto Ramsay, Waverley House, 7–12 Noel Street, London, W1F 8GQ, England (office). *Telephone:* (20) 7287-4450 (office). *Fax:* (20) 7287-9128 (office). *E-mail:* tom@casarotto.co.uk (office). *Website:* www.casarotto.co.uk (office).

BOND, J. Richard (Dick), OC, BSc, MS, PhD, FRS, FRSC, FAPS, FInstP, CPhys; Canadian astrophysicist and academic; *University Professor, University of Toronto;* b. 15 May 1950, Toronto; s. of Jack Parry Bond and Margaret Sandham Bond; m. Karin Giesbrecht; scientist, Gamma Ray Astronomy, Jet Propulsion Lab., Pasadena, Calif. 1975–76; Research Asst, Kellogg Radiation Lab., California Inst. of Tech. (Caltech) 1973–78; Postdoctoral Fellow/Lecturer in Astronomy, Univ. of California, Berkeley 1978–81; Research Fellow, Inst. of Astronomy, Univ. of Cambridge, UK 1982–83, Fellow of Churchill Coll.; mem. Inst. of Theoretical Physics, Univ. of California, Santa Barbara (UCSB) 1984, 1988–2000, 2002–; Directeur de Recherche Associée, 4ème échelon, Institut d'Astrophysique de Paris 1993–94, 1996; mem. Isaac Newton Inst., Cambridge, UK 1999; Moore Scholar, Caltech 2002; mem. Kavli Inst. for Theoretical Physics (KITP), USCB 2002, KITP China, Beijing 2007; Humboldt Fellow, Max Planck Inst. for Astrophysics 2006–07; Affiliate mem. Perimeter Inst. for Theoretical Physics 2002–; mem. Inst. for Advanced Study, Princeton Univ. 2012–18; Asst Prof. of Physics, Stanford Univ. 1981–85, Assoc. Prof. 1985–87; Assoc. Prof., Canadian Inst. for Theoretical Astrophysics (CITA) 1985–87, Prof. 1987–99, Acting Dir CITA 1990–91, 1994–95, Dir 1996–2001, 2001–06; Cross-appointed Prof., Depts of Astronomy and Physics, Univ. of Toronto 1985–, Univ. Prof. 2000–; Dir Canadian Inst. for Advanced Research (CIFAR) Cosmology and Gravity Program 2002–17, CIFAR Sr Fellow 1986–; Visiting Scientist, Nuclear Theory, Neils Bohr Inst. 1976–77; Visiting Research Physicist, Inst. for Theoretical Physics, Univ. of California, Santa Barbara Feb.–June 1995; Visiting Prof., 1ère class, Univ. of Paris/IAP/IAS 2003; Visiting Scientist, Inst. for Astronomy, Univ. of Hawaii 2008, Stanford Inst. for Theoretical Physics, Stanford Univ. 2008, KIPAC and SLAC 2008; Visiting Faculty Assoc., Caltech 2008; Sacker Visitor, Inst. of Astronomy, Univ. of Cambridge 2008; Hanna Distinguished Visiting Prof., Stanford Univ. 2018; mem. American Astronomical Soc., American Physical Soc., Canadian Astronomical Soc., Canadian Asscn of Physicists, Inst. of Physics, Int. Astronomical Union, RSC, Royal Soc. of London; Assoc., CIFAR 1985–85, Fellow 1986–; Foreign Assoc., NAS 2011; Fellow, American Physical Soc. 1998; Hon. Foreign mem. American Acad. of Arts and Sciences 2003; Order of Ontario; Hon. DSc (St Mary's Univ., Halifax) 2016; Richard P. Feynman Fellowship, Caltech 1974–75, Alfred P. Sloan Foundation Research Fellow 1985–89, E.W.R. Steacie Fellow, NSERC 1989–91, E.W.R. Steacie Prize, NRC 1989, Beals Prize, Canadian Astronomical Soc. 1995, CAP/CRM Prize in Theoretical and Math. Physics 1998, Exchange Lecturer, Institut de France, Acad. des Sciences/RSC 1998, Dannie Heineman Prize, AAS and AIP 2002, Moore Scholar, Caltech 2002, Inaugural mem. Etobian Gallery of Distinction, ECI, Toronto 2003, NSERC Award of Excellence 2003, Herzberg Gold Medal 2006, Killam Prize in the Natural Sciences 2007, Alexander von Humboldt Research Award 2007, Cosmology Prize, The Gruber Foundation 2008, RSC Henry Marshall Tory Medal 2009, Medal for Lifetime Achievement in Physics, Canadian Asscn of Physicists (first astrophysicist) 2010, Queen Elizabeth II Diamond Jubilee Medal 2012, Gruber Prize in Cosmology 2018, Royal Astronomical Soc. Group Award (with Planck Team) 2018. *Publications:* book chapters and reviews; more than 500 papers in peer-reviewed journals. *Address:* McLennan Phys Labs, 14th floor, Room 1408, Canadian Institute for Theoretical Astrophysics, 60 St George Street, University of Toronto, Toronto, ON M5S 3H8, Canada (office). *Telephone:* (416) 978-6874 (office). *Fax:* (416) 978-3921 (office). *E-mail:* bond@cita.utoronto.ca (office). *Website:* www.cita.utoronto.ca/~bond (office).

BOND, Sir John Reginald Hartnell, Kt; British business executive; b. 24 July 1941, Oxford, England; s. of Capt. R. H. A. Bond and E. C. A. Bond; m. Elizabeth Caroline Parker 1968; one s. two d.; ed Tonbridge School, Kent, Cate School, Calif., USA; joined The Hongkong and Shanghai Banking Corpn (later became HSBC) 1961; worked in Hong Kong, Thailand, Singapore, Indonesia and USA; Chief Exec. Wardley Ltd (Merchant Banking) 1984–87; Chair. Hongkong Bank of Canada 1987–98; Exec. Dir Hongkong and Shanghai Banking Corpn (responsible for the Americas) 1988–89, Commercial Banking, Hong Kong 1990–91; Pres. and CEO Marine Midland Bank, Inc., Buffalo, USA (subsidiary of HSBC Holdings PLC) 1991–92, Chair. HSBC Americas Inc. 1997; Deputy Chair. HSBC Bank PLC (fmrly Midland Bank) 1996–98 (Dir 1993), Chair. 1998–2006; Chair. HSBC Bank Middle East (fmrly British Bank of the Middle East) 1998–2006; Group CEO HSBC Holdings PLC 1993–98, Group Chair. 1998–2006 (Dir 1990–); Dir (non-exec.) Vodafone Group plc, Chair. 2006–11; Dir (non-exec.) and Chair. Xstrata plc 2011–13 (acquired by Glencore); Dir Hang Seng Bank Ltd 1990–96, Bank of England 2001–; Sr Adviser Kohlberg Kravis Roberts 2006–; Dir (non-exec.) London Stock Exchange 1994–99, British Steel 1994–98, Orange PLC 1996–99, Ford Motor Co., USA 2000–09 (adviser to Exec. Chair. 2006–09), A.P. Møller-Mærsk A/S (Denmark), Shui On Land Ltd (Hong Kong SAR); Chair. Inst. of Int. Finance, Washington, DC 1998–2003; adviser to Northern Trust, Chicago, KKR Asia; mem. of various advisory bodies in China: China Devt Forum, China Banking Regulatory Comm. Int. Advisory Bd, Tsinghua School of Econs and Man. at Tsinghua Univ.; Gov. The English-Speaking Union 1997–; Hon. Fellow, London Business School 2003; Hon. DEcon (Richmond American Univ., London) 1998; Hon. DLit (Loughborough) 2000, (Sheffield) 2002; Hon. LLD (South Bank) 2001; Foreign Policy Asscn Medal, New York 2003, Magnolia Gold Award, Shanghai Municipal People's Govt 2003. *Leisure interests:* golf, skiing, reading biographies. *Address:* c/o Glencore plc, Baarermattstrasse 3, 6340 Baar, Switzerland. *E-mail:* info@glencore.com.

BONDEVIK, Kjell Magne; Norwegian politician, diplomatist and clergyman; *President, The Oslo Center;* b. 3 Sept. 1947, Molde, Co. of Møre og Romsdal; s. of Margit Bondevik and Johs Bondevik; m. Bjørg Bondevik 1970; two s. one d.; ed Free Faculty of Theology, Univ. of Oslo; ordained minister in (Lutheran) Church of Norway 1979; Deputy Chair. Christian Democratic Youth Asscn 1968–70, Chair. 1970–73; Deputy mem. Storting 1969–73, mem. 1973–; Political Vice-Chair. Christian Democratic Party 1975–83, Chair. 1983–95; Minister of Church and Educ. 1983–86, Deputy Prime Minister 1985–86, Minister of Foreign Affairs 1989–90; Chair. Christian Democratic Party's Parl. Group 1981–83, 1986–89, 1993–97; Prime Minister of Norway 1997–2000, 2001–05; UN Sec.-Gen.'s Special Humanitarian Envoy for the Horn of Africa 2006–07; Founder and Pres. The Oslo Center 2006–; mem. Bd, Club of Madrid; Hon. mem. The Int. Raoul Wallenberg Foundation; Grand Cross of St Olav 2004, Grand Cross, Portuguese Order of Merit 2004; Hon. DTech (Brunel) 1997; Dr hc (Suffolk) 2000, (Wonkurang) 2000; Wittenberg Award, Luther Inst. 2000, King Harald V Anniversary Medal 2016. *Publication:* Et liv i spenning (A life of excitement/tension) 2006, Fortellingen om Aung San Suu Kyi (The story of Aung San Suu Kyi) (children's book) 2009. *Address:* The Oslo Center, Øvre Slottsgate 11, 0157 Oslo, Norway (office). *Telephone:* 23-13-66-70 (office). *Fax:* 23-13-66-77 (office). *E-mail:* post@oslocenter.no (office). *Website:* www.oslocenter.no (office).

BONDS, Barry Lamar; American fmr professional baseball player; b. 24 July 1964, Riverside, Calif.; s. of Bobby Bonds (fmr San Francisco Giants player); m.; three c.; ed Serra High School, San Mateo, Calif., Arizona State Univ.; outfielder; drafted by Pittsburgh Pirates in first round (6th pick) 1985 amateur draft, played with Pirates 1985–92, signed as free agent San Francisco Giants 1992–2007, filed for free agency status Oct. 2007; hit 73 home runs 2001 (single-season major league baseball home run record); hit 756th home run on 7 Aug. 2007 to set record of most career home runs; National League Most Valuable Player 1990, 1992, 1993, 2001, 2002, 2003, 2004; National League batting champion 2002 (.370 avg.), 2004 (.362 avg.); f. Bonds Family Foundation; hitting coach, Miami Marlins 2016–; Most Valuable Player (National League), Baseball Writers Asscn of America 1990, 1992, 1993, 2001, 2002, 2003, 2004, Maj. League Player of Year, Sporting News 1990, 2001, 2004, Nat. League Player of Year, Sporting News 1990, 1992, 1993, 2001, 2002, 2003, 2004. Gold Glove Award 1990–98, Silver Slugger Award 1990–94, 1996–97, 2000–04, 13 All-Star appearances. *E-mail:* contact@barrybonds.com. *Website:* www.barrybonds.com.

BONE, Sir Roger, KCMG, BA; British diplomatist and business executive (retd); ed Palmer's School, Grays, Essex, Univ. of Oxford; career diplomat, overseas assignments in Moscow, Washington, DC, and with UK Rep. to EU, Brussels; Pvt. Sec. to Foreign Sec. 1982–84; Visiting Fellow in Int. Relations, Harvard Univ., USA 1984–85; Asst Under-Sec. of State, FCO 1991–95, Amb. to Sweden 1995–99, to Brazil 1999–2004; Pres. Boeing UK Ltd 2005–14; mem. Bd of Dirs F & C Investment Trust plc, Continental Data Graphics Ltd, Nat. Centre for Univs and Business; Trustee, Royal United Services Inst.; Council mem. Air League, Brazilian Chamber of Commerce; apptd one of Prime Minister's UKTI Ambs for British Businesses.

BONELL, Carlos Antonio; British musician, teacher, guitarist and composer; b. 23 July 1949, London; s. of Carlos Bonell and Ana Bravo; m. Pinuccia Rossetti 1975; two s.; ed William Ellis School, Highgate and Royal Coll. of Music, under John Williams; debut as solo guitarist, Wigmore Hall, London 1971; concerto debut with Royal Philharmonic Orchestra 1975; American debut, Avery Fisher Hall, New York 1978; concert appearances with prin. British orchestras; appearances with John Williams, Teresa Berganza, Pinchas Zukerman 1975–; formed Carlos Bonell Ensemble 1983; Prof., Royal Coll. of Music 1972–, London Coll. of Music 1983–; Profesor Invitado, Univ. of Guanajuato, Mexico; Hon. ARCM. *Recordings include:* Guitar Music of Spain 1975, Guitar Music of the Baroque 1976, Showpieces 1981, Rodrigo Concerto 1981, Paganini Trios and Quartets 1983, Twentieth Century Music for Guitar 1987, Once Upon a Time, with Xer-Wai (violin) 1992, Walton Bagatelles and Anon in Love 1993, Britten Folksongs (with Philip Langridge) 1994, The Sea in Spring 1997, The Private Collection 1998, Kinkachoo I Love You (Millennium Guitar, The First 1000 Years) 2000, Trinity Coll. Grade pieces 2003, Carlos Bonell plays Gordon Mizzi 2003, Guitar Classics 2004. *Publications:* 20 First Pieces 1982, Tarrega: Fantasia on "La Traviata", 3 Spanish Folk Songs, Purcell: Music from the Fairy Queen, Fantasy for 3 Guitars 1995, Technique Builder 1997, Millennium Guitar, The First 1000 Years 2000. *Leisure interests:* reading, walking, snooker, films. *Address:* Patrick Allen, Connaught Artists Management Ltd, Penhurst House, 352–356 Battersea Park Road, London, SW11 3BY, England (office). *Telephone:* (20) 7978-0144 (office). *E-mail:* classicalmusic@connaughtartists.com (office); carlos@carlosbonell.com. *Website:* www.carlosbonell.com.

BONET, Pep; Spanish architect and designer; b. 19 Nov. 1941, Barcelona; m. Marta Monné 1964; three s.; ed High School of Architecture, Barcelona; f. Studio Per architectural practice, with Cristian Cirici, Lluis Clotet and Oscar Tusquets 1965; began producing furniture and bldg components, co-f. BD Ediciones de Diseño (now BD Barcelona Design) 1972; taught at School of Architecture, Barcelona 1975–78, Washington School of Architecture, St Louis, Mo., USA 1981; Deltas ADI-FAD Award 1967, 1976, 1986, 1990, 1991, Azulejo de Oro Award 1970, Nat. Restoration Award 1980, FAD Award for Architecture 1965, 1970, 1972, 1987, Architecture and Town Planning award 1987 for Triángulo de Oro Sports Centre, Madrid, Jarra Canal Isabel II Award 2001. *Major works include:* (Feria de Barcelona) Plaza Universo 1983–85, Rius i Taulet pavilion 1987, Iberia pavilion 1987, Lleida-Parallel pavilion 1989; Triángulo de Oro Sports Centre 1985, Canillejas civic centre 1985 (Madrid); Granollers Olympic sports centre, COOB-92. *Leisure interest:* playing jazz (tenor saxophone). *Address:* C/Pujades 63, 08005 Barcelona, Spain. *Telephone:* (93) 4855494. *Fax:* (93) 3091472.

BONETTI, Mattia; Swiss designer, decorator and artist; b. 2 May 1952, Lugano; s. of Giorgio Bonetti and Stella Frossard; m. Isabelle Forestier 1990; two d.; ed Centro Scolastico Industrie Artistiche, Lugano; decorated Bernard Picasso's Boisgeloup Castle 1987, Christian Lacroix Showroom and Graphics 1987–88; designs for cafeteria, Schloss Regensburg Thurn und Taxis Museum, Germany 1990; Banque Bruxelles-Lambert, Geneva 1991; packaging for Nina Ricci Cosmetics 1992, 1994; Water Carafe design for Ricard 1995; designed tramway for city of Montpellier 1998, designed second tramway 2006; Venetian Renaissance Glass show installation, Musée des Arts Décoratifs, Paris 2003; Emile Gallé show installation, Musée d'Orsay, Paris 2004; designed choir for Metz Cathedral 2006; Musée d'Orsay: Art Nouveau Revival installation 2009; designed Hôtel Cristal, Champs Elysées, Paris 2009; Hon. Citizen, City of Villeurbanne; Chevalier, Ordre des Arts et des Lettres 1995; 'Créateurs de l'Année 1991' (France). *Publications:* Mattia Bonetti and Elizabeth Garouste 1990, Garouste and Bonetti 1996, 1998, Elizabeth Garouste and Mattia Bonetti 1981–2001, Mattia Bonetti Drawings 2005, Mattia Bonetti 2008, Mattia Bonetti (by Rizzoli-Skira) 2010. *Leisure interests:* swimming, photography. *Address:* 10 rue Rochebrune, 75011 Paris (office); 1 rue Oberkampf, 75011 Paris, France (home). *Telephone:* 1-48-05-61-21 (office); 1-48-05-86-51 (home). *Fax:* 1-48-05-61-29 (office); 1-48-05-86-51 (home). *E-mail:* mattiabonetti@noos.fr (office).

BONFIELD, Sir Peter (Leahy), Kt, CBE, FREng, FIEE, FRSA; British business executive; *Chairman, NXP Semiconductors NV;* b. 3 June 1944; s. of George Bonfield and Patricia Bonfield; m. Josephine Houghton 1968; ed Hitchin Boys' Grammar School and Univ. of Loughborough; Div. Dir, Texas Instruments Inc., Dallas, Tex., USA 1966–81; Group Exec. Dir, Worldwide Operations, ICL 1981–84, Man. Dir 1984, Chair. and CEO ICL PLC 1987–97, Deputy Chair. 1997–2000; Deputy Chief Exec. STC PLC 1987–90; CEO British Telecommunications PLC 1996–2002; Chair. NXP Semiconductors NV; Chair. of Council and Sr Pro-Chancellor, Univ. of Loughborough; Chair. GlobalLogic Inc. 2015–18; mem. Bd of Dirs, L.M. Ericsson 2002–15, Mentor Graphics Corpn 2002–17, TSMC 2002–, Sony Corpn –2014; Board Mentor, CMi, Belgium; mem. Longreach Group Advisory Bd, Hong Kong; Sr Advisor, Rothschild, London –2015, Alix Partners, London 2015–, G3 Good Governance Group, London 2015–18, The Hampton Group, London 2017–19; Chair. East West Inst., UK; Vice-Pres. British Quality Foundation 1993–2012; Amb. for British Business; Fellow, British Computer Soc. 1990, Chartered Inst. of Marketing 1990, Inst. of Eng and Tech.; Liveryman, Information Technologists' Co. 1992; Freeman, City of London 1990; Hon. Citizen, Dallas, Tex.; Commdr, Order of the Lion (Finland) 1995; Dr hc (Open Univ.) 1997; Hon. DTech (Loughborough) 1988, (Brunel) 1997, (Nottingham) 1998, (Northumbria) 1999, (Royal Holloway) 2001, (Cranfield) 2001, (Essex) 2001; Nat. Electronics Council Mountbatten Medal 1995, Inst. of Man. Gold Medal 1996. *Leisure interests:* music, sailing, skiing, reading. *Address:* Truchas Associates Ltd, PO Box 129, Shepperton, Middx, TW17 9WL, England (office). *E-mail:* sirpeter@sirpeterbonfield.com (home). *Website:* www.sirpeterbonfield.com.

BONGO ONDIMBA, Ali; Gabonese politician and head of state; *President;* b. 9 Feb. 1959, Brazzaville, Repub. of Congo; s. of Omar Bongo (fmr Pres. of Gabon) and Patience Dabany; m. 2nd Sylvia Ajma Valentin; three s. one d.; ed Univ. of Paris Sorbonne I, France; High Personal Rep. of the Pres. of the Repub. 1987–89; Minister of Foreign Affairs and Cooperation 1989–91 (resgnd); Deputy (Parti démocratique gabonais) for Bongoville, Nat. Ass. 1991–99, for Haut-Ogooué Prov. 2001–09; Minister of Nat. Defence 1999–2009 (resgnd); Pres. of Gabon 2009–. *Leisure interests:* sports, music. *Address:* Présidence de la Republique, BP 546, Libreville, Gabon (office). *Telephone:* (1) 72-76-00 (office). *E-mail:* cabinetpr@presidence.ga (office). *Website:* www.presidentalibongo.com (office).

BONHAM CARTER, Helena, CBE; British actress; b. 26 May 1966, Golders Green, London; d. of Hon. Raymond Bonham Carter and Elena Bonham Carter; (great granddaughter of British Prime Minister Lord Asquith); partner Tim Burton; one s. one d. *Plays include:* The Barber of Seville 1992, Trelawny of the "Wells" 1992. *Films include:* A Room with a View 1985, Lady Jane 1986, Maurice (uncredited) 1987, La maschera 1988, Six Minutes with Ludwig (short) 1988, Francesco 1989, Getting it Right 1989, Hamlet 1990, Where Angels Fear to Tread 1991, Howards End 1992, Mary Shelley's Frankenstein 1994, The Glace Bay Miners' Museum 1994, A Little Loving 1995, Mighty Aphrodite 1995, Margaret's Museum 1995, Jeremy Hardy Gives Good Sex (video) 1995, Twelfth Night 1996, Portraits chinois 1996, The Petticoat Expeditions 1997, The Theory of Flight 1997, The Wings of the Dove (numerous awards including London Film Critics Circle Award for British Actress of the Year, Nat. Bd of Review Award for Best Actress, Toronto Film Critics Asscn Award for Best Actress) 1997, Keep the Aspidistra Flying 1997, The Revengers' Comedies 1998, The Theory of Flight 1998, Fight Club 1999, Women Talking Dirty 1999, Carnivale (voice) 2000, Football (short) 2001, Planet of the Apes 2001, Novocaine 2001, The Heart of Me 2002, Till Human Voices Wake Us 2002, Big Fish 2003, Charlie and the Chocolate Factory 2005, Conversations with Other Women 2005, Wallace & Gromit in the Curse of the Were-Rabbit (voice) 2005, Corpse Bride (voice) 2005, Sixty Six 2006, Harry Potter and the Order of the Phoenix 2007, Sweeney Todd: The Demon Barber of Fleet Street 2007, Terminator Salvation 2009, Harry Potter and the Half-Blood Prince 2009, Alice in Wonderland 2010, The King's Speech (BAFTA Award for Best Supporting Actress 2011) 2010, Harry Potter and the Deathly Hallows: Part 1 2010, Toast 2010, Harry Potter and the Deathly Hallows: Part 2 2011, Dark Shadows 2012, Les Misérables 2012, The Lone Ranger 2013, Suffragette 2015, Alice Through the Looking Glass 2016. *Television appearances include:* A Pattern of Roses (film) 1983, Miami Vice (series) 1987, Screen Two (series; The Vision) 1987, A Hazard of Hearts (film) 1987, Theatre Night (series; Arms and the Man) 1989, The Early Life of Beatrix Potter 1990, Jackanory (series) 1991, Brown Bear's Wedding (film) 1991, Dancing Queen (film) 1993, Fatal Deception: Mrs. Lee Harvey Oswald (film) 1993, A Dark Adapted Eye (film) 1994, Butter (short) 1994, Absolutely Fabulous (series) 1994, Humanoids from the Deep (film) 1996, 1914–1918 (series) 1996, Merlin (mini-series) 1998, The Nearly Complete and Utter History of Everything (film) 1999, Live from Baghdad (film) 2002, Henry VIII (film) 2003, Magnificent 7 (film) 2005, Enid (film) 2009, The Gruffalo (voice) 2009, The Gruffalo's Child (short) (voice) 2011, Burton & Taylor (film) 2013, Love. Nina (series) 2016. *Address:* c/o Nicola van Gelder, Conway van Gelder Grant Ltd, 8/12 Broadwick Street, London, W1F 8HW, England. *Telephone:* (20) 7287-1070. *E-mail:* nicki@conwayvg.co.uk. *Website:* www.conwayvangeldergrant.com.

BONHOEFFER, Tobias, PhD; German/American neurobiologist; *Director, Max Planck Institute of Neurobiology;* b. 9 Jan. 1960, Berkeley, Calif.; ed Max Planck Inst. for Biological Cybernetics, Tübingen; with Rockefeller Univ., New York, USA 1989–90; with Max Planck Inst. for Brain Research, Frankfurt 1991–93, Max Planck Inst. of Psychiatry, Martinsried, nr Munich 1993–98, Dir and Scientific Mem., Max Planck Inst. of Neurobiology 1998–; Assoc., Neuroscience Research Program, Neuroscience Inst. 2003–11; mem. German Neuroscience Soc., Faculty 1000, Academia Europaea, European Molecular Biology Org., Nat. Acad. of Sciences Leopoldina 2010–; Gov., Wellcome Trust, London 2014, Chan Zuckerberg Initiative, San Francisco 2016; Attempto Prize for Young Neuroscientists, Tübingen Univ., Ernst Jung Prize 2004. *Publications include:* numerous articles on visual system, cerebral cortex devt, neuronal plasticity and optical imaging. *Address:* Max Planck Institute of Neurobiology, Am Klopferspitz 18, 82152 Martinsried, Germany (office). *Telephone:* (89) 8578-3751 (office). *Fax:* (89) 8578-3700 (office). *E-mail:* office.bonhoeffer@neuro.mpg.de (office). *Website:* www.neuro.mpg.de (office).

BONIFACE, Pascal, PhD; French political scientist and academic; *Founding Director, Institut de Relations Internationales et Strategiques (IRIS);* b. 25 Feb. 1956, Paris; m.; three c.; ed Lycée Saint-Exupery, Mantes-la-Jolie, Univ. of Paris XIII Villetaneuse, Institut d'Études Politiques de Paris; Ed., Strategic Yearbook 1985–; worked with Socialist parl. group in Nat. Ass. 1986–88; Lecturer at Insts of Political Studies, Lille and Paris; currently Prof. of Int. Relations, Inst. for European Studies, Univ. of Paris VIII; currently columnist, La Croix (France), La Vanguardia (Spain), Al-Ittihad (UAE); Founding Dir Institut de Relations Internationales et Strategiques (IRIS) (Inst. for Int. and Strategic Relations) 1991–; Adviser to Ministers Jean-Pierre Chevenement and Pierre Joxe 1988–92; Chair. Cttee for Future of Football, French Fed. of Football; mem. Nat. Ethical Comm., Fédération française du football (French Football Fed.), Advisory Bd, Inst. for Nat. Defence Studies 1998–2004, High Council for Int. Co-operation 1999–2003, UN Advisory Bd on Disarmament Matters 2001–05; Chevalier, Légion d'honneur, Ordre nat. du Mérite. *Publications include:* over 40 books as author or ed., dealing with int. relations, nuclear deterrence and disarmament, European security, French int. policy, sport in int. relations. *Address:* Institut de Relations Internationales et Stratégiques (IRIS), 2 bis rue Mercoeur, 75011 Paris, France (office). *Telephone:* 1-53-27-60-72 (office). *Fax:* 1-53-27-60-70 (office). *E-mail:* boniface@iris-france.org (office). *Website:* www.iris-france.org (office).

BONILLA, Manuel Acosta; Honduran diplomatist and lawyer; b. 13 Jan. 1929, El Progreso, Yoro; Dr Isidoro Acosta, Prof. Adela Bonilla de Acosta; m. Dr Anna Lucia Marchetti de Acosta; four c.; ed Universidad Autónoma de Mexico, Universidad Autónoma de Honduras; Head Int. Relations, Civil Aviation Authority 1953–54; Dir-Gen. Welfare, Legal Adviser, Ministry Labour and Social Security 1954–56; Chair. Nat. Electoral Council 1964–65; Minister of Econ. Affairs and Finance 1965–71; Minister of Finance and Public Credit 1972–75; Minister and

Adviser, Pres. and Nat. Coordinator, State Modernization Programme 1990–94; mem. Central American Parl. 1991, First Vice-Chair., then Chair. Human Rights Cttee; Perm. Rep. to UN, New York 2002–06; Deputy Chair. Fundación Iras Ulargui (youth scholarship and children's home); mem. Nat. Law Acad. *Publications:* numerous articles, chapters, and co-authored works.

BONINGTON, Sir Christian John Storey (Chris), Kt, CVO, CBE, DL; British mountaineer, writer and photographer; b. 6 Aug. 1934, Hampstead, London; s. of Charles Bonington and Helen Anne Bonington (née Storey); m. Muriel Wendy Marchant 1962 (died 2014); three s. (one s. deceased); m. 2nd Loreto McNaught-Davis 2016; ed Univ. Coll. School, Hampstead, Royal Mil. Acad., Sandhurst; commissioned in Royal Tank Regt 1956–59; Instructor, Army Outward Bound School 1959–61; man. trainee, Unilever 1961–62; writer and photographer 1962–; Vice-Pres. Army Mountaineering Asscn 1980–; Pres. LEPRA 1985–, British Orienteering Fed. 1986– (now Hon. Pres.), British Mountaineering Council 1988–91 (Vice-Pres. 1976–79, 1985–88, now Patron), Council for Nat. Parks 1992–2000, The Alpine Club 1995–99; Chair. (non-exec.) Berghaus 1998–; Chair. Mountain Heritage Trust 2000–; Chancellor Univ. of Lancaster 2005–15; 19 expeditions to the Himalayas, including four to Mount Everest and first ascent of south face of Annapurna 1970, British Everest Expedition 1972, Brammah, Himalayas 1973, Changabang, Himalayas 1974, British Everest Expedition (first ascent, SW Face) 1975, Mount Vinson, Antarctica 1983, Panch chuli II, Himalayas (first ascent, W Ridge) 1992, Maslin, Greenland (first ascent) 1993, Rangrik Rang, India (first ascent) 1994, Drangnag-Ri, Nepal (first ascent) 1995, Danga II 2000, The Old Man of Hoy 2014; reached Everest summit 1985; motivational/after-dinner speaker; Hon. Fellow, UMIST, Lancashire Polytechnic; Hon. Pres. Hiking Club; Hon. MA (Salford); Hon. DSc (Sheffield) 1976, (Lancaster) 1983; Hon. DCL (Northumbria) 1996; Hon. DUniv (Sheffield Hallam) 1998; Hon. DLitt (Bradford) 2002; Founders Medal, Royal Geographical Soc. 1971, Lawrence of Arabia Medal 1986, Livingstone Medal 1991, David Livingstone Medal, Royal Scottish Geographical Soc. 1991. *Publications include:* I Chose to Climb (autobiog.) 1966, Annapurna South Face 1970, The Next Horizon (autobiog.) 1973, Everest South West Face 1973, Changabang 1974, Everest the Hard Way 1976, Quest for Adventure 1981, Kongur: China's Elusive Summit 1982, Everest: The Unclimbed Ridge (with Dr Charles Clarke) 1983, The Everest Years 1986, Mountaineer 1989, The Climbers 1992, Sea, Ice and Rock (with Robin Knox-Johnston) 1992, Great Climbs (co-ed. with Audrey Salkeld) 1994, Tibet's Secret Mountain: The Triumph of Sepu Kangri (with Dr Charles Clarke) 1999, Boundless Horizons 2000, Chris Bonington's Everest 2002, Chris Bonington's Lakeland Heritage (with Roly Smith) 2004, Mountaineer: Thirty Years of Climbing on the World's Great Peaks 2007, Ascent (memoir) 2017. *Leisure interests:* mountaineering, orienteering. *Address:* Badger Hill, Hesket, Newmarket, Wigton, Cumbria, CA7 8LA, England. *Telephone:* (16974) 78286. *Fax:* (16974) 78238. *E-mail:* margaret@bonington.com. *Website:* www.bonington.com.

BONINO, Emma, PhD; Italian politician; b. 9 March 1948, Bra, Turin; d. of Filippo Bonino and Catterina Barge; ed Bocconi Univ., Milan; mem. Camera dei Deputati (Chamber of Deputies, lower house of parl.) 1976–83, re-elected 1986, 1992, 1994, 2006; Pres. Parl. Group, Radical Party 1981; mem. European Parl. 1979–2006; Founder, Centro Informazione Sterilizzazione e Aborto 1975, No Peace without Justice; Pres. Transnational Radical Party 1991–93, Sec. 1993–94; EC Commr for Consumer Policy, EC Humanitarian Office and Fisheries 1995–99; Leader, Rosa nel Pungo party; unsuccessful cand. in presidential elections 1999, 2013; presented own list in general elections 2001; mem. Bd of Dirs Int. Crisis Group; Distinguished Visiting Prof., American Univ. of Cairo; Minister for EU Policies 2006–08; mem. Senate (upper house of parl.) 2008–13, Vice-Pres. 2008–13; Minister of Foreign Affairs 2013–14; Gran Cruz de la Orden de Mayo (Argentina) 1995, Order of the Prince Branimir (Croatia) 2002; European Personality of the Year 1996, European Communicator of the Year 1997, Premio Principe de Asturias (Spain) 1998, Gonfalone d'Argento Award 2002, Premio Presidente della Repubblica 2003, Premio Campione 2003, Prix Femmes d'Europe 2004, Open Soc. Prize 2004, Premio Galileo 2005. *Leisure interests:* sailing, diving. *Address:* c/o Ministry of Foreign Affairs, Piazzale della Farnesina 1, 00194 Rome, Italy.

BONNAFÉ, Jean-Laurent; French business executive; *CEO, BNP Paribas SA;* b. 14 July 1961; ed École Polytechnique and École des Mines; CEO Banca Nazionale Del Lavoro Spa 2006–11; COO BNP Paribas Securities Services S.C.A. Sept.–Dec. 2008, Chair. BNP Paribas Development, COO BNP Paribas SA 2008–11, mem. Exec. Bd and CEO BNP Paribas Fortis 2009–11, Dir of BNP Paribas SA 2010–, CEO BNP Paribas SA 2011–, French Retail Banking Exec. of BNP Paribas (Canada) Valeurs Mobilières Inc., Head of French Retail Banking, BNP Paribas North America, Inc., BNP Paribas Hungaria Bank Rt., COO BNP Paribas Wealth Management; mem. Bd of Dirs, Carrefour SA 2008–, BNP Paribas Personal Finance, Banca Nazionale del Lavoro (Italy), BNP Paribas Fortis (Belgium). *Address:* BNP Paribas SA, 3 rue d'Antin, 75002 Paris, France (office). *Telephone:* 1-42-98-12-34 (office). *Fax:* 1-40-14-45-46 (office). *E-mail:* info@bnpparibas.com (office). *Website:* www.bnpparibas.com (office).

BONNAIRE, Sandrine; French film actress; b. 31 May 1967, Gannat, Auvergne; m. Guillaume Laurant 2003; two d.; film debut in La Boum 1980; Chevalier des Art et des Lettres; Venice Film Festival Award 1995, Grand prix nat. du cinéma, Ministry of Culture 1987, César Award 1983, Best Actress Award 1986. *Plays include:* The Good Person of Sechuan 1989. *Films include:* A Nos Amours (César Award 1983) 1983, Le Meilleur de la Vie 1983, Vagabond (Best Actress Award 1986) 1985, La Puritaine 1986, Sous le Soleil de Satan 1987, Jaune Revolver 1987, Monsieur Hire 1989, Dans la Soirée 1990, Joan of Arc 1992, La Cérémonie 1995, Judgment in Stone, Circle of Passion 1996, Secret défense 1998, The Colour of Lies 1999, East–West 2000, Mademoiselle 2001, Femme fatale 2002, C'est la vie 2002, Confidences trop intimes 2003, L'equipier 2003, Le Cou de la Girafe 2003, Quelques jours avec moi, Les innocents, Peaux de vaches, Le ciel de Paris, Je crois que je l'aime 2007, Demandez la permission aux enfants 2007, Elle s'appelle Sabine (dir) (French Film Critics Award for Best First Film) 2007, Un coeur simple 2008, L'empreinte de l'ange 2008, Joueuse 2009, Adieu Paris 2013, Salaud, on t'aime 2014. *Television includes:* Une femme en blanc 1996, La maison des enfants 2002, Le Procès de Bobigny 2006, Signature (series) 2011, La ballade de Lucie (film) 2013, Rouge Sang 2014. *Publication:* Elle s'appelle Sabine 2007. *Address:* c/o Intertalent, 5 rue Clément Marot, 75008 Paris, France (office). *Telephone:* 1-47-23-40-00.

BONNELAME, Jérémie Emile Patrick; Seychelles politician and diplomatist; *Chairman, Constitutional Appointment Authority;* b. 24 Oct. 1938, Mahé; ed Inst. Catholique de Paris, Inst. Ecuménique pour les Développement des Peuples, Paris, France, Sion School of Theology, Lucerne School of Theology, Switzerland, Univ. of Québec in Montréal, Canada; teacher, Modern Secondary School of Seychelles 1967–75; Dir-Gen. of Information 1978–79; Prin.-Sec., Ministry of Educ. 1979–80, of External Relations 1981–83, of Educ. and Information 1983–86; Minister of Manpower 1986–88, of Transport 1988–89, of Agric. and Fisheries 1989–93, of Foreign Affairs 1997; Sec.-Gen. Indian Ocean Comm. 1993–97; Amb. and Perm. Rep. to UN, New York 1997–2007, Amb. to USA 2005–07; Chair. Constitutional Appointment Authority 2007–; mem. Constitutional Review Comm. 2008–; Ed.-in-Chief L'Echo des Iles; Pres. Ministerial Council, Tuna Asscn; Co-ordinator Western Indian Ocean Tuna Org. (WIOTO); Gov. Int. Fund for Agricultural Devt; Head of Del. of Seychelles to numerous int. meetings of UN, OAU, ECA, FAO, UNESCO, EU, UNDP. *Leisure interests:* reading, fishing. *Address:* Office of the Chairman, Constitutional Appointment Authority, PO Box 1087, Ground Floor, La Ciotat Building, Mont Fleuri, Mahé, Seychelles (office).

BONNEMAIN, François; French broadcasting executive and fmr journalist; b. 9 Oct. 1942, Paris; s. of Georges Bonnemain and Renée Charpentier; ed Centre de formation des journalistes de Paris; with Associated Press (AP), Agence France-Presse (AFP), then France-Soir; joined TF 1 TV channel, in charge of political news 1972; Ed. in Chief TF 1 1977; apptd Ed. FR 3 TV channel 1981; Dir News and Current Affairs, France-Inter 1982; Political Ed. Hebdo (weekly magazine); Tech. Adviser to Prime Minister Jacques Chirac on Audiovisual Information 1986–88, to Mayor of Paris (Chirac) 1988–94; Man. Dir Radio-Télévision française d'outre-mer (RFO) 1994–95; mem. Conseil Supérieur de l'audiovisuel (CSA) 1996–99; Dir Chaîne Parl.-Sénat 2000–; Dir Human Resources, France Télévision 2000–02; Adviser to Prime Minister Jean-Pierre Raffarin 2004–05; CEO TV5 Monde 2006–08. *Leisure interest:* fine cuisine. *Address:* Chaîne Parlementaire-Sénat, 15 rue de Vaugirard, 75291 Paris Cedex 06, France (home).

BONNER, Paul Max, OBE, FRTS; British television executive (retd); b. 30 Nov. 1934, Banstead, Surrey; s. of Frank Bonner and Jill Bonner; m. Jenifer Hubbard 1956 (died 2013); two s. one d.; ed Felsted School; with Longmans Green & Co., Publrs 1952; trainee reporter, Southend Standard 1953; Nat. Service 1953–55; Asst Press Officer, E. K. Cole Ltd 1955; freelance work for Evening Standard 1955; Trainee Studio Asst, BBC, Bristol 1955–56, Studio Man. 1956–58, Acting Asst Producer, Talks Dept, West Region 1958–59, Production Asst, Talks Dept, TV 1961–65, Sr Producer, Travel and Features Programmes 1965–74, Ed. BBC Community Programmes 1974–77, Special Asst to Controller BBC2 1977, Chair. Small Integrated Multi-Role Production Unit Study Group 1977, Head of Science and Features Dept, TV 1978–81; Channel Controller, Channel Four TV Co. Ltd 1981–83, Controller of Programmes and Exec. Dir 1983–87; Dir of Programme Planning Secr. ITV Asscn 1987–92, Dir ITV Network Centre Secr. 1993–94; Dir House of Commons Broadcasting Unit Ltd 1989–94; Chair. Edin. TV Festival 1979; a Man., Royal Inst. 1982–85; Gov. of Nat. Film and TV School 1981–88; Bd mem. Broadcasting Support Services 1981–93; Chair. Media Group, Cttee on Public Understanding of Science 1981–93; mem. Classic FM Consumer Panel 2009–11. *Television documentaries include:* Climb up to Hell 1967, The Search for the Real Che Guevara 1971, Who Sank the Lusitania? 1972. *Publications:* The Third Age of Broadcasting 1983, Independent TV in Britain (Vol. 5: ITV and IBA 1981–92 1998, (Vol. 6: C4, TV-am, Cable & Satellite 1981–92) 2002. *Leisure interests:* photography, music. *Address:* 9 Alan Road, London, SW19 7PT, England (home). *Telephone:* (20) 8947-6635 (home).

BONNET, Christian, DenD; French politician and business executive; b. 14 June 1921, Paris; s. of Pierre Bonnet and Suzanne Delebecque; m. Christiane Mertian 1943 (died 1999); five c. (one s. deceased); ed Univ. of Paris and Ecole des sciences politiques; Pres. Les Grandes Marques de la conserve 1952–61, Del. Conseil supérieur de la conserve; MRP Deputy for Morbihan 1956–58; Deputy for the second constituency of Morbihan 1956–83; Gen. Councillor, Belle-Ile 1958–2001; Mayor of Carnac 1964–96; fmr Sec.-Gen. Républicains Indépendants; Chair. Cttee on Merchant Marine budget; Pres. Supervisory Council, Caisse des dépots et consignations; Sec. of State for Supply, Housing and Territorial Devt 1972–74; Minister of Agric. 1974–77, of the Interior 1977–81; Senator for Morbihan 1983–2001. *Address:* 56340 Carnac, France (home).

BONNICI, Josef, MA, PhD; Maltese economist, academic, fmr politician and fmr central banker; *Professor of Economics, University of Malta;* b. 15 April 1953, Birzebbuga; m. Rita Oliva; two c.; ed Univ. of Malta, Simon Fraser Univ., Canada; Sr Lecturer in Econs, Deakin Univ., Australia 1980–88; Visiting Prof., Univ. of Malta 1988, Prof. of Econs 1988–2004, 2016–; Econ. Adviser to Prime Minister 1988–92; apptd adviser to Council of Europe in Co-ordinated Social Research Programme 1992; mem. Parl. 1992–2004; Parl. Sec., Ministry of Finance 1993–95, Minister of Econ. Services 1995–96, Shadow Minister and Opposition Spokesman for Econ. Devt 1996–98, Minister for Econ. Services 1998–2003; Gov. Central Bank of Malta 2011–16; mem. European Court of Auditors 2004–10; fmr mem. Del. to OSCE, Del. to Council of Europe, Jt Malta EU Parl. Cttee; apptd mem. Nat. Comm. for Higher Educ. in Malta 2006; mem. Nationalist Party; Dr hc (Rikkyo) 1996. *Publications include:* Macroeconomics 1996; articles on econs in Malta and in professional econ. journals. *Address:* Department of Economics, University of Malta, Msida MSD 2080, Malta (office). *Website:* www.um.edu.mt/fema/economics (office).

BONNICI, Ugo Mifsud (see Mifsud Bonnici, Ugo).

BONNIN, Didier; French business executive; b. 1959; ed Reims Man. School; began career at Arthur Andersen; held several sr positions with Louis Vuitton; CEO Céline Production, Florence 1999–2003; Industrial Dir Bottega Veneta, Gucci Group NV 2003–07, CEO Sergio Rossi SpA 2007–09; Man. Dir VBH Luxury Inc.; Man. Dir, Accessories Div., Roberto Cavalli 2011–13; CEO (ROVEDA) Chanel 2013–18, Man. Dir 2017–. *Address:* Chanel, 31 rue Cambon, 75001 Paris, France (office). *Telephone:* 1-44-50-66-00 (office). *Website:* www.chanel.com (office).

BONO; Irish rock singer, songwriter and humanitarian; *Lead Singer, U2;* b. (Paul Hewson), 10 May 1960, Dublin; m. Alison Stewart 1982; ed Mount Temple School; Founder-mem. and lead singer, the Feedback 1976, renamed the Hype, finally renamed U2 1978–; numerous concerts, including Live Aid Wembley 1985, Self Aid Dublin, A Conspiracy of Hope (Amnesty International Tour) 1986, Smile Jamaica (hurricane relief fundraiser) 1988, Very Special Arts Festival, White House, Washington, DC 1988; numerous tours world-wide; Foreign Hon. Fellow, American Acad. of Arts and Sciences 2009; Portuguese Order of Liberty 2005; Hon. KBE 2007; 22 Grammy Awards with U2, including Best Rock Performance by a Duo or Group with Vocal (for Desire) 1988, BRIT Awards for Best Int. Act 1988–90, 1992, 1998, 2001, Best Live Act 1993, Outstanding Contribution to the British Music Industry 2001, JUNO Award 1993, World Music Award 1993, Grammy Award for Song of the Year, Record of the Year, Best Rock Performance by a Duo or Group with Vocal (all for Beautiful Day) 2000, Grammy Awards for Best Pop Performance by a Duo or Group with Vocal (for Stuck In A Moment You Can't Get Out Of), for Record of the Year (for Walk On), for Best Rock Performance by a Duo or Group with Vocal (for Elevation) 2001, American Music Award for Favourite Internet Artist of the Year 2002, Ivor Novello Award for Best Song Musically and Lyrically (for Walk On) 2002, Golden Globe for Best Original Song (for The Hands That Built America, from film Gangs of New York) 2003, Grammy Awards for Best Rock Performance by a Duo or Group with Vocal, Best Rock Song, Best Short Form Music Video (all for Vertigo) 2004, TED Prize 2004, Nordoff-Robbins Silver Clef Award for lifetime achievement 2005, Q Awards for Best Live Act 2005, 2016, Digital Music Award for Favourite Download Single (for Vertigo) 2005, Meteor Ireland Music Award for Best Irish Band, Best Live Performance 2006, Grammy Awards for Song of the Year, for Best Rock Performance by a Duo or Group with Vocal (both for Sometimes You Can't Make it on Your Own), for Best Rock Song (for City of Blinding Lights) 2006, Ambassadors of Conscience Award, Amnesty International 2006, Liberty Medal 2007, Visionary Award, Palm Springs Film Festival 2014, Golden Globe Award for Best Original Song (Ordinary Love in Mandela: Long Walk to Freedom) 2014, Man of the Year, Glamour magazine 2016, MTV Europe Music Award for Global Icon 2017. *Plays include:* Spider-Man: Turn Off The Dark (music and lyrics by Bono and The Edge), Broadway, New York 2011–14. *Films include:* Rattle and Hum 1988, The Million Dollar Hotel (co-writer) 2000. *Recordings include:* albums: Boy 1980, October 1981, War 1983, Under a Blood Red Sky 1983, The Unforgettable Fire 1984, Wide Awake In America 1985, The Joshua Tree (Grammy Award for Album of the Year, Best Rock Performance by a Duo or Group with Vocal) 1987, Rattle and Hum 1988, Achtung Baby (Grammy Award for Best Rock Performance by a Duo or Group with Vocal 1992) 1991, Zooropa (Grammy Award for Best Alternative Music Album) 1993, Passengers (film soundtrack with Brian Eno) 1995, Pop 1997, The Best Of 1980–90 1998, All That You Can't Leave Behind (Grammy Award for Best Rock Album 2001) 2000, The Best Of 1990–2000 2002, How To Dismantle An Atomic Bomb (Meteor Ireland Music Award for Best Irish Album 2006, Grammy Awards for Album of the Year, for Best Rock Album 2006) 2004, No Line on the Horizon 2009, Songs of Innocence 2014, Songs of Experience 2017. *Address:* c/o Principle Management, 30–32 Sir John Rogersons Quay, Dublin 2, Ireland (office). *E-mail:* nadine@numb.ie (office). *Website:* www.u2.com.

BONO MARTÍNEZ, José; Spanish politician; b. 14 Dec. 1950, Salobre; m. Ana Maria Rodriguez Mosquera (divorced); four c.; ed Colegio de la Inmaculada, Alicante, Univ. of Deusto; worked as lawyer until 1979; mem. Congreso de los Diputados (Congress of Deputies) for Albacete 1979–83, for Toledo 2008–11, Pres. Congreso de los Diputados 2008–11; Pres. Castilla-La Mancha region 1983–2004; Minister of Defence 2004–06; fmr Prof. of Political Law, Universidad Complutense de Madrid; mem. Partido Socialista Obrero Español (Spanish Socialist Workers' Party).

BONSE-GEUKING, Wilhelm; German mining engineer and business executive; b. 26 Aug. 1941, Arnsberg, Sauerland; m. Annette Bonse-Geuking 1974; three s.; Chair. Veba Oel AG (following acquisition by BP) 1995–2002, Head of BP Germany –2004, European Head of BP Group, Group Vice-Pres. and mem. Exec. Man. of BP Group 2003–06, Chair. Supervisory Bd, BP Europa SE 2005–13; Chair. Supervisory Bd Evonik Industries AG 2007–12; Chair. Exec. Bd, RAG Foundation 2007–12; apptd to Energy and Climate Advice Panel of State Govt of North Rhine-Westphalia; Chair. Comm. on Econ. Growth and Innovation, Econ. Council of CDU; Chair. Bd of Trustees, Foundation of the Int. Charlemagne Prize, Aachen, Zollverein Foundation; mem. Zollverein Fed. of Catholic Entrepreneurs (BKU). *Address:* c/o Evonik Industries AG, Rellinghauser Straße 1–11, 45128 Essen, Germany. *E-mail:* info@evonik.com.

BOODAI, Marwan Marzouk; Kuwaiti business executive; *Chairman and CEO, Jazeera Airways;* CEO Boodai Corpn 1995–; f. Jazeera Airways 2005, currently Chair. and CEO; mem. Advisory Bd, World Econ. Forum's Global Growth Cos. *Address:* Jazeera Airways, PO Box 29288, Safat 13153, Kuwait City (office); Boodai Trading Co. Ltd WLL, PO Box 1287, Safat 13013, Airport Road, Shuwaikh, Kuwait (office). *Telephone:* (248) 43986 (office). *Fax:* (248) 48368 (office). *E-mail:* isdcmd@boodaitrading.com (office). *Website:* www.jazeeraairways.com (office); www.boodaitrading.com (office).

BOOLELL, Arvin, LLM, MB, BCH, BAO, MRCP, MRCS; Mauritian physician and politician; b. 26 May 1953; s. of Sir Satcam Boolell; ed Nat. Univ. of Ireland, Royal Coll. of Surgeons, Ireland; fmr medical practitioner; mem. Nat. Ass. 1987–; Minister of Agric. and Nat. Resources 1995–2000, of Agro-Industry and Fisheries 2005–08, of Foreign Affairs, Regional Integration and Int. Trade 2008–14. *Address:* c/o Ministry of Foreign Affairs, International Trade and Co-operation, New Government Centre, 5th Floor, Port Louis, Mauritius.

BOOMGAARDEN, Georg; German diplomatist; b. 24 June 1948, Emden; m.; three c.; ed Univ. of Kiel; entered Higher Foreign Service 1974, Desk Officer, Cultural Section, Embassy in Moscow 1976–80, Press Officer, Embassy in Buenos Aires 1980–83, Desk Officer, Cen. America Div., Fed. Foreign Office 1983–86, Head of the Information Processing Div. 1986–89, Amb. to Nicaragua 1989–92, Head of Econ. Service, Embassy in Moscow 1992–95, Head of Div. responsible for Southern Latin America, Fed. Foreign Office 1995–99, Dir for Latin American Affairs 1999–2003, Amb. to Spain 2003–05, State Sec., Fed. Foreign Office 2005–08, Amb. to UK 2008–13. *Address:* Federal Ministry of Foreign Affairs, 11013 Berlin, Germany (office). *Telephone:* (30) 18170 (office). *Fax:* (30) 18173402 (office). *E-mail:* poststelle@auswaertiges-amt.de (office). *Website:* www.auswaertiges-amt.de (office).

BOON, David Clarence, MBE, Dipl. Bus. Man.; Australian fmr professional cricketer; *International Match Referee, International Cricket Council;* b. 29 Dec. 1960, Launceston, Tasmania; s. of Clarence Leonard Boon and Lesley Mary Boon; m. Philippa Louise Wright 1983; one s. two d.; ed Launceston Church Grammar School; right-hand batsman; teams: Tasmania 1978–79 to 1998–99 (Capt. 1992–93 to 1998–99), Durham, England (Capt.) 1997–99, for Australia played 107 Test matches 1984–96, scoring 7,422 runs (average 43.65) including 21 hundreds and holding 99 catches, highest score 200; toured England 1985, 1989 and 1993; scored 23,413 First-class runs (68 hundreds), highest score 227; 181 limited-overs ints; Marketing Man. Trust Bank Australia 1991–; Marketing and Special Events Co-ordinator 1999; Australian selector 2000–11; Gen. Man. Cricket Operations Tasmania 2004–11; Int. Match Referee, Int. Cricket Council; Patron Road Trauma Support Group, World Vision; Int. Cricketer of the Year 1987–88, Wisden Cricketer of the Year 1994, inducted into Sport Australia Hall of Fame 2005, the Southern Stand at Bellerive Oval named David Boon Stand in his honour 2015. *Publications:* In the Firing Line (with A. Mark Thomas), Under the Southern Cross (autobiog.) 1996. *Leisure interests:* gardening, golf, music. *Address:* 113 King Street, Sandy Bay, Tasmania 7005, Australia. *Website:* www.davidboon.com.au.

BOONE, Laurence, DEA, MA, PhD; French economist, banking analyst and government official; b. 15 May 1969; two c.; ed Université Paris X Nanterre, Univ. of Reading and London Business School, UK; began career as an analyst at Merrill Lynch Asset Management 1995–96; Researcher, Centre d'études prospectives et d'informations internationales 1996–98; Economist, Dept of Econ. Affairs, OECD, Paris 1998–2004; Chief French Economist and Man. Dir, Barclays Capital 2004–11; Man. Dir and Head of Developed Europe Econs, Bank of America Merrill Lynch, London 2011–14; Econ. Adviser to Pres. François Hollande 2014–; Assoc. Prof., Institut d'études politiques (Sciences Po), Paris; taught at École Polytechnique at ENSAE ParisTech (École nationale de la statistique et de l'admin économique) and École Normale Superieure de Cachan; fmr mem. Competition Jury of École nat. d'admin; mem. Bd of Dirs Kering Group (fmrly Pinault-Printemps-Redoute and PPR) 2010–14; columnist, L'Opinion newspaper; mem. Cercle des Economistes. *Address:* c/o Office of the President, Palais de l'Elysée, 55–57 rue du Faubourg Saint Honoré, 75008 Paris, France (office). *E-mail:* info@elysee.fr (office). *Website:* www.elysee.fr (office).

BOONSITHI, Chokwatana, PhD; Thai business executive; b. 25 July 1937, Bangkok; ed Wat Suthat Secondary School; Chair. Saha Group (consumer goods conglomerate), Pipat Paniangvait 1973, Chair. Saha Tokyu Corpn Co. Ltd 2014, currently Hon. Chair. Sahapat Group; Pres. Thai President Foods 1995–2017, Chair. 2017–; Advisory Chair. International Laboratories Corpn Ltd; mem. Advisory Cttee Thai-Japanese Asscn; mem. Bd of Dirs Champ Ace Co. Ltd, I.C.C. International Public Co. Ltd; Chair. Thanulux Public Co. Ltd –2010, Advisory Dir 2016; Chair. Waseda Education (Thailand) Co. Ltd; Order of the Sacred Treasure, Gold Rays with Neck Ribbon (Govt of Japan) 2002; Dr hc (Burapha Univ.) (Thammasat Univ.), (National Institute of Development Administration), (Univ. of the Thai Chamber of Commerce), (Khon Kaen Univ.), (Waseda Univ., Japan), (Rajamangala Univ. of Technology). *Address:* Saha Group, 2156 New Petchburi Road, Bangkapi, Huay Kwang, Bangkok 10320, Thailand (office). *Website:* www.sahagroup.thailand.com (office).

BOONYARATGLIN, Gen. Sonthi; Thai army officer (retd) and politician; *Leader, Matubhum (Motherland) Party;* b. 2 Oct. 1946; m. two wives, Sukanya and Piyada; ed Armed Forces Academies Preparatory School, Chulachomklao, Royal Mil. Acad.; commissioned into Royal Army Infantry Corps, went on to lead several top units, including Special Warfare Command based in Lopburi Prov.; Deputy Army Commdr 2004–05, C-in-C Royal Thai Army (first Muslim) 2005–07 (retd); Pres. Admin. Reform Council (de facto head of govt) following overthrow of elected govt of Thaksin Shinawatra in coup d'état 19 Sept.–1 Oct. 2006; Chair. Council for Nat. Security (mil. junta that ruled the kingdom) 2006–07; Deputy Prime Minister in charge of nat. security 2007–09; Leader, Matubhum (Motherland) Party 2009–; US Army Commendation Medal, with Valor device 1970, Victory Medal, Viet Nam War 1972, Freeman Safeguarding Medal (Second Class) 1973, Companion (Fourth Class), Order of the Crown of Thailand 1976, Border Service Medal (Thailand) 1982, Commdr (Third Class) of The Most Noble Order of the Crown of Thailand 1984, Chakra Mala Medal (Thailand) 1989, Kt Commdr (Second Class) of The Most Noble Order of the Crown of Thailand 1989, Kt Commdr (Second Class) of the Most Exalted Order of the White Elephant 1991, Kt Grand Cross (First Class) of the Most Noble Order of the Crown of Thailand 1995, Kt Grand Cross (First Class) of the Most Exalted Order of the White Elephant 1999. *Address:* c/o Office of the Prime Minister, Government House, Thanon Nakhon Pathom, Bangkok 10300, Thailand. *E-mail:* webmaster@opm.go.th.

BOORMAN, John, CBE; British film director, producer and screenwriter; b. 18 Jan. 1933, Shepperton, Middlesex, England; s. of George Boorman and Ivy Boorman (née Chapman); m. 1st Christel Kruse 1956; one s. three d.; m. 2nd Isabella Weibrecht 1994; one s. two d.; ed Salesian Coll., Chertsey; Broadcaster and critic, BBC Radio, also contributor to Manchester Guardian and magazines 1950–54; army service 1951–53; Film Editor, ITN London 1955–58; Dir and Producer Southern TV 1958–60; Head of Documentaries, Bristol, BBC TV; left BBC to work as film dir; Chair. Nat. Film Studios of Ireland 1975–85; Gov. British Film Inst. 1983–94, co-f. Merlin Films Group 1989; f. magazine Day by Day; Chevalier, Ordre des Arts et des Lettres 1985; Best Dir Prize, Cannes Festival 1970, 1998, BAFTA Fellowship Award 2004, numerous film awards. *Films include:* Catch Us If You Can 1965, Point Blank 1967, Hell in the Pacific 1968, Leo the Last 1969, Deliverance 1970, Zardoz 1973, The Heretic 1976, Excalibur 1981, The Emerald Forest 1985, Hope and Glory (Golden Globe Award 1988) 1987, Where the Heart Is 1989, I Dreamt I Woke Up 1991, Beyond Rangoon 1994, Two Nudes Bathing 1995, The General 1998, The Tailor of Panama 2001, In My Country 2005, The Tiger's Tail 2006, Queen and Country 2014. *Television includes:* Dir Citizen 1963, The Newcomers 1960–64. *Publications:* The Legend of Zardoz 1973 (novel), Money into Light 1985, Hope and Glory 1987, Projections 1 1992, Projections 2 1993, Projections 3 1994, Projections $4\frac{1}{2}$ (co-ed.) 1995, Projections 5 1996, Projections 6 1997, Projections 7 1997, Projections 8 1998; co-ed. A Year in Film 1993, Adventures of a Suburban Boy (autobiog.) 2003. *Leisure interests:* hacking the Wicklow Hills, losing gracefully at tennis, planting trees. *Address:* Merlin Films Group, 16 Upper Pembroke Street, Dublin 2, Ireland. *Telephone:* (1) 6764373. *Fax:* (1) 6764368. *E-mail:* info@merlinfilms.com. *Website:* www.merlinfilms.com.

BOOS, Georgy Valentinovich, CandTechSc; Russian engineer, politician and business executive; *President, Boos Lighting Group International Lighting Corporation;* b. 22 Jan. 1963, Moscow; m. 1st Valentina Boos; m. 2nd Elena Vladimirovna Lerina; m. 3rd Anna Boos; seven c.; ed Moscow Energy Inst.; served in the Soviet Air Force 1986–88; Sr Engineer, All-Union Research Inst. of Light Tech., also teacher of math., secondary school 1988–91; Founder, Dir-Gen., then Pres., Svetoservis Co. 1991–96; mem. State Duma 1996–98, 1999–2005, Deputy Speaker 2003–05 (joined Yedinstvo and Otechestvo Union (later Yedibaya Rossiya) 2000); Head of State Taxation Service of Russian Fed. Sept.–Dec. 1998; Minister of Revenue Dec. 1998–May 1999; Gov. of Kaliningrad Oblast 2005–10; currently Pres. Boos Lighting Group Int. Lighting Corpn, Moscow; mem. Bd of Dirs IDGC Holding Jt Stock Co. 2012–; apptd Pres. Int. Acad. of Information Technologies 1999; Head of Public Council, Fed. Road Agency (Rosavtodor) 2015–; Prof. and Full Mem. Acad. of Security, Defence and Law-and-Order 2004–; mem. Int. Acad. of Social Sciences 2008–; Order of Honour 2004, Order of Holy Prince Daniel of Moscow (Russian Orthodox Church) 2006, 4th Class Order of Merit for the Fatherland 2008, 2nd Class Order of the Silver Cross of Philanthropist (IASS) 2008; Dr hc (Immanuel Kant Baltic Fed. Univ.) 2012; Medal for the Memory of the 850th Anniversary of Moscow 1997, Medal for Merit in the Implementation of the All-Russia Census 2002, Medal for the Memory of the 300th Anniversary of Saint Petersburg 2003, Medal of the 70th Anniversary of the Armed Forces of the USSR, Medal for the 15th Anniversary of the Council of Federation 2008. *Achievements include:* designer of architectural illumination of Moscow 1996. *Leisure interests:* hockey, motorcycling, tennis, football, music, singing. *Address:* Boos Lighting Group International Lighting Corporation, 129626 Moscow, 6, 1st Rizshkiy pereulok, Russia (office). *Telephone:* (495) 785-20-95 (office). *Fax:* (495) 785-20-96 (office). *E-mail:* info@bl-g.ru (office). *Website:* www.bl-g.ru (office).

BOOTH, Cherie, CBE, QC, LLD, FRSA; British barrister; *Queen's Counsel, Matrix Chambers;* b. 23 Sept. 1954, Bury; d. of Anthony Booth and Gale Booth (née Smith); m. Anthony Charles Lynton Blair (Tony Blair (q.v.)) 1980; three s. one d.; ed Seafield Grammar School, Crosby, Liverpool, London School of Econs; called to Bar (Lincoln's Inn) 1976, Asst Recorder 1996–99, Recorder 1999–, Bencher 1999–; pupillage with Alexander Irvine (now Lord Irvine of Lairg) 1976–77; Tenant New Court Chambers 1977–91, 4/5 Gray's Inn Square, London 1991–2000, Matrix Chambers 2000–; parl. cand. for Thanet 1983; apptd QC 1995; Gov. LSE 1998–; Chancellor John Moores Univ., Liverpool 1998–2008, Chancellor Emer. 2008–, Hon. Fellow; Pres. Comm. of Inquiry into UK Prison and Penal System 2007–; Pres. Barnardo's 2001–07 (currently Hon. Vice-Pres.), Kids Club Network, Family Mediators Asscn; Patron Refuge, The Citizenship Foundation, CLIC-Sargeant (Cancer Care for Children), Breast Cancer Care 1997–, Islington Music Centre 1999–, Victim Support London, SCOPE, Greater London Fund for the Blind, Home Start Islington, Mary Ward Legal Centre, Noah's Ark, NOJOS Awards, Downside Up, Age Exchange, The Merlyn Trust; Fellow, International Soc. of Lawyers for Public Service, Howard League for Penal Reform; Founder Cherie Blair Foundation for Women 2008, Africa Justice Foundation 2011; Patron Asian Univ. for Women, Chittagong, Bangladesh 2009–11, Chancellor 2011–; Hon. Bencher, King's Inn, Dublin 2002, Hon. Fellow, LSE 2003, Open Univ., Inst. of Advanced Legal Studies, Hon. Pres. Plater Coll., Hon. Patron Genesis Appeal; Hon. DUniv (Open) 1999, Hon. LLD (Westminster), (Liverpool) 2003, Hon. DLitt (UMIST) 2003. *Publications include:* The Goldfish Bowl 2004, The Negligence Liabilty of Public Authorities 2005, Speaking for Myself 2008. *Leisure interests:* family, reading, the arts, keeping fit. *Address:* Matrix Chambers, Griffin Building, Gray's Inn, London, WC1R 5LN, England (office). *Telephone:* (20) 7563-5050 (office); (20) 7298-0830 (home). *Fax:* (20) 7723-6525 (office). *E-mail:* boothc@matrixlaw.co.uk (office). *Website:* www.matrixlaw.co.uk (office).

BOOTH, Chris; New Zealand sculptor; b. 30 Dec. 1948, Kerikeri, Bay of Islands; m.; two s. one d.; ed Ilam School of Fine Arts, Univ. of Canterbury, Christchurch; undertook specialist sculpture studies with Barbara Hepworth, Denis Mitchell, John Milne and Quinto Ghermandi 1968–70; numerous solo and collective exhbs; rep. in public and pvt. collections including Int. Land Art Collections; Frances Hodgkins Fellowship, Univ. of Otago 1982; int. mem. Royal Soc. of British Sculptors 1990–2009, Int. Sculpture Centre, USA; elected for Art in Motion Biennale, Bos van Ypeij, Netherlands 2003; public and pvt. comm. in UK, Germany, Netherlands, Italy, France, Denmark, Australia, USA, Canada and New Zealand 1988–; Hon. Fellow, Northtec, Tai Tokerau Wānanga 2011; Christchurch/Seattle Sister City Comm. Award 1996, Greenham Common Trust Prize 1998, 10th Millfield Int. Sculpture Comm., Somerset 1998, Artists in Industry Project, Vic., Australia 1998–99, Hanover 2000 Expo, Steinbergen, Germany 2000, Kinetic Art Org. Int. Competition, USA 2002, Premium ASAA national sculpture award, Australia 2014. *Major commissions:* Gateway, Albert Park, Auckland 1990, Rainbow Warrior Memorial, Matauri Bay 1990, Tuuram Cairn, Deakin Univ., Warrnambool, Australia 1996, In Celebration of a Tor, Grizedale, Cumbria, UK 1993, Cave, Takahanga Marae, Kaikoura 1996, Wiyung Tchellungnai-Najil, Evandale Sculpture Walk, Gold Coast, Australia 1997, Tranekaer-Vader, Tickon, Langeland, Denmark 1998, Wairau Strata, Seresin Estate, Marlborough 2000, Bukker Tillibul, Swinburne Univ., Lilydale, Melbourne 2001, Waka and Wave (collaboration with Te Warihi Hetaraka), Whangarei District Council, NZ 2002–06, Kroller-Muller Museum Sculpture Garden, Netherlands 2004–05, Nga Uri O Hinetuparimaunga, Hamilton Gardens Entrance Sculpture (collaboration with Diggeress Te Kanawa), Hamilton City Council, NZ 2004–05, Echo van de Veluwe, Kröller-Müller Museum (Sculpture Park), Otterlo, Netherlands 2004–05, Subterranean Living Sculpture System, Eden Project, Cornwall, UK 2006–, Ciclo, San Miguel de Allende, Mexico 2007–, Te Whiringa o Manoko, Kerikeri, NZ 2007–09, JET commission for Royal Botanic Gardens, Sydney 2007–10, Kaitiaki, Rotoroa Island, Hauraki Gulf, NZ 2010–11, Transformation Plant, Van Dusen Gardens, Vancouver, Canada 2014, Earth Art, Royal Botanic Gardens, Burlington, Ontario, Canada 2014, Limestone Acacia, Mucsarnok/Kunsthalle, Budapest, Hungary 2016, Varder IV, Park Vijversbyurg, Tytsjerk, Netherlands, Varder IV 2016, Tauranga Kotuku, Kauri Cliffs, Northland, NZ 2017, The Farm, Margaret River, South West Australia, Waljin Beela 2017, Kinetic Fungi Tower, Waiheke Island, Auckland, NZ 2017, Te Wai U o te Atakura, Whangarei Quarry Gardens, Whangarei, NZ 2018. *Television documentaries include:* When a Warrior Dies (documentary on bombing of Greenpeace ship Rainbow Warrior and the creation of the memorial to the ship and its crew) 1995, Sculpture in the Park 1996, New in Netherlands (documentary on Kröller-Müller Museum Sculpture), Respecting the Earth (documentary for Maori TV on the making of Nga Uri o Hinetuparimaunga, entranceway sculpture to the Hamilton Gardens). *Publications include:* Chris Booth Sculpture 1993, Balanced Stone 1998, Chris Booth: Sculpture in Europe, Australia and New Zealand 2001, Woven Stone: The Sculpture of Chris Booth 2007. *Address:* PO Box 816, Kerikeri, 0245, New Zealand (office). *Fax:* (2) 145-5328 (office). *E-mail:* chris@chrisbooth.co.nz (office). *Website:* www.chrisbooth.co.nz (office).

BOOTH, Lewis William Killcross, CBE, BEng; British automotive industry executive; b. 7 Nov. 1948, Liverpool; m.; two c.; ed Univ. of Liverpool; chartered man. accountant; joined Ford Motor Co. 1978 as Financial Analysis Co-ordinator, Product Devt Div., later various man. positions with Ford Europe 1980–92, Finance Dept, Ford USA 1992–96, Group Man. Dir South Africa Motor Corpn (SAMCOR) 1997–2000, Pres. Ford Asia Pacific, Africa and Tech. Staffs 2000–02, Pres. and COO Ford of Europe GmbH 2003–08, Group Vice-Pres. Ford Motor Co. 2003–05, Exec. Vice-Pres. Ford Europe Operations 2005–08, Exec. Vice-Pres. Premier Automotive Group 2005–08, Chief Financial Officer and Exec. Vice-Pres. Ford Motor Co. 2008–12, Group Vice-Pres. Ford Motor Credit Co. LLC, Chair. Volvo Car Corpn, Ford Europe, fmr Chair. Jaguar Brand, Ford of Europe GmbH, Land Rover Brand, Ford Motor Co., Chair. (non-exec.) Cars Div. of Ford Motor Co., Vice-Chair. Ford Otomotiv Sanayi AS, Dir, Ford Motor Credit Co. LLC, Ford Motor Co., Ford of Europe GmbH, Land Volvo Brand, Mahindra & Mahindra Ltd 2000–, Ford Otosan 2003–, Mazda Motor Corpn 2003–08; Sr Advisor for Corp. Strategy, Mazda Motor Corpn 2002, Pres. and CEO 2002–03; Dir (non-exec.), Rolls-Royce 2011–. *Address:* Ford Motor Co., One American Road, Dearborn, MI 48126, USA (office). *Telephone:* (313) 322-3000 (office). *Fax:* (313) 845-7512 (office). *E-mail:* info@ford.com (office). *Website:* www.ford.com (office).

BOOTHROYD, Baroness (Life Peer), cr. 2000, of Sandwell in the County of West Midlands; **Rt Hon. Betty Boothroyd,** OM, PC; British parliamentarian; b. 8 Oct. 1929, Dewsbury, Yorks.; d. of Archibald Boothroyd and Mary Boothroyd; ed Dewsbury Coll. of Commerce and Art; sec., Labour Party HQ 1955–60; legis. asst to US congressman, Washington, DC 1960–62; sec. and personal asst to various sr Labour politicians 1962–73; mem. Hammersmith Borough Council 1965–68; contested various elections and by-elections 1957–70; MP (Labour) for West Bromwich 1973, for West Bromwich West 1974–2000; Asst Govt Whip 1974–76; mem. Labour Party Nat. Exec. 1981–87; Deputy Speaker 1987–92; Speaker of the House of Commons 1992–2000; currently Ind. Cross Bencher, House of Lords; Chancellor, Open Univ. 1994–2006; Hon. Bencher, Middle Temple 2011; several hon. degrees from British univs including Hon. LLD (Cambridge) 1994, Hon. DCL (Oxford) 1995, (St Andrews) 2002; Parliamentarian of the Year 1992, Personality of the Year, Communicator of the Year. *Publication:* Betty Boothroyd – The Autobiography 2001. *Address:* House of Lords, Westminster, London, SW1A 0PW, England. *Telephone:* (20) 7219-8673 (office). *E-mail:* boothroyd@parliament.uk.

BOOZMAN, John Nichols; American optometrist and politician; *Senator from Arkansas;* b. 10 Dec. 1950, Shreveport, Louisiana; s. of Fay Winford Boozman, Jr and Marie Boozman (née Nichols); m. Cathy Marley; three d.; ed Northside High School, Fort Smith, Univ. of Arkansas, Southern Coll. of Optometry; entered pvt. practice as Co-founder Boozman-Hof Regional Eye Clinic, Rogers, Ark. 1977; served two terms on Rogers Public School Bd; mem. US House of Reps for 3rd Congressional Dist of Ark. 2001–11, served as Asst Whip, as Chair. Veterans Affairs Econ. Opportunity Sub-cttee; Senator from Ark. 2011–, mem. Commerce, Science and Transportation Cttee 2011–13, Cttee on Agric., Nutrition and Forestry 2011–, Environment and Public Works Cttee 2011–, Cttee on Appropriations 2013–, Sr Senator 2015–; mem. NATO Parl. Ass., Rogers (Arkansas) Bd of Educ. 1994–2001; mem. Int. Acad. of Sports Vision, Arkansas Optometric Asscn, American Optometric Asscn, Fellowship of Christian Athletes; Republican; Spirit of Enterprise Award, US Chamber of Commerce 2001, 2002, 2003, Hero of the Taxpayer Award, American for Tax Reform 2001, 2002, 2003, Small Business Advocate Award, Small Business Survival Cttee 2004, Brighter Vision Award, Age-Related Macular Degeneration Alliance International 2006, Award for Manufacturing Legis. Excellence, Nat. Asscn of Mfrs 2010, A in English Award, US English, Inc. 2010, Distinguished Advocate Award, Asscn of Educ. & Rehabilitation of the Blind & Visually Impaired (Arkansas chapter). *Achievements include:* est. low vision programme at Arkansas School for the Blind, Little Rock; worked as volunteer optometrist at area clinic providing medical services to low-income families. *Address:* 320 Hart Senate Office Building, Washington, DC 20510, USA (office). *Telephone:* (202) 224-4843 (office). *Fax:* (202) 228-1371 (office). *Website:* www.boozman.senate.gov (office).

BORAH, Nayan Mani, BE; Indian business executive; ed Indian School of Mines, Dhanbad, Norwegian Inst. of Tech., Trondheim; Reservoir Engineer, Oil India Ltd 1974, later Group Gen. Man., Main Producing Area, Gen. Man. of Geosciences, Dir (Operations) 2004–10, Chair. and Man. Dir 2008–12, also mem. Business Devt Cttee; mem. Bd of Dirs Numaligarh Refinery Ltd 2006–11; mem. Academic Council, Dibrugarh Univ., Soc. of Petroleum Engineers, Soc. of Petroleum Geophysics. *Leisure interests:* reading, playing golf. *Address:* c/o Oil India Ltd, Plot No. 19, Near Film City, Sector 16A, Noida 201 301, India.

BORC, Costin, PhD; Romanian business executive and government official; ed Polytechnic Univ. of Bucharest, Univ. of Wisconsin, USA; Chief of Staff to the Prime Minister 1998–99; Project Manager, Lafarge North America 2000–01, Man. Dir A&C Romania 2002–06, Dir of Strategy and Devt 2006–08, CEO Lafarge Serbia 2008–13, CEO Lafarge Romania 2013–15; Man. Dir CRH Romania Aug.–Nov. 2015; Deputy Prime Minister and Minister of the Economy, Trade and Relations with the Business Environment Nov. 2015–17. *Address:* c/o Ministry of the Economy, Trade and Relations with the Business Environment, 010096 Bucharest 1, Calea Victoriei 152, Romania. *E-mail:* birou_presa@minind.ro.

BORCHERDS, Richard Ewen, PhD, FRS; British mathematician and academic; *Professor, Department of Mathematics, University of California, Berkeley;*

b. 29 Nov. 1959, South Africa; s. of Dr Peter Howard Borcherds and Margaret Elizabeth Borcherds (née Greenfield); m. Ursula Gritsch; ed Trinity Coll., Cambridge; Research Fellow, Trinity Coll. 1983–87; Morrey Asst Prof., Univ. of Calif., Berkeley 1987–88, Prof. of Math. 1993–96, 1999–, Miller Research Prof. 2000–01; Royal Soc. Univ. Residential Fellow, Univ. of Cambridge 1988–92, Lecturer 1992–93, Royal Soc. Prof., Dept of Math. 1996–99; mem. NAS 2014–; Fellow, American Mathematical Soc. 2013; Jr Whitehead Prize 1992, European Mathematical Soc. Prize 1992, Fields Medal 1998. *Publications:* numerous papers in mathematical journals. *Leisure interest:* films. *Address:* Department of Mathematics, 927 Evans Hall, University of California, Berkeley, CA 94720-3840, USA (office). *Telephone:* (510) 642-8464 (office). *Fax:* (510) 642-8204 (office). *E-mail:* reb@math.berkeley.edu (office). *Website:* math.berkeley.edu/people/faculty/richard-e-borcherds (office).

BORDA, Dionisio Cornelio, MA, PhD; Paraguayan economist, academic and politician; *Founder and Director, Centro de Análisis y Difusión de la Economía Paraguaya;* b. 12 Sept. 1949, San Juan, Misiones; ed Univs of Wisconsin and Massachusetts, USA; Prof., Dept of Econs, Universidad Nacional de Asunción; Adviser to Nat. Congress 1994–96; Minister of Finance 2003–05 (resgnd), 2008–12; Founder and Dir Centro de Análisis y Difusión de la Economía Paraguaya (CADEP); fmr Visiting Prof., Univ. of Indiana. *Publications:* Dos interpretaciones y perspectivas 1987, Una aproximación teórico-metodológica a la educación con producción 1988, Internalizing the Crisis of Cotton: Organizing small farmers in Eastern Paraguay 1988, Cambio y Continuismo: Persisten los grandes desafíos económicos para el Paraguay del 90 1990, Empresariado y Transición a la Democracia en Paraguay 1993, La estatización de la economía y la privatización del Estado 1993, Escenarios económicos y Reforma Educativa 2001, La crisis del modelo y su impacto sobre el empleo en Paraguay 2001, Paraguay, una marcha lenta: situación y perspectiva económica 2007, Situación económica y perspectivas en el Paraguay, Diplomacia, Estrategia Política 2007, La economía política del crecimiento, pobreza y desigualdad en el Paraguay 1968–2010 2013, Eficiencia y Equidad tributaria: Una tarea en construcción 2016, Desempeño e Institucionalidad Tributaria 2017, Una reforma tributaria para mejorar la equidad y la recaudación 2017, Empresariado y transición a la democracia en el Paraguay 2017, Demanda de graduados universitarios en el sector agroindustrial del Paraguay 2018, Escuchando a los jóvenes de América Latina y el Caribe: el caso de Paraguay 2018. *Address:* Centro de Análisis y Difusión de la Economía Paraguaya, Piribebuy 1058 entre Colón y Hernandarias, Asunción, Paraguay (home). *Telephone:* (21) 49-4140 (home). *Fax:* (21) 45-2520 (home). *E-mail:* cadep@cadep.org.py (home). *Website:* www.cadep.org.py/etiqueta/dionisio-borda (home).

BORDABERRY HERRÁN, Pedro; Uruguayan lawyer and politician; b. 28 April 1960, Montevideo; s. of Juan Maria Bordaberry (fmr Pres. of Uruguay); m.; three c.; ed British School de Montevideo, Universidad de la República; Nat. Dir of Industrial Property, Ministry of Industry, Energy and Mining 1993–94, Under-Sec., Ministry of Tourism 2000, Minister of Industry and Energy 2002–03, of Sports and Youth 2003–04, of Tourism 2004–05; unsuccessful cand. for Mayor of Montevideo 2005; f. Vamos Uruguay group within Partido Colorado 2007, Sec.-Gen. Partido Colorado 2009–11, unsuccessful cand. for Pres. of Uruguay 2009; Senator 2010–; fmr Pres. Uruguayan Rugby Union. *Publications:* El Principio de Irretroactividad de las Normas en la Jurisprudencia de la Suprema Corte de Justicia 1991; contrib. to: Diez Años de Seven 1998, Cuentos del Pueblo Faro de José Ignacio 1999, Que me Desmientan 2006. *Leisure interest:* rugby, novela. *Address:* Partido Colorado, Andrés Martínez Trueba 1271, 11100 Montevideo, Uruguay (office). *Telephone:* (2) 9247645 (office); (2) 2036099 (office). *E-mail:* pbordaberry@parlamento.gub.uy (office). *Website:* www.parlamento.gub.uy (office); www.vamosuruguay.com.uy (office).

BORDER, Allan Robert, AO; Australian fmr professional cricketer; b. 27 July 1955, Cremorne, Sydney, NSW; s. of John Border and Sheila Border; m. Jane Hiscox 1980; two c.; ed Mosman Primary School, N Sydney Tech. School, N Sydney Boys' High School; fmr clerk; work in motor trade; left-hand middle-order batsman, left-arm slow bowler; teams: NSW 1976–80, Glos., England 1977 (1 match), Queensland 1980–96 (Capt. 1983–89), Essex, England 1986–88; Capt. Australian Nat. Team 1984–94; 156 (record) Tests for Australia 1978–94, including record unbroken sequence of 153 matches, record 93 (unbroken sequence 1984–94) as Capt., scoring 11,174 runs (average 50.56) including 27 centuries and then holding record 156 catches; scored 27,131 first-class runs (70 centuries); toured England 1979 (World Cup), 1980, 1981, 1983 (World Cup), 1985, 1989, 1993 (last three as Capt.); then record 273 limited-overs ints, record 178 as Capt.; with Ronald McConnell Holdings 1980–84; mem. Nat. Cricket Selection Panel 1998–2005, 2006, Queensland Cricket Bd 2001–; Int. Cricket Council (ICC) Amb. to developing regions, mem. ICC Cttee; cricket commentator for Fox Sports Australia; Wisden Cricketer of the Year 1982, inducted into Sport Australia Hall of Fame 1990, Australian Sports Medal in 2000, Australian Cricket Hall of Fame 2000, inducted into ICC Cricket Hall of Fame 2009, Queensland Sport Hall of Fame 2009, Queensland Greats Awards 2016. *Publication:* A Peep at the Poms 1986. *Leisure interests:* golf, tennis, reading. *Website:* www.foxsports.com.au/cricket.

BORDYUZHA, Gen. Nikolai Nikolayevich; Russian politician, diplomatist and fmr army officer; b. 20 Oct. 1949, Orel, Orel Oblast; m.; one s.; ed Perm. Military Eng School, Moscow Inst. of Political Science, Military Acad. of the Gen. Staff of Armed Forces of the Russian Fed., Diplomatic Acad. of the Russian Fed.; service in army and state security forces 1972–91; Deputy Head, Personnel Dept, Fed. Agency of Govt Communications and Information of Russian Presidency 1991–92; Deputy Commdr, Frontier Forces 1992–94; Deputy Dir, Fed. Frontier Service 1995–98, Dir 1998; Chief of Staff of Presidential Exec. Office and Sec., Russian Fed. Security Council 1998–99; Head, State Customs Cttee 1999; Amb. to Denmark 2000–03; Sec.-Gen. Collective Security Treaty Org. 2003–17; Order of Services to the Motherland, Third Class (Russia), of Courage (Russia), of Friendship (Russia), of Friendship of Peoples (Belarus), Dostyk (Kazakhstan), Danaker (Kyrgyzstan), numerous medals. *Leisure interest:* fishing. *Address:* c/o Secretariat, Collective Security Treaty Organization, 3/2 Sverchkov per., 101000 Moscow, Russia (office). *Telephone:* (495) 621-37-86 (office). *Fax:* (495) 623-43-46 (office). *E-mail:* odkb@gov.ru (office). *Website:* www.odkb.gov.ru (office).

BOREL, Jacques Paul, MBA; French restaurant and hotel executive and consultant; b. 9 April 1927, Courbevoie; s. of William Borel and Marie Borel (née Le Monnier); m. Christiane Roubit 1949; two s. one d.; ed Lycées Condorcet and Carnot, Paris, Ecole des Hautes Etudes Commerciales; mem. Sales Force, IBM France 1950–57, Man. Saigon (Viet Nam) Br. Office, IBM; f. restaurant chain Jacques Borel 1957, became Compagnie des Restaurants Jacques Borel (CRJB) 1960, then Jacques Borel Int. (J.B. Int.) 1970, Pres., Dir-Gen. –1977; Pres. J.B. Enterprises Soc. 1977; Dir Sofitel Jacques Borel, Jacques Borel Belgie NV-Belgique SA, Jacques Borel Do Brasil, Jacques Borel Deutschland, Jacques Borel Italia, Jacques Borel Nederland, Jacques Borel Iran, Jacques Borel Misr (Egypt), Jacques Borel Venezuela, Hoteles Jacques Borel (Barcelona), Farah Maghreb (Casablanca); Founder Syndicat Nat. des Restaurants Economiques (now Syndicat Nat. des Chaînes d'Hôtels et de Restaurants de Tourisme et d'Entreprise) 1966; Pres. Groupement HEC Tourisme-Hôtellerie; f. Club VAT 1994, Club TVA (group campaigning for reduction of VAT in hotel and restaurant industry) 2000; Chevalier, Légion d'honneur 2008. *Leisure interests:* music, painting, sailing. *Address:* Jacques Borel VAT CLUB, 29 Champs-Elysées, 75008 Paris, France.

BOREN, David Lyle, MA, JD; American lawyer, university administrator and fmr politician; *President Emeritus, University of Oklahoma;* b. 21 April 1941, Washington, DC; s. of Lyle H. Boren and Christine Boren (née McKown); m. 1st; one s. one d.; m. 2nd Molly Shi 1977; ed Yale Univ., Univ. of Oxford, UK, Univ. of Oklahoma; mem. Okla House of Reps 1966–74; Chair. Govt Dept, Okla Baptist Univ. 1969–74; Gov. of Okla 1975–79; Senator from Okla 1979–94; Chair. Senate Select Cttee on Intelligence 1987–93; Pres. Univ. of Okla 1994–2018, then Pres. Emer.; co-Chair. President's Intelligence Advisory Bd 2009–13; Rhodes Scholar 1965; mem. Bd of Trustees, Yale Univ. 1988–97; Hon. mem. National Association for Urban Debate Leagues inducted into Oklahoma Hall of Fame 1988, Henry Yost Award as Educ. Advocate of the Year, American Assn of Univ. Profs 1993, Foreign Language Advocacy Award, Northeast Conf. on the Teaching of Foreign Languages 1996, Mory's Cup, Mory's Assn, Yale Univ. 2004. *Publications:* A Letter to America 2008. *Leisure interests:* family, reading, rowing, tennis. *Address:* University of Oklahoma, 660 Parrington Oval, Norman, OK 73019-3073 (office); 750 West Boyd, Norman, OK 73019, USA (home). *Telephone:* (405) 325-3916 (office). *Website:* www.ou.edu (office).

BORG, Alan Charles Nelson, CBE, PhD, FSA; British museum director; b. 21 Jan. 1942; s. of Charles J. N. Borg and Frances M. O. Hughes; m. 1st Anne Blackmore 1964 (divorced); one s. one d.; m. 2nd Lady Caroline Hill 1976; two d.; ed Westminster School, Brasenose Coll., Oxford, Courtauld Inst. of Art, London; Lecteur d'anglais, Univ. d'Aix-Marseille 1964–65; Lecturer, History of Art, Indiana Univ. 1967–69; Asst Prof. of History of Art, Princeton Univ. 1969–70; Asst Keeper of the Armouries, HM Tower of London 1970–78; Keeper, Sainsbury Centre for Visual Arts, Univ. of East Anglia 1978–82; Dir-Gen. Imperial War Museum 1982–95; Chair. Nat. Inventory of War Memorials 1988–95, Advisory Cttee on Public Records 1993, Vice-Pres. Foundling Museum 2010–; Dir Victoria and Albert Museum 1995–2001; Pres. Elizabethan Club 1994–2000; Gov. Westminster School 1997–2019; Librarian, Order of St John 2007–18; mem. Priory Council of Trustees, St John Ambulance; Hon. Liveryman, Worshipful Co. of Painters 1997; Hon. FRIBA 2001; Hon. Freeman, Worshipful Co. of Cooks 2011; Kt, Order of St John; Dr hc (Sheffield Hallam) 2000. *Publications include:* Architectural Sculpture in Romanesque Provence 1972, European Swords and Daggers in the Tower of London 1974, Torture and Punishment 1975, Heads and Horses 1976, Arms and Armour in Britain 1979, The Vanishing Past 1981, War Memorials 1991, History of the Painter-Stainers Company 2002, History of the Worshipful Company of Cooks 2011, A History of Vauxhall Gardens 2011; articles in learned journals. *Leisure interests:* fencing, music, travel. *Address:* 16 Devonshire House, Lindsay Square, London, SW1V 2HN, England (home).

BORG, Anders E.; Swedish economist and politician; b. 11 Jan. 1968, Stockholm; m. Sanna Borg; three c.; ed De Geer School, local authority adult secondary educ., Norrköping, Uppsala and Stockholm Univs; Chair. Uppsala Univ. Student Union 1989, Föreningen Heimdal 1989; leader writer, Svenska Dagbladet 1990–91; Political Adviser, Prime Minister's Office, Coordination Secr., with responsibility for coordination of Ministry of Health and Social Affairs, Ministry of Public Admin, Ministry of Culture and Ministry of Educ. and Science 1991–93; Political Adviser to Carl Bildt at Prime Minister's Office 1993–94; Chief Economist, Transferator Alfred Berg 1995–98; Chief Economist, ABN Amro Bank, Stockholm 1998–99; Head of Econ. Analysis Dept, Skandinaviska Enskilda Banken (SEB) 1999–2001; adviser on monetary policy issues to Exec. Bd Riksbank (Swedish Cen. Bank) 2001–02; Chief Economist and Admin. Dir Moderate Party 2002–06; Minister of Finance 2006–14; mem. Expert Group on Public Finance 1992–96, Bd Swedish Labour Market Admin 2005. *Address:* c/o Ministry of Finance, Drottninggatan 21, 103 33 Stockholm, Sweden (office).

BORG, Björn Rune; Swedish business executive and fmr professional tennis player; b. 6 June 1956, Stockholm; s. of Rune Borg; m. 1st Mariana Simionescu 1980 (divorced 1984); one s. by Jannike Bjorling; m. 2nd Loredana Berte 1989 (divorced 1992); ed Blombacka School; professional player since 1972; Italian Champion 1974, 1978; French Open Champion 1974, 1975, 1978, 1979, 1980, 1981; Wimbledon Champion 1976, 1977, 1978, 1979, 1980 (runner-up 1981); WCT Champion 1976; four times runner-up in US Open; Grand Prix Masters Champion 1980, 1981; World Champion 1979, 1980; played Davis Cup for Sweden 1972, 1973, 1974, 1975, 1976, 1977, 1978, 1979, 1980; Winner Stockholm Open 1980; announced retirement from tennis Jan. 1983, two brief comebacks 1984, 1992; ranked by ATP World No. 1 in six different periods 1977–81, total of 109 weeks; 77 career top-level singles wins (64 listed on ATP website) and four doubles titles; later played in srs tour; f. Björn Borg Enterprises Ltd; Sweden's Sportsperson of the Century, voted second-best tennis player ever by Sports Illustrated and l'Equipe newspaper, BBC Sports Personality of the Year Overseas Personality Award 1979, inducted into Int. Tennis Hall of Fame 1987, BBC Lifetime Achievement Award 2006, elected Sweden's top sportsperson of all time by Dagens Nyheter newspaper 2014. *Publication includes:* Bjorn Borg – My Life and Game (with Eugene Scott) 1980. *Leisure interest:* fishing. *Address:* c/o IMG, McCormack House, One Burlington Lane, Hogarth Business Park, Chiswick, London, W4 2TH, England (office). *Telephone:* (20) 8233-5300 (office). *Fax:* (20) 8233-5301 (office). *E-mail:* speakersuk@imgworld.com (office); www.img.com

(office). *Website:* www.imgspeakers.com/speaker/Bjorn-Borg (office); www.bjornborg.com.

BORG, Joseph (Joe), LLD; Maltese politician and lawyer; b. 19 March 1952; m. Isabelle Agius; one s. one d.; ed Lyceum, Univ. of Malta, Univ. of Wales, UK; practising lawyer 1976–; legal adviser to cos and corpns in Malta and abroad; Lecturer, Univ. of Malta 1979–88, Sr Lecturer 1988; adviser on EU matters to Minister of Foreign Affairs 1989–95; mem. Bd of Govs Malta Int. Business Authority 1989–92, Bd of Dirs of Cen. Bank 1992–95; MP 1995–2004; Shadow Minister for Industry and EU Impact on Malta 1996–98; mem. Foreign Affairs Parl. Cttee, EU-Malta Jt Cttee 1996–98; Parl. Sec., Ministry of Foreign Affairs 1998–99; Minister of Foreign Affairs 1999–2004; EU Commr without Portfolio 2004, for Fisheries and Maritime Affairs 2004–10; Special Adviser, Fipra (public relations consultancy), Brussels 2010; Hon. LLM (Wales).

BORG, Tonio, LLD; Maltese politician, lawyer and fmr EU official; b. 12 May 1957; s. of Carmelo Borg and Maria Gemma Zarb; m. Adele Galea 1982; one s. two d.; ed St Aloysius Coll. and Univ. of Malta; Lecturer in Public Law, Univ. of Malta; Exec. mem. European Union Young Christian Democrats 1983–85; Dir Mid-Med Bank 1987–92; Pres. of Nationalist Party Gen. Council 1988–95; mem. of European Cttee for Prevention of Torture and Inhuman or Degrading Punishment or Treatment 1990–95; MP 1992–; mem. Planning Authority 1992–95; mem. of Council of Europe Ass. 1992–95; mem. Jt Parl. Cttee of the European Parl. and Maltese House of Reps 1992–95, 1996–98; Minister for Home Affairs 1995–96, 1998–2003, for Justice and Home Affairs 2003–08, for Foreign Affairs and Deputy Prime Minister 2008–12; Commr for Health and Consumer Policy, EC, Brussels 2012–14; mem. Nationalist Party. *Leisure interests:* reading, cycling. *Address:* c/o European Commission, 200 Rue de la Loi/Wetstraat 200, 1049 Brussels, Belgium (office).

BORGEAUD, Pierre, DiplEng; Swiss business executive; b. 31 March 1934, Pompaples, Morges; m.; three c.; ed Swiss Fed. Inst. of Tech.; with Research Dept, Sulzer Bros Ltd 1959–73, Man. Sulzer Eng Works and Swiss Locomotive and Machine Works, Winterthur 1973–75, Gen. Man., Sulzer Bros Ltd (now Sulzer Man. Ltd) 1975–81, Pres. and CEO 1981–88 (Chair. 1988–2000, Del. 1999), fmr mem. Bd of Dirs; Chair. Presidential Bd of Swiss Fed. of Commerce and Industry 1987–93; Vice-Chair. Clariant Ltd 2000–03; fmr mem. Bd of Dirs Swiss Bank Corpn, Bühler Ltd, Pirelli Int. Ltd, Winterthur Insurance Co.; mem. Advisory Bd Brainforce AG.

BORGES, Jacobo; Venezuelan painter; b. 28 Nov. 1931, Caracas; ed Escuela de Artes Plásticas Cristóbal Rojas, Caracas and Ecole des Beaux Arts, Paris; mem. of Young Painters' Group and illustrator of magazines and record covers while in Paris 1951–56, also exhibited in French nat. exhbns; Prof. of Scenography and Plastic Analysis, Escuela de Artes Plásticas Cristóbal Rojas, Caracas 1958–65; Prof. of Scenography, Theatre School of Valencia and Dir Experimental Art Centre, Univ. Centre de Venezuela 1966–; has taught at Int. Summer Acad., Salzburg, Austria 1995–96, 1998–99, 2000–04; int. exhbns at Guggenheim Museum, New York 1964, 1965; Artist-in-Residence, Mexico City 1993; Museo Jacobo Borges created to house his work 1995; Nat. Painting Prize 1963, Armando Reverón Bienal Prize 1965. *Major works:* La Lámpara y la Silla 1951, La Pesca 1957, Sala de Espera 1960, Todos a la Fiesta 1962, Ha Comenzado el Espectáculo 1964, Altas Finanzas 1965; series of Las Jugadoras and Las Comedoras de Helados 1965–66. *Website:* www.museojacoboborges.org.ve.

BORGES, Jorge Alberto da Silva; Cabo Verde economist, diplomatist and politician; b. 17 April 1952; ed Univ. of Porto, Portugal; worked for several years with EU at HQ in Brussels and in Botswana and Zimbabwe; Adjunct State Sec. to Minister of Economy, Growth and Competitiveness 2007; with Ministry of Foreign Affairs, Sec. of State for Foreign Affairs –2011, Minister of Foreign Affairs 2011–14. *Address:* c/o Ministry of Foreign Affairs, Palácio das Comunidades, Achada de Santo António, CP 60, Praia, Santiago, Cabo Verde.

BORGES, Victor Manuel Barbosa; Cabo Verde politician; *Independent Consultant, EFG Consulting;* b. 24 May 1955, Assomada; s. of André Borges and Maria Luisa Barbosa Borges; m. Leopoldina Maria Varela Furtado; one s. two d.; fmr Minister of Educ., Culture and Sports with portfolio of Human Resources Devt; Minister of Foreign Affairs, Co-operation and Communities 2004–08; mem. Governing Bd of UNESCO Inst. for Lifelong Learning; Ind. Consultant, EFG Consulting. *Address:* Rua Cidade de Funchal, 8 CP 133-A ASA, Praia, Santiago, Cabo Verde (office). *Telephone:* (262) 2368 (office). *E-mail:* victorborges@sapo.cv (office).

BORGO BUSTAMANTE, Enrique, MA, JD; Salvadorean business executive, lawyer, politician and diplomatist; b. 1928; ed Universidad de El Salvador, Rome Univ., Italy; Judge, First Instance Criminal Court, San Vicente 1955–57; attorney, Salvadoran Social Security Inst. 1957–60; attorney, Cen. Bank of El Salvador 1961–63; Dir Banco Cuscatlán 1975–79; Legal Adviser, Taca Int. Airlines 1975–80, CEO 1981–94; Vice-Pres. of El Salvador 1994–99; mem. Cen. American Congress 1999–2000; apptd Amb. to Spain 2004; fmr Partner, Consortium Centro America Abogados, El Salvador; Borgo, Avila & Cordova; Gentleman of the Order of Santiago 2008, Gran Cruz, Orden de Isabel La Catolica 2011.

BORIES, Christel; French business executive; *Chairman and CEO, ERAMET;* b. 20 May 1964; ed Hautes Etudes Commerciales School of Management, Paris; worked for Booz Allen & Hamilton; Man. Corporate Value Assocs; joined Pechiney 1993, later Head of Packaging Div., Pres. and CEO Alcan Packaging and Sr Vice-Pres. Alcan Inc. (following takeover of Pechiney by Alcan) 2003–06, Pres. and CEO Engineered Products Group (now Rio Tinto Alcan Engineered Products Group) 2006–10; Chair. Exec. Cttee European Aluminium Asscn 2007–08; CEO Constellium 2011; Deputy CEO Ipsen 2013–16; Chair. and CEO ERAMET 2017–; mem. Bd of Dirs Atlas Copco AB 2008; mem. Bd Legrand 2012–, Smurfit Kappa Group 2012–. *Address:* ERAMET Group, Tour Maine Montparnasse 33, avenue du Maine, 75755 Paris, Cedex 15, France (office). *Website:* www.eramet.com (office).

BORISOV, Lt-Gen. Boyko Metodiev, DS; Bulgarian politician and professional footballer; *Prime Minister;* b. 13 June 1959, Bankya; m. Stela Borisova (divorced); one d.; partner Tsvetelina Borislavova; ed Higher Specialized School, Ministry of the Interior; early career as police officer, Sofia 1978, Platoon Commdr 1982, later Co. Commdr; Lecturer, Higher Inst. for Officer Training and Scientific Research, Ministry of the Interior 1985–90; f. WON-1 Ltd (security co.) 1991; mem. Balgarska Komunisticheska Partiya (Bulgarian Communist Party) –1990, Natsionalno Dvizhenie Simeon Vtori (Nat. Movt Simeon II) 2001–06; Sec.-Gen., Ministry of the Interior 2001–05; Mayor of Sofia 2005–09; Founder and Leader Grazhdani za Evropeysko Razvitie na Balgariya (GERB—Citizens for European Devt of Bulgaria) 2006–; Prime Minister 2009–13 (resgnd), 2014–17 (resgnd), 2017–; mem. World Org. of Security Co.; has actively participated in karate championships since 1978, currently has 7th dan black belt; Chair. Bulgarian Karate Fed., fmr Coach, Bulgarian Nat. Karate Team and int. karate referee; plays as a forward for Vitosha Bistritsa football team, became the oldest player ever to play for a Bulgarian professional club when he appeared for Vitosha in the B PFG (second div.) 2013; Sign of Honour (Second Degree), Bulgaria 2003, Cross for Police Contrib. with Red Star, Spain 2003, Medal of Honour of the French Police, Medal for Operational Friendship and Co-operation, Russia, Commdr, Order of the Star of Italian Solidarity 2006. *Address:* Office of the Council of Ministers, 1594 Sofia, bul. Dondukov 1 (office); Grazhdani za Evropeysko Razvitie na Balgariya (GERB), 1463 Sofia, pl. Balgariya 1, NDK Administration Building 17, Bulgaria (office). *Telephone:* (2) 940-29-99 (office); (2) 490-13-13 (GERB) (office). *Fax:* (2) 980-21-01 (office); (2) 490-09-51 (GERB) (office). *E-mail:* gis@government.bg (office); pr@gerb.bg (office). *Website:* www.government.bg (office); www.gerb.bg (office).

BORISOV, Yurii Ivanovich, DSc; Russian army officer and politician; *Deputy Chairman of the Government;* b. 31 Dec. 1956, Vyshnii Volochyok, Kalinin Oblast (now Tver Oblast), Russian SFSR, USSR; m.; two s.; ed Kalinin Mil. School, Radioelectronics Higher Command School of Air Defence, Pushkin City, Moscow State M.V. Lomonosov Univ.; mil. service in Armed Forces of USSR and Russian Fed. 1978–98; Gen. Dir, Module Research and Devt Centre (jt stock co.) 1998–2004; Chief, Dept of Electronic Industry and Control Systems, Federal Industrial Agency 2004–07, Deputy Head, Federal Industrial Agency 2007; Deputy Minister of Industry and Trade 2008–11; First Deputy Chair., Govt Mil.-Industrial Comm. 2011–12; Deputy Minister of Defence 2012–18; Deputy Chair. of Govt 2018–; Order of Service to the Homeland in the USSR Armed Forces (3rd degree), Order of Alexander Nevsky 2018. *Address:* Office of the Government, 103274 Moscow, Krasnopresnenskaya nab. 2, Russia (office). *Telephone:* (495) 985-42-80 (office). *Fax:* (495) 605-53-62 (office). *E-mail:* duty_press@aprf.gov.ru (office). *Website:* government.ru (office).

BORITH, Ouch; Cambodian diplomatist; *Secretary of State, Ministry of Foreign Affairs and International Cooperation;* b. 2 Nov. 1957, Phnom-Penh; m.; five c.; ed Medical Faculty, Phnom-Penh, Inst. of Sociology, Moscow; French trans., Ministry of Foreign Affairs 1979–80, Dir Dept of UN Humanitarian Org., Ministry of Foreign Affairs 1980–83, Dir Dept of Asia and Pacific Affairs 1987–90; Counsellor in charge of Political Affairs, Embassy in Moscow 1983–87; Amb. to Viet Nam 1990–92; Chargé d'affaires, Perm. Mission to UN, New York 1992–93, Deputy Perm. Rep. 1993–97, Perm. Rep. 1998; currently Sec. of State, Ministry of Foreign Affairs and Int. Co-operation. *Address:* Ministry of Foreign Affairs and International Co-operation, 3 rue Samdech Hun Sen, Khan Chamkarmon, Phnom-Penh, Cambodia (office). *Telephone:* (23) 214441 (office). *Fax:* (23) 216144 (office). *E-mail:* mfaicasean@online.com.kh (office). *Website:* www.mfaic.gov.kh (office).

BORJA CEVALLOS, Rodrigo, PhD, DJur; Ecuadorean politician and academic; b. 19 June 1937, Quito; s. of Luis Felipe Borja de Alcázar and Aurelia Cevallos; m. Carmen Calisto de Borja; one s. three d.; ed Cen. Univ. of Ecuador; Deputy in Nat. Congress 1962–82; founder and fmr Leader Partido Izquierda Democrática; Prof. of Political Sciences, Cen. Univ. of Ecuador 1963–88; Pres. of Ecuador 1988–92; presidential candidate 2002; Pres. Law School Asscn, Cen. Univ. of Ecuador 1958; mem. Special Comm. of Lawyers on Ecuador's Political Constitution 1966; Hon. Mem. Charles Darwin Foundation; Hon. Prof. Universidad Nacional de Mar del Plata, Argentina, Universidad Autónoma de Santo Domingo, Dominican Repub.; Dr hc (Sorbonne, Paris), (Universidad de Buenos Aires), (Universaidad de San Andrés de Bolivia), (Univ. of N Carolina, Ashville, USA), (Universidad Nacional de Santiago, Dominican Repub.), (Universidad Ricardo Palma, Lima); Cristóbal Gabarrón International Award for Thought and Humanities 2010. *Publications:* Political Constitutional Law (2 vols) 1964, 1971, Socialismo Democrático (Democratic Socialism) 1983, El Asilo Diplomático en América (Diplomatic Asylum in the Americas), La democracia en América Latina (Democracy in Latin America), A Political Dictionary, Historia de una Claudicación, Tratado de Derecho Político y Constitucional, La Etica del Poder, Desarrollo del Derecho Constitucional Ecuatoriano, Derechos Humanos: una nueva perspectiva, Democracia y Populismo, La lucha de América Latina por la Democracia, Recovecos de la Historia, Sociedad, Cultura y Derecho; numerous essays.

BORKO, Yuri Antonovich, DEcon; Russian economist; *Head, European Integration Department, Institute of Europe, Russian Academy of Sciences;* b. 6 Feb. 1929, Rostov-on-Don; m. Yelena Borisovna Borko; two s.; ed Moscow State Univ.; researcher, Inst. of World Econ. and Int. Relations USSR (now Russian) Acad. of Sciences 1962–63; Ed. and mem. of Bd journal World Econ. and Int. Relations 1963–69; Head of Div. Inst. of Information on Social Sciences, USSR (now Russian) Acad. of Sciences 1970–90; Head of Div., Deputy Dir, Head of Research Centre of European Integration, Head of Centre of European Documentation, Prof., Inst. of Europe, Russian Acad. of Sciences 1990–, Jean Monnet Chairholder 2001–; Pres. Russian Asscn of European Studies 1992–. *Publications include:* works on problems of European integration, European Community policy and int. relations between Russia and European Community. *Leisure interests:* skiing, books, music. *Address:* Institute of Europe, 125993 Moscow, Mokhovaya str. 11, stroenye 3B (office); 127018 Moscow, Sovetskoy Armii str. 13–43, Russia (home). *Telephone:* (495) 292-10-23 (office); (495) 289-21-66 (home). *Fax:* (495) 200-42-98 (office). *E-mail:* europe@ieras.ru (office). *Website:* www.ieras.ru (office); www.edc-aes.ru (office).

BORLOO, Jean-Louis, MBA; French lawyer and politician; b. 7 April 1951, Paris; m. Béatrice Schönberg 2005; ed Ecole des Hautes Etudes Commerciales-Institut Supérieur des Affaires (HEC-ISA), Univ. of Manchester, UK; began career as finance lawyer, Paris; est. own law firm; fmr teacher of Financial Analysis, HEC-ISA; Mayor of Valenciennes 1989–2002, Deputy Mayor 2002–08; mem. European Parl. 1989–92; Regional Counsellor for Nord-Pas-de-Calais 1992–93, 1998; mem. Assemblée Nationale for Nord region 1993–2002, 2007–14; Spokesman, Union pour la Démocratie Française (UDF) 2001–02; mem. and Pres. Municipal Council of Valenciennes 2001–08; joined Union pour la majorité présidentielle (now Union pour un Mouvement Populaire—UMP) 2002; Minister-Del. of Towns and Urban Redevelopment, attached to Minister of Social Affairs, Labour and Solidarity 2002–04; Minister of Employment, Labour and Social Cohesion 2004–05, of Employment, Social Cohesion and Housing 2005–07, of the Economy, Finance and Employment May–June 2007, for Ecology, Energy, Sustainable Devt and Spatial Planning June 2007–10; Pres. Parti Radical de Gauche (assoc. party of UMP) 2007–11; Pres. and Leader, Union des démocrates et indépendants (Union of Democrats and Independents) 2012–14. *Publications:* Un Homme en colère 2002, L'Architecte et l'Horologer 2007.

BORMAN, Frank; American business executive and fmr astronaut; b. 14 March 1928, Gary, Ind.; s. of Edwin Borman and Marjorie Borman; m. Susan Bugbee 1950; two s.; ed US Mil. Acad., California Inst. of Tech., USAF Aerospace Research Pilots' School; pilot training, Williams Air Force Base, Arizona; assigned to various fighter squadrons in US and Philippines; Instructor in Thermodynamics and Fluid Mechanics, US Mil. Acad. 1957; Instructor, USAF Aerospace Research Pilots' School 1960–62; selected by NASA as astronaut Sept. 1962, Command Pilot, Gemini VII 1965, Commdr Apollo VIII spacecraft which made flight round the moon Dec. 1968, Deputy Dir for Flight Operations, NASA, –1969, Field Dir NASA Space Station Task Group 1969–70; Vice-Pres. Eastern Airlines Inc. 1970–74, Vice-Pres. for Eastern Operations 1974–75, Pres. 1975–85, CEO 1975–86, Chair. of Bd 1976–86; Vice-Chair. Texas Air Corp. 1986–92; Chair. and CEO Patlex Corp. 1988–92, Chair. Bd Autofinance Group Inc. (parent of Patlex) 1992–95; NASA Exceptional Service Medal, Harmon Int. Aviation Trophy 1966, Gold Space Medal, Int. Aeronautics 1969, Encyclopedia Britannica Achievement in Life Award 1980. *Publication:* Countdown: An Autobiography 1988. *Leisure interests:* restoring aeroplanes, building model aeroplanes. *Address:* 4530 Blue Lake Drive, Boca Raton, FL 33431, USA (home).

BORNER, Silvio; Swiss economist and academic; b. 24 April 1941; s. of Walter Borner and Meta Borner; m. Verena Barth 1966; two d.; ed St Gall Grad. School and Yale Univ., USA; Prof. of Econs, Univ. of St Gallen 1974–78, of Political Econs, Univ. of Basle 1978–2009, currently Prof. Emer. and Program Dir of Summer School in Law, Econs and Public Policy; Sr Adviser, Hoffmann & Partner (consultancy), Basel; mem. Man. Bd Avenir Suisse; columnist, Weltwoche magazine. *Publications include:* Die 'sechste Schweiz'—überleben auf dem Weltmarkt, New Forms of Internationalization: An Assessment, Einführung in die Volkswirtschaftslehre, International Finance and Trade in a Polycentric World. *Leisure interests:* sports (active) and culture. *Address:* WWZ der Universität Basel, Abteilung Wirtschaft und Politik, Peter Merian-Weg 6, Postfach, 4002 Basle, Switzerland (office). *E-mail:* silvio.borner-at-unibas.ch (office). *Website:* wwz.unibas.ch/en/people/profile/person/borner (office).

BORODIN, Pavel Pavlovich; Russian politician and economist; b. 25 Oct. 1946, Shakhudya, Nizhnii-Novgorod region; m. Valentina Borodina; one d. three adopted s.; ed Higher CPSU School, Moscow Inst. of Chemical Machine Construction, Ulyanovsk Inst. of Agric.; joined Yakutskgeologiya co. as economist 1978, Deputy Dir-Gen. until 1990; Mayor of Yakutsk 1993; Russian Soviet Federated Socialist Repub. People's Deputy, mem. Cttee on Problems of Women, Family Protection and Childhood 1990–93; moved to Moscow 1993; mem., then Man., then Chair. of Presidential Admin. 1993–2000; State Sec. Union of Russia and Belarus 2000–11; detained in USA on request of Swiss Govt Prosecutor, extradited to Switzerland for money laundering 2002, case closed 2002; Leader, Great Russia—Eurasian Union electoral bloc, State Duma elections 2003; Hon. Citizen, City of London 2009; Order of Merit for the Fatherland 1996, 2nd Class 1996, Order of Merit, Moldova 2001, Order of Merit, Transnistria 2001, Order of Friendship of Peoples, Belarus 2006, Order of Francisc Skarina, Order for Service to Motherland, 3rd Class 2011; State Prize of Russian Fed. *Leisure interests:* football, pets. *Address:* Executive Committee of Union of Russia and Belarus, 220000 Minsk, Kirova str. 17, Belarus (office). *Telephone:* (17) 229-34-34 (office). *Website:* www.belarus.mid.ru (office).

BORODINA, Olga Vladimirovna; Russian singer (mezzo-soprano); b. Leningrad (now St Petersburg); d. of Vladimir Nikolaevich and Galina Fedorovna Borodin; m. Ildar Abdrazakov; three s.; ed Leningrad Conservatory (student of Irina Bogacheva); soloist of Kirov (now Mariinsky) Theatre of Opera and Ballet 1987–; debut as Delilah in Samson and Delilah at Royal Opera House, Covent Garden with Plácido Domingo 1992; leading roles in operas including Marfa in Khovanshchina, Konchakovna in Prince Igor, Poline in Queen of Spades, Lubava in Sadko, Marina Mnichek in Boris Godunov, Cinderella in La Cenerentola, Carmen, Amneris in Aïda, Eboli in Don Carlos, Isabella in The Italian Girl in Algiers, Laura in La Giocconda, Delilah in Samson and Delilah, La Principessa in Adriana Lecouvreur, Giulietta in Les Contes d'Hoffmann, Marguerite in La Damnation de Faust; regular performances in all major opera houses as well as recitals and concerts world-wide; winner of First Prizes: All-Union Glinka Competition 1987, Int. Rosa Poncell Competition, New York 1987, Int. Francisco Viñas Competition, Barcelona 1989, People's Artist of Russia 2002, State Prize of Russia 2007. *Recordings include:* Verdi Requiem, Chicago Symphony Orchestra, conductor Riccardo Muti (Grammy Award for Best Classical Album) 2011, Cilea's Adriana Lecouvreur (Int. Classical Music Award for DVD Performance 2013). *Leisure interest:* fishing. *Address:* c/o NFBM Ltd, 3 Fergus Road, London, N5 1JS, England (office). *Telephone:* (20) 7359-4771 (office). *Fax:* (20) 3292-1913 (office). *E-mail:* nicola-fee@nfbm.com (office). *Website:* www.nfbm.com (office); www.mariinsky.ru/en/company/opera/soloists/mezzo_soprano/borodina.

BORONOV, Maj.-Gen. Kubatbek; Kyrgyzstani engineer, politician and fmr army officer; *First Deputy Prime Minister;* b. 15 Dec. 1964, Uzgen Dist, Osh Oblast, Kyrgyz SSR, USSR; ed Frunze Polytechnic Inst. (now Iskhak Razzakov Kyrgyz State Technical University, Bishkek); served in Soviet Army 1983–85; Engineer and Deputy Head of Base, Kyrgyzkurulush Stroileskomplekt PBdö JSC (jt stock construction co.) 1992–96, Dir Kyrgyzkurulush woodworking factory JSC 1998–2000; Deputy Dir, Goktürk LLC (eng co.) 2001–02; called to active service, Dept of Civil Defence 2003–06; Deputy Head, Int. Dept, Ministry of Emergency Situations 2006–08, Dir, Dept of prevention of emergency situations and elimination of consequences Jan.–July 2010, Deputy Minister of Emergency Situations 2010–11, Minister of Emergency Situations 2011–18; Head, Chui Oblast 2009–10; First Deputy Prime Minister 2018–. *Address:* Office of the Government, 720003 Bishkek, Dom Pravitelstva, Kyrgyzstan (office). *Telephone:* (312) 62-53-78 (office). *Fax:* (312) 66-46-40 (office). *E-mail:* ps@mail.gov.kg (office). *Website:* www.gov.kg (office).

BOROS, Christian; German art collector and media executive; b. 1964, Zabrze (German: Hindenburg), Upper Silesia, Poland; m. Karen Lohmann; ed studied communication design with Bazon Brock in Wuppertal; f. Boros communication agency 1990; cr. ad campaign for music channel VIVA 1994; began collecting art aged 18; first purchase, Intuition Box, an early multiple of Joseph Beuys; discovered the photographer Wolfgang Tillmans in London 1990; collected the Young British Artists Damien Hirst, Tracey Emin, Steven Gontarski and Sarah Lucas, and the German Zeitgeist artists Michel Majerus, Daniel Pflumm, the American artists Elizabeth Peyton, Anselm Reyle and the Danish artist Olafur Eliasson; owns pvt. museum of contemporary art, Bunker in Berlin, comprises more than 700 works of contemporary art; mem. Bd, Zeppelin Univ., Friedrichshafen, Lecturer 2012–. *Address:* Boros Group, Hofaue 63, 42103 Wuppertal (office); Sammlung Boros, Bunker, Reinhardtstr. 20, 10117 Berlin -Mitte, Germany (office). *Telephone:* (202) 24843-0 (Wuppertal) (office); (30) 27594065 (Berlin) (office). *Fax:* (202) 24843-19 (Wuppertal) (office). *E-mail:* info@sammlung-boros.de (office). *Website:* www.sammlung-boros.de (office).

BOROSS, Péter, PhD; Hungarian lawyer and politician; b. 27 Aug. 1928, Nagybajom; m. Ilona Papp (died 2010); two c.; ed Eötvös Loránd Univ. of Budapest; with Budapest Metropolitan Council 1951–56; dismissed for membership of revolutionary cttee and revolutionary council 1956; kept under police surveillance until 1959; employed as unskilled worker 1964; organized catering and tourist coll. training; catering chain dir 1971; mem. Council Coll. of Trade and Catering; mem. Hungarian League of Human Rights, Hungarian Chamber of Economy; Founder, Nation Bldg Foundation 1988; Minister of State for Office of Information and Office of Nat. Security 1990–94; Minister of Interior 1990–93; Prime Minister of Hungary 1993–94; mem. Parl. (Hungarian Democratic Forum—MDF) 1994–98; Chair. Nat. Security Cttee of Parl. 1994–96; Sr Counsellor and Adviser to Prime Minister 1998–2009; mem. Hungarian Democratic Forum –2010.

BOROVKOV, Aleksandr Alekseyevich, DSc; Russian mathematician and academic; *Professor, Head of Probability and Statistics Chair, Novosibirsk University;* b. 6 March 1931, Moscow; s. of Aleksey and Klaudia Borovkov; m. Svetlana Borovkov 1975; two s.; ed Moscow Univ.; Postgraduate, Research Assoc. Steclev Math. Inst. 1954–60; Head of Probability and Statistics Dept, Sobolev Inst. of Math., Siberian Branch USSR (now Russian) Acad. of Sciences 1960–, Deputy Dir 1981–91; Prof., Head of Probability and Statistics Chair, Novosibirsk Univ. 1965–; Corresp. mem. USSR (now Russian) Acad. of Sciences 1966–90, full mem. 1990–; mem. Int. Statistical Inst., Bernulli Soc.; Friendship of Nations Order 1981, Order Merit to Fatherland, Fourth Degree 2002; Badge of Honours 1975, State Prize 1979, Russian Fed. Govt Prize in Educ. 2003, Russian Acad. of Science Markov Prize 2003. *Publications:* Stochastic Processes in Queuing Theory 1976, Wahrscheinlichkeitstheorie 1976, Asymptotic Methods in Queuing Theory 1980, Statistique Mathématique 1987, Ergodicity and Stability of Stochastic Processes, 1998, Probability Theory 1998, Mathematical Statistics 1998, Asymptotic Analysis of Random Walks: Heavy-Tailed Distributions (jtly with K.A.Borovkov) 2008; more than 200 works on contiguous problems of theory probabilities and mathematical statistics. *Address:* Sobolev Institute of Mathematics, Koptyug prospekt 4, Novosibirsk 630090 (office); 12/1 Trofimuk str., Novosibirsk 630090, Russia (home). *Telephone:* (383) 363-45-89 (office); (383) 330-23-53 (home). *Fax:* (383) 333-25-98 (office). *E-mail:* borovkov@math.nsc.ru (office). *Website:* www.math.nsc.ru (office).

BOROWSKI, Marek Stefan; Polish politician; b. 4 Jan. 1946, Warsaw; m.; one s.; ed Main School of Planning and Statistics (now Warsaw School of Econs), Warsaw; Sr Economist, Centrum Dept stores, Warsaw 1968–82; Ministry of Nat. Economy 1982–91, Deputy Minister 1989; deputy to Sejm (Parl.) 1991–2001, Vice-Marshal of Sejm 1996–2001, Marshal (Speaker) 2001–04; Deputy Prime Minister, Minister of Finance and Head Econ. Cttee of Council of Ministers 1993–94; Minister/Head Council of Ministers Office 1995–96; mem. Polish United Workers' Party (PZPR) 1967–68, 1975–90; mem. Social Democracy of Polish Repub. 1990–99, Democratic Left Alliance 1999–2004 (Vice-Chair.); Leader, Polish Social Democracy Party (Socjaldemokracja Polska—SDPL) 2004–08; Senator 2011–; Hon. Citizen, Piła 2002; Order of the Cross of Terra Mariana First Class, Estonia 2002, Companion of Honour of the Nat. Order of Merit, Malta 2002, Grand Cross of the Order "For Merits for Lithuania" 2005, Officier, Légion d'Honneur 2014. *Leisure interests:* brain teasers, bowling, board and card games, classical and light music, science fiction books by Stanislaw Lem. *Address:* Biuro Senatorskie Marka Borowskiego, 03-408 Warsaw, ul. Targowa 81 lok. 107A (office); Senat, 00-902 Warsaw, ul. Wiejska 6, Poland. *Telephone:* (22) 881-77-65 (office). *E-mail:* biurosenatorskie@marekborowski.pl. *Website:* www.marekborowski.pl (home).

BORRA TOLEDO DE JIMÉNEZ, Dora Virginia, MEconSc; Peruvian economist and politician; b. 1943, Lima; ed Universidad Nacional Mayor de San Marcos, Universidad Inca Garcilaso de la Vega, Universidad ESAN, Lima; Adviser to Office of the Presidency of the Council of Ministers 2008; Minister of State, Ministry of Women and Social Devt 2006–07, Head of Decentralized Public Inst. Direct Assistance Programme (DAP) 1988–90, Dir Presidency of the Council of Ministers DAP 1987–88; Exec. Dir Instituto Trabajo y Familia 2002–06, 2008–09; Minister of Women and Social Devt 2010–11; fmr Exec. Dir Sembrando Devt Programme; mem. Alianza Popular Revolucionaria Americana.

BORRELL FONTELLES, Josep, MA, DEconSci; Spanish politician and academic; *Minister of Foreign Affairs and Co-operation;* b. 24 April 1947, Pobla Segur, Lérida; divorced; two c.; ed Polytechnic Univ. and Complutense Univ. Madrid, Institut français du Pétrole, France, Stanford Univ., USA; engineer and Dir Dept of Systems, CESPA (Compañía Española de Petróleos) 1972–81, elected as trade-union rep.; mem. Socialist Workers' Party (PSOE) Madrid 1975–, mem. Partit dels Socialistes de Catalunya Nat. Exec. 1992–2004, mem. PSOE Fed. Exec. 1997–2004, won PSOE's primary elections to become party cand. for office of Prime Minister 1998; elected as councillor in Spain's first democratic municipal elections 1979; Deputy, Treasury and Econ. Planning for Prov. Del. Madrid 1979–82; Under-Sec. Budget and Public Spending 1982–84, Sec. of State for the Treasury 1984–91,

Deputy for Barcelona in Legis. Ass. 1986–91; Minister of Public Works and Transport 1991–96, of the Environment 1993–96; Chair. Parl. Cttee on European Affairs 1999–2004; mem. European Parl. 2004–09, Pres. 2004–07, Chair. European Parl. Devt Cttee 2007–09, mem. European Convention 2002–03; Minister of Foreign Affairs and Co-operation 2018–; Dir European Studies Seminar, International Univ. of Santander and of Malaga Univ. at Ronda 2000–08; Pres. European Univ. Inst. 2010–12; currently Research Assoc., Complutense Inst. of International Studies, Universidad Complutense de Madrid; mem. Bd of Dirs Abengoa, Notre Europe (Jacques Delors Inst.); Grand Cross, Order of Charles III. *Address:* Ministry of Foreign Affairs and Co-operation, Plaza de la Provincia 1, 28012 Madrid, Spain (office). *Telephone:* (91) 3799700 (office). *E-mail:* informaec@maec.es (office). *Website:* www.exteriores.gob.es (office).

BÖRSIG, Clemens, PhD; German banker and business executive; b. 1948, Achern/Baden; ed Univ. of Mannheim; Asst Prof., Univs of Mannheim and Munich 1973–77; held several positions at Mannesmann Group, Dusseldorf 1977–85, including Head of Corp. Planning at Mannesmann-Kienzle GmbH and Chief Financial and Admin. Officer at Mannesmann-Tally; Head of Corp. Planning and Controlling, Robert Bosch GmbH, Stuttgart 1985–97, mem. Man. Bd 1990–97; Chief Financial Officer and mem. Man. Bd RWE AG, Essen 1997–99; Chief Financial Officer, Deutsche Bank AG 1999–2006, mem. Man. Bd 2001–06, also Chief Risk Officer responsible for corp. governance, mem. Supervisory Bd 2006–12, Chair. 2006–12, mem. European Advisory Board 2012–; Deputy Chair. Supervisory Bd Eurohypo AG –2005; mem. Supervisory Bd, Bayer AG, Linde AG 2006–, Daimlerchrysler AG (now Daimler AG) 2007–; mem. Advisory Bd, Fed. Cultural Foundation; Chair. Cultural Cttee of German Economy in the Fed. of German Industry (BDI); mem. Bd of Trustees, Soc. of Friends of Bayreuth eV, Soc. for Advancement of the Munich Opera Festival Asscn, Cultural Foundation Festspielhaus Baden-Baden eV; Chair. Supervisory Bd, European School of Man. and Tech.; mem. Bd, Istituto per le Opere di Religione (Vatican Bank) 2014–. *Address:* Deutsche Bank AG, Taunusanlage 12, 60262 Frankfurt, Germany (office). *Telephone:* (69) 910-00 (office). *Fax:* (69) 910-34225 (office). *E-mail:* webmaster@db.com (office). *Website:* www.db.com (office).

BORSIK, János, DJur; Hungarian trade union official; b. 22 June 1946; m.; two s.; ed Janus Pannonius Univ. of Sciences, Pécs; locomotive fitter 1964–88; locomotive driver 1968–86; trade union officer 1986–; consultant on labour law; Pres. Autonomous Trade Union Confed. (Autonóm Szakszervezetek Szövetsége—ASZSZ) 2000–12; Vice-Pres. Mozdonyvezetok Szakszervezet (MoSZ) 2000. *Leisure interests:* literature, theatre, sports. *Address:* 1066 Budapest, Oktogon 3, Hungary.

BORST, Piet, MD, PhD; Dutch biochemist; *Staff Member, Netherlands Cancer Institute;* b. 5 July 1934, Amsterdam; s. of Prof. J. G. G. Borst and A. Borst-de Geus; m. Jinke C. S. Houwing 1957; two s. one d.; ed Gymnasium, Amsterdam, Univ. of Amsterdam; Research Asst, Lab. of Biochemistry, Univ. of Amsterdam 1958–61; Post-doctoral Research Fellow, Dept of Biochemistry, New York Univ. 1963–64; Prof. of Biochemistry and Molecular Biology, Univ. of Amsterdam 1965–83, Head of Section for Medical Enzymology, Lab. of Biochemistry 1966–83, Dir Inst. of Animal Physiology 1972–80, Extraordinary Prof. of Clinical Biochemistry 1983–2004; Dir of Research Netherlands Cancer Inst., Amsterdam 1983–99, staff mem. 1999–; mem. Royal Netherlands Acad. of Arts and Sciences 1978, Hollandsche Maatschappij der Wetenschappen 1983, Academia Europaea 1989; Foreign mem. Royal Soc. of GB 1986; Foreign Assoc. NAS 1991; Foreign Hon. mem. American Acad. of Arts and Sciences 1995; Commdr, Order of the Dutch Lion 1999, Hon. CBE; Dr hc (Leiden) 2003; Hon. LLD (Dundee); Royal Dutch/Shell Prize for the Life Sciences 1981, Federatie van Medisch Wetenschappelijke Verenigingen Prize 1984, Paul-Ehrlich and Ludwig-Darmstaedter Prize (jtly) 1984, Ricketts Award, Univ. of Chicago 1989, Dr G. Wander Award of the Wander Foundation, Berne 1990, Gold Medal, Genootschap voor Natuur-, Genees- en Heelkunde, Amsterdam 1990, Dr H.P. Heineken Prize for Biochemistry and Biophysics, Amsterdam 1992, Gold Medal, Koch Foundation, Cologne 1992, Hamilton Fairley Award for Clinical Research, ESMO 2000. *Publications include:* over 300 scientific articles in biochemistry, molecular biology and cell biology. *Leisure interests:* tennis, windsurfing, skiing, cello, bridge. *Address:* Netherlands Cancer Institute, Plesmanlaan 121, 1066 CX Amsterdam (office); Meentweg 87, 1406 KE Bussum, Netherlands (home). *Telephone:* (20) 5122087 (office); (35) 6914453 (home). *Fax:* (20) 6691383 (office). *E-mail:* p.borst@nki.nl (office). *Website:* www.nki.nl (office).

BORTNIKOV, Lt-Gen. Aleksandr Vasilyevich; Russian government security official; *Head, Federal Security Service (FSB);* b. 15 Nov. 1951, Perm, Russian SFSR, USSR; m.; one s.; ed Leningrad Inst. for Railway Eng; joined Leningrad KGB 1975, Deputy Head, Fed. Security Service (FSB) Directorate for St Petersburg and Leningrad Oblast in charge of counter-intelligence operations –2003, Head of Directorate 2003–04, Deputy Dir FSB and Head of Econ. Security Service 2004–08, Head of FSB 2008–; mem. Bd of Dirs, Sovkomflot; Order of Merit for the Fatherland (First, Second, Third and Fourth Classes), Order of Mil. Merit, Medal of Honour; Diploma of the Govt of the Russian Fed. 2006. *Address:* Federal Security Service (FSB), 107031 Moscow, ul. Bolshaya Lubyanka, Building 1/3, Russia (office). *Telephone:* (495) 914-43-69 (office). *E-mail:* fsb@fsb.ru (office). *Website:* www.fsb.ru (office).

BORUBAYEV, Altai; Kyrgyzstani mathematician and politician; *Vice-President, National Academy of Sciences of the Kyrgyz Republic (NAS KR);* b. 1950, Kara-oy, Kyrgyzia; ed Kyrgyz State Univ.; teacher, Frunze Polytechnic Inst. 1975–76; teacher, Sr Teacher, Head of Chair., Dean, Pro-Rector Kyrgyz State Univ. 1976–92, Rector 1998–2000; Rector, Kyrgyz State Pedagogical Inst. 1994–98; First Deputy Minister of Educ. 1992–94; Chair. (Speaker) Ass. of People's Reps Chamber of Zhogorku Kenesh (Parl.) 2000; Chair. Nat. Comm. for Academic Degrees and Titles 2007–12, State Comm. for Academic Degrees and Titles 2012–; Vice-Pres. Nat. Acad. of Sciences of the Kyrgyz Republic (NAS KR); mem. Nat. Acad. of Sciences 2000, Russian Acad. of Social and Pedagogical Sciences. *Publications:* three monographs, over 100 articles. *Address:* National Academy of Sciences of the Kyrgyz Republic (NAS KR), 720071 Bishkek, 265a, Prospect Chui, Kyrgyz Republic (office). *Telephone:* (312) 39-23-66 (office). *Fax:* (312) 39-20-62 (office). *E-mail:* fiztech-07@mail.ru (office). *Website:* www.interacademies.net (office).

BORUCKI, William J., PhD; American space scientist; *Principal Investigator, NASA Ames Research Center;* ed Univ. of Wisconsin, San Jose State Univ.; joined NASA 1962, designed heat shields for Apollo programme spacecraft, turned his attention to the optical efficiency of lightning strikes in the atmospheres of planets 1982, then to extrasolar planets and their detection 1984, currently Prin. Investigator, NASA Ames Research Center, Moffett Field, Calif., Prin. Investigator for NASA's Kepler mission 2009–; NASA Outstanding Leadership Award, Popular Mechanics Breakthrough Award 2009, NASA Systems Eng Excellence Award 2010, Lancelot M. Berkeley Prize for Meritorious Work in Astronomy 2011, NAS Henry Draper Medal for his work with Kepler 2013, World Technology Award (Space) 2013, Shaw Prize in Astronomy 2015. *Address:* NASA Ames Research Center, Moffett Field, CA 94035-1000, USA (office). *E-mail:* steve.b.howell@nasa.gov (office). *Website:* kepler.nasa.gov/Mission/team/williamBorucki (office).

BORYSIEWICZ, Sir Leszek, MA, PhD, FRS, FRCP, FMedSci; British physician, academic and university administrator; b. 13 April 1951, Cardiff, Wales; s. of Polish parents who settled in Wales after World War II; m. Gwenllian Borysiewicz; ed Cardiff High School, Welsh Nat. School of Medicine; postdoctoral research in London 1977; Registrar, Dept of Medicine, Hammersmith Hosp. 1979–80; joined Royal Postgraduate Medical School, London initially as MRC Clinical Training Fellow, then Lister Research Fellow and Sr Lecturer 1980–86; Wellcome Trust Sr Lecturer in Infectious Diseases, Addenbrooke's Hosp., Cambridge 1987–88; Lecturer in Medicine, Univ. of Cambridge 1988–91, Vice-Chancellor 2010–17, fmr Fellow, Wolfson Coll., now Hon. Fellow; Prof. of Medicine, Univ. of Wales Coll. of Medicine 1991–2001; Prin., Faculty of Medicine, Imperial Coll. London 2001–04, Deputy Rector, Imperial Coll. London 2004–07; mem. Council of MRC 1995–2000 Chief Exec. MRC 2007–10; Chair. UK Clinical Research Collaboration's Integrated Academic Training Awards Panel 2005–07, HEFCE RAE Main Panel A Assessment Panel; Gov. Wellcome Trust 2006–07; Chair. Nat. Health Service (Wales) R&D Grants Cttee; Acting Dir NHS (Wales) Research and Devt 1994–96; mem. Council, Cancer Research UK 2002–05; Dir (non-exec.) North Thames Regional Health Authority 2003–04; Founding Fellow, Acad. of Medical Sciences 1996, mem. Council 1997–2002. *Address:* c/o Vice-Chancellor's Office, University of Cambridge, The Old Schools, Trinity Lane, Cambridge, CB2 1TT, England (office).

BORZAKOVSKIY, Yuriy; Russian middle distance runner; b. 12 April 1981, Kratovo; m. Irina; two s.; winner 800m., European Cup Super League, Paris 1999, Annecy 2002; Gold Medal 800m., World Youth Games, Moscow 1998, European U20 Championships, Riga 1999, European U23 Championships, Amsterdam 2001, European Team Championship, Paris 1999, Annecy 2002, Bergen 2010, European Indoor Championships, Gent 2000, Torino 2009, World Indoor Championships, Lisbon 2001, Golden League, Brussels 2001, 2005, Paris 2003, Oslo 2009, Athens Olympics 2004, European Championships, Helsinki 2012; Gold Medal 400m. European U23 Championships, Amsterdam 2001; represented Russia Silver Medal 800m., IAAF Grand Prix Final, Melbourne 2001, IAAF World Championships, Paris 2003, Helsinki 2005; Silver Medal 4 x 400m. European Championships, Munich 2002; Bronze Medal 800m., IAAF World Indoor Championships, Moscow 2006, IAAF World Championships, Osaka 2007, Daegu 2011; retd 2013; Gold Medal in numerous Nat. Championships including 800m., Saransk 2010, Cheboksary 2011, Moscow 2013; Sr Coach, Nat. Endurance Team (juniors) 2015.

BORZOV, Valeriy Filippovich; Ukrainian sports administrator, politician and fmr athlete; b. 20 Oct. 1949, Sambor, Lvov Region, Ukraine; s. of Philipp Petrovich Borzov and Valentina Georgiyevna Borzova; m. Lyudmila Turishcheva 1978; one d.; ed Kiev State Inst. of Physical Culture; competed Olympic Games Munich 1972, winning gold medals at 100m and 200m; bronze medal at 100m, Montreal 1976; European Junior Champion 100m and 200m 1968; European Champion 100m 1969; 100m and 200m 1971, 100m 1974; European Indoor Champion 60m 1970, 1971, 1972, 50m 1974, 1975, 1976; held European record at 100m and 200m and world record at 60m; Minister of Sport and Youth Ukrainian Repub. 1991–97; mem. Int. Olympic Cttee, Jt Asscn of Summer Olympic Sports 1994–; Chair. State Cttee for Physical Culture and Sport 1996–97; Chair. Nat. Olympic Cttee of Ukraine 1990–98; mem. Parl. 1998–2006; f. Nat. Olympic Acad. of Ukraine; Merited Master of Sport. *Leisure interests:* fishing, hunting.

BOS, Caroline Elisabeth, BA, MSc; Dutch art historian and urban planner; *Founder and Director, UNStudio;* b. 17 June 1959, Rotterdam; d. of Peter Bos and Ellen Guibal; m. Ben van Berkel; one d.; ed Birkbeck Coll., London, UK, Utrecht Univ.; freelance journalist 1982–88; Co-founder (with Ben van Berkel) and Dir Van Berkel & Bos Architectur Bureau 1988–99; Co-founder and Dir UNStudio (network of specialists in architecture, urban devt and infrastructure), Amsterdam 1998–; has lectured at Princeton Univ., Berlage Inst., Amsterdam, Acad. of Fine Arts, Vienna, Acad. of Architecture, Arnhem, Liverpool Univ.; Int. FRIBA 2009; Hon. Prof. (Melbourne) 2012; Eileen Gray Award 1983, British Council Fellowship 1986, Charlotte Köhler Prize 1991; winning entry for Police HQ, Berlin 1995, Museum Het Valkof 1995, La Defense Offices Almere (Netherlands) 1999, Agora Theater, Lelystad 2003, Te Papa Museum, Wellington Waterfront, Waitangi, NZ 2005, Charles Jencks Award 2007. *Projects include:* switching substation, Amersfoort 1989–93, Erasmus Bridge, Rotterdam 1990–96, Villa Wilbrink, Amersfoort 1992–94, Möbius House, 't Gooi 1993–98, Rijksmuseum Twente, conversion and extension, Enschede 1992–96, Museum Het Valkhof, Nijmegen 1995–99, Masterplan of station area, Arnhem 1996–2005, Willemstunnel, Arnhem 1996–99, City Hall and Theatre, Ijsselstein 1996–2000, Lab. for NMR facilities, Utrecht 1996–2000, switching station, Innsbruck 1998–2001, Mercedes-Benz Museum, Stuttgart (Hugo Haring Prize 2008) 2006, VilLA NM 2007, Galleria Dept Store, Seoul, South Korea 2007, Theatre Agora, Lelystad 2007, Star Place Dept Store, Kaohsiung, Tawian 2008, Music Theater, Graz 2009, Grand Musée de l'Afrique, Algiers 2013, Three Museums One Square, Guangzhou, China 2013, The WIND House, Netherlands 2014, Nat. Inst. for Public Health and Environment and Dutch Medicines Evaluation Bd, Utrecht 2014; other projects include mixed-use devt in Hangzhou, China, Theatre, St Petersburg, restructuring of Harbour Ponte Parodi, Genoa. *Address:* UNStudio, Stadhouderskade 113, 1073 AX Amsterdam, The Netherlands (office). *Telephone:* (20) 5702040 (office). *Fax:* (20) 5702041 (office). *E-mail:* info@unstudio.com (office). *Website:* www.unstudio.com (office).

BOS, Wouter Jacob; Dutch business executive and fmr politician; *Chairman, VU University Medical Center Amsterdam;* b. 14 July 1963, Vlaardingen; ed Grammar

School, Zeist and Free Univ. of Amsterdam; Man. Consultant, Shell Netherlands Refinery BV 1988–90, Policy Adviser, Rotterdam 1990–92, Gen. Affairs Man. Shell Romania Exploration BV, Bucharest 1992–93, Staff Planning and Devt Man., Shell Cos in China, Hong Kong 1993–96, Consultant, New Markets, Shell International Oil Products, London 1996–98; mem. Parl. (Partij van de Arbeid) 1998–2000, 2002–07, Parl. Leader PvdA 2002–07; mem. Partij van de Arbeid (PvdA), Leader 2002–10; Sec. of State for Finance (Taxes) 2002–02; Deputy Prime Minister and Minister of Finance 2007–10; Partner, KPMG Advisory NV 2010–13; Chair. VU Univ. Medical Center Amsterdam 2013–. *Address:* VU University Medical Center, PO Box 7057, 1007 Amsterdam, Netherlands (office). *Website:* www.vumc.com (office).

BOSKIN, Michael Jay, MA, PhD; American economist, academic, consultant and fmr government official; *T. M. Friedman Professor of Economics and Hoover Institution Senior Fellow, Stanford University;* b. 23 Sept. 1945, New York; s. of Irving Boskin and Jean Boskin; m. Chris Dornin 1981; ed Univ. of California, Berkeley; Asst Prof., Stanford Univ., Calif. 1970–75, Assoc. Prof. 1976–78, Prof. 1978–86, Wohlford Prof. of Econs 1987–92, T. M. Friedman Prof. of Econs and Hoover Inst. Sr Fellow 1993–, Dir, Centre for Econ. Policy Research 1981–88; Chair. Pres.'s Council of Econ. Advisers 1989–93; Pres., Boskin & Co., Calif. 1993–; Research Assoc., Nat. Bureau of Econ. Research 1976–; Chair. Congressional Comm. on the Consumer Price Index 1995–96; Pres. International Atlantic Econ. Soc. 2005–06; mem. Advisory Bd Nat. Income and Product Accounts, US Dept of Commerce, Bureau of Econ. Analysis 2000–; mem. Governor's Council of Econ. Advisors 2003–; Visiting Prof., Harvard Univ. 1977–78; Faculty Research Fellow, Mellon Foundation 1973; Distinguished Faculty Fellow, Yale Univ. 1993; Visiting Scholar, American Enterprise Inst. 1993; mem. Bd of Dirs ExxonMobil Corpn, Oracle Corpn, Shinsei Bank; several prizes and awards including Abramson Award for Outstanding Research, Nat. Asscn of Business Economists 1987, Distinguished Teaching Award, Stanford Univ. 1987, W.S. Johnson Award for Contributions to Free Enterprise, Nat. Fed. of Ind. Business 1990, Medal of the Pres. of the Italian Repub. 1991, Distinguished Public Service Award, Stanford Univ. 1993, Adam Smith Prize, Nat. Asscn of Business Economists 1998. *Publications:* Too Many Promises: The Uncertain Future of Social Security 1986, Reagan and the Economy: Successes, Failures, Unfinished Agenda 1987, Frontiers of Tax Reform 1996, Capital Technology and Growth 1996, Toward a More Accurate Measure of the Cost of Living 1996; contrib. articles in various professional journals. *Leisure interests:* tennis, skiing, reading, theatre. *Address:* Stanford University, 213 HHMB, Stanford, CA 94305, USA (office). *Telephone:* (650) 723-6482 (office). *Fax:* (650) 723-6494 (office). *E-mail:* boskin@hoover.stanford.edu (office). *Website:* stanford.edu (office).

BOŠKOVIĆ, Predrag, MBA; Montenegrin politician; *Minister of Defence;* b. 12 March 1972, Pljevlja, Socialist Repub. of Montenegro, Socialist Fed. Repub. of Yugoslavia; s. of Milenko Bošković and Milana Bošković; m. Stela Bošković; ed Univ. of Montenegro, Univ. of Belgrade; fmr Teaching Asst, Faculty of Econs, Univ. of Montenegro; mem. Podgorica City Council 2000; mem. Montenegrin Parl. 2001–04; Deputy Minister of Foreign Affairs (Govt of Serbia and Montenegro) 2004–05, Minister of Economy (Govt of Montenegro) 2005–06, of Labour and Social Welfare 2012–15, of Educ. 2015–16, of Defence 2016–; Pres. Bd of Dirs, Montenegrobonus (oil and gas trade co.) 2006–08, Pljevlja Coal Mine 2008; Vice-Pres., European Handball Fed.; mem. Council, Int. Handball Fed.; mem. Demokratska Partija Socijalista (Democratic Party of Socialists) 1997–. *Address:* Ministry of Defence, 81000 Podgorica, ul. Jovana Tomaševića 29, Montenegro (office). *Telephone:* (20) 483561 (office). *Fax:* (20) 224702 (office). *E-mail:* kabinet@mod.gov.me (office). *Website:* www.odbrana.gov.me (office).

BOSSANO, Hon. Joseph (Joe) J., BSc (Econ), BA; Gibraltarian politician; *Minister of Enterprise, Training and Employment, and of Health and Safety;* b. 10 June 1939; m. 1st Judith Baker 1967 (divorced 1988); three s. one d.; m. 2nd Rose Torilla 1988; ed Gibraltar Grammar School, Univ. of Birmingham, London School of Econs, UK; factory worker 1958–60; merchant seaman 1960–64; Sec. Integration with Britain Movt 1964; mem. Man. Cttee Tottenham Constituency Labour Party 1965–68; fmr mem. IWBP Exec. Cttee; Leader, Gibraltar Socialist Labour Party 1977–2011; Leader of the Opposition 1984–88, 1996–2011; Sec. Gibraltar Br., Commonwealth Parl. Asscn 1980–88; Br. Officer TGWU (Gibraltar) 1974–88; Chief Minister of Gibraltar, with responsibility for Information 1988–96; Minister of Enterprise, Training and Employment, and of Health and Safety 2011–. *Leisure interests:* carpentry, fishing, thinking and linguistics. *Address:* Ministry of Enterprise, Training, Employment, and of Health and Safety, Unit 75, Harbours Walk, Rosia Road (office); 2 Gowland's Ramp, Gibraltar (home). *Telephone:* 2001100 (office). *Fax:* 20073981 (office). *E-mail:* employment.service@gibraltar.gov.gi (office); hqgslp@gibtelecom.net (home).

BOSSE, Christine (Stine), LLM; Danish lawyer and insurance industry executive; *CEO, TrygVesta A/S;* b. 1960; four c.; ed Univ. of Copenhagen, Institut Européen d'Admin des Affaires (INSEAD), France, Wharton School of Univ. of Pennsylvania, USA; served with Tryg Forsikring A/S 1987–2001, joined TrygVesta 1987, Head of Claims Dept 1988–90, Head of Underwriting Dept 1990–91, Deputy Functional Man. responsible for product and concept devt, Claims and Underwriting Dept 1991–93, Personnel Man. 1993–95, Human Resource Dir 1995–99, Sr Vice-Pres. 1999–2002, currently Group CEO TrygVesta A/S, also CEO Tryg i Danmark smba and Tryg Forsikring A/S (subsidiaries), Man. Dir TrygVesta Forsikring A/S; Chair. Danish Insurance Asscn, Hjertebarnsfonden, Ejendomsselskabet af 8. maj 2008 A/S; mem. Bd of Dirs Forsikring og Pension, Grundfos Management A/S, Poul Due Jensens Fond, TDC A/S 2004–06, Nordea Bank AB 2008–, Grundfos DK A/S –2009, Amlin plc; Ind. Dir, Flügger A/S 2002–; mem. Danish Welfare Comm.; mem. Supervisory Bd Forsikring & Pension (F&P), TDC; Chair. Supervisory Bd Vesta Forsikring AS, ApS KBIL 9 NR. 2032, Tryg Ejendomme A/S, TrygVesta IT A/S. *Address:* TrygVesta A/S, Klausdalsbrovej 601, 2750 Ballerup, Denmark (office). *Telephone:* 70-11-20-20 (office). *Fax:* 44-20-67-00 (office). *E-mail:* trygvesta@trygvesta.com (office). *Website:* www.trygvesta.com (office).

BOSSI, Umberto; Italian politician; *President, Lega Nord;* b. 19 Sept. 1941, Cassano Magnago, Varese; m.; four c. (two by Manuela Marrone); ed Pavia Univ.; f. Lombard Autonomy League 1982; Leader, Lombard League 1984–93; mem. European Parl. 1994–2001, 2004–08; Senator 1987–92; Fed. Sec., Lega Nord (Northern League) 1989–2012, Pres. for Life 2012–; mem. Chamber of Deputies 1992–2004, 2008–18; Minister without Portfolio, responsible for Reforms and Devolution 2001–04 (resgnd); Minister without Portfolio for Federal Reform 2008–11; convicted of fraud and sentenced to two years and three months in prison July 2017. *Address:* Lega Nord, via C. Bellerio 41, 20161 Milan, Italy (office). *Telephone:* (02) 662341 (office). *Fax:* (02) 6454475 (office). *E-mail:* webmaster@leganord.org (office). *Website:* www.leganord.org (office).

BOSSIDY, Lawrence Arthur, BA; American business executive and writer; b. 5 March 1935, Pittsfield, Mass.; m. Nancy Bossidy 1956; three s. six d.; ed Colgate Univ.; joined General Electric Co. 1957, Chief Operating Officer, General Electric Credit Corpn (now GE Capital Corpn) 1979–81, Exec. Vice-Pres. and Pres. Services and Materials Sector 1981–84, Vice-Chair. and Exec. Officer, General Electric Co. 1984–91, fmr Chair. and Dir-Gen. Electric Credit Corpn; Chair. and CEO Allied Signal Inc. 1991–99, Chair. Honeywell International Inc. (after merger of Allied Signal and Honeywell 1999) 1999–2000, 2001–02; mem. Bd of Dirs Merck & Co. 1992–2007, Champion Int. Corpn, J.P. Morgan & Co. Inc., Berkshire Hills Bancorp Inc.; mem. Exec. Bd Aurora Capital Group, Chair. Advisory Bd, Aurora Resurgence; CEO of the Year, Financial World magazine 1994, Chief Executive of the Year, CEO Magazine 1998. *Publications:* Execution: The Discipline of Getting Things Done 2002, Confronting Reality: Doing What Matters to Get Things Right (with Ram Charan) 2004. *Address:* c/o Aurora Capital Group, 10877 Wilshire Blvd, 21st Floor, Los Angeles, CA 90024, USA.

BOST, Eric M., BA, MA; American diplomatist (retd) and university administrator; *Assistant Director for External Relations and Special Assignments, Vice-President for Global Initiatives, Borlaug Institute of International Agriculture, Texas A&M University;* b. 8 Aug. 1952, Concord, NC; ed Univ. of North Carolina, Univ. of South Florida; served in a variety of positions in several state social welfare agencies and pvt. and non-profit orgs; Deputy Dir Ariz. Dept of Econ. Security 1994–97; Chief Exec. and Admin. Officer, Tex. Dept of Human Services 1997–2001; Under-Sec. for Food, Nutrition, and Consumer Services, US Dept of Agric., Washington, DC 2001–06; Amb. to South Africa 2006–09; Vice-Pres. for Global Initiatives, Texas A&M Univ. 2009–11, Asst Dir for External Relations and Special Assignments, Borlaug Inst. for Int. Agric. 2011–. *Leisure interest:* travelling. *Address:* Borlaug Institute of International Agriculture, Texas A&M University, 578 John Kimbrough Blvd, AGSV Building, Room 201, College Station, TX 77843-2477, USA (office). *Telephone:* (979) 458-3406 (office). *Fax:* (979) 845-5663 (office). *E-mail:* Eric.Bost@ag.tamu.edu (office). *Website:* borlaug.tamu.edu (office).

BOSTRÖM, Rolf Gustav, PhD; Swedish physicist and academic; *Professor Emeritus, Swedish Institute of Space Physics;* b. 15 April 1936, Kalmar; s. of Gustav Boström and Greta Boström (née Bergström); m. Barbro Karlsson 1962; one s.; ed Royal Inst. of Tech.; Research Assoc., Dept of Plasma Physics, Royal Inst. of Tech. 1961–71, Sr Physicist 1971–75, Assoc. Prof. 1975–76; Prof., Uppsala Div. of Swedish Inst. of Space Physics (fmrly Uppsala Ionospheric Observatory) 1976–2002, Prof. Emer. 2002–; Head Dept of Space Physics, Uppsala Univ. 1988–96; mem. Royal Swedish Acad. of Sciences. *Publications:* scientific papers on space plasma physics. *Leisure interests:* hiking, angling. *Address:* Klippvägen 22, 756 52 Uppsala, Sweden (home). *Telephone:* (18) 32-02-61 (home). *E-mail:* rolf.g.bostrom@telia.com (home).

BOT, Bernard Rudolf (Ben); Dutch diplomatist and politician; *Chairman, Carnegie Foundation;* b. 21 Nov. 1937, Jakarta, Indonesia; s. of Theo H. Bot and E. W. van Hal; m. Christine Bot-Pathy 1962 (deceased); three c.; ed St Aloysius Coll., The Hague, Univ. of Leiden, Acad. of Int. Law, The Hague and Harvard Law School, USA; Deputy Perm. Rep. of Netherlands to North Atlantic Council, Brussels 1982–86; Amb. to Turkey 1986–89; Sec.-Gen. Ministry of Foreign Affairs 1989–92; apptd Perm. Rep. to EU 1992; Minister of Foreign Affairs 2003–07; currently Chair. Carnegie Foundation, The Peace Palace, The Hague; Kt, Order of the Netherlands Lion; Officier, Order of Orange-Nassau and other decorations. *Publications include:* Non-recognition and Treaty Relations 1968; numerous articles on the Common Market, European political co-operation, NATO and other political matters. *Leisure interests:* cycling, painting, skiing. *Address:* Carnegie Foundation, Carnegieplein 2, 2517 KJ The Hague, The Netherlands (office). *Telephone:* (70) 3622552 (office). *E-mail:* bernardbot@meinesholla.nl (office). *Website:* www.vredespaleis.nl (office).

BOTCHWAY, Shirley Ayorkor, MA, MBA; Ghanaian communications consultant and politician; *Minister of Foreign Affairs and Regional Integration;* b. 8 Feb. 1963, Accra; m.; two c.; ed Univ. of Ghana, Univ. of Westminster; fmr journalist and public relations exec.; fmr Man. Dir, Dynacom Ltd (advertising agency); mem. Parl. for Anyaa Sowutuom 2013–; fmr Minister of State, Ministry of Water Resources, Works and Housing; fmr Deputy Minister of Foreign Affairs, for Information, for Trade and Industry, Ranking mem. on Foreign Affairs 2009–13, Minister of Foreign Affairs and Regional Integration 2017–; mem. ECOWAS Parliament 2013–17, Vice-Chair. NEPAD and APRM cttees, also mem. Communications Cttee, Gender and Children's Cttee; mem. New Patriotic Party. *Address:* Ministry of Foreign Affairs and Regional Integration, Treasury Road, POB M53, Accra, Ghana (office). *Telephone:* (30) 2999604 (office); (30) 2738473 (office). *E-mail:* info@mfa.gov.gh (office). *Website:* www.mfa.gov.gh (office).

BOTELHO, João; Portuguese film director; b. 11 May 1949, Lamego; m. Leonor Pinhão; three c.; ed Nat. Conservatory Film School, Lisbon; involved in film socs in Coimbra and Oporto; film critic for newspapers; f. film magazine M. *Films include:* Alexandre e Rosa (short, co-dir) 1978, Conversa acabada (The Other One) 1980, Um adeus português (A Portuguese Goodbye) 1985, Tempos difíceis (Hard Times) 1987, No dia dos meus anos (On my Birthday) 1992, Aqui na Terra (Here on Earth) 1993, Três Palmeiras (Three Palm Trees) 1994, Tráfico (Traffic) 1998, Se a Memória Existe (If Memories Exist) 1999, Quem és tu? (Who are you?) (Mimmo Rotella Foundation Prize, Venice Film Festival) 2001, O Fatalista 2005, A Luz na Ria Formosa 2005, True and Tender Is the North 2008, Para Que Este Mundo Não Acabe! 2009, Disquiet 2010, Anquanto la Lhéngua fur Cantada 2012. *Address:* c/o Associação Portuguesa de Realizadores, Rua de Palmeira 7, r/c, 1200 Lisbon, Portugal.

BOTELHO, Maurício; Brazilian business executive; Exec. Vice-Pres. Técnica Nacional de Engenharia Ltda. 1992; Exec. Officer, Cia. Bozano 1995; CEO CMW

Equipamentos SA 1985–95; CEO Stelar Telecom (fmrly Odebrecht Automação & Telecomunicações Ltda.) 1988–95; Pres. and CEO Empresa Brasiliera de Aeronautica SA (Embraer) 1995–2007, Chair. 2006–12; Pres. Mogno Consultoria de Negócios Ltda. (business consultancy); Commdr, Ordem do Rio Branco (Brazil); Chevalier, Legion d'Honneur; BACCF Excellence Award 1999.

BOTELHO, Urbino José Gonçalves; São Tomé and Príncipe politician; ed Liceu Nacional de São Tomé e Príncipe; several years with Ministry of Foreign Affairs and Communities, including as fmr Dir of External Policy, Minister of Foreign Affairs and Communities 2016–18; mem. Acção Democrática Independente. *Address:* c/o Ministry of Foreign Affairs and Communities, Av. 12 de Julho, CP 111, São Tomé, São Tomé and Príncipe (office).

BOTERO, Fernando; Colombian artist and sculptor; b. 19 April 1932, Medellín; s. of David Botero and Flora Botero; m. 2nd Cecilia Botero 1964; m. 3rd Sophia Vari; four c.; first group exhbn, Medellín 1948; first solo exhbn, Galería Leo Matiz, Bogotá 1951; studied at Acad. San Fernando and El Prado Museum, Madrid 1952; visited Paris and Italy and studied art history with Roberto Longhi, Univ. of Florence 1953–54; lived in Mexico 1956; solo exhbn Pan American Union, Washington, DC 1957, Colombia 1958–59; lived in New York 1960–; first solo exhbn in Europe, Baden-Baden and Munich 1966; visited Italy and Germany 1967, studied work of Dürer; travelling retrospective exhbn of 80 paintings in five German museums 1970; solo exhbn Hannover Gallery, London 1970; moved to Paris 1973; concentrated on Sculpture 1976–77, first solo exhbn of sculpture, Foire Int. d'Art Contemporain, Paris 1977; retrospective exhbn, Hirshorn Museum and Sculpture Garden, Washington, DC 1979; first solo exhbn in Japan, Tokyo, Osaka 1981; outdoor sculpture exhbn, Chicago 1994; Abu Ghraib series 2005; paintings in public collections in Belgium, Finland, Germany, Israel, Italy, S. America, Spain and USA; Guggenheim Nat. Prize for Colombia 1960, Lifetime Achievement in Contemporary Sculpture Award, International Sculpture Center 2012.

BOTERO NIETO, Guillermo; Colombian lawyer, business executive and politician; *Minister of National Defence;* b. 9 April 1948, Bogotá; s. of Lorenzo Botero Jaramillo; m. Margarita Jaramillo Ocampo; three c.; ed Univ. de los Andes; f. Hacienda Cuernavaca (later Agropecuaria Cuernavaca, flower farm and export business) 1979; co-f. Consimex SA (customs procedures firm), 11 years as Man.; mem. Bd of Dirs Federación Nacional de Comerciantes (FENALCO, Nat. Fed. of Merchants) 1985–, Pres. 2003–; Minister of Nat. Defence 2018–; fmr Lecturer, Univ. de los Andes; mem. Bd of Dirs La Nueva EPS, Chamber of Commerce of Bogotá. *Address:* Ministry of National Defence, Carrera 54, No 26-25, Centro Administrativo Nacional, 2°, Bogotá DC, Colombia (office). *Telephone:* (1) 266-0296 (office). *Fax:* (1) 315-0111 (office). *E-mail:* usuarios@mindefensa.gov.co (office). *Website:* www.mindefensa.gov.co (office).

BOTHAM, Sir Ian Terence, Kt, OBE; British business executive, cricket commentator and fmr professional cricketer; b. 24 Nov. 1955; s. of Leslie Botham and Marie Botham; m. Kathryn Waller 1976; one s. two d.; ed Buckler's Mead Secondary School, Yeovil; right-hand batsman, right-hand, fast-medium bowler; teams: Somerset 1974–86 (Capt. 1984–85), Worcs. 1987–91, Queensland 1987–88, Durham 1992–93; 102 Tests for England 1977–92, 12 as Capt., scoring 5,200 runs (average 33.54, highest score 208) including 14 hundreds, taking 383 wickets (average 28.40) and holding 120 catches; scored 1,673 runs and took 148 wickets v. Australia; became first player to score a century and take 8 wickets in an innings in a Test match, v. Pakistan (Lord's) 1978; took 100th wicket in Test cricket in record time of 2 years 9 days 1979; achieved double of 1,000 runs and 100 wickets in Tests to create world record of fewest Tests (21) and English records of shortest time (2 years 33 days) and at youngest age (23 years 279 days) 1979; became first player to have scored 3,000 runs and taken 250 wickets in Tests (55) Nov. 1982; first player to score a century and take 10 wickets in a Test match, v. India; scored 19,399 runs (38 hundreds) and took 1,172 wickets in first-class cricket; toured Australia 1978–79, 1979–80, 1982–83 and 1986–87; has also played soccer for Scunthorpe United and Yeovil; mem. Sky Sports cricket commentary team 1995–; team capt., BBC Question of Sport –1996; Tech. Advisor, England Cricket Team 1996; Chair. Mission Sports Management 2000–12; mem. MCC Cricket Cttee 1995, Sports Council 1995–, Laureus World Sports Acad.; columnist, Daily Mirror; first Pres. Leukaemia Research 2003, raised more than £3 million through long-distance walks; Hon. MSc (UMIST); Hon. LLD (Bath) 2008; Hon. Dr in Sports Science (Leeds Metropolitan) 2008; Hon. DSc (Lincoln) 2010; Wisden Cricketer of the Year 1978, BBC Sports Personality of the Year 1981, Pipe Smoker of the Year 1988, BBC Sports Personality of the Year Lifetime Achievement Award 2004, inducted into Int. Cricket Council Hall of Fame 2009, selected to deliver the MCC's Spirit of Cricket Cowdrey Lecture at Lord's 2014. *Publications include:* It Sort of Clicks 1986, Cricket My Way 1989, Botham: My Autobiography 1994, The Botham Report (with Peter Hayter) 1997, Head On: The Autobiography 2007. *Leisure interests:* shooting, golf, flying, fishing. *Address:* c/o Mission Sports Management Ltd, 11 Northfields Prospect, London, SW18 1PE, England. *E-mail:* adam@missionsportsmanagement.com.

BOTÍN-SANZ DE SAUTUOLA Y O'SHEA, Ana Patricia; Spanish banking executive; *Executive Chairman, Santander Group;* b. 4 Oct. 1960, Santander; d. of Emilio Botín-Sanz de Sautuola y García de los Ríos and Paloma O'Shea; m. Guillermo Morenés Mariátegui; three s.; ed Bryn Mawr Coll. and Harvard Univ., USA; began career with JP Morgan, New York and Madrid 1981, various positions in Latin American Div. including Vice-Pres. –1988; CEO Banco Santander de Negocios and Exec. Vice-Pres. Banco Santander 1994–99; Founder, Chair. and CEO Suala Capital Advisers 1999–2002; Jt Pres. Banco Santander Central Hispano (BSCH), Chair. of subsidiary Banco Banesto, Madrid 2002–10, CEO Santander UK plc 2010–14, Exec. Chair. Santander Group 2014–; Chair. coverlink.com; Exec. Chair. Razona (tech. consulting and systems integrations co.) 1999–; Dir The Coca-Cola Co. 2013–; mem. Foro Iberoamerica, Trilateral Comm.; mem. Int. Advisory Bd J.E. Robert Cos (int. real estate investment and asset man. firm) 2002–; mem. Int. Advisory Bd New York Stock Exchange, Council of Georgetown Univ.; Hon. DBE 2015. *Leisure interest:* golf. *Address:* Santander Group, City Av. de Cantabria s/n, 28660 Boadilla del Monte, Madrid, Spain (office). *Telephone:* (90) 2112211 (office). *E-mail:* comunicacion@gruposantander.com (office). *Website:* www.santander.com (office).

BOTNARU, Ion, PhD; Moldovan diplomatist and UN official; b. 19 Aug. 1954, Pitusca, Calarasi; s. of Toma Botnaru and Tatiana Sheremet; m. 1979; one s. one d.; ed Inst. of Oriental Studies, Moscow, Moscow State Univ.; fmr translator and interpreter of Turkish and English; Sr Researcher, Inst. of History Studies, Nat. Acad. of Science, Chişinău 1983–84; Prof. of Contemporary History of Asia and Africa, Chişinău State Univ. 1987–89; Deputy Dir-Gen. Dept of Protocol, Ministry of Foreign Affairs 1989–90, Dir-Gen. Dept of Political Affairs 1990–92, Deputy Minister 1992–93, Minister 1993–94; Amb. to Turkey (also accred to Kuwait and Egypt) 1994–98, 2002; Amb. and Perm. Rep. to UN, New York 1998–2002; fmr Chief, UN Gen. Ass. Affairs Br., Dept for Gen. Ass. and Conf. Man., Dir-Gen. Ass. and ECOSOC Affairs Div. 2011–16; mem. Moldovan del. to UN Gen. Ass. 1992; Head of Moldovan del. to UN World Conf. on Human Rights 1993; mem. Asscn of Orientalists 1985–. *Publications include:* The Army and Politics in Turkey 1986, Islam and Political Parties in Turkey 1989, The Process of Democratisation in Moldova—Political Aspects 1993; numerous papers and articles.

BOTSTEIN, David, BS, PhD; American biologist and academic; *Anthony B. Evnin '62 Professor of Genomics, Princeton University;* b. 8 Sept. 1942, Switzerland; ed Bronx High School of Science, Harvard Univ., Massachusetts Inst. of Tech., Univ. of Michigan; taught at MIT, later Prof. of Genetics; Vice-Pres. (Science), Genentech, Inc. 1987–90; Chair. Dept of Genetics, Stanford Univ. 1990–2003; Dir, Lewis-Sigler Inst., Princeton Univ. 2003–13, currently Anthony B. Evnin '62 Prof. of Genomics and Dir Integrated Science Program; Eli Lilly & Co. Award in Microbiology 1978, Genetics Soc. of America Medal (co-recipient) 1988, Allan Award, American Soc. of Human Genetics (co-recipient) 1989, Gruber Prize in Genetics 2003, Albany Medical Center Prize in Medicine and Biomedical Research (co-recipient) 2010, Agilent Thought Leader Award (co-recipient), Dan David Prize Laureate 2012, Breakthrough Prize in Life Sciences (co-recipient) 2013. *Publications:* numerous papers in professional journals. *Address:* Department of Molecular Biology, 119 Lewis Thomas Laboratory, Washington Road, Princeton University, Princeton, NJ 08544-1014, USA (office). *E-mail:* botstein@princeton.edu (office). *Website:* molbio.princeton.edu (office).

BOTTOMLEY OF NETTLESTONE, Baroness (Life Peer), cr. 2005, of St Helens in the County of Isle of Wight; **Rt Hon. Virginia (Hilda Brunette Maxwell) Bottomley,** PC, BA, MSc, DL; British politician and business executive; *Chair of the Board Practice, Odgers Berndtson;* b. 12 March 1948, Dunoon, Argyll, Scotland; d. of W. John Garnett and Barbara Garnett (née Rutherford-Smith); m. Sir Peter Bottomley, MP; one s. two d.; ed Putney High School, Univ. of Essex, London School of Econs; Behavioural Scientist 1971–84; Vice-Chair. Nat. Council of Carers and their Elderly Dependants 1982–88; Dir Mid Southern Water Co. 1987–88; mem. MRC 1987–88; MP for Surrey SW 1984–; Parl. Pvt. Sec. to Minister of State for Educ. and Science 1985–86, to Minister for Overseas Devt 1986–87, to Sec. of State for Foreign and Commonwealth Affairs 1987–88; Parl. Under-Sec. of State, Dept for the Environment 1988–89; Sec., Conservative Backbench Employment Cttee 1985; Fellow, Industry Parl. Trust 1987; Minister of State (Minister for Health) 1989–92; Sec. of State for Health 1992–95; Sec. of State for Nat. Heritage 1995–97; Pnr and Chair of the Bd Practice, Odgers Berndtson 2000–; mem. Supervisory Bd Akzo Nobel 2000–12; Nat. Pres. Abbeyfield Soc. 2003–09; Co-Chair. Women's Nat. Comm. 1991–92; mem. Court of Govs, LSE 1985–, British Council 1997–2001, House of Commons Select Cttee on Foreign Affairs 1997–99; Dir (non-exec.) BUPA 2009–, Smith & Nephew Plc 2012–; Gov. Ditchley Foundation 1991–, London Univ. of the Arts 1999–; JP, Inner London 1975 (Chair. Lambeth Juvenile Court 1981–84); Lay Canon, Guildford Cathedral; Pro-Chancellor Univ. of Surrey 2005–; Chancellor, Univ. of Hull 2006–; Trustee, The Economist; DL (Surrey) 2006; Freeman City of London 1989; Hon. LLD (Portsmouth) 1992; Hon. DSc (Aston) 2012. *Leisure interest:* family. *Address:* Odgers Berndtson, 20 Cannon Street, London, EC4M 6XD (office); House of Lords, Westminster, London, SW1A 0PW, England. *Telephone:* (20) 7529-1066 (office); (20) 7219-5060. *E-mail:* bottomleyv@parliament.uk.

BOUARÉ, Lassine; Malian politician; b. 1959, Massala, Ségou region; m.; ed École nat. d'admin publique, Rabat, Morocco, École nat. d'admin, Paris, France; began career with Admin Reform Comm. 1990–94; Head of Devt Unit, Office for Decentralization and Institutional Reform 1994–2000; Tech. Adviser, Ministry of Territorial Admin and Local Communities 2000–01; Tech. Adviser, Office of the Pres. 2002–03; Dir Nat. Inst. of Social Welfare 2003–09; Minister Del., Ministry of Economy and Finance 2009–11, Minister of the Economy and Finance 2011–12; mem. Bd of Govs, African Devt Bank. *Address:* c/o Ministry of the Economy and Finance, Bamako, Mali.

BOUASONE, Bouphavanh; Laotian politician; b. 3 June 1954, Ban Tao Poun, Salavan Prov.; m. Soumly Bouphavanh; ed secondary school, Champasak Prov., Communist Party Inst., Moscow, USSR; student activist 1970s; fmr Pres. State Planning Cttee; fmr Third Deputy Prime Minister, First Deputy Prime Minister 2003–06, Prime Minister 2006–10 (resgnd); removed from Politburo (and Cen. Cttee) of Lao People's Revolutionary Party 2011. *Address:* c/o Office of the Prime Minister, Ban Sisavat, Vientiane, Laos.

BOUBLIL, Alain Albert; French (b. Tunisian) writer and dramatist; b. 5 March 1941, Tunis, Tunisia; m. Marie Zamora; four s.; emigrated to France age 18; worked for several years in music publishing; wrote libretto and lyrics for La Révolution Française 1973, Les Misérables 1980, Abbacadabra 1984, Miss Saigon 1989, Martin Guerre 1996, The Pirate Queen 2006, Marguerite 2008; Le Journal d'Adam et Eve (play) 1994; two Tony Awards, Two Grammy Awards, two Victoire de la Musique Awards, Molière Award (all for Les Misérables), Evening Standard Drama Award (for Miss Saigon), Laurence Olivier Award (for Martin Guerre). *Leisure interests:* theatre, opera, cinema, tennis. *Website:* www.lesmis.com/uk/about/cast-and-creatives/alain-boublil.

BOUCHAIN, Patrick; French architect and designer; b. 31 May 1945, Paris; ed Acad. des Beaux-Arts, internships at Jacques Dumond (decorator), André Hermant (architect), Henry Malvaux (painter); Prof. of Drawing and Architecture, École Camondo, Paris 1972–74, École des Beaux-Arts de Bourges 1974–81, École de Création industrielle, Paris 1981–83; adviser to Jack Lang at Ministry of Culture, then to Pres. Établissement public du Grand Louvre 1992–94; Dir Atelier public d'architecture et d'urbanisme, Blois 1990–93; has a background in theatre, circuses and urban festivals; relies on collaborations to develop an alternative urban planning; projects use several specialists rather than a single contractor; leader, spectacle of the Grandes Roues on Champs-Elysées in Paris as part of the Millennium celebrations 1999–2000; curated French pavilion at the Venice Architecture Biennale 2006; architect of the Pompidou Centre travelling on tour 2011. *Works include:* Magasin, Grenoble 1985, Zingaro Theatre, Aubervilliers 1988, Dromesko Birdcage, Lausanne 1991, Admin. and Tech. Centre, Valeo à La Verrière 1995, registered office of Thomson Multimédia, Boulogne-Billancourt 1997, transformation of the old LU factories in Nantes for CRDC 1999, Musée int. des Arts modestes, Sète 2000, Capital of the Centaur Theatre, Marseille 2001, Academy Fratellini, St Denis 2002, La Condition Publique, Roubaix 2004, Pool Baths, Bègles 2005, French Pavilion at Venice Architecture Biennale 2006, National City of the history of immigration, Paris 2007, transformation of the slaughterhouses Channel, Calais 2007, Burgundy restaurant Michel Troisgros 'La Colline du Colombier' 2008, renovation of the restaurant La Grenouillère 2011; architectural installations 'L'amour de l'art' for first Biennale d'art contemporain de Lyon 1991, 'Tous, ils changent le monde', Lyon Bienniale 1993. *Collaborations include:* with numerous contemporary artists, including Daniel Buren ('Les deux plateaux', court of the Palais Royal) 1986, Sarkis, Ange Leccia, Bartabas (Celebration of the battle of Valmy) 1989, Joseph Kosuth (Figeac) 1989, Claes Oldenbourg ('Le vélo enseveli', Parc de la Villette) 1990, Jean-Luc Vilmouth ('Comme deux tours', Châtellerault) 1994. *Publications include:* La condition publique 2004, Construire autrement 2006, Construire ensemble le grand ensemble: habiter autrement 2010, Histoire du Palais Royal. Les Deux Plateaux/ Daniel Buren (with Daniel Buren, Edith Hallauer, Michel Nuridsany) 2010, Venise: métacité-métavilla 2011, Histoire de construire 2012, Histoire de faire 2012. *Address:* c/o Institut Français d'Architecture, 1 chemin de la Chapelle St Antoine, ZA Les Portes du Vexin, 95300 Ennery, France. *Telephone:* 1-30-38-03-89. *Fax:* 1-34-43-83-81. *E-mail:* ifa@veolia-proprete.fr. *Website:* www.ifa.fr.

BOUCHARD, Benoît, PC, CM, BA, LèsArts; Canadian fmr politician and fmr diplomatist; b. 16 April 1940, Roberval, Québec; m. Jeannine Lavoie; three c.; ed Laval Univ.; teacher, Coll. Classique, Coll. Notre-Dame, then Prin. Coll. Notre-Dame and Villa étudiante, Roberval; Dir-Gen. St Félicien CEGEP 1979; alderman, Roberval 1973–80; MP for Roberval, Québec 1984–93, served as Minister of State (Transport) 1984–85, Minister of Communications 1985–86, of Employment and Immigration 1986–88, of Transport 1988–90, of Industry, Science and Tech. 1990–91, of Nat. Health and Welfare 1991–93; Amb. to France 1993–96; Chair. Transportation Safety Bd of Canada 1996–2001; treaty negotiator for Canadian Govt with Innus people of Québec 2004–10; Commr, Int. Jt Comm. on Boundary Waters Canada-USA 2013–; Order of Canada 2012. *Address:* 1120 Rachelle, Roberval, QC G8H 2B9, Canada (home). *Telephone:* (418) 275-8365 (office). *E-mail:* benbouch@cgocable.ca (home); bouchardb@ottawa.ijc.org (office).

BOUCHARD, Lucien, BA, BSc, LLL; Canadian lawyer, diplomatist and fmr politician; *Partner, Davies Ward Phillips & Vineberg LLP;* b. 22 Dec. 1938, Saint-Coeur-de-Marie, Lac Saint-Jean, Québec; s. of Philippe Bouchard and Alice Simard; m. Audrey Best; two s.; ed Collège de Jonquière, Univ. of Laval; called to Québec Bar 1964; pvt law practice in Chicoutimi until 1985; mem. numerous comms and orgs connected with labour relations, both in public and pvt. sectors; Pres. Saguenay Bar 1978; Amb. to France 1985–88; Sec. of State of Canada 1988; MP 1988–2001; Minister of the Environment 1989–90; resgnd from Conservative Party 1990 to lead Bloc Québécois; Chair. and Leader, Bloc Québécois 1991–96; Leader Parti Québécois 1996–2001; Leader of Opposition, House of Commons 1993–95; Prime Minister of Québec 1996–2001; currently Partner, Davies Ward Phillips & Vineberg LLP (law firm); mem. Bd of Dirs Transcontinental Inc., Saputo Inc., Centre d'études et de recherches internationales de l'Université de Montréal, Groupe BMTC, TransForce Inc; Commdr, Légion d'Honneur 2002; Grand officier, Ordre national du Québec 2008. *Publications:* À visage découvert 1992; articles in legal and labour relations journals. *Address:* Davies Ward Phillips & Vineberg LLP, 26th Floor, 1501 McGill College Avenue, Montreal, PQ H3A 3N9, Canada (office). *Telephone:* (514) 841-6515 (office). *E-mail:* lbouchard@dwpv.com (office). *Website:* www.dwpv.com (office).

BOUCHÈNE, Abderrahmane; Algerian publisher; b. 1941, Algiers; m.; four c.; ed Algeria and Lausanne Univs; worked in family clothing shop; admin. posts at Société nat. d'édition et de diffusion, Entreprise nat. du livre and Ministry of Culture; f. Editions Bouchène publishing house, Kouba, in late 1980s; by 1990 owner of two bookshops in Algiers, one in Riad-El-Feth; forced to flee Algeria and close business 1994; exile in Tunisia 1994–96; moved to Paris and set up new co. specializing in Algerian historical texts and historical anthropology of Maghreb socs. *Address:* Editions Bouchène, 113–115 rue Danielle Casanova, 93200 Saint-Denis, Paris, France (office). *Telephone:* 1-48-20-93-75 (office). *Fax:* 1-48-20-20-78 (office). *E-mail:* edbouchene@wanadoo.fr (office). *Website:* www.bouchene.com (office).

BOUCHER, Mark Verdon; South African professional cricketer (retd); b. 3 Dec. 1976, East London, Cape Prov.; s. of Verdon Boucher and Heather Boucher; ed Selborne Coll.; wicketkeeper batsman; right-handed batsman; right-arm medium pace bowler; plays for Border 1995–2003, S Africa 1997–2012 (Capt. Test side 2001–02), Warriors 2004–, ICC (Int. Cricket Council) World XI, Royal Challengers Bangalore 2009–10, Kolkata Knight Riders 2011, Africa XI, Cape Cobras; First-class debut: 1995/96; Test debut: Pakistan v S Africa, Sheikhupura 17–21 Oct. 1997; One-Day Int. (ODI) debut: NZ v S Africa, Perth 16 Jan. 1998; T20I debut: S Africa v NZ, Johannesburg 21 Oct. 2005); played in 147 Tests, took 1 wicket and scored 5,515 runs (5 centuries, 35 half-centuries), highest score 125, average 30.30; played in 295 ODIs and scored 4,686 runs (1 century, 26 half-centuries), highest score 147 not out, average 28.57; played in 25 T20Is and scored 268 runs, highest score 36 not out, average 17.86; has played in 212 First-class matches, scored 8,803 runs (10 centuries, 53 half-centuries), highest score 134, average 33.34; put on, with Pat Symcox, 195 to set new Test ninth-wicket partnership record 1998; first wicketkeeper in Test cricket history to reach milestone of 400 dismissals 2007, holds Test record of 999 dismissals 2012; retd from int. cricket after sustaining eye injury during tour of England 10 July 2012; Head Coach Titans cricket franchise 2016–; South Africa Cricketer of the Year 1998, 2000, 2006, Wisden Cricketer of the Year 2009, Cricket South Africa Long Service Award; Coach of the Year, Cricket South Africa 2017. *Address:* Titans, Centurion West Road, Centurion, South Africa (office). *Telephone:* (12) 663 1005 (office). *Fax:* (12) 663 3329 (office). *E-mail:* ncureception@cricket.co.za (office). *Website:* www.titans.co.za (office); www.markboucher.co.za.

BOUCHEZ, Élodie; French actress; b. 5 April 1973, Montreuil-sous-Bois, Seine-Saint-Denis, Île-de-France; m. Thomas Bangalter; two c. *Films include:* Stan the Flasher 1990, Tous les garçons (short) 1992, Tango 1993, Le cahier volé 1993, Les mots de l'amour (short) 1994, Le péril jeune 1994, Les roseaux sauvages (Wild Reeds) (César Award for Most Promising Actress) 1994, Le plus bel âge… 1995, Mademoiselle Personne 1996, Clubbed to Death (Lola) 1996, À toute vitesse 1996, The Proprietor 1996, Les fantômes du samedi soir (voice) 1997, C'est Noël déjà (short) 1997, La divine poursuite 1997, Le ciel est à nous 1997, Flammen im Paradies 1997, Je veux descendre (short) 1998, La vie rêvée des anges (Best Actress Award, Cannes Film Festival 1998) 1998, Zonzon 1998, J'aimerais pas crever un dimanche 1998, Louise (Take 2) 1998, Les kidnappeurs 1998, Meurtre d'une petite grue 1999, Lovers 1999, Blame It on Voltaire 2000, Too Much Flesh 2000, CQ 2001, The Beatnicks 2001, Le petit poucet 2001, Being Light 2001, Dreams of Trespass 2002, La merveilleuse odyssée de l'idiot Toboggan (segment 'Les mots de l'amour') 2002, The War in Paris 2002, Le pacte du silence 2003, Stormy Weather 2003, À quoi ça sert de voter écolo? (short) 2004, America Brown 2004, Toi, vieux (short) 2004, Shooting Vegetarians 2005, The Brice Man 2005, Sorry, Haters 2005, Ma place au soleil 2007, Héros 2007, I Hate My Best Friends' Kids 2007, Après lui 2007, Tel père telle fille 2007, Seuls Two 2008, Driving Elodie (short) 2009, The Imperialists Are Still Alive! 2010, Happy Few 2010, Four Lovers 2010, In Memory of the Days to Come 2010, Anna et Jérôme (short) 2012, Juliette 2013, Tour de force 2013, Reality 2014, GHB: To Be or Not to Be 2014, Hard Drive (short) 2015. *Television includes:* Les compagnons de l'aventure (series) 1990–91, La lettre inachevée (film) 1993, 3000 scénarios contre un virus (series) 1994, Les Cordier, juge et flic (series) 1994, Les brouches (film) 1994, Tous les garçons et les filles de leur âge… (series) 1994, Premières neiges (film) 1999, Alias (series) 2005–06, The L Word (series) 2006–07, Douce France (film) 2009, Le débarquement (episode) 2013.

BOUCHIER, Ian Arthur Dennis, CBE, MB, ChB, MD, FRCP, FRCPE, FRSA, FRSE, FFPHM, FSB, FMedSci; British professor of medicine (retd); b. 7 Sept. 1932, Cape Town, S Africa; s. of E. A. Bouchier and May Bouchier; m. Patricia N. Henshilwood 1959; two s.; ed Rondebosch Boys' High School and Univ. of Cape Town; jr staff positions, Groote Schuur Hosp., Cape Town 1955–60; Registrar, Lecturer, Royal Free Hosp., London 1961–63; Research Fellow, Boston Univ. 1963–65; Sr Lecturer, Univ. of London 1965–70, Reader in Medicine 1970–73; Prof. of Medicine, Univ. of Dundee 1973–86, Univ. of Edinburgh 1986–97; Sec.-Gen. World Org. of Gastroenterology 1982–90, Pres. 1990–98; Chief Scientist for Scotland 1992–97; mem. Chief Scientist Cttee; Visiting Prof., Univ. of Michigan 1979, Madras Medical Coll. 1981, McGill Univ. 1983, Royal Postgraduate Medical School 1984, Univ. of Hong Kong 1988, China Medical Univ. 1988, Univ. of Dunedin 1989, Keio Univ. 1991; mem. Council, British Soc. of Gastroenterology 1987–90 (Pres. 1994–95); mem. Council, Royal Soc. of Edinburgh 1986–89, British Soc. of Gastroenterology 1992–; Corresp. mem. Italian Soc. of Gastroenterology, Royal Catalonian Acad. of Medicine; mem. numerous editorial bds; Hon. FCP(SA); Hon. mem. South African Soc. of Gastroenterology, Japanese Soc. of Gastroenterology; Hon. MD (Iasi). *Publications:* 28 textbooks and 600 articles mainly on gastroenterological topics. *Leisure interests:* music of Berlioz, history of whaling, cooking. *Address:* 8A Merchiston Park, Edinburgh, EH10 4PN, Scotland.

BOUDA, Jean Claude; Burkinabè politician; b. 28 Dec. 1959, Paris, France; m.; three d.; ed univ. in France; began career with Office nat. du commerce extérieur (Onac, Burkinabè foreign trade promotion agency); worked for Faso-Tours (nat. tourism agency); mem. Nat. Ass. (Congrès pour la démocratie et le progrès, CDP) 1992–97; Dir-Gen. Salon international de l'artisanat de Ouagadougou (Siao, handicraft trade promotion agency) 1997–2016; Minister of Youth, Training and Professional Integration 2016–17, Minister of Nat. Defence and War Veterans 2017–19. *Address:* c/o Ministry of National Defence and War Veterans, BP 496, Ouagadougou 01, Burkina Faso (office).

BOUDOU, Amado, DEcon, MEconSc; Argentine economist, business executive and politician; b. 19 Nov. 1962, Buenos Aires; m. Daniela Andriuolo 1993 (divorced 1998); ed Nat. Univ. of Mar del Plata, Centro de Estudio Macroeconómicos Argentinos; Asst Prof. of Econs, Univ. Nacional de Tres de Febrero 2000; Asst Prof., Centro de Estudio Macroeconómicos Argentinos 2001–02; Asst Prof., Univ. Argentina de la Empresa 2001–05; with Sales Dept, Venturino ESHIUR SA 1990–95; Project Man. ECOPLATA SA 1995–98; Co-ordinator, Administración Nacional de la Seguridad Social 2000, Gen. Man. Comptroller's Office 2001, later Finance Dir, Sec.-Gen. 2008–09; Sec. of Housing and Finance, Dist of La Costa 2003–05; Minister of Economy and Public Finance 2009–11; Vice-Pres. of Argentina 2011–15.

BOUDREAUX, Gail Koziara, BA, MBA; American business executive; *President and CEO, Anthem, Inc.;* m. Terry Boudreaux; two s.; ed Chicopee Comprehensive High School, Mass, Dartmouth Coll., Columbia Univ. Business School; fmr professional basketball player, including for Dartmouth Big Green Women's basketball team 1978–82; joined Aetna Inc. as Regional Man., becoming Gen. Man., Pacific Northwest Market, Vice-Pres., Customer Service, Sr Vice-Pres., later Pres. Group Insurance; Pres. Blue Cross and Blue Shield of Illinois 2002–05; Exec. Vice-Pres., External Operations, Health Care Services Corpn (HCSC) 2005–08, Pres. UnitedHealthcare 2008–11, CEO 2011–18, Exec. Vice-Pres. UnitedHealth Group 2008–18; CEO GKB Global Health LLC 2015–17; Pres. and CEO Anthem, Inc. 2017–; mem. Bd of Dirs Dental Network America, Health Care Services Corpn Insurance Services, Fort Dearborn Life Insurance Co., Metropolitan Planning Council; Dir Genzyme Corpn 2004–; named Ivy League Player of the Year for three consecutive seasons, twice an Academic All-American and third team All-American, NCAA Silver Anniversary Award 2007, Minneapolis/St Paul Business Journal Women in Business Industry Leader Award 2009, Billie-Jean King Leadership Award, Women's Sports Foundation 2018. *Leisure interest:* tennis. *Address:* Anthem, Inc., 220 Virginia Avenue, Indianapolis, IN 46204, USA (office). *Telephone:* (800) 331-1476 (office). *Website:* antheminc.com (office).

BOUDRIA, Don, PC, BA; Canadian fmr politician; *Senior Counsellor, Hill+-Knowlton Canada;* b. 30 Aug. 1949, Hull, Québec; m. Mary Ann Morris 1971; one s. one d.; ed Eastview High School, Univ. of Waterloo; entered Fed. Govt 1966, held various positions including Chief Purchasing Agent –1981; Councillor, Cumberland Township 1976–80, fmr mem. Cumberland Township Housing Corpn; mem. Ontario Legis. for Prescott-Russell 1981–84, Opposition Critic of Govt Services 1981–82, of Community and Social Services 1982–83, of Consumer and Commercial Relations 1983–84; mem. Parl. for Glengarry-Prescott-Russell 1984–2005 (retd); Opposition Critic on Fed. Supply and Services, mem. Standing Cttee on Agriculture 1984, Opposition Critic on Public Works 1985, Govt Operations 1987, Canada Post and Govt Operations 1988; Deputy Opposition Whip 1989, Asst House Leader for the Official Opposition and Govt Operations Critic 1990–93, Deputy Govt Whip 1994; mem. Ont. Liberal Caucus 1984, Chair. 1985–87; Minister of Int. Co-operation and Francophonie 1996–97, Minister of State and Leader of Govt in House of Commons 1997–2002, Minister of Public Works and Govt Services Jan.–May 2002, Minister of State and Leader of the Govt in House of Commons 2002–03; currently Sr Counsellor, Hill+Knowlton Canada; Founding Pres. Ont. Section, Int. Asscn of French-speaking Parliamentarians; mem. Bd of Dirs International Election Monitoring Inst., Canadian Asscn of Former Parliamentarians; Founding mem. Sarsfield Knights of Columbus; currently Chair. Canadian Section FIPA. *Publication:* Busboy: From Kitchen to Cabinet 2005. *Leisure interests:* history, music, downhill skiing. *Address:* Hill+Knowlton Canada, 55 Metcalfe Street, Suite 1100, Ottawa, ON K1P 6L5 (office); 3455 Dessaint Crescent, Sarsfield, ON K0A 3E0, Canada (home). *Telephone:* (613) 238-4371 (office). *Website:* hkstrategies.ca (office).

BOUGIE, Jacques, OC, LLL, DSA; Canadian business executive and academic; *Adjunct Professor, Department of Management, HEC Montréal;* b. 1947, Montreal; ed Univ. de Montréal; joined Alcan 1979, Man. Beauharnois Works, then various positions in Winnipeg, Toronto and Montreal in major project devt, planning and gen. man., responsible for fabricating operations in N America, Pres., COO Alcan Aluminium Ltd 1989–93, Pres., CEO 1993–2001; Adjunct Prof., HEC Montréal 2002–; fmr Vice-Chair. Business Council on Nat. Issues; mem. Bd of Dirs Abitibi-Consolidated Inc., Nova Chemicals Inc. 2001, McCain Foods Ltd, Rona Inc. 2003–05; Chair. Int. Advisory Council, CGI Group Inc. 2004; Businessman of the Year, Les Affaires newspaper 1999, Order of Merit graduates, Univ. de Montréal 2000, Academy of Great Montrealers 2001. *Address:* Department of Management, HEC Montréal, Côte-Sainte-Catherine Building, 3000 chemin de la Côte-Sainte-Catherine, Montréal, PQ H3T 2A7, Canada (office). *Fax:* (514) 340-5635 (office). *E-mail:* jacques.bougie@hec.ca (office). *Website:* www.hec.ca/en/profs/jacques.bougie.html (office).

BOUH, Yacin Elmi; Djibouti politician; b. 4 June 1962, Djibouti City; ed Univ. of Nantes, France; successively, Head of Dept of the Civil Service, Legal Adviser to the Minister of Public Service and Counsel for the State 1992–93; Dir Caisse Nationale de Retraite 1993–94; Vice-Chair. Cttee on Decentralization 1994–97, also participated in peace talks with Front pour la restauration de l'unité et la démocratie (FRUD) by signing of Ab'a agreement 1994–97; Minister of the Economy, Finance and Planning, in charge of privatization 1997–2005, Minister of Interior and Decentralization 2005–11; rank of Amb. 2011; fmr mem. Bd of Govs, Islamic Devt Bank. *Address:* c/o Ministry of the Interior, BP 33, Djibouti, Djibouti.

BOUHAMED CHAABOUNI, Habiba, DèsSc; Tunisian medical geneticist and academic; b. 1953; ed Faculty of Medicine, Tunis; est. first genetic counselling service and launched epidemiological studies on consanguinity in northern Tunisia 1981, set up medical genetics and consultation service to carry out antenatal diagnostic tests 1993; fmr Prof. of Medical Genetics, Univ. of Tunis, Head of Dept of Congenital and Hereditary Diseases, Charles Nicolle Hosp., Tunisia, Dir Human Genetics Research Lab. and Faculty of Medicine, Tunis, currently Prof.-Researcher in Human Genetics; fmr mem. Tech. Comm. of Arab League for Genetic Diseases Prevention and Genetic Counselling, represented Tunisia in Cttee of Governmental Experts to prepare UNESCO draft declaration on the Human Genome; mem. Soc. Tunisienne des Sciences Médicales, Soc. Tunisienne de Pédiatrie, American Soc. of Human Genetics, European Soc. of Cytogenetics; L'Oréal-UNESCO Women in Science Award 2006. *Publications:* more than 100 scientific papers on the analysis and prevention of hereditary disorders. *Address:* University of Tunis El Mar, BP 94, Tunis 1068, Tunisia (office). *Telephone:* (71) 873-366 (office). *Fax:* (71) 872-055 (office). *E-mail:* utm@utm.tn (office). *Website:* www.utm.rnu.tn (office).

BOUHIA, (Haya) Hynd, SM, MA, PhD; Moroccan economist and business executive; b. 21 Oct. 1972, Casablanca; m. Khalid Zerouali; one s.; ed Ecole Centrale, Paris, France, Johns Hopkins School for Advanced Int. Studies and Harvard Univ., USA; joined World Bank Young Professional Program, Washington, DC 1996, worked on Bank's lending operations 1996–2001, worked as Water and Environmental Economist in Middle East and N Africa (MENA) Region, in Latin America Region on water sector strategy for Argentina and water quality control in Brazil and SE Asia Region, Special Asst to Vice-Pres. for MENA Region –2001, Sr Financial Officer in Capital Market Operations unit of Banking, Capital Markets and Financial Eng Dept, World Bank Treasury 2001–04; econ. adviser to Prime Minister of Morocco 2004–08; Dir-Gen. Casablanca Stock Exchange 2008–11; currently CEO Global Nexus; mem. Washington Conservatory of Music (performs classical piano); Hon. Prize of Casablanca Conservatory of Music for Piano performances. *Publications:* Water in the Macro Economy: Application of an Integrated Analytical Model 2001; several academic papers and book chapters. *Leisure interest:* athletic and fitness activities.

BOUIS, Howarth (Howdy), BA, MA, PhD; American plant scientist; *Institute Fellow and HarvestPlus Advisor, International Food Policy Research Institute;* b. 1950, Berkeley, Calif.; ed Stanford Univ.; worked with Volunteers in Asia in the Philippines 1972–75; returned to Stanford Univ. to take a graduate programme at Food Research Inst. 1975; Postdoctoral position at Food Consumption and Nutrition Div., Int. Food Policy Research Inst. (IFPRI), Washington, DC to undertake a two-year research project on the Philippines 1982–84, subsequently Research Fellow and Sr Research Fellow; has promoted biofortification within the CGIAR (fmrly Consultative Group for Int. Agricultural Research) consortium since 1993; Founder and Dir HarvestPlus programme, co-ordinated by Int. Center for Tropical Agric. (CIAT), Cali, Colombia and IFPRI; World Food Prize (co-recipient) 2016. *Address:* International Food Policy Research Institute, 2033 K Street, NW, Washington, DC 20006-1002, USA (office). *Telephone:* (202) 862-5600 (office). *Fax:* (202) 467-4439 (office). *E-mail:* h.bouis@cgiar.org (office). *Website:* www.ifpri.org (office).

BOUKADOUM, Sabri; Algerian diplomatist and politician; *Minister of Foreign Affairs;* b. 1 Sept. 1958; m. Sabria Boukadoum; two c.; ed École Nationale d'Admin (Diplomatic Section); First Sec., Embassy in Budapest 1987–88, Counsellor, Perm. Mission of Algeria to UN, New York 1988–92, Asst Dir of Political Affairs, UN and Disarmament, Ministry of Foreign Affairs 1992–93, Dir of Political Affairs 1993–95, Amb. to Côte d'Ivoire 1996–2001, Chief of Protocol, Ministry of Foreign Affairs 2001–05, Amb. to Portugal 2005–09, Dir-Gen. for the Americas, Ministry of Foreign Affairs 2009–13, Amb. and Perm. Rep. to UN, New York 2014–19, Minister of Foreign Affairs 2019–. *Address:* Ministry of Foreign Affairs, place Mohamed Seddik Benyahia, el-Mouradia, Algiers, Algeria (office). *Telephone:* (21) 29-12-12 (office). *Fax:* (21) 50-43-63 (office). *Website:* www.mae.gov.dz (office).

BOULAMA, Kané Aïchatou, DESS; Niger politician; b. 24 April 1955, Keita, Tahoua Region; m.; three c.; ed Univ. Rennes I, Univ. of Paris (Sorbonne), France; del. to Nat. Conf. (which discussed political evolution of Niger following mil. regime) 1991; Sec. of State for Planning 1993; Dir, Salon Int. de l'artisanat pour la Femme (agency to promote women's business activities) 2006; fmr Dir, Cabinet of Prime Minister; Gov. Niamey Region 2011–15; Minister of State, Minister of Foreign Affairs, African Integration and Nigeriens Abroad 2015–16. *Address:* c/o Ministry of Foreign Affairs, African Integration and Nigeriens Abroad, BP 396, Niamey, Niger (office).

BOULLIER, Éric René; French motorsport manager; b. 9 Nov. 1973, Laval; ed Institut Polytechnique des Sciences Appliquées, Ivry-sur-Seine; Chief Engineer, Spanish Racing Engineering team 2002; Man. and Tech. Dir, Driot-Arnoux Motorsport (DAMS) team, France 2003–08, Team Prin. 2007–08; CEO Gravity Sport Man. 2008–10; Team Prin., Renault F1 Team 2010–11, Lotus F1 Formula Team 2012–14; Racing Dir McLaren Formula One Team 2014–18; Vice-Chair. Formula One Teams Asscn 2011–14. *Address:* c/o McLaren Technology Centre, Chertsey Road, Woking, Surrey, GU21 4YH, England (office).

BOULUD, Daniel; French chef and restaurateur; b. 25 March 1955, St Pierre de Chandieu, Rhône; began career as apprentice chef at age 14; spent two years as chef in Copenhagen; chef, European Comm., Washington DC 1981; opened first restaurants, The Polo Lounge, Westbury Hotel, and Le Régence, Hotel Plaza Athenée, New York; Exec. Chef Le Cirque, New York 1986–92; opened Daniel restaurant 1993 (Gourmet Magazine Top Table Award), Café Boulud, New York Sept. 1998, DB Bistro Moderne June 2001, Café Boulud, Florida 2003, numerous other restaurants; Founding Pnr, Payard Patisserie & Bistro –2000; Owner, Feast & Fêtes Catering and Daniel Boulud CONNOISSEUR (direct mail co.); mem. Bd of Dirs Citymeals-on-Wheels 1999–; contrib. Elle Décor; Bon Appétit Magazine Chef of the Year, Outstanding Restaurateur, James Beard Foundation 2006. *Publications include:* Cooking with Daniel Boulud 1993, Daniel Boulud's Café Boulud Cookbook 1999, Chef Daniel Boulud Cooking in New York City 2002, Letters to a Young Chef (jt author) 2003, Daniel's Dish: Entertaining at Home with a Four-Star Chef 2003, Braise: A Journey through International Cuisine 2006; Easy Cooking with Great Chefs (Ed.) monthly newsletter. *Address:* c/o Daniel, 60 East 65th Street, New York, NY 10065, USA (office). *Website:* www.danielboulud.com (office).

BOUMA, Johannes, PhD; Dutch soil scientist and academic; b. 29 Oct. 1940, 't Bildt; s. of S. Bouma and J. Bouma (née Werff); m. Marianne Wiebols 1969; one s. one d.; ed Agricultural Univ., Wageningen, Univ. of Wisconsin USA; Asst Prof., Soils Dept, Univ. of Wis., Madison 1969–73, Assoc. Prof. 1973–75; Head of Soil Physics Dept, Netherlands Soil Survey Inst., Wageningen 1975–82, Deputy Dir in charge of research 1982–86; Prof. of Soil Science, Agricultural Univ. of Wageningen 1986–2002, Scientific Dir Environmental Sciences Group Research Centre 2002–04; mem. Netherlands Scientific Council for Govt Policy 1998–2003; mem. Royal Dutch Acad. of Sciences 1989; Corresp. mem. German Soil Science Asscn 1982; Fellow, Soil Science Soc. of America 1985; Hon. mem., Int. Union of Soil Sciences 2006, Dutch Soil Science Soc. 2010; Officer of the Order of Orange-Nassau 2001; Alexander von Humboldt Medal 2017, Dukachaev Award 2017. *Publications:* several books and various articles in tech. journals. *Leisure interests:* jogging, cycling. *Address:* Alterra, PO Box 47, 6700 AA Wageningen (office); Spoorbaanweg 35, 3911 CA Rhenen, Netherlands (home). *Telephone:* (317) 613469 (home). *E-mail:* johan.bouma@wur.nl (office); johan.bouma@planet.nl (home).

BOUMTARI, Faraj Abderrahmane, MBA; Libyan accountant and politician; *Minister of Finance;* ed Benghazi Univ., Bentley Univ. Business School, Mass, USA; Assoc. Faculty mem., Faculty of Econs, Al-Asmariya Univ. 2009–12; Deputy Dir of Risk Man., Libya-Africa Investment Portfolio 2009–10, Dir of Risk Man. 2011–12; Deputy Dir, Audit Dept, Nat. Commercial Bank 2012; Asst Deputy Minister of Finance and Oil, Nat. Transitional Council March–Oct. 2011; Minister of Finance (in Govt of Nat. Accord) 2018–.

BOUNNHANG, Vorachith; Laotian politician, army officer and head of state; *President;* b. 15 Aug. 1937; m. Khammeung Vorachith; fmr army officer; fmr Gov. Savannaket, then Mayor Vientiane Municipality; Minister of Finance and Deputy Prime Minister 1999–2001; Prime Minister of Lao People's Democratic Repub. 2001–06, Vice-Pres. 2006–16, Pres. 2016–; mem. Lao People's Revolutionary Party, mem. Politburo 1996–, Sec.-Gen. 2016–. *Address:* Office of the President, ave Lane Xang, Vientiane, Laos. *Telephone:* (21) 214200 (office). *Fax:* (21) 214208 (office).

BOUQUET, Carole; French actress and director; b. 18 Aug. 1957, Neuilly-sur-Seine (Hauts-de-Seine); m. 1st Rodolfo Recrio 1980 (divorced 1981); m. 2nd Jean-Pierre Rassam 1982 (died 1985); one s.; m. 3rd Jacques Liebowitch 1992 (divorced 1996); partner Gérard Depardieu 1997–2005; partner Francis Giacobetti; fmr Face of Chanel No. 5; mem. Jury, Cannes Film Festival 2014. *Films include:* Cet Obscur Objet du Désir 1977, Buffet Froid 1979, Le Manteau d'Astrakan 1979, For Your Eyes Only 1981, Le Jour des Idiots 1981, Bingo Bango 1982, Dream One 1983, Mystère 1983, Dagobert 1984, Rive droite, Rive gauche 1984, Double Messieurs 1985, Special Police 1985, Le Mal d'Aimer 1986, Jenatsch 1986, On se dépêche d'en rire 1987, Bunker Palace Hotel 1988, Trop Belle pour toi (César for Best Actress) 1990, In All Innocence, The Bridge, Tango 1993, Grosse Fatigue 1994, A Business Affair 1994, Lucie Aubrac 1997, En plein cœur 1998, Un pont entre deux rives 1999, Le Pique-nique de Lulu Kreutz 2000, Embrassez qui vous voudrez 2002, Blanche 2002, Bienvenue chez les Rozes 2003, Feux Rouges 2004, Les Fautes d'orthographe 2004, Nordeste 2005, Travaux, on sait quand ça commence 2005, L'Enfer 2005, Aurore 2006, Un ami parfait 2006, Si c'était lui 2007, Les Enfants de Timpelbach 2007, Les Hauts murs 2008, You'll Miss Me 2009, Protéger et servir 2010, Libre échange 2010, Le mystère 2010, Impardonnables 2011, Bad Girl 2012, Une heure de tranquillité 2015. *Television:* Ruy Blas (film) 2002, L'éloignement (film) 2009, Le grand restaurant II (film) 2011, Rosemary's Baby (mini-series) 2014. *Plays include:* Phèdre, Théâtre Dejazet, Paris 2002. *Address:* c/o Intertalent, 5 rue Clément-Marot, 75008 Paris, France (office).

BOURCE, Ludovic; French composer and actor; b. 19 Aug. 1970, Pontivy. *Film scores include:* Mes amis 1999, OSS 117: Cairo, Nest of Spies 2006, Here to Stay (documentary) (original music) 2009, OSS 117: Lost in Rio 2009, The Artist (Broadcast Film Critics Asscn Award for Best Composer 2011, Chicago Film Critics Asscn Award for Best Original Score 2011, European Film Award for Best Composer 2011, Washington, DC Area Film Critics Asscn Award for Best Score 2011, Golden Globe Award for Best Original Score 2012) 2011, De l'autre côté du périph (On the Other Side of the Tracks) 2012. *Film roles in:* OSS 117: Lost in Rio 2009. *Television includes:* House Arrest (series) 2018, Clear History (movie) 2013.

BOURDAIS DE CHARBONNIÈRE, Eric; French business executive; b. 1939; began career with JP Morgan 1965, various positions, including commercial banker, Controller and Treas., New York and Paris 1965–81, Chair. and CEO JP Morgan (France) 1981–85, Sr Vice-Pres. JP Morgan Continental Europe 1985–87, Exec. Vice-Pres. JP Morgan Europe 1987–90; Chief Financial Officer, Compagnie Générale des Établissements Michelin 1990–2000, Chair. Supervisory Bd 2000–13; mem. Bd of Dirs, Thomson 2003–, also Chair. Audit Cttee; mem. Supervisory Bd, Oddo & Cie, ING Group 2004–09; Dir, Faurecia SA 2010–; Gov., American Hosp., Paris; Chevalier des Arts et des Lettres. *Address:* c/o Compagnie Générale des Établissements Michelin, 12 cours Sablon, 63000 Clermont-Ferrand, France. *E-mail:* info@michelin.com.

BOURDEAU, Philippe François, PhD, FAAS; Belgian academic and fmr European Community official; b. 25 Nov. 1926, Rabat, Morocco; s. of Michel Bourdeau and Lucienne Imbrecht; m. Flora Gorirossi 1954; three d.; ed Gembloux, Belgium and Duke Univ. USA; Asst Prof., State Univ. of North Carolina 1954–56, Yale Univ. 1956–58, 1960–62; Prof., Univ. of Belgian Congo 1958–60; Head, Radiobiology Dept, EURATOM, Jt Research Centre, Ispra, Italy 1962–71; Head of Div. then Dir research programmes in environment and in non-nuclear energy, Comm. of EC, Brussels 1971–91; Prof., Univ. Libre de Bruxelles 1972–96; Head, European Environment Agency Task Force 1991; Chair. Scientific Cttee, European Environmental Agency; mem. Belgian Royal Acad. *Publications include:* scientific papers in the fields of environment policy, ecophysiology, ecotoxicology. *Leisure interests:* reading, sport. *Address:* ULB, CP 130/02, 50 avenue F.D. Roosevelt, 1050 Brussels, Belgium (office). *E-mail:* bourdeau@ulb.ac.be (office).

BOURESLI, Amani Khaled; Kuwaiti academic, business executive and government official; ed Southern Illinois Univ., USA; fmr Asst Prof. then Prof., Dept of Finance, Kuwait Univ.; Founder and Chair. Capital Standards (regional credit ratings agency); Minister of Trade and Industry 2011–12; mem. Bd of Dirs Burgan Bank –2011; Economic Policy and Knowledge Devt Achiever Award, Middle East Excellence Awards Inst. 2010. *E-mail:* bouresli@cba.edu.kw (office).

BOURGES, Hervé; French administrator, diplomatist and journalist; b. 2 May 1933, Rennes, Ile-et-Vilaine; s. of Joseph Bourges and Marie-Magdeleine Desjeux; m. Marie-Thérèse Lapouille 1966; ed Lycée de Biarritz, Coll. Saint-Joseph, Reims, École supérieure de journalisme; Ed. then Ed.-in-Chief Témoignage Chrétien 1956–62; attached to Keeper of the Seals 1959–62, Dir Algerian Ministry of Youth and Popular Education, attached to Ministry of Information; Asst Lecturer Univ. de Paris II 1967–; Founder and Dir École supérieure de journalisme de Yaoundé, Cameroun 1970–76; Dir then Pres. Admin. Council École nat. supérieure de journalisme de Lille 1976–80; Dir Information Service and Dir-Gen.'s Messenger UNESCO 1980–81, Amb. to UNESCO 1994–95; Dir then Dir-Gen. Radio France Int. 1981–83; Chair. and Dir-Gen. TV Française 1 (TF1) 1983–87, Hon. Pres. 1987–93; Hon. Pres. Admin. Council, Ecole Supérieure de Journalisme de Lille 1992–; Dir-Gen. Radio Monte Carlo (RMC) 1988; Pres. and Dir-Gen. Société financière de radiodiffusion (Sofirad) 1989–91; Pres. Canal Horizon 1990–91, Conseil Supérieur de L'Audio-Visuel (CSA) 1995–2001; Pres. L'Union internationale des journalistes et de la presse de langue française (UIJPLF) 2001; apptd Pres. Comité permanent de la diversité de France Télévisions 2009; Commdr, Légion d'honneur 2011; Croix de la Valeur Militaire. *Film:* L'Algérie à l'épreuve du pouvoir (documentary). *Publications:* L'Algérie à l'épreuve du pouvoir 1967, La Révolte étudiante 1968, Décoloniser l'information 1978, Les cinquante Afriques (jtly) 1979, Le village planétaire (jtly) 1986, Une Chaîne sur les bras 1987, Un amour de télévision (jtly) 1989, La Télévision du Public 1993, De mémoire d'éléphant (autobiog.) 2000, Le règne de la terreur sacrée (with Liess Boukra) 2001, Entretiens (with Jean-Michel Djian) 2003, Léopold Sédar Senghor, lumière noire 2006, L'Afrique n'attend pas 2010. *Website:* www.ftv-diversite.fr.

BOURGUIGNON, François, DEcon, DEA, PhD; French economist and academic; *Emeritus Chair, Paris School of Economics;* b. 22 May 1945, Paris; m.; ed Ecole Nationale de la Statistique at des Analyses Economique (ENSEA), Univ. of Paris VI, Univ. of Western ON, Canada, Univ. of Orléans; Expert de coopération (VSN), Univ. of Chile 1969–70; Asst Prof., Univ. of Toronto, Canada 1975–78; Consultant, OECD Devt Center 1971–72; Research Fellow, Laboratoire d'économie politique de l'Ecole normale supérieure, CNRS, Paris 1978–85; Research Fellow, Centre d'observation économique, Chambre de Commerce et d'Industrie de Paris 1971–72; Prof. of Econs, Ecole des Hautes Etudes en Sciences Sociales (EHESS), Dir Centre d'Economie Quantitative et Comparative 1986–87, Founder and first Dir of Delta (jt research unit CNRS, EHESS and Ecole Nat. Supérieur) 1988; Advisor to Chief Economist, Banque Mondiale 1999–2000; fmr Dir and Assoc. Chair, Paris School of Econs 2007–13, Emer. Chair 2013–; mem. Conseil d'Analyse Economique (advisory group to Prime Minister), Paris; Visiting Prof., Concordia Univ., Montreal, Canada 1979, Birkbeck Coll., London, UK 1984, Univ. of Geneva, Switzerland 1989–90, Università Commerciale Luigi Bocconi, Milan, Italy 1992–95; Chief Economist and Sr Vice-Pres., Devt Econs, World Bank, Washington, DC 2003–07, Dir Devt Research Group 2003, est. Devt Impact Evaluation Initiative (DIME); Ed. World Bank Economic Review, European Economic Review; fmr consultant, UN, EC, ILO; Pres. European Soc. for Population Econs 1995, Comité d'évaluation du RSA (revenu de solidarité active); mem. Scientific Cttee of WIDER (UN, Helsinki), Universidad Torcuato di Tella (Argentina), Centro Luca d'Agliano, Turin, Council of Econ. Advisors of the French Prime Minister, Exec. Cttee of EUDN (European Devt Network), EC Advisory Group on Societal Analysis, Evaluation Cttee of European Research Council, Brussels, Copenhagen Consensus Panel; Fellow, Econometric Soc. 1986; Chevalier, Ordre nat. du Mérite 1991, Légion d'honneur 2010; Dr hc (Université du Québec à Montréal) 2001, (Geneva) 2005, (Western Ontario) 2009, (Liège) 2009 Merrit Brown Prize for the best thesis, Univ. of Western Ontario 1975, CNRS Bronze Medal 1982, El Fasi Prize for Devt Econs, Asscn des Universités de langue française (Aupelf/Uref), Médaille d'argent, CNRS 1997, Médaille d'honneur de la Santé et des Affaires Sociales 2012, Juan Luis Londono Prize, Lacea (Colombia) 2012. *Publications include:* Statistical Analysis of Incomes in Chile (in Spanish) 1970, International Labour Migrations and Economic Choices – The European Case (with G. Gallais-Hamonno) 1977, L'économie française au XIX[e]siècle – Analyse macroéconomique (with M. Lévy-Leboyer) 1985 (English trans.: A Macroeconomic Model of France during the 19th Century: An Essay in Econometric Analysis) 1990, Foreign Trade and Income Distribution (co-author) 1989, Théorie micro-économique: L'équilibre concurrentiel (co-author) 1992, Equity and Adjustment in Developing Economies (co-author) 1992, Growth and Macro-economic Crisis in Côte d'Ivoire (co-author) 1996, Handbook of Income Distribution (co-ed.) 2000, The Impact of Economic Policies on Poverty and Income Distribution: Evaluation Techniques and Tools (co-ed.) 2003, The Microeconomics of Income Distribution Dynamics in East Asia and Latin America (co-ed.) 2005, The Impact of Macroeconomic Policies on Poverty and Income Distribution (co-ed.) 2008, Trajectoires et enjeux de l'économie mondiale (co-author) 2010, La Mondialisation de l'inégalité 2012, Income Distribution in Computable General Equilibrium Modeling (co-author) 2013; several book chapters; numerous articles in specialist journals. *Address:* Paris School of Economics, Building B, 1st Floor, Office 112, 48 boulevard Jourdan, 75014 Paris, France (office). *Telephone:* 1-43-13-62-57 (office). *E-mail:* francois.bourguignon@psemail.eu (office). *Website:* www.parisschoolofeconomics.eu/en/bourguignon-francois (office).

BOURGUIGNON, Philippe Etienne, MScEcon, MBA; French business executive; *Chairman, Groupe Primonial;* b. 11 Jan. 1948, Salins les Bains; s. of Jacques Bourguignon and Paule Clément; m. Martine Lemardeley 1977; one s. one d.; ed Univ. of Aix; analyst, Synthèse Documentaire, Paris 1971–72; Project Man. Systembau, Munich 1973; Vice-Pres. Devt Accor, Novotel Asia, Middle East 1974–79; Exec. Vice-Pres. Accor North America, New York 1979–84; Pres. and CEO Accor Asia Pacific, Los Angeles 1984–88; Sr Vice-Pres. Real Estate Devt Euro Disney, Paris 1989–92; Pres. Euro Disney SA, Paris 1992, Chair. and CEO 1993–97; Exec. Vice-Pres. for Europe Walt Disney Co. 1996–97; Chair. Bd of Dirs Club Méditerranée 1997–2002; Man. Dir World Econ. Forum Aug.–Oct. 2003, Co-CEO 2003–04; Chair. Aegis Media France 2004–06; Vice-Chair. Revolution Resorts (div. of Revolution LLC) 2006–07, Vice-Chair. Revolution Places Group and CEO Revolution Places Development 2007–; CEO Miraval Resort 2009–; CEO Exclusive Resorts 2011–15; Chair. Groupe Primonial 2017–; Pres. Young Pres. Org. 1990; Pres. Exec. Comm. for Paris' bid for Olympic Games 2008 1998; mem. Bd of Dirs eBay Inc 1999–, American Chamber of Commerce in France; mem. Econ. Council Confed. of French Industries and Services; Chair. YPO French Chapter 1990; Chevalier, Légion d'honneur, Officier, Ordre nat. du Mérite, Wissam Al Alaoui Order (Morocco). *Leisure interests:* sailing, reading, tennis, skiing. *Website:* www.primonial.com (office).

BOURHANE, Nourdine; Comoran politician; b. 1958; Prime Minister of Comoros 1997–98; Vice-Pres., with responsibility for Land Settlement, Town Planning and Housing 2011–16. *Address:* c/o Ministry of Land Settlement, Town Planning and Housing, BP 12, Moroni, Comoros (office).

BOURITA, Nasser, CES, DES; Moroccan diplomatist and politician; *Minister of Foreign Affairs and International Cooperation;* b. 27 May 1969, Taounate; m.; two c.; ed Univ. of Rabat; several years with Ministry of Foreign Affairs and Cooperation (MFA), including with Directorate of Multilateral Cooperation 1992–95, First Sec., Embassy in Vienna 1995–2000, Adviser to Gen. Directorate of Multilateral Relations and Global Cooperation, MFA 2000–02, with UN Dept, MFA 2002, Adviser, Mission of Morocco to European Communities, Brussels 2002–13, Head, UN Div., MFA 2003–06, Dir of UN and Int. Orgs Dept 2006–09, Chef de Cabinet, Ministry of Foreign Affairs and Cooperation 2007–11, Amb. and Dir-Gen. of Multilateral Relations and Global Cooperation 2009–11, Sec.-Gen., MFA 2011–16, Minister Del. to Minister of Foreign Affairs and Cooperation 2016–17, Minister of Foreign Affairs and Int. Co-operation 2017–; ind. *Address:* Ministry of Foreign Affairs and International Cooperation, ave Franklin Roosevelt, Rabat, Morocco (office). *Telephone:* (53) 7761125 (office). *Fax:* (53) 7765508 (office). *Website:* www.diplomatie.ma (office).

BOURNE, Larry Stuart, BA, MA, PhD, FRSC, MCIP, RPP; Canadian geographer and academic; *Professor Emeritus of Geography and Planning, University of Toronto;* b. 24 Dec. 1939, London, Ont.; s. of Stuart H. Bourne and Florence Bourne; m. Paula T. O'Neill 1967; one s. one d.; ed Univs of Western Ontario, Alberta and Chicago; Asst Prof. of Geography, Univ. of Toronto 1967–69, Assoc. Prof. and Assoc. Dir, Centre for Urban and Community Studies (CUCS) 1969–82, Prof. and Dir 1973–78, 1979–84, Prof. of Geography and Planning, Co-ordinator of Grad. Studies 1985–89, 1991–94, Dir Grad. Planning Program 1996–98, 1999–2002, 2004–06, Prof. Emer. 2006–; Research Assoc., Centre for Urban and Community Studies and Global Cities Program; Visiting Scholar, Univ. of Monash, Australia and LSE, UK 1972–73, Centre for Environmental Studies, London, UK 1978–79; Visiting Prof., Univ. of Alberta, Univ. of Texas, USA 1984, Marburg (FRG) 1985, Melbourne 1988, Meiji Univ., Tokyo 1991, Univ. of Tokyo 1996, Ben Gurion Univ. 1998, Seoul Nat. Univ. 1999; Chair. Comm. on Urban Systems and Devt, Int. Geographical Union 1988–92; consultant to local, nat. and int. agencies; Pres. Canadian Asscn of Geographers 1993–94, North American Regional Science Council 1994–95; Hon. DES (Waterloo) 1999; Hon. DLitt (New Brunswick) 2008; Award for Scholarly Distinction, Canadian Asscn of Geographers 1985, Honors Award, Asscn of American Geographers 1985, Elected to Royal Soc. of Canada 1986, Award for Service to Geography (Ont. Div. Canadian Asscn of Geographers) 1990, Teaching Award, Univ. of Toronto 1999, Massey Medal, Royal Canadian Geographical Society 2004, Laureat d'honneur, Int. Geographical Union 2012.

Publications: 19 books, including Urban Systems: Strategies for Regulation 1975, The Geography of Housing 1981, Internal Structure of the City 1982, Urbanization and Settlement Systems 1984, Urban Systems in Transition 1986, The Changing Geography of Urban Systems 1989, Urbanization and Urban Growth 1991, Changing Social Geography of Canadian Cities 1993, People and Places 2000, Canadian Urban Regions 2011; over 250 articles in journals and professional reports. *Address:* Department of Geography, University of Toronto, 100 St George Street, Toronto, ON M5S 3G3 (office); 26 Anderson Avenue, Toronto, ON M5P 1H4, Canada (home). *Telephone:* (416) 978-1593 (office); (416) 486-7819 (home). *Fax:* (416) 946-3886 (office); (416) 978-6729 (home). *E-mail:* bourne@geog.utoronto.ca (office); larry.bourne@utoronto.ca (home). *Website:* www.geog.utoronto.ca (office).

BOURNE, Sir Matthew Christopher, Kt, OBE, BA; British dancer and choreographer; *Artistic Director, New Adventures;* b. 13 Jan. 1960, Walthamstow, London; s. of Harold Jeffrey (Jim) Bourne and June Lillian Bourne (née Handley); ed Laban Centre for Movt and Dance; Founder and Artistic Dir Adventures in Motion Pictures 1987–2002; Co-founder (with Robert Noble) New Adventures, Artistic Dir 2002–; Resident Artist, Sadler's Wells Theatre 2005–, Resident Co., Sadlers Wells Theatre 2006–; Artistic Dir Re:Bourne 2008–; Hon. Fellow, Laban Centre 1997, Companion, Trinity Laban Conservatoire of Music and Dance 2011, Companion, Liverpool Inst. of Performing Arts 2012; Dr hc (Open) 2007, (De Montford) 2007, (Plymouth) 2010, (Kingston) 2010, (Roehampton) 2011, (Royal Conservatoire of Scotland) 2016; Tony Award 1999, Astaire Award 1999 (for Swan Lake), Hamburg Shakespeare Prize for the Arts 2003, Theatre Managers Asscn Special Award 2007, British Inspiration Award (for Arts) 2010, De Valois Award for Outstanding Achievement, Nat. Dance Awards 2013, Dance in Focus Award, Dance Film Asscn 2013, The Sir George Monoux Founders Award, presented at dedication ceremony of The Matthew Bourne Theatre, Monoux Coll., Walthamstow 2014, Primio Ravenna Festical 2015, UK Theatre Award for Outstanding Contrib. to British Theatre 2015, Queen Elizabeth II Award 2016, The Gene Kelly Legacy Award 2016. *Dance:* Overlap Lovers 1987, Spitfire 1988, As You Like It (RSC) 1989, Show Boat (musical; Malmö, Sweden) 1989, The Infernal Galop 1989, 1992, Children of Eden (musical) 1990, Town and Country 1991, Deadly Serious 1992, Percy of Fitzrovia 1992, Nutcracker! 1992, 2002, Highland Fling 1994, Oliver! 1994, 2009, Matthew Bourne's Swan Lake 1995, Cinderella 1997, Swan Lake Broadway 1998, Matthew Bourne's The Car Man 2000–01 (also televised Channel 4), My Fair Lady (Olivier Award for Best Theatre Choreographer 2002) 2001, South Pacific 2002, Play Without Words (Olivier Awards for Best Entertainment and Best Theatre Choreographer 2003) 2002, Mary Poppins (with Stephen Mear) (Olivier Award for Best Theatre Choreographer 2005) 2004, Edward Scissorhands 2005, Dorian Gray 2008, Cinderella 2010, Lord of the Flies 2011, Nutcracker! – 20th Birthday 2012, Sleeping Beauty 2012–13, Early Adventures 2012, Play Without Words 2012, Swan Lake 2013–14, Lord of the Flies 2014, Edward Scissorhands 2014–15, The Car Man 2015, Sleeping Beauty 2015–16, The Red Shoes 2016–17, Lord of the Flies 2017, Early Adventures 2017, Cinderella 2017. *Films:* Swan Lake 3D 2011, The Car Man 2015. *Television includes:* Drip: a Narcissistic Love Story (BBC) 1993, Late Flowering Lust (BBC) 19933, Sleeping Beauty (BBC) 2013, Swan Lake 3D (Sky Arts) 2011, The Car Man (Sky Arts) 2015. *Publication:* Matthew Bourne & His Adventures in Motion Pictures 1999. *Leisure interests:* theatre, cinema, music. *Telephone:* (1252) 597050 (office). *E-mail:* office@new-adventures.net (office). *Website:* new-adventures.net (office).

BOURNE, Stephen, MA, FCA, FRSA; British publisher; *Vice-President, Clare Hall, Cambridge;* b. 20 March 1952, Kampala, Uganda; s. of Colyn M. Bourne and Kathleen Bourne; m. Stephanie Ann Bickford 1978; one s. one d.; ed Berkhamsted School, Univ. of Edinburgh; with Deloitte Haskins and Sells, London and Hong Kong 1974–80; with Exxon Chemical Asia-Pacific, Hong Kong 1980–86; Financial Dir Asia, Dow Jones Telerate, London and Hong Kong 1986–89, Gen. Man. Northern Europe 1989–94; Man. Dir, Financial Printing Div., St Ives PLC, London 1994–96; Devt Dir, Cambridge Univ. Press 1997–2000, Chair. of Printing Div. 2000, CEO 2002–12, Pres. 2012–13; Vice-Pres. Clare Hall, Cambridge 2015–; Chair. Britten Sinfonia Ltd 2010–, Theatre Royal, Bury St Edmunds 2010–; Cathedral Admin., Ely Cathedral 2013–; Bd mem. The Wine Soc. 2005–; mem. Publishing Studies Advisory Bd, Univ. Coll. London, City Univ., London Coll. of Communication; Fellow, Inst. of Printing; Liveryman, The Stationers' Co.; Prince of Wales' Amb. for East of England, Business in the Community 2009, China Special Book Award 2011. *Leisure interests:* fine wines, performing arts, cricket, skiing, Real Tennis. *Address:* Clare Hall, Herschel Road, Cambridge, CB3 9AL (office); Falmouth Lodge, Snailwell Road, Newmarket, CB8 7DN, England (home). *Website:* www.clarehall.cam.ac.uk (office).

BOURRIAUD, Nicolas; French curator and art critic; *Director, École Nationale Supérieure des Beaux-Arts;* b. 1965; Paris Corresp., Flash Art (magazine) 1987–1995; Co-founder, Documents sur l'art 1992–2000, Perpendiculaire 1995–98; Founding Dir Palais de Tokyo, Paris 1999–2005; Adviser to Ukrainian collector Victor Pinchuk 2006; Gulbenkian Curator of Contemporary Art, Tate Britain, London 2008–10; Dir École Nationale Supérieure des Beaux-Arts, Paris 2011–. *Publications:* Postproduction 2000, Relational Aesthetics 2002, Altermodern 2009, The Radicant 2009. *Address:* Ecole nationale supérieure des Beaux-arts, 14, rue Bonaparte, 75006 Paris, France (office). *Telephone:* 1-47-03-50-00 (office). *Website:* www.beauxartsparis.com (office).

BOUSNINA, Mongi; Tunisian academic, diplomatist and international organization executive; b. Tunis; ed Univ. of Paris (Sorbonne); fmr Minister of Culture; fmr Amb. to Morocco, to France; apptd Prof., Univ. of Tunis 1970, Prof. Lecturer 1981; Dir-Gen. Arab League Educational, Cultural and Scientific Org. (ALECSO) 2001–09; Gen. Co-ordinator for the Arab Participation Programme at the Frankfurt Book Fair 2004; Medal of the Republic, Seventh of November Medal, Alaoui Medal (Morocco), Higher Oscar Medal of Culture (Egypt).

BOUSQUET, Jean; French couturier and fmr politician; *President, Cacharel;* b. 30 March 1932, Nîmes; s. of Célestin Bousquet and Rosa Pyronnet; m. Dominique Sarrut 1965; one s. one d.; ed Ecole Tech. de Nîmes; dress cutter, Jean Jourdan, Paris 1955–57; Founder and Pres., Soc. Jean Cacharel 1962–, of subsidiaries abroad 1972–; Mayor of Nîmes 1983–95; Deputy (UDF) for Gard, Assemblée Nat. 1986–97; mem. Radical Party 1993–96; Acad. Award for export achievement 1969, Man of the Year, Jeune Chambre économique française 1985. *Leisure interests:* travel, football, golf, skiing. *Address:* Cacharel, 36 rue Tronchet, 75009 Paris, France (office). *Telephone:* 1-42-68-38-88 (office). *Fax:* 1-42-68-38-77 (office).

BOUSQUET, Rufus; Saint Lucia politician; Man. Dir Luxury Vacation Homes 1997–2006; mem. House of Ass. (Parl.) for Choiseul 2006–11; Minister for External Affairs, Int. Financial Services, Information and Broadcasting 2006–07, for Industry, Trade, Commerce, Investment and Consumer Affairs 2008–09, for External Affairs, Int. Trade and Investment 2009; mem. United Workers Party (UWP), fmr Deputy Leader and Chair. Public Relations Cttee.

BOUSSAID, Muhammad, DipEng, MBA; Moroccan engineer and politician; b. 26 Sept. 1961, Fez; ed Ecole Nat. des Ponts et Chaussées, Paris; worked as consulting engineer, Banque Commerciale du Maroc 1986–92; Deputy Man. Dir, chemical production and trading co. 1992–94; Portfolio Man., Moroccan Bank of Commerce and Industry 1994–95; Chef du cabinet of Minister of Public Works, later Chef du cabinet of Minister of Agric., Equipment and Environment 1995–98; Dir of Programmes and Studies, Ministry of Infrastructure 1998–2001; Dir of Public Institutions and Participation, later Dir of Public Enterprises and Privatization, Ministry of Finance and Privatization 2001–04; Minister in charge of Modernization of the Public Sector 2004–07; Minister of Tourism and Handicrafts 2007–10; Wali (Gov.), Souss-Massa-Draa Region and Gov., Agadir Idda Outanane Prefecture 2010–12; Wali of Grand Casablanca and Gov., Casablanca Prefecture 2012–13; Minister of the Economy and Finance 2013–18; mem. Rassemblement Nat. des Indépendants (RNI). *Address:* c/o Ministry of the Economy and Finance, blvd Muhammad V, Quartier Administratif, Chellah, Rabat, Morocco (office).

BOUTEFLIKA, Abdul Aziz; Algerian fmr head of state; b. 2 March 1937, Oujda; s. of Ahmed Bouteflika and Mansouria Ghezlaoui; m. Amal Triki 1990 (divorced); ed Morocco; Maj., Nat. Liberation Army and Sec. of Gen. Staff; mem. Parl. for Tlemcen 1962; Minister of Youth, Sports and Tourism 1962–63, of Foreign Affairs 1963–79; Counsellor to the Pres. March 1979–80; Pres. of Algeria and Minister of Nat. Defence 1999–2019; mem. FLN Political Bureau 1964–81, mem. Cen. Cttee 1989; mem. Revolutionary Council 1965–79; led negotiations with France 1963, 1966, for nationalization of hydrocarbons 1971; leader of dels to many confs of Arab League, OAU 1968, Group of 1977 1967, Non-aligned Countries 1973, Pres. Seventh Special Session of UN Gen. Ass. 1975, Int. Conf. on Econ. Co-operation, Paris 1975–76; Pres. 29th UN Gen. Ass. 1974; mem. Nat. Council Moujahidin (Nat. Liberation Army) 1990–; Grand Collar, Order of Prince Henry (Portugal) 2003. *Address:* c/o Office of the President, el-Mouradia, Algers, Algeria.

BOUTERSE, Col Désiré (Desi) Delano; Suriname politician and head of state; *President;* b. 13 Oct. 1945, Paramaribo; m. 1st Ingrid Figueira (divorced); one s. one d.; m. 2nd Ingrid Waldring; led mil. coup 1980, Chair. Nat. Mil. Council (de facto Leader) 1980–88 (resgnd); Pres. 1982; led mil. coup 1990, Chief of Army 1990–92 (resgnd); Pres. Nationale Democratische Partij 1992–99, 2006–; political adviser to Pres. 1996–99; convicted of drug trafficking in absentia, Netherlands 1999; mem. Parl. 2005–; unsuccessful cand. in presidential election 2005; Pres. of Suriname 2010–. *Address:* Office of the President, Kleine Combéweg 2–4, Centrum, Paramaribo, Suriname (office). *Telephone:* 472841 (office). *Fax:* 475266 (office). *E-mail:* kabpressur@sr.net (office). *Website:* www.kabinet.sr.org (office).

BOUTON, Daniel; French business executive; b. 10 April 1950, Paris; ed Ecole nat. d'Admin; Insp. of Finance, Ministry of Finance 1973–76, Budget Dept, Ministry of Finance 1977–86, Chief of Staff to Alain Juppé, Deputy Minister in charge of the Budget 1986–88; Exec. Vice-Pres. Société Générale 1991, CEO 1993–2008, Chair. 1997–2009 (resgnd), now Hon. Pres.; Founder and Pres. DMJB Conseil (consultancy) 2009; mem. Bd of Dirs Total SA 1997–, Veolia 2003–18; Sr Adviser, Rothschild & Cie Banque, CVC Capital Partners; Chevalier, Légion d'honneur, Ordre nat. du Mérite. *Address:* DMJB Conseil, 26 rue d'Artois, 75008 Paris, France (office).

BOUVET, Jean-Christophe; French actor, director and screenwriter; b. 24 March 1947, Paris. *Film appearances include:* La philosophie dans le boudoir 1969, Change pas de main 1975, Le pendule 1976, Les pornocrates 1976, Le théâtre des matières 1977, Le borgne 1980, C'est la vie 1981, Loin de Manhattan 1982, L'archipel des amours 1983, En haut des marches 1983, Sous le soleil de Satan 1987, Les dents de ma mère 1991, J'embarassa pas 1991, Krapatchouk 1992, Bouvet son texte 1992, Les nuits fauves 1992, Terre sainte 1994, Dadou 1994, La cité de la peur 1994, L'eau froide 1994, J'aime beaucoup ce que vous faites 1995, Dialogue au sommet 1996, Des progrès en amour 1996, Le complexe de Toulon 1996, Le rocher d'Acapulco 1996, L'@mour est à réinventer 1996, Vicious Circles 1997, Un arrangement 1997, Le passager 1997, Le Plaisir (et ses petits tracas) 1998, Pain au chocolat 1998, Le comte de Monte Cristo 1998, L'examen de minuit 1998, Out! 1999, Le domaine 1999, Glória 1999, Les passagers 1999, Recto/Verso 1999, Lovers 1999, Une rue dans sa longeur 2000, Taxi 2 2000, Cosmocrator 2000, Lise et André 2000, La chambre obscure 2000, Effraction 2001, Le chien, le chat et le cibachrome 2001, La boîte 2001, Being Light 2001, Jojo la frite 2002, Le nouveau Jean-Claude 2002, La sirène rouge 2002, Le cou de Clarisse 2003, Taxi 3 2003, Saltimbank 2003, En famille 2003, Notre musique 2004, Mensonges et trahisons 2004, Prisonnier 2004, Comme un frère 2005, Journal IV 2005, Il sera une fois 2005, La comédie du pouvoir 2005, Marie-Antoinette 2006, Les brigades du tigre 2006, La France 2007, Des Indes à la planète Mars 2008, The Wolberg Family 2009, Black Venus 2010, Let My People Go! 2011, Chaos 2012, Gare du Nord 2013, Hasta mañana 2013, Deux Rémi, deux 2015, 4 Days in France 2016, Sélection officielle 2016, We Are Tourists 2017, Tempting Devils 2018, La légende 2018. *Television:* Légitime défense (film) 1980, Un garçon de France 1985, Opération Mozart (film) 1988, Les grandes personnes (film) 1995, The Count of Monte Cristo (mini-series) 1998, Victor Schoelcher, l'abolition (film) 1998, Le monde à l'envers (film) 1999, Zone Reptile (film) 2002, The Mole (film) 2007, A votre service 2015–16. *Films directed and written include:* Le troisiéme wagon 1981, En veux-tu, en voilà (TV) 1982, Peinture à l'eau (TV) 1983, En voilà 2 (TV) 1983, Et de trois (TV) 1988, Les dents de ma mère 1991, Bouvet et son texte 1992. *Address:* Agence Artistique Terenga, 32, rue Yves Toudic, Paris 75010, France (office). *Telephone:* 1-53-36-72-91 (office). *Fax:* 1-53-36-71-85 (office). *E-mail:* terenga@noos.fr (office). *Website:* www.terenga.com (office).

BOUYGUES, Martin; French business executive; *Chairman and CEO, Bouygues SA;* b. 3 May 1952; s. of Francis Bouygues; three c.; ed Univ. of Paris Dauphine;

joined Bouygues Group 1974, site supervisor for Les Halles shopping complex, Paris 1974–78, f. Maison Bouygues 1978, Chair. and CEO Saur 1986, mem. Bd of Dirs Bouygues SA 1982–, Vice-Chair. 1987–89, Chair. and CEO 1989–; Chair. SCDM; mem. Bd of Dirs TF1, Sodeci, CIE; mem. Supervisory Bd Paris-Orléans; Chevalier, Légion d'honneur, Ordre nat. du Mérite. *Leisure interests:* hunting, boating. *Address:* Bouygues Headquarters, 32 avenue Hoche, 75378 Paris Cedex 08, France (office). *Telephone:* 1-44-20-10-00 (office). *Fax:* 1-44-20-14-99 (office). *E-mail:* presse@bouygues.com (office). *Website:* www.bouygues.com (office).

BOUZAT, Cecilia Beatriz, DSc; Argentine neuroscientist; *Deputy Director, Biochemical Research Institute of Bahia Blanca;* b. 1962; two c.; ed Colegio La Inmaculada, Universidad Nacional del Sur; Prof., Universidad Nacional del Sur; currently Deputy Dir, Biochemical Research Inst. of Bahia Blanca; mem. Nat. Scientific and Technical Research Council (CONICET), Buenos Aires; Laureate for Latin America, L'Oréal-UNESCO Women in Science Awards 2014. *Achievements include:* int. leader in neurotransmitter pharmacology. *Address:* Biochemical Research Institute of Bahia Blanca, Edificio E1, CONICET Bahía Blanca, Camino La Carrindanga km 7, 8000 Bahía Blanca,, Argentina (office). *E-mail:* inibibb@inibibb-conicet.gob.ar (office). *Website:* www.inibibb-conicet.gob.ar (office).

BOVENDER, Jack O., Jr, BSc; American health care industry executive (retd); ed Duke Univ.; served in Navy Service Medical Corps, attained rank of Lt; fmr Asst Admin., Community Gen. Hosp., Thomasville, NC; joined HCA (Hospital Corpn of America) Inc., CEO Medical Center Hosp., Largo, Fla and West Fla Regional Medical Center, Pensacola, later several man. positions 1985–92, including Vice-Pres. HCA Atlanta Div., Pres. HCA Eastern Group Operations, Exec. Vice-Pres. and COO HCA 1992–94, 1997–2001, Pres. and CEO 2001–02, Chair. and CEO 2002–09 (retd); mem. Bd of Dirs Bank of America 2012–; Founding mem. Nashville Health Care Council; fmr Dir Nashville Community Foundation, Frist Foundation, Tennessee Performing Arts Center, Center for Non-Profit Man.; mem. Duke Univ. Health System Bd; mem. Bd of Visitors, Duke Univ. Fuqua School of Business, Bd of Trustees, Duke Univ. 2007–; Hon. mem. Bd of Visitors, Duke Univ. Divinity School; Best CEO in America for healthcare facilities, Institutional Investor magazine 2003, 2004, 2005, Gold Medal Award, American Coll. of Healthcare Execs 2007, Distinguished Alumni Award, Duke Univ. 2012. *Address:* c/o Secretary, Duke University, PO Box 90030, Durham, NC 27708, USA.

BOWAO, Charles Zacharie, Dr.Sci.Hum.; Republic of the Congo professor of philosophy and politician; ed Université Cheikh Anta Diop, Dakar, Senegal; Prof., Dept of Philosophy, Université Marien Ngouabi, Brazzaville, also Dir of Philosophical Training; Official, Comm. nat. d'organisation des élections 2002; Minister at the Presidency in charge of Co-operation, Humanitarian Action and Solidarity –2009, Minister at the Presidency responsible for Nat. Defence 2009–12; mem. Parti congolais du travail (PCT), mem. Cen. Cttee; Dir Editorial Bd, Géopolitique Africaine (journal). *Publications:* Autour de la méthode (de Descartes à Feyerabend) 1997, Gaston Berger: Introduction à une philosophie de l'avenir 1997, Bonne gouvernance et développement 1997, La mondialité: entre histoire et avenir 2004, Pour la refondation du PCT: La refondation politique à l'aune de la nouvelle espérance 2006, L'imposture ethnocentrism 2014. *Website:* www.univ-mngb.net.

BOWE, Riddick Lamont; American fmr professional boxer; b. 10 Aug. 1967, Brooklyn, New York; s. of Dorothy Bowe; m. 1st Judy Bowe 1986 (divorced); five c.; m. 2nd Terri Blakney; amateur boxer 1982–89, professional boxer 1989–96, 2004–08, won World Boxing Asscn, World Boxing Confed., Int. Boxing Fed. titles 1992, World Boxing Asscn, Int. Boxing Fed. titles 1993, World Boxing Org. title 1995, defeating two challengers in that year to retain title; Silver Medal Super Heavyweight Div., Olympic Games, Seoul, 1988; ranked Undisputed Heavyweight Champion 1992–93, 1995; retd from boxing 1996; briefly with US Marine Corps; pleaded guilty to fed. charge of abduction June 1998, served 18 months, released 2004; announced resumption of boxing career 2004; 43 wins and one loss, with one no-contest, and 33 knockouts. *E-mail:* joemelendez@msn.com.

BOWEN, Gregory, BEng, MEng; Grenadian politician; *Minister of Infrastructure Development, Public Utilities, Energy, Transport and Implementation;* m.; five c.; ed Presentation Brothers Coll., Univ. of the West Indies, Univ. of Saskatchewan, Canada; several diplomas and certificates in Financial Man., Eng Man. and Business; taught at Presentation Brothers Coll. and Anglican High School; Lecturer, Inst. for Further Educ. 1980–81; Planning and Devt Engineer, Grenada Electricity Services Ltd 1983, later Man.; Senator and Minister for Communications, Works, Public Utilities, Energy and Transport 1995–2003; mem. Parl. for St George South East 1999–; apptd Deputy Prime Minister and Minister of Agric., Lands, Forestry and Fisheries, Public Utilities, Energy and The Marketing and Nat. Importing Bd 2003; Minister of Communications and Works, Physical Devt, Public Utilities and Information Communications Tech. 2013–18, of Infrastructure Development, Public Utilities, Energy, Transport and Implementation 2018–; mem. ASME, Inst. of Diesel and Gas Turbine Engineers, Grenada Inst. of Professional Engineers, American Soc. of Agricultural Engineers. *Leisure interest:* guitar playing. *Address:* Ministry of Infrastructure Development, Public Utilities, Energy, Transport and Implementation, Ministerial Complex, 4th Floor, Botanical Gardens, Tanteen, St George's, Grenada (office). *Telephone:* 440-2271 (office). *Fax:* 440-4122 (office). *E-mail:* ministryofworks@gov.gd (office).

BOWEN, Most Rev. Michael George, STL, PhL; British ecclesiastic; *Archbishop Emeritus of Southwark;* b. 23 April 1930, Gibraltar; s. of Maj. C. L. J. Bowen and Mary J. Pedley; ed Downside Abbey School, Trinity Coll., Cambridge and Gregorian Univ., Rome; army service 1948–49; in the wine trade 1951–52; Venerable English Coll., Rome 1952–59; ordained RC priest 1958; curate, Earlsfield and Walworth, Diocese of Southwark 1959–63; teacher of Theology, Pontifical Beda Coll., Rome 1963–66; Chancellor, Diocese of Arundel and Brighton 1966–70, Coadjutor Bishop 1970–71, Bishop of Arundel and Brighton 1971–77; Archbishop and Metropolitan, Diocese of Southwark 1977–2003, Archbishop Emer. 2003–; Vice-Pres. Catholic Bishops' Conf. England and Wales 1996–99; Pres. 1999–2000; Freeman City of London 1984. *Leisure interests:* golf, tennis. *Address:* c/o Archbishop's House, 150 St George's Road, London, SE1 6HX, England. *Telephone:* (20) 7928-2495. *Fax:* (20) 7928-7833.

BOWEN, Ray M., PhD; American engineer, academic and fmr university administrator; *Professor Emeritus, Department of Mechanical Engineering and President Emeritus, Texas A&M University;* b. 30 March 1936, Fort Worth, Tex.; s. of Winfred Herbert Bowen and Elizabeth Williams Bowen; m. Sara Elizabeth Gibbons Bowen 1958; one s. one d.; ed Texas A&M Univ., California Inst. of Tech.; Assoc. Prof. of Mechanical Eng, Louisiana State Univ. 1965–67; Prof. of Mechanical Eng, Rice Univ. 1967–83, Chair. Dept of Mechanical Eng 1972–77; Div. Dir, NSF 1982–83, Acting Asst Dir Eng to Deputy Asst Dir 1990–91; Prof. and Dean of Eng, Univ. of Kentucky 1983–89; Vice-Pres. for Academic Affairs, Oklahoma State Univ. 1991–93, Interim Pres. 1993–94; Pres. Texas A&M Univ. 1994–2002, Pres. Emer. 2002–, Prof., Dept of Mechanical Eng and Sara and John H. Lindsey '44 Chair 2002–10, Prof. Emer. 2010–; mem. Nat. Science Bd 2002–14 (Chair. 2010–12), Soc. of Scholars, Johns Hopkins Univ., Fellow, American Soc. for Eng Educ.; Hon. mem. American Soc. of Mechanical Eng; Corps Hall of Honor, Texas A&M Univ., Distinguished Alumni, Texas A&M Univ. *Publications:* Introduction to Continuum Mechanics for Engineers, Introduction to Vectors and Tensors (co-author), Rational Thermodynamics (contrib.); contrib. of numerous articles to professional journals. *Leisure interests:* travelling, opera. *Telephone:* (713) 622-4110 (home). *E-mail:* rbowen@tamu.edu (office). *Website:* www.mengr.tamu.edu (office).

BOWEN, Tim; British music industry executive; Head of Business Affairs, Sony Music UK, then Head, Sony Music Publishing Int., New York 1982–86; Man. Dir CBS/Columbia Records UK 1986–91; Sr Vice-Pres. Marketing and Business Affairs, Universal Music Int. 1994–99, Exec. Vice-Pres. 1999–2001; COO BMG Europe 2002–03, Chair. BMG Entertainment, UK and Ireland 2003–04, Chair. Sony BMG UK & Ireland, Canada, Australia, New Zealand, South Africa 2004–06, COO Sony BMG 2006–08; currently Prin., BPM Entertainment, London; Dir Hysteria Live Ltd 2016–. *Address:* Hysteria Live Ltd, 34 Woodside Close, Amersham, Bucks., HP6 5EF, England. *E-mail:* discos@bpmentertainment.co.uk. *Website:* www.bpmentertainment.co.uk.

BOWER, Gordon H., MS, PhD; American psychologist and academic; *Albert Ray Lang Professor Emeritus of Psychology, Stanford University;* b. 30 Dec. 1932, Scio, Ohio; s. of Clyde W. Bower and Mabelle Bosart Bower; m. Sharon Anthony 1957; one s. two d.; ed Western Reserve (now Case Western Reserve) and Yale Univs; Woodrow Wilson Fellowship for Grad. Study, Univ. of Minnesota 1954–55; NIMH Fellowship for Grad. Study, Yale Univ. 1956–59; Asst Prof., Stanford Univ. 1959–63, Assoc. Prof. 1963–65, Prof. 1965–75, Albert Ray Lang Prof. of Psychology 1975–2008, Prof. Emer. 2008–, Chair. Dept of Psychology 1978–82, Assoc. Dean, Stanford Univ. 1983–86; Ed. The Psychology of Learning and Motivation 1964–92; Sr Science Advisor to Dir of Nat. Insts of Mental Health 1991–92; Pres. Western Psychological Asscn 1990–91, 2004–05, American Psychological Soc. 1991–93; mem. NAS, American Acad. of Arts and Sciences, Soc. of Experimental Psychologists (Pres. 1989), American Philosophical Soc.; Distinguished Fellow and Founding Mem., Cognitive Science Soc. 2008; Dr hc (Univ. of Chicago) 1991, (Indiana State Univ.) 1993, (Univ. of Basel, Switzerland) 2003; Distinguished Scientist Contrib. Award, American Psychology Asscn 1979, Warren Medal, Soc. of Experimental Psychologists, Wilbur Cross Medal, Yale Univ. 1986, Presidential Citation for scientific contributions, American Psychological Asscn 2002, Nat. Medal of Science 2005, Lifetime Contributions Award, Western Psychological Asscn 2006, Outstanding Grad. Student Mentoring Award, Western Psychological Asscn 2011. *Publications:* co-author of five books and more than 250 scientific papers. *Leisure interests:* reading novels and history, American sports. *Address:* Department of Psychology, Jordan Hall, Building 420, Room 314, Stanford University, Stanford, CA 94305, USA (office). *Telephone:* (650) 283-1734 (mobile) (office); (650) 494-8163 (home). *Fax:* (650) 484-8163 (office). *E-mail:* gbower@stanford.edu (office). *Website:* www-psych.stanford.edu (office).

BOWERING, George Harry, OC, MA; Canadian writer, poet and academic; *Professor Emeritus, Simon Fraser University;* b. 1 Dec. 1936, Penticton, BC; s. of Ewart Bowering and Pearl Bowering (née Brinson); m. 1st Angela Luoma 1962 (died 1999); one d.; m. 2nd Jean Baird 2006; ed Victoria Coll., Univ. of British Columbia, Univ. of Western Ontario; served as Royal Canadian Air Force photographer 1954–57; Lecturer, Univ. of Calgary 1963–66; Writer-in-Residence, Sir George Williams Univ., Montreal 1967–68, Lecturer 1968–71; Prof., Simon Fraser Univ., Burnaby, BC 1972–2001, Prof. Emer. 2001–; First Parl. Poet Laureate 2002–04; Order of BC 2005; Hon. DLit (British Columbia) 1997, (Western Ontario) 2003; Gov.-Gen.'s Award for poetry 1967, for fiction 1980, bpNichol Chapbook Awards for Poetry 1991, 1992, Canadian Authors' Asscn Award for Poetry 1993, Lt-Gov.'s Award for Literary Excellence 2011, Alumni Award of Distinction, Univ. of British Columbia 2011. *Play:* The Home for Heroes 1962. *Radio plays:* George Vancouver (CBC) 1972, Sitting in Mexico (CBC) 1973, Music in the Park (CBC) 1986, The Great Grandchildren of Bill Bissett's Mice (CBC) 1989. *Television play:* What Does Eddie Williams Want? (CBC) 1966. *Publications include:* poetry collections: Sticks & Stones 1963, Points on the Grid 1964, The Man in Yellow Boots/El hombre de las botas amarillas 1965, Rocky Mountain Foot 1969, The Gangs of Kosmos 1969, Touch: Selected Poems 1960–1969 1971, In the Flesh 1974, The Catch 1976, Poem & Other Baseballs 1976, The Concrete Island 1977, Another Mouth 1979, West Window: Selected Poetry 1982, Smoking Mirror 1982, Seventy-One Poems for People 1985, Delayed Mercy & Other Poems 1986, George Bowering Selected: Poems 1961–1992 1993; chapbooks: How I Hear Howl 1967, Two Police Poems 1969, The Sensible 1972, Layers 1–13 1973, In Answer 1977, Uncle Louis 1980, Spencer & Groulx 1985, Quarters 1991, Do Sink 1992, A, You're Adorable 1998, 6 Little Poems in Alphabetical Order 2000, Joining the Lost Generation 2002; long poems: Sitting in Mexico 1965, George,Vancouver 1970, Geneve 1971, Autobiology 1972, Curious 1973, At War With the US 1974, Allophanes 1976, Kerrisdale Elegies 1984, His Life: A Poem 2000, Baseball: A poem in the magic number 9 2003, Changing on the Fly 2004, Vermeer's Light 2006, Fulgencio 2008, A Little Black Strap 2009, My Darling Nelly Grey 2010; novels: Mirror on the Floor 1967, A Short Sad Book 1977, Burning Water 1980, En eaux troubles 1982, Caprice 1987, Harry's Fragments 1990, Shoot! 1994, Parents from Space 1994, Piccolo Mondo 1998, Diamondback Dog 1998, Pinboy 2012; short story collections: Flycatcher & Other Stories 1974, Concentric Circles 1977, Protective Footwear 1978, A Place to Die 1983, Standing on Richards 2004, The Box 2009; non-fiction: Al Purdy 1970, Three Vancouver Writers 1979, The Mask in Place 1983, Craft Slices 1985, Imaginary Hand 1988, Bowering's B.C. 1996, Egotists and Autocrats – The Prime Ministers of Canada 1999, A Magpie Life (memoir) 2001, Cars (memoir) 2002, Stone Country (history)

2003, Left Hook (criticism) 2005, Baseball Love (memoirs) 2006, Horizontal Surfaces (chapbook) 2010, The Diamond Alphabet 2011, How I Wrote Certain of My Books (essays) 2011, Words, Words, Words (essays) 2012. *Leisure interests:* motor trips to see baseball games in Canada, USA, Mexico, Cuba, Italy, Australia, etc. *Address:* 4403 West 11th Avenue, Vancouver, BC V6R 2M2, Canada. *Telephone:* (604) 224-4898. *E-mail:* bowering@sfu.ca.

BOWERS-BROADBENT, Christopher Joseph, FRAM; British organist and composer; *Organist and Choirmaster of Gray's Inn and Organist of the West London Synagogue;* b. 13 Jan. 1945, Hemel Hempstead, Herts.; s. of Henry W. Bowers-Broadbent and Doris E. Mizen; m. Deirdre Cape 1970; one s. one d.; ed Berkhamsted School, King's Coll., Cambridge and Royal Acad. of Music; Organist and Choirmaster of St Pancras Parish Church 1965–88; Organist of West London Synagogue 1973–; Organist and Choirmaster of Gray's Inn 1983–; debut organ recital, Camden Festival 1966; Prof. of Organ, RAM, London 1976–92; Three Choirs Festival Composers' Competition Prize 1978. *Recordings include:* Trivium, O Domina Nostra, Méditations sur le Mystère de la Sainte Trinité, Mattins Music, Duets and Canons. *Operas include:* The Pied Piper 1972, The Seacock Bane 1979, The Last Man 1983–2000, The Face 2012. *Leisure interests:* sketching, silence. *Address:* 94 Colney Hatch Lane, Muswell Hill, London, N10 1EA, England. *Telephone:* (20) 8883-1933. *Fax:* (20) 8883-8434; (20) 8888-8434. *E-mail:* kitbb@btinternet.com. *Website:* www.graysinn.org.uk/chapel/organist.

BOWLES, Erskine, BS, MBA; American investment banker, fmr university administrator and fmr government official; *Senior Advisor, Carousel Capital;* b. 8 Aug. 1945, Greensboro, NC; s. of Hargrove 'Skipper' Bowles; m. Crandall Bowles 1971; three c.; ed Univ. of North Carolina, Columbia Univ. Grad. School of Business; with Morgan Stanley & Co. New York; Bowles Hollowell Conner & Co. Charlotte, NC 1975–93; Admin., Small Business Admin., Washington, DC 1993–94; Deputy Chief of Staff to Pres., The White House, Washington, DC 1994–97, Chief of Staff 1997–99; Pnr, Forstmann Little & Co., Charlotte 1999–2001; unsuccessful campaigns for US Senate from NC 2002, 2004; Pres. Univ. of NC 2006–10, Pres. Emer. 2010–; Co-founder and Sr Advisor, Carousel Capital 2006–; Co-Chair. (with Alan K. Simpson) Nat. Comm. on Fiscal Responsibility and Reform 2010; Co-founder (with Alan K. Simpson) The Campaign to Fix the Debt; mem. Bd of Dirs Morgan Stanley, Norfolk Southern Corpn, North Carolina Mutual Life Insurance Co., Cousins Properties, Inc., Belk, Inc., Facebook Inc. 2011–; apptd UN Deputy Special Envoy to tsunami affected countries in SE Asia 2005; fmr Pres. Juvenile Diabetes Foundation; fmr Trustee Duke Endowment, Golden LEAF Foundation; fmr Chair. Rural Prosperity Task Force, NC; Co-founder Dogwood Equity 2002; mem. North Carolina Advisory Bd DonorsChoose; eight hon. degrees from US univs. *Address:* Carousel Capital, 201 North Tryon Street, Suite 2450, Charlotte, NC 28202, USA (office). *Telephone:* (704) 372-2040 (office). *Website:* www.carouselcapital.com (office); www.fixthedebt.org.

BOWMAN, Philip, MA; Australian business executive; *Executive Chairman, The Miller Group (UK) Limited;* b. Melbourne; ed Westminster School and Pembroke Coll., Cambridge, UK; served in accountancy positions in venture devt in Iran, Australia and USA; fmr CEO and Chair. Bass Taverns; Dir of Finance and Admin Coles Myer Ltd, Australia 1995–98; Finance Dir Allied Domecq 1998–99, CEO 1999; fmr Chair. (non-exec.), Liberty plc, Coral Eurobet Ltd; CEO Scottish Power plc 2006–07; CEO Smiths Group plc 2007–15; Exec. Chair. The Miller Group (UK) Ltd 2012–; fmr Dir (non-exec.), Scottish & Newcastle plc, British Sky Broadcasting Group plc; Sr Ind. Dir (non-exec.), Burberry plc 2002–; Dir, Better Capital Ltd, Berry Bros. & Rudd Ltd. *Address:* Office of the Chairman, The Miller Group (UK) Ltd, Miller House, 2 Lochside View, Edinburgh Park, Edinburgh EH12 9DH, Scotland (office). *Telephone:* (870) 336-5000 (office). *Website:* www.miller.co.uk (office).

BOWMAN, William Scott (Scotty), OC; Canadian sports executive and fmr professional ice hockey coach; *Senior Advisor, Chicago Blackhawk Hockey Team, Inc.;* b. 18 Sept. 1933, Verdun, PQ; m. Suella Bowman; three s. two d.; early and short career as player then minor league coach in Montréal Canadiens system; began Nat. Hockey League (NHL) coaching career as Coach St Louis Blues 1967–71, then Montréal Canadiens 1971–79, winning Stanley Cups 1973, 1976–79; Coach and Gen. Man. Buffalo Sabres 1979–87; left NHL and worked as analyst for CBCs 'Hockey Night in Canada' TV programme 1987; returned to NHL as Dir of Player Personnel Pittsburgh Penguins 1987–91, then Coach 1991–93, winning Stanley Cup 1992; Coach Detroit Red Wings 1993–2002, winning Stanley Cup 1997, 1998, 2002; records include winning nine Stanley Cups, coaching 1,244 NHL regular-season wins (next highest total is 781), 223 post-season wins; retd at end of 2002 season, consultant, Detroit Red Wings 2002–08; Sr Advisor, Chicago Black Hawks 2008–; Order of Hockey in Canada, Hockey Canada Foundation, 2017; NHL Jack Adams Award for Outstanding Coach 1977, 1996, NHL Lester Patrick Award for outstanding service to hockey in the United States 2001; mem. Hockey Hall of Fame 1991, Mich. Sports Hall of Fame 1999, Greater Buffalo Sports Hall of Fame in 2000; Canada Walk of Fame 2003. *Address:* Chicago Blackhawk Hockey Team, Inc., 1901 West Madison Street, Chicago, IL 60612, USA (office). *Telephone:* (312) 455-7000 (office). *Fax:* (312) 455-7041 (office). *Website:* www.chicagoblackhawks.com (office).

BOWNESS, Sir Alan, Kt, CBE, MA; British art historian; b. 11 Jan. 1928; s. of George Bowness and Kathleen Bowness (née Benton); m. Sarah Hepworth-Nicholson 1957; one s. one d.; ed Univ. Coll. School, Downing Coll., Cambridge, Courtauld Inst. of Art, Univ. of London; with Friends' Ambulance Unit and Friends' Service Council 1946–50; Regional Art Officer, Arts Council of GB 1955–57; Courtauld Inst. 1957–79, Deputy Dir 1978–79; Reader, Univ. of London 1967–78, Prof. of History of Art 1978–79; Visiting Prof., Humanities Seminar, Johns Hopkins Univ., Baltimore 1969; Dir Tate Gallery 1980–88, Henry Moore Foundation 1988–94 (Trustee 1984–88, 1994–2003); mem. Arts Council 1973–75, 1978–80, Art Panel 1960–80 (Vice-Chair. 1973–75, Chair. 1978–80), Arts Film Cttee 1968–77 (Chair. 1972–75); mem. Fine Arts Cttee, British Council 1960–69, 1970–93 (Chair. 1981–93); mem. Exec. Cttee, Contemporary Art Soc. 1961–69, 1970–86, Cultural Advisory Cttee, UK Nat. Comm. for UNESCO 1973–82; Gov. Chelsea School of Art and London Inst. 1965–88; Hon. Sec. Asscn of Art Historians 1973–76; Dir Barbara Hepworth Museum, St Ives, Cornwall 1976–88; mem. Council Royal Coll. of Art 1978–99; Trustee, Yorkshire Sculpture Park 1979–, Handel House Museum 1994–2001 (Chair. 1997–2001); mem. int. juries for Premio Di Tella, Buenos Aires 1965, São Paulo Bienal 1967, Lehmbruck Prize, Duisburg 1970, Rembrandt Prize 1982, Venice Biennale 1986, Heiliger Prize 1998; Hon. Fellow, Downing Coll., Cambridge 1980, Univ. of the West of England, Bristol 1980, Courtauld Inst. of Art 1985; Chevalier, Ordre des Arts et des Lettres 1973; Hon. DLitt (Liverpool) 1988, (Leeds) 1995, (Exeter) 1996. *Publications:* William Scott Paintings 1964, Impressionists and Post Impressionists 1965, Henry Moore: Complete Sculpture 1955–64 1965, Modern Sculpture 1965, Barbara Hepworth Drawings 1966, Alan Davie 1967, Recent British Painting 1968, Gauguin 1971, Barbara Hepworth: complete sculpture 1960–69 1971, Modern European Art 1972, Ivon Hitchens 1973, Picasso 1881–1973 (contrib.) 1973, The Genius of British Painting (contrib.) 1975, Henry Moore: Complete Sculpture 1964–73 1977, Henry Moore: Complete Sculpture 1974–80 1983, Henry Moore: Complete Sculpture 1981–86 1988, The Conditions of Success 1989, British Contemporary Art 1910–1990 (contrib.) 1991, Bernard Meadows 1995. *Leisure interests:* going to concerts, opera, theatre. *Address:* 91 Castelnau, London, SW13 9EL; 16 Piazza, St Ives, Cornwall, TR26 1NQ, England. *Telephone:* (20) 8846-8520 (London); (1736) 795444 (St Ives).

BOWO, Fauzi, DrIng; Indonesian politician and diplomatist; b. 10 April 1948, Jakarta; s. of Djohari bin Adiputro and Nuraini binti Abdul Manaf; m. Sri Hartati Bowo; ed Canisius Coll., Jakarta, Univ. of Indonesia, Tech. Univ. at Brunswick and Univ. of Kaiserslautern, Germany; involved in Indonesian Students Action Front (KAMI) established to counter communist-influenced Indonesian Student Union; won scholarship to study in West Germany 1968, active in Indonesian Students Asscn in Germany; apptd Acting Head of Jakarta Regional Bureau 1979, Regional Sec. 1998; Treas. of govt Golkar org. 1983–97; Deputy Gov. of Jakarta 2002–07, Gov. 2007–12; Amb. to Germany 2013–18.

BOWOLEKSONO, Budi; Indonesian diplomatist; ed Krisnadwipayana Univ.; began diplomatic career at Ministry of Foreign Affairs 1986, assigned to Perm. Mission of Indonesia to UN, New York, to UN, Geneva, to UN, Vienna, assigned to various offices of Ministry of Foreign Affairs, including Directorate Gen. of Foreign Econ. Relations, Directorate Gen. of ASEAN Co-operation, Directorate Gen. of Multilateral Affairs and Sec.-Gen., Amb. to Kenya (also accred to Seychelles, Mauritius, Uganda, UNEP and UNHCR) 2008–10, Sec.-Gen. Ministry of Foreign Affairs –2013, Amb. to USA 2013–18.

BOWSER, Muriel Elizabeth, BA, MA; American politician; *Mayor of Washington, DC;* b. 2 Aug. 1972, Washington, DC; d. of Joe Bowser and Joan Bowser; ed Chatham Coll., American Univ.; Commr for Dist 4B09, Advisory Neighborhood Comm., Washington, DC 2004–07; Councilwoman for Ward 4, DC 2007–15; Mayor, Washington, DC 2015–; Democrat. *Address:* Office of the Mayor, John A. Wilson Building, 1350 Pennsylvania Avenue, NW, Washington, DC 20004, USA (office). *Telephone:* (202) 727-2980 (office). *E-mail:* eom@dc.gov (office). *Website:* mayor.dc.gov (office).

BOXER, Barbara, BA; American politician; b. 11 Nov. 1940, Brooklyn, NY; d. of Ira Levy and Sophie Levy (née Silvershein); m. Stewart Boxer 1962; one s. one d.; ed Brooklyn Coll.; stockbroker, New York 1962–65; journalist, then Assoc. Ed. Pacific Sun 1972–74; Congressional Aide, Democratic 5th Congressional Dist, San Francisco 1974–76; mem. Marin Co. Bd of Supervisors, San Rafael, Calif. 1976–82, Pres. 1980–81; mem. US House of Reps from 6th Calif. Dist, Washington, DC 1982–93; Senator from California 1993–2017; mem. Foreign Relations Cttee, Chair. Environment and Public Works Cttee, Chair. Sub-cttee on Near Eastern and S Asian Affairs, Democratic Chief Deputy Whip 2007–17; mem. Bd of Dirs Golden Gate Bridge Highway and Transport Dist, San Francisco 1978–82; Pres. Democratic New Mems Caucus 1983–; f. Senate Mil. Family Caucus 2010; Democrat; numerous awards. *Publications:* novels: A Time to Run 2005, Blind Trust 2009.

BOXSHALL, Geoffrey Allan, BSc, PhD, FRS; British/Canadian zoologist; *Merit Researcher (Band 1), Natural History Museum, London;* b. 13 June 1950, Oyen, Alberta; s. of John Edward Boxshall and Sybil Irene Baker; m. Roberta Gabriel Smith 1972; one s. three d.; ed Churcher's Coll., Univ. of Leeds; Higher Scientific Officer, British Museum (Natural History) 1974–76, Sr Scientific Officer 1976–80, Prin. Scientific Officer 1980–91, Sr Prin. Scientific Officer 1991–97, Merit Researcher (Band 2) 1997–2014, Merit Researcher (Band 1) 2014–; Visiting Prof., Queen Mary Coll., Univ. of London 1996; Vice-Chair. MarBEF (EU-funded Network of Excellence) 2004–09; Vice-Pres. World Asscn of Copepodologists 1990–93, Pres. 1999–2002; Pres. The Ray Soc. 2004–07; mem. Exec. Cttee Marine Biological Asscn 2003–07; mem. of Council, Sir Alister Hardy Foundation for Ocean Science 2010–13, The Linnean Soc. 2010–13 (Vice-Pres. 2012–13); Sec., Zoological Soc. of London 2011–; Chair. Steering Cttee, World Register of Marine Species 2013–16; Hon. Prof., Univ. of St Andrews 2006; Hon. Vice-Pres. Marine Biological Asscn of the UK 2007; Scientific Medal of the Zoological Soc. of London 1986, Excellence in Research Award, Crustacean Soc. 1998, Linnean Soc. Medal for Zoology 2004, Homage Award, Brazilian Crustacean Soc. 2004, Monoculus Award, World Asscn of Copepodologists 2008, Plymouth Marine Science Lecturer 2010. *Publications include:* co-author: Dictionary of Ecology, Evolution and Systematics, Illustrated Dictionary of Natural History, Copepod Evolution, An Introduction to Copepod Diversity. *Leisure interests:* travel, tennis, lexicography. *Address:* Department of Life Sciences, Natural History Museum, Cromwell Road, London, SW7 5BD, England (office). *Telephone:* (20) 7942-5749 (office). *Fax:* (20) 7942-5054 (office). *E-mail:* g.boxshall@nhm.ac.uk (office). *Website:* www.nhm.ac.uk/our-science/departments-and-staff/staff-directory/geoff-boxshall.html (office).

BOYARCHIKOV, Nikolai Nikolayevich; Russian ballet dancer, choreographer and ballet director; b. 27 Sept. 1935, Leningrad; s. of Maria Boyarchikova; m. Larissa Klimova; ed Leningrad Vaganova School of Choreography, Leningrad State Conservatory; soloist, Mussorgsky Academic Opera and Ballet Theatre (fmrly Leningrad Maly State Academic Opera and Ballet Theatre, renamed Mikhailovsky Theatre 2007) 1954–71, Artistic Dir 1977–2007 (retd); Chief Choreographer, Perm Opera and Ballet Theatre 1971–77; produced own ballet Orpheus and Eurydice 1979; Glinka Prize 1977, People's Artist of Russia 1985, State Prize of Russian Fed., Order of Friendship 1996. *Productions include:* The Three Musketeers (Maly Theatre) 1964, The Woodcut Prince or The Wooden Prince (Maly Theatre) 1965, The Queen of Spades (Leningrad Chamber Ballet) 1968, Romeo and Juliet (Perm) 1972, also West Berlin German Opera 1974, The

Miraculous Mandarin (Perm) 1973, Tsar Boris (Perm Theatre) 1975, Hercules 1980, The Robbers 1983, Macbeth 1984, The Marriage 1986, Quiet Flows the Don 1988, Petersburg 1992. *Address:* c/o Mikhailovsky Theatre, 1 Arts Square, 191011 St Petersburg, Russian Federation.

BOYARSKY, Mikhail Sergeyevich; Russian actor and singer; b. 26 Dec. 1949, Leningrad; s. of Sergei Boyarsky; m. Larisa Luppian; one s. one d.; ed Leningrad Inst. of Theatre, Music and Cinematography; fmrly with Lensovet Theatre, appeared in musicals Interview in Buenos Aires, Troubadour and His Friends; cinema debut 1974, more than 60 roles; Artistic Dir Benefice Theatre; People's Actor of Russian Fed. 1984, People's Artist of Russia 1995. *Films include:* Starshiy syn 1975, Sentimentalnyy roman 1976, Ma-ma 1976, Kak Ivanushka-durachok za chudom khodil 1976, Dikiy Gavrila 1976, Poka bezumstvuyet mechta 1978, Komissiya po rassledovaniyu 1978, Nesravnennyy Nakonechnikov 1981, Kuda on denetsya! 1981, Dusha 1981, Tamozhnya 1982, Lishniy bilet 1983, Geroy eyo romana 1984, Gum-gam 1985, Chelovek s bulvara Kaputsinov 1987, Uznik zamka If 1988, Iskusstvo zhit v Odesse 1989, Vivat, gardemariny! 1991, Choknute 1991, Mushketyory 20 let spustya 1992, Tayna korolevy Anny ili mushketyory 30 let spustya 1993, Plachu vperyod! 2001, Klyuchi ot smerti (Keys to Death 2) 2002, Novogodnyye muzhchiny (New Year's Men) 2004, Schastlivyi (Happy) 2005, Vy ne ostavte menya (Don't Leave Me) 2006. *Television includes:* Don Sezar de Bazan 1989, Tartyuf 1992, Koroleva Margo (series) 1996, Zal ozhidaniya (series) 1998, Idiot (miniseries) 2003. *Address:* Naberezhnaya Moiki 31, Apt. 2, 191186 St Petersburg; c/o Benefice Theatre, 24 Moyki reki nab, St. Petersburg, Russia. *Telephone:* (812) 311-37-97. *E-mail:* info@boyarskiy.su. *Website:* www.boyarskiy.su.

BOYCE, Baron (Life Peer), cr. 2003, of Pimlico in the City of Westminster; **The Adm. of the Fleet Michael (Cecil) Boyce,** Kt, KG, GCB, OBE, DL; British naval officer; *Lord Warden and Admiral of the Cinque Ports and Constable of Dover Castle;* b. 2 April 1943, Cape Town, S Africa; s. of Commdr Hugh Boyce and Madeline Boyce (née Manley); m. 1st Harriette Gail Fletcher 1971 (divorced 2005); one s. one d.; m. 2nd Fleur Margaret Ann Rutherford (née Smith) (died 2016); ed Hurstpierpoint Coll., Royal Naval Coll., Dartmouth Royal Coll. of Defence Studies; joined RN 1961; qualified submariner 1965, TAS 1970, served in HM submarines Anchorite, Valiant and Conqueror 1965–72, commanded HM submarines Oberon 1973–74, Opossum 1974–75, Superb 1979–81, frigate HMS Brilliant 1983–84, Capt. (SM) Submarine Sea Training 1984–86; Royal Coll. Defence Staff 1988; Sr Naval Officer ME 1989; Dir Naval Staff Duties 1989–91; Flag Officer, Sea Training 1991–92, Surface Flotilla 1992–95; Commdr Anti-Submarine Warfare Striking Force 1992–94; Second Sea Lord and C-in-C Naval Home Command 1995–97; Flag ADC to the Queen 1995–97; C-in-C Fleet, C-in-C Eastern Atlantic Area and Commdr Naval Forces NW Europe 1997–98; First Sea Lord 1998–2001; Chief of Defence Staff 2001–03; First and Prin. Naval ADC to the Queen 1998–2001, ADC 2001–03; Lord Warden and Adm. of the Cinque Ports and Constable of Dover Castle 2004–; Col Commdt SBS 2003–; Gov. Alleyn's School 1995–2005; mem. Bd of Dirs, W.S. Atkins 2004–13, VT Group PLC 2004–10; Chair. HMS Victory Preservation Co. 2012–; Pres. Officers Asscn 2003–12, London Dist St John Ambulance 2003–11, Submarine Museum 2005–; mem. Council White Ensign Asscn 2003–13 (Chair. 2007–10), Royal Nat. Lifeboat Inst. 2004– (Chair. 2008–13); Trustee, Nat. Maritime Museum 2004–13; King of Arms, Order of the Bath 2009–18; DL Greater London 2003–; Patron Sail4Cancer 2003–, Submarine Asscn 2003–, Forces in Mind Trust 2012–; Freeman of the City of London 1999; Younger Brother, Trinity House 1999–2006, Elder Brother 2006–; DL, Greater London 2003–; Hon. Freeman, Drapers' Co. 2005–08, Liveryman 2008–, Court 2011–, Master 2013–14; KStJ; Commdr, Legion of Merit (USA) 1999; Bronze Oak Leaf (USA) 2003; Hon. LLD (Portsmouth) 2005; Dr hc (Canterbury Christ Church Univ.) 2011; Hon. DCL (Kent) 2013; Hon. DSc (Imperial Coll.) 2016. *Leisure interests:* squash, tennis, real tennis, sailing, windsurfing, opera, ballet. *Address:* House of Lords, Westminster, London, SW1A 0PW, England (office). *E-mail:* boycem@parliament.uk (office). *Website:* www.parliament.uk/biographies/lords/lord-boyce/3630 (office).

BOYCE, Ralph L. (Skip), BA, MPA; American business executive and fmr diplomatist; *Vice-President, Boeing International;* b. 1 Feb. 1952, Washington, DC; m. Kathryn Sligh; two c.; ed George Washington Univ., Princeton Univ.; joined Foreign Service 1976, Staff Asst to Amb., Embassy in Tehran 1977–79, Commercial Attaché, Embassy in Tunis 1979–81, Financial Economist, Embassy in Islamabad 1981–84, Special Asst, then Adviser to Deputy Sec. of State, State Dept 1984–88, Political Counsellor, Embassy in Bangkok 1988–92, Deputy Chief of Mission, Embassy in Singapore 1992–93, Chargé d'affaires a.i. 1993–94, Deputy Chief of Mission, Embassy in Bangkok 1994–98, Deputy Asst Sec. for E Asia and Pacific Affairs 1998–2001, Amb. to Indonesia 2001–04, to Thailand 2004–07; Vice-Pres. Boeing Int. 2008–, Pres. Boeing Southeast Asia, The Boeing Co. 2008–; mem. Bd of Trustees The Asia Foundation 2014–16. *Address:* Boeing Corporate Offices, 100 North Riverside, Chicago, IL 60606, USA (office). *Telephone:* (312) 544-2000 (office). *Website:* www.boeing.com (office).

BOYCOTT, Geoffrey, OBE; British sports commentator and fmr professional cricketer; b. 21 Oct. 1940, Fitzwilliam, Yorks.; s. of Thomas Wilfred Boycott and Jane Boycott; m. Rachael Swinglehurst 2003; one d.; ed Kinsley Modern School, Hemsworth Grammar School; fmrly in civil service; right-hand opening batsman; teams: Yorkshire 1962–86 (Capt. 1971–78), Northern Transvaal 1971–72; 108 Tests for England 1964–82, 4 as Capt., scoring then record 8,114 runs (average 47.72) including 22 hundreds; scored 48,426 first-class runs (151 hundreds); completed 100 hundreds for Yorkshire 1985, 7th batsman to achieve this for a county; toured Australia 1965–66, 1970–71, 1978–79 and 1979–80; only Englishman to achieve average of 100 in English County season 1971; repeated this achievement in 1979; scored 100th hundred, England v. Australia, Headingley, Leeds Aug. 1977; became 18th batsman in history of game to score 100 hundreds and the first to achieve this in a Test match; mem. Gen. Cttee; served as coach for Pakistan's Nat. Acad. 2001; cricket commentator for BBC and Sky –1998, talkSPORT –2003, Channel 4 2004–05, BBC Test Match Special for England's tour of Pakistan 2005, Cricket on Five 2006–, Ten Sports 2006–, BBC Cricket Team for Ashes series 2006–07; Pres., Yorkshire County Cricket Club 2012–14; Wisden Cricketer of the Year 1965, Winner of Walter Lawrence Trophy 1970, inducted into Int. Cricket Council Hall of Fame 2009. *Publications:* Geoff Boycott's Book for Young Cricketers 1976, Put to the Test: Ashes Series in Australia 1978/79 1979, Geoff Boycott's Cricket Quiz 1979, Boycott on Batting 1980, Opening Up 1980, In the Fast Lane 1981, Master Class 1982, Boycott – The Autobiography 1987, Boycott on Cricket 1990, Geoffrey Boycott on Cricket 1999, The Best XI 2008. *Leisure interest:* golf. *Website:* www.geoffboycott.com.

BOYD, Sir John Dixon Iklé, Kt, KCMG, MA; British fmr diplomatist and fmr university administrator; b. 17 Jan. 1936, Cambridge; s. of Prof. James Dixon Boyd and Amélie Lowenthal; m. 1st Gunilla Kristina Ingregerd Rönngren 1968 (divorced 1977); one s. one d.; m. 2nd Julia Daphne Raynsford 1977; three d.; ed Westminster School, Clare Coll., Cambridge, Yale Univ., USA; joined HM Foreign Service 1962, in Hong Kong 1962–64, Third Sec., Embassy in Beijing 1965–67, at FCO 1967–69, Asst Under-Sec. of State 1984, Deputy Under-Sec. of State 1987–89, Chief Clerk 1989–92, at Embassy in Washington, DC 1969–73, First Sec., Embassy in Beijing 1973–75; on secondment to Treasury 1976; Econ. Counsellor, Embassy in Bonn 1977–81, Counsellor (Econ. and Social Affairs), Perm. Mission to UN, New York 1981–84; Political Adviser, Hong Kong 1985–87; Amb. to Japan 1992–96; Master of Churchill Coll., Cambridge 1996–2006; Chair. Bd of Govs, Bedales School 1966–2001, David Davies Memorial Inst. 1997–2001; Chair. Asia House 2010–16, Hon. Pres. 2017–; Co-Chair. Nuffield Languages Inquiry 1998–2000; Vice-Chair. Yehudi Menuhin Int. Violin Trust Ltd 1996–; Dir UK-Japan 21st Century Group 2006–15; Dir (non-exec.) British Nuclear Fuels PLC 1997–2000; Adviser, East Asia Inst., Univ. of Cambridge 1998–2005, Iran Heritage Foundation 2009–; mem. Advisory Cttee, London Symphony Orchestra 2009–; mem. ASEM (Asia-Europe Meeting) 'Vision Group' 1998–2000, ANA Advisory Group 2003–13; Trustee, British Museum 1996–2006 (Chair. 2002–06, Trustee Emer. 2007–), Sir Winston Churchill Archive Trust 1996–2006, Cambridge Union (also Chair.) 1997–2006, Margaret Thatcher Archive Trust 1997–2006, Cambridge Foundation 1997–2005, The Wordsworth Trust 1997–2013, Great Britain-Sasakawa Foundation 2001–, Council of Senate Cambridge Univ. 2001–04, Huang Hsing Foundation 2001–, RAND (Europe) UK 2001–, Joseph Needham Research Inst. 2005– (Chair. 2008–16); Syndic Fitzwilliam Museum 1997–2002; Gov. RSC 1996–2005; Patron, Thomas Wade Foundation 2017–; Hon. Fellow, Clare Coll., Cambridge 1994, Westminster School 2003, Life Fellow, Churchill Coll., Cambridge 2006; Grand Cordon Order of the Rising Sun (Japan) 2007. *Publications include:* contrib. of articles to Asian Affairs and others. *Leisure interests:* music, books, sheep farming, fly-fishing. *Address:* 87 Elizabeth Street, London, SW1W 9PG, England (home). *Telephone:* (20) 7730-8389 (home). *E-mail:* jul.boyd@gmail.com (home).

BOYD, Joseph Walker, BA; American music industry executive, film producer and writer; b. 5 Aug. 1942, Boston, Mass; s. of Joseph M. Boyd and Elizabeth Walker Boyd; m. Andrea Goertler-Boyd; ed Harvard Univ.; Gen. Man. Elektra Records UK 1965–66; Man. Dir Witchseason Productions Ltd 1966–71; Dir Music Services, Warner Bros Films 1971–73; Man. Dir Osiris Films 1976–79; Vice-Pres. Broadway Pictures, New York 1979–80; Man. Dir Hannibal Records Ltd 1980–91; Vice-Pres. A&R, Rykodisc Inc. 1991–98; A&R Dir Hannibal/Ryko Latino Labels 1999; Grammy Award 1974. *Radio:* Joe Boyd's A-Z podcast. *Publication:* White Bicycles: Making Music in the 1960s 2007. *Leisure interest:* history. *E-mail:* catherine@caterinesteinmann.co.uk (office); info@joeboyd.co.uk. *Website:* www.serpentstail.com (office); www.joeboyd.co.uk.

BOYD, Sir Michael, Kt, MA; British theatre director; b. 6 July 1955, Belfast, Northern Ireland; s. of John Truesdale Boyd and Sheila Boyd; partner Caroline Hall; one d.; one s. one d. (twins) with previous partner; ed Latymer Upper School, London, Daniel Stewart's Coll., Edinburgh and Univ. of Edinburgh; Trainee Dir, Malaya Bronnaya Theatre, Moscow; Trainee Asst Dir Belgrade Theatre, Coventry, Asst Dir 1980–82; Assoc. Dir Crucible Theatre, Sheffield 1982–84; Founding Artistic Dir Tron Theatre, Glasgow 1985–96; Assoc. Dir RSC 1996–2003, Artistic Dir 2002–12; projects with Royal Opera House and abroad 2014. *Productions include:* for Tron Theatre: The Trick is to Keep Breathing, Macbeth, Good, The Real World, Crow, Century's End, Salvation, The Baby, Clyde Nouveau, The Guid Sisters; for RSC: The Broken Heart 1994–95, Measure for Measure 1996–97, The Spanish Tragedy, Much Ado About Nothing 1997–98, Troilus and Cressida 1998–99, A Midsummer Night's Dream 1999–2000, Romeo and Juliet 2000–01, Henry VI, Parts I, II and III and Richard III (Olivier Award for Best Dir 2001, South Bank Award 2001) 2000–01, The Tempest 2002, Hamlet 2004, Twelfth Night 2005, The Histories (eight play cycle) 2006–08, The Grain Store 2009, As You Like It, 2009–11, Antony and Cleopatra 2010–11; other theatre productions include: Miss Julie (Haymarket Theatre, West End) 1999, Commedia (Lyric Hammersmith) 1983, Othello (Lyric Hammersmith) 1984, A Passion in Six Days (Crucible Theatre, Sheffield), Hard to Get (Traverse Theatre, Edinburgh), Hedda Gabler (Leicester Haymarket), The Alchemist (Cambridge Theatre Co.), The Big Meal (Ustinov Studio, Theatre Royal Bath) 2014. *Leisure interests:* walking, reading, music, cooking. *Address:* c/o Royal Shakespeare Company, Royal Shakespeare Theatre, Waterside, Stratford-upon-Avon, Warwicks., CV37 6BB, England.

BOYD, Sir Robert, Kt, MA, MB, BChir, FRCP, FFPHM, FRCPCH, FMedSci; British paediatrician; b. 14 May 1938, Cambridge; s. of James Dixon Boyd and Amélie Boyd; m. Meriel Cornelia Talbot 1966; one s. two d.; ed Ley's School, Clare Coll., Cambridge, Univ. Coll. Hosp., London; jr posts, Hosp. for Sick Children, Great Ormond Street, Brompton Hosp., Univ. Coll. Hosp. (UCH), London 1962–65; Sir Stuart Halley Research Fellow and Sr Registrar, UCH 1966–71; Goldsmiths MRC Travelling Fellow, Univ. of Colorado Medical Center, USA 1971–72; Sr Lecturer and Hon. Consultant, UCH Medical School 1972–80; Sec., Academic Bd, British Paediatric Asscn 1976–79, Chair. 1987–90; Asst Registrar Royal Coll. of Physicians 1980–81; Prof. of Paediatrics, Univ. of Manchester 1981–96, Dean 1989–93, Visiting Prof. 2003–; Prin. St George's Hosp. Medical School and Prof. of Paediatrics 1996–2003, Pro-Vice-Chancellor for Medicine, Univ. of London 2000–03, Deputy Vice-Chancellor 2002–03; Chair. Manchester Health Authority 1994–96, Nat. Primary Care R&D Centre, Univs of Manchester, Salford and York 1994–96, Dir Nat. Health Service (NHS) Research and Devt, Greater Manchester 2004–08; Chair. Council of Heads of UK Medical Schools 2001–03, Lloyds TSB Foundation for England and Wales 2003–, Council for Assisting Refugee Academics 2004–; Ed. Placenta 1989–95; mem. Health Cttee Universities UK 1997–2003, Asscn of Medical Research Charities Scientific Advisory Cttee

1996–2002, Task Force 'Supporting Research & Development in the NHS' 1994; mem. Council, Royal Veterinary Coll. 1999–2003; Gov. Kingston Univ. 1998–2003, Univ. of Manchester 2004–; Hon. Consultant, St Mary's Hosp., Manchester and Booth Hall Children's Hosp., Manchester 1981–96, St George's Healthcare Nat. Health Service Trust, London 1996–2003, Hon. Fellow, American Pediatric Soc.; Hon. DSc (Kingston, Keele). *Publications include:* Paediatric Problems in General Practice (co-author) 1982; contribs to Placental and Fetal Physiology and Paediatrics and Health Administration. *Leisure interests:* cooking, reading, holidays. *Address:* The Stone House, Skellorn Green, Adlington, Macclesfield, Cheshire, SK10 4NU, England (home). *Telephone:* (1625) 872400 (home). *E-mail:* rboyd@doctors.org.uk.

BOYD, William Andrew Murray, CBE, MA, FRSL; British novelist and screenwriter; b. 7 March 1952, Accra, Ghana; s. of Dr Alexander Murray Boyd and Evelyn Boyd; m. Susan Anne Boyd (née Wilson) 1975; ed Gordonstoun School, Glasgow Univ., Jesus Coll., Oxford; lecturer in English, St Hilda's Coll., Oxford 1980–83; TV critic, New Statesman 1981–83; Officier, Ordre des Arts et des Lettres; Hon. DLitt (St Andrews), (Glasgow), (Stirling), (Dundee). *Film appearance:* Rabbit Fever 2006. *Television:* adapted his novel Any Human Heart into a four-part drama for Channel 4 2010. *Publications include:* A Good Man in Africa (Whitbread Prize 1981, Somerset Maugham Award 1982) 1981 (screenplay 1994), On the Yankee Station 1981, An Ice-Cream War (John Llewellyn Rhys Prize) 1982, Stars and Bars 1984 (screenplay 1988), School Ties 1985, The New Confessions 1987, Scoop (screenplay) 1987, Brazzaville Beach (McVitie's Prize and James Tait Black Memorial Prize) 1990, Aunt Julia and the Scriptwriter (screenplay) 1990, Mr Johnson (screenplay) 1990, Chaplin (screenplay) 1992, The Blue Afternoon (novel) 1993, A Good Man in Africa (screenplay) 1994, The Destiny of Nathalie 'X' 1995, Armadillo 1998 (screenplay 2001), Nat Tate: An American Artist 1998, The Trench (screenplay, also dir) 1999, Sword of Honour (screenplay) 2001, Any Human Heart 2002, Fascination 2004, Bamboo (collection of literary reviews) 2005, A Waste of Shame (screenplay) 2005, Restless (novel) (Costa Book Award for Novel of the Year, Yorkshire Post Book of the Year 2007) 2006, Granta 100 (Ed.) 2008, The Dream Lover (short stories) 2008, Ordinary Thunderstorms (novel) 2009, Waiting for Sunrise (novel) 2012, Solo (novel) 2013, Sweet Caress (novel) 2015, Love is Blind 2018. *Leisure interests:* tennis, strolling. *Address:* c/o Bloomsbury Publishing, 50 Bedford Square, London, WC1B 3DP, England (office). *Website:* www.williamboyd.co.uk.

BOYD OF DUNCANSBY, Baron (Life Peer), cr. 2006, of Duncansby in the County of Caithness; **Colin Boyd,** PC, QC, BA (Econ), LLB, FRSA, LARTPI; British lawyer; b. 7 June 1953, Falkirk; s. of David Hugh Aird Boyd and Betty Meldrum Boyd; two s. one d.; ed Wick High School, George Watson's Coll., Edinburgh, Univ. of Manchester and Univ. of Edinburgh; qualified as solicitor 1978; called to Bar 1983; Legal Assoc. Royal Town Planning Inst. 1990; Advocate Depute (prosecutor) 1993–95; QC 1995; Solicitor-Gen. for Scotland, UK Govt 1997; Solicitor-Gen., Scottish Exec. 1999–2000; Lord Advocate of Scotland 2000–06; Senator of Coll. of Justice 2012–; Hon. Fellow, Inst. of Advanced Legal Studies 2001. *Leisure interests:* reading, walking, watching rugby. *Address:* House of Lords, London, SW1A 0PW, England (office). *Telephone:* (20) 7219-3000 (office). *E-mail:* boydcd@parliament.uk (office).

BOYD OF MERTON, 2nd Viscount, cr. 1960 of Merton-in-Penninghame, Co. Wigtown; **Simon Donald Rupert Neville Lennox-Boyd,** BA, MA; British business executive (retd); b. 7 Dec. 1939, London, England; s. of Alan Tindal Lennox-Boyd (1st Viscount Boyd of Merton) and Lady Patricia Florence Susan Guinness; m. Alice Mary Clive 1962; two s. two d.; ed Eton Coll., Christ Church, Oxford; Deputy Chair. Arthur Guinness & Sons 1981–86; Vice-Chair. Save the Children Fund 1979–82, Chair. 1987–93; Chair. Stonham Housing Asscn 1992–98, Trustee, Guinness Trust 1974–; Dir The Iveagh Trustees Ltd. *Leisure interest:* forestry. *Address:* Ince Castle, Saltash, Cornwall, PL12 4QZ, England. *Telephone:* (1752) 842672. *Fax:* (1752) 847134 (home). *E-mail:* boydince@aol.com (home).

BOYDEN, Edward (Ed) S., BS, BS, MEng, PhD; American neuroscientist and academic; *Y. Eva Tan Professor in Neurotechnology and Investigator, McGovern Institute, Massachusetts Institute of Technology;* b. 18 Aug. 1979, Plano, Tex.; m. Xue Han 2009; ed Massachusetts Inst. of Tech., Stanford Univ. (Hertz Fellow); Research Asst, Chem. Dept, Univ. of North Texas 1994–95; Research Programmer, Activision, Inc., Santa Monica, Calif. 1997; Research Asst, MIT Media Lab, MIT 1996–98, Grad. Research 1998–99, Visiting Scientist, MIT Media Lab, Leader, Neuroengineering and Neuromedia Group 2006–07, Asst Prof., MIT Media Lab (Benesse Career Devt Prof.), Jt Prof., Dept of Biological Eng and Dept of Brain and Cognitive Sciences, Leader, Synthetic Neurobiology Group 2007–11, Assoc. Prof., MIT Media Lab (Benesse Career Devt Prof. 2011–13, AT&T Career Devt Prof. 2013–14), Investigator, McGovern Inst., Jt Prof., Dept of Biological Eng and Dept of Brain and Cognitive Sciences, Assoc. mem. Broad Inst., Leader, Synthetic Neurobiology Group, Co-Dir, MIT Center for Neurobiological Eng 2011–14, Assoc. Prof. with Tenure, MIT Media Lab 2014–, Y. Eva Tan Prof. in Neurotechnology, MIT 2018–; Research Asst, Bell Labs, Lucent Technologies, Murray Hill, NJ 1998–99; Hertz Predoctoral Fellow, NIH NRSA Predoctoral Fellow, Program in Neurosciences, Depts of Molecular and Cellular Physiology and Neurobiology, Stanford Univ. 1999–2005, Helen Hay Whitney Fellow, Depts of Bioengineering, Applied Physics, Biological Sciences 2005–06; mem. Editorial Bd, Journal of Neural Engineering 2013–, Bioelectronic Medicines 2014–, Neural Computation 2014–; mem. Soc. for Neuroscience 2000; named to MIT Technology Review TR35 as one of the top 35 innovators in the world under the age of 35 2006, named by Discover Magazine as one of the top 20 scientists under 40 2008, work included in Nature Methods 'Method of the Year' 2010, Perl/UNC Neuroscience Prize 2011, NIH Director's Transformative Research Award 2012, 2013, Jacob Heskel Gabbay Award 2013, Grete Lundbeck European Brain Research Prize 2013, NIH Director's Pioneer Award 2013, Jacob Heskel Gabbay Award 2013, named to World Econ. Forum Young Scientist list 2013, Schuetze Award in Neuroscience 2014, Carnegie Prize in Mind and Brain Sciences 2015, Breakthrough Prize in Life Sciences (co-recipient) 2016, Drexel Prize in Biotechnology 2017, Gairdner Foundation Int. Award 2018, Rumford Prize, American Acad. of Arts and Sciences (co-recipient) 2019. *Publications:* Optogenetics: Tools for Controlling and Monitoring Neuronal Activity (co-ed.), Progress in Brain Research, Vol. 196; numerous articles in professional journals. *Address:* Room E15-485, MIT Media Lab, Massachusetts Institute of Technology, 20 Ames Street, Cambridge, MA 02139, USA (office). *Telephone:* (617) 324-3085 (office). *Fax:* (617) 258-6264 (office). *E-mail:* esb@media.mit.edu (office). *Website:* syntheticneurobiology.org (office); mcgovern.mit.edu (office); edboyden.org.

BOYER, Yves, PhD; French research institute director and academic; *Research Director, Forum du Futur;* b. 9 Oct. 1950, Blois; m. Isabelle Kraft 1978; one s. one d.; ed Inst. d'Etudes Politiques, Paris and Paris-Panthéon Univ.; Deputy Gen. Sec. SOFRESA, Paris 1978–80; Bureau des Etudes Stratégiques et des Négociations Internationales, Secr. Gén. de la Défense Nationale 1980–82; Defence Consultant and Research Assoc., IISS, London 1982–83; Sr Researcher, Inst. Français des Relations Internationales 1983–88; Research Fellow, Woodrow Wilson Center 1986; fmr Deputy Dir CREST, Ecole Polytechnique; Prof., Army Acad. 1986–, Staff Coll. 1992–; fmr Prof. of Int. Relations, Ecole polytechnique, Paris; currently Research Dir Forum du Futur; Chair. French Soc. for Mil. Studies (SFEM), Working Groups for the French Ministry of Defence's Scientific Advisers; mem. Editorial Bd, Annuaire Français de Relations Internationales; Chevalier, Ordre des Palmes académiques. *Publications:* Oxford Handbook of War (co-ed. with J. Lindley-French) 2012. *Address:* Forum du Futur, 11 Avenue Franklin Delano Roosevelt, 75008 Paris (office); 2 rue de Haut Bourg, 41000 Blois, France (home). *Telephone:* (1) 40-73-86-26 (office). *E-mail:* forumdufutur@orange.fr (office). *Website:* www.forumdufutur.fr (office).

BOYKO, Yuriy Anatoliyovych; Ukrainian engineer and politician; *Co-Chair, Opozytsiyny Blok (Opposition Bloc);* b. 9 Oct. 1958, Horlivka, Donetsk Oblast, Ukrainian SSR, USSR; m. Vera Dimitrievna Boyka; three s. three d.; ed Mendeleyev Moscow Inst. of Chemical Tech., Russian SFSR, East Ukraine Univ., Voroshylovhrad (now Luhansk—Lugansk); began career as Foreman and Gen. Man., Zorva Rubizhanskiy chemical plant 1981–89; various man. positions, including Dir Gen., with Lisichansknaftoorgsintez JSC (now LiNOS), and Ukrvybuhprom State Corpn 1999–2001; Chair. Man. Bd Ukrtatnafta (oil refining co.) and Chair. Supervisory Bd Ukrtransnafta (oil transportation co.) 2001–02; Head, Naftogaz of Ukraine (nat. oil and gas co.) 2002–05; Sr Deputy Minister of Fuel and Energy 2003–05, Minister of Fuel and Energy 2006–07, of Energy and Coal Industry 2010–12; Deputy Prime Minister 2012–14; mem. (Republican Party of Ukraine 2007–10, Partiya Rehioniv (Party of Regions) 2010–14; mem. Opozytsiyny Blok (OB—Opposition Bloc) 2014–, currently Co-Chair.;) mem. Verkhovna Rada (Supreme Council, Parl.) 2007–10, 2014–, Deputy Chair. Cttee on Fuel and Energy Complex, Nuclear Policy and Nuclear Safety; Leader of OB at legis. elections 2014; unsuccessful cand. in presidential elections 2014, 2019; Order of St Seraphim of Sarov (Second Class), Order of Merit (Third Class) 2003, Hero of Ukraine 2004, Order of the State 2004. *Leisure interests:* plays ice hockey and football, likes water-skiing and windsurfing. *Address:* Opozytsiyny Blok (Opposition Bloc), Kyiv, Ukraine (office). *Telephone:* (44) 223-32-12 (Press Service) (office). *E-mail:* pressa@opposition.org.ua (office). *Website:* opposition.org.ua (office).

BOYLE, Danny; British film director; b. 20 Oct. 1956, Bury, Lancs.; Artistic Dir, Royal Court Theatre 1982–87; Artistic Dir for Isles of Wonder, Opening Ceremony of London Summer Olympic Games 2012; Fellow, British Film Inst. 2010; Patron, HOME, Manchester 2014–; Golden Ephebe Award 1997. *Theatre includes:* Royal Court Theatre: The Grace of Mary Traverse, Genius, Saved; RSC: The Pretenders, The Last Days of Don Juan, The Silent Woman; Nat. Theatre: Frankenstein 2011. *Films include:* Shallow Grave 1994, Trainspotting 1996, A Life Less Ordinary 1996, Twin Town (exec. producer) 1996, The Beach 1999, Alien Love Triangle 1999, 28 Days Later 2002, Alien Love Triangle 2002, Millions 2004, Sunshine 2007, Slumdog Millionaire (Best Film Nat. Bd of Review 2008, Golden Globe Award for Best Dir 2009, BAFTA Award for Best Dir 2009, Acad. Award for Best Picture 2009, Acad. Award for Best Dir 2009) 2008, 127 Hours 2010, National Theatre Live: Frankenstein 2011, Trance 2013, Steve Jobs 2015. *Television includes:* Elephant (producer) 1989, The Greater Good (series) 1991, Mr Wroe's Virgins 1993, Not Even God is Wise Enough 1993, London 2012 Olympic Opening Ceremony: Isles of Wonder 2012, Babylon (mini-series) 2014. *Address:* c/o WME Entertainment, 9601 Wilshire Boulevard, Beverley Hills, CA 90210-5213, USA (office); c/o Independent Talent, 40 Whitfield Street, London, W1T 2RH, England (office); c/o D6A, 7920 West Sunset Boulevard, Los Angeles, CA 90046, USA. *Telephone:* (310) 859-4000 (office); (20) 7636-6565 (office). *Fax:* (310) 859-4440 (office); (20) 7323-0101 (office). *Website:* www.wmeentertainment.com (office); www.independenttalent.com (office). *E-mail:* info@independenttalent.com (office).

BOYLE, T(homas) C(oraghessan), BA, MFA, PhD; American academic and writer; *Writer-in-Residence and Distinguished Professor Emeritus of English, University of Southern California;* b. 2 Dec. 1948, Peekskill, NY; m. Karen Kvashay 1974; two s. one d.; ed State Univ. of New York at Potsdam, Univ. of Iowa; Founder-Dir, Creative Writing Program, Univ. of Southern California 1978–86, Asst Prof. of English 1978–82, Assoc. Prof. of English 1982–86, Prof. of English 1986, currently Writer-in-Residence and Distinguished Prof. Emer. of English; mem. Nat. Endowment of Arts literature panel 1986–87; Guggenheim Fellowship 1988, mem. American Acad. of Arts and Letters 2009–; Hon. DHumLitt (SUNY) 1991; Commonwealth Club of California Gold Medal for Literature 1988, O. Henry Short Story Award 1988, 1989, 1999, 2001, 2003, Prix Passion Publishers' Prize, France 1989, Harold D. Vursell Memorial Award, American Acad. of Arts and Letters 1993, Ross Macdonald Award for body of work by a California writer 2007, Henry David Thoreau Award for excellence in nature writing 2013, among others. *Publications include:* Descent of Man 1979, Water Music 1982, Budding Prospects 1984, Greasy Lake 1985, World's End (PEN/Faulkner Prize 1988) 1987, If the River was Whiskey 1989, East is East 1990, The Road to Wellville 1993, Without a Hero 1994, The Tortilla Curtain (Prix Médicis Étranger for best foreign novel 1997) 1995, Riven Rock 1998, T.C. Boyle Stories (PEN/Malamud Prize 1999) 1998, A Friend of the Earth 2000, After the Plague 2001, Drop City 2003, The Inner Circle 2004, Tooth and Claw 2006, Talk Talk 2006, The Women 2009, Wild Child 2010, When the Killing's Done 2011, San Miguel 2012, T. C. Boyle Stories II 2013, The Harder They Come 2015, The Terranauts 2016, The Relive Box and Other Stories 2017, Outside Looking In: A Novel 2019; contrib. to numerous anthologies and periodicals. *Address:* Department of English, THH 431, University of Southern California, Los Angeles, CA 90089, USA (office); c/o Georges Borchardt, Inc., 137 E 57th Street, New York, NY 10022, USA (office). *Telephone:* (213) 821-

0477 (office); (212) 753-5785 (office). *E-mail:* tcb@tcboyle.com (office). *Website:* dornsife.usc.edu/engl (office); www.tcboyle.com; gbagency.com (office).

BOZANGA, Georges; Central African Republic politician; Minister of Finance and Budget –June 2013, then Minister of Development Industries.

BOZANIĆ, HE Cardinal Josip, MTS, LLM; Croatian ecclesiastic; *Archbishop of Zagreb;* b. 20 March 1949, Rijeka; s. of Ivan Bosanić and Dinka Valković; ed Lower Seminary of Pazin, Faculties of Theology, Rijeka and Zagreb, Pontifical Gregorian Univ. and Pontifical Lateran Univ., Rome; ordained priest by Bishop of Krk, Karmelo Zazinović 1975; Sec. to Bishop of Krk 1975–76; Parish Priest 1976–78; Chancellor of Diocesan Curia in Krk 1986–87; Gen. Priest 1987–89; Prof. of Canon Law and Theology, Seminary of Rijeka 1988–97; elected Bishop of Krk 1989; consecrated by Cardinal Franjo Kuharić 1989; Admin. of Archdiocese of Rijeka-Senj 1996; Archbishop of Metropolitan See of Zagreb 1997–; Pres. Croatian Conf. of Bishops; Vice-Pres. Council of European Bishops' Confs; cr. Cardinal (Cardinal-Priest of San Girolamo dei Croati) 2003–; participated in Papal Conclave 2005, 2013; del. to Special Ass. for Europe, World Synod of Bishops, The Vatican 1999; mem. Congregation for Worship and Discipline of the Sacraments 2016. *Address:* Archdiocese of Zagreb, Kaptol 31, p.p. 553, 10001 Zagreb, Croatia (office). *Telephone:* 4894802 (office). *Fax:* 4816104 (office). *E-mail:* Josip.Bozanic@hbk.hr (office). *Website:* zagreb.hbk.hr (office).

BOZER, Ali Husrev, Dr in Law; Turkish academic, judge and government official; *Board Member, AxA A.S.;* b. 28 July 1925, Ankara; s. of Mustafa Fevzi Bozer and Zehra Bozer; m.; three s.; ed Ankara and Neuchâtel Univs and Harvard Law School; Asst judge, Ankara 1951; Asst, Faculty of Law, Ankara Univ. 1952–60, Agrégé 1955–60, Head of Dept 1961, apptd Prof. of Commercial Law 1965; Prof. of Law Çankaya Univ. 1992–, also Law Faculty, Ankara Univ., Law Faculty, Gazi Univ.; lawyer at bar, Ankara 1952–; Dir Inst. de Recherche sur le Droit commercial et bancaire 1960–; Judge, European Court of Human Rights 1974–76; mem. Admin. Council, Turkish Radio-TV Corpn 1968–71, Vice-Pres. 1971–73; Minister of Customs and Monopolies 1981–83, of State for Relations with EEC 1986–90; Deputy Prime Minister and Minister of State 1989–90; Minister of Foreign Affairs Feb.–Oct. 1990; fmr Pres., now Hon. Pres. European Asscn of Former Parliamentarians of the Member Countries of the European Council or the EU; mem. Bd AxA A.S.; fmr mem. Bd or legal adviser, various public and private enterprises; Officier Légion d'honneur 1993; Mérite Européen 1992, Esteemed Alumnus Ankara Univ. *Publications:* Les droits d'administration et de jouissance de père et mère sur les biens de l'enfant, Nantissement commercial, Aperçu général sur le droit des assurances sociales en droit turc, Droit commercial pour les employés de banques, Papiers valeurs pour les employés de banques, Droits des Assurances, Droit des Obligations, Insurance Law, Contracts Law, Negotiable Instruments; monographs and articles in several reviews in Turkish and French; articles published on Turkish relations with European Union. *Leisure interests:* theatre, music, sport, tennis, swimming. *Address:* Ahmet Rasim sok. 35/5, Çankaya, Ankara, Turkey (home). *Telephone:* (312) 4424112 (home). *Fax:* (312) 4424113 (home).

BOZIMBAEV, Qanat Aldabergenulı; Kazakhstani business executive and government official; *Minister of Energy;* b. 8 Jan. 1969, Almatı, Kazakh SSR, USSR; ed Kazakh State Acad. of Man.; worked for various govt agencies and pvt. cos 1993–97; Head of Dept of Regional Policy, Ministry of Economy and Trade Sept.–Nov. 1997; Head of Consolidated Financial Dept and Vice-Pres., Econ. Affairs, Nat. Oil Transportation Co. KazTransOil JSC 1997–98; Dir Dept of Oil and Gas and Vice-Minister of Energy, Industry and Trade 1998–2001; First Vice-Pres., Kazakhstan Co. on Man. of Electric Networks JSC Feb.–May 2001, Pres. 2001–07, 2008–; Dir, Kazakhstan Holding Co. for Man. of State Assets, Samruk JSC 2007–08; Akim (Gov.) of Jambıl Oblast 2009, of Pavlodar Oblast 2013–; Minister of Energy 2016–; Honoured Power Eng Specialist of the CIS. *Address:* Ministry of Energy, 010000 Nur-Sultan, Kabanbai batyr kösh. 19, Kazakhstan (office). *Telephone:* (7172) 97-68-01 (office). *Fax:* (7172) 97-68-88 (office). *E-mail:* info@energo.gov.kz (office). *Website:* kz.energo.gov.kz (office).

BOŽINOVIĆ, Davor, BA, MA, PhD; Croatian diplomatist and government official; *Minister of Internal Affairs;* b. 27 Dec. 1961, Pula; m.; two c.; ed Univ. of Zagreb, George C. Marshall European Center for Security Studies, Garmisch-Partenkirchen, Germany; Adviser, Secr. for Defence 1987–90; Chair. Draft Bd, Ministry of Defence 1990–94; Sr Adviser, Dept for Consular Affairs, Ministry of Foreign Affairs (MFA) 1994–96, Counsellor, Embassy in Sarajevo, Bosnia and Hercegovina, 1996, Deputy Head and Head of Dept on Neighbouring Countries, MFA 1997–99, Asst Minister of Foreign Affairs 1999, Coordinator for relations with Yugoslavia, MFA 2000, Chargé d'affaires a.i., Embassy in Belgrade, Yugoslavia (now Serbia) 2001, Amb. to Yugoslavia, then Serbia and Montenegro 2002–04; Chief of Staff, Office of the Pres. 2004; Perm. Rep. to NATO, Brussels 2005–08, State Sec. for European Integration, Ministry of Foreign Affairs and European Integration 2008–09, State Sec. for Political Affairs 2009, Special Envoy of the Prime Minister for SE Europe March–Dec. 2010; Minister of Defence 2010–11, of Internal Affairs 2017–; mem. Parl. (Hrvatska Demokratska Zajednica—Croatian Democratic Union) 2011–; negotiator during Croatia-EU accession negotiations; observer for Croatia, European Parl., Brussels 2012–13; fmr Lecturer, Faculty of Political Science, Univ. of Zagreb, MFAEI Diplomatic Acad., Ban Josip Jelacic War Coll.; has lectured at Woodrow Wilson Int. Scientific Center, Washington, DC, German Marshall Fund, Washington, DC, Johns Hopkins Univ., Baltimore, Md, USA, Diplomatic Acad. of Russian Ministry of Foreign Affairs, Moscow. *Publications include:* NATO-Euro-Atlantic Integration 2008, Mutual Transition NATO-EU-Southeast Europe 2010. *Address:* Ministry of Internal Affairs, 10000 Zagreb, ul. grada Vukovara 33, Croatia (office). *Telephone:* (1) 6122111 (office). *Fax:* (1) 6122452 (office). *E-mail:* pitanja@mup.hr (office). *Website:* www.mup.hr (office).

BOZIZÉ, Jean Francis; Central African Republic government official; b. 19 Feb. 1970, Bangui; s. of fmr Pres. François Bozizé Yangovounda; served in several positions in the Ministry of Nat. Defence, War Veterans, War Victims, Disarmament and the Restructuring of the Armed Forces, including Chief of Staff to the Minister, Deputy Minister, Minister-Del. at the Presidency in charge of Nat. Defence, War Veterans, War Victims, Disarmament and the Restructuring of the Armed Forces 2008–13; in exile in France following overthrow of his father March 2013.

BOZIZÉ YANGOVOUNDA, Gen. François; Central African Republic army officer and fmr head of state; opposition leader 1981–93, led unsuccessful coup 1983; spent many years in exile in Togo; presidential cand. 1993; supported Pres. Ange-Felix Patasse in suppressing coups 1996–97; sacked as Army Chief; participated in unsuccessful coup against Pres. 2001, took control of N Bangui before escaping to Chad with 300 supporters; launched several rebel attacks from base in Chad 2001–02; led successful coup March 2003, suspended constitution and dissolved Parl.; self-proclaimed Pres. of Cen. African Repub. 2003–05, elected 2005, Pres. 2005–13, Minister of Defence 2005–08, also Minister of Nat. Defence, War Veterans, War Victims, Disarmament and the Restructuring of the Armed Forces; fled to Democratic Repub. of Congo following attack by rebel forces March 2013; in exile in Cameroon.

BRABEC, Richard; Czech business executive and politician; *Deputy Prime Minister and Minister of the Environment;* b. 5 July 1966, Kladno,Czechoslovak Socialist Repub. (now Czech Repub.); m.; two s.; ed Charles Univ., Prague; mem. Kladno city council 1990–98; Analyst, Devt Dept, ČSA a.s. 1991–92; Dir Czech-Moravian Commodities Exchange, Kladno 1992–97; worked at UNIPETROL, a.s. 1997–2003; mem. Central Bohemian Regional Ass. 2000–04; Finance Dir and mem. Bd of Dirs, SPOLANA, a.s. 2003–05; Gen. Man. and Vice Chair. Lovochemie, a.s. 2005–10; Advisor, Czech Chemical Industries Asscn; mem. Chamber of Deputies (parl.) 2013–; Minister of the Environment 2014–, also Deputy Prime Minister 2017–; mem. Ano (Yes) 2012–, mem. Exec. Bd 2012–13, 2015–. *Address:* Office of the Government, náb. E. Beneše 4, 118 01 Prague 1, Czech Republic (office). *Telephone:* 224002111 (office). *Fax:* 257531283 (office). *E-mail:* posta@vlada.cz (office). *Website:* www.vlada.cz (office).

BRABECK-LETMATHE, Peter, BA; Austrian business executive; *Chairman, Nestlé SA;* b. 13 Nov. 1944, Villach; ed Univ. of World Trade, Vienna; fmrly with Findus Austria; joined Nestlé Group as salesman 1968, becoming new products specialist 1970, Nat. Sales Man. 1970, later Dir of Marketing, Nestlé Chile, frozen food and ice-cream specialist, Nestlé HQ 1975, Marketing and Sales Div. Man., Chiprodal (Chile) 1976, Asst to Regional Man. for S America, Nestlé HQ 1980, Man. Dir Nestlé Ecuador 1981, Nestlé Venezuela 1983, Sr Vice-Pres. and Head of Culinary Products Div., Nestlé SA, Vevey 1987, Exec. Vice-Pres. and Head of Strategic Business Group 2 1992, Group CEO (desig.) Nestlé SA, Vevey 1995–97, Group CEO 1997–2008, Vice-Chair. 2001–05, Chair. 2005–, also Chair. Chairman's and Corp. Governance Cttee, Nomination Cttee, Chair. Nestlé Health Science SA; Vice-Chair. L'Oréal SA 1997–, Crédit Suisse Group 2000–05, 2008–; mem. Bd of Dirs Exxon Mobil Corpn (USA) 2010–, Delta Topco Ltd (Formula 1), Jersey 2010– (Chair. 2012–); Chair. Int. Business Council of World Econ. Forum; Deputy Chair. The Prince of Wales Int. Business Leaders' Forum; mem. European Round Table of Industrialists, Int. Asscn for the Promotion and Protection of Pvt. Foreign Investments; mem. Foundation Bds World Econ. Forum, Foundation for the Int. Fed. of Red Cross and Red Crescent Socs; La Orden Mexicana del Aguila Azteca, Austrian Cross of Honour; Hon. LLD (Univ. of Alberta, Canada) 2012; Schumpeter Prize for outstanding contrib. in economics. *Address:* Nestlé, Avenue Nestlé 55, 1800 Vevey, Switzerland (office). *Telephone:* (21) 924-1111 (office). *Fax:* (21) 921-1885 (office). *E-mail:* info@nestle.com (office). *Website:* www.nestle.com (office).

BRACHES, Ernst; Dutch academic (retd); b. 8 Oct. 1930, Padang, Indonesia; s. of Godfried Daniel Ernst Braches and Zeni Jansz; m. Maartje van Hoorn 1961; three s. one foster s.; ed Univ. of Amsterdam; asst, Univ. of Amsterdam 1957–65; Keeper of Western Printed Books, Univ. Library, Leiden 1965–73; Dir Rijksmuseum Meermanno-Westreenianum, The Hague 1973–77; Dir Univ. of Amsterdam Library 1977–88, Prof. of History of the Printed Book, Univ. of Amsterdam; Hon. mem. Soc. de la Reliure Originale, Paris. *Publications include:* Henry James: Engel en Afgrond 1983, Lord Peter Wimsey as a Book Lover 1989, The Scheffers Type 1990, Gutenberg's Scriptorium 1991, The Steadfast Tin Soldier of Joh Enschede en Zonen 1992, Alle nieuwe kunst wordt eerst niet begrepen 2003, Nieuwe Kunst en het boek 2003, Nieuwe Kunst Documentatie 2006, Dutch Art Nouveau and Book Design 1892–1903 2009, Kommentar zum Tod in Venedig 2015. *Address:* Vrijburglaan 53, 2051 LB Overveen, Netherlands (home).

BRACKE, Siegfried; Belgian journalist and politician; *President, Chamber of Representatives;* b. 21 Feb. 1953, Ghent; m. Marina Nuyts; ed Univ. of Ghent, Sint-Lievens Coll.; Radio Producer, Radio 1, Vlaamse Radio-en Televisieomroep 1981–83, apptd journalist 1983, Ed. 2007–09; mem. Nieuw-Vlaamse Alliantie (N-VA) (East Flanders) 2010–; Leader Ghent City Council 2013–; Pres. Chamber of Reps 2014–; Perm. Mem. Comm. for Revision of the Constitution and the Reform of the Insts, Advisory Cttee on European Affairs (also Chair.), Parl. Consultation Cttee (also Chair.). *Radio:* Bow tie, Vlaamse Radio-en Televisieomroep (VRT) 1991, Bracke on Friday 2010. *Address:* Palais de la Nation, 1008 Brussels, Belgium (office). *Telephone:* (2) 549-81-11 (office). *E-mail:* info@lachambre.be (office); siegfried.bracke@dekamer.be. *Website:* www.lachambre.be (office).

BRACKEN, Richard M., BSc, MSc; American business executive; b. 14 Sept. 1952; m. Judith Bracken; four c.; ed San Diego State Univ., Medical Coll. of Virginia; joined HCA (Hospital Corpn of America) Inc. 1981, held numerous man. positions, including CEO Green Hospital, Scripps Clinic and Research Foundation, San Diego, Centennial Medical Center, Nashville, Pres. Pacific Div. 1995–97, Pres. Western Group 1997–2001, COO 2001–09, mem. Bd of Dirs, HCA, Inc. and HCA Holdings, Inc. 2002–14, Pres. 2002–09, Pres. and CEO Jan.–Dec. 2009, Chair. and CEO 2009–13, Chair. 2013–14; Ind. Dir, CVS Health Corpn 2015–; fmr mem. Bd of Dirs, California Hosp. Asscn, Fed. of American Hosp., St Luke's Community Center, United Way of Metropolitan Nashville; mem. American Soc. of Corp. Execs, Business Council, Nashville Healthcare Council, Community Foundation of Middle Tennessee Bd; Fellow, American Coll. of Healthcare Execs. *Address:* CVS Health, 1 CVS Drive, Woonsocket, RI 02895, USA (office). *Telephone:* (401) 765-1500 (office). *Fax:* (401) 766-2917 (office). *E-mail:* info@cvshealth.com (office). *Website:* cvshealth.com (office); www.cvs.com (office).

BRACKS, Hon. Stephen (Steve) Phillip, AC, DipBusStudies, GradDipEduc; Australian politician; b. 15 Oct. 1954, Ballarat, Vic.; m.; two s. one d.; ed Ballarat Univ.; secondary commerce teacher 1976–81; employment project worker and municipal recreation officer 1981–85; Exec. Dir Ballarat Educ. Centre 1985–89; Statewide Man. Victoria's Employment Programmes 1989–93; Adviser to Premier of Vic. 1990; Prin. Adviser to Fed. Parl. Sec. for Transport and Communications 1993; Exec. Dir Victorian Printing Industry Training Bd 1993–94; mem. Parl. (Labour) 1994–; Deputy Chair. Public Accounts and Estimates Cttee 1996–99; Shadow Minister for Employment, Industrial Relations and Tourism 1994–96; Shadow Treas., Shadow Minister for Finance and Industrial Relations 1996–99; Premier of Vic., Minister for Multicultural Affairs 1999–2007, Treas. of Vic. 1999–2000, Minister for Veterans' Affairs 2004–07; Adviser to Prime Minister of Timor-Leste (East Timor) 2007–; Chair. United Super Pty Ltd (Cbus) 2008–, Cycling Australia 2017–, Melbourne Cricket Ground Trust 2017–; Ind., Chair. Australian Subscription TV and Radio Asscn (ASTRA) 2008–13; Sr Adviser KPMG 2007–12, Nat. Australia Bank 2008–13; mem. Bd Jardine Lloyd Thompson Pty Ltd 2007–, Bank of Sydney 2010–; Australia Automotive Industry Envoy 2009–13; adviser to several major Australian finance and service sector corpns; Hon. Chair. 2010 Road World Cycling Championship. *Publication:* A Premier's State (with Ellen Whinnett) 2012. *Leisure interests:* camping, cycling, distance swimming, tennis. *Address:* Old Treasury Building, 20 Spring Street, Melbourne, Vic. 3000, Australia (office). *Telephone:* (3) 9651-2223 (office). *E-mail:* info@stevebracks.com.au (office). *Website:* www.stevebracks.com.au (office).

BRADBURY, Edward P. (see MOORCOCK, Michael John).

BRADFORD, Barbara Taylor, OBE; British writer and journalist; b. 10 May 1933, Leeds, Yorks.; d. of Winston Taylor and Freda Walker; m. Robert Bradford 1963; reporter, Yorkshire Evening Post 1949–51, Women's Ed. 1951–53; Fashion Ed. Woman's Own 1953–54; columnist, London Evening News 1955–57; Exec. Ed. London American 1959–62; Ed. Nat. Design Centre Magazine 1965–69; syndicated columnist, Newsday Specials, Long Island 1968–70; nat. syndicated columnist, Chicago Tribune-New York (News Syndicate), New York 1970–75, Los Angeles Times Syndicate 1975–81; Dir Library of Congress; Bd mem. American Heritage Dictionary, Police Athletic League, Author's Guild Foundation 1989–; Girls Inc.; Hon. DLit (Leeds) 1990, (Bradford) 1995, Hon. DHumLitt (Teikyo Post Univ.) 1996; numerous awards and prizes. *Television:* ten novels adapted into TV mini-series. *Publications include:* Complete Encyclopaedia of Homemaking Ideas 1968, A Garland of Children's Verse 1968, How to be the Perfect Wife 1969, Easy Steps to Successful Decorating 1971, How to Solve your Decorating Problems 1976, Decorating Ideas for Casual Living 1977, Making Space Grow 1979, A Woman of Substance (novel) 1979, Luxury Designs for Apartment Living 1981, Voice of the Heart 1983, Hold the Dream 1985, Act of Will (novel) 1986, To Be The Best 1988, The Women in his Life (novel) 1990, Remember (novel) 1991, Angel (novel) 1993, Everything to Gain (novel) 1994, Dangerous to Know (novel) 1995, Love in Another Town (novel) 1995, Her Own Rules 1996, A Secret Affair 1996, Power of a Woman 1997, A Sudden Change of Heart 1998, Where You Belong 2000, The Triumph of Katie Byrne 2001, Three Weeks in Paris 2002, Emma's Secret 2003, Unexpected Blessings 2004, Just Rewards 2006, The Ravenscar Dynasty 2007, Heirs of Ravenscar 2007, Being Elizabeth 2008, Breaking the Rules 2009, Playing the Game 2010, Letter from a Stranger 2011, Secrets from the Past 2013, Hidden 2013, Cavendon Hall 2014, The Cavendon Women 2015, The Cavendon Luck 2016. *Leisure interests:* fashion, travelling, art collecting, jewellery, reading. *Address:* Bradford Enterprises, 450 Park Avenue, New York, NY 10022, USA (office). *Telephone:* (212) 308-7390 (office). *Fax:* (212) 935-1636 (office). *E-mail:* maria@mbcomms.co.uk (office); btbreaders@aol.com (office). *Website:* www.barbarataylorbradford.com; barbarataylorbradford.blogspot.co.uk.

BRADFORD, Mark, BFA, MFA; American artist; b. 1961, Los Angeles; s. of Janice Banks; ed Calif. Inst. of the Arts; Joan Mitchell Foundation Award 2002, Louis Comfort Tiffany Foundation Award 2003, Bucksbaum Award 2006, MacArthur Fellowship 2009, Nat. Medal of Arts 2014, David C. Driskell Prize, High Museum of Art 2016 and numerous other awards. *Address:* c/o Sikkema Jenkins & Co., 530 W 22nd Street, New York, NY 10011, USA. *Telephone:* (212) 929-2262. *E-mail:* gallery@sikkemajenkinsco.com. *Website:* www.sikkemajenkinsco.com.

BRADFORD, Hon. Max, MCom (Hons); New Zealand economist, consultant and fmr politician; b. (Maxwell Robert Bradford), 19 Jan. 1942, Christchurch; s. of Robert Bradford and Ella Bradford; m. 1st Janet Grieve (divorced); m. 2nd Rosemary Bradford; two step-d.; ed Univ. of Canterbury, Melbourne Business School; fmr mem. staff, Treasury; fmr mem. staff IMF, Washington, DC; fmr Chief Exec. New Zealand Bankers' Asscn; MP (Nat. Party) for Tarawera (now for Rotorua) 1990–2002; Minister of Labour, Energy, Immigration and Business Devt 1996–98, of Labour, Energy, Defence, Enterprise and Commerce 1998–99, of Tertiary Educ. 1998–99; fmr Chief Exec. Nat. Party; fmr Dir Castalia Strategic Advisors Ltd; f. Bradford and Assocs (consultancy); fmr Assoc., Oxford Policy Man. (UK). *Leisure interests:* fishing, music, reading, sailing. *E-mail:* bradform@gmail.com (home).

BRADLEY, Clive, CBE, MA (Hons); British publishing and media executive and barrister; b. 25 July 1934, London, England; s. of Alfred Bradley and Annie Kathleen Bradley; ed Felsted School, Essex, Clare Coll., Cambridge, Yale Univ., USA; barrister (Middle Temple); with BBC 1961–63; Broadcasting Officer, Labour Party 1963–65; Political Ed., The Statist 1965–67; Group Labour Adviser, Int. Publishing Corpn and Deputy Gen. Man. Daily Mirror and Sunday Mirror 1967–73; Dir The Observer 1973–75; Chief Exec. The Publishers Asscn 1976–97; Convenor Confed. of Information Communication Industries 1984–2014; Chair. Central London Valuation Tribunal 1972–2006, Age Concern Richmond upon Thames 1999–2003, Richmond upon Thames Arts Council 2003–09, BookPower 2008–11; Gov. Felsted School 1972–2009. *Publications include:* many articles and broadcasts on politics, econs, industrial relations, industry media and current affairs. *Leisure interests:* politics, reading, walking. *Address:* 8 Northumberland Place, Richmond upon Thames, Surrey, TW10 6TS, England (home). *Telephone:* (20) 8940-7172 (home); (077) 1015-8877 (home). *E-mail:* bradley_clive@btopenworld.com.

BRADLEY, David John, MA, DM, FRCP, FRCPath, FFPHM, FIBiol, FMedSci; British medical scientist and academic; *Ross Professor Emeritus, Ross Institute of Tropical Hygiene, London School of Hygiene and Tropical Medicine, University of London;* b. 12 Jan. 1937; s. of Harold Robert Bradley and Mona Bradley; m. Lorne Marie Farquhar 1961 (divorced 1989); two s. two d.; ed Wyggeston Grammar School, Leicester, Selwyn Coll., Cambridge and Univ. Coll. Hosp. Medical School, London; Univ. Coll. Hosp. 1960–61; Medical Research Officer, Ross Inst. Bilharzia Research Unit, Mwanza, Tanzania 1961–64; Lecturer, Makerere Medical School, Univ. of East Africa 1964–66, Sr Lecturer in Preventive Medicine 1966–69; Royal Soc. Tropical Research Fellow 1969–73; Sr Research Fellow, Staines Medical Fellow, Exeter Coll., Oxford 1971–74; Clinical Reader in Pathology, Univ. of Oxford Clinical Medical School 1973–74; Prof. of Tropical Hygiene, Univ. of London, Dir and Head of Dept Ross Inst. of Tropical Hygiene, London School of Hygiene and Tropical Medicine 1974–2000, Ross Prof. Emer. 2000–, currently Distinguished Visiting Scientist, School of Geography and the Environment, Univ. of Oxford; Chair. Div. of Communicable and Tropical Diseases 1982–88; fmr Pres. Royal Soc. of Tropical Medicine and Hygiene; Visiting Prof., Univ. of Wales Coll. of Medicine 1995–; corresp. mem. German Tropenmedizingesellschaft; Foreign Corresp. mem. Royal Belgian Acad. of Medicine; Dr hc (Univ. of Leicester); Chalmers Medal, Royal Soc. of Tropical Medicine and Hygiene, Macdonald Medal, Royal Soc. of Tropical Medicine and Hygiene, Harben Gold Medal, Royal Inst. of Public Health. *Publications:* five books and more than 150 papers on tropical medicine and related topics. *Leisure interests:* natural history, landscape gardens, travel. *Address:* School of Geography and the Environment, South Parks Road, Oxford, OX1 3QY; Ross Institute, London School of Hygiene and Tropical Medicine, Keppel Street, London, WC1E 7HT (office); Flat 3, 1 Taviton Street, London, WC1H 0BT, England (home). *Telephone:* (20) 7927-2216 (office); (20) 7383-0228 (home). *Fax:* (20) 7580-9075 (office). *E-mail:* David.Bradley@lshtm.ac.uk (office); david.bradley@zoo.ox.ac.uk (office). *Website:* www.lshtm.ac.uk (office); www.geog.ox.ac.uk (office).

BRADLEY, Donal Donat Conor, CBE, BSc, PhD, ARCS, FRS, FInstP, FIET, FRSA, CEng; British physicist and academic; *Professor of Engineering Science and Physics and Head of Division of Mathematical, Physical and Life Sciences, University of Oxford;* b. 3 Jan. 1962, Windsor, Berkshire; ed Wimbledon Coll., Imperial Coll., London, Royal Coll. of Science, Univ. of Cambridge Cavendish Lab.; served as Royal Coll. of Science Union Departmental Rep. for Physics; BP-funded Research Assoc. 1987; Unilever Research Fellow in Chemical Physics, Corpus Christi Coll., Cambridge 1987–89; Toshiba Fellow within Chemical Lab., Toshiba R&D Center, Kawasaki, Japan 1987–88; Univ. Asst Lecturer in Physics, Cavendish Lab., Cambridge 1989–93, Coll. Lecturer in Physics and Title A Fellow, Churchill Coll. 1989–93, Dir of Studies in Physics 1992–93, Hon. Fellow, Churchill Coll. 2018–; Reader in Dept of Physics, Univ. of Sheffield 1993–95, Prof. 1995–2002, f. Molecular Electronic Materials and Devices Group, Warden of Tapton Hall of Residence 1994–99, Co-Dir Centre for Molecular Materials 1994–95, Dir 1995–2000, Royal Soc. Amersham Int. Sr Research Fellowship 1996–97, Leverhulme Research Fellowship 1997–98; Prof. of Experimental Solid State Physics, Imperial Coll. London 2000–06, Head of Experimental Solid State Physics Group 2001–04, 2005, Dir of Imperial College London Consultants Ltd 2005–06, Head of Dept 2005–08, Lee-Lucas Prof. 2006–15, Deputy Prin., Faculty of Natural Sciences 2008–11, Founder Dir Centre for Plastic Electronics 2009–15, Pro-Rector (Research) 2011–13, Chair. Coll.'s Research Cttee and mem. Coll. Man. Bd 2011–13, Vice-Provost (Research) and mem. Provost's Bd 2013–15, Visiting Prof., Dept of Physics 2015–; Prof. of Eng Science and Physics, Univ. of Oxford 2015–, Head of Div. of Math., Physical and Life Sciences 2015–, Chair. Div. Bd 2015–, mem. Planning and Resource Allocation Cttee 2015–, mem. Univ. Council 2015–, Professorial Fellow, Jesus Coll., Oxford 2015–; Adjunct Chair Prof., Dept of Physics and Inst. of Advanced Materials, Hong Kong Baptist Univ. 2012–; Chief Int. Academic Advisor, Faculty of Science, Harbin Inst. of Tech., China 2012–13; Trustee, Rank Prize Funds 2013–; Chair. Optoelectronics Cttee 2013–; mem. Bd of Dirs Molecular Vision Ltd 2001–12, Solar Press (UK) Ltd 2009–16, Oxford Advanced Research Centres Ltd 2017–; mem. Scientific and Medical Advisory Bd, Abingdon Health Group 2015–17; Hon. Prof., Nanjing Tech. Univ. 2013; Hon. DSc (Univ. of Sheffield) 2014, (Hong Kong Baptist Univ.) 2017; Silver Medal Royal Soc. of Arts 1983, Daiwa Award 1994, EU Descartes Prize 2003, Jan Rajchman Prize, Soc. for Information Display 2005, European Latsis Prize for Nanoengineering, European Science Foundation 2005, Research Excellence Award, Imperial Coll. London 2006, Brian Mercer Award for Innovation, Royal Soc. 2007, Faraday Medal, Inst. of Physics 2009, Faraday Medal, Inst. of Eng and Tech. 2010, Bakerian Lecturer, Royal Soc. 2010, Founders Prize, combined Inst. of Physics, RSC and Inst. of Materials, Minerals and Mining, Polymer Physics Group 2013, Gov.'s Award for Outstanding Contribution in Int. Cooperation (Jiangsu Prov.) 2016, Jinji Lake Talents Award 2017. *Publications include:* numerous papers in professional journals; numerous patents. *Address:* Mathematical, Physical and Life Sciences Division, University of Oxford, 9 Parks Road, Oxford, OX1 3PD, England (office). *Telephone:* (18) 6528-2572 (office). *E-mail:* donal.bradley@mpls.ox.ac.uk (office). *Website:* www.mpls.ox.ac.uk (office).

BRADLEY, Rt Hon. Karen Anne, BSc; British politician and fmr accountant; *Secretary of State for Northern Ireland;* b. (Karen Anne Howarth), 12 March 1970, Newcastle-under-Lyme; m. Neil Austin Bradley; two s.; ed Imperial Coll. London; qualified Chartered Accountant and Chartered Tax Adviser; Tax Man., Deloitte & Touche 1991–98; Sr Tax Man., KPMG 1998–2004, 2007; worked as fiscal and econ. consultant 2004–07; MP (Conservative) for Staffordshire Moorlands 2010–, mem. Work and Pensions Cttee 2010–12, Procedure Cttee 2011–12, Admin Cttee 2012–14; Asst Whip (HM Treasury) 2012–13, Lord Commr (HM Treasury) (Whip) 2013–14, Parl. Under-Sec. (Home Office) 2014–16, Sec. of State for Culture, Media and Sport 2016–18, Sec. of State for Northern Ireland 2018–. *Address:* Northern Ireland Office, 1 Horse Guards Road, London, SW1A 2HQ (office); House of Commons, London, SW1A 0AA, England (office). *Telephone:* (20) 7211-6000 (office); (28) 9052-0700 (Northern Ireland). *E-mail:* karen.bradley.mp@parliament.uk (office); comms@nio.gov.uk (office). *Website:* www.gov.uk/government/organisations/department-for-culture-media-sport (office); www.gov.uk/government/organisations/northern-ireland-office (office); www.karenbradley.co.uk.

BRADLEY, Michael Carl, MBE; British trade union official; b. 17 Feb. 1951, Birmingham; s. of Ronald William Bradley and Doris Florence Bradley (née Hill); m. Janice Bradley (née Holmes) 1973; ed Aldridge Grammar School, Brooklyn Coll., Birmingham; Exec. Officer, Inland Revenue 1971–74; Payroll Admin. Smedley H.P. Foods 1974–80; Researcher, Transport and Gen. Workers Union

(TGWU) 1980–82; Staff Section Organizer, Nat. Union of Lock and Metal Workers 1982–87, Gen. Sec. 1988–92; Gen. Sec., Gen. Fed. of Trade Unions 1993–2011; mem. Unity Trust Advisory Cttee 1986–, Social Security Appeals Tribunal 1986–98, Governing Council, Ruskin Coll., Oxford 1994–, Trade Union Labour Party Liaison Cttee 1996–; Chair. Trade Union Co-ordinating Cttee 2003–; Gov. The Northern Coll., Barnsley 2000–; Trustee, Trade Union Unit Charitable Trust 2000–; Hon. Fellow, Oxford Brookes Univ. 2006. *Leisure interests:* sport, reading, music. *Address:* c/o General Federation of Trade Unions, 4th Floor, Headland House, 308–312 Gray's Inn Road, London, WC1X 8DP, England. *E-mail:* mike@gftu.org.uk.

BRADLEY, Stephen Edward; British diplomatist and consultant; b. 4 April 1958; m. Elizabeth Bradley; one s. one d.; ed Balliol Coll., Oxford, Fudan Univ., Shanghai; joined FCO 1981, Afghan/Pakistan Desk, S Asian Dept 1981–83; Second Sec., Econ., later First Sec., Chancery, British Embassy, Tokyo 1983–87; Deputy Political Adviser to Hong Kong Govt 1988–93; FCO French Desk, W European Dept 1995; Deputy Head of Near East and N Africa FCO Dept 1996–97; Head of W Indian Atlantic Dept 1997–98; Dir of Trade and Investment Promotion, British Embassy, Paris 1999–2002; Minister, Deputy Head of Mission and Consul Gen., British Embassy, Beijing 2002; Consul-Gen., Hong Kong Special Admin. Region 2003–08; Independent Consultant to Grosvenor Ltd, Hong Kong; Marketing Dir, Guinness Peat Aviation, Hong Kong 1987–88, Assoc. Dir, Lloyd George Investment Man., Hong Kong 1993–95, New Millennium Experience Co. 1998–99; mem. Bd of Dirs Husky Energy Inc. 2010–, Swire Properties Ltd 2010–. *Leisure interests:* books, gardens, travel, hiking.

BRADLEY, William (Bill) W., BA, MA; American business executive, fmr politician and fmr professional basketball player; *Managing Director, Allen & Company LLC;* b. 28 July 1943, Crystal City, Mo.; s. of Warren W. Bradley and Susan Crowe; m. Ernestine Schlant 1974; one d.; ed Princeton Univ., Univ. of Oxford, UK; served in USAF Reserve 1967; after graduating from Princeton Univ., attended Univ. of Oxford as Rhodes Scholar; returned to USA to play professional basketball with New York Knickerbockers of Nat. Basketball Asscn (NBA) 1967–77; Senator from New Jersey 1979–96; Payne Dist Prof., Inst. for Int. Studies, Stanford Univ. 1997–98; Sr Advisor and Vice-Chair. of Int. Council, J.P. Morgan & Co. 1997–99; unsuccessful bid for Democratic Party nomination for President of US 2000; Chief Outside Advisor, McKinsey & Co.'s non-profit practice 2001–04; currently Man. Dir Allen & Company LLC (investment bank); mem. Bd of Dirs Quinstreet Inc. 2004–2015, Willis Towers Watson PLC 2002–12 (Presiding Dir 2011–12), Snap Kitchen LLC 2016–; Chair. Int. Advisory Bd, First Data Corporation 2015– (also mem.); mem. Advisory Bd Hakluyt & Co. (UK) 2005–, Eurasia Foundation; fmr Visiting Prof., Stanford Univ., Univ. of Notre Dame, Univ. of Maryland; host, American Voices radio show on Sirius Satellite Radio; Hon. DCL (Univ. of Oxford) 2003; elected mem. Basketball Hall of Fame. *Achievements include:* Olympic gold medalist (basketball) 1964. *Publications:* Life on the Run 1976, The Fair Tax 1984, Time Present, Time Past 1996, Values of the Game 1998, The New American Story 2007, We Can All Do Better 2012. *Address:* c/o Allen & Company LLC, 711 Fifth Avenue, 9th Floor, New York, NY 10022 (office); 1661 Page Mill Road, Palo Alto, CA 94304, USA (home). *Telephone:* (212) 832-8000 (office). *Fax:* (212) 832-8023 (office). *Website:* www.billbradley.com.

BRADMAN, Godfrey Michael, FCA; British business executive; b. 9 Sept. 1936; s. of William I. Bradman and Anne Bradman (née Goldsweig); m. Susan Bennett 1975; two s. three d.; Sr Pnr, Godfrey Bradman & Co. (chartered accountants) 1961; Chair. Bankers London Mercantile Corpn 1969; Jt Chair. Broadgate Devts 1984–91; Chair. European Land and Property Corpn PLC 1992–2003, Ashpost Finance Ltd 1993–2004, Vic. Quay 1993–2000, Pondbridge Europe Ltd 1994–2000; Founder CLEAR (Campaign for Lead-Free Air) 1981–91; Jt Founder and Pres. Campaign for Freedom of Information 1983–, Founder and Chair. Citizen Action and European Citizen Action 1983–91; Chair. Friends of the Earth Trust 1983–91; Founder and Dir AIDS Policy Unit 1987–90; Pres. Soc. for the Protection of Unborn Children Educational Research Trust 1987–2006; mem. Bd of Dirs Property and Land Investment Corpn 2001–11, Midatech Ltd 2004–13, Bridgehall Real Estate Ltd 2012–, UK Residential Properties Ltd 2013–; mem. Council UN Int. Year of Shelter for the Homeless 1987; mem. governing body London School of Hygiene and Tropical Medicine 1988–91; Founder and Jt Chair. Parents Against Tobacco Campaign; Founder Opren Victims Campaign; Trustee Right to Life Charitable Trust; Wilkins Fellow, Cambridge 1999; Hon. Fellow, King's Coll. London, Downing Coll., Cambridge; Hon. DSc (Salford). *Leisure interest:* reading. *Address:* 1 Berkeley Street, London, W1J 8DJ, England (home). *Telephone:* (20) 7706-0189 (home). *E-mail:* gb@godfreybradman.com (office).

BRADSHAW, Benjamin (Ben) Peter James; British journalist and politician; b. 30 Aug. 1960, London, England; civil partner Neal Dalgleish; ed Univ. of Sussex, Univ. of Freiburg, Germany; reporter, Exeter Express & Echo 1984, Eastern Daily Press, Norwich 1985, BBC Radio Devon 1986, BBC Radio Four (The World at One) 1991–97; MP (Labour) for Exeter 1997–, Parl. Pvt. Sec. to Minister of State at Dept of Health 2000–01, Parl. Under-Sec. of State at FCO 2001, Minister in the Foreign Office 2001, Deputy Leader of the Commons 2002, Under-Sec. of State at Dept of Environment, Food and Rural Affairs 2003–06, Sec. of State at Dept for Culture, Media and Sport 2009–10, also Minister for the South West; mem. GMB, NUJ, Usdaw (trade unions), Henry Jackson Soc. Advisory Council; Sony News Reporter Award 1993, Charity Champions Award for Animal Welfare. *Leisure interests:* hiking, theatre. *Address:* House of Commons, Westminster, London, SW1A 0AA, England (office). *Telephone:* (20) 7219-6597 (office). *Fax:* (20) 7219-0950 (office). *E-mail:* ben.bradshaw.mp@parliament.uk (office). *Website:* www.parliament.uk/biographies/commons/mr-ben-bradshaw/230 (office); www.benbradshaw.co.uk.

BRADSHAW, Peter, BA, FRS; American (b. British) professor of aerodynamics; *Professor Emeritus of Engineering, Stanford University;* b. 26 Dec. 1935, Torquay, Devon, England; s. of J. W. N. Bradshaw and F. W. G. Bradshaw (née Finch); m. Sheila Dorothy Brown 1968; ed Torquay Grammar School, St John's Coll., Cambridge; Scientific Officer, Aerodynamics Div., Nat. Physical Lab., Teddington 1957–69; Sr Lecturer, Dept of Aeronautics, Imperial Coll., London 1969–71, Reader 1971–78, Prof. of Experimental Aerodynamics 1978–88; Thomas V. Jones Prof. of Eng, Dept of Mechanical Eng, Stanford Univ. 1988–95, Prof. Emer. 1996–; Hon. DSc (Exeter) 1990; Royal Aeronautical Soc. Bronze Medal 1971, Royal Aeronautical Soc. Busk Prize 1972, AIAA Fluid Dynamics Award 1994. *Publications include:* Experimental Fluid Mechanics 1964, An Introduction to Turbulence 1971, Momentum Transfer in Boundary Layers (with T. Cebeci) 1977, Engineering Calculation Methods for Turbulent Flow (with T. Cebeci and J. H. Whitelaw) 1981, Convective Heat Transfer (with T. Cebeci) 1984. *Leisure interests:* ancient history, walking. *Address:* Flow Physics and Computational Engineering Group, Department of Mechanical Engineering, Stanford University, Stanford, CA 94305-3035, USA (office).

BRADY, Conor, BA, MA; Irish journalist and academic; b. 24 April 1949, Dublin; s. of Conor Brady and Amy MacCarthy; m. Ann Byron 1971; two s.; ed Mount St Joseph Cistercian Abbey, Univ. Coll. Dublin; reporter, Irish Times 1969–73, Asst Ed. 1977–81, Dir and Deputy Ed. 1984–86, Ed. and Group Editorial Dir 1986–2002, Ed. Emer. 2002–; Ed. Garda Review 1973–74; Tutor, Dept of Politics, Univ. Coll. Dublin 1973–74 Presenter/Reporter RTE News At One and This Week 1974–75; Ed. The Sunday Tribune 1981–82; Chair. Bd of Counsellors, European Journalism Centre, Maastricht 1993–98; Pres. World Eds' Forum, Paris 1995–2000; mem. Bd of Dirs World Press Freedom Cttee, Federation International des Editeurs de Journeaux 1995–2000; Commr, Garda Síochána Ombudsman Comm. 2006–11; fmr Chair. British-Irish Asscn; Visiting Prof., John Jay Coll., CUNY; Sr Teaching Fellow, Michael Smurfit Grad. School of Business, Univ. Coll. Dublin; Cttee Mem. UNESCO Int. Press Freedom; Award for Outstanding Work in Irish Journalism 1979. *Publications:* Guardian of the Peace 1974, Up With The Times 2005, Cead Bliain Faoi Rath: The Story of Cistercian College Roscrea 1905–2005 (co-ed.) 2005, A June of Ordinary Murders (fiction) 2012, The Eloquence of the Dead (fiction) 2013, The Guarding of Ireland: The Garda Siochana and the Irish State 1960–2014 2014. *Leisure interests:* travel, reading, swimming.

BRADY, Nicholas F., BA, MBA; American investment banker, financial executive and fmr government official; *Chairman, Darby Overseas Investment Ltd;* b. 11 April 1930, New York; s. of James C. Brady and Eliot Brady; m. Katherine Douglas 1952; three s. one d.; ed Yale and Harvard Univs; with Dillon, Read and Co. Ltd 1954–82, Chair. and CEO 1982–88; Chair. Purolater Inc. 1971–87; Vice-Chair. Breed Registry 1972–74, Chair. 1974–82; Sec. of the Treasury, Washington, Dc 1988–93; apptd to US Senate from NJ 1982; Chair. Templeton Latin American Investment Trust 1994–; Founder and Chair. Darby Overseas Investments 1994–; mem. Bd of Dir Amerada Hess Corpn, Holowesko Partners Ltd, Weatherford International; Dir/Trustee US Templeton Funds; served on five Presidential comms including Chair. Presidential Task Force on Market Mechanisms (known as Brady Comm.), mem. Scowcroft Comm. on Strategic Forces, Kissinger Comm. on Cen. America, Packard Comm. on Defense Man.; fmr US Gov. IMF, IDB, EBRD; fmr Chair. Jockey Club, New York. *Address:* Darby Overseas Investments Ltd 1133 Connecticut Avenue, NW, Suite 400, Washington, DC 20036, USA (office). *Telephone:* (202) 872-0500 (office). *Fax:* (202) 872-1816 (office). *E-mail:* contact@doil.com (office). *Website:* www.darbyoverseas.com (office).

BRADY, HE Cardinal Seán Baptist, DCL; Irish ecclesiastic; *Archbishop of Armagh and Primate of All Ireland;* b. 16 Aug. 1939, Laragh, Co. Cavan; s. of Andrew Brady and Teresa Smith; ed Caulfield Nat. School, St Patrick's Coll., Cavan, St Patrick's Coll., Maynooth, Irish Coll., Rome and Lateran Univ.; ordained priest 1964; language teacher, St Patrick's Coll., Cavan 1967–80; Diocesan Sec., Kilmore 1973–80; mem. Cavan Co. Bd of Gaelic Athletic Asscn; Vice-Rector Irish Coll., Rome 1980, Rector 1987–94; Parish Priest, Ballyhaise, Co. Cavan 1994; Coadjutor Archbishop of Armagh 1995–96, Archbishop of Armagh and Primate of All Ireland 1996–; cr. Cardinal (Cardinal-Priest of SS. Quirico e Giulitta) 2007; participated in Papal Conclave 2013; Chair. Irish Episcopal Conf. *Leisure interest:* Gaelic football. *Address:* 86 Maydown Road Benburb Dungannon Co, Tyrone, BT71 7LN, Northern Ireland (home). *Website:* www.archdioceseofarmagh.com (home).

BRADY, Stephen, AO, CVO, BA (Hons); Australian civil servant and diplomatist; b. 11 June 1959, London; partner Peter Stephens; ed Australian Nat. Univ.; worked in Dept of the Prime Minister and Cabinet 1991–96, Sr Adviser (Govt) to the Prime Minister 1996–98, 2003–04, also worked as Foreign Policy Adviser to Leaders of the Opposition and Shadow Foreign Ministers; now a sr career officer with Dept of Foreign Affairs and Trade (DFAT), Counsellor, then Chargé d'affaires a.i., Embassy in Dublin, Amb. to Sweden (also accred to Denmark, Norway, Finland, Estonia, Latvia, Lithuania and Iceland) 1998–2003, Amb. to the Netherlands and Perm. Rep. to OPCW 2004–08, seconded as Official Sec. to Gov.-Gen. 2008–14, Amb. to France 2014–17; mem. European Australian Business Council; Commdr, Legion of Honour 2017.

BRADY, Thomas (Tom) Edward Patrick, Jr; American football player; b. 3 Aug. 1977, San Mateo, Calif.; s. of Thomas Brady, Sr and Galynn Johnson-Brady; m. Gisele Bündchen 2009; one s. one d.; one s. with Bridget Moynahan; ed Junipero Serra High School, Univ. of Michigan; played coll. football for Univ. of Michigan and set record for completing 214 of 350 passes and 15 touchdowns 1999; drafted as quarterback by New England Patriots of Nat. Football League (NFL) 2000–, became youngest quarterback to win a Super Bowl 2001 season, won second Super Bowl 2003, third 2005, fourth 2015; picked in 1995 Major League Baseball draft in 18th round as a catcher by the Montreal Expos; Pro Bowl 2001, 2004, 2005, 2007, 2009, 2010, 2011, 2012, 2013, 2014, First-team All-Pro 2007, 2010, Second-team All-Pro 2005, Super Bowl MVP 2002, 2004, 2015, AFC Champion 2001, 2003, 2004, 2007, 2011, 2014, Sports Illustrated Sportsman of the Year 2005, Sporting News Sportsman of the Year 2004, 2007, AP Male Athlete of the Year 2007, AP NFL MVP 2007, 2010, AP NFL Offensive Player of the Year 2007, 2010, AFC Offensive Player of the Year 2007, 2010, 2011, NFL Comeback Player of the Year 2009, NFL 2000s All-Decade Team. *Leisure interests:* golf, reading. *Address:* New England Patriots, 1 Patriot Place, Foxborough, MA 02035-1388, USA. *Telephone:* (508) 543-8200. *Fax:* (508) 543-0285. *Website:* www.patriots.com; www.facebook.com/TomBrady.

BRAGG, Baron (Life Peer), cr. 1998, of Wigton in the County of Cumbria; **Melvyn Bragg,** CH, BA, MA, FRS, FRSL, FRTS; British author and television editor and presenter; *Director, Directors Cut Productions;* b. 6 Oct. 1939, Wigton, Cumbria, England; s. of Stanley Bragg and Mary E. Park; m. 1st Marie-Elisabeth Roche 1961 (deceased); one d.; m. 2nd Catherine (Cate) M. Haste 1973; one s. one d.; ed Nelson-Thomlinson Grammar School, Wigton and Wadham Coll., Oxford; Co-Dir (with wife Cate Haste) Melvyn Bragg Ltd (ind. programme maker for BBC Radio, BBC TV and Sky Arts 1965–; BBC Radio and TV Producer 1961–67; TV Presenter and Ed. The South Bank Show for ITV 1978–2010; Head of Arts, London Weekend TV 1982–90, Controller of Arts and Features 1990–2010; Co-Dir Directors Cut Productions 2010–; Deputy Chair. Border TV 1985–90, Chair. 1990–96; writer and presenter of BBC Radio Four's Start the Week 1988–98, In Our Time 1998–, Routes of English 1999–, The Adventure of English 2001; mem. Arts Council and Chair. Literature Panel of Arts Council 1977–80; Pres. Cumbrians for Peace 1982, Northern Arts 1983–87, Nat. Campaign for the Arts 1986–2005; Gov. LSE 1997–; Chancellor Univ. of Leeds 1999–2017; mem. Bd Really Useful Co. 1989–90; Pres. Nat. Acad. of Writing –2009; Chair. MIND 1997–2011; Appeal Chair. Royal Nat. Inst. for the Blind Talking Books Appeal 1998–2005; Domus Fellow, St Catherine's Coll., Oxford 1990; Hon. Fellow, Lancashire Polytechnic 1987, The Library Asscn 1994, Wadham Coll. Oxford 1995, Univ. of Wales, Cardiff 1996, Domus Fellow, St Catherine's Coll., Oxford 1990; Hon. DLitt (Liverpool) 1986, (CNAA) 1990, (Lancaster) 1990, (South Bank) 1997, (Leeds) 2000, (Bradford) 2000; Hon. DUniv (Open Univ.) 1988, Hon. DCL (Northumbria) 1994, Hon. DSc (UMIST) 1998, (Brunel) 2000; Dr hc (St Andrews) 1993, (Sunderland) 2001; John Llewellyn Rhys Memorial Award 1968, PEN Award for Fiction 1970, Richard Dimbleby Award for Outstanding Contribution to TV 1987, Ivor Novello Award for Best Musical 1985, VLV Award 2000, WHSmith Literary Award 2000, four Prix Italia Awards, various BAFTA Awards including Acad. Fellowship 2010, South Bank Show Life Achievement Award, Sandford St Martin Personal Award 2014. *Plays include:* Mardi Gras 1976, Orion 1977, The Hired Man 1985, King Lear in New York 1992. *Screenplays:* Play Dirty 1968, Isadora 1968, The Music Lovers 1970, Jesus Christ Superstar 1973, A Time to Dance (TV) 1992. *Publications include:* novels: For Want of a Nail 1965, The Second Inheritance 1966, Without a City Wall 1968, The Hired Man 1969, A Place in England 1970, The Nerve 1971, The Hunt 1972, Josh Lawton 1972, The Silken Net 1974, A Christmas Child 1976, Autumn Manoeuvres 1978, Kingdom Come 1980, Love and Glory 1983, The Maid of Buttermere 1987, A Time to Dance 1990, Crystal Rooms 1992, Credo 1996, The Sword and the Miracle 1997, The Soldier's Return 1999, A Son of War 2001, Crossing the Lines 2005, Remember Me 2008, Grace and Mary 2013, Now is the Time 2015; non-fiction: Speak for England 1976, Land of the Lakes 1983, Laurence Olivier 1984, Rich, The Life of Richard Burton 1988, The Seventh Seal: A Study on Ingmar Bergman 1993, On Giants' Shoulders 1998, The Adventure of English 2003, Twelve British Books That Changed the World 2006, The South Bank Show: Final Cut 2010, In Our Time (ed.) 2010, The Book of Books: The Radical Impact of the King James Bible 1611-2011 2011. *Leisure interests:* walking. *Address:* 12 Hampstead Hill Gardens, London, NW3 2PL, England. *Telephone:* (20) 7261-3128. *Fax:* (20) 7261-3299. *Website:* directorscutproductions.co.uk.

BRAGHIŞ, Dumitru; Moldovan politician, business executive and diplomatist; b. 28 Dec. 1957, Grătieşti village, Chişinău municipality; ed Institutul Politehnic din Chişinău; First Sec., Komsomol, Moldovan SSR 1989–91; Dir-Gen. Dept of Foreign Econ. Relations, Ministry of the Economy and Reform 1995; First Deputy Minister of Economy and Reform 1997–99; Prime Minister of Moldova 1999–2001; mem. Parl. 2001–13; Leader Social-Democratic Alliance 2001–03; Co-leader Alianţa Moldova Noastra (AMN–Our Moldova), following merger of Alliance of Independents, Liberal Party and Social Democratic Alliance 2003–05 (party disbanded 2011); left politics; Amb. to Russian Fed. 2015–17.

BRAHIMI, Abdelhamid, DEcon; Algerian politician and academic; b. 2 April 1936, Constantine; m.; one c.; officer, Nat. Liberation Army 1956–62; Wali of Annaba (Govt Rep. in province of Annaba) 1963–65; Dir OCI (Algerian-French Bd for promotion of industrial co-operation) 1968–70; Prof. of Econs, Univ. of Algiers 1970–75; Chair. SONATRACH Inc., USA 1976–78; Minister of Planning and Regional Devt 1979–83; Prime Minister of Algeria 1984–88; fled to UK after assassination attempt 1990s; later Dir-Gen. Maghreb Centre for Islamic Studies, London. *Publications include:* Dimensions et perspectives du monde arabe 1977, Stratégies de développement pour l'Algérie (1962–1991) 1992, Justice sociale et développement en économie islamique 1993, Le Maghreb à la croisée des chemins à l'ombre des transformations mondiales (1956–1995) 1996, Aux origines de la tragédie algérienne (1958–2000) 2000.

BRAHIMI, Lakhdar; Algerian UN official, diplomatist and politician; *Andrew D. White Professor-at-Large, Cornell University;* b. 1 Jan. 1934; m.; three c.; ed in Algeria and France; FLN Rep. in SE Asia 1956–61; Perm. Rep. to Arab League, Cairo 1963–70; Amb. to UK 1971–79, to Egypt and Sudan; Diplomatic Adviser to Pres. of Algeria 1982–84; Under-Sec.-Gen., League of Arab States 1984–91, Special Envoy Arab League Tripartite Cttee to Lebanon 1989–91; Minister of Foreign Affairs 1991–93; Rapporteur, UN Conf. on Environment and Devt (Earth Summit) 1992; Special Rep. of UN Sec.-Gen. in South Africa –1994, in Haiti 1994–96; Under-Sec.-Gen. for Special Assignments in Support of Preventive and Peace-making Efforts of the Sec.-Gen. 1997; Special Envoy of UN Sec.-Gen. in Afghanistan, UN Special Mission to Afghanistan 1997–99, Special Rep. 2001–04; Special Envoy of UN Sec.-Gen. in Angola 1998, Special Adviser to UN Sec.-Gen. 2004–05 (retd); Joint Special Rep. of the UN and the League of Arab States for Syria 2012–14, Chair. UN panel for evaluation of peace-keeping operations March–Aug. 2000, other special missions to Zaïre (now Democratic Repub. of the Congo), Yemen, Liberia, and Iraq; Special Rep. of the UN Sec.-Gen. for Afghanistan and Head, UN Assistance Mission in Afghanistan 2001–03; Andrew D. White Prof.-at-Large, Cornell Univ. 2007–; Dir Visitor Inst. for Advanced Study, Princeton 2007; Chair. Ind. Panel on Safety and Security of UN Personnel and Premises 2007; Distinguished Sr Fellow, Centre for the Study of Global Governance, LSE; mem. The Elders 2007–, Comm. on Legal Empowerment of the Poor (UNDP), Global Leadership Foundation; mem. Governing Bd Stockholm International Peace Research Inst.; Harvard Law School Great Negotiator Award 2002, Dag Hammarskjöld Hon. Medal, German UN Asscn 2004, Laureate of the Special Jury Prize for Conflict Prevention, Foundation Chirac 2010. *Address:* Cornell University, 114b Day Hall, Ithaca, NY 14853, USA (office). *Telephone:* (607) 255-0832 (office). *E-mail:* adwhitepal@cornell.edu (office). *Website:* adwhiteprofessors.cornell.edu/2013/04/22/lakhdar-brahimi (office).

BRAHMS, Hero Heinrich, B. Dipl.-Kfm; German business executive; *Senior Advisor, Société Générale Corporate & Investment Banking;* b. 6 July 1941, Munster; s. of Johannes Brahms and Ursula Brahams (née Stuhlmann); ed Univ. Munster; fmrly with SKET Schwermaschinenbau Magdeburg, Deutsche Waggonbau AG and Max-Planck-Institute; joined Hoesch AG, Dortmund 1969, Man. Dir 1982–91; Vice-Chair. Treuhandanstalt (privatization agency), Berlin 1991–94; Chief Financial Officer Kaufhof Holding AG, Cologne 1994–95; Chair. Supervisory Bd Bremer Vulkan (shipyard) 1995; mem. Exec. Cttee and Chief Financial Officer Linde AG 1996–2004; joined DRG Instruments GmbH 2002, currently Head of Production and Medical Security Man.; mem. Supervisory Bd Karstadtquelle AG (renamed Arcandor AG 2007) 2003–08, Chair. 2005–08; Sr Advisor (non-exec.) SG Corporate & Investment Banking (SG CIB) 2004–; Second Vice-Chair. Supervisory Bd Zumtobel AG 2008–10, First Vice-Chair. 2010–15; Chair. Supervisory Bd Telefunken Holding AG 2009; mem. Supervisory Bd and Vice-Chair. Georgsmarienhuette Holding GmbH; mem. Supervisory Bd Deutsche Post AG 2004–14, Wincor Nixdorf AG 2004–, Morgan Stanley AG, Madeleine Schickedanz Co. KG; mem. Shareholders' Cttee M.M. Warburg & Co. Holding KGaA. *Address:* SG Corporate & Investment Banking, Tour S.G., 17 cours Valmy, 92987 Paris, Île-de-France, France (office). *Telephone:* 1-42-14-20-20 (office). *Fax:* 1-42-13-30-17 (office). *E-mail:* fr-relations-medias@socgen.com (office). *Website:* www.sgcib.com (office).

BRAITHWAITE, Sir Rodric Quentin, GCMG; British fmr diplomatist; b. 17 May 1932, London; s. of Henry Warwick Braithwaite and Lorna Constance Davies; m. Gillian Mary Robinson 1961; four s. (one deceased) one d.; ed Bedales School, Christ's Coll., Cambridge; mil. service 1950–52; joined Foreign Service 1955, Third Sec., Embassy in Jakarta 1957–58, Second Sec., Embassy in Warsaw 1959–61, Foreign Office 1961–63, First Sec. (Commercial), Embassy in Moscow 1963–66, First Sec., Embassy in Rome 1966–69, Foreign Office 1969–72, Head of European Integration Dept (External) 1973–75, Head of Planning Staff 1979–80, Asst Under-Sec. of State 1981, Deputy Under-Sec. of State 1984–88, Head of Chancery, Office of Perm. Rep. to EEC, Brussels 1975–78, Minister (Commercial), Embassy in Washington, DC 1982–84, Amb. to Soviet Union 1988–92; Foreign Policy Adviser to Prime Minister 1992–93; Chair. Jt Intelligence Cttee 1992–93; currently Sr Research Fellow in Diplomacy and International Affairs, Univ. of Buckingham; currently Sr Consultant in Global Investment Banking, Deutsche Bank AG, London; Chair. Britain Russia Centre 1994–2000, Moscow School of Political Studies 1998–; mem. European Strategy Bd ICL 1994–2000, Supervisory Bd Deutsche Bank Moscow 1998–99, Bd Ural Mash Zavody (Moscow and Ekaterinburg) 1998–99; mem. Advisory Bd Sirocco Aerospace 2000–03; mem. RAM 1993–2002 (Chair. Bd of Govs 1998–2002); Visiting Fellow, All Souls Coll. Oxford 1972–73; Hon. Fellow, Christ's Coll. Cambridge; Hon. FRAM; Hon. Prof. (Birmingham) 2000; Dr hc (Birmingham) 1998. *Publications include:* Engaging Russia (with Blackwill and Tanaka) 1995, Russia in Europe 1999, NATO at Fifty: Perspectives of the Future of the Atlantic Alliance (jtly) 1999, Across the Moscow River 2002, Moscow 1941 2006, Afgantsy: The Russians in Afghanistan, 1979–89 2011, Armageddon and Paranoia 2017. *Leisure interests:* chamber music (viola), sailing, Russia. *Address:* Humanities Research Institute, University of Buckingham, Yeomanry House, Hunter Street, Buckingham, MK18 1EG, England. *E-mail:* info@buckingham.ac.uk. *Website:* www.buckingham.ac.uk/research/hri.

BRAJOVIĆ, Ivan; Montenegrin politician; *President (Speaker), Skupština (Parliament);* b. 9 March 1962, Podgorica; m.; one s. two d.; ed high school in Danilovgrad, Univ. of Podgorica; fmr del. to SO Danilovgrad; fmr mem. Presidency of Union of Socialist Youth of Yugoslavia; fmr Sec. of Youth of Montenegro; fmr Vice-Pres. Ass. of the Socialist Repub. of Montenegro; co-founder of Socijalistička Partija Crne Gore (Socialist Party of Montenegro), Saveza Reformskih Snaga Jugoslavije za Crnu Goru (Union of Reform Forces of Yugoslavia for Montenegro) and Socijaldemokratska Partija Crne Gore (SDP—Social Democratic Party of Montenegro); fmr Sec. Exec. Bd, SDP, elected Vice-Pres. SDP 2001; fmr Councillor and Vice-Pres., Municipality of Danilovgrad; fmr mem. Ass. of State Union of Serbia and Montenegro, Ass. of Montenegro; mem. Del. to Parl. Ass. of Council of Europe; mem. Skupština Crne Gore (Parl.) 2002–; Minister of the Interior and Public Admin 2009–12, of Transport and Maritime Affairs 2012–16; Leader, Socijaldemokrate Crne Gore (Social Democrats of Montenegro) 2015, Pres. 2016–; several awards, including 9 December Award on the Occasion of the Liberation of Danilovgrad, 19 December Student Award on the Occasion of the Liberation of Podgorica. *Address:* Office of the President, Skupština Crne Gore, 81000 Podgorica, bul. Svetog Petra Cetinjskog 10, Montenegro (office). *Telephone:* (20) 242182 (office); (20) 244759 (office). *Fax:* (20) 242192 (office). *E-mail:* predsjednik@skupstina.me (office). *Website:* www.skupstina.me (office).

BRALY, Angela Fick, BA, JD; American lawyer and business executive; b. 1 July 1961, Dallas, Tex.; m.; three c.; ed Texas Tech. Univ., Southern Methodist Univ. School of Law; Partner, Lewis, Rice & Fingersh LC (law firm), St Louis 1987–99; joined RightCHOICE Managed Care Inc. (now Blue Cross Blue Shield of Mo., an operating subsidiary of WellPoint Inc.) as Gen. Counsel 1999, Pres. and CEO 2003–05, Exec. Vice-Pres., Gen. Counsel and Chief Public Affairs Officer WellPoint, Inc. 2005–07, Pres. and CEO 2007–12, Chair. 2010–12 (resgnd); mem. Bd of Dirs The Procter & Gamble Co., Blue Cross Blue Shield Asscn, Council for Affordable Quality Healthcare, Nat. Inst. for Health Care Man., America's Health Insurance Plans, Cen. Indiana Corp. Partnership; mem. United Way Women's Initiative Cttee, ABA, American Health Lawyers Asscn. *Address:* c/o WellPoint, Inc., 120 Monument Circle, Indianapolis, IN 46204, USA. *E-mail:* boardofdirectors@wellpoint.com.

BRAMALL, Baron (Life Peer), cr. 1987, of Bushfield in the County of Hampshire; **Field Marshal The Lord Edwin Noel Westby Bramall,** KG, GCB, OBE, MC, KStJ; British army officer (retd); b. 18 Dec. 1923, Tunbridge Wells; s. of Maj. Edmund Haselden Bramall and Katherine Bridget Bramall (née Westby); m. Dorothy Avril Wentworth Vernon 1949; one s. one d.; ed Eton Coll.; commissioned in King's Royal Rifle Corps 1943, served in North-west Europe 1944–45, occupation of Japan 1946–47; Instructor, School of Infantry 1949–51; served Middle East 1953–58; Instructor, Army Staff Coll. 1958–61; on staff of Lord Mountbatten with special responsibility for reorg. of Ministry of Defence 1963–64; CO 2nd Green Jackets (King's Royal Rifle Corps) 1965–66; Commdr 5th Airportable Brigade 1967–69; GOC 1st Div. BAOR 1972–73; rank of Lt-Gen. 1973; Commdr British Forces Hong Kong 1973–76; Col Commdt 3rd Royal Green Jackets 1973–84; Col 2nd Gurkhas 1976–86; rank of Gen. 1976; C-in-C UK Land Forces 1976–78; Vice-Chief of Defence Staff (Personnel and Logistics) 1978–79;

Chief of Gen. Staff and ADC Gen. to HM The Queen 1979–82; rank of Field Marshal 1982; Chief of Defence Staff 1982–85; Lord Lt of Greater London 1986–98; Pres. of MCC 1988–89; Trustee Imperial War Museum 1983–98, Chair. 1989–98; JP London 1986; KStJ 1986; Golden Medallion for Service to Christian-Jewish Dialogue 2001; currently Network Participant for UK, European Leadership Network (ELN). *Publication:* The Chiefs: The Story of the United Kingdom Chiefs of Staff (co-author) 1993. *Leisure interests:* cricket, painting, travel, tennis. *Address:* European Leadership Network (ELN), Suite 7, Southbank House, Black Prince Road, London, SE1 7SJ, England. *Website:* www.europeanleadershipnetwork.org.

BRAMMERTZ, Baron; **Serge,** PhD; Belgian lawyer, UN official and author; *Prosecutor, UN Mechanism for International Criminal Tribunals;* b. 17 Feb. 1962, Eupen; ed Univ. of Louvain-la-Neuve, Univ. of Liège, Albert Ludwig Univ., Germany; Deputy Prosecutor, then Chief Deputy Prosecutor, Court of First Instance, Eupen 1996–97, before becoming Deputy to the Prosecutor-Gen., Liège Court of Appeal; Fed. Prosecutor of the Kingdom of Belgium 1997–2002; Scientific Asst, then Prof. of Law, Univ. of Liège –2002; Deputy Prosecutor, Int. Criminal Court in charge of Investigations Div. of Office of the Prosecutor 2003–07; Commr UN Int. Ind. Investigation Comm. into the murder of fmr Lebanese Prime Minister Rafiq Hariri 2006–07; Prosecutor, Int. Criminal Tribunal for the fmr Yugoslavia (ICTY) 2008–16; Prosecutor, UN Mechanism for Int. Criminal Tribunals 2016–; assisted Council of Europe as expert on organized crime; also served on Justice and Internal Affairs Cttee of EC and as adviser for Int. Org. for Migration, leading major research studies on cases of cross-border corruption and trafficking in human beings in Cen. Europe and the Balkans. *Publications include:* has published extensively in int. academic journals on global terrorism, organized crime, corruption, int. co-operation in criminal matters and corruption and int. criminal law. *Address:* United Nations Mechanism for International Criminal Tribunals, New York, NY 10017, USA (office). *Telephone:* (27) 2504207 (office). *Fax:* (27) 2504000 (office). *Website:* www.unmict.org (office).

BRANAGH, Sir Kenneth Charles, Kt; British actor and director; b. 10 Dec. 1960, Belfast, Northern Ireland; s. of William Branagh and Frances Branagh; m. 1st Emma Thompson 1989 (divorced 1998); m. 2nd Lindsay Brunnock 2003; ed Meadway Comprehensive School, Reading, Royal Acad. of Dramatic Art (RADA); f. Renaissance Theatre Co. 1987 (resgnd 1994), Renaissance Films PLC 1988 (resgnd 1994), Shakespeare Film Co. 1999; mem. Bd BFI 1993–97; Officier des Arts et des Lettres; Hon. DLitt (Queen's Univ., Belfast) 1990, (Univ. of Birmingham) 2001; Bancroft Gold Medal, RADA 1982. *Theatre includes:* Another Country (Soc. of W End Theatres Award for Most Promising Newcomer) 1982, The Madness 1983, Francis, Henry V, Hamlet, Love's Labour's Lost, Golden Girls, Tell Me Honestly (writer and dir) 1986, Romeo and Juliet (producer and dir) 1986, Public Enemy (writer, actor) 1986, Napoleon (dir) 1987, Twelfth Night (dir) 1987, Much Ado About Nothing, As You Like It, Hamlet, Look Back in Anger 1989, Napoleon: The American Story (dir) 1989, King Lear (actor, dir) 1989, Midsummer Night's Dream (actor, dir) 1989, Uncle Vanya (co-dir) 1991, Coriolanus (actor), Hamlet (actor, RSC) 1992, The Play What I Wrote (dir) 2001–03, Richard III (actor) 2002, Edmond (actor, Royal Nat. Theatre) 2003, Ducktastic (Albery Theatre, London, dir) 2005, Ivanov (actor, Wyndham's Theatre) 2008, Macbeth (actor, co-dir) (Manchester Theatre Award for Best Actor 2014) 2013. *Films include:* High Season, A Month in the Country, Henry V (actor, dir, writer) (Evening Standard Best Film, NY Film Critics' Circle Best Dir Award, BAFTA Award for Best Dir, European Film Award for Best Dir 1990, European Actor of the Year, European Film Awards 1990) 1989, Dead Again (actor, dir) 1991, Peter's Friends (actor, dir, producer) 1992, Swing Kids (actor) 1992, Swan Song (dir) 1992, Much Ado about Nothing (actor, dir, producer) (British Producer of the Year, London Film Critics' Circle 1993) 1993, Mary Shelley's Frankenstein (actor, dir) 1994, Othello (actor) 1995, In the Bleak Midwinter (dir, writer) 1995, Hamlet (actor, dir, producer) 1996, The Theory of Flight 1997, The Proposition 1997, The Gingerbread Man 1997, Celebrity 1998, Wild, Wild West 1998, Love's Labour's Lost (actor, dir, producer) 2000, How to Kill Your Neighbor's Dog 2002, Rabbit Proof Fence 2002, Harry Potter and the Chamber of Secrets (British Supporting Actor of the Year, London Film Critics' Circle) 2002, Five Children and It 2004, The Magic Flute (dir) 2006, As You Like It (dir) 2006, Sleuth (dir) 2007, Valkyrie 2008, The Boat That Rocked 2009, My Week with Marilyn (Supporting Actor of the Year, London Film Critics' Circle) 2011, Thor (dir) 2011, Jack Ryan: Shadow Recruit (dir and actor) 2014. *Radio includes:* Hamlet (actor, dir) 1992, Romeo and Juliet (actor, dir) 1993, King Lear (actor) 1994, Bequest to the Nation 2005. *Television includes:* The Boy in the Bush, Billy (Trilogy), To the Lighthouse, Maybury, Derek, Coming Through, Ghosts, Fortunes of War, Strange Interlude, The Lady's Not for Burning, Shadow of a Gunman, Conspiracy (Emmy Award for Best Actor 2001), Shackleton 2002, Warm Springs 2004, 10 Days to War (series) 2008, Wallander (series) (also exec. producer) (BAFTA Award for Best Actor 2009) 2008–12. *Publications include:* Public Enemy (play) 1988, Beginning (memoirs) 1989, The Making of Mary Shelley's Frankenstein 1994, In the Bleak Midwinter 1995, screenplays for Henry V, Much Ado About Nothing, Hamlet. *Address:* Shepperton Studios, Studio Road, Shepperton, Middx, TW17 0QD, England.

BRANCH, Taylor, AB; American writer; b. 14 Jan. 1947, Atlanta, Ga; m. Christina Macy; one s. one d.; ed Univ. of North Carolina, Princeton Univ.; mem. staff, The Washington Monthly magazine, Washington, DC 1971–73, Harper's magazine, New York 1973–75, Esquire magazine, New York 1975–76; Lecturer in Politics and History, Goucher Coll. 1998–2000; John S. Guggenheim Fellowship 1983; John D. and Catherine T. MacArthur Fellowship 1991; Christopher Award 1988, Nat. Humanities Medal 1999, Dayton Literary Peace Prize for Lifetime Achievement 2008. *Publications include:* Blowing the Whistle: Dissent in the Public Interest (with Charles Peters) 1972, Second Wind: The Memoirs of an Opinionated Man (with Bill Russell) 1979, The Empire Blues 1981, Labyrinth (with Eugene M. Propper) 1982, Parting the Waters: America in the King Years 1954–63 (Nat. Book Critics Circle Award for General Non-fiction 1988, Pulitzer Prize in History 1989, Los Angeles Times Book Award 1988, Melcher Book Award 1988, English-Speaking Union Book Award 1989, Anisfield-Wolf Book Award 1989) 1988, Pillar of Fire: America in the King Years 1963–65 (American Bar Association Silver Gavel Award 1999, Sidney Hillman Book Award 1999, Imus Book Award) 1998, At Canaan's Edge (Chicago Tribune Heartland Prize for Non-Fiction 2006, Search For Common Ground Book Award 2007) 2006, The Clinton Tapes: Wrestling History with the President 2009, The Cartel: Inside the Rise and Imminent Fall of the NCAA (e-book) 2011, The King Years: Historic Moments in the Civil Rights Movement 2013; other: Blind Ambition (ghostwriter for John Dean) 1976; contrib. of articles to magazines and journals, including 'The Shame of College Sports' in The Atlantic, 2011. *Address:* 1806 South Road, Baltimore, MD 21209, USA (office). *E-mail:* info@taylorbranch.com (office). *Website:* www.taylorbranch.com.

BRANCO, Joaquim Rafael; São Tomé and Príncipe politician; b. 1953; Minister of Foreign Affairs 2000–01, of Public Works 2003; Prime Minister 2008–10; fmr Pres. Movt for the Liberation of São Tomé and Príncipe–Social Democratic Party. *Address:* Movimento de Libertação de São Tomé e Príncipe—Partido Social Democrata (MLSTP—PSD), Estrada Riboque, Edif. Sede do MLSTP, São Tomé, São Tomé and Príncipe (office).

BRAND, Stewart, BS; American editor, writer and publisher; *Co-Chairman and President, The Long Now Foundation;* b. 14 Dec. 1938, Rockford, Ill.; m. 1st Lois Jennings 1966 (divorced 1972); m. 2nd Ryan Phelan 1983; one s. from a previous relationship; ed Phillips Exeter Acad., Stanford Univ.; served in US Army 1960–62; fmrly with Merry Pranksters; consultant to Gov. of Calif. 1976–78; research scientist Media Lab., MIT 1986; Visiting Scholar Royal Dutch/Shell 1986; f. America Needs Indians, Whole Earth Review 1985, Point Foundation, Hacker's Conf.; co-f. The Well (Whole Earth 'Lectronic Link—internet bulletin bd) 1985–, Global Business Network consultancy 1988–, The Long Now Foundation 1996– (currently Co-Chair. and Pres.), All Species project 2000–; Trustee, Santa Fe Inst. 1989–; Golden Gadfly Lifetime Achievement Award, Media Alliance 1989, Erdman Campbell Award for Creative Contributions to the Contemporary Mythopoetic Imagination, Joseph Campbell Foundation 2006, Gene Burd Urban Journalism Award, Urban Communication Foundation 2008, Cleantech Leader of the Year Award, Cleantech Group 2010. *Television:* How Buildings Learn (writer and presenter) 1997. *Publications include:* Two Cybernetic Frontiers 1974, The Media Lab: Inventing the Future at MIT 1987, How Buildings Learn 1994, The Clock of the Long Now 2000, Whole Earth Discipline: An Ecopragmatist Manifesto 2009, SALT Summaries, Condensed Ideas About Long-term Thinking (with Brian Eno) 2011; ed. (or co-ed.) and publr: The Last Whole Earth Catalog 1968–72 (Nat. Book Award), Whole Earth Epilog 1974, Whole Earth Epilog: Access to Tools 1974, The Co-Evolution Quarterly 1974–85, The Next Whole Earth Catalog 1980–81, The (Updated) Last Whole Earth Catalog: Access to Tools (16th edn) 1975, Space Colonies, Whole Earth Catalog 1977, Soft-Tech 1978, The Next Whole Earth Catalog: Access to Tools 1980, (revised 2nd edn) 1981, Whole Earth Software Catalog (Ed.-in-Chief) 1983–85, Whole Earth Software Catalog for 1986, '2.0 edition' of above title (Ed.-in-Chief) 1985, News That Stayed News 1974–1984: Ten Years of CoEvolution Quarterly 1986, SALT Summaries 2011. *Address:* 3E Gate 5 Road, Sausalito, CA 94965, USA (home). *Telephone:* (415) 561-6582 (office). *Fax:* (415) 561-6297 (office). *E-mail:* sb@longnow.org (office). *Website:* www.longnow.org (office); sb.longnow.org.

BRANDAUER, Klaus Maria; Austrian actor; b. 6 Feb. 1944, Bad Aussee; m. Karin Brandauer 1965 (died 1992); m. 2nd Natalie Krenn 2007; ed Acad. of Music and Dramatic Arts, Stuttgart; mem. Burgtheater, Vienna; extensive stage repertoire; Cannes Film Festival Prize for film Mephisto 1981; appeared as Jedermann at Salzburg Festival 1983, as Speer, Almeida Theatre, London 1999;. *Films include:* The Salzburg Connection 1972, A Sunday in October (Októberi vasárnap) 1979, Mephisto 1980, Never Say Never Again 1983, Kindergarten 1984, Colonel Redl 1985, The Lightship 1985, Out of Africa (National Board of Review Award for Best Supporting Actor 1985, Kansas City Film Critics Circle Award for Best Supporting Actor 1985, New York Film Critics Circle Award for Best Supporting Actor 1985, Golden Globe Award for Best Supporting Actor - Motion Picture 1986) 1985, Burning Secret (Golden Ciak 1988, Bavarian Film Awards 1989) 1988, Hanussen 1988, Russia House, Angel in Hell 1989, Streets of Gold 1989, The French Revolution 1989, The Artisan (also dir), Spider's Web 1989, La revolution francaise 1989, The Russia House 1990, Becoming Colette 1991, White Fang 1991, Mario und der Zauberer (also dir) 1994, The Resurrected, Seven Minutes (also dir) 1989, Felidae (voice) 1994, Balkan Island: The Last Story of the Century 1997, Mario and the Magician (also dir) (Andrei Tarkovsky Award 1995) 1994, Die Wand (dir), Rembrandt 1999, The Diver 2000, Vera, nadezhda, krov' 2000, The Gaul 2001, Druids 2001, Jedermanns Fest 2002, Between Strangers 2002, Poem - Ich setzte den Fuss in die Luft, und sie trug 2003, Tetro 2009, Manipulation 2011, The Strange Case of Wilhelm Reich 2012. *Television includes:* Die Ballade von Peckham Rye 1966, Das Käthchen von Heilbronn 1968, Zwei aus Verona 1969, Juno und der Pfau 1969, Das Wort 1970, Fast ein Hamlet 1970, Der alte Richter 1970, Der Tag des Krahenflügels 1970, Friede den Hutten! Krieg den Palasten! 1970, Der Widerspenstigen Zahmung 1971, Emilia Galotti 1971, Weh dem, der lugt 1972, Oscar Wilde 1972, Was Ihr wollt 1973, Wienerinnen 1974, Die Verschworung des Fiesco zu Genua 1975, Das Konzert 1975, Frag nach bei Casanova 1975, Leonce und Lena 1975, Die Babenberger in Österreich 1976, Kabale und Liebe 1976, Darf ich mitspielen? 1976, Jean-Christophe 1978, Jahreszeiten der Liebe 1979, Die Bräute des Kurt Roidl 1979, Die Weber 1980, Wochenendgeschichten 1980, La quinta donna (mini-series) 1982, Jedermann 1983, Roda Rodas rote Weste 1983, Der Weg ins Freie 1983, The Snob 1984, Quo Vadis? (mini-series) 1985, Europa und der zweite Apfel 1988, Jeremiah 1998, Speer (also dir) 1998, Introducing Dorothy Dandridge 1999, Cyrano von Bergerac 2000, Perlasca, un eroe italiano 2002, Die Entführung aus dem Serail 2003, Entrusted 2003, The Crown Prince 2006, Die Auslöschung 2013, Capelli Code 2016 (series). *Address:* Bartensteingasse 8/9, 1010 Vienna, Austria.

BRANDICOURT, Olivier, MSc, MD; French physician and business executive; *CEO, Sanofi SA;* b. 13 Feb. 1956, Casablanca, Morocco; ed Univ. of Paris V, Paris Descartes Univ., Univ. of Paris XII; has worked in pharmaceutical industry since 1987; began career as Medical Dir for the Africa Region, Warner-Lambert/Parke-Davis, also held other sr positions before appointment as Gen. Man., Canada; mem. staff, Inst. of Infectious and Tropical Diseases, Pitié-Salpêtrière Hosp., Paris for eight years, specialized in malaria research in West and Cen. Africa and practised medicine in Rep. of Congo for two years; mem. staff, Pfizer Inc. for 13 years, most recently as mem. Exec. Leadership Team and Pres. and Gen. Man. Emerging Markets and Established Products business units, Head of Global Specialty Care business unit 2008–09, Global Primary Care business unit

2009–12, led Cardiology business in USA, as well as several regional operations; CEO Bayer Healthcare AG 2013–15; CEO Sanofi SA 2015–; mem. Bd of Man., Pharmaceutical Research and Mfrs of America (PhRMA), Council of Int. Fed. of Pharmaceutical Mfrs and Asscn; mem. Bd, Children's Aid Soc., New York; Hon. FRCP. *Address:* Sanofi SA, 174 avenue de France, 75013 Paris Cedex 13, France (office). *Telephone:* 1-53-77-42-23 (office). *Fax:* 1-53-77-42-65 (office). *E-mail:* info@sanofi.com (office). *Website:* www.sanofi.com (office).

BRANDIS, George, BA, LLB, QC, BCL (Oxon); Australian lawyer, politician and diplomatist; *High Commissioner to United Kingdom;* b. 22 June 1957, Sydney; divorced; two c.; ed Univ. of Queensland, Magdalen Coll., Oxford, UK; called to Bar, Queensland 1985; apptd Sr Counsel, Supreme Court of Queensland 2006, QC 2013; mem. Senate for Sydney 2004–, Deputy Leader of Opposition in Senate 2010–13, Deputy Leader of Govt in Senate 2013–15, Leader of Govt in Senate 2015–; Minister for Arts and Sport Jan.–Dec. 2007; Shadow Attorney-Gen. 2007–13; Shadow Minister for the Arts 2010–13; Attorney-Gen. 2013–17, Minister for the Arts 2013–15; Vice-Pres. Exec. Council 2013–; High Commr to UK 2018–; mem. Liberal Party of Australia. *Publications:* Liberals Face the Future: Essays on Australian Liberalism (with T. Harley and D. Markwell) 1984, Australian Liberalism: The Continuing Vision (with Y. Thompson and T. Harley) 1986. *Address:* Australian High Commission, Australia House, Strand, London, WC2B 4LA, UK (office). *Telephone:* (20) 7379-4334 (office). *Fax:* (20) 7240-5333 (office). *E-mail:* GeneralEnquiries.LhLh@dfat.gov.au. *Website:* uk.embassy.gov.au (office).

BRANDMÜLLER, HE Cardinal Walter, Dr theol. habil.; German ecclesiastic, historian and academic; *President Emeritus, Pontifical Committee for Historical Sciences;* b. 5 Jan. 1929, Ansbach, Bavaria; ed Ludwig-Maximilians Univ., Munich; ordained priest, Diocese of Bamberg 1953; carried out pastoral work in Church of St John, Kronach 1953–57, Church of St Martin, Bamberg 1957–60; Prof. of Church History and Patrology, Univ. of Dillingen 1969–70; Prof. of Modern and Medieval Church History, Univ. of Augsburg 1970–97; Parish Priest of the Assumption, Walleshausen, Diocese of Augsburg 1971–98; Canon of the Chapter of St Peter's Basilica 1997–2010; specialist in the history of the Church Councils; Founder and Ed. Annuarium historiae conciliorum (journal) 1969, of series 'Konziliengeschichte' (37 vols) 1979–; mem. Pontifical Cttee for Historical Sciences 1981–98, Pres. 1998–2009, Pres. Emer. 2009–; Pres. Int. Comm. for Comparative Church History 2000–06; Titular Archbishop of Caesarea in Mauretania 2010–; cr. Cardinal (Cardinal-Deacon of S. Giuliano dei Fiamminghi) (non-voting) 20 Nov. 2010; Hon. Prelate 1983, Corresp. mem., Accad. degli Intronati, Siena, Ordinary mem. Pontifical Theological Acad., Rome, Hon. citizenship of Genazzano 2007, of Geltendorf 2011; Kt of Holy Sepulchre of Jerusalem 1981, Cross of the Order of Merit (FRG) 1990, First Class Cross of Honour, Pro litteris et artibus (Austria) 2001, Grand Cross, Order of Holy Sepulchre of Jerusalem 2010; František-Palacký-Medal, Czechoslovakian Acad. of Sciences 2001. *Publications:* The Council of Pavia-Siena 1423–1424 1974, Ignaz von Döllinger on the Eve of the First Vatican Council: A Provocation and the Answer 1977, Handbook of Bavarian Church History (three in four vols) 1991–99, The Council of Constance 1414-1418 (Vol I) 1991, (Vol II) 1997, Galilei and the Church 1994, Holocaust in Slovakia and the Catholic Church 2003, Light and Shadows: Church History Amid Faith, Fact and Legend 2008. *Address:* 00120 Città del Vaticano, Rome, Italy (office). *Website:* www.vatican.va (office).

BRANDT, Werner, MBA, PhD; German business executive and corporate consultant; *Chairman of the Supervisory Board, RWE International SE;* b. Jan. 1954, Herne, North Rhine-Westphalia; ed Univ. of Erlangen-Nuremberg, Darmstadt Tech. Univ.; with Price Waterhouse AG (now PricewaterhouseCoopers AG) 1981–92; mem. Bd of Dirs and Vice-Pres., European Operations, Baxter Deutschland GmbH 1992–99; Chief Financial Officer (CFO) and Labour Dir, Fresenius Medical Care AG 1999–2001; CFO, SAP SE 2001–14; corp. consultant 2014–; Chair. Supervisory Bd, RWE International SE 2016–; mem. Supervisory Bd, Deutsche Lufthansa AG, OSRAM Licht AG, ProSiebenSat.1 Media SE (Chair.). *Address:* RWE International SE, Opernplatz 1, 45128 Essen, Germany (office). *Telephone:* (201) 1215025 (office). *Fax:* (201) 1215265 (office). *E-mail:* info@rwe.com (office). *Website:* www.rwe.com (office).

BRANDTZAEG, Svein Richard, BEcons, PhD; Norwegian business executive; *President and CEO, Norsk Hydro ASA;* b. 23 Dec. 1957, Haugesund; s. of Svein Brandtzaeg and Kari Brandtzaeg (née Bjorlo); m. Turid Anita Merkesvik; three c.; ed Norwegian Univ. of Science and Tech., Trondheim, Norwegian School of Man., Univ. of Auckland, NZ; started career as Project Man., ASV Group; joined Norsk Hydro, Karmøy 1986, various positions within Hydro's aluminium business including Vice-Pres. Casthouses Norway 1998–2000, Pres. Hydro Magnesium, Brussels 2000–01, Pres. Hydro Aluminium Metal Products 2002–03, Pres. Hydro Aluminium Rolled Products 2003–06, Pres. Aluminium Products Business 2006–09, Pres. and CEO Norsk Hydro ASA 2009–; Chair. Int. Aluminium Inst. 2010–12; Chair. Norwegian Univ. of Science and Tech. 2014, mem. Bd 2017–; mem. European Round Table of Industrialists. *Address:* Office of the CEO, Norsk Hydro ASA, Drammensveien 260, 0283 Oslo, Norway (office). *Telephone:* 22-53-81-00 (office). *Fax:* 22-53-27-25 (office). *Website:* www.hydro.com/en (office).

BRANKOVIĆ, Nedžad, MSc, PhD; Bosnia and Herzegovina engineer, politician and professor; b. 28 Dec. 1962, Višegrad; m.; two c.; ed Univ. of Sarajevo; served with Bosnia-Herzegovina Army then apptd to head logistics team attached to Gen. Staff; with IPSA (Inst. for Transport and Communications), Sarajevo 1987–92; Dir-Gen. BiH Railways 1993–98; Dir-Gen. Energoinvest Co. (eng firm) 1998–2002; Sr Teaching Asst, Faculty for Transport and Communications, Univ. of Sarajevo; Minister of Transport and Communications, Fed. of Bosnia and Herzegovina 2003–07, Prime Minister of Fed. of Bosnia and Herzegovina 2007–09 (resgnd); mem. Stranka Demokratske Akcije (SDA—Party of Democratic Action). *Address:* c/o Stranka Demokratske Akcije (Party of Democratic Action), 71000 Sarajevo, Mehmeda Spahe 14, Bosnia and Herzegovina (office). *Telephone:* (33) 216906 (office). *Fax:* (33) 225363 (office). *E-mail:* sda@bih.net.ba (office). *Website:* www.sda.ba (office).

BRANSCOMB, Lewis McAdory, MS, PhD; American physicist and academic; *AETNA Professor Emeritus of Public Policy and Corporate Management and Director Emeritus, Public Policy Program, John F. Kennedy School of Government, Harvard University;* b. 17 Aug. 1926, Asheville, NC; s. of Bennett Harvie Branscomb and Margaret Vaughn Branscomb; m. 1st Anne Wells 1951 (died 1998); one s. one d.; m. 2nd Constance Hammond Mullin 2005; ed Duke and Harvard Univs; Instructor in Physics, Harvard Univ. 1950; Lecturer in Physics, Univ. of Maryland 1950–51; Chief, Atomic Physics Section, Nat. Bureau of Standards, Washington, DC 1954–60, Chief Atomic Physics Div. 1960–62; Chair. Jt Inst. for Lab. Astrophysics 1962–65, 1968–70; Chief, Lab. Astrophysics Div., Nat. Bureau of Standards, Boulder, Colo 1962–69; Dir Nat. Bureau of Standards 1969–72; Chief Scientist, Vice-Pres. IBM Corpn 1972–86; Prof., Dir Public Policy Program Kennedy School of Govt, Harvard Univ. 1986–96, now Dir Emer., AETNA Prof. of Public Policy and Corp. Man. 1988–96, Prof. Emer. 1996–; Adjunct Prof., Univ. of California, San Diego School of Int. Relations and Pacific Studies, Distinguished Research Fellow, Inst. for Global Conflict and Cooperation, Univ. of California; Visiting Prof., Vanderbilt Univ. 1999–2000; mem. tech. assessment advisory council, Office of Tech. Assessment, US Congress 1990–95; mem. Bd, Mobil Corpn, MITRE Corpn; mem. Nat. Acad. of Sciences (mem. Council 1972–75, 1998–), Inst. of Medicine, Nat. Acad. of Eng; Fellow, American Acad. of Arts and Sciences, American Philosophical Soc.; mem. Nat. Acad. of Public Admin, Harvard Univ. Bd of Overseers, Comm. on Global Information/Infrastructure 1995–; Trustee, Carnegie Inst. of Washington 1973–90, Vanderbilt Univ., Nat. Geographic Soc., Woods Hole Oceanographic Inst., LASPAU 1999–2004; 16 hon. degrees; several awards. *Publications:* Empowering Technology 1993, Confessions of a Technophile 1994, Korea at the Turning Point 1996, Investing in Innovation 1998, Taking Technical Risks 2000; numerous articles in professional journals. *Leisure interests:* skiing, sailing. *Address:* John F. Kennedy School of Government, Harvard University, Mailbox 57, 79 John F. Kennedy Street, Cambridge, MA 02138-5801 (office); 1600 Ludington Lane, La Jolla, CA 92037, USA (home). *Telephone:* (617) 495-1853 (office); (858) 454-6871 (home). *Fax:* (858) 456-1752 (home). *E-mail:* lewis_branscomb@harvard.edu (office); lbranscomb@branscomb.org (home). *Website:* ksgfaculty.harvard.edu/Lewis_Branscomb (office); www.branscomb.org (home).

BRANSON, Sir Richard Charles Nicholas, Kt; British business executive; *Chairman, Virgin Group Ltd;* b. 18 July 1950, Blackheath, London; s. of Edward James Branson and Eve Branson; m. 1st Kristen Tomassi 1969 (divorced 1979); m. 2nd Joan Templeman 1989; one s. one d.; ed Stowe School; est. Student Advisory Centre (now Help) 1970; f. Virgin mail-order co. 1969, first Virgin record shop 1971, recording co. 1973, nightclub (The Venue) 1976, Virgin Atlantic Airlines 1984; Founder and Chair. Virgin Retail Group, Virgin Communications, Virgin Travel Group, Voyager Group; took Virgin Music Group public 1986, bought back shares 1988 (rotating chairmanship 1991, Chair. 1991–92, now Life Pres. after sale of shares 1992); Group also includes publishing, broadcasting, construction, heating systems, holidays; Chair. UK 2000 1986–88, Pres. 1988–; Dir Intourist Moscow Ltd 1988–90; f. The Healthcare Foundation 1987, Virgin Books 1989 (sold to Random House 2007), Virgin Radio 1993, Virgin Rail Group Ltd 1996, Virgin Express 1996 (merged with SN Brussels Airlines forming Brussels Airlines 2006), V2 Records 1997 (sold to Universal Music Group 2007), Virgin Mobile (sold to NTL/NTL:Telewest 2006 and re-launched as Virgin Media 2007) 1999, Virgin Blue (Australia) 2000, Virgin Galactic (space tourism co.) 2004, Virgin Comics 2006, Virgin Animation 2006, Virgin Health Bank 2007, Virgin Nigeria 2007, Virgin America 2007, Virgin Fuels 2009; launched Virgin Cola (drink) 1994, Babylon (restaurant) 2001, Virgin Vodka (drink); crossed Pacific in hot air balloon with Per Lindstrand 1991; world record for fastest crossing of the Channel in amphibious vehicle 2004; made unsuccessful attempt with his children at eastbound record crossing of Atlantic Ocean under sail in 99ft (30m) sloop, Virgin Money (also known as Speedboat) 2008; Chair. jury of first Picnic Green Challenge 2007; est. global science and tech. prize, The Virgin Earth Challenge 2007; hosted environmental gathering at his pvt. island, Necker Island (part of British Virgin Islands) in Caribbean with several prominent entrepreneurs, celebrities and world leaders to discuss global warming-related problems March 2008; Patron Int. Rescue Corps, Prisoners Abroad; Commr Broadband Comm. for Digital Devt 2010, Global Comm. on Drug Policy 2011; Hon. DTech (Loughborough) 1993; Dr hc (Kaunas Technology Univ.) 2013; Blue Riband Title for Fastest Atlantic Crossing 1986, Segrave Trophy 1987, UN Correspondents Asscn Citizen of the World Award 2007, German Media Prize 2011, Pres.'s Merit Award, Nat. Acad. of Recording Arts and Sciences 2012, Business for Peace Foundation Award 2014. *Film and TV appearances:* Friends, Baywatch, Birds of a Feather, Only Fools and Horses, Goodness Gracious Me, Tripping Over, Live & Kicking, The Rebel Billionaire 2004, Around the World in 80 Days 2004, Casino Royale 2006, Superman Returns 2006, Rabbit Fever 2006. *Publications:* Losing My Virginity (autobiography) 1998, Screw It, Let's Do It 2006, Business Stripped Bare: Adventures of a Global Entrepreneur 2008, Reach for the Skies: Ballooning, Birdmen and Blasting into Space 2010, Screw Business as Usual 2011, Like a Virgin: Secrets They Won't Teach You at Business School 2013, The Virgin Way: How to Listen, Learn, Laugh and Lead 2014. *Leisure interest:* sailing. *Address:* Virgin Group Ltd, 120 Campden Hill Road, London, W8 7AR, England (office). *Telephone:* (20) 7229-1282 (office). *Fax:* (20) 7727-8200 (office). *Website:* www.virgin.com/richard-branson (office).

BRANSTAD, Terry Edward, BA, JD; American university administrator, health care administrator, politician, state governor and diplomatist; *Ambassador to People's Republic of China;* b. 17 Nov. 1946, Leland, Ia; s. of Edward Arnold Branstad and Rita Branstad (née Garland); m. Christine Ann Johnson 1972; two s. one d.; ed Univ. of Iowa, Drake Univ.; served in US Army 1969–71; admitted to Iowa Bar; Sr Partner, Branstad-Schwarm law firm, Lake Mills, Iowa –1982; mem. Iowa House of Reps 1973–78; Lt-Gov. of Iowa 1979–82; Gov. of Iowa 1983–99, 2011–17; Amb. to People's Repub. of China 2017–; Chair. Educ. Comm. of the US 1997–98; Founder Branstad & Assocs, West Des Moines 1999; fmr Partner, Kayfman, Patee, Branstad & Miller, Washington, DC; flomr financial adviser, Robert W. Baird & Co.; Chair. Pres.'s Comm. for Excellence in Special Educ. 2001–03; Pres. and CEO Des Moines Univ. Osteopathic Medical Center 2003–09; mem. Bd of Dirs American Legion of Iowa Foundation, Iowa Health Systems, Cementech, Featherlite, Liberty Bank, Living History Farms, Advanced Analytical Technologies, Inc., American Inst. of Certified Public Accountants; Chair. Nat. Govs Asscn 1989–90; Visiting Prof., Univ. Iowa; mem. Farm Bureau, American Inst. of Certified Public Accountants (public mem. 2003), Council of State Govts (Chair. 1991), Midwest Gov. Conf., Midwestern Govs' Asscn 1986–87, Republican Govs Asscn (Task Chair. 1997), Nat. Govs Asscn (Chair. 1989), Univ. of Iowa

Alumni Asscn (Distinguished Alumni Award 1999), American Legion, Sons of Norway, Kts of Columbus, Lions; Republican; Hon. mem. Des Moines Rotary; Army Commendation Medal; Hon. LHD (Univ. Osteopathic Medical and Health Service, Buena Vista Coll., Marycrest Coll.); Hon. LLD (Clarke Coll., Dubuque). *Address:* US Embassy in China, 55 An Jia Lou Lu, Beijing 100600, People's Republic of China (office). *Telephone:* (10) 85313000 (office). *Fax:* (10) 85314200 (office). *E-mail:* beijingwebmaster@state.gov (office). *Website:* beijing.usembassy-china.org.cn (office).

BRANTLEY, Mark, BCL; Saint Kitts and Nevis lawyer and politician; *Minister of Foreign Affairs and Aviation, and Premier of Nevis;* b. 11 Jan. 1969, Gingerland, Nevis; s. of Irving Brantley and Cynthia Williams; m.; two d.; ed Univ. of the West Indies, Norman Manley Law School, Jamaica, Univ. of Oxford, UK; began career as Legal Counsel for Nevis Island Admin; co-f. Daniel, Brantley & Associates (law firm), practised before High Court and Court of Appeal; mem. Bar St Christopher and Nevis 1994, Anguilla 1996, Grenada 2009, Antigua and Barbuda 2009; mem. Concerned Citizens Movt 2006–; mem. Nat. Ass. (Fed. Parl.) 2007–, Leader of the Opposition 2007–15, Deputy Premier and Minister of Tourism, Health, Culture, Youth, Sports, and Community Devt, Nevis Island Admin 2013–17, Premier of Nevis 2017–, also Minister of Foreign Affairs and Aviation, St Christopher and Nevis 2015–; host, weekly show on VON Radio. *Address:* Ministry of Foreign Affairs, 3rd Floor, Government Headquarters, Church Street, Basseterre, St Christopher and Nevis (office). *Telephone:* 467-1161 (office). *Fax:* 465-5202 (office). *E-mail:* infocom@sisterisles.kn (office). *Website:* www.gov.kn (office); foreign.gov.kn (office).

BRAR, Davinder Singh, BE, MBA; Indian business executive; *Chairman, GVK Biosciences Pvt Ltd;* ed Thapar Inst. of Eng and Tech., Univ. of Delhi; Systems and Business Analyst, Associated Cement Co. 1974–77; Pres. Ranbaxy Laboratories Ltd 1996–99, CEO and Man. Dir 1999–2004; Chair. GVK Biosciences Pvt. Ltd 2004–, Davix Man. Services Pvt. Ltd; mem. Bd of Dirs Central Bd Reserve Bank of India –2007, Mphasis-BFL Ltd 2004– (Chair. 2015–), moksha8 Pharmaceuticals, Maruti Suzuki India Ltd Inc. 2006–, Barista Coffee Co. Ltd, India Trade Promotion Org., Indian Inst. of Man., Lucknow, Suraj Hotels Pvt. Ltd, Madhubani Investments Pvt. Ltd, Suraj Overseas Pvt. Ltd, Green Valley Land and Devt Pvt. Ltd, Inogent Labs Pvt. Ltd, Confed. of Indian Industry, Nat. Inst. of Pharmaceutical Education and Research, VK Biosciences Pvt. Ltd, Mountain Trail Foods Pvt. Ltd 2014–; Advisor Bd of Dirs Codexis Inc., USA 2005–; fmr Special Advisor, Bd of Dirs Redwood City, USA; fmr Special Advisor, KKR & Co. L.P., Adamas Pharmaceuticals Inc.; mem. Advisory Bd Venture Factory; mem. Bd of Gov. IIM Lacknow; Dean's Medal, Tufts Univ. School of Medicine, Gold Medal, Faculty of Man. Studies, Univ. of Delhi 1974. *Address:* GVK Biosciences Pvt. Ltd., Plot No. 28 A, IDA Nacharam, Hyderabad 500076, India (office). *Telephone:* (40) 66929999 (office). *Fax:* (40) 66929900 (office). *Website:* www.gvkbio.com (office).

BRASH, Donald (Don) Thomas, MA, PhD; New Zealand banker, politician and consultant; *Chairman, Industrial and Commercial Bank of China (New Zealand) Ltd;* b. 24 Sept. 1940, Wanganui; s. of Rev. Dr Alan A. Brash and Eljean Brash; m. 1st Erica Beatty 1964; m. 2nd Je Lan Lee 1989; two s. one d.; ed Christchurch Boys' High School, Canterbury Univ. and Australian Nat. Univ.; Gen. Man. Broadbank Corpn Ltd 1971–81; Gen. Man. Finance and Computer Sector, Fletcher Challenge Ltd 1981–82; Man. Dir New Zealand Kiwifruit Authority 1982–86; Man. Dir Trust Bank Group 1986–88; Gov. Reserve Bank of New Zealand 1988–2002; mem. Parl. (Nat. Party) 2002–07; Nat. Spokesperson (Opposition) on Finance 2002–03; Leader, Nat. Party and Parl. Opposition 2003–06; Chair. Consultative Cttee on GST 1985–88; Chair. New Zealand Government 2025 Taskforce 2009–11; Chair. Industrial and Commercial Bank of China (New Zealand) Ltd 2013–; mem. New Zealand Monetary and Econ. Council 1974–78, New Zealand Planning Council 1977–80; fmr Adjunct Prof. of Banking, Business School, AUT Univ.; fmr Adjunct Prof., Faculty of Law and Management, La Trobe Univ.; Distinguished Fellow, New Zealand Asscn of Economists 2007; Hon. Prof., Univ. of International Business and Economics, Beijing 2012; Dr hc (Canterbury) 1999; NZIER-Qantas Econs Award 1999, inducted into New Zealand Business Hall of Fame 2002. *Publications include:* New Zealand's Debt Servicing Capacity 1964, American Investment in Australian Industry 1966, Incredible Luck 2014. *Leisure interest:* kiwifruit growing. *Address:* Unit 311, 184 Symonds Street, Auckland 1010, New Zealand (office). *Telephone:* (21) 420-144 (office). *E-mail:* mail@donbrash.com (home). *Website:* www.donbrash.com.

BRASSAC, Philippe; French business executive; *CEO, Crédit Agricole SA;* b. 31 Aug. 1959; ed École Nationale de la Statistique et de l'Admin Économique; joined Crédit Agricole du Gard 1982, held several exec. offices before being apptd Deputy CEO Crédit Agricole des Alpes Maritimes (now Crédit Agricole Provence Côte d'Azur) 1994–99, joined Caisse Nationale de Crédit Agricole as Dir of Relations with Regional Banks 1999–2001, CEO Crédit Agricole Provence Côte d'Azur 2001–08, Deputy Chair. Fédération Nationale du Crédit Agricole 2008–10, Sec.-Gen. 2010–15, Deputy Chair. SAS Rue La Boétie (Crédit Agricole SA's majority shareholder) 2010–15, CEO Crédit Agricole SA 2015–. *Address:* Crédit Agricole SA, 91–93 blvd Pasteur, 75015 Paris, France (office). *Telephone:* 1-43-23-52-02 (office). *Fax:* 1-43-23-34-48 (office). *E-mail:* info@credit-agricole-sa.fr (office). *Website:* www.credit-agricole-sa.fr (office).

BRASSARD, Gilles, OC, PhD, FRS, FRSC; Canadian quantum physicist, computer scientist and academic; *Canada Research Chair in Quantum Information Processing, Université de Montréal;* ed Cornell Univ., USA; Faculty mem. Université de Montréal since 1980s, currently Canada Research Chair in Quantum Information Processing 2001–; Foreign mem. Latvian Acad. of Sciences 1998; Fellow, Canadian Inst. for Advanced Research (CIFAR) 2002, Int. Asscn for Cryptologic Research 2006; Dr hc (ETH, Zurich) 2010; E.W.R. Steacie Memorial Fellowship 1992, Prix Urgel-Archambault 1992, 'Grand Débrouillard', Les Débrouillards 1993, Prix Steacie 1994, Scientist of the Year, La Presse 1995, Killam Research Fellow 1997, Prix Marie-Victorin 2000, Rank Prize in Optoelectronics 2006, NSERC Award of Excellence 2006, IACR Distinguished Lecturer 2008, Gerhard Herzberg Canada Gold Medal for Science and Eng 2009, Killam Prize for Natural Sciences, Canada Council for the Arts 2011, Wolf Prize for Physics (co–recipient) 2018. *Achievements include:* with Charles H. Bennett, developed the BB84 protocol, the most secure method of encrypting information for confidential transfer from one party to another 1984, discovery hailed as one of the "10 emerging technologies that will change the world" by MIT 2003. *Publications:* Algorithmique: Conception et analyse (with P. Bratley) 1987, Modern Cryptology, Lecture Notes in Computer Science, Vol. 325 1988, Advances in Cryptology – Proceedings of Crypto '89, Santa Barbara, Calif. Aug. 1989, Lecture Notes in Computer Science, Vol. 435 (ed.) 1990, Fundamentals of Algorithmics (with P. Bratley) 1996; numerous papers in professional journals. *Address:* Département d'informatique et de recherche opérationnelle, Pavillon André-Aisenstadt, 2215 chemin de la Tour, Montréal, PQ H3T 1J4, Canada (office). *Telephone:* (514) 343-6807 (office). *Fax:* (514) 343-5834 (office). *E-mail:* brassard@iro.umontreal.ca (office). *Website:* www-labs.iro.umontreal.ca/~brassard (office).

BRASSEUR, Claude; French actor; b. (Claude Espinasse), 15 June 1936, Paris; s. of Pierre Espinasse (known as Pierre Brasseur) and Odette Joyeux; m. 2nd Michèle Cambon 1970; one s.; ed René Girard and René Simon drama schools, Paris; Beatrix Dussane Trophy 1974, César Awards for Best Supporting Actor in Un éléphant ça trompe énormément 1976, Best Actor in La guerre des polices 1980; Chevalier, Ordre Nat. du Mérite. *Plays include:* Un ange passe, L'enfant du dimanche, Match 1964, La calèche 1966, Britannicus 1966, Du côté de chez l'autre 1971, Les jeux de la nuit 1974, George Dandin 1987, Le Souper 1989, Dîner de cons 1993, La Dernière salve 1995, À torts et à raisons 1999. *Films include:* Rue des prairies, Les yeux sans visage 1959, Le noeud de vipères, La verte moisson, Pierrot la tendresse 1960, Le caporal épinglé, La bride sur le cou 1961, Germinal 1962, Dragées au poivre, Peau de banane 1963, Bande à part, Lucky Joe 1964, L'enfer (unfinished), Le chien fou, Du rififi à Paname 1966, Un homme de trop, Caroline chérie 1967, La chasse royale, Catherine ou il suffit d'un amour 1968, Le viager, Le portrait de Marianne, Un cave 1971, Une belle fille comme moi 1972, Bel ordure 1973, Les seins de glace 1974, Il faut vivre dangereusement, L'agression 1975, Attention les yeux 1976, Barocco, Le grand Escogriffe, Un éléphant ça trompe énormément 1976, Monsieur papa, Nous irons au paradis, L'état sauvage 1977, L'argent des autres, Une histoire simple 1978, La guerre des polices 1979, La boume 1980, Une langouste au petit déjeuner, Une robe noire pour un tueur, L'ombre rouge, Une affaire d'hommes 1981, Josepha, Guy de Maupassant 1982, Légitime violence 1982, T'es heureuse? Moi toujours 1983, la Crime 1983, Signes extérieurs de richesse 1983, Souvenir, Le Léopard 1984, Palace 1985, Les loups entre eux 1985, La gitane 1986, Taxi Boy 1986, Descente aux enfers 1986, George Dandin 1988, Radio Corbeau 1989, l'Union sacrée 1989, l'Orchestre Rouge 1989, Dancing Machine 1990, Sale comme un Ange 1991, Le Bal des Casse-Pieds 1992, Le Souper 1992, le Fil de L'Horizon 1993, Le plus beau pays du monde et fait d'hiver 1999, Fait d'hiver 1999, La Taule 2000, Toreros et les Acteurs 2000, Malabar Princess 2004, L'Amour aux trousses 2005, Les Parrains (voice) 2005, Camping 2006, J'invente rien 2006, Les Petites Vacances 2006, Le Héros de la famille 2006, Fauteuils d'orchestre 2006. *Television appearances include:* Le paysan parvenu, La misère et la gloire, Don Juan, Le mystère de la chambre jaune (as Rouletabille), Les eaux mêlées, Vidocq, Les nouvelles aventures de Vidocq, l'Équipe, l'Argent, Véga 1999, Soraya 2003, Franck Keller 2003. *Leisure interests:* boxing, swimming, football, bobsleighing, skiing. *Address:* c/o Artmédia, 20 avenue Rapp, 75007 Paris, France.

BRATUŠEK, Alenka, BA, MA; Slovenian public official and politician; *President, Zavezništvo Alenke Bratušek (ZaAB—Alliance of Alenka Bratušek);* b. 31 March 1970, Celje; partner; one s. one d.; ed Faculty of Natural Sciences and Tech. and Faculty for Social Sciences, Univ. of Ljubljana; worked for a small textile co. following graduation; with Ministry of the Economy 1995–99, helped set up small business promotion network; moved to Ministry of Finance 1999, Head of Budget Directorate 2004, played active role in preparations for Slovenian EU Council presidency 2007–08; mem. Nat. Ass. 2011–, Chair. Comm. for Public Finance Control, mem. Cttee on Finance and Monetary Policy, Cttee on Justice, Public Admin and Local Self-Govt; Pres. Positive Slovenia party 2013–14; Prime Minister of Slovenia 2013–14 (resgnd); had nominated herself to position of Vice-Pres. of EC under the Juncker Presidency, nomination rejected Oct. 2014; Founder and Pres. Zavezništvo Alenke Bratušek (Alliance of Alenka Bratušek) 2014–. *Address:* Zavezništvo Alenke Bratušek, Štefanova ulica 5, 1000 Ljubljana, Slovenia (office). *Telephone:* (8) 3872617 (office). *E-mail:* info@zaveznistvo.si (office). *Website:* www.zaveznistvo.si (office).

BRAUER, Arik; Austrian artist; b. 4 Jan. 1929, Vienna; s. of Simon Moses Brauer and Hermine Brauer; m. Naomi Dahabani 1957; three d.; ed Wiener Kunstakademie; underground, Vienna 1942–45; after studies in Vienna travelled in Africa, France, Spain, Austria, Greece and Israel 1950–58, USA, E Africa, Ethiopia, Japan 1965–74; Prof. Acad. of Fine Arts Vienna 1986; one-man exhbns 1956–, in Austria, Germany, Switzerland, France, Denmark, Liechtenstein, Italy, Canada, Sweden, Yugoslavia, Bulgaria, Norway, Japan, Israel and USA; world travelling exhbn 1979–; group exhbns, including travelling exhbns with Wiener Schule des Phantastischen Realismus 1962–, in W Europe, USA, S. America, Poland, Yugoslavia, Israel, Iran, Turkey, Japan; Scenery for The Seven Mortal Sins (Vienna 1972), Bomarzo (Zürich 1970); scenery and costumes for Medea (Vienna 1972), The Magic Flute (Paris 1977); book, design and costumes for Sieben auf einen Streich (Vienna 1978); mural design for Univ. of Haifa, Israel 1982–; designer Brauerhaus, Vienna 1983–95; Guest Lecturer, Int. Summer Acad. for Fine Arts, Salzburg 1982, 83; two gold records for Erich Brauer LP (poetry, music and songs) 1971,. *Publications:* Zigeunerziege 1976, Runde Fliegt 1983, Der Teufel und der Maler 2000. *Leisure interests:* alpinism, skiing, windsurfing. *Address:* c/o Art Directory GmbH, An den Römerhügeln 1, 82031 Grünwald, Germany. *Telephone:* (89) 41074682. *E-mail:* info@art-directory.org. *Website:* www.art-directory.info; www.arikbrauer.com.

BRAUER, Stephen Franklin, BEcons; American business executive and diplomatist; *Chairman, President and CEO, Hunter Engineering Company;* b. 3 Sept. 1945, St Louis, Mo.; m. Camilla Thompson Brauer 1971; three c.; ed Westminster Coll.; First Lt, US Army Corps of Engineers 1967–70, tour of duty in Viet Nam; joined Hunter Engineering Co. 1971, Exec. Vice-Pres. and COO 1978–81, Pres. and CEO 1981–2001, Chair., Pres. and CEO 2003–; Amb. to Belgium 2001–03; mem. Bd of Dirs Ameren Corpn 2006–13; pnr and part-owner of St Louis Cardinals professional baseball team; Trustee St Louis Art Museum, Missouri Botanical Garden (Pres. Bd Trustees), Smithsonian Inst., Washington, DC, Washington Univ.; Hon. Consul of Belgium in Missouri state 1987–2001. *Leisure interest:* baseball. *Address:* Hunter Engineering Company, 11250 Hunter

Drive, Bridgeton, MO 63044, USA (office). *Telephone:* (314) 731-3020 (office). *Fax:* (314) 731-1776 (office). *Website:* www.hunter.com (office).

BRAUMAN, John I., PhD; American chemist and academic; *J.G. Jackson-C.J. Wood Professor Emeritus of Chemistry, Stanford University;* b. 7 Sept. 1937, Pittsburgh, Pa; s. of Milton Brauman and Freda S. Brauman; m. Sharon Lea Kruse 1964; one d.; ed Massachusetts Inst. of Tech., Univ. of California, Berkeley, Univ. of California, Los Angeles; Asst Prof., Stanford Univ. 1963–69, Assoc. Prof. 1969–72, Prof. 1972–80, J. G. Jackson-C. J. Wood Prof. 1980, now Prof. Emer., Chair. 1979–83, 1995–96, Assoc. Dean for Natural Sciences, Humanities and Sciences 1999–2003, apptd Assoc. Dean of Research 2005; Deputy Ed. Science 1985–2000, Chair. Sr Editorial Bd 2000–; mem. editorial bds several journals including Nouveau Journal de Chimie 1977–85, Chemical Physics Letters 1982–85, Chemical and Engineering News 1982–84, Journal of Physical Chemistry 1985–87; mem. Bd of Dirs, Camille and Henry Dreyfus Foundation 2006–; mem. Nat. Research Council Bd on Chemical Sciences and Tech., advisory panels of NASA, Nat. Science Found., Atomic Energy Comm.; mem. NAS (Home Sec. 2003–11), AAAS (Chair. Sr Editorial Bd 2001–11); ACS Award in Pure Chemistry 1973, Harrison-Howe Award 1976, ACS, James Flack Norris Award in Physical Organic Chemistry 1986, Arthur C. Cope Scholar Award 1986, R.C. Fuson Award 1986, NAS Award in Chemical Sciences 2001, Linus Pauling Award 2002, National Medal of Science Award 2002, Willard Gibbs Medal 2003, Charles Lathrop Parsons Award, American Chemical Soc. 2017. *Publications:* over 270 publs in scientific journals. *Address:* Department of Chemistry, Stanford University, Stanford, CA 94305-5080 (office); 849 Tolman Drive, Palo Alto, CA 94305, USA (home). *Telephone:* (415) 723-3023 (office); (415) 493-1378 (home). *Fax:* (650) 725-0259 (office). *E-mail:* brauman@stanford.edu (office). *Website:* www.stanford.edu/dept/chemistry/faculty/brauman (office).

BRAUN, Christian Frédéric; Luxembourg diplomatist; *Permanent Representative, United Nations;* b. 30 May 1958, Luxembourg; m.; four c.; ed Catholic Univ. of Louvain, Belgium; worked for Political Affairs Directorate, Ministry of Foreign Affairs (MFA) 1987–90, European Correspondent 1990–93; Exec. Sec. Peace Conference for Yugoslavia, The Hague 1992; Deputy Political Dir, MFA 1993–95, Counsellor, Perm. Representation to EU 1995–97, Enlargement Counsellor 1998–2002; Perm. Rep. to Int. Orgs in Vienna 2005–07; Amb. to Austria 2005–07; Dir for Int. Econ. Relations, MFA 2007–08; Perm. Rep. to EU 2008–16, Perm. Rep. to UN 2016–. *Address:* Permanent Mission of Luxembourg, 17 Beekman Place, New York, NY 10022, USA (office). *Telephone:* (212) 935-3589 (office). *Fax:* (212) 935-5896 (office). *E-mail:* newyork.rp@mae.etat.lu (office). *Website:* www.un.int/luxembourg (office).

BRAUN, Ewa, MA; Polish costume designer, production decorator and art director; *Lecturer, National Film, Television and Theatre School in Łódź;* b. 2 Aug. 1944, Kraków; ed Warsaw Univ.; costume designer, Documentary Film Producers 1967–72; interior decorator, Art Dir, Film Production Agency 1972–99; Lecturer, Nat. Film, TV and Theatre School, Łódź 1999–; mem. Polish Film Makers Acad., American Acad. of Motion Picture Arts and Sciences; Golden Medal for Merit to Culture 2014, Kt's Cross of the Order of Polonia Restituta 2014; Special Golden Dinosaur, Int. Film Festival Etiuda & Anima 2018. *Films:* interior decorations and designs in over 60 films including Illumination 1972, Jealousy and Medicine 1973, Hotel Pacific 1975, Camouflage 1977, Career of Nikodem Dyzma 1979, Queen Bona 1980, C.K. Dezerterzy 1985, Young Magician (Gdańsk Bronze Lions Gèrald1987) 1986, Europe, Europe 1990, Eminent Domain 1991, Coupable d'innocence 1992, The Silent Touch 1992, Schindler's List (Acad. Award for Art Direction/Set Decoration 1994) 1993, Les Milles 1995, Holy Week 1995, Bandit 1996, Palais de la Santé 1997, Brother of Our God 1997, Jacob the Liar 1997, Gold Deserts 1998, Capri Fischer 2014. *Leisure interests:* movies, travels, music, literature. *Address:* Polish National Film, Television and Theatre School, ul. Targowa 61/ 63, 90-323 Łódź, Poland (office). *Telephone:* (42) 2755800 (office); (22) 6428153 (home). *E-mail:* promo@filmschool.lodz.pl (office); braunewa@hotmail.com (home); ebraun@parta.onet.pl (home). *Website:* www.filmschool.lodz.pl.

BRAUN, Mike, BA, MBA; American business executive and politician; *Senator from Indiana;* b. 24 March 1954, Jasper, Ind.; m. Maureen Braun 1976; two s. two d.; ed Wabash Coll., Harvard Univ.; co-founder Crystal Farms, Inc. 1979; Founder and CEO, Meyer Distributing mid-1980s–; mem. State House of Reps, Ind. 2014–17; Senator from Indiana 2019–; mem. Bd Jasper School 2004–14; mem. Sub Cttees on Aging, Budget, Environment and Public Works, Health, Educ., Labor and Pensions; Republican; Distributor of the Year, Specialty Equipment Market Asscn, Entrepreneur of the Year Award, Dubois Strong. *Address:* United State Senate, B85 Russell Senate Office Building, Washington, DC 20510, USA (office). *Telephone:* (202) 224-4814 (office). *Website:* www.braun.senate.gov (office); www.meyerdistributing.com (office); www.mikebraunforindiana.com.

BRAUN, Volker; German poet and playwright; b. 7 May 1939, Dresden; ed Univ. of Leipzig; Asst Dir Deutsches Theater, Berlin 1972–77, Berlin Ensemble 1979–90; Brother Grimm Prof., Univ. of Kassel 1999–2000; mem. Akad. der Künste, Berlin, Deutsche Akademie für Sprache und Dichtung, Sächsischen Akademie der Künste; Heinrich Mann Prize 1980, Bremen Literature Prize 1986, Nat. Prize, First Class 1988, Berlin Prize 1989, Schiller Commemorative Prize 1992, Deutschen Kritikerpreis 1996, Erwin Schrittmatter Prize 1998, Georg Büchner Prize 2000. *Plays:* Die Kipper 1965, Grosser Frieden 1979, Dmitri 1982, Die Ubergangsgesellschaft 1987, Lenins Tod 1988, Transit Europa: Der Ausflug der Toten 1988, Böhmen am Meer 1992. *Publications:* Provokation für mich 1965, Vorläufiges 1966, KriegsErklärung 1967, Wir und nicht sie 1970, Gedichte 1972, Gegen die symmetrische Welt 1974, Es genügt nicht die einfache Wahrheit 1975, Unvollendete Geschichte 1977, Training des aufrechten Gangs 1979, Hinze-Kunze-Roman 1985, Langsamer knirschender Morgen 1987, Verheerende Folgen magnelnden Anscheins innerbetrieblicher Demokratie (essays) 1988, Der Stoff zum Leben 1990, Bodenloser Satz 1990, Der Wendehals: Eine Enterhaltung 1995, Lustgarten Preussen 1996, Wir befinden uns soweit wohl. Wir sind erst einmal am Ende 1998, Tumulus 1999, Das Wirklichgewollte 2000, Das unbesetzte Gebiet 2004, Auf die schönen Possen 2005, Das Mittagsmahl (Ver.di-Literature Prize) 2007, Machwerk oder Das Schichtbuch des Flick von Lauchhammer 2008, Die hellen Haufen 2011. *Address:* Wolfshagenerstrasse 68, 13187 Berlin, Germany (home).

BRAUNGART, Michael, PhD; German chemist and academic; *Professor of Process Engineering, University of Lüneburg;* b. 7 Feb. 1958, Schwäbisch Gmünd; ed Univs of Darmstadt, Konstanz and Hannover; fmr Greenpeace activist, led formation of Chem. Section of Greenpeace International, Leader of Greenpeace Chem. 1985; Prof. of Process Eng, Leuphana Univ. of Lüneburg 1994–, also Dir interdisciplinary materials flow man. Masters programme; Founder and Scientific Dir Environmental Protection Encouragement Agency International Umweltforschung GmbH, Hamburg 1987–; Co-founder and Prin. McDonough Braungart Design Chemistry, Charlottesville, Va, USA; Co-founder and Scientific Dir HUI Hamburger Umweltinstitut eV 1989; currently holds Cradle-to-Cradle for Innovation and Quality Chair, Rotterdam School of Man., Erasmus University; Visiting Prof., Univ. of Twente 2010–, TU Delft 2011–. *Publications:* Hannover Principles of Design: Design for Sustainability 2000, Cradle to Cradle: Remaking the Way We Make Things 2002, David Gottfried Global Green Building Entrepreneurship Award 2017. *Address:* Leuphana University of Lüneburg, Universitätsallee 1, C13.116, 21335 Lüneburg, Germany (office). *Telephone:* (41) 31677-2634 (office). *E-mail:* michael.braungart@euphana.de (office); braungart@braungart.com (office). *Website:* www.leuphana.de (office); www.braungart.com (office).

BRAUNWALD, Eugene, MD; American cardiologist and academic; *Hersey Distinguished Professor of Theory and Practice of Physical Medicine, Harvard Medical School;* b. 15 Aug. 1929, Vienna, Austria; s. of Wilhelm Braunwald and Clara Wallach; m. 1st Nina Starr 1952 (deceased); three d.; m. 2nd Elaine Smith 1994; ed New York Univ.; successively Chief of Section of Cardiology, Clinic of Surgery, Cardiology Br. and Clinical Dir Nat. Heart, Lung & Blood Inst. 1958–68; Prof. and Chair. Dept of Medicine, Univ. of Calif., San Diego School of Medicine 1968–72; Hersey Prof. of Theory and Practice of Physical Medicine, Harvard Medical School 1972–96, Hersey Distinguished Prof. of Theory and Practice of Physical Medicine 1996–, Faculty Dean for Academic Programs 1996–2003; Sr Consultant in Medicine, Mass. Gen. Hosp. 1994–; Vice-Pres. Academic Programs Partners Healthcare System 1996–2003; Herrmann Blumgart Prof. of Medicine 1980–89; Chair. Dept of Medicine, Peter Bent Brigham Hosp. (now Brigham & Women's Hosp.) 1972–96; Founding Chair. TIMI Study Group, Brigham & Women's Hosp. 1984–; more than 14 hon. degrees; J. Allyn Taylor Int. Prize in Medicine 1993, Warren Alpert Foundation Prize 2001, Libin/AHFMR Prize for Excellence in Cardiovascular Research 2004, and many other awards. *Publications:* over 1,200 articles, reviews and book chapters. *Address:* TIMI Study Group, 350 Longwood Avenue, Boston, MA 02215, USA (office). *Telephone:* (617) 732-8989 (office). *Fax:* (617) 975-0955 (office). *E-mail:* ebraunwald@partners.org (office). *Website:* www.timi.org (office).

BRÄUTIGAM, Hans Otto, DJur, LLM; German fmr diplomatist and fmr politician; b. 6 Feb. 1931, Völklingen, Saar; s. of Maximilian Bräutigam and Margarethe Sauerwald; m. Dr Hildegard Becker 1961; two s.; ed Bonn Univ. and Harvard Law School, USA; Research Asst in Int. Law, Heidelberg 1958–62; served in foreign service of FRG 1962–74; Deputy Head, Perm. Representation of FRG to GDR 1974–77, Dir Fed. Chancellor's Office, Bonn 1977–80; Foreign Office, Bonn 1980–82, Perm. Rep. to GDR 1982–89; Perm. Rep. of FRG to UN, New York 1989–90; Brandenburg Minister of Justice 1990–99; mem. Bd of Dirs Foundation for Remembrance, Responsibility and Future, Berlin 2000–02, Chair. 2004–06; Grosses Verdienstkreuz mit Stern der Bundesrepublik Deutschland. *Leisure interests:* arts, literature. *Address:* Eichenallee 37, 14050 Berlin, Germany (home). *Telephone:* (30) 3048037 (home). *Fax:* (30) 3048037 (home). *E-mail:* hobraeutigam@gmx.de (home).

BRAVO, Dwayne James John; Trinidad and Tobago professional cricketer; b. 7 Oct. 1983, Santa Cruz, Trinidad; s. of John Bravo and Joycelyn Bravo; m. Regina Ramjit; one s. one d.; all-rounder; right-handed batsman; right-arm medium-fast bowler; plays for Trinidad & Tobago 2002–, West Indies 2004–18, Kent 2006, Mumbai Indians 2008–10, Chennai Super Kings 2011–15, 2018–, Sydney Sixers 2011–12, Chittagong Vikings 2012–13, Melbourne Renegades 2014–, Trinbago Knight Riders 2013–, Gujarat Lions 2016–17, Melbourne Stars 2018–; First-class debut: 2001/02; Test debut: England v West Indies, Lord's 22–26 July 2004; One-Day Int. (ODI) debut: West Indies v England, Georgetown 18 April 2004; T20I debut: NZ v West Indies, Auckland 16 Feb. 2006; played 40 Tests (to Dec. 2010), scored 2,200 runs (average 31.42) and took 86 wickets (average 39.83) with 3 centuries, 13 fifties and two five-wicket performances, highest score 113 runs against Australia, Hobart 2005, best bowling 6/55 against England, Manchester 2004; played 164 ODIs (to Oct. 2014), scored 298 runs (average 25.36) and took 199 wickets (average 29.51) with two centuries, ten fifties and one five-wicket performance, highest score 112 not out against England, Ahmedabad 2006, best bowling 6/43 against Zimbabwe, St George's 2013; played 66 T20Is (to Sept. 2016), scored 1,142 runs (average 24.29) and took 52 wickets (average 28.26) with four fifties and two five-wicket performances, best score 66 not out against India, Lord's 2009, best bowling 4/28 against Sri Lanka, Colombo 2015; played 100 First-class matches (to March 2013), scored 5,302 runs (average 30.64) and took 177 wickets (average 33.43) with eight centuries, 30 fifties and seven five-wicket performances, highest score 197 runs, best bowling 6/11; retd from Test cricket 2015; retd from Int. cricket 2018. *Recordings include:* Go Gyal Go 2014, Chalo Chalo 2015, Champion Champion 2016. *Address:* c/o National Cricket Centre, Clifford Roach Drive, Balmain, Couva, Trinidad. *Website:* www.djbravo47.com.

BRAVO, Rose Marie; American retail executive; *Vice-Chairman, Burberry Ltd;* ed Bronx High School of Science and Fordham Univ., Bronx, New York; began retailing career at Abraham & Strauss 1971–74; joined R. H. Macy and Co., New York as assoc. buyer 1974, various positions 1974–87, Chair. and CEO I. Magnin Specialty Div. 1987–92; Pres. Saks Fifth Avenue, New York 1992–97; CEO Burberry Ltd, London, UK 1997–2006, Vice-Chair. 2006–, mem. Bd Burberry Group PLC 1997–; mem. Bd Tiffany & Co., The Estee Lauder Cos, Inc., Nat. Italian American Foundation; Vice-Chair. Kennedy Center's Corp. Fund Bd; mem Advisory Bd Fashion Group International, The Fashion Inst. of Tech., New York; Trustee Fordham Univ.; honoured for excellence in retailing by Nat. Italian American Foundation, March of Dimes, City of Hope, Eleanor Lambeth Award, Council of Fashion Design Awards, New York 2003. *Address:* Burberry Ltd, 18–22 Haymarket, London, SW1 4DQ, England (office). *Telephone:* (20) 7968-0412 (office). *Fax:* (20) 7318-2666 (office). *Website:* www.burberry.com (office).

BRAVO DE LA PARRA, María Alejandra, BSc, MSc, PhD; Mexican biochemist and academic; *Researcher, Institute of Biotechnology, National Autonomous University of Mexico (UNAM);* b. 29 April 1961; m. Dr Mario Soberon; ed Nat. Autonomous Univ. of Mexico (UNAM); Research Visitor, Plant Genetic Systems, Ghent, Belgium 1990–91; Researcher, Inst. of Biotechnology, UNAM; included in list of Experts on Biosafety under Cartagena Protocol Security and Convention on Biological Diversity, Univ. of Colombia 2003; mem. Nat. Acad. of Sciences 2002; Gabino Barreda Medal (Licenciatura) 1985, Gabino Barreda Medal (Doctorado) 1989, Award from Nat. Acad. of Sciences in Natural Sciences 1998, National Univ. Distinction for Young Academics, UNAM 2000, Award for Best Research in Agricultural Biotechnology, AgroBIO-Mexico 2003, Laureate for Latin America, L'Oréal-UNESCO Awards for Women in Science 2010. *Publications:* numerous papers in professional journals; six patents. *Address:* Instituto de Biotecnología, UNAM, Cuernavaca, Morelos, Mexico (office). *E-mail:* bravo@ibt.unam.mx (office). *Website:* www.ibt.unam.mx (office).

BRÁZ DE AVIZ, HE Cardinal João; Brazilian ecclesiastic and academic; *Prefect, Congregation for Institutes of Consecrated Life and Societies of Apostolic Life;* b. 24 April 1947, Matra; ed Major Seminary 'Rainha dos Apostolos', Curitiba, Faculty of Palmas, Pontifical Gregorian Univ. and Pontifical Lateran Univ., Rome; ordained priest, Diocese of Apucarana, Parana 1972; served as Rector of Major Seminary Apucarana and Londrina; fmr Prof. of Dogmatic Theology, Theological Inst. Paul VI, Londrina; fmr mem. Council of Priests and Coll. of Consultors and Gen. Coordinator of the Diocesan Pastoral Apucarana; apptd Auxiliary Bishop of Vitória, Espirito Santo and Titular Bishop of Flenucleta 1994, Bishop of Ponta Grossa, Parana 1998–2002, Archbishop of Maringá, Parana 2002–04, Archbishop of Brasília, DF 2004–11; Prefect of the Congregation for Institutes of Consecrated Life and Societies of Apostolic Life 2011–13, 2013–; cr. Cardinal (Cardinal-Deacon of Sant'Elena fuori Porta Prenestina) 2012; participated in Papal Conclave 2013. *Address:* Congregation for Institutes of Consecrated Life and Societies of Apostolic Life, Palazzo della Congregazioni, Piazza Pio XII 3, 00193 Rome, Italy (office). *Telephone:* (06) 69884121 (office); (06) 69892511 (office); (06) 69884128 (office). *Fax:* (06) 69884526 (office). *E-mail:* civcsva.pref@ccscrlife.va (office). *Website:* www.vatican.va/roman_curia/congregations/ccscrlife (office).

BREAM, Julian, CBE, FRCM, FRNCM; British classical guitarist and lutenist; b. 15 July 1933, London; s. of Henry G. Bream; m. 1st Margaret Williamson; one adopted s.; m. 2nd Isobel Sanchez 1980 (divorced); ed Royal Coll. of Music; began professional career at Cheltenham 1947, London debut, Wigmore Hall 1950; has made numerous transcriptions for guitar of Romantic and Baroque works; commissioned new works from Britten, Walton, Henze and Arnold; tours throughout the world, giving recitals as soloist and with the Julian Bream Consort (f. 1960); many recitals with Sir Peter Pears and Robert Tear, and as guitar duo with John Williams; 60th Birthday Concert, Wigmore Hall, London 1993; Hon. DUniv (Surrey) 1968; Hon. DMus (Leeds) 1984; Villa-Lobos Gold Medal 1976, Gramophone Award for Best DVD (for My Life in Music) 2007, Lifetime Achievement Award, Gramophone Classical Music Awards 2013; numerous recording awards. *Leisure interests:* playing the guitar, cricket, table tennis, gardening, backgammon. *Address:* Hazard Chase Ltd, 25 City Road, Cambridge, CB1 1DP, England (office). *Telephone:* (1223) 312400 (office). *Fax:* (1223) 460827 (office). *E-mail:* info@hazardchase.co.uk (office). *Website:* www.hazardchase.co.uk (office).

BREARLEY, John Michael (Mike), OBE; British psychoanalyst, author, journalist and fmr professional cricketer; b. 28 April 1942, Harrow, Middx; s. of Horace Brearley and Midge Brearley; partner, Mana Sarabhai; two c.; ed City of London School, St John's Coll., Cambridge, Univ. of California, Irvine, USA; right-hand opening batsman, occasional wicket-keeper; played for Univ. of Cambridge 1961–64, captained Univ. of Cambridge 1963, 1964; awarded county cap (Middx) 1964; Capt. of Middx (winning County Championships four times and Gillette Cup twice) 1971–82; Test debut 1976; Capt. of England in 31 Tests 1977–80, 1981; played in 39 Tests, scored 1,442 runs, highest score 91, average 22.88; went on tours of S Africa 1964–65, Pakistan 1967, India, Sri Lanka and Australia 1976–77, Pakistan 1977–78, Australia 1978–79, Australia and India 1979–80; holds record for most runs scored at Univ. of Cambridge (4,310 at an average of 38.48) 1964; scored 312 not out for MCC Under-25 v. North Zone, Peshawar 1967; Pres. MCC 2007–08; Chair. MCC World Cricket Cttee 2011–17; Lecturer in Philosophy, Univ. of Newcastle-upon-Tyne 1968–71; Assoc. mem. British Psycho-Analytical Soc. 1985, Full mem. 1990, Pres. 2008–10; part-time cricket journalist for The Times; Hon. Fellow, St John's Coll., Cambridge 1997; Hon. DCL (Newcastle) 1984, (Lancaster) 1999, Dr hc (Oxford Brookes) 2006; Wisden Cricketer of the Year 1977. *Publications:* (with Dudley Doust) The Return of the Ashes 1978, The Ashes Retained (with Dudley Doust) 1979, Phoenix: The Series That Rose from the Ashes 1982, The Art of Captaincy 1985, 2001, Arlott in Conversation with Mike Brearley (with John Arlott) 1986. *Address:* c/o Middlesex County Cricket Club, Lord's Cricket Ground, St John's Wood Road, London, NW8 8QN, England. *Telephone:* (20) 7289-1300. *Website:* www.middlesexccc.com.

BREAUX, John B., JD; American business executive and fmr politician; *Senior Counsel, Squire Patton Boggs LLP;* b. 1 March 1944, Crowley, La; s. of Ezra Breaux and Katie Breaux; m. Lois Gail Daigle 1964; two s. two d.; ed Southwestern Univ., State Univ. of Louisiana; called to La Bar 1967; Partner, Brown, McKernan, Ingram and Breaux 1967–68; Legislative Asst to US Congressman 1968–69; Dist Asst 1969–72; mem. US House of Reps from 7th Dist, La 1971–87; Senator from Louisiana 1987–2005 (retd), Chief Deputy Whip 1993–2005; Chair., Democratic Senatorial Campaign Cttee, Nat. Water Alliance 1987–88; Sr Man. Dir Clinton Group, Inc. (investment firm) 2005; f. Breaux-Lott Leadership Group 2008, acquired by Patton Boggs LLP, Sr Counsel, Squire Patton Boggs LLP 2005–; Sr Advisor, Riverstone Holdings LLC 2005; fmr Distinguished Prof., Manship School of Mass Communication, Louisiana State Univ.; mem. Bd of Dirs CSX Transportation; apptd by Pres. George W. Bush as Vice-Chair. nat. comm. to make recommendations or changes to current US tax laws 2005; Co-Chair. Nat. Bipartisan Comm. on Future of Medicare 1998–99; American Legion Award, Neptune Award, American Oceanic Org. 1980. *Address:* Squire Patton Boggs LLP, 2550 M Street, NW, Washington, DC 20037, USA (office). *Telephone:* (202) 457-5290 (office). *Fax:* (202) 457-6315 (office). *Website:* www.squirepattonboggs.com (office).

BRECHER, Michael, PhD, FRSC; Canadian political scientist and academic; *R.B. Angus Professor of Political Science, McGill University;* b. 14 March 1925, Montréal, Québec; s. of Nathan Brecher and Gisela Hopmeyer; m. Eva Danon 1950; three d.; ed McGill Univ., Yale Univ., USA; mem. Faculty, McGill Univ. 1952–, Prof. 1963–, R.B. Angus Prof. of Political Science 1993–; Pres. Int. Studies Asscn 1999–2000; Visiting Prof., Univ. of Chicago 1963, Hebrew Univ., Jerusalem 1970–75, Univ. of California, Berkeley 1979, Stanford Univ. 1980; Nuffield Fellow 1955–56; Rockefeller Fellow 1964–65; Guggenheim Fellow 1965–66; f. Shastri Indo-Canadian Inst. 1968 (Pres. 1969–71); Founder and Dir Int. Crisis Behavior (ICB) Project 1975–2015; Watumull Book Prize, American Hist. Asscn 1960, Killam Awards, Canada Council 1970–74, 1976–79, Woodrow Wilson Book Award, American Political Science Asscn 1973, Fieldhouse Award for Distinguished Teaching, McGill Univ. 1986, Distinguished Scholar Award, Int. Studies Asscn 1995, Prix Léon-Gérin in Social Sciences (Prix du Québec) 2000, Award for High Distinction in Research, McGill Univ. 2000, Lifetime Achievement Award, American Political Science Asscn 2009. *Publications include:* The Struggle for Kashmir 1953, Nehru: A Political Biography 1959, The New States of Asia 1963, Succession in India 1966, India and World Politics 1968, Political Leadership in India 1969, The Foreign Policy System of Israel 1972, Israel, the Korean War and China 1974, Decisions in Israel's Foreign Policy 1975, Studies in Crisis Behavior 1979, Decisions in Crisis 1980, Crisis and Change in World Politics 1986, Crises in the 20th Century (Vols I, II) 1988, Crisis, Conflict and Instability 1989, Crises in World Politics 1993, A Study of Crisis 1997, 2000, Millennial Reflections on International Studies (Vols 1–5) 2002, International Political Earthquakes 2008, The World of Protracted Conflicts 2016, Political Leadership and Charisma 2016, Dynamics of the Arab/Israel Conflict 2017; over 85 articles in journals. *Address:* Department of Political Science, McGill University, 855 Sherbrooke Street West, Montréal, PQ H3A 2T7 (office); 3450 Drummond Street, Apartment 1701, Montréal, PQ H3G 1Y3, Canada (home). *Telephone:* (514) 398-4800 (office); (514) 288-4060 (home). *Fax:* (514) 398-1759 (office). *E-mail:* michael.brecher@mcgill.ca (office). *Website:* www.mcgill.ca/politicalscience (office).

BRÉCHIGNAC, Catherine, DSc; French physicist; *Secrétaire perpétuel, French National Academy of Sciences;* b. 12 June 1946, Paris; d. of Jean Teillac and Andrée Teillac (née Kerleguer); m. Philippe Bréchignac 1969; two s. one d.; ed Ecole Normale Supérieure, Fontenay-aux-Roses; Research Asst, CNRS 1971–78, Supervisor 1978–85, Dir of Research 1985–91, Del. to the Scientific Dir, Dept of Physical and Math. Sciences 1985–89, Dir of Aimé Cotton Lab. 1989–95, Scientific Dir Dept of Physical and Math. Sciences 1995–97, Dir-Gen. CNRS 1997–2000, Exec. Pres. 2006–10; Assoc. Researcher Institut d'astrophysique d'Ottawa, Canada 1979–80; Visiting Prof., Ecole Polytechnique de Lausanne 1987–; Adjunct Prof. then Distinguished Visiting Scholar, Georgia Tech. Univ., USA 2001–; James Frank lecturer, Israel Acad. of Sciences and Humanities 2001; Pres. Int. Council for Science (ICSU) 2008–, High Council of Biotechnologies 2009–; Amb.-Del. for Science, Tech. and Innovation to Minister of Foreign Affairs; Assoc. mem. Royal Acad. of Sciences, Arts and Fine Arts, Belgium 2010, Hassan II Academy of Sciences and Techniques, Morocco 2015; Corresp. mem. French Acad. des Sciences 1997 (mem. 2005, Secrétaire perpétuel 2011–), American Acad. of Arts and Sciences 2011–; mem. French Acad. of Tech. 2000–; Humboldt Research Fellowship 2009; Officier, Légion d'honneur 2005, Commdr 2014, Commdr, Ordre nat. du Mérite 2011, Officer, Order of Arts and Letters 2013; Dr hc (Univ. of Berlin, Georgia Tech. Inst., Atlanta, Ecole polytechnique fédérale de Lausanne); Acad. des Sciences Prize 1991, CNRS Silver Medal 1994, Holweck Prize and Medal 2003, Prix Roberval 2008. *Leisure interests:* opera, painting, literature. *Address:* 23 quai de Conti, 75006 Paris, France (office). *Telephone:* 1-44-41-45-05 (office). *E-mail:* catherine.brechignac@academie-sciences.fr (office). *Website:* www.academie-sciences.fr (office).

BRÉCHOT, Christian, PhD; French medical researcher and professor of cell biology; *Director-General, Institut Pasteur;* b. 23 July 1952, Paris; s. of Claude Bréchot and Marie-Louise Bréchot (née Tisne); m. 1st (divorced); one s. two d.; m. 2nd Patrizia Paterlini; two s.; ed Lycée Montaigne, Paris, Lycée Louis le Grand, Paris, Univ. of Paris VII, Inst. Pasteur; Prof. of Cell Biology, Necker-Enfants Malades Faculty of Medicine, Univ. of Paris V 1989–2001; Head, Hybridotest Lab., Inst. Pasteur 1990–98; Head, Institut nat. de la santé et de la recherche médicale (INSERM) Research Unit U.370, Necker Hosp., Paris 1993–2001, Head, Liver Unit, Necker Hosp. 1997–2001, Head, Nat. Reference Centre on the molecular epidemiology of viral hepatitis, Inst. Pasteur and INSERM U.370 1998–2001, Dir-Gen. INSERM 2001–07 (resgnd); Vice-Pres. Institut Mérieux 2008; Dir-Gen. Inst. Pasteur 2013–; WHO study co-ordinator for standardization of PCR in diagnosis of HIV infections 1988–91; mem. Scientific Cttee, Asscn pour la Recherche sur le Cancer 1988–2001, Agence Française du Sang 1993–96; mem. Inst. Universitaire de France 1992–, European Asscn for Virological Diagnosis, American Asscn for the Study of Liver Diseases, French Asscn for the Study of the Liver, European Asscn for the Study of the Liver (Sec. 1993–97); Biotrol Award 1982, Fondation pour la Recherche Médicale Award 1982, Abott Award for research on viral hepatitis 1983, Ligue Française contre le cancer Paris Award for research on liver cancer and hepatitis B virus 1985, APMS Award for research on prevention of transmissible diseases 1987, French Medical Soc., René Fauvert Award 1987, French Acad. of Medicine Award 1996, Fondation de France Jean Valade Award 2000. *Leisure interests:* paintings, tennis, rugby. *Address:* Institut Pasteur, 25–28 rue du Docteur Roux, 75015 Paris, France (office). *Telephone:* 1-45-68-80-00 (office). *Fax:* 1-43-06-98-35 (office). *Website:* www.pasteur.fr (office).

BRECHTEFELD, Natan Teewe, BA, LLB; I-Kiribati lawyer and politician; *Attorney-General;* b. 27 May 1961, Abemama; s. of Teewe and Bwebweniti; m. Tebaraoi Tangimate; five c.; ed Univ. of the South Pacific, Fiji, Univ. of Papua New Guinea, Otago Univ., New Zealand; mem. Maneaba Ni Maungatabu (Parl.) for Abemama –2011, 2015–; Minister for Communications, Transport and Tourism Devt –2007, of Finance and Econ. Devt 2007–11; mem. Boutokaan Te Koaua Party; State Advocate, Office of Attorney-Gen., Kiribati; Asst Attorney-Gen., Marshall Islands –2014, Attorney-Gen. 2014–15; Attorney-Gen. of Kiribati 2016–; CEO Kiribati Oil Co. (KOIL). *Leisure interest:* cycling. *Address:* Attorney-General's Office, POB 62, PO Box 62, Bairiki, Tarawa (office); Asemama, Kiribati (home). *Telephone:* 21242 (office). *Fax:* 21025 (office). *E-mail:* n_teewe@yahoo.com (home).

BRECKENRIDGE, Sir Alasdair Muir, Kt, CBE, MD, MSc, FRCP, FRCPE, FRSE; British scientist and academic; *Chairman, Emerging Science and Bioethics Advisory Committee;* b. 7 May 1937, Arbroath, Scotland; s. of Thomas Breckenridge and Jane Breckenridge; m. Jean M. Boyle 1967; two s.; ed Bell-Baxter School, Cupar, Fife and Univ. of St Andrews; House Physician and Surgeon, Dundee Royal Infirmary 1961–62; House Physician, Registrar, Lecturer, Sr Lecturer, Hammersmith Hosp. and Royal Postgraduate Medical School 1963–74; Prof. of Clinical Pharmacology, Univ. of Liverpool 1974–2002, Prof. Emer. 2002–; mem. Cttee on Safety of Medicines 1981, Chair. 1999–2003; Chair. Medicines and Healthcare Products Regulatory Agency (MHRA) 2003–12; Chair. Emerging Science and Bioethics Advisory Cttee 2012–; Councillor Int. Union of Pharmacology 1981–87; Foreign Sec. British Pharmacological Soc. 1983–91, Dir Research and Devt, Mersey Region 1992–96; Vice-Chair. Advisory Cttee on Drugs 1985–98; mem. Council Royal Coll. of Physicians 1983–86, Panel of Tropical Diseases, Wellcome Trust 1984–88, WHO Steering Cttee on Chemotherapy of Malaria 1987–91, MRC Physiological Systems and Disorders Bd 1987–91, Council MRC 1992–96, Cen. Research and Devt Cttee, Nat. Health Service 1991–95, Council, Acad. of Medical Sciences; Chair. NW Regional Office of the Nat. Health Service 1996–99; Chair. Jt Medical Advisory Cttee of Higher Educ. Funding Councils of the UK 1998–2002; mem. Bd of Dirs Univ. Coll. London Hosps 2012–; Goulstonian Lecturer, Royal Coll. of Physicians 1975; Paul Martini Prize for Clinical Pharmacology 1974, Poulson Medal (Norwegian Pharmacological Soc.) 1988, Lilly Prize (British Pharmacological Soc.) 1993. *Publications:* articles in scientific and medical journals. *Leisure interest:* golf. *Address:* Cree Cottage, Feather Lane, Wirral, L69 3BX, England (home). *Telephone:* (151) 342-1096 (home).

BREDESEN, Philip Norman (Phil), Jr, AB; American politician, business executive and fmr state governor; b. 21 Nov. 1943, Oceanport, NJ; s. of Phillip Norman Bredesen, Sr and Norma Lucille Bredesen (née Walborn); m. 1st Susan Cleaves 1968 (divorced 1974); m. 2nd Andrea Conte 1974; one s.; ed Red Jacket Cen. School, NY, Harvard Coll.; computer programmer, Itek Corpn, Mass 1967–70; Dir of Systems Devt G.D. Seale & Co. 1971–73, Div. Man. 1973–75; Dir of Special Projects Hosp. Affiliates Int. Nashville 1976–80; f. Healthplans Corpn (later HealthAmerica Corpn) 1980, Chair. and CEO 1980–86 (sold co.); co-f. Coventry Corpn 1986, Chair. 1986–90; co-f. Clinical Pharmaceuticals 1986, Chair. 1986–93; Mayor of Nashville and Davidson Co. 1991–99; Pres. Bredex Corpn 2000–02; Gov. of Tenn. 2003–11; f. Nashville's Table 1989, mem. Bd of Dirs 1989–91; Founder Land Trust for Tenn. 1999, Chair. 1999–2001; Co-Chair. Achieve, Inc. (bipartisan and educ. reform org.) from 2009; mem. Bd of Dirs, United Cerebral Palsy 1988–92, United Way of Middle Tennessee 1985–90, Nashville Symphony 1985–91, Univ. School, Nashville 1986–95, Nashville Publrs' Library Foundation 1997–2007, Tennessee State Univ. Foundation; mem. Bd of Trustees, Frist Center for Visual Arts 1998–2003, Chair. Finance Cttee 2000–03; Democrat. *Leisure interests:* oil painting, flying glider planes, jogging, hunting, fishing, skiing, hiking, reading, computers. *Address:* 1724 Chickering Road, Nashville, TN 37215-4908, USA.

BREDIN, Jean-Denis, LèsL; French lawyer; b. 17 May 1929, Paris; m. Danièle Hervier; two c. (including Frédérique Bredin); ed Lycée Charlemagne and Facultés de Droit et des Lettres, Paris; called to the Bar 1950–; Prof. Faculté de Droit, Rennes 1958, Lille 1967; Founding Partner, Bredin Prat (law firm) 1965–; Adviser to Council for Higher Educ. 1968–69; Prof. of Pvt. Law, Univ. of Paris-Dauphine 1969; Prof. Univ. of Paris I 1971–93, Prof. Emer. 1993–; worked with Edgar Faure on higher educ. reform 1968; Vice-Pres. Mouvement des radicaux de gauche 1976–80; Pres. Man. Bd Bibliothèque Nationale 1983–88; Vice-Pres. Comm. Moinot 1981; Pres. Comm. for Reform of Cinema 1982; Adviser on Audiovisual Matters to Prime Minister 1985; mem. Acad. Française 1989–; Prix Gobert 1984. *Publications include:* Traité de droit commercial international 1967, La République de Monsieur Pompidou 1974, Eclats 1976, Les Français au pouvoir 1977, Joseph Cailleux 1980, L'Affaire 1983, Un coupable 1985, L'Absence 1986, La Tâche 1988, Weisbuch 1989, Un enfant sage 1990, Battements de coeur 1991, Bernard Lazare 1992, Comédie des Apparences 1994, Encore un peu de temps 1996, Convaincre, dialogues sur l'éloquence 1997, L'Affaire 1998, Une singulière famille 1999, Rien ne va plus 2000, Lettre à Dieu le fils 2001, Un tribunal au garde-à-vous 2002, Et des amours desquelles nous parlons 2004, Mots et pas perdus: images du Palais 2004, On ne meurt qu'une fois: Charlotte Corday 2006. *Address:* Bredin Prat, 130 rue du Faubourg Saint-Honoré, 75008 Paris, France (office). *Telephone:* 1-44-35-35-51 (office). *Fax:* 1-42-89-10-73 (office). *E-mail:* jdb@bredinprat.com (office). *Website:* www.bredinprat.fr (office).

BREEDLOVE, Gen. (retd) Philip M., BCE, MS; American air force officer (retd); b. 21 Sept. 1955; m. Cindy Breedlove; one s. one d.; ed Georgia Inst. of Tech., Arizona State Univ., Air Command and Staff Coll., Nat. War Coll.; commissioned 1977, First Lt 1979, Capt. 1981, F-16 Aircraft Commdr and Instructor Pilot, 614th Tactical Fighter Squadron, Torrejon AB, Spain 1983–85, Air Liaison Officer, 602nd Air Support Operations Group, Kitzingen AB, West Germany 1985–87, F-16 Pilot, 526th Tactical Fighter Squadron, Ramstein AB, West Germany 1987–88, F-16 Flight Commdr, then Asst Operations Officer, 512th Tactical Fighter Squadron, Ramstein AB, Germany 1988–90, Chief of Air Operations, UN Command and Korea/US Combined Forces Command, Yongsan Army Garrison, South Korea 1991–93, Commdr 80th Fighter Squadron, Kunsan AB, South Korea 1993–94, 27th Operations Group, Cannon AFB, New Mexico 1997–99, 8th Fighter Wing, Kunsan AB, South Korea 2000–01, 56th Fighter Wing, Luke AFB, Arizona 2002–04, 31st Fighter Wing, Aviano AB, Italy 2004–05, 3rd Air Force, Ramstein AB, Germany 2008–09, USAF in Europe, Air Forces HQ Allied Air Command, Ramstein 2012–13, Sr Mil. Asst to Sec. of Air Force 2001–02, Vice-Dir for Strategic Plans and Policy on the Jt Staff –2008, Deputy Chief of Staff for Operations, Plans and Requirements, Air Force HQ 2009–11, Vice-Chief of Staff, USAF 2011–12, Dir, Jt Air Power Competence Centre, Kalkar Germany 2012–13, NATO Supreme Allied Commdr, Europe and Commdr of US European Command 2013–16 (retd); attained rank of Maj. 1988, Lt-Col 1993, Col 1998, Brig.-Gen. 2003, Maj.-Gen. 2006, Lt-Gen. 2008, Gen. 2011; Seminar XXI Fellow, MIT; Legion of Merit (with three oak leaf clusters), Defense Meritorious Service Medal (with two oak leaf clusters), Meritorious Service Medal (with three oak leaf clusters), Air Force Distinguished Service Medal, Defense Superior Service Medal, Aerial Achievement Medal, Joint Service Commendation Medal, Air Force Achievement Medal, Combat Readiness Medal (with bronze oak leaf cluster), Nat. Defense Service Medal (with bronze service star), Global War on Terrorism Service Medal, Korea Defense Service Medal, Air Force Overseas Short Tour Service Ribbon (with two bronze oak leaf clusters), Air Force Overseas Long Tour Service Ribbon (with four bronze oak leaf clusters), Air Force Longevity Service Award (with one silver and three bronze oak leaf clusters), Air Force Training Ribbon, Inter-American Defense Board Medal (with gold award star); Jt Meritorious Unit Award (with bronze oak leaf cluster), Air Force Outstanding Unit Award (with four bronze oak leaf clusters).

BREEDON, Timothy (Tim) James, CBE, MA, MSc; British insurance industry executive; b. 1958; m.; three c.; ed Calthorpe Comprehensive School, Fleet, Hants., Farnborough Coll., Worcester Coll. Oxford, London Business School; began career with Standard Chartered Bank 1981–85; joined Legal & General Investment Man. Ltd 1987, Man. Quantitative Products and Index Funds 1987, Dir Index Funds 1994, Man. Dir (Index Funds) 2000–02, mem. Bd of Dirs and Group Dir (Investments) 2002–05, Deputy Group Chief Exec. Legal & General Group Plc 2005–06, Group Chief Exec. 2006–12; mem. Bd of Dirs Asscn of British Insurers, Chair. 2010–12; Chair. Bd of Dirs Apax Global Alpha Ltd, The Northview Group Ltd; mem. Bd of Dirs Barclays PLC 2012–, The Investment Man. Asscn, The Financial Reporting Council; mem. Bd of Trustees Marie Curie Cancer Care. *Address:* c/o Barclays Group Plc, 1 Churchill Place, London, E14 5HP, England. *Telephone:* (20) 7116-1000. *Website:* www.home.barclays.

BREEN, Edward D., Jr, BS; American business executive; *Chairman, Tyco International Inc.;* m.; three c.; ed Grove City Coll.; joined General Instrument (GI) Corpn 1978, Sr Vice-Pres. of Sales 1988–94, Pres. GI Broadband Networks Group 1994–97, Chair., Pres. and CEO GI 1997–2000; Vice-Pres. Motorola 2000–02, Pres. Motorola Broadband Communications Sector 2000–01, Pres. Motorola Networks Sector 2001–02, Pres. and COO Motorola Jan.–July 2002; Chair. and CEO Tyco International Inc. July 2002–12, Chair. (non-exec.) 2012–; Lead Dir Comcast Corpn 2005–11; mem. Advisory Bd New Mountain Capital (pvt. equity firm); Trustee Grove City Coll.; Vanguard Award, Nat. Cable TV Asscn 1998. *Address:* Tyco International Inc., 9 Roszel Road, Princeton, NJ 08540, USA (office). *Telephone:* (609) 720-4200 (office). *Website:* www.tyco.com (office).

BREGA, Gheorghe; Moldovan urologist and politician; b. 25 Sept. 1951, Drepcăuţi, Moldovan SSR, USSR; ed Nicolae Testemiţanu State Univ. of Medicine and Pharmacy, Chişinău; emergency nurse, hosp. in Chişinău 1972–74; intern and physician-surgeon urologist, Municipal Hosp. No. 1, Chişinău 1974–76; urologist, Municipal Hosp. No. 2, Chişinău 1976–78; clinical oncologist and urologist, Oncology Inst. of Moldova 1978–83, urologist-oncologist, Dept of Urology 1983–89, Head of Dept of Urology 1989–2004; surgeon-urologist, Family Health Centre 'Galaxia' 2004–09; mem. Parl. 2009–15; mem. Partidul Liberal (PL—Liberal Party); affiliated to Alliance for European Integration 2009–13, Pro-European Coalition 2013–15, Political Alliance for a European Moldova 2015, Alliance for European Integration III 2015–; Acting Prime Minister of Moldova Oct. 2015–Jan. 2016; Deputy Prime Minister, responsible for Social Affairs Jan. 2016–17.

BREGGIN, Peter Roger, BA, MD; American psychiatrist; b. 5 Nov. 1936, New York, NY; m. 3rd Ginger Ross 1984; one c. (and three c. from two previous marriages); ed Harvard Coll., Case Western Reserve School of Medicine, State Univ. of New York, Upstate Medical Center, Massachusetts Mental Health Centre; consultant, Nat. Inst. of Mental Health 1966–68; psychiatrist in pvt. practice 1968–; Founder and Dir Int. Center for Study of Psychiatry and Psychology 1972–2002, Dir Emer. 2002–; Adjunct Prof. of Conflict Resolution George Mason Univ. 1990–96; Faculty Assoc. Dept of Counselling Johns Hopkins Univ. 1996–99; Ed. numerous journals, including Journal of Mind and Behaviour, International Journal of Risk and Society in Medicine, The Humanistic Psychologist, Review of Existential Psychology and Psychiatry; Founding Ed. Ethical Human Sciences and Services 1999–; Ludwig von Mises Award of Merit 1987, Minn. Mental Health Asscn Advocacy Award 1990, honours from Harvard Coll. *Publications:* College Students in a Mental Hospital: Contribution to the Social Rehabilitation of the Mentally Ill (co-author) 1962, Electroshock: Its Brain-Disabling Effects 1979, Psychiatric Drugs: Hazards to the Brain 1983, Toxic Psychiatry 1991, Talking Back to Prozac (with Ginger Breggin) 1994, Brain-Disabling Treatments in Psychiatry 1997 (revised edn 2008), The Heart of Being Helpful 1997 (new paperback edn 2006), The War Against Children of Color (with Ginger Breggin) 1998, Talking Back to Ritalin 1998, Your Drug May Be Your Problem (with David Cohen) 1999 (revised edn 2007), Reclaiming Our Children: A Healing Solution for a Nation in Crisis 2000, Talking Back to Ritalin: What Doctors Aren't Telling You About Stimulants and ADHD 2001, The Anti-Depressant Fact Book: What Your Doctor Won't Tell You About Prozac, Zoloft, Paxil, Celexa, and Luvox 2001, The Ritalin Fact Book: What Your Doctor Won't Tell You 2002, Dimensions of Empathic Therapy (co-ed.) 2002, Medication Madness: A Psychiatrist Exposes the Dangers of Mood-Altering Medications 2008, Wow, I'm an American! How to Live Like Our Nation's Heroic Founders 2009, Psychiatric Drug Withdrawal: A Guide for Prescribers, Therapists, Patients and their Families 2012; numerous articles in scientific journals. *Address:* 101 East State Street, #112, Ithaca, NY 14850, USA. *Telephone:* (607) 272-5328; (607) 272-5354. *Fax:* (607) 272-5329. *E-mail:* psychiatricdrugfacts@hotmail.com. *Website:* www.breggin.com.

BRÉGIER, Fabrice; French aeronautics industry executive; *President, Palantir Technologies, France;* b. 16 July 1961, Dijon; ed École Polytechnique and École des Mines; began career as a test engineer at Creys-Malville nuclear power station 1983–84; Sales Man. for Péchiney (Japan) 1984–86; joined Directions Régionales de l'Industrie de la Recherche et de l'Environnement, Alsace, Ministry of Industry 1986–89; Dir of Econ. and Financial Affairs, Ministry of Agric. 1989–90; Tech. Advisor to Minister of Foreign Trade 1990–91, to Minister of Post and Telecommunications 1991–93; joined Matra Défense (later Matra BAe Dynamics) as Chair. Apache MAW GIE (co-operation with Dasa) and Eurodrone GIE (with STN-Atlas) 1993–96, Dir of Stand-Off activities (Apache, Scalp EG/Storm Shadow), Matra BAe Dynamics 1996–98, CEO Matra BAe Dynamics 1998–2001; CEO MBDA (European missile systems co. cr. by Aerospatiale Matra, British Aerospace and Finmeccanica) 2001–03; Pres. and CEO Eurocopter Group, European Aeronautic Defence and Space Co. (EADS) 2003–06, Head of EADS' Eurocopter Div. 2005–06, COO Airbus SAS 2006–12, Pres. and CEO 2012–18, mem. EADS Exec. Cttee, commissioned by Louis Gallois to improve overall operational performance of the Group, tasked with implementing the Power 8 reorganization plan and the A350

XWB programme; Pres. Palantir Technologies, France 2018–; Chevalier, Légion d'honneur. *Address:* Palantir, 1 Rue Bouquières, 31000 Toulouse, France (office). *E-mail:* info@palantir.com (office). *Website:* www.palantir.com (office).

BREGU, Majlinda Enver, PhD; Albanian politician; b. 19 May 1974, Tirana; m.; two c.; ed Sami Frashëri Gymnasium, Univ. of Tirana, Univ. of Urbino, Italy; worked for Albanian Radio-TV 1992–2002; interships, NOVA Inst. for Research and Social Policy Oslo, Norway, Viadrina Univ., Germany 1997–2004; Lecturer on Social Sciences and Gender Issues, Univ. of Tirana 1996–; Visiting Prof., McGill Univ., Canada 2000; mem. Partia Demokratike e Shqipërisë (Democratic Party of Albania), Co-ordinator of Social Policies at Political Orientation Cttee 2004, mem. Nat. Council 2004, Head of the sub-comm. on Minors and Gender Equality 2005–07; mem. Kuvendi Popullor (Parl.) 2005–, Head, Parl. Del. to European Parl. 2005–07, Chair. Parl. Sub-comm. for Juveniles and Equal Opportunities (in co-operation with Children's Human Rights Centre of Albania) 2006, mem. Health and Social Issues Parl. Comm. 2005–07; Minister of European Integration 2009–13; Spokesperson, Council of Ministers 2009–13. *Publications:* co-author: Qualitative Research for Social Sciences 2003, Media Monitoring on Domestic Violence 2003, Domestic Violence and Judiciary System 2005, Assesment of Health Care Workers 2006, National Strategy for Gender Equality 2006; ed.: Prostitute. Ci passerano davanto nel Regno dei Cieli 2004. *Address:* Kuvendi Popullor, Bulevardi Dëshmorët e Kombit 4, Tirana, Albania. *E-mail:* majlindabregu@yahoo .com. *Website:* www.parlament.al.

BREIEN, Anja; Norwegian film director; b. 1940; ed Inst. des hautes études cinématiques, France; mem. European Film Acad.; Aamot-statuetten Prize 1982, Hon. Amanda 2005. *Short films include:* Vokse opp (Part 1 of Dager fra 100 år) 1967, 17. Mai: en film om ritualer 1969, Ansikter 1971, Murer rundt fengslet 1972, Herbergister 1973, Mine Søsken, goddag 1974, Gamle 1975, Fjellet 1989, Solvorn 1997, Å se en båt med seil (To see a boat in sail; UIP/EFA Prize, Berlin Film Festival 2001, Best Short Feature, Toronto 2001) 2000, Uten Tittel (Untitled) 2005, Riss 2009, Fra tyggegummiens historie (From the History of the Chewing Gum) 2012. *Feature films include:* Voldtekt/Tilfellet Anders (Rape/Le viol) (Norsk Kritikerlags Pris) 1971, Hustruer (Wives) (Silver Hugo Award, Chicago 1976) 1975, Den Allvarsamme Leken (Games of Love and Loneliness) (Silver Hugo Award, Chicago 1977) 1977, The Swedish (Guldbogga) 1978, Arven (Next of Kin/ The Inheritance) (Norske kinosjefers Sølvklumpen Award) 1979, Forfølgelsen (Witch Hunt) 1981, Papirfuglen (Paper Bird) (Silver Hugo Award, Chicago 1984) 1984, Hustruer: ti år etter (Wives: Ten Years After) (Norwegian Film Prize Amanda for Best Film 1985) 1985, Smykketyven (Twice upon a Time) 1990, Hustruer III (Wives III) 1996, Solvorn 1997, Jezidi (Yezidi) 2009; has also written script for film Trollsyn (Second Sight) (dir by Ola Solum) 1994. *Publications:* Forfølgelsen (script) 1981, Trollsyn (script) 1995, Kaniaw (novel) 2006. *Leisure interest:* skiing. *Address:* Norwegian Film Institute, Dronningens 6T. 16, 0152 Oslo, Norway (office). *Telephone:* 95-21-49-49. *E-mail:* anja@mfu.no (office).

BREIMER, Douwe Durk, PhD; Dutch pharmacologist, academic and fmr university rector; b. 24 Nov. 1943, Gaasterland; m. Joan Breimer; four d.; ed Univ. of Groningen, Univ of Nijmegen; apptd Prof. of Pharmacology, Leiden Univ. 1975, mem. Bd, Rector Magnificus and Pres. Exec. Bd Leiden Univ. 2001–07, now Prof. Emer.; Foreign Assoc. mem. Inst. of Medicine of NAS, Nat. Innovation Platform; Kt, Order of the Dutch Lion; Dr hc (Ghent Univ., Uppsala Univ., Semmelweis Univ. (Budapest), Univ. of Navarra, Hoshi Univ. (Tokyo), Univ. of London, Université de Montréal). *Publications include:* more than 500 scientific papers on pharmacokinetics, pharmacodynamics and drug metabolism. *Telephone:* (71) 5176410 (home). *E-mail:* ddbreimer@lacdr.leidenuniv.nl (office).

BREJON DE LAVERGNÉE, Arnauld, DenL; French museum curator; b. 25 May 1945, Rennes; s. of Jacques Brejon de Lavergnèe and Monique Perquis; m. Barbara Mercillon 1977; four c.; ed Univ. of Sorbonne, Paris; trainee curator, Louvre Museum, Museums of Cluny and Dijon 1969–70; Visiting Fellow, Acad. of France in Rome 1971–72; Curator Museum of Cluny 1973–76; Curator Dept of Painting, Louvre Museum 1976–87; Gen. Curator of Heritage 1987; Curator Museum of Fine Arts, Lille 1987–2003 (oversaw 220 million French franc restoration project 1992–97); Dir of Collections, Mobilier Nat. 2003–12 (retd); Corresp. mem. Acad. des Beaux Arts 1993, Acad. of Bologne; Chevalier, Légion d'honneur, Ordre nat. du Mérite, Ordre des Arts et des Lettres; Fotillon Fellow, Yale Univ. 1977, Getty Center Art History Grant 1984, Prix nat. de Muséographie 1987. *Publications include:* L'art italien dans les collections françaises, La collection du Bailli de Breteuil, Une monographie sur Simon Vouet, La collection des tapissiers de Louis XIV, Catalogue sommaire illustré des peintures du Musée du Louvre. Vol. 1: Ecoles flamande et hollandaise 1979, Dijon, Musée Magnin, catalogue des tableaux et dessins italiens (XVe-XIXe siècles) (Inventaire des collections publiques françaises) 1980, L'inventaire Le Brun de 1683: La collection des tableaux de Louis XIV (Notes et documents des musées de France) 1987. *Address:* c/o Mobilier National, 42 avenue des Gobelins, 75013 Paris, France. *E-mail:* arnauld.brejon@culture.gouv.fr.

BREMAÏDOU, Christophe; Central African Republic politician; fmr mem. Commission Electorale Indépendante; fmr Minister of Econ. Reform; Minister of Finance and the Budget –2013; Pres. Alliance pour la Solidarité et le Développement 2011.

BREMAN, Jan; Dutch sociologist and academic; *Professor Emeritus, Institute of Social Studies, The Hague;* b. 24 July 1936, Amsterdam; staff mem., later Reader and Prof., Erasmus Univ. (fmrly Netherlands Econ. School), Rotterdam, held Chair in the Sociology of Devt 1974–87; Prof. of Comparative Sociology, Dir and Dean Centre of Asian Studies and Dean of Amsterdam School for Social Science Research, Univ. of Amsterdam 1987–98; Extraordinary Prof. of Devt Sociology, Inst. of Social Studies, The Hague 1998–2001, Prof. Emer. 2001–; Visiting Prof., Inst. of Econ. Growth, Delhi, Agricultural Univ., Bogor, Indonesia; extensive anthropological fieldwork in India (South Gujarat) and Indonesia (West Java), mainly on rural and urban labour and employment since 1962; has travelled widely on short-term academic visits to other Asian countries; consultancy missions in the Asian region for ILO, UN Research Inst. for Social Devt, ESCAP, Asian Devt Bank; devt consultant on social policies in Asia; mem. Nat. Advisory Council on Devt Co-operation, The Netherlands; mem. Royal Netherlands Acad. of Sciences and Humanities; Fellow, Int. Inst. for Asian Studies; Dr hc (Inst. of Social Studies) 2009. *Publications:* Of Patronage and Exploitation 1974, Landless Labour in Colonial Java 1984, Of Peasants, Migrants and Workers 1985, Taming the Coolie Beast 1989, Beyond Patronage and Exploitation 1993, Wage Hunters and Gatherers 1994, Footloose Labour: Working India's Informal Economy (Edgar Graham Prize 1998) 1996, The Labouring Poor in India 2003, The Making and Unmaking of an Industrial Working Class 2006, The Poverty Regime in Village India 2007, The Jan Breman Omnibus 2007, Outcast Labour in Asia 2010. *Address:* 48 Kloveniersburgwal, 1012 CX Amsterdam, The Netherlands (office). *Telephone:* (20) 5252262 (office). *E-mail:* j.c.breman@uva.nl (office).

BREMER, Kåre, PhD; Swedish botanist, academic and fmr university administrator; *Professor, Stockholm University;* b. 17 Jan. 1948, Lidingö; m. Birgitta Bremer; one s. one d.; ed Stockholm Univ.; Asst Prof., later Assoc. Prof. of Systematic Botany, Stockholm Univ. 1972–75, 1976–80, Vice-Chancellor (Rector) 2004–13, Prof. 2013–; Head of Curator Dept of Phanerogamic Botany, Swedish Museum of Natural History 1980–89; Research Assoc. and B.A. Krukoff Curator of African Botany, Mo. Botanical Garden, USA 1985–86; Prof. of Systematic Botany, Uppsala Univ. 1989–2004, Dean of Biology 1993–99; Foreign mem. Linnean Soc. of London 1998; Fellow, Royal Swedish Acad. of Sciences; Lund Royal Physiographic Soc. Linnaeus Prize 1999, HM The King's Gold Medal 2006. *Publications:* numerous papers in learned journals. *Address:* Stockholm University, 106 91 Stockholm, Sweden (office). *Telephone:* (8) 162000 (office). *E-mail:* kare.bremer@su .se (office). *Website:* karebremer.wordpress.com.

BREMER, L. Paul, III, BA, MBA; American business executive, fmr diplomatist and fmr government official; *Chairman, Board of Advisors, Global Secure Corporation;* ed Yale Univ., Institut d'études politiques, Paris, Harvard Grad. School of Business Admin; joined US State Dept, Special Asst to six Secs of State, service at US Embassies in Afghanistan and Malawi; fmr Deputy Chief of Mission, US Embassy, Norway; Amb. to Netherlands 1983–86; fmr Exec. Sec., State Dept and Amb. at Large for Counter Terrorism; Presidential Envoy to Iraq and Admin. Coalition Provisional Authority 2003–04; Man. Dir Kissinger Assocs 1989–2000; fmr Chair. and Chief Exec. Marsh Crisis Consulting Co.; Pres. and CEO World T.E.A.M. Sports 2010–12; currently Chair. Bd of Advisors, Global Secure Corpn; Chair. Nat. Comm. on Terrorism 1999; fmr Dir Air Products and Chemicals Inc., Akzo Nobel NV, Harvard Business School Club of New York, Netherland-America Foundation; fmr Trustee Econ. Club of New York; Founder and Pres. Lincoln/ Douglass Scholarship Foundation; mem. Pres.'s Homeland Security Advisory Council 2002; mem. IISS, Council on Foreign Relations; fmr mem. NAS Comm. on Science and Tech.; State Dept Superior Honor Award, two Presidential Meritorious Service Awards, Distinguished Honor Award, Presidential Medal of Freedom 2004. *Publications:* My Year in Iraq 2006. *Address:* Global Secure Corporation, 2600 Virginia Avenue, Suite 600, Washington, DC 20037, USA (office). *Telephone:* (202) 333-8400 (office). *Fax:* (202) 333-0082 (office). *E-mail:* info@globalsecurecorp .com (office). *Website:* www.globalsecurecorp.com (office).

BREMI, Ulrich; Swiss business executive and politician; b. 6 Nov. 1929, Zurich; s. of Heinrich Bremi-Sennhauser and Johanna Bremi-Sennhauser; m. Anja Bremi-Forrer; two d.; ed School of Mechanical Eng, Winterthur and Swiss Fed. Inst. of Tech., Zürich; CEO Kaba Holding Ltd Zürich 1962–90; Chair. Bd Neue Zürcher Zeitung 1988–99, Georg Fischer AG 1989–98, Swiss Reinsurance Co. 1992–2000, Flughafen-Immobilien-Gesellschaft 1992–2000; mem. Swiss Nat. Parl. 1975–91, Chair. 1990–91; Hon. Senator, Univ. of St Gallen 2000; Hon. Counsellor, ETH Zurich. *Address:* Zollikerstrasse 57, 8702 Zürich, Switzerland (office). *Telephone:* (44) 3952010 (office). *Fax:* (44) 3952019 (office). *E-mail:* ulrich.bremi@bremi.ch (office). *Website:* www.bremi.ch (office).

BREMKAMP, Detlev; German business executive; b. 2 March 1944, Hamburg; insurance apprenticeship, Allianz Versicherungs AG 1963–65, skills devt in UK Commercial Union Insurance, Willis Faber and Lloyd's of London 1969–70, posted to Munich HQ as First Clerk and dept dir 1971, apptd Head of Fire Dept and Dir of Insurance sector 1974, advanced to Exec. Bd of Allianz Versicherungs AG (holding co. for damage and casualty business) 1980; Sr Strategic Adviser to European Business, Lehman Brothers Inc. 2005–08, mem. European Advisory Council; mem. Man. Bd and Head of Europe II, Allianz SE 1991–, Allianz AG, Munich 2000–05, responsible for Western, Northern and Southern Europe, reinsurance, alternative risk transfer and assistance/travel insurance and served as Head of Europe II; Deputy mem. Man. Bd Allianz Versicherung 1981–82, Full mem. 1983–87, Man. Dir and Gen. Man. Allianz Europe Ltd, Amsterdam 1987–90; Chair. Supervisory Bd Hochtief AG –2011; Dir, Converium Holding AG 2006–, Allianz Portugal SA, Assurances Générales de France, Lloyd Adriatico, Allianz Nederland Group and vorstand of Allianz; mem. Supervisory Bd ABB AG, HSH Nordbank AG 2009–13, ACIF, AGF RAS Holding BV (Chair.), Allianz Financial & Insurance Services GmbH, Allianz General Insurance Co. SA, Allianz Life Insurance Co. SA, Allianz Portugal SA, Allianz Global Risks Rückversicherungs-AG, Allianz Risk Transfer, Reaseguros SA (Spain), Companhia de Seguros (Portugal), Cornhill Insurance PLC (UK), Dresdner ABD Securities Ltd (Hong Kong), Dresdner Kleinwort Wasserstein (Japan) Ltd, Elmonda Assistance (France, Chair.), Lloyd Adriatico (Italy), RAS International II BV, RINV (NewCo) (Chair.), Zwolsche Algemeene NV (Netherlands), Bayerische Hypovereinsbank AG (Germany), Royal Nederland Verzekeringsgroep NV; mem. Econ. Advisory Council Bayerische Landesbank 2005–09; Dir RAS International NV, Assurances Generales de France 1998–2005, SCOR Holding (Switzerland) Ltd 2006–; Dir (non-exec.) Riunione Adriatica Di Sicurtà SpA (RAS) 1997–. *Address:* c/o Hochtief AG, Opernplatz 2, 45128 Essen, Germany.

BREN, Donald L., BA; American real estate investment industry executive and philanthropist; *Chairman, The Irvine Company Inc.;* b. 11 May 1932, Los Angeles, Calif.; s. of Milton H. Bren and Marion Bren (née Newbert); m. 1st Diane Bren; three c.; m. 2nd Mardelle Bren 1977 (divorced); one d.; m. 3rd Brigitte Muller 1998; one s.; three c. by two fmr companions; ed Univ. of Washington; served as officer in US Marine Corps; f. Bren Co. to build homes in Orange Co., Calif. 1958, later renamed California Pacific Homes; Founder and Pres. Mission Viejo Co., Orange Co. 1963, sold interest in co. 1967; joined a group of investors to purchase The Irvine Co. from The Irvine Foundation 1977, later mem. Exec. Cttee and Vice-Chair., bought out partners and elected Chair. 1983–, sole shareholder 1996–; f. Donald Bren Foundation; mem. Bd of Trustees, Chapman Univ., California Inst. of Tech. (Caltech), LA County Museum of Art, Orange County Museum of Art;

Fellow, American Acad. of Arts and Sciences; Semper Fidelis Award, Marine Corps Univ. Foundation 1998, and its Gen. Leonard F. Chapman Medallion 2003, Univ. of California Presidential Medal 2004. *Leisure interests:* skiing, tennis, sailing, windsurfing. *Address:* The Irvine Company Inc., 550 Newport Center Drive, Newport Beach, CA 92660, USA (office). *Telephone:* (949) 720-2000 (office). *Fax:* (949) 720-2218 (office). *E-mail:* webmaster@irvinecompany.com (office). *Website:* www.irvinecompany.com (office); www.donaldbren.com.

BRENCIU, Marius; Romanian singer (tenor); b. 11 Nov. 1973, Braşov; s. of Radu Brenciu and Maria-Elena Brenciu; m.; ed Andrei Saguna High School, Univ. of Music, Bucharest; began singing in choir of local Orthodox church aged 12; teaching asst, Univ. of Music, Bucharest 1997–2000; debut as Don Ottavio in Mozart's Don Giovanni at Bucharest Opera 1997; Perm. Leading Singer, Romanian Nat. Opera, Bucharest; recent opera activities include Rodolfo (La Bohème) in Hamburg and Tel-Aviv, Alfredo (La traviata) in Berlin, Rome and Brussels, Almaviva (Il Barbiere di Siviglia) in Lyon and Lisbon, Adorno (Simon Boccanegra) in Hamburg, Macduff (Macbeth) at Edinburgh Festival and Amsterdam; debut at New York Met in La rondine (Puccini) 2008, also sang in Paris and Toulouse; sang Nemorino (L'elisir d'amore) in Berlin and Tel-Aviv, Edgardo (Lucia di Lammermoor) in Amsterdam and Lensky (Eugen Onegin) in Vienna, Munich, Berlin, Zurich, Toulouse, Lyon, Tokyo, Lisbon, Genf, Israel and Cardiff and title role in Idomeneo (Mozart) at Opéra Nat. de Paris; sang Prunier (La rondine) at New York Met 2013, Alfredo Germont (La traviata) in Sofia 2013–14, Lenski (Eugene Onegin) in Naples 2014; regular collaborations with conductors including Claudio Abbado, Seiji Ozawa, Lorin Maazel, Zubin Mehta, Simone Young, Ion Marin, Kent Nagano, Valéry Gergiev, Sylvain Cambreling, Marco Armiliato, Ton Koopman, Lothar Zagrosek, Sir Charles Mackerras, Stefan Soltesz, Gianandrea Noseda, Jacques Delacôte, Mstislav Rostropovich, Herbert Blomstedt, Kiril Petrenko, Dan Ettinger; with orchestras including Berlin Philharmonic, Gewandhaus Orchestra, Rotterdam Philharmonic Orchestra, NDR Symphony Orchestra, BBC Philharmonic, Academy of Ancient Music, Orchestre Philharmonique de Radio France and Orquesta Nacional de Espana; other repertoire includes Requiem (Verdi), Mass in C Minor (Mozart), Messa di Gloria (Puccini), Messe Solennelle (Gounod), A Child of our Time (Tippett); winner Julian Gayarre Int. Competition, Georges Enescu Int. Competition 1999, Second Prize and Opera Prize, Queen Elizabeth Competition, Brussels 2000, First Prize, Young Artists Int. Auditions, New York 2001, Winner Cardiff Singer of the World (also Song Prize) 2001. *Television:* Puccini's La Rondine, Metropolitan Opera, NY, Tchaikovsky's Eugene Onegin, BBC 2004, NHK, Japan 2008. *Recordings include:* George Enescu's Vox Maris, Verdi's Requiem, Lehár's Friederike, d'Indy's L'Étranger. *Leisure interests:* literature, foreign languages, history, history. *Address:* c/o Luisa Petrov, Glauburgstr. 95, 60318 Frankfurt, Germany (office). *Telephone:* (69) 5970377 (office). *Fax:* (69) 59748–08 (office). *E-mail:* luisapetrov@web.de (office).

BRENDE, Børge, BA; Norwegian politician and international organization official; *President, World Economic Forum;* b. 25 Sept. 1965, Odda; s. of Knut Brendeseter and Kari Wesche; m.; two s.; ed Norwegian Univ. of Science and Tech.; mem. Trondheim Municipal Exec. Bd (Kommunalråd) 1992–97; mem. Storting (Parl.) 1997–2007; Minister of the Environment 2001–04, of Trade and Industry 2004–05, of Foreign Affairs 2013–17; Chair. PD Burma (int. network of political leaders promoting democracy in Burma) 2005–07; Man. Dir World Econ. Forum, Geneva 2008–09, 2011–13; Sec.-Gen. Red Cross Norway 2009–11; Pres. World Econ. Forum 2017–; mem. Bd Norwegian School of Econs and Business Admin 2009–12; Trustee The Oslo Center for Peace and Human Rights 2009–12; Chair. Mesta (road maintenance co.) 2010–13; mem. Bd of Dirs Statoil 2012–13; mem. China Council for Int. Cooperation on Environment and Devt 2005–; mem. Foundation Bd Global Shapers Community 2012–; mem. Conservative Party (Høyre), Deputy Chair. 1994–98; Grand Cross, Order of Merit (Italy), Order of the Phoenix 2004, Commdr, Order of St Olav 2005. *Address:* World Economic Forum, 91–93 route de la Capite, CH-1223 Geneva, Switzerland (office). *Telephone:* 228691212 (office). *Fax:* 227862744 (office). *E-mail:* contact@weforum.org (office). *Website:* www.weforum.org (office).

BRENDEL, Alfred; Austrian pianist and writer; b. 5 Jan. 1931, Wiesenberg; s. of Ing. Albert Brendel and Ida Brendel (née Wieltschnig); m. 1st Iris Heymann-Gonzala 1960 (divorced 1972); one d.; m. 2nd Irene Semler 1975; one s. two d.; ed studied piano under Sofija Deželić, Zagreb, Ludovika v. Kaan, Graz, Edwin Fischer, Lucerne, Paul Baumgartner, Basel, Edward Steuermann, Salzburg; studied composition under A. Michl and harmony under Franjo Dugan; first piano recital Musikverein Graz 1948; concert tours through Europe, Latin America, North America 1963–2008, Australia 1963, 1966, 1969, 1976; has appeared at numerous music festivals, including Salzburg 1960–2008, Vienna, Edinburgh, Aldeburgh, Athens, Granada, Lucerne, Puerto Rico, London Proms and has performed with most major orchestras of Europe and USA; mem. American Acad. of Arts and Sciences; Hon. RAM; Hon. RCM; Hon. Fellow, Exeter Coll., Oxford 1987; Hon. KBE 1989, Hon. mem. Wiener Philharmoniker 1998; Commdr, Ordre des Arts et des Lettres 1985, Ordre pour le Mérite (Germany) 1991; Hon. DMus (London) 1978, (Oxford) 1983, (Warwick) 1991, (Yale) 1992, (Exeter) 1998, (Southampton) 2002; Hon. DLitt (Sussex) 1981; Dr hc (Cologne) 1995, (RAM 1999, (Hochschule Franz Liszt Weimar) 2009, (New England Conservatory 2009), (McGill) 2011, (Juilard School) 2011, (Cambridge) 2012; Premio Città de Bolzano, Concorso Busoni 1949, Grand Prix du Disque 1965, Edison Prize (five times 1973–87), Grand Prix des Disquaires de France 1975, Deutscher Schallplattenpreis (four times 1976–84, 1992), Wiener Flötenuhr (six times 1976–87), Gramophone Award (six times 1977–83), Japanese Record Acad. Award (five times 1977–84, with Scottish Symphony Orchestra/Sir Charles Mackerras 2002), Japanese Grand Prix 1978, Franz Liszt Prize (four times 1979–83), Frankfurter Musikpreis 1984, Diapason D'Or Award 1992, Heidsieck Award for Writing on Music 1990, Hans von Bülow-Medaille, Kameradschaft der Berliner Philharmoniker eV, 1992, Cannes Classical Award 1998, Léonie Sonnings Musikpris, Denmark 2002, Ernst von Siemens Musikpreis 2004, Premio Artur Rubinstein 2007, Prix Venezia 2007, Praemium Imperiale 2008, Herbert von Karajan Prize 2008, Gramophone Lifetime Achievement Award 2010, Franz Liszt Ehrenpreis 2011, Juillard Medal 2011, Golden Mozart Medal, Salzburg Mozarteum 2014. *Recordings include:* extensive repertoire; Beethoven's Complete Piano Works, Beethoven Sonatas, three sets of Beethoven Concertos (with Vienna Philharmonic Orchestra and Simon Rattle) 1998. *Publications:* essays on music and musicians in Phono, Fono Forum, Österreichische Musikzeit-schrift, Music and Musicians, Hi-Fi Stereophonie, New York Review of Books, Die Zeit, Frankfurter Allgemeine Zeitung, Musical Thoughts and Afterthoughts 1976, Nachdenken über Musik 1977, Music Sounded Out (essays) 1990, Musik beim Wort genommen 1992, Fingerzeig 1996, Störendes Lachen während des Jaworts 1997, One Finger Too Many 1998, Kleine Teufel 1999, Collected Essays on Music 2001, Augerechnet Ich (aka The Veil of Order: In Conversation with Martin Meyer) 2001, Spiegelbild und Schwarzer Spuk (poems) 2003, Cursing Bagels (poems) 2004, Alfred Brendel über Musik 2005, A bis Z eines Pianisten 2012. *Leisure interests:* books, theatre, the visual arts, films, baroque and romanesque architecture, unintentional humour, kitsch. *Address:* Maestro Arts, 1 Eastfields Avenue, London SW18 1FQ, England (office). *Telephone:* (20) 3637-2789 (office). *E-mail:* iain@maestroarts.com (office). *Website:* maestroarts.com (office); www.alfredbrendel.com.

BRENDISH, Clayton (Clay) M., CBE, BSc, MSc, CEng, FBCS, CMgr FCMI; British business executive; *President, Chartered Management Institute;* served as an Adviser to the Govt on the efficiency of the Civil Service, as an Adviser to the Chancellor of the Duchy of Lancaster and the Office of Public Services on their respective Next Steps Agencies 1993–2000; played key role in the privatization of HM's Stationery Office, Civil Service Occupational Health and Safety Agency, Recruitment and Assessment Services and Chessington Computer Centre; co-f. CMG Admiral PLC (acquired Admiral PLC) 1979, Exec. Chair. 1979–2000, Exec. Deputy Chair. CMG Plc (following CMG's merger with Admiral) 2000–01; Chair. (non-exec.) Close Beacon Investment Fund 1995–, Echo Research Ltd 2003–, Anite plc 2005–, SThree Plc 2010–; External Chair. The Meterological Office; Chair. GlobeOp Financial Services SA 2007–09; Dir (non-exec.), Ordnance Survey 1993–96, BT Group PLC 2002–11, Close Beacon Investment Fund 1995–, Elexon plc, Echo Research Ltd; Dir, Defence Logistics Organisation, Defence Communication Services Agency, Test and Itchen Asscn Ltd, Herald Investment Trust Plc 2001–12, Group NBT plc; fmr Chair. Exec. Bd Inst. of Man. (Chartered Man. Inst. since 2002), Pres. 2001–, Chair. Information Tech. Task Group, mem. Remuneration Cttee, Chartered Fellow; Trustee, Economist Newspapers Ltd 1999–; mem. Admin. Bd, Elster Group SE 2011–12; mem. Ind. TV Comm. 2000–, Council City Univ., London 2000–, Malaysian British Business Council –2001; Trustee, Economist Newspapers Ltd. *Address:* Chartered Management Institute, 2 Savoy Court, Strand, London, WC2R 0EZ, England (office). *Telephone:* (20) 7497-0580 (office). *Fax:* (20) 7497-0463 (office). *E-mail:* enquiries@managers.org.uk (office). *Website:* www.managers.org.uk (office).

BRENES SOLÓRZANO, HE Cardinal Leopoldo José; Nicaraguan ecclesiastic; *Archbishop of Managua;* b. 7 March 1949, Ticuantepe; ordained priest, Archdiocese of Managua 1974; consecrated Auxiliary Bishop of Managua 1988–91, Archbishop of Managua 2005–; apptd Titular Bishop of Maturba 1988; Bishop of Matagalpa 1991–2005; cr. Cardinal (Cardinal-Priest of San Gioacchino ai Prati di Castello) 2014–. *Address:* Archdiocese of Managua, Apartado 3058, Managua, Nicaragua (office). *Telephone:* (2) 277-17-54 (office). *Fax:* (2) 276-01-30 (office). *E-mail:* info@curiamanagua.org (office). *Website:* www.curiamanagua.org (office).

BRENNAN, David R., BBA; American pharmaceutical industry executive; m.; four c.; ed Gettysburg Coll.; joined Merck as sales rep. 1975, Gen. Man. Chibret Int. (French subsidiary) 1990–92; joined AstraMerck 1992, was responsible for business planning and devt at Astra Pharmaceuticals, Sr Vice-Pres. of Commercial Operations, AstraZeneca Pharmaceuticals LP (N America) 1999–2001, Pres. and CEO AstraZeneca LP (N America) 2001–06, Exec. Bd Dir AstraZeneca 2005–12, CEO AstraZeneca PLC 2006–12; Pres. Int. Fed. of Pharmaceutical Mfrs and Asscns; Past Chair. Pharmaceutical Research and Mfrs of America (PhRMA), Southeastern Pennsylvania Chapter of the American Heart Asscn; mem. Exec. Bd European Fed. of Pharmaceutical Industries and Asscns, European Roundtable of Industrialists, Nat. Inst. of Health Roundtable on Evidence Based Medicine; Commr UK Comm. for Employment and Skills 2007–; mem. Bd Philadelphia Orchestra; Hon. mem. Bd of Dirs CEO Roundtable on Cancer. *Leisure interests:* scuba diving, cycling, amateur photography.

BRENNAN, Hon. Sir (Francis) Gerard, Kt, AC, KBE, GBS (Hong Kong), LLB, QC; Australian judge (retd); b. 22 May 1928, Rockhampton, Queensland; s. of Hon. Mr Justice Frank T. Brennan and Gertrude Brennan; m. Patricia O'Hara 1953; three s. four d.; ed Christian Brothers' Coll., Rockhampton, Downlands Coll., Toowoomba and Univ. of Queensland, Brisbane; admitted to Bar 1951, QC 1965; Pres. Bar Asscn of Queensland 1974–76, Australian Bar Asscn 1975–76, Admin. Review Council 1976–79, Admin. Appeals Tribunal 1976–79; mem. Exec. Law Council of Australia 1975–76, Australian Law Reform Comm. 1975–77; Additional Judge, Supreme Court of ACT 1976–81; Judge, Australian Industrial Court 1976–81, Fed. Court of Australia 1977–81; Justice, High Court of Australia 1981–95; Chief Justice of Australia 1995–98; External Judge, Supreme Court of Fiji 1999–2000; Non-perm. Judge, Court of Final Appeal of Hong Kong 2000–12; Foundation Scientia Prof. of Law, Univ. of New South Wales 1998; Chancellor, Univ. of Tech., Sydney 1998–2004; Hon. LLD (Univ. of Dublin Trinity Coll.) 1988, (Univ. of Queensland) 1996, (ANU) 1996, (Melbourne Univ., Univ. of Tech., Sydney) 1998, (Univ. of New South Wales) 2005; Hon. DLitt (Central Queensland Univ.) 1996; Hon. DUniv (Griffiths Univ.) 1996, (Univ. of Tech., Sydney) 2005. *Address:* c/o Suite 3003, Piccadilly Tower, 133 Castlereagh Street, Sydney, NSW 2000, Australia. *Telephone:* (2) 9261-8704 (office). *Fax:* (2) 9261-8113 (office).

BRENNAN, John J. (Jack), AB, MBA; American business executive; *Chairman Emeritus and Senior Advisor, The Vanguard Group Inc.;* b. 1954, Boston, Mass; s. of Frank Brennan; m. Catherine Brennan; two s. one d.; ed Dartmouth Coll., Harvard Business School; Assoc., New York Bank for Savings 1976–78; Planning Assoc., S.C. Johnson & Son 1980–82; joined Vanguard Group Inc. 1982, Asst to Chair. 1982–85, Chief Financial Officer 1985–89, Pres. 1989–96, CEO 1996–2008, Chair. 1998–2009, Chair. Emer. and Sr Advisor 2010–; fmr Chair. Investment Company Inst., Financial Accounting Foundation; Dir, Guardian Life Insurance Co. of America, LPL Financial Holdings Inc.; fmr Dir, The Hanover Insurance Group; Lead Gov., FINRA Bd Govs; Trustee, The Vanguard Charitable Endowment Program, Univ. of Notre Dame. *Address:* The Vanguard Group Inc., PO Box 1110, Valley Forge, PA 19482-1110, USA (office). *Telephone:* (610) 648-6000 (office). *Fax:* (610) 669-6605 (office). *E-mail:* info@vanguard.com (office). *Website:* www.vanguard.com (office).

BRENNAN, John Owen, BA, MA; American government official; b. 22 Sept. 1955; m. Kathy Pokluda; three c.; ed Fordham Univ., American Univ., Cairo, Univ. of Texas, Austin; career trainee, Operations Directorate, CIA 1980, joined Directorate of Intelligence, CIA 1981, Political Officer, Embassy in Jeddah, Saudi Arabia 1982–84, various positions with Office of Near Eastern and South Asian Analysis, CIA 1984–89, Head of Terrorism Analysis, CIA Counterterrorist Center 1990–92, Daily intelligence briefer to Pres. Bill Clinton 1994–95, Exec. Asst to CIA Deputy Dir 1995–96, Station Chief, CIA, Riyadh, Saudi Arabia 1996–99, Chief of Staff to CIA Deputy Dir 1999–2001, Deputy Exec. Dir, CIA 2001–03, Dir, Terrorist Threat Integration Center 2003–04, Interim Dir, Nat. Counterterrorism Center 2004–05, Dir, CIA 2013–17; Asst to Pres., Deputy Nat. Security Adviser for Homeland Security and Counterterrorism, Nat. Security Council 2009–13; Pres. and CEO, The Analysis Corpn 2005–08; Chair. Intelligence and Nat. Security Alliance 2007–08; Nat. Security Medal, Distinguished Intelligence Medal, Distinguished Career Intelligence Medal.

BRENNAN, Megan J., MBA; American business executive and government official; *Postmaster-General and CEO, United States Postal Service;* ed Immaculata Coll., Massachusetts Inst. of Tech.; joined US Postal Service (USPS) as mail carrier, Lancaster, Pa 1986, held various positions including Dist Man., USPS, Springfield, Mass, Plant Man. (processing and distribution facilities), Lehigh Valley and Reading, Pa, Man. (field support and integration), Washington, DC, Delivery and Collection Supervisor, Man. (operations support), NE area 2003–05, Vice-Pres. of Area Operations, NE area 2005–06, Vice-Pres. of Area Operations, East area 2006–10, Exec. Vice-Pres. and COO, USPS, Washington, DC 2010–15, Postmaster-Gen. and CEO USPS (first woman) 2015–. *Address:* US Postal Service, 475 L'Enfant Plaza SW, Washington, DC 20260, USA (office). *Telephone:* (202) 268-3118 (office). *Website:* www.usps.com (office).

BRENNECKE, Joan F., BS, MS, PhD; American chemist and academic; *Keating-Crawford Professor of Chemical and Biomolecular Engineering, University of Notre Dame;* ed Univ. of Texas, Univ. of Illinois; mem. Faculty, Univ. of Notre Dame, Ind. 1989–, currently Keating-Crawford Prof. of Chemical and Biomolecular Eng, Dir Notre Dame's Energy Center; Past Chair. Council for Chemical Research; mem. Editorial Bd Green Chemistry; mem. AIChE, ACS, American Soc. for Eng Educ.; numerous awards, including NSF Presidential Young Investigator Award 1991, ACS Ipatieff Prize 2001, AIChE Professional Progress Award 2006, John M. Prausnitz Award, Conf. on Properties and Phase Equilibria for Product and Process Design 2007, Julius Stieglitz Lecturer, Chicago section of ACS and Univ. of Chicago 2008. *Publications:* numerous papers in professional journals on supercritical fluid tech., ionic liquids, thermodynamics, environmentally benign chemical processing and carbon dioxide separation, storage and usage. *Address:* 180 Fitzpatrick Hall, Department of Chemical and Biomolecular Engineering, University of Notre Dame, Notre Dame, IN 46556, USA (office). *Telephone:* (574) 631-5847 (office); (574) 631-7709 (Lab.) (office). *Fax:* (574) 631-8366 (office). *E-mail:* jfb@nd.edu (office). *Website:* www.nd.edu/~jfb (office).

BRENNEMAN, Ronald Alvin, BSc, MSc; Canadian petroleum industry executive; b. 1947; ed Univ. of Toronto, Univ. of Manchester, Sr Exec. Program, Sloan School of Business, Massachusetts Inst. of Tech.; joined Imperial Oil Ltd 1969, Operations Man. 1977, various man. roles 1978–83, with Exxon Corpn (parent co.), NY 1983–86, becoming Vice-Pres. then Pres. Imperial Oil Ltd 1992–94, CEO Esso Benelux 1994–97, Gen. Man. of Corp. Planning, Exxon, Dallas 1997–99; mem. Bd of Dirs, Pres. and CEO Petro-Canada 2000–09, Exec. Vice-Chair. Suncor Energy Inc. (following merger with Petro-Canada) 2009–10; mem. Bd of Dirs, The Bank of Novia Scotia (Scotiabank) 2000–(17), BCE Inc., WestJet Airlines Ltd, Syncrude Canada Ltd 2004–08; fmr mem. Canadian Petroleum Asscn, Canada Safety Council, United Way of Calgary and of Toronto; Trustee, United Way of Greater Toronto, Hosp. for Sick Children. *Address:* Office of the Chairman, Scotiabank, Scotia Plaza, 44 King Street West, Toronto, ON M5H 1H1, Canada (office). *Telephone:* (416) 866-6161 (office). *Fax:* (416) 866-3750 (office). *E-mail:* email@scotiabank.com (office). *Website:* www.scotiabank.com (office).

BRENNER, David J., BA, MSc, MA, PhD; British physicist and academic; *Higgins Professor of Radiation Biophysics, College of Physicians and Surgeons, Columbia University;* b. 9 June 1953, Liverpool, England; ed Merchant Taylors' School, Liverpool, St Edmund Hall, Oxford, St Bartholomew's Hosp., Univ. of London, Univ. of Surrey; Postdoctoral Fellow, Los Alamos Scientific Lab. 1979–81, Staff mem. 1981–83; Assoc Research Scientist, Radiological Research Lab., Coll. of Physicians and Surgeons, Columbia Univ., New York 1983–86, Asst Prof. of Radiation Oncology 1986–92, Assoc. Prof. 1992–93, Prof. and Dir Center for Radiological Research 1994–, Higgins Prof. of Radiation Biophysics 2008–, also Dir Columbia Univ. Radiological Research Accelerator Facility; Miller Prof., Univ. of California, Berkeley 2002; mem. Editorial Bd Radiation and Environmental Biophysics 2002–; mem. Nat. Council on Radiation Protection and Measurements; Hon. DSc (Oxford) 1996; Univ. of Oxford Carter Physics Prize 1974, Radiation Research Soc. Annual Research Award 1991, Robert D. Moseley Award for Radiation Protection in Medicine, Nat. Council on Radiation Protection and Measurements 1992, Jean Roy Memorial Lecturer, Canadian Asscn of Radiation Oncology 2002, G. William Morgan Lecturer, Health Physics Soc. 2008, Selby Lecturer, Memorial Sloan Kettering Cancer Center 2009, Douglas Lea Lecturer, UK Radiation Oncology Congress 2009, Herbert L. Abrams Lecturer, Brigham and Women's Hosp., Boston 2011, Failla Gold Medal Award, Radiation Research Soc. 2011. *Publications include:* Radon, Risk and Remedy 1989, Making the Radiotherapy Decision 1996; more than 300 articles in scientific journals; five US patents. *Address:* Center for Radiological Research, Columbia University, 630 West 168th Street, New York, NY 10032, USA (office). *Telephone:* (212) 305-5660 (office). *Fax:* (212) 305-3229 (office). *E-mail:* djb3@cumc.columbia.edu (office). *Website:* www.columbia.edu/~djb3 (office).

BRENT, Richard P., MA, PhD, DSc, FAA, FIEEE, FACM, FIMA, FAustMS, FSIAM; Australian computer scientist, mathematician and academic; *Professor Emeritus, Australian National University;* b. 1946, Melbourne, Vic.; s. of Oscar Brent and Nancy Brent; m. Erin O'Connor 1969 (died 2005), two s.; m. Judy-Anne Osborn 2007; one s.; ed Melbourne Grammar School, Monash Univ., Stanford Univ., USA; Research Scientist, IBM T.J. Watson Research Center, Yorktown Heights, New York, USA 1971–72; Research Fellow, ANU, Canberra 1972–78, Prof. of Computer Sciences 1978–98, Australian Research Council Fed Fellow and Prof., Math. Sciences Inst. 2005–10, Distinguished Prof. of Math. and Computer Science 2010–11, Prof. Emer. 2011–; Prof. of Computing Science, Univ. of Oxford 1998–2005, Fellow, St Hugh's Coll. 1998–2005; Conjoint Prof. of Math., CARMA, Univ. of Newcastle, NSW 2010–; Fellow, Inst. of Math. and its Applications, Asscn for Computing Machinery (USA), Soc. for Industrial and Applied Math. (USA), Australian Math. Soc.; Foreign Fellow, Bangladesh Acad. of Science; Australian Math. Soc. Medal 1984, Forsythe Memorial Lecturer 1990, Hannan Medal 2005, Moyal Medal 2014. *Publications include:* Algorithms for Minimization without Derivatives 1973, Topics in Computational Complexity and the Analysis of Algorithms 1980, Modern Computer Arithmetic (with Paul Zimmermann) 2010. *Leisure interests:* music, chess, bridge, sustainability. *Address:* Mathematical Sciences Institute, Australian National University, Canberra, ACT 2600, Australia (office). *E-mail:* europa@rpbrent.com (office). *Website:* maths-people.anu.edu.au/~brent (office).

BRENTON, Howard, BA, FRSL; British playwright; b. 13 Dec. 1942, Portsmouth, Hants.; s. of Donald Henry Brenton and Rose Lilian Brenton (née Lewis); m. Jane Fry 1970; two s.; ed Chichester High School for Boys and St Catharine's Coll., Cambridge; resident writer, Royal Court Theatre, London 1972–73; Writer-in-Residence, Univ. of Warwick 1978–79; Granada Artist-in-Residence, Univ. of Calif., Davis 1997; Arts and Humanities Research Bd Fellowship, Univ. of Birmingham 2000; Hon. Dr of Arts (North London) 1996, (Westminster), (Portsmouth); John Whiting Award 1970, Standard Best Play of the Year Award 1976, Standard Best Play of the Year (with David Hare) 1985. *Publications include:* Revenge (play) 1969, Christie in Love 1969, Scott of the Antarctic (or What God Didn't See) 1970, Lay By (co-author) 1972, Plays for Public Places 1972, Hitler Dances 1972, Magnificence 1973, Brassneck (with David Hare) 1973, The Churchill Play 1974, Government Property 1975, The Saliva Milkshake 1975, Weapons of Happiness 1976, The Paradise Run (TV play) 1976, Sore Throats 1979, Plays for the Poor Theatre 1980, The Romans in Britain 1980, Thirteenth Night 1981, The Genius 1983, Desert of Lies (TV play) 1983, Sleeping Policemen (with Tunde Ikoli) 1983, Bloody Poetry 1984, Pravda (with David Hare) 1985, Dead Head 1986, Greenland 1988, Diving for Pearls (novel) 1989, Iranian Nights (with Tariq Ali) 1989, Hess is Dead 1990, Moscow Gold (with Tariq Ali) 1990, Berlin Bertie 1992, Hot Irons (Essays and Diaries) 1995, Playing Away (opera) 1994, Goethe's Faust, Parts I and II (adaptation) 1995, Plays I 1996, Plays II 1996, In Extremis 1997, Ugly Rumours (with Tariq Ali) 1998, Collateral Damage (with Tariq Ali and Andy de la Tour), Nasser's Eden (play for radio) 1999, Snogging Ken (with Tariq Ali and Andy de la Tour) 2000, Kit's Play 2000, Spooks (TV series) 2002–05, Paul (play) 2005, In Extremis (play) 2006, Never So Good (play) 2008, Anne Boleyn (play) 2010, Danton's Death (version) 2010, The Ragged Trousered Philanthropists (adaptation) 2010, 55 Days (play) 2012, The Interrogation of Ai Weiwei (play) 2013, Dances Of Death (adaptation) 2013, The Guffin (play) 2013, Drawing the Line (play) 2013, Doctor Scroggy's War (play) 2014, Ransomed (play) 2015, Lawrence After Arabia (play) 2016, Miis Julie (adaptation) 2017, The Blinding Light (play) 2017, The Shadow Factory (play) 2018, Creditors (adaptation) 2019, Jude (play) 2019. *Leisure interest:* painting. *Address:* c/o Casarotto Ramsay Ltd, Waverley House, 7–12 Noel Street, London, W1F 8GQ, England (office). *Telephone:* (20) 7287-4450 (office). *Fax:* (20) 7287-9128 (office). *E-mail:* info@casarotto.co.uk (office). *Website:* www.casarotto.co.uk (office).

BRESCH, Heather, BA; American pharmaceutical company executive; *CEO, Mylan;* ed Univ. of West Virginia; joined Mylan (pharmaceutical co.) 1992, has held numerous positions including Head of North America operations, later COO and Chief Integration Officer, led integration of Matrix Laboratories and Merck KGaA's generics business, Pres. Mylan –2012, mem. Bd of Dirs and CEO 2012–; fmr Chair. and Vice-Chair. Generic Pharmaceutical. *Address:* Mylan, 1500 Corporate Drive, Canonsburg, PA 15317, USA (office). *Telephone:* (724) 514-1800 (office). *E-mail:* info@mylan.com (office). *Website:* www.mylan.com (office).

BRETH, Andrea; German theatre director; b. 31 Oct. 1952, Rieden, Allgau; d. of Herbert Breth and Maria Breth (née Noether); ed Darmstadt, Heidelberg; worked at numerous theatres including in Wiesbaden, Bochum, Bremen, Hamburg, Berlin Zürich, Freiburg, and Vienna; Artistic Dir Berliner Schaubühne am Leniner Platz 1992–97; Dir-in-Residence, Burgtheater Wien 1997; Prof. for Directing, Hochschule für Schauspielkunst Ernst Busch; mem. der Darstellenden Künste, Frankfurt, Akademie der Künste Berlin, Bayerische Akademie der Schönen Künste; Austrian Cross of Honour for Science and Art (1st class), Grand Cross of Merit, Federal Republic of Germany, Pour le Mérite 2018; Fritz-Kortner-Prize 1987, Nestroy-Award 2003, German Schiller-Preis 2015, and other awards. *Theatre productions include:* Städtische Bühnen Freiburg: Lorca's House of Bernarda Alba 1984; Bochum: Julien Green's Süden 1987, Gorki's The Last 1989; Schaubühne Berlin: Schnitzler's Der einsame Weg 1991, Gorki's Night Asylum 1992, Wampilow's Last Summer in Tschulimsk 1992, Ibsen's Hedda Gabler 1993, Chekhov's Uncle Vanya 1998; Burgtheater Wien: Kleist's Der zerbrochene Krug 1990, O'Casey's End of the Beginning 1992, Schiller's Maria Stuart 2001, Schiller's Don Carlos 2004, Shakespeare's Hamlet 2013, O'Neill's A Long Day's Journey into Night 2018; Salzburg Festival: Dostoyevsky's Crime and Punishment 2008, Kleist's Prinz Friedrich von Homburg 2012, Pinter's The BirthdayParty 2017. *Operas directed include:* Orfeo ed Euridice, Eugene Onegin, Kat'a Kabanova, Wozzeck, Lulu, La traviata, Jakob Lenz (German Faust-Preis for Best Opera Dir 2015), Médée 2018, Il prigioniero 2018. *Leisure interests:* literature, music, paintings, theatre. *Address:* c/o Burgtheater, Dr. Karl-Lueger-Ring 2, 1010 Vienna, Austria (office).

BRETON, Guy, CM, BA, MD; Canadian radiologist, academic and university administrator; *Rector, Université de Montréal;* b. 1 April 1950, Saint-Hyacinthe, Québec; ed Séminaire de Saint-Hyacinthe, Univ. of Sherbrooke; served residency in diagnostic radiology at McGill Univ., while obtaining additional training in neuroradiology at Montreal Neurological Inst. and Hosp.; Assoc. Clinical Prof., Dept of Radiology, Radio-Oncology and Nuclear Medicine, Faculty of Medicine, Université de Montréal 1979–94, Full Prof. 1994–, Head of Dept 1996–2003, Exec. Vice-Dean of Post-Doctoral Medical Studies and Hosp. Affairs, Faculty of Medicine 2003–06, helped establish integrated university health network (RUIS), Exec. Vice-Rector Université de Montréal 2006–10, Rector 2010–; involved in operations and admin of Hôpital Saint-Luc early 1980s, later of Centre hospitalier de l'Université de Montréal (CHUM), Head of hospital's Radiology Dept, Dir of

Planning for CHUM and Special Advisor to Chair. and CEO; played role in CHUM project 2000–06, Vice-Pres. SICHUM in planning of care, services, education and research, and Dir of Planning, CHUM 2010–; Pres. and CEO of pvt. radiology clinic in Québec 1983–97; Pres. Asscn des radiologistes du Québec 1987–97, Canadian Heads of Academic Radiology 1998–2000; fmr Chair. Medical Affairs Cttee of Conf. of Rectors and Prins of Quebec Univs; fmr mem. Bd CHUM, Fondation du CHUM, Hôpital Maisonneuve-Rosemont, Hôpital du Sacré-Cœur de Montréal, Canadian Asscn of Univ. Business Officers and Québec-Transplant; Hon. Prof., China Univ. of Political Science and Law; Dr hc (Shanghai Jiao Tong Univ.), (Université de Technologie Compiègne); Albert Jutras Prize, Asscn des radiologistes du Québec 2009. *Publications:* author or co-author of 100 scientific publs in professional journals. *Address:* Office of the Rector, Université de Montréal, PO Box 6128, Station Centre-ville, Montréal, PQ H3C 3J7, Canada (office). *Telephone:* (514) 343-6991 (office). *Fax:* (514) 343-2354 (office). *E-mail:* recteur@umontreal.ca (office). *Website:* www.umontreal.ca (office).

BRETON, Thierry; French government official and business executive; *CEO and Chairman of the Management Board, Atos Origin;* b. 15 Jan. 1955; m.; three c.; ed Lycée Louis Le Grand, Supelec Electrical Eng . School, Paris and French Inst. for Nat. Defence Studies (IHEDN); nat. mil. service as teacher of information tech. and math., French Lycée, New York 1979–81; Chair. and CEO Forma Systèmes 1981–86; Chief Adviser of Minister for Information and New Technologies, Ministry of Educ. and Research 1986–88; CEO Futuroscope de Poitiers (science and tech. theme park) and CEO Futuroscope Telecommunications Platform 1986–90; CEO CGI Group 1990–93; CEO and Vice-Chair. Bd Dirs Bull Group 1993–97; Chair. and CEO Thomson SA and Thomson Multimedia 1997–2002; Chair. and CEO France Telecom SA 2002–05; Minister of the Economy, Finance and Industry 2005–07; CEO and Chair. Man. Bd Atos Origin 2008–; mem. Bd of Dirs Carrefour SA 2008–; Chevalier, Légion d'honneur, Commdr, Ordre nat. du Mérite. *Publications include:* Softwar 1984, Vatican III 1985, Netwar 1987, La Dimension Invisible 1991, La Fin des Illusions 1992, Le Lievre et la Tortue 1994, Antidette 2007. *Address:* Atos Origin, Tour les Miroirs–Bat C, 18 avenue d'Alsace, 92926 Paris, La Défense 3 Cedex, France (office). *Telephone:* 1-55-91-20-00 (office). *Fax:* 1-55-91-20-05 (office). *Website:* www.atosorigin.com (office).

BRETSCHER, Mark Steven, MA, PhD, FRS; British/Swiss research scientist (retd); b. 8 Jan. 1940, Cambridge; s. of Egon Bretscher and Hanni Bretscher (née Greminger); m. Barbara M.F. Pearse 1978; one s. one d.; ed Abingdon School, Gonville and Caius Coll., Cambridge; research student, Gonville and Caius Coll., Cambridge 1961–64; Post-doctoral Visitor, Stanford Univ., USA 1964–65; Scientific Staff mem. MRC Lab. of Molecular Biology, Cambridge 1965–2012, Head, Div. of Cell Biology 1984–95; Visiting Prof., Harvard Coll., USA 1974–75, Stanford Univ. 1984–85; Friedrich-Miescher Prize 1979. *Television:* Bags of Life (Horizon, BBC) 1974. *Publications:* scientific papers in professional journals. *Leisure interest:* silviculture. *Address:* Ram Cottage, Commercial End, Swaffham Bulbeck, Cambs., CB25 0ND, England (home). *Telephone:* (1223) 811276 (home). *E-mail:* msb@mrc-lmb.cam.ac.uk (home). *Website:* www2.mrc-lmb.cam.ac.uk/personal/bretscher/msb_home.html (office).

BREUER, Michael; German accountant and politician; *President, Rheinische Sparkassen- und Giroverband (Rheinische Savings Bank and Giro Association);* b. 2 Oct. 1965, Brühl, North Rhine-Westphalia; m.; one s. one d.; ed Abitur in Lechenich, Univ. of Bonn; grew up in Erftstadt-Ahrem; mil. service in Munster and Lüneburg; mem. CDU 1983–, co. and dist chair. Jungen Union, mem. North Rhine-Westphalia State Parl. and mem. Bd CDU Parl. Group Cttee 1995, Spokesman for Budgetary Control 1995–2005; Dist Chair. CDU Cen. Rhine (Cologne, Bonn, Leverkusen, Rhine Erft) 1999, mem. regional-level Party Council of CDU North-Rhine-Westphalia; Minister for Fed., European and Int. Affairs, State of North Rhine-Westphalia 2005–07; worked for KPMG German trust 1993–2004; ind. certified public accountant and tax adviser 2004–05; Pres. Rheinische Sparkassen- und Giroverband (Rheinische Savings Bank and Giro Asscn), Düsseldorf 2008–; Chair. Supervisory Bd WestLB 2008–; mem. Bd of Dirs DekaBank Deutsche Girozentrale 2008–; Chair. Fördervereins der NRW-Stiftung; Order of Merit of North Rhine-Westphalia 2018. *Address:* Rheinischer Sparkassen-und Giroverband, Kirchfeldstraße 60, 40217 Düsseldorf, Germany (office). *Telephone:* (211) 3892-01 (office). *Fax:* (211) 3892-240 (office). *E-mail:* info@rsgv.de (office). *Website:* www.rsgv.de (office).

BREUER, Rolf-Ernst, DJur; German banker (retd); b. 1937; ed Univs of Lausanne, Munich and Bonn; joined Deutsche Bank as apprentice 1956, worked in Karlsruhe and Frankfurt, becoming Spokesman, Bd of Man. Dirs and Chair., Group Exec. Cttee, Deutsche Bank AG, Frankfurt 1997–2002, Chair. Supervisory Bd 2002–06 (resgnd); numerous other commercial appointments. *Address:* c/o Deutsche Bank, 60262 Frankfurt, Germany (office).

BREWER, Janice Kay (Jan); American politician and fmr state governor; b. 26 Sept. 1944, Los Angeles, Calif.; d. of Perry Wilford Drinkwine and Edna C. Drinkwine (née Bakken); m. Dr John Leon Brewer; three s. (one deceased); ed Glendale Community Coll.; qualified as radiological technologist; mem. Ariz. House of Reps from 19th Dist 1983–97; Chair. Bd of Supervisors, Maricopa Co. 2001–03; Sec. of State of Ariz. 2003–09; Gov. of Ariz. 2009–Jan. 2015; mem. or fmr mem. Nat. Org. of Women, American Legis. Exchange Council, Nat. Fed. of Republican Women, Luke Fighter Country Partnership, Hope and a Future, Child Help USA, Arizonans for Children, Arrowhead Republican Women's Club, Maricopa Co. SMI Comm., Arizona Rifle and Pistol Asscn, Japanese-American Citizens League; Republican; named Woman of Year, Chiropractic Asscn of Arizona 1983, Legislator of Year, Behaviour Health Asscn of Arizona 1991, Freedom Award, Veterans of Arizona 1994.

BREWER, Rosalind G., BS; American business executive; *President and Chief Operating Officer, Starbucks Corporation;* ed Spelman Coll., Advanced Man. Program at The Wharton School, Director's Coll. at Univ. of Chicago School of Business/Stanford School of Law; worked for Kimberly-Clark Corpn, starting as a scientist in non-woven technology and product devt before becoming Vice-Pres. Global Non-wovens sector 2004–06; joined Wal-Mart Stores, Inc. (now Walmart) as Regional Vice-Pres., responsible for operations in Georgia 2006, promoted to Pres. of SE Operating Div., later Exec. Vice-Pres. and Pres. South business unit of Walmart US, Exec. Vice-Pres. and Pres. Walmart East –2011, Pres. and CEO Sam's Club (first woman and first African American CEO of a Walmart business unit) 2012–17; Pres. and COO Starbucks Corpn 2017–; mem. Bd of Dirs Lockheed Martin, Molson Coors Brewing Co. 2006– (mem. Human Resources/Compensation Cttee); mem. Bd of Trustees Spelman Coll., Westminster Schools, Atlanta. *Address:* Starbucks Corporation, 2401 Utah Avenue S, SW 8th Street, Seattle, WA 98134, USA (office). *Telephone:* (206) 318-7100 (office). *E-mail:* press@starbucks.com (office). *Website:* www.starbucks.com (office).

BREYER, Stephen Gerald, AB, BA, LLB; American lawyer, academic and judge; *Associate Justice, Supreme Court;* b. 15 Aug. 1938, San Francisco, Calif.; s. of Irving Breyer and Anne Breyer; m. Joanna Hare 1967; one s. two d.; ed Stanford Univ., Magdalen Coll., Oxford, UK and Harvard Univ. Law School; law clerk to Mr Justice Arthur Goldberg, US Supreme Court 1964–65; Special Asst to Asst US Attorney-Gen., Antitrust Div. US Dept of Justice 1965–67; Asst Prof. of Law, Harvard Univ. 1967–70; Prof. of Law, Harvard Law School 1970–80; Prof., Kennedy School of Govt Harvard Univ. 1977–80; Lecturer, Harvard Law School 1981–; Asst Special Prosecutor, Watergate Special Prosecution Force 1973; Special Counsel, Admin. Practices Subcttee, US Senate Judiciary Cttee 1974–75, Chief Counsel, Senate Judiciary Cttee 1979–80; Circuit Judge, US Court of Appeals for the First Circuit 1980–94, Chief Judge 1990–94; mem. US Sentencing Comm. 1985–89; Judicial Conference of the US 1990–94; Assoc. Justice, US Supreme Court 1994–; Visiting Lecturer, Coll. of Law, Sydney, Australia 1975; Visiting Prof., Univ. of Rome 1993; Fellow, American Acad. of Arts and Sciences; Distinguished Eagle Scout Award, Boy Scouts of America 2007. *Publications:* The Federal Power Commission and the Regulation of Energy (with P. MacAvoy) 1974, Administrative Law and Regulatory Policy (with R. Stewart) 1979, Regulation and Its Reform 1982, Breaking the Vicious Circle: Towards Effective Risk Regulation 1993, Making our Democracy Work: A Judge's View 2010; numerous articles and book chapters. *Address:* Supreme Court of the United States, 1 First Street NE, Washington, DC 20543, USA (office). *Telephone:* (202) 479-2977 (office). *Fax:* (202) 479-2963 (office). *Website:* www.supremecourtus.gov (office).

BREYTENBACH, Breyten; South African/French poet and writer; b. 16 Sept. 1939, Bonnievale, Western Cape; m. Yolande Ngo Thi Hoang Lien 1962; ed Univ. of Cape Town; Visiting Prof., Graduate Program in Creative Writing, New York Univ. 1999–; Visiting Prof., Univ. of Cape Town 2000–02, also Univ. of Natal, Princeton Univ.; Dr hc (Univ. of Cape Town), (Univ. of Natal, Durban); Hertzog Prize 1984, 1999, Rapport Prize 1986, Alan Paton Award 1994, CNA Prize, Jan Campert Foundation Special Prize. *Publications include:* poetry: The Iron Cow Must Sweat (A.P.B. prize 1965) 1964, The House of the Deaf 1967, Gangrene 1969, Lotus 1970, The Remains 1970, Scrit: Painting Blue a Sinking Ship (Van der Hoogt Prize) 1972, In Other Words 1973, Foot Writing 1976, Sinking Ship Blues 1977, And Death White as Words – An Anthology 1978, In Africa Even the Flies Are Happy 1978, Flower Writing 1979, Eclipse 1983, YK 1983, Buffalo Bill 1984, Living Death 1985, Judas Eye 1989, As Like 1990, Nine Landscapes of our Times Bequeathed to a Beloved 1993, The Handful of Feathers 1995, The Remains. An Elegy 1997, Paper Flower 1998, Lady One 2000, Iron Cow Blues 2001, Lady One: Of Love and other Poems 2002, The Undanced Dance: Prison Poetry 1975–1983 2005, The Windcatcher (Hertzog Prize 2008) 2007, Voice Over: A Nomadic Conversation with Mahmoud Darwish (Max Jacob Prize 2010, Mahmoud Darwish Literature Prize 2010) 2009, In Africa Even the Flies Are Happy: Selected Poems 1964–1977 2011, Catalects 2012; prose: Catastrophes (A.P.B. Prize 1965) 1964, The Tree Behind the Moon 1974, The Anthill Bloats 1980, A Season in Paradise 1980, Mouroir: Mirror Notes of a Novel 1983, Mirror Death 1984, End Papers 1985, The True Confessions of an Albino Terrorist 1985, Memory of Snow and of Dust 1987, All One Horse. Fiction and Images 1989, Sweet Heart 1991, Return to Paradise – An African Journal (Alan Paton Award) 1992, The True Confessions of an Albino Terrorist 1994, The Memory of Birds in Times of Revolution 1996, Dog Heart: A Travel Memoir 1998, Word Work 1999, A Veil of Footsteps 2008, All One Horse 2008, Mouroir: Mirror Notes of a Novel 2008, Intimate Stranger 2009, Notes From The Middle World: Essays 2009, Notes from the Middle World 2009.

BREZIGAR, Barbara; Slovenian lawyer and government official; *State Secretary, Ministry of the Interior;* b. 1 Dec. 1953, Ljubljana; m.; two c.; ed Univ. of Ljubljana; Dist State Prosecutor, Ljubljana Public Prosecutor's Office 1980, Vice-Pres. 1994, Head of Office 1995, apptd head of special team of prosecutors dealing with organized crime 1996–99; Supreme State Prosecutor 1998–2000, 2000–05; Minister of Justice in caretaker Govt of Andrej Bajuk 2000; presidential cand. 2002; Nat. mem. for Slovenia at Eurojust 2004–05; State Prosecutor Gen., Repub. of Slovenia 2005–11; State Sec., Ministry of Interior 2012–. *Address:* Ministry of the Interior, 1501 Ljubljana, Štefanova 2, Slovenia (office). *Telephone:* (1) 4284000 (office). *Fax:* (1) 2514330 (office). *E-mail:* gp.mnz@gov.si (office). *Website:* www.mnz.gov.si (office).

BREZIS, Haïm; French mathematician and academic; *Professor Emeritus of Mathematics, Institut Universitaire de France;* b. 1 June 1944, Riom-ès-Montagnes (Cantal); s. of Jacob Brezis and Rebecca Brezis; m. Michal Govrin 1982; two d.; ed Univ. of Paris; Prof. of Math., Pierre et Marie Curie Univ. 1974–, Inst. Universitaire de France 1997–, now Emer.; Visiting Prof., New York Univ., Univ. of Chicago, Princeton Univ., MIT, Hebrew Univ.; Distinguished Visiting Prof. of Math., Rutgers Univ., Technion (Haifa); mem. Acad. des Sciences, Academia Europaea 1988; Fellow, American Math. Soc. 2012; Foreign Hon. mem. NAS 2003, American Acad. of Arts and Sciences; Hon. mem. Romanian Acad., Real Academia Madrid, Royal Acad. of Belgium; numerous hon. degrees; Prix Ampère 1985. *Publications:* Analyse Fonctionnelle 1983, Ginzburg-Landau vortices 1994, Un mathématicien juif 1999. *Leisure interest:* Hebraic studies. *Address:* Laboratoire Jacques-Louis Lions, Université Pierre et Marie Curie, boîte courrier 187, 4 place Jussieu, 75252 Paris Cedex 05 (office); 18 rue de la Glacière, 75013 Paris Cedex 13, France (home). *Telephone:* 1-44-27-63-04 (office); 1-43-36-15-10 (home). *Fax:* 1-44-27-72-00 (office). *E-mail:* haim.brezis@upmc.fr (office); brezis@ann.jussieu.fr (office). *Website:* www.ljll.math.upmc.fr/fr/membres/fiches/brezis.html (office); math.rutgers.edu/~brezis (office).

BRGLEZ, Milan, BA, MA, PhD; Slovenian politologist, academic, lawyer and politician; b. 1 Sept. 1967, Ljubljana, Socialist Repub. of Slovenia, Socialist Fed. Repub. of Yugoslavia; ed Univ. of Ljubljana; Teaching Asst in Diplomatic and Consular Relations, Int. Law Policy, Int. Relations, Faculty of Social Sciences,

Univ. of Ljubljana 1992–2006, Asst Prof. of Diplomatic and Consular Relations, Theory of Int. Relations, Selected Topics of Int. Law, Selected Topics of Diplomatic Law, European Protection of Human Rights 2006–14, Chair. Int. Relations Dept; joined newly est. Stranka Mira Cerarja (SMC—Party of Miro Cerar, renamed Stranka Modernega Centra—Modern Centre Party 2015) and became Vice-Pres. 2014–, expelled from party 2018; mem. Državni Zbor (Nat. Ass.) for IV Ljubljana – Bežigrad II 9 Electoral Dist 2014–, Speaker 2014–18; Vice-Pres. Slovenian Red Cross 2011–14; recipient of Best PhD Award, Univ. of Ljubljana 2006. *Address:* Državni Zbor (National Assembly), 1102 Ljubljana, Šubičeva 4, Slovenia (office). *Telephone:* (1) 4789400 (office). *Fax:* (1) 4789845 (office). *E-mail:* gp@dz-rs.si (office). *Website:* www.dz-rs.si (office).

BRICEÑO, Hon. Juan Antonio (Johnny), BBA; Belizean politician; b. 17 July 1960, Orange Walk Town; m. Rossana Briceño; three s.; ed Muffles High School, St John's Coll., Belize City, Univ. of Texas, Austin, USA; mem. Parl. for Orange Walk Cen. Div. (People's United Party) 1993–; Deputy Prime Minister 1998–2007, also Minister of Natural Resources and the Environment 1998–2007, of Commerce Trade and Industry 1999–2007, of Local Govt 2005–07; Deputy Leader People's United Party –2008, Leader 2008–11, Leader of the Opposition 2008–11. *Leisure interests:* reading, music, cinema. *Address:* People's United Party (PUP), 3 Queen Street, Belize City, Belize (office). *Telephone:* 223-2428 (office). *Fax:* 223-3476 (office). *Website:* www.nationalassembly.gov.bz/index.php/hor-lowerhouse/69-members-of-the-house/135-hon-juan-antonio-johnny-briceno-; www.pupbelize.bz (office).

BRIDÉ, Stéphane Christophe; Moldovan/French chartered accountant and government official; b. 30 Sept. 1971, Dakar, Senegal; m.; one c.; ed École des Cadres, France; Auditor/Adviser, Ernst & Young 1992–2001, Country Dir 2001–05, Prin. 2006–10; Project Dir, Via Lactia, Chişinău 2005–06; Man. Partner, Grant Thornton LLP, Bucharest, Romania 2010–15, Grant Thornton LLP, Chişinău 2010–15; Deputy Prime Minister and Minister of the Economy 2015–16; mem. Asscn of Professional Accountants and Auditors 2010; Censor, French Alliance 2010; Treas., Bd of Chamber of Commerce and Industry France-Moldova –2013, Vice-Pres. 2013, 2014; Counsellor for Foreign Trade of France in Moldova 2012–. *Achievements include:* Motocross Champion, Sixth African Championship, Senegal 1988, 1989, Motocross Champion, Moldova 2005. *Leisure interests:* sports, especially tennis and jogging, flying (pvt. aeroplane licence), Judo Master (black belt, first dan). *Address:* c/o Ministry of the Economy, 2033 Chişinău, Piaţa Marii Adunări Naţionale 1, Moldova. *E-mail:* mineconcom@mec.gov.md.

BRIDENSTINE, James (Jim) Frederick, BA, MBA; American naval officer, space research administrator and politician; *Administrator, National Aeronautics and Space Administration (NASA);* b. 15 June 1975, Ann Arbor, Mich.; s. of Wayne Bridenstine and Jane Bridenstine; m. Michelle Bridenstine (née Ivory) 2004; two s. one d.; ed Rice Univ., Cornell Univ.; Naval Aviator, US Navy 1998–2007, US Naval Reserve 2010–15; Defence Consultant, Wyle Labs., Inc. 2007, 2010; Exec. Dir, Tulsa Air and Space Museum & Planetarium 2008–10; subject matter expert, Deloitte Consulting 2010; Marketing Consultant, Dr Robert Zoellner and Assocs 2011; promoted to Lt-Commdr 2012; mem. US House of Reps, Oklahoma 2013–18; enlisted in Oklahoma Air Nat. Guard 2015–; Chair. Sub-Cttee on Environment 2015, House Cttee on Science, Space and Tech. 2017–18; Admin. NASA 2018–; introduced the American Space Renaissance Act for the 114th Congress 2016; various awards from US Navy and Marine Corps. *Address:* NASA Headquarters, 300 East Street SW, Suite 5R30, Washington, DC 20546, USA (office). *Telephone:* (202) 358-0001 (office). *Fax:* (202) 358-4338 (office). *Website:* www.nasa.gov (office).

BRIDGEMAN, John Stuart, CBE, TD, DL, BSc, CIMgt, FRGS, FRSA, FID; British business executive; b. 5 Oct. 1944; s. of James Alfred George Bridgeman and Edith Celia Bridgeman (née Watkins); m. Lindy Jane Fillmore 1967; three d.; ed Whitchurch School, Cardiff, Univ. Coll., Swansea, McGill Univ., Montreal; with Alcan Industries 1966–69, Aluminium Co. of Canada 1969–70, Alcan Australia 1970, Commercial Dir Alcan UK 1977–80, Vice-Pres. (Europe), Alcan Basic Raw Materials 1978–82, Man. Dir, Extrusion Div., British Alcan Aluminium PLC 1983–87, British Alcan Enterprises 1987–91, Dir of Corp. Planning, Alcan Aluminium Ltd, Montreal 1992–93, Man. Dir British Alcan Aluminium PLC 1993–95; Chair. Aluminium Extruders' Asscn 1987–88 (mem. Council 1982–91); mem. Monopolies and Mergers Comm. 1990–95; Dir-Gen. Office of Fair Trading 1995–2000; Dir Regulatory Impact Unit, Cardew & Co. Corp. Financial Advisers 2001–03; Chair. Direct Marketing Authority 2000–07 (currently Ind. Appeals Commr), Audit and Standards Cttee Warwicks. Co. Council 2000–, Howtocom-plain.com 2000–, Warwickshire Police Authority 2001–08, Regulatory Cttee British Horseracing Authority (BHA) 2007–08 (fmrly Chair. Jockey Club Regulatory Bd, Regulatory Dir BHA 2009–12); ind. complaints adjudicator, Asscn for TV on Demand 2007–10; consultant with law firm Norton Rose 2000–02; Chair. Standards Cttee, Worcs. Co. Council; Visiting Prof. of Man., Keele Univ. 1992–2010, Imperial Coll. London 2001–04, Univ. of Surrey 2004–07; Chair. N Oxon. Business Group 1984–92, Enterprise Cherwell Ltd 1985–91, N Oxon Coll. 1989 (also Gov. 1985–98), Oxfordshire Econ. Partnership 2000–07; Pres. Oxford Gliding Club 1998–2006; Vice-Pres. Aluminium Fed. 1995 (mem. Bauxite Advisory Group 1977–81), UK-Canada Chamber of Commerce 1995–96 (Pres. 1997–98); Deputy Chair. Heart of England Trading and Enterprise Council 1989–2002, Chair. 2000–02; mem. Bd British Waterways 2006– (Chair. Fair Trading Cttee 2007–, Wales Advisory Bd 2008–, Vice-Chair. British Waterways 2009–); Dir, Oxford Orchestra da Camera 1996–2000, Oxford Psychologists Press 2001–06; commissioned, TA and Reserve Forces 1978, Queen's Own Yeomanry 1981–84, Maj. REME (V) 1985–94, Staff Coll. 1986, mem. Territorial Auxiliary and Volunteer Reserve Asscn, Oxon. and E Wessex 1985–2000; Hon. Col 5 (Queen's Own Oxfordshire Hussars) Squadron 31 (City of London) Signal Regt 1996–, mem. South Eastern Reserve Forces and Cadets Assoc (SERFCA) 2001–09, Defence Science Advisory Council 1991–94; mem. British Airways NE Consumer Council 1978–81, Defence Science Advisory Council 1991–94, Nat. Employer Liaison Cttee for Reserve Forces 1992–2002 (Chair. 1997–2002), Council of UK-Canada Colloquia 1993–98, 2003– (Treas. 2005), Cttee Canada Club 1994–2010; Fellow, Univ. of Wales, Swansea 1997; Chair. of Trustees, Banbury Sunshine Centre 2003–; Trustee, Foundation for Canadian Studies 1995–2010 (Vice-Chair. 2005–10), Oxon. Community Foundation 1996–2002, Oxfordshire Yeomanry Trust 1997–, Canal and River Trust 2011–; DL (Oxon.) 1989; High Sheriff, Oxon. 1995–96; Hon. Fellow, Univ. of Wales, Swansea 1997, Inst. of Credit Man. 1998; Hon. mem. Inst. of Consumer Affairs 1999; mem. Court of Assts, Worshipful Co. of Turners 2004– (Master Steward 2011); Dr hc (Sheffield Hallam) 1996; US Aluminum Asscn Prize 1988. *Leisure interests:* horses, Oxfordshire affairs, Territorial Army, gardening, shooting, skiing. *Address:* c/o The Reform Club, 104 Pall Mall, London, SW1Y 5EW, England; c/o Glamorgan County Cricket Club, SWALEC Stadium, Cardiff, CF11 9XR, Wales.

BRIDGEMAN, Rt Hon. The Viscountess Victoria Harriet Lucy, (Harriet Bridgeman), CBE, MA, FRSA; British fine arts specialist, picture library executive, art historian and editor; *Executive Chairman, The Bridgeman Art Library;* b. (Victoria Harriet Lucy Turton), 30 March 1942, Co. Durham; d. of Ralph Meredyth Turton and Mary Blanche Turton (née Chetwynd Stapylton); m. Viscount Bridgeman 1966; four s. (one deceased); ed St Mary's School, Wantage, Trinity Coll., Dublin; worked as editorial trainee with The Lady magazine; Exec. Ed. The Masters 1965–69; Ed. Discovering Antiques 1970–72; est. own co. producing books and articles on fine and decorative arts; Founder and Exec. Chair. The Bridgeman Art Library 1971–; Cttee mem. British Asscn of Picture Libraries and Agencies; Founder Artists Collecting Soc. 2006; European Woman of the Year (Arts Section) Award 1997, Int. Business Woman of the Year 2005. *Publications include:* Encyclopaedia of Victoriana, Needlework: An Illustrated History, The British Eccentric 1975, Society Scandals 1977, Beside the Seaside 1977, Guide to the Gardens of Europe 1980, The Last Word 1982 (all jtly with Elizabeth Drury), eight titles in Connoisseur's Library series. *Leisure interests:* reading, family, travel. *Address:* The Bridgeman Art Library, 17–19 Garway Road, London, W2 4PH (office); 19 Chepstow Road, London, W2 5BP (home); Watley House, Sparsholt, Winchester, Hants., SO21 2LU, England (home). *Telephone:* (20) 7727-4065 (London) (office); (20) 7727-5400 (London) (home); (1962) 776297 (Winchester) (home). *Fax:* (20) 7792-8509 (London) (office); (20) 7792-9178 (London) (home); (1962) 776297 (Winchester) (home). *E-mail:* harriet.bridgeman@bridgemanart.co.uk (office). *Website:* www.bridgemanart.com (office).

BRIDGES, Jeff Leon; American actor, singer, producer and composer; b. 4 Dec. 1949, Los Angeles, Calif.; s. of Lloyd Bridges and Dorothy Bridges; m. Susan Geston 1977; three d.; acting debut aged eight; Career Achievement Award, Nat. Bd of Review 2004. *Films include:* Halls of Anger 1970, The Last Picture Show 1971, Fat City 1971, Bad Company 1972, The Last American Hero 1973, The Iceman Cometh 1973, Thunderbolt and Lightfoot 1974, Hearts of the West 1975, Rancho Deluxe 1975, King Kong 1976, Stay Hungry 1976, Somebody Killed her Husband 1978, Winter Kills 1979, The American Success Company 1980, Heaven's Gate 1980, Cutter's Way 1981, Tron 1982, Kiss Me Goodbye 1982, The Last Unicorn 1982, Against All Odds 1984, Jagged Edge 1985, 8 Million Ways to Die 1986, The Morning After 1986, Nadine 1987, See You in the Morning 1990, Texasville 1990, The Fabulous Baker Boys 1990, The Fisher King 1991, American Heart, The Vanishing, Blown Away 1994, Fearless 1994, Wild Bill, White Squall 1995, The Mirror Has Two Faces 1996, The Big Lebowski 1997, Arlington Road 1998, Simpatico 1999, The Muse 1999, The Contender 2000, K-Pax 2002, Lost in La Mancha (voice) 2002, Seabiscuit 2003, The Door in the Floor 2004, The Moguls 2005, Tideland 2005, Stick It 2006, Surf's Up (voice) 2007, How to Lose Friends & Alienate People 2008, Iron Man 2008, The Open Road 2009, A Dog Year 2009, The Men Who Stare at Goats 2009, Crazy Heart (Golden Globe for best performance by an actor in a motion picture—drama 2010, Academy Award for Best Actor in a Leading Role 2010) 2009, True Grit 2010, TRON: Legacy 2010, A Place at the Table (narrator) 2012, Pablo (voice) 2012, R.I.P.D. 2013, The Giver 2014, Seventh Son 2015, The Little Prince (voice) 2015, Hell or High Water (Best Supporting Actor, Nat. Bd of Review Awards 2017) 2016. *Television includes:* Raising the Hammoth (voice) 2000, National Geographic: Lewis and Clark - Great Journey West 2002, Saturday Night Live (host) 2011. *Recordings include:* albums: Be Here Soon 2000, Jeff Bridges 2011, Sleeping Tapes 2015; single: What a Little Bit of Love Can Do 2011. *Publication:* The Dude and the Zen Master (with Bernie Glassman) 2013. *Address:* c/o Rick Nicita, Creative Artists Agency, 2000 Avenue of the Stars, Los Angeles, CA 90067, USA (office). *Telephone:* (424) 288-2000 (office). *Fax:* (424) 288-2900 (office). *Website:* www.caa.com (office); www.jeffbridges.com.

BRIDGES, Simon Joseph, BA, LLB; New Zealand politician and lawyer; *Leader of the Opposition;* b. Oct. 1976, Auckland; s. of Heath Bridges; m. Natalie Bridges; two s. one d.; ed Univ. of Auckland, London School of Econs, Univ. of Oxford; Crown Prosecutor, Dist Court and High Court 2001; mem. House of Reps. (Parl.) (Nat. Party) for Tauranga 2008–; Minister for Consumer Affairs 2012–13, of Labour 2013, of Energy and Resources 2014, of Transport 2014–17, for Communications 2016–17, of Econ. Devt 2016–17; Minister outside Cabinet 2012; fmr Assoc. Minister of Transport, for Climate Change Issues, of Finance; Leader of the House 2017; Leader of the Opposition 2018–; mem. Nat. Party, Spokesperson for Nat. Security & Intelligence, Leader 2018–. *Leisure interests:* reading, music. *Address:* New Zealand National Party, 1 Molesworth Street, Pipitea, Wellington 6011, New Zealand (office). *Telephone:* (4) 817-8680 (office). *E-mail:* simon.bridges@national.org.nz (office). *Website:* simonbridges.national.org.nz (office).

BRIERLEY, Sir Ronald (Ron) Alfred, Kt; New Zealand business executive and investor; b. 2 Aug. 1937, Wellington; s. of J. R. Brierley; ed Wellington Coll.; Chair. Brierley Investments Ltd 1961–89 (Founder 1961, Founder Pres. 1990–); Deputy Chair. Bank of NZ 1987–89; Chair. Industrial Equity Pacific Ltd 1966–90, Guinness Peat Group PLC 1990–2010 (Dir (non-exec.) 2010–), Tozer Kemsley & Millbourn Holdings PLC 1986, The Citizens & Graziers Life Assurance Co. Ltd 1990–91; Dir Ariadne Australia Ltd 1989–91, The Australian Gas Light Co. 1987–, Australian Oil & Gas Corpn Ltd, Mid-East Minerals Ltd 1992–, Metals Exploration Ltd 1992–, Tyndall Australia Ltd 1992–, Advance Bank Australia 1990–; mem. NZ Cricket Council, NZ Cricket Foundation; Dir Sydney Cricket & Sports Ground Trust. *Leisure interests:* cricket, ballet, stamp collecting, chess. *Address:* Guinness Peat Group plc, 78 Pall Mall, London, SW1Y 5ES, England. *Telephone:* (20) 7663-3992.

BRIGGS, Raymond Redvers, CBE, NDD, DFA, FSCD, FRSL; British writer, illustrator and cartoonist; b. 18 Jan. 1934, Wimbledon, London, England; s. of Ernest R. Briggs and Ethel Bowyer; m. Jean Taprell Clark 1963 (died 1973); ed Rutlish School, Merton, Wimbledon School of Art and Slade School of Fine Art, London; freelance illustrator 1957–; part-time lecturer in illustration, Brighton School of Art 1961–87; children's author 1961–; mem. Soc. of Authors; Hon. Fellow,

Univ. of the Arts London; awards include Kate Greenaway Medal 1966, 1973, BAFTA Award, Francis Williams Illustration Award, Victoria & Albert Museum 1982, Broadcasting Press Guild Radio Award 1983, Children's Author of the Year 1992, Kurt Maschler Award 1992, Illustrated Book of the Year Award 1998, Smarties Silver Award 2001, Lifetime Achievement Award, Cartoon Art Museum. *Radio play:* When the Wind Blows, The Man. *Publications:* The Strange House 1961, Midnight Adventure 1961, Ring-a-Ring o' Roses 1962, Sledges to the Rescue 1963, The White Land 1963, Fee Fi Fo Fum 1964, The Mother Goose Treasury 1966, Jim and the Beanstalk 1970, The Fairy Tale Treasury 1972, Father Christmas 1973 (also film version), Father Christmas Goes on Holiday 1975, Fungus the Bogeyman 1977, The Snowman 1978 (also film version), Gentleman Jim 1980 (also stage version), When the Wind Blows 1982 (stage and radio versions 1983, animated film version 1987), The Tinpot Foreign General and the Old Iron Woman 1984, The Snowman Pop-Up 1986, Unlucky Wally 1987, Unlucky Wally Twenty Years On 1989, The Man 1992, The Bear 1994 (also film version), Ethel and Ernest 1998, UG 2001, Blooming Books (with Nicolette Jones) 2003, The Puddleman 2004. *Leisure interests:* second-hand books, walking, gardening, fishing. *Address:* Weston, Underhill Lane, Westmeston, nr Hassocks, Sussex, BN6 8XG, England.

BRIGHT, Roger, CB, MA (Cantab.); British civil servant and university administrator; *Deputy Pro-Chancellor, City University London;* ed Univ. of Cambridge; joined Dept of the Environment 1973, held series of sr positions, including Prin. Pvt. Sec. and Press Sec. to Sec. of State –1991; apptd Deputy CEO Housing Corpn 1991; held sr posts at Personal Investment Authority, including Chief Exec., and subsequently Head of Investment Business (Personal Investment Authority firms) Dept, Financial Services Authority; Dir of Finance and Admin, The Crown Estate 1999–2001, mem. Bd of Dirs 2000–11, Chief Exec. 2001–11; mem. Governing Council of City Univ., currently Deputy Pro-Chancellor; Chair. Advisory Bd, Curtin & Co. (public affairs consultants); Dir (non-exec.), London First, The Royal Parks; mem. Council of the Royal Veterinary Coll.; Public Mem. of Network Rail. *Address:* City University London, Northampton Square, London, EC1V 0HB, England (office). *Telephone:* (20) 7040-5060 (office). *Website:* www.city.ac.uk (office).

BRIGHTMAN, Sarah; British actress and singer; d. of Grenville Brightman and Pauline Brightman (née Hall); m. Andrew Lloyd Webber 1984 (divorced 1990); fmr mem. Pan's People and Hot Gossip groups; apptd UNESCO Artist for Peace 2012; f. Instinct Films (film production co.); Cavaliere, Ordine al Merito della Repubblica Italiana 2016. *Performances include:* Cats, Requiem, The Phantom of the Opera, Aspects of Love (music all by Andrew Lloyd Webber), I and Albert, The Nightingale, The Merry Widow, Trelawney of the Wells, Relative Values, Dangerous Obsession, The Innocents. *Recordings include:* albums: As I Came of Age 1990, Sarah Sings the Music of Andrew Lloyd Webber 1992, Dive 1993, Surrender 1995, Fly 1995, Timeless 1997, Eden 1999, La Luna 2000, Classics 2001, Harem 2003, Diva 2006, Symphony 2008, A Winter Symphony 2008, Dreamchaser 2013, Hymn 2018. *Address:* c/o Nat Farnham, Creative Artists Agency, 162 5th Avenue, 6th Floor, New York, NY 10010, USA (office). *E-mail:* nfarnhamasst@caa.com (office); sarahbrightman@cyoa.co.uk. *Website:* www.sarah-brightman.com.

BRIGHTY, (Anthony) David, CMG, CVO; British diplomatist (retd); *Chairman, Anglo-Spanish Cultural Foundation;* b. 7 Feb. 1939; m. 1st Diana Porteous 1963 (divorced 1979); two s. two d.; m. 2nd Jane Docherty 1982 (divorced 1996); m. 3rd Susan Olivier 1997; ed Clare Coll., Cambridge; joined FCO 1961, Third Sec., Embassy in Brussels 1962–64, Third Sec., Embassy in Havana 1964–66, Second Sec. 1966–67, with FCO 1967–69; Asst Man. S.G. Warburg & Co. 1969–71; at FCO 1971–73, Head of Chancery, Saigon 1973–75, First Sec., UK Mission, New York 1975–78; Royal Coll. of Defence Studies 1979; at FCO 1979–83, Counsellor, Embassy in Lisbon 1983–86, Dir of Cabinet of Sec.-Gen. to NATO, FCO 1986–87, Amb. to Cuba 1989–91, to Czech Repub. and Slovakia (non-resident) 1991–94, to Spain and Andorra (non-resident) 1994–98; Dir (non-exec.) EFG Pvt. Bank 1999–2006; Chair. Co-ordinating Cttee on Remuneration (NATO, OECD, etc.) 1999–2006; Dir (non-exec.) Henderson European Microcap Trust 2000–04; Chair. Anglo-Spanish Soc. 2001–07, Friends of the British Library 2004–07, Anglo-Spanish Cultural Foundation 2005–; Robin Humphries Fellow, Inst. of Latin American Studies, Univ. of London 2003. *Address:* 15 Provost Road, London, NW3 4ST, England (home).

BRIGMANIS, Augusts; Latvian agronomist and politician; *Chairman, Centre Party Latvian Farmers' Union;* b. 19 July 1952, Jelgava; m. Elita Brigmane; three c.; ed Latvian Acad. of Agric.; worked on his farm in Pūre following graduation; First Sec., Latvian Communist Party, Saldus Dist Cttee 1985–87; adviser to Minister for Agric., Aigars Kalvitis 1999; elected Pres. Latvian Farmers' Union 2000; unsuccessful cand. for Rīga City Council 2001; Chair. Centre Party Latvian Farmers' Union (forms part of the Greens' and Farmers' Union—ZZS) 2000–; mem. Saeima (Parl.) for Zemgale constituency 2010–, Chair. ZZS Parl. Group, Sec., Human Rights and Public Affairs Cttee (mem. Children and Youth Affairs Subcttee), Chair. Govt Review Cttee. *Address:* Centriskā partija Latvijas Zemnieku savienība (Centre Party Latvian Farmers' Union), Republikas lauk. 2, Rīga 1010, Latvia (office). *Telephone:* 6732-3628 (office). *Fax:* 6702-7467 (office). *E-mail:* augusts.brigmanis@lzs.lv (office); augusts.brigmanis@saeima.lv (office); lzs@latnet.lv (office). *Website:* www.lzs.lv (office).

BRILLINGER, David Ross, BA, MA, PhD, FRSC; Canadian professor of statistics; *Professor of Statistics, University of California, Berkeley;* b. 27 Oct. 1937, Toronto, Ont.; s. of Austin C. Brillinger and Winnifred E. Simpson; m. Lorie Silber 1961; two s.; ed Univ. of Toronto and Princeton Univ.; Woodrow Wilson Nat. Fellow 1959–60; Bell Telephone Laboratories Grad. Fellowship 1960–61; Social Science Research Council Fellow, LSE, UK 1961–62, Lecturer 1964–66, Reader 1966–69; Lecturer in Math., Princeton Univ., concurrently mem. Tech. Staff, Bell Telephone Labs 1962–64; Visiting Assoc. Prof., Univ. of California, Berkeley 1967–68, Prof. of Statistics 1969–, Miller Research Prof. 1973, Chair. Statistics Dept 1979–81; Instructional Lecturer, 12th Biennial Seminar, Canadian Math. Congress 1969; Visiting Prof. of Math., Univ. of Auckland, NZ 1976; Short Term Visitor, CSIRO, Australia 1977; Visiting Maclaurin Fellow, NZ Inst. of Math. and Its Applications 2010; Ed. International Statistical Review 1987–91; Assoc., Soc. of Actuaries; mem. Int. Statistical Inst. 1974, Royal Statistical Soc.; Foreign mem. Norwegian Acad. of Science and Letters 2004, Brazilian Acad. of Science 2006; Fellow, Inst. of Math. Statistics 1969, American Statistical Assn 1972, AAAS 1983, American Acad. of Arts and Sciences 1993; Founding Fellow, Fields Inst. for Research in Math. Sciences 2002; Hon. mem. Probability and Statistics Section, Cuban Soc. of Math. and Computation 2001, Statistical Soc. of Canada 2010; Hon. DMath (Waterloo) 2003; Hon. DSc (Western Ontario) 1999, (McMaster) 2008; S.H. Janes Medal, Victoria Univ., Toronto 1959, Canada Council Scholarship 1959, Guggenheim Fellow 1975–76, 1982–83, Wald Lecturer 1983, R.A. Fisher Award 1991, Gold Medal, Statistical Soc. of Canada 1992, Lecturer PIMS Inaugural Meeting 1997, Parzen Prize for Statistical Innovation 2001, Huggins Lecturer, Acadia Univ., NS 2004, Neyman Lecturer, IMS 2005, PIMS 10th Anniversary Distinguished Lecturer 2007. *Publications:* Time Series: Data Analysis and Theory 1975, Directions in Time Series 1980. *Address:* Department of Statistics, University of California, Berkeley, CA 94720-3860, USA (office). *Telephone:* (510) 642-0611 (office). *Fax:* (510) 642-7892 (office). *E-mail:* brill@stat.berkeley.edu (office). *Website:* www.stat.berkeley.edu/~brill (office).

BRIN, Sergey Mihailovich, BS, MS; American (b. Russian) computer scientist, computer software executive and entrepreneur; *President, Alphabet Inc.;* b. 21 Aug. 1973, Moscow, Russia; s. of Michael Brin and Eugenia Brin; m. Anne Wojcicki 2007 (divorced 2015); one s. one d.; ed Eleanor Roosevelt High School, Univ. of Maryland, College Park, Stanford Univ.; emigrated to USA aged six; interned at Wolfram Research, makers of Mathematica 1993; co-f. Google Inc. with Larry Page (q.v.), Co-Pres. 1998–2001, Pres. of Tech. 2001–11, Dir of Special Projects 2012–15, Pres. Alphabet Inc. (newly formed holding co. for Google and new ventures) 2015–; mem. AmBAR (networking org. for Russian-speaking business professionals in USA); mem. Nat. Acad. of Eng 2009; Fellow, NSF; Hon. MBA (IE Business School) 2003; Marconi Award (with Larry Page) 2004, named (with Larry Page) "Persons of the Week" by ABC World News Tonight 2004, Economist Innovation Award (with Larry Page) 2005. *Film:* Broken Arrows (exec. producer) 2009. *Publications:* more than a dozen academic papers including Extracting Patterns and Relations from the World Wide Web, Dynamic Data Mining: A New Architecture for Data with High Dimensionality (with Larry Page), Scalable Techniques for Mining Casual Structures, Dynamic Itemset Counting and Implication Rules for Market Basket Data, Beyond Market Baskets: Generalizing Association Rules to Correlations. *Address:* Office of the President, Alphabet Inc., 1600 Amphitheatre Parkway, Mountain View, CA 94043, USA (office). *Telephone:* (650) 253-0000 (office). *Fax:* (650) 253-0001 (office). *E-mail:* sergey.m.b@mysergeybrin.com. *Website:* www.google.com (office); plus.google.com/+SergeyBrin/posts.

BRINDLE, Ian, FCA, BA; British business executive; b. 17 Aug. 1943; s. of John Brindle and Mabel Brindle (née Walsh); m. Frances Elisabeth Moseby 1967; two s. one d.; ed Blundells School, Univ. of Manchester; articled, Price Waterhouse London 1965, Toronto 1975, Partner 1976–2001, mem. Supervisory Cttee 1988–98, Dir Auditing and Business Advisory Services 1990–91, Sr Partner 1991–98; Chair. PricewaterhouseCoopers UK (following merger with Coopers and Lybrand) 1998–2001, Sr Partner UK 1991–98; mem. Auditing Practices Cttee, Consultancy Cttee of Accounting Bodies 1986–90, Chair. 1990; mem. Accounting Standards Bd 1993–2001; mem. Council Inst. of Chartered Accountants in England and Wales 1994–97 (Chair. Financial Reporting Faculty Group 2008–13), mem. Financial Reporting Council from 1995; Deputy Chair. Financial Reporting Review Panel 2001–08; Chair. Sherborne Investors –2013, Elementis Plc 2005–14; Sr Ind. Dir (non-exec.), Spirent Communications plc 2006–; Dir (non-exec.), 4imprint Group PLC 2003–12, F&C Asset Management Plc 2011–13. *Leisure interests:* tennis, golf, classical music. *Address:* Spirent Communications plc, Northwood Park, Gatwick Road, Crawley, West Sussex, RH10 9XN (office); Milestones, Packhorse Road, Bessels Green, Sevenoaks, Kent, TN13 2QP, England (home). *Telephone:* (1293) 767676 (office). *Fax:* (1293) 767677 (office). *Website:* corporate.spirent.com (office).

BRINDLEY, Giles Skey, MA, MD, FRCP, FRS; British physiologist and academic; *Professor Emeritus, University of London Institute of Psychiatry;* b. (Giles Skey), 30 April 1926, Woking, Surrey, England; s. of Arthur James Benet Skey and Dr Margaret Beatrice Marion Skey (née Dewhurst), later Brindley; m. 1st Lucy Dunk Bennell 1959 (divorced); m. 2nd Dr Hilary Richards 1964; one s. one d.; ed Leyton Co. High School, Downing Coll., Cambridge, London Hosp. Medical School; clinical and research posts 1950–54; Russian Language Abstractor, British Abstracts of Medical Sciences 1953–56; Demonstrator, then Lecturer and Reader in Physiology, Univ. of Cambridge 1954–68; Prof. of Physiology, Univ. of London Inst. of Psychiatry 1968–91, Prof. Emer. 1991–; Hon. Dir MRC Neurological Prostheses Unit 1968–92; Partner, Brindley Surgical Implants 1991–2001; Hon. Consultant Physician, Maudsley Hosp. 1971–92; Fellow, King's Coll., Cambridge 1959–62, Trinity Coll., Cambridge 1963–68; Chair. Editorial Bd Journal of Physiology 1964–66; Visiting Prof., Univ. of Calif., Berkeley 1968; Hon. FRCS 1988; Hon. FRCSE 2000; Liebrecht-Franceschetti Prize, German Ophthalmological Soc. 1971, Feldberg Prize, Feldberg Foundation 1974, St Peter's Medal, British Assn of Urological Surgeons 1987. *Compositions:* Tyrolean Suite for wind quintet 1999, The Waterman's Daughter for soprano and woodwind quartet 2001, The Four Temperaments, variations on a theme from Schoenberg's wind quintet 2004, The Standard-bearer, the Wave-reader and the Milker of Goats for woodwind quartet and undilector 2004, Lantern Festival for mezzo-soprano and piano 2005, Lost is My Wallet for baritone and guitar 2006, The Sun on the Sea for soprano and piano 2007, Midnight Dance for fute choir 2008, Suite for Small Orchestra 2010. *Publications:* Physiology of the Retina and Visual Pathway 1960, numerous scientific papers. *Leisure interests:* designing and playing musical instruments, composing chamber music. *Address:* 102 Ferndene Road, London, SE24 0AA, England. *Telephone:* (20) 7274-2598. *E-mail:* gsbrindley@btinternet.com.

BRINDLEY, Dame Lynne Janie, DBE, MA, FLA, FRSA, CCMI; British librarian; *Master, Pembroke College, Oxford;* b. 2 July 1950, London; d. of Ivan Blowers and Janie Blowers (née Williams); adopted d. of Ronald Williams and Elaine Williams (née Chapman); m. Timothy Stuart Brindley 1972; ed Truro High School, Univ. of Reading, Univ. Coll., London; Head of Marketing and of Chief Exec.'s Office, British Library 1979–85, Chief Exec. British Library 2000–12; Dir of Library and Information Services, also Pro-Vice Chancellor, Univ. of Aston 1985–90; Prin. Consultant, KPMG 1990–92; Librarian and Dir of Information Services, LSE 1992–97; Librarian and Pro-Vice Chancellor, Univ. of Leeds 1997–2000, Visiting Prof. of Knowledge Man. 2000–10; Visiting Prof. of Information Man., Leeds Metropolitan Univ. 2000–03; Master, Pembroke Coll., Oxford

2013–; mem. Int. Cttee on Social Science Information, UNESCO 1992–97, Lord Chancellor's Advisory Cttee on Public Records 1992–98, Stanford Univ. Advisory Council for Libraries and Information Resources 1999–, Resource Bd 2002–05, Eng and Physical Sciences Research Council User Panel 2002–04, Ithaka Bd; non-exec. mem. Arts & Humanities Research Council 2008–, Ofcom (telecoms and media regulator) 2011–, Wolfson Trust Panel 2012–; Trustee, Thackray Medical Museum, Leeds 1999–2001; Freeman, City of London 1989, Liveryman, Goldsmiths' Co. 1993, Court of Assistants Goldsmiths' Co. 2006, Hon. Fellow, Univ. Coll., London 2002, Univ. of Wales 2007, British Acad. 2015; Hon. DLitt (Nottingham Trent) 2001, (Oxford) 2002, (Leicester) 2002, (Sheffield) 2004, (Reading) 2004, (Leeds) 2006, (Aston) 2008, Hon. DPhil (London Guildhall) 2002, Hon. DSc (City) 2005, 12 further hon. degrees, most recently from Trinity Coll., Dublin and Univ. of London. *Publications include:* numerous articles on the digital society, copyright and information man. *Leisure interests:* classical music, theatre, modern art, hill walking. *Address:* Pembroke College, Pembroke Square, St Aldates, Oxford, OX1 1DW, England (office). *E-mail:* lynne.brindley@pmb.ox.ac.uk (home). *Website:* www.pmb.ox.ac.uk (office).

BRINES, Francisco; Spanish poet; b. 1932, Oliva, Valencia; ed Univ. of Deusto, Univ. of Valencia, Univ. of Salamanca; fmr Reader of Spanish Literature, Univ. of Cambridge, UK; fmr Prof. of Spanish Literature, Univ. of Oxford, UK; mem. Royal Spanish Acad. 2001–; Valencian Literature Award 1967, Nat. Award for Spanish Literature 1999, Creativity Award 'Ricardo Marin' 2004, IV Poetry Prize Federico García Lorca 2007, Queen Sofia Award for Poetry 2010. *Publications include:* Las brasas (Premio Adonais 1959) 1960, El santo inocente 1965, Palabras a la oscuridad (Premio de la Crítica 1967) 1966, Aún no 1971, Ensayo de una despedida 1960–71 1974, Insistencias en Luzbel 1977, Poesía. 1960–81 1984, Poemas excluidos 1985, El otoño de las rosas (Premio Nacional de Literatura 1987) 1986, La rosa de las noches 1986, Poemas a DK 1986, Espejo Ciego 1993, La última costa (Fastenrath Prize 1998) 1995, Breve antología personal 1997, Selección de poemas 1997, Poesía completa (1960–97) 1997, Antología poética 1998, Ensayo de una despedida 1998, La Iluminada Rosa Negra 2003, Amada vida mía 2004, Todos los rostros del pasado 2007; contrib. to various anthologies and reviews. *Address:* Royal Spanish Acad., 4 Felipe IV, 28014 Madrid, Spain (office). *Telephone:* (91) 4201478 (office). *Fax:* (91) 4200079 (office). *E-mail:* prorae@rae.es (office). *Website:* www.rae.es (office).

BRINKHORST, Laurens Jan, LLM, MA; Dutch politician, academic, diplomatist and consultant; b. 18 March 1937, Zwolle; ed Leiden Univ., Columbia Univ., New York, USA; worked for Shearman & Sterling law firm, New York; worked at Europe Inst., Leiden Univ., Dir Europe Inst. and Sr Lecturer in the Law of Int. Orgs 1965, later Extraordinary Prof. of Int. Environmental Law; Chair of European Law, Groningen Univ. 1967–73; State Sec. for Foreign Affairs with European Affairs portfolio 1973–77; mem. House of Reps of States Gen. 1977–82; mem. Democraten 66 (D66), Leader Parl. Party 1981–82, now Hon. mem.; Head, Del. of Comm. of European Communities in Japan 1982; Dir-Gen. of Environment, Consumer Protection and Nuclear Safety, EC 1987–89, of Environment, Nuclear Safety and Civil Protection 1989; mem. European Parl. 1994–99; Minister of Agric., Nature Man. and Fisheries 1999–2002; European Affairs Adviser, NautaDutilh law firm, Brussels 2002; Minister of Econ. Affairs 2003–04; Deputy Prime Minister and Minister of Econ. Affairs 2004–06 (resgnd); mem. Bd of Dirs Salzburg Seminar, Int. Inst. of Sustainable Devt, LJB Europe Consult BV; Prof. of Int. and European Law and Governance, Univ. of Leiden –2011; Coordinator EC for the Project No. 6 Trans-eur. Network; Dr hc (Sofia). *Address:* Lange Houtstraat 23C, 2511 CV The Hague, Netherlands (office). *Telephone:* (70) 30-20-165 (office). *Fax:* (70) 42-77-345 (office). *E-mail:* l.j.brinkhorst@gmail.com (office); office@ljbeurope.eu (office).

BRINKLEY, Alan, BA, PhD; American historian and academic; *Allan Nevins Professor of History, Columbia University;* b. 2 June 1949, Washington, DC; s. of David Brinkley; m. Evangeline Morphos 1989; one d.; ed Princeton and Harvard Univs; Asst Prof. of History, MIT 1978–82; visiting position, Harvard Univ. 1980, Dunwalke Assoc. Prof. of American History 1982–88; Prof. of History, Grad. School and Univ. Center, CUNY 1988–91; visiting positions, Princeton Univ. 1991, Univ. of Turin 1992, New York Univ. 1993, École des Hautes Études en Sciences Sociales, Paris 1996; Prof. of History, Columbia Univ. 1991–98, Allan Nevins Prof. of History 1998–, Provost 2003–09; Harmsworth Prof. of American History, Univ. of Oxford 1998–99; Fellow, Soc. of American Historians 1984– (Exec. Bd mem. 1989–); Trustee, Oxford Univ. Press 2009–, The Dalton School 1995–2005; mem. American Historical Asscn, Org. of American Historians (Exec. Bd mem. 1990–93), Century Foundation (Trustee 1995–, Chair. 1999–), Nat. Humanities Center (Trustee 2004–), American Acad. of Arts and Sciences; Nat. Endowment for the Humanities Fellowship 1972–73, American Council of Learned Socs Fellowship 1981, Robert L. Brown Prize, Louisiana Historical Asscn 1982, Nat. Book Award for History 1983, Guggenheim Fellowship 1984–85, Woodrow Wilson Center for Int. Scholars Fellowship 1985, Joseph R. Levenson Memorial Teaching Prize, Harvard Univ. 1987, Nat. Humanities Center Fellowship 1988–89, Media Studies Center Fellowship 1993–94, Russell Sage Foundation Fellowship 1996–97, Great Teacher Award, Columbia Univ. 2003. *Publications include:* Voices of Protest: Huey Long, Father Coughlin, and the Great Depression 1982, American History: A Survey 1983, The Unfinished Nation: A Concise History of the American People 1993, The End of Reform: New Deal Liberalism in Recession and War 1995, Eyes of the Nation: A Visual History of the United States (with others) 1997, New Federalist Papers (with Kathleen Sullivan and Nelson Polsby) 1997, Liberalism and Its Discontents 1998, The Chicago Handbook for Teachers (co-ed.) 1999, The Reader's Companion to the American Presidency (co-ed.) 2000, Franklin Delano Roosevelt 2009, The Publisher: Henry Luce and His American Century 2010, Memories of the Bush Administration 2011, John F. Kennedy 2012; contribs to scholarly books and journals. *Address:* 622 Fayerweather Hall, Columbia University, 1180 Amsterdam Avenue, New York, NY 10027, USA (office). *Telephone:* (212) 854-5220 (office). *E-mail:* ab65@columbia.edu (office). *Website:* history.columbia.edu (office).

BRINKLEY, Robert Edward, CMG, MA; British independent consultant and fmr diplomatist; *Chairman of Steering Committee, Ukraine Forum, Chatham House;* b. 21 Jan. 1954; m. Mary Brinkley; three s.; ed Stonyhurst Coll., Lancs., Corpus Christi Coll., Oxford; joined FCO, London 1977, mem. staff 1982–88, 1992–96; mem. UK Del. to Comprehensive Test Ban Negotiations, Geneva 1978; assigned to Embassy in Moscow 1979–82, 1996–99, to Embassy in Bonn 1988–92; Head of FCO/Home Office Jt Entry Clearance Unit 2000–02; Amb. to Ukraine 2002–06; High Commr to Pakistan 2006–09; Business Devt Man., Associated British Foods plc (on secondment) 2010–11; int. affairs consultant 2011–18; currently Chair. Steering Cttee, Ukraine Forum, Chatham House; Senator, Ukrainian Catholic Univ., Chair. Ukrainian Inst., London; mem. Advisory Bd, School of Slavonic and East European Studies, Univ. Coll. London; Trustee, Keston Inst. *Leisure interests:* reading, walking, swimming, music (violin).

BRINKMAN, Leendert Cornelis (Elco), Dr rer. pol; Dutch politician and national organization official; b. 5 Feb. 1948, Dirksland; m. Janneke Salentijn; three c.; ed Gymnasium, Dordrecht, Free Univ., Amsterdam; research post, Public Admin. Dept, Free Univ. 1969–74; mem. Co-ordination Office for North of West Holland conurbation 1974–75; Head of Office of Sec.-Gen., Ministry of Home Affairs 1976–79, Dir-Gen. 1980–82; Minister for Welfare, Health and Cultural Affairs 1982–89; Chair. Civil Service Pension Fund (ABP) 2001–09; Pres. Het Nederlandse Rode Kruis (Netherlands Red Cross) 2001–11; mem. Christen-Democratisch Appèl (CDA—Christian Democratic Appeal), Parl. Leader of CDA in House of Reps 1989–94, Leader of CDA Jan.–Aug. 1994; mem. of the Senate 2011–, Parl. Leader of CDA in the Senate 2011–. *Publications:* articles on public admin. in specialist journals. *Address:* First Chamber (Eerste Kamer), PO Box 20017, 2513 AA The Hague, The Netherlands (office). *Telephone:* (70) 3129200 (office). *Fax:* (70) 3129390 (office). *E-mail:* postbus@eerstekamer.nl (office). *Website:* www.eerstekamer.nl/persoon/mr_drs_l_c_brinkman_cda (office).

BRINSTER, Ralph L., VMD, PhD; American physiologist and academic; *Richard King Mellon Professor of Reproductive Physiology, University of Pennsylvania;* b. 10 March 1932, Montclair, NJ; ed School of Agric., Rutgers Univ., New Brunswick, NJ, School of Veterinary Medicine and Grad. School of Arts and Sciences, Univ. of Pennsylvania; Postdoctoral Fellow, Jackson Lab., Bar Harbor, ME 1960, Marine Biological Lab., Woods Hole, Mass 1962; Teaching Fellow, Dept of Physiology, School of Medicine, Univ. of Pennsylvania 1960–64, Instructor 1964–65, Asst Prof. of Physiology, School of Veterinary Medicine 1965–66, Assoc. Prof. of Physiology, Dept of Animal Biology 1966–70, Program Dir, Reproductive Physiology Training Program 1968–83, Program Dir, Veterinary Medical Scientist Training Program 1969–84, Prof. of Physiology, School of Veterinary Medicine and Grad. School of Arts and Sciences and Grad. Faculty 1970–, Richard King Mellon Prof. of Reproductive Physiology, School of Veterinary Medicine and Grad. School 1975–; mem. Inst. of Medicine (NAS) 1986, NAS 1987, American Veterinary Medical Asscn, American Physiological Soc., American Soc. of Cell Biology, Soc. for the Study of Fertility (GB), Soc. for the Study of Reproduction; Fellow, American Acad. of Arts and Science 1986, AAAS 1989, American Acad. of Microbiology 1992; Hon. MD (Univ. of the Basque Country) 1994; Hon. DSc (Rutgers Univ.) 2000; Nat. Medal of Science, USA 2010; Distinguished Service Award, US Dept of Agric. 1989, Pioneer Award, Int. Embryo Transfer 1992, Charles-Leopold Mayer Prize, Acad. des Sciences (France) 1994, Alumni Award of Merit, Univ. of Pennsylvania School of Veterinary Medicine 1995, Prize in Developmental Biology, March of Dimes 1996, John Scott Award for Scientific Achievement, City Trusts of Philadelphia 1997, Bower Award and Prize for Achievement in Science, Franklin Inst. 1997, Carl Hartman Award, Soc. for the Study of Reproduction 1997, honoured by Special Festschrift Issue, Int. Journal of Developmental Biology 1998, Pioneer in Reproduction Research Award, Nat. Inst. of Child Health and Human Devt (NICHHD) 1998, George Hammel Cook Distinguished Alumni Award, Rutgers Univ. 1999, Charlton Lecturer, Tufts Univ. School of Medicine 2000, Ernst W. Bertner Award, Univ. of Texas M.D. Anderson Cancer Center 2001, selected for Hall of Honor, NICHHD 2003, Wolf Prize in Medicine (Israel) 2003, Gairdner Foundation Int. Award 2006, Int. Soc. for Transgenic Technology Prize 2011, Career Excellence in Theriogenology Award 2012. *Publications:* more than 360 articles in scientific journals. *Address:* 100E, School of Veterinary Medicine, University of Pennsylvania, 3800 Spruce Street, Philadelphia, PA 19104, USA (office). *Telephone:* (215) 898-8805 (office). *Fax:* (215) 898-0667 (office). *E-mail:* brinster@vet.upenn.edu (office). *Website:* www.vet.upenn.edu (office).

BRINTON, Baroness (Life Peer), cr. 2011, of Kenardington in the County of Kent; **Sarah (Sal) Brinton;** British politician and organization executive; b. 1 April 1955, Paddington, London; d. of Tim Brinton, fmr Conservative MP for Gravesend; m.; several c.; ed Benenden School, Kent, Churchill Coll., Cambridge, Cen. School of Speech and Drama, London; began career at BBC TV as a floor man. in mid-1970s, worked on programmes including Playschool, Grandstand and Doctor Who; has worked as a venture capitalist; joined Liberal Party 1975, served as Vice-Chair. Fed. Policy Cttee, fmr mem. Fed. Conf. Cttee; managed New Cambridge Research Co. Ltd 1984–87; Bursar Lucy Cavendish Coll., Cambridge 1992–97, Selwyn Coll., Cambridge 1997–2002; Cambridgeshire Co. Councillor 1993–2004; unsuccessful Parl. cand. (Liberal Democrat) for SE Cambridgeshire at Gen. Elections 1997, 2001, for Watford 2005, 2010; mem. Liberal Democrat Educ. and Higher Educ. Working Group 1993–97, Fed. Conf. Cttee 2004–, Fed. Policy Cttee 2004– (Vice-Chair. 2006–), Schools Working Group 2008–; Founder-mem. Bd East of England Devt Agency 1998–2004 (Deputy Chair. 2001–04); Chair. Cambridgeshire Learning and Skills Council 2000–06; regional skills champion and Chair. regional skills forum and Framework for Employment and Skills Action –2004; self-employed consultant in training and skills; Exec. Dir Asscn of Univs in the East of England 2006–11; Pres. Liberal Democrats 2014–; Dir (non-exec.) St John's Innovation Centre, Univ. for Industry (Learndirect), Ufi Ltd, East of England International; Dir and Trustee, Christian Blind Mission UK Ltd, Ufi Charitable Trust; Dir Joseph Rowntree Reform Trust; Fellow, Birkbeck Coll. 2013–; Patron, Christian Blind Mission UK; Trustee, UK Cttee of UNICEF; Hon. PhD (Anglia Ruskin Univ.) 2003; East Anglian Entrepreneurial Businesswoman of the Year Award 1997. *Address:* Liberal Democrats, 8–10 Great George Street, London, SW1P 3AE (office); 128 Langley Road, Watford, WD17 4RR, England (home). *Telephone:* (20) 7222-7999 (London) (office); 7768-821187 (mobile). *Fax:* (1223) 202822 (office). *E-mail:* sal@salbrinton.co.uk (office). *Website:* www.libdems.org.uk (office); www.salbrinton.co.uk.

BRIQUET MARMOL, Armando; Venezuelan politician; *President, Fundación Justicia y Democracia;* b. 3 June 1970, Caracas; s. of Juan Francisco Briquet and Dorisabel Marmol Briquet; m. Teresa Saavedra de Briquet; two s.; ed Colegio El

Peñón, Universidad Central de Venezuela, Universidad Católica Andrés Bello, Advanced Course IV Local Public Man., Zaragoza, Spain; mem. Nat. Swimming Team for ten years; Gen. Man. for Health and Social Issues, Caracas City Council 1996–98; Man. Dir Office of Pres. of Nat. Congress 1999; Man. Dir Municipality of Baruta 2000–03, Dir of Intergovernmental Affairs 2003–05; Gen. Co-ordinator in Caracas, Primero Justicia party 2002–04, Nat. Organizing Sec. 2004–06, Campaign Chief for presidential cand. Julio Borges 2005–06, Nat. Sec.-Gen. 2006–07, mem. Nat. Bd; currently Pres. Fundación Justicia y Democracia; elected mem. Legis. Council of Miranda State 2008; a campaign manager in presidential election 2012. *Address:* Primero Justicia, Planta de Oficianas, Centro Comercial Chacaito, Chacaito, Caracas, Venezuela (office). *Telephone:* (212) 952-9733 (office). *E-mail:* contacto@fjd.com.ve (office). *Website:* www.primerojusticia.org.ve (office); fjd.com.ve (office).

BRISON, Scott, PC, MP, BCom; Canadian business executive and politician; b. 10 May 1967, Windsor, Nova Scotia; s. of Clifford Brison and Verna Patricia Brison (née Salter); m. Maxime Saint-Pierre 2007; two d.; ed Dalhousie Univ.; worked in corporate sales for 10 years; mem. House of Commons for Kings-Hants 1997–2000, 2000–19; Parl. Sec. to Prime Minister 2003, Minister of Public Works and Govt Services 2004–06, Pres. of the Treasury Bd 2015–19, Minister of Digital Govt July 2018–Jan. 2019; Vice-Pres. of Investment Banking, Yorkton Securities Inc., Toronto 2000–03; Chair. Seafort Capital Inc.; mem. Canada-US Inter-Parl. Group; mem. Trilateral Comm. (non-govt discussion group); mem. Progressive Conservative Party 1997–2003, Liberal Party of Canada 2003–; Order of San Carlos (Colombia) 2010. *Leisure interests:* viniculture, economics, country music, kayaking. *Address:* c/o Treasury Board of Canada Secretariat, Strategic Communications and Ministerial Affairs, L'Esplanade Laurier, 9th Floor, East Tower, 140 O'Connor Street, Ottawa, ON K1A 0R5, Canada (office). *Website:* www.brison.ca.

BRISTOW, Laurence (Laurie) Stanley, CMG, BA, PhD; British diplomatist; *Ambassador to Russia;* b. 23 Nov. 1963; m. Fiona Bristow; two c.; ed Univ. of Cambridge; joined FCO 1990, posted to Bucharest, Romania 1992–95; Pvt. Sec. to Minister of State for Europe 1996–98; Head of Political Section, Ankara, Turkey 1999–2002; worked at NATO Defence Coll., Rome, Italy 2002–03; Amb. to Azerbaijan 2004–07; Deputy Head of Mission, Moscow 2007–10; Dir, Eastern Europe and Cen. Asia, FCO 2010–12, Dir, Nat. Security 2012–15, Amb. to Russia 2015–. *Address:* British Embassy, 121099 Moscow, Smolenskaya Naberezhnaya 10, Russia (office). *Telephone:* (495) 956-72-00 (office). *Fax:* (495) 956-74-81 (office). *E-mail:* ukinrussia@fco.gov.uk (office). *Website:* www.gov.uk/government/world/organisations/british-embassy-moscow (office); www.gov.uk/government/world/russia (office).

BRITO, Carlos, MBA; Brazilian business executive; *CEO, Anheuser-Busch InBev;* b. 1960; ed Fed. Univ. of Rio de Janeiro, Stanford Univ., USA; worked for Shell Oil and Daimler Benz –1989; Financial Analyst, Brahma, AmBev (now InBev) 1989–91, Plant Man. 1991–92, Head Softdrink Div. 1992–96, Head Beer Sales 1997–2001, Head Operations 2002–03, CEO Ambev Jan.–Aug. 2004, Zone Pres. for N America (after merger with Interbrew) 2004–05, CEO InBev 2005–08, CEO Anheuser-Busch InBev (following takeover of Anheuser-Busch) 2008–. *Address:* Anheuser-Busch InBev, Brouwerijplein 1, Leuven 3000, Belgium (office). *Telephone:* (16) 27-61-11 (office). *Fax:* (16) 50-61-11 (office). *E-mail:* info@ab-inbev.com (office). *Website:* www.ab-inbev.com (office).

BRITTAN, Sir Samuel, Kt, MA; British writer and journalist; *Columnist, Financial Times;* b. 29 Dec. 1933, London; brother of Lord Brittan of Spennithorne; ed Kilburn Grammar School, Jesus Coll., Cambridge; journalist on The Financial Times 1955–61, prin. economic commentator 1966–, Asst Ed. 1978–95; Econs Ed. The Observer 1961–64; Adviser, Dept of Econ. Affairs 1965; Research Fellow, Nuffield Coll., Oxford 1973–74, Visiting Fellow 1974–82; Visiting Prof., Chicago Law School, USA 1978; mem. Peacock Cttee on Finance of the BBC 1985–86; Hon. Prof. of Politics, Univ. of Warwick 1987–92; Hon. Fellow, Jesus Coll., Cambridge 1988; Chevalier, Légion d'honneur 1993; Hon. DLitt (Heriot-Watt) 1985; Hon. DUniv (Essex) 1995; first winner Sr Harold Wincott Award for financial journalists 1971, George Orwell Prize for political journalism 1980, Ludwig Erhard Prize 1987. *Publications:* Steering the Economy (3rd edn 1970), Left or Right: The Bogus Dilemma 1968, The Price of Economic Freedom: A Guide to Flexible Rates 1970, Is There an Economic Consensus? 1973, Capitalism and the Permissive Society 1973 (new edn A Restatement of Economic Liberalism 1988), The Delusion of Incomes Policy (with Peter Lilley) 1977, The Economic Consequences of Democracy 1977, How to End the 'Monetarist' Controversy 1981, Role and Limits of Government: Essays in Political Economy 1983, There Is No Such Thing As Society 1993, Capitalism with a Human Face 1995, Essays, Moral, Political and Economic 1998, Against the Flow 2005, Inside the Department of Economic Affairs: Samuel Brittan, the Diary of an 'Irregular' 2012. *Address:* The Financial Times, Number 1 Southwark Bridge, London, SE1 9HL, England (office). *Telephone:* (20) 7873-3000 (office). *Fax:* (20) 7873-4343 (office). *E-mail:* samuel.brittan@ft.com (office). *Website:* www.samuelbrittan.co.uk.

BRIX, Emil, Mag. phil, DPhil; Austrian historian and diplomatist; *Ambassador to Russia;* b. 1956, Vienna; ed Univ. of Vienna; joined Austrian Foreign Service 1982; Sec., Austrian People's Party (ÖVP) 1984–86; worked in office of Fed. Minister for Science and Research 1986–89; Gen. Consul in Kraków 1990–95, Man. Austrian Inst. for Culture, London 1995–99, Dir for Cultural Programmes 2000–02, Dir-Gen. for Foreign Cultural Policies, Fed. Ministry for European and Int. Affairs 2002–09, Amb. to Russia 2010–; Deputy Chair. Inst. for the Danube Region and Cen. Europe 1995–; Sec.-Gen. Austrian Research Inst. 2000–10; Pres. EU Nat. Insts of Culture 2007–08; Head of Civil Society in Austria (research group); mem. Presidium, Austrian Research Asscn 2009–; mem. Polish Acad. of Arts and Sciences 2011; Dr hc (Univ. of Drohobych) 2003, (Univ. of Cluj Napoca) 2005; Anton Gindely Prize, Vienna 1983, European Culture Prize 'New Cultures in the New Europe', Krynica 2008. *Publications include:* numerous books and articles on the Austrian and European history of the 19th and 20th centuries, including Die Frauen der Wiener Moderne (with Lisa Fischer) 1994, Schweiz und Österreich. Eine Nachbarschaft in Mitteleuropa (with Urs Altermatt) 1996, Liberalismus. Grundlagen und Perspektiven (with Wolfgang Mantl) 1996, Memoria Austriae 1 Menschen – Mythen – Zeiten (with Ernst Bruckmüller and Hannes Stekl) 2004. *Address:* Austrian Embassy, 115127, Moscow, Starokonyushennyi per. 1, Russia (office). *Telephone:* (495) 780-60-66 (office). *Fax:* (495) 937-42-69 (office). *E-mail:* moskau-ob@bmeia.gv.at. *Website:* www.aussenministerium.at/moskau.

BRIZ ABULARACH, Jorge; Guatemalan lawyer, politician and business executive; *President, Cámara de Comercio de Guatemala;* b. 27 Sept. 1955, Guatemala City; m.; ed Univ. Rafael Landívar de Guatemala; Dir Chamber of Commerce 1985–86, Vice-Pres. 1987–88, Pres. 1989–91, 1995–99, 2001–03; Leader Partido Movimento Reformador 2002–; mem. Parl. 2003–; Minister of Foreign Affairs 2004–06; Pres. Coordinating Cttee, Asscn of Agric., Commerce, Industry and Finance (CACIF) 1990–96, Dir 2000–03; Pres. Perm. Secr. of Latin American Chambers of Commerce and Industry 1997–98; currently Pres. Cámara de Comercio de Guatemala (Chamber of Commerce of Guatemala); fmr Dir Fed. of Chambers of Commerce of Central America; mem. Financial Bd of Guatemala 1992–2002; fmr del. to IMF, World Bank, IDB, EU; Gran Oficial, Orden al Mérito Bernardo O'Higgins (Chile) 1997, Orden José Cecilio del Valle (Guatemala) 1999. *Website:* www.negociosenguatemala.com.

BRNABIĆ, Ana, MBA; Serbian politician; *Prime Minister;* b. 28 Sept. 1975, Belgrade, Socialist Repub. of Serbia, Socialist Fed. Repub. of Yugoslavia; ed Northwood Univ., USA, Univ. of Hull, UK; more than 10 years working with int. orgs, foreign investors, local govts and the public sector; co-f. Nat. Alliance for Local Econ. Devt (NALED), Belgrade 2006; fmr Deputy Dir Booz Allen Hamilton/USAID Competitiveness Project, Acting Dir Aug.–Oct. 2011; fmr Exec. Dir and mem. Managing Bd, Pexim Foundation (non-profit foundation); Project Dir and Gen. Man., Continental Wind Serbia (CWS, renewable energy firm) –2015; entered politics as ind. 2016; Minister of Public Admin and Local Self Govt 2016–17; Prime Minister (first female) 2017–. *Address:* Office of the Prime Minister, 11000 Belgrade, Nemanjina 11, Serbia (office). *Telephone:* (11) 3617586 (office). *Fax:* (11) 3617586 (office). *E-mail:* predsednikvlade@gov.rs (office). *Website:* www.srbija.gov.rs (office).

BROAD, Eli, BA, CPA; American business executive and philanthropist; b. 6 June 1933, New York, NY; s. of Leon Broad and Rebecca Broad (née Jacobson); m. Edythe Lois Lawson 1954; two s.; ed Michigan State Univ.; Asst Prof., Detroit Inst. of Tech. 1956; Co-founder, Chair., Pres. and CEO AIG SunAmerica Life Insurance Co. (fmrly Kaufman & Broad, Inc.), LA 1957–2001; Chair. of numerous cos, including CalAmerica Life Insurance Co., KB Home (fmrly Kaufman & Broad Home Corpn) 1989–93, Stanford Ranch Co.; mem. Exec. Cttee Fed. Nat. Mortgage Asscn 1972–73; mem. California Business Roundtable 1986–2000; Regent Smithsonian Inst. 2004–09; Co-owner Sacramento Kings and Arco Arena 1992–99; Dir LA World Affairs Council 1988– (Chair. 1994–99), DARE America 1989–95 (Hon. Dir 1995–); Chair. Mayor's Housing Policy Comm. 1974–75; mem. Advisory Council, Town Hall of California 1985–87; mem. Contemporary Art Comm., Harvard Univ. Art Museum 1992–; mem. Bd of Overseers, Univ. of Southern California Keck School of Medicine 1999–, Bd of Dirs EdVoice 2001–; Trustee, Pitzer Coll., Claremont, Calif. 1970–82 (Chair. Bd of Trustees 1973–79, Life Trustee 1982–), Haifa Univ., Israel 1972–80, Windward School, Santa Monica, Calif. 1972–77, California State Univ. 1978–82 (Vice Chair. Bd of Trustees 1979–80, Trustee Emer. 1982–), Museum of Contemporary Art, LA 1980–93, UCLA Foundation 1986–, Caltech 1993–, Trustee, Comm. for Econ. Devt 1993–95; Founder and Trustee, The Broad Foundation 1999–; numerous philanthropic donations, including funds to build the Frank Gehry-designed Walt Disney Concert Hall 2003; mem. Bd Future Generation Art Prize; Fellow, American Acad. of Arts and Sciences 2001; Chevalier, Légion d'honneur 1994; Golden Plate Award, American Acad. of Achievement 1971, Humanitarian Award, NCCJ 1977, Public Affairs Award, Coro Foundation 1987, KCET-Los Angeles Visionary Award 1999, Julius Award, Univ. of Southern California 2001, Teach for America Educational Leadership Award 2001, United Way Alexis de Tocqueville Award 2002, Exemplary Leadership in Man. Award, Anderson School, UCLA 2002, Carnegie Medal of Philanthropy 2007, David Rockefeller Award, Museum of Modern Art 2009, William E. Simon Prize for Philanthropic Leadership, Philanthropy Roundtable (co-recipient with his wife) 2013. *Publication:* The Art of Being Unreasonable: Lessons in Unconventional Thinking 2012. *Address:* The Broad Foundations, 10900 Wilshire Boulevard, 12th Floor, Los Angeles, CA 90024, USA (office). *Telephone:* (310) 954-5000 (office). *Fax:* (310) 954-5051 (office). *E-mail:* info@broadfoundation.org (office). *Website:* www.broadfoundation.org (office); www.broadeducation.org (office).

BROADBENT, Jim; British actor and writer; b. 24 May 1949, Holton cum Beckering, Lincs.; s. of Roy Broadbent and Dee Broadbent; m. Anastasia Lewis 1987; two step-s.; ed Leighton Park School, Reading, Hammersmith Coll. of Art, London Acad. of Music and Dramatic Arts (LAMDA); actor 1972–; mem. Nat. Theatre and RSC; wrote and appeared in short film A Sense of History (Clermont-Ferrand Int. Film Festival Award); Richard Harris Award, British Ind. Film Awards 2007. *Theatre includes:* The Recruiting Officer, A Winter's Tale, The Government Inspector, A Flea in Her Ear, Goose Pimples, Our Friends in the North, Habeas Corpus. *Films include:* The Shout, Breaking Glass, The Dogs of War, The Good Father, Superman IV, Life is Sweet, Enchanted April, The Crying Game, Widow's Peak, Princess Caraboo, Richard III, The Borrowers, Little Voice, The Avengers, Topsy Turvy 1999, Moulin Rouge (Acad. Award for Best Supporting Actor 2002, BAFTA Award for Best Supporting Actor 2002) 2001, Bridget Jones's Diary 2001, Iris (Golden Globe for Best Supporting Actor) 2001, Gangs of New York 2002, Nicholas Nickleby 2002, Bright Young Things 2003, Around the World in Eighty Days 2004, Vanity Fair 2004, Vera Drake 2004, Bridget Jones: The Edge of Reason 2004, The Chronicles of Narnia: The Lion, the Witch and the Wardrobe 2005, Art School Confidential 2006, Free Jimmy (voice) 2006, Hot Fuzz 2007, And When Did You Last See Your Father? 2007, Indiana Jones and the Kingdom of the Crystal Skull 2008, Inkheart 2008, The Young Victoria 2009, The Damned United 2009, Harry Potter and the Half-Blood Prince 2009, Perrier's Bounty 2009, Another Year 2010, Harry Potter and the Deathly Hallows: Part 2 2011, Arthur Christmas (voice) 2011, The Iron Lady 2011, Filth 2012, Cloud Atlas 2012, Le Week-End 2013, The Harry Hill Movie 2013, Paddington 2014, Get Santa 2014, Big Game 2014, Brooklyn 2015, The Lady in the Van 2015, Cooking Cats 2015. *Television includes:* Not the Nine O'Clock News, Sense of History (also writer), Murder Most Horrid, Only Fools and Horses, The Victoria Wood Show, Silas Marner, Blackadder, Birth of a Nation, Gone to the Dogs, Gone to Seed, The Peter Principle, The Gathering Storm, The Young Visitors, Spider-Plant Man 2005,

Longford (BAFTA Award for Best Actor 2007) 2006, Einstein and Eddington 2008, Any Human Heart 2010, Exile 2011, The Great Train Robbery (mini-series) 2013, Lives of the Infamous Comedy Blaps (mini-series) 2014, London Spy (mini-series) 2015, The Go-Between (film) 2015. *Address:* c/o Harriet Robinson, ICM, 3rd Floor, Marlborough House, 10 Earlham Street, London, WC2H 9LN, England (office). *Telephone:* (20) 7836-8564 (office). *Website:* www.icmtalent.com (office).

BROADBENT, Hon. John Edward (Ed), OC, CC, PhD; Canadian politician and academic; b. 21 March 1936, Oshawa, Ont.; s. of Percy E. Broadbent and Mary A. Welsh; m. 1st Yvonne Yamaoka 1961 (divorced 1967); one s. one d.; m. 2nd Lucille Munroe 1971 (died 2006); one step-s. and one adopted d.; ed High School in Oshawa, Trinity Coll., Toronto, London School of Econs, UK; fmr mem. RCAF; Prof. of Political Science, York Univ., Ont. 1965–68; MP for Oshawa-Whitby 1968–79, for Oshawa 1979–90; Co-Chair. Policy Review Cttee for New Democratic Party Fed. Convention 1969; Chair. Fed. Caucus 1972–74, Parl. Leader of Fed. Caucus 1974–75; Nat. Leader of New Democratic Party (NDP) 1975–89; Vice-Pres. Socialist Int. 1978–90, Hon. Pres. 1991–; Pres. Int. Centre for Human Rights and Democratic Devt 1990–96; Fellow, All Souls Coll., Oxford 1996–97; J.S. Woodsworth Chair, Inst. for the Humanities, Simon Fraser Univ. 1997–99; Skelton-Clark Fellow, Queen's Univ. 1999–2000, Fellow, School of Policy Studies; MP representing riding of Ottawa Centre 2004–06 (retd); came out of retirement to help negotiate a formal coalition agreement between the Liberals and New Democratic Party 2008; announced creation of the Broadbent Inst. 2011; Hon. LLD (Dalhousie Univ.) 1990, (York Univ.) 1991; Hon. DLitt (Trinity Coll., Oxford) 1990, (Toronto Univ.) 1990; Nation Builder of the Year, Globe and Mail 2005. *Publication:* The Liberal Rip-Off 1970. *Leisure interests:* reading contemporary fiction, listening to music, skiing. *Address:* c/o New Democratic Party of Canada, 279 Laurier Avenue West, Suite 300, Ottawa, ON K1P 5J9, Canada. *E-mail:* info@ndp.ca.

BROADBENT, Sir Richard John, Kt, KCB, MA; British business executive; b. 22 April 1953, England; m. Jill Broadbent; two c.; ed Queen Mary, Univ. of London, Univ. of Manchester, Stanford Business School (Harkness Fellow), USA; began career at HM Treasury 1975, Pvt. Sec. to both Labour and Conservative Party ministers –1985; joined Schroders investment bank, London 1986, Head of European corp. finance business 1995–98, Global Head of Corp. Finance and mem. Group Exec. Cttee, New York 1998–99; Exec. Chair. HM Customs and Excise 2000–03; mem. Man. Bd of UK Civil Service 1999–2003; mem. Bd of Dirs, Barclays plc 2003–11, Sr Ind. Dir 2004–11, Deputy Chair. 2010–11; Dir (non-exec.), Arriva plc 2004–10, Chair. (non-exec.), 2004–10; Dir (non-exec.), Tesco plc July 2011–14, Chair. (non-exec.) Nov. 2011–14 (resgnd); mem. Securities Inst., Dir (non-exec.) 1995–97; mem. Council, Relate; Chair. GSB Trust; Partner, Centre for Compassionate Communication. *Address:* c/o Tesco plc, New Tesco House, PO Box 18, Delamare Road, Cheshunt, Herts., EN8 9SL, England.

BROCK, Gunnar, MBA; Swedish business executive; *Chairman, Stora Enso;* b. 1950, Skövde; ed Stockholm School of Econs; various positions with Tetra Pak including Man. Dir, Pres. Tetra Pak Europe and Exec. Vice Pres. Tetra Pak Group 1974–92, Pres. and CEO 1994–2000; Pres. and CEO Alfa Laval Group 1992–94; CEO Thule International 2001–02; Pres. and CEO Atlas Copco Group 2002–09; Chair. Stora Enso 2010–; Dir, OM-Gruppen, Lego AS, Denmark, Investor AB 2009–; mem. Royal Swedish Acad. of Eng Sciences (IVA) 2000. *Address:* Stora Enso, World Trade Center, Klarabergsviadukten 70, C4, PO Box 70395, 107 24 Stockholm, Sweden (office). *Telephone:* (10) 460-00-00 (office). *Fax:* (8) 10-60-20 (office). *Website:* www.storaenso.com (office).

BROCK, John F.; American business executive; *Chairman and CEO, Coca-Cola Enterprises Inc.;* b. 6 May 1948; with Procter & Gamble Inc. 1972–83; joined Cadbury Schweppes North America 1983, various sr positions, becoming mem. Bd and Man. Dir, Global Beverages Div. 1996, COO 1999–2002; CEO Interbrew (later InBev SA following merger with AmBev 2004) 2003–05; Dir, Pres. and CEO Coca-Cola Enterprises Inc. 2006–08, Chair. and CEO 2008–; Dir (non-exec.), Reed Elsevier PLC; Dir Georgia Inst. of Tech. Presidential Advisory Bd; USA Beverage Industry Exec. of the Year 2000, Business Leader of the Year, Ethical Corpn's Responsible Business Awards 2012. *Address:* Coca-Cola Enterprises Inc., 2500 Windy Ridge Parkway, Atlanta, GA 30339, USA (office). *Telephone:* (678) 260-3000 (office). *Fax:* (770) 989-3788 (office). *E-mail:* info@cokecce.com (office). *Website:* www.cokecce.com (office).

BROCKES, Jeremy Patrick, PhD, FRS; British biologist and academic; *Professor Emeritus, University College, London;* b. 29 Feb. 1948, Haslemere, Surrey; s. of Bernard Brockes and Edna Heaney; ed St John's Coll., Cambridge, Univ. of Edinburgh; Asst, then Assoc. Prof. of Biology, California Inst. of Tech. (Caltech), USA 1978–83; mem. MRC Biophysics Unit, King's Coll., London 1983–88; mem. Ludwig Inst. for Cancer Research 1988–97; Prof. of Cell Biology, Univ. Coll., London 1992–97, MRC Research Prof., Dept of Structural and Molecular Biology 1997–2016, Prof. Emer. 2016–; Scientific Medal, Zoological Soc. of London 1986, AAAS Newcomb Cleveland Prize 2008. *Publications:* Amphibian Limb Regeneration: Rebuilding a Complex Structure 1997, Plasticity and Reprogramming of Differentiated Cells in Amphibian Regeneration 2002, Molecular Basis for the Nerve Dependence of Limb Regeneration in an Adult Vertebrate 2007. *Leisure interests:* soprano saxophone, chess, cinema. *Address:* Department of Structural and Molecular Biology, Darwin Building, University College London, Gower Street, London, WC1E 6BT, England (office). *E-mail:* j.brockes@ucl.ac.uk (office). *Website:* www.ucl.ac.uk/biosciences/departments/smb (office).

BROCKINGTON, Ian Fraser, MP, MD, FRCP, FRCPsych; British psychiatrist and academic; *Professor Emeritus of Psychiatry, University of Birmingham;* b. 12 Dec. 1935, Chillington, Devon; s. of Fraser Brockington and Joyce Brockington; m. Diana Hilary Pink 1969; two s. two d.; ed Winchester Coll., Univ. of Cambridge, Univ. of Manchester Medical School; Wellcome Research Fellow, Royal Postgraduate Medical School and Univ. of Ibadan, Nigeria 1966–69; Visiting Prof., Univ. of Chicago, USA 1980–81, Washington Univ., St Louis 1981; Prof. of Psychiatry, Univ. of Birmingham 1983–2002, Prof. Emer. 2002–; Visiting Prof., Univ. of Nagoya, Japan 2002, Univ. of Kumamoto, Japan 2003, Inst. of Psychiatry, London 2009; Founder and fmr Pres. The Marcé Society 1982–84, now Chair.; Founder and first Pres. Women's Mental Health section, World Psychiatric Asscn; est. Eyry Press 2002; Cottman Fellow, Monash Univ. 1988. *Publications include:* monographs: Motherhood and Mental Health 1996, Eileithyia's Mischief: The Organic Psychoses of Pregnancy, Parturition and the Puerperium 2006, Menstrual Psychosis and the Catamenial Process 2008, What is Worth Knowing about Puerperal Psychosis 2014, The Psychoses of Menstruation and Childbearing 2017, Bonding Disorders: Emotional Rejection of the Infant 2018; papers on African heart diseases 1966–80, on schizoaffective psychosis, methods of clinical psychiatric research, pregnancy-related psychiatric disorders. *Leisure interests:* family activities, choral singing, French, Italian and German literature, publishing, bookbinding. *Address:* Lower Brockington Farm, Bredenbury, Bromyard, Herefords., HR7 4TE, England (home). *Telephone:* (1885) 3245 (home). *E-mail:* i.f.brockington@bham.ac.uk (home).

BRODER, Samuel E., BS, MD; American physician; b. 24 Feb. 1945, Łódź, Poland; m. Gail Broder; two d.; moved to USA 1949; ed Univ. of Michigan and Stanford Univ.; Clinical Assoc., Nat. Cancer Inst. (NCI), Bethesda, Md 1972, Investigator, Medicine Br. 1975, Sr Investigator, Metabolism Br. 1976, in charge of lab. overseeing new drug trials 1981–89, Dir NCI 1989–95; Sr Vice-Pres. for Research and Devt IVAX Corpn 1995–98; Chief Medical Officer, Celera Corpn 1998–2010; Sr Vice-Pres. of Health Sector, Intrexon Corpn 2012–16; mem. Inst. of Medicine; Arthur S. Flemming Award, Leopold Griffuel Award. *Publications:* AIDS: Modern Concepts and Therapeutic Challenges (ed.) 1987; more than 300 papers in scientific journals. *Leisure interests:* long walks, playing cards, cinema, dinner with friends.

BRODERICK, Matthew; American actor; b. 21 March 1962, New York; s. of James Broderick and Patricia Broderick; m. Sarah Jessica Parker (q.v.) 1997; one s. two d. *Theatre includes:* Valentine's Day (workshop production), Torch Song Trilogy 1981, Brighton Beach Memoirs (Tony Award) 1983, Biloxi Blues 1985, The Widow Claire, How to Succeed in Business Without Really Trying (Tony Award) 1995, Night Must Fall 1999, Taller Than a Dwarf 2000, The Producers 2001–02, 2003, Short Talks on the Universe 2002, The Foreigner 2004, The Odd Couple 2005, The Philanthropist 2009, The Starry Messenger 2009, Nice Work If You Can Get It 2012–13, It's Only a Play 2014–15. *Films include:* War Games, Ladyhawke, 1918, On Valentine's Day, Ferris Bueller's Day Off, Project X, Biloxi Blues, Torch Song Trilogy, Glory, Family Business, The Freshman, Lay This Laurel, Glory, Out on a Limb, The Night We Never Met, The Lion King (voice), Road to Welville, Mrs Parker and the Vicious Circle, Infinity (also dir), The Cable Guy, Addicted to Love, The Lion King II: Simba's Pride (voice), Godzilla, Election, Inspector Gadget 1999, Walking to the Waterline 1999, You Can Count on Me 2000, Suspicious Minds 2001, Good Boy! (voice) 2003, Marie and Bruce 2004, Lion King 1 1/2 (voice) 2004, Stepford Wives 2004, Last Shot 2004, Strangers with Candy 2005, The Producers: The Movie Musical 2005, Deck the Halls 2006, Then She Found Me 2007, Bee Movie (voice) 2007, Diminished Capacity 2008, Finding Amanda 2008, Wonderful World 2009, Margaret 2011, Tower Heist 2011, Skum Rocks! 2013, The American Side 2014, Dirty Weekend 2014, The Gettysburg Address (documentary) 2015. *Television includes:* Master Harold . . . and the Boys 1985, Cinderella, Jazz 2001, The Music Man 2003, 30 Rock (series) 2008, 2012, Cyberchase 2009, Who Do You Think You Are? 2009, Beach Lane (film) 2010, Louie (series) 2010, Adventure Time 2012, Modern Family 2012. *Address:* c/o Creative Artists Agency, 2000 Avenue of the Stars, Los Angeles, CA 90067, USA. *Telephone:* (424) 288-2000. *Fax:* (424) 288-2900. *Website:* www.caa.com.

BRODEUR, Yves; Canadian diplomatist; b. 1953, Montreal; m. Sylvie Gauvin; two c.; ed Université Laval, Québec; completed studies in Architecture at Université Laval, Québec and worked as architect; joined Dept of External Affairs and Int. Trade 1982, served in Media Relations Office, Ottawa 1982–83, Second Sec. and Vice-Consul, Embassy in Ankara 1983–85, Analyst, Political and Strategic Analysis Secr., Ottawa 1985–87, Analyst in South, SE Asia Relations Div. 1987, Chief of Staff to the Deputy Minister of Foreign Affairs 1988–89, First Sec., OECD, Paris 1989–93, Policy Advisor, Foreign Affairs and Defence, Privy Council Office 1993–95, Departmental Spokesperson and Press Secretary to the Minister of Foreign Affairs 1995–96, Counsellor (Political) and Head of Political Affairs Section, Perm. Mission of Canada to EU Brussels 1996–2000, Dir of Communications and Spokesperson, NATO 2001–03, Amb. to Turkey 2005–07, Dir Media Relations Office and Director General of the Communications Bureau 2003–05, Asst Deputy Minister for the Afghanistan Task Force 2007–09, Asst Deputy Minister of Int. Security Br. and Political Dir 2009–11, Amb. and Perm. Rep. to NATO, Brussels 2011–15.

BRODHEAD, Richard H., PhD; American university administrator and writer; *President, Duke University;* b. Dayton, Ohio; m. Cynthia Brodhead; one s.; ed Yale Univ.; mem. Faculty, Yale Univ. 1972–2004, later A. Bartlett Giamatti Prof. of English and American Studies –2004, served as Chair. Dept of English for six years, Dean of Yale Coll. 1993–2004; Prof. of English and Pres. Duke Univ. 2004–; spent eight summers teaching high school teachers at Bread Loaf School, Middlebury, Vt; has lectured widely in univs at home and in Europe and Asia; mem. Business-Higher Educ. Forum; Trustee Carnegie Corpn of New York; fmr Pres. J. William Fulbright Foreign Scholarship Bd; mem. American Acad. of Arts and Sciences; DeVane Medal for Outstanding Teaching, Yale Univ. *Publications:* The Good of This Place: Values and Challenges in College Education; has written or ed more than a dozen books on Nathaniel Hawthorne, Herman Melville, Charles W. Chestnutt, William Faulkner, Harriet Beecher Stowe, Louisa May Alcott, Richard Wright and Eudora Welty, among others. *Address:* Office of the President, Duke University, 207 Allen Building, Box 90001, Durham, NC 27708-0001, USA (office). *Telephone:* (919) 684-2424 (office). *Fax:* (919) 684-3050 (office). *E-mail:* president@duke.edu (office). *Website:* about.duke.edu/leadership/brodhead (office).

BRODJONEGORO, Bambang Permadi Soemantri, BEcons, PhD; Indonesian economist and politician; *Chairman, National Development Planning Agency;* b. 3 Oct. 1966, Senin; s. of Prof. Dr Ir. Soemantri Brodjonegoro; m. Irina Justina Zega; one s.; ed Univ. of Indonesia, Univ. of Illinois, USA; Research Partner, Faculty of Econs, Univ. of Indonesia 1997–2005, Sr Researcher, Lab. of Econs and Devt Studies 2002–, also Prof. of Econs, Dean, Faculty of Econs 2005–09; held several positions with Ministry of Finance including Adviser to Fiscal Decentralization Team 2005–06, Team Leader and Adviser to Minister of Finance for Fiscal Decentralization 2007–08, Deputy Minister of Finance 2009–14, Head of Fiscal Policy Office 2011–, Minister of Finance 2014–16; Chair., Nat. Devt Planning Agency 2016–; Dir-Gen. Islamic Research and Training Inst., Islamic Devt Bank 2009–11; Vice-Pres. Asscn of Indonesian Bachelors of Econs 2003–; Visiting

Fellow, Inst. of East Asian Studies, Thammasat Univ., Thailand 1999, ANU 2004, Hitotsubashi Univ., Japan; Chair. Audit Cttee, Bd Komisionaris PT PLN 2004–06; consultant to several int. bodies including UNDP and USAID. *Address:* Badan Perencanaan Pembangunan Nasional (Bappenas), Jalan Taman Suropati 2, Jakarta 10310, Indonesia (office). *Telephone:* (21) 3905650 (office). *Fax:* (21) 3145374 (office). *E-mail:* admin@bappenas.go.id (office). *Website:* www.bappenas.go.id (office).

BRODY, Adrien; American actor; b. 14 April 1973, Queens, New York; s. of Elliot Brody and Sylvia Plachy; ed American Acad. of Dramatic Arts, High School for the Performing Arts; first worked in off-Broadway productions; television debut in PBS movie Home at Last 1988; other TV appearances include Home at Last 1988, Annie McGuire (series) 1988. *Films include:* New York Stories 1989, King of the Hill 1993, Jailbreakers 1994, Angels in the Outfield 1994, Solo 1996, Bullet 1996, The Undertaker's Wedding 1997, The Last Time I Committed Suicide 1997, The Thin Red Line 1998, Sweet Jersey 1998, Ten Benny 1998, Summer of Sam 1999, Six Ways to Sunday 1999, Oxygen 1999, Liberty Heights 1999, Restaurant 2000, Harrison's Flowers 2000, Bread and Roses 2001, Love the Hard Way 2001, The Affair of the Necklace 2001, Dummy 2002, The Pianist (Acad. Award for Best Actor 2003) 2002, Harrison's Flowers 2002, The Singing Detective 2003, The Village 2004, The Jacket 2005, King Kong 2005, Hollywoodland 2006, The Tehuacan Project 2007, The Darjeeling Limited 2007, Giallo (also producer) 2009, Fantastic Mr Fox (voice) 2009, Predators 2010, Wrecked (also exec. producer) 2011, Detachment 2011, Third Person 2013, The Grand Budapest Hotel 2014. *Address:* c/o Jeff Kwatinetz, The Firm, 9465 Wilshire Blvd., 6th Floor, Beverly Hills, CA 90212; c/o Creative Artists Agency, 2000 Avenue of the Stars, Los Angeles, CA 90067, USA. *Telephone:* (310) 860-8000 (The Firm). *Fax:* (310) 860-8100 (The Firm).

BRODY, Alexander, BA; Hungarian/American advertising executive and writer; b. (Sándor Bródy), 28 Jan. 1933, Budapest, Hungary; s. of János Brody and Lilly Brody (née Pollatschek); ed Princeton Univ.; with Young & Rubicam Inc. 1953–83; Vice-Pres., Man. Young & Rubicam Inc., Frankfurt, Germany 1965–70; Sr Vice-Pres., Head, European Operations, Young & Rubicam Inc. 1967–70; Int. Pres. Young & Rubicam Inc., Brussels and New York 1970–82; Pres. and CEO DYR Worldwide, New York 1984–87; Pres. Int. Ogilvy & Mather Worldwide 1987–93; returned to Hungary to concentrate on writing 1993; organizer of the Sandor Brody Literary Award for journalists in honour of his grandfather 1995–; Order of Merit of the Hungarian Repub. 2004, Order of Merit of the Hungarian Repub., Civil Div. 2005. *Publications;* Gondok és gondolatok (Thoughts and Concerns) 1998, Húszezeregy éjszaka – Álmok és mesék a valóságról (Twenty Thousand and One Nights – Dreams and Tales of Reality) 2001, Alibi hat hónapra 1. Evés-ivás (Alibi for Six Months 1. Eating-drinking) 2001, Alibi hat hónapra 2. Kert (Alibi for Six Months 2. Garden) 2002, Alibi hat hónapra 3. (Alibi for Six Months 3. Horses) 2002, Később, mint soha… 2002, Alibi hat hónapra 4. Fürdő (Alibi for Six Months 4. Bath) 2003, Alibi hat hónapra 5. Urak – Dámák (Alibi for Six Months 5. Men – Queens) 2003, Alibi hat hónapra 1–4 (alibi for Six Months 1–4) 2003, Alibi hat hónapra 6. (Alibi for Six Months 6. Luck) 2004, Hunyady Margit (Margaret Hunyady) 2006, Hét évtized íze (Seven Decades of Flavours) 2008.

BRODY, Jane Ellen, MS; American journalist and author; b. 19 May 1941, Brooklyn, New York; d. of Sidney Brody and Lillian Kellner; m. Richard Engquist 1966; twin s.; ed New York State Coll. of Agric., Cornell Univ., Univ. of Wisconsin; reporter, Minneapolis Tribune 1963–65; science writer, personal health columnist, New York Times 1965–; mem. Advisory Council, New York State Coll. of Agric. 1971–77; Dr hc (Princeton Univ., Hamline Univ., Univ. of Minnesota School of Public Health, State Univ. of New York School of Public Health); Howard Blakeslee Award, American Heart Asscn 1971, Science Writers' Award, ADA 1978, J.C. Penney Univ. of Missouri Journalism Award 1978, Lifeline Award, American Health Foundation 1978. *Publications include:* Secrets of Good Health (with R. Engquist) 1970, You Can Fight Cancer and Win (with A. Holleb) 1977, Jane Brody's Nutrition Book 1981, Jane Brody's New York Times Guide to Personal Health 1982, Jane Brody's Good Food Book 1985, Jane Brody's Good Food Gourmet 1990, Jane Brody's Good Seafood Book (with Richard Flaste) 1994, Jane Brody's Cold and Flu Fighter 1995, Jane Brody's Allergy Fighter 1997, The New York Times Book of Health 1997, The New York Times Book of Women's Health 2000, The New York Times Book of Alternative Medicine 2001, Jane Brody's Guide to the Great Beyond 2009. *Address:* New York Times, 620 Eighth Avenue, New York, NY 10018, USA (office). *E-mail:* inquiries@janebrody.net (office). *Website:* www.nytimes.com (office); www.janebrody.net (home).

BRODY, Neville; British magazine designer, typographer and album cover designer; *Head of Communication Art and Design Department, Royal College of Art;* b. 23 April 1957, London, England; ed Hornsey Coll., London Coll. of Printing; designed record sleeves for Rocking Russian and Stiff Records; Art Dir, Fetish Records early 1980s, The Face magazine 1981–86, Arena magazine 1987–90; design work for City Limits, Lei, Per Lui, Actuel, The Observer; founder and Dir typographic design agencies, FontWorks and FontShop International 1990–; founder and Dir, Research Studios 1994–; involved in launch of FUSE quarterly design forum and publication; Head of Communication Art and Design Department, Royal College of Art 2011–. *Publications:* The Graphic Language of Neville Brody Vol. 1 (with Jon Wozencroft) 1988, Vol. 2 1994, G1: New Dimensions in Graphic Design (with Lewis Blackwell) 1996. *Address:* Research Studios, 94 Islington High Street, London, N1 8EG (office); Royal College of Art, Kensington Gore, London, SW7 2EU, England. *Telephone:* (20) 7590-4444. *Fax:* (20) 7590-4500. *E-mail:* info@researchstudios.com; info@rca.ac.uk. *Website:* www.researchstudios.com; www.rca.ac.uk.

BRODY, William R., BS, MS, PhD, MD; American physician, biomedical engineer, research institute director and fmr university administrator; b. 4 Jan. 1944, Stockton, Calif.; m. Wendy Brody; two c.; ed Massachusetts Inst. of Tech., Stanford Univ., Univ. of California, San Francisco; Fellow, Dept of Cardiovascular Surgery, Stanford Univ. School of Medicine 1970–71, Intern, Dept of Surgery 1971–72, Resident, Dept of Cardiovascular Surgery 1972–73; Clinical Assoc., Surgery Br., Nat. Heart, Lung, and Blood Inst., Bethesda, Md 1973–75; Resident, Dept of Radiology, Univ. of California, San Francisco 1975–77; Assoc. Prof. of Radiology and, by courtesy, Electrical Eng, Stanford Univ. School of Medicine 1977–82, Dir of Research Labs, Div. of Diagnostic Radiology 1977–84, Dir Advanced Imaging Techniques Lab., Dept of Radiology 1978–84, Prof. of Radiology and, by courtesy, Electrical Eng 1982–86, on unpaid leave of absence 1984–86; Martin Donner Prof. and Dir Dept of Radiology, The Johns Hopkins Univ. School of Medicine 1987–94, Prof. of Biomedical Eng 1987–94, Prof. of Electrical and Computer Eng 1987–94, Radiologist-in-Chief, The Johns Hopkins Hosp. 1987–94, Pres. The Johns Hopkins Univ. 1996–2008; Prof. of Radiology, Univ. of Minnesota 1994–96, Provost, Academic Health Center 1994–96; Pres. The Salk Inst., La Jolla, Calif. 2009–15; Founder and Consultant, Resonex, Inc. 1983–84, Pres. 1984–86, Pres. and CEO 1986–87, Chair. 1987–89; mem. Pres.'s Foreign Intelligence Advisory Bd 2003–05; mem. Bd of Dirs IBM, Biomed Realty Trust, T. Rowe Price Mutual Funds, W.M. Keck Foundation; fmr mem. Bd Minnesota Orchestra Asscn, Corpn of Massachusetts Inst. of Tech.; mem. Nat. Acad. of Eng, Inst. of Medicine, NAS, AAAS; Fellow, IEEE, American Coll. of Radiology, American Coll. of Cardiology, American Heart Asscn, Int. Soc. of Magnetic Resonance in Medicine, American Inst. of Biomedical Eng, American Acad. of Arts and Sciences; Founding Fellow, American Inst. of Medical and Biological Eng; Trustee Baltimore Museum of Art 1997–, Baltimore Community Foundation 2004–; Hon. mem. Canadian Asscn of Radiologists; Prize Manuscript Award, Western Thoracic Surgical Soc. 1974, Established Investigator Award, American Heart Asscn 1980–84, Outstanding Alumnus Award, Univ. of California, San Francisco 1994. *Publications:* Digital Radiography: Proceedings of the Stanford Conference on Digital Radiography. Society for Photooptical Instrumentation Engineers (SPIE). Proceedings Vol. 315 (ed.) 1981, Digital Radiography 1984, Computer Applications to Assist Radiology. Proceedings of the 11th S/CAR Symposium (co-ed.) 1992; more than 120 publs and one patent (US Patent No. 4,445,226, 1984) in the field of medical imaging; bimonthly columns for Diagnostic Imaging 1990–94.

BROERS, Baron (Life Peer), cr. 2004, of Cambridge in the County of Cambridgeshire; **Alec Nigel Broers,** Kt, ScD, FRS, FMedSci, FREng; British electrical engineer, academic and business executive; b. 17 Sept. 1938, Calcutta, India; s. of Alec W. Broers and of Constance A. Broers (née Cox); m. Mary T. Phelan 1964; two s.; ed Geelong Grammar School, Melbourne Univ. and Gonville & Caius Coll. Cambridge; moved to Sydney, Australia 1941, to UK 1944, to Melbourne, Australia 1948; mem. research staff and man. of photon and electron optics groups, IBM Thomas Watson Research Center 1965–80; Man., Semiconductor Lithography and Process Devt and Advanced Devt, IBM East Fishkill Lab. 1981–84; mem. Corp. Tech. Cttee, IBM Corp. HQ 1984; Prof. of Electrical Eng, Univ. of Cambridge 1984–96, Prof. Emer. 1996–, Head, Electrical Div. 1984–92, of Dept of Eng 1992–96; Chair. Diamond Light Source Ltd 2008–14, Bio Nano Consulting 2009–15, Tech. Strategy Bd Knowledge Transfer Network for Transport 2010–, Judging Panel of the Queen Elizabeth Prize for Eng 2012–; Dir (non-exec.), Vodafone Group 1998–2000, Vodafone PLC 2000–, Lucas Industries Group 1995–96, R.J. Mears 2003–; Adviser, Warburg Pincus 2003–; Chair. House of Lords Select Cttee on Science and Tech. 2004–; Fellow, Trinity Coll., Cambridge 1984–90; Master, Churchill Coll., Cambridge 1990–96, Fellow 1996–; Vice-Chancellor, Univ. of Cambridge 1996–2003; mem. (Crossbench), House of Lords 2004–; Pres. Royal Acad. of Eng 2001–06; Foreign Assoc. Nat. Acad. of Eng (USA), Chinese Acad. of Eng, Australian Acad. of Technological Sciences and Eng, and American Philosophical Soc.; Hon. Fellow, Gonville and Caius Coll. Cambridge 1996–, Trinity Coll. Cambridge 1999–, Univ. of Wales, Cardiff 2001–, St Edmund's Coll. Cambridge 2004–, Imperial Coll. London 2004–; Hon. DEng (Glasgow) 1996; Hon. DSc (Warwick) 1997; Hon. LLD (Melbourne) 2000; Hon. DUniv (Anglia Polytechnic) 2000; Dr hc (Greenwich) 2000, (UMIST) 2002, (Peking) 2002; IBM Fellow 1977, Prize for Industrial Applications of Physics, American Inst. of Physics 1982, Cledo Brunetti Award, Inst. of Electrical and Electronic Engineers 1985, BBC Reith Lecturer 2005. *Publications:* patents, papers and book chapters on electron microscopy, electron beam lithography and integrated circuit fabrication. *Leisure interests:* music, sailing, skiing. *Address:* House of Lords, London, SW1A 0PW, England (office). *Telephone:* (20) 7219-5353 (office). *Fax:* (20) 7219-5979 (office). *E-mail:* contactholmember@parliament.uk (office). *Website:* www.parliament.uk/biographies/lords/lord-broers/3695.

BROGGINI, Andrea, Dr iur, LLM; Swiss lawyer and business executive; *Chairman, Federation of Migros Cooperatives;* ed Univ. of Geneva, Harvard Law School, Univ. of Urbino; f. law firm focusing on corporate law 1992; mem. Bd of Dirs Migros-Genossenschafts-Bund (Fed. of Migros Cooperatives) 2004–, Chair. 2012–; Chair. Bd of Dirs Kieger AG; Dir, Generali Schweiz Holding AG, Fondiaria-SAI SpA, Banca Euromobiliare (Suisse) SpA, Florenz, March Ltd, Hamilton & Knorr-Bremse SfS GmbH, Munich, Leerink Partners; Ind. Dir Fastweb SpA 2008–. *Address:* Federation of Migros Cooperatives, Limmatstrasse 152, 8031 Zurich, Switzerland (office). *Telephone:* (44) 277-21-11 (office). *Fax:* (44) 277-25-25 (office). *E-mail:* media@migros.ch (office). *Website:* www.migros.ch (office).

BROKAW, Thomas (Tom) John, BA; American broadcast journalist and writer; b. 6 Feb. 1940, Webster, S Dakota; s. of Anthony O. Brokaw and Eugenia Conley; m. Meredith Lynn Auld 1962; three d.; ed Univ. of South Dakota; morning news KMTV, Omaha 1962–65; news ed., anchorman, WSB-TV, Atlanta 1965–66; reporter, corresp., anchorman KNBC-TV, Los Angeles 1966–73; White House corresp. NBC, Washington, DC 1973–76; anchorman, Saturday Night News, New York 1973–76; host, Today Show, New York 1976–82; anchor and Man. Ed., NBC Nightly News 1982–2004 (retd), Special Corresp. NBC News 2005–; mem. Bd of Dirs Council on Foreign Relations, Cttee to Protect Journalists, Int. Rescue Cttee; mem. advisory cttee Reporters Cttee for Freedom of Press, Gannett Journalism Center, Columbia Univ.; Trustee, Norton Simon Museum of Art, Pasadena, Calif.; mem. American Acad. of Arts and Sciences; Légion d'honneur 2016; Dr hc (Univ. of South Dakota), (Washington Univ., St. Louis), (Syracuse Univ.), (Hofstra Univ.), (Boston Coll.), (Emerson Coll.), (Simpson Coll.), (Duke Univ.) 1991, (Notre Dame Univ.) 1993; Hon. DHL (Dartmouth Coll.) 2005; two Dupont Awards, Peabody Award, Alfred I. duPont-Columbia Univ. Award for Excellence in Broadcast Journalism 1997, ten Emmy Awards including Emmy for Outstanding Interview 2003, Records of Achievement Award, Foundation for the Nat. Archives 2005, George Catlett Marshall Medal, Asscn of the US Army 2005, Edward R. Murrow Award for Lifetime Achievement in Broadcasting, Wash. State Univ. 2006, Sylvanus Thayer Award, US Military Acad. at West Point 2006, Walter Cronkite Award for Journalism Excellence, Ariz. State Univ. 2006, Presidential Medal of Freedom 2014; elected to TV Hall of Fame 1997. *Publications:* The Greatest Generation 1998, The Greatest Generation Speaks 1999, An Album of Memories

2001, A Long Way from Home 2002, Boom! Voices of the Sixties 2007, The Time of Our Lives: A Conversation about America 2011, Christmas from Heaven: The True Story of the Berlin Candy Bomber 2013, A Lucky Life Interrupted: A Memoir of Hope 2015. *Address:* c/o Board of Directors, Council on Foreign Relations, The Harold Pratt House, 58 East 68th Street, New York, NY 10021, USA (office).

BROKENSHIRE, Rt Hon. James Peter; British politician; *Secretary of State for Housing, Communities and Local Government;* b. 8 Jan. 1968, Southend-on-Sea; m. Cathrine Anne Mamelok; one s. two d.; ed Univ. of Exeter; 13 years as Of Counsel, later Partner, Jones Day (law firm), London; MP (Conservative) for Hornchurch 2005–10, for Old Bexley and Sidcup 2010–, mem. Constitutional Affairs Cttee 2005–06; Shadow Minister (Home Affairs) 2006–10, Parl. Under-Sec. (Home Office) 2010–14, Minister of State (Home Office) (Security and Immigration) 2014–16, Sec. of State for NI 2016–Jan. 18, for Housing, Communities and Local Government April 2018–. *Address:* Ministry of Housing, Communities and Local Government, 2 Marsham Street, London, SW1P 4DF, England (office). *Telephone:* (30) 3444-0000 (office). *E-mail:* contact@jamesbrokenshire.com; newsdesk@communities.gsi.gov.uk (office). *Website:* www.jamesbrokenshire.com; www.gov.uk/government/organisations/department-for-communities-and-local-government.

BROLIN, Josh; American actor; b. 12 Feb. 1968, Santa Monica, Calif.; s. of James Brolin and Jane Cameron Agee; m. 1st Alice Adair; two c.; m. 2nd Diane Lane. *Films include:* The Goonies 1985, Thrashin' 1986, Bed of Roses 1996, Flirting with Disaster 1996, Nightwatch 1997, Best Laid Plans 1999, Hollow Man 2000, Slow Burn 2000, Melinda and Melinda 2004, Into the Blue 2005, The Dead Girl 2006, Grindhouse - Planet Terror 2007, In the Valley of Elah 2007, No Country for Old Men 2007, American Gangster 2007, W. 2008, Milk 2008, Wall Street: Money Never Sleeps 2010, True Grit 2010, Men in Black III 2012, Gangster Squad 2012, Oldboy 2013, Sin City: A Dame to Kill For 2014, Inherent Vice 2014, Sicario 2015, Everest 2015, Hail, Caesar! 2016. *Television includes:* Picnic 2000, Mister Sterling 2003, Into the West 2005.

BROMBERG, Serge; French film collector, director and producer; *Founder and Chairman, Lobster Films;* b. 26 April 1961, Saint-Maur-des-Fossés (Val-de-Marne); ed École Supérieure de Commerce, Paris; Founder and Chair. Lobster Films 1985–; Project Man., Havas, Carrefour de la Communication 1985–86; Dir exhibitions, Cité des sciences et de l'industrie 1986–88; f. LE Diapason sound restoration lab. 2003; Founder Steamboat Films 2006; Artistic Dir Annecy Festival 1999–2012; Dir silent film DVD collection of Arte 2000–; mem. and Admin. Asscn française de lutte contre les myopathies, Institut de Myologie; Admin. Cinémathèque française 1999–2007, École de la Poudrière 2000–, Fondation GAN pour le cinéma 2004–; Officier, Ordre des Arts et des Lettres 2010; Prix Jean Mitry 1997, Telluride Silver Medallion 2010, National Society of Film Critics Award 2011, Mel Novikoff Award, San Francisco Film Festival 2011, Denver Silent Film Festival Lifetime Achievement Award 2012, History Maker Lifetime Achievement Award 2012, 6 Focal Award. *Films directed:* Inferno (documentary) (also writer and producer) (Int. Jury Award, São Paulo Int. Film Festival (co-recipient) 2009, Legacy of Cinema Award, Los Angeles Film Critics Asscn Awards 2010, Étoile d'Or, France (co-recipient) 2010, César Award for Best Documentary Film 2010) 2009, Le voyage extraordinaire (documentary) (also writer) 2011, The Birth of the Tramp (film documentary) (exec. producer) 2013. *Films produced:* The Lost World (producer of alternative version) 2000, Jean Vigo: Le son retrouvé (video documentary short) 2001, 8 mai 1945, la capitulation (documentary) 2005, Coster Bill of Paris (producer of alternative version) 2005, The Hunchback of Notre Dame (producer of alternative version) 2006, Poil de carotte (restoration producer of alternate version) 2007, The Flying House (short) (assoc. producer) 2011, A Rabbi, a Priest and an Ex-Gumba 2017, Sydney, the Other Chaplin (documentary) 2017. *Television includes:* Cellulo (series) (writer, producer and host) 1995–2001, Ça tourne Bromby (series) (writer, producer and host) 1997–99, Grande promesse du Téléthon (producer) 2000, Guérir (producer) 2001, le Vinyle fait de la résistance (producer) 2002, La mafia à Hollywood (documentary) (producer) 2002, Discovering Cinema: Learning to Talk (documentary) (writer and producer) 2003, Discovering Cinema: Movies Dream in Color (documentary) (writer and producer) 2004, Arletty, Lady Paname (documentary) (producer) 2007; dir: Chaplin Today: City Lights (documentary short) 2003, Robert Mitchum, le mauvais garçon d'Hollywood (film documentary) (assoc. producer) 2018. *Address:* Lobster Films, 13 rue Lacharrière, 75011 Paris, France (office). *Telephone:* 1-43-38-69-69 (office). *Fax:* 1-43-57-26-05 (office). *E-mail:* lobster@lobsterfilms.com (office). *Website:* www.lobsterfilms.com (office).

BRON, Eleanor, BA; British actress and author; b. 14 March 1938, Stanmore, Middx; d. of Sydney Bron and Fagah Bron; ed North London Collegiate School and Newnham Coll. Cambridge; started at Establishment Night Club, toured USA 1961; TV satire, Not So Much a Programme, More a Way of Life 1964–65; co-wrote and appeared in TV series Where Was Spring? 1969, Beyond a Joke 1972, After That This 1975; Dir Actors' Centre 1982–93, Soho Theatre Co. 1993–2000. *Stage appearances include:* Private Lives, Hedda Gabler, Antony and Cleopatra, Madwoman of Chaillot, Hamlet; appeared at Royal Exchange in Uncle Vanya, Heartbreak House, Oedipus, The Prime of Miss Jean Brodie, Present Laughter; appeared at Nat. Theatre in The Duchess of Malfi, The Cherry Orchard, The Real Inspector Hound, The Miser, The White Devil, Desdemona – If You Had Only Spoken! (one-woman show), Dona Rosita The Spinster, A Delicate Balance, Be My Baby, Making Noise Quietly, Twopence to Cross the Mersey 2005, The Clean House 2006, In Extremis 2007, All About My Mother 2007, The Late Middle Classes 2010. *Television appearances include:* BBC TV Play for Today: Nina 1978, Rumpole of the Bailey 1979, Dr Who 1979, 1985, A Month in the Country 1985, French & Saunders 1990, The Hour of the Lynx 1991, Absolutely Fabulous 1992, 1994, 2003, The Blue Boy 1994, Vanity Fair 1998, Fat Friends 2000–05, Ted and Alice 2002, Casualty 1909 2009, Foyle's War 2010, Midsomer Murders 2012. *Films:* Help!, Alfie, Two for the Road, Bedazzled, Women in Love, The National Health, Turtle Diary, Little Dorritt, The Attic, Deadly Advice 1994, Black Beauty 1993, A Little Princess 1994, The House of Mirth 2000, Iris 2001, The Heart of Me 2002, Love's Brother 2003, Wimbledon 2004, StreetDance 2010, Hyde Park on Hudson 2012. *Concert appearances (as narrator) include:* Façade, Carnival des Animaux, Peter and the Wolf, Bernstein's Symphony No. 3 with BBC Symphony Orchestra; with Counterpoise: works by Edward Rushton, David Matthews. *Publications include:* Song Cycle (with John Dankworth) 1973; verses for Saint-Saëns Carnival of the Animals 1975; Is Your Marriage Really Necessary? (with John Fortune) 1972, Life and Other Punctures 1978, The Pillow Book of Eleanor Bron 1985, Desdemona – If You Had Only Spoken! (trans. of original by Christine Brückner) 1992, Double Take (novel) 1996, Cedric Price Retriever (co-ed.) 2005. *Address:* c/o Rebecca Blond, 69A King's Road, London, SW3 4NX, England. *Telephone:* (20) 7351-4100. *Fax:* (20) 7351-4600.

BRON, Zakhar; Russian violinist and academic; *Professor of Violin, Hochschule für Musik Köln;* b. 1947, Uralsk; ed Stoliarski School of Music, Odessa, Gnessin Conservatoire, Moscow, Tchaikovsky Conservatoire; studied with Boris Goldstein and Igor Oistrakh; has taught at Musikhochschule, Lübeck, Glinka Conservatoire, Novosibirsk, RAM, London, Rotterdam Conservatory, Reina Sofia School, Madrid; currently Prof. of Violin, Hochschule für Musik, Cologne; lectures and gives masterclasses in many countries; has performed with many maj. int. orchestras; prizewinner Wieniawski Int. Violin Competition, Poznań, Queen Elizabeth Competition, Brussels; Verdienstkreuz am Bande (Germany). *Address:* Hochschule für Musik Köln, Dagobertstr. 38, 50668 Cologne, Germany. *Telephone:* (221) 9128180. *Fax:* (221) 131204. *E-mail:* zakharbron@gmail.com. *Website:* www.zakharbron.com.

BRONFMAN, Charles Rosner, PC, CC; Canadian/American business executive; b. 27 June 1931, Montreal, Québec; s. of Samuel Bronfman and Saidye Bronfman (née Rosner); m. 1st Barbara Baerwald; s. one d.; m. 2nd Andrea Morrison 1982 (died 2006); m. 3rd Bonita Rocheone 2008 (divorced 2012); m. 4th Rita Mayo 2012; ed Selwyn House School, Trinity Coll., McGill Univ.; joined The Seagram Co. Ltd 1951, Pres. and Co.-Chair. 1986–2000 9 co. sold to Vivendi); Chair., prin. owner Montreal Expos 1968–90; fmr Chair. Koor Industries Ltd; Chair. The Jerusalem Report, Andrea and Charles Bronfman Philanthropies, Claridge Israel LLC, The CRB Foundation, United Jewish Communities; mem. Int. Advisory Corpn of Canada; Hon. Pres. United Israel Appeal of Canada; mem. of Bd Washington Inst. for Near E Policy, The Kravis Center for Performing Arts, Fla; Co-founder and Co-Chair. Birthright Israel; Chair. (non-exec.) The Nat. Jewish Center for Learning and Leadership; Hon. DPhil (Hebrew Univ. of Jerusalem), Hon. DL (McGill Univ., Montreal), (Concordia Univ., Montreal), (Univ. of Waterloo), (Univ. of Toronto), Hon. DHumLitt (Branders). *Leisure interests:* tennis, golf. *Website:* www.acbp.net.

BRONFMAN, Edgar Miles, Jr; American business executive; *Managing Partner, Accretive, LLC;* b. 16 May 1955, Montreal, Quebec, Canada; s. of Edgar Miles Bronfman; m. 1st Sherri Brewer 1979 (divorced 1991); three c.; m. 2nd Clarissa Alcock 1994; three c.; began career working in British and US film industries as producer; joined family firm Seagram as Asst to Pres. 1982, Man. Dir Seagram Europe in London 1982–84, Pres. House of Seagram 1984–88, Exec. Vice-Pres. US Operations 1988–89; Pres. and COO J.E. Seagram Corpn New York 1989–94; Pres. and CEO Seagram Co. Ltd 1994–2000 (after merger with Vivendi to form Vivendi Universal), Vice-Chair. Bd of Dirs Vivendi Universal 2000–03; attempted to buy back Seagram assets in 2003 but failed; Chair. and CEO Lexa Partners LLC, then with Thomas H. Lee Partners acquired Warner Music Group, Chair. and CEO 2004–11, Chair. 2011–12; fmr Acting Pres. MCA Inc.; currently Man. Partner, Accretive LLC (venture capital firm), New York; Chair. Bd of Dirs Endeavor Global (non-profit); Co-Chair. Insureon; Exec. Chair. Global Thermostat LLC; mem. Bd of Dirs Arise, Accolade, Accumen, Everspring, AlphaStaff, New York Univ. Elaine A. and Kenneth G. Langone Medical Center; apptd Chair. Governing Bd, World Jewish Congress 2007; mem. Council on Foreign Relations. *Address:* Accretive, LLC, 51 Madison Avenue, 31st Floor, New York, NY 10010, USA (office). *Telephone:* (646) 282-1920 (office). *E-mail:* info@accretivellc.com (office). *Website:* www.accretivellc.com (office); www.endeavor.org; globalthermostat.com.

BRONNERT, Deborah Jane, CMG, BSc (Hons), MA; British diplomatist; b. Stockport, Greater Manchester; m. Alfonso Torrents; one s.; ed Univ. of Bristol, School of Slavonic and Eastern European Studies, University Coll., London; Fast Stream Trainee, Dept of the Environment 1989–90, mem. Secr., Royal Comm. on Environmental Pollution 1990–91, Second Sec. (Environment), UK Perm. Representation to the EU, Brussels 1991–93, mem. Secr., Sir Michael Latham's Review of the Construction Industry 1993–94, Team Leader, EU Dept (Internal), FCO 1994–95, mem. Neil Kinnock's Cabinet, EC 1995–99, Deputy Head, Southern European Dept, FCO 1999–2001, Russian language training 2001–02, Counsellor (Econ.), Embassy in Moscow 2002–05, School of Slavonic and Eastern European Studies 2005–06, Head, Future of Europe Dept, then Europe Delivery, FCO 2006–08, Dir, Prosperity (previously Global and Econ. Issues) 2008–11, Amb. to Zimbabwe 2011–14, COO, FCO 2014–15, Dir-Gen. Econ. and Consular, FCO 2016–19; mem. Bd of Dirs, Merlin (charity) 2010–13; Trustee, British Council 2014–. *Leisure interests:* politics, reading, running (Moscow marathon 2005, Victoria Falls 2012). *Address:* c/o Foreign and Commonwealth Office, King Charles Street, London, SW1A 2AH, England. *Telephone:* (20) 7008-2206 (office). *E-mail:* fcocorrespondence@fco.gov.uk (office). *Website:* www.gov.uk/government/fco (office).

BRONSTEIN, Alexander Semenovich, DrMed; Russian therapist (internist); *Director-General, Centre for Endosurgery and Lithotripsy;* b. 19 Sept. 1938, Khmelnitsky, Ukrainian SSR, USSR; s. of Semen Bronstein and Rebecca Yangarber; m. Inna Vladimirovna Kunina 1939; two d.; ed Moscow Sechenov Inst. of Medicine; gen. practitioner of polyclinic, therapist, Moscow hosp.; Intern, Jr, then Sr Researcher, Inst. of Proctology 1964–76; Head, Div. of Gastroenterology, Moscow clinic 1976–90; Pres., Dir-Gen. Centre for Endosurgery and Lithotripsy 1993–; Prof., Moscow Sechenov Acad. of Medicine; mem. Editorial Bd, International Medical Journal; Academician, Russian Acad. of Nat. Sciences; Order of St Constantine the Great; Merited Dr of Russian Fed. *Publications:* Clinical Medicine (two vols) and more than 150 scientific works. *Leisure interests:* classical music, tennis, singing. *Address:* Centre for Endosurgery and Lythotripsy, Entusiastov shosse 62, 111125 Moscow (office); Petrovsko-Razumovskaya Allea 20, Apt 18, Moscow, Russia (home). *Telephone:* (495) 305-15-83 (office). *Fax:* (495) 305-22-09 (office). *E-mail:* bronshtein@celt.ru (office). *Website:* www.celt.ru (office).

BROOK, Peter Stephen Paul, CH, CBE, MA; British theatre director, film director and writer; b. 21 March 1925, Chiswick, London; s. of Simon Brook; m. Natasha Parry 1951 (died 2015); one s. one d.; ed Westminster and Gresham's Schools and Magdalen Coll., Oxford; joined RSC as Dir 1962, Producer, Co-Dir

Royal Shakespeare Theatre; f. Centre for Theatre Research, Paris 1970, opened Théâtre des Bouffes du Nord, Paris 1974–2010, Co-Dir with Stéphane Lissner 1998–2005; Dir Int. Centre for Theatre Creations; Officier des Arts et des Lettres, Légion d'honneur 1995, Praemium Imperiale 1997, Commandeur, Légion d'honneur 2013; Hon. DLitt (Birmingham), (Strathclyde) 1990; Freiherr von Stein Foundation, Shakespeare Award 1973, Prix Italia 1984, Wexner Prize (Ohio State Univ.) 1991, Onassis Int. Award 1993, Times Award 1994, Dan David Prize 2005, Ibsen Award 2008. *Films include:* The Beggar's Opera 1952, Moderato Cantabile 1959, Lord of the Flies 1963, Marat/Sade 1967, Tell Me Lies 1967, King Lear 1969, Meetings With Remarkable Men 1976–77, La Tragédie de Carmen 1983, The Mahabharata 1989 (also producer), The Tragedy of Hamlet 2002. *Productions include:* Dr Faustus 1943, Pygmalion, King John, Lady from the Sea 1945, Romeo and Juliet (at Stratford) 1947, Dir of Productions at Covent Garden Opera 1949–50, Faust (at Metropolitan Opera, New York) 1953, The Dark is Light Enough (London) 1954, House of Flowers (New York) 1954, Cat on a Hot Tin Roof (Paris) 1956, Eugene Onegin (New York) 1958, View from the Bridge (Paris) 1958, The Fighting Cock (New York) 1959, Irma la Douce 1960, King Lear 1963, The Physicists (New York) 1964, The Marat/Sade (New York) 1965, US (London) 1966, Oedipus (Seneca) 1968, A Midsummer Night's Dream 1970, Orghast (Iran) 1971, The Conference of the Birds 1973, Timon of Athens (Paris) 1974, The Ik (Paris) 1975, (London) 1976, (USA) 1976, Ubu (Paris) 1977, Meetings with Remarkable Men (film, also dir screenplay) 1977, Antony and Cleopatra (Stratford and London) 1978, Measure for Measure (Paris) 1978, Conference of the Birds, L'os (Festival Avignon and Paris) 1979, (New York) 1980, The Cherry Orchard (Paris) 1981, (New York) 1988, (Moscow) 1989, La Tragédie de Carmen (opera) (Paris) 1981, (film) 1983, Le Mahabharata (Avignon and Paris) 1985, (world tour) 1988, Woza Albert! (Paris) 1989, La Tempête (Paris) 1990, Impressions de Pelléas (opera) 1992, L'Homme Qui (Paris) 1993, 1997, The Man Who 1994, Oh! Les Beaux Jours (Lausanne) 1995, (Paris) 1996, Don Giovanni (opera) 1998, Je suis un phénomène (Paris) 1998, Le Costume (Paris) 1999, The Tragedy of Hamlet (Paris) 2000, Far Away (Paris) 2002, La Tragédie d'Hamlet (Paris) 2002, La Mort de Krishna (Paris) 2002, Ta Main Dans La Mienne (Paris) 2003, Tierno Bokar (Paris) 2004, Le Grand Inquisiteur (Paris) 2004, Fragments (Paris, London, New York) 2008, Warum Warum 2008, Love Is My Sin (Paris), Eleven and Twelve (London) 2009, Une Flûte Enchantée (opera) (world tour) 2010–11, The Suit (Paris and world tour) 2012, Battlefield 2015. *Publications:* The Empty Space 1968, The Shifting Point: Forty years of theatrical exploration 1946–87, 1987, There Are No Secrets 1993 (appeared in USA as The Open Door: Thoughts on Acting and the Theatre), Threads of Time (autobiog.) 1998, Evoking Shakespeare 1999, The Quality of Mercy: Reflections on Shakespeare 2013. *Leisure interests:* painting, playing the piano, air travel. *Address:* CIRT, 37 bis boulevard de la Chapelle, 75010 Paris, France (office).

BROOK, Robert Henry, MD, ScD, FACP; American physician and professor of medicine; *Distinguished Chair in Health Care Services, RAND Corporation;* b. 3 July 1943, New York; s. of Benjamin N. Brook and Elizabeth Berg; m. 1st Susan Weiss 1966; m. 2nd Jacqueline Kosecoff 1981; one s. three d.; ed Univ. of Arizona, Johns Hopkins Medical School, Johns Hopkins School of Hygiene and Public Health; mil. service, US Public Health Services 1972–74; joined Health Program, RAND Corpn 1974, apptd Dir 1990, apptd Vice-Pres. 1998, now Distinguished Chair in Health Care Services and Prof., Pardee RAND Grad. School; Prof. of Medicine and Public Health, UCLA Center for Health Sciences 1974–; Dir Robert Wood Johnson Clinical Scholars Program 1974–; mem. Inst. of Medicine, NAS, American Soc. of Clinical Investigation, American Asscn of Physicians; Commendation Medal Richard and Hinda Rosenthal Foundation Award Baxter Health Services Research Prize 1988 Sonneborn Distinguished Lecturer, Univ. of Pa, Distinguished Health Services Researcher, Asscn of Health Services Research Robert J. Glaser Award of Soc. of Gen. Internal Medicine, Johns Hopkins Soc. of Scholars Hollister Univ. Lecturer, Northwestern Univ. Nat. Cttee for Quality Assurance Health Quality Award 2001, Research America 2000 Advocacy Award for Sustained Leadership 2001, Inst. of Medicine Gustav O. Lienhard Medal 2005, American Asscn of Medical Colls David Rogers Award 2007. *Publications:* over 300 articles on quality of medical care. *Leisure interests:* tennis, swimming, golf. *Address:* The RAND Corporation, PO Box 2138, 1776 Main Street, Santa Monica, CA 90401-3297 (office); 1474 Bienvenida Avenue, Pacific Palisades, CA 90272-2346, USA (home). *Telephone:* (310) 393-0411 (office); (310) 454-0766 (home). *Fax:* (310) 451-6917 (office); (310) 454-2797 (home). *E-mail:* brook@rand.org (office). *Website:* www.rand.org (office).

BROOKE-MARCINIAK, Beth A., BS; American business executive; *Global Vice-Chair, Public Policy, Ernst & Young LLP;* b. (Beth Millard), 9 June 1959; d. of Howard J. Millard and E. Mary Millard; m. 1st James Brooke 1983; m. 2nd Michelle M. Marciniak 2014; ed Purdue Univ.; joined Ernst & Young 1981, held several leadership roles including Dir, Ind. Insurance Tax Practice 1986–91, Nat. Dir, Insurance Tax Services 1991–93, Nat. Dir, Tax Vision 1996–98, Nat. Dir, Tax Consultant Services 1999–2000, Global and Americas Vice-Chair for Public Policy, Sustainability and Stakeholder Engagement, Global Vice-Chair, Public Policy, Ernst & Young LLP 2005–, also mem. Ernst & Young's Americas Exec. Bd; Nat. Dir, Office of Tax Policy, Dept of Treasury 1993–95; mem. Bd of Dirs TechnoServe Inc., Atlantic Council of United States, March of Dimes Public Policy Advisory Council, Nat. Women's Hall of Fame Advisory Council; Bd mem. The White House Project, Women's Leadership Bd, Harvard Kennedy School, Women's Advisory Bd, World Economic Forum; Fellow, Life Management Inst.; Henry Crown Fellow, Aspen Inst., also mem. Bd of Trustees; Pathways Envoy State Dept; mem. Committee of 200; mem. del. to UN Comm. on Status of Women; mem. Audit Advisory Cttee, Dept of Defence. *Address:* Ernst & Young, 1101 New York Avenue NW, Suite 601, Washington, DC 20005 (office); Ernst & Young, 5 Times Square, New York, NY 10036-6530, USA (office). *Telephone:* (202) 293-7500 (Washington, DC) (office); (212) 773-3000 (New York) (office). *Fax:* (202) 465-3149 (Washington, DC) (office); (212) 773-6350 (New York) (office). *Website:* www.ey.com (office).

BROOKHART, Maurice S., BA, PhD; American chemist and academic; *William R. Kenan, Jr Professor of Chemistry, University of North Carolina;* b. 28 Nov. 1942, Cumberland, Maryland; s. Maurice S. Brookhart and Martha Maurine Engle; ed Johns Hopkins Univ., Univ. of California, Los Angeles; NSF Postdoctoral Fellow, UCLA 1968; NATO Postdoctoral Fellowship, Univ. of Southampton, UK 1968–69; William R. Kenan, Jr Prof. of Chem., Univ. of North Carolina 1969–; Visiting Prof., Univ. of Wisconsin 1974, Univ. of Rennes, France 1981, 1987, Univ. of Oxford 1982–83, Univ. of Bordeaux 1989, CNRS Inst. for Co-ordination Chem., Toulouse 1989, Univ. of California, Berkeley 1996, Instituto de Investigaciones Quimicas, Seville 1997; Sr Humboldt Fellow, Univ. of Marburg 2001, Max Planck Inst., Muelheim 2003; Assoc. Ed., Organometallics 1990–96; Medicinal Chem. Study Section, DRG, NIH 1997–2001; mem. Editorial Advisory Bd, Organic Letters, Journal of Polymer Science, Advanced Synthesis and Catalysis; mem. NAS 2001; Fellow, American Acad. of Arts and Sciences 1996, AAAS 2001; Dr hc (Univ. of Rennes) 2000; ACS Award in Organometallic Chem. 1992, North Carolina Section ACS Distinguished Speaker Award 1992, ACS A.C. Cope Scholar Award 1994, Japan Soc. for the Promotion of Science Fellowship 1995, ACS Co-operative Research Award in Polymer Science and Eng (co-recipient) 1998, Charles H. Stone Award, Piedmont Section, ACS 1998, RSC Centenary Lecturer 2000, ACS Award in Polymer Chem. 2003, North Carolina Award in Science 2008, Willard Gibbs Medal, ACS Somorjai Award in Catalysis 2015. *Publications include:* more than 290 papers in professional journals; 22 US patents. *Address:* Department of Chemistry, University of North Carolina, Chapel Hill, NC 27599-3290 (office); 105 Rocky Point, Carrboro, NC 27510, USA. *Telephone:* (919) 962-0362 (office); (919) 933-0717 (office). *Fax:* (919) 962-2476 (office). *E-mail:* mbrookhart@unc.edu (office). *Website:* www.chem.unc.edu/people/faculty/brookhart (office).

BROOKS, Albert; American actor, writer and director; b. (Albert Einstein), 22 July 1947, Beverly Hills, Calif.; s. of Harry Brooks and Thelma (Leeds) Einstein; m. Kimberly Brooks; two c.; began career with several successful comedy albums then directing short comedy films for TV shown on Great American Dream Machine (PBS) and Saturday Night Live (NBC). *Films include:* (actor) Taxi Driver 1976, Private Benjamin 1980, Twilight Zone: The Movie 1983, Unfaithfully Yours 1983, Terms of Endearment 1983, Broadcast News 1987, I'll Do Anything 1994, The Scout 1994, Critical Care 1997, Out of Sight 1998, Dr Dolittle (voice) 1998, The Muse 1999; (dir, writer and actor) Real Life 1979, Modern Romance 1982, Lost in America 1985, Defending Your Life 1991, Mother 1996 (NY Soc. of Film Critics' Award, Nat. Soc. of Film Critics' Award for Best Screenplay), The Muse 1999, My First Mister 2000, Finding Nemo (voice) 2003, The In-Laws 2003, Looking for Comedy in the Muslim World 2006, The Simpsons Movie (voice) 2007, Drive 2011, This Is 40 2012. *Television includes:* The Simpsons (voice) 1990, 1993, 1996, 2005, 2011, 2015, Weeds (series) 2008. *Recordings include:* Comedy Minus One, A Star is Bought. *Publication:* 2030: The Real Story of What Happens to America (novel) 2011. *Address:* 1888 Century Drive Park East, Suite 900, Los Angeles, CA 90067-1609, USA. *Website:* www.albertbrooks.com.

BROOKS, (Troyal) Garth, BS; American country singer, songwriter and musician (guitar); b. 7 Feb. 1962, Tulsa, Okla; s. of Troyal Raymond and Colleen Carroll Brooks; m. 1st Sandra Mahl 1986; three c.; m. 2nd Trisha Yearwood 2005; ed Oklahoma State Univ.; mem. American Soc. of Composers, Authors and Publrs (ASCAP), Country Music Asscn, Acad. of Country Music; Acad. of Country Music Entertainer of the Year 1991, 1992, 1993, 1994, Male Vocalist of the Year Award 1991, Horizon Award 1991, Country Music Asscn Entertainer of the Year Awards 1991, 1992, 2016, 2017, Grammy Award for Best Male Country Vocalist 1992, Best Male Country Music Performer 1992, 1993, Best Male Musical Performer, People's Choice Awards 1992–95, Country Music Award for Artist of the Decade 1999, American Music Award for Favorite Country Artist 2000, Special Award of Merit 2002, inducted into Country Music Hall of Fame 2012, 50th Anniversary Milestone Award, Acad. of Country Music Awards 2015. *Recordings include:* albums: Garth Brooks 1989, No Fences (Acad. of Country Music Album of the Year 1991, CMA Award for Best Album 1991) 1990, Ropin' The Wind 1991, Beyond The Season 1992, The Chase 1992, In Pieces 1993, The Hits 1994, Fresh Horses 1995, Sevens 1997, In The Life Of Chris Gaines 1999, Garth Brooks & The Magic Of Christmas 1999, Double Live (American Music Award for Favorite Country Album 2001) 2000, Scarecrow 2001, The Entertainer 2006, Man Against Machine 2014, Gunslinger 2016, Christmas Together (with Trisha Yearwood) 2016; singles: If Tomorrow Never Comes 1989, The Dance (Acad. of Country Music Song of Year, CMA Award for Best Single) 1991, The Thunder Rolls 1991, Friends in Low Places (Acad. of Country Music Single Record of Year) 1991, If Tomorrow Never Comes (American Music Country Song of Year) 1991, We Shall Be Free 1992, Somewhere Other Than the Night 1992, Learning to Live Again 1993, Tour EP 1994, To Make You Feel My Love 1998, One Heart At A Time 1998, Lost In You 1999, Call Me Claus 2001. *Television specials:* This is Garth Brooks 1992, This is Garth Brooks Too 1994, Garth Brooks: The Hits 1995, Garth Brooks Live in Central Park 1997. *Address:* c/o Bob Doyle, Major Bob Music, 1111 17th Avenue S, Nashville, TN 37212, USA (office). *Telephone:* (615) 329-4150 (office). *Fax:* (615) 329-1021 (office). *Website:* majorbob.com (office); www.garthbrooks.com.

BROOKS, James Lawrence; American screenwriter, director and producer; b. 9 May 1940, Brooklyn, New York; s. of Edward M. Brooks and Dorothy Helen Sheinheit; m. 1st Marianne Catherine Morrissey 1964 (divorced); one d.; m. 2nd Holly Beth Holmberg 1978–99; three c.; ed New York Univ.; writer CBS News, New York 1964–66; writer-producer documentaries Wolper Productions, LA 1966–67; founder and owner Gracie Films 1984; mem. Guild of America, Writers' Guild of America, TV Acad. of Arts and Sciences, Acad. of Motion Picture Arts and Sciences. *Films include:* producer, writer, dir: Terms of Endearment (Golden Globe Best Screenplay and Best Picture Awards, Acad. Awards for Best Film, Best Dir, Best Screenplay, Dirs' Guild of America Award for Best Dir) 1983, Broadcast News (New York Film Critics' Awards for Best Picture, Best Dir, Best Screenplay) 1987, As Good As It Gets 1997, How Do You Know 2010; exec. producer: Big 1988, The War of the Roses 1989; producer: Jerry Maguire 1996, Riding in Cars With Boys 2001, The Simpsons Movie 2007, The Longest Daycare 2012. *Television series include:* creator: Room 222 (Emmy Award for Outstanding New Series) 1968–69; co-creator, producer: Mary Tyler Moore Show (Emmy Awards for Comedy Writing, Outstanding Comedy Series, Peabody Award, Writers' Guild of America Award, Humanitas Award and others) 1970–77; writer, producer: Paul Sand in Friends and Lovers 1974; co-creator, co-exec. producer: series Rhoda Show (Emmy and Humanitas Awards) 1974–75; co-creator, exec. producer: Taxi (Emmy, Film Critics' Circle, Golden Globe and Humanitas Awards) 1978–80; co-exec. producer, co-writer: Cindy 1978; co-creator, exec. producer: The Associates 1979; exec. producer, co-exec. producer, co-creator: The Tracey Ullman Show (three Emmy Awards for Outstanding Variety or Comedy Series, two Emmy Awards for Outstanding Writing Variety or Music Show) 1986–90, The Simpsons (three

Emmy Awards) 1990–, The Critic (exec. producer) 1994–95, What About Joan (exec. producer) 2001. *Address:* Gracie Films, 10201 West Pico Blvd, Building 41/42, Los Angeles, CA 90064, USA (office). *Telephone:* (310) 369-7222 (office). *Website:* www.graciefilms.com (office).

BROOKS, Mel; American actor, writer, producer and director; b. (Melvin Kaminsky), 28 June 1926, Brooklyn, New York City, NY; s. of James Kaminsky and Kate Kaminsky (née Brookman); m. 1st Florence Baum 1953 (divorced 1962); two s. one d.; m. 2nd Anne Bancroft 1964 (died 2005); one s.; scriptwriter for Your Show of Shows (TV series) 1950–54, Caesar's Hour 1954–57, Get Smart 1965; est. feature film production co. Brooksfilms; Kennedy Center Honor 2009, American Film Inst. Life Achievement Award 2013, BFI Fellowship 2015, Nat. Medal of Arts 2016, BAFTA Fellowship 2017. *Musicals include:* The Producers (producer, co-writer, composer) (Tony Awards for Best Book, Best Score, Best Musical 2001, Evening Standard Award for Best Musical 2004, Critics Circle Theatre Award for Best Musical 2005) 2001, Young Frankenstein 2007. *Films include:* The Critic (writer, cartoon) (Academy Award 1964) 1963, The Producers (writer, dir) (Acad. Award for Best Screenplay) 1968, The Twelve Chairs (writer, dir, actor) 1970, Shinbone Alley (writer) 1971, Blazing Saddles (writer, dir, actor) 1974, Young Frankenstein (writer, dir) 1974, Silent Movie (writer, dir, actor) 1976, High Anxiety (writer, dir, actor, producer) 1977, The Muppet Movie (actor) 1979, The Elephant Man (exec. producer) 1980, History of the World Part I (writer, dir, actor, producer) 1981, My Favourite Year 1982, To Be or Not to Be (actor, producer) 1983, The Doctor and the Devils (exec. producer) 1985, Solarbabies (exec. producer) 1986, Fly I 1986, Spaceballs (writer, dir, actor, producer) 1987, 84 Charing Cross Road (exec. producer) 1987, Fly II 1989, Life Stinks (writer, dir, actor, producer) 1991, The Vagrant (exec. producer) 1992, Robin Hood: Men in Tights (writer, dir, actor, producer) 1993, The Little Rascals (actor) 1994, Dracula: Dead and Loving It (writer, dir, actor, producer) 1995, Svitati (actor) 1999, The Producers: The Movie Musical (screenplay and producer) 2005, Get Smart (characters) 2008, Mr. Peabody & Sherman (voice) 2014, Hotel Transylvania 2 2015, Sam (exec. producer) 2015, The Guardian Brothers (voice) 2016, Blazing Samurai (actor and exec. producer) 2017. *Television includes:* Get Smart (writer) 1965–70, The Nutt House (writer) 1989, Mad About You (Emmy Award for Outstanding Guest Actor in a Comedy Series 1997, 1998, 1999) 1996–99, Jakers! The Adventures of Piggley Winks (series) 2003–07, Curb Your Enthusiasm 2004, Spaceballs: The Animated Series (series; writer and exec. producer) 2008–09, Ruby's Studio: The Feelings Show (video) 2010, Glenn Martin DDS (series) 2010, Special Agent Oso (series) 2011, The Paul Reiser Show (series) 2011, Inside Comedy 2012, Mel Brooks Strikes Back! (film; exec. producer) 2012, Dora the Explorer (series) 2014, Mel Brooks Live at the Geffen (special; writer and exec. producer) 2015, The Comedians (series) 2015. *Website:* www.melbrooks.com.

BROOKS, Rebekah Mary; British journalist and newspaper executive; *CEO, News UK;* b. 27 May 1968, Warrington, England; d. of Robert Wade and Deborah Wade; m. 1st Ross Kemp 2002 (divorced 2009); m. 2nd Charlie Brooks 2009; one d.; ed Appleton Hall, Cheshire and Univ. of Paris (Sorbonne); began career as Features Ed., later Assoc. Ed. and Deputy Ed. News of the World –1998, Ed. 2000–03; Deputy Ed. The Sun 1998–2000, Ed. 2003–09; CEO News International (now News UK) 2009–11 (resgnd), 2015–; Founder-mem. and Pres. Women in Journalism; arrested and charged with her husband in connection with UK phone hacking scandal 2011, 2012, tried and cleared of all charges June 2014. *Address:* News UK & Ireland Ltd, The News Building, 1 London Bridge Street, London, SE1 9GF, England (office). *Telephone:* (20) 7782-6000 (office). *E-mail:* info@news.co.uk (office). *Website:* www.news.co.uk (office).

BROOME, David McPherson, CBE; British fmr professional show jumper, sports administrator and farmer; b. 1 March 1940, Cardiff, Wales; s. of Fred Broome and Amelia Broome; brother of veteran show jumper Liz Edgar; m. Elizabeth Fletcher 1976; three s.; ed Monmouth Grammar School for Boys; European show jumping champion, riding Sunsalve, Aachen 1961, riding Mr Softee, Rotterdam 1967 and Hickstead 1969; world champion, riding Beethoven, La Baule (France) 1970; professional world champion, riding Sportsman and Philco, Cardiff 1974; mem. of six British Olympic teams (including Barcelona 1992); Master of Foxhounds. *Publications:* Jump-Off 1970, Horsemanship (with S. Hadley) 1983. *Leisure interests:* hunting, shooting, golf. *Address:* Mount Ballan Manor, Crick, Chepstow, Monmouthshire, NP26 5XP, Wales. *Telephone:* (1291) 420777; (1291) 418125. *E-mail:* charlotte@theshowground.com. *Website:* www.theshowground.com.

BROSNAN, Pierce Brendan; Irish/American actor, producer and environmentalist; b. 16 May 1953, Drogheda, Co. Louth; s. of Thomas Brosnan and May Brosnan (née Smith); m. 1st Cassandra Harris 1980 (died 1991); one s.; one step-s. one step-d. (died 2013); m. 2nd Keely Shaye Smith 2001; two s.; ed Drama Centre London; London stage appearances include Wait Until Dark, The Red Devil Battery Sign (cast in role of McCabe in British premiere by Tennessee Williams), Filumenia; co-f. (with Beau St. Clair) Irish Dreamtime (production co.) 1996; Hon. OBE 2003; hon. degrees from Dublin Inst. of Tech. 2002, Univ. Coll. Cork 2003. *Films include:* The Mirror Crack'd 1980, The Long Good Friday 1980, Nomads 1986, The Fourth Protocol 1987, Taffin 1988, The Deceivers 1988, Mister Johnson 1990, The Lawnmower Man 1992, Mrs Doubtfire 1993, Entangled 1993, Love Affair 1994, GoldenEye 1995, The Disappearance of Kevin Johnson 1996, Mars Attacks! 1996, The Mirror Has Two Faces 1996, Dante's Peak 1997, Robinson Crusoe 1997, Tomorrow Never Dies 1997, The Nephew 1998, The Magic Sword: Quest for Camelot 1998, The Thomas Crown Affair 1999, The Match 1999, The World Is Not Enough 1999, Grey Owl 2000, The Tailor of Panama 2001, Evelyn 2002, Die Another Day 2001, Laws of Attraction 2004, After the Sunset 2004, The Matador 2005, Seraphim Falls 2006, Shattered 2007, Married Life 2007, Mamma Mia! 2008, Thomas & Friends: The Great Discovery-The Movie 2008, The Greatest 2009, Percy Jackson & the Olympians: The Lightning Thief 2010, The Ghost Writer 2010, Remember Me 2010, Salvation Boulevard 2011, I Don't Know How She Does It 2011, The Bald Hairdresser 2012, Love Is All You Need 2013, The World's End 2013, The Love Punch 2014, A Long Way Down 2014, The November Man 2014, How to Make Love Like an Englishman 2014, Some Kind of Beautiful 2014, No Escape 2015, Survivor 2015, Urge 2015, The Moon and the Sun 2015, A Christmas Star 2015, I.T. 2016. *Television includes:* role of detective in Remington Steele (series), Murphy's Stroke (TV movie) 1980, Nancy Astor 1982, Noble House (mini-series) 1988, Around the World in Eighty Days 1989, The Heist 1990, Murder 101 (TV movie) 1991, Victim of Love 1991, Live Wire 1992, Detonator (TV movie) 1993, Detonator II: Night Watch (TV movie) 1995, The Broken Chain 1993, Don't Talk to Strangers (TV movie) 1994, Death Train 1993, Robinson Crusoe 1994, The James Bond Story 1999, The Simpsons 2001, Bag of Bones (mini-series) 2011. *Address:* c/o Guttman Associates, 118 South Beverly Drive, Suite 201, Beverly Hills, CA 90212, USA (office); Irish Dreamtime, 3110 Main Street, Suite 200, Santa Monica, CA 90405, USA. *Telephone:* (310) 449-3411. *Fax:* (310) 586-8138. *Website:* www.piercebrosnan.com.

BROTODININGRAT, Soemadi Djoko Moerdjono; Indonesian diplomatist; *Senior Adviser, Minister of Defence;* b. 13 June 1941, Solo, Cen. Javan Prov.; m.; one s. one d.; ed Gadjah Mada Univ., Int. Inst. of Public Admin, France; with Dept of Foreign Affairs 1965–, Head of Section (and later of Staff), Directorate of Information 1965–71; Third then Second Sec., Embassy in Brussels 1971–75; Deputy Dir of Social and Cultural Relations, Dept of Foreign Affairs 1975–78; First Sec., Counsellor, Perm. Mission to UN, New York 1978–82, Minister Counsellor 1984–88; Deputy Dept, Directorate of Multilateral Econ. Co-operation, Dept of Foreign Affairs 1982–84, Dept 1988–91; Amb. and Perm. Rep. to UN, Geneva 1991–95; Dir for Foreign Econ. Relations, Dept of Foreign Affairs 1995–98; Amb. to Japan and Federated States of Micronesia 1998–2002, to USA (also accred to Grenada, St Lucia, St Vincent and Dominica) 2002–05; apptd Chief Negotiator for the Econ. Partnership Agreement with Japan 2005–07; Special Envoy for Climate Change 2007; Lecturer, Center of Educ. and Training, Ministry of Foreign Affairs 2005–; mem. Bd of Govs Asia-Europe Foundation/ASEF 2009–; Sr Adviser, Minister of Defence 2009–; Chief Negotiator, Indonesia–EFTA Econ. Partnership Agreement 2010; Sr Advisor, HD Asia Advisory; mem. Bd of Commrs Astra International, DBS Bank Indonesia. *Address:* Ministry of Defence, Jalan Medan Grantham 13–14, Jakarta 10110, Indonesia (office). *Telephone:* (21) 3828500 (office). *E-mail:* ppid@kemhan.go.id (office). *Website:* www.kemhan.go.id (office).

BROU, Kassi Jean-Claude, MBA, PhD; Côte d'Ivoirian economist, politician and UN official; *President, Economic Community of West African States (ECOWAS);* m.; two c.; ed Univ. of Cincinnati; Prof. of Econs, Univ. of Cincinnati 1981–82; apptd Economist, IMF 1982, then Sr Economist, in-charge of Guinea-Bissau, Togo, Cabo Verde, Senegal, Resident Rep. 1990–91; Econ. Counsellor to Prime Minister 1991–95, Dir, Cabinet of Prime Minister 1996–99, apptd Adviser to Prime Minister 2009; Dir Int. Relations Dept, Banque Centrale des Etats de l'Afrique de l'Ouest 2000–03, Dir Research Dept 2003–05, Dir Econ. and Monetary Dept 2006–07, Sr Adviser and Comptroller-Gen. 2007–08; Resident Dir for Chad, World Bank 2010–13; Minister of Industry 2012–18, of Mines 2013–18; Pres. ECOWAS 2018–. *Address:* ECOWAS Executive Secretariat, 101 Yakubu Gowon Crescent, PMB 401, Asokoro, Abuja, Nigeria (office). *Telephone:* (9) 3147647 (office). *Fax:* (9) 3147646 (office). *E-mail:* info@ecowas.int (office). *Website:* www.ecowas.int (office).

BROUGHTON, Sir Martin Faulkner, Kt, FCA; British business executive and chartered accountant; *Deputy Chairman, International Airlines Group;* b. 15 April 1947, London; s. of Edward Broughton and Laura Faulkner; m. Jocelyn Mary Rodgers 1974; one s. one d.; ed Westminster City Grammar School; joined British-American Tobacco Co. (BAT) 1971, with group's Brazilian subsidiary Souza Cruz 1980–85, Finance Dir BAT Industries 1988–93, Group Chief Exec. and Deputy Chair. 1993–98, Chair. BAT PLC (following demerger) 1998–2004; Finance Dir Eagle Star 1985–88, Chair. 1992–93, Chair. Wiggins Teape Group 1989–90; Dir (non-exec.) Whitbread 1993–2000; Dir (non-exec.) British Airways PLC 2000–, Deputy Chair. (non-exec.) 2003–04, Chair. (non-exec.) 2004–13; Deputy Chair. International Airlines Group 2010–; Pres. CBI 2007–09, Deputy Pres. 2009–; Ind. Dir British Horseracing Bd 1999–2004, Chair. 2004–07; Co-Chair. Transatlantic Business Dialogue 2006–08, currently European Chair.; Chair. Liverpool Football Club April–Oct. 2010; mem. Financial Reporting Council 1998–, European Round Table of Industrialists. *Leisure interests:* golf, football, horse racing, the theatre. *Address:* International Airlines Group, 2 World Business Centre, Heathrow, Newall Road, London Heathrow Airport, Hounslow, TW6 2SF, England (office); Company Secretary, IAG Registered Office, Calle Velázquez 130, Madrid 28006, Spain (office). *Telephone:* (20) 8564-2800 (Hounslow) (office). *E-mail:* media.relations@iairgroup.com (office). *Website:* www.iairgroup.com (office).

BROUSSARD, Bruce D.; American business executive; *President and CEO, Humana Incorporated;* CEO McKesson Specialty/US Oncology, Inc. (purchased by McKesson in 2010) –2010, held several sr exec. roles, including Chief Financial Officer, Pres., CEO and Chair.; Pres. Humana Inc. 2011–12, mem. Bd of Dirs, Pres. and CEO 2013–; mem. Bd of Dirs, America's Health Insurance Plans and its Exec. Cttee; mem. Business Roundtable. *Address:* Humana Inc., 500 West Main Street, Louisville, KY 40202, USA (office). *Telephone:* (502) 580-1000 (office). *Fax:* (502) 580-3677 (office). *E-mail:* info@humana.com (office). *Website:* www.humana.com (office).

BROVTSEV, Vadim Vladimirovich; Russian business executive and politician; b. 26 July 1969, Chelyabinsk (now Ozyorsk), Russian SFSR, USSR; m.; two c.; served in Soviet Strategic Rocket Forces; Chair. Vermikulit (construction co.), Chelyabinsk 2005–09; Prime Minister of the 'Repub. of South Ossetia' 2009–12, also Acting Pres. Dec. 2011–12. *Address:* c/o Office of the Prime Minister of the 'Republic of South Ossetia', 100001 Tskhinvali, ul. Khetgurova 1, South Ossetia, Georgia. *E-mail:* ospress@yandex.ru.

BROWN, Adriane M., BSc, MA; American automotive industry executive; *President and CEO, Transportation Systems, Honeywell International Inc.;* ed Old Dominion Univ., Norfolk, Va, Massachusetts Inst. of Tech. (Sloan Fellow); Vice-Pres. and Gen. Man. Environmental Products Div., Corning Inc. 1980–94, Vice-Pres. and Gen. Man. Automotive Products business 1994–99; Vice-Pres. and Gen. Man. Aircraft Landing Systems, Honeywell Aerospace 1999, later Vice-Pres. and Gen. Man. Engine Systems and Accessories, Pres. and CEO Transportation Systems, Honeywell International Inc., Torrance, Calif. 2005–; mem. Bd of Dirs Jobs for America's Graduates; mem. Exec. Leadership Council, Arizona Women's Forum; named one of Top 100 Leading Women in the Automotive Industry 2005. *Address:* Honeywell Transportation Systems, 23326 Hawthorne Blvd, # 200, Torrance, CA 90505, USA (office). *Telephone:* (310) 791-9101 (office). *Website:* www.honeywell.com (office).

BROWN, Cedric Harold, FREng, FICE, CEng; British engineer and business executive; b. 7 March 1935; s. of William Herbert Brown and Constance Dorothy Brown (née Frances); m. Joan Hendry 1956; one s. three d.; ed Sheffield, Rotherham and Derby Colls of Tech.; East Midlands Gas Bd 1953–59; Eng Asst Tunbridge Wells Borough Council 1959–60; Eng posts, East Midlands Gas Bd 1960–75; Dir of Eng East Midlands Gas 1975–78; joined British Gas Corpn (now British Gas PLC) 1978; Dir Morecambe Bay Project 1980–87; Regional Chair. British Gas West Midlands 1987–89; Dir and Man. Dir Exploration and Production 1989; Man. Regional Services 1989–91; Sr Man. Dir 1991; Chief Exec. British Gas PLC 1992–96; Chair. CB Consultants 1996–, Atlantic Caspian Resources PLC 1999–2006, Business Champions-East Midlands Devt Agency 2001–, Lachesis Investment Advisory Cttee 2002–, Intellipower 2003–06; Dir, Bow Valley Industries 1988–92, Orb Estates 2000–; mem. Advisory Council on Business and the Environment 1993–95; Fellow, Inst. of Gas Engineers (Pres. 1996–97); Freeman, City of London 1989; Liveryman, Worshipful Co. of Engineers 1988. *Publications include:* tech. papers. *Leisure interests:* sport, countryside, places of historic interest.

BROWN, Christina Hambley (Tina), (Lady Evans), CBE, MA; American (b. British) magazine editor, television presenter and author; b. 21 Nov. 1953, Maidenhead, Berks., England; d. of George Hambley Brown and Bettina Iris Mary Brown (née Kohr); m. Sir Harold Matthew Evans (q.v.) 1981; one s. one d.; ed Univ. of Oxford; columnist, Punch magazine 1978; Ed.-in-Chief Tatler Magazine 1979–83, of Vanity Fair Magazine, New York 1984–92, London 1991–92; Ed. The New Yorker 1992–98, Talk magazine 1999–2002; Partner and Chair. Talk Media 1998–2002, Talk Miramax Books 1998–2002; columnist, Washington Post 2003–; Founder and Ed.-in-Chief The Daily Beast (internet news site) 2008–13, Ed.-in-Chief Newsweek (after jt venture with Daily Beast to form The Newsweek Daily Beast Co.) 2010–13; Founder and CEO Tina Brown Live Media 2013–; Most Promising Female Journalist, Katherine Pakenham Prize Sunday Times 1973, Young Journalist of the Year 1978, Univ. of Southern Calif. Distinguished Achievement in Journalism Award 1994, four George Polk Awards, five Overseas Press Club awards, ten National Magazine Awards, inducted into Magazine Editors' Hall of Fame 2007. *Publications include:* Under the Bamboo Tree (play) (Sunday Times Drama Award) 1973, Happy Yellow (play) 1977, Loose Talk – Adventures on the Street of Shame 1979, Life as a Party 1983, The Icarus Complex 2005, The Diana Chronicles 2007. *E-mail:* info@tinabrownmedia.com. *Website:* www.tinabrownmedia.com.

BROWN, Daniel (Dan) Gerhard; American writer; b. 22 June 1964, Exeter, NH; s. of Richard G. Brown and Constance (née Gerhard); m. Blythe Newlon 1997; ed Phillips Exeter Acad., Amherst Coll.; English teacher 1986–96. *Publications include:* 187 Men to Avoid (as Danielle Brown) 1995, Digital Fortress 1998, Angels and Demons 2001, Deception Point 2002, The Da Vinci Code (British Book Award for Book of the Year 2005) 2003, The Lost Symbol 2009, Inferno 2013, Origin 2017. *Address:* c/o Heide Lange, Sandford J. Greenburger Assocs Inc., 55 Fifth Avenue, New York, NY 10003, USA (office). *Telephone:* (212) 206-5600 (office). *Fax:* (212) 463-8718 (office). *E-mail:* queryHL@sjga.com (office). *Website:* www.greenburger.com (office); www.danbrown.com.

BROWN, Donald David, MS, MD; American biologist and academic; *Staff Member, Department of Embryology, Carnegie Institution and Adjunct Professor, Department of Biology, Johns Hopkins University;* b. 30 Dec. 1931, Cincinnati, Ohio; s. of Albert L. Brown and Louise R. Brown; m. Linda Weil 1957; one s. two d.; ed Walnut Hills High School, Cincinnati, Dartmouth Coll and Univ. of Chicago; Intern, Charity Hosp., New Orleans 1956–57, Sr Asst Surgeon, US Public Health Service, Bethesda, Md 1957–59; Postdoctoral Fellow, Pasteur Inst. 1959–60, Dept of Embryology, Carnegie Inst. of Washington, Baltimore, Md 1960–62, staff mem. 1963–, Dir 1976–94; Adjunct Prof., Dept of Biology, Johns Hopkins Univ. 1968–; Pres. Life Sciences Research Foundation 1981–, American Soc. of Cell Biology 1992; US Steel Award in Molecular Biology 1973, V.D. Mattia Award 1976, New York Acad. of Science Boris Pregel Award 1977, Ross Harrison-ISDB Award 1981, Ernst W. Bertner Award, Texas Univ. Cancer Center 1982, Louisa Gross Horwitz Award, Columbia Univ. 1985, Rosensteil Award 1985, Feodor Lynen Medal, Miami Winter Symposium 1987, E.B. Wilson Award 1996, Lifetime Achievement Award, American Soc. of Developmental Biology 2009. *Address:* Carnegie Institution, Department of Embryology, 3520 San Martin Drive, Baltimore, MD 21218 (office); 6511 Abbey View Way, Baltimore, MD 21212, USA (home). *Telephone:* (410) 246-3052 (office); (410) 377-0812 (home). *Fax:* (410) 243-6311 (office). *E-mail:* brown@ciwemb.edu (office). *Website:* emb.carnegiescience.edu/labs/donald-brown (office); www.bio.jhu.edu (office).

BROWN, Edmund Gerald (Jerry), Jr, AB, JD; American lawyer, politician and fmr state governor; b. 7 April 1938, San Francisco, Calif.; s. of Edmund Gerald Brown and Bernice Layne; m. Anne Gust 2005; ed Univ. of Santa Clara, Sacred Heart Novitiate, Univ. of California, Berkeley, Yale Law School; worked as a law clerk to Calif. Supreme Court Justice Mathew Tobriner 1964–65, Attorney, Tuttle & Taylor (law firm) Los Angeles 1966–69; mem. Bd of Trustees, Los Angeles Community Coll. 1969–70; Calif. Sec. of State 1971–74; Gov. of Calif. 1975–83, 2011–19; Chair. Calif. State Democratic Party 1989–90; unsuccessful Democratic presidential cand. 1992; Mayor of Oakland, Calif. 1999–2007; Attorney-Gen. of Calif. 2007–11; fmr Partner, Reavis & McGarth (law firm); f. Oakland School for the Arts, Oakland Mil. Inst. *Publication:* Dialogues 1988. *Address:* c/o Office of the Governor of California, State Capitol Building, Sacramento, CA 95814, USA (office). *Website:* www.jerrybrown.org.

BROWN, Hon. Ewart Frederick, Jr, BSc, MD, MPH, JP; Bermudian physician and politician; b. 1946; s. of Ewart Brown and Helene Brown; m. Wanda Henton Brown; four s. from previous m.; ed Berkeley Inst., Howard Univ., Washington DC, USA, Howard Coll. of Medicine, Univ. of California, Los Angeles; spent many years practising medicine in USA, including at Vermont-Century Medical Clinic, Los Angeles –1993; Medical Dir Bermuda HealthCare Services Ltd; MP for Warwick West 1993–98, for Warwick South Cen. 1998–; Minister of Transport 1998–2003, Deputy Premier and Minister of Transport 2003–04, Deputy Premier and Minister of Transport and Tourism 2004–06, Premier and Minister of Transport and Tourism 2006–10 (resgnd); Leader, Bermuda Progressive Labour Party 2006–10; fmr Vice-Pres. Union of American Physicians and Dentists; fmr Asst Prof., Dept of Family Practice, Charles R. Drew Univ. of Medicine and Science; fmr Dir, Marcus Garvey School, Los Angeles; fmr physician consultant of Rev. Jesse Jackson (1988 US presidential cand.); fmr mem. California State Comm. on Maternal, Child and Adolescent Health; Founding Commr Bd of Prevention Commrs for South Cen. Los Angeles Regional Centre for Devt Disabilities; Founder and Chair. Western Park Hosp., Calif.; fmr Coordinator Summer Health Task Force, Nat. Urban Coalition, Washington, DC; fmr Sec., Charles R. Drew Medical Soc., Los Angeles; mem. Nat. Medical Asscn, American Coll. of Utilization Review Physicians, Golden State Medical Asscn, American Medical Asscn, American Acad. of Family Physicians, American Public Health Asscn, Charles R. Drew Medical Soc.; fmr Trustee Howard Univ., Charles R. Drew Univ. of Medicine and Science; Howard Univ. Service Awards 1968, 1972, Physician's Recognition Award, American Medical Asscn 1977, Community Leadership Award, DuBois Academic Inst. 1982, Pacesetter Award, Nat. Asscn for the Advancement of Colored People 1984, Humanitarian of the Year Award, Marcus Garvey School, Los Angeles 1991, Scroll Award, Union of American Physicians and Dentists 1993. *Achievements include:* represented Bermuda at Commonwealth Games, Kingston, Jamaica, where he ran the 400m and 1600m relay 1966. *Leisure interests:* travel, exercising, golf.

BROWN, Gary W.; American banking executive; *CEO, FirstCaribbean International Bank Ltd;* ed Oral Roberts Univ.; began banking career with Chase Manhattan Bank as lending officer in Commodity Finance Div. 1976, then held various business devt positions 1976–80; Chief Credit Officer (Americas), UBS AG 1980–99; Pres., K2 Digital, Inc. 2000–07; Pres., Chief Financial Officer, Sec. and Prin. Accounting Officer, Accelerated Building Concepts Corpn 2001–07; joined Canadian Imperial Bank of Commerce (CIBC) as Sr Vice-Pres. and Man. Dir, Risk Management Div. 2001, Pres. and CEO CIBC World Markets Corpn 2004, Head, US Region 2004–13, Man. Dir and Global Head of Corp. Banking, CIBC 2013–15; CEO FirstCaribbean International Bank Ltd, Trinidad 2016–; mem. Bd of Trustees Oral Roberts Univ.; mem. Bd of Dirs Foreign Policy Asscn. *Address:* FirstCaribbean International Bank Ltd, 74 Long Circular Road, Maraval, Trinidad and Tobago (office). *Telephone:* 628-4685 (office). *Fax:* 628-8906 (office). *Website:* www.firstcaribbeanbank.com (office).

BROWN, Gavin; British art gallery owner; b. 1963, Croydon, London, England; m. Lucy Barnes (divorced); three d.; ed Newcastle-upon-Tyne Polytechnic, Whitney Museum of American Art, USA; moved to New York 1988; worked at several art galleries, including Pat Hearn Gallery, Brooke Alexander Editions, Lisa Spellman's 303 Gallery; opened Gavin Brown's Enterprise 1994, represents artists Franz Ackermann, James Angus, Uri Aran, Thomas Bayrle, Dirk Bell, Jennifer Bornstein, Joe Bradley, Kerstin Brätsch, Martin Creed, Verne Dawson, Jeremy Deller, Peter Doig, Urs Fischer, Dara Friedman, Mark Handforth, Jonathan Horowitz, Alex Katz, Christopher Knowles, Udomsak Krisanamis, Ella Kruglyanskaya, Mark Leckey, Bjarne Melgaard, Silke Otto-Knapp, Laura Owens, Oliver Payne, Oliver Payne & Nick Relph, Elizabeth Peyton, Steven Pippin, Rob Pruitt, Nick Relph, Steven Shearer, Frances Stark, Katja Strunz, Sturtevant, Spencer Sweeney and Rirkrit Tiravanija; Owner Passerby (bar) 1999–2008; expanded to the West Coast by opening a large warehouse in Los Angeles with gallery artist Laura Owens 2013; has also been running a project space from his own house, promoted only through Instagram. *Address:* Gavin Brown's Enterprise, 620 Greenwich Street, New York, NY 10014, USA (office). *Telephone:* (212) 627-5258 (office). *Fax:* (212) 627-5261 (office). *E-mail:* gallery@gavinbrown.biz (office). *Website:* www.gavinbrown.biz (office).

BROWN, Gregory Q., BA; American business executive; *Chairman and CEO, Motorola Solutions, Inc.;* b. 14 Aug. 1960; ed Rutgers Univ.; held several sales and marketing positions with AT&T 1983–87; joined Ameritech 1987, Pres. Custom Business Services and Ameritech New Media, Inc. 1994–96; Chair. and CEO Micromuse, Inc., San Francisco 1999–2003; joined Motorola 2003, held several exec. positions including Exec. Vice-Pres., CEO Commercial, Govt and Industrial Solutions 2003–05, Exec. Vice-Pres. Networks and Enterprise 2005–07, mem. Bd Dirs 2007–, Pres. and COO Motorola, Inc. March–Dec. 2007, Pres. and Co-CEO 2008–11, Chair. and CEO Motorola Solutions, Inc. (following separation of Motorola into Motorola Mobility and Motorola Solutions) 2011–; apptd by White House to serve on Nat. Security Telecommunications Advisory Cttee 2004–, Pres.'s Man. Advisory Bd 2011–, Skills for America's Future Bd 2011–; Deputy Chair. Fed. Reserve Bank of Chicago 2013–15, Chair. 2015–; mem. Bd Dirs, Cisco Systems, Inc. 2013–14, Commercial Club of Chicago, World Business Chicago, Northwestern Memorial Hosp.; mem. Business Council, Business Roundtable, Technology CEO Council, Exec. Cttee of the US-China Business Council, 2016 Chicago Olympic Cttee; mem. Bd of Trustees and Bd of Overseers, Rutgers Univ.; Hon. DHumLitt (Rutgers Univ.). *Address:* Motorola Solutions, Inc., 1303 East Algonquin Road, Schaumburg, IL 60196, USA (office). *Telephone:* (847) 576-5000 (office). *Fax:* (847) 576-5372 (office). *E-mail:* info@motorolasolutions.com (office). *Website:* www.motorolasolutions.com (office).

BROWN, Hank, JD, LLM, CPA; American lawyer, university administrator and fmr politician; *Senior Counsel, Brownstein Hyatt Farber Schreck, LLP;* b. 12 Feb. 1940, Denver, Colo; s. of Harry W. Brown and Anna M. Hanks; m. Nana Morrison 1967; one s. two d.; ed Univ. of Colorado, George Washington Univ.; Lt USN 1962–66; tax accountant, Arthur Andersen 1967–78; admitted to Colo Bar 1969; Asst to Pres., Monfort of Colo Inc., Greeley 1969–70, Counsel 1970–71, Vice-Pres. Monfort Food Distributing 1971–72, Vice-Pres. Corp. Devt 1973–75, Int. Operations 1975–78, Lamb Div. 1978–80; mem. Colo State Senate 1972–76, Asst Majority Leader 1974–76; mem. US House of Reps from Colo 4th Dist 1981–90; Senator from Colorado 1991–97, mem. Senate Judiciary, Budget and Foreign Affairs Cttees 1991–97; Pres. Univ. of Northern Colo 1998–2002; Pres. and CEO Daniels Fund 2002–05; Pres. Univ. of Colo 2005–08, now Quigg and Virginia S. Newton Endowed Chair; Sr Counsel, Brownstein Hyatt Farber Schreck, LLP 2008–; mem. Bd of Dirs Guaranty Bancorp 2008–; Republican; Order of Merit (Poland), Grand Cordon of the Order of the Brilliant Star (Repub. of China), Nishan-I-Quaid-I-Azam (Pakistan); Viet Nam Service Medal, Hungarian Presidential Gold Medal, Air Medal, Nat. Western Stock Show Citizen of the West Award 2008. *Leisure interest:* skiing. *Address:* Brownstein Hyatt Farber Schreck, LLP, 410 Seventeenth Street, Suite 2200, Denver, CO 80202-4432, USA (office). *Telephone:* (303) 223-1177 (office). *E-mail:* hbrown@bhfs.com (office). *Website:* www.bhfs.com (office).

BROWN, Rt Hon. (James) Gordon, PC, MA, PhD; British politician and UN official; b. 20 Feb. 1951, Glasgow, Scotland; s. of Rev. J. Brown and J. Elizabeth Brown; m. Sarah Macaulay 2000; two s. one d. (deceased); ed Kirkcaldy High School, Univ. of Edinburgh; Rector, Univ. of Edinburgh 1972–75, Temporary Lecturer 1976; Lecturer, Glasgow Coll. of Tech. 1976–80; journalist and Current Affairs Ed., Scottish TV 1980–83; MP (Labour) for Dunfermline East 1983–2005, for Kirkcaldy and Cowdenbeath 2005–15; Chair. Labour Party Scottish Council 1983–84; Opposition Chief Sec. to the Treasury 1987–89; Shadow Sec. of State for Trade and Industry 1989–92; Shadow Chancellor of the Exchequer 1992–97; Chancellor of the Exchequer 1997–2007; Prime Minister 2007–10; Minister for the Civil Service 2007–10; First Lord of the Treasury 2007–10; Leader, Labour Party 2007–10; Chair. Global Strategic Infrastructure Initiative, World Economic Forum; Distinguished Global Leader in Residence, New York Univ.; Jt Hon. Treas. (ex-officio), Commonwealth Parl. Asscn (UK Br.) 1997–99, fmr Jt Hon. Sec., Vice-Pres. 2007–10; Special Rep. of the Sec.-Gen. for Global Educ., UN 2012–; mem. Global Advisory Bd, Pacific Investment Management Co., LLC—Pimco (int. investment firm) 2015–; mem. Chair. Interim Cttee IMF 1999; mem. Transport and Gen. Workers' Union; Hon. DCL (Newcastle) 2007. *Publications include:* The Red Paper on Scotland (ed.) 1975, A Voter's Guide to the Scottish Assembly (with Christopher Harvie) 1979, The Politics of Nationalism and Devolution (with H. M. Drucker) 1980, Scotland: The Real Divide (co-ed. with Robin Cook) 1983, Maxton: A Biography 1986, Where There is Greed: Margaret Thatcher and the Betrayal of Britain's Future 1989, John Smith: Life and Soul of the Party (with J. Naughtie) 1994, Values, Visions and Voices (with T. Wright) 1995, Speeches 1997–2006 2006, Courage: Eight Portraits 2007, Britain's Everyday Heroes 2007, Wartime Courage 2008. *Leisure interests:* reading, writing, football and tennis. *Address:* Office of Gordon and Sarah Brown, The Broadgate Tower, 20 Primrose Street, London, EC2A 2RS, England. *Website:* gordonandsarahbrown.com.

BROWN, James (Jim) Nathaniel; American actor and fmr professional football player; b. 17 Feb. 1936, St Simons Island, Ga; s. of Swinton Brown and Theresa Brown; m. Sue Jones; two s. one d.; ed Manhasset High School Long Island, Syracuse Univ.; All-American running back and lacrosse player at Syracuse Univ.; fullback for Cleveland Browns 1957–65; played in nine straight NFL (Nat. Football League) Pro Bowls; NFL's leading rusher in eight of his nine seasons; NFL Most Valuable Player—MVP 1958, 1963, 1965; All-NFL 1957–61, 1963–65; career totals include: 118 games played, 12,312 rushing yards, 262 receptions, 15,459 combined net yards, 756 points scored, 126 touchdowns, 106 rushing touchdowns, average 104 yards per game, 5.2 yards per carry; retd from football to pursue acting career 1966; co-f. Negro Industrial Economic Union (NIEU) 1966; works with Coor Golden Door, Barriers and Vital Issues inmates and ex-convicts training programmes 1980–; Founder and Pres. Amer-I-Can Program Inc. 1988–, Chair. Amer-I-Can Foundation for Social Change 1993–; mem. Bd Rebuild LA Project 1992–; hired as sports analyst for the Ultimate Fighting Championship 1993; Exec. Advisor to the Cleveland Browns 2008–13, Special Advisor 2013–; Syracuse All-America 1956, NFL Rookie of the Year 1957, Hickok Belt Winner 1964, Jim Thorpe Trophy 1965, inducted into Pro Football Hall of Fame 1971 (second youngest ever, at 35), to Lacrosse Hall of Fame 1984, to Coll. Football Hall of Fame 1995, Walter Camp All-Century Team, named by The Sporting News as greatest professional football player ever 2002, chosen by NFL Network's NFL Films production The Top 100: NFL's Greatest Players as the second-greatest player in NFL history 2010. *Films include:* Rio Conchos 1964, Dirty Dozen 1967, Mercenaries 1968, Ice Station Zebra 1968, The Split 1968, Riot 1969, Kenner 1969, 100 Rifles 1969, . . .tick. . .tick. . .tick. . . 1970, Grasshopper 1970, Slaughter 1972, Black Gunn 1972, Slaughter's Big Rip-Off 1973, Slams 1973, I Escaped from Devil's Island 1973, Three the Hard Way 1975, Kid Vengeance 1977, Fingers 1978, Pacific Inferno 1979, One Down, Two to Go 1982, Running Man 1987, I'm Gonna Git You Sucka 1988, Crack House 1989, L.A. Heat 1989, Twisted Justice 1990, Killing American Style 1990, Divine Enforcer 1991, Original Gangstas 1996, Mars Attacks! 1996, He Got Game 1998, Any Given Sunday 1999, New Jersey Turnpikes 1999, On the Edge 2002, She Hate Me 2004, Animal (video) 2005, Dream Street 2010, Draft Day 2014. *Television includes:* I Spy (one episode) 1967, Cops and Robbers (one episode) 1967, Police Story (one episode) 1977, End of the Line (one episode) 1977, CHiPs (three episodes, High Times, Roller Disco: Part 1, Roller Disco: Part 2) 1979–83, T.J. Hooker (two episodes, Anatomy of a Killing, Raw Deal 1983–84, Knight Rider (one episode, Knight of the Drones 1984, Cover Up (one episode, Midnight Highway) 1984, Lady Blue (one episode) 1985, The A-Team (one episode, Quarterback Sneak) 1986, Highway to Heaven (one episode, Whose Trash Is It Anyway?) 1988, Hammer, Slammer, & Slade 1990, Soul Food (three episodes, Survival Techniques, The Son Also Rises, Pagan Poetry) 2004, Sucker Free City 2004, Sideliners (film) 2006. *Publication:* Out of Bounds (autobiog., with Steve Delsohn) 1989. *Address:* The Amer-I-Can Program, 269 South Beverly Drive, #1048, Los Angeles, CA 90212, USA. *Telephone:* (310) 652-7884. *Fax:* (310) 652-9353. *E-mail:* info@amer-i-can.org. *Website:* www.amer-i-can.org.

BROWN, John Joseph, AO; Australian politician; *Emeritus Chairman, Tourism Task Force Limited;* b. 19 Dec. 1931, Sydney, NSW; s. of Norman Leslie Brown and Eva May Spencer; m. Jan Murray 1963 (divorced); four s. one d.; ed St Patrick's Coll., Strathfield and Sydney Univ.; worked as distributor and co. dir in wholesale meat business; Alderman, Parramatta City Council 1970–77; MP for Parramatta, NSW 1977–90; Minister for Sport, Recreation and Tourism 1983–87 (also Minister assisting the Minister for Defence), for Admin. Services 1983–84; Chair. NSW Wholesale Meat Traders' Asscn 1974–76, Tourism Task Force Ltd 1989 (now Emer. Chair.), Environmental Choice 1992–94, London/Sydney Air Race; Dir Tourism Assets Ltd 1992–98, Sea World Man. Ltd 1993–98, Duty Free Operators Accreditation Bd 1998–, Sport Industry Australia, Macquarie Tourism and Leisure, Canterbury Bankstown Leagues Club; est. Sport and Tourism Youth Foundation (fmrly the John Brown Foundation); mem. Sydney Olympics 2000 Bid Cttee, Co-founding Dir Sydney Olympic Games Organizing Cttee; mem. Australasian Meat Industry Employees' Union, Sport and Tourism, Advisory Council of the Australian Opera, Advertising Standards Council; Labor Party; Patron Les Clefs d'Or; Olympic Silver Order of Merit 1986, Australian of the Year 1986, Gold Award, Australian Inst. of Marketing, Distinguished Service Award, US Sports Acad., Australian Sport Medal 2000. *Leisure interests:* golf, jogging, horse racing, theatre, opera, gardening. *Address:* c/o Tourism Task Force Ltd, PO Box R 1804, Royal Exchange, Sydney, NSW 1225, Australia. *Telephone:* (2) 9240-2000. *Fax:* (2) 9240-2020. *E-mail:* jj.brown@bigpond.com (home); jbrown@ttf.org.au (office). *Website:* www.ttf.org.au.

BROWN, Joyce F., BA, PhD; American educator and academic administrator; *President, Fashion Institute of Technology;* ed Marymount Coll., Inst. for Educational Man. at Harvard Univ., New York Univ.; held several sr admin. posts at CUNY, including Acting Pres. Bernard Baruch Coll. and Vice-Chancellor CUNY, Prof. of Clinical Psychology, Grad. School and Univ. Center –1998, Prof. Emer. 1998–, directed numerous special initiatives, including the Urban Summit of Big City Mayors, as well as collaborations between the New York City Bd of Educ. and the univ.; served as a New York City Deputy Mayor for Public and Community Affairs; cr. and directed programmes with Govt of South Africa, including the Professional Devt Program; Pres. (first woman) Fashion Inst. of Tech., State Univ. of NY 1998–; Pres. The FIT Foundation; mem. Bd of Dirs Ralph Lauren Corpn; served on state-wide comms and task forces on the black family, child care and domestic violence; Trustee, Marymount Coll. 1994–2000; honoured by numerous educational, cultural and civic orgs, including New York Univ., Marymount Coll., Clark Atlantic Univ., The Town Hall, Thurgood Marshall Coll. Fund, Brooklyn Chamber of Commerce, New York Co. Supreme Court, Staten Island Econ. Devt Corpn. *Address:* President's Office, Fashion Institute of Technology, 227 West 27th Street, New York, NY 10001-5992, USA (office). *Telephone:* (212) 217-4000 (office). *E-mail:* info@fitnyc.edu (office). *Website:* www.fitnyc.edu (office).

BROWN, Kate, BA, JD; American lawyer and politician; *Governor of Oregon;* b. 21 June 1960, Torrejón de Ardoth, Spain; m. Dan Little; two step-c.; ed Univ. of Colorado, Lewis & Clark Coll.; Attorney, Tennyson, Winemiller & Lavalle, Portland, Ore. 1991–94; mem. Oregon House of Reps for Dist 13 1991–97; mem. Oregon State Senate for Dist 21 1997–2009, Majority Leader 2004–09; Sec. of State, State of Oregon 2009–15; Gov., State of Oregon 2015–; Adjunct Prof. of Admin of Justice, Portland State Univ. 1994; Co-f. Oregon Women's Health and Wellness Alliance 1993; mem. Multnomah Bar Asscn, Oregon Trial Lawyers Asscn, Juvenile Rights Project, Women's Rights Coalition; Rodel Fellowship 2009, Outstanding Young Oregonian Award, Oregon Jaycees 1993, Woman of Achievement Award, Oregon Comm. for Women 1995, Nat. Public and Community Service Award, American Mental Health Counselors Asscn 2004, Pres.'s Award of Merit, Oregon State Bar 2007, Profiles in Courage Award, Basic Rights Oregon 2012. *Address:* Office of the Governor, State Capitol Building, 900 Court Street NE, Suite 254, Salem, OR 97301, USA (office). *Telephone:* (503) 378-4582 (office). *Website:* www.oregon.gov/gov (office).

BROWN, Lawrence (Larry); American basketball coach and fmr basketball player; b. Brooklyn, NY; m. Shelly Brown; one s. four d.; ed Long Beach High School, NY; Univ. of North Carolina; played college basketball Univ. of North Carolina 1960–63, asst coach 1965–67; played for Akron, OH (AAU) 1964–65, then began professional career in American Basketball Asscn (ABA) with New Orleans Buccaneers 1967–68, Oakland Oaks 1968–69, Washington Capitols 1969–70, Virginia Squires 1970–71, Denver Nuggets 1971–72; mem. gold-medal winning US Olympic basketball team 1964; ABA All-Star team 1968–70, Most Valuable Player ABA All-Star Game 1968; won ABA Championship with Oakland 1969; began coaching career as Head Coach of Carolina Cougars 1973–74, then Denver Rockets 1975–76, Denver Nuggets 1977–79 (all ABA), three-time ABA Coach of the Year 1973, 1975, 1976; switched to college coaching going to UCLA 1979–81, led team to Nat. Collegiate Athletic Asscn (NCAA) championship game 1980; returned to professional ranks as Head Coach with Nat. Basketball Asscn (NBA) New Jersey Nets 1981–83; returned to college coaching going to Univ. of Kansas 1983–88, won NCAA Championship 1988; returned to professional coaching going to NBA San Antonio Spurs 1988–93, Los Angeles Clippers 1991–93, Indiana Pacers 1993–97, Philadelphia 76ers 1997–2003, Detroit Pistons 2003–05 (won NBA championship 2004), New York Knicks 2005–06; Exec. Vice-Pres. Philadelphia 76ers 2007–08; Head Coach, Charlotte Bobcats 2008–10 (resgnd); returned to college coaching with Southern Methodist Univ. 2012–; won 900th NBA game 2003–04 (seventh coach to win 900 games); in 22 seasons as NBA coach has record of 987 wins and 741 losses (.571), ranking fourth all-time among NBA coaches and first amongst active coaches; only coach in NBA history to take seven different teams to play-offs; Asst Coach of gold-medal winning Team USA, Olympic Games, Sydney 2000, Head Coach of bronze-medal winning Team USA, Olympic Games, Athens 2004; winning Head Coach NBA All-Star Game 2001; NBA coach of the year 2001; elected Naismith Memorial Hall of Fame. *Leisure interests:* golf. *Address:* Moody Coliseum, 6024 Airline Road, University Park, TX 75205, USA. *Website:* www.smumustangs.com/sports/m-baskbl/smu-m-baskbl-body.html.

BROWN, Lawrence Michael, MA, PhD, ScD, FRS; British/Canadian physicist and academic; *Professor Emeritus of Physics, University of Cambridge;* b. 18 March 1936, Windsor, Ont., Canada; s. of B. W. Brown and Edith Brown; m. Susan Drucker 1965; one s. two d.; ed Univ. of Toronto, Univ. of Birmingham, UK; work in Cambridge 1960–, W.M. Tapp Fellow, Gonville and Caius Coll. 1963–77, Robinson Coll. 1977–2001. Emer. Fellow 2001–, Univ. Demonstrator in Physics 1966, Reader in Structure and Properties of Materials, Dept of Physics 1983–89, Prof. of Physics 1989–2001, Prof. Emer. 2001–; Rosenhain Medal, Inst. of Metals 1980, Robert Franklin Mehl Award, TMS 1991, Van Horn Distinguished Lecturer, Case Western Reserve Univ., USA 1994, Guthrie Medal and Prize, Inst. of Physics 2000, Frontiers of Electron Microscopy and Materials Science (FEMMS) Prize Lecturer 2007, Cook-Ablett Award, Inst. of Materials, Minerals and Mining 2013. *Publications include:* numerous papers in Philosophical Magazine and Acta Metallurgica (now Acta Materialia). *Leisure interests:* reading, gardening. *Address:* Cavendish Laboratory, J.J. Thomson Avenue, Cambridge, CB3 0HE (office); 74 Alpha Road, Cambridge, CB4 3DG, England (home). *Telephone:* (1223) 337200 (office); (1223) 362987 (home). *E-mail:* lmb12@cam.ac.uk (office).

BROWN, Mark, MBA; Cook Islands politician; *Minister of Finance and Economic Development;* m. Daphne Brown; one s. one d.; ed Univ. of the S. Pacific, Massey Univ., New Zealand; worked for Cook Islands Party 2000–10, currently Vice-Pres.; fmr Head of Ministry, Ministry of Agric.; fmr Sr Performance Man., Public Service Comm.; fmr Policy Adviser, Office of the Prime Minister; MP for Takuvaine-Tutakimoa 2010–; Minister of Finance and Economic Devt, also Minister of Seabed Minerals and Natural Resources, Commerce Comm., Financial Intelligence Unit, Telecommunications, Financial Services Devt Authority, Cook Islands Investment

Corpn, Nat. Superannuation Fund, Pearl Authority and Public Expenditure Review Cttee and Audit (PERCA) 2010–; fmr Vice-Pres. Cook Islands Chamber of Commerce, Cook Islands Sports and Nat. Olympic Cttee. *Address:* Ministry of Finance and Economic Management, POB 3255, Clarkes Building, Parekura, Rarotonga, Cook Islands (office). *Telephone:* 21175 (office). *Fax:* 23877 (office). *E-mail:* enquiry@fsda.gov.ck (office). *Website:* www.cookislandsfinance.com (office); www.mfem.gov.ck (office).

BROWN, Melanie Janice, (Mel B); British singer and actress; b. 29 May 1975, Leeds, England; m. 1st Jimmy Gulzar 1998 (divorced); two d.; m. 2nd Stephen Belafonte 2007; mem. Touch, later renamed The Spice Girls 1993–2001, as Melanie B (later Melanie G) or 'Scary Spice', reunion tour 2007–08, 2018–; numerous tours, concerts, television and radio appearances; world tours include UK, Europe, India, USA; solo artist 1998–; two Ivor Novello songwriting awards 1997, Smash Hits Award for Best Band 1997, BRIT Awards for Best Single (for Wannabe), for Best Video (for Say You'll Be There) 1997, for Best Performance of the last 30 years 2010, three American Music Awards 1998, Special BRIT Award for Int. Sales 1998. *Films include:* Spiceworld: The Movie 1997, The Seat Filler 2004, Telling Lies 2008. *Television includes:* as presenter: This is My Moment (ITV 1) 2001; Mel B: It's a Scary World 2010; as judge: America's Got Talent 2013–18, The X Factor UK (ITV) 2014, guest judge 2012, 2016, The X Factor Australia 2010–12, 2016; TV films: The Twelve Trees of Christmas 2013, The Pro 2014, Text Santa 2014 2014. *Recordings include:* albums: with The Spice Girls: Spice 1996, Spiceworld 1997, Forever 2000, Greatest Hits 2007; solo: Hot 2003, LA State of Mind 2005. *Website:* spicegirlsgem.com.

BROWN, Michael Stuart, BA, MD; American geneticist and academic; *The W.A. (Monty) Moncrief Distinguished Chair in Cholesterol and Arteriosclerosis Research, Regental Professor and Paul J. Thomas Chair in Medicine, Southwestern Medical Center, University of Texas;* b. 13 April 1941, Brooklyn, NY; s. of Harvey Brown and Evelyn Katz; m. Alice Lapin 1964; two d.; ed Univ. of Pennsylvania; Intern, then Resident, Massachusetts Gen. Hosp., Boston 1966–68; served with US Public Health Service 1968–70; Clinical Assoc., NIH 1968–71; Asst Prof., Univ. of Texas Southwestern Medical School, Dallas 1971–74, Paul J. Thomas, Prof. of Genetics and Dir Center of Genetic Diseases 1977–, now The W.A. (Monty) Moncrief Distinguished Chair in Cholesterol and Arteriosclerosis Research, Regental Prof. and Paul J. Thomas Chair in Medicine, Southwestern Medical Center; mem. NAS, American Soc. for Clinical Investigation, Asscn of American Physicians, Inst. of Medicine, Royal Soc. (London); numerous hon. degrees; Passano Award, Johns Hopkins Univ. 1978, Lita Annenberg Hazen Award 1982; co-recipient with Joseph L. Goldstein: ACS Pfizer Award 1976, NAS Lounsbery Award 1979, Gairdner Foundation Int. Award 1981, Louisa Gross Horwitz Prize 1984, William Allan Award, American Soc. of Human Genetics 1985, Albert Lasker Medical Research Award 1985, Nobel Prize in Medicine or Physiology 1985, Nat. Medal of Science USA 1988, Warren Alpert Foundation Prize, Harvard Medical School 1999, Kober Medal, Asscn of American Physician 2002, Albany Medical Center Prize 2003, Herbert Tabor Award, American Soc. for Biochemistry and Molecular Biology 2005, Woodrow Wilson Award for Public Service 2005, Builders of Science Award, Research!America 2007, Stadtman Distinguished Scientist Award, American Soc. for Biochemistry and Molecular Biology 2011. *Address:* The University of Texas Southwestern Medical Center, 5323 Harry Hines Boulevard, Dallas, TX 75390-9046, USA (office). *Telephone:* (214) 648-2179 (office). *E-mail:* mike.brown@utsouthwestern.edu (office). *Website:* profiles.utsouthwestern.edu/profile/10894/michael-brown.html (office); www4 .utsouthwestern.edu/moleculargenetics/pages/brown/lab.html (office).

BROWN, Rt Hon. Nicholas (Nick) Hugh, PC, BA; British politician; b. 13 June 1950; s. of R. C. Brown and G. K. Brown (née Tester); ed Swatenden Secondary Modern School, Tunbridge Wells Tech. High School, Univ. of Manchester; trade union officer, Gen. and Municipal Workers' Union, Northern Region 1978–83; mem. Newcastle-upon-Tyne City Council 1980–83; MP (Labour) for Newcastle-upon-Tyne E 1983–97, for Newcastle-upon-Tyne E and Wallsend 1997–2010, for Newcastle-upon-Tyne E 2010–; Labour spokesman on Legal Affairs 1987–92, on Treasury Affairs 1988–94, on Health 1994–95; Deputy Chief Opposition Whip 1995–97; Chief Whip and Parl. Sec. to the Treasury 1997–98, 2008–10, Shadow Parl. Sec. and Chief Whip May–Oct. 2010; Sec. of State for Agric., Fisheries and Food 1998–2001; Minister of State for Work, Dept for Work and Pensions 2001–03. *Address:* House of Commons, Westminster, London, SW1A 0AA, England (office). *Telephone:* (20) 7219-6814 (office). *Fax:* (20) 7219-5941 (office). *E-mail:* nickbrownmp@parliament.uk (office). *Website:* www.parliament.uk/biographies/commons/mr-nicholas-brown/523 (office); www.nickbrownmp.com.

BROWN, Paulette, BA, JD; American lawyer; b. 28 April 1951, Baltimore, Md; one s.; ed Howard Univ., Seton Hall Univ.; called to the NJ Bar 1976, admitted to practice US Supreme Court 1981, US Court Appeals (Third Circuit), US Dist Court (NJ); early career as in-house counsel at National Steel Corpn, Prudential Insurance Co. and Buck Consultants Inc.; Co-founder Brown & Childress, East Orange 1984, became Brown, Lofton, Childress & Wolf 1993 after merger with another firm, Man. Partner –1999; served as judge, Plainfield Municipal Court 1987–89; Partner, Duane Morris LLP 2000–05; joined Edwards & Angell, Short Hills 2005, now Locke Lord LLP after series of mergers, currently Partner, Labor and Employment Practice Group and Chief Diversity Officer; mem. ABA, has held numerous positions including Chair. Council on Racial and Ethnic Justice 1993–99, mem. House of Delegates 1997–, mem. Council on Legal Educ. and Admissions to the Bar 2010–, mem. Bd of Govs 2008–10, Pres.-elect 2014–15, Pres. 2015–16; mem. Nat. Bar Asscn, has held numerous positions including Regional Dir 1981–84, mem. Bd of Govs 1981–99, Vice-Pres. 1989–92, Chair. Judicial Selection Cttee 1994–97, Pres. 1993–94; mem. Asscn of Black Women Lawyers of NJ (Pres. 1983–86), Willard Heckel Inn of American Inns of Court (Master 1991–93), Asscn of Law Firm Diversity Professionals, NJ Fellows of American Bar Foundation, NJ State Bar Asscn; Founder NJ Women of Color Mentoring Group; mem. Advisory Bd Carter G. Woodson Foundation; mem. American Law Inst.; named one of The 50 Most Influential Minority Lawyers in America by Nat. Law Journal 2008, EBONY Power 100 2014; NJ Bar Foundation Medal of Honor, NJ Comm. on Professionalism Professional Lawyer of Year Award, Sheryl J. Willert Pioneer Diversity Award 2010, Margaret Brent Women Lawyers of Achievement Award, ABA Comm. on Women in the Profession 2011, ABA Spirit of Excellence Award, Gertrude Rush Award, Nat. Bar Asscn. *Publications include:* co-author of ABA report Visible Invisibility: Women of Color in Law Firms 2006; numerous articles in law journals. *Address:* Locke Lord LLP, 44 Whippany Road, Suite 280, Morristown, NJ 07960-4558, USA (office). *Telephone:* (973) 520-2365 (office). *E-mail:* paulette.brown@lockelord.com (office). *Website:* www.lockelord.com (office).

BROWN, Pauline; American business executive; *Chairman, LVMH Moët Hennessy Louis Vuitton Inc.;* began career as a man. consultant at Bain & Co.; fmr Vice-Pres. of Strategic Planning and New Business Devt, Estée Lauder Cos Inc.; held roles as Sr Vice-Pres. of Corp. Strategy and Global Business Devt, Avon Products Inc.; Man. Dir, The Carlyle Group, working on firm's global consumer and retail team 2006–10; ind. investor and adviser to emerging luxury brands 2010–12; Chair. LVMH Moët Hennessy Louis Vuitton Inc. 2013–. *Address:* LVMH Inc., 19 East 57th Street, New York, NY 10022, USA (office). *Telephone:* (212) 931-2700 (office). *Fax:* (212) 931-2730 (office). *Website:* www.lvmh.com (office).

BROWN, Richard H. (Dick), BSc; American business executive; *Executive Officer, Joseph E. Seagram & Sons, Inc.;* b. 3 June 1947, New Brunswick, NJ; ed Ohio Univ.; began working in telecommunications industry 1974; fmr Vice-Pres. Sprint Corpn; Pres. CEO Illinois Bell 1990; mem. Bd of Dirs and Vice-Chair. Ameritech Corpn 1993–94; fmr Pres. and CEO H & R Block Inc. 1995–96; mem. Bd of Dirs and CEO Cable & Wireless (C&W) PLC, London 1996–98; Chair. and CEO Electronic Data Systems Co. 1999–2003; Exec. Officer, Joseph E. Seagram & Sons, Inc.; mem. Bd of Dirs Vivendi Universal, Browz Group, LC and Browz, LLC, Pharmacia & Upjohn Co., LLC 1993–, The Seagram Co. Ltd 1997–2000, The Home Depot Inc. 2000–06, DuPont Qualicon, Inc. 2001–; Ind. Dir, EI DuPont de Nemours & Co. 2001–; mem. Business Roundtable, Business Council, Pres.'s Advisory Cttee on Trade and Policy Negotiations, US-Japan Business Council, French-American Business Council, Pres.'s Nat. Security Telecommunications Advisory Cttee, Pres.'s Council of Advisors on Science and Tech., Econ. Club of Chicago; Pres. Boston Univ.; fmr Provost and fmr Prof., MIT; Trustee, Southern Methodist Univ., Rush-Presbyterian-St Luke's Medical Center; Vice-Chair. Bd of Trustees, Ohio Univ. Foundation; mem. NAS, American Acad. of Arts and Sciences, Nat. Acad. of Eng; Hon. DrIur (Ohio Univ.); Hon. PhD (James Madison Univ.). *Address:* Joseph E. Seagram & Sons, Inc., 375 Park Avenue, New York, NY 10152, USA (office). *Telephone:* (212) 572-7000 (office). *Fax:* (212) 572-1022 (office).

BROWN, Robert A., BS, MS, PhD; American engineer, academic and university administrator; *President, Boston University;* b. 1951; m. Beverly Brown; two s.; ed Univ. of Texas at Austin; Instructor, Dept of Chemical Eng and Material Science, Univ. of Minnesota 1978; Asst Prof. of Chemical Eng, Massachusetts Inst. of Tech. (MIT) 1979–82, Assoc. Prof. 1982–84, Prof. 1984–2005, Arthur Dehun Little Prof. of Chemical Eng 1986–92, Warren K. Lewis Prof. 1992–2005, Dean of Eng 1996–98, Provost 1998–2005; Pres. Boston Univ. 2005–; Exec. Ed. Journal of Chemical Engineering Science 1991–2004; mem. Pres.'s Council of Advisors on Science and Tech. 2006–08, Council on Competitiveness 2011–, Exec. Cttee Asscn of Ind. Colls and Univs in Mass 2007– (Chair. 2010–11); mem. and Chair. Academic Research Council, Ministry of Educ., Singapore 2006–; mem. Bd Nat. Research Foundation, Singapore 2006–; Dir, E.I. du Pont de Nemours & Co. 2007–; Trustee, Aalto Univ. Foundation, Finland 2008–10, Universities Research Asscn, Washington, DC 2009–; mem. Nat. Acad. of Eng 1991, American Acad. of Arts and Sciences 1994, NAS 2001; Hon. Citizen of Singapore; numerous honours and awards, including Univ. of Texas at Austin Grad. School Outstanding Alumnus/a Award 2003, named by AIChE to list of 100 Most Influential Chemical Engineers of the Modern Era 2008. *Publications:* over 250 papers in areas related to mathematical modelling of transport phenomena in materials. *Address:* Office of the President, University of Boston, 8th Floor, 1 Silber Way, Boston, MA 02215, USA (office). *Telephone:* (617) 353-2200 (office). *Fax:* (617) 353-3278 (office). *E-mail:* president@bu.edu (office). *Website:* www.bu.edu/president (office).

BROWN, Robert (Bob) James, MB, BS; Australian physician and politician; b. 27 Dec. 1944, Oberon, NSW; partner, Paul Thomas 1996; ed Blacktown Boys High School, Univ. of Sydney; elected School Capt. in sr year; medical practice, Canberra, London, Sydney, Perth, Launceston 1969–80; moved to Tasmania to work in Launceston gen. practice 1972; cand. for United Tasmania Group 1975; Dir The Wilderness Soc. 1979–84; emerged as leader of campaign to prevent construction of Franklin Dam late 1970s, spent 19 days in Hobart's Risdon Prison 1983; elected to Tasmanian House of Ass. 1983–93, Leader of five Green inds, formed accord with Labor Party 1989–92; unsuccessful cand. for Fed. House of Reps 1993; extensive tours of Australian cities and towns as Australian Greens Nat. Spokesperson 1994–96; Senator for Tasmania (first Australian Greens Senator) 1996–2012; hosted first Global Greens Conf., Canberra 2001; Leader, Australian Greens 2005–12; elected first Fed. Parl. Leader of The Greens 2005–12; Founding Pres. Australian Bush Heritage Fund (now Bush Heritage Australia) 1990–96; Founding Pres. Bob Brown Foundation 2012–; Chair. Sea Shepherd Australia 2012–14, Sea Shepherd Australia Advisory Panel 2014–; Dr hc (La Trobe) 2013; Australian of the Year, The Australian newspaper 1983, UNEP Global 500 Award 1987, Goldman Environmental Prize (USA) 1990, World's Most Inspiring Politician, BBC Wildlife magazine 1996, Nat. Trust Australian Nat. Treasure 1998, Rainforest Action Network Environmental Hero 2006, My Favourite Australian 2008, Australian Geographic Award for Excellence: Lifetime of Conservation 2012. *Publications:* several books, including Wild Rivers 1983, Lake Pedder 1986, Tarkine Trails 1994, The Greens (with Peter Singer) 1996, Memo for a Saner World 2004, Tasmania's Recherche Bay 2005, Earth 2009, Optimism 2014, Green Nomads 2015. *Leisure interests:* photography, bushwalking, poetry, philosophy. *Address:* PO Box 4586, Hobart, Tasmania 7000, Australia (office). *Telephone:* (408) 855261 (office). *E-mail:* contact@bobbrown.org.au (office). *Website:* www.bobbrown.org.au (office).

BROWN, Scott Philip, BA, JD; American lawyer, politician and diplomatist; *Ambassador to New Zealand;* b. 12 Sept. 1959, Kittery, Maine; m. Gail Huff; two d.; ed Wakefield High School, Tufts Univ., Boston Coll. Law School; mem. US Army Nat. Guard 1979–2014, rank of Col in Judge Advocate Gen. Corps, head defence attorney for the New England States; began career in public service as mem. Wrentham, Mass Bd of Assessors 1987–90; mem. Wrentham Bd of Selectmen 1995–98; served in Mass House of Reps 1998–2004; elected three times to Mass Senate from Norfolk, Bristol & Middlesex Dist 2004–10; Senator from Mass

2010–13; Counsel, Nixon Peabody LLP (law firm), Boston 2013–14; commentator, Fox News 2013; unsuccessful cand. for Senator from New Hampshire 2014; Amb. to New Zealand 2017–; Republican; Army Commendation Medal for meritorious service in homeland security, Meritorious Service Medal. *Address:* US Embassy in New Zealand, 29 Fitzherbert Terrace, PO Box 1190, Wellington, New Zealand (office). *Telephone:* (4) 462-6000 (office). *Fax:* (4) 499-0490 (office). *Website:* nz.usembassy.gov (office).

BROWN, Sherrod Campbell, BA, MA; American politician; *Senator from Ohio;* b. 9 Nov. 1952, Mansfield, Ohio; m. Connie Schultz; two d. one step-s. one step-d.; ed Yale Univ. and Ohio State Univ.; taught at Mansfield br. campus, Ohio State Univ. 1979–81; Ohio State Rep. 1975–82; Ohio Sec. of State 1982–91; mem. US House of Reps for the 13th Dist 1993–2006, Ranking Minority mem. on House Energy and Commerce Cttee's Health Sub-cttee, also served on Sub-cttee on Telecommunications and the Internet and Sub-cttee on Commerce, Trade and Consumer Protection, mem. House Int. Relations Cttee, Sub-cttee on Asia and the Pacific; Senator from Ohio 2007–, Ranking Democratic mem. on the Cttee on Banking, Housing and Urban Affairs 2015–; mem. Congressional Progressive Caucus; Democrat; American Public Health Asscn Distinguished Public Health Legislator of 2002, Congressional Leadership Award, Nat. Asscn of Public Hosps and Health 2005, Congressional Leadership Award, American Coll. of Emergency Physicians 2002, Paul G. Rogers Award, Asscn of Academic Health Centers 2002, recognized by Acad. of Medicine of Cleveland and Northern Ohio Medical Asscn. *Publications:* Congress from the Inside: Observations from the Majority and the Minority 2004, Myths of Free Trade: Why American Trade Policy Has Failed 2006. *Address:* 713 Hart Senate Office Building, Washington, DC 20510, USA (office). *Telephone:* (202) 224-2315 (office). *Fax:* (202) 228-6321 (office). *Website:* www.brown.senate.gov (office); www.sherrodbrown.com (office).

BROWN, Shona L., PhD; American business executive; b. 1966; ed Carleton Univ., Canada, Univ. of Oxford, UK (Rhodes Scholar), Stanford Univ.; has taught in Dept of Industrial Eng and Grad. School of Business, Stanford Univ. and within McKinsey's mini-MBA programme; Pnr, McKinsey & Co., worked with tech. clients in Toronto and Los Angeles and Leader, Global Strategy Practice 1995–2003; Vice-Pres. Business Operations, Google Inc. 2003–06, Sr Vice-Pres. Business Operations 2006–11; Chair. Bd of Dirs Atlassian Corpn Plc 2015–; mem. Bd of Dirs PepsiCo Inc. 2009–, BetterWorks 2014–, ClearStory Data Inc., Paperless Post, The Nature Conservancy, Center for Advanced Study in the Behavioral Sciences (Stanford Univ.), The Gladstone Foundation, Code for America, San Francisco Jazz Org., Bridgespan Group. *Publications:* Competing on the Edge: Strategy as Structured Chaos (co-author) 1998, Blackford and Round About (co-author) 2004; numerous articles in both applied and academic journals. *Address:* Atlassian Corporation Plc, 1098 Harrison Street, San Francisco, CA 94103, USA (office). *Telephone:* (415) 701-1110 (office). *Website:* www.atlassian.com (office); shonalbrown.wordpress.com.

BROWN, William Charles Langdon, CBE; British banker (retd); b. 9 Sept. 1931, London; s. of Charles Leonard Brown and Kathleen May Tizzard; m. Nachiko Sagawa 1959; one s. two d.; ed John Ruskin School, Croydon, Ashbourne Grammar School, Derbyshire; with Chartered Bank of India, Australia and China, serving throughout Far East 1954–75, Area Gen. Man., Hong Kong 1975–87, Sr Gen. Man. (London) for Asia Pacific Region 1987; Exec. Dir Standard Chartered Bank PLC (SCB) 1987, Man. Dir 1988, Deputy Group Chief Exec. 1988, Group Deputy Chair. 1989–91, Dir (non-exec.) 1991–94; Dir and Treasurer Royal Commonwealth Soc. 1991–95, Commonwealth Trust 1991–95; Dir HongKong Investment Trust PLC 1991–97; Dir (non-exec.) Kexim Bank UK Ltd 1992–2003, Arbuthnot Latham & Co. Ltd 1993–99; Chair. (non-exec.) Atlantis Japan Growth Fund Ltd 1996–2002; Unofficial mem. Legis. Council of Hong Kong 1980–85; Hon. DScS (Chinese Univ., Hong Kong) 1987. *Leisure interests:* mountain walking, yoga, skiing, philately, photography, classical music. *Address:* Penthouse B, 15 Portman Square, London, W1H 6LJ (home); Appleshaw, 11 Central Avenue, Findon Valley, Worthing, Sussex, BN14 0DS, England (home). *Telephone:* (1903) 873175 (home). *Fax:* (20) 7486-3005 (home). *E-mail:* wclbrown@yahoo.co.uk (home).

BROWN OF CAMBRIDGE, Baroness (Life Peer), cr. 2015, of Cambridge in the County of Cambridgeshire; **Dame Julia Elizabeth King,** DBE, FRS, FInstP, FREng, CEng, PhD; British academic and engineer; *Chair, STEM Learning Board;* b. 11 Aug. 1954; m. Colin William Brown; ed New Hall, Cambridge; Lecturer, Univ. of Nottingham 1980–87; Sr Research Fellow, Royal Acad. of Eng 1987; several research and teaching positions, Cambridge Univ. 1987–94; with Rolls-Royce PLC 1994–2002, several sr positions including Head of Materials, Man. Dir of Fan Systems, Eng Dir of Marine Business; CEO, Inst. of Physics 2002–04; Prin. of Eng Faculty, Imperial Coll. London 2004–06; Vice-Chancellor, Aston Univ. 2006–16; Chair. Learning Bd, STEM Learning Ltd 2016–; UK Low Carbon Business Amb. 2010–; mem. Cttee on Climate Change, Chair., Adaptation Sub-Cttee 2017–; mem. Airports Comm.; inaugural mem. Governing Bd, European Inst. of Innovation and Tech.; fmr mem. World Econ. Forum (WEF) Automotive Council, mem. WEF Global Agenda Council on Decarbonising Energy; mem. Bd, Eng and Tech. Bd (now EngineeringUK) 2004–08; apptd by Chancellor of the Exchequer to lead the King Review on low-carbon vehicles 2007, final recommendations published March 2008; Chair. Sir Henry Royce Centre for Advanced Materials; Dir (non-exec.) Green Investment Bank, Offshore Renewable Energy Catapult; Non-exec. mem., Technology Strategy Bd 2004–09; fmr Dir (non-exec.), Dept for Business, Innovation and Skills; Liveryman of the Goldsmiths Co.; Hon. Fellow, Murray Edwards Coll., Cambridge, Cardiff Univ., Inst. of Eng and Tech., Soc. for the Environment, British Science Asscn. *Address:* House of Lords, London, SW1A 0PW, England (office). *Telephone:* (20) 7219-5353 (office). *E-mail:* kingje@parliament.uk. *Website:* www.parliament.uk/biographies/lords/baroness-brown-of-cambridge/4565.

BROWNBACK, Samuel Dale (Sam), BS, JD; American lawyer and government official; *US Ambassador-at-Large for International Religious Freedom;* b. 12 Sept. 1956, Garnett, Kan.; s. of Robert Brownback and Nancy Brownback; m. Mary S. Stauffer; two s. three d. (two c. adopted); ed Kansas State Univ. and Univ. of Kansas; raised in farming family in Parker, Kan.; elected student body pres., Kan. State Univ.; State Pres. Nat. FFA Org., Nat. Vice-Pres. 1976–77; spent a year working as a broadcaster, hosting a weekly half-hour show, KKSU; admitted to Kansas Bar 1982; Partner, law firm in New York; Instructor in Law, Kan. State Univ.; Sec. Agricultural State of Kansas, Topeka 1986–93; City Attorney, Ogden & Leonardville, Kan.; mem. US Congress from 2nd Kansas Dist 1995–96; Senator from Kan. 1996–2011 (retd), mem. Foreign Relations Cttee, Chair. Sub-cttee on East Asian and Pacific Affairs; unsuccessful campaign for Republican nomination for Pres. of US 2007; Gov. of Kansas 2011–18; US Amb.-at-Large for Int. Religious Freedom 2018–; Vice-Chair. Riley Co. Republican Cttee; Commr, US Helsinki Comm.; Pres. Kansas Prayer Breakfast; mem. ABA, Nat. Future Farmers of America (Vice-Pres. 1977), American Judicature Soc., American Agricultural Law Asscn, Riely Co. Bar Asscn, Kansas Bar Asscn; Republican; named a Kansan of Distinction 1988, Manufacturing Excellence Award, Nat. Asscn of Mfrs 2001, Honor Award, Oncology Nursing Soc. 2002, US Oncology Medal of Honor 2002, Pro Deo et Patria Medal, Christendom Coll., Va 2005. *Publication:* From Power to Purpose: A Remarkable Journey of Faith and Compassion (with Jim Nelson Black) 2007. *Address:* Office of International Religious Freedom, Department of State, 2201 C St, NW, Washington, DC 20520, USA (office). *Telephone:* (202) 647-4000 (office). *Fax:* (202) 647-6738 (office). *Website:* www.state.gov (office).

BROWNE, Anthony; British writer, artist and illustrator; b. 1946, Sheffield; m.; two c.; ed Leeds Coll. of Art; fmr medical illustrator, Leeds Royal Infirmary; fmr greetings card illustrator; Illustrator-in-Residence, Tate Britain 2001–02; Children's Laureate 2009–11; Hon. DEd (Kingston Univ.) 2005; Boston Globe Book Award, Hans Christian Andersen Award 2000. *Publications include:* Through the Magic Mirror 1976, A Walk in the Park 1977, Bear Hunt 1979, Look What I've Got! 1980, Hansel and Gretel 1981, Bear Goes to Town 1982, Gorilla (Kate Greenaway Medal, Kurt Maschler Emil Award) 1983, The Visitors Who Came to Stay 1984, Willy the Wimp 1985, Knock, Knock, Who's There 1985, Willy the Champ 1985, Piggybook 1986, Kirsty Knows Best 1988, Alice's Adventures in Wonderland (Kurt Maschler Emil Award) 1988, Little Bear Book 1988, I Like Books 1988, Things I Like 1989, A Bear-y Tale 1989, The Tunnel 1990, Trail of Stones 1990, Changes 1990, Willy and Hugh 1991, The Night Shimmy 1991, Zoo (Kate Greenaway Medal) 1992, The Big Baby 1993, The Topiary Garden 1993, The Daydreamer 1994, King Kong 1994, Willy the Wizard 1995, Willy the Dreamer 1997, Voices in the Park (Kurt Maschler Emil Award) 1998, My Dad 2000, Willy's Pictures 2000, The Animal Fair 2002, The Shape Game (Honor Book, Boston Globe-Horn Book Awards) 2003, Into the Forest 2004, Silly Billy 2006, My Brother 2007, My Mum 2008, Little Beauty 2008, Me and You 2011, How Do You Feel? 2011, One Gorilla, A Counting Book 2012, What If...? 2013, Willy's Stories 2014. *Address:* c/o Walker Books, 87 Vauxhall Walk, London, SE11 5HJ, England (office). *Website:* www.walker.co.uk/contributors/Anthony-Browne-1481.aspx (office).

BROWNE, Gaston Alphonso, MBA; Antigua and Barbuda business executive, fmr banker and politician; *Prime Minister;* b. 9 Feb. 1967, Potters Village, Antigua; m. Maria Browne; ed City Banking Coll., Univ. of Manchester, UK; fmr Sr Bank Man. with Swiss American Banking Group; mem. House of Reps (Parl.) for St John's City West 1999–; fmr Minister of Planning and Trade; Prime Minister 2014–; Chair. and CEO of construction and land devt co.; mem. Bd of Dirs of several cos including LIAT (1974) Ltd (aviation), Antigua Pier Group Ltd, Community Motors Ltd; mem. Antigua Labour Party (ALP), Leader 2012–. *Address:* Office of the Prime Minister, Queen Elizabeth Highway, St John's, Antigua and Barbuda (office). *Telephone:* 462-4610 (office). *Fax:* 462-3225 (office). *E-mail:* gaston@gastonbrowne.com. *Website:* www.antigua.gov.ag (office); gastonbrowne.com.

BROWNE, Jackson; American singer, songwriter and musician (guitar, piano); b. 9 Oct. 1948, Heidelberg, Germany; m. 1st Phyllis Major 1975 (died 1976); one s.; m. 2nd Lynne Sweeney 1981 (divorced 1983); one s.; fmr mem., Nitty Gritty Dirt Band 1966; solo singer, songwriter, musician 1967–; Co-founder Musicians United for Safe Energy (MUSE), Nukefree.org, Success through the Arts Foundation; numerous tours and concerts, festival appearances and benefit concerts; Hon. DMus (Occidental Coll.) 2004; John Steinbeck Award 2002, inducted into Rock and Roll Hall of Fame 2004, Songwriters Hall of Fame 2007, NARM Harry Chapin Humanitarian Award 2008. *Compositions include:* songs recorded by Tom Rush, Nico, Linda Ronstadt, The Eagles; co-writer with Glenn Frey, Take It Easy. *Recordings include:* albums: Jackson Browne 1972, For Everyman 1973, Late For The Sky 1974, The Pretender 1976, Running On Empty 1978, Hold Out 1980, Lawyers In Love 1983, Lives In The Balance 1987, World In Motion 1989, I'm Alive 1993, Looking East 1996, The Naked Ride Home 2002, Solo Acoustic Vol. 1 2005, Solo Acoustic Vol. 2 2008, Time the Conqueror 2008, Love Is Strange: En Vivo Con Tino (with David Lindley) 2010, Standing in the Breach 2014. *Telephone:* (818) 506-0898 (office). *Website:* www.insiderecordings.com (office); www.jacksonbrowne.com.

BROWNE, Hon. Michael (Mike) Rayfield Cornelius, BA (Hons), MEd; Saint Vincent and the Grenadines government official; b. 28 Sept. 1948, Layou, Saint Vincent; m. Zoila Browne; one s. three d.; ed Boys Grammar School, Teachers' Centre and Lakehead Univ., Canada; teacher, Emmanuel High School; Lecturer, St Vincent Teachers' Training Coll. 1973–75; Pres. St Vincent Union of Teachers 1976–80, Co-ordinator, St Vincent Union of Teachers Adult Educ. Programme 1983–91, Gen. Co-ordinator of New Horizons 1991–2001; political career began in univ. student unions; involved with Youlou United Liberation Movt (YULIMO) 1974–79, United People's Movt (UPM, East Kingstown) 1979; cand. for UPM, East Kingstown 1984, 1987, for Unity Labour Party (ULP), West St George 1994; ULP Senator 1994–97; MP (ULP) for West St George 1998–; Minister of Educ., Youth and Sport –2005, of Foreign Affairs and of Commerce and Trade May–Dec. 2005. *Address:* c/o Ministry of Foreign Affairs, Foreign Trade and Consumer Affairs, Administrative Building, Third Floor, Bay Street, Kingstown, Saint Vincent and the Grenadines. *E-mail:* office.foreignaffairs@mail.gov.vc.

BROWNE, Air Chief Marshal Norman Anil Kumar; Indian air force officer and diplomatist; b. 15 Dec. 1951; m. Kiran Browne; one s. one d.; ed St Joseph's Coll., Nat. Defence Acad., Air Force Acad., Air Command and Staff Coll., USA; joined Air Force as Operational Fighter Squadron 1972, mem. first two batches of pioneer pilots that went to train with Number 226 Operational Conversion Unit at RAF Lossiemouth on Jaguar Deep Penetration Strike Aircraft, Commdr Number 16 Squadron 'The Cobras' 1990–92, also Fighter Combat Leader, fmr Instructor, Tactics and Air Combat Devt Establishment and Defence Services Staff Coll., USA; has held various operational and staff positions including Jt Dir Air War

Strategy Cell, Air HQ, Chief Operations Officer and Air Officer Commanding SU-30 base, Air-I at Western Air Command, Asst Chief of the Air Staff (Intelligence), Deputy Chief of the Air Staff 2007–09, Vice-Chief of the Air Staff Jan.–July 2011, Chief of the Air Staff 2011–14; est. Indian Defence Wing in Tel Aviv, Israel 1997, Defence Attaché 1997–2000; Amb. to Norway 2014–16; Hon. ADC to Pres. of India; Param Vishist Seva Medal, Ati Vishist Seva Medal, Vayu Sena Medal.

BROWNE OF LADYTON, Baron (Life Peer), cr. 2010, of Ladyton in Ayrshire and Arran; **Des Browne,** PC, LLB; British politician and lawyer; b. 22 March 1952, Ayrshire, Scotland; m.; two s.; ed St Michael's Acad., Kilwinning, Univ. of Glasgow; admitted as solicitor 1976; joined Ross, Harper and Murphy (law firm), Kilmarnock; Co-founder McCluskey Browne (law firm) –1993; unsuccessful cand. for MP for Argyll and Bute 1992; called to the Bar 1993, served as specialist child law advocate; MP for Kilmarnock and Loudoun 1997–2005, for New Kilmarnock and Loudoun 2005–10; Parl. Pvt. Sec. to Sec. of State for Scotland Donald Dewar 1998–99, for Adam Ingram 2000; Parl. Under-Sec. of State, NI Office 2001–03; Minister of State, Dept for Work and Pensions (Work) 2003–04; Minister of State, Home Office (Citizenship, Immigration and Nationality) 2004–05; Chief Sec. to Treasury 2005–06; Sec. of State for Defence 2006–08, for Scotland 2007–08; Prime Minister's Special Envoy for Sri Lanka 2009–10; Convenor, The Top Level Group for Multilateral Nuclear Disarmament and Non-Proliferation; Vice-Chair. Nuclear Threat Initiative; Hon. Sec., Labour Party Departmental Cttee for Social Security 1997–2001. *Address:* House of Lords, London, SW1A 0PW, England (office).

BROWNE OF MADINGLEY, Baron (Life Peer), cr. 2001, of Madingley in the County of Cambridgeshire; **(Edmund) John (Philip) Browne,** BSc, MS, FRS, FREng, FInstP, FInstPet, CIMgt; British business executive; *Executive Chairman, L1 Energy;* b. 20 Feb. 1948, Hamburg, Germany; ed Univ. of Cambridge, Stanford Univ., USA; joined BP 1966, held various exploration and production posts in Anchorage, New York, San Francisco, London and Canada 1969–83, Group Treas. and Chief Exec. BP Finance Int. 1984–86, Exec. Vice-Pres. and Chief Financial Officer The Standard Oil Co., Cleveland, Ohio 1986–87, BP America and CEO Standard Oil Production Co. (following BP/Standard merger) 1987–89, Man. Dir and CEO BP Exploration, London 1989–91, Man. Dir The British Petroleum Co. PLC 1991–95, Group CEO 1995–98, Group CEO BP Amoco (now BP PLC) 1998–2007 (resgnd); Man. Dir and Man. Riverstone Holdings LLC 2007–15; Chair. Cuadrilla Resources 2007–15; Lead Non-Exec. Dir, Cabinet Office 2010–15; Exec. Chair. L1 Energy 2015–, also Chair. sister co. DEA 2015–; Chair. Huawei Technologies (UK) Ltd, Stanhope Capital Advisory Bd 2010–, Queen Elizabeth Prize Foundation 2011–, Blavatnik School of Government Advisory Bd, Oxford 2011–, Donmar Warehouse 2015–, Accenture Global Energy Board, Mubadala Oil and Gas International Advisory Board, Performance Theatre Advisory Group; Chair. Emer. Advisory Bd, Stanford Grad. School of Business; mem. Supervisory Bd Daimler Chrysler AG 1998–2001, Chair.'s Council 2001–04; Pres. Royal Acad. of Eng 2006–11; Vice-Pres. Prince of Wales Business Leaders Forum; mem. Bd of Dirs (non-exec.) Foster + Pnrs 2007–, Fairfield Energy Ltd, White Rose Energy Ventures LLP, Goldman Sachs 1999–2007, SmithKline Beecham 1996–99, Intel Corpn 1997–2006, Apax Pnrs Worldwide 2006–07; mem. Deutsche Bank Advisory Bd for Climate Change, Schlumberger Business Consulting Advisory Group, Deutsche Bank Europe Advisory Bd, British-American Business Council (also fmr Chair.), Cambridge Consultative Cttee and Chem. Appeal (also fmr Chair.), Guild of Cambridge Benefactors, Council of the Foundation for Science and Tech., Bd of Catalyst, School of Econs and Man., Tsinghua Univ. (Chair. Advisory Bd); Chair. Advisory Board, Russian Museum, St Petersburg, Advisory Bd Cambridge Business School; Global Counsellor, Conference Bd; Fellow, Inst. of Mining and Metallurgy, American Acad. of Arts and Sciences; Sr Mem. St Anthony's Coll., Oxford; Chair. Bd of Trustees Queen Elizabeth Prize Foundation 2011–, John Browne Charitable Trust; Trustee, British Museum 1995–2005, Tate Gallery 2007– (Chair. 2009–), Needham Research Inst., Cambridge China Development Trust, Cambridge Foundation; mem. Bd of Govs Folger Shakespeare Library; apptd by UK Prime Minister David Cameron to lead Whitehall efficiency initiative 2010; Hon. Fellow, St John's Coll. Cambridge; Hon. FIChemE; Hon. FGS; Hon. FIMechE; Hon. FRSC; Hon. Trustee, Chicago Symphony Orchestra; Hon. DEng (Heriot Watt, Colorado School of Mines, Belfast); Hon. DTech (Robert Gordon); Hon. LLD (Dundee, Thunderbird, Notre Dame); Hon. DUniv (Sheffield Hallam); Hon. DSc (Cranfield, Hull, Leuven, Warwick, Mendeleyev University of Chemical Technology—Moscow, Buckingham); Hon. DLitt (Arizona State Univ.); Prince Philip Medal, Royal Acad. of Eng 1999, Henry Shaw Medal, Missouri Botanical Gardens, Gold Medal, Inst. of Man., Ernest C. Arbuckle Award, Stanford Business School Alumni Asscn 2001, Soc. of Petroleum Engineers Public Service Award 2002. *Publications:* Beyond Business (memoir) 2010, Seven Elements that Have Changed the World 2013, The Glass Closet 2014. *Address:* House of Lords, London, SW1A 0PW; L1 Energy, Devonshire House, One Mayfair Place, London, W1J 8AJ, England (office). *Telephone:* (20) 3815-3130 (L1 Energy) (office); (20) 7219-5353 (House of Lords). *E-mail:* contact@l1energy.co.uk (office). *Website:* www.letterone.com/our-businesses/l1-energy (office).

BROWNER, Carol Martha, BA, JD; American lawyer and fmr government official; *Senior Counselor, Albright Stonebridge Group;* b. 16 Dec. 1955, Miami; d. of Michael Browner and Isabella Browner (née Hugues); m. 1st Michael Podhorzer (divorced); one s.; m. 2nd Thomas Joseph Downey 2007; two step-c.; ed Univ. of Florida; Assoc. Dir, Citizen Action, Washington, DC 1983–86; mem. staff of Senator Lawton Chiles 1986–89; mem. staff, Senate Cttee on Energy and Natural Resources 1989; Legis. Dir on staff of Senator Al Gore 1989–90; Head of Dept of Environmental Regulation, State of Fla 1990–93; Admin., Environmental Protection Agency 1993–2001; Co-founder and Prin. The Albright Group LLC (consulting firm), Washington, DC 2001–08, also Prin. Albright Capital Management (investment advisory firm); Sr Counselor, Albright Stonebridge Group 2011–; Coordinator for Energy and Climate, The White House, Washington, DC 2009–11; mem. Bd of Dirs Center for American Progress 2003–08; mem. Exec. Cttee and Distinguished Sr Fellow, Infosys Limited 2014–15, Blue292, Inc.; mem. Bd of Dirs, Bunge Limited 2013–, Global Oceans Comm.; mem. Advisory Board Opower 2013–, General Fusion, Inc. 2014–, Harvest Power, Inc., Constella Group, LLC; mem. Bd The Spectrum Solutions Co.; mem. Advisory Cttee Export-Import Bank; fmr mem. Bd of Dirs Audubon Soc., League of Conservation Voters, Alliance for Climate Protection; Sr Fellow Aspen Inst.; Woman of the Year, Glamour magazine 1998, Guy M. Bradley Lifetime Achievement Award, S Florida Chapter of Audubon Soc., Lifetime Environmental Achievement Award, New York State Bar Asscn. *Address:* Albright Stonebridge Group, 601, 13th Street NW, 10th Floor, Washington, DC 20005, USA (office). *Telephone:* (202) 759-5100 (office). *Fax:* (202) 759-5101 (office). *Website:* www.albrightstonebridge.com (office).

BROWNING, Keith Anthony, BSc, PhD, DIC, FRS, ARCS; British meteorologist and academic; *Professor Emeritus, Department of Meteorology, University of Reading;* b. 31 July 1938, Sunderland; s. of James Anthony Browning and Amy Hilda Greenwood; m. Ann Baish 1962; one s. two d.; ed Imperial Coll. of Science and Tech., Univ. of London; Research Atmospheric Physicist, Air Force Cambridge Research Labs, Mass, USA 1962–66; Prin. then Chief Meteorological Officer, Meteorological Office Radar Research Lab., Royal Signals and Radar Establishment, Malvern, Worcs. 1966–74, 1975–85; Chief Scientist, Nat. Hail Research Experiment, Nat. Center for Atmospheric Research, Boulder, Colo, USA 1974–75; Deputy Dir (Physical Research), Meteorological Office, Bracknell, Berks. 1985–89, Dir of Research 1989–91; Visiting Prof., Dept of Meteorology, Univ. of Reading 1988–94, Visiting Scientist, Jt Centre for Mesoscale Meteorology 1991–92, Dir 1992–2003, Prof. in Dept of Meteorology 1995–2003, Prof. Emer. 2003–; Visiting Prof. of Atmospheric Science, School of Earth and Environment, Univ. of Leeds 2006–; Dir Univs Weather Research Network 2000–03, Univs Facility for Atmospheric Measurements 2001–03; Chair. Meteorology & Atmospheric Physics Sub-cttee of British Cttee for Geodesy and Geophysics 1985–89, GEWEX Cloud System Study 1992–95; mem. Natural Environment Research Council 1984–87, Scientific Steering Group, Global Energy and Water Cycle Experiment 1988–97, Jt Scientific Cttee, World Climate Research Programme 1990–94, Scientific Steering Cttee, World Weather Research Programme 1996–2005; Pres. Royal Meteorological Soc. 1988–90; mem. Academia Europaea 1989–; Foreign Assoc., Nat. Acad. of Eng (USA) 1992–; Fellow, American Meteorological Soc. 1975–, Hon. mem. 2010–; fmr Chartered Meteorologist and now Fellow, Royal Meteorological Soc., Hon. mem. 2006–; Ministry of Defence L. G. Groves Memorial Prize 1969, Inst. of Physics Charles Chree Medal 1981, Symons Gold Medal 2001 and three other awards from Royal Meteorological Soc., Carl Gustaf Rossby Medal 2003 and two other awards from American Meteorological Soc. *Publications:* more than 200 articles on meteorology in learned journals since 1962. *Leisure interests:* meteorological research, photography, playing the piano, walking. *E-mail:* kandabrowning@googlemail.com (home).

BROWNLEE, Hon. Gerard (Gerry) Anthony; New Zealand teacher and politician; b. 4 Feb. 1956, Christchurch; ed St Bede's Coll.; worked in family's timber business, received training in carpentry; later qualified as a teacher and taught woodwork and crafts at high-school level at Ellesmere Coll. and later at St Bede's Coll.; unsuccessful cand. for Sydenham in general election 1993; mem. National Party, Deputy Leader 2003–06; MP for Ilam 1996–, served as National Party's Jr Whip and as its spokesperson on superannuation, energy, transport, local government and the ACC, Leader of the House 2008–17; Minister for Econ. Devt, of Energy and Resources and Assoc. Minister for the Rugby World Cup 2008–11, Minister for Canterbury Earthquake Recovery 2010–17, for Transport 2011–14, of Defence 2014–17, Minister Responsible for the Earthquake Comm. 2014–17, Minister of Foreign Affairs May–Oct. 2017. *Address:* New Zealand National Party, 41 Pipitea St, Thorndon, Wellington 6011, New Zealand (office). *Telephone:* (4) 894-7016 (office). *Fax:* (4) 894-7031 (office). *E-mail:* hq@national.org.nz (office). *Website:* www.national.org.nz (office); www.brownlee.co.nz.

BROWNLOW, Kevin; British film historian and television director; b. 2 June 1938, Crowborough, Sussex; s. of Robert Thomas Brownlow and Nina Fortnum; m. Virginia Keane 1969; one d.; ed Univ. Coll. School, Hampstead; joined World Wide Pictures 1955; became film ed., then co-dir 1964; with Thames TV 1975–90; Co-founder and Dir Photoplay Productions 1990–; Hon. Acad. Award, Acad. of Motion Picture Arts and Sciences 2010. *Films directed include:* It Happened Here 1964, Winstanley 1975 (both with Andrew Mollo). *Television includes:* 13-part series Hollywood 1980, three-part Unknown Chaplin 1983, three-part British Cinema (producer only) 1986, three-part Buster Keaton: A Hard Act to Follow 1987, two-part Harold Lloyd 1988, three-part D. W. Griffith 1993, six-part Cinema Europe: The Other Hollywood 1995 (all with David Gill), Universal Horror 1998, Lon Chaney: A Thousand Faces 2000, The Tramp and the Dictator (with Michael Kloft) 2002, Cecil B. De Mille: American Epic 2003; with Christopher Bird: Buster Keaton: So Funny It Hurt 2004, Garbo 2005, I'm King Kong: The Exploits of Merion C. Cooper 2005. *Publications:* Parade's Gone By 1968, The War, the West and the Wilderness 1978, Napoleon (Abel Gance's Classic Film) 1983, Behind the Mask of Innocence 1990, David Lean: A Biography 1996, Mary Pickford Rediscovered 1999, Winstanley: Warts and All 2009, The Search for Charlie Chaplin 2010. *Address:* Photoplay Productions, 21 Princess Road, London, NW1 8JR, England (office). *Telephone:* (20) 7722-2500 (office). *E-mail:* info@photoplay.co.uk (office). *Website:* www.photoplay.co.uk (office).

BROWSE, Sir Norman Leslie, Kt, MD, FRCP, FRCS; British government official and surgeon (retd); b. 1 Dec. 1931, London, England; s. of Reginald Browse and Margaret Browse; m. Jeanne Menage 1957; one s. one d.; ed St Bartholomew's Hosp. Medical Coll. and Univ. of Bristol; Capt. RAMC 1957–59; Sr House Officer and Registrar, Bristol 1959–62; Lecturer in Surgery, Westminster Hosp. 1962–65; Harkness Fellow, Research Assoc. Mayo Clinic, Rochester, Minn. 1964–65; Reader in Surgery and Consultant Surgeon, St Thomas' Hosp. 1965–72, Prof. of Vascular Surgery 1972–81, Prof. of Surgery 1981–96, Consulting Surgeon 1996–; Hon. Consultant to Army and RAF 1980–96; Prof. of Surgery, United Medical and Dental Schools 1981–96; Prof. Emer. Univ. of London 1996–; Pres. States of Alderney, CI 2002–11; Observer, Sark election 2012; Pres. Royal Coll. of Surgeons of England 1992–95; Chair., Jt Consultants Cttee 1994–98, Lord Brock Memorial Trust 1994–2001; Vice-Chair. British Vascular Foundation 1997–; Visiting Prof. and Lecturer, Cape Town, Johannesburg, Perth, Sydney, Melbourne, Brisbane, Boston, Ann Arbor, San Diego, Los Angeles, Vancouver, Seattle, Singapore, Hong Kong, Madras, Sri Lanka, Delhi, Kuwait, Paris, Marseille, Barcelona, Amsterdam, Copenhagen, Stockholm, Helsinki; mem. Council Marlborough Coll. 1990–2001; Gov. American Coll. of Surgeons 1997–2003; Fellow, King's Coll., London 2000–; Patron HOPE 2002–; Hon. Fellow, Royal Coll. of Physicians and Surgeons (Glasgow) 1993; Hon. FRACS 1994; Hon. Fellow in Dental Surgery 1994; Hon. Fellow, Royal Coll. of Surgeons in Ireland 1995; Hon. FACS 1995; Hon. Fellow,

Faculty of Accident and Emergency Medicine 1995; Hon. FRCSE 1996; Hon. Fellow, Coll. of Medicine of S Africa 1996; Distinguished Alumnus, Mayo Clinic 1993; Hon. Freeman, Worshipful Co. of Barbers 1997; Arris and Gale Medal 1968, Abraham Colles Medal 1990, Kinmouth Medal 1991, Vicary Medal 2000, Ratschow Medal 2007. *Publications:* Physiology and Pathology of Bed Rest 1964, Symptoms and Signs of Surgical Disease 1978, Reducing Operation for Lymphoedema 1986, Diseases of the Veins 1989, Diseases of the Lymphatics (co-author) 2003. *Leisure interests:* marine art, medieval history, sailing. *Address:* Corbet House, Butes Lane, Alderney, GY9 3UW, Channel Islands. *E-mail:* norman.browse@virgin.net (home).

BROYLES, William Dodson, Jr, MA; American journalist; b. 8 Oct. 1944, Houston, Tex.; s. of William Dodson Broyles and Elizabeth Broyles (née Bills); m. 1st Sybil Ann Newman 1973; one s. one d.; m. 2nd Linda Purl 1988 (divorced 1992); m. 3rd Andrea Bettina Berndt; three c.; ed Rice Univ., Univ. of Oxford, UK; Marine Corps Reserve 1969–71; teacher of philosophy, Naval Acad. 1970–71; Asst Supt, Houston Public Schools 1971–72; Ed.-in-Chief Texas Monthly 1972–82; Ed.-in-Chief California Magazine 1980–82; Ed.-in-Chief Newsweek Magazine 1982–84; columnist, US News and World Report 1986; fmr mem. Advisory Council, Harry Ransom Center, Univ. of Texas; Bronze Star, inducted into Texas Film Hall of Fame 2002. *Television:* China Beach (co-producer, exec. consultant) 1988–91. *Films:* as screewriter: Apollo 13 (with Al Reinert) 1995, Entrapment 1999, Cast Away 2000, Planet of the Apes 2001, Unfaithful 2002, The Polar Express 2004, Jarhead 2005, Flags of Our Fathers 2006. *Publications include:* Brothers in Arms: A Journey from War to Peace 1986, Cast Away: The Shooting Script 2001, All Aboard the Polar Express (Ed.) 2004. *Address:* Paradigm Talent Agency, 360 North Crescent Drive, North Building, Beverly Hills, CA 90210, USA.

BRUCE, Christopher, CBE; British ballet dancer and choreographer; *Associate Choreographer, Houston Ballet;* b. 3 Oct. 1945, Leicester, England; s. of Alexander Bruce and Ethel Parker; m. Marian Meadowcroft 1967; two s. one d.; ed Rambert School, London; dancer, Ballet Rambert, London 1963–80, Assoc. Dir 1975–79, Assoc. Choreographer 1979–87, Artistic Dir Rambert Dance Co. 1994–2003; Assoc. Choreographer, English Nat. Ballet (fmrly London Festival Ballet), London 1986–91; Assoc. Choreographer, Houston Ballet 1989–; choreographer for Kent Opera, Nederlands Dans Theater, Ballet du Grand Théâtre de Genève, and others; Hon. Life mem. Amnesty International 2010; Visiting Hon. Prof., Univ. of Exeter 2011; Dr hc (De Montfort) 2000; Hon. DLitt (Exeter) 2001; Evening Standard Inaugural Dance Award 1974, Int. Theatre Inst. Award 1993, Evening Standard Ballet Award 1996, Critic's Circle Award for Outstanding Achievement in Dance 2002, Critic's Circle Award for Best Choreography 2010. *Ballets include:* George Frideric 1969, For Those Who Die as Cattle 1971, There Was a Time 1972, Weekend 1974, Ancient Voices of Children 1975, Black Angels 1976, Cruel Garden 1977, Night with Waning Moon 1979, Dancing Day 1981, Ghost Dances 1981, Berlin Requiem 1982, Concertino 1983, Intimate Pages 1984, Ceremonies 1986, Swansong 1987, Symphony in Three Movements 1989, Rooster 1991, Waiting 1993, Crossing 1994, Meeting Point 1995 (for 'United We Dance' Int. Festival celebrating 50 years of UN), Quicksilver (tribute to Marie Rambert to celebrate Rambert Dance Co.'s 70th anniversary) 1996, Stream 1996, Four Scenes 1998, God's Plenty 1999, Hurricane 2000, Grinning in Your Face 2001, 3 Songs, 2 Voices 2005, A Steel Garden 2005, Hush 2006, Shift 2007, Dance at the Crossroads 2007, Ten Poems 2009, Für Alina 2011. *Address:* c/o Rambert Dance Company, 94 Chiswick High Road, London, W4 1SH, England; c/o Houston Ballet, Wortham Theater Center, 501 Texas Avenue at Smith Street, Houston, TX 77002, USA. *Telephone:* (713) 523-6300 (Houston). *E-mail:* info@houstonballet.org. *Website:* www.rambert.org.uk; www.houstonballet.org.

BRUCKHEIMER, Jerry, BA; American film and television producer; *Producer, Chairman and CEO, Jerry Bruckheimer Films & Television;* b. 1945, Detroit, Mich.; m. Linda Bruckheimer; ed Univ. of Arizona; fmr producer of TV commercials; formed Don Simpson/Jerry Bruckheimer Productions with the late Don Simpson 1983; formed Jerry Bruckheimer Films 1996, currently Chair. and CEO; entered into partnership with Paramount 2014; Hon. DFA (Univ. of Arizona Coll. of Fine Arts); ShoWest Producer of the Year 1999, David O. Selznick Lifetime Achievement Award 2000, Emmy Award 2004, 2005, 2006, Nat. Bd of Review Producers Award 2004, Variety Showman of the Year 2006, Salute to Excellence, Museum of TV and Radio 2006, Norman Lear Achievement in TV Award 2007, American Cinematheque Award 2013. *Films include:* Culpepper Cattle Company 1972, Rafferty and the Gold Dust Twins 1975, (producer) Farewell My Lovely 1975, March or Die 1977, Defiance 1980, American Gigolo 1980, Thief 1981, Cat People 1982, Young Doctors in Love 1982, Flashdance 1983, Beverly Hills Cop 1984, Thief of Hearts 1984, Top Gun 1986, Beverly Hills Cop II 1987, Days of Thunder 1990, The Ref (exec. producer) 1994, Dangerous Minds 1995, Bad Boys 1995, Crimson Tide 1995, The Rock 1996, Con Air 1997, Enemy of the State 1998, Armageddon 1998, Gone in 60 Seconds 2000, Coyote Ugly 2000, Remember the Titans 2000, Pearl Harbor 2001, Black Hawk Down 2002, Bad Company 2002, Kangaroo Jack 2003, Pirates of the Caribbean 2003, Bad Boys 2003, Veronica Guerin 2003, King Arthur 2004, National Treasure 2004, Pirates of the Caribbean: Dead Man's Chest 2006, Glory Road 2006, Deja Vu 2006, Pirates of the Caribbean: At World's End 2007, National Treasure: Book of Secrets 2007, Confessions of a Shopaholic 2009, G-Force 2009, Prince of Persia: The Sands of Time 2010, The Sorcerer's Apprentice 2010, Pirates of the Caribbean: On Stranger Tides 2011, The Lone Ranger 2013, Beware the Night 2014, Deliver Us From Evil 2014, Pirates of the Caribbean: Dead Men Tell No Tales 2017, Horse Soldiers 2017. *Television includes:* exec. producer CSI: Crime Scene Investigation 2000–13, The Amazing Race 2001–13, CSI: Miami 2002–12, Without a Trace 2002–09, Cold Case 2003–10, The Amazing Race Asia 2006–10, CSI: New York 2004–13, E-Ring 2005–06, Just Legal 2005–06, Close to Home 2005–07, Modern Men 2006, Justice 2006–07, Eleventh Hour 2008–09, The Forgotten 2009–10, Dark Blue 2009–10, Miami Medical 2010, The Amazing Race: China Rush 2010, The Whole Truth 2010, Jerry Bruckheimer's Chase 2010–11, The Amazing Race Australia 2011, Take the Money and Run 2011, Hostages 2013, Marshal Law: Texas 2013, CSI: Cyber 2015, Lucifer 2016, Training Day 2017. *Leisure interest:* ice hockey. *Website:* www.jbfilms.com (office).

BRUCKMANN, Gerhart, PhD; Austrian politician and statistician; b. 9 Jan. 1932, Vienna; s. of Friedrich Bruckmann and Anny Bruckmann (née Pötzl); m. Hilde Bartl 1961; two s.; ed Univ. of Graz, Vienna and Rome, Antioch Coll., USA; with Austrian Fed. Chamber of Commerce 1957–67; Prof. of Statistics, Univ. of Linz 1967–68, Univ. of Vienna 1968–92; Dir Inst. for Advanced Studies 1968–73; Consultant Int. Inst. for Applied Systems Analysis 1973–83, Council mem. 1983–86; mem. Parl. 1986–94, 1999–2002; Bd mem. Austrian Sr Citizens' Union 1998–; Exec. Officer European Sr Citizens' Union 1998–2001; mem. Austrian Acad. of Sciences; Hon. PhD (Linz) 1998. *Publications:* Auswege in die Zukunft 1974, Sonnenkraft statt Atomenergie 1978, Groping in the Dark (with D. Meadows and J. Richardson) 1982, Megatrends für Österreich 1988, Österreicher wer bist du? 1989. *Leisure interest:* collecting anchor building blocks. *Address:* Österr. Seniorenbund, Lichtenfelsgasse 7, 1010 Vienna (office); Zehenthofgasse 11, 1190 Vienna, Austria (home). *Telephone:* (431) 40126-151 (office). *Fax:* (431) 4066-266 (office).

BRUCKNER, Pascal, DèsSc, PhD; French writer and lecturer; b. 15 Dec. 1948, Paris; s. of René Bruckner and Monique Bruckner; m. Violaine Barret 1970 (divorced 1973); one s.; also one d. by Caroline Thompson; ed Lycée Henri IV, Univ. of Paris I (Sorbonne), Univ. of Paris VII (Jussieu); annual travels in Asia 1977–90; Lecturer, Inst. d'Etudes Politiques, Paris 1990–94; Visiting Prof., Univ. of San Diego and New York Univ. 1986–95; mem. Bd of Dirs Action contre la faim 1983–88; mem. Cercle de l'Oratoire (French think tank) 2001–; Chevalier des Arts et des Lettres, Légion d'honneur 2002. *Theatre:* many of his books have been played on stage throughout Europe and in India. *Publications include:* Le nouveau Désordre Amoureux 1977, Lune de Fiel 1982 (adapted for screen by Roman Polanski under the title Bitter Moon 1992), Le sanglot de l'homme blanc 1983, Le palais des claques 1986, Le divin enfant 1992, La tentation de l'innocence (Prix Médicis) 1995, Les voleurs de beauté (Prix Renaudot) 1997, Les ogres anonymes 1998, L'Euphorie perpétuelle, essai sur Le devóir de bonheur 2000, Misère de la prospérité. La religion marchande et ses ennemis (Sénat Prix du Livre d'économie) 2002, Au secours, le Père Noël revient 2003, L'amour du prochain 2006, La tyrannie de la pénitence: Essai sur le masochisme en Occident 2006, Perpetual Euphoria: On the Duty to Be Happy (trans. Steven Rendall) 2011, The Fanaticism of the Apocalypse: Save the Earth, Punish Human Beings (trans. Steven Rendall) 2013, Un bon fils (Prix Marcel Pagnol) 2014; translations in 25 countries. *Leisure interests:* piano, sports, fantasy films. *Address:* 8 rue Marie Stuart, 75002 Paris, (home); c/o Editions Denoel, 9 Rue de Cherche-Midi, 75248 Paris, France (office). *Telephone:* 1-40-26-68-79 (home). *Fax:* 1-40-56-34-37 (home). *E-mail:* bruckner@wanadoo.fr (home); contact@lemeilleurdesmondes.org (office). *Website:* www.lemeilleurdesmondes.org (office).

BRÜDERLE, Rainer, BEcons; German politician; b. 22 June 1945, Berlin; m.; ed Gutenberg Univ., Mainz; mem. FDP (Freie Demokratische Partei—Free Democratic Party) 1973–, becoming FDP Dist Chair. for Rheinhessen-Vorderpfalz, Deputy Chair. Mainz Dist FDP 1981–83, FDP Chair. in Land of Rhineland-Palatinate 1983–, mem. FDP Fed. Exec. Cttee (Bundesvorstand) 1983–; Dir Office of Econ. Affairs and Transport Devt, city of Mainz 1975–77, Dir Office of Econ. Affairs and Real Estate 1977–81, Full-time City Councillor and Head of Dept of Econ. Affairs 1981; mem. Rhineland-Palatinate Landtag (State Parl.) 1987–98, Rhineland-Palatinate Minister of Economy and Transport 1987–94, of Economy, Transport, Agric. and Viticulture 1994–98, Deputy Minister-Pres. of Rhineland-Palatinate 1988–98; mem. Bundestag (Parl.) 1998–2013, Deputy Chair. FDP Parl. Group 1998–2011, Chair. 2011–13; Fed. Minister of Econs and Tech. 2009–11; Chair. Bd of Supervisory Dirs KfW Bankengruppe 2010–11. *Address:* Freie Demokratische Partei, Thomas-Dehler-Haus, Reinhardtstr. 14, 10117 Berlin, Germany (office). *Telephone:* (30) 28495820 (office). *Fax:* (30) 28495822 (office). *E-mail:* fdp-point@fdp.de (office). *Website:* www.fdp-bundespartei.de (office); www.rainer-bruederle.de.

BRUDZIŃSKI, Joachim, PhD; Polish politician; *Minister of the Interior and Administration;* b. 4 Feb. 1968, Świerklaniec; s. of Władysław Brudziński and Ludwika Brudzińska; m. Arletta Brudzińska; one s. two d.; ed Univ. of Szczecin, Univ. of Poznań; early career as navigator technician; fmr co-worker and journalist, Polskie Radio Szczecin; fmr spokesman, Szczecin Maritime Office; mem. Sejm (parl.) (Prawo i Sprawiedliwość—PiS—Law and Justice) for 41 Szczecin Dist 2005–, Deputy Marshal (Speaker) 2015–18; Minister of the Interior and Admin 2018–; fmr mem. Porozumienia Centrum (Centre Agreement); mem. PiS, Sec.-Gen. 2006, Chair. Exec. Cttee 2009–18. *Address:* Ministry of the Interior and Administration, 02-591 Warsaw, ul. Stefana Batorego 5, Poland (office). *Telephone:* (22) 2500112 (office). *Fax:* (22) 6013988 (office). *E-mail:* kancelaria.glowna@mswia.gov.pl (office). *Website:* www.mswia.gov.pl (office); www.joachimbrudzinski.pl.

BRUEL, Jean-Marc André; French business executive; b. 18 Feb. 1936, Akbou, Algeria; s. of René Bruel and Jeanine Poirson; m. Anne-Mary Barthod 1962; two s. two d.; ed Ecole Centrale des Arts et Manufactures; Head of Tech. Services, Rhodiaceta, Brazil 1964; Dir nylon polyester factory, Rhône-Poulenc, Brazil 1968; Deputy Dir-Gen. of Textile Poduction Rhône-Poulenc, Brazil 1971; Deputy Dir-Gen. Div. of Plant Hygiene, Groupe Rhône-Poulenc 1975, Dir-Gen. 1976; Asst to Pres. and mem. Exec. Cttee Rhône-Poulenc 1979–80, Deputy Dir-Gen. 1980, Dir-Gen. 1982–84; mem. Exec. Cttee Sandoz, Basle 1985–87; Dir-Gen. Rhône Poulenc 1987–92, Vice-Pres. 1992–99; Pres. Rhône Poulenc Chimie 1987–92; Vice-Pres. European Council of Fed. of Chemical Industry (Cefic) 1988; Pres. Soc. of Chemical Industry 1993–94, Villette Enterprises 1995–2005, Institut Curie 1998–2002; mem. Supervisory Bd Sanofi-Aventis 1999–2004, Ind. Dir 2004–; Chair. Firmenich SA, Geneva 2000–08; mem. Bd of Dirs Rhodia 2002–05; Chevalier Légion d'honneur, Officier Ordre nat. du Mérite. *Leisure interests:* tennis, sailing. *Address:* 105 bis rue de Longchamp, 92200 Neuilly-sur-Seine, France (home).

BRUFAU NIUBÓ, Antonio, MBA; Spanish business executive; *Chairman, Repsol YPF SA;* b. 1948, Mollerussa, Lérida; ed Univ. of Barcelona, IESE Business School, Univ. of Navarra; fmr Partner and Head of Audit Div., Arthur Andersen; Asst Gen. Man. La Caixa 1998, Man. Dir La Caixa Group 1999–2004; mem. Bd of Dirs Repsol YPF SA 1996–, Chair. and CEO 2004–14, Chair. 2014–, Chair. Del. Cttee, mem. Global E&P Cttee, Global Downstream Cttee, Human Resources Cttee; Chair. Gas Natural Fenosa 1997–2004, Vice-Chair. 2004–; Chair. Comupet Madrid 2008, S.L., Fundación Repsol YPF; Pres. Círculo de Economía de Barcelona 2002–05; mem. European Round Table of Industrialists, Advisory Bd of CEIM Confederación Empresarial de Madrid – CEOE, Asociación Española de Directivos, Círculo de Economía, Foundation Privada Instituto Ildefons Cerdà, Foundation CEDE (Confederación Española de Directivos y Ejecutivos); Chair. Consorcio Interinstitucional GlobalLleida; fmr mem. Bd of Dirs, Enagás, Abertis, Aguas de Barcelona, Colonial, Suez, Caixa Holding, CaixaBank France, CaixaBank Andorra; mem. Exec. Cttee, ICC; Dr hc (Ramon Llull Univ.) 2011; Global Business Leader Award, American Chamber of Commerce in Spain (AmchamSpain) 2009, Best Businessman of the Year, Spanish Chamber of Commerce of the Repub. of Argentina (CECRA) 2010, Entrepreneur of the Year, Fed. of Spanish Chambers of Commerce in Europe (FEDECOM) 2010, CEO of the Year, Platts Global Energy Awards 2012, ESADE Award 2013, named by Institutional Investor magazine as Best CEO in the industry 2014, named by Petroleum Economist as Best CEO of the year 2014, Business Leader of the Year Award, Spain-US Chamber of Commerce 014, AED Director of the Year Award 2014. *Address:* Repsol YPF SA, Méndez Álvaro 44, 28045 Madrid, Spain (office). *Telephone:* (91) 7538100 (office). *Fax:* (902) 303145 (office). *E-mail:* info@repsol.com (office). *Website:* www.repsol.com (office).

BRUGUERA, Sergi; Spanish fmr professional tennis player; b. 16 Jan. 1971, Barcelona; s. of Luis Bruguera; coached by his father; turned professional 1988; winner French Open 1993, 1994, finalist 1997; Olympic silver medal, Atlanta, USA 1996; winner of 17 titles (three doubles); retd 2002; Delta Tour of Champions; coached Richard Gasquet 2014–17; Captain Spanish Davis Cup 2017–18; Advisor Bruguera Acad. *Address:* Bruguera Academy, Carrer de les Orenetes, Santa Coloma de Cervello, 08690 Barcelona, Spain (office). *Telephone:* (93) 6340330 (office). *E-mail:* info@brugueraacademy.com (office). *Website:* www.brugueraacademy.com (office).

BRUININKS, Robert H., MA, PhD; American university administrator, psychologist and academic; m. Dr Susan Andrea Hagstrum; three s.; ed Western Michigan Univ., George Peabody Coll. (now part of Vanderbilt Univ.); Asst Prof., Dept of Educational Psychology, Univ. of Minnesota 1968, later Prof., Dean, Exec. Vice-Pres. and Provost Univ. of Minnesota, Pres. 2002–11, Elmer L. Andersen President Emer. Chair in Civic Leadership and Emma M. Birkmaier Prof. in Educational Leadership, Coll. of Education and Human Development, Hubert H. Humphrey School of Public Affairs 2011–; Fellow, American Asscn on Mental Retardation, American Psychological Asscn, American Psychological Soc.; named Minnesotan of the Year by Minnesota Monthly magazine 2004, Executive of the Year, Minneapolis St. Paul Business Journal 2009. *Publications:* more than 90 journal articles and 70 book chapters, as well as training materials and several nationally standardized tests. *Address:* University of Minnesota Hubert H. Humphrey School of Public Affairs, 301 19th Avenue South, Minneapolis, MN 55455, USA (office). *Telephone:* (612) 626-1776 (office). *Fax:* (612) 625-3513 (office). *E-mail:* bruin001@umn.edu (office). *Website:* www.leadership.umn.edu (office).

BRUMMELL, Paul, CMG, BA, MA; British diplomatist; *Head of Soft Power and External Affairs Department, Communication Directorate, Foreign and Commonwealth Office;* b. 28 Aug. 1965, Harpenden, Herts., England; s. of Robert George Brummell and June Brummell; m. Adriana Mitsue Ivama Brummell; ed St Albans School, St Catharine's Coll., Cambridge; joined HM Diplomatic Service 1987, Third Sec., later Second Sec., Embassy in Islamabad 1989–92, with FCO, London 1993–94, First Sec., Embassy in Rome 1995–2000, Deputy Head Eastern Dept, FCO 2000–01, Amb. to Turkmenistan 2002–05, to Kazakhstan (also accred to Kyrgyzstan) 2005–09, High Commr to Barbados (also accred to Antigua and Barbuda, Dominica, Grenada, Saint Kitts and Nevis, Saint Lucia, and Saint Vincent and the Grenadines) 2009–13, concurrently UK Rep. to CARICOM and the Org. of Eastern Caribbean States 2010–13 and Consul Gen. to the Dutch Caribbean 2011–13, Amb. to Romania 2014–18; Head of Soft Power and External Affairs Dept, Communication Directorate, FCO 2018–. *Publications:* Turkmenistan: The Bradt Travel Guide 2005, Kazakhstan: The Bradt Travel Guide 2008. *Address:* Communication Directorate, Foreign and Commonwealth Office King Charles Street, London, SW1A 2AH, England (office). *Telephone:* (20) 7008-1500 (office). *E-mail:* fcocorrespondence@fco.gov.uk (office). *Website:* www.gov.uk/government/organisations/foreign-commonwealth-office (office).

BRUNDIN, Clark Lannerdahl, BS, PhD; American/British engineer, academic and university administrator (retd); b. 21 March 1931, Los Angeles, Calif.; s. of Ernest Brundin and Elinor Brundin (née Clark); m. Judith Anne Maloney 1959; two s. two d.; ed Whittier High School, California Inst. of Tech., Univ. of California, Berkeley; electronics petty officer, USN 1951–55; Assoc. in Mechanical Eng, Univ. of California, Berkeley 1956–57, Research Engineer, Inst. of Eng Research 1959–63; Demonstrator, Dept of Eng Science, Univ. of Oxford 1957–58, Lecturer 1963–85, Vice-Chair. Gen. Bd of Faculties, Univ. of Oxford 1984–85, Fellow and Tutor in Eng, Jesus Coll. Oxford 1964–85, Sr Tutor 1974–77, Estates Bursar 1978–84, Hon. Fellow 1985–; Gov. Oxford Polytechnic 1978–83, Cokethorpe School 1983–96, Magdalen Coll. School 1987–99, Coventry School Foundation; Vice-Chancellor Univ. of Warwick 1985–92; Visiting Prof., Univ. of California, Santa Barbara 1978; Visiting Scholar, Center for Higher Educ. Studies, Univ. of California, Berkeley 1997–2004; Liberal Democrat City Councillor, Oxford 2004–12; Chair. Anchor Housing Asscn 1985–91; Dir Blackwell Science Ltd 1990–98; Dir Heritage Projects (Oxford) 1986–97, Finsbury Growth Trust PLC 1995–2000, Charities Aid Foundation America 1997–2000 (Pres. 1998–2000); Founding Dir Oxford Univ. School of Man. Studies 1992–96; Pres. Templeton Coll., Oxford 1992–96; mem. Eng Bd, CNAA 1976–82; Hon. Fellow, Jesus Coll., Oxford 1985, Green Templeton Coll., Oxford 2011, Freeman, City of Oxford 2013; Hon. LLD (Warwick) 2005. *Publications include:* articles on rarefied gas dynamics and education. *Leisure interests:* sailing, mending old machinery, all types of music. *Address:* Jesus College, Oxford, OX1 3DW, England (office).

BRUNDTLAND, Gro Harlem, Cand. med, MPH; Norwegian politician, diplomatist, physician and international organization official; *Deputy Chair, The Elders;* b. 20 April 1939, Oslo; d. of Gudmund Harlem and Inga Harlem; m. Arne Olav Brundtland 1960; three s. (one deceased) one d.; ed Oslo Univ. and Harvard Univ., USA; Consultant, Ministry of Health and Social Affairs 1965–67; Medical Officer, Oslo City Health Dept 1968–69; Deputy Dir School Health Services, Oslo 1969; Minister for Environmental Affairs 1974–79; Deputy Leader Labour Party 1975–81, Leader Labour Parl. Group 1981–92; Prime Minister of Norway Feb.–Oct. 1981, 1986–89, 1990–96; mem. Parl. Standing Cttee on Foreign Affairs, fmr mem. Parl. Standing Cttee on Finance; mem. of Storting (Parl.) 1977–97; Dir-Gen. WHO 1998–2003; Chair. UN World Comm. on Environment and Devt 2003–05; UN Sec.-Gen.'s Special Envoy on Climate Change 2007–09, mem. UN Sec.-Gen.'s High Level Panel on Global Sustainability 2010–; Founding mem. The Elders group 2007–, Deputy Chair. 2013–; consultant, Pepsi Co.; fmr Vice-Chair. Sr Secondary Schools' Socialist Asscn, Students' Asscn of Labour Party; mem. Council of Women World Leaders, Club of Madrid; Dr hc (Oxford) 2001; Third World Prize for Work on Environmental Issues 1989, Indira Gandhi Prize 1990, Onassis Foundation Award 1992, Scientific American Policy Leader of the Year Award 2003, Thomas Jefferson Foundation Medal in Architecture 2008, Zayed Int. Prize for the Environment (Category 1) 2008, Premi Internacional Catalunya 2013, Weltwirtschaftliche Preis 2013, Tang Prize in Sustainable Devt 2014. *Publications:* articles on preventive medicine, school health and growth studies. *Leisure interest:* cross-country skiing. *Address:* The Elders Foundation, POB 67772, London, W14 4EH, England (office). *Telephone:* (20) 7013 4646 (office). *Website:* theelders.org (office).

BRUNEKREEF, Bert, BSc, MSc, PhD; Dutch environmental scientist and academic; *Professor of Environmental Epidemiology and Director of the Institute for Risk Assessment Sciences, University of Utrecht;* b. 3 March 1953, Utrecht; ed Univ. of Wageningen; worked at US Environmental Protection Agency (EPA) monitoring lab., Las Vegas, Nev., USA 1978–79; Asst Prof., Dept of Environmental and Tropical Health (later Dept of Environmental Sciences), Univ. of Wageningen 1979–86, Assoc. Prof. 1986–93, Prof. 1993–, Dept of Environmental and Occupational Health moved to Utrecht Univ. and merged with existing Research Inst. of Toxicology Div. to create Inst. for Risk Assessment Sciences (IRAS) 2000, IRAS absorbed Dept of Food Safety and Veterinary Public Health 2005, Dir IRAS 2005–, currently Prof. of Environmental Epidemiology in Faculty of Veterinary Medicine and in Faculty of Medicine; Academy Prof., Royal Netherlands Acad. of Arts and Sciences 2009; Visiting Prof., Harvard School of Public Health, USA 1986–87; Councillor, Int. Soc. for Environmental Epidemiology (ISEE) –1995, Pres. ISEE 2000–01; Co-ordinator European Study of Cohorts for Air Pollution Effects (ESCAPE) 2008–12; adviser on nat. and int. panels in the field of environmental health, including Dutch Nat. Health Council (also mem.), WHO, USA EPA; Kt, Order of the Netherlands Lion 2011; Dr hc (Catholic Univ. of Louvain) 2008; John Goldsmith Award, Int. Soc. for Environmental Epidemiology 2007, European Lung Foundation Award 2007, Dr A.H. Heineken Prize for Environmental Sciences, Royal Netherlands Acad. of Arts and Sciences 2008. *Publications:* co-author of more than 300 peer-reviewed journal articles in the field of environmental epidemiology and exposure assessment. *Address:* Institute for Risk Assessment Sciences, Faculty of Veterinary Medicine, PO Box 80.163, 3508 TD Utrecht, The Netherlands (office). *Telephone:* (30) 2539490 (office). *Fax:* (30) 2537727 (office). *E-mail:* b.brunekreef@uu.nl (office). *Website:* www.uu.nl (office).

BRUNET, Michel, LèsSc, PhD, DSc; French palaeontologist, palaeoanthropologist and academic; *Professor, Collège de France;* b. 6 April 1940, Vienne (Poitou); ed Lycée Hoche, Versailles, Univs of Paris and Poitiers; formed a team with colleague Emile Heintz to search for extinct apes in Afghanistan 1970s, expedition was unsuccessful; Founder and current Head of int. transdisciplinary team MPFT (Mission Paléoanthropologique Franco-Tchadienne), a scientific collaboration between Univs of Poitiers, N'Djamena and Centre Nationale d'Appui à la Recherche; Head, Institut Int. de Paléoprimatologie, Evolution et Paléoenvironnements, Univ. of Poiters 2000–07; Prof., Collège de France, Chair of Human Palaeontology 2007–11; Hon. mem. Soc. of Vertebrate Paleontology (USA) 2008; Officier, Légion d'honneur, Officier, Ordre nat. du Mérite, Commdr, Ordre des Palmes académiques, Officier, Ordre Nat. du Tchad; Prix Fontanes Prize 1977, Philip Morris Scientific Prize (Paleoanthropology) 1996, Dan David Prize 2003. *Achievements include:* moved to Africa 1980s, described a new Chadian hominid species, *Australopithecus bahrelghazali* (nicknamed Abel), dated around 3.5 Ma 1995, published in Nature an almost complete cranium of claimed oldest prehuman ancestor (7 Ma): *Sahelanthropus tchadensis* (nicknamed Toumai) discovered in Chad in 2001 and published in Nature 2002, 2005. *Address:* Collège de France, 3 rue d'Ulm, 75231 Paris Cedex 05, France (office). *Telephone:* 1-44-27-16-11 (office); 1-44-27-10-39 (Asst) (office). *Fax:* 1-44-27-10-59 (office). *E-mail:* michel.brunet@college-de-france.fr (office). *Website:* www.college-de-france.fr/site/en-michel-brunet (office).

BRUNETTA, Renato; Italian economist, academic and politician; b. 26 May 1950, Venice; ed Marco Foscarini Liceo Classico, Univ. of Padua, Univ. of Cambridge, UK, Univ. of Rotterdam, Netherlands; researcher in political sciences, Univ. of Padua 1975–77, Prof. of Labour Econs 1978–82; Gen. Sec. Fondazione G. Brodolini, Rome 1980–; Chief Consultant, Econ. Adviser to Ministry of Labour 1983–88; Sec., Italian Asscn of Labour Economists 1985–87; Vice-Pres., OECD Manpower and Social Affairs Cttee 1985–89; Prof. of Labour Econs, Rome Univ. II 'Tor Vergata' 1990; mem. European Parl. 1999–2008; mem. Parl. (for Veneto II constituency) 2008–; Econ. Adviser to Prime Minister 2004–06; Minister for Public Admin. and Innovation 2008–11; Program Man. Popolo della Libertà 2011–12; Ed. Economia & Lavoro (quarterly review), Rome 1980–; Founder and Ed. Labour (journal) 1987–; Pres. Fondazione Ravello 2011–; Pres. Comm. on Information for CNEL (Nat. Council of Economy and Labour) 1989–94, Councillor 1995; mem. ASPEN-Italy 1989–; columnist, Il Sole 24 Ore, Il Giornale; Premio St Vincent (for Econs) 1988, Premio Tarantelli (for Econs) 1993, Scanno Prize 1994, Rodolfo Valentino Int. Prize 2000. *Publications include:* Economia del Lavoro 1981, Multilocalizzazione produttiva come strategia d'impresa 1983, Squilibri, conflitto, piena occupazione 1983, Spesa pubblica e conflitto 1987, Microeconomia del lavoro: Teorie e analisi empiriche 1987, Labour Relations and Economic Performance (ed.) 1990, Il Modello Italia 1991, Economics for the New Europe 1991, Il conflitto e le relazioni di lavoro negli anni '90 1992, Disoccupazione, Isteresi, Irreversibilità 1992, Retribuzione, costo del lavoro. Regolazione e deregolazione; il capital umano; la destrutturazione del mercato (ed.) 1992, La fine della società dei salariati 1994, Sud: Alcune idee perché il Mezzogiorno non resti com'è 1995, Venezia XXI, Cronache di una transizione difficile 2004, Quindici piu Direci: Il difficile cammino dell'integrazione europea (jt author) 2004, Il coraggio e la paura, Scritti de economia e politica 1999–2003 2004, Sud 2009, Rivoluzione in corso 2009, La mia politica 2011, L'occasione della crisi 2011, Il grande imbroglio 2012, Il grande imbroglio 2 2013; articles and essays on labour econs and industrial relations. *Leisure interests:* photography, history of Venice, gastronomy. *Address:* Chamber of Deputies (Camera dei Deputati), Palazzo di Montecitorio, Piazza Montecitorio, 00186 Rome, Italy (office). *Telephone:* (06) 67601 (office). *E-mail:* r.brunetta@camera.it (office). *Website:* www.camera.it (office); www.renatobrunetta.it (office).

BRUNETTI, Wayne H., BSc; American energy industry executive (retd); ed Univ. of Florida, Harvard Business School; fmr Exec. Vice-Pres. Florida Power & Light Co.; fmr Pres. and CEO Man. Systems International; Chair., Pres. and CEO New Century Energies –2000; joined Public Service Co. of Colo 1994, Pres. and CEO 1994, later Chair., Pres. and CEO; Chair., Pres. and CEO Southwestern Public Service Co., Cheyenne Light, Fuel and Power Co.; Chair., Pres. and CEO Xcel Energy Inc. 2001–03, Chair. and CEO 2003–05 (retd); Dir, Cheyenne Light, Fuel and Power Co. 1994–, NRG Energy Inc. 2000–03, Synenco Energy Inc. 2006–, OGE Energy Corpn 2008–; fmr Chair. Colo Asscn of Commerce and Industry, 2000 Mile High United Way Campaign; Dir Capital City Partnership, Minn. Orchestral Asscn, Juran Center for Leadership and Quality, Labour Relations Cttee, Chamber of Commerce of the USA; mem. Nat. Petroleum Council, Minn. Business Partnership, Colo Renewable Energy Task Force; fmr Cttee mem., Electric Power Research Inst., Edison Electrical Inst. (EEI), also EEI First Vice-Chair. *Publications:* Achieving Total Quality in Integrated Business Strategy and Customer Needs. *Address:* c/o Xcel Energy Inc., 414 Nicollet Mall, Minneapolis, MN 55401-1993, USA. *E-mail:* info@xcelenergy.com.

BRUNI, Carla; Italian/French model and singer; b. (Carla Gilberta Bruni Tedeschi), 23 Dec. 1967, Turin; fmr partner of Raphaël Enthoven; one s.; m. Nicolas Sarközy de Nagy Bocsa 2008; one d.; ed Univ. of Paris; began career as model, City Models, Paris 1986; appeared in GUESS? advertising campaigns 1987; catwalk model for Chistian Dior, Paco Rabanne, Chanel, Givenchy, Yves Saint Laurent and John Galliano 1990s; listed as one of world's top 20 highest-paid models, Business Age 1998; retd from catwalk modelling 1998; signed to Versace to model fragrance advertisements 1998; signed to record label Naïve, launched singing career 2002; First Lady of France (as wife of Pres. of French Repub.) 2008–12; f. Carla Bruni-Sarkozy Foundation 2009. *Films include:* Prêt-à-Porter 1994, Catwalk 1996, Paparazzi 1998, Yves Saint Laurent: His Life and Times 2002, La caravane des enfoirés 2007, Starko! 2008, (500) Days of Summer 2009, Midnight in Paris 2011. *Film music:* En la ciudad (song Tout le monde) 2003, Le divorce (song Quelqu'un m'a dit) 2003, In the City (writer and performer Tout le monde) 2003, Conversations with Other Women (music Le Plus Beau du Quartier, J'en connais, L'excessive) 2005, The Lake House (performer La Noyée 1970) 2006, Colors en sèrie: Rosa: Enganxós o diví (song and lyrics and performer Quelqu'un m'a dit) 2007. *Television includes:* Die Schönsten Frauen der Welt – Carla Bruni 1995, Ombre et lumière 2003, Lo + plus 2003, Qui veut gagner des millions? 2004, Vivement dimanche prochain 2005, 2008, 2009, 2010, Le grand journal de Canal+ 2005, 2008, 2009, Campus, le magazine de l'écrit: Nouveau campus en direct! 2006, Turin 2006: XX Olympic Winter Games (mini-series) 2006, Symphonic show spécial Sidaction 2007, Stars of Europe 2007, Tenue de soirée: Cannes 2007, Later with Jools Holland 2008, Wetten, dass...? 2008, Somebody Told Me About... Carla Bruni (documentary) 2008, Late Show with David Letterman 2008, Sidaction 2009 2009, Chuck: Chuck vs First Class 2010, Melody Gardot: The Accidental Musician 2010. *Recordings include:* albums: Quelqu'un m'a dit 2002, No Promises 2007, Comme si de rien n'était 2008, Little French Songs 2013. *Leisure interests:* playing guitar, spending time with her cats. *Website:* www.carlabruni.com.

BRUNI MACHÍN, Jorge Ricardo; Uruguayan lawyer and politician; b. 1941; ed Univ. de la República, Montevideo; Lecturer, Dept of Law, Univ. de la República 1991–96; with Banco de Previsión Social 1992; fmr Co-ordinator, Legal Dept, Central Unica de Trabajadores del Uruguay (trade union); columnist, La República de Montevideo; Under-Sec., Ministry of Labour and Social Security 2005–09; Minister of the Interior 2009–10. *Address:* c/o Ministry of the Interior, Mercedes 953, 11100 Montevideo, Uruguay. *E-mail:* unicom@minterior.gub.uy.

BRUNNER, Han Grit (Henry), PhD; Dutch geneticist and academic; *Professor of Human Genetics and Head of Institute of Human Genetics, Nijmegen Medical Centre, Radbound University;* b. 18 Oct. 1956, Rotterdam; ed Univ. of Groningen Medical School; specialized in Clinical Genetics at Radboud Univ. Medical Center, Nijmegen 1984–88; board certified in Clinical Genetics 1988; joined Section of Clinical Genetics, Inst. of Human Genetics, Radboud Univ., Nijmegen Medical Centre 1988, Prof. of Human Genetics and Head of Inst. of Human Genetics 1998–, Chancellor for Human Genetics, Paediatrics and Medical Psychology 2004–08; Chair. Inst. of Clinical Genetics, Maastricht Univ. 2014–; mem. Scientific Advisory Bd, Koninklijke Nederlandse Akad. Wetenschappen Hubrecht Lab., Utrecht; fmr Chair. Dutch Nat. Org. for Scientific Research Cttee for VICI career devt grants, Quality Assurance Cttee of Dutch Clinical Genetic Soc.; fmr mem. Scientific Council of Dutch Org. for Research of Neuromuscular Diseases, Core Assessment Cttee for the Leiden UMC Science Review, Bd of Dirs of Dutch Soc. of Human Genetics, Medical Sciences Fellowship Cttee of Dutch Nat. Org. for Scientific Research; Pres. European Soc. of Human Genetics; Co-Chair. of Diagnostics, Int. Rare Diseases Research Consortium; Jt Organizer, European School of Medical Genetics; mem. Bd of Dirs, American Soc. of Human Genetics; mem. Scientific Advisory Bd, Sydney Brenner Inst. of Molecular Biology, Johannesburg, South Africa; fmr mem. Exec. Bd, European Soc. of Human Genetics, Scientific Cttee, Telethon, Italy, Scientific Program Cttee for World Congress of Human Genetics, Brisbane, Australia, Jury for Soderberg Professorship of Royal Swedish Acad. of Sciences; mem. Editorial Bd, Molecular Syndromology, Clinical Genetics, Journal of Medical Genetics; fmr mem. Editorial Bd Netherlands Journal of Medicine, Clinical Syndromology; Prize of Dutch Org. for Research of Neuromuscular Diseases 1994, Ben ter Haar Prize, Clinical Genetics Soc. of the Netherlands 1995, Frank Greenberg Memorial Lectureship, Baylor Coll. of Medicine, Houston, USA 2009, Radboud Science Award (with Joris Veltman), Radboud Univ. Medical Centre, Nijmegen 2011, Royal Coll. of Physicians, Edinburgh Endowed Lecturer, Edinburgh, UK 2012, King Faisal Int. Prize for Medicine (co-recipient) 2016. *Publications:* numerous papers in professional journals. *Address:* Department of Human Genetics, Radboud University Medical Centre, 855 Postbus 9101, 6500 HB Nijmegen, The Netherlands (office). *Telephone:* (24) 3614017 (office). *E-mail:* han.brunner@radboudumc.nl (office). *Website:* www.radboudumc.nl/OverhetRadboudumc (office).

BRUNO, Franklin (Frank) Roy, MBE; British fmr professional boxer; b. 16 Nov. 1961, Hammersmith, London, England; s. of Robert Bruno and Lynette Bruno (née Campbell); m. Laura Frances Mooney 1990 (divorced 2001); one s. four d.; ed Oak Hall School, Sussex; began boxing with Wandsworth Boys' Club, London 1970; mem. Sir Philip Game Amateur Boxing Club 1977–80; won 20 out of 21 contests as amateur; professional career 1982–96; won 38 out of 42 contests as professional 1982–89; European heavyweight champion 1985–86 (relinquished title), world heavyweight title challenges against Tim Witherspoon 1986, Mike Tyson 1989; staged comeback, won first contest 1991; lost fourth world title challenge against Lennox Lewis Oct. 1993; World Boxing Council (WBC) heavyweight champion 1995–96, lost title to Mike Tyson 1996; announced retirement Aug. 1996; numerous appearances in pantomimes; fmr presenter, BBC TV; DJ 2002–03; admitted to Goodmayes Hosp., Ilford Sept. 2003, subsequently diagnosed with bipolar disorder, later recovered; personal appearances, TV shows, voiceovers, adverts etc. throughout Europe 2004–12; held meetings with Minister of Health to discuss the stigma surrounding mental health issues 2013, out of which came The Crisis Care Concordat signed by more than 20 nat. orgs to drive up standards of care 2014; Patron The Shannon Bradshaw Trust; Dr hc (Bournemouth Univ.) 2018; SOS Sports Personality of the Year 1990; TV Times Sports Personality of the Year 1990, Lifetime Achievement Award, BBC Sports Personality of the Year Awards 1996. *Achievements include:* completed London Marathon 2011, has also run numerous half marathons including Newcastle 2015. *Television includes:* The Royal Variety Show, Trevor Macdonald Special, Sports Relief, Comic Relief, Fort Boyard 1999, Cass (crime drama) 2008, The Weakest Link 2009, Harry Hill's TV Burp 2011, The Alan Titchmarsh Show 2011, Sooty 2011, Piers Morgan's Life Stories 2012, featured in the BBC Three documentary Rachel Bruno: My Dad and Me 2013. *Recordings include:* cover version of Eye of the Tiger (theme song of film Rocky III) 1995, one of several celebrities recorded on World Cup song Who Do You Think You Are Kidding Jurgen Klinsmann? 2006. *Publications:* Know What I Mean; Eye of the Tiger; Personality: From Zero to Hero (with Norman Giller) 1996, Frank (autobiog., with Kevin Mitchell) (Sky Sports Autobiography of the Year 2006) 2005. *Leisure interests:* music, training, swimming, West Ham Football Club. *Address:* POB 99, Hockley, Essex, SS5 4TB, England (home). *Telephone:* (1702) 202036. *E-mail:* info@frankbruno.co.uk (home); dave@frankbruno.co.uk (office). *Website:* www.frankbruno.co.uk (home).

BRUS, Louis E., BA, PhD; American chemist and academic; *Samuel Latham Mitchill Professor, Columbia University;* b. 10 Aug. 1943; ed Rice Univ., Columbia Univ.; Lt, USN, US Naval Research Lab., Washington, DC 1969–73; Mem. Tech. Staff, AT&T Bell Labs, Murray Hill, New Jersey 1973–84, Distinguished Mem. Tech. Staff 1984–96; Prof. of Chem., Columbia Univ. 1996–, Prof. of Chemical Eng and Applied Chem. 1997–, Thomas Alva Edison Prof. 2001–04, Samuel Latham Mitchill Prof. 2004–, Scientific Head, Columbia NSF MRSEC IRG on Complex Films 1998–2008; Co-Dir Columbia Dept of Energy EFRC Energy Research Center 2009–14; Visiting Prof., Univ. of Paris VI (Pierre et Marie Curie) 2002; Vice Chair. Gordon Research Confs 1997, Chair. 1998; mem. Editorial Bd of several journals, including Journal of Chemical Physics 1988–91, Journal of Physical Chemistry 1990–93, 2003–06, Journal of the American Chemical Society 1990–96, Nano Letters 2000–04, ACS Nano 2007–, Accounts of Chemical Research 2012–15; mem. numerous review cttees; mem. NAS 2004–; Foreign mem. Norwegian Acad. of Science and Letters 2009; Fellow, American Physical Soc. 1980, American Acad. of Arts and Sciences 1998; NSF Predoctoral Fellow 1966–69, Univ. of Chicago Herman Bloch Award 1995, Irving Langmuir Prize in Chemical Physics, American Physical Soc. 2001, ACS E.I. Pont de Nemours & Co. Award in the Chem. of Materials 2005, R.W. Wood Prize, Optical Soc. of America (co-recipient) 2006, Inaugural Kavli Prize in Nanoscience (with S. Iijima) 2008, J. Willard Gibbs Medal, ACS (Chicago Section) 2009, NAS Prize in the Chemical Sciences 2010, R.T. Major Medal, Merck and Univ. of Connecticut 2010, Distinguished Alumnus Award Rice Univ. 2010, ACS Peter Debye Award in Physical Chem. 2011, Bower Award and Prize for Achievement in Science, Franklin Inst. 2012, Welch Foundation Award in Chem. 2013. *Address:* Department of Chemistry, Columbia University, Havemeyer Hall, MC 3125, 3000 Broadway, New York, NY 10027, USA (office). *Telephone:* (212) 854-4041 (office). *Fax:* (212) 932-1289 (office). *E-mail:* leb26@columbia.edu (office). *Website:* www.columbia.edu/cu/chemistry (office).

BRUSKIN, Grisha (Brouskine Grigori); Russian artist; b. 21 Oct. 1945, Moscow; s. of David Brouskin and Bassia Strunina; m. 1st Ludmila Dmitrieva 1975 (divorced 1978); m. 2nd Alexandra Makarova 1982; one d. one adopted s.; ed Art High School, Moscow, Moscow Textile Inst.; mem. Soviet Artists' Union 1969; work includes paintings, gouaches, drawings, sculptures, performances; work included in first Sotheby's auction in Moscow, designed poster for Chicago Art Exhbn 1988; lives and works in New York; Kandinsky Prize for 'H-Hour', Art Chronika Foundation 2012. *Public collections:* Museum of Modern Art, New York, Museum Ludwig, Cologne, State Tretyakoff Gallery, Moscow, State Russian Museum, St Petersburg, State Pushkin Museum of Fine Arts, Moscow, Reichstag, Berlin, Portland Museum of Art, Portland, Me Milwaukee Art Museum, Jane Voorhees Zimmerli Art Museum, Rutgers Univ., NJ, Kupferstichkabinett Staatliche Museen zu Berlin, Kunsthalle Emden, Germany, Jewish Museum, New York, Israel Museum, Jerusalem, Galeria de Arte Nacional, Caracas, Sydney Besthoff Sculpture Garden, New Orleans Museum, Art Inst. of Chicago, Arkansas Art Center, Little Rock, The Achenbach Foundation for Graphic Arts, Fine Arts Museums of San Francisco. *Publications:* Past Imperfect (memoir) 2001, Life is Everywhere 2001, Das Alphabet des Grisha Bruskin 2002, Yours Truly 2003, Letter Follows 2005, Alefbet 2006 (English and French edns 2010), Direct and Indirect Objects 2008, Past Imperfect: 318 Episodes from the Life of a Russian Artist 2009, Towards Bruskin (collection of articles) 2011, H-Hour 2012, Archaeologist's Collection 2013. *Leisure interests:* literature, music. *Address:* c/o Marlborough Galleries, 40 West 57th Street, New York, NY 10019, USA. *Telephone:* (212) 541-4900. *E-mail:* info@marlboroughgallery.com. *Website:* www.marlboroughgallery.com/galleries/chelsea/artists/grisha-bruskin/biography.

BRUSTEIN, Robert Sanford, MA, PhD; American drama critic, actor and producer; *Founding Director and Creative Consultant, American Repertory Theatre;* b. 21 April 1927, New York, NY; s. of Max Brustein and Blanche Brustein (née Haft); m. 1st Norma Cates 1962 (died 1979); one s. one step-s.; m. 2nd Doreen Beinart 1996; one step-s. one step-d.; ed Amherst Coll., Yale Univ. Drama School, Columbia Univ.; played about 70 roles in theatre groups and TV plays 1950–; Instructor, Cornell Univ. 1955–56, Vassar Coll. 1956–57; Lecturer, Columbia Univ. 1957–58, Asst Prof. 1958–63, Assoc. Prof. 1963–65, Prof. 1965–66; Prof. of English, Yale Univ., Dean of Yale Drama School, Artistic Dir and Founder Yale Repertory Theatre 1966–79; Founder and Artistic Dir, American Repertory

Theatre, Loeb Drama Center, Cambridge, Mass 1980–2002, Founding Dir and Creative Consultant 2002–; Prof. of English, Harvard Univ. 1979–2002; Sr Fellow, Nat. Arts Journalism Program, Columbia Univ. 2003, Nat. Endowment for the Arts Arts Journalism Inst. in Theatre and Musical Theatre, Univ. of Southern California 2004–05; Drama Critic, The New Republic 1959–67, 1978–, Contributing Ed. 1959–79; regular contrib. to New York Times 1972–, Huffington Post; Advisory Ed., Theatre Quarterly 1967–; Guest Critic, The Observer, UK 1972–73, 1978–, Contributing Ed. 1959–; Trustee, Sarah Lawrence Coll. 1973–77; panel mem. Nat. Endowment for the Arts 1970–72, 1981–84; mem. American Acad. of Arts and Sciences 1999; Hon. LittD (Lawrence Univ.) 1968, (Amherst Coll.) 1972; Hon. LHD (Beloit Coll.) 1975; Hon. Dr of Arts (Bard Coll.) 1981; Fulbright Fellow 1953–55, Guggenheim Fellow 1961–62, George G. Nathan Prize in Criticism 1962, Ford Fellow 1964–65, George Polk Memorial Award in Criticism 1964, Jersey City Journal Award in Theatre Criticism 1967, Eliot Norton Award for Theatre, New England Theatre Conf. Award for Excellence in Theme, Award, Outstanding Achievement in American Theater, New England Theater Council 1985, Tiffany Award for Excellence in Theater, Soc. for Performing Arts Administrators 1987, American Acad. of Arts and Letters Distinguished Services to Arts Award 1995, ATHE Award for Lifetime Achievement in the Theater 2000, inducted into American Theatre Hall of Fame 2002, Lifetime Achievement Award, US Inst. for Theatre Tech. 2003, Chair.'s Award for Achievement in Theatre, Nat. Corp. Theatre Fund 2003, Gann Academy Award for Excellence in the Performing Arts 2005, Tao House Award, Eugene O'Neill Foundation 2008, Nat. Medal of Arts 2010, inducted into Players Club Hall of Fame 2011, Pirandello Medal, Medal from Egyptian Govt for contribs to world theatre. *Plays:* Demons 1995, Nobody Dies on Friday 1996, The Face Lift 1999, Spring Forward, Fall Back, Shakespeare Trilogy: The English Channel, Mortal Terror, The Last Will; short plays: Poker Face 1999, Chekhov on Ice 2000, Divestiture, AnchorBimbo, Noises, Terrorist Skit, Airport Hell, Beachman's Last Poetry Reading, Sex For a Change, Kosher Kop. *Television:* writer and narrator of a WNET series called The Opposition Theatre 1966. *Publications:* Introduction to The Plays of Chekhov 1964; Ed. The Plays of Strindberg 1964; author: The Theatre of Revolt: An Approach to Modern Drama 1964, Seasons of Discontent: Dramatic Opinions 1959–1965 1965, The Third Theatre 1969, Revolution as Theatre: Notes on the New Radical Style 1971, The Culture Watch: Essays on Theatre and Society, 1969–1974 1975, The Plays and Prose of Strindberg (ed.), Critical Moments: Reflection on Theatre & Society, 1973–1979 1980, Making Scenes: A Personal History of the Turbulent Years at Yale, 1966–1979 1981, Who Needs Theatre: Dramatic Opinions 1987, Reimagining American Theatre 1991, Dumbocracy in America: Studies in the Theatre of Guilt, 1987–1994 1994, Culturak Calisthenics: Writings on Race, Politics, and Theatre 1998, Three Farces and a Funeral 2000, Divestiture 2001, The Siege of the Arts: Collected Writings, 1994–2001 2001, Letters to a Young Actor: A Universal Guide to Performance 2005, Millennial Stages: Essays and Reviews 2001–2005 2006, Doctor Hippocrates is Out: Please Leave a Message (anthology of theatrical and cinematic satire on medicine and physicians) 2008, The Tainted Muse: Prejudices and Preconceptions in Shakespeare's Works and Times 2009, Rants and Raves: Opinions, Tributes, and Elegies 2011, Winter Passages: Essays and Criticism 2014. *Address:* American Repertory Theatre, Loeb Drama Center, Harvard University, 64 Brattle Street, Cambridge, MA 02138, USA. *Telephone:* (617) 495-2668. *Fax:* (617) 495-1705. *E-mail:* info@americanrepertorytheater.org. *Website:* americanrepertorytheater.org.

BRUTON, John Gerard, BA, BL; Irish politician, diplomatist, barrister, farmer and company director; b. 18 May 1947, Dublin; s. of Matthew Joseph Bruton and Doris Mary Delany; m. Finola Gill 1981; one s. three d.; ed Clongowes Wood Coll., Univ. Coll., Dublin, King's Inn, Dublin; mem. Dáil Éireann (House of Reps) 1969–2004; Fine Gael Spokesman on Agric. 1972–73; Parl. Sec. to Minister for Educ. 1973–77, to Minister for Industry and Commerce 1975–77; Fine Gael Spokesman on Agric. 1977–81, on Finance Jan.–June 1981; Minister of Finance 1981–82, of Industry, Trade, Commerce and Tourism 1982–86, of Finance 1986–87; Deputy Leader of Fine Gael 1987–90, Leader 1990–2001, Fine Gael Spokesman on Industry and Commerce 1987–89, on Educ. 1989–90, Vice-Pres. 2010–; mem. Parl. Ass., Council of Europe 1989–91, British-Irish Parl. Body 1993–94, Parl. Ass., WEU 1997–; Prime Minister of Ireland 1994–97; Leader of Opposition 1997–2001; Amb. and Head of EU Del. to USA 2004–09; mem. Fine Gael Front Bench 2002; Pres. Int. Financial Services Centre Ireland 2010–15; Chair. European Sustainable Materials Platform 2012–14; mem. Bd of Dirs Ingersoll Rand, Irish Diaspora Loan Origination Fund, Irish Inst. for Int. and European Affairs 2017–; Gov. Ditchley Foundation 1999–2012; Hon. Citizen, Sioux City, Iowa, USA; Commdr, Grand Cross of the Royal Order of the Polar Star (Sweden), Kt Grand Cross with Gold Star, Sacred Mil. Constantinian Order of St George; Hon. LLD (Memorial Univ., St John's, Newfoundland), (Nat. Univ. of Ireland), (Univ. of Missouri). *Publications:* Reform of the Dail 1980, A Better Way to Plan the Nation's Finances 1981, Faith in Politics (essays) 2015. *Leisure interests:* history, folk music, tennis. *Address:* Cornelstown, Dunboyne, Co. Meath, Ireland (home). *E-mail:* jgbcor@gmail.com (office). *Website:* www.johnbruton.com.

BRUTUS, Duly; Haitian diplomatist and politician; elected to Chamber of Deputies (Parl.) 1990, Pres. 1991–92; Perm. Rep. to OAS 2004–14, Chair. OAS Cttee on Hemispheric Security 2013; Minister of Foreign Affairs and Religion 2014–15 (resgnd). *Address:* c/o Ministry of Foreign Affairs and Religion, boulevard Harry S Truman, Cité de l'Exposition, Port-au-Prince, Haiti (office).

BRUYNINCKX, Hans, MPS, PhD; Belgian political scientist; *Executive Director, European Environment Agency;* b. 20 March 1964, Schoten; ed Catholic Univ. Leuven, Colorado State Univ., USA; 20 years' research experience in environmental, sustainable devt and climate change policy; fmr Researcher and Lecturer, Colorado State Univ., Canisius Coll., Buffalo, NY and Wageningen Univ., Netherlands; Prof. of Int. and European Environmental Politics, Catholic Univ. Leuven –2013, also Dir HIVA Research Inst. for Work and Soc. 2010–13; Exec. Dir European Environment Agency 2013–; Founding mem. Leuven Centre for Global Governance Studies. *Address:* European Environment Agency, 6 Kongens Nytorv, 1050 Copenhagen K, Denmark (office). *Telephone:* 33-36-71-00 (office). *Fax:* 33-36-71-99 (office). *E-mail:* eea@eea.europa.eu (office). *Website:* www.eea.europa.eu (office).

BRYAN, Albert, BA, MBA; American business executive and politician; *Governor, United States Virgin Islands;* b. 21 Feb. 1968, St Thomas; s. of Albert Bryan, Sr and Genevieve Bryan (née Pilgrim); m. Yolanda Cabodevilla; two d.; ed Wittenberg Univ., Univ. of the Virgin Islands; fmr Analyst, HESS Oil Corpn; co-f. Generation Now! Inc. (non-profit org.) 2002; District Dir, Innovative Cable TV 2005–07; Commr of Labor 2007–14; Chair. Economic Devt Authority 2007–14; Chair. Government Devt Bank 2007–14; Pres. Aabra Group (econ. devt agency) 2015–; Exec. Dir Junior Achievement (int. org.) 2015–; Man. Partner Master Strategies USVI LLC 2015–; Gov., US Virgin Islands 2019–; mem. Bd of Dirs Virgin Islands Port Authority 2007–14, Virgin Islands Housing Authority, Region 2 Health Equity Council 2014–; fmr Dir of Business Offices and Liaison, Public Services Comm. for Innovative Communications; mem. Democratic Party of the Virgin Islands. *Address:* Office of the Governor, 21-22 Kongens Gade, 00802 St Thomas, US Virgin Islands (office). *Telephone:* (340) 774-0001 (office). *Website:* www.vi.gov (office).

BRYAN, Elizabeth, BA (Econ), MA (Econ); Australian business executive; *Non-Executive Chairman, Caltex Australia Limited;* ed Australian Nat. Univ., Univ. of Hawaii, USA; experience in financial services industry, in govt policy and admin, and on bds of cos and statutory orgs since late 1970s; served for six years as Man. Dir Deutsche Asset Man. and its predecessor org., NSW State Superannuation Investment and Man. Corpn; mem. Bd of Dirs Ridley Corpn Ltd 2001–07, Westpac Banking Corpn 2006–, Australian Inst. of Co. Dirs; mem. Bd of Dirs Caltex Australia Ltd 2002–, Ind. Chair. (non-exec.) 2007–, Chair. Nomination Cttee; mem. Bd of Dirs, later Chair. UniSuper Ltd 2002–11. *Address:* Caltex Australia Ltd, GPO Box 3916, Sydney, NSW 2001 (office); Caltex Australia Ltd, Level 24, Market Street, Sydney, NSW 2000, Australia (office). *Telephone:* (2) 9250-5000 (office). *Fax:* (2) 9250-5742 (office). *E-mail:* info@caltex.com.au (office). *Website:* www.caltex.com.au (office).

BRYAN, Richard H., LLB; American lawyer and fmr politician; *Director, Fennemore Craig, P.C.;* b. 16 July 1937, Washington, DC; m. Bonnie Fairchild; three c.; ed Univ. of Nevada, Hastings Coll. of Law, Univ. of California; admitted to Nev. Bar 1963, US Supreme Court Bar 1967; Deputy Dist Attorney, Clark Co., Nev. 1964–66; Public Defender, Clark Co. 1966–68; Counsel, Clark Co. Juvenile Court 1968–69; mem. Nev. Ass. 1969–71; Nev. Senate 1973–77; Attorney-Gen., Nev. 1979–83; Gov. of Nev. 1983–89; Senator from Nev. 1989–2001; Partner and mem. Exec. Cttee, Lionel, Sawyer & Collins (law firm) 2001–14 (dissolved); Dir Fennemore Craig, P.C. 2015–; mem. Bd of Trustees, Las Vegas Global Economic Alliance 2001–, Econ. Devt Authority of Western Nev. (EDAWN), Las Vegas Chamber of Commerce; mem. Bd of Dirs Las Vegas Performing Arts Center; mem. City of Las Vegas Centennial Cttee; Chair. Preserve Nevada; mem. Order of the Coif; rated in The Best Lawyers in America 2008–13, named Distinguished Nevadan by Nevada System of Higher Educ. 2011. *Address:* Fennemore Craig, P.C. 300 S Fourth Street, Suite 1400 Las Vegas, NV 89101, USA (office). *Telephone:* (702) 791-8249 (office). *Fax:* (702) 791-8250 (office). *E-mail:* rbryan@fclaw.com (office). *Website:* www.fclaw.com (office).

BRYANT, Andy D., BEcons, MBA; American business executive; *Chairman, Intel Corporation;* ed Univ. of Missouri, University of Kansas; held positions in finance at Ford Motor Co. and Chrysler Corpn –1981; joined Intel as Controller for the Commercial Memory Systems Operation 1981–83, Systems Group Controller 1983–87, Dir of Finance 1987–90, Vice-Pres. and Dir of Finance, Intel Products Group 1990–94, Chief Financial Officer 1994–99, Sr Vice-Pres. 1999–2007, Chief Financial and Enterprise Services Officer 1999–2007, Chief Admin. Officer 2007–11, Head of Tech. and Manufacturing Group 2009–11, mem. Bd of Dirs and Vice-Chair. Intel Corpn 2011–12, Chair. 2012–. *Address:* Intel Corporation, 2200 Mission College Boulevard, Santa Clara, CA 95054-1537, USA (office). *Telephone:* (408) 765-8080 (office). *Fax:* (408) 765-9904 (office). *E-mail:* info@intel.com (office). *Website:* www.intel.com (office).

BRYANT, (Dewey Phillip) Phil, BA, MA; American politician, state governor and educator; *Governor of Mississippi;* b. 9 Dec. 1954, Moorhead, Miss.; s. of Dewey C. Bryant and Estelle R. Bryant; m. Deborah Hays; one s. one d.; ed Hinds Community Coll., Univ. of Southern Mississippi, Mississippi Coll.; worked as Service Manager at Jackson Mack Sales; later insurance investigator; taught Mississippi political history at Mississippi Coll.; mem. Mississippi House of Reps 1990–95, Vice-Chair. Insurance Cttee; apptd State Auditor 1996–99, elected 1999–2008; Lt-Gov. 2008–12; Gov. of Mississippi 2012–; Republican. *Address:* Office of Governor, PO Box 139, Jackson, MS 39205, USA (office). *Telephone:* (601) 359-3150 (office). *Fax:* (601) 359-3741 (office). *Website:* www.governorbryant.com (office).

BRYANT, John Martin, MA, CEng, FIM; British business executive; b. 28 Sept. 1943, Cardiff, Wales; s. of William George Bryant and Doris Bryant; m. Andrea Irene Emmons 1965; two s. one d.; ed West Monmouth School, Pontypool, St Catharine's Coll., Cambridge; grad. trainee, Steel Co. of Wales 1965–68; various tech., production, personnel positions at British Steel 1968–78, Works Man. Hot Rolled Products 1978–87, Dir Coated Products 1987–90, Dir Tinplate 1990–92, Man. Dir Strip Products 1995–99, Exec. Dir 1996–98, Chief Exec. 1999; Chief Exec. Corus PLC 1999–2001; Chair. Actoris Group Ltd 2009–; mem. Bd of Dirs ASW PLC 1993–95, Bank of Wales PLC 1996–2001, Welsh Water PLC 2001–14, Glas Cymru Ltd 2001–14, Costain Group PLC 2002–13; Fellow, Royal Acad. of Eng; Hon. DSc (Wales) 2000. *Leisure interests:* all sports, particularly squash and rugby, opera, theatre, family. *Address:* Broadway Farm, 24 Roger Lane, Laleston, Bridgend, CF32 0LA, Wales. *Telephone:* (1656) 647558. *Fax:* (1656) 664348.

BRYANT, Kobe Bean; American professional basketball player (retd); b. 23 Aug. 1978, Philadelphia, Pa; s. of Joe 'Jellybean' Bryant and Pam Bryant; m. Vanessa Laine 2001; two d.; ed Lower Merion High School, Pa; position: guard; moved with family to Italy where he lived until 1992; selected from high school by Charlotte Hornets in first round (13th pick overall) 1996 Nat. Basketball Assn (NBA) draft, draft rights traded to LA Lakers; youngest-ever NBA all-star starter at 19 years of age 1998; five times NBA champion with Lakers (2000, 2001, 2002, 2009, 2010); played final NBA game, Lakers against Utah Jazz, April 2016; played in gold medal-winning US Nat. Team at FIBA Americas Championships, Las Vegas 2007; played in gold medal-winning Team USA, Olympic Games, Beijing 2008, London 2012; official Amb. for After-School All-Stars; est. Kobe Bryant China Fund, Kobe

Bryant Basketball Acad.; NBA All-Star 1998, 2000–15, All-NBA First Team 2002–04, 2006–13, NBA Most Valuable Player in All-Star Game 2002, 2007, 2009 (shared award with Shaquille O'Neal), 2011, NBA Scoring Champion 2005–06, 2006–07, NBA Most Valuable Player 2008, NBA Finals Most Valuable Player 2009, NBA Finals MVP Award 2009, 2010, honoured as one of the 35 Greatest McDonald's All-Americans 2012. *Television:* Moesha (series) 1996. *Address:* c/o Los Angeles Lakers, 555 North Nash Street, El Segundo, CA 90245, USA (office). *Website:* www.kb24.com; kobebryant.com.

BRYARS, Gavin, BA; British composer; b. 16 Jan. 1943, Goole, Yorks.; s. of Walter Joseph Bryars and Miriam Eleanor Bryars; m. 1st Angela Margaret Bigley 1971 (divorced 1993); two d.; m. 2nd Anna Tchernakova 1999; one s. one step d.; ed Goole Grammar School, Univ. of Sheffield, Northern School of Music and pvt composition study with Cyril Ramsey, George Linstead and Benjamin Johnston; freelance double bassist 1963–66; Lecturer in Liberal Studies, Northampton Coll. of Tech. 1966–67; freelance composer/performer 1968–70; Lecturer in Music, Portsmouth Polytechnic 1969–70; Sr Lecturer, School of Fine Art, Leicester Polytechnic 1970–78, Sr Lecturer and Head of Music, School of Performing Arts 1978–85; Prof. of Music, De Montfort Univ. 1985–96; Assoc. Research Fellow, Dartington Coll. of Arts 2004–08; collaborations with numerous artists, including Aphex Twin, John Cage, Brian Eno, Tom Waits, Father John Misty; mem. Collège de Pataphysique, France 1974–, Regent 2007–, Transcendent Satrap 2015–; Ed. Experimental Music Catalogue 1972–81; British Rep. Int. Soc. for Contemporary Music Festival 1977; Visiting Prof., Univ. of Hertfordshire 1999–2003, Leeds Coll. of Music 2015–17; Arts Council Comms 1970, 1980, 1982, Bursary 1982; Music Juror, Akad. Schloss Solitude, Stuttgart 1990–92; freelance composer 1994–; Hon. Fellow, Bath Spa Univ. 2008, Birmingham Conservatoire 2015; Dr hc (Plymouth) 2006. *Compositions include:* The Sinking of the Titanic 1969, Jesus' Blood Never Failed Me Yet 1971, Out of Zaleski's Gazebo 1977, The Vespertine Park 1980, Medea (opera with Robert Wilson) 1982, My First Homage for two pianos 1978, Effarene 1984, String Quartet No. 1 1985, Pico's Flight 1986, By the Vaar for double bass and ensemble 1987, The Invention of Tradition 1988, Glorious Hill 1988, Cadman Requiem 1989, String Quartet No. 2 1990, Four Elements (dance piece) 1990, The Black River for soprano and organ 1991, The White Lodge 1991, The War in Heaven for chorus and orchestra 1993, Epilogue from 'Wonderlawn' for four players 1994, Three Elegies for Nine Clarinets 1994, The North Shore for solo viola and small orchestra 1994, After Handel's Vesper 1995, Cello Concerto 1995, The Adnan Songbook 1996, Doctor Ox's Experiment (opera) 1997, String Quartet No. 3 1998, The Porazzi Fragment for strings 1998, Biped (ballet) 1999, First Book of Madrigals 2000, Violin Concerto 2000, G (opera) 2001, Second Book of Madrigals 2001, Double Bass Concerto 2002, Book of Laude 2003, Writings on Water (ballet) 2003, Third Book of Madrigals 2003, Eight Irish Madrigals 2004, New York (percussion concerto) 2004, From Egil's Saga 2004, Creamer Etudes 2005, New York 2005, Paper Nautilus 2006, The Stones of the Arch 2006, Nothing Like the Sun 2007, Amjad 2007, Nine Irish Madrigals 2007, To Define Happiness 2007, Sonnets from Scotland 2007–09, Trondúr I Gøtu 2008, Anail Dé 2008–09, St Brendan Arrives at the Happy Land of the Saints 2009, Four Songs from Northern Seas 2009, Four I Tatti Madrigals 2009, At Portage and Main 2009, The First Light (ballet) 2010, The Solway Canal 2010, The Morrison Songbook 2010, Ramble on Cortona 2010, Reverence (ballet) 2011, Dido and Orfeo (after Purcell and Gluck) (ballet) 2011, Lauda 40 and 41 2011, Four Battiferri Madrigals 2011, Children's Songs 2012, The Open Road 2012, Psalm 141 2012, Lauda 42 2012, Three Choral pieces from the Faroe Islands 2012, The Voice of St Columba 2012, After the Underworlds 2012, Through the Halls 2012, The Beckett Songbook 2012–13, Marilyn Forever (opera) 2013, Pneuma (ballet) 2014, The Seasons (ballet) 2014, 11th Floor (ballet) 2014, Peer Gynt (ballet) 2014, The Fifth Century (cantata) 2014, Fifth Book of Madrigals 2009–14, De Profundis Aquarium 2015, Sixth Book of Madrigals 2015–16, The Stopping Train 2016, Lauda 43/44/45 2016, Raga Dawn 2016, The Other Side of the River 2016, Jimmy Smith in Paradise 2016, Words for Music 2017, Lauda 46 2017, Winestead 2017, The Heart of August (ballet) 2017–18, The Collected Works of Billy the Kid (opera) 2018, Requiem (ballet) 2019, A Native Hill 2019. *Films:* Sea and Stars (Nat. Film Bd of Canada) 2003, Season of Mists 2008, Our Chekhov 2010, Proezd Serova 2012–13, A Tale of Us 2015–16. *Radio:* I Send You This Cadmium Red (BBC Radio 3, with John Berger and John Christie) 2002, Egil's Last Days (BBC Radio 3) 2004, The Pythagorean Comma (BBC Radio 3) 2012. *Television:* Last Summer (CBC, Dir Anna Tchernakova) 2000. *Publications:* contribs to Music and Musicians, Studio International, Art and Artists, Contact, The Guardian, Arcana, Modern Painters, Parkett, Open Space (Moscow). *Leisure interests:* cricket (mem. Yorks. Co. Cricket Club), football, Dalmatians. *Address:* c/o Schott & Co. Ltd, 48 Great Marlborough Street, London, W1F 7BB, England (office). *Telephone:* (20) 7534-0750 (office). *Fax:* (20) 7534-0759 (office). *E-mail:* sam.rigby@schott-music.com (office); gbproductions@gavinbryars.com (office). *Website:* www.schott-music.com (office); www.gavinbryars.com.

BRYCE ECHENIQUE, Alfredo; Peruvian writer; b. 19 Feb. 1939, Lima; Premio Nacional de Literatura de Perú 1972, Premio Passion, France 1983, Encomienda de Isabel la Católica, Spain 1993, Premio Nacional de Narrativa, Spain 1998, Encomienda de Alfonso X El Sabio, Spain 2000, Premio Grinzane Cavour, Piemonte, Italy 2002, Premio Planeta, Spain 2002; Commdr, Ordre des Arts et des Lettres 2000. *Publications include:* Huerto cerrado (short stories) 1968, Un mundo para Julius (novel) 1970, La felicidad ja ja (short stories) 1974, Tantas veces Pedro (novel) 1977, A vuelo de buen cubero y otras crónicas (non-fiction) 1977, La vida exagerada de Martín Romaña (novel) 1981, El hombre que hablaba de Octavia de Cádiz 1984, Magdalena peruana y otros cuentos (short stories) 1986, Crónicas personales 1986, La última mudanza de Felipe Carrillo (novel) 1988, Dos señoras conversan (novella) 1990, Permiso para vivir (Antimemorias) (memoir) 1993, No me esperen en abril (novel) 1995, A trancas y barrancas (articles) 1997, Reo de nocturnidad (novel) 1997, Guía triste de París (short stories) 1999, La amigdalitis de Tarzán (novel) 1999, El huerto de mi amada 2002, Doce cartas a dos amigos 2003, Entrevistas escogidas 2004, Entre la soledad y el amor 2005, Las obras infames de Pancho Marambio 2007, Dándole pena a la tristeza 2012. *Website:* www.clubcultura.com/clubliteratura/clubescritores/bryce/index.htm.

BRYDEN, Alan, Dipl. in Nuclear Physics; British/French international organization executive; b. 1945; m. Laurence Bryden; three c.; ed Ecole Polytechnique, Paris, Ecole des Mines, Paris and Univ. d'Orsay, France; began career in metrology with Nat. Bureau of Standards (now Nat. Inst. of Standards and Tech.), USA; Dir-Gen. Laboratoire Nat. d'Essais 1981–99; f. Eurolab (European Fed. of Measurement, Testing and Analytical Labs), Pres. 1990–96; Dir-Gen. AFNOR (French nat. standardization inst.) 1999–2003; mem. Council Int. Org. for Standardization (ISO) 1999–2003, Sec.-Gen. 2003–09; fmr Vice-Pres. European Cttee for Standardization Policy; fmr Vice-Pres. Cttee on Tech. Barriers to Trade in GATT (now WTO); fmr Chair. Labs Cttee of Int. Lab. Accreditation Co-operation; Chevalier, Ordre nat. du Mérite 1988, Légion d'honneur 1995. *Leisure interests:* riding, sailing. *Address:* c/o International Organization for Standardization, ISO Central Secretariat, Chemin de Blandonnet 8, CP 401, 1214 Vernier, Geneva, Switzerland. *E-mail:* central@iso.org.

BRYDON, Donald Hood, BSc, CBE; British business executive; *Chairman, Royal Mail Group;* b. 25 May 1945, Stirling, Scotland; s. of James Hood Brydon and Mary Duncanson Brydon (née Young); m. 1st Joan Victoria 1971 (divorced 1995), one s. one d.; m. 2nd Corinne Susan Jane Green 1996; ed George Watson's Coll., Edinburgh, Univ. of Edinburgh; with Econs Dept, Univ. of Edinburgh 1967–70; with British Airways Pensions Fund 1970–77; Barclays Investment Man.'s Office 1977–81, Deputy Man. Dir Barclays Investment Man. Ltd 1981–86; Dir BZW Investment Man. 1986–88, Man. Dir 1988–91, Chair., CEO BZW Asset Man. Ltd 1991–94, Chair. (non-exec.) 1994–95, Deputy Chief Exec. Barclays de Zoete Wedd 1994–96, Acting CEO 1996; Chair. and CEO AXA Investment Managers 1997–2002; Chair. Smiths Group 2004–13; Chair. Royal Mail Group 2009–; Chair. Sage Group 2012–; Chair. MRC 2012–; Chair. Chance to Shine 2014–; mem. Bd of Dirs Stock Exchange 1991–98, Edinburgh Inca Investment Trust 1996–2002, Allied Domecq 1997–2004, AXA UK (fmrly Sun Life and Provincial Holdings) 1997–2002, Amersham 1997–2004, Scottish Power 2003–07; Chair. European Children's Trust 1999–2001, Fund Man. Asscn 1999–2001, Financial Services Practitioner Panel 2001–03, TNS 2005–08, ifs School of Finance 2006–10, EveryChild 2002–08; Pres. European Asset Man. Asscn 1999–2001. *Publications:* Economics of Technical Information Services (co-author) 1972. *Leisure interests:* Cricket, football, theatre, opera, deltiology. *Address:* Royal Mail Group, 100 Victoria Embankment, London, EC4Y 0HQ, England (office). *Telephone:* (20) 7449-8099 (office). *E-mail:* donald.brydon@royalmail.com (office).

BRYMER, Charles E. (Chuck), BA; American advertising executive; *Chairman, DDB Worldwide;* b. 30 July 1959, Louisville, Ky; s. of Robert L. Brymer and Natalie Brymer; m. Tracy Brymer; four c.; ed Coll. of Communications & Information, Univ. of Kentucky; worked at various TV stations and advertising agencies while at coll.; opened and ran BBDO's Houston office 1982–85; joined Interbrand Group (int. consultancy specializing in brands and branding) 1985, served as Founding Pres. of the UK co.'s US div., Interbrand acquired by Omnicom Group 1993, Pres. and CEO Interbrand 1994–2006, Pres. and CEO Omnicom-owned DDB Worldwide 2006–18, Chair. 2018–; helped create Businessweek's World's Most Valuable Brands feature; has advised US State Dept on the USA's int. image; mem. Bd Regal Entertainment Group, Ad Council 2007, Chamber of Commerce of the US; named one of Fortune Magazine's People to Watch 1986. *Publications:* Brands and Branding (co-author) 2004, The Nature of Marketing: Marketing to the Swarm as Well as the Herd 2009. *Address:* Roberts+Langer DDB, 437 Madison Avenue, 8th Floor, New York, NY 10022, USA (office). *Telephone:* (212) 415-2000 (office). *Fax:* (212) 415-3550 (office). *E-mail:* info@ddb.com (office). *Website:* www.ddb.com (office).

BRYN, Kåre; Norwegian diplomatist; b. 12 March 1944; m.; four c.; ed Norwegian School of Econs and Business Admin; Trainee, Ministry of Foreign Affairs 1969, Attaché/Second Sec., Embassy in London 1971–74, First Sec., Embassy in Belgrade 1974–76, Exec. Officer, Ministry of Foreign Affairs 1976–79, First Sec., later Counsellor, Perm. Mission of Norway, Geneva 1979–84, Head of Div., Ministry of Foreign Affairs 1984, Asst Dir-Gen. 1985–89, Dir-Gen. Dept for Natural Resources and Environmental Affairs 1989–99, Norwegian Rep. to Int. Whaling Comm. (IWC) 1995–99, Amb. and Perm. Rep. to EFTA and WTO, Geneva 1999–2003 (Chair. WTO Gen. Council 2000–01), Amb. to the Netherlands 2003–06; Sec.-Gen. EFTA 2006–12. *Address:* c/o European Free Trade Association, 9–11 rue de Varembé, 1211 Geneva 20, Switzerland.

BRYNGDAHL, Olof, Dr rer. nat; Swedish scientist and academic; *Professor, University of Duisburg-Essen;* b. 26 Sept. 1933, Stockholm; s. of Carl Olof Bryngdahl and Ingeborg M. Pihlgren; m. Margaretha Schraut 1959; ed Royal Inst. of Tech., Stockholm; Research Assoc., Inst. for Optical Research, Stockholm 1956–64; staff mem., Xerox Research Lab. Rochester, NY, USA 1964–65; Man. IBM Research Lab. San José, Calif. 1966–69; Sr Scientist, IBM Research Lab., Yorktown Heights NY 1970; Prin. Scientist, Xerox Research Lab., Palo Alto, Calif. 1970–77; Prof., Inst. d'Optique, Univ. of Paris 1975–76; Prof., Univ. of Duisburg-Essen, Germany 1977–; Fellow, Optical Soc. of America. *Publications:* more than 200 scientific articles; 14 patents in optics. *Address:* University of Duisburg-Essen, 45117 Essen, Universitätsstrasse 2, Germany (office). *Telephone:* (201) 1832562 (office). *E-mail:* olof.bryngdahl@uni-essen.de (office). *Website:* www.uni-due.de (office).

BRYNTSALOV, Vladimir Alekseyevich; Russian business executive; b. 23 Nov. 1946, Cherkessk; m. 1st; one d.; m. 2nd Natalya Bryntsalova; one s. one d.; ed Inst. of Construction and Eng; engineer, then Head Construction Dept in Stavropol 1970–80; expelled from CPSU for 'petty bourgeois inclination'; pvt. enterprise activities started late 1980s; f. co-operative Pchelka (Bee) 1987; bought stock shares of pharmaceutical factories, f. Co. Ferein 1992 (produces over one third of all medicaments in Russia), Hon. Pres. 1996–; mem. State Duma (Parl.) 1995–1999 (joined Our Home–Russia faction 1997); f. Russian Socialist Party 1998; re-elected as ind. cand. 1999; Deputy Chair. Yedinstvo i Otechestvo party; cand. for Presidency of Russia 1996. *Address:* Ferein, 117105 Moscow, Nagatinskaya str. 1, Russia. *Telephone:* (499) 611-13-20 (office); (495) 111-00-79 (office). *E-mail:* info@ferain.ru (office). *Website:* www.ferain.ru (office).

BRYSON, Bill, OBE, Hon. FRS; American writer; b. 8 Dec. 1951, Des Moines, Ia; s. of Bill Bryson Sr and Agnes Mary (née McGuire); m.; four c.; ed Drake Univ.; travelled to UK and worked as orderly in mental hosp. 1973; worked as journalist for The Times and the Independent; returned with his family to USA 1993; apptd to selection panel, Book of the Month Club 2001; Commr for English Heritage 2003–07; Chancellor Durham Univ. 2005–11; Pres. Campaign to Protect Rural England 2007–12; Hon. DCL (Durham) 2004; Kenneth B. Myer Award, Florey

Inst. of Neuroscience 2012. *Publications include:* Penguin Dictionary of Troublesome Words (re-printed as Bryson's Dictionary of Troublesome Words) 1985, The Lost Continent 1987, The Mother Tongue: English and How It Got That Way, Made in America 1994, Neither Here Nor There: Travels in Europe 1995, Notes From a Small Island 1995, A Walk in the Woods 1998, I'm a Stranger Here Myself (essays, aka Notes From a Big Country) 1999, In a Sunburned Country (aka Down Under) 2000, The Best American Travel Writing (ed.), African Diary 2002, A Short History of Nearly Everything (Aventis Prize 2004, Descartes Science Communication Prize 2005) 2003, The Life and Times of the Thunderbolt Kid (memoirs) 2006, Shakespeare: A Short Life (biog.) 2007, Bryson's Dictionary for Writers and Editors 2008, At Home: A Short History of Private Life 2011, One Summer: America, 1927 2013, The Road to Little Dribbling 2015. *Address:* The Marsh Agency, 50 Ablemarle Street, London, W1S 4BD, England (office). *Telephone:* (20) 7493-4361 (office). *Fax:* (20) 7495-8961 (office). *Website:* www.marsh-agency.co.uk (office); www.billbryson.co.uk.

BRYSON, John E., LLB, JD; American energy industry executive and government official; b. 24 July 1943; m. Louise Bryson; four d.; ed Stanford Univ., Yale Law School; Dir Edison International 1990–, Chair. and CEO 1990–99, Chair., Pres. and CEO 2000–, Dir Southern California Edison (subsidiary) 1990–99, 2003–, Chair. and CEO 1990–99, Chair. 2003–, Chair., Edison Mission Energy (subsidiary) 2000–02; Sec. of Commerce 2011–12; Distinguished Public Policy Scholar, Woodrow Wilson Int. Center for Scholars 2012–14; fmr mem. Bd of Dirs The Boeing Co., Pacific American Income Shares Inc., Western Asset Funds Inc., The Walt Disney Co., W. M. Keck Foundation; Trustee, California Inst. of Tech.; fmr Chair. Calif. Business Roundtable; fmr Trustee, Stanford Univ. *Address:* c/o Woodrow Wilson International Center for Scholars, Ronald Reagan Building and International Trade Center, One Woodrow Wilson Plaza, 1300 Pennsylvania Avenue NW, Washington, DC 20004-3027, USA. *E-mail:* john.bryson@wilsoncenter.org.

BU, Changsen, BSc, MSc; Chinese business executive and academic; *Chairman and CEO, Shandong Energy Group Company Ltd;* ed Shandong Coll. of Mining Tech., China Univ. of Mining and Tech.; worked as Section Chief of Geology and Survey Div., Taoyang Mine, Feicheng Mining Group, subsequently Deputy Div. Chief of Geology and Survey Div., Feicheng Mining Group, later Dir Liangbaosi Mine Preparation Office, then Man. of Taoyang Mine, of Guojiazhuang Mine, then Deputy Chief Engineer, Feicheng Mining Group, later Deputy Chief Econ. Man., then Asst to the Gen. Man., Deputy Gen. Man. Feicheng Mining Group; fmr Deputy Dir Coal Industry Bureau of Shandong Prov., mem. Party Cttee of Shandong Prov. Econ. and Information Tech. Comm. and Dir of Coal Industry Bureau of Shandong Prov.; Chair. and CEO Shandong Energy Group Co. Ltd 2011–; Adjunct Prof. and Doctoral Supervisor, China Univ. of Mining and Tech., Shandong Univ. of Science and Tech.; mem. Special Talent Project 2010–11. *Address:* Shandong Energy Group Co. Ltd, 10777 Jingshi Road, Jinan City 250014, Shandong Province, People's Republic of China (office). *Telephone:* (531) 66597812 (office); (531) 66597799 (office). *Fax:* (531) 66597700 (office). *E-mail:* web@snjt.com (office). *Website:* www.snjt.com (office).

BUAINAIN, Ghanem bin Fadhil al-; Bahraini politician; *Minister for Shura Council and Parliament Affairs;* mem. Majlis al-Nuab (Council of Reps) for Muharraq Eighth Constituency –2012; Minister of State for Foreign Affairs 2012–14; Minister for Shura Council and Parl. Affairs 2014–; Pres. Al-Asala Islamic Soc. *Address:* Minister for Shura Council and Parliament Affairs, c/o Prime Minister's Court, PO Box 1000, Government House, Government Road, Manama, Bahrain (office). *Telephone:* 17253361 (office). *Fax:* 17533033 (office).

BUARQUE DE HOLLANDA, Anna Maria, (Ana de Hollanda); Brazilian singer, songwriter and politician; b. 12 Aug. 1948, São Paulo; d. of Sérgio Buarque de Hollanda and Maria Amélia Alvim Buarque de Hollanda; ed Int. School of Theater of Latin America and the Caribbean, Cuba; stage debut aged 16 at Coll. of Rio Branco; Dir Centro Cultural São Paulo 1983–85; Sec. of Culture, City of Osasco 1986–88; musical tours throughout Brazil and Angola, Cuba, Uruguay 1988–2000; Dir Centro de Música da Funarte (Fundação Nacional de Artes) 2003–07; Minister of Culture 2011–12; fmr mem. Partido Comunista Brasileiro. *Recordings:* solo albums: Tão Simples 1995, Um Filme 2001, Só na Canção 2009. *Website:* www.anadehollanda.com.

BUBALO, Predrag, LLM, LLD; Serbian politician; b. 14 Oct. 1954, Vladicin Han; m.; one s. one d.; ed Faculty of Law, Univ. of Novi Sad; joined Livnica Kikinda (foundry co.) as Adviser to Gen. Man. 1977, Eng Man. 1981–90, Financial Man. 1991–94, Head, office in Beijing 1994–2000, Man. AUTO-KUCA (Livnica Kikinda subsidiary) 2000–02, Gen. Man. Livnica Kikinda 2002–04; Minister of Int. Econ. Relations March–Oct. 2004, Co-ordinator, Ministry of Economy July–Oct. 2004, Minister of the Economy 2004–06, of Trade and Services 2007–08; mem. Democratic Party of Serbia (DPS); included by Anti-Corruption Council of Serbia on a list of people facing criminal charges related to the privatization of the Port of Belgrade co. Sept. 2010, arrested on orders of the Prosecutor's Office for Organized Crime June 2013, went on trial July 2014, acquitted Dec. 2017.

BUBKA, Sergey Nazarovich; Ukrainian politician, sports official and fmr athlete; *Vice-President, Council, International Association of Athletics Federations;* b. 4 Dec. 1963, Voroshilovgrad (now Lugansk); s. of Nazar Bubka and Valentina Bubka; m. Lilya Tioutiounik 1983; two s.; ed Kiev State Inst.; fmr pole vaulter; turned professional, represented USSR 1981–91, Ukraine 1991–2001 (retd); set 17 world records outdoors and 18 indoors; cleared 6m or better in more than 44 competitions; first man to clear 6m feet both indoors and out 1991; holds current world outdoor record of 6.14m (20 feet $1^3/_4$ inches) set in Sestriere, Italy July 1994 and current world indoor record of 6.15m set in Donetsk, Ukraine Feb. 1993; six-time Int. Asscn of Athletics Feds (IAAF) world champion Helsinki 1983, Rome 1987, Tokyo 1991, Stuttgart 1993, Gothenburg 1995, Athens 1997; gold medal, Olympic Games, Seoul, South Korea 1988; mem. IOC Exec. Bd, IOC Evaluation Comm. for 2008, IOC Athletes' Comm. –2008, IAAF Council 2001– (Vice-Pres. 2011–), Bd Nat. Olympic Cttee of Ukraine (Pres. 2005–); Chair. IOC Athletes' Comm.; Pres. S. Bubka Sports Club; mem. Parl. (For United Ukraine, Regions of Ukraine faction) 2002–06; unsuccessful cand. for IOC Pres. 2013; mem. Champions for Peace club; Best Sportsman of the Soviet Union 1984, 1985, 1986, Prince of Asturias Award in Sports 1991, L'Equipe Sportsman of the Year 1997, Track and Field Best Pole Vaulter of the Last Half-Century, UNESCO Champion for Sport 2003, Panathlon Int. Flambeau d'Or 2005, Marca Leyenda 2005, inducted into IAAF Hall of Fame 2012. *Publication:* An Attempt is Reserved (in Russian) 1987. *Address:* Ukrainian National Olympic Committee, 39–41 Khoryva Street, Kiev 04071, Ukraine (office). *Telephone:* (44) 379-12-77 (office). *E-mail:* office@noc-ukr.org (office). *Website:* www.noc-ukr.org (office); www.iaaf.org/athletes/ukraine/sergey-bubka-365; www.sergeybubka.com.

BUCHACHENKO, Anatoly Leonidovich, MSc, PhD; Russian chemical physicist; *Professor of Chemistry and Head of Dynamics Department, Institute of Chemical Physics, Russian Academy of Sciences;* b. 7 Sept. 1935, Plesetsk; s. of L. P. Buchachenko and A. S. Buchachenko; m. Maya S. Buchachenka 1960; one s. one d.; ed Gorky Univ.; postgraduate, Jr, then Sr Scientific Asst 1958–68; Prof. of Chem., Inst. of Chemical Physics, USSR (now Russian) Acad. of Sciences 1970–, Vice-Dir 1989–94, Dir 1994–96, Head of Dynamics Dept 1996–; Prof. of Chem. and Head of Dept of Chemical Kinetics, Moscow State Univ. 1988–; Ed.-in-Chief, Russian Journal of Physical Chemistry, Focus on Physics; mem. Advisory Bd, Chemical Physics Letters, Journal of Physical Chemistry, Russian Chemical Reviews, Russian Chemical Bulletin, Russian Journal of Physical Chemistry, Mendeleev Communications; mem. USSR (now Russian) Acad. of Sciences 1987; State Prize 1977, Lenin Prize 1986, Voevodsky Award 1997, Nat. Prize for Educ. Activity 2002, Nat. Prize Triumph 2008. *Publications:* Stable Radicals 1965, Chemically Induced Electron and Nuclear Polarization (in Russian) 1974 (in Czech 1979), Spin Polarization and Magnetic Effects in Radical Reactions (co-author) 1984, Complexes of Radicals and Molecular Oxygen with Organic Molecules (in Russian) 1984, Chemical Physics of Aging and Stabilization of Polymers (with N. Emanuel) 1987, Chemical Generation and Reception of Radio- and Microwaves (co-author) 1994, Magnetic Isotope Effect in Chemistry and Biochemistry 2009; articles on the physical chemistry of free radicals, chemical reactions, spin chemistry, molecular ferromagnets. *Leisure interest:* wood architecture modelling. *Address:* N.N. Semenov Institute of Chemical Physics, Russian Academy of Sciences, 1 Academyya Semenova Prospect, Chernogolovka, Noginskyy Region, 142432 Moscow Oblast (office); Chemistry Department, Moscow State University, 119991 Moscow, Russia (office). *Telephone:* (495) 939-71-28 (ICP) (office); (495) 331-31-70 (home). *Fax:* (496) 515-54-20 (MSU) (office). *E-mail:* abuchach@chph.ras.ru (office). *Website:* www.icp.ac.ru (office); www.chem.msu.ru/eng/people/buchach.html (office).

BUCHAN, Richard Duke, III, BA, MBA; American financier, business executive and diplomatist; *Ambassador to Spain;* b. 3 July 1963, Henderson, N Carolina; m. Hannah Flournoy; two s. one d.; ed Univ. of N Carolina at Chapel Hill, Harvard Business School, Univ. of Seville; started his career in corp. finance with NCNB National Bank, N Carolina and Florida; worked for Smith Barney & Co. and NationsBank; Vice Pres., Investment Banking, Global Financial Institutions Group, Merrill Lynch 1992–97; Man. Dir Maverick Capital Ltd (MCL Corpn, equity fund), Dallas, Texas and New York 1997–2001; mem. Bd of Dirs Scottish Annuity and Life 1998–2000; Founder and CEO, Hunter Global Investors LP (private investment management firm) 2001–; Amb. to Spain 2017–; Vice Chair, Univ. of N Carolina at Chapel Hill Arts and Sciences Foundation Bd of Dirs; Republican. *Address:* Embassy of the USA, Calle de Serrano, 75, 28006 Madrid, Spain (office). *Telephone:* 91-587-2200 (office). *Fax:* 91-587-2303 (office). *Website:* es.usembassy.gov (office).

BUCHANAN, Isobel Wilson, Dip.RSAMD; British singer (soprano); b. 15 March 1954, Glasgow, Scotland; d. of Stewart Buchanan and Mary Buchanan; m. Jonathan Stephen Geoffrey King (actor Jonathan Hyde) 1980; two d.; ed Cumbernauld Comprehensive High School and Royal Scottish Acad. of Music and Drama; professional debut in Sydney, Australia with Richard Bonynge and Joan Sutherland 1976–78; British debut, Glyndebourne 1978; US and German debuts 1979; Vienna Staatsoper debut 1979; ENO debut 1985, Paris Opera debut 1986; now freelance artist working with all major opera cos and orchestras and giving recitals; teaches and regularly gives master-classes and acts as adjudicator in music festivals and competitions; returned to the concert stage 2015. *Recordings:* Beethoven's Ninth Symphony, Werther, Mozart Arias and Duets, Mahler's 2nd Symphony, Handel's Rodelinda, Laudate pueri Dominum, Bellini's La Sonnambula, Bizet's Carmen, Vivaldi's Gloria. *Leisure interests:* cooking, reading, gardening, yoga, knitting. *E-mail:* isobel@totalfiasco.co.uk (office).

BUCHANAN, J. Robert, MD; American medical scientist and academic; *Professor of Medicine, School of Medicine, Harvard University;* b. 8 March 1928, Newark, NJ; m. Susan Carver; one s. one d.; ed Amherst Coll. and Cornell Univ. Medical School; Intern, then Asst Resident Physician, New York Hosp. 1954–58, Research Fellow in Medicine 1956–57; Research Fellow in Endocrinology, Cornell Univ. Medical Coll., New York 1960–61; WHO Travelling Fellow 1963; Instructor in Medicine, Cornell Univ. Medical Coll. 1961–63, Asst Prof. 1963–67, Asst to Chair. Dept of Medicine 1964–65, Assoc. Dean 1965–69, Clinical Assoc. Prof. 1967–69, Assoc. Prof. 1969–71, Prof. 1971–76, Acting Dean, then Dean 1969–76; Prof. of Medicine, Univ. of Chicago, Ill. 1977–82; Assoc. Dean, Pritzker School of Medicine, Chicago 1978–82; Prof. of Medicine, Harvard Medical School, Boston, Mass. 1982–; Gen. Dir, Mass. Gen. Hosp. 1982–94; Gen. Dir Emer. 1994–; physician at hosps in New York, Chicago and Boston 1956–; mem. Admin. Bd, Council of Teaching Hosps 1984–89, mem. Exec. Council 1985–; Dir Mass. Div., American Cancer Soc. 1984–; Bd of Dirs Bank of New England 1986–91, AMI Holdings 1991–, Exec. Cttee Mass. Hosp. Asscn 1987– (Chair. 1990–91), Charles River Labs; Chair. Council of Teaching Hosps, Asscn of American Medical Colls 1988–89; mem. NAS Cttee to review Inst. of Medicine, American Cancer Soc., Mass. Div., Soc. of Medical Admins; Chair. Educ. Comm. for Foreign Medical Grads 1994–; Fellow, American Coll. of Physicians; Founding Trustee, Aga Khan Univ.; Hon. ScD (Amherst Coll.); Hon. LHD (Rush Univ.); Hon. MD (Peking Union Medical Coll., Beijing, China). *Publications:* numerous papers and articles in journals. *Leisure interests:* boating, gardening. *Address:* 5 Chestnut Hill Road, POB 669, Killingworth, CT 06419, USA (office). *Telephone:* (860) 663-2637 (home). *Fax:* (860) 663-3058 (home). *E-mail:* jrobertbuchan@aol.com (home). *Website:* hms.harvard.edu/hms/home.asp (office).

BUCHANAN, Patrick (Pat) Joseph, MS; American journalist and fmr government official; b. 2 Nov. 1938, Washington, DC; s. of William Buchanan and Catherine Crum; m. Shelley A. Scarney 1971; ed Georgetown and Columbia Univs;

editorial writer, St Louis Globe Democrat 1962–64, asst editorial writer 1964–66; Exec. Asst to Richard Nixon 1966–69; Special Asst to Pres. Nixon 1969–73; consultant to Pres. Nixon and Pres. Ford 1973–74; Asst to Pres., Dir of Communications, White House, Washington, DC 1985–87; syndicated columnist, political commentator, New York Times special features 1975–78, Chicago Tribune-New York News Syndicate 1978–85, Tribune Media Services 1987–91, 1993–95; commentator, NBC Radio Network 1978–82; co-host Crossfire (TV Show) Cable News Network 1982–85, 1987–91, 1993–95, 1997; Ed. The American Conservative; Ed.-in-Chief PJB—From the Right (newsletter) 1990–91; moderator, Capital Gang TV show CNN 1988–92; Chair. The American Cause 1993–95, 1997–, Pat Buchanan & Co., Mutual Broadcasting System 1993–95; currently political analyst, MSNBC; unsuccessful cand. for Republican Presidential nomination 1992, 1996; Republican. *Publications include:* The New Majority 1973, Conservative Votes, Liberal Victories 1975, Right from the Beginning 1988, Barry Goldwater, The Conscience of A Conservative 1990, The Great Betrayal 1998, A Republic, not an Empire 2000, State of Emergency 2007, Day of Reckoning 2008, Churchill, Hitler, and The Unnecessary War: How Britain Lost Its Empire and the West Lost the World 2009, Suicide of a Superpower: Will America Survive to 2025? 2011, The Greatest Comeback: How Richard Nixon Rose from Defeat to Create the New Majority 2014. *Address:* Linda Muller, c/o Buchanan.org, 707 West Main Street, Smethport, PA 16749; 1017 Savile Lane, McLean, VA 22101, USA (home). *E-mail:* LindaMuller@buchanan.org. *Website:* buchanan.org/blog.

BUCHANAN, Robin William Turnbull, MBA, FCA, FRSA; American/British business executive and academic administrator; *Chairman, PageGroup (Michael Page International plc);* b. 2 April 1952; s. of Iain Buchanan and Gillian Pamela Buchanan (née Hughes-Hallett); m. Diana Tei Tanaka 1986; one s. one d.; ed Harvard Business School (Baker Scholar); with Mann Judd Landau (now Deloitte & Touche) 1970–77; with American Express Int. Banking Corpn 1979–82; with Bain & Co. Inc. 1982–, Bain Capital 1982–84, Man. Partner, London 1990–96, Sr Partner, London 1996–2007, Sr Adviser 2007–; Dean, then Pres. London Business School 2007–09; Chair. PageGroup (Michael Page International plc) 2011–; Dir (non-exec.), Liberty International plc 1997–2008, Shire plc (fmrly Shire Pharmaceuticals Group plc) 2003–08, Schroders plc 2010–; mem. Trilateral Comm., Northern Meeting, Highland Soc., Professional Standards Advisory Bd, Inst. of Dirs, Editorial Bd European Business Journal; mem. Advisory Council, Prince's Trust, Int. Advisory Council, Recipco; Fellow, Salzburg Seminar, Liveryman Worshipful Co. of Ironmongers. *Address:* PageGroup (Michael Page International plc), Page House, 1 Dashwood Lang Road, The Bourne Business Park, Addlestone, Weybridge, Surrey, KT15 2QW, England (office). *Telephone:* (20) 7831-2000 (office). *E-mail:* info@page.com (office). *Website:* www.page.com (office).

BÜCHELE, Wolfgang, Dr rer. nat; German chemist and business executive; *Chairman of the Executive Board and CEO, Linde AG;* b. 11 Aug. 1959, Geislingen; ed Univ. of Ulm; Research Chemist for industrial catalysts, BASF AG 1987–90, Research Group Head (industrial catalysts) 1990–93, Head of Regional Marketing Catalysts Asia, Hong Kong 1993–97, Head of Global Marketing Cosmetic Raw Materials 1997–99, Head of Business Man. Fine Chemicals Europe 1999–2001, Pres. Eastern Europe, Africa, West Asia Regional Div. 2001–03, Pres. Performance Chemicals Supervisory Bd and Chair. BASF Drucksysteme GmbH, Stuttgart 2003–05, mem. Site Man. Cttee, Ludwigshafen site 2003–07, Pres., Fine Chemicals 2005–07, apptd to Man. Bd 2007, responsibility for oil and gas, Europe Region as well as Global Procurement and Logistics, The Blackstone Group LLP 2008, Project Adviser (including minority interest in Evonik AG), Permira Beteiligungsberatung GmbH, Frankfurt 2008, Sr Adviser, BorsodChem Zrt., Kazincbarcika, Hungary 2008–11, CEO 2008–09, Chair. and CEO 2009–11, mem. Bd of Dirs Kemira Oyj., Helsinki, Finland 2009–11, CEO 2011, Adviser to the Chair. and mem. Bd of Dirs 2012–, CEO 2012–14; Chair. Exec. Bd and CEO Linde AG 2014–; mem. Supervisory Bd Merck KGaA 2009–, Chair. 2014–; mem. Baden-Badener Unternehmergespräche, Rotary International. *Address:* Linde AG, Head Office, Klosterhof Strasse 1, 80331 Munich, Germany (office). *Telephone:* (89) 35757-01 (office). *Fax:* (89) 35757-1075 (office). *E-mail:* info@the-linde-group.com (office). *Website:* www.the-linde-group.com (office).

BÜCHNER, Ton, MSc (CivilEng), MBA; Dutch engineer and business executive; b. 1965; ed Delft Univ. of Tech., Int. Inst. for Man. Devt, Switzerland, Stanford Univ. Exec. Program, USA; early career spent in oil and gas construction industry involving roles at Allseas Engineering in Europe and AkerKvaerner in SE Asia 1987–90; Project Design Engineer and Project Man., offshore pipelines, R.J. Brown and Assoc. (Far East) 1990–92, Project Man. 1992–94; Strategic Devt Man., Sulzer Man. 1994–96, Chief Rep. and Gen. Man. Compressors 1996–99, Div. Pres. Exec. Cttee 1999–2007, Pres. and CEO Sulzer Corpn 2007–12; Chair. Bd of Man. and Exec. Cttee and CEO Akzo Nobel NV 2012–17.

BUCHWALD, Christoph; German publishing executive; *Publisher, Uitgeverij Cossee;* b. 30 Nov. 1951, Tübingen; ed Freie Universität, Berlin, Technische Universität, Berlin; fmrly Ed. Hanser, Munich; fmrly Publr Luchterhand Literaturverlag; fmrly with Suhrkamp Verlag KG, Frankfurt; Co-founder and Publr Uitgeverij Cossee, Amsterdam; Kt, Orde van Oranje-Nassau (Netherlands) 2011. *Address:* Uitgeverij Cossee, Kerkstraat 361, 1017 HW Amsterdam, Netherlands (office). *Telephone:* (20) 5289911 (office). *Fax:* (20) 5289912 (office). *E-mail:* buchwald@cossee.com (home). *Website:* www.uitgeverijcossee.nl (office).

BUCHWALD, Stephen L., ScB, PhD; American chemist and academic; *Camille Dreyfus Professor of Chemistry, Massachusetts Institute of Technology;* b. 1955, Bloomington, Ind.; ed Brown, Columbia and Harvard Univs; NSF Predoctoral Fellow, Harvard Univ. 1977–82; Myron A. Bantrell Postdoctoral Fellow, California Inst. of Tech. 1982–84; Asst Prof. of Chem., MIT 1984–89, Assoc. Prof. 1989–93, Prof. 1993–, Camille Dreyfus Prof. 1997–, Assoc. Head Chemistry Dept 2015–; Assoc. Ed. Advanced Synthesis and Catalysis and Chemical Science; consultant to several cos; mem. NAS 2008; mem. National Acad. of Science 2008; Fellow, American Acad. of Arts and Sciences 2000; Dr hc (Univ. of South Florida); Harold Edgerton Faculty Achievement Award, MIT, ACS Arthur C. Cope Scholar Award, ACS Award in Organometallic Chem. 2000, NIH MERIT Award, Bristol-Myers Squibb Distinguished Achievement Award 2005, CAS Science Spotlight Award 2005, ACS Award for Creative Work in Synthetic Organic Chem. 2006, Siegfried Medal Award in Chemical Methods which Impact Process Chem. 2006, Gustavus J. Esselen Award for Chem. in the Public Interest 2010, ACS Arthur C. Cope Award 2013, Linus Pauling Medal 2014, William H. Nichols Medal 2016, Roger Adams Award 2018. *Publications:* more than 390 papers in professional journals and 43 issued patents. *Address:* Massachusetts Institute of Technology, Room 18-490, 77 Massachusetts Avenue, Cambridge, MA 02139, USA (office). *Telephone:* (617) 253-1885 (office). *Fax:* (617) 253-3297 (office). *E-mail:* sbuchwal@mit.edu (office). *Website:* web.mit.edu/chemistry/buchwald (office).

BUCK, Linda B., PhD; American physiologist and academic; *Affiliate Professor of Physiology and Biophysics, University of Washington;* ed Univ. of Wash., Univ. of Tex. Southwestern Medical Center, Dallas; Postdoctoral Fellow, Columbia Univ. Coll. of Physicians and Surgeons 1980–84; Assoc., Howard Hughes Medical Inst., Columbia Univ. 1984–91; Asst Prof., Dept of Neurobiology, Harvard Medical School 1991–96, Assoc. Prof. 1996–2001, Prof. 2001–02; Asst Investigator Howard Hughes Medical Inst. (HHMI) 1994–97, Assoc. Investigator, 1997–2000, Full Investigator 2001–; Affiliate Prof. of Physiology and Biophysics, Univ. of Wash. 2003–; Full Mem. Basic Sciences Div., Fred Hutchinson Cancer Research Center 2002–; Fellow, AAAS, American Acad. of Arts and Sciences; mem. NAS; mem. Bd of Dirs International Flavors and Fragrances Inc. 2007–; Lewis S. Rosenstiel Award, Unilever Science Award, Perl/UNC Neuroscience Prize, Gairdner Foundation Int. Award, Nobel Prize in Physiology or Medicine (jtly with Richard Axel) 2004. *Publications:* numerous articles in professional publs; books include The Human Olfactory Receptor Gene Family (co-author) 2004, The Mouse Olfactory Receptor Gene Family (co-author) 2004. *Address:* Fred Hutchinson Cancer Research Center, 1100 Fairview Avenue North, POB 19024, Seattle, WA 98109-1024 (office); Howard Hughes Medical Institute, 4000 Jones Bridge Road, Chevy Chase, MD, 20815-689, USA (office). *Telephone:* (206) 667-6316 (office); (301) 215-8500 (office). *Fax:* (206) 667-1031 (office). *E-mail:* lbuck@fhcrc.org (office); webmaster@hhmi.org (office). *Website:* www.fhcrc.org (office); www.hhmi.org (office).

BUCKINGHAM, (Amyand) David, CBE, FRS, FRSC, FInstP, FRACI; Australian/British chemist and academic; *Professor Emeritus of Chemistry, University of Cambridge;* b. 28 Jan. 1930, Sydney, NSW; s. of Reginald Joslin Buckingham and Florence Grace Buckingham; m. Jillian Bowles 1965; one. s. two d.; ed Barker Coll., Hornsby, NSW, Univ. of Sydney, Corpus Christi Coll., Cambridge; Lecturer, then Student and Tutor, Christ Church, Univ. of Oxford 1955–65, Univ. Lecturer in Inorganic Chem. 1958–65; Prof. of Theoretical Chem., Univ. of Bristol 1965–69; Prof. of Chem., Univ. of Cambridge 1969–97, Fellow, Pembroke Coll., Cambridge 1970–97, Prof. Emer. 1997–, Hon. Fellow 2005–; Pres. Faraday Div. of RSC 1987–89, Cambridge Univ. Cricket Club 1990–2009; mem. Council Royal Soc. 1999–2001; mem. ACS; Corresp. mem. Australian Acad. of Science; Foreign mem. American Acad. of Arts and Sciences, Royal Swedish Acad. of Sciences; Foreign Assoc., NAS; Fellow, Royal Australian Chemical Inst., American Physical Soc., Optical Soc. of America; Dr hc (Université de Nancy I) 1979; Hon. DSc (Sydney) 1993, (Antwerp) 2004; Harrie Massey Medal, Inst. of Physics 1995, Hughes Medal, Royal Soc. 1996, Faraday Medal, RSC 1998, Townes Medal, Optical Soc. of America 2001, Inaugural Ahmed Zewail Prize 2007. *Achievement:* Cricket Blue, Univ. of Sydney 1953. *Publications:* The Laws and Applications of Thermodynamics 1964, Organic Liquids: Structure, Dynamics and Chemical Properties 1978, The Principles of Molecular Recognition 1993; more than 330 papers in scientific journals. *Leisure interests:* cricket, woodwork, travel, walking. *Address:* Department of Chemistry, University of Cambridge, Cambridge, CB2 1EW (office); Crossways, 23 The Avenue, Newmarket, Cambs., CB8 9AA, England (home). *Telephone:* (1223) 336372 (office); (1638) 663799 (home). *Fax:* (1223) 336362 (office). *E-mail:* adb1000@cam.ac.uk (office). *Website:* www.ch.cam.ac.uk/person/adb1000 (office).

BUCKLAND, David John; British artist, theatre director and filmmaker; *Director, Cape Farewell;* b. 15 June 1949, London, England; s. of Denis Buckland and Valarie Buckland; partner Siobhan Davies 1978; one s. one d.; ed Dorchester Secondary Modern School, Dorset, Hardye's Grammar School, Dorchester, Deep River High School, Ottawa and London Coll. of Printing; has participated in group exhbns and work appears in public collections in London, New York, Chicago, Los Angeles, Paris etc.; Artistic Dir Siobhan Davies Dance Co.; Lecturer, RCA, London Coll. of Printing, Chicago Art Inst.; 21 set and costume designs for dance, including Rambert Dance Co., Siobhan Davies Dance Co., English Nat. Ballet and work for TV; Northern Arts Fellow 1972–73; Kodak Bursary 1978; Founder and Dir Cape Farewell environmental project 2000–; three commissions from MasterCard, Vanguard Insurance and Royal Caribbean completed; Minn. First Bank Award 1988–90. *Leisure interests:* multi-hull sailor, arts, theatre, travel, hill walking. *Address:* Cape Farewell, The Science Museum's Dana Centre, 165 Queen's Gate, South Kensington, London, SW7 5HD, England (office). *Telephone:* (20) 7620-6235 (office). *Fax:* (20) 7401-8231 (office). *E-mail:* davidbuckland@capefarewell.com (office). *Website:* www.capefarewell.com (office).

BUCKLAND, Robert James, QC; British barrister and politician; *Solicitor-General for England and Wales;* b. 22 Sept. 1968, Llanelli, Carmarthenshire, Wales; m. Sian Buckland 1997; two c. (twins); ed St Michael's School, Llanelli, Hatfield Coll., Durham, Inns of Court School of Law; Sec. Junior Common Room and Pres. Union Soc., Hatfield Coll.; called to the Bar at Inner Temple 1991; returned to practise in Wales, most recently as mem. Apex Chambers, Cardiff; door tenant, 23 Essex Street Chambers, London; Recorder of the Crown Court, sitting on the Midland Circuit 2009–10; mem. Dyfed Co. Council 1993–96; unsuccessful Conservative Party cand. for Islwyn constituency by-election 1995, for South Swindon 2005; MP (Conservative) for South Swindon 2010–, mem. Justice Select Cttee 2012–, Chair. All Party Group on Autism; Solicitor-Gen. for England and Wales 2014–; elected Jt Sec. 1922 Backbench Cttee 2012; Chair. Conservative Human Rights Comm.; prizewinner for Advocacy, Inns of Court School of Law. *Leisure interests:* music, wine, political history, watching rugby and cricket. *Address:* Solicitor-General's Office, 20 Victoria Street, London, SW1H 0NF (office); House of Commons, Westminster, London, SW1A 0AA, England (office). *Telephone:* (20) 7271-2406 (Solicitor-Gen.'s Office) (office); (20) 7219-7168 (Westminster) (office). *Fax:* (20) 7271-2429 (Solicitor-Gen.'s Office) (office); (20) 7219-4849 (Westminster) (office). *E-mail:* robert.buckland.mp@parliament.uk (office). *Website:* www.gov.uk/government/organisations/attorney-generals-office (office); www.parliament.uk/biographies/commons/mr-robert-buckland/4106 (office); www.robertbuckland.co.uk.

BUCKLEY, Sir George William, Kt, BSc, PhD; British business executive; *Chairman, Arle Capital Partners Limited;* b. 23 Feb. 1947; ed Univs of Southampton and Huddersfield; fmr Man. Dir Cen. Services Div., British Railways Bd, UK; fmr Pres. Electric Motors Div. and Automotive and Precision Motors Div., Emerson Electric Co., St Louis, Mo., USA; joined Brunswick Corpn 1997, Chair. and CEO 2000–05; Chair., Pres. and CEO 3M Company 2005–12; Chair. Arle Capital Partners Ltd 2012–; Chair. Expro International; Chair. (non-exec.) Smiths Group plc 2013–; Dir (non-exec.) Technogym; mem. Bd of Dirs, Stanley Black & Decker 2010–, Archer Daniels Midland 2008–13, PepsiCo 2012–, Hitachi 2012–, Technogym SpA 2012–; Hon. DSc (Huddersfield). *Address:* Arle Capital Partners Ltd, 12 Charles II Street, London, SW1Y 4QU, England (office). *Telephone:* (20) 7979-0000 (office). *E-mail:* info@arle.com (office). *Website:* www.arle.com (office).

BUCKLEY, James Lane, BA, LLB; American fmr politician and judge (retd); b. 9 March 1923, New York; s. of William F. Buckley and Aloise Steiner Buckley; brother of William F. Buckley, Jr; m. Ann F. Cooley 1953; five s. one d.; ed Yale Univ.; served in USN 1943–46; Senator from New York 1971–77; Under-Sec. of State for Security Assistance 1981–82; Pres. Radio Free Europe–Radio Liberty 1982–85; Circuit Judge, US Court of Appeals, DC Circuit 1985–2001, then Sr Judge, retd 2001; Co-Chair. US Del. to UN Conf. on Environment, Nairobi 1982; Chair. US Del. to UN Conf. on Population, Mexico City 1984; Republican. *Publications:* If Men Were Angels 1975, Gleanings from an Unplanned Life 2006, Freedom at Risk 2010. *Leisure interests:* natural history, American history. *Address:* PO Box 597, Sharon, CT 06069 (office); 28 Great Elm Drive, Sharon, CT 06069, USA (home). *Telephone:* (860) 364-2207 (home).

BUCKLEY, Michael, MA, LPh, MCSI; Irish banker; b. Cork; m. Anne Buckley; fmr stockbroker and civil servant in Ireland and EU; joined Allied Irish Bank PLC (AIB) 1991, Exec. Dir 1995–2001, Man. Dir Capital Markets Div. 1994–99, Head Polish Div. 1999–2001, Group Chief Exec. 2001–05; Chair. DCC PLC 2008–14; Adjunct Prof. and Chair. Advisory Bd, Dept of Econs, Nat. Univ. of Ireland, Univ. Coll. Cork; Chair. Irish Chamber Orchestra; Dir M&T Bank Corpn, UK Asset Resolution Ltd. *Address:* c/o DCC House, Brewery Road, Stillorgan, Blackrock, Co. Dublin, Ireland.

BUCKLEY, Stephen, MFA; British artist and university professor (retd); *Professor Emeritus, University of Reading;* b. 5 April 1944, Leicester; s. of Nancy Throsby and Leslie Buckley; m. Stephanie James 1973 (deceased 2017); one s. one d.; ed Durham Univ. (King's Coll., Newcastle-upon-Tyne), Univ. of Reading; taught at Canterbury Coll. of Art 1969, Leeds Coll. of Art 1970, Chelsea School of Art 1971–80; Artist in Residence, King's Coll., Cambridge 1972–74; Prof. of Fine Art, Univ. of Reading 1994–2009, currently Prof. Emer.; worked with Rambert Dance Co., London 1987–88; works in public collections in Chile, Sweden, UK, Venezuela, USA, NZ, Australia; comms include Neal Street Restaurant 1972, mural painting for Penguin Books 1972, Leith's Restaurant 1973; included in over 45 public collections world-wide; prizewinner, John Moores Exhbn 1974, 1985, Chichester Nat. Art Exhbn 1975, Tolly-Cobbold Exhbn 1977. *E-mail:* contact@stephenbuckley.com (office). *Website:* www.stephenbuckley.com.

BUČKOVSKI, Vlado, MA, PhD; Macedonian politician; b. 2 Dec. 1962, Skopje; ed Univ. of Skopje; expert legal collaborator for Parl. 1987–88; Jr Teaching Asst of Roman Law, Univ. of Skopje 1988–91, Sr Teaching Asst 1992–99, Docent 1999–, Assoc. Prof., Faculty of Law 2004–; mem. State Election Comm. 1998–2000; Party Spokesman, Socijaldemokratski Sojuz na Makedonije (SDSM—Social Democratic Alliance of Macedonia) 1999–2001, Vice-Pres. SDSM 1999–2004, Chair. 2004–06; Chair. Council of Skopje 2000–01; Minister of Defence May–Nov. 2001, Oct. 2002–04; Prime Minister of Fmr Yugoslav Repub. of Macedonia 2004–06; found guilty of abuse of power while serving as defence minister during an armed conflict in 2001 and sentenced to three and a half years in jail 2008. *Publications include:* academic papers on public law.

BUCKSTEIN, Mark Aaron, BS, JD; American lawyer, mediator and arbitrator; *President, Professional Dispute Resolutions, Inc.;* b. 1 July 1939, New York, NY; s. of Henry Buckstein and Minnie Buckstein; m. Rochelle J. Buchman 1960; one s. one d.; ed New York Univ. Law School and City Coll. of New York; with various New York law firms 1963–69; Sr Partner, Baer, Marks & Upham (law firm), New York 1969–86; Special Prof. of Law, Hofstra Univ. School of Law 1980–93; Adjunct Prof. of Law, Rutgers Univ. Law School 1993–96; Florida Adjunct Prof., Florida Atlantic Univ. 2004–07; Sr Vice-Pres., Gen. Counsel and mem. Bd of Dirs Trans World Airlines Inc. 1986–92; Exec. Vice-Pres., Gen. Counsel, GAF Corpn and International Speciality Products, Inc., NJ 1993–96; Counsel, Greenberg, Traurig, Fort Lauderdale, Fla 1996–99; Pres. Professional Dispute Resolutions, Inc., Boca Raton, Fla 1999–; Dir, Bayswater Realty and Capital Corpn, Travel Channel Inc.; mem. American Arbitration Assn 1970– (Exec. Vice-Pres. and Pres.-Designate 1992–93); mem. FINRA Dispute Resolution (fmrly NASD Regulation) 1996–. *Leisure interests:* tennis, puzzles, reading, music. *Address:* Professional Dispute Resolutions, Inc., 2424 North Federal Highway, Suite 150, Boca Raton, FL 33432-2803 (office); 5832 Waterford, Boca Raton, FL 33496, USA (home). *Telephone:* (561) 417-6602 (office); (561) 994-6067 (home). *Fax:* (561) 417-6604 (office); mabresolve@aol.com (office). *Website:* www.professionaldisputeresolutions.com (office).

BUCYANAYANDI, Hon. Tress, MSc; Ugandan agriculturalist and politician; *Minister of Agriculture, Animal Industry and Fisheries;* b. 1 Jan. 1938, Kisoro; m.; ed Bukalasa Agricultural Coll., Univ. of West Virginia and Univ. of Wisconsin-Madison, USA; Dist Agricultural Officer, Kabale and Masaka 1962–69, then Area Extension Adviser and Deputy Regional Agricultural Officer, Buganda; Gen. Man. Kinyara Sugar Works 1972–76; Asst Commr for Agric. 1982–87, Deputy Commr for Agric. 1988–91; Man. Dir Uganda Coffee Devt Authority 1993–2000; Farmer and Consultant on Agric. 2001–05; Dir of Agric., Entebbe HQ 1990–92; MP (Nat. Resistance Movt) for Bufumbira South; Minister of Agric., Animal Industry and Fisheries 2011–; mem. Nat. Resistance Movt. *Address:* Ministry of Agriculture, Animal Industry and Fisheries, PO Box 102, Entebbe (office); PO Box 77, Kisoro, Uganda (office). *Telephone:* (41) 4320987 (office); 77-2358186 (mobile). *Fax:* (41) 4321255 (office). *E-mail:* tbucyanayandi@parliament.go.ug (office); mosagr@hotmail.com (office). *Website:* www.agriculture.go.ug (office).

BUDAKIAN, Raffi Ohannes, BS, MS, PhD; American physicist and academic; *Associate Professor of Physics, University of Illinois at Urbana-Champaign;* b. 22 Aug. 1969, Istanbul, Turkey; s. of Sirahuys Budakian and Nazar Budak; m. Adrienne Lo; one s. one d.; ed Univ. of California, Los Angeles; fmr Researcher, Physics Dept, UCLA; currently Assoc. Prof. of Physics, Univ. of Illinois at Urbana-Champaign; Visiting Scientist, IBM Almaden Research Center, San Jose, Calif. 2002–05; Edwin Pauly Merit Fellowship, UCLA 1994–98, E. Lee Kinsey Award in Physics, UCLA 1994, IBM Research Div. Award for Single Spin Detection 2004, World Tech. Award in Materials, The World Tech. Network (co-recipient) 2005. *Achievements include:* part of team that made first demonstrations of magnetic resonance force microscopy (MRFM) 1992, work reached key milestone with manipulation and detection of individual electron spin 2004. *Publications:* numerous scientific papers in professional journals on experimental condensed matter physics, magnetic resonance force microscopy, ultra-sensitive force/displacement detection, design and fabrication of micro- and nanomechanical devices. *Address:* 106 Seitz Materials Research Lab, Department of Physics, University of Illinois at Urbana-Champaign, 1110 West Green Street, Urbana, IL 61801-3080, USA (office). *Telephone:* (217) 333-3065 (office). *Fax:* (217) 244-8544 (office). *E-mail:* budakian@illinois.edu (office). *Website:* physics.illinois.edu/people/profile.asp?budakian (office).

BUDD, Sir Alan Peter, Kt, GBE, BSc (Econ), PhD; British economist and academic; *Member of Council, Institute for Fiscal Studies;* b. 16 Nov. 1937, Kent, England; s. of Ernest Budd and Elsie Budd; m. Susan Millott 1964; three s.; ed Oundle School, London School of Econs, Univ. of Cambridge; Lecturer in Econs, Univ. of Southampton 1966–69; Ford Foundation Visiting Prof., Carnegie-Mellon Univ., USA 1969–70; Sr Econ. Adviser, HM Treasury 1970–74, Chief Econ. Adviser to HM Treasury 1991–97; Sr Research Fellow, London Business School 1974–81, Prof. of Econs 1981–88, Fellow 1997; Econ. Adviser, Barclays Bank 1988–91; Provost, The Queen's Coll., Oxford 1999–2008; Chair. Tax Law Review Cttee, Inst. for Fiscal Studies 2002–12, mem. Council; Chair. UK Office for Budget Responsibility May–Aug. 2010; mem. Bank of England Monetary Policy Cttee 1997–99; Visiting Prof., Univ. of New South Wales, Australia 1983; Grocers' Co. Scholarship; Leverhulme Undergraduate Scholarship; Chair. Gambling Review Body 2000–01; Gov. Nat. Inst. of Econ. and Social Research 1998–; Chair. (non-exec.) Oxford Biosensors Ltd 2001–02; Hon. Fellow, The Queen's Coll., Oxford; Hon. DSc (Salford). *Publication:* Politics of Economic Planning 1978. *Leisure interests:* music, gardening, reading. *Address:* Queen's College, Oxford, OX1 4AW, England (office). *Website:* www.ifs.org.uk (office).

BUDD, Sir Colin Richard, Kt, KCMG, BA; British diplomatist (retd); b. 31 Aug. 1945, Harpenden, Herts., England; s. of B. W. Budd, QC and M. A. Budd (née Burgin); m. Agnes Smit; one s. one d.; ed Univ. of Cambridge; joined Diplomatic Service 1967, overseas assignments in Warsaw, Islamabad, Bonn and Brussels, Head of Political Section, Embassy in The Hague 1980–84, various positions in European Div., FCO, Deputy Sec., Cabinet Office 1996–97, Deputy Under-Sec. of State and Dir of EU and Econ. Affairs 1997–2001, Amb. to the Netherlands 2001–05; Commr, Comm. for Racial Equality 2006–07; Lay mem. QC Selection Panel 2009–13; mem. Prime Minister's Advisory Cttee on Business Appointments 2010–15. *Telephone:* (20) 7223-7211 (home). *E-mail:* acbudd@hotmail.com (office).

BUDIMIR, Gen. (retd) Živko; Bosnia and Herzegovina politician and army officer (retd); b. 20 Nov. 1962, Vir, nr Posušje, Herzegovina; m. Darija Kuna; two s. one d.; ed Aeronautical Tech. Mil. Coll., Rajlovac, War Coll. of Armed Forces of Repub. of Croatia 'Ban Josip Jelačić'; mem. League of Communists of Yugoslavia 1979–84; mem. Yugoslav People's Army 1984–86; long career in army, positions included Bn Commdr, Logistics Adviser, Hrvatsko vijeće obrane (HVO, Croatian Defence Council), Deputy Commdr, Jt HQ of Fed. Army following Washington Agreement, Commdr-in-Chief HVO following Dayton Agreement; elected mem. City Council of Mostar 2008; Pres. Fed. of Bosnia and Herzegovina March 2011–15 (suspended April–May 2013); mem. Croatian Party of Rights (Hrvatska stranka prava) 2006–13; f. Party of Justice and Trust 2013. *Address:* 88000 Mostar, Ante Starčevića bb, Bosnia and Herzegovina. *Telephone:* (36) 318905. *Fax:* (36) 313255.

BUDIŠA, Dražen; Croatian linguist, editor and fmr politician; *Editor, Školska Knjiga;* b. 25 July 1948, Drniš; m. Nada Budiša; three s.; ed Zagreb Univ.; Pres. of Students' League of Zagreb 1971; Pres. Croatian Social-Liberal Party (Hrvatska socijalno-liberalna stranka—HSLS) 1990–96, 1997–2001, 2002–03; Minister in Croatian Govt 1991–92; mem. House of Reps (Parl.) 1992, 1995–2003, First Leader of the Opposition 1992–2000; presidential cand. 2000; currently Ed., Školska Knjiga. *Publications include:* Beginning of Printing in Europe 1984, Heritage of Croatian Reformers in Custody of the National and University Library 1985, Humanism in Croatia 1988, Croatian Books Published in Venice from 15th to 18th Centuries 1990, Talks on Free Croatia (co-author) 1991, The Talks on the State of Croatia 2001. *Leisure interest:* gardening. *Address:* Školska Knjiga, 28, 10000 Zagreb, Croatia (office). *Website:* www.skolska.com.hr (office).

BUERGENTHAL, Thomas, BA, LLM, JD, SJD; American judge and academic; *Lobingier Professor Emeritus of International and Comparative Law, George Washington University Law School;* b. 11 May 1934, Lubochna, Slovakia; s. of Mundek Buergenthal and Gerda Buergenthal; m. 2nd Marjorie Julia Buergenthal (née Bell); three s. from previous m.; ed Bethany Coll., W Va, New York Univ. Law School (Root Tilden Scholar), Harvard Law School; became US citizen 1957; mem. (Judge, then Pres.) Inter-American Court of Human Rights 1979–91; mem. (Judge, then Pres.) Admin. Tribunal, IDB 1989–94; mem. UN Truth Comm. for El Salvador 1992–93, UN Human Rights Comm. 1995–99; mem. Claims Resolution Tribunal for Dormant Accounts, Switzerland 1998–99, Vice-Chair. 1999; Judge, Int. Court of Justice 2000–10; mem. Faculty, George Washington Univ. Law School, Washington, DC 1989–2000, Lobingier Prof. Emer. of Int. and Comparative Law 2000–10, re-apptd Lobingier Prof. 2010–15, re-apptd Prof. Emer. 2015–; mem. New York Bar, Dist of Columbia Bar, US Supreme Court Bar; Hon. Pres., American Soc. of Int. Law 2001–09, Inter-American Inst. of Human Rights 2014–, Int. Acad. Nuremberg Principles 2017–; Olympic Order, Int. Olympic Cttee 2015, Das Grosse Verdienstkreuz 2016; Dr hc (Bethany Coll.) 1981, (Heidelberg Univ.) 1986, (Free Univ. of Brussels) 1994, (State Univ. of New York) 2000, (American Univ., Washington, DC) 2002, (Univ. of Minnesota) 2003, (George Washington Univ.) 2004, (Univ. of Gottingen) 2007, (New York Univ.) 2008, (Brandeis Univ.) 2011, (Univ. for Peace, Costa Rica) 2014; Manley O. Hudson Medal, American Soc. of Int. Law 2002, Gruber Foundation Int. Justice Prize 2008, Goler Butcher Human Rights Prize, Elie Wiesel Award, US Holocaust Memorial Council 2015, and numerous other awards. *Publications include:* Law-Making in the International Civil Aviation Organization 1969, International Protection of Human Rights (co-author) 1973, Protecting Human Rights in the Americas (co-author, fourth edn) 1995, International Human Rights (co-author, fourth edn) 2007, A Lucky Child (memoir) 2009, Menschnrechte (co-author) 2010, Public International Law (co-author, fifth edn) 2013. *Address:* George Washington University Law School, 2000 H Street NW, Washington, DC 20052, USA (office). *Telephone:* (202) 994-6120 (office). *Fax:* (202) 994-5654 (office). *E-mail:* tbuergen@law.gwu.edu (office). *Website:* www.law.gwu.edu (office).

BUFE, Uwe-Ernst, PhD; German business executive and chemist; *Deputy Chairman of the Supervisory Board, Akzo Nobel NV;* b. 22 May 1944, Teschen; m.; two c.; ed Technische Universität, Munich; with Spang and Co. 1971–74; Product Man., Degussa Frankfurt 1974, Corp. Devt and Inorganic Chemicals 1981, mem. Bd Degussa AG 1987, Corp. Devt Degussa Corpn 1977, Exec. Vice-Pres. Chemical Group 1985, Chair. and CEO 1996–99, Chair. Degussa-Hüls AG 1999–2003; Deputy Chair. Supervisory Bd, Akzo Nobel NV 2003–; mem. Supervisory Bd Solvay SA, Umicore SA, Kali + Salz AG; Dir (non-exec.) SunPower Inc. *Address:* Akzo Nobel NV, Strawinskylaan 2555, 1077 ZZ Amsterdam, The Netherlands. *Telephone:* (20) 502-7555. *Fax:* (20) 502-7604 (office). *E-mail:* info@akzonobel.com. *Website:* www.akzonobel.com.

BUFFET, Marie-George; French politician; b. 7 May 1949, Sceaux (Hauts-de-Seine); d. of Paul Kossellek and Raymonde Rayer; m. Jean-Pierre Buffet 1972; two c.; joined Parti Communiste Français (PCF) 1969, elected to PCF Cen. Cttee 1987, mem. Nat. Bureau 1994, Head Nat. Women's Cttee 1996, elected to Nat. Secr. 1997, Nat. Sec. 2001–10; municipal councillor, then Deputy Mayor Châtenay-Malabry (Hauts-de-Seine) 1977–83; Nat. Ass. Deputy for Seine-Saint-Denis 1997–; Minister for Youth and Sport 1997–2002; presidential candidate 2007; Vice-Pres. Comm. for Cultural Affairs and Education. *Address:* Parti Communiste Français, 2 place du Colonel Fabien, 75019 Paris, France (office). *Telephone:* 1-42-35-71-97 (office). *Fax:* 1-40-40-13-56 (office). *E-mail:* mgbuffet@assemblee-nationale.fr (office). *Website:* www.pcf.fr (office).

BUFFETT, Warren Edward; American financier and investor; *Chairman and CEO, Berkshire Hathaway Inc.;* b. 30 Aug. 1930, Omaha, Neb.; s. of Howard Homan Buffett and Leila Stahl; m. 1st Susan Thompson 1952 (died 2004); two s. one d.; m. 2nd Astrid Menks 2006; ed Wharton Business School, Univ. of Pennsylvania, Univ. of Nebraska, Columbia Univ. Business School; worked as investment salesman for father's brokerage firm 1951–54; Graham-Newman Corpn, New York City 1954–56; formed Buffett Partnership, Omaha 1956–69, Chair. and CEO Berkshire Hathaway Inc. (investment co.), Omaha, Neb. 1969–, Nat. Indemnity Co., Buffalo Evening News; mem. Bd of Dirs Salomon Brothers 1987, interim Chair. and CEO 1991–92; mem. Bd of Dirs Coca-Cola Co. (second largest stockholder in co.) 1989–2006; f. Buffet Foundation; Co-Chair. Goldman Sachs 10,000 Small Businesses initiative; Presidential Medal of Freedom 2010, named, along with Bill Gates, by Foreign Policy as the most influential global thinker 2010. *Address:* Berkshire Hathaway Inc., 3555 Farnam Street, Suite 1440, Omaha, NE 68131, USA (office). *Telephone:* (402) 346-1400 (office). *Fax:* (402) 346-3375 (office). *E-mail:* berkshire@berkshirehathaway.com (office). *Website:* www.berkshirehathaway.com (office).

BUFI, Ylli; Albanian chemical engineer and politician; b. 25 May 1948, Tiranë; m. Zana Bufi 1978; two d.; Minister of Foodstuff Industry 1990–91, of Food and Light Industry Feb.–May 1991, of Nutrition May–June 1991; Prime Minister of Albania June–Dec. 1991; Minister of the Public Economy and Privatization –2000; mem. Leading Cttee of Socialist Party; mem. (Socialist Party of Albania) of Parl., Chair. Cttee on Industry, Energetics, Transport and Telecommunications, Cttee on Economy, Finance and Privatization 2002–08. *Address:* c/o Ministry of Economic Development, Trade and Entrepreneurship, 1001 Tirana, Albania. *E-mail:* ybufi@hotmail.com.

BUGÁR, Béla; Slovak politician; *Chairman, Most-Híd (Bridge);* b. 7 July 1958, Bratislava, Czechoslovak Repub. (now Slovakia); ed Slovak Tech. Univ., Bratislava; early career as mechanical engineer in heavy engineering plants 1982–90; mem. Fed. Ass. of Czechoslovakia 1990–92; mem. Nat. Council of the Slovak Repub. (Parl.) 1992–, Deputy Speaker 1998–2006, 2010–, Acting Speaker Feb.–July 2006; mem. Magyar Kereszténydemokrata Mozgalom (Hungarian Christian-Democratic Movt) 1990–98, Chair. 1991–98; Leader, Strana Madarskej Koalície -Magyar Koalíció Pártja (Party of the Hungarian Coalition) 1998–2007; Co-founder and Chair. Most-Híd (Bridge) (promoting inter-ethnic co-operation) 2009–. *Address:* Most-Híd, Trnavská cesta 37, 831 04 Bratislava, Slovakia (office). *Telephone:* (2) 4911-4555 (office). *Fax:* (2) 4911-4500 (office). *E-mail:* bela_bugar@nrsr.sk (office); office@most-hid.sk (office). *Website:* www.most-hid.sk (office).

BUHARI, Maj.-Gen. Muhammadu; Nigerian army officer (retd), government official and head of state; *President and Commander-in-Chief of the Armed Forces;* b. 17 Dec. 1942, Daura, Katsina Prov. of Kaduna; m. 1st Safinatu Yusuf 1971 (divorced); one s. four d.; m. 2nd Aisha Halilu; one s. four d.; ed Katsina Prov. Secondary School, Nigerian Mil. Training Coll., Mons Officers' Cadet School, Aldershot, UK; joined Army 1962; commissioned 1963; served in 2nd Bn in Congo (now Zaïre) 1963–64; Army Service Corps 1964–66; staff and command appointments in 1st and 3rd Infantry Divs; Defence Service Staff Coll., Wellington, India 1972–73; Acting Dir of Supply and Transport, Nigerian Army 1974–75; Mil. Gov. of North Eastern State (divided into three States Feb. 1976) 1975–76, of Borno State Feb.–March 1976; Fed. Commr for Petroleum 1976–78; Chair. Nigerian Nat. Petroleum Corpn 1976–80; Mil. Sec. Nigerian Army 1978; mem. Supreme Mil. Council 1976–77; overthrew Govt of Shehu Shagari; Head of State, Chair. Supreme Mil. Council and C-in-C of Armed Forces 1983–85; detained 1985–88, released 1988; mem. All Nigeria's People's Party (ANPP), presidential cand. 2003, 2007, 2011; Pres. and C-in-C of the Armed Forces 2015–; Chair. Special Trust Fund 1994–; Chair. Econ. Community of West African States (ECOWAS) 2018–. *Leisure interests:* tennis, squash, golf. *Address:* Office of the Head of State, New Federal Secretariat Complex, Shehu Shagari Way, Central Area District, Abuja, Nigeria (office). *Telephone:* (9) 5233536 (office). *Website:* www.statehouse.gov.ng (office).

BUHL RASMUSSEN, Jørgen, BEcons, MBA; Danish business executive; *President and CEO, Carlsberg A/S;* b. 18 Aug. 1955; ed Copenhagen School of Econs and Business Admin; Research Man. and Consultant IFH Research Int. (Unilever), Denmark 1979–82; Product Group Man. A/S Lagerman, Slagelse 1982–85; Marketing Man. Pet Food, MasterFoods Denmark 1985–87; Nordic Marketing Dir Duracell Denmark 1987–88, Gen. Man. Duracell Denmark and Finland 1988–93, Gen. Man. Duracell UK and Ireland 1993–95, Area Dir Duracell N Europe 1995–97; Pres. Gillette Group N Europe 1997–99, Pres. Gillette Group AMEE (Africa, Middle East, E Europe) 2001–06; mem. Exec. Bd Carlsberg A/S 2006–, Exec. Vice-Pres. 2006–07, Pres. and CEO 2007–. *Address:* Carlsberg A/S, 100 Ny Carlsberg Vej, 1799 Copenhagen V, Denmark (office). *Telephone:* 33-27-33-00 (office). *Fax:* 33-27-48-08 (office). *Website:* www.carlsberggroup.com (office).

BUICAN, Denis, DèsScNat, DèsL et ScHum; Romanian/French academic, biologist and philosopher of biology; *Honorary Professor, Université de Paris X Nanterre;* b. 21 Dec. 1934, Bucharest; s. of Dumitru Peligrad and Elena Buican; ed Bucharest Univ., Faculté des Sciences de Paris, Univ. de Paris I-Sorbonne; teaching asst, Bucharest Univ. 1956–57, Prin. Scientific Researcher 1957–60, Course Leader Gen. Biology and Genetics with History of Science course 1960–69, Invited Prof. 1990–; Invited Prof. First Class, History of Sciences, Faculté des Sciences, Univ. de Paris 1969–70, Univ. de Paris-Sorbonne 1970–74, Assoc. Prof., History and Philosophy of Science 1970–74; Assoc. Prof., History and Philosophy of Science, Univ. of Dijon 1974–80; Assoc. Prof., History of Sciences, Univ. of Paris I Panthéon-Sorbonne 1980–83; Assoc. Prof. First Class, History of Sciences, Univ. of Paris X 1983–86; Invited Prof. Collège de France 1984, 1993; Prof. First Class, Univ. of Paris X Nanterre 1986–2003, Hon. Prof. 2003–; Hon. Citizen of Saliste (Romania) 2003; Grand Prix, Acad. Française 1989. *Achievements include:* developed new synergetic theory of evolution and Biognoseology theory of knowledge. *Publications include:* Histoire de la génétique et de l'évolutionnisme en France 1984, La Génétique et l'évolution 1986, Génétique et pensée évolutionniste 1987, Darwin et le darwinisme 1987, Lyssenko et le lyssenkisme 1988, L'Evolution et les évolutionnismes 1989, La Révolution de l'évolution 1989, L'Explosion biologique, du néant au Sur-être 1991, Dracula et ses avatars de Vlad l'Empaleur à Staline et Ceausescu 1991, Charles Darwin 1992, Mendel et la génétique d'hier et d'aujourd'hui 1993, Les Métamorphoses de Dracula 1993, Biognoséologie: Evolution et révolution de la connaissance 1993, Jean Rostand 1994, Histoire de la Biologie 1994, Evolution de la pensée biologique 1995, L'Evolution aujourd'hui 1995, L'Evolution: la grande aventure de la vie 1995, Ethologie comparée 1996, Dictionnaire de Biologie 1997, L'Evolution et les théories évolutionnistes 1997, L'Epopée du vivant, L'Evolution de la biosphère et les avatars de l'Homme 2003, Le Darwinisme et les évolutionnismes 2005, Memorii 2007, L'Odyssée de l'Evolution 2008, Darwin dans l'histoire de la pensée biologique 2008, Mendel dans l'histoire de la génétique 2008, Mosaïque profane 2010, Biologie, Histoire et Philosophie 2010, Darwin et l'épopée de l'évolutionnisme 2012; poetry books: Arbre seul 1974, Lumière aveugle 1976, Mamura 1993, Spice (poèmes anciens et nouveaux) 2006, Margaritare negre (Perles noires) 2008, Roue de torture-Roue de lumière 2009. *Leisure interests:* literature and the arts. *Address:* 15 rue Poliveau, 75005 Paris, France (home). *Telephone:* 1-43-36-33-97 (home).

BUIJNSTERS, Petrus Jacobus Adrianus Maria (Piet J.); Dutch historian and academic; *Professor Emeritus of Dutch Literature, Radboud University Nijmegen;* b. 18 Oct. 1933, Breda; s. of Adriaan Buijnsters and Johanna Wirken; m. Leontine Smet 1961; two s. two d.; ed Univs of Nijmegen and Tübingen; f. Werkgroep 18e Eeuw (with C. M. Geerars) 1968; apptd Prof. of Dutch Literature, Univ. of Nijmegen (now Radboud Univ. Nijmegen) 1971, now Prof. Emer.; mem. Royal Netherlands Acad. of Arts and Sciences; Anne Frank Foundation Prize 1964, Jan Campbert Stiching Prize 1974, Menno Hertzberg Prize 1981, GH 's-Gravesandestraat Prize 2005. *Publications include:* Tussen twee werelden: Rhijnvis Feith als dichter van 'Het Graf' 1963, Hiëronymus van Alphen 1746–1803 1973, Bibliografie der geschriften van en over Betje Wolff en Aagje Deken 1979, Levens van beruchte personen. Over de criminele biografie in Nederland gedurende de 18e eeuw 1980, Nederlandse literatuur van de achttiende eeuw 1984, Wolff en Deken, een biografie 1984, Het verzamelen van boeken. Een handleiding 1985, Briefwisseling van Betje Wolff en Aagje Deken 1987, Spectatoriale geschriften 1991, Justus van Effen (1684–1735). Leven en werk 1992, Bibliofilie in de kinderkamer. Over het verzamelen en bestuderen van oude kinderboeken 1995, Het Nederlandse antiquariaat tijdens de Tweede Wereldoorlog 1997, Bibliografie van Nederlandse school- en kinderboeken 1700–1800 (with Leontine Buijnsters-Smet) 1997, Lust en leering. Geschiedenis van het Nederlandse kinderboek in de negentiende eeuw (with Leontine Buijnsters-Smet) (Menno Hertzbergerprijs 2002) 2001, Papertoys. Speelprenten en papieren speelgoed in Nederland (1640–1920) (with Leontine Buijnsters-Smet) 2005, Geschiedenis van het Nederlandse antiquariaat: 1750–2006 2007, Sluikhandel met juffrouw Duizer 2007, Effectief verplegen 0: handboek voor evidence based verpleegkundig handelen (co-author) 2009, Geschiedenis van de Nederlandse bibliofilie: boeken prentverzamelaars 1750–2010 2010, Geschiedenis van antiquariaat en bibliofilie in België (1830–2012) 2013. *Leisure interest:* book collecting. *Address:* Centre for Language Studies, Radboud University Nijmegen, PO Box 9103, 6500 HD Nijmegen (office); Witsenburgselaan 35, 6524 TE Nijmegen, The Netherlands (home). *Telephone:* (80) 225466 (home).

BUIRA, Ariel, MA; Mexican economist and academic; *Professor of Economics, Universidad Iberoamericana;* b. 20 Sept. 1940, Chihuahua; s. of Antonio Buira and Enriqueta Seira de Buira; m. Janet Clark 1965; two s.; ed Univ. of Manchester, UK; Lecturer, Centre for Econ. and Demographic Studies, El Colegio de México 1966–68; Prof. of Econs, Grad. School of Business, Instituto Tecnológico de Monterrey 1968–70; Economist, IMF 1970–74; Econ. Adviser to Gov., Man. for Int. Research, Banco de México, SA 1975–78, Deputy Dir then Dir for Int. Orgs and Agreements 1982–94, then Deputy Gov. and mem. Bd of Govs; Del. to Conf. on Int. Econ. Co-operation (CIEC) (Financial Affairs Comm.) 1976–77; Alt. Exec. Dir, IMF 1978–80, Exec. Dir for Mexico, Spain, Venezuela, Cen. America 1980–82; Chair. Bd of Dirs BLADEX 1985–94; mem. Bd of Govs Bank of Mexico 1994–96; Amb. to Greece 1998–2001; Sr mem., St Antony's Coll., Oxford 2001–02; Special Envoy of Pres. of Mexico and Chair. of Panel, UN Int. Conf. on Financing for Devt 2002; Dir Secretariat, Intergovernmental Group of Twenty Four on Int. Monetary Affairs and Devt (G-24) 2002–06; currently Prof. of Econs, Univ. Iberoamericana, Mexico, DF; Order of the Phoenix (Greece) 2001; First Prize, Course on Econ. Integration, Coll. Européen des Sciences Sociales et Economiques 1963, Medal of the City of Athens 2001. *Publications include:* 50 Años de Banca Central (jtly) 1976, LDC External Debt and the World Economy 1978, Directions for Reform – The Future of the International Monetary System (jtly) 1984, México: Crisis Financiera y Programa de Ajuste en América Latina: Deuda, Crisis y Perspectivas 1984; Is There a Need for Reform? 1984; contrib.: Politics and Economics of External Debt Crisis – The Latin American Experience 1985, Incomes Policy (ed. V. L. Urquidi) 1987, Money and Finance Vol. I (R. Tandon) 1987, Adjustment with Growth and the Role of the IMF 1987, La Economía Mundial: Evolución y Perspectivas 1989, Una Evalución de la Estrategia de la Deuda 1989, Los Determinantes del Ahorro en México 1990, Evolución de la Estrategia de la Deuda 1990, International Liquidity and the Needs of the World Economy (Vol. IV) 1994, Reflections on the International Monetary System 1995, Can Currency Crises be Prevented or Better Managed? (co-ed. Jan Joost Teunissen) 1996, The Potential of the SDR for Improving the International Monetary System 1996, Reflections on the Mexican Crisis of 1994 1996; and numerous articles and essays; as ed.: The IMF and the World Bank at Sixty 2005, Reforming the Governance of the IMF and the World Bank 2005; as contrib. and ed.: The Governance of the IMF in a Global Economy, An Analysis of IMF Conditionality (in Challenges to the World Bank and the IMF: Developing Country Perspectives) 2003; as contrib.: Curbing the Impact of Shocks (in Protecting the Poor; ed. Jan Joost Teunissen and Age Akkerman) 2005, Does the IMF Need More Financial Resources? (in Reform of the IMF for the 21st Century; ed. Edwin M. Truman) 2006. *Leisure interests:* music, literature. *Address:* Ruben Dario 45, piso 9, Col. Ricon del Bosque, México, DF 11560, Mexico (home). *Telephone:* (55) 5250-1711 (home). *Fax:* (202) 623-6000 (office). *E-mail:* abuiras@yahoo.com.mx.

BUITER, Willem Hendrik, CBE, BA, PhD, FBA; American/British (b. Dutch) economist and academic; *Chief Economist, Citigroup Inc.;* b. 26 Sept. 1949, The Hague, Netherlands; s. of Hendrien Buiter van Schooten and Harm Geert Buiter; m. 1st Jean Archer 1988; two c.; m. 2nd Anne C. Sibert 1998; ed Univ. of Cambridge, Yale Univ.; Asst Prof. of Econs and Int. Affairs, Woodrow Wilson School, Princeton Univ. 1975–79; Prof. of Econs, Univ. of Bristol 1980–82; Cassel Prof. of Econs with Special Reference to Money and Banking, LSE 1982–85, Prof. of European Political Economy 2005–11; Prof. of Econs, Yale Univ. 1985–94, Juan T. Trippe Prof. of Int. Econs 1990–94; Prof. of Int. Macroeconomics, Univ. of Cambridge 1994–2000; external mem. Monetary Policy Cttee, Bank of England 1997–2000; Chief Economist and Special Counsellor to the Pres., EBRD 2000–05; Chair. Council of Econ. Advisers, Netherlands Parl. 2005–07; Chief Economist, Citigroup Inc. 2010–; Consultant IMF, IBRD, IDB 1979–; adviser, Goldman Sachs 2005–09; adviser to House of Commons Treasury Select Cttee, UK 1980–82, Netherlands Ministry of Educ. 1985–86, EC, DGII 1982–85; Fellow, British Acad. 1998, European Econ. Asscn 2004; Corresp. mem. Royal Netherlands Acad. of Sciences 1989–; Research Assoc., Nat. Bureau of Econ. Research 1979–2011; Research Fellow, Centre for Econ. Policy Research 1983–; Dr hc (Amsterdam) 2012; Royal Netherlands Acad. of Sciences Dr Hendrik Muller Prize for the behavioural and social sciences 1995, N.G. Pierson Medal (Netherlands) 2000. *Publications:* Temporary and Long-run Equilibrium 1979, Budgetary Policy, International and Intertemporal Trade in the Global Economy 1989, Macroeconomic Theory and Stabilization Policy 1989, Principles of Budgetary and Financial Policy 1990, International Macroeconomics 1990, Financial Markets and European Monetary Cooperation: The Lessons of the 92–93 ERM crisis (with Giancarlo Corsetti and Paolo Pesenti) 1997. *Leisure interests:* tennis, theatre, westerns, science fiction and fantasy novels, poetry. *Address:* Citigroup Centre, Canada Square, Canary Wharf, London, E14 5LB, England (office); Apt 1201, The Aldyn, 60 Riverside Blvd, New York, NY 10069, USA (home). *Telephone:* (20) 7986-5944 (office). *Fax:* (20) 7986-3221 (office). *E-mail:* willem.buiter@citi.com (office). *Website:* www.citigroup.com (office); www.willembuiter.com.

BUJAK, Zbigniew; Polish politician and trade union official; b. 29 Nov. 1954, Łopuszno; ed Warsaw Univ.; worked in Polfa Pharmaceutical plant, Grodzisk Mazowiecki, then Ursus Mechanical Works 1973–81; nat. service in airborne commando div. 1974–76; organizer of strike in Ursus Works in July 1980; assoc. Workers' Cttee for solidarity with striking coastal workers Aug. 1980; Chair. Founding Cttee Solidarity Trade Union, Mazowsze Region 1980; mem. Nat. Consultative Comm. of Solidarity, took part in negotiations with Govt 1981; under martial law in hiding, continued union activity 1981–86; Chair. Bd Mazowsze Region in Provisional Exec. Comm. of Solidarity 1982–86; arrested May 1986, pardoned Sept. 1986; mem. Nat. Exec. Comm. of Solidarity 1987–90; Chair. Citizens' Cttee of Solidarity 1988–90; took part in Round Table debates in Groups for Political Reform and for Economy and Social Policy Feb.–April 1989; Chair. Council of Warsaw Agreement of Citizens' Cttees 1990–91; Co-founder and Co-leader Citizens' Movt–Democratic Action (ROAD) 1990–91; Deputy to Sejm (Parl.) 1991–97, Chair. Sejm Comm. of Admin. and Internal Affairs 1993–97; Chair. Cen. Bd of Customs 1999–2001; Chair. of Democratic-Social Movt 1991; Co-founder and Vice-Chair. Union of Labour (UP) 1992–98; mem. Freedom Union (UW) Party 1998–; fmr mem. Socialist Rural Youth Union; co-f. Solidarity Citizens' Cttee of Ukraine 2014; Kt's Cross, Order of Polonia Restituta 1990, Grand Cross 2011; Robert F. Kennedy Human Rights Award 1988. *Publication:* Przepraszam za Solidarność 1991. *Address:* Główny Urząd Ceł, ul. Świętokrzyska 12, 00-916 Warsaw, Poland (office). *Telephone:* (22) 6944946 (office). *E-mail:* gabinet_prezesa_guc@guc.gov.pl (office). *Website:* www.guc.gov.pl (office); zbigniewbujak.natemat.pl.

BUJOLD, Genevieve; Canadian actress; b. 1 July 1942, Montreal; m. Paul Almond 1967 (divorced); one s.; ed Montréal Conservatory of Drama; fmr cinema usherette in Montreal. *Films include:* La guerre est finie, La fleur de l'age, Entre la mer et l'eau douce, King of Hearts, The Thief of Paris, Isabel, Anne of the Thousand Days, The Act of the Heart, The Trojan Women, The Journey, Earthquake, Alex and the Gypsy, Kamouraska, Obsession, Swashbuckler, Another Man Another Chance, Coma, Murder by Decree, Final Assignment, The Last Flight of Noah's Ark, Monsignor, Tightrope, Choose Me, Trouble in Mind, The Moderns, Dead Ringers, False Identity, Secret Places of the Heart, A Paper Wedding, Star Trek: Generations, An Ambush of Ghosts, Mon Ami Max, Dead Innocent 1996, The House of Yes 1997, Last Night 1998, Eye of the Beholder 1999, Alex in Wonder 2001, La Turbulence des fluides 2002, Jericho Mansions 2003, Finding Home 2003, Downtown: A Street Tale 2004, Mon petit doigt m'a dit 2005, Disappearances 2006, Délivrez-moi 2006, The Trotsky 2009, Pour l'amour de Dieu 2011, Still Mine 2012, The Legend of Sarila (voice) 2013, Northern Borders 2013, Chorus 2015. *Stage appearances include:* The Barber of Seville, A Midsummer Night's Dream, A House... A Day. *TV appearances include:* St Joan, Antony and Cleopatra, Mistress of Paradise, Red Earth, White Earth, Star Trek. *Address:* c/o WME, 9601 Wilshire Blvd, Beverly Hills, CA 90210, USA (office).

BUJON DE L'ESTANG, François; French diplomatist and business executive; *President, FBE International Consultants;* b. 21 Aug. 1940, Neuilly-sur-Seine, Hauts-de-Seine; s. of Henry Bujon de l'Estang and Vera Markels; m. Anne Jacquin de Margerie 1963; four c.; ed Institut Politique de Paris, Ecole Nat. d'Admin, Harvard Grad. School of Business Admin, USA; Office of Perm. Sec., Ministry of Foreign Affairs 1966; Special Adviser on staff of Pres. of Repub. 1966, Deputy to Pres.'s Diplomatic Adviser –1969; Second, then First Sec., Embassy in Washington, DC 1969–73; First Sec. and Second Counsellor in London 1973–75; Adviser on Int. Affairs to Del. Gen. for Energy, Ministry of Industry 1975–77; Dir for Int. Relations, Atomic Energy Commissariat 1978–79; French Rep. on Bd of Govs of IAEA 1979; Chief of Staff to Minister of Industry 1980–81; f. COGEMA Inc., Washington, DC 1982, Pres. and CEO 1982–86; apptd Amb. to Mexico 1986 (did not take up post); Sr Adviser to Prime Minister Jacques Chirac for Diplomatic Affairs, Defence and Co-operation 1986–88; Amb. to Canada 1989–91, to USA 1995–2002, rank of Amb. of France 1999; mem. Bd of Dirs Sofratome, Technicatome and Eurodif 1979–80, Copperweld Corpn (Imetal Group) 1982–86; Sr Vice-Pres. Compagnie de Navigation Mixte and Via Banque 1991–92; Chair. and CEO SFIM 1991–92, mem. Bd Dirs 1991–93; Pres. Harvard Business School Club of France 1992–95; Founder FBE International Consultants 1992, Pres. 1992–95, 2003–; mem. Bd Dirs Banque Indosuez 1993–95, CNES 2003–10, Institut Pasteur 2003–05, Tembec Inc. 2005–07, Thales 2003–09, IFRI 2003–09; mem. Int. Advisory Bd Total 2004–; Chair. Citigroup France 2003–10, Sr Int. Adviser 2010–12, mem. European Advisory Bd, Citigroup 2003–12; Vice-Chair. French-American Foundation US 2003–, mem. Bd French-American Foundation France 2008–; Chair. Bd of Trustees, MB American Center for Arts & Culture 2013–; Officier, Legion d'honneur; Commdr, Ordre nat. du Mérite. *Address:* FBE International Consultants, 38 rue Marbeuf, 75008 Paris, France (office). *Telephone:* 1-42-25-55-53 (office). *Fax:* 1-42-25-55-56 (office). *E-mail:* fbe@fbe-international.com (office). *Website:* www.fbe-international.com (office).

BUKEJLOVIĆ, Pero, MEng; Bosnia and Herzegovina politician and engineer; b. 9 Aug. 1946, Bušletic, Doboj municipality; m.; one s.; ed Univs of Sarajevo and Zagreb; various positions as engineer; Gen. Man. Trudbenik Co.; Minister of Industry and Tech. 2001–03; worked in private sector 2003–05, 2006–; Prime Minister of Republika Srpska 2005–06; represented the Serbian Democratic Party. *Address:* c/o Office of the Prime Minister, 78000 Banja Luka, trg Republike Srpske 1, Bosnia and Herzegovina. *E-mail:* kabinet@vladars.net.

BUKELE ORTEZ, Nayib Armando; Salvadorean business executive and politician; *President-elect;* b. 24 July 1981, San Salvador; s. of Armando Bukele Kattán and Olga Ortez de Bukele; m. Gabriela Rodríguez de Bukele 2014; ed José Simeón Cañas Central American Univ.; owner, Yamaha Motors El Salvador; Dir and Pres. OBERMET, SA de CV (advertising agency); Mayor of Nuevo Cuscatlán 2012–15; Mayor of San Salvador 2015–18; Pres.-elect of El Salvador (scheduled to assume office 1 June 2019); mem. Frente Farabundo Martí para la Liberación Nacional (FMLN) 2012–17 (expelled from party); mem. Gran Alianza por la Unidad Nacional (GANA) 2018–. *Address:* c/o Gran Alianza por la Unidad Nacional, 41 Avda Sur y 6a y 10a Calle Poniente 2143, Col. Flor Blanca, San Salvador, El Salvador (office). *Telephone:* 2279-0254 (office). *E-mail:* info@gana.org.sv (office). *Website:* gana.org.sv (office).

BUKENYA, Gilbert Balibaseka, MSc, MD, PhD; Ugandan professor of public health and politician; b. May 1949, Wakiso Dist; m.; three c.; ed Makerere Univ. Medical School, Royal Inst. of Public Health and Hygiene, UK, Ross Inst., London School of Hygiene and Tropical Medicine, UK, Univ. of Queensland, Australia; internship in Uganda; following studies in public health in London returned to Uganda in 1983; Lecturer, Inst. of Public Health, Makerere Univ. 1983–84, Dir 1989, Assoc. Prof. 1993, Dean Faculty of Medicine 1995; Lecturer, Dept of Community Medicine, Univ. of Papua New Guinea 1984–87, Head of Dept 1987–89; Assoc. Prof., Tulane Univ. School of Public Health, New Orleans, La, USA 1995; Adjunct Prof. of Int. Health, Case Western Reserve Univ., Cleveland, OH, USA 2004; MP for Busiro North 1996–, Chair. Movt Caucus; Minister of State for Trade and Minister in charge of the Presidency; Vice-Pres. of Uganda 2003–11; Chair. Nat. Advisory Cttee on Environmental Health and Maternal and Child Health, Papua New Guinea 1985–91, Bd of Examiners, Coll. of Allied Health Sciences Health Inspectors' Programme 1985–91; Vice-Chair. Network of African Postgraduate Public Health Training Schools, WHO-Afro Region 1992–94, Chair. 1994–96.

BUKHARY, Tan Sri Syed Mokhtar al-; Malaysian business executive; *Executive Chairman, Albukhary Foundation;* b. 1952, Alor Star; m. Puan Sri Sharifah Zarah Al-Bukhary; five c.; began career in meat and later rice trading; f. transport business 1973; owns stakes in numerous cos in Malaysia and abroad, including Malaysian Mining Corpn (MMC), Johor Port Bhd, Malakoff (ind. power producer), Gas Malaysia; investment interests include plantations, property devt, construction, power generation, retailing, information tech., infrastructure and ports; f. Syarikat Impian Teladan Sendirian Bhd; Owner SKS Ventures; Exec. Chair. Albukhary Foundation; mem. Bd, Syarikat Bina Puri Holdings Berhad; mem. United Malays Nat. Org.; Panglima Setia Mahkota, Dato' Setia Mahkota Kedah, announced and awarded Tokoh Ma'al Hijrah by The Yang Di Pertuan Agong of Malaysia in recognition of his contrib. to nation building 2008. *Address:* Albukhary Foundation, 30 Jalan Pahang Barat, 53000 Kuala Lumpur, Wilayah Persekutuan Kuala Lumpur, Malaysia (office). *Telephone:* 4032-2056 (office). *Fax:* 4032-2057 (office). *E-mail:* info@albukhary.org (office). *Website:* www.albukharyfoundation.org (office).

BUKOVAC, Martin J., PhD; American horticulturist and academic; *Distinguished Professor Emeritus, Department of Horticulture, Michigan State University;* b. 12 Nov. 1929, Johnston City, Ill.; s. of John Bukovac and Sadie Fak; m. Judith A. Kelley 1956; one d.; ed Mich. State Univ.; Asst Prof., Dept of Horticulture, Mich. State Univ. 1957–61, Assoc. Prof. 1961–63, Prof. 1963–92, Univ. Distinguished Prof. 1992–, now Distinguished Prof. Emer.; Biological Science Collaborator, USDA/Agricultural Research Service 1982–2003; Postdoctoral Fellow, Univs of Oxford and Bristol, UK 1965–66; Dir Mich. State Univ. Press

1983–91; Adviser, Eli Lilly Co. 1971–88; Pres. Martin J. Bukovac Inc. 1996–; Fellow, AAAS, American Soc. of Horticultural Science; mem. NAS, Editorial Advisory Bd Horticultural Abstracts 1990–2003, Editorial Bd Encyclopedia of Agricultural Science 1991–96, Int. Editorial Bd, Horticultural Science, Kertészetic Tudomány, Budapest 1989–2003; mem. Int. Advisory Bd, Life Sciences Div., Center for Nuclear Sciences, Grenoble 1993–2000; Hon. DrAgr (Bonn) 1995; Alexander von Humboldt Award for Sr Scientist 1995, Gold Veitch Memorial Medal, Hall of Fame, American Soc. for Horticultural Science 2001, Royal Horticultural Soc. 2003, Spiridon Brusina Medal, Croatian Soc. of Natural Sciences 2004. *Publications:* over 350 research articles. *Leisure interests:* photography, sports. *Address:* A390B Plant and Soil Sciences, Michigan State University, East Lansing, MI 48824-1325 (office); 4428 Seneca Drive, Okemos, MI 48864-2946, USA (home). *Telephone:* (517) 355-5191 (ext. 393) (office); (517) 349-1952 (home). *Fax:* (517) 353-0890 (office). *E-mail:* bukovacm@msu.edu (office). *Website:* www.hrt.msu.edu/faculty/bukovac.htm (office).

BUKOVSKY, Vladimir Konstantinovich, MA; Russian writer and scientist; b. 30 Dec. 1942, Belebey, Bashkirian ASSR, Russian SFSR (now Bashkortostan), USSR; s. of Konstantin Bukovsky and Nina Bukovsky; ed Moscow State Univ., Univ. of Cambridge; worked at Moscow Centre of Cybernetics; arrested for possessing banned literature 1963, confined to Leningrad Psychiatric Prison Hosp. for 15 months; arrested for demonstration on behalf of Soviet writers 1965, confined for eight months in psychiatric institutions; arrested for civil rights work 1967, on trial Sept. 1967 and sentenced to three years' corrective labour; arrested for delivering information on psychiatric abuse to the West 1971, on trial 1972 and sentenced to two years in prison, five in a labour camp and five in exile; after worldwide campaign for his release, was exchanged for Chilean Communist Party leader Luis Corvalán in Zurich Dec. 1976; citizenship restored 1992; research work, Stanford Univ., Calif. 1982–90; f. Centre for Democracy in Support of New Russia, New York; Co-founder political group 'Committee 2008' 2004 (aimed to promote free and fair 2008 presidential elections; last meeting 2005); nominated cand. for 2008 presidential elections 2007; mem. Int. Advisory Council Victims of Communism Memorial Foundation; hon. mem. several human rights orgs, several PEN clubs; has lived in Cambridge, UK since 1976; Konrad Adenauer Freedom and Literature Prize 1984, Truman-Reagan Medal of Freedom 2001. *Publications:* short stories in Russia's Other Writers 1970 and in Grani, Opposition – Eine neue Geisteskrankheit in der USSR (German edn) 1972, A Manual on Psychiatry for Dissenters (with Semyon Gluzman) 1974, To Build a Castle: My Life as a Dissenter (in English; trans. in Swedish, Italian, Spanish, French and German) 1978, Soul of Man Under Socialism 1979, Cette lancinante douleur de la liberté 1981, The Peace Movement and the Soviet Union 1982, Soviet Hypocrisy and Western Gullibility 1987, Judgement in Moscow 1987, EUSSR: The Soviet Roots of European Integration 2004, L'Union européenne, une nouvelle URSS? (co-author) 2005. *Leisure interests:* the arts, architecture. *Website:* www.bukovsky2008.org (office).

BULATHSINGHALA, Air Marshal Gagan, MSc, MPhil; Sri Lankan military commdr (retd), diplomatist; *Ambassador to Afghanistan;* b. 12 Sept. 1961; s. of Bulathsinghala Percy Marcus Perera and Dona Beatrice Perera; m. Samanthi Bulathsinghala; one s. one d.; ed Nalanda Coll., Colombo, Air Command and Staff Coll., Air Univ. (USAF), USA, Nat. Defence Coll. and Univ. of Madras, India; joined Sri Lanka Air Force (SLAF) as Officer Cadet Feb. 1981, commissioned as Pilot Officer, Gen. Duties Pilot Br. 1983, later becoming CO, No 6 Squadron, longest-serving CO of No 4 (VVIP/VIP) Helicopter Squadron SLAF, commanded Sri Lanka Air Force Base China Bay, various staff appointments at Air Force HQ including Aide de Camp to Commdr of Air Force, Overall Operations Commdr, Air Defence and Command Flight Safety Officer, Chief Instructor of Air Wing at Defence Service Command and Staff Coll., Dir of Air Operations 2011–12, Dir of Operations 2012–14, Chief of Staff of SLAF 2014–15, Commdr 2015–16; Ambassador to Afghanistan 2017–; Pres. Air Force Sports Council; Fellow, Asia-Pacific Center for Security Studies, Near East South Asia Center for Strategic Studies, USA; fmr mem. SLAF Sport Council; fmr Pres. Interim Cttee of Cycling Fed. of Sri Lanka; attained rank of Air Marshal 2015; numerous campaign and operational mil. awards including Combat Gallantry Medal, Combat Excellence Medal, Meritorious Service Medal. *Address:* Embassy of Sri Lanka, SQ Kabul Hotel and Business Complex, Taimany Wat, Sabequa Square, Kabul, Afghanistan (office). *Telephone:* (20) 2231952 (office). *Fax:* (20) 2231953 (office). *E-mail:* slembkabul@mea.gov.lk (office).

BULATOVIĆ, Momir, CandEconSc; Montenegrin politician; b. 21 Sept. 1956, Belgrade, Yugoslavia; ed Titograd Univ.; fmr mem. League of Communists of Montenegro, then Leader, Republican League of Communists; Chair. Democratic Party of Socialists 1990–98; Chair. Socialist People's Party of Montenegro 1998–2001; Pres. of Montenegro 1990–98; Prime Minister of Yugoslavia 1998–2001. *Address:* c/o Socialist People's Party of Montenegro, Podgorica, Montenegro.

BULATOVIĆ, Predrag; Montenegrin politician; b. 16 July 1956, Kolašin; m.; three d.; ed Faculty of Mechanical Eng, Univ. of Montenegro, Podgorica; various admin., teaching and exec. positions, Univ. of Montenegro 1975–80; Sec. of Montenegro Youth Org. and Socialist Fed. Repub. of Yugoslavia Youth Org. 1982–84; worked for Radoje Dakić Factory, Podgorica 1985–89; began career as professional politician 1989–; elected to Ass. of Repub. 1990–; elected to Fed. Ass. of Fmr Yugoslavia 2001–02, Chair. Foreign Policy Cttee 2000–03; Pres. Parl. Group of Democratic Party of Socialists (DPS) 1992–97; Vice-Pres. Socialist People's Party of Montenegro (SSPM—following division of DPS 1997) 1997–2001, Pres. 2001–02; Vice-Pres. Parl. Group of SSPM 1997–2001; mem. Montenegro Ass. 2006–, mem. Cttee for Int. Relation and European Integration; several Awards and Prizes from Univ. of Montenegro. *Address:* 13 Jula No. 49, Podgorica (home); Vaka Djurovica No. 5, Podgorica (office); Bulevar Svetog Petra Cetinjskog 10, Podgorica, Montenegro (office). *Telephone:* (20) 272-421 (office). *Fax:* (20) 272-421 (office). *E-mail:* predrag.bulatovic@skupstina.me (office). *Website:* www.skupstina.me (office).

BULC, Violeta, BSc, MBA; Slovenian politician and EU official; *Commissioner for Transport, European Union;* b. 24 Jan. 1964, Novo mesto, Socialist Repub. of Slovenia, Socialist Fed. Repub. of Yugoslavia; ed Univ. of Ljubljana, Golden Gate Univ., USA, IEDC-Bled School of Man.; Analyst, Wide Area Networks Performance Dept, DHL Systems, Burlingame, Calif., USA 1991–94; Man., Institutional Traffic, Telekom Slovenia 1994–97, Dir of Carrier Business 1997–99; Vice-Pres. Telemach Ltd (telecommunications provider) 1999–2000; Owner and CEO Vibacom Ltd (sustainable strategies and innovation ecosystems) 2000–14; Slovenian Rep., Advisory Group for ICT, European Comm. 2004–07; Minister without Portfolio (responsible for Devt, Strategic Projects and Cohesion) Sept.–Nov. 2014; Commr for Transport, EC, Brussels 2014–(19); Chair. Umanotera (sustainable devt NGO) 2009–14; Visiting Prof., Faculty of Design, Univ. of Ljubljana 2013–; mem. Stranka Modernega Centra (Modern Centre Party). *Address:* European Commission, 200 Rue de la Loi/Wetstraat 200, 1049 Brussels, Belgium (office). *Telephone:* (2) 299-11-11 (switchboard) (office). *Website:* ec.europa.eu/commission/2014-2019/bulc_en (office).

BULCKE, Paul; Belgian business executive; *CEO, Nestlé SA;* b. 1954, Roeselare; m.; three c.; ed Univs of Louvain and Ghent, Belgium, Program for Exec. Devt, IMD Business School, Switzerland; financial analyst, Scott Graphics International, Bornem, Belgium 1977–79; with Nestlé Group, Vevey, Switzerland 1979–, marketing trainee, Nestlé SA (Switzerland, Spain, Belgium) 1979–80, Marketing, Sales and Div. functions, Nestlé Peru, Nestlé Ecuador and Nestlé Chile 1980–96, Man. Dir Nestlé Portugal 1996–98, Man. Dir Nestlé Czech and Slovak Repubs 1998–2000, Man. Dir Nestlé Germany, Frankfurt am Main 2000–03, Exec. Vice-Pres. responsible for Zone Americas: USA, Canada, Latin America, Caribbean 2004–08, CEO Designate and mem. designate Bd Nestlé SA 2007–08, mem. Bd Dirs and CEO 2008–, Administrateur Délégué, Nestlé Health Science SA; Co-Chair. Supervisory Bd Cereal Partners Worldwide (Switzerland); Bd mem. and Co-Chair. Governance Cttee, Consumer Goods Forum; mem. Bd Roche Holding Ltd (Switzerland). *Address:* Nestlé, Avenue Nestlé 55, 1800 Vevey, Switzerland (office). *Telephone:* (21) 924-1111 (office). *Fax:* (21) 921-1885 (office). *E-mail:* info@nestle.com (office). *Website:* www.nestle.com (office).

BULGAK, Vladimir Borisovich, CandTechSc, DEconSc; Russian politician and business executive; b. 9 May 1941, Moscow; m.; one d.; ed Moscow Electrotech. Inst. of Communications, Inst. of Man. of Nat. Econ., USSR State Cttee on Science and Tech.; instructor, then sec. Moscow City Komsomol Cttee 1963–68; for 15 years worked in Moscow radio trans. network; head of depts USSR Ministry of Telecommunications 1983–90; Minister 1990–91; Minister of Telecommunications Russian Fed. 1991–97; Deputy Chair. Govt of Russian Fed. 1997–98, 1998–99; Minister of Science and Tech. April–Sept. 1998; Chair. TV-Holding Svyazinvest 1999–2001, Comincom-Combellga group 1999–2003; fmr Chair. Insurance Group Nasta; mem. Council of Dirs Sovintel (operating company of Golden Telecom) 2004–; mem. Int. Acad. of Informatization, Russian Acad. of Tech. Sciences, Russian Acad. of Natural Sciences; USSR State Prize. *Publications:* several textbooks on communication techniques; over 100 articles and papers. *Address:* c/o Golden Telecom, 115114 Moscow, 1 Kozhevnicheskii prospect, Russia.

BULGURLU, Bülent, MS, PhD; Turkish business executive; b. 1947, Ankara; m.; three c.; ed Ankara Eng and Architectural Faculty, Norwegian Tech. Univ., Trondheim; Construction Engineer, Elliot Strömme A/S, Oslo 1972; Asst Lecturer and Researcher, Norveç Tech. Univ. 1972–77; Project Man., Intes San. ve Tic. AŞ 1977–79; Construction Engineer, Garanti Insaat AŞ Oct.–Dec. 1979, Planning and Construction Man. 1979–81, Site Coordination Construction Man. 1981–82, Asst Gen. Man. 1982–84, Asst Gen. Man. (Tech.) 1984–86, Asst Gen. Man. (Production) Tech. Processes (by proxy) 1986–88, Gen. Man. 1988–90, Gen. Man. Garanti Koza Insaat AŞ 1990–96; Vice-Pres. Tourism and Services Group, Koç Holding AŞ 1996–2000, Pres. Tourism and Services Group 2000–01, Pres. Tourism and Construction Group 2001–03, Pres. Durable Goods and Construction Group 2004–07, mem. Bd of Dirs and CEO 2007–10, Dir 2010–; fmr Vice-Chair. Arcelik AŞ; fmr Deputy Chair. Izocam Ticaret ve Sanayi AŞ; mem. Bd of Dirs Grundig Elektronik AS, Aygaz AŞ, Arcelik AŞ, Ford Otomotiv Sanayi AŞ 2007–, Turkiye Petrol Rafinerileri AŞ 2007–, Yapi Kredi Koray 2007–, Otokar Otobus Karoseri Sanayi AŞ 2008–, TOFAS Turk Otomobil Fabrikasi AŞ –2011, Izocam; mem. Turkish Industrialists' and Businessmen's Asscn (TÜSIAD), Altunizade Rotary Club, T.E.D.Club, Anatolian Club, Turkish Marine Environment Protection Asscn, Turkish Tourism Investors Asscn, Chaîne de Rotisseurs. *Address:* Koç Holding AŞ, Nakkaştepe Aziz Bey Sok. 1, Kuzguncuk, 34674 Istanbul, Turkey (office). *Telephone:* (216) 5310000 (office). *Fax:* (216) 5310099 (office). *E-mail:* info@koc.com.tr (office). *Website:* www.koc.com.tr (office); www.rmk-museum.org.tr (office).

BULJEVIĆ, Josip, BSc; Croatian security adviser, politician and fmr journalist; b. 2 April 1971; m.; two c.; ed Univ. of Zagreb; journalist with culture dept, Večernji List (daily newspaper) 1992–95; Nat. Security Officer, Constitutional Order Protection Service, Split Regional Centre 1995–2000, Head of Analytics Dept 2000–01, Head of Operations Dept 2001–04; Head of Counterintelligence Dept, Nat. Counterintelligence Agency 2004, Asst Operations Dir 2004–06; Asst Operations Dir, Security and Intelligence Agency 2006–08, Dir, Security and Intelligence Agency 2008–12; Chair. Middle European Conf., Central European Asscn of Dirs of Security and Intelligence Services 2007–08; mem. NATO Intelligence Cttee 2008–12; Analyst, Office of Nat. Security Council 2012–13; Consul-Gen., Consulate Gen. of Croatia in Los Angeles 2013–15; Defence and Nat. Security Adviser, Office of the Pres. 2015–16; Minister of Defence Jan.–Oct. 2016; awarded Homeland War medals Operation Lightning, Operation Storm and Daring Feat 1995. *Address:* c/o Ministry of Defence, 10000 Zagreb, trg kralja Petra Krešimira IV, Croatia (office).

BULL, Baroness (Life Peer), cr. 2018, of Aldwych in the City of Westminster; **Deborah Clare Bull,** CBE; British ballerina, writer, broadcaster, creative director and cultural commentator; *Assistant Principal (London), King's College London;* b. 22 March 1963, Derby; d. of Rev. Michael John Bull and Doreen Audrey Franklin Bull (née Plumb); ed Royal Ballet School; joined Royal Ballet 1981, Prin. Dancer 1992–2001, teacher of Nutrition, Royal Ballet School 1996–99; Dir Clore Studio Upstairs, Royal Opera House 1999–2001, Creative Dir, ROH2, Royal Opera House 2002–08, Creative Dir, Royal Opera House 2008–12; Dir Cultural Partnerships, King's Coll., London 2012–15, Asst Prin. (London) 2015–; Vice-Pres. of Cultural Devt, British Science Asscn 2015–; mem. Dance Panel, Arts Council 1996–98, Arts Council 1998–2005; Gov. South Bank Centre 1997–2003, BBC Bd Govs 2003–06, Foundation, Prix de Lausanne 2012–, ARHC Cultural Value Project Advisory Group 2012–; Commr, Warwick Comm. on Cultural Value 2013–; mem. Council Arts & Humanities Research Council 2013–; mem. Bd of Dirs

Science Gallery Int. 2013–; Vice-Pres., Cultural Devt, British Science Asscn 2015–, Arts and Humanities Research Council; columnist, The Telegraph 1999–2002; Patron Nat. Osteoporosis Soc., Foundation for Community Dance, Journalism Foundation; Hon. Pres. Voices of British Ballet; Dr hc (Derby) 1998, (Sheffield) 2001, (Open Univ.) 2005, (Kent) 2010; Prix de Lausanne 1980, Dancer of the Year, Sunday Express and The Independent on Sunday 1996, Overall Prize Dancescreen Monaco 2002. *Dance includes:* appearances with Royal Ballet include leading roles in La Bayadère (Gamzatti), Swan Lake (Odette/Odile), The Sleeping Beauty (Aurora), Don Quixote (Kitri), Steptext (first staging in UK for her by William Forsythe) 1995; appeared in Harrogate Int. Festival 1993, 1995, An Evening of British Ballet, Sintra Festival, Portugal 1994, 1995, Diamonds of World Ballet Gala, Kremlin Palace, Moscow 1996, Rite of Spring, Teatro dell'Opera, Rome 2001–02. *Radio includes:* regular contrib. to BBC Radio 4 including Breaking the Law 2001, Law in Order 2002, A Dance Through Time 2002, Hothouse Kids 2009, After I Was Gorgeous 2011, Steps in Time 2011, Dance for Your Life 2012, Deborah Bull's Dance Nation 2012, Desert Island Discs (BBC Radio 4) 2013, The Essay (BBC Radio 3) 2013, Classic FM at the ballet 2014, Saturday Classics (BBC Radio 3). *Television includes:* Dance Ballerina Dance (writer, presenter) 1998, Travels with my Tutu (writer, presenter) 2000, Coppélia, Royal Ballet (live broadcast), Rambert Dance Co., Sadler's Wells (live broadcast), BBC 1 and BBC 2 Proms (live broadcast), The Dancer's Body (writer, presenter) 2002, Saved for the Nation (presenter) 2006, Bolshoi Unseen (presenter) 2013, Britten on Camera 2013, Dancing for Russia 2014. *Publications include:* The Vitality Plan 1998, Dancing Away 1998, The Faber Guide to Classical Ballets (with Luke Jennings) 2004, The Everyday Dancer 2011; numerous articles and reviews in newspapers and dance magazines. *Leisure interests:* reading, writing, walking, cycling, dancing, talking, theatrical and arts experiences, politics. *Address:* c/o Rosemary Scoular, United Agents, 12–26 Lexington Street, London, W1F 0LE, England (office). *Telephone:* (20) 3214-0893 (office). *E-mail:* rscoular@unitedagents.co.uk (office). *Website:* www.unitedagents.co.uk (office); www.deborahbull.com.

BULL, Sir George, Kt; British business executive; b. 16 July 1936, London; s. of Michael Bull and Hon. Noreen Hennessy; m. Tessa Freeland 1960; four s. one d.; ed Ampleforth Coll.; Coldstream Guards 1954–57; joined Twiss Browning & Hallowes 1958; Gilbey Vintners Ltd 1970; Dir Int. Distillers and Vintners (IDV) 1973; Man. Dir IDV Europe 1977; Deputy Man. Dir IDV Ltd 1982; Dir Grand Metropolitan Ltd 1985; Chief Exec. IDV Ltd 1987; Chair. and CEO IDV Ltd (Drinks Sector of Grand Metropolitan PLC) 1988; Chair. and CEO Grand Met Food Sector 1992; Group Chief Exec. Grand Metropolitan PLC 1993, Chair. Grand Metropolitan PLC 1996–97; Co.-Chair. Diageo (after merger with Guinness PLC) 1997–98; Chair. J Sainsbury PLC 1998–2004; Dir (non-exec.) BNP Paribas UK Holdings 2000–04, The Maersk Co. Ltd 2001–06, Marakon Assocs 2002–06; mem. Advisory Bd Marakon Assocs 2002; Chevalier, Légion d'honneur 1994. *Leisure interests:* golf, photography. *Address:* The Old Vicarage, Arkesden, Saffron Walden, Essex, CB11 4HB, England (home).

BULL, William V. S., MA; Liberian diplomatist; b. 1946, Monrovia; ed Univ. of Liberia, Univ. of Pittsburgh, USA; joined Bureau of African and Asian Affairs, Ministry of Foreign Affairs 1972; Counsellor and Deputy Chief of Mission, Washington, DC 1976, Chargé d'affaires 1980; Asst Minister for American Affairs, Monrovia 1981, for African and Asian Affairs 1982–86, Prin. Deputy to Minister of Foreign Affairs 1987–90; Amb. and Perm. Rep. to UN, New York 1990–98; Amb. to UK 1998–2000, to USA 2000–03, 2010–12; Acting Foreign Minister –2010. *Address:* Ministry of Foreign Affairs, Mamba Point, PO Box 10-9002, 1000 Monrovia 10, Liberia (office). *Telephone:* 226763 (office). *Website:* www.mofa.gov.lr (office).

BULLARD, Robert D., PhD; American sociologist and academic; *Dean, Barbara Jordan-Mickey Leland School of Public Affairs, Texas Southern University;* b. 21 Dec. 1946, Elba, Ala; s. of Nehemiah Bullard and Myrtle Bullard (née Brundidge); ed Iowa State Univ.; Asst Prof., then Assoc. Prof., Texas Southern Univ., Houston 1976–88, Dean, Barbara Jordan-Mickey Leland School of Public Affairs 2011–; Assoc. Prof., Univ. of Tennessee 1987–88; Assoc. Prof./Visiting Scholar, Univ. of California, Berkeley 1988–89; Assoc. Prof., then Prof., Dept of Sociology, Univ. of California-Riverside 1989–94; Edmund Asa Ware Distinguished Prof. of Sociology, Founder and Dir Environmental Justice Resource Center, Clark-Atlanta Univ., Atlanta, Ga 1994–2011; Conservation Achievement Award, Nat. Wildlife Fed. 1990, featured in CNN People You Should Know, Bullard: Green Issue is Black and White July 2007, named by Newsweek magazine as one of 13 Environmental Leaders of the Century 2008, Building Economic Alternatives Award, Co-op America 2008, John Muir Award, Sierra Club 2013. *Publications:* Invisible Houston: The Black Experience in Boom and Bust 1987, In Search of the New South: The Black Urban Experience in the 1970s and 1980s 1989, Houston: Growth and Decline in a Sunbelt Boomtown (co-author) 1989, Dumping in Dixie: Race, Class and Environmental Quality, 1990, Confronting Environmental Racism: Voices From the Grassroots (ed.) 1993, Unequal Protection: Environmental Justice and Communities of Color (ed.) 1994, Residential Apartheid: The American Legacy (co-ed.) 1994, Just Transportation: Dismantling Race and Class Barriers to Mobility (co-ed.) 1997, People of Color Environmental Groups Directory 2000, 2000, Sprawl City: Race, Politics and Planning in Atlanta, Washington, DC (co-ed.) 2000, Just Sustainabilities: Development in an Unequal World (co-author) 2003, Highway Robbery: Transportation Racism and New Routes to Equity (co-author) 2004, The Quest for Environmental Justice: Human Rights and the Politics of Pollution 2005, In the Wake of the Storm: Environment, Disaster and Race After Katrina (co-author) 2006, Toxic Wastes and Race at Twenty: 1987–2007 2007, Growing Smarter: Achieving Livable Communities, Environmental Justice, and Regional Equity 2007, The Black Metropolis in the Twenty-First Century: Race, Power, and the Politics of Place 2007, Deadly Waiting Game Beyond Hurricane Katrina: Government Response, Unnatural Disasters, and African Americans 2009, Race, Place and Environmental Justice After Hurricane Katrina: Struggles to Reclaim, Rebuild, and Revitalize New Orleans and the Gulf Coast 2009. *Address:* BJ-ML School of Public Affairs Dean, Public Affairs Building 415 F, Texas Southern University, 3100 Cleburne Street, Houston, TX 77004, USA (office). *Telephone:* (713) 313-6849 (office). *E-mail:* bullardrd@tsu.edu (office). *Website:* www.tsu.edu/academics/colleges__schools/publicaffairs/drbullard/bio.php (office); drrobertbullard.com.

BULLER, Arthur John, BA, MB, BSc, PhD, FRCP, FIBiol, FRSA; British physiologist and academic; *Professor Emeritus, Faculty of Medicine, University of Bristol;* b. 16 Oct. 1923; s. of Thomas Alfred Buller and Edith May Buller (née Wager); m. Helena Joan Pearson 1946; one s. two d. (one deceased); ed Duke of York's Royal Mil. School, Dover, St Thomas' Hosp. Medical School; Kitchener Scholar 1941–45; Lecturer in Physiology St Thomas' Hosp. 1946–49; Maj. RAMC, Specialist in Physiology, Jr Sec., Mil. Personnel Research Cttee 1949–53; Lecturer in Medicine, St Thomas' Hosp. 1953–57; Reader in Physiology, King's Coll., London 1961–65; Gresham Prof. of Physic 1963–65; Prof. of Physiology, Univ. of Bristol 1965–82, Dean Faculty of Medicine 1976–78, Prof. Emer. 1982–; Chief Scientist (on secondment), Dept of Health and Social Security 1978–81; Visiting Prof., Monash Univ., Australia 1972; Royal Soc. Commonwealth Fellow, Canberra, Australia 1958–59; mem. Bd of Govs Bristol Royal Infirmary 1968–74, Avon Health Authority 1974–78, MRC 1975–81; Chair. Neurosciences and Mental Health Bd, MRC 1975–77; External Scientific Adviser, Rayne Inst., St Thomas' Hosp. 1979–85; Research Devt Dir, Muscular Dystrophy Group of GB and NI 1982–90; mem. BBC, IBA Cen. Appeals Advice Cttee 1983–88; Hon. Consultant in Clinical Physiology, Bristol Dist Hospital 1970–85; Emergency Reserve Decoration (Army); Long Fox Memorial Lecturer, Univ. of Bristol 1978, Milroy Lecturer, Royal Coll. of Physicians 1983. *Publications:* articles in books and journals on normal and abnormal physiology. *Leisure interests:* clarets and conversation. *Address:* Flat 13, Turnpike Court, Hett Close, Ardingly, Haywards Heath, RH17 6GQ, England (home). *Telephone:* (1444) 891873 (home). *E-mail:* arthur.buller@btinternet.com.

BULLOCK, Sandra; American actress; b. 26 July 1964, Arlington, Va; d. of John Bullock and Helga Bullock; m. Jesse James 2005 (divorced 2010); ed East Carolina Univ.; grew up in Germany and Washington, DC; frequent appearances on European stage with opera-singer mother; appeared in off-Broadway productions including No Time Flat (WPA Theatre); f. Fortis Films (production co.). *Films include:* Hangmen 1987, A Fool and His Money 1988, Breakin' the Rules 1989, Religion, Inc. 1989, Love Potion No. 9 1992, The Vanishing 1993, When the Party's Over 1993, The Thing Called Love 1993, Fire on the Amazon 1993, Demolition Man 1993, Wrestling Ernest Hemingway 1993, Speed 1994, Who Do I Gotta Kill? 1994, While You Were Sleeping 1995, The Net 1995, Stolen Hearts 1996, Two If By Sea 1996, Moll Flanders, A Time to Kill 1996, In Love and War 1996, Speed 2 1997, Hope Floats (also exec. producer) 1998, Making Sandwiches (short, also writer) 1998, Practical Magic 1998, Prince of Egypt (voice) 1998, Forces of Nature 1999, Gun Shy 1999, 28 Days 2000, Famous 2000, Miss Congeniality 2000, Murder by Numbers 2001, Exactly 3:30 2001, Divine Secrets of the Ya-Ya Sisterhood 2002, Two Weeks' Notice 2002, Crash 2004, Loverboy 2005, Miss Congeniality 2: Armed and Fabulous 2005, The Lake House 2006, Infamous 2006, Premonition 2007, The Proposal 2009, All About Steve 2009, The Blind Side (Golden Globe for Performance by an Actress in a Motion Picture — Drama 2010, Acad. Award for Best Actress in a Leading Role 2010) 2009, Extremely Loud & Incredibly Close 2011, The Heat 2013, Gravity 2013, Aningaaq (short, voice) 2013. *Television includes:* Bionic Showdown: The Six Million Dollar Man and the Bionic Woman (film) 1989, Starting from Scratch (series) 1989, The Preppy Murder (film) 1989, Working Girl (NBC mini-series) 1990, Lucky Chances (mini-series) 1990, George Lopez (series) 2002–04. *Address:* c/o CAA, 2000 Avenue of the Stars, Los Angeles, CA 90067; Fortis Films, 8581 Santa Monica Blvd, Suite 1, West Hollywood, CA 90069, USA. *Telephone:* (310) 659-4533 (Fortis).

BULLOCK, Stephen (Steve) Clark, MA, JD; American lawyer, politician, state governor and academic; *Governor of Montana;* b. 11 April 1966, Missoula, Mont.; m. Lisa Bullock; ed Helena High School, Claremont McKenna Coll., Columbia Univ.; served as Chief Legal Counsel to Mont. Sec. of State Mike Cooney; worked with Montana Dept of Justice for four years, first as Exec. Asst Attorney-Gen., later as Acting Chief Deputy 1997–2001, also served as Legis. Dir; unsuccessful cand. for Mont. Attorney-Gen. 2000; practised law with Steptoe & Johnson, Washington, DC 2001–04; Adjunct Prof., George Washington Univ. Law School 2001–04; returned to Mont. to work in pvt. practice in Helena 2004–08; Attorney-Gen. of Mont. 2009–13; Gov. of Montana 2013–; Chair. Western Governors' Asscn 2016–17, Nat. Governors' Asscn 2018–19; Democrat. *Address:* Office of the Governor, PO Box 200801, State Capitol, Helena, MT 59620-0801, USA (office). *Telephone:* (406) 444-3111 (office). *Fax:* (406) 444-5529 (office). *E-mail:* governor@mt.gov (office). *Website:* governor.mt.gov (office).

BULMAHN, Edelgard, MA; German politician; *Deputy Chairman, Atlantik-Brücke;* b. 4 March 1951, Minden; m. Prof. Joachim Wolschke-Bulmahn; ed Petershagen Aufbaugymnasium and Hanover Univ.; high school teacher for seven years; mem. SPD 1969–; mem. Bundestag (SPD) 1987–2017, Vice-Pres. 2013–2017; SPD Parl. Group Deputy Spokesman on Research and Tech. 1990–94, mem. Exec. Cttee SPD Parl. Group 1991–98, Exec. Cttee SPD 1993–2011, Chair. Parl. Cttee on Educ., Science, Research, Tech. and Tech. Assessment 1995–96, Spokeswoman on Educ. and Research 1996–98, Study Commission on Growth, Wellbeing and Quality of Life, SPD 2011–13, mem. Cttee for Econ. Affairs and Tech. 2005–09, mem. Cttee on Foreign Affairs 2009–13; Fed. Minister of Educ. and Research 1998–2005; Chair. European Space Agency (ESA) at ministerial level 2001–05; currently Deputy Chair. Atlantik-Brücke; mem. Bd of Trustees Stiftung Lesen 2015–, Humboldt Univ., Deutsche Telekom Foundation, German Inst. for Econ. Research, Berghof Foundation, IMPULS Stiftung; Hon. Doctorate (German-Jordanian Univ., Amman) 2016; Christian-Peter-Beuth Prize 2008, Sophie-de-la-Roche Prize, German Asscn of Women Academics 2010. *Leisure interests include:* reading, sports, gardening. *Address:* Atlantik-Brücke, Magnus-Haus Am Kupfergraben 7, 101117 Berlin, Germany (office). *Telephone:* (30) 2039830 (office). *Fax:* (30) 20398320 (office). *E-mail:* info@atlantik-bruecke.org (office). *Website:* www.atlantik-bruecke.org (office).

BULMER-THOMAS, Victor Gerald, OBE, MA, DPhil; British economist, academic and international consultant; *Honorary Professor, Institute of the Americas, University College London;* b. 23 March 1948, London, England; s. of Ivor Bulmer-Thomas and Joan Bulmer; m. Barbara Swasey 1970; two s. one d.; ed Westminster School, New Coll. and St Antony's Coll., Oxford; Research Fellow, Fraser of Allander Inst., Univ. of Strathclyde 1975–78; Lecturer in Econs, Queen Mary Coll., London 1978–87, Reader, Queen Mary & Westfield Coll. 1987–90, Prof. of Latin American Econs 1990–98, Prof. Emer. 1998–, Dir Inst. of Latin American Studies 1992–98, Sr Research Fellow 1998–2001; Dir Chatham House (Royal Inst.

of Int. Affairs) 2001–06, Assoc. Fellow 2007–; Visiting Prof., Florida Int. Univ., Miami 2007–10; Sr Distinguished Fellow, School of Advanced Study 2007–; Dir (non-exec.), Schroders Emerging Countries Fund 1996–2003, Deutsche Latin America Companies Trust 2004, New India Investment Trust 2004–, JP Morgan Brazil Investment Trust 2010–; fmr Dir Gartmore Latin America New Growth Fund SA; Hon. Prof., Inst. of the Americas, University College London 2012–, Hon. Research Fellow, Inst. of Latin American Studies 2014–; Order of San Carlos (Colombia) 1998, Order of the Southern Cross (Brazil) 1998. *Publications include:* Input-Output Analysis for Developing Countries 1982, The Political Economy of Central America since 1920 1987, Studies in the Economics of Central America 1988, Britain and Latin America: A Changing Relationship (ed.) 1989, The Economic History of Latin America Since Independence 1994, The New Economic Model in Latin America and Its Impact on Income Distribution and Poverty (ed.) 1996, Thirty Years of Latin American Studies in the UK 1997, United States and Latin America: The New Agenda (ed.) 1999, Regional Integration in Latin America and the Caribbean: The Political Economy of Open Regionalism (ed.) 2001, The Cambridge Economic History of Latin America, Vol. I: The Colonial Era and the Short Nineteenth Century, Vol. II: The Long Twentieth Century (co-ed.) 2005, The Economic History of the Caribbean since the Napoleonic Wars 2012, The Economic History of Belize (with Barbara Bulmer-Thomas) 2012. *Leisure interests:* music (viola), tennis, walking, canoeing, underwater photography. *Address:* UCL Institute of the Americas, University College London, Gower Street, London, WC1E 6BT, England (office). *Telephone:* (20) 7679-9748 (office). *E-mail:* ucl-ia@ucl.ac.uk (office). *Website:* www.ucl.ac.uk/americas/people/academic-staff/Victor-Bulmer-Thomas (office).

BUMAYA, Al Hajj André Habib, MA; Rwandan diplomatist and politician; ed univ. in USA; fmr Amb. to Libya; Minister of Foreign Affairs and Regional Co-operation 2000–02, of Labour and Public Service 2003–06; Leader, Parti démocratique idéal (fmrly Parti démocratique islamique); left party and fled to Burundi Feb. 2010.

BUMÇI, Aldo Tonin, BA, MA; Albanian politician; b. 11 June 1974, Tirana; ed Eastern Mediterranean Univ., Northern Cyprus, Bilkent Univ., Turkey; Researcher, Albanian Inst. for Int. Studies, Tirana 1999, becoming Deputy Exec. Dir –2005; mem. Kuvendi Popullor (Parl.) for Tirana 2005–, mem. Cttee on Legal Affairs, Public Admin and Human Rights, Cttee on European Integration; Minister of Justice 2005–07, of Tourism, Culture, Youth and Sports 2011–12, of Foreign Affairs April–Sept. 2013; mem. Democratic Party of Albania. *Address:* Kuvendi Popullor, Bulevardi Dëshmorët e Kombit 4, Tirana, Albania (office). *E-mail:* info@parlament.al (office). *Website:* www.parlament.al (office).

BÜNDCHEN, Gisele Caroline; Brazilian model, actress and fashion designer; b. 20 July 1980, Três de Maio; d. of Valdir Bündchen and Vânia Bündchen (née Nonnenmacher); m. Tom Brady 2009; one s. one d.; grew up in Horizontina, Rio Grande do Sul; has participated in modelling campaigns for Valentino, Tommy Hilfiger, Chloe, Celine, Versace, Christian Dior, Michael Kors, Ralph Lauren, Victoria's Secret, Louis Vuitton and Dolce & Gabbana; introduced own skin care product line, Sejaa Pure Skincare 2010; currently owns a hotel in Brazil; UNEP Goodwill Amb.; announced retirement from modelling 2015; VH1/Vogue Model of the Year Award 1999. *Films:* Taxi 2004, The Devil Wears Prada 2006, cameo role in Apple Get a Mac campaign. *Address:* c/o img models NY, 304 Park Avenue South, 12 Floor, New York NY 10010, USA (office). *Website:* www.imgmodels.com (office); www.giselebundchen.com.br.

BUNDU, Abass Chernor, PhD; Sierra Leonean lawyer, diplomatist, politician and business executive; *Chairman, Afcan Holdings Limited;* b. 3 June 1948, Gbinti, Port Loko Dist; s. of Isatu Kallay Bundu and Pa Santigie; m. Khadija Allie 1976; two s. three d.; ed Australian Nat. Univ., Canberra, Univ. of Cambridge, UK; Asst Dir, Commonwealth Secr., London 1975–82; mem. Parl. for Port Loko NE 1982–90; Minister of Agric., Natural Resources and Forestry 1982–85; Exec. Sec., Econ. Community of W African States (ECOWAS) 1989–93; Sec. of State for Foreign Affairs and Int. Co-operation 1994–95; Leader, People's Progressive Party (PPP) 1996; unsuccessful presidential cand. (PPP) 1996; Co-founder and Chair. Afcan Holdings Ltd 1997–; Northern Regional Chair. Sierra Leone People's Party 2013–; Yorke Award, Univ. of Cambridge. *Leisure interests:* tennis, swimming. *Address:* Afcan Holdings Ltd, 40 UN Drive, Cockerill, South Freetown, Sierra Leone (office). *Telephone:* (22) 230581 (office); 76-766581 (mobile). *E-mail:* abassbundu@hotmail.com (office). *Website:* www.afcanholdings.com (office).

BUNDY, Colin James, BA, BA (Hons), MPhil, DPhil; South African historian, academic and fmr university administrator; b. 4 Oct. 1944; m.; two c.; ed Graeme Coll., Grahamstown, Univ. of Natal, Univ. of the Witwatersrand, Merton Coll., Oxford (Rhodes Scholar) and St Antony's Coll. (Beit Sr Research Scholar), UK; Research Fellow, Queen Elizabeth House, Oxford 1979–80, Dept for External Studies, Oxford 1980–84; fmr Sr Lecturer, Manchester Polytechnic; Dir Inst. for Historical Research, Univ. of the Western Cape 1992–94, Vice-Rector 1994–97; Vice-Chancellor and Prin. Univ. of the Witwatersrand 1997–2001; Dir and Prin. SOAS, London 2001–06; Deputy Vice-Chancellor Univ. of London 2003–06; Warden, Green Coll., Oxford 2006–08, first Prin. Green Templeton Coll. (following merger with Templeton Coll.) 2008–10; Trustee, Canon Collins Educational & Legal Assistance Trust; Hon. Fellow, Kellogg Coll., Oxford. *Publications:* History, Revolution and South Africa 1987, Remaking the Past: New Perspectives in South African History 1987, Hidden Struggles in Rural South Africa: Politics & Popular Movements in the Transkei & Eastern Cape 1890–1930 (co-author) 1987, The History of the South African Communist Party 1991. *Leisure interests:* cricket, chess, music, hiking. *Address:* c/o Office of the Principal, Green Templeton College, 43 Woodstock Road, Oxford, OX2 6HG, England. *E-mail:* info@gtc.ox.ac.uk.

BUNDY, James Abbott, AB, MFA; American theatre director and academic; *Dean, School of Drama and Artistic Director, Yale Repertory Theatre, Yale University;* b. 8 May 1959, Boston, Mass; s. of McGeorge Bundy and Mary L. Bundy; m. Anne Tofflemire 1988; two d.; ed Harvard Coll., London Acad. of Music and Dramatic Art, UK, Yale School of Drama; Man. Dir Cornerstone Theater Co., New York 1989–91; Assoc. Producing Dir The Acting Company 1996–98; Artistic Dir Great Lakes Theater Festival, Cleveland 1998–2002; Adjunct Prof. of Theatre, Case Western Reserve Univ., Cleveland –2002; Artistic Dir Yale Repertory Theatre, New Haven, Conn. 2002–, Prof. of Drama, Yale School of Drama 2002–, Dean 2002–; mem. Bd of Dirs, Theatre Communications Group 2007–13; fmr Dir California Shakespeare Festival, Alabama Shakespeare Festival, Lincoln Center Theater Dirs Lab., Juilliard School Drama Div.; Trustee, Groton School 2003–; Tom Killen Award, Conn. Critics Circle 2007. *Address:* Yale School of Drama, 222 York Street, New Haven, CT 06520 (office); Yale Repertory Theatre, PO Box 208244, 1120 Chapel Street (at York), New Haven, CT 06520-8244, USA (office). *Telephone:* (203) 432-1234 (office). *Fax:* (203) 432-6423 (office). *E-mail:* james.bundy@yale.edu (office); yalerep@yale.edu (office). *Website:* drama.yale.edu (office); www.yalerep.org (office).

BUNE, Poseci Wagalevu; Fijian politician and diplomatist; ed Queen Victoria School, Royal Coll. of Public Admin., London, UK; joined Public Service Dept 1966, apptd Sr Admin. Officer 1972, attached to Australian Embassy, Bangkok 1973, joined Perm. Mission to UN, New York 1973, apptd First Sec. 1973, Counsellor, Mission to EEC 1976–80; Western Divisional Commr, Ministry of Rural Devt 1981–85; Amb. to EEC (also accred to Belgium, Luxembourg, The Netherlands, France and Italy) 1985–87; Perm. Sec. for Public Service 1987–95, Perm. Sec. to Govt and for Public Service 1990–95; Amb. and Perm. Rep. to UN, New York 1995–2000; began political career with Veitokani ni Lewenivanua Vakarisito (VLV—Christian Democratic Alliance), co-f. 1998; mem. Parl. for Macuata Fijian Communal constituency on VLV ticket 1999–2001, for Labasa Open constituency on Fiji Labour Party ticket 2001–06; mem. and Deputy Leader, Fiji Labour Party 2004–06, Vice-Pres. 2005–06 (expelled); Minister for the Environment June–Dec. 2006, for Public Service and Public Sector Reform 2007–08.

BUNGEI, Wilfred Kipkemboi; Kenyan athlete; b. 24 July 1980, Kabirirsang, nr Kapsabet; second cousin of Kenyan-born Danish fmr athlete Wilson Kipketer; ed Samoei High School; middle distance runner; ranked World No. 1 over 800m in 2002 and 2003; set personal best of 1:42.34 in Rieti 2002; part of 4×800m relay team that holds world record 2008; Silver Medal, World Jr Championships, Annecy, France 1998, World Championships, Edmonton 2001; Bronze Medal, African Championships, Radès 2002, World Indoor Championships, Birmingham 2003; finished first at Int. Asscn of Athletics Feds (IAAF) World Athletics Final, Monaco 2003, fifth at Olympic Games, Athens 2004, fourth at World Championships, Helsinki 2005, first at IAAF World Athletics Final, Monaco 2005; Gold Medal, World Indoor Championships, Moscow 2006; Bronze Medal, IAAF World Athletics Final, Stuttgart 2006; finished first at World Championships, Osaka 2007; Gold Medal, Olympic Games, Beijing 2008. *Address:* c/o Kenya Athletics Federation, PO Box 46722-00100 GPO, Riadha House, Aerodrome Road, 00100 Nairobi West, Kenya. *Telephone:* (2) 605021. *Fax:* (2) 605020. *E-mail:* info@athleticskenya.or.ke. *Website:* www.athleticskenya.or.ke.

BUNNAG, Marut; Thai politician and lawyer; b. 21 Aug. 1925, Bangkok; s. of Phra Sutthikarnvinijchai and Mrs Phongsri; m. Phantipha Bunnag; two c.; ed Thammasat Univ.; with Ministry of Justice –1952; Marut Bunnag Int. Law Office law practice 1952–; Minister of Justice 1979; mem. Parl. (Democratic Party) 1983–, served as Speaker of the House of Reps and Pres. Nat. Ass.; Minister of Public Health 1983–86, Sept.–Dec. 1990, of Educ. 1988; Deputy Leader, Democrat Party, Sr Adviser; part-time Lecturer, Thai Bar Asscn, Thammasart Univ., Chulalongkorn Univ., Mahidol Univ., Ramkhamhaeng Univ., etc.; mem. World Peace Through Law Centre, Int. Bar Asscn, Law Asscn for Asia and the Pacific (Pres.). *Address:* c/o Marut Bunnag International Law Office, Forum Tower, 22nd Floor, 184/130–136 Ratchadaphisek Road, Huaykwang, Bangkok 10320 (office); 45/1 Pradipat Road, Kwaeng Samsane-nai, Khet Phyathai, Bangkok 10400, Thailand (home). *Telephone:* (2) 645-2556 (office); (2) 271-1081 (home). *Fax:* (2) 645-2568 (office). *E-mail:* marut@loxinfo.co.uk (office). *Website:* www.marut.th.com (office).

BUNSUMPUN, Prasert, BEng, MBA; Thai energy executive; b. 20 Feb. 1952; ed Churalongkorn Univ., Utah State Univ., Harvard Univ. and Nat. Defense Coll., USA, King Prajadhipoks Inst.; Dir Dept of Petroleum Procurements & Contracts, Petroleum Authority of Thailand (PTT) 1986–91, Asst Gov. of Marketing 1991–92, Sr Vice-Pres., Marketing Downstream Oil Business 1992–96, Pres. PTT Oil 1996–99, Pres. PTT Gas Business Group 2000–01, Sr Exec. Vice-Pres. PTT Gas Business Group 2001–03, Pres. and CEO PTT Public Co. Ltd 2003–11, Sec. 2007–11, Chair. PTT Global Chemical Public Co. Ltd Feb.–June 2010, 2011–, Vice-Chair. 2010–11; Chair. Thai Lube Base Public Co. Ltd 2005–; Chair. of the Bd and Chair. Exec. Cttee IRPC Public Co. Ltd 2011–14, Dir 2009–14; mem. Bd of Dirs, PTT Exploration and Production PLC (Chair. 2007–11), Trans Thai-Malaysia (Thailand) Co. Ltd, PTT Natural Gas Distribution Co. Ltd, PTT Aromatics and Refining Public Co. Ltd 2007–11, PTT Global Chemical Public Co. Ltd 2005–, Thai Olefin Public Co. Ltd, Thai Petroleum Pipeline Co. Ltd, Nat. Petrochemical PLC, Thaioil Co. Ltd –2010, Thaioil Power Co. Ltd, Independent Power (Thailand) Co. Ltd, Siam City Bank Public Co. Ltd –2010, Krungthai Bank Public Co. Ltd 2014–15; Ind. Dir Shin Corpn Public Co. Ltd 2011–; mem. Nat. Legis. Ass. 2006–08; Pres. Utah Univ. Alumni, USA; Chair. Thailand Business Council for Sustainable Devt 2011–, Community Enterprise Inst., Churalongkorn Univ. Eng Alumni; mem. Nat. Legis. Ass. 2006–08; Hon. DEng (Chulalongkorn Univ.); Hon. Dr of Man. (Nat. Inst. of Devt Admin); Hon. Dr of Man. Science (Petchaburi Rajabhat Univ.). *Address:* c/o IRPC Public Co. Ltd, 555/2 Energy Complex Building B, 6th Vibhavadi-Rangsit Road, Kwaeng Chatuchak Khet, Chatuchak, Bangkok 10900, Thailand. *E-mail:* info@irpc.co.th.

BUORA, Carlo Orazio; Italian business executive; b. 26 May 1946, Milan; m.; two s.; ed Bocconi Univ., Milan; began career at Banca Nazionale del Lavoro 1972; Head of Finance and Admin, Merloni Finanziaria 1979–82; Finance Dir SNIA Viscose 1982–89 (co. acquired by Fiat 1984), Deputy Dir-Gen. Telettra SpA 1989; Gen. Man. Benetton Group 1989–91; joined Pirelli SpA 1991, Dir and CEO 1999–2006; apptd Jt CEO Olivetti SpA 2001; CEO and Man. Dir Telecom Italia SpA 2001–11; Dir or fmr Dir, Riunione Adriatica Di Sicurta SpA, Olimpia SpA, RCS MediaGroup SpA, FC Internazionale SpA, Pirelli Labs SpA, Tecnost SpA, Mediobanca SpA, Salini Impregilo SpA 2008–12; mem. Bd of Man. HDP Holding di Partecipazioni SpA, Mediobanca SpA, RAS SpA, Tecnost SpA; mem. Advisory Cttee EuroQube Fund.

BURBIDGE, (Eleanor) Margaret Peachey, PhD, FRS; American (b. British) astronomer and academic; *Professor Emerita of Physics, University of California, San Diego;* b. 12 Aug. 1919, Davenport, England; d. of Stanley John Peachey and Marjorie Peachey (née Stott); m. Geoffrey Burbidge 1948 (died 2010); one d.; ed

Frances Holland School, London and Univ. Coll., London; Second Asst, Asst Dir and acting Dir Univ. of London Observatory 1946–51; Research Fellow, Yerkes Observatory, Harvard Coll. Observatory 1951–53, Calif. Inst. of Technology 1955–57; Research Fellow and Assoc. Prof. Univ. of Chicago 1957–62; Assoc. Research Physicist, Univ. of Calif., San Diego 1962–64, Prof. 1964, Univ. Prof. 1984–91, Prof. Emer. 1991–, Research Prof., Dept of Physics 1990–, Dir Center for Astrophysics and Space Sciences 1979–88; Dir Royal Greenwich Observatory 1971–73; Ed. Observatory 1948–51; mem. Editorial Bd Astronomy and Astrophysics 1969–85; Lindsay Memorial Lecture, NASA 1985; mem. Royal Astronomical Soc., American Astronomical Soc. (Pres. 1978), American Acad. of Arts and Science, NAS, AAAS (Fellow 1981, Pres. 1982), American Philosophical Soc., Soc. Royale des Sciences de Liège, Astronomical Soc. of the Pacific, New York Acad. of Sciences; Fellow, Univ. Coll., London, Lucy Cavendish Coll., Cambridge, Girton Coll., Cambridge; Hon. DSc (Smith Coll., Mass, Rensselaer Political Inst. and Univs of Sussex, Leicester, Bristol, Chicago, Mich., Mass, City Univ., London, Notre Dame, London and Williams Coll.); numerous prizes and awards including Helen B. Warner Prize (jtly with Geoffrey Burbidge) 1959, Karl G. Jansky Lectureship, Nat. Radio Astronomy Observatory 1977, Bruce Gold Medal, Astronomical Soc. of the Pacific 1982, Nat. Medal of Science, USA 1983, Einstein Medal 1988, Gold Medal, Royal Astronomical Soc. (jtly with Geoffrey Burbidge) 2005. *Publications:* Quasi-Stellar Objects (with Geoffrey Burbidge) 1967; numerous articles in scientific journals. *Address:* Center for Astrophysics and Space Sciences, University of California, Mail Code #0424, La Jolla, CA 92093, USA (office). *E-mail:* mburbidge@ucsd.edu (office).

BURBULIS, Gennady Eduardovich; Russian politician, academic and university administrator; *Vice-Rector for Innovative Development, International University, Moscow;* b. 4 Aug. 1945, Pervouralsk, Sverdlovsk (now Ekaterinburg); s. of Eduard Kazimirovich Burbulis and Valentina Ivanovna Belonogova; m. Natalia Kirsanova; one s.; ed Ural State Univ.; Lecturer, Ural Polytechnic Inst. 1974–83; Head of Chair and Deputy Dir Inst. of Non-Ferrous Metals 1983–89; organized Sverdlovsk Podium (open forum for discussing local and later nat., social, political and econ. problems) during perestroika period 1987; USSR People's Deputy 1989–90; formed Discussion Tribune, Sverdlovsk 1988; elected to Congress of People's Deputies 1989; mem. Inter-Regional Group; Chief of Staff to Boris Yeltsin 1991; State Sec. RSFSR (now Russian Fed.) 1991–92, State Council Sec. 1991–92; First Deputy Chair. Russian Govt 1991–92, Sec. of State May–Nov. 1992, Head of Advisors' Team Nov.–Dec. 1992; f. Strategy Centre for Humanitarian and Political Science 1993; Founder and Pres. Int. Humanitarian and Political Cen. Strategy 1993–; mem. State Duma (Parl.) 1994–2000, mem. Cttee for Geopolitics; Deputy Gov. Novgorod Region 2000–01; Chair. Observational Bd, Novotrubny factory, Pervouralsk 1997–98; Rep. of Novgorod Region to Council of Fed. 2001–07, Chair. Fed. Council Comm. on Methodology of Exercising the Fed. Council's Constitutional Powers 2002, later Adviser to Chair. of Fed. Council, First Deputy Head of Centre for Monitoring Law and Practice (Law Monitoring Centre) 2007–10; Founder, Prof. and Head of Dept of Politosophy and Philosophy, International Univ. in Moscow 2006–, Founder and Chair. Intercollegiate club 'Zub Mudrosti' (Wisdom Tooth), Vice-Rector for Innovative Devt 2011–; f. School of Politosophy 'Dostoinstvo' (Dignity) 2009; Pres. Youth Forum of Modernizers 'My Russia', Russian Fed. of Short Track Speed Skating; Medal 'In Commemoration of the 850th Anniversary of Moscow', Medal 'In Commemoration of the 1000th Anniversary of Kazan', Medal 'In Commemoration of the 300th Anniversary of St Petersburg', Jubilee Medal 'Twenty Years of Victory in the Great Patriotic War 1941–1945'. *Publication:* Profession – Politician 1999; lead author of annual report on the status of legislation in the Russian Fed. *Leisure interests:* poetry, playing soccer and tennis. *Address:* Rectorate, International University in Moscow, 125040 Moscow, Leningrad Prospect 17, Russia (office). *Telephone:* (495) 946-04-34 (office). *Fax:* (495) 946-03-29 (office). *E-mail:* burbulis@interun.ru (office). *Website:* www.interun.ru (office).

BURCH, Lt-Col (retd) David, OBE, JP, ED; Bermudian army officer (retd) and politician; ed Royal Mil. Acad., Sandhurst, UK; spent 20 years as Reinsurance Underwriting Man.; Commanding Officer, The Bermuda Regt 1994–97 (retd); Consultant to Ministry of Works and Eng and Housing 2005, Minister of Works and Eng and Housing 2005–06, Minister of Public Safety and Housing 2006–07, of Labour, Home Affairs and Housing 2007–10, of Nat. Security 2010–11; fmr Govt Leader in the Senate; host, weekly radio talk show Bermuda Speaks: Sundays with the Colonel; mem. Progressive Labour Party; mem. Bermuda Sea Cadet Asscn, Royal Artillery Asscn; Efficiency Decoration for outstanding mil. service 1990, First Clasp 1996. *E-mail:* dburch@plp.bm.

BURCH, Tory; American fashion designer, business executive and philanthropist; *Creative Director and CEO, Tory Burch LLC;* b. 17 June 1966, Valley Forge, Pa; d. of Buddy Robinson and Reva Robinson; m. 1st William Macklowe; m. 2nd Christopher Burch 1997 (divorced 2006); three s. (including twins) three step-d.; ed Agnes Irwin School, Rosemont, Pa, Univ. of Pennsylvania; moved to New York City and began career working with fashion designers, including Zoran, a Yugoslavian designer; worked at Harper's Bazaar magazine; copywriter for Polo Ralph Lauren and worked for Vera Wang; began fashion label, known as TRB by Tory Burch (later as Tory Burch) 2004, began as business operation in her Upper East Side apartment and then into free-standing boutiques, now numbering 26, opened flagship store in the NoLIta (North of Little Italy) neighbourhood of Manhattan, New York 2004; sold minority stake in co. to Mexican pvt. equity firm Tresalia Capital 2009; f. Tory Burch Foundation 2008; mem. Bd Memorial Sloan-Kettering Cancer Center; Chair. Spring Gala for the American Ballet Theatre 2006; inaugural mem. Presidential Ambassadors for Global Entrepreneurship (PAGE) 2014; Rising Star Award for Best New Retail Concept, Fashion Group International 2005, Accessory Brand Launch of the Year Award, Accessories Council of Excellence 2007, Council of Fashion Designers of America winner (Accessories Designer of the Year) 2008. *Television:* appeared as herself in fourth episode of Gossip Girl (teen drama series) 2009, Fashion King (cameo) 2012. *Address:* Tory Burch Corporate Offices & Showroom, 11 West 19th Street, 7th Floor, New York, NY 10011, USA (office). *Telephone:* (212) 683-2323 (office). *Fax:* (212) 683-3876 (office). *E-mail:* press@toryburch.com (office). *Website:* www.toryburch.com (office); www.toryburchfoundation.org; www.toryburchfoundation.org; www.toryburch.com.

BURCHULADZE, Paata; Georgian singer (bass) and politician; *Leader, Saxelmcipho Xalxistvis (State for the People);* b. 12 Feb. 1955, Tbilisi; ed Tbilisi State Conservatory, La Scala, Milan, Italy; debut in Tbilisi as Mephistopheles in Faust 1976; sang in Russia and Milan; further studies in Italy and began int. career after winning competitions 1981–82; roles include Basilio in Il Barbiere di Siviglia, Leporello, King Rene in Iolantha, Gremin in Eugene Onegin and Boris Godunov; guest appearances at the Bolshoi in Moscow; British debut in Elgar's Dream of Gerontius at Lichfield Festival 1983; Covent Garden debut as Ramfis in Aïda 1984; Salzburg Festival appearances as the Commendatore in Don Giovanni under von Karajan; Rossini's Basilio at the Metropolitan 1989, Khan Konchak in Prince Igor at Covent Garden 1990; Boris Godunov 1991, the Inquisitor in Prokofiev's The Fiery Angel 1992; King Philip in Don Carlos at Santiago 1994; Zaccaria in Nabucco at Verona Arena and Konchak in Prince Igor at San Francisco 1996; Walter in Luisa Miller for Royal Opera, Edinburgh 1998; apptd UN Goodwill Amb. 2006, UNICEF Goodwill Amb. 2010; f. Iavnana (charity foundation) 2004; est. Georgian Foundation (civic movt) 2015; Leader, centre-right Saxelmcipho Xalxistvis (State for the People) party 2016–; Honoured Artist of Georgia 1983, Kammersänger, State Opera of Stuttgart 1998, Hon. Citizen of Tbilisi 2001, Honoured Citizen of Tel Aviv 2010, Hon. Academician, Georgian Acad. of Science 2015, Georgian Business Acad. 2015; Order of Honour 1997, 2003, Order of the Star of Italy 2010, Golden Order of St George, Patriarchate of the Georgian Orthodox Church 2010, Austrian Cross of Honour (1st Class) for Science and Art 2014; Dr hc (SDASU) 2014, (Georgian Tech. Univ.) 2015; has won several competitions, including Voci Verdiane, Busseto 1981, Gold Medal and First Prize, Tchaikovsky Competition, Moscow 1982, First Prize, Int. Luciano Pavarotti Competition 1985, First Prize, Maria Callas Competition 1986; numerous awards, including Nat. Artist of Georgia 1985, Zakaria Paliashvili State Award 1991, Shota Rustaveli State Award 1991, Iakob Gogebashvili Award for Charity Activities for Orphans 1991, Vaja-Pshavela Award 1992, M. Tumanishvili Prize 2009, Presidential Order of Excellence of Georgia 2010. *Recordings include:* scenes from operas by Mussorgsky and Verdi; Don Giovanni; Fiesco in Simon Boccanegra; Sparafucile in Rigoletto; Ramfis in Aïda; Samson et Dalila. *Address:* c/o Camilla Wehmeyer, Askonas Holt Ltd, 15 Fetter Lane, London, EC4A 1BW, England (office); Markus Bendl, Künstleragentur Dr Raab & Dr Böhm GmbH, Plankengasse 7, 1010 Vienna, Austria (office); Angelo Gabrielli, Prima International Artists Management, Palazzo Zambeccari, Piazza Calderini 2/2, 40124 Bologna, Italy (office); Saxelmcipho Xalxistvis (State for the People), Tbilisi, Agmashenebeli 150, Georgia (office). *Telephone:* (20) 7400-1700 (London) (office); (1) 512050110 (Vienna) (office); (5) 1264056 (Bologna) (office); (32) 224-88-55 (Tbilisi) (office). *Fax:* (20) 7400-1799 (London) (office); (1) 5127743 (Vienna) (office); (5) 1230766 (Bologna) (office). *E-mail:* camilla.wehmeyer@askonasholt.co.uk (office); bendl@rbartists.at (office); prima@primartists.com (office); markusb@cso.at (office). *Website:* www.askonasholt.co.uk/artists/singers/bass/paata-burchuladze (office); www.rbartists.at (office); www.facebook.com/stateforpeople (office); burchuladze.com; www.primartists.com (office).

BURD, Steven A., BS, MA; American retail executive; *Founder and CEO, Burd Health;* b. 1949, Valley City, ND; m. Chris Burd; two c.; ed Carroll Coll., Univ. of Wisconsin; worked for Arthur D. Little, New York 1981–87; man., Safeway Stores, Kohlberg Kravis Roberts & Co. 1986–91; consultant Stop and Shop Cos, Boston 1988–89; consultant and interim CEO Fred Meyer Inc., Portland, Ore. 1991–92; Pres. Safeway Inc. 1992–2012, CEO 1993–2013, Chair. 1998–2013; Founder and CEO Burd Health 2013–; mem. Bd of Dirs Kohl's Corpn; mem. US Dept of Homeland Security's Pvt. Sector Sr Advisory Cttee 2003–. *Address:* Burd Health, 3201 Danville Blvd, Suite 215, Alamo, CA 94507, USA (office). *E-mail:* contact@burdhealth.com (office). *Website:* www.burdhealth.com (office).

BURDA, Hubert, DPhil; German publisher and author; *Managing Partner and Publisher, Hubert Burda Media;* b. 9 Feb. 1940, Heidelberg; s. of Franz Burda and Aenne Lemminger; m. Maria Furtwängler; ed Univ. of Munich; Man. Bild & Funk 1966–74; partner, Burda GmbH 1974, currently Man. Partner and Publisher, Hubert Burda Media; Co-Publr Elle-Verlag GmbH, Munich; Founder Hubert Burda Centre for Innovative Communications, Ben-Gurion Univ. in Beer Sheva, Israel; Co-founder Europe Online SA, Luxembourg, European Publishers Council; fmr Pres. Asscn of German Magazine Publishers; fmr Chair. of the Council, Munich Ludwig-Maximilians Univ.; est. Felix Burda Foundation 2001; f. Petrarca Prize (for poetry), Bambi (Media-Prize), Corp. Art Prize 1997; Publr Anna, Bunte, Burda Moden, Das Haus, ElleDecoration, Focus, Focus Online, Focus TV, Freundin, Freizeit Revue, InStyleLisa, Lisa Kochen & Backen, Mein schoener Garten, Meine Familie & ich; Great Cross of Merit (Germany); Interfaith Gold Medallion, Council of Christians and Jews 1999, European Print Media Prize, Gold Medal Freedom of Speech, European Asscn of Communications Agencies, Leo Baeck Prize, Cen. Council of Jews in Germany 2006, Jakob Fugger Medal. *Address:* Hubert Burda Media, Arabellastrasse 23, 81925 Munich, Germany (office). *E-mail:* info@hubert-burda-media.com (office). *Website:* www.burda.com (office); www.hubert-burda.de (office).

BURDETT-COUTTS, William Walter, MA; British artistic director and film and television producer; *Artistic Director and CEO, Riverside Studios;* b. 17 Feb. 1955, Harare, Zimbabwe; s. of William A. F. Burdett-Coutts and Nancy C. Burdett-Coutts (née Gervers); one s. two d.; ed Radley Coll., Oxford, Rhodes Univ., South Africa, Univ. of Essex; Artistic Dir Assembly Rooms, Edinburgh 1981–; Festival Dir Mayfest, Glasgow 1987–90; Head of Arts Granada TV 1990–93; Artistic Dir and CEO, Riverside Studios 1993–, Dir Riverside TV Studios Ltd 1998–, Chair. 2002–; Exec. Producer Assembly Film and TV 1994–2004, Dir Assembly Media Group Ltd 2007–11; Chair. Kiss 102 1993–97, Kiss 105 1996–97; Festival Dir Brighton Comedy Festival 2002–15; Chair. Red61 2006–. *Address:* Riverside Studios, 101 Queen Caroline Street, London, W6 9BN, England (office). *Telephone:* (20) 8237-1000 (office). *E-mail:* wbc@riversidestudios.co.uk (office). *Website:* www.riversidestudios.co.uk (office).

BUREAU, Jérôme, DHist; French journalist; *Head of News, Métropole Télévision 6 (M6);* b. 19 April 1956, Paris; m. Fabienne Pauly 1999; two c. (and two from previous m.); ed Sciences Po Paris; journalist with Libération 1978–81; Sr Reporter L'Equipe Magazine 1981–87, Ed.-in-Chief 1989–93; Ed.-in-Chief Le Sport 1987–88; Editorial Dir L'Équipe, L'Équipe-TV 1997–2003, L'Équipe Magazine, Vélo, XL, Tennis de France 1993–2003, lequipe.fr 1999–2003; TV and Radio

Producer, Sport FM 2004; apptd Dir of Communications, Métropole Télévision 6 (M6) 2004, currently Head of News. *Publications include:* L'Amour-Foot 1986, Les Géants du football 1996, L'année du football 2004, Euro 2004: la grande fête du football 2004, Les champions d'Athènes 2004, Braaasil: Les magiciens du football 2005. *Leisure interests:* cookery, bullfighting. *Address:* Métropole Télévision 6 (M6), 89 avenue Charles de Gaulle, 92575 Neuilly sur Seine cedex (office); 20 avenue Pernety, 75014 Paris, France (home). *E-mail:* jerome.bureau6@wanadoo.fr (home). *Website:* www.m6.fr (office).

BURES, Doris; Austrian politician; *Second President of National Council;* b. 3 Aug. 1962, Vienna; one d.; ed completed training as dental nurse; moved to Fed. Office of Austrian Socialist Youth Movt 1980, responsible for unemployed youth project 1985–86; active in Prov. Youth Information Office, Vienna 1987–88; Dist Councillor in Liesing (Vienna) 1987–90; Deputy Chair. Liesing Br., Sozialdemokratische Partei Österreichs (Austrian Socialist Party—SPÖ) 1995, held post of Chair. Dist Women's Org.; mem. Fed. Parl. 1990–, Fed. Party Man. SPÖ 2000–06, SPÖ Spokesperson on Building, Fed. Minister for Women, Media and Civil Service 2007–08, of Transport, Innovation and Technology 2008–14; Pres. National Council 2014–17, Second Pres. 2017–; Jt Acting Pres. of Austria 2016–17 (following annulment by Constitutional Court of presidential election result 1 July 2016); Pres. Austrian Tenants' Asscn 1997–. *Address:* Parliament, Dr. Karl Renner-Ring 3, 1017 Vienna, Austria (office). *E-mail:* doris.bures@parlament.gv.at (office). *Website:* www.parlament.gv.at (office).

BURG, Avraham (Avrum), BA; Israeli politician and author; b. 19 Jan. 1955, Jerusalem; s. of Dr Josef Burg and Rivka Burg (née Slonim); m. Yael Burg; six c.; ed Hebrew Univ. of Jerusalem; Lt in paratroopers brigade, Israel Defense Forces; mem. Knesset 1988–2004, Speaker 1999–2003, mem. Finance and State Control Cttees 1988–92, Chair. Educ. Cttee 1992–95, mem. Cttee for the Advancement of the Status of Women 1992–95; Chair. Jewish Agency for Israel 1995–99; fmr Chair. Zionist Movt, Co-Chair. World Jewish Restitution Org. 1995–99, Deputy Chair. World Jewish Congress; mem. int. cttee that negotiated settlement with Swiss banks 1995–99, mem. Bd of Claims Conf. 1995–99; Sr Fellow, Molad - The Center for Renewal of Democracy (think tank) 2012; mem. Hadash (Hachazit Hademokratit Leshalom Uleshivyon—Democratic Front for Peace and Equality) (leftist Jewish-Arab political party) 2015–. *Publications:* Brit Am: A Covenant of the People 1995, God Is Back 2006, Defeating Hitler 2007, The Holocaust Is Over: We Must Rise from Its Ashes 2008. *Address:* c/o Hadash, PO Box 26205, Tel-Aviv 61261, Israel. *Telephone:* 3-6293944. *Fax:* 3-6297263. *E-mail:* info@hadash.org.il. *Website:* hadash.org.il.

BURGEN, Sir Arnold (Stanley Vincent), Kt, MD, FRS; British scientist; b. 20 March 1922, London, England; s. of Peter Burgen and Elizabeth Burgen (née Wolfers); m. 1st Judith Browne 1946 (died 1993); two s. one d.; m. 2nd Olga Kennard 1993; ed Christ's Coll., Finchley, London, Middlesex Hosp. Medical School; Demonstrator, later Asst Lecturer, Middlesex Hosp. Medical School 1945–49; Prof. of Physiology, McGill Univ., Montreal 1949–62; Deputy Dir McGill Univ. Clinic, Montreal Gen. Hospital 1957–62; Sheild Prof. of Pharmacology, Univ. of Cambridge 1962–71; Dir Nat. Inst. of Medical Research, London 1971–82; Master Darwin Coll., Cambridge 1982–89, Deputy Vice-Chancellor, Univ. of Cambridge 1983–89; mem. MRC 1969–71, 1973–77, Hon. Dir MRC Molecular Pharmacology Unit 1967–72; Pres. Int. Union of Pharmacology 1972–75; Vice-Pres. Royal Soc. 1980–86, Foreign Sec. 1981–86; Fellow, Downing Coll., Cambridge 1962–71, Hon. Fellow 1972; mem. Bureau, European Science and Tech. Asscn 1994–; Ed. European Review 1993–; mem. Deutsche Akad. der Naturforscher Leopoldina 1984; Corresp. mem. Royal Acad. of Spain 1984; Foreign Assoc. NAS; Pres. Academia Europaea 1988–94; Academician of Finland; Hon. FRCP (Canada); Hon. DSc (McGill, Leeds, Liverpool), Hon. MD (Zurich) 1983, (Utrecht), Hon. DUniv (Surrey) 1983; Wellcome Gold Medal 1999. *Publications:* papers in journals of pharmacology and physiology. *Leisure interests:* sculpture, music. *Address:* 8A Hills Avenue, Cambridge, CB1 7XA, England. *Telephone:* (1223) 415381. *Fax:* (1223) 363852. *E-mail:* asvb@cam.ac.uk (office).

BURGESS, Sir Robert George, Kt, DL, BA, PhD; British academic administrator; b. 23 April 1947, Sherborne, Dorset; s. of George Burgess and Olive Burgess (née Andrews); m. Hilary Margaret Mary Joyce 1974; ed Durham Univ., Univ. of Warwick; Lecturer, Univ. of Warwick 1974–84, Sr Lecturer 1984–88, Dept Chair. 1985–88, Dir Centre for Educational Devt Appraisal and Research 1987–99, Chair. Faculty of Social Sciences 1988–91, Prof. of Sociology 1988–99, Founding Chair. Grad. School 1991–95, Pro-Vice-Chancellor 1995–99; Vice-Chancellor, Univ. of Leicester 1999–2014 (retd); mem. Research Resources Bd, Econ. and Social Research Council 1991–96, mem. Council 1996–2000, Chair. Postgraduate Training Bd 1997–2000 (mem. 1989–93, Vice-Chair. 1996–97); Founding Chair. UK Council for Grad. Educ. 1993–99; Chair. East Midlands Univs Asscn 2001–04; mem. Higher Educ. Funding Council for England (HEFCE) Review of Postgraduate Educ. 1995–96, HEFCE Quality Assessment, Learning and Teaching Cttee 2003–07, Bd UCAS 2001–11 (Chair. 2005–11), Jt Equality Steering Group 2001–03, Bd British Library 2003–10, School Teachers' Review Body 2015–; Trustee and Chair., Higher Educ. Acad. 2003–; apptd Deputy Lt of Leicestershire 2010; Chair. UUK/Guild HE Managing and Recording Student Achievement (The Burgess Groups) 2004–, Econ. and Social Research Council (ESRC) Teaching and Learning Research Programme 2004–09, Research Information Network 2005–11, Nat. Centre for Social Research 2012–; Chair. Bd of Govs, Greenwich School of Man., London 2017–; currently Pres. Soc. for Research into Higher Educ.; Academician, Acad. of Learned Socs in the Social Sciences 2000, Acad. of Social Sciences; DL 2010, UCEA Bd 2013–; Kt Bachelor for services to Higher Educ. locally and nationally 2010; Hon. DLitt (Staffordshire) 1998, Hon. DUniv (Northampton) 2007, Hon. EdD (De Montfort) 2013. *Publications include:* Experiencing Comprehensive Education 1983, In the Field 1984, Education, Schools and Schooling 1985, Sociology, Education and Schools 1986, Implementing In-Service Education (co-author) 1993, Research Methods 1993, Reflections of the University of Leicester (with Joanne Wood) 2010; ed. of more than 24 books on social research methodology and the sociology of educ. *Leisure interests:* some gardening, music, walking. *Address:* Society for Research into Higher Education, 73 Collier Street, London, N1 9BE, England (office). *Telephone:* (20) 7427-2350 (office). *Fax:* (20) 7278-1135 (office). *E-mail:* srhe@srhe.ac.uk (office). *Website:* www.srhe.ac.uk (office).

BURGHARDT, Günter, PhD, DrJur; German lawyer, academic, international organization official and fmr diplomatist; *Senior Counsel, Mayer Brown Europe-Brussels LLP;* b. 27 April 1941, Krosswitz; m. Rita Byl; three c.; ed Univs of Hamburg, Paris and Strasbourg; mem. of Legal Service, EC 1970, Desk Officer for External Relations (USA, Canada and Australia), for Devt of EC External Relations Network and Asst to Dir-Gen. Sir Roy Denman 1972–80, Deputy Head of Cabinet to Commr Karl-Heinz Narjes 1981–84, to Pres. Jacques Delors 1985–88, Political Dir, Sec.-Gen. of the Comm. under Pres. Delors 1988–93, Dir-Gen. of External Relations (Europe and Newly Ind. States), Common Foreign and Security Policy and External Service under Commr Hans van den Broek 1993–99, Dir-Gen. of External Relations for Commr Chris Patten 1999–2000; Amb. and Head Del. of EC to USA 2000–05; Visiting Prof., European Political and Admin. Studies Dept and EU Int. Relations and Diplomacy Studies Dept Coll. of Europe, Bruges 2005–; Sr Counsel, Mayer Brown Europe-Brussels LLP, Brussels 2005–; Bundesverdienstkreuz 1. Klasse. *Address:* Mayer Brown Europe-Brussels LLP, Avenue des Arts 52, 1000 Brussels (office); Vossenlaan 12, 3080 Tervuren (home); c/o Department of EU International Relations and Diplomacy Studies, College of Europe, Dijver 11, 8000 Bruges, Belgium (office). *Telephone:* (2) 502-55-17 (Mayer Brown) (office); (50) 47-72-51 (office). *Fax:* (2) 502-54-21 (Mayer Brown) (office); (50) 47-72-50 (office). *E-mail:* gburghardt@mayerbrown.com (office). *Website:* www.mayerbrown.com (office).

BURGIN, Victor, ARCA, MFA; British artist, writer and academic; *Emeritus Millard Chair of Fine Art, Goldsmiths College, London;* b. 24 July 1941, Sheffield; s. of Samuel Burgin and Gwendolyne A. Crowder; m. 1st Hazel P. Rowbotham 1964 (divorced 1975); m. 2nd Francette Pacteau 1988; two s.; ed Firth Park Grammar School, Sheffield, Sheffield Coll. of Art, Royal Coll. of Art, London, Yale Univ., USA; Sr Lecturer, Trent Polytechnic, Nottingham 1967–73; Prof. of History and Theory of Visual Arts, Faculty of Communication, Polytechnic of Cen. London 1973–88; Prof. of Art History, Univ. of Calif., Santa Cruz 1988–95, Prof. of History of Consciousness 1995–2001, Prof. Emer. of History of Consciousness 2001–; Millard Prof. of Fine Art, Goldsmiths Coll., Univ. of London 2001–06, Emer. Millard Chair of Fine Art 2006–; Prof. of Media Philosophy and History of Consciousness, European Grad. School; Picker Professorship, Colgate Univ., Hamilton, New York 1980; mem. arts advisory panel, Arts Council of Great Britain 1971–76, 1980–81; Artist-in-Residence, Institut Méditerranéen de Recherche et de Création, Marseille, France 1993, Soros Foundation Center for Culture and Communication, Budapest, Hungary 1997; Robert Gwathmey Chair. in Art and Architecture, The Cooper Union for Advancement of Science and Art, New York 2000; Josep Lluis Sert Practitioner in Arts, Carpenter Center for Visual Arts, Harvard Univ. 2007; apptd Visiting Prof., Dept of Cinema and Media Studies, Univ. of Chicago 2015; US/UK Bicentennial Arts Exchange Fellow 1976–77, Deutscher Akademischer Austauschdienst Fellowship 1978–79; Mellon Fellow, Univ. of Pennsylvania 2016; numerous mixed and solo exhbns at galleries around the world from 1965; Hon. DUniv (Sheffield Hallam) 2005, Dr hc (Université de Liège, Belgium) 2010. *Publications include:* Work and Commentary 1973, Thinking Photography 1982, The End of Art Theory 1986, Between 1986, Passages 1991, In/Different Spaces 1996, Some Cities 1996, Venice 1997, Shadowed 2000, The Remembered Film 2005, Voyage to Italy 2007, Incomplete Components of a Practice 2008, Situational Aesthetics 2009, Parallel Texts: Interviews and Interventions About Art 2011, Victor Burgin: Five Pieces for Projection 2014; contrib. to exhbn catalogues. *Address:* Department of Art, Goldsmiths College, Lewisham Way, New Cross, London, SE14 6NW, England (office). *Telephone:* (20) 7919-7671 (office). *Fax:* (20) 7919-7673 (office). *E-mail:* v.burgin@gold.ac.uk (office). *Website:* www.gold.ac.uk/art/staff (office).

BURGMANS, Antony, MA; Dutch business executive; b. 13 Feb. 1947, Rotterdam; one s. one d.; ed Nijenrode Univ., Univ. of Stockholm, Sweden, Univ. of Lancaster, UK; joined Unilever Netherlands 1972, Marketing Asst, Lever Netherlands and Indonesia, Marketing and Sales Dir Lever, Netherlands 1982–85, Lever Germany 1985–88, Chair. PT Unilever Indonesia 1988–91, Dir Unilever (Personal Care Products Div.) 1991–94, (Ice Cream and Frozen Foods—Europe) 1994–98, Chair. Unilever European Cttee 1994–98, Vice-Chair. Unilever Nevada 1998–99, Chair. 1999–2007 (retd); fmr Chair. Supervisory Bd Akzo Nobel; fmr Chair. TNT Express; fmr Dir (non-exec.), BP PLC; Commdr, Order of Orange Nassau 2007, Hon. KBE (UK) 2008; Dr hc (Lancaster) 2005; UN Humanitarian of the Year Award 2007. *Leisure interests:* skiing, Dutch painters, soccer, fly fishing. *Address:* BurGo BV, Hooikade 33-34, 2514 BJ The Hague, Netherlands (office). *Telephone:* (70) 5140382 (office). *E-mail:* antony.burgmans@burgobv.nl (office).

BURGO, Carlos Augusto Duarte, BEcons, MSc; Cabo Verde politician and central banker; *Governor, Banco de Cabo Verde;* b. 5 March 1958, Nova Sintra, Ilha da Brava; ed Martin Luther Univ., Halle-Wittenberg, Germany, Catholic Univ. of Louvain, Belgium, Univ. of Iowa, USA; Prof. of Econs, Instituto Amílcar Cabral 1983–90, Dir 1987–90; Deputy, Assembleia Nacional for Brava constituency 1991–2001, Pres. Special Perm. Comm. for Finance 2000; Pres. Municipal Ass. of Brava 2000–04; Minister of Finance, Planning and Regional Devt 2001–03; currently Gov. Banco de Cabo Verde (BCV—Central Bank of Cabo Verde); mem. Nat. Council and Political Comm., Partido Africano da Independência de Cabo Verde (PAICV). *Address:* Banco de Cabo Verde, Av. Amilcar Cabral, CP 101, Praia, Santiago, Cabo Verde (office). *Telephone:* (261) 7192 (office); (260) 7180 (office). *Fax:* (261) 4447 (office). *Website:* fevora@bcv.cv (office); www.bcv.cv (office).

BURGOS VARELA, Jorge; Chilean lawyer, fmr diplomatist and politician; b. 24 June 1956, Providencia; m. María Patricia Salas; three s.; ed Universidad de Chile; began career as Vice-Pres., Public Safety Coordinating Council; Chief of Staff and Legal Adviser to Minister of Interior 1990–93; Acting Mayor, Metropolitan Region 1992; Sec. of War 1993–96; Amb. to Ecuador 1996–2000; Sec. of the Interior 2000–01; mem. Camera de Diputados (Parl.) for Dist 21 (Ñuñoa y Providencia) 2002–14, Chair. Standing Cttee on Constitution, Legislation and Justice 2002–03, Special Cttee on Public Safety 2003–04, Leader, Christian Democrat Parl. Group 2005, First Vice-Pres. Chamber of Deputies 2006; Minister of Nat. Defence 2014–15, of the Interior and Public Security 2015–16 (resgnd); mem. Partido Demócrata Cristiano. *Address:* c/o Ministry of the Interior and Public Security, Palacio de la Moneda, Santiago, Chile (office). *Website:* www.jorgeburgos.cl.

BURGUBURU, Jean-Marie, LLM; French lawyer and international organization official; b. 19 Aug. 1945; m. Danièle Burguburu (née Combaldieu); two d.; ed Univ. of Paris, French Inst. for Higher Nat. Defence Studies, French Inst. for Higher Nat. Security Studies; lecturer at Univs of Paris and Bordeaux, in several law schools and at Industrial Property Centre, Univ. of Alicante, Spain; mem. Paris Bar 1966–, Chair. 2004–05, mem. Paris Bar Council 1991–; spent more than 40 years at Gide Loyrette Nouel (int. law firm), Partner 1976–2010; Chair. French Nat. Cttee of Union Internationale des Avocats (UIA) 2006–08, First Vice-Pres. UIA 2010–12, Pres. 2012–16, Pres. Int. Bar Leaders Senate (UIA consultative body and discussion forum) 2008–; Int. Counsel, Debevoise & Plimpton LLP, Paris 2011; currently working at Burguburu Blamoutier Charvet Gardel & Assocs. (BCG & A); mem. Conseil Nat. des Barreaux (French Law Soc.), Vice-Pres. of its int. comm.; fmr mem. French del. to Council of Bars and Law Socs of Europe, Int. Asscn for Protection of Intellectual Property, Conseil Supérieur de la Propriété Industrielle 1996–2010. *Leisure interests:* golf, music. *Address:* 18 Rue De Bievre, 75005 Paris (home); Burguburu Blamoutier Charvet Gardel & Associates, 12 place Dauphine, 75001 Paris, France (office). *Telephone:* 9-73-87-20-00 (office). *Fax:* 1-56-24-25-12 (office). *E-mail:* bat.burguburu@bcga.fr (office). *Website:* bcga.fr (office).

BURGUM, Douglas (Doug) J., BA, MPA; American business executive and politician; *Governor of North Dakota;* b. 1 Aug. 1956, Arthur, ND; three c.; ed North Dakota State Univ., Stanford Univ.; Consultant, McKinsey & Co., Chicago 1980–83; Chair. and CEO, Great Plains Software, Inc. 1984–2001 (co. acquired by Microsoft Corpn 2001), Sr Vice-Pres., Microsoft Business Solutions Group, Microsoft Business Div., Microsoft Corpn 2005–07; Founder Kilbourne Group, Fargo 2006; Co-Founder Arthur Ventures 2008; Gov. of North Dakota 2016–, Vice-Chair. Western Governors' Asscn 2018–19; mem. Bd of Dirs Avalara 2008, SuccessFactors, Inc. 2007– (Chair. 2010–12); Republican; North Dakota Business Innovator of the Year 1989, Theodore Roosevelt Rough Rider Award 2009. *Address:* Office of the Governor, 600 East Blvd Avenue, Bismarck, ND 58505-0001, USA (office). *Telephone:* (701) 328-2200 (office). *Fax:* (701) 328-2205 (office). *Website:* www.governor.nd.gov (office).

BURHAN, Lt-Gen. Abdel Fattah Abdelrahman; Sudanese army officer; *Head of Transitional Military Council;* b. 1960; m.; three c.; ed Sudanese Mil. Coll.; long service with Sudanese Armed Forces, beginning as soldier with Border Guard; fmr Mil. Attaché, People's Repub. of China; fmr Gen., Land Forces Command; Gen. Inspector of Sudanese Armed Forces 2018–19; Chief of Staff of Sudanese Army 2018–19; Head of Transitional Mil. Council and de facto head of state (following removal of fmr Pres. Omar al-Bashir) 2019–. *Address:* Transitional Military Council, Khartoum, Sudan (office).

BURJANADZE, Nino, JD, PhD; Georgian politician, lawyer and professor of international law; *Chairman, Demokratiuli Modzraoba-Ertiani Sakartvelo (DM-ES—Democratic Movement-United Georgia);* b. 16 July 1964, Kutaisi, Georgian SSR, USSR; d. of Anzor Burjanadze and Tina Morchadze; m. Badri Bitsadze 1960; two s.; ed Akaki Tsereteli School, Kutaisi, Tbilisi State Univ., Moscow Lomonosov State Univ., Russian SFSR; Prof. of Int. Relations and Int. Law, Tbilisi State Univ. 1991–; consultant to Ministry of Environmental Protection 1991–92, Parl. Cttee on Foreign Relations 1992–95; mem. Parl. 1995–, Deputy Chair. Cttee on Constitutional Legal Affairs and Rule of Law 1995–98, Chair. 1998–99, Chair. Cttee on Foreign Relations 2000–01, Chair. (Speaker) of Parl. 2001–04, 2004–08; Rapporteur, Gen. Cttee on Democracy, Human Rights and Humanitarian Issues, OSCE Parl. Ass. 1998–2000, Vice-Pres. OSCE Parl. Ass. 2000–; Pres. Parl. Ass. of Black Sea Econ. Co-operation 2001–02; fmr mem. Sakartvelos Mokalaketa Kavshiri (Citizens' Union of Georgia), initiated efforts to organize opposition alliance of Gaertianebuli Demokratebi (United Democrats), Natsionaluri Modzraoba (Nat. Movt) and Axali Memarjveneebi (New Rights) 2003; formed Burjanadze-Demokratebi (Burjanadze Democrats) electoral bloc Aug. 2003; Founder and Chair. Demokratiuli Modzraoba-Ertiani Sakartvelo (DM-ES—Democratic Movement-United Georgia) 2008–; Interim Pres. of Georgia Nov. 2003–Jan. 2004, Nov. 2007–Jan. 2008; Chair. Perm. Parl. Del. to UK 1995–98; Co-Chair. EU–Georgian Parl. Co-operation Cttee 1999–2000; Pres. Black Sea Econ. Co-operation Parl. Ass. 2001–02; mem. Young Lawyers Asscn, Int. Justice Asscn, Int. Marine Justice Asscn, US Int. Justice Asscn; participant in numerous int. confs; led protest demonstration in Tbilisi demanding resignation of Pres. Mikheil Saakashvili May 2011. *Publications include:* Legal Problems of International Organisations of a New Type; more than 40 articles on issues related to int. law and int. relations. *Address:* Demokratiuli Modzraoba-Ertiani Sakartvelo (Democratic Movement-United Georgia), 0160 Tbilisi, Abuladze 8, Georgia (office). *Telephone:* (32) 255-03-77 (office). *Fax:* (32) 255-03-77 (office). *E-mail:* nino.burjanadze64@gmail.com (office); mail@democrats.ge (office). *Website:* www.democrats.ge (office).

BURK, Martha, PhD; American psychologist and national organization official; b. 18 Oct. 1941, Houston, Texas; m. Ralph Estes; two s.; ed Univ. of Texas; political psychologist and women's equity expert; fmr Univ. Research Dir, Prof. of Man. and adviser to political campaigns and orgs; Chair. Nat. Council of Women's Orgs 2000–05; Sr Policy Advisor for Women's Issues to fmr Gov. of New Mexico Bill Richardson 2007–10; Co-Founder and Pres. Center for Advancement of Public Policy, Washington, DC; fmr mem. Comm. for Responsive Democracy, Advisory Cttee of Americans for Workplace Fairness, Sex Equity Caucus of Nat. Asscn for the Educ. of Young Children, Bd Dirs Nat. Org. for Women; mem. Bd Wider Opportunities for Women; Chair. Legislative Task Force for Nat. Cttee on Pay Equity; mem. advisory bd to several other nat. orgs including Univ. of Texas, US Bureau of Indian Affairs, US Dept of Educ., US Dept of State, NSF, Kansas House of Reps Smithsonian Inst., Women's Int. News Gathering Service, Nat. Educ. Asscn, Search for Common Ground and US Information Agency; numerous TV and radio broadcasts and frequent contrib. to major newspapers and magazines on public policy; Ed. Washington Feminist Faxnet, Money Ed. Ms. Magazine. *Telephone:* (202) 247-1300 (home). *E-mail:* martha@marthaburk.org. *Website:* marthaburk.org.

BURKE, Bernard Flood, PhD; American physicist and astrophysicist; *Professor Emeritus of Astrophysics, Massachusetts Institute of Technology;* b. 7 June 1928, Boston, Mass; s. of Vincent Paul Burke and Clare Aloyse Brine; m. 1st Jane Chapin Pann 1953 (died 1993); three s. one d.; m. 2nd Elizabeth King Platt 1998; ed Massachusetts Inst. of Tech.; mem. of staff, Carnegie Inst. of Washington 1953–65; Chair. Radio Astronomy Section, Carnegie Inst. of Washington, Dept of Terrestrial Magnetism 1962–65; Prof. of Physics, MIT 1965–2000, William Burden Prof. of Astrophysics 1981–2001, Prof. Emer. 2001–; Visiting Prof., Leiden Univ. 1971–72, Manchester Univ. 1992–93; Pres. American Astronomical Soc. 1986–88; Ed. Comments on Astrophysics 1984–87; Trustee Associated Univ. Inc. 1972–90; Trustee and Vice-Chair. NE Radio Observatory Corpn 1973–82, Chair. 1982–95; Oort Lecturer, Leiden Univ. 1993, Karl Jansky Lecturer, Nat. Radio Astronomy Observatory 1998; Visiting Scholar, Carnegie Inst. of Washington 1998; mem. Nat. Science Bd 1990–96; mem. Nat. Acad. of Science, American Acad. of Arts and Sciences; Sr Fellow, Carnegie Inst. of Washington 1997; Fellow, AAAS; Sherman Fairchild Scholar, Calif. Inst. of Tech. 1984–85; Smithsonian Regents Fellow 1985; Helen B. Warner Prize, American Astron. Soc. 1963, Rumford Prize, American Acad. of Arts and Sciences 1971, NASA Achievement Award 1989, 1998, Oort Lecturer, Univ. of Leiden 1997, Karl Jansky Lecturer, Nat. Radio Astronomy Observatory 1997. *Publications:* Microwave Spectroscopy 1953–54, Radio Noise from Jupiter 1955–61, Galactic Structure 1959–, Very Long Baseline Interferometry 1968–, Interstellar Masers 1968–, Gravitational Lenses 1980–, Interferometry in Space 1984–, Introduction to Radio Astronomy (2nd edn) (co-author) 2002; miscellaneous publs in radio astronomy 1955–. *Leisure interests:* skiing, sailing, hiking, chamber music. *Address:* Room 37-641, Massachusetts Institute of Technology, Department of Physics, Cambridge, MA 02139 (office); 34 Bradbury Street, Cambridge, MA, 02138 USA (home). *Telephone:* (617) 253-2572 (office); (617) 354-1209 (home). *Fax:* (617) 253-0861 (office). *E-mail:* bfburke@space.mit.edu (office); bfburke@comcast.net (home).

BURKE, Kathy; British actress and director; b. 13 June 1964, London; ed Anna Scher's Theatre School, London. *Play:* Smaller (dir) 2006. *TV includes:* Harry Enfield's Television Programme 1990–92, Absolutely Fabulous 1992–96, Mr Wroe's Virgins (Royal TV Soc. Award) 1993, Harry Enfield and Chums 1994–97, Common as Muck 1994–97, Tom Jones 1997, Gimme Gimme Gimme 1999–2001, The Catherine Tate Show 2007, Walking and Talking 2012, School of Roars 2017–18. *Films:* Scrubbers 1983, Nil by Mouth (Best Actress, Cannes Film Festival 1997, Best Actress, British Ind. Film Awards 1998) 1997, Elizabeth 1998, This Year's Love 1999, Love, Honour and Obey 2000, The Martins 2001, Once Upon a Time in the Midlands 2002, Anita and Me 2003, Flushed Away (voice) 2006, Tinker, Tailor, Soldier, Spy 2011, Pan 2015, Absolutely Fabulous: The Movie 2016. *Theatre includes:* Mr Thomas, London, Boom Bang-a-Bang, London (Dir), Once a Catholic 2014, Lady Windermere's Fan 2018. *Address:* c/o Hatton McEwan Penford, Studio 11.B.1, The Leather Market, Weston Street, London, SE1 3ER, England. *Telephone:* (20) 3735-8268. *E-mail:* mail@hattonmcewanpenford.com. *Website:* hattonmcewanpenford.com.

BURKE, Nazim, BA, MA, LLB, LLM; Grenadian lawyer and politician; ed Concordia Univ., Univ. of Windsor, York Univ., Queen's Univ., Canada; Perm. Sec., Ministry of Trade 1979–83; lawyer, Burke, Sealy-Burke (law firm), Toronto 1992–2000; Founding Pnr Ciboney Chambers Law Firm 2000; mem. Grenada House of Reps 2003–13, apptd mem. Senate 2013; Minister of Finance, Planning, Economy, Energy and Co-operatives 2008–13, also Minister of Foreign Trade 2008–2009; Co-founder Lex Fidelis Chambers (law firm) 2013; Sr Lecturer, Faculty of Law, Cave Hill Campus, Univ. of the West Indies 2014–; mem. Nat. Democratic Congress Party, fmr Public Relations Officer.

BURKE, (Ulick) Peter, MA, FRHistS, FBA; British historian and academic; *Professor Emeritus of Cultural History, University of Cambridge;* b. 16 Aug. 1937, Stanmore, Middx; s. of John Burke and Jenny Burke (née Colin); m. 1st Susan Patricia Dell 1972 (divorced 1983); m. 2nd Maria Lucía García Pallares 1989; ed St Ignatius' Coll., Stamford Hill, St John's Coll., Oxford, St Antony's Coll., Oxford; Asst Lecturer, then Lecturer, then Reader in History (later Intellectual History), School of European Studies, Univ. of Sussex 1962–78; Lecturer in History, Univ. of Cambridge 1979–88, Reader in Cultural History 1988–96, Prof. of Cultural History 1996–2004, Prof. Emer. 2004–; Fellow, Emmanuel Coll. Cambridge 1979–; Visiting Prof., Univ. of São Paulo, Brazil 1986, 1987, Nijmegen Univ. 1992–93 and Groningen Univ. 1998–99, The Netherlands, Heidelberg Univ., Germany 2002; Fellow, Wissenschaftskolleg, Berlin 1989–90, Netherlands Inst. for Advanced Study 2005; Hon. Fellow, St John's Coll., Oxford; Hon. Prof., Universidad Nacional de Colombia Hon. PhD (Lund), (Copenhagen), (Bucharest), (Zurich), (Brussels); Erasmus Prize, Academia Europaea 1999. *Publications include:* The Renaissance Sense of the Past 1969, Culture and Society in Renaissance Italy 1972, Venice and Amsterdam 1974, Popular Culture in Early Modern Europe 1978, Sociology and History 1980, Montaigne 1981, Vico 1985, Historical Anthropology of Early Modern Italy 1987, The Renaissance 1987, The French Historical Revolution: The Annales School 1929–1989 1990, The Fabrication of Louis XIV 1992, History and Social Theory 1992, Antwerp: A Metropolis in Europe 1993, The Art of Conversation 1993, The Fortunes of the Courtier 1995, Varieties of Cultural History 1997, The European Renaissance 1998, A Social History of Knowledge 2000, Eyewitnessing 2001, A Social History of the Media (co-author) 2002, Languages and Communities in Early Modern Europe 2004, A Social History of Knowledge Vol. 2 2011. *Leisure interest:* travel. *Address:* Emmanuel College, Cambridge, CB2 3AP (office); 14 Warkworth Street, Cambridge, CB1 1EG, England (home). *Telephone:* (1223) 334272 (home). *Fax:* (1223) 334426 (office). *E-mail:* upb1000@cam.ac.uk (office). *Website:* www.hist.cam.ac.uk (office).

BURKE, Philip George, CBE, PhD, FRS, FRAS, FInstP, MRIA; British mathematical physicist and academic; *Professor Emeritus, Queen's University, Belfast;* b. 18 Oct. 1932, London; s. of Henry Burke and Frances Mary Burke (née Sprague); m. Valerie Mona Martin 1959; four d.; ed Univ. Coll. of the South West of England, Exeter, Univ. Coll., London; Research Fellow, Univ. Coll. London 1956–57, Lecturer, Computer Unit 1957–59, Fellow 1986–; Research Physicist, Alvarez Bubble Chamber Group and Watson's Theory Group, Lawrence Radiation Lab., Berkeley, Calif. 1959–62; Research Fellow, later Prin. Scientific Officer, then Sr Prin. Scientific Officer, Atomic Energy Research Establishment, Harwell 1962–67; Prof. of Math. Physics, Queen's Univ., Belfast 1967–98, Prof. Emer. 1998–, Head Dept of Applied Math. and Theoretical Physics 1974–77, Dir School of Math. and Physics 1988–90; Chair. Inter-Council High Performance Computing Man. Cttee 1996–98; Head Div. Theory and Computational Science, Science and Eng Research Council, Daresbury Lab., Cheshire 1977–82 (jt appointment with Queen's Univ.); Founding and Prin. Ed., Computer Physics Communications 1969–79, Hon. Ed. 1980–; mem. UK Science and Eng Research Council 1989–94,

Chair. Supercomputing Man. Cttee 1991–94; mem. Council Royal Soc. 1990–92; mem. American Physical Soc.; Hon. DSc (Exeter) 1981, (Queens Univ., Belfast) 1999; Inst. of Physics' Guthrie Medal and Prize 1994, Sir David Bates Prize 2000, Will Allis Prize 2012. *Publications:* author or co-author of eight books; more than 350 articles in numerous specialist journals. *Leisure interests:* walking, books, music. *Address:* Brook House, Norley Lane, Crowton, Northwich, Cheshire, CW8 2RR, England (home); Department of Applied Mathematics and Theoretical Physics, David Bates Building, Queen's University, Belfast, BT7 1NN, Northern Ireland (office). *Telephone:* (28) 9097-6034 (office); (1928) 788301 (home). *E-mail:* p.burke@qub.ac.uk (office).

BURKE, HE Cardinal Raymond Leo, BA, MA, STB, MA, STL, STD; American ecclesiastic; *Patron, Sovereign Military Order of Malta;* b. 30 June 1948, Richland Center, Wis.; s. of Thomas Burke and Marie Burke; ed Holy Cross Seminary, La Crosse, Wis., Catholic Univ. of America (Basselin Scholar), Pontifical Gregorian Univ., Italy; ordained priest, Diocese of La Crosse 1975; served as Asst Rector, Cathedral of St Joseph the Workman, La Crosse; also taught religion at Aquinas High School, La Crosse; Moderator of the Curia and Vice-Chancellor of La Crosse Diocese 1984–89; Bishop of La Crosse 1994–2003; Archbishop of Saint Louis, Mo. 2004–08; apptd first American Defender of the Bond of the Supreme Tribunal of the Apostolic Signatura 1989, mem. Supreme Tribunal of the Apostolic Signatura 2006–, Prefect 2008–13, 2013–14 (resgnd); Pres. Comm. for Advocates 2008–13; Patron Sovereign Military Order of Malta (charity) 2014–; mem. Pontifical Council for Legis. Texts 2008, Congregation for the Clergy 2008, Congregation for Bishops 2009–13, Congregation for Divine Worship and the Discipline of the Sacraments 2010–, Congregation for the Causes of Saints 2010–; cr. Cardinal (Cardinal-Deacon of S. Agata de' Goti) 2010; participated in Papal Conclave 2013; Cardinal Prefect of the Supreme Tribunal of the Apostolic Signatura 2008–14; Patron, Sovereign Military Order of Malta 2014–; mem. Bd of Trustees, Catholic Univ. of America; Kt Commdr with Star, Order of the Holy Sepulchre 1997; Hon. DHumLitt (Ave Maria Univ.) 2005, (Christendom Coll.) 2007. *Address:* Apostolic Chamber, Palazzo Apostolico, 00120 Città del Vaticano, Rome, Italy (office). *Telephone:* (06) 69883554 (office). *Website:* www.vatican.va (office).

BURKE, Richard T.; American business executive; *Non-Executive Chairman, UnitedHealth Group;* b. 1944, Raleigh, NC; m. Jude Burke; five c.; ed Georgia State Univ., Univ. of Virginia; f. UnitedHealth Inc. (later UnitedHealth Group), Dir 1977–, Chair. and CEO 1974–88, Chair. (non-exec.) 2006–; CEO Physicians Health Plan of Minnesota (now MEDICA) 1977–87; Owner and CEO Phoenix Coyotes (professional sports franchise of Nat. Hockey League) 1995–2001; Dir First Cash Financial Services Inc. 1993–2009, Meritage Homes Corpn (fmrly Meritage Corpn) 2004–. *Address:* UnitedHealth Group, PO Box 1459, Minneapolis, MN 55440-1459, USA (office). *Telephone:* (952) 936-1300 (office). *E-mail:* info@www .unitedhealthgroup.com (office). *Website:* www.unitedhealthgroup.com (office).

BURKE, Stephen B., BA, MBA; American media executive; *CEO, NBCUniversal;* m.; five c.; ed Colgate Univ., Harvard Business School; joined The Walt Disney Co. 1986, helped develop and found The Disney Stores, Pres. and COO Euro Disney SA from 1992, later served as Pres. of ABC Broadcasting; joined Comcast as Pres. of Comcast Cable 1998, led integration of AT&T Broadband with Comcast, COO Comcast Corpn –2011, CEO NBCUniversal and Exec. Vice-Pres. Comcast Corpn 2011–; mem. Bd of Dirs NBCUniversal, Berkshire Hathaway Inc., JP Morgan Chase & Co., The Children's Hosp. of Philadelphia. *Address:* NBCUniversal Media LLC, 30 Rockefeller Plaza, New York, NY 10112, USA (office). *Telephone:* (212) 664-4444 (office). *Fax:* (212) 664-4085 (office). *E-mail:* info@ nbcuni.com (office). *Website:* www.nbcuni.com (office).

BURKE, Sir (Thomas) Kerry, Kt, BA; New Zealand politician; b. 24 March 1942, Christchurch; m. 1st Jennifer Shiel (divorced 1984); two s.; m. 2nd Helen Paske 1984 (died 1989); one s.; ed Univ. of Canterbury, Christchurch Teachers' Coll.; general labourer in Auckland 1965–66, Factory del., Auckland Labourers' Union; teacher, Rangiora High School 1967, Chair. Rangiora Post-Primary Teachers' Asscn 1969–71; MP for Rangiora 1972–75, for West Coast 1978–90; teacher, Greymouth High School 1975–78; Minister of Regional Devt and of Employment and Immigration 1984–87; Speaker, New Zealand Parl. 1987–90; mem. Bd Draco Foundation (NZ) Charitable Trust 2012–; Patron Cholmondeley Children's Home. *Leisure interests:* skiing, swimming. *Address:* c/o Cholmondeley Children's Home Inc., 6 Cholmondeley Lane, Governors Bay, Lyttelton 8971; c/o Draco Foundation (NZ) Charitable Trust, PO Box 291, Christchurch, New Zealand. *E-mail:* cholmondeley@cholmondeley.org.nz. *Website:* cholmondeley.org.nz.

BURKE, Tom, CBE, BA, FRSA; British/Irish environmental policy adviser; *Chairman, E3G;* b. (David Thomas Burke), 5 Jan. 1947, Cork, Ireland; s. of J. V. Burke and Mary Bradley; ed St Boniface's Coll., Plymouth, Univ. of Liverpool; Great George's Community Arts Project 1969–70; Lecturer, Carlett Park Coll., Cheshire 1970, Old Swan Tech. Coll. 1971–73; Local Groups Co-ordinator, Friends of the Earth 1973–75, Exec. Dir 1975–79, Dir of Special Projects 1979–80, Vice-Chair. 1980–81; Policy Adviser, European Environment Bureau 1978–88, mem. Exec. Cttee 1988–91; Sec.-Gen. Bergen 1990 NGO Conf. 1988–90; Dir The Green Alliance 1982–91 (mem. Exec. Cttee 1979–82, 1997–), Sustainability Ltd 1987–89; Sec. Ecological Studies Inst. 1987–92; Special Adviser to Sec. of State for Environment 1991–97; Environmental Policy Adviser, Rio Tinto plc 1996–, BP PLC 1997–2001; mem. Council English Nature 1999–2005; Adviser, Cen. Policy Group, Office of the Deputy Prime Minister 2002–, Sr Adviser to Special Rep. on Climate Change 2006–12; Founding Dir and Chair. E3G, London 2003–; Chair. Review of Environmental Governance in NI 2006–07; Chair. Editorial Advisory Bd ENDS 2005–; Visiting Fellow, Cranfield School of Man. 1990–94; Visiting Prof., Imperial Coll. London 1997–, Univ. Coll. London 2003–; mem. Bd of Dirs, Earth Resources Research 1975–87, Waste Man. Advisory Council 1976–80, Packaging Council 1978–82, Exec. Cttee Nat. Council for Voluntary Orgs and Chair. Planning and Environment Group 1984–89, UK Nat. Cttee for European Year of the Environment 1986–88, Council, Royal Soc. for Nature Conservation 1993–97; mem. Council Royal Soc. of Arts 1990–92 (mem. Environment Cttee 1989–96), Overseas Cttee, Save the Children Fund 1992–97, Exec. Bd World Energy Council Comm. 1990–93; Dir (non-exec.) Earth Resources Research 1975–88; Fellow Inst. of Energy; mem. Co-operative Insurance Services Environ Trust Advisory Cttee 1990–92, 1997–2001, OECD High Level Advisory Group on the Environment 1996–98; stood as SDP cand., Gen. Elections 1983, 1987; mem. Council London Sustainable Devt Comm. 2002–06, American Chem. Council Leadership Dialogue (USA) 2003–07, Advisory Bd Center for Environmental Leadership in Business (USA), Council Inst. of Environmental Man.; Patron UK Environmental Law Asscn 2008–; Hon. Visiting Fellow, Manchester Business School 1984–86; Hon. Prof., Faculty of Laws, Univ. Coll. London; Hon. Fellow, Soc. for the Environment 2010; Royal Humane Soc. Testimonials on Vellum 1966, on Parchment 1968, UNEP Global 500 Laureate 1991. *Publications:* Europe: Environment 1981, Pressure Groups in the Global System (co-author) 1982, Ecology 2000 (co-author) 1984, The Green Capitalists (co-author) 1987, Green Pages (co-author) 1988, Ethics, Environment and the Company (with Julie Hill) 1990, Connecting the Dots 2009. *Leisure interests:* photography, birdwatching. *Address:* E3G, 47 Great Guildford Street, London, SE1 0ES, England (office). *Telephone:* (20) 7593-2020 (office). *E-mail:* tom.burke@riotinto.com (office); tom@tomburke.co.uk. *Website:* e3g.org (office); tomburke.co.uk.

BURKHALTER, Didier Eric; Swiss politician; b. 17 April 1960, Neuchâtel; m.; three s.; ed Univ. of Neuchâtel; staff mem., Univ. of Neuchâtel 1981–82; Econs Ed., Soc. for Swiss Econ. Devt, Geneva 1984–86; mem. FDP-The Liberals 1985–, Ed. in Chief National (Neuchâtel FDP newspaper) 1985–89, FDP Cantonal Sec. for Neuchâtel 1986–89; mem. Hauterive NE Communal Council 1988–90, Neuchâtel Communal Council 1991–2005 (Pres. 1994, 1998, 2001); mem. Neuchâtel Cantonal Parl. 1990–2001; mem. Nat. Council 2003–07, Council of States 2007–09; mem. Swiss del. to Parl. Ass. of OSCE 2005–09; mem. Fed. Council 2009–17, Head of Fed. Dept of Home Affairs 2009–11, of Foreign Affairs 2012–17, Vice-Pres., Swiss Confed. 2013, Pres. (Head of State) 2014–15. *Leisure interests:* cycling, swimming, football, hiking, travel.

BURLAND, John Boscawen, CBE, DSc, FRS, FREng, FICE, FIStructE, NAE; British scientist, academic and civil engineer; *Professor Emeritus of Soil Mechanics, Imperial College London;* b. 4 March 1936, Little Chalfont, Bucks.; s. of John Whitmore Burland and Margaret Irene Burland (née Boscawen); m. Gillian Margaret Burland (née Miller) 1963; two s. one d.; ed Parktown Boys' High School, Univ. of the Witwatersrand, S Africa, Univ. of Cambridge; Engineer, Ove Arup and Partners, London 1961–63; Sr Scientific Officer then Prin. Scientific Officer, Bldg Research Station (BRS), Watford 1966–72, Head of Geotechnics Div. 1972–79, Asst Dir, BRS 1979–80; apptd Prof. of Soil Mechanics, Imperial Coll., London 1980, now Prof. Emer.; mem. Italian Prime Minister's Cttee for stabilizing the Leaning Tower of Pisa; Hon. Fellow, Imperial Coll., London, Emmanuel Coll., Cambridge, Cardiff Univ.; Kt Commdr, Royal Order of Francis I, Italy, Commendatore Ordine della Stella di Solidarietà Italiana; Hon. DEng (Heriot-Watt, Glasgow), Hon. DSc (Nottingham, Warwick, Hertfordshire), Hon. DSc (Eng) (Univ. of Witwatersrand); Kelvin Medal, Baker Medal, Kevin Nash Gold Medal, Gold Medal, Inst. of Structural Engineers, Gold Medal, Inst. of Civil Engineers, Public Promotion of Engineering Medal, Royal Acad. of Engineering. *Publications include:* numerous papers on soil mechanics and civil eng. *Leisure interests:* golf, painting, sailing. *Address:* Department of Civil and Environmental Engineering, Imperial College, South Kensington Campus, London, SW7 2AZ, England (office). *Telephone:* (20) 7594-6079 (office). *Fax:* (20) 7594-5934 (office). *E-mail:* j.burland@imperial.ac.uk (office). *Website:* www.cv.imperial.ac.uk (office).

BURNAT, Emad; Palestinian farmer and documentary filmmaker; m.; four c.; first film experience as cameraman for Israeli producer Guy Davidi on documentary Keywords 2010; film Five Broken Cameras nominated for Acad. Award 2013 (first nomination for a Palestinian). *Film:* Five Broken Cameras (documentary, co-produced with Guy Davidi) (Best Documentary, Jerusalem Film Festival, Sundance Film Festival Directing Award 2013, Int. Emmy Award 2013). *Website:* emadburnat.com (office).

BURNETT, Erin Isabelle, BA; American journalist, news broadcaster and television presenter; *Anchor, CNN Worldwide;* b. 1976, Mardela Springs, Md; m. David Rubulotta 2012; one s.; ed St Andrew's School, Middletown, Del., Williams Coll.; began career as a financial analyst for Goldman Sachs in investment banking div. 1998; was offered a position at CNN as writer and booker for CNN's Moneyline; moved to Citigroup to serve as Vice-Pres. for Citigroup/CitiMedia, responsible for all anchoring of Citigroup online financial news network; accepted position with Bloomberg Television 2003, anchor of Bloomberg on the Markets and In Focus 2003–05; host of CNBC's Street Signs and co-anchor of Squawk on the Street 2005–11, anchored several documentaries, including India Rising: The New Empire, City of Money and Mystery, The Russian Gamble, On Assignment: Iraq, and Dollars & Danger: Africa, The Final Investment Frontier, Big Money in the Middle East; contributed to NBC's Today 2001–11, Meet the Press 2008–11, MSNBC's Morning Joe; Chief Business and Econs Corresp. CNN Worldwide (div. of Turner Broadcasting System, Inc., a Time Warner Co.) 2011–12, Anchor 2011–, anchors weekday general news programme Erin Burnett OutFront and contributes to CNN's coverage of nat. and int. breaking news events, contributing reporter to CNN.com; mem. Council on Foreign Relations. *Television includes:* boardroom adviser, The Apprentice USA (series) 2008–10, co-host, Weekend Today (series) 2010, Too Big to Fail (film) 2011. *Address:* c/o Creative Artists Agency, 2000 Avenue of the Stars, Los Angeles, CA 90067, USA (office); CNN, 1 Time Warner Center, New York, NY 10019, USA (office). *Telephone:* (424) 288-2000 (office). *Fax:* (424) 288-2900 (office). *Website:* www.caa.com (office); edition.cnn.com (office).

BURNETT, Baron (Life Peer), cr. 2017, of Maldon in the County of Essex; **Rt Hon The Lord Burnett Ian Duncan Burnett,** QC, PC; British judge; *Lord Chief Justice;* b. 28 Feb. 1958; m.; one s. one d.; ed St John's Coll., Southsea, Pembroke Coll., Oxford; called to the bar, Middle Temple 1980; mem. Temple Garden Chambers 1982–2008, practised common law and public law, becoming Head of Chambers 2003–08; Jr Counsel for the Crown, Common Law 1992; apptd Queen's Counsel 1998; apptd Recorder 2000; Judge, High Court 2008–14; Presiding Judge, Western Circuit 2011–14; Lord Justice of Appeal 2014–17; Lord Chief Justice (most sr judicial position in England and Wales) Oct. 2017–; Deputy Chair. Security Vetting Appeals Panel; Vice Chair. independent Judicial Appointments Comm. 2015–17. *Address:* Royal Courts of Justice, Strand, London, WC2A 2LL, England (office). *Telephone:* 020 7947 6000 (office). *Website:* www.judiciary.gov.uk (office).

BURNETT, Sir Keith, Kt, CBE, BA, DPhil, FRS, DFInstP; British physicist, academic and university administrator; *Vice-Chancellor, University of Sheffield;* b. 1953, Llwynypia, Wales; m. Anne Burnett; one s. one d.; ed Univ. of Oxford; began career as Research Assoc., Jt Inst. for Lab. Astrophysics, Colo, USA; fmr Asst Prof. of Physics, Univ. of Colorado; Physics Lecturer, Imperial Coll., London 1984–87; Lecturer in Physics and Fellow of St John's Coll. Oxford 1987, becoming Chair. of Physics, Univ. of Oxford, Head of Div. of Math., Physical and Life Sciences 2005–07; Vice-Chancellor Univ. of Sheffield 2007–; Pres. The Science Council 2016–; mem. Universities UK, Yorkshire Univs, Russell Group; Dir Worldwide Univs Network, Sheffield Univ. Enterprises Ltd; mem. Man. Bd Higher Educ. Funding Council for England 2015–; Fellow, Inst. of Physics; Inst. of Physics Thomas Young Medal and Prize 1997, Royal Soc. Wolfson Merit Award 2003. *Publications:* Spectral Line Shapes 1983, Ultracold Atoms and Bose-Einstein-Condensation 1996; author or co-author of nearly 200 scientific papers in the fields of atomic, molecular and laser physics. *Leisure interests:* Chinese language and culture. *Address:* Office of the Vice-Chancellor, University of Sheffield, Western Bank, Sheffield, S10 2TN, England (office). *Telephone:* (114) 222-1000 (office). *E-mail:* vc@sheffield.ac.uk (office). *Website:* www.shef.ac.uk/vc (office).

BURNETT, Mark; British television producer; *President, Mark Burnett Productions, Inc.;* b. 17 July 1960, London, England; s. of Archie Burnett and Jean Burnett; m. 1st Dianne J. Valentine *c.* 1991 (divorced 2003); two s.; m. 2nd Roma Downey 2007; one step-d.; enlisted in British Army aged 17, Section Commdr in Parachute Regt, served with 3rd Bn, Parachute Regt (3 PARA) 1978–82, saw action during Falklands War; moved to USA 1982; worked as a security guard in Beverly Hills, Calif. for one year then later worked in an insurance office; rented plot at Venice Beach and sold T-shirts at weekends 1985; joined a French adventure competition Raid Gauloises 1991; bought format rights and brought a similar competition, Eco Challenge, to USA which launched career as TV producer; best known as producer of Survivor 2000– and creator of The Apprentice 2005–; has produced several other TV franchises, including The Apprentice, Are You Smarter Than a 5th Grader?, Shark Tank, The Voice, MTV Movie Awards 2007–11, annual People's Choice Awards 2010–, Spike Video Game Awards, the Primetime Emmy Awards 2011; past TV shows include Bully Beatdown, Combat Missions, The Contender, The Contender Asia, Expedition Africa, Expedition Impossible, How'd You Get So Rich?, Martha Stewart, My Dad Is Better Than Your Dad, On the Lot (a collaboration with Steven Spielberg), The Restaurant, Rock Star, Sarah Palin's Alaska, Stars Earn Stripes, Starmaker, Toughest Cowboy, Wedding Day, The Bible 2013; four Emmy Awards and four People's Choice Awards; Brandweek Marketer of the Year Award 2004, Reality Cares Foundation Philanthropist of the Year 2004, Brandon Tartikoff Legacy Award 2004, TIME 100 Most Influential People in the World Today 2004, Rose d'Or Frapa Format Award 2005, Producers' Guild of America Norman Lear Award 2009, Hollywood Walk of Fame Star Excellence in Television 2009, Producers' Guild of America Lifetime Achievement Award in Television 2010, TV Guide Magazine Producer of the Year 2013, The Dove Foundation Recognition of Son of God 2013, Anti-Defamation League Entertainment Award 2014. *Publications:* four books, including autobiographical self-help book Jump In!: Even If You Don't Know How to Swim 2005. *Address:* Mark Burnett Productions, Inc., 640 North Sepulveda Blvd, Los Angeles, CA 90049, USA (office). *Telephone:* (310) 903-5400 (office).

BURNHAM, Rt Hon. Andrew (Andy) Murray, PC, MA; British politician; *Mayor of Greater Manchester;* b. 7 Jan. 1970, Aintree, Merseyside, England; m. Marie-France Van Heel 2000; one s. two d.; ed St Aelred's Roman Catholic High School (now St Aelred's Catholic Tech. Coll.), Newton-le-Willows, Fitzwilliam Coll., Cambridge; joined Labour Party aged 15 during miners' strike 1984; researcher for Tessa Jowell MP 1994–97; joined Transport and Gen. Workers' Union 1995; researcher, Nat. Health Service Confed. Aug.–Dec. 1997; Admin. with Football Task Force 1998; Special Adviser to Chris Smith MP, Dept for Culture, Media and Sport 1998–2001; MP (Labour) for Leigh 2001–17, mem. Health Select Cttee 2001–03; Parl. Pvt. Sec. to Home Sec. David Blunkett 2003–04, Parl. Under-Sec. of State for Immigration, Citizenship and Nationality 2005–06, Minister of State at Dept of Health 2006–07, Chief Sec. to Treasury 2007–08, Sec. of State for Culture, Media and Sport 2008–09, for Health 2009–10; Shadow Sec. of State for Health May–Oct. 2010, 2011–15, for Educ. Oct. 2010–11, Shadow Home Sec. 2015–16; unsuccessful cand. in Labour Party leadership election Sept. 2010, 2015; Election Co-ordinator Oct. 2010–11; Mayor of Greater Manchester 2017–; Pres. Rugby Football League 2018–19; fmr Hon. Chair. Leigh Rugby League Club. *Leisure interest:* Everton Football Club. *Address:* Office of the Mayor, GMCA, Churchgate House, 56 Oxford Street, Manchester M1 6EU, England (office). *E-mail:* info@agma.gov.uk (office). *Website:* www.greatermanchester-ca.gov.uk/info/20077/the_mayor (office).

BURNHAM, Christopher Bancroft, BA, MPA; American investment banker and fmr UN official; *CEO, Cambridge Global Capital;* b. 1956, New York City; ed Washington & Lee Univ., Harvard Univ., Georgetown Univ. Nat. Security Studies Program; served in US Marine Corps Reserve, veteran of first Gulf War, led one of the first infantry units to reach and liberate Kuwait City in 1991; elected to Conn. House of Reps three times, served as Asst Minority Leader; fmr investment banker with Credit Suisse First Boston and Advest Corp. Finance; Treas. of Conn. 1994; fmr CEO PIMCO's Columbus Circle Investors (asset man. and mutual fund co.), fmr Vice-Chair. PIMCO's mutual fund group; Asst Sec. for Resource Man. and Chief Financial Officer, State Dept 2002–05; UN Under-Sec.-Gen. for Man. 2005–06; Man. Dir and Vice-Chair. Deutsche Asset Man. (DeAM), Deutsche Bank, New York 2006–12, Global Co-head DeAM's Climate Change Business 2008–12; Founder and CEO Cambridge Global Capital 2013–, Chair. Cambridge Global Advisors 2013–; Sr Adviser (Non-resident), Project on Prosperity and Devt, Center for Strategic & Int. Studies, Washington, DC; Legislator of the Year, Connecticut Children's Coalition 1988, Combat Action Ribbon, Navy Unit Citation, Marine Corps Unit Citation 1991, Friend of Democracy Award, Connecticut Common Cause for authoring legislation to stop 'Pay to Play' 1995, Outstanding Citizen Award, Greenwich Chambers of Commerce 1996, Nat. Govt Finance Officer's Asscn Award for excellence in financial reporting (first ever awarded to any state treasury) 1996, Individual Excellence Award, New England Asscn of Comptrollers 1997, Asscn of Govt Accountants 'CEAR' Award for excellence in financial reporting (first ever awarded to Dept of State) 2002, 2003, 2004, Presidential Award for Man. Excellence for "Innovative and Exemplary Practices in Budget and Performance Integration" 2004, US Sec. of State's Award for Distinguished Service (highest award in Dept) 2005, One To World Fulbright Award for Global Public Service 2007. *Address:* Cambridge Global Capital, 1700 North Moore Street, Suite 2100, Arlington, VA 22209, USA (office). *Telephone:* (703) 600-1933 (office). *E-mail:* info@cambridgeglobal.com (office). *Website:* www.cambridgeglobal.com (office).

BURNHAM, James B., AB, PhD; American economist, banker and academic; *Distinguished Service Professor of Finance, Palumbo Donahue School of Business, Duquesne University;* b. 22 Oct. 1939, New York, NY; s. of James Burnham and Marcia Burnham (née Lightner); m. Anne Mullin 1964; two s. two d.; ed Milton Acad., Princeton Univ., Washington Univ., St Louis; Economist and Special Asst, Federal Reserve Bd, Washington, DC 1969–71; Sr Economist, Mellon Bank, Pittsburgh, Pa 1971–74, Vice-Pres. 1974–81, Sr Vice-Pres. 1985, Office of Govt Affairs 1979–81, Chair. Country Review Cttee 1977–81; Staff Dir and Special Asst to Chair., Pres.'s Council of Econ. Advisors 1981–82; US Exec. Dir IBRD, Washington, DC 1982–85; John M. Olin Visiting Prof., Center for the Study of American Business, Washington Univ., St Louis 1989–90; Prof. of Finance, John F. Donahue Grad. School of Business, Duquesne Univ. 1990–, now Distinguished Service Prof. of Finance, Palumbo Donahue School of Business; mem. American Econs Asscn, Nat. Asscn of Business Economists; Fulbright Scholar, Univ. of São Paulo, Brazil 1962, Murrin Prof. in Global Competitiveness, Fulbright Sr Research Grant (Turkey) 2005. *Publications:* articles on contemporary economic subjects. *Leisure interests:* canoeing, bridge. *Address:* Palumbo Donahue School of Business, Duquesne University, 507 Rockwell Hall, Pittsburgh, PA 15282, USA (office). *Telephone:* (412) 396-5118 (office). *Fax:* (412) 396-1797 (office). *E-mail:* burnham@duq.edu (office). *Website:* www.duq.edu/academics/schools/business/faculty-and-research/faculty-directory/burnham-phd-james-j (office); www.jamesbburnham.typepad.com.

BURNS, Duncan Thorburn, BSc, MA, PhD, DSc, FICI, CChem, FRSC, FRSE, MRIA; British chemist and academic; *Professor Emeritus of Analytical Chemistry, The Queen's University of Belfast;* b. 30 May 1934, Wolverhampton; s. of James Thorburn Burns and Olive Mary Constance Burns (née Waugh); m. 1st Valerie Mary Vinton 1961 (divorced 1994); one s. two d.; m. 2nd Celia Mary Thorburn Burns 1994; ed Whitcliffe Mount School, Univ. of Leeds; Asst Lecturer in Physical Chem., Medway Coll. of Tech. 1958–59, Lecturer 1959–63; Sr Lecturer in Analytical Chem., Woolwich Polytechnic 1963–66, Loughborough Univ. 1966–71, Reader 1971–75; Prof. of Analytical Chem., Queen's Univ., Belfast 1975–99, Prof. Emer. 1999–, Sr Research Fellow, School of Chem. 2009–15; Redwood Lecturer, Royal Soc. of Chem. 1982, Pres. Analytical Div. 1988–90; Visiting Prof., Kasetsart Univ., Bangkok; Fellow, Inst. of Chem. in Ireland, European Chemist; Hon. mem. Pharmaceutical Soc. of Northern Ireland 2001–11 (Hon. Research Prof. 2013–), Asscn of Public Analysts; numerous awards including Boyle/Higgens Gold Medal, Inst. of Chem. of Ireland 1990, Ehren Nadel in Gold, Analytical Inst. Technische Univ. Wien 1990, AnalaR Gold Medal, Royal Soc. of Chem. 1990, SAC Gold Medal, Royal Soc. of Chem. 1993, Fritz Pregl Medal, Austrian Chemical Soc. 1993, Sigillum Magnum, Univ. of Bologna 1996, Div. of Analytical Chem. (DAC) Tribute, European Asscn for Chemical and Molecular Sciences 2005, Award for Service to Analytical Science, Royal Soc. of Chem. 2005, Award for Service, Royal Soc. of Chem. 2009. *Publications:* nine books and more than 450 papers. *Leisure interest:* history of chemistry. *Address:* The Institute for Global Food Security, Queen's University, Belfast, BT9 5AG (office); 318 Stranmillis Road, Belfast, BT9 5EB, Northern Ireland (home). *Telephone:* (28) 9097-4849 (office); (28) 9066-8567 (home). *E-mail:* d.t.burns@qub.ac.uk (office).

BURNS, John Fisher; British journalist; b. 4 Oct. 1944, Nottingham; s. of Air Cdre R. J. B. Burns and Dorothy Burns (née Fisher); m. 1st Jane Pequegnat 1972 (divorced 1989); m. 2nd Jane Scott-Long 1991; two s. one d.; ed Stowe School, McGill Univ., Canada and Harvard Univ., USA; China correspondent, Globe and Mail, Toronto, Canada; Foreign Corresp., New York Times 1975–80, Soviet Union 1981–84, China 1984–86, Canada 1987–88, Afghanistan 1989–90, Persian Gulf 1990, Balkans 1991–94, India 1994–98, Special Corresp. for Islamic Affairs 1999–2002, Chief of Bureau for Baghdad 2002–07, Chief of Bureau for London 2007–15; Chief of Bureau for Pakistan and Afghanistan, Washington Post 2002; Visiting Fellow, King's College, Cambridge 1998–99; Hon. LLD (Colby College) 2007; Pulitzer Prize for Int. Reporting 1993 (co-winner for reporting from Bosnia), 1997 (for coverage of the Taliban regime in Afghanistan); George Polk Prize for Foreign Correspondence 1978, 1997, Elijah Parish Lovejoy Award 2007. *Leisure interests:* golf, music, motor racing.

BURNS, Kenneth (Ken) Lauren, BA; American film director and film producer; b. 29 July 1953, New York; s. of Robert Burns and Lyla Burns; m. 1st Amy Stechler Burns 1982 (divorced 1993); two c.; m. 2nd Julie Deborah Brown 2003; ed Ann Arbor Pioneer High School, Mich., Hampshire Coll.; Co-founder Florentine Films; Dr hc (Bowdoin Coll.) 1991, (Amherst Coll.) 1991, (Univ. of New Hampshire), (Franklin Pierce Coll.), (Notre Dame Coll.), (Coll. of St Joseph), (Springfield Coll.), (Pace Univ.), (Univ. of North Carolina, Chapel Hill); S. Roger Horchow Award for Greatest Public Service by a Private Citizen, annual Jefferson Awards 2004, John Steinbeck Award 2013. *Films include:* Brooklyn Bridge 1981, The Shakers: Hands to Work, Hearts to God 1984, The Statue of Liberty 1985, Huey Long 1985, The Congress 1988, Thomas Hart Benton 1988, Empire of the Air: The Men Who Made Radio 1991, The West (producer, Erik Barnouw Prize) 1996, Lewis & Clark: The Journey of the Corps of Discovery 1997, Frank Lloyd Wright (Peabody Award) 1998, Unforgivable Blackness: The Rise and Fall of Jack Johnson (documentary) (three Primetime Emmy Awards) 2004, The Central Park Five (documentary) 2012, Two Who Dared: The Sharps' War (documentary) 2013. *Television includes:* Thomas Hart Benton (film) 1988, The Congress (film) 1988, The Civil War (mini-series) (more than 40 major film and TV awards, including two Emmy Awards, two Grammy Awards, Producer of the Year Award from Producers' Guild, People's Choice Award, Peabody Award, DuPont-Columbia Award, D.W. Griffiths Award, Lincoln Prize) 1990, Baseball (mini-series) (numerous awards, including Emmy, CINE Golden Eagle Award, Clarion Award, TV Critics' Awards for Outstanding Achievement in Sports and Special Programming) 1994, Thomas Jefferson (mini-series) 1997, Not for Ourselves Alone: The Story of Elizabeth Cady Stanton and Susan B. Anthony (mini-series) (Peabody Award) 1999, Biography (series documentary) 2000, Jazz (mini-series) 2001, Mark Twain (film documentary) (Leon Award for Best Documentary, St Louis Film Festival) 2001, Horatio's Drive:

America's First Road Trip (film documentary) 2003, The War (mini-series) 2007, Medal of Honor (film documentary) 2008, The National Parks: America's Best Idea (mini-series documentary) (Emmy Award for Outstanding Non-fiction Series 2010) 2009, The Tenth Inning (mini-series documentary) 2010, Prohibition (mini-series documentary) 2011, The Dust Bowl (mini-series documentary) 2012, The Roosevelts: An Intimate History (series documentary) 2014, Cancer: The Emperor of All Maladies (series documentary) 2015. *Publications:* The Civil War (with Geoffrey C. Ward), Baseball (with Geoffrey C. Ward), Lewis and Clark: The Journey of the Corps of Discovery (with Dayton Duncan), The War (with Geoffrey C. Ward) 2007. *Address:* Florentine Films, PO Box 613, Walpole, NH 03608, USA (office). *Telephone:* (603) 756-3038 (office). *Fax:* (603) 756-4389 (office). *Website:* www.florentinefilms.com (office); kenburns.com.

BURNS, R. Nicholas, MA; American diplomatist (retd) and academic; *Roy and Barbara Goodman Family Professor of the Practice of Diplomacy and International Relations, Belfer Center for Science and International Affairs, Harvard University;* b. 28 Jan. 1956, Buffalo, NY; m. Elizabeth Baylies; three d.; ed Univ. of Paris, France, Boston Coll., Johns Hopkins School of Advanced Int. Studies; before entering Foreign Service worked in US Embassy in Mauritania and as programme officer for AT Int.; Vice-Consul and Staff Asst to Amb., Cairo 1983–85, political officer, Consulate-Gen., Jerusalem 1985–87, staff officer, Operations Center and Secr., Dept of State 1987–88, Special Asst to Counsellor 1989–90; Adviser to Pres. George Bush on Greece, Turkey and Cyprus and Dir for Soviet (later Russian) Affairs; Special Asst to Pres. Clinton and Sr Dir for Russia, Ukraine and Eurasia Affairs; Spokesman, Dept of State and Acting Asst Sec. for Public Affairs 1995–97, Amb. to Greece 1997–2001, Perm. Rep. to NATO, Brussels 2001–05, Under-Sec. Of State for Political Affairs 2005–08 (resgnd); Visiting Scholar, Woodrow Wilson Center for Int. Scholars 2008; apptd Sultan of Oman Prof. of Int. Relations and Prof. of the Practice of Diplomacy and Int. Politics, then Roy and Barbara Goodman Family Prof. of the Practice of Diplomacy and Int. Relations, John F. Kennedy School of Govt, Harvard Univ., also Dir Future of Diplomacy Project and Faculty Chair for Programs on the Middle East and on India and South Asia, mem. Bd of Dirs Belfer Center for Science and Int. Affairs, Faculty Assoc., Weatherhead Center for International Affairs; Sr Counselor, Cohen Group; Vice-Chair. American Ditchley Foundation; mem. Bd of Dirs Aspen Strategy Group, Entegris, Inc., Council on Foreign Relations, Special Olympics, Rockefeller Brothers Fund, Center for the Study of the Presidency and Congress, Richard Lounsbery Foundation, Atlantic Council, American Media Abroad, Asscn of Diplomatic Studies and Training, Appeal of Conscience Foundation, Gennadius Library; mem. Panel of Sr Advisors, Chatham House; mem. Order of St John, IISS, Cttee on Conscience of the United States Holocaust Memorial Museum, American Acad. of Arts and Sciences, Trilateral Comm., Red Sox Nation; foreign affairs columnist, Boston Globe; Order of the Terra Mariana (Estonia); Dr hc (Worcester Polytechnic Inst.) 1997; Superior Honor Award (three times), James Clement Dunn Award for Excellence 1994, Charles E. Cobb Award for Trade Devt by an Amb. 2000, Woodrow Wilson Award for Distinguished Govt Service (Johns Hopkins Univ.) 2002. *Address:* Littauer 374, John F. Kennedy School of Government, 79 JFK Street, Cambridge, MA 02138, USA (office). *Telephone:* (617) 495-2495 (office). *E-mail:* nicholas_burns@hks.harvard.edu (office). *Website:* belfercenter.ksg.harvard.edu (office).

BURNS, Sir (Robert) Andrew, Kt, KCMG, MA, FRSA; British diplomatist; b. 21 July 1943, London; s. of Robert Burns CB, CMG and Mary Burns (née Goodland); m. Sarah Cadogan 1973; two s. one step-d.; ed Highgate School, Trinity Coll. Cambridge, School of Oriental and African Studies, Univ. of London; joined Diplomatic Service 1965, served in New Delhi 1967–71, FCO, London and UK Del. to CSCE 1971–75, First Sec. and Head of Chancery, Bucharest 1976–78, Pvt. Sec. to Perm. Under-Sec. and Head of Diplomatic Service, FCO 1979–82, Fellow, Center for Int. Affairs, Harvard Univ., USA 1982–83, Counsellor (Information) and Head of British Information Services, Washington, DC and New York 1983–86, Head of S Asian Dept, FCO 1986–88, Head of News Dept 1988–90, Asst Under-Sec. of State (Asia), FCO 1990–92, Amb. to Israel 1992–95, Deputy Under-Sec. of State (non-Europe, Trade and Investment Promotion) 1995–97, Consul-Gen., Hong Kong Special Admin. Region and Macao 1997–2000, High Commr to Canada 2000–03, UK Envoy for Post-Holocaust Issues 2010–15; Int. Gov. BBC 2005–06; Dir JP Morgan Chinese Investment Trust 2003–, Aberdeen All Asia Investment Trust 2008–13; Chair. Council, Royal Holloway, Univ. of London 2004–11, Anglo-Israel Asscn 2004–05, 2008–11, Hestercombe Gardens Trust 2005–, Advisory Council British Expertise 2006–10; Chair. Bar Standards Bd 2015–; mem. Cttee of Univ. Chairs 2009–11, British North America Cttee 2004–, Bd Govs Guildhall School of Music and Drama; Fellow, Portland Trust 2004–; Trustee, Canadian Studies Foundation; Patron, British Friends of the Abraham Fund Initiatives; Hon. Pres. Canada UK Colloquia 2003–, China Asscn 2009–14. *Publication:* Diplomacy, War and Parliamentary Democracy 1989. *Leisure interests:* music, theatre, Exmoor. *Address:* Foreign and Commonwealth Office, King Charles Street, London, SW1A 2AH, England (office). *Telephone:* (20) 7008-4340 (home). *E-mail:* andrew.burns@fco.gsi.gov.uk (office). *Website:* www.gov.uk/government/organisations/foreign-commonwealth-office (office).

BURNS, Stephanie A., PhD; American business executive; *Chairman, President and CEO, Dow Corning Corporation;* ed Iowa State Univ.; postdoctoral research in organic chemistry, Université Montpellier, Sciences et Techniques du Languedoc, France; joined Dow Corning Corpn 1983, Researcher 1983–87, Product Devt Man. for Electronics Industry 1987–94, Dir of Women's Health 1994–97, Science and Tech. Dir for Europe, Brussels, Belgium 1997–99, Industry Dir for Life Sciences in Europe 1999, European Electronics Industry Dir 1999–2000, Exec. Vice-Pres. 2000–03, apptd mem. Bd Dirs 2000, Pres. and COO 2003–04, Pres. and CEO 2004–06, Chair., Pres. and CEO 2006–; mem. Bd of Dirs GlaxoSmithKline plc, Manpower Inc., Michigan Molecular Inst., Chemical Bank Midland Area, American Chem. Council, Dow Corning/Genencor Int. Partnership, The Conference Board; mem. Advisory Bd Chemical and Engineering News; mem. Exec. Cttee Soc. of Chemical Industry; mem. ACS; Trustee Midland Community Center; Michigan Woman Exec. of the Year 2003, Vanguard Award, Chemical Educ. Foundation 2006. *Address:* Dow Corning Corporation, 2200 West Salzburg Road, Midland, MI 48686, USA (office). *Telephone:* (989) 496-4000 (office). *Fax:* (989) 496-4393 (office). *Website:* www.dowcorning.com (office).

BURNS, Baron (Life Peer), cr. 1998, of Pitshanger in the London Borough of Ealing; **Terence Burns,** GCB, BAEcon; British economist and business executive; *Chairman, Channel 4;* b. 13 March 1944, Durham; s. of Patrick Owen Burns and Doris Burns; m. Anne Elizabeth Powell 1969; one s. two d.; ed Houghton-le-Spring Grammar School and Victoria Univ. of Manchester; held various research positions at London Business School 1965–70, Lecturer in Econs 1970–74, Sr Lecturer in Econs 1974–79, Dir Centre for Econ. Forecasting 1976–79, Prof. of Econs 1979; Chief Econ. Adviser to HM Treasury and Head, Govt Econ. Service 1980–91; Perm. Sec. to Treasury 1991–98; Chair. Inquiry into Hunting 1999; Chair. Financial Services and Markets Jt Cttee 1999, Nat. Lottery Comm. 2000–01, Santander UK plc (formerly Abbey National plc) 2002–15, Channel 4 Television Corpn 2009–; Deputy Chair. Marks & Spencer Group 2005–06, Chair. 2006–08; Dir (non-exec.) Legal and General Group PLC 1999–2001, Pearson 1999–2010, British Land 2001–05, Banco Santander 2004–; Vice-Pres. Soc. of Business Economists 1985–99, Pres. 1999–; Fellow, London Business School 1989–; mem. Council Royal Econ. Soc. 1986–91, Vice-Pres. 1992–; Visiting Prof., Durham Univ. 1995–; Gov. RAM 1998–, Chair. Governing Body 2002–14; Hon. DScS (Manchester) 1992. *Leisure interests:* Dir Queen's Park Rangers football team 1996–2001, music and golf. *Address:* House of Lords, Westminster, London, SW1A 0PW (office); Santander UK plc, 2 Triton Square, Regent's Place, London, NW1 3AN, England. *Telephone:* (20) 7756-5550 (Santander). *Fax:* (20) 7756-5644 (Santander). *E-mail:* burnst@parliament.uk (office); terry.burns@santander.co.uk. *Website:* www.parliament.uk/biographies/lords/lord-burns/3351 (office).

BURNS, Ursula M., MSc (MechEng); American business executive; *Chairman and CEO, Xerox Corporation;* b. 20 Sept. 1958, New York; m. Lloyd Bean; two c.; ed Brooklyn Polytechnic Inst. of New York, Columbia Univ., New York; mechanical eng summer intern, Xerox Corpn in 1980, Exec. Asst to Chair. and CEO 1991–92, held several positions in eng, including product devt and planning, led several business teams, including office colour and fax business, office network copying business and departmental business unit 1992–2000, Sr Vice-Pres. Corp. Strategic Services 2000–01, Pres. Document Systems and Solutions Group 2001–02, Sr Vice-Pres. and Pres. Business Group Operations 2002–07, mem. Bd of Dirs 2007–, Pres. Xerox Corpn 2007–09, CEO 2009–, Chair. 2010–; mem. Bd of Dirs American Express Corpn, Boston Scientific Corpn, FIRST (For Inspiration and Recognition of Science and Tech.), Nat. Asscn of Manufacturers, PQ Corpn, Univ. of Rochester, The Rochester Business Alliance, CASA – The Nat. Center on Addiction and Substance Abuse at Columbia Univ.; named by Pres. Obama to help lead the White House nat. programme on STEM (science, tech., eng and math.) 2009–; Vice-Chair. President's Export Council 2010–. *Address:* Xerox Corporation, 45 Glover Avenue, Norwalk, CT 06856-4505, USA (office). *Telephone:* (203) 968-3000 (office). *Website:* www.xerox.com (office).

BURNS, William (Bill) Joseph, BA, MPhil, DPhil; American diplomatist; *President, Carnegie Endowment for International Peace;* b. 11 April 1956, Fort Bragg, NC; m. Lisa Carty; two d.; ed La Salle Univ., Univ. of Oxford, UK (Marshall Scholar); entered Foreign Service 1982; Political Officer, US Embassy, Amman; mem. staff, Bureau of Near E Affairs, Office of Deputy Sec. of State; Special Asst to the Pres., Sr Dir for Near E and S Asian Affairs, Nat. Security Council; Acting Dir and Prin. Deputy Dir State Dept's Policy Planning; Minister-Counsellor for Political Affairs, Moscow; Exec. Sec., State Dept and Special Asst to Sec. of State; Amb. to Jordan 1998–2001; Asst Sec. of State for Near Eastern Affairs 2001–05; Amb. to Russia 2005–08; Under-Sec. of State for Political Affairs 2008–11, Deputy Sec. of State 2011–14; Pres. Carnegie Endowment for Int. Peace 2014–; mem. American Acad. of Arts and Sciences; four hon. doctorate degrees; two Distinguished Honor Awards, James Clement Dunn Award, five Superior Honor Awards, two Presidential Distinguished Service Awards, and to TIME's list of 100 Young Global Leaders 1994, Robert C. Frasure Memorial Award 2005, Charles E. Cobb, Jr Ambassadorial Award for Initiative and Success in Trade Devt 2006, Diplomat of the Year, Foreign Policy journal 2013. *Publication:* Economic Aid and American Policy Toward Egypt, 1955–1981 1985. *Address:* Carnegie Endowment for International Peace, 1779 Massachusetts Avenue NW, Washington, DC 20036–2103, USA (office). *Telephone:* (202) 483-7600 (office). *Fax:* (202) 483-1840 (office). *Website:* carnegieendowment.org (office).

BURNSTOCK, Geoffrey, AC, PhD, DSc, FRS, FAA, FMedSci; Australian/British scientist and academic; *Professor Emeritus, Department of Pharmacology and Therapeutics, University of Melbourne;* b. 10 May 1929, London, England; s. of James Burnstock and Nancy Green; m. Nomi Hirschfeld 1957; three d.; ed London and Melbourne Univs; Nat. Inst. for Medical Research, London 1956–57; Post-Doctoral Fellow, King's Coll., London 1957; Dept of Pharmacology, Univ. of Oxford 1957–59; Dept of Physiology, Illinois Univ. 1959; Sr Lecturer, Dept of Zoology, Melbourne Univ. 1959–62, Reader 1962–64, Prof. and Chair. 1964–75, Assoc. Dean (Biological Sciences) 1969–72, Prof. Emer. 1993–; Visiting Prof., Dept of Pharmacology, Univ. of Calif. 1970; Vice-Dean, Faculty of Medical Sciences, Univ. Coll., London (UCL) 1980–83, Prof. of Anatomy 1975–, Head of Dept of Anatomy and Developmental Biology 1975–97, Convenor, Centre for Neuroscience 1979–, Fellow 1996, Dir Autonomic Neuroscience Inst., Royal Free and Univ. Coll. Medical School, UCL 1997–, then Pres. Autonomic Neuroscience Centre; currently Prof. Emer., Dept of Pharmacology and Therapeutics, Univ. of Melbourne; Contract Prof., Univ. of Siena 1985–87, Univ. of Milan 1993–94; Visiting Prof., Royal Soc. of Medicine Foundation, New York 1988; Chair. Scientific Advisory Bd, Eisai London Ltd 1990–96; Chair. Bd of Clinical Studies, Royal Nat. Orthopaedic Hosp. Trust 1996; Pres. Int. Soc. for Autonomic Neuroscience 1995–2000, Int. Neurovegetative Soc. 1995–, British Asscn (Medical), Purine Club 2009–; Founder FMedSci 1998; mem. Academia Europaea 1992; mem. Russian Soc. of Neuropathology 1993; Ed.-in-Chief, Journal of Autonomic Neuroscience, Purinergic Signalling, Open Pharmacology, Neuroscience Journals; mem. Bd of over 30 journals; Fellow, Real Academia Nacional de Farmacia, Spain 2003–; Hon. FRCS; Hon. FRCP; Hon. MRCP 1987; Hon. Fellow, British Pharmacological Soc. 2007; Hon. mem. Australian Physical Soc. 2008; Dr hc (Antwerp) 2002, (J.W. Goethe-Universität) 2007, (Leipzig) 2011; Royal Soc. of Vic. Silver Medal 1970, Special Award, NIH Conf., Bethesda 1989, Royal Medal, Royal Soc. 2000, Janssen Award for Lifetime Achievement 2000, Copernicus Gold Medal 2009, Annual Award, British Neuroscience Asscn 2009, Gaddum Memorial Award, British Pharmacological Soc. 2010, The Erasmus Medal, Academia Europaea 2012. *Publications include:* books: Adrenergic Neurons: Their Organisation, Function and Development in the Peripheral Nervous System 1975, An Atlas of the Fine Structure of Muscle and its Innervation 1976; Ed. Purinergic Receptors 1981, Somatic and Autonomic Nerve-Muscle Interactions 1983, Peptides: A Target for New Drug Development 1991, Cardiovascular Biology of Purines 1998; series Ed. The Autonomic Nervous System (Vols 1–14) 1992–97, Neural-Endothelial Interactions in the Control of Local Vascular Tone 1993, Nitric Oxide in Health and Disease 1997, Cardiovascular Biology of Purines 1998; also author of over 1,800 publs in scientific and medical journals and books. *Leisure interests:* wood sculpture, tennis. *Address:* Dept of Pharmacology and Therapeutics, Univ. of Melbourne, Australia (office). *Telephone:* (3) 9035-7580 (office). *E-mail:* g.burnstock@ucl.ac.uk (office).

BURNYEAT, Myles Fredric, CBE, BA, FBA; British academic; *Emeritus Fellow, All Souls College, University of Oxford;* b. 1 Jan. 1939; s. of Peter James Anthony Burnyeat and Cynthia Cherry Warburg; m. 1st Jane Elizabeth Buckley 1971 (divorced 1982); one s. one d.; m. 2nd Ruth Sophia Padel 1984 (divorced 2000); one d.; m. 3rd Heda Segvic 2002 (died 2003); ed Bryanston School and King's Coll., Cambridge; Russian Interpreter, RN 1959; Asst Lecturer in Philosophy, Univ. Coll., London 1964, Lecturer 1965; Lecturer in Classics, Univ. of Cambridge 1978, Lecturer in Philosophy, Robinson Coll. 1978, Fellow 1978–96, Hon. Fellow 2006–; Laurence Prof. of Ancient Philosophy, Univ. of Cambridge 1984–96, Sr Research Fellow in Philosophy, All Souls Coll., Oxford 1996–2006, Emer. Fellow 2006–; Foreign Hon. mem. American Acad. of Arts and Sciences 1992–; Hon. DLitt (St Andrews) 2012. *Publications:* Philosophy As It Is (co-ed.) 1979, Doubt and Dogmatism (co-ed.) 1980, Science and Speculation (co-ed.) 1982, The Sceptical Tradition (ed.) 1983, The Theaetetus of Plato 1990, The Original Sceptics (co-ed.) 1997, A Map of Metaphysics Zeta 2001, Aristotle's Divine Intellect 2008, Explorations in Ancient and Modern Philosophy (two vols) 2012. *Leisure interest:* travel. *Address:* All Souls College, Oxford, OX1 4AL, England (office). *Fax:* (1865) 279299 (office).

BURR, Richard; American politician; *Senator from North Carolina;* m. Brooke Burr; two s.; ed R.J. Reynolds High School, Wake Forest Univ.; family moved to Winston-Salem, NC when he was a young child; various positions with Carswell Distributing 1977–94; elected to US Congress from N Carolina 1994–2005, wrote Food and Drug Admin Modernization Act ('Burr Bill') 1997, Vice-Chair. House Energy and Commerce Cttee 2001, mem. House Select Cttee on Intelligence and Task Force on Terrorism 2001; Senator from N Carolina 2005–, Chair. Senate Intelligence Cttee 2015–; Co-Chair. Partnership for a Drug Free N Carolina; mem. Bd Brenner Children's Hosp., Idealliance; mem. Bd of Visitors, West Point; Republican. *Address:* 217 Russell Senate Office Building, Washington, DC 20510, USA (office). *Telephone:* (202) 224-3154 (office). *Fax:* (202) 228-2981 (office). *Website:* www.burr.senate.gov (office).

BURRELL, Leroy Russel; American athletics coach and fmr professional athlete; *Head Coach, Track and Field, University of Houston;* b. 21 Feb. 1967, Lansdowne, Philadelphia; m. Michelle Finn (fmr Olympic sprinter) 1994; three s.; ed Pen Wood High School, Lansdowne and Univ. of Houston, Tex.; fmr sprinter and long jumper; set world record, 100m in 9.90 seconds at US Championships, New York June 1991; set another world record 100m of 9.85 seconds July 1994; Olympic gold medal 4×100m relay, Barcelona 1992; Head Coach, Track and Field, Univ. of Houston 1998–. *Website:* www.uhcougars.com/sports/c-track/c-track-coaches.html.

BURRIS, Roland Wallace, BA, JD; American attorney, politician and fmr banker; b. 3 Aug. 1937, Centralia, Ill.; s. of Earl L. Burris and Emma M. Burris (née Curry); m. Berlean Miller 1961; one s. one d.; ed Centralia High School, Southern Illinois Univ., Carbondale, Univ. of Hamburg, Germany, Howard Univ., Washington, DC; Nat. Bank Examiner, Office of Comptroller, Currency for US Treasury Dept, Washington, DC 1963–64; called to Ill. Bar 1964; worked at Continental Illinois National Bank and Trust Company 1964–73, positions included tax accountant, tax consultant, commercial banking officer, Vice-Pres.; Dir Dept of Central Management Services, State of Ill. 1973–77, Comptroller 1979–91, Attorney-Gen. 1995–98; Nat. Exec. Dir and COO Operation Push Jan.–Oct. 1977; Man. Partner, Jones Ware & Grenard 1995–98; Of counsel, Buford & Peters LLC (law firm) 1999–2002, Burris, Wright, Slaughter & Tom LLC 2002–07; Sr Counsel, Gonzalez Saggio & Harlan LLP 2007–09; Man. and CEO Burris & Lebed Consulting LLC 2002–09; Senator from Ill. 2009–10 (retd); fmr Adjunct Prof., MPA Program, Southern Illinois Univ. 1995–98; Chair. Ill. Comm. of African-American Males 1992–94; Chair. Nat. Asscn of Attorneys Gen. Civil Rights Comm. 1993–95; Chair. Ill. State Justice Comm. 1994–96; Pres., Nat. Asscn of State Auditors, Comptrollers and Treasurers 1981–82; Founder and Pres. Nat. Forum on State Leaders 1982–; Trustee, Govt Finance Officers Asscn of US and Canada 1987–91, Financial Accounting Foundation Bd 1991–94; served three years on Exec. Bd as Trustee, Govt Finance Office of US and Canada; fmr Vice-Chair. Cttee on Illinois Govt; fmr mem. of Bd Ill. Criminal Justice Authority, Law Enforcement Foundation of Ill., Ill. Supreme Court Cttee for Civil Jury Instructions, mem. Nat. Center for Responsible Gaming 1996–2005, Auditorium Theater of Chicago 2001–06, Better Business Bureau 2008; mem. ABA, Ill. Bar Asscn, Cook Co. Bar Asscn (Public Service Award 1975), Chicago Bar Asscn, Nat. Asscn for Advancement of Colored People (Pres.'s Award 1991), Howard Univ. Law School Alumni Asscn, Southern Illinois Univ. Alumni Asscn, Southern Illinois Univ. Foundation, Mental Health Asscn of Greater Chicago, US Jaycees, Chicago Area Council of Boy Scouts of America; Hon. LLD (Nat. Louis Univ., Evanston, Ill., Tougaloo Coll., Miss.); Distinguished Service Award, Chicago South End Jaycees 1968, named as one of The Ten Outstanding Young Men of Chicago 1970, 1972, 1,000 Successful Black Men of America, Fortune magazine 1973, Blackbook's Outstanding Business Man of Year 1974, Community Service Award, Operation Push 1975, 100 Most Influential Black Americans, Ebony Magazine 1979–95, named Man of the Year, Goodwill Industries 1980, Outstanding Alumnus Award, Howard Univ. Law School Alumni Asscn 1980, 1989, Donald L. Scantlebury Memorial Award for State Leadership 1982, Award of Financial Reporting Achievement, Govt Finance Officers Asscn (USA and Canada) 1985, Three Outstanding Financial Officers, Crain's Chicago Business 1986, Distinguished Public Service Award, B'nai B'rith 1988, One of the Top Three Govt Financial Officers in the Nation, City and State Magazine 1989, State Auditors, Comptrollers, & Treasurers Service Award, Govt Finance Officers Asscn 1990, Outstanding Black Manitoba, 21st Century Comm. of African American Males 1991, Defender of Justice Award, Nat. Center for Juvenile Justice 1991, Peace & Justice Award, Kappa Alpha Psi 1991, Distinguished Accomplishments in the Field of Law, Nat. Bar Asscn 1993, Distinguished Service Award for Excellence in Crime Prevention, Chicagoland Chamber of Commerce 1993, Ten Most Distinguished Alumni in the History of the University Wall of Fame, Southern Illinois Univ., Carbondale 1997, Hall of Fame, Centralia, Ill., Centralia High School Alumni Asscn Award 2008. *Address:* Burris & Lebed Consulting, LLC, 35 East Wacker Drive, Suite #500, Chicago, IL 60601-2105, USA (office). *Telephone:* (312) 566-0202 (office). *Fax:* (312) 566-0041 (office).

BURROW, Sharan Leslie, BA; Australian international trade union official; *General Secretary, International Trade Union Confederation;* b. (Sharan Leslie Murphy), 27 May 1954, Warren, NSW; ed Univ. of New South Wales, Charles Sturt Univ.; became an organizer for NSW Teachers' Fed., Bathurst; Pres. Bathurst Trades and Labour Council 1980s; fmr Sr Vice-Pres. NSW Teachers' Fed.; fmr mem. Bd Curriculum Corpn; Vice-Pres. Education International 1995–2000; Pres. Australian Educ. Union 1993–2000; Pres. Australian Council of Trade Unions (second woman) 2000–10; Pres. (first woman) Int. Confed. of Free Trade Unions (ICFTU) Asia Pacific Region Org. 2000–04, Pres. ICFTU (first woman) 2004–06, Pres. Int. Trade Union Confed. (ITUC) 2006–10, Gen. Sec. 2010–; mem. Governing Body of ILO (chaired Workers' Group of Sub-cttee on Multinational Enterprises), Stakeholder Council of Global Reporting Initiative. *Address:* International Trade Union Confederation, Blvd du Roi Albert II 5, Bte 1, 1210 Brussels, Belgium (office). *Telephone:* (2) 224-02-11 (office). *Fax:* (2) 201-58-15 (office). *E-mail:* sharan.burrow@ituc-csi.org (office). *Website:* www.ituc-csi.org (office).

BURROWS, Richard; Irish business executive and banker; *Chairman, British American Tobacco plc;* b. 16 Jan. 1946, Dublin; m.; four c.; began career as chartered accountant; joined Irish Distillers 1971, Man. Dir Old Bushmills Distillery 1972–76, Gen. Man. Irish Distillers 1976–78, CEO 1978–91, Chair. and CEO Irish Distillers (acquired by Pernod Ricard SA 1988) 1978–2000, Dir-Gen. Pernod Ricard SA 2000, Co-CEO 2000–05, mem. Bd of Dirs 2004–; apptd to Court of Bank of Ireland 2000, Deputy Gov. 2002–05, Sr Ind. Dir 2003–09, Gov. 2005–09 (resgnd); Dir (non-exec.) British American Tobacco plc, London Sept. 2009–, Chair. Nov. 2009–; Dir Cityjet Ltd 2007–; Dir (non-exec.) Rentokil Initial, Carlsberg; Chair. Nat. Devt Corpn 1984–88, Scotch Whisky Asscn 2006–07, Craven House Capital, PLC 2016–18; Pres. Irish Business and Employers Confed. 1998–2000; mem. Trilateral Comm.; Royal Dublin Soc. Gold Medal Award for Excellence in Industry 2005. *Leisure interests:* sailing, watching rugby. *Address:* British American Tobacco plc, Globe House, 4 Temple Place, London, WC2R 2PG, England (office). *Telephone:* (20) 7845-1000 (office). *Fax:* (20) 7845-2118 (office). *Website:* www.bat.com (office).

BURSÍK, Martin, RNDr; Czech politician; *Chairman, Liberálně ekologická strana (Liberal Ecology Party);* b. 12 Aug. 1959, Prague; m. Ivana Buršíková 1998 (divorced 2008); two d.; partner Catherine Jacques 2009; one d.; ed Faculty of Natural Sciences, Charles Univ., Prague; signatory of civic initiative 'Civil Liberty Movement' 1989; involved in Civic Forum from outset, mem. and subsequently Deputy Chair. following split in party; switched to Free Democrats (Svobodní Demokraté) –2003; Chair. Environmental Protection Cttee, Prague City Ass. 1994–98, specialized in waste man. and transport, mem. Environment Protection Cttee 1998–2002; unsuccessful cand. for Mayor of Prague; later joined Christian and Democratic Union – Czechoslovak People's Party (KDU-ČSL); Minister for the Environment Feb.–July 1998; consultant in field of energy and environmental protection 1998–2005; external energy and environment adviser to Minister for the Environment 2002–05; mem. Strana zelených (Czech Green Party) 2004–13, Chair. 2005–09, Vice-Chair. 2012–13; mem. Parl. (Green Party) 2006–10; Acting Minister of Educ., Youth and Sports Oct.–Dec. 2007; Deputy Prime Minister and Minister for the Environment 2007–09; taught Environmental Policy, New York Univ., Prague 2010; taught a course on Renewable Energy, Czech Agricultural Univ., Prague 2012–13; Founder and Chair. Liberálně ekologická strana (Liberal Ecology Party) 2014–; cand. for Senate Dist No. 27 for TOP 09 with support of Liberal Ecology Party 2014; Dir, Ecoconsulting s.r.o.; Merit Prize of Josef Vavroušek 2012. *Leisure interest:* rock climbing. *Address:* Sněmovní 7, Prague 1, Czech Republic (office). *Telephone:* 77-6287745 (mobile). *E-mail:* senator@martinbursik.cz; martin.bursik@stranales.cz (office). *Website:* stranales.cz/?team=rndr-martin-bursik (office); www.martinbursik.cz.

BURSON, Harold, BA; American public relations executive and consultant; *Founding Chairman, Burson-Marsteller;* b. 15 Feb. 1921, Memphis; s. of Maurice Burson and Esther Burson; m. Bette Foster 1947; two s.; ed Univ. of Miss.; Acting Dir Ole Miss News Bureau 1938–40; reporter Memphis Commercial Appeal 1940; Asst to Pres. and Public Relations Dir, H. K. Ferguson Co. 1941–43; operated own public relations firm for six years; Founding Chair. Burson-Marsteller 1953–, CEO 1953–88; Public Relations Adviser to Pres. Reagan 1989–94; Dir World Environmental Center 1998–; Exec. Vice-Pres. Young and Rubicam Inc., mem. Exec. Cttee 1979–85; Garrett Lecturer on Social Responsibility, Columbia Univ., Grad. School of Business 1973; Exec.-in-Residence, Univ. of Ky Coll. Comm. 2000; Visiting Prof., Leeds Univ. 2001; Vice-Pres. and mem. Exec. Cttee, Nat. Safety Council 1964–77; Int. Trustee World Wildlife Fund 1977–81; Trustee and mem. Exec. Cttee Foundation for Public Relations Research and Educ. 1978–84; Founder and Sec. Corporate Fund, John F. Kennedy Centre for the Performing Arts 1977; Dir Kennedy Cen. Productions Inc. 1974–89; presidential appointee to Fine Arts Comm. 1981–85, to Exec. Cttee Young Astronauts Co. 1984–88; mem. Advisory Cttee, Medill School of Journalism, Northwestern Univ. 1985, Grad. School of Business, Emory Univ. 1986; mem. Public Relations Soc. of America, Int. Public Relations Asscn of Business Communicators, Overseas Press Club, NY Soc. of Security Analysts, Exec. Cttee, Catalyst Inc. 1977–88, Public Relations Advisory Cttee, US Information Agency 1981; assoc. mem. NY Acad. of Medicine; Counsellor, Nat. Press Foundation; Trustee The Economic Club of NY, Ray Simon Inst. of Public Relations, Syracuse Univ. 1985; Chair. Jt Council on Econ. Educ., Public Relations Seminar 1983; Hon. Prof. Fudan Univ., Shanghai 1999; Hon. DHumLitt (Boston Univ.) 1988; Public Relations Professional of the Year Award (Public Relations News) 1977, Gold Anvil Award (Public Relations Soc. of America) 1980, Univ. of Miss. Alumni Hall of Fame 1980, Silver Em Award (Miss. Press Asscn) 1982, Arthur Page Award, Univ. of Tex. 1986, Horatio Alger Award 1986,

Nat. Public Relations Achievement Award, (Ball State Univ.), Inside PR Life Achievement Award 1993. *Publications include:* The Making of Burson-Marsteller 2004. *Leisure interests:* stamp collection, West Highland White terriers. *Address:* Burson-Marsteller, 230 Park Avenue South, New York, NY 10003-1513, USA. *Telephone:* (212) 614-4444 (office). *Fax:* (212) 598-5679 (office). *E-mail:* harold_burson@nyc.bm.com (office). *Website:* www.bm.com; www.haroldburson.com.

BURSTYN, Ellen; American actress; b. (Edna Rae Gillooly), 7 Dec. 1932, Detroit, Mich.; d. of John Austin and Coriene Marie Gillooly (née Hamel); m. 1st William C. Alexander 1950 (divorced 1957); m. 2nd Paul Roberts 1958 (divorced 1962); m. 3rd Neil Burstyn 1964 (divorced 1972); one s. and one adopted s.; ed Cass Tech. High School, Detroit, study acting with Lee Strasberg at The Actor's Studio, New York; had several jobs before becoming an actress; went to Texas to model and then to New York as a showgirl on The Jackie Gleason Show 1952; worked as a nightclub dancer in Montreal; Broadway debut in Fair Game 1957; appeared on TV series The Doctors 1963; gained notice for her role in Goodbye Charlie 1964; cast as female lead in The Last Picture Show 1971; Co-Artistic Dir The Actor's Studio 1982–88; Pres. Actors' Equity Assen (first woman) 1982–85; Dir Judgement (off Broadway) 1981, Into Thin Air 1985; mem. jury, Berlin Int. Film Festival 1977 (Co-head of jury 1988), Cannes Film Festival 1981; ordained minister; mem. Bd of Selectors, Jefferson Awards Foundation; chosen by People Magazine as one of the 50 Most Beautiful People in the World 2001, Lifetime Achievement Award in Acting, Savannah Film Festival 2005, Career Achievement in Acting Award, the Hamptons Film Festival 2006, became the 20th person (and one of only 12 actresses) to have won the Triple Crown of Acting (Academy Award 1975, Tony Award 1975, Emmy Award 2009) 2009. *Stage productions include:* Fair Game 1957, Same Time Next Year 1975, 84 Charing Cross Road, Shirley Valentine 1989–90. *Films:* as Ellen McRae: For Those Who Think Young 1964, Goodbye Charlie 1964, Pit Stop 1969; as Ellen Burstyn: Tropic of Cancer (uncredited) 1970, Alex in Wonderland 1970, The Last Picture Show (Best Supporting Actress, New York Film Critics' Award, Nat. Soc. of Film Critics' Award) 1971, The King of Marvin Gardens 1972, The Exorcist 1973, Harry and Tonto 1974, Alice Doesn't Live Here Anymore (Best Actress, Acad. Awards, British Acad. Awards) 1974, Providence 1977, A Dream of Passion 1978, Same Time, Next Year 1978, Resurrection 1980, Silence of the North 1981, The Ambassador 1984, Twice in a Lifetime 1985, Hanna's War 1988, Dying Young 1991, Grand Isle 1991, The Cemetery Club 1993, The Color of Evening 1994, When a Man Loves a Woman 1994, Roommates 1995, The Baby-Sitters Club 1995, How to Make an American Quilt 1995, Cross the Line 1996, The Spitfire Grill 1996, Liar 1997, Playing by Heart 1998, The Yards 1999, You Can Thank Me Later 1999, Walking Across Egypt 1999, Requiem for a Dream 2000, Distance (short) (voice over) 2001, Divine Secrets of the Ya-Ya Sisterhood 2002, Red Dragon 2002 (voice) (uncredited), Cross the Line 2005, The Wicker Man 2006, The Fountain 2006, 30 Days 2006, Charlotte's Web 2006, The Elephant King 2006, The Stone Angel 2007, Lovely, Still 2008, The Loss of a Teardrop Diamond 2008, W. 2008, The Velveteen Rabbit 2009, Greta 2009, The Mighty Macs 2009, Main Street 2010, Another Happy Day 2011, Some Day This Pain Will Be Useful to You 2011, Wish You Well 2013, Two Men in Town 2014, Draft Day 2014, The Calling 2014, Interstellar 2014, The Age of Adaline 2014, Unity 2015, About Scout 2015, Wiener-Dog 2016, Custody 2016, The House of Tomorrow 2017, All I Wish 2017, Nostalgia 2018, The Tale 2018. *Television films:* Thursday's Game 1974, The People vs. Jean Harris 1981, Surviving 1985, Into Thin Air 1985, Act of Vengeance 1986, Something in Common 1986, Pack of Lies 1987, Look Away 1987, When You Remember Me 1990, Mrs. Lambert Remembers Love 1991, Taking Back My Life: The Nancy Ziegenmeyer Story 1992, Shattered Trust: The Shari Karney Story 1993, Getting Out 1994, Getting Gotti 1994, Primal Secrets 1994, My Brother's Keeper 1995, Follow the River 1995, Our Son, the Matchmaker 1996, Timepiece 1996, A Deadly Vision 1997, Flash 1997, The Patron Saint of Liars 1998, Night Ride Home 1999, Mermaid 2000, Dodson's Journey 2001, Within These Walls 2001, Brush with Fate 2003, The Madam's Family: The Truth About the Canal Street Brothel 2004, The Five People You Meet in Heaven 2004, Our Fathers 2005, Mrs. Harris 2005, Mitch Albom's For One More Day 2007, Possible Side Effects 2009, Flowers in the Attic 2014, Petals on the Wind 2014. *Television series:* as Ellen McRae: Kraft Television Theatre 1958, The Christmas Tree 1958, Westinghouse Desilu Playhouse 1960, The DuPont Show of the Month 1960, Michael Shayne 1961, Letter to Loretta 1961, Surfside 6 1961, The Dick Powell Show 1961, Dr. Kildare 1961, Cheyenne 1961, Bus Stop 1962, The Detectives 1962, Checkmate 1962, Kraft Mystery Theater 1962, Ben Casey 1962, I'm Dickens, He's Fenster 1962, The Many Loves of Dobie Gillis 1962, Perry Mason 1962, The Real McCoys 1962, Gun Law 1962, Laramie 1963, 77 Sunset Strip 1961–63, The Defenders 1963, Going My Way 1963, Wagon Train 1963, The Big Brain 1963, Kraft Suspense Theatre 1964, Theatre of Stars 1964, The Greatest Show on Earth 1964, The Doctors 1964–65, For the People 1965, The Time Tunnel 1966, The Big Valley 1967, Iron Horse 1967–68, Insight 1968, The Virginian 1969; as Ellen Burstyn: Gun Law 1971, The Bold Ones: The Lawyers 1972, The Ellen Burstyn Show 1986–87, A Will of Their Own (mini-series) 1998, That's Life 2000–02, The Book of Daniel 2006, Law & Order: Special Victims Unit 2008, Big Love 2007–11, Political Animals (Emmy Award for Outstanding Supporting Actress in a Miniseries or a Movie 2013)2012, Coma 2012, Louie 2014, Mom 2015, House of Cards. *Address:* c/o Creative Artists Agency, 2000 Avenue of the Stars, Los Angeles, CA 90067, USA. *Telephone:* (424) 288-2000. *Fax:* (424) 288-2900. *Website:* www.caa.com.

BURT, E. David, MSc; Bermudian business executive and politician; *Premier;* b. 1979; s. of Gerald and Merlin Burt m. Kristin Burt; one s. one d.; ed Florida Air Acad., George Washington Univ.; early career with family co. Burt Construction; Pres. GMD Consulting Ltd (IT consulting co.) 2004–10, 2011–16; co-f. HITCH Ltd (electronic taxi booking app) 2015; mem. Senate 2010–12; apptd Jr Minister for Finance, Environment and Planning, Infrastructure Strategy and Chief of Staff to Premier 2010; mem. House of Ass. (Parl.) for Pembroke West 2012–, Leader of the Opposition 2016–17; Premier of Bermuda 2017–, also Minister of Finance 2017–18; fmr mem. Tourism Bd, Nat. Training Bd; fmr mem. Bd of Dirs Bermuda Chamber of Commerce, Bermuda Econ. Devt Corpn; mem. Progressive Labour Party, Leader 2016–. *Address:* Office of the Premier, Cabinet Office, Cabinet Bldg, 105 Front Street, Hamilton, HM 12, Bermuda (office). *Telephone:* 292-5501 (office). *Fax:* 292-8397 (office). *E-mail:* premier@gov.bm (office). *Website:* www.gov.bm (office).

BURT, Robert Amsterdam, BA, BA (Oxon.), MA (Oxon.), JD; American lawyer and academic; *Alexander M. Bickel Professor of Law, Yale University;* b. 3 Feb. 1939, Philadelphia, Pa; s. of Samuel Mathew Burt and Esther Amsterdam Burt; m. Linda Gordon Rose 1964; two d.; ed Princeton and Yale Univs, Univ. of Oxford, UK; Law Clerk, US Court of Appeals, Dist of Columbia Circuit 1964–65; Asst Gen. Counsel, Exec. Office of the Pres. of USA 1965–66; Legis. Asst, US Senate 1966–68; Assoc. Prof. of Law, Chicago Univ. 1968–70; Assoc. Prof. of Law, Univ. of Michigan 1970–72, Prof. of Law 1972–73, Prof. of Law and Prof. of Law in Psychiatry 1973–76; Prof. of Law, Yale Univ. 1976–, Southmayd Prof. of Law 1982–93, Alexander M. Bickel Prof. 1993–; Special Master US Dist Court, Conn. 1987–92; Rockefeller Fellowship in Humanities 1976; mem. Bd of Dirs, Benhaven School for Autistic Persons 1977–, Chair. 1983–96, Mental Health Law Project 1985–, Chair. 1990–2000; Dir Yale Hillel Foundation 1996–; mem. Inst. of Medicine and NAS 1976, Advisory Bd Open Soc. Inst. Project on Death in America 1993–2003, Advisory Bd of Greenwall Foundation Bioethics Faculty Scholar Program 2003–12; Guggenheim Fellowship 1997. *Publications:* Taking Care of Strangers: The Rule of Law in Doctor-Patient Relations 1979, Two Jewish Justices: Outcasts in the Promised Land 1987, The Constitution in Conflict 1992, Death is That Man Taking Names 2002. *Leisure interests:* cello, swimming, bicycling. *Address:* Yale Law School, PO Box 208215, Room 216, 127 Wall Street, New Haven, CT 06520 (office); 66 Dogwood Circle, Woodbridge, CT 06525, USA (home). *Telephone:* (203) 432-4960 (office); (203) 393-3881 (home). *Fax:* (203) 432-4982 (office); (203) 393-1292 (home). *E-mail:* robert.burt@yale.edu (office). *Website:* www.law.yale.edu/faculty/RBurt.htm (office).

BURTON, Ian, (Burtoni), MA, PhD, FRSC; Canadian/British environmental scientist, geographer, scholar and consultant; *Scientist Emeritus, Meteorological Service of Canada;* b. 24 June 1935, Derby, England; s. of Frank Burton and Elsie Victoria Barnes; m. 1st Lydia Demodoff 1962 (divorced 1977); one s. one d.; m. 2nd Anne V. T. Whyte 1977 (divorced 1995); one s. two d.; m. 3rd Elizabeth May; one d.; ed Derby School, Univ. of Birmingham, Univ. of Chicago and Oberlin Coll., Ohio; Lecturer, Indiana Univ. 1960–61, Queen's Univ., Kingston, Ont. 1961; Consultant, Ford Foundation, India 1964–66; Prof., Univ. of Toronto 1968–90, Adjunct Prof. 1990–, Dir Inst. for Environmental Studies 1979–84, now Prof. Emer.; Prof. of Environmental Science, Univ. of East Anglia, UK 1972–73; Sr Adviser, Int. Devt Research Centre, Ottawa 1972–75; Sr Connaught Fellow, École des Hautes Études en Sciences Sociales, Paris 1984–86; Dir Int. Fed. of Insts for Advanced Study 1986–92; Dir Environmental Adaptation Research, Atmospheric Environmental Service, Meteorological Service of Canada 1990–96, Scientist Emer. 1996–; mem. Bd of Dirs Foundation for Int. Training 1994–; mem. Ind. World Comm. on the Oceans 1995–98; mem. Int. Soc. of Biometeorology, Vice-Pres. 1996–2002, Pres. 2002–05; numerous cttee and consultant assignments with UNESCO, WHO, UNEP, Rockefeller Foundation, UNDP, World Bank Global Environment Facility, World Resources Inst., Intergovernmental Panel on Climate Change, European Comm., Ford Foundation, projects in Sudan and Nigeria etc.; mem. Jury, St Francis Environment Prize; Fellow, TWAS—the acad. of sciences for the developing world; Order of Zvonkova (USSR) 1968; Burtoni Award 2003. *Publications:* co-author: The Human Ecology of Coastal Flood Hazard in Megalopolis 1968, The Hazardousness of a Place: A Regional Ecology of Damaging Events 1971, The Environment as Hazard 1978; co-ed.: Readings in Resource Management and Conservation 1986, Environmental Risk Assessment 1980, Living with Risk 1982, Geography, Resources and Environment 1986, Climate Change and Adaptation 2007. *Leisure interests:* swimming, hiking, cricket. *Address:* Meteorological Service of Canada, 4905 Dufferin Street, Downsview, ON M3H 5T4 (office); 26 St Anne's Road, Toronto, ON M6J 2C1, Canada (home). *Telephone:* (416) 739-4314 (office); (416) 538-2034 (home). *Fax:* (416) 739-4297 (office). *E-mail:* ian.burton@ec.gc.ca (office); burtoni.ian@gmail.com (home). *Website:* www.ec.gc.ca/meteo-weather (office).

BURTON, Hon. (Richard) Mark; New Zealand politician; b. 16 Jan. 1956, Northampton, England; m. Carol Burton; two s. one d.; ed Wanganui Boys' Coll., Univ. of Waikato, Massey Univ., NZ Council of Recreation and Sport; moved with family to NZ aged ten; began career in community and social work, adult educ. and recreation; fmr employee Red Cross, Dept of Social Welfare, Palmerston North City Council; fmr Community Educ. Organiser, Cen. N Island; MP for Tongariro 1993–96, for Taupo 1996–2008; Sr Labour Party Whip 1996–99; Minister of Defence, State-Owned Enterprises and Tourism 1999–2005, also Minister of Internal Affairs and Veterans' Affairs 1999–2002; Deputy Leader of the House 1999–2007; Minister Responsible for Fire Service Comm. 2004–05; Minister of Justice and of Local Govt and in Charge of Treaty of Waitanagi Negotiations and Minister Responsible for Law Comm. 2005–07; unsuccessful cand. for Mayor of Taupo Dist 2010; Pres. Japan Karate NZ; NZ 1990 Medal. *Leisure interests:* reading, listening to music, playing guitar, trained in Aikido. *Website:* www.parliament.nz/en-nz/mpp/mps/former/48PlibMPsFormerMarkBurton1/burton-hon-mark.

BURTON, Tim; American film director and screenwriter; b. 25 Aug. 1958, Burbank, Calif.; pnr Helena Bonham Carter; one s. one d.; ed California Arts Inst.; began career as animator, Walt Disney Studios (projects included The Fox and the Hound and The Black Cauldron); Chevalier, Ordre des Arts et des Lettres 2010; short-length film awards include two from Chicago Film Festival, Golden Lion Lifetime Achievement Award, Venice Int. Film Festival 2007. *Films as director include:* Vincent (also animator) 1982, Luau 1982, Hansel and Gretel (TV) 1982, Frankenweenie (short, for Disney) 1984, Pee-Wee's Big Adventure 1985, Alfred Hitchcock Presents (TV episode, The Jar) 1985, Beetlejuice 1988, Batman 1989, Edward Scissorhands (also producer) 1991, Batman Returns (also producer) 1992, Ed Wood (also producer) 1994, Mars Attacks! (also producer) 1996, Sleepy Hollow 1999, Planet of the Apes 2001, Big Fish 2003, Charlie and the Chocolate Factory 2005, Corpse Bride (also producer) 2005, Sweeney Todd: The Demon Barber of Fleet Street (Best Dir Nat. Bd of Review 2007, Golden Globe for Best Musical or Comedy 2008) 2007, Alice in Wonderland (also producer) 2010, Dark Shadows 2012, Frankenweenie (also producer) 2012, Big Eyes (also producer) 2014, Miss Peregrine's Home for Peculiar Children (also producer) 2016. *Films as producer include:* The Nightmare Before Christmas 1993, Cabin Boy 1994, Batman Forever

1996, James and the Giant Peach 1996, 9 2009, Abraham Lincoln: Vampire Hunter 2012, Alice Through the Looking Glass 2016. *Film screenplays include:* The Island of Doctor Agor 1971, Stalk of the Celery 1979, Vincent 1982, Luau 1982, Beetlejuice (story) 1988, Edward Scissorhands (story) 1990, The Nightmare Before Christmas (story) 1993. *Film appearance:* Men in Black III. *Publications:* My Art and Films 1993, The Melancholy Death of Oyster Boy and Other Stories 1997, Burton on Burton 2000; various film tie-in books. *Address:* Chapman, Bird & Grey, 1990 South Bundy Drive, Suite 200, Los Angeles, CA 90025, USA (office). *Website:* www.timburton.com (office); www.facebook.com/TimBurton (office).

BURTYNSKY, Edward, OC, BAA; Canadian photographer; b. 1955, St Catharines, Ont.; ed Ryerson Univ.; f. Toronto Image Works (darkroom rental facility, custom photo lab., digital imaging and new media computer-training centre) 1985; known for photographic depictions of global industrial landscapes; works are held in numerous collections worldwide; six hon. degrees; numerous awards including Roloff Beny Book Award 2003, Rencontres d'Arles Outreach Award 2004, Deutscher Fotobuchpreis 2008, Prix Pictet 2009, Kraszna-Krausz Book Award 2010, MOCCA Award 2011, Tiffany Mark Award 2012, Gov. Gen.'s Award in Visual and Media Arts 2016. *Address:* Edward Burtynsky Photography, 80 Spadina Avenue, Suite 207, Toronto, ON M5V 2J4, Canada (office). *E-mail:* karen@edwardburtynsky.com (office). *Website:* www.edwardburtynsky.com (office).

BURWELL, Sylvia Mathews, AB, BA; American foundation president and government official; b. 1965, Hinton, W Va; d. of Dr William Mathews and Cleo Mathews; m. Stephen Burwell; one c.; ed Harvard Univ., Oxford Univ., UK; Assoc., McKinsey & Co., New York 1990–92; Staff Dir, Nat. Econ. Council, Washington, DC 1993–94; Chief of Staff to Treasury Sec. Robert Rubin 1995–97; Deputy White House Chief of Staff to Pres. Bill Clinton 1997–98; Deputy Dir, Office of Man. and Budget (OMB) 1998–2001, Dir 2013–14; Sec. of Health and Human Services 2014–17; COO Bill and Melinda Gates Foundation 2001–05, Pres., Gates Foundation Global Devt Program 2006–11; Pres. Walmart Foundation 2012; Dir MetLife and Metropolitan Life Insurance Co. 2004; mem. Univ. of Washington Medicine Bd, Pacific Council on Int. Policy, Aspen Strategy Group, Nike Foundation Advisory Group; mem. Governing Council, Miller Center of Public Affairs, Univ. of Virginia.

BURWITZ, Nils, BA (Fine Arts); German freelance artist, sculptor and lecturer; b. 16 Oct. 1940, Swinemünde; s. of Ulrich Burwitz and Johanna Lohse; m. Marina Schwezova 1964; two s. one d.; ed Univ. of the Witwatersrand and postgrad. studies in London, Fribourg and Salzburg; emigrated to S Africa 1958; settled in Balearic Islands 1976; over 200 solo exhbns, including 36 Exposures 1971 and restrospective exhbn in Sollerich Palace, Palma, Majorca 1985, Pretoria Art Museum, Pretoria 1991, Nat. Gallery 1992, Kunsthalle Munich-Germering 1995; lecturer at Lessinghaus, Herzog Bibliothek, Wolfenbüttel 2002; visual concept for stage works Iconostasis 1967–68, 8 Birds 1969, 8 Beasts 1970, Gentlemen (with R. Kirby) 1972, Mobile (with V. Rodzianko), London 1972, Retalls de l'Ignorancia (with R. Esteras) 1978, Llagrimes del Vienès (with A. Ballester) 1995; stained glass windows in churches of St Philip and St James and Sta Eulalia, Palma de Mallorca, Monastery of Lluch, La Ermita de la Santísima Trinidad, Royal Carthusian Monastery, Valldemossa, Majorca, Cupola for Castillo Hotel Son Vida, Palma de Mallorca, Cathedral, Palma de Mallorca; Founder Libra Press 1984; opened Funda Art Centre, Soweto, SA 1986; works in around 90 public collections including: Albertinum, Vienna, Albertinum, Dresden, Fitzwilliam Museum, Cambridge, Museum Ludwig, Cologne, Nat. Gallery, Warsaw, Nat. Portrait Gallery, Washington, DC, Museum of Modern Art, Tokyo, State Museum of Prints and Drawings, Berlin, British Museum, London, Victoria and Albert Museum, London, Sculpture for Plaza de la Concordia, Sa Pobla; has collaborated in three video documentaries in SA and Namibia; posters for UNHCR 2001, OAU 2001, Max Planck Inst. (Einstein's Legacy) 2005; portfolios: Locust Variations 1967, It's About Time 1973, Tidal Zone 1974, Heads or Tails? 1981, 9 Terraces 1986, The Journey to Dresden 1989, Marinas Terraces 1995, The Invisible Miró 2000, Journey to Berlin 2014; numerous honours and awards, including Gold Medal (Design), Johannesburg 1963, African Arts Centre Award, Durban 1971, Art Critics' Award, XI Graphic Biennale, Ljubljana 1975, Prix de la Ville de Monaco 1981, Primer Premio 'Ciutat de Palma' 1982, Merit Award, II Biennale of Painting, Barcelona 1987, Balearic European Citizen Award 1999, Premio Importantes, Diario de Mallorca 2002, Bishop Teodor Ubeda Memorial Award 2004. *Publications:* On the Razor's Edge 1995, Walking the Tightrope 2002. *Leisure interests:* swimming, diving. *Address:* Calle Rosa 22, 07170 Valldemossa, Majorca, Balearic Isles, Spain (home). *Telephone:* (971) 612838 (home). *E-mail:* nils@burwitz-art.com (home). *Website:* www.burwitz-art.com.

BURZAN, Dragiša, MS, PhD; Montenegrin politician and diplomatist; b. 1950, Podgorica; m. Vesna Burzan; one s. two d.; ed Univ. of Montenegro, Univ. of Belgrade, Serbia, Univ. of Essex, UK; mem. staff, Dept of Natural Sciences, Univ. of Montenegro 1976–98; Founder Democratic Alternative 1989; mem. Reform Forces of Fmr Yugoslavia 1991; Co-founder Montenegro Party 1992; mem. Parl. (Montenegro) 1992–96; Deputy Prime Minister of Montenegro with portfolios of Educ., Labour and Welfare, Health, Culture, Sport, Secr. of Information, Secr. for Int. and Science Cooperation, Commissariat for Refugees, etc. 1998–2001, Minister of Labour and Social Welfare 2001–02, of Foreign Affairs 2003–04; Amb. of Serbia and Montenegro to UK 2004–06, Amb. of Montenegro to UK 2007–11; foreign policy adviser to Pres. of Montenegro 2011–14; apptd Amb. to Turkey 2014; Chair. Parl. Comm. investigating abduction of group of Muslims in Bosnia; mem. SDP (Vice-Pres. 1996–2000); Co-founder Monitor (weekly). *Publications:* numerous articles on physics in scientific journals.

BUSAIDI, Sayyid Badr bin Saud bin Hareb al-; Omani politician; currently Minister Responsible for Defence Affairs. *Address:* Ministry of Defence, POB 113, Muscat 113, Oman (office). *Telephone:* 24312605 (office). *Fax:* 24702521 (office).

BUSCEMI, Steven (Steve) Vincent; American actor and film director; b. 13 Dec. 1957, New York; m. Jo Andres 1987; one s.; ed Valley Stream Cen. High School, NY; moved to Manhattan following high school graduation to study acting with John Strasberg; worked as bartender, ice-cream truck driver, stand-up comedian; New York City Fireman, Engine Co. No. 55, Little Italy Section 1980–84; began writing and performing theatre pieces with Mark Boone, Jr; film debut in The Way It Is 1984; first lead role in Parting Glances 1986; directed several episodes of TV series The Sopranos 1999, appeared in series 2004; hosts and produces own web series talk show, Park Bench 2014–; currently volunteer fireman, New York. *Films include:* The Way It Is 1984, Tommy's 1985, Parting Glances 1986, Heart 1987, Kiss Daddy Goodnight 1988, Vibes 1988, New York Stories 1989, Slaves of New York 1989, Mystery Train 1989, Coffee and Cigarettes II 1989, Borders 1989, King of New York 1990, Miller's Crossing 1990, Barton Fink 1991, Zandalee 1991, Billy Bathgate 1991, In the Soup 1992, CrissCross 1992, Reservoir Dogs 1992, Who Do I Gotta Kill? 1992, Claude 1993, Rising Sun 1993, Twenty Bucks 1993, Ed and His Dead Mother 1993, Floundering 1994, The Hudsucker Proxy 1994, Airheads 1994, Somebody to Love 1994, Pulp Fiction 1994, Living in Oblivion 1995, Dead Man 1995, Things to Do in Denver When You're Dead 1995, Fargo 1996, Trees Lounge 1996, Kansas City 1996, Escape from L.A. 1996, Con Air 1997, The Real Blonde 1997, The Wedding Singer 1998, The Big Lebowski 1998, The Impostors 1998, Armageddon 1998, Louis & Frank 1998, Animal Factory 2000, 28 Days 2000, Ghost World 2000, Final Fantasy: The Spirits Within (voice) 2001, The Grey Zone 2001, Monsters Inc. (voice) 2001, The Laramie Project 2002, Love in the Time of Money 2002, 13 Moons 2002, Mr Deeds 2002, Spy Kids 2: Island of Lost Dreams 2002, Deadrockstar 2002, Spy Kids 3-D: Game Over 2003, Coffee and Cigarettes 2003, Big Fish 2003, Home on the Range 2004, The Sky is Green 2004, Romance & Cigarettes 2005, Art School Confidential 2004, The Island 2005, A License to Steal 2005, Cordless 2005, Delirious 2005, Paris, je t'aime 2006, Monster House 2006, Charlotte's Web (voice) 2006, Interview 2007, I Think I Love My Wife 2007, I Now Pronounce You Chuck & Larry 2007, I'm Dirty! (video short) 2008, Igor (voice) 2008, The Messenger 2009, City of War: The Story of John Rabe 2009, Rage 2009, Handsome Harry 2009, Saint John of Las Vegas 2009, G-Force (voice) 2009, Youth in Revolt 2009, Fight for Your Right Revisited (short) 2010, Grown Ups 2010, The Chosen One 2010, Pete Smalls Is Dead 2010, Rampart 2011, On the Road 2012, Hotel Transylvania (voice) 2012, The Incredible Burt Wonderstone 2013, Grown Ups 2 2013, The Cobbler 2014, Hotel Transylvania 2 (voice) 2015. *Films directed include:* What Happened to Pete? 1992, Trees Lounge 1996, Animal Factory 2000, Lonesome Jim 2005, Interview 2007. *Films produced include:* Animal Factory 2000, Symbiopsychotaxiplasm: Take 2 1/2 (documentary) (exec. producer) 2005, Lonesome Jim 2005, Saint John of Las Vegas (exec. producer) 2009. *Films written include:* What Happened to Pete? 1992, Trees Lounge 1996, Interview 2007. *Television includes:* The Simpsons (series) 2007, 30 Rock (series) 2007–13, ER (series) 2008, Boardwalk Empire (Golden Goble Award for Best Performance by an Actor in a TV Series – Drama 2011) 2010–14, Portlandia (series) 2011–, My Depression (film) 2014. *Address:* c/o WME Entertainment, 9601 Wilshire Boulevard, Beverly Hills, CA 90210-5213, USA (office). *Telephone:* (310) 285-9000 (office). *Fax:* (310) 285-9010 (office). *Website:* www.wmeentertainment.com (office).

BUSCH, August A., III; American brewery industy executive; *Director, Anheuser-Busch Companies Inc.;* b. 16 June 1937, St Louis, Mo.; s. of August A. Busch, Jr; one s.; ed Univ. of Arizona; began career with family-business Anheuser-Busch Cos Inc. (brewery, theme-park operator and mfr of alumnium cans), mem. Bd of Dirs 1963–, Pres. 1974–2002, CEO 1975–2002, Chair. 1977–2006; mem. Bd of Dirs Emerson Electric Co., SBC Communications Inc.; Beverage Forum Lifetime Achievement Award 2003. *Address:* Anheuser-Busch Companies Inc., 1 Busch Place, St Louis, MO 63118, USA (office). *Telephone:* (314) 577-2000 (office). *Fax:* (314) 577-2900 (office). *Website:* www.anheuser-busch.com (office).

BUSCH, August Adolphus, IV, MBA; American brewing industry executive; b. 15 June 1964, St Louis, Mo.; s. of August Busch, III and Susan Busch (née Hornibrook); m. Kathryn (Kate) Thatcher 2006 (divorced 2009); ed Parkway West High School, Ballwin, Mo., St Louis Univ., Int. Brewing Inst., Berlin; joined Anheuser-Busch as apprentice brewer 1985, Vice-Pres. Brand Man. 1994–96, Vice-Pres. Marketing 1996–2000, Group Vice-Pres. Marketing and Wholesale Operations 2000–02, Pres. 2002–08, CEO 2006–08 (co. sold to InBev), mem. Bd of Dirs 2006–08, of Anheuser-Busch InBev 2008–11; mem. Bd of Dirs FedEx Corpn 2003–08; f. Great Rivers Habitat Alliance; Hon. DBA (Webster Univ.) 2006. *Leisure interests:* holds advanced black belt degrees in Judo, Tae-Kwon-Do and Hapkido. *Address:* c/o Anheuser-Busch Companies, LLC, 1 Busch Place, St Louis, MO 63118, USA. *E-mail:* info@anheuser-busch.com.

BUSCH, May Chien, MBA; British/American investment banker; *Managing Director, May Busch & Associates Ltd;* ed Harvard Coll., Harvard Business School; joined Morgan Stanley Dean Witter 1985, later Head of Debt Capital Markets in Europe for Corporates, later Man. Dir and Co-Head of European Coverage of Global Capital Markets, Morgan Stanley & Co. Int. Ltd 2002–04, Head of Firm Relationship Man. 2004–06, COO 2006–07; Sr Advisor and Exec. in Residence, Office of the Pres. 2010–; Man. Dir May Busch & Assocs. Ltd 2013–; mem. Council for Industry and Higher Educ., Advisory Bd SEO London UK Internship Programme. *Publications include:* Accelerate: 9 Capabilities to Achieve Success at Any Career Stage 2016. *Address:* May Busch & Associates Ltd, 22a St James's Square, London, SW1Y 4JH, England (office). *Telephone:* (20) 7193-2468 (office); (858) 888-9045 (office). *E-mail:* connect@maybusch.com (office). *Website:* maybusch.com (office).

BUSEK, Erhard, DJur; Austrian politician and international organization official; *President, Institut für den Donauraum und Mitteleuropa (Institute for the Danube Region and Central Europe);* b. 25 March 1941, Vienna; m. Helga Busek; ed Univ. of Vienna; Sec., Parl. of the Austrian Nat. Council 1964–68; Gen. Sec., Austrian Federal Fed. of Trade and Commerce 1972–76; joined Fed. Exec. Cttee of Austrian Econ. Fed. 1968, Deputy Sec.-Gen. 1969, Sec.-Gen. 1972–76; Gen. Sec. ÖVP 1975–76; mem. Parl. 1975–78; Chair. Vienna's People's Party 1976–89; City Councillor, Vienna City Senate 1976–78, 1987–89; Deputy Mayor of Vienna 1978–87; Deputy Fed. Chair. ÖVP 1983–91, Chair. 1991–95; Pres. Austrian Research Community; Fed. Minister of Science and Research 1989–94, of Educ. and Culture 1994–95, Vice-Chancellor 1992–95; with Instituts für den Donauraum und Mitteleuropa (Inst. for the Danube Region and Central Europe—IDM) 1995–; Co-ordinator for Southeastern European Co-operative Initiative 1996–; Pres. European Forum Alpbach 2000–12; Special Co-ordinator, Stability Pact for SE Europe 2002–08; Vice-Pres., Vienna Economic Forum (VEF) 2004–05, Pres. 2005–16; Rector, Salzburg Univ. of Applied Sciences 2004–11; Chair. Advisory Bd ERSTE Foundation 2005–, Univ. Council, Medical Univ. of Vienna

2008–; Pres. Int. Centre for Advanced and Comparative EU, Russia 2009–11; Pres. EU-Russia Centre 2010–13; Visiting Prof. of the Practice of Public Policy Studies, Duke Univ., USA 1995–; Perm. Sr Fellow, Centre for Research into European Integration, Bonn; Pres. Gustav Mahler Youth Orchestra, Österreichischen Volksliedwerkes, Stipendienwerkes 'pro scientia'; Jt-Pres. Technologieforums Sloweniens; Adviser, Economic Initiative for Kosovo 2008–; Dr hc (Univs of Kraków, Bratislava, Czernowitz and Ruse). *Publications include:* Projekt Mitteleuropa 1986, Aufbruch nach Mitteleuropa (with G. Wilflinger) 1986, Wissenschaft, Ethik und Politik (with M. Peterlik) 1987, Wissenschaft und Freiheit – Ideen zu Universität und Universalität (with W. Mantl and M. Perterlik) 1989, Heimat – Politik mit sitz im Leben 1994, Mensch im Wort 1994, Mitteleuropa: Eine Spurensicherung 1997, Politik am Gängelband der Medien 1998, Österreich und der Balkan – Vom Umgang mit dem Pulverfass Europas 1999, Eine Reise ins Innere Europas – Protokoll eines Österreichers 2001, Offenes Tor nach Osten 2003, Die Europäische Union auf dem Weg nach Osten 2003. *Address:* Institut für den Donauraum und Mitteleuropa, Hahngasse 6/17, 1090 Vienna, Austria (office). *Telephone:* 431319725811 (office). *Fax:* 4313197258-50 (office). *E-mail:* idm@idm.at (office). *Website:* www.idm.at (office).

BUSER, Walter Emil, DrIur; Swiss government official; b. 14 April 1926, Lausen; s. of Emil Buser and Martha Buser; m. Renée Vuille 1947; ed Humanistic Gymnasium, Basel, Univs of Basel and Berne; Ed. Sozialdemokratische Bundeshauskorrespondenz 1950–61; legal consultant 1962–64; Head, legal and information service, Fed. Dept of Interior 1965–67; Vice-Chancellor of the Swiss Confed. 1968–81, Chancellor 1981–91; Hon. Dozent (Basel). *Publications:* Das Bundesgesetz über die Ordnung des Arbeitsverhaltnisses vom 27.6.19, Die Rolle der Verwaltung und der Interessengruppen im Entscheidungsprozess der Schweiz, Betrachtungen zum schweizerischen Petitionsrecht, Die Organisation der Rechtsetzung, in Hundert Jahre Bundesverfassung 1874–1974, Das Institut der Volksinitiative in rechtlicher und rechtspolitischer Sicht. *Address:* c/o Federal Chancellery, Swiss Confederation, 3003 Berne, Switzerland.

BUSH, George Walker, BA, MBA; American business executive, politician and fmr head of state; b. 6 July 1946, New Haven, Conn.; s. of George Herbert Walker Bush (fmr Pres. of USA) and Barbara Bush (née Pierce); brother of John Ellis (Jeb) Bush; m. Laura Welch Bush; twin d.; ed Yale Univ. and Harvard Business School; trained as F-102 fighter pilot, Tex. Air Nat. Guard 1968; CEO Bush Exploration, Midland, Tex. 1975–83; Chair. and CEO Spectrum 7 Energy Corpn (merged with Harken Energy Corpn 1986) 1983–87; worked in father's presidential campaign 1988; Man. Gen. Partner, Texas Rangers professional baseball team 1989–94; Gov. of Tex. 1995–2000; Pres. of USA 2001–09; Order of the Cross of Terra Mariana (Estonia) 2012; Isaiah Award, Int. Leadership Reunion Conference, Toronto 2017. *Publications:* A Charge To Keep (with Karen Hughes) 2000, Decision Points 2010, 41: A Portrait of My Father 2014, Portraits of Courage: A Commander in Chief's Tribute to America's Warriors 2017. *Address:* Office of George W. Bush, PO Box 259000, Dallas, TX 75225-9000, USA. *Website:* www.georgewbush.com.

BUSH, John Ellis (Jeb), BA; American business executive and fmr politician; b. 11 Feb. 1953, Midland, Tex.; s. of George Herbert Walker Bush, fmr Pres. of USA and Barbara Bush; brother of George W. Bush (q.v.), fmr Pres. of USA; m. Columba Bush; two s. one d.; ed Univ. of Texas; co-f. Codina Group (real estate devt co.), Miami, Fla 1981, served as Pres. and COO; Sec. of Commerce, State of Fla 1987–88; unsuccessful bid for Fla Gov.'s office 1994; Gov. of Florida 1999–2007; Founder and Man. Partner, Jeb Bush & Associates LLC (consultancy), Miami 2007–; mem. Pvt. Equity Advisory Bd, Lehman Brothers Holdings Inc. 2007–08; Co-founder Britton Hill Holdings (investment group) 2008; Founder and Chair. Foundation for Excellence in Education, Foundation for Florida's Future; Sr Advisor, Academic Partnerships –2014; Sr Advisor, Barclays Capital 2008–14; mem. Bd of Dirs Tenet Healthcare 2007–14, CNL Bancshares Inc. 2007–14, Rayonier Inc. 2008–14, Swisher Hygiene Inc. 2010–13; Co-Chair. Barbara Bush Foundation for Family Literacy; mem. Advisory Bd George W. Bush Inst.; Visiting Fellow, Inst. of Politics, Harvard Univ. 2010; announced candidacy for Republican Party nomination in 2016 presidential election June 2015; Republican. *Publications:* Profiles in Character (co-author) 1996, Immigration Wars: Forging an American Solution (co-author) 2013. *Address:* Jeb Bush & Associates LLC, The Biltmore Hotel, 1200 Anastasia Avenue, Coral Gables, FL 33134, USA (office).

BUSH, Kate, CBE; British singer, songwriter, musician and record producer; b. 30 July 1958, Bexleyheath, Kent; pnr Danny McIntosh; one s.; numerous live and TV appearances; Dir Novercia Ltd; Founder Fish People record label; guest and backing vocalist for numerous artists, including Peter Gabriel, Roy Harper, Prince, Midge Ure; BPI Awards for Best Vocalist 1979, 1987, Ivor Novello Award for Outstanding British Lyrics (for The Man With The Child In His Eyes) 1979, BRIT Award for Best Female Artist 1987, Q Magazine Award for Best Classic Songwriter 2001, Ivor Novello Award for Outstanding Contribution to British Music by a Songwriter 2002. *Film:* The Line, The Cross and The Curve (writer, dir and actor) 1993. *Stage:* live shows: The Tour of Life 1979, Before the Dawn (Evening Standard Theatre Editor's Award 2014) 2014. *Recordings include:* albums: The Kick Inside 1978, Lionheart 1978, Never for Ever 1980, The Dreaming 1982, Hounds Of Love 1985, The Whole Story 1986, The Sensual World 1989, This Woman's Work 1990, The Red Shoes 1993, Aerial 2005, Director's Cut 2011, 50 Words for Snow (South Bank Sky Arts Award 2012) 2011, Before The Dawn 2016. *Publications:* How to Be Invisible: Selected Lyrics 2018. *E-mail:* admin@katebush.com. *Website:* www.katebush.com.

BUSH, Laura Welch, BA, MLS; American public servant and teacher; b. Midland, Tex.; m. George W. Bush 1977; twin d.; ed Southern Methodist Univ., Univ. of Tex.; worked as teacher at Longfellow Elementary School, Dallas, Tex. 1968–69; teacher, John F. Kennedy Elementary School 1969–72; librarian, Houston Public Library 1973–74, Dawson Elementary School, Austin, Tex. 1974–77; First Lady of Tex. 1995–2000; First Lady of US 2001–09. *Publication:* Spoken from the Heart (autobiog.) 2010. *Address:* c/o Office of George W. Bush, PO Box 259000, Dallas, TX 75225-9000, USA (office).

BUSH, McKeeva, OBE, JP; Cayman Islands business executive and politician; *Speaker, Legislative Assembly;* b. 20 Jan. 1955, West Bay; s.; m. Kerry Bush 1975; one s. one d. (deceased); ed Cayman Islands Community Coll., George Town; mem. Legis. Ass. (parl.) for West Bay 1984–, Speaker Legis. Ass. of Cayman Islands 2017–; mem. Exec. Council (renamed Cabinet 2003) as Mem. (Minister) for Health and Human Services 1992–94, for Community Devt, Sports, Women's and Youth Affairs and Culture 1994–97, for Tourism, Environment and Transport 2000–01, for Tourism, Environment, Devt and Commerce 2001–05; Founding mem. United Democratic Party (now Cayman Islands Democratic Party—CDP) 2001–; Leader of the Opposition 2005–09, 2013–17; Leader of Govt Business 2001–05, May–Nov. 2009; Premier of the Cayman Islands and Minister responsible for Financial Services, Tourism and Devt Nov. 2009–12; Founder and Realtor, Cambridge Real Estate Corpn 1984–; Hon. MSc (Int. Coll. of the Cayman Islands); Cayman Islands Football Assen Order of Merit. *Leisure interests:* reading, music, fishing, dancing. *Address:* Cayman Islands Democratic Party (CDP), Unit 15, 2nd Floor, Rankin's Plaza, Eastern Avenue, Grand Cayman (office); PO Box 321, West Bay, Grand Cayman, Cayman Islands (office). *Telephone:* 943-3338 (office). *Fax:* 943-3339 (office). *Website:* www.legislativeassembly.ky (office).

BUSH, Wesley (Wes) G., BSc, MSc; American defence industry executive; *Chairman, Northrop Grumman Corporation;* b. 1961; m. Natalie Bush; three c.; ed Massachusetts Inst. of Tech., Univ. of California, Los Angeles; worked at Aerospace Corpn and Comsat Labs; joined TRW as systems engineer 1987, served in several man. positions including Vice-Pres. TRW Ventures, Vice-Pres. and Gen. Man. Telecommunications Programs Div., Pres. and CEO Aeronautical Systems UK; Corp. Vice-Pres. and Pres. of Space Tech., Northrop Grumman Corpn 2002–05, Vice-Pres. and Chief Financial Officer (CFO) 2005–06, Pres. 2006–18, also CFO 2006, COO 2007–10, mem. Bd of Dirs 2009–, CEO 2010–18, Chair. 2011–. *Address:* Northrop Grumman Corpn, 2980 Fairview Park Drive, Falls Church, VA 22042, USA (office). *Telephone:* (703) 280-2900 (office). *Website:* www.northropgrumman.com (office).

BUSHATI, Ditmir, LLM; Albanian lawyer and politician; b. 24 March 1977, Shkodër; m. Aida Bushati; one s. one d.; ed Faculty of Law, Univ. of Tirana, Univ. of Leiden, The Netherlands; fmr Researcher on European Affairs, European Centre for Public Law, Univ. of Athens, Greece; trained in int. affairs at several univs and research centres, including Harvard Univ., Acad. of Int. Law, Dallas, USA, Åbo Univ. Acad., Finland; Founding Dir European Movt in Albania; then Dir of Legal Approximation, Ministry of European Integration, part of team negotiating Stabilization and Assen Agreement with EU; worked as Advisor on European Affairs to Deputy Prime Minister, as Legal Advisor to Constitutional Court, Office of the Pres. of Albania and Int. Criminal Tribunal for the fmr Yugoslavia; Analyst for Freedom House for the Nations in Transition Report 2007–08; fmr Nat. Reporter for European Soc. of Int. Law; Nat. Co-ordinator, Open Society Foundation's project monitoring Albania's progress in European integration process 2006–08; worked as consultant for various projects of EU, World Bank, USAID, Deutsche Gesellschaft für Internationale Zusammen-arbeit, OSI, Friedrich Ebert Stiftung, Int. Org. for Migration, Netherlands Devt Org. (SNV); has lectured on European Law and EU enlargement process at different insts and univs in Albania and Kosovo; mem. Parl. (Partia Socialiste e Shqipërisë—Albanian Socialist Party) for Tirana Dist 2009–, Chair. Parl. Cttee for European Integration 2011–13, mem. Jt EU-Albania Parl. Cttee 2009–13; mem. Steering Cttee, PSSh 2011–; Minister of Foreign Affairs 2013–18; various fellowships and research grants, including TEMPUS, NUFFIC, Victor Folsom, Kokkalis, TMC Asser Inst., Gold Medal, Faculty of Law, Univ. of Tirana. *Publications include:* numerous scientific papers and articles in areas related to EU enlargement process, public int. law and European law. *Address:* c/o Ministry of Foreign Affairs, Bulevardi Gjergj Fishta 6, Tirana, Albania (office).

BUSQUIN, Philippe; Belgian politician; b. 6 Jan. 1941; m.; ed Université Libre de Bruxelles; fmr Prof. of Biology and Physics; Deputy for Hainaut 1977–78, for Charleroi 1978–; Minister of Nat. Educ. 1980–81, of the Interior and Nat. Educ. Feb.–Dec. 1981, for the Budget and Energy (French region) 1982–85, of the Economy and Employment (French region) Feb.–May 1988, of Social Affairs 1988–92; Chair. Parti Socialiste (PS) 1992–99; Vice-Pres. Socialist Int. 1992–, PES 1995–; EU Commr responsible for Science, Research and Devt and the Jt Research Centre 1999–2004, mem. European Parliament (MEP) 2004–09; Commdr of the Order of Leopold 1987, Civic Medal, First Class 1988, MEP Grand Cross of the Order of Leopold II 1995. *Address:* Place du Petit Moulin 22, 7181 Feluy, Belgium. *Telephone:* (67) 87-75-46. *Fax:* (67) 87-93-20.

BUSSEL, James Bruce, BS, MD; American paediatrician, haematologist, oncologist and academic; *Professor Emeritus of Pediatrics, Weill Cornell Medical College;* b. 199, New York; ed Yale Univ., Coll. of Physicians and Surgeons, Columbia Univ.; completed residency in paediatrics at Cincinnati Children's Hosp., Ohio; returned to New York City to undertake jt fellowship in Pediatric Hematology/Oncology at Memorial Sloan-Kettering Cancer Center and New York-Presbyterian Hosp., Chief Fellow 1980–81; Assoc. Prof. of Pediatrics, Weill Cornell Medical Coll. 1991–2000, Prof. of Pediatrics in Obstetrics and Gynecology 2000–17, Prof. of Pediatrics in Medicine 2004–17, Prof. Emer. of Pediatrics 2017–; Attending Pediatrician, New York-Presbyterian Hosp.; Ratnoff Prof. of Hematology, Case Western Reserve Univ. 2008; Alpha Award, American Blood Resources Assen for Contribs in Immunohematology 1998, selected as one of 15 reps of American Soc. of Hematology for SPARKII 2003, King Faisal Int. Prize for Medicine (co-recipient) 2012. *Publications:* more than 90 papers in professional journals. *Address:* Weill Cornell Medical College, 1300 York Avenue, New York, NY 10065, USA (office). *Telephone:* (212) 746-3474 (office). *Fax:* (212) 746-5981 (office). *E-mail:* jbussel@med.cornell.edu (office). *Website:* weill.cornell.edu (office).

BUSSELL, Dame Darcey Andrea, DBE, CBE, OBE; British ballet dancer (retd); b. 27 April 1969, London; d. of Philip M. Bussell and Andrea Williams; m. Angus Forbes 1997; two d.; ed Arts Educational School and Royal Ballet School; joined Sadler's Wells Royal Ballet (later Birmingham Royal Ballet) 1987; debut with leading role in The Prince of The Pagodas (Kenneth MacMillan) 1988; soloist, Royal Ballet 1988, first soloist 1989, prin. ballerina 1989–2006, guest artist 2006–07; appearances with Royal Ballet include leading roles in The Spirit of Fugue (created for her by David Bintley), first Royal Ballet performances of Balanchine's Rubies and Stravinsky Violin Concerto and leading roles in Agon, Symphony in C, Tchaikovsky pas de deux, Apollo (Terpsichore), Prodigal Son (Siren), Duo Concertante, Ballet Imperial and Serenade, Kenneth Macmillan's The Prince of the Pagodas (role of Princess Rose created for her), Winter Dreams (role of Masha created for her), Manon (title role), Song of the Earth, Elite

Syncopations, Raymonda, Romeo and Juliet, Requiem, Mayerling and Anastasia, Frederick Ashton's Cinderella (title role), Monotones II, Les Illuminations (Sacred Love), Birthday Offering, Les Rendezvous, William Forsyth's In the middle, somewhat elevated and Herman Scherman (pas de deux), Glen Tetley's La Ronde (Prostitute), Ninette de Valois' Checkmate (Black Queen), Ashley Page's Bloodlines (creator of leading role) and ...now languorous, now wild..., Twyla Tharp's Push Comes to Shove (co. premiere), Jerome Robbins' The Concert (Ballerina), Antony Tudor's Lilac Garden (Caroline), Roland Petit's Le Jeune Homme et La Mort, Balanchine's The Four Temperaments and Themes and Variations, Alistair Marriot's Kiss; classical repertory includes leading roles in Swan Lake (Odette/Odile), The Sleeping Beauty (Princess Aurora), The Nutcracker (Sugar Plum Fairy), La Bayadère (Nikiya and Gamzatti), Cinderella (title role), Giselle (title role), Raymonda Act III (title role); numerous appearances on TV and abroad as guest with other ballet cos in Paris, St Petersburg, New York, Australian Ballet, La Scala; in Viva La Diva touring production (with Katherine Jenkins) 2007–08; Pres. Royal Acad. of Dance 2010–; Patron Sydney Dance Co. 2008– (fmr mem. Bd of Dirs); Hon. Fellow, Arts Univ., Bournemouth; Hon. DLit (Oxford) 2009, Dr hc (Royal Conservatoire, Glasgow Scotland) 2017; Prix de Lausanne 1989, Dance and Dancers Magazine Dancer of the Year 1990, Variety Club of GB Sir James Carreras Award 1991, Evening Standard Ballet Award 1991, Jt Winner Cosmopolitan Achievement in the Performing Arts Award 1991, Olivier Award 1992, Carl Alan Award, Gold Medal, John F. Kennedy Center for the Performing Arts. *Television includes:* Judge, Strictly Come Dancing (UK) 2012–18, Dancing to Happiness 2018, Darcey Bussell: Looking for Audrey, Darcey Bussell: Looking for Margot, Darcey Bussell: Looking for Fred. *Publications include:* Life in Dance (with Judith Mackrell) 1998, Favourite Ballet Stories, The Young Dancer, Pilates for Life 2005, Darcey Bussell's Dance Body Workout 2007, Magic Ballerina children's book series 2008–, Life in Pictures 2012, Evolved 2018. *Leisure interests:* sketching/painting, arts. *Address:* c/o Royal Opera House, Bow Street, London, WC2E 9DD, England.

BUSSEREAU, Dominique; French politician; b. 13 July 1952, Tours (Indre-et-Loire); ed Institut d'études politiques, Paris; Conseiller Général, Charente-Maritime 1985–, Pres. Conseil Gen. 2008–; Deputy (4ème circonscription) for Charente-Maritime, Assemblée nationale 1986–88, 1993–2002, 2007–, mem. Comm. des Lois, comité directeur du fonds d'investissement pour le développement économique et social des territoires d'outre-mer (fidestom); Conseiller régional de Poitou-Charentes 1992–93, March–April 2004; Mayor of Saint-Georges-de-Didonne, Charente-Maritime 1989–2002, 1er adjoint au Maire 2002–08, Conseiller municipal 2008–; Sec. of State, Transport and Sea 2002–04, for the Budget and Budgetary Reform, Ministry of the Economy, Finances and Industry March–Nov. 2004; Minister of Agric., Food, Fishing and the Countryside 2004–05, of Agric. and Fishing 2005–07, Sec. of State for Ecology, Energy, Sustainable Devt and Spatial Planning, responsible for Transport 2007–10; mem. Union pour un Mouvement Populaire (UMP); Pres. Asscn Avenir Transports; Commdr, Ordre du Mérite agricole, Ordre du Mérite maritime, Ordre du Mérite Agricole (Senegal), Grand Cordon, Order of the Rising Sun (Japan) 2007. *Address:* Conseil général de Charente-Maritime, 88 boulevard de la République, 17000 La Rochelle Cedex 9 (office); Assemblée nationale, 126 rue de l'Université, 75355 Paris 07 SP, France. *Telephone:* 5-46-31-70-00. *Fax:* 5-46-31-76-00. *E-mail:* dominique.bussereau@cg17.fr. *Website:* www2.assemblee-nationale.fr/deputes/fiche/OMC_PA696.

BUSTAMANTE, Jean-Marc; French artist, sculptor and photographer; b. 1952, Toulouse; conceptual and installation artist, has incorporated ornamental design and architectural space in his works, has also worked with film; with Bernard Bazile operated under jt name BazileBustamante 1983–87; Prof., Rijksakademie, Amsterdam 1990–95, École nationale supérieure des Beaux-Arts de Paris 1996; lives and works in Paris. *Address:* 43 rue de la Bruyère, 75009 Paris, France (office).

BUSTAMANTE PONCE, Fernando, MPA, PhD; Ecuadorean sociologist, academic and politician; b. (Fernando Xavier Bustamante), 25 Dec. 1950, New York; s. of Teodoro Bustamante and Augusta Ponce; m. Maria Francisca Bustamante; one s. one d.; ed Catholic Univ. of Chile, Harvard Univ. and Massachusetts Inst. of Tech., USA; Asst Prof., Human Sciences Dept, Federico Santa María Univ. Valparaíso, Chile 1973; Teaching Asst, Sociology Dept, Catholic Univ., Santiago, Chile 1973–74, Asst Prof., Econs and Man., and at Social Sciences School 1975–77; Teaching Asst, Arts and Sciences Faculty, Harvard Univ. 1984–85, Political Sciences Dept, MIT 1984–85; Prof., Sociology Dept, Christian Humanism Acad. Univ. 1991–92; Prof., Sociology Dept, ARCIS Univ., Santiago 1992–93; Co-ordinator, Master's Program in Political Science, Latin American Faculty of Social Sciences (FLACSO), Quito 1993–95, Assoc. Prof., Int. Relations Master's Program 2001, 2002, Visiting Prof. 2012; Prof., Antonio J. Quevedo Diplomatic Acad., Ministry of Foreign Affairs 1994; Full Prof., Liberal Arts Coll., San Francisco de Quito Univ. 1996, Co-ordinator, Sociology Program and Asst Dean, Liberal Arts Coll. 1997–2000; Assoc. Prof., Nat. War Inst., Ministry of Defence 2000; Theory of Int. Relations Prof., Ministry of Foreign Affairs (Foreign Service Acad.) 2005; Minister of Internal and External Security Policy Co-ordination 2007–08, of Domestic Security 2008–09; mem. Nat. Ass. (Parl.) 2009–, Chair. Foreign Affairs and Security Cttee 2009–; Assoc. Vice-Pres. Second Standing Cttee of Inter-Parliamentary Union 2011–15, First Vice-Pres. Latin American and Caribbean Group (GRULAC) 2014–16; Chair. Drafting Cttee, 23th Ass. of the Asia Pacific Forum, Quito Jan. 2015; columnist, diario Hoy. *Address:* Avenida González Suárez N32-225, dpto. 6N, Quito, Ecuador (office). *Telephone:* (9) 8762-8754 (office); (2) 255-3108 (office). *E-mail:* febusta@pi.pro.ec (office). *Website:* www.asambleanacional.gob.ec/es/blogs/fernandobustamante (office).

BUSTANI, José Mauricio, LLB; Brazilian diplomatist and government official; b. 5 June 1945, Porto Velho, Rondônia; m. Janine-Monique Bustani; two s. one d.; ed Pontifício Universidade Católica (Law School), Rio de Janeiro, Rio Branco Inst.; joined Ministry of Foreign Relations 1967, Asst to Assoc. Sec.-Gen. for Int. Orgs 1967–70, 1975–77; posted to Brazilian Embassy in Moscow 1970–73, Vienna 1973–75, Brazilian Mission to the UN 1977–84, Embassy in Montevideo 1984–86, Consulate-Gen. Montreal 1987–92; Head Dept for Tech., Financial and Devt Policy, Ministry of Foreign Relations 1992–93; Dir-Gen. Dept for Int. Orgs 1993–97; Dir-Gen. UN OPCW, The Hague 1997–2002; Amb. to UK 2003–08, to France 2008–15; del. to numerous int. confs., including UNIDO, Vienna 1973–75, UN Conf. on the Law of the Sea (13 sessions 1974–93), UN Gen. Ass. 1977–83, UN Special Sessions on Disarmament 1978–82, UN Emergency Sessions on Afghanistan 1980, Namibia 1981. *Address:* Ministry of Foreign Affairs, Palácio do Itamaraty, Esplanada dos Ministérios, Bloco H, 70170-900 Brasília, DF, Brazil (office). *Telephone:* (61) 2030-6161 (office). *E-mail:* imprensa@itamaraty.gov.br (office). *Website:* www.itamaraty.gov.br (office).

BUSUJIMA, Kunio; Japanese business executive; *Founder, Sankyo Co. Ltd;* b. 1925; m.; four c.; began career with Heiwa Corpn (gaming co.); f. Sankyo Co. Ltd (pachinko slot machine co.) 1966, Chair. 1966–2008, currently Hon. Chair., Dir and Sr Adviser. *Address:* Sankyo Co. Ltd, 3-29-14 Shibuya, Shibuya-ku, Tokyo 150 8327, Japan (office). *Telephone:* (3) 5778-7773 (office). *Fax:* (3) 5778-6731 (office). *Website:* www.sankyo-fever.co.jp (office).

BUTAGIRA, Francis K., LLB, LLM; Ugandan diplomatist; b. 22 Nov. 1942, Bugamba; m.; seven c.; ed Dar es Salaam Univ. Coll., Harvard Univ., USA, School of Oriental and African Studies, London, UK; State Attorney, Ministry of Justice 1967; Lecturer in Law, Nsamizi Law School 1968; Head of Law Dept, Law Devt Center 1969–70; Chief Magistrate of Buganda Road Law Courts 1973, of Mbarara 1974; High Court Judge 1974–79; mem. Nat. Consultative Council 1979–80; mem. Parl. 1980–85, also served as Pres. Jt Ass. of the European Econ. Community and the African, Caribbean and Pacific Group of States 1981–83; Chair. Legal and Security Affairs Cttee Nat. Resistance Council (Parl.) 1989–96; Amb. to Ethiopia and Perm. Rep. to Org. of African Unity, Addis Ababa 1998; led team of Ugandan negotiators in talks leading to establishment of E African Community 1999; fmr High Commr in Kenya and Perm. Rep. to UNEP and UN–HABITAT, Nairobi; served as mediator in Sudanese peace talks sponsored by Intergovernmental Authority on Devt 2000–03; Amb. and Perm. Rep. to UN, New York 2003–09, Chair. UN Gen. Ass. Third Cttee (Social, Humanitarian and Cultural) 2005–09; Amb. to Germany 2009–13; Sr Partner, Butagira & Co. (law firm) 1989–; Uganda Investment Authority Golden Award for Attraction of Investment 2002. *Address:* c/o Embassy of Uganda, Axel-Springer-Str. 54A, 10117 Berlin, Germany.

BUTBA, Beslan, CandSci, DrSci; Georgian (Abkhaz) business executive and politician; b. 7 Feb. 1960, Chlou village, Ochamchira Oblast, Abkhazian ASSR; ed Inst. for Eng and Construction, Moscow, Russian Interdisciplinary Centre for Ergonomic Research and Devt, Tula; began working for Repair and Construction Dept No. 1 of Moscow 1983–86, Head of Dept 1986–89; f. a co-operative in Moscow 1989; returned to Abkhazia and also began to do business 1990; Head of Business Club Sukhum 2005; f. Abaza TV (first pvt. channel) 2007; Owner of Ekho Abkhazii newspaper; mem. People's Ass. of Abkhazia (Apsny zelar reizara) 2002–07, for Constituency No. 26, Chlou 2012–14, Chair. Cttee for Interparliamentary Relations; Founder and Chair. Apsny aekonomika apartia (Party of the Econ. Devt of Abkhazia) 2007–; unsuccessful cand. in presidential election Dec. 2009; apptd Special Rep. of the Pres. for co-operation with the countries of South and Central America 2013; Acting Vice-Premier June–Sept. 2014, Prime Minister of the 'Republic of Abkhazia' 2014–15. *Address:* c/o Office of the Cabinet of Ministers of the 'Republic of Abkhazia', 384900 Sukhumi, nab. Makhajirov 32, Georgia.

BUTCHER, Hon. David John, BA (Hons); New Zealand/British economist, consultant and fmr politician; *Consultant, David Butcher and Associates;* b. 19 Sept. 1948, England; s. of Frank George Butcher and Dorothy May Butcher; m. Mary Georgina Hall 1980; two d.; ed Victoria Univ. of Wellington; Research Economist, Dept of Labour 1972–74; Field Officer, Clerical Workers Union and New Zealand Labourers Union, Hawke's Bay, Wellington 1976–78; MP for Hastings 1978–90; Parl. Under-Sec. to Ministers of Agric., Lands and Forests 1984–87; Minister of Energy, of Regional Devt 1987–90, Assoc. Minister of Finance 1987–88, of Regional Devt 1987–90, of Commerce 1988–90; Consultant, David Butcher and Assocs (econ. consultancy) 1992–; Sr Man., Ernst & Young, Wellington 1995–96; mem. Labour Party; Fellow, New Zealand Inst. of Man.; mem., Inst. of Man. Consultants New Zealand, New Zealand Asscn of Former MPs; Commemorative Medal 1990. *Achievements include:* helped dismantle agricultural subsidies, new taxation regime for livestock, dismantled unnecessary protection for manufacturing, helped put in place deregulation of telecommunications, electricity; helped establish Information Communications Networking Co. Mongolia, first ever nationwide NETCO; employed by int. agencies to offer advice in more than 30 different countries. *Publications include:* Agriculture in a More Market Economy 1985, Lessons for the Future from the Free Market Economy, Open the Way to Competition 2007, Parliamentary Committees in Westminster Systems, UNDP Dhaka Bangladesh 2006, Electricity Sectors in CAREC Member Countries (co-author) 2005; contrib. to Privatization Yearbook 1993, 1994, 1995, 1999; numerous speeches and articles. *Leisure interests:* swimming, reading, classical music, family history, photography. *Address:* PO Box 5279, Wellington 6145, New Zealand (home). *Telephone:* (4) 476-9001 (office); 21-438630 (mobile) (office). *E-mail:* david@dba.org.nz (office). *Website:* www.dba.org.nz (office).

BUTCHER, Eugene (Gene) Corning, BS, MD; American immunologist and academic; *Klaus Bensch Professor in Pathology, Stanford University;* b. 6 Jan. 1950, St Louis, Mo.; ed Massachusetts Inst. of Tech., Washington Univ., St Louis; Residency in Pathology (Anatomic), Dept of Pathology, Stanford Univ., Calif. 1976–77, 1979–80, NIH Postdoctoral Fellowship, Dept of Pathology 1977–79, Sr Fellow, American Cancer Soc., Calif. Div., Dept of Pathology 1980–82, Asst Prof., Dept of Pathology, Stanford Univ. Medical Center 1982–89, Assoc. Prof. 1989–99, Prof. 1999–, currently Klaus Bensch Prof. in Pathology; Staff Physician, Veterans Admin Palo Alto Health Care System 1982–, Dir Serology and Immunology Section, Veterans Admin Palo Alto Health Care System 1982–; Co-Dir Immunohistologic Diagnosis Service, Surgical Pathology, Stanford 1983–93; Univ. Lecturer, Univ. of Texas Southwest Medical Center 1996; Burroughs-Wellcome Visiting Prof., Univ. of New Mexico 1996; mem. American Asscn of Pathologists, American Asscn of Immunologists, Asscn of American Physicians 2003, Fed. of American Socs for Experimental Biology, American Soc. for Investigative Pathology, Mars Soc., Planetary Soc.; Eloranta Award 1971, PLU (Hon. Chem. Soc.) 1972, Richard S. Brookings Award for Excellence in Medical Student Research 1976, Scholar, Leukemia Soc. of America 1982–87, Established Investigator, American Heart Asscn 1987–92, Warner-Lambert/Parke-Davis Award for meritorious research in experimental pathology, American Soc. for Investigative Pathology 1989, Marjorie J. Williams Lecturer, Asscn of Veterans Admin Pathologists 1989, AAI-Huang Foundation Meritorious Career Award, American

Asscn of Immunologists 1999, William S. Middleton Award (Highest Research Award from Dept of Veterans Affairs) 2001, Stanford Univ. Outstanding Inventor Award 2004, Crafoord Prize in Polyarthritis, Royal Swedish Acad. of Sciences (co-recipient) 2004, invited to membership of Scientific Advisory Bd, 'SystemsX' (Swiss nat. initiative in systems biology) 2005. *Publications:* more than 33 reviews and 280 scientific papers in professional journals on the trafficking of white blood cells, including their interactions with the endothelial lining of blood vessels at sites of leukocyte extravasation, and their chemotactic responses in tissues; nine US patents. *Address:* Department of Pathology, Stanford University School of Medicine, Lane Building, Mailcode 5324, Stanford, CA 94305-5324, USA (office). *Telephone:* (650) 852-3369 (office). *Fax:* (650) 858-3986 (office). *E-mail:* ebutcher@stanford.edu (office); marthas1@stanford.edu (office). *Website:* med.stanford.edu/profiles/eugene-butcher (office); butcherlab.stanford.edu (office).

BUTCHER, John Charles, ONZM, PhD, DSc, FRSNZ; New Zealand mathematician and academic; *Honorary Research Professor and Professor Emeritus of Mathematics, University of Auckland;* b. 31 March 1933, Auckland; s. of Charles Hastings Butcher and Alice Lilac Cornwall Butcher (née Richards); m. 1st Patricia Frances Nicolas 1957 (divorced 1989); two s. one d.; m. 2nd Jennifer Ann Wright (née Bowman) 1990; ed Dargaville, Taumarunui and Hamilton High Schools, Univ. of New Zealand (Auckland Univ. Coll.), Univ. of Sydney, Australia; Lecturer in Applied Math., Univ. of Sydney 1959–61; Sr Lecturer in Math., Univ. of Canterbury 1961–64; computer scientist, Stanford Linear Accelerator Center, USA 1965–66; Prof. of Math., Univ. of Auckland 1966–79 (Head of Math. Dept 1967–73), of Computer Science 1980–88 (f. Dept of Computer Science 1980), Head, Applied and Computational Math. Unit 1989–94, 1997–98, Prof. of Math. 1989–98, Hon. Research Prof. and Prof. Emer. 1999–; various visiting lectureships and professorships in USA, UK, Sweden, Austria, Germany, USSR, Netherlands 1965–; mem. Editorial Bd Acta Numerica, Applied Numerical Mathematics, Numerical Algorithms, Journal of Universal Computer Science; Life mem., Fellow and Past Pres. NZ Math. Soc.; mem. American Math. Soc. 1966, Soc. for Industrial and Applied Math. (USA), Australian and NZ Industrial and Applied Math.; Fellow, Inst. of Math. and its Applications (UK) 1972; Officer, New Zealand Order of Merit 2013; Award for Math. Research, NZ Math. Soc. 1991, Hector Medal, Royal Soc. of NZ 1996, Jones Medal, Royal Soc. of NZ 2010, Van Wijngaarden Award 2011. *Publications:* The Numerical Analysis of Ordinary Differential Equations: Runge-Kutta and General Linear Methods 1987 (second edn as Numerical Methods for Ordinary Differential Equations 2008); approx. 160 papers on numerical analysis and other topics. *Leisure interests:* classical music, bridge. *Address:* Room 424B, Department of Mathematics, University of Auckland, Private Bag 92019, Auckland (office); 16 Wallace Street, Herne Bay, Auckland, New Zealand (home). *Telephone:* (9) 3737599 (ext. 88747) (office); (9) 3762743 (home). *Fax:* (9) 3737457 (office). *E-mail:* butcher@math.auckland.ac.nz (office). *Website:* www.math.auckland.ac.nz/~butcher (office); jcbutcher.com.

BUTERIN, Vitalik; Russian computer programmer; b. 31 Jan. 1994; ed Abelard School, Toronto and Univ. of Waterloo, Canada; moved to Canada 2000; Developer Intern, NextThought, LLC 2012; Co-founder and lead writer, Bitcoin Magazine, Toronto 2011–; Founder Ethereum project (generalized blockchain platform) 2013, now Chief Scientist; Dr hc (Univ. of Basel) 2018; Thiel Fellowship 2014, World Tech. Award, World Tech. Network (Information Tech.– Software) 2014. *Publications include:* articles about Bitcoin-related topics for various publs, including Bitcoin Weekly. *Website:* ethereum.org (office); bitcoinmagazine.net (office); about.me/vitalik_buterin (office); ccrg.org/team/vitalik (office).

BUTHELEZI, Chief Mangosuthu Gatsha, BA; South African politician; b. 27 Aug. 1928, Mahlabatini; s. of Chief Mathole Buthelezi and Princess Magogo; m. Irene Audrey Thandekile Mzila 1952; three s. four d.; ed Adams Coll., Fort-Hare Univ.; installed as Chief of Buthelezi Tribe 1953; assisted King Cyprian in admin. of Zulu people 1953–68; elected leader of Zululand territorial authority 1970; Chief Minister of KwaZulu 1976–94; Minister of Home Affairs (in Gov. of Nat. Unity) 1994–2004; mem. Nat. Ass. 2009–; Pres. Inkatha Freedom Party; Kt Commdr Star of Africa (Liberia), Commdr Ordre Nat. du Mérite 1981; Hon. LLD (Zululand and Cape Town); George Meany Human Rights Award 1982. *Publications include:* South Africa: My Vision of the Future 1990. *Address:* Inkatha Freedom Party, Albany House North, 4th Floor, Albany Grove, PO Box 443, Durban 4000, South Africa. *Telephone:* (73) 9291418 (office); (21) 4033065 (office). *E-mail:* mbuthelezi@parliament.gov.za (office); lyndithw@ifp.co.za (office). *Website:* www.fp.org.za.

BUTIME, Col Tom; Ugandan government official; joined Nat. Resistance Army guerrillas 1981; mil. training in Libya 1982; Acting Minister of Foreign Affairs 2004–05, also served as Minister of State for Int. Affairs and Second Deputy Prime Minister; Minister of State for Karamoja Affairs 2006 (resgnd). *Address:* c/o Ministry of Foreign Affairs, 2a/b Apollo Kaggwa Road, PO Box 7048, Kampala, Uganda. *E-mail:* info@mofa.go.ug.

BUTKEVIČIUS, Algirdas, MS, DScS; Lithuanian politician and economist; b. 19 Nov. 1958, Paežeriai, Radviliškis dist; m. Janina Butkevičienė; one d.; ed Radviliškis, Šeduva dist high schools, Vilnius Eng Construction Inst., Lithuanian Acad. of Man., Kaunas Technological Univ., German Man. Acad., Würzburg, studies in Denmark and USA; construction site Man., Asscn Žemūktechnika, Vilkaviškis dist 1982–85, Architect, mem. Exec. Cttee 1985–90; Head of Dept of Econs and Finance, Deputy Gov. Vilkaviškis Region 1991–95; Marketing Dir, SC Vilkauta 1995–96; mem. Vilkaviškis Dist Council 1990–97, 2000–02, mem. Vilkaviškis Municipal Bd 1995–97; mem. Lietuvos Socialdemokratų Partiya (LSDP—Lithuanian Social Democratic Party) 1992–, Chair. Vilkaviškis Br. 1995–97, Deputy Chair. LSDP 1999–2005, Chair. 2009–17, Chair. LSDP Parl. Group 2009; mem. Seimas (Parl.) 1996–, Chair. Treasury Sub-cttee 1996–2001, Budget and Finance Cttee 2001–04, Family Budget and Finance Cttee and Cttee on European Affairs 2005–06; Minister of Finance 2004–05 (resgnd), of Transport and Communications 2006–08; Prime Minister 2012–16; unsuccessful LSDP cand. in presidential election 2009; Hon. Citizen, Vilkaviškis dist and Radviliškis dist 2008; Cross of Commdr, Order for Merits to Lithuania 2004. *Leisure interest:* sports, literature. *Address:* c/o Lietuvos Socialdemokratų Partija (Lithuanian Social Democratic Party), Barboros Radvilaites g. 1, Vilnius 01124 (office); Žirnūnus 38A -31, Vilnius, Lithuania (home). *Telephone:* (5) 261-3907 (office). *Fax:* (5) 261-5420 (office). *E-mail:* info@lsdp.lt (office). *Website:* www.lsdp.lt (office).

BUTLER, Basil Richard Ryland, CBE, MA, FREng; British business executive; b. 1 March 1930, Hexham, Northumberland, England; s. of Hugh Montagu Butler and Annie Isabel Butler (née Wiltshire); m. Lilian Joyce Haswell 1954; one s. two d.; ed Denstone Coll., Staffs., St John's Coll., Cambridge; 2nd Lt, 5th Royal Inniskilling Dragoon Guards; Operations Man. Sinclair and BP Colombian Inc. 1968–70, Operations Man. BP Alaska Inc. 1970–72, Gen. Man. BP Petroleum Devt Ltd 1978–81, Chief Exec. BP Exploration Co. Ltd 1981–86, Dir 1986–89, Man. Dir BP Co. PLC 1986–91; Dir BP Solar International 1991–98, Chair. 1991–95; Chair. European Council of Applied Sciences and Eng 1993–98; Dir Brown and Root Ltd 1991–97, Chair. 1993–97; Dir Murphy Oil Corpn 1991–2002; Gen. Man. Kuwait Oil Co. Ltd 1972–75, Sullom Voe Devt 1975–78; Chair. KS Biomedix Holdings PLC 1995–2001; Pres. Inst. of Petroleum 1990–92; mem. Council Royal Acad. of Eng 1993–2002, Hon. Sec. Int. Activities 1995–98, Sr Vice-Pres. 1996–99; Cdre, Royal Western Yacht Club of England 2004–08; Freeman, City of London. *Leisure interests:* sailing, music. *Address:* c/o Royal Academy of Engineering, London, SW1P 5DG, England.

BUTLER, Sir David Edgeworth, Kt, CBE, MA, DPhil, FBA; British psephologist and academic; b. 17 Oct. 1924; s. of Prof. Harold E. Butler and Margaret Pollard; m. Marilyn S. Evans 1962 (died 2014); three s.; ed St Paul's School, Princeton Univ., USA and New Coll., Oxford; J.E. Procter Visiting Fellow, Princeton Univ. 1947–48; student, Nuffield Coll. Oxford 1949–51, Research Fellow 1951–54, Fellow 1954–92, Emer. Fellow 1992–, Dean and Sr Tutor 1956–64; Personal Asst to British Amb. in Washington, DC 1955–56; Co-Ed. Electoral Studies 1982–92; Hon. DUniv (Paris) 1978, (Essex) 1993; Hon. DSc (Queen's Univ. Belfast) 1985, (Teesside) 1998; Hon. LLD (Plymouth) 1997. *Publications include:* The Study of Political Behaviour 1958, Elections Abroad (ed.) 1959, British Political Facts 1900–1960 (with J. Freeman), Political Change in Britain 1969, The Canberra Model 1973, Coalitions in British Politics (ed.) 1978, Policy and Politics (co-ed. with A. H. Halsey), Referendums (with A. Ranney) 1978, British Political Facts 1900–79 (with A. Sloman), European Elections and British Politics (with D. Marquand) 1981, Democracy at the Polls (with A. Ranney) 1981, Democracy and Elections (with V. Bogdanor) 1983, Governing without a Majority 1983, A Compendium of Indian Elections 1984, Party Strategies in Britain (with P. Jowett) 1985, Sovereigns and Surrogates (with A. Low) 1991, Failure in British Government (with others) 1994, India Decides (with P. Roy) 1995, Referendums Around the World (co-ed.) 1995, British Politics and European Elections (with Martin Westlake) 2000, British Political Facts 1900–2000 (with G. Butler) 2000, The British General Election of 2001 2001; also numerous books on the British electoral system and British elections since 1945. *Address:* Nuffield College, Oxford, OX1 1NF, England. *Telephone:* (1865) 278500.

BUTLER, Sir James (Jim), Kt, KCB, CBE, FCA; British chartered accountant; b. 15 March 1929, Batheaston, Somerset; m. Margaret Butler (née Copland); one s. two d.; ed Marlborough Coll., Clare Coll., Cambridge; Articled clerk, Peat Marwick (chartered accountants) 1952; negotiated Peat Marwick's merger with Klynveld Main Goerdeler to form KPMG 1986–87; Sr Partner, Peat Marwick (UK arm of KPMG) 1987–93; Chair. KPMG Int. 1991–93; Dir Camelot PLC 1994–2002 (Deputy Chair. 1995), Royal Opera House 1994–99, Wadworth and Co. Ltd 1994–, Nicholson, Graham & Jones 1994–2005. *Address:* Littleton House, Crawley, Winchester, Hants., SO21 2QF, England. *Telephone:* (1962) 880206. *Fax:* (1962) 886177. *E-mail:* jbutler603@aol.com.

BUTLER, James Walter, MBE, RA, RWA, FRBS; British sculptor; b. 25 July 1931, London; s. of Walter Arthur Butler and Rosina Kingman; m. Angela Elizabeth Berry 1975; five d.; ed Maidstone Grammar School, Maidstone School of Art, St Martin's School of Art, City & Guilds of London Art School, Royal Coll. of Art; worked as stone carver; taught sculpture and drawing, City & Guilds Art School; professional sculptor working on public and pvt. comms and exhbns; works in various galleries; mem. Soc. of Portrait Sculptors, Royal West of England Acad. *Leisure interest:* astronomy. *Address:* Valley Farm Studios, Radway, Warwickshire, CV35 0UJ, England (office). *Telephone:* (1926) 641938 (office); 7831-847129 (mobile) (office). *Fax:* (1926) 640624 (office). *E-mail:* info@jamesbutler-ra.com (office). *Website:* www.jamesbutler-ra.com (office).

BUTLER, Hon. Richard William, AC, DUniv; Australian diplomatist and academic; *Global Diplomat in Residence and Clinical Professor, Center for Global Affairs, New York University;* b. 13 May 1942; s. of H. H. Butler; m. Barbara Evans 1974; three s. one d.; ed Randwick Boys High School, Univ. of Sydney, Australian Nat. Univ.; Second Sec., Embassy and Perm. Mission to UN, Deputy Perm. Rep. IAEA, Vienna 1966–69; First Sec. Mission to UN, New York 1970–73; Deputy High Commr, Singapore, 1975–76; Prin. Pvt. Sec. to Leader of Opposition 1976–77; Counsellor, Bonn Embassy 1978–81; Minister-Del. to OECD, Paris, Amb. and Perm. Rep. to UN (Disarmament Matters), Geneva 1983–88; Amb. to Thailand 1989–92; Amb. and Perm. Rep. to Supreme Nat. Council of Cambodia 1991–92; Amb. and Perm. Rep. to UN, New York 1992–97; Exec. Chair. UN Special Comm. on Iraqi Disarmament 1997–99; Diplomat-in-Residence, Council on Foreign Relations, New York 1999–2002; Gov. of Tasmania 2003–04 (resgnd); Global Diplomat in Residence and Clinical Prof., Center for Global Affairs, School of Continuing and Professional Studies, New York University 2008–. *Publications:* The Greatest Threat 2000, Saddam Defiant 2000. *Leisure interests:* art, music, rugby. *Address:* Center for Global Affairs, School of Continuing and Professional Studies, New York University, 145 4th Avenue, New York, NY 10003, USA (office). *Website:* www.scps.nyu.edu/areas-of-study/global-affairs (office).

BUTLER, William Elliott, BA, MA, JD, LLM, PhD, LLD, FRSA, FSA; American/British legal scholar and academic; *John Edward Fowler Distinguished Professor of Law, Dickinson Law, Pennsylvania State University;* b. 20 Oct. 1939, Minneapolis, Minn., USA; s. of William E. Butler and Maxine Swan Elmberg; m. 1st Darlene Johnson (died 1989); two s.; m. 2nd Maryann Gashi 1991; ed Hibbing Junior Coll., The American Univ., Harvard Law School, Russian Acad. of Sciences, Johns Hopkins School of Advanced Int. Studies, Univ. of London, UK, Kyiv Univ. of Law, Ukraine, Acad. Int. Ind. Ecological-Politological Univ., Moscow, Russia, Uppsala Univ., Sweden; Research Asst, Washington Center for Foreign Policy Research, Johns Hopkins Univ. 1966–68; Research Assoc. in Law and Assoc., Russian Research Center, Harvard Univ. 1968–70; Reader in Comparative Law, Univ. of London 1970–76, Prof. of Comparative Law 1976–2005, Dean, Faculty of Laws 1988–90, Prof. Emer. 2005–, mem. Council, School of Slavonic and East

European Studies 1973–93, Dean, Faculty of Laws, Univ. Coll. London 1977–79, Vice-Dean 1979–81, Dir Vinogradoff Inst. 1982–2005, Professorial Research Assoc., SOAS, Univ. of London 2006–11; Dean, Faculty of Law and Speranskii Prof. of Int. and Comparative Law, Moscow Higher School of Social and Econ. Sciences 1995–2005; John Edward Fowler Distinguished Prof. of Law, Dickinson Law, Penn State Univ. 2005–, mem. Faculty Council, School of Int. Affairs 2007–, mem. Senate, Penn State Univ. 2008–; Professorial Lecturer in Int. Law, Johns Hopkins School of Advanced Int. Studies 2009; Of Counsel, Cole, Corette & Abrutyn 1989–92, Clifford Chance 1992–94; Partner, White & Case 1994–96, Price Waterhouse Coopers 1997–2001; Sr Partner, Phoenix Law Assocs, Moscow 2002–12; Special Counsel, Comm. on Econ. Reform, USSR Council of Ministers 1989–91; consultant, IBRD; adviser and consultant to govts of Russian Fed., Belarus, Ukraine, Kyrgyzstan, Kazakhstan, Tajikistan, Uzbekistan; Legal Adviser, UN Office on Drugs and Crime (UNODC) 2006–08; Visiting Scholar, Moscow State Univ. 1972, 1980, Mongolian State Univ. 1979, Inst. of State and Law, USSR Acad. of Sciences 1976, 1981, 1983, 1984, 1988, Harvard Law School 1982; Visiting Prof., New York Univ. Law School 1978, Ritsumeikan Univ. 1985, Harvard Law School 1986–87, Washington and Lee Univ. 2005; mem. Russian Court of Int. Commercial Arbitration 1995–, Expert Council on Reform of Corp. Man., Ministry of Econ. Devt and Trade of Russian Fed. 2004–06, Int. Commercial Arbitration Court of Kazakhstan 2012–, Court of Int. Commercial Arbitration of Ukraine 2013–; Academician, Int. Acad. of Comparative Law 1986, Russian Acad. of Natural Sciences 1992, Nat. Acad. of Sciences of Ukraine 1992, Nat. Acad. of Legal Sciences of Ukraine 2012, Int. Acad. of the Book and Art of the Book, Russian Acad. of Legal Sciences; mem. Sr Common Room, St Antony's Coll. Oxford, UK 2004–11; mem. Exec. Council, Russian Asscn of Maritime Law 2008, American Law Inst. 2009–; Chair. Fellowship of American Bibliophilic Socs. 2019–; George F Kennan Fellow, Kennan Inst., Washington DC 2019; Hon. LLD (Kyiv Univ. of Law) 2012; Dr hc (Acad. Int. Ind. Ecological-Politological Univ.) 2016, Hon. DJur (Univ. of Uppsala, Sweden) 2018; G.I. Tunkin Medal 2003, Ivan Fedorov Medal 2004, FISAE (Int. Fed. of Ex-libris Socs) Certificates of Honour, Medal 'For Fidelity of Law', Supreme Court of Ukraine 2012, Jubilee Medal, Kyiv Univ. of Law 2015, Gold Medal, Nat. Acad. of Legal Sciences of Ukraine 2016, Gold Medal, Nat. Acad. of Legal Sciences of Ukraine 2017. *Publications:* more than 5,000 books, articles, reviews and translations, including Soviet Law 1983, The Non-Use of Force in International Law 1989, Perestroika and International Law 1990, The History of International Law in Russia 1647–1917 1990, Foreign Investment Legislation in the Republics of the Former Soviet Union 1993, Russian Law of Treaties 1997, Russian Legal Texts 1998, Russian Law 1999, 2003, 2009, Constitutional Foundations of the CIS Countries 2000, American Bookplates 2000, Russian Company Law 2000, Russian-English Legal Dictionary 2001, Foreign Investment Laws in the CIS 2002, The Law of Treaties in Russia and the CIS 2002, Civil Code of the Russian Federation 2003, 2008, 2009, Russian Company and Commercial Law 2003, Narcotics and HIV in Russia 2005, Russian Intellectual Property Law (fourth edn) 2005, Russian Foreign Relations and Investment Law 2006, Russian Legal Biography (with V. A. Tomsinov) 2007, Civil Code of Uzbekistan 2007, Civil Code of Kazakhstan 2008, Russia and the Law of Nations in Historical Perspective 2009, The Nakaz of Catherine the Great (with V. A. Tomsinov) 2010, Russian Criminal Law and Procedure 2011, Russian Family Law 2014, Russian Inheritance Law, 2015, Russian Law and Legal Institutions 2014, Ukrainian Legal Doctrine (6 Vols) 2015–18. *Leisure interests:* book collecting, bookplate collecting. *Address:* 155 Mt Rock Road, Newville, PA 17241-8916 (home); Dickinson Law, Penn State University, Lewis Katz Hall, 150 South College Street, Carlisle, PA 17013, USA (office). *Telephone:* (717) 776-7359 (home); (717) 240-5227 (office). *Fax:* (717) 240-5126 (office). *E-mail:* webakademik@aol.com (home); web15@psu.edu (office). *Website:* dickinsonlaw.psu.edu/academics/faculty/resident-faculty/william-e-butler (office).

BUTLER, William T., BA, MD; American immunologist, academic, university administrator and petrochemical industry executive; *Chancellor Emeritus, Baylor College of Medicine;* ed Western Reserve Univ., Oberlin Coll.; served as Chief Clinical Assoc., Lab. of Clinical Medicine, Nat. Inst. of Allergy and Infectious Diseases, Washington, DC; joined faculty Baylor Coll. of Medicine, Houston 1966, served in several positions including Prof. of Internal Medicine and Microbiology and Immunology, Assoc. Dean, Dean of Admissions, Exec. Vice Pres. and Dean 1976–79, Pres. and CEO 1979–96, Chancellor 1996–2004, Chancellor Emer. 2004–, Interim Pres. 2008–10; mem. Bd of Dirs Lyondell Chemical Co., Houston 1989–2007, Chair. 1997–2007 (retd); mem. Bd of Dirs Browning-Ferris Industries, C.R. Bard Inc.; mem. Inst. of Medicine. *Publications:* numerous publications in the fields of immunology, infectious disease and medical admin. *Address:* Baylor College of Medicine, One Baylor Plaza, Houston, TX 77030, USA. *Telephone:* (713) 798-4951. *E-mail:* info@bcm.edu. *Website:* www.bcm.edu.

BUTLER OF BROCKWELL, Baron (Life Peer), cr. 1998, of Herne Hill in the London Borough of Lambeth; **Frederick Edward Robin Butler,** KG, GCB, CVO, PC, MA; British public servant; *Non-Executive Member, King's Health Partners;* b. 3 Jan. 1938, Poole, Dorset; s. of Bernard Butler and Nora Butler (née Jones); m. Gillian Lois Galley 1962; one s. two d.; ed Harrow School, University Coll., Oxford; with HM Treasury 1961–69, Pvt. Sec. to the Financial Sec. 1964–65, Sec. Budget Cttee 1965–69; seconded to Cabinet Office as mem. Cen. Policy Review Staff 1971–72; Pvt. Sec. to Prime Minister 1972–74, 1974–75, 1982–85; Head of General Expenditure Policy Group 1977–80; Principal Establishment Officer, HM Treasury 1980–82; Second Perm. Sec., Public Services 1985–87; Sec. to Cabinet and Head of Home Civil Service 1988–98; Master Univ. Coll., Oxford 1998–2008; Chair. Cttee to review intelligence on weapons of mass destruction 2004; mem. (non-exec.) King's Health Partners 2009–; Chair. of Govs Dulwich Coll. 1997–2003; Gov. Harrow School 1975–91 (Chair. of Govs 1988–91); mem. Royal Comm. for Lords' Reform 1999; Hon. Fellow, Univ. Coll. Oxford 1989, Kings Coll. London 2011; Hon. DSc (Cranfield) 1994, Hon. LLD (Exeter) 1998, Hon. DCL (London) 1999. *Leisure interests:* competitive games, opera. *Address:* House of Lords, London, SW1A 0PW, England. *E-mail:* lord.butler@univ.ox.ac.uk.

BUTLER-SLOSS, Baroness (Life Peer), cr. 2006, of Marsh Green in the County of Devon; **(Ann) Elizabeth (Oldfield) Butler-Sloss,** GBE, DBE, PC, FRSM; British judge (retd); b. 10 Aug. 1933, Bucks., England; d. of Sir Cecil Havers and Enid Snelling; m. Joseph William Alexander Butler-Sloss 1958; two s. one d.; ed Wycombe Abbey School; called to Bar, Inner Temple 1955, Bencher 1979; contested Lambeth, Vauxhall as Conservative Cand. 1959; practising barrister 1955–70; Registrar, Prin. Registry of Probate, later Family Div. 1970–79; Judge, High Court of Justice, Family Div. 1979–87; Lord Justice of Appeal 1988–99; Pres. of Family Div., High Court of Justice 1999–2005; Chair. Crown Appointments Comm. 2002; Lord of Appeal 2006–09; fmr Vice-Pres. Medico-Legal Soc.; Chair. Cleveland Child Abuse Inquiry 1987–88; Chair. Advisory Council, St Paul's Cathedral 2000–09; currently Chair. Nat. Comm. on Forced Marriage; Pres. Honiton Agricultural Show 1985–86; Treas. Inner Temple 1998; mem. Judicial Studies Bd 1985–89; Hon. Fellow, St Hilda's Coll., Oxford 1988, Visiting Fellow 2001–; Fellow, Kings Coll., London 1991, mem. Council 1992–98; Chancellor Univ. of the West of England 1993–2011; Trustee, Human Trafficking Foundation; mem. (Crossbench) House of Lords 2006–, Chair. Adoption Legislation Cttee 2012–13, mem. Ecclesiastical Cttee (Jt Cttee) 2010–, Draft Modern Slavery Bill 2014; announced as chair. of large-scale inquiry into cases of child sex abuse in previous decades July 2014, stepped down several days later under pressure to quit from MPs and victims concerned about her family links; Hon. FRCP; Hon. FRCPsych; Hon. FRCPaed; Hon. LLD (Hull) 1989, (Bristol) 1991, (Keele) 1991, (Brunel) 1992, (Exeter) 1992, (Manchester) 1995, (Cambridge) 2000, (Greenwich) 2000, (East Anglia) 2001, (Liverpool) 2001, (Ulster) 2004, (London) 2004; Hon. DLit (Loughborough Univ. of Tech.) 1993; Hon. DUniv (Univ. of Central England) 1994, (Open Univ.), (LSE) 2009. *Publications:* Jt Ed. Phipson on Evidence (tenth edn), Corpe on Road Haulage (second edn), fmr Ed. Supreme Court Practice 1976, 1976. *Address:* House of Lords, Westminster, London, SW1A 0PW, England. *Telephone:* (20) 7219-4044. *Fax:* (20) 7219-5979. *E-mail:* butlerslosse@parliament.uk.

BUTLER-WHEELHOUSE, Keith Oliver, BComm; British business executive; *Non-Executive Chairman, Chamberlin plc;* b. 29 March 1946, Walsall, West Midlands, England; s. of Kenneth Butler-Wheelhouse and May Butler-Wheelhouse; m. Pamela Anne Bosworth Smith 1973; two s.; ed Technicon, Port Elizabeth, Univ. of Witwatersrand and Univ. of Cape Town Grad. School of Business; Ford Motor Co. South Africa 1965–85; Dir of Tech. Operations, Gen. Motors South Africa 1985–86; Chair. and CEO Delta Motor Corpn 1987–92; Pres. and CEO Saab Automobile 1992–96; Chief Exec. Smiths Group (fmrly Smiths Industries) PLC 1996–2007; Chair. (non-exec.), Chamberlin plc 2012–. *Leisure interests:* golf, tennis, shooting, skiing, keeping fit. *Address:* Chamberlin plc, Chuckery Road, Walsall, WS1 2DU, England (office). *Telephone:* (1922) 707100 (office). *Fax:* (1922) 638370 (office). *Website:* www.chamberlin.co.uk (office).

BUTLIN, Martin Richard Fletcher, CBE, MA, DLit, FBA; British museum curator and art historian; b. 7 June 1929, Birmingham; s. of K. R. Butlin and Helen M. Butlin (née Fletcher); m. Frances C. Chodzko 1969; ed Trinity Coll., Cambridge and Courtauld Inst. of Art, Univ. of London; Asst Keeper, Tate Gallery, London 1955–67, Keeper of the Historic British Collection 1967–89; consultant, Christie's, London 1989; Mitchell Prize (jtly) 1978. *Publications:* A Catalogue of the Works of William Blake in the Tate Gallery 1957, 1971, 1990, Samuel Palmer's Sketchbook of 1824, 1962, 2005, Turner Watercolours 1962, Turner (with Sir John Rothenstein) 1964, Tate Gallery Catalogues: The Modern British Paintings, Drawings and Sculpture (with Mary Chamot and Dennis Farr) 1964, The Later Works of J. M. W. Turner 1965, William Blake 1966, The Blake-Varley Sketchbook of 1819 1969, The Paintings of J. M. W. Turner (with E. Joll) 1977, 1984, The Paintings and Drawings of William Blake 1981, Aspects of British Painting 1550–1800 1988, Turner at Petworth (with Mollie Luther and Ian Warrell) 1989, The Oxford Companion to J. M. W. Turner (co-ed. with Evelyn Joll and Luke Herrmann) 2001, William Blake's Watercolour Inventions in Illustration of The Grave by Robert Blair 2010; catalogues, articles, reviews etc. *Leisure interests:* music, travel. *Address:* 74C Eccleston Square, London, SW1V 1PJ, England (home). *Telephone:* (20) 7828-8245 (home).

BUTOLA, Ranbir Singh, BA, MBA; Indian oil industry executive; b. 5 May 1954; ed Faculty of Man. Studies, Univ. of Delhi; worked in a nationalized bank and also in Govt of India dept –1991; joined Oil And Natural Gas Corpn Ltd (ONGC) as Deputy Gen. Man. Finance and Accounts) 1991, Dir (Finance), ONGC Videsh Ltd (subsidiary of ONGC) 2002–04, Man. Dir and CEO ONGC Videsh Ltd 2004–11; Man. Dir Indian Oil Corpn Ltd (IndianOil) 2004–11, mem. Bd of Dirs and Chair. 2011–14; apptd mem. Bd of Dirs and Chair. Imperial Energy Corpn plc 2009; Chair. Chennai Petroleum Corpn Ltd 2011–14; Chair. Governing Council, Petroleum Fed. of India; Certified Assoc., Indian Inst. of Bankers. *Leisure interests:* travelling, reading. *Address:* c/o Indian Oil Corporation Ltd, Corporate Office, 3079/3, J.B. Tito Marg, Sadiq Nagar, New Delhi 110 049, India. *E-mail:* info@iocl.com.

BÚTORA, Martin, PhD; Slovak diplomatist, sociologist, academic and author; *Honorary President, Institute for Public Affairs;* b. 7 Oct. 1944; m.; four c.; Ed.-in-Chief, Bratislava student paper 1966–67, Deputy Ed.-in-Chief 1969; Ed. Kulturny Zivot 1968; Research Asst, Research Inst. of Labour and Social Studies 1971–77; sociologist and psychotherapist at outpatient clinic for alcohol and drug addiction, Bratislava 1978; freelance writer and researcher 1988–; Co-founder and Leader Public Against Violence; Co-founder and first Pres. Inst. for Public Affairs (IVO) 1997–99, Hon. Pres., Programme Dir and Analyst 2003–; Adviser to Pres. Havel on Human Rights Issues and Dir Human Rights Section, Office of Pres. of Fed. Repub. 1990–92; Sr Assoc. mem. St Anthony's Coll. 1993; taught at Faculty of Social Sciences, Charles Univ., Prague 1991–92, Trnava Univ. 1993–97; Amb. to USA 1999–2003; unsuccessful cand. in presidential election 2004; Order of Ľudovít Štúr 2000;German Marshall Fund Fellow 1993, Exec. Educ. Fellow, Woodrow Wilson School of Public and Int. Affairs 1993, Democracy Service Medal, Nat. Endowment for Democracy, Washington, DC 1999, Ján Papánek Medal 2000, Celebration of Freedom Award, American Jewish Cttee 2002, Czech and Slovak Freedom Lecturer, Woodrow Wilson Center, Washington, DC 2012. *Publications include:* Active Citizenship and the Nongovernmental Sector in Slovakia: Trends and Perspectives 2012; numerous journals and magazine articles on post-communist transition, civil society, NGOs, political behaviour, foreign policy issues, ethnicity, nationalism and anti-Semitism. *Address:* Institute for Public Affairs (Inštitút pre verejné otázky), Baštová 5, 811 03 Bratislava, Slovakia (office). *Telephone:* (2) 5443-4030 (office). *Fax:* (2) 5443-4041 (office). *E-mail:* butora@ivo.sk (office). *Website:* www.ivo.sk/166/en/people/martin-butora (office).

BUTROS, Albert Jamil, PhD; Jordanian academic and diplomatist; *Professor Emeritus of English, University of Jordan;* b. 25 March 1934, Jerusalem; s. of Jamil Issa Butros and Virginie Antoine Butros (née Albina); m. Ida Maria Albina 1962; four d.; ed Univs of London and Exeter, UK, Columbia Univ., USA; taught English and math. in two pvt. schools, Amman 1950–55; instructor, Teachers' Coll., Amman 1958–60; Lecturer in English, Hunter Coll., CUNY 1961; Instructor, Miami Univ., Oxford, Ohio 1962–63; Asst Prof. of English, Univ. of Jordan 1963–65, Assoc. Prof. 1965–67, Prof. 1967–79, Acting Chair. Dept of English 1964–67, Chair. 1967–73, 1974–76, Dean of Research and Graduate Studies 1973–76, Prof. of English 1985–2004, Prof. Emer. 2004–; Visiting Prof. of English, Ohio Wesleyan Univ., Delaware, Ohio 1971–72, Jordan Univ. for Women, Amman 1995–96; Dir-Gen. and Pres. Royal Scientific Soc., Amman 1976–84; Sr Research Fellow, Int. Devt Research Centre, Ottawa, Canada 1983–84, Gov. 1986–98; Special Adviser to HRH Crown Prince Hassan of Jordan 1984–85; Amb. to UK 1987–91, (also accred to Ireland 1988–91, to Iceland 1990–91); mem. Bd of Trustees, Philadelphia Univ., Amman 1995–2009; Rapporteur, Cttee on the Jordan Incentive State Prize in Trans. 2001, Cttee on Selection for the Shoman Foundation Prize for Young Arab scholars in the Humanities and Social Sciences 2002, Cttee on Selection of Outstanding Researchers in Jordan 2004; Fellow, World Acad. of Art and Science 1986–; mem., Int. Advisory Bd Jordan Journal of Modern Languages and Literature 2007–; Istiqlal Order, First Class 1987, Order of Merit (Grande Ufficiale), Italy 1983, KStJ 1991. *Publications:* Leaders of Arab Thought 1969; several articles in learned journals; several translations including parts of Chaucer into Arabic; long paper on the English language and non-native writers of fiction in English, published 2004, Geoffrey Chaucer, Introduction and Selected Translations (in Arabic) 2009. *Leisure interests:* reading, writing, translation, art, world affairs. *Address:* Department of English, University of Jordan, Amman, Jordan (office). *Telephone:* (6) 535-5000 (office); (6) 515-7870 (home). *Fax:* (6) 535-5511 (office); (6) 515-7870 (home). *E-mail:* albertbutros@gmail.com (home). *Website:* www.ju.edu.jo (office).

BUTSCHEK, Günter, MEcons; German automotive industry executive; *Managing Director and CEO, Tata Motors;* b. 21 Oct. 1960; m.; two d.; ed Univ. of Cooperative Educ. Stuttgart; started professional career at Mercedes-Benz AG, Stuttgart 1984; worked at Daimler AG for 25 years, holding various sr positions in production, industrialization and procurement; COO and mem. Group Exec. Cttee, Airbus Group 2011–16; Man. Dir and CEO Tata Motors 2016–, Additional Dir 2016–. *Leisure interests:* skiing, biking, canoeing, golfing, running. *Address:* Tata Motors, Bombay House, 24 Homi Mody Street, Fort, Mumbai 400001, India (office). *Telephone:* (22) 66658282 (office). *E-mail:* info@tatamotors.com (office). *Website:* www.tatamotors.com (office).

BUTT, Michael Acton, OBE, MA, MBA; British business executive; *Chairman, Axis Capital Holdings Ltd;* b. 25 May 1942, Thruxton, Hants.; s. of Leslie Acton Kingsford Butt and Mina Gascoigne Butt; m. 1st Diana Lorraine Brook 1964; two s.; m. 2nd Zoe Benson 1986; ed Rugby School, Magdalen Coll., Oxford and Institut Européen d'Admin des Affaires (INSEAD), France; joined Bland Welch Group 1964; Dir Bland Payne Holdings 1970; Chair. Sedgwick Ltd 1983–87; Deputy Chair. Sedgwick Group PLC 1985–87, Eagle Star Holdings PLC 1987–91; Chair. and CEO Eagle Star Insurance Co. 1987–91; Dir BAT Industries PLC 1987–91, Marceau Investissements SA (France) 1987–94, Phoenix International (Bermuda) 1992–97, Bank of N. T. Butterfield & Son Ltd (Bermuda) 1996–2002; Pres. and CEO Mid Ocean Ltd 1993–98, Chair. and CEO Mid Ocean Reinsurance Co. Ltd 1993–98; Dir Exel Capital Ltd 1998–99, XL Capital Ltd 1998–2002; Chair. Axis Capital Holdings Ltd 2002–; Dir Istituto Nazionale delle Assicurazioni 1994–97; Bd mem. and mem. Int. Advisory Council, INSEAD 1982–. *Leisure interests:* travel, tennis, opera, reading, family, the European movt. *Address:* Axis Capital Holdings Ltd, Axis House, 92 Pitts Bay Road, Pembroke, HM 08 (office); Leamington House, 50 Harrington Sound Road, Hamilton Parish, CR 04, Bermuda (home). *Telephone:* 496-2600 (office); 293-1378 (home). *Fax:* 405-2720 (office); 293-8511 (home). *E-mail:* michael.butt@axis.bm (office). *Website:* www.axiscapital.com (office).

BUTT, Noor Mohammed, PhD, DSc; Pakistani nuclear solid state physicist (retd); *Professor and Chairman, Preston Institute of Nano Science and Technology;* b. 3 June 1936, Sialkot City; s. of Ferozuddin Butt and Sardar Begum; m. Gulzar Butt; two s. one d.; ed Punjab Univ., Univ. of Birmingham, UK; fmrly Chief Scientist and Dir Gen., Pakistan Inst. of Nuclear Science and Tech.; currently Prof. and Chair. Preston Inst. of Nano Science and Tech. (PINSAT), Preston Univ., Islamabad; fmr Vice-Pres. Crystallography Soc. of Pakistan; Pres. Pakistan Nuclear Soc. 1995–97; Treas. Pakistan Acad. of Sciences 1994–98; Chair. Pakistan Science Foundation 2005–08, Nat. Comm. on Nano-Science and Tech.; mem., Expert Group, Ministry of Science and Technology; Visiting Scientist, AERE, Harwell, UK, Univ. of Oxford, Int. Centre for Theoretical Physics, Trieste, Reactor Inst., Stockholm, Sweden; IAEA nuclear energy consultant; occasional appearances on Pakistan radio and TV; Fellow, Islamic Acad. of Sciences; Sitara-i-Imtiaz from Pres. of Pakistan 1991; Open Gold Medal in Physical Sciences, Pakistan Acad. of Sciences 1990, 8th Kharazmi Prize (co-recipient) (Iran) 1995, Scientist Emer., PAEC, Life Title 1996. *Publications:* Waves and Oscillations (text book) 1973, International Seminar on Solid State Physics (ed.) 1974, CTBT and its Implications (ed.) 1996; ed. of eight books; more than 140 research papers on nuclear solid state physics; journals and conf. proceedings. *Leisure interests:* photography, playing with grandchildren. *Address:* Preston Institute of Nano Science and Technology (PINSAT), Preston University, Sector H-8/1, Islamabad (office); H: 155, St 15, Sector E-7, Islamabad, Pakistan (home). *Telephone:* (51) 4430597 (ext. 409) (office); (51) 2652242 (home). *Fax:* (51) 4430648 (office). *E-mail:* nmbutt36@yahoo.com (office). *Website:* www.preston.edu.pk (office).

BUTT, Salman Aslam, BA, LLB, LLM; Pakistani lawyer and fmr government official; *Partner, Cornelius, Lane and Mufti Advocates and Solicitors;* b. 16 July 1958; ed Government Coll., Lahore, Punjab Univ. Law Coll., Univ. of London, UK; est. own law practice 1982; joined Cornelius, Lane and Mufti Advocates and Solicitors (law firm), Lahore 1980s, Partner 2016–; Visiting Law Lecturer, Univ. of the Punjab 1985–88; Attorney-Gen. 2014–16; mem. Supreme Court Bar Asscn, Lahore High Court Bar Asscn, Lahore Dist Bar Asscn. *Address:* Cornelius, Lane and Mufti Advocates and Solicitors, Nawa-e-Waqt House, 4 Shahrah-e-Fatima Jinnah, Lahore 54000, Punjab, Pakistan (office). *E-mail:* salman.butt@clm.com.pk (office). *Website:* www.clm.com.pk (office).

BUTT, Air Chief Marshal Tahir Rafique, MSc; Pakistani air force officer (retd); b. 1955; m.; three c.; ed Punjab Univ., Staff Coll., Turkey, Nat. Defence Univ., Pakistan Air Force Acad.; joined Pakistan Air Force as Gen. Duty Pilot 1977, served as Deputy Dir Plans 1996–97, Dir Flight Safety 1997–99, Officer Commanding No 34 Flying Wing, PAF Base Rafiqui 1999–2000, Base Commdr, PAF Base Lower Topa 2001–02, Asst Chief of the Air Staff (Personnel Branch) 2002–04, Base Commdr,PAF Base Mianwali 2004–05, Asst Chief of the Air Staff (Training) Oct.–Dec. 2005, Dir-Gen. Nat. Accountability Bureau 2005–07, Commandant, Nat. Security Coll., Nat. Defence Univ., Islamabad 2007–08, Air Officer, Commdg Southern Air Command 2008–09, Deputy Chief of the Air Staff (Personnel) 2009–10, Vice-Chief of Air Staff 2010–12, Chief of Air Staff 2012–15 (retd); Hilal-i-Imtiaz, Sitara-i-Imtiaz, Tamgha-i-Basalat; Professional Excellence Badge, Chief of Air Staff Commendation Certificate.

BUTTENHEIM, Lisa M.; American UN official; *Assistant Secretary-General for Field Support, United Nations;* b. 1954; d. of Curtis R. Buttenheim; m. Jean-Claude Aimé; ed Stanford Univ., Johns Hopkins Univ. School of Advanced Int. Studies; joined UN 1983, served in various positions including in Exec. Office of Sec.-Gen., in Office of Under-Secs-Gen. for Special Political Affairs, New York and UN Truce Supervision Org., Jerusalem, Sr Political Adviser, Office of Dir-Gen., UN, Geneva 1997–2003, also assignments as Chief of Staff, Office of the Special Rep. of Sec.-Gen. UN Interim Admin Mission in Kosovo and Dir and Sr Adviser, Office of the Special Envoy for Balkans, Geneva, Dir and Head of UN Office, Belgrade 2003–04, Dir Asia and Middle East Div., Dept of Peacekeeping Operations 2004–07, Dir Asia and Pacific Div. 2008, Dir Middle East and West Asia Div., Dept of Political Affairs 2009–10, Special Rep. of UN Sec.-Gen. and Head of Mission, UN Peacekeeping Force in Cyprus (UNFICYP) 2010–16; Asst Sec.-Gen. for Field Support 2016–. *Address:* Office of the Secretary-General, United Nations, New York, NY 10017, USA (office). *Telephone:* (212) 963-1234 (office). *Fax:* (212) 963-4879 (office). *Website:* www.un.org (office).

BUTTERWORTH, David, Eur Ing, BSc (Eng), FREng, FIChemE, FRSA; British chemical engineer; *Director, Healthwatch Oxfordshire;* b. 24 Oct. 1943; m. Pauline Morgan 1966; one s.; ed Univ. Coll., London; Visiting Engineer, MIT, USA 1976–77; Group Leader, UKAEA 1977–89; Man. Dir Heat Transfer and Fluid Flow Service 1989–95, Sr Consultant in heat transfer 1995–; Visiting Prof., Univ. of Bristol 1993–, Cranfield Univ. 1995–2002, Aston Univ., Birmingham 1996–2001; Pres. UK Heat Transfer Soc. 1988–89; Gen. Sec. Aluminium Plate-Fin Heat Exchanger Mfrs Asscn (ALPEMA) 1995–2008; Dir Healthwatch Oxfordshire 2017–; AIChE Kern Award 1986. *Publications:* Introduction to Heat Transfer 1977, Two-Phase Flow and Heat Transfer 1977 (co-author) (Russian trans. 1980), Condensers, Theory and Practice 1983, Design and Operation of Heat Exchangers (co-ed.) 1992, New Developments in Heat Exchangers (co-ed.), The 8th UK National Conference on Heat Transfer 2004. *Leisure interests:* landscape painting, cooking. *Address:* 29 Clevelands, Abingdon, Oxon., OX14 2EQ, England (home). *Telephone:* (1235) 525955 (home). *E-mail:* davebutterworth@aol.com (home).

BUTTIGLIONE, Rocco; Italian academic and politician; b. 16 June 1948, Gallipoli, Lecce; m.; four d.; fmr Acting Chancellor, Int. Acad. of Philosophy, Liechtenstein; Prof. of Political Science, Saint Pius V Univ., Rome; Minister of European Union Affairs 2001–05, of Cultural Assets and Activities 2005–06; Sec.-Gen. Partito Popolare Italiano 1994–95, Cristiani Democratici Uniti 1995–2002; Pres. Unione dei Democratici Cristiani e di Centro (UDC) 2002–; unsuccessful cand. for Mayor of Turin 2006; mem. Camera dei Deputati, Vice-Pres. from 2008; Dr hc (Univ. Cattolica di Lublino), (Univ. Francisco Marroquin) 2005. *Publications:* Dialettica e nostalgia 1978, La crisi dell'economia marxista: Gli inizi della scuola di Francoforte 1979, Il pensiero di Karol Wojtyla 1982, Ethik der Leistung (co-ed.) 1988, La crisi della morale 1991, Die Verantwortung des Menschen in einem globalen Weltzeitalter (co-ed.) 1996, Wie erkennt man Naturrecht? (co-ed.) 1998, Karol Wojtyla: The Thought of the Man Who Became Pope John Paul II 1997, The Moral Mandate for Freedom: Reflections on Centesimus Annus 1997. *Address:* Camera dei Deputati, Palazzo di Montecitorio, Rome (office); Unione dei Democratici Cristiani e di Centro, Via dei Due Macelli 66, 00182 Rome, Italy (office). *Telephone:* (06) 67603316 (office); (06) 69791001 (office). *Fax:* (06) 6791574 (office). *E-mail:* dlwebmast@camera.it (office); info@udc-italia.it (office). *Website:* www.camera.it (office); www.udc-italia.it (office).

BUTTON, Jenson Alexander Lyons, MBE; British racing driver; b. 19 Jan. 1980, Frome, Somerset, England; s. of John Button (fmr Rallycross driver) and Simone Lyons; m. Jessica Michibata 2014; ed Selwood Middle School, Frome Community Coll.; began karting aged eight; Formula Ford Festival Winner 1998, British Formula Ford Champion 1998; first drove in Formula One in 2000 season, with Williams team; youngest driver to score points in Formula One aged 20 years, 67 days (Brazilian Grand Prix 2000); switched to Benetton 2001–03 (became Renault F1 2002); moved to BAR 2003 (renamed Honda for 2006 season), won first Grand Prix in Hungary after 113 races 6 Aug. 2006, Honda withdrew from sport Dec. 2008, man. buy-out of team by Ross Brawn Feb. 2009, drove Mercedes-engined car in 2009 Championship; Formula One World Champion 2009; signed for Vodafone McLaren Mercedes Nov. 2009–; runner-up, Formula One World Championship 2011; Australian Grand Prix 2012; won Belgian Grand Prix 2012; resides in Monaco; McLaren Autosport BRDC Award 1998, Lorenzo Bandini Trophy 2001, British Competition Driver of the Year 2003, Hawthorn Memorial Trophy 2004, 2005, 2006, Int. Driver of the Year 2004, British Competition Driver of the Year 2006, Laureus Breakthrough of the Year Award 2010. *Leisure interests:* triathlon, car collection includes a McLaren MP4-12c. *Address:* McLaren Technology Centre, Chertsey Road, Woking, GU21 4YH, England (office). *Telephone:* (1483) 261000 (office). *Fax:* (1483) 261010 (office). *E-mail:* info@mclaren.com (office). *Website:* www.mclaren.com (office); www.jensonbutton.com.

BUXTON, Andrew Robert Fowell, CMG, FIB; British banker; b. 5 April 1939, London, England; m. Jane Margery Grant 1965; two d.; ed Winchester Coll. and Pembroke Coll., Oxford; joined Barclays Bank Ltd 1963; Gen. Man. Barclays Bank PLC 1980, CEO 1992–93, Chair. 1993–99; Deputy Chair. (non-exec.) Xansa PLC 1999–2007; Chair. Heart of the City; Pres. British Bankers' Asscn 1997–2002; Dir (non-exec.), Capitaland Ltd 2003–07, DBS Group Holdings Ltd 2006–11; mem.

Court, Bank of England 1997–2001, Guild of Int. Bankers 2001, Panel on Takeovers and Mergers 2001; Gov. Imperial Coll. of Science and Tech.; fmr Visiting Prof., City Univ., London; currently Visiting Prof., Cass Business School; Patron, Nat. Educ. Business Partnership Network 2004–; Hon. DSc (City). *Address:* Cass Business School, City University London, 106 Bunhill Row, London, EC1Y 8TZ, England (office). *Telephone:* (20) 7040-8600 (office). *E-mail:* enquiries@city.ac.uk (office). *Website:* www.cass.city.ac.uk (office).

BUYOYA, Maj. Pierre; Burundian politician and fmr head of state; *President, Foundation for Unity, Peace and Democracy;* b. 24 Nov. 1949, Mutangaro, Rutovu; m. Sophie Buyoya 1978; one s. three d.; ed Royal Mil. Acad., Brussels, staff coll. in France, war coll. in Germany; mem. Cen. Cttee UPRONA Party 1979–87; fmr COO Ministry of Nat. Defence; led mil. coup against fmr Pres. Bagaza Sept. 1987; Pres. of Third Repub. and Minister of Nat. Defence 1987–93, Chair. Mil. Cttee for Nat. Salvation 1987–93; Pres. Foundation for Unity, Peace and Democracy 1994–; Pres. of Burundi 1996–2003; mem. Senate 2003–; African Union High Rep. for Mali and the Sahel (MISAHEL) 2013–. *Publications:* Building Peace in Burundi – Mission Impossible 1998. *Leisure interests:* reading, football, swimming. *Address:* BP 2006, Bujumbura, Burundi (office). *Telephone:* (2) 20796 (office); (2) 13208 (home). *Fax:* (2) 20816 (office). *E-mail:* fupd2003@yahoo.fr (office).

BUYSSE, Baron Paul Henri Maria; Belgian business executive; *Chairman, NV Bekaert SA;* b. 17 March 1945, Antwerp; m.; five c.; various marketing and sales functions, Ford Motor Co. 1966–76; Gen. Man. Car Sales & Marketing, Deputy Man. Dir British Leyland Belgium NV 1976–79, Exec. Dir Tenneco Belgium 1980–84, Man. Dir J.I. Case Benelux 1980–84, Gen. Man. Europe N, J.I. Case, Int. Harvester and Poclain 1984–88; Group Man. Dir Hansen Transmissions Int. 1988; Group Chief Exec. BTR Automotive & Eng Group (London) 1989, Group Chief Exec. BTR Eng and Dunlop Overseas 1991, Exec. Dir BTR PLC 1992–97; CEO Vickers PLC 1998–2000; Chair. NV Bekaert SA 2000–; Dir (non-exec.) Bd of Generale Bank, Censor Nat. Bank of Belgium; Chair., mem. Exec. Cttee and Dir King Baudouin Foundation; Chair. Prince Filip Foundation; Hon. Pres. Antwerp Chamber of Commerce & Industry; Hon. Dean of Labour, Emer. 2003–; Kt, Order of Leopold 1988; Officer, Order of Orange-Nassau 1994; Officier, Order nat. du Mérite 1996; Hon. CBE 1997; Commdr, Order of Leopold II 2001; Grand Officer, Order of Leopold II 2005; Hon. CMG 2005; UNIZO Prize 2003. *Publication:* main author of the Belgian Code for Corporate Governance (Code Buysse). *Leisure interests:* golf, reading. *Address:* NV Bekaert SA, President Kennedypark 18, 8500 Kortrijk, Belgium (office). *E-mail:* paul.buysse@bekaert.com (office). *Website:* www.bekaert.com (office).

BÜYÜKANIT, Gen. (Mehmet) Yaşar; Turkish army officer; b. 1 Sept. 1940, Istanbul; m. Filiz Büyükanit; one d.; ed Mil. Acad., Infantry School, Army Staff Coll., NATO Defence Coll.; served in different units of Land Forces as Platoon and Commando Co. Commdr 1963–70, then numerous leadership positions, including Chief of Operations, 6th Infantry Div., Instructor, Army Staff Coll., Intelligence Div. Basic Intelligence Br. Forces and Systems Section Chief, Supreme HQ Allied Powers Europe (SHAPE), Mons, Belgium, Section, then Br. Chief of Gen.-Adm. Br. at Turkish Gen. Staff (TGS) HQ, Commdr of Kuleli Mil. High School and of Presidential Guard Regiment; rank of Brig.-Gen. 1988; 2nd Armoured Brigade Commdr, then Chief of Intelligence Dept, AFSOUTH HQ, Naples, Italy; rank of Maj.-Gen. 1992; Sec.-Gen. Turkish Gen. Staff, then Supt Turkish Army Acad. 1992–96; rank of Lt-Gen. 1996; Commdr 7th Army Corps 1996–98; Chief of Operations, TGS 1998–2000, Deputy Chief 2000–03; rank of Gen. 2000; Commdr First Army 2003–04, Turkish Army 2004–06, Chief of the Gen. Staff, Turkish Armed Forces 2006–08; Turkish Armed Forces (TAF) Medal of Distinguished Service, TAF Medal of Distinguished Courage and Self-Sacrifice, TAF Medal of Honour, Italian Medal of Honour, USA Legion of Merit, Pakistani Nishan-ı Imtiaz. *Address:* Ministry of National Defence, Milli Savunma Bakanlığı, 06100 Ankara, Turkey (office). *Telephone:* (312) 4026100 (office). *Fax:* (312) 4184737 (office). *E-mail:* msb@msb.gov.tr (office). *Website:* www.msb.gov.tr (office).

BUZDAR, Sardar Usman Ahmad Khan, BA, LLB, MA; Pakistani politician; *Chief Minister of Punjab;* b. May 1969, Dera Ghazi Khan, Punjab; s. of Sardar Fateh Muhammad Khan Buzdar; ed Bahauddin Zakariya Univ., Law Coll.; elected as District Nazim, Taunsa Sharif 2001–08; mem. Pakistan Muslim League (Q) (PML-Q) 2001–07, 2008–13; elected to the provincial ass. as mem. Pakistan Tehreek-e-Insaf (PTI) political party 2018–; Chief Minister of Punjab 2018–. *Website:* www.insaf.pk/public/insafpk/leadership/usman-buzdar (office).

BUZEK, Jerzy Karol; Polish chemical engineer, politician and academic; b. 3 July 1940, Śmiłowice; m. Ludgarda Buzek; one d.; ed Silesian Tech. Univ.; Scientific Researcher and Prof., Chemical Eng Inst., Polish Acad. of Sciences, Gliwice 1963–97, Prof. of Tech. Science 1997–; mem. Solidarity Trade Union 1980–; organizer of Solidarity underground structures in Silesia; activist of union's regional and nat. leadership; expert and co-author economic program of the Solidarity Election Action (AWS), Chair. Nat. Bd of Social Movt of Solidarity Election Action 1999–2001, Chair. AWS coalition 2001; Deputy to Sejm (Parl.) 1997–2001; Prime Minister of Poland 1997–2001; Researcher and Pro-Rector Polonia Univ., Częstochowa 2002–04; Prof., Mechanical Div., Tech. Univ. of Opole; mem. European Parl. (Silesian Voivodship constituency) (Group of the European People's Party—Christian Democrats and European Democrats) 2004–, Pres. 2009–12, Chair. Industry, Research and Energy Cttee 2014–; Founder Polish Diaspora School of Diplomacy; Co-f. (with wife) Family Foundation 1998; est. Pro Publico Bono Prize 1999; Dr hc (Seoul, Dortmund); Laureate, Grzegorz Palka Award 1998. *Publications include:* several dozen articles and monographs on mathematical modelling, desulphurization of exhaust gases and optimization of processes. *Leisure interests:* poetry, theatre, horse riding, tennis, yachting. *Address:* European Parliament, Bâtiment Altiero Spinelli, 05F243, 60 rue Wiertz, 1047 Brussels, Belgium (office). *Telephone:* (2) 284-56-31 (office). *Fax:* (2) 284-97-69 (office). *E-mail:* jbuzek@europarl.eu.int (office). *Website:* www.buzek.pl (office).

BYAMBASÜREN, Dashiyn; Mongolian politician; b. 20 June 1942, Binder somon Dist, Hentii Prov.; s. of Lombyn Dash and Tsevegeen Perenlee; m. Sanjeen Dulamlkhand 1968; three s. three d.; ed Inst. of Economics and Statistics, Moscow, USSR; apptd Dept Chief, State Statistics Bd; Deputy Chair., then Chair. State Cttee for Prices and Standardization 1970–76; Chair. Construction and Repair Work Trust for Auto Transport 1984, Chief Research Officer, Research Inst. of Project Drafts for Automated Man. Systems 1985, Dir Manager Training Inst., Council of Ministers 1986; Deputy Chair. Council of Ministers 1989–90, First Deputy Chair. March–Sept. 1990, Prime Minister of Mongolia 1990–92; Pres. Mongolian Devt Foundation, World Mongolian Fed. 1993; fmr mem. Parl.; fmr Chair. Mongolian Democratic Renewal Party; Rector Inst. of Admin. and Man. 1998–2000; Rector Acad. of Man.; Dir Centre for Devt Strategy and System Research 2001; Prof. and Academician, Nat. Acad. of Science. *Publications:* Orchlongiin hurd, Sergen mandakh ireedui, Uuriin javar. *Address:* GPO Box 248, Ulan Bator, Mongolia (home). *Telephone:* 324167 (office). *Fax:* 320090 (office). *E-mail:* byambasuren@cdssr.mn (office). *Website:* www.cdssr.mn (office).

BYATT, Dame Antonia Susan (A.S.), (Dame Antonia Duffy), DBE, BA, FRSL; British writer; b. 24 Aug. 1936, Sheffield, Yorkshire; d. of John F. Drabble, QC and Kathleen M. Bloor; sister of Margaret Drabble; m. 1st Ian Charles Rayner Byatt (q.v.) 1959 (divorced 1969); one s. (deceased) one d.; m. 2nd Peter John Duffy 1969; two d.; ed Sheffield High School, The Mount School, York, Newnham Coll., Cambridge, Bryn Mawr Coll., USA, Somerville Coll., Oxford; Extra-Mural Lecturer, Univ. of London 1962–71; Lecturer in Literature, Cen. School of Art and Design 1965–69; Lecturer in English, Univ. Coll., London 1972–81, Sr Lecturer 1981–83; Assoc. Newnham Coll., Cambridge 1977–82; mem. BBC Social Effects of TV Advisory Group 1974–77; mem. Bd of Creative and Performing Arts 1985–87, Bd of British Council 1993–98; Kingman Cttee on English Language 1987–88; Man. Cttee Soc. of Authors 1984–88 (Chair. 1986–88); mem. Literature Advisory Panel of the British Council 1990–98; broadcaster, reviewer and judge of literary prizes; Fellow, English Asscn, British Acad. 2017; Hon. Fellow, Newnham Coll. Cambridge 1999, London Inst. 2000, Univ. Coll. London 2004, Somerville Coll. Oxford 2005, Foreign Hon. Mem. American Acad. of Arts and Sciences 2014; Chevalier, Ordre des Arts et Lettres 2003; Hon. DLitt (Bradford) 1987, (Durham, York) 1991, (Nottingham) 1992, (Liverpool) 1993, (Portsmouth) 1994, (London) 1995, (Cambridge) 1999, (Sheffield) 2000, (Kent at Canterbury) 2004, (Oxford) 2007, (Winchester) 2007, (Leiden, Holland) 2010; Premio Malaparte Award, Capri 1995, Toepfer Foundation Shakespeare Prize, Hamburg 2002, Grand Prix littéraire du Metropolis Bleu (Canada) 2009, Erasmus Prize 2016, Park Kyong-ni Prize 2017, Hans Christian Andersen Literature Award 2018. *Radio:* dramatization of quartet of novels (BBC Radio) 2002. *Television:* profile on Scribbling (series, BBC 2) 2002, interview with Mark Lawson (BBC 4) 2010. *Films:* Angels and Insects 1996, Possession 2002. *Publications:* fiction: The Shadow of the Sun 1964, The Game 1967, The Virgin in the Garden 1978, Still Life (PEN/Macmillan Silver Pen for Fiction 1986) 1985, Sugar and Other Stories 1987, Possession: A Romance (Booker Prize 1990, Irish Times-Aer Lingus Int. Fiction Prize 1990, Eurasian Regional Award of the Commonwealth Writers' Prize 1991) 1990 (filmed 2002), Angels and Insects (novellas) 1992 (filmed 1996), The Matisse Stories 1993, The Djinn in the Nightingale's Eye (Mythopoeic Fantasy Award 1998) 1994, Babel Tower 1996, Elementals, Stories of Fire and Ice 1998, The Biographer's Tale 2000, A Whistling Woman 2002, Little Black Book of Stories 2003, The Children's Book (James Tait Black Memorial Prize 2010) 2009, Ragnarok: the End of the Gods 2012; non-fiction: Degrees of Freedom: The Novels of Iris Murdoch (revised edn as Degrees of Freedom: The Early Novels of Iris Murdoch) 1965, Wordsworth and Coleridge in Their Time (revised edn as Unruly Times: Wordsworth and Coleridge in Their Time) 1970, Iris Murdoch 1976, Passions of the Mind (selected essays) 1991, Imagining Characters: Conversations About Women Writers (with Ignês Sodré) 1995, New Writing 4 (ed. with Alan Hollinghurst) 1995, New Writing 6 (co-ed.) 1997, The Oxford Book of English Short Stories (ed.) 1998, On Histories and Stories (essays) 2000, Portraits in Fiction 2001, Bird Hand Book (with V. Schrager) 2001, Memory (ed., anthology, with Harriet Harvey Wood) 2008, Peacock & Vine: On William Morris and Mariano Fortuny 2016; ed. and introduction to numerous works by other writers. *Address:* c/o Rogers, Coleridge & White, 20 Powis Mews, London, W11 1JN, England (office). *Telephone:* (20) 7221-3717 (office). *Fax:* (20) 7229-9084 (office). *Website:* www.asbyatt.com.

BYATT, Sir Ian Charles Rayner, Kt, BA, DPhil; British economist and government official; *Senior Associate, Frontier Economics;* b. 11 March 1932, Preston, Lancs.; s. of Charles Rayner Byatt and Enid Marjorie Annie Byatt (née Howat); m. 1st Antonia Susan Drabble (q.v.) 1959 (divorced 1969); one s. (deceased) one d.; m. 2nd Prof. Deirdre Kelly 1997; two step-s.; ed Kirkham Grammar School, St Edmund Hall and Nuffield Coll., Oxford, Harvard Univ.; Lecturer in Econs, Durham Coll., Univ. of Durham 1958–62, LSE 1964–67; Econ. Consultant, HM Treasury 1962–64; mem. Central Council of Educ. (England) 1965–66; Sr Econ. Adviser, Dept of Educ. and Science 1967–69; Dir of Econs, Ministry of Housing and Local Govt (and subsequently Dept of Environment) 1969–72; Under-Sec., HM Treasury 1972–78, Deputy Chief Econ. Adviser 1978–89, Chair. Advisory Cttee to HM Treasury on Accounting for Econ. Costs and Changing Prices 1986; Dir-Gen. of Water Services 1989–2000; Sr Assoc., Frontier Economics 2001–; Pres. Econs and Business Educ. Asscn 1998–2001; Co-Sec.-Gen. Foundation for Int. Studies in Social Security 2002–02; Adviser to Water Industry Commr for Scotland 2000–04, Chair. 2005–11; mem. Econ. Policy Cttee of EC 1978–89 (Chair. 1982–85), Econ. and Social Research Council 1983–89, Bd of Man., Int. Inst. of Public Finance 1987–90, 2001–06, Council, Royal Econ. Soc. 1983–90 (mem. Exec. Cttee 1987–89), Cttee on Water Services, Econ. and Financial Objectives 1970–73, Public Services Productivity Panel, HM Treasury 2000–02, Chief Sec.'s Advisory Panel on Better Public Services 2002–06, Bd of Public Finance Foundation 1984–89, Bd of Regulatory Policy Inst. 2001–07, Panel of Advisors to NI Govt in reform of water services 2003–06, Council of Man., Nat. Inst. of Econ. and Social Research 1996–2002, Advisory Bd Centre for Management Under Regulation, Warwick Business School 1996–2010, Governing Body of Birkbeck Coll. 1997–2005 (Chair. Finance and Gen. Purposes Cttee 2001–05, Fellow 2005–), Bd of Advisers, St Edmund Hall, Oxford 1998–2003, Int. Advisory Cttee Public Utilities Research Center, Univ. of Florida 2002–; Vice-Pres. Strategic Planning Soc. 1993–, Human City Inst., Birmingham 1999–2002; Treas., Holy Cross Centre Trust, London 1988–2002, Patron 2006–; Chair. Friends of Birmingham Cathedral 1999– (mem. Cathedral Council 2003–), Trustees of David Hume Inst., Edinburgh 2008–11; Trustee, Acad. of Youth, Birmingham 2001–05; Freeman, City of London 1995; Hon. Prof., Univ. of Birmingham; Hon. Fellow, St Edmund Hall, Oxford 2007–; Hon. DUniv (Brunel) 1994, (Univ. of Central England) 2000, (Aston) 2005. *Publications:* The British Electrical Industry

1875–1914 1979, Delivering Better Services to Citizens 2001; articles and book chapters on nationalized industries and public utilities; contribs to govt reports on micro-econ. policy. *Leisure interests:* painting, family life. *Address:* Frontier Economics, MidCity Place, 71 High Holborn, London, WC1V 6DA (office); 34 Frederick Road, Birmingham, B15 1JN, England (home). *Telephone:* (20) 7031-7000 (office); (121) 689-7946 (home). *Fax:* (20) 7031-7001 (office); (121) 454-6438 (home). *E-mail:* ianbyatt@blueyonder.co.uk (home); ian_byatt@yahoo.co.uk (home); ian.byatt@frontier-economics.com (office). *Website:* www.frontier-economics.com (office).

BYATT, Ronald (Robin) Archer Campbell, CMG; British diplomatist (retd); b. 14 Nov. 1930; s. of Sir Horace Byatt and Lady Byatt (née Olga Campbell); m. Ann Brereton Sharpe 1954; one s. one d.; ed Gordonstoun, New Coll., Oxford; joined Diplomatic Service 1959, at Foreign Office 1959, 1963, served in Havana 1961, Kampala 1970, Perm. Mission to UN, New York 1966, Counsellor and Head of Chancery 1977–79, Head of Rhodesia Dept, FCO 1972–75, Asst Under-Sec. of State for Africa 1979–80, High Commr to Zimbabwe 1980–83, Amb. to Morocco 1985–87, High Commr to NZ (also accred to Western Samoa and Gov. of Pitcairn Island) 1987–90; Visiting Fellow, Univ. of Glasgow 1975–76; Civilian Dir Royal Coll. of Defence Studies, London 1983–84; Panel Chair. Civil Service Selection Bd 1992–95; mem. Forestry Comm. Home-Grown Timber Advisory Cttee (Chair. Environment Sub-cttee) 1993–98; Trustee, Beit Trust 1987–2011, UK Antarctic Heritage Trust 1993–2001; Wissem Alaouite (First Class) (Morocco) 1987. *Leisure interests:* birdwatching, sailing, gardening. *Address:* Drim-na-Vullin, Lochgilphead, Argyll, Scotland (home). *E-mail:* byatt.drim@virgin.net (home).

BYCHKOV, Semyon; American conductor and academic; *Chief Conductor and Artistic Director, Czech Philharmonic Orchestra;* b. 30 Nov. 1952, Leningrad (now St Petersburg), Russia; brother of Yakov Kreizberg; m. Marielle Labèque; ed Leningrad Conservatory (pupil of Musin); invited to conduct Leningrad Philharmonic Orchestra; left USSR 1975; debut with Concertgebouw, Amsterdam and Berlin Philharmonic 1984–85; toured Germany with Berlin Philharmonic 1985; Music Dir Grand Rapid Symphony Orchestra 1980, Buffalo Philharmonic Orchestra 1986–87, Orchestre de Paris 1989–98, Semperoper, Dresden 1999–2003; Prin. Guest Conductor, Maggio Musicale Fiorentino 1992–96; Chief Conductor, WDR Sinfonieorchester Köln 1997–2010; Günter Wand Conducting Chair, BBC Symphony Orchestra 2012–; Chief Conductor and Artistic Dir Czech Philharmonic Orchestra 2017–; Otto Klemperer Chair of Conducting, RAM, London; apptd Chief Conductor and Music Dir, Czech Philharmonic 2018–; guest conductor with New York Philharmonic, Chicago Symphony, Cleveland Orchestra, Philadelphia Orchestra, Los Angeles Philharmonic, Vienna Philharmonic, Royal Concertgebouw Orchestra, Gewandhausorchester Leipzig, Berlin Philharmonic, Munich Philharmonic, London Symphony, Royal Opera House Covent Garden, Teatro Real Madrid, Metropolitan Opera New York, La Scala Milan, Opéra de Paris, Vienna State Opera; Franco Abbiati Prize 1996, Conductor of the Year, Int. Opera Awards 2015. *Recordings include:* R. Strauss's Daphne (with Cologne Radio Chorus and Symphony Orchestra) 2005, Elektra (with Chorus and Symphony Orchestra of Westdeutscher Rundfunk, Köln) 2005. *Address:* IMG Artists, Capital Tower, 91 Waterloo Road, London, SE1 8RT, England (office). *Telephone:* (20) 7957-5800 (office). *Fax:* (20) 7957-5801 (office). *E-mail:* jchadwick@imgartists.com (office). *Website:* www.imgartists.com (office); www.semyonbychkov.com.

BYCZEWSKI, Iwo, DrIur; Polish lawyer and diplomatist; *Ambassador to Tunisia;* b. 29 Feb. 1948, Poznań; m. Anna Nehrebecka; two d.; ed Adam Mickiewicz Univ., Poznań and Collège d'Europe, Bruges; mem. staff, Ministry of Justice 1977–82; researcher, Inst. of Econ. Sciences, Polish Acad. of Sciences (PAN) 1982–89; Prin. Expert, Sec. Comm. in Senate Chancellery; Ministerial Adviser, Vice-Dir Council of Minister's Office 1989–90; Dir Personnel Dept, Ministry of Foreign Affairs 1990–91, Under-Sec. of State 1991–95; Perm. Rep. to EU 2001–02; Amb. to Belgium and Luxembourg 2002–03, to Belgium 2005–07; Chair. Supervisory Bd Alcatel Polska SA 1995–; consultant, Hogan and Hartson (American law firm) 1996–; Chair. Centre of Int. Affairs Foundation 1997–; mem. cttee in support of Bronisław Komorowski before the pre-term presidential elections 2010; Amb. to Tunisia 2012–; Officer's Cross, Order of Polonia Restituta 1995, Commdr 2009. *Address:* Embassy of Poland, Le Grand Blvd de la Corniche, 2045 Les Berges du Lac II, Tunis, Tunisia (office). *Telephone:* (71) 196193 (office). *Fax:* (71) 196203 (office). *E-mail:* tunis.amb.sekretariat@msz.gov.pl (office). *Website:* tunis.msz.gov.pl (office).

BYDDER, Graeme M., PhD, MD, FRCR, FRCP; British (b. New Zealand) radiologist and academic; b. 1 May 1944, Motueka, New Zealand; m. Patricia Anne Hamilton 1970; ed Univ. of Canterbury, Univ. of Otago; fmrly with Robert Steiner Magnetic Resonance Unit, MRC Clinical Sciences Centre, Imaging Sciences Dept, Imperial Coll. Faculty of Medicine, Hammersmith Hosp., London, UK, later Prof. and Fellow, Acad. of Medical Sciences; apptd Prof. of Radiology and Dir Bydder Lab., Univ. of California, San Diego 2003, now mem. Recall Faculty; Pres. Int. Soc. for Magnetic Resonance in Medicine 1989–90; Hon. Fellow, Soc. for Magnetic Resonance Imaging 1991, Royal Australasian Coll. of Radiologists 1991; Hon. mem. Soc. for Magnetic Resonance Imaging 1992, American Soc. of Neuroradiology 1995, British Soc. of Neuroradiology 2003; McKenzie Davidson Medal, British Inst. of Radiology 1995, Taylor Prize, Robarts Research Inst. 1998, Gold Medal, Royal Coll. of Radiologists 2001,. *Publications include:* Magnetic Resonance Imaging Atlas of the Brain (co-author) 1989, MRI Atlas of the Brain (co-author) 1990, Advanced MR Imaging Techniques (co-author) 1997; more than 500 papers in professional journals. *Address:* Department of Radiology, School of Medicine, University of California, 9500 Gilman Drive, La Jolla, San Diego, CA 92093-0021, USA (office). *Telephone:* (619) 471-0506 (office). *E-mail:* gbydder@ucsd.edu (office). *Website:* medschool.ucsd.edu/som/radiology (office).

BYERS, Rt Hon. Stephen John, PC, LLB, FRSA; British politician and business executive; *Non-Executive Chairman, ACWA Services Limited;* b. 13 April 1953, Wolverhampton; s. of Robert Byers; ed Chester City Grammar School, Chester Coll., Liverpool Polytechnic; Sr Lecturer of Law Newcastle Polytechnic 1977–82; Labour Party MP for Wallsend 1992–97, for Tyneside N 1997–2010; Opposition Whip 1994–95, Frontbench Spokesman on Educ. and Employment 1995–97; Minister of State, Dept for Educ. and Employment 1997–98; Chief Sec. to the Treasury 1998–99; Sec. of State for Trade and Industry 1999–2001, for Transport, Local Govt and the Regions 2001–02; Chair. (non-exec.), ACWA Services Ltd. *Address:* ACWA Services Ltd, ACWA House, Keighley Road, Skipton, North Yorkshire, BD23 2UE, England (office). *Telephone:* (1756) 794794 (office). *Fax:* (1756) 790898 (office). *E-mail:* acwa@acwa.co.uk (office). *Website:* www.acwa.co.uk (office).

BYFORD, Mark, LLB; British broadcasting executive; b. 13 June 1958, Castleford, West Yorks., England; s. of Sir Lawrence Byford and Lady Muriel Byford (née Massey); m. Hilary Bleiker 1980; two s. three d.; ed Christ's Hosp. School, Lincoln, Univ. of Leeds; joined BBC as Holiday Relief Asst 1979, Controller, Regional Broadcasting 1991–94, Deputy Man. Dir 1994–96, Dir 1996–98, Dir BBC World Service and Global News 1998–2004, Deputy Dir-Gen. BBC 2003–11, Acting Dir-Gen. Jan.–June 2004, fmr mem. BBC Exec. Cttee; Fellow, Radio Acad. 2000; Royal TV Soc. Journalism Awards 1980, 1982, 1988, Webby Award (World Service) 2001, Sony Radio Special Award (World Service) 2002, One World Special Award (World Service) 2002. *Publication:* A Name on a Wall 2013. *Leisure interests:* family life, soccer, cricket, rock music, being surrounded by children. *Address:* Bolberry House, 1 Clifton Hill, Winchester, Hants., SO22 5BL, England (home). *Telephone:* (1962) 860197 (home).

BYNG, (James Edmund) Jamie, BA; British publishing director; *CEO, Canongate Books;* b. 27 June 1969, Winchester; s. of Thomas Edmund Byng (8th Earl of Strafford) and Jennifer May; m. 1st (divorced); one s. one d.; m. 2nd Elizabeth Sheinkman 2005; ed Univ. of Edinburgh; joined Canongate Books as unpaid worker 1992, bought the co. 1994, apptd Man. Dir 1994, now CEO; f. World Book Night. *Address:* Canongate Books, 14 High Street, Edinburgh, EH1 1TE, Scotland (office); Canongate Books, Basement, 151 Chesterton Road, London, W10 6ET, England (office). *Telephone:* (131) 557-5111 (office); (20) 8969-6011 (office). *Fax:* (131) 557-5211 (office); (20) 8969-8462 (office). *E-mail:* info@canongate.co.uk (office). *Website:* www.canongate.co.uk (office); www.worldbooknight.org.

BYRNE, David, BA, BL, SC; Irish barrister and politician; *Chancellor Emeritus, Dublin City University;* b. 6 April 1947; m.; three c.; ed Dominican Coll., Newbridge, Univ. Coll. Dublin, King's Inns, Dublin; Founder Free Legal Aid Centre (FLAC) (student org. providing legal services), Dublin 1968; called to the Bar 1970; mem. Bar Council 1974–87; mem. Exec. Cttee, Irish Maritime Law Asscn 1974–92; called to Inner Bar 1985; mem. Nat. Cttee, ICC 1988–97; mem. Govt Review Body on Social Welfare Law 1989, ICC Int. Court of Arbitration, Paris 1990–97, Constitution Review Group 1995–96; External Examiner for Arbitration and Competition Law, King's Inns 1995–97; Attorney-Gen. of Ireland 1997–99; mem. Council of State, Cabinet Sub-cttees on Social Inclusion, European Affairs, Child Abuse; EU Commr for Health and Consumer Protection (with particular responsibility for Food Safety, Public Health and Consumer Protection) 1999–2004; apptd Special Envoy, WHO 2004; apptd Chancellor, Dublin City Univ. 2006, now Chancellor Emer.; fmr Adjunct Prof. of Law, Univ. Coll. Dublin; Founder-mem. and Co-Chair. European Alliance for Personalised Medicine; Chair. Int. Prevention Research Inst. (iPRI) Ethics Cttee; Chair. Nat. Treasury Management Agency Advisory Cttee; Deputy Chair. DCC plc; mem. Bd of Dirs Kingspan Plc; mem. Barristers' Professional Practices and Ethics Cttee 1995–97, World Prevention Alliance; Fellow, Chartered Inst. of Arbitrators of England and Ireland 1998–; Patron Health First Europe; Hon. Treasurer, Bar Council 1982–83, Hon. Chair. World Justice Council, Hon. Fellow, FRCPI, FRCP; Dr hc (Univ. Coll. Dublin) 2004. *Achievements include:* while Attorney-Gen. participated in negotiation of Good Friday Agreement April 1998. *Publications:* numerous papers on legal affairs. *Address:* European Alliance for Personalised Medicine, Avenue de l'Armee, Legerlaan 10, 1040 Brussels, Belgium. *Website:* euapm.eu.

BYRNE, David; American musician, songwriter, composer, director and writer; b. 14 May 1952, Dumbarton, Scotland; s. of Thomas Byrne and Emily Anderson Byrne (née Brown); m. Adele Lutz 1987; one c.; ed Rhode Island School of Design, Maryland Inst. Coll. of Art; Founder-mem. Talking Heads 1974–92; solo artist, musician, composer, producer 1980–; producer for artists, including B-52s, Fun Boy 3, Margareth Menezes; producer Index Video 1983–; dir videotapes 1981–; designer stage sets, lighting, album covers and posters 1977–; f. Luaka Bop label 1988; Curator, Meltdown festival, Southbank Centre, London 2015; Film Critics Award for Best Documentary 1985, MTV Video Vanguard Award 1985, Music Video Producers Asscn Award 1992, inducted into Rock and Roll Hall of Fame 2002. *Compositions for film, television and theatre include:* Stop Making Sense 1984, The Knee Plays 1984, Alive from Off Center 1984, Dead End Kids 1986, True Stories 1986, Tribute 1986, The Kitchen Presents Two Moon July 1986, True Stories 1986, The Forest 1986, Something Wild 1986, The Last Emperor (Acad. Award for Best Music, Original Score 1988, Golden Globe Best Original Score - Motion Picture 1988, Grammy Award for Best Album of Original Instrumental Background Score Written for a Motion Picture or Television 1988, Los Angeles Film Critics Asscn Award for Best Music 1987) 1987, Married to the Mob 1988, A Rustling of Leaves: Inside the Philippine Revolution 1988, The Catherine Wheel 1988, Magicians of the Earth: The Giant Woman and The Lightning Man (TV) 1990, Magicians of the Earth: A Young Man's Dream and a Woman's Secret (TV) 1990, Blue in the Face 1995, In Spite of Wishing and Wanting 2002, Young Adam 2003, This Must be the Place (David di Donatello Award for Best Music and Best Song 2012) 2011. *Films include:* Stop Making Sense (actor) 1984, True Stories (actor, dir and co-screenwriter) 1986, Checking Out 1988, This Must Be the Place (as himself) 2011. *Recordings include:* albums: with Talking Heads: Talking Heads '77 1977, More Songs About Buildings And Food 1978, Fear Of Music 1979, Remain In Light 1980, The Name Of This Band Is Talking Heads 1982, Speaking In Tongues 1983, Stop Making Sense 1984, Little Creatures 1985, True Stories 1986, Naked 1988, Popular Favourites: Sand In The Vaseline 1992; solo: My Life In The Bush Of Ghosts (with Brian Eno) 1981, The Knee Plays 1985, The Forest 1988, Rei Momo 1989, Uh-Oh 1992, David Byrne 1994, Feelings 1997, Look Into The Eyeball 2001, Grown Backwards 2004, Big Love: Hymnal 2008, Everything that Happens will Happen Today (with Brian Eno) 2008, Here Lies Love (with Fatboy Slim) 2010, Love This Giant (with St Vincent) 2012, Caetano Veloso And David Byrne: Live At Carnegie Hall 2012, American Utopia 2018. *Publications include:* Stay Up Late 1987, What the Songs Look Like 1987, Strange Ritual 1995, Bicycle Diaries 2009, How Music Works 2012. *Address:* Maine Road Management, 195 Chrystie Street, Suite 901F, New York, NY 10002, USA (office). *Telephone:* (212) 979-9004 (office). *Fax:* (212) 979-0985 (office). *E-mail:* mailbox@maineroadmanagement.com (office). *Website:* www.maineroadmanagement.com (office); www.davidbyrne.com.

BYRNE, Edward, AO, AC, MB BS, MD, DSc, MBA, FRCP, FRCPE, FRACP; Australian neuroscientist, academic and university administrator; *President and Principal, King's College London;* b. 1952; m. Melissa Byrne; ed Univs of Tasmania, Melbourne, Adelaide and Queensland; Muscular Dystrophy Research Fellow, Univ. Coll. London (UCL) Inst. of Neurology 1980–82, Exec. Dean of Medicine, Univ. Coll. and Royal Free Medical School and Vice-Provost (Health), UCL 2007–09; Neurology Registrar, Royal Adelaide Hosp. 1978–80; Dir of Neurology, St Vincent's Hosp., Melbourne 1983; Founding Dir Melbourne Neuromuscular Research Unit, Centre for Neuroscience, Univ. of Melbourne, fmr Prof. of Experimental Neurology; Dean, Faculty of Medicine, Nursing and Health Sciences, Monash Univ. 2003–07, Vice-Chancellor and Pres. Monash Univ. 2009–14, now Prof. Emer.; Pres. and Prin., King's College London 2014–; Dir (non-Exec.) Cochlear Pty Ltd 2002–, BUPA 2008–09, BUPA Australia 2009–14; Hon. DSc (Univ. of Warwick) 2013, (Western Univ.) 2015; Hon. MD (Univ. od Adelaide) 2014; UCL Queen Square Prize for Neurological Research 1982, Bethlehem Griffith Research Medal 2003, Sir Louis Pyke Award for Contribution to Multiple Sclerosis 2004, John Sands Medal 2005, Alumnus of the Year, Univ. of Tasmania 2010. *Publications include:* 200 publs on neurology and neuroscience; Poems from the City, a London Interlude. *Leisure interests:* fly fishing, classical music. *Address:* Office of the Principal, 5th floor, James Clerk Maxwell Building, 57 Waterloo Road, London, SE1 8WA, England (office). *Telephone:* (20) 7848-3434 (office). *Fax:* (20) 7848-3430 (office). *E-mail:* principal@kcl.ac.uk (office). *Website:* www.kcl.ac.uk/aboutkings/principal/index.aspx (office).

BYRNE, Gabriel; Irish actor; b. 12 May 1950, Dublin; s. of Dan Byrne and Eileen Gannon; m. Ellen Barkin (q.v.) 1988 (divorced 1999); two c.; m. Hannah Beth King 2014; ed Univ. Coll. Dublin; archaeologist, then teacher, began acting in amateur productions; joined an experimental repertory co. 1980; first TV appearance in series The Riordans 1982; first cinema role in Excalibur; moved to New York 1987; f. Plurabelle Films (production co.) 1985; Patron, The West of Ireland Cardiology Foundation 1997–; apptd Amb. UNICEF Ireland 2004; Hon. Patron, Univ. Philosophical Soc., Trinity Coll. 2007; Hon. degree (Nat. Univ. of Ireland, Galway) 2007; Maverick Tribute Award, Cinequest San Jose Film Festival 1999, Volta Award, Jameson Dublin Int. Film Festival 2007, Lifetime Achievement Award, Irish Film and Television Awards 2018. *Theatre:* several roles Nat. Theatre, London; A Touch of the Poet (Broadway) 2005, Camelot (Avery Fisher Hall) 2008, Long Day's Journey into Night (Broadway) 2016. *Films include:* Hanna K 1983, Gothic (Int. Fantasy Film Award for Best Actor 1987) 1986, Julia and Julia 1987, Siesta 1987, Miller's Crossing 1990, Dark Obsession 1989, Cool World 1992, A Dangerous Woman 1993, Little Women 1994, The Usual Suspects (Awards Circuit Community Award for Best Cast Ensemble 1995) 1995, Frankie Starlight 1995, Dead Man 1995, Last of the High Kings 1996, Mad Dog Time 1996, Somebody is Waiting 1996, The End of Violence (dir) 1997, This is the Sea 1997, Polish Wedding 1998, The Man in the Iron Mask 1998, Quest for Camelot (voice) 1998, An Ideal Husband, Enemy of the State 1998, Stigmata 1999, End of Days 1999, Canone inverso – making love 2000, Spider 2002, Virginia's Run 2002, Emmett's Mark 2002, Ghost Ship 2002, Shade 2003, Vanity Fair 2004, P.S. 2004, The Bridge of San Luis Rey 2004, Assault on Precinct 13 2005, Wah-Wah 2005, Played 2006, Jindabyne 2006, Emotional Arithmetic (aka Autumn Hearts: A New Beginning) 2007, Attack on Leningrad 2009, Perrier's Bounty 2009, I, Anna 2012, Capital 2012, All Things to All Men 2013, Just a Sigh 2013, Vampire Academy 2014, The 33 2015, Louder Than Bombs 2015, Carrie Pilby 2016, No Pay, Nudity 2016, Mad to Be Normal 2017, Lies We Tell 2017, In the Cloud 2018, Hereditary (also Exec. producer) 2018; co-producer In the Name of the Father. *Television includes:* Bracken (Jacob's Award for Best Actor in a TV Series-Drama 1979) 1980–82, Madigan Men 2000, Patrick (voice) 2004, Live from Lincoln Center (episode, Camelot) 2008, In Treatment (Golden Globe Award for Best Actor in a TV Series – Drama 2009) 2008–10, Secret State (series) 2012, Quirke (mini-series) 2013, Vikings (series) 2013, Maniac 2018 (mini-series). *Publications:* Pictures in My Head (autobiog.) 1994. *Address:* c/o ICM, 8942 Wilshire Blvd, Beverly Hills, CA 96211, USA (office); Plurabelle Films, 10125 Washington Blvd, #205, Culver City, CA 90232, USA. *Telephone:* (310) 244-6782 (Plurabelle).

BYRNE, John V., BA, MA, PhD; American oceanographer and academic; *President Emeritus, Oregon State University;* b. 9 May 1928, Hempstead, NY; s. of Frank E. Byrne and Kathleen Barry Byrne; m. Shirley O'Connor 1954; one s. three d.; ed Hamilton Coll., Clinton, NY, Columbia Univ. and Univ. of Southern Calif.; research geologist, Humble Oil & Refining, Houston, Tex. 1957–60; Assoc. Prof., Oregon State Univ., Corvallis 1960–66, Prof. of Oceanography 1966–, Chair, Oceanography 1968–72, Dean, Oceanography 1972–76, Dean, Research 1976–80, Vice-Pres. Research and Grad. Studies 1980–81, Pres. 1984–95, now Pres. Emer.; Program Dir Oceanography, NSF 1966–67; US Commr to Int. Whaling Comm. 1982–85; Exec. Dir Kellogg Comm. on Future of State and Land Grant Univs 1996–2000; Admin. Nat. Oceanic & Atmospheric Admin., Washington, DC 1981–84; Hon. Assoc. of Arts (Lynn-Benton Community Coll., Ore.); Hon. JD (Hamilton Coll.) 1994; Distinguished Service Award, Oregon State Univ. 1996, Carter Inspirational Teaching Award. *Leisure interests:* music, painting. *Address:* 811 SW Jefferson Avenue, Corvallis, OR 97333, USA (office). *Telephone:* (541) 737-3542. *Fax:* (541) 737-4380. *E-mail:* john.byrne@oregonstate.edu (office).

BYRNE, Rt Hon. Liam Dominic, PC, BA (Hons), MBA; British politician; b. 2 Oct. 1970, Warrington, Cheshire, England; m.; three c.; ed Burnt Mill School, Harlow, Univ. of Manchester, Harvard Business School, USA (Fulbright Scholar); early positions at Accenture and N.M. Rothschild & Sons; f. e-Government Solutions Ltd computer co. 2000; adviser to Labour Party on re-organisation of Millbank and nat. business campaign 1996–97; MP (Labour) for Birmingham Hodge Hill (by-election) 2004–10, (revised boundary at Gen. Election) 2010–; Under-Sec. of State for Care Services, Dept of Health 2005; Minister of State for Borders and Immigration 2006–08; Minister for the Cabinet Office and Chancellor of the Duchy of Lancaster 2008–09, Chief Sec. to the Treasury 2009–10; Shadow Chief Sec. to the Treasury May–Oct. 2010, Shadow Minister for the Cabinet Office 2010–11, Shadow Sec. of State for Work and Pensions and Policy Review Co-ordinator 2011–13, Shadow Minister for Business, Innovation and Skills 2013–15; mem. Amicus, Christian Socialist Movt, Fabian Soc.; fmr Assoc. Fellow, Social Market Foundation. *Publications:* Local Government Transformed 1996, Information Age Government 1998, Cities of Enterprise 2002, Britain in 2020 2003, Reinventing Government Again (co-author) 2004, Why Labour Won 2005, A Common Place 2007. *Address:* House of Commons, Westminster, London, SW1A 0AA, England (office). *Telephone:* (20) 7219-6953 (London) (office); (121) 789-7287 (Birmingham) (office). *Fax:* (20) 7219-1431 (London) (office); (121) 789-9824 (Birmingham) (office). *E-mail:* byrnel@parliament.uk (office). *Website:* www.parliament.uk/biographies/commons/mr-liam-byrne/1171 (office); liambyrne.co.uk.

BYRON, Rt Hon. Sir (Charles Michael) Dennis, Kt, PC, LLB, MA; Saint Kitts and Nevis barrister and judge; b. 4 July 1943, Basseterre; m. Lady Norma Virgen Byron; ed Fitzwilliam Coll., Univ. of Cambridge, UK; called to the Bar, Hon. Soc. of the Inner Temple, London, Barrister-at-Law, High Court of Justice in England and Wales 1965; pvt. practice as barrister throughout Leeward Islands, with chambers in St Kitts, Nevis and Anguilla 1966–82; apptd High Court Judge 1982; High Court Judge, East Caribbean Supreme Court 1982–90, Acting Chief Justice 1996–99, Chief Justice 1999–2004; Perm. Judge, Int. Criminal Tribunal for Rwanda, Tanzania 2004–07, Pres. 2007–11; Pres. Caribbean Court of Justice, Trinidad and Tobago 2011–18; Pres. Commonwealth Judicial Educ. Inst. 2000–; Yogis and Keddy Chair in Human Rights Law, Dalhousie Univ., Nova Scotia, Canada.

BYZANTINE, Julian Sarkis, ARCM; British classical guitarist and academic; *Senior Lecturer and Head of Classical Guitar Studies, Queensland Conservatorium, Griffith University, Australia;* b. 11 June 1945, London, England; s. of Carl Byzantine and Mavis Harris; ed Royal Coll. of Music (RCM), London and Accad. Chigiana, Siena, Italy; studied with John Williams at RCM, subsequently with Julian Bream and with Andrés Segovia and Alirio Diaz in Siena; taught at RAM, London 1966–68; Sr Lecturer in Guitar, Queensland Conservatorium, Griffith Univ., Australia; London debut, Wigmore Hall 1969; New York debut, Carnegie Hall 1980; has performed in 77 countries; has given concerts with leading British orchestras, including Royal Philharmonic, City of Birmingham Symphony, Scottish Chamber, BBC Symphony; numerous radio and TV appearances; awarded first ARCM for guitar 1966; scholarships to study with Segovia from Vaughan Williams and Gilbert Foyle Trusts. *Recordings include:* five solo albums, two recordings with flautist Gerhard Mallon. *Publications:* Arrangements of Six Albéniz Piano Works for Guitar 1984, Guitar Technique Rationalised 2002. *Leisure interests:* collecting oriental art, archaeology, tennis. *Address:* Flat 1, 42 Ennismore Gardens, London, SW7 1AQ, England. *Telephone:* (20) 7584-7486. *E-mail:* j.byzantine@griffith.edu.au. *Website:* www.julianbyzantine.net (home).

C

CAAMAÑO DOMÍNGUEZ, Francisco, DIur; Spanish lawyer, politician and academic; b. 8 Jan. 1963, Cee, A Coruña Prov.; m.; two d.; ed Univ. de Santiago de Compostela; Adjunct Prof., then Prof. of Constitutional Law, Univ. de Santiago de Compostela; counsel to Constitutional Court 1993–2002; Prof. of Constitutional Law, Univ. of Valencia 2002, 2015–; Dir Democracy and Local Govt Foundation 2001–04; Sec. of State for Constitutional and Parl. Affairs 2004–09; Minister of Justice 2009–11; Deputy, Galician Parl. (Partido Socialista Obrero Español—PSOE) 2011–15 (resgnd). *Address:* Faculty of Law, University of Valencia, Edificio Departamental Occidental, Campus dels Tarongers, Avda. dels Tarongers, s/n, 46022 Valencia, Spain.

CAAN, James; American actor and director; b. 26 March 1940, Bronx, New York; s. of Arthur Caan and Sophie Caan; m. 1st DeeJay Mathis 1961 (divorced 1966); one d.; m. 2nd Sheila Ryan 1976 (divorced 1977); one s.; m. 3rd Linda O'Gara 1995; two c.; ed Michigan State Univ., Hofstra Coll.; made theatre debut in the off-Broadway production of La Ronde 1960; Broadway debut in Blood Sweat and Stanley Poole, 1961; Outstanding Achievement in Acting, Hollywood Film Festival 1999. *Films include:* Irma La Douce 1963, Lady in a Cage 1964, The Glory Guys 1965, Countdown 1967, Games 1967, Eldorado 1967, Journey to Shiloh 1968, Submarine XI 1968, Man Without Mercy 1969, The Rain People 1969, Rabbit Run 1970, T. R. Baskin 1971, The Godfather 1972, Slither 1973, Cinderella Liberty 1975, Freebie and the Bean 1975, The Gambler 1975, Funny Lady 1975, Rollerball 1975, The Killer Elite 1975, Harry and Walter Go to New York 1976, Silent Movie 1976, A Bridge Too Far 1977, Another Man, Another Chance 1977, Comes a Horseman 1978, Chapter Two 1980, Thief 1982, Kiss Me Goodbye 1983, Bolero 1983, Gardens of Stone 1988, Alien Nation 1989, Dad 1989, Dick Tracy 1990, Misery 1991, For the Boys 1991, Dark Backward 1991, Honeymoon in Vegas 1992, Flesh and Bone 1993, The Program 1994, North Star 1995, Boy Called Hate 1995, Eraser 1996, Bulletproof 1996, Bottle Rocket 1996, This Is My Father 1997, Poodle Springs 1997, Blue Eyes 1998, The Yards 1999, The Way of the Gun 1999, In the Boom Boom Room 2000, Luckytown 2000, Viva Las Nowhere 2000, In the Shadows 2001, Night at the Golden Eagle 2002, City of Ghosts 2002, Dogville 2003, This Thing of Ours 2003, Jericho Mansions 2003, Elf 2003, Get Smart 2008, Cloudy with a Chance of Meatballs (voice) 2009, Middle Men 2010, Henry's Crime 2010, Minkow 2011, Detachment 2011, Tower Heist 2011, Small Apartments 2012, That's My Boy 2010, For the Love of Money 2012, Blood Ties 2013, A Fighting Man 2014, Preggoland 2014, The Outsider 2014, The Throwaways 2015, Minkow 2015; dir and actor Hide in Plain Sight 1980, dir Violent Streets 1981. *Television includes:* Brian's Song (film) 1971, Las Vegas (series) 2003–07, Magic City (series) 2013, Back in the Game (series) 2013–14, and numerous other TV appearances.

CABALLERO GÓMEZ, Paula, MA; Colombian government official; *Director of Economic, Social and Environmental Affairs, Ministry of Foreign Affairs;* ed Phillips Acad. and Brown Univ., USA, Universidad Pontificia Javeriana, Int. Inst. for Climate and Society, Columbia Univ. and UNDP; Researcher, Centre for Int. Studies, Universidad de Los Andes, Bogotá 1986–87; Dir of Public Relations, Colombian Asscn of Flower Exporters (ASOCOLFLORES), Bogotá 1988–89; journalist, El Espectador newspaper, Bogotá 1990; Counsellor, Perm. Mission to UN, New York 1992–93; Adviser on Bilateral Issues, Council for Defence and Nat. Security, Presidency of the Repub. 1994; Adviser on Environmental Issues to Minister of Foreign Affairs 1994–96; Colombia Sub-Dir, Fundación para la Educación Superior (FES) Andean Program for Environment and Sustainable Devt 1997–99; Academic Dir, Environmental Area, School of Law, Universidad de Los Andes 1997–2000; Asst Exec. Dir, Advisory Cttee on Protection of the Sea (ACOPS), London (based in Bogotá) 2000–03, Sr Policy Consultant 2003–04; also worked for many years at UNDP, managing diverse projects on biodiversity, land degradation and territorial approaches to climate change, including as Regional Tech. Advisor in Natural Resource Man. for Latin America and the Caribbean, P5 level 2005–10; Dir of Econ., Social and Environmental Affairs, Ministry of Foreign Affairs 2010–; GEF Council mem. for the Colombia-Brazil-Ecuador Constituency 2010–12; mem. External Advisory Group, Vice-Presidency for Sustainable Devt, IBRD (World Bank) 2012–; Zayed Int. Prize - Category 3: Environmental action leading to positive change in society (co-recipient) 2014. *Leisure interests:* private pilot, diver. *Address:* Ministry of Foreign Affairs, Palacio de San Carlos, Calle 10, No 5-51, Bogotá, DC, Colombia (office). *Telephone:* (1) 381-4000 (office). *Fax:* (1) 381-4747 (office). *E-mail:* cancilleria@cancilleria.gov.co (office). *Website:* www.cancilleria.gov.co (office).

CABALLEROS, Rómulo Alfredo; Guatemalan economist, diplomatist and politician; b. 29 March 1941; m. Nora Wellmann de Caballeros; ed Univ. de San Carlos de Guatemala, Centro Interamericano de Enseñanza Estaística (CIENES), Instituto Latinoamericano de Planificación Economica y Social (ILPES), Univ. de Madrid, Spain; worked at Bank of Guatemala 1962–72; consultant to Dept of Gen. Studies, Secr. Gen. of Econ. Planning 1972–73, Dir 1973–75; consultant to UNDP 1975; Econ. Affairs Exec., Econ. Comm. for Latin America and the Caribbean (CEPAL) 1975–79, Deputy Head of Econ. Devt, Int. Trade and Statistics Section 1976–81, Head of Section 1983–90, Deputy Dir CEPAL Satellite Office, Mexico 1990–92, 1994–96, Dir Planning, Programmes and Operations Div. 1996–97, Dir Sub-regional Office, Mexico 1997–2000; Sec.-Gen. of Econ. Planning 1993; Amb. to Mexico 2000–02; consultant to EC, UN, IDB, World Bank 2002–07; Minister of the Economy 2008–09; currently consultant; Orden del Águila Azteca (Mexico).

CABALLEROS LÓPEZ, Harold Osberto, MA, MBA; Guatemalan lawyer, business executive and politician; *Secretary-General, Visión con Valores;* b. 20 June 1956, Guatemala City; s. of Osberto Caballeros and Coralia López; m. Cecilia Arimany; two s. two d.; ed Universidad Francisco Marroquin, Univ. of Miami, Harvard Univ., Fletcher School of Law and Diplomacy, Tufts Univ., USA; pvt practice as lawyer 1983–; f. El Shaddai Ministries, 20 years as pastor; f. Visión con Valores political party 2006, Sec.-Gen. 2009–; unsuccessful cand. for Pres. of Guatemala 2011; Minister of Foreign Affairs 2012–13; Chair. Bd of Trustees, Universidad San Pablo de Guatemala; Founder and Pres. Radios Vision Corpn. *Publications:* De Victoria en Victoria 1999, Dios te invita a soñar 2002, El poder transformador del evangelio de Jesucristo 2003, El poder transformador del avivamiento 2005. *Address:* Visión con Valores, 41 Calle 3-45, Zona 8, Guatemala City, Guatemala (office). *Telephone:* 2243-2999 (office). *E-mail:* contacto@visionconvalores.com (office). *Website:* www.visionconvalores.com (office).

CABEZAS MOLINA, Eduardo; Ecuadorean economist, diplomatist and fmr central banker; m. Berta Cabezas; ed Universidad Cen. del Ecuador, Queen's Coll., New York, USA; Minister, Embassy in Bonn 1981–84, Amb. to Uruguay 1994, to Guatemala –2003, to UK (also accred to Portugal) 2003–06, 2008–10; Pres. Cen. Bank of Ecuador 2006–08; Chair. Ministry of Foreign Relations Safety Improvement 2010–12, Pres. Administrative Improvement Fund of the Ministry of Foreign Affairs (pvt. entity) 2010–14.

CABEZAS MORALES, Rodrigo Eduardo; Venezuelan politician and economist; *Chairman, Grupo Parlamentario Venezolano;* b. 19 June 1956, Valera, Trujillo state; m.; ed Univ. of Zulia; mem. Faculty, Univ. of Zulia 1982–, currently Prof. and mem. Instituto de Investigaciones; Deputy, Congreso de la República 1990–93, 1994–98, Asamblea Nacional 2000–04, Vice-Chair. Asamblea Nacional Finance Comm. 2000–01, Chair. 2002–06; Minister of Finance 2007–08; Chair. Parlamento Latinoamericano, Grupo Parlamentario Venezolano 2011–; Bd mem. Nat. Council on Culture 2002; mem. Por la Democracia Social (PODEMOS) party. *Address:* Grupo Parlamentario Venezolano, Edificio La Perla, Mezzanina - Piso 1. Caracas Distrito Capital 1010, Correo de Carmelitas Caracas, 5971 Caracas, Venezuela (office). *E-mail:* contacto@podemos.org.ve (office). *Website:* www.parlatino.org.ve (office).

CABI, Martinho N'Dafa; Guinea-Bissau politician; b. 17 Sept. 1957, Nhacra, Oio Prov.; s. of Cabi Imbitna and Tchambu Insol; mem. Balanta ethnic group; joined Partido Africano da Independência da Guiné e Cabo Verde (PAIGC) 1974, various roles including Chair. Cttee for Autonomous Region of Guinea-Bissau, mem. Cen. Cttee 1999, Third Vice-Pres. 2002–07; fmr Minister of Energy; Minister of Nat. Defence 2004–05; Prime Minister 2007–08. *Website:* www.paigc.org (office).

CABLE, Sir (John) Vincent (Vince), Kt, BA, PhD; British politician and economist; *Leader, Liberal Democrat Party;* b. 9 May 1943, York, N Yorks.; m. 1st Olympia Rebelo 1968 (died 2001); three c.; m. 2nd Rachel Wenban Smith 2004; ed Nunthorpe Grammar School, Fitzwilliam Coll., Cambridge, Univ. of Glasgow; mem. Liberal Party 1963–65, Labour Party 1966–82, Social Democratic Party (SDP) 1982–88; Pres. Cambridge Union 1965; fmr Pres.-elect Cambridge Univ. Liberal Club (resgnd from Liberals before taking up office); Treasury Finance Officer for Govt of Kenya 1966–68; fmr Lecturer in Econs, Univ. of Glasgow, LSE; Councillor (Labour), Glasgow City Council 1971–74; First Sec., FCO 1974–76; Deputy Dir Overseas Devt Inst., including as a Special Adviser to then Sec. of State for Trade and Industry, John Smith MP 1970s; worked as Special Adviser on Econ. Affairs for Commonwealth Sec.-Gen., Sir Sonny Ramphal 1983–90; worked for Shell International from 1990, Chief Economist 1995–97; fmr Head of Econs Programme, Chatham House; contested Glasgow Hillhead (Labour) constituency 1970, York (SDP/Liberal Alliance) 1983, 1987, Twickenham (Liberal Democrat) 1992; MP for Twickenham 1997–2015, 2017–; Liberal Democrat Spokesperson for Treasury (EMU and The City) 1997–99, 2017–, Prin. Spokesperson for Trade and Industry 1999–2003, Shadow Chancellor of the Exchequer 2003–10; Sec. of State for Business, Innovation and Skills and Pres. Bd of Trade 2010–15; Deputy Leader, Liberal Democrat Party 2006–10, Acting Leader 2007, Leader 2017–; mem. (Select Cttees), Treasury (Treasury Sub-cttee) 1998–99, Treasury 1998–99; mem. Competitiveness Council, Council of the EU 2010–; Fellow, Nuffield Coll., Oxford; Visiting Research Fellow, Centre for the Study of Global Governance, LSE 2001–04; Patron, Polycystic Kidney Disease Charity; Liberal Democrat. *Publications:* Protectionism and Industrial Decline 1983, The New Giants: China and India 1994, The World's New Fissures: The Politics of Identity 1995, Globalisation and Global Governance 1999, Multiple Identities 2005, Public Services: Reform with a Purpose 2005, The Storm: The World Economic Crisis and What It Means 2009, Tackling the Fiscal Crisis: A Recovery Plan for the UK 2009. *Address:* Liberal Democrat Party, 8–10 Great George St, London, SW1P 3AE (office); Constituency Office, 2A Lion Road, Twickenham, TW1 4JQ, England (office). *Telephone:* (20) 7222-7999 (Liberal Democrats) (office). *Fax:* (20) 7799-2170 (Liberal Democrats) (office). *Website:* www.libdems.org.uk (office); vincentcable.org.uk.

CABRAAL, Ajith Nivard; Sri Lankan chartered accountant and fmr central banker; *Principal Consultant, Cabraal Consulting Group (Pvt) Ltd;* b. 14 Dec. 1954; est. own man. consultancy before taking up public service 2005; fmr Chair. and/or Dir of several quoted and unquoted public cos; Sec., Ministry of Plan Implementation and Adviser to Pres. on Econ. Affairs –2006, also served as mem. Bd Strategic Enterprises Man. Agency; mem. Govt Team at Geneva Talks with Liberation Tigers of Tamil Eelam Feb. 2006; represented Govt in Millennium Challenge Fund negotiations with US Govt; Gov. Cen. Bank of Sri Lanka 2006–15 (resgnd), also Chair. Monetary Bd; currently Prin. Consultant, Cabraal Consulting Group (Pvt) Ltd; Chair. Capital Reach Holdings Group; fmr Eisenhower Fellow; Founder-Chair. Corp. Governance Cttee; fmr Pres. Business Recovery and Insolvency Practitioners Asscn of Sri Lanka; Past Pres. Inst. of Chartered Accountants of Sri Lanka, S Asian Fed. of Accountants, St Peter's Coll. Old Boys Union; fmr mem. Bd Securities and Exchange Comm., Nat. Inst. of Business Man., Postgraduate Inst. of Man., Univ. of Moratuwa. *Publications include:* Towards a Sri Lankan Renaissance, Lak Mawata Muthu Potak (A String of Pearls for Mother Lanka, collection of more than 60 short essays submitted to popular nat. newspapers 2003–04). *Address:* Cabraal Consulting Group (Pvt) Ltd, 18/1, School Lane, Nawala, Sri Lanka (office). *E-mail:* nivard@eureka.lk (office).

CABRAL BARRETO, Ireneu; Portuguese judge and government official; *Representative of the Portuguese Republic in the Autonomous Region of Madeira;* b. 5 Feb. 1941, Ponta do Sol, Madeira; ed Coimbra Law Univ.; Asst to Dist Attorney for Ourique, S Vicente, Vila Nova de Famalicão, Vila Verde, Portimão and Lisbon 1964–70; Judge, São Jorge co. 1971–72; Asst to Dist Attorney for Bragança, Évora and Setúbal 1972–75; Deputy Attorney Gen. of Portugal 1975–97; Legal Adviser, Ministry of Trade and Tourism 1975–77; Judge, Supreme Court of Justice

1997–98; mem. European Comm. of Human Rights 1993–99; Judge, European Court of Human Rights, Strasbourg 1998–2011; Rep. of Portuguese Repub. in Autonomous Region of Madeira 2011–. *Publications:* A Convenção Europeia dos Direitos do Homen (fifth edition) 2015; numerous articles in professional journals. *Address:* Palácio de São Lourenço, Apat n.° 142, Avenida Zarco 9001-902 Funchal, Madeira (office). *Telephone:* (291) 202530 (office). *Fax:* (291) 234626 (office). *E-mail:* geral@representantedarepublica-madeira.pt (office). *Website:* www.representantedarepublica-madeira.pt (office).

CABREJAS, Santiago Cembrano; Colombian government official and international organization official; ed Jorge Tadeo Lozano Univ.; fmr Dir of Econ. Integration, Ministry of Foreign Trade and Tourism; CEO Gen. Secr., Andean Community (Comunidad Andina) 2008–13, Sec.-Gen. a.i. March–June 2013. *Address:* c/o Ministry of Foreign Affairs, Palacio de San Carlos, Calle 10, No 5-51, Bogotá, DC, Colombia.

CABRERA, Miguel; Venezuelan professional baseball player; b. 18 April 1983, Maracay, Aragua State; s. of Miguel Cabrera and Gregoria Cabrera; m. Rosangel Cabrera; one s. two d.; major league debut at age 20 with Florida Marlins 2003, playing as infielder 2003–07, traded to Detroit Tigers 2008–; mem. Venezuelan nat. team, World Baseball Classic 2009; f. Miguel Cabrera Foundation 2012. *Achievements include:* led American League in home runs 2008, 2012, RBI (runs batted in) 2010, 2012, batting average 2011, 2012, 2013, 2015 (won Triple Crown 2012, first player since 1967), American League Most Valuable Player 2012, 2013, mem. National League All-Star team 2004–07, American League All-Star team 2010–15. *Address:* c/o Detroit Tigers, Comerica Park, 2100 Woodward Avenue, Detroit, MI 48201-3470, USA (office). *Website:* detroit.tigers.mlb.com (office).

CACCIAVILLAN, HE Cardinal Agostino, DCnL, DCL; Italian ecclesiastic and diplomatist; b. 14 Aug. 1926, Novale; ordained priest of Vicenza 1949; joined Holy See diplomatic service 1959, served in Philippines, Spain, Portugal; Head Documentation and Information Office, Secr. of State, Vatican City 1969–76; Apostolic Pro-Nuncio to Kenya, Apostolic Del. to Seychelles 1976–81; Apostolic Pro-Nuncio to India 1981–90, to Nepal 1985–90, to USA 1990–98; Pres. Admin. Patrimony of the Apostolic See 1998–2002, now Pres. Emer.; mem. Pontifical Comm. for Vatican City State; Perm. Observer to OAS 1990–98; cr. Cardinal 2001, Cardinal-Deacon of Ss Angeli Custodi a Città Giardino; Kt Grand Cross, Order of the Holy Sepulchre. *Address:* c/o Patrimony of the Apostolic See, Palazzo Apostolico, 00120 Vatican City, Italy.

CÁCERES CHÁVEZ, Juan Ramón Carlos Enrique; Salvadorean banker and politician; ed Univ. of Leuven, Belgium, Universidad Tecnologica de El Salvador; f. Carlos Cáceres Soluciones Financieras (consulting firm); Exec. Dir Asociación Bancaria Salvadoreña (ABANSA) 2006–09; Minister of Finance 2009–18. *Address:* c/o Ministry of Finance, Blvd Los Héroes 1231, San Salvador, El Salvador (office).

ČAČIĆ, Radimir; Croatian business executive and politician; b. 11 May 1949, Zagreb; m.; ed Univ. of Zagreb; began career with Interpublic, Zagreb 1973–77; Founder, Dir and Prin. Pvt. Shareholder, Coning, Varaždin 1978–2000; Founder Zagal (now Croatia Airlines) 1990; served as Brig. in Croatian Army 1991; mem. Constitutional Comm. for drafting new constitution of Repub. of Croatia 1990; Founding mem. Croatian People's Party—Liberal Democrats (Hrvatska narodna stranka—liberalni demokrati, HNS) 1990–2013, mem. Presidency 1990, Vice-Pres. 1993, Pres. 1994–2000, 2008–13; Pres. People's Party - Reformists (Narodna stranka - Reformisti) 2014–; mem. Sabor (Parl.) 1995–; Minister for Public Works, Reconstruction and Devt 2000–03, Deputy Prime Minister and Minister of the Economy 2011–12 (resgnd); served prison sentence for causing traffic accident 2013–14; Pres. Croatian Tennis Fed. 2002–11; Independence War Medal, Order of Prince Domagoj with Neckband. *Leisure interests:* tennis, reading. *Address:* People's Party - Reformists, 10000 Zagreb, Pavla Hatza 12, Croatia (office). *Telephone:* (1) 5513687 (office). *E-mail:* reformisti@reformisti.hr (office). *Website:* www.reformisti.hr (office).

CADBURY, Sir (Nicholas) Dominic, Kt, KBE, MBA; British business executive; b. 12 May 1940; s. of Laurence John Cadbury and Joyce Cadbury (née Mathews); m. Cecilia Sarah Symes 1972; three d.; ed Eton Coll., Trinity Coll., Cambridge, Stanford Univ., USA; Chief Exec. Cadbury Schweppes PLC 1984–93, Chair. 1993–2000; Dir Economist Group 1990–2003, Chair. 1994–2003; Jt Deputy Chair. Guinness (now Diageo PLC) 1994–97, Deputy Chair. 1996; Jt Deputy Chair. EMI Group PLC 1999–2004; Chair. The Wellcome Trust 2000–06, Transense Techs 2000–03; Pres. Food and Drink Fed. 1999; apptd Dir (non-exec.) Misys PLC 2000, interim Chair. 2005, Chair. 2006–09; apptd Sr Adviser, Financial Services Authority (FSA) 2009 (FSA dissolved 2013); mem. Royal Mint Advisory Cttee 1986–94, Pres.'s Cttee CBI 1989–94, Food Asscn 1989–2000, Stanford Advisory Council 1989–95; Chancellor Univ. of Birmingham 2002–13; Trustee Heart of England Community Foundation 2015–. *Leisure interests:* tennis, golf, shooting. *Address:* c/o Board of Trustees, Heart of England Community Foundation, PO Box 126, Torrington Avenue, Coventry, CV4 0UX, England.

CADET, Jean, LLM; French fmr diplomatist; b. 15 Oct. 1942; m. Elisabeth Cadet; three c.; ed Inst. d'études politiques de Paris, Ecole Nat. d'Admin; Attaché, Cen. Admin, Ministry of Justice 1968–70, Cen. Admin, Econ. and Financial Affairs 1972–75; apptd Minister Plenipotentiary 1977; Second Sec., Perm. Rep. to EC, Brussels 1978–82, Minister Counsellor 1986–92, First Sec., Embassy in Abidjan 1982–84, in Bonn 1984–86, Amb. to Greece 1992–94, to Austria 1997–2001, to South Africa 2001–03, Amb. (non-resident) to Lesotho 2002–03, to Russian Fed. 2003–06; Sec.-Gen. Inter-ministerial Cttee on European Econ. Cooperation 1995–97; Counsellor for European Affairs, Cabinet of the Prime Minister 1995–97; Conseiller Maitre, Cour des Comptes 2006–11; Officier, Légion d'honneur, Officier, Ordre nat. du Mérite.

ČAĐO, Stanislav; Bosnia and Herzegovina politician; b. 1961, Bosanska Gradiška; m.; two c.; ed Faculty of Law, Univ. of Banja Luka; worked for Vuk Karadžić publishing co.; Civil Servant, Dept for Social-Political Orgs, Laktaši Municipal Council; fmr Commercial Man., Sim Prom (import and export co.); fmr Gen. Man. Technogas; Minister of Internal Affairs, Republika Srpska 2006–13.

CADOGAN, Sir John Ivan George, Kt, CBE, PhD, FRS, FRSE, CChem, FRSC; British chemist and academic; b. 8 Oct. 1930, Pembrey, Carmarthenshire; s. of Alfred Cadogan and Dilys Cadogan; m. 1st Margaret Jeanne Evans 1955 (deceased 1992); one s. one d.; m. 2nd Elizabeth Purnell 1997; ed Grammar School, Swansea and King's Coll., London; research at King's Coll., London 1951–54; Civil Service Research Fellow 1954–56; Lecturer in Chem., King's Coll., London 1956–63; Purdie Prof. of Chem. and Head of Dept, St Salvator's Coll., Univ. of St Andrews 1963–69; Forbes Prof. of Organic Chem., Univ. of Edin. 1969–79; Chief Scientist, BP Research Centre 1979–81; Dir of Research, British Petroleum 1981–92, CEO BP Ventures 1988–92; Dir Gen. Research Council 1994–99; Chair. DNA Research Innovations Ltd 1999–2004; Science Policy Adviser, Science Foundation Ireland 1999–2005; Dir BP Chemicals Int. Ltd, BP Venezuela Ltd; Visiting Prof., Imperial Coll., London 1979–2002; Professorial Fellow, Univ. Coll. of Swansea, Univ. of Wales 1979–2007; Pres. Royal Soc. of Chem. 1982–84; Founding Fellow, Learned Soc. of Wales, inaugural Pres. and Chair of Council 2010–14; mem. Council, Royal Inst. 1984–87, Royal Comm. on Criminal Justice 1991–93; Gov. Jt Research Centre, EC 1994–; Chair. Fusion Antibodies Ltd 2005; Hon. Fellow, Royal Acad. of Eng 1992, Royal Soc. of Chem.; recipient of 20 fellowships and hon. degrees; several prizes, including Corday Morgan Medal, Prize of the Chemical Soc., Meldola Medal, Royal Inst. of Chem., Soc. of Chemical Industry Medal 2001, Lord Lewis Prize 2010, Royal Medal of Royal Soc. of Edinburgh 2013. *Publications:* about 300 papers in professional journals. *Leisure interests:* supporting rugby football, being in France, gardening.

CADOT, Michel François Jacques; French civil servant and administrator; *Prefect, Préfecture de Police, Paris;* b. 22 May 1954, Suresnes, Seine; s. of Jean Cadot and Elsa Cadot (née Puiatti); m. Catherine Van Luchene 1981; three s. two d.; ed Lycées Charlemagne and Henri IV, Paris, Univ. of Paris II Panthéon, Ecole Nat. d'Admin.; Civil Admin., Ministry of the Interior 1980; Asst Prefect, Dir of Cabinet of Prefect of Oise 1980–82; Sec.-Gen. of Prefecture of Cantal 1982–85; Civil Admin., Embassy in Venezuela 1985–88; Asst Prefect of Saint-Julien-en-Genevois 1988–89; Civil Admin., Elf Aquitaine 1989–93; Sec.-Gen. Elf Trading S.A. 1989–93; Asst Prefect of Béziers 1993–95; Prefect of Languedoc-Roussillon 1993–95, of Meuse 1998–2000, of Martinique 2000–04; Chief of Staff, Office of Sec. of State for Rural Devt 1995; Dir for Man. of Region of Datar 1995–98; Chief of Staff, Minister for Agric., Food and Fisheries 2004–06, Adviser to Prime Minister Dominique de Villepin 2006, then Chief of Staff to Sec. of State of the Interior; Prefect of Brittany region 2009–13, Provence-Alpes-Côte d'Azur 2013–15; Prefect, Préfecture de Police, Paris 2015–; Pres. of Bd Institut national des hautes études de la Sécurité et de la Justice 2009–13; Chevalier, Ordre National du Mérite, Officier, Légion d'honneur. *Address:* Préfecture de Police, 71 Rue Albert, 75013 Paris, France (office). *Telephone:* 1-53-71-53-71 (office). *Website:* www.prefecturedepolice.interieur.gouv.fr (office).

CAETANI, Oleg; Italian conductor; b. 5 Oct. 1956, Lausanne, Switzerland; s. of Igor Markevitch and Topazia Caetani; m. Susanna Stefani Caetani; three d. (two from previous m.); ed studied with Nadia Boulanger, Franco Ferrara in Rome, Kyrill Kondrashin in Moscow and Ilia Mussin in Leningrad; Asst to Otmar Suitner, Staatsoper Berlin 1981–84; Deutsche Nat. Theater Weimar 1984–87; Kapellmeister, Städtische Buhnen Frankfurt am Main; Music Dir Wiesbaden 1992–95, leading the Ring, Tristan und Isolde, La Forza del Destino, Otello, Rimsky's Invisible City of Kitezh and Bluebeard's Castle; guest engagements with Semiramide in Vienna, Les Vêpres Siciliennes in Nice, Lucia di Lammermoor and Tosca at Trieste and Verdi's Falstaff at Stuttgart 1996–97; Zurich Opera with Rigoletto, The Nutcracker, La Bohème and Norma; led Tchaikovsky's Maid of Orleans at Strasbourg 1998, Otello and Turandot at La Scala, Don Pasquale in Florence, The Flying Dutchman in Rome etc.; Oslo Opera Madama Butterfly 2012, Lady Macbeth of Mtsensk 2014; with ENO Khovanshchina 2003, Sir John in Love 2006, Madam Butterfly 2012, La Bohème 2013, ROH London Tosca 2014; concert repertoire includes all symphonies by Beethoven, Brahms, Schubert, Schumann, Shostakovich and Tchaikovsky, with soloists such as Martha Argerich, Viktoria Mullova, Shlomo Mintz and the late Sviatoslav Richter; Music Dir, Chemnitz 1996–2001; Chief Conductor Desig., Melbourne Symphony Orchestra 2003–04, Chief Conductor and Artistic Dir 2005–09; winner RAI Competition, Turin 1979, Herbert von Karajan Competition 1982. *E-mail:* caetanioffice@gmail.com. *Website:* www.olegcaetani.com.

CAFFARELLI, Luis A., MSc, PhD; Argentine/American mathematician and academic; *Sid Richardson Chair, University of Texas, Austin;* b. 8 Dec. 1948, Buenos Aires, Argentina; m. Irene M. Gamba; three s.; ed Univ. of Buenos Aires; Postdoctoral Researcher, Univ. of Minnesota 1973–74, Asst Prof. 1975–77, Assoc. Prof. 1977–79, Prof. 1979–83; Prof., Courant Inst. of Math. Sciences, New York Univ. 1980–82, 1994–97; Prof., Univ. of Chicago 1983–86; Perm. Faculty mem., Inst. for Advanced Study, Princeton 1986–96; Prof., Univ. of Texas, Austin 1997–, currently holds Sid Richardson Chair; Pres. of the Jury, Int. Math. Olympiad 1997, 2012; mem. NAS 1991, American Math. Soc., Union Matematica Argentina, Pontifical Acad. of Sciences; Foreign mem. Accad. Nazionale delle Scienze (dei XL, Italy), Accad. Nazionale dei Lincei (Italy), Academia Nacional de Ciencias, Buenos Aires, Academia Nacional de Ciencias, Cordoba, Insituto Lombardo, Accad. di Scienze e Lettere (Italy); Fellow, American Acad. of Arts and Sciences 1986; Hon. Prof., Universidad de Buenos Aires, Universidad de Mar del Plata; Dr hc (Universidad Autónoma de Madrid) 1992, (École Normale Superieure, Paris) 2003, (Universidad de La Plata) 2003, (Universidad de San Luis) 2007), (Univ. of Buenos Aires) 2012; Hon. DSc (Univ. of Notre Dame) 2012, (Univ. of Chicago) 2013; Stampacchia Prize (jtly) 1982, Bocher Prize 1984, Guggenheim Fellowship 1984, Pius XI Gold Medal, Pontifical Acad. of Sciences 1988, Premio Konex, Platino y Brillantes (Argentina) 2003, Rolf Schock Prize, Royal Swedish Acad. of Sciences 2005, Leroy P. Steele Prize for Lifetime Achievement, American Math. Soc. 2009, Rouse Ball Lecturer, Univ. of Cambridge 2011, Wolf Prize in Math. (jtly with Michael Aschbacher) 2012, Shaw Prize in Mathematical Sciences 2018. *Publications include:* Fully Nonlinear Elliptic Equations (co-author) 1995, A Geometric Approach to Free Boundary Problems (co-author) 2005; more than 260 articles on partial differential equations and their applications. *Address:* RLM 8.100, Department of Mathematics, University of Texas at Austin, 1 University Station C1200, Austin, TX 78712-1202, USA (office). *Telephone:* (512) 475-8635 (office). *Fax:* (512) 471-9038 (office). *E-mail:* caffarel@math.utexas.edu (office). *Website:* www.ma.utexas.edu/users/caffarel (office).

CAFFARELLI, Paulo Rogério, BL, MBA, MA; Brazilian business executive; *President of the Executive Board and CEO, Banco do Brasil;* b. 19 Sept. 1965; m.;

three c.; ed Fundação Getúlio Vargas, Rio de Janeiro, FAE Centro Universitário, Curitiba, Instituto Brasileiro de Estudos Jurídicos-Cursos, Curitiba, Universidade de Brasília; began career at Banco do Brasil, worked for more than 30 years in several Exec. Bd positions, held positions as Vice-Pres. of Debt and Credit Cards and New Retail Business and Vice-Pres. of Wholesale Business, Int. Business and Private Banking, also held positions as Dir in Distribution, Logistics, Marketing and Communication and New Retail Business Directorships, Pres. Exec. Bd and CEO Banco do Brasil 2016–; Exec. Dir, Companhia Siderúrgica Nacional 2015–, Exec. Dir of Investor Relations 2016–; Exec. Sec., Ministry of Finance 2014–15. *Address:* Banco do Brasil SA, SAUN Qd 5 lt B - Torre I - Ed.BB - 13º andar, 70040-912 Brasília, DF, Brazil (office). *Telephone:* (61) 3493-1000 (office); (61) 3310-5920 (office). *Fax:* (61) 3310-3735 (office). *E-mail:* presidencia@bb.com.br (office). *Website:* www.bb.com.br (office).

CAFU; Brazilian professional footballer (retd); b. (Marcos Evangelista de Moraes), 7 June 1970, São Paulo; m. Regina de Morales; defender (right back); played with São Paulo 1989–94 (115 appearances, seven goals, won Campeonato Brasileiro Série A 1991, Copa Conmebol 1994, Supercopa Sudamericana 1993), Juventude 1995, Real Zaragoza 1995, Palmeiras 1996–97 (won Torneio Maria Quitéria 1997), Roma, Italy 1997–2003 (won Serie A 2000–01), AC Milan, Italy 2003–08 (won Serie A 2003–04, Supercoppa Italiana 2004, UEFA Champions League 2007, UEFA Super Cup 2007, FIFA Club World Cup 2007); mem. Brazil nat. team 1990–2006 (retd), 142 int. caps (record), scored five goals; only player to have played in three World Cup final matches, mem. winning team for FIFA World Cup 1994, 2002 (Capt.), FIFA Confederations Cup 1997, Copa América 1997, 1999; Brazilian record of 21 World Cup appearances; Officer, Order of Rio Branco 2008; South American Footballer of the Year 1994, named by Pelé as one of the top 125 greatest living footballers 2004. *Address:* Fundação Cafu, Rua Alves de Souza, 65 Jardim Amalia, São Paulo, SP 05890-010, Brazil (office). *Telephone:* (11) 5821-6786 (office). *E-mail:* cafu@fundacaocafu.org.br (office). *Website:* www.fundacaocafu.org.br (office).

CAGE, Nicolas; American actor and film company executive; b. (Nicolas Coppola), 7 Jan. 1964, Los Angeles, Calif.; s. of Prof. August Coppola and Joy Vogelsang; nephew of Francis Ford Coppola (q.v.); m. 1st Patricia Arquette (q.v.) 1995 (divorced 2001); m. 2nd Lisa Marie Presley 2002 (divorced 2004); m. 3rd Alice Kim 2004, one s.; one s. with Christina Fulton; ed studied theatre at Beverly Hills High; changed his name early in his career to make his own reputation; secured bit part in Fast Times at Ridgemont High 1982; took job selling popcorn at Fairfax Theater; then landed role in his uncle's film Rumble Fish 1983 followed by role as punk-rocker in Valley Girl 1983 (released first) which launched his career; f. Saturn Films (production co.); Dr hc (California State, Fullerton); numerous awards including Acad. Award for Best Actor 1996, Golden Globe Award for Best Actor 1996, Lifetime Achievement Award 1996, P. J. Owens Award 1998, Charles A. Crain Desert Palm Award 2001, UN Global Citizen of the Year Award for humanitarian endeavours 2009. *Films include:* Fast Times at Ridgemont High 1982, Valley Girl 1983, Rumble Fish 1983, Racing with the Moon 1984, The Cotton Club 1984, Birdy 1984, The Boy in Blue 1986, Peggy Sue Got Married 1986, Raising Arizona 1987, Moonstruck 1987, Vampire's Kiss 1989, Tempo di uccidere (aka Le raccourci, aka The Short Cut, aka Time to Kill) 1989, Fire Birds 1990, Wild at Heart 1990, Zandalee 1991, Red Rock West 1992, Honeymoon in Vegas 1992, Amos & Andrew 1993, Deadfall 1993, Guarding Tess 1994, It Could Happen to You 1994, Trapped in Paradise 1994, Kiss of Death 1995, Leaving Las Vegas (Golden Globe Award for Best Actor 1996, Acad. Award for Best Actor 1996) 1995, The Rock 1996, The Funeral 1996, Con Air 1997, Face/Off 1997, City of Angels 1998, Snake Eyes 1998, 8MM 1999, Bringing Out the Dead 1999, Gone in 60 Seconds 2000, The Family Man 2001, Captain Corelli's Mandolin 2001, Christmas Carol: The Movie (voice) 2001, Windtalkers 2002, Sonny 2002, Adaptation 2003, Matchstick Men 2003, National Treasure 2004, Lord of War 2005, The Weather Man 2005, The Ant Bully (voice) 2006, World Trade Center 2006, The Wicker Man 2006, Ghost Rider 2006, Grindhouse 2007, Next 2007, National Treasure: Book of Secrets 2007, Bangkok Dangerous 2007, Knowing 2009, G-Force (voice) 2009, The Bad Lieutenant: Port of Call – New Orleans 2009, Astro Boy (voice) 2009, Kick-Ass 2010, The Sorcerer's Apprentice 2010, Season of the Witch 2011, Angry 2011, Trespass 2011, Ghost Rider: Spirit of Vengeance 2011, Seeking Justice 2011, Stolen 2012, The Frozen Ground 2012, The Croods 2013, Joe 2014, Rage 2014, The Trust 2016, Mom and Dad 2017, Mandy 2018, Spider-Man: Into the Spider Verse 2018, Between Worlds 2018. *Television includes:* Best of Times 1981, Industrial Symphony No. 1: The Dream of the Brokenhearted 1990. *Address:* c/o Creative Artists Agency, 2000 Avenue of the Stars, Los Angeles, CA 90067, USA (office); Saturn Films, 9000 West Sunset Boulevard, Suite 911, West Hollywood, CA 90069, USA (office). *Website:* www.saturnfilms.com.

ÇAĞLAYAN, Zafer; Turkish business executive and politician; b. 1957, Muş; m.; two c.; ed Gazi Univ.; fmr Chair. Çağlayanlar Alüminyum Ltd, Akel Alüminyum A.Ş; Chair. Ankara Chamber of Industry (ASO) 1995–2007; Deputy Chair. Turkish Union of Chambers and Commodities Exchanges (TOBB) 2005–07; mem. Parl. (AKP) 2007–; Minister of Industry and Trade 2007–09, Minister of State 2009–11, Minister of Econ. Affairs 2011–13.

CAHILL, Teresa Mary, LRAM, AGSM; British singer (soprano); *Professor of Voice, Trinity Laban Conservatoire of Music and Dance;* b. 30 July 1944, Maidenhead, Berks.; d. of Henry D. Cahill and Florence Cahill (née Dallimore); m. 1st John Anthony Kiernander 1971 (divorced 1978); m. 2nd Prof. Robert Saxton 2005; ed Notre Dame High School, Southwark, Guildhall School of Music and Drama and London Opera Centre; debut at Glyndebourne 1969, Covent Garden 1970, La Scala, Milan 1976, Philadelphia Opera 1981; has given concerts with all London orchestras, Boston and Chicago Symphony Orchestras, at Berlin, Vienna and Bath Festivals and throughout Europe, USA and the Far East; regular adjudicator for Royal Overseas League Competition, Making Music, Live Music Now (Musical Adviser 2000–), YCAT, Boise Foundation, Allcard Awards, Great Elm Vocal Awards, Nat. Fed. of Music Socs Awards; Prof., Trinity Coll. of Music, London, now Prof., Vocal Dept, Trinity Laban Conservatoire of Music and Dance, London; Artistic Adviser, Nat. Mozart Competition 1997–2002; Gov. Royal Soc. of Music 2000, Royal Soc. of Musicians of Great Britain 2001–18; master-classes, Dartington Festival 1984, 1986, 's-Hertogenbosch 1988, 2000, Univ. of Oxford 1995–96, Peabody Inst. 1999, RAM 2002, Bowdoin Coll. 2004; Patron Opera/UK; Warden of Composers and Performers Section, Incorporated Soc. of Musicians 2007–08; specialises in works of Mozart, Strauss, Mahler, Elgar and Tippet; vocal consultant Worcester Coll., Oxford 2014–; Worshipful Company of Musicians Silver Medal 1966, John Christie Award 1970, Elgar Medal 2017. *Recordings include:* works by Elgar, Strauss, Mahler, Mozart, Rachmaninov, Saxton and Lutyens. *Publications:* contrib. to 'Divas in their Own Words', compiled by Andrew Palmer; career archive housed in British Library. *Leisure interests:* cinema, theatre, travel, photography, reading and going to sales, from car boots to Sothebys. *Address:* 65 Leyland Road, London, SE12 8DW, England (home). *Telephone:* (20) 8852-0847 (home). *E-mail:* tessitura@btopenworld.com (home). *Website:* teresacahill.net.

CAHUC, Pierre, DEcon; French economist and academic; *Professor of Economics, Ecole Polytechnique;* b. 18 Jan. 1962; three c.; ed Ecole polytechnique, Agrégation des Universités en Sciences Economiques; Prof. of Econs, Université des Antilles et de la Guyane 1990–92; Prof. of Econs, Univ. of Paris I-Panthéon-Sorbonne 1992–2003; Research Fellow, CREST-INSEE Laboratoire de Macroéconomie 1998–, Dir Macroeconomic Lab. 2011–; Asst Prof. (Professeur chargé de cours), École Polytechnique, Paris 1998–2007, Prof. of Econs 2007–; Research Fellow, Inst. for the Study of Labor (IZA), Bonn, Germany 1999–, Program Dir 'Labor Markets and Institutions' 2004–; Research Fellow, Centre for Econ. Policy Research 2001–; Dir Securisation des parcours professionnels 2012–; mem. Conseil d'Analyse Economique (advisory council of the Prime Minister 2006–10, 2012–; mem. Groupe d'experts sur le Smic 2013–; mem. Comm. d'étude des effets la loi pour la croissance et l'activité 2015–; mem. Comité d'orientation de l'Institut Montaigne 2013–; mem. Comm. Economique de la Nation 2005–09, Conseil de l'Emploi des Revenus et de la Cohésion Sociale 2005–10, Assoc. Ed. American Economic Journals: Macroeconomics, European Economic Review, Labour Economics, Journal of Economics/Zeitschrift für Nationalökonomie; mem. Scientific Cttee Problèmes Economiques, Economie et Statistique; Jr mem. Institut Universitaire de France 1998–2003; Chevalier des Palmes académiques 2004; Prix de thèse, Asscn Française de Science Economique 1989, Prix du 'Meilleur jeune economiste', Le Monde and Le Cercle des Economistes 2001, Prix Risque les Echos 2005, Prix Zerilli-Marimo 2006, Prix du livre d'Economie 2007, Lire magazine Best Essay Prize 2007, Prix du livre des dirigeants, essay section 2007. *Publications include:* Les negociations salariales, des fondements microéconomiques aux implications macroéconomiques 1991, La Nouvelle Microéconomie 1993, La réduction du temps de travail, une solution pour l'emploi? (co-ed.) 1997, Le marché du travail (with Andre Zylberberg) 2001, La microéconomie du marché du travail (with Andre Zylberberg) 2003, Le chômage, fatalité ou nécessité? (with Andre Zylberberg) (Prix Mutation et Travail 2004, Prix Européen du livre d'économie 2004, Prix ManPower 2005 de l'ouvrage de ressources humaines) 2004, Labor Economics (with Andre Zylberberg) 2004; numerous articles in professional journals. *Address:* CREST-INSEE, Timbre J 360, 15 Boulevard Gabriel-Peri, 92245 Malakoff Cedex, France (office). *Telephone:* 1-41-17-37-17 (office). *E-mail:* pierre.cahuc@gmail.com (office); cahuc@ensae.fr (office).

CAI, Guo-Qiang; Chinese artist; b. 8 Dec. 1957, Quanzhou City, Fujian Prov.; ed Shanghai Theatre Acad.; lived in Japan 1986–95; explored properties of gunpowder in his drawings, experimented with explosives including signature explosion events exemplified in his series Projects for Extraterrestrials; has collaborated with specialists and experts from various disciplines including Issey Miyake, Rafael Vinoly, Zaha Hadid, Tan Dun and Tsai Ming-liang; has lived in New York since 1995; core mem. creative team and Dir of Visual and Special Effects for opening and closing ceremonies of Beijing Olympics 2008; Dir of fireworks festivities for China's 60th Nat. Day, Beijing 2009; Fireworks Artistic Dir, Repub. of China Centennial; core mem. creative team for Taipei Int. Flora Exposition 2010; Japan Cultural Design Prize, Tokyo 1995, Benesse Prize of Transculture Exhbn, 46th Venice Biennial 1995, Oribe Award, Gifu (Japan) 1997, Golden Lion Prize, 48th Venice Biennial Int. 1999, CalArts/Alpert Award in the Arts (USA) 2001, Hiroshima Art Prize, Hiroshima City Culture Foundation (Japan) 2007, Best Monographic Museum Show, Best Installation or Single Work in a Museum, Int. Curators Asscn 20th Fukuoka Prize for Arts and Culture (Japan) 2009, First Place for Best Project in a Public Space (for Cai Guo-Qiang: Fallen Blossoms), AICA 2010, Lifetime Achievement in the Arts (Painting) 24th Praemium Imperiale (Japan) 2012, Medal of Arts, US Dept of State 2012; several awards for Best Exhbn and Best Installation from Int. Curators Asscn; repeatedly listed amongst the UK journal ArtReview's Power 100. *Works in permanent collections include:* Agnes Gund Collection, New York, Annie Wong Art Foundation, Vancouver, BC, Astrup Fernley Museum of Modern Art, Oslo, Centre Pompidou, Paris, City of New York, Cleveland Museum of Art, Contemporary Art Gallery, Art Tower Mito, Japan, Dentsu, Caretta Shiodome, Tokyo, Deste Foundation, Athens, Deutsche Bank Collection, Germany, Fogg Art Museum, Harvard Univ. Art Museums, Fondation Cartier pour l'art contemporain, Paris, Fonds Nat. d'art Contemporain and Musée d'art contemporain Lyon, Fukuoka Asia Art Museum, Fukuoka, Japan, Graphische Sammlung Albertina Wien, Vienna, Guangdong Museum of Art, Guangzhou, China, Hirshhorn Museum and Sculpture Garden, Smithsonian Inst., Washington, DC, Ho-Am Art Museum, Seoul, Issey Miyake Inc., Japan, Iwaki City Art Museum, Japan, The Japan Foundation, Tokyo, Modern Museum, Stockholm, Mori Art Center, Tokyo, Museo Navale di Venezia, Museu de Arte Moderna da Bahia, Bahia, Brazil, Museum of Contemporary Art, Tokyo, Museum of Modern Art, New York, Museum of Modern Art, Saitama, Japan, Queensland Art Gallery, Brisbane, Queens Museum of Art, New York, Riiksmuseum, Kroller-Muller, Netherlands, San Diego Museum of Art, Shiseido Co. Ltd, Tokyo, S.M.A.K.: Museum van Hedendaags Kunst Ghent, Solomon R. Guggenheim Museum, New York, Städtische Galerie Nordhorn, Germany, Takamatsu City Museum of Art, Japan, Taiwan Museum of Art, Taichung, Tate Collection, London. *Solo projects include:* Primeval Fireball: The Project for Projects, P3 art and environment, Tokyo 1991, Project to Extend the Great Wall of China by 10,000 Meters, Jiayuguan City 1993, The Century with Mushroom Clouds – Projects for the 20th Century, Nevada, Nuclear Test Site, Salt Lake, New York 1996, Cultural Melting Bath: Projects for the 20th Century, Queens Museum of Art, Queens, New York 1997, APEC Cityscape Fireworks Show, Asia Pacific Econ. Cooperation, Shanghai 2001, Explosion Project for Tate Modern, London 2003, Light Cycle Over Central Park, Asia Soc. and Museum, New York 2003, Explosion Project for Central Park, Creative Time, New York 2003, Kite Project for Siwa, Egypt 2003,

Explosion Project for the Festival of China, John F. Kennedy Center for the Performing Arts, Washington, DC 2005, Curator DMoCA, Echigo-Tsumari Triennial, Japan 2006. *Address:* Cai Studio, 40 East First Street #1B, New York, NY 10003, USA (office). *Telephone:* (212) 995-0908 (office). *Fax:* (212) 254-0336 (office). *E-mail:* studio@caiguoqiang.com (office). *Website:* www.caiguoqiang.com (office).

CAI, Jin-Yong, BS, PhD; Chinese economist, banker and fmr international organization official; *Executive Vice-President and CEO, TPG Capital Ltd;* b. 1959; ed Peking Univ., Boston Univ., USA; began career with World Bank Group 1990, worked as Economist in Cen. Europe and S Asia 1990–93; joined Morgan Stanley 1995, later seconded to China International Capital Corpn (CICC), Man. Dir CICC 1994–99; joined Goldman Sachs 2000, apptd Partner 2006, held numerous other sr positions including Participating Man. Dir, Chief Exec. Goldman Sachs Gao Hua Securities Co., Head of China Investment Banking Business –2012; Exec. Vice-Pres. and CEO, IFC 2012–16; Partner TPG Capital Ltd 2016–. *Address:* TPG Capital Ltd, 57th Floor, Two International Finance Centre, 8 Finance Street, Central, Hong Kong Special Administrative Region, People's Republic of China (office). *Telephone:* 3515-8883 (office). *E-mail:* inquiries@tpg.com (office). *Website:* www.tpg.com (office).

CAI, Qi; Chinese party official; *Secretary, Beijing CCP Municipal Committee;* b. Dec. 1955, Youxi County, Fujian Prov.; ed Fujian Normal Univ.; worked at rural commune during Cultural Revolution, Fujian Prov. 1973–75; joined CCP 1975; Cadre, Gen. Office, CCP Provincial Cttee, Fujian Prov. 1983–91; Deputy Sec., CCP City Cttee, Sanming City, Fujian Prov. 1996–99, Mayor, Sanming City 1997–99; Deputy Sec., CCP City Cttee, Quzhou City, Zhejiang Prov. 1999–2002, Sec. 2002–04, also Mayor of Quzhou City 1999–2002, Dir, Standing Cttee, Quzhou City People's Congress 2002–04; Sec., CCP City Cttee, Taizhou City, Zhejiang Prov. 2004–07; Mayor of Hangzhou 2007–10; Head, Organization Dept, Zhejiang Prov. CCP Cttee 2010–13; Exec. Vice-Gov., Zhejiang Prov. 2013–14; Exec. Dir, Nat. Security Comm., CCP Central Cttee Gen. Office 2014–16; Deputy Mayor of Beijing 2016–17, Mayor Jan.–May 2017; Sec., Beijing CCP Municipal Cttee 2017–; Pres., Organizing Cttee for Beijing 2022 Olympic and Paralympic Winter Games 2017–. *Address:* Chinese Communist Party, Municipal Committee, Beijing, People's Republic of China (office).

CAI, Wu, LLD; Chinese government official; b. Oct. 1949, Wedu Co., Gansu Prov.; ed Beijing Univ.; joined CCP 1973; mem. Communist Youth League of China (CYLC), Cen. Cttee, Standing Cttee 1983–95; fmr lecturer, Beijing Univ.; mem. All-China Youth Fed. and Deputy Sec.-Gen. then Prin. 1983–95; Dir Int. Liaison Dept 1983–95, Research Office, then Deputy Sec.-Gen. 1995–97, Vice-Minister Int. Liaison Dept 1997–2005; Dir Information Office, State Council 2005–08; mem. 17th CCP Cen. Cttee 2007–12, 18th CCP Cen. Cttee 2012–17; Minister of Culture 2008–14; Prof. of Int. Relations, Beijing Univ.

CAI, Xiyou, BA, MBA; Chinese economist and business executive; *President, Sinochem Group;* ed Fushun Petroleum Inst. (now Liaoning Shihua Univ.), Nat. Centre for Industrial Science and Tech. Man. Devt, Dalian; held series of positions at China Petrochemical Corpn (Sinopec Group), including Deputy Man. Jinzhou Petrochemical Co., Vice-Pres. Dalian West Pacific Petrochemical Co. Ltd (WEPEC), Acting Pres. WEPEC, Exec. Vice-Pres. Sinopec Refined Products Sales Co., Pres. and Party Chief, China International United Petrochemical Co. Ltd, and Chair. Sinopec Engineering (Group) Co. Ltd, mem. Party Cttee, China Petrochemical Corpn, Sr Vice-Pres. and Gen. Counsel, Sinopec Corpn –2014; Pres. Sinochem Group 2014–, Vice-Chair. Sinochem Corpn, Dir Strategic Planning Cttee, Investment Cttee, Risk Man. Cttee, HSE Cttee of Sinochem Corpn; Chair. Quanzhou Petrochemical Co. Ltd. *Address:* Sinochem Group, 11/F Central Tower, Chemsunny World Trade Centre 28 Fuxingmennei Street, 100031 Beijing, People's Republic of China (office). *Telephone:* (10) 59568888 (office). *Fax:* (10) 59568890 (office). *E-mail:* webmaster@sinochem.com (office). *Website:* www .sinochem.com (office).

CAI, Zhenhua, MA; Chinese fmr table tennis coach and sports official; b. 3 Sept. 1961, Wuxi, Jiangsu Prov.; ed Hebei Normal Univ.; Head Coach, Chinese men's table tennis team 1991–97, Chief Coach 1997–2004; Chief Coach, Italian table tennis team 1985–89; Deputy Head, Chinese Olympic Del. 2008; Vice-Pres. Chinese Olympic Cttee; Deputy Dir, State Gen. Admin of Sports 2007–18; Chair. All-China Ping-Pong Soc. 2009–, All-China Badminton Soc. 2009–, All-China Soccer Soc. 2014–; fmr Vice-Pres. All-China Youth Fed.; Alt. mem. 17th CCP Cen. Cttee 2007–12, 18th CCP Cen. Cttee 2012–17. *Coaching achievements include:* 2000 Olympic Games: 4 gold medals, 3 silver medals, 1 bronze medal; 2001 World Championships: gold medals, 4 silver medals, 5 bronze medals; 2003 World Championships: 4 gold medals; 2004 World Team Championships: 1st men's/ women's. *Address:* c/o State General Administration for Physical Culture and Sports, 9 Tiyuguan Road, Chongwen District, Beijing, 100061 People's Republic of China (office). *Telephone:* (10) 87183505 (office). *Fax:* (10) 67110248 (office).

CAIN, John, LLB; Australian politician; b. 26 April 1931; s. of John Cain; m. Nancye Williams 1955; two s. one d.; ed Northcote High School, Scotch Coll. and Melbourne Univ.; mem. Council Law Inst. of Victoria 1967–76, Exec. Law Council of Australia 1973–76; Vice-Chair. Vic. Br. Australian Labor Party 1973–75; Pres. Law Inst., Vic. 1972–73, Chair. Council 1971–72; mem. Legis. Ass. for Bundoora, Vic. 1976–92; Leader of Opposition 1981–82; Premier of Vic. 1982–90; Attorney-Gen. 1982–83; Minister for Fed. Affairs 1982, Minister for Women's Affairs 1982–90, for Ethnic Affairs 1990; Treas. Law Inst., Vic. 1969–70; Professorial Assoc., School of Social & Political Sciences, Melbourne Univ. 1994–; part-time mem. Law Reform Comm. of Australia 1975–77; mem. Commonwealth Secr. Observer Group, South African elections 1994; mem. Trust, Nat. Tennis Centre, Flinders Park 1990–94; Trustee, Melbourne Cricket Ground 1982–98, 1999–2013; Pres. Melbourne Univ. Grad. Union 2005–11; Chair. Hume Global Village Learning Advisory Bd 2004–14; mem. Faculty of Business and Law Academic Advisory Bd, Deakin Univ. 2004–, Melbourne and Olympic Parks Trust 2005–13, Library Bd of Vic. 2005–12 (Pres. 2006–12); Dir and Trustee, LUCRF Community Partnership Trust 2010–. *Publications include:* John Cain's Years: Power, Parties and Politics 1994, On With the Show 1998, Off Course (with John Hewitt) 2004. *Leisure interests:* tennis, swimming, jogging. *Address:* 9 Magnolia Road, Ivanhoe, Vic. 3079, Australia. *Telephone:* (03) 9651-1493 (office).

CAINE, Sir Michael, Kt, CBE; British actor; b. (Maurice Joseph Micklewhite Jr), 14 March 1933, London; s. of Maurice Joseph Micklewhite and Ellen Frances Marie Micklewhite (née Burchell); m. 1st Patricia Haines 1954 (divorced 1962); one d.; m. 2nd Shakira Khatoon Baksh 1973; one d.; ed Wilson's Grammar School, Peckham; army service, Berlin and Korea 1951–53; worked at repertory theatres, Horsham and Lowestoft 1953–55; Theatre Workshop, London 1955; mem. IBA 1984–; Hon. Fellow, Univ. of London 1994; Freeman of the City of London 2013; Commdr, Ordre des Arts et des Lettres 2011; BAFTA Fellowship 2000, Nat. Film Award for Global Contribution to Motion Picture 2019. *Films include:* A Hill in Korea 1956, How to Murder a Rich Uncle 1958, Zulu 1964, The Ipcress File 1965, Alfie 1966, The Wrong Box 1966, Gambit 1966, Funeral in Berlin 1966, Billion Dollar Brain 1967, Woman Times Seven 1967, Deadfall 1967, The Magus 1968, Battle of Britain 1968, Play Dirty 1968, The Italian Job 1969, Too Late the Hero 1970, The Last Valley 1970, Kidnapped 1971, Pulp 1971, Get Carter 1971, Zee and Co. 1972, Sleuth 1973, The Black Windmill 1974, The Wilby Conspiracy 1974, The Destructors (also known as The Marseilles Contract) 1974, Peeper (also known as Fat Chance) 1975, The Romantic Englishwoman 1975, The Man Who Would be King 1975, Harry and Walter Go to New York 1976, The Eagle has Landed 1976, A Bridge Too Far, The Silver Bears 1976, The Swarm, California Suite 1977, Ashanti 1978, Beyond the Poseidon Adventure 1979, The Island 1979, Dressed to Kill 1979, Escape to Victory 1979, Deathtrap 1981, The Hand 1981, Educating Rita (BAFTA Award for Best Actor in a Leading Role 1983, Golden Globe Award for Best Actor-Motion Picture Musical or Comedy 1983) 1982, Jigsaw Man 1982, The Honorary Consul 1982, Blame it on Rio 1983, Water 1984, The Holcroft Covenant 1984, Sweet Liberty 1985, Mona Lisa 1985, The Whistle Blower 1985, Half Moon Street 1986, The Fourth Protocol 1986, Hannah and Her Sisters (Academy Award for Best Supporting Actor 1986) 1986, Surrender 1987, Without a Clue 1988, Dirty Rotten Scoundrels 1988, A Shock to the System 1989, Mr. Destiny 1989, Bullseye 1989, Noises Off 1991, Blue Ice 1992, The Muppet Christmas Carol 1992, On Deadly Ground 1993, Bullet to Beijing 1994, Blood and Wine 1995, 20,000 Leagues under the Sea 1996, Mandela and De Klerk 1996, Curtain Call, Shadowrun, Little Voice (Golden Globe Award for Best Actor-Motion Picture Musical or Comedy 1998, London Film Critics' Circle Award for British Supporting Actor of the Year 1998) 1997, The Debtors 1998, The Cider House Rules (Academy Award for Best Supporting Actor 2000) 1999, Quills 1999, Shiner 2000, Last Orders 2000, Quick Sand 2000, Austin Powers: Gold Member 2002, The Actors 2002, The Quiet American (London Film Critics' Circle Award for Best Actor 2002) 2002, Secondhand Lions 2003, The Statement 2003, Around the Bend 2004, The Weather Man 2005, Bewitched 2005, Batman Begins 2005, Children of Men 2006, The Prestige (Best British Actor in a Supporting Role, London Film Critics' Circle Award for British Supporting Actor of the Year 2007) 2006, Flawless 2007, Sleuth 2007, The Dark Knight 2008, Harry Brown 2009, Is Anybody There? 2009, Inception 2010, Journey 2: The Mysterious Island 2011, Cars 2 2011, Gnomes and Juliet (voice) 2011, The Dark Knight Rises 2012, Mr. Morgan's Last Love 2013, Now You See Me 2013, Interstellar 2014, The Last Witch Hunter 2015, Now You See Me 2 2016, Dunkirk 2017, King of Thieves 2018. *Television includes:* over 100 TV plays 1957–63, Jack the Ripper (mini-series) (Golden Globe Award for Best Actor-Miniseries or Television Film 1988) 1988, World War 2: When Lions Roared (NBC TV) 1993. *Plays include:* Next Time I'll Sing to You 1963. *Publications:* Michael Caine's File of Facts 1987, Not Many People Know This 1988, What's It All About? 1992, Acting in Film 1993, The Elephant to Hollywood: The Autobiography 2010, Elephant to Castle 2011. *Leisure interests:* gardening, reading. *Address:* c/o Toni Howard, ICM Partners, 10250 Constellation Blvd, Los Angeles, CA 90067, USA (office). *Telephone:* (310) 550-4000 (office). *Website:* www.icmpartners.com (office).

CAINE, Uri; American jazz pianist and classical composer; b. 8 June 1956, Philadelphia; s. of Burton Caine; ed Univ. of Pennsylvania; began studying piano with Bernard Pfeiffer; played in bands led by Philly Joe Jones, Johnny Coles, Odean Pope, Hank Mobley, Grover Washington, Mickey Roker and Jymmie Merritt during high school; studied music composition with George Crumb and George Rochberg at Univ. of Pennsylvania and performed with Joe Henderson, Donald Byrd, J. J. Johnson, Stanley Turrentine, Lester Bowie and Freddie Hubbard; Composer-in-Residence, Los Angeles Chamber Orchestra 2006–09, Mannes Coll. 2013–14; performed in groups led by Don Byron, Dave Douglas, John Zorn, Terry Gibbs and Buddy DeFranco, Clark Terry, Rashid Ali, Arto Lindsay, Sam Rivers and Barry Altschul, Bobby Watson, Annie Ross, The Enja Band, Global Theory, The Woody Herman Band, The Master Musicians of Jajouka; performed at What is Jazz? Festival, New York, North Sea Jazz Festival, The Hague, Montréal Jazz Festival, Jazz Across the Borders, Berlin, Texaco Jazz Festival, NY, Umbria Jazz Festival, Gustav Mahler Festival, Toblach, Italy, Vittoria Jazz Festival, San Sebastian Jazz Festival, Newport Jazz Festival, Salzburg Festival, Munich Opera, Holland Festival, Israel Festival, IRCAM and others; numrous recordings with piano trio, Bedrock trio and versions of music by Mahler, Mozart,Verdi and others; Toblacher Komponierhäuschen Award for Best Mahler CD 1997. *Compositions include:* ballet composed for Vienna Volksoper 2000, version of Diabelli Variations for Concerto Köln 2001, Mahler Reimagined, London 2002. *Recordings include:* 25 CD recordings including albums: Sphere Music 1993, Toys 1995, Urlicht/Primal Light 1996, Wagner e Veneza 1997, Blue Wail 1998, Sidewalks of New York 1999, Love Fugue 2000, The Goldberg Variations 2000 (performed by Pennsylvania Ballet 2001), Solitaire 2001, Rio 2001, Bedrock 3 2001, Shelf-Life (with Bedrock) 2005, Closure (with Mark O'Leary and Ben Perowsky) 2006, Things (with Paolo Fresu) 2006, Uri Caine Ensemble Plays Mozart 2006, Pure Affection (with Gust Tsillis) 2007, The Othello Syndrome 2008, Secrets (with Mark Feldman, Greg Cohen and Joey Baron) 2009, Think (with Paolo Fresu and Alborada String Quartet) 2009, Plastic Temptation (with Bedrock) 2009, Twelve Caprices (with Arditti String Quartet) 2010, Siren 2011, Sonic Boom (with Han Bennink) 2012, Rhapsody in Blue 2013, Callithump 2014, Present Joys (with Dave Douglas) 2014. *E-mail:* uricaine@verizon.net. *Website:* www.uricaine.com.

CAIO, Francesco, MBA, MSc; Italian business executive; *CEO, Poste Italiane;* b. 23 Aug. 1957; m. Meryl Caio; two c.; ed Politecnico di Milano, INSEAD; consultant with McKinsey & Company, London 1986–1991; CEO Omnitel Pronto Italia (now Vodafone Italy) 1993–96; CEO Merloni (now Indesit) 1997–2000, Dir 2000–04, 2010–13; Founder and CEO Netscalibur (internet service provider) 2000–03; Group CEO Cable & Wireless 2003–06; Vice-Chair., Europe, Lehman Brothers

2006–08, Chair. European Advisory Bd 2008, Vice-Chair., Europe, Investment Banking, Nomura International plc (after acquisition by Nomura of Lehman Brothers' Europe and Middle East investment bank and equities businesses) 2008–11; CEO GE Avio Aero Srl 2011–13; CEO Poste Italiane 2014–; mem. Bd of Dirs Motorola Corpn 2000–03, Cable & Wireless PLC 2003–06, ENV International NV 1997–2000, Allied Domecq Limited 2005–, Invensys plc 2009–13, Alcatel-Lucent 2014–16; mem. Int. Advisory Bd, Univ. Bocconi, Milan; head of ind. review on next generation high speed broadband for UK Dept for Business Enterprise and Regulatory Reform 2008; mem. Steering Bd Digital Britain Report 2008. *Address:* Poste Italiane, Viale Europa, 190 Roma 00144, Italy (office). *Telephone:* (06) 59581. *Fax:* (06) 59589100. *Website:* (office).

CAIRNCROSS, Dame Frances Anne, DBE, CBE, BA, MA, FRSE; British journalist and academic; *Chair of the University Court, Heriot-Watt University;* b. 30 Aug. 1944, Otley, Yorks.; d. of Alexander Kirkland Cairncross and Mary Frances Cairncross; m. Hamish McRae 1971; two d.; ed St Anne's Coll., Oxford, Brown Univ., USA; staff mem. The Times 1967–69, The Banker 1969, The Observer 1969–71; Econs Corresp., The Guardian 1973–81, Women's Ed. 1981–84; Britain Ed., The Economist 1984–89, Environment Ed. 1989–2000, Communications Ed. 1995–2000, Man. Ed. 2000–04; Chair., Econ. and Social Research Council 2001–07; Rector, Exeter Coll., Oxford 2004–14, also Freedom of Information Officer; Chair Univ. Court, Heriot-Watt Univ., Edinburgh 2015–; Pres. BAAS 2005–06; Sr Fellow, School of Public Policy, UCLA; fmr Dir (non-exec.), Stramongate Ltd; Interim Dir, Nat. Inst. for Econ. and Social Research 2015–16; Trustee, Natural History Museum 2015–; High Sheriff of Greater London 2004–05; Hon. Fellow, St Anne's Coll., Oxford, St Peter's Coll., Oxford, Exeter Coll., Oxford, RSA; Dr hc (Univs of Glasgow, Birmingham, City, Loughborough, East Anglia, Trinity Coll. Dublin); Inst. of Internal Auditors award for business and management journalism 2003, British Acad. President's Medal 2018. *Publications:* Capital City (with Hamish McRae) 1971, The Second Great Crash (co-author) 1973, The Guardian Guide to the Economy 1981, Changing Perceptions of Economic Policy 1981, Second Guardian Guide to the Economy 1983, Guide to the Economy 1987, Costing the Earth 1991, Green, Inc. 1995, The Death of Distance 1997, The Company of the Future 2002. *Leisure interest:* winter swimming. *Address:* University Court, Heriot-Watt University, Edinburgh, EH14 4AS, Scotland (office). *Telephone:* (131) 449-5111 (office). *E-mail:* ann-marie.dalton@hw.ac.uk (office). *Website:* www.hw.ac.uk/about/governance/frances-cairncross.htm (office).

CAIRNS, Rt Hon. Alun Hugh, MBA; Welsh politician; *Secretary of State for Wales;* b. 30 July 1970, Swansea; m. Emma Cairns; one s.; ed Univ. of Wales; Business Devt Consultant, Lloyds Banking Group 1989–99; mem. Nat. Ass. for Wales for S Wales West 1999–2011; MP (Conservative) for Vale of Glamorgan 2010–, mem. Welsh Affairs Cttee 2010–11, Public Admin Cttee 2011–14; Lord Commr (HM Treasury) (Whip) 2014–16, also Parl. Under-Sec. (Wales Office) 2014–16, Sec. of State for Wales 2016–. *Address:* Wales Office, Gwydyr House, Whitehall, London, SW1A 2NP (office); House of Commons, London, SW1A 0AA, England (office). *Telephone:* (29) 2092-4220 (office). *E-mail:* alun.cairns.mp@parliament.uk (office); correspondence@walesoffice.gsi.gov.uk (office). *Website:* www.gov.uk/government/organisations/wales-office (office); www.aluncairns.com.

CAIRNS, Christopher (Chris) Lance; New Zealand professional cricketer (retd); b. 13 June 1970, Picton, Marlborough; s. of Lance Cairns; right-hand batsman, right-arm fast-medium bowler; teams: Northern Districts 1988–89, Notts. 1988–, Canterbury, New Zealand 1990–2006, Chandigarh Lions 2008 (Capt.); First-class debut: 1988/89; Test debut: Australia v NZ, Perth 24–28 Nov. 1989; ODI debut: NZ v England, Wellington 13 Feb. 1991; in 62 Tests scored 3,320 runs (average 33.53, highest score 158), 218 wickets (average 29.40); T20I debut: NZ v Australia, Auckland 17 Feb. 2005; in 215 One Day Ints (ODIs) scored 4,950 runs (average 29.46), 201 wickets (average 32.80); 10,702 first-class runs (average 35.32), 647 wickets (average 28.31) in 217 matches; with father Lance Cairns (fmr test player), the only father and son to have captured 10 wickets in single Test matches; retd from Test cricket 2004, from ODI cricket 2006; played for Notts. in Twenty20 League; arrested and charged with perjury and perverting the course of justice, London, acquitted Nov. 2015; Wisden Cricketer of the Year 2000, PricewaterhouseCoopers No 1 All-rounder in the World 2000, New Zealand Nat. Bank Player of the Year 2001, Redpath Cup for Batting, Windsor Cup for Bowling.

CAIRNS, David Adam, CBE, MA, FRSL; British journalist and musicologist; b. 8 June 1926, Loughton, Essex; s. of Sir Hugh William Bell Cairns and Barbara Cairns (née Smith); m. Rosemary Goodwin 1959; three s.; ed Dragon School, Winchester Coll., Oxford, Princeton Univ. Graduate Coll., USA; Library Clerk, House of Commons 1951–53; critic, Record News 1954–56; mem. editorial staff, Times Educational Supplement 1955–58; music critic, Spectator 1958–63, Evening Standard 1958–63; asst music critic, Financial Times 1963–67; music critic, New Statesman 1967–70; mem. staff, Philips Records, London 1968–70, Classic Programme Co-ordinator 1970–73; asst music critic, Sunday Times 1975–84, music critic 1985–92; Leverhulme Research Fellow 1972–74; Distinguished Visiting Prof., Univ. of California, Davis 1985; Distinguished Visiting Scholar, Getty Center for the History of Art and Humanities 1992; Visiting Resident Fellow, Merton Coll., Oxford 1993; Chair. The Berlioz Soc.; Pres. City Music Soc., Putney Music; Founder-Conductor, Thorington Players (amateur orchestra); Hon. mem., Royal Acad. of Music; Commdr, Ordre des Arts et des Lettres 2013; Hon. DLitt (Southampton) 2001; British Acad. Derek Allen Memorial Prize 1990, Royal Philharmonic Soc. Award 1990, 1999, Yorkshire Post Prize 1990. *Publications include:* The Memoirs of Hector Berlioz (ed. and trans.) 1969 (revised 2002), Responses: Musical Essays and Reviews 1973, The Magic Flute (co-author, ENO Opera Guide) 1980, Falstaff (co-author, ENO Opera Guide) 1982, Berlioz: The Making of an Artist 1803–1832 (ASCAP Deems Taylor Award 2001) 1989, Berlioz: Servitude and Greatness 1832–1869 (Whitbread Biog. of the Year 2000, Samuel Johnson Non-Fiction Prize 2000, Prix de l'Académie Charles Cros 2003) 1999, Mozart and his Operas 2006; contrib. of articles on Beethoven and Berlioz, in Viking Opera Guide 1993. *Leisure interests:* conducting, reading, walking, cinema, theatre, cricket, Shakespeare. *Address:* 49 Amerland Road, London, SW18 1QA, England (office). *Telephone:* (20) 8870-4931 (office). *E-mail:* d03.cairns@btinternet.com (office).

CAIRNS, Gordon, MA (Hons); Australian business executive; *Chairman, Woolworths Ltd;* m. Jane Cairns; two c.; ed Univ. of Edinburgh, UK; fmr CEO, Lion Nathan Ltd; served in sr man. positions in marketing, operations and finance with PepsiCo, Cadbury Ltd and Nestlé; mem. Bd of Dirs, Origin Energy Ltd 2007–, Chair. 2013–; Chair. David Jones Ltd March–Aug. 2014; Chair. Quick Service Restaurant Group Pty Ltd; Sr Advisor to McKinsey & Co.; Chair. Woolworths Ltd 2015–; mem. Bd of Dirs (non-exec.), Westpac Banking Corpn 2004–13, Macquarie Group Ltd 2014–, Macquarie Bank Ltd 2014–, Rebel Group Ltd, World Education Australia Ltd. *Address:* Woolworths Ltd, 1 Woolworths Way, Bella Vista, NSW 2153, Australia (office). *Telephone:* (2) 8885-0000 (office). *E-mail:* info@woolworthslimited.com.au (office). *Website:* www.woolworthslimited.com.au (office).

CAIRNS, 6th Earl; Simon Dallas Cairns, BA, CVO, CBE; British business executive; b. 27 May 1939; s. of 5th Earl Cairns and Barbara Jeanne Harrisson; m. Amanda Mary Heathcoat Amory 1964; three s.; ed Eton, Trinity Coll., Cambridge; Chair. VSO 1981–92 (Treas. 1974–81); mem. City Capital Markets Cttee 1989–95; Dir S.G. Warburg Group PLC (fmrly Mercury Int. Group) 1985–95, Vice-Chair. 1987–91; Jt Chair. S. G. Warburg and Co. 1987–95, CEO, Deputy Chair. 1991–95; Chair. Commonwealth Devt Corpn (CDC Group PLC) 1995–2004, BAT Industries 1996–98 (Deputy Chair. June–Dec. 1995); Chair. Allied Zurich 1998–2000, Actis Capital LLP 2004–05; Vice-Chair. Zurich Allied 1998–2000, Zurich Financial Services 1998–2000; Chair. Commonwealth Business Council 1997–2003, Chair. Charities Aid Foundation 2003–10; Overseas Devt Inst. 1994–2002; Receiver Gen. Duchy of Cornwall 1990–2000; Dir Fresnillo PLC 2008–14; mem. Bd of Dirs Celtel Int. (now Zain Africa BV 2I) 2005–10, Chair. 2007–10; mem. Bd of Dirs Mo Ibrahim Foundation 2006–, Africa's Voices Foundation. *Address:* Bolehyde Manor, Allington, nr Chippenham, Wilts., SN14 6LW, England (home). *Telephone:* (7733) 014570 (mobile) (home). *E-mail:* simon.cairns@gmail.com (home).

CAKTIONG, Tony Tan, BEng; Philippine business executive; *Chairman, President and CEO, Jollibee Foods Corporation;* m. Grace Tan Caktiong; three c.; ed Univ. of Santo Tomas, Manila; opened two ice cream parlours 1975; est. chain of seven hamburger outlets under name Jollibee Foods Corpn 1978 (now nat. and int. fast food chain), currently Chair., Pres. and CEO; corp. acquisitions include Greenwich Pizza Corpn 1994, Chowking 2000, Hongzhuangyuan 2007, Lao Dong, Taiwan 2008; mem. Bd of Dirs Philippine Long Distance Telephone Co. 2008–, First Gen. Corpn; Philippines Entrepreneur of the Year 2004, Ernst and Young World Entrepreneur of the Year 2004. *Address:* Jollibee Foods Corporation, 10th Floor, Jollibee Plaza Building, F. Ortigas Jr. Road, Ortigas Center, Pasig, Metro Manila 1605, Philippines (office). *Telephone:* (2) 6341111 (office). *Fax:* (2) 6339504 (office). *Website:* www.jollibee.com.ph (office).

CALABRESI, Guido, BS, LLB, MA; American judge and professor of law; b. 18 Oct. 1932, Milan, Italy; s. of Massimo Calabresi and Bianca Maria Finzi-Contini Calabresi; m. Anne Gordon Audubon Tyler 1961; one s. two d.; ed Yale Coll., Magdalen Coll., Oxford, UK and Yale Law School; Asst Instructor, Dept of Econs, Yale Coll. 1955–56; with Thacher & Bartlett (law firm), New York 1957; mem. Conn. Bar 1958; law clerk to Mr Justice Hugo Black, US Supreme Court 1958–59; Asst Prof. of Law, Yale Univ. School of Law 1959–61, Assoc. Prof. 1961–62, Prof. of Law 1962–70; John Thomas Smith Prof. of Law, Yale Univ. 1970–78, Sterling Prof. of Law 1978–95, Sterling Prof. of Law Emer. 1995–, Dean Yale Univ. Law School 1985–94; Judge, US Court of Appeals (Second Circuit) 1994–2009; Corresp. mem. British Acad.; mem. Royal Acad. of Sweden, Accademia delle Scienze di Torino, Accad. Nazionale dei Lincei, American Acad. of Arts and Sciences, American Philosophical Soc.; Commendatore, Repub. of Italy 1994; awarded more than 30 hon. degrees; awards include Laetare Medal, Univ. of Notre Dame 1985, Thomas Jefferson Medal in Law 2000. *Publications:* The Costs of Accidents: A Legal and Economic Analysis 1970, Tragic Choices (with P. Bobbit) 1978, A Common Law for the Age of Statutes 1982, Ideals, Beliefs, Attitudes and the Law: Private Law Perspectives on a Public Law Problem 1985; more than 80 articles on law and related subjects. *Leisure interests:* walking, reading (especially history), gardening, travel, bridge. *Address:* c/o United States Court of Appeals for the Second Circuit, 157 Church Street, New Haven, CT 06510-2100 (office); 639 Amity Road, Woodbridge, CT 06525-1206, USA (home). *Telephone:* (203) 393-0008 (home). *Fax:* (203) 393-1575 (home). *E-mail:* guido.calabresi@yale.edu (office).

CALANTZOPOULOS, André, MBA; Swiss (b. Greek) business executive; *CEO, Philip Morris International;* b. 1958, Pyrgos, Greece; ed Swiss Fed. Inst. of Tech., Institut Européen d'Admin des Affaires (INSEAD), France; served as design engineer in automotive industry –1985; joined Philip Morris Int. Inc. (PMI) as Business Devt Analyst 1985, transferred to Area Operations Dept 1987–90, Gen. Man. Philip Morris Finland 1990–91, Gen. Man. for PMI in Czechoslovakia 1991–92, Area Dir for Cen. Europe 1992–93, covering the fmr Yugoslavia, Romania and Bulgaria, Area Dir for Hungary and Cen. Europe South 1993–95, Area Dir for Poland and Hungary 1995–96, Man. Dir Poland 1996–99, Pres. Eastern Europe Region 1999–2002, Pres. and CEO Philip Morris Int. Man. SA 2002–08, COO Philip Morris Int. (following spin-off from Altria Group) 2008–13, mem. Bd of Dirs and CEO 2013–; mem. Advisory Bd American European Community Assen. *Address:* Philip Morris International, Avenue de Rhodanie 50, 1007 Lausanne, Switzerland (office). *Telephone:* 582420000 (office). *E-mail:* info@pmi.com (office). *Website:* www.pmi.com (office).

CALATRAVA VALLS, Santiago, PhD; Spanish architect, artist and civil engineer; *Principal, Santiago Calatrava LLC;* b. 28 July 1951, Benimamet, nr Valencia; m. Robertina Marangoni Calatrava; three s. one d.; ed Escuela Tecnica Superior de Arquitectura, Valencia, Fed. Inst. of Tech. (ETH), Zürich, Switzerland; asst, Fed. Inst. of Tech. (ETH), Zürich 1979; undertook small eng comms. 1980s; est. firm Santiago Calatrava LLC, Zürich, 1983, second office Paris 1989, third office Valencia 1991, fourth office New York 2004; won competitions to design and construct Stadelhofen Station, Zürich 1983, Bach de Roda Bridge (commissioned by Olympic Games), Barcelona 1984, Cathedral of St John the Divine, New York 1991; sculptural works include Shadow Machine (large-scale sculpture with undulating concrete fingers) 1993; recently selected to design the expansion of Museo dell'Opera del Duomo, Florence and Symphony Center for the Atlanta Symphony Orchestra, Georgia; mem. Acad. des Arts et Lettres, Paris; Creu Sant Jordi, Barcelona; several hon. degrees, including Dr hc (Columbia Univ.) 2007, (Tel-Aviv Univ.) 2008, (Univ. Camilo José Cela) 2009, (Université de Liège) 2010,

(Pratt Inst.) 2012, (Georgia Inst.) 2013; Gold Medal, Inst. of Structural Engineers (UK), City of Toronto Urban Design Award (Canada), Global Leader for Tomorrow, World Econ. Forum, Davos (Switzerland), Algur H. Meadows Award for Excellence in the Arts, Meadows School of the Arts, Gold Medal, Circolo de Bellas Artes, Valencia, Sir Misha Black Medal, Royal Coll. of Art (UK), Leonardo da Vinci Medal, Société pour les Formations des Ingénieurs (France); Principe de Asturias Art Prize; Eugene McDermott Award in the Arts, MIT, American Inst. of Architects Gold Medal, Gold Medal for Merit in the Fine Arts, Ministry of Culture (Granada). *Architectural works include:* Alamillo Bridge Viaduct, Seville 1987–92, BCE Place Mall, Toronto 1987–92, Campo Volantin Footbridge, Bilbao 1990–97, Alameda Bridge and Underground Station, Valencia 1991–95, Lyon Airport Station, France 1989–94, City of Arts and Sciences, Valencia 1991–, Oriente Railway Station, Lisbon, Portugal 1993–98, Sondica Airport, Bilbao 2000, The Bridge of Europe, Orléans, France 2000, Bodegas Ysios Winery, Laguardia 2001, Milwaukee Art Museum, USA (Time Magazine 'Best of 2001' designation) 2001, Tenerife Auditorium, Santa Cruz, Canary Islands, 2003, Turtle Bay Bridge, Redding, Calif., USA 2004, Athens Olympic Sports Complex, Greece 2004, World Trade Center Transportation Hub, New York 2004, Valencia Opera House 2005, Petach Tikvah Bridge, Israel 2005, Quarro Ponte sul Canal Grande, Venice, Italy 2005, Turning Torso Tower, Malmö, Sweden 2005. *Address:* Santiago Calatrava LLC, Parkring 11, 8002 Zürich, Switzerland (office). *Telephone:* (1) 2045000 (office). *Fax:* (1) 2045001 (office). *E-mail:* zurich@scsa-mail.com (office). *Website:* www.calatrava.com (office).

CALCAGNO, HE Cardinal Domenico; Italian ecclesiastic and academic; *President Emeritus, Administration of the Patrimony of the Apostolic See;* b. 3 Feb. 1943, Tramontana; ed diocesan seminary, Pontifical Gregorian Univ., Rome; ordained priest, Archdiocese of Genoa 1967; several years of parish ministry; fmr Prof. of Theology, Theological Faculty of Northern Italy and, later, at Higher Inst. of Religious Studies of Liguria; served as Pres. of Diocesan Clergy Inst. and was Episcopal Vicar for 'new activities'; held positions as Sec., Italian Priests Comm., Inspector of Italian Episcopal Conf. for Insts of Religious Sciences, Dir of Nat. Missionary Cooperation between Churches, Treas. of the Bishops' Conf., amongst others; taught Theology at Pontificia Università Urbaniana 1992; Bishop of Savona-Noli 2002–07; apptd Archbishop ad personam 2007; Sec., Admin of the Patrimony of the Apostolic See 2007–11, Pres. 2011–13, 2013–18, Pres. Emer. 2018–; cr. Cardinal (Cardinal-Deacon of Annunciazione della Beata Vergine Maria a Via Ardeatina) 2012; participated in Papal Conclave 2013; mem. Congregation for Institutes of Consecrated Life and Societies of Apostolic Life 2014–. *Address:* Administration of the Patrimony of the Apostolic See, Palazzo Apostolico, 00120 Città del Vaticano, Rome, Italy (office). *Telephone:* (06) 69893403 (office). *Fax:* (06) 69883141 (office). *E-mail:* info@apsa.va (office). *Website:* www.vatican.va (office).

CALDERA, Louis Edward, BS, MBA, JD; American lawyer, university administrator and government official; b. 1 April 1956, El Paso, Tex.; s. of Benjamin Luis Caldera and Soledad Siqueiros; m. Eva Orlebeke Caldera; ed US Mil. Acad., West Point and Harvard Univ.; called to Bar, Calif. 1987; Commdr 2nd Lt US Army 1978, advanced through ranks to Capt. 1982, resigned comm. 1983; Assoc. O'Melveny & Myers (law firm), LA 1987–89, Buchalter, Nemer, Fields & Younger, LA 1990–91; Deputy Co. Counsel, Co. of LA 1991–92; mem. Calif. State Ass., 46th Dist, LA 1992–97, Chair. Banking and Finance Cttee; Man. Dir and COO Corpn for Nat. Service, Washington, DC 1997–98; Sec. of US Army 1998–2001; Vice-Chancellor for Univ. Advancement, Calif. State Univ. System 2002–03; Pres. Univ. of New Mexico 2003–06, mem. Faculty, School of Law 2006–08; Dir White House Mil. Office, Washington, DC Jan.–May 2009; Sr Fellow, Center for American Progress 2009–10; Vice-Pres. of Programs, Jack Kent Cooke Foundation 2010–12; Pres. Caldera Associates LLC, Washington, DC (consultancy) 2012–; mem. Bd of Dirs IndyMac Bank 2002–08; mem. Bd of Trustees Claremont McKenna Coll., Nat. World War II Museum; mem. Council on Foreign Relations; Democrat; Dr hc (Norwich Univ.) 2000; Distinguished Civilian Service Award, US Department of Defense 2001, American Heritage Award, American Immigration Council 2011. *Address:* Caldera Associates LLC, 7012 Darby Road, Bethesda, MD 20817, USA (office).

CALDERA CARDENAL, Norman José, BBA, MBA, DPhil; Nicaraguan politician, economist and consultant; *President and CEO, Estudio Caldera, SA;* b. 21 Oct. 1946, Managua; m. Nora Maria Mayorga Arg Üello; one s. two d.; ed Wentworth Mil. Acad., Univ. of Texas and Columbia Univ., USA; fmr Marketing Supervisor, then Product Man., Kimberley Clark Co.; Finance Gen., Empresas Universales SA 1972, Exports Man. 1975, Gen. Man. 1976; consultant to Agricultural Devt of Latin America Investment Co. 1979, to OAS 1979, to UNCTAD/GATT 1980–96, to GUATEXPRO 1980–84 (apptd Chief Adviser 1984); Adjunct Sec.-Gen. SIECA and COMIECO (Cabinet of Integration and Commerce of Cen. America) 1992–95; consultant to IDB 1995–96, UNCTAD 1996; Econ. Adviser to Pres. of Nicaragua 1996–97; Exec. Sec., Cttee to Reform the Public Admin 1997; Pres. and CEO Estudio Caldera, SA (intellectual property services); Minister of Trade, Industry and Commerce 1999–2001, of Foreign Affairs 2002–07. *Address:* Estudio Caldera, SA, 7a Calle S.E, Managua, Nicaragua (office). *Website:* estudiocaldera.com (office).

CALDERÓN HINOJOSA, Felipe, MEcon, MPA; Mexican lawyer, politician and fmr head of state; b. 18 Aug. 1962, Morelia, Michoacan; s. of Luis Calderón Vega and María del Carmen Hinojosa González; m. Margarita Zavala; two s. one d.; ed Escuela Libre de Derecho, Mexico City, Instituto Tecnológico Autónomo de México (ITAM), Kennedy School of Govt, Harvard Univ., USA; Pres. Partido Acción Nacional (PAN) youth group 1986, Sec.-Gen. 1993, Nat. Pres. 1996–99, Leader Parl. Group 2000–03; Rep. to Mexico City Legis. Ass. 1988; mem. Cámara Federal de Diputados Mexico (Fed. Chamber of Deputies) 1991–94, 2000–03; Dir Banobras 2001–03; Sec. of Energy 2003–04 (resgnd); Pres. of Mexico 2006–12; Angelopoulos Global Public Leaders Fellow, Kennedy School of Govt, Harvard Univ. 2013–14; Pres. Sustainable Human Development Foundation; Chair. Global Comm. on the Economy and Climate; mem. Bd of Dirs World Resources Inst.; unsuccessful cand. for Gov. of Michoacan 1995; Hon. Chair. Green Growth Action Alliance; named as a Global Leader of Tomorrow, World Econ. Forum 1997. *Publication:* El Hijo Desobediente 2006. *Website:* www.fdhs.org.mx; newclimateeconomy.net.

CALDERÓN MARTÍNEZ, Rafael P.; Dominican Republic politician and sociologist; m.; ed Univ. Autónoma de Santo Domingo; lecturer on sociology at various insts in Dominican Repub. and Central America 1975–94; Dir-Gen. Planning and Programs, Dist Council of Santo Domingo 1994–95, mem. Comm. on Modernisation 1998–2000; Tech. Sec. of the Presidency 2000–03; Sec. of State for Finance 2003–04, Chair. Bank of Reserves of the Dominican Republic 2003–04; mem. Chamber of Deputies for Ázua (Partido Revolucionario Dominicano) 2006–10; Senator, 2010–16; Dir Dept of Studies and Programs, Caritas Dominicanas 1970–81; Dir-Gen. Centre of Scientific Investigation and Consultation (CENICC) 1973–2000; Gen. Co-ordinator for Area of Latin America, Mexico, Panama and the Caribbean, Carita International 1978–93; Pres. Dominican Asscn of Sociologists 1979–81, Recursos del Futuro Foundation (FUNDARE) 1990–99; Vice-Pres. Amigos de los Niños Foundation 1994–98; Presidente del Consejo de Directores de la Universidad Tecnológica del Sur-UTESUR-Azua 2009–11. *Publications:* numerous articles in periodicals and nat. journals.

CALDICOTT, Dame Fiona, DBE, BM, BChir, MA, FRCP, FRCPsych, FRCPI; British psychiatrist and psychotherapist; b. 12 Jan. 1941, Scotland; d. of Joseph Maurice Soesan and Elizabeth Jane Soesan (née Ransley); m. Robert Gordon Woodruff Caldicott 1965; one d. (one s. deceased); ed City of London School for Girls, St Hilda's Coll., Oxford Univ.; House Surgeon and Physician, Coventry Hosps 1966–67; GP, Family Planning and Child Welfare 1968–70; training in psychiatry 1970–76; Sr Registrar in Psychiatry, W Midlands Regional Training Scheme 1977–79; Consultant Psychiatrist, Univ. of Warwick 1979–85; Consultant Psychotherapist, Uffculme Clinic, Birmingham 1979–96; Sr Clinical Lecturer in Psychotherapy, Univ. of Birmingham 1982–96; Unit Gen. Man., Mental Health, Cen. Birmingham 1989–91; Clinical Dir Adult Psychiatric and Psychotherapy Service, Mental Health Unit, S Birmingham 1991–94; Medical Dir S Birmingham Mental Health Nat. Health Service (NHS) Trust 1994–96; mem. Sec. of State's Standing Advisory Cttee on Medical Manpower (now Workforce) Planning 1991–2001, on Postgrad. Medical Educ. 1993–99, Council Univ. of Oxford 1998–; Chair. Monospecialist Cttee for Psychiatry 1995– (Sec. 1991–95); Sec. European Bd of Psychiatry 1992–96; Sub-Dean Royal Coll. of Psychiatrists 1987–90, Dean 1990–93, Pres. 1993–96; Chair. Conf. of Medical Royal Colls. 1995–96; Prin. Somerville Coll., Oxford Univ. 1996–2010, Hon. Fellow 2010–; Pro-Vice-Chancellor Oxford Univ. 2001–02; mem. Union of European Medical Specialists, Broadcasting Standards Council 1996–, Czech Psychiatric Soc. 1994; Fellow Acad. of Medicine, Singapore 1994; Chevalier du Tastevin 1991; Hon. DSc (Warwick) 1997; Hon. MD (Birmingham) 1997. *Publications:* contrib. to Discussing Doctors' Careers (ed. Isobel Allen) 1988; papers in learned journals on psychiatry. *Leisure interests:* family, friends, reading, theatre, wine. *Address:* Somerville College, Oxford, OX2 6HD; The Old Rectory, Manor Farm Lane, Balscote, Banbury, OX15 6JJ, England (home). *Telephone:* (1295) 730293 (home). *Fax:* (1295) 730549 (home).

CALDWELL, John Bernard, OBE, PhD, DSc; British academic; *Professor Emeritus, Newcastle University;* b. 26 Sept. 1926, Northampton; s. of John R. Caldwell and Doris Caldwell (née Bolland); m. Jean M. F. Duddridge 1955; two s.; ed Bootham School, York, Univs of Liverpool and Bristol; Prin. Scientific Officer, RN Scientific Service 1957–60; Asst Prof., Royal Naval Coll., Greenwich 1960–66; Visiting Prof., MIT 1962–63; Prof. of Naval Architecture, Newcastle Univ. 1966–91, Prof. Emer. 1991–, Head, Dept of Naval Architecture 1966–83, Head, School of Marine Tech. 1975–80, 1986–88, Dean, Faculty of Eng 1983–86; Fellow, Royal Inst. of Naval Architects (RINA), Pres. 1984–87; Dir Nat. Maritime Inst. Ltd 1983–85, Marine Design Consultants Ltd 1985–89, Marine Tech. Directorate 1986–90; mem. Eng Council 1988–94; Founding Fellow, Royal Acad. of Eng 1976; Hon. DSc (Tech. Univ. of Gdansk); NECIS Gold Medal 1973, RINA Froude Medal 1984, Soc. of Naval Architects and Marine Engineers David Taylor Medal (USA) 1987, Eng Council Pres.'s Award of 1995. *Publications include:* more than 70 papers in various eng and scientific publs. *Leisure interests:* music, walking, reading. *Address:* Barkbooth, Winster, Windermere, Cumbria, LA23 3NZ, England (home). *Telephone:* (15395) 68222. *E-mail:* caldwell892@btinternet.com.

ČALFA, Marián, DrJur; Czech lawyer and politician; b. 7 May 1946, Trebišov, Slovakia; m. Jiřina Čalfová; two d.; ed Charles Univ.; studied law in Prague, subsequently worked in legal and admin. depts of official press agency CTK; Minister without portfolio 1988–89; resgnd from CP of Czechoslovakia; Prime Minister of Czechoslovakia 1989–92; Chair. State Defence Council 1990–92; Deputy to House of Nations of Fed. Ass. CSFR 1990–92, official, Fed. Govt of CSFR July–Oct. 1992; Deputy Chair. Civic Democratic Union—Public Against Violence 1991–92; Co-founder CTL Consulting, Prague 1992–95, Čalfa, Bartošík a partneři, Prague 1995–; Chair. Supervisory Bd I. Silas, Deputy Chair. Alia Chem. 1995; Ed.-in-Chief Legal Adviser 1993–95, Chair. Editorial Bd 1995–99; mem. Bd of Dirs Prazska energetika 2012–; mem. M. R. Štefánik Foundation 2000–; Grand Cross of the Order of the Crown (Belgium) 1990. *Address:* Čalfa, Bartošík a Partneři, Karlovo náměstí 24, 110 00 Prague 1, Czech Republic (office). *Telephone:* 222232380 (office). *Fax:* 222232388 (office). *E-mail:* kancelar@calfabartosik.cz (office). *Website:* www.calfabartosik.cz (office).

CALHEIROS, Renan; Brazilian politician; *President of the Federal Senate;* b. (José Renan Vasconcelos Calheiros), 16 Sept. 1955, Murici; s. of Olavo Calheiros Novais and Ivanilda Vasconcelos Calheiros; m. Verônica Calheiros; three c.; ed Universidade Federal da Alagoas; student Pres., Universidade Federal da Alagoas 1974; State Deputy for Alagoas, Movimento Democrático Brasileiro 1978–80; Leader, Alagoas Legis. Ass. 1980–82; Fed. Deputy (Partido do Movimento Democrático Brasileiro—PMDB) 1982–92, Leader of House of Deputies 1990–92; Vice-Pres. PMDB 1984–85; Senator for Alagoas state 1994–, Leader of PMBD in Fed. Senate 2001–02, 2009–, Pres. of Fed. Senate 2005–07 (resgnd), 2013–; Minister of State for Justice 1998–99; Exec. Vice-Pres. Petrobras Química 1992–94. *Address:* Senado Federal, Praça dos Três Poderes, Anexo 1, Edifício Principal, 15° andar, 70165-920 Brasília, DF, Brazil (office). *Telephone:* (61) 3303-2261 (office). *Fax:* (61) 3311-1695 (office). *E-mail:* renan.calheiros@senador.gov.br (office). *Website:* www.senado.gov.br/renan (office); www.renancalheiros.com.br.

CALIFANO, Joseph Anthony, Jr, AB, LLB; American lawyer, writer, academic and fmr government official; *Founder and Chairman Emeritus, National Center on Addiction and Substance Abuse, Columbia University;* b. 15 May 1931, New York; s. of Joseph A. Califano and Katherine Gill Califano; m. 2nd Hilary Paley Byers 1983; two s. one d. from previous marriage; one step-s. one step-d.; ed Holy Cross Coll. and Harvard Univ.; admitted to New York Bar 1955; served in USNR 1955–58; attorney, Dewey Ballantine, Bushby, Palmer Wood, New York 1958–61;

Special Asst to Gen. Counsel, US Dept of Defense, Washington, DC 1961–62; Special Asst to US Sec. of Army 1962–63, Gen. Counsel, US Dept of Army 1963–64; Special Asst to Sec. and Deputy Sec. of Defense 1964–65; Special Asst to Pres. 1965–69; US Sec. of Health, Educ. and Welfare 1977–79; Special Counsel to US House of Reps Cttee on Standards of Official Conduct 1982–83; admitted to US District Court; US Court of Appeals for 2nd Circuit; US Supreme Court Bar 1966; mem. ABA, Fed. Bar Asscn, American Judicature Soc.; attorney, Arnold & Porter 1969–71, Williams, Connolly & Califano 1971–77, Califano, Ross & Heineman 1980–82, Dewey, Ballantine, Bushby, Palmer & Wood 1983–92; General Counsel, Democratic Nat. Cttee 1971–72; Prof. of Public Health Policy, Schools of Medicine and Public Health, Columbia Univ. 1992–; Founder and Chair. Nat. Center on Addiction and Substance Abuse, Columbia Univ. 1992, now Chair. Emer.; mem. Democratic Party's Nat. Charter Comm. 1972–74; Founding Chair. Inst. for Social Policy in the Middle East, Kennedy School of Govt, Harvard Univ.; mem. Bd of Dirs Willis Group Holdings 2004–, CBS Corpn 2006–; fmr mem. Bd of Dirs Viacom Inc. 2003–05, Primerica Corpn, Automatic Data Processing Inc., K-Mart Corpn, True North Communications, Inc., Warnaco; Trustee Urban Inst., American Ditchley Foundation, LBJ Foundation, National Health Museum; Trustee Emer. John F. Kennedy Center for the Performing Arts; mem. Advisory Council, American Foundation for AIDS Research; mem. Council on Foreign Relations; numerous hon. degrees, including from Coll. of Holy Cross, Coll. of New Rochelle, Univ. of Michigan, Davis and Elkins Coll., Howard Univ., Univ. of Notre Dame, City Coll., New York; Distinguished Civilian Service Medal, Dept of Army 1964, Dept of Defense 1968; Man of Year Award, Justinian Soc. Lawyers 1966. *Publications:* The Student Revolution, A Global Confrontation 1969, A Presidential Nation 1975, The Media and the Law (with Howard Simons) 1976, The Media and Business (with Howard Simons) 1978, Governing America: An Insider's Report from the White House and the Cabinet 1981, Report on Drug Abuse and Alcoholism 1982, America's Health Care Revolution: Who Lives? Who Dies? Who Pays? 1985, Inside—A Public and Private Life (memoir) 2004, High Society: How Substance Abuse Ravages America and What to Do About It 2007, How To Raise A Drug Free Kid: The Straight Dope for Parents 2009; numerous articles for various newspapers and other publications. *Leisure interest:* jogging. *Address:* Center on Addiction and Substance Abuse, Columbia University, 633 Third Avenue, 19th Floor, New York, NY 10017-6706, USA. *Telephone:* (212) 841-5200. *Website:* www .casacolumbia.org.

CALIFF, Robert McKinnon, MD; American cardiologist and academic; b. 29 Sept. 1951, Columbia, SC; m. Lydia Carpenter 1974; two s. one d.; ed Duke Univ. and Duke Univ. Medical School; internship in cardiology, Univ. of Calif., San Francisco 1978–79, Resident 1979–80; fellowship in cardiology, Duke Univ. 1978, 1980–83, Attending Physician 1983, Donald F. Fortin Prof. of Cardiology and Prof. of Internal Medicine 1995, Dir Duke Clinical Research Inst. 1995–2006, Dir Translational Medicine Inst. 2006, Assoc. Vice-Chancellor for Clinical Research 1995–2005, Vice-Chancellor for Clinical Research 2005–15; Deputy Commr for Medical Products and Tobacco, US Food and Drug Admin, Washington, DC 2015–16, Commr of Food and Drugs 2016–17; mem. Health Sector Advisory Council, Fuqua School of Business; fmr mem. Cardiorenal Advisory Panel, US Food and Drug Admin., Pharmaceutical Roundtable of Inst. of Medicine (IOM), IOM Cttee; Dir Co-ordinating Center for Centers for Educ. and Research in Therapeutics; Ed.-in Chief Mosby's American Heart Journal; Contributing Ed. theheart.org; Fellow, American Coll. of Cardiology 1988. *Publications:* Acute Coronary Care (ed.), Textbook of Cardiovascular Medicine (section ed.); more than 600 articles in medical journals. *Leisure interests:* golf, basketball, listening to music.

CALLADINE, Christopher Reuben, ScD, FRS, FREng; British engineer and academic; *Professor Emeritus of Structural Mechanics, University of Cambridge;* b. 19 Jan. 1935, Derby; s. of Reuben Calladine and Mabel Calladine (née Boam); m. Mary Ruth Howard Webb 1964; two s. one d.; ed Nottingham High School, Peterhouse, Cambridge, Massachusetts Inst. of Tech., USA; early career as Devt Engineer, English Electric Company; Lecturer, Dept of Eng, Univ. of Cambridge 1963–79, Reader 1979–86, Prof. of Structural Mechanics 1986–2002, Prof. Emer. 2002–, Fellow, Peterhouse 1960–92, Sr Fellow 1992–2002, Emer. Fellow 2002–; Trustee, EMF Biological Research Trust 2005–19, Chair. 2007–19; mem. Gen. Bd Univ. of Cambridge 1984–88; Fellow, The Royal Soc., Inst. of Civil Engineers, Royal Acad. of Engineering; mem. Council The Royal Soc. 2000–02; Hon. DEng (Malaysian Univ. of Tech.) 2002; IMechE Ludwig Mond Prize 1966, ICE James Alfred Ewing Medal 1998, ICE Frederick Palmer Prize 2007. *Publications include:* Engineering Plasticity 1969, Theory of Shell Structures 1983, Understanding DNA (with H. R. Drew, B. F. Luisi and A. A. Travers) (3rd edn) 2004; many articles in eng and biological journals. *Leisure interests:* music, mending toys. *Address:* CRC, Department of Engineering, University of Cambridge, Trumpington Street, Cambridge, CB2 1PZ (office); 25 Almoners Avenue, Cambridge, CB1 8NZ, England (home). *Telephone:* (1223) 764099 (office). *Fax:* (1223) 332662 (office). *E-mail:* crc@ eng.cam.ac.uk (office). *Website:* www-civ.eng.cam.ac.uk/crc/crc_web.htm (office).

CALLEJAS ROMERO, Rafael Leonardo; Honduran politician, economist and fmr head of state; b. (Rafael Leonardo Callejas Romero), 14 Nov. 1943, Tegucigalpa; s. of Rafael Callejas Valentine and Emma Romero; m. 1st Nan López (divorced); m. 2nd Norma Regina Gaborit; ed Mississippi State Univ., USA; worked at Higher Council for Econ. Planning (CONSUPLANE) 1967–71, appointed Head of Govt Econ. Planning 1968; Under-Sec. for Natural Resources 1972–75; Minister for Agric. and Natural Resources 1978–81; Pres. Cen. Cttee Partido Nacional de Honduras 1982; unsuccessful cand. for Pres. of Honduras 1985, Pres. of Honduras 1990–94; Pres. Federación Nacional Autónoma de Fútbol de Honduras (Honduran Football Asscn) 2002–11; mem. FIFA Asscns Cttee; fmr Pres. Nat. Bank for Agricultural Devt (Banadesa), Honduran Inst. of Agricultural Marketing (IHMA); fmr Dir, Nat. Electricity Co. (ENEE), Nat. Port Co. (ENP), Nat. Autonomous Service of Aqueducts and Sewers (SANAA), Honduran Forest Devt Corpn (COHDEFOR), Honduran Banana Corpn (COHBANA); decorations from several countries; Hon. PhD (Mississippi State) 1989, (Georgetown) 1990, (Vermont) 1990, (Pepperdine) 1991, (Guadalajara) 1993, (Vermont, Escuela Agricola El Zamorano). *Publications:* Hog Production Opportunities in Mississippi 1966, Plan de Gobierno, 1990–1994: cambio: participación, bienestar y dignidad nacional 1990, Declaración del Gobierno de la República de Honduras sobre la prevención y el control del alcoholismo, la drogadicción y la farmacodependencia 1990, La Modernización del Estado: Exposiciones del Presidente de la República y los cuatro candidatos a la Presidencia, lunes 5 de julio de 1993 1993, Las Relaciones Entre Chile y Honduras: nuevas perspectivas a la luz del proceso de paz en Centroamérica 1993. *Leisure interest:* football. *Address:* El Hatillo, Calle Principal, Kilometro 9, Tegucigalpa (home); Edificio Palmira, 5 piso, Frente Hotel Honduras Maya, Tegucigalpa (office); c/o Partido Nacional, Tegucigalpa, Honduras. *Telephone:* 2239-1875 (office); 2211-9359 (home). *Fax:* 2239-2059 (office); 2211-9173 (home). *E-mail:* rcallejas2001@yahoo.com (home).

CALLESEN, Per, MSc; Danish economist, academic and central banker; *Governor, Danmarks Nationalbank;* b. 9 Nov. 1958, Gladsaxe; m. 1985; two c.; ed Univ. of Copenhagen; Head of Section, Fed. of Danish Industries 1979–86; Asst Lecturer, Univ. of Copenhagen 1984–88, External Assoc. Prof. 1988–93; Special Consultant and Head of Section, Ministry of Finance 1986–91, Head of Div. 1991–93, Deputy Perm. Sec. 1993–2010, responsible for Macroeconomic Policies 1993–2003, Int. Econ. Policies 2003–09; Chair. Climate Finance Working Group 2009; Exec. Dir IMF 2010–11; Gov. Danmarks Nationalbank 2011–; Chair. EU/EFC High Level Working Group on Regulatory of Sovereign Exposures 2015–16; Chair. Danish Payments Council 2015–; Chair. Nordic-Baltic Monetary and Financial Cttee 2016–; mem. Bd of Dirs. Green Climate Fund 2011–14, Bruegel 2012–14; mem. Systemic Risk Council 2013–; Visiting Fellow, ESRC Modelling Bureau, Univ. of Warwick 1991. *Address:* Office of the Governor, Danmarks Nationalbank, Havnegade 5, 1093 Copenhagen K, Denmark (office). *Telephone:* 33-63-63-63 (office). *Fax:* 33-63-71-03 (office). *E-mail:* nationalbanken@ nationalbanken.dk (office). *Website:* www.nationalbanken.dk (office).

CALLIL, Carmen Thérèse, BA, FRSA, FRSL, DBE; Australian/British publisher and writer; b. 15 July 1938, Melbourne, Vic.; d. of Frederick Alfred Louis Callil and Lorraine Claire Allen Callil; ed Star of the Sea Convent, Loreto Convent, Melbourne and Melbourne Univ.; settled in UK 1960; Buyer's Asst, Marks and Spencer 1963–65; Editorial Asst, Hutchinson Publishing Co. 1965–66, B.T. Batsford 1966–67, Publicity Man., Granada Publishing 1967–70, André Deutsch 1971–72; f. Carmen Callil Ltd, Book Publicity Co. and Virago Press 1972, Founder, Chair. and Man. Dir Virago 1972–83, Chair. 1982–95, Man. Dir Chatto and Windus, The Hogarth Press 1983–93; Co-founder-Dir The Groucho Club, London 1984–94; Publr-at-Large, Random House, UK 1993–94; Ed.-at-Large, Knopf, New York 1993–94; mem. Bd Channel 4 1985–91, Random Century 1989–94; mem. Cttee for The Booker Prize 1979–84, Chair. of Judges, Booker Prize for Fiction 1996; fmr judge, Int. IMPAC Dublin Literary Award, The Orwell Prize; Hon. DLitt (Sheffield) 1994, (Oxford Brookes Univ.) 1995; Hon. DUniv (York) 1995, (Open) 1997; Distinguished Service Award, Int. Women's Writing Guild 1989, Benson Medal 2017. *Publications include:* British Council's New Writing 7 (co-ed.) 1998, The Modern Library: The 200 Best Novels in England since 1950 (with Colm Toibín) 1999, Bad Faith: A Forgotten History of Family and Fatherland 2004. *Leisure interests:* friends, reading, animals, films, gardening, politics, France, Europe. *Address:* c/o Rogers, Coleridge & White Literary Agency, 20 Powis Mews, London, W11 1JN, England (office). *E-mail:* info@rcwlitagency.co.uk (office). *Website:* www.rcwlitagency.co.uk (office).

CALLOW, Simon Philip Hugh, CBE; British actor, director and writer; b. 15 June 1949, London; s. of Neil Callow and Yvonne Mary Callow; ed London Oratory Grammar School, Queen's Univ., Belfast, Drama Centre; debut Edinburgh Festival 1973; repertory seasons, Lincoln and Traverse Theatre, Edin.; work at the fringe theatre, the Bush, London; joined Joint Stock Theatre Group 1977, Nat. Theatre 1979; regular book reviewer The Guardian; Freedom of the City of London 2013; Hon. Fellow, Univ. of the Arts, London; Hon. DLitt (Queen's Univ., Belfast) 1999, (Birmingham) 2000, (Open Univ.) 2010; Evening Standard Patricia Rothermere Award 1999. *Stage appearances include:* Passing By 1975, Plumbers Progress 1975, Arturo Ui 1978, Titus Andronicus 1978, Mary Barnes 1978, As You Like It 1979, Amadeus 1979, Sisterly Feeling 1979, Total Eclipse 1982, Restoration 1982, The Beastly Beatitudes of Balthazar B 1982, The Relapse 1983, On The Spot 1984, Melancholy Jacques 1984, Kiss of the Spider Woman 1985, Faust 1988, Single Spies 1988, 1989, The Destiny of Me 1993, The Alchemist 1996, The Importance of Being Oscar 1997, Chimes at Midnight 1997, The Mystery of Charles Dickens 2000–02, Through the Leaves 2003, The Holy Terror 2004 (tour, Duke of York's Theatre, London 2004), The Woman in White (Palace Theatre, London) 2005, Aladdin (Richmond Theatre, London) 2005, Present Laughter (tour) 2006, Equus (tour) 2008, Dr Marigold and Mr Chops (Edinburgh Assembly Rooms and Riverside Studios) 2008–09, Peter Pan (Richmond) 2008, There Reigns Love (Stratford, Ontario) 2008, Waiting for Godot (tour, Theatre Royal, Haymarket) 2009, The Man from Stratford (tour) 2010, Twelfth Night (Nat. Theatre) 2011, Being Shakespeare (Trafalgar Studios) 2011, Tuesday at Tesco's (Assembly Hall, Edinburgh) 2011, Dr Marigold and Mr Chops (tour) 2011, A Christmas Carol (Arts Theatre, London) 2011, Being Shakespeare (Trafalgar Studios) 2012, The Mystery of Charles Dickens (Playhouse Theatre) 2012, A Christmas Carol (Arts Theatre, London) 2012, The Man Jesus (Lyric Theatre, Belfast) 2013, Inside Wagner's Head (Linbury Studios, Royal Opera House) 2013, Chin-Chin (tour) 2013. *Directed:* Loving Reno 1983, Passport 1985, Nicolson Fights Croydon 1986, Amadeus 1986, The Infernal Machine 1986, Così Fan Tutte 1987, Jacques and His Master 1987, Facades 1988, Single Spies 1988/89, Shirley Valentine (theatre production) 1988/89, Die Fledermaus 1989/90, Stevie Wants to Play the Blues 1990, The Ballad of the Sad Café (film) 1991, Carmen Jones (Evening Standard Olivier Award) 1991, My Fair Lady 1992, Shades 1992, The Destiny of Me 1993, Carmen Jones 1994, Il Trittico 1995, Les Enfants du Paradis (RSC) 1996, Stephen Oliver Trilogy 1996, La Calisto 1996, Il Turco in Italia 1997, HRH 1997, The Pajama Game 1999, The Consul 1999, Tomorrow Week (play for radio) 1999, Le Roi Malgré Lui 2003, Everyman 2003, Jus' Like That 2004, The Magic Flute 2008. *Films include:* Amadeus 1983, A Room with a View 1984, The Good Father 1985, Maurice 1986, Manifesto 1987, Mr and Mrs Bridge 1991, Postcards from the Edge 1991, Soft Top Hard Shoulder 1992, Four Weddings and A Funeral 1994, Jefferson in Paris 1994, Victory 1994, Le Passager Clandestin 1995, England, My England 1995, Ace Ventura: When Nature Calls 1995, James and the Giant Peach (voice) 1996, The Scarlet Tunic 1996, Woman In White 1997, Bedrooms and Hallways 1997, Shakespeare in Love 1997, No Man's Land 2000, Thunderpants 2001, A Christmas Carol 2001, George and the Dragon 2004, The Phantom of the Opera 2004, Rag Tale 2005, The Civilization of Maxwell Bright 2005, Bob The Butler 2005, Ripley Under Ground 2005, The Best Man 2005, Some Break (short) 2006, Surveillance

2007, Arn: The Knight Templar 2007, Chemical Wedding 2008, Natural Selection (short) 2010, The Mr. Men Movie (voice, UK version) 2010, Late Bloomers 2011, Save Our Bacon (short) 2011, No Ordinary Trifle 2011, Love's Kitchen 2011, Acts of Godfrey 2012, Miss in Her Teens 2014. *Television includes:* Wings of Song 1977, Instant Enlightenment inc. VAT 1979, La Ronde 1980, Man of Destiny 1982, Chance in a Million 1982–86, Deadhead 1984, Handel 1985, David Copperfield 1986, Cariani and the Courtesan 1987, Old Flames 1989, Patriot Witness 1989, Trial of Oz 1991, Bye Bye Columbus 1992, Femme Fatale 1993, Little Napoleons 1994, An Audience with Charles Dickens 1996, A Christmas Dickens 1997, The Woman in White 1998, Trial & Retribution 1999, 2000, Galileo's Daughter, The Mystery of Charles Dickens 2002, Angels in America (mini-series) 2003, Hans Christian Andersen: My Life as a Fairy Tale (film) 2003, Shoebox Zoo (series) 2004, Agatha Christie's Marple (series) 2004, Doctor Who (series) 2005, 2011, Rome (series) 2005, Midsomer Murders 2006, The Curse of King Tut's Tomb (film) 2007, The Roman Mysteries (series) 2007, The Company (mini-series) 2007, What's on Theatre (series) 2008, Anatomy of Hope (film) 2009, Lewis (series) 2009, The Sarah Jane Adventures (series) 2009, Ice (series) 2011, Comic Relief: Uptown Downstairs Abbey (film) 2011, This is Jinsy (series) 2011, Them from That Thing (mini-series) 2012, Best Possible Taste: The Kenny Everett Story (film) 2012, Agatha Christie's Poirot (series) 2013. *Publications:* Being An Actor 1984 (expanded edn 2004), A Difficult Actor: Charles Laughton 1987, Shooting the Actor, or the Choreography of Confusion (with Dusan Makevejev) 1990 (expanded edn 2004), Acting in Restoration Comedy 1991, Orson Welles: The Road to Xanadu 1995, Les Enfants du Paradis 1996, Snowdon – On Stage 1996, The National 1997, Love is Where it Falls 1999, Shakespeare on Love 2000, Charles Laughton's the Night of the Hunter 2000, Oscar Wilde and His Circle 2000, The Nights of the Hunter 2001, Henry IV Part 1 2002, Henry IV Part 2 2003, Dickens' Christmas: A Victorian Celebration 2003, Orson Welles: Hello Americans 2006, My Life in Pieces: An Alternative Autobiography 2010, Charles Dickens and the Great Theatre of the World 2012; translations of works of Cocteau, Kundera, Prévert, Chabrier; weekly column in Sunday Express, Independent, Country Life; contrib. to The Times, The Sunday Times, The Guardian, The Observer, Evening Standard etc. *Address:* c/o Brebners, The Quadrangle, 130 Wardour Street, London, W1D 5AR, England. *Telephone:* (20) 7413-0869. *Fax:* (20) 7413-0870. *E-mail:* simon.callow@yahoo.co.uk. *Website:* www.simoncallow.com.

CALMAN, Sir Kenneth (Charles), DL, MD, PhD, KCB, FRCP, FMedSci, FRCPE, FRCS, FFPHM, FRSE; British chief medical officer and university administrator; *Chancellor, University of Glasgow;* b. 25 Dec. 1941; s. of Arthur McIntosh Calman and Grace Douglas Don; m. Ann Wilkie 1967; one s. two d.; ed Allan Glen's School, Glasgow, Univ. of Glasgow; Hall Fellow in Surgery, Western Infirmary, Glasgow 1968; Lecturer in Surgery, Univ. of Glasgow 1969, Prof. of Clinical Oncology 1974, Dean of Postgraduate Medicine and Prof. of Postgraduate Medical Educ. 1984–88, Chancellor 2006–; MRC Clinical Research Fellow, Inst. of Cancer Research, London 1972; Chief Medical Officer, Scottish Office Home and Health Dept 1989–91, (at Dept of Health and Social Security) Dept of Educ. and Science (later Dept for Employment, then Dept for Educ. and Employment) 1991–98; Vice-Chancellor and Warden, Durham Univ. 1998–2007 (retd); Deputy Chair. British Library 2008–15; Chair. Nat. Trust for Scotland 2010–15; mem. Statistics Comm. 2000–; Fellow, Royal Coll. of Surgeons (Glasgow) 1971, Royal Coll. of Gen. Practitioners 1989; Hon. Fellow, Inst. of Cancer Research; Hon. MD (Nottingham) 1994, (Newcastle) 1995, (Birmingham) 1996; Hon. DSc (Strathclyde) 1993, (Westminster) 1995, (Glasgow Caledonian) 1995, (Glasgow) 1996, (Birmingham) 1996, (Brighton) 2000; Hon. DUniv (Stirling) 1992, (Open Univ.) 1996, (Paisley) 1997; Sir Thomas and Lady Dixon Medal, Belfast 1994, Francis Bissett Hawkins Medal, RCP 1995, Crookshanks Medal, RCR 1995, Alexander Hutchinson Medal, Royal Soc. of Medicine (RCS) 1995, Gold Medal, Macmillan Cancer Relief 1996, Heberden (also Orator), British Soc. of Rheumatology 1996, Silver Medal, Royal Coll. of Surgeons in Ireland 1997, Allwyn Smith Medal, Faculty of Public Health Medicine 1998, Bradlaw Medal, RCS Dental Faculty 1999, Thomas Graham Medal, Royal Philosophical Soc., Glasgow 1999. *Publications:* Basic Skills for Clinical Housemen 1971, Basic Principles of Cancer Chemotherapy 1982, Invasion 1984, Healthy Respect 1987, The Potential for Health 1998, Storytelling, Humour & Learning in Medicine 2000, A Doctor's Line: Poetry and Prescriptions in Health and Healing 2014; contrib. to Handing on Learning. *Leisure interests:* gardening, golf, collecting cartoons, Scottish literature, sundials. *Address:* University of Glasgow, Glasgow, G12 8QQ, Scotland (office). *Telephone:* (141) 330-2000 (office). *Website:* www.gla.ac.uk/about/facts/whoswho/chancellor (office).

CALMELS, Virginie; French business executive and fmr politician; *President, Barnes France;* b. 11 Feb. 1971, Talence (Gironde); ed Lycée Marceau, Chartres, Lycée Claude Bernard, Paris, Groupe ESC Toulouse, Institut Européen d'Admin des Affaires (INSEAD); began career as financial auditor, then as Dir, Salustro Reydel 1993–98; Chief Financial Officer (CFO), NC Numericable (Canal+) 1998–99; Admin. and Financial Dir Sky Gate BV, Amsterdam 1999–2000; Financial Dir, Int. and Devt, Canal+ SA, CFO Canal+ SA 2000–02, Deputy CEO and Co-Deputy Gen. Man. Canal+ SA 2002–03; Gen. Man. Endemol France 2003–07, CEO 2007–13, Exec. Dir and COO Endemol Group Worldwide 2012–13; Founder and Pres. SHOWER Co. 2013–; First Deputy Mayor of Bordeaux 2014–19; Vice-Pres. Bordeaux Metropolitan District 2015–19; Founder and Pres. DroiteLib 2017–; mem. Supervisory Bd Euro Disney SCA and Euro Disney Associés 2011–13, Chair. 2013–17; mem. Bd of Dirs Iliad SA 2009–, Assystem 2016–, Technicolor 2014–17; Vice-Pres. Syndicat des Producteurs et Créateurs d'Emissions de Télévision (ind. TV producers' union) 2004–13; Pres. Barnes France (real estate group) 2019–, also CEO Barnes International and Barnes Hospitality; Chevalier, Ordre nat. du Mérite 2008. *Address:* Barnes France, 120–122 rue du faubourg Saint Honoré, 75008 Paris, France (office). *Website:* www.barnes-international.com (office).

CALMÎC, Octavian; Moldovan economist and politician; b. 9 Oct. 1974, Bardar, Moldovan SSR, USSR; m.; one c.; ed State Univ. of Moldova, Acad. of Econ. Studies of Moldova, WTO Inst. for Training and Tech. Cooperation, Geneva, Switzerland; main specialist, Bilateral Div., Ministry of the Economy 1996–98, Deputy Head of WTO Div. 1996–2001, Head of Multilateral Trade and WTO Regimes Div. 2001–05, Dir, Directorate Gen. of Trade Policy 2005–09, Deputy Minister of the Economy 2009–16, Deputy Negotiator of Assen Agreement Between Repub. of Moldova and EU, Main Negotiator of Deep and Comprehensive Free Trade Agreement with EU, Bilateral and Multilateral Co-operation with Int. Orgs and Donors Financial, Rep. of Moldova to WTO and Cen. European Free Trade Agreement, Deputy Prime Minister 2016–17, Minister of the Economy and Infrastructure 2016–17.

CALMY-REY, Micheline; Swiss politician; b. 8 July 1945, Sion, Valais canton; m. André Calmy; two c.; ed Ecole de commerce, St Maurice, Valais, Grad. Inst. of Int. Studies, Geneva; ran family books business 1977–97; joined Social Democratic Party 1979, Pres. 1986–90; elected Deputy Geneva Grand Council 1981–97, fmr Pres. Finance Comm., fmr Pres. Grand Council; elected to Geneva Conseil d'Etat (Head Dept of Finances) 1997–, Vice-Pres. 2000–01, Pres. 2001–02; mem. Fed. Council 2002–11, Head, Fed. Dept of Foreign Affairs 2002–11; Vice-Pres. of the Swiss Confed. 2006, 2010; Pres. 2007, 2011; mem. Bd of Dirs Caisse d'épargne, Geneva 1986–93, Geneva Int. Airport 1994–97; Vice-Pres., later Pres. Caisse de la pension des employées de la fonction publique 1998–2002; mem. Bd of Dirs Fonds d'équipement communal 1998–2002, Banque Nat. Suisse 2002–.

CALNE, Sir Roy Yorke, Kt, MA, MS, FRCP, FRS; British surgeon, academic and artist; *Professor Emeritus, University of Cambridge;* b. 30 Dec. 1930; s. of Joseph R. Calne and Eileen Calne; m. Patricia D. Whelan 1956; two s. four d.; ed Lancing Coll. and Guy's Hosp. Medical School, London; with RAMC 1954–56; Departmental Anatomy Demonstrator, Univ. of Oxford 1957–58; Sr House Officer, Nuffield Orthopaedic Centre, Oxford 1958; Surgical Registrar, Royal Free Hosp. 1958–60; Harkness Fellow in Surgery, Peter Bent Brigham Hosp., Harvard Medical School 1960–61; Lecturer in Surgery, St Mary's Hosp. London 1961–62; Sr Lecturer and Consulting Surgeon, Westminster Hosp. 1962–65; Prof. of Surgery, Univ. of Cambridge 1965–98, Prof. Emer. 1998–, Fellow, Trinity Hall, Cambridge 1965–98, Emer. 1998–; Ghim Seng Prof. of Surgery, Nat. Univ. of Singapore 1998–2003, Visiting Prof., Dept of Surgery and Medicine 2004–; Pres. Int. Transplantation Soc. 1992–94; mem. Group 90 art group, Singapore; Hon. Consulting Surgeon, Addenbrooke's Hosp., Cambridge 1965–98; Hon. FRCS (Edinburgh) 1992; Grand Officer of the Repub. of Italy 2000, Encomienda con Placa de la Orde Civil de Sanidad (Spain) 2008; Hon. MD (Oslo) 1986, (Athens) 1990, (Hanover) 1991, (Thailand) 1993, (Belfast) 1994, (Edinburgh) 2001; Royal Coll. of Surgeons: Hallet Prize, Jacksonian Prize, Hunterian Prof. 1962, Cecil Joll Prize 1966; numerous other honours and awards, including Lister Medal 1984, Hunterian Oration 1989, Cameron Prize 1990, Ellison-Cliffe Medal 1990, Ernst-Jung Prize, Gold Medal of Catalan Transplantation Soc. 1996, King Faisal Int. Prize for Medicine 2001, Prince Mahidol Prize for Medicine 2002, Thomas E. Starzl Prize in Surgery & Immunology 2002, Felix T. Rapaport Memorial Award 2005, Hamdan Award for Medical Research Excellence 2008, Marharshi Sushruta Ginyaanpeeth Prize for advancement of transplantation biology 2009, ASTS-Roche Pioneer Award 2009, Lasker-DeBakey Clinical Medical Research Award (co-recipient) 2012, Pride of Britain Lifetime Achievement Award 2014. *Achievements include:* performed first liver transplant in Europe 1968, world's first liver, heart and lung transplant 1987; first surgeon to perform a pancreas transplant in UK 1979, first to perform an intestinal transplant in UK 1992; first to use drugs to control the rejection of donated organs; first to develop and use Azathioprine, Cyclosporine, Rapamycin and Campath in organ transplantation. *Television:* talk on immunosuppression. *Publications include:* Renal Transplantation 1963, Too Many People 1994, Art, Surgery and Transplantation 1996, The Ultimate Gift 1998; books and scientific papers on renal and liver transplantation and gen. surgery. *Leisure interests:* painting, tennis, squash, sculpture. *Address:* 22 Barrow Road, Cambridge, CB2 8AS (home); Department of Surgery, Strangeways Laboratory, 2 Worts Causeway, Cambridge, CB1 8RN, England (office). *Telephone:* (1223) 248777 (office); (1223) 359831 (home). *Fax:* (1223) 740147 (office). *E-mail:* ryc1000@cam.ac.uk (office).

CALOW, Peter, OBE, DSc, PhD, FSB; British zoologist and academic; *Research Professor, University of Nebraska-Lincoln;* b. 23 May 1947; two c.; ed Univ. of Leeds; Lecturer, Reader, Univ. of Glasgow 1972–84, Warden Wolfson Hall 1975–84; Prof. of Zoology, Univ. of Sheffield 1984–2004, Prof. Emer. 2004–; Dir Inst. of Environmental Sciences and Tech. 1991–96; Dir Environmental Businesses Network 1998–2000; Founding Ed. Functional Ecology 1986–1999; Pres. SETAC (Europe) 1990–91; Chair. UK Govt Advisory Cttee on Hazardous Substances 1991–2000; Trustee Health and Environmental Sciences Inst. 1996–2002, Int. Life Sciences Inst. 1999–2001; Dir Danish Nat. Environmental Assessment Inst. 2004–06; Prof. of Zoology, Roskilde Univ., Denmark, 2004–12; Research Prof., Univ. of Nebraska-Lincoln 2012–; mem. Council Freshwater Biology Assen 1995–99, Univ. of Buckingham 1997–2002. *Publications:* author, jt author of 20 books; more than 300 articles in tech. journals. *Leisure interests:* running, reading, writing. *Address:* Office of Research and Economic Development, 230 Whittier Research Center, 2200 Vine Street, PO Box 830857, Lincoln, NE 68583-0857, USA (office). *Telephone:* (402) 472-6035 (office); (402) 405-2892 (mobile). *Fax:* (402) 472-9277 (office). *E-mail:* pcalow2@unl.edu (office). *Website:* www.unl.edu (office).

CALTAGIRONE, Francesco Gaetano; Italian business executive; *Chairman, Caltagirone SpA;* b. 1943, Rome; m.; three c.; developed family construction firm into large holding co. with interests in cement manufacturing, real estate, media and construction, currently Chair. Caltagirone SpA, also Chair. of subsidiaries Caltagirone Editore SpA, Il Messaggero SpA, Il Gazzettino SpA, Eurostazioni SpA; Vice-Chair. Assicurazioni Generali 2010–; mem. Bd of Dirs Grandi Stazioni SpA, Ical SpA; Cavaliere del Lavoro 2006. *Address:* Caltagirone SpA, Via Barberini 28, 00187 Rome, Italy (office). *Telephone:* (06) 4541-2293 (office). *Fax:* (06) 4541-2299 (office). *E-mail:* info@caltagironespa.it (office). *Website:* www.caltagironespa.it (office).

CALVANI, Sandro, Dottorato in Scienze Biologiche; Italian academic, diplomatist, international organization official and UN official; *Senior Adviser on Strategic Planning, Mae Fah Luang Foundation;* b. 16 Aug. 1952, Genoa; m.; four c.; ed Univ. of Genoa, Colorado State Univ. and Kennedy School of Govt, Harvard Univ., USA; fmr Asst Prof., Univ. of Genoa; Chief of Devt Aid Dept of Caritas, Italy 1980, went on to lead the Caritas Int. del. at FAO, WFP and IFAD and was a mem. of del. of Italian non-governmental orgs to the EC 1985–87, Coordinator for Caritas Foreign Aid Programme 1987, mem. Governing Bd, Devt Cooperation Directorate, Ministry of Foreign Affairs; Founder and first Exec. Dir WHO Pan-African Centre for Disaster Reduction, Addis Ababa, Ethiopia 1988–90, Asst Dir WHO African regional office, Brazzaville, Repub. of the Congo 1990; joined UN System 1992,

Country Dir of UN Office on Drugs and Crime (UNODC) Office in Bolivia 1992–95, Dir Barbados-based UNODC Regional Office for the Caribbean 1995–98, Rep. of UNODC to Insts of EU 1998–99, with UNODC Regional Centre in Bangkok, Thailand 1999–2002, Chair. UN Regional working group with remit to contain AIDS epidemic for 30 countries of SE Asia and Pacific 2002, Head of UNODC Office in Colombia 2002–07, Dir UN Interregional Crime and Justice Research Inst., Turin, Italy 2007–10; Dir ASEAN Center of Excellence on Millennium Devt Goals, Asian Inst. of Tech., Bangkok 2010–13; Sr Adviser on Strategic Planning, Mae Fah Luang Foundation, Bangkok 2013–; Prof., Politics of Devt, Webster Univ. Thailand 2014–; mem. Int. Faculty, Coll. of Politics, Culture and Devt, Univ. of Calabria 2014–; fmr Visiting Scientist, Colorado State and Harvard Univs, USA, Louvain Univ., Belgium; mem. Global Agenda Council on Illicit Trade, World Econ. Forum 2008; mem. Scientific Council, Istituto di diritto internazionale della pace Giuseppe Toniolo of Italian Catholic Action, Rome; mem. American Asscn for the Advancement of Science, Asscn of Change Man. Professionals. *Publications:* 24 books and more than 800 articles on sustainable development, human security, human rights, leadership and management of behavioural change. *Address:* Mae Fah Luang Foundation, 1875/1 Rama IV Road, Lumpini, Pathumwan, Bangkok 10330, Thailand (office). *Telephone:* 2252-7114 (office). *Fax:* 2253-6999 (office). *E-mail:* sandro@doitung.org (office). *Website:* www.maefahluang.org (office); www .sandrocalvani.it.

CALVERT, Rev. Lorne Albert, SOM, BA, BDiv; Canadian fmr politician and college principal; b. 24 Dec. 1952, Moose Jaw, Sask.; m. Betty Sluzalo; two c.; ed St Andrew's Coll. Seminary, Saskatoon, Univ. of Regina, Univ. of Sasketchewan; ordained in United Church of Canada 1976, served congregations in Perdue, Gravelbourg, Bateman, Shamrock, Coderre, Palmer; Minister Zion United Church, Moose Jaw 1979–86; MLA Sask. 1986–2009; apptd to Cabinet as Assoc. Minister of Health and Minister Responsible for Wakamow Valley Authority 1992; fmr Minister Responsible for SaskPower and SaskEnergy, Minister of Health, Minister of Social Services, Minister Responsible for Public Service Comm., Minister Responsible for Srs, Minister Responsible for Office of Disabilities; Leader, New Democratic Party of Sask. 2001–09; Premier of Sask. and Pres. Exec. Council 2001–07; Leader of the Opposition, Saskatchewan Legis. Ass. 2007–09; Prin., St Andrew's Coll., Saskatoon 2009–18 (retd); Saskatchewan Order of Merit; Hon. DD (St Andrew's Coll., Saskatoon) 2019. *Address:* c/o St Andrew's College, 1121 College Drive, Saskatoon, Sask. S7N 0W3, Canada.

CALVERT, Peter Anthony Richard, BA, MA, PhD, FRHistS; British political scientist, writer and academic; *Professor Emeritus of Comparative and International Politics, School of Social Sciences, University of Southampton;* b. 19 Nov. 1936, Islandmagee, Co. Antrim, Northern Ireland; s. of Raymond Calvert and Irene Calvert; m. 1st Diana Elizabeth Farrow 1962; two c.; m. 2nd Susan Ann Milbank 1987; two s.; ed Campbell Coll., Belfast, Queens' Coll., Cambridge, Univ. of Michigan, USA; Lecturer, Univ. of Southampton 1964–71, Sr Lecturer 1971–74, Reader 1974–83, Prof. of Comparative and Int. Politics 1984–2002, Prof. Emer. 2002–; Research Fellow, Charles Warren Center, Harvard Univ. 1969–70; Visiting Lecturer/Prof., Birkbeck Coll., London, 1983–84; Co-Ed. Democratization (journal) 1996–2007; Fulbright Scholar 1960, 1969, Ford Foundation grantee 1984–88. *Publications include:* The Mexican Revolution 1910–1914 1968, 2008, A Study of Revolution 1970, The Falklands Crisis 1982, The Concept of Class 1982, The Foreign Policy of New States 1986, Argentina: Political Culture and Instability (with Susan Calvert) 1989, Revolution and Counter Revolution 1990, Latin America in the 20th Century (with Susan Calvert) 1990, 1993, International Politics of Latin America 1994, Politics and Society in the Third World (with Susan Calvert) 1995, The South, the North and the Environment (with Susan Calvert) 1999, Comparative Politics: An Introduction 2002, A Political and Economic Dictionary of Latin America 2004, Politics and Society in the Developing World (with Susan Calvert) 2007, Terrorism, Civil War, and Revolution 2010, Mexico – A Hundred Years of Revolution 2012; editor: The Process of Political Succession 1987, The Central American Security System 1988, 2008, Political and Economic Encyclopedia of South America and the Caribbean 1991, The Resilience of Democracy (with Peter Burnell) 1999, Civil Society in Democratization (with Peter Burnell) 2004, Border and Territorial Disputes of the World (fourth edn) 2004; fiction: The King of the Land of Flopdoodle 2012. *Leisure interest:* non-jarring exercise. *E-mail:* peter@pcalvert24.fsnet.co.uk.

CALVET, Jacques, LenD; French business executive and banker (retd); b. 19 Sept. 1931, Boulogne-sur-Seine; s. of Prof. Louis Calvet and Yvonne Olmières; m. Françoise Rondot 1956; two s. one d.; ed Paris Univ. and Nat. School of Admin., Diplomé d'études supérieures d'économie politique et de sciences économiques, Diplomé de l'Institut Politique de Paris; at Cour des Comptes 1957–63; Chargé de mission to office of Valéry Giscard d'Estaing (Sec. of State for Finance) 1959–62, Dir 1962–66; Dir Financial Affairs, Paris Dist 1966–68; Prin. Pvt. Sec. to Minister of Finance 1968–74; Deputy Gen. Man. Banque Nat. de Paris (BNP) 1974–75, Gen. Man. 1975–79, Chair. 1979–82, Hon. Chair. 1997–; Vice-Chair. Peugeot SA 1982–84, Pres. 1984–97; Chair. Automobiles Peugeot 1982–84, Bd Pres. from 1984, Vice-Pres., Dir-Gen. 1984–89, Pres. 1990–97; Pres. Citroën 1983–97; Pres. Conseil d'Admin. de la Publicité Française 1991–97; unsuccessful cand. in parl. elections in constituency of Levallois-Perret 1997; Dir, Petrofina; Chair. European Automobiles Mfrs Asscn 1996; Chair. and Pres. Supervisory Bd, Bazar de l'Hôtel de Ville (BHV) from 2000; Vice-Chair. Galeries Lafayette, also Chair. Audit CTTEE; mem. or fmr mem. Bd of Dirs, Icade (Chair. Audit Cttee), Censor, Société Foncière Lyonnaise, Cottin Frères, Soc. Européenne de Participations Industrielles, Enjoy; mem. Advisory Council Banque de France; mem. Institut Montaigne (think tank); Commdr, Légion d'honneur; Officier, Ordre nat. du Mérite, du Mérite agricole; Italian Order of Merit; Chevalier des Palmes académiques. *Publication:* La Grande faillite: Comment l'éviter 1998. *Leisure interests:* tennis, gardening. *Address:* 31 avenue Victor Hugo, 75116 Paris, France (home). *Telephone:* 1-40-67-16-25 (home). *E-mail:* jaccalvet@wanadoo.fr (office).

CALVIÑ, Nadia; Spanish economist; *Minister of Economy and Business;* b. 3 Oct. 1968, La Coruña; d. of José María Calviño; three c.; ed Complutense University of Madrid, National University of Distance Education; joined EC 2006, positions held include Dir-Gen., Directorate-Gen. for Competition, Directorate-Gen. for Internal Market, Industry, Entrepreneurship and SMEs, Directorate-Gen. for Financial Stability, Financial Services and Capital Markets Union, Dir-Gen. of Budget 2014–18; Minister of Economy and Business 2018–; Ex-officio mem. Bd of Govs., EIB 2018–, European Stability Mechanism 2018–, Asian Infrastructure Investment Bank 2018–, Central American Bank for Econ. Integration 2018–, EBRD 2018–, Inter-American Investment Corpn 2018–, IMF 2018–, Multilateral Investment Guarantee Agency 2018–, World Bank 2018–; mem. Sr Corps of State Economists and Trade Advisors. *Address:* Ministry of Economic Affairs, Industry and Competitiveness, Alcalá 9, Paseo de la Castellana 162, 28046 Madrid, Spain (office). *Telephone:* (91) 5837400 (office). *Website:* www.mineco.gob.es (office).

CALVO, Eddie Baza, BBA; Guam lawyer, business executive, politician and fmr state governor; b. 29 Aug. 1961, Tamuning, Guam; s. of fmr Gov. Paul McDonald Calvo and fmr Guam First Lady Rosa Herrero Baza; m. Christine Lujan Sonido; three s. three d.; ed Father Duenas Memorial School, Saint Francis High School, Mountain View, Calif. and Notre Dame de Namur Univ., Belmont, Calif., USA; worked as Gen. Man. Pacific Construction Co. and as Vice-Pres. and Gen. Man. Pepsi Bottling Co. of Guam before entering politics late 1990s; Senator in Guam Legis. 1999–2002, Maite Dist 2004–10, served as Vice-Speaker and Acting Speaker of Legis., Minority Leader in 30th Guam Legislature 2009–11; ran for Lt Gov. of Guam as running mate of Republican gubernatorial cand., Tony Unpingco 2002; Gov. of Guam 2011–19; Republican. *Address:* c/o Executive Chamber, PO Box 2950, Hagåtña, GU 96932, Guam (office).

CALZAGHE, Joseph William (Joe), CBE; British fmr professional boxer; b. 23 March 1972, London; s. of Enzo Calzaghe and Jackie Calzaghe; m. Mandy Davies 1994 (divorced 2005); two s.; ed Roots School System; southpaw; family moved to Wales when he was two years old; joined Newbridge Boxing Club aged nine; won British Amateur Boxing Asscn (ABA) titles 1991 (welterweight), 1992 (light-middleweight), 1993 (middleweight); second to win three ABA titles in consecutive years; professional debut Oct. 1993; won British Super-Middleweight Championship Oct. 1995; World Boxing Organization World Super-Middleweight Champion 1997–2008; Int. Boxing Fed. Champion March–Nov. 2006; Inaugural The Ring Super Middleweight Champion 2006–08; World Boxing Council Super Middleweight Champion 2007–08; World Boxing Asscn Super Middleweight Champion Super Title 2007–08; Lineal Super Middleweight Champion 2007–08; The Ring Light Heavyweight Champion 2008–09; 18 defences; won 46 fights including 32 knock-outs; retd with an undefeated record and as a reigning world champion 2009; est. own boxing promotion co., Calzaghe Promotions, with his father 2009 (now dissolved); Freedom of Caerphilly 2009; Professional Boxing Asscn and Boxing Writers' Club Young Boxer of the Year 1995, BBC Wales Sports Personality of the Year 2001, 2006, 2007, rated by The Ring as a top ten pound for pound boxer 2006–08, BBC Sports Personality of the Year Award 2007, ranked by The Ring No. 3 in the world 2009, inducted into Int. Boxing Hall of Fame 2014. *Television:* contestant (with Kristina Rihanoff) in Strictly Come Dancing (BBC 1) 2009; cameo appearance as himself in episode of UK comedy drama Stella 2012. *Achievement:* won the 2010 Soccer Aid, a British charity football match with the Rest of the World team beating England. *Publication:* No Ordinary Joe (autobiog.) 2007. *E-mail:* joe@joecalzaghe.com. *Website:* www.joecalzaghe.com.

CAMACHO, Felix Perez, BBA; American computer software executive and politician; b. 30 Oct. 1957, Camp Zama, Japan; s. of fmr Gov. of Guam, the late Carlos Garcia Camacho and Lourdes Perez Camacho; m. Joann Gumataotao Garcia Camacho; one s. two d.; ed Father Duenas Memorial School, Marquette Univ.; fmr Insurance Man., Property Casualty Div., Pacific Financial Corpn; Account Admin., IBM Corpn; Deputy Dir Public Utility Agency, Guam 1988–92; Senator, Legislature of Guam 1992–2002, Chair. Cttee on Tourism, Transportation and Econ. Devt 2000–02; Gov. Commonwealth of Guam 2003–11; fmr mem. and Exec. Dir Civil Service Comm.; mem. Nat. Council of State Legislators, Asian Pacific Parliamentarian Union, Kts of Columbus; Republican; Dr hc (Marquette Univ.) 2004.

CAMAÑO, Eduardo Oscar; Argentine lawyer and politician; b. 17 June 1946, Buenos Aires; fmr Pres. Partido Justicialista de Quilmes; Pres. of Bloc in Consejal 1983–85; Prov. Deputy 1985–87; Mayor of Quilmes Partido 1987–91; Deputy to Nat. Ass. 1991–2007, Vice-Pres. Bloc Justicialista 1994–98, Second Vice-Pres. Chamber of Deputies 1999–2001, Pres. 2001–07, Acting Head of Exec. Br. 31 Dec. 2001–1 Jan. 2002. *Address:* c/o Partido Justicialista, Domingo Matheu 128/130, C1082ABD Buenos Aires, Argentina. *E-mail:* contacto@pj.org.ar.

CAMARA, Almamy Kabèlè; Guinean economist and government official; *Second Vice-President, Confederation of African Football;* ed Univ. of Conakry; intern, Ministry of State Supervision 1979; Deputy Dir Gen. Alimag (supply co.) 1980–85; Dir Commercial Operations, SNG (govt maritime transport co.) 1986–97; Deputy Gen. Man. 1997–2000, Dir Gen. 2000–01; fmr Dir Gen. Port Autonome De Conakry; Minister of Nat. Defence 2008–09; mem. Exec. Cttee Confed. of African Football, currently Second Vice-Pres. *Address:* Confédération Africaine de Football, 3 Abdel Khalek Sarwat Street, El Hay El Motamayez, PO Box 23, 6th October City, Egypt (office).

CAMARA, Amedi; Mauritanian economist and politician; *Minister of the Environment and Sustainable Development;* b. 31 Dec. 1966, Dafort; m.; four c.; ed Univ. Sidi Mohamed Ben Abdallah, Fez, Morocco, Ecole Nat. de l'Aviation Civile, Toulouse, France; Adviser to Dir-Gen. Société des Aéroports de Mauritanie (SAM), later Financial Dir, SAM 2007–08; Sec.-Gen. Ministry of Industry and Mines 2008–10; Minister of Finance 2010, of the Environment and Sustainable Devt 2011–. *Address:* c/o Office of the Secretary-General of the Government, BP 184, Nouakchott, Mauritania (office).

CAMARA, Commdr Abdoul Kabèlè; Guinean lawyer and politician; fmr lawyer, Court of Appeal, Conakry; Overseer of Senegal elections for Parl. Ass. of Francophone Countries 2000; Pres. Bar Asscn of Guinea 2000–06; Minister of Foreign Affairs, Int. Co-operation, African Integration and Guineans Abroad 2007–08, Minister Delegate, Ministry of Defence 2010–15, Minister of State, Minister of Security and Civil Protection 2015–18.

CAMARA, Kamissa, MA; Malian/American consultant and politician; b. 1983, Grenoble, France; ed Univ. Pierre Mendès France, Grenoble, Univ. Denis Diderot, Paris; Adviser, US Dept of State Foreign Service Inst. 2015–18; Fellow, Harvard Univ. Center for African Studies 2017; Co-Founder, Sahel Strategic Forum; Adviser to Hillary Clinton's electoral campaign, also mem. Clinton's Africa Policy

Group as strategic adviser on Sahel region 2016–17; fmr Sr Program Officer for West & Central Africa, Nat. Endowment for Democracy (NED), Washington, DC; fmr consultant, Int. Foundation for Electoral Systems (IFES); Africa Dir, PartnersGlobal (NGO), Washington, DC 2017–18; Diplomatic Adviser to Pres. Ibrahim Boubacar Keïta 2018; Minister of Foreign Affairs and Int. Co-operation 2018–19. *Address:* c/o Ministry of Foreign Affairs and International Co-operation, Koulouba, Bamako, Mali (office). *Website:* www.kamissacamara.com.

CAMARA, Mady Kaba; Guinean government official; *Minister Counsellor for Economic and Financial Issues;* fmr Minister of Trade, Minister of Finance 2004, of the Economy and Finance 2004–07, Gov. for Guinea, IMF Bd of Govs 2006; Minister Counsellor for Econ. and Financial Issues 2014–. *Address:* Ministry of the Economy and Finance, Boulevarde du Commerce, Kaloum, Conakry 579, Guinea (office). *Telephone:* 300-45-17-95 (office). *Fax:* 300-41-30-59 (office). *E-mail:* mef.mdb@finances.gov.gn (office). *Website:* www.finances.gov.gn (office).

CAMARA, Makalé, LLM; Guinean diplomatist and politician; b. 1956, Mamou; ed Univ. Gamal Abdel Nasser, Conakry, Int. Labour Office, ILO, Paris, American Univ., USA; Asst to Prosecutor-Gen. of the Repub., Ministry of Justice 1980–81; Head of Div. responsible for control of Ministerial Depts, Ministry of Labour and Public Service 1981–82, Head of Dept, responsible for Int. Relations, Ministry of Public Service 1982–84, Nat. Dir, Public Service Training Centre 1985, Inspector-Gen. of Labour, Ministry of Public Service 1986–91; mem. Comité Transitoire de Redressement Nat. (CTRN, legislative body responsible for implementing new constitution) 1991–92; Sec. of State for Social Affairs and the Promotion of Women and Children 1992–94; Minister of Agric., Livestock and Forests 1994–96; Man. Dir Bangouraya Sansi 1995–; Chair. Office Nat. de l'Emploi et de la Main d'Œuvre (nat. labour and workforce office) 1997–2000; mem. High Council for Electoral Affairs (overseeing transparency of presidential election) 1998; Sec.-Gen., Réseau des femmes africaines ministres et parlementaires de Guinée 1997–2002, 2012–15; Amb. to Senegal, Gambia, Cabo Verde and Mauritania 2002–07, to France, Spain, Portugal and Monaco 2007–11; Minister of Foreign Affairs and Guineans Abroad 2016–17; Del. to 59th Session, Conf. Int. des Femmes 2015; f. Mouvement de Femmes et de Jeunes de Guinée pour la Paix 2015; mem. Steering Cttee, Lutte contre les Mutilations Génitales; Chevalière, Ordre Nat. du Mérite 2008. *Address:* c/o Ministry of Foreign Affairs and Guineans Abroad, Quartier Almamya, face au Port Autonome de Conakry, Commune de Kaloum, BP 2519, Conakry, Guinea (office).

CAMARA, Col-Maj. Yamoussa; Malian army officer and politician; b. 1953, Bancoumana; ed Ecole normale supérieure, Bamako, Ecole supérieure de guerre de Tunis; joined Malian army 1981, Dist Commdr 1991–93, Instructor, Jt Mil. School 1982–83, Deputy Commdr, 133rd Div. 1983–84, Dir Nat. Youth Service Training Centre 1986–88, Head of Operations Div., Army Gen. Staff 1994–96, Adviser to Minister of Armed Forces and War Veterans 2001–03, Commdr, Third Mil. Region 2003, First Mil. Region 2003–05, Operational Controller, Army Gen. Staff 2005, Deputy Chief of Staff Operations 2008, later Chief of Staff of Nat. Guard; rank of Sub-Lt 1981, Lt 1983, Capt. 1988, Commdr 1992, Lt-Col 1997, Col 2002, Col-Maj. 2011; mem. of mil. command group which led coup d'état March 2012; Minister of Defence and War Veterans 2012–13; imprisoned on charge of complicity in murder (during uprising of Sept. 2013) Feb. 2014; Silver Star of Nat. Merit with Bee, Chevalier, Ordre nat. du Mali; Assalam-2 Campaign Commemorative Medal, Medal of Mil. Merit. *Leisure interests:* running, walking, badminton.

CAMARENA BADÍA, Vicente, PhD; Spanish mathematician and academic; *Professor of Applied Mathematics, University of Zaragoza;* b. 26 Aug. 1941, Xátiva, Valencia; s. of Vicente Camarena and Victoria Badía; m. Carmen Grau; one s. four d.; ed Universidad de Zaragoza; Asst Prof. of Math., Universidad de Zaragoza 1966–81, Prof. 1981–84, Rector 1984–92, Prof. of Applied Math. 1992–; mem. Spanish Asscn of Math., Spanish Soc. of Gen. Systems, American Math. Soc., Soc. for Industries and Applied Math., Int. Astronomical Union. *Publications:* Curso de Mecánica 1977–78, Optimización de Trayectorias y efecto de Trampolín Lunar 1972, Formulación Sistemática de la Teoría de Perturbaciones en el Movimiento Orbital 1976, Determinación del Vector Primer de Lawden en Forma Universal y su Aplicación a Problemas de Optimización 1979–83, Elementos Orbitales y Osculadores en Teoría de Perturbaciones, Uniformización de Métodos Canónicos de Perturbaciones 1984, Números y Cálculo con Números: Del 1 al 0, hasta el ∞ 1999. *Leisure interests:* cycling and swimming. *Address:* Universidad de Zaragoza, Centro Politécnico Superior, María de Luna 3, Campus Rio Ebro, Zaragoza 50018 (office); Latassa 17, Zaragoza, Spain (home). *E-mail:* camarena@unizar.es (office). *Website:* www.cps.unizar.es (office).

CAMBRELING, Sylvain; French conductor; *Principal Conductor, Yomiuri Nippon Symphony Orchestra;* b. 2 July 1948, Amiens; conducting debut with Orchestre de Lyon 1975; Prin. Guest Conductor, Ensemble Intercontemporain, Paris 1976; subsequent appearances in Paris with Orchestre de Paris, Nat. Orchestra of France and Ensemble Intercontemporain; has worked regularly at Paris Opéra since conducting Chéreau's production of Les Contes d'Hoffmann; debuts with Glyndebourne Opera (The Barber of Seville) 1981, La Scala (Lucio Silla) 1984, Metropolitan Opera, New York (Roméo et Juliette) 1986; Musical Dir Nat. Opera, Théâtre Royal de la Monnaie, Brussels 1981–91; Music Dir Frankfurt Opera 1990s; Chief Conductor, SWR Sinfonieorchester Baden-Baden und Freiburg 1999–2012; Prin. Conductor, Yomiuri Nippon Symphony Orchestra 2010–(19); Gen. Music Dir Staatsoper Stuttgart 2012–18; Prin. Conductor, Symphoniker Hamburg 2018–; has also appeared at Salzburg, Aix-en-Provence and Bregenz festivals; has worked in UK with Hallé and Royal Liverpool Philharmonic orchestras, in Germany with Berlin Philharmonic, Berlin Radio Symphony and other orchestras and in USA; Echo Klassik Conductor of the Year Award 2009, Deutsche Schallplatten Jahres-preis for best orchestral CD (for his recording of Messiaen with the SWR Freiburg and Baden-Baden Symphony Orchestra) 2009, MIDEM Contemporary Music Award (for his recording of Messiaen with the SWR Freiburg and Baden-Baden Symphony Orchestra) 2010, Int. Classical Music Award for Contemporary 2011. *Address:* c/o Peter Railton, Hazard Chase Ltd, 48–49 Russell Square, London, WC1B 4JP, England (office). *E-mail:* info@hazardchase.co.uk (office). *Website:* www.sylvaincambreling.com; yomikyo.or.jp/e; www.sylvaincambreling.com; www.oper-stuttgart.com.

CAMBRIDGE, HRH The Duchess of, MA; British royal; b. (Catherine Kate Elizabeth Middleton), 9 Jan. 1982, Reading, Berks.; d. of Michael Francis Middleton and Carole Elizabeth Middleton (née Goldsmith); m. HRH The Duke of Cambridge 2011; two s., one d.; ed St Andrew's School, Pangbourne, Berks., Downe House, Marlborough Coll., Univ. of St Andrews, Scotland; worked for Party Pieces (co. owned by her parents); buyer with Jigsaw Junior (clothing chain) 2006–08; Patron, Action on Addiction, East Anglia's Children's Hospices, The Art Room, Nat. Portrait Gallery 2012–; volunteer in Scout Asscn. *Address:* Clarence House, London, SW1A 1BA, England. *Website:* www.royal.gov.uk.

CAMBRIDGE, HRH The Duke of William Arthur Philip Louis, (Earl of Strathearn and Baron Carrickfergus), KG, PC, ADC (P), FRS; British royal; b. 21 June 1982, London; s. of HRH The Prince of Wales and Diana, Princess of Wales; m. Catherine Middleton 2011; two s. one d.; ed Mrs Mynors' Nursery School, Wetherby School, Ludgrove School, Eton Coll., St Andrews Univ., Royal Mil. Acad., Sandhurst, Royal Air Force Coll., Cranwell, Univ. of Cambridge; commissioned as Lt, Blues and Royals Regt, Household Cavalry 2006–09; promoted to Flight Lt with RAF 2009–13, helicopter pilot with Search and Rescue Force, RAF Valley, Anglesey, Wales 2010–13; Patron of youth homelessness charity, Centrepoint 2005–; Pres. Football Asscn 2006–; Patron Tusk Trust 2005–; Pres. British Sub-Aqua Club 2014; Pilot, East Anglian Air Ambulance 2015–17; Queen Elizabeth II Golden Jubilee Medal 2002, Queen Elizabeth II Diamond Jubilee Medal 2012. *Address:* Clarence House, London, SW1A 1BA, England. *Website:* www.royal.gov.uk.

CAMDESSUS, Michel Jean; French international civil servant; *Honorary Governor, Banque de France;* b. 1 May 1933, Bayonne; s. of Alfred Camdessus and Madeleine Cassembon; m. Brigitte d'Arcy 1957; two s. four d.; ed Notre Dame Coll., Betharram, Inst. of Political Studies, Paris, Nat. School of Admin.; civil servant, Treasury, Ministry of Finance 1960–66; Chief, Bureau of Industrial Affairs, Treasury, Ministry of Econ. and Finance 1969–70; Chair. 'Investissements' Sub-cttee of Treasury 1971; Deputy Dir of Treasury 1974–82, Dir 1982–84; Financial Attaché, Perm. Representation, EEC, Brussels 1966–69; mem. Monetary Cttee, EEC 1978, Pres. 1982; Sec. Conseil de Direction du Fonds de Développement Economique et Social 1971; Asst Dir 'Epargne et Crédit' Sub-cttee 1972; Deputy Gov. Banque de France 1984, Gov. 1984–87, Hon. Gov. 1987–; Man. Dir IMF 1987–2000; Pres. Club de Paris 1978–84; Chair. Centre d'études prospectives et d'informations internationales 2000–04, Semaines Sociales de France 2001–07; UN Sec.-Gen. Special Envoy to the Monterrey Conf. 2002; Dir Banque Européenne d'Investissements, Banque Cen. des États de l'Afrique de l'Ouest, Air France, Soc. Nat. des Chemins de fer Français, Crédit Lyonnais (all 1978); Personal Rep. to Africa for French Govt and G8 Heads of State 2002; Grand Officier, Légion d'honneur; Chevalier, Ordre nat. du Mérite; Croix de la Valeur militaire. *Publications include:* Notre foi dans ce siècle (with M. Albert, J. Boissonnat), Eau (with Bertrand Badré, Ivan Chéret, Pierre-Frédéric Tenière-Buchot) 2004, Le Sursaut: Vers une nouvelle croissance pour la France 2004, Lettre ouverte aux candidats à l'élection présidentielle 2006, Rapport de la mission sur la modernisation de la distribution du livret A et des circuits de financement du logement social 2007, Réaliser l'objectif constitutionnel d'équilibre des finances publiques 2010, Contrôle des Rémunérations des professionnels de marché 2011, Reform of the International Monetary System (Palais-Royal Initiative) 2011, La Scène de ce Drame est le Monde-Treize ans à la tête du FMI 2014, Vers le Monde de 2050 2017. *Address:* Banque de France, 09–1060, 75049 Paris Cedex 01, France (office). *Telephone:* 1-42-97-73-38 (office). *E-mail:* lyliane.huot@banque-france.fr (home); office.camdessus@banque-france.fr.

CAMERON, Dame Averil Millicent, DBE, CBE, MA, DLitt, FBA, FSA, FRHistS; British historian of late antiquity and Byzantine studies and writer; *Professor of Late Antique and Byzantine History and Chair, Oxford Centre for Byzantine Research, University of Oxford;* b. (Averil Millicent Sutton), 8 Feb. 1940, Leek, Staffs.; d. of Tom Roy Sutton and Millicent Drew; m. Alan Douglas Edward Cameron 1962 (divorced 1980); one s. one d.; ed Somerville Coll., Oxford, Univ. Coll., London; Asst Lecturer in Classics, King's Coll., London 1965, Lecturer 1968, Reader in Ancient History 1970, Prof. 1978–88, Prof. of Late Antique and Byzantine Studies 1988–94, Dir Centre for Hellenic Studies 1989–94, Fellow 1987–; Warden of Keble Coll., Oxford 1994–2010, Prof. of Late Antique and Byzantine History, Univ. of Oxford 1997–, Pro-Vice-Chancellor, Univ. of Oxford 2001–, Leverhulme Emer. Fellowship, Faculty of Theology 2011–13, Chair. Oxford Centre for Byzantine Research 2010–; Corresp. Fellow, Centre for Byzantine Research, Aristotelian Univ., Thessaloniki 2013; Visiting Prof., Columbia Univ., New York 1967–68; Visiting mem. Inst. for Advanced Study, Princeton, NJ 1977–78, Distinguished Visitor 1992; Summer Fellow, Dumbarton Oaks 1980; Sather Prof. of Classical Literature, Univ. of California, Berkeley 1985–86; Visiting Prof., Collège de France 1987, Lansdowne Lecturer, Victoria, BC 1992; Ed. Journal of Roman Studies 1985–90; Pres. Soc. for the Promotion of Roman Studies 1995–98, Ecclesiastical History Soc. 2005–06, Council for British Research in the Levant 2005–17, Fédération internationale des asscns d'études classiques (FIEC) 2009–14, Soc. for the Promotion of Byzantine Studies 2017–; Natalie Zemon Davis Lecturer, Cen. European Univ., Budapest 2014; Ptarmigan Lecturer, Univ. of Oxford 2018; Chair. Cathedrals Fabric Comm. for England 1999–2005, Review Group on the Royal Peculiars 1999–2000; Corresp. mem. Akad. der Wissenschaften zu Göttingen 2006; Fellow, King's Coll. London 1987; Corresponding Fellow, Medieval Acad. of America 2017; Hon. Fellow, Somerville Coll., Oxford, Keble Coll., Oxford; Hon. Fellow, Ecclesiastical History Soc., Inst. of Classical Studies; Hon. DLitt (Warwick, St Andrews, Queen's, Belfast, Aberdeen, London); Hon. DTheol (Lund). *Publications:* Procopius 1967, Agathias 1970, Corippus, In laudem Iustini minoris 1976, Images of Women in Antiquity (ed.) 1983, Continuity and Change in Sixth-Century Byzantium 1981, Constantinople in the Eighth Century (ed.) 1984, Procopius and the Sixth Century 1985, 1996, History as Text (ed.) 1989, The Greek Renaissance in the Roman Empire (ed.) 1990, Christianity and the Rhetoric of Empire 1991, The Byzantine and Early Islamic Near East I (ed.) 1992, II (ed.) 1994, III (ed.) 1995, The Later Roman Empire 1993, The Mediterranean World in Late Antiquity A.D. 395–600 1993 (second edn 2011), Changing Cultures in Early Byzantium (ed.) 1996, Cambridge Ancient History Vol. XIII. The Late Empire (ed.) 1998, Eusebius, Life of Constantine (ed. and trans.) 1999, Cambridge Ancient History Vol. XIV. Late Antiquity: Empire and Successors (ed.) 2000, Fifty Years of Prosopography (ed.) 2003, Cambridge Ancient History Vol. XII. The Crisis of Empire (ed.) 2005, The Byzantines 2006, Doctrine and Debate in the East Christian World (ed.) 2011, Late Antiquity and Early Islam (ed.) 2012, Byzantine Matters 2014, Dialoguing in Late Antiquity 2014, Arguing it Out 2016, Dialogues and Debates from Late Antiquity to Late Byzantium (co-ed.) 2017, Byzantine Christianity 2017. *Address:* Keble College, Oxford, OX1 3PG, England (office). *E-mail:* averil.cameron@keble.ox.ac.uk (office). *Website:* www.classics.ox.ac.uk/averilcameron.html (office); ocbr.history.ox.ac.uk//Oxford_Centre_for_Byzantine_Research/Home.html (office).

CÁMERON, Daniel Omar; Argentine government official; b. 28 March 1954, Río Gallegos, Santa Cruz Prov.; m.; three c.; ed Colegio Nuestrea Señora de Luján, Universidad Nacional del Sur, Bahía Blanca, Buenos Aires Technological Inst.; fmr Gen. Man. then Dir state-owned SPSE; fmr adviser to state energy bd of Santa Cruz, then chief adviser to state economy minister and public works ministry; Minister of Economy and Public Works, State of Santa Cruz 1991; Rep. for Santa Cruz to Ofephi (fed. org. of hydrocarbon-producing states) 1991–99 (later Exec. Sec.), also Rep. of Ofephi to fed. govt ministries of economy and public works during privatization of state-owned oil co. YPF (mem. Bd 1998–200); mem. govt comm. that drafted basic energy law 1993, fed. electricity comm. 1998–2002, Man. Cttee, Fed. Trust for Electricity 2002; Minister of Energy 2003–14 (resgnd). *Address:* c/o Ministry of Energy, av. Paseo Colón 171, Capital Federal – CP (C1063ACB), Argentina. *E-mail:* energia@minplan.gov.ar.

CAMERON, Rt Hon. David William Donald, PC, BA (Hons); British politician; b. 9 Oct. 1966, London; s. of Ian Donald Cameron and Mary Fleur Cameron (née Mount); m. Samantha Gwendoline Sheffield 1996; two s. (one deceased) two d.; ed Eton Coll., Brasenose Coll., Oxford; raised at Peasemore, Berks.; Head of Political Section, Conservative Research Dept 1988–92; Special Adviser to Chancellor of the Exchequer 1992–93, to Home Sec. 1993–94; Dir of Corp. Affairs and mem. Exec. Bd Carlton Communications plc 1994–2001; unsuccessful parl. cand. for Stafford 1997; MP (Conservative) for Witney 2001–16, fmr mem. Home Affairs Select Cttee, Modernisation Cttee, All Party Cttee on Drugs, All Party Media Cttee, Shadow Minister, Privy Council Office July–Nov. 2003, Shadow Minister for Communities and Local Govt April–Oct. 2004, Shadow Sec. of State for Educ. May–Dec. 2005, Leader of the Opposition 2005–10, Prime Minister 2010–16, Minister for the Civil Service 2010–16, First Lord of the Treasury 2010–16; Deputy Chair. Conservative Party 2003–04, Leader, Conservative Party 2005–16; Chair. NCS (National Citizen Service) Patrons 2016–; Pres. Alzheimer's Research UK 2017–; mem. Exec. British-American Parl. Group; Patron St Mary's Church, Witney, Carterton Educational Trust, Oxon., Victoria County History Trust, Mulberry Bush School, Standlake; Order of Abdulaziz al Saud Medal of Excellence 2012. *Leisure interests:* tennis, growing vegetables, cooking, supports Aston Villa Football Club.

CAMERON, Ian Rennell, CBE, MA, DM, FRCP, FMedSci, FLSW; British professor of medicine (retd); b. 20 May 1936, London; s. of James Cameron and Frances Cameron; m. 1st Jayne Bustard 1964 (divorced); one s. one d.; m. 2nd Jennifer Payne 1980; ed Westminster School, Corpus Christi Coll. Oxford and St Thomas' Hosp. Medical School; jr appointments at St Thomas' Hosp. 1961–64; Lecturer, St Thomas' Hosp. Medical School 1967, Sr Lecturer 1969, Reader 1975, Prof. of Medicine 1979–94, Dean 1986–89; Research Asst, Dept of Physiology, Univ. Coll., London 1966–68; NIH Postdoctoral Fellowship, Cedars-Sinai Medical Center, Los Angeles and Asst Prof., Dept of Physiology, UCLA 1968–69; Prin. United Medical and Dental Schools of Guy's and St Thomas' Hosps 1989–92; Dir Research and Devt South-East Thames Health Authority 1993–94, Bro Taf Health Authority (non-exec.) 1996–99; Provost and Vice-Chancellor, Univ. of Wales Coll. of Medicine 1994–2001; mem. and Treas. GMC 1995–2001; mem. Comm. for Health Improvement 1999–2004; Founder Acad. of Medical Sciences 1998; Fellow, Learned Soc. of Wales; Hon. Fellow, King's Coll. London 1998, Corpus Christi Coll., Oxford 2000; Hon. LLD (Univ. of Wales) 2001, Hon. DSc (Univ. of Glamorgan) 2001, Hon. PhD (Tokyo Women's Medical Univ., Kobe Gakuin Univ., Japan) 2001. *Publications:* Respiratory Disorders (co-author) 1983; papers in medical and physiological journals. *Leisure interests:* collecting paintings, books and ceramics. *Address:* 8 Weigall Road, London, SE12 8HE, England (home).

CAMERON, James Francis; Canadian film director, producer, screenwriter, editor and inventor; *Chairman and CEO, Lightstorm Entertainment;* b. 16 Aug. 1954, Kapuskasing, Ont.; s. of Phillip Cameron and Shirley Cameron; m. 1st Sharon Williams 1978 (divorced 1984); m. 2nd Gale Anne Hurd 1985 (divorced 1989); m. 3rd Kathryn Bigelow 1989 (divorced 1991); m. 4th Linda Hamilton 1997 (divorced 1999); one d.; m. 5th Suzy Amis 2000; two d.; ed Stamford Collegiate, Niagara Falls, Fullerton Jr Coll., Calif., California State Univ., Fullerton; f. Lightstorm Entertainment 1990, Head 1992–; CEO Digital Domain 1993–; mem. Advisory Bd Science Fiction Museum and Hall of Fame; Hon. DFA (Carleton Univ.) 1998, Hon. LLD (Ryerson Univ., Toronto) 1998, Hon. DUniv (Univ. of Southampton) 2004; Bradbury Award, Science Fiction and Fantasy Writers of America 1991. *Achievements include:* co-developed the digital 3-D Fusion Camera System; completed only the second manned (solo) expedition to the deepest place in the ocean, the Mariana Trench in the western Pacific March 2012. *Films include:* Xenogenesis 1978, Piranha II – The Spawning (dir), The Terminator (dir and screenplay) 1984, Rambo – First Blood Part II (co-screenwriter) 1985, Aliens (dir and screenplay) 1986, The Abyss (dir and screenplay) 1989, Terminator 2 – Judgment Day (co-screenwriter, dir and producer) 1991, Point Break (exec. producer) 1994, True Lies 1994, Strange Days (writer) 1995, Titanic (Acad. Award for Best Dir, film won 11 Acad. Awards equalling record) 1997, Solaris 2002, Ghosts of the Abyss (documentary short; dir and producer) 2003, Volcanoes of the Deep Sea (exec. producer) 2003, Aliens of the Deep (dir and producer) 2005, Avatar (writer, dir and producer) (Golden Globe for Best Motion Picture–Drama 2010, Golden Globe for Best Dir–Motion Picture 2010) 2009, Sanctum (producer) 2010, Cirque du Soleil: Worlds Away (producer) 2012, Terminator Genisys (writer, characters) 2015. *Television includes:* Dark Angel (series, exec. producer) 2000, Expedition: Bismarck (producer) 2002, The Lost Tomb of Jesus 2007, Terminator: The Sarah Connor Chronicles (series, writer) 2008–09, Titanic: The Final Word with James Cameron (documentary, exec. producer) 2012, Years of Living Dangerously (series documentary, exec. producer) 2014, Deepsea Challenge 3D (documentary, producer) 2014. *Publication:* Strange Days 1995. *Address:* Lightstorm Entertainment, 919 Santa Monica Boulevard, Santa Monica, CA 90401, USA (office). *Telephone:* (310) 656-6100 (office). *Fax:* (310) 656-6102 (office).

CAMERON, Peter Duncanson, LLB, PhD, FCIArb, FRSE; British academic and barrister; *Professor of International Energy Law and Policy and Director, Centre for Energy, Petroleum & Mineral Law, University of Dundee;* b. 21 June 1952, Glasgow, Scotland; s. of Stewart Cameron and Margaret Cameron; m. Qiumin Li 2004; one s. one d.; ed Bishop Vesey Grammar School, High School of Stirling and Univ. of Edinburgh; Lecturer in Law, Univ. of Dundee 1977–86, Prof. of Int. Energy Law and Policy 1997–, also Dir, Centre for Energy, Petroleum & Mineral Law; Visiting Research Assoc., Oxford Univ. Centre for Socio-Legal Studies 1980; Visiting Scholar, Stanford Law School 1985; Adviser, UN Centre on Transnational Corpns 1985–86; Dir Int. Inst. of Energy Law, Univ. of Leiden 1986–97; Chair. Academic Advisory Group and mem. Council, Int. Bar Asscn Section on Energy and Natural Resources Law 1996–2001; Jean Monnet Fellow, European Univ. Inst., Florence, Italy 2001–02, Prof. 2002–05; adviser, UN ESCAP 1988–89; consultant, World Bank 1990–; Visiting Prof., Univ. Autónoma de Madrid 1997–2000; Professorial Fellow, Univ. of Edinburgh Law School 2008–; Visiting Prof., Nat. Univ. of Singapore 2012; mem. Editorial Bd Journal of World Energy Law & Business 2012–; barrister, Middle Temple; door tenant, Tanfield Chambers, London; Fellow, Chartered Inst. of Arbitrators; Fellow, Royal Soc. of Edinburgh 2013–; Research Awards from Asscn of Int. Petroleum Negotiators 1996, 2005. *Publications include:* Property Rights and Sovereign Rights: The Case of North Sea Oil 1983, Petroleum Licensing 1984, The Oil Supplies Industry: A Comparative Study of Legislative Restrictions and Their Impact 1986, Nuclear Energy Law After Chernobyl (ed.) 1988, The Regulation of Gas in Europe 1995, Gas Regulation in Western and Central Europe 1998, Kyoto: From Principles to Practice (ed.) 2001, Competition in Energy Markets 2002, 2007, Legal Aspects of EU Energy Regulation (ed.) 2005, International Energy Investment Law: The Pursuit of Stability 2010. *Leisure interests:* long-distance running (marathons: New York, Stockholm, Amsterdam), travel, film. *Address:* Centre for Energy, Petroleum and Mineral Law and Policy, University of Dundee, Park Place, Dundee, DD1 4HN (office); 23 Ainslie Place, Edinburgh, EH3 6AJ, Scotland (home). *Telephone:* (1382) 344388 (office). *E-mail:* p.d.cameron@dundee.ac.uk (office). *Website:* www.cepmlp.org (office); www.eisourcebook.org (office).

CAMERON OF LOCHBROOM, Baron (Life Peer), cr. 1984, of Lochbroom in the District of Ross and Cromarty; **Kenneth John Cameron,** LLB, MA, QC, FRSE, FRSA; British lawyer; b. 11 June 1931, Edinburgh, Scotland; s. of Lord Cameron and Eileen Dorothea Burrell; m. Jean Pamela Murray 1964; two d.; ed The Edinburgh Acad., Corpus Christi Coll., Oxford and Univ. of Edinburgh; called to Bar 1958; QC 1972; Chair. Industrial Tribunals (Scotland) 1966–81; Pres. Pensions Appeal Tribunal (Scotland) 1976–84; Chair. Cttee for Investigation in Scotland of Agricultural Marketing Schemes 1980–84; Advocate Depute 1981–84; Lord Advocate 1984–89; Senator of Coll. of Justice in Scotland 1989–2003; Chair. Royal Fine Art Comm. for Scotland 1994–2005; Pres. Scottish Council for Voluntary Orgs 1989–2001; Chancellor's Assessor, Univ. of Edinburgh 1997–2010; Hon. Bencher, Lincoln's Inn, London; Hon. Fellow, Corpus Christi Coll. Oxford, Royal Incorporation of Architects in Scotland, Royal Scottish Acad. *Leisure interest:* fishing. *Address:* Stoneyhill House, Musselburgh, Edinburgh, EH21 6RP, Scotland. *Telephone:* (131) 665-1081.

CAMILLERI, Louis C., BA; British business executive; *Chairman, Philip Morris International; CEO, Ferrari SpA;* b. 1955, Alexandria, Egypt; m. (divorced); three c.; ed Univ. of Lausanne, Switzerland; business analyst with W.R. Grace & Co., Lausanne –1978; joined Philip Morris Europe as a Business Devt Analyst 1978–82, Dir, Business Devt and Planning 1982–86, Vice-Pres., Eastern Europe, Middle East and Africa (EEMA) Region 1986–90, Vice-Pres., Cen. and Eastern Europe 1990–93, Sr Vice-Pres., EU Region 1993–95, Vice-Pres., Corp. Business Strategy Feb.–Aug. 1995, Sr Vice-Pres., Corp. Planning, Philip Morris Cos Inc. (later Altria Group, Inc.), New York Aug.–Dec. 1995, Sr Vice-Pres. and Chief Financial Officer 1996–2002, Pres. and CEO April–Aug. 2002, Chair. and CEO Aug. 2002–08, Chair. and CEO Philip Morris International (following spin-off from Altria Group, Inc. March 2008) 2008–13, Chair. 2013–; Pres. and CEO Kraft Foods Int. 1995–2002, mem. Bd of Dirs 2001–07, Chair. 2002–07; CEO Ferrari SpA 2018–; Dir (non-exec.) SABMiller 2002–; mem. Bd of Dirs Telmex International SAB 2009–11, América Móvil, SAB de CV 2011–. *Leisure interests:* motorsports, scuba diving. *Address:* Philip Morris International, Avenue de Cour 107, 1171 Lausanne, Switzerland (office); Ferrari SpA, Via Abetone Inferiore n. 4, 41053 Maranello, Italy (office). *Telephone:* (21) 618-61-11 (office); (05) 36949111 (Ferrari) (office). *E-mail:* info@pmi.com (office). *Website:* www.pmi.com (office); www.auto.ferrari.com (office).

CAMILO, Michel; Dominican Republic jazz musician (piano) and composer; b. 4 April 1954, Santo Domingo; m. Sandra Camilo 1975; ed Nat. Conservatory, Santo Domingo, Mannes and Juilliard School of Music, New York; mem. Nat. Symphony Orchestra, Santo Domingo 1970, apptd Conductor 1987; moved to New York 1979; debut at Carnegie Hall with trio 1985; Musical Dir Heineken Jazz Festival, Dominican Rep. 1987–92; guest soloist with numerous orchestras 1994–; Co-Artistic Dir Latin-Caribbean Music Festival, Washington, DC 1998; toured internationally with Paquito D'Rivera; Prof. Emer., Univ. Autónoma de Santo Domingo 1992–; Jazz Creative Director Chair, Detroit Symphony Orchestra 2009–10; fmr Artist-in-Residence, Klavier Piano Festival Ruhr; Herb Alpert Visiting Professorship, Berklee College of Music 2003–06; mem. AfofM, RMA, American Music Center; Dr hc (Univ. Tecnológica de Santiago) 1994, (Berklee Coll. of Music) 2000, (Universidad Autónoma de Santo Domingo); Clearwater Jazz Holiday Int. Jazz Award 1993, Emmy Award 1986, Artist of the Year, JazzWeek 2004, Outstanding Dominican-American, New York City 2008; Kt Heraldic Order of Christopher Columbus, Silver Cross of the Order of Duarte, Sanchez y Mella 2001. *Recordings include:* albums: The Goodwill Games (theme) (Grammy Award), Calle 54 (OST), Amo mi cama rica (OST) 1970, Why Not! (Grammy Award) 1986, Suntan/Michel Camilo in Trio 1987, Michel Camilo 1988, On Fire 1991, On The Other Hand 1991, Amo tu cama rica (OST) 1992, Rhapsody for two pianos 1992, Suntan 1992, Rendezvous 1993, Los Peores años de nuestra vida (OST) 1994, One More Once 1994, Two Much (OST) 1996, Hands of Rhythm (with Giovanni Hidalgo) 1997, Thru My Eyes 1997, Piano Concerto and Suite 1998, Spain (with Tomatito) 2000, Calle 54 2001, Triangulo 2002, Concerto for piano and orchestra 2002, Solo 2005, Live at the Blue Note 2005, Rhapsody in Blue 2006, Spain Again (with Tomatito) 2006, Spirit of the Moment 2007, Mano a Mano 2011, What's Up? (Latin Grammy Award for Best Latin Jazz Album 2013) 2013. *Address:* c/o Sandra Camilo, Redondo Music & Management Co., PO Box 216, Katonah, NY 10536, USA (office). *Telephone:* (914) 234-6030 (office). *Fax:* (914) 205-3082 (office). *E-mail:* Mijazz@ix.netcom.com (office). *Website:* www.michelcamilo.com.

CAMMARATA, Bernard (Ben); American retail executive; b. 1941; f. The TJX Cos Inc. (owns TJ Maxx, Marshalls, Home Goods and A.J. Wright dept stores) 1976, Pres. –1999, Chair. and CEO –2000, Acting CEO 2005–06, Chair. 2000–15, Exec. Advisor 2015–; Co-Chair. Inner-City Scholarship Fund, The Catholic Schools Foundation Inc. 2003–04; mem. Bd of Trustees, Bentley Coll. (Trustee Emer. 2004–), Lahey Clinic, Burlington, Mass; Dir, Heritage Property Investment Trust Inc. (gen. partner of Bradley Operating LP) 1999. *Leisure interest:* golf. *Address:* The TJX Companies Inc., 770 Cochituate Road, Framingham, MA 01701, USA (office). *Telephone:* (508) 390-1000 (office). *Fax:* (508) 390-2828 (office). *E-mail:* info@tjx.com (office). *Website:* www.tjx.com (office).

CAMOYS, 7th Baron (cr. 1264, called out of abeyance 1839); **(Ralph) Thomas Campion George Sherman Stonor,** GCVO, PC, MA; British banker; b. 16 April 1940; s. of 6th Baron Camoys and Mary Jeanne Stourton; m. Elisabeth Mary Hyde Parker 1966; one s. three d.; ed Eton Coll., Balliol Coll., Oxford; Man. Dir Rothschild Intercontinental Bank Ltd 1969–75; with Amex Bank Ltd 1975–78; Man. Dir Barclays Merchant Bank 1978–84, Exec. Vice.-Chair. 1984–86; Dir Barclays Bank PLC 1984–94; Chief Exec. Barclays de Zoete Wedd Holdings Ltd 1986–87, Deputy Chair. 1987–98; Deputy Chair. Sotheby's Holdings Inc. 1994–97; Dir 3i Group 1991–2002, Perpetual PLC 1994–2000, British Grolux Ltd 1994–; Lord Chamberlain of HM Household 1998–2000; Lord-in-Waiting to HM the Queen 1992–98, Perm. Lord in Waiting 2000–; Pres. River and Rowing Museum, Henley-on-Thames 1998–; mem. Court of Assistants, Fishmongers' Co. 1980–; Consultor Extraordinary Section of Admin. of the Patrimony of the Holy See 1991–2006; Chair. The Tablet Trust 2009–; DL Oxon. 1994–; Order of Gorkha Dakshina Bahu, 1st Class (Nepal), Kt Grand Cross of the Order of St Gregory the Great 2006; Hon. DLitt (Sheffield) 2001. *Leisure interests:* the arts, family. *Address:* Stonor Park, Henley-on-Thames, Oxon., RG9 6HF, England. *Telephone:* (1491) 638644. *Fax:* (1491) 639348.

CAMP, Garrett M., BSc, MSc; Canadian business executive; *Co-Founder and Chair, Uber Technologies Inc.;* b. 4 Oct. 1978, Calgary, Alberta; ed Univ. of Calgary; co-f. StumbleUpon (web-discovery platform) 2002, CEO 2002–12, Chair. 2012–14; co-f. (with Travis Kalanick) Uber Technologies Inc. (mobile application for on-demand car-sharing service) 2009, currently Chair. and Adviser; f. Expa (start-up studio) 2013; panel mem. and judge, DEMO Mobile, San Francisco 2013; MIT Technology Review TR35 Award 2007, named by Bloomberg Businessweek as one of Tech's Best Young Entrepreneurs 2008, Tribeca Disruptive Innovation Award 2013. *Address:* Expa HQ, 555 Mission Street, San Francisco, CA 94105, USA (office). *Website:* expa.com (office).

CAMP, Jeffery Bruce, RA; British artist; b. 1923, Oulton Broad, Suffolk; s. of George Camp and Caroline Denny; m. Laetitia Yhap 1963; ed Lowestoft and Ipswich Art Schools and Edin. Coll. of Art (under William Gillies); Andrew Grant Scholarship for travelling and study 1944, 1945, David Murray Bursary for landscape painting 1946; painted altarpiece for St Alban's Church, Norwich 1955; Lecturer, Slade School of Fine Art, London 1963–88; mem. London Group 1961; numerous solo and mixed exhbns 1958–; works in numerous public collections in UK; Athena Art Award 1987. *Publications include:* Draw 1981, Paint 1996. *Address:* 27 Stirling Road, London, SW9 9EF, England.

ČAMPARA, Aljoša; Bosnia and Herzegovina lawyer, government official and politician; *Minister of Internal Affairs, Federation of Bosnia and Herzegovina;* b. 20 Jan. 1975, Dubrovnik, Socialist Repub. of Croatia, Socialist Fed. Repub. of Yugoslavia; s. of Avdo Čampara; m. Amela Čampara; two c.; ed Faculty of Law, Univ. of Sarajevo; fmr Assoc., Dept for Personnel Issues and Dept for Protocols of Parl. Ass. of Bosnia and Herzegovina; held various admin. posts, including Sec., Constitutional-Legal Comm. of Dom Naroda (House of Peoples of Bosnia and Herzegovina), later Sec., Dom Naroda, later Sec., Jt Service of Parl. Ass. of Bosnia and Herzegovina, later adviser to Chair. of Dom Naroda, later mem. Legis.-Legal Comm. of Dom Naroda (external expert); mem. Steering Cttee, Faculty of Political Sciences, Univ. of Sarajevo; mem. Ass. of Islamic Community of Bosnia and Herzegovina; Deputy Mayor of Sarajevo 2013–; Minister of Internal Affairs, Fed. of Bosnia and Herzegovina 2015–; mem. Stranka Demokratske Akcije (Party of Democratic Action). *Address:* Ministry of Internal Affairs, 71000 Sarajevo, Mehmeda Spahe 7, Bosnia and Herzegovina (office). *Telephone:* (33) 280020 (office). *Fax:* (33) 280020 (office). *E-mail:* info@fmup.gov.ba (office). *Website:* www.fmup.gov.ba (office).

CAMPBELL, Alastair John, MA; British journalist, broadcaster, political aide and writer; *Strategic Counsel, Portland Communications;* b. 25 May 1957, Keighley, West Riding of Yorks., England; s. of Donald Campbell and Elizabeth Campbell (née Caldwell); partner Fiona Millar; two s. one d.; ed City of Leicester Boys School, Gonville and Caius Coll., Cambridge; trainee reporter, Tavistock Times and Sunday Independent 1980–82; freelance reporter 1982–83; reporter, Daily Mirror 1982–86, Political Ed. 1989–93; News Ed. Sunday Today 1985–86; Political Corresp., Sunday Mirror 1986–87, Political Ed. 1987–89, columnist 1989–91; Asst Ed. and columnist, Today 1993–95; Press Sec. to Leader of the Opposition 1994–97; Press Sec. to Prime Minister 1997–2001, Dir of Communications and Strategy 2001–03, mem. election campaign team 2005; Strategic Counsel, Portland Communications (PR agency) 2012–; Pres. Keighley Br., Burnley Football Supporters' Club; Visiting Fellow, Inst. of Politics, Harvard Univ. 2004; Mind Champion of the Year Award 2009. *Television includes:* Cracking Up (BBC 2) 2008, Top Gear (BBC 1) 2010, Jamie's Dream School (Channel Four) 2011, Have I Got News For You (BBC 1, guest presenter) 2012, Panorama – Britain's Hidden Alcoholics (BBC 1, presented and narrator) 2012, acting role in episode of BBC drama Accused 2012. *Publications:* The Blair Years 2007, All in the Mind (novel) 2008, Maya (novel) 2010, The Alastair Campbell Diaries Volume One: Prelude to Power 1994–1997 2010, The Alastair Campbell Diaries Volume Two: Power and the People 1997–1999 2011, The Alastair Campbell Diaries Volume Three: Power and Responsibility 1999–2001 2012, The Happy Depressive: In Pursuit of Personal and Political Happiness 2012, The Happy Depressive 2012, Burden of Power 2012, My Name Is... 2013, The Irish Diaries (1994–2003) 2013, Winners: And How They Succeed 2015. *Leisure interests:* running, cycling, bagpipes, Burnley Football Club. *Address:* Portland Communications, 85 Strand, London, WC2R 0DW, England (office). *Telephone:* (20) 7554-1600 (office). *E-mail:* speaker@alastaircampbell.org (office). *Website:* www.portland-communications.com (office); www.alastaircampbell.org.

CAMPBELL, Hon. Alexander Bradshaw, OC, PC, QC, LLD; Canadian lawyer and politician; b. 1 Dec. 1933, Summerside, PEI; s. of Thane A. Campbell and Cecilia Bradshaw; m. Marilyn Gilmour 1961; two s. one d.; practised law in Summerside, PEI 1959–66; mem. PEI Legislature 1965–78, Leader of Liberal Party for PEI Dec. 1965–78; Premier of PEI 1966–78; Minister of Devt 1969–72, of Agric. and Forestry 1972–74, Pres. Exec. Council, Minister of Justice, Attorney and Advocate-Gen. 1974–78; Justice, Supreme Court of PEI 1978–94; mem. Privy Council for Canada 1967; mem. and fmr Sec. Summerside Bd of Trade; Past Pres. Y's Men's Club; fmr Vice-Pres. and Exec. mem. PEI Young Liberal Asscn; Pres. Summerside YMCA 1981–91; Elder, United Church, Summerside; Founding Pres. Summerside Area Historical Soc. 1983–88; Founding Chair. Duke of Edinburgh's Awards Cttee (PEI) 1984; Trustee Wyatt Foundation 1990; mem. Heedless Hoarsemen Men's Chorus, Largo, Fla; Co-founder Prince Edward Island Day, Fla; Hon. LLD (McGill, PEI). *Leisure interests:* golf, swimming, gardening. *Address:* Stanley Bridge, Kensington, R.R. #6, Prince Edward Island, C0B 1M0, Canada; 7100 Ulmerton Road, Lot 314, Largo, FL 33771, USA (Winter). *Telephone:* (902) 886-2081 (Summer); (727) 530-9499 (Winter). *E-mail:* alexbcampbell@auracom.com (home).

CAMPBELL, Ben Nighthorse, BA; American lawyer and fmr politician; *President, Ben Nighthorse Consultants;* b. 13 April 1933, Auburn, Calif.; m. Linda Price; two c.; ed Univ. of California, San José; educator, Sacramento Law Enforcement Agency; mem. (Democrat) Colo Gen. Ass. 1983–86; mem. US House of Reps 1987–93; Senator from Colo 1993–2005; Sr Policy Advisor, Holland & Knight LLP (law firm), Washington, DC 2005–12; Founder and Pres. Ben Nighthorse Consultants, Pueblo, Colo 2012–; one of 44 chiefs Northern Cheyenne Tribe; mem. American Quarter Horse Asscn, American Indian Educ. Asscn, Aircraft Owners and Pilots Asscn; Ellis Island Medal of Honor 2008. *Address:* Ben Nighthorse Consultants, PO Box 11201, Pueblo, CO 81001, USA (office). *Telephone:* (719) 250-0541 (office). *E-mail:* NighthorseConsultants@gmail.com (office). *Website:* bennighthorseconsultants.com (office).

CAMPBELL, Sir Colin Murray, Kt, LLB; British academic and fmr university administrator; b. 26 Dec. 1944, Aberdeen, Scotland; s. of Donald Campbell and Isobel Campbell; m. 1st Elaine Carlisle 1974 (divorced 1999); one s. one d.; m. 2nd Maria Day 2002 (divorced 2004); ed Robert Gordon's Coll., Aberdeen and Univ. of Aberdeen; Lecturer, Faculty of Law, Univ. of Dundee 1967–69, Univ. of Edinburgh 1969–73; Prof. of Jurisprudence, Queen's Univ., Belfast 1974–88, now Prof. Emer.; Vice-Chancellor, Univ. of Nottingham 1988–2008; mem. Council, Soc. for Computers and Law 1973–88, Standing Advisory Comm. on Human Rights 1977–80, Legal Aid Advisory Cttee, Northern Ireland 1978–82, Mental Health Legislation Review Cttee, Northern Ireland 1978–82, Nottingham Devt Enterprise 1988–91, Inquiry into Police Responsibilities and Rewards 1992–93; Chair. Ind. Advisory Group on Consumers' Protection in Northern Ireland 1984, Northern Ireland Econ. Council 1987–94 (mem. 1985–94), Lace Market Devt Co. 1989–97, Human Fertilisation and Embryology Authority 1990–94, Medical Workforce Standing Advisory Cttee 1991–2001, Food Advisory Cttee 1994–2001, Human Genetics Advisory Comm. 1996–99; Chair. QUBIS Ltd 1983–88, Zeton Ltd 1990; Dir (non-exec.) Swiss Re GB 1999–2005; HM's First Commr for Judicial Appointments 2001–06; Hon. Freeman, City of Nottingham; Hon. LLD (Aberdeen) 2001, (Shanghai Jia-Tong), (Lincoln), (Nottingham). *Publications include:* Law and Society (co-author) 1979, Do We Need a Bill of Rights? (ed.) 1980, Data Processing and the Law (ed.) 1984; numerous articles in books and journals. *Leisure interests:* walking, sport, music, reading.

CAMPBELL, Finley Alexander, PhD, FRSC; Canadian geologist and academic; *Professor Emeritus, Department of Geology and Geophysics, University of Calgary;* b. 5 Jan. 1927, Kenora, Ont.; s. of Finley McLeod Campbell and Vivian Delve; m. Barbara E. Cromarty 1953; two s. one d.; ed Kenora High School, Portland Univ., Brandon Coll., Univ. of Manitoba, Queen's Univ. Kingston, Ont. and Princeton Univ.; exploration and mine geologist 1950–58; Asst, Assoc. Prof., Univ. of Alberta 1958–65; Prof. and Head, Dept of Geology, Univ. of Calgary 1965–69; Vice-Pres. Capital Resources, Univ. of Calgary 1969–71, Vice-Pres. (Academic) 1971–76, Prof. of Geology 1976–84, Vice-Pres. Priorities and Planning 1984–88, Prof. Emer., Dept of Geology and Geophysics 1988–; Vice-Chair. Canadian Energy Research Inst.; Pres. Emer. Asscn, Univ. of Calgary; Queen's Jubilee Medal 1977, Commemorative Medal for 125th Anniversary of Canada, Distinguished Service Award (Brandon Univ.) 1993 and other awards and distinctions. *Publications:* over 50 publs on geological topics. *Leisure interests:* sailing, golf, music, skiing, ballet. *Address:* Department of Geology and Geophysics, University of Calgary, 2500 University Drive NW, Calgary, AB T2N 1N4 (office); 3408 Benton Drive NW, Calgary AB T2L 1W8, Canada (home). *Telephone:* (403) 220-3258 (office). *E-mail:* campbelf@ucalgary.ca (office). *Website:* www.geo.ucalgary.ca (office).

CAMPBELL, Hon. Gordon Muir, BA, MBA; Canadian politician and diplomatist; b. 12 Jan. 1948, Vancouver, BC; s. of Dr Charles Gordon (Chargo) Campbell and Peg Campbell; m. Nancy Campbell; two s.; ed University Hill Secondary School, Dartmouth Coll., Simon Fraser Univ.; taught secondary school in Yola, Nigeria 1970s; Asst to Vancouver Mayor Art Phillips; Gen. Man. of Devt, Marathon Realty 1976–81; f. Citycore Devt Corpn 1981; mem. Vancouver City Council 1984–86; Mayor of Vancouver 1986–93; Leader BC Liberal Party 1993; mem. BC Legislature for Vancouver-Quilchena 1994–2011, for Vancouver-Point Grey 2001; Premier of BC 2001–11; High Commr to UK 2011–16; Dir (non-Exec.) Grosvenor Americas 2016–; Queen's Golden Jubilee Medal 2002, Order of British Columbia 2011, Queen's Diamond Jubilee Medal 2012; Canadian Olympic Order, Canadian Olympic Cttee 2010, Interfaith Brotherhood Man of the Year, Harald Merilees Tourism Award, Modern Makers of Canada Award. *Address:* Grosvenor Americas, One California Street, Suite 2500, San Francisco, CA 94111, USA (office). *Telephone:* (415) 434-0175 (office). *E-mail:* americas@grosvenor.com (office). *Website:* www.grosvenor.com (office).

CAMPBELL, Juliet Jeanne d'Auvergne, CMG, MA; British fmr diplomatist and university administrator (retd); *Life Fellow, Girton College, Cambridge;* b. 23 May 1935, London; d. of Wilfred d'Auvergne Collings and Harriet Nancy Draper

Bishop; m. Alexander Elmslie Campbell 1983 (died 2002); ed schools in S Africa, Palestine, Lebanon and UK, Lady Margaret Hall, Oxford; joined Foreign Office, London 1957, Del. to Conf. negotiating Britain's proposed entry to EC 1961–63, Second Sec., Bangkok 1964–67, First Sec. Paris (NATO) 1966, First Sec., FCO News Dept 1967–70, Head of Chancery, The Hague 1970–74, First Sec. then Counsellor FCO 1974–77, Counsellor, Paris 1977–80, Royal Coll. Defence Studies 1981, Counsellor, Jakarta 1982–83, Head, Training Dept 1983–87; Amb. to Luxembourg 1987–91; mem. Wilton Park Acad. Council 1992–2000; Mistress Girton Coll., Cambridge 1992–98, Life Fellow 1998–; Deputy Vice-Chancellor, Cambridge Univ. 1993–98; mem. Council Queen's Coll., Harley St 1992–2002; Gov. Marlborough Coll. 1999–2007; Trustee Cambridge European Trust 1994–98, Kurt Hahn Trust 1995–98, Changing Faces (Charity) 1994–2006, Council Royal Soc. for Asian Affairs 2008–14; Hon. Fellow, Lady Margaret Hall, Oxford 1992. *Address:* 3 Belbroughton Road, Oxford, OX2 6UZ, England (home). *Telephone:* (1865) 558685 (home). *E-mail:* jencampbell@aol.com.

CAMPBELL, Rt Hon Kim Avril Phaedra, BA, LLB, PC QC; Canadian politician and lawyer; b. 10 March 1947, Port Alberni, BC; m. Hershey Felder; ed Univ. of British Columbia, London School of Econs, UK; Lecturer in Science and History, Vancouver Community Coll., in Political Science, Univ. of British Columbia; mem. BC Legis.; elected (Progressive Conservative) House of Commons 1988, Progressive Conservative leader June–Nov. 1993; Minister of State Affairs and Northern Devt 1989–90, Minister of Justice and Attorney-Gen. of Canada 1990–93; Minister of Defence 1993; Prime Minister (first female) June–Nov. 1993; mem. Visiting Cttee Center for Int. Affairs, Harvard Univ. 1995; Consul Gen. of Canada in Los Angeles serving states of California, Utah, Nevada, Arizona, Hawaii and territory of Guam 1996–2000; Visiting Prof. of Practice, John F. Kennedy School of Govt, Harvard Univ. 2001–04; Chair. Council of Women World Leaders 1999–2003, Chair. Emer. 2003–; Pres. Int. Women's Forum 2003–05; Sec.-Gen. Club of Madrid 2004–06; Sr Fellow, Gorbachev Foundation of North America; Fellow, John F. Kennedy School of Govt, Harvard Univ.; mem. Int. Council of Asia Soc.; Hon. Fellow, LSE 1994; Dr hc (Brock Univ.) 1998, (Univ. of British Columbia) 2000, (Mt Holyoke Coll., South Hadley, Mass) 2004, (DPS Northeastern Univ., Boston) 1999. *Publications:* Sayings of Chairman Kim 1995, Time and Chance: A Political Memoir of Canada's First Woman Prime Minister (autobiog.) 1996. *Address:* c/o American Program Bureau, 313 Washington Street, Suite 225, Newton, MA 02458, USA. *Telephone:* (800) 225-4575 (office). *Fax:* (617) 965-6610 (office). *E-mail:* kim_campbell@ksg.harvard.edu. *Website:* www.apbspeakers.com (office).

CAMPBELL, Lewis B., BEng; American business executive; b. 1946, Winchester, Va; ed Duke Univ.; 24 years at Gen. Motors, including Gen. Mfg Man., Rochester Products Div., Mfg Man., Chevrolet-Pontiac, Exec. Dir GM/UAW Quality Network, Vice-Pres. Gen. Motors and Gen. Man. Flint Automotive Group 1988–91, Gen. Man. GMC Truck 1991–92; joined Textron Inc. 1992 as Exec. Vice-Pres. and COO, Pres. and COO 1994–98, CEO 1998, also Chair. 1999–2009 and Pres. 2001–09; interim CEO and Chair., Navistar International Corpn 2012–13; mem. Bd of Dirs Bristol-Myers Squibb, Sensata Technologies Holding NV; mem. Business Roundtable, Business Council; mem. Bd of Visitors, Fuqua School of Business, Duke Univ.

CAMPBELL, Naomi; British model; b. 22 May 1970, London; d. of Valerie Morris; ed Barbara Speake Stage School, Italia Conti; fashion model 1985–; showed collections of designers including Chanel, Azzedine Alaia, Christian Dior and Versace; established Fashion For Relief, presenting shows in New York, London, Cannes, Moscow, Mumbai and Dar es Salaam to raise funds first for victims of Hurricane Katrina in New Orleans, then various other causes; named Ed.-at-Large, Interview Russia and Interview Germany 2011; Women Leading Change Award 2016. *Film appearances include:* Ready To Wear 1994, Miami Rhapsody 1995, Catwalk 1995, Invasion of Privacy 1996, Beautopia 1996, Prisoner of Love 1999, Destinazione Verna 2000, Ali G Indahouse 2002, Fastlane 2003, Fat Slags 2004, The Call 2006, Karma, Confessions and Holi 2009, Rose, c'est Paris 2010, Por el Camino 2010; music videos: Madonna's Erotica, Bob Marley's Is This Love, Michael Jackson's In The Closet. *Television includes:* appearances on Ugly Betty 2008, The Cosby Show, The Fresh Prince of Bel-Air; The Face (series exec. producer), shown in USA, UK, Australia. *Albums include:* Baby Woman 1994, Love and Tears 1994. *Publications include:* That Wild Lie 1992, Swan 1994, Naomi 2001. *Address:* TESS Management, 9–10 Market Place, 4th Floor, London, W1W 8AQ, England (office). *Website:* www.naomicampbell.com.

CAMPBELL, Neve Adrienne; Canadian actress; b. 3 Oct. 1973, Guelph, Ont.; m. 1st Jeff Colt 1995 (divorced 1997); m. 2nd John Light 2007; ed Nat. Ballet School, Canada. *Dance includes:* The Phantom of the Opera, The Nutcracker, Sleeping Beauty. *Films include:* Paint Cans 1994, The Dark 1994, Love Child 1995, The Craft 1996, Scream (Saturn Award for Best Actress 1996, MTV Movie Award for Best Female Performance 1996) 1996, A Time to Kill 1996, Simba's Pride 1997, Scream 2 (MTV Movie Award for Best Female Performance 1996, Blockbuster Entertainment Award for Favourite Actress – Horror 1997) 1997, Wild Things 1998, Hairshirt 1998, 54 1998, Three to Tango 1999, Scream 3 2000, Panic 2000, A Lust for Life 2000, Drowning Mona 2000, Last Call 2003, Blind Horizon 2003, Lost Junction 2003, The Company 2003, When Will I Be Loved 2004, Churchill: The Hollywood Years 2004, Partition 2006, Relative Strangers 2006, Closing the Ring 2006, Love Bites 2007, I Really Hate My Job 2007, Owl Song 2009, Vivaldi 2009, Scream 4 2011, The Glass Man 2011, Singularity 2012, Walter 2015. *Television includes:* Catwalk 1992–93, Web of Deceit 1993, Baree 1994, The Forget-Me-Not Murders 1994, Party of Five 1994–98, The Canterville Ghost 1996, Reefer Madness: The Movie Musical 2005, Medium 2007, Burn Up 2008, Sea Wolf (mini-series) 2009, The Philanthropist 2009, Titanic: Blood and Steel (series) 2012, Sworn to Silence (film) 2012, Grey's Anatomy (2 episodes) 2012, An Amish Murder (film) 2013. *Address:* Creative Artists Agency, 2000 Avenue of the Stars, Los Angeles, CA 90067, USA. *Telephone:* (424) 288-2000. *Fax:* (424) 288-2900. *Website:* www.caa.com.

CAMPBELL, Sir Philip Henry Montgomery, Kt, BSc, MSc, PhD, FInstP, FRAS; British astrophysicist, academic and editor; *Editor-in-Chief, Nature;* b. 19 April 1951; s. of Hugh Campbell and Mary Montgomery Campbell; m. Judie Yelton 1980 (died 1992); two s.; ed Shrewsbury School, Univ. of Bristol, Queen Mary Coll., London, Univ. of Leicester; postdoctoral research asst, Dept of Physics, Univ. of Leicester 1977–79; Asst Ed. Nature journal 1979–82, Physical Sciences Ed. 1982–88, Ed., Nature journal and Ed.-in-Chief Nature journal and Nature publs 1995–, also Ed.-in-Chief Nature Publishing Group; Founding Ed. Physics World magazine 1988–95; Visiting Scholar, Rockefeller Univ., New York; Assoc., Clare Hall, Cambridge, Life mem. 2009; Trustee, Cancer Research UK; Hon. Prof., Peking Union Medical Coll.; Hon. Fellow, Queen Mary, Univ. of London 2009; Hon. DSc (Leicester) 1999, (Bristol) 2008. *Radio:* broadcasts on BBC World Service; guest on Private Passions (BBC Radio 3) 2010. *Publications include:* numerous papers and articles in journals, magazines and newspapers. *Leisure interest:* music. *Address:* Nature Publishing Group, The Macmillan Building, 4 Crinan Street, London, N1 9XW, England (office). *Telephone:* (20) 7833-4000 (office). *Fax:* (20) 7843-4640 (office). *E-mail:* exec@nature.com (office). *Website:* www.nature.com/nature/about/editors (office).

CAMPBELL, Sydney, MA (Econ); Belizean fmr central banker; ed Florida Int. Univ., USA; joined Cen. Bank of Belize 1981, served in various posts, including Deputy Gov. –2003, Gov. and Vice-Chair. 2003–08. *Address:* c/o Central Bank of Belize, Gabourel Lane, PO Box 852, Belize City, Belize. *E-mail:* cenbank@btl.net.

CAMPBELL, William Cecil, BA, MSc, PhD; Irish/American biologist, parasitologist and academic; *Research Institute for Scientists Emeriti (RISE) Associate, Drew University;* b. 28 June 1930, Derry, Northern Ireland; s. of Robert John Campbell and Sarah Jane Campbell (née Patterson); m. Mary Mastin 1962; one s. two d.; ed Trinity Coll., Dublin, Univ. of Wisconsin, USA; Research Assoc., Merck Sharp & Dohme Research Labs, Rahway, NJ 1957–63, Research Fellow 1963–66, Sr Research Fellow 1966, Dir, Parasitology 1966–72, Dir, Merck Sharp & Dohme Veterinary R&D Lab., Ingleburn, Australia 1972–73, Sr Investigator, Rahway, NJ 1973–76, Dir, Basic Parasitology 1977–78, Sr Dir 1978–84, Sr Scientist 1984–90; Adjunct Prof., New York Medical Coll., Valhalla 1985–, Univ. of Pennsylvania 1981–; Dana Fellow, Drew Univ., Madison, NJ 1990–2010, Research Inst. for Scientists Emeriti (RISE) Assoc. 2010–; mem. Editorial Bd Experimental Parasitology, and others; mem. NAS, New York Soc. of Tropical Medicine (Pres. 1970–71), New Jersey Soc. of Parasitology (Pres. 1976–77), Int. Comm. on Trichinellosis (Pres. 1980–84), American Soc. of Parasitology (Pres. 1987), Summit Playhouse Asscn (Pres. 1991–94), Medical History Soc. of New Jersey (Pres. 1994–96); Fellow, Royal Soc. of Tropical Medicine and Hygiene; Fulbright Grantee 1953, Kohler Fellow, Univ. Wisconsin 1955, Directors Science Award, Merck & Co. Inc. 1987, Discoverers Award, Pharmaceutical Manufacturing Asscn 1989, Kitasato Medal 1990, Nobel Prize in Physiology or Medicine (co-recipient with Satoshi Ōmura and Youyou Tu) 2015. *Achievement:* known for his discoveries concerning a novel therapy against infections caused by roundworms. *Publications:* Trichinella and Trichinosis (ed.) 1983, Chemotherapy of Parasitic Diseases (ed.) 1986, Ivermectin and Abamectin (ed.) 1989; numerous papers in professional journals. *Leisure interests:* community theatre, poetry, painting. *Address:* Research Institute for Scientists Emeriti (RISE), Hall of Sciences, Drew University, 36 Madison Avenue, Madison, NJ 07940, USA (office). *Telephone:* (973) 408-3096 (office); (973) 408-3180 (office). *E-mail:* wcampbel@drew.edu (office). *Website:* www.drew.edu/rise/rise-fellows-and-associates (office); www.germtheorycalendar.com.

CAMPBELL BARR, Epsy, BA, MA; Costa Rican economist and politician; *First Vice-President;* b. 4 July 1963, San José; d. of Luis Campbell Barr and Shirley Campbell Barr Aird Patterson; m.; two d.; ed Franco Costarricense Lyceum, Colegio Superior de Señoritas, San José, Univ. of Costa Rica, Universidad Latina de Costa Rica, Fundación Cultural y de Ciencias Sociales de España; fmr student leader and musician (played flute and saxophone in Symphonic Youth Orchestra 1976–83); began univ. studies and later moved to Regional HQ of Limón Prov. to study and work; lived in Caribbean for 10 years, then returned to San José; fmr researcher and activist, Human Rights of Women and People of African Descent; Deputy, Legis. Ass. 2002–06, 2014–18; Co-founder (with Ottón Solís) Partido Acción Ciudadana (PAC) 2000, head of PAC party faction 2003–05, Pres. PAC 2005–09, PAC vice-presidential nominee (first ever female) 2006; First Vice-Pres. 2018–, also Minister of Foreign Affairs and Worship May–Dec. 2018; has been involved in several women's and Afro-Latin American groups, including Women's Forum for Cen. American Integration, Centre for Afro-Costa Rican Women, Alliance of Latin American and Caribbean Leaders of African Descent, Black Parl. of the Americas, amongst others. *Publications include:* several books and articles on democracy, inclusion, political and econ. participation of women, people of African descent, sexism and racism. *Address:* Presidency of the Republic of Costa Rica, Zapote, San José; Legislative Assembly, Avenida Central y Primera entre calles 15 y 17, San José (office); Partido Acción Ciudadana, 25 San Pedro, 425 m sur del Templo Parroquial, San José, Costa Rica. *Telephone:* 2207-9100 (office). *Website:* www.asamblea.go.cr (office); pac.cr.

CAMPBELL-BROWN, Veronica; Jamaican athlete; b. 15 May 1982, Trelawny; d. of Cecil Campbell and Pamella Bailey; m. Omar Brown 2007; ed Vere Tech. High School, Clarendon, Barton Co. Community Coll., Great Bend, Kan. and Univ. of Arkansas, USA; track and field sprint athlete; six-time Olympic medallist, Olympic 200m and World 100m Champion; gold medals, 100m and 4×100m, inaugural Int. Asscn of Athletics Feds (IAAF) World Youth Championships 1999; first female to win sprint double at IAAF World Jr Championships 2000; silver medal, 4×100m relay, Olympic Games, Sydney 2000; only female athlete to win both 100m and 200m sprints at same World Youth Championships; silver medal, 100m, Commonwealth Games, Manchester 2002; gold medals, 200m and 4×100m, bronze medal, 100m, Olympic Games, Athens 2004; silver medals, 100m and 4×100m relay, World Championships, Helsinki 2005; silver medal, 200m, Commonwealth Games, Melbourne 2006; gold medal, 100m, World Championships, Osaka 2007, silver medals, 200m and 4×100m relay; gold medal, 200m, Olympic Games, Beijing 2008 (set new personal best time of 21.74 seconds; only second woman in history to win Olympic 200m twice and successfully defend her title); Jamaica Nat. Champion 200m 2009; World Championships 200m (silver medal) 2009; gold medal, 200m, World Championships, Daegu 2011; silver medal, 4×100m relay, bronze medal, 100m, London Olympics 2012; gold medal, 4×100m relay, Commonwealth Games, Glasgow 2014; gold medal, 4×100m relay, bronze medal, 200m, World Championships, Beijing 2015; silver medal, 4×100m relay, Olympic Games, Rio de Janeiro 2016; World Indoor Champion, 60m 2010; World Leader 100m & 200m 2010; Founder-Chair. Veronica Campbell-Brown Foundation 2011–; apptd UNESCO Champion for Sport Amb. 2009; Jamaica's Sportswoman of the Year Award 2004, 2007, 2008, 2010, 2011, Courtney Walsh Award for Excellence 2012, Children of Jamaica Outreach (COJO) Humanitarian Award 2015. *Publication:* A Better You, Inspirations for Life's Journey. *Address:* On Track Management, PO Box 43023, Atlanta, GA 30336, USA. *Telephone:* (770) 420-1075. *Fax:* (770) 420-1076. *E-mail:* veronica@veronicacampbellbrown.com. *Website:* www.veronicacampbellbrown.com.

CAMPBELL OF PITTENWEEM, Baron (Life Peer), cr. 2015, of Pittenweem in the County of Fife; **Rt Hon. Walter Menzies (Ming) Campbell,** Kt, CH, CBE, QC, MA, LLB, LLD; British politician and university administrator; b. 22 May 1941, Glasgow; m. Elspeth Urquart; ed Hillhead High School, Univ. of Glasgow, Stanford Univ., USA; ran 200m at Tokyo Olympic Games 1964 and Commonwealth Games 1966, Capt. UK Athletics Team 1965–66; called to Scottish Bar as Advocate 1968; Chair. Scottish Liberal Party 1975; MP for Fife North East 1987–2015, Spokesman on Sport and Defence 1988–94, Shadow Foreign Sec. 1997–2006; Deputy Leader, Liberal Democrat Party 2003–06, Leader 2006–07; Chancellor St Andrews Univ. 2006–; mem. (Liberal Democrat), House of Lords 2015–; Dr hc (Glasgow), (Strathclyde); Hon. LLD (St Andrews) 2006. *Achievements include:* held British 100m record 1967–74. *Publication:* Menzies Campbell: My Autobiography 2008. *Address:* House of Lords, Westminster, London, SW1A 0PW, England (office). *Telephone:* (20) 7219-6910 (office). *E-mail:* contactholmember@parliament.uk (office). *Website:* www.parliament.uk/biographies/lords/lord-campbell-of-pittenweem/627 (office).

CAMPBELL OF SURBITON, Baroness (Life Peer), cr. 2007, of Surbiton in the Royal Borough of Kingston upon Thames; **Jane Susan Campbell,** DBE; British politician; b. 19 April 1959; d. of Ronald James Campbell and Jessie Mary Campbell (née Ball); m. Roger Symes; progressed through several local govt equal opportunities roles, principally focusing on disability human rights issues before becoming an Ind. Consultant on Direct Payments 1994–96; co-directed Nat. Centre for Ind. Living 1996–2001; Founding Chair. Social Care Inst. for Excellence 2001–05; Commr, Disability Rights Comm. 2000–07, Equalities and Human Rights Comm. 2007–09; Consultant to Office of Disability Issues in role of Chair. of Right to Control Working Group, Dept of Work and Pensions 2007–12, also in role of Chair. of Ind. Living Scrutiny Group; Chair. All-Party Parl. Disability Group, Ind. mem. House of Lords Appointments Comm. 2008–; Pres. Nat. Disability Archive 2013–. *Address:* House of Lords, Westminster, London, SW1A 0PW, England (office). *Telephone:* (20) 7219-5124 (office). *Fax:* (20) 7219-1303 (office). *E-mail:* campbelljs@parliament.uk (office).

CAMPBELL-WHITE, Martin Andrew, MBE, FRSA; British business executive; *Consultant, Askonas Holt Ltd;* b. 11 July 1943; s. of John Vernon Campbell-White and Hilda Doris Ash; m. Margaret Mary Miles 1969; three s.; ed Dean Close School, Cheltenham, St John's Coll., Oxford, Univ. of Strasbourg, France; with Thomas Skinner & Co. Ltd (Publrs) 1964–66, Ibbs & Tillett Ltd (Concert Agents) 1966–72, Dir 1969–72, Harold Holt Ltd (Concert Agents), subsequently Askonas Holt Ltd 1972–, Dir 1973–2014, Deputy Chair. 1989–92, Chief Exec. 1992–98, Jt Chief Exec. 1998–2014, Consultant 2014–; Chair. British Asscn of Concert Agents 1978–81; Council mem. London Sinfonietta 1973–86; Dir Chamber Orchestras of Europe 1983–93; Asst Dir Festival of German Arts 1987; Founding Dir Japan Festival 1991; mem. Bd Première Ensemble 1991–, Riverside Studios 1998–2000; Trustee, Abbado Trust for Young Musicians 1987–2006, Salzburg Festival Trust 1996–2000; Exec. Trustee, Musicians Benevolent Fund 2006–; Hon. mem. Royal Philharmonic Soc. 2014; Sebetia Ter prize for Culture, Naples, Italy 1999. *Leisure interests:* golf, watching cricket, classical music, travel. *Address:* Askonas Holt Ltd, 15 Fetter Lane, London, EC4A 1BW, England (office). *Telephone:* (20) 7400-1700 (office). *Fax:* (20) 7400-1799 (office). *E-mail:* martin.campbell-white@askonasholt.co.uk (office). *Website:* www.askonasholt.co.uk (office).

CAMPESE, David Ian, AM; Australian fmr professional rugby union player and business executive; *Managing Director, Goosestep Pty Ltd;* b. 21 Oct. 1962, Queanbeyan, NSW; s. of Tony Campese and Joan Campese; m. Lara Berkenstein 2003; partner, Campo's Sports Store; played with ACT 1981–85, Queanbeyan Whites 1982–86, Petrarca Padova 1984–88, Randwick 1987–98, NSW 1987–98, Amatori Rugby Milano 1988–93; int. debut for Australia versus NZ 1982; Capt. Australia team; winner World Cup 1991; world's leading int. try scorer with 64; scored 310 points for Australia; fmrly Australia's most capped player (represented Australia 101 times) 1982–96; played for Australia Sevens nat. team, Commonwealth Games 1998; coach, Singapore 1998, Murray Mexted Int. Acad. 2004–05, Natal Sharks 2005–08, Tonga 7s 2010; Dir David Campese Man. Group 1997–; Man. Dir Goosestep Pty Ltd; Australian Writers Player of the Year 1991, inducted into Sport Australia Hall of Fame 1997, English Rugby Writers Player of the Year 1991, Australian Sports Medal 2000, Int. Rugby Hall of Fame 2001, Order of Australia Medal (for services to rugby union) 2002, inducted into Australian Rugby Union Hall of Fame 2007, inducted into IRB Hall of Fame 2013. *Publications:* On a Wing and a Prayer (biog.), My Game, Your Game 1994, Still Entertaining 2003. *Leisure interests:* golf, cooking, music, reading. *Address:* 13 Nicholas Avenue, Concord, Sydney, NSW 2137, Australia (home). *E-mail:* dcampese@bigpond.net.au (office).

CAMPION, Dame Jane, BA; New Zealand film director and writer; b. 30 April 1954, Wellington; d. of Richard Campion and Edith Campion; ed Victoria Univ., Chelsea School of Arts, London, Australian Film, TV and Radio School, Sydney Coll. of the Arts; Adjunct Prof., Sydney Coll. of the Arts, Univ. of Sydney 2000; Pres. Int. Jury of 54th Mostra Internazionale d'Arte Cinematografica Festival, Venice Film Festival; Hon. DLitt (Victoria Univ. of Wellington) 1999; Women in Hollywood Icon Award, Taormina Arte Diamond Award (Italy), Taormina Arte Award for Cinematic Excellence (Italy) 2004, Vanguard Dir Award 2005, Byron Kennedy Award for Excellence and contrib. to Australian Cinema, Special Career Award 2010, Golden Coach Award, Cannes Film Festival 2013. *Films directed include:* Peel (Palme d'Or for Best Short Film, Cannes Film Festival) 1981–82, Girl's Own Story (Best Dir, Best Telemovie, Best Screenplay at Australian Film Inst. (AFI) Awards, Rouben Mamoulian Award for Best Overall Short Film, Sydney Film Festival, Best Direction, Best Screenplay, Best Cinematography, AFI Awards, First Prize, Cinestud (Press Prize), Amsterdam Film Festival, voted Best Film by critics at Cinestud 1985) 1984, Two Friends (Best Dir, Best Telemovie, Best Screenplay, AFI Awards 1987) 1985, Sweetie (also co-writer) 1988, The Piano (more than 30 int. international awards, including the Palme d'Or (only female winner), Cannes Film Festival, three Acad. Awards, including Best Screenplay, winner Best Dir, New York Film Critics' Circle, Los Angeles Film Critics' Asscn, Australian Film Critics, winner Best Picture, Australian Film Inst.) 1993, The Portrait of a Lady (Best Film, Venice Film Festival) 1996, Holy Smoke 1999, In the Cut 2003, The Water Diary (short film for UNDP) 2005, The Lady Bug (short) 2006, Bright Star (NSW Premier's Literary Award 2010) 2009, 2017. *Television includes:* Top of the Lake (series) (Australian Film Inst. Award, New Zealand Film and TV Award 2014) 2013, Top of the Lake: Chine Girl (series) 2017. *Address:* c/o HLA Management Theatrical Agency Australia, PO Box 1536, Strawberry Hills, Sydney, NSW 2012, Australia (office). *Telephone:* (2) 9549-3000 (office). *Fax:* (2) 9310-4113 (office). *E-mail:* hla@hlamgt.com.au (office).

CAMPOS E CUNHA, Luis; Portuguese economist, academic and fmr government official; b. 6 Feb. 1954; m.; three c.; ed Univ. Católica Portuguesa, Columbia Univ., USA; Asst Prof. of Econs, School of Econs, Universidade Nova de Lisboa 1985–91, Assoc. Prof. 1991–95, Prof. 1995–, Dean, School of Econs 2002–05; Prof., Universidade Católica Portuguesa 1992–95; Vice-Gov. Banco de Portugal 1996–2002; Minister of Finance and Public Admin, Minister of State March–July 2005; mem. Int. Relations Cttee, European Cen. Bank, Frankfurt 1998–2002; mem. Econ. and Finance Cttee, Brussels 1998–2001; Chair. SEDES, Associação para o Desenvolvimento Económico e Social; Vice-Pres. Fundação Serralves; mem. Bd of Dirs (non-exec.) Fundação Serralves 2006–; mem. Bd of Govs Centro Cultural de Belém. *Address:* School of Business and Economics, Universidade Nova de Lisboa, Campus de Campolide, 1099-032 Lisbon, Portugal (office). *E-mail:* lccunha@novasbe.pt (office). *Website:* www.novasbe.unl.pt (office).

CAMUS, Philippe; French business executive; *Chairman and Interim CEO, Alcatel-Lucent;* b. 28 June 1948, Paris; ed Ecole Normale Supérieure, Paris, Institut des Etudes Politiques de Paris; Special Project Man. Caisse des Dépôts et Consignations 1972–82; Dir, Sr Man. Lagardère Groupe, Co-Pres. Chair. Financial Cttee 1993–98, Co-Man. Partner Lagardère SCA 1998–2012, Chair. and CEO Arjil Commanditée – ARCO (Gen. Partner, Group) 1992, later Vice-Chair. and Deputy CEO, Chair. and CEO Lagardère North America, Inc.; Chair. Financial Cttee Matra Group 1982–92; CEO and Chair. Man. Bd Aérospatiale Matra 1999–2000; Co-CEO European Aeronautic Defence and Space Co. (EADS) 2000–05; Chair. Supervisory Bd Banque Arjil 1987–93; Pres. Groupement des Industries Françaises Aéreonautiques et Spatiales (GIFAS) 2001–05, Hon. Chair. 2005–; Sr Man. Dir Evercore Partners Inc. (investment man. co.) from 2006, now Sr Advisor; Chair. (non-exec.), Alcatel-Lucent 2008–15, Chair. and Interim CEO 2015–; mem. or fmr mem. Bd of Dirs, Crédit Agricole SA, Accor SA, Institut d'Expertise et de Prospective of Ecole Normale Supérieure, Paris Ueroplace Asscn; Perm. Rep. of Lagardère SCA to Bd of Dirs Hachette SA, of Hachette SA to Bd of Dirs, Lagardère Services; mem. Supervisory Bd Lagardère Active; Dir, Éditions P. Amaury, Schlumberger, Cellfish Media LLC; Chevalier, Légion d'honneur 2000, Officier 2005; Bundesverdienstkreuz 2004; Aviation Week Aerospace Laureate 1989, Prix de la meilleure opération financière 2000. *Address:* Alcatel-Lucent, 148–152 route de la Reine, 92100 Boulogne-Billancourt, France (office); Evercore Partners, 10 Hill Street, London, W1J 5NQ, England (office). *Telephone:* 1-55-14-10-10 (Paris) (office); (20) 7268-2700 (London) (office). *Fax:* (20) 7268-2710 (London) (office). *E-mail:* execoffice@alcatel-lucent.com (office). *Website:* www.alcatel-lucent.com (office); www.evercore.com (office).

CANAHUATI, Mario Miguel, BE; Honduran diplomatist and politician; b. 12 Sept. 1955, San Pedro Sula; m.; four c.; ed Georgia Inst. of Tech., USA; Gen. Man. for cos Creations Vantage, Industries Pacer, Genesis Apparel; Pres. Distribudora la Bobina; Pres. Chamber of Commerce and Industries of Cortes, Directorate of the Commerce Econ. System; Vice-Pres. Fed. of Chambers of Commerce and Industry; Dir Honduran Council for Pvt. Enterprise, Council for Sustainable Devt, Nat. Asscn for Industry; pvt. sector rep. Negotiation Cttee of Bilateral Treaties; mem. Bd of Dirs San Pedro Sula Int. Airport, Sula Valley Nat. Comm.; Founder and Pres. Mhotivo Foundation; Vice-Pres. Nueva Vida Foundation; mem. Inter-American Devt Bank's Comm. for Dialogue and Social Politics; Amb. to USA 2002–05; Minister of Foreign Affairs 2010–11.

CANALES CLARIOND, Fernando de Jesús, MBA; Mexican lawyer, business executive and politician; b. 21 July 1946, Monterrey, Nuevo León; m. Angela Stelzer; two s. two d.; ed Escuela Libre de Derecho, Instituto Tecnológico y de Estudios Superiores de Monterrey, Univ. of the Sorbonne, Paris, France, Instituto de Altos Estudios en La Haya, Holanda; fmr Pres. Grupo IMSA SA de CV, also fmr Man. Dir Corporativo Grupo IMSA, SA de CV; mem. Partido Accion Nacional 1978–; mem. Congress for First Dist of Nuevo León 1979–81; Gov. of Nuevo León 1997–2003; Minister for the Economy 2003–05; Sec. of Energy 2005–06 (by law also Pres. of Bd of PEMEX, CFE and Luz y Fuerza del Centro); currently Pres. Corporación Finestra SA de CV, Monterrey; Ind. Dir, Compañía Minera Autlán SAB de CV 2009–; Dir, Grupo Aeromexico SAB de CV 2007–; Pres. Chamber of Commerce of Nuevo León, Monterrey Chamber of Commerce; Vice-Pres. Nat. Confed. of Chambers of Commerce in Mexico; mem. Nuevo Leon Business Council, IMSS Ass., Movimiento de Promocion Rural, AC, Consejo Coordinador Empresarial; mem. Mexico–USA Comm. of the Ford Foundation. *Address:* c/o Partido Acción Nacional, Avenida Coyoacán 1546, Col. del Valle, Del. Benito Juárez, 03100 México, DF, Mexico. *E-mail:* correo@cen.pan.org.mx.

CANÇADO TRINDADE, Antônio A., LLB, LLM, PhD; Brazilian professor of international law and judge; *Judge, International Court of Justice;* b. 17 Sept. 1947, Belo Horizonte; ed Fed. Univ. of Minas Gerais, Univ. of Cambridge, UK; Prof. of Public Int. Law, Univ. of Brasilia 1978–, Diplomatic Acad. Rio Branco of Brazil 1979–; Lecturer, Hague Acad. of Int. Law 1987, 2005, Lecturer, annual courses of Int. Law organized by OAS Inter-American Juridical Cttee, Rio de Janeiro 1981–82, 1985, 1990–92, 1995–97, 2000–07; Lecturer, annual study sessions of Int. Inst. of Human Rights, Strasbourg, France 1988, 1991, 1993–2007; Lecturer, Interdisciplinary Courses of Inter-American Inst. of Human Rights (IIHA) 1986, 1989, 1991–2001, 2004, 2007; External Legal Adviser to IIHA 1991–94; Head of Del. of IIHA to Cen. American Conf. on Peace and Devt, Tegucigalpa 1994, mem. Bd of Dirs IIHA 1988–91, 1991–94, 1996–, *ad hoc* Judge, Inter-American Court of Human Rights 1990–94, Exec. IIHA 1994–96, Judge 1995–, Vice-Pres. 1997–99, Pres. 1999–; Judge, Int. Court of Justice, The Hague 2009–; Special Envoy of Minister of External Relations for Questions Pertaining to Human Rights,

Santiago, Chile 1993–94; Dir Brazilian Journal of International Law 1985–; Co-Dir Brazilian Journal of Human Rights 2001–; Brazilian Ed. International Legal Materials, American Soc. of Int. Law 1981–; mem. Editorial Council, Review "Arquivos" of Ministry of Justice of Brazil 1987–2002; mem. Editorial Bd Brazilian Journal of International Politics 1993–, International Newsletter of University of São Paulo, Brazil 1997–; mem. Bd of Dirs IIHA, San José, Int. Inst. of Human Rights, Strasbourg; mem. Brazilian Bar Asscn, Inst. of Int. Law 1997, Int. Inst. of Humanitarian Law, Soc. Française pour le Droit Int., American Soc. of Int. Law, British Inst. of Int. and Comparative Law, Indian Soc. of Int. Law, Asscn des Anciens Auditeurs of Hague Acad. of Int. Law; Assoc. mem. Asociación Argentina de Derecho Internacional; Hon. Pres. Brazilian Inst. of Human Rights; 'Professor Homenageado' (elected by the students), Univ. of Brasilia, Catholic Univ. of Minas Gerais, Brazil 2002, Tuiuti Univ. of Curitiba, Brazil 2002, Diplomatic Acad. Rio Branco 1999, 2006; holder of many academic and other distinctions; several prizes. *Publications:* numerous books and other publs on int. law. *Address:* International Court of Justice, Peace Palace, Carnegieplein 2, 2517 KJ, The Hague, The Netherlands (office). *Telephone:* (70) 302-2323 (office). *Fax:* (70) 364-9928 (office). *E-mail:* info@icj-cij.org (office). *Website:* www.icj-cij.org (office).

CANCELA, Walter; Uruguayan economist, diplomatist and fmr central banker; b. 1950, Montevideo; four c.; ed Universidad de la República; worked at Cen. Bank of Uruguay 1970–78, Centro Cooperativo Uruguayo 1978–85; Researcher, Centro Latinoamericano de Economía Humana (CLAEH) 1975–90; Prof., Universidad de la República 1987–2002, Dir Econ. Inst. 2003; adviser on Uruguay to UN and EC 1990–2000; Pres. Cen. Bank of Uruguay 2005–08; Amb. and Perm. Rep. to EU, Brussels 2010–15.

CANCELLIERI, Anna Maria; Italian government official; b. 22 Oct. 1943, Rome; ed La Sapienza Univ., Rome; joined Ministry of Interior 1972, extensive career in local govt, becoming Prefect of several cities including Vicenza, Bergamo and Brescia 1993–2003, Catania 2003, Head of Genoa Prefecture 2008, Special Commr of Bologna 2010–11, of Parma 2011; Minister of the Interior 2011–13; Minister of Justice 2013–14; Ufficiale dell'Ordine al merito della Repubblica Italiana 1992, Commdr 1993, Grande Ufficiale 2001. *Address:* c/o Ministry of Justice, Via Arenula 71, 00186 Rome, Italy.

CANDU, Andrian, LLB; Moldovan lawyer, business executive and politician; *Chairman, Parliament (Parlamentul);* b. 27 Nov. 1975, Chişinău, Moldovan SSR, USSR; m. Zuzana Candu; three c.; ed T. Popoviciu Lyceum of Informatics, Cluj-Napoca, Romania, Babes-Bolyai Univ., Cluj-Napoca, Vienna Univ. of Econs and Business Admin, Austria, Inst. for Austrian and Int. Tax Law; lawyer, Aric SRL, Romania 1994–98; Sr Consultant, Foreign Policy Comm., Parl. of Moldova 1998–2002; Lecturer, Acad. of Public Admin under the Pres. of the Repub. 2000–04; lawyer, Jt Venture English Compudava LLC 2001–02; Exec. Dir Moldovan–Italian jt enterprise Isimbardi International LLC 2002–03; Sr Man., PricewaterhouseCoopers Moldova 2002–10; Dir-Gen. Prime Management SRL 2010; mem. Parl. (Parlamentul) (Partidul Democrat din Moldova—Democratic Party of Moldova) 2010–, Deputy Chair. 2013–14, Chair. 2015–; Deputy Prime Minister and Minister of the Economy 2014–15; Gen. Dir Moldovan Asscn of Business People; mem. Moldovan Asscn of Int. Law. *Publications:* several publs on law and taxation. *Address:* Office of the Chairman, Parlamentul Republicii Moldova, 2073 Chişinău, bd. Ştefan cel Mare şi Sfânt 105, Moldova (office). *Telephone:* (22) 26-82-44 (office). *Fax:* (22) 23-30-12 (office). *E-mail:* inform@parlament.md (office). *Website:* www.parlament.md (office); www.candu.md.

CANE, Louis Paul Joseph; French painter and sculptor; b. 13 Dec. 1943, Beaulieu-sur-Mer (Alpes-Maritimes); s. of Albert Cane and Andrée Cane (née Pasquier); m. Nicole Rondinella 1970; two d.; ed Collège des Frères Dominicains de Sorèze, Lycée Gassendi de Digne, Ecole Nationale des Arts Décoratifs, Nice, Ecole Nationale Supérieure des Arts Décoratifs, Paris; first exhbn, Galerie Givaudan, Paris 1969; regular exhbns in Germany, Sweden, Spain, Belgium, Italy, Australia, Japan, fmr USSR, UK; perm. exhbn at La Galerie 14, Paris; Officier des Arts et des Lettres. *Publications:* Louis Cane, artiste-peintre 1967, Toiles découpées 1971, Toiles sol/mur 1972, Annonciations 1982, Déluges 1983, Accouchements 1983, Déjeuners sur l'herbe 1985, Trois graces 1987, 1988, Fleurs et tampons 1989, Nymphéas 1992. *Leisure interests:* 18th-century France, studying 18th-century French bronzes. *Address:* 184 rue Saint-Maur, 75010 Paris (office); 37 rue d'Enghien, 75010 Paris, France (home). *Telephone:* 1-42-03-73-31. *Fax:* 1-42-03-01-19. *E-mail:* info@louis-cane.com. *Website:* www.louis-cane.com.

CANET, Guillaume; French actor, film director and screenwriter; b. 10 April 1973, Boulogne-Billancourt; m. Diane Kruger 2001 (divorced 2006); partner Marion Cotillard 2007–; one s.; ed Saint-Louis-Notre-Dame-Du-Bel-Air school, briefly studied at Cours Florent; was engaged in a circus aged ten; parents were horse breeders, briefly followed a professional career in horse riding until an accident aged 18 forced him to take up acting. *Films include:* Fils unique 1995, Barracuda 1997, Sentimental Education 1998, Ceux qui m'aiment prendront le train (Those Who Love Me Can Take the Train) 1998, En plein cœur (In All Innocence) 1998, Trait d'union (short) 1999, Je règle mon pas sur le pas de mon père (Walking in My Father's Footsteps) 1999, J'peux pas dormir... (short) (also dir) 2000, The Beach (La Plage) 2000, La Fidélité 2000, The Day the Ponies Come Back 2000, Les Morsures de l'aube (Love Bites) 2001, Vidocq (aka Dark Portals) 2001, Le Frère du guerrier (The Warrior's Brother) 2002, Mille millièmes (aka The Landlords) 2002, Mon idole (My Idol) (also dir and assoc. producer) 2002, Jeux d'enfants (Love Me if You Dare) 2003, Les Clefs de bagnole (cameo, as himself) 2003, Narco (aka The Secret Adventures of Gustave Klopp) 2004, Joyeux Noël (Merry Christmas) 2005, L'Enfer (Hell) 2005, Un ticket pour l'espace (A Ticket to Space) 2005, Ne le dis à personne (Tell No One) 2006, Cars (French voice of Flash McQueen) 2006, Ensemble, c'est tout (aka Hunting and Gathering) 2007, Darling 2007, La Clef (The Key) 2007, Les Liens du sang (Rivals) 2008, Spy(ies) 2009, Farewell 2009, The Last Flight 2009, Last Night 2010, A Better Life 2011, War of the Buttons 2011, The Players 2012, Thibault 2012, Jappeloup 2013, Turning Tide 2013, In the Name of My Daughter 2014, Next Time I'll Aim for the Heart 2014, The Program 2015, Minions 2015; as dir: Sans regrets 1996, Je taim 1998, Ne le dis à personne (Tell No One) (César Award for Best Dir) 2007, Little White Lies 2010, La nouvelle guerre des boutons (War of the Buttons) 2011, Ivresse (short) 2013, Blood Ties 2013. *Television includes:* La colline aux mille enfants 1994, Jeanne 1994, Ils n'ont pas 20 ans 1995, Le juge est une femme (episode Le secret de Marion) 1995, 17 ans et des poussières 1996, Le voyage de Pénélope (The Voyage of Penelope) 1996, Je m'appelle Régine 1996, Le cheval de coeur 1996, Pardaillan 1997, La vocation d'Adrienne (episode Pilot) 1997, Le porteur de destins 1999, Electrochoc 2004, Platane (series) 2011–13, Le débarquement (series) 2013; as dir: Scénarios sur la drogue (episode Avalanche) 2000. *Address:* c/o Cécile Felsenberg, UBBA, 6 rue de Braque, 75003 Paris, France (office). *Telephone:* 1-44-54-26-40 (office). *Fax:* 1-44-54-08-44 (office). *E-mail:* assistantecf@ubba.eu (office). *Website:* www.ubba.eu/fiche.cfm/182843-guillaume-canet.html?lng=en& (office); www.guillaumecanet.net.

CANGEMI, Joseph P., BS, MS, EdD; American psychologist, academic, consultant and editor; *Professor Emeritus of Psychology/Scholar-in-Residence, Western Kentucky University;* b. 26 June 1936, Syracuse, NY; s. of Samuel Cangemi and Marion Cangemi; m. Amelia Elena Santalo' 1962; two d.; ed State Univ. of NY (SUNY), Oswego, Syracuse and Indiana Univs; taught in Syracuse public schools and in Dominican Repub. 1960–64; Chair. and Lecturer in Psychology, SUNY and Community Coll., Syracuse 1962–65; Supervisor of Educ. and of Training and Devt, US Steel Corpn, Venezuela 1965–68; Teaching Assoc., Indiana Univ., Bloomington 1972, 1973; Asst Prof. to Assoc. Prof., Western Kentucky Univ., Bowling Green 1968–79, Prof. of Psychology and Full mem. Grad. Faculty 1979, now Scholar-in-Residence and Prof. Emer.; Chair. Nat. Bd of Visitors/Advisors, School of Educ., Syracuse Univ.; mem. Bd of Visitors, School of Educ., Indiana Univ.; currently Dir Creative Leadership and Change Inc.; consultant to Firestone, General Motors and numerous cos; Ed. Journal of Human Behavior and Learning 1983–90, Psychology: A Journal of Human Behavior 1977–, Organization Development Journal 1983–88, International Journal of Leadership and Change; mem. Editorial Bd Education and several other publs; mem. American Psychological Asscn, Inter-American Soc. of Psychology, Int. Registry of Org. Devt Professionals, Psychologists in Man.; mem. Bd of Trustees, William Woods Univ. 1988–; Diplomate in Professional Counselling, Int. Acad. of Behavioural Medicine, Counselling and Psychotherapy 1994; Hon. LLD (William Woods Univ.) 1996; Dr hc (State Univ. of Humanities, Moscow) 2001; Distinguished Public Service Award, Western Kentucky Univ. 1983, Distinguished Alumnus Award, SUNY 1983, Diplomate American Coll. of Counsellors, American Coll. of Forensic Examiners 1996, Excellence in Productive Teaching Award, Coll. of Educ. and Behavioral Sciences, Western Kentucky Univ. 1977, 1991, 1999, Excellence in Research/Creativity Award, Western Kentucky Univ. Coll. of Ed. and Behavioral Sciences 1987. *Publications:* author, ed. or co-ed. of 20 books and monographs in French, Spanish, Italian, Portuguese, Romanian, Polish, Russian and Chinese and more than 300 papers and articles published in over 80 periodicals, including 31 foreign journals. *Leisure interests:* Latin American music, foreign travel, international exchanges. *Address:* Gary Ransdell Hall 3051, Western Kentucky University, 1906 College Heights Blvd, #21030, Bowling Green, KY 42101-1030 (office); Effective Leadership and Change Inc., 1409 Mount Ayr Circle, Bowling Green, KY 42103-4708, USA (home). *Telephone:* (270) 745-2343 (office); (270) 842-3436 (home). *Fax:* (270) 842-0432 (office); (270) 842-0432 (home). *E-mail:* joseph.cangemi@wku.edu (office). *Website:* www.wku.edu/psychology/staff/joseph_cangemi (office); edtech.wku.edu/~jcangemi (office).

CANI, Shkëlqim, DEcon, PhD; Albanian central banker, economist, politician and academic; b. 6 May 1956, Tirana; m. Merita Cani; ed Univ. of Tirana; Credit Officer, State Bank of Albania (SBA), Tirana br. 1979–81, Export-Import Officer, SBA Head Office 1981–83, Chief Economist, Research Div. 1984–85, Dir Overseas Dept, mem. Bd of Dirs Cen. Bank 1985–90; Exec. Gen. Man. Commercial Bank of Albania 1990–91, Deputy Gen. Man. 1991–92; ind. financial adviser 1996–97; Gov. Bank of Albania 1997–2004, also Gov. IMF for Albania; currently Prof., Inst. for Econ. and Juridical Consultations, Univ. of Tirana; Project Man. jt Italian-Albanian project L'Aquila e il Falcone volano insieme 2008; Chair. Tirana Stock Exchange 1997–2002; mem. People's Ass. 1991–96, July–Aug. 1997, 2013–; Vice-Pres. Council of Ministers 1991; Deputy Prime Minister of Albania 1991; Minister of Finance 2013–16; mem. Econ. Policies Comm.; mem. Socialist Party of Albania. *Address:* Faculty of Economics, University of Tirana, Bulevardi Dëshmorët e Kombit, Sheshi Nen Tereza, Tirana, Albania. *Telephone:* (4) 2230803 (office). *Fax:* (4) 2228405 (office). *Website:* www.unitir.edu.al.

CANIKLI, Nurettin; Turkish accountant and politician; b. 15 May 1069, Alucra, Giresun Prov.; s. of Şevket Canikli and Aiche Canikli; m. Hatice Canikli; four c.; ed Ankara Univ., Sheffield Univ.; various positions in Ministry of Finance, including Finance Inspector 1982, Chief Inspector of Finance 1993, Gen. Dir, Revenue Dept 1993–96, Asst Gen. Man. 1996, apptd to Istanbul Treasury Jan. 1997; columnist on econs and finance, Yeni Şafak (daily newspaper) 1997–2002; mem. Grand Nat. Ass. (Parl.) for Giresun 2002–15, 2015–, Chair. Parl. Comm. on State Econ. Enterprises (SEEs); Minister of Customs and Trade 2014–15; Deputy Prime Minister 2016–17; Minister of Nat. Defence 2017–18; Founder mem. Adalet ve Kalkınma Partisi (AKP, Justice and Devt Party). *Website:* www.nurettincanikli.com.tr.

CANIVET, Guy, JD, FBA; French judge and academic; *Member, Constitutional Council;* b. 23 Sept. 1943, Lons-le-Saunier, Jura; s. of Pierre Canivet and Henriette Barthélémy; m. Françoise Beuzit 1981; two s. two d.; ed Univ. of Dijon; judge, Trial Court of Chartres 1972–75; Public Prosecutor, Paris 1975–77; Sec.-Gen., Trial Court of Paris 1977–83, judge 1983–86; Justice, Court of Appeal, Paris 1986–94, Chief Justice 1996–99; Justice, Cour de Cassation 1994–96, Chief Justice 1999–2007; mem. Constitutional Council (Conseil constitutionnel) 2007–; Assoc. Prof., Institut d'études politiques, Paris 2004–; Founder and Pres. Network of the Pres of the Supreme Judicial Courts of the EU 2004–07; Hon. Bencher, Gray's Inn, London, King's Inn, Dublin; Officier, Ordre nat. du Mérite des Palmes académiques, Commdr, Légion d'honneur, Commdr, Ordre des Arts et des Lettres; Hon. LLD (London, Laval, Manila, St Kliment Ohridski, Sofia, Tulane, New Orleans, Leicester). *Publication:* Droit français de la concurrence 1995. *Leisure interests:* music, outdoor recreational activities. *Address:* Conseil constitutionnel, 2 rue de Montpensier, 75001 Paris (office); 8 rue Nicolas Charlet, 75015 Paris, France (home). *Telephone:* 1-40-15-30-03 (office). *Fax:* 1-40-20-93-27 (office). *E-mail:* guy.canivet@conseil-constitutionnel.fr (office). *Website:* www.conseil-constitutionnel.fr (office).

CAÑIZARES LLOVERA, HE Cardinal Antonio, DTheol; Spanish ecclesiastic; *Archbishop of Valencia;* b. 15 Oct. 1945, Utiel; ed minor and major seminaries in

Valencia, Pontifical Univ. of Salamanca; ordained priest 1970; served as asst pastor and del. for catechesis in Archdiocese of Valencia; taught Catechetical Theology at Univ. of Salamanca and Fundamental Theology at Conciliar Seminary of Madrid; later became Dir and a Prof. of the Inst. of Religious Science and Catechesis, Madrid; sat on several comms and secrs of Spanish Episcopal Conf.; Dir Secr. of Episcopal Comm. for Doctrine of the Faith 1985–92; Founder and first Pres. Asociación Española de Catequistas; fmr Dir Teología y Catequesis (review); Bishop of Ávila 1992–96; mem. Congregation for Doctrine of the Faith, Roman Curia 1996; Archbishop of Granada 1996–2002, also Apostolic Admin. of Cartagena Jan.–Oct. 1998, elected Pres. Episcopal Comm. of Educ. and Catechesis 1999; Archbishop of Toledo and Primate of Spain 2002–08; Vice-Pres. Spanish Episcopal Conf. 2008; cr. Cardinal (Cardinal-Priest of San Pancrazio) 2006; Prefect of the Congregation for Divine Worship and the Discipline of the Sacraments 2008–13, 2013–14; mem. Pontifical Cttee for Int. Eucharistic Congresses 2010–, Congregation for Doctrine of the Faith, Congregation for Bishops, Pontifical Comm. Ecclesia Dei, Congregation for the Evangelization of Peoples 2013–; Archbishop of Valencia 2014–; mem. Real Academia de la Historia de España 2008–; Dr hc (Universidad CEU Cardenal Herrera) 2006, (Universidad Católica de Valencia) 2010. *Address:* Arzobispado, C/Palau 2, 46003 Valencia, Spain (office). *Telephone:* (96) 3829700 (office). *Fax:* (96) 3918120 (office). *E-mail:* archivalencia@archivalencia.org (office). *Website:* www.archivalencia.org (office).

CANNADINE, Sir David Nicholas, Kt, DPhil, LittD, FRHistS, FBA, FRSA, FRSL; British historian and academic; *Dodge Professor of History, Princeton University;* b. 7 Sept. 1950; s. of Sydney Douglas Cannadine and Dorothy Mary Hughes; m. Linda Jane Colley (q.v.) 1982; one d. (deceased); ed King Edward's Five Ways School, Birmingham, Clare Coll., Cambridge, St John's Coll., Oxford, Princeton Univ., USA; Resident Fellow, St John's Coll. Cambridge 1975–77, Asst Lecturer in History 1976–80, Lecturer 1980–88; Fellow, Christ's Coll. Cambridge 1977–88, Dir of Studies in History 1977–83, Tutor 1979–81; Prof. of History, Columbia Univ., New York 1988–92, Moore Collegiate Prof. 1992–98; Dir Inst. of Historical Research Univ. of London 1998–2003, Prof. 1998–2003, Queen Elizabeth the Queen Mother Prof. of British History 2003–08, Hon. Fellow 2005–, Consultant, History in Educ. 2008–; Visiting mem., Inst. for Advanced Study, Princeton, New Jersey 1980–81; Visiting Fellow, Council of the Humanities 2003–05, Whitney J. Oates Sr Research Scholar 2008–11, Dodge Prof. of History 2011–; Visiting Prof., Birkbeck Coll., London 1995–97; Visiting Fellow, Whitney Humanities Center, Yale Univ. 1995–96; Visiting Scholar, Pembroke Coll., Cambridge 1997; Visiting Prof., Stern Business School, New York Univ. 2013–14; Pres. Worcs. Historical Soc. 1999–; Vice-Pres. British Records Soc. 1998–, Royal Historical Soc. 1998–2002; Chair. IHR Trust 1999–2003; mem. Advisory Bd Centre for Study of Soc. and Politics, Kingston Univ. 1998–2003, ICBH 1998–2003, Advisory Council Warburg Inst. 1998–2003, Inst. of US Studies 1999–2004, Public Record Office 1999–2004, Inst. of English Studies 2000–03, Inst. of Latin American Studies 2000–04, Kennedy Memorial Trust 2000–, Nat. Trust Eastern Regional Cttee 2000–, Royal Mint Advisory Cttee 2004–, Editorial Bd History of Parliament 2004–, Advisory Council Inst. for the Study of the Americas 2004–; Gov. Ipswich School 1982–88; Fellow, Berkeley Coll., Yale Univ. 1985, J.P. Morgan Library, New York 1992–98; American Council of Learned Socs Fellowship 1990–91; regular radio and TV broadcaster; Ed.-in-Chief Journal of Maritime History 1999–; Ed. Oxford Dictionary of National Biography 2014–; Gen. Ed. Studies in Modern History 1979–2002, Penguin History of Britain 1989–, Penguin History of Europe 1991–, Historical Research 1998–2003; Trustee, Kennedy Memorial Scholarship Fund 1999–, Nat. Portrait Gallery 2000– (Chair. of Trustees 2005–), British Empire and Commonwealth Museum 2003–, Commr English Heritage 2001–; Visiting Fellow, ANU, Canberra 2005 (Adjunct Prof. 2006), Nat. Humanities Center, North Carolina 2006; Chair. Blue Plaques Panel, English Heritage; Hon. Fellow, Christ's Coll. Cambridge 2005, Hon. Prof., Univ. of London 2008; Hon. DLitt (East Anglia, South Bank) 2001, (Birmingham) 2002; T.S. Ashton Prize, Econ. History Soc. 1977, Silver Jubilee Prize, Agric. History Soc. 1977, Governors' Award 1991, Dean's Distinguished Award in the Humanities, Columbia Univ. 1996. *Radio:* A Point of View (BBC Radio 4) 2005–06. *Publications include:* Lords and Landlords: The Aristocracy and the Towns 1774–1967 1980, Patricians, Power and Politics in Nineteenth-Century Towns (ed. and contrib.) 1982, H.J. Dyos, Exploring the Urban Past (co-ed. and contrib.) 1982, Rituals of Royalty: Power and Ceremonial in Traditional Societies (co-ed. and contrib.) 1987, The Pleasures of the Past 1989, The Decline and Fall of the British Aristocracy (Lionel Trilling Prize 1991) 1990, G.M. Trevelyan: A Life in History 1992, Aspects of Aristocracy: Grandeur and Decline in Modern Britain 1994, Class in Britain 1998, History in Our Time 1998, Making History Now 1999, Ornamentalism: How the British Saw Their Empire 2001, In Churchill's Shadow: Confronting the Past in Modern Britain 2002, What is History Now? (ed.) 2002, History and the Media (ed.) 2004, Winston Churchill in the 21st Century (co-ed. and contrib.) 2004, Admiral Lord Nelson, his context and legacy (ed.) 2005, Trafalgar: A Battle and its Afterlife (ed.) 2006, National Portrait Gallery: A Brief History 2007, Empire, the Sea and Global History: Britain's Maritime World c. 1763–1840 (ed.) 2007, History and Philanthropy: Past Present Future (co-ed. and contrib.) 2008, Making History Now and Then: Discoveries, Controversies and Explanations 2008, The Undivided Past: Humanity Beyond our Differences 2013, King George V 2014; numerous contribs to other books and learned journals. *Leisure interests:* life, laughter. *Address:* Institute of Historical Research, Senate House, Malet Street, London, WC1E 7HU, England (office). *Fax:* (20) 7862-8754 (office). *E-mail:* martha.vandrei@sas.ac.uk (office). *Website:* www.history.ac.uk (office).

CANNAVARO, Fabio Mamerto; Italian football coach and fmr professional footballer; b. 13 Sept. 1973, Naples; s. of Pasquale Cannavaro and Gelsomina Cannavaro; m. Daniela Arenoso 1996; two s. one d.; centre-back; played for S.S.C. Napoli 1992–95, Italy U21 1993–96, Parma FC 1995–2002, Italy 1997–2010, FC Internazionale Milano 2002–04, Juventus FC 2004–06, 2009–10, Real Madrid (in Spanish Primera Divisiòn, wearing No. 5 jersey) 2006–09, Al-Ahli, Dubai 2010–11 (retd); Serie A debut at Turin's Stadio Delle Alpi against Juventus 1993; mem. two European championship-winning Italy Under-21 teams 1992–94, 1994–96; debut for full nat. team 1997, played in World Cup, France 1998; helped Juventus win Serie A titles 2004/05, 2005/06 (club was stripped of titles and demoted to Serie B by a sports tribunal investigating claims of match fixing); Capt. FIFA World Cup-winning team, Germany 2006; 136 caps for Italy (all-time most capped player); mem. coaching staff, Al-Ahli, notably as Global Amb. and Tech. Dir 2011–13, Asst Coach 2013–14; Head Coach of Chinese club Guangzhou Evergrande 2014–15; nicknames: Il muro di Berlino (The Berlin Wall), Il umano bus (The Human Bus); has helped establish charity foundation FCF (Fondazione Cannavaro Ferrara), specialising in the procurement of cancer research equipment and surgery for special cases of cancer for a hosp. in Naples; worked as a pundit on ITV during FIFA World Cup 2014; Euro 2000 Team of the Tournament 2000, Oscar del calcio: Serie A Defender of the Year 2005, 2006, Serie A Footballer of the Year 2006, Italian Footballer of the Year 2006; selected in FIFPro World XI 2005–06, 2006–07, European Footballer of the Year 2006, Ballon d'Or, France Football magazine 2006, UEFA Team of the Year 2006, FIFA World Player of the Year (second ever defender) 2006, FIFA World Cup Silver Ball Award 2006, FIFA World Cup Team of the Tournament 2006. *Address:* c/o Juventus FC SpA, Corso Galileo Ferraris, 32, 10128 Turin, Italy. *E-mail:* fabio@fabiocannavaro.it. *Website:* www.fabiocannavaro.it.

CANNELL, Melvin Gilbert Richard, BSc, PhD, DSc, FRSE; British research scientist; b. 12 Aug. 1944, Bungay, Suffolk; s. of Charles Cannell and Joyce Cannell; m. Maria Rietdijk 1966; two d.; ed Bungay Grammar School and Univ. of Reading; research officer, coffee research station, Kenya 1966–71; NERC Inst. of Tree Biology Edin. 1971–74, NERC Inst. of Terrestrial Ecology (now Centre for Ecology and Hydrology) 1974–87, Dir 1987, Prof. (retd), now consultant; Co-Investigators, Grid Enabled Integrated Earth systems model (GENIE), London e-Science Centre, Imperial Coll. London; Fellow, Inst. of Chartered Foresters; Founder Bd mem. European Forest Inst. *Publications:* Joint Tree Physiology and Yield Improvement 1976, Trees as Crop Plants 1985; over 100 other scientific publs. *Address:* Centre for Ecology and Hydrology, Bush Estate, Penicuik, Midlothian, EH26 0QB (office); Easter Greyfield, Eddleston Road, Peebles, Tweeddale, EH45 9JB, Scotland (home). *Telephone:* (131) 445-4343 (office); (1721) 720144 (home). *Fax:* (131) 445-3943 (office). *E-mail:* mgrc@ceh.ac.uk (office). *Website:* www.ceh.ac.uk (office).

CANNING, Mark, CMG; British diplomatist (retd) and business executive; *Senior Adviser, Bell Pottinger;* b. 15 Dec. 1954; m. Cecilia Canning; one d.; Migration and Visa Dept, FCO 1974–76, Registry/Communications, Freetown 1976–78, Middle Eastern Dept, FCO 1978, Consular Dept 1981–82, Third Sec. (Chancery and Information), Georgetown 1982–85, Man. Review Staff, FCO 1985–86, Vice-Consul (Commercial), Chicago 1986–88, Counter-Terrorism Dept, FCO 1988–92, W Africa Dept 1992-93, First Sec. (Commercial), Jakarta 1993–97, Head of Personnel Div. 1 (Postings Div.), FCO 1997–2001, Deputy High Commr, Kuala Lumpur 2001–06, Amb. to Myanmar 2006–09, to Zimbabwe 2009–11, to Indonesia (also accred to Timor Leste and ASEAN) 2011–14; Sr Adviser, Bell Pottinger 2014–. *Address:* Bell Pottinger, Holborn Gate, 330 High Holborn, London, WC1V 7QD, England (office). *E-mail:* info@bellpottinger.com (office). *Website:* www.bellpottinger.com (office).

CANNON, John; American business executive; *Executive Vice-President and Chief Administrative Officer, Health Care Service Corporation (HCSC);* ed Denison Univ., Ohio, The Dickinson School of Law at Pennsylvania State Univ.; attorney with Rawle & Henderson, Philadelphia, specialized in litigation and securities law; joined CIGNA Corpn 1988, roles included Sr Vice-Pres. and Deputy Gen. Counsel, Pres. CIGNA Foundation and Chief Counsel for CIGNA Healthcare and CIGNA Int. –2007; joined WellPoint, Inc. 2007, Exec. Vice-Pres., Gen. Counsel, Corp. Sec. and Chief Public Affairs Officer –2012, Interim Pres. and CEO 2012–13; Exec. Vice-Pres. and Chief Admin. Officer Health Care Service Corpn (HCSC) 2014–; mem. Bd of Dirs US Chamber of Commerce, Indianapolis Symphony Orchestra. *Address:* Health Care Service Corporation, 300 E. Randolph Street., Chicago, IL 60601, USA (office). *Telephone:* (800) 654-7385 (office). *Website:* www.hcsc.com (office).

CANNON, Hon. Lawrence, BA, MBA; Canadian politician and diplomatist; b. 6 Dec. 1947; s. of Louis Cannon and Rosemary Power; ed Université de Montréal, Université Laval; Councillor Cap-Rouge 1979–85; mem. Quebec Nat. Ass. 1985–94, Deputy Speaker 1989–94; Minister of Communications 1991–94; fmr Parl. Sec. to Minister of External Trade; fmr consultant; City Councillor, Gastineau 2001; Chair. Outaouais Urban Transit Corpn 2001, Strategic Choices Comm., City of Gatineau; apptd Pres. Asscn du transport urbain du Québec 2004; MP for Pontiac 2006–11; Minister of Transport, Infrastructure and Communities 2006–08, of Foreign Affairs 2008–11; Amb. to France 2012–17; mem. Bd LiveWell Foods Canada Inc. 2018–, Hull Bicentennial Corpn (also, fmr Gen. Man.).

CANNON, Michael R., BEng; American computer industry executive; *General Partner, MRC & LBC Partners, LLC;* b. 1952; ed Michigan State Univ., Harvard Business School; began career with Boeing Corpn, various man. positions in Mfg Research and Devt Group; fmr Man. Imprimis Tech., Singapore; fmr Vice Pres., IBM Personal Storage Systems Div., also becoming Vice Pres. of IBM Product Design and Worldwide Mfg; Pres., Dir and CEO Maxtor Corpn 1997–2003; Pres. and CEO Solectron Corpn 2003–07; Pres. of Global Operations, Dell Inc. 2007–09 (retd), served as consultant 2009–11; currently Gen. Partner, MRC & LBC Partners, LLC; mem. Bd of Dirs Adobe Systems 2003–, Elster Group SE 2010–, Seagate Technology LLC 2011–, Lam Research Corpn 2011–. *Address:* MRC & LBC Partners, LLC, 7912 Cava Place, Austin, TX 78735-1560, USA (office).

CANNONIER, Craig, BSc, JP; Bermudian business executive and politician; b. 1963, St David's; m. Antoinette Cannonier; four c.; ed Towson State Univ., Baltimore, USA; began career working in retail man.; fmrly with human resources, training and purchasing depts, MarketPlace Group (grocery chain); 10 years as Gen. Man. People's Pharmacy; fmr Relationship Man. Cable & Wireless Bermuda; propr three petrol stations (Esso City Tigermarket, Collector's Hill Esso, Warwick Esso); entered politics 2009, joined Bermuda Democratic Alliance, becoming Leader –2011 (merged into One Bermuda Alliance—OBA 2011), Leader OBA 2011–14; mem. House of Ass. (Parl.) for Devonshire S constituency 2011–, Opposition Leader 2018–; Premier of Bermuda 2012–14 (resgnd); fmr Minister of Public Works. *Leisure interests:* sports, travelling, boating. *Address:* One Bermuda Alliance, 58 Reid Street, Hamilton HM 11, Bermuda (office). *Telephone:* 294-3212 (office). *E-mail:* ccannonier@oba.bm (office). *Website:* www.oba.bm (office).

CANNY, Nicholas Patrick, PhD, FRHistS, FBA, MRIA; Irish historian and academic; *Professor Emeritus, National University of Ireland, Galway;* b. 4 Jan. 1944, Clifden, Co. Galway; s. of Cecil Canny and Helen Joyce; m. Morwena Denis 1974; one s. one d.; ed St Flannan's Coll., Ennis, Co. Clare, Univ. Coll., Galway, Univ. of London, UK, Univs of Pennsylvania, Harvard and Yale, USA; Lecturer in History, Univ. Coll., Galway (now Nat. Univ. of Ireland, Galway) 1972–79, Prof. of History 1980, now Prof. Emer., Dir Moore Inst. for Research in the Humanities 2000–11; mem. Inst. for Advanced Study, Princeton 1979–80; Fellow, Nat. Humanities Center, NC 1985–86; mem. Irish Manuscripts Comm. 1980–, Nat. Archives Advisory Council 1986–96; Chair. Irish Comm. on Historical Sciences 1991–97; Distinguished Visiting Prof., New York Univ. 1995; Fellow-in-Residence, Netherlands Inst. for Advanced Study 2000–01; Prof. invité, École des Hautes Études en Sciences Sociales, Paris 2005; Sr Parnell Research Fellow, Magdalene Coll., Cambridge 2005–06; Pres. Royal Irish Acad. 2008–11; mem. Scientific Council, European Research Council 2011; Corresponding Fellow, British Acad. 2005; mem. Academia Europaea 1995; Foreign mem. American Philosophical Soc. 2007; Irish Historical Research Prize 1976, 2003. *Publications include:* The Elizabethan Conquest of Ireland 1976, The Upstart Earl: The Social and Mental World of Richard Boyle 1982, From Reformation to Restoration: Ireland 1534–1660 1987, Colonial Identity in the Atlantic World 1500–1800 1987, Kingdom and Colony: Ireland in the Atlantic World 1560–1800 1988, Europeans on the Move: Studies on European Migration 1500–1800 1994, The Oxford History of the British Empire (Vol. I): The Origins of Empire 1998, Making Ireland British 1580–1650 2001, Oxford Handbook of the History of the Atlantic World 1450–1840 2011. *Leisure interests:* reading, walking, music. *Address:* Furramelia West, Barna, Co. Galway, Ireland (home). *Website:* www.nuigalway.ie/mooreinstitute/site/view/24 (office).

CANO FERNÁNEZ, Ángel; Spanish business executive; b. 1961, Santander; m.; ed graduate in Econ. and Business Sciences; began career at Arthur Andersen, specializing in finance 1984–91; joined Argentaria as Controller 1991, mem. Exec. Cttee 1998, held various man. positions in Banco Bilbao Vizcaya Argentaria (BBVA) Group SA (following merger between BBV and Argentaria), mem. Exec. Cttee 2000, Group Financial Dir 2001–03, Head of Human Resources and Services Dept 2003–05, Head of Resources 2005–09, Pres. and COO 2009–15. *Address:* c/o Banco Bilbao Vizcaya Argentaria SA, Paseo de la Castellana 81, 28046 Madrid, Spain.

CANOGAR, Rafael, BA; Spanish painter; b. 17 May 1935, Toledo; s. of Genaro Rafael Garcia-Cano and Alfonsa Canogar (née Gómez); m. 1st Ann Jane McKenzie 1960; m. 2nd Purificación Chaves 1992; six c.; studied under Daniel Vázquez Díaz 1949–54; Founder-mem. El Paso group 1957–60; Visiting Prof., Milles Coll., Oakland, Calif. 1965–66; Artist-in-Residence, DAAD, Berlin 1972, 1974; mem. Exec. Cttee Círculo de Bellas Artes, Madrid 1983–86, Advisory Bd Dept of Fine Arts, Ministry of Culture 1981–82, 1983–84, Bd of Trustees, Museo Nacional de Arte Contemporáneo, Madrid 1983, Admin. Bd Nat. Art Collections 1984–90, Exec. Cttee Fundación de Gremios, Madrid 1984–87; more than 120 solo shows and numerous group exhbns; works held in many public art collections world-wide; mem. Real Academia de Bellas Artes de San Fernando, Madrid 1996; nominated 'Hijo predilecto' (Favourite Son) of City of Toledo 2002; Chevalier, Ordre des Arts et des Lettres 1985, Special Commendation, Orden de Isabel la Católica 1991; Dr hc (Universidad Nacional de Educación a Distancia, Madrid) 2001; Third Prize, Primer Concurso para estampados sobre tejidos de tapicería Gastón y Daniela, Bilbao/Madrid 1955, Premio de Instalación de trabajos concedido por la Revista Nacional de Arquitectura 1955, Second Prize, XVII Exposición Manchega de Artes Plásticas, Valdepeñas, Ciudad Real 1956, Prix de la Critique, Brussels 1960, Palette d'Or, XI Festival Int. de la Peinture, Cagnes-sur-Mer, France 1969, Gran Premio Itamaraty, XI Bienal de São Paulo, Brazil 1971, Premio Sol de Oro, lberian Daily Sun, Palma de Mallorca 1972, Grand Prix, Int. Triennial of Painting, Sofia, Bulgaria 1982, Premio Nacional de Artes Plásticas, Ministry of Culture 1982, Premio Vídeo Castilla-La Mancha, Consejería de Educación y Cultura 1991, IX Premio de Plástica Cultura Viva de la Asociación Cultura Viva, Madrid 1998, Tomislav Krizman Prize of Honour, Second Hrvatski Trijenale Grafike, Zagreb 2000, XIII Premio Tomás Francisco Prieto, Fundación Casa de la Moneda, Madrid 2002, Placa de Pintor Ilustre, Asociación de Escritores y Artistas Españoles, Madrid 2002, Medalla de Oro al Merito en las Bellas Artes, Ministry of Culture 2003, Premio de Cultura de la Comunidad de Madrid 2005, Medalla de Oro, Feria de Arte Contemporáneo Artesevilla 06 2006, Premio Extraordinario del Jurado, III edición de los Premios Castellano-manchegos del Mundo 2008, XVII Premio Ignazio Silone per La Cultura, Rome 2009, Premio AECA al mejor artista vivo español representado en ARCO Madrid 2010 2010, Premio Nacional de Arte Gráfico, otorgado por la Calcografía Nacional, Real Academia de Bellas Artes de San Fernando XV Premio Real Fundación Toledo 2011, VI Premio 'Juanelo Turriano', Toledo 2011. *Publications:* 'Rafael Canogar, Espejismo y Realidad', Editorial Síntesis, Madrid 2011. *Address:* c/o Bernardino Obregón, 6 Local, 28012 Madrid, Spain (office). *Telephone:* (91) 5287729 (office). *Fax:* (91) 5287729 (office). *E-mail:* info@rafaelcanogar.com (office). *Website:* www.rafaelcanogar.com; catalogo.rafaelcanogar.com/home.aspx/ rafael canogar.

CANTACUZÈNE, Jean Michel, DS; French director of research (retd); b. 15 Dec. 1933, Bucharest, Romania; s. of Dr Alexandre Cantacuzène and Marianne Cantacuzène (née Labeyrie); m. 1st Anne-Marie Szekely 1956 (divorced); one s. one d.; m. 2nd Danièle Ricard 1971; one s.; ed Ecole Supérieure Chem. Industry, Lyon, Ecole Normale Supérieure, Paris; Asst Prof., Ecole Normale Supérieure, Paris 1960–62, Deputy Dir, Lab. Chimie 1964–67; Scientific attaché, French Embassy, Moscow 1962–64, Counsellor for Science and Tech., Washington, DC 1977–80; Prof. of Organic Chem., Univ. of Paris 1967–73, Titular Prof. 1972–; Counsellor for Scientific Affairs, Ministry of Foreign Affairs, Paris 1971–77; Dir Chem. Scientific Dept, CNRS Paris 1973–77, Sr Counsellor for Industrial Affairs 1988; Scientific Dir Total Co. Française des Pétroles, Paris 1980–90; Chair. Bd SOLEMS 1983–86, AVRIST 1982; mem. Conseil pour l'innovation industrielle 1989–91, Applications Cttee, Acad. of Science (Cadas) 1989–2000, Exec. Cttee groupe Climents français 1990–92; mem. Advisory Comm. for Science and Tech. 1971–75, Chair. Industrial R&D Advisory Cttee, EEC, Brussels 1983–86; mem. Council Nuclear Safety Cttee, 1981–90; Pres. Adit 1992–95; mem. Acad. des Technologies (Paris) 2001; Officier, Légion d'honneur, Ordre nat. du Mérite, Grand Cross, Merit Nat. Order (Romania) 2000; Le Bel Award of the Chemical Soc. of France 1968. *Publications:* Chimie Organique (three vols) (co-author) 1971–75, America, Science and Technology in the 80s (two vols) 1981, Mille Ans dans les Balkans, Chronique des Cantacuzène dans la Tourmente des Siècles 1992; historical papers in Archiva Genealogica and Biblos and over 100 papers in scientific journals. *Leisure interests:* book collecting, history. *Address:* 52 bis route de Damiette, 91190 Gif-sur-Yvette (home); Académie des Technologies, 28 rue Saint Dominique, 75007 Paris, France (office). *E-mail:* jcantacuzene@wanadoo.fr.

CANTARELLA, Paolo; Italian business executive; b. 4 Dec. 1944, Varallo Sesia/Vercelli; m. Clara Cantarella; ed Turin Polytechnic; began working in car components industry 1977; Commercial Dir Ages (Fiat Group) 1978; Intersectoral Co-ordinator and Asst to Man. Dir, Fiat Group 1980; Man. Dir Comau (machine tools) 1983; Man. of Supplies and Distribution, Fiat Auto SpA 1989; Vice-Chair. Maserati SpA (luxury sports cars), Modena 1989, Chair. 1993–96; Man. Dir and Gen. Man. Fiat Auto SpA 1990–96, Chair. 1996–2002; Pres. and CEO Fiat SpA 1996–2002; Pres. European Automobile Mfrs Asscn (ACEA) 2000–02; Co-Chair. EU-Russia Industrialists' Round Table (IRT) 2001; Chair. IVECO NV, Business Solutions (Fiat Group) 2001–02; Dir Polaroid Holding 2003–08; Operating Partner, Advent International from 2008; mem. Bd of Dirs, Iride, Inpartner (Investitori & Partner Immobiliari); Ind. Dir and Chair. Control & Risks Cttee, Finmeccanica SpA 2011–, Lead Ind. Dir 2014–; fmr mem. Bd of Dirs, Organizing Cttee of the Winter Olympics, Turin 2006; Kt, Order of Labour Merit 1997. *Address:* Finmeccanica SpA, Piazza Monte Grappa n. 4, 00195 Rome, Italy (office). *Telephone:* (06) 324731 (office). *Fax:* (06) 3208621 (office). *E-mail:* webeditor@finmeccanica.it (office). *Website:* www.finmeccanica.com (office).

CANTLEY, Lewis C., BS, MA, PhD; American cell biologist, biochemist and academic; *Professor of Cancer Biology in Medicine and Meyer Director, Sandra and Edward Meyer Cancer Center, Weill Cornell Medical College/Ronald P. Stanton Clinical Cancer Program at New York-Presbyterian;* b. 20 Feb. 1949, West Virginia; m. Vicki Sato; ed West Virginia Wesleyan Coll., Cornell Univ., Harvard Coll.; Postdoctoral Researcher, Harvard Univ. 1975–78, Asst Prof. of Biochemistry and Molecular Biology, Faculty of Arts and Sciences 1978–85, Prof. of Cell Biology, Harvard Medical School 1992–2003, William Bosworth Castle Chair in Medicine and Prof. of Systems Biology 2003–12, Dir Cancer Center and Chief of Div. of Signal Transduction, Beth Israel Deaconess Medical Center, Boston, Mass 2007–12; Prof. of Physiology, Tufts Univ. 1985–92; Margaret and Herman Sokol Prof. in Oncology Research, Joan and Sanford I. Weill Dept of Medicine, Weill Cornell Medical Coll./Ronald P. Stanton Clinical Cancer Program at New York-Presbyterian 2011–14, Prof. of Cancer Biology in Medicine 2011–, Dir Sandra and Edward Meyer Cancer Center 2014–; Co-founder Agios Pharmaceuticals; mem. Advisory Bd AVEO Pharmaceuticals, TransMolecular, Inc.; mem. NAS 2001, Institute of Medicine of the National Academies 2014, European life sciences academy EMBO 2015; Fellow, American Acad. of Arts and Sciences 1999; ASBMB Avanti Award for Lipid Research 1998, Heinrich Wieland Prize for Lipid Research 2000, Caledonian Prize, Royal Soc. of Edinburgh 2002, Pezcoller-AACR Int. Award for Cancer Research 2005, Rolf Luft Award, Karolinska Inst. 2009, Breakthrough Prize in Life Sciences (co-recipient) 2013, Jacobaeus Prize for Diabetes Research, Karolinska Inst. 2013, AACR Princess Takamatsu Memorial Lectureship 2015, Ross Prize in Molecular Medicine 2015, Canada Gairdner Int. 2015, Distinguished Scientist Award, Asscn of American Cancer Insts 2015, Thomson Reuters The World's Most Influential Scientific Minds 2015, Wolf Prize in Medicine (co-recipient) 2016. *Publications:* numerous papers in professional journals. *Address:* Meyer Cancer Center, Belfer Research Building, 413 East 69th Street, Room 1362, Box 50, New York, NY 10021, USA (office). *Telephone:* (646) 962-6297 (office). *E-mail:* lcantley@med.cornell.edu (office). *Website:* meyercancer.weill.cornell.edu/about/leadership (office); cantleylab.weill.cornell.edu (office).

CANTO-SPERBER, Monique, PhD; French philosopher, academic and academic administrator; *President, Paris Sciences et Lettres;* b. 14 May 1954, Algeria; m. Dan Sperber (divorced); ed École normale supérieure Paris, Univ. Paris I; Asst, Dept of Philosophy, Univ. de Haute-Normandie 1980–84; Prof., Univ. de Picardie 1984–91; Visiting Researcher, King's Coll. London 1988, Princeton Univ., USA 1989, 1990; Visiting Fellow, Inst. for Advanced Study, Princeton, NJ 1993; Dir of Research, CNRS 1993–95; Visiting Prof., Univ. de Caen 1993–96; Visiting Prof., Institut franco-argentin, Buenos Aires 2000, Stanford Univ. 2001, 2002, 2003; fmr Prof., École des Hautes Études en Sciences Sociales; Head of Dir's Office, École normale supérieure Paris 2003–05, Dir 2005–12; Pres. Paris Sciences et Lettres and PSL Foundation 2012–; mem. Editorial Bd European Journal of Philosophy 1993–96; mem. Comité Consultatif Nat. d'Ethique 2001– (Vice-Pres. 2005–); mem. Commissions 'Violence et télévision' 2002, 'Ethique et justice' 2003, du Grand Emprunt nat. 2009; mem. Acad. royale de Belgique 2008; Chevalier, Ordre des Arts et des Lettres 1997, Légion d'honneur 2000, Officier 2009; Officier, Ordre nat. du Mérite 2005; Prix Marcelle Blum, Acad. française 1991, Prix Philippe Habert des professeurs de sciences politiques 2005. *Radio:* host, Questions d'éthique (France Culture) 2006–. *Publications:* Platon, Menon 1991, Les paradoxes de la connaissance 1991, La Philosophie morale britannique 1994, Dictionnaire d'éthique et philosophie morales (ed.) 1996 (revised 2004), La Philosophie grecque 1997, Les Ethiques grecques 2001, L'Inquiétude morale et la vie humaine 2001 (trans. as Moral Disquiet and Human Life 2008), Le style de la pensée 2002, Les règles de la liberté 2003, Le socialisme libéral 2003, La Bien, la guerre et la terreur 2005, La philosophie morale 2006, Faut-il sauver le libéralisme? (co-author) 2006, Platon Gorgias 2007, Le libéralisme et la gauche 2008, Essai sur la vie humaine 2008, Naissance et liberté 2008, Que devons-nous faire face aux nouvelles questions d'éthique? 2008, Vies et destins 2009, L'idée de guerre juste 2010, La Morale du monde 2010, Sans foi ni loi 2015, L'oligarchie de l'excellence: les meilleures études pour le plus grand nombre 2017. *Leisure interests:* sport, music. *Address:* Office of the President, Paris Sciences et Lettres, 62 bis rue Gay Lussac, 75005 Paris, France (office). *Telephone:* 1-75-00-02-89 (office). *E-mail:* contact@univ-psl.fr (office). *Website:* www.parissciencesetlettres.org (office).

CANTONA, Eric Daniel Pierre; French actor and fmr professional footballer; b. 24 May 1966, Marseille; s. of Albert Cantona and Léonor Raurich; m. 1st Isabelle Ferrer 1987 (divorced 2003); one s. one d.; m. 2nd Rachida Brakni 2007; player, Auxerre 1983–88, Martigues 1985–86, Marseille 1988–91 (won Coupe de France 1988, Ligue 1 1989, 1991), Bordeaux (loan) 1989, Montpellier (loan) 1989–90 (won Coupe de France 1990), Nîmes 1991, Leeds United 1992 (League Champions 1992, won Charity Shield 1992), Manchester United 1992–97 (League Champions 1993, 1994, 1996, 1997, Football Asscn Cup 1994, 1996, Charity Shield 1993, 1994, 1996), Capt. 1996–97 (scoring 80 goals in 182 appearances); played for French nat. team 1987–95 (45 appearances, 20 goals), Capt. 1993–96; retd 1997; apptd Capt. French Nat. Beach Football team 1997, Man. 2005–11; Dir of Soccer, New York Cosmos 2011–; Professional Footballers' Asscn Player of the Year 1994, Football Writers' Asscn Footballer of the Year 1996, Premier League 10 Seasons Awards (1992/93–2001/02): Overseas Player of the Decade and Overall Team of the Decade. *Play:* Face au Paradis, Théâtre Marigny, Paris 2010. *Films include:* Le Bonheur est dans le Pré 1995, Elizabeth 1998, Mookie 1998, Les Enfants du Marais 1999, La Grande Vie 2001, L'Outremangeur 2003, Les Clefs de bagnole 2003, Une belle histoire 2005, La Vie est à nous! 2005, Le Deuxième souffle 2007, Jack Says 2007, French Film 2008, Looking for Eric 2009, Together Is Too Much 2010, Switch 2011, De force 2011, Porn in the Hood 2012, Les mouvements du bassin 2012. *Television includes:* Le grand journal de Canal+ 2006–12, Papillon noir 2008, La liste 2009. *Leisure interest:* painting. *Address:* c/o Mikado, 36 rue Montorgueil, 75001 Paris, France. *Website:* www.fff.fr; www.nycosmos.com.

CANTOR, Anthony John James; British diplomatist (retd); b. 1 Feb. 1946, London; m. Patricia Cantor; one s. two d.; joined Diplomatic Service 1965, Desk Officer, Finance Dept 1966–68, Third Sec., Rangoon, Burma 1968–71, Third Sec., later Second Sec. (Commercial), Tokyo, Japan 1972–76, Second Sec. (Consular), Accra, Ghana, Lomé, Togo 1977–80, Desk Officer, Aid Policy Dept, FCO 1980–82, Desk Officer, West Indian Atlantic Dept 1982–83, Consul (Commercial), Osaka, Japan 1983–89, Deputy Head of Mission, Hanoi, Vietnam 1990–92, on loan to Dept of Trade and Industry 1992–94, First Sec. (Commercial), Tokyo 1994–95, Deputy Consul Gen., Osaka 1995–98, Desk Officer, EU Dept (Bilateral), FCO 1999–2000, Deputy Commr Gen., Expo 2000, Hanover, Germany 2000, Head of Expo Section, Public Diplomacy Dept, FCO 2000–01; Amb. to Paraguay 2001–05, to Armenia 2006–08; mem. Britain-Burma Soc., Kobe Club (Japan). *Leisure interests:* travel, languages, World War II in Asia.

CANTOR, Charles Robert, PhD, FAAS; American molecular biologist and academic; *Chief Scientific Officer, Sequenom Inc.;* b. 26 Aug. 1942, New York; s. of Louis Cantor and Ida Diane Banks; ed Columbia Coll. and Univ. of California, Berkeley; Asst Prof. of Chem., Columbia Univ. 1966–69, Assoc. Prof. of Chem. and Biological Sciences 1969–72, Prof. 1972–81, Prof. of Genetics and Devt; Sherman Fairchild Scholar, Calif. Inst. of Tech. 1975–76; Deputy Dir Comprehensive Cancer Center, Coll. of Physicians and Surgeons 1981–89; Dir Human Genome Center, Lawrence Berkeley Lab. 1989–90; Prof. of Molecular Biology, Univ. of Calif., Berkeley 1989–92; Prof. of Biomedical Eng, Boston Univ. 1992–, Chair. 1994–98, Dir Center for Advanced Biotech. 1992–; Prof. of Pharmacology 1995–; Prin. Scientist, Human Genome Project, US Dept of Energy 1990–92; Chief Scientific Officer, Sequenon Inc. 1998–, mem. Bd of Dirs 2000–; Assoc. Ed. Annual Review of Biophysics and Biophysical Chemistry 1983–93; Pres. Americas Human Genome Org. 1991–98; mem. Biophysics and Biophysical Chem. Study Section, NIH 1971–75, Proposal Review Panel, Stanford Sychrotron Radiation Lab. 1976–88, Ozone Update Comm., NRC 1983, Research Opportunities in Biology Comm. 1985–89, Comm. on Human Genome 1986–89, Scientific Advisory Bd, Hereditary Disease Foundation 1987–89; mem. Council, Human Genome Org. 1989–92, Vice-Pres. 1990–92, Pres. 1991–98; mem. US Nat. Cttee of Int. Union of Pure and Applied Biophysics 1986–94, Vice-Chair. 1988–91, Chair. 1991–94; Chair. US Dept of Energy Human Genome Coordinating Comm. 1989–92; mem. Advisory Cttee Searle Scholars Program 1987–93, Chair. 1993–94; mem. Advisory Cttee Program in Parasite Biology, MacArthur Foundation 1990–93, Scientific Advisory Council Rosewell Park Cancer Inst. 1992–98, Scientific Advisory Cttee European Molecular Biology Lab. 1989–94, Bd of Scientific Counsellors, Nat. Centre for Biotechnology Information, Nat. Library of Medicine 1990–95; consultant, Incyte Pharmaceuticals Inc. 1992–98, Genelabs Inc. 1988–, Samsung Advanced Inst. of Tech. 2000–; mem. Bd of Dirs Applied Biophysics 1993–99, Visiting Cttee for Biology, Brookhaven Nat. Lab. 1986–89; mem. Bd of Dirs and Chair. Scientific Advisory Cttee Avitech Diagnostics Inc. (fmrly ATGC Inc.) 1992–97, Nomenclature Cttee IUBMB 1989–; Chair. Advisory Cttee European Bioinformatics Inst. 1993–94; mem. USDA Genome Advisory Cttee 1992–98; Co-Chair. Biotechnology Advisory Cttee Fisher Scientific 1994–, Biology Advisory Cttee Lawrence Livermore Nat. Lab. 1995–, Chair. 2000–04; mem. Scientific Advisory Cttee Aclara Inc. 1996–2003, Caliper Inc. 1996–; mem. Bd of Dirs ExSar Inc. (fmrly Carta Inc.) 1999–2004, SIGA Inc. (fmrly Plexus Inc.), The Molecular Sciences Inst. SelectX Pharmaceuticals 2003–04 (Chair. Scientific Advisory Bd 2003–), Keystone Conferences 1999–2006; mem. Scientific Advisory Cttee Odyssey Inc. 2002–; Pres. Biochemist Inc. 2001–02; Quest Scholar, Quest Diagnostics Inc. 1997–99; mem. Biotech Council, Dept of Energy 1996–99; mem. Unconventional Pathogen Countermeasures Advisory Cttee 1996–2000; mem. Advisory Cttee Uppsala Bio-X 2004–06; Adjunct Prof. of Biomedical Eng, Univ. of Calif., San Diego 2002–; mem. NAS, American Acad. of Arts and Sciences, Biophysics Soc., American Soc. of Biological Chemists, ACS, Analytical Cytology Soc., Harvey Soc., American Soc. of Human Genetics, Biomedical Eng Soc., Biophysical Soc.; Fellow, Alfred P. Sloan Foundation 1969–71; Hon. mem. Japanese Biochemical Soc.; Fresenius Award 1972, Guggenheim Fellow 1973–74, Eli Lilly Award in Biological Chem., ACS 1978, Nat. Cancer Inst. Outstanding Investigator Grantee 1985, Analytica Prize 1988, ISCO Prize 1989, Sober Prize 1990, Emily Gray Prize 2000. *Achievements include:* helped sequence the human genome and developed methods to non-invasively determine the genes in human foetuses. *Publications include:* Biophysical Chemistry (three vols, with Paul Schimmel), Genomics: The Science and Technology Behind the Human Genome Project. *Leisure interests:* gastronomy, running, skiing. *Address:* Sequenom Inc., 3595 John Hopkins Court, San Diego, CA 92121 (office); 526 Stratford Court, Apt E, Del Mar, CA 92014-2767, USA (home). *Telephone:* (858) 202-9012 (office). *Fax:* (858) 858-9020 (office). *E-mail:* ccantor@sequenom.com (office). *Website:* www.sequenom.com (office).

CANTWELL, Maria E., BA; American politician; *Senator from Washington;* b. 13 Oct. 1958, Indianapolis, IN; d. of Paul Cantwell and Rose Cantwell; ed Univ. of Miami, Ohio; with Cantwell and Assocs (public relations firm) 1981–87; mem. Washington State House of Reps 1987–92; mem. US House of Reps from Wash. 1st Congressional Dist 1993–95; Vice-Pres. of Marketing Progressive Networks (now RealNetworks) 1994–97, Sr Vice-Pres. 1997–2000; Senator from Wash. 2001–, mem. Cttees on Commerce, Science and Transportation, Energy and Natural Resources, Finance, Indian Affairs, Small Business and Entrepreneurship. *Address:* 311 Hart Senate Office Building, Washington, DC 20510, USA (office). *Telephone:* (202) 224-3441 (office). *Fax:* (202) 228-0514 (office). *Website:* cantwell.senate.gov (office).

CAO, Bochun; Chinese politician; *Deputy Director, NPC Environment and Resources Protection Committee;* b. Nov. 1941, Zhuzhou City, Hunan Prov.; ed Zhuzhou School of Aeronautical Industry; teacher, Zhuzhou School of Aeronautical Industry 1963; joined CCP 1966; Deputy Chief No. 331 Factory, Aircraft Engine Factory, Political Div., Jiangnan, Zhejiang Prov. 1970–83, Dir No. 331 Factory, Political Dept 1970–83, Deputy Dir No. 331 Factory 1980–83; Deputy Sec. and Head CCP Publicity Dept, Zhuzhou City Cttee 1983, Sec. Zhuzhou City Cttee 1984; Sec. CCP Xiangtan City Cttee 1990; Vice-Gov. Hunan Prov. 1991; Deputy Sec. CCP Liaoning Prov. Cttee 1992–95, Sec. Dalian City Cttee 1992–95; Alt. mem. 14th CCP Cen. Cttee 1992; mem. 15th CCP Cen. Cttee 1997–2002, 16th CCP Cen. Cttee 2002–07, Sec. CCP Guangxi Zhuang Autonomous Regional Cttee 1997–2002; Chair. Standing Cttee Guangxi Zhuang Autonomous Regional People's Congress 2002–06; Deputy Dir 10th NPC Environment and Resources Protection Cttee 2006–. *Address:* Environment and Resources Protection Committee, National People's Congress, Beijing, People's Republic of China.

CAO, Dewang; Chinese business executive and philanthropist; *Chairman, Fuyao Glass Industry Group;* b. 1948, Fuqing, Fujian Prov.; s. of He Ren; left school early and worked as herdsman, chef and fruit seller; started own business as tobacco seller at age 16; joined Fuqing Gao Shan Special Glass Factory as merchandiser 1976, f. Fuyao Group 1987, currently Chair. Fuyao Glass Industry Group; mem. Fujian Prov. CPPCC Cttee; f. Heren Charitable Foundation 2011; Chair. China Automobile Glass Asscn; Pres. Fujian Golf Asscn; Ernst & Young World Entrepreneur of the Year 2009, listed among Top 10 Economic Figures in China's Economy 2009, named by Ministry of Civil Affairs among China's Top 10 Charitable Persons. *Leisure interest:* golf. *Address:* Office of the Chairman, Fuyao Glass Industry Group, Fuyao Industrial Park, Fuqing 350301, Fujian Province, People's Republic of China (office). *Telephone:* (591) 8538-3777 (office). *Fax:* (591) 8538-2719 (office). *Website:* www.fuyaogroup.com (office).

CAO, Đuc Phát, MPA; Vietnamese agronomist and politician; *Minister of Agriculture and Rural Development;* b. 25 May 1956, Yen Khang, Y Yen Dist, Nam Dinh Prov.; ed Univ. of Belarus, Harvard Univ., USA; joined Agriculture Planning and Design Inst., Ho Chi Minh City 1982, becoming Dir, Centre for Agric. Devt, later Deputy Dir and Dir, Centre for Agric. Devt 1995; with Policy and Financial Planning Dept, Ministry of Agric. and Rural Devt 1995–99, Deputy Minister of Agric. and Rural Devt 1999–2004, Minister of Agric. and Rural Devt 2004–; mem. Cen. Cttee, Communist Party of Viet Nam. *Publications:* author or co-author of several scientific articles published in int. journals. *Address:* Ministry of Agriculture and Rural Development, 2 Ngoc Ha, Ba Dinh District, Hanoi, Viet Nam (home). *Telephone:* (4) 37341635 (office). *Fax:* (4) 38230381 (office). *E-mail:* trangtin@mard.gov.vn (office). *Website:* www.mard.gov.vn (office).

CAO, Gen. Gangchuan; Chinese politician and army officer; b. Dec. 1935, Wuyang Co., Henan Prov.; ed Third Artillery Tech. School, Zhengzhou City, PLA Russian Tech. School, Dalian, Artillery Mil. Eng Acad. Moscow and PLA Univ. of Nat. Defence; joined PLA 1954; teacher, No. 1 Ordnance Tech. School 1956; mem. CCP 1956–; Asst, PLA Gen. Logistics Dept, Ordinance Dept, Ammunition Div. 1963–69, Gen. Logistics Dept, Mil. Equipment Dept, Munitions Div. 1969–75; Staff Officer and Deputy Dir Gen. Planning Div., Mil. Equipment Dept Gen. Staff HQ 1975–82; Deputy Commdr artillery troops during Sino-Vietnamese border conflict 1979; Deputy Dir Mil. Equipment Dept Gen. Staff HQ 1982–89; Maj. Gen., PLA 1988–93, Lieutenant Gen. 1993–98; Dir Mil. Affairs Dept Gen. Staff HQ 1989–90; Dir Mil. Products Trade Office of Mil. Cttee of Cen. Cttee of CCP 1990–92; Deputy Dir Leading Group for Placement of Demobilized Army Officers; Deputy Sec. Comm. for Disciplinary Inspection; Deputy Chief of Gen. Staff, PLA 1992–96; Minister, State Comm. of Science, Tech. and Industry for Nat. Defence 1996–98; rank of Gen. 1996; mem. Central Military Comm. CCP 1998–; Dir and Sec. PLA Gen. Armaments Dept 1998–; mem. 15th Cen. Cttee CCP 1997–2002, 15th Cen. Cttee CCP Cen. Mil. Comm. 1997–2002, 16th Cen. Cttee CCP 2002–07, 16th Cen. Cttee CCP Politburo 2002–07; Vice-Chair. 16th Cen. Cttee CCP Cen. Mil. Comm. 2002–07; State Councillor 2003–08; Minister of Nat. Defence 2003–08. *Address:* c/o Ministry of National Defence, 20 Jingshanqian Jie, Beijing 100009, People's Republic of China.

CAO, Peixi, MEcon, MEng; Chinese engineer and business executive; *Chairman and President, China Huaneng Group;* b. Aug. 1955; ed Party School of CCP Cen. Cttee, Shandong Univ.; has worked in power generation, operation and man. and capital operations since mid-1970s; joined Qingdao Plant, China Huadian Corpn 1972, held positions of technician, Deputy Chief Engineer, Deputy Head and Head of the plant, Asst to Gen. Man., Deputy Gen. Man., Chair. and Party Sec. and Gen. Man. of Shandong Electric Power (Group) Corpn 1995–2002, Deputy Gen. Man. and Party mem. China Huadian Corpn 2002–06, Chair. Huadian Power International Corpn Ltd 2007–08; Chair. China Huaneng Group 2008–, Pres. 2009–, also Chair. Huaneng International Power Devt Corpn, Huaneng Power International, Inc., Huaneng Renewables Corpn Ltd 2013–, Vice-Sec. CCP Huaneng Cttee. *Address:* China Huaneng Group, 6 Fuxingmennei Street, Xicheng District, Beijing 100031, People's Republic of China (office). *Telephone:* (10) 63228800 (office). *Fax:* (10) 63228866 (office). *E-mail:* info@chng.com.cn (office). *Website:* www.chng.com.cn (office).

CAO, Lt-Gen. Shuangming; Chinese army officer (retd) and party official; b. 1929, Linxian Co., Henan Prov.; joined CCP 1946; Deputy Commdr PLA Shengyang Mil. Area Command 1987–92, Commdr PLA Air Force 1992–94; rank of Lt-Gen. 1988; mem. 14th CCP Cen. Cttee 1992–97. *Address:* c/o Shengyang Military Area Command, People's Liberation Army, Shengyang City, Liaoning Province, People's Republic of China.

CAO, Zhi; Chinese politician; b. May 1928, Anqiu, Shandong Prov.; joined CCP 1947; Dir Acheng News Report, Acheng Co., Heilongjiang Prov. 1947–48; Sec. CCP Co. Cttee, Acheng Co. 1948–49, Deputy Head CCP Co. Cttee Publicity Dept 1949–51, Head 1951–52; Deputy Section Chief CCP Prov. Cttee Publicity Dept, Heilongjiang Prov. 1952–53, Div. Chief 1953–60, Deputy Dir CCP Prov. Cttee Gen. Office 1960–66; Deputy Sec. CCP Prefectural Cttee, Hejiang Prefecture,

Heilongjiang Prov. 1966–70; Vice-Chair. CCP Revolutionary Cttee, Heilongjiang Prov. 1970–77; Leading mem. State Devt and Reform Comm. 1977–78; Head CCP Cen. Cttee Research Office 1978–83; Deputy Head CCP Cen. Cttee Org. Dept 1983–87; Deputy Dir Research Office, Secr. CCP Cen. Cttee 1987–88; Sec.-Gen. 7th Standing Cttee NPC 1988–93, 8th Standing Cttee NPC 1993–98; Vice-Chair. Standing Cttee 9th NPC 1998–2003; Del. 14th CCP Nat. Congress 1992–97, 15th CCP Nat. Congress 1997–2002; Vice-Pres. Cen. Cttee for Comprehensive Man. of Public Security 1993; mem. Hong Kong Special Admin. Region Preparatory Cttee Govt Del. for Hong Kong Hand-Over Ceremony 1997. *Address:* c/o Standing Committee, National People's Congress, Tian'anmen Square, Beijing, People's Republic of China.

CAO, Zhi'an; Chinese economist and business executive; *General Manager and President, China Southern Power Grid Company Ltd;* Dir Human Resources Dept, Asst Pres., then Vice-Pres. and Deputy Gen. Man. State Grid Corpn –2015; Gen. Man. and Pres. China Southern Power Grid Co. Ltd 2015–. *Address:* China Southern Power Grid Co. Ltd, 6 Huasui Road, Zhujiang Xincheng, Tianhe District, Guangzhou 510623, People's Republic of China (office). *Telephone:* (20) 3812-1958 (office); (20) 3812-1080 (office). *Fax:* (20) 3886-5670 (office); (20) 3812-0189 (office). *E-mail:* international@csg.cn (office). *Website:* www.csg.cn (office); eng.csg.cn (office).

CAPASSO, Federico, PhD, FInstP; Italian/American mathematician, physicist, computer scientist and academic; *Robert L. Wallace Professor of Applied Physics and Vinton Hayes Senior Research Fellow in Electrical Engineering, Harvard University;* b. 1949, Rome, Italy; m.; two c.; ed Univ. of Rome; Postdoctoral Fellow Fondazione Bordoni, Rome 1973–74, Research Physicist 1974–76; Visiting Scientist, Bell Labs, Holmdel, NJ 1976–77, mem. Tech. Staff, Bell Labs, Murray Hill, NJ 1977–84, Distinguished Mem. of Tech. Staff 1984–87, Dept Head, Quantum Phenomena and Device Research, Bell Labs Lucent Technologies (fmrly AT&T Bell Labs –1996) 1987–97, Dept Head, Semiconductor Physics Research 1997–2000, Vice-Pres. of Physical Research 2000–02; Robert L. Wallace Prof. of Applied Physics, Harvard Univ. 2003–, Vinton Hayes Sr Research Fellow in Electrical Eng, School of Eng and Applied Sciences (fmrly, Div.); Adjunct Researcher, Inst. for Quantum Studies, Texas A&M Univ. 2009–; mem. NAS 1995, Nat. Acad. of Eng 1995; Fellow, American Physical Soc. 1986, IEEE 1987, Optical Soc. of America 1989, Int. Soc. for Optical Eng (SPIE) 1991, AAAS 1992, American Acad. of Arts and Sciences 1998; US citizenship 1992; Hon. mem. Franklin Inst. 1997; Commendatore of Italian Repub. 2004; Hon. Dr of Electrical Eng (Bologna) 2003; Distinguished Mem. of Technical Staff Award, Bell Labs 1984, IEEE David Sarnoff Award in Electronics 1991, New York Acad. of Sciences Award 1993, Heinrich Welker Memorial Medal (Germany) and Int. Compound Semiconductors Symposium Award 1994, Electronics Letters Prize, IEE (UK) 1995, Newcomb Cleveland Prize, AAAS 1995, Moët Hennessy-Louis Vuitton 'Leonardo da Vinci' Award of Excellence (France) 1995, Medal of Materials Research Soc. 1995, Fellow Award, Bell Labs 1997, Wetherill Medal, Franklin Inst. 1997, Capitolium Prize, Mayor of Rome 1998, Rank Prize in Optoelectronics (UK) 1998, W. Streifer Award for Scientific Achievement, IEEE/Laser & Electro-Optics Soc. 1998, Alessandro Volta Memorial Medal, Univ. of Pavia 1999, NASA Group Achievement Award 2000, Willis E. Lamb Medal for Laser Physics and Quantum Optics 2000, Robert Wood Prize, Optical Soc. of America 2001, Silver Seal, Univ. of Bari 2001, Duddell Medal and Prize, Inst. of Physics (UK) 2002, Goff Smith Prize and Lecture, Univ. of Michigan 2003, Tommasoni & Chisesi Prize for Outstanding Achievements in Physics 2004, Arhur Schawlow Prize in Laser Science, American Physical Soc. 2004, IEEE Edison Medal 2004, Gold Medal, Pres. of Italy 2005, King Faisal Int. Prize for Science 2005, Berthold Leibinger Zukunft Prize (Future Prize) 2010, Julius Springer Prize for Applied Physics 2010, Enrico Fermi Prize of the Italian Physical Soc. 2018. *Publications:* Problems of General Physics (co-ed.) 1976, Picosecond Electronics and Optoelectronics (co-ed.) 1987, Heterojunction Band Discontinuities: Physics and Device Applications (co-ed.) 1987, Quantum Well and Superlattice Physics II. Proceedings SPIE (co-ed.) 1988, Physics of Quantum Electron Devices; Springer Series in Electronics and Photonics, Vol. 28 (ed.) 1990, Intersubband Transitions in Quantum Wells: Physics and Applications, Part I (co-ed.) 2000, Intersubband Transitions in Quantum Wells: Physics and Applications, Part II (co-ed.) 2000; numerous book chapters and more than 450 papers in peer-reviewed journals. *Address:* School of Engineering and Applied Sciences, Harvard University, 205A Pierce Hall, 29 Oxford Street, Cambridge, MA 02138, USA (office). *Telephone:* (617) 384-7611 (office); (617) 495-5909 (lab.) (office). *Fax:* (617) 495-2875 (office). *E-mail:* capasso@seas.harvard.edu (office). *Website:* www.seas.harvard.edu/directory/capasso (office).

CAPECCHI, Mario Renato, PhD; American (b. Italian) geneticist and academic; *Distinguished Professor of Human Genetics, School of Medicine and Investigator, Howard Hughes Medical Institute, University of Utah;* b. 6 Oct. 1937, Verona, Italy; m. 2nd Laurie Fraser 1985; one d.; ed Antioch Coll., Harvard Univ.; Jr Fellow in Biophysics, Harvard Univ. 1966–69, Asst Prof. to Assoc. Prof. of Biochemistry, Medical School 1969–73; Prof. of Biology, Univ. of Utah 1973–88, Prof. of Human Genetics, School of Medicine 1989–, Distinguished Prof. 1993–, Investigator, Howard Hughes Medical Inst., Univ. of Utah 1988–; mem. Bd Scientific Counselors, Nat. Cancer Inst.; mem. NAS, American Biochemial Soc., American Soc. of Microbiology, New York Acad. of Science, Int. Genome Soc., Genetics Soc. of America, AAAS, Soc. for Developmental Biology, European Acad. of Sciences, American Acad. of Arts and Sciences 2009–; ACS Biochemistry Award 1969, Bristol-Myers Squibb Award for Distinguished Achievement in Neuroscience Research 1992, Gairdner Foundation Int. 1993, Gen. Motors Corpn Alfred P. Sloan Jr Prize 1994, Kyoto Prize in Basic Sciences 1996, Franklin Medal 1997, Baxter Award 1998, Lasker Award 2001, Nat. Medal of Science 2001, John Scott Medal Award 2002, Pezcoller Foundation–AACR Int. Award 2003, Wolf Prize in Medicine 2002–03, March of Dimes Prize in Developmental Biology 2005, Nobel Prize in Physiology or Medicine (with Sir Martin Evans and Oliver Smithies) 2007 for the discovery of principles for introducing specific gene modifications in mice by the use of embryonic stem cells; American Heart Asscn Distinguished Scientist Award 2008. *Publications include:* Targeted Gene Replacement 1994, The Making of a Scientist (Howard Hughes Medical Inst. Bulletin) 1997, Generating Mice with Targeted Mutations 2001, and a total of 141 peer-reviewed manuscripts, books and book chapters. *Address:* Howard Hughes Medical Institute, University of Utah, 15 N 2030 E, Room 5100, Salt Lake City, UT 84112-5331 (office); 778 East 13800 South, Draper, UT 84020, USA (home). *Telephone:* (801) 581-7096 (office). *Fax:* (801) 585-3425 (office). *E-mail:* mario.capecchi@genetics.utah.edu (office). *Website:* capecchi.genetics.utah.edu (office).

CAPELLAS, Michael D., BBA; American business executive; *Principal, Capellas Strategic Partners;* b. 19 Aug. 1954; m. Marie Capellas; two c.; ed Kent State Univ.; systems analyst, Republic Steel Corpn 1976–81; joined Schlumberger Ltd 1981, holding successive posts as First Corp. Dir for Information Systems, Controller and Treas. of Asia Pacific Operations, Chief Financial Officer Dowell Schlumberger, Operations Man. Schlumberger's Fairchild Semiconductor unit 1981–96; Founder and Man. Pnr, Benchmarking Partners, Cambridge, Mass 1996; Dir of Supply-Chain Man., SAP America 1996–97; Sr Vice-Pres. and Gen. Man. Global Energy Business, Oracle Corpn 1997–98; Chief Information Officer Compaq Computer Corpn 1998–99, Pres. and CEO 1999–2000, Chair. and CEO 2000–02; Pres. Hewlett-Packard Co. (following acquisition of Compaq by Hewlett-Packard) 2002; Chair. and CEO WorldCom (now MCI Group) 2002–04, Pres. and CEO 2004–06; Acting Pres. and CEO Serena Software Inc. 2006–07; Sr Advisor, Silver Lake Partners (investment firm) 2007–; Chair. and CEO First Data Corpn 2007–10; Chair. and CEO VCE 2010–11; Prin., Capellas Strategic Partners 2012–; mem. Bd of Dirs Cisco Systems Inc. 2006–; Trustee American Univ., Washington, DC. *Leisure interests:* community leadership and charity work, golf. *Website:* www .capellaspartners.com.

CAPELLE, Alfred, MA; Marshall Islands civil servant and diplomatist; b. 20 March 1940; m. Mwejo term; five s. three d.; ed Univ. of Hawaii at Manoa; Admin. Aide, Global Assocs, Inc., Kwajalein 1964–66; Mayor, Likiep Atoll 1966–68; elementary school teacher 1968–77; Educ. Specialist, Dept of Educ. 1977–79; Continuing Educ. Programme Co-ordinator, Coll. of Micronesia 1979–82; Chief of Post-Secondary Educ., Ministry of Educ. 1982–83, Language Consultant and Researcher 1996; Dir of Assumption Schools, Assumption Parish, Majuro 1983–86; Resource Protection Officer and CEO, Alele Museum 1986–96; Pres., Coll. of Marshall Islands 1996–2002; Amb. and Perm. Rep. to UN, New York 2002–08; currently Adviser, Pacific Aquaculture Cooperatives International Inc. *Publications include:* Marshallese-English Dictionary (co-author) 1976. *Address:* c/o Pacific Aquaculture Cooperatives International Inc., 6 South Lakeview Drive, Jackson, NJ 08527, USA. *E-mail:* info@pacinternational.org.

CAPELLINO, Ally, BA; British fashion designer; b. (Alison Lloyd), 1956; ed Middlesex Univ.; worked in Courtaulds Cen. Design Studio 1978–79; est. Ally Capellino Little Hat, initially selling hats and accessories 1979; developed clothing line with accessories for Moscow Olympics collection 1979–80; began selling Ally Capellino label to int. markets 1980; launched menswear collection 1986; first London fashion show 1986; opened shop in Soho, London 1988; launched Hearts of Oak sportswear collection 1990, Mini Capellino children's wear 1991; signed promotional and licensing agreement with Coats Viyella PLC 1992; launched 'ao' collection 1996; opened Ally Capellino shop, London 1997; opened flagship store Tokyo, Japan 1998. *Address:* c/o Goodley PR, 41 Dover Street, Mayfair, London, W1S 4NS, England. *Telephone:* (20) 7493-9600 (office). *E-mail:* info@allycapellino .co.uk (office). *Website:* www.allycapellino.co.uk (office).

CAPELLO, Fabio; Italian fmr professional football manager and fmr professional footballer; b. 18 June 1946, San Canzian d'Isonzo; s. of Guerrino Capello and Evelina Capello; m. Laura Capello; two c.; played for SPAL 1964–67, A.S. Roma 1967–69 (won Coppa Italia 1969), Juventus 1969–76 (won Serie A 1972, 1973, 1975), Associazione Calcio (A.C.) Milan 1976–80 (won Coppa Italia 1977, Serie A 1979), Italian nat. team 1972–76 (32 caps, eight goals); Man. AC Milan 1991–96, 1997–98 (won Serie A 1992, 1993, 1994, 1996, Supercoppa Italiana 1992, 1993, 1994, UEFA Champions League 1994, European Super Cup 1994), Real Madrid 1996–97, 2006–07 (winner La Liga 1997, 2007), A.S. Roma 1999–2004 (won Serie A 2001, Supercoppa Italiana 2001), Juventus 2004–06 (won Serie A 2005, 2006 (Trophy revoked due to Calciopoli scandal)), England Nat. Football Team 2008–12 (qualified for 2010 World Cup 2009), Russia Nat. Football Team 2012–15, Jiangsu Suning 2017–18; apptd Pres. League Managers Asscn 2008; Serie A Coach of the Year 2005, BBC Sports Personality Coach of the Year 2009-10. *Leisure interests:* fine art enthusiast and collector, opera and classical music.

CAPITANICH, Jorge Milton, MEconSc; Argentine accountant and politician; *Governor, Chaco Province;* b. 28 Nov. 1964, Roque Saenz Peña, Chaco Prov.; ed Universidad Nacional del Nordeste, Instituto Universitario Escuela Superior de Economía y Administración de Empresas (ESEADE); Head of Private Employment Generation Program, Secr. of Assistance in Provincial Econ. Reforms 1994; Under-Sec. of Admin. Co-ordination, Nat. Secr. for Social Devt 1995, Under-Sec. of Social Planning 1998; Acting Minister of Infrastructure and Housing, of Social Devt and Environment, of Public Health, of Work, Employment and Human Resources, and of Social Security 2001; Cabinet Chief, Govt of Argentina 2002; Nat. Senator for Chaco Prov. 2002–07; Gov. of Chaco Prov. 2007–13, 2015–; Chief, Cabinet of Ministers 2013–15. *Publications:* Investigación Sobre El Orígen de las Crisis Provinciales, Federalismo Fiscal y Coparticipación, La Sumergida. Chaco, Propuestas para la Integración. *Address:* Office of the Governor, 0362 Resistencia, Chaco Province, Argentina (office). *Website:* chaco.gov.ar/ (office).

CAPITO, Shelley Wellons Moore, BSc, MEd; American politician; *Senator from West Virginia;* b. 26 Nov. 1953, Glen Dale, W Virginia; d. of Arch Alfred Moore, Jr and Shelley Moore (née Riley); m. Charles L. Capito; two s. one d.; ed Duke Univ., Univ. of Virginia; Dir, Educational Information Center, W Virginia Bd of Regents 1978–81; mem. W Virginia House of Dels for Dist 30 1996–2000; mem. US House of Reps from W Virginia 2nd Dist, Washington, DC 2001–15, mem. House Cttee on Financial Services, House Cttee on Transportation and Infrastructure, fmr Chair. Congressional Caucus for Women's Issues; Senator from W Virginia 2015–; Republican. *Address:* Senate Office Building, Russell Courtyard 5, Washington, DC 20510, USA (office). *Telephone:* (202) 224-6472 (office). *Website:* www.capito .senate.gov (office).

CAPLIN, Mortimer Maxwell, BS, LLB, JSD; American lawyer, government official and academic; *Senior Partner, Caplin & Drysdale Attorneys;* b. 11 July 1916, New York; s. of Daniel Caplin and Lillian Epstein; m. Ruth Sacks 1942 (died 2014); three s. one d.; ed Univ. of Virginia and New York Univ. Law School; law Clerk to US Circuit Judge 1940–41; legal practice with Paul, Weiss, Rifkind, Wharton & Garrison, New York 1941–50; with USNR, Beachmaster in Normandy landings 1942–45; Prof. of Law, Univ. of Virginia 1950–61, Lecturer and Visiting Prof. 1965–87, Prof. Emer. 1988–; Counsel, Perkins, Battle & Minor 1952–61; US Commr of Internal Revenue 1961–64; Founder and Sr Pnr, Caplin & Drysdale, Washington, DC 1964–; Chair. Nat. Civil Service League 1965–80, American Council on Int. Sports 1975–80, Nat. Citizens' Advisory Cttee 1975–80, Asscn of American Medical Colls., Univ. of Virginia Council of the Arts; Dir Fairchild Corpn, Presidential Reality Corpn, Danaher Corpn 1990–2013; mem. Public Review Bd, Arthur Andersen & Co. 1980–88; mem. House of Dels 1980–92, DC and Fed. Bar Asscns, Va and New York State Bars, American Law Inst.; Ed.-in-Chief Virginia Law Review 1939–40; mem. Bd of Trustees, George Washington Univ. 1964, Bd of Visitors, Univ. of Virginia Law School Foundation 1982–; Emer. Trustee Shakespeare Theatre, Wolf Trap Foundation and Arena Stage; Hon. LLD (St Michael Coll.) 1964; Raven Award, Alexander Hamilton Award, Univ. of Virgina/Thomas Jefferson Memorial Foundation Medal in Law 2001 and other awards; Order of the Coif. *Publications include:* Doing Business in Other States, Proxies, Annual Meetings and Corporate Democracy; numerous articles on tax and corporate matters. *Leisure interests:* swimming, horseback riding, gardening. *Address:* Caplin & Drysdale, One Thomas Circle, NW, Washington, DC 20005-5802 (office); Apartment 18E, 5610 Wisconsin Avenue, Chevy Chase, MD 20815-4415, USA (home). *Telephone:* (202) 862-5050 (office). *E-mail:* mcaplin@capdale.com (office). *Website:* www.capdale.com (office).

ČAPLOVIČ, Dušan, DrSci; Slovak archaeologist and politician; b. 18 Sept. 1946, Bratislava; ed Comenius Univ.; Head of Historical Dept, East Slovak Museum, Košice 1969–79; The East Regional Nat. Cttee– Culture Košice 1979–80; Head of Inst. of Archaeology of Nitra, Košice, Slovak Acad. of Sciences 1980–86, Scientific Sec. 1986–90, Deputy Dir 1990–91, mem. Presidium and Deputy Vice-Chair. 1992–2001, Deputy Chair. 1995–2001, Inst. of Archaeology of Nitra 2001–02; mem. Nat. Council 2002–06; Deputy Prime Minister for Knowledge-Based Soc., European Affairs, Human Rights and Minorities 2006–10; interim Minister of the Environment 2008; mem. Parl. and Chair. Parl. Cttee for Educ., Science, Youth and Sport 2010–12; Minister of Educ., Science, Research and Sport 2012–14 (resgnd); mem. Council for Science and Tech. 1992–95; mem. Advisory Bd Ministry of Culture 1995–98; mem. Arbeitskreis für genetische Siedlungforschung in Mitteleuropa, Bonn, Germany 1995, Medieval Settlement Research Group, Leicester/Durham, UK 1998, European Acad. of Sciences and Arts, Salzburg 2008; mem. of domestic and foreign editorial boards; Hon. Citizen of Kovačica (Slovak village), Imeľ (Slovakia-Hungarian village); Silver Dionýz Stuř Honorary Plaque of Merit in Social Sciences, Slovak Acad. of Sciences, Medal of the Slovak Acad. of Sciences – Nummum Academiae Memorialen Tribune for scientific research and organizational activities, Pax International Guardian di Pace – con dall'albero di Palme d'Olivo, Assisi, Italy. *Publications:* several articles in scientific journals. *Address:* c/o Ministry of Education, Science, Research and Sport, Stromová 1, 813 30 Bratislava, Slovakia. *E-mail:* info@minedu.sk. *Website:* www.caplovic.sk.

CAPPE, Mel, OC, MA; Canadian economist and fmr diplomatist; *Professor, Munk School of Global Affairs and Public Policy, University of Toronto;* b. 3 Dec. 1948, Toronto; s. of David Cappe and Patricia Cappe; m. Marline (Marni) Cappe (née Pliskin); one s. one d.; ed Univs of Toronto and Western Ontario; joined Canadian public service as a policy analyst 1975; with Treasury Bd 1975–78, Deputy Sec. 1990–94; with Dept of Finance 1978–82; Deputy Dir Investigation and Research, Dept of Consumer and Corp. Affairs 1982–90; Deputy Asst Sec. Dept of Finance 1990, Deputy Sec. Program Br. 1990; fmr Asst Deputy Minister Competition Policy; fmr Asst Deputy Minister Policy Co-ordination; fmr Asst Deputy Minister Corp. Affairs and Legis. Policy; Deputy Minister of the Environment 1994–96, of Human Resources Devt 1996–99; Chair. Employment Insurance Comm. 1996–99; Deputy Minister of Labour 1996–99; Clerk of the Privy Council, Sec. to Cabinet and Head of the Public Service 1999–2002; Special Adviser to Prime Minister 2002; High Commr to UK 2002–06; Pres. and CEO Inst. for Research on Public Policy, Montreal 2006–12; Prof., School of Public Policy and Governance (now Munk School of Global Affairs and Public Policy), Univ of Toronto 2012–; Chair. Health Research Foundation 2014; Mentor, Pierre Elliott Trudeau Foundation 2016; Chair. Canadian Blood Services 2018–; Queen's Golden Jubilee Medal 2002, Queen's Diamond Jubilee Medal 2012; Hon. PhD (Univ. of Western Ontario, Univ. of Toronto); Hon. LLD. *Address:* Munk School of Global Affairs and Public Policy, University of Toronto, 14 Queen's Park Crescent, West Toronto, ON M5S 3K9, Canada (office). *Telephone:* (416) 978-2875 (office). *Fax:* (416) 978-5079 (office). *E-mail:* mel.cappe@utoronto.ca (office).

CAPPELLAZZO, Amy, BA, MA; American art dealer; *Deputy Chairman, Christie's Americas and Co-Head of Post-War and Contemporary Art, Christie's International;* ed New York Univ. (Presidential Trustee Scholar), Pratt Inst.; Sr Vice-Pres. and Int. Co-Head of Postwar and Contemporary Art, Christie's auction house 2001–, played key role in historic sale which was the first ever Post-War and Contemporary auction to break the $100 million mark May 2004, Deputy Chair. Christie's Americas 2008–; taught and lectured at New York Univ., Museum of Modern Art, New York, Univ. of Miami, Museum of Fine Arts Boston and at UCLA; Trustee, Pratt Inst.; featured in Crain's Business New York 40 under 40 2006. *Address:* Christie's International, 20 Rockefeller Plaza, New York, NY 10020, USA (office). *Telephone:* (212) 636-2000 (office). *Fax:* (212) 636-2399 (office). *E-mail:* info@christies.com (office). *Website:* www.christies.com (office).

CAPPON, Claudio; Italian broadcasting executive; b. 9 July 1952, Rome; m. Antonella Riccio Cobucci; three c.; ed Univ. of Rome; worked for Istituto per la Ricostruzione Industriale for 20 years, specializing in control and man.; Dir of Industrial Activities, Fintecna 1994–96, Dir-Gen. and CEO 1996–98; Deputy Dir-Gen. Radiotelevisione Italiana SpA (RAI) 1998–2001, Dir-Gen. 2001–02, 2006–09; CEO Consap (Concessionaria dei servizi assicurativi pubblici) from 2002; Pres. APT (Asscn of TV Producers) from 2002; mem. Bd of Dirs, Dada SpA 2010–13; Pres. Rai World 2012–13; Vice-Pres. European Broadcasting Union 2009–14; Prof. and Maitre de conference of a course on Public Service Media in Europe, Sciences-Po, Paris; mem. Bd, Roma Tre Univ., Rome. *Address:* c/o European Broadcasting Union, L'Ancienne-Route 17A, PO Box 45, 1218 Le Grand-Saconnex/ Geneva, Switzerland. *E-mail:* ebu@ebu.ch.

CAPPS, Thomas E., BA, JD; American business executive; b. 31 Oct. 1935, Wilmington, North Carolina; s. of Edward S. Capps Jr and Agnes Rhodes; m. 1st Jane Paden 1963; two c.; m. 2nd Sandra Lee Hurley; four c.; ed Univ. of North Carolina; in pvt. legal practice, N Carolina and Fla 1966–70; held positions in legal depts of two electric utilities; joined Dominion Resources Inc. 1984, apptd Pres. 1990, Vice-Chair., Pres. and CEO 2000, Chair., Pres. and CEO 2000–03, Chair. and CEO 2003–06, Chair. 2006–07 (retd); Chair. and Dir Virginia Electric and Power Co., Consolidated Natural Gas Co.; mem. Bd of Dirs Amerigroup Corpn 2004–, Associated Electric and Gas Insurance Services Ltd, Shaw Group Inc. 2007–; mem. Bd of Visitors Coll. of William and Mary; Trustee Univ. of Richmond, Virginia Foundation of Ind. Colls.

CAPRA, Carlo; Italian historian and academic (retd); b. 14 Nov. 1938, Quartu S. Elena, Cagliari; s. of Agostino Capra and Maria Maxia; m. Maria Grazia Bosi 1964; one s.; ed Università degli Studi, Milan; teacher of English in state secondary schools –1970; Asst Lecturer in History, Università degli Studi, Milan 1970–72, Reader 1972–81, Assoc. Prof. 1981–86, Prof. 1986–2008, Head, Dept of History 1989–92; mem. Scientific Council, Società Italiana di Studi sul XVIII Secolo; Gen. Ed. Edizione Nazionale delle Opere di Pietro Verri; Co-ed. Società e storia (journal), Storia (series), Settecento italiano (series). *Publications:* Giovanni Ristori da illuminista a funzionario (1755–1830) 1968, Il giornalismo nell'età rivoluzionaria e napoleonica 1976, La Lombardia austriaca nell'età delle riforme 1984, 1987, Cesare Beccaria, Carleggio Vols IV–V of Edizione Nazionale delle Opere (ed.) 1995, I progressi della ragione: Vita di Pietro Verri 2002, Storia moderna 2004, Pietro Verri, Scritti politici della maturità (ed.) 2010. *Leisure interests:* music, cinema. *Address:* Corso Garibaldi 71, Milan 20121, Italy (home). *Telephone:* (02) 86461509 (home). *E-mail:* carlo.capra1@unimi.it (home).

CAPRIATI, Jennifer Maria; American fmr professional tennis player; b. 29 March 1976, New York; d. of Stefano Capriati and Denise Capriati; ed Pasco High School, Fla; coached by her father; winner, French Open Jr 1989, US Open Jr 1989, Wimbledon and US Open Jr Doubles 1989; youngest player in Whiteman Cup 1989; youngest player to reach a professional final (aged 13 years and 11 months at Boca Raton 1990); gold medal (Olympic Games of 1992); Wimbledon debut 1990; semi-finalist French Open 1990, 2002, US Open 1991, 2001, 2003, Wimbledon 1991 (youngest Grand Slam semi-finalist in tennis history), 2001; won Australian Open 2001, 2002, French Open 2001; 15 career professional titles in total (one doubles title); Int. Tennis Fed. World Champion 2001; retd 2004. *Leisure interests:* dancing, golf, music, reading, writing.

CAPRILES RADONSKI, Henrique; Venezuelan lawyer and politician; b. 11 July 1972, Caracas; ed Universidad Católica Andrés Bello, Cen. Univ. of Venezuela, IBFD Int. Tax Acad., Amsterdam, Centro Interamericano de Administradores Tributarios, Viterbo, Italy, Columbia Univ., USA; worked for several law firms in private sector, including Nevett & Mezquita Abogados and Hoet, Pelaez, Castillo & Duque; Vice-Pres. Chamber of Deputies (COPEI Party) 1998–99; Mayor, Baruta Municipality of Caracas 2000–08; Gov. of Miranda 2008–June 2012, Dec. 2012–17; unsuccessful cand. in presidential elections 2012, 2013; mem. Int. Fiscal Asscn, World Asscn of Young Jurors, Cttee of Taxes, Venezuelan American Chamber of Industry and Commerce.

CAPRON, Alexander Morgan, LLB; American academic and lawyer; *University Professor and Scott H. Bice Chair in Healthcare Law, Policy and Ethics, University of Southern California;* b. 16 Aug. 1944, Hartford, Conn.; s. of William M. Capron and Margaret Capron (née Morgan); m. 1st Barbara A. Brown 1969 (divorced 1985); m. 2nd Kathleen M. West 1989; four c.; ed Palo Alto High School, Swarthmore Coll. and Yale Law School; law clerk to Chief Judge, US Court of Appeals, DC Circuit 1969–70; Lecturer and Research Assoc., Yale Law School 1970–72; Asst Prof. to Prof. of Law and Prof. of Human Genetics, Univ. of Pennsylvania 1972–82; Exec. Dir Pres.'s Comm. for Study of Ethical Problems in Medicine and Biomedical and Behavioural Research 1979–83; Prof. of Law, Ethics and Public Policy, Georgetown Univ. 1983–84; Topping Prof. of Law, Medicine and Public Policy, Univ. of Southern California 1985–89, Univ. Prof. 1989–, Co-Dir Pacific Center for Health Policy and Ethics 1990–, Henry W. Bruce Prof. of Law 1991–2006, Scott H. Bice Chair in Healthcare Law, Policy and Ethics 2006–, Pres. Univ. Faculty 2009–10, Vice-Dean Law School 2011–13; Dir Ethics, Trade, Human Rights and Health Law, WHO 2002–06; Pres. American Soc. of Law and Medicine 1988–89; Pres. Int. Asscn of Bioethics 2005–07; Chair. Biomedical Ethics Advisory Cttee, US Congress 1988–91, Public Responsibility in Medicine and Research (PRIM&R) 2013–; mem. Nat. Bioethics Advisory Comm. 1996–2001; Hon. Fellow, American Coll. of Legal Medicine; Hon. MA (Univ. of Pennsylvania); several honours and awards. *Publications include:* books including Catastrophic Diseases: Who Decides What? (with J. Katz) 1975, Law, Science and Medicine (with others) 1984, Treatise on Health Care Law (with others) 1991; 300 articles in journals and books. *Leisure interests:* gardening, films, travel. *Address:* Gould School of Law, University of Southern California, 699 Exposition Blvd, Los Angeles, CA 90089-0071, USA (office). *Telephone:* (213) 740-2557 (office). *Fax:* (213) 740-5502 (office). *E-mail:* acapron@law.usc.edu (office). *Website:* lawweb.usc.edu/who/faculty/directory/contactInfo.cfm?detailID=205 (office).

CAPUÑAY, Juan Carlos, BEcons; Peruvian diplomatist and international organization official; *Ambassador to the People's Republic of China;* b. 1948; ed Nat. Univ. of San Marcos; joined Ministry of Foreign Affairs 1972, Third Sec., Embassy in Tokyo 1973–76, Second Sec. 1976, Second Sec., Perm. Mission to UN, New York 1976–79, First Sec. 1979–82, First Sec., Perm. Mission to OAS 1982–83, Counsellor 1983–86, Minister Counsellor and Alt. Rep. 1986–91, Minister, Embassy in Tokyo and Alt. Rep. to Int. Org. for Tropical Woods 1991–94, Minister, Embassy in Beijing 1994–97, Minister, Chargé d'Affaires to Singapore 1997–98, Amb. to Singapore and Brunei 1998–2003, Amb. and Dir-Gen. Asia-Pacific Econ. Co-operation (APEC) Div., also Sr Official of Peru in APEC Under-Secr. for Asia and Pacific Basin Affairs 2003–07, Amb. and Deputy Exec. Dir APEC Secr. 2007, Exec. Dir 2008; Amb. to Japan 2009–14, to the People's Republic of China 2014–; official decorations from Japan, Repub. of Korea and Chile. *Address:* Embassy of Peru, 1-91 San Li Tun, Chaoyang Qu, Beijing 100600, The People's Republic of China (office). *Telephone:* (10) 65323477 (office). *Fax:* (10) 65322178 (office). *E-mail:* info@embaperuchina.com.cn (office). *Website:* www.embperuchina.com (office).

CAPUS, Steve, BA; American media executive; b. 4 Oct. 1963; m. Sophia Faskianos; two s. one d.; ed Temple Univ.; with WCAU-TV, Philadelphia 1986;

joined KYW-TV, Philadelphia 1987, Exec. Producer 1990–93; joined NBC as Sr Producer NBC Nightside, 1993, Broadcast Producer NBC News Sunrise 1994, Supervising Producer Today Show 1995, Sr Producer MSNBC daytime news 1996–97, Exec. Producer The News with Brian Williams (MSNBC) 1997–2001, Exec. Producer, Nightly News show 2001–05, Sr Vice-Pres., News Division June–Nov. 2005, Pres. NBC News Nov. 2005–13; Exec. Ed. CBS News 2014–18, Exec. Producer CBS Evening News 2014–18; Alfred I. DuPont-Columbia Award, four Emmys, six Edward R. Murrow Awards, six Nat. Headliner Awards.

CAPUTO, Luis Andrés (Toto); Argentine economist, politician and central banker; b. 21 April 1965, Buenos Aires; s. of Luis Nicolás Caputo Oliveto and María Rosa d'Alvia; m. Ximena Ruiz Hanglin; four s. two d.; ed Univ. of Buenos Aires; Man. Dir JP Morgan 1994–98, Head of Emerging Markets Fixed Income Trading for Latin America, Eastern Europe and Asia 1997–2002; Pres., CEO and Country Man. Deutsche Bank 2003–08; Co-Founder Noctua Partners 2009; fmr Prof. Pontifical Catholic Univ. of Argentina; fmr Dir Empresa Distribuidora y Comercializadora Norte S.A.; Independent Dir Pampa Energía S.A 2010–; Sec. of Finance 2015–16; Minister of Finance 2016–18; mem. Board of Governors, Central American Bank for Economic Integration 2017–; Pres. Banco Central de la República Argentina June–Sept. 2018; Gov. Inter-American Devt Bank. *Address:* c/o Central Bank of Argentina, Reconquista 266, C1003ABF, Buenos Aires, Argentina (office).

ČAPUTOVÁ, Zuzana, LLB; Slovak lawyer and politician; b. 21 June 1973, Bratislava; m. Ivan Čaputá (divorced 2018); two d.; ed Comenius Univ.; fmr Asst of Legal Dept and Deputy of Municipal Office, local govt of Bratislava, project man., EQ Klub 1998; joined VIA IURIS 2001, Attorney 2010–17; co-founder Progressive Slovakia 2017, Vice-Chair. 2018–19; Pres.-elect 2019 (June–); Fellow, Environmental Law Alliance Worldwide; Goldman Environmental Prize 2016. *Publications include:* Zodpovednosť verejných činitelov : Právna úprava a aplikačná prax disciplinárnej a trestnej zodpovednosti za škodu 2011, Profesijná etika sudcov v etických kódexoch, judikatúre a stanoviskách etických poradných komisií 2012, Vybrané aspekty disciplinárneho súdnictva 2012. *Website:* www.zuzanacaputova.sk.

CARACCIOLO DI VIETRI, Giovanni; Italian diplomatist; *Secretary General, Central European Initiative;* b. 5 Dec. 1947, Rome; ed Lycée Châteaubriand, Rome, Univ. of Rome; entered Foreign Service 1971, held several positions, including assignment to Directorate Gen. for Personnel and Admin and Minister's Pvt. Office, First Sec., Embassy in Addis Ababa 1977–80, in Washington, DC 1980–86, assigned to Secr. Gen. of Presidency of the Repub., Office of Diplomatic Affairs 1986–87, Adjunct Diplomatic Advisor to Pres. of the Repub. 1987–92, Consul Gen. in Paris 1992–96, Deputy Dir Gen. for Emigration and Social Affairs, Rome 1996–2000, Minister Plenipotentiary and Amb. to Serbia and Montenegro 2000–04, Dir Gen. for the Countries of Europe 2004–06, Amb. and Perm. Rep. to UN and other Int. Orgs, Geneva 2006–09, Amb. to France 2009–12; Sec. Gen. Cen. European Initiative 2013–. *Address:* Central European Initiative Secretariat, Via Genova 9, 34121 Trieste, Italy (office). *Telephone:* (040) 7786777 (office). *Fax:* (040) 360640 (office). *E-mail:* cei@cei.int (office). *Website:* www.cei.int (office).

CARAMITRU, Ion Horia Leonida; Romanian actor, theatre director and politician; *General Director, National Theatre of Bucharest;* b. 9 March 1942, Bucharest; s. of Aristide Caramitru and Maria Caramitru; m. Michaela Caracaş 1975; three s.; ed Theatre and Cinema Art Inst., Bucharest; actor and dir, Lucia Sturdza Bulandra Theatre, Bucharest 1965–90, Artistic Dir 1990–93, 1996–2000; Acting Prof., I.L. Caragiale Acad. of Drama and Film, Bucharest 1976–81; mem. Exec. Bureau, Council of Nat. Salvation Front 1989, Pres. of Cultural Cttee 1990; Vice-Pres. of Prov. Council for Nat. Unity (responsibility for cultural and youth problems) Feb.–May 1990; Founder and Pres. ITI Romanian Centre, Romanian Theatre Union (UNITER) 1990–; Minister of Culture 1996–2000; currently Gen. Dir Nat. Theatre of Bucharest; Vice-Pres. PNTCD 2001–06 (resgnd); Hon. OBE 1995; Chevalier des Arts et des Lettres 1997; Order of Merit, Grand Cross of Romania 2000; Dr hc (George Enescu Univ. of Arts, Iaşi) 2008; Best Actor of the Year 1975, 1979, 1981, 1985, Cinema magazine FIlm Award 1976, Filmmakers Asscn Award 1980. *Principal roles include:* Romeo, Hamlet, Julius Caesar, Feste, Brutus, Leonce (Büchner), Eugene Marchbanks (Bernard Shaw), Cotrone (Pirandello), Perdican (Musset), Riccardo Fontana (Rolf Hochhuth) etc. *Directed:* Remembrances (Aleksei Arbuzov), Insignificance (Terry Johnson), Dialogues (author's performance), The Third Stake (Marin Sorescu), The Shape of the Table (David Edgar), Home (David Storey); musical theatre: Eminescu (Paul Urmuzescu), My Fair Lady; opera: The Little Sweep (Benjamin Britten), Carmen (Bizet) for Belfast Opera 1993, Eugene Onegin (Tchaikovsky) for Belfast Opera 1994, Bastien and Bastienne (Mozart) for Tăndărică puppet theatre, Bucharest. *Films include:* The Treasure from Old River Bed, The City Blue Gates, Stefan Luchian (Special Award of the Jury for leading part, Nat. Film Festival, Costinesti 1984) 1981, Oak – Extreme Urgency, The Purse with Dragonflies, High-School Pupils, Civic Education Test-Write, Darkness, Kafka 1991, Mission Impossible 1996, Amen. 2002, Adam & Paul 2004, Two Point Five Billion (short) 2008, The Necessary Death of Charlie Countryman 2013, Herman: The Man Behind the Terror 2016. *Television includes:* Jute City (BBC serial) 1991, A Question of Guilt (film) 1993, An Exchange of Fire (series) 1993, Citizen X (film) 1995, Two Deaths (BBC) 1995, Deep Secrets (film) 1996. *Leisure interests:* collecting icons, tennis, writing, painted popular eggs. *Address:* National Theatre of Bucharest, 2, Nicolae Bălcescu boulevard, 010051, Sector 1, Bucharest (office); UNITER, 2–4, George Enescu Str., Bucharest; 16, Caderea Bastiliei, Sector 1, Bucharest, Romania (home). *Telephone:* (21) 313 9437 (office); (21) 3113214 (UNITER); (21) 2106337 (home). *Fax:* (21) 3123169 (office); (21) 3120913 (UNITER); (21) 2105783 (home). *E-mail:* contact@tncaragiale.ro (office). *Website:* www.tnb.ro (office).

CARATTONI, Enrico, LLB; San Marino lawyer and politician; b. 18 May 1985, Borgo Maggiore; ed Univ. of Bologna; mem. Consulta for Educ. 2003–06; mem. Junta of Castello di Città 2003–09, Sec. 2009–14; mem. Supervisory Comm. 2012–15; mem. Consiglio Grande e Generale 2015–, Perm. Council Cttee; Capt. Regent (head of state) Oct. 2017–April 2018; lawyer and notary at a law firm in San Marino 2013–. *Address:* Campettino, Murata, 47890, San Marino (home).

CARBONEZ, Luc, LLD; Belgian fmr diplomatist; b. 1946; m. Marie-Claire Carbonez-deJager; four d.; ed Univ. of Louvain; joined Diplomatic Corps 1978, served in numerous positions including Attaché, Embassy in Dublin 1979–80, Embassy Sec., Abidjan 1980–84, Consul, Lille 1984–88, Deputy Head of Mission, Vienna 1988–92; Counsellor for Foreign Affairs, Brussels 1992–94, Minister-Counsellor and Perm. Deputy Rep. of Belgium to EU 1994–97, Amb. to Canada 1997–2002; Dir European Security, Ministry of Foreign Affairs 2002–06; Amb. to the Netherlands 2006–11; Adviser, WalloniaInvest 2011–17; mem. Inner Circle, Investinfuture 2011–14; mem. Bd of Dirs Nederlandse kamer van Koophandel 2014. *Address:* Investinfuture, Stationsweg 147, 2515 The Hague, Netherlands (office). *Telephone:* (70) 3699-699 (office). *E-mail:* info@investinfuture.nl (office). *Website:* investinfuture.nl (office).

CARCASSES, Moana Jacques Raymond Kalosil; Ni-Vanuatu politician; b. 12 Jan. 1959, Tahiti; m. Marie Louise Milne; Leader, Green Confederation Party 2001–; mem. Parl. (Green Confederation Party) for Port Vila constituency 2002–15; Minister of Foreign Affairs 2003–04, for Finance and Econ. Devt 2004–05; Deputy Leader of the Opposition 2006–08; Minister of Internal Affairs 2009–10, of Finance and Econ. Man. 2010–11, 2011–12; Prime Minister 2013–14; sentenced to four years' imprisonment for bribery and corruption Oct. 2015. *Leisure interests:* rock and roll, dance (especially Bolero), Elvis Presley, golf, rugby.

CARCIERI, Donald (Don) L., BA; American business executive, fmr politician and fmr teacher; b. 16 Dec. 1942, East Greenwich, RI; s. of Nicola J. Carcieri and Marguerite E. Carcieri (née Anderson); m. Suzanne Owren; one s. three d.; ed East Greenwich High School, Brown Univ.; fmr math. teacher, Rogers High School, Newport, RI, Concord Carlisle Regional High School, Concord, Mass; held various positions at Old Stone Bank 1971–81, including Exec. Vice-Pres.; Head of Catholic Relief Service's West Indies operation, Kingston, Jamaica 1981–83; joined Cookson America 1983, rising to CEO and Jt Man. Dir Cookson Group Worldwide; Gov. of RI 2003–11; co-f. (with his wife) Academy Children's Science Center, East Greenwich; fmr Chair. Rhode Island Math./Science Educ. Coalition; Dir Providence Center, RI; mem. Catholic Relief Services Leadership Council; Republican.

CARD, Andrew (Andy) H., Jr, BS; American business executive, university administrator and fmr government official; *President, Franklin Pierce University;* b. 10 May 1947, Brockton, Mass.; m. Kathleene Card; three c.; ed USA Merchant Marine Acad., Univ. of South Carolina; served in USN 1965–67; Engineer, Maurice Reidy Engineers, Inc. 1971–72, David M. Berg Inc. 1972–75; mem. Mass. House of Reps 1975–83; Special Asst for Inter-governmental Affairs, The White House, Washington, DC 1983–87, Dir Office of Intergovernmental Affairs 1988, Asst to Pres. George H. W. Bush and Deputy Chief of Staff 1989–92; New Hampshire Campaign Man. for George H. W. Bush 1987–88; Sec. of Transportation 1992–93; Pres. and CEO American Automobile Mfrs Asscn 1993–98; Vice-Pres. for Governmental Relations, Gen. Motors Corpn 1999–2000; Chief of Staff to US Pres. George W. Bush 2000–06 (resgnd); Acting Dean, Bush School of Govt and Public Service, Texas A&M Univ. 2011–14, also Exec. Dir in Office of the Provost; Pres. Franklin Pierce Univ. 2014–; Co-founder Lonsdale Group; mem. Bd of Dirs Union Pacific Corpn 2006–; mem. Bd of Trustees Franklin Pierce Univ. 1996–2000; numerous hon. degrees, including from Franklin Pierce Univ. 2002, Univ. of Massachusetts 2007; named Legislator of the Year by Nat. Republican Legislators Asscn 1982, Mass. Municipal Asscn Distinguished Legislator Award 1982. *Address:* Office of the President, Franklin Pierce University, 40 University Drive, Rindge, NH 03461-0060, USA (office). *Website:* www.franklinpierce.edu/about/president_card.htm (office).

CARDEN, Joan Maralyn, AO, OBE; Australian opera singer (soprano); b. 9 Oct. 1937, Richmond, Vic.; d. of Frank Carden and Margaret Carden (née Cooke); m. William Coyne 1962 (divorced 1980); two d.; ed Trinity Coll. of Music, UK, Stuyvesant Scholar at London Opera Centre, voice studies with Thea Phillips and Henry Portnoj, Melbourne, Vida Harford, London, and David Harper, UK/Australia; nat. debut as Grisette in The Merry Widow with June Bronhill, Melbourne 1960; int. debut, world premiere of Malcolm Williamson's Our Man in Havana, Sadler's Wells 1963; joined Australian Opera (Opera Australia) 1971: Royal Opera, Covent Garden as Gilda in Rigoletto 1974, Glyndebourne as Anna in Don Giovanni 1977, Scottish Opera as Constanze 1977; soloist, Sydney Opera House from opening 1974–2003; US debut at Houston as Amenaide in Tancredi 1977; Metropolitan Opera tour as Anna in Don Giovanni 1978, Kennedy Center 1980, Miami Opera 1981; Singapore Festival 1983; Adelaide Festival 1984; other appearances include Victoria State Opera, Lyric Opera of Queensland, State Opera of South Australia; over 50 major roles including most Mozart heroines, Liu in Turandot, Marguerite in Faust, Gilda in Rigoletto, four heroines in Contes d'Hoffmann, Natasha in War and Peace, Tatyana in Onegin, Lakmé, Leonora in Forza del Destino/Il Trovatore, Violetta in La Traviata, Alice in Falstaff, Mimi, Musetta in La Bohème, Madama Butterfly, Eva in Die Meistersinger, Feldmarschallin in Der Rosenkavalier, Elisabetta in Maria Stuarda, Médée, Tosca, Public Opinion in Orpheus in the Underworld, Mother Abbess in Sound of Music, Ida Straus in Titanic 2006, Mother Superior in Harp on the Willow 2007; concerts with Australian, Sydney, Melbourne, and Queensland Symphony Orchestras and for Australian Broadcasting Corpn, Sydney Univ. Graduates Choir (sponsors of Joan Carden Award, Sydney Conservatorium 2004–14), then independent; repertoire includes Mozart Masses, concert arias, choral works, Vier Letzte Lieder (R. Strauss), Britten, works by Australian composers including Peter Sculthorpe, Nigel Butterley, Barry Conyngham, Ross Edwards, Moya Henderson; soloist at numerous state and fed. events, including 1988 bicentenary, royal and presidential state visits; est. Joan Carden Award, Sydney Conservatorium of Music 2004; known as The People's Diva; Hon. DUniv (Swinburne Univ. of Tech., Melbourne) 2000, (Australian Catholic Univ., Sydney); Dame Joan Hammond Award for Outstanding Service to Opera in Australia 1987, Australian Govt Creative Fellowship 1993, Australian Govt Fed. Centenary Medal 2001. *Recordings include:* Joan Carden Sings Mozart, Great Opera Heroines: Joan Carden, The Australian Opera, Mozart: A Bicentennial Celebration, Stars of The Australian Opera Sing Verdi; Verdi aria in Priscilla, Queen of the Desert, film score, From Melba to Sutherland (boxed set). *Leisure interests:* dogs, walking, writing, gardening, reading, history. *Address:* Opera Australia, PO Box 291, Strawberry Hills, NSW 2012, Australia (office). *Telephone:* (2) 9699-1099 (office). *E-mail:* tonepainter@optusnet.com.au. *Website:* www.opera-australia.org.au (office).

CARDENAL, Ernesto; Nicaraguan poet, fmr priest and fmr government official; b. 20 Jan. 1925, Granada; s. of Rodolfo Cardenal and Esmerelda Cardenal (née

Martinez); ed Univ. of Mexico, Columbia Univ., USA; ordained RC priest 1965–84; Minister of Culture 1979–90; Co-founder and Hon. Pres. Casa de los Tres Mundos (literary org.); Austrian Cross of Honour for Science and Art, 1st class 2010; Premio de la Paz 1980, Queen Sofia Ibero-American Poetry Award 2012. *Publications include:* Proclama del conquistador 1947, Gethsemani Ky 1960, Hora 0 1960, Epigramas 1961, Poemas 1961, Salmos 1964, Oración por Marilyn Monroe y otros poemas 1965, La voz de un monje en la era nuclear 1965, El estrecho dudoso 1966, Homenaje a los Indios Americanos 1969, Mayapán 1970, Vida en el amor 1971, La hora cero y otros poemas 1971, Canto nacional al F.S.L.N. 1972, Oráculo sobre Managua 1973, El evangelio en solentiname 1975, La santidad de la revolución 1976, Cátulo marcial 1978, Nueva antología poética 1978, Viaje a New York 1980, Nostalgia del futuro 1982, Crónica de un reencuentro 1982, Waslala 1983, Vuelos de victoria 1984, With Walker in Nicaragua and other early poems 1949–54 1984, Quetzalcoatl 1985, Nuevo cielo y tierra nueva 1985, From Nicaragua with Love: Poems 1976–1986 1986, Cántico cósmico 1989, La noche iluminada de palabras 1991, Los ovnis de oro 1991, El telescopio en la noche oscura 1993, Del monasterio al mundo: correspondencia entre Ernesto Cardenal y Thomas Merton 1998, Vida perdida 1999, Los años de Granada 2002, Las ínsulas extrañas 2002, La revolución perdida 2003, Thomas Merton–Ernesto Cardenal: Correspondencia (1959–1968) 2004, Versos del pluriverso 2005, Love: A Glimpse of Eternity 2006, Pluriverse: New and Selected Poems 2009, The Gospel in Solentiname 2010, The Origin of Species and Other Poems 2011. *E-mail:* escritor@ibw.com.ni (office).

CÁRDENAS CONDE, Victor Hugo, BA; Bolivian politician and academic; *Leader, Tupac Katari Revolutionary Liberation Movement Party;* b. 4 June 1951, Achica Abajo Aymara Indian community, Omasuyos Prov., Dept of La Paz; m. Lidia Katari 1980; one s. two d.; ed Ayacucho High School, Universidad Mayor de San Andrés; Lecturer, then Prof. in Educ. Sciences, Linguistics and Languages, Faculty of Humanities and Educ., Universidad Mayor de San Andrés 1975–92; Chair. First Nat. Congress for Peasant Unity 1979; consultant on educational issues UNESCO and UNICEF 1990, various other orgs 1992; Prof., Latin American Coll. of Social Sciences 1992–93; Nat. Rep. Tupac Katari Revolutionary Liberation Movt party (MRTKL), Exec. Sec. (Nat. Exec. Cttee) 1993, currently Leader; Pres. Nat. Congress 1993–94, Andean Parl. 1993–94, Science and Tech. Nat. Council 1993–94; Vice-Pres. of Bolivia 1993–97; unsuccessful cand. in Bolivian presidential election 2009; mem. Culture and Educ. Comm., Bolivian Workers Union 1979, Educ. and Culture Comm., House of Reps 1985–86, political forum of Latin American Inst. for Social Research 1992–93, Exec. Council UNESCO 1995–2000; Fray Bartolomé de las Casas Award (Spain) 1994. *Publications include:* articles on culture, educ. and history in local and foreign books, journals and newspapers. *Address:* Movimiento Revolucionario Túpac Katarí de Liberación, Avenida Baptista 939, Casilla 9133, La Paz, Bolivia. *Telephone:* (2) 235-4784.

CÁRDENAS SANTA MARIA, Mauricio, BA, MA, PhD; Colombian economist, academic and politician; b. 9 July 1962, Bogotá; ed Univ. de los Andes, Univ. of California, Berkeley; Assoc. Prof. of Econs, Univ. de los Andes 1981–84, Prof. 1985–87, Adjunct Prof. 1992–; Research Assoc., Centre for Econ. Devt Studies 1983; Researcher, Fedesarrollo (Foundation for Higher Educ. and Devt) 1985–87, Asst Dir 1992–93, Assoc. Researcher 1994–96, Exec. Dir 1996–98, 2003–08; intern, Int. Debt and Finance Div., World Bank 1990; Gen. Man. Empresa de Energía de Bogotá 1993; Minister for Econ. Devt 1994; Minister for Transport 1998–99; Dir Nat. Planning Dept 1999–2000; consultant to IDB and IFC 2000–01; Visiting Prof., Center for Int. Devt, Harvard Univ. 2001; Pres. Titularizadora Colombiana 2001–03; Pres. Latin American and Caribbean Econ. Asscn (LACEA) 2008–09; Sr Fellow and Dir Latin American Initiative, Brookings Inst., Washington, DC 2008–12; Minister of Finance and Public Credit 2012–18; Order of the Aztec Eagle (Mexico); Lauchlin Currie Scholarship, Nat. Bank of Colombia 1987–89. *Publications:* Diez Años de Reformas Tributarias en Colombia (co-author) 1986, Movimiento Internacional de Capitales en los Años Noventa: la experiencia colombiana bajo análisis (co-author) 1993, El Crecimiento Económico en América Latina (ed.) 1996, Inflación, Estabilización y Política Cambiaria en América Latina: Lecciones de los años noventa (co-author) 1997, Empleo y Distribución del Ingreso en América Latina: ¿Hemos avanzado? (ed.) 1997, La Tasa de Cambio en Colombia 1997, Corrupción, Crimen y Justicia (co-author) 1998, Pobreza y Desigualdad en América Latina (co-author) 1999, Reflexiones sobre el aporte social y económico del sector cooperativo colombiano (co-author) 2005, La infraestructura de transporte en Colombia (co-author) 2005, Un pacto nacional para Colombia: crecimiento, estabilidad y progreso social (co-author) 2005, Análisis del sistema tributario colombiano y su impacto sobre la competitividad (co-author) 2006, Introducción a la Economía Colombiana 2007; numerous journal articles.

CÁRDENAS SOLÓRZANO, Cuauhtémoc; Mexican politician; *President, Fundación para la democracia;* b. 1 May 1934, Mexico City; s. of Lázaro Cárdenas and Amalia Solórzano; m. Celeste Batel; two s. one d.; ed Escuela Nacional de Ingenieros, Universidad Nacional Autónoma de México; Senator from Michoacán 1976–82; Under-Sec. for Forestry and Wildlife 1976–80; Gov. of Michoacán 1980–86; cand. for presidency (Frente Democrático Nacional) 1988, (Partido de la Revolución Democrática—PRD) 1994, (Allianza por México) 2000; mem. PRD 1989–2014, Pres. 1989–93; Pres. Fundación para la democracia—alternativa y debate 1995–; Mayor of Mexico City 1997–99; Vice-Pres. Socialist International 2003–; Co-ordinator of Int. Affairs of the Fed. Dist 2012–; Grand officier, Ordre nat. du Mérite (France) 1999; Cardenal Cisneros Medal, Universidad Complutense, Madrid (Spain) 1991, Belisario Dominguez Medal 2011. *Publications include:* Nuestra lucha a penas comienza 1988, Nace—una esperanza 1990, El proyecto nacional de la Revolució mexicana, un camino a retomar 1990, La esperanza en marcha. Ideario politico 1998, Palabras de Cárdenas 1999, Un México para Todos 2005, Sobre mis Pasos 2010. *Leisure interests:* reading, travel. *Address:* Fundación para la democracia, Diego Rivera #140, Colonia San Angel Inn, delegación Alvaro Obregón, México, DF, CP 01060 (office); Edgar Allan Poe No. 28-1102, 11560 México, DF, Mexico (home). *Telephone:* (55) 5202-1219 (direct) (office); (55) 6553-2261 (office). *E-mail:* c_cardenas@mexico.com (office); contacto@fundaciondemocracia.org (office). *Website:* fundaciondemocracia.org/sobre-la-fundacion/#equipo (office); www.ccardenass.org.

CARDIN, Benjamin L., BA, LLB, JD; American politician; *Senator from Maryland;* b. 5 Oct. 1943, Baltimore, Md; s. of Meyer M. Cardin and Dora Cardin (née Green); m. Myrna Edelman; one s. (died 1998) one d.; ed Baltimore public schools, Univ. of Pittsburgh and Univ. of Maryland School of Law; admitted to Maryland Bar 1967; mem. US House of Reps, 3rd Congressional Dist of Md 1987–2007, House Speaker 1979–86, Chair. Ways and Means Cttee 1974–79, Savings and Loan Oversight Cttee 1986, State Fed. Ass., Nat. Conf. of State Legislatures 1980–81, mem. several other cttees, Chair. Democratic Transition Team 1994; mem. House of Dels, representing Dist 5 and Dist 42 (Baltimore City) 1967–86, Asst Democratic Whip 1987–2003, Sr Democratic Whip 2003–07; Senator from Maryland 2007–, mem. numerous cttees, Chair. Int. Devt and Foreign Assistance, Econ. Affairs and Int. Environmental Protection Sub-cttee 2011–12, Chair. East Asian and Pacific Affairs Sub-cttee 2013–, Co-Chair. CSCE (Helsinki Comm.) 2007–; mem. Gov.'s Comm. on Domestic Relations Laws 1976–86 and numerous other comms; mem. Bd of Trustees, St Mary's Coll. of Maryland 1988–99, mem. Advisory Bd, Center for the Study of Democracy 2002–; mem. Bd of Visitors, Univ. of Maryland School of Law 1989–, Univ. of Maryland, Baltimore Co. 1998–, US Naval Acad. 2007–; Democrat; hon. degrees (Univ. of Baltimore School of Law) 1990, (Univ. of Maryland at Baltimore) 1993, (Baltimore Hebrew Univ.) 1994, (Goucher Coll.) 1996; numerous awards including Israel Freedom Award 1992, Congressional Award, Small Business Council of America 1993, 1999, H. Vernon Eney Award, Maryland Bar Foundation 1996, Representative of the Year Award, Nat. Asscn of Police Organizations 1998, Arthur W. Machen, Jr., Award, Maryland Legal Services Corpn 1998, Dr. Nathan Davis Award for Outstanding Government Service, American Medical Asscn 1999, Jacob K. Javits Award, American Psychiatric Asscn 1999, Congressional Advocate of the Year Award, Child Welfare League of America 2000, 2005, named by Worth Magazine amongst top "100 people who have influenced the way Americans think about money" 2001, Congressional Leadership Award, American Coll. of Emergency Physicians 2001, Public Sector Distinguished Service Award, Tax Foundation 2003, named by Treasury and Risk Management Magazine amongst the 100 Most Influential People in Finance 2004, Congressional Award, Small Business Council of America 2005, Friend of Farm Bureau Award, Maryland Farm Bureau 2009, Lifetime Achievement Award, Law and Health Care Program, Univ. of Maryland School of Law 2009, Anti-Poverty Award, Frederick Co. Community Action Agency 2009, Whitney M. Young, Jr Award, Greater Baltimore Urban League 2011, Conservation Champion, Audubon Soc. 2011, Bird Conservation Leader of the Year Award, American Bird Conservancy 2011, Friend of the Nat. Parks Award, Nat. Parks Conservation Asscn 2011, Congressional Champion Award, Nat. Asscn for Equal Opportunity in Higher Educ. 2012, Chesapeake Conservation Hero Award, Chesapeake Conservancy 2012, Congressional Award, Devt Dist Asscn of Appalachia 2012, Legislator of the Year Award 2016. *Address:* 509 Hart Senate Office Building, Washington, DC 20510, USA (office). *Telephone:* (202) 224-4524 (office). *Fax:* (202) 224-1651 (office). *Website:* cardin.senate.gov (office); www.bencardin.com.

CARDIN, Pierre; French couturier; b. 2 July 1922, San Biagio di Callatla, Italy; fmrly worked with Christian Dior; f. fashion house 1949; f. Espace Pierre Cardin (theatre group); Dir Ambassadeurs-Pierre Cardin Theatre (now Espace Pierre Cardin Theatre) 1970–; Man. Société Pierre Cardin 1973; Chair. Maxims 1982–; Exhbn at Victoria and Albert Museum 1990; FAO Goodwill Amb. 2009; mem. Acad. des Beaux-Arts; Hon. UNESCO Amb. 1991–; Grand Officer, Order of Merit (Italy) 1988; Order of the Sacred Treasure (Gold and Silver Star) 1991; Officier, Légion d'honneur 1997; Fashion Oscar 1985; Council of Fashion Designers of America International Award 2007. *Publications:* Fernand Léger, Sa vie, Son oeuvre, Son rêve 1971, Le Conte du Ver à Soie 1992 (Prix Saint-Exupéry valeurs-jeunesse 1992). *Address:* Haute Couture 14, place François-1er, 8e, 75008 Paris (office); 27 avenue Marigny, 75008 Paris (office); Pierre Cardin, 7 rue Royale, 75008 Paris, France (office); Institut de France, 23 quai Conti, 75006 Paris (office). *Website:* www.pierrecardin.com; www.maxims-de-paris.com.

CARDINAL, Douglas Joseph, OC, BArch, FRAIC, RCA; Canadian architect; b. 7 March 1934, Calgary, Alberta; s. of Joseph Treffle Cardinal and Frances Margarete Rach; m. 1st Marilyn Zahar 1973; three s. three d.; m. 2nd Idoia Arana-Beobide 1996; ed Univ. of British Columbia, Univ. of Texas; design architect, Bissell & Halman, Red Deer 1963–64; Prin., Douglas Cardinal Architect, Red Deer 1964–67, Edmonton 1967–76, Douglas J. Cardinal Architect Ltd, Edmonton 1976–85, Ottawa 1985–; 15 hon. doctorates; Honour Award, Alberta Asscn of Architects, for St Mary's Church 1969 and Award of Excellence, Canadian Architect Magazine, for Grande Prairie Regional Coll. 1972, Governor General's Award in Visual and Media Arts in March 2001. *Major works include:* St Mary's Church, Red Deer, Alberta 1968, Grande Prairie Regional Coll., Alberta 1976, Ponoka Provincial Bldg, Ponoka, Alberta 1976, St Albert Place and City Hall, St Albert, Alberta 1976, Spruce Grove City Hall, Spruce Grove, Alberta 1981, Edmonton Space and Science Centre, Coronation Park, Edmonton 1984 (renovated and rebranded as the Telus World of Science), Leighton Artist Colony, Banff Centre, Alberta 1985, Canadian Museum of Civilization, Gatineau, Quebec 1989, York Region Admin. Centre, Newmarket, Ont. 1992, Nat. Museum of the American Indian, Washington, DC 1993–98, Cultural Inst., Oujé-Bougoumou, Québec 1996, Saskatchewan Indian Federated Coll., Regina, Sask. 2003, Maynidoowahak AIDS Hospice, Minneapolis, Minn. 2004, Discovery Museum, Design Concept, Tenn. 2008, Kitigan Zibi Cultural Centre, Maniwaki, Quebec 2009, Meno-ya-win Health Centre, Sioux Lookout, Ont. 2010, Public Works Building, Blind River, Ont. 2010, Dawson Creek Native Housing Project, Dawson Creek, BC 2010, Asinabka Nat. Indigenous Centre, Victoria Island, Ottawa, Ont., Blue Quills First Nations Coll., St Paul, Alberta, Wabano Aboriginal Health Centre, Ottawa, Ontario. *Publications include:* contribs to Of the Spirit 1977 and Human Values: A Primary Motive in Planning 1981. *Address:* Douglas Cardinal Architect Inc., 14 Lodge Road, Suite 200, Ottawa, ON K2C 3H1, Canada (office). *Telephone:* (613) 440-2262 (office). *Fax:* (613) 440-2187 (office). *E-mail:* d.cardinal@djcarchitect.com (office). *Website:* www.djcarchitect.com (office).

CARDINALE, Claudia; Italian actress; b. 15 April 1939, Tunis, Tunisia; d. of Franco Cardinale and Yolanda Cardinale; m. Franco Cristaldi 1966; one s.; ed Lycée Carnot and Collège Paul Cambon, Tunis; made first film 1958; awards include Nastro d'Argento, David di Donatello, Grolla d'Oro; UNESCO Goodwill Amb. 2000–; Golden Apple for Contrib. to European Cinema, European Actors'

Awards 2003. *Television:* Hold Up à l'Italienne (film) 2008, Il giorno della Shoah (film) 2010, Il bello delle donne... alcuni anni dopo (mini-series) 2017. *Films include:* 8½, The Pink Panther, The Leopard, The Professionals, Once Upon a Time in the West, Fury, The Magnificent Showman, La Scoumoune, Fitzcarraldo 1982, Le Ruffian 1982, History (TV), A Man in Love 1988, The French Revolution 1989, Hiver '54, L'abbé Pierre, Mother, 588 Rue Paradis, Son of the Pink Panther 1993, Women Only Have One Thing On Their Minds, Un café... l'addition 1999, Li chiamarono... briganti! 1999, And Now... Ladies and Gentlemen 2002, Le Démon de midi 2005, Cherche fiancé tous frais payés 2007, Le fil 2009, Sinyora Enrica ile Italyan Olmak 2010, Father 2011, Gebo et l'ombre 2012, Joy de V. 2013, Ultima fermata 2014, All Roads Lead to Rome 2015, Una gita a Roma 2017, Niente di Serio 2017. *Address:* c/o Carole Levi, Via Pisanelli 2, 00196 Rome, Italy.

CARDOSO, Fernando Henrique, BA, MA, PhD; Brazilian sociologist, academic and fmr head of state; *Professor Emeritus, University of São Paulo;* b. 18 June 1931, Rio de Janeiro; m. 1st Ruth Corrêa Leite Cardoso 1953 (died 2008); three c.; m. 2nd Patrícia Kundrát 2014; ed Univs of São Paulo and Paris, France; Prof., Latin American Inst. for Econ. and Social Planning (ILPES/CEPAL), Santiago 1964–67; Prof. of Sociological Theory, Univ. of Paris-Nanterre 1967–68; Prof. of Political Science, Univ. of São Paulo 1968–69, now Prof. Emer.; Visiting Prof., Stanford Univ., USA 1972, Inst. for Econ. and Social Devt Univ. of Paris 1977, Univ. of California 1981; Simon Bolivar Prof., Univ. of Cambridge, UK 1976; Assoc. Dir of Studies, Inst. for Higher Studies in Social Sciences, Univ. of Paris 1980–81; Prof., Collège de France 1981; Prof. at Large, Watson Inst. for Int. Studies, Brown Univ., USA 2003–; Fed. Senator for State of São Paulo 1983–94; fmr Leader, Brazilian Social Democratic Party (PSDB) in Fed. Senate; Govt Leader in Congress 1985–86; Minister of Foreign Affairs 1992–93, of Economy and Finance 1993–94; Pres. of Brazil 1995–2002; Founder, Pres. Fundação Instituto Fernando Henrique Cardoso (think-tank) 2004, currently Lifetime mem. Bd of Trustees; Pres. Global Comm. on Drug Policy; mem. The Elders 2007–; Co-Pres. Inter-American Dialogue; mem. of Consultative Comm., Inst. for Advanced Study, Princeton Univ. and Rockefeller Foundation, New York; Pres. of Fundação Osesp; mem. Academia Brasileira de Letras 2013; Foreign Hon. mem. American Acad. of Arts and Sciences; Grand Cross, Order of Rio Branco, Chevalier, Légion d'honneur, Grand Cross, Order of Merit of Portugal, Order of the Bath (UK), Order of Infante D. Henrique (Portugal), Order of Liberty (Portugal), Order of the Elephant (Denmark), Order of the Star of Romania, Grand Cross (or 1st Class), Order of the White Double Cross (Slovakia) 2001, Order of the White Eagle (Poland) 2002; Dr hc (Rutgers) 1978, (Notre Dame, Ill.) 1991, (Santiago) 1993, (Central of Caracas), (Porto and Coimbra), (Sophia, Japan), (Free Univ. of Berlin), (Lumière Lyon 2), (Bologna), (Cambridge), (London), (Hebrew Univ. of Jerusalem) 2001; Hon. Dr of Sociology (ISCTE-IUL, Portugal) 2012; Fulbright Award for Int. Understanding, Prince of Asturias Award for Int. Co-operation 2000, John W. Kluge Prize for Lifetime Achievement in the Study of Humanity, Library of Congress 2012. *Publications:* São Paulo Growth and Poverty 1978, Dependency and Development in Latin America (co-author) 1979, Fernando Henrique Cardoso: Reinventing Democracy in Brazil 1999, The New Global Economy in the Information Age 1993, Charting a New Course: The Politics of Globalization and Social Transformation (co-ed.) 2001, A Arte da Política 2006, Carta a jovem político 2006, The Accidental President of Brazil 2006. *Address:* c/o Fundação Instituto Fernando Henrique Cardoso, Rua Formosa, 367, Centro, São Paulo 01049-000, Brazil (office). *E-mail:* info@ifhc.org.br. *Website:* www.ifhc.org.br.

CARDOSO, Nuno; Portuguese artistic director; *Artistic Director, São João National Theatre (TNSJ);* b. 1970, Canas de Senhorim; ed Univ. of Coimbra; theatre actor, conductor and director; co-f. Visões Úteis 1994; Artistic Dir, Carlos Alberto Theatre 1998–2003, Programming Coordinator 2003–07; Artistic Dir Ao Cabo Teatro 2007–, São João National Theatre (TNSJ), Porto 2019–; collaborations with F. Ribeiro; directed plays by Aeschylus, Euripides, Shakespeare, Gorky, Milton, Lessing, Goethe, Schiller, Bulgakov, Brecht, Büchner, Beckett, Koltès, Camus, Dagerman, Handke, Sartre, Bergman, Müller, Richter, Norén, Callaghan, Fassbinder, Fernando Pessoa, Miguel Torga, Al Berto, Luis de Sttau Monteiro, Pedro Eiras, Mickael de Oliveira, José Maria Vieira Mendes, Tiago Rodrigues, António Pedro, Hugo Curado, Sarah Kane, Don Dellilo, Marius von Mayenburg, Lars Norén; performed in numerous plays by Luís Araújo and John Romão among others; Authors Prize, Portuguese Soc. of Authors 2016. *Productions directed include:* The Adventures of João Sem Medo by José Gomes Ferreira 1994, The Adventures of John Fearless by José Gomes Ferreira 1995, House of Women by Dacia Maraini 1996, Sixth Sense by Regina Guimarães 1999, Pas de Cinq+1 by Mauricio Kagel 1999, De Miragem in Miragem Did Travel by Carlos J. Pessoa 2000, Before Lizards by Pedro Eiras 2001, The Spring Awakening by Frank Wedekind 2004, Woyzeck by Georg Büchner 2005, Plasticina by Vassili Sigarev 2006, Ricardo II by Shakespeare 2007, Platónov by Chekhov 2008, The Seagull by Chekhov 2010, The Three Sisters by Chekhov 2011, Measure by Measure by Shakespeare 2012, The Visit of the Old Lady by Friedrich Dürrenmatt 2013, British by Jean Racine 2015, The Misanthrope by Molière 2016, Timon of Athens by Shakespeare 2018. *Address:* Teatro Nacional São João, Batalha Square, 4000-102 Porto, Portugal (office). *Telephone:* (22) 3401900 (office). *E-mail:* geral@tnsj.pt (office). *Website:* www.tnsj.pt (office).

CARDOSO, Santina José Rodrigues Ferreira Viegas; Timor-Leste politician; b. 24 Nov. 1975; ed Widya Mandira Univ., Indonesia; began career with Children Recovery and Resilience Program (non-govt org. dealing with Timorese children's issues); worked in Secretariat, Constituent Ass. 2001; joined Timor-Leste Public Admin late 2001, becoming Programme Officer, Planning and Monitoring Div., Nat. Directorate for Planning and External Assistance Coordination (NDPEAC), Ministry of Planning and Finance 2002–07, Program Implementation Officer, Planning and Financial Man. Capacity Building Project 2007, also Dir-Gen. for Corp. Services 2007, Vice-Minister of Finance 2012–15, Minister of Finance 2015–17. *Address:* c/o Ministry of Finance, Palácio do Governo, Edif. 5, Av. Presidente Nicolau Lobato, Dili, Timor-Leste (office).

CARELL, Steve; American comedian and actor; b. 16 Aug. 1963, Acton, Mass; s. of Edwin A. Carell and Harriet T. Koch; m. Nancy Walls; one s. one d.; ed Denison Univ.; fmr mem. Second City, Chicago. *Films include:* Bruce Almighty 2003, Anchorman: The Legend of Ron Burgundy 2004, The 40 Year-Old Virgin 2005 (also co-writer) (MTV Movie Award for Best Comedic Performance 2006), Bewitched 2005, Little Miss Sunshine 2006, Evan Almighty 2007, Dan in Real Life 2007, Horton Hears a Who! (voice) 2008, Get Smart 2008, Dinner for Schmucks 2010, Despicable Me 2010, Date Night 2010, Seeking a Friend for the End of the World 2012, Hope Springs 2012, The Way, Way Back 2013, The Incredible Burt Wonderstone 2013, Foxcatcher 2014, Alexander and the Terrible, Horrible, No Good, Very Bad Day 2014, Minions (voice) 2015, Freeheld 2015, The Big Short 2015. *Television includes:* The Daily Show 1999–2004, The Office 2005–11 (also co-writer) (2006 Golden Globe Award for Best Actor in Television Comedy), Web Therapy (series) 2013. *Address:* William Morris Endeavor (WME), 9601 Wilshire Blvd, Beverly Hills, CA 90212, USA (office). *Telephone:* (310) 859-4085 (office).

CARENÇO, Jean-François Claude, LLL; French administrator; *Prefect of région d'Île-de-France and Paris;* b. 7 July 1952, Talence (Gironde); s. of Guy Carenco and Roselyne Carenco (née Dalmas); m. Magali Serre 1977; two d.; ed Lycée Thiers, Marseille, Stanislas Coll., Paris and Univ. of the Sorbonne, Ecole Nat. d'Admin; Councillor of Admin. Tribunal, Marseille 1979–83; Dir Gen. Dist of Montpellier 1983–88, Sec.-Gen. 1988–90; Sec.-Gen. of New Caledonia 1990–91; Sec.-Gen. of Pref. of Yvelines 1991–96; Prefect of Saint-Pierre et Miquelon 1996–97, of Tarn-et-Garonne 1997–99, of Guadeloupe 1999–2002, of Haute-Savoie 2002–04, of Haute-Normandie and Seine-Maritime 2006–10, of région de la Rhône-Alpes and Rhône 2010–15, of région d'Île-de-France and Paris 2015–; Chief of Staff Minister of Employment, Labour and Social Cohesion, then Employment, Social Cohesion and Housing 2004–06; Chevalier, Légion d'honneur, Ordre nat. du Mérite, des Palmes académiques; Chevalier du Mérite de l'Ordre souverain de Malte. *Publications include:* L'Espérance occitane (co-author) 1979. *Address:* La préfecture de Paris et d'Île-de-France, 5 rue Leblanc, 75015 Paris, France (office). *Telephone:* 1-82-52-40-00 (office). *Website:* www.ile-de-france.gouv.fr (office).

CAREW, David Omashola, BSc (Econ); Sierra Leonean chartered accountant and politician; b. Freetown; m.; two c.; ed Univ. of Sierra Leone; joined KPMG accounting and man. consultancy firm as grad. accountant in 1979, seconded to KPMG Nigeria 1979–86, Audit Supervisor in charge of KPMG's clients in banking and financial insts. industry, Kanu, Asst Man., KPMG, Freetown 1986, Asst Man., then Deputy Man., then Man. and later Sr Man. 1986–88, Partner, KPMG-Sierra Leone 1989, Partner, KPMG-Gambia 1991, Man. Partner for KPMG-Sierra Leone and for delivering KPMG services to clients in The Gambia and Liberia –2007, fmr Dir KPMG Peat Marwick, Freetown; Minister of Finance and Devt 2007–09, of Trade and Industry 2009–10; CEO Freetown Nominees Ltd 2010–; Man. Dir Omagbemi Holdings; Fellow, Inst. of Chartered Accountants (Nigeria); Fellow and Past Pres. Inst. of Chartered Accountants (Sierra Leone); Partner Moore Stephens (Sierra Leone) 2017–. *Leisure interests:* golf, philanthropy. *Address:* Freetown Nominees Ltd, 1st Floor, 55 Sir Samuel Lewis Road, Freetown (office); Moore Stephens, 55 Sir Samuel Lewis Road, Aberdeen, Freetown, Sierra Leone (office). *Telephone:* (88) 886691 (office). *E-mail:* docarew@moorestephens-sl.com (office). *Website:* www.moorestephens.com (office).

CAREY, Chase; American business executive; *Executive Chairman and CEO, Formula One Group;* fmr mem. Bd of Dirs, Pres. and CEO Sky Global Networks, Inc.; worked at Columbia Pictures 1981–87; Co-COO Fox Entertainment Group 1998–2002, Inc., also Chair. and CEO Fox TV, mem. Bd of Dirs 1992–2002; Exec. Dir and Co-COO News Corporation 1996–2002, Deputy Chair., Pres. and COO 2009–13 (co. restructured with News Corporation's publishing assets spun off into similarly named News Corp while existing News Corporation renamed 21st Century Fox as its legal successor 2013), CEO The DIRECTV Group, Inc. 2003–09, apptd Pres. and COO 21st Century Fox 2009, then Vice-Chair. 2015–17; Exec. Chair. and CEO Formula One Group 2017–; Trustee Emer., Colgate Univ. *Website:* www.formula1.com (office).

CAREY, John, MA, DPhil, FRSL, FBA; British literary critic and academic; *Merton Professor Emeritus of English Literature, University of Oxford;* b. 5 April 1934, London; s. of Charles William Carey and Winifred Ethel Carey (née Cook); m. Gillian Mary Florence Booth 1960; two s.; ed Richmond and East Sheen County Grammar School, St John's Coll., Oxford; served in East Surrey Regt 1953–54; Harmsworth Sr Scholar, Merton Coll., Oxford 1957–58; Lecturer, Christ Church, Oxford 1958–59; Andrew Bradley Jr Research Fellow, Balliol Coll., Oxford 1959–60; Tutorial Fellow, Keble Coll., Oxford 1960–64, St John's Coll. 1964–75; Merton Prof. of English Literature, Univ. of Oxford 1976–2001, Prof. Emer. 2001–; Chief Book Reviewer, Sunday Times (London) 1976–; T.S. Eliot Memorial Lecturer, Univ. of Kent 1989; Northcliffe Lecturer, Univ. Coll., London 2004; Chair. Booker Prize Judges 1982, 2003, Int. Booker Prize Judges 2005; Judge, WH Smith Prize 1989–95; Hon. Fellow, St John's Coll. Oxford 1991, Balliol Coll. Oxford 1992; Hon. Prof. Univ. of Liverpool 2004–. *Publications include:* The Poems of John Milton (co-ed. with Alastair Fowler) 1968, Milton 1969, The Violent Effigy: A Study of Dickens' Imagination 1973, Thackeray: Prodigal Genius 1977, John Donne: Life, Mind and Art 1981, The Private Memoirs and Confessions of a Justified Sinner, by James Hogg (ed.), William Golding: The Man and His Books (ed.) 1986, Original Copy: Selected Reviews and Journalism 1987, The Faber Book of Reportage (ed.) 1987, John Donne (Oxford Authors) (ed.) 1990, The Intellectuals and the Masses 1992, The Faber Book of Science (ed.) 1995, The Faber Book of Utopias (ed.) 1999, Pure Pleasure 2000, What Good are the Arts? 2005, William Golding: The Man Who Wrote Lord of the Flies (James Tait Black Memorial Prize 2010) 2009, The Unexpected Professor: An Oxford Life in Books (memoir) 2014, The Essential 'Paradise Lost' 2017; articles in Review of English Studies, Modern Language Review etc. *Leisure interests:* beekeeping, swimming, gardening, etching. *Address:* Merton College, Oxford, OX1 4JD (office); Brasenose Cottage, Lyneham, Oxon., OX7 6QL (home); 57 Stapleton Road, Headington, Oxford, OX3 7LX, England (home). *Telephone:* (1865) 764304 (home). *E-mail:* john.carey@appleinter.net (home). *Website:* johncarey.org.

CAREY, Mariah; American singer and songwriter; b. 22 March 1970, Long Island, NY; m. 1st Tommy Mottola 1993 (divorced 1998); m. 2nd Nick Cannon 2008 (divorced 2014); two s.; fmr backing singer, Brenda K. Starr, New York 1988; solo artist 1988–; f. Crave record label 1997; f. Camp Mariah holiday project for inner-city children; Grammy Awards for Best New Artist, Best New Pop Vocal by a Female Artist 1990, Soul Train Awards for Best New Artist, Best Single by a Female Artist 1990, Rolling Stone Award for Best Female Singer 1991, eight World Music Awards 1991–95, seven Billboard Awards 1991–96, four American Music Awards 1992–96, Int. Dance Music Award for Best Solo Artist 1996, American

Music Awards Special Award of Achievement 2000, Lady of Soul Award for Best Solo R&B/Soul Single (for We Belong Together) 2005, Vibe Awards for Artist of the Year, for R&B Voice of the Year, for Best R&B Song (for We Belong Together) 2005, American Music Award for Favorite Female Soul/R&B Artist 2005, Female Billboard 200 Album Artist of the Year 2005, Billboard Music Awards for Hot 100 Song of the Year, Hot 100 Airplay of the Year, Rhythmic Top 40 Title of the Year (all for We Belong Together) 2005, Billboard Music Award for Female R&B/Hip-Hop Artist of the Year 2005, Grammy Award for Best Female R&B Vocal Performance (for We Belong Together) 2006. *Recordings include:* albums: Mariah Carey (Soul Train Award for Best Album by a Female Artist) 1990, Emotions 1991, MTV Unplugged (EP) 1992, Music Box 1993, Merry Christmas 1994, Daydream 1995, Butterfly 1997, #1s 1998, Rainbow 1999, Glitter 2001, Charmbracelet 2002, The Remixes 2003, The Emancipation of Mimi (Lady of Soul Award for Best Solo R&B/Soul Album, Vibe Award for Album of the Year, Grammy Award for Best Contemporary R&B Album 2006, Image Award for Best Album 2006) 2005, E=MC2 2008, Memoirs of an Imperfect Angel 2009, Merry Christmas II You 2010, Me. I Am Mariah, The Elusive Chanteuse 2014, Caution 2018. *Television includes:* judge, American Idol 2013. *Films include:* The Bachelor 1999, Glitter (also soundtrack) 2001, WiseGirls 2002, State Property 2 2005, Tennessee 2008, Precious 2009, The Butler 2013. *Website:* www.mariahcarey.com.

CAREY, Peter Philip, AO, FRSL; Australian/American writer and teacher; *Executive Director, Creative Writing Program, Hunter College, City University of New York;* b. 7 May 1943, Bacchus Marsh, Vic., Australia; s. of Percival Stanley Carey and Helen Jean Warriner; m. 2nd Alison Summers 1985 (divorced); two s.; m. 3rd Frances Rachel Coady 2007; ed Geelong Grammar School and Monash Univ.; fmr Teacher of Creative Writing, New York Univ., New School, New York, Columbia Univ., Princeton Univ., Barnard Coll.; currently Exec. Dir Creative Writing Program, Hunter Coll., CUNY; Hon. LittD (Queensland); Hon. DLit (Monash), (New School, New York), (Univ. of Sydney). *Film screenplays:* Bliss (co-author), Until the End of the World (co-author). *Publications include:* The Fat Man in History (short stories, aka Exotic Pleasures 1981) 1974, War Crimes (short stories) (NSW Premier's Award) 1979, Bliss (novel) (Miles Franklin Award, Nat. Book Council Award, NSW Premier's Award) 1981, Illywhacker (novel) (Age Book of the Year Award, Nat. Book Council Award, Victorian Premier's Award) 1985, Oscar and Lucinda (Booker Prize for Fiction 1988, Miles Franklin Award, Nat. Book Council Award, Adelaide Festival Award, Foundation for Australian Literary Studies Award) 1988, Until the End of the World 1990, The Tax Inspector (novel) 1991, The Unusual Life of Tristan Smith (novel) (Age Book of the Year Award) 1994, Collected Stories 1995, The Big Bazoohley (children's novel) 1995, Jack Maggs 1997, The True History of the Kelly Gang (Booker Prize 2001) 2000, 30 Days in Sydney: A Wildly Distorted Account 2001, My Life as a Fake 2003, Wrong About Japan 2005, Theft: A Love Story 2006, His Illegal Self 2008, Parrot and Olivier in America 2009, The Chemistry of Tears 2012, Amnesia 2014, A Long Way From Home 2017. *Address:* c/o Amanda Urban, ICM, 825 Eighth Avenue, New York, NY 10019, USA (office). *Telephone:* (212) 556-5764 (office). *E-mail:* aurban@icmtalent.com (office). *Website:* www.hunter.cuny.edu/creativewriting (office); petercareybooks.com.

CAREY OF CLIFTON, Baron (Life Peer), cr. 2002, of Clifton in the City and County of Bristol; **Most Rev. and Rt Hon. George Leonard Carey,** RVO, PC, MTh, PhD, FRSA; British ecclesiastic and university chancellor; b. 13 Nov. 1935, London; s. of George Thomas Carey and Ruby Catherine Carey; m. Eileen Harmsworth Hood 1960; two s. two d.; ed Bifrons Secondary Modern School, Barking, Essex, King's Coll., London Univ.; Nat. Service, RAF 1954–56; univ. studies and theological training 1957–62; Curate, St Mary's, Islington 1962–66; Lecturer, Oak Hill Theological Coll. 1966–70, St John's Coll., Nottingham 1970–75; Vicar, St Nicholas' Church, Durham 1975–82; Prin., Trinity Theological Coll., Bristol 1982–87; Bishop of Bath and Wells 1987–91; Archbishop of Canterbury 1991–2002; Chancellor, Univ. of Gloucestershire 2003–10; Chair. United Church School Trust, World Faiths Development Dialogue; Chaplain, Christian Responsibility in Public Affairs; fmr Pres. London School of Theology; Vice-Pres. Tearfund; Fellow, King's Coll., London; Hon. Bencher, Inner Temple; Freeman, Cities of London and of Wells 1990; Kt Grand Cross, Royal Order of Francis I (House of Bourbon-Two Sicilies) 2009; Hon. DLitt (Polytechnic of East London) 1991; Hon. DD (Kent) 1991, (Nottingham) 1992, (Bristol) 1992, (Durham) 1994, (Open Univ.) 1995, (Univ. of the South, USA) 1999, (City Univ.) 1999, (Univ. of Notre Dame, USA) 1999, (Southern Methodist Univ., USA) 2000, (Wycliffe Coll., Canada) 2002, (Cambridge) 2006; Hon. LLD (Bath) 1992; Hon. DHL (Univ. of Cambodia) 2005; Greek, Hebrew and theological prizes. *Publications:* I Believe in Man 1978, The Great Acquittal 1981, The Church in the Market Place 1983, The Meeting of the Waters 1985, The Gate of Glory 1986, The Great God Robbery 1988, I Believe 1991, Spiritual Journey 1994, My Journey Your Journey 1996, Canterbury – Letters to the Future 1998, Jesus 2000, Know The Truth 2004, We Don't Do God: The Marginalisation of Public Faith (with Andrew Carey) 2012. *Leisure interests:* walking, football, poetry, music. *Address:* House of Lords, Westminster, London, SW1A 0PW, England. *Telephone:* (20) 7219-5353. *E-mail:* carey.andr@gmail.com. *Website:* www.parliament.uk/biographies/lords/lord-carey-of-clifton/2205; www.glcarey.co.uk.

CARL XVI GUSTAF, HM The King of Sweden (Carl Gustaf Folke Hubertus); b. 30 April 1946; s. of Prince Gustaf Adolf and Sibylla, Princess of Saxe-Coburg-Gotha; m. Silvia Sommerlath (HM Queen Silvia) 1976; two d., Crown Princess Victoria Ingrid Alice Désirée b. 14 July 1977, Princess Madeleine Thérèse Amelie Josephine b. 10 June 1982; one s., Prince Carl Philip Edmund Bertil b. 13 May 1979; ed studied in Sigtuna and Univs of Uppsala and Stockholm; cr. Duke of Jämtland; became Crown Prince 1950; succeeded to the throne on death of his grandfather, King Gustaf VI Adolf 15 Sept. 1973; Chair. Swedish Branch, World Wide Fund for Nature; Hon. Pres. World Scout Foundation; Kt of the Royal Order of the Seraphim, Kt Grand Cross of the Royal Order of the Sword, Kt Grand Cross of the Royal Order of the Polar Star, Kt Grand Cross of the Royal Order of Vasa, Royal Kt of the Royal Order of Charles XIII, Hon. Kt of the Order of Saint John in Sweden, Grand Cross with Collar of the Order of the Liberator General San Martín, Argentina, Grand Cross of the Order of Honour for Services to the Republic of Austria, Special Class, Austria, Kt Grand Cross of the Order of Leopold, Belgium, Grand Cross with Collar of the Order of the Southern Cross, Brazil, Knight Grand Cross of the Royal Family Order of the Crown of Brunei, Brunei, Grand Cross of the Order of the Balkan Mountains, Bulgaria, Grand Cross with Collar of the Order of Merit, Chile, Kt Grand Cross with Collar of the Order of the Elephant, Denmark, Grand Cross with Collar of the Order of the Nile, Egypt, Grand Cross with Collar of the Order of the Cross of Terra Mariana, Estonia, Grand Cross with Collar of the Order of the White Rose, Finland, Grand Cross of the Order of the Legion of Honour, France, Grand Cross of the Order of Merit of the Federal Republic of Germany, Special Class, Germany, Grand Cross with Collar of the Order of Merit of the Republic of Hungary, Grand Cross with Collar of the Order of Merit of the Italian Republic, Kt Grand Cordon with Collar of the Order of the Chrysanthemum, Japan; Dr hc (Swedish Univ. of Agricultural Sciences, Stockholm Inst. of Tech., Åbo Acad., Finland, Stockholm School of Econ.); US Environmental Protection Agency Award, 90th Birthday Medal of King Gustaf V, 85th Birthday Medal of King Gustaf VI Adolf. *Leisure interests:* hunting, sailing and water sports, motor sport, cross-country and downhill skiing, art, music and food. *Address:* The Royal Palace, 111 30 Stockholm, Sweden (office). *Telephone:* (8) 402-60-00 (office). *Fax:* (8) 402-60-05 (office). *E-mail:* info@royalcourt.se (office). *Website:* www.royalcourt.se (office).

CARLESON, Lennart Axel Edvard, PhD; Swedish mathematician and academic; *Professor Emeritus, Mathematics Department, Uppsala University;* b. 18 March 1928, Stockholm; m. Sylvia Elmstedt 1978 (died 2009); one s.; ed Uppsala Univ.; Dir Mittag-Leffler Inst., Djursholm, Stockholm 1968–84; now Prof. Emer., Math. Dept, Uppsala Univ.; frmly at Royal Inst. of Tech., Stockholm, UCLA, USA; Pres. Int. Math. Union 1978–82; Wolf Prize 1992, Lomonosov Gold Medal 2002, Sylvester Medal 2003, Abel Prize for outstanding work in the field of maths, particularly for his proof of the convergence of the Fourier series 2006. *Publications:* Selected Problems on Exceptional Sets 1967, Complex Dynamics (with T. W. Gamelin) 1993, Matematik för vår tid (Mathematics for Our Time); numerous articles in professional journals on harmonic analysis. *Address:* Vendev 9E, 18269 Djursholm, Sweden (home). *Telephone:* (8) 51241588 (home). *Fax:* (8) 7231788 (office). *E-mail:* carleson@math.kth.se (office); lennart.carleson@gmail.com (home).

CARLIN, John William, BS; American business executive, archivist, academic and fmr state governor; *Visiting Professor/Executive in Residence, School of Leadership Studies, Kansas State University;* b. 3 Aug. 1940, Salina, Kan.; s. of Jack W. Carlin and Hazel L. Carlin (née Johnson); m. 1st Ramona Hawkinson 1962 (divorced 1980); one s. one d.; m. 2nd Lynn Carlin 1997; ed Lindsborg High School, Kansas State Univ.; farmer and dairyman, Smolan, Kan. 1962–80; mem. Kan. House of Reps for 93rd Dist 1970–73, 73rd Dist 1973–79, Minority Leader 1975–77, Speaker 1977–79; Gov. of Kan. 1979–87; Visiting Prof. of Public Admin. and Int. Trade, Wichita State Univ. 1987–88; Visiting Fellow, Univ. of Kansas 1987–88; Pres. Econ. Devt Assocs Inc. 1987–92; Pnr, Carlin and Assocs, Topeka 1989–95; Vice-Chair. and CEO Midwest Superconductivity Inc., Lawrence 1990–94; Pnr, Clark Publishing Inc., Topeka 1991–95; Archivist of the US, Nat. Archives and Records Admin., Washington, DC 1995–2005; Visiting Prof./Exec. in Residence, School of Leadership Studies, Kansas State Univ., also Co-Chair. Advancement Council for School of Leadership Studies; Pres. Econ. Devt Asscn 1987–92, Vice-Chair. Midwest Superconductivity Inc. 1990–94; mem. Kan. Bioscience Authority 2006–; Chair. Nat. Historical Publications and Records Comm. 1995–2005, Nat. Comm. for Industrialized Farm Animal Production 2006–08; fmr Chair. Nat. Govs Asscn, mem. Nat. Govs Asscn (NGA) Exec. Cttee; fmr Chair. Midwestern Govs Conf.; Democrat; Hon. DIur (Kan.). *Leisure interests:* golf, swimming. *Address:* School of Leadership Studies, Kansas State University, 107 Leadership Studies Building, Manhattan, KS 66506, USA (office). *Telephone:* (785) 532-6346 (office). *E-mail:* jwcarlin@k-state.edu (office). *Website:* www.k-state.edu/leadership (office).

CARLING, William (Will) David Charles, BA, OBE; British sports commentator and fmr rugby union player; b. 12 Dec. 1965, Bradford-on-Avon, Wilts.; m. 1st Julia Carling 1994 (divorced 1996); m. 2nd Lisa Cooke 1999; one s. one step-s. one step-d.; ed Durham Univ.; centre; fmr mem. Durham Univ. Club; mem. Harlequins club; int. debut England versus France 1988; Capt. England team 1988–96; announced retirement from int. rugby 1997 (brief return to the game with Harlequins 1999); played 72 times for England, Capt. 59 times (world record), including as Capt. of runner-up team in Rugby World Cup 1991, Five Nations Champions 1991 (Grand Slam and Triple Crown), 1992 (Grand Slam and Triple Crown), 1995 (Grand Slam and Triple Crown), 1996 (Triple Crown), Calcutta Cup Winners 1989, 1991–96, Millennium Trophy Winners 1989–92, 1995–96; rugby football commentator 1997–; Owner Inspirational Horizons Co., Insights Ltd (now dissolved), Will Carling Management 2001. *Publications:* Captain's Diary 1991, Will Carling (autobiog.) 1994, The Way to Win (with Robert Heller) 1995, My Autobiography 1998. *Leisure interests:* painting and sketching. *Address:* Will Carling Management, 3000 Hillswood Drive, Chertsey, Surrey, KT16 0RS, England. *Telephone:* (1932) 895322. *Fax:* (1932) 796642. *E-mail:* info@wcmltd.com. *Website:* www.wcmltd.com.

CARLISLE, Sir James (Beethoven), Kt, GCMG, BDS; Antiguan/British dental surgeon and fmr administrator; b. 5 Aug. 1937; s. of James Carlisle and Jestina Jones; m. 1st Umilta Mercer 1963 (divorced 1973); one s. one d.; m. 2nd Anne Jenkins 1973 (divorced 1984); one d.; m. 3rd Nalda Amelia Meade 1984; one s. one d.; m. 4th Emma Carlisle; ed Univ. of Dundee; dentist 1972–93; Gov.-Gen. Antigua and Barbuda 1993–2007; Chair. Nat. Parks Authority 1986–90; Chief Scout Antigua and Barbuda 1986–90; mem. American Acad. of Laser Dentistry, Int. Asscn of Laser Dentistry; Hon. Fellow, Dental Surgery Royal Coll. of Surgeons of Edin. 1995; Hon. mem. British Dental Asscn; Kt Grand Cross, Order of Queen of Sheba (Ethiopia) 1995, Kt Grand Collar, Most Distinguished Order of the Nation (Antigua and Barbuda) 2000, Kt of Grace, Kt of Justice, Order of St John; Hon. LLD (Andrews Univ., USA) 1996. *Leisure interests:* gardening, reading, music. *Address:* PO Box W1644, St John's, Antigua. *Telephone:* (305) 396-3542. *E-mail:* govg@hotmail.com.

CARLOS, Roberto; Brazilian singer and songwriter; b. 19 April 1941, Cachoeiro de Itapemirim; s. of Robertino Braga and Laura Moreira Braga; m. 1st Cleonice Rossi 1968 (divorced 1978); one d.; m. 2nd Myrian Rios 1980 (divorced 1989); m. 3rd Maria Rita Simões Braga 1996 (died 1999); two s. one d.; ed Conservatório Musical de Cachoeiro; started performing professionally in 1958; has presented numerous radio and TV programmes; pioneered Jovem Guarda movt in 1970s, influenced by American rock and roll; numerous tours in South America; has performed with Maria Bethânia, Tom Jobim, Chico Buarque, Caetano Veloso, Dorival Caymmi, Jennifer Lopez; First Prize, San Remo Festival 1968, Latin Grammy Awards for Best Singer 1989, for Best Brazilian Romantic Album 2005, for Best Brazilian Song 2013. *Recordings include:* Louco por Você 1961, O Inimitável 1968, À Janela, A Distância e Por Amor 1971, Honestly 1981, Se Diverte e já não Pensa em Mim 1988, Amor sem limite 2000, Pra sempre 2003; over 45 albums including Para Sempre Ao Vivo No Pacaembu (Latin Grammy Award for Best Brazilian Romantic Album), Roberto Carlos 2006 (Latin Grammy Award for Best Brazilian Romantic Album), Roberto Carlos-En Vivo 2008, Elas Cantam Roberto Carlos 2009, Esse Cara Sou Eu 2012. *Website:* www.robertocarlos.com.

CARLOS, Roberto (see ROBERTO CARLOS).

CARLOT, Alfred, BA; Ni-Vanuatu diplomatist and politician; b. 11 June 1959; ed Univ. of the South Pacific, Australian Nat. Univ.; early career as secondary school teacher and salesman, Asco Motors Co.; fmr Perm. Sec., Ministry of Foreign Affairs and Perm. Rep. to UN, New York; mem. Parl. for Efate rural 2008–12; fmr Minister of Lands and Natural Resources, of Justice 2010–11, of Foreign Affairs and External Trade 2011–13; mem. Vanuatu Republikan Pati. *Address:* c/o Ministry of Foreign Affairs and External Trade, PMB 9051, Port Vila, Vanuatu (office).

CARLOT KORMAN, Maxime; Ni-Vanuatu politician; *Leader, Vanuatu Republikan Pati;* b. 26 April 1941, Erakor, Efate; mem. Parl. for Port Vila Constituency 1979–, Speaker 1980–83, 1995–96, 2009–10, 2010–11; Prime Minister of Vanuatu 1991–95, Feb.–Oct. 1996; Minister of Foreign Affairs and Trade 1993, Minister for Lands, Geology and Mines 1998–2001, for Agric. 2002–04; Deputy Prime Minister Aug. 2004; Minister for Public Works and Public Utilities Dec. 2004, for Lands and Mineral Resources 2007–08; Acting Pres. Aug.–Sept. 2009; cand. in presidential election 2017; fmr Leader, Union of Moderate Parties; Founder and Leader Vanuatu Republikan Pati 1995–. *Address:* Vanuatu Republikan Pati, Port Vila (office); Parliament of Vanuatu, PMB 9052, Port Vila, Vanuatu (office). *Telephone:* 33060 (office).

CARLSEN, (Sven) Magnus Øen; Norwegian chess grandmaster; b. 30 Nov. 1990, Tønsberg; s. of Henrik Albert Carlsen and Sigrun Øen; started playing chess aged five; played first tournament, Norwegian Chess Championship 1999; won title of Int. Master aged 12 years 7 months and 25 days 2003; became second-youngest grandmaster in chess history (behind Sergey Karjakin) aged 13 years 4 months and 27 days 2004; qualified first time for World Chess Fed. (FIDE) World Championship Knockout Tournament 2004 (eliminated in first round tiebreaker); placed tenth at World Chess Fed. (FIDE) World Cup 2005, becoming youngest player ever to qualify for Candidates Tournament; coached by Garry Kasparov 2009–10; ranked No. 1 by FIDE for first time Jan. 2010; undisputed World Chess Champion 2013–; won FIDE World Rapid Championship, thus becoming first player to simultaneously hold the title in all three FIDE rated time controls (Standard, Rapid and Blitz) 2014; represented Norway at Chess Olympiads in 2004, 2006, 2008, 2010, 2014, 2016; beat Sergey Karjakin to retain No. 1 ranking at World Chess Championship, New York City 2016; f. Play Magnus AS (selling digital chess training tools), Oslo 2013; Hon. Chair. American Foundation for Chess; Chess Oscars 2009, 2010, 2011, 2012, 2013; Verdens Gang (Norwegian newspaper) Name of the Year 2009, 2013, Verdens Gang Sportsman of the Year 2009, Peer Gynt Prize 2011. *Tournament victories include:* Norwegian Under 11 Championship 2000, Under 10 Nordic Championship 2001, Gausdal Bygger'n Masters 2005, Norwegian Chess Championship 2006, Biel Chess Festival 2007, Baku Grand Prix (jt first place) 2008, London Chess Classic 2009, Nanjing Pearl Spring Tournament 2010, Bilbao Masters 2012, London Chess Classic 2012, World Championship Candidates, London 2013, Sinquefield Cup 2013, World Chess Championship, Chennai 2013, Zurich Chess Challenge 2014, FIDE World Rapid Championship 2014, World Chess Championship, Sochi 2014, Tata Steel Tournament 2015, 2016, 2019, Gashimov Memorial 2015, London Chess Classic 2015, Grand Chess Tour 2015, Qatar Masters 2015, World Chess Championship, New York 2016, London 2018. *Publications include:* Lær sjakk med Magnus 2004. *Address:* c/o Espen Agdestein, POB 143, Bogstadveien, 0323 Oslo, Norway (office). *Website:* magnuscarlsen.com (office).

CARLSON, Arne Helge, BA; American politician and business executive; b. 24 Sept. 1934, New York; s. of Helge William and Kerstin Carlson (née Magnusson); m. 1st Barbara Carlson (divorced); one s. two d.; m. 2nd Joanne (divorced); m. 3rd Susan Shepard 1985; one d.; ed Williams Coll., Univ. of Minnesota; with Control Data, Bloomington, Minn. 1962–64; Councilman, Minneapolis City Council 1965–67; in pvt. business, Minneapolis 1968–69; Legislator, Minn. House of Reps, St Paul 1970–78; State Auditor, State of Minn. 1978–90; Sec., Minn. Housing Finance Agency 1979–91; Gov. of Minn. 1991–98; Chair. IDS Mutual Fund Group, Minneapolis 1999; Ind. Chair. American Express Funds (now RiverSource Funds) 1999–2006, mem. Bd 2006–; mem. Bd of Dirs Minn. Land Exchange Bd, Exec. Council St Paul; Trustee, Minn. State Bd Investment; several awards including Small Business Guardian Award, Nat. Fed. of Ind. Businesses 1994. *Leisure interests:* reading, squash, Univ. of Minnesota basketball and football games. *E-mail:* govarne@gmail.com. *Website:* govarnecarlson.blogspot.co.uk.

CARLSON, Lawrence Evan, (Bear), BS, MS, DEng; American engineer and academic; *Professor Emeritus of Mechanical Engineering, University of Colorado;* b. 22 Dec. 1944, Milwaukee, Wis.; s. of John W. Carlson and Louise M. Altseimer; m. Poppy C. Copeland; one s. two d.; ed Univ. of Wisconsin, Univ. of California, Berkeley; Asst Prof., Dept of Materials Eng, Univ. of Illinois at Chicago 1971–74; Asst Prof., Dept of Eng Design and Econ. Evaluation, Univ. of Colorado, Boulder 1974–78, Dept of Mechanical Eng 1978–, now Prof. Emer. of Mechanical Eng, Founding Co-Dir Integrated Teaching and Learning Lab. 1995–2007 (retd 2010); numerous awards, including Charles Hutchinson Outstanding Teaching Award, Coll. of Eng and Applied Science 2001, John and Mercedes Peebles Innovation in Educ. Award 2004, Bernard M. Gordon Prize (with Jacquelyn Sullivan), Nat. Acad. of Eng 2008, Excellence in Teaching Award, Boulder Faculty Assembly 2009. *Publications:* numerous papers in academic journals. *Leisure interests:* hiking, fishing, camping, biking, tennis, handball, racquetball, skiing, photography, music. *Address:* University of Colorado, College of Engineering and Applied Science, 1111 Engineering Drive 422, Boulder, CO 80309-0422, USA (office). *Telephone:* (303) 304-9308 (home). *Fax:* (303) 492-2498 (office). *E-mail:* lawrence .carlson@colorado.edu (office). *Website:* www.me.colorado.edu/#!emeritus-faculty-/c24y5 (office).

CARLSSON, Gunilla; Swedish politician; b. 11 May 1963, Vadstena, Östergötland; ed Linköping Univ.; accountant 1984–90, accounting man. 1990–94; mem. Vadstena Municipal Council 1989; mem. European Parl. (Group of the European People's Party (Christian Democrats) and European Democrats—EPP-ED) 1995–2002, Leader Moderate Party Del., mem. Cttee on Foreign Affairs, Human Rights, Common Security and Defence Policy 1999–2002, Vice-Chair. EPP 2004–06; mem. Parl. (Riksdag) 2002–13, mem. War Del. 2002–, mem. Cttee on Educ. 2002–03, Cttee on EU Affairs 2002–04, Cttee on Foreign Affairs 2003–04, Deputy Chair. Cttee on Foreign Affairs 2004–, Deputy mem. Cttee on EU Affairs 2004–; Minister for Int. Devt Cooperation 2006–13; mem. UN High-Level Panel on Global Sustainability 2010–; Vice-Chair. Moderate Party Youth League 1992–95, apptd mem. Bd of Moderate Party 1999, Second Vice-Chair. Moderate Party 1999–2003, First Vice-Chair. 2003–15; Vice-Chair. Nordic Young Conservative Union 1993–94; Vice-Chair. Int. Young Democratic Union 1994–98; Alt. mem. Swedish Del. to Nordic Council 2004; mem. Bd Gavi (Vaccine Alliance) 2014–. *Address:* c/o Gavi, 2 Chemin des Mines, 1201 Geneva, Switzerland (office). *Website:* www.gavi.org (home).

CARLSSON, Ingvar Gösta, MA; Swedish politician; b. 9 Nov. 1934, Borås, Älvsborg Co.; m. Ingrid Melander 1957; two d.; ed Lund Univ. and Northwestern Univ. USA; Sec. in Statsradsberedningen (Prime Minister's Office) 1958–60; Pres. Social Democratic Youth League 1961–67; mem. Parl. 1964–; Under-Sec. of State, Statsradsberedningen 1967–69; Minister of Educ. 1969–73, of Housing and Physical Planning 1973–76, Deputy Prime Minister 1982–86, Minister of the Environment 1985–86, Prime Minister 1986–91, 1994–96; Co-Chair. Comm. on Global Governance 1995–2001, Inter Action Council 2005–; Chair. Anna Lindh Memorial Fund 2003–; mem. Exec. Cttee Social Democratic Party, Chair. 1972–96; Dr hc (Lund Univ.) 1989, (Northwestern Univ.) 1991. *Publications:* Ur skuggan av Olof Palme 1999, Så tänkte jag 2003. *Leisure interest:* supporting IF Elfsborg and Wolverhampton Wanderers Football Club. *Address:* c/o Anna Lindhs Minnesfond (Anna Lindh Memorial Fund), Kulturhuset Box 16414, 10327 Stockholm, Sweden. *Telephone:* (8) 411-90-91. *E-mail:* annalindhsminnesfond.se. *Website:* www .annalindhsminnesfond.se.

CARLSTROM, John E., BA, PhD; American astrophysicist and academic; *Subramanyan Chandrasekhar Distinguished Service Professor, Departments of Astronomy and Astrophysics, and Physics, University of Chicago;* b. 1957, Hyde Park, New York; ed Vassar Coll., Univ. of California, Berkeley; Subramanyan Chandrasekhar Distinguished Service Prof., Depts of Astronomy and Astrophysics, and Physics, Univ. of Chicago 2001–, Deputy Dir Kavli Inst. for Cosmological Physics; Dir Center for Astrophysical Research in Antarctica; has led several experiments, including Degree Angular Scale Interferometer, Interferometric Sunyaev-Zel'dovich Effect Imaging Experiment, Sunyaev-Zel'dovich Array, South Pole Telescope; MacArthur Fellows Program 1998, NASA Medal for Exceptional Scientific Achievement 1997, Magellanic Gold Medal 2004, Beatrice M. Tinsley Prize, American Astronomical Soc. 2006, Cosmology Prize, Peter Gruber Foundation (co-recipient) 2015. *Publications:* numerous papers in professional journals on measurements of the cosmic microwave background. *Address:* Room ERC 341, Department of Astronomy and Astrophysics, University of Chicago, 5640 S. Ellis Avenue, Chicago, IL 60637, USA (office). *Telephone:* (773) 834-0269 (office). *E-mail:* jckicp.uchicago.edu (office). *Website:* astro.uchicago.edu/people/john-e-carlstrom.php (office); kicp.uchicago.edu/people/profile/john_carlstrom.html (office).

CARLYLE, Joan Hildred; British singer (soprano) and teacher; b. 6 April 1931; d. of Edgar J. Carlyle and Margaret M. Carlyle; m.; two d.; ed Howell's School, Denbigh, N Wales; studied singing with Madame Bertha Nichlass Kempner; Prin. Lyric Soprano, Covent Garden 1955–79; has sung at La Scala Milan, Staatsoper Vienna, Munich, Berlin, Teatro Colón Buenos Aires, San Carlo Naples, Monet Monte Carlo, Nico Milan, Cape Town, Brussels, Geneva, Zurich, Amsterdam, Boston, New York; teaches privately and also in London; gives master-classes, promotes young singers and judges prestigious competitions. *Major roles sung in UK include:* Oscar, Un Ballo in Maschera 1957–58, Sophie, Der Rosenkavalier 1958–59, Nedda, Pagliacci (Zeffirelli production) 1959, Mimi, La Bohème 1960, Titania, Midsummer Night's Dream, Britten (Gielgud production) 1960, Pamina, Magic Flute 1962, 1966, Countess, Marriage of Figaro 1963, Zdenka, Arabella (Hartman Production) 1964, Suor Angelica 1965, Desdemona, Othello 1965, Arabella 1967, Marschallin, Der Rosenkavalier 1968, Jenifer, Midsummer Marriage 1969, Donna Anna, Don Giovanni 1970, Reiza, Oberon 1970, Adriana Lecouvreur 1970, Rusalka, Elisabetta, Don Carlos 1975. *Major roles sung abroad include:* Oscar, Nedda, Mimi, Pamina, Zdenka, Micaela, Donna Anna, Arabella, Elisabetta and Desdemona. *Recordings include:* Von Karajan's production of Pagliacci as Nedda, Midsummer Marriage as Jenifer, Medea, Pagliacci from Buenos Aires, Mavra, Purcell Anthology, Voice from the Old House (1/11) 2002, (12/29), (30/42) 2003, Complete versions of Otello, Arabella, Suor Angelica, Highlights from La Bohème 2003, complete versions of Arabella and Adriana Lecouvreur, Rusalka, Oberon, Complete Ballo 1962, 1971, Benvenuto Cellini 2004, Die Zauberflöte, Samson. *Leisure interests:* gardening, travel, preservation of the countryside, interior design, cooking. *Address:* Laundry Cottage, Hanmer, SY13 3DQ, Clwyd, Wales. *Telephone:* (1948) 830265. *E-mail:* joan@joancarlyle.co.uk (home). *Website:* www.joancarlyle.co.uk (home).

CARLYLE, Robert, OBE; British actor; b. 14 April 1961, Glasgow, Scotland; s. of Joseph Carlyle and Elizabeth Carlyle; m. Anastasia Shirley 1997; three c.; ed N Kelvinside Secondary School, Royal Scottish Acad. of Music and Drama; f. Rain Dog Theatre Co. 1990, productions include: Wasted, One Flew Over the Cuckoo's Nest (Paper Boat Award), Conquest of the South Pole, Macbeth (Paper Boat Award 1992); Scottish BAFTA Award 1995, Royal TV Award 1996, Salerno Film Festival Award 1997, Evening Standard Outstanding British Actor Award 1998, Film Critics' Circle Award for Best Actor 1998, Variety Club Actor of the Year 1998, Bowmore Whisky/Scottish Screen Award for Best Actor 2001, Michael Elliot Award for Best Actor 2001, David Puttnam Patrons Award. *Stage appearances include:* Twelfth Night, Dead Dad Dog, Nae Problem, City, No Mean City, Cuttin' a Rug, Othello. *Films include:* Marooned, Riff Raff 1990, Silent Scream 1990, Safe 1993, Being Human 1993, Priest 1994, Go Now 1995, Trainspotting 1996, Carla's

Song 1996, Face 1997, The Full Monty (BAFTA Award for Best Actor 1998) 1997, Ravenous 1999, Apprentices, Plunkett and Macleane 1999, The World is Not Enough 1999, Angela's Ashes 2000, The Beach 2000, There's Only One Jimmy Grimble 2000, To End All Wars 2000, 51st State 2001, Once Upon a Time in the Midlands 2002, Black and White 2002, Dead Fish 2004, Marilyn Hotchkiss' Ballroom Dancing and Charm School 2005, The Mighty Celt 2005, Eragon 2006, 28 Weeks Later 2007, Stone of Destiny 2008, Summer 2008, The Tournament 2009, California Solo 2012, The Legend of Barney Thomson (also dir) (BAFTA Scotland Award for Best Film 2015) 2015. *Television includes:* The Part of Valour 1981, Safe 1993, Cracker 1994, Hamish Macbeth 1995, The Advocates, Arena, Byrne on Byrne, Taggart, The Bill, Looking After Jo Jo 1998, Hitler: The Rise of Evil 2003, Gunpowder, Treason and Plot 2004, Class of '76 2005, Human Trafficking 2005, Born Equal 2006, The Last Enemy (series) 2008, 24: Redemption 2008, Zig Zag Love 2009, The Unloved (Scottish BAFTA for Best TV Actor) 2009, SGU Stargate Universe (series) 2009–11, Once Upon a Time (series) 2011–12.

CARMACK, John D.; American software industry executive; *Chief Technology Officer, Oculus VR;* b. 20 Aug. 1970; m. Katherine Anna Kang; one s.; ed Univ. of Missouri, Kansas City; worked for Softdisk Publishing, Shreveport, La; Co-founder and Technical Dir id Software 1991–2012, created computer games, including Wolfenstein 3-D, Doom and Quake; Chief Tech. Officer, Oculus VR 2013–; Founder Armadillo Aerospace 2000; inducted into Acad. of Interactive Arts and Sciences Hall of Fame 2001, numerous awards from gaming publs. *Address:* Oculus Inc., 3131 Turtle Creek Blvd, Suite 1020, Dallas, TX 75219; Armadillo Aerospace LP, 201 Laurence Drive, PMB# 512, Heath, TX 75032, USA (office). *Website:* oculusinc.com; armadilloaerospace.com.

CARMENA CASTILLO, Manuela, Licenciatura in Law; Spanish politician, judge and lawyer; *Mayor of Madrid;* b. 9 Feb. 1944; m. Eduardo Leira; two c.; ed Complutense Univ. of Madrid; labour lawyer for 15 years and judge for 30 years, Sr Judge of Madrid 1993–2010 (retd); Founder, Judges for Democracy 1984; mem. Patronato de la Fundación Alternativas 2010–15; Founder, Yaos emprendedores (sponsors retail business selling items made by Alcala de Guadaira prisoners, Seville) 2011; apptd Adviser to Basque govt of Patxi Lopez 2011; Mayor of Madrid 2015–; fmr mem. PCE (Spanish Communist Party); apptd mem. General Council Judiciary 1996; Trustee Alternatives Foundation; APDHE Nat. Human Rights Award 1986. *Address:* Palacio de Cibeles, Calle de Montalbán 1, 28014 Madrid, Spain (office). *Website:* www.munimadrid.es (office).

CARMI, Rivka, MD; Israeli paediatrician, geneticist and university administrator; *President, Ben-Gurion University;* ed Hebrew Univ. Medical School, Jerusalem, Harvard Univ., USA; Sr Faculty mem. Faculty of Health Sciences and Soroka Medical Center, Be'ersheva, Dir Clinical Genetics Unit, Soroka Hosp., Prof. and Dean, Faculty of Health Sciences (first woman dean of a faculty of health sciences in Israel) 2000– (fmr Assoc. Dean of Student Affairs), Acting Pres. Ben-Gurion Univ. of the Negev (first woman pres. of Israeli univ.) Feb.–May 2006, Pres. May 2006–, Chair. Bd of Dirs Aug.–Dec. 2012; fmr Chair. Selection Cttee Joyce and Irving Goldman Medical School, Instructional Cttee Recanati School for Community Health Professions, Ben-Gurion Univ.; fmr Acting Dir Nat. Inst. for Biotechnology in the Negev; mem. Editorial Bd American Journal for Medical Genetics; mem. and adviser in local and nat. cttees and in int. insts; Dr hc (Dalhousie, Nova Scotia, Canada) 2013; Lifetime Achievement Award, Yated organization for children with Down's Syndrome, Women of Distinction Award, Hadassah Women's Zionist Org. of America 2008. *Achievements include:* identified 12 new genes and delineated three new syndromes, one named after her. *Publications:* more than 120 scientific papers on molecular genetics of rare recessive diseases and on community genetics. *Address:* Office of the President, Ben-Gurion University of the Negev, PO Box 653, Be'ersheva 84105, Israel (office). *Telephone:* (8) 6461111 (office). *Fax:* (8) 6479434 (office). *E-mail:* rcarmi@bgumail.bgu.ac.il (office). *Website:* www.bgu.ac.il (office).

CARMICHAEL, Rt Hon. Alexander Morrison (Alistair), PC, LLB; British lawyer and politician; b. 15 July 1965, Islay, Scotland; m. Kathryn Jane Eastham 1987; two s.; ed Islay High School, Univs of Glasgow and Aberdeen; Pres. Liberal Club, Univ. of Glasgow; hotel manager 1984–89; contested Paisley South in Gen. Election 1987; qualified as solicitor 1993; Procurator Fiscal Depute for Edinburgh and Aberdeen 1993–96; solicitor, Aberdeen & Macduff 1996–2001; MP for Orkney and Shetland 2001–, mem. Commons Scottish Affairs Cttee 2001–05, 2008–10, Int. Devt Cttee 2001–02, Public Accounts Cttee 2005–06, Consolidation etc. Bills (Jt Cttee) 2008–10, Draft Constitutional Renewal Bill (Jt Cttee) 2008–10, Members' Allowances 2009–10; Liberal Democrat Spokesperson on Energy and Climate Change 2001–05, on Home Affairs 2005–06, on Transport 2006–07, on NI 2007–10, on Scotland 2008–10; Comptroller, HM Household and Deputy Chief Whip, House of Commons 2010–13; Sec. of State for Scotland 2013–15; Deputy Leader of Scottish Liberal Democrats; Elder, Church of Scotland; Liberal Democrat; Hon. Pres. Liberal Youth Scotland 2011–. *Leisure interests:* listening to music, theatre, cooking. *Address:* House of Commons, Westminster, London, SW1A 0AA, England (office); Constituency Office, 14 Palace Road, Kirkwall, KW15 1PA, Orkney; Constituency Office, 171 Commercial Street, Lerwick, ZE1 0HX, Shetland, Scotland. *Telephone:* (20) 7219-8181 (Westminster); (1856) 876541 (Kirkwall); (1595) 690044 (Lerwick). *Fax:* (1595) 690055 (Lerwick). *E-mail:* carmichaela@parliament.uk (office). *Website:* www.parliament.uk/biographies/commons/mr-alistair-carmichael/1442; www.alistaircarmichael.co.uk.

CARMONA, Anthony Thomas Aquinas, SC, BA, LLB; Trinidad and Tobago fmr judge and fmr head of state; b. 7 March 1953, Fyzabad; s. of Dennis Stephen Carmona and Barbara Carmona; m. Reema Carmona; one s. one d.; ed Presentation Coll., San Fernando, Univ. of the West Indies; began career as teacher at primary and secondary school levels 1972–75, first at St Hugh's High School and Merle Grove High School, Kingston, Jamaica, later at Palo Seco Govt Secondary and Fyzabad Anglican Secondary Schools; Lecturer in Business Law, San Fernando Technical Inst. 1983–85, also Lecturer, Dept of Language and Linguistics and Sr Tutor, Dept of Govt, Univ. of the West Indies, St Augustine, Trinidad and Tobago; called to the Bar of Trinidad and Tobago 1983, Sr State Attorney 1989, Asst, then Deputy Dir of Public Prosecutions 1994–99; Judge, Supreme Court of Trinidad and Tobago 2004–12; Appeals Counsel at Office of the Prosecutor, Int. Criminal Tribunal for fmr Yugoslavia, The Hague and Int. Criminal Tribunal for Rwanda, Arusha 2001–04; Judge, Int. Criminal Court 2011–13; Pres. of Trinidad and Tobago 2013–18. *Address:* c/o Office of the President, President's House, Circular Road, St Ann's, Port of Spain, Trinidad and Tobago (office).

CARMONA ESTANGA, Pedro Francisco; Venezuelan politician, economist and oil industry executive; b. 6 June 1941, Barquisimeto, Lara; ed Universidad Católica Andrés Bello, Université Libre de Bruxelles, Belgium; with Aditivos Orinoco 1989–93, Química Venoco 1989–2000, Industrias Venoco 1990–2000, Promotora Venoco 2001; First Vice-Pres. Fedecamaras 1999–2001, Pres. 2001–02; Pres. Andean Enterprise Consultative Council 2000–01; also worked for Venezuelan Confed. of Industry–Conindustria, Venezuelan Asscn of the Chemical and Petrochemical Industries, Venezuelan Asscn of Exporters (AVEX), Chamber of Commerce, Venezuelan–Columbian Integration (CAVECOL); fmr mem. Directive Council Instituto de Estudios Superiores de la Administración de Empresas; fmr mem. Junta del Acuerdo de Cartagena, fmr Pres. Venezuelan Del. to Comisión del Acuerdo de Cartagena; fmr mem. Corporación Andina de Fomento; fmr Dir Instituto de Comercio Exterior, Sistema Económico Latinoamericano; fmr adviser to Directorate of Econ. Policy, Ministry of Foreign Affairs; installed by army as interim Pres. of Venezuela following anti-govt protests against Pres. Chávez 12–13 April 2002, placed under house arrest 14 April 2002, accused of rebellion and usurping the presidency, later granted asylum by Colombian Govt; Order of the Sun (Peru), Nat. Order of Merit (Colombia), Bernardo O'Higgins Order (Chile).

CARNEGIE, Sir Roderick Howard, Kt, AC, BSc, BA, MA, MBA, DipAgrEcon, FTSE; Australian business executive; *Chairman, Pacific Edge Group;* b. 27 Nov. 1932, Melbourne, Vic.; s. of D. H. Carnegie and Margaret F. Carnegie; m. Carmen Clarke 1959 (died 2008); three s.; ed Geelong GS, Trinity Coll., Melbourne, New Coll., Oxford, Harvard Business School; Assoc., McKinsey and Co., Melbourne and New York 1959–64, Prin. 1964–68, Dir 1968–70; Dir CRA 1970, Jt Man. Dir 1971–72, Man. Dir and Chief Exec. 1972–74, Chair. and Man. Dir 1974–83, Chair. and Chief Exec. 1983–86; Dir Comalco Ltd, CRA Ltd, Rio Tinto-Zinc Corpn Ltd; Chair. Consultative Cttee on Relations with Japan 1984–87; Pres. German-Australian Chamber of Industry and Commerce 1985; Pres. Business Council of Australia 1987–88; Chair. Hudson Conway Ltd 1987–2000; currently Chair. Pacific Edge Group; Vice-Pres. Australian Mining Industry Council 1985; Chair. Salvation Army Council 1992–96, G10 Australia Holdings Ltd 1992–94, Valiant Consolidated Ltd 1993–98, Adacel Techs Ltd 1998–2003, Newcrest Mining Ltd 1994–98; Dir John Fairfax Holdings Pty Ltd 1992–94, Lexmark Holdings Inc. (USA) 1994–98; Patron Australian Centre for Blood Diseases; Commdr's Cross, Order of Merit (Germany) 1991, Centenary Medal 2003; Hon. DSc (Newcastle); Hon. LLD (Monash). *Address:* Pacific Edge Group, PO Box 7458, St Kilda Road, Melbourne, Vic. 8004, Australia (office). *Telephone:* (3) 9863-7242 (office). *Fax:* (3) 9863-7241 (office). *E-mail:* rod@carboniron.com.au (office).

CARNEY, John Charles, Jr, BA, MPA; American politician; *Governor of Delaware;* b. 20 May 1956, Wilmington, Del.; s. of Jack Carney and Ann Carney; m. Tracey Quillen; two s.; ed Dartmouth Coll., Univ. of Delaware; Staff Asst to US Senator from Del. Joseph R. Biden 1986–89; Deputy Chief Admin. Officer, New Castle County, Del. 1989–94; Deputy Chief of Staff to Gov. of Del. 1994–97; Sec. of Finance, State of Del. 1997–2000; Lt Gov. of Del. 2001–09; mem. US House of Reps from Del. at-large Dist, Washington, DC 2011–, mem. House Financial Services Cttee 2011–; Gov.-elect of Delaware Nov. 2016, Gov. 2017–; fmr Chair. Delaware Health Care Comm., Interagency Council on Adult Literacy, Criminal Justice Council, Center for Educ. Tech., Livable Delaware Advisory Council; Democrat. *Address:* Office of the Governor, Legislative Hall, 150 Martin Luther King Jr Blvd South, 2nd Floor, Dover, DE 19901, USA (office). *Telephone:* (302) 744-4101 (office). *Fax:* (302) 739-2775 (office). *Website:* governor.delaware.gov (office); johncarney.house.gov.

CARNEY, Mark, OC, BA, MA, PhD; Canadian central banker; *Governor, Bank of England;* b. 16 March 1965, Fort Smith, NWT; m. Diana Fox 1994; four c.; ed Harvard Univ., USA, Univ. of Oxford, UK; worked at Goldman Sachs 1988–2001, as analyst in London, later working in Tokyo and New York before becoming Man. Dir Goldman's investment banking div., based in Toronto; Deputy Gov., Bank of Canada, responsible for int. issues 2003–04, Adviser to the Gov. 2007–08, Gov. Bank of Canada 2008–12; Sr Assoc. Deputy Minister, Dept of Finance 2004–07; served as Canada's Finance Deputy at G7, G20 and Financial Stability Forum, Chair. G20 Financial Stability Forum 2011–; Gov.-Elect Bank of England Nov. 2012–June 2013, Gov. July 2013–(20), also Chair. Monetary Policy Cttee, Financial Policy Cttee, Bd of Prudential Regulation Authority; Chair. Financial Stability Bd (FSB) 2011–18; First Vice-Chair. European Systemic Risk Board; Chair. Global Economy Meeting, Bank for Int. Settlements 2017–, Economic Consultative Cttee 2017–; mem. Group of Thirty, Foundation Bd of World Economic Forum. *Address:* Bank of England, Threadneedle Street, London, EC2R 8AH, England (office). *Telephone:* (20) 7601-4444 (office). *Fax:* (20) 7601-5460 (office). *E-mail:* enquiries@bankofengland.co.uk (office). *Website:* www.bankofengland.co.uk (office).

CARNEY, Rt Hon. Patricia (Pat), CM, BA, PC, MA; Canadian politician and economist; b. 26 May 1935, Shanghai, China; d. of James Carney and Dora Sanders; m. 2nd Paul S. White 1998; one s. one d. from previous marriage; ed Univ. of British Columbia; Adjunct Prof., Univ. of British Columbia; fmrly econ. journalist; f. Gemini North Ltd (consulting firm for socio-econ. impact studies) 1970; elected MP 1980; Minister of State for Finance, Minister of Finance, Energy, Mines and Resources; Minister of Energy, Mines and Resources 1984–86, of Int. Trade 1986–88; Pres. Treasury Bd April–Oct. 1988; Chair. Cabinet Cttee on Trade; mem. Senate 1990–2008; fmr Chair. Standing Senate Cttee on Energy, the Environment and Natural Resources; mem. Standing Senate Cttee on Foreign Affairs, Aboriginal Peoples, Fisheries; Adjunct Prof., School of Community and Regional Planning, Univ. of British Columbia; mem. Canadian Inst. of Planners, Asscn of Professional Economists of BC; fmr mem. Econ. Council of Canada; Hon. Fellow, Royal Architectural Inst. of Canada 1989; Hon. LLD (Univ. of British Columbia) 1990, (British Columbia Open Univ.) 1991. *Publication:* Trade Secrets: A Memoir 2000. *Website:* www.patcarney.ca.

CARNLEY, Most Rev. Peter Frederick, AC, DD, PhD; Australian theologian and ecclesiastic (retd); b. 17 Oct. 1937, New Lambton, NSW; s. of F. Carnley; m. Carol Ann Dunstan, 1966; one s. one d.; ed St John's Theological Coll., NSW, Trinity Coll., Melbourne Univ., St John's Coll., Univ. of Cambridge; Deacon 1962;

Priest 1964; Chaplain, Mitchell Coll. of Advanced Educ., NSW 1970–72; Research Fellow, St John's Coll., Cambridge 1971–72; Warden St John's Coll., Univ. of Queensland 1973–81; Anglican Archbishop of Perth and Metropolitan of the Prov. of Western Australia 1981–2005, Primate of the Anglican Church of Australia 2000–05; mem. Archbishop of Canterbury's Comm. on Communion and Women in the Episcopate 1988, Int. Anglican Theological and Doctrinal Comm. 1994; Visiting Prof. of Anglican Studies, Gen. Theological Seminary, New York 1993, 1996, 1999; Anglican Co-Chair. Anglican-Roman Catholic Int. Comm. 2003–; Adjunct Prof. of Theology, Murdoch Univ. 2004–; fmr GTS Distinguished Visiting Prof. of Systematic Theology; Scholar in Residence, St Peter's Church, Morristown, NJ 2013; Patron, Australian Council of Christians and Jews 2004–; Lady Margaret Preacher, Univ. of Cambridge 2010; Hon. Fellow, Trinity Coll., Univ. of Melbourne 2000, St John's Coll., Cambridge 2000, Emmanuel Coll., Cambridge 2006; Dr hc (Newcastle) 2000, (Western Australia) 2000, (Queensland) 2002; Hon. DUniv (Charles Sturt) 2001; Hon. DST (Melbourne Coll. of Divinity) 2004. *Publications:* The Structure of Resurrection Belief 1987, The Yellow Wallpaper and Other Sermons 2001, Faithfulness in Fellowship: Reflections on Homosexuality and the Church 2001, Reflections in Glass: Trends and Tensions in the Contemporary Anglican Church 2004. *Leisure interests:* gardening, music. *Address:* GPO Box 221, Nannup, WA 6275, Australia. *Telephone:* (4) 1188-8203. *E-mail:* pluspeter@westnet.com.au.

ČARNOGURSKÝ, Ján, LLD, JUDr; Slovak politician and lawyer; b. 1 Jan. 1944, Bratislava; s. of Pavol Čarnogurský and Kristína Čarnogurská (née Fašungová); m. Marta Stachová 1970; two s. two d.; ed Charles Univ., Prague; lawyer, Bratislava 1970–81; mem. of Slovak Lawyers' Cen. Office and Czech Lawyers' Cen. Office; banned from legal profession after defence in a political trial 1981; driver, lawyer for a co. Bratislava 1982–86; unemployed, after expulsion from legal profession, continued giving legal advice to mems of the political opposition and religious activists 1987–89; held in custody, released and pardoned Aug.–Nov. 1989; First Deputy Premier, Govt of Czechoslovakia 1989–90, Deputy Premier June 1990; Chair. Legis. Council Feb.–Aug. 1990; Chair. Christian Democratic Movt 1990–2000; First Deputy Premier, Govt of Slovak Repub. 1990–91, Prime Minister of Slovak Govt 1991–92; mem. State Defence Council 1991–92; Deputy to Slovak Nat. Council (Slovak Parl.) for KDH (Christian Democratic Movt) 1992–98; Deputy Chair. Parl. Ass. of CSCE 1993–95; Minister of Justice 1998–2002; advocate in pvt sector 2002–; Chair. Slovak–Russian Asscn 2006–; Trustee, Order of the German Kts 1994–; mem. Valdai Discussion Club; Grand Cross, Order of Merit (Poland) 2008; Hon. Kt, Order of St George 2015; Slovak Literary Fund Prize (Journalists' Section) 1992, Mechitar Gosh Medal (Armenia) 2008, Medal of Friendship (Russia) 2010. *Publications include:* The Bratislava Letters (samizdat), Suffered for the Faith 1987, Seen from Danube 1997, By the Roads of KDH 2007, Diary 1994–2007 2013, Yes and No of Ján Čarnogurský 2014. *Leisure interests:* history, jogging. *Address:* Law Office, Dostojevského rad 1, 81109 Bratislava, Slovakia (office). *Telephone:* (2) 2072-2099 (office). *E-mail:* jancarnogursky@slovanet.sk (office). *Website:* www.jancarnogursky.sk.

CAROLUS, Cheryl, BA; South African organization executive and diplomatist; *Chairperson, Sibanye Gold Limited;* b. 27 May 1958, Silvertown; m. Graeme Bloch 1989; ed Univ. of the Western Cape; Gen. Sec. Nat. Exec. Cttee, United Democratic Front (UDF) 1983–87, Fed. of S African Women (FedSAW) 1987, UDF Western Cape Region 1983; UDF Del. Int. Centre for Swedish Labour Movt 1986; mem. Interim Leadership Group, S African Communist Party 1990; mem. Interim Leadership Cttee, African Nat. Congress (ANC) 1990, ANC Rep. at talks with Govt at Groote Schur, Cape Town 1990, Deputy Sec.-Gen. ANC 1994; High Commr to UK 1998–2001; CEO South African Tourism Bd (SATOUR) 2001–04; Chair. South African National Parks (SANPARKS) 2004–10; Exec. Chair. Peotona Holdings Ltd; Chair. of the Bd, South African Airways 2009; Chair. Sibanye Gold Ltd 2013–; mem. Congress of S African Trade Unions, Nat. Educ. Crisis Cttee 1989, OAU, Harare, Bd of Dirs Int. Inst. for Democracy and Electoral Assistance; detained under emergency regulations 1986, 1989; mem. Bd of Dirs Gold Fields Ltd 2009–, Investec Ltd; fmr mem. Bd of Dirs De Beers Consolidated Mines Ltd, Fenner Conveyor Belting SA Ltd, Macsteel Service Centres SA, IQ Business Group, Investec PLC, Constitution Hill Trust (Proprietary) Ltd; Bd mem. International Marketing Council of South Africa, International Crisis Group, World Wildlife Fund International 2005–, Nat. Parks Trust, Soul City Health Inst.; Dr hc (Univ. of Cape Town) 2004. *Address:* International Crisis Group, 149 Avenue Louise, Level 24, 1050 Brussels, Belgium (office). *Telephone:* (2) 502-90-38 (office). *Fax:* (2) 502-50-38 (office). *E-mail:* brussels@crisisgroup.org (office). *Website:* www.crisisgroup.org/en (office).

CARON, Leslie Claire Margaret; French actress and ballet dancer; b. 1 July 1931, Boulogne-Billancourt; m. 1st George Hormel; m. 2nd Peter Reginald Frederick Hall 1956 (divorced 1965); one s. one d.; m. 3rd Michael Laughlin 1969 (divorced); ed Convent of the Assumption, Paris and Conservatoire de Danse; with Ballet des Champs Elysées 1947–50, Ballet de Paris 1954; Chevalier Légion d'honneur; Officier Ordre nat. du Mérite. *Films include:* An American in Paris 1951, Man with a Cloak 1951, Glory Alley 1952, Story of Three Loves 1953, Lili 1953, Glass Slipper 1955, Daddy Long Legs 1955, Gaby 1956, Gigi 1958, The Doctor's Dilemma 1958, The Man Who Understood Women 1959, The Subterranean 1960, Austerlitz 1960, Fanny 1961, Guns of Darkness 1962, The L-Shaped Room 1962, Father Goose 1964, A Very Special Favor 1965, Promise Her Anything 1965, Is Paris Burning? 1966, Head of the Family 1969, Madron 1970, Chandler 1971, Purple Night 1972, Surreal Estate 1976, The Man Who Loved Women 1977, Valentino 1977, Nicole 1978, Golden Girl 1979, The Contract 1980, All Stars 1980, Chanel Solitaire 1981, Imperative 1982, Deathly Moves 1983, The Train 1987, Courage Mountain 1990, Guns 1990, Damage 1992, The Genius 1993, Guerriers et Captives 1994, Funny Bones 1995, Let It Be Me 1995, The Reef 1996, Chocolat 2000, Le Divorce 2003. *Television includes:* The Wild Bird 1959, Les Fables de La Fontaine 1964, Carola 1973, QB VII 1974, Docteur Erika Werner 1978, Run, Rabbit, Run 1982, Tales of the Unexpected 1982, The Unapproachable 1982, Le Château faible 1983, Master of the Game 1984, La Génie du Faux 1984, L'oiseau bleu 1985, Mon meilleur Noël 1985, Falcon Crest 1987, The Man Who Lived at the Ritz 1988, Lenin: The Train 1990, The Ring 1996, The Last of the Blonde Bombshells 2000, Murder on the Orient Express 2001, Law and Order (Primetime Emmy Award for Outstanding Guest Actress 2007) 2006, Jo 2013. *Plays include:* Orvet (Jean Renoir), La Sauvage (Anouilh), Gigi (Anita Loos), 13 rue de l'Amour (Feydan), Ondine (Giraudoux), Carola (Renoir), La Répétition (Anouilh), On Your Toes (Rogers and Hart), Apprends-moi Céline (Maria Pacôme) (played in English in USA as One for the Tango 1985), Grand Hotel (Vicky Baum), George Sand (Bruno Villien), Le Martyre de Saint Sébastien (Debussy), Nocturne for Lovers (Villien), Babar the Elephant (Poulenc); toured France in Apprends-moi Céline 1998–99, Little Night Music, Châtelet, Paris 2010; stage appearances in Paris, London, USA, Germany and Australia; readings of Colette, USA and Australia. *Publication:* Vengeance 1983, Thank Heaven: A Memoir 2009. *Address:* c/o Clifford Stevens, Paradigm Agency, 360 Park Avenue South, New York, NY 10010, USA (office). *Telephone:* (212) 897-6408 (office). *E-mail:* cstevens@paradigmagency.com (office). *Website:* www.paradigmagency.com (office).

CARP, Daniel A., MS, MBA; American business executive; b. 1948, Wytheville, Va; ed Ohio Univ., Rochester Inst. of Tech., Sloan School of Man., Massachusetts Inst. of Tech.; with Kodak 1970–2005, Asst Gen. Man. Latin American Region 1986–88, Vice-Pres., Gen. Man. 1988–90, Gen. Man. European Marketing Cos 1991, Gen. Man. European, African and Middle Eastern Region 1991, Exec. Vice-Pres. and Asst COO Eastman Kodak Co. 1995–97, Dir, Pres. and COO 1997–2000, Chair., Pres. and CEO 2000–01, Chair. and CEO 2001–05; Chair. (non-exec.) Delta Air Lines, Inc. 2007–16; mem. Bd Dirs Texas Instruments Inc. 1997–, Liz Claiborne Inc. 2006–09, Norfolk Southern Corpn 2006–; mem. Business Roundtable, Business Council; Trustee, Nat. Urban League, George Eastman House; Human Relations Award from American Jewish Cttee Photographic Imaging Div. 1997, Photographic and Imaging Manufacturers Asscn Leadership Award 2001, Diversity Best Practices CEO Leadership Award 2003, PhotoImaging Manufacturers and Distributors Asscn Person of the Year Award 2004. *Address:* c/o Norfolk Southern Corp. 3 Commercial Place, Norfolk, VA 23510, USA. *Website:* www.nscorp.com.

CARPENTER, John Howard; American film director and screenwriter; b. 16 Jan. 1948, Carthage, NY; s. of Howard Ralph Carpenter and Milton Jean Carpenter (née Carter); m. 1st Adrienne Barbeau 1979; m. 2nd Sandy King 1990; ed Univ. of Southern California; mem. American Soc. of Composers, Authors and Publrs, Acad. of Motion Picture Arts and Sciences, Dirs Guild of America, West, Writers Guild of America. *Films directed:* The Resurrection of Bronco Billy 1970, Dark Star 1974, Assault on Precinct 13 1976, Halloween 1978, Elvis 1978, The Fog 1979, Escape from New York 1980, The Thing 1982, Christine 1983, Starman 1984, Big Trouble in Little China 1986, Prince of Darkness 1987, They Live 1987, Memoirs of an Invisible Man 1992, In the Mouth of Madness 1995, Village of the Damned 1995, Escape from LA 1996, Vampires 1998, Ghosts of Mars 2001, The Ward 2010. *Television includes:* Someone's Watching Me! 1978, Elvis 1979, Body Bags 1993, Masters of Horror 2005–06. *Leisure interests:* music, helicopter piloting. *Address:* c/o International Creative Management, 8942 Wilshire Boulevard, Beverly Hills, CA 90211, USA.

CARPENTER, Michael A., BSc, MBA; British business executive; ed Univ. of Nottingham, Harvard Business School (Baker Scholar), USA; spent nine years as Vice-Pres. and Dir Boston Consulting Group and three years with ICI, UK; Vice-Pres. Corp. Business Devt and Planning, General Electric (GE) Co. 1983–86, Exec. Vice-Pres. GE Capital Corpn 1986–89, Chair., Pres. and CEO Kidder Peabody Group Inc. (subsidiary of GE) 1989–94; Chair. and CEO Travelers Life & Annuity and Vice-Chair. Travelers Group Inc. 1994–98; Chair. and CEO Salomon Smith Barney (following merger that created Citigroup) 1998–2002, Chair. and CEO Citigroup's Global Corp. & Investment Bank, with responsibility for Salomon Smith Barney Inc. and Citibank's corp. banking activities globally 1998–2002, Chair. and CEO Citigroup Alternative Investments 2002–06; f. Southgate Alternative Investments 2007; mem. Bd of Dirs, GMAC Financial Services (renamed Ally Financial Inc. 2009) May 2009–15, CEO Nov. 2009–15, Consultant 2015–; Dir, Mikronite Technologies Group Inc. 2004–, Autobytel Inc. 2012–; mem. Bd, US Retirement Partners, New York City Investment Fund; fmr mem. Bd New York Stock Exchange, General Signal, Loews Cineplex and various other pvt. and public cos; Hon. LLD (Nottingham). *Address:* Ally Financial Inc., 200 Renaissance Center, Detroit, MI 48265-2000, USA (office). *Telephone:* (313) 556-5000 (office). *Fax:* (815) 282-6156 (office). *E-mail:* info@ally.com (office). *Website:* www.ally.com (office).

CARPENTIER, Alain Frédéric, DenM, DèsSc; French cardiac surgeon; *Head, Department of Cardiovascular Surgery and Organ Transplantation, Hôpital Européen Georges-Pompidou;* b. 11 Aug. 1933, Toulouse (Haute-Garonne); Lab. Researcher, CNRS 1963–66; Founder and Dir, Lab. for the Study of Cardiac Grafts and Prostheses 1967–; apptd Lab. Dir, Univ. of Paris VI 1978, now Prof. Emer.; Head of Dept of Cardiovascular Surgery, l'Hôpital Broussais 1982, of Cardiovascular Surgery and Organ Transplantation, Hôpital Européen Georges-Pompidou 1999–; Visiting Prof., New York Univ. 1983, 2001–05, Adjunct Prof., Mount Sinai School of Medicine, New York Univ. 2002–; Visiting Prof., Univ. of Oregon 1986, 1989, Univ. of London 1989, 1996–2002, Cleveland Clinic Foundation 1990, Harvard Univ. 1991, 1996, 1999, 2002, 2005, Univ. of Montreal 1991, 2004–06, Baylor Univ. 1992, Univ. of Washington 1994, 2000, Florida Heart Inst. 1996, 1999, Univ. of Padua 1996, Hôtel Dieu de France de Beyrouth 1996, Univ. of Virginia 1997, Univ. of North Carolina 1998, Univ. of Tokyo 1998, 2000, 2003, Univ. of Bangkok 2000, Univ. of Pavia 2000, Univ. of Mexico 2004, Univ. of Delhi 2006; Scientific Adviser, Edwards LifeSciences Research Centre, Calif. 1975–; Founder and Pres. Heart Inst., Ho Chi Minh City 1991–; Pres. Cttee Télémédecine et technologies pour la santé, Ministry of Nat. Educ., Research and Tech. 1999; mem. Conseil nat. de la science 1998, Acad. des sciences 2000 (Vice-Pres., then Pres. 2009–12), Haut conseil de la science et de la technologie 2006, Cardiothoracic Surgery Network, European Asscn for Cardio-Thoracic Surgery, French Soc. for Thoracic and Cardiovascular Surgery, Soc. for Heart Valve Disease, American Asscn for Thoracic Surgery, Western Thoracic Surgical Asscn; mem. Bd of Dirs, World Heart Foundation; Hon. mem. Mexican Cardiology Soc. 1978, American Surgical Asscn 1985, Soc. of Cardiothoracic Surgeons of GB and Ireland 1986, American Coll. of Surgeons 1988, American Coll. of Cardiology 1990, Royal Coll. of Doctors and Surgeons of Canada 1991, Royal Coll. of Surgeons of England 1992; Officier, Légion d'honneur; Commdr, Ordre nat. du Mérite, du Mérite de l'Ordre de Malte, Ordre du Cèdre (Lebanon), Grand Croix, Ordre de Léopold (Belgium); Dr hc (Univ. of Bucharest, Romania) 2001, (Univ. of Pavia, Italy) 2001; Prix de l'Internat, Médaille d'argent 1965, Bronze Medal, CNRS 1967, Prix de l'Asscn française de chirurgie 1967, Grand Prix, Acad. des sciences 1986, Prix Médecine-Sciences du Rayonnement français 1990, Grand prix mondial Cino del Duca 1996, Grand Prize, The Foundation for Medical Research 1998, Fifth Scientific Achievement Award, American Asscn for Thoracic Surgery 2005, Lasker Prize 2007. *Achievements include:* developed the first 100% artificial heart, using biomaterials and electronic sensors, device was successfully implanted by a team at Hôpital Européen Georges-Pompidou Dec. 2013. *Publications include:* Le Mal Universitaire 1988, La Transplantation d'Organes 1994, Philosophie du Progrès en Cardiologie (co-author) 2002. *Address:* Hôpital Européen Georges-Pompidou, 20 rue Leblanc, Paris 75908 Cedex 15, France (office). *Telephone:* 1-56-09-36-01 (office). *Fax:* 1-56-09-36-04 (office). *E-mail:* alain.carpentier@hop.egp.ap-hop-paris.fr (office); prcarpentier@europost.org (office).

CARPENTIER, Jean Claude Gabriel; French aeronautical engineer; *Scientific Adviser, Office Nationale d'études et de recherches aérospatiales (ONERA);* b. 13 April 1926, Haspres; m. Micheline Robinet 1950; ed Ecole Polytechnique, Ecole Nationale Supérieure Aéronautique et Espace; Service technique de l'aéronautique 1950; Direction des recherches et moyens d'essais 1961; Dir Direction des recherches, études et techniques, Ministry of Defence 1977; Pres. Office Nat. d'études et de recherches aérospatiales (ONERA) 1984–91, Sr Consultant 1991–, Scientific Adviser 1991–; Pres. Man. Cttee Nat. Meteorological Bureau 1989–94; Pres. Comité Avion-Ozone 1992–96; Ed. Aerospace Research 1994–; Co-Ed.-in-Chief Aerospace Science and Technology 1997–, Revue Scientifique et Technique de la Défense; mem. Acad. Nat. de l'Air et de l'Espace; Commdr Légion d'honneur, Ordre Nat. du Mérite; Médaille de l'Aéronautique. *Publications:* Flight Mechanics 1952, Autopilots 1953, Inertial Navigation 1962, Recherche Aéronautique et Progrès de l'Aviation 1999. *Leisure interest:* history. *Address:* Office National d'études et de recherches aérospatiales, 29 avenue de la Division Leclerc, PO Box 72, 92322 Chatillon Cedex, France (office). *Telephone:* 1-46-73-40-01 (office). *Fax:* 1-46-73-41-65 (office). *Website:* www.onera.fr (office).

CARPER, Thomas Richard, BA, MBA; American politician; *Senator from Delaware;* b. 23 Jan. 1947, Beckley, W Va; s. of Wallace Richard Carper and Mary Jean Carper (née Patton); m. Martha Stacy 1986; two s.; ed Ohio State Univ. (Navy ROTC scholarship), Univ. of Delaware; raised in Va; Commdr in USN 1968–73, Capt., USN Reserve 1973–91; industrial devt specialist, then State Treasurer, State of Del., Dover 1976–83; mem. US House of Reps from Del. 1983–93; Gov. of Delaware 1993–2001; Senator from Delaware 2001–, Deputy Whip 2004–11, Co-Chair. Senate Nuclear Caucus, Senate Recycling Caucus, Congressional Fire Services Caucus, Co-Chair. Senate Moderate Democrats Working Group; fmr mem. Nat. Govs Asscn (Vice-Chair. 1997–98, Chair. 1998–99); Hon. Chair. Delaware Special Olympics 1987–; Hon. Co-Chair. Third Way. *Leisure interests:* physical fitness, running, weightlifting, tennis, reading, raising two sons. *Address:* 513 Hart Senate Office Building, Washington, DC 20510 (office); 600 West Matson Run Parkway, Wilmington, DE 19802, USA (home). *Telephone:* (202) 224-2441 (office). *Fax:* (202) 228-2190 (office). *E-mail:* carper@senate.gov (office). *Website:* carper.senate.gov (office).

CARR, Jack, DPhil, FRSE; British mathematician and academic; *Professor Emeritus of Mathematics, Heriot-Watt University;* b. 29 Aug. 1948, Newcastle-upon-Tyne; s. of John George Carr and Elizabeth Eleanor Carr; m. Teresa Nancy Thorpe 1976; one s. two d.; ed Walbottle Secondary School, Univ. of Bath, St Catherine's Coll., Oxford; Lecturer, Heriot-Watt Univ., Edin. 1974–83, Prof. of Math. 1983–, now Emer.; Visiting Prof., Brown Univ., USA 1978–79, Michigan State Univ., USA 1982, Ecole Polytechnique, Lausanne, Switzerland 1983; Chair. Programme Man. Cttee, Int. Congress on Industrial and Applied Math., Edinburgh 1999. *Publication:* Applications of Centre Manifolds 1981. *Leisure interest:* cricket. *Address:* Room S.11, Colin Maclaurin Building, School of Mathematical & Computer Sciences; Mathematics, Heriot-Watt University, Riccarton, Edinburgh, EH14 4AS (office); 42 Balgreen Avenue, Edinburgh, EH12 5SU, Scotland (home). *Telephone:* (131) 451-3220 (office). *Fax:* (131) 451-3249 (office). *E-mail:* j.carr@hw.ac.uk (office). *Website:* www.hw.ac.uk/schools/mathematical-computer-sciences (office).

CARR, James (Jim) Gordon, PC, MP; Canadian journalist, business executive and politician; *Minister of International Trade Diversification;* b. 11 Oct. 1951, Winnipeg; ed Univ. of Manitoba, McGill Univ.; fmr oboe player with Winnipeg Symphony Orchestra (WSO), later becoming WSO Dir of Devt; Exec. Dir Manitoba Arts Council 1973–74; mem. Legis. Ass. of Manitoba 1988–90, 1990–92; mem. Editorial Bd, Winnipeg Free Press 1992–97; Pres. and CEO Business Council of Manitoba 1998–2014; mem. House of Commons (Parl.) for Winnipeg South Centre 2015–; Minister of Natural Resources 2015–18, of Int. Trade Diversification 2018–; Founding Co-Chair., Winnipeg Poverty Reduction Council; fmr Exec. Dir of External Relations, Univ. of Winnipeg; mem. Bd of Dirs Univ. of Manitoba Arthur V. Mauro Centre for Peace and Justice; mem. Liberal Party of Canada, Deputy Leader, Manitoba Liberal Party 1988–92; Dir Emer. Canada West Foundation; Order of Manitoba; Canada 125 Medal, Queen Elizabeth II Diamond Jubilee Medal. *Website:* www.international.gc.ca (office).

CARR, Robert (Bob) John, BA; Australian politician; b. 28 Sept. 1947; s. of Edward Carr and Phyllis Carr; m. Helena Carr; ed Univ. of New South Wales; journalist, ABC Radio 1969–71; Educ. Officer, NSW Council 1972–78; mem. NSW Parl. for Maroubra 1983–2005, Leader of the Opposition of NSW 1988–95, Premier of NSW 1995–2005 (resgnd); Senator for NSW 2012–13; Minister of Foreign Affairs 2012–13; mem. Int. Task Force on Climate Change 2004; mem. Labor Party; Life mem. Wilderness Soc. 2003–; Kt Grand Cross, Order of Merit of the Italian Repub. 2008; World Conservation Union Int. Parks Merit Award. *Publications include:* Thoughtlines 2002, What Australia Means to Me 2003, My Reading Life 2008. *Address:* Australian Labor Party (ALP), POB 6222, Kingston, ACT 2604, Australia (office). *Telephone:* (2) 6120-0800 (office). *Fax:* (2) 6120-0801 (office). *E-mail:* info@cbr.alp.org.au (office). *Website:* www.alp.org.au (office).

CARR, Roderick (Rod) M., LLB, BCom, MA, MBA, PhD; New Zealand central banker, business executive and university administrator; *Vice-Chancellor, University of Canterbury;* b. 26 Nov. 1958; m.; four c.; ed Wharton Business School, Univ. of Pennsylvania, Columbia Univ., New York, USA, Otago Univ.; fmr Head of Global Payments, Nat. Australian Bank, Melbourne; Deputy CEO and Deputy Gov. Reserve Bank of New Zealand –2003, fmr Acting Gov., re-apptd to Reserve Bank Board of Dirs 2012, Chair. 2013–; Man. Dir Jade Software Corpn Ltd 2003–09; Vice-Chancellor, Univ. of Canterbury 2009–; Chair. National Infrastructure Advisory Bd; mem. Bd of Dirs Lyttelton Port Company Ltd, Taranaki Investment Management Ltd, Canterbury Employers' Chamber of Commerce, New Zealand International Business Forum; mem. Otago Business School Bd of Advisers, Univ. of Canterbury Coll. of Business and Econs; Dir Canterbury Employers' Chamber of Commerce 2006–; Fellow, NZ Inst. of Man.; NZ Hi-Tech Co. Leader of the Year 2006. *Publication:* Productivity and Efficiency in the US Life Insurance Industry. *Leisure interests:* running, swimming, hiking. *Address:* Vice-Chancellor's Office, Private Bag 4800, University of Canterbury, Christchurch 8140, New Zealand (office). *Website:* www.canterbury.ac.nz/vco.

CARR, Sir Roger Martyn, Kt, FRSA; British business executive; *Chairman, BAE Systems plc;* b. 22 Dec. 1946; various sr positions, including CEO Williams PLC and Chair. Thames Water PLC 1984–2000; Chair. Chubb PLC 2000–02; mem. Bd of Dirs Centrica plc 2001–14, Chair. 2004–14, also Chair. Nominations Cttee; mem. Bd of Dirs Cadbury-Schweppes plc 2001–, Deputy Chair. 2003–08, Chair. 2008–10; Chair. Mitchells & Butlers plc –2008; Dir (non-exec.) and Chair. BAE Systems plc 2014–; Dir (non-exec.) Six Continents PLC 2002; Pres. CBI 2011–13; Deputy Chair. and Sr Ind. Dir Court of the Bank of England; Sr Adviser, Kohlberg Kravis Roberts Co. Ltd; mem. or fmr mem. Industrial Devt Advisory Bd, Manufacture Council of the CBI, Higgs Cttee on Corp. Governance, Business for New Europe; Trustee, Landau Forte Charitable Trust; Visiting Fellow, Said Business School, Oxford, Companion of the Inst. of Man.; Fellow, Royal Soc. for Encouragement of the Arts, Manufacturers and Commerce; Hon. Fellow, Inst. of Chartered Secretaries and Administrators. *Address:* BAE Systems plc, Stirling Square, 6 Carlton Gardens, London SW1Y 5AD, England (office). *Telephone:* (1252) 373232 (office). *Website:* www.baesystems.com (office).

CARRANZA UGARTE, Luis, BA, LicEcon, MA, PhD; Peruvian economist, banker, government official and academic; *Director, Escuela Profesional de Economía, Universidad de San Martín de Porres;* b. 21 Dec. 1966, Lima; ed Pontifical Catholic Univ. of Peru, Lima, Univ. of Minnesota, USA; worked as official at IMF for several years 1990s; worked in Dept of Econ. Investigation, US Fed. Reserve Bank of Minneapolis 1990s; apptd Deputy Finance Minister and Dir Cen. Bank by Pres. Alejandro Toledo 2004–05 (resgnd); Chief Economist for Latin America and Emerging Markets, Banco Bilbao Vizcaya Argentaria 2005–06; consultant, IDB; Minister of Economy and Finance 2006–08, Jan.–Dec. 2009 (resgnd); Visiting Prof., Univ. of Navarra, Spain; currently Dir Escuela Profesional de Economía, Universidad de San Martín de Porres; named by America Economia magazine as Best Finance Minister of Latin America Nov. 2007. *Address:* Ciudad Universitaria, Jr Las Calandrias 151–291, Santa Anita, Lima 1, Peru (office). *Telephone:* (511) 362-0064 (office). *E-mail:* escuela_economia@usmp.pe (office). *Website:* www.usmp.edu.pe/contabilidadyeconomia/economia.php (office).

CARRARD, François Denis Etienne, Dr iur; Swiss lawyer and fmr international organization official; *Partner, Kellerhals Carrard;* b. 19 Jan. 1938, Lausanne; ed Lausanne, John Muir High School, Pasadena, Calif., USA, Univ. of Lausanne; attorney with audit co., Lausanne 1962–63; with law firm, Stockholm, Sweden 1963–64; attorney, Lausanne 1965–, admitted to Bar of Vaud (Swiss Bar) 1967, Sr Partner, Etude Carrard, Paschoud, Heim et Associés (renamed Carrard & Associés, now Kellerhals Carrard) 1967–; Dir-Gen. IOC 1989–2003, currently Sr Adviser in charge of legal affairs; Pres. Presses Centrales Lausanne SA; regularly involved in int. arbitration proceedings, including before the Court of Arbitration for Sport and various chambers of commerce; Chair. Montreux Jazz Festival Foundation; fmr Pres. Automobile-Club de Suisse; fmr Vice-Pres. Bd of Vintage Brands of Vaud; fmr mem. Swiss Fed. Comm. of Foreign Indemnities; mem. Ordre des Avocats Vaudois, Fédération Suisse des Avocats, Int. Bar Asscn, Asscn Suisse de l'Arbitrage, Union Internationale des Avocats; Chair. and Dir of various cos; Commdr, Orden del Mérito Civil (Spain) 1992, Officier, Ordre de Saint-Charles (Monaco) 1993. *Address:* Kellerhals Carrard, PO Box 7191, Place Saint-François 1, 1002 Lausanne, Switzerland (office). *Telephone:* (58) 2003300 (office). *Fax:* (58) 2003311 (office). *E-mail:* francois.carrard@kellerhals-carrard.ch (office). *Website:* www.kellerhals-carrard.ch (office).

CARRARO, Franco; Italian sports administrator, business executive and politician; b. 6 Dec. 1939, Padua; m.; two c.; Pres. Italian Water-skiing Fed. 1962–65, Chair. Tech. Comm. 1963–67; Chair. World Water-skiing Union 1967–73; Chair. Associazione Calcio (AC) Milan football team 1967–71; with Italian Football Fed. (FIGC) 1970s, Pres. Italian League of Serie A and B 1973–76, Pres. Italian Football Fed. (Federazione Italiana Gioco Calcio) 1976–78, 1997–2001, 2001–06, Extraordinary Commr 1986–87; Pres. CONI 1978–87; fmr Chair. Comm. for Amateur and Professional Football; fmr Chair. Sub-comm. for Professional Football, UEFA, mem. UEFA Exec. Cttee 2004–09; Vice-Pres. Italian Nat. Olympic Cttee 1976–78, Pres. 1978–; Vice-Pres. Alitalia 1981–87; Minister of Tourism and Performing Arts 1987–90; Mayor of Rome 1989–93; Chair. Impregilio 1994–99; Pres. MCC—Mediocredito Centrale SpA (bank) from 2000; mem. Int. Olympic Cttee 1982–, Vice-Chair. Comm. for the Olympic Programme 1983–94, Chair. Olympic Programme Working Group 1998–2001, mem. Exec. Bd 2000–04, Chair. Olympic Programme Comm. 2002–; Chair. Asscn of European Olympic Cttees 1980–87; Chair. Organizing Cttee World Cup Football Championship 1990; mem. Italian Socialist Party 1980s–94, The People of Freedom 2009–13, Forza Italia 2013–18; Senator for Emilia Romagna 2013–18. *Achievements include:* fmr champion water skier, Italian jr champion 1953–54, Italian Open champion 1955–60, European champion, slalom and combined 1956 and 1961, European team champion 1958, 1959, 1960; bronze medallist, World Championships 1957. *Address:* Senato Della Repubblica, Piazza Madama, 00186 Rome, Italy (office). *Telephone:* (06) 67061 (switchboard) (office). *E-mail:* franco.carraro@senato.it (office). *Website:* www.senato.it/leg/17/BGT/Schede/Attsen/00000500.htm (office).

CARRASQUILLA BARRERA, Alberto, BS, MS, PhD; Colombian economist, politician and business executive; *Minister of Finance and Public Credit;* b. 24 April 1957, Bogotá; ed Univ. of Los Andes, Univ. of Illinois, USA; Tech. Man., Banco de la República 1993–97; Prin. Economist, Investigation Div., IDB, Washington, DC 1997–99; Econ. Adviser, Gen. Republic Controllership 1999–2000; fmr Assoc. Teacher, Univ. of Los Andes, Dean Faculty of Econs 2000–02; Deputy Minister of Finance 2002–03, Minister of Finance 2003–07, of Finance and Public Credit 2018–; fmr Partner and CEO Capital Konfigura; Chair.

Textiles Fabricato Tejicondor. *Address:* Ministry of Finance and Public Credit, Carrera 8, No 6c-38, Of. 305, Bogotá, DC, Colombia (office). *Telephone:* (1) 381-1700 (office). *Fax:* (1) 381-2863 (office). *E-mail:* atencioncliente@minhacienda.gov.co (office). *Website:* www.minhacienda.gov.co (office).

CARRELL, Robin Wayne, MA, PhD, DSc, FRS, FRCP, FRSNZ; New Zealand haematologist and academic; *Professor of Haematology, University of Cambridge;* b. 5 April 1936, Christchurch; s. of Ruane George Carrell and Constance Gwendoline Carrell (née Rowe); m. Susan Wyatt Rogers 1962; two s. two d.; ed Christchurch Boys' High School, Univs of Otago and Canterbury, Univ. of Cambridge, UK; mem. MRC Haemoglobin Unit, Cambridge 1965–68; Dir Clinical Biochemistry, Christchurch Hosp., NZ 1968–75; Lecturer in Clinical Biochemistry, Univ. of Cambridge 1976–78, Prof. of Haematology 1986–; Prof. of Clinical Biochemistry and Dir Molecular Research Lab., Christchurch Clinical School of Medicine, Otago Univ. 1978–86; Commonwealth Fellow, St John's Coll., Cambridge and Visiting Scientist, MRC Lab. of Molecular Biology 1985; Gov. Imperial Coll. London 1997–98, mem. Court 1999–2003; Pres. British Soc. of Thrombosis and Haemostasis 1999; Fellow, Trinity Coll., Cambridge 1987–; Royal Soc. of New Zealand Hector Medal 1986. *Publications:* articles in scientific journals on genetic abnormalities of human proteins and new protein family, serpins. *Leisure interests:* topiary, walking. *Address:* 19 Madingley Road, Cambridge, CB3 0EG (home); Trinity College, Cambridge, CB2 1TP, England (office). *Telephone:* (1223) 312970 (office). *E-mail:* rwc1000@cam.ac.uk (office).

CARREÑO, José Manuel; Cuban ballet dancer; *Artistic Director, Silicon Valley Ballet;* b. 25 May 1968, Havana; ed Prov. School of Ballet and Nat. Ballet School, Cuba; with Nat. Ballet of Cuba 1986–90; joined English Nat. Ballet 1990; Prin. Dancer, The Royal Ballet 1993–95; Prin. Dancer, American Ballet Theatre 1995–2011; numerous appearances in Europe, Latin America, USA and Japan; Artistic Dir The Carreño-Barbieri Festival, Sarasota, Fla; Artistic Dir Ballet San Jose (renamed Silicon Valley Ballet 2015) 2013–; Gold Medal, NY Int. Ballet Competition 1987, Grand Prix, Int. Ballet Competetition, Jackson, MS 1990, Dance Magazine Award 2004. *Repertoire as dancer:* (with English Nat. Ballet): Solor in La Bayadère, the Prince in Cinderella, Franz in Coppélia, Albrecht in Giselle, the Prince and the Gopak in The Nutcracker, Romeo in Romeo and Juliet, Petruchio in The Taming of the Shrew, pas de deux in A Stranger I Came, Graduation Ball and Prince Igor; (with The Royal Ballet): Bluebird in The Sleeping Beauty, Basilio in Don Quixote, Oberon and Puck in The Dream, leading role in Caught Dance and Herman Schmerman; (with American Ballet Theatre): title role in Apollo, leading role in Ballet Imperial, Conrad, Ali, the Slave and Lanckendem in Le Corsaire, third sailor in Fancy Free, Danilo in The Merry Widow, pas de deux in The Nutcracker, leading role in Push Comes to Shove, the Son in Prodigal Son, Romeo and Mercutio in Romeo and Juliet, Prince Desire in The Sleeping Beauty, Misgir in The Snow Maiden, Prince Siegfield in Swan Lake, leading role Études, Themes and Variations, Stepping Stones, Raymonda, Petit Mort. *Film:* Born to be Wild (PBS). *Address:* Silicon Valley Ballet, 40 North First Street, San Jose, CA 95113, USA (office). *Telephone:* (408) 288-2820 (office). *Fax:* (408) 993-9570 (office). *E-mail:* jcarreno@aol.com (home). *Website:* siliconvalleyballet.org (office).

CARRERAS, José; Spanish singer (tenor); b. (Josep Maria Carreras i Coll), 5 Dec. 1947, Barcelona; s. of José Carreras and Antonia Carreras; m. Ana Elisa Carreras; one s. one d.; opera debut as Gennaro in Lucrezia Borgia, Liceo Opera House, Barcelona 1970–71 season; appeared in La Bohème, Un Ballo in Maschera and I Lombardi alla Prima Crociata at Teatro Regio, Parma, Italy 1972; US debut as Pinkerton in Madame Butterfly with New York City Opera 1972; debut at Metropolitan Opera as Cavaradossi 1974; debut at La Scala as Riccardo in Un Ballo in Maschera 1975; has appeared at major opera houses and festivals including Teatro Colón, Buenos Aires, Covent Garden, London, Vienna Staatsoper, Easter Festival and Summer Festival, Salzburg, Lyric Opera of Chicago; Founding mem. (with the late Luciano Pavorotti and Plácido Domingo) Three Tenors 1990; Founder and Pres. Josep Carreras Int. Leukaemia Foundation 1988–; Hon. Pres. London Arts Orchestra; Hon. mem. RAM 1990, European Soc. for Medicine, Leukaemia Support Group, European Haematology Asscn, German Soc. of Paediatric Oncology and Haematology; Hon. Patron European Soc. for Medical Oncology; Hon. Rector, Hyunghee Hon.; Commdr des Arts et des Lettres, Chevalier, Légion d'honneur, Gran Croce di Cavaliere (Italy), Komandor's Cross of Order of Merit (Poland), Commandeur de la Médaille du Sahametrei (Cambodia), Civil Order Golden Cross of Social Solidarity (Spain), Nat. Order Steaua Romaniei (Romania), Grand Cross, Order of Merit (Germany); Dr hc (Univ. of Barcelona), (Univ. of Loughborough), (Univ. of Sheffield), (Univ. Mendeleyev of Moscow), (Univ. of Camerino), (Napier Univ., Edinburgh), (Rutgers Univ.), (Miguel Hernández Univ. of Elche), (Univ. of Coimbra), (National Univ. of Music, Bucharest), Univ. of Marburg), (Univ. of Pécs), (Univ. of Porto); Grammy Award 1991, Sir Laurence Olivier Award 1993, Gold Medal of City of Barcelona, Albert Schweizer Music Award 1996, ECHO Klassik Lifetime Achievement Award 2008, Classical BRIT Lifetime Achievement Award 2009, Honour Medal of Bavarian Govt, Grand Honour Award of Austrian Republic, Gold Medal of New York Spanish Inst., Hon. Gold Medal of Vienna and Medal of Honour in Gold of the Federal Capital of Vienna, Gold Medal of Fine Arts of Spain, Gold Medal of the Generalitat of Catalunya, Gold Medal of the Gran Teatre del Liceu, Hon. Medal of the City of Leipzig, Prince of Asturias Award 1991, among numerous other awards and prizes. *Recordings include:* Un Ballo in Maschera, La Battaglia di Legnano, Il Corsaro, Un Giorno di Regno, I Due Foscari, Simone Boccanegra, Macbeth, Don Carlos, Tosca, Thais, Aida, Cavalleria Rusticana, Pagliacci, Lucia di Lammermoor, Turandot, Elisabetta, regina d'Inghilterra, Otello (Rossini). *Films include:* La Bohème, I Lombardi, Andrea Chenier, Turandot, Carmen, Don Carlos, La Forza del Destino, Fedora, Jerusalem, My Life. *Publication:* Singing from the Soul 1991. *Address:* c/o Josep Carreras International Leukaemia Foundation, Muntaner 383, 2nd Floor, 08021 Barcelona, Spain (office). *E-mail:* info@fcarreras.es (office). *Website:* www.fcarreras.org/en (office).

CARRÈRE D'ENCAUSSE, Hélène, DèsSc; French political scientist; *Perpetual Secretary, Académie française;* b. 6 July 1929, Paris; d. of Georges Zourabichvili and Nathalie von Pelken; m. Louis Carrère 1952; one s. two d.; ed Univ. of Paris (Sorbonne); fmr Prof., Univ. of Paris (Sorbonne); currently Prof., Inst. d'Etudes Politiques, Paris and Dir of Research, Fondation Nationale des Sciences Politiques; Pres. Radio Sorbonne-Radio France 1984–87; Advisor on Reconstruction and Devt, European Bank 1992; fmr mem. Bd of Dirs East-West Inst. for Security Studies; Visiting Prof. at numerous univs in USA; mem. Acad. française 1990–, Perpetual Sec. 1999–; Foreign mem. Russian Acad. of Sciences 2003–, Acad. of Georgia; Assoc. mem. Acad. Royale de Belgique; mem. European Parl. 1994–99; fmr Vice-Pres. Comm. on Foreign Affairs and Defence, on French Diplomatic Archives; mem. Nat. Council for New Devts in Human and Social Sciences 1998; Pres. Statistical Observatory on Immigration and Integration 2004; Hon. mem. Acad. of Georgia; Commdr, Order of Cultural Merit (Monaco) 1999; Grand-Croix de la Légion d'honneur 2011; Officier, Ordre nat. du Mérite; Commdr des Palmes académiques, des Arts et des Lettres, Ordre de Léopold de Belgique; Dr hc (Montréal, Louvain); Prix de la Fondation Louis-Weiss 1986, Prix Comenius 1992, Lomonosov Gold Medal, Russian Acad. of Sciences 2008. *Publications include:* Le marxisme et l'Asie 1965, Réforme et révolution chez les musulmans de l'Empire russe 1966, L'URSS et la Chine devant les révolutions dans les sociétés pré-industrielles 1970, L'Empire éclaté (Prix Aujourd'hui) 1978, Lénine: la révolution et le pouvoir 1979, Staline: l'ordre par la terreur 1979, Le pouvoir confisqué 1982, Le Grand Frère 1983, La déstalinisation commence 1984, Ni paix ni guerre 1986, Le Grand Défi: bolcheviks et nations 1917–30 1987, Le Malheur russe 1988, La Gloire des nations ou la fin de l'Empire soviétique 1991, Victorieuse Russie 1992, Nicholas II: la transition interrompue (Prix des Ambassadeurs) 1996, Lénine 1998, La Russie inachevée 2000, Catherine II 2002, L'Impératrice et l'abbé un duel littéraire ivédit 2003, L'Empire d'Eurasie 2005, La Deuxième Mort de Staline 2006, Alexandre II. Le printemps de la Russie 2008, La Russie entre deux mondes 2010, Des siècles d'immortalité. L'Académie française 1635–. . . 2011, Les Romanov – Une dynastie sous le règne du sang 2013, Six années qui ont changé le monde 1985–1991 2015, Le général de Gaulle et la Russie 2017. *Address:* Académie française, 23 quai Conti, 75270 Paris Cedex 06 – CS 90618, France (office). *Telephone:* 1-44-41-43-00 (office). *Fax:* 1-43-29-47-45 (office). *E-mail:* contact@academie-francaise.fr (office). *Website:* www.academie-francaise.fr (office).

CARREY, James Eugene Redmond (Jim); Canadian/American film actor; b. 17 Jan. 1962, Newmarket, Ont., Canada; s. of Percy Carrey and Kathleen Carrey; m. 1st Melissa Worner 1987 (divorced 1995); one d.; m. 2nd Lauren Holly 1996 (divorced 1997); began performing in comedy clubs in Toronto aged 17, before moving to Los Angeles 1979; American Film Inst. Star Award 2005. *Films include:* All in Good Taste 1983, The Sex and Violence Family Hour 1983, Introducing. . . Janet 1983, Copper Mountain 1983, Finders Keepers 1984, Once Bitten 1985, Peggy Sue Got Married 1986, The Dead Pool 1988, Earth Girls Are Easy 1988, Pink Cadillac 1989, The Itsy Bitsy Spider (voice) 1992, Ace Ventura: Pet Detective (also screenplay) (London Critics' Circle Film Award for Newcomer of the Year) 1994, The Mask 1994, High Strung 1994, Dumb & Dumber 1994, Batman Forever 1995, Ace Ventura: When Nature Calls 1995, The Cable Guy (MTV Movie Award) 1996, Liar Liar (Blockbuster Entertainment Award) 1997, The Truman Show (Golden Globe for Best Performance 1999) 1998, Simon Birch 1998, Man on the Moon (Golden Globe for Best Performance 2000) 1999, Me, Myself & Irene 2000, How the Grinch Stole Christmas 2000, The Majestic 2001, Bruce Almighty 2003, Pecan Pie 2003, Eternal Sunshine of the Spotless Mind 2004, Lemony Snicket's A Series of Unfortunate Events 2004, Fun with Dick and Jane 2005, The Number 23 2007, Horton Hears a Who! (voice) 2008, Yes Man (MTV Movie Award for Best Comedic Performance) 2008, I Love You Phillip Morris 2009, A Christmas Carol (Kids' Choice Award) 2009, Mr Popper's Penguins 2011, The Incredible Burt Wonderstone 2013, Kick-Ass 2 2013, Dumb and Dumber To 2014, The Bad Batch 2016. *Television includes:* The Duck Factory (series) 1984, Mike Hammer: Murder Takes All 1989, In Living Color (series, also writer) (TV Land Award for Groundbreaking Show 2012) 1990–94, Doing Time on Maple Drive 1992, The Office (series) 2011, 30 Rock (series) 2012. *Address:* c/o WME Entertainment, 9601 Wilshire Boulevard, Beverley Hills, CA 90210-5213, USA (office). *Telephone:* (310) 285-9000 (office). *Fax:* (310) 285-9010 (office). *Website:* www.wmeentertainment.com (office); www.jimcarrey.com.

CARRICK, Sir Roger John, Kt, KCMG, LVO; British international consultant and fmr diplomatist; *Chairman, Lime Finance;* b. 13 Oct. 1937, Middx, England; s. of John Carrick and Florence Carrick; m. Hilary E. Blinman 1962; two s.; ed Isleworth Grammar School, Jt Services School for Linguists and School of Slavonic and E European Studies, Univ. of London; RN 1956–58; joined HM Diplomatic Service 1956; served in Sofia 1962, FCO 1965, Paris 1967, Singapore 1971, FCO 1973–77; Visiting Fellow, Inst. of Int. Affairs, Univ. of Calif., Berkeley 1977–78; Counsellor, Washington, DC 1978; Head, Overseas Estate Dept FCO 1982; Consul-Gen., Chicago 1985–88; Asst Under-Sec. of State (Econ.), FCO 1988–90; Amb. to Indonesia 1990–94; High Commr to Australia 1994–97 (retd); currently Chair. Lime Finance; Deputy Chair. Britain-Australia Soc. 1998–99, Chair. 1999–2002, Vice-Pres. 2003–, Pres. West Country Br. 2003–; Dir (non-exec.) cmb technologies 2000–02; Chair. (non-exec.), Charteris Mackie & Baillie Ltd 2001–03; Deputy Chair. The D Group 1999–2007; Dir Strategy International Ltd 2001–07, Chair. 2007–09; Trustee, Chevening Estate 1998–2003, Britain-Australia Bicentennial Trust; Churchill Fellow, Westminster Coll., Mo. 1986; Freeman of the City of London 2002. *Publications:* East-West Technology Transfer in Perspective 1978, RolleroundOz: Reflections on a Journey Around Australia 1998, Admiral Arthur Phillip RN, Founder and First Governor of Australia: A British View 2011, Diplomatic Anecdotage: Around the World in 40 Years 2012. *Leisure interests:* sailing, reading, music, theatre, travel, public speaking, avoiding gardening. *Address:* Lime Finance, Queen's Gardens, 31 Ironmarket, Newcastle-under-Lyme, Staffs., ST5 1RP, England (office). *Telephone:* (1782) 638500 (office). *Fax:* (1782) 617577 (office). *E-mail:* info@lime-finance.com (office). *Website:* lime-finance.com (office).

CARRIER, Jean-Guy; Canadian business executive and international organization official; various positions with Int. Inst. for Systems Analysis, Vienna, Austria, Econ. Council of Canada, CBC and with several global communications consulting firms; several sr positions with WTO 1996–2008, including Publr and Chief Ed.; Acting Sec.-Gen., ICC 2010–11, Sec.-Gen. 2011–14, also Dir of Programmes, ICC Research Foundation; mem. UN Global Compact Bd. *Publications include:* My Father's House 1974, Family 1977, A Cage of Bone 1978, The Trudeau Decade (co-author) 1979, Patriots and Traitors 1992, The End of War 1992; numerous articles in nat. and int. media. *Address:* c/o International Chamber of Commerce, 38 cours Albert 1er, 75008 Paris, France.

CARRIÈRE, J. A. Berthold (Bert), OC, BMus, MMus; Canadian composer and music director; b. 27 Feb. 1940, Ottawa; s. of Rolland Carrière and Berthe Carrière (Paradis); m. Nancy Carpenter 1969; ed Univs of Montreal and Western Ontario; began piano studies aged four; played trombone at Ottawa Tech. High School; early work as arranger and conductor of music for CBC radio and TV 1960–63, 1966–68; school teacher, Ottawa area 1965–68; directing several shows for Orpheus Operatic Soc., Ottawa 1965–69; Conductor/Arranger, Dominion Day Celebrations before HM Queen Elizabeth 1967; Musical Dir, Banff School of Fine Arts 1968–72; Resident Musical Dir, Theatre London 1972–74, Dir of Music 1976–77, Assoc. Dir 1976; Dir of Music, Stratford Festival 1976–83, 1985–2007, conducted The Music Man 2008; Musical Dir, Talk of Toronto 1980–82; Mem. Order of Canada 2001; Man of the Year, City of Ottawa 1967, Special Tribute Guthrie Award, Stratford Shakespearean Festival 1975, Dora Mavor Moore Musical Dir Award 1981, 1982, 1987, Alumni Professional Achievement Award, Univ. of Western Ontario 2000, Queen's Golden Jubilee Medal 2003. *Address:* Box 1273, St Mary's, Ont., N0M 2V0 (home); c/o Stratford Festival, PO Box 1013, Stratford, Ont., N5A 6W4, Canada.

CARRILLO ZÜRCHER, Federico, LLB; Costa Rican lawyer, banker and fmr government official; b. 29 Sept. 1964, San José; m.; four c.; ed Austin Community Coll. and Univ. of Texas, USA, Univ. of Costa Rica, Saïd Business School, Oxford, UK; attorney, Zurcher, Odio y Raven 1982–90; Fulbright-Hats Scholarship, Northwestern Univ., Evanston, Ill., USA 1990; Sr Vice-Pres. (Exec. Dir), Lehman Brothers, New York 1992–2000; CEO Bolsa Nacional de Valores (Costa Rican Stock Exchange) 2000–04; Dir Tech. Advisory Cttee on Civil Aviation 2004; Minister of Finance and Chair. Econ. Council 2004–05; Exec. Vice-Pres. Central American Bank for Econ. Integration 2005–06; CEO Banco Internacional de Costa Rica SA, Panama City 2007–13; CEO, Sponsor and Investor, New Trade Finance Bank (In Formation) 2013–. *Website:* federicocarrillo.com; www.facebook.com/pages/FCZ-Federico-Carrillo-Zürcher/138587166327996.

CARRINGTON, Edwin Wilberforce, MSc; Trinidad and Tobago economist and international organization official; *Ambassador, Caribbean Community and Common Market (CARICOM);* b. 23 June 1938; m.; two s. one d.; ed Univ. of the West Indies, McGill Univ., Montreal, Canada; Admin. Cadet, Cen. Planning Unit, Prime Minister's Office 1964; Chief of Econs and Statistics, Caribbean Community and Common Market (CARICOM) 1973–76, Dir Trade and Integration Div. 1973–76, Sec.-Gen. CARICOM 1992–2010 (retd), Amb. to CARICOM 2011–; Deputy Sec.-Gen. African, Caribbean and Pacific (ACP) states 1976–85, Sec.-Gen. 1985; High Commr to Guyana 1991; Sec.-Gen. Caribbean Forum ACP states; Duarte Sanchez y Mella, Gran Cruz de Plata (Dominican Repub.) 1993, Trinity Cross (Trinidad and Tobago 2005, Chaconia Medal Gold (Trinidad and Tobago) 1987, Order of Distinction (Belize) 2001, Companion of Honour (Barbados) 2002, Order of Jamaica (Jamaica) 2003, Cacique Crown of Honour (Guyana) 2003, Cacique's Crown of Honour (Guyana) 2004, Kt Commdr of Most Distinguished Order of Nation (Antigua and Barbuda) 2010, Order of Caribbean Community 2011; Dr hc (Univ. of the West Indies) 2005, (Medgar Evers Coll., CUNY) 1995; Pinnacle Award Nat. Coalition of Caribbean Affairs. *Publications include:* Industrialization by Invitation: The Case of Trinidad and Tobago 1968, The Solution of Economic Problems through Regional Groupings (jtly), Tourism as a Vehicle for Economic Development 1975. *Address:* Colgrain House, 205 Camp Street, Georgetown, Guyana (home).

CARRINGTON, Ruth (see JAMES, Michael Leonard).

CARRIZALES RENGIFO, Col (retd) Rámon Alonso; Venezuelan army officer (retd) and politician; *Governor of Apure;* b. 8 Nov. 1952, Zaraza, Guarico; m. Yuviri del Carmen Ortega Lovera; three c.; ed Venezuelan Acad. of Mil. Sciences; fmr Col of Venezuelan Armed Forces, retd 1994; Chair. Fondo Nacional de Transporte Urbano (Fontur) 2000–04; Minister of Infrastructure 2004–07, of Housing 2007–08, of Nat. Defence 2009–10 and Vice-Pres. of Venezuela 2008–10 (resgnd); Acting Gov. of Apure 2011–12, Gov. of Apure 2012–. *Address:* Office of the Governor, San Fernando de Apure, Apure, Venezuela (office). *E-mail:* info@apure.gob.ve (office). *Website:* www.apure.gob.ve (office).

CARROLL, Cynthia, MSc, MBA; American business executive; m.; four c.; ed Skidmore Coll., Univ. of Kansas, Harvard Univ.; fmr Sr Petroleum Geologist, Amoco, USA; joined Rolled Products Group, Alcan 1988, apptd Gen. Man. Foil Products, USA 1991, Man. Dir Aughinish Alumina, Ireland, Pres. Bauxite, Alumina and Speciality Chemicals Group 1998–2002, Pres. and CEO Alcan Primary Metal Group 2002–06, also Officer, Alcan Inc., Montreal; Chief Exec. Anglo American plc, London 2007–13, Chair. Exec. Cttee, Chief Exec.'s Cttee, mem. Safety Cttee, Sustainable Devt Cttee; fmr mem. Bd of Dirs AngloGold Ashanti Ltd, Sara Lee Corpn; Chair. Anglo Platinum Ltd; Dir (non-exec.) BP plc, De Beers; Hon. DSc.

CARRON, René Joseph; French banking executive; b. 13 June 1942, Yenne, Savoie; s. of Albert Carron and Claudine Philippe Carron (née Genoud); m. Françoise Dupasquier 1963; three s. one d.; fmr dairy farmer in Yenne; Pres. Yenne br. Crédit Agricole 1981–, Pres. regional br. in Savoie 1992, all Savoie 1994, mem. Bureau 1995–2010, Pres. Fédération nationale du crédit agricole 2000–03, Vice-Pres. 2003–10, Dir 1999–2010, Vice-Pres. Caisse nationale de crédit agricole (CNCA, renamed Crédit Agricole SA 2000) 2000–10, mem. Supervisory Council, Crédit Agricole Indosuez 2000–, Chair. Crédit Agricole SA 2002–10; Chair. SAS Rue La Boétie 2001–03; Deputy Chair. Confédération Nationale de la Mutualité, de la Coopération et du Crédit Agricole; Pres. Int. Confed. for Agricultural Credit (CICA) 2005–; fmr Co-Deputy Chair. Intesa Sanpaolo SpA (fmrly Banca Intesa SpA); mem. or fmr mem. Bd of Dirs, GDF Suez, Crédit Agricole Indosuez SA, Soc. de banque de financement pour le commerce (Sofinco), Rue Impériale, Crédit Agricole Solidarité et Développement, Fondation du Crédit Agricole Pays de France, Sacam (SAS), Sapacam (SAS), Suez SA, Fiat SpA 2007–14, Caisse Locale de Crédit Agricole de Yenne, Gecam (GIE); mem. Supervisory Bd Lagardere SCA 2004–, Lagardere Active Broadcast 2008–; Pres. Savoie Chamber of Agric. 1983–92, Savoie 92 (asscn to promote Winter Olympics in Albertville 1992) 1988–92, Mission prospective du département de la Savoie 1988–98, Groupe d'étude et de mobilisation Espaces ruraux 1991, Steering Cttee for Savoie Strategic Plan Year 2000 1991–98; Counsellor Banque de France de la Savoie 1991– (mem. 1992–, mem. Perm. Comm. 1992–), Conseil d'admin de l'org. du dialogue et de l'intelligence sociale dans la société et l'entreprise (Odisée) 2006–; Vice-Pres. Conseil géneral of Savoie 1995–98; Mayor of Yenne 1995–2001; mem. Econ. and Social Council 2000–03, Man. Bd. Groupement Européen des Banques Coopératives; Officier, Légion d'honneur, Ordre nat. du Mérite; Chevalier des Arts et des Lettres; Commdr du Mérite agricole. *Address:* Crédit Agricole SA, 91–93 boulevard Pasteur, 75015 Paris, France (office). *Telephone:* 1-43-23-52-02 (office). *Fax:* 1-43-23-34-48 (office). *E-mail:* info@credit-agricole-sa.fr (office). *Website:* www.credit-agricole-sa.fr (office).

CARSBERG, Sir Bryan (Victor), Kt, MSc(Econ); British public servant, academic and chartered accountant; b. 3 Jan. 1939, London; s. of Alfred Victor Carsberg and Maryllia Ciceley Carsberg (née Collins); m. Margaret Linda Graham 1960; two d.; ed London School of Econs; accounting practice 1962–64; Lecturer in Accounting, LSE 1964–68, Arthur Andersen Prof. of Accounting 1981–87, Visiting Prof. 1987–89; Visiting Lecturer, Grad. School of Business, Univ. of Chicago 1968–69; Prof. of Accounting, Univ. of Manchester 1969–78; Visiting Prof. of Business Admin., Univ. of California, Berkeley 1974; Asst Dir Research and Tech. Activities, US Financial Accounting Standards Bd 1978–81; Dir of Research, Inst. of Chartered Accountants in England and Wales 1981–87; Dir-Gen. of Telecommunications, Oftel 1984–92; mem. Accounting Standards Bd 1990–94 (Vice-Chair. 1990–92); Dir-Gen. of Fair Trading 1992–95; Sec.-Gen. Int. Accounting Standards Cttee 1995–2001; Chair. Pensions Compensation Bd 2001–04; Chair. MLL Telecoms Ltd 1999–2002; Pres. Locus 2005–12, e-Homebuying Forum 2010–12; mem. Bd of Dir Nynex Cable Communications 1996–97, Cable & Wireless Communications 1997–2000, RM plc 2002–12, Philip Allan (publrs), Novae Group plc 2003–15, Inmarsat plc 2005–, Actual Experience plc 2014–; mem. Bd Radio Communications Agency 1990–92, Council of Univ. of Surrey 1990–92, Council of Loughborough Univ. 1999–2011 (Chair. 2001–11), Equality of Access Bd at BT plc 2005–13, Governing Council, Royal Inst. of Chartered Surveyors 2010–13; Hon. Fellow, LSE, Hon. FIA, Hon. RICS; Hon. DSc (East Anglia) 1992, Hon. DLitt (Loughborough) 1994, Hon. DUniv (Essex) 1995, Hon. LLD (Bath) 1990, Dr hc (Nottingham Trent) 2008; Inst. Medal, W.B. Peat Medal and Prize, Inst. of Chartered Accountants, England, Chartered Accountants Founding Socs Centenary Award 1988, Blaew Prize for Telecommunications 1992, Sempier Award, Int. Fed. of Accountants 2002. *Publications include:* An Introduction to Mathematical Programming for Accountants 1969, Analysis for Investment Decisions 1974, Economics of Business Decisions 1975 and others. *Leisure interests:* theatre, music, opera, physics. *E-mail:* bryan.carsberg@ntlworld.com (home).

CARSON, Anne, BA, MA, PhD; Canadian academic, poet and writer; b. 21 June 1950, Toronto, Ont.; m. Robert Currie; ed St Michael's Coll., Univ. of Toronto, Univ. of St Andrews, Scotland; Prof. of Classics, Univ. of Calgary 1979–80, Princeton Univ. 1980–87, Emory Univ. 1987–88; fmr John MacNaughton Prof. of Classics, McGill Univ. and Dir of Grad. Studies, Classics; fmr Prof., Dept of English, Univ. of Michigan; Fellow, John D. and Catherine T. MacArthur Foundation 2001; Anna-Maria Kellen Fellow, American Acad., Berlin, Germany 2007; Inga Maren Otto Fellowship, Watermill Center 2018; Dr hc (Univ. of Toronto) 2012; Lannan Literary Award 1996, Pushcart Prize for Poetry 1997, Guggenheim Fellowship 1999. *Publications include:* Eros the Bittersweet: An Essay 1986, Short Talks 1992, Plainwater 1995, Glass, Irony and God 1995, Autobiography of Red 1998, Economy of the Unlost 1999, Men in the Off Hours (Griffin Poetry Prize 2001) 2000, The Beauty of the Husband (Poetry Book Soc. T. S. Eliot Prize 2001) 2001, Sophocles' Electra 2001, If Not, Winter: Fragments of Sappho (trans.) 2002, Decreation 2005, Grief Lessons: Four Plays by Euripides (trans.) 2006, An Oresteia (trans.) (PEN Award for Poetry in Translation 2010) 2009, Nox 2010, Antigonick 2012, Red Doc (Griffin Poetry Prize 2014) 2013, The Albertine Workout 2014, Nay Rather 2014, Float 2016, Bakkhai 2017; poetry: The Glass Essay 1997, Short Talk on Herbology 2013, Pronoun Envy 2014, Saturday Night as an Adult 2017; contrib. to anthologies and journals. *Address:* c/o Academy of American Poets, 75 Maiden Lane, Suite 901, New York, NY 10038, USA.

CARSON, Benjamin (Ben) Solomon, Sr, MD; American author and neurosurgeon (retd) and government official; *Secretary of Housing and Urban Development;* b. 18 Sept. 1951, Detroit, Mich.; s. of Robert Solomon Carson and Sonya Carson (née Copeland); m. Candy Carson; three c.; ed Yale Univ., Univ. of Michigan Medical School; surgical intern, Johns Hopkins Hosp., Baltimore, Md 1977–78, neurosurgery resident 1978–82, Chief Resident, Fellow of Neurological Surgery 1982–83, Dir, Div. of Pediatric Neurosurgery 1984–2013, Co-Dir Johns Hopkins Cleft & Craniofacial Center 1991–2013; Asst Prof. of Neurological Surgery and of Oncology, Johns Hopkins School of Medicine 1984–91, Asst Prof. of Pediatrics 1987–96, Assoc. Prof. of Neurological Surgery, Oncology, Plastic Surgery and Pediatrics 1991–99, Prof. 1999–2013; Sr Neurosurgical Resident, Loch Raven Hosp., Baltimore 1980, Baltimore City Hospitals 1981; Sr Registrar, Sir Charles Gairdner Hosp., Perth, W Australia 1983–84; mem. Bd of Dirs Kellogg Co. 1997–, Costco Wholesale Corpn 1999–; mem. Advisory Bd Vaccinogen, Inc. 2014–, Chair. 2014–; weekly columnist, The Washington Times 2013–; contributor, FOX News 2013–14; announced candidacy for Republican nomination for Pres. of US May 2015 (withdrew March 2016); Sec. of Housing and Urban Devt 2017–; Emer. Fellow, Yale Corpn; mem. American Acad. of Achievement, Horatio Alger Asscn of Distinguished Americans, NAS Inst. of Medicine, American Medical Asscn, AAAS, American Asscn of Neurological Surgeons, Nat. Medical Asscn; more than 60 hon. doctorate degrees; numerous awards including Liberty Bell Award, Philadelphia 1987, Loyola Coll. Andrew White Medal 1989, George Washington Carver Award 1993, Johns Hopkins Hosp. Martin Luther King, Jr Award for Community Service 1994, Jefferson Award for Greatest Public Service Benefiting the Disadvantaged 2000, Fords Theatre Lincoln Medal, The White House 2008, Presidential Medal of Freedom 2008. *Achievements include:* first surgeon to successfully separate conjoined twins joined at the head 1987. *Publications include:* Gifted Hands 1989, Think Big 1996, The Big Picture 1999, Take the Risk: Learning to Identify, Choose, and Live with Acceptable Risk 2008, America the Beautiful: Rediscovering What Made This Nation Great 2011, One Nation: What We Can All Do to Save America's Future 2014; numerous book chapters and articles in professional journals. *Address:* Department of Housing and Urban Development, 451 Seventh St, SW, Washington, DC 20410, USA (office). *Telephone:* (202) 708-1112 (office). *Fax:* (202) 708-3106 (office). *Website:* www.hud.gov (office); www.bencarson.com (office).

CARSON, William (Willy) Fisher Hunter, OBE; British thoroughbred horse breeder and fmr professional jockey; b. 16 Nov. 1942, Stirling, Scotland; s. of Thomas Whelan and Mary Hay Carson (née Hunter); m. 1st Carole Jane Sutton 1962 (divorced 1979); three s.; m. 2nd Elaine Williams 1982; ed Riverside School, Stirling, Scotland; apprentice with Capt. Gerald Armstrong 1957–62; rode first winner Pinker's Pond at Catterick 1962; first jockey to Lord Derby 1968, to Bernard van Cutsem 1971–75, to Maj. Dick Hern 1977–89, to HM The Queen 1977; champion jockey 1972, 1973, 1978, 1980, 1983; rode the winners of 18 English Classics, eight Irish Classics and 68 English Group One races; rode six winners at one meeting July 1990; best horses ridden Nashwan and Dayjur; bred and rode St Leger winner Minster Son 1988; 3,828 career winners in UK (1997); retd 1997 as fourth-most successful ever UK jockey; racing pundit, BBC 1997–2012; Owner Minster Stud; Dir, Swindon Town Football Club 1997–98, Head of Public Relations 1997–2001, Chair. 2001–07; Dr hc (Stirling 1998); Hon. DSc (Chester) 2010. *Television:* a team capt. (with Bill Beaumont), A Question of Sport (BBC) 1982–83, co-presenter (with Clare Balding), BBC horse racing on BBC 1 1997–2012, came 5th in I'm a Celebrity. . .Get Me Out of Here! (ITV) 2011. *Publication:* Willie Carson Up Front: A Racing Autobiography 1993. *Leisure interests:* golf, football. *Address:* Minster House, Barnsley, Cirencester, Glos., GL7 5DZ, England. *Telephone:* (1285) 658919. *E-mail:* carson_w@sky.com.

CARSTENS CARSTENS, Agustín Guillermo, BA, MA, PhD; Mexican economist, government official and international banker; *General Manager, Bank for International Settlements;* b. 9 June 1958, Mexico City; m. Catherine Mansell; ed Instituto Tecnológico Autónomo de México, Univ. of Chicago, USA; Intern, Banco de México 1983; left for studies in USA; rejoined Banco de México 1986, Treas. 1987, Dir-Gen. Econ. Research and Chief of Staff in Gov.'s office 1991–94, Chief Economist and Research Dir 1994–98, Gov. 2010–17; Chair. Global Economy Meeting, Bank for Int. Settlements (BIS) 2013–17, Economic Consultative Cttee 2013–17, Gen. Man. of BIS 2017–; Alt. Gov. for Mexico at IDB and World Bank 1998–2000; Deputy Sec. of Finance 2000–03, organized UN Conf. on Financing for Devt, Monterrey, meetings of Group of 20 2002; Second Deputy Man. Dir IMF 2003–06, Chair. Policy Advisory Cttee 2015–17; Sec. (Minister) of Finance and Public Credit 2006–09. *Publications:* has published articles in collections edited by Fed. Reserve Bank of Boston, Univ. of London, OECD, IMF and World Bank and in journals including Columbia Journal of World Business, American Economic Review, Journal of Asian Economics, Journal of International Finance, Cuadernos Económicos del ICE (Spain) and Gaceta de Economía del ITAM (Mexico). *Address:* Bank for International Settlements, Centralbahnplatz 2, 4002 Basel, Switzerland (office). *Telephone:* 612808080 (office). *Fax:* 612809100 (office). *E-mail:* email@bis.org (office). *Website:* www.bis.org (office).

CARSWELL, Baron (Life Peer), cr. 2004, of Killeen in the County of Down; **Rt Hon. Robert Douglas Carswell,** PC; British judge (retd); b. 28 June 1934, Belfast, Northern Ireland; s. of Alan E. Carswell and Nance E. Carswell; m. Romayne Winifred Ferris 1961; two d.; ed Royal Belfast Academical Inst., Pembroke Coll., Oxford, Univ. of Chicago Law School, USA; called to the Bar, NI 1957, to English Bar, Gray's Inn 1972; Counsel to Attorney-Gen. for NI 1970–71; QC 1971; Sr Crown Counsel for NI 1979–84; Judge High Court of Justice in NI 1984–93; Lord Justice of Appeal, Supreme Court of Judicature 1993–97; Lord Chief Justice of NI 1997–2004; Lord of Appeal in Ordinary 2004–09; Chancellor, Dioceses of Armagh and of Down and Dromore 1990–97; Chair. Council of Law Reporting for NI 1987–97, Law Reform Advisory Cttee for NI 1989–97, Distinction and Meritorious Service Awards Cttee, DHSS 1995–97; Pres. NI Scout Council 1993–; Pro-Chancellor, Chair. Council, Univ. of Ulster 1984–94; mem. (Crossbench), House of Lords 2004–, mem. Consolidation Bills (Jt Cttee) 2009–15, Chair. 2010–15; Hon. DLitt (Ulster) 1994. *Publications:* Trustee Acts (NI) 1964; articles in legal periodicals. *Leisure interests:* golf, hillwalking, music, architecture, antiques and conservation, wildlife. *Address:* House of Lords, Westminster, London, SW1A 0PW, England (office). *Website:* www.parliament.uk/biographies/lords/lord-carswell/3653 (office).

CARTELLIERI, Ulrich; German lawyer and banker; b. 21 Sept. 1937; ed Univs of Munich and Cologne; joined Deutsche Bank AG, Frankfurt 1970, Man. Dir 1975–77, CEO 1977 82, Chair. Chair. Supervisory Bd European Asian Bank 1982, then Chair. Deutsche Bank (Asia Credit) Ltd, Singapore, DB Finance (Hong Kong) Ltd, Hong Kong; AG 1990–98, mem. Deutsche Bank Man. Bd 1981–97, also served as Deputy Chair. Deutsche Bank North America, mem. Supervisory Bd 1997–2004; Chair. Supervisory Bd, Karstadt 1988–97; Vice-Chair. Supervisory Bd, Siemens 1990–98; mem. Supervisory Bd, Thyssen-Krupp 1986–97, Solvay Germany 1990–97, Henkel –2003, Ruhrgas AG 1991–98; fmr mem. Supervisory Bd, Robert Bosch GmbH, Deutsche Solvay-Werke GmbH, Solingen, Deutsche Telephonwerke und Kabelindustrie AG, Berlin, Euro-Pacific Finance Corpn Ltd, Melbourne, Girmes-Werke AG, Grefrath-Oedt, Th. Goldschmidt AG, Essen, Wilhelm Karmann GmbH, Osnabrück, Thyssen Edelstahlwerke AG, Düsseldorf, G. M. Pfaff AG, Kaiserslautern; Dir (non-exec.), BAE Systems 1999–2007; fmr Pres. German Soc. on Foreign Affairs; fmr German Co-Chair. German-Japanese Forum; Chair. Univ. Council, Heidelberg Univ. from 2001. *Leisure interest:* climbing. *Address:* c/o Board of Directors, BAE Systems, Stirling Square, Carlton Gardens, London, SW1Y 5AD, England.

CARTER, Ashton (Ash) B., BA, PhD; American physicist, academic and fmr government official; *Belfer Professor of Technology and Global Affairs and Director, Belfer Center for Science and International Affairs, Harvard University;* b. 24 Sept. 1954, Philadelphia, Pa; m. 1st Ava Clayton Spencer 1983 (divorced); one s. one d.; m. 2nd Stephanie Carter; ed Yale Univ., Univ. of Oxford, UK; early career positions at MIT, US Congressional Office of Tech. Assessment, Rockefeller Univ.; served as Asst Sec. of Defense for Int. Security Policy, US Dept of Defense, Washington, DC 1993–96; Co-Dir Preventive Defense Project and Ford Foundation Prof. of Science and Int. Affairs, Harvard Univ. –2011, 2013, Dir, Belfer Center for Science and Int. Affairs 2017–, also Belfer Prof. of Technology and Global Affairs 2017–; Deputy Sec. of Defense 2011–13, Sec. of Defense 2015–17; Distinguished Visiting Fellow, Hoover Inst., Stanford Univ. 2014–15; Sr Exec. Markle Foundation 2014–15; fmr Sr Pnr, Global Technology Partners; fmr Chair. Advisory Bd MIT Lincoln Labs; fmr Chair. Editorial Bd International Security (journal); fmr mem. Bd of Dirs Mitretek Systems; fmr mem. Defense Science Bd, Defense Policy Bd, Draper Lab. Corpn, Aspen Strategy Group, Council on Foreign Relations, American Physical Soc., IISS, Nat. Cttee on US-China Relations; Fellow, American Acad. of Arts and Sciences; mem. American Acad. of Diplomacy 2009–; Ten Outstanding Young Americans 1987, US Dept of Defense Distinguished Service Medal (twice), Defense Intelligence Medal, Chair. of the Joint Chiefs of Staff Joint Distinguished Civilian Service Award 2013. *Publications include:* Directed Energy Missile Defense in Space 1984, Ballistic Missile Defense 1984, Managing Nuclear Operations 1987, Soviet Nuclear Fusion: Control of the Nuclear Arsenal in a Disintegrating Soviet Union 1991, Beyond Spinoff: Military and Commercial Technologies in a Changing World 1992, A New Concept of Cooperative Security 1992, Cooperative Denuclearization: From Pledges to Deeds 1993, Preventive Defense (jtly) 1997, Keeping the Edge: Managing Defense for the Future (co-ed.) 2001. *Address:* Belfer Center for Science and International Affairs, 79 John F. Kennedy Street, Cambridge, MA 02138, USA (office). *Telephone:* (617) 496-6099 (office). *Fax:* (617) 495-1905 (office). *Website:* www.belfercenter.org (office).

CARTER, Brandon, DSc, FRS; British (b. Australian) theoretical physicist and academic; *Director Emeritus, Centre National de la Recherche Scientifique (CNRS);* b. 26 May 1942, Sydney, NSW, Australia; s. of Harold B. Carter and Mary Brandon-Jones; m. Lucette Defrise 1969; three d.; ed George Watson's Coll., Edinburgh, Univ. of St Andrews, Pembroke Coll., Cambridge; Research Fellow, Pembroke Coll., Cambridge 1967–72; staff mem., Inst. of Astronomy, Cambridge 1968–72; Asst Lecturer, Dept of Applied Math. and Theoretical Physics, Univ. of Cambridge 1973, Lecturer 1974; Maître de Recherche, CNRS, Paris 1975–85, Dir-Adjoint, Group d'Astrophysique Relativiste, Observatoire de Paris-Meudon 1975–82, Dir 1987–2001, Dir of Research, Laboratoire de l'Univers Théorique 2002–08, Dir Emer. 2009–. *Publications:* Global Structure of the Kerr Family of Gravitational Fields 1968, Black Hole Equilibrium States 1973, Large Number Coincidences and the Anthropic Principle in Cosmology 1974, The General Theory of the Mechanical Electromagnetic and Thermodynamic Properties of Black Holes 1979, The Anthropic Principle and its Implications for Biological Evolution 1983, Covariant Mechanics of Simple and Conducting Strings and Membranes 1990. *Address:* L.U.T.H., 259, Observatoire de Paris-Meudon, 92195 Meudon (office); 19 rue de la Borne au Diable, 92310 Sèvres, France (home). *Telephone:* 1-45-07-74-34 (office). *Fax:* 1-45-07-79-71 (office). *E-mail:* brandon.carter@obspm.fr (office). *Website:* www.luth.obspm.fr (office).

CARTER, Daniel William (Dan); New Zealand professional rugby union player; b. 5 March 1982, Southbridge, Canterbury, South Island; s. of Neville Carter and Bev Carter; m. Honor Dillon 2011; ed Ellesmere Coll., Christchurch Boys' High School; plays as fly-half; played for Southbridge Rugby Club as a scrum half from age five; prov. debut for Canterbury against Marlborough 2002–12; selected to play in the Super 12 (now Super Rugby) franchise for the Crusaders against the Hurricanes 2003–15; reached final of competition with the Crusaders 2003, 2004, 2005, 2006; scored the most individual points (221) for a player in one season; signed six-month contract with French club side Perpignan 2008, ruptured Achilles tendon playing against Stade Français Jan. 2009; played for Canterbury in opening game of Air New Zealand Cup 2009; is now the top scorer in Super 12/14 rugby history; Test debut for New Zealand Nat. Rugby Union Team (All Blacks) in Hamilton scoring 20 points against Wales 2003; capped against France in Christchurch, winning 31–23; included in New Zealand's 2003 Rugby World Cup squad, only secured a permanent position as the first five-eighth in the team during tour to UK and France 2004; mem. winning All Blacks side against British and Irish Lions 2005, in first Test scored two tries, five penalties and four conversions and ended the match with 33 points, passing the previous All Blacks record of 18 points in a Lions Test; became the highest points scorer of all time after scoring a halfway penalty against Wales 27 Nov. 2010, overtook England's Jonny Wilkinson's previous record of 1,178 points although Wilkinson took the record back on 26 Feb. 2011 against France, reclaimed record on 30 July 2011 when he moved to 1,204 points in first Tri Nations match against South Africa, scored a record 1,598 points by end of int. career; Vice-Capt. for more than 50 tests under Richie McCaw, announced as captain of All Blacks for the first time against Canada Oct. 2011; missed most of Rugby World Cup following a groin injury 2011; has won four Super Rugby titles with the Crusaders 2002, 2005, 2006, 2008 and nine Tri-Nations/The Rugby Championships with the All Blacks 2003, 2005, 2006, 2007, 2008, 2010, 2012, 2013, 2014; became fifth All Black to win 100 caps Nov. 2013; mem. winning All Blacks team and named Man of the Match against Australia, Rugby World Cup 2015; retd from int. rugby with 112 caps following World Cup win Oct. 2015; plays for Racing 92 (fmrly Racing Métro), Paris 2015–; Kelvin Tremain Memorial Trophy (NZ Player of the Year) 2004, 2005, Rebel Sport Super 14 Player of the Year 2004, 2006, voted sexiest New Zealand male in a survey 2004, 2005, Int. Rugby Bd (IRB, now World Rugby) Int. Player of the Year 2005, 2012, judged by US Cable Channel E! Entertainment to be 11th on their list of Sexiest Men in the World 2008, voted by E! as third Sexiest Male Athlete in the World 2010, BBC Overseas Sports Personality of the Year 2015. *Publication:* Dan Carter: Skills & Performance 2006. *Address:* Racing Metro 92, 11 avenue Paul Langevin, 92350 Le Plessis Robinson, France (office); c/o New Zealand Rugby Union, PO Box 2172, Wellington 6140, New Zealand. *Telephone:* 1-41-87-51-10 (office); (4) 499-4995. *Fax:* 1-41-87-51-39 (office); (4) 499-4224. *E-mail:* contact@racing-metro92.fr (office); info@nzrugby.co.nz. *Website:* www.racing92.fr (office); www.nzru.co.nz; www.dancarter.com; www.allblacks.com.

CARTER, David, BAS; New Zealand politician; b. 3 April 1952, Christchurch; ed Lincoln Univ.; MP 1994–; Minister for Senior Citizens 1998–99; Assoc. Minister for Revenue 1998–99; Assoc. Minister for Food, Fibre, Biosecurity and Border Control 1998–99; mem. Nat. Party 1999; Minister for Forestry 2008–11; Biosecurity Minister 2008–11; Minister for Agric. 2008–11; Minister for Primary Industries 2011–13; Speaker, House of Reps 2013–17, mem. Finance and Expenditure Cttee 2017–, Privileges Cttee 2019–. *Address:* Parliament Office, Private Bag 18888, Parliament Buildings, Wellington 6160, New Zealand (office). *Telephone:* (4) 817-9999 (office). *E-mail:* david.carter@parliament.govt.nz (office). *Website:* www.parliament.nz (office).

CARTER, (Edward) Graydon, CM; Canadian magazine editor; b. 14 July 1949; s. of E.P. Carter and Margaret Ellen Carter; m. 2nd Cynthia Williamson 1982 (divorced 2000); four c.; m. Anna Scott 2005; one d.; ed Carleton Univ., Univ. of Ottawa; Ed. Canadian Review 1973–77; writer, Time 1978–83, Life 1983–86;

Founder, Ed. Spy 1986–91; Ed. New York Observer 1991–92; Ed.-in-Chief, Vanity Fair 1992–Dec. 2017; Co-owner Waverly Inn, Monkey Bar; Hon. Ed. Harvard Lampoon 1989; Advertising Age Editor of the Year 1996, Nat. Magazine Award for Gen. Excellence 1997, 1999, Nat. Magazine Award for Photography 2000, 2002, Nat. Magazine Award for Reviews and Criticism 2003. *Television:* 9/11 (CBS) (Emmy Award, Peabody Award) (executive producer) 2002. *Film:* The Kid Stays in the Picture (producer) 2002. *Publications:* Vanity Fair's Hollywood (ed.) 2000, Tom Ford: Ten Years (co-author) 2004, What We've Lost 2004, Oscar Night: 75 Years of Hollywood Parties (ed.) 2004, Spy: The Funny Years (co-author, ed.) 2006, Vanity Fair Portraits (ed.) 2008, Vintage Postcards from Vanity Fair: One Hundred Classic Covers, 1913–1936 2011. *Leisure interest:* fly fishing. *Address:* Monkey Bar, 60 East, 54th Street, New York, NY 10022, USA (office). *Telephone:* (212) 288-1010 (office). *Website:* www.monkeybarnewyork.com (office).

CARTER, James (Jimmy) Earl, Jr, BSc; American politician, international political consultant, farmer and fmr head of state; *Chairman, Carter Center;* b. 1 Oct. 1924, Plains, Ga; s. of James Earl Carter, Sr and Lillian Gordy; m. Eleanor Rosalynn Smith 1946; three s. one d.; ed Plains High School, Georgia Southwestern Coll., Georgia Inst. of Tech., US Naval Acad., Annapolis, Md, Union Coll., New York State; served in USN 1946–53, attained rank of Lt (submarine service); peanut farmer, warehouseman 1953–77, businesses include Carter Farms, Carter Warehouses, Plains, Ga; mem. Sumter Co., Ga, School Bd 1955–62 (Chair. 1960–62); State Senator, Ga 1962–66; Gov. of Georgia 1971–74; Pres. of USA 1977–81; Distinguished Prof., Emory Univ., Atlanta 1982–; leader of int. observer teams in Panama 1989, Nicaragua 1990, Dominican Repub. 1990, Haiti 1990; hosted peace negotiations in Ethiopia 1989; visited Democratic People's Repub. of Korea (in pvt. capacity) June 1994; negotiator in Haitian crisis Sept. 1994; visit to Bosnia Dec. 1994; f. Carter Presidential Center 1982; est. Jimmy and Rosalynn Carter Work Project for Habitat for Humanity International 1984; Chair. Bd of Trustees, Carter Center Inc. 1986–, Carter-Menil Human Rights Foundation 1986–, Global 2000 Inc. 1986–, Council of Freely Elected Heads of Govt 1986–, Council of Int. Negotiation Network 1991–; joined The Elders 2007; mem. Americus and Sumter Co. Hosp. Authority 1956–70, Sumter Co. Library Bd 1961; Pres. Plains Devt Corpn 1963; Georgia Planning Asscn 1968; Dir Ga Crop Improvement Asscn 1957–63 (Pres. 1961); Chair. West Cen. Ga Area Planning and Devt Comm. 1964; State Chair. March of Dimes 1968–70; Dist Gov. Lions Club 1968–69; Chair. Congressional Campaign Cttee, Democratic Nat. Cttee 1974; Democrat; several hon. degrees; Ansel Adams Conservation Award, Wilderness Society 1982, World Methodist Peace Award 1984, Albert Schweitzer Prize for Humanitarianism 1987, Onassis Foundation Award 1991, Notre Dame Univ. Award 1992, Matsunaga Medal of Peace 1993, J. William Fulbright Prize for Int. Understanding 1994, Houphouët Boigny Peace Prize, UNESCO (jtly) 1995, UNICEF Int. Child Survival Award (jtly with Rosalynn Carter) 1999, Presidential Medal of Freedom 1999, Eisenhower Medallion 2000, Nobel Peace Prize 2002, American Peace Award (jtly with Rosalynn Carter) 2009, among numerous other awards. *Recordings:* Living Faith 1996, The Virtues Of Aging 1998, An Hour Before Daylight 2001, Sunday Mornings In Plains: Bringing Peace To A Changing World 2007, Our Endangered Values: America's Moral Crisis (Grammy Award for Best Spoken Word Album 2007) 2005, We Can Have Peace In The Holy Land 2009, A Call To Action 2014, A Full Life: Reflections at Ninety (Grammy Award for Best Spoken Word Album 2016) 2015, Faith: A Journey For All (Grammy Award for Best Spoken Word Album 2019) 2019. *Publications include:* Why Not the Best? 1975, A Government as Good as Its People 1977, Keeping Faith: Memoirs of a President 1982, The Blood of Abraham: Insights into the Middle East 1985, Everything to Gain: Making the Most of the Rest of Your Life 1987, An Outdoor Journal 1988, Turning Point: A Candidate, a State and a Nation Come of Age 1992, Always a Reckoning (poems) 1995, Sources of Strength 1997, The Virtues of Ageing 1998, An Hour Before Daylight 2001, The Hornet's Nest (novel) 2003, Our Endangered Values 2005, Palestine: Peace Not Apartheid 2006, We Can Have Peace in the Holy Land: A Plan that Will Work 2009, White House Diary 2010, Call to Action: Women, Religion, Violence, and Power 2014. *Leisure interests:* reading, tennis. *Address:* The Carter Center, 453 Freedom Parkway, 1 Copenhill Avenue NE, Atlanta, GA 30307, USA (office). *Telephone:* (404) 420-5100 (office). *E-mail:* carterweb@emory.edu (office); info@cartercenter.org (office). *Website:* www.cartercenter.org (office).

CARTER, Marshall, BS, MS, MA; American business executive; *Chairman of the Board of Directors, NYSE Group Inc.;* b. 23 April 1940, Newport News, Va; m. Mary Meehan 1964; one s. one d.; ed US Mil. Acad. at West Point, US Naval Postgraduate School, Monterey, George Washington Univ.; fmr Marine Corps officer; White House Fellow, State Dept and Agency for Int. Devt 1975–76; with Chase Manhattan Bank –1992; Chair. and CEO State Street Bank and Trust Co., State Street Corp. 1992–2001; Fellow, Center for Public Leadership, Kennedy School of Govt, Harvard Univ. 2001–05; Lecturer in leadership and man., Sloan School of Man., MIT; mem. Bd of Dirs New York Stock Exchange 2003–, Chair. 2005–06, Chair. NYSE Group Inc. 2006–; Chair. Bd of Trustees, Boston Medical Center; Fellow, American Acad. of Arts and Sciences 2006; Navy Cross, Bronze Star, Purple Heart. *Address:* NYSE Group Inc., 11 Wall Street, New York, NY 10005, USA (office). *Telephone:* (212) 656-3000 (office). *Website:* www.nyse.com (office).

CARTER, Stephen Lisle, BA, JD; American academic and lawyer; *William Nelson Cromwell Professor of Law, Yale University;* b. 26 Oct. 1954, Washington, DC; s. of Lisle C. Carter; m. Enola G. Aird; two c.; ed Stanford and Yale Univs; fmr Note Ed. Yale Law Journal; admitted to Bar, Washington, DC 1981; law clerk, Judge Spottswood W. Robinson III, US Court of Appeal, Washington, DC 1979–80; law clerk, Justice Thurgood Marshall, US Supreme Court 1980–81; Assoc. Shea & Gardner, Washington, DC 1981–82; Asst Prof. of Law, Yale Univ. 1982–84, Assoc. Prof. 1984–85, Prof. 1986–91, William Nelson Cromwell Prof. of Law 1991–; Advisor to US Pres. Bill Clinton 1993; Hon. LLD (Univ. of Notre Dame) 1996, (Bates Coll.) 2015. *Publications include:* non-fiction: Reflections of an Affirmative Action Baby 1991, The Culture of Disbelief 1991, The Confirmation Mess 1994, Integrity 1997, The Dissent of the Governed 1998, Civility 1998, God's Name in Vain 2001, The Violence of Peace: America's Wars in the Age of Obama 2011; novels: The Emperor of Ocean Park 2002, New England White 2007, Palace Council 2008, Jericho's Fall 2009, The Impeachment of Abraham Lincoln 2012, The Church Builder 2013, Back Channel 2014. *Address:* Yale Law School, POB 208215, New Haven, CT 06520, USA (office). *E-mail:* stephen.carter@yale.edu (office). *Website:* www.law.yale.edu (office); www.stephencarterbooks.com.

CARTER OF BARNES, Baron (Life Peer), cr. 2008, of Barnes in the London Borough of Richmond upon Thames; **Stephen A. Carter**, CBE, LLB; British business executive; *Group Chief Executive, Informa PLC;* b. 12 Feb. 1964, Scotland; m. Anna Carter; two c.; ed Currie High School, Edinburgh, Univ. of Aberdeen; began career as trainee, J. Walter Thompson UK (advertising agency), Man. Dir 1995–97, CEO 1997–2000; Man. Dir of UK Operations, NTL (cable TV co.) 2000–02; CEO Ofcom (telecommunications regulatory authority) 2003–06; CEO Brunswick Group LLP 2006–08; Downing Street Chief of Staff 2008; Minister for Communications, Tech. and Broadcasting 2008–09; Chief Marketing, Strategy and Communications Officer, Alcatel-Lucent 2010–13; Group Chief Exec., Informa PLC 2013–; mem. House of Lords 2008–; Chair. Ashridge Business School 2008–15; Trustee RSC 2007–; Dir (non-Exec.) NED United Utilities 2014–. *Leisure interest:* running. *Address:* House of Lords, London, SW1A 0PW; Informa PLC, 5 Howick Place, London, SW1P 1WG, England (office). *Telephone:* (20) 7219-4776 (House of Lords); (20) 7017-5000 (office). *E-mail:* carterst@parliament.uk. *Website:* informa.com (office).

CARTES JARA, Horacio Manuel; Paraguayan business executive, politician and fmr head of state; b. 5 July 1956, Asunción; s. of Ramón Telmo Cartes Lind; ed Colegio Goethe, Colegio Internacional, Colegio Cristo Rey, Asunción; began career with internship at Cessna (aircraft co.), Kansas, USA; returned to Paraguay, f. Cambios Amambay (currency exchange co.) 1989 (renamed Banco Amambay 1992); joined Tabacalera del Este SA (tobacco co.) as Partner 1994, f. Tobacco del Paraguay SA 1996, f. Compañía Agrotabacalera del Paraguay SA 2002; now Owner, Grupo Cartes conglomerate (active in fields of tobacco, soft drinks, meat production, transport and banking); imprisoned 1989 for currency dealings, later acquitted; mem. Colorado Party 2009–, selected as Colorado Party cand. for presidential elections 2012; Pres. of Paraguay 2013–18; elected to Cámara de Senadores (Senate) April 2018, but withdrew June 2018; Pres. Club Libertad (football club) 2001–; fmr Selection Dir Paraguayan Football Asscn. *Address:* Partido Colorado, Casa de los Colorados, 25 de Mayo 842, Asunción, Paraguay (office). *Telephone:* (595) 414-5000 (office).

CARTWRIGHT, Gen. (retd) James E., MA; American military officer (retd); *Harold Brown Chair in Defense Policy Studies, Center for Strategic and International Studies;* b. 22 Sept. 1949, Rockford, Ill.; ed Univ. of Iowa, Maxwell Air Command and Staff Coll., Naval War Coll., Massachusetts Inst. of Tech.; commissioned Second Lt in US Marine Corps 1971, Naval Flight Officer, graduated 1973, Naval Aviator, graduated 1977, operational assignments as an NFO in the F-4 and as a pilot in the F-4, OA-4 and F/A-18, has served in numerous leadership positions including Commdr Marine Aviation Logistics Squadron 12 1989–90, Marine Fighter Attack Squadron 232 1992, Marine Aircraft Group 31 1994–96, Deputy Commanding Gen., Marine Forces Atlantic 1999–2000, Commanding Gen., First Marine Aircraft Wing 2000–02; Commdr US Strategic Command, Offutt Air Force Base, Neb. 2004–07, command areas include full-spectrum global strike, space operations, computer network operations, Dept of Defense information operations, strategic warning, integrated missile defense, combating weapons of mass destruction, staff assignments included Asst Program Man. for Eng, F/A-18 Naval Air Systems Command 1986–89, Deputy Aviation Plans, Policy and Budgets HQ, US Marine Corps 1993–94, Directorate for Force Structure, Resources and Assessment, J-8 the Jt Chiefs of Staff 1996–99, Dir for Force Structure, Resources and Assessment, J-8 the Jt Chiefs of Staff 2002–04, Vice-Chair. Jt Chiefs of Staff 2007–11 (retd); currently Harold Brown Chair in Defense Policy Studies, Center for Strategic and Int. Studies; Strategic Advisor, IxReveal Inc. 2012–; mem. Advisory Bd Opera Solutions, LLC, TASC, Inc., Enlightenment Capital, Logos Technologies; Sr Fellow, Belfer Center for Science and International Affairs, Kennedy School, Harvard Univ.; mem. Bd of Dirs Raytheon Co. 2012–; consultant, ABC News; agreed to plead guilty to lying to FBI about discussions with reporters about Iran's nuclear programme Oct. 2016; Outstanding Carrier Aviator, Asscn of Naval Aviation 1983, Naval War College Distinguished Graduate Leadership Award. *Address:* Center for Strategic and International Studies, 1616 Rhode Island Avenue, NW, Washington, DC 20036, USA (office). *Telephone:* (202) 644-5644 (office). *E-mail:* jcartwright@csis.org (office). *Website:* csis.org/expert/james-e-cartwright (office).

CARTWRIGHT, Nancy Delaney, PhD, FBA; American/British academic; *Professor, Department of Philosophy, Durham University;* b. 24 June 1944, Pennsylvania; d. of Claudis Delaney and Eva Delaney; m. 1st Bliss Cartwright 1966 (divorced); m. 2nd Ian Hacking 1974 (divorced); m. 3rd Sir Stuart Hampshire 1985 (died 2004); two d.; ed Univs of Pittsburgh and Illinois; Prof. of Philosophy, Stanford Univ. 1983–91; Prof. of Philosophy, Logic and Scientific Method, LSE 1991–2012 (currently Emer. Prof. of Philosophy), Dir Centre for the Philosophy of the Natural and Social Sciences 1993–2001; Prof. of Philosophy, Univ. of California, San Diego 1997–; also currently Prof. of Philosophy, Durham Univ., Dir Centre for Humanities Engaging Science and Soc.; Hon. DLitt (Univ of St Andrews), Hon. DHumLitt (Southern Methodist Univ); Macarthur Foundation Award 1993, Leopoldina 1999. *Publications include:* How the Laws of Physics Lie 1983, Nature's Capacities and Their Measurement 1989, Otto Neurath: Between Science and Politics (with others) 1995, The Dappled World: A Study of the Boundaries of Science 2000, Measuring Causes: Invariance, Modularity and the Causal Markov Condition 2000, Causal Powers: What Are They? Why Do We Need Them? What Can be Done with Them and What Cannot? 2007, Hunting Causes and Using Them: Approaches in Philosophy and Economics 2007, Evidence Based Policy: A Practical Guide to Doing it Better (with Jeremy Hardie) 2012, Evidence: For Policy and Wheresoever Rigor is a Must 2013, Improving Child Safety: Deliberation, Judgement and Empirical Research (with others) 2017. *Address:* Department of Philosophy, University of Durham, 50 Old Elvet, Durham, DH1 3HN, England (office); Department of Philosophy, University of California, San Diego, 9500 Gilman Drive, La Jolla, CA 92093-0302, USA (office). *E-mail:* nancy.cartwright@durham.ac.uk (office). *Website:* www.dur.ac.uk/philosophy (office); www.profnancycartwright.com.

CARTWRIGHT, The Hon. Dame Silvia Rose, PCNZM, DBE, QSO, LLB; New Zealand judge; b. 7 Nov. 1943, Dunedin; d. of Monteith Poulter and Eileen Jane Poulter; m. Peter John Cartwright 1969; ed Univ. of Otago; Partner, Harkness

Henry & Co. barristers and solicitors, Hamilton 1971–81; Dist Court and Family Court Judge 1981–89, Chief Dist Court Judge 1989–93; Judge High Court of NZ 1993–2001; Gov.-Gen. of NZ 2001–06; Judge in Trial Chamber, Extraordinary Chambers in the Courts of Cambodia for the Prosecution of Crimes Committed during the Period of Democratic Kampuchea 2007–14; apptd to UN Human Rights Council investigation into war crimes and human rights abuses in Sri Lanka 2014–; mem. Comm. for the Future 1975–80, Cttee UN Human Rights Convention to eliminate discrimination against women 1992–2000; Chair. Comm. of Inquiry into the Treatment of Cervical Cancer and Other Related Matters, Nat. Women's Hosp. 1987–88; Fellow, Hastings Center (USA); Int. Hon. Mem., Zonta International 2001, The Int. Raoul Wallenberg Foundation; Hon. LLD (Otago) 1993, (Waikato) 1994, (Canterbury) 2002; NZ Medal 1990, NZ Suffrage Centennial Medal 1993. *Address:* Office of the United Nations High Commissioner for Human Rights (OHCHR), Palais des Nations, 1211 Geneva 10, Switzerland (office). *Telephone:* (22) 9179220 (office). *E-mail:* infodesk@ohchr.org (office). *Website:* www.ohchr.org/HRC (office).

CARTWRIGHT-ROBINSON, Sharlene Linette, LLB, JP; Turks and Caicos lawyer and politician; *Premier and Minister of Finance, Trade and Investment;* b. 1971, Bahamas; m. Lorne Robinson; two d.; ed Coll. of the Bahamas, Norman Manley Law School, Univ. of the West Indies, Jamaica; legal practice with Dempsey & Co. and Misick & Stanbrook (law firms); f. own legal firm Cartwright & Co. 2002; Law Tutor, TCI Community Coll. 2004–08; apptd mem. Legis. Council (renamed House of Ass. 2006) 1999–2003, elected mem. (All-Island Dist) 2012–, Chair. Public Accounts Cttee, Appropriations Cttee, mem. Constitutional Review Cttees 2002, 2006, 2014; mem. Consultative Forum (apptd by Gov.) 2009–12; Premier and Minister of Finance, Trade and Investment 2016–; mem. People's Democratic Movement, Leader 2012–. *Address:* Office of the Premier, N. J. S. Francis Bldg, Goverment Square, Grand Turk, Turks and Caicos (office). *Telephone:* 946-2801 (office). *Fax:* 946-2777 (office). *E-mail:* premier@gov.tc (office). *Website:* www.gov.tc (office).

CARTY, Donald J., OC; Canadian business executive; *Chairman, Virgin America Airlines;* m. Ana Carty; ed Queen's Univ., Kingston, Ont., Harvard Grad. School of Business Admin., USA; various man. positions at Celanese Canada Ltd, Air Canada, Canadian Pacific Railway, American Airlines Inc.; Pres. and CEO CP Air 1985–87; Sr Vice-Pres. (Airline Planning) AMR Corpn 1987–89, Exec. Vice-Pres. (Finance and Planning) AMR Corpn and American Airlines Inc. 1989–95, Pres. AMR Airline Group and American Airlines Inc. 1995–98, Chair., Pres. and CEO AMR Corpn and American Airlines Inc. 1998–2003 (resgnd); Chair. Virgin America Airlines 2006–; Chair. Porter Airlines, Toronto 2006–; mem. Bd of Dirs Dell Computer Inc. 1992–, Vice-Chair. and Chief Financial Officer 2007, Vice-Chair. 2008–; mem. Bd of Dirs CHC Helicopter Corpn, Barrick Gold Corpn, Brinker Int., Canada-US Foundation for Educational Exchange, Hawaiian Holdings Inc.; mem. Nat. Infrastructure Advisory Council 2002–05. *Address:* Virgin America, 555 Airport Blvd., Fl. 2, Burlingame, CA 94010, USA (office). *Telephone:* (650) 762-7000 (office). *Fax:* (650) 762-7001 (office). *Website:* www.virginamerica.com (office).

CARUANA, Sir Peter Richard, Kt, KCMG, QC; Gibraltarian politician, lawyer and fmr government official; b. 15 Oct. 1956; m.; six c.; ed Christian Brothers School, Grace Dieu Manor, Leicester, Ratcliffe Coll. Leicester, Queen Mary Coll., Univ. of London, Council of Legal Educ., London; joined Triay & Triay (law firm), Gibraltar 1979, Pnr specializing in commercial and shipping law 1990–95; joined Gibraltar Social Democrats 1990, Leader 1991–2012; elected in Gibraltar's first-ever by-election to House of Ass. May 1991; Leader of Opposition 1992–96; QC for Gibraltar 1998; Chief Minister of Gibraltar 1996–2011 (re-elected 2000, 2003, 2007); Hon. Fellow, Queen Mary Coll., Univ. of London. *Leisure interests:* golf, political and current affairs. *Address:* 10/3 Irish Town, Gibraltar (home); c/o Office of the Chief Minister, 6 Convent Place, Gibraltar (office).

CARUANA LACORTE, Jaime; Spanish central bank governor; b. 14 March 1952, Valencia; ed Univ. Complutense Madrid; fmr telecommunications engineer; various posts with Ministry of Trade 1979–84; Commercial attaché to the Spanish Commercial Office, New York 1984–87; Man. Dir and CEO Renta 4, SA, SVB 1987–91, Pres. 1991–96; Gen. Dir of the Treasury and Financial Policy 1996–99; mem. Bd SEPP (State Holding Co.) 1996–99; mem. EU Monetary Cttee 1996–99; Pres. SETE (Euro State Co.) 1997–99; Gen. Dir for Supervision, Banco de España 1999–2000, Gov. 2000–06; Counsellor and Dir Monetary and Capital Markets Dept, IMF 2006–09, Gen. Man. BIS 2009–17; Chair. Basel Cttee for Banking Supervision 2003–06, Int. Org. of Securities Comms (IOSCO) 2004–06, Int. Asscn of Insurance Supervisors 2004–06, Jt Forum 2004–06; mem. Governing Council, European Cen. Bank 2000–, Financial Stability Forum 2003–, Group of Thirty Consultative Group on Int. Econ. and Monetary Affairs, Inc. (G-30), Washington, DC 2003–. *Publications:* numerous articles on the Spanish financial system, the financing of public admins and the man. of public debt. *Address:* c/o Bank for International Settlements, Centralbahnplatz 2, 4002 Basel, Switzerland (office). *Telephone:* 612808080 (office). *Fax:* 612809100 (office). *E-mail:* email@bis.org (office). *Website:* www.bis.org (office).

CARVAJAL AGUIRRE, Miguel Ángel; Ecuadorean sociologist and politician; *Minister of National Defence;* b. 23 Feb. 1960, Quito; divorced; ed Univ. Central del Ecuador, Facultad Latinoamericana de Ciencias Sociales (FLACSO); fmr Prof., FLACSO and Univ. Politécnica Salesiana, Cuenca; Adviser to Ministry of Tourism and Ministry of the Environment 2003; Nat. Operations Coordinator, Poverty Reduction and Devt Project 2003–07; Deputy Minister of Defence 2007–09, Minister Coordinator of Internal and External Security 2009–10, Deputy Minister of Agric. 2010–12, Minister of Nat. Defence 2012, 2017–; mem. Nat. Ass. (parl.) 2012–17; mem. Alianza País (Patria Altiva i Soberana), mem. Exec. Cttee. *Address:* Ministry of National Defence, Calle Exposición S4-71 y Benigno Vela, Quito, Ecuador (office). *Telephone:* (2) 295-1951 (office). *Fax:* (2) 258-0941 (office). *E-mail:* comunicacion@midena.gob.ec (office). *Website:* www.defensa.gob.ec (office).

CARVALHO, Evaristo do Espírito Santo de; São Tomé and Príncipe politician and head of state; *President;* b. 22 Oct. 1941; mem. Nat. Ass. (Parl.) 1975–90, 2006–, Pres. (Speaker) 2010–12; Sec. of State for Territorial Admin 1977–78; Minister of Construction, Transport and Communications 1978–80; Deputy Dir of Social Security 1982–86; Ombudsman 1986–88; mem. Admin Council, Bela Vista 1988–91; Sec.-Gen. of the Presidency 1991–92; Minister of Defence and Internal Order 1992–94; Prime Minister July–Oct. 1994, Sept. 2001–March 2002; Dir, Office of Pres. Miguel Trovoady 1997–2001; cand. in presidential election 2011, 2016; Pres. of São Tomé and Príncipe 2016–; mem. Acção Democrática Independente. *Address:* Palácio Presidêncial, CP 38, São Tomé, São Tomé e Príncipe (office). *Website:* www.presidencia.st (office).

CARVALHO DE ANDRADE, Marcelo, PhD; Brazilian banker and international organization official; *President, Earth Council Alliance;* s. of Atabalipa de Andrade and Maria Carvalho de Andrade; m. Lisa Bjornson 1995; ed Univ. Gama Filho, Rio de Janeiro; Partner, T.W.P. Ltd (investment firm), Rio de Janeiro; Co-founder, Partner and Prin., Earth Capital Partners LLP (responsible for external relations); Co-founder Terra Capital; Founder and Chair. Pro-Natura International (first int. NGO based in Southern Hemisphere to specialize in sustainable devt), Rio de Janeiro 1980s; Advisor (non-exec.), BHP Billiton, DuPont, Shell; mem. Biotechnology Advisory Panel, E.I. du Pont de Nemours & Co. 2004–; Pres. and mem. Bd, Earth Council Alliance 2005–; mem. CONCEC (pvt.-sector advisory panel for Brazilian Govt), Counterpart International, Earth Restoration Corps; George and Cynthia Mitchell Int. Prize for Sustainable Devt 1997. *Address:* Earth Council Alliance, 1250 24th Street NW, Suite 300, Washington, DC 20037, USA (office). *Telephone:* (202) 467-2786 (office). *E-mail:* contact@earthcouncil1.org (office). *Website:* earthcouncilalliance.org (office).

CARVALHO DE AZEVÊDO, Roberto; Brazilian diplomatist and international organization official; *Director-General, World Trade Organization;* b. 3 Oct. 1957, Salvador; m. Maria Nazareth Farani Azevêdo; two d.; ed Univ. of Brasília, Instituto Rio Branco; joined Foreign Service 1984, served at Embassies in Washington, DC 1988–91 and Montevideo 1992–94, Perm. Mission in Geneva 1997–2001, Deputy Chief of Staff for Econ. Affairs to the Foreign Minister 1995–96, Head, Dispute Settlement Unit 2001–05, Dir Dept of Econ. Affairs 2005–06, Vice-Minister for Econ. and Technological Affairs, Ministry of Foreign Relations 2006–08, Perm. Rep. to WTO, WIPO, UNCTAD, ITU 2008–13; Dir-Gen. WTO 2013–; fmr Rep. to FAO Codex Alimentarius Comm., Int. Cotton Council, Int. Cotton Advisory Cttee, OECD Trade Cttee. *Address:* World Trade Organization, Centre William Rappard, Rue de Lausanne 154, 1211 Geneva 21, Switzerland (office). *Telephone:* 227395111 (office). *Fax:* 227314206 (office). *E-mail:* enquiries@wto.org (office). *Website:* www.wto.org (office).

CARVILLE, James, BA, JD; American political consultant; *Professional-in-Residence Manship School of Mass Communication, Louisiana State University;* b. 25 Oct. 1944, Fort Benning, Ga; s. of Chester James Carville and Lucille Carville (née Normand); m. Mary Matalin 1993; two d.; ed Louisiana State Univ.; litigator Baton Rouge 1973–79; managed first campaign 1982, then managed campaign for Gov. of Texas 1983; subsequent successful campaigns included Robert Casey for Penn. Gov. 1986, Wallace Wilkinson for Ky Gov. 1987, Frank Lautenberg for NJ Sen. 1988, Zell Miller for Ga Lt.-Gov. 1990, Harris Wofford for Penn. Sen. 1991; co-f. Carville and Begala (political consulting co.) 1989; co-managed Clinton Presidential Campaign 1992, later sr political adviser to Pres.; numerous int. political clients 1993–, including successful campaign for Ehud Barak for PM Israel 1999; Prof. of Political Science, Tulane Univ. 2009–17; Co-host, Crossfire (television show), CNN 2002–14, 60/20 Sports (sports radio show) 2006–; Professional-in-Residence, Manship School of Mass Communication, Louisiana State Univ. 2017–; joined Fox News as Contrib. 2014; Co-f. Democracy Corps (consultancy and polling co.); mem. Bd of Dirs Gaslight Inc.; Campaign Man. of the Year 1993. *Films include:* The People vs. Larry Flynt 1996, Old School 2003, Wedding Crashers 2005, All the King's Men (exec. producer) 2006, G.I. Joe: Retaliation 2013. *Publications include:* All's Fair: Love, War and Running for President (with Mary Matalin) 1995, We're Right, They're Wrong (with Mary Matalin) 1996, And The Horse He Rode In On: The People v. Ken Starr 1998, Stickin': The Case for Loyalty 2000, Take It Back: Our Party, Our Country, Our Future (with Paul Begala) 2006, 40 More Years: How the Democrats Will Rule the Next Generation (with Rebecca Buckwalter-Poza) 2009, It's the Middle Class, Stupid! (with Stan Greenberg) 2012, Love & War: Twenty Years, Three Presidents, Two Daughters and One Louisiana Home (with Mary Matalin) 2014, We're Still Right, They're Still Wrong: The Democrats' Case for 2016 2016. *Address:* Democracy Corps, 10 G Street, NE, Suite 400, Washington, DC 20002 (office); Manship School of Mass Communication, Louisiana State University, Journalism Building, Baton Rouge, LA 70803, USA (office). *Telephone:* (202) 478-8330 (DC) (office); (225) 578-7309 (office). *Fax:* (202) 289-8648 (DC) (office); (225) 578-2125 (office). *E-mail:* james@carville.info (office). *Website:* www.democracycorps.com (office); www.carville.info (office).

CARY, Anthony Joyce, CMG, MA, MBA; British fmr diplomatist and administrator; *Commissioner, Commonwealth Scholarship Commission;* b. 1 July 1951; m. Clare Cary; three s. one d.; ed Univ. of Oxford, Stanford Business School, USA; entered British Diplomatic Service 1973; with British Mil. Govt in Berlin 1975–78; mem. Policy Planning Staff, FCO 1978–80, EC Dept 1982–84; Pvt. Sec. to Ministers of State Malcolm Rifkind, then Lynda Chalker 1984–86; Head of Chancery, Kuala Lumpur 1986–89; Deputy Chef de Cabinet to Leon Brittan, EC, Brussels 1989–93; Head of EU Dept, FCO 1993–97; Counsellor, Political and Public Affairs, Embassy in Washington, DC 1997–99; Chef de Cabinet to Chris Patten, European Commr for External Relations 1999–2003; Amb. to Sweden 2003–07; High Commr to Canada 2007–10; Int. Juror, Cundill History Prize, McGill Univ. 2011; Exec. Dir Queen's-Blyth Worldwide (partnership between Queen's Univ., Ont. and Blyth Education) 2011–13; Commr, Commonwealth Scholarship Comm. 2012–; Harkness Fellow, Stanford Univ. 1980; Hon. Pres. British Cttee of the Canada UK Colloquia 2011–. *Address:* c/o Commonwealth Scholarship Commission, Woburn House, 20–24 Tavistock Square, London WC1H 9HF, England (office). *Telephone:* (866) 960-3552 (office). *Website:* cscuk.dfid.gov.uk (office).

CASADESUS, Jean Claude; French conductor; b. (Jean Claude Probst), 7 Dec. 1935, Paris; s. of Lucien Probst and Gisèle Casadesus; two s. one d.; ed Paris Nat. Conservatoire and Ecole Normale, Paris; solo timpanist, Concert Colonne 1959–68; percussion soloist, Domaine Musical (with Boulez); Conductor, Paris Opéra 1969–71; Co-Dir Orchestre Pays de Loire 1971–76; Founder and Dir Orchestre Nat. de Lille 1976–2016; appearances as guest conductor with leading orchestras in UK, USA, France, Germany, Norway, Russia, Czech Repub., int. music festivals etc.; Pres. Musique Nouvelle en Liberté; Musical Dir, Lille Piano Festival; Commdr, Légion d'honneur, Ordre nat. du Mérite, Grand Officier des Arts et des Lettres; Chevalier, Ordre des Palmes académiques; Commdr, Order of Orange Nassau (Netherlands); Officer, Order of Léopold (Belgium); Grand Prix de la SACEM, First Prize in Percussion and Conducting, and several other prizes and awards for recordings. *Recordings include:* works by Dutilleux (1st Symphony), Berlioz, Mahler, Bizet, Stravinsky, Mozart, Beethoven, Ravel, Debussy, Poulenc, Groupe des Six, Prokofiev, Dukas, Massenet, Milhaud, Honneger, Mussorgsky, Franck, Canteloube – Songs of the Auvergne. *Publications include:* Le plus court chemin d'un coeur à un autre 1998, La partition d'une vie 2012. *Leisure interests:* yachting, sailing, skiing, tennis. *Address:* c/o Orchestre National de Lille, 30 place Mendès-France, BP 119, 59027 Lille Cedex (office); 2 rue de Steinkerque, 75018 Paris, France (home).

CASAJUANA I PALET, Carles; Spanish diplomatist and writer; b. 24 Oct. 1954, Sant Cugat del Vallès, Barcelona; m. Margarita Massanet; two d.; ed Univ. of Barcelona; entered Spanish Diplomatic Service 1980, posted to Embassies in Colombia 1980–82, the Philippines 1982–84, with Ministry of Foreign Affairs 1984–87, Perm. Mission to UN, New York 1987–91, Chief of Staff to Sec. Gen. for Foreign Policy, Ministry of Foreign Affairs 1991–96, Amb. to Malaysia 1996–2001 (also accred to Brunei Darussalam 1996–2001, to Viet Nam 1997–98), Amb. Rep. to Political and Security Cttee of EU 2001–04, Sr Diplomatic Adviser to the Prime Minister 2004–08, Amb. to UK 2008–12. *Publications include:* novels: Tap d'escopeta 1987, Bondag 1989, La puresa del porc 1990, Punt de fuga 1992, Esperit d'evasió 1998, Diumenge de temptació 2001, Kuala Lumpur 2005, L'últim home que parlava català (XXIX Premi de les Lletres Catalanes Ramon Llull 2009) 2009, El melic del món 2013; essays: Pla i Nietzsche: afinitats i coincidències 1996, Les lleis del castell (Premi Godó de Reporterisme i Assaig Periodístic) 2014. *Address:* Ministry of Foreign Affairs and Co-operation, Plaza de la Provincia 1, 28012 Madrid, Spain (office). *Telephone:* (91) 3799700 (office); (91) 3798300 (office). *E-mail:* informae@maec.es (office). *Website:* www.maec.es (office).

CASALE, Carl M., BS, MBA; American business executive; *President and CEO, CHS Inc.;* b. Willamette Valley, Ore.; m. Kim Casale; ed Oregon State Univ., Washington Univ., St Louis, Mo.; joined Monsanto as a sales rep. in eastern Wash. 1984, held numerous sales, strategy, marketing and tech.-related positions, later Exec. Vice-Pres., North American Commercial Operations, Exec. Vice-Pres., Strategy and Operations –2009, Chief Financial Officer 2009–10; Pres. and CEO CHS Inc. (agricultural cooperative) 2011–; fmr mem. Bd National 4-H Council; Alumni Fellow, Oregon State Univ. Coll. of Agric. 2009. *Address:* CHS, PO Box 64089, St Paul, MN 55164-0089 (office); CHS, 5500 Cenex Drive, Inver Grove Heights, MN 55077, USA (office). *Telephone:* (651) 355-6000 (office). *E-mail:* info@chsinc.com (office). *Website:* www.chsinc.com (office).

CASANOVA, Corina, Lic. iur.; Swiss lawyer and politician; b. 4 Jan. 1956, Ilanz, Graubünden; ed Univ. of Fribourg; admitted to the Bar, Graubünden 1984, pvt. practice as lawyer 1984–86; Red Cross Del. in S Africa, Angola, Nicaragua and El Salvador 1986–90; Del. for Information, Parl. Service of Fed. Ass. 1992–96; joined staff of Fed. Councillor Flavio Cotti, Fed. Dept of Foreign Affairs (DFA) 1996, Adviser to Fed. Councillor Joseph Deiss 1999, Deputy Sec.-Gen., DFA 2002–05; Vice-Chancellor of Switzerland 2005–07, Fed. Chancellor 2008–15; mem. Christian Democratic People's Party. *Address:* c/o Federal Chancellery, Bundeshaus West, 3003 Bern, Switzerland (office).

CASANOVA, Jean-Claude, DEcon; French economist, academic and journalist; *Editor, Commentaire;* b. 11 June 1934, Ajaccio, Corsica; s. of Jean Casanova and Marie-Antoinette Luciani; m. Marie-Thérèse Demargne 1962; two s.; ed Lycée Carnot, Inst. des Hautes Etudes, Tunis, Univ. of Paris, Harvard Univ.; Asst Fondation nat. des sciences politiques 1958; Chief of Staff to Minister of Industry 1958–61; Asst in Law Faculty, Univ. of Dijon 1963; Sr Lecturer then Prof., Faculty of Law and Econ. Sciences, Univ. of Nancy 1964–68; with Univ. of Paris-Nanterre 1968; with Inst. d'Etudes politiques, Paris 1969–; Dir of Studies and Research, Fondation nationale des sciences politiques 1965–90, Pres. 2007–; Tech. Adviser to Minister of Educ. 1972–74; Adviser to Prime Minister Raymond Barre 1976–81; Ed. Commentaire 1978–; leader writer, L'Express 1985–95; regular contrib. to Le Figaro 1996–2001; mem. Comm. on Renovation and Ethics of Public Life 2012–; mem. Econ. and Social Council 1994–2004, Acad. des Sciences morales et politiques 1996–; columnist, Le Monde 2002–; Pres. Fondation nationale des sciences politiques 2007–16; Officier, Ordre nat. du Mérite 1996, Commdr, Légion d'honneur 2008. *Address:* Commentaire, 116 rue du Bac, 75007 Paris (office); Casa Strenna, 20275, Botticella, Ersa, Corsica (home); 11–13 rue de l'Aude, 75014 Paris, France (home). *Telephone:* 1-45-49-37-82 (office); 1-43-26-51-95 (home). *Fax:* 1-45-44-32-18 (office). *E-mail:* jcc@commentaire.fr (office); jccasanova@icloud.com (home). *Website:* www.commentaire.fr (office).

CASAS-GONZALEZ, Antonio, BA, MA, PhD; Venezuelan economist, business executive and fmr government official; *Economic Adviser and Board Member, Tecnoconsult SA;* b. 24 July 1933, Mérida; m. Carmen Elena Granadino de Casas; five s. one d.; ed George Washington Univ., Georgetown Univ., USA; fmrly Prof. of Econs at various insts; Adviser, Venezuelan Petrochemical Inst. and Asst to Minister of Mines and Hydrocarbons 1957–59; Petroleum and Econ. Counsellor, Embassy in Washington, DC 1959–61; with Inter-American Devt Bank 1961–69; Vice-Minister of Devt 1969; Minister for Nat. Planning Office (CORDIPLAN) 1972; Man. Dir Petróleos de Venezuela (UK) SA 1990–94; Gov. Banco Cen. de Venezuela 1994–99; Vice-Pres. Intergovernmental Group of Twenty-Four on Int. Monetary Affairs 1996–; mem. Bd of Dirs Venezolana de Aviación (VIASA) 1970–73, Corp. Andina de Fomento 1970–73, Banco Cen. de Venezuela 1972–75, Corp. Venezolana de Guyana 1979–82, Petróleos de Venezuela SA 1979–90; currently Econ. Adviser and Bd mem., Tecnoconsult SA; mem. Int. Council Elliot School of Int. Affairs, George Washington Univ.; 16 decorations from nine countries. *Publications include:* América Latina y los problemas de Desarrollo (co-author) 1974, Venezuela y el CIAP (co-author) 1974, La planificación en América Latina (co-author) 1975, World Development (co-author) 1977; articles for various publs. *Leisure interest:* golf. *Address:* Tecnoconsult SA, Av. Rómulo Gallegos, Urbanización. Los Dos Caminos, No. 23, Caracas, Venezuela (office). *Telephone:* (212) 273 8000 (office). *E-mail:* comercial@tecnoconsult.com (office). *Website:* www.tecnoconsult.com (office).

CASE, Stephen M., MA; American business executive; b. 21 Aug. 1958, Honolulu, Hawaii; m. 1st Joanne Case 1985 (divorced 1996); three d.; m. 2nd Jean Case 1998; ed Williams Coll.; worked in marketing dept, Procter & Gamble 1980–82; Man. of New Pizza Devt, Pizza Hut Div., PepsiCo 1982–83; Marketing Asst, Control Video Corpn, Va 1983–85, Marketing Dir Quantum Computer Services (fmrly Control Video then renamed America Online (AOL)) 1985–92, CEO AOL 1992–2001, Chair. 1995–2001; Chair. AOL Time Warner (cr. after merger of Time Warner and AOL) 2001–03, Dir with jt responsibility for corp. strategy 2003, mem. Bd of Dirs –2005 (resgnd); f. Revolution LLC 2005; prin. investor and Chair. Exclusive Resorts LLC, Denver, Colo 2004; prin. investor, Maui Land and Pineapple, HI; f. Case Foundation 1997; f. ABC2, Accelerate Brain Cancer Cure 2001; Entrepreneur of the Year, Incorporated Magazine 1994. *Leisure interests:* reading political science and history. *Address:* c/o The Case Foundation, 1717 Rhode Island Avenue, NW, Seventh Floor, Washington, DC 20036, USA. *Website:* casefoundation.org; www.abc2.org.

CASEY, Robert (Bob) Patrick, Jr, JD; American lawyer and politician; *Senator from Pennsylvania;* b. 13 April 1960, Scranton, Pa; eldest s. of Pa Gov. Robert P. Casey and Ellen Casey; m. Terese Foppiano Casey 1985; four d.; ed The Coll. of the Holy Cross, Catholic Univ. of America; taught fifth grade and coached eighth grade basketball team for Jesuit Volunteer Corps, Gesu School, Philadelphia 1983; began practising law in Scranton 1988; Pa State Auditor Gen. 1997–2005; cand. for State Gov. 2002; State Treas. 2005–06; Senator from Pa 2007–, mem. Foreign Relations Cttee, Agric., Nutrition and Forestry Cttee, Health, Educ., Labor and Pensions Cttee, Special Cttee on Aging, Jt Econ. Cttee; Democrat. *Address:* 393 Russell Senate Office Building, Washington, DC 20510, USA (office). *Telephone:* (202) 224-6324 (office). *Fax:* (202) 228-0604 (office). *Website:* casey.senate.gov (office); bobcasey.com (office).

CASH, Patrick (Pat) Hart; Australian sports commentator, tennis coach and fmr professional tennis player; b. 27 May 1965, Melbourne, Vic.; s. of Patrick Cussen and Dorothy Hart Cash; one s. one d. with Anne-Britt Kristiansen; m. Emily Bendit 1990 (divorced 2002); twin s.; ed Whitefriars Coll.; winner, US Open Jr Championship 1982; mem. winning Australian Davis Cup team 1983, 1986; in quarter-finals at Wimbledon 1985; finalist, Australian Open 1987, 1988; Wimbledon Champion 1987; retd 1997; plays on Masters Tennis circuit; co-f. Pat Cash Tennis Acad.; currently BBC Wimbledon analyst; lives in London; Australian Tennis Hall of Fame 2003. *Leisure interests:* music, football. *Address:* c/o Duncan March, Academies and Global Management, Once Upon A Time, Golden House, 30 Great Pulteney Street, London, W1F 9NN, England (office); c/o Marina Paul, Australian Management (office). *Telephone:* 7956-447811 (mobile) (office); (20) 7534-8804 (office); (411) 423826 (office). *E-mail:* duncan@patcash.co.uk (office); marina@marinapaul.com (office). *Website:* www.onceuponlondon.com (office); www.atpworldtour.com/en/players/enwiki/C023/overview; www.patcash.net; www.patcash.co.uk.

CASHMORE, Roger John, CMG, MA, DPhil, FRS, FInstP; British physicist and academic; *Chairman, UK Atomic Energy Authority (UKAEA);* b. 22 Aug. 1944, Birmingham; s. of C. J. C. Cashmore and E. M. Cashmore; m. Elizabeth Ann Lindsay 1971; one s.; ed Dudley Grammar School, St John's Coll., Cambridge, Balliol Coll., Oxford; Weir Jr Research Fellow, Univ. Coll., Oxford 1967–69; 1851 Research Fellow 1968; Research Assoc. Stanford Linear Accelerator, Calif. 1969–74; Research Officer, Univ. of Oxford 1974–79, Lecturer 1979–90, Reader in Experimental Physics 1990–91, Prof. 1991–98; Research Dir, CERN 1999–2003, Deputy Dir Gen. 2002–03; Prin. Brasenose Coll. Oxford 2002–; Chair. UKAEA 2010–; Boys Prize, Inst. of Physics 1983, Humboldt Research Award 1995. *Publications:* contribs to Physics Review. *Leisure interests:* sports, wine. *Address:* Culham Science Centre, Abingdon, Oxon., OX14 3DB, England (office). *Telephone:* (1235) 466700 (office). *E-mail:* roger.cashmore@physics.ox.ac.uk (office).

CASIMIR, Pierre-Richard, LLB; Haitian lawyer, diplomatist and politician; b. 19 Feb. 1970, Port-au-Prince; ed Haiti State Univ., Univ. of Montreal, Canada; admitted to the Bar 1999; Instructor in Civic Educ., Amicale des Juristes 1994; Dir Legal Assistance Dept, Staff Training and Improvement Acad. 1995–; Program Dir USAID Poor Detainees Legal Assistance Program 1995–99; fmr Legal Asst and Interpreter, US Embassy Ministerial Advisory Team on Justice; fmr Assoc., Cabinet Lissade (law firm), Port-au-Prince; Legal Counsel to Pres. of Haiti 1999; Deputy Dir Pvt. Office of Minister of Justice 2001; mem. Pvt. Office of Pres. of Haiti 2004–05; Consul-Gen. in Montreal 2005–11; Sec. of State for Foreign Affairs 2011–12, Minister of Foreign Affairs and Religion 2012–14; mem. Bar Asscn of Port-au-Prince. *Address:* c/o Ministry of Foreign Affairs and Religion, boulevard Harry S. Truman, Cité de l'Exposition, Port-au-Prince, Haiti (office).

CASINI, Pier Ferdinando; Italian politician; b. 3 Dec. 1955, Bologna; m. Roberta Lubich (divorced); two d.; m. Azzurra Caltagirone 2007; one d.; joined Unione dei Democratici Cristiani e di Centro (UDC) 1980, Leader from 2002; elected Town Councillor, Bologna 1980; mem. Chamber of Deputies 1983–2013, Pres. 2001–06, Group Leader 2008–12; mem. Senate 2013–; mem. European Parl. 1994–2001 (PPE-DE Group); Pres. Inter-Parl. Union 2005–08; Co-Pres. Centrist Democrat International (CDI) (fmrly Christian Democrat International) from 2006, now Honorific Pres.; fmr Pres. Christian Democratic Centre, Sec. 1994–2001; Order of Merit from Austria, Brazil, Chile, France, Germany, Hungary, Lithuania, Luxembourg, Malaysia, Malta, Norway, Peru, Poland, San Marino, Spain. *Address:* Unione dei Democratici Cristiani e di Centro, Via dei Due Macelli 66, 00182 Roma, Italy (office). *Telephone:* (06) 69791001 (office). *Fax:* (06) 6791574 (office). *E-mail:* pier@pierferdinandocasini.it; info@udc-italia.it (office). *Website:* www.udc-italia.it (office); www.pierferdinandocasini.it.

CASPERSEN, Sven Lars, MEcon; Danish academic; b. 30 June 1935, Åabenraa; s. of Jes P. Caspersen and Carla Caspersen; m. Eva Caspersen 1962; three s.; Asst Sec., Danish Cen. Bureau of Statistics 1962–64; Deputy Chief, Cen. Statistical Centre of Danish Insurance Cos at Danish Insurance Asscn 1964–68; Assoc. Prof. of Statistics, Copenhagen School of Econs and Business Admin. 1968–73, Head of Dept of Statistics 1970–73; Dean of Social Sciences, Ålborg Univ. 2004, Rector 1976–2004, Chair. 2004–06; Chair. Bd Copenhagen Stock Exchange 1989–96; Chair. Liaison Cttee of Rectors' Confs of mem. states of the EC 1992–94; Chair. Govt Advisory Council on EU Matters 1993–2001; Chair. European Capital Markets Inst. 1993–95; Vice-Pres. Fed. of Stock Exchanges of the EC 1993–95,

Pres. 1995–96; Pres. Int. Asscn of Univ. Presidents 1999–2002; Chair. Aalborg Theatre 1986; Dr hc (Vilnius Tech. Univ.) 1999; recipient, Tribute of Appreciation, US Dept of State 1981. *Leisure interests:* chess, bridge, tennis. *Address:* Duebrødrevej 6, 9000 Aalborg, Denmark.

CASS, Sir Geoffrey Arthur, Kt, MA (Oxon.), MA (Cantab.), CCMI; British publishing executive and arts and lawn tennis administrator; b. 11 Aug. 1932, Bishop Auckland; s. of Arthur Cass and Jessie Cass (née Simpson); m. Olwen Mary Richards, MBE, JP, DL 1957; four d.; ed Queen Elizabeth Grammar School, Darlington and Jesus Coll., Oxford; Nuffield Coll., Oxford 1957–58; RAF 1958–60; ed. Automation 1960–61; Consultant, PA Man. Consultants Ltd 1960–65; Pvt. Man. Consultant, British Communications Corpn and Controls and Communications Ltd 1965; Dir Controls and Communications Ltd 1966–69; Dir George Allen & Unwin 1965–67, Man. Dir 1967–71; Dir Weidenfeld Publrs. 1972–74, Univ. of Chicago Press, UK 1971–86; Chief Exec. Cambridge Univ. Press 1972–92, Consultant 1992–; Sec. Press Syndicate, Univ. of Cambridge 1974–92; Univ. Printer 1982–83, 1991–92; Fellow, Clare Hall, Cambridge 1979–; Trustee Shakespeare Birthplace Trust 1982–94 (Life Trustee 1994–); Chair. Royal Shakespeare Co. 1985–2000 (Deputy Pres. 2000–11), Royal Theatrical Support Trust (fmrly Royal Shakespeare Theatre Trust) 1983–, British Int. Tennis and Nat. Training 1985–90, Nat. Ranking Cttee; mem. Bd of Man., Lawn Tennis Asscn of GB 1985–90, 1993–2000, Deputy Pres. 1994–96, Pres. 1997–99; Chair. Tennis Foundation 2003–07, Pres. 2007–; mem. Cttee of Man., Wimbledon Championships 1990–2002; Pres., Chair. or mem. numerous other trusts, bds, cttees, charitable appeals and advisory bodies particularly in connection with theatre, sport and medicine; Oxford tennis Blue and badminton; Hon. Fellow, Jesus Coll., Oxford 1998; Chevalier, Ordre des Arts et Lettres. *Achievements include:* played in Wimbledon Tennis Championships 1954, 1955, 1956, 1959; British Veterans Singles Champion, Wimbledon 1978. *Publications:* articles in professional journals. *Leisure interests:* tennis, theatre. *Address:* Middlefield, Huntingdon Road, Cambridge, CB3 0LH, England (home). *Website:* www.tennisfoundation.org.uk.

CASSEL, Vincent; French actor; b. 23 Nov. 1966, Paris; s. of Jean-Pierre Cassel; m. 1st Monica Bellucci 1999 (divorced 2013); two d.; m. 2nd Tina Kunakey 2018; Patrick Dewaere Hon. Award, Valenciennes Int. Festival of Action and Adventure Films 2002. *Films include* Les Clés du paradis 1991, Hot Chocolate 1992, Café au Lait 1993, Jefferson in Paris 1995, La Haine 1995, Blood of the Hunter 1995, Adultery: A User's Guide 1995, L'Appartement 1996, L'Elève 1996, Come mi vuoi 1996, Dobermann 1997, Compromis 1998, Mediterranée 1998, Le Plaisir (et ses petits tracas) 1998, Elizabeth 1998, Guest House Paradiso 1999, Messenger: The Story of Joan of Arc 1999, Les Rivières pourpres (Crimson Rivers) 2000, Birthday Girl 2000, The Reckoning 2001, Le Pacte des loups (Brotherhood of the Wolf) 2001, Sur mes lèvres 2001, Shrek 2001, Irréversible (also co-producer) 2002, Ice Age 2002, Blueberry 2004, Spy Bound 2004, Ocean's Twelve 2004, Robots (voice) 2005, Derailed 2005, Sheitan 2006, Ocean's Thirteen 2007, Eastern Promises 2007, Sa majesté Minor 2007, L'instinct de mort (Best Actor Award, Tokyo Int. Film Festival 2008, César Award for Best Actor 2009, Globes de Cristal Award for Best Actor 2009, Golden Globe Award for Best European Actor 2009, Étoile d'Or for Best Actor 2009) 2008, L'ennemi public no. 1 (Best Actor Award, Tokyo Int. Film Festival 2008, César Award for Best Actor 2009, Golden Globe Award for Best European Actor 2009, Lumiere Award for Best Actor 2009, Étoile d'Or for Best Actor 2009) 2008, Lascars (voice) 2009, À deriva 2009, Black Swan 2010, Our Day Will Come 2010, The Monk 2011, A Dangerous Method 2011, Trance 2013, Rio, I Love You 2014, Beauty and the Beast 2014, Child 44 2015, Partisan 2015, Tale of Tales 2015, My King 2015, One Wild Moment 2015, The Little Prince (voice) 2015, It's Only the End of the World (Canadian Screen Award for Performance by an Actor in a Supporting Role 2017) 2016, Jason Bourne 2016, The Movie of My Life 2017, Gauguin: Voyage to Tahiti 2017, Black Tide 2018, The World Is Yours 2018, The Great Mystical Circus 2018, The Emperor of Paris 2018. *Address:* c/o Laurent Grégoire, Adéquat, 21 rue d'uzés, 75002 Paris, France (office). *Telephone:* 1-42-80-00-42 (Paris) (office); (424) 288-2000 (Los Angeles) (office). *Fax:* 1-42-80-00-43 (Paris) (office). *E-mail:* agence@agence-adequat.com (office). *Website:* www.agence-adequat.com (office).

CASSESE, Sabino; Italian lawyer, judge and academic; *Professor Emeritus, Scuola Normale Superiore di Pisa;* b. 20 Oct. 1935, Atripalda; Prof., Faculté Int. de droit comparé, Luxembourg 1966; Prof. of Public Admin. and Prof. of Govt, Dept of Econs, Univs of Ancona and Naples, Political Science Dept, Univ. of Rome, School for Higher Civil Servants, Rome; Dir Inst. of Public Law, Law Dept, Univ. of Rome 'La Sapienza' 1991–93, Prof. of Admin. Law 1993–2005; Judge, Corte costituzionale (Constitutional Court) 2005–; Prof., Univ. de Paris I 1986, 1994; Assoc. Prof., Univ. of Nantes 1987; now Prof. Emer., Scuola Normale Superiore di Pisa, teaches History of Political Inst.; Visiting Prof., Inst. d'Etudes Politiques, Paris 1991, 2005–07; Visiting Scholar, Law School, Univ. of California, Berkeley 1965, LSE 1969, Law School, Stanford Univ., USA 1970, 1975, 1981, 1986; Guest Scholar, Wilson Int. Center for Scholars, Washington, DC 1983; Visiting Scholar and Jemolo Fellow, Nuffield Coll., Oxford 1987–89, 1995; Pres. European Group of Public Admin (Int. Inst. of Admin. Sciences) 1987–91; Co-founder Istituto di Ricerche sulla Pubblica Amministrazione, Rome 2004, Fellow; mem. editorial bds of several journals, including Rivista di Diritto Pubblico, International Review of Administrative Sciences, Revue européenne de droit administratif, Western European Politics, Revue française d'administration publique; mem. Prime Minister's policy unit 1988–89; fmr consultant to several Govt ministries and Bank of Italy; Minister for the Public Service 1993–94; Fellow, European Inst. of Public Admin., Maastricht 1985–86; Grande Ufficiale della Repubblica Italiana, Cavaliere di Gran Croce, Ordino al Merito della Repubblica Italiana; Dr hc (Aix-en-Provence) 1987, (Cordoba) 1995, (Panthéon-Assas) 1998, (Castilla-La Mancha) 2002, (Athens) 2002, (Macerata) 2002, (European Univ. Inst., Florence) 2010; Campano d'Oro, Associazione Laureati Ateneo Pisano 1994, Premio Tarantelli 1993, Prix Alexis de Tocqueville, Institut européen d'admin publique 1997. *Publications:* Lo Stato introvabile 1998, Maggioranza e Minoranza. Il problema della democrazia in Italia 1995, La nuova Costituzione economica 2000, Le basi del diritto amministrativo 2000, Il mondo nuovo del diritto 2008, I tribunali di Babele 2009, Il diritto globale 2009, Massimo Severo Giannini 2010, Il diritto amministrativo: storia e prospettive 2010, Lo stato fascista 2010, When Legal Orders Collide: The Role of Courts 2010, L'Italia una società senza Stato 2011, Governare gli italiani: Storia dello stato 2014, and many other books. *E-mail:* s.cassese@www.irpa.eu (office). *Website:* www.irpa.eu (office).

CASSIDY, (Charles) Michael Ardagh, BD, MA; South African evangelist and author; b. 24 Sept. 1936, Johannesburg; s. of Charles Stewart Cassidy and Mary Craufurd Cassidy; m. Carol Bam 1969; one s. two d.; ed Parktown School, Johannesburg, Michaelhouse, Natal, Cambridge Univ., UK, Fuller Theological Seminary, Calif., USA; Founder and Int. Team Leader, interdenominational evangelistic mission team African Enterprise 1962–2002; conducted missions in cities including Cape Town, Johannesburg, Nairobi, Cairo, Lusaka, Gaborone, Monrovia (Liberia), Mbabane (Eswatini); initiated SA Congress on Mission and Evangelism 1973, Pan African Christian Leadership Ass. 1976, SA Christian Leadership Ass. 1979, 2003, Nat. Initiative for Reconciliation 1985, Nat. Initiative for Reformation of S Africa 2003; speaker at events including Lausanne II conf., Manila, Philippines 1989, Missionsfest 1990, N American Renewal Conf. 1990, UN 50th Anniversary, Dublin Castle, Repub. of Ireland 1995; admitted to Anglican Order of Simon of Cyrene 1983; Patron Transformation Africa Prayer Initiative, Christians for Peace in Africa; Hon. Co-Chair. of Lausanne Movement 2012; Hon. HLD (Azusa Pacific Univ., USA) 1993; Paul Harris Fellow, Rotary Award 1997, Michaelhouse St Michael's Award 1997, Fuller Seminary Distinguished Alumnus 2012. *Publications:* Decade of Decisions 1970, Where Are You Taking the World Anyway? 1971, Prisoners of Hope 1974, Relationship Tangle 1974, Bursting the Wineskins 1983, Chasing the Wind 1985, The Passing Summer 1989, The Politics of Love 1991, A Witness For Ever 1995, Window on the Word 1997, Getting to the Heart of Things 2005, What on Earth Are You Thinking for Heaven's Sake? 2006, So You Want to Get Married? 2010, The Church Jesus Prayed For 2012. *Leisure interests:* music, photography, scrapbooks, sport, jogging. *Address:* African Enterprise, PO Box 13140, Cascades 3202, South Africa (office). *Telephone:* (33) 347-7037 (office). *Fax:* (33) 347-1915 (office). *E-mail:* mcassidy@pobox.com (office). *Website:* www.africanenterprise.org.za (office).

CASSIDY, HE Cardinal Edward Idris, AC, DCnL; Australian fmr ecclesiastic; b. 5 July 1924, Sydney, NSW; s. of Harold Cassidy and Dorothy Phillips; ed Parramatta High School, Sydney, St Columba's Seminary, Springwood, St Patrick's Coll. Manly, Lateran Univ. and Pontifical Ecclesiastical Acad., Rome, Vatican City; ordained priest 1949; Asst Priest, Yenda 1950–52; diplomatic service in India 1955–62, Ireland 1962–67, El Salvador 1967–69, Argentina 1969–70; consecrated Archbishop 1970; Titular Archbishop of Amantia 1970; Apostolic Pro-Nuncio in Taiwan 1970–79 (also accred to Bangladesh and Burma 1973–79); Apostolic Del. to Southern Africa and Apostolic Pro-Nuncio to Lesotho 1979–84; Apostolic Pro-Nuncio to the Netherlands 1984–88; Substitute of the Secr. of State 1988–89; Pres. Pontifical Council for Promoting Christian Unity and Comm. for Religious Relations with the Jews 1989–2001; cr. Cardinal-Deacon of S. Maria in Via Lata 1991, Cardinal Priest 2001; Cavaliere, Gran Croce dell'Ordine al Merito della Repubblica Italiana; decorations from El Salvador, Taiwan, Netherlands, Australia, France, Sweden and Germany. *Publications include:* Vatican II – Ecumenism and Interreligious Dialogue 2005, My Years in Vatican Service 2009. *Leisure interests:* tennis, golf, music. *Address:* 16 Coachwood Drive, Warabrook, NSW 2304, Australia (home). *Telephone:* (2) 4968-9025 (home). *Fax:* (2) 4968-9064 (home). *E-mail:* icassidy4@bigpond.com.

CASSIDY, Kathryn A., BA, MBA; American business executive; *Vice-President, Corporate Treasury, General Electric Company;* m.; three c.; ed Univ. of Connecticut, Fordham Univ.; joined General Electric (GE) 1980, serving in several positions including Man. Dir GE Capital Real Estate, led Real Estate Capital Markets 1996–2000, Vice-Pres. and Treas. General Electric Co. 2001–; mem. Bd of Dirs UCONN Foundation, Building with Books; mem. Treasury Leadership Roundtable, Washington, DC. *Address:* 152 Canyon Road, Wilton, CT 06897-2639; General Electric Company, 3135 Easton Turnpike, Fairfield, CT 06828-0001, USA (office). *Telephone:* (203) 373-2211 (office). *Fax:* (203) 373-3131 (office). *Website:* www.ge.com (office).

CASSIDY, William (Bill) Morgan, BS, MD; American physician and politician; *Senator from Louisiana;* b. 28 Sept. 1957, Chicago, Ill.; m. Laura Layden; one s. two d.; ed Louisiana State Univ.; co-f. Greater Baton Rouge Community Clinic 1998; mem., Louisiana State Senate from Dist 16 2006–09; mem. US House of Reps from 6th Louisiana Dist 2009–14, Vice-Chair. Health and Welfare Cttee, mem. Educ. & Environmental Quality Cttee; Senator from Louisiana 2015–; fmr Assoc. Prof. of Medicine, Louisiana State Univ.; Sunday school teacher, Chapel on the Campus; mem. American Coll. of Physicians, Louisiana State Medical Soc. (mem. Bd of Dirs), East Baton Rouge Parish Medical Soc. (Pres. 1998), American Asscn for Study of Liver Diseases, Gastroenterology Soc.; Republican. *Address:* Senate Office Building, Washington, DC 20510, USA (office). *Website:* www.senate.gov (office).

CASSIS, Ignazio, MD, MPH; Swiss physician and politician; *Head, Federal Department of Foreign Affairs;* b. 1961, Malcanto; s. of Gion Cassis and Mariarosa Cassis; m. Paola Cassis; ed Univ. of Zurich, Univ. of Geneva; worked as a doctor 1988–96; Cantonal Officer of Public Health, Ticino 1996–2008; mem. Legis. Council, Collina d'Oro, Ticino 2004–12; mem. Nat. Council 2007–17, Chair. Social Security and Health Cttee 2015–17, Pres. FDP Parl. Group 2015–17; mem. Fed. Council 2017–; Head, Fed. Dept of Foreign Affairs 2017–; lecturer at various Swiss univs 2001–; Pres. Fourchette Verte Ticino 2009–15; Vice-Pres., Swiss Medical Association (FMH) 2008–12; mem. FDP.The Liberals. *Address:* Federal Department of Foreign Affairs, Bundeshaus West, 3003 Bern, Switzerland (office). *Telephone:* 584653333 (office). *Fax:* 584627866 (office). *E-mail:* info@eda.admin.ch (office). *Website:* www.eda.admin.ch (office).

CASSON, Mark Christopher, BA, FRSA, FBA; British economist and academic; *Professor of Economics, University of Reading;* b. 17 Dec. 1945, Grappenhall, Cheshire; s. of Stanley Christopher Casson and Dorothy Nowell Barlow; m. Janet Penelope Close 1975; one d.; ed Manchester Grammar School, Univ. of Bristol, Churchill Coll., Cambridge; Lecturer in Econs, Univ. of Reading 1969–77, Reader 1977–81, Prof. 1981–, Head Dept of Econs 1987–94, Dir Centre for Institutional Performance 2003–; Pres., Asscn of Business Historians 2007–09; Fellow, Acad. of Int. Business, Univ. of Leeds 1993, Visiting Prof. of Int. Business 1995–; Visiting Prof. of Man., Univ. of London 2004–, Univ. of York 2010–; Visiting Fellow, Lancaster Univ. 2009–; Leverhulme Major Research Fellow 2006–09; mem.

Council Royal Econ. Soc. 1985–90; Chair. Business Enterprise Heritage Trust 2000–. *Publications include:* The Future of the Multinational Enterprise 1976, The Entrepreneur: An Economic Theory 1982, Economics of Unemployment: An Historical Perspective 1983, The Firm and the Market: Studies in Multinational Enterprise and the Scope of the Firm 1987, The Economics of Business Culture: Game Theory, Transaction Costs and Economic Welfare 1981, Entrepreneurship and Business Culture 1995, Information and Organization: A New Perspective on the Theory of the Firm 1997, Economics of International Business 2000, Enterprise and Leadership 2000, Oxford Handbook of Entrepreneurship 2006, Economics of Networks 2008, The World's First Railway System 2009, The Multinational Enterprise Revisited 2009, Entrepreneurship: Theory, Networks, History 2010, Markets and Market Institutions 2011, History of Entrepreneurship 2013, The Entrepreneur in History 2013, Large Databases in Economic History 2013, Theory of International Business: Economic Models and Methods 2016, The Multinational Enterprise: Theory and History 2017. *Leisure interests:* railway history, Church of England activities, book collecting, drawing in pastel. *Address:* Department of Economics, University of Reading, PO Box 218, Reading, Berks., RG6 6AA (office); 6 Wayside Green, Woodcote, Reading, Berks., RG8 0QJ, England (home). *Telephone:* (118) 931-8227 (office); (1491) 681483 (home). *Fax:* (118) 975-0236 (office). *E-mail:* m.c.casson@reading.ac.uk (office). *Website:* www.reading.ac.uk/economics/about/staff/m-c-casson.aspx (office).

CASTA, Laetitia; French model and actress; b. 11 May 1978, Pont-Audemer; d. of Dominique Casta and Line Casta; one d. (with pnr Stephane Sednaoui); launched by Yves Saint Laurent; first maj. advertising campaign for Guess jeans 1993; model, Victoria's Secret 1996–99; appeared in Sports Illustrated 1997, 1998, 1999, on covers of Vogue, Elle, Cosmopolitan, Rolling Stone; contracts with L'Oréal, Galeries Lafayette; chosen to represent Marianne (nat. emblem of France) 2000. *Films include:* Astérix et Obélix contre César 1999, La bicyclette bleue, Les ames fortes (TV miniseries) 2000, Gitano 2000, Rue des plaisirs 2002, Errance 2003, Luisa Sanfelice (TV miniseries) 2004, La déraison du Louvre 2006, Le grand appartement 2006, La jeune fille et les loups 2008, Nés en 68 2008, Visage 2009, La nouvelle guerre des boutons (War of the Buttons) 2011, Arbitrage 2012, Do Not Disturb 2012, Tied 2013, Una donna per amica 2014, Sous les jupes des filles 2014, Des lendemains qui chantent 2014, Arletty, une passion coupable (TV film) 2014, Des Apaches 2015. *Address:* c/o Artmedia, 10 ave Georges V, 75008 Paris, France (office).

CASTANEDA GUTMAN, Jorge Germán, BA, MA, PhD; Mexican politician, academic and writer; *Global Distinguished Professor of Politics and Latin American and Caribbean Studies, New York University;* b. 24 May 1953, Mexico City; s. of Jorge Castañeda y Álvarez de la Rosa; m. Miriam Morales; one s.; ed Princeton Univ., USA, Université de Paris-I (Panthéon-Sorbonne), Ecole Pratique des Hautes Etudes, Paris I, Univ. of Paris, France; has taught at Nat. Autonomous Univ. of Mexico, Princeton Univ., Univ. of California, Berkeley; Sr Assoc. Carnegie Endowment for Int. Peace 1985–87; f. San Angel Group 1994; Global Distinguished Prof. of Politics and Latin American and Caribbean Studies, New York Univ. 1997–; Sec. of State for Foreign Affairs 2000–03 (resgnd); began travelling around the country, giving lectures and promoting his ideas; announced campaign for candidacy for 2006 presidential election 2004, Supreme Court ruled he could not run without support of a registered political party, took case to Inter-American Court of Human Rights; mem. Bd of Dirs Human Rights Watch; regular columnist for Reforma (Mexican daily newspaper), Los Angeles Times, Newsweek International, Project Syndicate; John D. and Catherine T. MacArthur Foundation Research and Writing Grant Recipient 1989–91. *Publications:* Nicaragua: Contradicciones en la Revolución 1980, Los últimos capitalismos. El capital financiero: México y los 'nuevos países industrializados' 1982, México: El futuro en juego 1987, Limits on Friendship: United States and Mexico (with Robert A. Pastor) 1989, La casa por la ventana 1993, Utopia Unarmed: The Latin American Left After the Cold War 1993, The Mexican Shock 1995, The Estados Unidos Affair. Cinco ensayos sobre un 'amor' oblicuo 1996, Compañero: The Life and Death of Che Guevara 1997, Perpetuating Power: How Mexican Presidents Were Chosen 2000, Somos Muchos: Ideas para el Mañana 2004, La diferencia: Radiografía de un sexenio (with Rubén Aguilar) 2007, Y Mexico Por Que No? 2008, Ex Mex: From Migrants to Immigrants 2008, Mañana Forever?: Mexico and the Mexicans 2011; numerous articles. *Address:* Center for Latin American and Caribbean Studies, King Juan Carlos I of Spain Center, New York University, 53 Washington Square South, Floor 4W, New York, NY 10012, USA (office). *Telephone:* (212) 998-8686 (office). *Fax:* (212) 995-4163 (office). *E-mail:* jorge.castaneda@nyu.edu (office). *Website:* clacs.as.nyu.edu/page/home (office).

CASTAÑEDA LOSSIO, Oscar Luis; Peruvian lawyer and politician; *Mayor of Lima;* b. 21 June 1945, Chiclayo, Lambayeque; s. of Carlos Castañeda Iparraguire; ed Colegio Manuel Pardo, Chiclayo, Pontificia Universidad Católica del Perú; began career with Empresa Municipal Administradora del Peaje de Lima (Metropolitan Inst. for Public Transportation); fmr Man. Dir Banco Industrial del Perú; Exec. Pres. Instituto Peruano de Seguridad Social (Nat. Inst. of Public Health) 1990–96; fmr Dir several private and public cos including COFIDE, EMMSA, ENATA, ESMIL, ENACO; mem. Solidaridad Nacional (SN) party, SN presidential cand. 2000; Mayor of Lima 2003–10, 2015–. *Address:* Office of the Mayor, Municipalidad Metropolitana de Lima, Jirón de la Unión 300/Jirón Conde de Superunda 141, Lima, Peru (office). *Telephone:* (1) 632-1300 (switchboard) (office). *E-mail:* webmaster@munlima.gob.pe (office). *Website:* www.munlima.gob.pe (office).

CASTANEDA MAGAÑA, Carlos Alfredo; Salvadorean politician; *Minister of Foreign Affairs;* b. 24 April 1954, Chalchuapa, Santa Ana Dept; ed Kiev State Univ.; mem. Legis. Ass. (FMLN) for Sonsonate constituency 2000–03, 2003–06, 2006–09; fmr Prof., Dept of Law, Univ. Modular Abierta; Deputy Minister of Foreign Affairs 2009–18, Minister of Foreign Affairs 2018–; mem. Frente Farabundo Marti para la Liberación Nacional (FMLN), FMLN Rep. in Cuba 1990–93, Regional Dir, FMLN Sonsonate Br. 1994–2009. *Address:* Ministry of Foreign Affairs, Calle El Pedregal, Blvd Cancillería, Ciudad Merliot, Antiguo Cuscatlán, La Libertad, San Salvador, El Salvador (office). *Telephone:* 2231-1001 (office). *Fax:* 2289-8016 (office). *E-mail:* webmaster@rree.gob.sv (office). *Website:* www.rree.gob.sv (office).

CASTEEN, John Thomas, III, BA, MA, PhD, FACLS; American writer, academic and fmr university administrator; *University Professor and President Emeritus, University of Virginia;* b. 11 Dec. 1943, Portsmouth, Va; s. of John T. Casteen, Jr and Naomi Irene Casteen; m. Elizabeth F. Casteen; two s. three d.; ed Univ. of Virginia; Asst Prof. of English, Univ. of California, Berkeley 1970–75; Assoc. Prof. and Dean, Univ. of Virginia 1975–81, Pres. Univ. of Virginia 1990–2010, also George M. Kaufman Presidential Prof. and Prof. of English, Pres. Emer. 2010–; Sec. of Educ., Commonwealth of Va 1982–85; Pres. and Prof., Univ. of Connecticut 1985–90; Chair. Jefferson Science Assocs LLC, Universitas 21; mem. Bd of Dirs, Wachovia Corpn, Altria Group, Strayer, Inc., Echo360, U21 Global Pte Ltd, SAGE Publs Inc.; Trustee, Chesapeake Bay Foundation, Mariner's Museum, Jamestown-Yorktown Foundation, Woodrow Wilson Int. Center for Scholars; Fellow, American Acad. of Arts and Sciences 2009, American Council of Learned Socs; Hon. LLD (Shenandoah Coll.), (Bentley Coll.) 1992, (Piedmont Community Coll.) 1992, (Bridgewater Coll.) 1993, Transylvania Univ.) 1999; Hon. PhD (Univ. of Edinburgh) 2011; Dr hc (Athens) 1996; Mishima Award 1987, Raven Award, Univ. of Virginia, Outstanding Virginian of 1993, American Assn of Univ. Profs Jackson Davis Award 1993, Gold Medal, Nat. Inst. of Social Sciences 1998, Higher Educ. Center for Alcohol and Other Drug Prevention President's Leadership Group Award 2002, Architecture Medal for Virginia Service, Virginia Soc. of the AIA 2004, Virginian of the Year 2010, John Hope Franklin Award 2013. *Publications:* 16 stories 1982; numerous essays and articles 1970–. *Leisure interests:* sailing, walking. *Address:* Office of the President Emeritus, University of Virginia, Alderman Library, PO Box 400283, Charlottesville, VA 22904, USA (office). *Telephone:* (434) 924-6243 (office). *Fax:* (434) 243-6688 (office). *E-mail:* jtc@virginia.edu (office). *Website:* www.virginia.edu/presidentemeritus (office).

CASTEL, Charles, MA, LLM; Haitian lawyer, economist and fmr central banker; ed Haiti State Univ., Port-au-Prince, Columbia Univ. and State Univ. of New York, Albany, USA; Head of Commercial and Industrial Law, Ministry of Commerce and Industry 1987–89; fmr Economist, Govt Dept of Central Planning and Demand; Economist, Managerial Support Unit, Electricité d'Haïti 1991–92; Prof. of Finance and Econs, Inst. of Nat. Admin, Man. and Higher Int. Studies, Faculty of Law and Econ. Sciences, Haiti State Univ. 1991–95; Consultant, Nat. Econ. Mission under coordination of UNDP April–June 1993; with Sogebank SA (Société Générale Haïtienne de Banque), Port-au-Prince 1994–95; joined Banque de la République d'Haïti (central bank) 1995, Adviser to Gov. 1995–96, mem. Monetary Policy Cttee 1996, Dir of Legal Affairs 1996–2004, Dir of Banking Supervision 1998–99, Dir-Gen. 2004–07, Gov. 2007–15; mem. Bar Assn of Port-au-Prince; mem. World Jurist Assn, Assn des Economistes Haïtiens, Fondation Haïtienne de l'Environnement.

CASTELLANETA, Giovanni; Italian diplomatist and business executive; *Chairman, SACE SpA;* b. 11 Sept. 1942, Puglia; ed Faculty of Law, Univ. of Rome 'La Sapienza'; joined Foreign Service 1967, assigned to Embassy in Mogadishu, Somalia 1969–72, Consul, Chambery, France 1972–74, Head of Econ. and Trade Office, Embassy in Lisbon 1974–76, European Affairs Desk, Ministry of Foreign Affairs 1976–78, Chief of Staff to Sec.-Gen., Ministry of Foreign Affairs 1978–81, Head of Press, Information and Cultural Office, Embassy in Paris 1981–84, on special assignment to Prime Minister's Office 1984–85, Deputy Perm. Rep., Mission to UN and Int. Orgs, Geneva 1985–89, Diplomatic Adviser to Treasury Minister, then Spokesman, Ministry of Foreign Affairs 1989–92, Amb. to Iran 1992–95, Head, Office for Coordination of Int. Activity of Italian Regions 1995–97, Special Coordinator, Italian Reconstruction Program for Albania 1997–98, Amb. to Australia (also accred to various insular States in Pacific Ocean) 1998–2001, Foreign Policy Adviser to Prime Minister 2001–05, rank of Amb. of Italy 2002, Personal Rep. of Prime Minister for G8 Summits, Amb. to USA and Perm. Observer to OAS, Washington, DC 2005–09; Deputy Chair. Finmeccanica Group 2002–05; Chair. SACE SpA 2009–, Italfondiario SpA 2013–; Pres. Torre SGR SpA 2013–; Great Cross, Order of Merit of the Italian Repub. *Address:* SACE SpA, Piazza Poli 37/42, 00187 Rome, Italy (office). *Telephone:* (06) 67361 (office). *Fax:* (06) 6736225 (office). *E-mail:* info@sace.it (office). *Website:* www.sace.it (office).

CASTELLI, Roberto; Italian engineer and politician; b. 12 July 1946, Lecco, Lombardy; m.; one s.; ed Alessandro Manzoni School, Lecco, Politecnico di Milano; worked as researcher developing technological system of electronic noise reduction; adviser to EC on environmental affairs; joined Lega Nord 1986, elected Deputy for Lecco 1992, 1994, fmr Vice-Pres. of Lega Nord in Chamber of Deputies; elected Senator for Lecco e Bergamo 1996–2013, Pres. Lega Nord Parl. Group 1999–2001; Minister of Justice 2001–06; Group Leader, Transport Cttee; mem. Budget Cttee of Senate, Parl. Cttee for Impeachments; mem. Jt Cttee on Regional Affairs, Supervision over RAI TV and Radio, Investigations over Terrorism and Massacres; fmr mem. Comm. for Regional Affairs, Comm. on Terrorism; voluntary mem. Nat. Alpine and Speleological Rescue Corps; Hon. Pres. Alpe (Assn of Free Padan Hikers). *Leisure interests:* ski-alpinism, hiking, sailing, reading. *Address:* c/o Lega Nord, Via C. Bellerio 41, 20161 Milan, Italy. *E-mail:* sen.robertocastelli@tin.it. *Website:* www.leganord.org.

CASTELLINA, Luciana; Italian journalist, politician and writer; *Honorary President, Unione Circoli Cinematografici ARCI;* b. 9 Aug. 1929, Rome; m. (divorced); one s. one d.; ed Univ. of Rome; Ed. Nuova Generazione (weekly) 1958–62, Il Manifesto (daily) 1972–78, Pace e Guerra (weekly) then Liberazione (weekly) 1992–94; elected mem. Parl. 1976, 1979, 1983; elected mem. European Parl. 1979, 1984, 1989, 1994, Chair. Culture and Media Cttee 1994–96, later Chair. External Econ. Relations Cttee; fmr mem. directorate Italian CP; Pres. Cineuropa.org, Italia Cinema Srl; fmr Pres. Unione Circoli Cinematografici ARCI, Hon. Pres. 2014–; Vice-Pres. Eurovisioni Bd, Eurosolar International; Lecturer, Pisa State Univ.; mem. Bd of Dirs, Lelio Basso Foundation; Officier des Arts et des Lettres; Kt Commdr of the Argentine Repub.; European Personality of the Year, San Sebastian Film Festival 2006. *Publications include:* Che c'è in America (reports from America) 1972, Family and Society in Marxist Analysis 1974, Il Commino Dei Movimenti 2003, 50 Anni d'Europa 2007, Eurollywood 2009, La scoperta del mondo 2011, Siberiana 2012, Guardati dalla mia fame 2014, Manuale Antiretorico dell'UE 2016. *Leisure interest:* films. *Address:* Via di San Valentino 32, 00197 Rome (home); c/o Board of Directors, ARCI, Via dei Monti di

Pietralata 16, 00182 Rome, Italy (office). *Telephone:* (06) 41609220 (office). *E-mail:* lcastellina@gmail.com (home).

CASTIGLIONI SORIA, Luis Alberto; Paraguayan politician; *Minister of Foreign Affairs;* b. 31 July 1962, Itacurubí del Rosario, San Pedro; s. of Idilio Castiglioni and Adelina Soria de Castiglioni; m. Miriam Ayala; two s. one d.; joined Asociación Nacional Republicana (ANR—Partido Colorado) 1979; Perm. mem. Partido Colorado Nat. Constituent Convention 1991–92, Partido Colorado Govt Bd 1992–95; Pres. Capital Sectional Cttee No. 4 1996–2000; Vice-Pres. of Paraguay 2003–07 (resgnd); unsuccessful presidential cand. (Partido Colorado) 2008; Gen. Sec. Supreme Council of Int. Parl. for Safety and Peace; Special Advisor, with Bill Richardson, to Election Observation Mission of general elections in Nicaragua 2011; Senator and Caucus Leader 2013–18; Minister of Foreign Affairs 2018–. *Address:* Ministry of Foreign Affairs, Edif. Benigno López, Palma, esq. 14 de Mayo, Asunción, Paraguay (office). *Telephone:* (21) 49-3872 (office). *Fax:* (21) 49-3910 (office). *E-mail:* sistemas@mre.gov.py (office). *Website:* www.mre.gov.py (office).

CASTILLA RUBIO, Luis Miguel, BA, PhD; Peruvian economist, academic, government official and diplomatist; widowed; two d.; ed McGill Univ., Canada, Johns Hopkins Univ., USA; Head of Practice, Macroeconomics and Econ. Devt, Johns Hopkins Univ. 1992–93; several positions with World Bank, Washington, DC including Vice-Pres., Latin America and the Caribbean, Country Operations Analyst 1994, Vice-Pres. North Africa and the Middle East, Chief Economist, Consultant 1996; Economist, Corporación Andina de Fomento, Caracas 1996–2000, Lima 2000–02, Dir of Econ. Studies 2003–05, Chief Economist and Head of Public Policy and Competitiveness 2006–09, Adviser to Exec. Presidency 2009; Prof. of Intermediate Macroeconomics, Universidad del Pacifico, Lima 2001–02; Deputy Minister of Finance 2010–11, Minister of Economy and Finance 2011–14; Amb. to USA 2015–16.

CASTILLO, Eva; Spanish investment banker and business executive; *Chair and CEO, Telefónica Europe;* b. 1962, Madrid; ed Universidad Pontificia de Comillas of Madrid; equity researcher, Beta Capital Sociedad de Valores, SA 1987–92; with Goldman Sachs Int., London, UK in Int. Equities Dept 1992–97; Head of Equity Markets for Spain and Portugal, Merrill Lynch Spain, Madrid 1997–99, Gen. Man. for Spain and Portugal 1999–2000, CEO Merrill Lynch Capital Markets Spain 2000, then COO Europe, Middle East and Africa (EMEA) Equity Markets, then Head of Global Markets and Investment Banking in Spain and Portugal 2003, also Pres. Merrill Lynch Spain, Head of Global Wealth Man. EMEA 2009, including Merrill Lynch Bank and Int. Trust and Wealth Structuring; mem. Bd Telefónica Europe 2008–, Chair. and CEO 2012–; mem. Bd of Dirs Telefónica SA. *Address:* Telefónica Europe, Distrito Telefónica Edificio Central, 2ª planta Ronda de la Comunicación s/n, 28050 Madrid, Spain (office). *Telephone:* (91) 4823800 (office). *Website:* pressoffice.telefonica.com (office).

CASTILLO BARRANTES, José Enrique, BA, MA, JD; Costa Rican lawyer, diplomatist and politician; b. 27 Aug. 1945, San José; ed Univ. of Costa Rica, Univ. of Bordeaux, France; Lecturer in Criminology and Criminal Law, Univ. of Costa Rica 1971–, Prof. 1986–2000, Founder and first Dir of Graduate Studies in Law, 1981–86, 1995–2004; Dir Gen. UN Latin American Inst. for the Prevention of Crime 1975–94; Partner, Facio y Cañas (law firm) 1980–, Chair. 2006–07; Amb. to France 1986–2000; Minister of Justice 1994–95; Perm. Rep. of Costa Rica to OAS 2007–11; Minister of Foreign Relations 2011–14; mem. Bar Asscn of Costa Rica, Sec. of the Bd 1986; mem. Int. Asscn of Penal Law, Int. Asscn of French Language Criminologists, Int. Asscn of Criminal Law; mem. Scientific Cttee, Int. Soc. of Criminology, Paris 1978–2005, Deputy Sec.-Gen. 1995–2000; Chevalier, Ordre des Palmes académiques 1999. *Publications:* five books including Ensayos sobre la nueva legislación procesal penal (essays) (Bar Asscn of Costa Rica Alberto Brenes Córdoba Award) 1977, Pesadillas de un hombre urbano (Nightmares of an Urban Man, short stories) (Aquileo J.Echeverría Prize) 2003. *Address:* c/o Ministry of Foreign Relations, Avda 7 y 9, Calle 11 y 13, Apdo 10027, 1000 San José, Costa Rica (office).

CASTLE, Michael (Mike) N., BA, LLB; American lawyer and fmr politician; *Partner, DLA Piper LLP;* b. 2 July 1939, Wilmington, Del.; s. of J. Manderson Castle and Louisa B. Castle; m. Jane Castle; ed Hamilton Coll., Georgetown Univ.; called to Del. Bar 1964, DC Bar 1964; Assoc., Connolly, Bove and Lodge (law firm), Wilmington 1964–73, Pnr 1973–75; Deputy Attorney-Gen., State of Del. 1965–66; mem. Del. House of Reps 1966–67; mem. Del. Senate 1968–77; Pnr, Schnee & Castle PA 1975–80; Lt-Gov. State of Del. 1981–85; Gov. of Delaware 1985–93; mem. US House of Reps 1993–2011; Partner, DLA Piper 2011–; Prin. Michael N. Castle 1981–; Co-founder and mem. Republican Main Street Partnership (fmr Pres.); Republican; Josiah Marvel Cup Award, Delaware Chamber of Commerce 2011. *Address:* DLA Piper LLP, 1201 North Market Street, Suite 2100, Wilmington, DE 19801, USA (office). *Telephone:* (302) 468-5630 (office). *E-mail:* michael.castle@dlapiper.com (office). *Website:* www.dlapiper.com (office).

CASTRESANA FERNÁNDEZ, Carlos; Spanish jurist and international organization official; *Head of Criminal Law, Ejaso, Madrid;* b. 12 July 1957, Madrid; ed Universidad Complutense de Madrid, Institut Int. de Droits de l'Homme, Strasbourg, France; Assoc. Prof. of Criminal Law, Univ. of San Francisco (Dir Human Rights Program, Center for Law and Global Justice) and Universidad Carlos III, Madrid 2003–06; served as prosecutor in circuit courts of Madrid and Catalunya, temporarily dist and investigating judge and magistrate of territorial court of Madrid before being assigned to Special Prosecutor's Office against drug smuggling and money laundering 1993–95; Special Anti-Corruption Prosecutor for Spain's nat. court 1995–2005; Public Prosecutor for Spanish Supreme Court 2005–15; work for Mexico and Cen. America regional office of UN Office on Drugs and Crime (UNODC) 2006–07, also for UNDP; Commr with rank of UN Asst Sec. Gen., Comisión Internacional contra la Impunidad en Guatemala (Int. Comm. Against Impunity in Guatemala—CICIG, body est. under agreement between UN and Guatemalan Govt) 2007–10 (resgnd); currently Head of Criminal Law Dept, Ejaso, Madrid (law firm); Guest Prof., Haverford Coll., Pa, USA 2014; mem. Bd of Trustees, UN Interregional Crime and Justice Research Inst. of Int., Bd of Harald Edelstam Foundation (Sweden); has lectured in Europe and the Americas, at univs including Harvard, Yale, Stanford, Berkeley and New York, and collaborated with insts including Max Planck Inst., World Bank, Int. Comm. of Jurists, US Depts of State and Justice, Swiss Ministry of Foreign Affairs, Gen. Prosecutor's Office, Mexico and Bahrain, among many others; Commdr, Order of Civilian Merit; Officier, Légion d'honneur; Commdr, Order of the Star of Solidarity (Italy); Great Cross, Order of the Quetzal (Guatemala); Dr hc (Universidad de Guadalajara, Mexico) 2003, (Universidad Central, Chile) 2006, (Instituto Nacional Ciencias Penales, Mexico) 2018; Nat. Human Rights Award (Spain) 1997, Certificate of Honor, City of San Francisco 2004, Medal of Honour, Vice-Presidency of the Senate (Chile) 2006, Transparency, Integrity and Anticorruption Prize, General Counsel of Advocacy and Transparency Int., Spain 2016. *Address:* Ejaso Madrid, C/ Goya nº 15 – 1º y 2ªp (esquina calle Serrano), CP 28001 Madrid, Spain (office). *Telephone:* (915) 341480 (office). *Fax:* (915) 347791 (office). *E-mail:* ccastresana@ejaso.com (office). *Website:* www.ejaso.es (office).

CASTRO, Julián, BA, JD; American lawyer and politician; b. 16 Sept. 1974, San Antonio, Tex.; s. of Jessie Guzman and Maria Rosie Castro; m. Erica Lira Castro; one d.; ed Stanford Univ., Harvard Law School; began career with Akin Gump Strauss Hauer & Feld, San Antonio (law firm) 2002; co-f. law firm (with twin brother) Julian Castro PLLC, San Antonio 2005; mem. San Antonio city council (youngest councilman) 2001–05; Mayor of San Antonio 2009–14; Sec. of Housing and Urban Devt 2014–17; mem. Inter-American Dialogue, LBJ Foundation Bd; Fellow, Aspen Inst.-Rodel; keynote speaker at Democratic Nat. Convention 2012; Democrat.

CASTRO, Gen. Raúl (see CASTRO RUZ, Gen. Raúl Modesto).

CASTRO CALDAS, Júlio de Lemos de; Portuguese politician and lawyer; *Partner, Correia, Seara, Caldas, Simões e Associados;* b. 19 Nov. 1943, Lisbon; s. of Eugénio Queiroz de Castro Caldas and Maria Lusitana Mascarenhas de Lemos de Castro Caldas; m. Ana Cristina Ribeiro Sobral Cid; one s. two d.; ed Classic Univ. of Lisbon; Leader, Students' Asscn, Classic Univ. of Lisbon 1963; mil. service in Portuguese Army 1967–70; f. Associação para o Desenvolvimento Económico e Social (SEDES) 1970, Partido Popular Democrático 1974; Legal Adviser to Pres. of Portugal 1976–78; Democratic Alliance mem. Parl. for Viana do Castelo 1979; Leader Parl. Group of Democratic Alliance 1979–82; Minister of Defence, Socialist Party 1999–2001; fmr Partner, Almeida Sampaio & Associados (law firm), Lisbon; currently Partner, Correia, Seara, Caldas, Simões e Associados (law firm); mem. Supreme Council of Public Prosecutor's Dept 1980–92, Superior Council of the Public Ministry 2005–11; Chair. Bilbao Vizcaya Bank (Portugal) 1995–99, EGEO – Tecnologia e Ambiente, SA; fmr chair. several cos; mem. Portuguese Bar Asscn, Treas. 1988–91, Pres. 1993–99; Pres. European Bar Fed. 1997–99; Dir (non-exec.) OGMA – Indústria Aeronáutica de Portugal. *Address:* Correia, Seara, Caldas, Simões e Associados, Avenida 5 de Outubro, n.º 17, 7º Andar, 1050-047 Lisbon, Portugal (office). *Telephone:* (21) 3552250 (office). *Fax:* (21) 3552268 (office). *E-mail:* csa_lisboa@csca.pt (office). *Website:* www.csca.pt (office).

CASTRO GONZÁLEZ, Sonia; Nicaraguan physician and politician; *Minister of Health;* trained as obstetrician-gynaecologist; worked at several hospitals 1990–2010; Minister of Health 2010–. *Address:* Ministry of Health, Complejo Nacional de Salud 'Dra Concepción Palacios', costado oeste Colonia Primero de Mayo, Apdo 107, Managua, Nicaragua (office). *Telephone:* 2289-7164 (office). *E-mail:* dirprensa@minsa.gob.ni (office). *Website:* www.minsa.gob.ni (office).

CASTRO PÉREZ, Olivier, BEcons, MA; Costa Rican economist and central banker; *President, Banco Central de Costa Rica;* b. Feb. 1941, Valverde Vega, Alajuela; ed Univ. of Costa Rica, Univ. of Kansas, USA; held various positions within int. operations and credit, Banco de Costa Rica 1962–69; joined Banco Cen. de Costa Rica 1969, Primer Official for Money and Credit, Dept of Econ. Studies 1972–78, Chief Economist 1978–79, Dir Finance Dept 1979–81, Man. Dir 1983–85; Exec. Dir Consejo Monetario Centroamericano 1985–92; Superintendent of Pensions 1996–2002; apptd mem. Legis. Ass. 2002; apptd Man. Bd, BN Vital, Pension Operator 2006; Pres. Banco Central de Costa Rica 2014–; fmr mem. Bd of Dirs Soc. of Investment Funds, Banco Nacional de Costa Rica, Banco Internacional de Costa Rica, SA; mem. Regional Consultive Group for America, Financial Stability Bd; mem. Bd of Govs Inter-American Devt Bank. *Address:* Banco Central de Costa Rica, Avdas Central y Primera, Calles 2 y 4, Apdo 10058, 1000 San José, Costa Rica (office). *Telephone:* 2243-3333 (office). *Fax:* 2243-4566 (office). *Website:* www.bccr.fi.cr (office).

CASTRO RUZ, Gen. Raúl Modesto; Cuban politician and fmr head of state; *First Secretary, Communist Party of Cuba;* b. 3 June 1931, Birán; brother of Fidel Alejandro Castro Ruz; m. Vilma Espín 1959 (died 2007); one s. three d.; ed Jesuit School of Colegio Dolores, Santiago, Colegio de Belén, Havana; sentenced to 15 years' imprisonment for insurrection 1953; amnestied 1954; assisted his brother's movement in Mexico and in Cuba after Dec. 1956, made Commdt 1957; Maximum Gen. of the Revolutionary Armed Forces 1959–2008; led Cuban mil. in repulsing force of Cuban exiles in Bay of Pigs invasion April 1961; Second Sec. CP of Cuba Cen. Cttee 1965–2011, First Sec. 2011–; Deputy, Asamblea Nacional del Poder Popular 1976; First Vice-Pres. of the Councils of State and Ministers 1976–2008, Acting Pres. Council of State 2006–08, Pres. Council of State and Council of Ministers (head of state) 2008–18; Acting C-in-C of the Revolutionary Armed Forces 2006–08, C-in-C 2008–; Acting Sec.-Gen. Non-Aligned Movt 2006–08, Sec.-Gen. 2008–09; Order of Lenin 1979, Order of the October Revolution 1981, Orden Máximo Gómez 1998; Medal for Strengthening of Brotherhood in Arms 1977. *Address:* Palacio del Gobierno, Havana, Cuba (office). *Website:* www.pcc.cu.

CASTRO SALAZAR, René, BE, MA, PhD; Costa Rican government official and politician; b. 25 Aug. 1957, St Louis, Mo., USA; ed Univ. of Costa Rica, Harvard Univ., USA; fmr Vice-Minister of the Interior; Minister of Environment and Energy 1994–98, of the Environment, Energy and Telecommunications 2011–14; consultant with UNDP 1998–2010; Minister of Foreign Affairs 2010–11; fmr Prof., INCAE Business School; mem. Bd of Dirs, Inter Press Service 2001–; fmr Pres. San José City Council; fmr Nat. Dir of Transport; fmr Sec. Gen. Partido Liberacion Nacional; Visiting Prof. and Lecturer, Harvard, Yale and Columbia Univs, USA, Valencia Polytechnic and Univ. of Zaragoza, Spain, ETH Zurich, Switzerland, LSE, UK and UN Univ., Tokyo, Japan; has taught at schools and insts of eng in Central America and organized REDICA Network since 2003; int. consultant for IDB, World Bank, UN; has worked in most Latin American countries, USA, Canada, Spain, Switzerland, Macedonia, Albania, Montenegro and Serbia and acted as consultant to govts of Mexico, Argentina, South Africa, El Salvador, Ecuador, Peru, Paraguay, Macedonia, Croatia and Montenegro; mem. Advisory

Bd, SEE Change Net Foundation (think-tank). *Publications include:* Evaluación de Proyectos Ambientales, Evaluación de Impacto Ambiental y Sostenibilidad del Desarrollo, Valoración de los servicios ambientales del Bosque: El Caso de Cambio Climático. *Address:* c/o SEE Change Net Foundation, Branilaca Sarajeva 20/I, 71000 Sarajevo, Bosnia and Herzegovina. *Telephone:* (33) 213716. *Fax:* (33) 213716. *E-mail:* info@seechangenet.org. *Website:* seechangenetwork.org.

CATERIANO BELLIDO, Pedro Alvaro; Peruvian lawyer, academic and politician; b. 26 June 1958; ed Pontifical Catholic Univ. of Peru, Univ. Complutense, Madrid, Spain; fmr Dir of External Cooperation and Prof. of Constitutional Law, Univ. of Lima; mem. Congreso (Parl.) for Lima (Movimiento Libertad) 1990–92, mem. Parl. Constitution Cttee, External Relations Cttee; fmr Deputy Minister of Justice and mem. Ministry of Justice Advisory Cttee; Rep. of Peruvian Govt to Inter-American Court of Human Rights, San José, Costa Rica 2012; Minister of Defence 2012–15; Pres. Council of Ministers (Prime Minister) 2015–16. *Address:* c/o Office of the President of the Council of Ministers, Jirón Carabaya, cuadra 1 s/n, Anexo, Lima 1105-1107, Peru (office).

CATHCART, Kevin James, MA, PhD, MRIA; Irish academic; *Professor Emeritus of Near Eastern Languages, University College, Dublin;* b. 9 Oct. 1939, Derrylin, Co. Fermanagh, Northern Ireland; s. of Andrew Cathcart and Elizabeth Cathcart (née Flannery); m. Ann McDermott 1968; two s.; ed Salesian Coll., Cheshire, UK, Mellifont Abbey, Co. Louth, Trinity Coll., Dublin, Pontifical Biblical Inst., Rome, Italy; Lecturer in Hebrew, Pontifical Biblical Inst., Rome 1968; Lecturer in Near Eastern Studies, Univ. of Ottawa, Canada 1968–71, Asst Prof. 1971–73, Assoc. Prof. 1973–74; Sr Lecturer in Semitic Languages and Dept Head, Univ. Coll. Dublin 1974–79, Prof. of Near Eastern Languages and Dept Head 1979–2001, Prof. Emer. of Near Eastern Languages 2001–; Fellow, Campion Hall, Oxford 2001–13, Sr Research Fellow 2013–; Visiting Fellow, St Edmund's Coll., Cambridge 1987–88, 1993–94; Visiting Academic, St Benet's Hall, Oxford 1994; Visiting Prof., Heidelberg 1981, 1986, 1992, Ottawa 1983, Århus 1986, Toronto 1989, Mainz 1992; mem. Bd of Electors (Regius Professorship of Hebrew), Univ. of Cambridge 1989–2009; editorial consultant, Journal of Semitic Studies 1991–; mem. Advisory Cttee, Vetus Testamentum (journal) 1997–; mem. Royal Danish Acad.; Trustee, Chester Beatty Library, Dublin 1974–89, Chair. Bd of Trustees 1984–86. *Publications include:* Nahum in the Light of Northwest Semitic 1973, Back to the Sources: Biblical and Near Eastern Studies (with J. F. Healey) 1989, The Targum of the Minor Prophets (with R.P. Gordon) 1989, The Aramaic Bible (22 vols, co-ed.), The Edward Hincks Bicentenary Lectures 1994, Targumic and Cognate Studies (with M. Maher) 1996, The Letters of Peter le Page Renouf (1822–97) (four vols) 2002–04, The Correspondence of Edward Hincks (three vols) 2007–09. *Leisure interests:* birdwatching, medieval architecture. *Address:* 8 Friarsland Road, Clonskeagh, Dublin 14, Ireland (home). *Telephone:* (1) 2981589 (home). *E-mail:* kevin.cathcart@ucd.ie (home).

CATHCART, (William) Alun; British business executive; *Chairman, Avis Europe;* b. 9 Dec. 1943; mem. Bd of Dirs (non-exec.) Avis Rent A Car Inc. 1980–98, CEO and Deputy Chair. Avis Europe PLC 1999–2003, Chair. (non-exec.) 2004–; Deputy Chair. (non-exec.) Nat. Express Group PLC 1992; Deputy Chair. Belron Int.; Chair. (non-exec.) Selfridges 1998–2003; Chair. (non-exec.) The Rank Group 2001–07; mem. Bd of Dirs Emap plc 2005, Exec. Chair. 2006–08, Chair. (non-exec.) 2008–; Dir Tikkun UK Ltd (charity). *Address:* Avis Europe plc, Avis House, Park Road, Bracknell, Berks., RG12 2EW, England (office). *Telephone:* (1344) 426-644 (office). *Website:* www.avis-europe.com (office).

CATLOW, (Charles) Richard Arthur, MA, DPhil, FRS, FRSC, FInstP; British chemist and academic; *Dean of Faculty of Mathematical and Physical Sciences, University College London;* b. 24 April 1947, Simonstone, Lancs.; s. of Rolf M. Catlow and Constance Catlow (née Aldred); m. 1st Carey Anne Chapman 1978; one s.; m. 2nd Nora de Leeuw 2000; ed Clitheroe Royal Grammar School and St John's Coll., Oxford; Grad. Scholar, Jesus Coll. Oxford 1970–73; Research Fellow, St John's Coll., Oxford 1970–76; Lecturer, Univ. Coll. London 1976–85, Head, Dept of Chem. 2002–07, Dean of Faculty of Math. and Physical Sciences 2007–; Prof. of Chem., Univ. of Keele 1985–89; Wolfson Prof. of Natural Philosophy, Royal Inst. of GB 1989–, Dir Davy Faraday Research Lab. 1998–2002; Fellow, Acad. of Science 2006; RSC Medal (Solid State Chem.) 1992, RSC Award (Interdisciplinary Science) 1992, 1998, RSC Liversidge Medal 2009, Gerhard Ertl Lecturer, Fritz-Haber-Institut, Berlin 2014. *Publications:* co-author: Computer Simulation of Solids 1982, Mass Transport in Solids 1983, Computer Simulation of Fluids, Polymers and Solids 1989, Applications of Synchrotron Radiation 1990, New Frontiers in Materials Chemistry 1997, Microscopic Properties or Processes in Minerals 1999, Computational Materials Science 2003; more than 850 research papers and several monographs. *Leisure interests:* reading, walking, music. *Address:* MAPS Faculty Office, University College London, Gower Street, London, WC1E 6BT, England (office). *Telephone:* (20) 7679-2818 (office). *Fax:* (20) 7679-7463 (office). *E-mail:* c.r.a.catlow@ucl.ac.uk (office). *Website:* www.ucl.ac.uk/chemistry/staff/academic_pages/richard_catlow (office).

CATMULL, Edwin, BS, PhD; American studio executive and computer graphics designer; *President, Pixar Animation Studios;* b. 31 March 1945, Parkersburg, W Va; m. Susan Catmull; five c.; ed Univ. of Utah; Vice-Pres. Computer Div., Lucasfilm Ltd 1979–86, managed devt in areas of computer graphics, video editing, video games and digital audio, key developer of RenderMan programme; Co-Founder Pixar Animation Studios 1986, Chief Tech. Officer and exec. mem. 1986–2001, Pres. 2001–, Pres. Pixar and Disney animation studios after acquisition by Walt Disney Co. 2006–; mem. Acad. of Motion Picture Arts and Sciences, Science and Tech. Awards Cttee, Nat. Acad. of Eng, Visual Effects Soc., Univ. of California President's Bd on Science and Innovation; Dr hc (Univ. of Utah) 2005; Scientific and Tech. Eng Awards (three), Acad. of Motion Picture Arts and Sciences Award, Coons Award for Lifetime Contrib. to Computer Graphics Industry, Randy Pausch Prize, Carnegie Mellon Univ. Entertainment Technology Center 2008, Computer Entrepreneur Award, IEEE Computer Soc. 2008, Gordon E. Sawyer Award, Acad. of Motion Picture Arts and Sciences 2009. *Address:* Pixar Animation Studios, 1200 Park Avenue, Emeryville, CA 94608, USA (office). *Telephone:* (510) 752-3000 (office). *Fax:* (510) 752-3151 (office). *Website:* www.pixar.com (office).

CATON-JONES, Michael; British film director; b. 15 Oct. 1957, Broxburn, West Lothian, Scotland; m. 1st Beverly Caton (divorced); one d.; m. 2nd Laura Viederman 2000; one c.; ed Nat. Film School; worked as stagehand in London West End theatres, wrote and directed first film The Sanatorium and several other short films before being accepted by Nat. Film School; films made while a student include: Liebe Mutter (first prize European film school competition), The Making of Absolute Beginners (for Palace Productions), The Riveter; left school to make serial Brond for Channel 4 TV, then Lucky Sunil (BBC TV). *Films include:* Scandal 1989, Memphis Belle 1990, Doc Hollywood 1991, This Boy's Life 1993, Rob Roy 1995, The Jackal 1997, City By The Sea 2002, Shooting Dogs 2005, Basic Instinct 2 2006. *Television:* World Without End (mini-series) 2012. *Address:* c/o United Agents, 12–26 Lexington Street, London, W1F 0LE, England (office). *Telephone:* (20) 3214-0800 (office). *Fax:* (20) 3214-0802 (office). *E-mail:* info@unitedagents.co.uk (office). *Website:* unitedagents.co.uk (office).

CATTANACH, Bruce Macintosh, BSc, PhD, DSc, FRS; British geneticist (retd); b. 5 Nov. 1932, Glasgow, Scotland; s. of James Cattanach and Margaretta May Cattanach (née Fyfe); m. 1st Margaret Bouchier Crewe 1966 (died 1996); two d.; m. 2nd Josephine Peters 1999; ed Heaton Grammar School, Newcastle-upon-Tyne, King's Coll., Durham and Univ. of Edinburgh; mem. scientific staff, MRC Induced Mutagenesis Unit, Edinburgh 1959–62, 1964–66; NIH Post-Doctoral Research Fellow, Biology Div., Oak Ridge, Tenn., USA 1962–64; Sr Scientist, City of Hope Medical Centre, Duarte, Calif. 1966–69; Sr Scientist, MRC Radiobiology Unit, Chilton, Oxon. 1969–86, Head of Genetics Div. 1987–96; Acting Dir MRC Mammalian Genetics Unit, Harwell, Oxon. 1996–97. *Publications:* numerous papers in scientific journals. *Leisure interests:* control of inherited disease in pedigree dogs, Boxer dog breeding, exhibiting and judging. *Address:* Downs Edge, Reading Road, Harwell, Oxon., OX11 0JJ, England (home). *Telephone:* (1235) 835410 (home). *E-mail:* bcattanach@steynmere.freeserve.co.uk (home).

CATTANEO, Elena, DrSc; Italian professor of pharmaceutical biotechnology; *Professor of Pharmaceutical Biotechnology, University of Milan;* b. 22 Oct. 1962, Milan; m. Enzo Rivolta; one s. one d.; ed Univ. of Milan, Massachusetts Inst. of Tech., USA; researcher of neutral stem cells, MIT, USA; joined Dept of Pharmacological Science, Univ. of Milan 1994, Prof. of Pharmaceutical Biotechnology 2003–, also Dir Lab. of Stem Cell Biology and Pharmacology of Neurodegenerative Diseases, Co-founder and Dir UniStem, the Centre for Stem Cell Research; Coalition Investigator, Huntington's Disease Soc. of America 1997–2008; Coordinator FIRB (Fondo Investimento per la Ricerca di Base) research programme 2002–05; mem. Italian Del., Genomics and Biotechnology Work Programme, EU, Brussels 2002; mem. Bd of Dirs EuroStemCell, NeuroNE; mem. Scientific Advisory Bd Hereditary Disease Foundation, Euro-HD Network; mem. Accademia dei Lincei; Cavaliere Ufficiale (Kt) of the Italian Repub. 2006, Senator for Life (highest Italian honour) 2013; Cure Huntington's Disease Initiative Award, Hereditary Disease Foundation 1997, Le Scienze Prize for Medicine 2001, Presidential Medal, Italy 2001, Marisa Bellisario and Chiara D'Onofrio prizes 2005, Grande Ippocrate Prize for Medical Researcher of the Year 2008, Premio Tartufari Prize, Accademia dei Lincei 2012, Public Service Award, Int. Soc. for Stem Cell Research 2014. *Publications:* more than 150 papers in professional journals. *Leisure interest:* cooking. *Address:* Department of Biosciences, University of Milan, via Francesco Sforza 35, 20122 Milan, Italy (office). *Telephone:* 0250318333 (office). *Fax:* 0250318284 (office). *E-mail:* elena.cattaneo@unimi.it (office); cattaneolab@unimi.it (office). *Website:* www.cattaneolab.it (office).

CATTAUI, Maria Livanos, BA; Swiss international organization official; b. 25 June 1941, New York, USA; m. Stéphane Cattaui (deceased); two s.; ed Harvard Univ., USA; writer/researcher, Encyclopedia Britannica 1965–67; Ed. Time Life Books 1967–69; Dir, then Man. Dir World Econ. Forum 1977–96; Sec.-Gen. ICC 1996–2005; fmr Dir, Petroplus Holdings; mem. Bd or Advisory Bd, Int. Crisis Group, EastWest Inst., Soros Economic Devt Fund, Inst. of Int. Educ., Nat. Bureau of Asian Research (NBR), The Resolution Project, Schulich School of Business, York Univ., Elliott School of Int. Affairs, Inst. for Integrated Transitions, Shift Project; fmr mem. Bd ICT4Peace; Hon. LLD (York Univ., Toronto), Hon. DCS (Univ. of Hartford).

CATTELAN, Maurizio; Italian artist; b. 21 Sept. 1960, Padua; self-taught artist, works include sculpture, multimedia and installations; known especially for his satirical sculptures; hon. degree in Sociology (Univ. of Trento) 2004; Arnold Bode Prize, Kunstverein Kassel, Germany 2004, Career Prize (Gold Medal), 15th Rome Quadriennale 2009. *Television:* appeared on 60 Minutes (USA). *Address:* c/o Galerie Emmanuel Perrotin, 5 & 20, rue Louise Weiss, 75013 Paris, France. *Telephone:* 1-42-16-79-79. *Fax:* 1-42-16-79-74. *E-mail:* mauriziocattelan@katamail.com. *Website:* www.perrotin.com/artiste-Maurizio_Cattelan-2.html; www.guggenheim.org/new-york/exhibitions/past/exhibit/3961; mauriziocattelan.altervista.org.

CATTO, Sir Graeme Robertson Dawson, Kt, DSc, MD, FRCP, FRSE, FMedSci; British academic; *Professor Emeritus, Universities of London and Aberdeen;* b. 24 April 1945, Aberdeen, Scotland; s. of William D. Catto and Dora E. Catto (née Spiby); m. Joan Sievewright 1967; one s. one d.; ed Robert Gordon's Coll., Univ. of Aberdeen, Harvard Univ.; House Officer, Aberdeen Royal Infirmary 1969–70, Hon. Consultant Physician and Nephrologist 1977–2000; Research Fellow, then Lecturer, Univ. of Aberdeen 1970–75, Sr Lecturer, then Reader in Medicine 1977–88, Prof. of Medicine and Therapeutics 1988–2000, Dean, Faculty of Medicine and Medical Sciences 1992–98, Vice-Prin. 1995–2000, Prof. of Medicine 2005–09, now Prof. Emer.; Chief Scientist, Scottish Exec. (fmrly Scottish Office) Health Dept 1997–2000; Vice-Prin. King's Coll. London 2000–05; Dean, Guy's, King's Coll. and St Thomas' Hosps Medical and Dental School 2000–05, Hon. Nephrologist, Guy's and St Thomas' Hosps NHS Trust 2000–05; Pro-Vice-Chancellor Univ. of London 2003–05, now Prof. Emer.; Vice-Chair. Aberdeen Royal Hosps NHS Trust 1992–99; mem. Gen. Medical Council (GMC) 1994–2009, Chair. GMC Educ. Cttee 1999–2002, Pres. GMC 2002–09; Chair. Robert Gordon's Coll. Aberdeen 1995–2005, Scottish Stem Cell Network 2008–11; Pres. Asscn for the Study of Medicine 2009–13, Coll. of Medicine 2010–14; Chair. Dignity in Dying 2012–15, Lathallan School 2012–16; mem. Scottish Higher Educ. Funding Council 1996–2002, Specialist Training Authority 1999–2002, Lambeth, Southwark and Lewisham Health Authority 2000–02, South East London Strategic Health Authority 2002–05, Council for the Regulation of Healthcare Professionals 2003–08; Founder-mem. Acad. of Medical Sciences 1998, Treas. 1998–2001, Qatar Council for Healthcare Practitioners 2014–; Harkness Fellow, Commonwealth

Fund of New York; Fellow in Medicine, Harvard Univ. and Peter Bent Brigham Hosp., Boston 1975–77; Fellow, King's Coll. London 2005; mem. Jt Advisory Bd, Weill Cornell Medicine, Qatar 2017–; Hon. Fellow, Royal Coll. of Gen. Practitioners 2001, Royal Coll. of Surgeons of Edinburgh 2002, Faculty of Pharmaceutical Medicine 2008, Acad. of Medical Educators 2012; Hon. LLD (Aberdeen) 2002, Hon. DSc (St Andrews) 2003, (Robert Gordon) 2004, (Kent) 2007, (London South Bank) 2008, (London) 2009, (Buckingham) 2015, Hon. MD (Southampton) 2004, (Brighton) 2010. *Leisure interest:* hills and glens. *Address:* 4 Woodend Avenue, Aberdeen, AB15 6YL (home); Maryfield, Glenbuchat, Strathdon, Aberdeenshire, AB36 8TS, Scotland (home). *Telephone:* (1224) 310509 (Aberdeen) (home); (1975) 641317 (Strathdon) (home). *E-mail:* gcatto@btinternet.com (home).

CATTORETTI, Marco; Italian fashion designer and business executive; *Vice-President, Global Wholesale, J. Mendel;* partner, Bryan Bradley; moved to New York and co-f. and co-designed, with Luca Mosca, own fashion collection 'Luca+Marco' 1994; Retail Man., Gucci by Tom Ford 1996–98; Sales and Merchandising Dir, Blumarine-Blufin USA 1998–2006; Vice-Pres. Malo-Ittierre USA, New York 2006–07; Pres. Tuleh LLC fashion co., New York 2007–10; Pres. Kevork Kiledjian 2010–12; Vice-Pres., Wholesale and Merchandising, Amsale Group 2012–13; Global Sales Dir, Naeem Khan 2013–15; Vice-Pres., Global Wholesale, J. Mendel, New York 2015–. *Films:* costume designer: Hostage 1999, Girlfight 2000, Hamlet 2000, Happy Here and Now 2002, When Will I Be Loved 2004. *Television:* costume designer: The Education of Max Bickford (series) 2001. *Address:* J. Mendel Boutiques, Bergdorf Goodman, 754 Fifth Avenue, 4th Floor, New York, NY 10019, USA (office). *Telephone:* (212) 872-8963 (office). *E-mail:* info@jmendel.com (office). *Website:* www.jmendel.com (office).

CATZ, Safra Ada, BA, JD; Israeli/American business executive; *Co-CEO and Chief Financial Officer, Oracle Corporation;* b. 1 Dec. 1961, Holon, Israel; m. Gal Tirosh 1997; two s.; ed Brookline High School, Wharton School of Univ. of Pennsylvania and Univ. of Pennsylvania Law School; held various investment banking positions 1986–94; Sr Vice-Pres. Donaldson, Lufkin & Jenrette (global investment bank) 1994–97, Man. Dir 1997–99; Sr Vice-Pres. Oracle Corpn April–Oct. 1999, Exec. Vice-Pres. 1999–2004, mem. Bd of Dirs 2001–, Co-Pres. Oracle Corpn with responsibility for global operations 2004–14, Co-CEO 2014–, Chief Financial Officer 2005–08, 2011–, mem. Exec. Man. Cttee; Lecturer in Accounting, Stanford Business School; mem. Bd of Dirs (non-exec.) HSBC Holdings plc 2008–15. *Address:* Oracle Corporation, 500 Oracle Parkway, Redwood City, CA 94065-1675, USA (office). *Telephone:* (650) 506-7000 (office). *Fax:* (650) 506-7200 (office). *E-mail:* info@oracle.com (office). *Website:* www.oracle.com (office).

CAUBET, Marie-Christine; French automotive industry executive; b. (Marie-Christine Bourgignon), 4 Dec. 1950, Salins Les Bains; m.; three c.; ed Institut d'Etudes Politiques, Aix-en-Provence, Centre Européen d'Educ. Permanente (CEDEP), Fontainebleau, Institut Européen d'Admin des Affaires (INSEAD); joined Renault SA as financial analyst in 1973–85, Dir Mantes sales br. 1985–88, Regional Br. Dir 1988–90, Regional Dir Île de France region 1990–93, Marketing Dir for France 1993–97, Regional Dir Renault France Automobiles 1997–2000, Sr Vice-Pres. Market Area France and mem. Renault Man. Cttee 2000–05, Sr Vice-Pres. Market Area Europe 2005–08; Chair. Groupe Volkswagen France 2009–12, Advisor Volkswagen Group 2013–; Chevalier, Ordre nat. du Mérite. *Leisure interests:* sailing, family life. *Address:* Groupe Volkswagen France, 11 avenue de la Boursonne, 02601 Villers-Cotterêt Cedex, France (office). *Telephone:* (3) 23-73-58-00 (office). *E-mail:* marie-christine.caubet@gr-vw.fr (office).

CAUCHON, Hon. Martin, PC, DCL, LLM; Canadian politician and lawyer; *Counsel, DS Welch Bussières;* b. 23 Aug. 1962, La Malbaie, Québec; ed Univ. of Ottawa, Bar School of Québec, Univ. of Exeter, UK, Inst. of Corporate Dirs; practised as civil and commercial lawyer 1985–93; MP for Outremont 1993–2004 (resgnd); apptd Sec. of State responsible for the Econ. Devt Agency of Canada for the Regions of Québec 1996–2002, Minister of Nat. Revenue (responsible for Canada Customs) 1999–2002, Minister of Justice, Attorney-Gen. 2002–03; Pres. Canada-France Inter-parl. Asscn 1994–95; Pres. Liberal Party of Canada (Québec) 1993–95; Vice-Chair. Standing Cttee on Public Accounts 1994; mem. Standing Cttee on Human Resources Devt 1994–96; Partner, Gowling Lafleur Henderson LLP (law firm), Montreal 2004–12; Partner and Leader, China Group, Heenan Blaikie (law firm), Montreal 2012–14; unsuccessful cand. for leadership of Liberal Party of Canada 2013; Counsel, DS Welch Bussières, Montreal 2014–; Strategic Advisor, Martin Cauchon 2014–. *Publications:* articles in Revue du Barreau and Bulletin de la Société de droit int. économique. *Address:* DS Welch Bussières, 1080 Côte du Beaver Hall, Bureau 2100, Montreal, PQ H2Z 1S8, Canada (office). *Telephone:* (514) 360-4321 (office). *Fax:* (514) 284-3235 (office). *E-mail:* mcauchon@dsavocats.ca (office). *Website:* www.dswelchbussieres.com/Cauchon-Martin.html (office); martincauchon.ca.

CAUTE, (John) David, (John Salisbury), MA, DPhil, JP, FRSL, FRHistS; British writer; b. 16 Dec. 1936, Alexandria, Egypt; s. of Edward H. C. Caute and Rebecca Perlzweig; m. 1st Catherine Shuckburgh 1961 (divorced 1970); two s.; m. 2nd Martha Bates 1973; two d.; ed Edinburgh Acad., Wellington, Wadham Coll., Oxford; St Antony's Coll., Oxford 1959; army service in Gold Coast 1955–56; Henry Fellow, Harvard Univ. 1960–61; Fellow, All Souls Coll., Oxford 1959–65; Visiting Prof., New York Univ. and Columbia Univ. 1966–67; Reader in Social and Political Theory, Brunel Univ. 1967–70; Regents' Lecturer, Univ. of California 1974, Visiting Prof. Univ. of Bristol 1985; Literary Ed. New Statesman 1979–80; Co-Chair. Writers' Guild 1982. *Plays:* Songs for an Autumn Rifle 1961, The Demonstration 1969, The Fourth World 1973, Brecht and Company (BBC TV) 1979. *Radio plays:* The Demonstration 1971, Fallout 1972, The Zimbabwe Tapes 1983, Henry and the Dogs 1986, Sanctions 1988, Animal Fun Park 1995. *Publications include:* Novels: At Fever Pitch (Authors' Club Award 1960, John Llewellyn Rhys Award 1960) 1959, Comrade Jacob 1961, The Decline of the West 1966, The Occupation 1972, The Baby-Sitters (as John Salisbury) 1978, Moscow Gold (as John Salisbury) 1980, The K-Factor 1983, News from Nowhere 1986, Veronica or the Two Nations 1989, The Women's Hour 1991, Dr Orwell and Mr Blair 1994, Fatima's Scarf 1998; Non-fiction: Communism and the French Intellectuals 1914–1960 1964, The Left in Europe Since 1789 1966, Essential Writings of Karl Marx (ed.) 1967, The Confrontation: A Trilogy, The Demonstration (play), The Illusion 1971, The Fellow-Travellers 1973, Collisions: Essays and Reviews 1974, The Great Fear: The Anti-Communist Purge Under Truman and Eisenhower 1978, Under the Skin: The Death of White Rhodesia 1983, The Espionage of the Saints 1986, Sixty Eight: The Year of the Barricades 1988, Joseph Losey: A Revenge on Life 1994, The Dancer Defects: The Struggle for Cultural Supremacy During the Cold War 2003, Marechera and the Colonel 2009, Politics and the Novel During the Cold War 2010, Isaac and Isaiah: the Covert Punishment of a Cold War Heretic 2013. *Address:* 41 Westcroft Square, London, W6 0TA, England (home).

CAUTHEN, Stephen (Steve) Mark; American professional jockey (retd); b. 1 May 1960, Walton, Ky; s. of Ronald Cauthen and Myra Cauthen; m. Amy Rothfuss 1992; three d.; rode first race 1976, first winner 1976, top jockey, USA with 487 winners 1977; at 18, youngest person to win US racing's Triple Crown; moved to UK 1979; champion jockey 1984, 1985, 1987; won Derby on Slip Anchor 1985, on Reference Point 1987; rode 1,704 winners including 10 classics 1979–93 (retd); only jockey to have won Kentucky, Epsom, Irish, French and Italian Derbys; now works on family farm, Ky and as racing commentator on TV; Vice-Pres. Turfway Racing Asscn, Ky; Seagram Prize 1977, Eclipse Award 1977; youngest person to be elected to Racing Hall of Fame. *Address:* 167 South Main Street, Walton, KY 41094, USA.

CAVACO SILVA, Aníbal António, PhD; Portuguese politician, economist, academic and fmr head of state; b. 15 July 1939, Loulé; s. of Teodoro Silva and Maria do Nascimento Cavaco; m. Maria Alves da Silva 1964; one s. one d.; ed Univ. of York, UK and Inst. of Econ. and Financial Studies; taught Public Econs and Political Economy, Inst. of Econ. and Financial Studies 1965–67, then at Catholic Univ. 1975–2006 and New Univ. of Lisbon 1977–2002; Research Fellow, Calouste Gulbenkian Foundation 1967–77; Dir of Research and Statistical Dept, Bank of Portugal 1977–85; Minister of Finance and Planning 1980–81; Pres. Council for Nat. Planning 1981–84; Leader, PSD 1985–95; Prime Minister of Portugal 1985–95; mem. Real Academia de Ciencias Morales y Políticas, Spain; Econ. Adviser to Bank of Portugal (Cen. Bank) 1995–2004; Pres. of Portugal 2006–16; Social Democrat (PSD) mem. Exec. Cttee Club of Madrid in Democratic Transition and Consolidation; Dr hc (Univ. of York, UK, Universidade da Coruña, Spain); Joseph Bech Prize 1991, Max Schmidleinz Foundation Prize, Carl Bertelsmann Prize. *Publications:* Budgetary Policy and Economic Stabilization 1976, Economic Effects of Public Debt 1977, The Economic Policy of Sá Carneiro's Government 1982, Public Finance and Macroeconomic Policy 1992, A Decade of Reforms 1995, Portugal and the Single Currency 1997, European Monetary Union 1999, Political Autobiography 2002; over 20 articles on financial markets, public economics and Portuguese economic policy. *Leisure interests:* golf, gardening. *Address:* c/o Office of the President, Presidência da República, Palácio de Belém, Calçada da Ajuda, 1349-022 Lisbon, Portugal (office).

CAVALIER-SMITH, Thomas (Tom), PhD, FRS, FRSC, FLS, FIBiol; British/Canadian biologist and academic; *Professor Emeritus of Evolutionary Biology, University of Oxford;* b. 21 Oct. 1942, London, England, UK; s. of Alan Hailes Spencer Cavalier-Smith and Mary Maude Cavalier-Smith (née Bratt); m. 1st Gillian Glaysher 1967 (divorced); one s. one d.; m. 2nd Ema E-Yung Chao 1991; one d.; ed Norwich School, Gonville and Caius Coll., Cambridge, King's Coll., London; Guest Investigator and Damon Runyon Memorial Fellow, Rockefeller Univ., New York 1967–69; Lecturer in Biophysics, King's Coll., Univ. of London 1969–82, Reader 1982–89; Prof. of Botany, Univ. of British Columbia 1989–99; Natural Environment Research Council Research Prof., Dept of Zoology, Univ. of Oxford 1999–2007, Prof. of Evolutionary Biology 2000–, now Emer.; Pres. British Soc. for Protist Biology; mem. Council of Int. Congress of Systematic and Evolutionary Biology, Advisory Cttee of Canadian Inst. for Advanced Research's Programme on Integrated Microbial Biodiversity; Fellow, Canadian Inst. for Advanced Research Evolutionary Biology Programme 1988–2007; Int. Prize for Biology 2004, Linnean Medal for Zoology 2007, Frink Medal, Zoological Soc. of London 2008. *Publications:* Biology, Society and Choice (ed.) 1982, The Evolution of Genome Size (ed.) 1985; more than 180 scientific papers on cell and genome evolution, large scale phylogeny and the tree of life, understanding major evolutionary transitions, molecular evolution, cell biology, ultrastructure, ecology, and classification of Protozoa. *Leisure interests:* reading, natural history. *Address:* Department of Zoology, University of Oxford, The Tinbergen Building, South Parks Road, Oxford, OX1 3PS (office); 54 Warwick Street, Oxford, Oxon., OX14 1SX, England (home). *Telephone:* (1865) 281065 (office). *Fax:* (1865) 281310 (office). *E-mail:* tom.cavalier-smith@zoo.ox.ac.uk (office). *Website:* www.zoo.ox.ac.uk/people/view/cavaliersmith_t.htm (office).

CAVALLI, Roberto; Italian fashion designer; b. 15 Nov. 1940, Florence, Tuscany; ed Accad. di Belle Arti, Florence; first collection, Palazzo Pitti, Florence 1972; known for exotic prints and for creating the sand-blasted look for jeans; judge, Miss Universe pageant 1977; Hon. Master Diploma in Fashion Man. (Domus Acad., Milan) 2013. *Fashion lines include:* Just Cavalli, Class, Freedom, Timewear, Angels. *Address:* Press Office, Via Gesu 19, Milan, Italy (office). *Telephone:* (02) 784416 (office). *Fax:* (02) 782361 (office). *E-mail:* press@robertocavalli.it (office). *Website:* www.robertocavalli.it (office).

CAVALLO, Domingo Felipe (Mingo), DEcon, PhD; Argentine politician, economist, academic and business executive; *Chairman and CEO, DFC Associates LLC;* b. 21 July 1946, San Francisco, Córdoba; s. of Felipe Cavallo and Florencia Cavallo; m. Sonia Abrazián; three s.; ed Nat. Univ. of Córdoba, Harvard Univ., USA; Under-Sec. for Devt , Govt of Prov. of Córdoba 1969–70; Prof. of Econs and Statistics, Nat. Univ. of Córdoba 1969–84; Prof. of Econs, Catholic Univ. of Córdoba 1970–74; Vice-Pres. Bd of Dirs Banco de la Provincia de Córdoba 1971–72; Founding Dir Instituto de Estudios Económicos sobre la Realidad Argentina y Latinoamericana (IEERAL), Fundación Mediterránea 1977–87, Academic Adviser, IEERAL 1987–, now Hon. Pres.; fmr Pres., then Gov. Argentine Cen. Bank; mem. World Bank Research Observer Editorial Bd 1987–88, Advisory Cttee Inst. for Econ. Devt of World Bank 1988; Nat. Deputy for Córdoba 1987–91; Minister of Foreign Affairs and Worship 1989–91, of the Economy 1991–92, of the Economy and Public Works 1992–96, March–Dec. 2001; Visiting Prof., Stern School of Business, New York Univ. 1996–97, 2002–03; Founder and Pres. Acción por la República party 1997–2001; Nat. Deputy for Buenos Aires 1997–2001; Publr Forbes Global 1998–99; unsuccessful cand. for Pres. 1999, for Mayor of Buenos Aires 2000, for Chamber of Deputies 2013; Founder Fundación Novum Millenium; arrested for alleged involvement in arms smuggling April 2002, released June

2002, exonerated of all charges 2005; Robert Kennedy Visiting Prof. in Latin American Studies, Harvard Univ. 2003–04; Chair. and CEO DFC Associates LLC 2003–; Partner, GlobalSource Partners, Inc. 2009–; Sr Fellow, Jackson Inst. for Global Affairs, Yale Univ. 2011–13, also Visiting Lecturer, Dept of Econs; mem. Group of Thirty Consultative Group on Int. Econ. and Monetary Affairs, Inc., Washington, DC; Corresp. mem. Royal Acad. of Moral and Political Sciences of Spain 1993; Hon. Pres. Fundación Mediterránea (Argentina) 1996; Dr hc in Jurisprudence (Univ. of Genoa, Italy) 1994; Honour Diploma as Academic mem. Econ., Legal and Social Research Inst. of Argentina) 1995; Dr hc in Philosophy (Ben Gurion Univ., Negev, Israel) 1995, Dr hc in Econs (Univ. of Turin, Italy) 1995, Dr hc (Univ. of Paris 1, Panthéon-Sorbonne, France) 1999, Dr hc in Political Sciencies (Univ. of Bologna, Italy) 2000; Premio Universidad Gold Medal and Honor Diploma for Best Student in Univ. of Córdoba 1968, scholarships from OAS and the Ford Foundation for grad. studies at Harvard Univ. 1975–76, American Agricultural Econs Asscn 1983, Man of the Year Award, Latin Finance Magazine, Santo Domingo 1992, Minister of Finance of the Year Award, Euromoney magazine 1992, Economist of the Year Award, Inst. of Contemporary Studies, Buenos Aires, Argentina 1992, Eagle of the Americas Award, Asscn of American Chambers of Commerce in Latin America (declaring Dr Cavallo Promoter of Int. Trade) 1995, Americas Award, The Americas Foundation, New York 1999. *Publications:* Volver a Crecer 1984, El Desafío Federal 1986, Economía en Tiempos de Crisis 1989, La Argentina Que Pudo Ser; jtly with Roberto Domenech and Yair Mundlack) 1989, El Peso de la Verdad 1997, Pasion por Crear (with Juan Carlos De Pablo) 2001, Estanflacion (Stagflation) 2008, Camino a la Estabilidad 2014; numerous tech. publs and articles in Argentine and foreign newspapers. *Address:* Hipólito Yrigoyen 250, 1310 Buenos Aires; DFC Associates LLC, Buenos Aires, C1425EEH, Argentina (office); GlobalSource Partners, Inc., 708 Third Avenue, 18th Floor, Suite 1801, New York, NY 10017, USA (office). *Telephone:* (11) 4804-0862 (Buenos Aires) (office); (212) 207-8465 (DFC Associates) (office); (212) 317-8015 (GlobalSource Partners) (office). *Fax:* (11) 4804-0865 (Buenos Aires) (office); (212) 888-9512 (DFC Associates) (office); (212) 317-8318 (GlobalSource Partners) (office). *E-mail:* team@globalsourcepartners.com (office); info@dfcassociates.com (office). *Website:* www.globalsourcepartners.com (office); www.cavallo.com.ar (office).

ČAVARA, Marinko; Bosnia and Herzegovina engineer, politician and head of state; *President, Federation of Bosnia and Herzegovina;* b. 2 Feb. 1967, Busovača, Socialist Repub. of Bosnia and Herzegovina, Socialist Fed. Repub. of Yugoslavia; s. of Nico Čavara and Anđa Čavara; m. Ivanka Čavara; two s. one d.; ed Univ. of Zenica; began career as teacher of physics and eng, Busovača High School 1991–92; Postmaster, Busovača 1992; Municipal Commr for war production in central Bosnia and Head of Municipal Civil Protection Dept during Bosnian War 1992–95; mem. Busovača Municipal Council 1997–2000; mem. Central Bosnia Canton Ass. 2000; Deputy Minister for Traffic and Communications, Central Bosnia Canton Govt 1996–2001, Deputy Dir, later Dir, Cantonal Directorate for Roads 2001–05; Adviser to Croat mem. of Presidency of Bosnia and Herzegovina Ivo Miro Jović 2005–06; mem. Fed. House of Peoples (Dom Naroda Federacije) 2006–07; mem. Fed. House of Reps (Predstavnički Dom Federacije/Zastupnički Dom Federacije) 2006–14, Co-Speaker 2014–15; Pres. Fed. of Bosnia and Herzegovina 2015–; mem. Hrvatska Demokratska Zajednica Bosne i Hercegovine (HDZ BiH—Croatian Democratic Union of Bosnia and Herzegovina) 1990–, Vice-Pres. 1994–96, 2002–, also Pres. HDZ BiH in Busovača 2002–. *Address:* Office of the Federation Presidency, 71000 Sarajevo, Musala 9 (office); 88000 Mostar, Ante Starčevića bb, Bosnia and Herzegovina. *Telephone:* (33) 212986 (Sarajevo) (office); (36) 318905 (Mostar). *Fax:* (33) 220437 (Sarajevo) (office); (36) 313255 (Mostar). *E-mail:* info@fbihvlada.gov.ba (office). *Website:* www.fbihvlada.gov.ba (office).

ČAVIĆ, Dragan; Bosnia and Herzegovina politician and fmr head of state; b. 10 March 1958, Zenica; m.; one s. one d.; ed Banja Luka Univ.; worked as man. at several state and pvt. enterprises; mem. Parl. 1998–2000; Vice-Pres. Republika Srpska 2000–02, Pres. 2002–06; mem. Serbian Democratic Party of Bosnia and Herzegovina (SDP) (Srpska Demokratska Stranka Bosne i Hercegovine) (SDS BiH), Deputy Pres. 2002–04, Pres. 2004–06. *Address:* c/o Serbian Democratic Party of Bosnia and Herzegovina (SDP) (Srpska Demokratska Stranka Bosne i Hercegovine) (SDS BiH), 78000 Banja Luka, Nikole Tesle 1B, Bosnia and Herzegovina.

CAVIEZEL, James (Jim) Patrick; American actor; b. 26 Sept. 1968, Mount Vernon, Wash.; s. of Jim Caviezel and Maggie Caviezel; m. Kerri Browitt 1997; one s. (adopted); ed Mount Vernon High School, O'Dea High School, Burien Kennedy High School, Seattle, Bellevue Community Coll., Univ. of Wash.; moved to LA and worked as waiter between auditions 1992; modelled for The Gap; Spokesperson for Redeem the Vote; Dr hc (King's Coll., Wilkes-Barre, Pa) 2003. *Films include:* My Own Private Idaho 1991, Diggstown 1992, Wyatt Earp 1994, Ed 1996, The Rock 1996, G.I. Jane 1997, The Thin Red Line 1998, Ride with the Devil 1999, Resurrection 2000, Frequency 2000, Pay It Forward 2000, Madison 2001, Angel Eyes 2001, The Count of Monte Cristo 2002, High Crimes 2002, Highwaymen 2003, I Am David 2003, The Final Cut 2004, The Passion of the Christ 2004, Bobby Jones: Stroke of Genius 2004, Unknown 2006, Deja Vu 2006, Outlander 2008, The Stoning of Soraya M. 2008, Long Weekend 2008, Transit 2012, Savannah 2013, Escape Plan 2013, When the Game Stands Tall 2014. *Television includes:* Murder, She Wrote 1984, The Wonder Years 1988, The Prisoner (mini-series) 2009, Person of Interest (series) 2011–15. *Leisure interests:* basketball, Indy car racing. *Address:* c/o United Talent Agency, 9560 Wilshire Boulevard, Suite 500, Beverly Hills, CA 90212, USA (office).

CAVINESS, Madeline Harrison, BA, MA, PhD, FSA; American medieval art historian and academic; *Mary Richardson Professor Emerita, Department of Art History, Tufts University;* b. 1938, London, UK; d. of Eric Vernon Harrison and Gwendoline Fownes Rigden; m. Verne Strudwick Caviness, Jr 1962; two d.; ed Newnham Coll., Cambridge, Harvard Univ.; Prof. of Medieval Art, Tufts Univ. 1981–2007, Mary Richardson Prof. 1987–2007, Prof. Emer. 2007–; Pres., Int. Acad. Union 1998–2001, Int. Center for Medieval Art 1984–87, Medieval Acad. of America 1993–94, Int. Council for Philosophy and Humanistic Studies 2001–04; Vice-Pres. Corpus Vitrearum Int. Bd 1983–87, Pres. 1987–95, Hon. Pres. 2000–; Vice-Pres. New England Medieval Conference 1985, Pres. 1986; Fellow, Soc. of Antiquaries, London 1980; mem. American Acad. of Arts and Sciences 2007–; Fellow, Medieval Acad. of America 1992–; Hon. Phi Beta Kappa, Radcliffe Coll. 1977; Hon. DLitt (Bristol, UK) 2000; John Nicholas Brown Prize, Medieval Acad. 1981, Haskins Medal, Medieval Acad. 1993, Distinguished Sr Scholar Award, American Asscn of Univ. Women Educational Foundation 2005, Tufts Univ. Award for Distinguished Research and Seymour Simches Award for Teaching and Advising 2005. *Publications include:* Early Stained Glass of Canterbury Cathedral (John Nicholas Brown Prize, Medieval Acad. 1981) 1977, Sumptuous Arts at the Royal Abbeys in Reims and Braine (Charles Homer Haskins Medal, Medieval Acad. of America 1993) 1980, Visualizing Women in the Middle Ages: Sight, Spectacle and Scopic Economy 2001, Medieval Art in the West and its Audience 2001, Reframing Medieval Art: Difference, Margins, Boundaries (e-book) 2001. *Leisure interests:* travel, archaeology, gardens. *Address:* 8 Whittier Place, 24H, Boston MA 02114-1497 (home); Department of Art and Art History, Tufts University, 11 Talbot Avenue, Medford, MA 02155, USA (office). *Telephone:* (617) 627-3567 (office); (617) 670-4008 (home). *Fax:* (617) 627-3890 (office). *E-mail:* mhcaviness@comcast.net (office); madeline.caviness@tufts.edu (home). *Website:* ase.tufts.edu/art (office); nils.lib.tufts.edu/Caviness (office).

ČAVKOV, Mitko, MA; Macedonian police officer and government official; b. 24 Jan. 1963, Novo Selo; m.; ed Faculty of Security, Skopje; following graduation, employed in Ministry of Interior; Head of Dept of Criminal Police, SIA Strumica 1992–99, Deputy Chief of SIA Strumica 1999–2001; Chief Insp., Financial Crime Dept for Organized Crime 2005–06; Head of Dept for Organized Crime (now Centre to Combat Organized and Serious Crime) 2006–12; Head of Cen. Police Services 2012–13; Dir Public Security Bureau 2013–15; Minister of Internal Affairs May–Nov. 2015, 2016; mem. Vnatrešno-Makedonska Revolucionerna Organizacija-Demokratska Partija za Makedonsko Nacionalno Edinstvo (VMRO-DPMNE—Internal Macedonian Revolutionary Organization-Democratic Party for Macedonian National Unity). *Address:* c/o Ministry of Internal Affairs, 1000 Skopje, ul. Dimče Mirčev 9, North Macedonia. *E-mail:* kontakt@mvr.gov.mk.

ÇAVUŞOĞLU, Mevlüt, BA, MEcons, PhD; Turkish politician; *Minister of Foreign Affairs;* b. 5 Feb. 1968, Alanya; s. of Osman and Fatima Çavuşoğlu; m.; one c.; ed Ankara Univ., Long Island Univ., USA, Bilkent Univ.; mem. Grand Nat. Ass. (Parl.) for Antalya 2002–; Chair. Turkey-USA and Turkey-Japan Inter-Parl. Friendship Caucuses; Chair. Turkish Del., Parl. Ass. of Council of Europe (PACE) 2003–14, PACE Pres. 2010–12, Hon. Pres. 2014–, also Chair. or mem. several cttees and 2nd Vice-Chair. and Chief Whip, European Democrat Group; Chair. Turkish Del. to European Security and Defence Ass. (Ass. of WEU) 2007–10; Minister for EU Affairs and Chief Negotiator of Repub. of Turkey 2013–14; Minister of Foreign Affairs 2014–15, 2015–; mem. Venice Comm. of Council of Europe 2012–14; Founding mem. Adalet ve Kalkınma Partisi (Justice and Devt Party), Vice-Chair. for Foreign Affairs 2013, mem. Central Decision-making and Admin. Cttee 2012–. *Address:* Ministry of Foreign Affairs, Dr Sadık Ahmet Cadesi 8, 06100 Balgat, Ankara, Turkey (office). *Telephone:* (312) 2921000 (office). *Fax:* (312) 2873869 (office). *E-mail:* info@mfa.gov.tr (office). *Website:* www.mfa.gov.tr (office).

CAWLEY, Evonne Fay Goolagong, AO, MBE; Australian fmr professional tennis player; b. 31 July 1951, Griffith, NSW; d. of Kenneth Goolagong and Linda Hamilton; m. Roger Anson Cawley 1975; one s. one d.; ed Willoughby High School, Sydney; professional tennis player 1970–83; Wimbledon Champion 1971, 1980 (singles), 1974 (doubles); Australian Open Champion 1974, 1975, 1976, 1977; French Open Champion 1971; Italian Open Champion 1973; S African Champion 1972; Virginia Slims Circuit Champion 1975, 1976; played Fed. Cup for Australia 1971, 1972, 1973, 1974, 1975, 1976; Capt. Australian Fed. Cup Team 2001–04; consultant to Indigenous Sports Programme; Sports Amb. to Aboriginal and Torres Strait Island Communities 1997–; Amb. and Exec. Dir Evonne Goolagong Sports Trust; f. Evonne Goolagong Getting Started Programme for young girls; Hon. DUniv (Charles Sturt) 2000; Australian of the Year 1982, Int. Tennis Hall of Fame 1988. *Publications:* Evonne Goolagong (with Bud Collins) 1975, Home: The Evonne Goolagong Story (with Phil Jarratt) 1993. *Leisure interests:* fishing, reading, researching Aboriginal heritage, movies, soccer. *Address:* c/o IMG, 281 Clarence Street, Sydney, NSW 2000; PO Box 1347, Noosa Heads, Queensland 4567, Australia. *Telephone:* (7) 5474-0112. *Fax:* (7) 5474-0113.

CAYETANO, Alan Peter Schramm, BA, JD; Philippine lawyer and politician; b. 28 Oct. 1970, Taguig; s. of Renato Cayetano and Sandra Schramm Cayetano; m. Laarni Lopez-Cayetano; ed Univ. of the Philippines, Ateneo School of Law; Councillor, Municipality of Taguig 1992–95, Vice Mayor 1995–98; admitted to Philippine Bar May 1998; mem. House of Reps (lower house of parl.) for Taguig-Pateros Dist 1998–2007; mem. Senate (upper house of parl.) 2007–17, Senate minority floor leader 2010–13, majority floor leader 2013–16, Chair. Foreign Relations Cttee 2016–17, Agrarian Reform Cttee 2016–17; Sec. (Minister) of Foreign Affairs 2017–18; fmr Columnist, Compañero y Compañera (public affairs TV discussion show); mem. Nacionalista Party 2005–16; mem. Partido Demokratiko Pilipino-Lakas ng Bayan (PDP-Laban) 2016–. *Address:* c/o Partido Demokratiko Pilipino-Lakas ng Bayan (PDP-Laban), 721 J. P. Rizal St, Makati City, Metro Manila, Philippines. *Website:* alanpetercayetano.com.

CAYETANO, Benjamin Jerome, BA, JD; American lawyer and politician; b. 14 Nov. 1939, Honolulu, Hawaii; m. 1st Lorraine Gueco 1958; m. 2nd Vicky Tiu 1997; two s. three d.; ed Farrington High School, Honolulu, Univ. of California, Los Angeles, Loyola Law School, Los Angeles; practising lawyer 1971–86; Pnr, Schutter Cayetano Playdon (law firm) 1983–86; mem. Hawaii State Legis. 1975–78, 1979–86; Lt-Gov. of Hawaii 1986–94, Gov. 1994–2002; Chair. Western Govs Asscn 1999; Democrat; Legion of Honor (Philippines) 2002; Hon. LLD (Univ. of the Philippines) 1995, Hon. Dr of Public Service (Loyola Marymount Univ.) 1998; numerous awards for public service including Medal of UCLA 1995, The Aloha Council Boy Scouts of America Harvard Foundation Leadership Award 1996, Distinguished Citizens Award 1997, Edward A. Dickson Alumnus of the Year Award, UCLA 1998, Distinguished Alumnus of the Year, Loyola Law School 2002. *Publication:* Ben: A Memoir, From Street Kid to Governor 2007. *Address:* PO Box 161060, Honolulu, HI 96816, USA (office). *E-mail:* bjcayetano@aol.com. *Website:* bencayetano.com.

CAYGILL, Hon. David Francis, CNZM, BA, LLB (Hons); New Zealand politician, lawyer and government official; *Deputy Chairman, Environment*

Canterbury Regional Council; b. 15 Nov. 1948, Christchurch; s. of Bruce Allott Caygill and Gwyneth Mary Caygill; m. Eileen E Boyd 1974; one s. three d.; ed Univ. of Canterbury; practised law in Christchurch legal firm 1974–78; mem. Christchurch City Council 1971–80; mem. House of Reps (Labour) 1978–90; Minister of Trade and Industry, Minister of Nat. Devt, Assoc. Minister of Finance 1984–87, of Health, Trade and Industry 1987–88, Deputy Minister of Finance 1988, Minister of Finance 1988–90, of Revenue 1988–89, Deputy Leader of the Opposition 1994–96; Partner, Buddle Findlay, Barristers and Solicitors 1996–; Chair. Accident Compensation Corpn 1998–; Chair. Ministerial Inquiry into the Electricity Ind. 2000; Deputy Chair. Commerce Comm. 2004–; Chair. Electricity Comm. 2007–10; Chair. Educ. NZ Trust, Advisory Cttee on Official Statistics; Deputy Chair. Environment Canterbury Regional Council, responsible for Water Portfolio 2010–; mem. Canterbury Regional Planning Authority 1977–80; led panel that reviewed operation and effectiveness of NZ Emissions Trading Scheme; fmr mem. Bd of Dirs, Infratil Ltd; Companion, NZ Order of Merit. *Leisure interests:* collecting classical music records, science fiction, following American politics. *Address:* Environment Canterbury Regional Council, PO Box 345, Matthew Fraser House, 5 Sir William Pickering Drive, Burnside, Christchurch 8140, New Zealand (office). *Telephone:* (3) 365-3828 (office). *Fax:* (3) 365-3194 (office). *E-mail:* ecinfo@ecan.govt.nz (office). *Website:* ecan.govt.nz (office).

CAYLA, Véronique; French civil servant and television executive; *President of Arte GEIE and President and CEO, Arte France;* b. 5 July 1950, Saint-Cloud, Paris; m. Philippe Cayla; ed Institut d'Études Politiques, Paris; joined Ministry of Culture 1973, began as Special Asst to Cultural Intervention Fund, joined Office of Sec. of State for Culture 1974, worked at Legal and Tech. Information Service 1976–78, returned to Ministry as a tech. adviser in charge of cinema 1978–85, apptd Deputy Dir Video Library, Paris 1982, Dir 1983–89, Gen. Man. 1989–92; Deputy Head of MK2 and CEO Images LMK SA 1992–99; apptd to Higher Audiovisual Council 1999–2000; joined trio at head of Cannes Film Festival, as CEO, in tandem with Thierry Fremaux, chaired by Gilles Jacob 2000–05; Head of Centre nat. de la cinématographie 2005–11; Pres. Man. Bd Arte GEIE(Arte—Asscn Relative à la Télévision Européenne, f. 1991 and composed of ARTE Deutschland TV GmbH and ARTE France) Jan. 2011–, Pres. and CEO Arte France (new name of La Sept—French TV) March 2011–; Officier, Légion d'honneur, des Arts et des Lettres. *Address:* Arte GEIE, 4 Quai du Chanoine Winterer, BP 20035, 67080 Strasbourg Cedex (office); Arte France, 8 rue Marceau, 92785 Issy-les-Moulineaux Cedex 9, France (office). *Telephone:* (3) 88-14-22-22 (Strasbourg) (office); 1-55-00-77-77 (Issy-les-Moulineaux) (office). *Fax:* (3) 88-14-22-00 (Strasbourg) (office); 1-55-00-77-00 (Issy-les-Moulineaux) (office). *E-mail:* info@arte.tv (office). *Website:* www.arte.tv (office).

CAYLEY, Andrew Thomas, CMG, QC, LLM; British solicitor and barrister; b. 24 March 1964, Rustington, West Sussex; s. of Granville Cayley and Elizabeth Cayley; m. Andrea von Matacic; two s. two d.; ed Brighton Coll., Univ. Coll., London, Coll. of Law, Guildford, Royal Mil. Acad., Sandhurst; Asst Solicitor and Articled Clerk with Thomas Eggar, London 1987–91; Legal Officer, British Army 1991–98; Prosecuting Counsel, Office of the Prosecutor, Int. Criminal Tribunal for the Former Yugoslavia (ICTY), The Hague 1994–2001, Sr Prosecuting Counsel 2001–05, Sr Prosecuting Counsel, Int. Criminal Court, The Hague 2005–07; called to the Bar of England & Wales by the Inner Temple 2007; counsel on the defence team for Charles Ghankay Taylor before Special Court for Sierra Leone and also for Ivan Cermak before ICTY 2007–09; Chief Int. Co-Prosecutor, Extraordinary Chambers in the Courts of Cambodia (Khmer Rouge Tribunal) 2009–13; took Silk 2012; Assoc. Tenant, Doughty Street Chambers, London 2011–13; Barrister, Temple Garden Chambers, London 2013–, Dir of Service Prosecutions; Governing Bencher, Hon. Soc. of the Inner Temple 2014–. *Address:* Temple Garden Chambers, 1 Harcourt Buildings, Temple, London, EC4Y 9DA, England (office). *Telephone:* (20) 7583-1315 (office). *Fax:* (20) 7353-3969 (office). *E-mail:* acayley@tgchambers.com (office). *Website:* tgchambers.com (office).

CAYROL, Roland; French researcher, opinion pollster and producer; b. (Marc Gilbert Roland Cayrol), 11 Aug. 1941, Rabat, Morocco; m. Annabelle Gomez 1989; two s. two d.; Prof. and Researcher, Nat. Foundation of Political Sciences, Centre de Recherches Politiques de Sciences Po (CEVIPOF) 1968, Research Dir 1978–, now Sr Research Assoc.; Scientific Adviser, Louis Harris France 1977–86; Dir CSA (Opinion polling and market research co.) 1986–98, Dir Gen. CSA Group 1998–2006, Special Adviser 2006–; Special Adviser, Bolloré Group 2006–; Chevalier du Mérite agricole. *Television productions include:* Portrait d'un Président: François Mitterrand (with A. Gaillard) 1985. *Publications:* François Mitterrand 1967, Le Député Français (with J. L. Parodi and C. Ysmal) 1970, La Presse écrite et audiovisuelle 1973, La télévision fait-elle l'élection? (with G. Blumler and G. Thoveron) 1974, La nouvelle communication politique 1986, Les médias 1991, Le grand malentendu, Les Français et la politique 1994, Médias et démocratie: la dérive 1997, Sondages mode d'emploi 2000, La nuit des politiques 2006, La revanche de l'opinion: Médias, sondages, Internet (with Pascal Delannoy) 2007, Tenez enfin vos promesses! – Essai sur les pathologies politiques françaises 2012; political fiction novels under the pseudonym Jean Duchateau: Meurtre à l'Elysée 1987, Meurtre à l'Elysée II 1994, Meurtre à TF1 1998. *Address:* CSA, 2 rue de Choiseul, 75002 Paris, France (office). *Telephone:* 1-44-94-59-57 (office). *E-mail:* cetan.rc@me.com (office); roland.cayrol@csa.eu (office); roland.cayrol@wanadoo.fr (home). *Website:* www.cevipof.com (office).

CAZALET, Sir Peter Grenville, Kt, MA; British business executive (retd); b. 26 Feb. 1929, Weymouth, England; s. of Vice-Adm. Sir Peter Cazalet, KBE, CB, DSO, DSC and Lady (Elise) Cazalet (née Winterbotham); m. Jane Jennifer Rew 1957; three s.; ed Uppingham School and Magdalene Coll., Cambridge; Gen. Man. BP Tanker Co. Ltd 1968–70, Regional Co-ordinator, Australasia and Far East, BP Trading Ltd 1970–72, Pres. BP North America Inc. 1972–75, Dir BP Trading Ltd 1975–81, Chair. BP Oil Int. Ltd 1981–89, Man. Dir BP 1981–89, Deputy Chair. 1986–89; Chair. APV PLC 1989–96, Hakluyt & Co. 1998–99, Breamar Seascope Group PLC 2001–02; Chair. Armed Forces Pay Review Body 1989–93; Deputy Chair. (non-exec.) GKN PLC 1989–96; Dir Standard Oil Co., Cleveland, Ohio 1973–76, Peninsular & Oriental Steam Navigation Co. Ltd 1980–99, De La Rue Co. PLC 1983–95, Energy Capital Investment Co. 1995–98, Seascope Shipping Holdings PLC 1997–2001 (Chair. 2000–01); Dir Gen. Maritime Corpn (US) 2000–02; mem. Top Salaries Review Body 1989–94, Lloyds Register of Shipping Bd 1981–86 and Gen. Cttee 1981–99; Vice-Pres. ME Asscn 1982–, China–Britain Trade Group 1993–96 (Pres. 1996–98); Trustee, Uppingham School 1976–95; Trustee, The Wellcome Trust 1989–92, Gov. The Wellcome Trust Ltd 1992–96; Hon. Sec. King George's Fund for Sailors 1989–2000; Liveryman, Tallow Chandlers' Co. (Master 1991–92), Shipwrights' Co. *Leisure interests:* golf, theatre, fishing.

CAZALOT, Clarence P., Jr, BS; American energy industry executive (retd); b. 1 Feb. 1951; ed Louisiana State Univ.; joined Texaco Inc. as Geophysicist 1972, becoming Vice-Pres. 1992, also Pres. of Texaco Latin America/W Africa 1992, Pres. Texaco Exploration and Production Inc. 1994–97, Pres. Texaco Int. Marketing and Mfg 1997, Pres. Int. Production 1998, Chair. Texaco Ltd, London 1998–99, Chair. Texaco Worldwide Production 1999–2000; Vice-Chair. USX Corpn 2000, apptd mem. Bd Dirs Marathon Oil Co. (later Corpn) 2000, Pres. 2000–12, CEO 2002–12, Exec. Chair. 2012–13 (retd); mem. Bd Dirs Baker Hughes Inc., Spectra Energy Corpn 2013–, FMC Technologies, Inc. 2013–; mem. The Business Council, Advisory Bd of the World Affairs Council of Houston, James A. Baker III Inst. for Public Policy, Bd of Visitors of Univ. of Texas M.D. Anderson Cancer Center, Exec. Advisory Bd of the Houston Minority Supplier Devt Council, Bd of the Bipartisan Policy Cttee Energy Project; mem. American Asscn of Petroleum Geologists, Nat. Petroleum Council, All-American Wildcatters org.; Hon. DHumLitt (Louisiana State Univ.) 2007.

CAZANCIUC, Robert-Marius; Romanian magistrate and government official; ed Faculty of Law, Univ. of Bucharest, Nat. Inst. of Magistracy; prosecutor, within Prosecutor's Office attached to Ilfov Court 1995–98; Prosecutor, Prosecutor's Office attached to Supreme Court of Justice, Office for Relations with mass-media 1998–2000; Chief Prosecutor and Head of Press Office, Prosecutor's Office attached to High Court of Cassation and Justice 2000–01, 2005–09; trainer for Nat. Inst. of Magistracy and Nat. School of Court Clerks (on communication and public relations) 2007–; Dir Gen., Govt Control Unit and Under-Sec. of State 2001–04; Sec. of State, Dept of Programmes Implementation and Structural Adjustment 2004; Deputy Dir Gen., Ministry of Justice –Nat. Admin of Penitentiaries 2005; Sec. Gen., Ministry of Foreign Affairs 2009; Minister of Justice April–Nov. 2015; Ind.; Judicial Merit Order (Fifth Class) 2001, Romanian Mil. Emblem of Honour, Ministry of Defence 2011; Collective Award granted by Minister of Foreign Affairs 2012. *Publications include:* Colecta Publica – Pro Lege Review No. 3 2005, General and Particular Training of the Magistrate Spokesperson (co-author) 2007, Illustrated History of Romanian Diplomacy 2010; several papers. *Address:* c/o Ministry of Justice, 050741 Bucharest 5, Str. Apolodor 17, Romania. *E-mail:* relatiipublice@just.ro.

CAZENEUVE, Bernard, BA, MA; French lawyer and politician; b. 2 June 1963, Senlis (Oise); m. Véronique Cazeneuve; two c.; Gen. Councillor, La Manche 1994–98; Judge, Cour de justice de la République and Haute Cour de Justice 1997–2002; Mayor of Octeville 1995–2000; Second Deputy Mayor of Cherbourg, responsible for port affairs and for fmr territory of Octeville 2000–01, Mayor of Cherbourg 2001–12; called to the bar of Cherbourg-Octeville 2003; First Vice-Pres. Regional Council of Lower Normandy for Econ. Devt, Maritime Policy and Tourism 2004–07; First Vice-Pres. Urban Community of Cherbourg 2004–08, Pres. 2008–12; Councillor, Cherbourg-Octeville 2012–14; mem. (Parti socialiste) Nat. Ass. for 5th constituency of La Manche 1997–2002, 2007–12, for 4th constituency of La Manche June–July 2012; Jr Minister for European Affairs 2012–14, Minister of the Interior 2014–16, Prime Minister 2016–17. *Publications:* Première manche 1993, La Politique retrouvée 1994, La Responsabilité du fait des produits en France et en Europe 2005, Karachi – L'enquête impossible 2011. *Address:* Parti Socialiste, 10 rue de Solférino, 75333 Paris Cedex 07, France (office). *Telephone:* 1-45-56-77-00 (office). *Fax:* 1-47-05-15-78 (office). *E-mail:* interps@parti-socialiste.fr (office). *Website:* www.parti-socialiste.fr (office).

CÉANT, Jean Henry; Haitian politician and lawyer; b. 27 Sept. 1956, Port-au-Prince; s. of Célima Céant; m. Chantal Volcy; two s. two d.; ed École de Commerce Julien Craan, Institut Haitien de Statistique et d'Informatique, Institut Lope de Vega, Universidad Pontificia Comillas; fmr notary and accountant; lecturer at Quisqueya Univ., GOC Univ., Nat. School of Financial Admin; f. Collectif Aimer Haiti 2009, Tout Moun Ladan'l 2014, Fondation Institut Dwa Pou Tout Moun and numerous other orgs.; Prime Minister 2018–19 (resgnd); mem. Renmen Ayiti Political Party, Int. Union of Notaries. *Publications include:* Vade-Mecum du notaire et de ses clients 2005, Analyse sur le processus électoral 2005, Vade-Mecum de l'agent de la fonction publique et de l'administré Volume I and II), 2006–08, Dictionnaire juridique 2008, 20 ans de législation haïtienne 2009, Loi du 15 avril 2010: état d'urgence, un cheval de Troie 2010. *Address:* c/o Office of the Prime Minister, 33 blvd Harry Truman, HT 6110, Port-au-Prince, Haiti (office).

CEBRIÁN ECHARRI, Juan Luis, BS; Spanish writer, journalist and publisher; *Executive Chairman, PRISA;* b. 30 Oct. 1944, Madrid; s. of Vicente Cebrián and Carmen Echarri; m. 1st María Gema Torallas 1966 (divorced); two s. two d.; m. 2nd Teresa Aranda 1988; one s. one d.; ed Universidad Complutense de Madrid; Founding mem. Cuadernos para el diálogo (political monthly) 1963; Chief Reporter and Deputy Ed. of Madrid newspapers Pueblo and Informaciones de Madrid 1963–75; was also Head of News at Televisión Española; Founding Ed. El País (global Spanish-language newspaper) 1976–88, Chair. and Publr 2011–; Exec. Chair. PRISA (news, educ. and entertainment group in Spanish and Portuguese) 2012–; mem. Bd Le Monde newspaper; CEO Sogecable 1989–99; Pres. Int. Press Inst. 1986–88, Asscn of Spanish Newspaper Publrs (AEDE) 2004–05; mem. Advisory Bd, Dept of Spanish and Portuguese Languages and Cultures, Princeton Univ. (USA), Advisory Council for the degree in Journalism, Faculty of Humanities, Univ. of Coimbra (Portugal); Trustee, Alfonso Reyes Chair, Technological Inst. of Monterrey (Mexico); mem. Real Academia Española 1966; Corresp. mem. Chilean Acad. of Language; Hon. Prof., Universidad Iberoamericana de Santo Domingo, Dominican Repub. 1988, Hon. Visiting Prof., Univ. of La Plata (Argentina) 2003; Chevalier, Ordre des Arts et des Lettres, Grand Officer, Order of Bernardo O'Higgins (Chile) 2014, decorations from Dominican Repub. and Bolivia; Dr hc (Iberoamericana Univ., Santo Domingo) 1988, (La Plata Univ., Argentina) 2003; numerous prizes in journalism include Int. Ed. of the Year Award, World Press Review, New York 1980, Premio Nacional de Periodismo de España 1983, Freedom of Expression Medal, F.D. Roosevelt Four Freedoms Foundation, Medal of Honour, Univ. of Missouri 1986, Joaquin Chamorro Prize for Freedom of Expression (Chile), Honor Medal for Distinguished Service in

Journalism, Univ. of Missouri 1986, Trento Int. Prize in Journalism and Communication 1987, Rector's Medal, Univ. of Chile 2001, Medal of Merit, Universidad Veracruzana (Mexico) 2003, Washington the First Amendment Award, Spanish Asscn of Eisenhower Fellows 2014. *Publications include:* La Prensa y la Calle 1980, La España que bosteza 1980, ¿Qué pasa en el mundo? 1981, Crónicas de mi país 1985, La rusa Alfaguara (novel) 1986, El Tamaño del elefante 1987, Red Doll 1987, La isla del viento (novel) 1990, El siglo de las sombras 1994, Cartas a un joven periodista 1997, Exaltación del vino, y de la alegría 1998, La red 1998, La agonía del dragón (novel) 2000, El futuro no es lo que era 2001, Francomoribundia (novel) 2003, El Fundamentalismo Democrático 2004; literary works published in compilations: Retrato de un Siglo, De Madrid… al cielo; essays included in Prensa para la democracia: Reto del Siglo XXI, Transición Española. *Leisure interests:* music, literature. *Address:* PRISA, Avenida de los Artesanos 6, 28760 Tres Cantos Madrid, Spain (office). *Telephone:* (91) 3301009 (office); (91) 3301020 (office). *Fax:* (91) 3301070 (office). *E-mail:* presidencia@prisa.com (office). *Website:* www.prisa.com (office).

CECCHI GORI, Vittorio; Italian film producer and politician; *Head of Gruppo Cecchi Gori;* b. 27 April 1943, Florence, Tuscany; s. of Mario Cecchi Gori; ed Univ. of Rome; began cinematographic career in father's co. Gruppo Cecchi Gori (previously Casa di Produzione Cinematografica); apptd Head of Group 1993, purchased Telemontecarlo and Videomusic (now TMC2) 1995; has produced more than 180 films; Senator (Partido Populare Italiano) 1996–2001, mem. Perm. Comm. for Labour and Social Welfare; Owned ACF Fiorentina football club 1993–2002, La7 pvt. TV channel. *Films produced include:* Il bisbetico domato 1980, Asso 1981, Innamorato pazzo 1981, Grand Hotel Excelsior 1982, Attila 1982, La casa stregata 1982, Acqua e Sapone 1983, Softly Softly 1984, Pizza Connection 1985, Joan Lui 1986, Sono un fenomeno paranormale 1985, Scuola di Ladri 1986, Me and My Sister 1987, Il Burbero 1987, Il volpone 1988, La leggenda del santo bevitore (Best Film, Venice Film Festival) 1988, La chiesa 1989, Russicum 1989, La voce della luna 1990, Il segreto 1990, La Femme Nikita 1990, Che ora è? 1990, Il sole buio 1990, La setta 1991, Atlantis 1991, Volere volare 1991, Mediterraneo 1991, Piedipiatti 1991, Miliardi 1991, Johnny Stecchino 1991, Maledetto il giorno che t'ho incontrato 1992, Folks! 1992, Puerto escondido 1992, Man Trouble 1992, Al lupo, al lupo 1992, L'angelo con la pistola 1992, House of Cards 1993, Io speriamo che me la cavo 1993, Caino e Caino 1993, Una pura formalità 1994, Il postino 1994, Occhio Pinocchio 1994, Pisolini, un delitto italiano 1995, Al di là delle nuvole 1995, La scuola 1995, L'uomo delle stelle 1995, Viaggi di nozze 1995, I laureati 1995, Vite strozzate 1996, Tre 1996, Il ciclone 1996, Sono pazzo di Iris Blond 1996, Nirvana 1997, Ovosodo 1997, Le bossu 1997, Naja 1997, I piccoli maestri 1998, La seconda moglie 1998, Viola bacia tittu 1998, La fame e la sete 1999, Canone inverso – Making Love 2000, Denti 2000, Faccia di Ricasso 2000, Almost Blue 2000, Commedia sexy 2001, E adesso sesso 2001, Figli 2001, Momo 2001, Imperial Treasures 2001, My Name is Tanino 2002, L'anima gemella 2002, La vita come viene 2003, Opopomoz 2003, L'Amore è eterno finché dura 2004, In questo mondo di ladri 2004, Cose da pazzi 2005, Il Ritorno del Monnezza 2005, Towards the Moon with Fellini 2006, Scusa ma ti chiamo amore 2008, Everybody's Fine 2009, La brutta copia (TV film) 2013, Silence 2016. *Address:* c/o Gruppo Cecchi Gori, Via Valadier, 00193 Rome, Italy (office). *Telephone:* (06) 324721 (office). *E-mail:* webmaster@cecchigori.com (office). *Website:* www.cecchigori.com (office).

CECH, Thomas Robert, PhD; American professor of chemistry and biochemistry; *Distinguished Professor, Department of Chemistry and Biochemistry, University of Colorado;* b. 8 Dec. 1947, Chicago, Ill.; s. of Robert Franklin Cech and Annette Marie Cech (née Cerveny); m. Carol Lynn Martinson 1970; two d.; ed Grinnell Coll., Univ. of California, Berkeley; Postdoctoral Fellow, Dept of Biology, MIT, Cambridge, Mass. 1975–77; Asst Prof., then Assoc. Prof. of Chem., Univ. of Colorado, Boulder 1978–83, Prof. of Chem. and Biochemistry and of Molecular, Cellular and Devt Biology 1983–, Distinguished Prof. 1990–, Dir BioFrontiers Inst. 2009–; Research Prof., American Cancer Soc. 1987–; Investigator, Howard Hughes Medical Inst. 1988–99, 2009–, Pres. 2000–09; Deputy Ed. Science 1990–99; mem. Editorial Bd Genes and Devt 1987–; Assoc. Ed. Cell 1986–87, RNA 1994–; mem. Bd of Dirs Merck, Inc., 2009–, Mount Desert Island Biological Laboratory 2009–; Nat. Science Foundation Fellow 1970–75; Public Health Service Research Fellow, Nat. Cancer Inst. 1975–77; Guggenheim Fellow 1985–86; mem. American Acad. of Arts and Sciences, NAS 1987–, American Soc. of Biochemistry and Molecular Biology; Foreign mem. Academia Europaea 1999–; Hon. mem. Japanese Biochemical Soc. 1990–; Hon. DSc (Grinnell Coll.) 1987, (Univ. of Chicago) 1991, (Drury Coll.) 1994, (Colorado Coll.) 1999, (Univ. of Maryland) 2000, (Williams Coll.) 2000, (Charles Univ., Prague) 2002, (Ohio State Univ.) 2003, (Moscow State Univ., Russia) 2004, (Univ. of Vermont) 2005, (Univ. of Buenos Aires, Argentina) 2007, (Dartmouth Coll.) 2008, (Rockefeller Univ.) 2009, (Harvard Univ.) 2010, (Watson School of Biological Sciences, Cold Spring Harbor Laboratories) 2010; Medal of American Inst. of Chemists 1970, Research Career Devt Award, Nat. Cancer Inst. 1980–85, Young Scientist Award, Passano Foundation 1984, Harrison Howe Award 1984, Pfizer Award 1985, US Steel Award 1987, V.D. Mattia Award 1987, Heineken Prize 1988, Gairdner Foundation Award 1988, Lasker Award 1988, Warren Triennial Prize 1989, Nobel Prize in Chem. (with Sidney Altman) 1989, Rosenstiel Award 1989, Nat. Medal of Science 1995, Gregor Mendel Medal 2002, Rolf Sammet Prize, Goethe Univ., Frankfurt, Germany 2004, Award for Exemplary Contribution to Educ., American Soc. for Biochemistry and Molecular Biology 2006, Othmer Gold Medal, Chemical Heritage Foundation 2007, Lifetime Achievement Award, RNA Soc. 2009; numerous lectureships. *Leisure interest:* skiing. *Address:* Cristol Chemistry 334B, Department of Chemistry and Biochemistry, University of Colorado, Boulder, CO 80309-0215, USA (office). *Telephone:* (303) 492-8606 (office). *E-mail:* Thomas.Cech@colorado.edu (office). *Website:* www.colorado.edu/chem (office); cechlab.colorado.edu (office).

CEDAIN, Zhoima, (Tseten Dolma); Chinese singer; b. 1 Aug. 1937, Xigaze, Xizang (Tibet); m. Namgyal Dorje 1957; one s. one d.; ed Shanghai Music Coll.; joined CCP 1961; performed in USSR 1963; in political disgrace during Proletarian Cultural Revolution 1966–76; rehabilitated 1977; mem. Standing Cttee 5th NPC 1978–83; Vice-Chair. 6th CPPCC Tibet Regional Cttee 1987; Vice-Chair. Chinese Musicians' Asscn 1979–; apptd consultant, Tibetan Art Troupe 1994; mem. Standing Cttee 6th NPC 1983–88, 7th CPPCC 1988–92; Exec. Vice-Chair. China Fed. of Literary and Art Circles 1988–; Gold Record award, Wuzhou Cup Golden Melody Award, Everest Literature and Art Fund Award, Chinese Arts Award 2013. *Songs:* On the Golden Mountain of Beijing, Emancipated Serfs Sing Proudly, Flying Goose, Heart Song, Happy Songs, Spring Wind Waves in My Heart, Lhobas are Flying High. *Address:* Chinese Musicians' Association, Beijing, People's Republic of China.

CEDAR, Howard, BS, MD, PhD; Israeli/American biochemist and academic; *Edmond J. Safra Distinguished Professor Emeritus, Hebrew University of Jerusalem;* b. (Haim Cedar), 12 Jan. 1943, New York; m. Zipporah Cedar; six c.; ed Massachusetts Inst. of Tech., New York Univ.; worked for US Army's Public Health Service and NIH, Bethesda, Md 1970–73; emigrated to Israel with his family 1973; joined Dept of Biochemistry, Hebrew Univ. of Jeruslaem-Hadassah Medical School, first Edmond J. Safra Distinguished Prof. 2008–11, Prof. Emer. 2011–; Prof., Dept for Biochemistry and Genetics of Human Cell and Chair. Dept for Developmental Biology and Cancer Research, Inst. for Medical Research, Israel-Canada; mem. Israel Acad. of Sciences and Humanities 2003; Israel Prize 1999, Wolf Prize in Medicine (with Aharon Razin) 2008, EMET Prize 2009, Canada Gairdner Award (with Aharon Razin), Gairdner Int. Award 2011, Rothschild Prize 2012, Louisa Gross Horwitz Prize (co-recipient with Aharon Razin and Gary Felsenfeld) 2016. *Publications:* numerous papers in professional journals. *Address:* Department of Developmental Biology and Cancer Research, Faculty of Medicine, Hebrew University of Jerusalem, Ein Kerem, PO Box 12272, 91120 Jerusalem, Israel (office). *Telephone:* 2-6758167 (office). *Fax:* 2-6415848 (office). *E-mail:* haimc@ekmd.huji.ac.il (office); cedar@cc.huji.ac.il (office). *Website:* medicine.ekmd .huji.ac.il/En/Publications/ResearchersPages/pages/haimc.aspx (office).

CEDAR, Joseph (Yossef); Israeli film director and screenwriter; b. 31 Aug. 1968, New York City, NY; s. of Howard (Haim) Cedar and Zipporah Cedar; m. Rose Kellner; three c.; ed Hebrew Univ. of Jerusalem, New York Univ., USA; moved to Israel with family aged six; began career as lighting designer and stage manager with Telad studios, Jerusalem; gained recognition with debut film Time of Favor. *Films include:* Time of Favor (six Ophir Acad. Awards including Best Picture) 2000, Campfire (five Ophir Acad. Awards including Best Picture, Best Dir and Best Screenplay) 2004, Beaufort (Silver Bear Award for Best Dir, 2007 Berlin Int. Film Festival, four Ophir Acad. Awards) 2007, Sharon Amrani: Remember His Name (documentary) 2010, Footnote (Best Screenplay Award, 2011 Cannes Film Festival) 2011, Oppenheimer Strategies 2015. *Address:* c/o ICM, 730 Fifth Avenue, New York, NY 10019, USA (office). *Telephone:* (212) 556-5600 (office). *Fax:* (212) 556-5677 (office). *Website:* www.icmtalent.com (office).

ÇEKU, Agim; Kosovo politician and military officer; *President, Partia Social Demokrate (PSD—Social Democratic Party);* b. 29 Oct. 1960, Qyshk, Pejë/Peć; s. of Hasan Çeku; m. Dragica Çeku; two s. one d.; ed Mil. High School, Belgrade, Zadar Mil. Acad., Croatia, Sr Exec. Course, George Marshall Centre, Germany; began career as Platoon Commdr, Yugoslav People's Army 1984, graduated as an Artillery Officer 1984; Platoon Commdr and Lecturer, School of Reserve Officers of the Artillery Centre, Mil. Acad., Zadar 1986–87, Lecturer and Commdr of Cadets' Co. 1989–91; joined newly formed Croatian Army as Capt. 1991, served as Commdr of an Infantry Bn and rose to rank of Maj. 1992, rank of Col 1993, rank of Brig. Gen. 1995; Chief of Staff of Mil. Dist of Gospiq 1995–99; released from Croatian Army to join Kosovo Liberation Army (KLA) and apptd Chief of Gen. Staff 1999, oversaw KLA demilitarization and formation of Kosovo Protection Corps, Commdr 1999–2006, rank of Lt Gen. 2006; Prime Minister of Kosovo 2006–08; Pres. Partia Social Demokrate (PSD—Social Democratic Party) 2008–; Minister of the Kosovo Security Force 2011–14; Order 'Adem Jashari', Medal of Mil. Service (Kosovo); Croatian decorations: Order 'Ban Jelačić', Nikola Šubić Zrinski, Hrvatskog Križa, Hrvatskog Trolista, Hrvatskog Pletera, Medal for Extraordinary Enterprise, Award for Operation 'Oluja' and 'Domovinske Zahvalnosti'; Award of Excellence from Supreme Allied Commdr Europe Gen. Wesley Clark. *Address:* Partia Social Demokrate (Social Democratic Party), 10000 Prishtina, Rruga Gustav Meyer 1, Kosovo (office). *Telephone:* (38) 225645 (office). *E-mail:* info@psd-ks.org (office). *Website:* www.psd-ks.org (office).

CELANT, Germano, PhD; Italian art historian, art critic and curator; *Senior Curator of Contemporary Art, Solomon R. Guggenheim Museum;* b. 1940, Genoa; m. Paris Murray; ed Univ. of Genoa; fmr Asst Ed., Marcatrè, Genoa magazine 1963; coined term Arte Povera (poor art) 1967; Jt Artistic Dir First Florence Biennale 1996; Curator, 47th Int. Art Exhbn, Venice Biennale 1997; Contributing Ed., Artforum 1977–, Interview (art reviews) 1991–; Sr Curator of Contemporary Art, Solomon R. Guggenheim Museum, New York 1989–; Artistic Dir Prada Foundation, Milan 1993–. *Publications include:* Arte povera: Appunti per una guerriglia 1967, The European Iceberg: Creativity in Germany and Italy Today 1985, The Italian Metamorphosis 1943–1968 1994, Mariko Mori: Dream Temple 1999, Carla Accardi 2001, Jim Dine: Walking Memory 1959–1969 (co-author) 2003, Giulio Paolini 1960–1972 2004, Anselm Kiefer 2007, Mimmo Rotella: Selected Works 2007, Vertigo: A Century of Multimedia Art from Futurism to the Web (co-author) 2008, The American Tornado: Art in Power 1949–2008 2008, Luigi Ghirri: It's Beautiful Here, Isn't It … 2008, Frank O. Gehry: Since 1997 2010, Carla Accardi: Catalogue Raisonné 2010, Louise Bourgeois: The Fabric Works 2011, Arte Povera: History and Stories 2011. *Address:* Solomon R. Guggenheim Museum, 1071 Fifth Avenue, New York, NY 100128-0173, USA (office). *Telephone:* (212) 423-3500 (office). *E-mail:* pressoffice@guggenheim.org (office). *Website:* www .guggenheim.org (office).

CELESTE, Richard (Dick) F., PhB; American diplomatist, university administrator and fmr state governor; b. 11 Nov. 1937, Cleveland, Ohio; s. of Frank Celeste; m. 1st Dagmar Braun 1962; three s. three d.; m. 2nd Jacqueline Lundquist; one s.; ed Yale Univ. and Univ. of Oxford, UK; Staff Liaison Officer, US Peace Corps 1963; Special Asst to US Amb. to India 1963–67; Officer with Nat. Housing Consultants, Cleveland 1967–74; mem. Ohio House of Reps 1970–74, Majority Whip 1972–74; Lt-Gov. of Ohio 1975–79, Gov. 1983–91; Dir US Peace Corps, Washington, DC 1979–81; Man. Pnr, Celeste and Sabety Ltd (econ. devt consultancy), Cleveland 1991–97; Amb. to India 1997–2001; Pres. Colorado Coll. 2002–11; Chair. Midwestern Govs' Conf. 1987–88; Great Lakes Govs' Asscn 1987–89; Chair. Bd of Trustees Health Effects Inst., Boston; Lifetime Nat. Assoc., The Nat. Acads; Visiting Fellow in Public Policy, Case Western Reserve Univ. 1995–97; mem. Bd of Dirs Nat. Asscn of Ind. Colls and Univs 2006–08, Garden City Co. 2007–; Pres. Colorado Springs Downtown Partnership; Trustee Glimcher Realty Trust 2007–, the CHF International 2012–; mem. Advisory Bd Inst. of Int.

Educ. 2003–, Leadership Council of ServiceNation 2008–; mem. Council on Foreign Relations; Hatch Prize, Yale Univ. 1959, Delta Sigma Rho-Tau Kappa Alpha Speaker of the Year Award 2006.

CELIŃSKI, Andrzej, MA; Polish politician; *Chairman, Partia Demokratyczna (PD—Democratic Party);* b. 26 Feb. 1950, Warsaw; s. of Zofia Celińska; three s.; ed Warsaw Univ.; co-f. Underground Soc. for Scholarly Courses; mem. Workers' Defence Cttee (KOR) and Solidarity Ind. Self-governing Trade Union; mem. Civic Cttee attached to Solidarity leader Lech Wałęsa (q.v.) 1988–90; participant in Round Table plenary debates 1989; Senator 1989–93 (mem. Civic Parl. Caucus, then Democratic Union Caucus); Deputy to Sejm (Parl.) 1993–2005, 2007–11 (Ind.); Vice-Chair. Democratic Union (UD) 1993–94; mem. Freedom Union (UW) 1994–99; Chair. Programme Comm., then Vice-Chair. Democratic Left Alliance (SLD) 1999–2004; Minister of Culture and Nat. Heritage 2001–02; mem. Mazowieckie Voivodship regional parl. 2006–07; Co-founder Polish Social Democracy (SDPL) 2004 (left party 2008); Chair. Partia Demokratyczna (PD—Democratic Party) 2012–; Commdr's Cross, Order of Polonia Restituta 2006 (returned 2007). *Address:* Partia Demokratyczna, 00-581 Warsaw, ul. Marszałkowska 2 lok. 4, Poland (office). *Telephone:* (22) 3355800 (office). *Fax:* (22) 3355801 (office). *E-mail:* sekretariat@demokraci.pl (office). *Website:* demokraci.pl (office); www.andrzejcelinski.pl.

CEMIL, Mustafa, (Mustafa Dzhemilov); Ukrainian politician; b. 13 Nov. 1943, Ay-Serez, Crimean ASSR, Russian SFSR, USSR; m.; several c.; deported by Soviet authorities May 1944, grew up in exile in Uzbek SSR; co-f. Union of Young Crimean Tatars 1962; arrested six times for anti-Soviet activities and spent time in Soviet prisons and labour camps 1966–86, underwent hunger strike lasting 303 days; elected Head of newly founded Crimean Tatar Nat. Movt 1989; returned to Crimea (then part of Ukrainian SSR) with his family 1989; Chair. Mejlis (Assembly) of the Crimean Tatar People 1991–2013; elected to Verkhovna Rada (Parl.) on Rukh (People's Movt of Ukraine) list 1998, re-elected as mem. of Nasha Ukraina (Our Ukraine) 2002, 2006, 2007, announced retirement from politics 2011, however joined All-Ukrainian Union 'Fatherland' election list and re-elected to Verkhovna Rada 2012, re-elected on electoral list of Bloc Petra Poroshenka (Petro Poroshenko Bloc) 2014; banned by fed. law from entering Russian territory for five years following Russian annexation of Crimea April 2014, warrant issued for his arrest and placed on Russian Fed. wanted list; Order of Prince Yaroslav the Wise (Ukraine); Kt's Cross, Order for Merits (Lithuania); Order of the Repub. (Turkey) 2014; Nansen Medal, UN High Commr for Refugees 1998, first recipient of Lech Wałęsa Prize of Solidarity 2014. *Address:* Verkhovna Rada, 01008 Kyiv, vul. M. Hrushevskoho 5, Ukraine (office). *Telephone:* (44) 255-21-15 (office). *Fax:* (44) 253-32-17 (office). *E-mail:* umz@rada.gov.ua (office). *Website:* www.rada.gov.ua (office).

CENAC, Sir Emmanuel Neville, GCMG; Saint Lucia politician; *Governor-General;* b. 24 Nov. 1939; s. of Frank Cenac and Leanese Cenac (née King); m. Julita Cenac; Councillor, Castries City Corpn 1971–75, Chair. 1980–82; co-f. St Lucia Labour Action Movement 1972; mem. House of Ass. (lower house of parl.) for Laborie constituency 1987–92; Minister of External Affairs 1987–92; Pres. Senate (upper house of parl.) 1993–97; retired from active politics 2006; Gov.-Gen. 2018–; mem. Civil Service Asscn (Sec. 1961–67); mem. Saint Lucia Labour Party (SLP) 1980–87 (Sec. 1980–82, Leader 1982–84); mem. United Workers Party 1987–; Dir St Lucia Electricity Services Ltd 1980–82. *Address:* Government House, Morne Fortune, Castries, Saint Lucia, West Indies (office). *Telephone:* 452-2481 (office). *Fax:* 453-2731 (office). *E-mail:* govgenslu@candw.lc (office). *Website:* www.governorgeneral.govt.lc (office).

CENNETOĞLU, Banu, BA; Turkish artist; b. 1970, Ankara; ed Bogazici Univ., Istanbul; lived in New York 1996–2002 and Amsterdam 2002–04; guest artist, Rijksakademie, Amsterdam; moved to Istanbul 2006; works with photography, installation and printed media; f. BAS (innovative project space), Istanbul 2006; chosen to represent Turkey at 53rd Int. Venice Biennial 2009. *Address:* BAS, Necati Bey Caddesi no 32/2, Karakoy, Istanbul, Turkey (office). *E-mail:* bcennetoglu@hotmail.com (office). *Website:* www.b-a-s.info (office).

CENTENO, Mário, MA, MSc, PhD; Portuguese economist and politician; *Minister of Finance;* b. 9 Dec. 1966, Olhão; m.; three c.; ed Technical Univ. Lisbon, Harvard Univ., USA; Prof., Universidade Tecnica de Lisboa 1993–; Research Asst, later Teaching Asst, Harvard Univ. 1998–2000; Research Economist, Banco de Portugal 2000–04, Asst Dir, Econs Dept 2004–13, Consultant to Banco de Portugal 2014–; mem. EC Econ. Policy Cttee 2004–13; Prof., ISEG, Universidade de Lisboa 2006–; Researcher, Macroeconomics Statistics Devt Group, Conselho Superior de Estatística (Statistical Council) 2007–13; mem. Assembleia da República (Parl.) 2015–; Minister of Finance 2015–; Pres. Eurogroup (informal gathering of eurozone finance ministers) 2018–; mem. Editorial Bd, Portuguese Economic Journal 2001–; Research Fellow, IZA Inst. for the Study of Labour, Bonn 2009–; mem. Exec. Cttee, European Asscn of Labour Economists 2003–05; European Econ. Asscn Young Economist Award 2001, União Latina Award for Scientific Merit 2006. *Publications:* author or co-author of several scientific publications, books and book chapters in the areas of labour economy, econometrics, microeconomics and theory of contract. *Address:* Ministry of Finance, Av. Infante D. Henrique 1, 1149-009 Lisbon, Portugal (office); European Council, Rue de la Loi, Wetstraat 175, 1048 Brussels, Belgium (office). *Telephone:* (21) 8816800 (office); (2) 281-61-11 (EC). *Fax:* (21) 8816862 (office); (2) 281-69-34 (EC). *E-mail:* gabinete.ministro@mf.gov.pt (office). *Website:* www.portugal.gov.pt/en/ministries/mf/the-team/minister/mario-centeno.aspx (office); www.consilium.europa.eu (office).

CENTENO, Pavel; Guatemalan economist, academic and government official; ed Univ. of Guadalajara, Mexico; Founding mem. Partido Patriota; economist, Universidad de San Carlos de Guatemala (USAC); econ. and financial adviser to numerous pvt. cos and banking insts; fmr adviser to Vice-Pres., Faculty of Social Sciences, Latin American School of Social Sciences (FLACSO), Guatemala; has taught in Guatemala, Mexico, the Netherlands and Norway at various academic insts including Centro Universitario de Ciencias Económico Administrativas, Univ. of Guadalajara, Univ. of San Carlos, Inst. of European–Latin American Relations, Univ. of Central Netherlands (HMN); fmr adviser to various govt bodies including Planning Secr., Presidency of the Repub.; Minister of Public Finance 2012–13. *Address:* c/o Ministry of Public Finance, Centro Cívico, 8A Avenida y 21 Calle, Zona 1, Guatemala City, Guatemala.

CENTENO NAJARRO, Humberto; Salvadorean politician and fmr trade unionist; *Minister of Labour and Social Security;* b. 14 Dec. 1941, Concepcion Ataco, Ahuachapán; m.; ed Univ. of El Salvador; served in army 1984–86; fmr mem. Partido Comunista; co-f. Salvadorean Asscn of Telecommunications Workers (trade union) 1984; mem. Asamblea Legislativa (parl.) for Ahuachapán (Frente Farabundo Martí para la Liberación Nacional, FMLN) 1994–2009; Minister of Internal Affairs 2009–11, of Labour and Social Security 2011–; founding mem. FMLN 1992–. *Address:* Ministry of Labour and Social Security, Edifs 2 y 3, Alameda Juan Pablo II y 17 Avda Norte, San Salvador, El Salvador (office). *Telephone:* 2209-3700 (office). *Fax:* 2209-3756 (office). *E-mail:* asesorialaboral@mtps.gob.sv (office). *Website:* www.mtps.gob.sv (office).

CENTERMAN, Jörgen, MSc; Swedish business executive; *Chairman, Gunnebo Industrier AB;* b. 1951; ed Univ. of Tech. of Lund; joined ABB 1976, worked in Singapore, Sweden, Germany, USA, Switzerland, Head of Automation –2000, Pres. and CEO 2001–02 (resgnd); Chair. HMS Industrial Networks AB 2004–09; Chair. Gunnebo Industrier AB 2008–, also Chair. Dacke PMC, Kemetyl Holding AB; mem. Bd of Dirs, Micronic Laser Systems AB 2004–, Telelogic, XPonCard, Segulah Advisor AB (Industrial Partner and Dir) 2004–; mem. Int. Advisory Group, Blekinge Inst. of Technology. *Address:* Gunnebo Industrier AB, Vasagatan 20A, 722 15 Västerås, Sweden (office). *Telephone:* (21) 838200 (office). *Fax:* (21) 838228 (office). *E-mail:* info@gunneboindustries.com (office). *Website:* www.gunneboindustries.com (office).

ČEPĀNIS, Alfreds; Latvian banker and fmr politician; *Deputy Chairman, Trasta komercbanka—TKB (Trust Commercial Bank);* b. 3 Aug. 1943, Kalsnava, Madona Region; m. Ilma Čepane; one d.; ed Jaungolbene School of Agric., Higher CP School in Moscow by correspondence; Comsomol functionary 1968–74; Deputy Chair., Chair. Ventspils District Exec. Cttee 1975–79; Sec. Preili Regional Cttee Latvian CP 1979–84; First Sec. Liepaja Regional CP Cttee 1983–88; Deputy Chair. Council of Ministers 1989–90; mem. Supreme Soviet of Latvia 1990–93; mem. Saeima (Parl.), Deputy Speaker 1993–95; mem. faction Demikratiska Partija Samnieks 1995, Speaker 1996–98; Gen. Man. Euroconsultant (consultancy) 1998–2006; mem. Council, Trasta komercbanka—TKB (Trust Commercial Bank), Rīga 1999–, now Deputy Chair.; fmr Head of Soc. for the Promotion of Latvian–Belarusian Econ. Relations, now mem. Bd of Dirs; Kt, Three Star Order. *Leisure interests:* hunting, literature, theatre. *Address:* Trasta komercbanka, Miesnieku iela 9, Rīga 1050, Latvia (office). *Telephone:* 6702-7777 (office). *Fax:* 6702-7700 (office). *E-mail:* info@tkb.lv (office). *Website:* www.tkb.lv (office).

CERAR, Miroslav (Miro), PhD; Slovenian lawyer and politician; *Minister of Foreign Affairs;* b. 25 Aug. 1963, Ljubljana, Socialist Repub. of Slovenia, Socialist Fed. Repub. of Yugoslavia; s. of Miroslav Cerar, Sr and Zdenka Cerar; m.; two d.; ed Univ. of Ljubljana; participant in drafting new Slovenian constitution following split from Yugoslavia 1991; Prof., Faculty of Law, Univ. of Ljubljana; Legal Adviser to Slovenian Parl.; Fulbright Visiting Prof., Golden Gate Univ., San Francisco, USA 2008; fmr Visiting Prof., Univ. of California, Berkeley; f. new political party Stranka Mira Cerarja (Party of Miro Cerar) 2014, renamed Stranka Modernega Centra (Modern Centre Party) 2015; Prime Minister of Slovenia 2014–18 (resgnd); Minister of Foreign Affairs 2018–. *Address:* Ministry of Foreign Affairs, 1001 Ljubljana, Prešernova 25 (office); Stranka Modernega Centra, Beethovnova 2, 1000 Ljubljana, Slovenia (office). *Telephone:* (1) 4782231 (office). *Fax:* (1) 4782170 (office). *E-mail:* info@strankasmc.si (office). *Website:* www.mzz.gov.si (office); www.strankasmc.si (office).

CEREZO ARÉVALO, Marco Vinicio; Guatemalan politician and lawyer; *Secretary-General, Central American Integration System (SICA);* b. 26 Dec. 1942, Guatemala City; s. of Marco Vinicio Cerezo Sierra; m. Raquel Blandón (divorced 2006); ed Univ. of San Carlos of Guatemala, Loyola Univ., New Orleans, USA; joined Guatemalan Christian Democrats (DCG) 1964, apptd Sec. 1970; Deputy Nat. Congress 1974–91, 1999–2008; Pres. 1986–91; Deputy Cen. American Parl. 1991–96; Sec.-Gen. Central American Integration System (SICA) 2017–; Perm. mem. Forum of Biarritz (France) and Int. Lecturer; mem. Carter Center. *Address:* Central American Integration System (SICA), Final Bulevar Cancillería, Distrito El Espino, Ciudad Merliot, Antiguo Cuscatlán, La Libertad, El Salvador (office). *Telephone:* 2248-8800 (office). *E-mail:* info@sica.int (office). *Website:* www.sica.int (office).

CERF, Vinton (Vint) Gray, MSc, PhD; American computer scientist; *Chief Internet Evangelist, Google Inc.;* b. 23 June 1943, New Haven, Conn.; s. of Vinton T. Cerf and Muriel G. Cerf; m. Sigrid Cerf; two s.; ed Van Nuys High School, Stanford Univ., Univ. of California, Los Angeles; began career working for N American Aviation, Rocketdyne, then IBM; Prof. of Computer Science, Stanford Univ. 1972–76, worked on ARPANET (earliest packet switched computer network); Head of Internet, Packet Radio, Packet Satellite and Network Security Research and Devt Program, Advanced Research Projects Agency (DARPA), US Dept of Defense 1976–82; played key role in devt of the Internet and TCP/IP protocols; Vice-Pres. MCI Digital Information Services 1982–86, led eng of MCI Mail (first commercial email service on internet), Sr Vice-Pres. of Internet Architecture and Tech. 1994–2005; headed several research projects including digital libraries, Corpn for Nat. Research Initiatives 1986–94; f. Internet Soc. (ISOC) 1992, Pres. 1992–95, Chair. 1999–2007; Vice-Pres. and Chief Internet Evangelist, Google Inc. 2005–; Chair. American Registry for Internet Numbers 2012–; currently consultant on Interplanetary Protocol, Jet Propulsion Lab., NASA; mem. US Presidential Information Tech. Advisory Cttee (PITAC) 1997–2001; mem. Bd, Internet Corpn for Assigned Names and Numbers (ICANN) 1999–2007 (Chair. –2007), Nat. Science Bd 2012–; Commr, Broadband Comm. for Digital Devt 2010–; serves on several nat., state and industry cttees focused on cyber-security; mem. Bd of Dirs, Endowment for Excellence in Educ.; mem. Asscn for Computing Machinery (ACM) 1967, Fellow 1993, Pres. 2012–14; mem. Bulgarian Pres. Georgi Parvanov's IT Advisory Council 2002–12, Advisory Bd of Eurasia Group, Bd of Advisors of The Liquid Information Co. Ltd (UK); Chair. StopBadware; Co-Chair. Campus Party Silicon Valley; Foreign mem. Royal Swedish Acad. of Eng; Fellow, IEEE, AAAS, American Acad. of Arts and Sciences, Int. Eng Consortium, Computer History Museum, Nat. Acad. of Eng, American

Philosophical Soc.; Hon. Chair. IPv6 Forum; Freeman of the City of London; Distinguished Fellow, British Computer Soc. 2011; Freeman of the Worshipful Co. of Information Technologists, London 2015; Hon. Liveryman, Stationers' Guild, London 2015; Officier, Légion d'honneur 2014; Order of the Cross of Terra Mariana (Estonia) 2014; Dr hc from 25 univs; numerous awards including Marconi Fellowship, NEC Computer and Communications Prize, ITU Silver Medal, IEEE Alexander Graham Bell Medal, IEEE Kobi Kobayahsi Award, ACM Software and Systems Award, Yuri Rubinsky Memorial Award 1995, ACM SIGCOMM Award 1996, US Nat. Medal of Tech. 1997, Kilby Award, Lifetime Achievement Award, Yankee Group/Network World/Interop, IEEE Third Millennium Medal, Computerworld/Smithsonian Leadership Award, J.D. Edwards Leadership Award, Charles Stark Draper Prize, Nat. Acad. of Eng 2001, Premio Principe de Asturias de Investigacion Cientifica (Spain) 2002, Alexander Graham Bell Asscn for the Deaf and Hard of Hearing Award, World Inst. on Disability Annual Award, Library of Congress Bicentennial Living Legend Medal, ACM Turing Award 2005, US Presidential Medal of Freedom 2005, Medal of Science (Tunisia), St Cyril and St Methodius Medal (Bulgaria), Dickinson Coll. Joseph Priestley Award, Japan Prize 2008, HPI Fellowship 2011, inducted into Internet Hall of Fame 2012, Queen Elizabeth Prize for Eng (co-recipient) 2013. *Publications include:* A Protocol for Packet Network Intercommunication (co-author with Bob Kahn) 1974, Networks, Scientific American Special Issue on Communications, Computers, and Networks 1991, Guidelines for Internet Measurement Activities 1991; numerous articles in professional journals. *Leisure interests:* fine wine, gourmet cooking, science fiction. *Address:* Google Inc., 1875 Explore Street, Reston, VA 20190, USA (office). *Telephone:* (202) 370-5637 (office). *Fax:* (703) 935-0228 (office). *E-mail:* vint@google.com (office). *Website:* www.google.com (office).

CERIĆ, Mustafa, PhD; Bosnia and Herzegovina ecclesiastic; *President, World Bosniak Congress;* b. 5 Feb. 1952, Veliko Cajno, Visoko; m.; one s. two d.; ed Medressa, Sarajevo, Al-Azhar Univ., Cairo, Egypt, Univ. of Chicago, USA; returned to Bosnia from Egypt and became an imam; Imam of US Islamic Cultural Center of Greater Chicago 1981–87; Grand Imam of Zagreb, Croatia from 1987, of Sanjak, Croatia and Slovenia; Grand Mufti of Bosnia-Herzegovina and Reis-ul-Ulema (Pres. Council of Ulema) 1993–2012; Co-founder Bosniak Acad. of Sciences and Arts 2011; Co-founder and Pres. World Bosniak Congress 2012–; Prof., Int. Inst. of Islamic Thought and Civilization, Kuala Lumpur 1991–92; has delivered numerous lectures and led several workshops on inter-religious and inter-faith issues at local and int. confs; cand. for a Bosniak mem. of Presidency of Bosnia and Herzegovina in general election 2014; mem. Interreligious Council of Bosnia-Herzegovina, Council of 100 Leaders of the World Econ. Forum, European Council for Fatwas and Research, World Conf. on Religion and Peace, European Council of Religious Leaders; mem. Exec. Bd Foundation for Srebrenica/Potocari Memorial and Cemetery, Sarajevo; mem. Sharia'h Bd Bosnia Bank Int., Fiqh Acad., Mecca, Aal Albayt Foundation for Islamic Thought, Jordan, Int. Comm. for Peace Research; mem. Advisory Council Tony Blair Faith Foundation; Trustee, Int. Islamic Univ., Islamabad; co-recipient UNESCO Félix Houphouët-Boigny Peace Prize for Contrib. to World Peace 2003, Int. Council of Christians and Jews Sir Sigmund Sternberg Award for Exceptional Contrib. to Inter-faith Understanding 2003, Theodor-Heuss-Stiftung Award 2007, Lifetime Achievement Award, Asscn of Muslim Social Scientists (UK) 2007, 2008. *Publications:* several books in Bosnian, including Roots of Synthetic Theology in Islam, A Choice Between War and Peace, A Declaration of European Muslims by Reis-ul-Ulama Dr. Mustafa Ceric 2006, The Challenge of a Single Muslim Authority in Europe 2007. *Address:* c/o European Council of Religious Leaders, PO Box 6820, 0130 Oslo, Norway.

ČERNÁK, Ľudovít, Ing., PhDr; Slovak politician and business executive; *President, Sitno Holding a.s.;* b. 12 Oct. 1951, Hliník nad Hronom; s. of Ľudovít Černák and Gabriela Černákova (née Chmelova); m. (divorced); three c.; ed Univ. of Tech., Bratislava, Technical Univ., Kosicee, Univ. of Birmingham, UK; man. training in UK 1990; fmr Chair. Slovak Nat. Party (SNP); Minister of Economy 1992–93, 1998–2000; Vice-Chair. Nat. Council 1993–94; fmr mem. Parl. of Slovakia; fmr Vice-Chair. Democratic Union; mem. Int. Cttee for Econ. Reform and Co-operation 2000; in pvt business (investment, finance, offsets) 2000–, Pres. Sitno Holding a.s.; Pres. Slovak Defence Industry Asscn 2005–07, 2010–14; Owner and Pres. Sk Slovan Bratislava Football Club 2005–08; Pres., Slovak-Russian Business Council 2006–12; Hon. Chancellor of Uzbekistan in Slovakia 2009–. *Leisure interests:* family, detective novels, tourism, football. *Address:* Sitno Holding a.s., Zechenterova 328/5, 67 01 Kremnica (office); Sitno Holding a.s., Rybne namestie 1, Bratislava (office); Buková 8, 811 01 Bratislava, Slovakia (home). *Telephone:* (2) 39900007 (office). *Fax:* (2) 39900008 (office). *E-mail:* lcernak@sitno.sk (office). *Website:* www.sitnobusiness.com (office).

CEROVSKÝ, Gen. Milan, DipEng; Slovak army officer; b. 10 Oct. 1949, Kalinovo; m.; two c.; ed Mil. Acad., Vyškov; Mil. Acad., Brno, Royal Coll. of Defence, London, UK; began career with Hungarian armed forces 1971, positions include platoon and co. Commdr 1971–74; Deputy Chief of Staff 60th Tank Regt, 14th Tank Div., E Mil. Dist, Commdr Tank Battalion; Chief of Staff 63rd Mechanized Regt, 14th Tank Div., Commdr; Chief of Staff 13th Tank Div., Deputy Commdr of Operations, Commdr 1993–94; Commdr 1st Army Corps 1994–98; Chief of Integration and Standardization Admin. of Army Gen. Staff 1998, Chief of Gen. Staff of Army 1998–2002, of Armed Forces 2002–04; rank of Lt Gen. 1999, Gen. 2003. *Leisure interest:* sport. *Address:* c/o Ministry of Defence, Kutuzovova 7, 832 28 Bratislava, Slovakia (office). *Telephone:* (2) 4425-0329 (office). *Fax:* (2) 4425-3242 (office). *Website:* www.mod.gov.sk (office).

CERRATO RODRIGUEZ, Wilfredo Rafael; Honduran economist, politician and central banker; *President, Banco Central de Honduras;* b. 1971; s. of Wilfredo Cerrato; ed Universidad Tecnológica Centroamericana, Central American Inst. of Business Admin (INCAE); held positions in pvt. banking and agribusiness cos and public admin, including as Pres. Coalianza—Comisionado para la Promoción de las Alianzas Público Privadas (Comm. for the Promotion of Public-Private Partnerships) –2012; Minister of Finance 2012–18; Pres., Banco Central de Honduras 2018–. *Address:* Banco Central de Honduras (BANTRAL), Avda Juan Ramón Molina, 7a Avda y 1a Calle, Apdo 3165, Tegucigalpa, Honduras (office). *Telephone:* 2222-3422 (office). *Fax:* 2237-4502 (office). *E-mail:* transparencia@bch.hn (office). *Website:* www.bch.hn (office).

CERUTTI, Dominique; French business executive; *Chairman and CEO, Altran;* b. 3 Jan. 1961, Manosque; m.; two c.; with Bouygues (civil eng co.), Saudi Arabia 1994–96; joined IBM 1986, served in various man. roles in sales eng and sales man., becoming Dir Personal Systems Group, W Region 1996–98, Exec. Asst to IBM Chair. and CEO, New York 1998–99, Gen. Man. IBM Global Services, W Region 2000, later Gen. Man., IBM Global Services in Europe, Middle East and Africa, Paris, mem. IBM Sr Leadership Team and Gen. Man. IBM SW Europe 2005–09; Deputy CEO and Pres. NYSE Euronext Paris SA 2009–13, Global Head of Tech. 2009–10, also Pres. Euronext Paris and Chair. Managing Bd, Euronext NV, Group CEO Euronext NV 2013–15; Chair. and CEO Altran 2015–. *Leisure interests:* jogging, diving. *Address:* Altran, 96 avenue Charles de Gaulle, 92200 Neuilly-sur-Seine, France (office). *Telephone:* 1-46-41-70-00 (office). *Fax:* 1-46-41-70-01 (office). *E-mail:* info@altran.com (office). *Website:* www.altran.com (office).

CERUTTI, Guillaume; French business executive and fmr civil servant; *Chief Executive Officer, Christie's;* b. 20 March 1966, La Ciotat; ed École Nationale d'Admin, Strasbourg, Institut d'Études Politiques de Paris; began career in French Treasury's Dept for Auditing Public Bodies 1991; served as Financial Advisor to the Secrétariat Général pour les Affaires Européennes (Office for European Affairs); Man. Dir Centre Pompidou, Paris 1996–2001; Chief of Staff to the Minister for Culture and Communication, Jean-Jacques Aillagon 2002–04; Head of Dept of Competition Policy, Consumer Affairs and Fraud Control, Ministry for the Economy and Finance 2004–07; CEO Sotheby's France 2007–15, Deputy Chair. Sotheby's Europe 2011–15; CEO Christie's 2016–; mem. Bd of Dirs Ingenico SA 2010–12, Flamel Technologies SA 2011–17, Avadel Pharmaceuticals 2011; Chair. Accentus vocal ensemble; Pres. Inst. for Financing Film and Cultural Industries; mem. Cttee of Honour of the Friends of the French Cinémathèque. *Publication:* Création et Internet (report, with Patrick Zelnik and Jacques Toubon) 2010, La politique culturelle, un enjeu du XXIème siècle, 20 propositions 2016; contrib. numerous articles to newspapers like Le Monde, Les Échos, l'Opinion. *Address:* Christie's, 8 King Street, St James's, London SW1Y 6QT, England (office). *Telephone:* (20) 7839-9060 (office). *Fax:* (20) 7389-2869 (office). *E-mail:* info@christies.com (office). *Website:* christies.com (office).

CÉSAR, Carlos Manuel Martins do Vale; Portuguese politician and government official; b. 30 Oct. 1956, Ponta Delgada, Azores; s. of Aurélio Augusto César and Maria Natália Martins do Vale César; m. Luísa Maria Assís Vital Gomes; one s.; ed Antero de Quental High School, Faculty of Law, Lisbon; f. Socialist Youth and Socialist Party 1974, mem. Nat. Exec. Socialist Party 1975–; Asst to State Sec. for Public Admin 1977–78; Deputy, Regional Ass. 1980–96, Vice-Pres. –1996; Pres. Regional Govt of the Azores 1996–2012 (retd); mem. Council of State, Higher Nat. Defence Council, Higher Internal Security Council, Cttee of the Regions, Ass. of European Regions, Conf. of Presidents of Ultra-peripheral Regions, Conf. of Peripheral Maritime Regions of Europe, Congress of Local Regional Authorities of Europe. *Address:* c/o Residência do Presidente, Governo Regional, Palácio de Santana, 9500-077 Ponta Delgada, The Azores. *E-mail:* presidencia@azores.gov.pt.

CESARSKY, Catherine Jeanne, PhD; French astrophysicist and government official; *High Commissioner for Atomic Energy, Commissariat à l'énergie atomique;* b. 24 Feb. 1943, Ambazac (Haute-Vienne); m.; two c.; ed Univ. of Buenos Aires, Argentina, Harvard Univ., USA; raised largely in Argentina; Research Fellow, Instituto Argentino de Radioastronomia 1965–66; Teaching Fellow, Harvard Univ. 1966–70; Research Fellow, Astronomy Dept, California Inst. of Tech. 1971–74; moved to France 1974; staff mem. Service d'Astrophysique (SAp), Direction des Sciences de la Matière (DSM), Commissariat à l'Energie Atomique (CEA), Saclay 1974–78, Head of Theoretical Group of SAp 1978–85, Head of SAp 1985–93, Dir DSM 1994–99; Dir Gen. European Southern Observatory 1999–2007; High Commr for Atomic Energy, CEA, Saclay 2007–; adviser to French Govt on science and energy issues; Chair. Science Program Cttee, Centre Nat. d'Etudes Spatiales, Consultative Cttee EURATOM-Fusion (CCE-FU); Pres. French Soc. of Professional Astronomers 1994–96, Comité des Programmes Scientifiques du CNES (Centre Nat. d'Etudes Spatiales) 2005–; Vice-Pres. European Astronomical Soc. 1993–97, Int. Astronomical Union 1997–2003 (Pres.-Elect 2003–06, Pres. 2006–09); mem. European Research Advisory Bd 2004–; Ed.-in-Chief Journal Astronomy and Astrophysics 1982–85; mem. Acad. des sciences, Academia Europaea, Int. Acad. of Astronautics; Foreign Assoc., NAS; Foreign mem. Royal Swedish Acad. of Sciences, Royal Soc. of London; Hon. mem. American Astronomical Soc. 2002; Chevalier, Ordre nat. du Mérite 1989, Officier 1999, Commdr, Grand Officier 2014; Chevalier, Légion d'honneur 1994, Officier 2004, Commdr 2011; Dr hc (Geneva) 2010; COSPAR Space Science Award 1998, Prix Jules Janssen, French Astronomical Soc. *Achievements include:* designed the ISOCAM camera on board the Infrared Space Observatory. *Publications:* more than 350 scientific papers in professional journals. *Address:* Commissariat à l'Energie Atomique, Centre d'études de Saclay, 91191 Gif-sur-Yvette Cedex, France (office). *E-mail:* info@cea.fr (office). *Website:* www.cea.fr (office).

CESCAU, Patrick Jean-Pierre, MBA; French business executive; *Non-Executive Chairman, InterContinental Hotels Group;* b. 27 Sept. 1948, Paris; s. of Pierre Cescau and Louise Cescau; m. Ursula Kadanski; one s. one d.; ed Institut Européen d'Admin des Affaires (INSEAD); joined Unilever France as org. officer 1973, sr consultant –1977, held post at Astra-Calvé and served as Chief Accountant, UDL Germany 1980–84, Commercial mem. Edible Fats and Dairy Co-ordination, Rotterdam, Netherlands 1984–86, Financial Dir Unilever Indonesia 1986–89, Nat. Man., Unilever Portugal 1989–91, Chair. PT Unilever Indonesia 1991–95, Pres. and CEO Van den Bergh Foods, USA 1995–96, Pres. and CEO Lipton, USA (following merger of Van den Bergh and Lipton) 1997–98, Controller and Deputy Financial Dir Unilever 1998–99, Financial Dir 1999–2000, Head, Bestfoods integration team 2000–01, Dir Unilever Global Foods Div. 2001, Chair. Unilever PLC and mem. Exec. Cttee, Unilever NV 2004–05, Group CEO 2005–08; Chair. (non-exec.) InterContinental Hotels Group 2013–; Chair. Nat. Asscn of Margarine Mfrs 1996–98; mem. Bd of Dirs, Pearson PLC from 2002, from INSEAD 2009; Dir (non-exec.), International Consolidated Airlines Group SA; mem. Exec. Cttee, Tea Council 1997–98; Trustee, The Leverhulme Trust; Chevalier, Légion d'honneur 200. *Leisure interests:* arts, reading, photography, theatre. *Address:* InterContinental Hotels Group PLC, Broadwater Park, Denham, UB9 5HR,

Bucks., England (office). *Telephone:* (1895) 512000 (office). *E-mail:* info@ihgplc.com (office). *Website:* www.ihgplc.com (office).

ÇETİN, Hikmet, BA; Turkish politician; b. 1937, Lice, Diyarbakır Prov.; m. İnci Çetın; two c.; ed Ankara Univ. Political Sciences Faculty, Williams Coll., Mass and Stanford Univ., Calif., USA; completed mil. service 1970; Head of Econs Planning Dept, Devlet Planlama Teşkilatı (State Planning Org.) –1977; part-time Lecturer, Middle East Tech. Univ., Ankara; 1970s; Deputy for Istanbul (Republican People's Party—CHP) from 1977–80; Minister of State 1978–79, later Deputy Prime Minister in cabinet of Prime Minister Bülent Ecevit; adviser in planning to Govt of Yemen following military coup in Turkey 1980; mem. Parl. for Diyarbakır (Sosyal Demokrat Halkçı Parti (SHP)—Social Democratic Populist Party, successor to banned CHP) 1987–91, for Gaziantep (SHP) 1991–; mem. Bd SHP, later Sec.-Gen., Chair. 1995; Minister of Foreign Affairs 1991–94; Deputy Prime Minister and Minister of State 1995–96; Speaker, Turkish Parl. 1997–99; Sr Civilian Rep. for Afghanistan, NATO 2003–06. *Address:* Rafet Canitez Cad. No. 3/47, Oran, Ankara, Turkey (home). *Telephone:* (312) 4903696 (home). *E-mail:* hikmetcetin@superonline.com.

ÇETINKAYA, Murat; Turkish economist, banking executive and central banker; *Governor, Türkiye Cumhuriyet Merkez Bankası AŞ;* b. 1976, Çorlu; ed Boğaziçi Univ.; started career at Albaraka Türk Participation Bank, held a range of posts in Dept of Foreign Transactions, Int. Banking and Treasury Depts; joined Türkiye Halk Bankası AŞ 2003, apptd Head, Int. Banking and Structured Finance Dept, then Deputy Gen. Man., Int. Banking and Investor Relations, also mem. Bd of Dirs Halk Investment; Deputy Dir Treasury, Int. Banking and Investment Banking, Kuveyt Turk Participation Bank 2008–12; Deputy Gov. Türkiye Cumhuriyet Merkez Bankası AŞ (Cen. Bank of the Republic of Turkey) 2012–16, Gov. 2016–; Dir KT Sukuk Varlik Kiralama AŞ. *Address:* Türkiye Cumhuriyet Merkez Bankası AŞ, Head Office, 10 Anafartalar Mah., İstiklal Cad., 06050 Ankara, Turkey (office). *Telephone:* (312) 5075000 (office). *Fax:* (312) 5075640 (office). *E-mail:* iletisimbilgi@tcmb.gov.tr (office). *Website:* www.tcmb.gov.tr (office).

CEYER, Sylvia T., AB, PhD; American physical chemist and academic; *John C. Sheehan Professor of Chemistry, Massachusetts Institute of Technology;* b. Chicago, Ill.; ed Hope Coll., Univ. of California, Berkeley; Post-doctoral Fellow, Nat. Bureau of Standards (now Nat. Inst. of Standards and Tech.) 1979–81; joined MIT Faculty 1981, Class of 1943 Career Devt Chair 1985–88, tenure 1987, W.M. Keck Foundation Professorship in Energy 1991–96, John C. Sheehan Prof. of Chem. 1996–, Assoc. Head of Dept of Chem. 2005–10, Head 2010–; held Chem. Chair of NAS 2002–05; Class I Chair of NAS 2009–12; Fellow, NAS, American Physical Soc., American Acad. of Arts and Sciences; Harold E. Edgerton Award 1988, Baker Memorial Award for Excellence in Undergraduate Teaching 1988, Young Scholar Award, American Assn of Univ. Women 1988, ACS Nobel Laureate Signature Award 1993, MIT School of Science Teaching Prize 1993, MacVicar Faculty Fellow 1998, ACS Willard Gibbs Award 2007, Arthur Smith Award 2008, ACS Langmuir Lectureship, Welch Foundation Lectureship. *Publications:* numerous scientific papers in professional journals on dynamics of interactions of molecules with surfaces of materials. *Address:* Room 6-217, Department of Chemistry, Massachusetts Institute of Technology, 77 Massachusetts Avenue, Cambridge, MA 02139-4307, USA (office). *Telephone:* (617) 253-4537 (office). *Fax:* (617) 253-7030 (office). *E-mail:* stceyer@mit.edu (office). *Website:* ceyer.mit.edu (office).

CEYLAN, Nurı Bılge; Turkish photographer, screenwriter, actor and film director; b. 26 Jan. 1959, Bakırköy, Istanbul; s. of Emin Ceylan and Fatma Ceylan; m. Ebru Ceylan; one s.; ed Istanbul Technical Univ., Boğaziçi Univ., Mimar Sinan Univ.; began career as commercial photographer; juror, Cannes Int. Film Competition 2009. *Films include:* Koza (Cocoon) (short) 1995, Kasaba (The Small Town) 1997, Mayis Sikintisi (Clouds of May) 1999, Uzak (Distant) (Cannes Film Festival Grand Jury Prize and Best Actor Prize 2003) 2002, Iklimler (Climates) (Cannes Film Festival FIPRESCI Movie Critics' Award 2006, five awards at 2006 Antalya Golden Orange Film Festival including Best Dir) 2006, Üç Maymun (Three Monkeys) (Cannes Film Festival Best Dir Award 2008) 2008, Bir Zamanlar Anadolu'da (Once Upon a Time in Anatolia) (Cannes Film Festival Grand Jury Prize) 2011, Kış Uykusu (Winter Sleep) (Palme d'Or, Cannes Film Festival) 2014. *Publication:* Turkey Cinemascope (photography). *Address:* NBC Film, Başkurt sok. 19/4, Ürgüp Palas apt, Cihangir, 34422 Istanbul, Turkey (office). *E-mail:* info@nbcfilm.com (office). *Website:* www.nuribilgeceylan.com (office).

CHA, Laura M., BA, JD, JP; Chinese politician, lawyer and business executive; *Member, Executive Council, Government of the Hong Kong Special Administrative Region;* b. 1949; m.; ed Univ. of Wisconsin, Santa Clara Univ., USA; began career as attorney with Pillsbury, Madison & Sutro, San Francisco, Calif. and Coudert Brothers, Hong Kong 1982–90; joined Securities and Futures Comm. (SFC), Hong Kong 1991, Asst Dir then Sr Dir 1991–94, Exec. Dir 1994–2001, Deputy Chair. 1998–2001; Vice-Chair. China Securities Regulatory Comm. 2001–04, Vice-Chair. Int. Advisory Cttee 2004–; apptd to Exec. Council of Govt of Hong Kong Special Admin. Region (HKSAR) 2004–; mem. Shanghai Int. Financial Advisory Council, Shanghai Municipal Govt 2007–; HKSAR Deputy for 11th NPC, People's Repub. of China 2008–13; Standing mem. CPPCC Shanghai Cttee 2008–; Dir (non-exec.) The Hong Kong and Shanghai Banking Corpn Ltd 2004–, Hong Kong Exchanges and Clearing Ltd 2006–12, Tata Consultancy Services Ltd 2006–12, China Telecom Corpn Ltd 2008–, HSBC Holdings Plc 2011–; Sr Int. Adviser, Foundation Asset Man. AB, Sweden; Chair. Univ. Grants Cttee, Hong Kong 2007–11, Advisory Cttee on Corruption, Ind. Comm. Against Corruption in Hong Kong 2007–; mem. Advisory Bd, Yale Center for Corp. Governance, Yale Univ., USA 2006–13, Yale School of Man. 2010–13; mem. ABA, State Bar of Calif., Int. Council of Asian Soc., New York; JP 1995–2001, 2006; Silver Bauhinia Star Medal 2001, Gold Bauhinia Star Medal 2009. *Address:* 23/F China Merchants Tower, Shun Tak Centre, 168 Connaught Road Central, Hong Kong Special Administrative Region, People's Republic of China (office). *Telephone:* 22381217 (office). *Fax:* 29873538 (office). *E-mail:* anita.yiu@hkri.com (office).

CHAABANE, Sadok, PhD; Tunisian professor of law and government official; b. 23 Feb. 1950, Sfax; s. of Jilani Chaabane; m. Dalenda Nouri 1974; one s. two d.; ed Univ. of Tunis; Prof. of Law, Univ. of Tunis 1973, now Assoc. Prof. of Public Law and Political Science; Dir of Studies, Research and Publ. Centre 1975–82; Perm. Sec. of RCD 1988; Sec. of State for Higher Educ. and Scientific Research 1989; Adviser to the Pres. on Political Affairs 1990; Sec. of State for Scientific Research 1991; Prin. Adviser to the Pres. on Human Rights 1991; Minister of Justice 1992–97, of Higher Educ., Scientific Research and Tech. 1999–2004; Minister Counsellor to the Pres., responsible for Political Affairs and Human Rights; Pres. Econ. and Social Council (Conseil Economique et social) 2007–11; currently mem. Arbitration Cabinet; fmr Dir Tunisian Inst. of Strategic Studies; Founder-mem. Int. Acad. of Constitutional Law, Int. Law Assn; Commdr, Order of Nov. 7; Great Cordon, Order of the Repub. *Publications:* Hannibal Redux: The Renewal of Modern Tunisia 1977, The Law of International Institutions 1985, The Way to Pluralism in Tunisia 1997, Fin de la géographie et retour de l'histoire. La Tunisie face à la globalisation 1998, Ben Ali: bâtir une démocratie. De la lutte des croyances à la compétition des programmes 2005, Le système politique tunisien 2006. *Leisure interests:* law, political affairs. *Address:* 30 Rue Mannoubia Ben Nasr, Manar 3, 2092 Tunis, Tunisia. *Telephone:* (71) 889690; 98-848485 (mobile).

CHABON, Michael, (Leon Chaim Bach, Malachi B. Cohen, August Van Zorn), MFA; American writer; b. 24 May 1963, Columbia, Md; m. Ayelet Waldman; two s. two d.; ed Univ. of Pittsburgh, Univ. of California, Irvine; Chair. MacDowell Colony 2010–; Fellow, American Acad. of Arts and Sciences 2009, mem. 2012–; O. Henry Award (for Son of the Wolfman) 1999, Pulitzer Prize for Fiction 2001, Fernanda Pivano Award for American Literature 2013. *Publications include:* The Mysteries of Pittsburgh 1988, A Model World (short stories) 1991, The Wonder Boys 1995, Werewolves in Their Youth (short stories) 1995, The Amazing Adventures of Kavalier & Clay (Pulitzer Prize for fiction 2001) 2000, Summerland (Mythopoeic Fantasy Award for Children's Literature 2003) 2002, The Final Solution (National Jewish Book Award 2005, Aga Khan Prize for Fiction) 2004, The Yiddish Policemen's Union (novel) (Nebula Award for Best Novel 2008, Hugo Award for Best Novel 2008) 2007, Gentlemen of the Road 2007, Maps and Legends: Reading and Writing along the Borderlands (essays) 2008, Manhood for Amateurs: The Pleasures and Regrets of a Husband, Father, and Son (essays) 2009, Telegraph Avenue 2012, Moonglow: A Novel (Gold Prize, California Book Award 2017) 2016; contrib. short stories to several magazines. *Address:* Steven Barclay Agency, 12 Western Avenue, Petaluma, CA 94952, USA (office). *Telephone:* (707) 773-0654 (office). *Fax:* (707) 778-1868 (office). *Website:* michaelchabon.com.

CHABRAJA, Nicholas D., BA, JD; American lawyer and defence industry executive; *Chairman, Tower International;* b. 6 Nov. 1942, Gary, Ind.; ed Northwestern Univ.; lawyer, Jenner and Block (law firm), Chicago 1968–1997, Partner 1984–93; Special Counsel to US House of Reps, Washington, DC 1986; Sr Vice-Pres. and Gen. Counsel, Gen. Dynamics Corpn 1993–94, mem. Bd of Dirs 1994–, Exec. Vice-Pres. 1994–96, Vice-Chair. 1996–97, Chair. and CEO 1997–2009, Chair. 2009–10; Chair. Tower International 2010–; mem. Bd of Dirs Ceridian Corpn 2001–07, Northern Trust Co. 2007–; mem. Kennedy Center Corp. Fund Bd; Trustee Northwestern Univ. *Address:* Tower International, 17672 North Laurel Park Drive, Suite 400E, Livonia, MI 48152, USA (office). *Website:* www.towerinternational.com (office).

CHADERTON MATOS, Roy; Venezuelan politician, lawyer and diplomatist; b. 17 Aug. 1942; ed Cen. Univ. of Venezuela, Instituto de Altos Estudios de Defensa Nacional; Second Sec., Embassy in Warsaw 1969–72, First Sec., Embassy in Bonn 1973, Embassy in Ottawa 1975, Counsellor, Embassy in Brussels 1977–78, Counsellor, Perm. Mission to UN, New York 1978–79, Counsellor, Embassy in Ottawa 1979, Minister-Counsellor 1979–82, Deputy Perm. Rep. 1982–83, Amb. to Canada 1983–85, to Gabon 1985–87, to Norway (also accred to Iceland) 1987–90, Gen. Dir of Int. Political Affairs, Ministry of Foreign Affairs 1990–93, Amb. to Canada 1993–94, Gen. Dir (Vice-Pres.), Ministry of Foreign Affairs 1994–95, Amb. to UK (also accred to Ireland) 1996–2000, to Colombia 2000–02, to USA 2002, Minister of Foreign Affairs 2002–04, Amb. to France 2004–07, to Mexico 2007–08, to OAS, Washington, DC 2008–09; mem. Social Christian Party of Venezuela 1958–, Official Rep. 1994; Caballero de Madara Order (Bulgaria), Francisco de Miranda Order, First Class (Venezuela), Bernardo O'Higgins Order (Chile), Great Cross, May Order (Argentina), Great Cross, San Olav Order (Norway), Great Cross, Cruceiro do Sul National Order (Brazil), Gran Cordon Orden Libertador (Venezuela). *Address:* Ministry of Foreign Affairs, Torre MRE, al lado del Correo de Carmelitas, Avenida Urdaneta, Caracas 1010, Venezuela (office). *Telephone:* (212) 806-4400 (office). *Fax:* (212) 861-2505 (office). *E-mail:* web.master@mre.gov.ve (office). *Website:* www.mre.gov.ve (office).

CHADIRJI, Rifat Kamil, DipArch, FRIBA; Iraqi architect; b. 6 Dec. 1926, Baghdad; s. of Kamil Chadirji; m. Balkis Sharara 1954; ed Hammersmith School of Arts and Crafts, London; Founder and Sr Partner and Dir Iraq Consult 1952–; Section Head, Baghdad Bldg Dept Waqaf Org. 1954–57; Dir-Gen. of Housing, Ministry of Planning, Baghdad 1958–59, Head of Planning Cttee Ministry of Housing 1959–63; returned to full-time pvt. practice with Iraq Consult 1963–78; apptd Counsellor to Mayoralty of Baghdad 1980–82; mem. Iraqi Tourist Bd 1970–75; Loeb Fellow, Harvard Univ. 1983; Hon. Fellow, RIBA, AIA; numerous awards, including First Prize for Council of Ministers Bldg, Baghdad 1975, First Prize New Theatre, Abu Dhabi, UAE 1977, First Prize, Council of Ministers, Abu Dhabi, UAE 1978, Chairman's Award, Aga Khan Awards for Architecture 1986. *Works include:* Council of Ministers Bldg, Baghdad 1975, Cabinet Ministers' Bldg, UAE 1976, Nat. Theatre, Abu Dhabi, UAE 1977, Al-Ain Public Library, UAE 1978. *Publications include:* Concepts and Influences: Towards a Regionalized International Architecture 1987, Internationalised Tradition in Architecture 1988, al-Ukhaidar and the Crystal Palace 1991, A Dialogue on the Structure of Art and Architecture 1995. *Leisure interests:* photography, travel.

CHADLINGTON, Baron (Life Peer), cr. 1996, of Dean in the County of Oxfordshire; **Peter Selwyn Gummer,** MA, FCIPR, FID, FCIM, FRSA; British business executive; *President, Witney Conservative Constituency Association;* b. 24 Aug. 1942, Bexley, London; s. of Rev. Canon Selwyn Gummer and (Margaret) Sybille Gummer (née Mason); brother of The Rt Hon Lord Deben (John Selwyn Gummer (q.v.)); m. Lucy Rachel Dudley-Hill 1982; one s. three d.; ed King's School, Rochester, Selwyn Coll., Cambridge; with Portsmouth & Sunderland Newspaper Group 1964–65, Viyella Int. 1965–66, Hodgkinson & Partners 1966–67, Industrial & Commercial Finance Corpn (3i Group) 1967–74; Founder, Chair. and Chief Exec. Shandwick PLC 1974–94, Chair. 1994–2000; Dir (non-exec.) CIA Group PLC

1990–94, non-exec. mem. Halifax Building Society London Bd 1990–94, Dir (non-exec.) Halifax PLC 1994–2001, Black Box Music Ltd 1999–2001, Oxford Resources 1999–2002, Chair. Hotcourses Ltd 2000–04, Britax Childcare Holdings Ltd 2005–; CEO Huntsworth PLC 2000–05; mem. EU Select Sub-cttee B (Energy, Industry and Transport), House of Lords 2000–03; Chair. Action on Addiction 2000–07; mem. Nat. Health Service Policy Bd 1991–95, Chair. Royal Opera House 1996–97, Understanding Industry Trust 1991–96, Arts Council of England (fmrly GB) 1991–96, Marketing Group of GB 1993–95, Nat. Lottery Advisory Bd for the Arts and Film 1994–96; Int. Public Relations 1998–2000, Guideforlife.com 2000–02; Dir Walbrook Club 1999–2004; Chair. Chadlington Consultancy 1999–, LAPADA 2011–; mem. Council, Cheltenham Ladies Coll. 1998–2003, Bd of Trustees, American Univ. 1999–2001, British Heart Foundation Mending Broken Hearts Appeal Cttee 2010–; currently Pres. Witney Conservative Constituency Asscn; Trustee, Atlantic Partnership 1999–; Gov., The Ditchley Foundation 2008–; Fellow, Chartered Inst. of Public Relations, Chartered Inst. of Marketing; Hon. Fellow, Bournemouth Univ. 1999–; Inst. of Public Relations Pres.'s Medal 1988, PR Week Award for Outstanding Individual Contrib. to Public Relations 1994, Ernst & Young Entrepreneur of the Year 2008. *Publications:* articles and booklets on public relations and marketing. *Leisure interests:* opera, cricket, rugby. *Address:* West Oxfordshire Conservative Association, Waterloo House, 58–60 High Street, Witney, Oxon., OX28 6HJ, England (office). *Telephone:* (1993) 702302 (office). *E-mail:* info@witneyconservatives.com (office). *Website:* www.witneyconservatives.com (office); www.parliament.uk/biographies/lords/lord-chadlington/3318.

CHADWICK, Michael J. (Mike), MA, PhD; British environmental scientist and academic; b. 13 Sept. 1934, Leicester; s. of John Chadwick and Hilda Corman; m. Josephine Worrall 1958; one s. two d.; ed Godalming Co. Grammar School and Univ. Coll. of North Wales, Bangor; Lecturer, Dept of Botany, Univ. of Khartoum, Sudan 1959–62; Univ. Demonstrator, School of Agric., Univ. of Cambridge 1962–66; Lecturer and Prof., Dept of Biology, Univ. of York 1966–91; Dir Stockholm Environment Inst., Stockholm, Sweden 1991–96; Dir LEAD-Europe, Geneva, Switzerland 1996–; Sr Research Assoc., Stockholm Environment Inst.'s York Centre; now works as pvt. consultant on environmental matters, most recently with MISTRA in Sweden, Intergovernmental Panel on Climate Change, EU projects and with Rockefeller Foundation on poverty alleviation and sustainable livelihoods; fmr Sec., British Ecological Soc.; Hon. Visiting Prof., Depts of Environment and Biology, Univ. of York; Award for Contributing to Nobel Peace Prize 2007 given to Intergovernmental Panel on Climate Change. *Publications:* Restoration of Land (with A. D. Bradshaw) 1980, The Relative Sensitivity of Ecosystems in Europe to Acidic Depositions (with J. C. I. Kuylenstierna) 1990, A Perspective on Global Air Pollution Problems (with J. C. I. Kuylenstierna and W. K. Hicks) 2002. *Leisure interests:* music, gardening, travel. *Address:* Stockholm Environment Institute, Grimston House, University of York, Heslington, York, YO10 5DD (office); 3 Skipwith Road, Escrick, York, YO19 6JT, England (home). *Telephone:* (1904) 728025 (office); (1904) 728234 (home). *Fax:* (1904) 728025 (office). *E-mail:* cmjchadwick@aol.com (office).

CHAFEE, Lincoln (Linc) Davenport, BA; American academic, politician and fmr state governor; b. 26 March 1953, Providence, RI; s. of John Lester Hubbard Chafee and Virginia Chafee (née Coates); m. Stephanie Danforth; one s. two d.; ed Brown Univ., Montana State Univ. Horseshoeing School, Bozeman; farrier, various harness racktracks 1977–83; planner, General Dynamics, Quonset Point 1983; Exec. Dir Northeast Corridor Initiative 1980s; began political career as del. to RI Constitutional Convention 1985–86; with Warwick City Council 1986–92, Mayor of Warwick 1993–99; apptd by Gov. of RI to fill the unexpired term of his father, the late Senator John H. Chafee Nov. 1999, elected Senator from RI 2000–07, mem. Cttee on the Environment and Public Works, Cttee on Foreign Relations, Chair. Sub-cttee on Near Eastern and South Asian Affairs, Jt Econ. Cttee, Sub-cttee on Superfund, Waste Control and Risk Assessment, Sub-cttee on Western Hemisphere, Peace Corps, Narcotics and Terrorism; Gov. of Rhode Island 2011–Jan. 2015; Distinguished Visiting Fellow, Thomas J. Watson, Jr Inst. for Int. Studies, Brown Univ. 2007–; mem. Republican Party –2007 (resgnd), Ind. 2007–; Francis M. Driscoll Award for Leadership, Scholarship and Athletics, Brown Univ., Fiscal Responsibility Award, Concord Coalition 2003, Congressional Award, Nat. Breast Cancer Coalition 2004. *Publication:* Against the Tide: How a Compliant Congress Empowered a Reckless President 2008. *Leisure interests:* skiing, horseback trail riding. *Address:* Democratic National Committee, 430 South Capitol Street SE, Washington, DC 20003, USA (office). *Telephone:* (202) 863-8000 (office). *Fax:* (202) 863-8174 (office). *Website:* www.democrats.org (office).

CHAGGER, Bardish, PC, MP, BSc; Canadian politician; *Minister of Small Business and Tourism;* b. 1980; d. of Gurminder (Gogi) Chagger; ed Univ. of Waterloo; Exec. Asst to MP Andrew Telegdi –2008; Dir of Special Events, Kitchener-Waterloo Multicultural Centre 2008–15; mem. House of Commons (Parl.) for Waterloo 2015–, Leader of Govt 2018–; Minister of Small Business and Tourism 2015–; fmr mem. Bd of Dirs Workforce Planning Bd of Waterloo Wellington Dufferin, MT Space (Multicultural Theatre Space); mem. Liberal Party of Canada. *Address:* Industry Canada, C. D. Howe Bldg, 11th Floor, East Tower, 235 Queen Street, Ottawa, ON K1A 0H5, Canada (office). *Telephone:* (613) 954-5031 (office). *Fax:* (613) 954-2340 (office). *E-mail:* info@ic.gc.ca (office); Bardish.Chagger@parl.gc.ca (office). *Website:* www.ic.gc.ca (office); bardishchagger.liberal.ca (office).

CHAGOURY, Gilbert; Nigerian/Lebanese business executive and diplomatist; *Co-Founder, Chagoury Group;* b. 8 Jan. 1946, Lagos; s. of Ramez Chagoury and Alice Chagoury; m. Rose Marie Chamchoum 1969; four c.; ed Coll. des Frères Chrétiens, Lebanon; f. Grands Moulins du Bénin Flour Mills, Cotonou 1971 (later part of Chagoury Group); co-f. Chagoury Group (large diversified conglomerate with interests in manufacturing, construction, real estate, hospitality and health care), Lagos 1971; Amb. of St Lucia to UNESCO and to Holy See 2004–; fmr econ. adviser to Pres. of Benin; Hon. Chair. In Defence of Christians 2014; Commdr, Order of St Gregory The Great 1990, Ordre des Arts et des Lettres 2000, Ordre Nat. du Benin 2001, Ordre National du Tchad 2005, Order of the National Cedar 2005, Grand Cross, Order of Saint Gregory The Great 2009. *Address:* Chagoury Group, Plot 1684, Sanusi Fafunwa Street, Victoria Island, Lagos, Nigeria (office). *Website:* www.chagourygroup.com (office); www.gilbertchagoury.com (office).

CHAHED, Youssef, BAgr, MAgr, PhD; Tunisian politician, engineer and academic; *Prime Minister;* b. 18 Sept. 1975, Tunis; ed Nat. Agric. Inst. of Tunisia, Institut Nat. Agronomique Paris-Grignon; int. expert in agricultural policies, FAO 2000–05; Asst Prof. Univ. of Rennes 1, France 2002–03; Visiting Prof. Higher Inst. of Agriculture –2009; Co-f. Wifak al-Jomhouri (political party) 2011; mem. Nidaa Tounes 2012–; Sec. of State for Fishing 2015–16; Minister of Local Affairs Jan.–Aug. 2016; Prime Minister 2016–. *Address:* Office of the Prime Minister, Place du Gouvernement, La Kasbah, 1030 Tunis, Tunisia (office). *Telephone:* (71) 565-400 (office). *E-mail:* boc@pm.gov.tn (office). *Website:* www.pm.gov.tn (office).

CHAI, Jing, MFA; Chinese journalist and broadcaster; b. 1 Jan. 1976, Linfen, Shanxi Prov.; m. Zhao Jia; one d.; ed Changsha Railway Inst. (now Central South Univ.), Beijing Broadcasting Inst. (now Communication Univ. of China), Peking Univ.; began career in broadcasting with radio station in Hunan Prov. 1995, as host of radio programmes Gentle Moonlight and New Youth; worked for China Central Television (CCTV) 2001–13, including as investigative reporter and presenter, Horizon Connection, presenter, 24 Hours, host, One on One for CCTV News and Insight 2009, also presenter and producer, weekend edition of Seeing 2011; currently ind. investigative reporter; Corresp. of the Year (for investigative journalism on the fight against SARS) 2003, Green China Person of the Year Award 2007, Soc. of Entrepreneurs and Ecology Award 2015. *Television includes:* Seven Days at Yangping (documentary on Sichuan earthquake) 2008, Under the Dome 2015. *Achievements include:* received widespread int. recognition for her self-financed documentary on pollution, Under the Dome, which was viewed more than 150 million times over the internet within three days of its release in 2015. *Publications include:* Use My Lifetime To Forget 2001, Insight (autobiography) 2012.

CHAI, Songyue; Chinese politician; b. Nov. 1941, Putuo Co., Zhejiang Prov.; joined CCP 1961; Sec. CCP Party Cttee, Changguang Coal Mine Co. 1982–84, Deputy Sec. CCP Provincial Cttee Comm. for Discipline Inspection, Zhejiang Province 1986–88; Vice-Gov. Zhejiang Prov. 1988–97, Acting Gov. 1997–98, Gov. 1998–2002; mem. CCP Zhejiang Provincial Cttee Standing Cttee 1993–2002; Deputy Sec. CCP Zhejiang Provincial Cttee 1993–2002; Alt. mem. 14th CCP Cen. Cttee 1992–97; mem. 15th CCP Cen. Cttee 1997–2002, 16th CCP Cen. Cttee 2002–07; Chair. State Electricity Regulatory Comm. 2002–07; Vice-Chair. 11th CPPCC Nat. Cttee, Econs Cttee 2008–13. *Address:* c/o State Electricity Regulatory Commission, Chang'an Street 86, Xicheng District, West Beijing 100031, People's Republic of China (office). *Telephone:* (10) 58681803 (office). *E-mail:* manager@serc.gov.cn (office). *Website:* www.serc.gov.cn (office).

CHAI, Zhifang, FRSC; Chinese nuclear physicist; ed Fudan Univ.; Alexander von Humboldt Foundation Fellow, Cologne Univ., Germany 1980–82; fmr Visiting Prof., Purdue Univ., USA, Strasbourg Nuclear Research Centre, France, Delft Univ. and ECN, Netherlands, Tokyo Metropolitan Univ., Japan; currently Prof. and Dir Lab. of Nuclear Analytical Techniques, Inst. of High Energy Physics, Chinese Acad. of Sciences; currently Dean, School of Radiation Medicine and Protection, School for Radiological and Interdisciplinary Science, Soochow Univ.; Titular mem. Int. Union of Pure and Applied Chemistry; mem. Hevesy Medal Selection Panel 2006; George Hevesy Medal 2005, Nat. Science Award. *Publications:* author or co-author of around 450 papers in peer-reviewed journals, including Nature, Nature Nanotechnology, Chemical Society Review, JACS, PNAS, Nano Letter, Analytical Chemistry, Environmental Science and Technology, etc and 10 books. *Address:* Room B302, Building 402, Soochow Univ., 199 Ren'ai Road, Suzhou 215123 (office); Laboratory of Nuclear Analytical Techniques, Institute of High Energy Physics, Chinese Academy of Sciences, 19B YuquanLu, Shijingshan District, PO Box 918, Beijing 100049, People's Republic of China (office). *Telephone:* (10) 88233197 (office); (12) 65880035 (Suzhou) (office). *Fax:* (10) 88233374 (office); (12) 65880035 (Suzhou) (office). *E-mail:* chaizf@ihep.ac.cn (office); zfchai@suda.edu.cn (office). *Website:* www.ihep.ac.cn (office); eng.suda.edu.cn (office).

CHAIGNEAU, Pascal Gérard Joël, DèsSc, DenScPol, DenScEcon, DenD; French academic; *Dean, Centre d'Etudes Diplomatiques et Stratégiques (CEDS);* b. 8 Feb. 1956, Paris; s. of André Chaigneau and Hélène Alexandre; m. Marie-Claude Ratsarazaka-Ratsimandresy 1983; three s.; ed Collège St Michel de Picpus and Facultés de Droit et des Lettres, Paris; practical work 1974–75; Asst, Ecole des Hautes Etudes Internationales and Ecole Supérieure de Journalisme 1976–78, Prof. 1978–, Dir of Studies 1984–85, Dir-Gen. 1985–90, Admin.-Gen. 1990; Research, Fondation pour les Etudes de Défense Nationale 1980–82; in charge of course, Univ. de Paris II 1982–90; Maître de conférences, Univ. de Paris V 1990–2000, Professeur des universités 2000–; Professeur des Universités, Directeur du Département de Science Politique, Université Paris Descartes 2001–; Sec.-Gen. Centre de Recherches Droit et Défense, Univ. de Paris V 1985–; Founder and Dir Centre d'Études Diplomatiques et Stratégiques (CEDS) 1986–, now Dean; Advocate, Court of Appeal, Paris 1990–; Prof., Centre des Hautes Etudes sur l'Afrique et l'Asie Modernes; Lecturer, Inst. des Hautes Etudes de Défense Nationale; in charge of course, Ecole des Hautes Etudes Commerciales (HEC) 1990–92, Prof. 1992–, Scientific Dir (masters degrees), Sustainable Devt, Int. Business, Man. des risques internationaux 2012–, currently Co-Dir Centre HEC Paris de Geopolitique; Prof., Collège Interarmes de Défense 1994–; with Bolivian Consulate in France 1994–97; Foreign Trade Counsellor 1995–; mem. bd of devt of higher mil. educ. 2010–14; Dir Chair of Geopolitics and Int. Relations MBA created by the Gendarmerie Nationale 2014–; Founding mem. Universitaires sans frontières 2012; numerous other public appointments; mem. Acad. des Sciences d'Outre-mer, Soc. d'Economie Politique, Royal Soc. of Arts (London) 2006; Commdr des Arts et des Lettres 1999, des Palmes académiques 2002; Chevalier, Légion d'honneur, Officier 2006; Officier, Ordre nat. du mérite, Commdr 2011; Officier du Mérite maritime 2008; decorations from Bolivia, Burkina Faso, Belgium, Honduras, Chad, Madagascar, Niger, etc.; Hon. LLD (Richmond, USA); Dr hc (Nat. Univ. of Bolivia, Université Nationale Mayor de San Andres); Grand Prix de l'Asscn des Ecrivains de Langue Française 1987, Prix de l'Acad. des Sciences Morales et Politiques 1993, Lauréat de l'Institut de France 2012, Prix Vernimmen, HEC 2012 and other prizes, awards and distinctions. *Publications:* La Stratégie soviétique 1978, La Politique militaire de la France en Afrique 1984, Rivalités politiques et socialisme à Madagascar 1985, Les Pays de l'Est et l'Afrique 1985, France-océan indien-mer rouge (with others) 1986, Pour une analyse du commerce international 1987, La Guerre du Golfe 1991, Europe: la nouvelle donne stratégique 1993, Les grands Enjeux du monde contemporain 1997, Dictionnaire des Relations Internationales 1998, Gestion des Risques internationaux 2001, Dictionnaire biographique des relations internationales depuis 1945 (co-author) 2007, Enjeux diplomatique et stratégiques 2008, Enjeux diplomatiques et stratégiques 2010, La déclaration universelle des droits de l'Homme, fondement d'une nouvelle justice mondiale (co-ed.) 2010, Conflictualités et politiques de sécurité et de défense en Afrique (co-ed.) 2012, Agir dans l'incertitude (co-ed.) 2012, Dictionnaire de l'Europe (co-author) 2013, La sécurité Euro-Méditerranéenne (co-ed.) 2013; chapters in books. *Address:* Centre d'Études Diplomatiques et Stratégiques (CEDS), 37 quai de Grenelle, 75015 Paris (office); Ecole des Hautes Etudes Commerciales (HEC), 1 Rue de la Libération, 78350 Jouy-en-Josas (office); 68 avenue de Gravelle, 94220 Charenton-le-Pont, France (home). *Telephone:* 1-47-20-78-47 (CEDS) (office); 1-39-67-70-00 (HEC) (office). *Fax:* 1-47-20-57-30 (CEDS) (office); 1-39-67-74-40 (HEC) (office). *E-mail:* contact@ceds.fr (office); chaigneau@hec.fr (office). *Website:* www.ceds.fr (office); www.hec.edu (office).

CHAIKA, Yurii Yakovlevich; Russian lawyer and government official; *Prosecutor-General;* b. 1951, Nikolayevsk-on-Amur, Khabarovsk Krai, Russian SFSR, USSR; m.; two c.; ed Sverdlovsk (now Yekaterinburg) Inst. of Law; electrician at shipbuilding factory, Nikolayevsk-on-Amur 1970; joined Prosecutor's Office, Irkutsk Oblast 1976, held several positions including investigator, Deputy Oblast Public Prosecutor, Taishetsk Transport Public Prosecutor, Head, Investigative Div. of East Siberian Transport Public Prosecutor's Office 1983–92, Public Prosecutor of Irkutsk Oblast 1992–95; instructor, Admin. Div., Irkutsk Oblast CPSU Cttee 1984–92; First Deputy Prosecutor-Gen. of Russian Fed. 1995–99, Prosecutor-Gen. April–July 1999, 2006–; Minister of Justice 1999–2006; Hon. Lawyer of the Russian Fed., Hon. Officer, Prosecution Service of the Russian Fed.; Order of Merit for Country, IV Degree; Order of Honour (Armenia); Order of Friendship (Armenia) 2016. *Address:* Office of the Prosecutor-General, 125993 Moscow, ul. B. Dmitrovka 15A, Russia (office). *Telephone:* (495) 987-56-56 (office). *Fax:* (495) 292-88-48 (office). *Website:* www.genproc.gov.ru (office); eng.genproc.gov.ru/management/genprokuror (office).

CHAILLY, Riccardo; Italian conductor; *Music Director and Principal Conductor, Teatro alla Scala;* b. 20 Feb. 1953, Milan; s. of Luciano Chailly and Anna Marie Motta; m. Gabriella Terragni 1987; two s.; ed Giuseppe Verdi and Perugia Conservatories and with Franco Caracciolo and Franco Ferrara; Asst to Claudio Abbado, La Scala, Milan 1972–74; debut as Conductor with Chicago Opera 1974; debut, La Scala 1978, Covent Garden (operatic debut) 1979; concert debut with London Symphony Orchestra and Edin. Festival 1979; American concert debut, Los Angeles Philharmonic, CA 1980; Metropolitan Opera debut 1982; Prin. Guest Conductor, London Philharmonic Orchestra 1982–85; Chief Conductor, Radio Symphony Orchestra, Berlin 1982–89; Vienna State Opera debut 1983; appearances at Salzburg Festival 1984, 1985, 1986; Japan debut with Royal Philharmonic Orchestra 1984; New York Philharmonic Orchestra debut 1984; Music Dir Bologna Orchestra, Teatro Comunale 1986–93; Chief Conductor, Royal Concertgebouw Orchestra, Amsterdam 1988–2004, Conductor Emer. 2004–; Prin. Conductor and Music Dir Giuseppe Verdi Symphony Orchestra, Milan 1999–2005, Conductor Laureate 2005–; Chief Conductor, Gewandhausorchester Leipzig 2005–15; Music Dir Lucerne Festival Orchestra 2015–; apptd Prin. Conductor, La Scala, Milan 2015, also Music Dir 2017–; Grande Ufficiale della Repubblica Italiana 1994; Hon. mem. RAM 1996; Kt, Order of Netherlands Lion 1998, Cavaliere di Gran Croce 1998, Abrogino d'Oro, Comune Milano; Gramophone Award Artist of the Year 1998, Diapason d'Or Artist of the Year 1999. *Recordings include:* Beethoven: The Symphonies (ECHO Klassik Award for Conductor of the Year 2012) 2011, Brahms: The Symphonies (Gramophone Award for Recording of the Year, Int. Classical Music Award for Symphonic Music 2014) 2014, Mahler Symphony No 7 (Int. Classical Music Award for Video Performance 2016). *Leisure interests:* music, paintings, the arts in general. *Address:* Teatro alla Scala, Via Filodrammatici, 2, 20121 Milan, Italy (office). *Telephone:* (02) 88791 (office). *Website:* www.teatroallascala.org/en (office).

CHAISANG, Chaturon, MA; Thai politician; b. 1 Jan. 1956, Chachoengsao; ed State Univ. of New York at Buffalo, American Univ., Washington DC; Asst Sec. to Minister of Finance 1986–87; Sec. Econ. Cttee, House of Reps 1986–88; mem. Parl. for Chachoengsao 1986–92, 1995–; Sec. Cttee on Finance, Banking and Financial Insts, House of Reps 1988–91 (mem. 1992); Sec. to Minister of Commerce and adviser to Minister of Agric. 1991; adviser to Minister of Science, Tech. and Environment 1992, Ministry of Labour and Social Welfare 1995; Spokesman for New Aspiration Party 1992–95, fmr Sec.-Gen.; Deputy Minister of Finance 1996–2001; Minister attached to Prime Minister's Office 2001; Minister of Justice 2002; Deputy Prime Minister 2003–05; Minister of Educ. 2005–06, 2013–14 (removed by mil. coup); Acting Leader Thai Rak Thai party (now banned) 2006–07; banned from political activity for five years 2007–12; fmr Chair. Cttee of Science and Tech., House of Reps; Kt Grand Cross (First Class) of Crown of Thailand. *Address:* 441/12 Supakij Road, Maung, Chachoengsao 24000, Thailand.

CHAIYAWAN, Vanich; Thai business executive; *Founder and Chairman, Thai Life Insurance Co. Ltd;* b. 1932; m.; eight c.; Founder and Chair. Thai Life Insurance Co. Ltd; Chair. Thai Credit Retail Bank Public Co. Ltd; Dir Thai Asia Pacific Brewery Co. Ltd, fmr Vice-Chair.; Dr hc (Srinakarinvirot Univ.), (Sripatum Univ.). *Address:* Thai Life Insurance Co. Ltd, 121/89 RS Tower, 31st Floor, Ratchadaphisek Road, Dindaeng, Bangkok 10400, Thailand (office). *Website:* www.thailife.com (office).

CHAKARI, Mohammad Sediq; Afghan politician; studied in Saudi Arabia, returned to join fight against invasion by Soviets; served as Minister of Information in early 1990s; currently Deputy, Wolasi Jirga (Lower House of Parl.) (Jamiat-i Islami); Acting Minister of Hajj and Islamic Affairs 2009. *Address:* c/o Ministry of Hajj and Islamic Affairs, nr District 10, Shir Pur, Shar-i-Nau, Kabul, Afghanistan. *Telephone:* (20) 2201338.

CHAKMA, Amit, MASc, PhD; Canadian (b. Bangladeshi) chemical engineer and university administrator; *President and Vice-Chancellor, University of Western Ontario;* b. 25 April 1959, Chittagong Hill Tracts, Bangladesh; ed Institut Algerien du Petrole, Boumerdès, Algeria, Univ. of British Columbia; Asst Prof. of Chemical and Petroleum Eng, Univ. of Calgary 1988–90, Assoc. Prof. 1990–94, Prof. 1994–96; Prof. of Environmental Eng, Univ. of Regina 1996–2001, Dean of Eng 1996–99, Vice-Pres. (Research) 1999–2001; Prof. of Chemical Eng, Univ. of Waterloo 2001–09, also Vice-Pres. (Academic) and Provost 2001–09; Pres. and Vice-Chancellor, Univ. of Western Ontario 2009–; Chair., World Univ. Service of Canada, Council of Asscn of Commonwealth Univs; Visiting Prof., Petroleum and Petrochemical Coll., Chulalongkorn Univ., Thailand 1997; Adjunct Prof., Hunan Univ., Changsha, People's Repub. of China 1998, Consulting Prof., Huazhong Univ. of Science & Tech. 1998, Wuhan Univ. of Hydraulic and Electrical Eng 2000; Guest Prof., Peking Univ. 2001; Assoc. Ed. Journal of Environmental Informatics 2003; Founding Chair. HealthForce Ontario Marketing and Recruitment Agency 2007–10; mem. Canada's Science and Tech. Innovation Council 2011–17; Dir Ont. Centres of Excellence; mem. Science, Tech. & Innovation Council of Canada; fmr Chair. Advisory Panel on Canada's Int. Educ. Strategy; Fellow, Canadian Acad. of Eng; Hon. DS (Univ. of Dhaka) 2017; Queen's Diamond Jubilee Medal 2012. *Publications:* more than 100 articles especially in the field of natural gas eng and petroleum waste management. *Address:* Office of the President, University of Western Ontario, Stevenson Hall, Suite 2107, London, ON N6A 5B8, Canada (office). *Telephone:* (519) 661-3104 (office). *Website:* president.uwo.ca (office).

CHAKRABARTI, Sir Sumantra, Kt, KCB, BA, MA; British (b. Indian) economist, banking executive and international organisation official; *President, European Bank for Reconstruction and Development (EBRD);* b. 12 Jan. 1959, West Bengal, India; s. of Hirendranath Chakrabarti and Gayatri Chakrabarti (née Rudra); m. Mari Sako 1983; one d.; ed City of London School for Boys, New Coll., Oxford, Univ. of Sussex; started career with IMF and World Bank in 1980s; Sr Econ. Asst, British Overseas Devt Admin 1984; fmr Private Sec. to the then Minister of State for Overseas Devt Lynda Chalker; fmr Head of Aid Policy and Resources; worked with HM Treasury 1996; fmr Head of Econ. and Domestic Affairs Secr., Cabinet Office; Dir-Gen. for Regional Devt Programmes, Dept for International Development 2001–02, Perm. Sec. 2002–07; Perm. Sec., Ministry of Justice 2007–12; Pres. EBRD 2012–; mem. Advisory Council, Oxford Dept of Int. Devt; Fellow, Overseas Devt Inst.; Hon. Fellow, New Coll., Oxford 2004, Hon. Master of the Bench 2009; Dr hc (Univ. of East Anglia) 2010, (Bucharest Univ. of Economic Studies) 2013; Kazakhstan's 25th Anniversary of Independence Medal 2016. *Address:* Office of the President, European Bank for Reconstruction and Development, One Exchange Square, London, EC2A 2JN, England (office). *Telephone:* (20) 7338-8548 (office). *Fax:* (20) 7338-6112 (office). *E-mail:* president@ebrd.com (office). *Website:* www.ebrd.com (office).

CHALANDON, Sorj; French writer and journalist; b. 16 May 1952, Tunis, Tunisia; ed ; writer and journalist for Libération 1973–2007, covered events in Lebanon, Iran, Iraq, Somalia and Afghanistan; has worked for the satirical-investigative newspaper Le Canard enchaîné 1988–; Albert Londres Prize for his articles on Northern Ireland and the Klaus Barbie trial 1988. *Publications:* Le petit Bonzi (Prix du premier roman de l'Université d'Artois, Prix de l'Ecole Normale Supérieure de Cachan, Prix du premier roman du Touquet) 2005, Une promesse (Prix Médicis 2006) 2006, Mon traître (My Traitor) (Prix Jean Freustié, Prix Joseph Kessel, Prix Marguerite Puhl-Demange, Prix Simenon, Prix littéraire de la ville des Sables d'Olonne, Prix Gabrielle d'Estrées, Prix Lettres Frontière 2008) 2008, La légende de nos pères (Prix Ouest du Printemps du Livre 2010) 2009, Retour à Killybegs (Return to Killybegs) (Grand Prix du roman de l'Acad. française 2011) 2011, The Fourth Wall (Prix Goncourt des Lycéens) 2013, Profession du père (Father's Profession) (Prix du Style 2015) 2015, Le Jour d'avant (The Day Before) 2017. *Address:* c/o Éditions Grasset, 61 rue des Saint-Pères, 75006 Paris, France (office). *Telephone:* 1-44-39-22-00 (office). *Fax:* 1-42-22-64-18 (office). *E-mail:* info@grasset.fr (office). *Website:* www.grasset.fr (office).

CHALAYAN, Hussein, MBE, BA; British fashion designer; ed Cyprus and Cen. St Martin's School of Art, London; final year graduation collection featured in luxury boutique Browns' window display; set up own label; exhbn of first solo collection, West Soho Galleries, London 1994; second collection shown during London Fashion Week and in Kobe and Tokyo; fourth collection received Absolut Vodka's Absolut Creation Sponsorship Award (first recipient) 1996; solo exhbn (key pieces from past collections), The Window Gallery, Prague 1996; exhibited Buried and Path dresses, Jam (style, music and media) exhbn, Barbican Art Gallery 1996; designs selected for Cutting Edge exhbn, Victoria and Albert Museum 1997; invited to exhibit in Challenge of Materials exhbn, Science Museum 1997; talk at Tate Gallery (with Zaha Hadid, Michael Bracewell and Georgina Starr) on parallels between fashion, art and architecture 1997; Creative Dir, Puma 2008–; Designer of the Year, London Fashion Awards 1998, 2000. *Address:* 71 Endell Road, London, WC2 9AJ, England. *E-mail:* enquiries@husseinchalayan.com. *Website:* www.husseinchalayan.com.

CHALFIE, Martin Lee, PhD; American biochemist and academic; *William R. Kenan, Jr Professor of Biological Sciences, Columbia University;* b. 15 Jan. 1947; s. of Eli Chalfie and Vivian Chalfie (née Friedlen); ed Harvard Univ.; teacher, Hamden Hall Country Day School, Conn. 1970–71; postdoctoral research at Lab. of Molecular Biology, Univ. of Cambridge, UK 1977–82; William R. Kenan, Jr Prof. of Biological Sciences, Columbia Univ. 1982–, also Chair. of Biological Sciences; mem. NAS 2004; Nobel Prize in Chem. (jtly) 2008. *Publications:* numerous articles in academic journals. *Address:* Columbia University, Biological Sciences, 1018 Fairchild Center, MC 2446, New York, NY 10027, USA (office). *Telephone:* (212) 854-8870 (office). *Fax:* (212) 865-8246 (office). *E-mail:* mc21@columbia.edu (office). *Website:* www.columbia.edu/cu/biology/faculty/chalfie (office).

CHALFONT, Baron (Life Peer), cr. 1964, of Llantarnam in the County of Monmouthshire; **(Arthur) Alun Gwynne Jones,** PC, OBE, MC, FRSA; British politician and writer; b. 5 Dec. 1919, Llantarnam, Wales; s. of Arthur Gwynne Jones and Eliza Alice Hardman; m. Dr Mona Mitchell 1948; one d. (deceased); ed West Monmouth School; commissioned into S. Wales Borderers (24th Foot) 1940; served in Burma 1941–44, Malaya 1955–57, Cyprus 1958–59; resgnd comm. 1961; Defence Corresp. The Times, London 1961–64; consultant on foreign affairs to BBC TV, London 1961–64; Minister of State for Foreign Affairs 1964–70, Minister for Disarmament 1964–67, 1969–70, in charge of day-to-day negotiations for Britain's entry into Common Market 1967–69; Perm. Rep. to WEU 1969–70; Foreign Ed. New Statesman 1970–71; Chair. All-Party Defence Group House of Lords 1980–96, Pres. 1996–; Chair. Industrial Cleaning Papers 1979–86, Peter Hamilton Security Consultants Ltd 1984–86, UK Cttee for Free World 1981–89,

European Atlantic Group 1983–, VSEL Consortium PLC 1987–93, Marlborough Stirling Group 1994–99; Deputy Chair. IBA 1989–90; Chair. Radio Authority 1991–94; Pres. Hispanic and Luso Brazilian Council 1975–80, Royal Nat. Inst. for Deaf 1980–87, Llangollen Int. Music Festival 1979–90; Chair. Abington Corpn (Consultants) Ltd 1981–, Nottingham Building Soc. 1983–90, Southern Mining Corpn 1997–99; Dir W. S. Atkins Int. 1979–83, IBM UK Ltd 1973–90 (mem. IBM Europe Advisory Council 1973–90), Lazard Brothers and Co. Ltd 1983–90, Shandwick PLC 1985–95, Triangle Holdings 1986–90, TV Corpn PLC 1996–2001; Pres. Freedom in Sport Int.; mem. IISS, Royal Inst.; Hon. Fellow, Univ. Coll. Wales, Aberystwyth 1974. *Publications:* The Sword and the Spirit 1963, The Great Commanders (ed.) 1973, Montgomery of Alamein 1976, Waterloo: Battle of Three Armies (ed.) 1979, Star Wars: Suicide or Survival 1985, Defence of the Realm 1987, By God's Will: A Portrait of the Sultan of Brunei 1989, The Shadow of My Hand (autobiog.) 2000; contrib. to The Times and nat. and professional journals. *Leisure interests:* music, theatre. *Address:* House of Lords, London, SW1A 0PW, England (office).

CHALGHOUM, Mohamed Ridha; Tunisian politician and business executive; *Minister of Finance;* b. 1962, Gafsa; m.; three c.; ed Institut de Défense Nationale; various positions within Ministry of Finance including fmr Bureau Chief, Dir Gen. of Tax Benefits, Dir of Savings and Financial Markets, Pres. Conseil du marché financier (financial services regulatory authority) –2010, Minister of Finance 2010–11, 2017–; mem. Nat. Econ. and Social Council 2006–11; Pres. and Dir-Gen. Société tunisienne de garantie (SOTUGAR) 2011–16; Adviser to the Pres. 2016–17; Chef du Cabinet to Prime Minister June–Sept. 2017; Chevalier, Ordre de la République. *Address:* Ministry of Finance, pl. du Gouvernement, La Kasbah, 1008 Tunis, Tunisia (office). *Telephone:* (71) 561-782 (office). *Fax:* (71) 575-680 (office). *E-mail:* pcontenu@finances.gov.tn (office). *Website:* www.finances.gov.tn (office).

CHALHOUB, Patrick, BEcons; French (b. Syrian) business executive; *CEO, Chalhoub Group;* b. 20 Dec. 1957, Damas; s. of Michel Chalhoub and Widad Chalhoub; m. Ingie Chalhoub; two c.; ed Institut d'Etudes Politiques (Sciences Po), Paris; joined Chalhoub Group (family retail business) 1979, currently CEO; distributor of luxury brands throughout Middle East, including LVMH, L'Oréal, Chanel, Ralph Lauren; fmr Chair. French Business Council in Dubai; Founding mem. Rotary Club Dubai, Capital Club; mem. Young Presidents' Org.; Chevalier, Ordre nat. du Mérite. *Address:* Chalhoub Group, PO Box 261075, Jebel Ali, Dubai, United Arab Emirates (office). *Telephone:* (4) 8045000 (office). *Website:* www.chalhoub-group.com (office).

CHALIAND, Gérard, PhD; French academic and writer; ed Institut National des Langues et Civilisations Orientales, Univ. of Paris V; f. magazine Partisans during Algerian war; Prof., École nat. d'admin (ENA), Collège interarmes de défense 1980–89; taught at l'École Supérieure de Guerre 1993–99; Visiting Prof., Harvard Univ., Univ. of Calif., Berkeley, Military Acad., Bogota, Colombia, Univ. of Capetown, SA, Univ. of Salamanca, Spain, Univ. of Manchester, UK; Visiting Fellow, Centre for Conflict and Peace studies; advisor to Centre for Analysis and Planning, Ministry of Foreign Affairs 1984–94; Dir Centre européen d'étude des conflits 1997–2000. *Publications include:* Armed Struggle in Africa 1969, Mythes révolutionnaires du tiers-monde 1977, Atlas stratégique (with J.-P. Rageau) 1987, Anthologie mondiale de la stratégie 1996, Voyage dans le demi-siècle (with Jean Lacouture) 2001, Atlas du nouvel ordre mondial 2003, Histoire du terrorisme: de l'Antiquité à Al-Qaïda 2004, Guerres et civilisations: de l'Assyrie à l'époque contemporaine 2005, L'Amérique en guerre: Irak-Afghanistan 2007, L'impasse afghane 2011, Le Crime de silence 2015. *Address:* 63 Rue Pascal, 75013 Paris, France (home). *Telephone:* 1-43-31-09-12 (home). *E-mail:* gchaliand@aol.com (home).

CHALKER OF WALLASEY, Baroness (Life Peer), cr. 1992, of Leigh-on-Sea in the County of Essex; **Lynda Chalker,** PC; British politician and consultant on business and development in Africa; *Chairman, Africa Matters Ltd;* b. (Lynda Bates), 29 April 1942, Hitchin, Herts.; d. of Sidney Henry James Bates and Marjorie Kathleen Randell; m. 1st Eric Robert Chalker 1967 (divorced 1973); m. 2nd Clive Landa 1981 (divorced 2003); ed Heidelberg Univ., Germany, London Univ., Cen. London Polytechnic; statistician with Research Bureau Ltd (Unilever) 1963–69; Deputy Market Research Man., Shell Mex & BP Ltd 1969–72; Chief Exec. Int. Div. of Louis Harris Int. 1972–74; MP for Wallasey 1974–92; Parl. Under-Sec. of State, Dept of Health and Social Security 1979–82, Dept of Transport 1982–83; Minister of State, Dept of Transport 1983–86, FCO 1986–97, Minister for Overseas Devt 1989–97; ind. consultant on Africa and Devt 1997–; Chair. Africa Matters Ltd 1998–; Dir (non-exec.) Capital Shopping Centres 1997–2000, Unilever PLC and NV 1998–2007, Landell Mills Ltd 1999–2001, Ashanti Goldfields Co. 2000–04, Group 5 (Pty) Ltd 2001–, Devt Consultants Int. 2001–05, Equator Exploration Ltd 2005–07; Chair. Greater London Young Conservatives (GLYC) 1969–70; Nat. Vice-Chair. Young Conservatives 1970–71; Chair. London School of Hygiene and Tropical Medicine 1998–2006; Chair. Bd of Medicines for Malaria Venture 2006–; mem. Advisory Bds Lafarge et Cie 2003–, MerchantBridge Int. 2005–, Renaissance Africa 2008–; mem. BBC Gen. Advisory Cttee 1975–79; Hon. Fellow, Queen Mary and Westfield Coll., Inst. of Transportation; Dr hc (Bradford) 1995, (Liverpool), (John Moores), (Cranfield), (Warwick), (Westminster), (East London). *Publications:* We Are Richer Than We Think 1978 (co-author), Africa: Turning the Tide 1989. *Leisure interests:* music, cooking, theatre, driving. *Address:* House of Lords, London, SW1A 0PW; Africa Matters Ltd, 51 Causton Street, London, SW1P 4AT, England (office). *Telephone:* (20) 7976-6850 (office). *Fax:* (20) 7976-4999 (office). *E-mail:* bstendall@africamatters.com (office). *Website:* (office).

CHALMERS, Sir Neil Robert, Kt, MA, PhD; British biologist and museum director; b. 19 June 1942, Surrey; s. of William King Chalmers and Irene Margaret Chalmers (née Pemberton); m. Monica Elizabeth Byanjeru Rusoke 1970; two d.; ed King's Coll. School, Wimbledon, Magdalen Coll., Oxford, St John's Coll., Cambridge; Lecturer in Zoology, Makerere Univ. Coll., Kampala, Uganda 1966–69; Scientific Dir Natural Primate Research Centre, Nairobi, Kenya 1969–70; Lecturer, subsequently Sr Lecturer then Reader in Biology, Open Univ. 1970–85, Dean of Science 1985–88; Dir Natural History Museum, London 1988–2004; Warden, Wadham Coll., Oxford 2004–12; fmr Chair. Bd Trustees Nat. Biodiversity Network; Hon. Fellow, Wadham Coll., Oxford 2012–. *Publications:* Social Behaviour in Primates 1979, and other books on animal behaviour; numerous papers in Animal Behaviour and other learned journals. *Leisure interests:* music, golf, swimming.

CHALUPEC, Igor Adam, BEcons; Polish economist and business executive; *Executive Partner, President of the Management Board, Icentis Corporate Solutions;* b. 29 May 1966, Warsaw; ed Warsaw School of Econs, Warsaw Univ.; consultant, Polexpert Sp. z oo 1989–90; consultant, Proexim Sp. z oo 1990; licensed stockbroker 1991–; Founder and CEO Cen. Brokerage House, Bank Pekao SA (later CDM Pekao) 1991–95, mem. Man. Bd 1995–2000, Vice-Pres. 2000–03; Under-Sec. of State and Gen. Insp. of Financial Information, Ministry of Finance 2003–04; Pres. and CEO PKN Orlen SA 2004–07, fmr Chair., Man. Bd; Chair. Supervisory Bd, Unipetrol AS, Prague 2005–07; Exec. Partner and Pres. Man. Bd, Icentis Corporate Solutions SKA and Icentis Capital Sp. z oo 2007–; Chair. Brokerage Houses Asscn 1994–95; mem. Supervisory Bd, Warsaw Stock Exchange 1994–2003, Pioneer Pekao Investment Management 2001–03, Budimex 2007–, PZU Zycie 2008–10, Bank Handlowy (Citigroup) 2009–, Ruch SA (Chair. 2010–, Pres. Man. Bd 2013–, also CEO); principal shareholder, Lurena Investments B.V.; Deputy Finance Minister and Chair. Financial Supervision Authority 2003–04; Deputy Chair. Insurance and Pensions Funds Supervisory Comm. 2003–04, Comm. for Banking Supervision 2003–04; owner, Solum Verbum Ltd; mem. European Corp. Governance Forum 2004–, Capital Market Council 2005–; Founder and Chair. Bd of Trustees, Evangelical Educational Asscn; Vice-Pres. Polish Asscn of Sports Bridge; Deputy Pres. Man. Bd, Polish Contract Bridge Asscn; mem. European Financial Cttee, Brussels, Programme Council of Econ. Forum in Krynica, Polish Business Roundtable, Inst. of Public Affairs; mem. Bd of Trustees, Polish Inst. of Dirs; mem. Jury Prize Foundation Lesław A. Paga; Shareholder, Fincores Business Solutions Ltd 2004–07; HERMES Award, Warsaw Stock Exchange Bd 1996, VECTOR Prize, Confed. of Polish Employers 2006, Lesław A. Paga Prize 2007, Manager Award 2010. *Publication:* Russia Petroleum Policy (co-author) 2009. *Leisure interests:* literature, cinema, politics, tennis, bridge. *Address:* ICENTIS Sp. z oo Corporate Solutions SKA, Plac Trzech Krzyży 3, 00-535 Warsaw, Poland (office). *E-mail:* office@icentis.com (office). *Website:* www.icentiscorporatesolutions.pl (office).

CHALYI, Aleksei Mikhailovich, DTechSc; Russian politician; *de facto Mayor of Sevastopol;* b. 13 June 1961, Sevastopol; ed Sevastopol Tech. Inst.; Founder, Chief Tech. Officer and CEO Tauris Electric group 1990–; Chief of Exec. Cttee, Sevastopol City Council (*de facto* Mayor) Feb. 2014–; built and operates the 35th Coastal Battery museum in Sevastopol; involved with restoration of World War II memorials; produced documentary series Sevastopol Tales; mem. Russian Acad. of Electrotechnology; 'For Faith and Fidelity' Award 2011. *Address:* Division of Media Relations, Legislative Assembly of Sevastopol, 99011 Sevastopol, Lenina 3, Crimea, Ukraine (office). *Telephone:* (692) 54-05-38 (office). *Fax:* (692) 54-03-53 (office). *E-mail:* press@sevsovet.com.ua (office). *Website:* sevsovet.com.ua (office).

CHAM, Prasidh; Cambodian politician; *Minister of Industry and Handicrafts;* b. (Ung You Teckhor), 15 May 1951, Phnom Penh; s. of Ung You Y; m. Tep Bopha; one s. two d.; ed Lycée Descartes, Phnom Penh, Univ. of Phnom Penh; mem. Cambodian People's Party (CPP); mem. Parl. for Siem Reap 1998–2003; Minister of Commerce 1998–2013, of Industry and Handicrafts 2013–; Sr Adviser to HH Samdech Preah Sometheatheppadey Tep Vong, Supreme Patriarch of the Mohanjkhay Buddhist Clergy 2004–; Order of the Sowathara, Moha Sereywadaan class, Order of the Kingdom of Cambodia Assarith Class 1998, Thipadin Class 2001, Oknha 2002. *Leisure interests:* golf, tennis, volleyball. *Address:* Ministry of Industry and Handicrafts, 45 boulevard Preah Norodom, Khan Duan Penh, Phnom Penh, Cambodia (office). *Telephone:* (23) 222504 (office). *Fax:* (23) 991438 (office).

CHAMA, Davies; Zambian agriculturist and politician; *Minister of Defence;* b. 21 Aug. 1964; unsuccessful parl. cand. (PF) for Kabwe Central 2006; Chair. Zambia Railways Ltd 2014; nominated mem. Nat. Ass. (parl.) 2016–; Minister of Defence 2016–; mem. Patriotic Front (PF), fmr Sec.-Gen., fmr Chair., Lusaka Prov. PF. *Leisure interests:* playing games, watching soccer. *Address:* Ministry of Defence, Independence Avenue, POB RW 17X, Lusaka, Zambia (office). *Telephone:* (21) 251211 (office). *Fax:* (21) 254670 (office). *E-mail:* info@mod.gov.zm (office). *Website:* www.mod.gov.zm (office).

CHAMBAS, Mohamed Ibn, BA, MA, PhD; Ghanaian lawyer, politician and international organization official; *Special Representative of the Secretary-General and Head of UNOWA, United Nations;* b. 7 Dec. 1950; m.; three c.; ed Univ. of Ghana, Legon, Cornell Univ., Ithaca, USA, Case Western Reserve Univ., Cleveland, USA; fmr Lecturer, Oberlin Coll., Ohio; admitted to practise law in Ghana and State of Ohio, USA; legal practice with Forbes, Forbes & Teamor, Cleveland, Ohio; also practised law with The Greater Cleveland Legal Aid Soc.; Deputy Foreign Sec. of Ghana 1987; MP for Bimbilla (Nat. Democratic Congress) 1993–96, 2000–02, First Deputy Speaker of Parl. 1993–94, mem. Select Cttee on Educ., Cttee on Subsidiary Legislation, Chair. Foreign Affairs Cttee 1993–94; Deputy Foreign Minister 1994; Deputy Minister of Educ. 1997–2000; Exec. Sec. Econ. Community of West African States (ECOWAS) 2002–06, Pres. 2007–10; Sec.-Gen., Secr. of the African, Caribbean and Pacific Group of States, Brussels, Belgium 2010–12; Jt Special Rep. of UN Sec.-Gen. and African Union Comm. Chair. for Darfur 2013–14, also Head African Union-UN Hybrid Mission in Darfur (UNAMID) and Jt Chief Mediator 2013–13; Special Rep. and Head of UN Office for West Africa (UNOWA) 2014–; mem. Cornell Univ. Council 1997–2001, 2003–07, 2009–; Commdr of the Nat. Order of Cote d'Ivoire 2002, Highest Nat. Award (for the restoration of Democracy and putting Nation on Path of Sustainable Econ. Devt) 2005, Order of Volta, 2nd Category (For Distinguished Diplomatic and Public Service to the Country) 2006, Kt Grand Band in the Humane Order of African Redemption (Liberia) 2009, Commdr, Ordre Nat. du Bénin 2010, Grand Officer of the Nat. Order of Merit of the Repub. of Guinea 2010; Hon. LLD (Univ. of Ghana) 2008; Nat. Legis. Ass. Certificate of Appreciation (for role in signing of Accra Comprehensive Peace Agreement that ended civil war in Liberia) 2006, German Africa Foundation Africa Prize 2010. *Leisure interests:* soccer, horse riding. *Address:* United Nations Office for West Africa (UNOWA), Ngor Diarama, BP 23851, Dakar, Senegal (office). *Telephone:* (33) 869-85-85 (office). *Fax:* (33) 820-46-38 (office). *Website:* unowa.unmissions.org (office).

CHAMBERLAIN, (George) Richard; American actor; b. 31 March 1935, Los Angeles, Calif.; s. of Charles Chamberlain and Elsa Chamberlain; ed Los Angeles Conservatory of Music and drama studies with Jeff Corey. *Films include:* Secret of Purple Reef 1960, Thunder of Drums 1961, Twilight of Honor 1963, Joy in the Morning 1965, Petulia 1968, The Madwoman of Chaillot 1969, The Music Lovers 1971, Julius Caesar 1971, Lady Caroline Lamb 1971, The Three Musketeers 1974, Towering Inferno 1974, The Four Musketeers 1975, The Slipper and the Rose 1977, The Swarm 1978, Murder by Phone 1982, King Solomon's Mines 1985, Alan Quartermain and The Lost City of Gold 1987, The Return of the Musketeers 1989, Bird of Prey 1996, River To Drown In 1997, All the Winters That Have Been 1997, The Pavilion 1999, Strength and Honour 2007, I Now Pronounce You Chuck and Larry 2007, Endless Bummer 2008, The Perfect Family 2011, We Are the Hartmans 2011. *Stage appearances include:* King Lear, Hamlet, Richard II, The Lady's Not for Burning, Night of the Iguana, Cyrano de Bergerac, My Fair Lady. *Television includes:* Dr. Kildare (series) 1961–65, Portrait of a Lady 1968, The Woman I Love 1973, The Count of Monte Cristo 1975, Centennial (mini-series) 1978, The Good Doctor 1978, The Man in the Iron Mask 1978, Shogun 1980 (Golden Globe Award), The Thorn Birds (mini-series) 1983, Cook & Peary: The Race to the Pole 1983, The Miracle 1985, Wallenberg: A Hero's Story 1985, Dream West (mini-series) 1986, Casanova 1987, The Bourne Identity 1988, Ordeal in the Arctic 1993, The Thorn Birds, The Missing Year 1996, The Lost Daughter 1997, All the Winters That Have Been 1997, Too Rich: The Secret Life of Doris Duke 1999, Blackbeard (mini-series) 2006, Brothers & Sisters (series) 2010–11.

CHAMBERLIN, Wendy J., MS; American diplomatist, international organization official and fmr UN official; *President, Middle East Institute;* b. 12 Oct. 1948, Bethesda, Md; two d.; ed Northwestern, Boston and Harvard Univs; joined Foreign Service, Dept of State, Washington, DC 1975, Consular and Econ. Officer, Vientiane 1976–78, Staff Aide, E Asia Bureau, Dept of State 1978–79, Special Asst to Deputy Sec. of State 1979, Political Officer, Kinshasa 1980–82, Pearson Fellow, US Senate, Washington, DC 1982–83, Political-Mil. Officer, Office of Israel Affairs, Dept of State 1983–85, Dir (acting) Office of Regional Affairs, Bureau of Near East-S Asian Affairs 1985–87, Asst Gen. Service Officer, Rabat 1988–89, Special Asst to Under-Sec. for Political Affairs, Dept of State 1989–90; Dir of Counter-Terrorism, Nat. Security Council, Washington, DC 1990–91; Dir Office of Press–Public Affairs, Bureau of Near East-S Asian Affairs 1991–93, Deputy Chief of Mission, Kuala Lumpur 1993–96, Amb. to Laos 1996–99; Prin. Deputy Asst Bureau of Int. Narcotics and Law Enforcement Programs, Washington, DC 1999–2001, Amb. to Pakistan 2001–02, Asst Admin. for Asia and Near East, USAID 2002–04, Deputy UN High Commr for Refugees 2004–Feb. 2005, June 2005–06, Acting High Commr Feb.–June 2005; Pres. Middle East Inst. 2007–; Nat. Security Fellow 1984; mem. Bd of Dirs American Acad. of Diplomacy, The Hollings Center, Sultan Qaboos Cultural Center; Hon. PhD (Northwestern Univ.); numerous meritorious awards from US State Dept. *Address:* Middle East Institute, 1761 N Street, NW, Washington, DC 20036-2882, USA (office). *Telephone:* (202) 785-1141 (office). *Fax:* (202) 331-8861 (office). *E-mail:* executiveassist@mei.edu (office). *Website:* www.mei.edu (office).

CHAMBERS, Anne Cox; American media proprietor and fmr diplomatist; *Co-Director, Cox Enterprises Inc.;* b. 1 Dec. 1919, Ga; d. of James M. Cox; sister of late Barbara Cox Anthony; m. (divorced); three c.; fmr Dir Fulton Nat. Bank 1973; Amb. to Belgium 1977–81; currently Co-Dir (with sister) Cox Enterprises Inc., parent co. of Cox Radio Inc., Cox Communications Inc., AutoTrader.com LLC, Mannheim Auctions Inc., The Atlanta-Journal Constitution, Atlanta Beat, other enterprises; Chair. Atlanta Newspapers Inc.; Vice-Chair. American Advisory Bd Pasteur Foundation; mem. Bd of Dirs Bank of the South 1977–82, Coca-Cola Co. 1981–91, American Soc. French Legion of Honor, MacDowell Gallery, Cities in Schools, High Museum of Art, Atlanta, Friends of Art and Preservation in Embassies, French American Foundation; Pres. American Friends Int. Lyric Art Festival, Aix-en-Provence; Trustee Int. Council Museum of Modern Art, Nat. Cttee Whitney Museum, Council of American Ambs, Council on Foreign Relations; Ordre de la Couronne, Officier, Légion d'honneur; YMCA Women of Achievement Award 1985. *Address:* Cox Enterprises Inc., 6205 Dunwoody Road, Atlanta, GA 30328, USA (office). *Website:* www.coxenterprises.com (office).

CHAMBERS, John T., BL, BA, BSc, MBA; American computer industry executive; *Chairman Emeritus, Cisco Systems, Inc.;* m. Elaine Chambers; two c.; ed West Virginia Univ., Indiana Univ.; with IBM 1976–82; with Wang Labs 1982–90; Sr Vice-Pres., Worldwide Sales and Operations, Cisco Systems, Inc., San Jose, Calif. 1991–94, Exec. Vice-Pres. 1994–95, Pres. 1995, CEO 1995–2015, Chair. 2006–15, Exec. Chair. 2015–17, Chair. Emer. 2017–; Chair. NetAid 1999–; mem. Bd of Dirs Clarify Inc., Arbor Software; co-sponsored Jordan Educ. Initiative in partnership with HM King Abdullah II of Jordan and World Econ. Forum; spearheaded 21st Century Schools initiative in Gulf Coast Region affected by Hurricane Katrina 2005; co-led del. of US business leaders, in partnership with US State Dept, to form the Partnership for Lebanon 2006; formed public-pvt. partnership to help rebuild health care and education models in Sichuan, China following earthquake of May 2008; fmr Vice-Chair. Nat. Infrastructure Advisory Council; also served on Pres. George W. Bush's Transition Team and Educ. Cttee and on Pres. Clinton's Trade Policy Cttee; Award for Lifetime Achievement, PricewaterhouseCoopers 1999, Mr Internet, Top 25 Executives Worldwide, Business Week 1999, Internet Industry Leader Award, US Internet Council 2000, CEO of the Year, Chief Executive Magazine 2000, Top 10 Most Influential Leaders Shaping Technology, Time Digital 2000, three-time winner, Best Investor Relations by a CEO, Investor Relations Magazine 2002, 2004, 2007, six-time winner, Best CEO, Telecommunications, Data Networking, Institutional Investor Magazine 2003–08, Scholars of the Smithsonian Inst. 2004, Presidential Award: Ron Brown Award for Corp. Leadership, The Business Council 2004, Award for Corp. Excellence, US State Dept 2005, 2010, Excellence in Corp. Philanthropy Award, Cttee to Encourage Corp. Philanthropy 2005, Woodrow Wilson Award for Corp. Citizenship, Woodrow Wilson Center for Excellence in Workplace Volunteer Programs, Points of Light Foundation 2005, Int. Community Service Award, US Chamber of Commerce, Business Civic Leadership Center 2007, Clinton Global Citizen Award (pvt. sector), Clinton Global Initiative 2007, Business Leadership Award, NASSCOM (India) 2007–08, 20th Anniversary Leadership Award, City Year 2008, Diversity Leadership Award, Diversity Best Practices 2009, Bower Award for Business Leadership, Franklin Inst. 2012. *Publications:* John Chambers and The Cisco Way 2002, The Eye of the Storm: How John Chambers Steered Cisco Through the Technology Collapse 2003, Connecting the Dots: Lessons for Leadership in a Startup World 2018. *Address:* Cisco Systems, Inc., Building 10, 170 West Tasman Drive, San Jose, CA 95134-1706, USA (office). *Telephone:* (408) 526-4000 (office). *Fax:* (408) 526-4100 (office). *E-mail:* jochambe@cisco.com (office). *Website:* www.cisco.com (office).

CHAMBERS, M. Susan; American retail executive; *Executive Vice-President, Global People Division, Walmart;* ed William Jewell Coll., Liberty, Mo.; began career with Amoco Oil Corpn; Dir of Applications Devt, Hallmark Cards Inc. 1985–99; joined Wal-Mart Stores Inc. (now known as Walmart) 1999, Store Club Man. 1999, becoming Vice-Pres., Applications Devt Merchandising, Information Systems Div., Sr Vice-Pres. CMI Benefits and Insurance Admin 2002–03, Exec. Vice-Pres., Risk Man. Benefits Admin 2004–06, Exec. Vice-Pres., Global People Div. 2006–, Dir of Wal-Mart de Mexico SAB De CV 2006–; mem. Business Advisory Bd, Kansas State Univ.; mem. Advisory Council, Women Impacting Public Policy; mem. Philanthropy Roundtable. *Address:* Wal-Mart Stores, Inc., 702 SW 8th Street, Bentonville, AR 72716-8611, USA (office). *Telephone:* (479) 273-4000 (office). *Fax:* (479) 277-1830 (office). *Website:* walmartstores.com (office).

CHAMBERS, Raymond G (Ray), MBA; American business executive and UN official; *Special Envoy for Health in Agenda 2030 and for Malaria, United Nations;* b. 1942, Newark, New Jersey; m. Patti Chambers; one s. two d.; ed Rutgers Univ., Seton Hall Univ.; Co-f. Wesray Capital Corpn 1981; after successful career in field of leveraged buyouts, left Wall Street to concentrate on philanthropic projects 1989; Founding Chair. Points of Light Foundation 1990; Co-f. (with Colin Powell) America's Promise – The Alliance for Youth; Co-f. The Millennium Promise Alliance 2005, Malaria No More (with Peter Chernin) 2006, Nat. Mentoring Partnership, New Jersey Performing Arts Center; UN Sec.-Gen.'s Special Envoy for Malaria 2008–16, also for Financing of Health-Related Millennium Devt Goals 2013–16, Special Envoy for Health in Agenda 2030 and for Malaria 2016–; f. Millennium Devt Goals Health Alliance 2012; Co-Chair. GBCHealth 2013–; Dir Population Services Int., Communities in Schools, Univ. of Notre Dame, American Museum of Natural History; f. (with William E. Simoand) Wesray Capital Corpn (also fmr Chair.); mem. Pres.'s Council on Service and Civic Participation; mem. Synergos Inst. Global Philanthropists Circle; William E. Simon Prize for Philanthropic Leadership 2002, UN Correspondents' Asscn Citizen of the Year 2011. *Address:* Office of the Secretary-General, United Nations, New York, NY 10017, USA (office). *Telephone:* (212) 963-1234 (office). *Fax:* (212) 963-4879 (office). *E-mail:* info@malariaenvoy.com (office). *Website:* www.mdghealthenvoy.org (office); www.malariaenvoy.com (office).

CHAMBERS, Richard Dickinson, PhD, DSc, FRS; British chemist and academic; *Professor Emeritus of Chemistry, Durham University;* b. 16 March 1935, West Stanley, Co. Durham; s. of Alfred Chambers and Elizabeth Chambers (née Allsop); m. Anne Boyd 1959; one s. one d. (deceased); ed Stanley Grammar School, Durham Univ.; postdoctoral research at Univ. of British Columbia, Vancouver 1959–60; Lecturer, Durham Univ. 1960–69, Reader 1969–76, Prof. of Chem. 1976–2003, Chair. and Head of Dept of Chem. 1983–86, Sir Derman Christopherson Research Fellow 1988–89, Research Prof. 2000–03, Prof. Emer. 2003–; Tarrant Visiting Prof., Univ. of Florida, Gainesville 1999; Fulbright Scholar, Case Western Reserve Univ., Ohio 1966–67; Dir (non-exec.) BNFL Fluorochemicals Ltd 1995–2000; ACS Award for Creative Work in Fluorine Chemistry 1991, Moissan Int. Prize 2003. *Publications:* Fluorine in Organic Chemistry 1973, 2004; also numerous articles in scientific journals. *Leisure interests:* opera, golf, watching soccer. *Address:* 5 Aykley Green, Durham, DH1 4LN, England (home). *Telephone:* (191) 386-5791 (home). *E-mail:* r.d.chambers@durham.ac.uk (office). *Website:* www.dur.ac.uk/directory/profile/?id=3271 (office).

CHAMBLISS, Saxby, BA, JD; American lawyer and politician; *Partner, DLA Piper;* b. 10 Nov. 1943, Warrenton, NC; m. Julianne Chambliss (née Frohbert) 1966; two c.; ed Univ. of Georgia, Univ. of Tennessee; fmr small businessman and attorney, Moultrie; mem. US House of Reps from 8th Dist of Georgia 1994–2003, mem. House Perm. Select Cttee on Intelligence 2001, Chair. Intelligence Sub-Cttee on Terrorism and Homeland Security, Chair. Agric. Gen. Farm Commodities and Risk-Man. Cttee 2001, mem. Armed Services Cttee (f. Congressional Air Power Cttee); Senator from Ga 2003–Jan. 2015 (retd), Vice-Chair. Select Cttee on Intelligence, mem. Armed Services Cttee, Cttee on Agric., Nutrition and Forestry, Rules Cttee, Special Cttee on Aging; fmr Chair. Congressional Sportsmen's Caucus; Republican; Partner, DLA Piper 2015–; Friend of the Farmer Award, Georgia Farm Bureau 1995, Distinguished Service Award, Georgia Peanut Comm. 1997, W. Stuart Symington Award, Air Force Asscn, named Fed. Legislator of the Year, Safari Club Int. 1999, Minuteman of the Year Award, Reserve Officers Asscn 2005, Harry S. Truman Award, Nat. Guard Asscn 2008, Nat. Legis. Advocacy Award, Naval Reserve Asscn 2008. *Leisure interests:* Little League baseball volunteer, YMCA basketball coach. *Address:* DLA Piper LLP, One Atlantic Center, 1201 West Peachtree Street, Suite 2800, Atlanta, GA 30309-3450, USA (office). *Telephone:* (404) 736-7800 (office). *Fax:* (404) 682-7786 (office). *E-mail:* saxby.chambliss@dlapiper.com (office). *Website:* www.dlapiper.com (office).

CHAMBON, Pierre, LèsSc, MD; French biochemist and academic; *Director, Institut Clinique de la Souris;* b. 7 Feb. 1931, Mulhouse; s. of Henri Chambon and Yvonne Weill; m. Brigitte Andersson 1957; two s. one d.; ed Univ. of Strasbourg; Research Asst, Strasbourg Medical School 1956–61, Assoc. Prof. 1962–66; Sabbatical, Dept of Biochemistry, Stanford Univ. Medical School, USA 1966–67; Prof. of Biochemistry, Inst. de Chimie Biologique, Faculté de Médecine, Strasbourg 1967–91; Prof., Universitaire de France, Faculté de Médecine, Louis Pasteur Univ., Strasbourg 1991–93; Prof., Collège de France 1993–2002, Hon. Prof. 2002–; Dir Lab. de Génétique Moléculaire des Eucaryotes (LGME), CNRS 1977–2002; Dir Unité 184 de Biologie Moléculaire et de Génie Génétique, Inst. Nat. de la Santé et de la Recherche Médicale (INSERM) 1978–2002; Dir Inst. of Genetics and Molecular and Cellular Biology (IGBMC), CNRS 1994–2002, Emer. Dir 2002–; Dir Génopôle de Strasbourg Alsace-Lorraine 1999–; Pres. Scientific Bd, Genome Programme, Ministry of Research 1999–2002; Founder and Dir Inst. Clinique de la Souris (ICS) 2002–; mem. numerous scientific and editorial bds etc.; mem. Acad. des Sciences; Foreign mem. NAS, Royal Swedish Acad.; Corresp. mem. Liège Acad.; Hon. mem. Chinese Soc. of Genetics; Foreign Hon. mem. American Acad. of Arts and Science, Acad. Royale de Médecine, Belgium; Officier, Ordre nat. du

Mérite 1987, Commdr 1995, Officier, Légion d'honneur 1991; Dr hc (Univ. de Liège, Belgium, Univ. of Sapporo, Japan); Prix Rosen 1976, CNRS Gold Medal 1979, Freeman Foundation Prize of New York Acad. 1981, Lounsbery Prize, NAS and Acad. des sciences 1982, Oberling Prize 1986, Prix Griffuel 1987, Prix Harvey, Israeli Inst. of Tech. 1987, Prix Henry et Mary Jane Mitjavile, Acad. Nat. de Médecine, Paris 1987, King Faisal Int. Prize 1988, Krebs Medal 1990, Prix Roussel 1990, Prix Louis Jeantet 1991, Grand Prix, Fondation for Medical Research 1996, Robert A. Welch Award in Chem. 1998, Louisa Gross Horwitz Prize 1999, Prix AFRT 1999, Albert Lasker Award for Basic Medical Research (co-recipient) 2004, Gairdner Foundation Int. Award 2010. *Publications:* 400 articles in scientific reviews. *Address:* Institut Clinique de la Souris, 1 rue Laurent Fries, BP 10142, Parc d'Innovation, 67404 Illkirch Cedex, Strasbourg (office); IGBMC, 1 rue Laurent Fries, BP 163, 67404 Illkirch Cedex, Strasbourg, France (office). *Telephone:* 3-88-65-32-15 (office). *Fax:* 3-88-65-32-99 (office). *E-mail:* ics@titus.u-strasbg.fr (office); chambon@igbmc.u-strasbg.fr (office). *Website:* www.ics-mci.fr/en (office).

CHAMEAU, Jean-Lou, PhD; French civil engineer, academic and university administrator; *President Emeritus, California Institute of Technology;* b. 1953; m. Dr Carol Carmichael; ed École Nat. Supérieure d'Arts et Métiers (ENSAM), France, Stanford Univ.; Prof. of Civil Eng, Purdue Univ. 1980; Dir School of Civil and Environmental Eng, Georgia Inst. of Tech. 1991–94, 1995–2001, Provost 2001–06; Pres. Golder Associates Inc. 1994–95; Pres. California Inst. of Tech. 2006–13, Pres. Emer. 2013–; Pres. King Abdullah Univ. of Science and Tech. 2013–17; mem. Bd Council on Competitiveness, John Wiley & Sons, MTS Systems, Safran, Academic Research Council of Singapore, Advisory Cttee of InterWest Partners; mem. Acad. des Technologies, Nat. Acad. of Eng; Chevalier, Légion d'honneur 2010; Dr hc (Polytechnique Montreal, Canada) 2009; ENSAM Prix Nessim Habif, Nat. Science Foundation Presidential Young Investigator Award, American Soc. of Civil Engineers Arthur Casagrande Award, Soc. of Women Engineers Rodney Chipp Memorial Award. *Address:* California Institute of Technology, 1200 E, California Blvd, Pasadena, CA 91125, USA (office). *E-mail:* chameau@caltech.edu (office). *Website:* www.directory.caltech.edu (office).

CHAMLING, Pawan Kumar; Indian politician, poet and writer; *Chief Minister of Sikkim;* b. 22 Sept. 1950, Yangang Busty, South Sikkim; s. of Shri Ash Bahadur Chamling and Smt. Asharani Chamling; m. Tika Maya Chamling; four s. four d.; early career as ind. farmer; entered politics in 1973; Vice-Pres. Dist Youth Congress 1975; Pres. Sikkim Handicapped Persons Welfare Mission 1976–77; Ed. Nava Jyoti 1976–77, Founder Nirman Prakashan 1977, Ed. Nirman (quarterly literary magazine) 1977–; Gen. Sec. and Vice-Pres. Sikkim Prajatantra Congress 1978–84; Pres., Yangang Gram Panchayat 1982; mem. Sikkim Legis. Ass. 1985–; Minister for Industries, Printing and Information and Public Relations 1989–92; f. Sikkim Democratic Front party 1993, Leader 1993–; Chief Minister of Sikkim 1994–; Chair. Sikkim Distilleries Ltd 1985–; Hon. PhD (Manipal Univ.) 2003; numerous awards including Chinton Puraskar 1987, Bharat Shiromani 1996, Man of the Year 1998, The Greenest Chief Minister of India 1998, Secular India Harmony Award 1998, Man of Dedication 1999, Manav Sewa Puraskar 1999, Pride of India Gold Award 1999, Best Citizen of India 1999, Poets' Foundation Award 2001, Nat. Citizens of India Award 2002, Bhanu Puraskar 2010. *Publications include:* Veer koh Parichaya (poem) 1967, Antahin Sapana Meroh Bipana 1985, Perennial Dreams and My Reality, Prarambhek Kabitaharu 1991, Pratiwad 1992, Damthang Heejah ra Aajah 1992, Ma koh Hun 1992, Sikkim ra Narikon Maryadha 1994, Crucified Prashna Aur Anya Kabitaye 1996, Sikkim ra Prajatantra 1996, Democracy Redeemed 1997, Prajatantra koh Mirmireymah 1997, Meroh Sapana Ko Sikkim 2002, Perspectives and Vision 2002. *Leisure interests:* reading, writing. *Address:* CM Secretariat, Tashiling, Gangtok, Sikkim 737 101 (office); Ghurpisay, Namchi, South Sikkim 737 126, India (home). *Telephone:* (3592) 222263 (office); (3592) 222536 (home). *Fax:* (3592) 222245 (office); (3592) 224710 (home). *E-mail:* cm-skm@nic.in (office). *Website:* sikkim.nic.in (office); sikkim.nic.in/cmonline/homepage.htm.

CHAMORRO, Violeta Barrios de (see BARRIOS de CHAMORRO, Violeta).

CHAN, Agnes, PhD; Japanese singer and academic; b. 20 Aug. 1955, Hong Kong; m. Tsutomu Kaneko 1985; three c.; ed Sophia Univ., Univ. of Toronto, Canada, Stanford Univ., USA; debut single Circle Game released in Hong Kong 1969; Japan debut single Hinagesi no Hana released 1972; performed charity concerts for Cambodia in Hong Kong and Japan 1980, Beijing 1985; Lecturer, Shinshui and Reitaku Univs 1986; Lecturer on Cross-Cultural Communication, Nagoya Women's Cultural Coll. 1993–97, Prof. 1997–; Asst Prof., Mejiro Univ. 1994–97, Prof. 1997–; Prof., Kyouei Univ. 2001; Amb. of Japan Cttee, UNICEF 1998–, travelled to Viet Nam, Cambodia, Thailand, Sudan and Philippines on issues of child prostitution and child soldiers; lobbied the law against child prostitution and won its passage in the Diet 1999; named Amb. of Hong Kong and Japan 2001; cr. new clothing line called Dear Agnes 1990; opened Chan's Boutique, Odaiba, Tokyo 2001; mem. Bd of Dirs, Wild Bird Asscn of Japan, Children's Dream Foundation, Children's Earth Club, Blue Sky Foundation, Kaijo Hoan Tomo no Kai; mem. Bd of Trustees, Day of Peace of Tokyo, Yokohama Museum, Sung Kei Ling Foundation, Japan and China Goodwill Asscn; TV talk show personality; regular contribs to newspapers and magazines; makes over 100 concert performances and speech tours throughout Japan each year; Hong Kong Top Ten Singers Award 1971, Japan Records Grand Prize 1973, New Artist Award 1973, Shinjuku Music Award 1973, Best New Artist Award 1974, Golden Arrow Award 1974, Japan Cable Music Award 1974, Int. Year of Youth Award (for essay on world peace) 1984, S. J. Grand Prize Winner, Asscn of Women Working in Broadcasting 1986, Asscn of Japanese Journalists Special Award 1986, Galaxy Award 1986; numerous gold and platinum discs. *Television:* Agnes' Music Salon 2006, Kitajima Wink Heart 2007. *Radio:* Agnes' Sunny Side Up, City Snapshot. *Albums include:* more than 100 albums in several different languages. *Publications include:* My Chinese Dishes 1983, Be Peaceful With Songs 1984, We All Are the People Who Live on the Earth 1984, Neo Woman 1993, Mama You Don't Need To Be a Doctor 1994, Hong Kong Guide 1997, The Road Winds Uphill All The Way (co-author) 1999, Positive Child Care 2001, Perfection Couple, Ring of Cullet 2002, This Road Leads to the Hill 2003, Cheers to the World! 2004, The Right Track – To People Who Live For the Future 2005, What the Marriage Life Is? (co-author), Agnes' Style Aging 2006. *Address:* Japan Committee for UNICEF, UNICEF House, 4-6-12 Takanawa, Minato-ku, Tokyo 108-8607, Japan (office). *Telephone:* (3) 5789-2032 (office); (3) 5789-2011 (office). *E-mail:* unicefjc@unicef.or.jp (office). *Website:* www.unicef.or.jp (office); www.agneschan.gr.jp.

CHAN, Chauto, BA; Chinese business executive; *President and Executive Director, CEFC China Energy Company Ltd;* b. March 1975, Zhangping, Fujian Prov.; ed Jimei Univ.; joined CEFC Petroleum (Fujian) Co. Ltd 2002, Pres. and Exec. Dir, CEFC China Energy Co. Ltd 2011–, mem. Strategic Decision Cttee, Pres. Exec. Cttee, China Energy Fund Cttee (Hong Kong) 2011–; Vice-Chair. of the Council, China Centre for Contemporary World Studies; Vice-Pres. All China Private Enterprises Fed., Shanghai Fed. of Enterprises, Shanghai Entrepreneur Asscn, Shanghai Youth Volunteer Asscn; mem. 11th Standing Cttee, Shanghai Youth Fed., 12th CPPCC Shanghai Municipal Cttee; Hon. Sec.-Gen., Inst. for Advanced Study of the Humanities and Religion, Beijing Normal Univ., Hon. Pres. Czech-China Chamber of Collaboration; ABLF Business Excellence Award 2015. *Address:* CEFC China Energy, 111 Xingguo Road, Xuhui District, Shanghai 200031, People's Republic of China (office). *Telephone:* (21) 23576747 (office). *E-mail:* enquiry@cefc.co (office). *Website:* en.cefc.co (office).

CHAN, Chuen-po, BA, MA; Taiwanese politician; b. 30 Oct. 1941; ed Tunghai Univ., Harvard Univ., USA; fmr Gen. Man. Taiwan TV; fmr Vice-Chair. Kuanghwa Investment Holdings Co.; mem. Nationalist Party of China (Kuomintang, KMT), numerous positions including Vice-Chair., Sec.-Gen. Cen. Cttee, Deputy Exec. Dir and Chief Exec. Policy Cttee, Vice-Chair., Chair. and Sec.-Gen. Taipei Municipal Cttee, Deputy Dir Secr., Cen. Cttee, Deputy Dir Dept of Policy Research, Dept of Organizational Affairs, Vice-Chair. Taiwan Prov. Cttee, Sec.-Gen. 2005–07, 2009, Vice-Chair. 2007–14; Sec.-Gen. of Presidential Office 2008–09.

CHAN, Maj.-Gen. Chun Sing; Singaporean army officer (retd) and politician; *Minister for Trade and Industry;* b. 9 Oct. 1969, Singapore; s. of Kwong Kait Fong; m.; two s. one d.; ed Christ's Coll., Cambridge, MIT Sloan School of Man.; served in Singapore Armed Forces 1987–2011, becoming CO 2nd Battalion, Singapore Infantry Regiment 1998–2001, Army Attaché 2001–03, Commdr 10th Singapore Infantry Brigade 2003–04, Head of Jt Plans and Transformation Dept 2005–07, Chief Infantry Office/Commdr 9th Div. 2007–09, Chief of Staff, Jt Staff 2009–10, Chief of Army 2010–11; mem. Parl. (Tanjong Pagar Group Representation Constituency) 2011–, Acting Minister for Community Devt, Youth and Sports 2011–12, Minister of State for Information, Communication and Arts 2011–12, for Social and Family Devt and Second Minister for Defence 2013–15, Minister in Prime Minister's Office 2015–18, Minister for Trade and Industry 2018–; mem. Nat. Trades Union Congress (NTUC) 2015–, Sec.-Gen. 2015–18; Deputy Chair. People's Asscn 2015–; mem. People's Action Party (PAP). *Address:* Ministry of Trade and Industry, 100 High Street, 09-01 The Treasury, Singapore 179434, Singapore (office). *Telephone:* 62259911 (office). *Fax:* 63327260 (office). *E-mail:* mti_email@mti.gov.sg (office). *Website:* www.mti.gov.sg (office).

CHAN, Florinda da Rosa Silva, MBA; Chinese government official; *Secretary for Administration and Justice, Macao Special Administrative Region;* b. June 1954, Macao; ed Int. Open Univ. of Asia (Macao), Univ. of Languages and Culture, Beijing, Nat. Inst. of Public Admin., Beijing; joined Macao Govt 1974, Deputy Dir Macao Economic Services Bureau 1995–98, Dir Macao Economic Services Bureau 1998–99, Sec. for Admin. and Justice, Macao Special Admin. Region 1999–; Commr Exec. Council Macao Special Admin. Region 1999–; Medal of Professional Merit 1987, Medal of Dedication 1988. *Address:* Office of the Secretary for Administration and Justice, Headquarters of the Government, Avenida da Praia Grande, Macao Special Administrative Region, People's Republic of China (office). *Telephone:* 89895179 (office). *Fax:* 28726880 (office). *E-mail:* florindachan.saj@raem.gov.mo (office). *Website:* www.gov.mo (office).

CHAN, Heng Chee, BSocSc (Hons), MA, PhD; Singaporean diplomatist, political scientist and academic; *Ambassador-at-Large;* b. 19 April 1942, Singapore; ed Nat. Univ. of Singapore, Cornell Univ., USA; Asst Lecturer, Nat. Univ. of Singapore 1967–70, Lecturer 1970–75, Sr Lecturer 1976–80, Assoc. Prof. of Political Science 1981–, Head, Dept of Political Science 1985–88, Prof. 1990; Dir Inst. of Policy Studies, Singapore Jan.–Dec. 1988; Amb. and Perm. Rep. to UN, New York 1989–91 (also accred as Amb. to Mexico 1989–91 and High Commr to Canada 1989–91); Exec. Dir Singapore Int. Foundation 1991–96; Amb. to USA 1996–2012, Amb.-at-Large 2012–, Rep. to ASEAN Intergovernmental Comm. on Human Rights 2012–; Dir Inst. of SE Asian Studies 1993; Chair. Nat. Arts Council, Lee Kuan Yew Centre for Innovative Cities at Singapore Univ. of Tech. and Design; mem. Int. Council of Asia Soc. 1991–, Singapore Nat. Cttee of Council for Security Co-operation in the Asia-Pacific 1993–, IISS Council, Hong Kong 1995–, Int. Advisory Bd of Council on Foreign Relations, New York 1995–, Presidential Council for Minority Rights 2012–, Bd of Trustees Nat. Univ. of Singapore 2012–, Bd Govs S. Rajaratnam School of Int. Studies at Nanyang Technological Univ. 2013–, Bd of Lowy Inst. for Int. Policy; Trustee, Asia Soc.; Hon. DLit (Newcastle, Australia) 1994, (Buckingham, UK) 1998; Distinguished Service Order 2011; Woman of the Year (Singapore) 1991, Public Admin Medal (Gold) 1999, Meritorious Service Medal 2005, Inaugural Asia Soc. Outstanding Diplomatic Achievement Award 2012, Inaugural Foreign Policy Outstanding Diplomatic Achievement Award 2012, USN Distinguished Public Service Award 2012. *Publications:* The Dynamics of One Party Dominance: The PAP at the Grassroots (Nat. Book Award (non-fiction) 1978) 1976, A Sensation of Independence: A Political Biography of David Marshall (Nat. Book Award (non-fiction) 1986) 1984, Government and Politics of Singapore (co-ed.), The Prophetic and the Political 1987. *Address:* Ministry of Foreign Affairs, MFA Bldg, Tanglin, off Napier Road, Singapore 248163, Singapore (office). *Telephone:* 63798000 (office). *Fax:* 64747885 (office). *E-mail:* mfa@mfa.gov.sg (office). *Website:* www.mfa.gov.sg (office).

CHAN, Jackie, MBE; Chinese actor, martial artist, film director and film producer; b. (Chan Kong-Sang), 7 April 1954, Hong Kong; s. of Chi-Ping Chan and Lee-Lee Chan; m. Lin Feng-Jiao 1982; one s.; ed Chinese Opera Research Inst.; attached to Beijing opera troupe at age of six; began film career as stuntman; worked in Australia; returned to Hong Kong, roles as stuntman or extra, Shaw Brothers Studios; signed with Golden Harvest 1980; est. The Jackie Chan Charitable Foundation 1988, The Jackie Chan Civil Aviation Foundation 2006; Amb., Hong Kong Tourism Board 2003–, Asia Pacific Tourism 2006–; UN Goodwill

Amb. 2004–; Cultural Amb., People's Repub. of China 2006–; mem. Faculty, School of Hotel and Tourism Man., Hong Kong Polytechnic Univ.; Dean of Jackie Chan Film and Television Acad., Wuhan Inst. of Design and Sciences; Appeal Patron Save China's Tigers Campaign 2006–; took part in Beijing Olympics closing ceremony 2008; Fellow, Hong Kong Acad. of Performing Arts 1998–; Hon. Prin. Qiannan Normal Coll. for Nationalities, People's Repub. of China; Silver Bauhinia Star (Hong Kong) 1999; title of Panglima Mahkota Wilayah (carries with it the title of Datuk) (Malaysia) 2015; Hon. DScS (Baptist Univ. Hong Kong) 1996; numerous awards, including Best Picture Award, Hong Kong Film 1989, Best Actor, Golden Horse Awards (Taiwan) 1992, 1993, MTV Lifetime Achievement Award 1995, Best Action Choreography, Hong Kong Film 1996, 1999, Maverick Tribute Award Cinequest San Jose Film Festival 1998, Third Hollywood Film Festival Actor of the Year 1999, Indian Film Awards Int. Achievement Award 2000, Montreal World Film Festival Grand Prix of the Americas 2001, MTV Movie Awards Best Fight Scene 2002, Golden Horse Best Action Choreography (Taiwan) 2004, Hong Kong Film Award for Professional Achievement 2005, mem. American Red Cross Nat. Celebrity Cabinet 2006, Laureus Friends and Ambs Certificate, Laureus Sport for Good 2006, Goodwill Amb., Beijing Olympics 2008. *Films include:* child roles: Big and Little Wong Tin-Bar 1962, The Lover Eternal 1963, The Story of Qui Xiang Lin 1964, Come Drink with Me 1966, A Touch of Zen 1968; adult roles: Fist of Fury (stuntman) 1971, The Little Tiger of Canton 1971, The Heroine 1971, Not Scared to Die 1973, Enter the Dragon (stuntman) 1973, All in the Family 1975, The Himalayan (stuntman) 1975, Hand of Death 1976, New Fist of Fury 1976, Shaolin Wooden Men 1976, Killer Meteors 1977, To Kill with Intrigue 1977, Snake and Crane Arts of Shaolin 1978, Magnificent Bodyguards 1978, Spiritual Kung Fu 1978, Dragon Fist 1978, Snake in Eagle's Shadow 1978, Drunken Master 1978, Fearless Hyena 1979, Fearless Hyena II 1980, The Young Master (also dir) 1980, Battle Creek Brawl 1980, The Cannonball Run 1980, Dragon Lord (dir and actor) 1982, Fantasy Mission Force (stuntman) 1982, Winners and Sinners 1983, Cannonball Run II 1983, Project A (also dir) 1983, Wheels on Meals 1984, My Lucky Stars 1985, Twinkle, Twinkle, Lucky Stars 1985, The Protector 1985, Heart of Dragon 1985, Police Story (Hong Kong Best Film Award) 1985, Armour of God (also co-dir) 1986, Project A II (also dir and writer) 1987, Dragons Forever 1987, Police Story II (also dir, writer and stunt coordinator) 1988, Miracles: Mr. Canton and Lady Rose (also dir, writer and stunt coordinator) 1989, Armour of God II: Operation Condor (also dir, producer, writer and stunt coordinator) 1990, Island of Fire 1991, Twin Dragons 1991 (also stunt choreographer), Police Story III: Supercop (also exec. producer and stunt coordinator) 1992, City Hunter (also producer and stunt coordinator) 1993, Crime Story (also producer and stunt coordinator) 1993, Rumble in the Bronx (also producer, writer, jt stunt coordinator and martial arts dir) 1994, Thunderbolt (also producer and stunt coordinator) 1995, Police Story IV: First Strike (also producer and jt stunt coordinator) 1996, Mr Nice Guy (also producer) 1997, An Alan Smithee Film: Burn Hollywood Burn (special appearance) 1997, Who Am I? (also dir, co-producer, co-writer and stunt coordinator) 1998, Rush Hour (also stunt coordinator) 1999, Gorgeous (also co-producer, co-writer and action choreographer) 1999, Shanghai Noon (also co-producer and exec. producer) 2000, Accidental Spy (also co-producer and stunt choreographer) 2001, Rush Hour II (also stunt choreographer) 2001, The Tuxedo 2002, Shanghai Knights (also stunt choreographer) 2003, The Medallion (also exec. producer) 2003, The Twins Effect 2003, Enter the Phoenix (also exec. producer) 2004, Around the World in 80 Days (exec. producer, actor, stunt coordinator) 2004, New Police Story (also exec. producer, stunt choreographer and action dir) 2004, The Huadu Chronicles: Blade of the Rose 2004, Rice Rhapsody (exec. producer) 2005, The Myth (also exec. producer and stunt dir) 2005, Everlasting Regret (co-producer) 2005, Rob-B-Hood (also exec. producer, writer, stunt choreographer and action dir) 2006, Rush Hour 3 2007, Kung Fu Panda (voice) 2008, The Forbidden Kingdom 2008, Shinjuku Incident 2008, The Spy Next Door 2010, The Karate Kid 2010, Kung Fu Panda 2 (voice) 2011, 1911 2011, Chinese Zodiac also (stunt choreographer/stunt double) (Best Action Choreography, Hong Kong Film Awards 2013) 2012, Personal Tailor 2013, Police Story: Lockdown (also action coordinator) 2013, As the Light Goes Out 2014, Dragon Blade 2015, Skiptrace 2015, Kung Fu Panda 3 (voice) 2016. *Publication:* I'm Jackie Chan (autobiog.). *Address:* The Jackie Chan Group, 145 Waterloo Road, Kowloon-Tong, Kowloon, Hong Kong Special Administrative Region, People's Republic of China (office). *Telephone:* 27940388 (office). *Fax:* 23387742 (office). *E-mail:* jcgroup@jackiechan.com (office). *Website:* www.jackiechan.com (office).

CHAN, Rt Hon. Sir Julius, PC, GCMG, KBE, CBE, GCL; Papua New Guinea politician; *Governor, New Ireland Province;* b. 29 Aug. 1939, Tanga, New Ireland; s. of Chin Pak and Tingoris Chan; m. Stella Ahmat 1966; one d. three s.; ed Marist Brothers Coll., Ashgrove, Queensland and Univ. of Queensland, Australia; Co-operative Officer, Papua New Guinea Admin. 1960–62; Man. Dir Coastal Shipping Co. Pty Ltd; mem. House of Ass. 1968–75, 1982–97, Deputy Speaker, Vice-Chair. Public Accounts Cttee 1968–72; Founder and Parl. Leader of People's Progress Party 1970–97; Minister of Finance and Parl. Leader of Govt Business 1972–77; Deputy Prime Minister and Minister for Primary Industry 1977–78, Prime Minister 1980–82, Deputy Prime Minister 1986–88, Minister of Trade and Industry 1986–88, Deputy Prime Minister 1992–94, Minister for Finance and Planning 1992–94, for Foreign Affairs and Trade 1994–96; Prime Minister 1994–97; mem. Parl. 2007–; Gov. New Ireland Prov. 2007–; Gov. for Papua New Guinea and Vice-Chair. Asian Devt Bank 1975–77; Chair. Eminent Person Group 2003–04; Chancellor Univ. of Vudal 2004–07; Fellowship mem. Int. Bankers' Asscn Inc., USA 1976; Hon. DEcon (Dankook Univ., Seoul) 1978; Hon. DTech (Univ. of Tech., Papua New Guinea) 1983. *Leisure interests:* boating, swimming, travel. *Address:* Office of the Governor, PO Box 130, Kavieng, New Ireland Province, Papua New Guinea.

CHAN, Kwok-Bun, PhD; Canadian sociologist and academic; *Professor and Head, Department of Sociology, Hong Kong Baptist University;* b. 9 April 1950, China; m. Wong Suk-yee; two c.; ed York Univ., Canada; currently Prof. and Head of Dept of Sociology, Hong Kong Baptist Univ.; fmr Dir David C. Lam Inst. for East-West Studies; Sr Lecturer in Sociology, Nat. Univ. of Singapore; mem. Hong Kong Central Policy Unit; Ed. Social Transformation of Chinese Society. *Publications:* Stepping Out: The Making of Chinese Entrepreneurs (co-author) 1995, Chinese Business Networks: State, Economy and Culture (ed.) 2000, Alternate Identities: the Chinese of Contemporary Thailand (co-ed.) 2001, Past Times: A Social History of Singapore (co-ed.) 2003, Chinese Identities, Ethnicity and Cosmopolitanism 2005, Migration, Ethnic Relations and Chinese Business 2005, Conflict and Innovation: Joint Ventures in China (co-ed.) 2006, Work Stress and Coping Among Professionals (ed.) 2007, East-West Identities: Globalization, Localization, and Hybridization (co-ed.) 2007, Circuit Entrepreneurs: A Study of Mobile Chinese Immigrant Entrepreneurs (in Chinese) (co-author) 2007, Our Families, Our Homes: Sociological Studies of Families in Hong Kong and China (in Chinese) (ed.) 2008; several articles in journals, contribs to books. *Address:* Department of Sociology, Hong Kong Baptist University, Kowloon Tong, Hong Kong Special Administrative Region, People's Republic of China (office). *Telephone:* 3411-7130 (office). *Fax:* 3411-7893 (office). *E-mail:* ckb@hkbu.edu.hk (office). *Website:* socweb.hkbu.edu.hk (office).

CHAN, Laiwa, (Chen Lihua); Chinese real estate executive; *President, Fu Wah International Group;* b. 1941, Bejiing; started furniture maintenance business 1976; moved to Hong Kong 1982, f. Fu Wah International Group (real estate developer) 1988, becoming Pres.; returned to mainland late 1980s; property devts include Changan Club, Beijing, Jinbao Street (luxury shopping district); f. China Red Sandalwood Museum 1999, now curator; mem. CPPCC. *Address:* Fu Wah International Group, 89 Jin Bao Street, Beijing, People's Republic of China (office). *Telephone:* (10) 85229988 (office). *Fax:* (10) 85221386 (office). *E-mail:* gmoffice@fuwahgroup.com (office). *Website:* www.fuwahgroup.com (office).

CHAN, Laurie; Solomon Islands politician and diplomatist; b. 6 April 1965; s. of Sir Thomas Chan; mem. Nat. Parl. for W Guadalcanal Constituency 2001–, mem. Bills and Legislation Cttee 2006, Chair. Foreign Relations Cttee 2008; Minister of Finance and Treasury 2002, of Foreign Affairs, Commerce and Tourism 2002–06, of Justice and Legal Affairs 2009; Amb. to Taiwan 2012–14.

CHAN, Margaret Fung Fu-chun, OBE, MSc, MScPH, MD, DSc, FFPHM; Chinese physician and international organization executive; b. 1947, Hong Kong; m.; one s.; ed Northcote Coll. of Educ., Hong Kong, Univ. of Western Ontario, Canada, Nat. Univ. of Singapore, Harvard Business School, USA, Tsinghua Univ., Beijing, Nat. School of Admin, Beijing; Rotating Internship, Victoria Hosp., London, Ont. 1977–78; Medical Officer (Maternal and Child Health Services), Dept of Health, Hong Kong 1978–85, Sr Medical Officer (Family Health Services) 1985–87, Prin. Medical Officer (Health Admin) 1987–89, Asst Dir (Personal Health Services) 1989–92, Deputy Dir 1992–94, Dir Dept of Health, Hong Kong Special Admin. Region 1994–2003; Dir Dept of Protection of the Human Environment, WHO 2003–05, Asst Dir-Gen. of Communicable Diseases and Rep. of Dir-Gen. for Pandemic Influenza 2005–06, Dir-Gen. WHO 2006–17, Organizer 43rd Session WHO Regional Cttee for the Western Pacific 1992, Chair. 49th Session WHO Regional Cttee for the Western Pacific 1998, WHO Guidelines on Methodologies for Research and Evaluation of Traditional Medicine 2000, WHO Int. Conf. for Drug Regulatory Authorities 2001 Planning Cttee 2000–02, Vice-Chair. WHO Working Group on Framework Convention on Tobacco Control 1999–2000, Moderator WHO Western Pacific Region Ministerial Roundtable on Social Safety Net 1999; Prince Mahidol Award in Public Health (Thailand) 1999. *Address:* c/o World Health Organization, Ave Appia 20, 1211 Geneva 27, Switzerland (office).

CHAN, Norman T., GBS, JP; Hong Kong civil servant and banking executive; *Chief Executive, Hong Kong Monetary Authority;* b. 1954; two c.; ed Queen's Coll., Chinese Univ. of Hong Kong; Admin. Officer, Hong Kong Civil Service 1976; apptd Deputy Dir of Monetary Man., Exchange Fund of Hong Kong 1991; Exec. Dir Hong Kong Monetary Authority 1993–96, Deputy Chief Exec. 1996–2005, Chief Exec. 2009–; Vice-Chair. Asia Region, Standard Chartered Bank 2005–07; Dir of Chief Exec., Office of the Hong Kong Special Administrative Region Govt 2007–09; currently Co-Chair. Regional Consultative Group for Asia, Financial Stability Bd; Founding Chair. Bauhinia Foundation Research Centre (think-tank) 2006. *Address:* Hong Kong Monetary Authority, 55/F, Two International Finance Centre, 8 Finance Street, Hong Kong Special Administrative Region, People's Republic of China (office). *Telephone:* 28788196 (office). *Fax:* 28788197 (office). *E-mail:* hkma@hkma.gov.hk (office). *Website:* www.hkma.gov.hk (office).

CHAN, Patrick Lewis, (Chan Wai-Kuan); Canadian fmr figure skater; b. 31 Dec. 1990, Ottawa, Ont.; s. of Lewis Chan and Karen Chan; ed École secondaire Étienne-Brûlé, Toronto, Colorado Coll., USA; began figure skating aged five; invited and/or participated in skating tours, shows and competitions in Canada, USA, China, Taiwan, S Korea, Japan, Europe and elsewhere; Pre-novice Men's Champion, Canadian nat. championships 2003, Men's Novice Champion 2004, Men's Jr Champion 2005; silver medal, World Jr Championships 2007; Men's Champion, Grand Prix of France (Trophée Eric-Bompard) 2007 (youngest in history aged 16), 2008, 2011, 2013; Four Continents Men's Champion, Vancouver 2009, 2012, 2016; Canadian Men's Champion (youngest in history aged 17) 2008–13, 2016–18; Men's Champion, Skate Canada Int. Grand Prix 2008, 2010, 2011, 2013, 2015, 2016, 2017; silver medal, World Championships, Los Angeles 2009, Turin 2010, gold medal, Moscow 2011, gold medal, Nice 2012, gold medal, London, Ont. 2013; winner, Grand Prix Final, Beijing 2011, Quebec City 2012, third, Sochi 2012, second, Fukuoka 2013; gold medal, Grand Prix Rostelecom Cup 2012; gold medal, Grand Prix Cup of China 2016; gold medal, Sr Men's Championship 2017; gold medal (Men's team) Olympic Games, Pyeongchang 2018; retd from competition 2018; finished fifth in Men's Event at Winter Olympics, Vancouver 2010; Japan Open Champion 2011; set world record of 93.02 points for the highest score in a short programme, at World Championships in Moscow, eclipsing record of 91.30 set by Olympic champion, Evgeni Plushenko 2006, also set world records for highest score in long programme (187.96) and highest overall score (280.98) 27 April 2011; set new world record of 98.37 points in the short programme under the ISU Judging System at World Championships, London, Ont. 2013; mem. Canadian Olympic Cttee Adopt-an-Athlete programme 2008–; Amb. and supporter, Ronald McDonald House Charities of Canada 2008–; Athlete Amb., Right to Play Canada 2010–; featured guest speaker for various figure skating asscns and clubs, nat. tennis youth squad, synchronized swimming teams, etc.; TD Canada Trust Chinese Canadian Youth of the Year, Chinese Cultural Centre of Greater Toronto 2007, named by Asia Network magazine as Asian of the Year in arts and sports 2008, Ontario Male Athlete of the Year 2009, named by The Globe and Mail as one of the most prominent sports personalities in their annual Power List in Canadian sports 2009, Guinness World Records – for short programme, long programme and combined score 2011, Distinguished

Canadian Leadership Award, Univ. of Ottawa 2011, Sportsnet's Canadian Athlete of the Year 2011, QMI Agency Canadian Male Athlete of the Year 2011, Lionel Conacher Award (The Canadian Press' Canadian male athlete of the year) 2011, Lou Marsh Trophy as Canada's top athlete 2011. *Leisure interests:* golf, tennis, skiing, music, video games, cars. *Address:* c/o Ryan Dus, Landmark Sport Group, 5500 Rose Cherry Place, Mississauga, ON L4Z 4B6, Canada (office). *Telephone:* (905) 949-1910 (office). *E-mail:* rdus@landmarksport.com (office). *Website:* www.landmarksport.com (office); www.patrickchan.ca.

CHAN, Tony F., BS, MS, PhD; American mathematician, computer scientist, academic and university administrator; *President, Hong Kong University of Science and Technology;* ed California Inst. of Tech., Stanford Univ.; fmr Research Fellow, California Inst. of Tech.; taught Computer Science at Yale Univ.; Prof. of Math., UCLA 1986, Chair. Dept of Math. 1997–2001, Dean of Physical Science 2001–06, held hon. jt appointments with Univ.'s BioEngineering Dept and Computer Science Dept, one of the principal investigators who made successful proposal to NSF to form Inst. for Pure and Applied Math. (IPAM) at UCLA, Dir IPAM 2000–01; Asst Dir Math. and Physical Sciences Directorate, NSF 2006–09; Pres. Hong Kong Univ. of Science and Tech. 2009–; fmr mem. NSF Math. and Physical Sciences Advisory Cttee, US Nat. Cttee for Math.; one of five US reps to Gen. Ass. of the Int. Union of Mathematicians 2006; mem. Bd of Trustees King Abdullah Univ. of Science and Tech. (KAUST), Saudi Arabia, Pres.'s Advisory Council of Korea Advanced Inst. of Science and Tech. (KAIST), US Cttee of 100, Selection Cttee for Shaw Prize in Math. Sciences, Steering Cttee of Innovation and Tech. Comm. of Hong Kong Govt; mem. Editorial Bd SIAM Review, SIAM Journal of Scientific Computing, SIAM Journal of Imaging Sciences –2012, Asian Journal of Mathematics; an Ed.-in-Chief of Numerische Mathematik; mem. American Math. Soc., IEEE; Fellow, Soc. of Industrial and Applied Math. (SIAM), AAAS. *Publications:* more than 200 papers in peer-reviewed journals on mathematical image processing and computer vision, Very Large-Scale Integration (VLSI) physical design and computational brain mapping. *Address:* Office of the President, Hong Kong University of Science and Technology, Clear Water Bay, Kowloon, Hong Kong Special Administrative Region, People's Republic of China (office). *Telephone:* 2358-6113 (office). *Fax:* 2358-0029 (office). *E-mail:* ophkust@ust.hk (office). *Website:* president.ust.hk (office).

CHAN FANG ON SANG, Hon. Anson, GBM, GCMG, CBE, JP, BA; Chinese fmr government official; b. 17 Jan. 1940, Shanghai; d. of Fang Zhaoling; m. Archibald Chan Tai-wing 1963; two c.; ed Hong Kong Univ.; held numerous positions at Govt Secr. including Asst Sec. 1963, 1966, Sec. 1988, Asst Financial Sec. 1970, Prin. Financial Sec. 1972, Deputy Sec. for NT 1975, for Social Services 1976–79, Dir Social Welfare Dept 1980, 1982–84, Sec. for Econ. Services 1987–93, Chief Sec. of Hong Kong 1993–2001 (retd); MP in Hong Kong Parl. for Hong Kong Island 2007–08; Founding mem. UNICEF Hong Kong Cttee; Patron and Hon. Adviser, Children's Cancer Foundation; Patron, Enlighten Hong Kong Ltd, SoulTalk Foundation; Dir Reuters Founders Share Co. Ltd; mem. Salvation Army Advisory Bd; Patron Hong Kong Br. and mem. Bd of Dirs Royal Over-Seas League; Hon. Prof., Jiao Tong Univ. Shanghai, Hon. Fellow, SOAS, London; Grand Bauhinia Medal, Chevalier, Nat. Order of the Legion d'Honneur; Hon. LLD (Hong Kong, Liverpool, Open Univ. of Hong Kong, Hong Kong Chinese Univ., Sheffield), Hon. DHumLitt (Tufts). *Leisure interests:* music, reading, cooking. *Address:* 10B Park Avenue Tower, 5 Moreton Terrace, Causeway Bay, Hong Kong Special Administrative Region, People's Republic of China. *Telephone:* 2520-2383 (home). *Fax:* 2520-2380 (home). *E-mail:* chanfanganson@gmail.com (office).

CHAN MO PO, Paul, JP, MBA; Hong Kong accountant and politician; *Financial Secretary;* b. 18 March 1955; m. Frieda Hui; one s., one d.; ed Chinese Univ. of Hong Kong, Harvard Business School; mem. Legis. Council 2008–12; Sec. of Devt 2012–17; Financial Sec. 2017–; Chair. Legal Aid Services Council 2006–, The Hong Kong Mortgage Corpn Ltd (also Exec. Dir) 2017–; fmr Chair. ACCA, Hong Kong, mem. World Council of ACCA; fmr Pres. Hong Kong Inst. of Certified Public Accountants; Man. Dir Paul Chan & Partner, Hong Kong Ltd; Ind. Dir Kinetana Int. Biotech Pharma Ltd 2001–, China Resources Cement Holdings Ltd 2003–, Kingmaker Footwear Holdings Ltd –2011, Wharf (Holdings) Ltd 2004–12, Hong Kong Economic Times Holdings Ltd 2005–12, China Resources Land Ltd 2006–09, China Communications Services Corpn Ltd 2006–12, China Vanke Co. Ltd 2011–12, China Construction Bank (Asia) Corpn Ltd –2012; Adjunct Assoc. Prof., Chinese Univ. of Hong Kong; Gov., Asian Devt Bank 2017–; mem. Commission on Strategic Devt, Transport Advisory Cttee, Copyright Tribunal, Governing Cttee of Beat Drugs Fund Asscn; Fellow mem. The Inst. of Chartered Secs. and Administrators, The Taxation Inst. of Hong Kong, The Soc. of Chinese Accountants and Auditors, The Hong Kong Inst. of Co. Secs.; Medal of Honour 2006, Justice of Peace 2007, Grand Bauhinia Medal, Gold Bauhinia Star. *Address:* Office of the Financial Secretary, 25/F, Central Government Offices, 2 Tim Mei Ave, Tamar, Hong Kong, People's Republic of China (office). *Fax:* 28400569 (office). *E-mail:* fso@fso.gov.hk (office). *Website:* www.fso.gov.hk (office).

CHAN-OCHA, Gen. Prayuth; Thai army officer and government official; *Prime Minister;* b. 21 March 1954, Bangkok; m. Naraporn Chan-ocha; two d.; ed Armed Forces Acads Preparatory School, Bangkok, Chulachomklao Royal Mil. Acad., Nakhon Nayok Prov.; fmr commdr of several army divs including Commdr, 2nd Bn, 21st Infantry Regt (Queen's Guard), Chief of Staff, 21st Infantry Regt (Queen's Guard), Deputy Commdr, later Commdr, 21st Infantry Regt (Queen's Guard), Deputy Commdr-Gen., later Commdr-Gen., 2nd Infantry Div. (Queen's Guard), Deputy Army Area Commdr, Region 1, Army Area Commdr, Region 1 2006–08, Chief of Staff, Royal Thai Army 2008–14; proclaimed martial law 20 May 2014, declaring himself head of new Peace and Order Maintaining Council (junta); nominated by Nat. Legis. Ass. as Prime Minister, endorsed by King 25 Aug. 2014. *Address:* Office of the Prime Minister, Government House, Thanon Phitsanulok, Dusit, Bangkok 10300, Thailand (office). *Telephone:* (2) 281-4040 (office). *Fax:* (2) 282-5131 (office). *E-mail:* opm@opm.go.th (office). *Website:* www.opm.go.th (office).

CHAN SUK-CHONG, Tanya, LLB, LLM; Hong Kong barrister, actress and politician; b. 14 Sept. 1971; ed Univ. of Hong Kong; mem. Legis. Council for Hong Kong Island constituency 2008–12; mem. Central and Western Dist Council of Hong Kong for Peak constituency, Vice-Chair. Culture, Leisure and Social Affairs Cttee; Founding mem. Civic Party, Vice-Chair. 2012–; Dir Hong Kong Mortgage Corpn Ltd, Urban Renewal Authority. *Play:* East Wing, West Wing (political satire). *Address:* Civic Party, Unit 202, 2/F, Blk B, Sea View Bldg, 4–6 Watson Road, North Point, Hong Kong Special Administrative Region, People's Republic of China (office). *Telephone:* 28657111 (office). *Fax:* 28652771 (office). *E-mail:* chantanya@civicparty.hk (office). *Website:* www.civicparty.hk (office).

CHAND, Lokendra Bahadur, BA, LLB; Nepalese politician; b. 15 Feb. 1940, Kurkuriya Village, Bashulinga Village Devt Cttee, Baitadi; s. of Mahavir Chand and Laxmi Chand; m.; seven c.; ed Pithauragarh, India, Tri-Chandra Coll., Kathmandu, DSB Degree Coll., Nainital, India and DAV Post-Grad. Coll., Dehradun, India; Founding mem. Shree Basudev High School, Liskita, served voluntarily as teacher 1961–64; practising advocate 1964–68; Vice-Chair. Lisakita Village Panchayat, Baitadi Dist 1968, Chair. Baitadi Dist Panchayat 1970, Pres. Mahakali Zonal Panchayat 1973, Vice-Chair. and Chair. Rastriya Panchayat (Nat. Ass.) 1974; Founder Rastriya Prajatantra Party (RPP), Chair. 1991, Leader and Pres. Parl. Bd after unification of Thapa and Chand Group 1994, declared himself as Chair. 2014 (party leadership still under dispute); elected mem. Parl. (RPP) for both constituencies of Baitadi Dist 1995, 2008–; Prime Minister of Nepal 1983–85, 1990, 1997, 2002–03; Founding Chair. Mahakali Sewa Samaj 1967; mem. Nepal Red Cross Soc. Cen. Exec. Cttee 1970. *Publications include:* Bahraun Kheladi (Twelfth Player), Visarjan (short stories) (Madan Puruskar Prize), Hiunko Tanna, Indra Dhanush, Aparichit Netako Saathi; also satirical essays, humorous plays and collections of short stories. *Leisure interest:* reading books on contemporary literature. *Address:* Rashtriya Prajatantra Party (RPP), Charumati Bahal, Chabahil, Kathmandu, Nepal (office). *Telephone:* (1) 4471071 (office). *Fax:* (1) 4460324 (office). *E-mail:* info@rppnepal.com (office). *Website:* www.rppnepal.org.

CHANDERPAUL, Shivnarine; Guyanese professional cricketer; b. 16 Aug. 1974, Unity Village, East Coast, Demerara; left-handed batsman; right-arm leg-break bowler; played for Guyana 1991–, West Indies (Capt. 2004–06) 1994–2015, Durham 2007–09, Royal Challengers Bangalore 2008, Lancashire 2010, Warwickshire 2011–12, Khulna Royal Bengal 2012–13, Derbyshire 2013–14, Guyana 2013–14, Amazon Warriors 2015; First-class debut: 1991/92; Test debut: West Indies v England, Georgetown 17–22 March 1994; One-Day Int. (ODI) debut: India v West Indies, Faridabad 17 Oct. 1994; T20I debut: NZ v West Indies, Auckland 16 Feb. 2006; played 164 Tests (to May 2015), scored 11,867 runs (average 51.37) with two double centuries, 30 centuries and 66 fifties, highest score 203 not out against Bangladesh, Dhaka 2012; played 268 ODIs (to March 2011), scored 8,778 runs (average 41.40) with 11 centuries and 59 fifties, highest score 150 against South Africa, East London 1999; played 22 T20Is (to May 2010), scored 343 runs (average 20.17), highest score 41 against England, The Oval 2007; played 385 First-class matches (to Aug. 2018), scored 27,545 runs (average 53.17) with 77 hundreds and 144 fifties, highest score 303 not out; retd from int. cricket 2016; Sir Garfield Sobers Trophy 2008, Wisden Cricketer of the Year 2008, ICC Player of the Year 2008. *Achievements include:* first Indo-Caribbean in West Indies team to play 100 Tests for the West Indies and has captained them in 14 Tests and 16 ODIs; made sixth fastest century in Test cricket, in 69 balls, 2002–03; only second player to make a double century on debut as Test Capt., March 2005; eight highest scorer of runs in Test cricket (second highest West Indian, after Brian Lara). *Address:* c/o West Indies Cricket Board Inc., PO Box 616 W, St John's, Antigua. *Telephone:* 481-2450. *Fax:* 481-2498. *E-mail:* wicb@windiescricket.com.

CHANDRA, Subhash; Indian media executive; *Chairman, Essel Group;* b. 30 Nov. 1950, Hissar, Haryana; m.; three c.; fmr rice packer in Hissar, Haryana; Founder-Chair. Essel Group 1976, comprising media, packaging, entertainment, tech.-enabled services, infrastructure devt and educ. assets, Group cos include Zee Entertainment Enterprise Ltd, Zee News Ltd, Zee Telefilms Ltd, Zee Turner Ltd, Zee Educ. Learning Systems, Dish TV, Wire & Wireless India Ltd, Essel Propack Ltd, ETC Networks Ltd, E-City Property Man. Services, Essel Infraprojects Ltd, Agrani Satellite Services Ltd, fmr jt owner (with Rupert Murdoch q.v.) of Zee Cinema, Zee TV and Zee India TV; Chair. Ekal Vidyalaya Foundation of India; est. Transnational Alternate Learning for Emancipation and Empowerment through Multimedia (TALEEM) 1996; Founder and Chair. Global Foundation for Civilizational Harmony; fmr Chair. Confed. of Indian Industry; f. Brain Trust of India; Trustee Global Vipassana Foundation; est. Indian Cricket League 2007; Ernst & Young Entrepreneur of the Year Award 1999, Business Standard's Businessman of the Year 1999, Global Indian Entertainment Personality of the Year, Fed. of Indian Chambers of Commerce and Industry 2004, Lifetime Achievement Award, Cable and Satellite Broadcasting Asscn of Asia 2009, The Hall of Fame – Entrepreneur 2010, Int. Emmy Directorate Award (first Indian) 2011. *Address:* Essel Group, 135 Continental Building, Dr Annie Besant Road, Worli, Mumbai 400 018, India (office). *Telephone:* (22) 24903926 (office). *Fax:* (22) 24988728 (office). *E-mail:* feedback@esselgroup.com (office). *Website:* www.esselgroup.com (office).

CHANDRASEKARAN, Natarajan, BSc; Indian business executive; *Chairman, Tata Sons Limited;* b. 1963, Mohanur, Tamil Nadu; m. Lalitha Chandrasekaran; one s.; ed Coimbatore Inst. of Tech., Tamil Nadu, Regional Eng Coll., Trichy; joined Tata Consultancy Services 1987, Head of Global Sales 2002, COO –2009, CEO and Man. Dir 2009–17, also Chair. Tata Consulting Services Luxembourg SA; Chair. TCS e-Serve Ltd (fmrly Citigroup Global Services Ltd), Dir 2008–; Chair. Tata Sons Ltd 2017–, Tata Global Beverages Ltd (also, Additional Dir) 2017–, Tata Steel, Tata Motors, Tata Power, Indian Hotels; Dir (non-exec.), Diligenta Ltd, Business Support Services, Reserve Bank of India 2016–; mem. Exec. Council, Nat. Asscn of Software and Service Cos, Vice-Chair. 2011–12, Chair. 2012–13; Chair. NASSCOM 2012–13, IT Industry Govs, World Econ. Forum, Davos 2015–16; mem. Indo–US CEO Forum; mem. IEEE, Computer Soc. of India, British Computer Soc.; hon. degrees from Indian univs, including SRM Univ., Chennai, Tamil Nadu 2010, KIIT Univ., Bhubaneswar, Odisha 2012, Gitam, Vishakapatnam and Andhra Pradesh Univs 2013; Dr hc (Nyenrode Business Univ., Netherlands) 2013, (JNTU, Hyderabad) 2014; Business Leader Award, All India Man. Asscn 2011, NDTV Business Leader of the Year IT 2012, Asia Business Leader of the Year, CNBC Asia 2012, Indian of the Year 2012, Business Visionary of the Year, NDTV Profit 2012, recognised by Forbes India as their CEO of the Year 2012, Distinguished Alumni Award, NIT Trichy 2013, Man of the Year Award, Bombay Man. Asscn 2013, named Best CEO in Tech., IT Services and Software sector, Institutional Investors Annual All-Asia Exec. Team Rankings 2013, CNN-IBN Indian of the Year (business category) 2014, Best CEO for 2013, 2014, Business Today, Medal of the

City of Amsterdam – Frans Banninck Coqc. *Leisure interests:* photography, music, running marathons (Amsterdam, Boston, Chicago, Berlin, Mumbai, New York, Prague, Stockholm, Salzburg and Tokyo). *Address:* Tata Sons Limited, Bombay House, 24 Homi Mody Street, Mumbai 400 001, India (office). *Telephone:* (22) 66658282 (office). *Fax:* (22) 66658080 (office). *E-mail:* tatasons@tata.com (office). *Website:* www.tata.com (office).

CHANDRASIRI, Maj.-Gen. G. A.; Sri Lankan army officer (retd) and government official; *Governor of Northern Province;* b. 1954; m.; three d.; ed St Mary's Coll., Chilaw, mil. training at Sri Lanka Mil. Acad., Diyatalawa; nat. class soccer player at time of enlistment into Sri Lanka Army; joined Sri Lanka Army Regular Force as Officer Cadet 1974; commissioned as Second Lt to 1st Recce Regt, Sri Lanka Armoured Corps 1976; first cavalry officer to deploy in Jaffna peninsula with a Troop of Armour (wheeled armoured cars) to assist infantry in counter-insurgency operations 1977–81, held appointments of Troop Leader, Regimental Signals Officer and Assistant Adjutant of 1st Recce Regt, Adjutant of 1st Recce Regt, Sri Lanka Armoured Corps 1981–83; apptd Squadron Commdr in own regt 1983–89; went to USA to follow Advance Armour Officers course at Armoured Warfare School, Fort Knox 1989; apptd Instructor at Sir John Kotelawala Defence Univ.; Gen. Staff Officer (Grade I), Operational HQ, Ministry of Defence 1991–92; followed Army Command and Staff Course at Tri Services Command and Staff Coll., Bangladesh 1993; assumed command of 4th Armoured Regt, Sri Lanka Armoured Corps 1994; Sr Command Course, Coll. of Combat Mhow, India; apptd Col of Gen. Staff of 51 Infantry Div., Jaffna 1995, took over command of 511 Infantry Brigade, Jaffna 1996, given command of only Armoured Brigade in Sri Lanka Army 1997–2000, participated in Operation Jayasikuru to link Vavuniya with Jaffna along main supply route (A9) and succeeded in capturing Omanthei Township; apptd Deputy GOC 21 Div. and Area Commdr, Mannar 2002, assigned command of 52 Infantry Div., Jaffna 2002–04, Dir Gen., Gen. Staff of Jt Operations HQ 2004–05, assisted Chief of Defence Staff on decision-making process at jt operational level in counter-terrorist operations; went to India to follow Nat. Defence Coll. course in New Delhi 2005; Commdr Security Forces HQ, Jaffna 2005–09, Chief of Staff of Sri Lanka Army March–July 2009; Gov. Northern Prov. July 2009–; several decorations and gallantry awards; recipient of Sri Lanka schools soccer colours 1972, awarded trophy for most outstanding officer cadet for mil. tactics at commissioning parade 1976. *Address:* Governor's Secretariat, Kanniya Rd, Varothayanagar, Trincomalee, Sri Lanka (office). *Telephone:* (26) 2226970 (office). *E-mail:* governornp@sltnet.lk (office). *Website:* www.np.gov.lk (office).

CHANDY, Oommen, BA, BL; Indian politician; b. 31 Oct. 1943, Kumarakom, Kottayam Dist; s. of Puthupally Karottu Vallakkalil K. O. Chandy and Baby Chandy; m. Mariamma Oommen; one s. two d.; ed St George High School, Puthupally, CMS Kottayam, SB Coll. Changanassery, Law Coll., Ernakulam; Pres. All Kerala Balajana Sakhyam 1961–62; State Pres. Kerala Students Union 1967–69; Pres. Youth Congress 1970–71; mem. Kerala Legis. Ass. 1970–, Leader of the Opposition 2006–11; Minister for Labour 1977–78, for Home Affairs 1981–82, for Finance 1991–94; Convenor United Democratic Front 1991, 2001; Chief Minister of Kerala 2004–05, 2011–16; Leader of the Opposition, Kerala 2005–11. *Address:* Cliff House, Nanthancode, Thiruvananthapuram 686 003, India (home). *Telephone:* (471) 2314853 (home). *E-mail:* oc@oommenchandy.net; office@oommenchandy.net. *Website:* www.oommenchandy.net.

CHANEY, Frederick Michael, AO, LLB; Australian lawyer and politician; b. 28 Oct. 1941, Perth, WA; s. of Frederick Charles Chaney and Mavis Mary Bond; m. Angela Margaret Clifton 1964; three s.; ed Univ. of Western Australia; in public service, Papua New Guinea 1964–66; pvt. law practice 1966–74; Senator from WA 1974–90, Senate Opposition Whip 1975, Govt Whip 1976–78; Minister for Admin. Services 1978, Assisting the Minister for Educ. 1978–79, for Aboriginal Affairs 1978–80, Assisting the Minister for Nat. Devt and Energy 1979–80, for Social Security 1980–83; Leader of Opposition in Senate 1983–90; Shadow Minister for Industrial Relations 1987–88, 1989–90, for the Environment 1990–92; Deputy Leader of the Opposition 1989–90; mem. House of Reps for Pearce 1990–93; Chair. Fightback! (Co-ordination and Marketing Group) 1992–93; Researcher and Lecturer, Grad. School of Man., Univ. of Western Australia 1993–95; Chancellor Murdoch Univ., Washington 1995–2003; Pres. Graham (Polly) Farmer Foundation 1995–; Chair. Desert Knowledge Australia 2005–14; mem. Nat. Native Title Tribunal 1995–2000, Deputy Pres. 2000–07; Co-Chair. Reconciliation Australia 2000–05, mem. Bd of Dirs 2000–14; Deputy Pres. Cen. Desert Native Title Services 2007–; Hon. LLD (Murdoch Univ.), Hon. DUniv (Australian Catholic Univ.) 2007, Hon. DLitt (Univ. of Western Australia), Hon. DIur (ANU); Sr Australian of the Year 2014. *Leisure interests:* swimming, reading. *Address:* 23B Brown Street, Claremont, WA 6010, Australia. *E-mail:* fredchaney@iinet.net.au.

CHANEY, Michael A., AO, BSc, MBA, FAIM, FAICD; Australian business executive; *Non-Executive Chairman, Wesfarmers Limited;* ed Univ. of Western Australia and Harvard Business School, USA; fmr adviser on corp. lending and finance, Australian Industry Devt Corpn; worked in finance and petroleum industries in Australia and USA –1983; joined Wesfarmers Ltd 1983, Chief Financial Officer 1984–92, mem. Bd 1988–2005, 2015–, Man. Dir and CEO 1992–2004, Man. Dir 1992–2005, Dir (non-exec.) 2004–05, 2015–, Chair. (non-exec.) 2015–; mem. Bd of Dirs, Gresham Partners Holdings Ltd 1985–, Chair. 2005–; Chair. National Australia Bank 2005–15 (resgnd); mem. Bd of Dirs, BHP Billiton Ltd 1995–2005, BHP Billiton PLC 2001–05; Dir (non-exec.), Woodside Petroleum Ltd 2005–, Chair. 2007–17; Chancellor Univ. of Western Australia 2006–; Dir Centre for Ind. Studies 2000–; Chair. Australian Research Alliance for Children and Youth Ltd 2002–07; Pres. Business Council of Australia 2005–07; mem. Council of Nat. Gallery of Australia 2000–06, JP Morgan Int. Advisory Council 2004–15, Fellow, Australian Inst. of Co. Dirs; Hon. Pres. Business Council of Australia; Hon. LLD (Univ. of Western Australia). *Address:* Wesfarmers Ltd, 12th Floor, Wesfarmers House, 40 The Esplanade, Perth, WA 6000, Australia (office). *Telephone:* (8) 9327-4211 (office). *Fax:* (8) 9327-4216 (office). *E-mail:* info@wesfarmers.com.au (office). *Website:* www.wesfarmers.com.au (office).

CHANFIOU, Mzé Aboudou Mohamed; Comoran central banker; *Governor, Banque Centrale des Comores;* Deputy Gov., Banque Centrale des Comores –2011, Gov. 2011–. *Address:* Office of the Governor, Banque Centrale des Comores, pl. de France, BP 405, Moroni, Comoros (office). *Telephone:* 7731814 (office). *Fax:* 7730349 (office). *E-mail:* bancecom@comorestelecom.com (office). *Website:* www.banque-comores.km (office).

CHANG, Datuk Brian; Singaporean shipping industry executive; *Executive Deputy Chairman, CIMC Raffles Offshore (Singapore) Ltd;* b. South Africa; m. Annie Chang; three c.; ed City Univ., London, UK; started career with Vosper Thorneycroft, Singapore, then with Far East Levingston Shipbuilding Pte Ltd (now Kepfels) 1967–70; f. Promet Group (civil and marine eng contractor) 1970, Exec. Chair. –1994; Founder and Exec. Chair. Yantai Raffles Shipyard Pte Ltd (shipyard located in Yantai, Shandong, People's Repub. of China and subsidiary of CIMC Offshore Holdings Ltd since 2013) 1994–2008, Exec. Deputy Chair. CIMC Raffles Offshore (Singapore) Ltd 2008–; Dir, Bergen Group 2010–15, Deputy Chair. –2015; Dir (non-exec.), TSC Group Holdings Ltd 2009–. *Address:* CIMC Raffles Offshore (Singapore) Ltd, No. 1 Claymore Drive #08-04, Orchard Towers, Singapore 229594 (office). *Telephone:* 6735-8690 (office). *Fax:* 6734-5449 (office). *E-mail:* enquire@cimc-raffles.com (office). *Website:* www.cimc-raffles.com (office).

CHANG, Chin-chen, PhD, FIEE; Taiwanese computer scientist and academic; *Professor and Dean of Academic Affairs, National Chung Cheng University;* b. 12 Nov. 1954, Taiwan; m. Ling-Hui Hwang 1981; one s. two d.; ed Nat. Tsing Hua Univ., Hsinchu and Nat. Chiao Tung Univ., Hsinchu; Assoc. Prof., Dept of Computer Eng, Nat. Chiao Tung Univ. 1982–83; Assoc. Prof., Dept of Applied Math., Nat. Chung Hsin Univ. 1983–85, Prof. 1985–89; Prof. and Chair. Dept of Computer Eng, Nat. Chung Cheng Univ. 1989–92, Prof. and Dean Coll. of Eng 1992–95, Prof. and Dean of Academic Affairs 1995–, Acting Pres. 1996–99; Ed. Journal of Information Science and Engineering 1988–93, Journal of the Chinese Institute of Engineers 1990–93, Information Science Applications 1994–; Ed.-in-Chief Information and Education 1987–; reviewer for numerous int. journals of information science; Fellow, Inst. of Eng and Tech.; Outstanding Talent in Information Science Award of Repub. of China 1984, several Distinguished Research Awards of Nat. Science Council 1986–. *Publications:* more than 300 tech. papers on database design and information security in leading scientific journals and conf. proceedings; 12 books in Chinese on database design, data structures, computer viruses, information security, cryptography etc.; Ed. Advanced Database Research and Development Series (Vols 1, 2, 3) 1992. *Address:* Room EA409, Multimedia and Network Security Laboratory, Department of Computer Science and Information Engineering, National Chung Cheng University, 168 University Road, Min-Hsiung Chiayi, Taiwan (office). *Telephone:* (5) 272-0411 (office); (4) 325-9100 (home); (5) 272-0405. *Fax:* (5) 272-0839; (4) 327-7423 (home); (5) 272-0404. *E-mail:* ccc@cs.ccu.edu.tw (office). *Website:* www.cs.ccu.edu.tw/~ccc (office).

CHANG, Chun-hsiung, LLB; Taiwanese politician; b. 23 March 1938, Kagi, Formosa (now Chiayi Co., Taiwan); m. 1st Hsu Jui-ying (divorced); three s. one d.; m. 2nd Chu A-ying 2007; ed Nat. Taiwan Univ.; defence lawyer in mil. trial following Kaohsiung Incident 1980; mem. Legis. Yuan 1983–2000; Founder-mem. Democratic Progressive Party (DPP) 1986, mem. Cen. Standing Cttee and Cen. Exec. Cttee DPP 1986–2000, Exec. Dir DPP Caucus in Legis. Yuan 1987–88, Gen. Convenor 1990, 1998–99, Sec.-Gen. DPP 2002–05; Sec.-Gen. Office of Pres. 2000; Vice-Premier of Taiwan July–Oct. 2000, Premier 2000–02, 2007–08, Vice-Premier 6–20 May 2008; Chair. Strait Exchange Foundation 2005–07; currently volunteer with Christian Born Anew Fellowship. *Address:* c/o Democratic Progressive Party, 10/F, 30 Beiping East Road, Taipei, 10051, Taiwan. *E-mail:* dppforeign@gmail.com. *Website:* www.dpp.org.tw.

CHANG, Dae-whan, (Chang Dae-hwan), MA, PhD; South Korean business executive and politician; *Chairman, Maekyung Media Group;* b. 21 March 1952; m.; two c.; ed Univ. of Rochester, USA, Coll. of Europe, Belgium, George Washington Univ., New York Univ., USA; Instructor and Capt., Korea Air Force Acad. 1977–83; mem. Acad. of Int. Business, USA 1984; Dir Planning Office, Maeil Business Newspaper 1986, mem. Bd of Dirs and Dir of Business Devt HQ 1986, Man. Dir 1987, Exec. Dir 1988, Pres. and Publr 1988–2002, Pres. Maeil Business News TV Co. 1993–2002, currently Chair. Maekyung Media Group (includes Maeil Business Newspaper and Maeil Broadcasting Network); Acting Prime Minister of Repub. of Korea 9–28 Aug. 2002; Lecturer in Int. Business Man., Grad. School of Seoul Nat. Univ. 1988–97; Auditor IPI Korean Nat. Cttee 1988–2002, PFA Korean Nat. Cttee 1991–2002; Dir, Korea Newspapers Asscn 1986–2002, Auditor 1996–2002, Chair. 2005–10; Founder Vision Korea Campaign 1997–2002; Founder and Exec. Chair. World Knowledge Forum 1998–; Chair. Press Foundation of Asia March–Aug. 2002, New York Univ. Korean Alumni Asscn, Sejong Centre for the Performing Arts 2008–11, Hong Reung Forum; mem. Advisory Bd Sungkyunkwan Univ. Grad. School of Business, World Asscn of Newspapers 1986–2002, Bd of World Asscn of Newspapers 2004–, Nat. Competitiveness Council 2008–13, Global Comm. on Internet Governance 2014–; Order of Civil Merit 1992, Dong-bag Medal 1992. *Publications include:* (in Korean): International Business Negotiation 1989, New Product Millennium (co-author) 1997. *Address:* Maekyung Media Centre Building, 51-9, 1-ga, Bil-dong, Jung-gu, Seoul 100-728 (office); World Knowledge Forum Secretariat, 5th Floor, Maekyung Media Centre Building 30, 1-ga, Bil-dong, Jung-gu, Seoul 100-728, Republic of Korea. *Telephone:* (2) 2000-2114 (office); (2) 2000-2411. *Fax:* (2) 2000-2419. *E-mail:* knowledge@mk.co.kr (office). *Website:* www.mk.co.kr (office).

CHANG, Fa-Te, BA; Taiwanese business executive; *Chief Representative of Greater China, Cathay Life Insurance Company Limited;* ed Nat. Chung Hsing Univ.; Pres. and Co-CEO Cathay Life Insurance Co. Ltd 2008–11, Chief Rep. of Greater China 2011–, Chair. –2013, mem. Bd of Dirs, Cathay Financial Holding Co. Ltd 2007–13. *Address:* The Lin-Yuan Group, Cathay Life Insurance Co. Ltd, 296 Jen-Ai Road, Section 4, Taipei 106, Taiwan (office). *Telephone:* (2) 2755-1399 (office). *Fax:* (2) 2708-2166 (office). *E-mail:* service@cathaylife.com.tw (office); service@cathayholdings.com.tw (office). *Website:* www.cathaylife.com.tw (office).

CHANG, Hsin-kang (H. K.), BS, MS, PhD; Chinese university administrator and academic; *Yeh-Lu Xun Chair Professor in Social Sciences, Peking University;* ed Nat. Taiwan Univ., Stanford and Northwestern Univs, USA; Asst Prof. of Civil Eng, Coll. of Eng and Applied Sciences, State Univ. of New York, Buffalo, USA 1969–75, Assoc. Prof. 1975–76; Assoc. Prof. of Biomedical Eng and Physiology, Faculty of Medicine, McGill Univ., Montreal, Canada 1976–80, Prof. 1980–84, Adjunct Prof. of Chemical Eng 1980–84; Visiting Prof., Faculté de Médecine, Université Paris-Val de Marne, Créteil, France 1981–82; Prof. of Biomedical Eng,

School of Eng and Prof. of Physiology and Biophysics, School of Medicine, Univ. of Southern California, Los Angeles, USA 1984–90, Chair. Dept of Biomedical Eng 1985–90; Prof. of Chemical Eng and Founding Dean, School of Eng, Hong Kong Univ. of Science and Tech. 1990–94; Prof. of Chemical Eng and Dean, School of Eng and Prof. of Medicine, School of Medicine, Univ. of Pittsburgh 1994–96; Univ. Prof. and Pres. City Univ. of Hong Kong 1996–2007; Hon. Prof. and Wei Lun Sr Visiting Scholar, Tsinghua Univ. 2007–; Yeh-Lu Xun Chair Prof. in Social Sciences, Peking Univ. 2007–; Chair. Culture and Heritage Comm., Govt of Hong Kong Special Admin. Region (SAR) 2000–03; Dir (Non-Exec.) Hon Kwok Land Investment Co. Ltd 2007–, PCCW Ltd; mem. Judicial Officers Recommendation Comm., Govt of Hong Kong SAR 1999–2005, Council of Advisors on Innovation and Tech., Govt of Hong Kong SAR 2000–04, CPPCC 2003–; Foreign mem. Royal Acad. of Eng (UK); Gold Bauhinia Star (Hong Kong SAR) 2002; Justice of Peace (Hong Kong SAR) 1999; Chevalier, Légion d'honneur, Commdr, Ordre des Palmes Académiques (France). *Publications:* five books and many articles in Chinese; more than 100 scientific articles, two research monographs and one Canadian patent. *Address:* Department of Sociology, Peking University, Haidian District, Beijing, People's Republic of China (office). *Website:* www.pku.edu.cn (office).

CHANG, Jin Sook; American/South Korean business executive; *Co-founder and Chief Merchandising Officer, Forever 21;* b. Pusan, S Korea; m. Do Won Chang; two c.; emigrated with her husband from S Korea 1981; co-f. (with her husband) Forever 21 retail chain and opened first store 1984, currently Chief Merchandising Officer; operates more than 480 stores world-wide with more than 34,000 employees. *Address:* Forever 21, Inc., 2001 South Alameda Street, Los Angeles, CA 90058, USA (office). *Telephone:* (213) 741-5100 (office). *Fax:* (213) 741-5161 (office). *E-mail:* info@forever21.com (office). *Website:* www.forever21.com (office).

CHANG, John H., (Chiang Hsiao-yen), BA, MS; Taiwanese politician; b. 1 March 1942, Guilin, Kwangsi; s. of Chiang Ching-kuo and Chang Ya-juo; grandson of Chiang Kai-shek, fmr leader of Repub. of China; m. Helen Huang; three c.; ed Soochow Univ., Georgetown Univ., USA; Third then Second Sec., Embassy in Washington, DC 1974–78; Section Chief Dept of N American Affairs, Ministry of Foreign Affairs 1978, Deputy Dir 1980–81; Sec.-Gen. Coordination Council of N American Affairs (now TECO/TECRO) 1981–82, Dir of Dept 1982–86; Admin. Vice-Minister of Foreign Affairs 1986–90; Dir-Gen. Dept of Overseas Affairs, Kuomintang Cen. Cttee 1990; Political Vice-Minister of Foreign Affairs 1990–93; Minister of Overseas Chinese Affairs Comm. and Minister of State 1993–96; Minister of Foreign Affairs 1996–97, Deputy Prime Minister Sept.–Dec. 1997; Sec.-Gen. Presidential Office 1999–2000; mem. Li-Fa Yuan (Legis. Yuan) for Taipei City South 2002–05, Taipei City North 2005–12, Chair. Interior Affairs Cttee; mem. Kuomintang Cen. Cttee and Cen. Standing Cttee 1993–, Sec.-Gen. 1997–99, Vice-Chair. 2008–14. *Publication:* Damansky Island Incident. *Address:* c/o Kuomintang (Nationalist Party of China), 232–234, Sec. 2, BaDe Road, Zhongshan District, Taipei, Taiwan. *Website:* www1.kmt.org.tw/english.

CHANG, Jung, PhD; British writer; b. 25 March 1952, Yibin, Sichuan Prov., China; d. of Chang Shou-Yu and Xia De-Hong; m. Jon Halliday 1991; ed Sichuan Univ., Univ. of York; fmrly worked as a peasant, a 'barefoot doctor', a steelworker and an electrician; Asst Lecturer, Sichuan Univ.; moved to UK to study linguistics 1978; now full-time writer; Dr hc (Buckingham) 1996, (Warwick, York) 1997, (Open Univ.) 1998, (Bowdoin Coll., USA) 2005; Bjørnsonordenen, Den Norske Orden for Literature, Norway 1995. *Publications:* Madame Sun Yat-sen (with Jon Halliday) 1986, Wild Swans: Three Daughters of China (NCR Book Award 1992, UK Writers' Guild Best Non-Fiction Book 1992, Fawcett Soc. Book Award 1992, Book of the Year 1993, Golden Bookmark Award, Belgium 1993, 1994, Best Book Award, Humo, Belgium 1993) 1991, Mao: the Unknown Story (with Jon Halliday) 2005, Empress Dowager Cixi: The Concubine Who Launched Modern China 2013. *Address:* Aitken Alexander Associates Ltd, 18–21 Cavaye Place, London, SW10 9PT, England (office). *E-mail:* enquiries@jungchang.co.uk. *Website:* www.jungchang.net.

CHANG, King-yuh, LLM, PhD; Taiwanese government official and academic; *Chairman, Foundation on International and Cross-Strait Studies;* b. 27 April 1937, Hsiangtan County, Hunan; s. of Shao Chu Chang and Hsi-chen Huang; m. Grace Yu 1964; two s.; ed Nat. Taiwan Univ., Nat. Chengchi Univ., Columbia Univ., USA; Lecturer, Hofstra Univ., USA 1968–69; Asst Prof., Western Illinois Univ., USA 1972; Assoc. Prof., Nat. Chengchi Univ. 1972–75, Chair. Dept of Diplomacy 1974–77, Dir Grad. School of Int. Law and Diplomacy 1975–77, Prof. 1975–, Deputy Dir Inst. of Int. Relations 1977–81, Dir 1981–84, 1987–90, Pres. Nat. Chengchi Univ. 1989–94; currently Prof. of Int. Affairs and Strategic Studies, Tamkang Univ.; fmr Chair. Mainland Affairs Council, Exec. Yuan; currently Chair. Foundation on Int. and Cross-Strait Studies; Visiting Fellow, Johns Hopkins Univ. 1976–77; Distinguished Visiting Scholar, Inst. of East Asian Studies, Univ. of California, Berkeley, USA 1983; Dir-Gen. Govt Information Office, Exec. Yuan 1984–87, Minister of State 1994–96, Minister of the Mainland Affairs Council 1996–99. *Publications include:* Sino-American Relations: Review and Analysis 1979, The Emerging Teng System Orientation Policies and Implications 1982, Perspectives on Development in the People's Republic of China 1984, A Framework for China's Unification 1986, Ideology and Politics in Twentieth Century China (ed.) 1988, ROC-US Relations under the Taiwan Relations Act: Practice and Prospects 1988, Political and Social Changes in Taiwan and Mainland China 1989, Mainland China after the Thirteenth Party Congress 1990. *Leisure interests:* reading, mountain climbing and sports. *Address:* Foundation on International and Cross-Strait Studies, 10050 Taipei (office); 1 Chung Hsiao East Road, Sec. 1, Taipei, Taiwan. *Telephone:* (2) 3968760 (office). *Fax:* (2) 3917850 (office). *E-mail:* webfics@gmail.com (office).

CHANG, Manuel, MPhil; Mozambican government official; b. 22 Aug. 1955, Gaza; s. of Chang Dai Fão and Angelina Mugabe; m. Lizete Izilda Adriano Simões Maia; three c.; ed Escola Industrial Mouzinho de Albuquerque, Universidade Eduardo Mondlane, Univ. of London, UK; joined Ministry of Finance 1974, Section Head 1977, Section Head, Service Comm. 1979, Acting Head, Dept of the Treasury 1987, Head, Dept of the Treasury 1988–89, Adjunct Nat. Dir of the Treasury 1989–93, Dir of Nat. Budget 1993–96, Vice-Minister of Planning and Finance –2005, Minister of Finance 2005–15; mem. Frente de Libertação de Moçambique (Frelimo) party; Vice-Pres. Fund for the Promotion of Fishing; Pres. of Audit Council, Banco de Moçambique; mem. Bd of Dirs, Pipeline Moçambique-Zimbabwe, Admin. Council of Correios de Moçambique 1994–96, Silos Granoleiros de Matola. *Leisure interests:* playing football, reading, watching television. *Address:* c/o Ministério das Finanças, Praça da Marinha, 929 Popular, CP 272, Maputo, Mozambique.

CHANG, Michael; American fmr professional tennis player and tennis coach; b. 22 Feb. 1972, Hoboken, NJ; s. of Joe Chang and Betty Chang; m. Amber Liu; three c.; ed Biola Univ.; coached by his brother Carl and others; aged 15 was youngest player since 1918 to compete in men's singles at US Open 1987; turned professional 1988; first played at Wimbledon 1988; winner, French Open 1989, becoming youngest male winner of a Grand Slam tournament; Davis Cup debut 1989; winner, Canadian Open 1990; semifinalist, US Open 1992, finalist 1996; finalist, French Open 1995, semi-finalist, Australian Open 1995, finalist 1996; won 34 singles titles; retd Aug. 2003; highest singles ranking: 2nd (1996); apptd USA Tennis High Performance Cttee, US Tennis Asscn 2005–06; coach to Kei Nishikori of Japan 2014–; Trustee, Biola Univ.; est. Chang Family Foundation 1999; inducted into Int. Tennis Hall of Fame 2008. *Publication:* Holding Serve: Persevering On and Off the Court 2001. *Address:* c/o Chang Family Foundation, 30242 Esperanza, Rancho Santa Margarita, CA 92688, USA (office). *E-mail:* cffoundation@mchang.com (office). *Website:* mchang.com (office).

CHANG, Richard M., BS; Chinese/American business executive and art collector; *Director, Tira Holdings;* ed Stern School of Business, New York Univ.; Dir Tira Holdings (investment firm with interests in media, real estate, hospitality, and fashion); Founder Domus Collection, Beijing (foundation to advance global contemporary art in China) 2008; has sponsored numerous exhbns, including Anish Kapoor at Royal Acad. of Arts, London; Roundtrip: Beijing–New York Now, a selection of works (among them commissioned pieces by Terence Koh and Matthew Day Jackson) from his Domus Collection, presented at Ullens Centre for Contemporary Art, Beijing May 2010; mem. Advisory Group, Asian Art Fairs Ltd; mem. Int. Council, Asia Pacific Acquisitions Cttee at the Tate; Trustee, MoMA for PS1. *Address:* Tira Holdings (Pty) Ltd, 7th Floor Prop Net Building, Cape Town, Western Cape 7530, South Africa (office). *Telephone:* (21) 9497181 (office). *E-mail:* rosy@domuscollection.com. *Website:* domuscollection.com.

CHANG, San-cheng (Simon), BS, MS, PhD; Taiwanese engineer and politician; b. 24 June 1954; ed Nat. Taiwan Univ., Stanford Univ. and Cornell Univ., USA; Lecturer, later Assoc. Prof. and Prof., Dept of Civil Eng, Nat. Taiwan Univ. 1981–90; Dir, Nat. Center for High-Performance Computing 1991–97; Dir, Dept of Planning and Evaluation, Nat. Science Council 1998–2000; Vice-Pres., e-Enabling Services Business Group, Acer, Inc. 2000–10; Regional Dir of Hardware Operations in Asia, Google, Inc. 2010–12; Minister without Portfolio, Exec. Yuan 2012–14, Minister of Science and Tech. March–Dec. 2014, Vice-Premier 2014–16, Premier Feb.–May 2016; Ind. *Address:* c/o Executive Yuan Headquarters, No.1, Sec. 1, Zhongxiao E. Road, Zhongzheng District, Taipei 10058, Taiwan (office).

CHANG, Shana; Chinese artist; b. 26 March 1931, Lyon, France; d. of Chang Shuhong and Chen Zhixiu; m. 2nd Cui Taishan; one s.; ed Dunhuang, Boston Museum of Fine Art School and New York; returned to China 1950; asst to architect Liang Sicheng, Qinghua Univ. 1951–56; Prof., Cen. Acad. of Arts and Design 1957–85, Deputy Dean 1982–83, Dean 1983–98; Del. 12th CCP Cen. Cttee 1982, 13th CCP Cen. Cttee; mem. New York Students League 1953; mem. Educ., Science, Culture and Public Health Cttee 8th NPC; mem. Standing Cttee 9th NPC; fmr Vice-Pres. China Artists Asscn. *Address:* c/o Central Academy of Arts and Design, 34 North Dong Huan Road, Beijing 100020, People's Republic of China.

CHANG, Steve, MSc; Taiwanese software industry executive; *Chairman, Trend Micro Inc.;* ed Fu-Jen Catholic Univ., Taiwan, Lehigh Univ., Pa, USA; fmr engineer, Hewlett-Packard; f. AsiaTek Inc. (UNIX software design co.), Taiwan; Co-founder, Chair. and CEO Trend Micro Inc. (software co. specializing in network virus protection and internet security), Calif., USA (now based in Japan) 1988–2004, Chair. 2004–; mem. Bd of Dirs, AsiaInfo Holdings, Inc. 2001–; Business Week Star of Asia Award (twice), named as one of Asia's 25 Movers and Shakers, ZDNet Asia 2001, named Innovator of the Year, Asia Business Leader Awards 2004, Lifetime Achievement Award, Asia Business Leader Awards 2009. *Address:* Trend Micro Inc., Shinjuku MAYNDS Tower, 1-1, Yoyogi 2-Chome, Shibuya-ku, Tokyo 151-0053, Japan (office). *Telephone:* (3) 5334-3618 (office). *Fax:* (3) 5334-3651 (office). *Website:* www.trendmicro.com (office).

CHANG, Gen. Wanquan; Chinese military commander and government official; b. 1949, Nanyang City, Henan Prov.; ed Univ. of Nat. Defence; joined PLA 1968, Platoon Leader, Services and Arms, Army 1969–70, Chief of Staff, Army Combat Training Section 1970–74, Chief of Staff, Operations Dept, Lanzhou Mil. Region, Gansu Prov. 1978, Deputy Dir Combat Training Section, Services and Arms, Army 1980–81, Chief of Staff, Div. Command, Services and Arms, Army 1983–85, Deputy Commdr 1985–90, Commdr 1992–94, Dir, Operations Dept, Lanzhou Mil. Region 1990–92, Chief-of-Staff, PLA Services and Arms, Group Army 1994–98, Commdr 2000–02; Dir Campaign Research Dept, Univ. of Nat. Defence 1998–2000; Chief of Staff, Lanzhou Mil. Region 2002–03, Beijing Mil. Region 2003–04, Commdr, Shenyang Mil. Region, Liaoning Prov. 2004–07; attained rank of Maj.-Gen. 1997, Lt-Gen. 2003, Gen. 2007; Dir PLA Gen. Armaments Dept 2007–; Minister of Nat. Defence 2013–18; mem. State Council 2013–18; mem. State Cen. Mil. Comm. 2008–; mem. 16th CCP Cen. Cttee 2002–07, 17th CCP Cen. Cttee 2007–12, also 17th CCP Cen. Comm. 2007–12, mem. 18th CCP Cen. Cttee 2012–17, also 18th CCP Cen. Mil. Comm. 2012–17. *Address:* c/o Ministry of National Defence, 20 Jingshanqian Jie, Beijing 100009, People's Republic of China (office).

CHANG, Xiaobing, BEng, MBA, DBA; Chinese engineer and telecommunications executive; *Executive Director, Chairman and CEO, China United Network Communications Group Company Limited (China Unicom);* b. 1958; ed Nanjing Inst. of Posts and Telecommunications, Tsinghua Univ., Hong Kong Polytechnic Univ.; Deputy Dir Nanjing Municipal Posts and Telecommunications (MPT) Bureau, Jiangsu Prov. 1993–96; Deputy Dir-Gen. Dept of Telecommunications Admin, Ministry of Information Industry 1996–2000, Dir 2000–04; Vice-Pres. China Telecom Group –2004, Pres. 2004–; Exec. Dir, Chair. and CEO China United Network Communications Group Co. Ltd (China Unicom) 2004–, Sec. of Party Leadership Group, CEO and Chair. China Unicom Ltd, Chair. China United Telecommunications Corpn Ltd. *Address:* China Unicom Ltd, 75th Floor, The

Center, 99 Queen's Road Central, Hong Kong Special Administrative Region (office); China United Telecommunications Corpn Ltd, No. 133A, Xidan North Street, Xicheng District, Beijing 100032, People's Republic of China (office). *Telephone:* 2126-2018 (Hong Kong) (office); (10) 66505588 (Beijing) (office); (21) 52732228 (Shanghai) (office). *Fax:* 2126-2016 (Hong Kong) (office); (21) 52732220 (Shanghai) (office). *E-mail:* info@chinaunicom.com.hk (office). *Website:* eng.chinaunicom.com (office); www.chinaunicom.com.hk (office); www.chinaunicom.com.cn (office).

CHANG, Yung Ho, BS, MArch; Chinese architect and academic; *Professor, Department of Architecture, Massachusetts Institute of Technology;* b. 1956, Beijing; m. Lijia Lu; ed Najing Inst. of Tech., Beijing, Ball State Univ., USA, Univ. of California, Berkeley; taught at Ball State Univ., Muncie, Ind. 1985–88, Univ. of Michigan (Walter B. Sanders Fellow) 1988–90, Univ. of California, Berkeley 1990–92, Rice Univ. 1993–96; co-f. Atelier Feichang Jianzhu Architects, Beijing 1993; f. Grad. Centre of Architecture, Peking Univ. 1999, Head and Prof. 2004–05; Kenzo Tange Chair, Harvard Univ. Grad. School of Design 2002–03; Prof., MIT 2005–, also Head, Dept of Architecture 2005–10; fmr Eliel Saarinen Chair Prof., University of Michigan; Steedman Travelling Fellowship, Washington Univ., St Louis 1992; First Place, Shinkenchiku Residential Design Competition, Japan Architect 1986, First Prize, From Table to Tablescape Design Competition, Formica Corpn 1988, Winner, Young Architects Forum, Architectural League of New York 1992, Progressive Architecture Citation Award 1996, UNESCO Prize for Promotion of the Arts 2000, China Architectural Arts Award 2004, Acad. Award in Architecture, American Acad. of Arts and Letters 2006, Distinguished Alumnus Award, Coll. of Environmental Design. *Publications:* Yung Ho Chang/Atelier Feichang Jianzhu: A Chinese Practice (contrib.) 2002, Yung Ho Chang: Luce Chiara, camera oscura 2005, Architecture: Verb (with Feichang Jianzhu Gongzuoshi) 2006. *Address:* Room 7-337D, Department of Architecture, Massachusetts Institute of Technology, 77 Massachusetts Avenue, Cambridge, MA 02139-4307, USA (office); Atelier Feichang Jianzhu Architects, Yuan Ming Yuan East Gate Nei, Yard No. 1 on northside, Yuan Ming Yuan Dong Lu, Beijing 100084, People's Republic of China (office). *Telephone:* (617) 253-4411 (office). *E-mail:* yungho@mit.edu (office); fcjz@fcjz.com (office). *Website:* architecture.mit.edu (office); www.fcjz.com (office).

CHANG, Zhenming, MBA; Chinese economist and banking executive; *Chairman, CITIC Group Corporation;* b. Oct. 1956; ed New York Insurance Inst., USA; joined China International Trust & Investment Corpn (CITIC) Group 1983, Deputy Dir, Capital Dept 1992, seconded to USA as Trader 1992–93, Deputy Man. 1993–94, Deputy Chief Man. in charge of Financial Business 1994–95, apptd Chair. and Pres. CITIC Securities 1995, Dir CITIC Pacific (Hong Kong) Ltd 2000–05, apptd Pres., CEO and Dir CITIC Ka Wah Bank Ltd (CKWB) 2001, Exec. Vice-Chair. 2002–04, Dir and CEO CITIC Int. Financial Holdings Ltd 2002–04, Vice-Chair. 2006–, Dir Capital Market Holdings Ltd, Dir and Exec. Vice-Pres. CITIC Group Corpn –2004, Vice-Chair. and Pres. 2006–10, Chair. 2011–; Pres. China Construction Bank 2004–06. *Address:* CITIC Group Corporation, Capital Mansion, 6 Xinuan Nanlu, Beijing 10004, People's Republic of China (office). *Telephone:* (10) 64660088 (office). *Fax:* (10) 64661186 (office). *Website:* www.citic.com (office); www.citic.com.cn (office); www.group.citic (office).

CHANG-BRITT, Irene, BA, MBA; Canadian business executive; b. 1963; ed Univ. of Toronto, Richard Ivey School of Business at Univ. of Western Ontario; with Kimberly-Clark 1986–99, held progressive marketing positions and assignments in Sales and Research and Devt leadership, later Dir Washroom Systems business; Vice-Pres., Nabisco Biscuits and Snacks, Nabisco Ltd 1999–2000; with Kraft Foods 1999–2005, positions including Sr Vice-Pres. and Gen. Man. Salted Snacks Div. and Post Cereal Div.; Vice-Pres. and Gen. Man., Sauces and Beverages, Campbell Soup Co. 2005–08, Pres., North America Food Service 2008–10, Sr Vice-Pres. and Chief Strategy Officer 2010–12, Sr Vice-Pres. of Global Baking and Snacking April 2010–12 Pres. Pepperidge Farm Aug. 2012–15; Chair. Bd of Dirs TerraVia Holdings Inc. 2016–18, BayBridge Senior Living 2017–; mem. Bd of Dirs Sunoco, Inc. 2011–12, Dunkin' Brands 2014–, Tailored Brands, Inc. 2015–, Brighthouse Financial 2017–; mem. Bd of Advisors, Catalyst; mem. US Exec. Advisory Bd, Enactus (fmrly Students In Free Enterprise); fmr Chair. NJ Kraft Employee Fund (twice); led two United Way campaigns as Co-Chair. and Exec. sponsor; Corp. Achievement Award, Org. of Chinese Americans 2002, recognized by NJBiz as one of the Best 50 Women in Business 2008, by Pink magazine as a Top 15 Innovator 2008, by Progressive Grocer as a Top Women in Grocery 2008, Laureate, New Jersey Business Hall of Fame 2011, named by The Philadelphia Business Journal amongst its Women of Distinction 2011. *Address:* c/o Dunkin' Brands, 130 Royall Street, Canton, MA 02021, USA. *E-mail:* press@dunkinbrands.com. *Website:* www.dunkinbrands.com.

CHANG ESCOBEDO, José Antonio, MEd; Peruvian university administrator and politician; *Rector, Universidad de San Martín de Porres;* b. 19 May 1958; ed Gran Unidad Escolar Melitón Carvajal, Univ. Nacional Federico Villarreal, Hartford Univ., Conn., USA; Gen. Co-ordinator, Dept of Computer Eng and Systems, Universidad de San Martín de Porres, Lima 1984, Dir of Academic Programme, Dept of Computer Eng and Systems 1984–85, Dir School of Computer Eng and Systems 1985–86, Dean, Faculty of Computer Eng and Systems 1986–96, Univ. Rector 1996–2006, 2011–; Cen. Devt Man., Banco de la Nación 1988–89, Cen. Information Man. 1989; Minister of Educ. 2006–10, Pres., Council of Ministers (Prime Minister) and Minister of Educ. 2010–11; mem. Alianza Popular Revolucionaria Americana; Dr hc (Univ. Nacional de Huacho) 2000, (Univ. Nacional Federico Villarreal) 2006; Gran Oficial, Policia Nacional del Perú 2005. *Address:* Ciudad Universitaria, Avenida Las Calandrias s/n Santa Anita, Lima, Peru (office). *Telephone:* (511) 362-0064 (office). *Website:* www.usmp.edu.pe (office).

CHANG-HIM, Most Rev. French Kitchener, MPhil, LTh; Seychelles ecclesiastic; *Archbishop Emeritus, Province of the Indian Ocean;* b. 10 May 1938; s. of Francis Chang-Him and Amelia Zoé; m. Susan Talma 1975 (died 1996); twin d.; ed Seychelles Coll., Lichfield Theological Coll. and St Augustine's Coll., Canterbury, UK, Univ. of Trinity Coll., Toronto, Canada, Oxford Centre for Mission Studies, UK; primary school teacher 1958; man. of schools 1973–77; Chair. Bd of Govs, Teacher Training Coll. 1976–77; Vicar-Gen., Diocese of Seychelles 1973–79, Archdeacon of Seychelles 1973–79, Bishop of Seychelles 1979–2004, Dean, Prov. of the Indian Ocean 1983–84, Archbishop 1984–95, Archbishop Emer. 2013–; Hon. DD (Univ. of Trinity Coll., Toronto) 1991; Rajiv Ghandi Foundation Lifetime Achievement Award 2003. *Publications include:* The Seychellois: In Search of an Identity 1975. *Leisure interests:* international affairs, cooking, gardening, reading. *Address:* PO Box 44, Victoria, Seychelles (home). *Telephone:* 4248151 (home). *Fax:* 4248151 (home). *E-mail:* bishop@seychelles.net (home).

CHANG TSONG-ZUNG, Johnson; Chinese art critic and gallery curator; *Founding Director, Hanart TZ Gallery;* b. 1951, Hong Kong; two s.; has curated Chinese exhbns since 1980s; pioneered participation of Chinese art at int. exhbns; adviser to numerous art collectors, including David Tang; Founding Dir Hanart TZ Gallery 1983–; Curator, Co-founder and mem. Bd Asia Art Archive, Hong Kong 2000; Co-founder Hong Kong chapter of AICA (Int. Asscn of Art Critics); Guest Prof., China Art Acad.; named by Art Review to The Power 100 listing. *Address:* Hanart TZ Gallery, 401 Pedder Building, 12 Pedder Street, Hong Kong Special Administrative Region, People's Republic of China (office). *Telephone:* 2526-9019 (office). *Fax:* 2521-2001 (office). *E-mail:* tzchang@hanart.com (office). *Website:* www.hanart.com (office); www.facebook.com/Hanart.TZ.Gallery.

CHANGEUX, Jean-Pierre, DèsSc; French medical scientist and academic; *Professor Emeritus, Laboratoire de Neurobiologie Moléculaire, Institut Pasteur;* b. 6 April 1936, Domont; s. of Marcel Changeux and Jeanne Benoît; m. Annie Dupont 1962; one s.; ed Lycées Montaigne, Louis le Grand and St Louis, Paris and Ecole Normale Supérieure, Ulm; research asst 1958–60; Asst Lecturer, Science Faculty, Univ. of Paris 1960–66; post-doctoral Fellow, Univ. of Calif. 1966, Columbia Univ., New York 1967; Vice-Dir Coll. de France (Chair. of Molecular Biology) 1967; apptd Prof., Laboratoire de Neurobiologie Moléculaire, Institut Pasteur 1974–, now Prof. Emer., also Hon. Pres. Neuroscience Dept; Prof., Coll. de France 1975–; Pres. Interministerial Comm. for Preservation of Nat. Artistic Heritage 1989–, Consultative Cttee on Ethics for Life and Medical Sciences 1993–99 (Hon. Pres. 1999–); mem. Soc. Des Amis du Louvre 2004–, Vice-Pres. 2006–; mem. Scientific Bd World Knowledge Dialogue 2007–, Bd Scientific Govs, The Scripps Research Inst., USA; Co-Chair. Ethics and Society Div., European Human Brain Programme 2013–; mem. European Molecular Biology Org.; mem. or Corresp. mem. Acad. des Sciences, Akad. Leopoldina, Halle 1974, Turin Acad. of Medicine 1976; Foreign Assoc. NAS, 1983, Inst. of Medicine of the Nat. Acads 2000, Istituto Veneto di Scienze, Lettere Ed Arti 2001, European Acad. of Sciences 2004, Int. Acad. of Humanism; Foreign mem. Royal Acad. of Sciences, Stockholm 1985, Acad. des Sciences 1988, American Acad. of Arts and Sciences 1994, Romanian Acad. of Medical Sciences 1996, Acad. Royale des Sciences, des Lettres et des Beaux-Arts de Belgique 2010, Accad. Nazionale dei Lincei 2010; Founding mem. Academia Europaea 1988; Foreign Assoc. mem. Hungarian Acad. of Sciences 2004; Hon. mem. Neurosciences Research Program, MIT and Rockefeller Univ. 1984–, Japanese Biochemical Soc. 1985, American Neurology Asscn 1988, Univ. Coll. London 1990; Membre d'honneur à titre étranger, Soc. Belge de Neurologie 1991; Foreign Hon. mem. Acad. Royale de Médecine de Belgique 1988; Commdr, Légion d'honneur, Grand Croix 2010; Commdr, Ordre des Arts et des Lettres 1994; Grand Croix, Ordre nat. du Mérite 1995; Dr hc (Torino) 1989, (Dundee) 1992, (Geneva) 1994, (Stockholm) 1994, (Liège) 1996, (Ecole Polytechnique Fédérale of Lausanne) 1996, (Southern California) 1997, (Bath) 1997, (Montreal) 2000, (Hebrew Univ. of Jerusalem) 2004, (Ohio State) 2007, (Buenos Aires) 2010; Alexandre Joannidès Prize, Acad. des Sciences, Gairdner Foundation Award 1978, NAS Lounsbery Prize 1982, Co-recipient Wolf Foundation Prize 1982, Céline Prize 1985, F.O. Schmitt Prize, Neurosciences Research Inst., New York 1985, Fidia Neuroscience Award 1989, Bristol-Myers-Squibb Award in Neuroscience 1990, Carl-Gustav Bernhard Medal, Swedish Acad. of Sciences 1991, CNRS Médaille d'Or 1992, Prix Jeantet, Geneva 1993, Goodman and Gilman Award 1994, Camillo Golgi Medal, Accad. Nazionale dei Lincei, Rome 1994, Sir Hans Krebs Medal, Helsinki 1994, Grand Prix, Fondation de la Recherche Médicale 1997, Eli Lilly Award 1999, Langley Award, Washington 2000, Prix Balzan 2001, Lewis Thomas Prize for Writing about Science, Rockefeller Univ. 2005, Biotechnology Study Center Award, New York Univ. 2006, NAS Award in the Neurosciences 2007, Award for Eminent Scientists, Japanese Soc. for the Promotion of Science 2012, Int. Research Award, Olav Thon Foundation 2016, World Award of Science, World Cultural Council 2018. *Publications include:* L'homme neuronal 1983, Matière à pensée 1989 (with Alain Connes), Raison et Plaisir 1994, Conversations on Mind, Matter and Mathematics (with Alain Connes) 1995, La Nature et la Règle (with Paul Ricoeur) 1998, L'Homme de vérité 2002, Les passions de l'âme 2006, Du vrai, du beau, du bien: Une nouvelle approche neuronale 2008, Les neurones enchantés 2014; author and co-author of more than 600 research papers on allosteric proteins, on the acetylcholine receptor and on the devt of the nervous system. *Leisure interests:* baroque paintings, organ music. *Address:* Laboratoire de Neurobiologie Moléculaire, Institut Pasteur, 25 rue du Docteur Roux, 75015 Paris (office); 47 rue du Four, 75006 Paris, France (home). *Telephone:* 1-45-68-88-05 (office); 1-45-48-44-64 (home). *Fax:* 1-45-68-88-36 (office). *E-mail:* changeux@pasteur.fr (office). *Website:* www.pasteur.fr (office).

CHANNING, Stockard, BA; American actress; b. (Susan Stockard), 13 Feb. 1944, New York; m. four times; ed Harvard Univ.; performed in experimental drama with Theatre Co. of Boston 1967. *Films include:* Comforts of the Home 1970, The Fortune 1975, Sweet Revenge 1975, The Big Bus 1976, Grease 1978, The Cheap Detective 1978, Boys Life 1978, Without A Trace 1983, Heartburn 1986, Men's Club 1986, Staying Together 1987, Meet the Applegates 1987, Married to It 1993, Six Degrees of Separation 1993, Bitter Moon 1994, Smoke 1995, Up Close and Personal 1996, Moll Flanders, Edie and Pen, The First Wives Club 1996, Practical Magic 1998, Twilight 1998, Lulu on the Bridge (voice) 1998, The Red Door 1999, Other Voices 1999, Isn't She Great 1999, The Venice Project 1999, Where the Heart Is 2000, The Business of Strangers 2001, Life or Something Like It 2002, Behind the Red Door 2002, Bright Young Things 2003, Le Divorce 2003, Anything Else 2003, Red Mercury 2005, Must Love Dogs 2005, 3 Needles 2005, Sparkle 2007, Multiple Sarcasms 2010, Pulling Strings 2013. *Stage appearances include:* Two Gentlemen of Verona, New York, San Francisco, LA 1972–73, No Hard Feelings, New York 1973, Vanities, LA 1976, As You Like It 1978, They're Playing Our Song, Lady and the Clarinet 1983, The Golden Age 1983, A Day in the Death of Joe Egg 1985 (Tony Award for Best Actress), House of Blue Leaves 1986, Woman in Mind 1988, Love Letters 1989, Six Degrees of Separation, New York 1990 (also London stage début, Royal Court Theatre 1992), Four Baboons Adoring the Sun 1992, Hapgood 1994, The Little Foxes 1997, The Lion in Winter 1999, Pal Joey 2008, Other Desert Cities 2011, It's Only a Play 2014. *Television appearances include:* The Stockard Channing Show 1979–80, The West Wing (Primetime Emmy for Outstanding Supporting Actress 2002) 1999–2006, Batman Beyond 1999–2000, Out of Practice 2005–06, The Cleveland Show (voice) 2009, The Good Wife (series) 2012–14, and various television movies including The Truth About Jane 2000, The Piano Man's Daughter 2000, Confessions of an Ugly Stepsister 2002, Hitler: The Rise of Evil 2003, Jack 2004, Sundays at Tiffany's 2010, 17th Precinct 2011, Family Trap 2012. *Address:* ICM, c/o Andrea Eastman, 40 West 57th Street, New York, NY 10019, USA.

CHANTLER, Sir Cyril, Kt, GBE, FRCP, FRCPCH, FMedSci; British paediatric nephrologist and health care administrator; *Honorary Fellow, UCLPartners;* b. 12 May 1939; m. Shireen Chantler; Consultant Paediatrician, Guy's Hosp. 1971–2000, Gen. Man. 1985–88, Prin. United Medical and Dental School, Guy's and St Thomas' Hosps 1992–98, also Prof. of Paediatric Nephrology –2000 (retd), Prof. Emer. 2001–; Pro-Vice Chancellor, Univ. of London 1997–2000; Chair. Great Ormond Street Hosp. for Children NHS Trust 2001–09; Chair. UCLPartners 2009–14, Hon. Fellow 2014–; Chair. King's Fund; Chair. Strategic Devt Group for Dulwich Community Hosp.; Chair. Council of Heads of UK Medical Schools and Faculties 1998–99; Chair. Beit Memorial Fellowships Bd; Pres. British Asscn of Medical Mans 1991–97; Medical Dir, Well Child Medical Research Fund; mem. Bd of Govs South Bank Univ.; Trustee, Dunhill Medical Trust; mem. Advisory Panel, Assoc. Parl. Health Group; mem. NHS Policy Bd 1989–96; mem. Gen. Medical Council 1994–2003; Fellow, Royal Coll. of Paediatrics and Child Health. *Address:* UCLPartners, 3rd Floor, 170 Tottenham Court Road, London, W1T 7HA, England (office). *Telephone:* (20) 7679-6633 (office). *E-mail:* barbara.cummins@uclpartners.com (office). *Website:* www.uclpartners.com (office).

CHANTURIA, Lado; Georgian lawyer, judge, academic and diplomatist; *Ambassador to Germany;* b. 14 April 1963, Jvari; m. Dali Chanturia; two c.; ed Iv. Javakhishvili Tbilisi State Univ., Moscow Legislation Inst., Göttingen Univ., Germany; Asst Prof., Assoc. Prof., Faculty of Law, Tbilisi State Univ. 1985–95, Prof. 1995–; co-ordinator Civil and Econ. Law Reform Project 1993–96; Research Fellow, Max Planck Inst. for Foreign and Int. Pvt. Law 1996; mem. Council of Justice 1997; Minister of Justice 1998–99; Chief Justice of the Supreme Court of Georgia 1999–2004; Humbolt Fellow and Prof., Faculty of Law, Univ. of Bremen, Germany 2004–06, Head of Research Project 2006–09; Sr Advisor of German Soc. for Int. Co-operation (GIZ) for issues of legal reform in the countries of the Caucasus and Cen. Asia 2009–11; Visiting Prof., Inst. of East European Law, Christian Albrechts Univ., Kiel 2011–13; legal adviser to Pres. Mikheil Saakashvili 2004–14; Amb. to Germany 2014–; mem. Int. Advisory Bd, ABA/CEELI Inst., Prague; Great Cross of Merit, Order of Merit of the FRG 2006; Dr hc (David Agmashenebeli Univ. of Georgia) 2012, (Univ. of Kiel) 2013; George Shultz Award for Young Scientists 1996, ABA Reformer's Award 2004. *Publications:* more than 180 publs, including Introduction to the General Part of the Georgian Civil Law (in Georgian) 1997, Property as a Means of Credit Insurance (in Georgian) 1999, Private Law in the Caucasus and Central Asia: Inventory and Development 2010, Commentary on the Civil Code of Georgia in Six Volumes (in Georgian) 1999–2000, Judicial Reform: The Georgian Experience 2002, Commentary on the Law on Commercial Operators (in Georgian) 2003, Freedom and Responsibility: Law and Jurisdiction of the post-Soviet Era (in Russian) 2004, Corporate Governance and Director Liability in Company Law (in Georgian) 2006, Introduction to the General Part of the Civil Code (in Russian) 2006. *Leisure interests:* literature, football, travel. *Address:* Embassy of Georgia, Rauchstr. 11, 10787 Berlin, Germany (office); Phanaskerteli st. 9/97, 0110 Tbilisi, Georgia (home). *Telephone:* (30) 4849070 (office); (32) 36-02-08 (home). *Fax:* (30) 48490720 (office). *E-mail:* berlin.emb@mfa.gov.ge (office); chanturialado@yahoo.com (home). *Website:* germany.mfa.gov.ge (office).

CHANTURIYA, Valentin Alekseyevich; Russian metallurgist and researcher; *Chief Scientific Officer, Research Institute of Complex Exploitation of Mineral Resources, Russian Academy of Sciences;* b. 15 Oct. 1938; s. of Aleksey Chanturiya and Maria Chanturiya; m. 2nd Yelena Leonidovna Chanturiya; two s. two d.; ed Moscow Inst. of Steel and Alloys; Jr, Sr Researcher, Head of Lab. Moscow Inst. of Earth Sciences 1969–74; Sr Researcher, Head of Lab., Inst. for Problems of Complex Exploitation of Mineral Resources, Russian Acad. of Sciences 1974–, Deputy Dir 1993–2003, Dir 2003, now Chief Scientific Officer; Prof., Moscow State Mining Inst. 1997–; Corresp. mem. Russian (fmrly USSR) Acad. of Sciences 1990, mem. 1994–; research in physical and chemical aspects of processing mineral raw materials; Prize of USSR Council of Ministers, Govt Prize, Russian Fed. 1983, 1990, 1998, Melnikov Gold Medal, Presidium Russian Acad. of Sciences 1992, Prize of Pres. of Russian Fed. in Educ. 2001. *Publications include:* Chemistry of Surfacial Phenomena at Flotation 1983, Electrochemistry of Sulphides 1993, Mining Sciences 1997, Modern Problems of Primary Processing of Minerals in Russia 2004, Nanoparticles in Geological Materials Destruction and Extraction Processes 2006, Full-field Development and Mineral Processing 2010. *Leisure interest:* fishing. *Address:* Research Institute of Complex Exploitation of Mineral Resources (IPKON), Russian Academy of Sciences, 111020 Moscow, Kryukovsky tupic 4, Russia (office). *Telephone:* (495) 360-06-06 (office); (495) 348-93-94 (home). *E-mail:* ipkon-dir@ipkonran.ru (office). *Website:* www.ipkonran.ru (office).

CHANYALATH, Lt-Gen. Chansamone; Laotian government official and fmr army officer; *Minister of National Defence;* m.; two s. two d.; fmr Dir, Gen. Political Dept, Lao People's Army; fmr Dir, Kaisone Phomvihane Mil. Acad.; fmr Head, Govt Special Task Cttee; Deputy Minister of Nat. Defence –2016, Minister of Nat. Defence 2016–; mem. Lao People's Revolutionary Party, mem. Cen. Cttee. *Address:* Ministry of National Defence, ave Kaysone Phomvihane, Ban Phone Kheng, Vientiane, Laos (office). *Telephone:* (21) 911550 (office). *Fax:* (21) 911118 (office). *E-mail:* kongthap@yahoo.com (office). *Website:* www.kongthap.gov.la (office).

CHAO, Charles, BA, MA, MAcc; Chinese business executive; *Chairman and CEO, SINA Corporation;* b. 1965, Shanghai; ed Univ. of Texas, Austin and Univ. of Oklahoma, USA, Fudan Univ., Shanghai; fmr news correspondent, Shanghai Media Group; fmr Audit Man., PricewaterhouseCoopers LLP 1993–99; Vice-Pres. of Finance, SINA Corpn 1999–2001, Chief Financial Officer 2001–06, Exec. Vice-Pres. 2002–03, Co-COO 2004–05, Pres. 2005–13, CEO 2006–, Chair. 2012–; current Co-Chair. China Real Estate Information Corpn; Dir Focus Media; Dir NetDragon Websoft Inc. *Address:* SINA Corporation, 20F Beijing Ideal International Plaza, No. 58 Northwest 4th Ring Road, Haidian District, Beijing 100080, People's Republic of China (office). *Telephone:* (10) 82628888 (office). *Fax:* (10) 82607166 (office). *Website:* corp.sina.com.cn/eng/sina_mng_eng.htm (office).

CHAO, Elaine L., BEcons, MBA; American government official and charity executive; *Secretary, US Department of Transportation;* b. 26 March 1953, Taiwan; d. of James S. C. Chao and Ruth Mulan Chu Chao; m. Mitch McConnell 1993; ed Mount Holyoke, Harvard Business School, Dartmouth Coll., Columbia Univ.; banker, Citicorp 1979–83; White House Fellow 1983–84; Vice-Pres. Syndications Bank America Capital Markets Group, San Francisco 1984–86; Deputy Admin. US Maritime Admin. 1986–88, Chair. Fed. Maritime Comm. 1988–89; Deputy Sec., US Dept of Transportation 1989–91, Sec., Dept of Transportation Nov. 2017–; Dir Peace Corps 1991–92, est. first Peace Corps in Baltic nations and newly ind. states of fmr USSR; Pres. and CEO United Way America 1992–96; US Sec. of Labor 2001–09; Fellow, Heritage Foundation, Washington, DC 1996–2001, Distinguished Fellow 2009–; mem. Bd of Dirs Wells Fargo & Co. 2011–, Protective Life Corpn 2011–; contrib. to Fox News 2009–; 34 hon. degrees including Hon. LLD (Villanova Univ.) 1989, (Sacred Heart Univ., St John's Univ.) 1991, (Notre Dame) 1998, (St Mary's Coll.) 2002, (N Alabama, Fu-Jen Catholic Univ.) 2003; Hon. LHD (Drexel Univ., Niagara Univ.) 1992, (Thomas More Coll.) 1994, (Bellarmine Coll., Univ. of Toledo) 1995, (Univ. of Louisville, Goucher Coll.) 1996, (Centre Coll.) 2003; Outstanding Young Achiever Award, Nat. Council of Women 1986, Harvard Univ. Grad. School of Business Alumni Achievement Award 1994, Woodrow Wilson Award for Public Service 2011. *Address:* Department of Transportation, 1200 New Jersey Avenue, SE, Washington, DC 20590, USA (office). *Telephone:* (202) 366-1100 (office). *Fax:* (202) 366-8979 (office). *E-mail:* elaine.l.chao@dot.gov (office). *Website:* www.elainelchao.com.

CHAO, Manu; French singer and songwriter; b. (José-Manuel Thomas Arthur Chao), 26 June 1961, Paris; one s.; as teenager played in various bands, including Les Hot Pants; formed Mano Negra 1987, band split 1993; first single earned group contract with Virgin; toured Latin America; moved to Spain 1995; formed 10-mem. Radio Bemba Sound System; spent next few years recording in South and Central America; King of Bongo recording featured on soundtrack to Madonna's The Next Big Thing film; British tour 2002; producer for Amadou and Mariam, Akli D; BBC Radio 3 World Music Innovator award 2002, Latin Grammy Award for Best Alternative Song (for Me Llaman Calle) 2007. *Recordings include:* with Mano Negra: Patchanka 1988, Puta's Fever 1989, King Of The Bongo 1991, Hell Of Patchinko 1992, Casa Babylon 1994; solo: Clandestino 1998, Próxima Estación: Esperanza 2001, Sibérie m'était contée 2004, La Radiolina 2007, Estación México 2008, Baionarena 2009. *Address:* c/o Management Corida, 120 boulevard Rochechouard, 75018 Paris, France (office). *Fax:* (1) 42-23-67-04 (office). *Website:* www.manuchao.net.

CHAOVARAT, Chanweerakul, BSc; Thai business executive and politician; b. 7 June 1936, Bangkok; m. Tassanee Chanrvirakul; three c.; ed Thammasat Univ.; Man. Dir Sino-Thai Eng & Construction PLC 1962–94, Dir and Chair. Advisory Bd 1998–2007; Chair. Bd of Dirs Stp&I PLC 1975–94, 1998–2007; Deputy Minister of Finance 1994–95, 1996–97; Minister of Public Health Feb.–Sept. 2008; Deputy Prime Minister of Thailand Sept.–Nov. 2008, Acting Prime Minister Nov.–Dec. 2008; Minister of the Interior 2008–11; Leader Bhum Jai Thai (Thai Pride Party) 2009–; mem. (Fifth Class) of the Most Exalted Order of the White Elephant 1982, Commdr (Third Class) 1992, Kt Grand Cross (First Class) 1996, (Special Class) 2004; Commdr (Third Class) of the Most Noble Order of the Crown of Thailand 1991, Kt Grand Cross (First Class) 1995, Kt Grand Cordon (Special Class) 1997; Hon. PhD (Ramkhamhaeng Univ.) 2006. *Address:* Bhum Jai Thai, Suite 2159, 11 Thanon Phaholyothin, Chatuchak, Bangkok 10900, Thailand (office). *Telephone:* (2) 940-6999 (office). *Website:* www.bhumjaithai.com (office).

CHAPLIN, Edward Graham Mellish, CMG, OBE, BA, MA; British diplomatist; *Prime Minister's Secretary for Senior Church of England Appointments;* b. 21 Feb. 1951, Hitchin, Herts.; m. Nicola Chaplin; one s. two d.; ed Univ. of Cambridge, Ecole Nationale d'Admin, France; joined FCO 1973, served with Middle East Dept 1973–74, Third Sec., Chancery, Oman 1975–77, Second Sec., Chancery, Brussels 1977–78; on secondment as Pvt. Sec. to Lord Pres. of the Council and Leader of the House of Lords 1979–81; with Near East and N Africa Dept, FCO 1981–85, Head of Chancery, Tehran, Iran 1985–87, Personnel Operations Dept 1987–89; on secondment with Price Waterhouse as man. consultant 1990–92; Deputy Head, Perm. Mission to UN and Int. Orgs, Geneva 1992–96, Head of Middle East Dept, FCO 1996–99, Amb. to Jordan 2000–02, Dir Middle East and N Africa, FCO 2002–04, Amb. to Iraq 2004–05, to Italy (also accred to San Marino) 2006–11; Sr Adviser, Good Governance Group (G3) 2011–17; Commr Commonwealth War Graves Comm. 2011–; Prime Minister's Sec. for Sr Church of England Appointments 2013–; mem. Council, British Inst. for the Study of Iraq 2012–18; Trustee, Mowgli Foundation 2011–18; Gov., Wellington Coll. 2011–; Visiting Fellow, Centre for Int. Studies, Univ. of Cambridge 2005–06.

CHAPLIN, Geraldine; American actress; b. 31 July 1944, Santa Monica, Calif.; d. of Charles Chaplin and Oona (O'Neill) Chaplin; m. Patricio Castilla; two c.; ed pvt. schools, Royal Ballet School, London, UK. *Films include:* Doctor Zhivago 1965, Stranger in the House 1967, I Killed Rasputin 1968, The Hawaiians 1970, Innocent Bystanders 1973, Buffalo Bill and the Indians or Sitting Bull's History Lesson, The Three Musketeers 1974, The Four Musketeers, Nashville 1975, Raise Ravens 1975, Welcome to LA Cria, Roseland 1977, Remember My Name, A Wedding 1978, The Mirror Crack'd 1980, Voyage en Douce 1981, Bolero 1982, Corsican Brothers, The Word, L'Amour Par Terre, White Mischief 1988, The Moderns 1988, The Return of the Musketeers, I Want To Go Home, The Children, Chaplin 1992, Jane Eyre, In the Name of God's Poor 1997, Cousin Bette 1998, In the Beginning 2000, Las Caras de la Luna 2001, En la Ciudad sin Límites 2002, Talk to Her 2002, El Puente de San Luis Rey 2004, Without Love 2004, Disappearances 2004, Oculto 2005, Heidi 2005, BloodRayne 2005, Melissa P. 2005, The Orphanage 2006, Miguel and William 2007, Teresa, el cuerpo de Cristo 2007, Miguel and William 2007, Los Totenwackers 2007, Diario de una Ninfómana 2008, Imago Mortis 2008, The Wolfman 2010, There Be Dragons 2011, ¿Para qué sirve un oso? 2011, The Monk 2011, Et si on vivait tous ensemble? 2011, Americano 2011, Memoria de mis putas tristes 2011, O Apóstolo (voice) 2012, Hostias 2012,

The Impossible 2012, es:Tres 60 2013, Dólares de Arena 2014, Valentin Valentin 2015, A Monster Calls 2016, Jurassic World: Fallen Kingdom 2018. *Television appearances include:* My Cousin Rachel, A Foreign Field 1994, Gulliver's Travels 1996, The Odyssey 1997, To Walk With Lions 1999, Dinotopia (series) 2002, Winter Solstice 2003, A Christmas Carol 2004, The Bridge of San Luis Rey 2004, Les Aventuriers des mers du Sud 2006, The Hollow Crown 2012, Electric Dreams 2017. *Address:* c/o Isabelle Gaudin, Artcine, 8–10 Rue de Normandie, 75003 Paris, France. *Telephone:* 9-81-28-22-27. *E-mail:* artcine@me.com.

CHAPMAN, Sir Frank Joseph, Kt, BSc; British engineer and business executive; *Chairman, Golar LNG;* b. 17 June 1953, London; m. 1st Evelyn Hill 1975 (divorced 1995); two d.; m. 2nd Kari Theodorsen 1996; one s. one d.; ed East Ham Tech. Coll. (now Newham Coll. of Further Educ.), Queen Mary Coll., London; worked for BP 1974–78, initially at research centre, Sunbury-on-Thames; with Shell 1978–96; joined British Gas plc as Man. Dir, Exploration and Production 1996, mem. Bd of Dirs, BG International 1997–2012, Pres. BG International 1999–2000, Chief Exec. BG Group plc (following de-merger of Transco from BG International) 2000–12, mem. Group Exec. Cttee, Chair.'s Cttee, Finance Cttee, Sustainability Cttee; Chair. Golar LNG 2014–; Dir (non-exec.), Rolls-Royce plc 2011–. *Achievements include:* won Global Challenge from Boston to Portsmouth via La Rochelle in BG Spirit in 2004–05. *Leisure interest:* sailing yachts. *Address:* Golar LNG, Second Floor, S.E. Pearman Building, 9 Par-la-Ville Road, Hamilton, HM11, Bermuda (office); Golar Management Ltd 13th Floor, One America Square, 17 Crosswall, London, EC3N 2LB, England (office). *Telephone:* (441) 295-4705 (Hamilton) (office); (20) 7063-7900 (London) (office). *Fax:* (441) 295-3494 (Hamilton) (office); (20) 7063-7901 (London) (office). *E-mail:* golarlng@golar.com (office). *Website:* www.golarlng.com (office).

CHAPMAN, (Francis) Ian, CBE, CBIM, FRSA, FFCS; British publisher; b. 26 Oct. 1925, St Fergus, Aberdeenshire, Scotland; s. of Rev. Peter Chapman and Frances Burdett; m. Marjory Stewart Swinton 1953; one s. one d.; ed Shawlands Acad., Ommer School of Music, Glasgow; served in RAF 1943–44; miner (nat. service) 1945–47; with William Collins Sons & Co. Ltd (fmrly W.M. Collins Holdings PLC, now Harper Collins) 1947, man. trainee, New York br. 1950–51, Sales Man., London br. 1955, mem. main operating Bd, Group Sales Dir 1959, Jt Man. Dir 1967–76, Deputy Chair. 1976–81, Chair. CEO 1981–89; Deputy Chair. Orion Publishing Group 1993–94, Dir William Collins overseas cos 1968–89, Canada 1968–89, USA 1974–89, South Africa 1978–89, NZ 1978–89, William Collins Int. Ltd 1975–89; Chair. Scottish Radio Holdings PLC (fmrly Radio Clyde) 1972–96 (Hon. Pres. 1996–2000), Harvill Press 1976–89, Hatchards Ltd 1976–89, William Collins Publrs Ltd 1979–81, The Listener Publs PLC 1988–93, RadioTrust PLC 1997–2001, Guinness Publrs Ltd 1991–98; Dir Pan Books Ltd 1962–84 (Chair. 1973–76), Book Tokens Ltd 1981–94, Ind. Radio News 1984–85, Stanley Botes Ltd 1986–89, Guinness PLC (non-exec.) 1986–91; Pres.-Dir Gen. Guinness Media SAS, Paris 1996–99; f. Chapmans Publrs, Chair. and Man. Dir 1989–94; Trustee, Book Trade Benevolent Soc. 1982–2003, The Publishers Asscn 1989–97; mem. Gov. Council SCOTBIC; mem. Council Publishers Asscn 1962–77, Vice-Pres. 1978, Pres. 1979–81; Chair. Nat. Acad. of Writing 2000–03, Vice-Pres. 2003; mem. Bd Book Devt Council 1967, Ancient House Bookshop 1972–89, Scottish Opera, Theatre Royal Ltd 1974–79, IRN Ltd 1983–85; Chair. Advisory Bd Strathclyde Univ. Business School 1985–88; Hon. DLitt (Strathclyde) 1990; Scottish Free Enterprise Award 1985. *Leisure interests:* grandchildren, music, golf, reading. *Address:* Kenmore, 46 The Avenue, Cheam, Surrey, SM2 7QE, England (home). *Telephone:* (20) 8642-1820 (home).

CHAPMAN, Jake, MA; British artist; b. (Iakovos Chapman), 1966, Cheltenham; brother of Dinos Chapman (q.v.); ed North East London Polytechnic, RCA; studied sculpture at RCA; now works jtly with brother Dinos; Charles Wollaston Award (for The Marriage of Reason and Squalor), RA Summer Exhbn 2003. *Publications:* articles in Frieze art magazine. *Address:* Chapman Fine Arts, 39 Fashion Street, London, E1 6PX; c/o White Cube, 48 Hoxton Street, London, N1 6PB, England. *Telephone:* (20) 7930-5373 (White Cube). *Fax:* (20) 7247-6914 (Chapman Fine Arts). *E-mail:* enquiries@whitecube.com. *Website:* whitecube.com/artists/jake_dinos_chapman; jakeanddinoschapman.com.

CHAPMAN, Dinos, MA; British artist; b. (Konstantinos Chapman), 1962, London; brother of Jake Chapman (q.v.); m. Tiphaine de Lussy; two d.; ed Ravensbourne Coll. of Art, RCA; studied painting at RCA; teacher of textiles in boys' school; worked as asst to artists Gilbert and George; now works jtly with brother Jake; Charles Wollaston Award (for The Marriage of Reason and Squalor), RA Summer Exhbn 2003. *Leisure interests:* cooking, pilates, rowing. *Address:* Chapman Fine Arts, 39 Fashion Street, London, E1 6PX; c/o White Cube, 48 Hoxton Street, London, N1 6PB, England. *Telephone:* (20) 7930-5373 (White Cube). *Fax:* (20) 7247-6914 (Chapman Fine Arts). *E-mail:* enquiries@whitecube.com. *Website:* whitecube.com/artists/jake_dinos_chapman; jakeanddinoschapman.com.

CHAPONDA, George Thapatula; Malawi lawyer and politician; b. 1 Nov. 1942, Mulanje; m.; ed Univ. of Delhi, India, Univ. of Zambia, Yale Univ., USA; lawyer, UNHCR, positions included Deputy Regional Dir for East and Horn of Africa, Addis Ababa, Ethiopia, also worked in Tanzania, Switzerland, Bangladesh, Thailand, Kenya, Somalia 1984–2002; Chair. Univ. Council, Univ. of Malawi 2003–04; mem. Parl. (United Democratic Front) for Mulanje South West constituency 2004–; Minister of Foreign Affairs 2004–05, of Local Govt and Rural Devt 2005, of Educ. 2009, Minister for Justice and Constitutional Affairs 2010–11, Minister of Educ., Science and Tech. 2011, of Foreign Affairs and Int. Cooperation 2014–16. *Leisure interests:* jogging, reading and football. *Address:* c/o Ministry of Foreign Affairs and International Co-operation, POB 30315, Lilongwe 3, Malawi (office).

CHAPOUTHIER, Georges, PhD (Science), PhD (Arts); French neuroscientist and philosopher; *Emeritus Research Director, Centre National de la Recherche Scientifique (CNRS);* b. 27 March 1945, Libourne; s. of Fernand Chapouthier and Odette Mazaubert; m. Wan Hua Goh; four c.; ed Lycée Montaigne, Lycée Louis-le-Grand and Lycée Saint-Louis, Paris, École normale supérieure, Univs of Paris, Strasbourg and Lyon; long career at CNRS, now Emer. Research Dir. *Publications include:* Psychophysiologie – Le système nerveux et le Comportement (with M. Kreutzer and C. Menini) 1980, L'inné et l'acquis des structures biologiques (co-ed.) 1981, Introduction au fonctionnement du système nerveux (codage et traitement de l'information) (with J. J. Matras) 1982, Mémoire et Cerveau – Biologie de l'apprentissage 1988, Au bon vouloir de l'homme, l'animal 1990, Les droits de l'animal 1992, La biologie de la mémoire, 1994, Les droits de l'animal aujourd'hui (co-ed.) 1997, The Universal Declaration of Animal Rights – Comments and Intentions (co-ed.) 1998, L'homme, ce singe en mosaïque 2001, Qu'est-ce que l'animal? 2004, Biologie de la mémoire 2006, L'être humain, l'animal et la technique (co-ed.) 2007, Plasticity and Anxiety (co-ed.) 2007, La cognition réparée? Perturbations et récupérations des fonctions cognitives (co-ed.) 2008, Kant et le chimpanzé – Essai sur l'être humain, la morale et l'art 2009, La création – définitions et défis contemporains (co-ed.) 2009, O faut bin rigoler in p'tit! (in Saintongeais) 2010, L'homme, l'animal et la machine – Perpétuelles redéfinitions (with F. Kaplan) 2011, La question animale – Entre science, littérature et philosophie (co-ed.) 2011, Le chercheur et la souris (co-ed.) 2013, Mondes Mosaïques (co-ed.) 2015, L'invention de la mémoire: Ecrire, enregistrer, numériser (co-ed.) 2017, The Mosaic Theory of Natural Complexity: A Scientific and Philosophical Approach 2018; numerous papers in professional journals. *Address:* Pavillon Clérambault, Institut du Cerveau et de la Moelle, 47 Blvd de l'Hôpital, Centre National de la Recherche Scientifique, 75013 Paris, France. *Telephone:* 1-42-16-16-51 (office). *E-mail:* georges.chapouthier@upmc.fr (office). *Website:* www.cnrs.fr (office).

CHAPPELL, Gregory (Greg) Stephen; Australian business executive, cricket coach and fmr professional cricketer; *Managing Director, Holdfast Consulting Services PLC;* b. 7 Aug. 1948, Unley, Adelaide, S Australia; s. of Arthur Martin Chappell and Jeanne Ellen Chappell (née Richardson); grandson of V. Y. Richardson (Australian Cricket Capt. 1935–36); brother of I. M. Chappell (Australian Cricket Capt. 1971–75); m. Judith Elizabeth Donaldson 1971; two s. one d.; ed St Leonard's Primary School and Plympton High School, Adelaide and Prince Alfred Coll., Adelaide; teams: South Australia 1966–73, Somerset 1968–69, Australia 1970–84 (Capt. Test side 1975–77, 1979–81, 1981/82, 1982/83, ODI side 1975–83), Queensland 1973–84 (Capt. 1970–77, 1979–80); played in 87 Tests, 48 as Capt., scoring 7,110 runs (average 53.86, highest score 247 not out), including 24 hundreds, taking 47 wickets and holding 122 catches, best bowling 5/61; scored 108 on Test debut v England, Perth 1970; only player to have scored a century in each innings of 1st Test as Capt. (v West Indies, Brisbane 1975); holds record for most catches in a Test match (seven, versus England, Perth 1975); scored 24,535 First-class runs (74 hundreds); toured England 1972, 1975, 1977, 1980; joined breakaway World Series Cricket org. 1977–79; Man. Dir AD Sports Technologies (fmrly Fundamental Golf and Leisure Ltd) 1993–95 (Dir 1992–95), Greg Chappell Sports Marketing 1995–98; mem. Australian Cricket Bd 1984–88; State Man. of Cricket, South Australian Cricket Asscn 1998–2003; coach, South Australian Redbacks 1998–2003; Man. Dir Greg Chappell Promotions PLC 2003–07; Man. Dir Holdfast Consulting Services PLC; contracted coaching tours in Pakistan 2005; coach India nat. team 2005–07; Head Coach Cricket Australia Centre of Excellence 2008–10; Chair. Cricket Australia Nat. Youth Selection Panel 2009–, currently Nat. Talent Man.; Chair. Expatland Global Network 2018–; mem. Bd of Dirs Greg Chappell Cricket Acad.; Patron Leukaemia Foundation of SA 1998–2003, Happi Foundation 2001–03, LBW Foundation 2008–, Chappell Foundation 2017–; Hon. Life mem. MCC 1985; Hon. MBE 1979; Wisden Cricketer of the Year 1973, Australian Sportsman of the Year 1976, chosen for Australian Team of the Century 2000, elected to Australian Cricket Hall of Fame 2002, to ICC Cricket Hall of Fame 2009. *Publications:* Greg Chappell's Health and Fitness Repair Manual 1998, Greg Chappell's Family Health and Fitness Manual 1999, Greg Chappell, Cricket, The Making of Champions 2004, Fierce Focus (autobiog.) 2011. *Leisure interests:* golf, reading, listening to music. *Address:* Cricket Australia National Cricket Centre, 20 Greg Chappell Street, Albion, Qld 4010, Australia (office). *Telephone:* (7) 3199-9329 (office). *E-mail:* greg.chappell@cricket.com.au (office).

CHAPPELLAZ, Jérôme, MSc, PhD Habil.; French geoscientist and research institute director; *Senior Scientist and Director of Research, Laboratoire de Glaciologie et Géophysique de l'Environnement, Centre National de la Recherche Scientifique (CNRS);* b. 22 Dec. 1964; m.; three c.; ed Joseph Fourier Univ., Grenoble; Researcher (Second Class), CNRS 1990–94, CNRS Researcher (First Class) 1994–2002, CNRS Research Dir (equivalent to Full Prof.) (Second Class) 2002–09, CNRS Research Dir (First Class) 2009, currently Sr Scientist and Dir of Research, Laboratoire de Glaciologie et Géophysique de l'Environnement; Nat. Research Council Resident Research Assoc., NASA/Goddard Inst. for Space Studies, New York, USA 1990–91; mem. American Geophysical Union, European Geosciences Union, Int. Union for Quaternary Research, Comité Nat. français pour la Recherche Arctique et Antarctique; Chevalier, Ordre nat. du Mérite 2010; US Nat. Research Council Postdoctoral Fellowship 1990, Nat. Bronze Medal, CNRS 1993, Grand Prix Jaffé, French Acad. of Sciences (with Jean-Marc Barnola) 2001, EU Descartes Prize for collaborative research (European Project for Ice Coring in Antarctica) 2008, Paul Gast Award, Geochemical Soc. and European Asscn of Geochemistry 2010, European Research Council Advanced Grant 2011. *Publications:* numerous articles in professional journals. *Address:* LGGE, 54 rue Molière, BP96, 38402 Saint Martin d'Hères Cedex, France (office). *Telephone:* (4) 76-82-42-64 (office). *Fax:* (4) 76-82-42-01 (office). *E-mail:* chappellaz@lgge.obs.ujf-grenoble.fr (office). *Website:* www-lgge.obs.ujf-grenoble.fr (office).

CHAPPLE, Field Marshal Sir John (Lyon), GCB, CBE, MA, FZS, FLS, FRGS; British army officer (retd); b. 27 May 1931; s. of C. H. Chapple; m. Annabel Hill 1959; one s. three d.; ed Haileybury and Trinity Coll., Cambridge; joined 2nd King Edward's Own Gurkhas 1954, served Malaya, Hong Kong, Borneo; Staff Coll. 1962, Jt Services Staff Coll. 1969; Commdr 1st Bn 2nd Gurkhas 1970–72; Directing Staff, Staff Coll. 1972–73; Commdr 48 Gurkha Infantry Brigade 1976; Gurkha Field Force 1977; Prin. Staff Officer to Chief of Defence Staff 1978–79; Commdr British Forces, Hong Kong and Maj.-Gen. Brigade of Gurkhas 1980–82; Dir of Mil. Operations 1982–84; Deputy Chief of Defence Staff (Programmes and Personnel) 1985–87; Col 2nd Gurkhas 1986–94; C-in-C UK Land Forces 1987–88; Aide-de-Camp Gen. to the Queen 1987–92; Chief of Gen. Staff 1988–92; Gov. and C-in-C Gibraltar 1993–95; Pres. Zoological Soc. of London 1991–94; Vice-Lord Lt of Greater London 1997–; Services Fellow, Fitzwilliam Coll., Cambridge 1973; mem. Council Nat. Army Museum 1980–93; Pres. Combined Services Polo Asscn 1991–, Indian Mil. History Soc. 1991–, Mil. History Soc. 1992–, Soc. for Army Historical Research 1993–, Trekforce 1998–, Sir Oswald Stoll Foundation 1998–, British

Schools Exploring Soc. Expeditions 1999–; Trustee,World Wide Fund for Nature (UK) 198893, Chair. WWF-UK Ambassadors 2002–11; mem. Council, Conservation Foundation; mem. Bd of Trustees, King Mahendra Trust for Nature Conservation 1993, currently Chair. King Mahendra United Kingdom Trust for Nature Conservation; Patron, Gap Activity Projects (now Lattitude Global Volunteering). *Address:* c/o Lattitude Global Volunteering, 44 Queen's Road, Reading, Berks. RG1 4BB, England. *Website:* lattitude.org.uk.

CHARA; Japanese singer; b. (Miwa Watabiki), 13 Jan. 1968, Kawaguchi-shi, Saitama Co.; m. Tadanobu Asano 1994 (divorced 2009); one d. one s.; began taking piano lessons aged four; signed contract with Epic/Sony Records 1990; first performance debut at Quattro Club, Tokyo 1991; released debut single Heaven and debut album Sweet 1991; TV commercials for Suntory, Shiseido and Marui 1990s; formed Mean Machine duo (with Yuki) 2001–05. *Films:* Swallowtail Butterfly (Best Actress Award, Japanese Acad. Awards) 1996. *Recordings include:* albums: Sweet 1991, Soul Kiss 1992, Violet Blue 1993, Happy Toy 1994, Baby, Baby, Baby XXX 1995, Yen Town Band (soundtrack album for film Swallowtail Butterfly) 1996, Junior Sweet 1997, Strange Fruits 1999, Mood 2000, Caramel Milk 2000, Cream (with Mean Machine) 2001, Madrigal 2001, Yokae Mae 2003, Sweet 2004, A Scenery Like Me 2004, Something Blue 2005, Union 2007, Sugar Hunter 2007, Honey 2008, Kiss 2008, Carol 2009, Dark Candy 2011, Cocoon 2012, Jewel 2013, Secret Garden 2015. *Website:* www.charaweb.net.

CHARASSE, Michel Joseph; French politician; *Member, Conseil Constitutionnel;* b. 8 July 1941, Chamalières; s. of Martial Henri Charasse and Lucie Castellani; m. Danièle Bas 1978; ed Lycée Blaise Pascal, Clermont-Ferrand, Institut d'Etudes Politiques and Faculté de Droit de Paris; mem. staff, Ministry of Finance 1965–92; Asst Sec.-Gen. Socialist group in Nat. Ass. 1962–67, 1968–81 and FGDS group 1967–68; Principal Executive Officer, Ministry of Economy and Finance 1976; Mayor Puy-Guillaume, Puy-de-Dôme 1977–; Sec.-Gen., Puy-de-Dôme Mayors' Association 1978–2001, Pres. 2001–; Regional Councillor, Auvergne 1979–87; Adviser to Pres. of the Repub. 1982–95; Senator for Puy-de-Dôme 1981–88, 1992–2010; Sec. of Senate 1995–98; Minister-Del. for Budget 1988–92, Minister for Budget April–Oct. 1992; Substitute Judge, High Court of Justice 2004–08; Vice-Pres., Puy-de-Dôme Departmental Council 1988–92, 1998–2001; Treas. Asscn of Mayors of France 1998–2008; full mem. Local Finance Cttee 1995–; mem. High Council for Int. Co-operation 2000–03; mem. Conseil Constitutionnel, Paris 2010–; Founder, François Mitterrand Inst. 1996– (Pres. 2003–); Chevalier, Légion d'honneur 2011. *Publications:* 55 Faubourg St Honoré 1996, Pensées, Répliques et Anecdotes de François Mitterrand 1998. *Leisure interests:* hunting, fishing, reading. *Address:* c/o Conseil Constitutionnel, 2 rue de Montpensier, 75001 Paris (office); Terre Dieu, 63290 Puy-Guillaume, France (home). *Telephone:* 1-40-15-30-06 (office); 1-40-15-30-31 (office). *Fax:* 1-40-20-93-27 (office); 4-73-94-77-54 (home). *Website:* www.conseil-constitutionnel.fr.

CHARBONNEAU, Hubert, MA, PhD; Canadian demographer and academic; *Professor Emeritus, Department of Demography, University of Montréal;* b. 2 Sept. 1936, Montréal, Québec; s. of Léonel Charbonneau and Jeanne Durand; m. Marie-Christiane Hellot 1961; one d.; ed Univ. of Montréal, Univ. of Paris, France; Sr Lecturer, Dept of Demography, Univ. of Montréal 1962–68, Asst Prof. 1968–70, Assoc. Prof. 1970–76, Prof. 1976–97, Prof. Emer. 1997–; Visiting Prof., Univ. do Paraná, Brazil 1978, 1980, 1983, Univ. de Buenos Aires, Argentina 1994, 1997; Killam Sr Research Scholarship 1974, 1975, 1976; J.B. Tyrrell Historical Medal, Royal Soc. of Canada 1990. *Publications include:* author or co-author of several books on demographic topics. *Leisure interests:* genealogy, billiards, cross-country skiing. *Address:* Département de démographie, Université de Montréal, CP 6128, succ. 'Centre-Ville', Montréal, PQ H3C 3J7 (office); 19 avenue Robert, Outremont, PQ H3S 2P1, Canada (home). *Telephone:* (514) 731-5503 (home). *E-mail:* hubert.charbonneau@umontreal.ca (office); hubert.charbonneau@videotron.ca (home). *Website:* www.125.umontreal.ca/Pionniers/Charbonneau.html (office).

CHARBONNEAUX, Anne-Marie, DESS; French arts administrator and art museum director; *Administrator, Établissement Public du Musée Picasso;* Pres. Magasin-CNAC (Nat. Centre for Contemporary Art), Grenoble 2013–14; Admin. Établissement Public du Musée Picasso, Paris 2014–. *Publications include:* Architectures de lumière. Vitraux d'artistes 1975–2000 (co-author) 2000, Oeuvre et lieu. Essais et documents (co-author) 2002, Les vanités dans l'art contemporain (co-author) 2005, Les vanités dans l'art contemporain 2010, L'or dans l'art contemporain (co-author) 2010. *Address:* Musée Picasso Paris, Hôtel Salé, 5 rue de Thorigny, 75003 Paris, France (office). *Telephone:* 1-85-56-00-36 (office). *Fax:* 1-48-04-75-46 (office). *E-mail:* contact@museepicassoparis.fr (office). *Website:* www.museepicassoparis.fr (office).

CHAREST, The Hon. Jean, PC, LLB; Canadian lawyer and fmr politician; *Partner, McCarthy Tétrault LLP;* b. 24 June 1958, Sherbrooke, Québec; m. Michèle Dionne 1980; one s. two d.; ed Université de Sherbrooke; mem. Sherbrooke Legal Aid Office 1981; Assoc. Beauchemin, Dussault et Charest 1981–84; Progressive Conservative MP for Sherbrooke 1984–2012; Asst Deputy Speaker, House of Commons 1984; Minister of State for Youth 1986–90, for Fitness and Amateur Sport 1988–90; Deputy Govt Leader in House of Commons 1989–90; Minister for the Environment 1991–93; Deputy Prime Minister of Canada and Minister of Industry; Leader Progressive Conservative Party 1993–98; Leader Liberal Party in Québec 1998–2012, Leader of the Opposition 1998–2002; Premier of Québec 2003–12; Partner, McCarthy Tétrault LLP (law firm) 2013–; mem. numerous Cabinet cttees; mem. Queen's Privy Council for Canada 1986; mem. Québec Bar Asscn, Canadian Bar Asscn; Grand Croix of Ordre de la Pléiade 2007, Bavarian Order of Merit 2007, Commdr, Légion d'honneur 2009; Medal of the Acad. of Distinguished Canadians and Americans of the Maple Leaf Foundation 2009, South Australian International Climate Change Leadership Award 2010, Statesman Award, Foreign Policy Asscn 2011, Woodrow Wilson Award for Public Service 2011. *Leisure interests:* skiing, sailing. *Address:* McCarthy Tétrault LLP, Suite 2500, 1000 De La Gauchetière Street West, Montréal, PQ H3B 0A2, Canada (office). *Telephone:* (514) 397-4100 (office). *E-mail:* jcharest@mccarthy.ca (office). *Website:* www.mccarthy.ca (office).

CHARETTE, Janice, BCom; Canadian diplomatist; *High Commissioner to UK;* b. Ottawa, Ontario; m. Reg Charette; two c.; ed Carleton Univ.; Prin. Ernst & Young 1996–99; Deputy Minister of Citizenship and Immigration 2004–06, of Human Resources and Skills Devt 2006–10, of Intergovernmental Affairs 2010–13; Assoc. Sec. to the Cabinet, Ministry of Foreign Affairs 2010–13, Deputy Clerk of the Privy Council 2013–14, Sec. to Cabinet 2014–16, Clerk of the Privy Council 2014–16; Public Service Advisor to Prime Minister 2014–16; High Commr to UK 2016–; Chair. Govt of Canada Workplace Charitable Campaign 2008; fmr Dir, Transition Team, Canada Pension Plan Investment Bd; mem. Bd Trustees Royal Ottawa Health Care Group. *Address:* High Commission of Canada, Canada House, Trafalgar Square, London SW1Y 5BJ, England (office). *Telephone:* (20) 7004-6000 (office). *Fax:* (20) 7004-6050 (office). *E-mail:* LDN.publicaffairs@international.gc.ca (office). *Website:* www.canadainternational.gc.ca/united_kingdom-royaume_uni (office).

CHARKIN, Richard Denis Paul, MA; British publishing executive; b. 17 June 1949, London; s. of Frank Charkin and Mabel Doreen Charkin (née Rosen); m. Susan Mary Poole 1972; one s. two d.; ed Haileybury, Imperial Service Coll., Univ. of Cambridge, Harvard Business School, USA; Science Ed. Harrap & Co. 1972; Sr Publishing Man. Pergamon Press 1973; Medical Ed. Oxford University Press 1974, Head of Science and Medicine 1976, Head of Reference 1980; Man. Dir Academic and Gen. 1984; joined Octopus Publishing Group (Reed Books Int.) 1988, Chief Exec. Reed Consumer Books 1989–94, Exec. Dir Reed Books International 1988–96, Chief Exec. 1994–96; CEO Current Science Group 1996–97; CEO Macmillan Ltd 1998–2007; Exec. Dir Bloomsbury PLC 2007–18; Non-Exec. Dir, Inst. of Physics Publishing 2009–, Liverpool Univ. Press 2017–; f. Mensch Publishing 2019; Visiting Prof., Univ. of Arts, London 2004–; Visiting Fellow, Green Coll., Oxford 1987; Chair. Common Purpose 1998–2008; mem. man. cttee John Wisden; mem. Publishers Asscn (Vice-Pres. 2004–05, Pres. 2005–06); Vice-Pres. Int. Publrs Asscn 2012–15, Pres. 2015–17; Dir, Fed. of European Publrs 2011–14. *Publication:* Charkin Blog: The Archive 2008. *Leisure interests:* music, cricket. *Address:* Mensch Publishing, 51 Northchurch Road, London, N1 4EE, England (office). *Telephone:* (20) 7631-5628 (office). *E-mail:* rcharkin@gmail.com (office). *Website:* www.menschpublishing.com (office).

CHARKVIANI, Gela; Georgian politician and fmr diplomatist; b. 1 March 1939, Tbilisi, Georgia; s. of Candide Charkviani and Tamar Djaoshvili; m. Nana Toidze-Charkviani; one s. one d.; ed Tbilisi Inst. of Foreign Languages, Univ. of Michigan, USA; teacher, Tbilisi Inst. of Foreign Languages; author and narrator, TV monthly programme Globe, Georgian TV 1976–94; Vice-Pres. Georgian Soc. for Cultural Relations with Foreign Countries 1984–92; apptd Chief Adviser to Pres. Shevardnadze on Foreign Affairs, Head of Int. Relations, Georgian State Chancellery 1992; teacher of sociology at Tbilisi State Univ. 1982–; Asst to Pres. Saakashvili of Georgia and Presidential Spokesperson 2005–06; Amb. to UK (also accred to Ireland) 2006–09, Perm. Rep., IMO, London 2009–11 (retd); Chair. Presidential Comm. on Peaceful Caucasus; has lectured in Austria, Germany, Sweden, UK and USA; Order of Honour 1998, Presidential Order of Excellence 2011, Victory Order of St George 2013. *Music:* CD of piano miniatures released 2001. *Television:* author and dir of five-part documentary The Georgians in the Kremlin (Rustavi-II TV) 2004. *Publications include:* trans. of King Lear; G. Charkviani – Lectures, Speeches and a Toast 2008; articles in numerous journals. *Leisure interests:* piano music, exotic cuisines. *Address:* Gamsakhurdia str. 14, Tbilisi, Georgia (home). *Telephone:* (32) 380776 (home).

CHARLES, Caroline, OBE; British fashion designer; b. 18 May 1942, Cairo, Egypt; d. of Noel St John Fairhurst and Helen T. Williams; m. Malcolm Valentine 1966; one s. one d.; ed Sacred Heart Convent, Woldingham, Surrey, Swindon Art School; f. Caroline Charles 1963; established retail outlet in London selling Caroline Charles Collection 1979; wholesale business suppliers to leading British shops and stores and exports to USA, Japan, Australia and Europe; Evening Standard Design Award 1983 and other design awards. *Publications:* Weekend Wardrobe, 50 Years in Fashion 2012. *Leisure interests:* travel, theatre, gardening, tennis, reading. *Address:* 56–57 Beauchamp Place, London, SW3 1NY, England (office). *Telephone:* (20) 7225-3197. *Website:* www.carolinecharles.co.uk.

CHARLESWORTH, Brian, BA, PhD, FRS, FRSE; British biologist and academic; *Senior Honorary Professorial Fellow, Institute of Evolutionary Biology, University of Edinburgh;* b. 29 April 1945, Brighton, Sussex, England; s. of Francis Gustave Charlesworth and Mary Ryan; m. Deborah Charlesworth; one d.; ed Queens' Coll., Cambridge; Post-doctoral Fellow in Population Biology, Univ. of Chicago 1969–71, Prof. of Ecology and Evolution 1985–92, George Wells Beadle Distinguished Service Prof. of Ecology and Evolution 1992–97; Lecturer in Genetics, Univ. of Liverpool 1971–74; Lecturer in Biology, Univ. of Sussex, Brighton 1974–82, Reader in Biology 1982–84; Royal Soc. Research Professorship, Univ. of Edinburgh 1997–2007, Professorial Fellow and Head of Inst. of Evolutionary Biology 2007–10, Sr Hon. Professorial Fellow 2010–; Pres. Genetics Soc. (UK) 2006–09, European Soc. for Evolutionary Biology 2011–13; mem. Genetics Soc. of GB 1966– (mem. Cttee 1981–84), Soc. for the Study of Evolution 1985–2005, 2013– (Pres. 1999), Genetics Soc. of America 1986–99, Soc. for Molecular Biology and Evolution 1995–97, 2001–, European Soc. for Evolutionary Biology 1997–99, 2010–, Research Fellowships Cttee, Royal Soc. 1999– (mem. Awards Cttee 2001–04), Functional Genomics Cttee Wellcome Trust 2000–03, Sectional Cttee A3, Royal Soc. of Edinburgh 2000–03, ERA Initiative Cttee Biotechnology and Biological Sciences Research Council 2001; Assoc. Ed. Current Biology 1992–; mem. Editorial Bd Genetical Research 1996–2000, Philosophical Transactions of the Royal Society 1999–2004; Ed. Biology Letters 2004–; mem. Advisory Bd Journal of Theoretical Biology 1996–2005; Reviewer, Nature, Science, Evolution, Genetics, Genetical Research, Journal of Theoretical Biology, American Naturalist, Molecular Biology and Evolution; Hon. Fellow, American Acad. of Arts and Sciences 1996, Foreign Associate, Nat. Acad. of Sciences USA 2013; Darwin Prize, Univ. of Edinburgh 1994, Darwin Medal, Royal Soc. 2000, Sewall Wright Award, American Soc. of Naturalists 2006, Frink Award, Zoological Soc. of London 2007, Weldon Memorial Award, Univ. of Oxford 2007, Fisher Memorial Lecturer 2009, Darwin-Wallace Medal, Linnaean Soc. 2010. *Publications:* Evolution: A Very Short Introduction (with Deborah Charlesworth) 2003, Elements of Evolutionary Genetics (with Deborah Charlesworth) 2010; more than 300 publs in scientific journals on population genetics and evolutionary biology. *Leisure interests:* reading, classical music, hill-walking. *Address:* Institute of Evolutionary Biology, University of Edinburgh, Ashworth Laboratories, West Mains Road, Edinburgh, Midlothian, EH9 3JT, Scotland (office). *Telephone:* (131) 650-5751 (office). *Fax:*

(131) 650-6564 (office). *E-mail:* brian.charlesworth@ed.ac.uk (office). *Website:* www.ed.ac.uk/schools-departments/biology/evolutionary-biology (office).

CHARLTON, John (Jack), OBE, DL; British fmr professional football manager and fmr professional football player; b. 8 May 1935, Ashington, Northumberland; s. of Robert Charlton and Elizabeth Charlton; brother of Sir Robert Charlton (q.v.); m. Patricia Charlton 1958; two s. one d.; ed Hirst Park School, Ashington; player for Leeds United youth team 1950–52, sr team 1952–73 (made 629 appearances, scored 70 goals); 35 full England caps 1965–70, scored six goals; played with winning teams League Championship 1969, Football Asscn Cup 1972, League Cup 1968, Fairs Cup 1968, 1971, Charity Shield 1969, World Cup (England v. Germany) 1966; Man. Middlesbrough (Div. 2 Champions 1974) 1973–77, Sheffield Wednesday 1977–83, Newcastle United 1984–85, Repub. of Ireland (qualified for European Championships, West Germany 1988, World Cup, Italy 1990, USA 1994) 1986–96; Football Writers' Asscn Footballer of the Year 1967, inducted into English Football Hall of Fame 2005, voted by Leeds United supporters into the club's greatest ever XI 2006. *Publications:* Jack Charlton's American World Cup Diary 1994, Jack Charlton: The Autobiography (with Peter Byrne) 1996. *Leisure interests:* shooting, fishing. *Address:* Cairn Lodge, Dalton, Ponteland, Northumbria, England.

CHARLTON, Sir Robert (Bobby), Kt, CBE, OBE; British sports official, fmr professional football player and fmr professional football manager; b. 11 Oct. 1937, Ashington, Northumberland; s. of Robert Charlton and Elizabeth Charlton; brother of Jack Charlton (q.v.); m. Norma Charlton 1961; two d.; ed Bedlington Grammar School, Northumberland; professional footballer with Manchester United 1954–73, played 751 games, scored 245 goals; FA Cup winners' medal 1963; First Div. championship medals 1956–57, 1964–65, 1966–67; World Cup winners' medal (with England) 1966; European Cup winners' medal 1968; 106 appearances for England 1957–73, scored a then record 49 goals (surpassed by Wayne Rooney Sept. 2015); Man. Preston North End 1973–75; Chair. NW Council for Sport and Recreation 1982–; Dir, Manchester United Football Club 1984–; mem. Laureus World Sports Acad.; Hon. Fellow, Manchester Polytechnic 1979; Hon. Pres. Nat. Football Museum; Freedom of the City of Manchester 2009; Order of the Rising Sun (Fourth Class) 2012; Hon. MA (Univ. of Manchester); FWA Footballer of the Year 1965–66, FIFA World Cup Golden Ball 1966, FIFA World Cup All-Star Team 1966, 1970, Ballon d'Or 1966, PFA Merit Award 1974, FWA Tribute Award 1989, FIFA World Cup All-Time Team 1994, Football League 100 Legends 1998, inducted into English Football Hall of Fame 2002, FIFA 100 2004, UEFA Golden Jubilee Poll 2004, BBC Sports Personality of the Year Lifetime Achievement Award 2008, voted the 4th greatest Manchester United player of all time by the readers of Inside United and ManUtd.com, behind Ryan Giggs, Eric Cantona and George Best 2011, Laureus Lifetime Achievement Award 2012. *Publications include:* My Soccer Life 1965, Forward for England 1967, This Game of Soccer 1967, Book of European Football, Books 1–4 1969–72, My Manchester United Years: The Autobiography 2007, My Life in Football 2009. *Leisure interest:* golf. *Website:* www.ifhof.com/hof/charlton.asp.

CHARNLEY, Irene; South African business executive; b. 6 May 1960; m. Clement Charnley; two s. one d.; ed Univ. of the Witwatersrand, Harvard Univ., USA; negotiator and strategist, Nat. Union of Mineworkers 1996; Commercial Dir MTN Group (fmrly M-Cell Ltd) 2001–05, Group Exec. Vice-Pres. 2005–07, mem. Bd of Dirs (non-exec.) 2008–, fmr Exec. Dir Johnnic Holdings, fmr Chair. M-Cell (subsidiary); Chair. Orbicom; mem. Bd of Dirs FirstRand Bank 2004–, Pontso Investment Holdings, Time Media Ltd, Metropolitan Life Ltd, Int. Marketing Council of South Africa, Black Econ. Empowerment Task Team; mem. King Committee on Corp. Governance; Trustee Eskom Pension Fund, Johnnic Ikageng Share Trust, Vaal Reefs Trust; World Econ. Forum Global Leader for Tomorrow, Businesswoman of the Year 2000. *Address:* MTN Group Limited, Innovation Centre, 216 14th Avenue, Fairlands (office); Private Bag X9955, Sandton, Johannesburg 2146, South Africa. *Website:* www.mtn.com (office).

CHARPENTIER, Emmanuelle Marie, PhD; French microbiologist and academic; *Alexander von Humboldt Professor, Helmholtz Centre for Infection Research;* b. 1968, Juvisy-sur-Orge (Essonne); ed Univ. Pierre and Marie Curie and Pasteur Inst., Paris; moved to USA upon graduation, held Research Assoc. positions at Rockefeller Univ., New York Univ. Langone Medical Center, Skirball Inst. of Biomolecular Medicine, St Jude Children's Research Hosp.; returned to Europe and est. research group, Max F. Perutz Labs, Univ. of Vienna 2002, apptd Prof. of Microbiology 2006; Assoc. Prof., Lab. for Molecular Infection Medicine Sweden (MIMS), Umeå Univ., Sweden 2009–14, Visiting Prof. 2014–17; Prof., Hannover Medical School 2013–15, Alexander von Humboldt Prof. 2014–; Prof. and Head, Regulation in Infection Biology Dept, Helmholtz Centre for Infection Research 2013–; Scientific mem. and Dir Max Planck Inst. for Infection Biology 2015–; Scientific Founder, CRISPR Therapeutics; mem. European Molecular Biology Org. (EMBO) 2014–; Hon. Prof., Humboldt University, Berlin 2016–; Dr hc (Catholic University, Leuven, Belgium) 2016, (New York University, USA) 2016, (Umeå University, Sweden) 2017, (Western University, London, Canada) 2017, (Hong Kong University of Science and Technology) 2017, (Université catholique de Louvain) 2018; Grand Prix Jean-Pierre LeCocq, Eric K. Fernström Prize 2011, Göran Gustafsson Prize 2014, Dr Paul Janssen Award for Biomedical Research (with Jennifer Doudna) 2014, Jacob Heskel Gabbay Award (with Feng Zhang and Jennifer Doudna) 2014, Hansen Family Award 2015, Breakthrough Prize in Life Sciences 2015, Princess of Asturias Award for Tech. and Scientific Research (with Jennifer Doudna) 2015, Ernst Jung Prize for Medicine 2015, Louis-Jeantet Prize for Medicine 2015, World Technology Awards (Biotechnology) (co-recipient) 2015, Canada Gairdner Int. Award (co recipient) 2016, L'Oréal-UNESCO Award for Women in Science (Europe) 2016, Int. Ellis Island Medal of Honor 2017, Japan Prize (co recipient) 2017, Kavli Prize 2018, Aachen Engineering Award 2018. *Achievements include:* research in the molecular structures of Ribonucleic acid (RNA) molecules and devt of gene-editing tech. allowing the modification of genetic material (Crispr-Cas9 genome editing technique). *Address:* Helmholtz Centre for Infection Research, Inhoffenstraße 7, 38124 Brunswick, Germany (office). *Telephone:* (531) 6181-5500 (office). *E-mail:* emmanuelle.charpentier@mims.umu.se (office); info@helmholtz-hzi.de (office). *Website:* www.helmholtz-hzi.de (office).

CHARPENTIER, Georg, MEcons; Finnish economist and UN official; *Senior Advisor, Crisis Management Initiative;* b. 11 Aug. 1956, El Salvador; m.; three c.; ed Univ. of Helsinki; fmr Secr., Programme de Restructuration du Marché Céréalier, Mali; joined UN in 1984 as Programme Officer, Viet Nam, has held numerous posts including Sr Deputy Resident Rep. in Ethiopia, Deputy Resident Rep. in Lesotho and São Tomé, Asst Resident Rep. in Mauritania, UNDP Rep., ad interim and Humanitarian Coordinator, ad interim, in Congo, UNDP Deputy Dir Bureau for Crisis Prevention and Recovery, Geneva 2002–04, UN Resident Coordinator and UNDP Resident Rep. in Burkina Faso 2004–06, UN Resident and Humanitarian Coordinator and UNDP Resident Rep. in Burundi 2006, Deputy Special Rep. in Côte d'Ivoire 2007–11, Deputy Special Rep. and UN Resident Coordinator and Humanitarian Coordinator for the Sudan 2010–11, Deputy Special Rep. of Sec.-Gen., Resident and Humanitarian Coordinator, UN Support Mission in Libya (UNSMIL) 2011–14; Sr Advisor, Crisis Man. Initiative 2014–. *Address:* Eteläranta 12, 2nd floor, 00130 Helsinki, Finland (office). *Telephone:* (9) 4242-8110 (office). *E-mail:* cmi.helsinki@cmi.fi (office). *Website:* cmi.fi (office).

CHARPY, Christian; French government official; *Secretary-General, Commission des comptes de la Sécurité sociale;* ed Ecole nat. d'admin; auditor, then public auditor, Cour des Comptes 1986–90, now Conseiller-maître; Counsellor, Embassy in Beijing 1990–92, Deputy Head of Service of Humanitarian Action, Ministry of Foreign Affairs 1992–93; Tech. Advisor to Simone Veil, Minister of Social Affairs, Health and the City 1993–94; Head of Cabinet of Philippe Douste-Blazy, Minister of Health 1994–95; Dir Radio France Internationale 1995–98; Chair. Agence française du sang 1998–2003; Social Advisor to the Prime Minister 2003–05; mem. Conseil d'Orientation pour l'Emploi (Employment Policy Council); Dir-Gen. Agence Nationale Pour l'Emploi 2005–11; Sec.-Gen. Comm. des comptes de la Sécurité sociale 2014–; Pres. World Asscn of Public Employment Service 2006–. *Address:* Commission des comptes de la Sécurité sociale, Ministère des Affaires sociales, de la Santé et des Droits des femmes, 14 avenue Duquesne 75350 Paris 07 SP, France (office). *E-mail:* info@securite-sociale.fr (office). *Website:* www.securite-sociale.fr (office).

CHARTIER, Roger; French historian and academic; *Professor Emeritus, Collège de France;* b. 9 Dec. 1945, Lyon; s. of Georges Chartier and Laurence Fonvielle; m. Anne-Marie Trépier 1967; one s. one d.; ed Ecole Normale Supérieure, St Cloud; Prof., Lycée Louis-Le-Grand, Paris 1969–70; Asst Prof., Univ. Paris I, Panthéon-Sorbonne 1970–75; Assoc. Prof., Ecole des Hautes Etudes en Sciences Sociales 1975–83, Dir of Studies 1984–; Prof., Collège de France 2007, now Prof. Emer.; Visiting Prof., Univ. of California, Berkeley 1987, Cornell Univ. 1988, Johns Hopkins Univ. 1992; currently Annenberg Visiting Prof. in History, Univ. of Pennsylvania, USA; Corresp. FBA; Dr hc (Universidad Carlos III, Madrid); Annual Award, American Printing History Asscn 1990, Grand Prix d'histoire, Acad. française 1992. *Publications include:* L'Education en France du XVIe au XVIIIe siècle (co-author) 1976, La Nouvelle Histoire (co-ed.) 1978, Histoire de l'Edition Française (ed.) 1982–86, Figures de la gueuserie 1982, Représentation et vouloir politique: Autour des Etats Généraux de 1614 (co-author) 1982, Figure della furfanteria, Marginalità e cultura popolare in Francia tra Cinque e Seicento 1984, Pratiques de la lecture (ed.) 1985, The Cultural Uses of Print in Early Modern France 1987, The Culture of Print (ed.) 1987, Cultural History: Between Practices and Representations 1988, The Cultural Origins of the French Revolution 1991, Correspondence: Models of Letter Writing from the Middle Ages to the Nineteenth Century 1991, The Order of Books 1994, Forms and Meanings: Texts, Performances, and Audiences from Codex to Computer 1995, A History of Reading in the West 1995, Culture écrite et société. L'ordre des livres 1996, On the Edge of the Cliff: History, Language, and Practices 1998, Publishing Drama in Early Modern Europe: The Panizzi Lectures 1998, Le Jeu de la règles 2000, Identités d'auteur dans l'Antiquité et la tradition européenne (co-ed.) 2004, Inscrire et effacer: Culture écrite et littérature 2005, Cardenio between Cervantes and Shakespeare: The Story of a Lost Play 2013, The Sociologist and the Historian (co-author) 2015. *Address:* Ecole des Hautes Etudes en Sciences Sociales, 54 boulevard Raspail, 75006 Paris (office); Collège de France, 11, Place Marcelin Berthelot, 75231 Paris, France (office); College Hall 206D, Department of History, University of Pennsylvania, Pennsylvania, PA 19104-6379, USA. *Telephone:* 1-44-27-12-11 (Paris) (office); 1-49-54-25-25 (Paris) (office); (215) 898-2747 (Pennsylvania) (office). *E-mail:* chartier@history.upenn.edu (office); webmestre@ehess.fr (office). *Website:* www.ehess.fr (office); www.history.upenn.edu/people/faculty/roger-chartier (office).

CHARTRES, Baron (Life Peer), cr. 2017, of Wilton in the County of Wiltshire; **Rt Rev. and Rt Hon. The Lord Chartres Richard John Carew Chartres,** KCVO, PC, DD, DLitt, FSA; British ecclesiastic (retd); b. 11 July 1947, Ware, Herts.; s. of Richard Chartres and Charlotte Chartres; m. Caroline Mary McLintock 1982; two s. two d.; ed Hertford Grammar School, Trinity Coll. Cambridge, Cuddesdon Theological Coll. Oxford and Lincoln Theological Coll.; ordained deacon 1973, priest 1974; Asst Curate, St Andrew's, Bedford 1973–75; Domestic Chaplain to Bishop of St Albans 1975–80; Chaplain to Archbishop of Canterbury 1980–84; Vicar, St Stephen with St John, Westminster 1984–92; Dir of Ordinands for London Area 1985–92; Gresham Prof. of Divinity 1986–92; Bishop of Stepney 1992–95, of London 1996–2017; Dean of the Chapels Royal 1995–; Ecclesiastical Patron Prayer Book Soc.; Prelate of Imperial Soc. of Kts Bachelor; Prelate of OBE 1995–; Chair. Churches Main Cttee 1998–2001, Church Bldgs Div.; Hon. Bencher, Middle Temple; Liveryman, Merchant Taylors' Co.; Hon. Freeman, Weavers' Co. 1998, Leathersellers' Co. 1999, Woolmen's Co. 2000, Vintners' Co. 2001, Drapers' Co.; Commdr of the Order of St John; Hon. DLitt (London Guildhall) 1998, Hon. DD (London) 1999, (City) 1999, (Brunel) 1999, (Surrey) 1999, (King's Coll. London) 2010. *Publications:* The History of Gresham College 1597–1997 1998, Tree of Knowledge Tree of Life 2005. *Address:* The Old Deanery, Dean's Court, London, EC4V 5AA, England (home). *Telephone:* (20) 7248-6233 (home). *Fax:* (20) 7248-9721 (home). *E-mail:* communications@london.anglican.org (office). *Website:* www.london.anglican.org (office).

CHASE, Chevy (Cornelius Crane), MA; American comedian, actor and writer; b. 8 Oct. 1943, New York, NY; s. of Edward Tinsley Chase and Cathalene Crane Chase (née Widdoes); m. 1st Jacqueline Carlin 1976 (divorced 1980); m. 2nd Jayni Chase; three d.; ed Bard Coll., Inst. of Audio Research, Massachusetts Inst. of Tech.; writer and actor, Channel One (satirical revue), The Great American Dream Machine, co-writer and actor, Lemmings (Nat. Lampoon satirical musical), writer and performer Nat. Lampoon Radio Hour, Saturday Night Live (TV series); writer

Mad magazine 1969; mem. American Fed. of Musicians, Stage Actors Guild, Actors Equity, American Fed. of TV and Radio Artists; three Emmy Awards, Writers Guild of America Award, Man of the Year, Harvard Univ. Theatrical Group 1992. *Films include:* The Groove Tube 1974, Tunnelvision 1976, Foul Play 1978, Oh Heavenly Dog 1980, Caddyshack 1980, Seems Like Old Times 1980, Under the Rainbow 1981, Modern Problems 1981, Vacation 1983, Deal of the Century 1983, Fletch 1985, European Vacation 1985, Sesame Street Presents: Follow that Bird 1985, Spies Like Us 1985, ¡Three Amigos! 1986, The Couch Trip 1988, Funny Farm 1988, Caddyshack II 1988, Christmas Vacation 1989, Fletch Lives 1989, National Lampoon's Winter Holiday 1989, Nothing But Trouble 1991, Memoirs of an Invisible Man 1992, Last Action Hero (cameo) 1993, Cops and Robbersons 1994, Man of the House 1995, National Lampoon's Vegas Vacation 1997, Dirty Work 1998, Snow Day 2000, Orange County 2002, Vacuums 2003, Mariti in affitto 2004, Bad Meat 2004, Ellie Parker 2005, Goose on the Loose 2006, Doogal (voice) 2006, Funny Money 2006, Zoom 2006, Stay Cool 2009, Jack and the Beanstalk 2010, 2010, Hot Tub Time Machine 2010, Not Another Not Another Movie 2011, Before I Sleep 2013, Lovesick 2014, Shelby 2014, Hot Tub Time Machine 2 2015, Vacation 2015. *Television includes:* The Great American Dream Machine (series) 1971, Saturday Night Live (series) 1975–2007, It's Garry Shandling's Show (series) 1989, The Larry Sanders Show (series) 1995, The Nanny (series) 1997, America's Most Terrible Things (film) 2002, Freedom: A History of Us (series documentary) 2003, The Karate Dog (film) (voice) 2004, The Secret Policeman's Ball (film) 2006, Law & Order (series) 2006, Brothers & Sisters (series) 2007, Family Guy (series) 2007–09, Hjälp! (series) 2009, Chuck (series) 2009, Community (series) 2009–14.

CHASE, David, MA; American scriptwriter, television director and producer; b. (David DeCesare), 22 Aug. 1945, Mount Vernon, NY; s. of Henry DeCesare and Norma DeCesare; m. Denise Kelly; one d.; ed Wake Forest Univ., School of Visual Arts, New York, Stanford Univ.; produced episodes of Northern Exposure and The Rockford Files, among other series; cr. TV series The Sopranos; Mystery Writers of America Special Edgar Award for his body of work. *Television includes:* Grave of the Vampire (film) 1972, Kolchak: The Night Stalker (series) (writer) 1974–75, The Rockford Files (series) (writer, producer) (Emmy Award 1977) 1976–80, Off the Minnesota Strip (film) (writer, producer) (Emmy Award 1979, Writers Guild of America Award 1980) 1980, Moonlight 1982, Alfred Hitchcock Presents (series) (dir) 1985, Almost Grown (series) (writer, dir) 1988–89, I'll Fly Away (writer, exec. producer) (Norman Felton Award, Producers Guild of America 1993) 1992–93, Northern Exposure (series) (exec. producer) 1993–95, The Rockford Files: A Blessing in Disguise (film) (producer) 1995, The Rockford Files: The Punishment and Crime (writer, producer, dir) 1996, The Sopranos (series) (writer, exec. producer, dir) (Emmy Award for College episode 1998, Golden Globe Award 1999, Norman Felton Award, Producers Guild of America 2000, Outstanding Directorial Achievement Award, Directors Guild of America 1999, Peabody Award 2000, Drama Series of the Year Award, American Film Inst. 2001, Primetime Emmy for Outstanding Writing for a Drama Series & Outstanding Drama Series, Acad. of TV Arts and Sciences 2007) 1999–2007. *Address:* c/o David Harbert, United Talent Agency, 9560 Wilshire Blvd, Suite 500, Beverly Hills, CA 90212-2401, USA (office). *Telephone:* (310) 273-6700 (office). *Fax:* (310) 247-1111 (office). *E-mail:* webmaster@unitedtalent.com (office). *Website:* www.unitedtalent.com (office).

CHASE, Robin M.; American entrepreneur; *Chairman, Veniam Inc.;* m. Roy Russell; three c.; ed Wellesley Coll., Sloan School of Man., Massachusetts Inst. of Tech., Harvard Grad. School of Design (Loeb Fellowship); consultant, JSI (firm working on public health USAID contracts), Boston 1981–91; Co-founder and CEO Zipcar (car-sharing service) 2000–03, Buzzcar (peer-to-peer car-sharing service in France, now merged with Drivy) 2011, GoLoco (online ride-sharing community) 2006–10; Founder and CEO Meadow Networks (transportation consulting firm) 2005–09; Co-founder and Chair. Veniam Inc. 2012–; mem. Bd of Dirs Tucows, World Resources Inst.; fmr mem. Bd of Dirs Mass Dept of Transportation, Nat. Advisory Council for Innovation and Entrepreneurship (US Dept of Commerce) 2010–13, Intelligent Transportations Systems Program Advisory Cttee (US Dept of Transportation) 2008–11, OECD Int. Transport Forum Advisory Bd 2010–13, Mass Gov.'s Transportation Transition Working Group, Boston Mayor's Wireless Task Force 2006; Dr hc (Illinois Inst. of Tech.); numerous honours and awards, including Massachusetts Gov.'s Award for Entrepreneurial Spirit, Start-up Woman of the Year, Business Week's Top 10 Designers, Fast Company's Fast 50 Champions of Innovation, tech. and innovation awards from Fortune, CIO and InfoWorld magazines, and numerous environmental awards from nat., state and local govts and orgs. *Publication:* Peers Inc: How People and Platforms Are Inventing the Collaborative Economy and Reinventing Capitalism 2015. *Address:* Veniam Inc., 331 West Evelyn Avenue, Mountain View, CA 94041, USA (office). *Telephone:* (650) 440-8999 (office). *E-mail:* rchase@alum.mit.edu; info@venaim .com (office). *Website:* veniam.com (office); www.robinchase.org; networkmusings .blogspot.com.

CHASTAIN, Jessica Michelle, BFA; American theatre, film and television actress, model and singer; b. 24 March 1977, Sacramento, Calif.; ed El Camino High School, Sacramento City Coll., Juilliard School; appeared as Juliet in a production of Romeo and Juliet staged by TheatreWorks, San Francisco 1998; Broadway debut playing Catherine Sloper in The Heiress at the Walter Kerr Theatre 2012. *Films include:* Jolene (Best Actress, Seattle Int. Film Festival) 2008, Stolen Lives 2009, The Westerner (short) (also producer) 2010, The Debt 2010, Take Shelter (Best Supporting Actress, Austin Film Critics Asscn) 2011, Coriolanus 2011, The Tree of Life (Best Supporting Actress, Satellite Awards, amongst others) 2011, The Help (Breakthrough Actress and Ensemble of the Year Award, Hollywood Film Festival, Spotlight Award, Palm Springs Int. Film Festival, Best Ensemble – Motion Picture, Satellite Awards, Outstanding Cast, Screen Actors Guild Awards, amongst others) 2011, Wilde Salome 2011, Texas Killing Fields 2011, Madagascar 3: Europe's Most Wanted (voice) 2012, Lawless 2012, Tar 2012, Zero Dark Thirty (Best Actress – Motion Picture, Drama, Golden Globe Awards, Best Actress in a Movie, Critics' Choice Movie Awards, Best Actress, Boston Online Film Critics Asscn, Best Actress, Broadcast Film Critics Asscn (Critics Choice Awards), Best Actress, Chicago Film Critics Asscn, Best Actress, Nat. Bd of Review, Best Actress, Washington DC Area Film Critics Asscn, amongst many others) 2012, Mama (Best Actress, Fantasporto) 2013, The Disappearance of Eleanor Rigby: His 2013, The Disappearance of Eleanor Rigby: Hers 2013, Miss Julie 2014. *Television includes:* Dark Shadows (movie) 2005, Law & Order: Trial by Jury (series) 2005–06, Close to Home (series) 2006, The Evidence (series) 2006, Pirates: The True Story of Blackbeard (movie) 2006, Journeyman (series) 2007, Agatha Christie: Poirot (series) – Murder on the Orient Express 2010. *Address:* c/o Mosaic Media Group, 9200 West Sunset Blvd, 10th Floor, Los Angeles, CA 90069, USA (office).

CHASTANET, Allen Michael, BA, MA; Saint Lucia business executive and politician; *Prime Minister;* s. of Michael Chastanet; m. Raquel DuBoulay-Chastanet; two c.; ed Bishop's Univ., Quebec, Canada, American Univ., USA; Vice-Pres. of Marketing and Sales, Windjammer Landing Villa Beach Resort 1990–91; Dir, St Lucia Tourist Bd 1991–93; Dir of Sales and Marketing, Island Outpost, Miami Fla 1994–96; Vice-Pres. of Marketing and Sales, Air Jamaica 1996–2003; Man. Dir, Coco Resorts 2003–06, Chair. 2012–; mem. Senate (upper house of parl.) 2006–11; Minister of Tourism and Civil Aviation 2006–11; mem. House of Ass. (lower house of parl.) for Micoud South constituency 2016–; Prime Minister 2016–; Pres., St Lucia Hotel Asscn 2005–06; First Vice-Pres., Caribbean Hotel Asscn 2005–06; Chair., Caribbean Tourism Org. 2006–08; mem. United Workers Party, Leader 2013–. *Address:* Office of the Prime Minister, Greaham Louisy Administrative Bldg, 5th Floor, Waterfront, Castries LC04 301, Saint Lucia (office). *Telephone:* 468-2111 (office). *Fax:* 453-7352 (office). *Website:* opm.govt.lc (office).

CHATEL, Luc Marie; French politician; *Secretary-General, Union pour un Mouvement Populaire;* b. 15 Aug. 1964, Bethesda, Md, USA; m. Astrid Herrenschmidt (died 2012); Municipal Councillor, Bayard-sur-Marne (Haute-Marne) 1993–95, Chaumont (Haute-Marne) 1996–2001; mem. Regional Council, Champagne-Ardenne 1998–2008, Vice-Pres. 1998–2004; mem. Assemblée nationale (Parl.) for Haute-Marne 2002–10, 2012–; Mayor of Chaumont 2008–13; Sec. of State for Consumer Affairs and Tourism 2007–08, for Industry and Consumer Affairs 2008–09, also Govt Spokesman 2009–10, Minister of Nat. Educ. 2009–10, of Nat. Educ., Youth and Voluntary Orgs 2010–12; mem. Union pour un Mouvement Populaire (UMP), Nat. Sec. 2002–05, Departmental Sec. 2002–07, Spokesman 2002–07, Deputy Vice-Pres. 2012–14, Sec.-Gen. 2014–; Commdr des Palmes académiques 2012; Grand Cross of the Order of Merit of FRG 2012. *Address:* Union pour un Mouvement Populaire (UMP), 238 rue de Vaugirard, 75015 Paris, France (office). *Telephone:* 1-40-76-60-00 (office). *E-mail:* webmaster@u-m-p.org (office). *Website:* www.u-m-p.org (office).

CHATER, Keith Frederick, PhD, FRS; British geneticist and academic; *Emeritus Fellow, Department of Molecular Microbiology, The John Innes Centre;* b. 23 April 1944, Croydon, Surrey; s. of Frederick Ernest Chater and Marjorie Inez Chater (née Palmer); m. Jean Wallbridge 1966; three s. one d.; ed Trinity School of John Whitgift, Croydon, Univ. of Birmingham; scientist, The John Innes Centre, Norwich 1969–, Deputy Head, Dept of Genetics 1989–98, Head 1998–2001, Head, Dept of Molecular Microbiology 2001–04, Emer. Fellow 2004–; Hon. Prof., Univ. of East Anglia 1988–, Chinese Acad. of Sciences Inst. of Microbiology, Beijing 1998–, Huazhong Agricultural Univ., Wuhan 2000–, Newcastle Univ. 2006–09, Fred Griffith Review Lecturer, Soc. for Gen. Microbiology 1997, Leeuwenhoek Lecturer, Royal Soc. 2005. *Publications include:* Genetic Manipulation of Streptomyces (co-ed) 1985, Genetics of Bacterial Diversity (co-ed) 1989, Practical Streptomyces Genetics (co-author) 2000. *Leisure interests:* art, bird-watching, gardening, cooking. *Address:* Department of Molecular Microbiology, The John Innes Centre, Norwich Research Park, Colney, Norwich, NR4 7UH (office); 6 Coach House Court, Norwich, NR4 7QR, England (home). *Telephone:* (1603) 450297 (office); (1603) 506145 (home). *Fax:* (1603) 450045 (home). *E-mail:* keith.chater@nbi.ac.uk (office); keithchater@yahoo.com. *Website:* www.nbi.ac.uk/staff/keith-chater (home).

CHATIKAVANIJ, Korn, BA (Hons), MA; Thai politician; *Deputy Leader, Democrat Party;* b. 19 Feb. 1964; m. Vorakorn Chatikavanij; ed Satit Srinakarinwirot Demonstration School, Old Malthouse School, Winchester Coll. and St John's Coll., Oxford, UK; worked for S.G. Warburg & Co., London 1985–88; Co-founder and Pres. JF Thanakom Securities Ltd 1988–99; Pres. JPMorgan (Thailand) Ltd (following takeover of JF Thanakom Securities Ltd) 2000–04; mem. Sapha Poothaen Rassadorn (House of Reps) for Bangkok 2005–06, 2007–10; Minister of Finance 2008–11; mem. Democrat Party, currently Deputy Leader and Shadow Deputy Prime Minister; Kt Grand Cordon (Special Class), Most Exalted Order of the White Elephant; The Banker Global Finance Minister of the Year 2010, Asia-Pacific Finance Minister of the Year 2010. *Address:* Democrat Party, 67 Thanon Setsiri, Samsen Nai, Phaya Thai, Bangkok 10400, Thailand (office). *Telephone:* 678-9777 (office). *Fax:* 678-9757 (office). *E-mail:* korn@democrat.or.th (office). *Website:* www.facebook.com/KornChatikavanijDP.

CHATT, Amares, BSc, MSc, MSc, PhD; Canadian (b. Indian) nuclear chemist and academic; *Adjunct Professor, Department of Chemistry, Dalhousie University;* b. (Amares Chattopadhyay), S India; ed Univ. of Calcutta, Indian Inst. of Tech., Roorkee, Univ. of Waterloo, Univ. of Toronto; joined Dept of Chem., Univ. of Dalhousie, Halifax, Nova Scotia *c.* 1975, becoming Prof., also Dir Dalhousie Slowpoke-2 Nuclear Research Reactor, Faculty of Science Killam Prof. in Chem. 2001–06, now Adjunct Prof.; fmr Adviser, IAEA, Vienna; Pres. Int. Cttee for Activation Analysis 1999–; Fellow, Chemical Inst. of Canada 1985, American Nuclear Soc. 1993; Francis W. Karasek Award 1993, Radiation Science and Tech. Award 1996, William D. Ehmann Award 1999, American Nuclear Soc., George Hevesy Medal 2001. *Publications include:* Hair Analysis: Applications in the Biomedical and Environmental Sciences (co-author) 1988. *Address:* Department of Chemistry, Dalhousie University, Halifax, NS B3H 4J3, Canada (office). *Telephone:* (902) 494-2474 (office). *Fax:* (902) 494-1310 (office). *E-mail:* a.chatt@dal.ca (office). *Website:* chemistry.dal.ca (office); myweb.dal.ca/chatt (office).

CHATTERJEE, Soumitra, (Soumitra Chattopadhyay), MA; Indian actor; b. 19 Jan. 1935, Krishnanagar Dist, West Bengal; s. of Mohitkumar Chatterjee; m. Dipa Chatterjee; one s. one d.; ed Univ. of Calcutta; worked at AIR before pursuing film career; Chair. Kolkata Film Festival Cttee 2007; Padma Bhushan 2004, Banglalive Legendary Award, Dadasaheb Phalke Award 2012. *Films include:* Apur Sansar (The World of Apu) 1959, Kshudista Pashan (Hungry Stones) 1960, Devi (The Goddess) 1960, Teen Kanya 1961, Punasha (Over Again) 1961, Atal Jaler Ahwan (1962), Abhijaan (The Expedition) 1962, Saat Pake Bandha 1963, Charulata (The Lonely Wife) 1964, Kapurush (The Coward) 1965, Kanch Kata Hirey 1965, Ek Tuku Basa 1965, Akash Kusum (Up in the Clouds) 1965, Prastar Swakshar 1967,

Mahashweta 1967, Baghini 1968, Teen Bhuboner Porey 1969, Parineeta (The Fiancee) 1969, Aparachita 1969, Aranyer Din Ratri (Days and Nights in the Forest, USA) 1970, Malyadaan 1971, KhunjeyBerai 1971, Stree 1972, Ashani Sanket (Distant Thunder, USA) 1973, Basanata Bilap 1973, Jadi Jantem 1974, Sonar Kella (The Golden Fortress, USA) 1974, Sangini 1974, Asati 1974, Sansar Seemantey 1975, Datta 1976, Joi Baba Felunath (The Elephant God) 1978, Ganadevata 1979, Naukadubi 1979, Debdas 1979, Heerak Rajar Deshe (The Kingdom of Diamonds) (TV) 1980, Khelar Putul 1981, Amar Geeti 1983, Ghare-Baire (The Home and the World) 1984, Kony 1984, Shyam Saheb 1986, Ekti Jiban (Portrait of a Life) 1987, La Nuit Bengali (Bengali Night) 1988, Ganashatru (An Enemy of the People, UK) 1989, Shakha Proshakha (The Branches of the Tree) 1990, Mahaprithivi (World Within, World Without) 1992, Wheel Chair 1994, Uttoran (The Broken Journey) 1994, Sopan 1994, Vrindavan Film Studios 1996, Gaach (The Tree) (as himself) 1998, Asukh (Malaise) 1999, Paromitar Ek Din 2000, Dekha 2001, Saanjhbatir Roopkathara (Strokes and Silhouettes) 2002, Abar Aranye (In the Forest Again) 2003, Patalghar 2003, Nil Sanket (Tryst of Blue) 2004, Schatten der Zeit 2004, Faltu 2005, Nishijapon 2005, 15 Park Avenue 2005, The Bong Connection 2006, Podokkhep (Rajat Kamal Nat. Film Award for Best Actor 2007) 2007, Minister Fatakesto 2007, Krishnakanter Will 2007, Jara Brishtite Bhijechhilo 2007, Chaader Baari 2007, Ballygunge Court 2007, 10:10 2008, Angshumaner Chhobi 2009, Sugar Baby 2009, Bodhisattva 2010, Nobel Chor 2012, The Nowhere Son 2012, Astra 2012, Life in Park Street 2012, Maach Mishti & More 2013, Shunyo Awnko 2013, Alik Sukh 2013, Rupkatha Noy (Filmfare Awards East for Best Male Actor (Critics) 2014) 2013, Nirbhoya 2013, Doorbeen 2014, Room No. 103 2015, Belaseshe 2015. *Publications:* fmrly co-ed. Ekshan (monthly journal); wrote several poems and plays. *Leisure interest:* reciting poetry.

CHAU, Solina, BA; Hong Kong business executive; *Director, Li Ka Shing Foundation;* b. (Solina Chau Hoi Shuen), 1961, Hong Kong; ed Diocesan Girls' School, Hong Kong, Univ. of New South Wales, Australia; co-f., with Li Ka-shing, Tom Group (Beijing digital media co.) 1997; business partner in Cheung Kong Group; Dir Li Ka Shing Foundation, makes investments through its business unit, provides grants for medical research and disaster relief in countries world-wide; co-f. Horizon Ventures; launched own foundation to focus on educ. and women's initiatives 1996. *Address:* Li Ka Shing Foundation, 7/F Cheung Kong Centre, 2 Queen's Road, Central, Hong Kong Special Administrative Region, People's Republic of China (office). *E-mail:* general@lksf.org (office). *Website:* www.lksf.org (office).

CHAUDHRY, Amir Husain; Pakistani lawyer and politician; b. 22 June 1942, Sialkot, British Raj (now Pakistan); ed Univ. of the Punjab; mem. Nat. Ass. 1985–2008, Speaker 2002–08; mem. Council, Azad Jammu and Kashmir Council 1985–90; Vice-Pres. Muslim Conf., Azad Jammu 1985–90; mem. Pakistan Muslim League –1985, Pakistan Muslim League—Functional 1985–88, Pakistan Muslim League—Nawaz 1988–2002, Pakistan Muslim League—Quaid e Azam Group 2002–. *Address:* c/o Pakistan Muslim League—Quaid e Azam Group, PML House, 4 Margalla Road, F-7/3, Islamabad, Pakistan. *Telephone:* (51) 9102469. *Fax:* (51) 2611061. *E-mail:* sqazi@pml.org.pk. *Website:* pml.org.pk.

CHAUDHRY, Asif J., PhD; American diplomatist (retd) and university administrator; *Vice-President for International Programs, Washington State University;* b. Nindowal, Pakistan; m. Charla Chaudhry; two s. one d.; ed Univ. of Punjab, Pakistan, American Univ. of Beirut, Lebanon, Washington State Univ.; early position as Asst Prof. of Econs, Montana State Univ.; Agriculture Attaché, Embassy in Warsaw 1992–95, Counselor, Agricultural Affairs, Embassy in Moscow 1996–99, Asst to Gen. Sales Man., Foreign Agricultural Service 1999–2002, Prin. Advisor, Dept of Agric. Commodity Assistance, Minister Counselor, Agricultural Affairs, Embassy in Cairo 2002–06, fmr Deputy Admin., Office of Global Analysis, Foreign Agricultural Service, Amb. to Moldova 2008–11, Foreign Policy Advisor to Chief of Naval Operations, Pentagon 2011–15 (retd); Vice-Pres. for Int. Programs, Washington State Univ. 2015–; three certificates of merit and three administrator's special awards from US Dept of Agric., US Presidential Award for Meritorious Service for foreign policy 2006, Washington State Univ. Alumni Asscn Alumni Achievement Award 2015. *Leisure interest:* playing squash. *Address:* Office of International Programs, Washington State University, Kruegel Hall, PO Box 643251, Pullman, WA 99164-3251, USA (office). *Website:* ip.wsu.edu (office).

CHAUDHRY, Iftikhar Mohammad, BA, LLB; Pakistani lawyer, politician and fmr judge; *President, Pakistan Justice Democratic Critic Party;* b. 12 Dec. 1948, Quetta; s. of Jan Muhammad Chaudhry; called to Bar 1974; enrolled as Advocate of the High Court 1976, Advocate of the Supreme Court 1985; Advocate Gen., Balochistan 1989–90; Additional Judge, Balochistan High Court 1990–99, also served as Banking Judge, Judge of Special Court for Speedy Trials, Judge of Customs Appellate Courts and Company Judge; Chief Justice, High Court of Balochistan 1999–2000; elevated to Supreme Court 2000, Chief Justice of Pakistan 2005–07, reinstated July–Nov. 2007 (suspended for refusing to ratify Pres. Musharraf's emergency rule), reinstated March 2009–13 (retd); Founder and Pres. Pakistan Justice Democratic Critic Party 2015–; fmr Pres. High Court Bar Asscn, Quetta; fmr Chair. Balochistan Local Council Election Authority, Prov. Review Bd for Balochistan, Enrolment Cttee of Pakistan Bar Council, Supreme Court Bldg Cttee; fmr Chair. Pakistan Red Crescent Soc., Balochistan; mem. Bar Council; Hon. mem. Asscn New York City Bar 2008; Hon. LLD (Nova Southeastern Univ.) 2009; Lawyer of the Year, National Law Journal, USA 2007, Medal of Freedom, Harvard Law School 2008, Lifetime Achievement Award, Karachi Tax Bar Asscn 2012, Hero to Animals Award, PETA, India, Int. Jurists Award, Int. Jurists Council 2012, Lifetime Achievement Award, Sindh High Court Bar Asscn 2012. *Address:* Pakistan Justice Democratic Critic Party, Office 17, First Floor, Rose I Plaza, I-8 Center, Islamabad (office); 54-B Zarghon Road, Quetta, Pakistan (home). *Telephone:* (51) 4862363 (office). *Website:* www.pjdp.org.pk (office).

CHAUDHRY, Mahendra Pal; Fijian politician and trade unionist; *Secretary General (Leader), Fiji Labour Party;* b. 2 Sept. 1942, Ba; s. of Ram Gopal Chaudhry and Devi Chaudhry (née Nair); two s. one d.; Sr Auditor, Office of the Auditor Gen. 1960–75; Gen. Sec. Fiji Public Service Asscn 1970–99; Gen. Sec. Nat. Farmers' Union 1978–; Nat. Sec. Fiji Trades Union Congress 1988–92; Minister of Finance April–May 1987 (ousted in May 1987 coup), Founding mem. Fiji Labour Party 1985, Parl. Leader 1992, Sec.-Gen. (Leader) 1994–; Prime Minister and Minister of Finance, Public Enterprise, Sugar Industry and Information 1999–2000; ousted in coup May 2000; re-assumed post of Prime Minister 1 March 2001, dismissed 14 March 2001 by Pres. of Fiji; Leader of the Opposition 2004–; Minister of Finance, Nat. Planning, Public Enterprise and Sugar Reform (in Cdre Josaia Bainimarama's interim govt) Jan. 2007–08 (resgnd); Bharatiya Samman Award, Govt of India 2004. *Leisure interests:* reading, music, gardening, social work. *Address:* Fiji Labour Party, PO Box 2162, Suva (office); 30 Varani Street, Suva (office); 3 Hutson Street, Suva, Fiji (home). *Telephone:* 3373317 (office); 3301865 (home). *Fax:* 3373173 (office). *E-mail:* flp@connect.com.fj (office); mahendrachaudhry42@hotmail.com (home). *Website:* www.flp.org.fj (office).

CHAUDHRY, Muhammad Ejaz, MA; Pakistani civil servant and business executive; b. 8 Oct. 1955; ed Govt Coll., Admin. Staff Coll., Lahore, George Washington Univ., Harvard Univ., USA, Univ. of Dundee, UK, Civil Service Coll., Singapore, Nat. Defence Univ., Islamabad; joined civil service in Dist Man. Group 1980; served in Public Admin in Sindh and Punjab Provinces and Fed. Govt; Asst Commr Larkana, Jakobabad and Liaquatabad 1981–86; Deputy Commr Thatta 1988–89, Karachi Cen. 1989–90, Nawabshah 1990–93; Additional Sec., Home 1994–96; Labour 1996–98, Registrar Cooperatives Punjab 1998–2002; Dist Coordination Officer, Multan 2003–05; Jt Sec., Ministry of Educ. 2005–06; Dir-Gen. Nat. Inst. of Public Admin, Lahore 2007–08; Additional Sec., Ministry of Petroleum and Natural Resources 2008–10, fmr Fed. Sec.; Fed. Sec., Ministry of Privatisation 2010–11; Chair. Oil and Gas Devt Co. Ltd 2011–13; Chair. Bd Inter State Gas System, Govt Holding Pvt. Ltd, Saindak Metals Ltd; mem. Bd of Dirs Hydrocarbon Devt Inst. of Pakistan, Pakistan Gems and Jewellery Devt Corpn, Mari Gas Co. Ltd; mem. Pvt. Power Infrastructure Bd, Alternate Energy Devt Bd. *Address:* c/o Ministry of Petroleum and Natural Resources, 3rd Floor, Block A, Pakistan Secretariat, Islamabad, Pakistan (office).

CHAUDHRY, Air Vice-Marshal Shahzad Aslam, MSc; Pakistani air force officer (retd) and diplomatist; m.; five c.; ed Air Command and Staff Coll., USA, Nat. Defence Coll., Islamabad; served in various command/staff and instructional roles during air force career, including Officer Commdg F-16 Squadron 1987–89, Officer Commdg F-16 Wing 1996–97, Base Commdr, Pakistan Air Force Base, Rafiqui 2000–02, Air Officer Commdg Southern Air Command 2003, Deputy Chief of Air Staff (Operations), Pakistan Air Force 2003–06; Air Attaché, Pakistan High Comm., London 1992–96; High Commr to Sri Lanka 2006–10; mem. UN Asscn of Sri Lanka; Hilal-e-Imtiaz (Mil.), Sitara-e-Imtiaz (Mil.), Tamgha-e-Basalat, Professional Efficiency Badge.

CHAUDHURI, Pratip, MSc; Indian fmr banking executive; b. 1954; m.; one s. one d.; ed Univ. of Rajasthan; joined State Bank of India as Probationary Officer 1974, has served in several positions, credited with merger of State Bank of Saurashtra 2008, fmr Group Exec. of Int. Banking and Deputy Man. Dir, later Man. Dir Int. Banking, State Bank of India –2011, Chief Gen. Man. Chennai, State Bank of India –2011, Chair. State Bank of India (and subsidiaries) 2011–13 (retd); apptd Man. Dir State Bank of Saurashtra 2007; Hon. Sec., Indian Banks Asscn.

CHAUDHURY, Shirin Sharmin, LLB (Hons), LLM, PhD; Bangladeshi lawyer and politician; *Speaker of the Jatiyo Sangshad (Parliament);* b. 6 Oct. 1966, Dhaka; d. of Rafiqullah Chaudhury and Naiyar Sultana; m. Syed Ishtiaque Hossain; one s. one d.; ed Univ. of Dhaka, Univ. of Essex, UK; Advocate, Bangladesh Bar Council 1992–94; Advocate, High Court Div., Bangladesh Supreme Court 1994–2008, Appellate Div., Bangladesh Supreme Court 2008–09; mem. of lawyers' panel that conducted cases filed against Sheikh Hasina during the army-backed caretaker govt 2007–08; mem. Bangladesh Awami League, Int. Affairs Sec. –2013; mem. Jatiyo Sangshad (Parl.) 2009–, Speaker (first woman) 2013–; State Minister, Ministry of Women and Children Affairs 2009–13; Chair., CPA 2014–17; mem. Dhaka Bar Asscn, Supreme Court Bar Asscn; Dr hc (Univ. of Essex) 2014; Best Student of the Year Award, Holy Cross Girl Award 1982, Humanitarian Service Award for Leadership Role in Prevention of Violence against Women, Asia Soc. 2010, Women Leadership Achievement Award 2015. *Publications include:* Ed., Bangladesh Legal Decisions Law Report Series (monthly) 2003–08; numerous articles in professional journals. *Leisure interest:* listening to music. *Address:* Speaker's Chamber, Room No. 521, Level-5, West Block, Sangsad Bhaban, Bangladesh Parliament, Shere-Bangla-Nagar, Dhaka, Bangladesh (office). *Telephone:* (2) 9111999 (Bangladesh) (office). *Fax:* (2) 9122254 (Bangladesh) (office). *E-mail:* speaker@parliament.gov.bd (office).

CHAUSSADE, Jean-Louis, MEcon; French business executive; *CEO, Suez;* b. 2 Dec. 1951; ed Ecole Spéciale des Travaux Publics, Univ. of the Sorbonne, Paris, Institut d'Etudes Politiques de Paris, Advanced Man. Program at Harvard Business School, USA; joined Degrémont 1978, apptd COO Degrémont Spain, Bilbao 1989, Dir Aguas de Barcelona, apptd CEO Dumez Copisa Spain 1992, COO Lyonnaise des Eaux in S America and COO Suez for S America 1997–2000, Chair. and CEO Degrémont 2000–04, Deputy CEO Suez 2004, CEO Suez Environnement (renamed Suez 2015) 2008–; Chair. Lyonnaise des Eaux (France), SITA France; Pres. Supervisory Bd, Institut de Prospective Economique du Monde Méditerranéen 2011–; mem. Bd of Dirs Criteria Caixa Holding SAU 2011–; Co-Chair. France–China Cttee; Chair. MEDEF (employers' Fed.) France–Arabian Peninsula Council of Businessmen. *Address:* Suez, Tour CB21 16, place de l'Iris, 92040 Paris La Défense Cedex, France (office). *Telephone:* 1-58-18-20-00 (office). *Fax:* 1-58-18-25-00 (office). *E-mail:* suez.media@suez-env.com (office). *Website:* www.suez-environnement.com (office).

CHAUTALA, Om Prakash; Indian politician; *Leader, Indian National Lok Dal;* b. 1 Jan. 1935, Sirsa Dist, Haryana; s. of Chaudhari Devi Lal; m. Sneh Lata; two s. three d.; Chief Minister of Haryana 1989, 1990, 1999, 2000–05; Pres. Haryana Unit, Indian Nat. Lok Dal 1999; Pres. Haryana State Janata Dal; Nat. Gen. Sec. Samajwadi Janata Party; currently Leader, Indian Nat. Lok Dal party (later United Nat. Progressive Alliance, after merger with other regional parties), Leader of Opposition, Haryana Vidhan Sabha; found guilty of illegally recruiting more than 3,000 unqualified teachers and sentenced by New Delhi court to ten years imprisonment Jan. 2013, sentence upheld by Delhi High Court and the Supreme Court; Hon. Citizen of Texas, USA. *Address:* c/o Indian National Lok Dal, 18 Janpath, New Delhi 110 001 (office); Chautala House, Barnala Road, Sirsa, Haryana, India (home). *Telephone:* (11) 23782650 (office); (98121) 36777 (home);

(172) 2704977 (home). *E-mail:* inldchandigarh@gmail.com (office). *Website:* www.inld.org (office).

CHAVALIT, Gen. Yongchaiyudh; Thai politician and army officer (retd); b. 15 May 1932, Bangkok; m. Khunying Phankrua Yongchaiyudh; ed Chulachomklao Royal Mil. Acad., Army Command and Gen. Staff Coll., Fort Leavenworth, Kan., USA; Dir of Operations 1981, Chief of Staff 1985, C-in-C 1986–90, Acting Supreme Commdr 1987–90; Deputy Prime Minister and Minister of Defence 30 March–21 June 1990; Opposition Leader May–Sept. 1992; Minister of Interior 1992–94, of Labour and Social Welfare 1993–94; Deputy Prime Minister July–Oct 1994, Deputy Prime Minister and Minister of Defence 1995–96, 2001–02, 2008 (resgnd); Prime Minister and Minister of Defence 1996–97 (resgnd); Deputy Prime Minister 2008 (resgnd); fmr Leader New Aspiration Party (now Muan Chon party); mem. Pheu Thai Party 2009–; Kt Grand Cordon (Special Class) of the Most Exalted Order of the White Elephant; Kt Grand Cordon (Special Class) of The Most Noble Order of the Crown of Thailand; Kt Grand Cross (First Class) of the Most Admirable Order of the Direkgunabhorn; Kt Grand Commdr (Second Class, Higher Grade) of the Most Illustrious Order of Chula Chom Klao; Kt Commdr (Second Class) of the Hon. Order of Rama; The Order of Symbolic Propitiousness Ramkeerati (Special Class) – Boy Scout Citation Medal; The Victory Medal – Vietnam War; The Freeman Safeguarding Medal (First Class); The Border Service Medal; Chakra Mala Medal; King Rama IX Royal Cypher Medal, 4th Class. *Address:* c/o Muan Chon, 630/182 Thanon Prapinklao, Bangkok 10700, Thailand. *Website:* www.ptp.or.th.

CHAVAN, Ashok Shankarrao, MBA; Indian politician; b. 28 Oct. 1958, Bombay (now Mumbai); s. of Shankarrao B. Chavan and Kusumtai Chavan; m. Ameeta Ashok Chavan; two d.; MP (Indian Nat. Congress) for Nanded constituency 1987–; MLC from Maharashtra Legis. Ass. Constituency 1992–, Minister of State for Public Works, Urban Devt and Home 1993, Minister for Transport, Ports, Cultural Affairs and Protocol 2003; Minister of Revenue, Maharashtra Region 1999–2004, also Minister of Cultural Affairs 2004–10, of Industries 2004–10, of Mines 2004–10, of Protocol 2004–10, Chief Minister 2008–10 (resgnd); Gen. Sec. Maharashtra Pradesh Youth Congress Cttee 1986–89, Maharashtra Pradesh Congress Cttee 1995–99; mem. Consultative Cttee, Ministry of Environment and Forests, Ministry of Personnel, Public Grievances and Pensions; Chair. Sanjay Gandhi Niradhar Yojna 1985; mem. Divisional Rail Users Advisory Cttee S-Cen. Railways 1987–89; mem. Advisory Panel, Cen. Film Censor Bd 1991–92; Pres. Sai Sevabhavi Trust, Nanded. *Leisure interests:* table tennis, reading, travelling. *Address:* Shivaji Nagar, Nanded 431 602, India. *Telephone:* (24) 62234081. *Fax:* (24) 62237732.

CHAVAN, Prithviraj, BE, MS; Indian politician; b. 17 March 1946, Indore, Madhya Pradesh; s. of D. R. Chavan; m. Satvasheela Chavan; one s. one d.; ed Birla Inst. of Tech. and Science, Pilani, Univ. of California, Berkeley, USA; began career in the field of aircraft instrumentation and anti-submarine warfare in USA; returned to India 1974; elected to 10th Lok Sabha (lower house of Parl.) for Karad Dist 1991, becoming Sec., Congress Party in Parl.; entered Rajya Sabha (upper house of Parl.) 2002; Minister of State in Prime Minister's Office 2004; Minister of State (Additional charge), Ministry of Personnel, Public Grievances and Pensions 2008–09, Minister of State 2009; Minister of State (Ind. Charge), Ministry of Science and Tech. 2009; Minister of State (Ind. Charge), Ministry of Earth Sciences 2009; Minister of State, Ministry of Parl. Affairs 2009; Chief Minister of Maharashtra 2010–14 (resgnd); mem. Maharashtra Legis. Ass. for Karad South 2014–; Visiting Prof., Birla Inst. of Tech. and Science, Pilani; Founding mem. Indo-US Parl. Forum; mem. Indian Nat. Congress party; Jt Sec., Constitution Club, New Delhi; mem. Atomic Energy Comm., Space Comm., Council of Indian Inst. of Tech.; mem. Consultative Cttee, Ministry of Finance 1996–97, Prime Minister's Cttee on Infrastructure, Energy Coordination Cttee, Trade and Econ. Relations Cttee, Cttee on Trade and Industry; mem. Prime Ministerial delegation to USA 2005. *Leisure interests:* cricket, reading, photography. *Address:* Patan Colony, Shaniwar Peth, Karad 415 410, India (home). *Telephone:* (2164) 220222 (home). *Website:* maharashtralegislature.org.in (office).

CHAVANAVIRAJ, Saroj, BA, MA; Thai government official and diplomatist; b. 11 May 1942; ed Univ. of California, Los Angeles, USA, Nat. Defence Coll. of Thailand; joined Ministry of Foreign Affairs 1967, Third Sec., Protocol Div. 1967–69, Asst Sec. to Minister, Office of Sec. to the Minister 1969–72; Second Sec., Perm. Mission to UN, New York 1972–76; Chief of East Asian Div., Political Dept, Ministry of Foreign Affairs 1976–77, Asst Sec. to the Minister, Office of the Sec. to the Minister 1977–79, Deputy Dir Gen. Dept of Political Affairs 1979–80, Dir Gen. Dept of Int. Orgs 1980–83, Chair. Social Cttee, 38th Session of UN Gen. Ass., New York 1983, Amb. to Singapore 1983–86, Dir Gen. Dept of Information, Ministry of Foreign Affairs 1986–88, Dir Gen. Dept of ASEAN Affairs 1988–90, Dir Gen. Dept of Political Affairs 1990–92, Deputy Perm. Sec., Office of Perm. Sec. 1992–96, Perm. Sec., Ministry of Foreign Affairs 1996–2000, Amb. to France 2000–02, Adviser to Minister of Foreign Affairs 2002–08; Minister of Foreign Affairs Sept. 2008; Amb. to Indonesia *c.* 2012; Hon. MBE (UK) 1972; Kt Grand Cordon (Special Class) of the Most Noble Order of the Crown of Thailand 1988; Order of the Sacred Treasure, Gold and Silver Star (Japan) 1991; Kt Grand Cordon (Special Class) of the Most Exalted Order of the White Elephant 1993; Hon. KCMG (UK) 1997; Kt Commdr (Second Class, Lower Grade) of the Most Illustrious Order of Chula Chom Klao 2002. *Address:* Ministry of Foreign Affairs, 443 Thanon Sri Ayudhya, Bangkok 10400, Thailand (office). *Telephone:* (2) 643-5000 (office). *Fax:* (2) 643-5102 (office). *E-mail:* information01@mfa.go.th (office). *Website:* www.mfa.go.th (office).

CHÁVEZ, Anna Maria, BA, JD; American lawyer and national organization official; *CEO, Girl Scouts of the USA;* b. 1968, Eloy, Ariz.; m. Robert Chávez; one s.; ed Yale Univ., James E. Rogers College of Law at Univ. of Arizona; following graduation, clerked for an Ariz. attorney and then attended Univ. of Arizona Law School; admitted to Bar of US Dist Court for Dist of Ariz., Ariz. Supreme Court, US Supreme Court; Chief of Staff to Deputy Admin., US Small Business Admin (SBA), Washington, DC, Chief of Staff for SBA's Office of Govt Contracting and Minority Enterprise Devt, served as adviser to sr SBA and White House officials on a variety of policy issues; legal counsel for Fed. Highway Admin, Washington, DC 1996–98; also served as an attorney adviser in Office of the Counsel to the Pres., Washington, DC; Sr Policy Advisor to fmr US Sec. of Transportation Rodney E. Slater; returned to Arizona as in-house Counsel and Asst Dir for Div. of Aging and Community Services, Arizona Dept of Econ. Security; Dir of Intergovernmental Affairs under Gov. Janet Napolitano 2003–07, later Deputy Chief of Staff for Urban Relations and Community Devt 2007–09; Head of Girl Scouts of SW Texas 2009–11, CEO Girl Scouts of the USA 2011–; Chair.'s Award, US Hispanic Chamber of Commerce 2012, Women of Excellence Award, Women of the Asscn of Latino Professionals in Finance and Accounting 2012, Adjutant Gen.'s Medal and Diversity Champion Leadership Award, Ariz. Nat. Guard. *Address:* Girl Scouts of the USA, 420 Fifth Avenue, New York, NY 10018-2798, USA (office). *Telephone:* (212) 852-8000 (office). *E-mail:* info@girlscouts.org (office). *Website:* www.girlscouts.org (office).

CHÁVEZ CHÁVEZ, Arturo, LicenDer; Mexican lawyer and government official; b. 4 Sept. 1960, Chihuahua; ed Inst. Tecnológico de Estudios Superiores de Monterrey; fmr Under-Sec. of Legal Affairs and Human Rights, Secr. of the Interior; fmr Chief Adviser to Senator Diego Fernández de Cevallos; Procurator Gen. (Attorney Gen.), Chihuahua State 1996–98; subsequently worked in Interior Secr. where positions included Dir of Internal Control, Under-Sec. of Legal Affairs and Human Rights, Under-Sec. of the Interior; Partner, law firm of Diego Fernández de Cevallos; Procurator Gen. of Mexico 2009–11 (resgnd); mem. Partido Acción Nacional. *Address:* c/o Office of the Procurator-General, Avenida Paseo de la Reforma 211–213, Col. Cuauhtémoc, Del. Cuauhtémoc, 06500 México DF, Mexico.

CHÁVEZ FRIAS, Adán, BSc, MA; Venezuelan government official; b. 11 April 1953, Estado de Mérida; brother of Hugo Chávez Frias (fmr Pres.); ed Univ. of the Andes; fmr mem. Ruptura political movt; Founding mem. Movimento Bolivariano Revolucionario 2000, Movimento Quinta República 2000 (MVR); Nat. Dir MVR 2001–, also responsible for electoral policy; elected to Nat. Constituent Ass. for Meridá 2001, served as Vice-Pres. Comisión de Disposiciones Transitorias, Pres. Sub-Comm. for Domestic Policy in Comisión Legislativa Nacional, Pvt. Sec. to Pres. Hugo Chávez; Amb. to Cuba –2006; Presidential Chief of Staff 2006–07; Minister of Educ. 2007–08; Gov. of Barinas 2008–17; Pres. Inst. Nacional de Tierras 2001; Minister of Culture Jan.–June 2017.

CHAWLA, Navin B., BA, MA; Indian civil servant; b. 30 July 1945, New Delhi; m. Rupika Chawla; two d.; ed St Stephen's Coll., New Delhi, Univ. of London, London School of Econs; entered Admin. Service 1969; Sub-Div. Magistrate, Delhi 1971–73, Additional Dist Magistrate, Delhi 1973–75; Dir, Delhi Financial Corp. 1975–77, Delhi Tourism Devt Corp., Delhi State Industrial Devt Corp. 1975–77; Sec. to Lt Gov., Delhi 1975–77; Collector, Lakshadweep 1977–79; Finance Sec., Pondicherry 1979–80; Additional Sec., later Sec., Town Planning 1979–80; Deputy Sec., Ministry of Labour 1980–81; Dir, Ministry of Labour 1981–84, mem. del. to ILO Conf., Geneva 1982–84; on assignment to ILO, Bangkok 1984–86; on study leave for nine months to study leprosy situation in India 1986–87; Gen. Man. Super Bazar, Delhi 1987–89; Sec., Medical and Public Health, New Delhi Admin 1989–90; Resident Rep. of Govt of Goa in New Delhi 1991–92; Jt Sec., Ministry of Home Affairs, New Delhi Nov. 1992; Jt Sec. (Broadcasting), Ministry of Information and Broadcasting, with special responsibility for Doordarshan and AIR 1992–96; Chair. Delhi Vidyut (Electricity) Bd 1997–98; Prin. Sec., Govt of New Delhi with responsibilities for Services, Gen. Admin Dept, and Information and Publicity 1998–2000; Div. Commr, New Delhi 2000; Prin. Sec., Govt of Pondicherry with responsibilities for Power, Ports, Tourism and Art and Culture Depts and Chair. Pondicherry Tourism Devt Corp. Ltd 2000–01; Special Sec. (with rank of Sec. to Union Govt), Ministry of Environment and Forests July–Sept. 2003; Sec., Union Public Service Comm., New Delhi 2001–03; Sec. (Food and Public Distribution), Dept of Consumer Affairs, Ministry of Consumer Affairs 2003–04; Election Commr 2005–09, Chief Election Commr 2009–10; Chair. Governing Body, Coll. of Vocational Studies, New Delhi 2015–16; Fellow, Queen Elizabeth House, Univ. of Oxford 1995–96; Award from Inst. of Dirs, New Delhi 2004, Mazzini Award, Govt of Italy 2005, NDTV-Icon of the Year 2009, 2013, Mumbai Award, Bhartiya Vidhya Bhavan 2014. *Publications include:* The Vocational Rehabilitation and Social Re-integration of the Leprosy Affected in India (report) 1988, Mother Teresa (official biog.) 1992, Faith and Compassion – The Life and Work of Mother Teresa (with photographer Raghu Rai) 1996. *Leisure interests:* social service, reading. *Address:* c/o Office of the Chief Election Commissioner, Nirvachan Sadan, Ashoka Road, New Delhi 110 001, India. *Website:* www.navinchawla.com.

CHAYHANE, Said Ali Said; Comoran politician; *Minister of Finance and the Budget;* mem. Ass. of the Union (Parl.) (CRC) for Bambao/Ngazidja constituency 2015–; Campaign Dir for Azali Assoumani during presidential election campaign 2016; Minister of Finance and the Budget 2016–; mem. Bd of Govs., Arab Fund for Econ. & Social Devt; mem. Convention pour le Renouveau des Comores (CRC). *Address:* Ministry of Finance, the Economy, the Budget and Investments and External Trading (Privatization), BP 324, Moroni, Comoros (office). *Telephone:* 7744140 (office). *Fax:* 7744141 (office). *Website:* www.finances.gouv.km (office).

CHAZAL, Gilles; French museum director and curator; b. 4 Sept. 1946, Paris; s. of Robert Chazal and Raymonde Teulon; m. Martine Flevet 1981; two d.; ed Ecole du Louvre, Univ. of Paris-Sorbonne; Asst to Gallery Dir, Galerie Haut Pavé, Paris 1970–78; Asst, Engravings Collections, Bibliothèque Nationale 1972, Chief Curator, Petit Palais, Musée des Beaux-Arts de la Ville de Paris 1979–98, Museum Dir 1998–2012; Tutor, Ecole du Louvre 1982–, Institut français de restauration des oeuvres d'art 1987–97, Institut Catholique de Paris 1995–2008; Chevalier, Légion d'honneur, Ordre des Palmes académiques; Officier, Ordre des Arts et des Lettres. *Leisure interest:* running races. *Address:* c/o Petit Palais, Musée des Beaux-Arts de la Ville de Paris, Avenue Dutuit, 75008 Paris, France. *E-mail:* info@paris.fr.

CHAZELLE, Damien Sayre; American film director and screenwriter; b. 19 Feb. 1985, Providence, Rhode Island; s. of Bernard Chazelle and Celia Chazelle (née Martin); m. Jasmine McGlade 2010 (divorced 2014); m. Olivia Hamilton 2018; ed Harvard Univ. *Films include:* Guy and Madeline on a Park Bench (dir, writer and producer) 2009, The Last Exorcism Part II (dir) 2013, Grand Piano (dir) 2013, Whiplash (dir and writer) (London Film Critics' Circle Award for Screenwriter of the Year 2014, Sundance Film Festival Grand Jury Prize 2014) 2014, 10 Cloverfield Lane (dir) 2016, La La Land (dir and writer) (Golden Globe Awards for Best Screenplay and Best Dir 2016, Toronto Int. Film Festival People's Choice Award 2016, Critics' Choice Movie Award for Best Director 2016, Directors Guild of America Award for Outstanding Directorial Achievement-Feature Film 2017, Acad. Award for Best Dir 2017, BAFTA for Best Dir 2017) 2016, First Man (dir and producer) 2018. *Address:* c/o Gary Ungar, Exile Entertainment, 1223 Wilshire Blvd, Suite 593, Santa Monica, CA 90403, USA (office). *Telephone:* (310) 573-1523 (office). *Fax:* (310) 573-0109 (office).

CHAZEN, Stephen I., BSc, MA, PhD; American business executive; b. 1946; ed Rutgers Coll., Univ. of Houston, Michigan State Univ.; Man. Dir and Head of Corp. Finance, Merrill Lynch 1982–94; Exec. Vice-Pres., Corp. Devt, Occidental Petroleum Corpn 1994–99, Exec. Vice-Pres., Corp. Devt and Chief Financial Officer (CFO) 1999–2004, Sr Exec. Vice-Pres. and CFO 2004–07, Pres. and CFO 2007–16, Dir, Pres. and COO 2010–11, Pres. and CEO 2011–16; fmr Investment Banker, Man. Dir and Head of Corporate Finance at Merrill Lynch; mem. Bd of Dirs Premcor Inc. 1995–99, Lyondell Chemical Co. 2002–, Washington Mutual, Inc. 2008–09, American Petroleum Inst. (fmr Chair.) 2011–, Ecolab Inc. 2013–, The Williams Cos., Inc. 2016–, TPG Capital, Port Arthur Finance Corp; mem. Bd of Trustees Aquarium of the Pacific, Catalina Island Conservancy; American Petroleum Inst. Gold Medal for Distinguished Achievement 2016.

CHAZOT, Georges-Christian; French business executive; b. 19 March 1939, Algiers; s. of Raymond Chazot and Suzanne Monnet; m. Marie-Dominique Tremois 1962; one s. two d.; ed Lycée Bugeaud, Algiers, Ecole Polytechnique, Paris, Harvard Int. Marketing Inst. and MSEE Univ. of Florida; electronic engineer EMR Sarasota, Florida 1962; Man., Space Electronics, Schlumberger 1965–68, Tech. Dir for Industrial Control 1968–70, Commercial Dir for Instruments and Systems 1970–74, Audio-professional Dir-Gen. 1974–76; Dir-Gen. for Alkaline Accumulators, SAFT 1976–80, Dir-Gen. 1981–83, Pres., Dir-Gen. 1983–88, Hon. Pres. and Admin. 1989; Pres., Dir-Gen. Centre d'Etudes et de Services pour le Développement Industriel (CEI) 1983–86; Vice-Pres., Dir-Gen. Télic Alcatel and Opus Alcatel 1989–90; Pres., Dir-Gen. Alcatel Business Systems 1990–91; Pres. Business Systems Group, Vice-Pres. Alcatel NV 1990–92; Pres., Dir-Gen. Adia France 1992–94; Group Man. Dir Eurotunnel 1994–2000, Chair. Eurotunnel Developments Ltd 2002–04; Chair. GCC Consultants from 2001, Prosegur France from 2003; Vice-Pres. French Chamber of Commerce in GB –2000; Chair. Paris Notre-Dame magazine from 2001; Vice-Chair. Radio Notre Dame from 2001; Dir, X-PM Transition Partners from 2001, Giat Industries from 2002; Fellow, Chartered Inst. of Transport; Chevalier, Légion d'honneur 1990; Officier, Ordre nat. du Mérite 1996. *Leisure interests:* opera, sailing, skiing. *Address:* 24 rue de Réservoirs, 78000 Versailles, France (home). *Telephone:* 1-30-21-83-14 (home). *Fax:* 1-30-21-83-14 (home). *E-mail:* georges-christian.chazot@wanadoo.fr (home).

CHAZOV, Yevgeny Ivanovich, MD, PhD; Russian politician and cardiologist; *General Director, Russian Cardiology Research Complex, Federal Health and Social Development Agency;* b. 10 June 1929, Gorky; ed Kiev Medical Inst.; mem. CPSU 1962–91, mem. Cen. Cttee 1982–90; Sr Scientific Worker, Inst. of Therapy 1959; Deputy Dir Inst. of Therapy, USSR Acad. of Medical Science 1963–65, Dir Inst. of Cardiology 1965–67; Deputy Minister of Public Health 1967–87, Minister 1987–91; mem. Supreme Soviet 1974–89; Gen. Dir, Russian Cardiology Research Complex, Fed. Health and Social Devt Agency 1975–; personal physician to Presidents Brezhnev, Andropov, Chernenko and Gorbachev; mem. USSR (now Russian) Acad. of Medical Sciences 1971, USSR (now Russian) Acad. of Sciences 1979; Pres. USSR (now Russian) Soc. of Cardiology 1975; Co-Pres. International Physicians for Prevention of Nuclear War 1980–87; mem. acads of USA, Germany, Hungary, Serbia, Mexico, Poland, Romania; Hon. mem. World Albert Schweitzer Medical Acad., European Acad. of Arts and Science; State Prize 1969, 1976, Hero of Socialist Labour 1978, Lenin Prize 1982, UNESCO Peace Prize 1984, State Prize 2004. *Publications include:* Myocardial Infarction (with others) 1971, Cardiac Rhythm Disorders 1972, Anti-coagulants and Fibrinolytics 1977, Health and Power (memoirs) and other monographs; over 500 articles on cardiology. *Leisure interests:* hunting, photography. *Address:* Russian Cardiology Research Complex, 121552 Moscow, 3D Cherepkovskaya Street 15A, Russia (office). *Telephone:* (495) 415-00-25 (office). *Fax:* (495) 414-61-13 (office). *E-mail:* rcardio-chazov@list.ru (office).

CHE, Yingxin, BA; Chinese banking executive; b. 1954, Henan Prov.; ed Henan Banking School, Henan CCP Party School; held posts at various local brs of People's Bank of China (PBC), Henan Prov., including Lushi Co. Br. and Luoyang, Sanmenxia and Xinyang Municipal Brs 1980–92, Vice-Pres. Prov. Br., PBC, Henan Prov. 1992–97, Deputy Dir-Gen. Auditing Dept, PBC 1997–98, Dir-Gen. Staff Compliance Dept, PBC 1998–2003, Deputy Disciplinary Officer, Staff Compliance Department 1998–2003; Deputy Dir State Adm. of Foreign Exchange, Prov. Office, Henan Prov. 1992–97; Dir-Gen. Banking Supervision Dept, China Banking Regulatory Comm. 2003–05, Vice-Chair. China Banking Regulatory Comm. 2005–; Chair. Bd of Supervisors, Agricultural Bank of China 2009–15. *Address:* c/o Agricultural Bank of China, 69 Jianguomen Nei Avenue, Dongcheng District, Beijing 100005, People's Republic of China. *E-mail:* ir@abchina.com.

CHEA, Chanto, PhD; Cambodian central banker and politician; *Governor, National Bank of Cambodia;* b. 9 Oct. 1951, Kompon Thom Prov.; m.; ed secondary school, Kampong Thom, Univ. of Commerce, Phnom Penh, Hanoi Univ., Viet Nam; Dir Phnom Penh Municipality Bank 1979–81; Deputy Gov. Nat. Bank of Cambodia 1981–86, Gov. 1998–, Gov. for IMF 1998–; First Vice-Minister, Ministry of Planning 1986, Minister of Planning 1986–98; mem. Parl. (Kampong Thom Constituency) 1993–98; Resident Adjunct Prof., Univ. of Southern California, USA 1995; Hon. PhD (Univ. of Southern California) 1995. *Publications:* Socio-Economic Rehabilitation Plan, 1994–1995 1994, Socio-Economic Survey of Cambodia, 1993–1994 1995, Survey of Industrial Establishment, 1993 1996, First Five Year Socio-Economic Development Plan, 1996–2000 1997, Cambodian Human Resource Development Report 1997, Law on Banking and Financial Institutions 1999, Financial Sector Blueprint for 2001–2010 2001, Law on Negotiable Instruments and Payment Transactions 2005, Draft Law on Financial Leasing 2006, Draft Law on Anti-Money Laundering and Financial Terrorism 2006. *Address:* National Bank of Cambodia, 22–24 boulevard Preah Norodom, BP 25, Phnom Penh, Cambodia (office). *Telephone:* (23) 722189 (office). *Fax:* (23) 426117 (office). *E-mail:* info@nbc.org.kh (office). *Website:* www.nbc.org.kh (office).

CHEA, Leang, MA; Cambodian lawyer and international organization official; *National Co-Prosecutor, Extraordinary Chambers in the Courts of Cambodia (ECCC);* ed Martin Luther Univ., Halle-Wittenberg, Germany; with Ministry of Justice 1996–2002, posts include Deputy, Training Office and mem. Cambodian Cttee for the Penal Code; Prosecutor, Cambodian Court of Appeals 2002–09; Prosecutor-Gen. Supreme Court 2009–; Nat. Co-Prosecutor, Extraordinary Chambers in the Courts of Cambodia 2006–. *Address:* Office of the Co-Prosecutors, Extraordinary Chambers in the Courts of Cambodia, National Road 4, Chaom Chau Commune, Dangkao District, PO Box 71, Phnom Penh, Cambodia (office). *Telephone:* (23) 219814 (office). *Fax:* (23) 219841 (office). *E-mail:* info@eccc.gov.kh (office). *Website:* www.eccc.gov.kh/en (office).

CHEADLE, Don, BFA; American actor; b. 29 Nov. 1964, Kansas City, Mo.; s. of Donald Frank Cheadle, Sr and Bettye North; pnr Bridgid Coulter; one s. one d.; ed California Calif. Inst. of the Arts; apptd UN Goodwill Ambassador for Environment 2010; BET Humanitarian Award 2007, Summit Peace Award 2007, Joel Siegel Award 2007, Spirit of Independence Award 2008, BAFTA/LA Humanitarian Award 2008. *Films include:* Moving Violations 1985, Punk 1986, Hamburger Hill 1987, Colors 1988, Roadside Prophets 1992, The Meteor Man 1993, Things to Do in Denver When You're Dead 1995, Devil in a Blue Dress (Los Angeles Film Critics Asscn Award for Best Supporting Actor 1995, Nat. Soc. of Film Critics Award for Best Supporting Actor 1996) 1995, Rosewood 1997, Volcano 1997, Boogie Nights 1997, Bulworth 1998, Out of Sight 1998, Mission to Mars, 2000, The Family Man 2000, Traffic (Black Reel Award for Theatrical-Best Supporting Actor) 2000, Things Behind the Sun 2001, Manic, 2001, Swordfish 2001, The Hire: Ticker 2002, The United States of Leland 2003, The Assassination of Richard Nixon 2004, Crash 2004 (also producer), Hotel Rwanda (Golden Satellite Award for Best Actor in a Motion Picture, Drama 2005) 2004, After the Sunset 2004, Ocean's Twelve 2004, Other Side of Simple 2006, The Dog Problem 2006, Reign Over Me 2007, Talk to Me (African-American Film Critics Asscn Award for Best Actor) 2007, Ocean's Thirteen 2007, Traitor 2008, Hotel for Dogs 2009, Brooklyn's Finest 2009, Iron Man 2 2010, The Guard (Black Reel Award for Outstanding Supporting Actor 2012) 2011, Sacks West (short) 2011, Don Cheadle Is Captain Planet (short) 2011, Flight 2012, Captain Planet 3 (short) 2012, Iron Man 3 2013, Avengers: Age of Ultron 2015, Miles Ahead (Dir) 2015, Captain America: Civil War 2016, Kevin Hart: What Now? (documentary) 2016, Avengers: Infinity War 2018. *Television includes:* The Golden Palace (series) 1992, Picket Fences (series) 1993–95, Lush Life 1993, Rebound: The Legend of Earl 'The Goat' Manigault (film) 1996, The Rat Pack (film) (Golden Globe Award for Best Performance by an Actor in a Supporting Role in a Series, Miniseries or Motion Picture Made for Television) 1998, A Lesson Before Dying (film) (Black Reel Award for Network/Cable—Best Actor 2000) 1999, Animated Tales of the World (series) 2000, The Simpsons (series) (voice) 2000, Fail Safe (film) 2000, The Bernie Mac Show (series) 2002, ER (series) 2002, Biography (series documentary) 2003, Independent Lens (series documentary) 2003, Make Your Own Superbowl Ad (film) 2006, Drunk History (series) 2010, House of Lies (series) (Golden Globe Award for Best Performance by an Actor in a Television Series—Comedy or Musical) 2012–16. *Publications:* Not On Our Watch (with John Prendergast) 2007, The Enough Moment: Fighting to End Africa's Worst Human Rights Crimes (with John Prendergast) 2010. *Address:* c/o Creative Artists Agency, 2000 Avenue of the Stars, Los Angeles, CA 90067, USA (office). *Telephone:* (424) 288-2000 (office). *Fax:* (424) 288-2900 (office). *Website:* www.caa.com (office).

CHEARAVANONT, Dhanin; Thai business executive; *Chairman and CEO, Charoen Pokphand (CP) Group;* b. April 1939, Bangkok; m. Vatanalikit Tawee (Khunying); five c.; ed secondary school, Shantou, China and commercial school, Hong Kong; Chair. Charoen Pokphand (CP) Group (conglomerate of 250 cos involved in agribusiness and food, telecommunications, retail and distribution and other industries) and Chia Tai Group, China 1989–; Chair. True Corpn 1993–; major shareholder in BD Bank, Shanghai (first foreign-owned bank with head office in China); adviser to Chinese Govt during Hong Kong negotiations with UK; Pres. China Asscn of Overseas Chinese Entrepreneurs Asscn 2008–; Businessman of The Year, Forbes Asia Magazine 2011. *Address:* 18 True Tower, Ratchadapisek Road, Huai Kwang, Bangkok 10320, Thailand (office). *Telephone:* (2) 643-1111 (office). *Fax:* (2) 643-1651 (office). *E-mail:* cp@cpthailand.com (office). *Website:* www.cpthailand.com (office).

CHECA CREMADES, Fernando, DenFil y Letras, LicEnD; Spanish professor of art history, arts administrator and writer; *Professor of Art History, Universidad Complutense de Madrid;* b. 14 May 1952, Madrid; s. of Francisco Checa and Concepción Cremades; Lecturer in Art History, Univ. Complutense de Madrid 1976–, Prof. of Art History –1996, 2002–; Dir Prado Museum 1996–2002; Summer Visiting Prof., Inst. of Advanced Studies, Princeton, NJ 1988; Paul Mellon Sr Fellow, Center of Advanced Studies in Visual Arts, Nat. Gallery of Art, Washington, DC 1989; Fae Norton Prof., Oklahoma State Univ. 1995; fmr mem. Ministerial Comm. for Classification of State Collections; organizer of several major exhbns; Premio Extraordinario de Doctorado 1981, Nat. Prize for History 1993. *Publications include:* Pintura y escultura del Renacimiento en España 1983, El coleccionismo en España (co-author) 1984, Las casas del Rey: Casas reales, cazaderos, jardines. Siglos XVI y XVII (co-author) 1986, La imagen impresa en el Renacimiento y el Manierismo 1987, Carlos V y la imagen del héroe en el Renacimiento 1987, Felipe II: mecenas de las artes (Nat. History Prize, Spain) 1992, Tiziano y la Monarquía Hispánica 1994, Carlos V. La imagen del poder en el Renacimiento 1999, Carlos V, a caballo, en Muhlberg de Tiziano 2000, Guia para el estudio de la historia del arte 2004, Pintura y escultura del renacimiento en Espana, 1450–1600 2007, Velazquez: The Complete Paintings 2008. *Address:* Departamento de Historia del Arte II (Moderno), Universidad Complutense de Madrid, Ciudad Universitaria, Avenida Seneca 2, 28040 Madrid, Spain (office). *Telephone:* (91) 394-5870 (office). *Fax:* (91) 394-6040 (office). *E-mail:* fcheca@ghis.ucm.es (office). *Website:* www.ucm.es/departamentoartemoderno (office).

CHECHELASHVILI, Valeri, PhD; Georgian diplomatist and international organization official; *Secretary-General, Organization for Democracy and Economic Development (GUAM);* b. 17 March 1961, Tbilisi; s. of Karlo Chechelashvili and Tina Chechelashvili; m. Marine Neparidze; two s. one d.; ed Kiev State Univ., Ukraine; mem. staff, Foreign Econ. Relations Dept, Ministry of Light Industry 1987–88; Deputy Head of Foreign Econ. Relations section, Jt Stock Co. Gruzkurort 1988–89; First Sec. Dept of Int. Econ. Relations, Ministry of Foreign Affairs

1989–90, Deputy Dir 1990–91, First Deputy Dir 1991–92, Dir 1992–94, Deputy Minister of Foreign Affairs 1998–2000; Amb. to Ukraine 1994–98, to Moldova 1996–98; Sec.-Gen. Black Sea Econ. Co-operation 2000–04; Amb. to Russian Fed. 2004–05; Minister of Finance Feb.–June 2005; Amb. to Switzerland and Perm. Rep. to UN and Other Int. Orgs, Geneva July–Nov. 2005; First Deputy Foreign Minister of Georgia 2005–07; Sec.-Gen. Org. for Democracy and Econ. Devt 2007–; Second Degree Order for Service, Ukraine 1998, Order for Merit (1st Degree), Ukraine 2002. *Publications:* several articles on econ. co-operation in learned journals. *Leisure interests:* classical music, fiction, tennis. *Address:* GUAM Secretariat, 01001 Kyiv, Sofiyska 2-A, Ukraine (office). *Telephone:* (44) 206-37-37 (office). *Fax:* (44) 206-30-06 (office). *E-mail:* secretariat@guam-organization.org (office). *Website:* guam-organization.org (office).

CHECKLAND, Sir Michael, Kt, BA, CCMI, FCMA; British broadcasting executive; b. 13 March 1936, Birmingham; s. of Leslie Checkland and Ivy Florence Checkland; m. 1st Shirley Checkland 1960 (divorced 1983); two s. one d.; m. 2nd Sue Zetter 1987; ed King Edward's Grammar School, Five Ways, Birmingham and Wadham Coll., Oxford; accountant, Parkinson Cowan Ltd 1959–62, Thorn Electronics Ltd 1962–64; Sr Cost Accountant, BBC 1964–67, Head, Cen. Finance Unit 1967, Chief Accountant, Cen. Finance Services 1969, Chief Accountant, BBC TV 1971, Controller, Finance 1976, Controller, Planning and Resource Man., BBC TV 1977, Dir of Resources, BBC TV 1982, Deputy Dir-Gen. BBC 1985–87, Dir-Gen. 1987–92, Dir BBC Enterprises 1979–92 (Chair. 1986–87); Dir Visnews 1980–85; Vice-Pres. RTS 1985–94, Fellow 1987–; Trustee Reuters 1994–2009; Pres. Commonwealth Broadcasting Asscn 1987–88; Vice-Pres. EBU 1991–92; Chair. NCH (fmrly Nat. Children's Home) 1991–2001; Gov. Westminster Coll. Oxford 1992–97, Birkbeck Coll. London 1993–97, Brighton Univ. 1996–97; Dir Nat. Youth Music Theatre 1991–2002, Nynex Cablecomms 1995–97, Wales Millennium Centre 2003–09; Chair. City of Birmingham Symphony Orchestra 1993–2001, Brighton Int. Festival 1993–2002, Higher Educ. Funding Council for England 1997–2001, Brighton Univ. 2002–07; Vice-Pres. Methodist Conf. 1997; mem. Ind. TV Comm. 1997–2003; numerous other appointments; Hon. Fellow Wadham Coll. Oxford 1989; Dr hc (Open Univ.) 1993, (Birmingham) 1999, (Brighton) 2008. *Leisure interests:* sport, music, travel. *Address:* Orchard Cottage, Park Lane, Maplehurst, West Sussex, RH13 6LL, England (home).

CHEE, Soon Juan, PhD; Singaporean neuropsychologist and politician; *Secretary-General, Singapore Democratic Party;* b. 20 July 1962; m. Huang Chih-Mei; three c.; ed Univ. of Georgia and Mansfield Univ. of Pennsylvania, USA; Lecturer in Psychology, Nat. Univ. of Singapore –1993; joined Singapore Democratic Party 1992, currently Sec.-Gen.; Chair. Alliance for Reform and Democracy in Asia; Reagan Fellow, Nat. Endowment for Democracy, Washington, DC; participated in numerous int. orgs, including World Movt for Democracy, Forum of Democratic Leaders in Asia Pacific; participated in Reagan-Fascell Democracy Program at Nat. Endowment for Democracy, Washington, DC 2004; declared a bankrupt by High Court after failing to pay S$500,000 in damages awarded to Prime Minister Goh Chok Tong and Sr Minister Lee Kuan Yew, not allowed to stand for elections until Feb. 2011; fined S$6,000 and sentenced to Queenstown Remand Prison for eight days for contempt of court after he criticized independence of Singapore judiciary; offered to pay reduced sum of S$30,000 to annul bankruptcy Sept. 2012, bankruptcy annulled Nov. 2012, allowing him to contest Singaporean general election 2015; Visiting Fellow, Sydney Democracy Network, Univ. of Sydney, Australia 2014; Chair. Asian Alliance for Reforms and Democracy; recognised by Amnesty International as a prisoner of conscience; Hon. Research Assoc., Monash Asia Inst. 1997, Human Rights Fellow, Univ. of Chicago 2001, Washington, DC 2004; Hellman/Hammett Writers Grant, Human Rights Watch, Parliamentarians for Global Action Defender of Democracy Award 2003, Prize for Freedom, Liberal International 2011. *Publications include:* Dare to Change: An Alternative Vision for Singapore 1994, Singapore, My Home Too 1995, To Be Free: Stories from Asia's Struggle Against Oppression 1998, Your Future, My Faith, Our Freedom: A Democratic Blueprint for Singapore 2001, The Power of Courage: Effecting Political Change in Singapore Through Nonviolence 2005, A Nation Cheated 2008, Democratically Speaking 2012. *Address:* Singapore Democratic Party, 3 Ang Mo Kio Street 62, 2-30 Link at AMK, Singapore 569139, Singapore (office). *Telephone:* 64564531 (office). *Fax:* 64564531 (office). *E-mail:* sdp@yoursdp.org (office). *Website:* www.yoursdp.org (office); cheesoonjuan.blogspot.co.uk; www.cheesoonjuan.com.

CHEETHAM, Anthony Kevin, BA, DPhil, FRS; British materials scientist and academic; b. 16 Nov. 1946, Stockport; ed St Catherine's Coll. and Wadham Coll., Oxford; Lecturer, Lincoln Coll., Oxford 1971–74, Lecturer in Chemical Crystallography 1974–90, Reader in Organic Materials 1990–91; Prof. of Materials and Chem., Univ. of California, Santa Barbara, USA 1991–2007; Goldsmiths' Prof. of Materials Science, Univ. of Cambridge 2007–17, currently Distinguished Research Fellow and Visiting Prof.; Distinguished Visiting Prof., Nat. Univ. of Singapore; Dr hc (Versailles 2006, Tumkur 2011, St. Andrews 2011, Warwick 2015), Hon. Fellow, Indian Acad. of Sciences 2001, Trinity Coll., Univ. of Cambridge 2017, Singapore Nat. Acad. of Science 2018; RSC Corday-Morgan Medal and Prize 1982, Solid State Chem. Award, Royal Soc. 1988, IUMRS Sômiya Award 2004, Leverhulme Medal, Royal Soc. 2008, Chemical Pioneer Award, American Inst. of Chemists 2014, Basolo Medal 2017. *Publications:* numerous papers in professional journals. *Address:* Department of Materials Science and Metallurgy, University of Cambridge, 27 Charles Babbage Road, Cambridge, CB3 0FS, England (office). *Telephone:* (1223) 334300 (office). *Fax:* (1223) 334567 (office). *E-mail:* akc30@cam.ac.uk (office). *Website:* www.msm.cam.ac.uk (office).

CHEF, Genia, MA; Russian artist; b. 28 Jan. 1954, Aktyubinsk, Kazakhstan; s. of Vladimir Scheffer and Sinaida Scheffer; m. Elke Schwab 1983; ed Polygraphic Inst., Moscow, Acad. of Fine Arts, Vienna, Austria; painter, graphic and computer artist; has provided illustrations for publs including Edgar Allan Poe, Prose and Poetry 1983, American Romantic Tales 1984, Finger World 1993, American Alphabet 1998, M. Lederer's Nothing Lasts Forever Anymore 1999, Great Game 2012, Cadaqués 2014; numerous appearances on radio and TV in New York, Berlin and Moscow, including Insight Germany (Deutsche Welle TV) 2014, Pavilion Telluria at Venice Biennale, Arts 21 (Deutsche Welle TV) 2015; Academician, Int. Acad. of Culture and Art 2016, Amb. for Germany; Hon. mem. Russian Acad. of Arts 2017; Kt Commdr, Order of St John, Russian Grand Priory, Imperial Order of St Anna, Third Degree, Imperial Order of St Stanislas, Second Degree; Fueger Gold Prize, Acad. of Fine Arts, Vienna 1993, Delfina Studio Trust Award, New York 1994, First Prize for Painting at Xth Int. Biennial of Miniature Art, Gornij Milanovac, Serbia 2010. *Publications include:* Manifesto of Degeneration 1988, Manifesto of Post-Historicism 1989, Viva Canova! 1995, New Computer Renaissance 2002, Glory of a New Century 2011. *Leisure interests:* music, books, collecting insects and coins. *Address:* Schustehrusstr. 1, 10585 Berlin, Germany (home). *Telephone:* (30) 3246479 (home); 173-6162940 (mobile) (home). *E-mail:* gêniachef@gmx.de (home). *Website:* www.artslant.com/global/artists/show/223967-genia-chef (home); www.geniachef.de.

CHEHADE MOYA, Omar Karim; Peruvian lawyer and politician; b. 8 Nov. 1970, Lima; m. Ursula Galdos; ed Univ. Inca Garcilaso de la Vega, Lima; Legal Adviser, Nat. Univ. of San Marcos, Lima 2003–05; consultant lawyer, Ad-hoc Anti-corruption Prosecution 2005–08; Partner, Omar Chehade & Torres la Torre (law firm), Lima 2008–; mem. Congreso (Parl.) for Lima (Gana Perú list) 2011–; Second Vice-Pres. of Peru 2011–12. *Address:* Omar Chehade & Torres la Torre Abogados, Calle los Pinos 156, Of. 203, Miraflores, Lima, Peru (office). *Telephone:* (1) 445-3376 (office).

CHEIFFOU, Amadou; Niger politician and civil servant; *President, Rassemblement social-démocratique—Gaskiya;* b. 1 Dec. 1942, Kornaka, Maradi Dept; fmr regional official, Int. Civil Aviation Org., then Regional Dir Western and Cen. African Office, Dakar; Prime Minister and Minister of Defence 1991–93; fmr Vice-Pres. Convention démocratique et social—Rahama; Founder and Pres. Rassemblement social-démocratique—Gaskiya (RSD) 2004; mem. Assemblée nationale 2004–; unsuccessful cand. in presidential election 2004, 2011; Pres. Econ., Social and Cultural Council of Niger (CESOC) 2006–10; elected municipal councillor in Kornaka 2009; Ombudsman 2011–. *Address:* Rassemblement social-démocratique–Gaskiya, Quartier Poudrière, Niamey, Niger (office). *Telephone:* 20-74-00-90 (office).

CHEMETOV, Paul; French architect and academic; b. 6 Sept. 1928, Paris; s. of Alexandre Chemetoff and Tamara Blumine; m. Christine Soupault 1958; one s. two d.; ed Ecole Nationale Supérieure des Beaux Arts; participated in founding of Atelier d'urbanisme et l'architecture 1961; Prof., Ecole d'architecture, Strasbourg 1968–72; Visiting Prof., UP8 1973; exhibited in the Venice Bienniale 1976; Prof. of Architecture, Ecole Nationale des Ponts et Chaussées 1978–89; mem. Directorial Cttee, then Vice-Pres. Plan Construction 1979–87; Visiting Prof., Ecole Polytechnique Fédérale, Lausanne 1993–98; mem. Acad. d'Architecture 1996; Officier, Légion d'honneur, Ordre nat. du Mérite, Ordre des Arts et des Lettres; Prix d'architecture, Cercle d'études architecturales 1965, Grand Prix Nat. d'architecture 1980, Médaille d'honneur d'Architecture 1991. *Publications include:* Architectures – Paris 1848–1914 (jtly) 1980, Cinq projets 1979–82 (jtly) 1983, Paris – Banlieue 1919–1939 (with B. Marrey and M. J. Dumont) 1989, La Fabrique des villes 1992, Le Territoire de L'Architecte 1995, Vingt Mille Mots pour la Ville 1996, Un architecte dans le siècle 2002, Mecano-factures (jtly) 2006; numerous articles in professional journals. *Address:* Chemetov, 4 square Masséna, 75013 Paris, France. *Telephone:* 1-45-82-85-48. *Fax:* 1-45-86-89-14. *E-mail:* cplush@compuserve.com.

CHEMEZOV, Sergei, PhD; Russian business executive; *CEO, Rostec Corporation;* b. 20 Aug. 1952, Cheremkhovo, Irkutsk; m. Yekaterina Ignatova; four c.; ed Irkutsk Inst. of Nat. Economy, Mil. Acad. of the Gen. Staff of Russian Fed.; worked in Irkutsk Scientific Research Inst. of Rare and Nonferrous Metals; worked with Experimental-Industrial Asscn Beam, represented Beam in GDR 1983–88; Asst to Gen. Dir Sovintersport 1989–96; Head, Dept of Foreign Econ. Relations, Admin of the Pres. of Russian Fed. 1996–99; First Deputy CEO Rosoboronexport (Russian Defence Export) State Corpn 2000–04, CEO 2004–07; CEO Russian Technologies Corpn (now Rostec Corpn) 2007–; Deputy Chair. Rosneft JSC 2013–; mem. Bd of Dirs MMC Norilsk Nickel, OJSC Aeroflot, National Information and Settlement Systems LLC, RUSNANO. *Address:* Rostec Corporation, 119048, Moscow, 24 Usacheva Ul., Russia (office). *Telephone:* (495) 287-25-25 (office). *E-mail:* info@rostec.ru (office). *Website:* rostec.ru (office).

CHEN, Ailian; Chinese dancer, academic and choreographer; b. 24 Dec. 1939, Shanghai; d. of Chen Xi Kang and Yu Xiu Ying; m. Wei Dao Ning; two d.; ed First Coll. of Chinese Dancing; teacher, Beijing Coll. of Dancing 1959–63; Chief Actress, China Opera and Dancing House 1963–; fmr Prof., Arts Dept, Nan Kai Univ., Hainan Univ., Wang Kan Arts Coll.; demonstrations and lectures in Shangdong Prov., Shaanxi Prov., Beijing Univ., Foreign Languages Inst., Post and Telegraph Inst., Light Industry Inst. and Municipal Dancers' Unions; Chief Dancer, Chinese Art Del. to USSR, USA, France, Spain, Belgium, Denmark, Finland, Sweden, Italy, Norway, Hong Kong, Germany, etc.; f. Chen Ailian Artistic Troupe 1989 (first non-governmental performing org. in China); est. Chen Ailian Dancing School, Beijing 1995; mem. CPPCC Nat. Cttee; mem. Exec. Cttee Chinese Dancers' Asscn; won four gold medals as a traditional dancer at 8th World Youth Festival in Helsinki 1962; Excellent Performance Award, First Nat. Dance Concert, First Prize, Ministry of Culture for Dance Soirée and Princess Wenzhen. *Performances include:* The Peony Pavilion, In the Dusk of Evening, The Oriental Melody, The Lantern Dance, Water, The Sword Dance, Ball Dance, The Song of the Serfs, Women Militia in the Grassland, The Red Silk Dance, The Dream of the Red Chamber 2007, 2012. *Publications:* I Came From An Orphanage; articles and commentaries on dance. *Leisure interests:* literature, music, traditional opera, travel, mountain climbing. *Address:* Chinese Dancers Association, No.10, Nanli, Nong Zhanguan (Agricultural Exhibition Hall), Beijing 100026, People's Republic of China; Room 101/7, 2 Nanhuadong Street, Hufang Road, Beijing 100050.

CHEN, B. L.; Taiwanese oil industry executive; fmr Dir and Pres. CPC Corpn, Taiwan (fmrly Chinese Petroleum Corpn). *Address:* c/o CPC Corpn, No. 3, Songren Road, Sinyi District, Taipei City 11010, Taiwan. *Telephone:* (2) 87898989. *E-mail:* ir@cpc.com.tw.

CHEN, Bangzhu; Chinese politician; b. Sept. 1934, Jiujiang City, Jiangxi Prov.; ed Chonqing Civil Eng Coll.; engineer, Jilin Chemical Industrial Dist Construction Co. 1954–65; engineer, Ministry of Chemical Industry No. 9 Chemical Industrial Construction Co. 1975–78, Chief Engineer 1978–80, Deputy Man. 1978–80, Man. 1980–83; joined CCP 1975; Chief Engineer, Man. Jiuhua Bldg Co. 1980–84; Chair. Foreign Econ. Relations Cttee, Hunan Province 1980–83; Mayor of Yueyang and Deputy Sec. CCP Yueyang City Cttee 1983–84; mem. CCP Provincial Cttee, Standing Cttee, Hunan Province 1984–85; Vice-Gov. Hunan Prov. 1984–89, Acting

Gov. 1989–93, Gov. 1993–95; Deputy Sec. CCP Provincial Cttee Hunan Province 1989–93; Minister of Internal Trade 1995–98; Vice-Minister State Econ. and Trade Comm. 1998–2000; Alt. mem. 13th CCP Cen. Cttee 1987–92; Deputy Sec. CCP 6th Hunan Provincial Cttee 1989–93; mem. 14th CCP Cen. Cttee 1992–97, 15th CCP Cen. Cttee 1997–2002; Vice-Minister State Econ. and Trade Comm. 1998–2000; mem. Macao Special Admin. Region Preparatory Cttee 1998–99, 9th CPPCC Nat. Cttee Standing Cttee 1998–2003 (Chair. CPPCC Sub-cttee on Human Resources and Environment 2003–08); Hon. Pres. Chinese Asscn for Materials Circulation 1995–. *Address:* c/o Chinese People's Political Consultative Conference, Beijing, People's Republic of China.

CHEN, Bao-lang, BS; Taiwanese business executive; *Chairman, Formosa Petrochemical Corporation;* ed Nat. Cheng Kung Univ.; fmr Pres. CPC Corpn, Taiwan; fmr Chair. Kuokuang Petrochemical Technology Co.; Chair. Formosa Petrochemical Corpn (FPC) 2011– (also mem. Bd Dirs 2006–); mem. Special Govt Cttee formed under Industrial Devt Bureau of Ministry of Econ. Affairs assigned to oversee safety at FPC petrochemical complex in Mailiao, Yunlin Co. –2011; mem. Bd of Dirs Mai-Liao Power Corpn 2011–; Nat. Cheng Kung Univ. Outstanding Alumni Award 2008. *Address:* Formosa Petrochemical Corporation, 1-1, Formosa Plastics Group Industrial Zone, Mailiao, Yunlin, Taiwan (office). *Telephone:* (5) 6812345 (office). *Website:* www.fpcc.com.tw (office); www.fpg.com.tw (office).

CHEN, Gen. Bingde; Chinese army officer (retd) and politician; b. July 1941, Nantong City, Jiangsu Prov.; ed Mil. Acad. of the Chinese PLA; joined PLA 1961, then Squadron Leader, Platoon Leader, Staff mem. PLA Services and Arms, Army (or Ground Force), Combat Training Section, Regt Chief of Staff, Div. Deputy Chief of Staff, Div. Chief of Staff 1979–81, Div. Commdr 1981–83, Deputy Commdr PLA Services and Arms, Army (or Ground Force) 1983, Maj.-Gen. 1988–95, Lt-Gen. 1995–2002, Chief of Staff, PLA, Nanjing Mil. Region 1985, C-in-C 1996–99, C-in-C Jinan Mil. Region 1999–2004, rank of Gen. 2002–; Dir-Gen. PLA Gen. Armaments Dept 2004–07, Chief of Gen. Staff, PLA 2007–12; joined CCP 1962, Deputy Sec. CCP Party Cttee PLA, Nanjing Mil. Region 1996–99; mem. 15th CCP Cen. Cttee 1997–2002, 16th CCP Cen. Cttee 2002–07, 17th CCP Cen. Cttee 2007–12; mem. Cen. Mil. Comm. 2005–. *Address:* c/o PLA General Staff Headquarters, 21, North Andeli Street, Beijing, People's Republic of China.

CHEN, Chao-min; Taiwanese air force officer and government official; b. 10 July 1940; ed Armed Forces Univ. (now Nat. Defence Univ.), Repub. of China Air Force Acad.; Dir of Operations, Office of the Deputy Chief of Gen. Staff for Operations, Ministry of Nat. Defence 1986–88, Commdr 443rd Tactical Fighter Wing 1988–89, Dir 4th Dept 1990–91, Dir Operations Div., Air Force Gen. HQ 1991–92, Insp.-Gen. Inspection Office 1992–93, Gen. Commdr Eastern Command 1993–94, Commdr Air Force Operations Command 1995–97, Deputy Commdr Air Force Gen. HQ 1997–98, C-in-C 1998–2002; strategic adviser to Pres. of Taiwan 2002, Deputy Minister for Armaments 2002–04, Minister of Nat. Defence 2008–09 (resgnd); Exec. Dir Repub. of China Air Force Acad. 1989–90, Supt 1994–95. *Address:* c/o Ministry of National Defence, 2/F, 164 Po Ai Road, Taipei 10048, Taiwan.

CHEN, Char-Nie, OBE, JP, MB, MSc, FHKAM (Psychiatry), FRCPsych, FRANZCP, FAPA (Int.), DPM; British (b. Chinese) physician, academic and fmr college principal; b. 19 July 1938, Fujian Prov., China; s. of Kam-Heng Chen and Mei-Ai Chen-Hsu; m. Chou-May Chien 1970; one s. two d.; ed Nat. Taiwan Univ., Taipei and Univ. Coll., London; Rotating Intern, Nat. Taiwan Univ. Hosp. 1964–65, Resident Physician, Dept of Neurology and Psychiatry 1965–68; Sr House Officer, Morgannwg Hosp., Wales 1968–69; Registrar, St George's Hosp. Medical School, London 1969–71, Lecturer and Hon. Sr Registrar 1971–72, 1973–78, Sr Lecturer and Hon. Consultant Psychiatrist 1978–80; Foundation Prof. of Psychiatry, Chinese Univ. of Hong Kong 1981–98, Chair. Dept of Psychiatry 1981–93, mem. Univ. Senate 1981, Head of Shaw Coll. 1987–94, mem. Univ. Council 1987–94; Specialist in Psychiatry, Chen Char-Nie Specialist Clinic 1999–; mem. Coll. Council, Hong Kong Baptist Coll. 1984–95; Pres. Hong Kong Psychiatric Asscn 1982–84, Hong Kong Soc. of Neurosciences 1983–84, 1988–89; Exec. Chair. Hong Kong Mental Health Asscn 1983–98; Pres. Pacific Rim Coll. of Psychiatrists 1988–90, Dir 1990–; Chair. Action Comm. Against Narcotics 1992–98, Hong Kong Advisory Council on AIDS; Pres. Hong Kong Coll. of Psychiatrists 1993–98; Fellow, Royal Coll. of Psychiatrists 1985–, Royal Australian and NZ Coll. of Psychiatrists 1983–, Royal Soc. of Medicine 1975–, Hong Kong Acad. of Medicine 1993–, Hong Kong Soc. of Sleep Medicine (Pres. 1993–), Hong Kong Coll. of Psychiatrists (Pres. 1994–98, Chief Examiner 1998–); mem. British Asscn for Psychopharmacology 1974–, European Sleep Research Soc. 1976–, British Medical Asscn 1979–, Collegium Internationale Neuro-psycho-pharmacologium 1981–, Hong Kong Medical Asscn 1981–, Int. Brain Research Org. 1985–, Mental Health Asscn, Hong Kong (Chair. 1983–98, Vice-Pres. 1998–); Corresp. Fellow, American Psychiatric Asscn 1991; Visiting Prof., St George's Hosp. Medical School, London 1984; JP, Hong Kong 1993–; Hon. Fellow, Shaw Coll., Chinese Univ. of Hong Kong, Hong Kong Psychological Soc. 1986, Hong Kong Coll. of Psychiatrists; Special Contrib. Award, Chinese Nat. Sleep Soc. 2016. *Publications:* over 90 scientific papers. *Leisure interests:* reading, poetry, travelling, good food. *Address:* Chen Char-Nie Clinic, Room 709, 7/F, Melbourne Plaza, 33 Queen's Road C, Central, Hong Kong Special Administrative Region (office); Flat 16B, Block 3, Villa Athena, 600 Sai Sha Road, Ma On Shan, Hong Kong Special Administrative Region, People's Republic of China (home). *Telephone:* 2899-2587 (office); 9500-2878 (home). *Fax:* 2899-2592 (office). *E-mail:* cnc@cuhk.edu.hk (office).

CHEN, Chien-Jen, ScD; Taiwanese politician and epidemiologist; *Vice-President;* b. 6 June 1951, Cishan Township, Kaohsiung Co.; s. of Hsin-an Chen and Wei Lien-chih Chen; ed Nat. Taiwan Univ., Johns Hopkins Univ.; Assoc. Prof., Coll. of Public Health, Nat. Taiwan Univ. 1983–86, Prof. 1986–2015, Dean 1999–2000, Dir Grad. Inst. of Public Health 1993–94, Founding Dir Grad. Inst. of Epidemiology 1994–97; Nat. Chair-Prof., Ministry of Educ. 1997–2002; Adjunct Prof., School of Public Health and Tropical Medicine, Tulane Univ. 1994; Dir Gen. Div. of Life Sciences, Nat. Science Council 1997–99, Deputy Minister 2002–03, Minister 2006–08; Minister of Health 2003–05; Distinguished Research Fellow, Genomics Research Center, Academia Sinica 2006–15, apptd Vice-Pres. 2011; Vice-Pres. 2016–; Cutter Lecturer on Preventive Medicine, Harvard Univ. 2008; Chair-Prof. Kaohsiung Medical Univ. 2008–15, Catholic Fu-Jen Univ. 2009–15; 14th Prof. Vikit Viranuvatti Lecturer, Gastroenterological Asscn of Thailand 2011; mem. Acad. of Sciences for the Developing World 2005, Delta Omega Hon. Soc. in Public Health 2010; Fogarty Int. Research Fellowship, US Nat. Inst. of Health 1989; Foreign Assoc., Nat. Acad. of Sciences 2017; Hon. mem. Mongolian Acad. of Sciences 2001, Hon. Chair-Prof. China Medical Univ. 2008–15; Officier dans l'Ordre des Palmes Academiques, Ministry of Educ., France 2009, Kt of the Order of St Gregory the Great, Vatican 2010, Kt of the Order of the Holy Sepulchre 2013; Outstanding Teaching Award, Ministry of Educ. 1992, Academic Award, Ministry of Educ. 1997, Inst. for Scientific Information Citation Classic Award 2001, Outstanding Research Fellow Award, Nat. Science Council 2003, Health Medal (First Rank), Dept of Health 2005, Achievement Medal (First Rank), Exec. Yuan 2005, Presidential Science Prize 2005, Science and Eng Achievement Award, Taiwanese-American Foundation, USA 2009, Outstanding Merit Award, Wang Ming-Ning Memorial Foundation 2010, Science Profession Medal (First Prize), Nat. Science Council 2012, Knowledge for the World Award, Johns Hopkins Univ. 2012. *Address:* Office of President, 122 Chungking South Rd, Zhongzheng District, Taipei 10048, Taiwan (office). *Telephone:* (2) 23113731 (office). *Fax:* (2) 23311604 (office). *E-mail:* public@mail.oop.gov.tw (office). *Website:* www.president.gov.tw (office).

CHEN, Deming, BA, PhD; Chinese government official; *President, Association for Relations Across the Taiwan Straits;* b. March 1949, Shanghai; ed Jiangxi Communist Labor Univ. (now Jiangxi Agricultural Univ.); began career in 1969 in Jiangxi, working five years for production team; joined CCP 1974; worked for three years for Jiangxi Agricultural Machinery Bureau, then worked for Jiangsu Food Products Corpn; Asst Dir, Gen. Office, Jiangsu Bureau of Commerce 1984, Deputy Dir 1985; fmr Sec.-Gen., Gen. Office, Jiangsu Prov. Govt; Mayor of Suzhou City 1998–2003; Vice-Gov. Shaanxi Prov. 1998–2003, Acting Gov. 2004–05, Gov. 2005–06; Vice-Chair. State Devt and Reform Comm. 2006–07; Vice-Minister of Commerce 2007, Minister of Commerce 2007–13; Pres. Asscn for Relations Across the Taiwan Straits 2013–; Deputy to 9th NPC 1998–2003, Del. to 16th CCP Cen. Cttee 2002–07, Alt. mem. 17th CCP Cen. Cttee 2007–12. *Website:* www.arats.com.cn.

CHEN, Derong; Chinese business executive; *President and General Manager, Baosteel Group Corporation;* mem. Standing Cttee, City Cttee, CCP, Jiaxing City, Zhejiang Prov. 1998–2002, Exec. Vice-Mayor, People's Govt, Jiaxing City 1998–2002, Deputy Sec., City Cttee 2002–07, Sec. 2007–10, Acting Mayor, People's Govt, Jiaxing City 2002, Mayor 2002–07; Deputy, 10th NPC 2003–08; Sec., Wenzhou City, CCP, Jiaxing City 2010–14, Vice-Gov., People's Govt, Jiaxing City 2010–14; Pres. and Gen. Man. Baosteel Group Corpn 2014–. *Address:* Baosteel Group Corporation, Baosteel Tower, 370 Pudian Road, Shanghai 200122, People's Republic of China (office). *Telephone:* (21) 58350000 (office). *Fax:* (21) 68404832 (office). *E-mail:* info@baosteel.com (office); ir@baosteel.com (office). *Website:* www.baosteel.com (office).

CHEN, Ding-Shinn, MD; Taiwanese physician and academic; *Principle Investigator, Hepatitis Research Centre, National Taiwan University Hospital;* b. 6 July 1943, Yin-Ge; ed Coll. of Medicine, Nat. Taiwan Univ.; Researcher, Nat. Cancer Center Research Inst., Tokyo, Japan 1975; Lecturer, Dept of Internal Medicine, Coll. of Medicine, Nat. Taiwan Univ. 1975, Assoc. Prof. 1978, Prof. 1983, Dean, Coll. of Medicine 2001–07, Founding Dir Hepatitis Research Centre, Nat. Taiwan Univ. Hosp. 1987–2001, now Prin. Investigator; Chair. Taiwanese Govt's Hepatitis Control Cttee; Pres. Taiwan Asscn for the Study of the Liver 1996–98, Gastroenterological Soc. of Taiwan 1997–2003, Formosan Medical Asscn 2001–04, Int. Asscn for the Study of the Liver, Munich, Germany 2004–06; Vice-Pres. Int. Asscn for the Study of the Liver 2000; Ed. or Assoc. Ed., Journal of Biomedical Science 1994–, Journal of Internal Medicine 1999–2005, Hepatology 2002–06, Molecular Carcinogenesis 2005–, Clinical Journal of Gastroenterology, 2008–; mem. Editorial Bd, Journal of the Formosan Medical Association 1985–2004, Journal of Gastroenterology and Hepatology 1986–, Viral Immunology 1996–99, Journal of Hepatology 2000–06, Journal of Gastroenterology 1996–2006, Hepatology Research 2002, Annual Review of Cancer Research in the Asia-Pacific 2002–; mem. NIH 1979–80; Academician, Academia Sinica 1992 (Distinguished Chair Prof.); Foreign Assoc. NAS 2005; Fellow, Third World Acad. of Sciences (now Acad. of Sciences for the Developing World) 2001; Hon. PhD (Kaohsiung Medical Univ.) 2002; Nat. Outstanding Science and Tech. Award, Exec. Yuan 1984, Abbott Laboratories Research Award 1986, Outstanding Research Award in Biology and Medicine, Nat. Science Council 1987–93, Outstanding Academic Award (Medicine), Ministry of Educ. 1989, Grand Award, Soc. of Chinese Bioscientists in America 1993, Hou Jin-Duei Outstanding Contrib. Award in Basic Science 1994, Outstanding Scholar Award, Foundation for the Advancement of Outstanding Scholarship 1995–99, Nat. Chair-Prof. of Medicine, Ministry of Educ. 1997–2003, Lifetime Nat. Chair-Prof. of Medicine, Ministry of Educ. 2004–, Caring Physicians of the World, World Medical Asscn (France) 2005, Outstanding Achievement Award, Foundation for the Advancement of Outstanding Scholarship 2005, Trieste Science Prize (co-recipient), Acad. of Sciences for the Developing World 2006, Presidential Science Prize of Taiwan 2007, EASL Int. Recognition Award, Copenhagen 2009, Okuda Lectureship Award, JGH Foundation, Australia 2009, Nikkei Asia Prize 2010. *Achievements include:* leading role in uncovering the factors responsible for the transmission of Hepatitis B virus from mothers to infants and for proving that viral disease is associated not only with liver cirrhosis but also with liver cancer, leading to a programme of mass vaccination against Hepatitis B. *Publications:* more than 600 articles in scientific journals on internal medicine, gastroenterology, viral hepatitis and liver disease. *Address:* Hepatitis Research Centre, National Taiwan University Hospital, No. 1 Changde Street, Zhongzheng Dist, Taipei 100, Taiwan (office). *Telephone:* (2) 23123456 (ext. 67176) (office). *E-mail:* 030003@ntuh.gov.tw (office). *Website:* www.ntuh.gov.tw/en/HRC (office).

CHEN, Dun; Chinese business executive; b. Dec. 1928, Tianjin City; Vice-Minister for Coal 1985–90; Gen. Man. China Nat. Coal Corpn 1993; fmr Pres. China Electric Green Technology Group; mem. 7th CPPCC 1987–92, 8th 1993–97.

CHEN, Enxiang; Chinese business executive; Pres. Henan Coal and Chemical Industry Group Co. Ltd. *Address:* Henan Coal and Chemical Industry Group Co. Ltd, Guo Long Mansion, Zhengzhou 450046, Hebei Province, People's Republic of China (office). *E-mail:* info@hnccgc.com (office).

CHEN, Feihu, BA; Chinese accountant and business executive; *President, China Guodian Corporation;* ed Renmin Univ.; has worked in Ministry of Electric Power Industry, Ministry of Water Resources and Electric Power, Ministry of Energy and China Electricity Council; Asst to Dir, Fujian Provincial Bureau of Electricity Industry 1995–96; Deputy Chief of Dept of Economy Adjustment and State-owned Assets Supervision, Ministry of Electric Power 1996–97; Deputy Head of Dept of Finance and Asset Operation, State Power Corpn 1997–99, Deputy Head and Head of Working Dept of Pres., Head, Office for Structural Reform 1999–2002; Chair. (non-exec.) Guodian Technology & Environment Group Corpn Ltd 2013–14, Chair. Strategic Cttee, mem. Remuneration and Appraisal Cttee; Dir, Pres. and mem. Party Cttee, China Guodian Corpn 2013–; Pres. China Datang Corpn 2016–, Chair. Bd (non-exec.) 2017–; Dir (non-exec.), Huadian Power International Corpn Ltd 2005–14, Vice-Chair. 2008–13; Vice-Pres. and mem. Party Cttee, China Huadian Corpn; Chair. GD Power Devt Co. Ltd 2013–16, China Huadian Capital Holdings Co. Ltd, China Huadian Finance Corpn Ltd, Huadian Energy Co. Ltd. *Address:* China Guodian Corporation, 6–8 Fuchengmen Bei Street, Beijing 100034, People's Republic of China (office). *Telephone:* (10) 58682000 (office). *Fax:* (10) 58553900 (office). *E-mail:* cgdcb@cgdc.com.cn (office). *Website:* www.cgdc.com.cn (office).

CHEN, Fenjian, BEng; Chinese engineer and business executive; *Executive Director and President, China Communications Construction Company Limited;* ed Changsha Communications Univ.; Deputy Gen. Man. Fourth Navigational Eng Bureau, fmr China Harbour Engineering Co. (Group) 2000–02, Gen. Man. 2002–05; Vice-Pres. China Communications Construction Group 2005–06, Vice-Pres. China Communications Construction Co. Ltd 2006–14, Exec. Dir and Pres. 2014–. *Address:* China Communications Construction Co. Ltd, 85 Deshengmenwai Street, Xicheng District, Beijing 100088, People's Republic of China (office). *Telephone:* (10) 82016655 (office). *Fax:* (10) 82016500 (office). *E-mail:* webmaster@ccgrp.com.cn (office). *Website:* en.ccccltd.cn (office).

CHEN, Gang; Chinese composer; b. 10 March 1935, Shanghai; s. of Chen Ge-Xin and Jin Jiao-Li; m. (divorced); two d.; ed Shanghai Conservatory of Music; now Prof. of Composition, Shanghai Conservatory of Music; mem. Council of Chinese Musicians' Asscn; Art Dir Shanghai Chamber Orchestra; Guest Prof., USA, France, Canada and Hong Kong; Sec. Chinese Dramatist Asscn 1987–; Golden Record Prize (five times). *Compositions include:* The Butterfly Lovers (with He Zhan Hao), Violin Concerto 1959, The Sun Shines on Tashikuergan, Violin Solo 1973, Morning on the Miao Mountains, Violin Solo 1975; A Moonlight Spring Night on the Flower-surrounded River, Symphonic Picture 1976, Concerto for Oboe 1985, Wang Zhaojun, Violin Concerto 1986, Chamber Music Ensemble 1989, Dragon Symphony 1991. *Leisure interests:* literature, writing. *Address:* Shanghai Conservatory of Music, 20 Fen Yang Road, Shanghai, People's Republic of China (office). *Telephone:* 4370689 (office).

CHEN, Gang, BE, ME, PhD; American (b. Chinese) engineer and academic; *Carl Richard Soderberg Professor of Power Engineering and Head, Department of Mechanical Engineering, Massachusetts Institute of Technology;* b. 20 June 1964; ed Huazhong Inst. of Tech. (now Huazhong Univ. of Science and Tech.—HUST), China, Univ. of California, Berkeley; Lecturer, HUST 1987–89; Grad. Student Research Asst, Univ. of California, Irvine 1989–90, Univ. of California, Berkeley 1990–93; Asst Prof., Dept of Mechanical Eng and Materials Science, Duke Univ. 1993–97; Assoc. Prof., UCLA 1997–2001; Assoc. Prof., Mechanical Eng Dept, MIT 2001–04, Prof. 2004–, Warren and Towneley Rohsenow Professorship 2006–09, Carl Richard Soderberg Prof. of Power Eng 2009–, Head of Dept of Mechanical Eng 2013–, Dir Pappalardo Micro and Nano Eng Labs; Springer Prof., Univ. of California, Berkeley 2012; Guest Prof. in China: HUST 1999–, Xian Jiaotong Univ. 2005–09, Wuhan Univ. of Science and Tech. 2007, Tsinghua Univ. 2012; fmr Chair. Advisory Bd of ASME Nanotechnology Inst.; led first US Dept of Defense Multidisciplinary Univ. Research Initiative (MURI) on thermoelectric materials, currently serves as Dir of Solid-State Solar-Thermal Energy Conversion Center (S3TEC) (Energy Frontier Research Center funded by Dept of Energy); mem. or fmr mem. Editorial/Advisory Bd of nine journals; mem. Nat. Acad. of Eng 2010; Academician, Academia Sinica, Taiwan 2014; Fellow, ASME 2006, AAAS 2009, American Physical Soc. 2012; Hon. Prof., Huanan Univ. of Science and Tech. 2007, Shanghai Univ. 2010, Hubei Univ. of Arts and Science 2011; Scholarship, K.C. Wong Educ. Foundation, Hong Kong 1989–92, Warren Faculty Scholar, Duke Univ. 1994–2001, NSF Young Investigator Award 1996–97, Guggenheim Fellowship 2002–03, NASA Space Act Tech Brief Award 2004, Dusinberre Distinguished Lecturer, Penn State Univ., College Station 2009, JALA Ten 2010 for High Thermal Conductivity Polymers 2010, Distinguished Lecturer, School of Eng, Univ. of Connecticut 2011, Capers and Marion McDonald Award for Excellence in Mentoring and Advising, MIT School of Eng 2011, Distinguished Lecturer, Mechanical Eng Dept, Carnegie Mellon Univ. 2011, Disinguished Seminar, Mechanical Eng Dept, Univ. of Toronto 2012, Hawkins Lecturer, Purdue Univ. 2012, George Persall Lecturer, Duke Univ. 2013, 75th Anniversary Medal, ASME Heat Transfer Div. 2013, Distinguished Lecturer, ME8888 Seminar, Ohio State Univ. 2014, Penner Lecturer, Dept of Mechanical Eng, Univ. of California, San Diego 2014, Nukiyama Memorial Award, Heat Transfer Soc. of Japan 2014, HUST Outstanding Alumni Award 2014, Inst. of Advanced Studies Distinguished Seminar, Hong Kong Univ. of Science and Tech. 2015, William Mong Distinguished Lecturer, Univ. of Hong Kong 2015, World Tech. Award (Energy) 2015. *Publications include:* Nanoscale Energy Transfer and Conversion 2005, In Memory of Chang-Lin Tien, Annual Review of Heat Transfer, Vol. 14 (co-ed.) 2005, Vol. 15 (co-ed.) 2012, Vol. 16 (co-ed.) 2013, Vol. 17 (co-ed.) 2014, Vol. 18 (co-ed.) 2015; numerous book chapters and more than 330 papers in professional journals; more than 40 patents. *Address:* Room 3-174, Massachusetts Institute of Technology, 77 Massachusetts Avenue, Cambridge, MA 02139, USA (office). *Telephone:* (617) 253-3523 (office). *Fax:* (617) 324-5519 (office). *E-mail:* gchen2@mit.edu (office). *Website:* meche.mit.edu/people/faculty/gchen2@mit.edu (office); web.mit.edu/nanoengineering (office).

CHEN, Geng; Chinese petroleum industry executive; b. May 1946; ed Beijing Econs Inst.; Deputy Dir Changqing Petroleum Exploration Bureau 1983–85; Deputy Dir Labour Dept, Ministry of Petroleum Industry 1985–88; Dir Labour Bureau, China Nat. Petroleum Corpn 1988–93, Asst to Gen. Man. 1993–97, Deputy Gen. Man. 1997–98, Gen. Man. 2004–06, also Pres.; Dir PetroChina 2001–06, Pres. 2002–04, Chair. 2004–06; currently External Dir China Ocean Shipping (Group) Co. (COSCO). *Address:* China Ocean Shipping (Group) Company, Ocean Plaza, 158 Fuxingmennei Street, Beijing 100031, People's Republic of China (office). *Telephone:* (10) 6649-3388 (office). *Fax:* (10) 6649-2288 (office). *E-mail:* internet@cosco.com (office). *Website:* www.cosco.com (office).

CHEN, Guangyi; Chinese government official; b. 7 Aug. 1933, Putian City, Fujian Prov.; s. of Chen Zhaohe and Li Muxin; m. Chen Xiuyun 1961; two s. one d.; ed Northeast China Engineering Coll.; joined CCP 1959; Deputy Div. Chief Prov. Heavy Industry Dept, Gansu Prov. 1960–64; Dir Production Office, Northwest China Nonferrous Metallurgical Design Acad. 1964–75; Div. Chief Prov. Metallurgical Bureau, Gansu Prov. 1977–80; Deputy Dir Prov. Planning Cttee, Gansu Prov. 1980–83; Deputy Sec. CCP Prov. Cttee, Gansu Prov. 1980–83; Gov. of Gansu Prov. 1983–86; Sec. 5th CCP Cttee, Fujian 1986; Chair. CPPCC 6th Fujian Provincial Cttee 1988; Chair. Fujian Prov. People's Congress Standing Committee 1993–94; mem. 12th CCP Cen. Cttee 1982–87, 13th CCP Cen. Cttee 1987–92, 14th CCP Cen. Cttee 1992–97, 15th CCP Cen. Cttee 1997–2002; Party Cttee Sec. and Head Civil Aviation Gen. Admin. of China 1993–98; mem. 9th Standing Cttee of the NPC 1998–2003, Chair. Financial and Econ. Cttee of 9th NPC 1998–2003, Overseas Chinese Affairs Cttee of 10th NPC 2003–08; Hon. Pres. Nanjing Aerospace Inst. *Address:* c/o Standing Committee of National People's Congress, Beijing, People's Republic of China.

CHEN, Hong, BSc; Chinese automotive executive; *Chairman, SAIC Motor Corporation Limited;* b. March 1961, Jiashan, Zhejiang Prov.; ed Tongji Univ., Shanghai; joined Shanghai Tractor and Automobile Co. (later Shanghai Automotive Industry Group Corpn—SAIC) 1984, with Shanghai-Volkswagen Automobile Co. Ltd (S-VW) project, Asst to Exec. Vice-Pres. of Human Resources, S-VW 1985–92, also Dir of Policy Research and Pres. S-VW Engine Factory, with Shanghai General Motors Co. Ltd (Shanghai-GM) Sedan Project 1995–97, Vice-Pres. Shanghai-GM 1997–99, later Pres., currently Vice-Chair. and Vice-Sec. Party Cttee of SAIC (Group), Pres. SAIC Motor Corpn Ltd 2004–14, Deputy Chair. and Deputy Sec. Party Cttee 2006–14, Chair. and Sec. Party Cttee 2014–; Chair. SsangYong Motor Co. 2005–; mem. CCP 1984–. *Address:* SAIC Motor Corporation Ltd, 5/F Building A, 563 Songtao Road, Zhangjiang, High Technology Park, Pu Dong, Shanghai 201203 (office); SAIC Motor Corporation Ltd, No. 489, Weihai Road, Shanghai 200041, People's Republic of China (office). *Telephone:* (21) 50803757 (office); (21) 22011688 (office). *Fax:* (21) 50803780 (office); (21) 22011188 (office). *E-mail:* info@saicgroup.com (office). *Website:* www.saicgroup.com (office); www.saicmotor.com (office).

CHEN, Houqun; Chinese geologist; *Research Professor and Chairman of the Academic Committee, Institute of Water Resources and Hydropower Research;* b. 3 May 1932, Wuxi, Jiangsu Prov.; ed Tsinghua Univ., Moscow Power Mechanics Inst., USSR; made original contrib. to the theoretical study of seismic hardening of concrete dams and to solving key problems of seismic resistance in maj. civil eng projects such as Xinfengjiang, Ertan and Xiaolangdi dams; presided over the compiling, editing and revising of many nat. standards, including Standard for the Anti-Seismic Design of Hydraulic Structures; built China's first large-scale three-dimensional and six-free-degree earthquake simulation platform; Chair. Standing Cttee, Dept of Civil Eng, Hydraulic and Constructional Eng, Chinese Acad. of Eng; Sr Engineer and Dir Eng Anti-Seismic Research Centre, China Water Conservancy and Hydroelectric Science Research Inst.; currently Research Prof. and Chair. Acad. Cttee, Inst. of Water Resources and Hydropower Research; Fellow Chinese Acad. of Eng; Chair. Seismic Cttee, Int. Comm. on Large Dams, Earthquake Eng and Disaster Prevention Chapter, Architectural Soc. of China; Deputy Dir Nat. Technical Cttee on Earthquake Standardization; Vice-Pres., Chinese Hydraulic Eng Soc.; currently Lead, Expert Group for S- to -N Water Diversion Project, Expert Examination Panel for Three Gorges Project; mem. Standing Cttee, National Earthquake Safety Assessment Cttee, Standing Cttee, Chinese Soc. for Vibration Eng, 9th Chinese People's Political Consultative Conf., Standing Cttee, Chinese Acad. of Eng; Hon. mem. Int. Comm on Large Dams 2011; 20 nat., ministerial and provincial awards for science and tech., including Prize of Progress in Science and Technology, Ho Leung Ho Lee Prize 2001. *Publications:* over 150 research papers. *Address:* Institute of Water Resources and Hydropower Research, A–1 Fuxing Road, Haidian District, Beijing 100038, People's Republic of China (office). *Telephone:* (10) 68781650 (office). *Fax:* (10) 68412316 (home). *E-mail:* wangyw@iwhr.com (office); dic@iwhr.com; (office). *Website:* www.iwhr.com (office).

CHEN, Hualan, MSc, PhD; Chinese animal virologist and academic; *Professor, Harbin Veterinary Research Institute, Chinese Academy of Agricultural Sciences;* b. 1969, Baiyin, Gansu Prov.; m.; one s.; ed Gansu Agricultural Univ., Grad. School of Chinese Acad. of Agricultural Sciences; Research Asst, Harbin Veterinary Research Inst., Chinese Acad. of Agricultural Sciences 1997–99, Researcher and PhD Supervisor 2002–, Dir Key Lab. of Animal Influenza and Dir Nat. Bird Flu Research Lab. 2002–, also Prof.; studied at Centers for Disease Control and Prevention (CDC), USA 1999–2002; mem. World Org. for Animal Health (OIE); mem. FAO Org. Corp. Statistical Database (FAOSTAT); First Class Nat. Science and Tech. Progress Award, Second Class Nat. Tech. Invention Award, Chinese Agricultural Elites Award, China Youth Science and Tech. Award, China Young Female Scientists Award 2011, Nat. 'May 1' Labour Medal, China Youth 'May 4' Medal, ranked among the Ten Scientific Figures of the Year by Nature journal) 2013, L'Oréal-UNESCO Award for Women in Science (Asia/Pacific) 2016. *Publications:* more than 50 papers in professional journals; seven Chinese patents. *Address:* Harbin Veterinary Research Institute, 427 Maduan Street, Nangang District, Harbin, 150001, People's Republic of China (office). *Telephone:* (451) 5199-7168 (office). *Fax:* (451) 5199-7166 (office). *E-mail:* chenhualan@caas.cn (office). *Website:* www.hvri.ac.cn (office).

CHEN, Huanyou; Chinese administrator; *Chairman, Standing Committee of Jiangsu Provincial People's Congress;* b. 1934, Nantong City, Jiangsu Prov.; ed East China Military and Political Acad., People's Univ. of China; joined PLA, CCP 1954; Lecturer, Jilin Industrial Univ. 1959–65 (also Sec., Teaching Office 1959–65 and Deputy Sec. CCP Gen. Br. 1959–65); Dir Wuxi Diesel Engine Plant, Jiangsu Prov. 1975–81 (also Deputy Sec. and Sec. CCP Party Cttee 1975–81); Deputy Dir Prov. Econ. Cttee and Nat. Defence Industry Cttee, Jiangsu Prov. 1981–83; Dir Planning Cttee, Jiangsu Province 1983–84; mem. Standing Cttee of Jiangsu CCP

Prov. Cttee 1984, later Chair. People's Armament Cttee; Deputy to 8th NPC Jiangsu Prov.; Vice-Gov. Jiangsu Prov. 1983–84, Exec. Vice-Gov. 1984–89, Gov. 1989–94; Deputy Sec. CCP Jiangsu Prov. Cttee 1986–93, Sec. CCP Jiangsu Prov. Cttee 1993–2000; Del., 13th CCP Nat. Congress 1987–92, 14th CCP Nat. Congress 1992–97, 15th CCP Nat. Congress 1997–2002; Deputy, 7th NPC 1988–92, 8th NPC 1993–98; Chair. Standing Cttee, Jiangsu Prov. People's Congress 1998–; Hon. Pres. Red Cross Soc. of China, Jiangsu Prov. 1994–. *Address:* 70 W Beijing Road, Nanjing 210000, Jiangsu Province, People's Republic of China. *Telephone:* 025-663 5164.

CHEN, Huiguang; Chinese politician; b. 1938, Yulin City, Guangxi Zhuang Autonomous Region; ed Guangxi Inst. of Coal Mining; successively, Engineer, Mining Technician, Head of Production Section, Deputy Head and Head Dongluo Mining Admin, Guangxi Zhuang Autonomous Region 1961–80 (also Deputy Sec. CCP Party Cttee 1961–80); joined CCP 1965; Deputy Dir Coal Industry Bureau, Guangxi Zhuang Autonomous Region 1980–83; Sec. CCP Municipal Cttee, Nanning 1983–85; Deputy Sec. CCP Cttee, Guangxi Zhuang 1983–85, (Leading) Sec. 1985–88; mem. 12th CCP Cen. Cttee 1982–87, 13th CCP Cen. Cttee 1987–92; Chair. CPPCC Guangxi Zhuang Autonomous Regional Cttee 1983–; Del. 14th CCP Nat. Congress 1992–97, 15th CCP Nat. Congress 1997–2002; mem. 8th CPPCC Nat. Cttee 1993–98, 9th CPPCC Nat. Cttee 1998–2003. *Address:* 1 Minlelu Road, Nanning City, Guangxi, People's Republic of China.

CHEN, Jiaer; Chinese professor of physics; b. 1 Oct. 1934, Shanghai; ed Jilin Univ.; joined CCP 1952; Lecturer in Physics, Peking Univ. 1955 (also Dir Teaching Staff Office and Deputy Dean), later Assoc. Prof., Prof. of Physics and Doctorate Dir 1984–, Vice-Pres. and Pres. Postgraduate School 1984–96, Pres. Beijing Univ. 1996–99, Vice-Pres. Council of Capital Devt Inst. 1999–; Visiting Scholar, Univ. of Oxford, UK 1963–66; fmr Dir Teaching Staff Office, Hanzhong School, Shaanxi Prov.; Visiting Scientist, South Africa 1982–84; Dir Heavy Ion Physics Research Inst. 1986–2001; Deputy Dir Nat. Natural Sciences Foundation of China 1991–99, Dir 1999–2003; Pres. Beijing Asscn of Science and Tech. 1997–, Asscn of Asia Pacific Physical Socs 1998–2001; Bd Dir China Physics Soc. 1996–99; Academician, Chinese Acad. of Sciences 1993– (mem. 4th Presidium of Depts, Chinese Acad. of Sciences 2000–02); Alt. mem. 15th CCP Cen. Cttee 1997–2002; mem. Third World Academy of Sciences 2002; Fellow Inst. of Physics 2001; Hon. SSc (Menlo Coll., Calif.) 1999, (Waseda Univ., Japan) 2000, (Chinese Univ. of Hong Kong) 2000, (Loughborough) 2002; numerous awards including First Grade Prize, State Educ. Comm. for Progress in Science and Tech. 1992, 1995, Zhou Pei-yuan Physics Award 1997, Ho Leung Ho Lee Foundation Award 2001. *Address:* National Natural Science Foundation of China, 83 Shuangqing Road, Haidian District, 100085 Beijing (office); Room 4–501, Bldg 12, Lanqiying, Peking University, Beijing, People's Republic of China (home). *Telephone:* (10) 62326876 (office); (10) 62758868 (home). *Fax:* (10) 62327082 (office); (10) 62758868 (home). *E-mail:* chenjer@rose.nsfc.gov.cn (office); chenje@pku.edu.cn (home). *Website:* www.nsfc.gov.cn (office).

CHEN, Jian; Chinese diplomatist and UN official; b. 2 Feb. 1942; m.; one d.; ed Fudan Univ., Beijing Foreign Studies Univ.; attaché, Perm. Mission of China to the UN 1972–77, Third, Second then First Sec. 1980–84, Amb. and Deputy Perm. Rep. to UN 1992–94; attaché, Dept of Int. Orgs and Confs, Ministry of Foreign Affairs 1977–80, Dir, Counsellor then Deputy Dir-Gen. 1985–92; Asst, Office of Exec. Dir representing China at IMF 1984–85; Dir-Gen. Dept of Information and Spokesperson Ministry of Foreign Affairs 1994–96; Asst Minister of Foreign Affairs 1996–98; Amb. to Japan 1998–2001; Under-Sec.-Gen. for Gen. Ass. and Conf Man., UN, New York 2001–07; Pres. UN Asscn of China 2007–12; fmr Rep. to UN Gen. Ass., Security Council, ECOSOC, UNEP, ESCAP and numerous confs and meetings. *Address:* c/o United Nations Association of China, 71 Nanchizi Street, Beijing, 100006, People's Republic of China.

CHEN, Jiangong; Chinese writer; b. Nov. 1949, Beihai, Guangxi Prov.; ed Peking Univ.; started career as coal miner in Jingxi Mine; joined Beijing Writers' Asscn 1981; Sec. of Secr., Chinese Writers' Asscn 1995–2001, 2003–, Vice-Chair. 2001–; currently Curator, Nat. Museum of Modern Chinese Literature, Beijing; mem. Exec. Council, China Overseas Friendship Asscn. *Television:* dramas: Haung Cheng Gen Er, Song of Youth, When We Were Still Young. *Publications:* The Meandering Stream 1980, The Fluttering Flowered Scarf 1981, A Girl with the Eyes of a Red Phoenix 1981, Selected Novels by Chen Jiangong, No. 9 Huluba Alley, Letting Go, Curly Hair, Previous Offence, Phoenix Eyes, Manic Starry Sky, At the Foot of Imperial City, The Selection of Chen Jiangong, Imperial City Wall (co-author) (Excellence Saga Novel Award), Sun Stone (Best Novella Award), Confusion Star Sky, Frizzle (Literature Award), Criminal Record, Slim Eyes (Nat. Award for Best Short Story), Colorful Turban Along with Wind (Nat. Award for Best Short Story), Free Captive Animals (Excellence Novella Award); essays: Be honest to Me, The Flavor of Beijing, Essay Selection of Chen Jiangong, Fess Up. *Address:* National Museum of Modern Chinese Literature, 45 Wenxueguan Lu, Shaoyaoju, Chaoyang District, Beijing 100029, People's Republic of China. *Website:* www.wxg.org.cn.

CHEN, Jinhang; Chinese engineer and business executive; *Chairman, China Datang Corporation;* ed Shandong Univ.; Deputy Chief of Shandong Heze Electric Power Bureau 1985–91; Deputy Chief and Chief of Tai'an Electric Power Bureau 1991–96; successively worked as Chief of Accounting Dept, Asst to the Chief, Chair. of Trade Union and Vice-Pres. Shandong Electric Power Corpn 1996–2000; Vice-Pres., later Pres. Shanxi Electric Power Corpn, 2000–01, Chair. Shanxi Zhangze Electric Power Corpn Ltd and Shanxi Yangcheng International Electric Power Co. Ltd 2001–02; Exec. Vice-Pres. State Grid Corpn of China 2002–10; Chair. China Datang Corpn 2010–, Chair. China Datang Corpn Renewable Power Co. Ltd 2010–. *Address:* China Datang Corporation, 1 Guangningbo Street, Xicheng District, Beijing 100032, People's Republic of China (office). *E-mail:* webmaster@china-cdt.com (office). *Website:* www.china-cdt.com (office).

CHEN, Jining, BSc, PhD; Chinese professor of environmental system analysis and university administrator; *Acting Mayor of Beijing;* b. 1964, Lishu Co., Jilin Prov.; ed Tsinghua Univ., Imperial Coll. London, UK; joined CCP 1984; Asst Researcher, Imperial Coll. London 1994–98; Vice-Dean Dept of Environmental Eng, Tsinghua Univ. 1998–99, Dean 1999–2006, Vice-Pres. Tsinghua Univ. 2006–07, Deputy Pres. 2007, Exec. Vice-Pres. 2007–12, Pres. 2012–15; Minister of Environmental Protection 2015–17; Acting Mayor of Beijing 2017–18, Mayor 2018–; mem. Nat. Environmental Advisory Comm.; Deputy Chair. Science and Tech. Cttee of Ministry of Environmental Protection; Vice-Pres. Chinese Soc. for Environmental Sciences; mem. Bd Chinese Environmental Foundation, and other scientific cttees, professional asscns and advisory councils related to water and environment; mem. or fmr mem. editorial bds of several environmental journals; several scientific prizes. *Publications:* author or co-editor of several books; more than 200 papers in professional journals; owner of more than a dozen registered environmental and software patents. *E-mail:* contact@ebeijing.gov.cn. *Website:* www.ebeijing.gov.cn/Government/Mayor_office (office).

CHEN, Jui-Tsung (Ray); Taiwanese business executive; *President and CEO, Compal Electronics, Inc.;* ed Nat. Cheng Kung Univ.; Pres. and CEO Compal Electronics, Inc. 1992–, Chair. and CEO Compal Communications Inc. 2000–, also Gen. Man. in four other cos; fmr Exec. Vice-Pres. Kinpo Electronics Inc.; Chair. TPO Displays Corpn, Arcadyan Technology Corpn; fmr Chair. Royal Philips Electronics NV, Mobile Display Systems Unit; Dir Compal Digital Technology (Kunshan) Co. Ltd, Chunghwa Picture Tubes Ltd 2009–, Compal Electronics, Inc. 2009–; Man. Dir Taipei Computer Asscn; named The Best CEO in Taiwan by Institutional Investors 2004, Outstanding Alumni with Exceptional Accomplishment Award, Nat. Cheng Kung Univ. 2006, International Entrepreneur, Entrepreneur of The Year 2010 Award, Ernst & Young Taiwan 2010. *Address:* Compal Electronics, Inc., 581 Ruiguang Road, Neihu District, Taipei 11492, Taiwan (office). *Telephone:* (2) 87978588 (office). *Fax:* (2) 26585001 (office). *E-mail:* info@compal.com (office). *Website:* www.compal.com (office).

CHEN, Jun, PhD; Chinese geochemist, academic and university administrator; *Vice-Chancellor and President, Nanjing University;* b. 1954, Yangzhou, Jiangsu Prov.; ed Nanjing Univ.; Prof. of Geochemistry, Dept of Earth Sciences, Nanjing Univ. 1992–, becoming Dean, Dept of Earth Sciences, Vice-Pres. and Exec. Vice-Pres. Nanjing Univ., Pres. 2006–17, Vice-Chancellor and Pres. 2017–; Standing Dir Chinese Geological Soc., Chinese Soc. for Quaternary Research; Vice-Pres. Chinese Soc. for Mineralogy, Petrology and Geochemistry; mem. Fifth Cttee of Science and Tech., Ministry of Educ.; Academician, Chinese Acad. of Sciences 2013; mem. 11th NPC Standing Cttee 2008–13; Dr hc (Univ. of Southampton) 2009, (Univ. of York) 2012; several Ministry of Educ. prizes for science and tech. *Address:* Office of the President, University of Nanjing, No. 22 Hankou Road, Nanjing, Jiangsu 210093, People's Republic of China (office). *Telephone:* (025) 3593186 (office). *E-mail:* chenjun@nju.edu.cn (office). *Website:* www.nju.edu.cn/cps/site/NJU/njue/profile/profile/president.htm (office).

CHEN, Kaige; Chinese film director; b. 12 Aug. 1952, Beijing; m. 1st Sun Jialin 1983; m. 2nd Hong Huang; m. 3rd Chen Hong 1996; ed Beijing Cinema Coll., New York Univ.; worker, rubber plantation, Yunnan; soldier for four years; Golden Palm Award 1993, New York Film Critics' Best Foreign Film 1993, 28th Moscow Int. Film Festival Lifetime Achievement Award 2006. *Films include:* The Yellow Earth (Best Film, Berlin Film Festival), Life on a String, King of the Children 1988, Farewell My Concubine 1993, The Assassin 1998, The Emperor and the Assassin 1999, Killing Me Softly 2002, He ni zai yi qi (Together with You) 2002, Ten Minutes Older: The Trumpet (segment) 2002, Mo gik (The Promise) 2004, Zhanxiou Village 2007, Mei Lanfang 2008, Sacrifice 2010, Caught in the Web 2012, The Monk 2015. *Publications include:* King of the Children, The New Chinese Cinema (with Tony Raynes) 1989, Bawang bieji 1992, The Emperor and the Assassin 1999, Together 2002, The Promise 2005. *Address:* c/o ICM Partners, 10250 Constellation Blvd, 9th Floor, Los Angeles, CA 90067-6209, USA (office). *Telephone:* (310) 550-4000 (office). *Fax:* (310) 550-4100 (office). *Website:* www.icmtalent.com (office).

CHEN, Kuiyuan; Chinese party official; b. Jan. 1941; ed Inner Mongolia Teachers' Univ.; joined CCP 1965; fmr mem., Deputy Sec.-Gen., Sec.-Gen. CCP League Cttee Standing Cttee, Hulun Buir League, Inner Mongolia Autonomous Region, Deputy Sec. and Sec. 1983–89; mem. CCP Autonomous Regional Cttee Standing Cttee, Inner Mongolia Autonomous Region 1989–92: Vice-Chair. Inner Mongolia Autonomous Regional People's Congress 1989–92; Deputy Sec. CCP Tibet Autonomous Region Cttee 1992, Sec. 1992–2000; mem. 14th CCP Cen. Cttee 1992–97, 15th CCP Cen. Cttee 1997–2002, 16th CCP Cen. Cttee 2002–07, 17th CCP Cen. Cttee 2007–12; apptd First Sec. CCP Party Cttee PLA, Tibet Mil. Region 1996; Sec. CCP Henan Prov. Cttee 2000–02; Pres. Chinese Acad. of Social Sciences 2002–13; Vice-Chair. 10th CPPCC Nat. Cttee 2003–08, 11th CPPCC Nat. Cttee 2008–13. *Address:* c/o Chinese Academy of Social Sciences, 5 Jianguomennei Dajie, Beijing 100732, People's Republic of China. *E-mail:* cssnenglish@cass.org.cn.

CHEN, Lei; Chinese politician; *Minister of Water Resources;* b. 1954, Beijing; ed North China Inst. of Water Conservancy and Hydroelectric Power; joined CCP 1980; Teacher, N China Inst. of Water Resources and Hydroelectric Power 1980–82; Clerk, Tech. Dept, China Irrigation and Drainage Co., Ministry of Water Resources 1985–89, Assoc. Man., Project Planning Dept 1989–92, Man. 1992–93, Deputy Gen. Man. 1993–95, Gen. Man. 1995, Dir, Rural Water Conservancy Dept, Ministry of Water Resources 1996–2000, Dir, Planning Dept 2000–01, Vice-Minister of Water Resources 2001–04, Minister 2007–; mem. Three Gorges Project Construction Cttee 2004–05; Vice-Chair., Autonomous Region People's Govt, Xinjiang Uygur Autonomous Region 2005, Exec. Vice-Chair. 2005–07; mem. 17th CCP Cen. Cttee 2007–12, 18th CCP Cen. Cttee 2012–17. *Address:* Ministry of Water Resources, 2 Baiguang Lu, Xiang 2, Xuanwu Qu, Beijing 100053, People's Republic of China (office). *Telephone:* (10) 63202114 (office). *E-mail:* webmaster@mwr.gov.cn (office). *Website:* www.mwr.gov.cn (office).

CHEN, Liangyu; Chinese politician; b. Oct. 1946, Ningbo, Zhejiang Prov.; ed PLA Logistics Engineering Inst., Tongji Univ., Shanghai, Party School, First Bureau of Electrical Machinery, Univ. of Birmingham, UK; joined PLA 1963, soldier, Services and Arms Group Army Unit No. 6716 1968–70; worker, designer, Deputy Section Chief of Infrastructure, Shanghai Pengpu Machinery Factory 1970–83; joined CCP 1980; designer, Shanghai Pengpu Machine Bldg Factory, Deputy Dir 1983–84; Deputy Sec., CCP Shanghai Metallurgical and Mining Machinery Corpn Cttee 1983–84; Sec. CCP Shanghai Electric Appliances Corpn Cttee 1984–85; Vice-Dir, then Dir Veteran Cadre Dept, Shanghai Municipal Cttee 1985–87, Deputy Dir and Dir Shanghai Dist Cttee 1987–92, Vice-Sec.-Gen., then Vice-Sec. Shanghai Municipal Cttee 1992–2002; Vice-Sec., then Dist Magistrate Huangpu Dist Cttee

1985–92; Exec. Vice-Mayor of Shanghai 1996–2001, Acting Mayor 2001–02, Mayor 2002–03; Alt. mem. 15th CCP Cen. Cttee 1997–2002, 16th CCP Cen. Cttee 2002–07, Politburo 2002–07, Sec. CCP Municipal Cttee, Shanghai 2002–06 (dismissed for misuse of Shanghai pension fund), expelled from CCP and sentenced to 18 years' imprisonment on corruption charges 2008.

CHEN, Lu Yu; Chinese television presenter; b. 12 June 1970, Beijing; known as "the Chinese Oprah"; host of daily chat show A Date with Lu Yu on Hong Kong-based Phoenix Satellite TV station; working with Sina.com to develop new daily Oprah Winfrey-style of talk show; China TV Programme Award for the Best Female Presenter of the Year 2000, named as Most Successful Woman 2007 by Jessica magazine. *Television includes:* Good Morning China, Phoenix Afternoon Express. *Address:* A Date with Lu Yu, Phoenix Satellite TV, Room 306, No. 165 Haidian Road, Haidian District, Beijing, 100080, People's Republic of China (office). *Telephone:* (10) 62510868 (office); (10) 62510511 (office). *Fax:* (10) 62510484 (office). *Website:* www.phoenixtv.com (office).

CHEN, Min'er, LLM; Chinese politician; *Communist Party Secretary, Chongqing municipality;* b. Sept. 1960, Zhuji, Zhejiang Prov.; ed Shaoxing Univ.; mem. CCP 1982–; Magistrate, Shaoxing County People's Court, Zhejiang Prov. 1991–95; Chief Ed. Zhejiang Daily 1999–2001; Dir, Propaganda Dept, Zhejiang Prov. CCP 2001–07; mem. CCP Standing Cttee, Zhejiang Prov. 2002–12; Pres., Zhejiang Admin Coll. 2007–12; Vice Gov., Zhejiang Prov. 2007–12; Gov., Guizhou Prov. 2012–15; CCP Sec., Guizhou Prov. 2015–17; CCP Sec., Chongqing municipality 2017–; alt. mem. 17th CCP Cen. Cttee 2007–12; mem. 18th CCP Cen. Cttee 2012–17; mem. 19th CCP Cen. Cttee 2017–, also mem. 19th CCP Politburo 2017–. *Address:* CCP Municipal Committee, Chongqing, People's Republic of China (office). *Website:* en.cq.gov.cn (office).

CHEN, Mingyi; Chinese administrator; *Chairman, Fujian Provincial Committee, Chinese People's Political Consultative Conference;* b. 1940, Fuzhou City, Fujian Prov.; ed Jiaotong Univ., Shanghai; joined CCP 1960; teacher, Jiaotong Univ.; Vice-Gov. Fujian Prov. 1993–94, Gov. 1994–96; Deputy Sec. CCP Fujian Prov. Cttee 1993–95, Sec. 1996–2000; Chair. CPPCC Fujian Prov. Cttee 2001–; Alt. mem. 12th CCP Cen. Cttee 1982–87, 13th CCP Cen. Cttee 1987–92, 14th CCP Cen. Cttee 1992–97, mem. 15th CCP Cen. Cttee 1997–2002; Deputy to 8th NPC 1996. *Address:* Fujian Provincial People's Political Consultative Conference, Fuzhou City, People's Republic of China.

CHEN, Ningning, (Diana Chen Ningning), MBA; Chinese business executive; *Chairman, Pioneer Metals Holdings;* b. 1971, Beijing; d. of Lu Hui; ed New York Inst. of Tech.; fmr Fund Man. Prudential Securities, New York; fmr Vice-Pres. Winease Investment, Hong Kong; fmr Exec. Dir and Vice-Chair. China Oriental Group Co. Ltd; Founder and Chair. Pioneer Metals Holdings 1996. *Address:* Pioneer Metals Holdings, 5F China Textile Building, No. 19 Jianguomennei Street, Beijing 100005, People's Republic of China (office). *Telephone:* (10) 65129966 (office). *Fax:* (10) 65285085 (office). *E-mail:* webmaster@pioneer-metals .com (office). *Website:* www.pioneer-metals.com (office).

CHEN, Peiqiu; Chinese artist; b. 29 Dec. 1922, Nanyang, Henan; m. Xie Zhiliu (died 1997); ed Nat. Acad. of Art; specialises in painting landscapes, birds and flowers in decorative style; also occasionally collaborated with her late husband, famous artist Xie Zhiliu; Shanghai Municipal People's Govt opened a museum in Nanhui New City in their name 2015; Council mem. Xiling Seal Art Soc.; Shanghai Art and Literature Prize Lifetime Achievement Award 2014. *Address:* c/o Huangjie Gallery, 356 Yuyuan Road, Jingan Qu, Shanghai 200000, People's Republic of China. *Telephone:* (21) 62514084.

CHEN, Peisi; Chinese comedian and actor; b. 1953, Ningjin, Hebei; s. of Chen Qiang; worked in Nei Monggo Production and Construction Corps 1969–73; with PLA Bayi Film Studio 1973–; f. Hainan Comedy Film and TV Ltd Co. (later renamed as Dadao Film and TV Ltd Co.) 1991; comic sketches in collaboration with Zhu Shimao, at successive Chinese New Year Gala Nights on Chinese Cen. TV; took part in Olympic Torch Relay, Nanjing May 2008. *Films:* Look at This Family, Inside and Outside the Law Court, Sunset Boulevard, Erzi Running a Shop, A Stupid Manager, A Chivalrous Ball-Game Star in the Capital, A Young Master's Misfortune, A Millionaire from the South China Sea, Make a Bomb 1993, Sub-Husband 1993, Her Majesty is Fine 1995, Bao lian deng (voice) 2000, The Secret of the Magic Gourd (voice) 2007. *Plays:* A Dou (producer and lead actor) 2008. *Address:* People's Liberation Army Bayi Film Studio, Beijing, People's Republic of China (office).

CHEN, Qingtai, BSc; Chinese politician and business executive; b. 1937, Fengrun, Hebei Prov.; ed Tsinghua Univ., Beijing; joined CCP 1956; Dir Design Dept, Vice-Chief Engineer, Chief Engineer, Gen. Man., then Chair. Aeolus United Automotive Industry Corpn 1962–88, Chair. Aeolus-Citroen Automobile Co. Ltd; Chair. and CEO Dongfeng Peugeot Citroen Automobile Ltd 1985–92; Chair. Shenlong Automobile Co., Ltd 1982–92; Deputy Dir State Econ. and Trade Comm. 1992–93, Vice-Minister 1993–98; mem. Chinese Monetary Policy Cttee 1997–; Dir Devt Research Centre of the State Council 1993–98, Deputy Dir 1998–2001; mem. 9th CPPCC Nat. Cttee 1998–2003; Dir Chardan North China Acquisition Corpn 2008–; Dir (non-Exec.) Bank of Communications Co. Ltd 2005–11, China Petroleum & Chemical Corpn 2003–06; Independent Dir Sinopec Corpn 2000–06, Mindray Medical Int. Ltd 2006–, Hollysys Automation Technologies, Ltd 2008–14; Dir China Europe Int. Business School 2011–, Public Man. Coll.; Nat. Excellent Entrepreneur 1988. *Address:* Development Research Centre of the State Council, Beijing, People's Republic of China (office).

CHEN, Qiqi; Chinese administrator; b. 26 April 1941, Guangdong Prov.; m. Prof. Zheng Sheu Xen; one s.; ed Guangdong Medical School, Medical Coll. of Italy; doctor, Guangdong Leprosy Hosp. 1965–75; teacher, Guangzhou Medical School 1975–81; Vice-Mayor of Guangzhou Municipality 1985; Pres. Guangdong Red Cross; Dir China Red Cross; Vice-Pres. Guangzhou People's Asscn for Friendship with Foreign Countries. *Address:* 86 Yue Hwa Road, Guangzhou, Guangdong (home); 1 Fuqian Road, Guangzhou, Guangdong, People's Republic of China (office). *Telephone:* (20) 330360 (office); (20) 3333100 (home). *Fax:* (20) 340347.

CHEN, Qiufa; Chinese aerospace engineer and politician; *CCP Secretary, Liaoning Province;* b. Dec. 1954, Chengbu, Hunan Prov.; ed Nat. Univ. of Defence Tech.; began career as teacher, Lianxing Elementary School, Chengbu 1973; joined CCP 1974; joined Ministry of Aerospace Industry as engineer 1978, becoming Man. –1994; worked for China Aerospace Science and Tech. Corpn 1994–98; Dir, Educ. Dept, Comm. for Science, Tech. and Industry for Nat. Defence (COSTIND) 1998–2000, Head, COSTIND Comm. for Discipline Inspection 2000–05, Deputy Dir, COSTIND 2005–08; Vice Minister of Industry and Information Tech. 2008–13; Dir, China Atomic Energy Authority 2008–13; Dir, State Admin for Science, Tech. and Industry for Nat. Defence (SASTIND) 2009–13; Dir, China Nat. Space Admin 2010–13; Chair. Hunan People's Political Consultative Conf. 2015–16; Acting Gov., Liaoning Prov. 2015, Gov. 2015–17; Deputy CCP Sec., Liaoning Prov. 2015–17, CCP Sec. 2017–; mem. 18th CCP Cen. Cttee 2012–17, 19th CCP Cen. Cttee 2017–. *Address:* CPC Provincial Committee, Liaoning Province, Shenyang 110000, People's Republic of China (office). *Website:* www.ln.gov.cn (office).

CHEN, Quanguo; Chinese politician; *CCP Secretary, Xinjiang Uyghur Autonomous Region;* b. Nov. 1955, Pingyu County, Zhumadian prefecture, Henan Prov.; ed Zhengzhou Univ., Wuhan Univ. of Tech.; enlisted in PLA Dec. 1973; joined CCP Feb. 1976; CCP Cttee Sec., Suiping city 1988–94; Head of Org. Dept, Pingdingshan city 1994–96; Mayor and Deputy CCP Sec., Luohe city, Henan Prov. 1996–98; Vice-Gov., Henan Prov. 1998–2001, Head, Henan Prov. Org. Dept 2000–04, Deputy CCP Sec. 2003–09; Acting Gov. and Deputy CCP Sec., Hebei Prov. 2009–10, Gov., Hebei Prov. 2010–11; CCP Sec., Tibet Autonomous Region 2011–16; CCP Sec., Xinjiang Uygur Autonomous Region 2016–; Alt. mem. 17th CCP Cen. Cttee 2007–12, mem. 18th CCP Cen. Cttee 2012–17. *Address:* Autonomous Regional Committee, Xinjiang Uygur Autonomous Region, Ürümqi 830000, People's Republic of China (office). *Website:* www.urumqi.gov.cn (office).

CHEN, Quanxun; Chinese business executive; *Chairman, China Nonferrous Metals Industry Association;* fmr Chair. Supervisory Bd, Shanghai Baosteel Group Corpn; Chair. Supervisory Panel, state-owned enterprise –2008; currently Chair. China Nonferrous Metals Industry Asscn; mem. Bd of Dirs Sichuan Chuantou Energy Co. Ltd 2008. *Address:* China Nonferrous Metals Industry Association, Fuxing Road, Haidian District, Beijing 100814, People's Republic of China (office). *Telephone:* (10) 63971798 (office). *E-mail:* public@chinania.org.cn (office). *Website:* www.chinania.org.cn/ (office).

CHEN, Rongzhen; Chinese business executive (retd); b. Aug. 1938, Feidong, Anhui Prov.; Dir Hefei Washing Machine Gen. Factory (later renamed Rongshida Group) 1986–2002, Chair. and Pres. Rongshida Group –2002 (retd). *Address:* c/o Rongshida Group, 669 Changjian Road, Hefei 230088, Anhui Province, People's Republic of China (office).

CHEN, Sean, (Chen Chun), LLB, LLM; Taiwanese banking executive and politician; b. 13 Oct. 1949; ed Nat. Taiwan Univ., Frankfurt Univ., Germany; man. positions with TaipeiBank and Farmers Bank of China 1975–84, Vice-Pres. and Head of Loan Cttee, Farmers Bank of China 1985–88, Sr Vice-Pres. and Gen. Man. of Strategic Planning 1988–89; Exec. Sec., Legal Affairs Cttee, Ministry of Finance (MOF) 1989, Deputy Dir-Gen., MOF Bureau of Monetary Affairs 1989–94, Dir-Gen., MOF Dept of Insurance 1994–95, Dir-Gen., Bureau of Monetary Affairs 1995–98, Deputy Minister of Finance 1998–2002, Minister of Financial Supervisory Comm. 2008–10, Vice-Premier and concurrently Minister of Consumer Protection Comm. 2010–12, Premier 2012–13; Chair. Taiwan Stock Exchange Corpn 2002–04, Taiwan Cooperative Bank 2004–07, KGI Securities Co. Ltd 2007–08, SinoPac Holdings 2008; mem. Kuomingtang. *Address:* c/o Kuomintang, 232–234 Bade Road, Sec. 2, Taipei 10492, Taiwan.

CHEN, Shineng; Chinese administrator; b. 1938, Jiaxing Co., Zhejiang Prov.; ed Qinghua Univ.; joined CCP 1962; Vice-Minister of Light Industry 1984–93; Gov., Guizhou Prov. 1993–96; Deputy Sec., CCP 7th Guizhou Prov. Cttee 1993–96, Dir Cttee for Comprehensive Man.; Vice-Minister of Chemical Industry 1996–98; Vice-Chair. NPC Ethnic Affairs Cttee 2003–; Pres. China National Light Industry Council. *Address:* Ethnic Affairs Committee, National People's Congress, Beijing 100723, People's Republic of China.

CHEN, Shui-bian, LLB; Taiwanese lawyer, politician, civil servant and fmr head of state; b. 12 Oct. 1950, Guantian, Tainan Co.; s. of Chen Sung-ken and Chen Li Shen; m. Wu Shu-jen 1975; one s. one d.; ed Nat. Taiwan Univ.; attorney-at-law 1974, Chief Attorney-at-Law, Formosa Int. Marine and Commercial Law Office 1976–89; mem. Taipei City Council 1981–85; Publr Free Time serial magazines 1984; Exec. mem. Taiwan Asscn for Human Rights 1984; in jail 1986–87; mem. Democratic Progressive Party (DPP) 1987–2008, Cen. Standing Cttee 1987–89, 1996–2000, Cen. Exec. 1987–89, 1991–96, Chair. 2002–04 (resgnd), 2007–08 (resgnd), 2013–; Ind. 2008–13; mem. Legis. Yuan (Parl.) 1989–94, Exec. Dir DPP Caucus 1990–93, Convener Nat. Defence Cttee 1992–94, Convener Rules Cttee 1993, mem. Judiciary Cttee 1994; Chair. Formosa Foundation 1990–94, 1999–2000; Mayor of Taipei City 1994–98; Pres. of Taiwan 2000–08; arrested and charged with graft Nov. 2008, sentenced to life imprisonment on charges of embezzlement, accepting bribes and money laundering Sept. 2009, found not guilty by Taipei Dist Court of embezzling diplomatic funds and life sentence reduced by High Court to 20 years June 2010; Hon. DEcons (Plekhanov Russian Acad. of Econs) 1995; Hon. LLD (Kyungnam Univ., Repub. of Korea) 1995; Hon. DPolSc (Yong-In Univ., Repub. of Korea) 2000; Dr hc (Nat. Asuncion Univ., Paraguay 2001, (Nat. Autonomous Univ., Honduras) 2001; Man of the Taiwan Parl. 1993, Newsweek magazine Global Young Leaders for the New Millennium 1994, Asiaweek magazine Asia's 20 Young Political Stars 1999, Prize for Freedom, Liberal International 2001, Int. League for Human Rights Award 2003. *Publications:* National Defense Black Box and White Paper (co-author), Series on Justice (four vols), Conflict, Compromise and Progress, Through the Line Between Life and Death, The Son of Taiwan, The First Voyage of the Century: Reflections on Taiwan's First Alternation of Political Power, Believe in Taiwan: Chen Shui-bian's Report to the People, President A-bian: Up Close and Personal, Taiwan, Young and Vibrant: Journeying Down the Road of Progress, The New Middle Road for Taiwan: A New Political Perspective (speech). *Address:* c/o Democratic Progressive Party, 10F, 30 Beiping East Road, Taipei 10051, Taiwan. *E-mail:* dppforeign@ gmail.com. *Website:* www.dpp.org.tw.

CHEN, Siqing, MBA; Chinese certified public accountant and business executive; *Chairman, Bank of China Ltd;* ed Hubei Inst. of Finance and Econs, Murdoch Univ., Australia; joined Bank of China (BOC) Ltd 1990, worked in Hunan Br. before being seconded to Hong Kong Br. of China and South Sea Bank Ltd as Asst

Gen. Man., held various other positions, including Vice-Gen. Man. Fujian Br., Gen. Man. Risk Man. Dept of Head Office and Gen. Man. Guangdong Br. 2000–08, Exec. Vice-Pres. BOC Ltd 2008–14, Pres. 2014–17, Vice-Chair. 2014–17, Chair. 2017–; Dir (non-exec.) BOC Hong Kong (Holdings) Ltd 2011–, Vice-Chair. 2014–17, Chair. 2017–; Chair. BOC Aviation 2011–, China Culture Industrial Investment Fund Co. Ltd; Vice-Chair. China Chamber of Int. Commerce; mem. Bd of Dirs of Trade Finance Cttee, China Banking Asscn. *Address:* Bank of China Ltd, 1 Fuxingmen Nei Dajie, Beijing 100818, People's Republic of China (office). *Telephone:* (10) 6659-6688 (office). *Fax:* (10) 6659-3777 (office). *E-mail:* info@boc.cn (office). *Website:* www.boc.cn (office).

CHEN, Suzhi; Chinese politician; b. 1931, Shengyang City, Liaoning Prov.; ed Liaoning Univ.; joined the CCP 1949; factory dir 1978; Vice-Gov. Liaoning in charge of industrial work 1982; Alt. mem. 12th CCP Cen. Cttee 1982–87, 13th Cen. Cttee 1987–92; mem. Standing Cttee CCP Prov. Cttee Liaoning 1982; Dir Liaoning Prov. Trade Union Council 1986; Alt. mem. CCP 12th and 13th Cen. Cttee; mem. Standing Cttee, 7th CCP Liaoning Prov. Cttee from 1985; Rep. to CCP 13th Nat. Congress; Vice-Gov. Liaoning Prov. from 1988; Deputy to 8th NPC Liaoning Prov.; Vice-Chair. Liaoning Prov. 8th People's Congress Standing Cttee from 1992, Cttee for Comprehensive Man. of Social Security; mem. NPC Internal and Judicial Affairs Cttee. *Address:* c/o Liaoning Trade Union Offices, Shenyang, People's Republic of China.

CHEN, Tan-sun (Mark), BA, PhD, PhD; Taiwanese politician; b. 1935, Tainan Co.; m. June Chen; three s.; ed Nat. Taiwan Univ., Purdue Univ. and Univ. of Oklahoma, USA; with US Dept of Commerce, Washington, DC 1973–92; mem. Legis. Yuan 1992, 2001–04, for 5th Electoral Dist, Tainan City 2012–; Magistrate of Tainan Co. 1993–2001; Minister of Foreign Affairs 2004–06; Sec.-Gen. Office of the Pres. 2006–07; Sec.-Gen. Nat. Security Council 2007; indicted on corruption and forgery charges Sept. 2007; Chair. Taiwanese Asscn of America 1979, World Fed. of Taiwanese Asscns 1979, Formosan Asscn for Public Affairs 1982, Int. Cooperation and Devt Fund 2004; fmr Vice-Chair. Taiwan Foundation for Democracy; mem. Democratic Progressive Party; Prof., Chang Jung Christian Univ.; Hon. Prof., Nat. Taiwan Univ.; Dr hc (Purdue Univ.) 2006. *Leisure interests:* hiking, tennis, swimming, reading, music. *Address:* Legislator Office, Room 3205, No. 1 Qingdao East Road, Zhongzheng Dist, Taipei 1005 (office); Tainan Service Office, No. 259, Sec. 1, Yongda Road, Yongkang Dist, Tainan 710; c/o Democratic Progressive Party, 10F, 30 Beiping East Road, Taipei 10051, Taiwan. *Telephone:* (2) 23929989 (DPP). *Fax:* (2) 23929989 (DPP). *E-mail:* dppforeign@gmail.com. *Website:* www.ly.gov.tw (office); www.dpp.org.tw.

CHEN, Tian-jy, BSc, PhD; Taiwanese economist, academic and government official; *Professor, Department of Economics, National Taiwan University;* ed Nat. Taiwan Univ., Pennsylvania State Univ., USA; Asst Prof., Dept of Econs, Univ. of Mississippi, USA 1983–85, Drexel Univ. 1986–87; Prof., Dept of Econs, Nat. Taiwan Univ. 1995–; Assoc. Research Fellow, Int. Div., Chung-Hua Inst. for Econ. Research 1985–88, Research Fellow 1988–95, Dir 1991–95, Acting Pres. 2002–03, Pres. 2003–05; Minister of the Council for Econ. Planning and Devt, Exec. Yuan 2008–09; Pres. Chung-Hua Inst. for Econ. Research; Ind. Dir, Darfon Electronics Corpn, Optimax Technology Corpn 2004–, Bank SinoPac 2010–, AU Optronics Corpn 2013–, Chunghwa Telecom Co. Ltd 2013–; fmr Dir, Taiwan Semiconductor Manufacturing Co. Ltd, Mega Financial Holding Co. Ltd –2008, TECO Electric & Machinery Co. Ltd, Lextar Electronics Corpn; fmr Resident Supervisor, China Development Financial Holding Corpn. *Address:* Department of Economics, National Taiwan University, 21 Hsu-Chow Road, Taipei 100, Taiwan (office). *Telephone:* (2) 2351-9641 (switchboard) (office). *Fax:* (2) 2351-1826 (office). *E-mail:* econman@ntu.edu.tw (office). *Website:* www.econ.ntu.edu.tw (office).

CHEN, Tsu-Pei, BA; Taiwanese business executive; *Chairman, Cathay United Bank Company Limited;* ed Nat. Chengchi Univ.; Pres. and CEO Cathay United Commercial Bank (subsidiary of Cathay Financial Holding Co. Ltd) 2005–11, Pres. Cathay United Bank, Pres. Cathay Financial Holding Co. Ltd –2011, Dir 2011–, Chair. Cathay United Bank Co. Ltd 2013–, Man. Taiwan Finance Corpn, Financial Information Service Co. Ltd; Dir, Seaward Card Co. Ltd, Indovina Bank, Nat. Credit Card Center of Repub. of China, Cathay Charity Foundation, Cathay Cultural Foundation; mem. Turnaround Man. Asscn. *Address:* Cathay United Bank Co. Ltd, 7 Sung Jen Road, Taipei, Taiwan (office). *Telephone:* (2) 8722-6666 (office). *Fax:* (2) 8789-8789 (office). *E-mail:* info@cathaybk.com.tw (office). *Website:* www.cathaybk.com.tw (office).

CHEN, Wei-jao, MD, MPH, DMSc; Taiwanese surgeon and academic; *Professor Emeritus of Surgery and Public Health, National Taiwan University;* b. 15 Nov. 1939, Taichung; s. of Chen Wen-Chiang and Chen Wu-Ping; m. Shiang Yang Tang 1970; one s. one d.; ed Coll. of Medicine, Nat. Taiwan Univ., Postgraduate Medical School, Tohoku Univ., Japan and School of Hygiene and Public Health, Johns Hopkins Univ., USA; Resident, Dept of Surgery, Nat. Taiwan Univ. Hosp. 1966–70, Visiting Surgeon (Pediatric Surgery) 1975–, Deputy Dir 1989–91; mem. Faculty, Coll. of Medicine, Nat. Taiwan Univ. 1975–, Dean 1991–93, Pres. Nat. Taiwan Univ. 1993–2005, also Prof. of Surgery and Public Health, now Emer.; Fellow in Pediatric Surgery, Tohoku Univ., Japan 1972–75; Visiting Research Assoc. Prof., Univ. of Cincinnati 1981–82; recipient of numerous awards. *Publications include:* Story of Separation of Conjoined Twins 1980, Unilateral Occlusion of Duplicated Mullerian Ducts with Renal Anomaly (jtly) 2000, New Advances in Clinical Nutrition 2004, Taiwan Higher Education: Its Problems and Treatment 2008, National Taiwan University: Prospective for the New Century 2008, I See and I Think 2008, Memoir of Wei Jao Chen 2009; more than 230 scientific papers on surgery, nutrition and public health. *Leisure interest:* hiking. *Address:* 7 Chung-shan South Road, Taipei 100 (office); No. 15, Sec. II, Hsin-Yi Road, Taipei, Taiwan (home). *Telephone:* (2) 2356-2122 (office); (2) 2351-6380 (home). *Fax:* (2) 2341-2969 (office). *E-mail:* chenwjh@ntu.edu.tw (office).

CHEN, Wenchi, MS; Taiwanese business executive; *President and CEO, VIA Technologies, Inc.;* b. 16 Nov. 1955; m. Cher Wang; two c.; ed Nat. Taiwan Univ., California Inst. of Tech., USA; held positions of Vice-Pres. Sales and Marketing, ULSI Systems Technology and Sr Architect, Intel; Co-founder, Pres. and CEO Symphony Laboratories, Santa Clara, Calif. –1992; Pres. and CEO VIA Technologies, Inc. 1992–; named Top Star in Asia by Business Week 1999, ranked No. 1 Entrepreneur in Asia by Business Week 2001. *Address:* VIA Technologies, Inc., 8F, 533 Zhongzheng Road, Xindian Dist, Taipei 231, Taiwan (office). *Telephone:* (2) 22185452 (office). *Fax:* (2) 22185453 (office). *E-mail:* embedded@via.com.tw (office). *Website:* www.viatech.com (office).

CHEN, Xianglin; Chinese automobile executive; fmr Gen. Man. Shanghai Donghai Valve Plant; Pres. Shanghai Automotive Industry Corpn (SAIC) 1983–86, 1995–2006; Dir Shanghai Planning Comm. 1986–93; Vice-Party Sec., Shanghai CP Cttee 1993–94; Vice-Exec. Chair., Shanghai Huaxia Econ. and Cultural Promotion Council, Shanghai Fed. of Econ. Organizations, Shanghai Fed. of Industrial Econs.; Dir (non-Exec. and independent) China Yongda Automobiles Services Holdings Ltd 2012–, Bank of Shanghai Co. 2013–. *Address:* SAIC Motor Corporation Ltd, 489 Weihai Road, Shanghai 200041, People's Republic of China (office).

CHEN, Xieyang; Chinese conductor; *Guest Conductor, China National Symphony Orchestra;* b. 4 May 1939, Shanghai; s. of Chen Dieyi and Liang Peiqiong; m. Wang Jianying 1973; ed Music High School, Shanghai Conservatory; Conductor, Shanghai Ballet 1965–84; studied with Prof. Otto Mueller, Yale Univ., USA 1981–82; Conductor, Aspen Music Festival, Group for Contemporary Music, New York, Brooklyn Philharmonia, Honolulu Symphony, Philippines State Orchestra, Hong Kong Philharmonic, Shanghai Symphony Orchestra, Cen. Philharmonic, Beijing 1981–83, Symphony Orchestra of Vilnius, Kaunas, Novosibirsk, USSR 1985, Tokyo Symphony Orchestra 1986, Orchestre Regional de Cannes 2003; Music Dir and Prin. Conductor, Shanghai Symphony Orchestra 1984–2009, Hon. Music Dir 2009–; Guest Conductor, China National Symphony Orchestra; Vice-Chair. Shanghai Asscn of Musicians; Dir China Musicians Asscn; Pres. Shanghai Symphonic Music Lovers Soc.; Excellent Conducting Prize, Shanghai Music Festival 1986. *E-mail:* cnsomail@126.com. *Website:* www.cnso.com.cn/english.

CHEN, Yao; Chinese actress; b. 5 Oct. 1979, Shishi City, Fujian Prov.; m. 1st Ling Xiao Su (divorced); m. 2nd Cao Yu; one s.; ed Beijing Dance Acad., Beijing Film Acad.; acting debut in 'City Man and Woman' (TV drama) 2002; UNHCR Goodwill Amb. 2013–; Hua Ding Award (Best Actress and Best TV Actress) 2010, Golden Phoenix Award 2011. *Films include:* Undercover 2008, A Story of Lala's Promotion 2009, Sophie's Revenge 2009, If You Are the One 2 2010, Color Me Love 2010, Love in Cosmo 2010, Caught in the Web 2012, My Lucky Star 2013, Control 2013, Firestorm 2013, The Ghouls 2014, Monster Hunt 2015, Chronicles of the Ghostly Tribe 2015, Everybody's Fine 2016, MBA Partners 2016, Journey to the West: The Demons Strike Back 2017. *Television includes:* My Own Swordsman 2005, Ambush 2008, Firewall 2009, Lurk 2009, Niu Tiehan and His Children 2010, Latent (Golden Eagle Award for Best Actress in a TV Series 2010) 2010. *Address:* c/o Huayi Brothers Media Corporation, Room 903, Building A, Full Link Plaza, 18 Chao Wei St, Chaoyang District, Beijing, People's Republic of China (office). *Telephone:* (10) 65805888 (office). *Website:* www.huayimedia.com (office).

CHEN, Yaobang; Chinese politician; b. 1935, Panyu City, Guangdong Prov.; ed Cen. China Agricultural Coll.; Asst, Cen. China Agricultural Coll. 1957–62; Deputy Chief Div. of Cash Crops Bureau, Ministry of Agriculture 1979–82; joined CCP 1982; Deputy Dir Animal Husbandry and Fisheries, Agricultural Bureau, Ministry of Agric. 1982–84, Vice-Minister 1986–88, Vice-Minister of Agric. 1988–93, Minister of Forestry 1997–98, Minister of Agric. 1998–2003; Deputy Sec. CCP Wuxi City Cttee 1984–86; Del., 13th CCP Nat. Congress 1987–92, 14th CCP Nat. Congress 1992–97; Vice-Minister State Devt and Reform Comm. 1993–97; mem. Science and Tech. Sub-cttee, CPPCC Nat. Cttee 1993–98; Deputy Chief State Flood Control and Drought Relief HQ 1993–98; Deputy Dir Nat. Afforestation Cttee 1993–98, Nat. Cttee on Mineral Reserves 1995–97; Vice-Pres. China Mining Industry Asscn 1997; Deputy Dir Beijing Afforestation Cttee 1997; mem. 15th CCP Cen. Cttee 1997–2002. *Address:* c/o Ministry of Agriculture, Nongzhanguan Nan Li, Chaoyang Qu, Beijing 100026, People's Republic of China (office).

CHEN, Yong; Chinese seismologist; b. Dec. 1942, Chongqing; ed Chinese Univ. of Science and Tech.; Assoc. Research Fellow, Research Fellow, Dir Geophysics Research Inst. of Nat. Bureau of Seismology 1965–85, Vice-Dir Nat. Bureau of Seismology 1985–96; Dean, School of Earth and Space Science, Chinese Univ. of Science and Tech. 2005–; mem. Chinese Acad. of Sciences 1993–, also Deputy Dir-Gen., Seismology Div. and Vice-Pres. Soc. of Seismology of China Academician; fmr Chair. Comm. on Earthquake Prediction and Hazard, Int. Asscn of Seismology and Physics of the Earth's Interior; mem. Executive Cttee Int. Seismological Center 1989–97, Exec. Dir –2005; Vice-Pres. Chinese Geophysical Soc., Chinese Seismological Soc.; Fellow Third World Acad. of Sciences 2000–; award for Progress in Science and Technology (several times); Ho Leung Ho Lee Foundation Earth Sciences Prize 2006. *Publications:* seven monographs and over 100 essays; The Great Tangshan Earthquake of 1976. *Address:* National Bureau of Seismology, 61 Fuxing Lu, Beijing 100036, People's Republic of China (office).

CHEN, Yuan, BS, MA; Chinese banker; b. 13 Jan. 1945, Shanghai; s. of Chen Yun; ed China Acad. of Social Sciences, Tsinghua Univ., Beijing; Sec. CCP Cttee of Xicheng Dist, Beijing 1982–84; Dir-Gen. Dept of Commerce and Trade, Beijing Municipal Govt 1984–88; Vice-Gov. People's Bank of China 1988–98; Gov. China Devt Bank 1998–2013; mem. Preparatory Cttee of Hong Kong Special Admin. Region, Vice-Pres. Financial Soc.; mem. Securities Comm. of the State Council; Sec. CCP Xicheng Dist Cttee, Beijing; Alt. Mem. 16th CCP Cen. Cttee 2002–07, 17th CCP Cen. Cttee 2007–12; Vice-Chair. 12th CPPCC Nat. Cttee 2013–18; involved with planning proposed BRICS Devt Bank 2013; Dir Inst. for Int. Econs, USA (mem. Advisory Cttee and the Financial Stability Inst.); Deputy Gov., Dir Business and Trade Activities Dept, and Adviser to Postgraduates, People's Bank of China (also Deputy Sec. CCP Party Cttee). *Publications:* The Underlying Problems and Options in China's Economy, Macroeconomic Management: The Need for Deepening Reform, Collected Works. *Address:* c/o China Development Bank, 29 Fuchengmenwai Lu, Xicheng Qu, Beijing 100037, People's Republic of China (office).

CHEN, Yunlin; Chinese politician; b. Dec. 1941, Heishan Co., Liaoling Prov.; ed Beijing Agricultural Univ.; joined CCP 1966; technician, Deputy Dir, Dir Yucuntun Chemical Works, Qiqihar City, Heilongjiang Prov. 1960s–70s (also Deputy Sec. CCP Party Cttee); Deputy Sec. CCP Qiqihar City Cttee 1983; Mayor Qiqihar City 1983; Deputy Sec. CCP Heilongjiang Prov. Cttee 1984 (also mem. Standing Cttee, CCP Prov. Cttee); Dir Comm. for Restructuring the Economy,

Heilongjiang Prov. 1984; Vice-Gov. Heilongjiang Prov. 1987–94; Del., 13th CCP Nat. Congress 1987–92; Deputy Dir Cen. Office for Taiwan Affairs of State Council 1999–2003, Dir 2003–08; Pres. Asscn for Relations Across the Taiwan Straits 2008–13; Alt. mem. 14th CCP Cen. Cttee 1992–97, mem. 15th CCP Cen. Cttee 1997–2002, 16th CCP Cen. Cttee 2002–07; mem. CCP Qiqihar City Standing Cttee. *Address:* c/o Association for Relations Across the Taiwan Straits, No. 6-1, Guang'anmen Nanjie, Xuanwu District, Beijing, People's Republic of China (office).

CHEN, Zhangliang, PhD; Chinese professor of biology and government official; *Executive Secretary, China Association for Science and Technology;* b. 3 Feb. 1961; ed Huanan Tropical Crops Coll., Washington Univ., USA; Prof., Head of Plant Gene Eng Lab., Biology Dept, Beijing Univ. 1987–92 (youngest full Prof. in China at age of 27), Vice-Pres. Beijing Univ. 1995–2002; Pres. China Agricultural Univ., Beijing 2002–07; Vice-Chair. Guangxi Zhuang Autonomous Region People's Govt 2008–13; Exec. Sec. China Asscn for Science and Technology 2013–; mem. Council of Advisors, World Food Prize 2007–; mem. Advisory Bd, Belfer Center for Science and Int. Affairs, Harvard Univ.; UNESCO Javed Husain Prize for Young Scientists 1991. *Publications:* several books and more than 150 research papers; holder of seven patents. *Address:* China Association for Science and Technology, 3 Fuxing Road, Beijing 100863, People's Republic of China (office). *Telephone:* (10) 68571898 (office). *E-mail:* english@cast.org.cn (office). *Website:* english.cast.org.cn (office).

CHEN, Zhili; Chinese government official, academic and fmr physicist; b. 21 Nov. 1942, Xianyou Co., Fujian Prov.; ed Fudan Univ., Shanghai Inst. of Ceramics, Chinese Acad. of Sciences; joined CCP 1961; served in People's Liberation Army, No. 6409 Army Unit, Danyang Lake Farm 1968–70; Assoc. Research Fellow, Chinese Acad. of Sciences 1970–80, 1982–84, Deputy Sec., CP Cttee of the Inst. 1982–84; Visiting Scholar, Materials Research Lab., Pa State Univ., USA 1980–82; Deputy Sec. CCP Party Cttee, Shanghai Inst. of Ceramics 1983–84; Deputy Sec. and Sec. Science and Tech. Work Cttee, Shanghai CCP Municipal Cttee 1984–86; Alt. mem. 13th CCP Cen. Cttee 1987–92, 14th CCP Cen. Cttee 1992–97; mem. Standing Cttee, Shanghai CCP Municipal Cttee 1988–89, Head Publicity Dept 1988–91, Deputy Sec. Publicity Dept 1989–91; Deputy Sec. CCP Shanghai Municipal Cttee 1991–97; Vice-Minister and Sec. CCP Leading Party Group, State Educ. Comm. 1997–98; Minister of Educ. 1998–2003; apptd mem. State Steering Group of Science, Tech. and Educ. 1998; apptd Vice-Chair. State Academic Degree Cttee 1999; State Councillor 2003–08; mem. 15th CCP Cen. Cttee 1997–2002, 16th CCP Cen. Cttee 2002–07, 17th CCP Cen. Cttee 2007–12; Vice-Chair. 11th NPC Standing Cttee 2008–13; Pres. All-China Women's Fed. 2008–13; Chair. Children's Foundation of China 2010–; Hon. Pres. Shanghai Inst. of Int. Friendship. *E-mail:* womenofchina@163.com (office). *Website:* www.womenofchina.cn (office).

CHEN, Zhixin, MA, PhD; Chinese engineer and business executive; *President, SAIC Motor Corporation Limited;* b. May 1959; mem. CCP; fmr Gen. Man. Nanjing Automotive Corpn (Group), fmr Exec. Vice-Pres. Shanghai Automotive Industry Corpn (SAIC) Motor, fmr Gen. Man. Shanghai Volkswagen Automotive Co. and SAIC-Volkswagen Sales Co., fmr Vice-Pres. SAIC Motor, Vice-Pres. Shanghai Automotive Industry Corpn (Group) –2014, Pres. and Deputy Party Sec. SAIC Motor Corpn Ltd 2014–, Gen. Man. SAIC Motor Passenger Vehicle Co. *Address:* SAIC Motor Corporation Ltd, 5/F Building A, 563 Songtao Road, Zhangjiang, High Technology Park, Pudong, Shanghai 201203, People's Republic of China (office). *Telephone:* (21) 50803757 (office). *Fax:* (21) 50803780 (office). *E-mail:* info@saicgroup.com (office). *Website:* www.saicgroup.com (office); www.saicmotor.com (office).

CHEN, Zhu, PhD; Chinese haematologist and government official; b. Aug. 1953, Zhenjiang, Jiangsu Prov.; m. Chen Saijuan; one s.; ed Shanghai No. 2 Medical Sciences Univ., St Louis Hosp., Univ. de Paris 7, France; apptd Foreign Resident Doctor, St Louis Hosp., Paris 1984; Research Fellow, Chinese Acad. of Sciences (Div. of Biological Sciences) 1990–; Dir Shanghai Haematology Research Inst. 1995; Deputy Dir Shanghai Research Centre of Life Sciences 1996; Deputy Dir Jt Genetics and Medical Sciences Centre, Shanghai No. 2 Medical Sciences Univ.; undertook over 20 nat. key scientific research projects and int. research projects and achieved results on the treatment of leukaemia with diarsenic trioxide and its molecular mechanism, providing a representative model for cancer research; academician, Chinese Acad. of Sciences 1995–, Vice-Pres. 2000–07; Minister of Health 2007–13; Chair. Cen. Cttee 15th Chinese Peasants and Workers Democratic Party 2012–, Vice-Chair. Standing Cttee, NPC; Pres. Red Cross Soc. of China; Prof., Shanghai Jiao Tong Univ.; Hon. DrSc (Univ. of Hong Kong) 2002, Hon. DUniv (York) 2010; Légion d'honneur 2002; Laureate, First Shanghai Honour Award of Medical Science 1994, China Youth Scientists' Prize 1994, Ho Lee Ho Leung Foundation Prize for Medicine 1996, Shanghai Science Elite Nat. Model Worker 1996, Nat. Outstanding Science and Technology Worker 1996, Yangtze Scholar Awarding Program Top Grade Prize 1999, Outstanding Technician Medal, Ministry of Personnel 1999, US Nat. Foundation for Cancer Research Szent-Györgyi Prize for Progress in Cancer Research 2012. *Address:* National People's Congress, No. 23, Xijiaominxiang, Xicheng Dist, Beijing 1100805, People's Republic of China (office). *E-mail:* english@npc.gov.cn (office). *Website:* www.npc.gov.cn (office).

CHEN, Zhuo Lin; Chinese business executive; *Chairman and President, Agile Property Holdings Ltd;* b. Guangdong Prov.; m. Luk Sin Fong; Pres. Zhongshan Agile Co. 1992–96, Zhongshan Group Co. 1997–; Gen. Man. Zhongshan Dynasty Furniture Factory 1989–92; Co-founder Agile Property brand name, Chair. Agile Property Holdings Ltd 2005–, Chair. and Pres. 2014–; Vice-Chair. Zhongshan Qiaozi Enterprise Asscn; Chair. Kong-Zhongshan Sanxiang Fellowship Asscn; Vice-Chair. China Overseas Chinese Entrepreneurs Asscn, Guangdong Overseas Chinese Enterprises Asscn, Sun Yat-sen Foundation; Vice-Pres. Chinese Language and Culture Educ. Foundation of China; Hon. DBA (Armstrong, Univ., USA) 2007; World Outstanding Chinese Award 2007, China Philanthropy Outstanding Contribution Individual Award 2009. *Address:* Agile Property Holdings Ltd, 20/F, 238 Nathan Road, Kowloon, Hong Kong Special Administrative Region, People's Republic of China (office). *Telephone:* (760) 6686868 (office). *Fax:* (760) 6683913 (office). *Website:* www.agile.com.cn (office).

CHEN, Zuohuang, MM, DMA; Chinese/American conductor (retd); b. 2 April 1947, Shanghai, China; s. of Chen Ru Hui and Li He Zhen; m. Zaiyi Wang 1969; one c.; ed Cen. Conservatory of Music, Beijing, Univ. of Michigan, USA; Conductor, All China Trade Union Performing Group 1965–77 (also pianist), China Film Philharmonic 1974–76; Assoc. Prof. in Conducting, Univ. of Kansas, USA 1985–87; Prin. Conductor Cen. Philharmonic Orchestra of China 1987–96; Music Dir Wichita Symphony Orchestra 1990–2000, Rhode Island Philharmonic Orchestra 1992–96, Guiyang Symphony Orchestra 2010–16; Founding Artistic Dir/Conductor China Nat. Symphony Orchestra 1996–2000; Music Dir Orquesta Filarmónica de la UNAM (OFUNAM), Mexico 2002–06, Incheon Philharmonic Orchestra, South Korea 2006–10, Guiyang Symphony Orchestra 2010–16; Artistic Dir Shanghai Philharmonic Orchestra 2004–08, China Nat. Centre for the Performing Arts, Beijing 2007–16; Founding Chief Conductor, China NCPA Orchestra 2010–12; guest conductor with numerous orchestras including Zurich Tonhalle Orchestra, Czechoslovak Radio Symphony Orchestra, Budapest Philharmonic Orchestra and State Symphony, Symphony Orchestra of Hungary, Gulbenkian Orchestra, Iceland Symphony Orchestra, Stavanger Symfoniorkester (Norway), Orchester Akademie Hamburg (Germany), Vancouver, Tanglewood Inst. Young Artists Orchestra, Colorado Symphony Orchestra, Pacific Symphony Orchestra, Virginia Symphony Orchestra, Alabama Symphony Orchestra, Hong Kong Philharmonic Orchestra, East Lansing Symphony Orchestra, Long Beach Symphony Orchestra, Russian Philharmonic Orchestra, Haifa Symphony Orchestra, Slovak Radio Symphony Orchestra, Hong Kong Philharmonic Orchestra, Singapore Symphony Orchestra, Pusan Philharmonic Orchestra, Yamagota Symphony Orchestra, Mexico Nat. Symphony Orchestra, Mexico City Philharmonic Orchestra, Taipei Symphony Orchestra, Macao Symphony Orchestra, Buffalo Philharmonic Orchestra, Hong Kong Chinese Orchestra, Nat. Taiwan Symphony Orchestra, Taipei Symphony Orchestra, Shanghai Symphony Orchestra, among others.

CHEN, Zuolin; Chinese politician; b. 1923, Wuwei Co., Anhui Prov.; Vice-Chair. Revolutionary Cttee, Zhejiang Prov. 1975–79; Deputy Sec. CCP Cttee, Zhejiang 1976, Sec. 1977–83; Alt. mem. 11th CCP Cen. Cttee 1977, 12th Cen. Cttee 1982–87; Vice-Gov., Zhejiang 1979–83; Sec.-Gen. Cen. Comm. for Discipline Inspection 1985–87, Deputy Sec. 1987; apptd Deputy Sec. CCP Cen. Discipline Inspection Comm. 1992; mem. Presidium of 14th CCP Nat. Congress 1992, CCP Standing Cttee, Cen. Leading Group for Party Building Work, Internal and Judicial Affairs Cttee; Deputy to 8th NPC Jiangxi Prov. *Address:* Zhejiang Government Office, 28 Reuminlu Road, Hangzhou, People's Republic of China. *Telephone:* 24911.

CHEN, Zutao; Chinese automobile executive (retired); b. 20 Jan. 1928; s. of Chen Changhao; ed Moscow Baumann Highest Tech. Inst.; joined CCP 1960; First Chief Engineer and Vice Dir for Techniques, Dongfeng Motor Corpn 1965–80; First Chief Engineer, Deputy Man. and Gen. Man., China Nat. Automotive Industry Corpn (CNAIC) 1981–88 (retd); Commr, Ministry of Science and Tech. 1989. *Address:* c/o China National Automotive Industry Corporation, 46 Fucheng Lu, Haidian Qu, Beijing 100036, People's Republic of China.

CHEN TIANQIAO, Timothy, BEcons; Chinese business executive; *Chairman and CEO, Shanda Entertainment;* b. 1973, Xinchang County, Zhejiang; ed Fudan Univ.; various man. positions with Shanghai Lujiazui Group 1994–98; Deputy Dir Office of the Pres. Kinghing Trust & Investment Co. Ltd 1998–99; Co-founder, Chair. and CEO Shanghai Shanda Networking Co. Ltd (now Shanda Entertainment) 1999–, Chair. and CEO Shanda Interactive Entertainment Ltd 1999–; Independent Non-Executive Dir SinoMedia Holding Ltd 2008–11; mem. 11th CPPCC Nat. Cttee 2008–13, 12th CPPCC Nat. Cttee 2013–; Alt. mem. 15th Chinese Communist Youth League Cen. Cttee; youngest mem. China Top 50, Rising Business Star Award, China Central TV 2003. *Address:* Shanda Entertainment, No. 1 Intelligent Office, Building No. 690, Bibo Road, Shanghai 201203, People's Republic of China (office). *Telephone:* (21) 50504740 (office). *Fax:* (21) 50508088 (office). *E-mail:* info@shanda.com.cn (office). *Website:* www.shanda.com (office).

CHENAULT, Kenneth Irvine, BA, JD; American financial services company executive; *Chairman and Managing Director, General Catalyst;* b. 2 June 1951, Long Island, NY; s. of Hortensius Chenault and Anne N. Chenault (née Quick); m. Kathryn Cassell 1977; two s.; ed Waldorf School of Garden City, Bowdoin Coll., Harvard Univ. Law School; called to Bar, Mass 1981; Assoc., Rogers & Wells, New York 1977–79; consultant, Bain & Co., Boston 1979–81; Dir Strategic Planning, American Express Co., New York 1981–83, Vice-Pres. American Express Travel Related Services Co. Inc., New York 1983–84, Sr Vice-Pres. 1984–86, Exec. Vice-Pres. Platinum Card/Gold 1986–88, Personal Card Div. 1988–89, Pres. Consumer Card and Financial Services Group 1990–93, Pres. (USA) 1993–95, Vice-Chair. American Express Co., New York 1995–97, Pres. and COO 1997–2000, Chair. and CEO 2001–18; Chair. and Man. Dir General Catalyst 2018–; Chair. Advisory Council, Smithsonian Nat. Museum of African American History and Culture 2017–; mem. Bd of Dirs Brooklyn Union Gas 1988, IBM 1998–2019, Quaker Oats Co. 1992–, Procter & Gamble 2008–19, Airbnb 2018–, Facebook 2018–, New York Univ. Medical Center; mem. Council of Foreign Relations, New York 1988, ABA; several hon. degrees; W. E. B. Du Bois Medal, Hutchins Center for African & African American Research, Harvard Univ. 2018. *Address:* General Catalyst, 434 Broadway Sixth Floor, New York, NY 10013, USA (office). *Telephone:* (212) 775-4000 (office). *E-mail:* info@generalcatalyst.com (office). *Website:* generalcatalyst.com/team/ken-chenault (home).

CHÊNEVERT, Louis R., BCom; Canadian business executive; b. 25 June 1957; m. Debra Chênevert; ed Univ. of Montreal, École des Hautes Études Commerciales (HEC), Montreal; worked at General Motors 1979–93, served as Production Gen. Man., St Therese; Vice-Pres. for Operations, Pratt & Whitney Canada 1993–97, Exec. Vice-Pres. 1998–99, Pres. 1999–2006; mem. Bd of Dirs, Pres. and COO United Technologies Corpn 2006–08, Pres. and CEO 2008–10, Chair. and CEO 2010–14; mem. The US-India CEO Forum, Business Council, Business Roundtable; Founding and current mem. Bd of Dirs Friends of HEC Montréal and Pres. HEC Advisory Bd; mem. Bd of Dirs Congressional Medal of Honor Foundation, Yale Cancer Center's Advisory Bd; Fellow, AIAA 2005; Dr hc (HEC Montréal) 2011; Nouveaux Performant, Quebec 1995, Quebec Quality Movement Harrington Medal 1997, Honor Award, Nat. Building Museum 2009, Pace Award for Leadership in Business Ethics 2010, FDNY Fire Commissioner's Humanitarian

Award 2010, named by Aviation Week & Space Technology magazine as Person of the Year 2011. *Address:* c/o United Technologies Corpn, 1 Financial Plaza, Suite 22, Hartford, CT 06103-2608, USA. *E-mail:* invrelations@corphq.utc.com.

CHENEY, Lynne Vincent, BA, MA, PhD; American academic and writer; *Senior Fellow, American Enterprise Institute for Public Policy Research (AEI);* b. 14 Aug. 1941, Casper, Wyo.; d. of Wayne Vincent and Edna Vincent (née Lybyer); m. Richard B. Cheney (q.v.) 1964; two d.; ed Colorado Coll., Univ. of Colorado, Univ. of Wisconsin; freelance writer 1970–83; Lecturer, George Washington Univ. 1972–77, Univ. of Wyoming 1977–78; researcher and writer Md Public Broadcasting 1982–83; Sr Ed. Washingtonian magazine 1983–86; Chair. Nat. Endowment for Humanities 1986–93; W. H. Brady Fellow, American Enterprise Inst. for Public Policy Research, Washington, DC 1993–95, Sr Fellow 1996–; Commr US Constitution Bicentennial Comm. 1985–87; cr. James Madison Book Award Fund 2003. *Publications:* Executive Privilege 1978, Sisters 1981, Kings of the Hill (jtly) 1983, The Body Politic 1988, Telling the Truth 1995, America: A Patriotic Primer 2002, A is for Abigail: An Almanac of Amazing American Women 2003, We the People: The Story of Our Constitution 2008. *Address:* American Enterprise Institute, 1150 17th Street, NW, Washington, DC 20036, USA (office). *Telephone:* (202) 862-5800 (office). *Fax:* (202) 862-7177 (office). *E-mail:* lcheney@aei.org (office). *Website:* www.aei.org (office).

CHENEY, Richard (Dick) B., BA, MA; American politician and fmr business executive; b. 30 Jan. 1941, Lincoln, Neb.; s. of Richard H. Cheney and Marjorie Dickey Cheney; m. Lynne Vincent Cheney (q.v.); two d.; ed Univ. of Wyoming, Univ. of Wisconsin; engaged on staff of Gov. of Wis.; Special Asst to Dir White House Office of Econ. Opportunity 1969–70; Deputy to White House Presidential Counselor 1970–71; Asst Dir of Operations, White House Cost of Living Council 1971–73; partner, Bradley, Woods & Co. 1973–74; Deputy Asst to the Pres. 1974–75, White House Chief of Staff 1975–77; Congressman, At-large District, Wyoming, 1978–89; Chair. Republican Policy Cttee 1981–87; Chair. House Republican Conf. 1987; House Minority Whip 1988; Sec. of Defense 1989–93; Sr Fellow American Enterprise Inst. 1993–95; Chair. Bd and CEO Halliburton Co., Dallas, Tex. 1995–2000 (Pres. 1997); Vice-Pres. of USA 2001–09; Presidential Medal of Freedom 1991. *Publication:* In My Time: A Personal and Political Memoir 2011, Exceptional: Why the World Needs a Powerful America 2015.

CHENG, Andong; Chinese politician; b. Oct. 1936, Huainan City, Anhui Prov.; ed Hefei Polytechnical Univ.; engineer, Mining Admin, Pingxiang City, Jiangxi Prov. 1965–67, Chief Engineer and Deputy Dir 1977–83; Chief Engineer and Deputy Dir Gaokeng Coal Mine, Jiangxi Prov. 1967–77; mem. CCP 1980–; Mayor of Pingxiang City and Deputy Sec. CCP City Cttee 1983–84; Mayor of Nanchang City, Jiangxi Prov. 1984–90; Asst to Gov. Jiangxi Prov. 1990; Sec. CCP Xian Municipal Cttee 1990; mem. Standing Cttee CCP Shaanxi Prov. Cttee 1990–94, 1998–, Deputy Sec. Provincial Cttee 1994–2003; Chair. City People's Congress Standing Cttee, Xi'an City, Shaanxi Prov. 1992; Alt. mem. 14th CCP Cen. Cttee 1992–97, mem. 15th CCP Cen. Cttee 1997–2002; Vice-Gov. Shaanxi Prov. 1994, Gov. 1995–2003; Hon. Pres. Bd Hefei Polytechnical Univ. 1995. *Address:* c/o Office of the Governor, Xi'an City, Shaanxi Province, People's Republic of China.

CHENG, Eva, BA, MBA; Chinese business executive; b. 1952; ed Univ. of Hong Kong; govt official in Hong Kong –1977; joined Amway Hong Kong as an Exec. Asst 1977, apptd Pres. Amway Hong Kong 1980, Exec. Vice-Pres. Amway, responsible for markets in Greater China (Amway (China) Co. Ltd) and SE Asia 2005–11, Chair. Amway China and Exec. Vice-Pres. Amway Corpn (global parent firm) –2011, currently Chair. Amway Charity Foundation in China; Exec. Dir Our Hong Kong Foundation 2015–; mem. Bd of Dirs Nestlé, Trinity Ltd, Amway (Malaysia) Holdings Berhad, Haier Electronics Group Co. Ltd, Esprit International 2012–; mem. Exec. Cttee All-China Women's Fed.; mem. CPPCC–Guangdong Comm.; mem. Council on Human Reproductive Tech.; Hon. Pres. All-China Women's Fed. Hong Kong Delegates Asscn, Hong Kong Fed. of Women; Perm. Hon. Cttee Mem. Chinese General Chamber of Commerce. *Leisure interest:* Cantonese opera. *Address:* Our Hong Kong Foundation, 19/F., Nan Fung Tower, 88 Connaught Road, Central, Hong Kong Special Administrative Region, People's Republic of China.

CHENG, Eva, (Eva Cheng Yu-wah), JP; Hong Kong politician, civil servant and non-executive director; b. 1960, Hong Kong; ed Diocesan Girls' School, Univ. of Hong Kong; joined Admin. Service 1983, served in various bureaux and depts, including Financial Sec.'s Office, Transport Br., Educ. and Manpower Br., Standing Comm. on Civil Service Salaries and Conditions of Service, as Deputy Head of Cen. Policy Unit 1996–98, Deputy Dir of Admin 1997, Deputy Sec. for Information Tech. and Broadcasting (later renamed Deputy Sec. for Commerce, Industry and Tech.) 1998–2003, Commr for Tourism 2003–06, Perm. Sec. for Econ. Devt and Labour (Econ. Devt) 2006–07, Sec. for Transport and Housing 2007–12; fmr Chair. Hong Kong Housing Authority; Dir (non-exec.) MTR Corpn 2007–12, BOC Hong Kong 2014–; Gold Bauhinia Star 2011. *Address:* c/o BOC Hong Kong, 52/F Bank of China Tower, 1 Garden Road, Hong Kong Special Administrative Region, People's Repub. of China (office).

CHENG, Jason, MEng; Taiwanese business executive; *Chairman, Casetek Holdings Limited;* ed Univ. of Southern California, USA; fmr Vice-Pres. Asustek; Pres. and CEO Pegatron 2008–16, Vice Chair. 2016– (also, mem. Bd of Dirs); currently Chair. Casetek Holdings Ltd; mem. Bd of Dirs Unihan, AzureWave. *Address:* Casetek Holdings, 2F, No. 96 Ligong Street, Beitou District, Taipei City, Taiwan (office). *Telephone:* (2) 55630588 (office). *E-mail:* ir@casetekholdings.com (office). *Website:* www.casetekholdings.com (office).

CHENG, Jingye; Chinese diplomatist; *Ambassador to Australia;* b. 1959; m.; one s.; Attaché and Third Sec., Dept of Int. Orgs. and Confs, Ministry of Foreign Affairs 1985–90, Third, then Second, Sec. Perm. Mission to UN 1990–93, Minister Counsellor 2003–05, Second Sec., Dept of Int. Orgs. and Confs (also Deputy Div. Dir, Div. Dir, Counsellor) 1993–2000, Deputy Dir-Gen., Dept of Arms Control 2000–03, Dir-Gen. 2007–11, Deputy Perm. Rep. to UN, Geneva 2005–07, Amb. Extraordinary and Plenipotentiary for Disarmament Affairs 2005–07, Perm. Rep. to UN, Vienna 2011–16, Amb. to Australia 2016–. *Address:* Embassy of People's Republic of China, 15 Coronation Drive, Yarralumla, ACT 2600, Australia (office). *Telephone:* (2) 6228-3999 (office). *Fax:* (2) 6228-3990 (office). *E-mail:* chinaemb_au@mfa.gov.cn (office). *Website:* au.china-embassy.org/eng (office).

CHENG, Lianchang; Chinese government official (retd); b. 14 May 1931, Jilin; m. Huang Shulan; one s. one d.; ed Jilin Industrial School, People's Univ. of China; joined CCP 1950; Vice-Minister of 7th Ministry of Machine Building 1975–82; Vice-Minister, Exec. Vice-Minister of Astronautical Ind. 1982–88; Sr Engineer and Researcher 1988–; Exec. Vice-Minister of Personnel 1988–94; mem. State Educational Comm. 1988–94; Vice-Pres. Nat. School of Admin. 1994–96; Vice-Chair. Steering Cttee for Enterprise; Standing mem. 8th Nat. Cttee CPCCC 1993–97, 9th Nat. Cttee CPPCC 1998–2003; Prof., China People's Univ.; Fellow, World Acad. of Productivity Science 2001; First-class Award, Ministry of Astronautical Ind. 1984, State Council Award for Outstanding Contribution in High-energy Physics 1991. *Publications:* Selected Works (two vols), Textbook for State Public Servant Examination (20 vols). *Leisure interest:* swimming. *Address:* c/o Ministry of Personnel, Hepingli Zhongjie, Beijing 100013 (office); Room 1501, No. 13 Building, Cuiwei Xili, Haidian District, Beijing 100036, People's Republic of China (home). *Telephone:* (10) 68462628 (office); (10) 68258072 (home). *Fax:* (10) 84233851 (office). *E-mail:* chenglch@izb.com (home).

CHENG, Yanan; Chinese sculptor; b. 15 Jan. 1936, Tianjin; d. of Cheng Goliang and Liuo Shijing; m. Zhang Zuoming 1962 (died 1989); one s. one d.; ed Cen. Acad. of Fine Arts, Beijing; sculptor Beijing Architectural Artistic Sculpture Factory 1961–84, Sculpture Studio, Cen. Acad. of Fine Arts 1984–; work included in Nat. Art Museum of China; mem. China Artists' Asscn. *Address:* 452 New Building of Central Institute of Fine Arts, No 5 Shuaifuyan Lane, East District, Beijing, People's Republic of China.

CHENG, Yonghua, BA; Chinese diplomatist; *Ambassador to Japan;* b. Sept. 1954, Jilin Prov.; m.; one d.; ed Soka Univ., Japan; joined Foreign Service 1977, served in various positions, including Attaché, Embassy in Tokyo 1996–2000, Deputy Dir Asia Dept, Ministry of Foreign Affairs 2000–03, Deputy Chief of Mission, Embassy in Tokyo 2003–06, Amb. to Malaysia 2006–08, to South Korea 2008–10, to Japan 2010–. *Address:* Embassy of the People's Republic of China, 3-4-33, Moto-Azabu, Minato-ku, Tokyo 106-0046, Japan (office). *Telephone:* (3) 3403-3380 (office). *Fax:* (3) 3403-3345 (office). *E-mail:* info@china-embassy.or.jp (office). *Website:* www.china-embassy.or.jp (office).

CHEONG, Yip Seng; Singaporean journalist and editor; *Editorial Advisor, Singapore Press Holdings;* b. June 1943; trainee journalist, The Straits Times Press 1963, then Ed. The New Nation, then Ed. The Straits Times, Deputy Ed.-in-Chief English/Malay Newspapers Div., Singapore Press Holdings (including The Straits Times, Business Times, Berita Harian and The New Paper) late 1970s–87, Ed.-in-Chief English/Malay Newspapers Div. 1987–2007, Editorial Advisor, Singapore Press Holdings 2007–; mem. Bd of Dirs, SBS Transit Ltd; mem. Nat. Univ. of Singapore Council 2004–; Founding mem. Singapore Press Club 1971–; ASEAN Award for Information 1997. *Publication:* OB Markers: My Straits Times Story (memoir) 2012. *Address:* The Straits Times, 1000 Toa Payoh North News Centre, Singapore City 318994, Singapore (office). *Telephone:* 6319-6319 (office). *Fax:* 6737-5576 (office). *E-mail:* cheong@sph.com.sg (office). *Website:* www.straitstimes.com (office); www.sph.com.sg (office).

CHER; American singer and actress; b. (Cherilyn Lapierre Sarkisian), 20 May 1946, El Centro, Calif.; d. of John Sarkisian and Georgina Holt; m. 1st Sonny Bono 1964 (divorced 1975, died 1998); one d.; m. 2nd Gregg Allman 1975 (divorced); one s.; formed singing duo Sonny & Cher with Sonny Bono 1964–74, with TV series; solo artist 1964–, with own TV variety series and night club act; VH1 First Music Award for achievements within the music industry 2005, Lifetime Achievement Award, Glamour Women of the Year Awards 2010, Billboard Music Icon Award 2017, Kennedy Center Honor for Lifetime Contribution to American culture through the performing arts 2018. *Theatre:* Come Back to the Five and Dime, Jimmy Dean, Jimmy Dean. *Television:* Sonny & Cher Comedy Hour (CBS) 1971–74, Cher (CBS) 1975–76, Sonny & Cher Show (CBS) 1976–77. *Films include:* Chastity 1969, Come Back To The Five and Dime, Jimmy Dean Jimmy Dean 1982, Silkwood 1983, Mask (Cannes Film Festival Best Actress Award) 1985, The Witches of Eastwick 1987, Suspect 1987, Moonstruck (Acad. Award for Best Actress 1988) 1987, Mermaids 1989, Club Rhino 1990, Faithful 1996, If These Walls Could Talk 1996, Nine 1996, Tea with Mussolini 1999, Stuck on You 2003, Burlesque 2010, Zookeeper (voice) 2011, Mamma Mia! Here We Go Again 2018. *Recordings include:* albums: as Sonny & Cher: Baby Don't Go 1965, Look At Us 1965, The Wondrous World Of Sonny & Cher 1966, Good Times 1967, In Case You're In Love 1967, Sonny & Cher Live 1971, All I Ever Need Is You 1972, Live In Las Vegas 1974, Mama Was A Rock 'N' Roll Singer 1974; solo: All I Really Want To Do 1965, Cher 1966, The Sonny Side Of Cher 1966, With Love 1967, Backstage 1968, 3614 Jackson Highway 1969, Cher 1971, Gypsies Tramps and Thieves 1971, Foxy Lady 1972, Half Breed 1973, Bittersweet White Light 1974, Dark Lady 1974, Stars 1975, I'd Rather Believe In You 1976, Cherished 1977, Two The Hard Way 1977, This Is Cher 1978, Take Me Home 1979, Prisoner 1982, I Paralyze 1984, Cher 1987, Heart Of Stone 1989, Outrageous 1989, Love Hurts 1991, It's A Man's World 1995, Believe 1998, Black Rose 1999, Not.Com.mercial 2000, Holdin' Out For Love 2001, Believe 2001, Living Proof 2001, Live: The Farewell Tour 2003, Closer to the Truth 2013, Dancing Queen 2018; singles: as Sonny & Cher: I Got You Babe 1975, Baby Don't Go 1965, Just You 1965, But You're Mine 1965, What Now My Love 1966, Little Man 1966, The Beat Goes On 1967, All I Ever Need Is You 1971, A Cowboy's Work Is Never Done 1972; solo: All I Really Want To Do 1965, Bang Bang 1966, Gypsies Tramps And Thieves 1971, The Way Of Love 1972, Half Breed 1973, Dark Lady 1974, Take Me Home 1979, Dead Ringer For Love (duet with Meatloaf) 1981, I Found Someone 1987, We All Sleep Alone 1988, After All (duet with Peter Cetera, for film Chances Are) 1989, If I Could Turn Back Time 1989, Jesse James 1989, Heart of Stone 1990, The Shoop Shoop Song (for film Mermaids) 1990, Love And Understanding 1991, Save Up All Your Tears 1991, Oh No Not My Baby 1992, Love Can Build A Bridge (with Neneh Cherry and Chrissie Hynde) 1995, Walking In Memphis 1995, One By One 1996, Paradise Is Here 1996, Believe (Grammy Award for Best Dance Recording 2000) 1998, Strong Enough 1999, All Or Nothing 1999, Dov'e l'Amore 1999, The Music's No Good Without You 2001, Alive Again 2002, A Different Kind Of Love 2002, When The Money's Gone 2003. *Website:* www.cher.com.

CHERESHNEV, Valery Aleksandrovich, DMed; Russian immunologist and academic; *Director, Institute of Ecology and Microorganism Genetics, Russian Academy of Sciences;* b. 24 Oct. 1944, Khabarovsk; m.; two c.; ed Medical Inst.,

Perm, Russian Acad. of Sciences; researcher, Medical Inst., Perm State Univ. –1988, Dir Inst. of Ecology and Microorganisms Genetics, Russian Acad. of Sciences, Ural, Perm State Univ. 1988–, Organizer and Head of Perm Inst. of Ecology and Microorganisms Genetics, Ural Br. of Russian Acad. of Sciences, Yekaterinburg 2000–03, Dir Inst. of Immunology and Physiology, Ural Br. of Russian Acad. of Sciences 2003–; Corresp. mem. Russian Acad. of Sciences 1990–97, mem. 1997–, Vice-Pres. Russian Acad. of Sciences 1999–2001 (mem. Presidium 1999–), Chair. Ural Br., Russian Acad. of Sciences 1999–2008 (mem. Presidium 1997–); mem. State Duma of the Russian Federation 2007, Chair. Cttee on Science and High Technologies; mem. Russian Acad. of Medical Sciences 2005; Fellow, World Acad. of Art and Science 2005; Order of Friendship 1998, Order 'For Merits for the Fatherland' IV Class 2004; Medal for Merits in Labour; Medal 'For Work Distinction' 1981, Gold Medal, All-Union Exhbn of Achievements of Nat. Economy of USSR 1981, Gold Badge 'For Merit for the City of Perm' 1999, P.L. Kapitza Silver Medal 2001, 2003, I.P. Pavlov Silver Medal 2003, A.D. Speransky Silver Medal 2003, I.I. Mechnikov Silver Medal 2002, V.V. Pashutin Medal, Russian Acad. of Medical Sciences 2003, V.V. Parin Prize, Ural Br. of Russian Acad. of Sciences 2003, Prize of Ural Br. of Russian Acad. of Science 2004, P. Ehrlich and R. Virchow Gold Medals, European Acad. of Natural Sciences, Hanover 2004, winner, scientific schools contest: Development of Bioactive Compounds of Bacterial Origin as Promising for Creating New Medicinal Products 2005–08, Prize of Russian Acad. of Sciences 2006, Stroganov's Prize, Perm Fraternity 2007, V.B. Parin Prize, Russian Acad. of Medical Sciences 2008, S.S. Schwartz Prize, Ural Br. of Russian Acad. of Sciences 2010, UNESCO Gold Medal 2010, UNESCO Silver Medal 'Avicenna' 2011. *Publications:* 14 books, 30 monographs, four textbooks, 13 school textbooks, more than 500 scientific articles; two inventions and 36 patents. *Leisure interest:* khatkha yoga. *Address:* Presidium, Ural Branch, Russian Academy of Sciences, Permovmayskaya str., 91, 620219 Yekaterinburg (office); Institute of Ecology and Genetics of Microorganisms, Golev str. 13, 614081 Perm, Russia (office). *Telephone:* (343) 280-74-42 (office); (343) 233-54-54 (home). *Fax:* (342) 280-92-11 (office). *E-mail:* info@iegm.ru (office); chereshnev@prm.uran.ru (office); conf@iegm.ru (office). *Website:* prm.uran.ru (office).

CHÉRIF, Taïeb, MSc, PhD; Algerian aviation official; b. 29 Dec. 1941, Kasr El Boukhari; m.; three c.; ed Univ. of Algiers, Ecole Nationale de l'aviation civile, France, Cranfield Inst. of Tech., UK; Eng Officer, Civil Aviation Directorate, Ministry of Transport, Algiers 1970–71, Deputy Dir of Transport and Aerial Activities 1971–74, Deputy Dir of Air Navigation 1974–75, Dir of Air Transport 1985–87, Dir aeronautical construction project 1987–92; State Sec. for Higher Educ. 1992–94; Algerian Rep., ICAO Council 1998–2003, Sec.-Gen. ICAO 2003–09; Dir Algiers Int. Airport 1975–76; Civil Aviation Consultant 1982–85, 1995–97; Visiting Lecturer, Inst. for Civil Aviation and Meteorology, Algiers 1970–71, Ecole Nationale des Techniciens de l'Aéronautique, Blida 1973–74, Econ. Science Inst., Algiers 1984–85. *Address:* c/o International Civil Aviation Organization, External Relations and Public Information Office, 999 University Street, Montreal, H3C 5H7, Canada.

CHERITON, David Ross, BA, MS, PhD; Canadian computer scientist, academic, venture capitalist and philanthropist; *Professor of Computer Science, Stanford University;* b. 29 March 1951, Vancouver, BC; m. Iris Fraser 1980 (divorced 1994); four c.; ed Univs of British Columbia and Waterloo; began career as Asst Prof., Univ. of British Columbia 1978–81; Prof. of Computer Science, Stanford Univ. 1981–, Founder and Leader, Distributed Systems Group; Co-founder computer networking equipment cos Granite Systems (acquired by Cisco Systems 1995), Kealia Inc. (acquired by Sun Microsystems 2004), Arastra (now Arista Networks); early investor in Google, Inc.; mem. Advisory Bd Aster Data Systems; Founder OptumSoft; SIGCOMM Lifetime Achievement Award 2003, University of Waterloo School of Computer Science renamed the David R. Cheriton School of Computer Science 2005. *Address:* Computer Science Department, Stanford University, 353 Serra Mall, Stanford, CA 94305-9025, USA (office). *Telephone:* (650) 723-1131 (office). *E-mail:* cheriton@cs.stanford.edu (office). *Website:* web.stanford.edu/~cheriton (office); gregorio.stanford.edu (office).

CHERKAOUI EL MOURSLI, Rajaà, BA, PhD; Moroccan nuclear physicist and academic; *Professor, Université Mohammed V-Agdal de Rabat;* b. 12 May 1954, Salé; ed Lycée Descartes, Rabat, Laboratoire de physique subatomique et cosmologie, Joseph Fourier Univ., Grenoble, France; returned to Rabat 1982; Prof., Université Mohammed V-Agdal, Rabat 1982–, Head of Nuclear Physics Lab. 1996–, est. first master's degree in medical physics, Vice-Pres. for Research, Co-operation and Partnership 2013–; mem. Scientific Council, Nat. Science Studies Centre and Nuclear Techniques; Pres. Moroccan Asscn for Radiation Protection; Vice-Pres. Asscn of Engineers in Nuclear Eng; Corresp. mem. Hassan II Acad. of Science and Tech. 2006; Laureate, L'Oréal-UNESCO Awards for Women in Science (Africa and the Arab States) for her contrib. to the proof of the existence of the Higgs Boson 2015. *Publications:* numerous papers in professional journals. *Address:* Université Mohammed V-Agdal de Rabat, Faculté des Sciences, 4 Avenue Ibn Battouta, BP 1014 RP, Rabat, Morocco (office). *Telephone:* (37) 771834 (office). *Fax:* (37) 774261 (office). *Website:* www.fsr.um5a.ac.ma (office).

CHERKASKY, Michael G., BA, JD; American lawyer and business executive; *Executive Chairman, Exiger;* b. 2 March 1950, Bronx, New York; m. Betsy Cherkasky; four c.; ed Case Western Reserve Univ.; began career as law clerk in US Dist Court, Northern Dist of Ohio; Asst Dist Attorney, NY Co. Dist Attorney's Office 1978–85, 1985–93, Deputy Chief of Trial Bureau 40 1983–84, Chief of Trial Bureau 1984–85, Head of Rackets Bureau 1986–90, Chief of Investigations Div. 1990–94; Head of Re-election Campaign of Robert Morgenthau 1985; joined Kroll Assocs 1994, Head of New York Office 1994–96, Head of N America Region 1996–97, COO and Exec. Man. Dir 1997, Pres. and COO The Kroll-O'Gara Co. (following merger with O'Gara-Hess & Eisenstadt 1997, renamed Kroll Inc. 2001) 1997–2001, Pres. and CEO Kroll Inc. 2001–04, Chair. and CEO Marsh Kroll Inc. (after acquisition of Kroll by Marsh & McLennan Cos) 2004; Pres. and CEO Marsh & McLennan Inc. 2004–08; CEO US Investigations Services Inc., Falls Church, Va 2008; CEO Altegrity 2008–11; Monitor (apptd by US Dept of Justice), HSBC 2013–; Chair. BrightLineGRC 2013–; Co-founder and Exec. Chair. Exiger (consulting firm that helps cos with legal and regulatory issues) 2014–. *Publication:* Forewarned: Why the Government is Failing to Protect Us and What We Must Do to Protect Ourselves 2002. *Address:* Exiger, 600 Third Avenue, 10th Floor, New York, NY 10016, USA (office). *Telephone:* (212) 833-3427 (office). *E-mail:* mcherkasky@exiger.com (office). *Website:* www.exiger.com (office).

CHERKESOV, Col-Gen. Viktor Vasilyevich; Russian security officer and lawyer; b. 13 July 1950, Leningrad; m. Natalya Sergejvna Cherkesova (née Chaplina); two d.; ed Leningrad State Univ.; investigator, KGB Dept, Leningrad 1975–91; Head, Dept of Fed. Security Service, St Petersburg and Leningrad Region 1992–98; First Deputy Dir Russian Fed. Security Service 1998–2000; Rep. of Russian Pres. to NW Fed. Okrug 2000–03; mem. Russian Federation Security Council; Dir Fed. Service for Control over Drugs and Psychotropic Substances 2003–08; Dir Fed. Agency for the Procurement of Mil. and Special Equipment 2008–10; Order of the Red Star 1985, Order of Honour 2000; 14 medals including Honoured Lawyer of the Russian Fed., Honourable Domestic Intelligence Officer of the Russian Fed., Honourable External Intelligence Officer of the Russian Fed.

CHERMAYEFF, Peter, AB, MArch, FAIA; American architect; *President, Peter Chermayeff LLC;* b. 4 May 1936, London, England, UK; s. of Serge Ivan Chermayeff and Barbara Chermayeff; m. 1st Clare Brandt (née Scott) 1960; m. 2nd Jane Borden (née Batchelder) 1966; one s. two step-s.; m. 3rd Andrea Petersen 1983; one d.; ed Phillips Acad., Andover, Harvard Coll., Harvard Graduate School of Design; Co-founder Cambridge Seven Assocs Inc. 1962, resigned 1998; Co-founder (with Peter Sollogub and Bobby Poole) Chermayeff, Sollogub & Poole, Inc. 1998–2005, continuing as Chermayeff & Poole, Inc. 2005–09; Founder Peter Chermayeff LLC 2009–; Co-founder, Pres. and CEO of affiliated firm International Design for the Environment Assocs Inc. 1990–2009; mem. Mass Council on Arts and Humanities 1969–72, Bd of Advisers, School of Visual Arts, Boston Univ. 1976–80, Visiting Cttee, Rhode Island School of Design, Providence 1969–75, Bd of Design Consultants, Univ. of Pennsylvania 1976–80; Claude M. Fuess Award for Distinguished Contribution to the Public Service, Phillips Acad., Andover 1979, AIA Firm of the Year Award (with others at Cambridge Seven Assocs) 1992. *Films include:* producer: Orange and Blue 1962, Cheetah, Zebra, Lion, Elephant & Giraffe (with Jane Borden) 1971, Wildebeest, Rhino, Impala, Gazelle, Baboon & Ostrich (with Andrea Petersen) 1984; exec. producer: Where's Boston? 1975. *Major complete works include:* design: Guidelines and Standards, Mass Bay Transportation Authority 1967, US Exhibition Expo '67 Montreal 1967, New England Aquarium, Boston 1969, Where's Boston? exhbn and show, Boston 1975, San Antonio Museum of Art, San Antonio, Tex. 1981, Nat. Aquarium, Baltimore, Md 1981, 2005, Ring of Fire Aquarium, Osaka, Japan 1990, Tennessee Aquarium, Chattanooga 1992, Genoa Aquarium, Italy 1992, Nivola Museum, Orani, Sardinia 1996, Lisbon Oceanarium 1998, Expansion Nat. Aquarium, Baltimore, Md 2005, Expansion Tennessee Aquarium, Chattanooga 2005; start-up operations: Genoa Aquarium 1992, Lisbon Oceanarium 1998, Scientific Centre of Kuwait 2000. *Work in progress includes:* New Bedford Aquarium, LA, Child (Rainforest) Cedar Rapids, Mammal Partition, Virginia Marine Science Museum, Oberhausen Aquarium, Germany, Cala Gonone Aquarium, Sardinia, Mindelo Aquarium, São Vicente, Cabo Verde, WetLand Master Plan, Homestead, Fla, Hartford Discovery Center, Conn., New Songdo Ecotarium, New Songdo City, South Korea. *Address:* Peter Chermayeff LLC, 111 Highland Road, Andover, MA 01810, USA (office). *Telephone:* (617) 226-1827 (office); (978) 289-5800 (office). *Fax:* (978) 289-5801 (office). *E-mail:* pchermayeff@peterchermayeff.com (office); peter@chermayeff.com (home). *Website:* www.peterchermayeff.com (office); www.idea-aquariums.com (office).

CHERNIN, Peter F.; American media executive; *Chairman and CEO, The Chernin Group;* b. 29 May 1951, Harrison, New York; early career as Assoc. Publicity Dir St Martin's Press and Ed. Warner Books; fmr Vice-Pres. of Devt and Production, David Gerber Co.; fmr Exec. Vice-Pres. of Programming and Marketing, Showtime/The Movie Channel Inc.; Pres. and COO Lorimar Film Entertainment 1988–89; joined Fox Broadcasting Co. 1989, Pres. of Entertainment Group 1989–92, Chair. Twentieth Century Fox Film Corpn (now Fox Filmed Entertainment) 1992–2009, Pres. and COO News Corpn 1996–2009, Chair. and CEO Fox Entertainment Group 1998–2009; Chair. and CEO The Chernin Group 2009–; Chair. Malaria No More; mem. Bd of Dirs Gemstar-TV Guide 2002–, DirecTV 2003–, American Express Co. 2006–. *Address:* The Chernin Group, 1733 Ocean Avenue, #300, Santa Monica, CA 90401, USA (office). *Telephone:* (310) 899-1205 (office).

CHERNOBROVKINA, Tatyana Anatolyevna; Russian ballerina; b. 14 Aug. 1965; m. Dmitry Zababurin; one s.; ed Saratov Ballet School; soloist, Saratov Theatre of Opera and Ballet 1983–86; soloist, Stanislavsky and Nemirovich-Danchenko Moscow Academic Music Theatre 1987–; prizewinner, 5th Moscow Int. Competition of Ballet Dancers 1985, Merited Artist of Russia 1994, People's Artist of Russia 1999. *Main ballet roles:* Odette/Odile (Swan Lake), Masha (The Nutcracker), Aurora (Sleeping Beauty), Juliet (Romeo and Juliet), Kitry (Don Quixote), Giselle (Giselle). *Address:* Moscow Academic Music Theatre, 103009 Moscow, B. Dmitrovka str. 17, Russia (office). *Telephone:* (495) 229-19-57 (office); (495) 954-14-26 (home). *Fax:* (495) 954-14-26 (home). *Website:* www.stanislavskymusic.ru (office).

CHERNOFF, Herman, PhD; American mathematician and academic; *Professor Emeritus of Statistics, Harvard University;* b. 1 July 1923, New York, NY; s. of Max Chernoff and Pauline Markowitz; m. Judith Ullman 1947; two d.; ed Townsend Harris High School, City Coll. of New York, Brown and Columbia Univs; Research Assoc., Cowles Comm. for Research in Econs, Univ. of Chicago 1947–49; Asst Prof. of Math., Univ. of Illinois 1949–51, Assoc. Prof. 1951–52; Assoc. Prof. of Statistics, Stanford Univ. 1952–56, Prof. 1956–74; Prof. of Applied Math., MIT 1974–85, now Prof. Emer.; Prof. of Statistics, Harvard Univ. 1985–97, Prof. Emer. 1997–; mem. NAS, American Acad. of Arts and Sciences; Dr hc (Ohio State) 1983, (Technion) 1984, (Univ. of Rome, La Sapienza) 1995, (Athens) 1999; Townsend Harris Prize 1982, Wilks Medal 1987. *Publications:* Elementary Decision Theory (with L. E. Moses) 1959, Sequential Analysis and Optimal Design 1972; numerous articles in scientific journals. *Address:* Department of Statistics, SC711, Harvard University, Cambridge, MA 02138 (office); 75 Crowninshield Road, Brookline, MA 02446, USA (home). *Telephone:* (617) 495-5462 (office); (617) 232-8256 (home). *Fax:* (617) 496-8057 (office). *E-mail:* chernoff@stat.harvard.edu (office). *Website:* www.fas.harvard.edu/~stats (office).

CHERNOV, Hon. Alex, AC, AO, QC, BCom, LLB; Australian (b. Lithuanian) lawyer and government official; m. Elizabeth Chernov; three c.; ed Melbourne High School, Univ. of Melbourne; emigrated with family to Australia as a young boy; fmr part-time tutor, Ormond and Newman Colls and at Monash Univ.; signed Roll of Counsel at Victoria Bar 1968; QC 1980; practised almost exclusively in commercial and co. law and equity, appearing in Supreme Courts in most states and in Supreme Court of Fiji, at trial and appellate levels, and before High Court of Australia and Privy Council; Ind. Lecturer in Equity for Council of Legal Educ. 1971–75; Hon. Consultant to Australian Law Reform Comm. 1985–87; Chair. Victorian Bar 1985–86; Vice-Pres. Australian Bar Asscn 1985–86; Pres. Australian Law Council 1990–91; Vice-Pres. LawAsia 1995–97; mem. Council of Presbyterian Ladies Coll. 1981–90; Chair. Australian Motor Sport Court of Appeal 1985–97; apptd a Judge of Trial Div. of Supreme Court of Victoria 1997, apptd to its Court of Appeal 1998; mem. Council of Univ. of Melbourne 1992–2011, chaired several of its major cttees, Deputy Chancellor 2004–10, Chancellor 2010–11; Gov. of Victoria 2011–15; Dr hc (Univ. of Melbourne) 2012. *Publication:* Brooking and Chernov, Tenancy Law and Practice in Victoria (co-author, and ed. of second edn). *Leisure interests:* music, theatre, reading, golf, walking, farming. *Address:* c/o Government House, Government House Drive, Melbourne, VIC 3004, Australia.

CHERNOV, Vladimir Kirillovich; Russian singer (baritone) and academic; *Professor of Vocal Studies, University of California, Los Angeles;* b. 1956, Belorechensk; m. Olga Chernova; one s.; ed Moscow Conservatory with Georgy Seleznev and Hugo Titz; winner of All-Union Glinka Competition, int. competitions: Tchaikovsky (Moscow), Voci Virdiagni (Vercelli), M. Helin (Helsinki); soloist of Kirov (now Mariinsky) Theatre 1990–; debut in USA 1988 (La Bohème, Boston), in UK 1990 (Forza del Destino, Glasgow); perm. soloist of Metropolitan Opera 1990–, Wiener Staatsoper 1991–; guest singer at La Scala, Chicago Lyric Opera, Mariinsky Opera, La Monnaie (Brussels) and other theatres of Europe and USA; leading parts in operas Queen of Spades, Boris Godunov, Barber of Seville, La Traviata, Eugene Onegin, Don Carlos, War and Peace, The Masked Ball, Faust, Rigoletto, Falstaff, Hérodiade (Hérod), La Cenerentola (Dandini), Nabucco (title role); in concerts and recitals performs opera arias, song cycles of Mahler, Tchaikovsky, romances; Regents' Lecturer, Voice and Opera, UCLA 2005, Prof. of Vocal Studies 2006–; mem. Faculty, Opera Ischia. *Address:* Robert Lombardo and Associates, 61 West 62nd Street, Suite 6f, New York, NY 10023, USA (office); 310 Ostin Music Center, UCLA Department of Music, 45 Charles E Young Drive East, Los Angeles, CA 90095, USA (office). *Telephone:* (212) 586-4453 (office). *Fax:* (212) 581-5771 (office). *E-mail:* robert@robertlombardo.com (office); vchernov@schoolofmusic.ucla.edu (office). *Website:* www.rlombardo.com (office); www.music.ucla.edu (office); www.vchernov.com.

CHERNUKHIN, Vladimir Anatolyevich; Russian business executive and fmr government official; b. 31 Dec. 1968, Moscow; m. Lubov Chernukhin; ed Acad. of Int. Business, Acad. of Finance, Russian Fed. Govt; with Techmashexport Co., Ministry of Foreign Trade 1986–87; with Chimmashexport Co., Ministry of Chemical Machine Construction 1986–87; army service 1987–89; Sr Expert, Technomashimport Ministry of External Econ. Relations 1989–96; Vice-Pres. Dept of Credits, Vnesheconombank 1996, mem. Bd of Dirs Vnesheconombank (Foreign Economic Bank) 1998–2004, Deputy Finance Minister and Vice-Chair. 2000–02, Chair. 2002–04; acquired 27/35 Poultry, London EC2 for devt 2006; Dir (non-exec.), Polyus Gold International –2013 (resgnd); Badge of Honour 2004. *Address:* c/o Vnesheconombank, Adademika Sakharova prosp. 9, 103810 Moscow, Russia.

CHERPITEL, Didier J., MPol, MA; French international organization official and investment banker; b. 24 Dec. 1944, Paris; s. of Bernard Cherpitel and Denise Cherpitel (née Lange); m. Nicole Estrangin 1973; one s. two d.; ed Inst. d'Etudes Politiques, Paris, Univ. of Paris; joined JP Morgan/Morgan Guaranty Trust 1972, various posts in Paris 1972–80, Man. Dir of Investment Banking Operations, Morgan Guaranty Pacific, Singapore 1980–83, Head of Commercial Banking Activities, Brussels 1983–84, Exec. Dir and Head of Capital Markets Activities, London 1984–88, Man. Dir Soc. de Bourse JP Morgan SA, Paris 1988–96, mem. Bd JP Morgan Europe 1994–97, Man. Dir of Pvt. Banking Activities Europe, JP Morgan, London 1977–98; mem. Bd French Stock Exchange (CBV) 1991–96; Admin. and Treas. American Chamber of Commerce in France 1991–96; Man. Dir Security Capital Markets Group Ltd, London 1998–99; Admin. Cie générale d'industrie et de participations (CGIP) from 1999; Sec.-Gen. Int. Fed. of Red Cross and Red Crescent Socs, Geneva 1999–2004; Chair. Atos Origin 2004–08; f. Managers sans Frontières 2005; Treas., François Xavier Bagnoud Int.; mem. Bd, Wendel Investissements 2002–05 (mem. Supervisory Bd 2005–), Foundation Mérieux, FXB International, Swiss Philanthropic Foundation, Int. Finance Facility for Immunisation (IFFIm), Porticus Global; fmr mem. Bd, Foundation Médecins sans Frontières (MSF/France), Fidelity International (Bermuda/Luxembourg), Prologis European Real Estate (Luxembourg). *Leisure interests:* travel, photography, opera, golf. *Address:* Porticus Global, PO Box 7867, 1008 AB 92926 Amsterdam, The Netherlands (office). *Telephone:* (20) 621-3871 (office). *E-mail:* communications@porticus.com (office). *Website:* www.porticus.com (office).

CHERTOFF, Michael, BA, JD; American judge and fmr government official; *Co-Founder and Executive Chairman, Chertoff Group;* b. 28 Nov. 1953, Elizabeth, NJ; ed Harvard Univ.; Summer Assoc., Miller, Cassidy, Larroca & Lewin (law firm) 1978; Law Clerk, Court of Appeals Second Circuit 1978–79, Supreme Court 1979–80; Assoc., Latham & Watkins 1980–83, Pnr 1994–2001; Asst US Attorney, Attorney's Office, Southern Dist of NY 1983–87, First Asst US Attorney, Dist of NJ 1987–90, US Attorney 1990–94; Special Counsel, US Senate Whitewater Cttee 1994–96; Asst Attorney-Gen., Criminal Div., US Dept of Justice 2001–03; Judge, Court of Appeals Third Circuit 2003–05; US Sec. of Homeland Security, Washington, DC 2005–09; Co-founder and Exec. Chair. The Chertoff Group, Washington, DC 2009–; also currently Senior Of Counsel, Covington & Burling LLP, Washington, DC; Chair. BAE Systems, Inc. 2012–; mem. American Law Inst.; numerous awards, including John Marshall Award for Trial of Litigation, US Dept of Justice 1987, Henry E. Petersen Memorial Award, US Dept of Justice 2006, Benjamin L. Hooks Award for Distinguished Service, NAACP 2007, European Inst. Transatlantic Leadership Award 2008. *Address:* The Chertoff Group, 1399 New York Avenue, NW, Suite 900, Washington, DC 20005 (office); Covington & Burling LLP, One City Center, 850 Tenth Street, NW, Washington, DC 20001-4956, USA (office). *Telephone:* (202) 552-5280 (The Chertoff Group) (office); (202) 662-5060 (Covington & Burling LLP) (office). *E-mail:* mchertoff@cov.com (office). *Website:* chertoffgroup.com (office); www.cov.com (office).

CHERUIYOT, Vivian Jepkemoi; Kenyan athlete; b. 11 Sept. 1983, Keiyo Dist, Rift Valley Prov.; specializes in long-distance running; represented Kenya at the Summer Olympic Games, Sydney 2000, Beijing 2008, London 2012; World Champion 2009, 2011, African Champion 2010, Commonwealth Games Champion 2010, Int. Asscn of Athletics Feds (IAAF) Continental Cup Champion 2010; also won IAAF Diamond League title 2010; Bronze Medal, 3,000m, World Youth Championships, Bydgoszcz 1999, 5,000m, All-Africa Games, Johannesburg 1999, 5,000m, World Junior Championships, Kingston 2002; World Championships: Gold Medal, 5,000m, Berlin 2009, Gold Medal, 10,000m, Daegu 2011, Gold Medal, 5,000m, Daegu 2011, Silver Medal, 5,000m, Osaka 2007; Commonwealth Games: Gold Medal, 5,000m, Delhi 2010; Olympic Games: Silver Medal, 5,000m, London 2012, Bronze Medal, 10,000m, London 2012, Gold Medal 5,000m, Rio 2016, Silver Medal 10,000m, Rio 2016; World Athletics Final: Gold Medal, 5,000m, Stuttgart 2007, Silver Medal, 3,000m, Stuttgart 2007, Silver Medal, 5,000m, Stuttgart 2008, Silver Medal, 3,000m, Stuttgart 2008, Silver Medal, 3,000m, Thessaloniki 2009, Bronze Medal, 3,000m, Stuttgart 2006, Bronze medal, 5,000m, Thessaloniki 2009; World Indoor Championships: Silver Medal, 3,000m, Doha 2010; World Cross Country Championships: Gold Medal, Sr Race, Punta Umbría 2011, Gold Medal, Jr Race, Vilamoura 2000, Silver Medal, Jr Race, Belfast 1999, Bronze Medal, Jr Race, Dublin 2002; competed for Africa and won Gold Medal, 5,000m, Continental Cup Gold, Split 2010; with a time of 14:20.89, set at DN Galan 2011; coached by Ricky Simms; Kenyan Sportswoman of the Year 2011, Women's Track & Field Athlete of the Year 2011, Laureus World Sportswoman of the Year 2011. *Website:* www.viviancheruiyot.com.

CHESHIRE, Sir Ian Michael, Kt; British retail executive; *Chairman, Maisons du monde SA;* b. 6 Aug. 1959, Miri, Malaysia; m. Kate Cheshire; three c.; ed Univ. of Cambridge; worked at Guinness and the Piper Trust; more than 20 years' retail experience, including Group Commercial Dir Sears plc; joined Kingfisher as Group Strategy Dir in 1998, subsequently joined main Bd as Chief Exec. of Kingfisher's e-Commerce Div. 2000–02, CEO Int. and Devt, with responsibility for all retail operations outside the UK and France 2002–05, CEO B&Q UK 2005–08, Group Chief Exec. Kingfisher plc 2008–15; Chair. and mem. Bd of Dirs Debenhams plc 2016–19; Chair. Maisons du monde SA 2017–; mem. Bd of Dirs, Whitbread plc 2011–17, Barclays Plc 2017–18; mem. Prince of Wales Corp. Leaders Group on Climate Change; mem. Employers' Forum on Disability Pres.'s Group. *Address:* Maisons du Monde, Le Portereau, Route des Ports aux Meules, Vertou, 44120, France (office). *Telephone:* 2-51-71-17-17 (office). *Website:* www.maisonsdumonde.com (office).

CHESHIRE, Air Chief Marshal Sir John Anthony, KBE, CB, KStJ, FRAeS; British air force commander and government official; b. 4 Sept. 1943; s. of Air Chief Marshal Sir Walter Cheshire; m. Shirley Ann Stevens 1964; one s. one d.; ed Ipswich School, Worksop Coll., RAF Coll., Cranwell; joined RAF as a cadet 1961; commissioned as a pilot officer 1963, promoted to Flying Officer 1964, Flight Lt 1966, Squadron Leader 1971, Wing Commdr 1977; specialist in air support, Special Forces –1980; Commdr Air Wing, Brunei 1980–82, RAF Lyneham 1983–85, Plans Br. HQ Strike Command 1986–87; Defence and Air Attaché, Moscow 1988–90; Deputy Commdt RAF Staff Coll. 1991–92; Asst Chief of Staff for Policy Supreme HQ, Allied Powers, Europe 1992–94; Mil. Rep. to NATO HQ 1995–97; C-in-C Allied Forces NW Europe 1997–2000; Lt-Gov. and C-in-C of Jersey (Channel Islands) 2001–06; Chair. Royal Air Force Charitable Trust and Pres. Royal Int. Air Tattoo 2008–13. *Leisure interests:* int. and defence affairs, creative writing, collecting (affordable) antiques, golf, squash, tennis. *Address:* c/o Royal Air Force Charitable Trust Enterprises, Douglas Bader House, Horcott Hill, Fairford, Glos., GL7 4RB, England. *Website:* www.airtattoo.com/our-parent-charity/the-trust (office).

CHESKY, Brian Joseph, BFA; American business executive; *Co-Founder and CEO Airbnb, Inc.;* b. 29 Aug. 1981, Niskayuna, New York; s. of Robert H. Chesky and Deborah Chesky; ed Rhode Island School of Design; Industrial Designer, 3DID, Inc., Los Angeles 2005–07; Prin., Brian Chesky, Inc. June–Oct. 2007; Co-founder and CEO, Airbnb, Inc. 2007–; named Amb. of Global Entrepreneurship by Pres. Barack Obama 2015. *Address:* Airbnb Inc., 888 Brannan Street, Suite 400, San Francisco, CA 94103-4932, USA (office). *Website:* www.airbnb.com (office).

CHESNAKOV, Aleksei Aleksandrovich, PhD; Russian political scientist; *Director, Centre for Current Politics in Russia;* b. 1 Sept. 1970, Baku, Azerbaijan; m.; one d.; ed Moscow State Univ.; Jr, then Sr Researcher, Inst. of Mass Political Movts, Russian-American Univ. 1991–93; Researcher, then Head of Collective of Political Lectures, Centre for Current Politics in Russia 1993–97, Dir 1997–; Dir Centre of Social-Political Information, Inst. of Social-Political Studies, Russian Acad. of Sciences 1997; currently Deputy Pres. Domestic Policy Directorate; mem. Presidium Ind. Assoc. Civil Soc.; mem. United Russia party –2013, Deputy Sec. Gen. Council; briefly mem. Kasimov City Council. *Publications:* numerous scientific publs on social and political problems; monographs: One Hundred Political Leaders of Russia 1993, Azerbaijan: Political Parties and Organizations 1993, Russia: Power and Elections 1996, Social and Political Situation in Russia in 1996 1997, Russia: New Stage of Neo-liberal Reforms 1998. *Address:* Centre for Current Politics in Russia, 105064 Moscow, 16 Kazakova ul., Russia (office). *Telephone:* (495) 775-14-10 (office). *Fax:* (495) 748-08-09 (office).

CHET, Ilan, PhD; Israeli microbiologist, academic and university administrator; *Francis Ariowitsch Chair of Agricultural Biotechnology, Hebrew University of Jerusalem;* b. 12 April 1939, Haifa; m. Ruth Geffen; two s. three d.; ed Hebrew Univ. of Jerusalem; teacher of microbiology (specializing in soil microbiology, fungal physiology and biological control of plant diseases), Faculty of Agric., Hebrew Univ. of Jerusalem 1965–2001, Assoc. Prof. of Microbiology 1975–78, Prof. 1978–2001, Head Dept of Plant Pathology and Microbiology 1981–83, Dean Faculty of Agric. 1986–89, currently Francis Ariowitsch Chair of Agricultural Biotechnology; mem. Senate, Hebrew Univ. of Jerusalem 1978, mem. Exec. Cttee of Hebrew Univ. 1990–92, Bd of Man. 1990–2001, Vice-Pres. for Research and Devt 1992–2001, Chair. Univ. Authority for Research and Devt 1992–2001; Prof., Dept of Biological Chem., Weizmann Inst., Rehovot 2001–, Pres. Weizmann Inst. 2001–06; Dir Otto Warburg Center of Biotechnology in Agric., Rehovot 1983–86, 1990–92; mem. Bd Scientific Incubators Co. 1992–94, Yissum R&D Co. 1992–2001;

Chair. Nat. Cttee for Strategic Infrastructure 1998–2001; Chair. Cttee for Agric. and Biotechnology, Nat. Council of Research and Devt 1984–86, Special Projects Cttee, Int. Soc. for Plant Pathology 1989–93; Deputy Sec.-Gen. Union for the Mediterranean 2010–; mem. Nat. Cttee for Biotechnology 1985–92, 1996–97, IUPAC Comm. on Biotechnology 1986–92, Editorial Bd, European Journal of Plant Pathology 1995–; mem. External Adviser to EU Group 1998–2002; panel mem. NATO 2000–03; numerous visiting professorships and lectureships; mem. Israeli Nat. Acad. of Sciences and Humanities 1998; Fellow, American Phytopathological Soc. 1991; Officer's Cross, Order of Merit (Germany) 2001, Ordre national de la Légion d'honneur 2014; Dr hc (Lund) 1991, (Naples), (Haifa Univ.); Max-Planck Research Award 1994, Israel Prize for Agricultural Research 1996, Wolf Prize 1998, E.M.T Prize, European Acad. of Science & Art 2003, Invited Speaker, World Econ. Forum, Davos, Switzerland 2003 and numerous other prizes. *Publications include:* Soil-Plant Interaction (co-ed.) 1986, Innovative Approaches to Plant Disease Control (ed.) 1987, Biotechnology in Plant Disease Control (ed.) 1993; 350 chapters, reviews and articles; 32 patents. *Leisure interest:* antique microscopes and scales. *Address:* Faculty of Agriculture, Hebrew University of Jerusalem, Rehovot 76100, Israel (office). *Telephone:* (8) 9489236 (office); (8) 934219077 (home); (8) 3453032 (home). *Fax:* (8) 9468785 (office). *E-mail:* chet@huji.ac.il (office). *Website:* ufmsecretariat.org (office).

CHEUNG, Barry, BSc, MBA, JP; Hong Kong business executive and fmr government official; b. (Cheung Chun-yuen), 15 Feb. 1958, Hong Kong; ed Univ. of Sussex, UK, Harvard Business School, USA; consultant with McKinsey & Co., Los Angeles and Hong Kong 1987–94; mem. Hong Kong Govt Cen. Policy Unit (on secondment from McKinsey & Co.) 1993–94; CEO Titan Petrochemicals Group Ltd 2004–08, later becoming Deputy Chair.; Chair. Hong Kong Mercantile Exchange (HKMEx) 2008–13; Dir (non-exec.), UC Rusal 2010–13, Chair. 2012–13; fmr CEO Camelot Oil Co. Ltd; Exec. Councillor –2013; mem. Bd, Hong Kong Urban Renewal Authority 2001–13, Chair. 2007–13, Chair. Standing Cttee on Disciplined Services Salaries and Conditions of Service 2009, Alt. Chair. Pay Trend Survey Cttee, mem. Standing Comm. on Civil Service Salaries and Conditions of Service 2008, Comm. on Strategic Devt 2009–12; fmr Chair. Corruption Prevention Advisory Cttee, Hong Kong Ind. Comm. against Corruption; declared bankrupt April 2015; found guilty of failing to pay an employee HK $340,000 while chair. of HKMEx and later defaulting on payment, sentenced to six months in prison April 2015, sentence downgraded on appeal to 160 hours community service Sept. 2015; Gold Bauhinia Star 2010.

CHEUNG, Maggie; Hong Kong actress; b. 20 Sept. 1964, Hong Kong; m. Olivier Assayas 1998 (divorced 2001); grew up in Bromley, Kent, UK; fmr fashion model; jury mem., Berlin International Film Festival 1997, Venice Film Festival 1999, Cannes Film Festival 2007, Marrakech International Film Festival 2010; apptd UNICEF Amb. to China 2010; Dr hc (Univ. of Edinburgh) 2011. *Films include:* Yuen fan (Behind the Yellow Line) 1984, Ching wa wong ji (Prince Charming) 1984, Ging chaat goo si (Jackie Chan's Police Force) 1985, Xin tiao yi bai (Heartbeat) 1987, Yue liang, xing xing, tai yang (Moon, Stars & Sun) 1988, Wong gok ka moon (As Tears Go By) 1988, Nan bei ma da (Mother vs Mother) 1988, Liu jin sui yue (Golden Years) 1988, Qiu ai ye jing hun (In Between Love) 1989, Xiao xiao xiao jing cha (Little Cop) 1989, Ketu qiuhen (Song of Exile) 1990, Hong chang fei long (Crying Freeman: Dragon from Russia) 1990, Hei xue (Will of Iron) 1990, Gungun hongchen (Red Dust) 1990, A Fei jing juen (Days of Being Wild) 1991, Yuen Ling-yuk (Centre Stage) (Best Actress Award, Berlin Int. Film Festival) 1992, Shuan long hui (Brother vs Brother) 1992, Jia you xi shi 1992, Dung fong saam hap 1993, Wu xia qi gong zhu (Holy Weapon) 1993, Shen Jing Dao yu Fei Tian Mao (Flying Dagger) 1993, Fei yue mi qing (Enigma of Love) 1993, Chai gong 1993, Bai mei gui (Blue Valentine) 1993, Tian mi mi (Comrades: Almost a Love Story) 1996, Irma Vep 1996, Song jia huang chao (The Soong Sisters) 1997, Augustin, roi du Kung-fu 1999, Fa yeung nin wa (In the Mood for Love) 2000, Ying xiong (Hero) 2002, 2046 2004, Clean (Best Actress Award, Cannes Film Festival) 2004, Ashes of Time Redux 2008, Hot Summer Days 2010, Ten Thousand Waves 2010, Playtime 2013. *Address:* c/o Golden Harvest, 16/F Peninsula Office Tower, 18 Middle Road, Tsumshatsui/Rowlon, Hong Kong Special Administrative Region, People's Republic of China.

CHEUNG, Yan, (Zhang Nin); Chinese business executive; *Founder and Chairperson, Nine Dragons Paper (Holdings) Ltd;* b. Heilongjiang Prov.; m. Liu Ming Chung; two s.; worked in paper products co. in Shenzhen in early 1980s; moved to Hong Kong 1985, est. waste-paper trading business; moved to Los Angeles 1990, est. paper recycling plant; returned to China 1995, est. Nine Dragons Paper (Holdings) Ltd (packaging manufacturer), Chair. 2006–; mem. Nat. Cttee CPPCC; Exec. Vice-Chair. Overseas Chinese Entrepreneurs Asscn, Guangdong Federation of Industry and Commerce; Vice-Chair. Women's Fed. of Commerce; Pres. Guangdong Overseas Chinese Enterprises Asscn; Exec. Vice-Pres. Hong Kong China Chamber of Commerce; Vice-Pres. China Paper Asscn, China Paper Industry Chamber of Commerce; Hon. Pres. World Dongguan Entrepreneurs, Hon. Citizen, City of Dongguan; Entrepreneur of the Year in China, Ernst & Young 2007, Leader Figure, China Cailun Awards, China Paper Industry Chamber of Commerce 2008, China Charity Award, Ministry of Civil Affairs 2008, Outstanding Entrepreneur in Pulp and Paper Manufacturing Industry in China, China Paper Asscn 2009, Chinese Chamber of Commerce Contributions Award 2010, Outstanding Person on Energy Saving and Emission Reduction in China 2009, All-China Environment Federation 2010, Outstanding Contribution Award on Poverty Alleviation and Benefiting the Community by a Businessman in the Private Sector in Guangdong Province 2010. *Address:* Nine Dragons Paper (Holdings) Ltd, 31st Floor, Sun Hung Kai Centre, 30 Harbour Road, Wanchai, Hong Kong Special Administrative Region, People's Republic of China (office). *Telephone:* 25116338 (office). *E-mail:* info@ndpaper.com (office). *Website:* www.ndpaper.com (office).

CHEUNG WING LAM, Linus, JP, BSocSc; Chinese business executive; ed Univ. of Hong Kong; Deputy Man. Dir Cathay Pacific Airways Ltd 1971–94; apptd Exec. Dir Cable & Wireless PLC 1995; Chief Exec. and Exec. Dir Hongkong Telecom (HKT) Ltd 1995–2000; Deputy Chair. and Exec. Dir PCCW Ltd (fmrly Pacific Century CyberWorks Ltd) (merged with Cable & Wireless HKT Ltd 2000) 2000–04; Chair. Companhia de Telecomunicações de Macao 1996; Dir China Unicom Ltd 2004–; currently mem. Chinese People's Political Consultative Conference, Tianjin Municipal Govt; Chair. Man. Bd, School of Business, Univ. of Hong Kong, Poon Kam Kai Inst. of Man., Advisory Bd HKU SPACE Community Coll.; Univ. apptd adviser to Chinese Soc. of Macroeconomics of the State Planning Comm., People's Repub. of China 1995; Adjunct Prof., Chinese Univ. of Hong Kong; mem. Council Univ. of Hong Kong. *Address:* China Unicom Limited, 75th Floor, The Center, 99 Queen's Road, Central, Hong Kong Special Administrative Region, People's Republic of China (office).

CHEVALIER, Tracy, MA, FRSL; American writer; b. 19 Oct. 1962, Washington, DC; m.; one s.; ed Oberlin Coll., Univ. of East Anglia, UK; moved to London, England 1984; fmr reference book ed. –1993; mem. Council, Soc. of Authors; Trustee, British Library 2015–; President, Royal Literary Fund 2015–; Dr hc (Oberlin Coll.) 2013, (Univ. of East Anglia) 2013; Barnes & Noble Discover Award 2000, Ohioana Award 2013. *Publications include:* novels: The Virgin Blue 1997, Girl with a Pearl Earring 1999, Falling Angels 2001, The Lady and the Unicorn 2003, Burning Bright 2007, Remarkable Creatures 2009, The Last Runaway 2013, At the Edge of the Orchard 2016, Reader, I Married Him (short stories) 2016, New Boy 2017. *Address:* c/o Jonny Geller, Curtis Brown, Haymarket House, 28–29 Haymarket, London, SW1Y 4SP, England (office). *Telephone:* (20) 7393-4400 (office). *E-mail:* hello@tchevalier.com. *Website:* www.tchevalier.com.

CHEVÈNEMENT, Jean-Pierre; French politician; *President, Fondation Res Publica;* b. 9 March 1939, Belfort; s. of Pierre Chevènement and Juliette Garessus; m. Nisa Grünberg 1970; two s.; ed Lycée Victor-Hugo, Besançon, Univ. de Paris, Ecole Nationale d'Admin.; joined Section française de l'Int. ouvrière (SFIO) 1964; Commercial Attaché, Ministry of Econ. and Finance 1965–68; Sec.-Gen. Centre d'études, de recherches et d'éducation socialistes (CERES) 1965–71; Commercial Adviser, Jakarta, Indonesia 1969; Political Sec. Fédération socialiste de Paris 1969–70; Dir of Studies, Soc. Eres 1969–71; Co-founder Parti Socialiste (PS) 1971, Nat. Sec. PS 1971–75, 1979–80, mem. Exec. Bureau 1971–81, 1986–93, Steering Cttee 1971–92; Deputy (Territoire de Belfort) to Nat. Ass. 1973–81, 1986–2002; Regional Councillor, Franche-Comté 1974–88; Minister of State, Minister of Research and Tech. 1981–82, of Industry 1982–83, of Nat. Educ. 1984–86, of Defence 1988–91, of the Interior 1997–2000; unsuccessful cand. in presidential elections 2002, 2007, 2012; First Asst to Mayor of Belfort 1977–83, 1997–2001, Mayor 1983–97, 2001–07; Pres. République Moderne 1983–, Conseil Régional de Franche-Comté 1981–82, mem. 1986–88, fmr Vice-Pres.; Founder and Pres. Citizens Movt (MDC) 1992–2003, renamed Citizen and Republican Movt (MRC) 2003, Hon. Pres. 2003–08, Pres. 2008–15 (resgnd and left party); Senator from Territoire de Belfort 2008–14; mem. Foreign Affairs Comm. Nat. Ass. 1986–88, 1991–93, Finance Comm. 1993–97, 2001–02; Founder and Pres. Fondation Res Publica (research foundation) 2005–; mem. Bd Dirs, Repères magazine; Croix de la valeur militaire. *Publications:* (as Jacques Mandrin): L'énarchie ou les mandarins de la société bourgeoise 1967, Socialisme ou socialmédiocratie 1969, Clefs pour le socialisme 1973, Le vieux, la crise, le neuf 1975, Les socialistes, les communistes et les autres, Le service militaire 1977, Etre socialiste aujourd'hui 1979, Apprendre pour entreprendre 1985, Le pari sur l'intelligence 1985, Une certaine idée de la République m'amène à 1992, le Temps des citoyens 1993, Le Vert et Le Noir. Intégrisme, Pétrole, Dollar 1995, France–Allemagne: parlons franc 1996, La République contre les bien-pensants 1999, Défis républicains 2004, Pour l'Europe votez non 2005, La Faute de M. Monnet. La République et l'Europe 2006. *Leisure interest:* chess. *Address:* Fondation Res Publica, 52 rue de Bourgogne, 75007 Paris, France (office). *Telephone:* 1-45-50-39-50 (office). *Fax:* 1-45-55-68-73 (office). *E-mail:* info@fondation-res-publica.org (office). *Website:* www.fondation-res-publica.org (office).

CHEVRIER, Francis, PhD; French economist, academic and institute director; *Director, Institut Européen d'Histoire et des Cultures de l'Alimentation;* b. 1965, Belfort; ed Univ. of Strasbourg, Univ. of the Sorbonne, Paris, Sciences Po, Paris, Univ. of Oxford, UK; est. Int. Festival of Geography of St-Dié-of-Vosges 1990; Creator and Dir Rendez-vous de l'Histoire (annual int. meeting in Blois bringing together researchers, educators, journalists, artists and publrs); Founder and Dir Institut Européen d'Histoire et des Cultures de l'Alimentation 2002–. *Publications include:* Les cahiers de la Gastronomie, N° 5, Hiver 2010/2011 2010, Notre gastronomie est une culture: Le repas gastronomique des Français au patrimoine de l'humanité 2011. *Address:* Institut Européen d'Histoire et des Cultures de l'Alimentation, 16 rue Briçonnet, 37000 Tours, France (office). *Telephone:* (2) 47-05-90-30 (office). *Fax:* (2) 47-60-90-75 (office). *E-mail:* contact@iehca.eu (office). *Website:* www.iehca.eu (office).

CHEW, Choon Seng, BMechEng (Hons), MSc; Singaporean business executive; ed Univ. of Singapore and Imperial Coll. of Science and Tech., Univ. of London, UK; joined Singapore Airlines 1972, man. assignments in Japan and Italy, regional appointments as Sr Vice-Pres. SW Pacific, the Americas and Europe, head of Planning, Marketing and Finance Divs, Sr Exec. Vice-Pres. (Admin) for Corp. Affairs, Auditing and Finance 2001–03, CEO 2003–10, Deputy Chair. SIA Engineering Co. Ltd (subsidiary); fmr Chair. SMRT Corpn Ltd, Singapore Aircraft Leasing Enterprise; Dir (non-exec.), Singapore Exchange (SGX) 2004–, Chair. (non-exec.) 2011–16; Chair. Singapore Tourism Bd 2011–; mem. Bd, Govt of Singapore Investment Corpn; mem. Bd of Dirs, GIC Pvt. Ltd, Nat. Gallery Singapore; fmr mem. Bd Govs, Int. Air Transport Asscn. *Address:* Singapore Exchange (SGX), 2 Shenton Way, #02-02 SGX Centre 1, Singapore 068804 (office); Singapore Tourism Board, Tourism Court, 1 Orchard Spring Lane, Singapore 247729, Singapore (office). *Telephone:* 62368888 (SGX) (office). *Fax:* 65356994 (SGX) (office). *E-mail:* info@sgx.com (office). *Website:* www.sgx.com (office); www.stb.gov.sg (office).

CHEY, Jae-won, BSc, MSc, MA; South Korean business executive; brother of Tae-won Chey; ed Brown, Stanford and Harvard Univs, USA; began career working in research position with Raychem Corpn; held positions in SK-USA, Vice-Pres. at Yamaichi International (America) Inc.; later Sr Man. Dir at SK C&C and Man. Dir at SKC Ltd, Exec. Vice-Pres., SK Telecom 2001–05, Vice-Chair. and Co-CEO SK Holdings Co. Ltd 2005–13. *Address:* c/o SK Holdings Co. Ltd, 99 Seorin-Dong, Jongru-Gu, Seoul 110-110, Republic of Korea.

CHEY, Tae-won, BS, MA, PhD; South Korean energy industry executive; *Chairman and Co-CEO, SK Holdings Company Limited;* b. 1961, brother of Jae-won Chey; m.; three c.; ed Korea Univ., Univ. of Chicago, USA; Man. Business

Devt, METRA Co., Calif., USA –1991; Gen. Man. SK Networks (fmrly SK Global) Co. Ltd 1991–93, with SK Global America Inc. 1993–96, Man. Dir SK Corpn 1996–97, Exec. Vice-Pres. 1997–98, Chair. 1998–2007, mem. Bd of Dirs, Chair. and CEO SK Holdings Co. Ltd 2007–08, Chair. and Co-CEO 2008–, Chair. and CEO SK Energy Co. Ltd 2007–; Exec. Dir Okedongmu; mem. Int. Business Leaders' Advisory Council; Co-Chair. East Asia Econ. Summit in Malaysia, Asian regional forum of WEF; Invited Prof., Seoul Nat. Univ. 2002, PhD programme in Econs, Univ. of Chicago; arrested on charges of fraud 2003, jailed for seven months in connection with accounting fraud at affiliate SK Networks; indicted for embezzling more than US $40 million from SK cos to cover up trading losses Jan. 2012, found guilty and sentenced to four years in prison by Seoul Dist Court Jan. 2013, pardoned Aug. 2015; selected as one of The Next 100 Leaders, World Econ. Forum 1998, WEF Global Leader for Tomorrow. *Address:* SK Holdings Co. Ltd, 99 Seorin-Dong, Jongru-Gu, Seoul 110-110, Republic of Korea (office). *Telephone:* (2) 2121-5114 (office). *Fax:* (2) 2121-7001 (office). *E-mail:* Byc778@sk.com (office). *Website:* www.sk.com (office); www.sk.co.kr/gateway/en (office); www.skenergy.com (office).

CHHABRIA, Vidya M.; Indian business executive; *Chairperson, Jumbo Group;* b. Bangalore; m. Manohar (Manu) Rajaram Chhabria (deceased); three d.; Chair. Jumbo Group 2002–, cos in group include Shaw Wallace & Co., Maharashtra Distilleries, SKOL Breweries, Shaw Wallace Distilleries, Shaw Wallace Breweries, Hindustan Dorr-Oliver, Mather & Platt, Falcon Tyres, Gordon Woodroffe and Shaw Wallace Hedges; Patron-in-Chief Confed. of Indian Alcoholic Beverage Cos 2003. *Leisure interests:* reading, travelling, Indian music. *Address:* Jumbo Group, PO Box 3426, Union Towers, Sheikh Zayed Road, Dubai, United Arab Emirates (office). *Fax:* (4) 343-7397 (office). *E-mail:* chairman@jumbocorp.com (office). *Website:* www.jumbocorp.com (office).

CHHETRI, Gen. Rajendra; Nepalese army officer; *Chief of Army Staff;* b. 15 Nov. 1960, Dudhekuna, Tanahun Dist; s. of Col Gopal Bahadur Khatri Chhetri and Pramila Khatri Chhetri; m. Rita Chhetri; two s.; ed Tribhuwan Univ., Royal Nepalese Military Acad., Army War Coll., and Command and Gen. Staff Coll., USA, School of Army Air Defense, Pakistan, Defense Inst. of Psychological Research, India; commissioned into Rajdal (Artillery) Battalion, Nepalese Army in 1978, numerous command positions including No.4 Air Defense Battery, Jagadal (Air Defense) Battalion, No. 7 (Infantry) Brigade, No.3 (Infantry) Brigade, Mid Division, staff positions have included Brigade Major of No. 1 Brigade, Asst Chief of Staff (Operations) of Mid Division HQ, Army HQ posts include serving in Research and Devt Directorate, Inspector Gen. Dept, Operations Br., Military Sec. Br., served as Dir of Recruiting and Selections and as Military Asst to Chief of the Army Staff, served as Analyst, Nat. Security Council Secretariat, other positions included Quarter Master Gen., Dir-Gen. of Military Training, Chief of Staff and Chief of Gen. Staff, Chief of Army Staff 2015–; Founding mem. and Col Commdt, Jagadal Battalion; Gorkha Dakshin Bahu Trishakti Patta Class IV; COAS Commendation Badge, two US Army Achievement Medals, four different UN Medals for service in various UN missions. *Leisure interests:* trekking, travelling, reading. *Address:* Nepal Army Headquarters, Bhadrakali, Kathmandu 44600, Nepal (office). *Telephone:* (1) 4269624 (office). *E-mail:* armyhq@gmail.com (office). *Website:* www.nepalarmy.mil.np (office).

CHI, Gen. Haotian; Chinese politician and army officer; b. 1929, Zhaoyuan Co., Shandong Prov.; m. Jiang Qingping; ed Anti-Japanese Mil. and Political Coll., Nanjing Mil. Acad., Political Acad. of the Chinese PLA, PLA High Infantry School, Mil. Acad. of the Chinese PLA; joined PLA 1945, CCP 1946; Company Instructor, Field Army, PLA Services and Arms 1946–49; joined Chinese People's Volunteers during Korean War 1951, bn instructor and Deputy Dir PLA Regimental Political Dept; Maj., unit, Nanjing Mil. Region 1958; Deputy Political Commissar, Beijing Mil. Region 1975–77; Deputy Ed.-in-Chief, People's Daily 1977–82; Deputy Chief of Staff PLA 1977–82; Political Commissar, Jinan Mil. Region 1985–87; PLA Chief of Staff 1987–92; Minister of Nat. Defence 1993–98, 1998–2003, State Councillor 2000–03; Chair. Drafting Cttee for Nat. Defence Law of People's Repub. of China; mem. PRC Cen. Cttee 1992–95, Vice-Chair 1995–2003; rank of Gen. 1988; mem. 14th CCP Cen. Cttee 1992–97, 15th CCP Cen. Cttee 1997–2002; mem. 8th NPC 1993–98, Politburo; State Councillor 1992–95; mem. Macao Special Admin. Region Preparatory Cttee, Govt Del., Macao Hand-Over Ceremony 1999; Hon. Pres. Wrestling Asscn of China; Third-Class People's Hero of East China; World Harmony Award 2010. *Address:* c/o Ministry of National Defence, Jingshanqian Jie, Beijing 100009, People's Republic of China (office).

CHIABRA LEÓN, Gen. (retd) Roberto; Peruvian army officer (retd) and government official; b. 15 July 1949, Callao; ed Escuela Militar de Chorrillos, Inst. Int. de Derechos Humanos, Costa Rica, Univ. of Piura; fmr instructor, Escuela Militar de Chorrillos, Escuela Superior de Guerra, Centro de Altos Estudios Militares (CAEM); C-in-C, Cenepa conflict 1995, Gen. Commdr Second Mil. Region 2002, Commdr Gen. of Armed Forces 2002–03, attained rank of Col 1995, later Brig.-Gen.; Minister of Defence 2003–05; numerous mil. awards including Medalla Académica del Ejército (Merit, Honour and Distinction), Peruvian Cross of Merit, Marshal Andrés Avelino Cáceres Medal, Grand Cross of Mil. Order Francisco Bolognesi.

CHIANG, Antonio; Taiwanese journalist and editor; fmr Ed. and Publr The Eighties magazine; fmr Publr The Journalist (weekly political magazine) 1980s; Co-founder and sr journalist, Taipei Times 1998, later Ed.-in-Chief and Publr; Deputy Sec.-Gen. Nat. Security Council 2000–04. *Address:* c/o Taipei Times, 14/F, 399 Ruiguang Road, Neihu District, Taipei City 11492, Taiwan. *E-mail:* letters@taipeitimes.com.

CHIASSON, Herménégilde, BA, BFA, MA, MFA; Canadian writer, artist, academic and fmr politician; b. 7 April 1946, Saint-Simon, New Brunswick; m. Marcia Chiasson; one d.; ed Université de Moncton, Mount Allison Univ., Université de Paris 1, France, State Univ. of New York, USA Univ. of Paris (Sorbonne); Dir Galerie d'art de l'Université de Moncton 1974; Pres. Galerie Sans Nom 1980; Founding Pres. Éditions Perce-Neige (publishing house) 1984; Pres. Asscn acadienne des artistes professionnels du Nouveau Brunswick 1993–95; Founding Pres. Productions du Phare-Est 1998; invited curator, Anecdotes and Enigmas: The Marion McCain Atlantic Art Exhbn, Beaverbrook Art Gallery 1994; Lt-Gov. of New Brunswick 2003–09; Artist-in-Residence, Univ. of Ottawa 2003; Casino New Brunswick Artist-in-Residence, Université de Moncton and Mount Allison Univ. 2013–; mem. RSC; Chevalier, Ordre des Arts et des Lettres 1990, Ordre des francophones d'Amérique 1993, Grand Officer of the Nat. Order of Merit (France) 2011, Kt Order of la Pléiade; Dr hc (de Moncton) 1999, Hon. DLit (de Moncton) 2009; Prix France-Acadie 1986, 1992, Grand Prix de la francophonie canadienne 1999, Prix quinquennal Antonine-Maillet-Acadie Vie 2003, Prix Montfort 2004, Molson Prize 2011. *Films:* has directed 17 films, including Toutes les photos finissent par se ressembler 1985, Le Grand Jack 1987, Robichaud 1989, Taxi Cormier 1990, Épopée 1996. *Publications include:* numerous books, including Mourir à Scoudouc 1974, Claude Roussel/Sculpteur/Sculptor 1985 (in collaboration with Patrick Condon Laurette), Vous (France-Acadie Prize 1992) 1991, Climats 1996, Conversations (Gov.-Gen.'s Literary Award) 1999; and 15 poetry collections; has written 25 plays, including Pierre, Hélène et Michael 1990, L'exil d'Alexa 1993, Aliénor 1997, Le Christ est apparu au Gun Club 2005. *Address:* 2, Roma Hélène, Grand Barachois, NB E4P 8B8, Canada.

CHIBA, Keiko; Japanese lawyer and politician; b. 11 May 1948; ed Chuo Univ., Tokyo; pvt. practice as lawyer; mem. Japan Socialist Party –1997; mem. Democratic Party of Japan (DPJ) 1997–, fmr Vice-Pres., also Chair. DPJ Admin Cttee; mem. House of Councillors for Kanagawa constituency 1986–2010, Dir Parl. Judicial Cttee; Minister of Justice 2009–10; Sec.-Gen. Japanese Parl. Group for Amnesty International; mem. Yokohama Bar Asscn. *Address:* c/o Democratic Party of Japan, 1-11-1, Nagata-cho, Chiyoda-ku, Tokyo 100-0014, Japan.

CHIBESAKUNDA, Hon. Justice Lombe Phyllis, BL; Zambian lawyer, judge and diplomatist; b. 5 May 1944; one s.; ed Chipembi Girls' School, Nat. Inst. of Public Admin, Lusaka, Australian Nat. Univ.; called to the Bar, Gray's Inn, UK 1969; State Advocate Ministry of Legal Affairs 1969–77; pvt legal practice with Jacques and Partners 1972–73; mem. Nat. Ass. (Parl.) for Matero 1973–75; Solicitor Gen. and Deputy Minister of Legal Affairs 1973–75; Chief Zambian Del., UN Law of the Sea Conf. 1974–79; Amb. to Japan 1975–77; High Commr to UK (also accred Amb. to FRG, the Netherlands and the Holy See) 1977–82; Chair. Industrial Relations Court 1981–86; Rep. UN Comm. on the Status of Women, Vienna, Austria 1984–88; Judge, High Court, Lusaka 1986–94; Judge in charge of Copperbelt, Luapula, Northern and Northwestern Provs 1994–97; apptd Judge, Supreme Court 1997, Acting Chief Justice 2012–15; Chair. Perm. Human Rights Comm. 1997–2003; Judge Admin. Tribunal of African Devt Bank 1997, Vice-Pres. 2005; Pres. Common Market for Eastern and Southern Africa 2015; Assessor of external examinations, Zambia Inst. of Advanced Legal Educ., Lusaka 2005; Pres. Zambia Asscn of Women Judges 2005–; Chair. Equality Cttee Sub-Cttee, UN Independence Party's Women's League; f. Social Action Charity, Lusaka; Founder-mem. Link Voluntary Org. 1979, Rotary Club 1994–97, Int. Asscn of Women Judges 1994–97; life mem. Commonwealth Parl. Asscn; Kt Grand Cross, Order of Pope Pius IX 1979. *Achievements include:* first woman lawyer in Zambia; first woman Solicitor Gen. in Zambia and Africa.

CHICAGO, Judy, MFA; American artist, author and academic; b. (Judy Cohen), 20 July 1939, Chicago, Ill.; m. 1st Jerry Gerowitz 1961 (died 1962); m. 2nd Lloyd Hamrol 1969; m. 3rd Donald Woodman 1985; ed Univ. of California, Los Angeles; taught art at Univ. of California Extension, Los Angeles 1963–69, Univ. of Calif. Inst. Extension, Irvine 1966–69, California State Univ., Fresno (f. art programme for women) 1969–71, Calif. Inst. of the Arts, Valencia (f. first Feminist Art Programme) 1971–73; co-f. Feminist Studio Workshop and Woman's Bldg, Through the Flower Corpn, Los Angeles 1977; Presidential Appt. in Art and Gender Studies, Indiana Univ. 1999; Robb Lecturer, Univ. of Auckland, NZ 1999; Visiting Prof., Artist-in-Residence, Duke Univ. and Univ. of North Carolina, Chapel Hill 2000; Prof. in Residence, Western Kentucky Univ., Bowling Green 2001; "Envisioning the Future" (interdisciplinary and multi-exhbn site project), Pomona Arts Colony/Cal Poly Pomona/Pitzer Coll., Pomona and Claremont, Calif. 2003; First Chancellor's Artists in Residence (with photographer Donald Woodman), Vanderbilt Univ. 2006; her work The Dinner Party in perm. collection of Elizabeth A. Sackler Center for Feminist Art at the Brooklyn Museum, New York 2007–; Hon. DFA (Smith Coll., Northampton, Mass.) 2000, (Duke Univ., Durham, NC) 2003; Hon. DHumLitt (Lehigh Univ., Bethlehem, Pa) 2000; Int. Lion of Judah Conference Award For Pioneering American Women Jewish Artists 2004, Visionary Woman Award Moore Coll. of Art, Philadelphia 2004; numerous other awards. *Publications:* Through the Flower: My Struggle as a Woman Artist 1975, The Dinner Party: A Symbol of Our Heritage 1979, Embroidering Our Heritage: The Dinner Party Needlework 1980, The Birth Project 1985, Holocaust Project: From Darkness into Light 1993, The Dinner Party/Judy Chicago 1996, Beyond the Flower: The Autobiography of a Feminist Artist 1996, Women and Art: Contested Territory 1999, Fragments from the Delta of Venus 2004, Kitty City: A Feline Book of Hours 2005, The Dinner Party: From Creation to Preservation 2007, Face to Face: Frida Kahlo (with Frances Borzello) 2010. *Leisure interests:* cats and exercise. *Address:* PO Box 1327, Belen, NM 87002, USA (office). *Telephone:* (505) 861-1499 (office). *E-mail:* info@judychicago.com (office). *Website:* www.judychicago.com (office).

CHICO PARDO, Jaime, BEng, MBA; Mexican telecommunications executive; *Chairman and CEO, ENESA;* m.; several c.; ed Universidad Iberoamericana, Univ. of Chicago Grad. School of Business, USA; spent six years doing M&A work at Banamex Int. Div., later managed operations of cos acquired by bank; then Deputy Man. Dir International Mexican Bank (INTERMEX), London, UK; f. International Financial Engineering (investment bank); Sr Exec. Euzkadi, Gen. Tire de México –1993, Fimbursa –1993; Pres. and CEO Grupo Condumex SA de CV 1993–95; joined Teléfonos de México SA (Telmex) 1995, Vice-Chair. and CEO 1995–2006, Chair. 2006–09, Co-Chair. 2009–10; Founder, Chair. and CEO ENESA (pvt. fund) 2010–; Chair. Carso Global Telecom SA de CV 1996–2010; Co-Chair. IDEAL (Impulsora del Desarrollo y el Empleo en America Latina SA de CV) 2006–10; Dir, AT&T, Inc. 2008– (Chair. Corp. Devt and Finance Cttee), Grupo Bimbo, SAB de CV, Honeywell International, Inc., Grupo Carso SA de CV 1991–2010 and the following of its affiliates: Telmex 1991–2010, Carso Global Telecom SA de CV 1996–2010, América Móvil, SAB de CV 2001–09, IDEAL 2006–11, Telmex Internacional SAB de CV 2008–10, CICSA (Carso Infraestructura y Construccíon) 2008–11; Distinguished Corp. Alumni Award 2005. *Address:* Grupo ENESA, Miguel de Cervantes, Saavedra 255, Col. Ampliacion Granada, Mexico City, DF, 11520, Mexico (office). *Telephone:* (55) 5626-3707 (office). *E-mail:* contacto@enesa.com.mx (office). *Website:* enesa.com.mx (office).

CHIDAMBARAM, Palaniappan, BSc, LLB, MBA; Indian lawyer and politician; b. 16 Sept. 1945, Kanadukathan, Tamil Nadu; s. of Shri Palaniappan and Lakshmi Achi; m. Nalini Chidambaram; one s.; ed Presidency Coll., Madras Univ., Harvard Business School, USA; mem. Lok Sabha (Lower House of Parl.) for Sivaganga constituency 1984–99, 2004–14; Deputy Minister, Dept of Commerce and Dept of Personnel 1985; Minister of State, Depts of Personnel and Home Affairs 1986–89; Minister of State, Dept of Commerce 1991–92, 1995–96; Minister of Finance 1996–98, 2004–08, 2012–14, of Home Affairs 2008–12; Trustee, Rajiv Gandhi Foundation, Indian Literary Asscn. *Publication:* A View from the Outside: Why Good Economics Works for Everyone. *Address:* Indian National Congress (Congress), 24 Akbar Road, New Delhi 110 001, India (office). *Telephone:* (11)-23019080 (office). *Fax:* (11)-23017047 (office). *E-mail:* connect@inc.in (office). *Website:* www.inc.in (office).

CHIEN, Eugene Y. H., BS, MS, PhD; Taiwanese politician and professor of engineering; *President and Chairman, Taiwan Institute for Sustainable Energy;* b. 4 Feb. 1946, Taoyuan Co.; m. Wang Kuei-Jung (Gwendolyn Chien); two s. one d.; ed Nat. Taiwan Univ., New York Univ., USA; Assoc. Prof., Tamkang Univ. 1973–76, Prof. and Chair. Dept of Aeronautical Eng 1976–78, Prof. and Dean Coll. of Eng 1978–84; Prof. Emer., Catholic Univ. of Honduras 2002; mem. Legis. Yuan (Parl.) 1984–87, Chair. Nat. Defense Cttee 1984–85, Educ. Cttee 1986; Minister of State, Environmental Protection Admin. 1987–91; Minister of Transportation and Communications 1991–93; Nat. Policy Adviser to Pres. 1993–96; Rep., Taipei Rep. Office, UK 1993–97; project consultant, EBRD 1997; Sr Adviser, Nat. Security Council 1997–2000; Deputy Sec.-Gen., Office of the Pres. 2000–02; Minister of Foreign Affairs 2002–04; Chair. Int. Co-operation and Devt Fund 2002–; consultant to various hi-tech cos 2004–; Pres. and Chair. Taiwan Inst. for Sustainable Energy 2007–; Pres. Chinese Inst. of Environmental Eng 1988–91, Chinese Inst. of Engineers 1991–92, Sino-British Cultural and Econ. Asscn 1998–; Hon. Fellow, Cardiff Univ., UK 1998; Ten Outstanding Young Persons of the World Award, Jaycees Int. and Osaka Jaycees, Japan 1985, Chinese Inst. of Environmental Eng Award 1991, Environment Protection Admin Medal 1998, Global Views Environmental Heroes Award 2010. *Publication:* The Asian Regional Economy (co-ed.) 1993. *Leisure interests:* horse riding, reading, swimming, jogging, chess. *Address:* Taiwan Institute for Sustainable Energy, 5F, No. 35 Kwang Fu N. Road, Taipei, Taiwan (office). *Telephone:* (2) 2768-2655 (office). *Fax:* (2) 2768-7522 (office). *E-mail:* eugenechien@gmail.com (office). *Website:* www.tise.org.tw (office).

CH'IEN, Kuo-fung Raymond, CBE, PhD, JP; Chinese business executive and fmr politician; *Non-Executive Chairman, MTR Corporation Limited;* b. 26 Jan. 1952, Tokyo, Japan; s. of James Ch'ien and Ellen Ma; m. Whang Hwee Leng; one s. two d.; ed schools in Hong Kong, Rockford Coll., Ill., Univ. of Pennsylvania, USA; Second Vice-Pres. and Economist, Chase Manhattan Bank, New York 1978–81; Vice-Pres. and Dir Spencer Stuart & Assocs, Hong Kong 1981–84; Group Man. Dir Lam Soon Hong Kong Group 1984–97; Dir (non-exec.), MTR Corpn Ltd 1998–, Chair. (non-exec.) 2003–; Ind. Dir (non-exec.), Hang Seng Bank Ltd, The Wharf (Holdings) Ltd, Swiss Re Ltd, China Resources Power Holdings Co.; Dir, HSBC Holdings –2007, Convenience Retail Asia Ltd –2014; mem. Standing Cttee, CPPCC Tianjin Municipal Cttee; fmr Chair. Fed. of Hong Kong Industries, now Hon. Pres.; mem. Exec. Council 1992–97, Exec. Council Hong Kong Special Admin. Region 1997–2002; mem. Econ. Devt Comm., Hong Kong Special Admin. Region (HKSAR) Govt, Standing Cttee, Tianjin Municipal Cttee of CPPCC; Trustee, Univ. of Pennsylvania 2006–; Hon. Adviser, China Aerospace Corpn; Hon. Pres. and Past Chair. Fed. of Hong Kong Industries; Hon. Prof., Nanjing Univ.; Gold Bauhinia Star (Hong Kong) 1999; Chevalier, Ordre du Mérite agricole 2008; Young Industrialist Award, Fed. of Hong Kong Industrialists 1988, Global Leader for Tomorrow, World Econ. Forum 1993. *Leisure interests:* hiking, tennis, scuba diving, Chinese paintings and ceramics. *Address:* MTR Corporation Ltd, GPO Box 9916, MTR Headquarters Building, Telford Plaza, 33 Wai Yip Street, Kowloon Bay, Kowloon, Hong Kong Special Administrative Region, People's Republic of China (office). *Telephone:* 29933333 (office). *Fax:* 27959991 (office). *E-mail:* info@mtr.com.hk (office). *Website:* www.mtr.com.hk/en/corporate/main/index.html (office).

CHIEN FU, Fredrick, BA, MA, PhD; Taiwanese fmr politician; *Chairman, Cathay Charity Foundation;* b. 17 Feb. 1935, Beijing; m. Julie Tien; one s. one d.; ed Nat. Taiwan Univ., Yale Univ., USA; Sec. to Premier, Exec. Yuan 1962–63; Visiting Assoc. Prof., Nat. Chengchi Univ. 1962–64; Section Chief, Dept of N American Affairs, Ministry of Foreign Affairs 1964–67, Deputy Dir 1967–69, Dir 1969–72, Dir-Gen. Govt Information Office 1972–75; Visiting Prof., Nat. Taiwan Univ. 1970–72; Admin. Vice-Minister of Foreign Affairs 1975–79, Political Vice-Minister 1979–82; Rep., CCNAA Office in USA 1983–88; Minister of State and Chair. Council for Econ. Planning and Devt, Exec. Yuan 1988–90; Minister of Foreign Affairs 1990–96; apptd mem. Kuomintang (KMT) Cen. Standing Cttee 1988–98; Speaker, Nat. Ass. 1996–98; Visiting Prof., Law School, Soochow Univ. 1997–98, Nat. Taiwan Univ. 1997–99; Pres. Control Yuan 1999–2005; Chair. Pacific Cultural Foundation 2011–; also currently Chair. Cathay Charity Foundation; numerous decorations from more than 25 countries, including Order of Brilliant Star with Grand Cordon 1975, Order of Good Hope, Grand Cross Class (South Africa) 1979, Order of Propitious Cloud with Special Grand Cordon (Taiwan) 2000, Order of Chung Cheng 2005; Hon. DLit (Wilson Coll.), Hon. LLD (Boston Univ., Idaho State Univ., Sun Kyun Kwan Univ., Caribbean American Univ.), Dr hc (Florida Int. Univ.). *Publications include:* The Opening of Korea: A Study of Chinese Diplomacy 1876–1885, Speaking as a Friend, More Views of a Friend, Faith and Resilience: The ROC Forges Ahead, Opportunity and Challenge, Memoir of Fredrick F. Chien. *Leisure interests:* reading, golf. *Address:* Cathay Financial Centre, 19th Floor, No. 7, Sung Ren Road, Hsin-yi District, Taipei 11073, Taiwan (office). *Telephone:* (2) 8722-6701 (office). *Fax:* (2) 8789-4242 (office). *E-mail:* fredrickchien@cathaybk.com.tw (office). *Website:* www.cathaybk.com.tw (office).

CHIFFLET, Jean-Paul; French banking executive; b. 1949, Tournon-sur-Rhône; ed Institut des Hautes Finances de Paris; joined Crédit Agricole du Sud-Est as Head of Sales Man. 1973, Corp. Sec. Crédit Agricole de la Drôme 1980–86, Corp. Sec. Crédit Agricole du Sud-Est 1986–90, Head of Devt and Lending 1990–92, Deputy CEO Crédit Agricole Ain Saône-et-Loire 1992–95, Deputy CEO Crédit Agricole Centre-Est 1995–97, Head of Relations with Regional Banks, Caisse Nationale de Crédit Agricole 1997–2000, CEO Crédit Agricole Centre-Est 2000–10, CEO Crédit Agricole SA 2010–15, also Chair. LCL (Le Crédit Lyonnais) and Chair. Crédit Agricole Corp. and Investment Bank; Chair. Fédération Bancaire Française 2012–13; Chair. Amundi Group 2011–16; mem. Conseil Economique et Social, Paris 2007–; mem. and Officer of the Bd of Confédération Nationale de la Mutualité, de la Coopération et du Crédit Agricole; Chevalier, Ordre nat. du Mérite; Officier du Mérite agricole. *Address:* c/o Crédit Agricole SA, 91–93 boulevard Pasteur, 75015 Paris, France. *E-mail:* info@credit-agricole-sa.fr.

CHIHARA, Charles Seiyo, BA, MS, PhD; American academic; *Professor Emeritus of Philosophy, University of California, Berkeley;* b. 19 July 1932, Seattle, Wash.; s. of George Chihara and Mary Chihara; m. Carol Rosen 1964; one d.; ed Seattle Univ., Purdue Univ., Univ. of Washington, Univ. of Oxford, UK; Instructor, Univ. of Washington 1961–62; Asst Prof., Univ. of Illinois 1962–63; Asst Prof., Univ. of California, Berkeley 1963–69, Assoc. Prof. 1969–75, Prof. 1975–2000, Prof. Emer. 2000–; Mellon Postdoctoral Fellowship 1964–65, Humanities Research Fellowship 1967–68, Nat. Endowment for the Humanities Fellowship 1985–86, 1994–95, Univ. of California President's Research Fellowship in the Humanities 1996–97. *Publications:* Ontology and the Vicious-Circle Principle 1973, Constructibility and Mathematical Existence 1990, The Worlds of Possibility: Modal Realism and the Semantics of Modal Logic 1998, A Structural Account of Mathematics 2004. *Leisure interests:* tennis, travel. *Address:* Department of Philosophy, University of California, Berkeley, CA 94720 (office); 567 Cragmont Avenue, Berkeley, CA 94708, USA (home). *Telephone:* (510) 525-4023 (home). *Fax:* (510) 525-4103 (home). *E-mail:* charles1@socrates.berkeley.edu (office). *Website:* philosophy.berkeley.edu (office).

CHIK, Tan Sri Sabbaruddin, BA, MPA; Malaysian business executive and fmr politician; *Chairman, Priceworth Wood Products Bhd;* b. 11 Dec. 1941, Temerloh, Penang; ed Abu Bakar Secondary School, Temerloh, Malay Coll., Kuala Kangser, Perak, Univ. of Malaya and Inst. of Social Studies, The Hague; Asst State Sec. Negri Sembilan, Prin. Asst Sec. JPM, Dir Planning, GPU/SERU, Dir Int. Trade, Ministry of Trade and Industry, Deputy State Sec. Selangor 1966–81; Gen. Man. Pernes Trading Sdn. Bhd 1981–82; mem. Parl. for Temerloh 1982–99; Deputy Minister of Finance 1982; Minister of Culture, Arts and Tourism 1987–99; mem. UMNO Supreme Council 1984; mem. Bd of Dirs Priceworth Wood Products Bhd (Chair. 2001–), EDEN Inc. Bhd 2002–. *Address:* Priceworth Wood Products Berhad, Suite 04-01A and 04-01B, 4th Floor, Menara Keck Seng, 203 Jalan Bukit Bintang, 55100 Kuala Lumpur, Malaysia (office). *Telephone:* (3) 21443299 (office). *Website:* www.pwpmalaysia.com.my (office).

CHIKÁN, Attila, PhD; Hungarian economist, academic and politician; *Professor Emeritus, Corvinus University of Budapest;* b. 4 April 1944, Budapest; s. of Zoltan Chikan and Klara Deak; m. Márta Nagy; one s. one d.; ed Karl Marx Univ. of Econ. Sciences, Budapest, Grad. School of Business, Stanford Univ., USA; Prof., Budapest Univ. of Econ. Sciences and Public Admin (Corvinus Univ. of Budapest since 2004) 1968–, Rector 2000–03, now Prof. Emer.; Founder Rajk Laszlo Coll. for Advanced Studies (Dir 1970–2010, Pres. 2010–), Dir Competitiveness Research Centre 2003–; Minister of Econ. Affairs 1998–99; Chair. Council of Econ. Advisers of the Prime Minister 2000–02; Exec. Vice-Pres. Int. Soc. for Inventory Research 1982–; Pres. Fed. of European Production and Industrial Man. Socs 1996, Int. Fed. of Purchasing and Supply Man. 2000–01; Chair. Supervisory Bd, Gedeon Richter Pharmaceutical Plc; Vice-Chair. Supervisory Bd, MOL Plc (oil co.); Pres. and/or CEO of several nat. asscn; mem. editorial bds of several int. journals; mem. Royal Swedish Acad. of Eng; mem. Bd Cen. European Univ.; Corresp. mem. Hungarian Acad. of Sciences; Middle Cross, Order of Merit of the Repub. of Hungary; Dr hc (Lappeenranta Univ. of Tech., Finland, Cluj Univ., Romania, Babes-Bolyai Univ.); Garner Themoin Award, Int. Fed. of Purchasing and Supply Man., Lifetime Achievement Award, Int. Purchasing and Supply Educ. and Research Asscn. *Publications include:* author or ed. of several books Inventory Models (co-ed) 1991, National Competitiveness in Global Economy (co-ed with Czako, E and Zoltay-Paprika, Z) 2002. *Leisure interest:* sports. *Address:* Corvinus University of Budapest, 1093 Budapest IX, Fővám tér 8, Hungary (office). *Telephone:* (1) 482-5569 (office). *Fax:* (1) 482-5290 (office). *E-mail:* chikan@uni-corvinus.hu (office). *Website:* www.uni-corvinus.hu (office).

CHIKANE, Rev. Frank, MA; South African ecclesiastic and government official; *President, Apostolic Faith Mission International;* b. 3 Jan. 1951, Bushbuckridge, Transvaal; s. of James Mashi and Erenia Chikane; m. Kagiso Oglobry 1980; three s.; ed Turfloop Univ. and Univs of S Africa, Durban and Pietermaritzburg, Harvard Univ., USA; worked with Christ for All Nations 1975–76; ordained Minister 1980; part-time Research Officer, Inst. of Contextual Theology 1981, Gen. Sec. 1983; Gen. Sec. S African Council of Churches 1987–94; Dir-Gen. in Office of the Deputy Pres. 1994–99, Dir-Gen. of The Presidency 1999–2010, also Chancellor of Nat. Orders, also Chair. Forum of S Africa's Dirs-Gen.; currently Pres. Apostolic Faith Mission International; mem. Nat. Exec. Cttee, African Nat. Congress 1997–; Sr Research Fellow, Dept of Religious Studies, Univ. of Cape Town 1995–; mem. Ecumenical Asscn of Third World Theologians; Hon. Pres. Nebo Youth Congress 1987–; Hon. DTheol (Groningen); Swedish Diakonia Peace Prize, Inst. for Contextual Theology 1986, Star Crystal Award 1987, Third World Prize 1989, Peace and Freedom Prize, Swedish Labour Movement, honoured by African-American Inst. at its Annual Awards Dinner. *Publications:* Doing Theology in a Situation of Conflict 1983, The Incarnation in the Life of People in South Africa 1985, Children in Turmoil: Effect of the Unrest on Township Children 1986, Kairos Document – A Challenge to Churches, No Life of my Own (autobiog.). *Leisure interests:* reading, keeping fit (mentally, spiritually, physically). *Address:* Apostolic Faith Mission International, PO Box 9450, Building No. 14, Central Office Park, 257 Jean Avenue, Centurion 0046 (office); University of Cape Town, Private Bag, Rondebosch 7700, South Africa. *Telephone:* (12) 6440490 (office). *Fax:* (12) 6440732 (office). *E-mail:* afmint@afm-ags.org (office). *Website:* www.afm-ags.org/afm-international (office).

CHIKIN, Valentin Vasilevich; Russian journalist; b. 25 Jan. 1932; ed Moscow Univ.; literary corresp. for Moscow Komsomol newspaper 1951–58; mem. CPSU 1956–91, CP of Russian Fed. 1992–; literary corresp., Deputy Ed., Ed. of Komsomolskaya Pravda 1958–71; Deputy then First Deputy Ed.-in-Chief of Sovietskaya Rossiya 1971–84, Ed.-in-Chief 1986–91; First Deputy Pres. of State Cttee on Publishing, Printing and the Book Trade 1984–86; Sec. of USSR Union of

Journalists 1986–90; cand. mem. of CPSU Cen. Cttee 1986–91; mem. State Duma (CP faction) 1993–. *Address:* Gosudarstvennaya Duma, 103265 Moscow, Okhotnyi ryad 1 (office); Communist Party of the Russian Federation (Kommunisticheskaya partiya Rossiiskoi Federatsii), 103051 Moscow, per. M. Sukharevskii 3/1, Russia. *Telephone:* (495) 692-80-00 (office); (495) 628-04-90. *Fax:* (495) 203-42-58 (office); (495) 292-90-50. *E-mail:* stateduma@duma.ru (office); kprf2005@yandex.ru. *Website:* www.duma.ru (office); kprf.ru.

CHIKWANDA, Alexander Bwalya; Zambian business executive and politician; b. 1938; ed Lund Univ., Sweden; fmr Minister of Health, Planning and Finance, and of Agric.; Minister of Finance 2011–16; Dir Sigma Enterprises Ltd; fmr mem. United Nat. Independence Party. *Address:* c/o Ministry of Finance, PO Box 50062, Chimanga Road, Lusaka, Zambia (office).

CHILDS, David M., BA, MArch, FAIA; American architect; *Consulting Design Partner, Skidmore, Owings and Merrill LLP;* b. 1 April 1941, Princeton, NJ; two c.; ed Yale Univ., Yale School of Art and Architecture; Design Dir Pennsylvania Avenue Comm., Washington, DC 1968–71; joined Skidmore, Owings and Merrill LLP, Washington, DC 1971, moved to New York City office 1984, currently Consulting Design Pnr; Chair. Nat. Capital Planning Comm. 1975–81; Chair. US Comm. of Fine Arts 2003–08; mem. Bd of Dirs Municipal Arts Soc. of New York; Trustee American Acad. in Rome, Museum of Modern Art, Smithsonian Nat. Portrait Gallery, Nat. Bldg Museum; Fellow, AIA. *Completed projects include:* in Washington, DC: Washington Mall master plan and Constitution Gardens, Nat. Geographic HQ, 1300 New York Avenue, Metro Center, US News and World Report HQ, Dulles Airport Extension, Four Seasons, Park Hyatt and Regent hotels; in New York: Worldwide Plaza on 8th Avenue, 450 Lexington Avenue, Bertelsmann Tower, NY Mercantile Exchange, JFK Airport Arrivals Bldg, Bear Stearns HQ, Stuyvesant School Bridge; other projects include Swiss Bank Center, Stamford, Conn., Deerfield Acad. Natatorium, US Courthouse, Charleston, WV, Lester B. Pearson Int. Airport, Toronto, Canada, Ben Gurion Int. Airport, Tel-Aviv, Israel, West Ferry Circus at Canary Wharf, London, England, US Embassy in Ottawa, Canada. *Address:* Skidmore, Owings and Merrill, 14 Wall Street, 24th Floor, New York, NY 10005, USA (office). *Telephone:* (212) 298-9300 (office). *Fax:* (212) 298-9500 (office). *E-mail:* somnewyork@som.com (office). *Website:* www.som.com (office).

CHILINGAROV, Artur Nikolayevich, CandGeoSc; Russian polar explorer and politician; *President, Association of Polar Explorers of the Russian Federation;* b. 25 Sept. 1939, Leningrad; m.; one s. one d.; ed Adm. Makarov Higher Marine School of Eng; worked as metalworker in Baltic vessel repair plant; First Sec. Regional Comsomol Cttee in Yakutya; headed drifting station N Pole 19, organized station N Pole 22, head Bellingshausen station in Antarctica, head expedition to free scientific vessel Mikhail Somol in Antarctic, expedition on board atomic ice-breaker Sibir; Deputy Chair. USSR State Cttee on Meteorology 1986–92; counsellor, Chair. Russian Supreme Soviet on problems of Arctic and Antarctic 1991–93; Pres. Asscn of Polar Explorers of the Russian Fed. 1991–, mem. Co-ordinating Council Polus Expeditionary Centre (organizes expeditions for the Asscn) 2002–; mem. State Duma (Parl.) 1993–2011, apptd Deputy Speaker 1994; Rep. for Tula Oblast, Federation Council 2011–14; mem. Bd of Dirs, Rosneft 2014–; mem. Org. Cttee, Otechestvo Movt 1999, joined Yedinstvo and Otechestvo Union (later Yedinaya Rossiya party); Corresp. mem. Russian Acad. of Natural Sciences; Co-Chair. Russian Foundation of int. humanitarian aid and co-operation; Hero of the Soviet Union 1986, Order of Lenin, Order of the Red Banner of Labour, Order of the Badge of Honour, Medal of Anania Shirakatsi (Armenia) 2000, Order of Polar Star (Yakutia) 2002, Order of Naval Merit 2003, Commdr, Order of Bernardo O'Higgins (Chile) 2006, Order of Merit for the Fatherland, Third Class 2007, Hero of the Russian Fed. 2008, Order of St Mashtots (Armenia) 2008, Order of Friendship (South Ossetia) 2009, Order of St Prince Daniil Moskovsky, Second Class (Russian Orthodox Church) 2009, Chevalier, Légion d'honneur 2010; numerous awards, including USSR State Prize, Honoured Meteorologist of the Russian Fed. 2005, Medal 'Symbol of Science' 2007. *Publications:* more than 50 scientific publs. *Leisure interest:* football. *Address:* c/o Coordinating Council, Polus Expeditionary Centre, 119027 Moscow, 2 Reysovaya Street, 2A, PGK Airport Vnukovo, Russia (office). *Telephone:* (495) 436-28-47 (office). *E-mail:* mail@polus.org (office). *Website:* www.polus.ru (office).

CHILINGIRIAN, Levon, OBE, FRCM, ARCM; British violinist and academic; *Chamber Musician in Residence, Royal Academy of Music;* b. 28 May 1948, Nicosia, Cyprus; m. Susan Paul Pattie 1983; one s.; ed Royal Coll. of Music; co-f. Chilingirian String Quartet 1971; has performed in N and S America, Africa, Australasia, Europe and Far East; apptd Prof., RAM 1980, currently Chamber Musician in Residence; mem. teaching staff, Guildhall School of Music and Drama; Musical Dir Camerata Nordica of Sweden, Mendelessohn on Mull Festival, Pharos Festival; BBC Beethoven Competition 1969, Munich Duo Competition (with Clifford Benson) 1971; Hon. DMus (Sussex) 1992; First Prize, BBC Beethoven Competition 1969, First Prize, Munich Duo International Competition 1971, Cobbett Medal 1995, Royal Philharmonic Soc. Chamber Music Award 1995. *Recordings include:* 10 Mozart quartets, last three Schubert quartets and complete viola quintets, Debussy and Ravel quartets, Schubert octet and quintet, six Bartók quartets and piano quintet, late and middle Dvořák quartets, Tippett Triple Concerto; music by Panufnik, Tavener, Pärt, Chausson, Grieg, Vierne, Hahn, Komitas, McEwen, Michael & Lennox Berkeley (Chilingirian Quartet), Mozart and Eliasson (with Camerata Nordica). *Publications:* Edvard Grieg's F Major Quartet 1999, The Classical Music Book 2018. *Leisure interests:* chess, backgammon, football. *Address:* Royal Academy of Music, Marylebone Road, London NW1 5HT, England (office). *E-mail:* levon@chilingirianquartet.co.uk. *Website:* www.ram.ac.uk/about-us/staff/levon-chilingirian (office); www.chilingirianquartet.co.uk.

CHILOSI, Alberto, PhD; Italian economist and academic; b. 14 Jan. 1942, Modena; s. of Giuseppe Chilosi and Clara Trabucchi; m. Lucia Ponzini; one s.; ed La Spezia Liceo Classico, Univ. of Pisa, Warsaw Cen. School of Planning and Statistics, Poland; Asst, Univ. of Pisa 1966–69, Lecturer in Theory and Policy of Econ. Devt 1972–81, Prof. of Econ. Policy 1981–2012; Lecturer, then Assoc. Prof. of Econs, Univ. Officielle du Congo, Lubumbashi 1969–72; Pres. Asscn Italiana per lo Studio dei Sistemi Economici Comparati 1988–89. *Publications include:* Growth Maximization, Equality and Wage Differentials in the Socialist Economy 1976, Kalecki 1979, Self-Managed Market Socialism with Free Mobility of Labour 1986, L'Economia del Periodo di Transizione 1992, Entrepreneurship and Transition 2002, Stakeholders vs Shareholders in Corporate Governance 2007, The European Union and Its Neighbours 2007, The Long March of Italian Communists from Revolution to Neoliberalism 2010, Stakeholder Protection, Varieties of Capitalism, and Long-Term Unemployment 2012. *Leisure interests:* cycling, swimming. *Address:* Via S. Andrea 48, 56127 Pisa, Italy. *Telephone:* (050) 544184. *E-mail:* chilosi@specon.unipi.it (office). *Website:* www.chilosi.it.

CHILTON, Mary-Dell, PhD; American plant biotechnologist and business executive; *Vice-President of Agricultural Biotechnology, Distinguished Science Fellow and Principal Scientist, Syngenta Biotechnology Inc.;* b. 2 Feb. 1939, Indianapolis, Ind.; ed Univ. of Illinois; Postdoctoral Researcher in Microbiology, Univ. of Washington, Seattle; mem. Faculty, Washington Univ. in St Louis 1979–83; hired by Syngenta Biotechnology Inc. (fmrly Ciba-Geigy) 1983, f. biotech research centre at Research Triangle Park 1984, later Vice-Pres. of Agricultural Biotechnology, Distinguished Science Fellow and Prin. Scientist; mem. North Carolina Bd of Science and Tech. 1986; mem. NAS 1985; Fellow, American Acad. of Arts and Sciences 1993, American Acad. of Microbiology 1994; Rank Prize in Nutrition (UK) 1986, David Gottlieb Medal, Univ. of Illinois 1986, ACS Hendricks Medal 1987, John Scott Award, City of Philadelphia 2000, Benjamin Franklin Medal in Life Sciences, Franklin Inst. 2002, CSSA Presidential Award, Crop Science Soc. of America 2011, World Food Prize (co-recipient) 2013. *Publications:* more than 100 scientific publs. *Address:* Syngenta Biotechnology Inc., PO Box 12257, 3054 East Cornwallis Road, Research Triangle Park, NC 27709-2257, USA (office). *Telephone:* (919) 541-8500 (office). *E-mail:* info@syngentabiotech.com (office). *Website:* www.syngentabiotech.com (office).

CHILTON, Tutii, BS, MS; Palauan academic and government official; *Chairman of the Governing Board, Financial Institutions Commission;* b. Koror; ed Rutgers Univ. and Univ. of Hawaii, USA; Assoc. Prof., Social Science and Humanities, Palau Community Coll.; Chair. Governing Bd, Financial Institutions Comm. 2009–; served on Palau Nat. Olympic Cttee Bd. *Address:* Financial Institutions Commission, PO Box 10243, Koror, PW 96940, Palau (office). *Telephone:* 488-3560 (office). *Fax:* 488-3564 (office). *E-mail:* info@ropfic.org (office). *Website:* www.ropfic.org (office).

CHILUMPHA, Cassim, PhD; Malawi politician; *President, People's Assembly for Democracy and Development;* b. Nkhotakota City; ed Univ. of Hull, UK; worked at Univ. of Malawi as Head of Business Admin, then Dean, Faculty of Commerce, later Assoc. Prof. of Commercial Law; Minister of Admin 1994–2000, 2003–06; Minister of Finance 1998–2000; Vice-Pres. and Minister responsible for Statutory Corpns 2004–09; Minister of Energy and Mining April–Dec. 2012; mem. People's Party 2012; Pres. People's Ass. for Democracy and Devt 2015–.

CHIMPHAMBA, Brown B., BSc, MSc, PhD; Malawi diplomatist, academic and university administrator; *Chairman of the Council, Mzuzu University;* b. 1939, Ntcheu; m.; four c.; ed Fourah Bay Coll., Univ. of Sierra Leone, Univ. Coll. London; various positions at Bunda Coll. of Agric., Univ. of Malawi 1961–81, including Research Assoc., Sr Lecturer, Prof. of Biology, Dean of Faculty of Science, Prin. 1981–90; Prin., Malawi Polytechnic 1991–92; Acting Vice-Chancellor, Univ. of Malawi 1991–92, Vice-Chancellor 1992–2000; Presidential Advisor on Educ. 2000–04; Chair. Nat. AIDS Comm. 2000–04; Amb. and Perm. Rep. to UN, New York 2004–06; currently Chair. Mzuzu Univ. Council; Head of Academic Freedom Comm. 2011; Fulbright Hayes Fellow; Hon. DLitt (Univ. of Malawi); Certificate of Merit for Devt Work. *Publications include:* numerous scientific publs. *Address:* Mzuzu University, Private Bag 201, Luwinga, Mzuzu 2, Malawi (office). *Telephone:* (1) 320722 (office). *E-mail:* ur@mzuni.ac.mw (office). *Website:* www.mzuni.ac.mw (office).

CHIMUTENGWENDE, Chenhamo (Chen) Chakezha, MA; Zimbabwean writer, activist and politician; b. 28 Aug. 1943, Mazowe Dist; m. Edith Matore; three s. two d.; ed Univ. of Bradford, UK; Exec. Dir Europe–Third World Research Centre, London 1969–74; Pres. Kwame Nkrumah Inst. of Writers and Journalists, London 1969–77; Deputy Dir and Sr Lecturer in Mass Communications and Int. Affairs, City Univ., London 1978–79; UNESCO Consultant on Mass Communications (Broadcasting) 1979–80; Corresp. for East and Southern Africa, Inter Press Service, Rome 1980–83; Sr Lecturer and Head, School of Journalism, Univ. of Nairobi 1980–82; MP 1985–2008; fmr Minister of Environment and Tourism, of Information, Posts and Telecommunications, of Public and Interactive Affairs; fmr Zanu PF Prov. Chair. for Mashonaland Central; fmr Pres. United New Africa Global Network; corresp., UNESCO's Int. Social Science Journal 1980–2003; Chair. Africa Star Holdings Ltd 1986; Pres. UN Convention on Climate Change 1996–98; Chair. UN High Level Cttee of Ministers and Sr Officials 1997–98. *Publications:* South Africa: The Press and the Politics of Liberation 1978, South Africa: the Press and the Politics 1989. *Leisure interests:* music, travelling, reading, public speaking. *Address:* 6 Duthie Road, Belgravia, Harare, Zimbabwe (home). *Telephone:* (4) 704586 (home). *E-mail:* chenchim@yahoo.com (home).

CHIN, Lt-Col Elias Camsek, AA, BA; Palauan army officer and politician; b. 11 Oct. 1949, Peleliu; s. of Taktai Chin and Takeko Kuratomi Chin; m. Miriam Rudimch 1977; one s. one d.; ed Farrington High School, Honolulu, Hawaii, Univ. of Hawaii, Electronic Inst. of Hawaii, Univ. of Hawaii at Manoa, Armor Officer Basic and Advanced Course, US Army Flight School, Air Ground Operations School, US Army Command and Gen. Staff Coll., US Army War Coll., US Army Airborne School, US Army Ranger School, US Army Motor Officer School, US Army Computer School; served for 23 years in army, achieving rank of Lt-Col in US Army before retiring in 1977, commissioned in Armor Corps of US Army 1975, later transferred to Aviation Corps, spent more than 20 years as US Army combat aviator; Minister of Justice 1997–2000, designed and built three-story BRT Building to house Ministry of Justice Office and Bureau of Public Safety Admin; participated in design, building and fund-raising for construction of Father Felix Yaoch Gymnasium 2000; Senator to Sixth Olbiil Era Kelulau (Palau Nat. Congress) 2000–04; Vice-Pres. of Palau 2005–09; Legion of Merit, Meritorious Service Medal with Second Oak Leaf Cluster, Army Commendation Medal with Second Oak Leaf Cluster, Army Achievement Medal with Oak Leaf Cluster, Nat. Defense Service Medal, Army Service Ribbon, Overseas Ribbon, Parachutist Badge, Army Master Aviator Badge, Ranger Tab. *Leisure interests:* baseball, spear fishing. *Address:* c/o Office of the Vice-President, PO Box 10284, Koror 96940, Palau.

CHINAMASA, Patrick Anthony, LLB; Zimbabwean politician; b. 25 Jan. 1947, Nyanga; s. of Anthony Chinamasa and Regina Maunga; m. 1st Monica Chinamasa; two s. two d.; m. 2nd Chiedza Faith Velemu; mem. Zimbabwe African Nat. Union–Patriotic Front (ZANU—PF); fmr Attorney-Gen.; Minister of Justice, Legal and Parl. Affairs 2000–13, Acting Minister of Finance Feb. 2009, Minister of Finance 2013–17, Minister of Cyber Security, Threat Detection and Mitigation Oct.–Nov. 2017, Minister of Finance and Econ. Devt 2017–18. *Leisure interests:* watching sport, jogging, reading. *Address:* c/o Ministry of Finance and Economic Development, Blocks B, E and G, Composite Bldg, cnr Samora Machel Ave and Fourth St, Private Bag 7705, Causeway, Harare, Zimbabwe (office).

CHINCHILLA MIRANDA, Laura, BA, MA; Costa Rican politician and fmr head of state; b. 28 March 1959, Carmen Central, San José; d. of Rafael Ángel Chinchilla Fallas and Emilce Miranda Castillo; m. 1st Mario Alberto Madrigal Díaz 1982 (divorced 1985); one s. with José María Rico Cueto 1996, m. 2000; ed Univ. of Costa Rica, Georgetown Univ., USA; adviser, Ministry of Planning and Political Economy 1989–90; consultant on state reform and structural adjustment programmes 1994–96, including with UNDP, IDB, USAID; Vice-Minister for Public Security and Governance 1994–96, Minister of Public Security 1996–98; Deputy, Asamblea Legislativa (Parl.) 2002–06; Vice-Pres. and Minister for Justice 2006–08, Interim Minister of Public Security April 2008 (resgnd); Pres. of Costa Rica (first woman) 2010–14; mem. Bd Nat. Drugs Council; Pres. Nat. Council on Migration 1996–98; mem. Comm. on Judicial Affairs, Comm. on Int. Affairs 2006–. *Publications:* various publs on admin of justice, public security and police reform. *Address:* Partido Liberación Nacional, Mata Redonda, 125 m oeste del Ministerio de Agricultura y Ganadería, Casa Liberacionista José Figueres Ferrer, Apdo 10051, 1000 San José, Costa Rica.

CHINOFOTIS, Adm. Panagiotis, MA; Greek politician, fmr naval officer and fmr chief of defence; b. 12 Aug. 1949, Athens; m. Maria Chinofotis; ed Hellenic Naval Acad., Hellenic Naval War Coll., Naval War Coll., USA, Salve Regina Univ., Newport, Rhode Island, USA; commissioned as Ensign, Hellenic Navy 1971; fmr Head, Hellenic Navy Gen. Staff (HNGS), NATO and Nat. Exercises and Operational Training; fmr Dir of Studies, Hellenic Naval War Coll.; Commdr, HS Lemnos (warship) 1991–93; worked for Mil. Rep. to NATO 1993–95; Asst Dir Strategic Plans and Policy Directorate, Hellenic Nat. Defence Gen. Staff (HNDGS) 1995–96; Commdr, First Div. of Destroyers and Frigates 1996–97; Deputy Mil. Rep. to WEU, Brussels 1997–98, concurrently Chair. Mil. Reps Working Group during Greek presidency of WEU; promoted to Commodore 1998; Deputy Chief of Staff, Hellenic Fleet Command 1998–99; Commdr and Flag Officer, Destroyers and Frigates 1999–2001; Dir A Div. HNGS 2001–02; promoted to Rear-Adm. 2002; Dir D Div. HNDGS 2002–04; C-in-C of Hellenic Fleet 2004–05; promoted to Adm. 2005; Chief of Defence 2005–07; Deputy Minister of Interior 2007–09; mem. New Democracy Party; mem. Parl.; Hon. Freeman of Newport, Rhode Island, USA, of Gavdos Island, Greece; Navy Force Formation Command Medal A' and C' Class, Navy Force Meritorious Command Medal A', B' and C' Class, Staff Officer Service Commendation Medal A' and B' Class, Chief of Defence Command Medal, Grand Cross of the Order of Phoenix, Grand Commdr of the Order of Honour. *Address:* 17 Aphroditis Street, Palaio Faliro, Athens 175 61, Greece (home). *Telephone:* (210) 9838797 (home). *E-mail:* chinofotis@yahoo.gr.

CHIOU, I-jen, MA; Taiwanese politician; *President, Chinese Taipei Football Association;* b. 9 May 1950, Pingtung Co.; ed Nat. Taiwan Univ. and Univ. of Chicago, USA; Deputy Chief of Staff, Nat. Security Council 2000–02, Sec.-Gen. 2002–03, 2004–07; Sec.-Gen. Exec. Yuan 2000–02, Vice-Pres. 2007–08 (resgnd); Minister without portfolio 2002; Chief of Staff, Office of the Pres. 2003–04, 2007; Minister responsible for Consumer Protection Comm. 2007–08 (resgnd); found not guilty by Taiwan High Court of defrauding the govt of US$500,000 of secret diplomatic funds used to promote diplomatic relations June 2012; Pres. Chinese Taipei Football Asscn 2005–10, 2018–; Head, Asscn of Taiwan-Japan Relations (fmrly Asscn of East Asian Relations 2016–. *Address:* Chinese Taipei Football Association, Room 210, 2nd Floor, 55 Changji Street, Datong District, Taipei 100, Taiwan (office). *Telephone:* (2) 25961185 (office). *Fax:* (2) 25951594 (office). *E-mail:* tpe@the-afc.com (office). *Website:* www.ctfa.com.tw (office).

CHIPMAN, John Miguel Warwick, CMG, BA, MA, DPhil; British administrator and academic; *Director-General and Chief Executive, International Institute for Strategic Studies (IISS);* b. 10 Feb. 1957, Montreal, Canada; s. of Lawrence Carroll Chipman and Maria Isabel Prados; m. Lady Theresa Manners 1997; two s.; ed Westmount High School, Montreal, El Estudio, Madrid, Harvard Univ., USA, London School of Econs and Balliol Coll., Oxford; Research Assoc. IISS, London 1983–84; Asst Dir for Regional Security, IISS 1987–91, Dir of Studies 1991–93, Dir IISS 1993, now Dir-Gen. and Chief Exec., Founder IISS Publ Strategic Comments; Research Assoc. Atlantic Inst. for Int. Affairs, Paris 1985–87; Dir Arundel House Enterprises, US Office IISS, Washington, DC, Asia Office IISS, Singapore; mem. Int. Advisory Bd Reliance Industries Ltd, Mumbai; NATO Fellowship 1983. *Achievements include:* was Capt. of Harvard Fencing Team and earned Full Blue while fencing at Oxford. *Publications:* Cinquième République et Défense de l'Afrique 1986, French Power in Africa 1989; ed. and prin. contrib. to NATO's Southern Allies: Internal and External Challenges 1988; articles in journals and book chapters. *Leisure interests:* tennis, skiing, scuba diving, collecting travel books, music. *Address:* International Institute for Strategic Studies, Arundel House, 6 Temple Place, London, WC2R 3DX, England (office). *Telephone:* (20) 7379-7676 (office). *Fax:* (20) 7836-3108 (office). *E-mail:* iiss@iiss.org (office). *Website:* www.iiss.org (office).

CHIPPERFIELD, Sir David Alan, Kt, CBE, DipArch, RA, RDI, RIBA; British architect; *Principal, David Chipperfield Architects;* b. 18 Dec. 1953, London, England; s. of Alan John Chipperfield and Peggy Chipperfield (née Singleton); m. Dr Evelyn Stern; two s. one d. and one s. from previous m.; ed Architectural Asscn; Prin. David Chipperfield Architects 1984–; Visiting Prof., Harvard Univ., USA 1987–88, Univ. of Naples, Italy 1992, Univ. of Graz, Austria 1992, Ecole Polytechnique Fedérale de Lausanne, Switzerland 1993–94, London Inst. 1997, Università degli Studi Federico II, Naples 2003, Art Inst., Chicago, USA 2003, Università degli Studi di Sassari, Alghero, Italy 2003, Illinois Inst. of Tech., Chicago 2006; Design Tutor, RCA 1988–89; Prof. of Architecture, Staatliche Akad. der Bildenden Künste, Stuttgart, Germany 1995–2001; Mies van der Rohe Chair, Barcelona School of Architecture, Spain 2001; first British architect to curate the Venice Biennale of Architecture 2012; Hon. Prof., Univ. of the Arts, London 2004–; Royal Designer for Industry 2006; Hon. FAIA 2007; Hon. mem. Bund Deutscher Architekten 2007; Order of Merit (Germany) 2009; Andrea Palladio Prize 1993, RIBA Regional Award 1996, 1998, RIBA Award 1998, 1999, 2002, 2003, 2004, Heinrich Tessenow Gold Medal 1999, Royal Fine Art Comm. Trust/BSkyB Best Building Award 1999, RIBA European and Int. Awards 2007, RIBA Nat. and European Awards 2008, Royal Gold Medal for Architecture 2010, Wolf Foundation Prize in the Arts (Architecture) (co-recipient) 2010, EU Prize for Contemporary Architecture (Mies van der Rohe Award) 2011, Deutscher Architekturpreis 2011, Praemium Imperiale, Japan Art Asscn 2013, winner, Nobel Centre architectural competition 2014. *Completed projects include:* TAK Design Centre, Kyoto 1990, pvt. museum, Japan 1991, Matsumoto Corp. HQ, Okayama 1992, River and Rowing Museum, Henley-on-Thames, UK 1997, Joseph Menswear, Sloane Avenue, London 1997, Kaistrasse Studios, Düsseldorf 1997, Joseph Store, Sloane Avenue, London 1997, Landeszentralbank HQ, Gera, Germany 2001, Shore Club Hotel, Miami, Ernsting Service Centre, Coesfeld-Lette, Germany 2001, Bryant Park Hotel, New York 2001, Gormley Studio, London 2003, Friedrichstrasse 126, Berlin 2004, Dolce & Gabbana Stores, world-wide 2004, housing, Villaverde, Madrid, Pantaenius House, Hamburg 2005, Hotel Beaumont, Maastricht 2005, Figge Art Museum, Davenport, Ia 2005, Hotel Puerta America, Madrid 2005, Museum of Modern Literature, Marbach am Neckar (RIBA Stirling Prize 2007) 2006, Des Moines Public Library, Ia 2006, America's Cup Bldg 'Veles e Vents', Valencia 2006, BBC Scotland Pacific Quay, Glasgow 2006, Freshfields Bruckhaus Deringer office bldg, Amsterdam 2006, Liangzhu Culture Museum, China 2007, Empire Riverside Hotel, Hamburg 2007, Gallery 'Hinter dem Giesshaus 1', Berlin 2007, Penn Museum Masterplan, Philadelphia 2007, Am Kupfergraben 10, Berlin 2007, Ninetree Village, China, Campus Audiovisual, Barcelona 2008, Kivik Pavilion, Sweden 2008, MW Orthopaedic Centre, Munich 2008, Neues Museum, Berlin 2009, Anchorage Museum, Rasmuson Center, Alaska 2009, City of Justice, Barcelona 2009, Museum Folkwang, Essen 2010, Laboratory bldg, Basel 2010, Kaufhaus Tyrol Dept Store, Innsbruck 2010, Ansaldo City of Cultures, Milan 2011, Salerno Palace of Justice, Italy 2011, The Hepworth Wakefield, W Yorks., UK 2011, Turner Contempary, Margate, UK 2011, Gesellschaftshaus Palmengarten, Frankfurt am Main 2011, Peek & Cloppenburg Flagship Store, Vienna 2011, Aust-Agder Cultural Historic Centre, Arendal, Norway 2012, St Louis, Mo. 2012, Seal House, London 2012, Café Royal Hotel, London 2012, Saint Louis Art Museum, Mo. 2013, Museo Jumex, Mexico 2013, James Simon Gallery, Berlin 2013, Valentino New York Flagship Store 2014, Valentino Rome Flagship Store 2015, Villa Eden, Gardone 2015. *Publications:* El Croquis (monograph) 1998, 2001, 2004, 2006, David Chipperfield, Idea e Realta 2005, David Chipperfield Architectural Works 1990–2002 2003, David Chipperfield Architects – Form Matters 2009, Neues Museum Berlin 2009. *Address:* David Chipperfield Architects Ltd, 11 York Road, London, SE1 7NX, England (office). *Telephone:* (20) 7620-4800 (office). *Fax:* (20) 7620-4801 (office). *E-mail:* info@davidchipperfield.co.uk (office). *Website:* www.davidchipperfield.co.uk (office).

CHIQUET, Maureen, BA; American business executive; *Global CEO, Chanel SA;* b. 9 March 1963, St Louis, Mo.; m. Antoine Chiquet; two d.; ed Yale Univ.; early career as intern then brand man., L'Oreal, Paris; Merchandise Trainee, Gap Inc., San Francisco 1988, then exec. positions including building Old Navy brand 1994–2002, Pres. Banana Repub. div. 2002–03; Pres. and COO Chanel SA, France 2004–, Global CEO 2007–; mem. Supervisory Bd Vivendi 2009–; mem. Bd of Dirs Peek... Aren't You Curious 2008–. *Address:* Chanel SA, 135 avenue Charles de Gaulle, 92521 Neuilly-sur-Seine, France (office). *Telephone:* 1-46-43-40-00 (office). *Fax:* 1-47-47-60-34 (office). *Website:* www.chanel.com (office).

CHIRAC, Jacques René; French politician and fmr head of state; b. 29 Nov. 1932, Paris; s. of François Chirac and Marie-Louise Valette; m. Bernadette Chodron de Courcel 1956; two d.; ed Lycée Carnot, Lycée Louis-le-Grand, Ecole Nationale d'Admin and Inst. d'Etudes Politiques, Paris; mil. service in Algeria; auditor, Cour des Comptes 1959–62; Special Asst, Secr.-Gen. of Govt 1962; Special Asst, Pvt. Office of M. Pompidou 1962–65; Counsellor, Cour des Comptes 1965–94; Sec. of State for Employment Problems 1967–68; Sec. of State for Economy and Finance 1968–71; Minister for Parl. Relations 1971–72, of Agriculture and Rural Devt 1972–73, 1973–74, of the Interior March–May 1974; Prime Minister of France 1974–76, 1986–88; Sec.-Gen. UDR 1974–75, Hon. Sec.-Gen. 1975–76; Pres. RPR (fmrly UDR) 1976–94, Hon. Sec.-Gen. 1977–80; mem. European Parl. 1979; Pres. Regional Council, La Corrèze 1970–79; Municipal Counsellor, Sainte-Féréole 1965–77; Mayor of Paris 1977–95; Pres. of France May 1995–2007; Co-Prince of Andorra 1995–2007; Deputy for Corrèze March–May 1967, June–Aug. 1968, March–May 1973, 1976–79, 1981–86, 1988–95; mem. Comm. on Nat. Defence, Nat. Ass. 1980–86; mem. (ex officio) Conseil Constitutionnel 2007–; f. Fondation Jacques Chirac (for sustainable devt and cultural dialogue) 2008; on trial for corruption (first fmr French head of state to stand trial since Philippe Pétain) involving the misuse of public money during his time as Mayor of Paris March 2011, declared guilty by Paris court of diverting public funds and abusing public confidence, given two-year suspended prison sentence Dec. 2011; Hon. Canon of the Basilica of St John Lateran 1995–2007; Grand-Croix, Légion d'honneur, Ordre nat. du Mérite, Croix de la Valeur Militaire, Chevalier du Mérite agricole, des Arts et des Lettres, de l'Étoile noire, du Mérite sportif, du Mérite touristique, Grand Cross of Merit, Sovereign Order of Malta; Hon. KCB (UK); Prix Louise Michel 1986, Médaille de l'Aéronautique, State Prize of the Russian Federation 2008. *Publications:* La Nouvelle-Orléans et son port en 1954, Discours pour la France à l'heure du choix, La lueur de l'espérance: réflexion du soir pour le matin 1978, Une Nouvelle France, Réflexions 1 1994, La France pour Tous 1995. *Address:* c/o Conseil Constitutionnel, 2 rue de Montpensier, 75001 Paris, France. *Telephone:* 1-40-15-30-00. *Fax:* 1-40-20-93-27. *E-mail:* relations-exterieures@conseil-constitutionnel.fr. *Website:* www.conseil-constitutionnel.fr.

CHIRICĂ, Andrei; Romanian telecommunications engineer, business executive and organization official; *Chairman, Orange România SA;* b. 14 June 1939, Ploieşti; ed Electronics and Telecommunications Coll. of Bucharest; engineer in Radio and TV Dept 1961–68; Chief Engineer, Gen. Direction of Post and Telecommunications 1968–84, then Asst Gen. Dir for matters of research and information in telecommunications, Minister of Communications 1990–94; Pres. Romtelecom SA 1994–95; Chair. MobilRom 1997–, Orange România SA; Chair. Romanian Asscn of Telecommunications Engineers (AITR) 2003–. *Publications:* numerous specialized works. *Address:* Orange România SA, Bd Lascar Catargiu 51–53, Europa House, Bucharest, Romania (office). *Telephone:* (21) 2033008 (office). *E-mail:* andrei.chirica@orange.ro (office).

CHIRTOACĂ, Dorin; Moldovan politician and government official; *Mayor of Chişinău;* b. 9 Aug. 1978, Chişinău, Moldovan SSR, USSR; s. of Valentina Ghimpu; ed Liceul 'Gheorghe Asachi', Chişinău, C. Negruzzi Liceul, Iaşi and Univ. of Bucharest, Romania, Univ. of Paris I Panthéon-Sorbonne, France; worked for Surprize, Surprize (show broadcast on TVR1, Romania) 2001–03; worked for Helsinki Cttee for Human Rights in Moldova 2003–05; Vice-Pres. Partidul Liberal (Liberal Party) 2005–; contested Chişinău mayoral elections 2005, elected Mayor 2007, re-elected 2011, 2015. *Address:* Office of the Mayor, bd Ştefan cel Mare şi Sfânt 83, Chişinău 2012, Moldova (office). *Telephone:* (22) 221002 (office). *Fax:* (22) 221289 (office). *E-mail:* dorin.chirtoaca@pmc.md (office). *Website:* www.chisinau.md (office).

CHIRTOACĂ, Nicolae; Moldovan architect, politician, fmr diplomatist and fmr army officer; *Leader, Partidul Forţa Poporului;* b. 22 March 1953, Glodeni; m.; two c.; ed Technical Univ. of Moldova; mil. service 1977–90, served in different structures of armed forces of fmr Soviet Union; joined Movt for Democracy and Nat. Liberation of Moldova 1990; apptd Dir-Gen. Dept of State for Mil. Problems of Moldova (became Ministry of Defence 1991) 1991–94, active role in creation of Nat. Army of Moldova with rank of Col, Nat. Security Adviser to Pres. of Moldova 1992–94, Rep. of Moldova at ambassadorial level at meetings of N Atlantic Co-operation Council at NATO; Co-founder Liberal Party of Moldova, Vice-Chair. and mem. Man. Bd 1994–98; Sr State Adviser to Prime Minister (Press Sec. of Govt) 1999–2006; Amb. to USA 2006–10; mem. Man. Bd Soros Foundation Moldova; Dir Invisible Coll. of Moldova; Pres. Man. Bd Euro-Atlantic Center of Moldova 1994–2006; Leader, Partidul Forţa Poporului party 2013–; Hon. Pres. European Movt of Moldova 2003. *Website:* www.pfp.md (office).

CHISHOLM, Sir John, Kt, KBE, MSc, FREng, CEng, FIEE; British business executive and international organization official; *Chairman, Nesta;* b. 1946; m. Kitty Chisholm; two c.; ed Univ. of Cambridge; began career with General Motors; fmr Man. Scicon Ltd (part of BP); f. CAP Scientific 1979, fmr Dir CAP Group PLC; Man. Dir Sema Group PLC 1988–91; Chief Exec. DERA 1991–2001; Chief Exec. QinetiQ 2001–05, Exec. Chair. 2005–10; Chair. Medical Research Council 2009–12; Chair. Nesta (charity) 2009–; Pres. Inst. of Eng and Tech. 2005–06; Dir (non-exec.) Expro International PLC 1994–2003, Bespack PLC 1999–2005; Fellow, IEE (Pres. 2005–06), Royal Acad. of Eng, Royal Aeronautical Soc., Inst. of Physics. *Leisure interest:* historic motor racing. *Address:* Nesta, 1 Plough Place, London, EC4A 1DE, England (office). *Website:* www.nesta.org.uk (office).

CHISSANO, Joaquim Alberto; Mozambican politician and fmr head of state; *Chairman, Joaquim Chissano Foundation;* b. 22 Oct. 1939, Malehice, Chibuto Dist, Gaza Prov., Portuguese colony of Mozambique (then Portuguese East Africa); m. Marcelina Rafael Chissano; four c.; faculty of medicine in Lisbon, Portugal and Poitiers, France; Founding mem. Frente de Libertação de Moçambique (FRELIMO), Asst Sec. to Pres., FRELIMO in charge of Educ. 1963–66, Sec. to Pres., FRELIMO 1966–69; Chief Rep. FRELIMO in Dar es Salaam 1969–74; Prime Minister, Transitional Govt of Mozambique 1974–75; Minister of Foreign Affairs 1975–86; Pres. of Mozambique and C-in-C of Armed Forces 1986–2005; Pres. FRELIMO 1991–2004; Chair. African Union 2002–04; Special Envoy of the UN Sec.-Gen. for the Lord's Resistance Army-affected areas (Northern Uganda, Democratic Repub. of Congo and Southern Sudan) 2006–09; Chair. Joaquim Chissano Foundation, Forum of Fmr African Heads of State and Govt; mem. Club of Madrid; Order, Augusto César Sandino (Nicaragua) 1988; numerous awards including Chatham House Prize 2006, inaugural US $5 million Prize for Achievement in African Leadership, Mo Ibrahim Foundation (given to a fmr African leader who has shown good governance) 2007, Athens Democracy Award 2018. *Address:* Fundação Joaquim Chissano, Av. do Zimbabwe 954, Caixa Postal 63, Maputo, Mozambique (office); Africa Forum, 351 Schoeman Street, PO Box 6541, Pretoria 0001, South Africa. *Telephone:* (21) 484000 (office); (12) 354-8073. *Fax:* (21) 484001 (office); (12) 354-0857. *E-mail:* info@fjchissano.org.mz (office); info@africaforum.org.za. *Website:* www.fjchissano.org.mz (office).

CHITANAVA, Nodari Amrosievich, PhD; Georgian politician, agricultural specialist and economist; b. 10 March 1936, Zugdidi Region, Georgia; s. of Ambrose Chitanava and Tina Chitanava; m. Keto Dimitrovna 1964; two d.; ed Georgian Polytechnic Inst., Moscow High Political School; mem. CPSU 1958–91; Komsomol and party work 1959–; Second Sec. Adzhar obkom 1973–74; Minister of Agric. for Georgian SSR 1974–79; First Deputy Chair., Georgian Council of Ministers 1979–85; Party Sec. for Agric. 1985–89; Chair. Council of Ministers, Georgian SSR 1989–90; Minister of Agric. 1991–93; Dir Econ. and Social Problems Research Inst. 1993; Chair. Georgian Economists' Soc. *Publications:* 70 scientific works of which there are seven monographs including Social-Economic Problems During Transition Period (three vols). *Leisure interest:* spending time in the country.

CHIŢOIU, Daniel, PhD; Romanian accountant and politician; b. 11 July 1967, Păusesti; ed Academy of Economic Studies, Bucharest, Inst. of Chartered Accountants of Scotland, UK, Nat. Defence Coll.; Special Insp., Gen. Directorate of State Financial Control, Ministry of Economy and Finance 1990–94; Financial Controller, Court of Accounts of Romania (NAFA) 1994–98, 2001–05; Deputy Gen. Dir, Gen. Directorate of Public Finance and State Financial Control, Ministry of Economy and Finance 1998–2001, Deputy Chair. (with rank of Sec. of State), Nat. Agency for Fiscal Admin, Co-ordinator of Dept for Admin of State Income, Ministry of Economy and Finance 2005–07, Interim Chair. Nat. Agency for Fiscal Admin Jan.–April 2007, Chair. 2007–08; mem. Nat. Liberal Party (Partidul Naţional Liberal—PNL) –2014; mem. Parl. 2008–, Deputy Chair. Comm. for Budget, Finance and Banks 2008–12, mem. 2012–; Minister of the Economy, Trade and the Business Environment May–Dec. 2012; Deputy Prime Minister and Minister of Public Finance 2012–14; Pres. Romanian Chamber of Fiscal Consultants; mem. Alianţa Liberalilor şi Democraţilor (ALDE) (political party). *Address:* Alliance of Liberals and Democrats (ALDE), Bucharest Soseaua Pavel Dimitrievici Kiseleff 57, Sector 1, Romania (office). *Telephone:* (31) 4251101 (office). *Fax:* (21) 2220594 (office). *E-mail:* dre@pnl.ro (office); contact@alde.ro. *Website:* www.alde.ro (office).

CHITTISTER, Joan D., MA, PhD; American social psychologist, writer and lecturer; *Executive Director, Benetvision;* b. 26 April 1936, Dubois, Pa; d. of Harold C. Chittister and Loretta Cuneo Chittister; ed St Benedict Acad. Erie, Mercyhurst Coll. Erie, Pa, Univ. of Notre Dame and Penn State Univ.; elementary teacher, 1955–59, secondary teacher 1959–74; teacher, Penn State Univ. 1969–71; Pres. Fed. of St Scholastica 1971–78; Prioress, Benedictine Sisters of Erie 1978–90; Pres. Conf. of American Benedictine Prioresses 1974–90; Invited Visiting Fellow, St Edmund's Coll., Cambridge, UK 1995–96; mem. Exec. Bd Ecumenical and Cultural Inst. St John's Univ., Collegeville 1976–98; Exec. Dir Benetvision 1990–; mem. Bd of Dirs Nat. Catholic Reporter 1983–2000; Co-Chair. Global Initiative of Women Religious and Spiritual Leaders 2002–, Network of Spiritual Progressives/Tikkun Community 2005–10; mem. Niwano Peace Foundation, Tokyo 2003–06; 12 hon. degrees; numerous awards, including Notre Dame Alumni Asscn Women's Award of Achievement 1997, Distinguished Alumni Award, Penn State Univ. 2000, Catholic Press Asscn Book Award 1996, 1997, 2001, 2004, 2005 (two), 2006, 2008, 2009, 2011, 2012 (three), 2014. *Publications include:* Climb along the Cutting Edge: An Analysis of Change in Religious Life 1977, Women, Church and Ministry 1983, Winds of Change: Women Challenge the Church 1986, The Fire in These Ashes: A Spirituality of Contemporary Religious Life 1995, The Psalms: Meditations for Every Day of the Year 1996, Beyond Beijing: The Next Step for Women 1996, Songs of Joy: New Meditations on the Psalms 1997, Light in the Darkness: New Reflections on the Psalms 1998, Heart of Flesh: A Feminist Spirituality for Women and Men 1998, Gospel Days: Reflections for Every Day of the Year 1999, The Story of Ruth: Twelve Moments in Every Woman's Life 2000, The Illuminated Life: Monastic Wisdom for Seekers of Light 2000, Living Well: Scriptural Reflections for Every Day 2000, The Friendship of Women: A Spiritual Tradition 2000, Scarred by Struggle, Transformed by Hope (Asscn of Theological Booksellers Award) 2003, Twelve Steps to Inner Freedom 2003, In the Heart of the Temple 2004, The Way We Were: A Story of Conversion and Renewal 2005, The Tent of Abraham (co-author) 2006, How Shall We Live? 2006, The Ten Commandments 2006, 25 Windows into the Soul 2007, Welcome to the Wisdom of the World 2007, The Gift of Years 2008, The Breath of the Soul 2009, The Liturgical Year 2009, Uncommon Gratitude (with Rowan Williams) 2010, God's Tender Mercy 2010, The Rule of Benedict: A Spirituality for the 21st Century (second edn) 2010, The Monastery of the Heart 2011, Songs of the Heart 2011, The Radical Christian Life 2011, Happiness 2011, Following the Path 2012, Aspects of the Heart 2012, The Art of Life 2012, The Way of the Cross 2013, The Sacred In Between 2013, Our Holy Yearnings 2014, Between the Dark and the Daylight 2015, In God's Holy Light 2015, Two Dogs and a Parrot 2015; more than 700 articles and lectures on religious life, peace and justice and on women in church and society. *Leisure interests:* computers, music, reading. *Address:* St Scholastica Priory, 355 East 9th Street, Erie, PA 16503, USA. *Telephone:* (814) 454-4052. *Fax:* (814) 459-8066. *E-mail:* office@benetvision.org. *Website:* www.joanchittister.org; www.eriebenedictines.org.

CHITTOLINI, Giorgio; Italian historian and academic; b. 9 Dec. 1940, Parma; s. of Gino Chittolini and Diva Scotti; m. Franca Leverotti 1977; one d.; Assoc. Prof. of History, Univ. of Pisa 1974–76, Univ. of Pavia 1976–79; Fellow at Villa I Tatti, Florence 1980; Prof. of Medieval History, Univ. of Parma 1981–84; apptd Prof. Univ. of Milan 1985; mem. Bd of Eds, Società e Storia 1979–; mem. Scientific Cttee, Istituto Storico Italo-Germanico, Trento 1989–; Pres. Centro Studi Civiltà del tardo Medioevo 1990–; mem. Int. Comm. for the History of Towns 1995; mem. Giunta storica nazionale. *Publications include:* La formazione dello stato regionale e le istituzioni del contado 1979, Gli Sforza, la chiesa lombarda e la corte di Roma (1450–1535) 1990, Comunità, Governi e Feudi nell'Italia Centrosettentrionale 1995, Materiali di storia ecclesiastica lombarda (series ed.) 1995, Piccole città, grandi città, territori urbani. *Address:* Via Madre Cabrini 7, 20122 Milan, Italy (home).

CHIU, Cheng-hsiung, BA, MA, PhD; Taiwanese banker and politician; b. 23 March 1938; ed Nat. Taiwan Univ., Ohio State Univ., USA; Assoc. Prof., Nat. Taiwan Univ. 1973–75, Adjunct Assoc. Prof. 1975–81; Deputy Dir-Gen., Dept of Banking, Cen. Bank of the Repub. of China, Exec. Yuan 1975–76, Deputy Dir-Gen., Dept of Foreign Exchange 1976–81, Dir-Gen., Dept of Banking 1981–88, Deputy Gov. 1989–96; Pres. Hua Nan Commercial Bank 1988; Minister of Finance 1996–2000; Man. Dir China Development Financial Holding Corpn 2003–04; Chair. Grand Cathay Securities Corpn 2000–04, EnTie Commercial Bank 2004–07, Hon. Chair. 2007–08; Vice-Premier and Minister of the Consumer Protection Comm. 2008–09; Man. Dir SinoPac Financial Holdings Co. Ltd 2008–, Chair. Bank SinoPac 2017 (resgnd); mem. Bd, Financial Service Information Co. *Address:* Bank Sinopac, No. 9-1, Sec 2, Chienkuo North Road, Chungshan District, Taipei 104, Taiwan (office). *Telephone:* (2) 2508-2288 (office). *Fax:* (2) 2517-2761 (office). *E-mail:* info@banksinopac.com.tw (office). *Website:* www.banksinopac.com.tw (office).

CHIUARIU, Tudor, LLB; Romanian lawyer, academic and politician; *Senior Partner, Chiuariu & Associates - Attorneys at Law;* b. 13 July 1976, Botoşani; ed Al. I. Cuza Univ., Iaşi, Police Acad., Bucharest, Cen. European Univ., Budapest, Acad. of European Law, Trier, Germany, Leiden Univ., The Netherlands; attorney at law, Iaşi 2000–; mem. Partidul Naţional Liberal (Nat. Liberal Party) 1997–, Vice-Pres. of Youth Org., Iaşi br. 1997–2002, mem. Political Cttee, Iaşi br. 2001–02; Vice-Pres. Court of Honour and Arbitration 2005–09; Lecturer in Law, Petre Andrei Univ., Iaşi 2000–07, George Bacovia Univ., Bacău 2008–; Sec. of State, Office of the Prime Minister 2005–07; Minister of Justice 2007; mem. Parlamentul României 2008–; Pres. Inter-Ministerial Comm. on Civil Servants' Pay System 2005–06; Vice-Pres. Justice and Human Rights Comm. 2002–05; mem. Implementation of Nat. Anticorruption Strategy Cttee 2005–07; currently Sr Pnr, Chiuariu & Assocs; mem. Romanian Bar Asscn 2000–. *Publications include:* numerous articles on Romanian law in professional journals. *Address:* Bd Aviatorilor 52, Etaj 3, Sector 1, 011864 Bucharest, Romania (office). *Telephone:* (21) 3161074 (office). *Fax:* (21) 3161075 (office). *E-mail:* tudor@chiuariulawyers.ro (office). *Website:* www.chiuariulawyers.ro (office); www.cdep.ro (office).

CHIWENGA, Gen. (retd) Constantino; Zimbabwean politician and fmr army officer; *Vice-President;* b. 1956, Wedza Dist, Mashonaland East Prov.; m. 1st

Jocelyn Chiwenga (divorced); m. 2nd Mary Chiwenga; fmr resistance fighter; trained in Mozambique with Zimbabwe African Nat. Liberation Army (ZANLA), becoming Provincial Commdr, Masvingo/Gaza Prov., ZANLA Deputy Political Commissar 1978; joined newly-formed Zimbabwe Nat. Army as Brig., First Brigade, Bulawayo 1981, becoming Commdr, Zimbabwe Nat. Army 1994–2003; Commdr, Zimbabwe Defence Forces 2003–17; rank of Lt Gen. 1994, Gen. 2004; retd from army Dec. 2017; fmr Chair. Jt Operations Command (state security body); Vice-Pres. of Zimbabwe 2017–, also Minister of Defence and War Veterans 2017–18.

CHIZEN, Bruce R., BS; American business executive; *Venture Partner, Voyager Capital Ltd;* b. 5 Sept. 1955; m.; one s. one d.; ed Brooklyn Coll., City Univ. of New York; Retail Merchandising Man. (Eastern Region), Mattel Electronics 1980–83; Sales Dir (Eastern Region), Microsoft Corpn 1983–87; Founding Sr Man. Claris Corpn 1987, later Vice-Pres. Sales, Worldwide Marketing, Vice-Pres. and Gen. Man. Claris Clear Choice; joined Adobe Systems Inc. 1994, Vice-Pres. and Gen. Man. Graphics Professional Div. and Consumer Div., later Exec. Vice-Pres. Worldwide Products and Marketing, Pres. Adobe Systems Inc. 1999–2005, CEO 2000–07, Strategic Advisor 2007–08; Sr Advisor, Permira Advisers Ltd 2009–; Venture Partner, Voyager Capital Ltd 2009–; Chair. Ancestry.com 2013–; mem. Bd of Dirs Synopsys, Inc. 2000–, PBS Foundation 2005–, Oracle Corpn 2008–, Elemental Technologies 2008–, ChargePoint, Inc. 2014–, Children's Discovery Museum of San Jose. *Address:* Voyager Silicon Valley, 3000 Sand Hill Road, 3-100, Menlo Park, CA 94025, USA (office). *Telephone:* (650) 854-4300 (office). *Fax:* (650) 854-4399 (office). *Website:* www.voyagercapital.com (office).

CHIZHOV, Ludvig Aleksandrovich; Russian diplomatist; b. 25 April 1936, Radornishl, Zhitomir Region; m.; one s. one d.; ed Moscow Inst. of Int. Relations; fmr mem. CPSU; attaché, Embassy in Tokyo 1960–65, First Sec., Counsellor, 1971–77; Third Sec., Second Sec., Second Far Eastern Dept, Ministry of Foreign Affairs 1966–70, Counsellor, Second Far Eastern Dept 1978–80; Minister Counsellor, Embassy in Tokyo 1980–86; Head of Pacific Ocean Countries Dept, Ministry of Foreign Affairs 1986–89; Russian Amb. to Japan 1990–96; Amb.-at-Large 1996–98; Dir 3rd European Dept, Ministry of Foreign Affairs 1998–2001, on staff of Ministry 2001–03, Deputy Minister 2003–. *Leisure interests:* fishing, reading. *Address:* c/o Ministry of Foreign Affairs, 119200 Moscow, Smolenskaya-Sennaya pl. 32/34, Russia (office). *Telephone:* (495) 244-16-06 (office). *Fax:* (495) 230-21-30 (office). *E-mail:* ministry@mid.ru (office). *Website:* www.mid.ru (office).

CHIZHOV, Vladimir A.; Russian diplomatist; *Permanent Representative, European Union;* b. 3 Dec. 1953, Moscow; m.; one s. one d.; ed Moscow State Inst. of Int. Relations; joined diplomatic service in 1976, numerous posts with Ministry of Foreign Affairs, Moscow, including at Embassy in Athens 1976–81, at 5th European Dept 1981–85, Embassy in Nicosia 1985–92, Counsellor, 2nd European Dept 1992, Head UK and Ireland Div. 1992–93, Deputy Dir 2nd European Dept 1993–95, Deputy Head of Del. to OSCE, Vienna, Austria 1995–96, Deputy High Rep. for Bosnia Peace Implementation, Sarajevo 1996–97, Dir 3rd European Dept 1997–99, Dir European Multilateral Co-operation Dept 1999, rank of Amb. 2000, Special Rep. for the Balkans 2000–02, Deputy Minister of Foreign Affairs 2002–05, Perm. Rep. to the European Communities, Brussels 2005–10, Amb. and Perm. Rep. to EU, Brussels 2010–; Order of Friendship 2003, Order of Merit (Luxembourg) 2006, Order of Honour 2013. *Leisure interests:* reading, travel. *Address:* Permanent Mission of the Russian Federation to the European Union, 45 Dreve de Lorraine, 1180 Brussels, Belgium (office). *Telephone:* (2) 502-17-91 (diplomatic chancellery) (office); (2) 375-66-29 (office). *Fax:* (2) 513-76-49 (diplomatic chancellery) (office); (2) 375-66-50 (office). *E-mail:* misrusce@numericable.be (office). *Website:* www.russianmission.eu (office).

CHKHEIDZE, Prince; **Peter,** Dr of Law; Georgian lawyer and diplomatist; *President, Foundation For Russian–Georgian Cooperation;* b. 22 Oct. 1941, Tbilisi; s. of Peter Chkheidze and Julia Chkheidze; m. Manana Chkheidze 1963; two s.; ed Tbilisi Nat. Univ., Diplomatic Acad. of USSR Ministry of Foreign Affairs and Inst. of State and Law, USSR Acad. of Sciences; various positions with Attorney Service of Repub. of Georgia 1963–75; First Sec., Dept of Int. Orgs, Ministry of Foreign Affairs of USSR 1978; First Sec., Counsellor, then Chief of Dept, Perm. Mission of USSR to the UN 1978–84; leading posts in nat. state and public insts 1984–89; Chair. Ind. Trade Unions Confed. of Repub. of Georgia 1989–91; Deputy Prime Minister of Repub. of Georgia and Perm. Rep. of Govt of Georgia to USSR, later to Russian Fed. 1991–92; Chargé d'affaires a.i., Moscow 1992–93; Amb. to USA 1993–94; Amb. and Perm. Rep. to UN 1993–2002; Amb. to Turkmenistan (also accred to Afghanistan) 2002–04; Vice-Pres. and Exec. Dir Int. Public Org. 'Ass. of Georgian Peoples' 2009–11; Pres. Foundation for Russian–Georgian Cooperation 2014–; mem. Int. Informatization Acad. 1994–. *Publications:* various publs in fields of law and int. relations 1975–95. *Leisure interests:* literature, art, horse riding. *Address:* Picasso 50, Tbilisi 0183, Georgia (home). *Telephone:* (32) 2537595 (home); (32) 2537595 (home); 7903-1047033 (mobile); 59-9405375 (mobile). *Fax:* (32) 2537593 (home). *E-mail:* frgc251@gmail.com; chkheidze7@hotmail.com.

CHKHEIDZE, Temur Georgyevich; Georgian theatre director; b. 18 Nov. 1943, Tbilisi; ed Tbilisi Rustaveli State Theatre Inst.; Dir Municipal Zugdidi Drama Theatre 1965–67; Dir Georgia Young Spectators Theatre, Tbilisi 1967–70; Dir Tbilisi Academic Rustaveli Theatre 1970–80; Artistic Dir Academic Mardzhanishvili Theatre, Tbilisi 1980–91; Dir Bolshoi Tovstonogov Drama Theatre 1991–2004, Prin. Dir 2004–07, Artistic Dir 2007–13; appeared as a producer at Mariinsky Theatre, St Petersburg and La Scala, Milan; People's Artist of Russia and Georgia, Lenin Prize 1986. *Production include:* Bolshoi Tovstonogov Drama Theatre: Schiller's Kabale und Liebe 1990, Arthur Miller's The Crucible 1991, O'Neill's Under the Elms 1992, de Filippo's Questi fantasmi 1993, Shakespeare's Macbeth 1995, Anouilh's Antigone 1996, Dumbadze's The Sunny Night 1997, Pushkin's Boris Godunov 1999, Shaw's Heartbreak House 2002, Lermontov's Masquerade 2003, Michael Frayn's Copenhagen 2004, Schiller's Maria Stuart 2005, Tolstoy's The Power of Darkness, or When the Claw is Caught the Whole Bird is Lost 2006. *Address:* c/o Bolshoi Tovstonogov Drama Theatre, 190023 St Petersburg, ul. Fontanka 65, Russia. *E-mail:* bdt@bdt.spb.ru.

CHO, Dae-sik, BA, MBA; South Korean business executive; *Co-CEO and President, SK Holdings Company Limited;* ed Korea Univ., Clark Univ., USA; Sr Vice-Pres. of Finance Man. and Strategy Office, SK Holdings Co. Ltd 2007–08, Head of Business Man. Office 2010–11, Chief Financial Officer, Head of Finance Team, Risk Man. and Corp. Auditing Office 2012–13, Co-CEO and Pres. 2013–, Chair. and Sr Man. Dir SK Securities Co. Ltd, Inside Dir, SK Telecom Co. Ltd 2013–. *Address:* SK Holdings Co. Ltd, 26 Jong-ro, Jongno-gu, Seoul 03188, Republic of Korea (office). *Telephone:* (2) 2121-5114 (office). *Fax:* (2) 2121-7001 (office). *E-mail:* Byc778@sk.com (office). *Website:* www.sk.com (office); www.sk.co.kr/gateway/en (office); www.skenergy.com (office).

CHO, Fujio; Japanese automobile industry executive; *Honorary Chairman, Toyota Motor Corporation;* b. 2 Feb. 1937, Tokyo; m. Emiko Cho; two s.; ed Tokyo Univ.; joined Toyota Motor Corpn 1960, apprentice 1960–66, Production Control Div. 1966–74 (Man. 1974–84), Man. Logistics Admin and Project Man., Production Control Div. 1984–86, Admin Man. 1986–87, Man. Toyota N America Project and Exec. Vice-Pres., Toyota Motor Manufacturing USA 1987–88, Pres. Toyota Motor Manufacturing USA 1988–94, Man. Dir Toyota Motor Corpn 1994–96, Sr Man. Dir 1996–98, Exec. Vice-Pres. 1998–99, Pres. and CEO 1999–2005, Vice-Chair., then Chair. and Rep. Dir 2006–13, Hon. Chair. 2013–; Ind. Dir, Sony Corpn 2006–12; Vice-Chair. Japan Business Fed. (Nippon Keidanren) 2005–; Chair. Japan Automobile Mfrs Asscn 2006–08, Aioi Insurance Co. Ltd; mem. Advisory Bd Development Bank of Japan Inc.; Hon. British Consul Gen. for Prefectures of Gifu, Mie and Aichi 2007; Officier, Légion d'honneur 2004; Hon. KBE 2006; Grand Cordon, Order of the Rising Sun 2009; Grand Decoration of Honour in Silver with Star of Austria 2009; included by TIME magazine in list of 100 Most Influential People of 2004. *Leisure interests:* golf, fishing, listening to classical music. *Address:* Toyota Motor Corpn, 1 Toyota-Cho, Toyota City, Aichi Prefecture 471-8571, Japan (office). *Telephone:* (5) 6528-2121 (office). *Fax:* (5) 6523-5800 (office). *Website:* www.toyota-global.com (office); www.toyota.co.jp (office).

CHO, Hwan-eik, BA, MBA, PhD; South Korean politician, academic and business executive; *President and CEO, Korea Electric Power Corporation;* ed Choongang High School, Seoul Nat. Univ., New York Univ., USA, Hanyang Univ.; fmr Pres. Korea Trade-Investment Promotion Agency; fmr Vice-Minister of Commerce, Industry and Energy; fmr CEO Korea Export Insurance Corpn; mem. Bd of Dirs, Pres. and CEO Korea Electric Power Corpn 2012–; Dir, Samsung Electro-Mechanics Co. Ltd; Chair-Prof., Hanyang Univ., Ansan Campus. *Address:* Korea Electric Power Corporation, 512 Yeongdong-daero, Gangnam-gu, Seoul 135-791, Republic of Korea (office). *Telephone:* (61) 345-3114 (office). *Fax:* (2) 848-0013 (office). *E-mail:* info@kepco.co.kr (office). *Website:* home.kepco.co.kr (office).

CHO, Tae-yul; South Korean politician and diplomatist; *Permanent Representative to UN;* b. 10 Nov. 1951; m.; two c.; ed Seoul Nat. Univ., Oxford Univ.; joined Ministry of Foreign Affairs 1979, Asst to Minister for Foreign Affairs 1994–95, Second Vice-Minister of Foreign Affairs 2013–16; Counsellor, Embassy of South Korea in Saudi Arabia 1992–94, Dir Int. Trade Div. 1995–96, Counsellor, Perm. Mission to UN and other int. orgs in Geneva 1996–2000, Embassy of South Korea in USA 2000–02, Dir Int. Trade Div. 1995–96, Deputy Dir-Gen. for North American and European Trade and for Trade Policy Planning, Multilateral Trade Bureau 2002, Dir-Gen. Bilateral Trade Bureau and Special Commr of Presidential Transition Cttee 2003, Perm. Rep. to UN and other int. orgs in Geneva 2005–06, Amb. to Spain 2008–11, Amb. for Devt Coordination 2011–12, for Int. Relations of Gyeonggi Province 2012–13, Perm. Rep. to UN 2016–, Chair. UN Peacebuilding Comm. 2017, Pres. Exec. Bd UNDP, UN Population Fund, UN Office for Project Services 2018–; Deputy Minister for Trade 2006–08. *Address:* Permanent Mission of Republic of Korea, 335 E 45th Street, New York, NY 10017, USA (office). *Telephone:* (212) 439-4000 (office). *Fax:* (212) 986-1083 (office). *E-mail:* korea.un@mofa.go.kr (office). *Website:* un.mofat.go.kr (office).

CHO, Yung-kil; South Korean army officer (retd) and politician; b. 9 May 1940, Yongkwangkun, Chollanamdo Prov.; m. Kang Suk; one s. two d.; ed Kwangju Soongil High School, Army Coll., Nat. Defence Coll., Grad. School of Public Admin, Dongkuk Univ.; commissioned Second Lt 1962; Co. Commdr Tiger Unit, Viet Nam War 1962–70; Commdr 26th Brigade, Capital Mechanized Div. 1983–84; Chief of Strategic Planning, Policy Planning Office, Army HQ 1984–87, Dir Special Inspection Group 1987–88, Dir of Strategic Planning 1989–91; Dean of Faculty, Nat. Defence Univ. 1988–89; Commdg Gen. 2nd Corps 1995–97, 2nd Repub. of Korea Army 1998–99; Chair. of Jt Chiefs of Staff 1999–2001; Minister of Nat. Defence 2003–04 (resgnd); Order of Mil. Merit Hwarang Medal 1970, Vietnam Hero Medal (Silver) and Bronze Star 1970, United States Bronze Star 1970, Order of Nat. Security Medal (Cheonsu) 1987, (Gukson) 1996, (Tongil) 1999, US Legion of Merit 2000, 2001. *Address:* c/o Ministry of National Defence, 1, 3-ga, Yonsan-dong, Yeongsan-gu, Seoul, Republic of Korea.

CHOBANOV, Petar Pandushev, MA, PhD; Bulgarian economist, academic and government official; *Associate Professor, Faculty of Finance and Accounting, University of National and World Economy;* b. 20 July 1976, Yambol; s. of Pandush Petrov Chobanov and Dona Dimitrova Chobanova; ed Univ. of Nat. and World Economy, Sofia; Assoc. Prof., Faculty of Finance and Accounting, Univ. of Nat. and World Economy; Sr Expert at Analysis Unit, Treasury Directorate, Bulgarian Nat. Bank –2005; Exec. Dir Agency for Econ. Analysis and Forecasting 2005–09, participated in the drafting of strategic programme documents, including Convergence Programme and Nat. Strategic Reference Framework; Chair. Financial Supervision Comm. 2009–10; Minister of Finance 2013–14 (resgnd); mem. Parl. 2014–, mem. Budget and Finance Cttee, Science and Educ. Cttee. *Publications:* several book chapters and numerous papers in professional journals. *Address:* Office 2020, Department of Finance, University of National and World Economy, 1700 Sofia, Students Town, Bulgaria (office). *Telephone:* (2) 8195635 (office). *E-mail:* pchoby@gmail.com (office). *Website:* blogs.unwe.bg/pchobanov/en (office).

CHOE, Jin Su; North Korean diplomatist; b. 1941, S Hwanghae Prov.; ed Univ. of Int. Affairs, Pyongyang; began career in Ministry of Foreign Affairs, posted to Embassy in Brunei 1969, in Burkina Faso 1974, to Trade Rep. Office, Paris 1978, later Head of W European Affairs, Ministry of Foreign Affairs, Amb. to Switzerland 1986–89, to China 2000–10; Deputy Chief, Workers' Party Cen. Cttee Int. Dept 1995–2000. *Address:* Ministry of Foreign Affairs, Pyongyang, Democratic People's Republic of Korea.

CHOE, Vice-Marshall Ryong-hae; North Korean military official and politician; *President, Presidium of the Supreme People's Assembly;* b. 15 Jan. 1950, Sinchon

County, South Hwanghae Prov.; s. of Choe Hyon; m. Kang Kyong-sil; two s. one d.; ed Kim Il-sung Univ.; joined Korean People's Army (KPA) 1967; Vice-Chair. Socialist Working Youth League 1981–86, Chair. 1986–96 (renamed Kim Il-sung Socialist Youth League 1996), Sec. 1996; Deputy, 8th Supreme People's Ass. (SPA, parl.) 1986, 9th SPA 1990, 12th SPA 2009; Chief Sec., North Hwanghae Korean Workers' Party (KWP) Provincial Cttee 2006; Dir KPA Gen. Political Bureau 2012–14; Vice Chair. Central Mil. Comm. 2012–14; Vice Chair. Nat. Defence Comm. April–Sept. 2014; Dir KWP Organization and Guidance Dept 2017–; Pres., SPA Presidium 2019–; First Vice Chair., State Affairs Comm. 2019–; mem. Korean Workers' Party (KWP), Alt. (candidate) mem. KWP Political Bureau 2010, mem. Political Bureau Presidium 2012, Vice Chair., KWP 2016, mem. Political Bureau Presidium (standing cttee) 2016. *Address:* Supreme People's Assembly, Somun-don, Pyongyang, Democratic People's Republic of Korea (office).

CHOE, Tae-bok; North Korean engineer, academic and government official; *Chairman of Supreme People's Assembly;* b. 1929, N Hamgyong Prov.; ed Mangyongdae Revolutionary School and studies in GDR; Prof. of Chemical Eng, Hamhung Tech. Eng Coll. 1961; Dean of Kimcahek Eng Coll. 1978, Chair. Educ. Comm. 1981; Minister of Higher Educ. 1985; Sec., Worker's Party Cen. Cttee 1986–; Assoc. mem. Politburo 1990–; Chair. Choe Ko In Min Hoe Ui (Supreme People's Ass.) 1998–. *Address:* Choe Ko In Min Hoe Ui, Pyongyang, Democratic People's Republic of Korea (office).

CHOE, Yong-rim; North Korean politician; b. 20 Nov. 1930; ed Mangyongdae Revolutionary School, Kim Il-sung Univ., Lomonosov Moscow State Univ., USSR; fmr Chief Public Prosecutor; Sec.-Gen., Presidium of Supreme People's Ass. 2005–09; mem. Korean Workers' Party (KWP), Alt. mem. KWP Political Bureau, Chief Sec., Pyongyang City Cttee 2009–10; Premier, Democratic People's Repub. of Korea 2010–13. *Address:* c/o Korean Workers' Party, Pyongyang, Democratic People's Republic of Korea (office).

CHOEDRA, His Holiness the 70th Je Khenpo Trulku Jigme; Bhutanese ecclesiastic; *Chairman, Council for Ecclesiastical Affairs;* followers believe him to be reincarnation of Maitreya, as well as Mahasiddha Saraha, Hungchen Kara, Kheuchung Lotsawa and His Holiness Pema Tsering; elected 70th Je Khenpo of Bhutan 1996, title given to highest religious official of Bhutan, Leader of Cen. Monk Body, also formally leader of Drukpa sect of Kagyupa School of Tibetan Buddhism; adviser to the King; Chair. Council for Ecclesiastical Affairs (Dratshang Lhentshog). *Address:* Council for Ecclesiastical Affairs (Dratshang Lhentshog), POB 254, Thimphu, Bhutan (office). *Telephone:* (2) 322754 (office). *Fax:* 2) 323867 (office). *E-mail:* dratsang@druknet.bt (office).

CHOI, Gee-sung; South Korean business executive; b. 2 Feb. 1951; ed Seoul Nat. Univ.; began career at Samsung C&T's Int. Trade Div. 1977, Chief Design Officer and est. co.'s chip business in Europe 1980s, Head, Memory Sales and Marketing, Semiconductor Business, Samsung Electronics 1994–98, Head, Visual Display Div. 1998–2003, Head, Digital Media Business 2003–07, Head, Corp. Design Centre 2007–09, Head, Mobile Communications Div., Head, Telecommunications Networks Business, Pres. and Head, Digital Media and Communications Business 2009, Pres. and CEO Samsung Electronics 2010, Vice-Chair. and CEO 2010–12, Vice-Chair., Corp. Strategy Office 2012; sentenced to four years in prison for corruption Aug. 2017.

CHOI, Kil-seon; South Korean business executive; *Chairman and Co-CEO, Hyundai Heavy Industries;* s. of Choi Ma-am and Yu Ok-soon; m. Yang Yang-ja 1971; two c.; ed Seoul Nat. Univ.; Lt in Korean Army 1969–71; Exec. Vice-Pres. Hyundai Heavy Industries Co. Ltd (HHI) 1972–92, Pres. Halla Engineering and Heavy Industries (subsidiary co.) 1993–99, Pres. Hyundai Mipo Dockyard, Ulsan 2004–05, Pres. and Co-CEO HHI 2005–11, mem. Bd Dirs 2008–11, 2014–, Chair. and Co-CEO 2014–; Chair. Korea Shipbuilders' Asscn 2003–05; Korean Govt Order of Industrial Merit 1977, Korea CEO Forum Grand Prix Award 2006. *Address:* Hyundai Heavy Industries Co. Ltd, 1000 Bangeojinsunhwan-doro Dong-gu, Ulsan 682-792, Republic of Korea (office). *Telephone:* (52) 230-2114 (office). *Fax:* (52) 230-3470 (office). *E-mail:* ir@hhi.co.kr (office); webzine@hhi.co.kr (office). *Website:* www.hhi.co.kr (office).

CHOI, Kyung-hwan, BEcons, PhD; South Korean economist and politician; b. 22 June 1955, Seoul; ed Yonsei Univ., Univ. of Wisconsin, USA; 20 years as civil servant 1979–99, including positions at Econ. Planning Bd, Office of the Pres. and Ministry of Planning and Budget (now Ministry of Strategy and Finance); Researcher, EBRD, London 1995; worked as journalist 1999–2004, as editorial writer and Deputy Ed.-in-Chief, Korea Economic Daily; Special Adviser on Econs to presidential cand. Lee Hoi-chang 2002; Dir Korea Econ. Inst. 2003; mem. Nat. Ass. (Parl.) for Gyeongsangbuk-do, Gyeongsan-Cheongdo 2004–, Saenuri Party Parl. leader; fmr Minister of Commerce, Industry and Energy, Minister of Knowledge Economy 2009; Deputy Prime Minister and Minister of Strategy and Finance 2014–15, Acting Prime Minister April-June 2015; Pres. Women's Korea Basketball League; mem. Saenuri Party (New Frontier Party). *Address:* c/o Ministry of Strategy and Finance, Government Complex, 477, Galmae-ro, Sejong City, 339-012, Republic of Korea (office).

CHOI, Man-Duen, PhD, FRSC; Canadian mathematician and academic; *Professor Emeritus of Mathematics, University of Toronto;* b. 13 June 1945, Nanking, China; m. Pui-Wah Ip 1972; two s. one d.; ed Chinese Univ. of Hong Kong, Univ. of Toronto; Lecturer, Dept of Math., Univ. of California, Berkeley 1973–76; Asst Prof., Dept of Math., Univ. of Toronto 1976–79, Assoc. Prof. 1979–82, Prof. of Math. 1982–, now Emer.; mem. American Math. Soc., Canadian Math. Soc., Math. Asscn of America; Israel Halperin Prize 1980, Coxeter-James Prize, Canadian Math. Soc. 1983. *Publications:* numerous articles in mathematical journals on operator theory, operator algebras and matrix theory. *Leisure interests:* yoga, stamps. *Address:* Department of Mathematics, BA6176, Bahen Centre, University of Toronto, Toronto, ON M5S 2E4, Canada (office). *Telephone:* (416) 978-3462 (office). *Fax:* (416) 978-4107 (office). *E-mail:* choi@math.utoronto.ca (office). *Website:* www.math.toronto.edu (office).

CHOI, Seok-young, BA, MBA; South Korean diplomatist and international organization official; *Permanent Representative to World Trade Organization;* b. 1955, Kangleung; m. Kim Young In; one s. one d.; ed Seoul Nat. Univ., Univ. of Heidelberg, Germany, Korea Devt Inst. School of Public Policy and Man.; joined Ministry of Foreign Affairs (MFA) 1979, Consul in Hamburg, Germany 1986–88, First Sec., Embassy in Nairobi 1988–91, Asst Dir Environmental Cooperation Div., MFA 1991–94, Counsellor for Econ. and Trade Affairs, Perm. Mission to UN, Geneva 1994–97, Dir for Environment and Science and Chief Negotiator for 1997 UNGA Special Session, MFA 1997–99, Counsellor and Chief of Econ. Section, Perm. Mission to UN, New York 1999–2002, Adviser to Pres. of UN Gen. Ass. 2001, Deputy Dir-Gen. Multilateral Trade Bureau, MFA 2002–03, Deputy Sr Official to APEC 2002–03, Deputy Exec.-Dir APEC Secr. 2004, Exec.-Dir 2005, Minister of Econ. Affairs, Embassy in Washington, DC 2006, also Deputy Chief of Mission, fmr Deputy Minister for Trade, Amb. and Perm. Rep. to UN Office and Other Int. Orgs in Geneva, Switzerland; currently Perm. Rep. to WTO, also Chair. WTO Council for Trade in Services, Chair. WTO Working Party 2013–18; del. to numerous int. and multilateral forums including UN, WTO and APEC. *Publications include:* numerous articles on trade, environmental issues and climate change negotiations.

CHOI, Maj.-Gen. Young-bum; South Korean army officer and UN official; b. 1959; m.; two c.; ed Army Infantry School, Army War Coll., Jt Staff Coll., US Defense System Man. Coll., USA; commissioned into Repub. of Korean Army 1982, Commdr Medical Support Group, UN Mission for Referendum in Western Sahara (MINURSO) 2000, Chief, Civil Mil. Cooperation, Centre of Repub. of Korea contingent in Iraq 2006, has also served as Chief Dir, Wartime Operational Control Transition Group, Chief, Ground Forces Br., Korea-US Combined Forces Command, Commdr 111th Regt, 37th Infantry Div.; Chief Mil. Observer and Head, UN Mil. Observer Group in India and Pakistan (UNMOGIP) 2012–14; Visiting Scholar, Univ. of Maryland, George Washington Univ. *Address:* c/o Ministry of Foreign Affairs, 37, Sejong-no, Seoul 110 787, Republic of Korea.

CHOI, Young-jin; South Korean diplomatist and UN official; b. 29 March 1948, Seoul; m.; two s.; ed Dept of International Relations, Yonsei Univ., Univ. of Paris I (Panthéon-Sorbonne), Fletcher School of Law, Tufts Univ., Boston; Political Officer, Embassy in Dakar 1977–78, in Paris 1979–81; Dir Cultural Exchanges Div., Ministry of Foreign Affairs, Seoul 1981; Political Counsellor, Embassy in Tunis 1983–85; Dir Int. Orgs Div., Ministry of Foreign Affairs, Seoul 1986, Sr Asst to Minister for Foreign Affairs 1987; Econ. Counsellor, Embassy in Washington, DC 1988–90; First Sr Coordinator, Office of Policy Planning, Ministry of Foreign Affairs, Seoul 1991–93, Dir-Gen. Int. Econ. Affairs Bureau 1994–95; Deputy Exec. Dir, Korean Peninsula Energy Devt Org., New York 1995–97; UN Asst Sec.-Gen. for Peacekeeping Operations 1998–99; Deputy Minister for Policy Planning and Int. Orgs, Seoul 2000–01; Amb. to Austria and Solvenia 2002, also Perm. Rep. to all int. orgs in Vienna 2002; Chancellor, Inst. of Foreign Affairs and Nat. Security (IFANS), Ministry of Foreign Affairs and Trade 2003; Vice-Minister for Foreign Affairs and Trade 2004–05; Perm. Rep. to UN, New York 2005–07; Special Rep. of the UN Sec.-Gen. in Côte d'Ivoire 2007–12; Amb. to USA 2012–13.

CHOIJILSUREN, Battogtokh; Mongolian business executive and politician; ed Tech. Inst. of the Urals, Yekaterinburg, Russia; Dir, SK Kaman Co., Yekaterinburg 1993–95; Dir, Hurd Ch LLC (trading co.) 1995–99, Dir, Hurd Huns LLC 1999–2006; Deputy Chief, Office of the Pres. 2006–08; mem. State Great Hural (Parl.) 2008–; Minister of Finance 2016–17; Order of the Polar Star 2009. *Address:* Office of the State Great Hural, State Palace, Dukhbaatar Square 1, Sukhbaatar, 14201, Mongolia (office). *Telephone:* (51) 267016 (office). *Fax:* (11) 327016 (office). *E-mail:* choijilsuren@parliament.mn (office). *Website:* choijilsuren.parliament.mn (office).

CHOLING, Padma, (Pema Thinley, Pelma Chiley, Baima Chilin); Chinese (Tibetan) government official; b. Oct. 1952, Dengqen, Qamdo Pref.; ed Graduate School, CCP Central Party School; served in People's Liberation Army 1969–86; joined CCP 1970; joined regional govt, Tibet (Xizang) Autonomous Region 1986, Vice-Chair. (Deputy Gov.), Tibet Autonomous Region People's Govt 2003–10, Gov. of Tibet 2010–13, also Deputy Sec. CCP Tibet Autonomous Regional Cttee 2010–13; Pres. Tibet Autonomous Region People's Congress Standing Cttee 2013–17; mem. 18th CCP Cen. Cttee 2012–17. *Address:* Tibet Autonomous Region People's Congress, 85000 Lhasa, Tibet, People's Republic of China.

CHOMBO, Ignatius Morgan, PhD; Zimbabwean politician; b. 1 Aug. 1952; m. Marion Mhloyi (divorced); three s.; ed Kutama Teachers Coll., Vanderbilt Univ.; Lecturer and Dept Chair., Univ. of Zimbabwe 1988–92; Gov., Mashonaland West 1995; mem. House of Ass. (parl.) for Zvimba North 2008–; Minister of Local Govt, Public Works and Urban Devt 2000–09, of Local Govt, Rural and Urban Devt 2009–13, of Local Govt, Public Works and Nat. Housing 2013–16, of Home Affairs 2015–17, of Finance and Econ. Devt Oct.–Nov. 2017; removed from office and charged with three counts of corruption following resignation of Pres. Robert Mugabe Nov. 2017; mem. Zimbabwe African Nat. Union—Patriotic Front (ZANU-PF).

CHOMSKY, (Avram) Noam, MA, PhD; American theoretical linguist and writer; *Professor Emeritus, Department of Linguistics, Massachusetts Institute of Technology;* b. 7 Dec. 1928, Philadelphia, Pa; s. of William Chomsky and Elsie Simonofsky; m. Carol Schatz 1949 (died 2008); one s. two d.; m. Valeria Wasserman 2014; ed Univ. of Pennsylvania; Asst Prof., MIT 1955–58, Assoc. Prof. 1958–61, Prof. of Modern Languages 1961–66, Ferrari P. Ward Prof. of Modern Languages and Linguistics 1966–76, Inst. Prof. 1976–, now Prof. Emer.; Visiting Prof., Columbia Univ. 1957–58; NSF Fellow, Inst. for Advanced Study, Princeton, NJ 1958–59; American Council of Learned Socs Fellow, Center for Cognitive Studies, Harvard Univ. 1964–65; Linguistics Soc. of America Prof., UCLA 1966; Beckman Prof., Univ. of California, Berkeley 1966–67; John Locke Lecturer, Univ. of Oxford 1969; Shearman Lecturer, Univ. Coll., London 1969; Bertrand Russell Memorial Lecturer, Univ. of Cambridge 1971; Nehru Memorial Lecturer, Univ. of Delhi 1972; Whidden Lecturer, McMaster Univ. 1975; Huizinga Memorial Lecturer, Univ. of Leiden 1977; Woodbridge Lecturer, Columbia Univ. 1978; Kant Lecturer, Stanford Univ. 1979; Jeanette K. Watson Distinguished Visiting Prof., Syracuse Univ. 1982; Pauling Memorial Lecturer, Oregon State Univ. 1995; mem. American Acad. of Arts and Sciences, Linguistic Soc. of America, American Philosophical Asscn, American Acad. of Political and Social Science, NAS, Bertrand Russell Peace Foundation, Deutsche Akademie der Naturforscher Leopoldina, Nat. Acad. of Sciences, Royal Anthropological Inst., Utrecht Soc. of Arts and Sciences; Fellow, AAAS; Corresp. Fellow, British Acad.; Hon. Fellow, British Psychological Soc.

1985, Royal Anthropological Inst.; Hon. DHL (Chicago) 1967, (Loyola Univ., Swarthmore Coll.) 1970, (Bard Coll.) 1971, (Massachusetts) 1973, (Maine, Gettysburg Coll.) 1992, (Amherst Coll.) 1995, (Buenos Aires) 1996; Hon. DLitt (London) 1967, (Delhi) 1972, Visva-Bharati (West Bengal) 1980, (Pennsylvania) 1984, (Cambridge) 1995; Dr hc (Tarragona) 1998, (Guelph) 1999, (Columbia) 1999, (Connecticut) 1999, (Pisa) 1999, (Harvard) 2000, (Toronto) 2000, (Western Ontario) 2000, (Kolkata) 2001; George Orwell Award, Nat. Council of Teachers of English 1987, Kyoto Prize in Basic Sciences 1988, James Killian Award, MIT 1992, Helmholtz Medal, Berlin Brandenburgische Akad. Wissenschaften 1996, Benjamin Franklin Medal, Franklin Inst., Philadelphia 1999, Rabindranath Tagore Centenary Award, Asiatic Soc. 2000, Peace Award, Turkish Publrs Asscn 2002, UCD Ulysses Medal, University Coll. Dublin 2013. *Film appearance:* Four Horsemen (documentary) 2012. *Publications include:* Syntactic Structures 1957, Current Issues in Linguistic Theory 1964, Aspects of the Theory of Syntax 1965, Cartesian Linguistics 1966, Topics in the Theory of Generative Grammar 1966, Language and Mind 1968, The Sound Pattern of English (with Morris Halle) 1968, American Power and the New Mandarins 1969, At War with Asia 1970, Problems of Knowledge and Freedom 1971, Studies on Semantics in Generative Grammar 1972, For Reasons of State 1973, The Backroom Boys 1973, Counter-revolutionary Violence (with Edward Herman) 1973, Peace in the Middle East? 1974, Reflections on Language 1975, The Logical Structure of Linguistic Theory 1975, Essays on Form and Interpretation 1977, Human Rights and American Foreign Policy 1978, Language and Responsibility 1979, The Political Economy of Human Rights (two vols, with Edward Herman) 1979, Rules and Representations 1980, Lectures on Government and Binding 1981, Radical Priorities 1981, Towards a New Cold War 1982, Concepts and Consequences of the Theory of Government and Binding 1982, Fateful Triangle: The United States, Israel and the Palestinians 1983, Modular Approaches to the Study of the Mind 1984, Turning the Tide 1985, Knowledge of Language: Its Nature, Origins and Use 1986, Barriers 1986, Pirates and Emperors 1986, Generative Grammar: Its Basis, Development and Prospects 1987, On Power and Ideology 1987, Language and Problems of Knowledge 1987, Language in a Psychological Setting 1987, The Chomsky Reader 1987, The Culture of Terrorism 1988, Manufacturing Consent (with Edward Herman) 1988, Language and Politics 1988, Necessary Illusions 1989, Deterring Democracy 1991, What Uncle Sam Really Wants 1992, Chronicles of Dissent 1992, Year 501: The Conquest Continues 1993, Rethinking Camelot: JFK, the Vietnam War and US Political Culture 1993, Letters from Lexington: Reflections on Propaganda 1993, The Prosperous Few and the Restless Many 1993, Language and Thought 1994, World Orders, Old and New 1994, The Minimalist Program 1995, Powers and Prospects 1996, Class Warfare 1996, The Common Good 1998, Profit over People 1998, The New Military Humanism 1999, New Horizons in the Study of Language and Mind 2000, Rogue States: The Rule of Force in World Affairs 2000, A New Generation Draws the Line 2000, Architecture of Language 2000, Propaganda and the Public Mind 2001, 9-11 2001, Understanding Power 2002, On Nature and Language 2002, Middle East Illusions 2003, Hegemony or Survival: America's Quest for Global Dominance 2003, Failed States: America 2006, Interventions 2007, What We Say Goes 2008, Perilous Power (with Gilbert Achcar) 2008, Hopes and Prospects 2010, Gaza in Crisis: Reflections on Israel's War Against the Palestinians (with Ilan Pappé) 2010, The Quotable Chomsky 2014, What Kind of Creatures Are We? 2015, Because We Say So 2015; numerous lectures, contribs to scholarly journals. *Address:* Department of Linguistics and Philosophy, Massachusetts Institute of Technology, 77 Massachusetts Avenue, 32-D808, Cambridge, MA 02139 (office); 15 Suzanne Road, Lexington, MA 02420, USA (home). *Telephone:* (617) 253-7819 (office); (781) 862-6160 (home). *Fax:* (617) 253-9425 (office). *E-mail:* chomsky@mit.edu (office). *Website:* web.mit.edu/linguistics/index.html (office).

CHONG, Michael David, PC, BA; Canadian politician; b. 22 Nov. 1971, Windsor; m. Carrie Davidson 2002; three s.; ed Centre Wellington Dist High School, Fergus, Univ. of Toronto; fmrly with Barclays Bank, Research Capital Corpn; fmr Chief Information Officer Nat. Hockey League Players' Asscn; fmr sr tech. consultant for redevelopment of Pearson Int. Airport, Greater Toronto Airports Authority; co-f. Dominion Inst. 1997, mem. Bd Govs; MP 2004–, Chair. House of Commons Standing Cttee on Industry, Science and Tech. 2009–10, Standing Cttee on Canadian Heritage 2010–11, Standing Cttee on Official Languages 2011–; Pres. Queen's Privy Council for Canada, Minister of Intergovernmental Affairs and of Sport 2006 (resgnd); mem. Corpn Trinity Coll., Univ. of Toronto; mem. Bd Elora Festival. *Address:* House of Commons, Ottawa, ON K1A 0A6, Canada (office). *Telephone:* (613) 992-4179 (office). *E-mail:* michael.chong@parl.gc.ca (office). *Website:* michaelchong.ca.

CHONG WONG, William, DrLic; Honduran politician; b. Puerto Cortés; ed Univ. of Southern Mississippi, USA; fmr Prof. and Vice-Pres. La Universidad Tecnologica Centroamericana (UNITEC); Dir Internal Revenue Service 1990–92; Deputy Minister of Finance 2002–04, Minister of Finance 2004–06, 2010–12 (resgnd); fmr Gov. IDB; fmr mem. Bd of Govs, Central American Bank for Econ. Integration; mem. Partido Nacional. *Address:* c/o Secretariat of Finance, Edif. SEFIN, Avenida Cervantes, Barrio El Jazmín, Tegucigalpa, Honduras. *E-mail:* sgeneral@sefin.gob.hn.

CHONGWE, Rodger Masauso Alivas, LLB, SC; Zambian lawyer and politician; *President, Liberal Progressive Front;* b. 2 Oct. 1940, Chipata; m. Gwenda Fay Eaton 1967; one s. one d.; ed St Mark's Coll., Mapanza, Choma, Munali Secondary School, Lusaka, Univ. of Western Australia School of Law, Perth; Native Courts Asst and Dist Asst, Govt of Northern Rhodesia 1962–63; admitted to practise as barrister, solicitor and Proctor of the Supreme Court of Western Australia and the High Court of the Commonwealth of Australia 1968; admitted as solicitor and barrister before all courts, Zambia 1969; Asst Solicitor, Martin & Co., Lusaka 1969–70, Partner 1979; Partner, Mwisiya Chongwe & Co., Lusaka 1970–77; owner, RMA Chongwe & Co., Lusaka 1987; apptd State Counsel 1985; mem. Industrial Relations Court of Zambia 1976–87; Lecturer, Law Practice Inst. 1974–83, Examiner 1975; Dir Tazama Pipelines Ltd 1974–89; Local Dir Jos Hansen & Soehne Zambia Ltd 1983; Dir Standard Chartered Bank of Zambia Ltd 1985; Pres. Liberal Progressive Front party 1993–; Minister of Local Govt and Housing and Legal Affairs 1997, shot by police 1997, fled Zambia and lived in exile in Australia, returned to Zambia 2003; mem. Int. Bar Asscn 1978, mem. Council 1984–86; Councillor Law Asscn of Zambia 1979, Vice-Chair. 1980, Chair. 1981–86, Councillor 1986, Chair. Human Rights Cttee 1986; Chair. African Bar Asscn 1985; mem. Council of Legal Educ. of Zambia 1982; Commr Law Devt Comm. of Zambia 1981; Exec. mem. Commonwealth Lawyers' Asscn 1983, Sec.-Gen. 1986, Pres. 1990; Gov. Art Centre Foundation 1977; Treas., Int. Asscn of Artists 1983. *Publications:* numerous papers on legal topics, particularly concerning human rights, the legal profession and legal education. *Address:* Liberal Progressive Front, PO Box 31190, Lusaka (office); Subdivision 36, Farm Number 34A, Great East Road, Lusaka, Zambia (home). *Website:* rodgerchongwe.com.

CHOO, Kangsoo, BSc, MSc, PhD; South Korean business executive; *Chairman, Korea Gas Corporation (KOGAS);* b. 9 Feb. 1945; ed Seoul Nat. Univ., Dalhousie Univ., NS, Canada, Korea Univ., Seoul; Man., Hyundai Heavy Industries Co. Ltd 1978; Dir and Sr Vice-Pres., Hyundai Corpn 1980–89, Exec. Vice-Pres., Hyundai Resources Devt Inc. 1990–92, Vice-Pres. and CEO 1993–94, Vice-Pres., Hyundai Corpn 1993–98; Korean Pnr, McKnight & Assocs 1999–2006; Advisor, Korea Resources Corpn Jan.–Dec. 2007; Sr Advisor, STX Energy Inc. 2007–08; Pres. and CEO Korea Gas Corpn (KOGAS) 2008–13, Chair. 2013–; Hon. LLD (Dalhousie) 2013; Tin Tower Order of Industrial Service Merit 1987. *Address:* Korea Gas Corpn, 93 Dolmaro, 215 Jeongja-dong, Bundang-gu, Seongnam, Gyeonggi-do, 463-754, Republic of Korea (office). *Telephone:* (31) 710-0114 (office). *Fax:* (31) 710-0117 (office). *E-mail:* kogasmaster@kogas.or.kr (office). *Website:* www.kogas.or.kr (office).

CHOPLIN, Jean-Luc; French arts management executive; *Director-General, Théâtre du Châtelet;* b. 1951; m.; three d.; Gen. Dir Roland Petit Ballet 1980–84; Man. Dir Paris Opéra Ballet 1984–89; Vice Pres. of Entertainment, Disneyland Paris 1989–95, Vice-Pres. Creative Devt, Walt Disney Co., Los Angeles 1995–2001; Artistic Consultant 2001–02; Programme and Devt Advisor, Robert Wilson's Watermill Center, New York 2001–02; CEO Sadler's Wells, London 2002–04; Dir-Gen. Théâtre du Châtelet, Paris 2006–. *Theatre includes:* new opera projects: Bintou Wéré (Sahel opera, first African opera), La Pietra del Paragone with Giorgio Barberio Corsetti and Pierrick Sorin, Monkey Journey to the West (Xi Yu Ji) with Damon Albarn and Jamie Hewlett (Gorillaz pop group), Welcome to the Voice with Sting, Verfügbar aux Enfers by Germaine Tillon (deportee from concentration camp of Ravensbrück), Magdalena (musical by Heitor Villa-Lobos), Die Feen (unknown opera by the young Wagner), Pastorale (contemporary opera by Gérard Pesson), The Fly (opera with David Cronenberg and Howard Shore (Lord of the Ring)), Padmavati (opera by Albert Roussel with Sanjay Leela Bhansali), Impempe Yomlingo (Mozart's Magic Flute on marimbas from a South African co.), Treemonisha by Scott Joplin, Vespro della beata Vergine by Monteverdi with Oleg Kulik, Il Postino by Daniel Catán, with Plácido Domingo as Pablo Neruda; introduced musicals to French audiences, including Candide, The Sound of Music, My Fair Lady, Showboat, A Little Night Music 2009, Sweeney Todd 2010. *Address:* Théâtre du Châtelet, 2 rue Edouard Colonne, 75001 Paris, France (office). *Telephone:* 1-40-28-28-28 (office). *Website:* chatelet-theatre.com (office).

CHOPPIN, Purnell Whittington, MD; American scientist and academic; *President Emeritus, Howard Hughes Medical Institute;* b. 4 July 1929, Baton Rouge, La.; s. of Arthur Richard Choppin and Eunice Dolores Choppin (née Bolin); m. Joan H. Macdonald 1959; one d.; ed La State Univ.; Intern, Barnes Hosp., St Louis 1953–54, Asst Resident 1956–57; Postdoctoral Fellow, Research Assoc., Rockefeller Univ., New York 1957–60, Asst Prof. 1960–64, Assoc. Prof. 1964–70, Prof., Sr Physician 1970–85, Leon Hess Prof. of Virology 1980–85, Vice-Pres. Acad. Programs 1983–85, Dean of Grad. Studies 1985; Vice-Pres. and Chief Scientific Officer, Howard Hughes Medical Inst. 1985–87, Pres. 1987–99, Pres. Emer. 2000–, Virology 1973–82; Chair. Virology Study Section, NIH 1975–78; mem. Bd of Dirs Royal Soc. of Medicine Foundation Inc., New York 1978–93, Advisory Cttee on Fundamental Research, Nat. Multiple Sclerosis Soc. 1979–84 (Chair. 1983–84), Advisory Council Nat. Inst. of Allergy and Infectious Diseases 1980–83, Sloan-Kettering Cancer Cttee, New York 1983–84, Comm. on Life Sciences, Nat. Research Council 1982–87, Council for Research and Clinical Investigation, American Cancer Soc. 1983–85; Pres. American Soc. of Virology 1985–86; Fellow, AAAS; mem. NAS (Chair. Class IV medical sciences 1983–86, Section 43 microbiology and immunology 1989–93), mem. council 2000–02, mem. Governing Bd NAS Nat. Research Council 1990–92; mem. Council Inst. of Medicine 1986–92, Exec. Cttee 1988–91; mem. American Philosophical Soc. (mem. Council 1999–2001, Vice-Pres. 2000–06); mem. Asscn of American Physicians, American Soc. of Microbiology, American Asscn of Immunologists and other professional orgs; numerous hon. degrees; Howard Taylor Ricketts Award, Univ. of Chicago 1978, Waksman Award for Excellence in Microbiology, NAS 1984. *Publications:* numerous articles and chapters on virology, cell biology, infectious diseases. *Leisure interests:* fly fishing, stamp collecting. *Address:* Howard Hughes Medical Institute, 4000 Jones Bridge Road, Chevy Chase, MD 20815 (office); 2700 Calvert Street, NW, Washington, DC 20008, USA (home). *Telephone:* (301) 215-8554 (office). *Website:* www.hhmi.org (office).

CHOPRA, Deepak; American writer; b. India; Founder Chopra Foundation, Co-founder and Dir of Educational Programs, Chopra Center for Wellbeing 1955–; Adjunct Prof., Kellogg School of Man., Northwestern Univ., Columbia Univ. Business School; Asst Clinical Prof., Family and Preventive Medicine Dept, Univ. of California, San Diego; mem. Faculty, Walt Disney Imagineering; Sr Scientist, The Gallup Organization; Fellow, American Coll. of Physicians; mem. American Asscn of Clinical Endocrinologists; numerous awards, including Einstein Humanitarian Award 2002, Trailblazer Award, Scripps Center for Integrative Medicine 2006, Ellis Island Medal of Honor 2006, Oceana Partners Award, Nat. Ethnic Coalition of Organizations Foundation 2009, Starlite Humanitarian Award 2010, GOI Peace Award 2010, Art for Life Honoree 2010. *Publications include:* Return of the Rishi 1989, Quantum Healing 1990, Perfect Health 1990, Unconditional Life 1991, Creating Health 1991, Creating Affluence 1993, Ageless Body, Timeless Mind 1993, Restful Sleep 1994, Perfect Weight 1994, The Seven Spiritual Laws of Success 1995, The Path of Love 1996, How to Create Wealth 1999, Everyday Immortality: A Concise Course in Spiritual Transformation 1999, How to Know God: The Soul's Journey into the Mystery of Mysteries 2000, How to Know God 2001, Grow Younger, Live Longer 2002, Golf for Enlightenment 2003, Book of Secrets 2004, Peace is the Way 2005, Buddha 2007, The Third Jesus: The Christ We Cannot Ignore 2008, Muhammad 2010. *Address:* Chopra Centre at La Costa Resort and Spa, 2013 Costa del Mar Road, Carlsbad, CA 92009, USA (office).

Telephone: (760) 494-1600 (office). *Fax:* (760) 494-1608 (office). *E-mail:* felicia@chopra.com (office). *Website:* www.deepakchopra.com.

CHOQUEHUANCA CÉSPEDES, David; Bolivian government official; b. 7 May 1961, Cota Cota Baja; ed Colegio General José Miguel Lanza, Escuela Nacional de Formación de Cuadros Niceto Pérez, Cuba, Universidad Cordillera; Nat. Coordinator NINA 1998; Minister of Foreign Affairs and Worship 2006–17.

CHORY, Joanne, AB, PhD; American biologist and academic; *Professor and Director, Plant Molecular and Cellular Biology Laboratory, Salk Institute for Biological Studies;* ed Oberlin Coll., Ohio and Univ. of Illinois at Urbana-Champaign; Postdoctoral Research, Harvard Medical School, Boston, Mass 1984–88; Asst Prof., Plant Biology Lab., Salk Inst., La Jolla, Calif. 1988–94, Assoc. Prof. 1994–98, Dir Plant Molecular and Cellular Biology Lab. 1998–, Prof. 1998– (mem. Academic Council Salk Inst. 1992–94, 1995–97, 2000–03); Adjunct Asst Prof., Biology Dept, Univ. of California, San Diego, La Jolla 1992–94, Adjunct Assoc. Prof. 1994–99, Adjunct Prof. 1999–; Assoc. Investigator, Howard Hughes Medical Inst., La Jolla 1997–; mem. Bd of Dirs Int. Soc. for Plant Molecular Biology 1995–98, Boyce Thompson Inst. for Plant Research 2001–03; mem. Bd on Life Sciences, Nat. Research Council 2001–04, Int. Advisory Cttee 7th Int. Congress of Plant Molecular Biology 2003; mem. Editorial Review Bd Plant Journal 1991–99, Plant Physiology 1992–95, 1998–, Genetics 1993–98, Developmental Genetics 1993–99, Cell 1994–97, 2001–, Genes to Cells 1995–, Current Opinion in Plant Biology 1998–, Science 1998–, BioProtocol 2000–01, Faculty of 1000 Section Head 2001–; Fellow, American Acad. of Arts and Sciences 1998–, AAAS; mem. NAS 1999–, German Nat. Acad. of Sciences (Leopoldina); Assoc. mem. European Molecular Biology Org.; Foreign mem. Royal Soc., UK 2011–; Foreign Assoc. French Acad. of Sciences; Trustees' Scholarship, Oberlin Coll. 1975–77, Anna Fuller Fund Jr Research Fellow, Harvard School of Public Health 1977, Award for Initiatives in Research, NAS 1994, Charles Albert Schull Award, American Soc. of Plant Physiologists 1995, Edna Roe Lecturer, Int. Congress of Photobiology 1996, Gatsby Foundation Flying Fellow 1997, L'Oreal-Helena Rubenstein Award for Women in Science 2000, Kumho Award in Plant Molecular Biology, Breakthrough Prize in Life Sciences 2018. *Publications:* more than 130 publs in scientific journals. *Address:* Plant Biology Laboratory, Salk Institute for Biological Studies, 10010 N Torrey Pines Road, San Diego, CA 92037, USA (office). *Telephone:* (858) 552-1148 (office). *Fax:* (858) 558-6379 (office). *E-mail:* chory@salk.edu (office). *Website:* www.salk.edu/faculty/chory.html (office).

CHOU, Chang-Hung, BS, MS, PhD; Taiwanese researcher and academic; *Chair Professor and Director, Research Centre for Biodiversity, China Medical University;* b. 5 Sept. 1942, Tainan, Taiwan; s. of F. K. Chou and C. Y. Shih Chou; m. Ruth L. H. Yang Chou 1970; one s. one d.; ed Nat. Taiwan Univ., Taipei, Univ. of Calif., Santa Barbara, USA, Univ. of Toronto, Canada; Assoc. Research Fellow, Inst. of Botany, Academia Sinica, Taipei 1972–76, Research Fellow 1976–2002, Dir 1989–96; Prof., Dept of Botany, Nat. Taiwan Univ. 1976–99; Vice-Pres. Nat. Sun Yat-sen Univ. 1999–2002; Pres. Nat. Pingtung Univ. of Science and Tech. 2002–06; Nat. Chair Prof., Ministry of Educ. 2001–04; Chair Prof. and Dir Research Centre for Biodiversity, China Medical Univ. 2006–; mem. various nat. cttees for Int. Council of Scientific Unions (ICSU) 1974–; Sec. for Int. Affairs, Academia Sinica 1988–, mem. Council, Academia Sinica 1989–, Pacific Science Asscn 1989; mem. Cttee for Science Educ., Ministry of Educ. 1986–, Cttee for Environmental Educ. 1991–, Cttee for Cultural and Natural Preservation Council of Agric. 1990; mem. Council Taiwan Livestock Research Inst. 1976–, Taiwan Forestry Research Inst. 1989–, Council Nat. Sustainable Devt 1997–; Dir Life Science Research Promotion Centre Nat. Science Council 1989–; Visiting Scholar, Oklahoma Univ., Univ. of Texas, Washington State Univ. 1979–80; Pres. Botanical Soc. of Repub. of China (Taiwan) 1983–84, Biological Soc. of Repub. of China (Taiwan) 1987–88; Chair. Nat. Cttee, Int. Union of Biological Sciences (IUBS) 1990–, Vice-Pres. IUBS 1997, mem. Exec. Cttee 2007–; Chair. SCOPE Nat. Cttee; Exec. mem. Pacific Science Asscn; Ed. Botanical Bulletin of Academia Sinica 1989–; mem. Academia Sinica, Taipei; Fellow, Third World Acad. of Sciences (now Acad. of Sciences for the Developing World); Highest Honour, Soka Univ., Japan 2003; awards from Ministry of Educ. and Science Council of Taiwan. *Publications:* one univ. textbook, ten monographs and more than 200 scientific papers. *Leisure interest:* listening to classical music. *Address:* College of Life Sciences, China Medical University, 91 Hsueh-Shih Road, Taichung 40402, Taiwan (office). *Telephone:* (4) 2205-3366 (ext. 1633) (office). *Fax:* (4) 2207-1507 (office). *E-mail:* choumasa@mail.cmu.edu.tw (office). *Website:* www.cmu.edu.tw (office).

CHOUDHURY, Subir Roy; Indian engineer and business executive; ed Univ. of Assam; began career in petroleum industry with Assam Oil Co., Digboi (subsidiary of Burma Oil Co.); joined Hindustan Petroleum Corpn Ltd as a construction engineer 1982, held various positions in co., including Gen. Man. (Supply, Operations and Distribution), Gen. Man. (Pipelines), Gen. Man. Sales (West Zone), Exec. Dir Direct Sales, Dir, Marketing 2004–10, Chair. and Man. Dir Hindustan Petroleum Corpn Ltd 2010–14; mem. Bd of Dirs Mangalore Refinery and Petrochemicals Ltd 2005–10, Prize Petroleum Co. Ltd –2010, (also fmr Chair.), Tide Water Oil Co. (India) 2014– (also fmr Chair.), HPCL Biofuels Ltd; mem. Governing Council, Petroleum Fed. of India.

CHOUHAN, Shivraj Singh, MA; Indian politician; b. 5 March 1959, Jait village, Sehore Dist; s. of Prem Singh Chouhan and Sundar Bai Chouhan; m. Smt. Sadhana Singh 1992; two s.; ed Barkatullah Univ., Bhopal; participated in underground movt against Emergency 1976–77, imprisoned in Bhopal Jail; joined Rashtriya Swayamsevak Sangh (Nat. Volunteers' Union—Hindu nationalist org.) 1977; Organizing Sec. Akhil Bhartiya Vidyarthi Parishad (ABVP) 1977–78, Jt Sec. ABVP 1978–80, Gen. Sec. 1980–83, mem. Nat. Exec. of ABVP 1982–83; Jt Sec. Bhartiya Janta Yuva Morcha (BJYM) 1984–85, Gen. Sec. BJYM, Madhya Pradesh (MP) 1985–88, Pres. BJYM, MP 1988–91, Gen. Sec. All India BJYM 1992, Nat. Pres. 2000–03; mem. Bharatiya Janata Party (BJP), fmr Pres. MP state party unit, Gen. Sec. BJP, MP 1992–94, 1997–98, later Nat. Sec. BJP, Pres. BJP, MP 2005–; elected to State Ass. from Budhni Constituency 1990–91; a convener of Akhil Bhartiya Keshariya Vahini 1991–92; mem. Lok Sabha (lower house of Parl.) 1991–2006, first representing Vidisha, later representing Budhni, Sehore Dist; MP in State Ass.; Chair. House Cttee (Lok Sabha), mem. Consultative Cttee, Ministry of Communications 2000–04, Sec. Parl. Bd 2004; Chief Minister of MP 2005–18. *Leisure interests:* music, spiritual literature, debates and discussions with friends, sight-seeing, watching movies, Kabaddi, cricket, volleyball. *Address:* 1 Shyamla Hills, Bhopal, Madhya Pradesh, India (home). *Telephone:* (755) 2442231 (home).

CHOUINARD, Yvon; American mountaineer, surfer, sportsman, business executive and writer; *Founder, Patagonia, Inc.;* b. 9 Nov. 1938, Lewiston, Me; m. Malinda Pennoyer 1970; two c.; served in US Army 1962–64; f. Chouinard Equipment for Alpinists (CEA), Inc. 1960; f. Lost Arrow Corpn 1974; Founder, Patagonia Inc. 1976–; also a kayaker, falconer and fisherman; writer on climbing issues and ethics and also on mixing environmentalism and sound business practice; mem. American Alpine Club; inducted into American Marketing Asscn's Marketing Hall of Fame 2015. *Achievements include:* participated in second ascent of The Nose on El Capitán 1960, ascent of North American Wall using no fixed ropes 1964; visited Canadian Rockies with Fred Beckey 1961, made several important first ascents, including North Face of Mount Edith Cavell, Beckey-Chouinard Route on South Howser Tower in the Bugaboos, and North Face of Mount Sir Donald; freeclimbed first pitch of Matinee in the Gunks 1961; climbed Cerro Fitzroy in Patagonia by a new route (The Californian Route) 1968. *Publications:* Climbing Ice 1982, Let My People Go Surfing 2005. *Address:* 259 West Santa Clara Street, Ventura, CA 93001, USA (office). *Telephone:* (805) 643-8616 (office). *Fax:* (800) 543-5522 (office). *E-mail:* info@patagonia.com (office). *Website:* www.patagonia.com (office).

CHOUMMALY, Lt-Gen. Sayasone; Laotian army officer, politician and fmr head of state; b. 6 March 1936, Attapu; m. Keosaychay Sayasone; mem. Nat. Ass.; Minister of Defence 1991–93, Deputy Prime Minister and Minister of Nat. Defence 1999–2001; Vice-Pres. of Laos 2001–06, Pres. 2006–16; mem. Cen. Cttee of Phak Pasason Pativat Lao (Lao People's Revolutionary Party) 1982, alt. mem. of Politburo and Sec. of the Secr. of the Cen. Cttee 1986, Sec.-Gen. 2006–16. *Address:* c/o Office of the President, ave Lane Xang, Vientiane, Laos.

CHOVANEC, Milan; Czech business executive and politician; b. 31 Jan. 1970, Plzeň; m.; two c.; ed Central School of Econs, Plzeň, Univ. of West Bohemia, Plzeň; worked in Czechoslovak bank –1989; owned business in retail, wholesale and services 1989–99; Partner, Miller-Sü sro 1999–2000; Dir and sole shareholder in Plzeň Furniture Ltd 2001–07; sold share in co. 2007; mem. Česká Strana Sociálně Demokratická (ČSSD—Czech Social Democratic Party), Chair. Regional Exec. Cttee 2011–13, Vice-Chair. ČSSD 2013–15, Acting Chair. June 2017–Feb. 2018; mem. Ass., City of Plzeň 2002–10, Chair. Audit Cttee 2006–08, First Deputy for region's economy and property 2008–10, Pres. (Gov.) Plzeň Region 2010–14; mem. Chamber of Deputies for Plzeňský (ČSSD) 2013–; Minister of the Interior 2014–17. *Address:* Česká Strana Sociálně Demokratická, Lidový dům, Hybernská 7, 110 00 Prague 1, Czech Republic (office). *Telephone:* 296522111 (office). *Fax:* 224222190 (office). *E-mail:* info@socdem.cz (office). *Website:* www.cssd.cz (office).

CHOW, Alan Y., BA, MD; American paediatric ophthalmologist and academic; b. Glen Ellyn, Ill.; brother of Vincent Y. Chow; ed Univ. of Chicago, Loyola Univ. Stritch School of Medicine; completed internships in Paediatrics at Cincinnati Children's/GSH and in Gen. Surgery at Loyola Univ. where he also completed his ophthalmology residency; fmr Knapp Fellow in Ophthalmic Genetics, Wilmer Eye Inst., Johns Hopkins Univ.; fmr Heed Fellow in Paediatric Ophthalmology, Children's Hosp. Nat. Medical Center; Asst Prof., Rush Univ. Medical Center, Chicago; Visiting Assoc. Prof., Univ. of Illinois Eye Center, Chicago; Adjunct Asst Prof., Tulane Univ. Eye Center; Co-founder (with his brother) and COO Optobionics Corpn, led devt of Artificial Silicon Retina 1990; Paediatric Ophthalmology Specialist, Hauser-Ross Eye Inst. and Surgicenter, Sycamore 2007–; spokesperson for American Acad. of Ophthalmology; grants and awards from NASA, Westinghouse Foundation, NSF, NIH and SBA, Chicago Inventor of the Year (together with his brother Vincent) for work in developing Artificial Silicon Retinal Prosthesis 1996, Tibbetts Award, Small Business Innovation Research Program 2000, RP International's Vision Award (with his brother) 2002, Ernst & Young Entrepreneur of the Year Award in the Chicago area 2003, World Tech. Award in Health and Medicine, The World Tech. Network (with his brother) 2004, Pioneer Research Award, Chinese American Ophthalmological Soc. 2006. *Publications:* numerous articles, book chapters and patents. *Address:* 386 Pennsylvania Avenue, Suite 3N, Glen Ellyn, IL 60137-4323 (office); Hauser-Ross Eye Institute and Surgicenter, 2240 Gateway Drive, Sycamore, IL 60178, USA (office). *Telephone:* (630) 858-4411 (Glen Ellyn) (office). *Website:* www.hauserross.org (office); alanchowmd.com.

CHOW, Sir C. K. (Chung Kong), Kt., CEng, BSc, MSc, DEng, FREng, FCGI, FIChemE, FHKEng; British (b. Hong Kong) business executive; *CEO, MTR Corporation Ltd;* b. 9 Sept. 1950; ed Univs of Wisconsin and California, USA, Chinese Univ. of Hong Kong, Harvard Univ., USA; Research Engineer, Climax Chemical Co., New Mexico 1974–76; Process Engineer, Sybron Asia Ltd, Hong Kong 1976–77; joined BOC Group 1977, with Hong Kong Oxygen, Hong Kong and BOC Australia 1977–84, Man. Dir Hong Kong Oxygen 1984–86, Pres. BOC Japan 1986–89, Group Man. Gases Business Devt, BOC Group PLC, UK and USA 1989–91, Regional Dir N Pacific, Tokyo and Hong Kong 1991–93, CEO Gases 1993–96, apptd to Main Bd 1994, Man. Dir 1994–97; CEO GKN PLC 1997–2001, CEO Brambles Industries Ltd 2001–03, CEO MTR Corpn Ltd 2003–; Dir (non-exec.) Standard Chartered PLC 1997–2008; Chair. Standard Chartered Bank (Hong Kong) Ltd 2004–10; fmr Pres. Soc. of British Aerospace Cos; mem. Governing Body London Business School; Fellow, Inst. of Chemical Engineers, Chartered Inst. of Logistics and Transport; Hon. Fellow, Inst. of Eng and Tech.; Int. Exec., Acad. of Int. Man. 2001, Exec. of the Year, DHL/South China Morning Post Business Award 2006, Dir of the Year, Hong Kong Inst. of Dirs 2006, Best CEO in Hong Kong Award, FinanceAsia Magazine 2009, 2011. *Address:* MTR Corporation Ltd, GPO Box 9916, Hong Kong Special Administrative Region, People's Republic of China (office). *Telephone:* 29932111 (office). *Fax:* 27988822 (office). *Website:* www.mtr.com.hk (office).

CHOW, Vincent Y., BS; American electrical engineer and business executive; *President, Vega Technology and Systems, Inc.;* brother of Dr Alan Chow; ed Illinois Inst. of Tech.; fmr Dir of Operations, Telco Systems; fmr Man. of Reliability Devt, AT&T Bell Labs/Teletype; Dir of Tech. Operations, Autotech Corpn 1985–89; Dir of Research and Devt, MDA Scientific 1989–94; Co-founder and Vice-Pres., Research and Devt, Optobionics Corpn 1990–94; Pres. Vega Technology and Systems, Inc. (eng consulting firm for optical sensing products and ASIC applications) 1994–;

Chicago Inventor of the Year Award (with his brother Alan) for work in developing Artificial Silicon Retina Microchip 1996, Vision Award, RP International (with his brother) 2002, Ernst & Young Entrepreneur of the Year Award in the Chicago area (with his brother) 2003, World Tech. Award in Health and Medicine, The World Tech. Network (with his brother) 2004. *Publications:* more than 220 papers in scientific journals and named inventor on 11 patents. *Address:* Vega Technology and Systems, Inc., 7980 Kingsbury Drive, Bartlett, IL 60133-2348, USA (office). *Telephone:* (630) 855-5068 (office).

CHOW, Yun-fat, (Donald Chow Yun-fat); Chinese film actor; b. 18 May 1955, Lamma Island, British Hong Kong; m. 1st Candice Yu 1983 (divorced 1983); m. 2nd Jasmine Chow 1986; began acting career at TV station TVB, Hong Kong 1973, appearing in over 1,000 TV series; Silver Bauhinia Star; Dr hc (City Univ. of Hong Kong) 2001. *Films include:* The Story of Woo Viet, A Better Tomorrow 1986, God of Gamblers 1989, The Killer 1989, Eighth Happiness, Once a Thief 1991, Full Contact 1992, Hard Boiled 1992, Peace Hotel 1995, Broken Arrow, Anna and the King 1999, Crouching Tiger, Hidden Dragon 2000, King's Ransom 2001, Bulletproof Monk 2003, Yi ma de hou xian dai sheng huo 2006, Man cheng jin dai huang jin jia (Curse of the Golden Flower) 2006, Pirates of the Caribbean: At World's End 2007, The Children of Huang Shi 2008, Dragonball Evolution 2009, Confucius 2010, Shanghai 2010, Let the Bullets Fly 2010, Beginning of the Great Revival 2011, The Assassins 2012, The Last Tycoon 2012, The Monkey King 2014, The Man from Macau 2014, From Vegas to Macau II 2015, The Office 2015. *Address:* c/o WME Entertainment, 9601 Wilshire Boulevard, Beverly Hills, CA 90210-5213, USA (office); Chow Yun Fat International, PO Box 71288, Kowloon Central, Hong Kong Special Administrative Region, People's Republic of China (office). *Telephone:* (310) 285-9000 (office). *Fax:* (310) 285-9010 (office). *Website:* www.wmeentertainment.com (office).

CHOW MAN YIU, Paul, JP; Chinese business executive; fmr Exec. Dir Sun Hung Kai Securities Ltd; CEO Hong Kong Securities Clearing Corpn 1990–91; CEO Hong Kong Stock Exchange 1991–97; mem. Global Man. Cttee, Dir (non-Exec.) HSBC Insurance (Hong Kong) Co. Ltd; CEO HSBC Asset Management (Hong Kong) Ltd 1997–2003; Chair. Hong Kong Investment Funds Asscn 2000–01; Exec. Dir and CEO Hong Kong Exchanges and Clearing Ltd 2003–10; Dir Hong Kong Cyberport Management Co. Ltd 2003–07, Chair. 2010–16; mem. Advisory Cttee Securities and Futures Comm. 2001–07; Independent non-Exec. Dir China Mobile Ltd 2013–, CITIC Ltd; mem. Bd of Dirs Julius Baer Group Ltd 2015–, Bank Julius Baer & Co. Ltd 2015–; mem. Advisory Cttee on Innovation and Tech., Govt of the Hong Kong Special Admin. Region 2015–17; Hon. Fellow, Univ. of Hong Kong; Silver Bauhinia Star 2005, Gold Bauhinia Star 2010. *Address:* c/o The Stock Exchange of Hong Kong Ltd, 1/F One and Two Exchange Square, Central, Hong Kong Special Administrative Region, People's Republic of China.

CHOWDHURY, A. Q. M. Badruddoza, FRCPE, FRCP (CLAS), TDD; Bangladeshi surgeon, politician and fmr head of state; b. 1 Nov. 1932; s. of Kafil Uddin Chowdhury and Sufia Khatun; m. Hasina Chowdhury; one s. two d.; ed St Gregory High School, Dhaka Coll., Dhaka Medical Coll., Univ. of Wales, UK; practised as physician specializing in treatment of tuberculosis; Founding Sec.-Gen. Bangladesh Nationalist Party 1978–90, fmr Deputy Leader, mem. until 2002; fmr Sr Deputy Prime Minister, Minister of Health and Family Planning, of Foreign Affairs 2001; Pres. of Bangladesh 2001–02; Co-founder and Pres. Liberal Democratic Party 2006–13; fmr Pres. Nat. Anti-Tuberculosis Asscn of Bangladesh, Int. Union Against Tuberculosis; led Bangladesh del. to World Health Conf., Geneva 1978, 1979 and many dels to int. confs on tuberculosis and chest diseases; Hon. Fellow, Coll. of Physicians and Surgeons (Bangladesh); Nat. TV Award 1976. *Publications:* many research papers in nat. and int. journals; essays and plays. *Address:* Residence Bari Dhar, near Gulshan, Dhaka, Bangladesh (home).

CHOWDHURY, Anwarul Karim, MA; Bangladeshi diplomatist and UN official; b. 5 Feb. 1943, Dhaka; m.; three c.; ed Univ. of Dhaka; Dir-Gen. for S and SE Asia, Ministry of Foreign Affairs 1979–80, for Multilateral Econ. Co-operation 1986–90, Deputy Perm. Rep. to UN, New York 1980–86, Amb. and Perm. Rep. 1996–2001, Chair. Fifth Cttee (Admin. and Budgetary) of UN 1997–98; UNICEF Dir for Japan, Australia and NZ 1990–93, Sec. Exec. Bd UNICEF, New York 1993–96 (Chair. Bd 1985–86), UN Under-Sec.-Gen. for Least Developed Countries, Landlocked Developing Countries and Small Island Developing States 2002–07 (retd), currently emissary for UN Culture of Peace Initiative; fmr Adjunct Prof., School of Diplomacy, Seton Hall Univ., USA; Hon. Patron Cttee on Teaching About the UN (CTAUN), New York; Ordre Nacionale (Burkina Faso) 2007; Dr hc (Soka Univ., Tokyo) 2003; U Thant Peace Award, UNESCO Gandhi Gold Medal for Culture and Peace, Chancellor's Medal for Global Leadership for Peace, Univ. of Massachusetts Boston 2012. *Publications:* contribs to journals on peace, devt and human rights issues. *Address:* Culture of Peace Initiative, Pathways To Peace, PO Box 1507, Larkspur, CA 94977, USA. *Telephone:* (415) 461-0500. *Fax:* (415) 925-0330. *E-mail:* info@pathwaystopeace.org. *Website:* pathwaystopeace.org/culture-of-peace-initiative.

CHOWDHURY, M. Nurunnabi; Bangladeshi business executive; fmr Chair. Bangladesh Textile Mills Corpn. *Address:* c/o Bangladesh Textile Mills Corpn, Bastra Bhaban, 7–9 Kawran Bazar, Dhaka 1215, Bangladesh.

CHOWDHURY, Shamsher Mobin, BA; Bangladeshi diplomatist and politician; *Vice-Chairman, Bangladesh Jatiyatabadi Dal (Bangladesh Nationalist Party);* ed Pakistan Mil. Acad.; joined Pakistan army 1969, promoted to rank of Maj. 1973; joined Bangladesh Civil Service 1975; Deputy Chief of Protocol and Dir West Europe, Ministry of Foreign Affairs 1975–77, with Embassy in Rome 1977–81, Counsellor, Embassy in Washington, DC 1981–83, Counsellor and Minister, High Comm. in Ottawa 1983–86, Deputy Chief of Mission, Embassy in Beijing 1986–88, Dir-Gen. SAARC Div., Ministry of Foreign Affairs 1988–91, High Commr to Sri Lanka 1991–95, Amb. to Germany 1995–98, to Viet Nam 1998–2001, Foreign Sec. 2001–05, Amb. to USA 2005–07; currently Vice-Chair. Bangladesh Jatiyatabadi Dal (Bangladesh Nationalist Party), also head of Int. Dept; Gallantry Award Bir Bikram (BB). *Address:* Bangladesh Jatiyatabadi Dal (Bangladesh Nationalist Party), 28/1 Naya Paltan, 8 VIP Road, Dhaka 1000, Bangladesh (office). *Telephone:* (2) 8351929 (office). *Fax:* (2) 8318678 (office). *E-mail:* info@bnpbd.org (office). *Website:* www.bnpbd.com (office).

CHRAPLYVY, Andrew R., BA, MS, PhD; American physicist and business executive; *Optical Technologies Research Vice-President, Bell Labs, Alcatel-Lucent;* ed Washington Univ. in St Louis, Cornell Univ.; with Bell Laboratories 1980–, currently Optical Technologies Research Vice-Pres., Bell Labs, Alcatel-Lucent, Bell Labs Fellow; mem. Nat. Acad. of Eng; Marconi Fellow; Fellow, Optical Soc. of America (OSA), IEEE; Bell Laboratories Pres.'s Gold Award (four times), Lucent Technologies Patent Award 1998, New Jersey Inventor of the Year Award 1999, Thomas Alva Edison Patent Award 1999, IEEE John Tyndall Award 2003, OSA John Tyndall Award 2008, Marconi Prize and Fellowship (co-recipient) 2009, inducted into New Jersey Inventors Hall of Fame 2010, IEEE Alexander Graham Bell Medal (co-recipient) 2013. *Publications:* numerous papers in professional journals. *Address:* Bell Labs, Alcatel-Lucent, 600 Mountain Avenue, Murray Hill, NJ 07974-0636, USA (office). *Telephone:* (732) 888-7255 (office). *E-mail:* andrew.chraplyvy@nokia-bell-labs.com. *Website:* www.bell-labs.com (office).

CHRÉTIEN, Rt Hon. Joseph Jacques Jean, PC, OM, CC, QC, BA, LLD; Canadian lawyer and fmr politician; b. 11 Jan. 1934, Shawinigan; s. of Wellie Chrétien and Marie Boisvert; m. Aline Chaîné 1957; two s. one d.; ed Laval Univ., Québec; Dir Bar of Trois-Rivières 1962; mem. House of Commons (Liberal) 1963–86; Parl. Sec. to Prime Minister 1965, to Minister of Finance 1966; Minister without Portfolio 1967–68, of Nat. Revenue Jan.–July 1968, of Indian Affairs and Northern Devt 1968–74; Pres. Treas. Bd 1974–76; Minister of Industry, Trade and Commerce 1976–77, of Finance 1977–79, of Justice, Attorney-Gen. of Canada and Minister of State for Social Devt 1980–82, of Energy, Mines and Resources 1982–84, Sec. of State for External Affairs, Deputy Prime Minister June–Sept. 1984; MP for Beauséjour 1990–93, for St Maurice 1993–2003, Prime Minister of Canada 1993–2003, Leader Nat. Liberal Party 1990–2003; Legal Counsel, Lang, Michener, Laurence & Shaw, Ottawa, Toronto and Vancouver 1984–90; special adviser on int. energy and power, Bennett Jones LLP 2004; Of Counsel, Heenan Blaikie LLP, Ottawa 2004–14 (defunct); mem. Barreau du Québec, Ont. Bar Asscn, Club de Madrid, Honour Cttee of Fondation Chirac 2008–; Hon. LLD (Wilfred Laurier Univ.) 1981, (Laurentian Univ.) 1982, (W Ont.) 1982, (York Univ.) 1986, (Alberta) 1987, (Lakehead) 1988, (Ottawa) 1994, (Meiji) 1996, (Queen's Univ.) 2004, (McMaster Univ.) 2005; Dr hc (Ottawa Univ.) 1994, (Meiji Univ., Japan) 1996, (Warsaw School of Econs, Poland) 1999, (Michigan State Univ.) 1999, (Hebrew Univ., Jerusalem) 2000 (Memorial Univ.) 2000, (Université Catholique Pontificate Madre y Maestra in Santiago de los Caballeros, Dominican Repub.) 2003, (Nat. Univ. of Kyiv-Mohyla Acad., Ukraine) 2007, (Univ. of Western Ontario) 2008; Int. Role Model Award, Equality Forum 2005. *Publications:* Straight from the Heart 1985, Finding a Common Ground 1992. *Leisure interests:* skiing, fishing, golf.

CHRÉTIEN, Raymond A. J., OC, BA, LLL; Canadian lawyer, government official and diplomatist (retd); *Partner and Strategic Advisor, Fasken Martineau;* b. 20 May 1942, Shawinigan, Quebec; s. of Maurice Chrétien and Cécille Chrétien (née Marcotte); m. Kay Rousseau; one s. one d.; ed Séminaire de Joliette and Laval Univ.; Quebec Bar Exams 1966; mem. Legal Affairs Div., Div. of External Affairs, Govt of Canada 1966–67, Policy Dir Industry, Investments and Competition 1981–82; Asst Under-Sec. for Manufacturing, Tech. and Transportation 1982–83; Insp.-Gen. 1983–85, Assoc. Under-Sec. of State for External Affairs 1988–91; Third Sec., Perm. Mission to UN, New York 1967–68; Asst Sec., Fed. and Provincial Relations Comm., Privy Council Office 1968–70, Exec. Asst to Sec., mem. Treasury Bd 1970–71; Exec. Asst to Pres., Canadian Int. Devt Agency 1971–72; First Sec., Embassy in Beirut 1972–75; First Sec. and Counsellor, Embassy in Paris 1975–78; Amb. to Zaïre 1978–81, to Mexico 1985–88, to Belgium and Luxembourg 1991–94, to USA 1994–2000, to France 2000–03; Partner and Strategic Advisor, Fasken Martineau (law firm), Montreal 2004–; UN Sec.-Gen.'s Special Envoy to Cen. Africa 1996; Chair. Centre d'études et de recherches internationales de l'Université de Montréal (CERIUM) 2004–; Pres. Comité des gouverneurs des corridors de commerce Québec-Canada-États-Unis of the Fédération des chambres de commerce du Québec; mem. Bd of Dirs, Institut de recherches cliniques de Montréal; mem. Trilateral Comm., Pierre Elliott Trudeau Foundation 2005–; Hon. mem. Bar of US Court of Appeal for the Armed Forces 1998; Officer, Nat. Order of the Leopard (Zaïre, now Democratic Repub. of the Congo) 1981; Order of Aztec Eagle, Mexico 1989; Commdr, Légion d'honneur 2003; Hon. DLitt (Brock) 1999; Hon. DJur (Laval) 2001, (State Univ. of New York) 2002. *Address:* Fasken Martineau Dumoulin, PO Box 242, The Stock Exchange Tower, Suite 3700, 800 Place Victoria, Montreal, PQ H4Z 1E9, Canada (office). *Telephone:* (514) 397-5230 (office). *Fax:* (514) 397-7600 (office). *E-mail:* rchretien@fasken.com (office). *Website:* www.fasken.com/raymond-chretien (office).

CHRIQUI, Vincent; French government official; *Mayor of Bourgoin-Jallieu;* b. 2 Dec. 1971; two c.; ed École Polytechnique, École Nationale d'Admin; responsible for environmental and agricultural budgets as part of overall Budget 1997–99; responsible for econ. and monetary union to Ministry for the Economy and Finances and, for this reason, mem. EU Econ. Policy Cttee 1999–2001; Finance Man. CDC-Ixis (groupe Caisse des dépôts et consignations—CDC) 2001–02; Budgetary Advisor, Office of François Fillon, Minister of Social Affairs, Labour and Solidarity 2002–04, then to Minister for State Educ., Higher Educ. and Research 2004–05; Parl. Pvt. Sec. to Gérard Larcher, Deputy Sec. for Employment, Labour and Youth Training, Asst Dir, Office of Jean-Louis Borloo, Minister of Employment, Social Cohesion and Housing 2005–07; Adviser in charge of analysis, then Parl. Advisor to Cabinet of François Fillon (Prime Minister) 2007–10; Dir-Gen. Centre d'analyse stratégique (Strategic Analysis Centre) 2010–13; Auditor, Cour des comptes 2013–16; Lecturer in Econs, Institut d'études politiques de Paris 1998–2000, Univ. of Paris II Panthéon-Assas 2005; Mayor of Bourgoin-Jallieu 2014–; campaign man. for presidential cand. François Fillon 2017.

CHRISOCHOIDIS, Michalis; Greek lawyer and politician; b. 31 Oct. 1955, Nisi, Imathia; s. of Vasilis Chrisochoidhis and Anna Chrisochoidhis; m. Aggeliu Hondromelidois; one s. one d.; ed Faculty of Law, Aristotle Univ. of Thessaloníki; attorney-at-law, Veria, Imathia 1978–87; Founding mem. Panhellenic Socialist Movement (PASOK) 1974–, held numerous elected posts at local level, elected mem. Cen. Cttee 1990, Sec.-Gen. 2003–; mem. Hellenic Parl. 1989–; Deputy Minister of Commerce 1994–96, of Devt 1996–99; Minister for Public Order 1999–2004, for Civic Protection 2009–10, for Regional Devt and Competitiveness 2010–11, for Devt, Competitiveness and Shipping 2011–12, for Civic Protection

March–May 2012, for Infrastructure, Transport and Networks 2013–15; mem. Bd, Party of European Socialists 1994–96. *Website:* www.chrisochoidis.gr; www.facebook.com/chrisochoidis.

CHRISTENSEN, Helena; Danish model and photographer; b. 25 Dec. 1968, Copenhagen; d. of Flemming Christensen and Elsa Christensen; one s.; grad. in arithmetic and sociology course; fmr child model; began adult modelling career in Paris 1988; has since worked as one of world's leading models in promotions for Versace, Rykiel, Chanel, Lagerfeld, Revlon, Dior, Prada etc.; has appeared on all major magazine covers working for photographers including Herb Ritts, Bruce Weber, Patrick DeMarchelier, Penn, Steven Meisel, Helmut Newton, and others; Co-founder and fmr Creative Dir Nylon Magazine. *Films include:* Inferno (TV) 1992, March of the Anal Sadistic Warrior 1998, Allegro 2005, The Christmas Party 2009, The Reunion 3 2016. *Leisure interests:* photography (black and white), oil/watercolour painting. *Address:* One Management, 42 Bond Street, #2, New York, NY 10012, USA (office). *Telephone:* (212) 431-0054 (office).

CHRISTENSEN, Lars Saabye; Norwegian poet, writer and playwright; b. 21 Sept. 1953, Oslo; Ed., Signaler 1986–90; Commdr, Order of St Olaf 2006, Chevalier, Ordre des Arts et des Lettres 2008; Tarjei Vesaas debutantpris 1976, Cappelenprisen 1984, Rivertonprisen 1987, Kritikerprisen 1988, Sarpsborgprisen 1988, Bokhandlerprisen 1990, Amandaprisen 1991, Doblougprisen 1993, Riksmålsforbundets litteraturpris 1997, Sarpsborgprisen 1999, Aamot-statuetten 2001, Bokhandlerprisen 2001, Brageprisen 2001, Den norske leserprisen 2001, Natt & Dags bokpris 2001, Nordisk Råds Litteraturpris 2002. *Plays:* Columbus' ankomst 1981, Kvitt eller dobbelt 1984, Jokeren 1987, Til pengene tar slutt, Al 1988, Mekka 1994, Lyset på yttersida 2001, Chet baker spiller ikke her 2010. *Publications:* Historien om Gly 1976, Amatøren 1977, Kamelen i mitt hjerte 1978, Jaktmarker 1979, Billettene 1980, Jokeren 1981, Paraply 1982, Beatles 1984, Blodets bånd 1985, Åsteder 1986, Sneglene 1987, Herman 1988, Stempler 1989, Versterålen 1989, Bly 1990, Gutten som ville være en av gutta 1992, Ingens 1992, Den akustiske skyggen 1993, Jubel 1995, Den andre siden av blått 1996, Den misunnelige frisøren 1997, Noen som elsker hverandre 1999, Falleferdig himmel 1999, Pasninger 1999, Kongen som ville ha mer enn en krone 1999, Under en sort paraply 1999, Pinnsvinsol 2000, Mann for sin katt 2000, Halvbroren 2001, Maskeblomstfamilien 2003, Sanger og steiner 2003, SATS 2003, Oscar Wildes heis 2004, Modellen 2005, Norske omveier i blues og bilder 2005, Saabyes sirkus 2006, Den arktiske drømmen 2007, Ordiord 2007, Bisettelsen 2008, Visning 2009, Men buicken står der fremdeles 2009, Bernhard Hvals forsnakkelser 2010, Sluk 2012, Stedsans 2013. *Address:* c/o Cappelen Damm AS, 0055 Oslo, Norway. *Telephone:* 22-61-65-00. *E-mail:* rights@cappelendamm.no. *Website:* www.cappelendamm.no.

CHRISTENSEN, Peter; Danish electrician and politician; b. 23 April 1975, Sønderborg; mem. Venstre (Liberal Party), mem. Exec. Cttee 1997–2001, Pres., Venstre Youth Div. 1999–2001; mem. Folketing (Parl.) (Venstre) for South Jutland constituency 2001–07, 2007–15, mem. Taxation Cttee 2001–11 (Deputy Chair. 2005–07), mem. Finance Cttee 2004–09, 2011–15; Auditor of Public Accounts 2010–11; Minister of Taxation March–Oct. 2011, Minister of Defence and Nordic Co-operation 2015–16; Kt of the Dannebrog 2012. *Address:* c/o Ministry of Defence, Holmens Kanal 42, 1060 Copenhagen K, Denmark. *Website:* peterc.dk.

CHRISTIAN, Peter M.; Micronesian politician and head of state; *President;* b. 16 Oct. 1947, Pohnpei; m. Maurina Weilbache; two c.; ed Univ. of Hawaii, USA; started public career as Ponape Dist Employment Service Officer, Pohnpei State Govt 1970–71, Ponape Field Services Officer 1971; mem. Pohnpei State Legislature for Kolonia Town 1975–79; mem. First Federated States of Micronesia Congress (Parl.) for Third Pohnpei Congressional Dist 1979–2007, 2009–15, fmr Speaker of Congress and Chair. numerous Congress Cttees including Cttee on Health, Educ. and Social Affairs, Cttee on Ways and Means, Cttee on Transportation and Communication, Cttee on Resources and Devt; Pres. of Federated States of Micronesia 2015–; Chief Negotiator, Amended Compact of Free Asscn with USA 1999. *Address:* Office of the President, POB PS-53, Palikir, Pohnpei FM 96941, Micronesia (office). *Telephone:* 320-2228 (office). *Fax:* 320-2785 (office). *E-mail:* ppetrus@mail.fm (office). *Website:* www.fsmpio.fm (office).

CHRISTIANSEN, Michael, Cand. jur. (LLM); Danish judge, academic, university administrator and fmr civil servant; *Chairman, Danish Broadcasting Corporation;* b. 5 June 1945; ed Univ. of Copenhagen; Sec., Ministry of Justice 1970–73, Acting Deputy Judge, Silkeborg 1973–74, Head of Section, Ministry of Justice 1974–77, consultant 1978–96, Head of Dept 1986–88, Perm. Sec. 1988–92; coach in constitutional law and criminal law and Assoc. Prof. of Criminal Law, Univ. of Copenhagen 1977–83, External Examiner 1999–; mem. Bd Aarhus Univ. 2009–17, Chair. 2011–17; Man. Dir Royal Danish Theatre 1992–2008; Chair. Sund og Bælt Holding A/S 1991–2000, Øresundskonsortiet 1993–96, Dan Computer Management 1994–2000, J. Lauritzen Holding A/S 1996–2001, A/S Øresundsforbindelsen 1998–2000, A/S Storebæltsforbindelsen 1998–2000, Schmidt Hammer Lassen Architects 2005–, Roshield A/S 2005–, Danish Broadcasting Corporation—DR 2008–; Chair. Laval Cttee, European Spallation Source Cttee; mem. Bd of Dirs A/S Politiken 1993–96, Lead Agency A/S 2007–, Have A/S 2008–, Danske Retursystem A/S 2008–, Boxer AB (Denmark) 2008–; Chair. Naturama, Svendborg, Copenhagen Film Festivals Foundation, Nørre Vosborg Manor Inst.; Vice-Chair. Holstebro Concert Hall; Commdr, First Class, Order of the Dannebrog. *Address:* Danish Broadcasting Corporation, Emil Holms Kanal 20, 0999 Copenhagen, Denmark (office). *Telephone:* 35-20-30-40 (office). *Website:* www.dr.custhelp.com (office).

CHRISTIANSEN, Niels B., BEng, MEng, MBA; Danish business executive; *CEO, Lego Group;* b. 12 April 1966, Sønderborg; m. Lene Grodt Christiansen; one s. one d.; ed Univ. of Southern Denmark, Tech. Univ. of Denmark, INSEAD; Man. Consultant, McKinsey & Co. 1991–95; Vice Pres., Corp. Devt, Hilti Corpn 1995–97; joined GN Netcom 1997, becoming Pres. and CEO 2000–03; Group Exec. Vice Pres., GN Store Nord 2003–04; Exec. Vice Pres. and mem. Exec. Cttee, Danfoss A/S 2004–05, COO 2005–06, Vice-CEO 2006–08, Pres. and CEO 2008–17; CEO LEGO Group 2017–; Chair. Energy Comm. 2017–; mem. Bd of Dirs William Demant Holding A/S 2008–, Axcel, Maersk Group 2014–, Tech. Univ. of Denmark. *Address:* The Lego Group, Aastvej 1, 7190 Billund, Denmark (office). *Telephone:* 79-50-60-70 (office). *Website:* www.lego.com (office).

CHRISTIANSON, Wei Sun, BA, JD; American/Chinese lawyer and business executive; *Co-CEO of Asia Pacific and CEO of China, Morgan Stanley;* b. 21 Aug. 1956; m. Jon Christianson; three s.; ed Amherst Coll. and Columbia Univ. Law School, USA; fmr attorney, Orrick Herrington & Sutcliffe, New York, USA; Assoc. Dir of Corp. Finance, Securities and Futures Comm. of Hong Kong 1993–98; Exec. Dir and Beijing Chief Rep., Morgan Stanley 1998–2002, Co-CEO of Asia Pacific and CEO Morgan Stanley China 2006–; Country Man., China, Credit Suisse First Boston 2002–04, Chair. China 2004–06; mem. Bd of Dirs Estee Lauder Co. 2011–; Co-Chair. Int. Advisory Bd, Columbia Law School; Trustee, Amherst Coll. 2010–; Columbia Law School Medal of Excellence 2006, named by The Wall Street Journal as one of 50 Women to Watch 2006. *Address:* Morgan Stanley China, 2905 First Avenue, Trade Building 2, Jian'guo Gate, Beijing 100004, People's Republic of China (office). *Telephone:* (10) 65058383 (office). *Fax:* (10) 65058220 (office). *E-mail:* infochina@morganstanley.com (office). *Website:* www.morganstanleychina.com (office).

CHRISTIDES, Michael B.; Greek diplomatist and international organization official; *Secretary-General, Permanent International Secretariat, Black Sea Economic Cooperation Organisation;* b. 1949, Thessaloniki; s. of Basil Christides; m.; two d.; ed Aristotelian Univ. of Thessaloniki, Acad. of Int. Law, The Hague, Netherlands; joined Ministry for Foreign Affairs (MFA) 1976, becoming Amb. to Bulgaria 2000–02, to Turkey 2002–05, to Argentina 2007–11, Special Envoy of Minister for Foreign Affairs on Balkan Issues 2008, fmr Political Dir for South East Europe, Dir-Gen. for Int. Orgs., Int. Security & Cooperation, Dir-Gen. for Int. Econ. Affairs 2012–14 (retd); Nat. Coordinator of Hellenic Chairmanship-in-Office of Black Sea Econ. Cooperation Org. 2014–15, Sec.-Gen., Perm. Int. Sec., Black Sea Econ. Cooperation Org. 2015–; Grand Commdr, Order of Phoenix (Greece), Order of Madara Horseman – First Class (Bulgaria), Gran Cruz, Orden de Mayo (Argentina). *Address:* Office of the Secretary-General, Black Sea Economic Cooperation Organisation, Sakıp Sabancı Cad., Müşir Fuad Paşa Yalısı, Eski Tersane 34460, İstinye, Istanbul, Turkey (office). *Telephone:* (212) 229-63-30 (office). *Fax:* (212) 229-63-36 (office). *E-mail:* info@bsec-organization.org (office). *Website:* www.bsec-organization.org (office).

CHRISTIE, Christopher (Chris) James, BA, JD; American lawyer, politician and state governor; b. 6 Sept. 1962, Mendham, NJ; s. of Bill Christie and Sandra Christie; m. Mary Pat Foster 1986; two s. two d.; ed Livingston High School, Univ. of Delaware, Seton Hall Univ. School of Law; admitted to State Bar of NJ and Bar of US Dist Court, Dist of NJ 1987; Assoc., Dughi, Hewit & Palatucci (law firm), Cranford, NJ 1987–93, Pnr 1993–2002, registered as lobbyist 1998–2001; mem. Morris Co., NJ Bd of Chosen Freeholders 1995–97; unsuccessful bid for a seat in NJ Gen. Ass. 1995; US Attorney for Dist of NJ, US Dept Justice 2002–08; Gov. of New Jersey 2010–18; Chair. Opioid and Drug Abuse Comm. 2017–; mem. Bd of Trustees, Daytop Village-NJ, Mendham 1998–2002; Officer, Christie Family Foundation 2001–; Chair. Republican Governors Asscn 2013–; Chair. Morris Co. Insurance Comm.; mem. Bd of Dirs United Way of Morris Co., Family Services, Morris Co., Morris Bd Social Services; mem. ABA, NJ State Bar Asscn (fmr mem. Election Law Cttee); Republican. *Address:* c/o Office of National Drug Control Policy, The White House, 1600 Pennsylvania Ave, NW, Washington, DC 20500, USA (office). *Telephone:* (202) 456-1111 (office). *Website:* www.usa.gov/federal-agencies/office-of-national-drug-control-policy (office).

CHRISTIE, Julie (Frances); British actress; b. 14 April 1940, Assam, India; d. of Frank St John Christie and Rosemary Christie (née Ramsden); ed Brighton Technical Coll. and Central School of Speech and Drama; Dr hc (Warwick) 1994; Motion Picture Laurel Award, Best Dramatic Actress 1967, Motion Picture Herald Award 1967; Fellow BAFTA 1997. *Films include:* Crooks Anonymous 1962, The Fast Lady 1962, Billy Liar 1963, Young Cassidy 1964, Darling (Acad. Award 1966, BAFTA Award for Best Actress, Laurel Award for Top Female Dramatic Performance, Best Actress, Nat. Bd of Review, New York Film Critics Circle) 1964, Doctor Zhivago (Donatello Award) 1965, Fahrenheit 451 1966, Far From the Madding Crowd 1966, Petulia 1967, In Search of Gregory 1969, The Go-Between 1971, McCabe & Mrs. Miller 1972, Don't Look Now 1973, Shampoo 1974, Demon Seed, Heaven Can Wait 1978, Memoirs of a Survivor 1980, Gold 1980, The Return of the Soldier 1981, Les Quarantièmes rugissants 1981, The Animals Film (voice-over) 1981, Heat and Dust 1982, The Gold Diggers 1984, Miss Mary 1986, The Tattooed Memory 1986, Power 1987, Fathers and Sons 1988, Dadah is Death (TV) 1988, Fools of Fortune 1989, McCabe and Mrs Miller 1990, The Railway Station 1992, Hamlet 1995, Afterglow (New York Film Critics Circle Award for Best Actress, Best Actress, Nat. Soc. of Film Critics, Best Actress, San Sebastián Int. Film Festival) 1998, The Miracle Maker (voice) 2000, No Such Thing 2001, Snapshots 2001, I'm With Lucy 2002, A Letter to True 2003, Harry Potter and the Prisoner of Azkaban 2004, Finding Neverland 2004, Troy 2004, The Secret Life of Words (Best Actress, Dublin Film Critics' Circle, Nat. Bd of Review, New York Film Critics Circle, Houston Film Critics Soc., Nat. Soc. of Film Critics, Golden Globe Award for Best Actress) 2005, Away From Her (Best Actress, Nat. Bd of Review 2007, Golden Globe for Best Actress in a Drama 2008, Outstanding Performance by a Female Actor in a Leading Role, Screen Actors Guild 2008) 2007, New York, I Love You 2009, Glorious 39 2009, The Company You Keep 2010, Red Riding Hood 2011, The Company You Keep 2012. *Plays:* Old Times 1995, Suzanna Andler 1997, Afterglow 1998.

CHRISTIE, Linford, OBE; British athletics coach, business executive and fmr athlete; b. 2 April 1960, Saint Andrew, Jamaica; s. of James Christie and Mabel Christie; one d.; fmr cashier, Wandsworth Co-op; mem. Thames Valley Harriers; winner, UK 100m 1985, 1987, 200m 1985 (tie), 1988; winner, Amateur Athletics Asscn 100m 1986, 1988, 200m 1988; winner, European 100m record; silver medal, 100m, Seoul Olympic Games 1988, gold medal, 100m, Commonwealth Games 1990, Olympic Games 1992, World Athletic Championships 1993, Weltklasse Grand Prix Games 1994, European Games 1994; winner, 100m Zurich 1995; Capt. British Athletics Team 1995–97; officially retd 1997; Co-founder (with Colin Jackson q.v. and Man. Dir Nuff Respect sports man. co. 1992–; successful coach to prominent UK athletes, including Katharine Merry and Darren Campbell; Hon. MSc (Portsmouth) 1993; Male Athlete of the Year 1988, 1992, BBC Sports Personality of the Year 1993, inducted into London Youth Games Hall of Fame 2009, inducted into England Athletics Hall of Fame 2010. *Television includes:* participant in I'm a Celebrity… Get Me Out of Here! (ITV) 2010. *Publications:*

Linford Christie (autobiog.) 1989, To be Honest With You 1995, A Year in the Life of Linford Christie 1996. *Leisure interests:* cooking, gardening. *Address:* Nuff Respect, 1 Constable's Boatyard, 15 Thames Street, Hampton, Middx, TW12 2EW, England (office). *Telephone:* (20) 8891-4145 (office). *Fax:* (20) 8891-4140 (office). *E-mail:* nuff_respect@msn.com (office). *Website:* www.nuff-respect.co.uk (office); www.iaaf.org/athletes/great-britain-ni/linford-christie-496.

CHRISTIE, Rt Hon. Perry Gladstone, LLB; Bahamian lawyer and politician; b. 21 Aug. 1943, Nassau; s. of Gladstone L. Christie and Naomi Christie; m. Bernadette Hanna; two s. one d.; ed Eastern Senior School, New Providence, Univs of London and Birmingham, UK; fmr athlete; attorney with McKinney Bancroft and Hughes; f. own law practice Christie Ingraham & Co. (now Christie Davis & Co.); mem. Bd of Dirs Broadcasting Corpn of The Bahamas 1973; mem. Progressive Liberal Party (PLP), Co-Deputy Leader 1993–97, Leader 1997–; Senator 1974–77; mem. House of Ass. (PLP) for Centerville and Farm Road, New Providence 1977–2017; Minister of Health and Nat. Insurance 1977–82, of Tourism 1977–82, of Agric., Trade and Industry 1990–93; Prime Minister and Minister of Finance 2002–07, 2012–17. *Address:* Progressive Liberal Party, Sir Lynden Pindling Centre, PLP House, Farrington Road, PO Box N-547, Nassau, Bahamas (office). *Telephone:* 325-5492 (office). *Fax:* 328-0808 (office). *Website:* www.myplp.com (office).

CHRISTIE, William Lincoln, BA; French/American harpsichordist, conductor and musicologist; *Founder and Musical Director, Les Arts Florissants;* b. 19 Dec. 1944, Buffalo, NY; s. of William Christie and Ida Jones; ed Harvard Univ., Yale School of Music, studied harpsichord with Ralph Kirkpatrick, Kenneth Gilbert and David Fuller; moved to France 1970; mem. Five Centuries Ensemble 1971–75, René Jacobs' Concerto vocale 1976–80; Founder and Musical Dir Les Arts Florissants vocal and instrumental ensemble 1979–; Prof., Conservatoire Nat. Supérieur de Musique, Paris 1982–95; conducts his own orchestra as well as many leading int. orchestras (Orchestra of the Age of Enlightenment, Glyndebourne 1996, 2005, Berlin Philharmonic, Zurich Opera, Opéra Nat. de Lyon); career highlights include Handel's Theodora, Glyndebourne 1996, Handel's Semele, Aix-en-Provence Festival 1996, Rameau's Hippolyte et Aricie, Paris 1996–97, Lully's Thésée, Barbican, London 1998, Monteverdi's Il ritorno d'Ulisse in patria, Aix-en-Provence 2002, Hercules, Aix-en-Provence 2004, Rameau's Les Paladins, Théâtre du Châtelet 2004, 2006, Brooklyn Acad. of Music 2006, Il Sant'Alessio 2007, The Fairy Queen 2010, Così fan tutte at the Met, etc., Lully's Atys at the Opéra Comique and worldwide tour 2011, La Didone (Théâtre de Caen, Théâtre des Champs Elysées) 2011–12, Charpentier's David et Jonathas (Aix, Edinburgh, Opéra Comique, Théâtre de Caen, Brooklyn Acad. of Music) 2012–13, Rameau's Hippolyte et Aricie, Glyndebourne 2013; Pres. Jury, Concours de Chant Baroque de Chimay, Belgium 2000–; cr. Le Jardin des Voix acad. for young singers in Caen, int. tours 2002, 2005, 2007, 2009, 2011, 2013; Artist-in-Residence (with Les Arts Florissants), Juilliard School, New York 2007–; mem. RAM, Acad. des Beaux-Arts 2008, Institut de France 2010; Commdr, Légion d'honneur 2010; Officier des Arts et des Lettres, Grand Officier, Ordre National du Mérite; Hon. DMus (State Univ. of New York, Buffalo) 1999, (Juilliard School); Prix Edison, Netherlands 1981, Grand prix du disque, Prix mondial de Montreux, Switzerland 1982, Gramophone Record of the Year, UK 1984, 1995, 1997, Deutscher Schallplattenpreis 1987, Grand prix de la Critique (best opera performance) 1987, Prix Opus, USA 1987, Prix int. de musique classique 1992, Prix Grand Siècle Laurent Perrier 1997, Grammy Award for Handel's Acis and Galatea 2000, Grammy and Cannes Classical Awards for Alcina 2001, Harvard Univ. Arts Medal 2002, Royal Philarmonic Award 2003, Liliane Bettencourt Choral Singing Prize, Acad. des Beaux Arts 2004, Prix Georges Pompidou 2005. *Recordings:* numerous recordings including all works for harpsichord by Rameau, works by Monteverdi, Purcell, Handel, Couperin, Charpentier, Desmarest, Mozart, etc. *Leisure interests:* gardening, old houses, cooking. *Address:* Les Arts Florissants, 46 rue Fortuny, 75017 Paris (office); Secrétariat de William Christie, 11 rue de la Cerisaie, 75004 Paris (office); 32 rue du Bâtiment, Thiré, 85210 Sainte-Hermine, France (home). *Telephone:* 1-43-87-98-88 (Arts Florissants) (office). *E-mail:* w.christie@orange.fr (home). *Website:* www.arts-florissants.com (office); www.jardindewilliamchristie.fr.

CHRISTO; American (naturalized) artist; b. (Christo Vladimirov Javacheff), 13 June 1935, Gabrovo, Bulgaria; m. Jeanne-Claude Denat de Guillebon (Jeanne-Claude) (died 2009); one s.; ed Acad. of Fine Arts, Sofia and Vienna; went to Paris 1958; mem. Nat. Acad. of Design 2011; hon. degrees (Franklin & Marshall Coll.) 2008, (Occidental Coll.) 2011; Doris C. Freedman Award for Public Art, Praemium Imperiale 1995, Achievement in Contemporary Sculpture Award, Int. Sculpture Center, Hamilton, NJ 2004, Best Project in a Public Space for The Gates, Central Park, New York 1979–2005, AICA-USA Awards 2006. *Solo works include:* Wrapped Objects 1958; project for Packaging of Public Building 1960; works with Jeanne-Claude 1961–: Stacked Oil Barrels and Dockside Packages, Cologne 1961–, Iron Curtain Wall of Oil Barrels blocking rue Visconti, Paris, Wrapping a Girl, London 1962, Showcases 1963, Store Front 1964, Air Package and Wrapped Tree, Eindhoven, Netherlands 1966, 42,390 cubic foot Package, Walker Art Center, Minneapolis School of Art 1966, Wrapped Kunsthalle, Bern 1968, 5,600 cubic m. Package for Kassel Documenta 4 1968, Wrapped Museum of Contemporary Art, Chicago 1969, Wrapped Coast, Little Bay, Sydney, Australia, 1969, Valley Curtain, Grand Hogback, Rifle, Colo, suspended fabric curtain 1970–72, Running Fence, Calif. 1972–76, Wrapped Roman Wall, Rome 1974, Ocean Front, Newport 1974, Wrapped Walk-Ways, Kansas City 1977–78, Surrounded Islands, Biscayne Bay, Miami, Fla 1980–83, The Pont Neuf Wrapped, Paris 1975–85, The Umbrellas, Japan-USA 1984–91, Wrapped Reichstag, Berlin 1971–95, Wrapped Trees, Fondation Beyeler and Berower Park, Riehen, Switzerland 1997–98, The Wall, 13,000 oil barrels, Gasometer, Oberhausen, Germany, indoor installation 1999, The Gates, Central Park, New York City 1979–2005, Over the River, Colo, The Mastaba, UAE, Big Air Package, Gasometer Oberhausen 2013, The Floating Piers, Lake Iseo nr Brescia (northern Italy) 2016. *Website:* christojeanneclaude.net.

CHRISTODOULAKIS, Nikos M., EngDipl, MPhil, PhD; Greek engineer, academic and politician; *Professor of Economic Analysis, Athens University of Economics;* b. 27 Oct. 1952, Chania, Crete; ed Nat. Tech. Univ. of Athens and Univ. of Cambridge, UK; fmr mem. Euro-Communist party, linked with student uprising at Athens polytechnic 1973; Sr Research Officer, Dept of Applied Econs, Univ. of Cambridge 1984–86; Fellow, European Univ. of Florence 1989–90; apptd Prof. of Econ. Analysis, Athens Univ. of Econs 1990, Vice-Rector 1992–94, Prof. of Econ. Analysis 2007–; fmr Visiting Research Fellow, London Business School, Tinbergen Inst.; Prof. of Econs, Grad. School, Charles Univ., Prague 1992–93, Univ. of Cyprus 1996; Sec.-Gen. Research and Tech. 1993–96; Econ. Adviser to Prime Minister 1996; Deputy Minister of Finance 1996–2000; Minister of Devt with portfolios of Energy, Industry, Tech., Tourism and Commerce 2000–01; Minister of Economy and Finance 2001–04; mem. Parl. (Socialist Party) for Chania, Crete 2004–07; First Prize, Greek Math. Soc. 1970, Winbolt Prize 1985. *Publications include:* The New Terrain for Growth (in Greek) 1998, Growth, Employment and the Environment 2002, The Pendulum of Convergence (in Greek) 2006, several books and articles on econ. policy, business cycles, growth, forecasting and econ. models. *Leisure interest:* art, swimming, trekking. *Address:* Athens University of Economics and Business, 76 Patission Street, Athens 10434 (office); 9 Kolokotroni Street, Athens 10562, Greece (office). *Telephone:* (210) 3313488 (office). *Fax:* (210) 3313428 (office). *E-mail:* nchris@aueb.gr (office).

CHRISTODOULIDES, Nikos, BA, DSc; Cypriot diplomatist, politician and academic; *Minister of Foreign Affairs;* b. 6 Dec. 1973, Paphos; m. Philippa Karsera; four d.; ed Queens Coll., City Univ. of New York, New York Univ., Univ. of Athens; joined Ministry of Foreign Affairs (MFA) 1999, roles include Dir, Office of the Minister of Foreign Affairs, Spokesperson of Cyprus Presidency of the Council of the EU, Brussels, Deputy Chief of Mission, Embassy in Athens, Dir, Office of the MFA Perm. Sec., Consul Gen. at High Comm. of Cyprus in London, Dir, Diplomatic Office of the Pres. of Cyprus 2013–18, Govt Spokesman 2014–18, Minister of Foreign Affairs 2018–; Lecturer and Research Assoc., Dept of History and Archaeology, Univ. of Cyprus 2007–10. *Publications:* numerous articles in domestic and int. journals; books: Plans for Solution of the Cyprus Problem 1948-1978 2009, Relations between Athens and Nicosia and the Cyprus Problem 1977-1988 2013. *Address:* Ministry of Foreign Affairs, Presidential Palace Ave, 1447 Nicosia, Cyprus (office). *Telephone:* 22651000 (office). *Fax:* 22661881 (office). *E-mail:* info@mfa.gov.cy (office). *Website:* www.mfa.gov.cy (office).

CHRISTODOULOU, Christodoulos, BA, BL, PhD; Cypriot business consultant, fmr government official and fmr central banker; b. 13 April 1939, Avgorou; m.; one d.; ed Pedagogical Acad. of Cyprus, Nicosia, Pantios High School of Political Sciences, Athens and Aristotelian Univ. of Salonica, Greece, Univ. of Wales, UK; Dir Govt Printing Office 1972–85; Perm. Sec., Ministry of Labour and Social Insurance 1985–89; Perm. Sec., Ministry of Agric. and Natural Resources 1989–94; Minister of Finance 1994–99, of the Interior 1999–2002; Gov. of Cen. Bank of Cyprus 2002–07; business consultant 2007–; several awards. *Publications include:* several books and articles on legal, social, econ. and political matters. *Leisure interests:* reading, gardening. *Address:* 20 Ionos Street, Office 501, 2406 Nicosia (office); 12 Pritagora Street, 2406 Nicosia, Cyprus (home). *Telephone:* 22673400 (office). *Fax:* 22670400 (office). *E-mail:* a.c.consultants@cytanet.com.cy (office).

CHRISTODOULOU, Demetrios, MA, PhD; Greek/American mathematician, physicist and academic; *Emeritus Professor of Mathematics and Physics, Eidgenössische Technische Hochschule (ETH), Zürich;* b. 19 Oct. 1951, Athens; s. of Lambros Christodoulou and Maria Christodoulou; m. Nikoleta Sigala; two d.; ed Princeton Univ.; Research Fellow, California Inst. of Tech. 1971–72; Prof. of Physics, Univ. of Athens 1972–73; Visiting Scientist, CERN, Geneva, Switzerland 1973–74; at Int. Centre for Theoretical Physics, Trieste 1974–76; Humboldt Fellow, Max Planck Inst., Munich, Germany 1976–81; Visiting mem., Courant Inst. 1981–83, Prof. of Math. 1988–92; Assoc. Prof. of Physics, Syracuse Univ. 1983–85, Prof. of Math. 1985–87; Prof. of Math., Princeton Univ. 1992–2001; Prof. of Math. and Physics, ETH, LOCZürich 2001–17, Emer. Prof. 2017–; Minerva Distinguished Visiting Prof., Princeton Univ. 2017; mem. American Acad. of Arts and Sciences 2001, European Acad. of Sciences 2003, NAS 2012, Academia Europea 2016; Hon. Prof. of Physics, Univ. of Crete 2011; Taxiarchis of the Order of Phoenix 2000; Dr hc (Athens) 1996, (Nat. Tech. Univ., Athens) 2000, (Brown Univ.) 2001, (Univ. of Cyprus) 2003, (Aristotle Univ. of Thessaloniki) 2010; Otto Hahn Medal, Max Planck Soc. 1981, Invited Address, Int. Congress of Mathematicians, Kyoto 1990, Basilis Xanthopoulos Award, GRG Soc. 1991, MacArthur Fellows Award, MacArthur Foundation 1993, Excellence in the Sciences Award, Acad. of Athens 1996, Guggenheim Fellow 1998, Bôcher Memorial Prize, American Soc. 1999, Zenon Prize, Math. Soc. of Cyprus 2000, Leonardo da Vinci Lecturer, Univ. of Milan 2003, Aristeio Bodossaki, Bodossaki Foundation 2006, Mordell Lecturer, Univ. of Cambridge 2007, Tomalla Prize 2008, Chaire d'État, Collège de France 2009, Plenary Lecturer, Int. Congress of Math. Physics, Prague 2009, Shaw Prize in Math. Sciences (co-recipient) 2012, Calderon-Zygmund Lecturer, Univ. of Chicago 2012, Hon. Plaque, Hellenic Soc. of Relativity, Gravitation and Cosmology 2012, Prize in Science, Letters and Arts, Tech. Univ. of Crete 2012, Inaugural Class of Fellows, American Math. Soc. 2012, Honorary Plaque, Hellenic Math. Soc. 2013, Plenary Lecturer, Int. Congress of Mathematicians, Seoul 2014, Nemitsas Prize in Math. 2016. *Publications:* six research monographs: The Global Nonlinear Stability of Minkowski Space 1993, The Action Principle and Partial Differential Equations 2000, The Formation of Shocks in 3-Dimensional Fluids 2007, The Formation of Black Holes in General Relativity 2009, Compressible Flow and Euler's Equations 2014, The Shock Development Problem 2019; numerous papers in professional journals. *Address:* Kennedy Pl 1, Ekali, 145 78 Athens, Greece (home). *Telephone:* (210) 8135595 (office). *E-mail:* demetri@math.ethz.ch (office). *Website:* www.math.ethz.ch/~demetri (office).

CHRISTOFIAS, Demetris, PhD; Cypriot politician and fmr head of state; b. 29 Aug. 1946, Kyrenia; ed Nicosia Commercial Lyceum, Inst. of Social Sciences and Acad. of Social Sciences, Moscow; joined United Democratic Youth Org. (EDON) 1964, elected mem. Central Council 1969, Cen. Organisational Sec. 1974–77, Sec.-Gen. 1977–87; mem. Anorthotiko Komma Ergazomenou Laou (AKEL) 1964–, Sec.-Gen. 1988–; mem. House of Reps representing Kyrenia 1991–, Pres. House of Reps 2001–08; Pres. of Cyprus 2008–13; Dr hc (Univ. of Macedonia) 2004, (Inst. of Int. Relations, Moscow) 2008, (Univ. for Foreigners of Perugia) 2009, (Univ. of Patra-Greece) 2010, (Nat. and Kapodistrian Univ. of Athens) 2010, (European Univ. of Cyprus) 2011, (Univ. of Mariupol, Ukraine) 2011. *Address:* Anorthotiko Komma Ergazomenou Laou, PO Box 21827, 4 East Papaioannou Street, 1075 Nicosia, Cyprus (office). *Telephone:* 22761121 (office). *Fax:* 22761574 (office). *E-mail:* k.e.akel@cytanet.com.cy (office). *Website:* www.akel.org.cy (office).

CHRISTOPHER, Ann, BA, RA, FRBS; British sculptor; b. 4 Dec. 1947, Watford, Herts.; d. of William Christopher and Phyllis Christopher; m. Kenneth Cook 1969; ed Watford Girls' Grammar School, Harrow School of Art, West of England Coll. of Art; works include: bronze sculpture, Castle Park, Bristol 1993, bronze sculpture, Georgetown, Washington, DC, USA 1994, Corten sculpture, Marsh Mills, Plymouth 1996, bronze sculpture for Linklaters, London 1997, bronze sculpture, Great Barrington, USA 1998, Corten sculpture, Port Marine, UK 2001, medal for British Art Medal Soc. 2004; represented by Pangolin, London; RBS Silver Medal for Sculpture of Outstanding Merit 1994, Frampton Award 1996, Otto Beit Medal for Sculpture of Outstanding Merit 1997. *Publications include:* Sculpture and Drawings 1969–89, Sculpture 1989–94, Selected Work 1995–2007, Marks on the Edge of Space 2010, To Know Without Remembering 2013, Drawing Lines 2015, All the Cages Have Open Doors 2016. *Leisure interests:* cinema, travel, architecture. *Address:* c/o Pangolin London, Kings Place, 90 York Way, London, N1 9AG, England (office); c/o Royal Academy of Arts, Burlington House, Piccadilly, London, W1J 0BD, England. *Telephone:* (20) 7520-1480 (office). *Website:* www.pangolinlondon.com (office); www.annchristopher.co.uk.

CHRISTOPHER, Sir (Duncan) Robin Carmichael, Kt, KBE, CMG, MA, MALD; British international organization executive and diplomatist (retd); *Projects Director, GLF Global Leadership Foundation;* b. 13 Oct. 1944, Sussex; m. Merril Stevenson 1980; two d.; ed Keble Coll., Oxford and Fletcher School, Tufts Univ., USA; VSO volunteer in Bolivia; philosophy teacher, Univ. of Sussex 1969; joined FCO 1970, served in Embassy in New Delhi 1972–76, FCO 1976, Deputy High Commr, Lusaka 1980–83, FCO and Cabinet Office 1983–87, Counsellor (Econ. and Commercial), Embassy in Madrid 1987–91, Head, Southern African Dept, FCO 1991–94, Amb. to Ethiopia 1994–97, to Indonesia 1997–2000, to Argentina 2000–04; Sec.-Gen. GLF Global Leadership Foundation 2007–10, Projects Dir 2010–; Trustee, Prospect Burma, Partners for Change (Ethiopia), Redress. *Publications include:* Indonesia in Transition: Democracy or Disintegration? 2000, Justice and Peace 2000 (Czech edn 2007), Remembrance Day 2007. *Leisure interests:* motorcycling, skiing, music. *Address:* GLF Global Leadership Foundation, 25 Knightsbridge, London, SW1X 7LY, England (office). *Telephone:* (20) 7838-7054 (office). *Fax:* (20) 7681-2263 (office). *E-mail:* robin.christopher@g-l-f.org (office); rchristopher2@yahoo.co.uk. *Website:* www.g-l-f.org (office).

CHRISTOV-BAKARGIEV, Carolyn; American/Italian writer, art historian and curator; *Director Castello di Rivoli Museum of Contemporary Art;* b. 2 Dec. 1957, Ridgewood, NJ; m. Cesare Pietroiusti; two d.; ed Univ. of Pisa, Italy; began career as art critic and ind. curator; Sr Curator of Exhbns, P.S.1 Contemporary Art Center, New York 1999–2001; Chief Curator, Castello di Rivoli Museum of Contemporary Art, Turin, Italy 2002–08, Interim Dir 2009, Dir 2016–; Artistic Dir Sydney Biennale 2008; Artistic Dir dOCUMENTA (13), Kassel, Germany 2008–12; Dir GAM-Galleria Civica di Arte Moderna e Contemporanea 2016–17; currently Dir Fondazione Francesco Federico Cerruti; Pernod Ricard Visiting Prof., Goethe-Universität 2013; Menschel Visiting Prof. in Art, The Cooper Union 2013; Leverhulme Visiting Prof., Univ. of Leeds 2013–14; Edith Kreeger Wolf Distinguished Visiting Prof. Northwestern Univ. 2013–15, Distinguished Visiting Prof. 2016–; Guest Prof. Lesley Univ. 2013; Visiting Scholar, Getty Research Inst. 2015; mem. jury, 49th Venice Biennale 2001, mem. Artistic Advisory Bd Istanbul Bienniale 2010–14; Audrey Irmas Award for Curatorial Excellence 2019. *Publications:* Arte Povera (Themes and Movements) 1999, The Moderns 2003, Pierre Huyghe 2004. *Address:* c/o Castello di Rivoli Museum of Contemporary Art, Pazza Mafalda di Savoia, 10098, Turin, Italy (office). *Telephone:* (011) 9565222 (office). *E-mail:* info@castellodirivoli.org (office). *Website:* www.castellodirivoli.org.

CHRONOWSKI, Andrzej; Polish politician; b. 9 April 1961, Grybów, Nowy Sącz Dist; m. Barbara Chronowski; two s.; ed Acad. of Mining and Metallurgy, Kraków; helped organize student strikes in univ. cities including Kraków 1980–81; railway repair factory, Nowy Sącz 1987, later Head of Production, Chair. Employees' Council 1991–93; mem. Solidarity Trade Union; Sec. Solidarity Senate Club Presidium 1993–97; Vice-Marshal of Senate 1997–2000; Chair. Nowy Sącz Region of Social Movt of Solidarity Electoral Action (RS AWS) 1997, Chair. Małopolski Region, Chair. Senators' Club 2001; Chair. Council of Sądecki Club; Minister of State Treasury 2000–01; Senator 1993–2005, Deputy Speaker of 5th term Senate 2001–05; mem. European Parl. (Group of the European People's Party—Christian Democrats and European Democrats) 2004, mem. Cttee on Budgets; mem. Solidarity Trade Union, Nat. Econ. Cttee, Cttee for Human Rights and Lawfulness, Cttee of Initiatives and Legislative Work. *Leisure interests:* skiing, climbing, time with family. *Address:* ul. Pijarska 17A, 33-300 Nowy Sącz S5C2, Poland (office).

CHSHMARITIAN, Karen, PhD; Armenian economist and politician; *Minister of the Economy;* b. 12 Sept. 1959, Yerevan; m.; two c.; ed Yerevan Inst. of Nat. Economy; trained as economist, Georgetown Univ. and Int. Law Inst., Washington, DC 1995; economist, Armenian Br., Research Inst. of Standards and State Planning, USSR 1980; mil. service in Soviet Army 1981–82; Sr Economist, Chief Specialist and Head of Financial Sub-Div., State Supply Cttee, Armenia 1985–90; Deputy Dir-Gen., Haielectramekenametzar (state co.), Armenia 1990–91; Head of Dept, Ministry of Material Resources, Repub. of Armenia 1991–93, Deputy Minister 1993–96; Head of Foreign Trade Dept, Ministry of Trade, Services and Tourism 1996–97; First Deputy Minister, Ministry of Industry and Trade 1997–98; adviser to Azgayin Zhoghov (Nat. Ass.) 1998–99; Minister of Industry and Trade 1999–2000, of Trade and Econ. Devt 2002–07, of the Economy 2014–; mem. Azgayin Zhoghov (Nat. Ass.) (Republican Party of Armenia) 2007–. *Address:* Ministry of the Economy, 0010 Yerevan, M. Mkrtchyan poghots 5 (office); Azgayin Zhoghov (National Assembly), 0095 Yerevan, Marshal Baghramian St 19, Armenia (office). *Telephone:* (10) 59-72-05 (Ministry) (office); (10) 58-82-25 (Nat. Ass.) (office). *Fax:* (10) 52-65-77 (Ministry) (office); (10) 52-98-26 (Nat. Ass.) (office). *E-mail:* secretariat@mineconomy.am (office); karen.chshmaritian@parliament.am (office). *Website:* www.mineconomy.am (office); www.parliament.am (office).

CHU, Bo; Chinese politician; b. Oct. 1944, Tongcheng, Anhui Prov.; ed Tianjin Univ.; joined CCP 1969; Deputy Dir and Deputy Sec. CCP Party Cttee, Yueyang Chemical Works 1975–84; fmr Mayor Yueyang City; Del., 13th CCP Nat. Congress 1987–92; mem. Standing Cttee, CCP Hunan Prov. Cttee 1990, Deputy Sec. CCP Hunan Prov. Cttee 1994–99; Exec. Vice-Gov. Hunan Prov. 1993–94, Vice-Gov. (also Acting Gov.) 1998–99, Gov. 1999–2001; Deputy, 9th NPC 1998–2003; Sec. CCP Cttee of Inner Mongolian Autonomous Region 2001–09; Alt. mem. 15th CCP Cen. Cttee 1997–2002, mem. 16th CCP Cen. Cttee 2002–07, mem. 17th CCP Cen. Cttee 2007–12; Hon. Pres. Hunan Prov. Merchants' Asscn.

CHU, Ivan (Kwok-leung), BSc, MCom; Hong Kong airline industry executive; *Chairman, John Swire & Sons (China) Limited;* b. 1962; ed Univ. of Hong Kong, Univ. of New South Wales, Australia; joined Cathay Pacific Airways Ltd as man. trainee 1984, has served in Hong Kong, China, Taiwan, Thailand and Australia, Gen. Man., Southwest Pacific Div. –2008, Dir of Service Delivery 2008–11, Dir 2011–, Chief Operating Officer 2011–14, CEO, Cathay Pacific Airways Ltd 2014–17; Chair. Hong Kong Dragon Airlines Ltd –2017, AHK Air Hong Kong; Dir John Swire & Sons (HK) Ltd 2014–, Swire Pacific 2014–, Chair. John Swire & Sons (China) Ltd 2017–; fmr Chair. Bd of Airline Rep., Hong Kong; fmr mem. Business Facilitation Advisory Cttee, Govt of Hong Kong. *Address:* John Swire & Sons (China) Ltd, 33/F, Unit 1405 14/F One Indigo, 20 Jiuxianqiao Road, Chaoyang District, Beijing 100016, People's Republic of China (office). *Telephone:* (10) 84863321 (office). *Fax:* (10) 84863221 (office). *Website:* www.swirepacific.com (office).

CHU, Lam Yiu; Chinese business executive; *Chairman and President, Huabao International Holdings Ltd;* b. 1971, Sichuan; m. Lam Kwok Man; f. Huabao Food and Flavours and Fragrances Co. Ltd, Shanghai 1996, made public 2006, now called Huabao International Holdings Ltd, Chair. and Pres. 2004–; Deputy Dir China Asscn of Fragrance, Flavour and Cosmetic Industry, China Food Additive Production and Application Industry Asscn; mem. 4th CPPCC Cttee. *Address:* Huabao International Holdings Ltd, Suite 1103, Central Plaza, 18 Harbour Road., Wanchai, Hong Kong Special Administrative Region, People's Republic of China (office). *Telephone:* 28276677 (office). *Fax:* 28278866 (office). *Website:* www.huabao.com.hk (office).

CHU, Li-luan (Eric), BBA, MA, PhD; Taiwanese politician; b. 7 June 1961; ed Nat. Taiwan Univ., New York Univ., USA; Asst Prof., CUNY, USA 1990–92; Assoc. Prof., later Prof., Nat. Taiwan Univ. 1992–2001; mem., Legis. Yuan (Parl.) 1999–2001, Convener, Budget Cttee 2000, Convener, Finance Cttee 2001; Magistrate, Taoyuan Co. 2001–09; Vice-Premier of Taiwan 2009–10; Minister of the Consumer Protection Comm. 2009–10; Mayor of New Taipei City 2010–15; mem. Kuomintang (KMT), Chair. 2015–16; KMT cand. in presidential election 2016. *Address:* Kuomintang, 232–234 Bade Rd, Sec. 2, Taipei 10492, Taiwan (office). *Telephone:* (2) 87711234 (office). *Website:* www.kmt.org.tw (office).

CHU, Paul Ching-Wu, BS, MS, PhD, JP; American (b. Chinese) physicist and academic; *T.L.L. Temple Chair of Science, Professor of Physics and Founding Director and Chief Scientist, Texas Center for Superconductivity, University of Houston;* b. 2 Dec. 1940, Hunan, China; ed Cheng-Kung Univ., Taiwan, Fordham Univ., Univ. of California, San Diego; Teaching Asst, Fordham Univ. 1963–65; Research Asst, Univ. of Calif., San Diego 1965–68; mem. Tech. Staff, Bell Labs, Murray Hill, NJ 1968–70; Asst Prof. of Physics, Cleveland State Univ. 1970–73, Assoc. Prof. 1973–75, Prof. 1975–79; Resident Research Assoc., Argonne Nat. Lab., Argonne, Ill. 1972; Visiting Scientist, Stanford Univ., Hansens Physics Lab. 1973; Visiting Staff mem., Los Alamos Scientific Lab., NM 1975–80; Prof. of Physics, Univ. of Houston, Tex. 1979–, also Dir Magnetic Information Research Lab. 1984–88, Dir Space Vacuum Epitaxy Center 1986–88, M.D. Anderson Chair. of Physics 1987–89, Dir Tex. Center for Superconductivity 1987–2001 (Exec. Dir 2005–11, Founding Dir and Chief Scientist 2011–), T.L.L. Temple Chair. of Science 1987–; Pres. and Prof. of Physics, Hong Kong Univ. of Science and Tech. 2001–09, Pres. Emer. and Univ. Prof. Emer. 2009–; Visiting Miller Research Prof., Univ. of Calif., Berkeley 1991; Prin. Investigator, Lawrence Berkeley Nat. Lab., Berkeley 1999–2005 (Guest Scientist 2005–); Adjunct Prof. of Physics, Sharif Univ. of Tech., Tehran, Iran 2014–; mem. Editorial Bd numerous journals, including Indian Journal of Pure and Applied Physics 1992–, Brazilian Journal of Physics 1995–, Science in China 1997–, Chinese Science Bulletin 1997–, Materials Today Physics 2017–; mem. numerous advisory bds and cttees, including Coalition for the Commercial Application of Superconductors 1989–, Int. Advisory Cttee, Innovative Center for Frontier Sciences, Ministry of Educ., China 2012 (apptd); mem. AAAS 1987, Academia Sinica 1988, NAS 1989, American Acad. of Arts and Sciences 1989, RSA 1989, Electromagnetic Acad. 1990, Acad. of Medicine, Eng and Science of Texas 2004; Foreign mem. Chinese Acad. of Sciences 1996, Russian Acad. of Eng 2005; Founding mem. Acad. of Sciences of Hong Kong 2015; Fellow, American Physical Soc. 1978, Tex. Acad. of Sciences 1992, Hong Kong Inst. of Science 2011; Charter Fellow, Nat. Acad. of Inventors 2013; Hon. Pres. Jiaxing Univ. 2006; Hon. Prof., Physics Inst., Chinese Acad. of Sciences 1979, Zhongshan Univ. 1988, Nankai Univ. 1991, Chinese Univ. of Science and Tech. 1991, Nanjing Univ. 1996, Dongnan Univ. 2003, Nat. Tsinghua Univ. 2009; Hon. Citizen, State of Texas 1987, City of Houston 1987; Hon. Chancellor, Taiwan Comprehensive Univ. System 2012–; Dr hc (Chinese Univ. of Hong Kong) 1988, (Northwestern Univ.) 1988, (Fordham) 1988, (Florida Int. Univ.) 1989, (State Univ. of New York at Farmingdale) 1989, (Whittier Coll.) 1991, (Hong Kong Baptist Univ.) 1999, (Providence Univ.) 2005, (Univ. of Macau) 2006, (Loughborough) 2007; numerous awards including Grumman Corpn Leroy Randle Grumman Medal for Outstanding Scientific Achievement 1987, NASA Achievement Award 1987, Univ. of Houston Faculty Research Award 1987, New York Acad. of Sciences Physical and Math. Science Award 1987, APS Int. Prize for New Materials 1988, Nat. Medal of Science 1988, NAS Comstock Award 1988, World Cultural Council Medal of Scientific Merit 1989, St Martin de Porres Award 1990, Texas Instruments Founders' Prize 1990, Int. Conf. on Materials and Mechanisms of Superconductivity, High Temperature Superconductors Bernd Matthias Prize 1994, Sharif Univ. Award 1999, Asscn of American-Chinese Professionals (AACP) Distinguished Achievement Award 2001, American Asscn of Eng Socs John Fritz Medal 2001, Univ. of Houston Esther Farfel Award 2000, Prize Ettore Majorana – Erice/Science for Peace 2007, Chinese Inst. of Engineers Lifetime Achievement Award 2008, Hong Kong Inst. of Engineers Hall of Fame Award 2010, Int. Leadership Foundation Inspirational Award 2014, Max Swerdlow Award for Sustained Service to the Applied Superconductivity Community, IEEE 2014. *Publications include:* more than 690 scientific papers in professional journals. *Address:* Texas Center for Superconductivity, University of Houston, 3369 Cullen Blvd, Room 202, Houston, TX 77204-5002, USA (office). *Telephone:* (713) 743-8222 (home). *Fax:*

(713) 743-8201 (office). *E-mail:* cwchu@uh.edu (office). *Website:* www.uh.edu/nsm/physics/people/profiles/paul-chu (office).

CHU, Steven, BA, PhD; American physicist, academic and government official; b. 28 Feb. 1948, St Louis; s. of Ju Chin Chu and Ching Chen Li; m. 1st Lisa Chu-Thielbar; two s.; m. 2nd Jean Fetter 1997; ed Garden City High School, Univ. of Rochester, Univ. of California, Berkeley; Post-doctoral Fellow, Univ. of California, Berkeley 1976–78; with Bell Labs, Murray Hill, New Jersey 1978–83, Head of Quantum Electronics Research Dept, Bell Labs, Holmdell, New Jersey 1983–87; Prof. of Physics and Applied Physics, Stanford Univ. 1987–2004, Frances and Theodore Geballe Prof. of Physics and Applied Physics 1990–2004, Chair. Physics Dept 1990–93, 1999–2001; apptd Prof. of Physics and Prof. of Molecular and Cell Biology, Univ. of California, Berkeley 2004, Dir Lawrence Berkeley Nat. Lab. 2004–08; US Sec. of Energy, Washington, DC 2009–13; Visiting Prof., Collège de France 1990; Fellow, American Physics Soc. (Chair. Laser Science Topical Group 1989), Optical Soc. of America, American Acad. of Arts and Sciences; Woodrow Wilson Fellow 1970, NSF Doctoral Fellow 1970–74; mem. NAS, American Philosophical Soc., Academia Sinica; Foreign mem. Chinese Acad. of Sciences, Korean Acad. of Science and Eng; Herbert P. Broida Prize for laser spectroscopy 1987, King Faisal Prize for Science 1993, Schawlow Prize 1994, Meggars Award 1994, Humboldt Sr Scientist Award 1995, Science for Art Prize 1995, shared Nobel Prize for Physics 1997 for developing methods of cooling matter to very low temperatures using lasers. *Publications include:* numerous papers on atomic physics and laser spectroscopy. *Leisure interests:* baseball, swimming, cycling, tennis. *Address:* c/o Department of Energy, Forrestal Building, 1000 Independence Avenue, SW, Washington, DC 20585, USA.

CHUA, Amy, AB, JD; American lawyer, academic and writer; *John M. Duff, Jr Professor of Law, Yale Law School;* b. 26 Oct. 1962, Champaign, Ill.; m. Jed Rubenfeld; two d.; ed Harvard Univ., Harvard Law School; served as Exec. Ed. Harvard Law Review while at Harvard Law School; clerked for Chief Judge Patricia M. Wald on US Court of Appeals, DC Circuit 1987–88; Assoc., Cleary, Gottlieb, Steen & Hamilton, New York 1988–93; Assoc. Prof. of Law, Duke Univ. 1994–99, Prof. of Law 1999–2001; Prof. of Law, Yale Univ. 2001–05, John M. Duff, Jr Prof. of Law 2005–; Visiting Prof. of Law, Columbia Univ. 1999, Stanford Univ. 2000, New York Univ. School of Law 2000. *Publications include:* World On Fire: How Exporting Free Market Democracy Breeds Ethnic Hatred and Global Instability 2002, Day of Empire: How Hyperpowers Rise to Global Dominance—and Why They Fall 2009, Battle Hymn of the Tiger Mother 2011, The Triple Package: How Three Unlikely Traits Explain the Rise and Fall of Cultural Groups in America (with Jed Rubenfeld) 2014. *Address:* c/o Juliana Kiyan, The Penguin Press, 375 Hudson Street, New York, NY 10014, USA (office); Yale Law School, PO Box 208215, New Haven, CT 06520, USA (office). *E-mail:* amy.chua@yale.edu (office). *Website:* www.law.yale.edu (office); amychua.com.

CHUA, Nam-Hai, PhD, FRS; Singaporean biologist and academic; *Andrew W. Mellon Professor and Head, Laboratory of Plant Molecular Biology, Rockefeller University;* b. 8 April 1944; m. Suat-Choo Pearl Chua 1970; two d.; ed Univ. of Singapore and Harvard Univ.; Lecturer, Dept of Biochemistry, Univ. of Singapore 1969–71; Research Assoc., Dept of Cell Biology, Rockefeller Univ., USA 1971–73, Asst Prof., Dept of Cell Biology 1973–77, Prof. and Head, Lab. of Plant Molecular Biology 1988–, Andrew W. Mellon Prof. 1988–; consultant, Shanghai Research Centre for Life Sciences, Chinese Acad. of Sciences 1996–, Global Tech. Centre and Nutrition, Monsanto Co. 1997–; numerous consultancies and bd memberships; mem. Academia Sinica (Taiwan); Foreign mem. Chinese Acad. of Sciences; Hon. mem. Japan Biochemical Soc., Japanese Soc. of Plant Physiologists; Singapore Nat. Science and Tech. Gold Medal 1998, Singapore Public Administration Gold Medal 2002, Int. Prize for Biology, Japan Soc. for the Promotion of Science 2005, Lawrence Bogorad Award for Excellence in Plant Biology Research, American Soc. for Plant Biologists 2010. *Publications:* more than 400 scientific publs. *Leisure interests:* squash, skiing. *Address:* Laboratory of Plant Molecular Biology, Rockefeller University, 1230 York Avenue, New York, NY 10065, USA (office). *Telephone:* (212) 327-8126 (office). *E-mail:* nam-hai.chua@rockefeller.edu (office). *Website:* www.rockefeller.edu/research/faculty/labheads/Nam-HaiChua (office).

CHUA, Sock Koong, CPA; Singaporean accountant and telecommunications industry executive; *Group CEO, Singapore Telecommunications Limited (SingTel);* m.; two d.; ed Univ. of Singapore; Certified Public Accountant and Chartered Financial Analyst; joined Singapore Telecommunications Ltd (SingTel) as Treas. in 1989, Chief Financial Officer 1999–2006, Group Chief Financial Officer and CEO Int. Feb.–Oct. 2006, Deputy Group CEO 2006–07, Group CEO 2007–; mem. Bd of Dirs JTC Corpn, Bharti Tele-Ventures Ltd; Trustee, Singapore Man. Univ.; FinanceAsia magazine's Best Chief Financial Officer 2004, Best Managed Companies poll 2002, 2003, 2004. *Leisure interest:* keeping fit. *Address:* SingTel, 31 Exeter Road, Comcentre #19-00, Singapore 239732 (office). *Telephone:* 68383388 (office). *Fax:* 67328248 (office). *E-mail:* contact@singtel.com (office). *Website:* info.singtel.com (office).

CHUAN, Leekpai, LLB; Thai lawyer and politician; b. 28 July 1938, Muang Dist, Trang Prov.; ed Trang Wittaya School, Silapakorn Pre-Univ. and Thammasat Univ.; studied for two years with Bar Asscn of Thailand; mem. Parl. for Trang Prov. 1969–; Deputy Minister of Justice 1975; Deputy Minister of Justice and Minister, Prime Minister's Office 1976; Minister of Justice 1980, of Commerce 1981, of Agric. and Co-operatives 1982–83, of Educ. 1983–86; Speaker, House of Reps 1986–88; Minister of Public Health 1988–89, of Agric. and Co-operatives 1990–91; Deputy Prime Minister 1990, Prime Minister of Thailand 1992–95, 1997–2001; Leader Prachatipat (Democrat Party—DP) 1992–2003; Leader of Opposition 1995–96, 1996–97, 2001–; Minister of Defence 1997–2001; Vice-Pres. Prince of Songkhla Univ. Council; Kt Grand Cordon (Special Class) of the Most Noble Order of the Crown of Thailand 1981, Kt Grand Cordon (Special Class) of the Most Exalted Order of the White Elephant 1982, Grand Collar (Raja) of the Order of Sikatuna (Philippines) 1993, Kt Grand Commdr (Second Class, Higher Grade) of the Most Illustrious Order of Chula Chom Klao 1998, Grand Cross, Order of the Sun (Peru) 1999, Grand Cross, Order of Christ (Portugal) 1999, Grand Cross, Gen. Order of José Dolores Estrada, Batalla de San Jacinto (Nicaragua) 2000, Grand Cross, Order of the Star of Romania 2000; six hon. degrees. *Leisure interest:* drawing. *Address:* Prachatipat (Democrat Party), 67 Thanon Setsiri, Samsen Nai, Phyathai, 10400, Bangkok 10300 (office); 471/2 Rajaprasop Road, Magasasam, Rajatheri District, Metropolitan 10400, Bangkok, Thailand (home). *Telephone:* (2) 278-4042 (office); (2) 245-4415 (home). *Fax:* (2) 279-6086; (2) 278-4218 (office). *E-mail:* admin@democrat.or.th (office). *Website:* www.democrat.or.th (office); www.chuan.org (office).

CHUBACHI, Ryoji, BA, MA, PhD; Japanese business executive; *President, National Institute of Advanced Industrial Science and Technology;* b. 4 Sept. 1947; ed Tohoku Univ.; joined Sony Corpn 1977, with Sony Magnetic Products Inc., Ala, USA 1989–92, Gen. Man. Video Tape Div., Recording Media Products Group, Tokyo 1992–94, Gen. Man. Video Tape Dept, Recording Media Div. 1994–98, Pres. Recording Media Co. 1999–2002, Pres. Core Tech. & Network Co. 2002–03, Pres. Micro Systems Network Co. 2003–04, COO in charge of Micro Systems Network Co. June 2004, Pres. Production Strategy Group 2004–05, mem. Bd of Dirs Sony Corpn 2005–, also Rep. Corp. Exec. Officer 2005–, Pres. 2005–09, CEO Global Electronics Business 2005–09, Vice-Chair. and Rep. Corp. Exec. Officer 2009–13; Pres. Nat. Inst. of Advanced Industrial Science and Tech. 2013–; mem. Asscn of Radio Industries and Businesses (Dir 2005–), Japan Electronics and Information Tech. Industries Asscn (Vice-Chair. Exec. Bd, Trade Affairs). *Address:* National Institute of Advanced Industrial Science and Technology, 1-3-1 Kasumigaseki, Chiyoda-ku, Tokyo 100-8921, Japan (office). *Telephone:* (3) 5501-0900 (office). *E-mail:* webmaster-ml@aist.go.jp (office). *Website:* www.aist.go.jp (office).

CHUBAIS, Anatolii Borisovich, CEconSc, PhD; Russian economist, business executive and politician; *CEO, Russian State Nanotechnology Corporation (Rosnanotech);* b. 16 June 1955, Borisov, Belarusian SSR; m. 1st Ludmila Chubais; one s. one d.; m. 2nd Maria Vishnevskaya; m. 3rd Avdotya Smirnova 2012; ed Leningrad Inst. of Eng and Econs; engineer and Asst to Chair. Leningrad (now St Petersburg) Inst. of Econs and Eng 1977–82, Asst Prof. 1982–90; Leader, The Young Economists 1984–87; Deputy, then First Deputy Chair. of Leningrad Municipal Council Jan.–Nov. 1991; Minister of Russia and Chair. State Cttee for Man. of State Property 1991–98; Deputy Prime Minister and Chair. Co-ordination Council for Privatization 1992–94; First Deputy Prime Minister responsible for economy 1994–96; mem. State Duma (Parl.) 1993–95; Chief of Staff of Presidential Exec. Office 1996–97; First Deputy Prime Minister 1997–98, Minister of Finance March–Nov. 1997; Russian Dir EBRD 1997–98; mem. Russian Security Council 1997–98; Head of Russian Fed. Interdepartmental Comm. on Co-operation with Int. Financial and Econ. Orgs and Group of Seven 1998; CEO Unified Energy Systems of Russia 1998–2001, CEO and Chair. Bd of Man. 2001–08; CEO Russian State Nanotechnology Corpn (Rosnanotech) 2008–; Co-Chair. Round Table of Russian and EU Producers 2000–; Pres. Electric Power Council of CIS 2000–07; mem. Int. Advisory Bd, JP Morgan Chase 2008–, Man. Bd, Russian Union of Mfrs and Entrepreneurs 2000–, Govt Comm. on Co-operation with EU 2000–, Global Bd of Advisers, Council on Foreign Relations 2012–; joined Union of Rightist Forces 1999, Co-Chair. 2001–04 (resgnd); Order 'For Merit to the Fatherland' (IV Degree) 2010; Hon. PhD (St Petersburg State Eng, Econ. Univ.); Best Minister of Finance Award, Euromoney magazine 1997, three commendations from Pres. of Russian Fed. 1995, 1997, 1998, 2008, Int. Award, Int. Union of Economists Int. Award 2001. *Leisure interests:* music, literature. *Address:* Russian State Nanotechnology Corpn (Rosnanotech), 117036 Moscow, 10A, Prospekt 60-letiya Oktyabrya, Russia (office). *Telephone:* (495) 988-53-88 (office). *Fax:* (495) 988-53-99 (office). *E-mail:* info@rusnano.com (office). *Website:* www.rusnano.com (office).

CHUBB, Ian William, AC, MSc, DPhil, FAA, FACE; Australian neuroscientist, government official and fmr university administrator; *Emeritus Professor, Australian National University (ANU);* b. 17 Oct. 1943, Melbourne, Vic.; JF & C Heymans Research Fellow, Univ. of Ghent, Belgium 1969–71; Wellcome Foundation Scholar, then Jr Research Fellow of St John's Coll., later Royal Soc. Research Fellow, Univ. of Oxford, UK 1971–77; Lecturer, then Sr Lecturer, later Assoc. Prof., School of Medicine, Flinders Univ. 1978–85, Vice-Chancellor Flinders Univ. 1995–2000; Deputy Vice-Chancellor Univ. of Wollongong 1986–90, Hon. Prof. of Biology; Chair. Higher Educ. Council 1990–94, part-time Chair. 1994–97; Deputy Chair. Nat. Bd of Employment, Educ. and Training 1990–94; Sr Deputy Vice-Chancellor and Foundation Dean Faculty of Business and Econs, Monash Univ. 1993–95; Interim Chair., then Deputy Chair. Nat. Cttee for Quality in Higher Educ. 1993–94; Vice-Chancellor ANU 2001–11, Emer. Prof.; Chief Scientist of Australia 2011–16; mem. Ministerial Task Force 1989, Prime Minister's Science, Eng and Innovation Council 2000–02, Foreign Affairs Council; mem. Bd of Dirs Australia-New Zealand School of Govt, Australian Vice-Chancellors' Cttee 1996–2006 (later Deputy Pres., Pres. 2000–01); Chair. Group of Eight Univs 2003–05; also served in various capacities on Nat. Health and Medical Research Council and Australian Research Cttee; Hon. DSc (Flinders) 2000, Hon. DUniv (ANU) 2011, Hon. DLitt (Charles Darwin Univ.) 2011, (Univ. of the Sunshine Coast) 2014, Hon. LLD (Monash) 2012, (Univ. of Melbourne) 2016; Fellow Acad. of Technological Sciences and Eng 2014, Royal Soc. of NSW 2014; several academic awards, grants from Nat. Health and MRC, Australian Research Grants Scheme and from various foundations, Centenary Medal 2003, ACT's Australian of the Year 2011, Acad. of Science Medal 2016. *Publications:* numerous articles in scientific journals. *Address:* Australian National University, Acton, Canberra, ACT 2601, Australia (office). *E-mail:* ian.chubb@anu.edu.au. *Website:* www.anu.edu.au (office).

CHUBUK, Ion, DrEcon; Moldovan politician; b. 20 May 1943; ed Odessa Inst. of Agric.; First Deputy Chair. Moldovan State Planning Cttee 1984–86; Head of Div. Research Inst. of Agric. 1986–89; Deputy Chair. Moldovan Agricultural-Industrial Council 1989–90; First Deputy Minister of Econs 1990–91; Deputy Prime Minister, Perm. Rep. of Moldovan Govt in USSR Council of Ministers 1991–92; First Deputy Minister of Foreign Affairs 1992–94; First Deputy Minister of Econs April–Dec. 1994; Chair. Moldovan Accountant Chamber 1994–97, Deputy Chair. Accountant Chamber 1999–; Prime Minister of Moldova 1997–99; Deputy Chair. Centrist Union 2000–. *Address:* c/o Centrist Union of Moldova, (Uniunea Centristă din Moldova), Chişinău, str. Tricolorului 35, Moldova. *Website:* ucm.md.

CHUCHOTTAWORN, Pailin, MEng, DEng; Thai business executive; b. 8 July 1956; ed Chulalongkorn Univ., Tokyo Inst. of Tech., Japan; Exec. Vice-Pres., Petrochemicals and Refining Business Unit, PTT Public Co. Ltd, Pres. PTT Asahi Chemical Co. Ltd 2006–08, Sr Exec. Vice-Pres., Pres. PTT Polymer Marketing Co. Ltd, PTT Asahi Chemical Co. Ltd 2008–09, Sr Exec. Vice-Pres., PTT, CEO IRPC Public Co. Ltd 2009–11, Chief Operations Officer, Upstream Petroleum and Gas

Business Group, Acting CEO IRPC Public Co. Ltd June–Sept. 2011, Pres. and CEO PTT Public Co. Ltd 2011–15, also Dir and Sec. to the Bd, mem. Nominating Cttee; Dir, Fraser & Neave Ltd 2013; Dr hc in Sustainable Energy and Environment Tech. and Man. (Rajamangala Univ. of Tech. Rattanakosin, Thailand); Asia Talent Management Award, CNBC Asia Business Leaders Award, Leadership Achievement Award, Asia-Pacific region 2012, Asian Banker Magazine, Best CEO 2012, Finance Asia Magazine. *Address:* c/o PTT Public Co. Ltd, 555 Vibhavadi Rangsit Road, Chatuchak, Bangkok 10900, Thailand. *E-mail:* info@pttplc.com.

CHUCK D, BFA; American rap artist; b. (Carlton Ridenhour), 1 Aug. 1960, Long Island, NY; m. Gaye Theresa Johnson; ed Adelphi Univ.; Super Special Mix Show, radio WBAU 1982; own mobile DJ and concert promotion co., Spectrum City; Founder mem. rap group, Public Enemy 1982–; Man. and Promoter, The Entourage (hip hop venue), Long Island, New York 1986; Founder, Offda Books, Under the Radar Publishing 2003; MOBO Award for Outstanding Contrib. to Black Music 2005, inducted into Rock and Roll Hall of Fame 2013. *Recordings include:* albums: with Public Enemy: Yo! Bum Rush The Show 1987, It Takes A Nation of Millions To Hold Us Back 1988, Fear of a Black Planet 1990, Apocalypse 91... The Enemy Strikes Black (Soul Train Music Award for Best Rap Album 1992) 1991, Greatest Misses 1992, Muse Sick-n-Hour Mess Age 1994, He Got Game (film soundtrack) 1998, There's a Poison Goin' On... 1999, Revolverlution 2002, Rebirth of a Nation 2005, New Whirl Odor 2005, How you Sell a Soul to a Soulless People who Sold their Soul??? 2007, Most of My Heroes Still Don't Appear on No Stamp 2012, The Evil Empire of Everything 2012, Man Plans God Laughs 2015; solo: No 1996, The Autobiography of Mistachuck 1996, The Black in Man 2014. *Publications include:* Public Enemy (autobiography) 1994, Fight the Power: Rap, Race and Reality (non-fiction, with Yusuf Jah) 1997. *E-mail:* Mistachuck@rapstation.com (office). *Website:* www.rapstation.com; www.publicenemy.com.

CHUDAKOVA, Marietta Omarovna, DLit, PhD; Russian academic; *Professor of Literature, Moscow Literary Institute;* b. (Marietta Khan-Magomedova), 2 Jan. 1937, Moscow; m. Alexander Pavlovich Chudakov (died 2005); one d.; ed Moscow State Univ.; school teacher in Moscow 1959–61; Sr Researcher, Div. of Manuscripts, Div. of Rare Books, Div. of Library Research All-Union Lenin's Public Library 1965–84; Ed.-in-Chief Tynyanovski sborniki 1984–; teacher, Moscow Literary Inst. 1986–, Prof. 1992–; Visiting Prof., Stanford Univ. 1989, Univ. of Southern Calif. 1990, Ecole Normale Supérieure, Paris 1991, Geneva Univ. and European Inst. in Geneva 1994, Ottawa Univ. 1995, Cologne Univ. 1999; Chair. All-Russian Mikhail Bulgakov Fund; mem. Academia Europaea; Prize of Moscow Komsomol for research on Yuri Olesha 1970. *Publications:* Effendi Kapiev (biog.) 1970, Craftsmanship of Yuri Olesha 1972, Talks about Archives 1975, Poetics of Mikhail Zoshchenko 1979, Life of Mikhail Bulgakov 1988, Literature of the Soviet Past 2001, Yeltsin and the Cult 2000, Results and Perspectives of the Contemporary Russian Revolution 2002; more than 350 publs in magazines on literary subjects and political essays. *Leisure interests:* rowing, skiing. *Address:* Moscow Literary Institute, Miklukho-Maklaia str. 39, korp. 2, Apt. 380, 117485 Moscow, Russia (home). *Telephone:* (495) 202-84-44 (office); (495) 335-92-57 (home). *Fax:* (495) 375-78-03 (office). *E-mail:* marietta@online.ru (home).

CHUDINOV, Igor Vitalyevich; Kyrgyzstani politician; b. 21 Aug. 1961, Frunze (now Bishkek); ed Kyrgyz State Univ., Int. Business School, Moscow, Russia; held high-ranking positions in Komsomol; early career as computer programmer; worked in a variety of positions as business exec. 1991–2005; Dir-Gen. Kyrgyzgaz (state co. that procures gas supplies for Kyrgyzstan) 2005–07; Minister of Industry, Energy and Fuel Resources Feb.–Dec. 2007; Prime Minister of Kyrgyzstan 2007–09 (resgnd); mem. Bd Creative Alliance International; mem. Ak Zhol party (Bright Road People's Party); Hon. Pres. Kyrgyz-North America Trade Council 2008–. *Address:* c/o Ak Zhol, 720000 Bishkek, Toktogul 175/15, Kyrgyzstan (office); Creative Alliance International, 582 Market Street, Suite 315, San Francisco, CA 94104, USA. *Telephone:* (312) 62-82-45 (office); (202) 656-0770 (Washington, DC). *E-mail:* info@callintern.com. *Website:* www.akjolnarod.kg (office); www.creallint.com.

CHUI, Benjamin W., PhD; American electrical engineer; *Consulting Associate, Alissa M. Fitzgerald & Associates;* ed Stanford Univ.; extensive experience in micro-device design and prototyping; has worked for Lightconnect, Inc. (optical Microelectromechanical systems (MEMS) startup co.); fmr Researcher, IBM Almaden Research Center, San Jose, Calif.; fmr Researcher, Inst. of Microtechnology, Neuchatel, Switzerland; Consulting Assoc., Alissa M. Fitzgerald & Assocs tech. consulting 2005–; World Tech. Award in Materials, The World Tech. Network (co-recipient) 2005. *Achievements include:* part of team that made first demonstrations of magnetic resonance force microscopy (MRFM) 1992, work reached key milestone with manipulation and detection of individual electron spin 2004, designed and fabricated micro-cantilevers used to measure single electron spins. *Publications:* one book and numerous papers on MEMS-related subjects. *Address:* A.M. Fitzgerald & Assocs, LLC, 655 Skyway Road, Suite 118, San Carlos, CA 94070, USA (office). *Telephone:* (650) 592-6100 (office). *Fax:* (650) 592-6111 (office). *E-mail:* info@amfitzgerald.com (office). *Website:* www.amfitzgerald.com (office).

CHUI, Sai On (Fernando Chui), BS, MS, PhD; Chinese government official and fmr public health official; *Chief Executive, Macao Special Administrative Region;* b. 1957, Macao; ed Ling Nam School, Macao, California State Univ., Sacramento and School of Public Health, Univ. of Oklahoma, USA; mem. 5th Legis. Ass., Macao Govt 1992–96; played active role in various local community orgs, including as Exec. Dir Macao Kiang Wu Hosp. Charitable Asscn, as Hon. Pres. Macao Nursing Asscn, and as Chair. Supervisory Bd Macao Asscn for the Mentally Handicapped –1999; apptd by Cen. People's Govt as Sec. for Social Affairs and Culture of Macao Special Admin. Region (SAR) Govt 1999–2009; Chief Exec. Macao SAR 2009–; Guest Prof., Huanan Teachers' Training Univ.; tutor in Chamber of Commerce for Int. Youth; mem. Youth Cttee of Macao Govt; Headmaster of Kiang Ping School; Pres. Youth Asscn of Kiang Wu Hosp.; mem. and Standing Cttee mem. All-China Youth Fed.; Exec. Man. and Dir of Medical and Health Dept of Tung Sin Tong Charitable Inst.; Pres. Macau Jaycee; Exec. Dir Macao Kiang Wu Hosp. Charitable Asscn; mem. Bd Macau Eye-Bank Foundation; Vice-Pres. Asscn of the Man. Professionals; mem. American Asscn of Public Hygiene, American Asscn for the Man. of Medical Affairs; Hon. Pres. Asscn of Nursing Staff of Macao. *Address:* Office of the Chief Executive, Headquarters of the Government of the Macao SAR, Av. da Praia Grande, Macao Special Administrative Region, People's Republic of China (office). *Telephone:* 28726886 (office). *Fax:* 28725468 (office); 28726168 (office). *E-mail:* info@gov.mo (office). *Website:* www.gov.mo (office).

CHUICHENKO, Konstantin Anatolyevich; Russian lawyer, business executive and politician; *Deputy Chairman of Government and Head of Government Administration;* b. 12 July 1965, Lipetsk, Lipetsk Oblast, Russian SFSR, USSR; m. Kristina Tikhonova; ed Leningrad State Univ. (now St Petersburg State Univ.); began career as trainee investigator, Kalinin Dist Prosecutor's Office, Leningrad (now St Petersburg) 1987–89; served in KGB 1989–92; Head of Legal Dept, Gazprom 2001–02, mem. Man. Cttee 2002–, Chair. Bd of Dirs Gazprom Media Holding 2003–04; mem. Bd of Dirs TNT TV network 2003–, Sibneft (now Gazprom Neft) 2005–; Exec. Dir RosUkrEnergo 2004–; Head of Control Dept, Presidential Admin 2008–18; Deputy Chair. of Govt and Head of Govt Admin 2018–; Order of Honour 2006, Order 'For Services to the Fatherland' (4th degree) 2011. *Address:* Office of the Government, 103274 Moscow, Krasnopresnenskaya nab. 2, Russia (office). *Telephone:* (495) 985-42-80 (office). *Fax:* (495) 605-53-62 (office). *E-mail:* duty_press@aprf.gov.ru (office). *Website:* government.ru (office).

CHUKA, Charles, BSc, MPhil; Malawi economist and central banker; *Chairman, Petroleum Importers Limited (PIL);* ed Chancellor Coll., Univ. of Malawi, Univ. of Glasgow, Scotland; joined Reserve Bank of Malawi 1979, served in various capacities and depts, becoming Gen. Man. for Econ. Services 1997–2003, Gov. Reserve Bank of Malawi 2012–17; Sr Adviser to Exec. Dir, World Bank, Washington, DC 2003–11; CEO Malawi Telecommunications Ltd 2010–12; Chair. Asscn of African Central Banks 2011–12; Chair. Petroleum Importers Limited (PIL) 2018–. *Leisure interest:* long-distance running. *Address:* Petroleum Importers Limited, Unit House, 6th Floor, Victoria Ave, Private Bag 200, Blantyre, Malawi (office). *Telephone:* 1822886. *E-mail:* petroleum@pilmalawi.mw.

CHUKHRAI, Pavel Grigoryevich; Russian film director and screenwriter; b. 14 Oct. 1946, Bykovo, Moscow; s. of Grigoriy Chukhrai; m. Maria Zvereva; two d.; ed All-Union State Inst. of Cinematography; actor, cameraman, scriptwriter; mem. Union of Cinematographers, European Acad. of Cinema and TV; Lenin's Komsomol Prize 1981, All-Union Film Festival Prize 1981, four Kinoshock Festival prizes, six Russian Acad. prizes, four Golden Oven Festival prizes, Grand Prix Prague Film Festival, Jury Prize, Int. Film Festival, Japan. *Films include:* Lyudi v okeane (also writer) 1980, Kto zaplatit za udachu? (writer) 1980, Kletka dlya kanareek (also writer) 1983, Zina-Zinulya 1986, Vor (also writer) 1997, Klassik (writer) 1998, Voditel dlya Very (also writer) 2004, Russkaya igra (The Russian Game) (also writer) 2007. *Television includes:* Zapomnite menya takoy (film) 1987, La clef (film) 1996, Broken Silence (mini-series documentary, segment 'Children from the Abyss') 2002. *Address:* Bolshaya Pirogovskaya str. 53/55, Apt 177, Moscow, Russia (home). *Telephone:* (495) 246-98-61 (home). *Fax:* (495) 246-98-61 (home). *E-mail:* pavel@girmet.ru (home).

CHULANONT, Gen. Surayud; Thai army officer and politician; b. 28 Aug. 1943, Prachinburi; s. of Lt Col Payom Chulanont and Ampoch Tharab; m. 1st Duang Chulanont; one s.; m. 2nd Thanpuying Chitravadee Chulanont; two s.; ed Chulachomklao Royal Mil. Acad., Jt Staff Coll., USA, Jt Staff Coll. and Nat. Defence Coll., Thailand; started career as Jr Lt, Royal Thai Army 1965, served in infantry, artillery and counter-insurgency units; Instructor, Special Warfare School 1974–76; Aide to C-in-C 1976; Commdr Gen., Special Warfare Command 1992–94, Second Army Area 1994–97, C-in-C 1998–2002, Supreme Commdr 2002–03; PC 2003–06, 2008–16; Interim Prime Minister 2006–08, also Minister of the Interior 2007–08; mem. Exec. Cttee Anandamahidol Foundation 2003–; Kt, Order of the Crown of Thailand 1992, Kt, Order of the White Elephant 1995, Kt Grand Commdr, Order of Chula Chom Klao 2001; Freeman Safeguarding Medal 1974, Rama Medal of the Hon. Order of Rama 1990. *Leisure interests:* reading, playing golf, jet skiing, trekking. *Address:* c/o Privy Council Chambers, Sanamchai Road, Pranakorn District, Bangkok 10200, Thailand (office). *Telephone:* (2) 220-7400 (office).

CHUMA, Kouki; Japanese politician; b. 8 Oct. 1936; ed Univ. of Tokyo; with Sumitomo Heavy Industries Ltd 1961; with Research Bureau, Econ. Planning Agency –1969; mem. House of Reps (Osaka 1st Dist) 1976–, Chair. House of Reps Standing Cttee on Science and Tech. 1991, on Local Admin Div. 1993, Special Cttee on Election Laws 1996, Standing Cttee on Foreign Affairs 1997, Special Cttee on Political Ethics and Election Laws 2001, Dir Special Cttee on Decentralization of Govt 1993; Chair. Policy Bd, New Liberal Club 1981; State Sec. for Environment 1984; Parl. Vice-Minister for Home Affairs 1990; Dir Local Admin Div., Liberal Democratic Party (LDP) 1991, Acting Head, Nat. Campaign HQ, LDP 1993, Deputy Chair. Policy Research Council, LDP (Local Admin and Transport) 1995, Chief Deputy Sec.-Gen. LDP 2000, Chair. Research Comm. on Local Govt Admin, LDP 2001, 2003, mem. Gen. Council LDP 2002, Deputy Chair. Gen. Council 2004; Chair. Special Cttee to Promote the Devt of Osaka Bay Area 1996; Sr State Sec. for Transport 1999–02; Sr Vice-Minister of Land, Infrastructure and Transport 2002–05; mem. Research Comm. on Local Admin Systems 2004; Minister of State for Admin. Reform, Regulatory Reform, Special Zones for Structural Reform, and Regional Revitalization 2005–06, for Special Assignment (Special Envoy of the Prime Minister) July 2006. *Address:* c/o Liberal-Democratic Party (Jiyu-Minshuto), 1-11-23, Nagata-cho, Chiyoda-ku, Tokyo 100-8910, Japan. *Telephone:* (3) 3581-6211. *E-mail:* koho@ldp.jimin.or.jp. *Website:* www.jimin.jp; www.chuma-koki.jp.

CHUN, Jung-bae, LLM; South Korean lawyer and politician; b. 12 Dec. 1954; ed Seoul Nat. Univ.; Founding mem. Minbyun (Lawyers for a Democratic Soc.) 1988, Co-ordinator, Chair. Int. Human Rights Cttee; elected mem. Nat. Ass. 1996, 2000, 2004, Chair. House Steering Cttee 2004, mem. Commerce, Industry and Energy Cttee 2005; Chief Sec. to Pres., Nat. Congress for New Politics (NCNP) 1998; Vice-Chair. Policy Cttee, Vice-Floor Leader, Millennium Democratic Party 2000, Special Advisor on State Affairs to Presidential Cand. 2002, Chief Sec. Advisory Cttee on Political Reform for Presidential Cand. 2002; Chair. Nat. Security and Int. Relations Cttee, Korea-Japan Parliamentarians' Union 2003, Adviser 2005; Chair. Special Cttee on Political Reform, Uri Party 2003, Chair. Gen. Election Planning Cttee, Clean Election Campaign Cttee 2004, Floor Leader 2004; Minister of Justice 2005–06 (resgnd); mem. UNDP (renamed Democratic Party, merged with ind. Ahn Cheol-Soo's prospective New Political Vision Party to form New Politics Alliance for Democracy 2014) 2007–15; declared intention to form new political party Sept. 2015; Pres. Korea-UK Parliamentarians' Friendship Asscn 2005; Baek-Bong Memorial Foundation Clean & Gentle Politician Award 1999, Asscn of Korean Journalists Politician of the Year Award 2001.

CHUNG, Dong-soo, BA, MA; South Korean academic and banking executive; b. 24 Sept. 1945; ed Seoul Nat. Univ., Univ. of Wisconsin, USA; fmr Asst Minister, Planning and Man. Office, Ministry of Planning and Budget; Deputy Minister, Ministry of Environment 2001–02; mem. Bd of Dirs, Kookmin Bank from 2002, fmr Chair.; Prof., Sangmyung Univ.; Dir Daewoo Shipbuilding and Marine Eng Co. Ltd. *Address:* c/o Board of Directors, KB Kookmin Bank, 9-1 Namdaemunro 2-ga, Jung-gu, Seoul 100-703, Republic of Korea.

CHUNG, Dong-young, MA; South Korean politician; b. 27 July 1953, Sunchang Co., N Jeolla Prov.; m.; two s.; ed Jeonju High School, Seoul Nat. Univ. and Cardiff Grad. School, Univ. of Wales, UK; imprisoned for involvement in Mincheong Hakryeon Case 1973; reporter, Moonhwa Broadcasting Corpn (MBC) 1978–88, Anchor, MBC Midnight News 1988–89, MBC Los Angeles Corresp., USA 1989–93, Main Anchor, 9 O'Clock News Desk, MBC 1994–96; mem. 15th Nat. Ass. 1996–2000, Cen. Party Affairs Cttee, Nat. Congress for New Politics (NCNP), 16th Nat. Ass. 2000–04, mem. Science, Tech., Information and Telecommunications Cttee, mem. 18th Nat. Ass. 2009–12; Special Asst to NCNP Pres. Kim Dae-jung and Campaign Planner; Seoul Mayor Electoral Campaign 1998; Spokesman, NCNP 1998–99; mem. and Spokesman, Millennium Democratic Party 2000; mem. Cen. Cttee Uri Party (subsequently renamed United Nat. Democratic Party—UNDP, renamed Democratic Party, merged with ind. Ahn Cheol-Soo's prospective New Political Vision Party to form New Politics Alliance for Democracy 2014) 2003–14, Chair. Uri Party Jan.–May 2004, Feb.–June 2006 (resgnd), unsuccessful UNDP cand. in presidential election 2007; Minister of Unification 2004–06; unsuccessful cand. in by-election April 2015.

CHUNG, Eui-sun, MBA; South Korean business executive; *Vice-Chairman, Hyundai Motors Co.;* b. 18 Oct. 1970; s. of Chung Mong-koo; m.; two c.; ed Korea Univ., Univ. of San Francisco, USA; CEO and Pres. Kia Motors Corpn 2005–09, also Dir Hyundai Mobis and Deputy Head, Hyundai-Kia Planning Div., Vice-Chair. Hyundai Motors Co., Dir 2009–, Vice-Chair. Hyundai Steel 2012–, Vice-Chair. of Hyundai Mobis; Pres. Asian Archery Fed. *Address:* Hyundai Motors Co., 231 Yangjae-dong, Seocho-gu, Seoul 137-938, Republic of Korea (office). *Telephone:* (2) 3464-1114 (office). *Fax:* (2) 965-3148 (office). *Website:* worldwide.hyundai.com (office).

CHUNG, Hong-won, LLB; South Korean lawyer and politician; b. 9 Oct. 1944, Hadong, South Gyeongsang Prov.; ed Sungkyunkwan Univ.; began career as teacher, Inwang elementary school 1963–70; 30-year career as state prosecutor, roles include Prosecutor, Seoul-Busan Public Prosecutor's Office 1974–83, Prosecutor, Legal Affairs Div., Ministry of Justice 1983–86, Chief Prosecutor, Geochang Br., Masan Dist 1986–87, Sr Prosecutor, E Secr., Busan Dist Public Prosecutor's Office 1988–89, Dir for Violent Crime, Supreme Public Prosecutor's Office 1990–93, Sr Prosecutor, Seoul Dist Public Prosecutor's Office 1993–95, Supt Prosecutor, Gwangju Dist Public Prosecutor's Office 2000–02, Busan Dist Public Prosecutor's Office 2002–03; Dir of Planning, Judicial Research and Training Inst. 1987–88, Supt 2003–04; Standing mem. Nat. Election Comm. 2004–06; Pres. Korea Legal Aid Corpn 2008–11; Prime Minister 2013–April 2014 (resgnd following criticism of Govt's handling of the sinking of a passenger ferry), reinstated June 2014–Feb. 2015; mem. Saenuri Party (New Frontier Party). *Address:* c/o Office of the Prime Minister, 55, Sejong-no, Jongno-gu, Seoul 110-760, Republic of Korea.

CHUNG, Joon-yang; South Korean business executive; b. 3 Feb. 1948; ed Seoul Nat. Univ.; joined POSCO (Pohang Iron and Steel Co.) 1975, Gen. Man. Steelmaking Dept 1991–98, Deputy Gen. Supt POSCO Tech. Research Lab. 1998–99, Man. Dir POSCO EU Office 1999–2004, Gen. Supt Gwangyang Works 2004–06, Sr Exec. Vice-Pres., COO and Chief Tech. Officer 2006–07, Pres., COO and Chief Tech. Officer 2007–08, Pres. POSCO Eng & Construction Co. Ltd 2008–09, CEO, Exec. Dir and Chair. Exec. Man. Cttee POSCO 2009–14, Chair. Posco-China Co. Ltd; Chair. Fed. of Korean Industries, Korea-Australia Econ. Co-operation 2007–, 7th Korea Iron & Steel Asscn 2009–; Pres. Korean Inst. of Metal and Materials 2008–, Nat. Acad. of Eng of Korea 2011–; mem. Exec. Cttee Int. Iron and Steel Inst. 2009–; Rep. of Multi-cultural Families Forum 2011–; Presidential Citation 1992, Technological Prize, Korean Inst. of Metal and Materials 1994, Gold Tower Order of Industrial Service Merit 2007, 8th Prize of Honoured Citizen 2008, CEO of the Year, Maegyeong Economy 2009, 9th Most Honoured Entrepreneur 2011, Grand Prized CEO of Korea in Manufacturing Industry 2011, The Figure of Moving Korean Economy 2012. *Address:* c/o POSCO Head Office, 1 Goedong-dong, Nam-gu, Pohang, Kyongsangbuk-do, 790-600, Republic of Korea. *E-mail:* info@posco.com.

CHUNG, Kyung-wha; South Korean violinist; b. 26 March 1948, Seoul; sister of Chung Myung-whun and Chung Myung-wha; m. Geoffrey Leggett 1984; two s.; ed Juilliard School, New York with Ivan Galamian; started career in USA; European debut 1970; has played with major orchestras, including all London orchestras, Chicago, Boston and Pittsburgh Symphony Orchestra, New York, Cleveland, Philadelphia, Berlin, Israel and Vienna Philharmonics, Orchestre de Paris, Royal Concertegebouw Orchestra, Deutsche Grammophon, San Francisco Symphony, Orchestre National de Lyon, Pittsburgh Symphony Orchestra, Orchestre Philharmonique de Radio-France, Tonhalle-Orchester Zurich; has toured world; played at Salzburg Festival with London Symphony Orchestra 1973, Vienna Festival 1981, 1984, Edinburgh Festival 1981 and at 80th birthday concert of Sir William Walton March 1982; with Hallé Orchestra, BBC Proms, London 1999; Co-Artistic Dir Great Mountain Music Festival; mem. Faculty of Music, Juilliard School, New York 2007–; Chair Prof. of Music, Ewha Womans Univ. 2012–; apptd Hon. Amb., UN Drug Control Programme, Charity Amb. for Better World; winner, Leventritt Competition 1968, Medal of Civil Merit (South Korea) 1972, Ho-am Prize 2011. *Recordings include:* Concertos by Bartók, Beethoven, Bruch, Mendelssohn, Stravinsky, Tchaikovsky, Vieuxtemps, Walton, Vivaldi's The Four Seasons 2001, Beau Soir 2018. *Leisure interests:* arts, family. *Address:* Opus 3 Artists, 470 Park Avenue South, 9th Floor North, New York, NY 10016, USA (office); The Juilliard School, 60 Lincoln Center Plaza, New York, NY 10023-6588, USA (office). *Telephone:* (212) 584-7500 (office); (212) 799-5000. *Fax:* (646) 300-8200 (office). *E-mail:* info@opus3artists.com (office). *Website:* www.opus3artists.com (office); www.juilliard.edu (office).

CHUNG, Mong-joon, MA, PhD; South Korean politician, sports administrator and business executive; b. 17 Oct. 1951, Busan; s. of Chung Ju-yung; brother of Chung Mong-koo; m.; two s. two d.; ed Joongang High School, Coll. of Commerce, Seoul Nat. Univ., Massachusetts Inst. of Tech. and Johns Hopkins Univ., USA; First Lt Reserve Officers Training Corps; joined Hyundai Heavy Industries 1978, Man. Dir 1980, CEO 1982, Adviser 1990–2002; Pres. Hyundai Heavy Industries Co. Ltd (HHI) 1982–87, Chair. 1987; Chair. Ulsan Inst. of Tech. Foundation 1999–; elected mem. (Ind.) Nat. Ass. 1988–2014; f. Nat. Unity 21 party Nov. 2002; Pres. Korea Football Asscn 1993–2009, Hon. Pres. 2009–; Vice-Pres. FIFA 1994–2011, Co-Chair. Korean Organizing Cttee for 2002 FIFA World Cup, Korea-Japan 2002, Hon. Vice-Pres. FIFA 2011–, 2016 FIFA presidential cand., banned for six years over corruption allegations Oct. 2015; Chair. Bd of Trustees, Ulsan Univ. 1983–2014, Asan Foundation 2001– (Hon. Chair. The Asan Inst. for Policy Studies 2010–, Hon. Chair. The Asan Nanum Foundation 2011–); Chair. Grand Nat. Party, mem. Supreme Council, Grand Nat. Party; cand. in nat. presidential election 2002; mem. Bd of Trustees, Johns Hopkins Univ., USA 1995–2000, Korea Univ.; mem. Bd of Dirs Salzburg Global Seminar; Hon. PhD (Myongji Univ.) 1998, Hon. LLD (Univ. of Maryland) 1999. *Publications include:* Corporate Management Ideology 1982, Relations Between the Government and the Corporate in Japan 1995, This I Say to Japan 2001. *Leisure interests:* football, tennis, golf, equestrianism, hiking. *Address:* 345-1, Pyeongchang-dong, Jongno-gu, Seoul, Republic of Korea. *Telephone:* (2) 741-1122 (office). *Fax:* (2) 741-1154 (office). *E-mail:* mongjoonc@naver.com. *Website:* www.mjchung.com (office).

CHUNG, Mong-koo, BA, PhD; South Korean automotive industry executive; *Chairman and CEO, Hyundai-Kia Automotive Group;* b. 19 March 1938, Seoul; s. of Chung Ju-yung (Founder of Hyundai); brother of Chung Mong-joon and Chung Mong-hun; m.; four c.; ed Hanyang Univ.; began career in family-owned business Hyundai Automotive Group 1970, various positions include Man. Hyundai Motor Co. 1983, Head of Hyundai Motor Service, Chair. Hyundai Group 1996–99 (Hyundai-Kia Automotive Group following purchase of Kia Motors 1998), Chair. and Co-CEO Hyundai Motor Co. and Kia Motor Co. 1999–2009, Chair. and CEO Hyundai-Kia Automotive Group 2009–; CEO Hyundai Automotive Group (holding co. of Hyundai Mobis Ameron International Corpn); received three-year suspended jail sentence for embezzling co. funds and breach of duty 2007, pardoned by Pres. of Repub. of Korea; Prof. Emer. of Business Admin, Qinghua Univ., China; Vice-Chair. Fed. of Korean Industries; Hon. Professorship in Business Admin, Tsinghua Univ.; Hon. PhD (Cen. Connecticut State Univ., USA, Nat. Univ. of Mongolia); Automotive Hall of Fame Distinguished Service Citation, Nat. Automobile Dealers Asscn 2001, named by BusinessWeek magazine as one of the top managers of 2004, named by Automotive News as one of its three Auto Executives of the Year (Asian award) 2010. *Address:* Hyundai-Kia Automotive Group, 231 Yangjae-dong, Seocho-gu, Seoul 137-1115, Republic of Korea (office). *Telephone:* (2) 3464-1114 (office). *E-mail:* dmkim@hyundai-motor.com (office). *Website:* worldwide.hyundai.com (office).

CHUNG, Moon Soul, BA; South Korean business executive; b. 7 March 1938, Chonbuk Imsil; ed Iksan Men's High School, Won Kwang Univ.; Sr Man. Planning and Coordinating Div., Korea Cen. Intelligence Agency 1962–80; Founder, Chair. and CEO Mirae Corpn 1983–2001, Consultant 2001–, Founder and CEO Lycos Korea 1999–2001; apptd Dir (non-exec.) Kookmin Bank 2001, Chair. 2004; Dir (non-exec.) Dongwon Securities; Dr hc (Korea Advanced Inst. of Science and Tech.) 2009. *Address:* c/o Mirae Corporation, 9-2 Cha-Am-dong, Chonan, Chungcheongnam 330-200, Republic of Korea.

CHUNG, Myung-whun; South Korean conductor and pianist; b. 22 Jan. 1953, Seoul; brother of Chung Kyung-wha and Chung Myung-wha; ed Mannes Coll. of Music and Juilliard School, New York, USA; asst to Carlo Maria Giulini as Assoc. Conductor, Los Angeles Philharmonic 1978–81; moved to Europe 1981, conducting Berlin Philharmonic, Munich Philharmonic, Amsterdam Concertgebouw, Orchestre de Paris, major London orchestras; Music Dir and Prin. Conductor, Radio Orchestra of Saarbrücken 1984–89; in USA has conducted the New York Philharmonic, Nat. Symphony, Washington, DC, Boston Symphony, Cleveland and Chicago Orchestras, Metropolitan Opera, San Francisco Opera 1986–; Guest Conductor, Teatro Comunale, Florence 1987; Musical Dir Opéra de la Bastille, Paris 1989–94; Covent Garden debut, conducting Otello 1997; Music Dir and Prin. Conductor, Orchestra of the Nat. Acad. of Santa Cecilia, Rome 1997–2005; conducted Swedish Radio Symphony Orchestra at London Proms, playing Beethoven's Fourth Piano Concerto and Nielsen's Fifth 1999; Music Dir Asia Philharmonic Orchestra 1997–; Music Dir Radio France Philharmonic Orchestra 2000–; Special Artistic Adviser, Tokyo Philharmonic Orchestra 2001–; Music Dir Seoul Philharmonic Orchestra 2005–15; Prin. Guest Conductor, Staatskapelle Dresden 2012–; Goodwill Amb. for UNICEF 2008–; Hon. Cultural Amb. for Korea; Legion d'honneur 1992; Second Prize, Tchaikovsky Competition, Moscow 1974, Abbiati Prize (Italian critics) 1988, Arturo Toscanini Prize 1989, Victoires de la Musique Best Conductor, Best Lyrical Production, Best French Classical Recording 1995, Record Acad. Prize (Japan), Kumkwan (South Korea). *Recordings include:* Chin: Piano and Cello Concertos (Int. Classical Music Award for Contemporary Music 2015). *Address:* Askonas Holt Ltd, 15 Fetter Lane, London, EC4A 1BW, England (office). *Website:* www.askonasholt.co.uk/artists/conductors/myung-whun-chung (office).

CHUNG, Shui-ming (Timpson), BSc, MBA; Chinese business executive and fmr government official; *CEO, Shimao Property Holdings Ltd;* b. 23 Nov. 1951, Hong Kong; two c.; ed Univ. of Hong Kong, Chinese Univ. of Hong Kong; fmr Hong Kong Affairs Adviser to Chinese Govt; fmr mem. Exec. Council, Hong Kong Special Admin. Region, Hong Kong Housing Soc. Exec. Cttee, now Chair., fmr mem. Housing Authority Finance Cttee; fmr Chief Exec. Hong Kong Special Admin. Region Land Fund; Exec. Dir and CEO Shimao Property Holdings Ltd 2004–; mem. Bd of Dirs Hantec Investment Holdings Ltd 2004–06, Man. Dir, Exec. Dir and Deputy Chair. 2006–; Dir (non-exec.) China Everbright Ltd 2012–; External Dir COSCO; Dir China Construction Bank Corpn 2013–; mem. Nat. Cttee, 10th, 11th and 12th CPPCC; Deputy Chair. Council of City Univ. of Hong Kong; mem. Hong Kong Housing Authority; Court mem. Univ. of Hong Kong; Fellow, Hong Kong Inst. of CPAs, Asscn of Chartered Certified Accountants, Hong Kong Soc. of

Accountants; fmr Chinese mem. Sino-British Land Comm.; Justice of the Peace 1998; Hon. DScS (City Univ. of Hong Kong) 2010; Gold Bauhinia Star 2000. *Address:* Shimao Property Holdings Ltd, 43/F, Convention Plaza, 1 Harbor Road, Wan Chai, Hong Kong Special Administrative Region, People's Republic of China (office). *Telephone:* (21) 86213861 (office). *Website:* www.shimaogroup.com (office).

CHUNG, Sye-Kyun, MBA; South Korean politician; b. 5 Nov. 1950, Jinan, North Jeolla; ed Korea Univ., New York Univ., Pepperdine Univ., USA, Kyung Hee Univ.; mem. Nat. Ass. 1996–2012 (Jinan–Muju–Jangsu), 2012– (Seoul Jongno), Speaker 2016–18; Minister of Commerce, Industry and Energy 2006–07; Chair. Uri Party Feb.–Aug. 2007, Democratic Party 2008–10; currently Chair. Korea-France Parl. Friendship Group. *Leisure interest:* reading. *Address:* National Assembly, 1 Uisadang-daero, Yeongdeungpo-gu, Seoul 07233, Republic of Korea (office). *Telephone:* (2) 788-2895 (office). *E-mail:* skchung@assembly.go.kr (office). *Website:* www.assembly.go.kr (office).

CHUNG, Un-chan, BA, MA, PhD; South Korean economist and politician; b. 29 Feb. 1948, Gongju City, S Chungcheong Prov.; m. Choi Sun-Ju; one s. one d.; ed Seoul Nat. Univ., Miami Univ., Princeton Univ., USA; clerk, Bank of Korea 1970–71; Business Assoc. and Asst Prof. of Money and Financial Markets, Columbia Univ., USA 1976–78; Asst, later Assoc. and Full Prof. of Econs, Seoul Nat. Univ. 1978–2009, Dean, Coll. of Social Sciences 2002, Pres. Seoul Nat. Univ. 2002–06, Dir Inst. for Research in Finance and Econs 2008–09, Hon. Pres. Seoul Nat. Univ. 2011–; Prime Minister of South Korea 2009–10; Chair. Presidential Comm. for Shared Growth for Large and Small Cos 2010–; Head of Nat. Cttee for New7Wonders of Nature 2010–; Visiting Assoc. Prof. of Econs, Univ. of Hawaii, USA 1983; Visiting Scholar, LSE, UK 1986; Visiting Prof., Ruhr-Universität Bochum, Germany 1999; Chair. Financial Devt Cttee, Ministry of Finance and Economy 2000–01, Cttee on Nat. Pension Devt, Ministry of Health and Welfare 2002; Pres. Korean Money and Finance Asscn 1998–99, Korean Econ. Asscn 2006–07, Korean Social Science Research Council 2008–09; Dir Korea Council of Econ. and Social Research Insts 1999–2001; mem. Pres.'s Council, Univ. of Tokyo 2006–09; first Hon. Mayor of Jeju Global Educ. City 2012; Hon. DUniv (Far Eastern Nat. Univ., Russia) 2004. *Publications:* numerous publs on econs in both Korean and English. *Leisure interest:* baseball. *Address:* c/o Prime Minister's Office, 55 Sejong-no, Jongno-gu, Seoul 110-760, Republic of Korea. *E-mail:* webmaster@pmo.go.kr.

CHUNG, Won-shik; South Korean fmr army officer, academic and politician; *President, Paradise Welfare Foundation;* b. 5 Aug. 1928; officer in South Korean Army 1951–55; Prof., Seoul Nat. Univ. 1955–60; Minister of Educ. 1988–90; Acting Prime Minister of South Korea 1991, Prime Minister 1991–92; Pres. Paradise Welfare Foundation (charity associated with Paradise Group); Adviser, Korea Support Cttee for Int. Vaccine Inst.; mem. Democratic Liberal Party. *Address:* Paradise Welfare Foundation, 186-39, Jangchoong Building, Jangchoong-dong 2ga, Joong-gu, Seoul 100-855, Republic of Korea (office). *Telephone:* (2) 2277-3296 (office). *Fax:* (2) 2277-3124 (office). *Website:* paradise.or.kr (office).

CHUNGONG, Martin, BA, MA; Cameroonian international organization official; *Secretary-General, Inter-Parliamentary Union;* b. 17 Feb. 1957; m.; two c.; ed Univ. of Yaoundé, Univ. of Ottawa, Canada, Central London Polytechnic, UK; held several positions at Nat. Ass. (Parl.) of Cameroon, including as Sr Trans./Interpreter, Research Man., Prof., Language Training Centre; Admin. Sec., Cameroon rep. office, IPU 1979–93, Programme Officer, Tech. Cooperation, IPU 1993–2000, Sec., Cttee on Parl., Juridical and Human Rights Questions and Cttee on Democracy and Human Rights 1995–2013, Programme Man. Study and Promotion of Representative Insts 2000–05, Dir Div. for the Promotion of Democracy 2005–11, Dir of Programmes 2011–14, Deputy Sec.-Gen. 2012–14, Sec.-Gen. 2014–, Chair. Man. Cttee on Accountability of the OECD Governance Network 2011–14, Parliamentary Rep., Steering Cttee, Global Partnership for Effective Devt Cooperation 2012–14; fmr Visiting Prof. of Trans., Interpretation and Applied Linguistics, Univ. of Yaoundé, Univ. of Buea, Cameroon; Chevalier, Ordre de la Pléiade, Ordre de la Francophonie. *Publications include:* handbook for UNESCO on how to work with parliaments, numerous technical papers and studies. *Address:* Office of the Secretary-General, Inter-Parliamentary Union, 5 chemin du Pommier, Case postale 330, Le Grand-Saconnex, 1218 Geneva, Switzerland (office). *Telephone:* (22) 9194150 (office). *Fax:* (22) 9194160 (office). *E-mail:* postbox@ipu.org (office); martinchungong@yahoo.com. *Website:* www.ipu.org (office).

CHURCHILL, Caryl, BA; British playwright; b. 3 Sept. 1938, London; d. of Robert Churchill and Jan Churchill (née Brown); m. David Harter 1961; three s.; ed Trafalgar School, Montréal, Canada, Lady Margaret Hall, Oxford; first play, Downstairs, performed at Nat. Union of Students Drama Festival 1958; writes mainly for theatre but has also written numerous radio plays and several TV plays. *Stage plays include:* Having a Wonderful Time (Oxford Players, 1960), Owners (Royal Court, London) 1972, Objections to Sex and Violence (Royal Court) 1975, Vinegar Tom (Monstrous Regiment toured 1976), Light Shining in Buckinghamshire (performed by Joint Stock Co., Edinburgh Festival 1976, then Royal Court), Traps (Royal Court) 1977, Cloud Nine (Joint Stock Co., Royal Court) 1979, 1980, Lucille Lortel Theater, New York 1981–83, Top Girls (Royal Court) 1982, 1983, Public Theater, New York 1983, Fen (Joint Stock Co., Almeida Theatre, London 1983, Royal Court 1983, Public Theater, New York 1983), Softcops (RSC 1984), A Mouthful of Birds (Joint Stock, Royal Court and tour 1986), Serious Money (Royal Court 1987, Wyndham's Theatre 1987, Public Theater New York 1988), Icecream (Royal Court 1989, Public Theater New York 1990), Mad Forest (Cen. School of Drama, Nat. Theatre Bucharest, Royal Court 1990), Lives of the Great Poisoners (Second Stride Co. Riverside Studios, London and tour 1991), The Skriker (Nat. Theatre 1994), Thyestes (by Seneca, translation; Royal Court Theatre Upstairs 1994); Hotel (Second Stride Co., The Place) 1997, This Is A Chair (Royal Court) 1997, Blue Heart (Out of Joint, Royal Court) 1997, Far Away (Royal Court) 2000, (Albery) 2001, A Number (Royal Court) 2002, Drunk Enough to Say I Love You? (Royal Court) 2006, Seven Jewish Children (Royal Court) 2009, Love and Information (Royal Court) 2012, Ding Dong the Wicked (Royal Court) 2013, Here We Go (Nat. Theatre) 2015, Escaped Alone (Royal Court) 2016. *Radio includes:* The Ants, Not . . Not . . not . . not enough Oxygen, Abortive, Schreiber's Nervous Illness, Identical Twins, Perfect Happiness, Henry's Past. *Television:* The Judge's Wife, The After Dinner Joke, The Legion Hall Bombing, Fugue (jtly). *Publications include:* Owners 1973, Light Shining 1976, Traps 1977, Vinegar Tom 1978, Cloud Nine 1979, Top Girls 1982, Fen 1983, Fen and Softcops 1984, A Mouthful of Birds 1986, Serious Money 1987, Plays I 1985, Plays II 1988, Objections to Sex and Violence in Plays by Women Vol. 4 1985, Ice Cream 1989, Mad Forest 1990, Lives of the Great Poisoners 1992, The Skriker 1994, Thyestes 1994, Blue Heart 1997, This is a Chair 1999, Far Away 2000, A Number 2002, Drunk Enough to Say I Love You? 2006, Bliss (Trans. Olivier Choinère) 2008, Seven Jewish Children 2009; anthologies. *Address:* c/o Mel Kenyon, Casarotto Ramsay & Associates, Waverley House, 7–12 Noel Street, London, W1F 8GQ, England (office). *Telephone:* (20) 7287-4450 (office). *Fax:* (20) 7734-9128 (office). *E-mail:* mel@casarotto.co.uk (office). *Website:* www.casarotto.co.uk (office).

CHUROV, Vladimir Yevgenyevich; Russian politician and engineer; b. 17 March 1953, St Petersburg; s. of Yevgeny Petrovich Churov and Irina Vladimirovna Churova; m. Larisa Nikolayeva Churova; one s.; ed Leningrad State Univ.; began career working in aerospace design 1977–91; worked for Cttee of Int. Relations of City of St Petersburg 1992–2003, Vice Chair. 1995–2003; Deputy in State Duma 2003–07, Deputy Chair. of the Cttee on CIS and Russian Diaspora; Chair. Cen. Electoral Comm. 2007–16; Prof. of Econs, Humanitarian Univ. of Trade Unions, St Petersburg; mem. Liberal Democratic Party of Russia (Liberalno-demokraticheskaya partiya Rossii); Order of Merit for Service to the Fatherland, Order of Friendship 2004. *Publications include:* several books on mil., including the history of the imperial army and White Movement, also popular maritime novels for children. *Leisure interests:* photography, military history, history of architecture. *Address:* c/o Central Election Commission, 109012 Moscow, Bolshoi Cherkassky per. 9, Russia.

CHUTE, Robert Maurice, ScD; American poet, biologist and academic (retd); *Professor Emeritus of Biology, Bates College;* b. 13 Feb. 1926, Bridgton, Me; s. of James Cleveland Chute and Elizabeth Davis Chute; m. Virginia Hinds 1946; one s. one d.; ed Fryeburg Acad., Univ. of Maine, Johns Hopkins Univ. School of Hygiene and Public Health; Instructor and Asst Prof., Middlebury Coll. 1953–59; Asst Prof. Northridge State Coll. 1959–61; Assoc. Prof. and Chair. of Biology, Lincoln Univ. 1961; Prof. and Chair. of Biology, then Dana Prof. of Biology, Bates Coll. 1962–93, Prof. Emer. 1993–; Fellow, AAAS; Maine Arts and Humanities Award 1978, Chad Walsh Award (Beloit Poetry Journal) 1997, Maine Writers and Publrs Alliance Poetry Competition 2001, Maine Writers and Publrs Lifetime Distinguished Achievement Award 2011. *Publications:* Environmental Insight 1971, Introduction to Biology 1976, Sweeping the Sky: Soviet Women Flyers in Combat 1999; poetry: Quiet Thunder 1975, Uncle George 1977, Voices Great and Small 1977, Thirteen Moons/Treize Lunes 1982, Samuel Sewell Sails for Home 1986, When Grandmother Decides to Die 1989, Woodshed on the Moon: Thoreau Poems, Barely Time to Study Jesus 1996, Androscoggin Too 1997, Bent Offerings 2003, Reading Nature 2006, Cat Tales, Constellations: Collected Story Poems 2013; novel: Coming Home 2009, Return to Sender 2011, Roadside Rest: Another Maine Mystery from Wyman Falls 2012; trans.: Thirteen Moons into Micmac Maliseet (native American) 2002; contribs to Kansas Quarterly, Beloit Poetry Review, Bitterroot, South Florida Poetry Review, North Dakota Review, Cape Rock, Fiddlehead, Greenfield Review, Literary Review, Poet Pore, Sow's Ear Poetry Review. *Leisure interests:* walking, reading, films, Thoreau studies. *Address:* 68 Schellinger Road, Poland Spring, ME 04274, USA (home). *Telephone:* (207) 998-1073 (home). *E-mail:* vrchute@gmail.com.

CHYLEK, Petr, PhD; American (b. Czech) atmospheric scientist and academic; *Technical Staff Member, Space and Remote Sensing Sciences, Los Alamos National Laboratory;* ed Charles Univ., Prague, Czech Repub., Univ. of California, Riverside; Research Assoc., Dept of Physics, Indiana Univ., Bloomington 1970–72; Post-doctoral Fellow, Advanced Study Program, Nat. Center for Atmospheric Research, Boulder, Colo 1972–73; Asst Prof., Dept of Atmospheric Science, State Univ. of NY, Albany 1973–75, Research Prof. 1978–86; Assoc. Prof., Dept of Geosciences, Purdue Univ., West Lafayette, Ind. 1975–78; Prof., School of Meteorology, Univ. of Oklahoma, Norman 1986–90; Founder and Co-ordinator Atmospheric Science Program, Dalhousie Univ., Halifax, NS, Canada, Prof. of Physics and Atmospheric Science –2001, Sr Chair in Climate Research 1990–2001, Adjunct Prof. of Physics and Atmospheric Science 2001–; Adjunct Prof. of Physics, New Mexico State Univ., Las Cruces 1990–; Tech. Staff Mem. Space and Remote Sensing Sciences, Los Alamos Nat. Lab., Santa Fe, NM 2001–; Visiting Scientist, Instituto di Fisica de la Atmosfera, Frascati, Italy March–May 1966; Visiting Scientist, Air Resources Laboratory, Nat. Oceanic and Atmospheric Admin, Boulder, Colo 2000–01; Chair. Scientific Program Cttee, Second Int. Conf. on Global Warming and the Next Ice Age, Los Alamos Nat. Lab. 2006; mem. American Meteorological Soc.; Fellow, Optical Soc. of America 1991, Los Alamos Nat. Lab. 2006, American Geophysical Union 2006; Hon. Fellow, Center for Earth and Planetary Physics, Harvard Univ. 1976–78; Univ. of California Grad. Fellowship 1968–70, Advanced Study Program Post-doctoral Fellowship, Nat. Center for Atmospheric Research 1972–73, Nat. Research Council Sr Fellowship, White Sands Missile Range 1984–85, paper by Chylek, Kiehl & Ko (1978) reprinted in SPIE Milestone Series as one of milestone papers in field of Light Scattering 1988, Sr Research Chair in Climate Research, Natural Sciences and Eng Research Council of Canada 1990–2000, Distinguished Faculty Summer Fellowship, Naval Research Lab. April–June 1992, paper by Chylek and Srivastava (1983) reprinted in SPIE Milestone Series as one of milestone papers in field of linear optical composite materials 1996, paper by Chylek and Borel (2004) selected by American Geophysical Union Eds as a Journal Highlight 2004, Los Alamos Nat. Lab. Award for Scientific and Tech. Leadership 2004. *Publications:* more than 100 scientific papers in professional journals on remote sensing, atmospheric radiation, climate change, cloud and aerosol physics, applied laser physics and ice-core analysis. *Address:* Space and Remote Sensing Sciences (ISR-2), PO Box 1663, MS B241, Los Alamos, NM 87545, USA (office). *Telephone:* (505) 667-2801 (office). *Fax:* (505) 665-4414 (office). *E-mail:* chylek@lanl.gov (office). *Website:* www.lanl.gov/org/padgs/adtr/intelligence-space-research/space-remote-sensing (office).

CHYNOWETH, Alan Gerald, BSc, PhD, FIEEE, FInstP; British physicist (retd); b. 18 Nov. 1927, Harrow, Middx; s. of James Charles Chynoweth and Marjorie Fairhurst; m. Betty Freda Edith Boyce 1950; two s.; ed King's Coll., London; Postdoctoral Fellow, Nat. Research Council of Canada, Chem. Div., Ottawa 1950–52; mem. Tech. Staff, Bell Telephone Labs 1953–60, Head of Crystal

Electronics Dept 1960–65, Asst Dir Metallurgical Research Lab. 1965–73, Dir Materials Research Lab. 1973–76, Exec. Dir Electronic and Photonic Devices Div. 1976–83, Vice-Pres. Applied Research, Bell Communications Research 1983–92; Survey Dir of NAS Cttee on Survey of Materials Science and Eng 1971–73, Comm. on Mineral Resources and the Environment 1973–75; mem. Nat. Materials Advisory Bd 1975–79, NATO Special Programme Panel on Materials 1977–82, consultant to NATO Advanced Study Inst. Panel 1982–89; mem. Materials Research Soc., Metallurgical Soc.; Alt. Dir Microelectronics and Computer Tech. Corpn 1985–92; Dir Industrial Research Inst. 1990–92; Chair. Tech. Transfer Merit Program, NJ Comm. on Science and Tech. 1992–98; consultant to EC Telecommunications Directorate 1995; Lecturer, Electrochemical Soc. 1983; Co.-Ed. Optical Fiber Telecommunications 1979; Assoc. Ed. Solid State Comm. 1975–83; mem. Visiting Cttee, Cornell Univ. Materials Science Centre 1973–76, Natural Sciences Advisory Bd, Univ. of Pennsylvania 1988–92, Advisory Bd Dept of Electrical Eng and Computer Science, Univ. of California, Berkeley 1987–90, Advisory Bd, Dept of Electrical Eng, Univ. of Southern California 1988–90, Advisory Council Electrical Eng Dept, Pennsylvania State Univ. 1993–98; mem. Office of Science and Tech. Policy Panel on High Performance Computing and Communications 1991–92; mem. IEEE Frederik Philips Award Cttee 1997–2000, Corp. Recognitions Cttee 1999–; Chair. IEEE Recognitions Council IEEE 2003–06; Chair. IEEE Awards Review Cttee 2007–12; Fellow, IEEE, American Physical Soc., Int. Eng Consortium, Inst. of Physics, London; IEEE W. R. G. Baker Prize 1967, IEEE Frederik Philips Award 1992, American Physical Soc. George E. Pake Prize 1992, IEEE Eng Leadership Recognition 1996. *Publications include:* Optical Fiber Telecommunications (with Stewart E. Miller) 1979; over 60 papers in professional journals on solid state physics, 11 patents on solid state devices, NAS reports: Materials and Man's Needs, Materials Conservation through Technology, Resource Recovery from Municipal Solid Wastes. *Leisure interests:* travel, boating. *Address:* 6 Londonderry Way, Summit, NJ 07901, USA (home); 17 Mill Close, Fishbourne, Chichester, PO19 3JW, England (home). *Telephone:* (908) 273-3956 (USA) (home); (01243) 775928 (UK) (home). *E-mail:* algchy@aol.com.

CIACCI, Matteo, LLB; San Marino lawyer and politician; b. 5 May 1990, Borgo Maggiore; ed Univ. of Urbino; Rep. ISISS Inst. Morciano di Romagna 2007–09; mem. City of Venice Council 2009–14; Radio Announcer San Marino Rtv 2010; Collaborator LoSportivo.sm 2010; Sports Man. Fiorentino Calcio 2014–15; co-f. Movimento Civico Dieci (C10) 2012, Coordinator 2013–17, Pres. 2017–; MP Grand and General Council 2016–; mem. Youth Policy Cttee 2013–14, Council of XII, of Finance Comm., of Health Comm., of Anti-Mafia Comm., of Parl. Ass. of Mediterranean; Co-Captain-Regent (head of state) April–Oct. 2018. *Address:* Movimento Civico Dieci (C10), Via Ca' dei Lunghi 4, 47893 Borgo Maggiore (office); Via Della Carrare 74, 47890 Murata, San Marino (home). *Telephone:* (549) 909833 (office). *E-mail:* msciacci@omniway.com. *Website:* www.civico10.org (office); www.sanmarino.sm (office).

CIANCHETTE, Peter, BS; American business executive, politician and fmr diplomatist; *President and Chief Operating Officer, Starcon International Inc.;* b. 21 June 1961, Waterville, Me; m. Carolyn Cianchette; one s. one d.; ed Univ. of Maine, Roger Williams Univ.; more than 20 years of business experience, from serving as sr exec. in Dragon Products Co., to running his own business, Cianchette Enterprises, Inc.; joined consulting firm Pierce Atwood Consulting 1998, served as COO and Exec. Vice-Pres.; Pres. The Cianchette Group (public affairs man. and business consulting firm) 2002–08; Partner, CHK Capital Partners, Portland; served in Maine's State Legislature representing South Portland and Cape Elizabeth in Maine's House of Reps 1996–2000, mem. Jt Standing Cttee on Taxation; Republican nominee for Gov. of Maine 2002; currently Maine's Nat. Republican Committeeman, served as Maine Gen. Chair. of Bush-Cheney 2004 campaign; Amb. to Costa Rica 2008–09; Vice-Pres., Business Devt, Cianbro Companies 2009–14; Pres. and COO Starcon Int., Inc. 2014–; Dir Make-A-Wish Foundation of Maine and YES! to Youth, Maine Education Services; mem. George and Barbara Bush Maine Cultural Center Cttee, Finance Cttee of American Lighthouse Foundation, MaineHealth Corporator; fmr Tech. Greater Portland Big Brothers/Big Sisters, Boy Scouts of America/Pine Tree Council, Portland Chamber of Commerce, Southern Maine Community Coll. Foundation; fmr Pres. Maine Better Transportation Asscn; fmr Chair. Maine Advancement Program. *Address:* Starcon International Inc., 10610 Fairmont Parkway, La Porte, TX 77571, USA. *Telephone:* (281) 291-5200 (office). *Fax:* (281) 291-8851 (office). *Website:* starconinternational.com (office).

CIAVATTA, Valeria; San Marino politician and fmr head of state; b. 16 Jan. 1959; m. Giovanni Pacelli; two c.; ed Univ. of Urbino; mem. Consiglio Grande e Generale (Parl.) 1993–; Co-Capt. Regent (jt head of state) Oct. 2003–April 2004, April–Oct. 2014; Sec. of State for Internal Affairs and Civil Protection 2006–12; mem. Popular Alliance of Democrats (Alleanza Popolare dei Democratici Sammarinese). *Address:* Alleanza Popolare dei Democratici Sammarinese (APDS), Via Luigi Cibrario 25, 47893 Cailungo, San Marino (office). *Telephone:* (0549) 907080 (office). *Fax:* (0549) 907082 (office).

CIBOTARU, Viorel; Moldovan journalist and politician; *Leader, Partidul Liberal Democrat din Moldova (Liberal Democratic Party of Moldova);* b. 19 April 1958, Chişinău, Moldovan SSR, USSR; m.; ed Moldova State Univ., Lomonosov Moscow State Univ., Russia, George C. Marshall European Center for Security Studies, Germany; Lecturer, Faculty of Journalism, Moldova State Univ. 1985–88, Sr Lecturer 1999, Assoc. Prof. 1999–2013; various roles with Nat. Congress of Trade Unions 1988–92, including First Deputy Head, Dept of Educ. and Culture and Chief of Int. and Interethnic Affairs Div. 1988–90, Deputy Ed. Voice of the People (weekly newspaper) 1990–92; Ed.-in-Chief Oastea Moldovei (Moldova's Troops, weekly newspaper) 1992–95; Head of Press Div., Ministry of Defence 1995–97, Head of External Relations 1997–99, Deputy Commdr of Peacekeeping Forces Feb.–May 1999, Minister of Defence Feb.–July 2015; Leader, Partidul Liberal Democrat din Moldova (Liberal Democratic Party of Moldova) 2016–; Program Dir, Inst. for Public Policy, Chişinău 2000–06; Head, NATO Information and Documentation Centre, Chişinău 2008–10; Visiting Prof., School of Journalism, Univ. of Missouri, USA 2005; mem. Partidul Liberal Democrat din Moldova (PLDM); Service to the Fatherland Medal, First Class, Nat. Army Impeccable Service Medal, First Class, 20 Years Mil. Service Medal. *Address:* Partidul Liberal Democrat din Moldova (Liberal Democratic Party of Moldova), 2012 Chişinău, str. Bucureşti 88, Moldova (office). *Telephone:* (22) 81-51-54 (office). *Fax:* (22) 81-51-63 (office). *E-mail:* info@pldm.md (office). *Website:* www.pldm.md (office).

ÇIÇEK, Cemil; Turkish lawyer and politician; b. 15 Nov. 1946, Yozgat; m.; three c.; ed Faculty of Law, Istanbul Univ.; Mayor of Yozgat 1984–88; co-f. Motherland Party (now ANAVATAN); mem. Grand Nat. Ass. (Parl.) (Justice and Devt Party), Speaker 2011–15; fmr State Minister; Minister of Justice 2003–07; Deputy Prime Minister 2007–11. *Address:* c/o Büyük Millet Meclisi (Grand National Assembly), TBMM 06543, Bakanlıklar, Ankara, Turkey (office).

CICHOCKI, Jacek; Polish sociologist, political scientist and politician; *Head of the Chancellery of the Prime Minister;* b. 17 Dec. 1971, Warsaw; m.; one s. three d.; ed XLII Grad. High School, Faculty of Philosophy and Sociology, Warsaw Univ.; worked at Centre for Eastern Studies in Warsaw 1992–2008, first as an expert in armed conflicts and ethnic problems in the post-Soviet states and subsequently as the Head of the Unit for Dept for the Caucasus and Cen. Asia and Head of Dept for Ukraine, Belarus and the Baltic States, Deputy Dir of the Centre 2001–04, Dir 2007–08; worked as programme asst at the programme of Cen. and Eastern Europe Forum, Stefan Batory Foundation 1995–97; Sec., Office of the Cttee for Special and Intelligence Services, Chancellery of the Prime Minister 2008–11; Minister of the Interior 2011–13; mem. Council of Ministers and Head of the Chancellery of the Prime Minister 2013–; Gold Cross of Merit 2006. *Address:* Chancellery of the Prime Minister, 00-583 Warsaw, Al. Ujazdowskie 1/3, Poland (office). *Telephone:* (22) 6946000 (office). *Fax:* (22) 6252637 (office). *E-mail:* kontakt@kprm.gov.pl (office). *Website:* www.kprm.gov.pl (office); www.premier.gov.pl (office).

CICHY, Leszek; Polish bank executive and mountaineer; b. 14 Nov. 1951, Pruszków; m. Maria Gierałtowska; two s.; ed Warsaw Univ. of Tech.; researcher, Geodesic Dept, Warsaw Univ. of Tech. 1977–90; engineer in Syria 1990–92; mem. of staff, Housing Investments, Warsaw 1992–93, Polski Bank Rozwoju 1993–98; Vice-Chair. Dom Inwestycyjny BRE Banku, Warsaw 1998–99, Bank Współpracy Europejskiej, Warsaw 1999–2000; Dir Kredyt Bank, Warsaw 2000–01; Vice-Chair. and Finance Dir, Capital Group ERGIS 2001–; mem. Polish Alpine Club, Pres. 1995–2000; mountaineering expeditions include Tatra, Alps, Andes, Caucasus, Karakoram and Himalayas; first person to climb Mount Everest in the winter (with partner Krzysztof Wielicki q.v.) 1980; first Pole to climb the Crown of the Earth (highest peaks on every continent) 1980–99; Kt's Cross, Order of Polonia Restituta 2004. *Publication:* Discussing Everest (co-author) 1982. *Leisure interests:* tennis, skiing, astronomy. *Address:* ul. Na Uboczu 16/49, 02-791 Warsaw, Poland.

CICUTTO, Frank J., BCom, MPA, FAIBF, FAICD, FCIOSB; Australian (b. Italian) business executive; *Chairman, ORIX Australia Corporation Limited;* b. Italy; ed Univ. of New South Wales, Harvard Univ., USA; joined Nat. Bank of Australia (later Nat. Australia Bank) as grad. trainee 1968, served in various man. positions including accountant, Gen. Man., State Man., NSW, Exec. Gen. Man., Products and Services 1994–96, Chief Gen. Man., Australian Financial Services 1996–98, also CEO, Clydesdale Bank, Scotland (subsidiary of Nat. Australia Bank), Man. Dir and CEO Nat. Australia Bank 1999–2004 (resgnd); Chair. ORIX Australia Corpn Ltd 2004–, also Chair. ORIX New Zealand Ltd; Chair. Run Corpn Ltd 2005–07; fmr Chair. Chord Capital Management Pty Ltd; mem. Bd of Dirs, St Vincent's Health Australia from 2004, Melbourne Business School; Fellow, Australian Inst. of Banking and Finance, Australian Inst. of Co. Dirs. *Leisure interests:* theatre, rugby, squash, golf. *Address:* ORIX Australia Corpn Ltd, Locked Bag 2068, North Ryde, NSW 1670 (office); ORIX Australia Corpn Ltd, 1 Eden Park Drive, Macquarie Park, NSW 2113, Australia. *Telephone:* (2) 9856-6000 (office). *Fax:* (2) 9856-6500 (office). *E-mail:* info@orix.com.au (office). *Website:* www.orix.com.au (office).

CIECHANOVER, Aaron J., MSc, MD, DSc; Israeli physician, molecular biologist and academic; *University Distinguished Research Professor, Technion-Israel Institute of Technology;* b. 1 Oct. 1947, Haifa; m. Menucha Ciechanover; ed Hebrew Univ. of Jerusalem; mil. service as a doctor in Israeli army 1974–77; studied protein degradation at biochemical level with Avram Hershko (q.v.) 1976–81; collaborated with Alexander Varshavsky (q.v.) at MIT; internship, 'Rambam' Univ. Medical Center and Faculty of Medicine, Technion-Israel Inst. of Tech., Haifa 1973–74, partial training, Dept of Surgery B 1974–79, Research Fellow, Dept of Biochemistry, Faculty of Medicine 1977–79, Lecturer 1979–81, Sr Lecturer (with tenure) 1984–87, Assoc. Prof. 1987–92, Full Prof. 1992–, Dir The Rappaport Family Inst. for Research in the Medical Sciences 1993–2000, Janet and David Polak Prof. of Life Sciences 1996–, Univ. Distinguished Research Prof. 2002–, Founder and Dir The Lorry Lokey Interdisciplinary Center for Life Sciences and Eng 2004–09; Prof., Israel Cancer Research Fund, USA 2003–; Adjunct Prof. and Dir Inst. for Chemical and Biomedical Studies, Nanjing Univ., China 2011–; Distinguished Visiting Research Prof., Nat. Cheng Kung Univ., Taiwan 2007–; Dir The Center for Protein Dynamics, Seoul Nat. Univ., South Korea 2014–; mem. or fmr mem. Scientific Advisory Bd, Rosetta Genomics (Chair.), BioLineRx Ltd, StemRad Ltd, Allosterix Ltd, Proteologics, Inc., MultiGene Vascular Systems Ltd, Protalix BioTherapeutics, BioTheryX, Inc.; mem. Editorial Bd, Israel Medical Association Journal 1999–, Experimental Biology and Medicine 2006–, Cell Death and Differentiation 2007–, Science China – Life Sciences 2008–, Structural Chemistry 2005–; mem. Council of European Molecular Biology Org. 1996–; mem. AAAS 1984, Asia-Pacific Int. Molecular Biology Network 1999, European Acad. of Sciences 2004 (Fellow 2004), Israel Nat. Acad. of Sciences and Humanities 2004, Pontifical Acad. of Sciences 2007, Polish Acad. of Medicine 2007, Albert Schweitzer World Acad. of Medicine 2007, Nat. Acad. of Science and Tech. of South Korea 2007, Inst. for Advanced Studies, Honk Kong Univ. of Science and Tech. 2007, Academia Europaea 2009, American Asscn for Cancer Research Acad. 2012; Foreign mem. American Philosophical Soc. 2005, Ukrainian Academy of Sciences 2009, Russian Acad. of Sciences 2011, Georgian Acad. of Sciences 2012, Chinese Acad. of Sciences 2013; Founding mem. European Acad. of Cancer Sciences 2009; Foreign Assoc. NAS 2007, Inst. of Medicine of the Nat. Acads of the USA 2008; Fellow, Fed. of Asian Chemical Socs 2006, American Acad. for Cancer Research 2013; Hon. mem. ACS 2004, Soc. for Experimental Biology and Medicine 2006, Hellenic Soc. for Biochemistry and Molecular Biology 2011, World Immunopathology Org. 2011, Georgian Asscn of Allergology and Clinical Immunology 2012; Distinguished Life mem. Cell Stress Soc. International (CSSI) 2005;

Hon. FRSC 2005; Hon. Foreign Fellow, American Acad. of Arts and Sciences 2008; Hon. Pres. Israel Cancer Soc. 2010–, Israel Amyotrophic Lateral Sclerosis Soc. 2014–; Hon. Distinguished Univ. Prof., Kyushu Univ., Japan 2012; Extraordinary Prof., TEFAF Oncology Chair, Maastricht Univ., The Netherlands 2013; 44 hon. doctorates; Austria Ilse and Helmut Wachter Prize, Univ. of Innsbruck (co-recipient) 1999, Jewish Nat. Fund Alkales Award for Distinguished Scientific Achievements 2000, Albert Lasker Basic Medical Research Award 2000, Michael Landau (Mifa'al Ha'Peis) Award in Medical Ssciences (co-recipient) 2001, EMET (Truth) Prize (Israeli Prime Minister Prize) for Arts, Sciences and Culture (in Life Sciences and Medicine, AMAN Foundation (co-recipient) 2002, Israel Prize for Biology 2003, Eminent Scientist Award, Japan Soc. for the Promotion of Science 2003–06, Nobel Prize in Chem. (co-recipient) 2004, CSSI Medal 2005, Sir Hans Krebs Medal 2006, Medical Magnus Medal, Polish Acad. of Medicine 2007, Lee Kuan Yew Visiting Professorship and Award, Singapore 2010, Medal for Distinct Contrib. to Science, Int. Union of Biochemistry and Molecular Biology 2011, Alexander von Humboldt Fellow, Alexander von Humboldt Stiftung, Bonn, Germany 2011–. *Publications include:* Modern Cell Biology: Cellular Proteolytic Systems (co-ed.) 1994, The Ubiquitin-Proteasome Proteolytic System: From Classical Biochemistry to Human Diseases (co-ed.) 2002, Protein Degradation Handbook, Vol. 1 (co-ed.) 2005, Vol. 2 2006, Vol. 3 2006, Vol. 4 2008; 37 book chapters, 73 review articles and more than 160 papers in scientific journals; two patents. *Address:* Cancer and Vascular Biology Research Center, Ruth and Bruce Rappaport Faculty of Medicine, Technion – Israel Institute of Technology, 1 Efron Street, PO Box 9697, Bat Galim, Haifa, 31096, Israel (office). *Telephone:* 4-8295427 (office); 4-8295379 (Lab.) (office). *Fax:* 4-8521193 (office). *E-mail:* aaroncie@tx.technion.ac.il (office). *Website:* md.technion.ac.il/faculty_member/ciechanover-aaron (office); www.technioncancer.co.il/lab.php?id=1 (office).

CIELO FILHO, César Augusto; Brazilian swimmer; b. 10 Jan. 1987, Santa Bárbara d'Oeste, São Paulo; s. of César Cielo and Flaria Cielo; m. Kelly Gisch; one s.; ed Colegio Avanco de Ensino Programado, Auburn Univ., USA; began career at small swimming clubs in his native state; trained at Esporte Clube Barbarense under coach Mario Francisco Sobrinho; later trained at Clube de Campo de Piracicaba under Reinaldo Rosa 2000; transferred to Esporte Clube Pinheiros, São Paulo under Alberto Silva and Gustavo Borges 2003; trained under Australian coach Brett Hawke at Auburn Univ.; competed for eight-time NCAA Nat. Champion Auburn Tigers' Swimming and Diving team; also tutored by short-distance specialist Fernando Scherer 2008; World Championships (short course), Indianapolis 2004: silver medal, 4×100m freestyle; Pan American Games, Rio de Janeiro 2007: gold medal, 50m freestyle, 100m freestyle, 4×100m freestyle, silver medal, 4×100m medley; Olympic Games, Beijing 2008: gold medal, 50m freestyle, bronze medal, 100m freestyle; World Championships (long course), Rome 2009: gold medal, 50m freestyle, 100m freestyle; World Championships, Dubai 2010: gold medal, 50m freestyle, 100m freestyle, bronze medal, 4×100m freestyle, 4×100m medley; World Championships (short course), Guadalajara 2011: gold medal, 50m freestyle, 100m freestyle, 4×100m freestyle, 4×100m medley; World Championships (long course), Shanghai 2011: gold medal, 50m freestyle, 50m butterfly; Pan Pacific Championships, Irvine 2010: gold medal, 50m butterfly, silver medal, 50m freestyle, bronze medal, 100m freestyle; Olympic Games, London 2012: gold medal, 50m freestyle; World Championships (long course), Barcelona 2013: gold medal, 50m freestyle, 50m butterfly; bronze medal, 50m freestyle Olympic Games, Rio 2016; silver medal, 4×100m freestyle relay, World Aquatics Championships, Budapest 2017; set world long course record in 50m (20.91s) and 100m freestyle (46.91s) 2009; coll. team: Auburn Tigers 2005–08; swims for Clube de Regatas do Flamengo/Auburn Aquatics; coach Alberto Pinto; Brazilian Swimmer of the Year, TV Globo 2006, NCAA Swimmer of the Year 2007, Athlete of the Year in 2008, 2009. *Leisure interests:* resting, playing video games. *Address:* Auburn Athletics Department, PO Box 351, Auburn, AL 36831-0351, USA. *Telephone:* (334) 844-9750. *E-mail:* athletics@auburn.edu; fcielo@terra.com.br. *Website:* www.auburntigers.com/sports/c-swim/mtt/cielo_cesar00.html; www.cesarcielo.com.br.

CIEMNIEWSKI, Jerzy, JuD; Polish lawyer and politician; b. 2 Aug. 1939, Warsaw; m.; one s.; ed Faculty of Law, Warsaw Univ.; Lecturer, Warsaw Univ. 1962–68; scientific worker, Inst. of Law Studies, Polish Acad. of Sciences, Warsaw 1969–, Lecturer 1972–; mem. Solidarity Independent Self-governing Trade Union 1980–89; Assoc. Understanding Cttee of Creative and Scientific Asscns and Teachers' Solidarity, also scientific worker Social and Labour Study Centre attached to Nat. Comm. of Solidarity 1980–81; mem. Helsinki Cttee in Poland 1983; participant, Round Table debates, mem. group for law and judicature reform, expert group for political reforms Feb.–April 1989; mem. State Election Comm. during election to the Sejm (Parl.) and Senate 1989; Under-Sec. of State in Office of the Council of Ministers, Sec. of Council of Ministers 1989–91; Deputy to Sejm 1991–98; Judge, Constitutional Court 1998–2007; mem. Democratic Freedom Union 1990–94, Freedom Union 1994–, Helsinki Foundation for Human Rights, Centre for Human Rights in Eastern Europe; Commdr's Cross, Order of Polonia Restituta 2011; Awards of Gen. Sec. of Polish Acad. of Sciences 1974, 1976. *Publications:* numerous scientific works, mainly on constitutional law, including Ustawa o systemie konstytucyjnym SFR Jugosławii 1976, Sejm Ustawodawczy RP (1947–1952) 1978 (co-author), Studia nad rządem 1985 (co-author), System delegacki na tle ewolucji ustroju politycznego SFR Jugosławii 1988, Draft of the Constitution of the Republic of Poland (co-author) 1990. *Leisure interests:* family life, walking with dog, general history, painting. *Address:* c/o Tribunał Konstytucyjny, al. J. Ch. Szucha 12A, 00-198 Warsaw, Poland. *Website:* www.trybunal.gov.pl.

CIENFUEGOS ZEPEDA, Gen. Salvador; Mexican army officer and government official; b. 14 June 1948, México City; ed Heroico Colegio Militar; entered Mexican military Jan. 1964, positions include Military and Air Attaché, Embassies in Tokyo and Seoul; fmr Commdr of several Mil. Dists including 7th (Chiapas), 1st (México City), 9th (Guerrero), 5th (Jalisico) 2005; fmr Inspector and Comptroller-Gen. of Army and Air Force; fmr Deputy Dir-Gen., Fed. Register of Firearms and Explosives Control; fmr Dir Center for the Study of the Army and Air Force; Sec. (Minister) of Nat. Defence 2012–18; several decorations including mem. Legion of Mil. Honour. *Address:* c/o Secretariat of State for National Defence, Blvd Manuel Avila Camacho, esq. Avda Industria Militar, 3°, Col. Lomas de Sotelo, Del. Miguel Hidalgo, 11640 México DF, Mexico (office).

CIKOTIĆ, Selmo, PhD; Bosnia and Herzegovina government official and army officer (retd); b. 25 Jan. 1964, Berane-Ivangrad, Montenegro; m. Tanja Cikotić; one s. one d.; ed Bratstvo i Jedinstvo Mil. High School, Belgrade, Zadar Mil. Acad., Sarajevo Univ.; Duty Officer, Air Defence Educ. Centre, Zadar 1986–92; mem. Bosnia and Herzegovina Army 1992–94; Defence Attaché in Washington, DC 1994–97; Head of Training and Educ. Centre, Joint Command of Fed. of Bosnia and Herzegovina Army 1997–99; Head of Cabinet, Deputy Minister of Defence of Fed. of Bosnia and Herzegovina 1999–2000; Deputy Commdr of 1st Corps, Fed. of Bosnia and Herzegovina Army 2000–01, Commdr 2001–04; retd from active mil. duty 2004 (rank of Brig.-Gen.); CEO OKI Ltd, Sarajevo 2004–07; Minister of Defence 2007–12; mem. Party of Democratic Action (SDA). *Publications:* numerous articles and two books on defence and security. *Leisure interests:* sharpshooting, skiing, mountain biking, swimming, reading. *Address:* c/o Ministry of Defence, 71000 Sarajevo, H. Kreševljakovića 98, Bosnia and Herzegovina.

ÇILLER, Tansu Penbe, PhD; Turkish economist, academic and politician; b. 24 May 1946, Istanbul; m. Özer Uçuran Çiller; two s.; ed Robert Coll., Boğaziçi Univ., Univ. of Connecticut and Yale Univ., USA; Assoc. Prof. 1978, Prof. 1983; served on academic bds of various univs, mainly in Dept of Econs Boğaziçi Univ.; joined True Path Party (DYP) 1990, Leader 1993–2002; mem. Parl. 1991–2002; Minister of State for the Economy 1991–93; Prime Minister of Turkey 1993–96; Deputy Prime Minister and Minister of Foreign Affairs 1996–97; mem. Council of Women World Leaders, Washington, DC. *Publications:* nine publs on econs. *Address:* Council of Women World Leaders, United Nations Foundation, 1750 Pennsylvania Avenue NW, Suite 300, Washington, DC 20006, USA (office). *Telephone:* (202) 887-9040 (office). *Fax:* (202) 887-9021 (office). *Website:* www.unfoundation.org/features/cwwl-bios/current-cwwl-members/Tansu-Ciller.html (office).

CIMOLI, Giancarlo; Italian administrator and airline industry executive; b. 12 Dec. 1939, Fivizzano; with SNIA Viscosa 1968–74; Chair. and Man. Dir Ferrovie dello Stato (state railways) 1996–2004; Chair. and CEO Alitalia 2004–07; mem. Bd of Dirs, Air France-KLM –2007; mem. Aspen Inst.; found guilty of bankruptcy and stock manipulation by Sixth Criminal Chamber of the Court of Rome (trial related to collapse of Alitalia) and sentenced to eight years and eight months' imprisonment, banned for life from public office, and to pay 160 million euros to Alitalia group cos that he administered and 1,000 pvt. shareholders and depositors Sept. 2015; Commdr, Order of Merit of the Italian Repub. 1993, Kt Grand Cross 2002; Cavaliere del lavoro 2003.

CIMOSZEWICZ, Włodzimierz, MA, PhD, DJur; Polish lawyer, politician and farmer; b. 13 Sept. 1950, Warsaw; m.; one s. one d.; ed Faculty of Law, Warsaw Univ.; Research Assoc. and then Asst Prof., Warsaw Univ. 1972–85; Fullbright Scholar, Columbia Univ., New York, USA 1980–81; farm owner and operator 1985–89; mem. Union of Socialist Youth 1968–73 (Chair. Bd, Warsaw Univ. 1972–73), Union of Polish Students/Socialist Union of Polish Students 1968–75 (Chair. Univ. Council 1973), PZPR 1971–90; Deputy to Sejm (Parl.) 1989–2005, (mem. PZPR caucus 1989–90, Chair. SLD Parl. Group 1990–93, Vice-Chair. Nat. and Ethnic Minorities Comm. 1989–91, mem. Parl. Foreign Affairs Comm. 1989, Special Comm. on Territorial Self-Government 1990, Chair. Constitutional Cttee 1995–96), Deputy Speaker 1995–96; mem. Bd Interparliamentary Union 1989–91; presidential cand. for Democratic Left Alliance (SLD) 1990; mem. Parl. Ass. Council of Europe 1992–96; Deputy Chair. Council of Ministers and Minister of Justice and Attorney-Gen. 1993–95; Prime Minister of Poland 1996–97; Chair. European Integration Cttee 1996–97; mem. Podlaskie Prov. Council 1998–2000; Minister of Foreign Affairs 2001–04; elected Marshal (Speaker) Sejm Jan.–Oct. 2005; teacher, Univ. of Białystok 2006–; mem. Senate for Białystok 2007–; workstream leader for Agency for the Modernisation of Ukraine 2015–; Fullbright Scholar, Columbia Univ., New York, USA 1980–81; Chevalier Ordre nat. du Mérite 1997; Kt Order of the Greek Repub. 1997; Dr hc (Univ. of South Carolina) 1997, (Appalachian Univ.) 1998, (Odessa Univ., Ukraine). *Leisure interests:* family, reading, handiwork, hunting, angling, crafts, ecology. *Address:* Senat (Senate), 00-902 Warsaw, ul. Wiejska 6 (office); Biuro Senatorskie, ul. Henryka Sienkiewicza 22, lok. 3, 15-950 Białystok, Poland; The Agency for the Modernisation of Ukraine, Renngasse 6–8, Top 504, 1010 Vienna, Austria. *Telephone:* (22) 6949265 (Warsaw) (office); (85) 6523333 (Białystok); (1) 535-07-65-204 (Vienna). *Fax:* (22) 6949428 (Warsaw) (office). *E-mail:* biuro@cimoszewicz.eu (office); bernhard.schragl@amukraine.org. *Website:* www.senat.gov.pl (office); www.amukraine.org; www.cimoszewicz.eu.

CINCA MATEOS, Jordi; Andorran banker and politician; *Minister of Finance and Public Service;* b. 26 July 1965, Andorra la Vella; m.; one s. two d.; worked for 14 years in Andorran financial sector, including various responsibilities within Dept of Banking; Dir of Marketing and Commercial Banking and mem. Exec. Bd Credit Andorra 2009–11; Govt Gen. Sec. and Spokesman 1990–93; mem. Gen. Council (Consell Gen.) 1993–96; Minister of Finance and Public Service 2011–; mem. Bd of dirs of several cos in Andorra in the areas of entertainment, insurance, health services and textiles. *Leisure interests:* basketball, running marathons, travel. *Address:* Ministry of Finance and Public Service, Carrer Prat de la Creu 62–64, Edif. Administratiu, Andorra la Vella AD500, Andorra (office). *Telephone:* 875700 (office). *Fax:* 860962 (office). *E-mail:* finances.gov@andorra.ad (office). *Website:* www.finances.ad (office).

CINTRA FRÍAS, Gen. Leopoldo; Cuban army officer and government official; *Minister of the Revolutionary Armed Forces;* b. 17 July 1941, Yara, Granma Prov.; joined Rebel Army 1957, took part alongside Fidel Castro in guerrilla advance and overthrow of Batista regime; ended war with rank of Lt; subsequent army roles include Brigade Chief of Land Artillery, Chief of Army Motorized Div., Chief of Artillery Div., Revolutionary Army Forces Div. 3234, Tank Div. UM-1011, Head of W Army Region 1990–2011; roles abroad include Chief of Tanks Third Brigade, Int. Cuban Troops, Ethiopia, Head of Cuban Mil. Mission, Angola; mem. Asamblea Nacional del Poder Popular (Parl.) 1976–; Minister of the Revolutionary Armed Forces 2011–; mem. Partido Comunista de Cuba, mem. Cen. Cttee and Political Bureau; Repub. of Cuba Nat. Hero Award. *Address:* Ministry of the Revolutionary Armed Forces, Plaza de la Revolución, Havana, Cuba (office). *Website:* www.cubagob.cu/otras_info/minfar/far/minfar.htm (office).

CIOCCA, Pierluigi, DIur; Italian economist, fmr central banker and academic; b. 17 Oct. 1941, Pescara; m. Maria Campolungh 1970; one d.; ed Univ. of Rome,

Fondazione Einaudi (Univ. of Turin) and Balliol Coll., Oxford, UK; economist, Research Dept Banca d'Italia (Bank of Italy) 1969–82, Cen. Man. for Cen. Bank Operations 1982–88, Cen. Man. for Econ. Research 1988–95, Deputy Dir-Gen. Bank of Italy 1995–2006; mem. Working Party 3 OECD Econ. Policy Cttee 1997; substitute for Gov. Bank of Italy, Governing Council, European Cen. Bank 1998; mem. Financial Stability Forum 1999, EU Econ. and Financial Cttee 2003; Prof. of Econ. History, Dept of Econs, Università degli Studi di Roma 'la Sapienza' 2006–11; Prof. of Political Economy and Devt Econs, Faculty of Political Science, LUISS Guido Carli Univ., Rome 2006–11; mem. Bd, Foundation Luigi Einaudi, Rome 2008–12, Liberal mem. of the Council 2012–; mem. Bd of Trustees for the celebrations of the 150th anniversary of Italy 2008–11; Corresp. mem. Accad. nazionale dei Lincei 2008; Corresp. Academician, Accad. dei Georgofili, Florence 2009; Grand Officer, Order of Merit of the Italian Repub. 1989; hon. degree from Univ. of Macerata 2013; Lao Silesu Award 1983, Book of the Year Award, Club of Jurists 2000, Canova Award 2001, Menichella Award 2003, Capalbio Award 2003, Aprutium Award 2004, Anassilaos Award 2007. *Publications include:* La nuova finanza in Italia, Una difficile metamorfosi (1980–2000) 2000, Ricchi per sempre? Una storia economica d'Italia (1796–2005) 2007, La banca che ci manca. Le banche centrali, l'Europa, l'instabilità del capitalismo 2014. *Address:* Via Cesalpino 12, 00161, Rome, Italy. *Telephone:* (06) 4991-7065.

CIOCLEA, Sergiu, MEconSc PhD; Moldovan economist, banking executive and central banker; b. 12 Sept. 1974, Chişinău; ed Academia de Studii Economice din Moldova, Université Panthéon Assas (Paris II), France; Sr Economist, BNP Paribas, Paris 1997, in charge of Cen. and Eastern Europe, Russia and Turkey, Country Risk Div.-Econ. Research Dept, Bond Analyst, Cen. and Eastern Europe, Emerging Market Desk, Fixed Income Dept, London Jan.–Aug. 1998, Assoc., Vice-Pres. and Dir Cen. and Eastern Europe Div., Corp. Finance Dept, Paris 2000–07, Man. Dir and Head of Corp. Finance for Russia and CIS 2008–15; Gov. Banca Naţională a Moldovei (Nat. Bank of Moldova) 2016–18 (resgnd).

CIOFFI, John M., BS, MS, PhD; American electrical engineer and academic; *Hitachi America Professor Emeritus of Engineering, Stanford University;* b. 7 Nov. 1956, Chicago, Ill.; s. of John M. Cioffi Jr and Lorraine M. Cioffi; m. Assia Cioffi; one s. five d.; ed Univ. of Illinois, Urbana-Champaign, Stanford Univ., Calif.; Bell Laboratories 1978–84; IBM Research 1984–86; EE Prof., Stanford Univ. 1986–2008, Hitachi America Prof. of Eng 2002–09, Prof. Emer. 2009–; Co-founder and Chief Tech. Officer, Amati Communications Inc. 1991–97 (acquired by Texas Instruments 1997); Chair. and CEO ASSIA Inc., Redwood City, Calif. (dynamic broadband-connection management software); mem. Bd of Dirs Alto Beam, Marconi Foundation; fmr Dir Marvell Semiconductor, Teknovus, ITEX, and others; mem. Nat. Acad. of Eng 2001; Fellow, IEEE 1996; Int. Fellow, Royal Soc. of Eng (UK) 2009; Dr hc (Edinburgh) 2010; NSF Presidential Investigator 1987–92, Faculty Devt Award, IBM Research 1986–88, Best Paper Award, IEEE Communications Soc. 1990, Outstanding Achievment Award, American Nat. Standards Inst. for contribs to ADSL 1995, Outstanding Alumnus, Univ. of Illinois 1999, IEE J.J. Thomson Medal 2000, IEEE Third Millennium Medal 2000, IEEE Kobayashi Medal 2001, ISSLS Best Paper Prize, IEE 2004, Marconi Prize and Int. Fellowship, Marconi Foundation 2006, Best Paper Award, IEEE ICC (co-recipient) 2006, Best Paper Award, IEEE ICC (co-recipient) 2007, Best Paper Award, IEEE Communications Magazine (co-recipient) 2007, Best Paper Award, IEEE ICC (co-recipient) 2008, IEEE Alexander Graham Bell Medal 2010, Innovation Award, Economist Magazine 2010, Distinguished Alumnus, Univ. of Illinois 2010, Edwin H. Armstrong Award 2013, Kirchmayer Award 2014. *Achievement:* designed world's first ADSL and VDSL modems (design accounts for 98% of world's more than 400 million DSL connections). *Publications:* more than 200 journal papers and 400 conf. papers and more than 100 licensed patents. *Address:* Room 363, David Packard Electrical Engineering Building, Stanford University, 350 Serra Mall, MC 9515, Stanford, CA 94305-9515, USA (office). *Telephone:* (650) 723-2150 (office). *Fax:* (650) 724-3652 (office). *E-mail:* cioffi@stanford.edu (office). *Website:* www.stanford.edu/group/cioffi (office).

CIOLOŞ, Dacian Julien; Romanian agricultural engineer, politician and fmr EU official; b. 27 July 1969, Zalău; m.; ed Univ. of Agricultural Sciences and Veterinary Medicine, Cluj-Napoca, École nationale supérieure agronomique de Rennes, Univ. of Montpellier 1, France; agro-economist intern, EC Directorate-Gen. for Agriculture and Rural Devt, Brussels 1997, 1999, mem. EC del. to Romania (worked on EU SAPARD agricultural devt programme) 2002–03; Dir, local rural devt programme, Argeş Co. 1998–99; adviser to Minister of Agric. 2005–07, Under-Sec. of State for European Affairs, Ministry of Agric. May–Oct. 2007, Minister for Agric. and Rural Devt 2007–08; Prime Minister of Romania 2015–17; Head of Presidential Comm. on Agricultural Devt Public Policy of Romania 2009–10; Commr for Agric. and Rural Devt, EC, Brussels 2010–14; mem. Groupe de Bruges (agricultural think-tank) 2000–; Ind. *Address:* c/o Office of the Prime Minister, 011791 Bucharest 1, Piaţa Victoriei 1, Romania.

CIORBEA, Victor; Romanian lawyer and politician; *Avocatul Poporului (Ombudsman);* b. 26 Oct. 1954, Ponor Village; s. of Vasile Ciorbea and Eugenia Ciorbea; m. 1977; one d.; ed Law School, Cluj-Napoca, Case Western Reserve Univ., Cleveland, Ohio, USA; judge, Court of Bucharest 1979–84; Prosecutor, Dept Civil Cases, Gen. Prosecutor's Office 1984–87; Asst to Lecturer Law School, Bucharest 1987–90; Pres. Free Trade Unions Fed. in Educ. 1990–96, CNSLR 1990–93, CNSLR-FRĂTIA 1993–94, Democratic Union Confed., Romania 1994–96; Mayor of Bucharest 1996; Prime Minister of Romania 1996–98; mem. Exec. Bd ICFTU, ETUC, CES 1993–94, Congress of Local and Regional Powers, Council of Europe, Strasbourg 1996, European Hon. Senate 1999; rep. of Romania at OIM confs; Vice-Pres. PNTCD 1997–99, Pres. 2001; mem. Christian Democratic Nat. Peasants' Party (now Popular Christian-Democratic Party of Romania) 1989–2012, Chair. 1999–2004; Pres. and Lawyer, SCPA Ciorbea Victor & Ciorbea Lacrima, Bucharest Bar Asscn 2004–14; mem. Nat. Liberal Party 2012–14; Senator 2012–14; Vice-Pres. Nat. Alliance for the Restoration of the Monarchy 2012–14; Avocatul Poporului (Ombudsman) 2014–; mem. Bd, Alianta Civica 1996; Founding mem. Int. Christian Coalition 1999; numerous decorations by various states and awards from nat. and int. orgs, foundations, etc. since 1990. *Address:* Office of the Avocatul Poporului, 3 St. Eugeniu Carada, Sector 3, Bucharest 71204, Romania (office). *Telephone:* (21) 3127134 (office). *Fax:* (21) 3124921 (office). *E-mail:* avp@avp.ro (office). *Website:* www.avp.ro (office).

CIOROIANU, Adrian Mihai, PhD; Romanian academic and politician; b. 5 Jan. 1967, Craiova; ed Univ. of Bucharest and Laval Univ., Canada; Lecturer, History Dept, Univ. of Bucharest 2002–; Adviser to Pres. of Nat. Liberal Party (PNL) 2002; elected to Romanian Senate (PNL) 2004–; Observer, European Parl. 2005–07; mem. European Parl. 2007; Minister of Foreign Affairs 2007–08 (resgnd); mem. editorial team, Dilema Veche 1998–, Gazeta Sporturilor, Interpres, Scrisul Romanesc (newspapers); TV presenter on TVR1, Realitatea TV, Pax TV 2000–04. *Publications include:* The Ashes of a Century: A Hundred and One Superimposed Stories 2001, The Fire Hidden in Stone: On History, Memory and Other Contemporary Vanities 2002, This Ceauşescu Who Is Haunting the Romanians: The Myth, the Images and the Cult of the Leader in Communist Romania 2005, On the Shoulders of Marx: An Incursion into the History of Romanian Communism 2005, Sic Transit Gloria: The Subjective Chronicle of a Five-Year Plan Completed over Three and a Half Years 2006. *Address:* Partidul Naţional Liberal (National Liberal Party), 011866, Bucharest, Boulevard Aviatorilor 86, Romania (office). *Telephone:* (21) 2310795 (office). *Fax:* (21) 2310796 (office). *E-mail:* dre@pnl.ro (office). *Website:* www.pnl.ro (office); www.cioroianu.ro (home).

CIOSEK, Stanisław, MA; Polish politician and diplomatist; b. 2 May 1939, Pawłowice, Radom Prov.; s. of Józef Ciosek and Janina Ciosek; m. Anna Ciosek 1969; two d.; ed Higher School of Econs, Sopot; spent time as activist in youth orgs 1957–75; Chair. Regional Council of Polish Students' Asscn (ZSP), Gdańsk, Deputy Chair. and Chair. Chief Council, ZSP 1957–73; Chair. Chief Council of Fed. of Socialist Unions of Polish Youth (FSZMP) 1974–75; mem. Polish United Workers' Party (PZPR) 1959–90, Deputy mem. PZPR Cen. Cttee 1971–80, First Sec., Voivodship Cttee PZPR and Chair. Presidium of Voivodship Nat. Council, Jelenia Góra 1975–80, mem. PZPR Cen. Cttee 1980–81, 1986–90, Sec., PZPR Cen. Cttee 1986–88, Alt. mem. Political Bureau of PZPR Cen. Cttee 1988, mem. Political Bureau 1988–89; Deputy to Sejm (Parl.) 1972–85; Minister for Co-operation with Trade Unions 1980–85, for Labour, for Wages and Social Affairs 1983–84, Vice-Chair. Cttee of Council of Ministers for Co-operation with Trade Unions 1983–85; Sec., Socio-Political Cttee of Council of Ministers 1981–85; Sec.-Gen. Nat. Council of Patriotic Movt for Rebirth (PRON) 1988–89; Co-organizer and participant, Round Table debates 1989; Amb. to USSR 1989–91, to Russia 1991–96; Foreign Policy Adviser to Pres. of Poland 1997–2005; Sec.-Gen. Eastern Club; Chair. Council, Polish-Russian Chamber of Commerce and Industry; Commdr's Cross, Order of Polonia Restituta. *Address:* 01-138 Warsaw, ul. Zimna 2/2, Poland (office). *Telephone:* (22) 654-7373 (office). *Fax:* (22) 654-7388 (office). *E-mail:* ciosek@ipgroup.pl (office). *Website:* prihp.pl (office).

CIPRIANI THORNE, HE Cardinal Juan Luis; Peruvian ecclesiastic; *Archbishop of Lima;* b. 28 Dec. 1943, Lima; ed St Mary's Catholic High School, Nat. Univ. of Eng, Univ. of Navarra, Spain; mem. Peruvian nat. basketball team in his youth; ordained priest 1977; apptd Coadjutor Bishop of Ayacucho 1988, Bishop of Turuzi 1988–95, Archbishop of Ayacucho 1995–99, Archbishop of Lima 1999–; cr. Cardinal (Cardinal-Priest of S. Camillo de Lellis) 2001; participated in Papal Conclave 2013; Great Chancellor Pontificia Universidad Católica del Perú; mem. Secr. for the Economy 2014–; mem. Opus Dei; Class of Grand Cross, Order of the Sun 2009. *Address:* Arzobispado, Plaza de Armas s/n, Apdo. 1512, Lima 100 (office); Calle Los Nogales 249, San Isidro, Lima 27, Peru. *Telephone:* (14) 427-5980 (office); (14) 441-1977. *Fax:* (14) 427-1967 (office); (14) 440-9134. *E-mail:* arzolimas@amauta.rcpnet.pe (office).

CIPUTRA, BEng; Indonesian real estate executive; *Chairman and President Commissioner, Ciputra Group;* b. (Tjie Tjin Hoan), 1931; m.; four c.; ed Bandung Inst. of Tech.; co-f. PT Pembangunan Jaya 1961, now Commr; Pres. Commr Ciputra Group 1984–90, 2002–, Pres. Dir 1990–2002, now also Chair.; f. PT Metropolitan Devt 1971, now Pres. Commr; Chair. Ciputra Foundation 1986–; Head of Jaya Raya Foundation; Man. Jaya Raya Badminton Club; Dr hc (Univ. Tarumanagara) 2008; Ernst and Young Indonesian Entrepreneur of the Year Award 2007, Lifetime Achievement Luminary Award, Channel NewsAsia Singapore 2013, Golden Life Time Achievement, Property & Bank Award 2013, Begawan Properti Indonesia, Housing Estate magazine 2013. *Address:* Ciputra Head Office, Prof. Dr. Satrio Kav 6, Jakarta 12940, Indonesia (office). *Telephone:* (21) 5225858 (office). *Fax:* (21) 5274125 (office). *Website:* www.ciputra.com (office).

CIRAC SASTURAIN, Juan Ignacio, LicTheorPhys, PhD; Spanish physicist and academic; *Director of the Theory Division, Max Planck Institute for Quantum Optics;* b. 11 Oct. 1965, Manresa, Catalonia; ed Universidad Complutense de Madrid; Fellow, Formación del Personal Investigador (Prog. Gen.), Dept of Optics, Universidad Complutense de Madrid 1989–91; Titular Univ. Prof., Dept of Applied Physics, Universidad de Castilla-La Mancha 1991–96; Research Assoc., Jt Inst. for Lab. Astrophysics, Univ. of Colorado, USA 1993–94; Prof., Institut für Theoretische Physik, Leopold Franzens Universität Innsbruck 1996–2001; Dir Theory Div., Max Planck Inst. for Quantum Optics and mem. Max Planck Soc. 2001–; Assoc. Ed., Physical Review A 2000–03, Revista Española de Física 2002–05, Review of Modern Physics 2005–; Founding Man. Ed., Quantum Information and Computation 2001–; mem. Advisory Bd Annalen der Physik journal 2012–; mem. Advisory Council, Fundación La Caixa 2015–; mem. Bd of Dirs Telefónica SA 2016–; Corresp. Spanish Acad. of Sciences 2002, Austrian Acad. of Sciences 2003; Fellow, American Physical Soc. 2002; Hon. Prof. of Physics, Tech. Univ. of Munich 2002–; Distinguished Guest Prof., Institut de Ciències Fotòniques (Barcelona) 2003; Distinguished Research Chair, Perimeter Inst., Waterloo, Canada 2009; Dr hc (Universidad Castilla-La Mancha) 2005, (Universidad Politecnica de Catalunya, Barcelona) 2007; Premio Nacional a Investigadores Noveles, Royal Physical Soc. of Spain 1992, Felix Kuschenitz Prize, Austrian Acad. of Sciences 2001, Medal of the Royal Physical Soc. of Spain 2002, Quantum Electronics Prize, European Science Foundation 2005, Prince of Asturias Award for Tech. and Scientific Research 2006, 6th Int. Quantum Communication Award 2006, Nat. 'Blas Cabrera' Prize for Physical, Material and Earth Sciences 2007, 'Académico de Honor', Academia de Ciencias de la Región de Murcia 2007, 'Premios de las artes y de la ciencia' – Castellano-Manchegos del Mundo, Junta Castilla-La Mancha 2009, Carl Zeiss Research Award 2009, BBVA Foundation Frontiers of Knowledge Award 2009, Benjamin Franklin Medal, Franklin Inst. (co-recipient) 2010, Premi Nacional de Pensament i Cultura Científica 2010, Wolf Prize in Physics (co-recipient) 2013, Max Planck Medal, German Physical Soc. 2018. *Publications:*

more than 440 papers in professional journals. *Address:* Room B1.41, Max-Planck-Institut für Quantenoptik, Hans-Kopfermann-Str. 1, 85748 Garching, Germany (office). *Telephone:* (89) 32905-705 (office). *Fax:* (89) 32905-336 (office). *E-mail:* ignacio.cirac@mpq.mpg.de (office). *Website:* www.mpq.mpg.de (office).

CIRELLI, Jean-François; French energy industry executive; *Vice-Chairman and President, in charge of the Energy Europe Business line, GDF Suez SA;* b. 9 July 1958, Chambéry; ed Institut d'Etudes Politiques, Ecole Nationale d'Admin, Paris; with Treasury Dept, Ministry of Economy and Finance 1985–95; Tech. Adviser to Pres. of France 1995–97, Econ. Adviser 1997–2002; Deputy Dir Office of the Prime Minister 2002–04; Chair. and CEO Gaz de France Group 2004–08, Vice-Chair. and Pres., in charge of the Energy Europe Business line, GDF Suez SA 2008–, Chair. GDF Suez Trading (France), Eurogas (Belgium), Vice-Chair. GDF Suez Corp. Foundation, Electrabel (Belgium), Dir of GDF Suez Energy Services, Suez Environnement Co. (France), GDF Suez Belgium, International Power (UK); mem. Supervisory Bd Vallourec; mem. Bd of Dirs Neuf Cegetel, Atos. *Address:* GDF Suez SA, 1 place Samuel de Champlain, 92400 Courbevoie, France (office). *Telephone:* 1-44-22-00-00 (office). *E-mail:* info@gdfsuez.com (office). *Website:* www.gdfsuez.com (office); www.suez-environnement.com (office).

CIRIANI, Henri Edouard; French architect and academic; b. 30 Dec. 1936, Lima, Peru; s. of Enrique Ciriani and Caridad Suito; m. Marcelle Espejo 1962; two d.; ed Santa Maria School, Nat. Univ. of Eng and Town Planning Inst., Lima; Asst Architect, Dept of Architecture, Ministry of Devt and Public Works, Lima, Project Architect 1961–64; pvt. practice with Crousse and Paez 1961–63; Asst Prof. of Design, Nat. Univ. of Eng, Lima 1962–64; emigrated to France 1964; f. pvt. practice 1968; Prof. Ecole des Beaux-Arts de Paris 1969–83; Prof. of Architecture, Ecole d'Architecture de Paris-Belleville 1984–2002; Dist Prof., Univ. Nacional de Ingeniería, Lima 1985–; Visiting Prof., Tulane Univ., New Orleans 1984, Univ. Coll., Dublin 1985, Ecole d'Architecture de Grenoble 1988, Univ. of Pennsylvania 1989 and many others; Sir Banister Fletcher Visiting Lecturer, Univ. Coll., London 1986; Prof., Univ. of Navarra 2006–07; Dir Acad. de France, Rome 1987–91; Fondation Le Corbusier 1989–; mem. Int. Acad. of Architecture; Hon. Fellow, RIBA; Chevalier, Légion d'honneur 1997; Dr hc (Universidad Nacional de Ingeniería of Peru) 2009; Nat. Grand Prix of Architecture 1983, Equerre d'Argent 1983, Palme d'Or de l'Habitat 1988, Brunner Memorial Prize 1997, Gold Medal, Acad. of Architecture 2012, Gold Medal, Colegio de Arquitectos Regional, Lima, Peru 2012. *Public works include:* public housing at Ventanilla Matute 1963, San Felipe 1964, Rimac Mirones 1965, Marne-la-vallée Noisy II 1980, Noisy III 1981, St Denis 1982, Evry 1985, Lognes 1986, Charcot 1991, Bercy 1994, Colombes 1995, urban landscape at Grenoble 1968–74, public facilities at St Denis Child-care Centre 1983, Cen. kitchen for St Antoine Hosp., Paris 1985, Torcy Child-care Centre 1989, Museum of the First World War, Péronne 1992, extension to Ministry of Finance Bldg, Paris 1993, Arles Archaeological Museum 1995, pvt. bldgs at The Hague Apartment Tower 1995, Stadspoort College 2000, Conf. Centre, French Nat. Inst. for Research in Computer Science and Control 2001, Palais de Justice 2006, retrospective exhbns at Institut Français d'Architecture, Paris 1984, Figueira da Foz, Oporto and Lisbon 1985, New York 1985, Tokyo 1987, Lima 1996, New York 1997, Montreal 1997, Venice 1999, São Paulo 2005, Pôle universitaire et culturel, Nancy 2006, extension and renovation of villa, San Isidro 2013, Maison à Señoritas, Punta Hermosa 2013. *Publications:* Pratique de la pièce urbaine 1996, Paroles d'architecte (ed. by Jean Petit Lugano) 1997. *Leisure interests:* drawing, collecting postcards. *Address:* Atelier Ciriani, 61 rue Pascal, 75013 Paris, France (office). *Telephone:* 1-43-37-41-00 (office). *Website:* henriciriani.blogspot.co.uk.

ĆIRIĆ, Nebojša, MBA; Serbian economist and politician; *CEO, East Point Holdings;* b. 12 Jan. 1974, Bor; m. Jelena Galic; two c.; ed London School of Econs, London Inst. of Chartered Accountants, HEC School of Man., Paris, France, Univ. of Belgrade; Jr Account Man., Ogilvy & Mather, Belgrade 1996–97; expert assoc., Consulting Dept, Econ. Inst., Belgrade 1997–2001; Special Foreign Investment Adviser, Ministry of Int. Econ. Relations 2001–02; Dir for Financial Consulting, Deloitte, Belgrade 2002–07; Asst Minister of the Economy, responsible for Industry and Privatization 2007–08; State Sec., Ministry of the Economy 2008–11, Minister of the Economy and Regional Devt 2011–12; Pvt. Practice, PJ Advisory Co. 2013–; CEO, East Point Holdings 2014–. *Address:* East Point Holdings, 11000 Belgrade, 115d Mihajla Pupina Blvd, Serbia (office). *Telephone:* (11) 7348482 (office). *E-mail:* info@eastpointholding.com (office). *Website:* www.eastpointholding.com (office).

CISNEROS, Henry G., BA, Master of Urban & Regional Planning, MPA, DPA; American real estate industry executive and fmr politician; *Executive Chairman, CityView;* b. 11 June 1947, San Antonio, Tex.; s. of J. George Cisneros and Elvira Munguia; m. Mary-Alice Perez; one s. two d.; ed Texas A&M Univ., Harvard Univ., George Washington Univ.; Admin. Asst, Office of the City Man., San Antonio, Tex. May–Sept. 1968, Office of the City Man., Bryan, Tex. 1968–69; Asst Dir, Dept of Model Cities, San Antonio, Tex. 1969–70; Asst to the Exec. Vice-Pres., Nat. League of Cities, Washington, DC 1970–71; Teaching Asst, Dept of Urban Studies and Planning, MIT 1972–74; Faculty mem., Dept of Urban Studies, Trinity Univ. 1974–87, Public Admin program, Univ. of Texas, San Antonio 1974–87; mem. City Council, City of San Antonio 1975–81, Mayor of San Antonio 1981–89; Chair. Cisneros Asset Management Co. 1989–93, Chair. Cisneros Benefit Group, Cisneros Communications; Sec., US Dept of Housing and Urban Devt 1993–97; Pres. and COO Univision Communications, Inc. 1997–2000; Chair. American Sunrise Non-Profit Corpn 2000–; Exec. Chair. CityView, LLC 2000–; Earthquake Assistance Hon. mem. AIA 1986; 23 hon. degrees; numerous awards including White House Fellow, Office of the Sec. of Health, Educ., and Welfare, Washington, DC 1971–72, Ford Foundation Grant recipient, John F. Kennedy School of Govt, Harvard Univ. 1972–74, Jefferson Award, American Inst. of Public Service 1982, Distinguished Leadership Award, American Inst. of Planners 1985, Nat. Recognition Award, Mexican Govt 1985, Pres.'s Award, Nat. League of Cities 1989, First Annual John A. Wilson Public Service Award 1993, Humanitarian Award, Los Angeles Inner City Law Center 2001, Lifetime Achievement Award, Para Los Niños 2001, Congressional Hispanic Caucus Medallion of Excellence for Leadership 2002, Aguila Azteca, Govt of Mexico 2003, Catherine Powell Distinguished Service Award, Texas City Planners Asscn 2004, James W. Rouse Civic Medal of Honor, Enterprise Foundation 2004, Martin Luther King Distinguished Leadership Award, San Antonio 2005, Excellence in Affordable Housing Initiatives, City of San Antonio 2005, Business Man of the Year, Texas Asscn of Mexican-American Chambers of Commerce (TAMACC) 2006, Lifetime Achievement Award, San Antonio Hispanic Chamber of Commerce 2006, listed in the Top 50 Most Influential People in Home Building, Builder Magazine 2006, listed in the Top 101 Top Leaders of the Hispanic Community, Latino Leaders Magazine 2006, Cesar Chavez Award, American Asscn for Affirmative Action 2007, Housing Person of the Year, Nat. Housing Conf. 2007, Builders Hall of Fame Inductee, Nat. Asscn of Home Builders 2007, Nat. Leadership Honoree, Hispanic Elected Local Officials 2008, Hubert H. Humphrey Award, American Political Science Asscn 2008, Habitat for Humanity, Visionary Award 2008, Walter F. Mondale and Edward W. Brooke Fair Housing Award, Nat. Alliance for Fair Housing 2009, Urban Leadership Award, Penn Inst. for Urban Research 2011, Jack Kemp Award, Terwilliger Center, Urban Land Inst. 2011, Leadership Award, Council of Large Public Housing Authorities 2011 Outstanding Corp. Citizen, Hispanic Chamber 2012. *Publications include:* San Antonio's Place in the Technology Economy: A Review of Opportunities and a Blueprint for Action 1982, Target 1990, US Dept of Housing and Urban Devt 1994–97, Opportunity and Progress: A Bipartisan Platform for National Housing Policy (with Jack Kemp, Nick Retsinas and Kent Colton) 2004, Casa y Comunidad: Latino Home and Neighborhood Design (co-ed. with John Rosales) 2006, BuilderBooks (Silver Award, Benjamin Franklin Awards, Publrs Marketing Asscn 2007) 2007, Our Communities, Our Homes: Pathways to Housing and Homeownership in America's Cities and States (with Jack Kemp, Nick Retsinas and Kent Colton) 2007, Latinos and the Nation's Future (ed.) 2008, From Despair to Hope: HOPE VI and the Transformation of America's Public Housing (ed.) 2009, Independent for Life (co-ed. with Jane Hickie) 2012. *Leisure interests:* reading, going to the cinema, spending time with his family. *Address:* CityView, 454 Soledad Street, Suite 300, San Antonio, TX 78205 (office); 2002 West Houston Street, San Antonio, TX 78207, USA (home). *Telephone:* (210) 228-9574 (office). *Fax:* (210) 224-7888 (home). *E-mail:* info@cityview.com (office). *Website:* www.cityview.com (office).

CISNEROS RENDILES, Gustavo A., BS; Venezuelan/Dominican Republic media executive; *Chairman, Cisneros Group;* b. 20 Nov. 1945, Caracas; s. of Diego Cisneros; m. Patricia Phelps; one s. two d.; ed Babson Coll., Wellesley, Mass, USA; Chair. and CEO Cisneros Group (family-owned co. holding stakes in over 70 cos in 39 countries, including Venevisión, Univisión, Chilevisión, Caracol Televisión de Colombia, Playboy TV Latin America, Caribbean Communications Network, Direct TV Latin America and American Online Latin America (AOLA) –2013, Chair. 2013–; Dir, Panamco Bottling Co., AOL Latin America, Pueblo International, Inc., Ibero-American Media Partners 1997–; Owner, Los Leones del Caracas baseball team 2001–; Co-founder (with wife Patricia and brother Ricardo) Fundación Cisneros; mem. Bd of Dirs, Barrick Gold Corpn, RRE Ventures LLC; Commr Global Information Infrastructure Comm.; Charter mem. UN Information and Communications Technologies Task Force; mem. World Business Council, World Econ. Forum; mem. Int. Advisory Councils, Columbia Univ., Babson Coll.; mem. Int. Advisory Bd Barrick Gold Corpn, Council on Foreign Relations; mem. Advisory Cttee, David Rockefeller Center for Latin American Studies, Harvard Univ.; mem. Bd of Advisers for Panama Canal; mem. Chair.'s Int. Advisory Council, Americas Soc.; mem. Bd of Overseers, Int. Center for Econ. Growth; mem. Bd Govs, Joseph H. Lauder Inst. of Man., Wharton School at Univ. of Pennsylvania; mem. Chair.'s Council, Museum of Modern Art; mem. Bd Trustees, Museum of TV and Radio; Kt, Order of Malta, Order of the Liberator (First Degree); Gran Cordón, Order of Andrés Bello; Order of Francisco Miranda (Second and First Class), among others; Americas Soc. Distinguished Service Award 2003, Woodrow Wilson Award for Public Service 2004. *Address:* Cisneros Group, 36 East 61st Street, New York, NY 10021, USA (office); Edeficio Venevisión, Final Avenida La Salle, Colina de los Caobos, Caracas 1050 (office); Fundación Cisneros, Centro Mozarteum, Final Avenida La Salle, Colina de los Caobos, Caracas 1050, Venezuela (office). *Telephone:* (212) 708-9444 (USA) (office); (582) 708-9697 (Venezuela) (office). *E-mail:* info@cisneros.com (office); info@fundacion.cisneros.org (office). *Website:* www.cisneros.com (office); www.venevision.net (office); www.gustavocisneros.com.

CISSÉ, Alioune Badara; Senegalese lawyer and politician; b. 1953; ed legal studies in USA; fmr English teacher; mem. Nat. Ass. (Parl.) for Saint-Louis Nord; Chef de Cabinet for Prime Minister Macky Sall 2005; Local Councillor, Saint-Louis 2009–12, First Deputy Mayor 2009; Minister of Foreign Affairs April–Oct. 2012; fmr mem. Parti démocratique sénégalais (PDS); Founding mem. Alliance pour la république (APR), currently Nat. Co-ordinator.

CISSÉ, Amadou Boubacar, BA, MEcon, PhD; Niger civil engineer, politician and banker; b. 29 June 1948; m.; five c.; ed Ecole Nationale des Ponts et Chaussées and Institut des Sciences Politiques, Paris; fmr sr staff mem. in various capacities with World Bank, including Infrastructure Specialist, Prin. Operations Officer, IFC for Privatization and Financial Adviser to Vice-Pres. Africa Region, Resident Rep. of World Bank in several African countries 1983–96; Prime Minister of Niger 1996–97, 2005; Minister for Finance, Econ. Reforms and Privatization 1996–98; fmr Managing Dir Public Works Dept; fmr Exec. Sec. Railway Authority of Benin-Niger; Vice-Pres. (Operations), Islamic Devt Bank, Jeddah, Saudi Arabia 2002–08; participated in symposium on Global Devt and Faith-Inspired Orgs in the Muslim World, co-sponsored by the Berkeley Center Dec. 2007. *Address:* c/o Islamic Development Bank, PO Box 5925, Jeddah 21432, Saudi Arabia.

CISSÉ, Boubou, PhD; Malian economist and politician; *Prime Minister and Minister of Economy and Finance;* b. 31 Jan. 1974, Bamako; m.; two c.; ed Centre d'Etudes et de Recherches sur le Développement Int., Univ. d'Auvergne, France, Univ. de la Méditerranée, Aix-Marseille; Socioeconomic Consultant, Regional Office for West and Central Africa, UNICEF, Abidjan, Côte d'Ivoire 1999–2000; Economist/Research Asst, Nat. Inst. for Health and Medical Research 2001–04; Economist, Human Devt Div., World Bank, Washington, DC 2005–09, Sr Economist and Project Man. with rank of Adviser to Group Gen. Man. 2009–12, Acting Resident Rep. of World Bank in Nigeria and Niger 2012; Minister of Industry and Mines 2013–15, of the Economy and Finance 2016–, also Prime Minister 2019–; mem. Bd of Dirs Nelson Mandela Foundation. *Publications:* numerous books on economic and human devt. *Leisure interests:* reading, football. *Address:* Office of the Prime Minister, Quartier du Fleuve, BP 790, Bamako, Mali (office). *Telephone:* 2022-4310 (office). *Fax:* 2023-9595 (office). *E-mail:* primature@primature.gouv.ml (office). *Website:* www.primature.gov.ml (office).

CISSÉ, Mahmoudou; Guinean judge and politician; *Minister of Security and Civil Protection;* b. 1955, Siguiri; m.; six c.; ed Inst. Polytechnique Gamal Abdel Nasser; fmr judge; fmr Chair. Admin and Finance Sub-Cttee, Nat. Comm. against the Proliferation and Illicit Traffic of Small Arms; served on Gen. State Inspectorate; fmr legal adviser to Dept of Audits, Econ. and Financial Control; fmr Sec.-Gen., Ministry of Labour, Admin. Reform and Civil Service; Minister of Security and Civil Protection 2014–. *Address:* Ministry of Security and Civil Protection, Coléah-Domino, Conakry, Guinea (office). *Telephone:* 300-41-45-50 (office).

CISSÉ, Soumaïla; Malian software engineer and politician; *President, Union pour la République et la Démocratie;* b. 20 Dec. 1949, Tombouctou; m. Astan Traoré 1972; four s.; ed Univ. of Dakar, Senegal, Univ. of Montpellier, France; software engineer with IBM-France, Groupe Pechiney-France and Groupe Thomson-France 1980–84; Analyst and Project Man. Air Inter, France 1984; Project Co-ordinator, Compagnie Malienne pour le Développement de Textile 1984, becoming Dir of Programs and Man. Control, Acting Gen. Man. 1991; fmr Gen. Man. Agence de Cessions Immobilières, Mali; Co-founder Alliance pour la démocratie au Mali 1991; Sec.-Gen. of the Presidency 1992–93; Minister of Finance 1993–2000, also of Trade 1994–97, of Equipment, Physical Planning, Environment and Urban Devt 2000–02; unsuccessful cand. in presidential elections 2002, 2012, 2013, 2018; Commr for Mali, Union Economique et Monétaire Ouest Africain (UEMOA) 2001, Pres. UEMOA Comm. 2004–12; f. Union pour la République et la Démocratie 2003, Pres. 2014–; Chevalier, Officer and Commdr, Nat. Order of Mali. *Address:* Union pour la République et la Démocratie, Niaréla, rue 268, porte 41, Bamako, Mali (office). *Telephone:* 2021-8642 (office). *E-mail:* contact@urd-mali.net (office). *Website:* www.urd-mali.net (office).

CISSOKO, Diango, LLD; Malian government official; b. 1948; ed Ecole Nat. d'Admin du Mali, Univ. of Caen, France, Inst. Int. d'Admin Publique, Paris, Univ. of Rouen; fmr Lecturer, Ecole des Hautes Etudes, Bamako, Ecole Nat. d'Ingénieurs, Inst. Int. d'Admin, Centre de Formation et d'Appui pour le Développement Local 1985–; Civil Admin., Nat. Directorate of Interior and Correctional Services 1971–72, Deputy Dir of Correctional Services April–Oct. 1972, Dir of Correctional Services, also Dir Bamako Central Prison 1972–79, Nat. Dir of Public Service and Personnel 1982–83; Dir of Cabinet of Minister of Labour and Public Service 1983–84; Minister of Justice and Keeper of the Seals 1984–88; Sec.-Gen., Presidency of the Repub. (with rank of Minister) 1988–89, 2008–11, Minister Sec.-Gen. of the Presidency 1989–91; Deputy Gov. Islamic Devt Bank in Mali 1989–90; Gov. World Bank in Mali 1990–91; consultant 1994–2002; Dir, Office of the Prime Minister (with rank of Minister) 2002–08; Ombudsman 2011–12; Prime Minister 2012–13; mem. Nat. Comm. for Admin. Reform 1983–84; Officer, Ordre Nat. du Mali. *Address:* c/o Office of the Prime Minister, Quartier du Fleuve, BP 790, Bamako, Mali (office).

ÇITAKU, Vlora, MA; Kosovo politician and diplomatist; *Ambassador to USA;* b. 10 Oct. 1980, Prishtina; as a teenager, became an interpreter and a stringer for major Western news outlets at onset of Kosovo war, later a refugee during the war; initially became spokesperson for Kosovo Liberation Army and then joined Democratic Party of Kosovo after its formation; mem. staff, Office of Public Relations, OSCE Verification Mission 1998–99; Govt Chief of Protocol and PDK Spokesperson, Provisional Govt of Kosovo 1999–2000; mem. Kosovo Ass. 2002–11; Deputy Foreign Minister 2007–09, Acting Foreign Minister 2009–10, Minister of European Integration 2010–14; Consul General in New York 2014–15, Amb. to USA 2015–; Bd mem. Kosovo charity involved in protecting women against domestic violence. *Address:* Embassy of Kosovo, 2175 K Street, Suite 300, Washington, DC 20037, USA (office). *Telephone:* (202) 450-2130 (office). *Fax:* (202) 735-0609 (office). *E-mail:* embassy.usa@rks-gov.net (office). *Website:* ambasada-ks.net/us (office).

CITERNE, Philippe, BEcons, PhD; French banker; *Vice-President of the Board, Accor SA;* b. 1949; ed Ecole Centrale de Paris; Project Man., Business Dept, INSEE 1972–74; Project Man., Forecasting Dept, Ministry of Finance, becoming Bureau Chief, Energy, Transport and Equipment Div. 1974–79; joined Econ. Research Dept, Société Générale 1979, Dir Econ. Research Dept 1984–86, Dir Financial Man. 1986–90, Dir of Human Resources 1990–95, Deputy CEO in charge of Resources and Services Div. 1995–97, CEO Société Générale 1997–2006, Dir and Co-CEO 2006–08; Dir (non-exec.), Accor SA 2006–, Vice-Pres. of the Bd 2013–; Ind. Dir, Edenred SA 2010–; Dir, Sopra Group (fmrly Sopra SA) 2006–12. *Address:* Accor SA, 110 avenue de France, 75210 Paris Cedex 13, France (office). *Telephone:* 1-45-38-86-00 (office). *E-mail:* info@accor.com (office). *Website:* www.accor.com (office).

ČIUPAILA, Regimantas, PhD; Lithuanian mathematician, engineer, academic and politician; *Vice-Chairman, Lietuvos laisvės sąjunga (LLS—Lithuanian Freedom Union);* b. 20 Aug. 1956; m. Dalia Čiupaila; two d.; ed Vilnius Univ.; engineer-programmer, Computation Centre, Vilnius Univ. 1991–92; Dir of Foreign Relations, Vilnius Gediminas Tech. Univ. 1992–96, Docent 1992–; Docent, Mykolas Riomeris Univ. 2001–; mem. Liberal and Centre Union (LCU—Liberalų Centro Sąjunga), mem. LCU Bd 2003–; mem. Council of Vilnius City Municipality 1990–96, 2010–11, Vice-Pres. Vilnius City Council 1990–91; mem. Seimas (Parl.), Vice-Pres. European Affairs Cttee, mem. Foreign Affairs Cttee 1996–2000; mem. Parl. Ass. of Council of Europe 1996–2000; mem. European Parl. Jt Cttee 1997–2000; Vice-Pres. Lithuanian Cen. Union 2001–03; Vice-Minister of the Interior 2006–07, Minister of the Interior 2007–08; Vice-Chair. Lietuvos laisvės sąjunga (LLS—Lithuanian Freedom Union) 2014–. *Address:* Lietuvos laisvės sąjunga (Lithuanian Freedom Union), Vilniaus g. 22, 01402 Vilnius, Lithuania (office). *Telephone:* (5) 231-3264 (office). *Fax:* (5) 261-9363 (office). *E-mail:* info@lls.lt (office). *Website:* www.lls.lt (office).

CIVILETTI, Benjamin R., AB, LLB; American lawyer and fmr government official; *Chairman Emeritus and Retired Partner, Venable, Baetjer, Howard & Civiletti LLP;* b. 17 July 1935, Peekskill, NY; s. of Benjamin C. Civiletti and Virginia I. Civiletti; m. Gaile Lundgren 1958; two s. one d.; ed Johns Hopkins Univ., Columbia Univ., Univ. of Maryland School of Law; admitted Md Bar 1961; law clerk to Hon. W. Calvin Chesnut, US District Court for Md 1961–62; Asst US Attorney, Md 1962–64; Pnr Venable, Baetjer & Howard (now Venable, Baetjer, Howard & Civiletti LLP) 1964–77, 1981, fmr Sr Partner, currently Chair. Emer. and Retd Partner; fmr Chair.; Asst Attorney-Gen., Criminal Div., US Dept of Justice, Washington, DC 1977–79, US Attorney-Gen. 1979–81; Chair. and Dir Healthcorp Inc.; Dir Bethlehem Steel Corpn, Wackenhut Corrections Corpn, MBNA America, MBNA International; Trustee Johns Hopkins Univ. 1980–98; mem. Legal Advisory Bd Martindale-Lexus; mem. Bd of Eds Federal Litigation Guide Reporter; mem. ABA, Federal Bar Asscn, Md State Bar, DC Bar Asscn, Bar Asscn of Baltimore City; Fellow, American Bar Foundation, American Law Inst., American Coll. of Trial Lawyers; Kt-Commdr, Order of Merit of the Italian Repub.; Hon. LLD (Univ. of Baltimore), (New York Law School), (St John's Coll.), (Tulane Univ.) (Univ. of Notre Dame), (Univ. of Maryland); Hon. DHumLitt (Towson State Univ.); Equal Justice Award, Baltimore Urban League 1997, Justice Award, American Judicature Soc. 2005. *Leisure interests:* golf, gardening, antiques. *Address:* Venable, Baetjer, Howard & Civiletti LLP, 1800 Mercantile Bank and Trust Building, 2 Hopkins Plaza, Baltimore, MD 21201, USA (office). *Telephone:* (410) 244-7600 (home). *Fax:* (410) 244-7742 (office). *E-mail:* brciviletti@venable.com (office). *Website:* www.venable.com (office).

CIXOUS, Hélène, DèsSc; French academic and author; b. 5 June 1937, Oran, Algeria; d. of Georges Cixous and Eve Klein; one s. one d.; ed Lycée d'Alger, Lycée de Sceaux, Univ. of Paris (Sorbonne); mem. staff, Univ. of Bordeaux 1962–65; Asst Lecturer, Univ. of Paris (Sorbonne) 1965–67; Lecturer, Univ. of Paris X (Nanterre) 1967–68; helped found Univ. of Paris VIII (Vincennes) 1968, Chair. and Prof. of Literature 1968–, Founder and Dir Centre d'Etudes Féminines 1974–; Co-Founder of journal Poétique 1969; currently Prof., European Graduate School, Switzerland; Southern Cross of Brazil 1989; Chevalier, Légion d'honneur 1994; Officier, Ordre nat. du Mérite 1998; Dr hc (Queen's Univ., Canada) 1991, (Edmonton, Canada) 1992, (York, UK) 1993, (Georgetown, USA) 1995, (Northwestern, USA) 1996; Prix Médicis 1969, Prix des critiques for best theatrical work of the year 1994, 2000, Amb. of Star Awards, Pakistan 1997. *Theatre:* Portrait de Dora 1976, Le nom d'Oedipe 1978, La prise de l'école de Madhubaï 1984, L'Histoire terrible mais inachevée de Norodom Sihanouk, roi du Cambodge 1985, L'Indiade ou l'Inde de leurs rêves 1987, On ne part pas on ne revient pas 1991, Voile noire voile blanche 1994, L'Histoire qu'on ne connaîtra jamais 1994, La Ville Parjure ou le Réveil des Erinyes 1994, Tambours sur la digue 1999 (Molière Award 2000), Rouen la trentième nuit de mai 31 2001. *Publications include:* Le Prénom de Dieu 1967, Dedans 1969, Le Troisième corps, Les Commencements 1970, Un vrai jardin 1971, Neutre 1972, Tombe, Portrait du Soleil 1973, Révolutions pour plus d'un Faust 1975, Souffles 1975, La 1976, Partie 1976, Angst 1977, Préparatifs de noces au-delà de l'abîme 1978, Vivre l'orange 1979, Anankè 1979, Illa 1980, With ou l'art de l'innocence 1981, Limonade tout était si infini 1982, Le Livre de Promethea 1983, Manne 1988, Jours de l'An 1990, L'Ange au secret 1991, Déluge 1992, Beethoven à jamais 1993, La fiancée juive 1995, Messie 1996, Or, les lettres de mon père 1997, Osnabrück 1999, Les Rêveries de la femme sauvage 2000, Le Jour où je n'étais pas là 2000, Portrait de Jacques Derrida en jeune saint juif 2001, Benjamin à Montaigne, il ne faut pas le dire 2001, Manhattan. Lettres de la Préhistoire 2002; essays: L'exil de James Joyce 1969, Prénoms de personne 1974, La Jeune née 1975, La venue à l'écriture 1977, Entre l'écriture 1986, L'heure de Clarice Lispector 1989, Reading with Clarice Lispector 1990, Readings, the Poetics of Blanchot, Joyce, Kafka, Lispector, Tsvetaeva 1992, Three Steps on the Ladder of Writing 1993, Photos de racines 1994, Stigmata 1998, Escaping Texts 1998. *Address:* European Graduate School, Ringacker, 3953 Leuk-Stadt, Switzerland. *Website:* www.egs.edu/faculty/helene-cixous/biography.

CIZA, Jean; Burundian economist and central banker; *Governor, Banque de la République du Burundi;* b. 8 Dec. 1966, Rubanga, Muhanga Dist, Kayanza Prov.; m.; two c.; ed Univ. du Burundi; worked with USAID on BEST project 1995–96; with Africare Burundi (US non-govt org.) 1996–98; joined Interbank Burundi 1999, becoming Dir Central Market Agency; Dir and CEO Banque Commerciale du Burundi (BANCOBU) –2012; Gov. Banque de la République du Burundi and Gov. of IMF 2012–. *Address:* Office of the Governor, Banque de la République du Burundi, BP 705, avenue de la Revolution, Bujumbura, Burundi (office). *Telephone:* 22222744 (office). *Fax:* 22223128 (office). *E-mail:* brb@brb.bi (office). *Website:* www.brb.bi (office).

CLAES, Willem (Willy) Werner Hubert; Belgian politician and pianist; b. 24 Nov. 1938, Hasselt; m. Suzanne Meynen 1965 (divorced 2005); one s. one d.; ed Univ. Libre de Bruxelles; mem. Exec. Cttee Belgian Socialist Party, Jt Pres. 1975–77; mem. Limbourg Council 1964; mem. Chamber of Deputies 1968–94; Minister of Educ. (Flemish) 1972–73, of Econ. Affairs 1973–74, 1977–81, Deputy Prime Minister 1979–81, 1988–94, Minister of Econ. Affairs, Planning and Educ. (Flemish Sector) 1988–91, of Foreign Affairs 1991–94; Sec.-Gen. NATO 1994–95 (resgnd), given suspended three-year prison sentence for corruption Dec. 1998; Pres. European Socialist Party 1992–94; f. Willy Claes Quartet; Chair. De Scheepvaart NV –2014. *Publications include:* Tussen droom en werkelijkheid 1979, La Chine et l'Europe 1980, Livre Blanc de l'Energie 1980, Elementen voor een nieuw energiebeleid 1980, De Derde Weg: beschouwingen over de Wereldcrisis 1987. *Address:* c/o Thienpont: Artiestenbureau, Leernsesteenweg 243A, 9800 Bachte-Maria-Leerne, Deinze; Berkenlaan 62, 3500 Hasselt, Belgium.

CLAIR, Louis Serge; Mauritian politician; *Chief Commissioner, Rodrigues Regional Assembly;* b. 1 April 1940, Rodrigues; s. of Emmanuel Clair and Willida Clair; m. Danielle Limock 1984; two c.; studied philosophy, theology and social sciences in France and TV production in Australia; Leader Org. du Peuple Rodriguais 1976–; Dir and Ed. L'Organisation (first local newspaper on island of Rodrigues) 1976–86; mem. Legis. Ass. 1982–2002, Minister for Rodrigues 1982–89, 1989–95, Chief Commr, Rodrigues Regional Ass. 2003–06, 2012–; Grand Commdr of the Star and Key of the Indian Ocean. *Leisure interests:* sight-seeing, gardening. *Address:* Organisation du Peuple Rodriguais, Mont Lubin, Rodrigues, Mauritius (office). *Telephone:* (230) 8310882 (office). *Fax:* (230) 8312404 (office). *E-mail:* chiefcom@mtnet.mn (office).

CLANCY, James, BA; Canadian trade union official; *President, National Union of Public and General Employees;* b. 10 March 1950, Kingston, Ont.; m.; three c.; ed Carleton Univ., Ottawa; social worker in Toronto 1976–84; Pres. Ont. Public Services Employees Union 1984–90; Pres. Nat. Union of Public and Gen. Employees 1990–; Gen. Vice-Pres. Canadian Labour Congress 1990–. *Address:*

National Union of Public and General Employees, 15 Auriga Drive, Nepean, ON K2E 1B7, Canada (office). *Telephone:* (613) 228-9800 (office). *Fax:* (613) 228-9801 (office). *E-mail:* national@nupge.ca (office). *Website:* nupge.ca (office).

CLAPPER, James R., Jr, BS, MA; American air force officer and government official (retd); b. 14 March 1941; m. Sue Clapper 1965; one d.; ed Univ. of Maryland, St Mary's Univ., Tex., Air Command and Staff Coll., Maxwell Air Force Base, Montgomery, Ala, Armed Forces Staff Coll., Norfolk, Va, Air War Coll., Maxwell Air Force Base, Montgomery, Ala, Nat. War Coll., Fort Lesley J. McNair, Washington, DC, Program for Sr Execs in Nat. and Int. Security, Harvard Univ., Harvard Defense Policy Seminar, Harvard Univ.; brief enlistment in US Marine Corps Reserve, transferred to Air Force Reserve Officer Training Corps Program; commissioned as a distinguished mil. grad. from Univ. of Maryland 1963; student, Signal Intelligence Officers Course, Goodfellow Air Force Base, Tex. 1963–64; Analytic Br. Chief, Air Force Special Communications Center, Kelly Air Force Base, Tex. 1964–65; Watch Officer and Air Defense Analyst, 2nd Air Div. (later, 7th Air Force), Tan Son Nhut Air Base, S Viet Nam 1965–66; aide to Commdr and command Briefer, Air Force Security Service, Kelly Air Force Base, Tex. 1966–70; Commdr Detachment 3, 6994th Security Squadron, Nakhon Phanom Royal Thai Air Force Base, Thailand 1970–71; Mil. Asst to the Dir Nat. Security Agency, Fort George G. Meade, Md 1971–73; aide to Commdr and Intelligence Staff Officer, HQ Air Force Systems Command, Andrews Air Force Base, Md 1973–74; Distinguished Grad., Armed Forces Staff Coll., Norfolk, Va 1974–75; Chief, Signal Intelligence Br., HQ US Pacific Command, Camp H.M. Smith, HI 1975–76, Chief, Signal Intelligence Br., J-23 1976–78; Washington, DC area rep. for electronic security command, Deputy Commdr Fort George G. Meade, Md 1979–80, Commdr 6940th Electronic Security Wing 1980–81; Dir for Intelligence Plans and Systems, Office of the Asst Chief of Staff for Intelligence, HQ USAF, Washington, DC 1981–84; Commdr Air Force Tech. Applications Center, Patrick Air Force Base, Fla 1984–85; Asst Chief of Staff for Intelligence, US Forces Korea, and Deputy Asst Chief of Staff for Intelligence, Repub. of Korea and US Combined Forces Command 1985–87; Dir for Intelligence, HQ US Pacific Command, Camp H.M. Smith, HI 1987–89; Deputy Chief of Staff for Intelligence, HQ Strategic Air Command, Offutt Air Force Base, Neb. 1989–90; Asst Chief of Staff for Intelligence, HQ USAF, Washington, DC 1990–91; Dir Defense Intelligence Agency and Gen. Defense Intelligence Program, Washington, DC 1991–95 (retd); promoted Second Lt 1963, First Lt 1965, Capt. 1967, Maj. 1973, Lt Col 1976, Col 1980, Brig.-Gen. 1985, Maj.-Gen. 1988, Lt-Gen. 1991; briefly served as exec. in several pvt. cos, including Booz Allen Hamilton and SRA International; Dir Nat. Geospatial-Intelligence Agency 2001–06; briefly served as COO Detica DFI (now a US-based subsidiary of BAe Systems) 2006; Intelligence and Nat. Security Alliance Distinguished Prof. in the Practice of Intelligence, Georgetown Univ. 2006–07; Under-Sec. of Defense for Intelligence 2007–10; Dir of Nat. Intelligence 2010–17; Defense Distinguished Service Medal, Air Force Distinguished Service Medal, Defense Superior Service Medal, Legion of Merit with two oak leaf clusters, Bronze Star with oak leaf cluster, Defense Meritorious Service Medal, Meritorious Service Medal with oak leaf cluster, Air Medal with oak leaf cluster, Jt Service Commendation Medal, Air Force Commendation Medal, Commdr, Ordre nat. du Mérite, Repub. of Korea Order of Nat. Security of Merit, Nat. Intelligence Distinguished Service Medal. *Address:* c/o Office of the Director of National Intelligence, Washington, DC 20511, USA (office).

CLAPTON, Eric Patrick, CBE; British musician (guitar), singer and songwriter; b. (Eric Patrick Clapp), 30 March 1945, Ripley, Surrey; m. 1st Patti Harrison (née Boyd) 1979 (divorced 1988); one s. (deceased) by Lori Delsanto one d.; m. 2nd Melia McEnery 2002; three c.; guitarist with Roosters 1963, Yardbirds 1963–65, John Mayall's Bluesbreakers 1965–66, Cream 1966–68, Blind Faith 1969, Derek and the Dominoes 1970, Delaney and Bonnie 1970–72; solo artist 1972–; Dir Clouds House 1993; mem. Bd of Dirs Chemical Dependency Centre 1994–99; f. Crossroads Center 1998; Silver Clef Award for Outstanding contrib. to British Music 1983, six Grammy Awards 1993, Grammy Award for Best Rock Performance by Duo or Group (for The Calling, with Santana) 2000, Grammy Award for Best Male Pop Vocalist 1996, Grammy Lifetime Achievement Award 2006, inducted into Rock and Roll Hall of Fame 2000. *Film appearances:* Tommy 1974, Blues Brothers 2000 1998. *Recordings include:* albums: Disraeli Gears 1967, Wheels of Fire 1968, Goodbye Cream 1969, Blind Faith 1969, Layla 1970, Eric Clapton 1970, Concert For Bangladesh 1971, Eric Clapton's Rainbow Concert 1973, 461 Ocean Boulevard 1974, There's One In Every Crowd 1975, E. C. Was Here 1975, No Reason To Cry 1976, Slowhand 1977, Backless 1978, Just One Night 1980, Another Ticket 1981, Money and Cigarettes 1983, Behind The Sun 1985, August 1986, Homeboy 1989, Journeyman 1989, 24 Nights 1991, Rush 1992, Unplugged 1992, From The Cradle 1994, Crossroads 2 1996, Live In Montreux 1997, Pilgrim 1998, Riding With The King (with B. B. King) (Grammy Award for Best Traditional Blues Album 2001) 2000, Reptile (Grammy Award for Best Pop Instrumental Performance 2002) 2001, One More Car One More Rider 2002, Me And Mr Johnson 2004, Sessions For Robert J. 2004, Back Home 2005, The Road to Escondido (with J. J. Cale; Grammy Award for Best Contemporary Blues Album 2008) 2006, Clapton 2010, Old Sock 2013, The Breeze 2014, Forever Man 2015, I Still Do 2016. *Publication:* Eric Clapton: The Autobiography 2007. *Website:* www.ericclapton.com.

CLARDY, Jon Christel, BS, PhD; American chemist and academic; *Co-Director, Institute of Chemistry and Cell Biology, Harvard Medical School;* b. 16 May 1943, Washington, DC; m. Andrea Clardy 1966; two s.; ed Yale Univ., Harvard Univ.; Asst Prof., Iowa State Univ. 1969–72, Assoc. Prof. 1972–75, Prof. 1975–77; Prof., Cornell Univ. 1978–90, Chair. Dept of Chem. 1988–93, Horace White Prof. of Chem. and Chemical Biology 1990–2002, Sr Assoc. Dean, Cornell Coll. of Arts and Sciences 2000–02; Prof., Dept of Biological Chem. and Molecular Pharmacology, Harvard Medical School 2003–, Co-Dir Inst. of Chem. and Cell Biology 2003–; mem. Editorial Advisory Bd Chemistry and Biology 1994–; mem. US Nat. Cttee on Crystallography 1994–98, Vice-Chair. 2000–02, Chair. 2003–; mem. Exec. Cttee American Soc. of Pharmacognosy 1999–2002, Pres. 2003–04, mem. Research Achievement Cttee 1997–2000; mem. Review Cttee Novartis Core Technologies 1997, NIH Nat. Cancer Inst. Developmental Therapeutics 1997–98, mem. Bd of Scientific Counselors 1999–2004; Fellow, Camille and Henry Dreyfus Foundation 1972–77, Alfred P. Sloan Foundation 1973–75, John Simon Guggenheim Memorial Foundation 1984–85, AAAS 1985–, American Acad. of Arts and Sciences 1995–; Hon. Fellow, Woodrow Wilson Nat. Fellowship Foundation 1964–; ACS Akron Section Award 1987, Cornell Univ. Clark Distinguished Teaching Award 1990, ACS Arthur C. Cope Scholar Award 1997, Paul J Scheuer Award 1998, American Soc. of Pharmacognosy Research Achievement Award 2004. *Publications:* over 600 papers in scientific journals. *Address:* Department of Biological Chemistry and Molecular Pharmacology, Harvard Medical School, 240 Longwood Avenue, Boston, MA 02115, USA (office). *Telephone:* (617) 432-2845 (office). *Fax:* (617) 432-3702 (office). *E-mail:* jon_clardy@hms.harvard.edu (office). *Website:* www.iccb.med.harvard.edu (office).

CLARK, Rt Hon. (Charles) Joseph (Joe), CC, PC; Canadian politician, business executive, academic and author; *President, Joe Clark & Associates Limited;* b. 5 June 1939, High River, Alberta; s. of Charles A. Clark and Grace R. Welch; m. Maureen Anne (née McTeer) 1973; one d.; ed Univ. of Alberta, Dalhousie Univ.; began career as a journalist; Nat. Pres. Progressive Conservative Party of Canada (PCP) Student Fed. 1963–65; First Vice-Pres. PCP Asscn of Alberta 1966–67; Lecturer, Univ. of Alberta 1965–67; Special Asst to Davie Fulton 1967; Exec. Asst to PCP Leader Robert Stanfield 1967–70; MP for Rocky Mountain 1972–79, for Yellowhead 1979–93, for Kings Hants 2000, for Calgary Centre 2000–04; Leader of PCP 1976–83, 1998–2003; Prime Minister of Canada 1979–80; Sec. of State for External Affairs 1984–91, Minister responsible for Constitutional Affairs, Pres. of Queen's Privy Council 1991–93; UN Sec.-Gen.'s Special Rep. for Cyprus 1993–96; Founder-Pres. Joe Clark & Assocs Ltd, Ottawa (consulting firm) 1993–; mem. Bd of Dirs Triton Inc., Globescan Inc., Stratus Royalty Corp, Lumenix, Supervisory Board Meridiam Infrastructure, chair Supervisory Board Meridiam Infrastructure Africa, Biotechnologie pour le développement durable en Afrique (BDA) 2006–09; Trustee, Lester B. Pearson Coll. of the Pacific 2007–13; Visiting Fellow, Univ. of California, Berkeley 1993–94; Distinguished Statesman-in-Residence, School of Int. Service and Sr Fellow, Center for North American Studies, American Univ., Washington, DC 2004–05; Public Policy Scholar, Woodrow Wilson Int. Center for Scholars 2004; Prof. of Practice for Public–Private Sector Partnerships, Inst. for the Study of Int. Devt, McGill Univ. 2006–; mem. Founding Bd Pacific Council on Int. Policy; Vice-Chair. Global Leadership Foundation 2006–; mem. Inter-American Dialogue 2006–; Hon. Chief, Samson Cree Nation 1992, Hon. Witness Truth and Reconciliation Comm.; mem. Alberta Order of Excellence 1983, Commdr, Ordre de la Pléiade; Hon. LLD (New Brunswick) 1976, (Calgary) 1984, (Alberta) 1985, (Univ. of King's Coll., Concordia Univ.) 1994, (St Thomas, Minn.) 1995, (York) 2009, (Carleton) 2010, (Univ. of British Columbia) 2011; Vimy Award 1992. *Publications include:* A Nation Too Good to Lose 1994, How We Lead: Canada in a Century of Change 2014. *Address:* Joe Clark & Associates Ltd, 65 Whitemarl, Unit 3, Ottawa, ON K1L 8J9, Canada (office). *Telephone:* (613) 244-0202 (office). *E-mail:* joeclark@cchambers.com (office). *Website:* www.joeclarkandassociates.ca (office).

CLARK, Christina (Christy) Joan; Canadian politician; b. 29 Oct. 1965, Burnaby; d. of Jim Clark and Mavis Clark; m. Mark Marissen (divorced); one s.; ed Simon Fraser Univ., Univ. of Paris (Sorbonne), France, Univ. of Edinburgh, UK; mem. BC Legis. Ass. for Port Moody-Burnaby Mountain 1996–2001, for Port Moody-Westwood 2001–05, for Vancouver-Point Grey 2011–13, for Kelowna West 2013–; Deputy Premier of BC and Minister of Educ. 2001–04, Minister of Children and Family Devt Jan.–Sept. 2004, also Vice-Chair. of Treasury Bd, Premier of BC and Pres. of Exec. Council 2011–17; host of Christy Clark Show, CKNW 2007–10; mem. BC Liberal Party, Leader 2011–; YWCA Woman of Distinction Award, Consumer Choice Awards Woman of the Year in BC 2009. *Address:* Parliament Buildings, Victoria, BC V8W 1X4, Canada (office). *Website:* www.leg.bc.ca (office).

CLARK, Sir Christopher (Chris) Munro, Kt, PhD, FAHA; Australian historian and academic; *Regius Professor of History, University of Cambridge;* b. 14 March 1960, Sydney, NSW; m. Nina Lübbren; two s.; ed Sydney Grammar School, Univ. of Sydney, Freie Universität, Berlin, Germany, Univ. of Cambridge, UK; mem. staff, Pembroke Coll., Cambridge 1987–91, Fellow, St Catharine's Coll. 1991–, also Dir of Studies in History, Univ. Lecturer in Modern European History 2003–06, Reader 2006–08, Prof. 2008–, Regius Prof. of History 2014–; mem. Arbeitsgemeinschaft zur Preußischen Geschichte (Prussian History Working Group), Mannheim, Preußischen Historischen Kommission (Prussian Historical Comm.) 2009–; Sr Advisory mem. (non-voting), German Historical Inst., London 2010–, Otto-von-Bismarck-Stiftung (Bismarck Foundation), Friedrichsruh 2010–; mem. British Acad. 2010; Officer's Cross, Order of Merit (FRG) 2010; European Prize for Political Culture 2018. *Publications include:* The Politics of Conversion: Missionary Protestantism and the Jews in Prussia 1728–1941 1995, Correspondence, by Paul Celan and Nelly Sach (trans.) 1995, Kaiser Wilhelm II 2000, Culture Wars: Catholic-Secular Conflict in Nineteenth-Century Europe (co-ed.) 2004, Iron Kingdom: The Rise and Downfall of Prussia, 1600–1947 (Wolfson History Prize 2007, and other prizes, including, for the German language version entitled Preußen. Aufstieg und Niedergang 1600–1947, German Historians' Prize 2010) 2006, The Sleepwalkers: How Europe Went to War in 1914 (Germans trans. 2013) (Los Angeles Times Book Prize (History) 2013, Laura Shannon Prize 2015) 2012; Series Ed. New Studies in European History, Cambridge University Press 1998–; numerous articles and essays in professional journals. *Address:* St Catharine's College, Cambridge, CB2 1RL, England (office). *Telephone:* (1223) 338351 (office). *E-mail:* cmc11@cam.ac.uk (office). *Website:* www.hist.cam.ac.uk (office).

CLARK, Christopher Richard Nigel, CBE, MIM; British business executive (retd); b. 29 Jan. 1942, St Austell, Cornwall, England; m. Catherine Ann Mather 1964; two s., one d.; ed Marlborough Coll., Cambridge Univ., Brunel Univ.; career spans 40 years at Johnson Matthey plc (speciality chemicals and precious metals group), Chief Exec. 1998–2004, led Group into FTSE 100 in 2002; several non-exec. positions since 2004; Chair. Associated British Ports 2004–11, Urenco Ltd (int. supplier of enriched uranium to power generating industry) 2005–12, Wagon Plc; Ind. Chair. (non-exec.), Severstal OAO 2006–, Ruspetro PLC 2011–13. *Leisure interests:* reading, films. *Address:* 30 Marryat Road, London, SW19 5BD, England (office). *Telephone:* (79) 6727-8462 (office); (20) 8946-5887. *E-mail:* christopher.clark64@gmail.com.

CLARK, Colin Whitcomb, PhD, FRS, FRSC; Canadian mathematician and academic; *Professor Emeritus of Mathematics, University of British Columbia;* b. 18 June 1931, Vancouver; s. of George Savage Clark and Irene Clark (née Stewart); m. Janet Arlene Davidson 1955; one s. two d.; ed Univ. of British Columbia, Univ. of Washington, USA; instructor, Univ. of California, Berkeley 1958–60; Asst Prof., then Assoc. Prof., Prof. of Math., Univ. of British Columbia 1960–94, Prof. Emer. 1994–; Regents' Prof., Univ. of California, Davis 1986; Visiting Prof., Cornell Univ. 1987, Princeton Univ. 1997; Hon. DSc (Univ. of Victoria) 2001. *Publications include:* Dynamic Modelling in Behavioral Ecology (with M. Mangel) 1988, Mathematical Bioeconomics 1990, 2010, Dynamic State Variable Models in Ecology (with M. Mangel) 2000, Worldwide Crisis in Fisheries 2006, Math Overboard! 2012. *Leisure interests:* natural history, hiking, gardening. *Address:* Mathematics Department, University of British Columbia, Vancouver, BC V6T 1Z2 (office); 10995 Springmont Gate, Richmond, BC V7E 1Y5, Canada (home). *Fax:* (604) 822-6074 (office). *E-mail:* colin_clark@shaw.ca.

CLARK, Graeme M., AC, MB BS, MSurgery, PhD, MD, FRCSE, FRACS, FAA; Australian surgeon, medical scientist and academic; *Distinguished Researcher at ICT for Life Sciences, Electrical and Electronic Engineering, University of Melbourne;* b. Camden, NSW; ed Scots Coll., Sydney, Univ. of Sydney, Univ. of Keele, UK; Resident Medical Officer, Royal Prince Alfred Hosp., Sydney 1958–61, Lecturer in Anatomy, Faculty of Medicine 1960–61, Registrar in Neurosurgery and Otolaryngology 1961; apptd Sr House Surgeon, Royal Nat. Ear, Nose and Throat Hospital, Hosp. London, UK 1962; worked at Bristol Gen. Hosp. and Royal Victorian Eye and Ear Hosp.; Asst Ear, Nose and Throat (ENT) Surgeon, Alfred Hosp., Melbourne 1966–67, later Sr Hon. ENT Surgeon; Lecturer in Physiology, Univ. of Sydney 1967–69; Sr Research Officer, Nat. Health and MRC of Australia 1969–70; Foundation Prof. of Otolaryngology, Univ. of Melbourne 1970–2004, Hon. Laureate Professorial Fellow, Dir Bionic Ear Inst. 2004–, currently Distinguished Researcher at ICT for Life Sciences, Electrical and Electronic Eng; Co-founder MED-EL Medical Electronics GmbH; Fellow, Australian Acad. of Technological Sciences and Eng; Hon. mem. American Otological Soc. 2002; Hon. FRCS, FAudSA, FRSM 2003; Hon. LLD (Monash); Hon. DSc (Wollongong) 2002; Hon. DEng (Chung Yuan Christian Univ., Taiwan) 2003; Hon. MD (Sydney), (Medizinische Hochschule, Hanover); Dr hc (Univ. of Zaragoza, Spain) 2010; Prime Minister's Prize for Science 1985, Australian Achiever's Award, Nat. Australia Day Council 2005, Sr Australian of the Year 2006, Australian Father of the Year Award 2007, Lister Medal 2010, Florey Medal 2011, Lasker~DeBakey Clinical Medical Research Award (co-recipient) 2013, Russ Prize, Nat. Acad. of Eng (co-recipient) 2015. *Achievements include:* pioneered the multiple-channel cochlear implant. *Publications:* Sounds from Silence (autobiog.) 2000, Cochlear Implants: Fundamentals and Applications 2003; numerous papers in professional journals and several patents. *Address:* The Graeme Clark Foundation, PO Box 2031, East Ivanhoe, Vic. 3079, Australia (office). *Telephone:* (3) 8677-2513 (office). *Fax:* (3) 8677-2513 (office). *E-mail:* enquiries@graemeclarkfoundation.org (office). *Website:* graemeclarkfoundation.org (office).

CLARK, Rt Hon. Gregory (Greg) David, PhD; British politician; *Secretary of State for Business, Energy and Industrial Strategy;* b. 28 Aug. 1967, Middlesbrough; m. Helen Clark; three c.; ed Magdalene Coll., Cambridge, London School of Econs; Special Adviser to Sec. of State for Trade & Industry Ian Lang 1996–97; Dir of Policy, Conservative Party 2001–05; MP (Conservative) for Tunbridge Wells 2005–, mem. Public Accounts Cttee 2005–07; Shadow Minister for Charities, Voluntary Bodies and Social Enterprise 2006–07, Shadow Minister (Cabinet Office) 2007–08, Shadow Sec. of State for Energy and Climate Change 2008–10, Minister of State (Dept for Communities and Local Govt) (Decentralisation and Cities) 2010–12, Minister of State (Dept for Business, Innovation and Skills) (Decentralisation and Cities) 2011–12, Financial Sec. (HM Treasury) 2012–13, Minister of State (Cabinet Office) 2013–15, Minister of State (Dept for Business, Innovation and Skills) (Univs and Science) 2014–15, Sec. of State for Communities and Local Govt 2015–16, Sec. of State for Business, Energy and Industrial Strategy 2016–; mem. Conservative Party 1988–. *Address:* Department for Business, Energy and Industrial Strategy, 1 Victoria Street, London, SW1H 0ET (office); House of Commons, Westminster, London, SW1A 0AA, England (office). *Telephone:* (300) 060-4000 (office). *E-mail:* greg.clark.mp@parliament.uk (office). *Website:* www.gov.uk/government/organisations/department-for-business-energy-and-industrial-strategy (office); www.gregclark.org.

CLARK, Rt Hon. Helen Elizabeth, ONZ, PC, MA; New Zealand politician and international organization official; b. 26 Feb. 1950, Hamilton; d. of George Clark and Margaret Clark; m. Peter Davis; ed Epsom Girls' Grammar School, Auckland, Auckland Univ.; Jr Lecturer, Dept of Political Studies, Auckland Univ. 1973–75, Lecturer 1977–81; MP for Mount Albert 1981–96, 1999–, for Owairaka 1996–99, mem. Foreign Affairs, Defence and Trade Cttee; Minister of Housing and Minister of Conservation 1987–89, of Health 1989–90, of Labour 1989–90; Deputy Prime Minister 1989–90, Prime Minister of New Zealand Nov. 1999–2008, also Minister for Arts, Culture and Heritage; Deputy Leader of the Opposition 1990–93, Spokesperson on Health and Labour 1990–93, Leader of the Opposition 1993–99; Leader NZ Labour Party 1993–2008; mem. Labour Party 1971–, Spokesperson on Foreign Affairs, on Arts, Culture and Heritage 2008–; Admin. UNDP 2009–17, also Chair. UN Devt Group; Hon. DJur (Univ. of Auckland) 2009; Peace Prize, Danish Peace Foundation 1986. *Leisure interests:* film, theatre, classical music, opera, cross-country skiing, trekking, reading.

CLARK, Ian D., OC, BSc, DPhil, MPP; Canadian government official, international civil servant and academic; *Professor, School of Public Policy and Governance, University of Toronto;* b. 15 April 1946, Co. Antrim, Northern Ireland; s. of Sidney Clark and Zella I. Stade; m. Marjorie Sweet 1968; ed Univ. of British Columbia, Univ. of Oxford, UK, Harvard Univ., USA; Exec. Asst to Minister of Urban Affairs 1972–74; Dir then Dir-Gen. Analysis and Liaison Br. Dept of Regional Econ. Expansion 1974–79; Dir then Deputy Sec. Ministry of State for Econ. Devt 1979–82; Deputy Sec. Privy Council Office 1982–87; Deputy Minister, Dept of Consumer and Corp. Affairs 1987–89; Sec. Treas. Bd 1989–94, also Comptroller-Gen. of Canada 1993–94; Exec. Dir IMF 1994–96; Partner, KPMG, Toronto 1996–98; Pres. and CEO Council of Ont. Univs 1998–2007; Prof., School of Public Policy and Governance, Univ. of Toronto 2007–; Order of Canada; Hon. LLD (Univ. of Victoria) 2008; Harvard Kennedy School Alumni Achievement Award 1997. *Publications:* Academic Transformation: The Forces Reshaping Higher Education in Ontario (co-author) 2009, Academic Reform: Policy Options for Improving the Quality and Cost-Effectiveness of Undergraduate Education in Ontario (co-author) 2011; numerous articles in professional journals. *Address:* School of Public Policy and Governance, University of Toronto, Canadiana Building, Room 316, 14 Queen's Park Crescent West, Toronto, ON M5S 3K9 (office); 44 Glenview Avenue, Toronto, ON, M4R 1P6, Canada (home). *Telephone:* (416) 978-2841 (office). *Fax:* (416) 978-5079 (office). *E-mail:* id.clark@utoronto.ca (office). *Website:* portal.publicpolicy.utoronto.ca/en/ianclark/Pages/default.aspx (office).

CLARK, Janet F., BEcons, MBA; American business executive; *Executive Vice-President and Chief Financial Officer, Marathon Oil Corporation;* b. New Orleans, La; d. of Bud Clark; ed Harvard Univ., Wharton School, Univ. of Pennsylvania; began career as investment banker, First Boston Corpn –1990; Chief Financial Officer, Santa Fe Energy Resources/Snyder Oil 1997–99, Exec. Vice Pres. of Corp. Devt and Admin 1999–2001; Sr Vice-Pres. and Chief Financial Officer, Nuevo Energy Co. 2001–04; Chief Financial Officer, Marathon Oil 2004–, also Exec. Vice-Pres. 2005–; mem. Bd of Dirs Dell, Inc, Houston Symphony, YES Prep Public Schools, Teach for America—Houston Regional, Greater Houston Community Foundation; mem. Council of Overseers, Rice Univ.- Jones Graduate School of Man.; mem. Business and Community Advisory Council, Federal Reserve Bank of Dallas. *Leisure interest:* tennis. *Address:* Marathon Oil Corporation, 5555 San Felipe Road, Houston, TX 77056-2723, USA (office). *Telephone:* (713) 629-6600 (office). *Fax:* (713) 296-2952 (office). *Website:* www.marathon.com (office).

CLARK, Johnson (John) Pepper, BA; Nigerian poet, dramatist and academic; b. 3 April 1935, Kiagbodo; s. of Fuludu Bekederemo Clark; m. Ebunoluwa Bolajoko Odutola; one s. three d.; ed Govt Coll. Ughelli, Univ. Coll. Ibadan, Princeton Univ., USA; Ed. The Horn (Ibadan) 1958; Head of Features and editorial writer, Express Group of Newspapers, Lagos 1961–62; Research Fellow, Inst. of African Studies, Univ. of Lagos 1963–64, Lecturer, Dept of English 1965–69, Sr Lecturer 1969–72, Prof. of English 1972–80; consultant to UNESCO 1965–67; Ed. Black Orpheus (journal) 1965–78; Visiting Distinguished Fellow, Center for Humanities, Wesleyan Univ., Conn., USA 1975–76; Visiting Research Prof., Inst. of African Studies, Univ. of Ibadan 1979–80; Distinguished Visiting Prof. of English and Writer-in-Residence, Lincoln Univ., Pa 1989; Visiting Prof. of English, Yale Univ. 1990; Trustee and mem. Petroleum (Special) Trust Fund and Man. Bd, Abuja 1995–; mem. Nat. Council of Laureates (Nigeria) 1992; Foundation Fellow, Nigerian Acad. of Letters 1996; Nigerian Nat. Order of Merit; Nigerian Nat. Merit Award. *Drama includes:* Song of a Goat 1961, Three Plays 1964, Ozidi 1968, The Bikoroa Plays 1985, The Wives' Revolt 1991. *Poetry published includes:* Poems 1962, A Reed in the Tide 1965, Casualties 1970, A Decade of Tongues 1981, State of the Union 1985, Mandela and Other Poems 1988, A Lot From Paradise 1997. *Other publications:* America, Their America 1964, The Example of Shakespeare 1970, Transcription and Translation from the Oral Tradition of the Izon of the Niger Delta; The Ozidi Saga (trans.) 1977, The Hero as a Villain 1978. *Leisure interests:* walking, swimming, collecting classical European and traditional African music. *Address:* 23 Oduduwa Crescent, GRA, Ikeja, Lagos; Okemeji Place, Funama, Kiagbodo, Burutu Local Government Area, Delta State, Nigeria. *Telephone:* (1) 497-8436 (Lagos). *Fax:* (1) 497-8463 (Lagos).

CLARK, Jonathan Charles Douglas, PhD, FRHistS; British historian and academic; *Joyce and Elizabeth Hall Distinguished Professor of British History, University of Kansas;* b. 28 Feb. 1951, London, England; s. of Ronald James Clark and Dorothy Margaret Clark; m. Katherine Redwood Penovich 1996; ed Univ. of Cambridge; Research Fellow, Peterhouse, Cambridge 1977–81; Research Fellow, The Leverhulme Trust; Fellow, All Souls Coll., Oxford 1986–95, Sr Research Fellow 1995; Joyce and Elizabeth Hall Distinguished Prof. of British History, Univ. of Kansas, USA 1995–; Visiting Prof., Cttee on Social Thought, Univ. of Chicago 1993; Visiting Prof., Forschungszentrum Europäische Aufklärung, Potsdam 2000, Univ. of Northumbria 2001–03, Oxford Brookes Univ. 2009–; Visiting Distinguished Lecturer, Univ. of Manitoba 1999; mem. Ecclesiastical History Soc., Church of England Record Soc., N American Conf. on British Studies, British Soc. for Eighteenth Century Studies. *Publications include:* The Dynamics of Change 1982, English Society 1688–1832 1985, Revolution and Rebellion 1986, The Memoirs and Speeches of James, 2nd Earl Waldegrave (ed.) 1988, Ideas and Politics in Modern Britain (ed.) 1990, The Language of Liberty 1660–1832 1993, Samuel Johnson 1994, Edmund Burke's Reflections on the Revolution in France (ed.) 2001, English Society 1660–1832 (revised edn) 2000, Samuel Johnson in Historical Context (co-ed.) 2002, Our Shadowed Present 2003, A World by Itself: A History of the British Isles (ed.) 2010, The Politics of Samuel Johnson (co-ed.) 2012, The Interpretation of Samuel Johnson (co-ed.) 2012, From Restoration to Reform 2014; articles on British and American history. *Leisure interest:* history. *Address:* Department of History, University of Kansas, 1445 Jayhawk Boulevard, Lawrence, KS 66045-7590, USA (office). *Telephone:* (785) 864-3569 (office). *Fax:* (785) 864-5046 (office). *E-mail:* jcdclark@ku.edu (office). *Website:* www.history.ku.edu (office).

CLARK, Rt Hon. Joseph (see CLARK, Rt Hon. (Charles) Joseph (Joe)).

CLARK, Mary Higgins, BA; American writer and business executive; b. 24 Dec. 1931, New York; d. of Luke Higgins and Nora Durkin; m. 1st Warren Clark 1949 (died 1964); two s. three d.; m. 2nd Raymond Ploetz (annulled 1986); m. 3rd John J. Conheeney 1996 (died 2018); ed Fordham Univ.; advertising asst, Remington Rand 1946; stewardess, Pan Am 1949–50; radio scriptwriter, producer, Robert G. Jennings 1965–70; Vice-Pres., Partner, Creative Dir, Producer Radio Programming, Aerial Communications, New York 1970–80; Chair. and Creative Dir D.J. Clark Enterprises, New York; mem. American Acad. of Arts and Sciences, Mystery Writers of America, Authors League; Grand Prix de Littérature Policière, France 1980; several hon. degrees; Gold Medal of Honor, American-Irish Historical Soc. 1993, Spirit of Achievement Award, Albert Einstein Coll. of Medicine, Yeshiva Univ. 1994, Gold Medal in Education, National Arts Club 1994, Horatio Alger Award 1997, Outstanding Mother of the Year Award 1998, Catholic Big Sisters Distinguished Service Award 1998, Graymoor Award, Franciscan Friars 1999, Bronx Legend Award 1999, Ellis Island Medal of Honor 2001, Passionists' Ethics in Literature Award 2002, Reader's Digest Author of the Year Award 2002, Christopher Life Achievement Award 2003, Ellis Island Family Heritage Award 2008; chosen by Mystery Writers of America as Grand Master of Edgar Awards 2000. *Publications include:* Aspire to the Heavens, A Biography of George Washington 1969, Where Are the Children? 1976, A Stranger is Watching 1978, The Cradle Will Fall 1980, A Cry in the Night 1982, Stillwatch 1984, Weep No More, My Lady 1987, While My Pretty One Sleeps 1989, The Anastasia Syndrome

1989, Loves Music, Loves to Dance 1991, All Around the Town 1992, I'll Be Seeing You 1993, Remember Me 1994, The Lottery Winner 1994, Bad Behavior 1995, Let Me Call You Sweetheart 1995, Silent Night 1996, Moonlight Becomes You 1996, My Gal Sunday 1996, Pretend You Don't See Her 1997, The Plot Thickens 1997, You Belong to Me 1998, All Through the Night 1998, We'll Meet Again 1999, Before I Say Good-Bye 2000, Deck the Halls (with Carol Higgins Clark) 2000, Daddy's Little Girl 2002, On the Street Where You Live 2002, Mount Vernon Love Story: A Novel of George and Martha Washington 2002, The Second Time Around 2003, Nighttime is My Time 2004, No Place Like Home 2005, Little Girls in Blue 2006, Santa Cruise 2006, Ghost Ship: A Cape Cod Story 2007, I Heard that Song Before 2007, Where Are You Now? 2008, Just Take my Heart 2009, The Shadow of Your Smile 2010, The Lost Years 2012, Daddy's Gone A Hunting 2013, I've Got You Under My Skin 2014, The Melody Lingers On 2015, Death Wears a Beauty Mask and Other Stories 2016, I've Got My Eyes on You 2018, Kiss the Girls and Make Them Cry 2019. *Address:* c/o Simon and Schuster, Inc., 1230 Avenue of the Americas, New York, NY 10020, USA (office); 15 Werimus Brook Road, Saddle River, NJ 07458, USA (home). *Telephone:* (212) 698-7000. *Website:* www.simonandschuster.com; www.maryhigginsclark.com.

CLARK, The Hon. Maureen Harding, BCL; Irish criminal lawyer and judge; *Judge, High Court of Ireland;* b. 3 Jan. 1946; ed Bukit Nanas School, Kuala Lumpur, Malaysia, Muckross Park School, Dublin, Trinity Coll. Dublin, Univ. Coll. Dublin, Univ. of Lyon, France; called to Irish Bar 1975, Irish Inner Bar 1991; criminal defence practice 1976–2001; Regional State Prosecutor 1985–91; Lead Counsel, Court of Criminal Appeal, Dublin 1991–2001; elected Judge Int. Criminal Tribunal for the Fmr Yugoslavia (ICTY) 2001; Judge, Int. Criminal Court, The Hague 2003–06; Judge, High Court of Ireland 2006–; governmental adviser on issues relating to victims' rights in sexual offence cases; Sec. and elected mem. Bar Council of Ireland; mem. Int. Asscn of Prosecutors, Irish Women Lawyers Asscn, Irish Human Rights Comm. 2004–; Assoc. mem. ABA; Rep. of Irish Bar to numerous int. legal confs. *Address:* Central Office of the High Court, Four Courts, Ground Floor (East Wing), Inns Quay, Dublin 7, Ireland (office). *Telephone:* (1) 8886000 (office). *Fax:* (1) 8886125 (office). *E-mail:* HighCourtCentralOffice@courts.ie (office). *Website:* www.courts.ie (office).

CLARK, Petula, CBE; British singer and actress; b. (Sally Olwen), 15 Nov. 1932, Epsom, Surrey; d. of Leslie Norman Clarke and Doris Olwen; m. Claude Wolff 1961; one s. two d.; started career as child singer entertaining troops during Second World War; early appearances in films under contract to Rank Organization; made numerous recordings and television appearances in both England and France; success of single Downtown started career in USA; Patron Art-Therapie Foundation; Commdr, Ordre des Arts et des Lettres 2012; two Grammy Awards, Francis Carco Prize 1962, Grand Prix de la Chanson 1964, Radio Caroline Bell Award 1965, Radio Luxembourg Golden Lion Award 1965, Fry's Shooting Star Award 1965, Cash Box Award 1966, Hon. Citizen Award, Greater Reno Chamber of Commerce 1965, Int. Award 1966, Midem Int. Award 1967, Médaille de Vermeil de Paris 1970, Waldorf Astoria Award 1975, Achievement in Arts Award 1994, Grammy Hall of Fame Award 2003, Gold Badge Award 2003, Heritage Foundation Pres.'s Award 2004. *Recordings include:* Petula Clark Sings 1956, A Date with Pet 1956, You Are My Lucky Star 1957, Tête à Tête avec Petula Clark 1961, In Other Words 1962, Le Soleil dans les Yeux 1963, Hello Paris 1964, Le James Dean 1964, Downtown 1965, The International Hits 1965, My Love 1966, Just Say Goodbye 1966, I Couldn't Live Without Your Love 1966, The Many Faces of Petula Clark 1967, These Are My Songs 1967, The Other Man's Grass Is Always Greener 1967, Just Pet 1969, Memphis 1970, Today 1971, La Chanson de Marie Madeleine 1972, Come on Home 1974, Live in London 1974, Just Petula 1975, Destiny 1978, Portrait of a Song Stylist 1991, Treasures 1992, Where the Heart Is 1998, Sign of the Times 2001, The Ultimate Collection 2002, In Her Own Write 2007, Then & Now: The Very Best of Petula Clark 2008, Lost in You 2013, From Now On 2016. *Films include:* Medal for the General 1944, Murder in Reverse 1945, London Town 1946, Strawberry Roan 1947, Here Come the Huggets, Vice Versa, Easy Money 1948, Don't Ever Leave Me 1949, Vote for Huggett 1949, The Huggetts Abroad, Dance Hall, The Romantic Age 1950, White Corridors, Madame Louise 1951, Made in Heaven 1952, The Card 1952, The Runaway Bus 1954, My Gay Dog 1954, The Happiness of Three Women 1955, Track the Man Down 1956, That Woman Opposite 1957, Calling All Cats 1958, Daggers Drawn 1964, Finian's Rainbow 1968, Goodbye Mr Chips 1969, Dame dans l'auto avec des lunettes et un fusil 1970, Drôle De Zèbres 1977, Second Star to the Right 1980, Twin Town 1997, Billy's Hollywood Screen Kiss 1998, Girl Interrupted 1999, The Yards 2000, How To Kill Your Neighbour's Dog 2002. *Stage appearances:* Sound of Music 1981, Someone Like You (also wrote) 1989, Blood Brothers (Broadway) 1993, Sunset Boulevard 1995–96; nat. tour 1994–95, Sunset Boulevard 1995, 1996, New York 1998, US tour 1998–2000, London 2000. *Website:* www.petulaclark.net.

CLARK, R. Kerry, BCom; Canadian health care industry executive; b. 29 April 1952, Ottawa, Ont.; ed Queen's Univ.; joined Procter & Gamble Co. 1974, held various man. positions including Group Vice-Pres. Laundry and Cleaning Products, Pres. Procter & Gamble Asia, Pres. of Global Market Devt and Business Operations, Vice-Chair. and Pres. Global Health, Baby and Family Care 2004–06; Pres. and CEO Cardinal Health Inc. 2006–07, Chair. and CEO 2007–09; mem. Bd of Dirs, Avnet, Textron Inc., General Mills 2009–; Partner, Hauser Private Equity, LLC; mem. The Business Council, Healthcare Leadership Council, Ohio Business Roundtable, The Columbus Partnership, Dean's Advisory Council for Ohio State Univ.'s Fisher Coll. of Business; Hon. Doctor of Commercial Science (St Bonaventure Univ.); Chapman Leadershsip Lecturer, Florida Int. Univ. 2014. *Address:* General Mills Inc., 1 General Mills Blvd, Minneapolis, MN 55426, USA (office). *Telephone:* (763) 764-7600 (office). *Fax:* (763) 764-7384 (office). *E-mail:* info@generalmills.com (office). *Website:* www.generalmills.com (office).

CLARK, Richard T., BA, MBA; American pharmaceutical industry executive; ed Washington and Jefferson Coll., American Univ.; Lt in US Army 1970–72; Quality Control Inspector, Industrial Engineer, Quality Control Analyst, Lead Supervisor (Pharmaceutical Production), MSD Pharmaceutical 1972–78, Sr New Products Planner 1978–81, Production Man., Elkton Pharmaceutical Labs 1981–83, Man. Industrial Eng, West Point 1983–84, Sr Man. Industrial Eng, MPMD 1984–85, Dir Operations Improvement, MPMD 1985–86, Sr Dir, Man. Eng, MSD/MPMD 1986–89, Exec. Dir, Man. Eng, Merck Pharmaceutical Mfg Div. 1989–91, Vice-Pres., Materials Man. and Man. Eng, Merck Mfg Div. (MMD) 1991–93, Vice-Pres., Procurement and Materials Man., MMD 1993–94, Vice-Pres., N American Operations, MMD 1994–96, Sr Vice-Pres. 1996–97, Sr Vice-Pres., Quality Commercial Affairs, MMD 1997, Exec. Vice-Pres. and COO, Merck-Medco Managed Care 1997–2000, Pres. Medco Health Solutions Inc. 2000–02, Chair. and CEO 2002–03, Pres. MMD 2003–05, mem. Bd of Dirs, Pres. and CEO Merck & Co., Inc. 2005–07, Chair., Pres. and CEO 2007–09, Chair. and CEO 2009–10, Chair. 2010–11 (retd); Chair. Bd of Trustees, Catholic Foundation of Greater Philadelphia 2013–; Trustee, Penn Medicine. *Address:* The Catholic Foundation of Greater Philadelphia, 100 North 20th Street, Suite 301, Philadelphia, PA 19103-1454, USA. *Website:* www.catholicfoundationphila.org.

CLARK, Robin Jon Hawes, CNZM, PhD, DSc, FRS, FRSC, FRSA; British chemist and academic; *Sir William Ramsay Professor Emeritus of Chemistry, University College, London;* b. 16 Feb. 1935, Rangiora, NZ; s. of Reginald Hawes Clark, JP and Marjorie Alice Clark (née Thomas); m. Beatrice Rawdin Brown, JP 1964; one s. one d.; ed Marlborough Coll., Blenheim, NZ, Christ's Coll., Christchurch, NZ, Canterbury Univ. Coll., Univ. of New Zealand, Univ. of Otago, NZ, Univ. Coll., London; Asst Lecturer in Chem., Univ. Coll. London 1962, Lecturer 1963–71, Reader 1972–81, Prof. 1982–88, Head of Dept of Chem. 1989–99, Dean, Faculty of Science 1987–89, Sir William Ramsay Prof. 1989–2009, now Prof. Emer., mem. Council 1991–94, Fellow, Univ. Coll. London 1992–, mem. Senate and Acad. Council, Univ. of London 1988–93; Visiting Prof., Columbia Univ. 1965, Padua 1967, Western Ontario 1968, Texas A&M 1978, Bern and Fribourg 1979, Auckland 1981, Odense 1983, Sydney 1985, Bordeaux 1988, Pretoria 1991, Würzburg 1997, Indiana 1998, Thessaloniki 1999; mem. Dalton Council Royal Soc. of Chem. 1985–88, Vice-Pres. 1988–90; mem. SRC Inorganic Chem. Panel 1977–80, Science and Eng Research Council (SERC) Post-Doctoral Fellowships Panel 1983, SERC Inorganic Chem. Panel 1993–94; Chair. Steering Cttee Int. Confs on Raman Spectroscopy 1990–92, 11th Int. Conf. on Raman Spectroscopy, London 1988, Advisory Council, Ramsay Memorial Fellowships Trust 1989– (Trustee 1994–); mem. Council, Royal Soc. 1993–94, Royal Inst. 1996– (Vice-Pres. 1997–, Sec. 1998–2004), Tilden 1983, Nyholm 1989, Thomas Graham 1991, Harry Hallam 1993, 2000, Liversidge 2003 and Sir George Stokes 2009 Lecturer and Medallist, Royal Soc. of Chem.; Chair. Univ. of Canterbury, NZ Trust (UK Br.) 2004–; mem. Academia Europaea 1990; Foreign Fellow, Nat. Acad. of Sciences (India) 2007; Int. mem. American Philosophical Soc. 2010; numerous radio and TV interviews on arts/science subjects in UK, Italy, France and NZ; invited lectures in over 360 insts in 36 countries; Hon. Fellow, Royal Soc. of NZ 1989, Royal Inst. of GB 2004; Companion of the NZ Order of Merit 2004; Hon. DSc (Canterbury, NZ) 2001; Joannes Marcus Marci Medal, Czech Spectroscopy Soc. 1998, UK-Canada Rutherford Lecturer 2000, T.J. Sidey Medal, Royal Soc. of NZ 2001, Ralph Anderson Lecturer-Horners' Co. 2003, Lifetime Achievement Award, New Zealand Soc. 2004, Royal Soc. of London Bakerian Lecturer 2008, Inaugural Franklin-Lavoisier Prize, Maison de la Chimie/Chemical Heritage Foundation 2009, Barber-Surgeons' Co. Denny Lecturer 2009, Rutherford Lecturer, Univ. of Canterbury 2010, Scientific Instruments Co. Minerva Lecturer 2011, Distinguished Lecturer, Royal Soc. of NZ 2011. *Publications include:* The Chemistry of Titanium and Vanadium 1968, The Chemistry of Titanium, Zirconium and Hafnium (co-author) 1973, The Chemistry of Vanadium, Niobium and Tantalum (co-author) 1973, Advances in Spectroscopy Vols 1–26 (co-ed.) 1975–98, Raman Spectroscopy (co-ed.) 1988; more than 525 scientific papers in learned journals on topics in transition metal chemistry, spectroscopy and scientific investigation of artwork and archaeological artefacts. *Leisure interests:* golf, long distance walking, travel, bridge, music, theatre, wine. *Address:* Christopher Ingold Laboratories, University College London, 20 Gordon Street, London, WC1H 0AJ, England (office). *Telephone:* (1923) 857899 (home); (20) 7679-7457 (office). *Fax:* (20) 7679-7463 (office). *E-mail:* r.j.h.clark@ucl.ac.uk (office). *Website:* www.chem.ucl.ac.uk (office).

CLARK, T(imothy) J(ames), BA, PhD; British art historian, academic and author; *Professor Emeritus of Art History, University of California, Berkeley;* b. 12 April 1943, Bristol; m. Anne Wagner; ed Bristol Grammar School, St John's Coll., Cambridge, Courtauld Inst. of Art, Univ. of London; Lecturer, Univ. of Essex 1967–69; Sr Lecturer, Camberwell Coll. of Arts 1970–74; mem. British Section of Situationist International (expelled) 1966–67; was also involved in the group King Mob; taught at UCLA 1974–76; Founding mem. Caucus for Marxism and Art, College Art Asscn 1976; returned to UK 1976; apptd Prof. and Head of Dept of Fine Art, Univ. of Leeds 1976–80; joined Dept of Fine Arts, Harvard Univ. 1980–88; mem. Faculty, Univ. of California, Berkeley 1988–, George C. and Helen N. Pardee Chair and Prof. of Art History 1988–2010, Prof. Emer. 2010–; Visiting Prof., Dept of History of Art, Univ. of York 2010–13; Visiting Prof. Inst. for the Humanities, Birkbeck Coll. 2016–; Co-curator, Lowry and the Painting of Modern Life, Tate Britain 2013, Pity and Terror: Picasso's Path to Guernica, Reina Sofia Museum, Madrid 2017; mem. American Acad. of Arts and Sciences 1992; Fellow, American Philosophical Soc. 2007; hon. degree from Courtauld Inst. of Art 2006; Distinguished Teaching of Art History Award, College Art Asscn 1991, Mellon Foundation Distinguished Achievement Award 2005, CAA Lifetime Achievement Award 2013. *Publications include:* The Absolute Bourgeois: Artists and Politics in France, 1848–51 1973, Image of the People: Gustave Courbet and the 1848 Revolution 1973, The Painting of Modern Life: Paris in the Art of Manet and his Followers 1985, Farewell to an Idea: Episodes from a History of Modernism 1999, Afflicted Powers: Capital and Spectacle in a New Age of War (with Iain Boal, Joseph Matthews and Michael Watts: under the name 'Retort') 2005, The Sight of Death: An Experiment in Art Writing 2006, The Painting of Postmodern Life? 2009, Picasso and Truth: From Cubism to Guernica 2013; numerous essays, and articles in London Review of Books and New Left Review. *Address:* Department of Art History, 416 Doe Library #6020, Berkeley, CA 94720, USA (office). *Telephone:* (510) 643-7290 (Berkeley) (office). *E-mail:* travesty@berkeley.edu (office). *Website:* arthistory.berkeley.edu (office).

CLARK, W. Edmund (Ed), OC, MA, DEcon; Canadian banker; b. 1947; m. Frances Clark; four c.; ed Univ. of Toronto, Harvard Univ., USA; various sr positions in Fed. Govt of Canada, Ottawa 1974–84, including heading Nat. Energy Program 1980; Head of Corp. and Govt Finance, Merrill Lynch, Toronto 1985–88, Chair. and CEO Morgan Financial Corpn 1988–91; Vice-Chair. and COO CT Financial Services Inc. 1991–94, Pres. and CEO 1994–2000; Chair. and CEO

Toronto-Dominion (TD) Canada Trust (following acquisition of CT Financial Services Inc. by TD Bank 2000) 2000, Pres. and COO TD Bank Financial Group 2000–02, Pres. and CEO 2002–14 (retd), also Chair. TD Bank US Holding Co. (and its subsidiary banks), Vice-Chair. TD Ameritrade Holding Corpn; Chair. United Way for the Greater Toronto Area 2010, Liquor Control Bd of Ontario –2018; mem. Bd of Dirs C.D. Howe Inst.; mem. Chair.'s Advisory Council for Habitat for Humanity Toronto; Trustee, Brookings Inst. 2014–; Egale's Leadership Award, inaugural Catalyst Canada Honour, Canada's Outstanding CEO of the Year 2010, Ivey Business Leader of the Year, Richard Ivey School of Business, Univ. of Western Ontario 2011, Outstanding Philanthropist, GTA Asscn of Fundraising Professionals 2011, among Barron's list of the world's 30 best CEOs 2012, 2013.

CLARK, Gen. (retd) Wesley Kanne, MA; American army officer (retd) and politician; *Chairman and CEO, Wesley K. Clark & Associates, LLC;* b. 23 Dec. 1944, Little Rock, Ark.; m. Gertrude Clark 1967 (divorced); one s.; ed US Mil. Acad., West Point, Univ. of Oxford (Rhodes Scholar), UK, Nat. War Coll., Command and Gen. Staff Coll., Armor Officer Advanced and Basic Courses, Ranger and Airborne School; served in US Army 1966–2000, held numerous staff and command positions and rose to rank of four-star Gen., served in Viet Nam; fmr Sr mil. Asst to Gen. Alexander Haig; fmr Head Nat. Army Training Center; fmr Dir of Strategy Dept of Defense; Sr mem. American negotiating team at Bosnian peace negotiations, Dayton, OH 1995; fmr Head of US Southern Command, Panama; NATO Supreme Allied Commdr in Europe (SACEUR) 1997–2000; Head of US Forces in Europe (USEUCOM) 1997–2000 (retd); consultant, Stephens Inc., Little Rock, Ark. 2000–01, Man. Dir Stephens Group 2001–03; Distinguished Advisor, Center for Strategic and Int. Studies, Washington, DC 2000; Chair. and CEO Wesley K. Clark & Assocs, LLC (consulting firm), Little Rock, Ark. 2003–; Vice-Chair. and Sr Advisor, James Lee Witt Assocs LLC, Washington, DC 2004–; Chair. Rodman & Renshaw LLC, New York 2006–; unsuccessful cand. for Democratic presidential nomination 2003; mil. analyst for CNN 2001–03; Sr Fellow and Lecturer, Ronald W. Burkle Center for Int. Relations, UCLA 2006–, Chair. and Dir Aerobic Creations, Inc. 2007–; Chair. Summit Global Logistics Inc. Jan.–Dec. 2007, Direct Markets Holdings Corp. 2007–12; Vice-Chair. and Senior Veterans Advisor, The Grilled Cheese Truck, Inc. 2013–; Dir Juhl Energy, Inc. 2009–14, Solace Systems, Inc. 2010–15, Torvec, Inc. 2011–14, root9B Technologies, Inc. 2012–16; Hon. Special Advisor to Prime Minister of Romania on econ. and security matters 2012–; Hon. OBE; Commdr, Légion d'honneur; Kt Grand Cross, Order of Orange-Nassau (The Netherlands); Hon. DHumLitt (Seton Hall Univ.) 2002; Hon. LLD (Univ. of Arkansas) 2002, (Ripon Coll.) 2005, (Lyon Coll.) 2005; Dr hc (Drake Univ.) 2002; Decorated Defense Distinguished Service Medal (three), Distinguished Service Medal, Silver Star, Legion of Merit (four), Bronze Star Medal (two), Purple Heart, Meritorious Service Medal (two), Army Commendation Medal (two), Presidential Medal of Freedom 2000. *Publications:* Waging Modern War: Bosnia, Kosovo and the Future of Combat 2001, Winning Modern Wars: Iraq, Terrorism, and the American Empire 2003, Time to Lead: For Duty, Honor and Country (co-author) 2007. *Address:* Wesley K. Clark & Associates, LLC, PO Box 3276, Little Rock, AR 72203, USA (office). *Telephone:* (501) 244-9522 (office). *Fax:* (501) 244-2203 (office). *E-mail:* wes@wesleykclark.com (office). *Website:* wesleykclark.com (office); www.rodm.com (office).

CLARK OF CALTON, Baroness (Life Peer), cr. 2005; **Lynda Margaret Clark,** QC, LLB, PhD; British lawyer, former law officer and judge; *Senator of the College of Justice;* b. 26 Feb. 1949, Dundee; ed Univ. of St Andrews and Univ. of Edinburgh; Lecturer Univ. of Dundee 1973–76; admitted as Advocate of the Scots Bar 1977; called to the English Bar, Inner Temple 1988, Bencher 2000; contested constituency of Fife NE (Labour Party) 1992; MP (Labour) for Edinburgh Pentlands 1997–2005; Advocate Gen. for Scotland 1999–2006; Senator, Coll. of Justice 2006–; Chancellor's Assessor, Edinburgh Napier Univ. 2008–; appointed to Inner House of Court of Sessions 2013–; Chair., Scottish Law Comm. 2012–13; mem. Court Univ. of Edinburgh 1995–97; Hon. LLD (Napier) 2007, (Dundee) 2007. *Leisure interests:* reading, arts, swimming. *Address:* Parliament House, Edinburgh, EH7 5BL, Scotland (office).

CLARK OF WINDERMERE, Baron (Life Peer), cr. 2001, of Windermere in the County of Cumbria; **David George Clark,** DL, PC, BA, MSc, PhD; British politician; b. 19 Oct. 1939, Castle Douglas, Dumfries and Galloway, Scotland; s. of George Clark and Janet Clark; m. Christine Kirkby 1970; one d.; ed Univs of Manchester, Sheffield; fmr forester, lab. asst and student teacher; Pres. Univ. of Manchester Union 1963–64; trainee man., USA 1964; univ. lecturer 1965–70; MP for Colne Valley 1970–74, for S. Shields 1979–2001; Labour spokesman on Agric. and Food 1973–74, on Defence 1980–81, on Environment 1981–86, on Environmental Protection and Devt 1986–87, on Food, Agric. and Rural Affairs 1987–92, on Defence, Disarmament and Arms Control 1992–97; Pres. Open Spaces Soc. 1979–88; mem. Parl. Ass., NATO 1981–2005; Chancellor of Duchy of Lancaster 1997–98; Chair. Atlantic Council of UK 1998–2001, Forestry Comm. 2001–10; Leader UK Del. to NATO-PA 2001–05; mem. House of Lords 2001–; Visiting Prof. in History and Politics, Univ. of Huddersfield; Freeman of South Tyneside 1999; Hon. Fellow, Univ. of Cumbria. *Publications include:* The Industrial Manager 1966, Colne Valley: Radicalisation to Socialism 1981, Victor Grayson: Labour's Lost Leader 1985, We Do Not Want the Earth 1992, The Labour Movement in Westmorland 2012. *Leisure interests:* walking, gardening, watching football. *Address:* House of Lords, Westminster, London, SW1A 0PW, England (office). *Telephone:* (20) 7219-2558 (office). *Fax:* (20) 7219-4885 (office). *E-mail:* clarkd@parliament.uk (office). *Website:* www.parliament.uk/biographies/lords/lord-clark-of-windermere/525.

CLARKE, Aidan, PhD; Irish historian and academic; *Fellow Emeritus, Trinity College, Dublin;* b. 2 May 1933, Watford, Herts., England; s. of Austin Clarke and Nora Walker; m. Mary Hughes 1962; two s. two d.; ed The High School, Dublin and Trinity Coll., Dublin; Lecturer in Modern History and Politics, Magee Univ. Coll., Derry 1959–65; Lecturer in Modern History, Trinity Coll., Dublin 1965–78, Assoc. Prof. 1978–86, Erasmus Smith's Prof. 1986–2001, Sr Tutor 1971–73, Registrar 1974–76, Bursar 1980–81, Vice-Provost 1981–87, 1989–91, Fellow 1970, now Fellow Emer.; Research Fellow, The 1641 Project 2007–10; Prin. Ed. 1641 depositions online; Chair. Irish Historical Soc. 1978–80; mem. Royal Irish Acad. 1982–, Sr Vice-Pres. 1988–89, Sec. Cttee of Polite Literature and Antiquities 1989–90, Pres. 1990–93; Hon. LittD (Dublin) 1992. *Publications include:* The Old English in Ireland 1625–42 1966, Letterbook of George, Earl of Kildare (ed) 2013, 1641 Depositions, Vols 1-3 (ed) 2015; contribs to The New History of Ireland, Vol. III: Early Modern Ireland 1976, Prelude to Restoration in Ireland: The End of the Commonwealth 1659–1660 1999; numerous articles and essays on early modern Irish history. *Address:* 160 Rathfarnham Road, Dublin 14, Ireland (home). *Telephone:* (1) 490-3223 (home). *E-mail:* aclarke@tcd.ie (office).

CLARKE, Brian, FRSA; British artist; b. 2 July 1953, Oldham, Lancs.; s. of Edward Ord Clarke and Lilian Clarke (née Whitehead); m. Elizabeth Cecilia Finch 1972; one s.; ed Oldham School of Arts and Crafts, Burnley School of Art, The North Devon Coll. of Art and Design; Visiting Prof. of Architectural Art, Univ. Coll. London 1993; mem. Council Winston Churchill Memorial Trust 1985–; Trustee and mem. Cttee Robert Fraser Foundation 1990–; Judge, Royal Fine Art Comm. and Sunday Times Architecture Award 1991, BBC Design Awards 1990; mem. Comm. for Architecture and the Built Environment 1999–2005; Chair. The Architecture Foundation 2007–13; Sole Executor, Estate of Francis Bacon 1998–; Gov. for Capital City Acad. 2001; Trustee, The Stained Glass Museum 1995–2008, The Lowe Educational Charitable Foundation 2001, Architecture Foundation 2002–07, Winston Churchill Memorial Trust 2007; Hon. FRIBA 1993; Hon. Liveryman, Worshipful Co. of Glaziers and Master Glass Painters 2012; Hon. DLitt (Huddersfield) 2007; Churchill Fellowship in Architectural Art 1974, Art and Work Award Special Commendation 1989, Europa Nostra Award 1990, The Leeds Award for Architecture Special Award for Stained Glass 1990, European Shopping Centre Award 1995, BDA Auszeichnung guter Bauten, Heildelberg 1996, Cttee of Honour: Foundation Vincent Van Gogh, Arles, France 2001. *Major works include:* St Gabriel's Church, Blackburn 1976, All Saints Church, Habergham 1976, Laver's & Barraud Bldg, London 1981, Olympus Optical Europa GmbH HQ Bldg, Hamburg 1981, King Khaled Int. Airport, Riyadh, Saudi Arabia 1982, Lake Sagami Country Club, Yamanishi, Japan (in asscn with Arata Isozaki) 1988, New Synagogue, Darmstadt, Germany 1988, Victoria Quarter, Leeds 1989, Glaxo Pharmaceuticals, Stockley Park, Uxbridge 1990, Stansted Airport, Essex (in asscn with Sir Norman Foster) 1991, España Telefónica, Barcelona 1991, Number One America Square, London 1991, 35–38 Chancery Lane, London 1991, The Carmelite, London 1992, 100 New Bridge Street, London 1992, façade of Hôtel de Ville des Bouches-du-Rhône, Marseille (with Will Alsop) 1992–94, Glass Dune, Hamburg (with Future Systems) 1992, EAM Bldg, Kassel, Germany 1992–93, New Synagogue, Heidelberg, Germany 1993, SMS Lowe The Grace Bldg, New York 1994, Cliveden Hotel 1994, Schadow Arkaden, Düsseldorf 1994, Norte Shopping, Rio de Janeiro 1995, Rye Hosp., Sussex (with Linda McCartney) 1995, Valentino Village, Noci Italy 1996, Kinderhaus Regensburg Germany 1996, Pfizer Pharmaceuticals, New York 1997, 2001, Willis Corroon Bldg, Ipswich 1997, Offenbach Synagogue 1997, New Catholic Church Obersalbach 1997, Praça Norte Clock Tower 1997, Warburg Dillon Read Stamford CT (stained glass cone) 1998, Al Faisaliah Centre, Riyadh (in asscn with Lord Norman Foster) 2000, Olympus Optical Europa GmbH New HQ Building, Hamburg 2000, Hotel and Thalassotherapy Centre, Nova Yardinia, Italy 2002, Pfizer Security Lobby, New York 2003, Pyramid of Peace, Astana, Kazakhstan (with Norman Foster) 2006, Mosaic Path From Life to Life, a Garden for George Harrison, Chelsea Flower Show, London 2008, stained glass for the Papal Chapel, Apostolic Nunciature, London 2010, stained glass, mosaic, painting, carpet and door furniture for a private house, London 2010, Love Him More (stained glass, paintings and works on paper), Kristy Stubbs Gallery, Texas 2011, The Quick and the Dead – New Paintings, Gemeentesmuseum Den Haag, Netherlands 2011, Works on Paper, Phillips de Pury & Co., space at the Saatchi Gallery, London 2011. *Design:* Hammersmith Hosp., London 1993, Crossrail, Paddington, London (with Will Alsop) 1994, Q206 Berlin 1994, Frankfurter Allee Plaza, Berlin 1994, New Synagogue, Aachen 1994, Hungerford Bridge, London (with Alsop and Störmer) 1996, Center Villa-Lobos, São Paulo 1997, Future Systems Tower NEC 1997, Heidelberg Cathedral 1997, Chep Lap Kok Airport, Hong Kong 1997, West Winter Garden, Heron Quays, London 2001, Design for Stained Glass and Rooflight, Ascot Racecourse 2003, Apax Partners, London 2007, The Watchtower, Point Village, Dublin, Eire (design) 2008. *Leisure interests:* reading, hoarding. *Address:* Brian Clarke Studio, 6A Trading Estate Road, London, NW10 7LU, England (office). *Telephone:* (20) 8961-9636 (office). *E-mail:* mail@brianclarke.co.uk (office). *Website:* www.brianclarke.co.uk (office).

CLARKE, Rt Hon. Charles Rodway, BA, FRSS; British politician; b. 21 Sept. 1950, London; s. of Sir Richard Clarke and Brenda Clarke (née Skinner); m. Carol Marika Pearson 1984; two s.; ed Highgate School and King's Coll., Cambridge; Pres. Nat. Union of Students 1975–77; various admin. posts 1977–80; Head, Office of Rt Hon Neil Kinnock, MP 1981–92; Chief Exec. Quality Public Affairs 1992–97; mem. Hackney London Borough Council 1980–86; MP (Labour) for Norwich S 1997–2010; Parl. Under-Sec. of State, Dept for Educ. and Employment 1998–99; Minister of State, Home Office 1999–2001; Chair. Labour Party and Minister without Portfolio 2001–02; Sec. of State for Educ. and Skills 2002–04, Home Sec. 2004–06; mem. Treasury Select Cttee 1997–98, mem. Parl. Cttee 2001, Labour Party Nat. Policy Forum 2001–; Chair. Labour Party Donations Cttee 2002–. *Leisure interests:* chess, reading, walking. *Address:* c/o The Labour Party, Eldon House, Regent Centre, Newcastle upon Tyne, NE3 3PW, England. *Telephone:* (870) 5900200.

CLARKE, (Christopher) Michael, CBE, FRSE; British art gallery director; *Director, Scottish National Gallery;* m. Deborah Clarke; two s. one d.; ed Univ. of Manchester; worked at British Museum, London and Univ. of Manchester –1987; Keeper, then Dir Nat. Gallery of Scotland (now the Scottish Nat. Gallery), Edinburgh 1987–, Dir Playfair Project 1999–2004; Trustee, Lakeland Arts Trust, Cumbria 2010–; Chevalier, Ordre des Arts et des Lettres 2004. *Publications:* The Tempting Prospect: A Social History of English Watercolours 1981, Corot and the Art of Landscape 1991, The Oxford Concise Dictionary of Art Terms 2001 (second edn 2010). *Leisure interests:* golf, cycling. *Address:* Curatorial Department, Scottish National Gallery, The Mound, Edinburgh, EH2 2EL, Scotland (office). *Telephone:* (131) 624-6200 (office). *Fax:* (131) 220-0917 (office). *E-mail:* nginfo@nationalgalleries.org (office). *Website:* www.nationalgalleries.org (office).

CLARKE, Sir Christopher Simon Courtenay Stephenson, Kt, QC, FRSA; British judge; *Lord Justice of Appeal, Court of Appeal of England and Wales;* b. 14 March 1947, Plymouth, Devon; s. of Rev. John Stephenson Clarke and Enid

Courtenay Clarke; m. Caroline Anne Fletcher 1974; one s. two d.; ed Marlborough Coll. and Gonville and Caius Coll., Cambridge; called to the Bar, Middle Temple 1969; apptd QC 1984; Recorder of the Crown Court 1990–, Deputy High Court Judge 1993–2005, High Court Judge, Queen's Bench Div., Commercial Court 2005–13, Lord Justice of Appeal, Court of Appeal of England and Wales 2013–; Attorney of the Supreme Court of Turks and Caicos Islands 1975–; Bencher of the Middle Temple 1991; mem. Courts of Appeal of Jersey and Guernsey 1998; Counsel for the Bloody Sunday Inquiry 1998–2004; Councillor, Int. Bar Assen 1988–90; Chair. Commercial Bar Assen 1993–95; mem. Bar Council 1993–99; Harmsworth Memorial Scholar, Middle Temple 1969, Lloyd Stott Memorial Prizeman (Middle Temple) 1969, J.J. Powell Prizeman (Middle Temple) 1969. *Leisure interest:* opera. *Address:* 11th Floor, Thomas More Building, Royal Courts of Justice, Strand, London, WC2A 2LL, England (office).

CLARKE, Darren Christopher, OBE; British professional golfer; b. 14 Aug. 1968, Dungannon, Co. Tyrone, NI; m. 1st Heather Clarke 1996 (died 2006); two s.; m. 2nd Alison Campbell 2012; ed Wake Forest Univ., USA; fmr jr mem. Dungannon Golf Club; won East of Ireland Championship 1989, Spanish Amateur Open Championship 1990, Irish Amateur Championship 1990, South of Ireland Championship 1990; turned professional 1990; won Ulster Professional Championship 1992, Irish PGA Championship 1994; won Alfred Dunhill Open 1993, Linde German Masters 1996, Benson & Hedges International Open 1998, Volvo Masters 1998, Compass Group English Open 1999, 2000, 2002, Andersen Consulting Match Play Championship 2000, Smurfit European Open 2001, The Crowns 2001, Dimension Data Pro-Am 2001, NEC Invitational 2003, Benmore Developments Northern Ireland Masters 2003, Mitsui Sumitomo VISA Taiheiyo Masters 2004, 2005, BMW Asian Open 2008, KLM Open 2008, JP McManus Invitational Pro-Am 2010, Iberdrola Open 2011; won Open Championship at Royal St George's 2011; currently plays on European Tour and has previously played on PGA Tour; highest finish of second on European Tour money list 1998, 2000, 2003; rep. Ireland as both an amateur and as a professional, at World Cup and Alfred Dunhill Cup; mem. European Ryder Cup teams 1997, 1999, 2002, 2004, 2006, winning on four occasions, non-playing Vice-Capt. 2010, 2012, 2014, Capt. European team, Hazeltine Nat. Golf Club, Chaska, Minn. 2016; Texaco Ireland Sportstar Golf Award 1993, 1997, 1998, 2000, 2003, 2004 (shared), Laureus World Comeback of the Year 2012. *Television:* appeared as himself in Kelly (series) 2000. *Leisure interest:* fishing, cigars, fine wines, cars, Liverpool Football Club. *Address:* c/o Andrew Chandler, International Sports Management Ltd, Cherry Tree Farm, Cherry Tree Lane, Rostherne, Cheshire, WA14 3RZ, England (office). *Telephone:* (1565) 832100 (office). *Fax:* (1565) 832222 (office). *E-mail:* ism@golfism.net (office). *Website:* sportism.net (office); www.darrenclarke.com.

CLARKE, Edmund M., BA, MA, PhD; American computer scientist and academic; *FORE Systems University Professor of Computer Science and Professor of Electrical and Computer Engineering, Carnegie-Mellon University;* ed Univ. of Virginia, Duke Univ., Cornell Univ.; taught in Dept of Computer Science, Duke Univ. –1978; Asst Prof. of Computer Science, Div. of Applied Sciences, Harvard Univ. 1978–82; joined Faculty of Computer Science, Carnegie-Mellon Univ. 1982, Full Prof. 1989–, first recipient of FORE Systems Professorship, School of Computer Science 1995, Univ. Prof. 2008–; fmr Ed.-in-Chief Formal Methods in Systems Design; fmr mem. Editorial Bd Distributed Computing, Logic and Computation, IEEE Transactions in Software Engineering; mem. Organizing Cttee Logic in Computer Science, Steering Cttee Computer-Aided Verification; mem. Nat. Acad. of Eng 2005; Fellow, Assen for Computing Machinery (ACM), IEEE; Tech. Excellence Award, Semiconductor Research Corpn 1995, ACM Kanellakis Award (co-recipient) 1998, Allen Newell Award for Excellence in Research, Carnegie Mellon Computer Science Dept 1999, IEEE Harry H. Goode Memorial Award 2004, ACM A.M. Turing Award (co-recipient) 2007, CADE Herbrand Award for Distinguished Contribs to Automated Reasoning 2008. *Publications:* numerous scientific papers in professional journals on software and hardware verification and automatic theorem proving. *Address:* School of Computer Science, Carnegie Mellon University, 5000 Forbes Avenue, Pittsburgh, PA 15213-3891, USA (office). *Telephone:* (412) 268-2628 (office). *Fax:* (412) 268-5576 (office). *E-mail:* emc@cs.cmu.edu (office). *Website:* www.cs.cmu.edu/~emc (office).

CLARKE, Graeme Wilber, AO, MA, LittD, FAHA, FSA; Australian professor of classics; *Professor Emeritus, Australian National University;* b. 31 Oct. 1934, Nelson, New Zealand; s. of Wilber P. Clarke and Marjorie E. Clarke (née Le May); m. Nancy J. Jordan 1963; three s. one d.; ed Sacred Heart Coll., Auckland, NZ, Univ. of Auckland, Balliol Coll., Oxford, UK; Lecturer, Dept of Classics, ANU 1957, 1961–63, Deputy Dir Humanities Research Centre 1982–90, Dir 1991–99, Prof. Emer. 2000–, Visiting Fellow, Dept of History 2000–; Sr Lecturer, Dept of Classics and Ancient History, Univ. of Western Australia 1964–66, Assoc. Prof., Dept of Classical Studies, Monash Univ. 1967–68; Prof., Dept of Classical Studies, Univ. of Melbourne 1969–81, Prof. Emer. 1981–; Dir archaeological excavation in N Syria at Jebel Khalid 1984–2010. *Publications include:* The Octavius of Marcus Minucius Felix 1974, The Letters of St Cyprian (four vols) 1984–88, Rediscovering Hellenism (ed.) 1988, Reading the Past in Late Antiquity (ed.) 1990, Identities in the Eastern Mediterranean in Antiquity (ed.) 1998, Jebel Khalid on the Euphrates. Report on Excavations 1986–1996 (Vol. I) 2002, The Terracotta Figurines (ed.) (Vol. 2) 2006, The Pottery (ed.) (Vol. 3) 2011, The Houses (Vol. 4) 2014, Excavations 2000-2010 (Vol. 5) 2016. *Leisure interest:* gardening. *Address:* School of Classical Studies, Australian National University, Canberra, ACT 0200 (office); 62 Wybalena Grove, Cook, ACT 2614, Australia (home). *Telephone:* (2) 6125-4789 (office); (2) 6251-4576 (home). *Fax:* (2) 6125-3969 (office). *E-mail:* graeme.clarke@anu.edu.au (office).

CLARKE, John, MA, PhD, ScD, FRS; British physicist and academic; *Professor of Physics, University of California, Berkeley;* b. 10 Feb. 1942, Cambridge; s. of Victor P. Clarke and Ethel M. Clarke; m. Grethe Fog Pedersen 1979; one d.; ed Perse School, Cambridge and Univ. of Cambridge; Postdoctoral Scholar, Dept of Physics, Univ. of California, Berkeley 1968–69, Asst Prof. 1969–71, Assoc. Prof. 1971–73, Prof. 1973–, Faculty Research Lecturer 2005, The Berkeley Citation 2011; Luis W. Alvarez Memorial Chair in Experimental Physics 1994–99; Faculty Sr Scientist, Lawrence Berkeley Nat. Lab., Berkeley 1969–; Visiting Fellow, Clare Hall, Cambridge 1989; Fellow, AAAS, American Physical Soc., Inst. of Physics; Alfred P. Sloan Foundation Fellowship 1970–72; Adolph C. and Mary Sprague Miller Research Professorship 1975–76, 1994–95, 2007–08; Vice-Chair., Chair.-Elect, Chair. and Immediate Past Chair. Div. of Condensed Matter Physics, American Physical Soc. 1998–2002; Foreign mem. Royal Soc. of Arts and Sciences, Gothenburg, Sweden 2007; Foreign Assoc., NAS 2012; mem. American Philosophical Soc. 2017; Fellow, American Acad. of Arts and Sciences 2015; Hon. Fellow, Christ's Coll., Cambridge; Guggenheim Fellowship 1977–78, Calif. Scientist of the Year 1987, Fritz London Memorial Award 1987, Joseph F. Keithley Award, American Physical Soc. 1998, Comstock Prize in Physics, NAS 1999, IEEE Council on Superconductivity Award for Significant and Continuing Contribs to Applied Superconductivity 2002, Hughes Medal, Royal Soc. 2004, Lounasmaa Prize, Finnish Acad. of Arts and Sciences 2004. *Publications:* approx. 475 publs in learned journals. *Address:* Department of Physics, 366 LeConte Hall, University of California, Berkeley, CA 94720-7300, USA (office). *Telephone:* (510) 642-3069 (office). *E-mail:* jclarke@berkeley.edu (office). *Website:* www.physics.berkeley.edu/research/faculty/clarke.html (office); physics.berkeley.edu/research/clarke (office).

CLARKE, Rt Hon. Kenneth (Ken) Harry, CH, PC, QC, BA, LLB; British politician; b. 2 July 1940, West Bridgford, Notts.; s. of Kenneth Clarke and Doris Clarke (née Smith); m. Gillian Mary Edwards 1964 (died 2015); one s. one d.; ed Nottingham High School, Gonville and Caius Coll., Cambridge; called to the Bar, Gray's Inn 1963; practising mem. Midland circuit 1963–79; Research Sec. Birmingham Bow Group 1965–66; contested Mansfield, Notts. in General Elections 1964, 1966, MP for Rushcliffe Div. of Notts. 1970–; Parl. Pvt. Sec. to Solicitor Gen. 1971–72; an Asst Govt Whip 1972–74, Govt Whip for Europe 1973–74; Lord Commr, HM Treasury 1974; Opposition Spokesman on Social Services 1974–76, on Industry 1976–79; Parl. Sec., Dept of Transport, later Parl. Under-Sec. of State for Transport 1979–82; Minister of State (Minister for Health), Dept of Health and Social Security 1982–85; Paymaster-Gen. and Minister for Employment 1985–87; Chancellor of Duchy of Lancaster and Minister for Trade and Industry 1987–88, Minister for the Inner Cities 1987–88; Sec. of State for Health 1988–90, for Educ. and Science 1990–92, for the Home Dept 1992–93; Chancellor of the Exchequer 1993–97; Shadow Sec. of State for Business, Enterprise and Regulatory Reform 2009–10; Lord Chancellor and Sec. of State for Justice 2010–12; Govt Anti-Corruption Champion 2010–; Minister without Portfolio, Cabinet Office 2012–14; mem. Parl. Del. to Council of Europe and WEU 1973–74; Dir Alliance UniChem PLC 1997–2001, Deputy Chair. (non-exec.) 2001–08; Dir Foreign and Colonial Investment Trust 1997–2008, Deputy Chair. British American Tobacco 1998–2009; Dir Ind. News and Media (VIC) 1999–2009; Chair. Savoy Asset Man. PLC 2000–08; participant at meeting of the Bilderberg Group 1993, 1998, 2006–08, 2012; wrote a monthly column for Financial Mail on Sunday; wrote a weekly commentary or interview for Bloomberg TV; mem. Campaign for Real Ale (CAMRA); Master of Bench, Gray's Inn; Liveryman, Clockmakers' Co. 2001–; Hon. LLD (Nottingham) 1989, (Huddersfield) 1993; Hon. DUniv (Nottingham Trent) 1996. *Television:* presented several series of jazz programmes on BBC Radio Four, including one on his namesake, bebop drummer Kenny Clarke. *Publication:* New Hope for the Regions 1969. *Leisure interests:* birdwatching, jazz, cricket, football. *Address:* House of Commons, Westminster, London, SW1A 0AA (office); Constituency Office, Rushcliffe House, 17–19 Rectory Road, West Bridgford, Nottingham, NG2 6BE, England. *Telephone:* (20) 7219-5189 (office); (115) 981-7224. *Fax:* (20) 7219-4841 (office); (115) 981-7273. *E-mail:* clarkek@parliament.uk (office). *Website:* www.parliament.uk/biographies/commons/mr-kenneth-clarke/366 (office); www.rushcliffeconservatives.com.

CLARKE, Michael John; Australian fmr professional cricketer; b. 2 April 1981, Liverpool, NSW; m. Kyly Boldy 2012; lower middle order batsman; right-handed batsman; slow left-arm orthodox bowler; plays for NSW 2000–15, Hants. 2004, Australia 2004–15 (Vice-Capt. Test and ODI sides –2011, Capt. Test side 2011–15, Capt. ODI side 2011–15, Capt. Twenty20 side 2009–11), Sydney Thunder 2011–14, Pune Warriors India 2012–13, Melbourne Stars 2015; First-class debut: for NSW 1999/2000; Test debut: India v Australia, Bangalore 6–10 Oct. 2004; One-Day Int. (ODI) debut: Australia v England, Adelaide 19 Jan. 2003, T20I debut: NZ v Australia, Auckland 17 Feb. 2005; played in 115 Tests, took 31 wickets and scored 8,643 runs (28 centuries, 27 half-centuries), highest score 329 not out, average 49.10, best bowling 6/9; ODIs: 245 matches, scored 7,981 runs, average 44.58, highest score 130, took 57 wickets, average 37.64, best bowling 5/35; First-class: 188 matches, 13,826 runs, average 47.02, highest score 329 not out, took 42 wickets, average 44.90, best bowling 6/9; only Australian to score a century on both home and away debuts 2004; only Test batsman to reach four double centuries in a single calendar year 2012; Capt. Ashes-winning team against England 2013–14, Australia vs NZ to win final of ICC Cricket World Cup 2015; lost four successive Ashes series in England (two as capt.); retd from all forms of cricket 23 Aug. 2015; Allan Border Medal 2005, 2009, 2012, Australian Man of the Series in Ashes Series (nominated by England team Dir Andy Flower for his "excellent batting") 2009, Test Cricketer of the Year 2009, 2012, named by Wisden as Leading Cricketer in the World for his performances in 2012, 2013, Sir Garfield Sobers Trophy (as world cricketer of the year) 2013. *Address:* c/o Level 3, 243 Liverpool Street, East Sydney, NSW 2010, Australia (office); c/o Cricket NSW, PO Box 333, Paddington, NSW 2021; c/o Cricket NSW, Driver Avenue, Moore Park, NSW 2021 Australia. *Telephone:* (2) 8353-7777 (office); (2) 8302-6000. *Fax:* (2) 8353-7788 (office); (2) 8302-6080. *E-mail:* we@sel.com.au (office); info@cricketnsw.com. *Website:* www.sel.com.au (office); www.cricketnsw.com.

CLARKE, Nigel, BSc, MSc, DPhil; Jamaican business executive and politician; *Minister of Finance and Public Service;* b. 20 Oct. 1971; ed Univ. of the West Indies, Univ. of Oxford; Equity Derivatives Trader, Goldman Sachs, London 1997–99; Founding Pnr and Man Dir, Caribbean Investment Fund, Caribbean Equity Partners, Kingston 1999–2002; COO Musson Group 2003–13, Vice Chair. and CFO 2013–18; Dir Facey Group 2003–18, CEO 2009–13; Vice-Chair. Productive Business Solutions 2009–18; Chair. Eppley Ltd 2013–18; mem. Senate (upper house of parl.) 2013–15; mem. House of Reps (lower house of parl.) (JLP) for St Andrew North Western 2018–; Jamaican Amb.-at-Large 2016–; Minister of Finance and Public Service 2018–; Chair. Heart Trust Nat. Training Agency 2007–11, Nat. Housing Trust, Jamaica 2016–18, Port Authority of Jamaica 2016–18; Dir (non-exec.) Jamaica Broilers Group 2000–03, Red Stripe 2000–04, Nat. Commercial Bank of Jamaica Ltd 2000–10, NCB Capital Markets 2002–10, Seprod Ltd 2003–18, Radius Communications 2006–18, Oceanic Communications Ltd 2007–18, General Accident Insurance Co. (Jamaica) Ltd 2009–18, Bank of

Jamaica 2010–12; mem. Jamaica Labour Party (JLP). *Address:* Ministry of Finance and Public Service, 30 National Heroes Circle, Kingston 4, Jamaica (office). *Telephone:* 922-8600 (office). *Fax:* 922-7097 (office). *E-mail:* hmf@mof.gov.jm (office). *Website:* www.mof.gov.jm (office).

CLARKE, Philip Andrew; British retail executive; b. 8 March 1960, Liverpool; m. Linda Clarke; two c.; ed Liverpool Blue Coat School, Univ. of Liverpool; worked shelf-stacking shift for Tesco supermarket as a schoolboy 1974; joined Tesco plc as grad. trainee 1981, held several roles in store operations, commercial and marketing, Regional Man. in Scotland and North of England 1995, mem. Bd of Dirs 1998–, Int. & IT Dir of Supermarket Group 2004–11, Group Chief Exec. March 2011–14; mem. Bd of Dirs Whitbread plc 2006–11. *Leisure interests:* horse riding, sailing, Liverpool Football Club. *Address:* c/o Tesco plc, New Tesco House, PO Box 18, Delamare Road, Cheshunt, Herts., EN8 9SL, England. *E-mail:* info@tesco.com.

CLARKSON, Rt Hon. Adrienne, PC, CC, CMM, COM, CD, MA, FRSC, FRAIC, FRCPSC; Canadian broadcaster and fmr government official; *Co-Chair, Institute for Canadian Citizenship;* b. 10 Feb. 1939, Hong Kong; d. of William Poy; m. John Ralston Saul; ed Univ. of Toronto, Univ. of Paris (Sorbonne), France; broadcaster with CBC TV 1965–82, 1988–98; Ont.'s Agent-Gen. in Paris 1982–87; Pres. McClelland & Stewart Publishing 1987–88; fmr Chair. Bd of Trustees, Canadian Museum of Civilization, Hull, Quebec; fmr Pres. Exec. Bd IMZ, Vienna (int. audio-visual asscn of music, dance and cultural programmers); Gov.-Gen. of Canada 1999–2005; Co-founder and Co-Chair. Inst. for Canadian Citizenship; Chair. of jury, Man Asian Literary Prize 2007; fmr Bencher of Law Soc. of Upper Canada; Colonel-in-Chief of Princess Patricia's Canadian Light Infantry on February 7, 2007; Order of Friendship of the Russian Fed. 2003; numerous Canadian decorations; 32 hon. doctorates. *TV includes:* Take Thirty, Adrienne at Large, The Fifth Estate, Adrienne Clarkson's Summer Festival, Adrienne Clarkson Presents, Something Special. *Publications include:* A Lover More Condoling 1968, True to You in My Fashion 1971, Heart Matters (memoirs) 2006, Dying to be Sick 2007, Norman Bethune 2009, Room for All of Us 2011; numerous magazine and newspaper articles. *Address:* Institute for Canadian Citizenship, 260 Spadina Avenue, Suite 500, Toronto, ON M5T 2E4, Canada (office). *Telephone:* (416) 593-6998 (office). *Fax:* (416) 593-9028 (office). *E-mail:* icc@icc-icc.ca (office). *Website:* www.icc-icc.ca (office); adrienneclarkson.com.

CLARKSON, Thomas William, BS, PhD; British toxicologist and academic; *J. Lowell Orbison Distinguished Alumni Professor Emeritus, Department of Environmental Medicine and Professor of Biochemistry and Biophysics, and Pharmacology and Physiology, University of Rochester;* b. 1 Aug. 1932, Blackburn, Lancs.; s. of William Clarkson and Olive Jackson; m. Winifred Browne 1957; one s. two d.; ed Univ. of Manchester; Instructor, Univ. of Rochester School of Medicine, USA 1958–61, Asst Prof. 1961–62, Assoc. Prof. 1965–71, Prof. of Biochemistry and Biophysics, and Pharmacology and Physiology 1971–, Head of Div. of Toxicology 1980–86, J. Lowell Orbison Distinguished Alumni Prof. 1983–2008, now Emer., Dir Environmental Health Sciences Center 1986–98, Chair. Dept of Environmental Medicine 1992–98; Scientific Officer, MRC, UK 1962–64; Sterling Drug Visiting Prof., Albany Medical Coll. 1989; Sr Fellowship, Weizmann Inst. of Science, Israel 1964–65; Post-Doctoral Fellow, Nuffield Foundation 1956–57 and US Atomic Energy Comm., Univ. of Rochester, NY 1957–58; mem. Inst. of Medicine of NAS; Dir NASA Center in Space Environmental Health 1991–95; mem. La Academia Nacional de Medicina de Buenos Aires 1984; mem. Collegium Ramazzini 1983; Hon. Dr Med. (Umeå Univ., Sweden) 1986; Merit Award, SOT 1999, Arthur Kornberg Award, Univ. of Rochester 1999. *Publications:* Reproductive and Developmental Toxicology (co-ed.), The Cytoskeleton as a Target for Toxic Agents (co-ed.), Biological Monitoring of Toxic Metals (co-ed.), Advances in Mercury Toxicology (co-ed.); more than 200 published papers. *Address:* Department of Environmental Medicine, University of Rochester School of Medicine, Box EHSC, Rochester, NY 14642 (office); 124 Rossiter Road, Rochester, NY 14620, USA (home). *Telephone:* (716) 275-3911 (office). *Fax:* (716) 256-2591 (office). *E-mail:* tom_clarkson@urmc.rochester.edu (office). *Website:* www.urmc.rochester.edu/people/20019143-thomas-w-clarkson (office).

CLARY, Sir David Charles, Kt, OBE, PhD, ScD, FRS, FRSC, FInstP, FRSA; British chemist and academic; *President, Magdalen College, Oxford;* b. 14 Jan. 1953, Halesworth, Suffolk; s. of Cecil Clary and Mary Clary; m. Heather Ann Clary 1975; three s.; ed Colchester Royal Grammar School, Univ. of Sussex, Corpus Christi Coll., Cambridge; researcher, IBM Research Lab., San Jose, Calif. 1977–78; post-doctoral research at Univ. of Manchester 1978–80; Research Lecturer in Chem., UMIST 1980–83; Lecturer, then Reader in Theoretical Chem., Dept of Chem., Univ. of Cambridge 1983–96; Fellow, Magdalene Coll., Cambridge 1983–96, Sr Tutor 1989–93, Fellow Commoner 1996–2002, Hon. Fellow 2002; Prof. of Chem., Dir of Centre for Theoretical and Computational Chem., Univ. Coll. London 1996–2002; Head of Math. and Physical Sciences, Univ. of Oxford 2002–05, Professorial Fellow, St John's Coll., Oxford 2002–05, Pres. Magdalen Coll., Oxford 2005–; Miller Fellow, Univ. of California, Berkeley 2001; Pres. Faraday Div., RSC 2006–09; Ed. Chemical Physics Letters 2000–; Chief Scientific Advisor, FCO 2009–13; mem. Int. Acad. of Quantum Molecular Science 1998, Council Royal Soc. 2004–05; Fellow, AAAS 2003, American Physical Soc. 2003; Foreign Hon. mem. American Acad. of Arts and Sciences 2003; Einstein Prof., Chinese Acad. of Sciences 2014; Hon. DSc (Sussex) 2011; Annual Medal of Int. Acad. of Quantum Molecular Science 1989, medals of the Royal Soc. of Chem.: Meldola 1981, Marlow 1986 Corday-Morgan 1989, Tilden 1998, Chemical Dynamics 1998, Polanyi 2004, Liversidge 2010, Spiers 2018; Kistiakowsky Lecturer, Harvard 2002, Pitzer Lecturer, Berkeley 2003, Coulson Lecturer, Georgia 2011. *Achievements include:* developed quantum theory for chemical reactions of polyatomic molecules. *Publications include:* more than 350 research papers on chemical physics and theoretical chem. in learned journals. *Leisure interests:* family, football. *Address:* Magdalen College, Oxford, OX1 4AU, England (office). *Telephone:* (1865) 276100 (office). *Website:* research.chem.ox.ac.uk/david-clary.aspx (office); www.magd.ox.ac.uk/member-of-staff/david-clary (office).

CLASPER, Michael (Mike), CBE, BEng; British business executive; *Chairman, Coats Group plc;* b. 21 April 1953, Sunderland; s. of Douglas Clasper and Hilda Clasper; m. Susan Rosemary Shore 1975; two s. one d.; ed Bede School, Sunderland, St John's Coll., Cambridge; with British Rail 1974–78; joined Proctor & Gamble 1978, Advertising Dir 1985–88, Gen. Man. Proctor & Gamble Holland 1988–91, Man. Dir and Vice-Pres. Proctor & Gamble UK 1991–95, Regional Vice-Pres. Laundry Products, Proctor & Gamble Europe 1995–99, Pres. Global Home Care and New Business Devt, Proctor & Gamble, Brussels 1999–2001; Deputy CEO and Chair. Airports Bd, BAA PLC 2001–03, CEO 2003–06; Head of EVP Marketing Sales and Operations, EMI Group 2008, mem. Investor Bd 2007; Chair. HM Revenue and Customs 2008–12 (resgnd); Chair. Which? Ltd 2008–; Chair. Guinness Peat Group plc (renamed Coats Group plc 2014) 2013–; Sr Ind. Dir, Serco Group plc; Sr Ind. Dir (non-exec.), ITV plc 2006–15; Pres. Chartered Man. Inst. 2014–; mem. Advisory Council on Business and the Environment 1993–99, Man. Cttee Business and Environment Programme, Univ. of Cambridge Programme for Industry 2000–, Prince of Wales Business and Environment Programme; Gov., RSC; Fellow, Inst. of Grocery Distribution; Hon. PhD (Sunderland). *Leisure interests:* swimming, cycling, skiing, tennis, golf. *Address:* Coats Group plc, 1 The Square, Stockley Park, Uxbridge, Middx, UB11 1TD, England (office). *Telephone:* (20) 8210-5000 (office). *Fax:* (20) 8210-5025 (office). *E-mail:* group.legal@coats.com (office). *Website:* www.coats.com (office).

CLAUSEN, Christian, MSc (Econs); Danish banking executive; *President and Group CEO, Nordea Bank AB;* b. 6 March 1955, Copenhagen; ed Univ. of Copenhagen; with United Credit Unions 1975–79; Exec. Sec. Henriques Bank 1979–82; Deputy, Andelsbanken 1982–87; Man. Dir Privatbørsen, Privatbanken 1988–90, Man. Dir and CEO Unibørs Securities (later Nordea) 1990–96, Man. Dir and CEO Unibank Markets 1996–98, mem. Exec. Bd Unibank 1998–2000, mem. Group Exec. Man. Nordea Bank AB (parent co.) 2001–, also Exec. Vice-Pres., Head of Asset Man. & Life 2000–07, Pres. and Group CEO Nordea Bank AB 2007–; Dir, OMX Nordic Exchange Group Oy 2005–; Chair. European Banking Fed. 2012–. *Address:* Nordea Bank AB, Smålandsgatan 17, 105 71 Stockholm, Sweden (office). *Telephone:* (8) 614-7000 (office). *Fax:* (8) 105-069 (office). *E-mail:* info@nordea.com (office). *Website:* www.nordea.com (office).

CLAUSER, John Francis, BS, MA, PhD; American physicist and consultant; b. 1 Dec. 1942, Pasadena, Calif.; s. of Francis H. Clauser and Catharine M. Clauser; m. Barbara A. Tosse 1996; ed California Inst. of Tech., Columbia Univ., New York; Postdoctoral Research Assoc., Lawrence Berkeley Nat. Lab., Berkeley, Calif. 1969–75; Research Physicist, Lawrence Livermore Nat. Lab. 1975–86; Sr Scientist, Science Applications International Corpn 1986–87; Research Physicist, Consultant and Inventor, J.F. Clauser & Assocs 1988–89, 1997; Research Physicist, Berkeley Fundamental Fysiks Group, Univ. of California 1990–97; mem. Berkeley Fundamental Fysiks Group (informal group of physicists who met weekly to discuss philosophy and quantum physics) 1975–; working with Stuart Freedman, carried out first experimental test of the CHSH-Bell's theorem predictions 1972, first ever observation of quantum entanglement and the first experimental observation of a violation of a Bell inequality; carried out the world's second experimental test of CHSH-Bell's Theorem predictions 1976; Reality Foundation Prize (jtly) 1982, Wolf Prize in Physics (jtly) 2010, named a Thomson Reuters Citation Laureate in Physics with Alain Aspect and Anton Zeilinger 2011. *Achievement:* known for contribs to the foundations of quantum mechanics, in particular the Clauser-Horne-Shimony-Holt (CHSH) inequality. *Publications:* numerous papers in professional journals. *Leisure interest:* sailboat racing. *Address:* 817 Hawthorne Drive, Walnut Creek, CA 94596-6112, USA.

CLAUSS, Michael; German diplomatist; *Ambassador to China;* b. 1961; m.; four c.; joined Fed. Foreign Service 1988, Crisis Team, Gulf War 1990–91, Political Speaker, Embassy in Tel-Aviv 1991–94, Personal Rep., Higher Service, Fed. Foreign Office 1994–97, Counsellor, Perm. Representation to EU, Brussels 1997–99, Personal Asst to Sec. of State, Berlin 1999–2001, Head of Office of State Secs 2001–02, Head of EU Convention Secr. of Fed. Govt 2002–05, Deputy Head of European Dept, Fed. Foreign Ministry 2005–07, German Rep. on EU Council Presidency 2007–10, Head of Europe Dept, Fed. Foreign Ministry 2010–13, Amb. to China 2013–. *Address:* Embassy of Germany, 17 Dongzhimenwai Dajie, San Li Tun, Chaoyang District, Beijing 100600, People's Republic of China (office). *Telephone:* (10) 85329000 (office). *Fax:* (10) 65325336 (office). *E-mail:* embassy@peking.diplo.de (office). *Website:* www.china.diplo.de (office).

CLAUSSEN, Holger, DiplIng (FH), MEng, PhD; German telecommunications engineer; *Department Head, Small Cells Research, Bell Labs, Alcatel-Lucent;* ed Univ. of Applied Sciences Kempten, Germany, Univ. of Ulster and Univ. of Edinburgh, UK; Research Engineer, Bell Labs, Alcatel-Lucent, UK 2004–09, Head of Autonomous Networks and Systems Research Dept, Bell Labs, Alcatel-Lucent, Ireland 2009–13, Dept Head, Small Cells Research 2013–; Sr mem. IEEE; mem. Inst. of Eng and Tech.; Fellow, World Tech. Network; Best Paper Award, 5th European Personal Mobile Communications Conf., EPMCC, Glasgow 2003, Excellent Paper Award, 14th IEEE Int. Symposium on Personal, Indoor and Mobile Radio Communications, PIMRC, Beijing 2003, Corp. Social Responsibility Champions Award 2008, mem. Alcatel-Lucent Tech. Acad. for exceptional contribs to Alcatel-Lucent's tech. leadership 2008–13, Eckermann-TJA Prize, Telecommunications Journal of Australia 2008, Bell Labs Inventors Award 2009, Alcatel-Lucent CEO Excellence 'Game Changer' Award (co-recipient) 2011, World Tech. Award, World Tech. Network (Communications Tech.) 2014. *Publications:* several book chapters and more than 80 papers in professional journals; more than 100 patent applications. *Address:* Bell Labs, Alcatel-Lucent, Blanchardstown Business and Technology Park, Dublin, Ireland (office). *Telephone:* (1) 8864444 (office). *E-mail:* holger.claussen@alcatel-lucent.com (office). *Website:* www.bell-labs.com/usr/holger.claussen# (office).

CLAVIER, Christian Jean-Marie; French actor and film producer; b. 6 May 1952, Paris; s. of Jean-Claude Clavier and Phanette Rousset-Rouard; one d. by Marie-Anne Chazel; ed Lycée Pasteur, Neuilly; began career with comedic theatre troupe Splendid; f. Ouille Productions; Chevalier, Ordre nat. du Mérite 1998, Officier 2005; Officier des Arts et des Lettres; Chevalier, Légion d'honneur 2008. *Theatre includes:* Ginette Lacaze, La Dame de chez Maxim's, Non Georges pas ici 1972, Ma tête est malade 1976, Le Pot de terre contre le pot de vin 1977, Amours, coquillages et crustacés 1978, Le Père Noël est une ordure 1979–80, Papy fait de la résistance 1981, Double Mixte 1986–88, Un fil à la patte 1989, Panique au plaza 1995. *Films include:* Que la fête commence 1974, F. comme Fairbanks 1976, Le Diable dans la boîte 1976, L'Amour en herbe 1977, Des enfants gâtés 1977, Dîtes-lui que je l'aime 1977, Les Bronzés font du ski (also co-writer) 1979, Cocktail

Molotov 1980, Je vais craquer 1980, Clara et les chics types 1980, Quand tu seras débloqué, fais-moi signe 1981, Elle voit des nains partout 1981, Le Père Noël est une ordure (also co-writer) 1982, Rock and Torah 1982, La Vengeance d'une blonde 1993, Les Anges gardiens (also co-writer) 1994, Les Couloirs du temps (also co-writer) 1998, Astérix et Obélix contre César 1999, The Visitors 2000, Astérix et Obélix: Mission Cleopatra 2002, Lovely Rita, sainte patronne des cas désespérés 2003, Albert est méchant 2004, L'Enquête corse 2004, L'Antidote 2005, Les Bronzés 3: amis pour la vie 2006, L'Entente cordiale 2006, Le Prix à payer 2006, L'Auberge rouge 2007, La sainte Victoire 2009, On ne choisit pas sa famille 2011, Les profs 2013, Qu'est-ce qu'on a fait au Bon Dieu? 2014, Serial (Bad) Weddings 2014, Le grimoire d'Arkandias 2014, Une heure de tranquillité 2014, Babysitting 2 2015, Les Visiteurs 3: la Terreur 2016. *Television includes:* l'Été 1985, Sueurs froides 1988, Palace 1988, Si Guitry m'était conté 1989, Bougez pas j'arrive 1989, Mieux vaut courir 1989, Fantôme sur l'oreiller (co-writer 1989), Charmante soirée (co-writer 1990), Les Misérables (mini-series) 2000, Napoléon 2002, Kronprinz Rudolf 2006, Kaamelott 2007, Le malade imaginaire (film) 2008, Le bourgeois gentilhomme (film) 2009, La cage aux folles (film) 2010, Les affaires sont les affaires (film) 2011, Le Boeuf clandestin (film) 2013. *Leisure interests:* skiing, cycling, swimming. *Address:* Ouille Productions, 7 rue des Dames Augustines, 92200 Neuilly, France (office). *Telephone:* 1-41-34-13-34 (office). *Fax:* 1-41-34-13-10 (office). *E-mail:* ouille2@wanadoo.fr (office).

CLAYTON, Adam Charles; British musician (bass guitar); b. 13 March 1960, Chinnor, Oxon., England; s. of Brian Clayton and Jo Clayton; ed Castle Park School, Dalkey, St Columba's, Rathfarnham, Mount Temple Comprehensive School, Dublin; family moved to Malahide, Co. Dublin 1965; Founder-mem. Feedback 1976, renamed The Hype, finally renamed U2 1978–; numerous concerts, including Live Aid Wembley 1985, Self Aid Dublin, A Conspiracy of Hope (Amnesty International Tour) 1986, Smile Jamaica (hurricane relief fundraiser) 1988, Very Special Arts Festival, White House, Washington, DC 1988; numerous tours world-wide; 22 Grammy Awards with U2, including Album of the Year and Best Rock Performance by a Duo or Group with Vocal (for The Joshua Tree) 1987, Grammy Awards for Best Rock Performance by a Duo or Group with Vocal (for Desire) and Best Performance Video, short form (for Where the Streets Have No Name) 1988, BRIT Awards for Best Int. Act 1988–90, 1992, 1998, 2001, Best Live Act 1993, Outstanding Contribution to the British Music Industry 2001, JUNO Award 1992, World Music Award 1992, Grammy Award for Best Rock Vocal by a Duo or Group (for Achtung Baby) 1992, Grammy Award for Best Alternative Music Album (for Zooropa) 1993, Grammy Award for Best Music Video, long form (for Zoo TV Live from Sydney) 1994, Grammy Award for Song of the Year, Record of the Year, Best Rock Performance by a Duo or Group with Vocal (all for Beautiful Day) 2000, Grammy Awards for Best Pop Performance by a Duo or Group with Vocal (for Stuck In A Moment You Can't Get Out Of), for Record of the Year (for Walk On), for Best Rock Performance by a Duo or Group with Vocal (for Elevation), for Rock Album of the Year (All That You Can't Leave Behind) 2001, American Music Award for Favorite Internet Artist of the Year 2002, Ivor Novello Award for Best Song Musically and Lyrically (for Walk On) 2002, Golden Globe for Best Original Song (for The Hands That Built America, from film Gangs of New York) 2003, Grammy Awards for Best Rock Performance by a Duo or Group with Vocal, Best Rock Song, Best Short Form Music Video (all for Vertigo) 2004, TED Prize 2004, Nordoff-Robbins Silver Clef Award for lifetime achievement 2005, Q Awards for Best Live Act 2005, Digital Music Award for Favourite Download Single (for Vertigo) 2005, 2016, Meteor Ireland Music Award for Best Irish Band, Best Live Performance 2006, Grammy Awards for Song of the Year, for Best Rock Performance by a Duo or Group with Vocal (both for Sometimes You Can't Make it on Your Own), for Best Rock Song (for City of Blinding Lights), for Album of the Year and Best Rock Album of the Year (both for How to Dismantle an Atomic Bomb) 2006, Golden Globe Award for Best Original Song, Motion Picture (Ordinary Love in Mandela: Long Walk to Freedom) 2014, MTV Europe Music Award for Global Icons 2017; Portuguese Order of Liberty 2005; Ambassadors of Conscience Award, Amnesty International 2006. *Film:* Rattle and Hum 1988. *Recordings include:* albums: Boy 1980, October 1981, War 1983, Under a Blood Red Sky 1983, The Unforgettable Fire 1984, Wide Awake In America 1985, The Joshua Tree 1987, Rattle and Hum 1988, Achtung Baby 1991, Zooropa 1993, Passengers (film soundtrack with Brian Eno) 1995, Pop 1997, The Best Of 1980–90 1998, All That You Can't Leave Behind 2000, The Best Of 1990–2000 2002, How To Dismantle An Atomic Bomb (Meteor Ireland Music Award for Best Irish Album 2006, Grammy Awards for Album of the Year, for Best Rock Album 2006) 2004, No Line on the Horizon 2009, Songs of Innocence 2014, Songs of Experience 2017. *Address:* c/o Principle Management, 30–32 Sir John Rogerson's Quay, Dublin 2, Ireland (office). *E-mail:* candida@numb.ie (office). *Website:* www.u2.com.

CLAYTON, (Walter) Jay, BS, BA, JD; American lawyer; *Chairman, Securities and Exchange Commission;* m. Gretchen Butler Clayton; three c.; ed Univ. of Pennsylvania, Univ. of Cambridge, UK; clerk for judge Marvin Katz, US Dist Court for Pennsylvania Eastern Dist 1993–95; Pnr, Sullivan & Cromwell (law firm), New York; Lecturer in Law, Univ. of Pennsylvania Law School 2009–15; Chair., Securities and Exchange Comm. 2017–; mem. bar, DC, Pennsylvania, New York. *Address:* US Securities and Exchange Commission, 100 F Street, NE, Washington, DC 20549, USA (office). *Telephone:* (202) 942-8088 (office). *Website:* www.sec.gov.

CLEAVER, Sir Anthony Brian, Kt, MA; British business executive; *Chairman, Natural Environment Research Council;* b. 10 April 1938, London; s. of William Brian Cleaver and Dorothea Early Cleaver (née Peeks); m. Mary Teresa Cotter 1962 (died 1999); one s. one d.; m. 2nd Jennifer Lloyd Graham 2000; ed Berkhamsted School and Trinity Coll. Oxford; nat. service in Intelligence Corps 1956–58; joined IBM 1962, UK Sales Dir 1976–77, DP Dir, mem. Bd, IBM UK (Holdings) 1977–80, Vice-Pres. of Marketing IBM Europe 1981–82, Asst Gen. Man. IBM UK 1982–84, Gen. Man. 1984–85, Chief Exec. 1986–91, Chair. 1990–94 (retd); Chair. UK Atomic Energy Authority (UKAEA) 1993–96, Chair. Atomic Energy Authority Tech. PLC (after privatisation and flotation of UKAEA) 1996–2001; Chair. Industrial Devt Advisory Bd Dept of Trade and Industry 1993–99, UKAEA 1993–96, The Strategic Partnership 1996–2000, Medical Research Council 1998, IX Holdings Ltd 1999, Baxi Partnership 1999–2000, SThree 2000, UK eUniversities Worldwide Ltd 2000, Working Links (Employment) Ltd 2002, Royal Coll. of Music, EngineeringUK 2007–11; Deputy Chair. ENO –2000; Pres. Involvement and Participation Asscn 1997–2002, Inst. of Man. 1998–2000; mem. Bd of Dirs Nat. Computing Centre 1977–80, Gen. Accident PLC (fmrly Gen. Accident) Fire and Life Assurance Corpn 1988–98, Gen. Cable PLC 1994–98 (Chair. 1995–98), Smith and Nephew PLC 1993; mem. Council, Templeton Coll. Oxford 1982–93, Asscn for Business Sponsorship of the Arts 1985–97; mem. Bd Centre for Economic and Environmental Development 1985–98 (Deputy Chair. 1992–98); apptd mem. Cttee on Standards in Public Life, British Govt Panel on Sustainable Devt 1998–2000; Chair. Nuclear Decommissioning Authority 2004–07; Chair. Exec. Bd Caithness and North Sutherland Regeneration Partnership 2008–; Chair. Bd of Govs, Birkbeck Coll. 1989–98, Natural Environment Research Council 2014–; Patron Big Bang Fair 2008–14; Fellow, British Computer Soc.; Hon. Fellow, Birkbeck Coll. 1999; Hon. FREng; Hon. LLD (Nottingham) 1991, (Portsmouth) 1996; Hon. DSc (Cranfield) 1995, (City) 2001, (Hull) 2001; Global 500 Roll of Honour (UNEP) 1989. *Leisure interests:* sports, especially cricket, music, especially opera and reading. *Address:* Natural Environment Research Council, Polaris House, North Star Avenue, Swindon, SN2 1EU, England (office); c/o Caithness and North Sutherland Regeneration Partnership, c/o Highland Council Offices, Rotterdam Street, Thurso, KW14 8AB, Caithness, Scotland (office). *Telephone:* (1793) 411500 (Swindon) (office); (1847) 805520 (Thurso) (office). *Fax:* (1793) 411501 (Swindon) (office). *E-mail:* eann.sinclair@hient.co.uk (office). *Website:* www.cnsrp.org.uk (office); www.nerc.ac.uk (office).

CLEESE, John Marwood, MA; British actor and writer; b. 27 Oct. 1939, Weston-super-Mare, Somerset; s. of Reginald Cleese and Muriel Cleese; m. 1st Connie Booth 1968 (divorced 1978); one d.; m. 2nd Barbara Trentham 1981 (divorced 1990); one d.; m. 3rd Alyce Faye Eichelberger 1992 (divorced 2009); 4th m. Jennifer Wade 2012; two d.; ed Clifton Sports Acad. and Downing Coll., Cambridge; started writing and making jokes professionally 1963; first appearance on British TV 1966; appeared in and co-wrote TV series: The Frost Report, At Last the 1948 Show, Monty Python's Flying Circus, Fawlty Towers, The Human Face; Founder and Dir Video Arts Ltd 1972–89; appeared as Petruchio in The Taming of the Shrew, BBC TV Shakespeare cycle 1981; appeared in Cheers, for which he received an Emmy Award; guest appearances in Third Rock From the Sun, Will and Grace; toured Scandinavia and USA with his Alimony Tour Year One and Year Two 2009, 2010, extended to UK (first tour), visiting Cambridge, Birmingham, Salford, Liverpool, Oxford, Leeds, Edinburgh and finishing in Palmerston North, New Zealand May–July 2011; Hon. A.D. White Prof.-at-Large, Cornell Univ. 1999–, Hon. LLD (St Andrews); Lifetime Achievement Award, Sarajevo Film Festival 2017. *Films include:* Interlude, The Magic Christian, And Now For Something Completely Different, Monty Python and the Holy Grail, Romance with a Double Bass, Life of Brian, Time Bandits, Privates on Parade, Yellowbeard 1982, The Meaning of Life 1983, Silverado 1985, Clockwise 1986, A Fish Called Wanda (BAFTA Award for Best Film Actor) 1988, Erik the Viking 1988, Splitting Heirs 1992, Mary Shelley's Frankenstein 1993, The Jungle Book 1994, Fierce Creatures 1996, The Out of Towners 1998, Isn't She Great 1998, The World Is Not Enough 1999, The Quantum Project 2000, Rat Race 2000, Pluto Nash 2000, Harry Potter and the Philosopher's Stone 2001, Scorched 2002, Die Another Day 2002, Harry Potter and the Chamber of Secrets 2002, Charlie's Angels: Full Throttle 2003, George of the Jungle 2 (voice) 2003, Shrek 2 (voice) 2004, Around the World in 80 Days 2004, Valiant (voice) 2005, Man About Town 2006, Complete Guide to Guys 2006, L'Entente cordiale 2006, Charlotte's Web (voice) 2006, Shrek the Third (voice) 2007, Igor (voice) 2008, The Day the Earth Stood Still 2008, The Pink Panther 2 2009, The Princess and the Frog (voice) 2009, Shrek Forever After (voice) 2010, Spud 2010, Winnie the Pooh (narrator) 2011, God Loves Caviar 2012, The Last Impresario 2013, The Croods 2013, Planes (voice) 2013, Absolutely Anything (voice) 2015. *Publications:* Families and How to Survive Them and Life and How to Survive It (both with Robin Skynner) 1993, The Human Face (with Brian Bates) 2001, The Pythons Autobiography (co-author) 2003, So, Anyway...: The Autobiography 2014. *Leisure interests:* gluttony, sloth. *Address:* c/o Lucy Ansbro, Phil McIntyre Entertainments, 3rd Floor, 85 Newman Street, London, W1T 3EU, England (office). *Telephone:* (20) 7291-9000 (office). *Fax:* (20) 7291-9001 (office). *E-mail:* info@mcintyre-ents.com (office). *Website:* www.mcintyre-ents.com (office); www.thejohncleese.com.

CLEGG, Rt Hon. Sir Nicholas (Nick) William Peter, Kt, PC, MA; British politician; b. 7 Jan. 1967, Amersham, Bucks.; s. of Nicholas Clegg CBE and Hermance van den Wall Bake; m. Miriam González Durántez; three s.; ed Westminster School, Robinson Coll., Cambridge, Univ. of Minnesota, USA, Coll. d'Europe, Belgium; began career as trainee journalist at The Nation magazine, Washington, DC; Aid and Trade Adviser, EC, Brussels, Belgium 1994–96; Adviser to Sir Leon Brittan 1996–99; Liberal Democrat MEP for E Midlands 1999–2004; joined political lobbying firm GPlus as a fifth partner 2004; part-time Lecturer, Univ. of Sheffield 2004; gave series of seminar lectures in Int. Relations Dept, Univ. of Cambridge 2004; MP (Liberal Democrats) for Sheffield Hallam 2005–17, Shadow Spokesperson on Foreign Affairs 2005–06, Shadow Home Sec. 2006–07; Leader, Liberal Democratic Party 2007–15; Deputy Prime Minister (in coalition with the Conservative Party under Prime Minister David Cameron) and Lord Pres. Privy Council 2010–15; Chair. Comm. on Inequality in Educ., Social Market Foundation 2016–; Founding mem. Campaign for Parliamentary Reform; columnist, Guardian Politics Unlimited; first David Thomas Prize, Financial Times 1993. *Publications include:* Doing Less to Do More: A New Focus for the EU 2000, Trading for the Future: Reforming the WTO (with Duncan Brack) 2001, Learning from Europe: Lessons in Education (with Richard Grayson) 2002, The Liberal Moment 2009, Change That Works for You: Liberal Democrat General Election Manifesto: Building a Fairer Britain (ed.) 2010, Politics: Between the Extremes 2016, How to Stop Brexit (And Make Britain Great Again) (Best Non-Fiction by a Parliamentarian, Parliamentary Book Awards 2017) 2017; numerous articles in nat. newspapers. *Leisure interests:* skiing, mountaineering. *Address:* Liberal Democrats, 8–10 Great George St, London, SW1P 3AE, England (office). *Telephone:* (20) 7222-7999 (office). *Fax:* (20) 7799-2170 (office). *Website:* www.libdems.org.uk (office); www.nickclegg.org.uk (office); www.nickclegg.com (office).

CLEGHORN, John Edward, OC, FCA, BComm, CA; Canadian banker and business executive; b. 7 July 1941, Montreal, PQ; s. of H. W. Edward Cleghorn and Hazel Miriam Dunham; m. Pattie E. Hart 1963; two s. one d.; ed McGill Univ.; Clarkson Gordon & Co. (chartered accountants) 1962–64; sugar buyer and futures trader, St Lawrence Sugar Ltd, Montréal 1964–66; Mercantile Bank of Canada

1966–74; joined Royal Bank of Canada 1974, various sr exec. positions 1975–83, including Pres. 1983, Pres., COO 1986, Pres. CEO 1994–95, Chair. CEO 1995–2001; Chair. SNC-Lavalin Group 2002–07 (retd); mem. Bd of Dirs, Canadian Pacific Railway Ltd 2001–12, Chair. 2006–12; Dir, Molson Coors Brewing Co.) from 2003; fmr mem. McGill Univ. Bd of Govs, now Govs Emer. and mem. McGill Desautels Faculty of Man.'s Int. Advisory Bd; Chancellor Wilfrid Laurier Univ. 1996–2003; mem. Canadian and British Columbia Insts of Chartered Accountants; Fellow, Ordre des Comptables Agréés du Québec, Inst. of Chartered Accountants of Ont.; Hon. DCL (Bishop's Univ.) 1989, (Acadia Univ.) 1996; Hon. LLD (Wilfrid Laurier Univ.) 1991; Hon. Assoc. Award, The Conf. Bd of Canada 2007, inducted into Canadian Business Hall of Fame 2008. *Leisure interests:* skiing, jogging, tennis, fishing. *Address:* c/o Canadian Pacific Railway Ltd, Gulf Canada Square, 401 9th Avenue SW, Calgary, Alberta, T2P 4Z4, Canada.

CLELAND, Joseph Maxwell (Max), MA; American fmr politician; b. 24 Aug. 1942, Atlanta, Ga; s. of Joseph Cleland and Juanita Kesler; ed Stetson Univ. Deland, Fla, Emory Univ.; served in US Army during Vietnam War, lost both legs and part of one arm 1968; mem. Ga Senate, Atlanta 1971–75; consultant, Comm. on Veterans Affairs, US Senate 1975–77; Admin. Veterans Affairs, Washington, DC 1977–81; Sec. of State, State of Ga 1982–95; Senator from Georgia 1997–2003; mem. Senate Armed Services Cttee 1997–2002, Cttee on Governmental Affairs 1997–2002, Cttee on Small Businesses 1997–2002, Commerce Cttee 1999–2002; mem. Nat. Comm. on Terrorist Attacks Upon the US 2002–03 (resgnd); Distinguished Adjunct Prof., American Univ. Washington Semester Program and Fellow, Center for Congressional and Presidential Studies 2003; mem. Bd of Dirs Export-Import Bank of the United States 2003–07; Sec., American Battle Monuments Comm. 2009–; Democrat; Silver Star and Bronze Star for valorous action in combat. *Publications:* Strong at the Broken Places 2000, Going for the Max!: 12 Principles for Living Life to the Fullest 2000, Heart of a Patriot: How I Found the Courage to Survive Vietnam, Walter Reed and Karl Rove 2009. *Address:* American Battle Monuments Commission, Courthouse Plaza II, Suite 500, 2300 Clarendon Boulevard, Arlington, VA 22201, USA. *Website:* www.abmc.gov.

CLÉMENT, Jérôme; French broadcasting and media executive and writer; *President, Fondation Alliance française;* b. 18 May 1945; m.; four c.; ed Institut d'Études Politiques de Paris, École Nat. d'Admin; began career at Ministry of Culture; Cultural and Scientific Councillor, Embassy in Cairo 1980–81; Advisor to the Prime Minister, Pierre Mauroy, in charge of Culture and Communication 1981–84; Gen. Man. Nat. Cinematography Centre 1984–89; Pres. La Sept (today ARTE France) 1989–2011, took part in negotiations with German reps that resulted in creation of ARTE 1991, Pres. ARTE France 1992–2011, Vice-Pres. ARTE GEIE and Chair. ARTE 1992–99, 2003–11; Pres. and Gen. Man. la Cinquième 1997–2000 (before it became France 5); Admin. for several cultural ventures, including Orchestre de Paris and Théâtre du Châtelet; mem. Senate of Deutsche Nationalstiftung 2007–, Council of Admin of Musée d'Orsay 2010–; Municipal Councillor, town of Clamart, in charge of Culture and Architecture 2000–; fmr Lecturer, Univ. of Paris I, École Nat. Supérieure, Sciences Politiques; Pres. Bd of Théâtre du Châtelet 2011–, PIASA action house 2011–, 15th Festival of Deauville Asian Film 2013, Fondation Alliance française 2014–; Officier, Légion d'honneur 2003; Chevalier, Ordre nat. du Mérite, Commdr 2012; Commdr des Arts et des Lettres; Commdr, Order of Merit of FRG. *Publications:* Socialisme et Multinationales 1978, Un Homme en Quête de Vertu 1992, Lettres à Pierre Bérégovoy 1993, La culture expliquée à ma fille 2000, Les Femmes et l'Amour 2002, Plus tard, tu comprendras 2005, Dictionnaire Des Papous dans la Tête 2007, Plus tard, tu comprendras suivi de Maintenant je sais 2008, Le choix d'ARTE 2011. *Address:* Fondation Alliance française, 101 boulevard Raspail, 75006 Paris, France (office). *E-mail:* mflageul@fondation-alliancefr.org (office). *Website:* www.fondation-alliancefr.org (office).

CLÉMENT, Pascal; French government official and barrister; b. 12 May 1945, Boulogne-Billancourt (Hauts-de-Seine); ed Sciences Po, Paris; fmr Marketing Dir, Rank-Xerox; mem. Union pour un Mouvement Populaire; Mayor of Saint-Marcel-de-Félines (Loire) 1977–2001, mem. Municipal Council 2001–08; Deputy, Nat. Ass. 1978–93, 1995–2005, 2007–12, fmr Chair. Cttee on Constitutional Laws and Legislation; Vice-Chair. Loire Gen. Council 1982–94, Chair. 1994–2008; Minister Del. attached to the Prime Minister, responsible for relations with the Nat. Ass. 1993–95; Keeper of the Seals and Minister of Justice 2005–07; Pres. Community of Communes in Balbigny –2008; Officier, Ordre de Saint-Charles de Monaco 2011. *Publications:* Les Partis politiques minoritaires aux États-Unis 2000, Persigny, L'homme qui a inventé Napoléon III 2006, La VIe République ou la Confusion des esprits 2007. *Address:* c/o Ministry of Justice, 13 place Vendôme, 75042 Paris Cedex 01, France.

CLEMENT, The Hon. Tony, PC, BA, LLB; Canadian politician; b. 1961, Manchester, UK; m. Lynne Golding; three c.; ed Univ. of Toronto; fmr Pres. Progressive Conservative Party of Ont.; Prov. Minister of Transportation 1997–99, of the Environment 1999–2000, of Municipal Affairs and Housing 1999–2001, of Health and Long-Term Care 2001–03; defeated in 2003 election; Counsel, Bennett Jones LLP 2003–06; mem. House of Commons for Parry Sound–Muskoka 2006–; Minister of Health and Minister for the Fed. Econ. Devt Initiative for Northern Ont. 2006–08, of Industry 2008–11, Pres. of the Treasury Bd 2011–15, Minister for the Federal Econ. Initiative for Northern Ont. 2011–13; Founding Pres. Canadian Alliance 2000. *Address:* Conservative Party of Canada, 130 Albert Street, Suite 1720, Ottawa, ON K1P 5G4, Canada (office). *Telephone:* (613) 755-2000 (office). *Fax:* (613) 755-2001 (office). *E-mail:* info@conservative.ca (office). *Website:* www.conservative.ca (office).

CLEMENT, Wolfgang; German politician; b. 7 July 1940, Bochum; m.; five d.; ed Graf-Engelbert-Schule, Bochum, Univ. of Münster; journalist, Westfälische Rundschau newspaper –1967, various positions including Deputy Ed.-in-Chief 1968–81; Research Asst, Inst. for Procedural Law, Univ. of Marburg 1967–68; Press Spokesman, SPD Nat. Exec., Bonn 1981–86, resgnd over campaign controversy 1986; Ed.-in-Chief Hamburger Morgenpost newspaper 1986–88; Chief-of-Staff N Rhine-Westphalia State Chancellery 1989–90, Minister without Portfolio 1990–95, Head of Ministry of Industry, Small Business, Tech. and Transport 1995–96; mem. N Rhine-Westphalia State Ass. 1993–2001; elected Deputy Chair. SPD Exec. for State of N Rhine-Westphalia 1996, Deputy Chair. SPD Nat. Exec. 1999–2008 (resgnd); Premier of State of N Rhine-Westphalia 1998–2002; Fed. Minister of Econs and Labour 2002–05; Visiting Prof. of Political Man., NRW School of Governance, Duisburg Univ., Duisburg-Essen 2008; Chair. Advisory Bd, Advice Kloepfel Consulting 2011; Chair. Bd of Trustees, Initiative Neue Soziale Marktwirtschaft 2012–; mem. Bd, Deutsche Wohnen 2011–; Hon. mem. Int. Raoul Wallenberg Foundation; Großes Bundesverdienstkreuz 2004; Grand Officer of the Star of Romania 2004; Dr hc (Ruhr Univ., Bochum) 2004; Dr Kurt Neven DuMont Medal, West German Acad. of Communications 1997, Georg Schulhoff Prize 1997, Bröckemännche Prize, Bonner Medienclubs 2010, Ludwig Erhard Prize for Econ. Journalism 2014. *Address:* c/o Federal Ministry of Economics and Labour, Scharnhorststrasse 34–37, 10115 Berlin, Germany.

CLEMENTE, Francesco; Italian painter; b. 23 March 1952, Naples; s. of Marquess Lorenzo Clemente; m. Alba Primiceri 1974; four c.; ed Univ. degli Studi di Roma, La Sapienza; collaborated with Andy Warhol and Jean-Michel Basquiat 1984; mem. American Acad. of Arts and Letters. *Address:* c/o Gagosian Gallery, 980 Madison Avenue, New York, NY 10021, USA. *Website:* www.gagosian.com/artists/francesco-clemente; francescoclemente.net.

CLEMENTI, Sir David Cecil, Kt, MA, MBA; British financial services executive and media executive; *Chairman, BBC;* b. 25 Feb. 1949, Hunts.; s. of Air Vice-Marshal Creswell Montagu Clementi and Susan Clementi (née Pelham); m. Sarah Louise (Sally) Cowley 1972; one s. one d.; ed Winchester Coll., Lincoln Coll., Oxford, Harvard Business School, USA; with Corp. Finance Div. Kleinwort Benson Ltd 1975–87, Head 1989–94; Head, Kleinwort Benson Securities 1987–89; Chief Exec. Kleinwort Benson Ltd 1994–97; Vice-Chair. Kleinwort Benson Group PLC 1997; Deputy Gov. Bank of England 1997–2002, mem. Monetary Policy Cttee, mem. Financial Capability Steering Group; Chair. Prudential plc 2002–08; apptd Chair. King's Cross Central (partnership to develop 67-acre central London scheme) 2008; Chair. Virgin Money Holdings 2011–15; Sr Adviser, World First UK Ltd 2006–11, apptd Chair. 2011; apptd by Govt to carry out an independent review into the way the BBC is governed and regulated 2015–16; Chair. BBC 2017–; apptd by Sec. of State for Constitutional Affairs to carry out review of regulation of legal services in England and Wales (completed 2004); mem. Bd of Dirs (non-exec.), Rio Tinto plc 2003–10, Foreign & Colonial Investment Trust PLC 2008; Pres. Investment Property Forum 2005; Warden of Winchester College 2008; Master of the Mercers Co.; Trustee, Royal Opera House. *Leisure interest:* sailing. *Address:* BBC, Broadcasting House, Portland Place, London, W1A 1AA, England (office). *Website:* www.bbc.co.uk (office).

CLEMENTS, John Allen, MD, FRCP; American paediatrician, physiologist and academic; *Professor of Pulmonary Biology and Professor of Pediatrics Emeritus, University of California, San Francisco;* b. 16 March 1923, Auburn, New York; s. of Harry Vernon Clements and May Victoria Porter; m. Margot Sloan Power; two c.; ed Cornell Univ. Medical Coll.; Research Asst, Cornell Univ. Medical Coll. 1947–49; with US Army studying defences against war gases 1949–61; with Cardiovascular Research Inst., Univ. of California 1961–; Julius H. Comroe, Jr Prof. of Pulmonary Biology, Univ. of California, San Francisco 1987, currently Prof. of Pulmonary Biology and Prof. of Pediatrics Emer.; Distinguished Lecturer in Medical Science, Mayo Clinic 1993; mem. Nat. Heart, Lung and Blood Inst. Advisory Council 1990–93; mem. NAS 1974; Fellow, American Acad. of Arts and Sciences 2002; Hon. Fellow, American Coll. of Chest Physicians 1978; Hon. Dir La Sociedad Chilena de Enfermedades del Thorax y Tuberculosis 1982; Hon. Life Mem. American Lung Asscn 1983; Hon. MD (Universität Bern) 1990, (Philipps Universität Marburg) 1992; Hon. ScD (Univ. of Manitoba) 1993; Bowditch Lecturer, American Physiological Soc. 1961, Modern Medicine Distinguished Achievement Award 1973, Howard Taylor Ricketts Medal and Award, Univ. of Chicago 1975, 57th Mellon Award, Univ. of Pittsburgh 1976, Edward Livingston Trudeau Medal, American Lung Asscn 1982, Gairdner Foundation Int. Award 1983, Research Achievement Award, American Heart Asscn 1991, Harold and Marilyn Menkes Memorial Lecturer, Johns Hopkins Univ. 1991, Christopher Columbus Discovery Award in Biomedical Research, NIH Christopher Columbus Quincentenary Jubilee Comm. of US Congress 1992, Nat. Medical Research Award, Nat. Health Council 1992, American Acad. of Pediatrics Virginia Apgar Award for Distinguished Contribs to Neonatology 1994, Albert Lasker Award for Clinical Research 1994, Warren Alpert Foundation Prize, Harvard Medical School 1996, Ulf von Euler Memorial Lecturer, Karolinska Inst., Nobel Foundation 1996, Pollin Prize for Pediatric Research 2008. *Achievements include:* independent discoverer of lung surfactant and elucidator of its composition and functions 1955–; inventor of synthetic surfactant replacements 1980. *Publications:* numerous scholarly articles in journals and books. *Leisure interests:* piano, musical concerts, tennis, swimming, biography, history of science. *Address:* Box 1245, University of California, San Francisco, 513 Parnassus Avenue, San Francisco, CA 94143-1245, USA (office). *Telephone:* (415) 476-2864 (office). *E-mail:* john.clements@ucsf.edu (office).

CLEOBURY, Nicholas Randall, MA, FRCO; British conductor and academic; *Associate Professor and Head of Opera, Queensland Conservatorium;* b. 23 June 1950, Bromley, Kent; s. of John Frank Cleobury and Brenda Julie Cleobury (née Randall); brother of Stephen Cleobury; m. Heather Kay 1978; one s. one d.; ed King's School, Worcester and Worcester Coll., Oxford; Asst Organist, Chichester Cathedral 1971–72, Christ Church, Oxford 1972–76; Conductor, Schola Cantorum of Oxford 1973–76; Chorus Master, Glyndebourne Festival Opera 1977–79; Asst Dir, BBC Singers 1977–79; Prin. Opera Conductor, RAM 1980–87; Prin. Guest Conductor, Gayle Orchestra 1983–85; Guest Conductor, Zurich Opera House 1992–2006; Music Dir, Oxford Bach Choir 1997–2015; Artistic Dir, Aquarius 1983–92, Cambridge Symphony Soloists 1990–92, Britten Sinfonia 1992–2005, Sounds New 1996–2009; Music Dir, Broomhill 1990–94, Artistic Dir, Cambridge Festival 1992, Mozart Ways Canterbury 2003; Artistic Adviser, Berkshire Choral Festival 2002–; Assoc. Dir, Orchestra of the Swan 2004–08; Prin. Conductor, Jam 2007–; Artistic Dir, Mid Wales Opera 2009–; Founder and Artistic Dir Britten in Oxford (festival) 2013; Assoc. Prof. and Head of Opera, Queensland Conservatorium, Griffith Univ., Australia 2015–; Fellow, Christ Church Univ. Coll., Canterbury 2005; Hon. RAM 1985. *Leisure interests:* cricket, food, wine, reading, theatre. *Address:* Queensland Conservatorium, Griffith University, 140 Grey Street, South Brisbane, Queensland 4101, Australia. *E-mail:* nicholascleobury@btinternet.com (home). *Website:* www.griffith.edu.au/music/queensland-conservatorium (office); www.nicholascleobury.net.

CLEOBURY, Stephen John, CBE, MusB, MA, FRCM, FRCO, FRSCM, FRSA; British conductor and organist; *Fellow, Director of Music and Organist, King's College, Cambridge;* b. 31 Dec. 1948, Bromley, Kent; s. of John Frank Cleobury and Brenda Julie Cleobury (née Randall); brother of Nicholas Cleobury; m. 2nd Emma Sian Disley; four d. (two from previous m.); ed King's School, Worcester and St John's Coll., Cambridge; Organist, St Matthew's, Northampton 1971–74; sub-organist, Westminster Abbey 1974–78; Master of Music, Westminster Cathedral 1979–82; Dir of Music, King's Coll. Cambridge 1982–(2019), Organist to the Univ. of Cambridge 1991–2016, also Fellow, King's Coll.; Conductor, Cambridge Univ. Music Soc. 1983–2009, Chorus Dir 2009–16, Conductor Laureate 2016–; frequent appearances on BBC 2, BBC Radio 3 and Classic FM; freelance conducting and organ playing; mem. Council, Royal School of Church Music 1982–2005; Pres. Inc. Asscn of Organists 1985–87, Cathedral Organists' Asscn 1988–90; mem. Royal Coll. of Organists 1967–2008, Hon. Sec. 1981–90, Pres. 1990–92; Chief Conductor BBC Singers 1995–2007, Conductor Laureate 2007–; Pres. Friends of Cathedral Music 2016–, Herbert Howells Soc. 2016–; Fellow, Royal School of Church Music 2008; Hon. DMus (Anglia Polytechnic) 2001. *Radio:* A Festival of Nine Lessons and Carols (BBC Radio 3). *Television:* Carols from King's (BBC 2), Easter from King's (BBC 2). *Recordings include:* directing Choir of King's Coll. Cambridge and BBC Singers (Decca, EMI, Priory, King's Coll. Cambridge own label). *Publications:* various musical arrangements and writings. *Leisure interests:* reading, opera. *Address:* c/o Robin Tyson, Edition Peters Artist Management Ltd, Edition Peters UK, 2–6 Baches Street, London, N1 6DN, England (office); King's College, Cambridge, CB2 1ST, England (office). *E-mail:* robin.tyson@editionpeters.com (office); choir@kings.cam.ac.uk (office). *Website:* www.editionpeters.com/london/epamstephencleobury.php (office); www.stephencleobury.com. *Telephone:* (1223) 331224 (office).

CLEVERS, Johannes Carolus (Hans), MD, PhD; Dutch geneticist and academic; *President, Royal Netherlands Academy of Arts and Sciences;* b. 27 March 1957, Eindhoven; ed Univ. of Utrecht; postdoctoral work, Dana-Farber Cancer Inst., Harvard Univ., USA 1986–89; Prof. of Immunology, Univ. of Utrecht 1991–2002, Prof. of Molecular Genetics 2002–; Prof. of Molecular Genetics and Dir Hubrecht Inst. for Developmental Biology and Stem Cell Research, Royal Netherlands Acad. of Arts and Sciences (KNAW), Utrecht 2002–12, Pres. KNAW 2012–; Dir Research, Princess Máxima Center for Pediatric Oncology 2012–; mem. KNAW 2000, American Acad. of Arts and Sciences 2012; Chevalier, Légion d'honneur 2005; Kt, Order of the Netherlands Lion 2012; Spinoza Award (Netherlands) 2001, Louis Jeantet Prize (Switzerland) 2004, Memorial Sloan-Kettering Katharine Berkan Judd Award 2005, Rabbi Shai Shacknai Memorial Prize (Israel) 2006, Josephine Nefkens Prize for Cancer Research (Netherlands) 2008, Meyenburg Cancer Research Award (Germany) 2008, Cancer Soc. Award (Netherlands) 2009, Research Prize, United European Gastroenterology Fed. 2010, Ernst Jung Prize for Medicine (Germany) 2011, Léopold Griffuel Prize, Asscn pour la Recherche sur le Cancer (France) 2012, Dr A.H. Heineken Prize for Medicine 2012, Breakthrough Prize in Life Sciences (co-recipient) 2013, Massachusetts Gen. Hosp. Award in Cancer Research 2014, TEFAF Oncology Chair 2014, Nat. Icon of the Netherlands 2014, Acad. Professor Prize of Royal Netherlands Acad. 2016, Körber European Science Prize, Germany 2016, Princess Takamatsu Award of Merit, Tokyo 2017; Fellow, American Asscn for Cancer Research Acad. 2014. *Publications:* numerous papers in professional journals. *Address:* Hubrecht Institute, Uppsalalaan 8, 3584 CT Utrecht, The Netherlands (office). *Telephone:* (30) 2121831 (office). *Fax:* (30) 2121801 (office). *E-mail:* h.clevers@hubrecht.eu (office). *Website:* www.hubrecht.eu/research/clevers (office).

CLEWLOW, Warren (Alexander Morten); South African business executive and chartered accountant; b. 13 July 1936, Durban; s. of Percy Edward Clewlow; m. Margaret Brokensha 1964; two s. three d.; ed Glenwood High School, Univ. of Natal; joined Barlow Group as Co. Sec. Barlow's (OFS) Ltd 1963; Alt. Dir Barlow Rand Ltd 1974, Dir 1975; mem. Exec. Cttee with various responsibilities Barlow Group 1978–83; CEO Barlow Rand Ltd (now Barloworld) 1983–86, Deputy Chair. and Chief Exec. 1985, Chair. 1991–2007 (resgnd); Chair. Nedbank Ltd and Nedcor Ltd 2004–06; Chair. Pretoria Portland Cement 1993–2004; fmr Dir SA Mutual Life Assurance Soc., Sasol Ltd; Regional Gov. Univ. of Cape Town Foundation; Council mem. South Africa Foundation; Chair. State Pres. Econ. Advisory Council 1985; mem. Bd Asscn of Marketers; Trustee Project South African Trust, Nelson Mandela Children's Fund; Chair. Duke of Edinburgh's South African Foundation, The President's Award for Youth Empowerment Trust; Chair. Bd of Trustees Carl & Emily Fuchs Foundation; Hon. Treas. African Children's Feeding Scheme; Hon. Prof. Univ. of Stellenbosch 1986; Order for Meritorious Service (Gold Class) 1988; Hon. DEcon (Natal) 1988; Businessman of the Year, Sunday Times 1984, Marketing Man of the Year, SA Inst. of Marketing 1984, Dr G. Malherbe Award, Univ. of Natal 1986. *Leisure interests:* tennis, horticulture, historical reading, sugar plantation farmering. *Address:* c/o Carl & Emily Fuchs Foundation, 1st Floor, Block 2, Waterfall Terraces, Waterfall Park, Bekker Road, Midrand, South Africa (office).

CLIFF, Ian Cameron, CMG, OBE, MA; British diplomatist; b. 11 Sept. 1952, Twickenham, Greater London; s. of Gerald Shaw Cliff and Dorothy Cliff; m. Caroline Redman 1988; one s. two d.; ed Hampton Grammar School, Univ. of Oxford; history teacher, Dr Challoner's Grammar School, Amersham 1975–79; joined FCO 1979; First Sec., Khartoum 1982–85, FCO 1985–89, UK Mission to UN, New York 1989–93; Dir Exports to Middle East, Near East and N Africa, Dept of Trade and Industry 1993–96; Deputy Head of Mission, Embassy in Vienna 1995–2001; Amb. to Bosnia and Herzegovina 2001–05, to Sudan 2005–07, Amb. and Head of Del. to OSCE, Vienna 2007–11, Amb. to Kosovo 2011–15, Chargé d'affaires a.i., Embassy in Zagreb 2015–16. *Leisure interests:* music, railways, philately. *Address:* Foreign and Commonwealth Office, King Charles Street, London, SW1A 2AH, England (office). *Telephone:* (20) 7008-1500 (office). *E-mail:* ian.cliff@fco.gov.uk (office). *Website:* www.gov.uk/government/organisations/foreign-commonwealth-office (office).

CLIFF, Jimmy; Jamaican reggae singer and composer; b. (James Chambers), 1 April 1948, St Catherine; one s.; ed Kingston Tech. School; singer, songwriter 1960s–; backing vocalist, London 1963; tours world-wide; concerts include Montreux Jazz Festival 1980, World Music Festival, Jamaica 1982, Rock In Rio II, Brazil 1991, Worlds Beat Reggae Festival, Portland, USA 1992; formed own record label, Cliff Records 1989, own production co. Cliff Sounds and Films 1990; Grammy Award, Best Reggae Recording 1985, MOBO Award for contrib. to Urban Music 2002, inducted into Rock and Roll Hall of Fame 2010. *Films include:* The Harder They Come 1972, Bongo Man 1980, Club Paradise 1986. *Compositions include:* You Can Get It If You Really Want (recorded by Desmond Dekker), Let Your Yeah Be Yeah (recorded by The Pioneers), Trapped (recorded by Bruce Springsteen). *Recordings include:* albums: Hard Road 1967, Jimmy Cliff 1969, Can't Get Enough 1969, Wonderful World 1970, Another Cycle 1971, The Harder They Come 1972, Struggling Man 1974, Follow My Mind 1975, Give Thanx 1978, I Am The Living 1980, Give The People What They Want 1981, Special 1982, The Power and The Glory 1983, Cliff Hanger 1985, Hanging Fire 1988, Images 1990, Breakout 1992, 100% Pure Reggae 1997, Shout for Freedom 1999, Humanitarian 1999, Live And In The Studio 2000, Wanted (compilation) 2000, Best of Jimmy Cliff 2001, Fantastic Plastic People 2002, Sunshine in the Music 2003, Black Magic 2005, Rebirth (Grammy Award for Best Reggae Album 2013) 2012. *E-mail:* bedelman@wmeentertainment.com (office). *Website:* www.jimmycliff.com.

CLIFFORD, R. Leigh, BEng, MEng Sci; Australian business executive; ed Univ. of Melbourne; joined Rio Tinto Group 1970, has held posts including Man. Dir Rio Tinto Ltd, Chief Exec. Energy Div., CEO Rio Tinto Group 2000–07 (retd), mem. Bd of Dirs 1994–2007; mem. Bd of Dirs Qantas Airways Aug. 2007, Chair. Nov. 2007–18; mem. Bd of Dirs Bechtel Group Inc. (Chair. Bechtel Australia Pty Ltd), Murdoch Childrens Research Inst., Nat. Gallery of Victoria Foundation; fmr mem. Bd of Dirs Barclays PLC; Sr Advisor to Kohlberg Kravis Roberts & Co.; mem. Council of Trustees of the Nat. Gallery of Victoria; Chair. IEA Coal Industry Advisory Bd 1998–2000. *Address:* c/o Qantas Airways Ltd, Level 12, Exhibition Street, Melbourne, Vic. 3000, Australia (office).

CLIFFORD, Sir Timothy Peter Plint, Kt, BA, FRSA, FRSE, FSA; British art historian, consultant and fmr museum director; b. 26 Jan. 1946; s. of Derek Plint Clifford and Anne Clifford (née Pierson); m. Jane Olivia Paterson 1968; one d.; ed Sherborne, Dorset, Perugia Univ., Courtauld Inst., Univ. of London; Asst Keeper, Dept of Paintings, Manchester City Art Galleries 1968–72, Acting Keeper 1972; Asst Keeper, Dept of Ceramics, Victoria and Albert Museum, London 1972–76; Dir Manchester City Art Galleries 1978–84; Dir Nat. Galleries of Scotland 1984–2001, Dir Gen. 2001–05; mem. Cttee ICOM (UK) 1980–82, Chair. Int. Cttee for Museums of Fine Art 1980–83, mem. Exec. Cttee 1983–88; mem. Bd Museums and Galleries Comm. 1983–88, British Council 1987–92, Exec. Cttee Scottish Museums Council 1984; Vice-Pres. Turner Soc. 1984–86, 1989–; mem. Advisory Council, Friends of the Courtauld Inst.; Pres. Nat. Asscn of Decorative and Fine Arts Socs 1996–2006; Consultant, Simon C. Dickinson Ltd, London 2007–; Comitatio Scientifico, Foundation of Civic Museums of Venice 2009–; Opificio delle Pietre Dure, Florence; Trustee, Royal Yacht Britannia 1998–2011, Hermitage Devt Trust 1999–2003, Wallace Collection 2003–11, Attingham Summer School, The American Friends of the Nat. Galleries of Scotland; Patron, Friends of Sherborne House 1997–, Olympia Art and Antiques Fair 2008–10; Freeman, Goldsmiths Co. 1989, City of London 1989, Liveryman 2007; Cavaliere al Ordine della Repubblica Italiana 1988, Commendatore 1999, Grand Ufficiale della Solidarietà Italiana 2004; Hon. LLD (St Andrews) 1996, (Aberdeen) 2005; Hon. DLitt (Glasgow) 2001; Special Award, BIM 1991, Ateneo Veneto, Italy 1997, Gulbenkian Prize for Charles Jenck's Landform 2004, Garrett Lifetime Award for Business Sponsorship for the Arts 2005. *Publications include:* John Crome (with Derek Clifford) 1968, The Man at Hyde Park Corner: Sculpture by John Cheere (with T. Friedmann) 1974, Vues pittoresques de Luxembourg ... par J.M.W. Turner 1977, Ceramics of Derbyshire 1750–1975 1978, J.M.W. Turner, Acquerelli e incisioni 1980, The Nat. Gallery of Scotland: an Architectural and Decorative History (with Ian Gow) 1988, Raphael: the Pursuit of Perfection (co-author) 1994, Effigies and Ecstasies: Roman Baroque Sculpture and Design in the Age of Bernini (with A. Weston-Lewis) 1998, Designs of Desire: Architectural and Ornament Prints and Drawings 1500–1850 2000, (co-author) A Poet in Paradise: Lord Lindsay and Christian Art 2000, The Age of Titian (co-author) 2004, Choice: Twenty-One Years of Collecting in Scotland 2005, Croatia: Aspects of Art and Architecture 2009. *Leisure interests:* bird watching, entomology.

CLINTON, George; American singer and bandleader; b. 22 July 1941, Kannapolis, NC; one s.; founder and leader, The Parliaments in 1950s, changed name to Funkadelic 1969, also performed and recorded as Parliament; solo artist 1982–; Owner, Bridgeport Music; regular worldwide concerts and tours; formed record label, The C Kunspyruhzy 2003–; Hon. DMus (Berklee Coll. of Music) 2012, Lifetime Achievement Award, Nat. Asscn for Advancement of Colored People, Vanguard Award, Oxfam America 2013. *Recordings include:* albums: with The Parliaments: I Wanna Testify 1967, Osmium 1970, Up for the Down Stroke 1974, Chocolate City 1975, Clones of Dr Funkenstein 1976, Mothership Connection 1976, Funkentelechy Vs The Placebo Syndrome 1977, Get Down & Boogie 1977, Live Earth Tour 1977, Motor Booty Affair 1978, Gloryhallastoopid (Pin The Tale On The Funky) 1979, Trombipulation 1980; with Funkadelic: Funkadelic 1970, Free Your Mind... And Your Ass Will Follow 1970, Maggot Brain 1971, America Eats Its Young 1972, Cosmic Slop 1973, Standing On The Verge of Getting It On 1974, Let's Take It to the Stage 1975, Hardcore Jollies 1976, Tales of Kidd Funkadelic 1976, One Nation Under A Groove 1978, Uncle Jam Wants You 1979, The Electric Spanking of War Babies 1981, First Ya Gotta Shake the Gate 2014; solo: Computer Games 1982, You Shouldn't Nuf Bit, Fish! 1983, Some of My Best Jokes Are Friends 1985, R&B Skeletons In The Closet 1986, Mothership Connection 1986, The Cinderella Theory 1989, Hey Man... Smell My Finger 1993, Go Fer Yer Funk 1995, P is the Funk 1995, Plush Funk 1995, Testing Positive 4 The Funk 1995, A Fifth of Funk 1995, The Awesome Power of a Fully Operation Mothership 1996, Live & Kickin' 1997, Dope Dogs 1998, Six Degrees of P-Funk 2003, How Late Do You Have 2BB4UR Absent 2006, George Clinton and His Gangsters of Love 2008. *E-mail:* unclejam@georgeclinton.com (office). *Website:* www.georgeclinton.com.

CLINTON, Hillary Rodham, MA, DJur; American lawyer, politician and governmment official; b. 26 Oct. 1947, Chicago, Ill.; d. of Hugh Ellsworth and Dorothy Howell Rodham; m. William (Bill) Jefferson Clinton (q.v.) (fmr Pres. of USA) 1975; one d.; ed Wellesley Coll. and Yale Univ.; joined Rose Law Firm 1977, fmr Sr Partner; Legal Counsel, Nixon impeachment staff, US House Judiciary Cttee, Washington, DC 1974; Asst Prof. of Law, Univ. of Arkansas, Fayetteville and Dir Legal Aid Clinic 1974–77; Lecturer in Law, Univ. of Arkansas, Little Rock 1979–80; Chair. Comm. on Women in the Profession, ABA 1987–91; First Lady of USA 1993–2001; Head of Pres.'s Task Force on Nat. Health Reform 1993–94; newspaper columnist 1995; Senator from New York 2001–09, mem. Armed Services Cttee, Environment and Public Works Cttee, Health, Educ., Labor and Pensions Cttee, Special Cttee on Aging; Co-Chair. Children's Defense Fund 1973–74; unsuccessful cand. for Democratic party nomination for US Pres. 2008; US Sec. of State, Washington, DC 2009–13; unsuccessful cand. (Democrat) for US Pres. 2016; mem. Bd of Dirs Southern Devt Bancorpn 1986, Nat. Center on Educ. and the Economy 1987, Franklin and Eleanor Roosevelt Inst. 1988, Children's TV Workshop 1989, Public/Pvt. Ventures 1990, Arkansas Single Parent Scholarship Fund Program 1990, Clinton Presidential Center 2004; Hon. LLD (Arkansas, Little Rock) 1985, (Arkansas Coll.) 1988, (Hendrix Coll.) 1992; Hon. DHL (Drew) 1996; numerous awards and distinctions including One of the Most Influential Lawyers in America, Nat. Law Journal 1988, 1991, Outstanding Lawyer-Citizen Award, Ark. Bar Asscn 1992, Lewis Hine Award, Nat. Child Labor Law Comm. 1993, Friend of Family Award, American Home Econs Foundation 1993, Humanitarian Award, Alzheimer's Asscn 1994, Elie Wiesel Foundation 1994, AIDS Awareness Award 1994, Grammy Award 1996, Alice Award 2009, Founders Award, Elton John AIDS Foundation 2013, ABA Medal 2013, American Patriot Award, National Defense Univ. Foundation 2013. *Publications include:* It Takes a Village 1996, Dear Socks, Dear Buddy 1998, An Invitation to the White House 2000, Living History (memoirs) 2003, Hard Choices (memoirs) 2014; numerous contribs to magazines and journals. *Leisure interests:* reading, walking, tennis. *Website:* www.hillaryclinton.com.

CLINTON, William (Bill) Jefferson, JD; American lawyer, fmr politician and fmr head of state; b. 19 Aug. 1946, Hope, Ark.; s. of William Jefferson Blythe, III and Virginia Dwire Kelley; m. Hillary Rodham Clinton (q.v.) 1975; one d.; ed Hot Springs High School, Ark., Georgetown Univ., Univ. Coll., Oxford, UK, Yale Law School; Prof., Univ. of Arkansas Law School 1974–76; Democratic nominee for US House of Reps from Third Ark. Dist 1974; Attorney-Gen. of Ark. 1977–79, Gov. of Ark. 1979–81, 1983–93; mem. counsel, Wright, Lindsey & Jennings (law firm) 1981–83; Pres. of USA, The White House, Washington, DC 1993–2001; impeached by US House of Reps for perjury and obstruction of justice Dec. 1998, acquitted in US Senate on both counts Jan. 1999; suspended from practising law in US Supreme Court 2001–06; UN Special Envoy for Tsunami Recovery 2005–07, to Haiti 2009–; Chair. Nat. Constitution Center, Philadelphia 2009–; headed mission to N Korea to free US journalists 2009; Chair. Southern Growth Policies Bd 1985–86; Chair. Nat. Govs Asscn 1987, Co-Chair. Task Force on Educ. 1990–91; Vice-Chair. Democratic Govs Asscn 1987–88, Chair. (elect) 1988–89, Chair. 1989–90; Chair. Educ. Comm. of the States 1987; Chair. Democratic Party Affirmative Action 1975, Southern Growth Policies Bd 1980; Chair. Democratic Leadership Council 1990–91; mem. US Supreme Court Bar, Bd of Trustees, Southern Center for Int. Studies of Atlanta, Ga; Chair. Bd of Dirs Global Fairness Initiative; Founder William J. Clinton Foundation, New York and Clinton Presidential Center, Ark.; Hon. Co-Chair. Club of Madrid; Hon. Fellow, Univ. Coll., Oxford 1992; Hon. DCL (Oxford) 1994; Hon. DLitt (Ulster) 1995; Dr hc (Northeastern Univ.) 1993, (Pace Univ.) 2006, (Univ. of New Hampshire) 2007; co-recipient TED (Tech. Entertainment Design) Prize 2007. *Recordings include:* Peter and the Wolf: Wolf Tracks (Grammy Award, Best Spoken Word Album for Children (jtly) 2004) 2003, My Life (Grammy Award, Best Spoken Word Album) 2005. *Publications include:* Between Hope and History 1996, My Life (memoir) (British Book Award for Biography of the Year 2005) 2004, Giving: How Each of Us Can Change the World 2008, Back to Work: Why We Need Smart Government for a Strong Economy 2011, The President is Missing (with James Patterson) 2018. *Leisure interests:* jogging, swimming, golf, reading. *Address:* William J. Clinton Foundation, 55 West 125th Street, New York, NY 10027; Clinton Presidential Center, 1200 President Clinton Avenue, Little Rock, AR 72201, USA. *Website:* www.clintonpresidentialcenter.org; www.clintonfoundation.org.

CLINTON-DAVIS, Baron (Life Peer), cr. 1990, of Hackney in the London Borough of Hackney; **Stanley Clinton-Davis,** PC, LLB; British politician, solicitor and international organization official; b. 6 Dec. 1928, London; s. of Sidney Davis and Lily Davis; m. Frances Jane Lucas 1954; one s. three d.; ed Hackney Downs School, Bournemouth School, Mercers' School and King's Coll., London; fmr Councillor and Mayor, London Borough of Hackney; MP for Hackney Cen. 1970–83; Parl. Under-Sec. of State for Trade 1974–79; Opposition Spokesman for Trade 1979–81, for Transport, House of Lords 1990–97; Minister of State, Dept of Trade and Industry 1997–98; Deputy Opposition Spokesman for Foreign Affairs 1981–83; Commr EC for the Environment, Consumer Protection, Nuclear Safety, Forests and Transport 1985–86, for Environment, Transport and Nuclear Safety 1986–88; Chair. Refugee Council 1989–97, Advisory Cttee on Protection of the Sea 1989–97, 1998–2001 (Pres. 2001–03); consultant on European affairs and law, S. J. Berwin & Co. 1989–97, 1998–2003, European Cockpit Asscn 1995–97; Pres. Asscn of Metropolitan Authorities 1992–97, 1998–2003, Airfields Environment Fed. 1994–97, British Airline Pilots Asscn 1994–; Deputy Chair. Labour Finance and Industry Group 1993–; Fellow, King's Coll. and Queen Mary and Westfield Coll., London Metropolitan Univ.; Labour; Grand Cross, Order of Leopold II, for services to EC (Belgium) 1990; Dr hc (Polytechnical Inst., Bucharest) 1993; First Medal for Outstanding Services to Animal Welfare in Europe (Eurogroup for Animal Welfare) 1988. *Publication:* Good Neighbours? Nicaragua, Central America and the United States (co-author) 1982. *Leisure interests:* reading political biographies, golf. *Address:* House of Lords, Westminster, London, SW1A 0PW (office); 22 Bracknell Gate, Frognal Lane, Hampstead, London, NW3 7EP, England (home). *Telephone:* (20) 7435-0541 (home).

CLODUMAR, Hon. Kinza Godfrey; Nauruan politician; b. 8 Feb. 1945, Boe; mem. Parl. for Aiwo 1971–79, 1983–89, for Boe 1995–2003; Prin. Financial Adviser to the Pres. 1992–95; Pres. of Nauru 1997–98, Jan.–May 2003; Minister of Finance several times between 1977–92, also 2003–04; Minister of the Environment 2004; Founded and fmr Leader of Centre Party; fmr Chair. Nauru Insurance Corpn.

CLONINGER, Kriss, III, BBA, MBA; American insurance industry executive; *Consultant, Aflac Inc.;* b. 21 Oct. 1947, Houston, Tex.; m. Lisa Cloninger (neé Welch); two c. two step-c.; ed Univ. of Texas, Austin; served as First Lt, USAF 1971–73; Consulting Actuary and Partner, Rudd & Wisdom, Austin, Tex. 1974–77; Prin., KPMG, Atlanta, Ga 1977–92; joined Aflac Inc. as Sr Vice-Pres. and Chief Financial Officer 1992, Sr Vice-Pres. 1992–93, Exec. Vice-Pres. 1993–2001, Pres. and Chief Financial Officer, Treas. and Dir 2001–17, Consultant 2018–; Lead Dir Total System Services, Inc. 2017–; mem. Bd of Dirs Total System Services Inc., Tupperware Brands Corpn 2003–, RiverCenter for the Performing Arts, Historic Columbus Foundation, Little Blessings Nurturing Center, Columbus, Ga; Fellow, Soc. of Actuaries; named Best CFO in America (insurance/life category) by Institutional Investor magazine (three times). *Address:* Aflac Inc., 1932 Wynnton Road, Columbus, GA 31999, USA (office). *Telephone:* (706) 323-3431 (office). *Fax:* (706) 324-6330 (office). *E-mail:* info@aflac.com (office). *Website:* www.aflac.com (office).

CLOONEY, George Timothy; American actor and film director; b. 6 May 1961, Georgetown, Ky; s. of Nick Clooney and Nina Bruce (née Warren); m. 1st Talia Balsam 1989 (divorced 1993); m. 2nd Amal Alamuddin 2014; one s., one d.; ed Northern Kentucky Univ.; acting debut on TV 1978; gained recognition by portraying Dr Douglas 'Doug' Ross on long-running medical drama ER 1994–99; Founder Section Eight (production co.) –2006; Co-founder Smoke House (production co.) 2006–; Chevalier des Arts et des Lettres 2007; Spirit of Independence Award 2005, Modern Master Award, Santa Barbara Film Festival 2006, American Cinemathèque Award 2006, Humanitarian Laureate, Robert F. Kennedy for Justice and Human Rights 2010, Cecil B. DeMille Lifetime Achievement Award, Hollywood Foreign Press Asscn 2015. *Films include:* And They Are Off 1982, Grizzly II: The Predator 1987, Return to Horror High 1987, Return of the Killer Tomatoes 1988, Red Surf 1990, Unbecoming Age 1992, The Harvest 1993, From Dusk Till Dawn 1996, Curdled 1996, One Fine Day 1996, Batman & Robin 1997, The Peacemaker 1997, Out of Sight 1998, The Thin Red Line 1998, South Park: Bigger Longer & Uncut (voice) 1999, Three Kings 1999, O Brother, Where Art Thou? (Golden Globe Award for Best Actor – Musical or Comedy 2000) 2000, The Perfect Storm 2000, Rock Star (exec. producer) 2001, Spy Kids 2001, Ocean's Eleven 2001, Insomnia (exec. producer) 2002, Far From Heaven (exec. producer) 2002, Welcome to Collinwood (also producer) 2002, Solaris 2002, Confessions of a Dangerous Mind (also dir) 2002, Spy Kids 3-D: Game Over 2003, Intolerable Cruelty 2003, Criminal (producer) 2004, Ocean's Twelve (also exec. producer) 2004, The Big Empty (exec. producer) 2005, The Jacket (producer) 2005, Good Night, and Good Luck (also dir, co-writer, Satellite Award for Best Original Screenplay 2005, Freedom Award, Critics' Choice Awards 2006, Best Director, Bratislava Film Festival 2005, several awards at Venice Film Festival 2005) 2005, Syriana (also producer, Golden Globe Award for Best Supporting Actor 2006, Acad. Award for Best Supporting Actor 2006) 2006, The Good German 2006, Ocean's Thirteen 2007, Michael Clayton (also exec. producer) (Best Actor, Nat. Bd of Review 2007) 2007, Leatherheads 2008, Burn After Reading 2008, Fantastic Mr Fox (voice) 2009, The Men Who Stare At Goats (also producer) 2009, Up in the Air (New York Film Critics Circle Award for Best Actor, Nat. Bd of Review Award for Best Actor) 2009, The American (also producer) 2010, Touch of Evil (short) 2011, The Ides of March 2011, The Descendants (Golden Globe Award for Best Performance by an Actor in a Motion Picture – Drama 2012) 2011, Gravity (also producer) 2012, The Monuments Men (also dir) 2014, Tomorrowland 2015, Hail, Caesar! 2016, Money Monster 2016, Suburbicon 2017. *Television includes:* The Nick Clooney Show (series) 1968, Centennial (mini-series) 1978, Riptide (series) 1984, Street Hawk (series) 1984, E/R (series) 1984–85, The Facts of Life (series) 1985–86, Combat High (film) 1986, Roseanne (series) 1988–89, Knights of the Kitchen Table (film) 1990, Sunset Beat (series) 1990, Rewrite for Murder (film) 1991, Baby Talk (series) 1991, Bodies of Evidence (series) 1992–93, Sisters (series) 1993–94, ER (series) 1994–2009, Kilroy (film, writer and producer) 1999, Fail Safe (film, also exec. producer) 2000, K Street (series, exec. producer) 2003, Unscripted (series, dir and exec. producer) 2005, Hope for Haiti Now: A Global Benefit for Earthquake Relief (film, exec. producer) 2010, Memphis Beat (series, exec. producer) 2010–11. *Address:* c/o Bryan Lourd, Creative Artists Agency, 2000 Avenue of the Stars, Los Angeles, CA 90067, USA (office); Stan Rosenfield & Associates Ltd, 2029 Century Park East, Suite 1190, Los Angeles, CA 90067-2931, USA (office); Smoke House, 4000 Warner Blvd, Bldg 15, Burbank, CA 91522, USA. *Telephone:* (424) 288-2000 (office); (310) 286-7474 (office); (818) 954-4840. *Fax:* (424) 288-2900 (office); (310) 286-2255 (office); (818) 954-4860. *Website:* www.caa.com (office).

CLOS, Joan; Spanish physician, politician, diplomatist and UN official; b. 29 June 1949, Parets del Vallés, Barcelona; m.; two c.; ed Universidad Autónoma de Barcelona, Univ. of Edinburgh, UK; worked as anaesthetist; apptd Dir of Public Health 1979; Chair. Spanish Soc. of Epidemiology and Healthcare Admin 1981–91; City Councillor, Barcelona 1983–87, Deputy Mayor in charge of Finance and Budgeting 1990–94; elected Councillor, Barcelona Council for Socialists' Party of Catalonia 1993; Mayor of Barcelona and Chair. Metropolitan Greater Area of Barcelona 1997–2006; apptd Pres. Metropolis 1998, World Asscn of Cities and Local Authorities 2000; Chair. UN Advisory Cttee of Local Authorities 2000–07; Minister of Industry, Tourism and Trade 2006–08; Amb. to Turkey and Azerbaijan 2008–10; Exec. Dir UN Human Settlements Programme 2010–17, also Sec.-Gen. Habitat III –2016; mem. Council of European Municipalities and Regions 1997–2003; Gold Medal, RIBA 1999, Scroll of Honour Award, UN Human Settlements Programme 2002. *Address:* c/o United Nations Human Settlements Programme (UN-Habitat), POB 30030, Nairobi, Kenya (office). *Telephone:* (20) 621234 (office). *Fax:* (20) 624266 (office). *E-mail:* infohabitat@unhabitat.org (office). *Website:* www.unhabitat.org (office).

CLOSE, Chuck, BA, MFA; American artist; b. (Charles Thomas Close), 1940, Monroe, Wash.; ed Univ. of Washington, Seattle, Yale Univ., Akad. der Bildenden Kunste, Vienna, Austria; works in perm. collections of Museum of Modern Art, New York, Louisiana Museum of Modern Art, Denmark, Centres George Pompidou, Paris, France, Tate Modern, London, UK; works include Big Self-Portrait 1967–68, Self-Portrait/White Ink 1977, Phil/Fingerprint 1978, John/Color Fingerprint 1983, Georgia/Fingerpainting 1984, Leslie 1986, Self-Portrait (spitbite aquatint) 1988, Lucas (seven-step reduction block/linoleum cut print) 1988, Alex/Reduction Block (silk screen print) 1993, Lucas/Rug 1993, Self-Portrait I 1999, Self-Portrait II 1999, Lyle (etching) 2000, Self-Portrait/Scribble/Etching Portfolio (etching) 2000, Emma (woodblock print) 2002; mem. American Acad. and Inst. of Arts and Letters 1992, President's Cttee on the Arts and the Humanities 2010–17 (resgnd); Hon. DFA (Colby Coll., Me) 1994, (Univ. of Massachusetts) 1995, (Yale

Univ.) 1996; Dr hc (Rhode Island School of Design) 1997; Acad.-Inst. Award in Art, American Acad. and Inst. of Arts and Letters 1991, Univ. of Washington Alumnus Summa Laude Dignatus 1997, Dieu Donné Art Award (jtly) 2000, Nat. Medal of Arts 2000. *Address:* c/o Pace Gallery, 32 East 57th Street, New York, NY 10022, USA (office). *Telephone:* (212) 421-3292. *Fax:* (212) 421-0835. *Website:* chuckclose .com.

CLOSE, Glenn; American actress; b. (Glenda Veronica Close), 19 March 1947, Greenwich, Conn.; d. of William Close and Bettine Close; m. 1st Cabot Wade 1969 (divorced 1971); m. 2nd James Marlas 1984 (divorced 1987); m. 3rd David Shaw 2006 (divorced 2015); one d. with John Starke; ed William and Mary Coll.; joined New Phoenix Repertory Co. 1974; Co-owner The Leaf and Bean Coffee House, Bozeman, Mont. 1991–. *Stage appearances include:* Love for Love 1974, The Rules of the Game 1974, King Lear 1975, The Singular Life of Albert Nobbs 1982, Childhood 1985, The Real Thing (Tony Award for Best Actress in a Play 1984) 1983, Death and the Maiden 1992, Sunset Boulevard 1993, 1994, 2016, 2017, A Streetcar Named Desire (Royal Nat. Theatre) 2002, The Normal Heart 2010, Into the Woods 2012, Mother of the Maid 2018. *Films include:* The World According to Garp 1982, The Big Chill 1983, The Natural 1984, The Stone Boy 1984, Maxie 1985, Jagged Edge 1985, Fatal Attraction 1987, Dangerous Liaisons 1989, Hamlet 1989, Reversal of Fortune 1989, The House of Spirits 1990, Meeting Venus 1990, Immediate Family 1991, The Paper 1994, Mary Reilly 1994, Serving in Silence: The Margaret Cammermeyer Story 1995, 101 Dalmatians 1996, Mars Attacks! 1996, Air Force One 1997, Paradise Road 1997, Tarzan 1999, Cookie's Fortune 1999, 102 Dalmatians 2000, The Safety of Objects 2001, Pinocchio (voice) 2002, Le Divorce 2003, The Stepford Wives 2004, Heights 2004, Nine Lives 2005, The Chumscrubber 2005, Tarzan II (voice) 2005, Hoodwinked (voice) 2006, Evening 2007, Hoodwinked Too!: Hood vs Evil (voice) 2011, Albert Nobbs 2011, Guardians of the Galaxy 2014, The Great Gilly Hopkins 2015, The Girl with All the Gifts 2016, The Wife (Screen Actors Guild Award for Outstanding Performance by a Female Actor in a Leading Role 2019) 2017, Father Figures 2017. *Television includes:* The Simpsons 1995–2018, The Lion in Winter (TV film) (Best Actress in a Miniseries or TV Movie, Golden Globe Awards 2005, Screen Actors Guild Awards 2005) 2004, The Shield (series) 2005, Damages (series) (Golden Globe for Best Actress in a TV series 2008, Emmy Award for Outstanding Lead Actress in a Drama Series 2009) 2007–12, Pokémon 2010, Sea Oak (TV film) 2017. *Address:* c/o Creative Artists Agency, 2000 Avenue of the Stars, Los Angeles, CA 90067, USA. *Telephone:* (424) 288-2000. *Fax:* (424) 288-2900. *Website:* www.caa.com.

CLOSETS, François de; French writer, journalist and producer; b. 25 Dec. 1933, Enghien-les-Bains; s. of Louis-Xavier de Closets and Marie-Antoinette Masson; m. 1st Danièle Lebrun; one s.; m. 2nd Janick Jossin 1970; one s. one d.; ed Lycée d'Enghien, Faculté de Droit de Paris and Inst. d'Etudes Politiques, Paris; Ed. then special envoy of Agence France-Presse in Algeria 1961–65; scientific journalist, Sciences et Avenir 1964–, Acualités Télévisées 1965–68; contrib. L'Express 1968–69; Head of Scientific Service, TV Channel 1 1969–72; Head of Scientific and Tech. Service of TV Channel 2 1972; contrib. to Channel 1 1974; Asst Ed.-in-Chief TF1; Co-producer l'Enjeu (econ. magazine) 1978–88; Dir of Econ. Affairs, TFI 1987; Co-producer, Médiations magazine 1987–93; producer, illustrator Savoir Plus for France 2 1992–2000, Les Grandes Enigmes de la Science for France 2 1992–2003; Grand Prix du reportage du Syndicat des journalistes et écrivains 1966, Prix Cazes 1974, 7 d'or du meilleur journaliste 1985, Prix Aujourd'hui 1985, Roland Dorgelès Prize 1997. *Publications imclude:* L'Espace, terre des hommes, La lune est à vendre 1969, En danger de progrès 1970, Le Bonheur en plus 1974, La France et ses mensonges 1977, Scénarios du futur (Vol. I) 1978, Le monde de l'an 2000 (Vol. II) 1979, Le Système EPM 1980, Toujours plus 1982, Tous ensemble pour en finir avec la syndicatrie 1985, La Grande Manip 1990, Tant et Plus 1992, Le Bonheur d'apprendre, et comment on l'assassine 1996, Le compte à Rebours 1998, L'Imposture informatique 2000, La dernière liberté 2001, Ne dites pas à Dieu ce qu'il doit faire 2004, Plus encore 2006, Le divorce français 2008, Zéro Faute: L'orthographe, une passion française 2009, L'échéance: Français, vous n'avez encore rien vu (with Irène Inchauspé) 2011, Le Monde était à nous (autobiography) 2012, Maintenant ou jamais 2013, La France à quitte ou double 2015, Ils ont écrit ton nom: Liberté 2016. *Address:* c/o Editions Fayard, 13 rue de la Montparnasse, 75006 Paris, France. *E-mail:* fclosets@noos.fr.

CLOTET, Lluís; Spanish architect and designer; *Principal, Clotet, Paricio i Associats SL;* b. 31 July 1941, Barcelona; s. of Jaime Clotet and Concepción Clotet; ed Barcelona Escuela Técnica Superior de Arquitectura; worked for Federico Correa and Alfonso Milás's Studio 1961–64; co-f. (with Pep Bonet, Cristian Cirici and Oscar Tusquets) Studio PER 1964; co-f. B.D. Ediciones de Diseño; collaborator, XV Triennale de Milano 1973, Festival of Fine Architecture, Paris 1978, Transformations in Modern Architecture, Museum of Modern Art, New York 1979, Forum Design, Linz 1980, Biennale de Venezia 1980, The House as Image, Louisiana Museum of Modern Art 1981, The Presence of the Past, San Francisco 1982, Ten New Buildings, Inst. of Contemporary Art, London 1983, Contemporary Spanish Architecture, New York 1986; associated with Ignacio Paricio 1983–; Prof. in Drawing, Barcelona Higher Tech. School in Architecture 1977–84; numerous prizes. *Major works include:* Banco España 1981–89, Water Cistern Ciutadella Park, Barcelona 1985–88, SIMON SA Bldg, Canovelles 1987–88, Museum of Art, Convent dels Angels, Barcelona (Restoration and extension plan) 1984–89, Teleport, Castellbisbal, Barcelona (plan) 1988, Sport Pavilion in Granada, 100 dwellings at Olympic Village 1992. *Address:* Clotet, Paricio i Associats SL, Pujades 63, 3 pl., 08005 Barcelona, Spain (office). *Telephone:* (93) 4853625 (office). *Fax:* (93) 3090567 (office). *E-mail:* cpa@coac.es (office).

CLUFF, Hon. Col John Gordon (Algy); British business executive; *Executive Chairman and CEO, Cluff Natural Resources Plc;* b. 19 April 1940, Bucklow, Cheshire; s. of Harold Cluff and Freda Cluff; m. Blondel Hodge 1993; three s.; ed Stowe School; army officer, served W Africa, Cyprus, Malaysia 1959–64; Chief Exec. Cluff Resources (fmrly Cluff Oil) 1971, Chair. (and Chair. Zimbabwe) 1979, Chair. and CEO Cluff Mining 1996–2003 (acquired by Ashanti Goldfields), Exec. Chair. and CEO Cluff Gold plc 2004–10, Exec. Chair. 2010–11, Chair. (non-exec.) 2011–12, Chair. Cluff Geothermal Plc 2010–, Cluff Natural Resources Plc 2012–, also CEO; Propr, The Spectator 1981–85, Chair. 1985–2004; Chair. Apollo Magazine Ltd 1985; Trustee, Anglo-Hong Kong Trust 1989–, Stowe House Preservation Trust 1999–; Dir Centre for Policy Studies 1998–; Gov. Commonwealth Inst. 1995–, Chair. Conservative Comm. on the Commonwealth 2001; mem. Bd of Govs Stowe School 1998–; Chair. Trustees, War Memorial Trust 2003–. *Publication:* Get On With It: A Memoir 2016. *Leisure interests:* collecting books and paintings, golf, shooting. *Address:* Cluff Natural Resources Plc, Third Floor, 5/8 The Sanctuary, Westminster, London, SW1P 3JS, England (office). *Telephone:* (20) 7887-2630 (office). *Fax:* (20) 7887-2639 (office). *E-mail:* admin@ cluffnaturalresources.com (office). *Website:* www.cluffnaturalresources.com (office).

CLUGSTON, Mackenzie, BA, MPA; Canadian diplomatist; *Professor, Kwansei Gakuin University;* b. Kobe, Japan; m. Paula Bowers; two s.; ed Trent Univ., Queen's Univ.; joined Dept of Foreign Affairs and Int. Trade 1982, served abroad twice in Tokyo as a Public Affairs Officer as well as Trade Commr 1985–97, seconded as Policy Adviser to Privy Council Office 1997–2000, Consul-Gen. in Osaka 2000–03, also held assignments, including with Southern Africa Task Force, Int. Financial and Investment Affairs Div., US Trade and Econ. Policy Div., Int. Econ. Relations Div., Minister and Deputy Head of Mission, Embassy in Tokyo 2003–06, Dir-Gen. Assignments and Exec. Man. Bureau 2006–09, Amb. to Indonesia 2009–12, Amb. to Japan 2012–16; Prof. Kwansei Gakuin Univ. *Address:* Kwansei Gakuin University, Uegahara, Nishinomiya, Hyogo 662-8501, Japan (office). *Website:* www.global.kwansei.ac.jp (office).

CLUNES, (Alexander) Martin, OBE; British actor; b. 28 Nov. 1961, Wimbledon, Surrey; s. of Alec Clunes and Daphne Acott; m. 1st Lucy Aston 1990 (divorced 1997); m. 2nd Philippa Braithwaite 1997; one d.; ed Royal Russell School, Croydon, The Arts Educational Schools; first role in rep at Mercury Theatre, Colchester; worked as photo model for artists Gilbert and George, including in World 1983;. *Films include:* The Russia House 1990, Carry on Columbus 1992, The Ballad of Kid Divine: The Cockney Cowboy 1992, Swing Kids 1993, Staggered 1994, The Revengers' Comedies 1998, The Acid House 1998, Shakespeare in Love 1998, Saving Grace 2000, Rock My World 2002, Me or the Dog (short) (voice) 2011, Nativity 3: Dude, Where's My Donkey?! 2014. *Television includes:* No Place Like Home (series) 1983–86, All at Number 20 (series) 1986–87, Jeeves and Wooster (series) 1991, Gone to the Dogs (mini-series) 1991, Men Behaving Badly (series) 1992–99, Dancing Queen (film) 1993, An Evening with Gary Lineker (film) 1994, Harry Enfield and Chums (series) 1994, Lord of Misrule (film) 1996, Over Here (film) 1996, Roger and the Rottentrolls (series) (voice) 1996, Never Mind the Horrocks (film) 1996, Hospital! (film) 1997, Touch and Go (film) 1998, Neville's Island (film) 1998, Born to Be Wild (film) 1999, Hunting Venus (film) 1999, Sex 'n' Death (film) 1999, The Nearly Complete and Utter History of Everything (film) 1999, Gormenghast (mini-series) 2000, Randall & Hopkirk (Deceased) (series) 2000, Dirty Tricks (film) 2000, Lorna Doone (film) 2000, Aladdin (film) 2000, Doc Martin (film) 2001, A Is for Acid (film) 2002, Goodbye, Mr. Chips (film) 2002, Doc Martin and the Legend of the Cloutie (film) 2003, The Booze Cruise (film) 2003, William and Mary (series) 2003–05, Beauty (film) 2004, Fungus the Bogeyman (series) 2004, Doc Martin (series) 2004–, Losing It (film) 2006, The Man Who Lost His Head (film) 2007, Reggie Perrin (series) 2009–10, A Mother's Son (mini-series) 2012, The Town (mini-series) 2012, Strike Back (series) 2013, The Feeling Nuts Comedy Night (film) 2014, Arthur & George (series) 2015, Manhunt 2019, Warren (series) 2019, has narrated several TV documentaries. *Address:* c/o Independent Talent, 40 Whitfield Street, London, W1T 2RH, England (office). *Telephone:* (20) 7636-6565 (office). *Fax:* (20) 7323-0101 (office). *E-mail:* info@independenttalent .com (office). *Website:* www.independenttalent.com (office).

CLUTTON-BROCK, Timothy (Tim) Hugh, MA, PhD, ScD, FRS; British zoologist and academic; *Director of Research, Department of Zoology, University of Cambridge;* b. 13 Aug. 1946; fmrly Prince Philip Prof. of Ecology and Evolutionary Biology and Head of the Large Animal Research Group, Dept of Zoology, Univ. of Cambridge, currently Dir of Research; Fellow of Magdalene Coll.; also holds extraordinary professorships in Dept of Zoology and Entomology and Mammal Research Inst. of Univ. of Pretoria, South Africa; Co-founder Kalahari Meerkat Project; Frink Medal, Zoological Soc. of London 1997, Darwin Medal, Royal Soc. 2012. *Publications:* Readings in Sociobiology (co-ed.) 1978, Red Deer: Behavior and Ecology of Two Sexes (co-author) 1982, Rhum: The Natural History of an Island (Edinburgh Island Biology) (co-ed.) 1987, Reproductive Success: Studies of Individual Variation in Contrasting Breeding Systems (ed.) 1990, The Evolution of Parental Care 1991, Changes and Disturbance in Tropical Rainforest in SouthEast Asia (co-ed.) 2000, Wildlife Population Growth Rates (co-ed.) 2003, Soay Sheep: Dynamics and Selection in an Island Population (co-ed.) 2004, Meerkat Manor – The Story of Flower of the Kalahari 2007; numerous papers in professional journals. *Address:* Room T14, Department of Zoology, University of Cambridge, Downing Street, Cambridge, CB2 3EJ, England (office). *Telephone:* (1223) 336618 (office). *Fax:* (1223) 336676 (office). *E-mail:* thcb@cam.ac.uk (office). *Website:* www.zoo.cam.ac.uk (office).

CLUZEL, Jean, LenD; French politician and business executive; *President, Canal Académie;* b. 18 Nov. 1923, Moulins; s. of Pierre Cluzel and Jeanne Cluzel (née Dumont); m. Madeleine Bonnaud 1947; three s. one d.; ed Lycée de Vichy and Univ. of Paris; Pres. and Dir-Gen. Cluzel-Dumont 1947–71; Municipal Councillor St Pourcain/Sioule 1959–65; Admin., later Senator, Allier 1971, 1980, 1989; Conseiller Général, Moulins-Ouest 1967, 1973, 1979, 1985; Pres. Conseil Général, Allier 1970–76, 1985–92; Senator, Allier 1971, 1980, 1989; mem. l'Union Centriste, Spokesman and Vice-Pres. Comm. des Finances du Senat; Pres. Cttee for Econ. Expansion of Allier 1959–67; Pres. 'Positions' and 'L'Allier Demain', Fed. des Elus Bourbonnais 1972, Univ. Populaire de Bransat 1981, Comité Français pour l'Audiovisuel 1993; Dir Cahiers de l'audiovisuel 1994; Admin. France 2 1998, Singer Polignac Foundation 1999; Perm. Sec. Académie des Sciences Morales et Politiques 1999–2004, now mem. Morale et sociologie, Section II; Founder and Pres. Canal Académie, Institut de France (internet radio service) 2004–; Council mem. Admin. du conseil mondial pour la Radio et la Télévision; mem. Supervisory Cttee European Business School; Officier Légion d'honneur. *Publications:* Horizons Bourbonnais 1973, Les boutiques en colère 1975, Elu de peuple 1977, Télé Violence 1978, L'argent de la télévision 1979, Finances publiques et pouvoir local 1980, Les pouvoirs publics et la transmission de la culture 1983, Les pouvoirs publics et les caisses d'épargne 1984, Les anti-monarque de la Vème 1985, Un projet pour la presse 1986, La loi de 1987 sur l'épargne 1987, La télévision après six réformes 1988, Les finances locales decentralisées 1989, Le Sénat dans la société française 1990, Une ambition pour l'Allier 1992, Une autre bataille de France 1993, Mots pour Mots 1993, Pour qui sont ces tuyaux qui sifflent sur nos têtes? 1993, Feu d'artifices pour fin de législature 1993, L'age de la télévision 1993, Lettre à mes collègues représentants du peuple 1993, Education, culture et télévision 1994, Du modèle canadien à l'appel sud-africain 1996, L'audiovisuel en Europe centrale et orientale 1996, La télévision 1996, Presse et démocratie 1997, L'indispensable Sénat 1998, A propos du Sénat et de ceux qui voudraient en finir avec lui 1999, Anne de France 2002, Propos impertinents sur le cinéma français 2003. *Address:* Canal Académie, 23, quai Conti, 75006 Paris; 12 villa Dupont, 75116 Paris (home); c/o L'Académie des Sciences Morales et Politiques, 23, quai Conti, 75006 Paris, France. *Website:* www.canalacademie.com.

CLUZEL, Jean-Paul, MA; French civil servant and government official; *President, Etablissement public de la Réunion des musées nationaux et du Grand Palais des Champs-Elysées;* b. 29 Jan. 1947, Paris; m. Nicolas Droin 2013; ed École nationale d'admin, Institut d'Études Politiques de Paris, Panthéon-Assas Paris II Univ., Univ. of Chicago, USA; lived in Paris suburb of Le Kremlin-Bicêtre –1961; Insp. of Finance 1972–76, 1981–82; adviser to Minister of Foreign Affairs 1979–81, adviser for Africa at Treasury Dept 1982–84; with insurance group GAN 1985–92, responsible for research and devt and int. affairs; Gen. Man. and Dir of the Paris Opera 1992–95; CEO Radio France Internationale 1995–2004; CEO Radio France 2004–09; Pres. Radios francophones publiques 2009–; Pres. Établissement public de la Réunion des musées nationaux et du Grand Palais des Champs-Elysées (administers 34 nat. museums under authority of Ministry of Culture) 2009–; mem. Bd of Dirs, Agence France-Presse, Arte France, Médiamétrie (polling org.), Théâtre du Châtelet; Officier, Légion d'honneur, Ordre nat. du Mérite; Commdr des Arts et des Lettres; Offizierkreuz, Verdienstkreuz 1. Klasse (Germany); Kt, Order of Infante Dom Enrique (Portugal). *Address:* Réunion des Musées Nationaux, 254/256 rue de Bercy, 75577 Paris Cedex 12, France (office). *Telephone:* 1-40-13-48-00 (office). *Fax:* 1-40-13-44-00 (office). *E-mail:* info@rmn.fr (office). *Website:* www.rmn.fr (office); www.grandpalais.fr (office).

CLUZET, François; French actor; b. 21 Sept. 1955, Paris; four c. and one s. with actress Marie Trintignant; ed acting lessons at Cours Simon and Cours de Périmony et Cochet; Prix Jean Gabin 1984. *Theatre includes:* Belgicae by Anita Van Belle, directed by Pierre Pradinas, at Festival d'Avignon 1992. *Films include:* Un enfant sans histoire 1979, Cocktail Molotov 1980, Le cheval d'orgueil (The Horse of Pride) 1980, Les fantômes du chapelier (The Hatter's Ghost) 1982, Coup de foudre (Between Us) 1983, L'Été meurtrier (One Deadly Summer) 1983, Les enragés 1985, Elsa, Elsa 1985, États d'âme 1986, 'Round Midnight (Autour de minuit) 1986, Rue du Départ 1986, Association de malfaiteurs 1987, Chocolat 1988, Une affaire de femmes (Story of Women) 1988, Deux (Two) 1989, Un tour de manège (Roundabout) 1989, Force majeure (Uncontrollable Circumstances) 1989, Trop belle pour toi (Too Beautiful for You) 1989, La Révolution française (The French Revolution) 1989, Olivier, Olivier 1992, À demain (See You Tomorrow) 1992, L'Instinct de l'ange 1993, L'Enfer (Hell) 1994, Le vent du Wyoming (Wind from Wyoming) 1994, Prêt-à-Porter (Ready to Wear) 1994, French Kiss (Paris Match) 1995, Le hussard sur le toit (The Horseman on the Roof) 1995, Enfants de salaud (Bastard Brood) 1996, Le silence de Rak (Best Actor Award, Paris Film Festival 1996) 1997, Rien ne va plus (The Swindle) 1997, La Voie est libre 1998, Fin août, début septembre (Late August, Early September) 1998, Dolce far niente (Sweet Idleness) 1998, L'Examen de minuit (Midnight Exam) 1998, L'Adversaire (The Adversary) 2002, Quand je vois le soleil 2003, Janis et John (Janis and John) 2003, Je suis un assassin (The Hook) 2004, Le domaine perdu (The Lost Domain) 2005, La cloche a sonné 2005, Quatre étoiles (Four Stars) 2006, Ne le dis à personne (Tell No One) (César Award for Best Actor 2007, Étoile d'Or for Best Actor 2007) 2006, Ma place au soleil (My Place in the Sun) 2007, La vérité ou presque 2007, Détrompez-vous 2007, Les liens du sang (Rivals) 2008, Paris 2008, Les liens du sang 2008, À l'origine (Étoile d'Or 2010) 2009, One for the Road 2009, White Snow 2010, Little White Lies 2010, Mon père est femme de ménage 2011, The Art of Love 2011, A Monster in Paris 2011, Intouchables 2011, Do Not Disturb 2012, 11.6 2013, Turning Tide 2013, Quantum Love 2014, One Wild Moment 2015, Irreplaceable 2016. *Television includes:* Au théâtre ce soir (episode Madame Jonas dans la baleine) 1977, Histoires de voyous: L'élégant 1979, Chère Olga 1980, Le gros oiseau 1981, Le boulanger de Suresnes 1981, Paris-Saint-Lazare (mini-series) 1982, Julien Fontanes, magistrat (episode Perpète) 1983, Un manteau de chinchilla 1983, Le bout du lac 1984, Série noire (episode Aveugle, que veux-tu?) 1984, La mèche en bataille 1984, Manipulations 1984, Sueurs froides (episode À la mémoire d'un ange) 1988, Lucas 1993, Sweet home 1995, L'huile sur le feu 1996, Le goût des fraises 1998, La cape et l'épée (episode La mise à mort) 1999, Les enfants du printemps (mini-series) 2000, L'Algérie des chimères (mini-series) 2001, Un mois à nous 2002, La famille Guérin (series) 2002, Vénus & Apollon (Venus and Apollo (episode Soin ultime) 2005, La forteresse assiégée (film documentary) 2006. *Address:* c/o Isabelle de la Patellière, VMA, 20 avenue Rapp, 75007 Paris, France (home). *Telephone:* 1-43-17-37-00. *Fax:* 1-47-20-15-86. *E-mail:* d.leprestre@vma.fr. *Website:* www.vma.fr.

CLWYD, Rt Hon. Ann, PC; British politician, journalist and broadcaster; b. 21 March 1937, Denbighshire, Wales; d. of Gwilym Henri Lewis and Elizabeth Ann Lewis; m. Owen Dryhurst Roberts 1963 (died 2012); ed Holywell Grammar School, The Queen's School, Chester and Univ. Coll., Bangor; fmr BBC studio man., freelance reporter and producer; Welsh corresp. The Guardian and The Observer 1964–79; Vice-Chair. Welsh Arts Council 1975–79; mem. Royal Comm. on NHS 1976–79, Arts Council of GB 1975–80; various public and political appointments; MEP for Mid- and West Wales 1979–84; MP (Labour) for Cynon Valley 1984–; Opposition Front Bench Spokesperson on Women 1987–88, on Educ. 1987–88; Shadow Sec. of State on Overseas Devt and Co-operation 1989–92, on Wales 1992, for Nat. Heritage 1992–93; Opposition Front Bench Spokesperson on Employment 1993–94, on Foreign Affairs 1994–95; mem. Select Cttee on Int. Devt 1997–, on Foreign Affairs 2010–; Chair. All-Party Group on Human Rights 1997–; Chair. INDICT 1997–2003; Prime Minister's Special Envoy on Human Rights in Iraq 2003–10; apptd by Prime Minister to lead review into Nat. Health Service Complaints Procedure 2013–; Hon. Fellow, North East Wales Inst. of Educ. 1996, Univ. of Wales, Bangor 2004; White Robed Bard of the Nat. Eisteddfod 1991; Hon. LLD (Univ. of Wales) 2007. *Address:* House of Commons, Westminster, London, SW1A 0AA, England (office); 6 Deans Court, Dean Street, Aberdare, Mid Glamorgan, CF44 7BN, Wales (office). *Telephone:* (1685) 871394 (Aberdare) (office); (20) 7219-6609 (London) (office). *Fax:* (20) 7219-5943 (London) (office); (1685) 883006 (Aberdare) (office). *E-mail:* clwyda@parliament.uk (office). *Website:* www.parliament.uk/biographies/commons/ann-clwyd/553 (office).

CLYNE, Cameron; Australian banking executive; *Executive Director, Managing Director and Group CEO, National Australia Bank;* Man. Partner, PricewaterhouseCoopers financial services consulting practice across Asia-Pacific 1993–2005, also worked in their financial services practices in New York; Exec. Gen., Group Devt, National Australia Bank Group 2005–07, Man. Dir and CEO Bank of New Zealand 2007–09, Exec. Dir, Man. Dir and Group CEO National Australia Bank 2009–, Chair. National Australia Group Europe Ltd 2012–; selected as a Young Global Leader by the World Econ. Forum 2008. *Address:* National Australia Bank Ltd, 500 Bourke Street, Melbourne, Victoria 3000, Australia (office). *Telephone:* (3) 8641-3500 (office). *Fax:* (3) 9208-5695 (office). *E-mail:* info@nabgroup.com (office). *Website:* www.nabgroup.com (office).

COAKLEY, Rev. Sarah Anne, MA, ThM, PhD; British academic; *Emeritus Norris-Hulse Professor of Divinity, University of Cambridge;* b. 10 Sept. 1951, London; d. of F. Robert Furber and Anne McArthur; m. James F. Coakley 1975; two d.; ed Blackheath High School for Girls, New Hall, Cambridge and Harvard Divinity School, USA; Lecturer in Religious Studies, Univ. of Lancaster 1976–90, Sr Lecturer 1990–91; Tutorial Fellow in Theology and Univ. Lecturer, Oriel Coll., Oxford 1991–93 (also Life Fellow); Prof. of Christian Theology, The Divinity School, Harvard Univ., USA 1993–95, Chair. Cttee on Academic Programs 1995–98, Edward Mallinckrodt, Jr, Prof. of Divinity 1995–2007, Chair. Dept of Theology 1999–2000; Co-founder The Littlemore Group 2005–; Norris-Hulse Professor of Divinity, Univ. of Cambridge 2007–18, now Emer.; Select Preacher, Univ. of Oxford 1991; Visiting Professorial Fellow, Princeton Univ., USA 2003–04, Australian Catholic Univ., Melbourne and Rome 2019–; Deputy Chair., Arts and Humanities, Univ. of Cambridge 2011–14; mem. Church of England Doctrine Comm. 1982–92; mem. Editorial Bd Modern Theology 1994–, Spiritus 2001–, Anglican Theological Review 2004–, Ecclesiology 2004–, Harvard Theological Review 2004–07, Anglican Studies 2008–, Zeitschrift für Systematische Theologie und Religionsphilosophie 2009–; mem. Advisorial Bd Center of Theological Inquiry, Princeton Univ. 1994–96; mem. Steering Cttee Christian Systematics Theology Group 1996–2002, Philosophy of Religion Group 2005–10, American Acad. of Religion; mem. Editorial Council Theology Today 2003–; mem. Int. Advisory Bd Templeton Foundation 2004–07, 2009; mem. Bd of Judges annual Templeton Prize 2007–10; mem. Resourcing Theological Education Cttee, Synod of the Church of England 2014–15, Crown Nominations Comm. review Cttee, Lambeth Palace, Church of England 2016–17; Leverhulme Foundation Major Research Fellowship 2014–17; Hon. Canon Ely cathedral 2011–, Hon. Prof., Logos Inst., St Andrews Univ. 2018–; Hon. DTheol (Lund Univ.) 2006, Dr hc (St Michael's Coll., Toronto) 2015, Hon. DD (Heythrop Coll.) 2017; Hulsean Prize, Univ. of Cambridge 1977, Hulsean Lecturer, Univ. of Cambridge 1991–92, Hulsean Preacher 1996, Samuel Ferguson Lecturer, Univ. of Manchester 1997, Riddell Lecturer, Univ. of Newcastle 1999, Tate-Wilson Lecturer, Southern Methodist Univ. 1999, Prideaux Lecturer, Univ. of Exeter 2000, Jellema Lecturer, Calvin Coll. 2001, Stone Lecturer, Princeton Theological Seminary 2002, Cheney Lecturer, Berkeley Divinity School at Yale 2002, Reynolds Lecturer, Princeton Univ. 2005, Hensley Henson Lecturer, Univ. of Oxford 2005, Harvard Univ. Award for Teaching 2005, Gifford Lecturer, Aberdeen Univ. 2012, Hickman Lecturer, Duke Divinity School 2012, Templeton Foundation grant 2005–08. *Publications include:* Christ Without Absolutes: A Study of the Christology of Ernst Troeltsch 1988, The Making and Remaking of Christian Doctrine (co-ed. with David Pailin) 1993, Religion and the Body (ed.) 1997, Powers and Submissions: Spirituality, Philosophy and Gender 2002, Praying for England: Priestly Presence in Contemporary Culture (co-ed with Sam Wells) 2008, The Spiritual Senses: Perceiving God in Western Christianity (co-ed.) 2012, Sacrifice Regained: Reconsidering the Rationality of Religious Belief 2012, Fear and Friendship: Anglicans Engaging with Islam (co-ed) 2012, Faith, Rationality and the Passions (ed.) 2012; contribs to Church of England Doctrine Comm. Reports 1987, 1991; articles in theological journals. *Leisure interests:* musical activities, thinking about the garden. *Address:* Faculty of Divinity, West Road, University of Cambridge, Cambridge, CB3 9BS, England (office). *Telephone:* (1223) 763002 (office). *Fax:* (1223) 763003 (office). *E-mail:* sc545@cam.ac.uk (office). *Website:* www.divinity.cam.ac.uk (office).

COATES, John Dowling, AC; Australian lawyer and business executive; *President, Court of Arbitration for Sport;* b. 7 May 1950, Sydney, NSW; Special Counsel, Kemp Strang Lawyers. Sydney; Pres. Australian Olympic Cttee 1990–; Council mem. Int. Rowing Fed. 1992–; mem. Int. Council of Arbitration for Sport 1994–, Vice-Pres. 1995–2010, Pres. 2011–, Pres. Court of Arbitration for Sport 2011–; mem. IOC 2001–, Exec. Bd 2009–, Juridical, TV Rights and New Media, 2012 London and 2016 Rio Olympic Games Coordination Comms. *Address:* Court of Arbitration for Sport, Château de Béthusy, Avenue de Beaumont 2, 1012 Lausanne, Switzerland (office). *Telephone:* (21) 613-50-00 (office). *Fax:* (21) 613-50-01 (office). *E-mail:* info@tas-cas.org (office). *Website:* www.tas-cas.org (office).

COATES, John Henry, BA, PhD, FRS; Australian mathematician and academic; *Sadleirian Professor Emeritus of Pure Mathematics, University of Cambridge;* b. 26 Jan. 1945, New South Wales; s. of J. H. Coates and B. L. Lee; m. Julie Turner 1966; three s.; ed Australian Nat. Univ., Ecole Normale Supérieure, Paris, France, Univ. of Cambridge, UK; Asst Prof., Harvard Univ., USA 1969–72; Assoc. Prof. (with tenure), Stanford Univ., USA 1972–75; Lecturer, Univ. of Cambridge, UK 1975–77, Sadleirian Prof. of Pure Math. 1986–2012, Prof. Emer. 2012–, Head of Dept of Pure Math. and Math. Statistics 1991–97; Prof., ANU 1977–78, Université de Paris XI (Orsay) 1978–85; Prof. and Dir of Math., Ecole Normale Supérieure, Paris 1985–86; Professorial Fellow, Emmanuel Coll., Cambridge 1975–77, 1986–; Vice-Pres. Int. Math. Union 1991–95; Fellow, Academia Europa 2008; Dr hc (Ecole Normale Supérieure) 1997, (Heidelberg) 2012; Senior Whitehead Prize 1997. *Leisure interests:* reading, early Japanese porcelain, Oriental art. *Address:* Emmanuel College, Cambridge, CB2 3AP (office); Department of Pure Mathematics and Mathematical Statistics, University of Cambridge, Wilberforce Road, Cambridge, CB3 0WB, England (office). *Telephone:* (1223) 337989 (office). *E-mail:* j.h.coates@dpmms.cam.ac.uk (office). *Website:* www.dpmms.cam.ac.uk (office).

COATS, Daniel (Dan) Ray, BA, JD; American lawyer, politician, diplomatist and government official; *Director of National Intelligence;* b. 16 May 1943, Jackson,

Mich.; s. of Edward R. Coats and Vera E. Coats; m. Marsha Ann Crawford 1965; one s. two d.; ed Wheaton Coll., Ill., Univ. of Indiana; served in US Army 1966–68; Asst Vice-Pres. and Counsel, Mutual Security Life Insurance Co., Fort Wayne, Ind. 1969–75; called to Bar of Ind. 1972; mem. US House of Reps from 4th Dist of Ind. 1981–89; Dist Rep. for Congressman Dan Quayle 1976–80; apptd to fill seat vacated by Senator Quayle following Quayle's election as Vice-Pres. of USA 1988, won 1990 special election to serve remainder of Quayle's unexpired term, as well as 1992 election for full six-year term, Senator from Indiana 1989–99, 2011–17, mem. Appropriations Cttee, Energy and Natural Resources Cttee, Select Cttee on Intelligence, Jt Econ. Cttee; Special Counsel, Verner, Liipfert, Bernhard, McPherson & Hand 1999–2001; Amb. to Germany 2001–05; Sr Policy Advisor, Govt Advocacy and Public Policy Practice Group, King & Spalding LLP, Washington, DC 2005–10; Dir of Nat. Intelligence 2017–; fmr lobbyist, Pharmaceutical Research and Mfrs of America; mem. Bd of Trustees American Inst. For Contemporary German Studies 2005–; mem. Bd of Dirs IPALCO, Lear Siegler Services Inc., Int. Republic Inst., The Empowerment Network; Pres. Big Brothers/ Big Sisters of America, Ind.; Republican. *Publication:* Mending Fences: Renewing Justice Between Government and Civil Society 1998. *Address:* Office of the Director of National Intelligence, Washington, DC 20511, USA (office). *Telephone:* (703) 733-8600 (office). *E-mail:* info@dni.gov (office). *Website:* www.dni.gov (office).

COBBOLD, Rear Adm. Richard, CB, FRAeS; British fmr research institute director and military analyst; b. 1942, Dartmouth, Devon; s. of Geoffrey Francis Cobbold and Elizabeth Mary Mallett; m. Anne Marika Hjorne; one s. one d.; served in RN 1961–94, first as seaman officer and helicopter observer, commanded frigates HMS Mohawk and HMS Brazen, then Capt. of 2nd Frigate Squadron in HMS Brilliant; promoted Rear Adm. 1991; Asst Chief Defence Staff Operational Requirements for Sea Systems –1994, ACDS (Jt Systems) 1992–94; mem. Royal Coll. of Defence Studies 1984; Dir of Defence Concepts, Ministry of Defence 1987; Dir Royal United Services Inst. for Defence Studies 1994–2007 (retd); apptd Gov. London Nautical School 1997; specialist adviser to House of Commons Defence Cttee 1997–2007, to Foreign Affairs Cttee 2002; apptd Vice Pres., Strategic Devt, Duos Technologies Group, Inc. 2007; Advisor, Int. Energy Advisory Council 2003; Foreign Minister's Certificate of Commendation 2017. *Publications:* numerous articles on defence and security issues. *Address:* c/o Royal United Services Institute for Defence Studies, Whitehall, London, SW1 2ET, England.

COBEN, Harlan, BA; American writer; b. 4 Jan. 1962, Newark, New Jersey; m. Anne Armstrong 1988; two s. two d.; ed Amherst Coll.; mem. MWA (pres. 2008–09), Sisters in Crime. *Television:* as scriptwriter: The Five 2016, Safe 2018. *Publications include:* novels: Play Dead 1990, Miracle Cure 1991, Deal Breaker (World Mystery Conference Anthony Award for Best Paperback Original Novel 1996) 1995, Drop Shot 1996, Fade Away (MWA Edgar Award for Best Paperback Original Mystery Novel, Shamus Award for Best Paperback Original Novel, Private Eye Writers of America 1997) 1996, Back Spin 1997, One False Move (WHSmith Fresh Talent Award) 1997, The Final Detail 1999, Darkest Fear 2000, Tell No One 2001, Gone For Good (WHSmith Thumping Good Read Award) 2002, No Second Chance 2003, Just One Look 2004, The Innocent 2005, Promise Me 2006, The Woods 2007, Hold Tight 2008, Long Lost 2009, Caught 2010, Shelter 2011, Live Wire 2011, Seconds Away 2012, Stay Close 2012, Six Years 2013, Missing You 2014, Found 2014, The Stranger 2015, Fool Me Once 2016, Home 2016, Don't Let Go 2017; short stories: A Simple Philosophy 1999, The Key to My Father 2003. *Address:* Aaron Priest Literary Agency, 708 Third Avenue, New York, NY 10017, USA (office). *E-mail:* me@harlancoben.com (office). *Website:* www.harlancoben.com.

COBOS, Julio César Cleto; Argentine engineer and politician; b. 30 April 1955, Godoy Cruz, Mendoza; m. María Cristina Cerutti; one s. two d.; ed Universidad Tecnológica Nacional; taught at Universidad Tecnológica Nacional and at Universidad Nacional de Cuyo, Universidad de Mendoza, Dean of Prov. Faculty, Universidad Tecnológica Nacional 1997–2003; joined Unión Cívica Radical 1991, has been involved in Mendoza local politics since early 1990s; Minister of Environment and Public Works, Mendoza Prov. 1999–2000; Gov. of Mendoza Prov. (in a coalition with Recrear Liberals and Federalists) 2003–07; Vice-Pres. of Argentina 2007–11; Deputy for Mendoza 2013–. *Publications include:* Principios fundamentales de la hidráulica, Materias integradoras en ingeniería civil. *Address:* Cámara de Diputados de la Nación, Congreso de la Nación, Avenida Rivadavia 1864, CPC1033AAV, Buenos Aires, Argentina (office). *Telephone:* (11) 4127-7100 (switchboard) (office). *E-mail:* jcobos@diputados.gob.ar (office). *Website:* www.hcdn.gob.ar/diputados/jcobos (office).

COBURN, Thomas (Tom) Allen, BS, MD; American physician, obstetrician and politician; b. 14 March 1948, Muskogee, Okla; m. Carolyn Coburn 1968; three c.; ed Oklahoma State Univ.; fmr Pres. Coll. of Business Student Council, Oklahoma State Univ.; Mfg Man., Ophthalmic Div., Coburn Optical Industries (family-owned co.), Colonial Heights, Va 1970–78; trained as physician 1978–83; internship in gen. surgery, St Anthony's Hosp., Oklahoma City 1983–84; family practice residency, Univ. of Arkansas, Fort Smith 1984–86; family practice physician, specializing in obstetrics and allergy, Muskogee 1986–94; mem. US House of Reps from Okla 2nd Dist, Washington, DC 1995–2001, mem. House Commerce Cttee; Co-Chair. Pres.'s Advisory Council on HIV/AIDS 2001–; f. Family Caucus; Senator from Okla 2005–15; mem. Ark. Medical Soc., Okla Medical Asscn, American Medical Asscn, American Acad. of Otolaryngic Allergy, American Acad. of Family Practice; Republican. *Publication:* Breach of Trust: How Washington Turns Outsiders Into Insiders (with John Hart) 2003.

COCCOPALMERIO, HE Cardinal Francesco, LTh, DCL; Italian ecclesiastic and academic; b. 6 March 1938, San Giuliano Milanese; ed Pontifical Gregorian Univ., Università Cattolica del Sacro Cuore, Milan; ordained priest, Archdiocese of Milan 1962; Prof. of Canon Law, Faculty of Theology, northern Italy 1966–99; Prof., Faculty of Canon Law, Pontifical Gregorian Univ. 1981–; apptd Auxiliary Bishop of Milan and Titular Bishop of Coeliana 1993, Titular Archbishop of Coeliana 2007; mem. Supreme Tribunal of the Apostolic Signatura 2000–, Congregation for the Doctrine of the Faith 2010–; Pres. Pontifical Council for Legis. Texts 2007–13, 2013–18; cr. Cardinal (Cardinal-Deacon of San Giuseppe dei Falegnami) 2012; participated in Papal Conclave 2013. *Address:* c/o Pontifical Council for Legislative Texts, Palazzo delle Congregazioni, Piazza Pio XII 10, 00193 Rome, Italy (office). *E-mail:* info@vatican.va (office). *Website:* www.vatican.va (office).

COCHRAN, (William) Thad, BA, JD; American politician; *Senator from Mississippi;* b. 7 Dec. 1937, Pontotoc, Miss.; s. of William Holmes Cochran and Emma Grace Cochran (née Berry); m. Rose Clayton 1964; two c.; ed Univ. of Mississippi and School of Law, Univ. of Dublin, Ireland; served as Lt in USNR 1959–61; called to the Bar 1995, pvt. law practice in Jackson, Miss. 1965–72; mem. US House of Reps, Washington, DC 1973–78; Senator from Miss. 1979–, Sec. Republican Conf. 1985–90, Chair. Republican Conf. 1990–96, mem. Agric., Nutrition and Forestry Cttee, Appropriations Cttee, Govt Affairs Cttee, Rules and Admin. Cttee and Select Cttee on Indian Affairs; mem. Bd of Dirs US Naval Acad.; mem. Bd of Regents, Smithsonian Inst.; fmr Pres. Young Lawyers' section of Miss. State Bar; fmr Chair. Miss. Law Inst.; mem. ABA; Trustee, Kennedy Center, Washington, DC; Republican; Dr hc (Kentucky Wesleyan Coll., Mississippi Coll., Blue Mountain Coll., Univ. of Richmond, Tougaloo Coll.). *Address:* 113 Dirksen Senate Office Building, Washington, DC 20510-2402, USA (office). *Telephone:* (202) 224-5054 (office). *Website:* cochran.senate.gov (office).

COCHRANE, John H., SB, PhD; American economist and academic; *AQR Capital Management Professor of Finance, Booth School of Business, University of Chicago;* b. 26 Nov. 1957, Chicago, Ill.; m. Elizabeth Fama; two s. two d.; ed Massachusetts Inst. of Tech., Univ. of California, Berkeley; Jr Economist, Council of Econ. Advisors 1982–83; Asst Prof., Dept of Econs, Univ. of Chicago 1985–90, Assoc. Prof. 1990–94, Prof. of Finance and Econs, Booth School of Business 1994–, currently AQR Capital Man. Prof. of Finance; Visiting Prof., UCLA Anderson School of Man. 2000–01; Consultant, Research Dept, Fed. Reserve Bank of Chicago 1995–; Research Assoc., Nat. Bureau of Econ. Research; Adjunct Scholar, Cato Inst., Washington, DC; Ed. Journal of Political Economy 1998–2003; Assoc. Ed. of several journals including Journal of Monetary Economics, Journal of Business, Journal of Economic Dynamics and Control; Fellow, Econometric Soc. 2001–; mem. American Finance Asscn (Pres. 2010); Dr hc (Univ. of St Gallen, Switzerland) 2014; Chookaszian Endowed Risk Man. Prize. *Publications include:* Asset Pricing (TIAA-CREF Inst. Paul A. Samuelson Award) 2001. *Leisure interest:* windsurfing. *Address:* Graduate School of Business, University of Chicago, 1101 E. 58th St, Chicago, IL 60637-1610, USA (office). *Telephone:* (773) 7020-3059 (office). *E-mail:* john.cochrane@gsb.uchicago.edu (office). *Website:* faculty.chicagobooth.edu/john.cochrane (office); johnhcochrane.blogspot.co.uk.

COCKBURN, William, CBE, TD, FRSA; British business executive; b. 28 Feb. 1943, Edinburgh, Scotland; joined Post Office 1961, Personal Asst to Chair. 1971–73, Asst Dir of Planning and Finance 1973–77, Dir Cen. Finance Planning 1977–78, Dir Postal Finance 1978–79, Dir London Postal Region 1979–82, mem. Bd 1981–95, Man. Dir Royal Mail 1986–92, Chief Exec. The Post Office 1992–95; Chair. Int. Post Corpn 1994–95; Group Chief Exec., WH Smith Group PLC 1995–97; Group Man. Dir British Telecommunications PLC 1997–2001; Chair. Parity Group PLC 2001–04; apptd Deputy Chair. UK Mail Group plc 2002; Deputy Chair. AWG PLC 2003–06, now Dir (non-exec.); Dir (non-exec.), Watkins Holdings Ltd 1985–93, Lex Service PLC 1993–2002, Centrica PLC 1997–99; Dir, Business in the Community from 1990; fmr Sr Ind. Dir, AWG PLC, Dir (non-exec.) 2003–06; Chair. Schoolteachers' Review Body 2002–08; Chair. Senior Salaries Review Body 2008–; Pres. Inst. of Direct Marketing 2001–05; Dir (non-exec.), Army Bd; Fellow, Chartered Inst. of Transport; Freeman, City of London. *Address:* 9 Avenue Road, Farnborough, Hants., GU14 7BW, England (home). *E-mail:* ws.cockburn@btinternet.com (home).

CODRON, Sir Michael Victor, Kt, CBE, MA; British theatre producer; b. 8 June 1930, London; s. of Isaac A. Codron and Lily Codron (née Morgenstern); ed St Paul's School, Worcester Coll., Oxford; Dir Aldwych Theatre (also Owner), Hampstead Theatre, Royal Nat. Theatre; known for his productions of the early work of Harold Pinter, Christopher Hampton, David Hare, Simon Gray and Tom Stoppard; Cameron Mackintosh Prof., Univ. of Oxford 1993; mem. Bd of Trustees, Oxford School of Drama; Laurence Olivier Award for Lifetime Achievement. *Plays:* has produced over 300 shows in West End, London including: The Birthday Party 1958, The Caretaker 1960, The Killing of Sister George, Little Malcolm and his Struggle against the Eunuchs, Big Bad Mouse 1966, The Boyfriend (revival) 1967, A Voyage Round My Father, The Homecoming (revival), Dr. Faustus, The Dresser, Three Sisters, Uncle Vanya, The Cherry Orchard 1989, Man of the Moment, Private Lives 1990, The Rise and Fall of Little Voice 1992, Time of My Life, Jamais Vu 1993, Kit and the Widow, Dead Funny, Arcadia, The Sisters Rosensweig 1994, Indian Ink, Dealer's Choice 1995, The Shakespeare Revue 1996, A Talent to Amuse 1996, Tom and Clem 1997, Silhouette 1997, Heritage 1997, Things We Do For Love, The Invention of Love, Alarms and Excursions 1998, Copenhagen 1999, Quartet, Comic Potential 1999, Peggy for You 2000, Blue/Orange 2001, Life After George 2002, Bedroom Farce 2002. *Film:* Clockwise 1986. *Leisure interest:* collecting Caroline of Brunswick memorabilia. *Address:* Aldwych Theatre Offices, Aldwych, London, WC2B 4DF (office); 12 Tower Bridge Wharf, London, E1 9UR, England (home). *Telephone:* (20) 7240-8291 (office); (20) 7925-6243. *Fax:* (20) 7240-8467 (office); (20) 7240-8467.

COE, Jonathan, BA, MA, PhD; British writer; b. 19 Aug. 1961, Birmingham, England; m. Janine McKeown 1989; two d.; ed Trinity Coll., Cambridge, Univ. of Warwick; fmr legal proofreader; Chevalier, Ordre des Arts et des Lettres 2004. *Publications:* The Accidental Woman 1987, A Touch of Love 1989, The Dwarves of Death 1990, Humphrey Bogart: Take It and Like It 1991, James Stewart: Leading Man 1994, What A Carve Up! (John Llewellyn Rhys Prize 1995, Prix du Meilleur Livre Étranger 1996) 1994, The House of Sleep (Writers' Guild Best Fiction Award 1997, Prix Médicis Étranger 1998) 1997, The Rotters' Club (Bollinger Everyman Wodehouse Prize 2001, Premio Arcebispo Juan de San Clemente 2004) 2001, The Closed Circle 2004, Like a Fiery Elephant: The Story of B. S. Johnson (BBC Four Samuel Johnson Prize for non-fiction 2005) 2004, The Rain Before It Falls (Prix de l'Europe de la médiatheque de Bussy Saint-Georges 2010) 2007, The Terrible Privacy of Maxwell Sim 2010, Expo 58 2013, Marginal Notes, Doubtful Statements: Non-fiction 1990–2013 2013, Loggerheads and Other Stories 2014, Number 11 2015, The Broken Mirror 2017, Middle England 2018; contrib. to periodicals. *Address:* c/o Caroline Wood, Felicity Bryan Associates, 2A North Parade Avenue, Oxford, OX2 6LX, England (office). *Website:* felicitybryan.com (office).

COE, Baron (Life Peer), cr. 2000, of Ranmore in the County of Surrey; **Sebastian (Seb) Newbold Coe,** Kt, CH, KBE, MBE, OBE, BSc; British fmr politician and fmr athlete; *President, International Association of Athletics Federations;* b. 29 Sept. 1956, Hammersmith, London; s. of Peter Coe and Angela Coe; m. 1st Nicola Susan Elliott 1990 (divorced 2002); two s. two d.; m. 2nd Carole Annett 2011; ed Loughborough Univ.; competed in Olympic Games, Moscow 1980, won Gold Medal at 1500m and Silver Medal at 800m and repeated this in Los Angeles 1984; European Jr Bronze Medallist at 1500m 1975; European Bronze Medallist at 800m 1978; European Silver Medallist at 800m 1982; European 800m Champion 1986; held world records at 800m, 1000m, 1500m and mile; est. new records at 800m, 1000m and mile 1981; mem. 4×400m world record relay squad 1982; only athlete to hold world records at 800m, 1000m, 1500m and mile simultaneously; Pres. first athletes' del. to IOC, Baden-Baden 1981 and mem. first athletes' comm. set up after Congress by IOC 1981–; Conservative MP for Falmouth and Camborne 1992–97; mem. Employment Select Cttee 1992–94, Nat. Heritage Select Cttee 1995–97; Parl. Pvt. Sec. to Chancellor of Duchy of Lancaster 1994–95, to Michael Heseltine 1995–96; Jr Govt Whip 1996–97; Deputy Chief of Staff then Pvt. Sec. to William Hague, Leader of the Opposition 1997–2001; Chair. Diadora UK 1987–94, ADT Health Quest Charitable Trust 1991–; Vice-Chair. Sports Council 1986–89, Sports Aid Trust 1987; Vice-Chair. London 2012 Olympic Games Bid 2003–04, Chair. and Pres. London 2012 Olympic and Paralympic Bid 2004–05, London Organizing Cttee of the Olympic Games and Paralympic Games (in 2012) 2005–13; apptd Chair. FIFA Ethics Cttee 2006; Chair. British Olympic Asscn 2012–16; Founder and Exec. Chair. CSM Sports and Entertainment (marketing firm) 2013–; Vice-Chair. Int. Asscn of Athletics Feds (IAAF) 2007–15, Pres. 2015–; Dir, London 2017 Ltd (set up to run World Athletic Championships in London in 2017); mem. Health Educ. Authority 1987–92, apptd Health Educ. Council (now Authority) 1986; Global Adviser, NIKE Inc. 2000–15 (resgnd); Vice-Patron Sharon Allen Leukemia Trust 1987–, Olympic Cttee Medical Comm. 1987–95, Sport for All Comm. 1997–; Admin. Steward, British Boxing Bd of Control 1995–; Founding mem. World Sports Acad. 2000–; sports columnist, Daily Telegraph 2000; Trustee, Youth Sports Trust, British Univ. in Egypt, Sebastian Coe Foundation; Hon. Fellow, RIBA 2009; Hon. D. Tech. (Loughborough) 1985; Hon. DSc (Hull) 1988, (East London) 2009; Hon. LLB (Sheffield) 1991; Hon. DLit (Sunderland) 2011; BBC Sports Personality of 1979, Sir John Cohen Memorial Award 1981, Príncipe de Asturias Award (Spain) 1987, BBC Sports Personality of the Year Special Award 2005, BBC Sports Personality of the Year Lifetime Achievement Award 2012, Lifetime Achievement Award, Laureus World Sports Awards 2013. *Publications include:* Running Free (with David Miller) 1981, Running for Fitness 1983, The Olympians 1984, More Than a Game 1992, Born to Run (autobiog.) 1992. *Leisure interests:* jazz, theatre, reading, some writing. *Address:* International Association of Athletics Federations, 6–8 Quai Antoine 1er, BP 359, MC 98007, Monaco (office); CSM Sports and Entertainment, 3rd Floor, 62 Buckingham Gate, London, SW1E 6AJ (office); House of Lords, Westminster, London, SW1A 0PW, England. *Telephone:* 93-10-88-88 (Monaco) (office); (20) 7593-5231 (London) (office); (20) 7219-5353 (House of Lords). *Fax:* 93-15-95-15 (Monaco) (office). *E-mail:* sara@iaaf.org (office). *Website:* www.iaaf.org (office); www.csm.com (office); www.parliament.uk/biographies/lords/lord-coe/783.

COELHO, Hernâni; Timor-Leste politician; b. 27 Aug. 1964, Uatucarbau, Portuguese Timor; s. of Adelino da Silva und Zulmira Coelho; ed Magelamg Agric. Devt Coll., Gen. Soedirman Univ., Java, Islamic Univ., Malang; Student Asst, Faculty of Animal Science, Gen. Soedirman Univ. 1987–89; journalist, ASOHI-INFOVET (veterinary journal) 1992–93; Sr Program Officer, Islands Council 1995–99; Sr Research Officer, Nat. Inst. of Agrararian Research, Portugal 1999–2002; Adviser, Econ. and Infrastructure Dept, UN Transitional Admin, Nat. Council of Timor-Leste May–Nov. 2001; Lecturer, Timor-Leste Nat. Univ. 2001–05; Head of Environment and Natural Resources Dept, UNDP, Dili 2002–05; Amb., Ministry of Foreign Affairs 2006–09; Amb./Deputy Chief of Staff, Office of Pres. of the Repub. 2009–12; Amb., Ministry of Foreign Affairs and Co-operation 2013–15, Minister of Foreign Affairs and Co-operation 2015–17; mem. Frente Revolucionária do Timor Leste Independente (FRETILIN, Revolutionary Front for an Independent East Timor). *Address:* c/o Ministry of Foreign Affairs and Co-operation, Edif. 1, Av. Presidente Nicolau Lobato, POB 6, Dili, Timor-Leste (office).

COELHO, Paulo; Brazilian writer; b. 24 Aug. 1947, Rio de Janeiro; m. Christina Oiticica; ed law school; worked as a dir, theatre actor, songwriter and journalist; collaborated with Brazilian composer and singer Raúl Seixas; imprisoned for alleged subversive activities against Brazilian Govt 1974; made pilgrimage to Santiago de Compostela, Spain 1986; regular columnist for O Globo (newspaper) 2007– and other newspapers world-wide; elected mem. Brazilian Acad. of Arts 2002, UN Messenger of Peace 2007; f. Paulo Coelho Inst. (non-profit for children), Paulo Coelho and Christina Oticica Foundation 2016; Chevalier, Ordre des Arts et des Lettres 1996, Comendador de Ordem do Rio Branco 1998, Chevalier, Légion d'honneur 2000, Order of St Sophia (Ukraine) 2004, Cruz do Mérito do Empreendedor Juscelino Kubitschek 2006; numerous awards, including Prix Lectrices d'Elle, France 1995, Golden Book Awards, Yugoslavia 1995, 1996, 1997, 1998, 1999, 2000, Flaiano Int. Award, Italy 1996, Super Grinzane Cavour Book Award, Italy 1996, Golden Medal of Galicia, Spain 1999, Crystal Mirror Award, Poland 2000, XXIII Premio Internazionale Fregene, Italy 2001, Bambi Award, Germany 2001, Budapest Prize, Hungary 2005, Goldene Feder Award, Germany 2005, Religion Communicators Council Wilbur Award, USA 2006, Premio Álava en el Corazón, Spain 2006, Asscn of Mexican Booksellers Pergolas Prize 2006, Distinction of Honour from the City of Odense (Hans Christian Andersen Award), Denmark 2007, best selling foreign book in Poland 2007, Best Int. Writer Award, ELLE Awards (Spain) 2008, Guinness World Record for the Most Translated Author for the same book (The Alchemist) 2009. *Publications include:* Arquivos do inferno 1982, O Diário de um mago (The Pilgrimage, aka The Diary of a Magus: The Road to Santiago) 1987, O Alquimista (The Alchemist) 1988, Brida 1990, O Dom Supremo (The Gift) 1991, As Valkírias (The Valkyries) 1992, Maktub 1994, Na margem do rio Piedra eu sentei e chorei (By the River Piedra I Sat Down and Wept) 1994, Frases 1995, O Monte Cinco (The Fifth Mountain) 1996, Cartas de Amor do Profeta (Love Letters from a Prophet) 1997, Manual do guerreiro da luz (Manual of the Warrior of Light) 1997, Veronika decide morrer (Veronika Decides to Die) 1998, Palavras essenciais (The Confessions of a Pilgrim) 1999, O demônio e a Srta Prym (The Devil and Miss Prym) 2000, Histórias para pais, filhos e netos (Fathers, Sons and Grandsons) 2001, Onze minutos (Eleven Minutes) 2003, O Gênio e as Rosas (The Genie and the Roses, juvenile) 2004, O Zahir (The Zahir) (Kiklop Literary Award, Croatia 2006, Austrian Booksellers' Platin Book Award 2006) 2005, Like the Flowing River (thoughts and short stories) 2006, A Bruxa do Portobello (The Witch of Portobello) (EMPiK's Ace Award) 2006, O Vencedor está Só (The Winner Stands Alone) 2008, O Aleph (The Aleph) 2010, Manuscrito encontrado em Accra (Manuscript Found in Accra) 2012, Adultério (Adultery) 2014, A Espiã (The Spy) 2016, Hippie 2018. *Address:* c/o Sant Jordi Asociados Agencia Literaria SL, Paseo de García Faria, 73–75, 08019 Barcelona, Spain (office). *Telephone:* (93) 2240107 (office). *E-mail:* mail@santjordi-asociados.com (office). *Website:* www.santjordi-asociados.com (office); www.paulocoelhoblog.com (home).

COËME, Guy; Belgian politician; b. 21 Aug. 1946, Bettincourt; m.; two c.; ed Univ. of Liège; mem. Nat. Office, Parti Socialiste (PS) 1970–74, Vice-Pres. PS 1983–; Deputy Mayor, Waremme 1971–74, 1982–87; Prov. Councillor, Liège 1971–74; Deputy, Liège 1974–81, Huy-Waremme 1982–96, 2007–12; apptd Burgomaster, Waremme 1987; Sec. of State for the Walloon Region, with responsibility for the Environment and Planning 1981–82; Minister-Pres. Wallonne Regional Exec., with responsibility for Water, Rural Devt, Conservation and Admin. Feb.–May 1988; Minister of Nat. Defence 1988–92; Deputy Prime Minister and Minister of Communications and Public Services 1992–94 (resgnd); convicted in government bribery case and received suspended sentence 1998; cand. in regional elections Huy-Waremme 2004; Pres. Soc. for the Regional Devt of Walloon 1978; Vice-Pres. Socialist Party 1983; Admin. Soc. for Regional Investment in Walloon 1979; Grand Officer, Order of Leopold. *Address:* c/o Office of the Mayor, Rue Joseph Wauters 2, 4300 Waremme, Belgium.

COEN, Enrico Sandro, CBE, PhD, FRS, FLS; British geneticist; *Project Leader, Department of Cell and Developmental Biology, John Innes Centre;* b. 29 Sept. 1957, Southport, Lancs.; s. of Ernesto Coen and Dorothea Coen (née Cattani); m. Lucinda Poliakoff 1984; two s. one d.; ed King's Coll., Cambridge; joined John Innes Centre, Norwich 1984, Project Leader 1995–98, Deputy Head Dept of Genetics 1998–2000, Project Leader, Dept of Cell and Developmental Biology 2000–; Foreign Assoc. mem. NAS 2001; Corresp. mem. Botanical Soc. of America 2003; Hon. Lecturer Univ. of E Anglia 1989, Hon. Reader 1994, Hon. Prof. 1998; EMBO Medal, Rome 1996, Science for Art Prize, Paris 1996, Linnean Gold Medal, London 1997, Darwin Medal (jtly), Royal Soc. 2004. *Publications include:* The Art of Genes 1999, Cells to Civilizations 2012; 80 articles in int. scientific research journals. *Leisure interests:* painting, children. *Address:* John Innes Centre, Norwich Research Park, Norwich, NR4 7UH, England (office). *Telephone:* (1603) 450000 (office). *Fax:* (1603) 450045 (office). *E-mail:* enrico.coen@jic.ac.uk (office). *Website:* www.jic.ac.uk (office).

COEN, Ethan; American film producer and screenwriter; b. 21 Sept. 1957, St Louis Park, Minn.; s. of Ed Coen and Rena Coen; brother of Joel Coen (q.v.); m.; ed Princeton Univ.; screenwriter (with Joel Coen) Crime Wave (fmrly XYZ Murders); producer, screenplay; ed. Blood Simple 1984; Dan David Prize (with Joel Coen), Tel-Aviv Univ. 2011. *Films include:* Raising Arizona 1987, Miller's Crossing 1990, Barton Fink (Palme d'Or, Cannes Festival) 1991, The Hudsucker Proxy 1994, Fargo 1996, The Naked Man, The Big Lebowski 1998, O Brother, Where Art Thou? 2000, The Man Who Wasn't There 2001, A Fever in the Blood 2002, Intolerable Cruelty 2003, The Ladykillers 2004, Paris, je t'aime (segment) 2006, No Country for Old Men (Best Film, Nat. Bd of Review 2007, Academy Awards for Best Film, Best Direction, Best Adapted Screenplay 2008) 2007, Burn After Reading 2008, A Serious Man 2009, True Grit 2010, Inside Llewyn Davis (Best Dir (with Joel Coen), Best Film, Nat. Soc. of Film Critics) 2013, Hail, Caesar! 2016, Suburbicon 2017. *Publication:* Gates of Eden 1998. *Address:* c/o United Talent Agency, 9336 Civic Center Drive, Beverly Hills, CA 90210, USA (office). *Telephone:* (310) 273-6700 (office). *Fax:* (310) 247-1111 (office). *Website:* www.unitedtalent.com (office).

COEN, Joel Daniel; American film director and screenwriter; b. 29 Nov. 1954, St Louis Park, Minn.; s. of Ed Coen and Rena Coen; brother of Ethan Coen (q.v.); m. Frances McDormand 1984; ed Simon's Rock Coll. and New York Univ.; Asst Ed. Fear No Evil, Evil Dead; worked with rock video crews; screenwriter (with Ethan Coen) Crime Wave (fmrly XYZ Murders); Dan David Prize (with Ethan Coen), Tel-Aviv Univ. 2011. *Films include:* (with Ethan Coen): Blood Simple 1984, Raising Arizona 1987, Miller's Crossing 1990, Barton Fink (Palme d'Or, Cannes Festival) 1991, The Hudsucker Proxy 1994, Fargo (Best Dir Award, Cannes Int. Film Festival 1996) 1996, The Big Lebowski 1998, O Brother, Where Art Thou? 2000, The Man Who Wasn't There 2001, Intolerable Cruelty 2003, The Ladykillers 2004, Paris, je t'aime (segment) 2006, No Country for Old Men (Best Film, Nat. Bd of Review 2007, Academy Awards for Best Film, Best Direction, Best Adapted Screenplay 2008) 2007, Burn After Reading 2008, A Serious Man 2009, True Grit 2010, Inside Llewyn Davis (Best Dir (with Ethan Coen), Best Film, Nat. Soc. of Film Critics) 2013, Hail, Caesar! 2016, Suburbicon 2017. *Address:* c/o United Talent Agency, 9336 Civic Center Drive, Beverly Hills, CA 90210, USA (office). *Telephone:* (310) 273-6700 (office). *Fax:* (310) 247-1111 (office). *Website:* www.unitedtalent.com (office).

COENE, Luc; Belgian government official and fmr central banker; b. 11 March 1947, Ghent; ed Ghent Univ., Coll. of Europe, Bruges; with Research Dept and Foreign Dept, Nat. Bank of Belgium 1973–79, Adviser to Head of Foreign Dept 1992–95, Vice-Gov. 2003–11, Gov. 2011–15, Hon. Gov. 2015–, mem. Governing Council and Gen. Council, European Central Bank 2011, Dir, BIS 2011 (apptd Chair. Audit Cttee 2013, apptd mem. Bd of Govs and High Council of Finance, G-10 2006, Chair. Public Sector Borrowing Requirements Dept 2006, mem. Bureau of the High Council of Finance 2006, IFC 2014, Alt. Gov., IBRD 2014, IDA 2014; Asst, Belgian Admin., IMF 1979–85; Deputy Chef de Cabinet to Minister of Finance 1985; Chef de Cabinet to Vice-Premier and Minister for the Budget 1988; Visiting Scholar, IMF 1988; Econ. Adviser, DG II, EC 1989–92; Senator 1995–99; Chef de Cabinet to the Prime Minister and Sec. to the Council of Ministers 1999–2001, Chair. Chancellery of the Prime Minister and Sec. of the Council of Ministers 2001–03; apptd Minister of State 2003; apptd mem. Bd of Dirs, Nat. Accounts Inst. 2011, SN Airholding 2015–; mem. Supervisory Bd, Single Supervisory Mechanism of the European Cen. Bank 2015–; apptd mem. Exec. Cttee, Belgian-American Educ. Foundation 2014; mem. Exec. Cttee King Baudouin Foundation, Madariaga European Foundation; Chair. Fulbright Fund Man. Cttee; Deputy Chair. Exec. Bd,

Théâtre Royal de la Monnaie/Koninklijke Muntschouwburg. *Address:* European Central Bank, 60640 Frankfurt, Germany (office). *Telephone:* (69) 13440 (office). *E-mail:* info@ecb.europa.eu (office). *Website:* www.bankingsupervision.europa.eu (office).

COETZEE, J(ohn) M(axwell), MA, PhD; South African/Australian writer and academic; b. 9 Feb. 1940, Cape Town; s. of Zacharias Coetzee and Vera Coetzee (née Wehmeyer); m. Philippa Jubber 1963 (divorced 1980); one s. one d.; partner Dorothy Driver; ed Univ. of Cape Town, Univ. of Texas, USA; Asst Prof. of English, State Univ. of NY (SUNY), Buffalo 1968–71; Lecturer, Univ. of Cape Town 1972–76, Sr Lecturer 1977–80, Assoc. Prof. 1981–83, Prof. of Gen. Literature 1984–2001; Prof. of Social Thought, Univ. of Chicago, USA 1995–2000, Distinguished Service Prof. 2001–03; Professorial Research Fellow, Univ. of Adelaide, Australia 2002–, Patron J.M. Coetzee Centre for Creative Practice 2011–; Chevalier des Arts et des Lettres, Ridder van de Orde van de Leeuw (Netherlands), Order of Mapungubwe (South Africa); Dr hc (Oxford) 2002; Nobel Prize for Literature 2003. *Publications include:* Dusklands 1974, In the Heart of the Country 1977, Waiting for the Barbarians 1980, Life and Times of Michael K (Booker-McConnell Prize 1983, Prix Femina Etranger 1985) 1983, Foe 1986, White Writing (essays) 1988, Age of Iron (Sunday Express Book of the Year Prize 1990) 1990, Doubling the Point: Essays and Interviews (ed. by David Attwell) 1992, The Master of Petersburg (Irish Times Int. Fiction Prize 1995) 1994, Giving Offence: Essays on Censorship 1996, Boyhood 1997, The Lives of Animals 1999, Disgrace (Booker Prize 1999, Commonwealth Writers Prize 2000) 1999, The Humanities in Africa 2001, Stranger Shores (essays) 1986–1999 2001, Youth 2002, Elizabeth Costello: Eight Lessons 2003, Slow Man 2005, Inner Workings (essays) 2007, Diary of a Bad Year 2007, Summertime 2009, Scenes from Provincial Life 2011, The Childhood of Jesus 2013, The Schooldays of Jesus 2016; short stories: A House in Spain 2000, The African Experience 2002, He and His Man 2003, As a Woman Grows Older 2004, Nietverloren 2014, The Dog 2017; also translator of Dutch and Afrikaans literature. *Address:* PO Box 3045, Newton, SA 5074, Australia (office). *E-mail:* john.coetzee@adelaide.edu.au (office). *Website:* www.adelaide.edu.au/jmcoetzeecentre (office).

COEY, John Michael David, DSc, FRS; Irish physicist and academic; *Professor Emeritus, Trinity College Dublin;* b. 24 Feb. 1945, Belfast, Northern Ireland; s. of David S. Coey and Joan E. Newsam; m. Wong May 1973; two s.; ed Tonbridge School, Jesus Coll. Cambridge, UK and Univ. of Manitoba, Canada; Chargé de Recherches, CNRS, Grenoble 1974–78; Lecturer/Prof., Trinity Coll. Dublin 1978–, Prof. of Experimental Physics 1987–2007, Head, Dept of Physics 1989–92, apptd Erasmus Smith's Prof. of Natural and Experimental Philosophy 2007, now Prof. Emer.; Visiting Scientist, IBM Research Center, Yorktown Heights, New York 1976–77, 1988, Univ. of Bordeaux 1984, Centre d'Etudes Nucléaires de Grenoble 1985–86, Johns Hopkins Univ. Applied Physics Lab. 1986, Univ. de Paris 7 1992, Univ. of California, San Diego 1997, Florida State Univ. 1998, National Univ. of Singapore 2012–, Beihang Univ. 2014–; Co-inventor, thermopiezic analyser 1986, nitromag 1990; Chief Coordinator, Concerted European Action on Magnets 1987–94; Dir Magnetic Solutions Ltd 1994–; mem. mem. Royal Irish Acad., Vice-Pres. 1989; mem. Fulbright Fellow 1997–98; Fellow, American Physical Soc. 2000, Royal Society 2002; Foreign Assoc. NAS 2005; Hon. DSc (Inst. Nat. Polytechnique de Grenoble) 1994; Charles Chree Prize and Medal, Inst. of Physics, London, Gold Medal, Royal Irish Acad. 2005, Humboldt Prize 2013. *Publications include:* Magnetic Glasses (with K. Moorjani) 1984, Structural and Magnetic Phase Transitions in Minerals (with S. Ghose and E. Salje) 1988, Rare-Earth Iron Permanent Magnets 1996, Permanent Magnetism (with R. Skomski) 1999, Magnetism and Magnetic Materials 2010; numerous papers on magnetic and electronic properties of solids. *Leisure interest:* gardening. *Address:* School of Physics, University of Dublin Trinity College, Dublin 2, Ireland (office). *Telephone:* (1) 8961470 (office). *Fax:* (1) 6711759 (office). *E-mail:* jcoey@tcd.ie (office). *Website:* www.tcd.ie/Physics (office).

COFFEY, Brian (see KOONTZ, Dean Ray).

COFFEY, Rev. David Roy, OBE, BA; British Baptist leader and minister of religion; *Global Ambassador, BMS World Mission;* b. 13 Nov. 1941, Purley, Surrey; s. of Arthur Coffey and Elsie Maud Willis; m. Janet Anne Dunbar 1966; one s. one d.; ed Spurgeon's Coll., London; ordained to Baptist ministry 1967; Minister, Whetstone Baptist Church, Leicester 1967–72, N Cheam Baptist Church, London 1972–80; Sr Minister, Upton Vale Baptist Church, Torquay 1980–88; Sec. for Evangelism, Baptist Union of GB 1988–91, Gen. Sec. 1991–2005; Pres. Baptist Union 1986–87; Vice-Pres. European Baptist Fed. 1995–97, Pres. 1997–99; Vice-Pres. Baptist World Alliance 2000–05, Pres. 2005–10; Free Churches Moderator and Co-Pres. Churches Together in England 2003–07; Co-Pres. Council for Christians and Jews 2003–07; Vice-Pres. Council for Christians and Jews 2009–; Chair. Spurgeon's Coll. Council 2012–15, Gov. 2007–15; Global Amb. for BMS World Mission 2009–; Patron, Embrace 2008–, SAT-7 2007–; Hon. DD (Dallas Baptist Univ.) 2008, (Palmer Seminary) 2009. *Publications include:* Build That Bridge: A Study in Conflict and Reconciliation 1986, Discovering Romans: A Crossway Bible Guide 2000, Joy to the World 2008, All One in Christ Jesus 2009. *Leisure interests:* grandchildren, music, soccer, bookshops, Elgar Soc. *Address:* BMS World Mission, Baptist House, 129 Broadway, Didcot, Oxon., OX11 8XA, England (office). *Telephone:* (1235) 517604 (office).

COFFMAN, Robert L., AB, PhD; American medical scientist and business executive; *Vice-President and Chief Scientific Officer, Dynavax Technologies;* ed Indiana Univ., Univ. of California, San Diego; fmr Postdoctoral Fellow, Stanford Univ. Medical School; joined DNAX Research Inst. 1981, later Distinguished Research Fellow; Vice-Pres. and Chief Scientific Officer, Dynavax Technologies 2000–; mem. NAS 2006; William S. Coley Award for Research in Immunology (jtly with Dr Tim Mosmann of Univ. of Rochester). *Achievements include:* made fundamental discoveries about the regulation of immune responses in allergic and infectious diseases including discovery of the TH1 and TH2 subsets of T-lymphocytes, the two major types of T-cells that control immune responses. *Address:* Dynavax Technologies, 2929 Seventh Street, Suite 100, Berkeley, CA 94710, USA (office). *Telephone:* (510) 848-5100 (office). *Fax:* (510) 848-1327 (office). *E-mail:* contact@dynavax.com (office). *Website:* www.dvax.com (office).

COFFMAN, Vance D., BS, MS, PhD; American aerospace industry executive (retd); b. 3 April 1944; m. Arlene Coffman; two d.; ed Iowa State Univ., Stanford Univ.; joined Lockheed Corpn as guidance and control systems analyst, Space Systems Div. (led devt of several major space programmes) 1967, apptd Div. Vice-Pres. 1985, Div. Vice-Pres. and Asst Gen. Man. 1987, Div. Pres. (responsible for Hubble Space Telescope and MILSTAR satellite communications programme) 1988, Pres. Space Systems Div. Lockheed Missiles & Space Co. and Vice-Pres. Corpn, Exec. Vice-Pres. Corpn –1995; Pres. and COO Space & Strategic Missiles Sector, Lockheed Martin Corpn (following merger of Lockheed and Martin Marietta Corpns) 1995, Pres., COO and Exec. Vice-Pres. –1997, Vice-Chair. 1997–98, CEO 1997–2004, Chair. 1998–2005 (retd); mem. Bd of Dirs Bristol-Myers Squibb 1998–2007, United Negro Coll. Fund 2001–, 3M Co. 2002–, Amgen Inc. 2007–; mem. Nat. Acad. of Eng, Security Affairs Support Asscn; Fellow, American Astronomical Soc. 1991, AIAA 1996; Hon. Dr Aerospace Eng (Embry-Riddle Univ.) 1998; Hon. DEng (Stevens Inst. of Tech.) 1998; Hon. LLD (Pepperdine Univ.) 2000; Professional Progress in Engineering Award, Iowa State Univ. 1989, Distinguished Achievement Citation, Iowa State 1999, Rear Admiral John J. Bergen Industry Award, New York Council of the Navy League 2000, Fleet Admiral Chester W. Nimitz Award, Navy League of USA 2001, Executive of the Year, Washington Techway 2001, Bob Hope Distinguished Citizen Award, Nat. Defense Industrial Asscn (Los Angeles Chapter) 2002. *Address:* POB 1785, Pebble Beach, CA 93953, USA.

COHAN, Robert Paul, CBE; British choreographer; b. 27 March 1925; s. of Walter Cohan and Billie Cohan; ed Martha Graham School, New York; Partner, Martha Graham School 1950, Co-Dir Martha Graham Co. 1966; Artistic Dir Contemporary Dance Trust Ltd, London 1967–; Artistic Dir and Prin. Choreographer, London Contemporary Dance Theatre 1969–87, Founder-Artistic Dir 1987–89; Artistic Adviser, Batsheva Co., Israel 1980–89; Dir York Univ., Toronto Choreographic Summer School 1977, Gulbenkian Choreographic Summer School, Univ. of Surrey 1978, 1979, 1982 and other int. courses; Gov. Contemporary Dance Trust; Ed., Choreography and Dance (journal) 1988–; Chair. Robin Howard Foundation; with London Contemporary Dance Theatre has toured Europe, S. America, N Africa, USA; maj. works created: Cell 1969, Stages 1971, Waterless Method of Swimming Instruction 1974, Class 1975, Stabat Mater 1975, Masque of Separation 1975, Khamsin 1976, Nympheas 1976, Forest 1977, Eos 1978, Songs, Lamentations and Praises 1979, Dances of Love and Death 1981, Agora 1984, A Mass for Man 1985, Ceremony 1986, Interrogations 1986, Video Life 1986, Phantasmagoria 1987, A Midsummer Night's Dream 1993, The Four Seasons 1996, Aladdin 2000; Hon. Fellow, York Univ., Toronto; Hon. DLitt (Exeter Univ.) 1993, (Univ. of Kent) 1996; Dr. hc (Middx) 1994, (Winchester) 2006; Evening Standard Award for outstanding achievement in ballet 1975, Soc. of West End Theatres Award for outstanding achievement in ballet 1978, UK Dance Critics Circle Award for Lifetime Achievement 2005, De Valois Award for Outstanding Achievement, Critics' Circle National Dance Awards 2013. *Publication:* The Dance Workshop 1986. *Leisure interest:* dancing. *Address:* The Place, 17 Duke's Road, London WC1H 9PY, England; Saussine, Bouquet, Lussan 30580, France. *Website:* www.theplace.org.uk/robertcohan.

COHEN, Abby Joseph, BA, MS, CFA; American economist and investment bank executive; *Senior Investment Strategist and President, Global Markets Institute, Goldman Sachs Group, Inc.;* b. 29 Feb. 1952, Queens, New York; d. of Raymond Joseph Cohen and Shirley Joseph (née Silverstein); m. David M. Cohen 1973; two d.; ed Martin Van Buren High School, Cornell Univ., George Washington Univ.; Jr Economist, Fed. Reserve Bd, Washington, DC 1973–76; Economist/Analyst, T. Rowe Price Assocs, Baltimore, Md 1976–83; Investment Strategist, Drexel Burnham Lambert, New York 1983–90, BZW, New York 1990; Investment Strategist, Goldman, Sachs & Co. 1990–, Man. Dir 1996–, Man. Pnr 1998–, Chair. Investment Policy Cttee, also Chief US Portfolio Strategist, currently Sr Investment Strategist and Pres. Global Markets Inst.; Chair. Inst. of Chartered Financial Analysts; mem. Bd Govs Nat. Economists Club, New York Soc. of Security Analysts; Vice-Chair. Asscn for Investment Man. Research; mem. Nat. Asscn of Business Economists; Trustee/Fellow, Cornell Univ.; Trustee Jewish Theological Seminary of America; Woman Achiever (Woman of the Year) Award, YWCA, New York 1989. *Address:* Goldman Sachs Group, Inc., 85 Broad Street, New York, NY 10004, USA (office). *Telephone:* (212) 902-1000 (office). *Fax:* (212) 902-3000 (office). *Website:* www.goldmansachs.com (office).

COHEN, Ben; American business executive; b. 1951, Brooklyn, New York; ed Calhoun High School, Merrick, Long Island, Colgate Univ., Skidmore Coll., New School, New York, New York Univ.; various jobs whilst studying pottery and jewellery, including pottery wheel delivery person, paediatric emergency room clerk, taxi cab driver; fmr craft therapist intern, Jacobi Hosp., Bronx, New York and Grand Street Settlement House, Manhattan; craft teacher, Highland Community School, Paradox, NY 1974–77; Co-founder Ben & Jerry's Homemade Inc. (with Jerry Greenfield) 1977, opened first Ice Cream Parlour in Burlington, Vt 1978, held various positions including Marketing Dir, Salesperson, Pres., CEO and Chair., est. Ben & Jerry's Foundation (to oversee donation of 7.5% of profits to non-profit orgs), co. sold to Unilever; f. TrueMajority.org (non-profit educ. and advocacy group), merged with USAction 2007; Founding mem. Businesses for Social Responsibility (org. that promotes socially responsible business practices); mem. numerous non-profit orgs; Corp. Giving Award, Council on Econ. Priorities 1988, US Small Business Persons of the Year, US Small Business Admin 1988. *Publications include:* Ben & Jerry's Homemade Ice Cream and Dessert Book (co-author with Jerry Greenfield) 1987.

COHEN, Bernard Woolf, DFA; British artist and academic; *Slade Professor Emeritus, University College London;* b. 28 July 1933, London, England; m. Jean Britton 1959; one s. one d.; ed South West Essex School of Art, St Martin's School of Art, London and Slade School of Fine Art, London; held teaching appointments at several art schools 1957–67; teacher of painting and drawing, Slade School of Fine Art 1967–73, 1977; Visiting Prof., Univ. of New Mexico 1969–70, Faculty Alumnus 1974; Guest Lecturer, Royal Coll. of Art 1974–75; Visiting Artist, Minneapolis School of Art 1964, 1969, 1971, 1975, Ont. Coll. of Art 1971, San Francisco Art Inst., Univ. of Victoria, BC 1975; has lectured at several Canadian univs since 1969; fmr Prin. Lecturer (Painting), Wimbledon School of Art 1980–84; Slade Prof., Chair. of Fine Art, Univ. Coll. London 1988–2000, Prof. Emer. 2000–, Fellow, Univ.

Coll. London 1992; Hon. DFA (Univ. of London, Slade School). *Publications:* articles and statements in journals and catalogues. *Leisure interests:* music, cinema, travel, museums. *Address:* 80 Camberwell Grove, London, SE5 8RF, England (home). *Telephone:* (20) 7708-4480 (home). *Fax:* (20) 7708-4480 (home). *E-mail:* bwc44@hotmail.com (home).

COHEN, Jared, BA, MPhil; American author, business executive and fmr government official; *Director, Jigsaw;* b. 24 Nov. 1981, Weston, Conn.; m. Rebecca Zubaty; ed Stanford Univ., Univ. of Oxford, UK; mem. Policy Planning Staff, Office of the Sec. of State, US Dept of State, Washington, DC (fmr adviser to Condoleezza Rice and Hillary Clinton) 2006–10; Dir Google Ideas (renamed Jigsaw 2015), Google, Inc. 2010–; Adjunct Sr Fellow, Council on Foreign Relations; mem. jury, Tribeca Film Festival; Sec. of State's Meritorious Honor Award 2008, 2010, Tribeca Film Festival Innovation Award 2010, Washington Post and John F. Kennedy School Center for Public Leadership Top American Leaders Award 2011. *Publications include:* One Hundred Days of Silence: America and the Rwanda Genocide 2006, Children of Jihad: A Young American's Travels Among the Youth of the Middle East 2007, The New Digital Age: Re-shaping the Future of People, Nations and Business (co-author) 2013. *Address:* Jigsaw, 76 Ninth Avenue, 4th Floor, New York, NY 10011, USA (office). *Telephone:* (212) 565-0000 (office). *Fax:* (212) 565-0001 (office). *E-mail:* jacohen@cfr.org (office). *Website:* www.igsaw .google.com (office).

COHEN, Joel E., BA, MA, PhD, MPh, DrPH; American mathematical biologist and academic; *Abby Rockefeller Mauzé Professor of Populations, The Rockefeller University* and*Professor of Populations, Columbia University;* b. 10 Feb. 1944; ed Harvard Univ.; taught at Harvard Univ. 1971–75; Prof., The Rockefeller Univ. 1975–, currently Abby Rockefeller Mauzé Prof. of Populations; also Prof. of Populations, Earth Inst., Columbia Univ., New York 1995–; fmr mem. Bd of Dirs The Nature Conservancy; fmr mem. Bd of Trustees Population Reference Bureau; mem. NAS, American Acad. of Arts and Sciences, American Philosophical Soc.; MacArthur Foundation Fellow; Olivia Schieffelin Nordberg Award for excellence in writing in the population sciences 1997, Fred L. Soper Prize, Pan American Health Org., Washington, DC 1998 for work on Chagas disease, Tyler Prize for Environmental Achievement 1999, City of New York Mayor's Award for Excellence in Science and Tech. 2002. *Publications:* author or ed. of 14 books; numerous scientific papers in professional journals on demography, epidemiology, ecology, pure and applied math., and ecology. *Address:* Laboratory of Populations, The Rockefeller University, 1230 York Avenue, Box 20, New York, NY 10065, USA (office). *Telephone:* (212) 327-8884 (office). *E-mail:* cohen@rockefeller.edu (office). *Website:* lab.rockefeller.edu/cohenje (office).

COHEN, Lyor; American music company executive; *Global Head of Music, YouTube;* b. 3 Oct. 1959, New York; ed Univ. of Miami; financial officer, Bank Leumi; Hip-Hop Performance Promoter, Mix Club, Los Angeles; joined Rush Entertainment 1985, later Partner; Pres. and CEO Island Def Jam Records 1988–2004; Vice-Chair. and CEO US and UK Recorded Music, Warner Music Group 2004–12; founder 300 Entertainment record label 2013–; Global Head of Music, YouTube. *Website:* 300ent.com; youtube.com.

COHEN, Marius (Job), PhD; Dutch politician and academic; b. 18 Oct. 1947, Haarlem; s. of Adolf Emiel Cohen and Hetty Koster; m. Lidie Cohen 1972 (died 2015); one s. one d.; ed Stedelijk Gymnasium Haarlem and Univ. of Groningen; joined PvDA (Netherlands Labour Party) 1967; held a scientific position at Bureau Research of Educ., Leiden Univ. 1971–81; Lecturer, Maastricht Univ. 1981–83, Chair. Comm. that prepared establishment of faculty of law, Prof. of Methods and Techniques, Faculty of Law 1983, Rector Magnificus 1991–93; State Sec. (Deputy Minister) of Educ. 1993–94; mem. Eerste Kamer (Upper House) 1995–98, Parl. Leader of Labour Party 2010–12; Interim Dir VRPO TV station Feb.–Aug. 1998; State Sec., Ministry of Justice, with responsibility for Immigration 1998–2000; Mayor of Amsterdam 2001–10; Labour Party cand. for Prime Minister in gen. elections 2003; mem. Parl. and Parl. Leader of Labour Party 2010–12; Kt, Order of the Netherlands Lion 1994, Order of Orange-Nassau 2003; Cross of Recognition, Second Class (Latvia) 2008; Dr hc (Univ. of Windsor) 2007, (Radboud Univ. Nijmegen) 2008; Cleveringa Lecturer, Univ. of Leiden 2002, named a TIME magazine 'European Hero' 2005, Best Mayor of the Last 25 Years, Binnenlands Bestuur 2005, Citizenship Award, P&V Foundation 2005, Advertising Man of the Year, Marketing Tribune 2007, Martin Luther King Award, DutchVersity 2008, Gold Medal, City Council of Amsterdam 2010. *Publications:* Binden (collection of speeches and lectures) 2009; audio books (as narrator): Het grijze kind (novel by Theo Thijssen) 2007, De Uitvreter (novella by Nescio) 2008), Lijmen/Het Been (two novellas by Willem Elsschot) 2009, Kaas (novella by Willem Elsschot) 2009, Titaantjes (novella by Nescio) 2010, Max Havelaar (novel by Multatuli) 2010. *Address:* c/o Office of the Mayor, Postbus 202, 1000 AE Amsterdam, Netherlands.

COHEN, Marvin Lou, PhD; American (b. Canadian) physicist and academic; *University Professor of Physics, University of California, Berkeley;* b. 3 March 1935, Montreal, Canada; s. of Elmo Cohen and Molly Zaritsky; m. 1st Merrill Leigh Gardner 1958 (died 1994); one s. one d.; m. 2nd Suzy R. Locke 1996; ed Univs of California, Berkeley and Chicago; mem. Tech. Staff, Bell Labs, Murray Hill, NJ 1963–64; Asst Prof. of Physics, Univ. of California, Berkeley 1964–66, Assoc. Prof. 1966–68, Prof. 1969–95, Univ. Prof. 1995–; Prof., Miller Inst. Basic Research in Science, Univ. of California1969–70, 1976–77, 1988, Chair. 1977–81, Univ. Prof. 1995–, Faculty Research Lecturer 1996–97, Faculty Research Prof., Lecturer 1997–; Distinguished Lecturer in Physics and Electrical Eng, Columbia Univ. 1996; US Rep., Semiconductor Comm., IUPAP 1975–81; Visiting Prof., Univ. of Cambridge, UK 1966, Univ. of Paris 1972–73, Univ. of Hawaii 1978–79, Technion, Haifa, Israel 1987–88; Alfred P. Sloan Fellow, Univ. of Cambridge 1965–67; Guggenheim Fellow 1978–79, 1990–91; Fellow, American Physics Soc. Exec. Council 1975–79, Chair. 1977–78; mem. NAS 1980, American Acad. of Arts and Sciences, Oliver E. Buckley Prize Comm. 1980–81 (Chair. 1981); mem. Govt-Univ.-Industry Research Round Table 1984–, Vice-Chair. Working Group on Science and Eng Talent 1984–, Advisory Bd Tex. Center for Superconductivity 1991– (mem. 1988–90), mem. Research Briefing Panels NAS on Funding and on High Temperature Superconductivity 1987, US–Japan Workshop on Univ. Research 1988–89, Science Policy Bd Stanford Synchrotron Radiation Lab. 1990–92, Visiting Cttee, The Ginzton Lab., Stanford Univ. 1991, American Acad. of Arts and Sciences 1993, Scientific Policy Cttee, Stanford Linear Accelerator Center 1993–95; Assoc. Ed. Materials Science and Engineering 1987, Chair. Exec. Bd Council, Panel on Public Affairs, Investment Cttee, American Physical Soc. Fellowship Cttee, Congressional Fellowship Cttee, 2003; mem. Advisory Bd, International Journal of Modern Physics B 1987–, Editorial Bd, Perspectives in Condensed Matter Physics 1987–, AAAS 1993–, mem. Bd of Advisors, Discover Magazine 1998–2000, Prize Cttee for Nanoscience Prize, ACSIN 1999, 2001, Int. Advisory Bd, Nanonetwork Materials, Kamakura, Japan 2000, Advisory Cttee, Inst. of Nano Science and Tech., Hong Kong Univ. of Science and Tech. 2001–; mem. Bd of Govs Weizmann Inst. of Science 2002–; mem. Governing Bd American Inst. of Physics 2003–07; Loeb Lecturer, Harvard Univ. 2004; Chief Scientific Officer, Nanomix Inc. 2006–; Inst. Advisor, Daegu Gyeongbuk Inst. of Science and Tech., Daegu, South Korea 2006–; Organizer of Nobel Symposium, Int. Conf. on the Physics of Semiconductors, Rio de Janeiro, Brazil 2008; mem. Advisory Cttee to the Simons Foundation (Physics, Math. and Computer Science) 2009–10; mem. numerous advisory bds including Korean Inst. for Advanced Study 2011–14, School of Science Advisory Cttee, Hong Kong Univ. of Science and Tech. 2012–14, Cttee and Academic Advisory Cttee to review Atomic, Molecular and Optical Physics, Weizmann Inst. of Science 2012, Advisory Bd, Texas Center for Superconductivity, Univ. of Houston 2012–, Advisory Panel, Samsung Science and Tech. Foundation 2013–; Visiting mem. Inst. for Advanced Study, Hong Kong Univ. of Science and Tech. 2010–15; mem. American Physical Soc. 2002 (Pres. 2005), American Philosophical Soc. 2003, The Berkeley Fellows, Univ. of California 2009; Fellow, AAAS 1997; Hon. Chair. Int. Conf. on the Physics of Semiconductors 2014; Dr hc (Montreal) 2005, (Weizmann Inst., Israel) 2014; Hon. DSc (Hong Kong Univ. of Science and Tech.) 2013; numerous awards, including Oliver E. Buckley Prize for Solid State Physics 1979, US Dept of Energy Award 1981, 1990, Julius Edgar Lilienfeld Prize, American Physical Soc. 1994, Outstanding Performance Award, Lawrence Berkeley Nat. Lab. 1995, Invited Speaker, Nobel Symposium 1996, Inauguration Speaker, Korea Inst. for Advanced Study 1996, Nat. Medal of Science 2001, Presidential Award 2002, Technology Pioneer Award, World Econ. Forum 2007, Basic Energy Sciences (DOE) Distinguished Lecturer, Brookhaven Nat. Lab. 2008, Berkeley Citation, Univ. of California 2011, Public Lecture, Fudan Univ., Shanghai, People's Repub. of China 2012, Dickson Prize in Science 2012, Oppenheimer Lecturer, Univ. of California, Berkeley 2013, Von Hippel Award, Materials Research Soc. 2014, dedication of Marvin L. Cohen Condensed Matter Physics Interaction Area, Univ. of California, Berkeley 2015, Symposium in honour of Marvin L. Cohen and Yuen Ron Shen, Univ. of California, Berkeley 2015, Thomson Reuters Citation Laureate 2016, Benjamin Franklin Medal in Physics 2017. *Publications:* over 800 articles on research topics. *Leisure interests:* music (clarinet), running. *Address:* Department of Physics, 366 Le Conte Hall, #7300, Berkeley, CA 94720-7300 (office); 201 Estates Drive, Piedmont, CA 94611, USA (home). *Telephone:* (510) 642-4753 (office). *Fax:* (510) 643-9473 (office). *E-mail:* mlcohen@berkeley.edu (office). *Website:* civet .berkeley.edu/cohen/index.html (office).

COHEN, Sir Philip, PhD, FRS, FRSE; British research biochemist and academic; *Professor of Enzymology and Deputy Director, Division of Signal Transduction Therapy, University of Dundee;* b. 22 July 1945, Edgware, Middx, England; s. of Jacob Davis Cohen and Fanny Bragman; m. Patricia T. Wade 1969; one s. one d.; ed Hendon County Grammar School, Univ. Coll., London; SRC/NATO Postdoctoral Fellow, Univ. of Washington, Seattle, USA 1969–71; Lecturer in Biochemistry, Univ. of Dundee 1971–77, Reader 1977–81, Prof. of Enzymology 1981–84, Royal Soc. Research Prof. 1984–2010, Dir MRC Protein Phosphorylation Unit 1990–2012, Dir Scottish Inst. for Cell Signalling 2008–12, currently Prof. of Enzymology and Deputy Dir Div. of Signal Transduction Therapy; Dir Wellcome Trust Biocentre 1997–2007; Fellow, Univ. Coll. London 1993, Acad. of Medical Sciences 1998; mem. Discovery Advisory Bd SmithKline Beecham Pharmaceutical Co. 1993–97; mem. European Molecular Biology Org. 1982, Academia Europaea 1990; Croonian Lecturer, Royal Soc. 1998; Foreign Assoc., NAS 2008; Fellow, American Acad. of Microbiology; Corresponding mem. Australian Acad. of Science 2014; Hon. Fellow, Royal Coll. of Pathologists 1998; Hon. mem. British Biochemical Soc. 2003 (Pres. 2006–08), American Soc. of Toxicology 2010; Hon. DSc (Abertay) 1998, (Strathclyde) 1999, (Debrecen, Hungary) 2004, Hon. MD (Linkoping, Sweden) 2004, (St Andrews) 2005, (Dundee) 2007, (Madrid) 2016; Anniversary Prize, Fed. of European Biochemical Socs 1977, Colworth Medal 1977, CIBA Medal and Prize 1991, British Biochemical Soc., Prix Van Gysel, Belgian Royal Acads of Medicine 1992, Bruce Preller Prize, Royal Soc. of Edin. 1993, Louis Jeantet Prize for Medicine 1997, Pfizer Award for Innovative Science in Europe 1999, Sir Hans Krebs Medal, Fed. of European Biochemical Socs 2001, Bristol-Myers Squibb Distinguished Achievement Award for Metabolic Research 2002, Royal Medal, Royal Soc. of Edin. 2004, Debrecen Award for Molecular Medicine 2004, Rolf Luft Prize, Karolinska Inst., Sweden 2006, Royal Medal, Royal Soc. 2008, Scottish Enterprise Leading Individual Achievement in the Life Sciences in Scotland 2009, MRC Millennium Medal 2013, Albert Einstein World Award of Science 2014. *Publications:* Control of Enzyme Activity 1976; more than 500 articles in scientific journals. *Leisure interests:* bridge, chess, golf, ornithology, picking wild mushrooms, cooking. *Address:* MRC Protein Phosphorylation and Ubiquitylation Unit, College of Life Sciences, MSI/WTB Complex, University of Dundee, Dow Street, Dundee, DD1 5EH (office); Inverbay Bramblings, Waterside, Invergowrie, Dundee, DD2 5DQ, Scotland (home). *Telephone:* (1382) 388446 (office); (1382) 562328 (home). *Fax:* (1382) 223778 (office). *E-mail:* p.cohen@dundee .ac.uk (office). *Website:* www.lifesci.dundee.ac.uk/people/philip-cohen (office); www .ppu.mrc.ac.uk/research/?pid=1 (office).

COHEN, Preston Scott, MArch; American architect and academic; *Gerald M. McCue Professor of Architecture and Chair, Department of Architecture, Graduate School of Design, Harvard University;* b. 1961, Asheville, North Carolina; ed Rhode Island School of Design, Harvard Univ. Grad. School of Design; Adjunct Asst Prof. of Architecture, Ohio State Univ. 1989; f. Preston Scott Cohen (architectural firm), Cambridge, Mass 1989; Design Critic in Architecture, Harvard Univ. Grad. School of Design 1989–92, Asst Prof. of Architecture 1992–95, Assoc. Prof. of Architecture 1995–2001, Prof. of Architecture 2002–03, Dir Master of Architecture Degree Programs 2003–08, Gerald M. McCue Prof. of Architecture 2003–, Chair Dept of Architecture 2008–; Visiting Faculty Mem., Rhode Island School of Design 1993–98; Visiting Assoc. Prof. of Architecture, Princeton Univ. 1997; Perloff Visiting Prof., UCLA 2002; Frank Gehry Int. Visiting Chair, Univ. of Toronto 2004;

Young Architects Award, Architectural League of New York 1992, Progressive Architecture Award 1998, 2000, First Prize, Herta and Paul Amir Int. Competition 2003, PA Award, Architecture, Tel Aviv Museum of Art 2004, Acad. Award in Architecture, American Acad. of Arts and Letters 2004. *Publications:* Contested Symmetries and Other Predicaments in Architecture 2001, Permutations of Descriptive Geometry 2002. *Address:* Preston Scott Cohen Inc., 77 Pleasant Street, Cambridge, MA 02139 (office); Harvard University Graduate School of Design, 48 Quincy Street, Gund Hall, Cambridge, MA 02138, USA (office). *Telephone:* (617) 441-2110 (Preston Scott Cohen Inc.) (office); (617) 495-2591 (office). *Fax:* (617) 441-2113 (Preston Scott Cohen Inc.) (office); (617) 495-8916 (office). *E-mail:* scott@pscohen.com (office). *Website:* www.pscohen.com (office); www.gsd.harvard.edu (office).

COHEN, Robert; British cellist, conductor and teacher; *Professor of Cello, Royal Academy of Music;* b. 15 June 1959, London; s. of Raymond Cohen and Anthya Rael; m. Rachel Smith 1987; four s.; ed Purcell School and Guildhall School of Music (Diploma of Advanced Solo Studies), cello studies with William Pleeth, André Navarra, Jacqueline du Pré and Mstislav Rostropovich; started playing cello aged five; Royal Festival Hall debut (Boccherini Concerto) aged 12; London recital debut, Wigmore Hall, aged 17; Tanglewood Festival, USA 1978; recording debut (Elgar concerto) 1979; concerts USA, Europe and Eastern Europe 1979; since 1980, concerts world-wide with major orchestras and with conductors including Muti, Abbado, Dorati, Sinopoli, Otaka, Mazur, Davis, Tilson-Thomas, Marriner and Rattle; Dir Charleston Manor Festival, E Sussex 1989–; regular int. radio broadcasts and numerous int. TV appearances; plays on the 'Ex-Roser' David Tecchler of Rome cello dated 1723; conductor, various chamber orchestras 1990–, symphony orchestras 1997–; Prof. of Advanced Cello Studies, Conservatorio della Svizzera Italiana di Lugano 2000–12; apptd Visiting Prof., RAM 1998, Prof. 2009–; launched Cello Clinic 2009; cellist, Fine Arts Quartet 2012–18; performance/choreographic projects in collaboration with Royal Ballet School 2010–11; Fellow, Purcell School for Young Musicians 1992; Hon. RAM 2009; winner, Suggia Award 1968–72, winner, Young Concert Artists Int. Competition, New York 1978, English Speaking Union Fellowship 1978, Piatigorsky Prize, Tanglewood Festival 1978, winner, UNESCO Int. Competition, Czechoslovakia 1981, Robert Helpmann Award, Australia 2005. *Recordings include:* Elgar Concerto (new Elgar concerto 1993), Dvořák Concerto, Tchaikovsky Rococo Variations, Rodrigo Concierto en modo Galante, Beethoven Triple Concerto, Grieg Sonata, Franck Sonata, Virtuoso Cello Music record, Dvořák Complete Piano trios with Cohen Trio, Schubert String Quintet with Amadeus Quartet, Complete Bach Solo Cello Suites, Howard Blake Diversions, Bliss Concerto 1992, Walton Concerto 1995, Britten Cello Suites 1997, Morton Feldman Concerto 1998, Britten Cello Symphony 1998, Sally Beamish Cello Concerto River 1999, HK Gruber Cello Concerto 2003, Lutoslawski Cello Concerto 2013. *Television includes:* Bach Sarabandes (BBC), Elgar Cello Concerto (BBC), Beamish Cello Concerto (BBC). *Leisure interests:* photography, alternative therapy, philosophy. *Address:* Royal Academy of Music, Marylebone Road, London, NW1 5HT, England (office). *Telephone:* (20) 8444-1065 (office). *E-mail:* office@robertcohen.info (office). *Website:* www.robertcohen.info; www.fineartsquartet.com; www.robertcohen.info; www.celloclinic.com.

COHEN, Sir Ronald, Kt, MA, MBA; British venture capital executive; *Founder and Chairman, The Portland Trust;* b. 1 Aug. 1945, Egypt; s. of Michael Mourad Cohen and Sonia Sophie Cohen (née Douek); m. 1st Carol Marylene Belmont 1972 (divorced 1975); m. 2nd Claire Whitmore Enders 1983 (divorced 1986); m. 3rd Sharon Ruth Harel; one s. one d.; ed Orange Hill Grammar School, Exeter Coll., Oxford (Exhibitioner and Pres. Oxford Union Soc.), Harvard Business School, USA; consultant, McKinsey & Co. (UK and Italy) 1969–71; Chargé de mission, Institut de Developpement Industriel, France 1971–72; Founder, Apax Partners Worldwide LLP (fmrly Apax Partners Holdings Ltd) 1972, Chair. 1972–2005; contested (Labour) Kensington North constituency, Gen. Election 1974, London West, European Parl. election 1979; Founder-Dir British Venture Capital Asscn 1983 (Chair. 1985–86), European Venture Capital Asscn 1985, City Group for Smaller Cos 1992; a Founder and Vice-Chair. European Asscn of Securities Dealers Automated Quotation 1995–2001; Founder and Chair. The Portland Trust 2003–; Founder and Dir, Social Finance Ltd 2009–11, Social Finance US 2011–; Chair. Big Society Capital 2012–; Dir, NASDAQ Europe 2001–03; Chair. Tech. Stars Steering Cttee, Dept of Trade and Industry (DTI) 1997–2000, Social Investment Task Force 2000–10, Bridges Ventures Ltd 2002–, Comm. on Unclaimed Assets 2005–07; mem. Advisory Bd, InterAction 1986–, Finance and Industry Cttee, NEDC 1988–90, Wider Share Ownership Cttee 1988–90, City Advisory Group 1993–99, CBI Working Party on Smaller Cos, London Stock Exchange 1993, UK Competitiveness Cttee, DTI 1998–2000, Exec. Cttee Centre for Econ. Policy Research 1996–99, Finance Cttee Inst. for Social and Econ. Policy in ME, Kennedy School of Govt, Harvard Univ. 1997–98, Advisory Bd Fullbright Comm., Harvard Univ. 2007–, Investment Cttee Univ. of Oxford 2007–, Int. Council, Tate Gallery 2004–; Vice-Chair. Ben-Gurion Univ.; Trustee and mem. Exec. Cttee, IISS 2005–10; Trustee, BM 2005–; Hon. Fellow, Exeter Coll., Oxford 2000; Hon. Pres. Community Devt Finance Asscn 2005–07; Henry Fellowship, Harvard Business School, Jubilee Award for services to Israeli business, Alumni Achievement Award 2006. *Publication:* The Second Bounce of the Ball: Turning Risk into Opportunity 2007. *Leisure interests:* music, art, theatre, cinema, tennis. *Address:* The Portland Trust, 42 Portland Place, London, W1B 1NB, England (office). *Telephone:* (20) 7182-7780 (office). *Fax:* (20) 7182-7895 (office). *Website:* www.portlandtrust.org (office).

COHEN, Stanley, BA, PhD; American biochemist and academic; *Distinguished Professor Emeritus, School of Medicine, Vanderbilt University;* b. 17 Nov. 1922, Brooklyn, New York; s. of Louis Cohen and Fruma Feitel; m. 1st Olivia Larson 1951; m. 2nd Jan Elizabeth Jordan 1981; three s.; ed Brooklyn and Oberlin Colls., Univ. of Michigan; Teaching Fellow, Dept of Biochemistry, Univ. of Michigan 1946–48; Instructor, Depts of Biochemistry and Pediatrics, Univ. of Colorado School of Medicine, Denver 1948–52; Postdoctoral Fellow, American Cancer Soc., Dept of Radiology, Washington Univ., St Louis 1952–53; Research Prof. of Biochemistry, American Cancer Soc., Nashville 1976–; Asst Prof. of Biochemistry, Vanderbilt Univ. School of Medicine, Nashville 1959–62, Assoc. Prof. 1962–67, Prof. 1967–86, Distinguished Prof. 1986–2000, Distinguished Prof. Emer. 2000–; mem. Editorial Bds Excerpta Medica, Abstracts of Human Developmental Biology, Journal of Cellular Physiology; mem. NAS, American Soc. of Biological Chemists, Int. Inst. of Embryology, American Acad. of Arts and Sciences; Hon. DSc (Chicago) 1985; Nobel Prize for Physiology and Medicine 1986, and many other prizes and awards. *Leisure interests:* camping, tennis. *Address:* 11306 East Limberlost Road, Tucson, AZ 85749 (home); Department of Biochemistry, Vanderbilt University School of Medicine, 607 Light Hall, Nashville, TN 37232, USA (office). *Telephone:* (615) 322-3318 (office). *Fax:* (615) 322-4349 (office). *Website:* medschool.mc.vanderbilt.edu/biochemistry (office).

COHEN, Stanley, MD; American pathologist and academic; *Professor Emeritus, Department of Pathology and Laboratory Medicine, New Jersey Medical School;* b. 4 June 1937, New York; s. of Herman Joseph Cohen and Eva Lapidus; m. Marion Doris Cantor 1959; two s. one d.; ed Stuyvesant High School, Columbia Coll. and Columbia Univ. Coll. of Physicians and Surgeons; Internship and Residency, Albert Einstein Medical Center and Harvard-Mass. Gen. 1962–64; Instructor, Dept of Pathology, New York Univ. Medical Center 1965–66; Captain, MC, USA, Walter Reed Inst. of Research 1966–68; Assoc. Prof., State Univ. of New York at Buffalo 1968–72, Assoc. Dir, Center for Immunology 1972–74, Prof. of Pathology 1972–74; Assoc. Chair. Dept of Pathology, Univ. of Conn. Health Center 1976–80, Prof. of Pathology 1974–87; Prof., Chair. Bd Hahnemann Univ., Philadelphia 1987–94; Chair. Dept of Pathology, Hahnemann Medical Center 1986–94; Prof. and Chair., Dept of Pathology and Laboratory Medicine, NJ Medical School 1994, now Prof. Emer.; Vice-Pres. American Soc. for Investigative Pathology; Treasurer, Fed. of Socs of Experimental Biology; Kinne Award 1954; Borden Award 1961; Parke-Davis Award in Experimental Pathology 1977; Outstanding Investigator Award, Nat. Cancer Inst. 1986; Co-Chair. Int. Lymphokine Workshop 1979, 1982 and 1984. *Publications:* 200 scientific articles on cellular immunity; ed. 7 books including Mechanisms of Cell-Medicated Immunity 1977, Mechanisms of Immunopathology 1979, The Biology of the Lymphokines 1979, Interleukins, Lymphokines and Cytokines 1983, Molecular Basis of Lymphatic Action 1986, The Role of Lymphatics in the Immune Response 1989. *Leisure interests:* music, photography, karate. *Address:* c/o Department of Pathology and Laboratory Medicine, UMDNJ-New Jersey Medical School, 185 South Orange Avenue, Newark, NJ 07103 (office); 79 Ettl Circle, Princeton, NJ 08540-2334, USA (home). *Telephone:* (973) 972-4520 (office). *Fax:* (973) 972-5909 (office). *E-mail:* cohenst@umdnj.com (office).

COHEN, Stanley Norman, BS, MD; American physician, geneticist and academic; *Kwoh-Ting Li Professor, School of Medicine, Stanford University;* b. 17 Feb. 1935, Perth Amboy, New Jersey; s. of Bernard Cohen and Ida Cohen (née Stolz); m. Joanna Lucy Wolter 1961; one s. one d.; ed Rutgers Univ. and Univ. of Pennsylvania School of Medicine; intern, Mount Sinai Hosp., New York 1960–61; Asst Resident in Medicine, Univ. Hosp., Ann Arbor, Mich. 1961–62; Clinical Assoc., Arthritis and Rheumatism Br., Nat. Inst. of Arthritis and Metabolic Diseases 1962–64; Sr Resident in Medicine, Duke Univ. Hosp., Durham, North Carolina 1964–65; American Cancer Soc. Postdoctoral Research Fellow, Dept of Molecular Biology and Dept of Developmental Biology and Cancer, Albert Einstein Coll. of Medicine, Bronx, New York 1965–67, Asst Prof. 1967–68; Asst Prof. of Medicine, Stanford Univ. School of Medicine 1968–71, Head, Div. of Clinical Pharmacology 1969–78, Assoc. Prof. of Medicine 1971–75, Prof. of Genetics 1977 and Prof. of Medicine 1975–, Chair. Dept of Genetics 1978–86, Kwoh-Ting Li Prof. of Genetics 1993–, Prof. and Prin. Investigator, Stanley N. Cohen Lab. –2011; mem. Editorial Bd Proceedings of the National Academy of Sciences, Current Opinion in Microbiology; Trustee, Univ. of Pa 1997–2002; mem. of various scientific orgs, including NAS, Inst. of Medicine, American Philosophical Soc. 2006; Fellow, American Acad. of Arts and Sciences (Chair. Genetics Section 1988–91), American Acad. of Microbiology, AAAS; Einstein Prof., Chinese Acad. of Sciences 2006; Hon. ScD (Rutgers) 1994, (Pennsylvania) 1995; numerous awards including Baldouin Lucke Research Award, Univ. of Pennsylvania School of Medicine 1960, Research Career Devt Award, US Public Health Service 1969, Burroughs Wellcome Scholar Award 1970, Mattia Award, Roche Inst. for Molecular Biology 1977, Albert Lasker Basic Medical Research Award 1980, Wolf Prize in Medicine 1981, Marvin J. Johnson Award, Nat. Biotechnology Award 1989, Nat. Medal of Tech. 1989, ACS Special Award 1992, Lemelson-MIT Prize 1996, Nat. Inventors Hall of Fame 2001, Albany Medical Center Prize in Medicine and Biomedical Research (co-recipient) 2004, Shaw Prize in Life Science and Medicine 2004, New York Acad. of Medicine John Stearns Award for Lifetime Achievement in Medicine 2007, Cold Spring Harbor Lab. Double Helix Medal for Scientific Research 2009, Dean's Medal, Stanford Univ. School of Medicine 2011, Fellow of the Inaugural Class of Acad. of American Asscn for Cancer Research 2013, BayBio DINA Lifetime Achievement Award 2013. *Address:* Department of Genetics, School of Medicine, Stanford University, Stanford, CA 94305-5120, USA (office). *Telephone:* (650) 723-5315 (office). *Fax:* (650) 725-1536 (office). *E-mail:* sncohen@stanford.edu (office). *Website:* sncohenlab.stanford.edu (office).

COHEN, Steven A., BS; American investment manager and art collector; b. 11 June 1956, Great Neck, NY; m. 1st Patricia Cohen; two c.; m. 2nd Alexandra Cohen; five c.; ed Wharton School, Univ. of Pennsylvania; early career on Wall Street as jr trader in options arbitrage dept at Gruntal & Co. 1978, later ran own trading group 1984–92; f. SAC Capital Partners, Stamford, Conn. 1992; began collecting art in 2000; mem. Bd of Trustees Brown Univ., Robin Hood Foundation, New York; has appeared on Art News magazine's Top 10 list of biggest-spending art collectors around the world each year since 2002, named by Forbes magazine amongst its Top Billionaire Art Collectors 2005. *Address:* SAC Capital Advisors, LP, 72 Cummings Point Road, Stamford, CT 06902, USA (office). *E-mail:* info@sac.com (office). *Website:* www.careers.sac.com (office).

COHEN, William Sebastian, BA, LLB; American consultant, fmr politician and fmr government official; *Chairman and CEO, Cohen Group;* b. 28 Aug. 1940, Bangor, Me; s. of Reuben Cohen and Clara Cohen (née Hartley); two s.; ed Bangor High School, Bowdoin Coll., Boston Univ. Law School; admitted to Maine Bar, Mass. Bar, DC Bar; Pnr, Prairie, Cohen, Lynch, Weatherbee and Kobritz, Bangor 1966–72; Asst Co. Attorney, Penobscot Co., Me 1968–70, instructor, Univ. of Maine at Orono 1968–72; mem. Bd of Overseers, Bowdoin Coll. 1973–85; City Councillor, Bangor 1969–72, Mayor of Bangor 1971–72; mem. US House of Reps, Washington, DC 1972–78; Senator from Maine 1979–96; US Sec. of Defense 1997–2001; Chair. and CEO The Cohen Group (consulting firm), Washington, DC 2001–; Trustee and Counselor, Center Strategic and Int. Studies 2001–; Fellow of John F. Kennedy

Inst. of Politics, Harvard Univ. 1972; mem. Bd of Dirs AIG –2006; Dir CBS Corpn 2003–, Viacom Inc. 2003–06, RLJ Acquisition, Inc. 2011–; mem. Supervisory Board of Head NV 2001–07; Distinguished Public Service, Boston Univ. Alumni Asscn 1976, L. Mendel Rivers Award, Non-Commissioned Officers' Asscn 1983, Pres.'s Award, New England Asscn of School Superintendents 1984, Silver Anniversary Award, Nat. Collegiate Athletic Asscn 1987, Nat. Asscn Basketball Coaches, US 1987, numerous other awards. *Publications:* Of Sons and Seasons 1978, Roll Call 1981, Getting the Most Out of Washington (with Prof. Kenneth Lasson) 1982, The Double Man (with Senator Gary Hart) 1985, A Baker's Nickel 1986, Men of Zeal (with Senator George Mitchell) 1988, One-Eyed Kings 1991, Murder in the Senate (with Thomas B. Allen) 1993. *Leisure interests:* poetry, sport. *Address:* The Cohen Group, 1200 19th Street, NW, Suite 400, Washington, DC 20036, USA (office). *Telephone:* (202) 689-7900 (office). *Fax:* (202) 689-7910 (office). *E-mail:* wsc@cohengroup.net (office). *Website:* www.cohengroup.net (office).

COHEN STUART, Martien A., BSc, PhD; Dutch physical chemist and academic; *Professor, East China University of Science and Technology;* b. 25 April 1948, Haarlem; ed Groningen State Univ., Wageningen Univ.; apptd Asst Prof., Physical Chem. and Colloid Science Group, Wageningen Univ. 1980, later Assoc. Prof., Prof. of Physical Chem. and Colloid Science 1996–2013, currently Head of Lab. of Physical Chem. and Colloid Science, Dept of Agrotechnology and Food Sciences; Visiting Prof. Twente Univ. 2011–16; sabbatical/postdoctoral year in group of Pierre Gilles de Gennes, Paris, worked on wetting and spreading experiments; Prof., East China Univ. of Science and Tech. 2016–; Scientific Dir, Dutch Polymer Inst., Univ. of Twente; adviser to AkzoNobel in area of colloid and physical chem.; Ed. European Physical Journal E (Soft Matter); mem. Royal Dutch Acad. of Sciences, Royal Netherlands Acad. of Arts and Science; Wolfgang Ostwald Medal, German Kolloid Gesellschaft 2007, AkzoNobel Science Award, Royal Holland Soc. of Sciences and Humanities 2008, Langmuir Lectureship Award 2008, American Chemical Soc. *Publications include:* more than 400 papers in scientific journals on statics and dynamics of macromolecules, interfaces, wetting, phase behaviour, self-assembly, networks and gels, emulsions and coalescence, and the physics of macromolecules in living cells. *Address:* Hartenseweg 44, 6705 BK Wageningen, The Netherlands (home). *Telephone:* (317) 426249 (office); (6) 26077388 (office). *E-mail:* martien.cohenstuart@wur.nl (office).

COHEN-TANNOUDJI, Claude Nessim, PhD; French academic; *Honorary Fellow, Indian Academy of Sciences;* b. 1 April 1933, Constantine, Algeria; s. of Abraham Cohen-Tannoudji and Sarah Sebbah; m. Jacqueline Veyrat 1958; two s. one d.; ed Ecole Normale Supérieure; Research Assoc., CNRS 1962–64; Maître de Conférences, then Prof., Faculté des Sciences, Paris 1964–73; Prof., Collège de France 1973–2004, Hon. Prof. 2004–; Hon. Fellow Indian Acad. of Sciences 1999; Hon. Prof. Peking Univ. 2002, Southeast Univ. 2009, Beihang University 2011; Hon. mem. European Physical Society 2010; mem. Acad. des Sciences; Fellow, American Physical Soc.; Foreign Hon. mem. American Acad. of Arts and Sciences, Accademia dei Lincei, Russian Acad. of Sciences, NAS, Pontifical Acad. of Sciences, Indian Nat. Acad. of Sciences, Brazilian Acad. of Sciences; Kt, Ordre nat. Légion d'honneur, Commdr, Ordre nat. du Mérite, Grand'Croix, Nat. Order of Scientific Merit (Brazil), Grand Officier, Légion d'honneur; Dr hc (Uppsala) 1994, (Jerusalem) 1998, (Brussels) 1999, (Liege) 2000, (Tel-Aviv) 2004, (Hong Kong) 2007, (Santiago) 2013, (Buenos Aires) 2014, (Rio de Janeiro) 2016, Hon. DrSc (Sussex) 1999, Hon. DTech (Stockholm) 1998; Ampère Prize, Acad. des Sciences 1980, Lilienfeld Prize, American Physical Soc., Charles Townes Award, Optical Soc. of America 1993, Harvey Prize, Technion, Haifa, CNRS Gold Medal 1996, Nobel Prize in Physics 1997. *Publications:* in collaboration: Quantum Optics and Electronic 1965, Quantum Mechanics (two vols) 1973, Photons and Atoms, Introduction to Quantum Electrodynamics 1987, Atom-Photon Interactions: Basic Processes and Applications 1988, Atoms in Electromagnetic Fields 1994, Lévy Statistics and Laser Cooling: How Rare Events Bring Atoms to Rest 2001, Advances in Atomic Physics: An Overview 2011. *Leisure interest:* music. *Address:* Indian Academy of Sciences, C V Raman Avenue, PO Box 8005, Sadashivanagar, Bengaluru 560 080, India (office); 38 rue des Cordelières, 75013 Paris, France (home). *Telephone:* (80)-22661200 (office); 1-45-35-02-18 (home). *Fax:* (80) 23616094 (office). *E-mail:* claudect@gmail.com (home); claude.cohen-tannoudji@lkb.ens.fr (office). *Website:* www.ias.ac.in (office).

COHN, Gary D.; American financial services industry executive; b. 27 Aug. 1960, Cleveland, Ohio; m. Lisa Pevaroff Cohn; ed American Univ.; has served in various sr man. positions with Goldman Sachs Group including Head of Commodities Div. 1996–99, managed Fixed Income, Currency and Commodities (FICC) macro businesses 1999–2002, Co-COO FICC 2002, Co-Head FICC 2002–, Co-Head Equities 2003–, Co-Head Global Securities 2004–06, mem. Bd of Dirs, Pres. and COO 2006–16; mem. Bd of Dirs New York Mercantile Exchange 1998–2000; Dir Nat. Econ. Council 2017–18; mem. Treasury Borrowing Advisory Cttee, Bond Market Asscn; Chair. Advisory Bd New York Univ. (NYU) Hosp. for Joint Diseases; Trustee, NYU Hosp., NYU School of Medicine, Harlem Children's Zone, American Univ.; est. Gary D. Cohn Endowed Research Professorship in Finance, American Univ.; Effecting Change Award, 100 Women in Hedge Funds 2005. *Address:* c/o National Economic Council, The White House Office, 1600 Pennsylvania Avenue, NW, Washington, DC 20500, USA (office).

COHN-BENDIT, Daniel Marc; French/German politician; b. 4 April 1945, Montauban, Tarn-et-Garonne, France; s. of Erich Cohn-Bendit and Herta Cohn-Bendit (née David); m. Ingrid Voigt 1997; one c.; ed Odenwaldschule, Heppenheim, Germany, Univ. de Paris X–Nanterre; moved to Germany 1958; student movt's spokesman, Paris 1968; deported from France May 1968; nursery school teacher, Frankfurt 1968–73; co-f. German students' group Revolutionärer Kampf, Bockenheim 1970; co-f. cultural magazine Pflasterstrand 1970, Ed.-in-Chief 1978–84; Deputy Mayor of Frankfurt 1989–97; mem. European Parl. (Greens) 1994–99, (Ecology Greens) 1999–2004, (Alliance 90/Greens) 2004–14, Vice-Pres. Parl. Comm. on Culture, Youth, Media and Sport 1994–95, mem. Foreign Affairs Comm., Public Freedoms Comm., N Africa Comm., Deputy mem. Budget Comm., Rapporteur on regional co-operation between states of Fmr Yugoslavia 1996, Rapporteur for Foreign Affairs Parl. Comm. on Jt EU-Mediterranean Accord, mem. Steering Cttee SOS Europe 1997, Chair. Del. to Jt EU-Turkey Parl. Comm. 1999–2002, Pres. Green Parl. Group 2001–04, Co-Pres. European Greens–European Free Alliance 2004–14; Adviser to Joschka Fischer, Vice-Chancellor and Minister of Foreign Affairs 1998; mem. German Green Party 1984, French Green Party 1998–; co-f. Forum Européen de Prévention Active des Conflicts (Fepac) 1994; presenter monthly literary programme Literaturclub, Swiss German TV 1995; f. monthly Eurospeed 1997; Dr hc (Catholic Univ. of Tilburg, Netherlands) 1997; Trombinoscope 'Political Discovery' Award 1998. *Documentary films:* (writer) A chacun son allemagne 1976, Nous l'avons tant aimée, la révolution (four films) 1983, C'est la vie (full-length film) 1990, Angst im Rüchen hat jeder von uns 1992, Juden in Frankfurt 1993. *Publications include:* Obsolete Communism: The Left-Wing Alternative (co-author) 1968, La Révolte étudiante 1968, Le Gauchisme, remède à la maladie sénile du communisme (co-author) 1972, Le Grand bazar 1976, De l'écologie à l'autonomie (co-author) 1981, Nous l'avons tant aimée, la révolution 1987, 1968: die letzte Revolution, die noch nichts vom Ozonloch wusste (co-author) 1988, Rechtsstaat und ziviler Ungehorsam, ein Streitgespräch (co-author) 1988, Einwanderbares Deutschland oder Vertreibung aus dem Wohlstandsparadies? (co-author) 1991, Heimat Babylon, das Wagnis der multikulturellen Demokratie (co-author) 1993, Une envie de politique: entretiens avec Lucas Delattre et Guy Herzlich 1998, Petit dictionnaire de l'euro (co-author) 1998, Xénophobies: histoires d'Europe (co-author) 1998, Sois jeune et tais-toi!, Un pavé dans la mare et la France est-elle soluble dans l'Europe? (co-author) 1999, Quand tu seras président (co-author) 2004. *Leisure interest:* football. *Website:* www.cohn-bendit.eu.

COHN-SHERBOK, Daniel (Dan) Mark, BA, BHL, MAHL, MLitt, PhD, DD; American/British rabbi and academic; *Professor Emeritus of Judaism, University of Wales Trinity Saint David, Lampeter;* b. 1 Feb. 1945, Denver, Colo; s. of Bernard Sherbok and Ruth Sherbok; m. Lavinia C. Heath 1976; ed Williams Coll., Hebrew Union Coll. and Univ. of Cambridge, UK; rabbi in USA, UK, Australia and South Africa 1968–74; Chaplain, Colorado State House of Reps 1971; Univ. Lecturer in Theology, Univ. of Kent, UK 1975–97, Dir Centre for Study of Religion and Society 1982–90; Visiting Prof. of Judaism, Univ. of Wales Trinity Saint David, Lampeter 1995–97, Prof. 1997–2009, Prof. Emer. 2010–, Dir Centre for the Study of the World's Religions 2003–09; Visiting Prof., Univ. of Essex, UK 1993–94, Middlesex Univ., UK 1994–, Univ. of St Andrews, UK 1995–96, St Andrew's Biblical Theological Coll., Moscow, Russia 1996, Univ. of Wales, Bangor, Univ. of Vilnius, Lithuania 1999, Durham Univ., UK 2002; Visiting Scholar, Sarum Coll. 2006–; Visiting Prof., St Mary's Univ. Coll. 2008–, York St John Univ. 2012–; Visiting Fellow, Heythrop Coll., Univ. of London 2010–; Pres., London Soc. for the Study of Religion 2012–14; Visiting Fellow, Centre for Religions for Peace and Reconciliation, Univ. of Winchester 2013–16; Fellow, Hebrew Union Coll., Acad. of Jewish Philosophy; Hon. Prof., Aberystwyth Univ. 2010–; Hon. DD (Hebrew Union Coll., Jewish Inst. of Religion) 1995; Winner, Royal Acad. Friends Competition. *Drawings:* The Athenaeum: Sketches (book) 2014. *Publications include:* The Jewish Heritage 1988, Jewish Petitionary Prayer 1989, God and the Holocaust 1989, Rabbinic Perspectives on the New Testament 1990, Issues in Contemporary Judaism 1991, Dictionary of Judaism and Christianity (with Lavinia Cohn-Sherbok) 1991, The Crucified Jew 1992, The Blackwell Dictionary of Judaica 1992, Exodus: An Agenda for Jewish-Christian Dialogue 1992, Not a Nice Job for a Nice Jewish Boy 1993, The Future of Judaism 1994, The American Jew (with Lavinia Cohn-Sherbok) 1994, Jewish and Christian Mysticism (with Lavinia Cohn-Sherbok) 1994, Jewish Mysticism 1995, Atlas of Jewish History 1996, Medieval Jewish Philosophy 1996, Fifty Key Jewish Thinkers 1996, The Jewish Messiah 1997, After Noah: Animals and the Liberation of Theology (with Andrew Linzey) 1997, A Concise Encyclopaedia of Judaism 1998, Understanding the Holocaust 1999, Jews, Christians and Religious Pluralism 1999, Messianic Judaism 2000, Holocaust Theology: A Reader 2001, The Palestinian-Israeli Conflict (with Dawoud El-Alami) 2001, Anti-Semitism 2002, Judaism: History, Belief, Practice 2003, The Dictionary of Jewish Biography 2005, Pursuing the Dream: Jewish Christian Dialogue (with Mary Grey) 2005, The Paradox of Antisemitism 2006, Politics of Apocalypse 2006, Kabbalah and Jewish Mysticism 2006, Dictionary of Kabbalah and Kabbalists 2009, Judaism Today 2011, Introduction to Zionism and Israel 2012, The Palestinian State: A Jewish Justification 2012, Love, Sex and Marriage 2013, Why Can't They Get Along 2014, Illustrated History of Judaism 2014, Debating Israel and Palestine 2014, Sensible Religion (with Christopher Lewis) 2014, Illustrated History of the Jewish Faith 2015, Dictionary of Jews and Judaism 2018, Jews: Nearly Everything You Wanted to Know but Were Too Afraid to Ask (with Peter Cave) 2018. *Leisure interests:* keeping cats, walking, drawing cartoons. *E-mail:* cohnsherbok@gmail.com. *Website:* dancohnsherbok.com.

COHON, Jared L., BS, PhD; American academic and university administrator; *President Emeritus, Carnegie Mellon University;* b. 1947, Cleveland, Ohio; m. Maureen Cohon; ed Univ. of Pennsylvania, Massachusetts Inst. of Tech.; mem. Faculty, Dept of Geography and Environmental Eng, Johns Hopkins Univ. 1973–92, later Asst and Assoc. Dean of Eng and Vice-Provost for Research; Prof. of Environmental Systems Analysis and Dean of School of Forestry and Environmental Studies, Yale Univ. 1992–97; Pres. Carnegie Mellon Univ. 1997–2013, Pres. Emer. 2013–, Univ. Prof., Civil and Environmental Engineering and Engineering and Public Policy 2013–; Legis. Asst for Energy and the Environment to the late Daniel Patrick Moynihan, US Senator from NY 1977–78; mem. Nuclear Waste Tech. Review Bd 1995– (Chair. 1997–2002), Homeland Security Advisory Council 2002– (Chair. Sr Advisory Cttee on Academia and Policy Research); mem. Bd of Dirs Mellon Financial Corpn, American Standard, Inc.; serves on bds of several nat. and local non-profit orgs, including Health Effects Inst., Heinz Center for Science, Econs and the Environment, Council for Competitiveness, Carnegie Museums of Pittsburgh, Pittsburgh Cultural Trust, Urban League of Pittsburgh, Allegheny Conf. on Community Devt; mem. Nat. Acad. of Engineering 2012–; Dr hc (Korean Advanced Inst. for Science and Technology) 2012, (Univ. of Pittsburgh) 2013, (Carnegie Mellon Univ.) 2013; named Distinguished Mem. American Soc. of Civil Engineering 2009, National Engineering Award, American Asscn of Engineering Socs 2011. *Publications include:* Multiobjective Programming and Planning 1978 (re-issued as a Classic of Operations Research 2004); author, co-author or editor of more than 80 professional publs on environmental and water resource systems analysis. *Address:* Civil and Environmental Engineering, Carnegie Mellon University, Pittsburgh, PA 15213-3890, USA (office). *Telephone:* (412) 268-1765 (office). *E-mail:* cohon@andrew.cmu.edu (office). *Website:* www.cmu.edu/cee (office).

ČOLAK, Bariša; Bosnia and Herzegovina politician and lawyer; *Minister of Justice;* b. 1 Jan. 1956, Široki Brijeg; m. Anela Čolak; one s. two d.; ed Univ. of Mostar; Judge, Magistrates Court, Široki Brijeg 1988–93; Deputy Minister of Justice 1993–96; Prime Minister of West Herzegovina Canton 1996–99; Minister of Justice 1999–2001, 2007–; mem. Parl., Fed. of Bosnia and Herzegovina 2001–02; Vice-Pres. and Minister of Security, Bosnia and Herzegovina 2003–07; mem. Croatian Democratic Union of Bosnia and Herzegovina (HDZ BiH). *Address:* Ministry of Justice, 71000 Sarajevo, trg Bosne i Hercegovine 1, Bosnia and Herzegovina (office). *Telephone:* (33) 223501 (office). *Fax:* (33) 223504 (office). *E-mail:* info@mpr.gov.ba (office). *Website:* www.mpr.gov.ba (office).

ÇOLAK, Emine; Turkish-Cypriot lawyer and politician; b. 9 March 1958, Lefkoşa (Nicosia); three c.; ed School of Oriental and African Studies, Univ. of London, UK; qualified as barrister 1980; practised as lawyer with own firm, specializing in administrative, commercial, family, heritage, human rights and property law 1982–; mem. Lefkoşa (Nicosia) Turkish Municipal Council 1994–2002; mem. High Judicial Bd (responsible for appointment of judges and functioning of courts in N Cyprus) 2007–11; Minister of Foreign Affairs 2015–16; f. Turkish Cypriot Human Rights Foundation; mem. Turkish-Greek Forum 2002. *Address:* c/o Ministry of Foreign Affairs, Selçuklu Rd, Lefkoşa (Nicosia), Mersin 10, Turkey (office).

COLANINNO, Roberto; Italian business executive; *Chairman and CEO, Piaggio & Company SpA;* b. 16 Aug. 1943, Mantua; began career with Fiamm SpA, fmr Chief Exec.; Co-founder Sogefi SpA (finance co.) 1981; mem. Bd several regional and nat. banks in Italy, including Mediobanco, Efibanca SpA, Gruppo Bancario Capitalia; CEO Olivetti & Co. 1996–2001; Chair. and CEO Telecom Italia 1999–2001, also Chair. Telecom Italia Mobile SpA 1999–2001; f. Omniaholding SpA 1998; Chair. IMMSI SpA 2002–; Chair. and CEO Piaggio & Co. SpA 2006–; mem. Bd, Alitalia; mem. Man. Cttee and Nat. Advisory Cttee Confindustria 1997–2002; Hon. Chair. Alitalia Società Aerea Italiana; Hon. DEcon (Lecce) 2001; Cavaliere del Lavoro. *Address:* Piaggio Group, Viale Rinaldo Piaggio 25, 56025 Pontedera, Italy (office). *Telephone:* (05) 87272111 (office). *Website:* www .piaggiogroup.com (office).

COLAO, Vittorio, MBA; Italian business executive; *Chief Executive, Vodafone Group Plc;* b. 3 Oct. 1961, Brescia; m. 1992; two c.; ed Bocconi Univ., Milan, Harvard Business School, USA; spent time at Morgan Stanley investment bankers, London, UK; Pnr, McKinsey & Co., Milan 1986–96; joined Omnitel Pronto Italia (now Vodafone Italy) 1996, later COO, CEO 1999–2001, Regional CEO, Southern Europe, Middle East and Africa, Vodafone Group Plc 2001–04, Exec. Dir on main Bd 2002–04, 2006–, Chief Exec., Europe, and Deputy Group Chief Exec. 2006–, Chief Exec. 2008–; CEO RCS MediaGroup, Milan 2004–06; Dir (non-exec.), Unilever 2015–; mem. Int. Advisory Bd, Bocconi Univ.; reserve officer in the Carabinieri. *Address:* Vodafone Group Plc, Vodafone House, The Connection, Newbury, Berks., RG14 2FN, England (office). *Telephone:* (1635) 33251 (office). *Fax:* (1635) 686111 (office). *E-mail:* info@vodafone.com (office). *Website:* www.vodafone.com (office).

COLARIČ, Jože, BEcons; Slovenian business executive; *President of the Management Board and CEO, KrKa d.d.;* b. 27 Aug. 1955, Brežice; ed Faculty of Econs, Univ. of Ljubljana; joined KrKa d.d. (pharmaceutical co.) 1982, Head of Foreign Exchange Trade Dept and later Asst Dir 1982–89, Head of Export Service, Export-Import Div. 1989–91, Deputy Dir 1991–93, Deputy to CEO for Marketing and Finance 1993–97, mem. Man. Bd 1997–, Deputy Pres. 1998–2004, Pres. of Man. Bd and CEO 2005–. *Address:* KrKa d.d., Šmarješka cesto 6, 8501 Novo Mesto, Slovenia (office). *Telephone:* (7) 3312111 (office). *Fax:* (7) 3321537 (office). *E-mail:* info@krka.biz (office). *Website:* www.krka.si (office).

COLAU BALLANO, Carli; Spanish activist and politician; *Mayor of Barcelona;* b. 3 March 1974, Barcelona; m. Adrià Alemany Salafranca; one s.; began career as political activist during protests against Gulf War early 1990s and G8 summits 2001; co-f. V de Vivienda (housing activist movt) 2006; mem. Associació de Veïns del Casc Antic (AVCA, neighbourhood asscn); mem. Bd of Dirs Catalan Confed. of Residents' Asscns, Barcelona Fed. of Residents' Asscns; Founding mem. and spokesperson Plataforma de Afectados por la Hipoteca (PAH, Platform for People Affected by Mortgages) 2009–14; Spokesperson for Barcelona en Comú (Barcelona in Common, citizens' platform group) 2014–; Mayor of Barcelona (first woman) 2015–; Barcelona Human Rights Film Festival Award for Human Rights 2013, European Citizens' Prize (with PAH) 2013, Artistas Intérpretes, Sociedad de Gestión United Women Prize 2013. *Publication:* Vidas Hipotecadas (with Adrià Alemany) 2012. *Address:* City Hall, Rambla de Catalunya, 2-4, 08007 Barcelona, Spain (office). *Telephone:* (932) 38-07-22 (office). *E-mail:* alcaldessa@bcn.cat (office). *Website:* ajuntament.barcelona.cat/alcaldessa (office); adacolau.cat.

COLBORN, Theodora Emily Decker (Theo), BS, MA, PhD; American zoologist, academic and environmental health analyst; *Professor Emerita of Zoology, University of Florida;* ed Western State Coll. of Colorado, Rutgers Univ., Univ. of Wisconsin; Congressional Fellow 1985–86, Science Analyst, Office of Tech. Assessment, US Congress, Washington, DC 1986–87; Assoc., Conservation Foundation, Washington, DC 1987–88, Consultant, Environmental Health Analysis 1987–90; Sr Fellow, World Wildlife Fund 1988–93 (on sabbatical 1990–93); Sr Fellow, W. Alton Jones Foundation 1990–93; Sr Scientist and Dir Wildlife and Contaminants Program, World Wildlife Fund 1993–2003; Prof. of Zoology, Univ. of Florida, Gainesville 2004–07, Prof. Emer. 2008–; Founder and Pres. The Endocrine Disruption Exchange, Paonia, Colo 2003–08; has served on numerous advisory panels, including US Environmental Protection Agency (EPA) Science Advisory Bd, Ecosystem Health Cttee of Int. Jt Comm. of US and Canada, Science Man. Cttee of Toxic Substances Research Initiative of Canada, EPA Endocrine Disruptor Screening and Testing Advisory Cttee, EPA Endocrine Disruption Methods and Validation Sub-cttee; mem. Bd of Dirs Rachel Carson Council 2006–; mem. Bd of Scientific Advisors, Children's Health Environmental Coalition 2006–; est. and directed Wildlife and Contaminants Program at World Wildlife Fund US; Nat. Water Alliance Award for Excellence in Protecting the Nation's Aquatic Resources 1991, Pew Fellows Award 1993–96, Nat. Conservation Achievement Award in Science, Nat. Wildlife Fed. 1994, Rachel Carson Award, Chatham Coll. 1997, Norwegian Int. Rachel Carson Prize 1999, UNEP Women Leadership for the Environment Award 1997, State of the World Forum, Mikhail Gorbachev, Change Makers Award 1997, Audubon Magazine: A Century of Conservation, 100 Champions of Conservation 1998, Int. Blue Planet Prize, Asahi Glass Foundation, Japan 2000, Rachel Carson Award, Soc. of Toxicology and Environmental Chem. 2003, Rachel Carson Award, Center for Science in the Public Interest 2004, Beyond Pesticides Dragonfly Award 2006, Woman on the Forefront: Leadership and Integrity in Science 2007, Lifetime Achievement Award, Nat. Council for Science and the Environment 2007, Time magazine Global Environmental Heroes Award 2007. *Publications:* Chemically Induced Alterations in Sexual and Functional Development: The Wildlife/Human Connection (ed.) 1992, Our Stolen Future: How We Are Threatening Our Fertility, Intelligence and Survival (co-author) 1996; numerous scientific papers in professional journals on the consequences of prenatal exposure to synthetic chemicals by the developing embryo and foetus in wildlife, lab. animals and humans. *Address:* PO Box 1253, 121 Main Avenue Paonia, CO 81428; University of Florida, PO Box 118525, Gainesville, FL 32611-8525 (office); The Endocrine Disruption Exchange, PO Box 1407, Paonia, CO 81428, USA (office). *Telephone:* (352) 392-1107 (Gainesville) (office); (970) 527-4082 (TEDX) (office); (970) 527-6548. *Fax:* (970) 527-6548. *E-mail:* colborn@tds.net (office). *Website:* www.endocrinedisruption.org (office); www.ourstolenfuture.org (office).

COLCLEUGH, David (Dave) W., BASc, MASc, PhD; Canadian business executive (retd) and academic; *Faculty Leadership Development Professor, Institute for Leadership Education in Engineering, University of Toronto;* b. Fort Erie, Ont.; m.; two c.; ed Univ. of Toronto and Univ. of Cambridge, UK; research engineer, DuPont Canada, Kingston 1963–68, polymer tech. supervisor, Fibres Div. 1968–73, tech. supt, Explosives Div., North Bay 1973–75, Tech. and Planning Man., Explosives Div., Montreal 1975–79, Rubber Industry Man., Tyre and Industrial Div. 1979–82, Man. of Gen. Products, Mississauga 1982–85, Prin. Consultant, Corp. Planning Div., Wilmington April–Dec. 1985, Gen. Man. of Finishes, Toronto 1985–89, Dir of Corp. Planning and Devt April–Nov. 1989, Vice-Pres. of Mfg and Eng 1989–92, Sr Vice-Pres. with responsibility for Fibres and Intermediates, Eng Polymers Units and Mfg and Eng 1992–94, Vice-Pres., Gen. Man. of Nylon, DuPont Asia-Pacific 1994–95, Pres. 1995–97, Pres. and CEO DuPont Canada Inc. 1997–2003, Chair. 1998–2003 (retd); Faculty Leadership Devt Prof., Inst. for Leadership Educ. in Eng, Faculty of Applied Science and Eng, Univ. of Toronto 2006–; mem. Bd of Dirs, Let's Talk Science 2003– (Chair. 2005–), ZENON Environmental Inc. 2000–, Hudson's Bay Co., Canadian Chemicals Producers Asscn, Textiles Human Resources Council, Art Gallery of Mississauga, EcoSynthetix Inc. 2008– (Chair. 2012–); mem. Dean's Advisory Bd Univ. of Toronto. *Address:* Institute for Leadership Education in Engineering, Wallberg Building, 200 College Street, Suite 240, Toronto, ON M5S 3E5, Canada (office). *Telephone:* (416) 978-3018 (office). *E-mail:* davidcolcleugh@yahoo.ca (office). *Website:* ilead.engineering.utoronto.ca/people/david-colcleugh-faculty-leadership -development-professor (office).

COLDITZ, Graham A., BSc (Med.), MBBS, MPH, DrPH, MD; Australian/ American epidemiologist and academic; *Niess-Gain Professor, Department of Surgery, School of Medicine, Washington University in St Louis;* b. 1 Nov. 1954, Sydney; ed Univ. of Queensland, Brisbane, Australia, and Harvard School of Public Health, Boston, Mass, USA; Instructor in Medicine, Harvard Medical School 1986–88, Asst Prof. of Medicine 1988–91, Assoc. Prof. 1991–98, Prof. 1998–2006, Prof. of Epidemiology, Grad. School of Public Health 1998–2006, Program Leader, Cancer Epidemiology, Dana-Farber/Harvard Cancer Center, Dir of Educ., Harvard Center for Cancer Prevention; Niess-Gain Prof., Dept of Surgery, Washington Univ. School of Medicine, St Louis 2006–, also Assoc. Dir for Prevention and Control, Alvin J. Siteman Cancer Center; Raine Visiting Prof., Univ. of Western Australia 1997; Adjunct Prof., Univ. of Queensland School of Population Health 2001–; fmr Dir, American Cancer Soc. New England Div., Inc., Dir, American Cancer Soc. 2010–13; mem. Inst. of Medicine 2006–; mem. Advisory Cttee on Research, Alberta Cancer Bd 2000–03; Fellow, Australian Faculty of Public Health Medicine, Royal Australian Coll. of Physicians 1990, American Asscn for the Advancement of Science; Frank Knox Memorial Fellowship, Harvard Univ. 1981–83, Faculty Research Award, American Cancer Soc. 1991–96, ACS Clinical Research Professorship Award 2003–, DeWitt S. Goodman Lectureship, American Asscn for Cancer Research (AACR) 2003, American Cancer Soc. Medal of Honor for Cancer Prevention and Control 2011, Award for Excellence in Cancer Epidemiology and Prevention, American Asscn for Cancer Research-American Cancer Soc. 2012, American Soc. of Clinical Oncology–American Cancer Soc. Award and Lecture 2014, AACR Award for Cancer Prevention Research 2014. *Publications:* more than 1,000 publs in medical journals. *Leisure interests:* vegetable gardening, forest conservation. *Address:* Washington University School of Medicine, 660 South Euclid Avenue, Campus Box 8100, St Louis, MO 63108, USA (office). *Telephone:* (314) 454-7940 (office). *E-mail:* colditzg@wustl.edu (office). *Website:* www.publichealthsciences.wustl.edu (office).

COLDWELL, Pedro Joaquín; Mexican lawyer, politician and company chairman; *Secretary (Minister) of Energy; Chairman, Petróleos Mexicanos (PEMEX);* b. 5 Aug. 1950, Cozumel, Quintana Roo; s. of Nassin Joaquín Ibarra; ed Universidad Iberoamericana; mem. Institutional Revolutionary Party (PRI), has occupied different positions, including Pres. 2011–12; fmr Dir Gen. Fondo Nacional para el Desarrollo Turístico (FONATUR); held seat in Chamber of Deputies, representing First Dist of Quintana Roo 1979–80; Gov. of Quintana Roo; fmr Peace and Reconciliation Commr in Chiapas; apptd Amb. to Cuba 1998; Senator (PRI) for Quintana Roo 2006–12; Sec. of Energy 2012–; Chair. Petróleos Mexicanos (PEMEX) 2012–. *Address:* Petróleos Mexicanos (PEMEX), Avenida Marina Nacional 329, Col. Huasteca, 11311 México DF (office); Secretariat of State for Energy, Insurgentes Sur 890, 17°, Col. del Valle, Del. Benito Juárez, 03100 México DF, Mexico (office). *Telephone:* (55) 1944-2500 (PEMEX) (office); (55) 5000-6000 (Secretariat) (office). *Fax:* (55) 5531-6354 (PEMEX) (office); (55) 5000-6222 (Secretariat) (office). *E-mail:* calidad@energia.gob.mx (office). *Website:* www .pemex.com (office); www.energia.gob.mx (office).

COLE, Shaun, BA, PhD; British astrophysicist and academic; *Professor, Institute for Computational Cosmology, Department of Physics, Durham University;* b. Nov. 1963; m. Margaret Cole 1992; one s. one d.; ed Clitheroe Royal Grammar School, Lancs., Jesus Coll., Oxford, Clare Coll., Cambridge; Asst Man., Seacroft Camping Park, Cromer, Norfolk 1983; Asst Oiler and Greaser, Nelson's Acetate, Lancaster 1986; Supervisor in Physics for Natural Sciences, Clare Coll., Cambridge 1986–88;

Tutor in Math. for Physics, Jesus Coll., Oxford and Tutor in Astrophysics for Physics, Wadham and Univ. Colls, Oxford 1988–89; postdoctoral research at Dept of Astronomy, Univ. of California, Berkeley 1989–91; Temporary Lecturer, Durham Univ. 1991–94, PPARC Advanced Fellow 1994–2001, Reader in Physics 2001–05, Prof. in Physics, Inst. for Computational Cosmology, Dept of Physics 2005–, Deputy Dir of the Inst.; Shaw Prize in Astronomy (co-recipient) 2014. *Publications:* more than 160 papers in professional journals. *Leisure interests:* family, DIY projects, five-a-side football. *Address:* Room OC306, Institute for Computational Cosmology, Department of Physics, Durham University, South Road, Durham, DH1 3LE, England (office). *Telephone:* (191) 334-3593 (office). *Fax:* (191) 334-3645 (office). *E-mail:* shaun.cole@durham.ac.uk (office). *Website:* www.dur.ac.uk/physics (office); astro.dur.ac.uk/~cole (office).

COLE-HAMILTON, David John, PhD, CChem, FRSC, FRSE; British chemist and academic; *Irvine Professor of Chemistry, University of St Andrews;* b. 22 May 1948, Bovey Tracey, Devon, England; s. of A. M. Cole-Hamilton and M. M Cartwright; m. 1st Elizabeth A. Brown 1973 (divorced); two s. two d.; m. 2nd Rosemary E. Macrae (née Semple) 2008; ed Haileybury & Imperial Service Coll. and Univ. of Edinburgh; Research Asst and temporary Lecturer, Imperial Coll. London 1974–78; Lecturer, Univ. of Liverpool 1978–83, Sr Lecturer 1983–85; Irvine Prof. of Chem., St Andrews Univ. 1985–, Chair. of Chem. 1985–90; Sir Edward Frankland Fellowship 1985, Corday Morgan Medal and Prize 1983, Industrial Award for Organo-metallic Chem. 1998, Sir Geoffrey Wilkinson Prize, Tilden Lecturer, Royal Soc. of Chem. 2000–01, Eminent Visitor, Catalysis Soc. of S Africa 2004, Sir Geoffrey Wilkinson Prize Lecturer, Royal Soc. of Chem. 2005–06. *Publications:* more than 360 articles on homogeneous catalysis and organometallic chem. *Address:* School of Chemistry, Purdie 340, University of St Andrews, St Andrews, Fife, KY16 9ST (office); 22 Buchanan Gardens, St Andrews, Fife, KY16 9LU, Scotland (home). *Telephone:* (1334) 463805 (office). *Fax:* (1334) 463808 (office). *E-mail:* djc@st-and.ac.uk (office). *Website:* ch-www.st-andrews.ac.uk (office).

COLEIRO PRECA, Marie-Louise, BA; Maltese politician and fmr head of state; b. 7 Dec. 1958, Qormi; m. Edgar Preca; one d.; ed Univ. of Malta; mem. House of Reps 1998–2014, mem. Parl. Perm. Cttee for Social Affairs 1998, also for Family Affairs; fmr Shadow Minister for Social Policy, for Tourism, for Health; Minister of the Family and Social Solidarity 2013–14; Pres. of Malta 2014–19; mem. Nat. Comm. for Fiscal Morality; f. President's Foundation for the Wellbeing of Soc. 2014; Patron, Mediterranean Tourism Foundation; Dir Strategy and Planning, Tourism Ministry; mem. Del. to Council of Europe; fmr Dir Maltacom PLC, Libyan Arab Maltese Holding Co.; fmr mem. National Bureau of Socialist Youths; mem. Labour Party, Nat. Exec., Asst Gen. Sec., Gen. Sec. 1982–91; mem. Advisory Bd Global Forum of Women Political Leaders; Hon. Life Pres. Arab-European Forum for Dialogue and Devt, UN Special Ambassador of the Int. Year of Sustainable Tourism for Devt 2017; Collar de Compañeros de Honor, Orden del Mérito de Malta; Hon. Prof. (Univ. of Warwick, UK) 2015; Crans Montana Prix de la Fondation 2014, Agent of Change Award 2016. *Address:* c/o Office of the President, The Palace, Valletta VLT 1190, Malta (office).

COLEMAN, David, BA; American business executive and educator; *President and CEO, College Board, New York City;* b. 1970; s. of Aaron Coleman and Elizabeth Coleman; ed Yale Univ., Univ. of Oxford, UK; began career as Consultant with McKinsey & Co. for five years; with McGraw-Hill 2005–07; Co-founder Student Achievement Partners 2007–12; Pres. and CEO, College Board, New York City 2012–; Co-founder, Grow Network; Founding mem. StudentsFirst. *Address:* The College Board, 45 Columbus Avenue, New York, NY 10023, USA (office). *Telephone:* (212) 713-8000 (office). *Website:* www.collegeboard.org (office).

COLEMAN, Lewis W., BA; American business executive; ed Stanford Univ.; with Wells Fargo & Co. in a variety of wholesale and retail positions, including as Head of Int. Banking, Chief Personnel Officer and Chair. Credit Policy Cttee 1973–86; joined Bank of America as Chief Credit Officer 1986, roles included Head of Capital Markets, Head of World Banking Group and Vice-Chair. Bd and Chief Financial Officer, Sr Man. Dir Banc of America Securities LLC (fmr known as Montgomery Securities, and a subsidiary of Bank of America Corpn), San Francisco 1995–98, Chair. 1998–2000; mem. Bd of Dirs Northrop Grumman 2001–12, Chair. (non-exec.) 2010–11, Lead Ind. Dir 2011–12; mem. Bd of Dirs DreamWorks Animation SKG 2004, Pres. 2005–14, Acting Chief Financial Officer June–Sept. 2014, Vice-Chair. 2014–15; mem. Bd of Dirs Immune Design 2015–; Pres. Gordon E. and Betty I. Moore Foundation, San Francisco, Calif. 2000–04; mem. Nat. Acads Bd on Science, Tech. and Econ. Policy, Bd of Global Crop Diversity Trust; Fellow, Nat. Acad. of Arts and Sciences.

COLEMAN, Mary Sue, BA, PhD; American fmr university administrator and academic; b. 2 Oct. 1943, Ky; m. Dr Kenneth Coleman; one s.; ed Grinnell Coll., Univ. of North Carolina, Univ. of Texas; mem. Biochemistry Faculty, Univ. of Kentucky 1971–90, Cancer Care Admin 1982–90; Assoc. Provost and Dean of Research, Univ. of North Carolina 1990–92, Vice-Chancellor Grad. Studies and Research 1992–93; Provost and Vice-Pres. of Academic Affairs Univ. of New Mexico 1993–95; Pres. Univ. of Iowa 1995–2002; Pres. Univ. of Michigan 2002–14, also Prof. of Biological Chem. and Medical School Prof.; elected to NAS Inst. of Medicine 1997, Co-Chair. Cttee on Consequences of Uninsurance; Chair. Hitchings-Elion Postdoctoral Fellowship Program, Burroughs-Wellcome Fund 1997; Co-Chair. Nat. Advisory Council on Innovation and Entrepreneurship 2010–; mem. Bd of Dirs Johnson & Johnson 2003–, Meredith Corpn, American Council of Educ. (ACE), Nat. Collegiate Athletic Asscn (NCAA); mem. Knight Comm. on Intercollegiate Athletics 2000–01, Michigan Strategic Econ. Investment and Commercialization Bd; mem. Bd of Trustees Univs Research Asscn, ACE Task Force on Teacher Educ. and Comm. Minorities in Higher Educ., Business-Higher Educ. Forum, Imagining America Pres.'s Council, Asscn of American Univs (AAU) Task Force Research Accountability, NCAA Standards for Success Advisory Bd, Pres.'s Leadership Group for Higher Educ., Center for Alcohol and Other Drug Prevention; fmr mem. Exec. Cttee Asscn AAU; Trustee, Knight Foundation 2005–, Gerald R. Ford Foundation; Fellow, American Acad. Arts and Sciences, AAAS; Dr hc (Grinnell Coll., Luther Coll., Univ. of Kentucky, Albion Coll., Dartmouth Coll., Shanghai Jiao Tong Univ., Northeastern Univ., Univ. of Toledo, Univ. of Notre Dame, Grand Valley State Univ., Univ. of North Carolina, Eastern Kentucky Univ., California Inst. of Tech.); Distinguished Alumnus Award, Univ. of North Carolina, Alumni Award, Grinnell Coll., Humanitarian of the Year, The Michigan Roundtable for Diversity and Inclusion, Trillium Lifetime Achievement Award, Michigan Women's Foundation, named by TIME magazine one of the nation's "10 best college presidents" 2009. *Address:* c/o Office of the President, University of Michigan, 2074 Fleming Administration Building, 503 Thompson Street, Ann Arbor, MI 41809-1340, USA.

COLEMAN, Norm, BA, JD; American lawyer and fmr politician; *Of Counsel, Hogan Lovells US LLP;* b. Brooklyn, New York; m. Laurie Coleman; one s. one d.; ed Hofstra Univ., Univ. of Iowa; served in Office of Attorney-Gen. of Minn. in various positions including Chief Prosecutor and Solicitor-Gen. of State of Minn. 1976–93; elected Mayor of St Paul (Conservative Democrat) 1993, re-elected 1997 (Republican); unsuccessful Republican cand. for Gov. of Minn. 1998; Senator from Minn. 2003–09; Of Counsel, Hogan Lovells US LLP, Washington, DC 2009–; Chair. American Action Network; Advisor, Republican Jewish Coalition, Washington, DC 2009–. *Leisure interests:* playing basketball with daughter, juggling, Bob Dylan's music. *Address:* Hogan Lovells US LLP, Columbia Square, 555 Thirteenth Street, NW, Washington, DC 20004, USA (office). *Telephone:* (202) 637-5440 (office). *Fax:* (202) 637-5910 (office). *E-mail:* norm.coleman@hoganlovells.com (office). *Website:* www.hoganlovells.com (office).

COLEMAN, Sir Robert John, Kt, KCMG, MA, JD; British lawyer, academic and international organization official; b. 8 Sept. 1943; m. Malinda Tigay Cutler 1966; two d.; ed Devonport High School for Boys, Plymouth, Jesus Coll. Oxford and Univ. of Chicago Law School, USA; Lecturer in Law, Univ. of Birmingham 1967–70; called to the Bar 1969; in practice as barrister-at-law, London 1970–73; Admin., subsequently Prin. Admin., EC 1974–82, Deputy Head of Div. 1983, Head of Div. 1984–87, Dir Public Procurement 1987–90, Dir Approximation of Laws, Freedom of Establishment and Freedom to Provide Services, the Professions 1990–91, Dir-Gen. Transport, EC 1991–99; Dir-Gen. Health and Consumer Protection 1999–2003; Sr Practitioner Fellow, Inst. of Governance, Queen's Univ., Belfast 2003–04, Visiting Research Fellow 2004–07; Visiting Prof., School of Law and Social Science, Univ. of Plymouth 2005–12; taught at World Maritime Univ., Malmo, Sweden and Inst. of Int. Maritime Law, Malta 2005–11; EU Liaison Officer, Baltic and Int. Maritime Council 2005–12; mem. Admin. Bd European Maritime Safety Agency, Lisbon 2008–12. *Publications include:* numerous articles in professional journals. *Leisure interest:* singing. *Address:* Flete House 3, Ivybridge, PL21 9NX, England (home). *Telephone:* (1752) 830147 (home). *E-mail:* robert.coleman18@btinternet.com.

COLEMAN, Terence (Terry) Francis Frank, LLB, FRSA; British journalist and writer; b. 13 Feb. 1931, Bournemouth; s. of Jack Coleman and D. I. B. Coleman; m. 1st Lesley Fox-Strangeways Vane 1954 (divorced); two d.; m. 2nd Vivien Rosemary Lumsdaine Wallace 1981; one s. one d.; ed 14 schools, latterly Poole Grammar School, Univ. of London; fmr reporter, Poole Herald; fmr Ed. Savoir Faire; fmr Sub-Ed. Sunday Mercury, Birmingham Post; Reporter then Arts Corresp. The Guardian 1961–70, Chief Feature Writer 1970–74, 1976–79, New York Corresp. 1981, Special Corresp. 1982–89; Special Writer with Daily Mail 1974–76; Assoc. Ed. The Independent 1989–91; columnist, The Guardian 1992–; Feature Writer of the Year, British Press Awards 1982, Journalist of the Year (What the Papers Say Award) 1988. *Publications include:* The Railway Navvies (Yorkshire Post Prize for Best First Book of the Year) 1965, A Girl for the Afternoons 1965, Providence and Mr Hardy (with Lois Deacon) 1966, The Only True History: Collected Journalism 1969, Passage to America 1972, An Indiscretion in the Life of an Heiress (Hardy's first novel) (ed.) 1976, The Liners 1976, The Scented Brawl: Collected Journalism 1978, Southern Cross 1979, Thanksgiving 1981, Movers and Shakers: Collected Interviews 1987, Thatcher's Britain 1987, Empire 1994, W. G. Grace: A Biography 1997, Nelson: The Man and the Legend (biog.) 2001, Olivier: The Authorised Biography 2005, Great Interviews of the 20th Century 2008, The Old Vic: The Story of a Great Theatre 2014. *Leisure interests:* cricket, opera and circumnavigation. *Address:* c/o Fiona Pethram, Peters Fraser + Dunlop, 55 New Oxford Street, London, WC1A 1BS, England (office). *Telephone:* (20) 7344-1064 (office); (20) 7720-2651 (home). *Fax:* (20) 7836-9539 (office). *E-mail:* fpetheram@pfd.co.uk (office). *Website:* www.petersfraserdunlop.com (office).

COLERIDGE, David Ean; British fmr insurance executive; b. 7 June 1932; s. of Guy Cecil Richard Coleridge and Katherine Cicely Stewart Smith; m. Susan Senior 1955; three s.; ed Eton Coll.; with Glanvill Enthoven 1950–57; joined R. W. Sturge & Co. 1957, Dir 1966–95; Chair. A. L. Sturge (Holdings) Ltd (now Sturge Holdings PLC) 1978–95; mem. Cttee of Lloyd's Underwriting Agents Asscn 1974–82, Chair. 1981–82; mem. Council and Cttee of Lloyd's 1983–86, 1988–92; Deputy Chair. Lloyd's 1985, 1988, 1989, Chair. 1991–92; Dir Wise Speke Holdings Ltd 1987–94, Ockham Holdings PLC (now Highway Insurance PLC) 1996– (Chair. 1995). *Leisure interests:* golf, racing, gardening, family. *Address:* 37 Egerton Terrace, London, SW3 2BU, England (home). *Telephone:* (1730) 813277 (home).

COLERIDGE, Nicholas David, CBE; British publisher, journalist and author; *President, Condé Nast International;* b. 4 March 1957, London; s. of David Ean Coleridge (q.v.) and Susan Coleridge (née Senior); m. Georgia Metcalfe 1989; three s. one d.; ed Eton, Trinity Coll., Cambridge; Assoc. Ed. Tatler 1979–81; columnist Evening Standard 1981–84; Features Ed. Harpers and Queen 1985–86, Ed. 1986–89; Editorial Dir Condé Nast Publs 1989–91, Man. Dir Condé Nast UK 1992–, Vice-Pres. Condé Nast International 1999–2012, Pres. 2012–, Dir Condé Nast France, Condé Nast India; Chair. British Fashion Council 2000–03, Fashion Rocks for The Prince's Trust 2003, Periodical Publrs Asscn 2004–07; Vice-Chair. The Campaign for Wool 2009–13, Chair. 2013–; mem. Council RCA 1995–2000; Trustee, Victoria and Albert Museum 2013–; Young Journalist of the Year, British Press Awards 1983, Mark Boxer Award for Editorial Excellence 2001, Professional Publrs Asscn Marcus Morris Lifetime Achievement Award 2013. *Publications include:* Tunnel Vision 1982, Around the World in 78 Days 1984, Shooting Stars 1984, The Fashion Conspiracy 1988, How I Met My Wife and Other Stories 1991, Paper Tigers 1993, With Friends Like These 1997, Streetsmart 1999, Godchildren 2002, A Much Married Man 2006, Deadly Sins 2009, The Adventuress 2012. *Address:* Condé Nast, Vogue House, Hanover Square, London, W1S 1JU (office); 29 Royal Avenue, London, SW3 4QE (home); Wolverton Hall, nr Pershore, Worcs., WR10 2AU, England (home). *Telephone:* (20) 7499-9080 (office). *Website:* www.condenast.co.uk (office).

COLES, Sir (Arthur) John, MA, GCMG; British diplomatist (retd); b. 13 Nov. 1937; s. of Arthur S. Coles and Doris G. Coles; m. Anne M. S. Graham 1965; two s. one d.; ed Magdalen Coll. School, Brackley and Magdalen Coll., Oxford; joined HM Diplomatic Service 1960; Middle Eastern Centre for Arabic Studies, Lebanon 1960–62; Third Sec., Embassy in Khartoum 1962–64; Asst Political Agent, Trucial States (Dubai) 1968–71; Head of Chancery, Cairo 1975–77; Counsellor, Perm. Mission to EEC 1977–80, Head of S Asian Dept, FCO 1980–81, Pvt. Sec. to Prime Minister 1981–84, Amb. to Jordan 1984–88, High Commr to Australia 1988–91, Deputy Under-Sec. of State, FCO 1991–94, Perm. Under-Sec. of State and Head of HM Diplomatic Service 1994–97; Dir B.G. PLC 1998–2009; Visiting Fellow, All Souls Coll. Oxford 1998–99; Trustee, Imperial War Museum 1999–2004; Chair. Sight Savers International 2001–07. *Publications include:* British Influence and the Euro 1999, Making Foreign Policy: A Certain Idea of Britain 2000, Blindness and the Visionary: The Life and Work of John Wilson 2006. *Leisure interests:* walking, cricket, bird-watching, reading, music. *Address:* Kelham, Dock Lane, Beaulieu, SO42 7YH, England.

COLES, John Morton, MA, PhD, ScD, FBA, FSA, FRSA, FRIA; British/Canadian archaeologist and academic; b. 25 March 1930, Canada; s. of John L. Coles and Alice M. Brown; m. 1st Mona Shiach 1958 (divorced 1985); two s. two d.; m. 2nd Bryony Orme 1985; ed Univ. of Toronto, Canada, Univs of Edinburgh and Cambridge, UK; Carnegie Scholar 1959–60; Research Fellow, Univ. of Edinburgh 1959–60; Univ. Lecturer and Reader, Univ. of Cambridge 1960–80, Prof. of European Prehistory 1980–86; Visiting Prof., Centre for Maritime Archaeology, Nat. Museum of Denmark 1994; Pres. The Prehistoric Soc. 1978–82; mem. Academia Europaea 1989–, Royal Comm. on Ancient and Historical Monuments of Scotland 1992–2002, Discovery Programme Ireland 2001–05; Corresp. mem. Deutsches Archaeologisches Institut 1979; Fellow, Fitzwilliam Coll. Cambridge 1963–; British Acad. Fellow, Royal Swedish Acad. of Letters, History and Antiquities 1990, 1998, 2002; Visiting Fellow, Japan Asscn for the Promotion of Science 1994–95; Fellow, Royal Irish Acad.; Hon. Prof., Univ. of Exeter 1993–2003, Univ. of Hull 1996–99, Hon. FSA, Scotland 2000, Hon. mem. Inst. of Field Archaeologists 1991; Dr hc (Uppsala) 1997; Chalmers-Jervise Prize 1960, Rhind Lecturer (with B. Coles), Soc. of Antiquaries of Scotland 1994–95, Grahame Clark Medal, British Acad. 1995, ICI Medal (jtly), British Archaeological Awards 1998, Europa Prize for Prehistory 2000, Gold Medal, Soc. of Antiquaries of London 2002, European Archaeological Heritage Prize 2006, Gold Medal, Royal Swedish Acad. of Letters, History and Antiquities 2009. *Publications include:* The Archaeology of Early Man (with E. Higgs) 1969, Field Archaeology in Britain 1972, The Bronze Age in Europe (with A. Harding) 1979, Experimental Archaeology 1979, Prehistory of the Somerset Levels (with B. Orme) 1980, The Archaeology of Wetlands 1984, Sweet Track to Glastonbury (with B. Coles) 1986, People of the Wetlands (with B. Coles) 1989, From the Waters of Oblivion 1991, Arthur Bulleid and the Glastonbury Lake Village 1892–1992 (with A. Goodall and S. Minnitt) 1992, Fenland Survey (with D. Hall) 1994, Rock Carvings of Uppland 1995, Industrious and Fairly Civilised: The Glastonbury Lake Village (with S. Minnitt) 1995, Enlarging the Past (with B. Coles) 1996, Lake Villages of Somerset (with S. Minnitt) 1996, Changing Landscapes: The Ancient Fenland (with D. Hall) 1998, Patterns in a Rocky Land: Rock Carvings in South-West Uppland, Sweden 2000, Shadows of a Northern Past: Rock Carvings of Bohuslän and Østfold 2005; numerous papers on European prehistory, field archaeology, experimental archaeology, wetland archaeology. *Leisure interests:* music, travel, wetlands. *E-mail:* johnmcoles85@gmail.com (home).

COLES, Robert Martin, AB, LHD, MD; American child psychiatrist, writer and academic; *Professor Emeritus of Psychiatry and Medical Humanities, Department of Psychiatry, Harvard Medical School;* b. 12 Oct. 1929, Boston, Mass.; s. of Philip W. Coles and Sandra Coles (née Young); m. Jane Hallowell 1960; three s.; ed Harvard Coll. and Columbia Univ.; Intern, Univ. of Chicago clinics 1954–55; Resident in Psychiatry, Mass. Gen. Hosp., Boston 1955–56, McLean Hosp., Belmont 1956–57; Resident in Child Psychiatry, Judge Baker Guidance Center, Children's Hosp., Roxbury, Mass. 1957–58, Fellow 1960–61; mem. psychiatric staff, Mass. Gen. Hosp. 1960–62, Clinical Asst in Psychiatry, Harvard Univ. Medical School 1960–62, apptd Research Psychiatrist in Health Services, Harvard Univ. 1963, Lecturer in Gen. Educ. 1966–, Prof. of Psychiatry and Medical Humanities, Harvard Univ. Medical School 1977, now Prof. Emer.; mem. American Psychiatric Asscn; Fellow, American Acad. of Arts and Sciences; Hon. DrSci (North Carolina) 1979; MacArthur Award 1981, Sara Josepha Hale Award 1986, Presidential Medal of Freedom 1998, National Humanities Medal 2001. *Publications include:* William Carlos Williams: The Knack of Survival in America 1975, Walker Percy: An American Search 1979, Harvard Diary 1988, Times of Surrender: Selected Essays 1989, The Moral Intelligence of Children 1997, The Spiritual Life of Children, Bruce Springsteen's America: The People Listening, a Poet Singing 2004, Minding the Store: Great Writing About Business from Tolstoy to Now (co-ed) 2008, Handing One Another Along: Literature and Social Reflection 2010; Children of Crisis series (Anisfield-Wolf Book Award 1968, Pulitzer Prize for General Non-Fiction for vols II and III 1973); numerous articles in professional journals. *Leisure interests:* tennis, bicycle riding, skiing. *Address:* 81 Carr Road, Concord, MA 01742, USA (home). *Telephone:* (617) 591-9389 (office); (617) 369-6498 (home). *E-mail:* Robert_Coles@hms.harvard.edu.

COLES, Sadie; British gallery owner; b. Feb. 1963; m. Juergen Teller 2003; one c.; ed Middlesex Univ. London; first worked as gallery dir for Anthony d'Offay; opened own gallery, Sadie Coles HQ, with paintings by John Currin and an installation by Sarah Lucas (one of the original Young British Artists) 1997, artists represented include Carl Andre, Darren Bader, Matthew Barney, Dirk Bell, Avner Ben Gal, Frank Benson, John Bock, Don Brown, Spartacus Chetwynd, Steven Claydon, William N. Copley, John Currin, Sam Durant, Shannon Ebner, Angus Fairhurst, Urs Fischer, Florian Hecker, Georg Herold, Jonathan Horowitz, David Korty, Gabriel Kuri, Jim Lambie, Hilary Lloyd, Sarah Lucas, Helen Marten, Victoria Morton, J. P. Munro, Laura Owens, Simon Periton, Raymond Pettibon, Elizabeth Peyton, Richard Prince, Ugo Rondinone, Wilhelm Sasnal, Gregor Schneider, Daniel Sinsel, Andreas Slominski, Christiana Soulou, Rudolf Stingel, Nicola Tyson, Paloma Varga Weisz, T. J. Wilcox, Michele Abeles, Uri Aran and Andrea Zittel. *Films:* as a producer: About Sarah 2014, Parasite 2014. *Address:* Sadie Coles HQ, 62 Kingly Street, London, W1B 5QN, England (office). *Telephone:* (20) 7493-8611 (office). *E-mail:* info@sadiecoles.com (office). *Website:* www.sadiecoles.com (office).

COLFER, Eoin; Irish children's writer; b. 14 May 1965, Wexford; m. Jackie Colfer; two s.; fmr teacher; invited to write new novel in Hitchhiker's Guide to the Galaxy series 2008; Irish Children's Laureate (Laureate na nOg) 2014–16; British Book Awards WH Smith Children's Book of the Year 2001, WH Smith Book Award 2002, German Children's Book Award 2004. *Publications include:* juvenile: Benny and Omar 1998, Benny and Babe 1999, The Wish List 2000, Artemis Fowl 2001, Artemis Fowl: The Arctic Incident 2002, Artemis Fowl: The Eternity Code 2003, The Seventh Dwarf (novella) 2004, The Legend of Spud Murphy 2004, The Supernaturalist 2004, The Artemis Fowl Files 2004, Artemis Fowl: The Opal Deception 2005, Artemis Fowl and the Lost Colony 2006, Half Moon Investigations 2006, Airman 2008, Artemis Fowl and the Atlantis Complex 2010, Artemis Fowl: The Last Guardian 2012; for younger children: Going Potty 1999, Ed's Funny Feet 2000, Ed's Bed 2001; has also written plays; other: And Another Thing: Douglas Adams' Hitchhiker's Guide to the Galaxy: Part Six of Three 2009, Plugged 2011, Doctor Who: A Big Hand For The Doctor 2013. *Address:* 1 Priory Hall, Spawell Road, Wexford, Ireland (office); Brookes Batchellor LLP, 102–108 Clerkenwell Road, London, EC1M 5SA, England. *Website:* www.eoincolfer.com; childrenslaureate.ie.

COLGAN, Michael Anthony, OBE, BA; Irish theatre, film and television producer; b. 17 July 1950, Dublin; s. of James Joseph Colgan and Josephine Patricia Colgan (née Geoghegan); ed Trinity Coll., Dublin; Dir Abbey Theatre, Dublin 1974–78; Co-Man. Irish Theatre Co. 1977–78; Man. Dublin Theatre Festival 1978–80, Artistic Dir 1981–83, mem. Bd of Dirs 1983–; Artistic Dir Gate Theatre, Dublin 1983–2016 (also mem. Bd of Dirs); Exec. Dir Little Bird Films 1986–; Co-founder Blue Angel Film Co. 1999 (producers of The Beckett Film Project with RTÉ and Channel 4 2000 and Celebration by Harold Pinter with Channel 4 2006); Artistic Dir Parma Festival, Italy 1982; Chair. St Patrick's Festival 1996–99; mem. Bd Millennium Festivals Ltd, Laura Pels Foundation, New York 2000–04, Irish Arts Council 1989–94, Governing Authority, Dublin City Univ. 1998–2001; Chevalier des Arts et des Lettres 2007; Hon. LLD (Trinity Coll. Dublin) 2000; Sunday Independent Arts Award 1985, 1987, Nat. Entertainment Award 1996, People of the Year Award 1999, Irish Times Theatre Lifetime Achievement Award 2006. *Plays produced:* Faith Healer (Dublin, New York, Edinburgh), No Man's Land (Dublin, London), I'll Go On (Samuel Beckett), Dublin, Paris, London, New York; Juno and the Paycock (Sean O'Casey), Dublin, New York; Salomé (Oscar Wilde), Dublin, Edin., Charleston, SC; Three Sisters (Anton Chekhov), Dublin and Royal Court Theatre, London; six Beckett Festivals, Dublin, London, New York (all 19 Samuel Beckett stage plays); four Pinter Festivals, Dublin and New York; director: First Love, Faith Healer, Krapp's Last Tape. *World premieres include:* The Birds, Molly Sweeney (Brian Friel), Dublin, London and New York; Port Authority (Conor McPherson); Afterplay (Brian Friel); See You Next Tuesday (Francis Veber); Shining City (Conor McPherson); The Home Place (Brian Friel). *Film:* Beckett on Film (co-producer) 2000: all 19 of Beckett's plays filmed using internationally known dirs and actors (Best Drama Award, South Bank Show 2002, US Peabody Award 2002). *Television includes:* Two Lives (exec. producer) for RTÉ 1986, Troubles (two two-hour films) for LWT 1996. *Leisure interests:* Schubert, Beckett, New York City, middle distance running, chamber music.

MONCADA COLINDRES, Denis; Nicaraguan government official, diplomatist and politician; *Minister of Foreign Affairs;* b. 28 Nov. 1948, Murra, Nueva Segovia; s. Jorge Adan Moncada Irías and Emma Esperanza Colindres Barahona; m. María Delia Guadamuz Núñez; four c.; ed Universidad Autónoma De Barcelona, Unan; Head Political and Military Regional Section, Sandinista Popular Army (Matagalpa) 1979–81; Substitute Magistrate Supreme Court of Justice 1981–83; Deputy Head Dirección Contrainteligencia Militar 1983; Auditor-Gen. Armed Forces Gen. Command 1983–85; Exec. Asst to Vice-Minister of Defense and Chief of Gen. Staff 1985–87; Military Attaché Embassy of Nicaragua, Mexico 2003–05; Perm. Rep. to OAS 2007–17; Minister of Foreign Affairs 2017–. *Address:* Ministry of Foreign Affairs, Del Antiguo Cine González, 1 c. al sur, sobre Avda Bolívar, Managua, Nicaragua (office). *Telephone:* 2244-8000 (office). *Fax:* 2228-5102 (office). *E-mail:* despacho.ministro@cancilleria.gob.ni (office). *Website:* www.cancilleria.gob.ni (office).

ÇOLLAKU, Bekim, MA; Kosovo political scientist, academic and politician; m. Aferdita Çollaku; two c.; ed Newcastle Univ., UK, Univ. of Ghent, Belgium; Asst Lecturer, Dept of Political Sciences, Prishtina Univ. and Researcher, Kosovar Inst. for Policy Research and Devt (KIPRED) –2007; mem. Partia Demokratike e Kosovës (PDK—Democratic Party of Kosovo); Political Adviser to Prime Minister Bajram Rexhepi 2003–04; Chief of Staff to Prime Minister Hashim Thaçi 2007–14; mem. Kosovo negotiating team in Political Dialogue for Normalization of Relations between Kosovo and Serbia 2011–14; Minister of European Integration 2014–17. *Publications:* Kosovo's Capacity for EU Integration: Don't Let the Grass Grow Under Your Feet!, Ethnic Centralization and the Perils of Confusing Solutions. *Address:* c/o Ministry of European Integration, 10000 Prishtina, Rruga Nënë Terezë, Ndërtesa e Qeverisë, Kati 9, Kosovo. *E-mail:* gresa.statovci@rks-gov.net.

COLLARD, Jean Philippe; French pianist; b. 27 Jan. 1948, Mareuil-sur-Aÿ (Marne); s. of Michel Collard and Monique Collard (née Philipponnat); m. 2nd Ariane de Brion; three s. (two from previous m.) one d.; ed Conservatoire Nat. de Musique de Paris; has appeared as soloist with numerous orchestras, including Zürich Tonhalle, Cleveland Orchestra, Philadelphia Orchestra, Minnesota Orchestra, Orchestre de Paris, Orchestre National de Lyon, London Philharmonia Orchestra, Orchestra of St. Luke's, New York Philharmonic Orchestra, BBC Philharmonic Orchestra, Royal Philharmonic Orchestra, Los Angeles Philharmonic Orchestra, Royal Liverpool Philharmonic Orchestra, BBC Scottish Symphony Orchestra, San Francisco Symphony Orchestra, London Symphony Orchestra, Vienna Symphony Orchestra, Pittsburgh Symphony Orchestra, Detroit Symphony Orchestra, Atlanta Symphony Orchestra, Indianapolis Symphony Orchestra, Boston Symphony Orchestra, NHK Symphony Orchestra; has collaborated with numerous conductors, including Semyon Bychkov, Marek Janowski, Eugen Jochum, Seiji Ozawa, André Previn, Simon Rattle, Charles Dutoit; Chevalier, Ordre des Arts et des Lettres, Chevalier, Ordre nat. du Mérite, Chevalier Légion d'honneur 2003. *Recordings include:* music by Bach, Brahms,

Debussy, Fauré, Franck, Rachmaninov, Ravel, Saint-Saëns, Schubert, Chopin, Mozart. *Leisure interests:* windsurfing, tennis. *Address:* c/o Angela Sulivan, Sulivan Sweetland Artists Management, 1 Hillgate Place, Balham Hill, London, SW12 9ER, England (office). *Telephone:* (20) 8772-3470 (office). *E-mail:* as@sulivansweetland.co.uk (office); pianojpc@aol.com (home). *Website:* www.jeanphilippecollard.com.

COLLENETTE, Hon. David Michael, PC, BA (Hons), MA; Canadian academic, business adviser and fmr politician; *Senior Counsel, Hill & Knowlton;* b. 24 June 1946, London; s. of David H. Collenette and Sarah M. Collenette; m. Penny Collenette 1975; one s.; ed Glendon Coll., York Univ.; fmrly worked in life insurance, plastics and exec. recruitment; fmr Exec. Vice-Pres. Mandrake Man. Consultants; elected to House of Commons 1974, 1980, 1993, 1997, 2000, retd 2004; Parl. Sec. to Postmaster-Gen. 1978–79, to Pres. of Privy Council 1980–81; Minister of State (Multiculturalism) 1983–84; Minister of Nat. Defence and Minister of Veterans Affairs 1993–96, of Transport 1997–2003; mem. Liberal Party; Minister responsible for Crown Corpns 2002–03; Chancellor Royal Mil. Coll. of Canada 1993–96; mem. Int. Advisory Council, Inst. of Int. Studies, Stanford Univ. 1999–2005; Distinguished Fellow, Dept of Political Science, Glendon Coll., York Univ. from 2004, now mem. Advisory Cttee; currently Sr Counsel, Hill & Knowlton (consultancy), Canada; Sr Advisor, Intergraph Corpn; Head of Ottawa Transportation Task Force 2007; Fellow and Chair. Chartered Inst. of Logistics and Transport (North America), Vice-Pres. CILT International; mem. Bd of Dirs, Harbourfront Corpn; mem. Advisory Bd, Parsons Brinkerhoff; Queen's Silver Jubilee Medal 1977, Canada 125 Medal 1992, Queen's Golden Jubilee Medal 2003. *Leisure interests:* swimming, weight lifting, classical music, theatre. *Address:* Hill & Knowlton Strategies, Suite 1100, 55 Metcalfe Street, Ottawa, ON K1P 6L5, Canada (office). *Telephone:* (613) 238-4371 (office). *Fax:* (613) 238-8642 (office). *E-mail:* david.collenette@hkstrategies.ca (office); david.collenette@rogers.com (office); dcollenette@glendon.yorku.ca (office). *Website:* hkstrategies.ca/expert/hon-david-collenette (office); www.glendon.yorku.ca/publicaffairs (office); www.davidcollenette.com.

COLLETTE, Toni; Australian actress; b. 1 Dec. 1972, Sydney; m. Dave Galafassi 2003; one d.; ed Nat. Inst. for Dramatic Art, Sydney; jury mem. Cannes Film Festival 2007. *Films include:* Spotswood 1991, Muriel's Wedding 1994, This Marching Girl Thing 1994, Arabian Knight (voice) 1995, Lilian's Story 1995, Cosí 1996, The Pallbearer 1996, Emma 1996, Clockwatchers 1997, The James Gang 1997, Diana & Me 1997, The Boys 1997, Velvet Goldmine 1998, 8½ Women 1999, The Sixth Sense 1999, Shaft 2000, Hotel Splendide 2000, Changing Lanes 2002, Dirty Deeds 2002, About a Boy 2002, The Hours 2003, Japanese Story 2003, Connie and Carla 2004, The Last Shot 2004, In Her Shoes 2005, The Night Listener 2006, Little Miss Sunshine (Screen Actors' Guild Award for Outstanding Performance by a Cast 2007) 2006, Like Minds 2006, The Dead Girl 2006, Evening 2007, Nothing is Private 2007, The Black Balloon 2008, Hey Hey It's Esther Blueburger 2008, Mary and Max (voice) 2009, Foster 2011, Friday Night 2011, Jesus Henry Christ 2012, Mental 2012, Hitchcock 2012, The Way Way Back 2013, Lucky Them 2013, Enough Said 2013, A Long Way Down 2014, Tammy 2014, Glassland 2014, Hector and the Search for Happiness 2014, The Boxtrolls (voice) 2014, Miss You Already 2015, Imperium 2016, xXx: Return of Xander Cage 2017, The Yellow Birds 2017, Madame 2017, Hereditary (also, Exec. Producer) (North Texas Film Critics Assn Award for Best Actress 2018, Georgia Film Critics Assn Award for Best Actress 2018) 2018, Hearts Beat Loud 2018. *Television includes:* Tsunami: The Aftermath 2006, United States of Tara (Emmy Award for Outstanding Lead Actress in a Comedy Series 2009, Golden Globe for Best Performance by an Actress in a Television Series—Comedy or Musical 2010) 2009–, Rake (series) 2012, Hostages (mini-series) 2013–14, Devil's Playground (mini-series) 2014. *Leisure interests:* yoga, mental and spiritual retreats in India, climbing Tibetan Himalayas. *Address:* c/o United Management, Marlborough House, Suite 45, Level 4, 61 Marlborough Street, Surry Hills, NSW 2010, Australia. *Telephone:* (2) 8096-0620. *Fax:* (2) 8096-0622. *E-mail:* agents@unitedmanagement.net.au. *Website:* unitedmanagement.net.au.

COLLEY, Amadou, BSc, MBA; Gambian central banker; *Governor and Chairman, Central Bank of The Gambia;* b. 10 Oct. 1962, Sanchaba Sulay Jobe, Kombo North Dist, West Coast Region; ed Fourah Bay Coll., Univ. of Sierra Leone, Birmingham Business School, UK; Dir, Banking Dept, Cen. Bank of The Gambia –2010, Gov. and Chair. 2010–. *Address:* Office of the Governor, Central Bank of The Gambia, 1–2 Ecowas Avenue, Banjul, The Gambia (office). *Telephone:* 4228103 (office). *Fax:* 4226969 (office). *E-mail:* info@cbg.gm (office). *Website:* www.cbg.gm (office).

COLLEY, Linda Jane, CBE, PhD, FRSL, FBA; British academic, writer and broadcaster; *Shelby M.C. Davis 1958 Professor of History, Princeton University;* b. 13 Sept. 1949, Chester; d. of Roy Colley and Marjorie Colley (née Hughes); m. David Nicholas Cannadine (q.v.) 1982; one d. (deceased); ed Univs of Bristol and Cambridge; Eugenie Strong Research Fellow, Girton Coll., Cambridge 1975–78, Fellow, Newnham Coll., Cambridge 1978–79, Christ's Coll., Cambridge 1979–81; Asst Prof. of History, Yale Univ., USA 1982–85, Assoc. Prof. 1985–90, Prof. of History 1990–92, Richard M. Colgate Prof. of History 1992–98, Dir Lewis Walpole Library 1982–96; Prof., School of History, LSE 1998–2003, Leverhulme Personal Research Prof., European Inst. 1998–2003; Shelby M.C. Davis 1958 Prof. of History, Princeton Univ., USA 2003–; mem. Bd British Library 1999–2003, Princeton University Press 2007–; mem. Advisory Bd Tate Britain 1999–2003, Paul Mellon Centre for British Art 1999–2003, Research Cttee, British Museum 2012–; Visiting Fellowship, Humanities Research Centre, ANU, Canberra 2005; Glaxo-Smith-Kline Sr Fellowship Nat. Humanities Center, North Carolina 2006; Fletcher Jones Distinguished Fellowship, Huntington Library, Calif. 2010; Birkelund Fellowship, Cullman Center for Scholars and Writers, New York Public Library 2013–14; Research Advisory Council, New York Public Library 2016–; Sr Fellow, Swedish Collegium for Advanced Study 2017; Hon. Fellow, Christ's Coll., Cambridge 2005; Dr hc (South Bank, London) 1999, (Essex) 2004, (East Anglia) 2005, (Bristol) 2006, (Hull) 2012; Wolfson Prize 1993, Anstey Lecturer, Univ. of Kent 1994, William Church Memorial Lecturer, Brown Univ. 1994, Distinguished Lecturer in British History, Univ. of Texas 1995, Trevelyan Lecturer, Univ. of Cambridge 1997, Wiles Lecturer, Queen's Univ. Belfast 1997, Prime Minister's Millennium Lecture 2000, Raleigh Lecturer, British Acad. 2002, Nehru Lecturer 2002, Bateson Lecturer, Oxford 2003, Chancellor Dunning Trust Lecturer, Queen's Univ., Ont. 2004, Byrn Lecturer, Vanderbilt Univ. 2005, Annual Lecture in Int. History, LSE 2006, C.P. Snow Lecture, Cambridge 2007, Pres's Lecture, Princeton Univ. 2007, Political Science Quarterly Lecture 2007, Gordon B. Hinkley Lecturer 2010, Univ. of Utah, Bosley-Warnock Lecturer, Univ. of Delaware 2010, Annual ISEHR Lecturer, Delhi 2011, Keyser Lecturer, George Washington Univ. 2011, Margaret Macmillan Memorial Lecturer, Univ. of Toronto 2013, Ralph Miliband Lecturer, London School of Economics, Magna Carta Lecturer, Royal Holloway, London Univ., Robbs Lecturer, Univ. of Auckland 2015, Gomes Lecturer, Emmanuel Coll., Cambridge 2015, Aylmer Lecturer, Univ. of York 2015, John Mackintosh Lecturer 2016, Lowell Humanities Lecturer 2016, Thomas Jefferson Foundation Lecturer, Univ. of Virginia 2016. *Radio:* Acts of Union, Acts of Disunion (BBC Radio 4) 15 talks 2014. *Publications include:* In Defiance of Oligarchy: The Tory Party 1714–60 1982, Namier 1989, Crown Pictorial: Art and the British Monarchy 1990, Britons: Forging the Nation 1707–1837 (Wolfson Prize 1993) 1992, Captives: Britain, Empire and the World 1600–1850 2002, The Ordeal of Elizabeth Marsh: A Woman in World History 2007, Taking Stock of Taking Liberties (catalogue of British Library exhbn) 2008, Acts of Union and Disunion 2013; numerous articles and reviews in UK and American learned journals. *Leisure interests:* travel, looking at art, politics. *Address:* c/o Gill Coleridge, Rogers, Coleridge & White Ltd, 20 Powis Mews, London, W11 1JN, England (office); Department of History, Princeton University, 129 Dickinson Hall, Princeton, NJ 08544-1017, USA (office). *Telephone:* (609) 258-8076 (office). *E-mail:* lcolley@princeton.edu (office). *Website:* www.lindacolley.com.

COLLIER, John P., AB, BE, ME, DE; American biomedical engineer and academic; *Myron Tribus Professor of Engineering Innovation, Thayer School of Engineering, Dartmouth College;* ed Dartmouth Coll. and Thayer School of Eng; currently Myron Tribus Prof. of Eng Innovation, Thayer School of Eng, Dartmouth Coll.; Research Consultant, Canadian Oxygen Ltd, DuPont Inc., DePuy (a Johnson & Johnson co.); mem. Soc. for Biomaterials, Orthopaedic Research Soc., American Acad. of Orthopaedic Surgeons, Hip Soc.; NH Professor of the Year 2010, Gordon Prize, Nat. Acad. of Eng (co-recipient) 2014. *Publications:* more than 30 papers in professional journals on aspects of orthopedic implant design and engineering; three patents. *Address:* Thayer School of Engineering, Dartmouth College, 14 Engineering Drive, Hanover, NH 03755, USA (office). *Telephone:* (603) 646-2355 (office). *Fax:* (603) 646-3856 (office). *E-mail:* john.p.collier@dartmouth.edu (office). *Website:* engineering.dartmouth.edu/people/faculty/john-collier (office); engineering.dartmouth.edu/dbec/people.html (office).

COLLIGNON, Stefan Colin, PhD; German economist and academic; *Professor of Political Economy, Sant'Anna School of Advanced Studies;* b. 11 Dec. 1951, Munich; s. of Klaus Collignon and Rosemarie Collignon; m. Judith Zahler 1984; ed Institut d'Etudes Politiques, Paris, Free Univ. of Berlin, Univ. of Dar es Salaam, Tanzania, Queen Elizabeth House, Oxford, UK, London School of Econs; financial analyst, First Nat. Bank in Dallas, Paris 1975–76; teacher, Lindi Secondary School, Deutscher Entwicklungsdienst (German Volunteer Service), Tanzania 1977–79; Man. Dir and Chair. Dorcas Ltd, London 1981–88; Dir Research and Communication, Asscn for the Monetary Union of Europe, Paris 1989–98; Lecturer, Institut d'Etudes Politiques, Paris 1990–95, Free Univ. of Berlin 1997–2000; Prof., Collège d'Europe, Bruges 1998–2005; Centennial Prof. of European Political Economy, LSE 2001–05, Visiting Prof. 2013–14; Faculty Political Sciences, IMT, Lucca 2007–10; Visiting Prof., Institut d'Etudes Politiques, Lille 2005–, Harvard Univ. 2005–07 (also Assoc., Minda de Gunzburg Center for European Studies), Univ. of Hamburg 2007–, Beijing Normal Univ. 2010–; Prof. of Political Economy, Sant'Anna School of Advanced Studies, Pisa 2007–, Founder Euro-Asia Forum; Int. Chief Economist, Centro Europa Ricerche, Rome 2007–; Pres. Asscn France-Birmanie 1990–; mem. Bd of Dirs Glunz AG 1999–2010, Sonae Industria SGPS, Portugal 2003–05. *Publications:* Europe's Monetary Future (Vol. I) 1994, The Monetary Economics of Europe: Causes of the EMS Crisis (Vol. II) 1994, European Monetary Policy (ed.) 1997, Exchange Rate Policies in Emerging Asian Countries 1999, Monetary Stability in Europe 2002, Private Sector Involvement in the Euro 2003, Vive la République européenne (The European Republic) (Prix du meilleur livre politique 2004) 2003, Bundesrepublik Europa? 2007, Viva la Repubblica europea! 2007, Pour la République européenne (co-author) 2008, Rebalancing the Global Economy. Four Perspectives on the Future of the International Monetary System (co-author) 2010, Macroeconomic imbalances and comparative advantages in the Euro Area 2012, Competitiveness in the European Economy (co-author) 2014; several book chapters and numerous articles on monetary union. *Address:* 11 rue d'Ormesson, 75004 Paris, France (home); Scuola Superiore Sant'Anna, Piazza Martiri della Libertà, 33, 56127 Pisa, Italy (office). *Telephone:* 1-40-27-95-63 (home); (050) 883241 (office); 6-18-04-26-40 (mobile). *Fax:* 1-40-27-90-45 (home); (050) 883241 (office). *E-mail:* s.collignon@lse.ac.uk (office); stefan.collignon@sssup.it (office). *Website:* www.stefancollignon.eu (home).

COLLIN, Jean-Philippe, MEng; French business executive; *Chief Procurement Officer, Sanofi;* b. 28 May 1956; ed Ecole Supérieure d'Electricité (Supelec); began career with IBM in 1982, served as man. of components procurement centre in USA and Chair. of one of co.'s Global Purchasing Councils, was also in charge of Tech. and Quality Lab.; joined Valeo 1995, Vice-Pres., Purchasing, for Electronics Div., later promoted to Vice-Pres. Purchasing Valeo Group; Sr Vice-Pres., Sourcing, Thomson 1999–2002, put in charge of spring cost reduction programme 2002, later served as Sr Vice-Pres., Integrated Circuits, Thomson Optical Systems, mem. Thomson Exec. Cttee; Vice-Pres., Purchasing, for PSA Peugeot Citroën, as part of Group's Platforms, Eng and Purchasing Dept 2004–07, reported directly to Chair. and Pres. PSA Peugeot Citroën Group as mem. Extended Exec. Cttee 2007, mem. PSA Peugeot Citroën Man. Bd and Sr Exec. Vice-Pres. Automobiles Peugeot 2007–09; Chief Procurement Officer, Sanofi 2010–. *Address:* Sanofi, 54 rue La Boétie, 75008 Paris, France (office). *Telephone:* 1-53-77-40-00 (office). *E-mail:* info@sanofi.com (office). *Website:* suppliers.sanofi.com/web (office); www.sanofi.com (office).

COLLINGWOOD, Paul David, MBE; British professional cricketer; b. 26 May 1976, Shotley Bridge, Co. Durham, England; s. of David Collingwood and Janet Collingwood; m. Vicki Collingwood; two d.; ed Blackfyne Comprehensive School (now Consett Community Sports Coll.); all-rounder; right-handed batsman; right-arm medium pace bowler; plays for Durham 1995– (Capt./Ass. Coach 2014–, won LV County Championship 2013, inaugural Royal London One-Day Cup 2014), England 2001–11 (ODI (One-Day Int.) Capt. 2007–08, T20I Capt. 2007–11), Delhi Daredevils 2009–10, Rajasthan Royals 2011–12, Perth Scorchers 2011; First-class debut: against Northants., Riverside, Durham 1996; Test debut: Sri Lanka v England, Galle 2–6 Dec. 2003; ODI debut: England v Pakistan, Birmingham 7 June 2001; T20I debut: England v Australia, Southampton 13 June 2005; has played in 68 Tests, scored 4,259 runs (ten centuries, 20 half-centuries), average 40.56, highest score 206, took 17 wickets, best bowling (innings) 3/23, (match) 3/35; ODIs: 197 matches, scored 5,092 runs, average 35.36, highest score 120 not out, took 111 wickets, average 38.68, best bowling 6/31; First-class: 266 matches, 14,912 runs, average 36.01, highest score 206, took 154 wickets, average 38.59, best bowling 5/52; played for Richmond Cricket Club in Melbourne Premier League 2000–01; 1,000+ Test runs in a calendar year 2006; only third English batsman to score a double century in Australia 2007; first Durham player to score a Test century for England and first to hit one at Riverside Ground 2007; played in three winning Ashes Test series 2005, 2009, 2010–11; most capped ODI cricketer for England; captained England Twenty20 team to World Twenty20 championship 2010; announced retirement from Test cricket Jan. 2011; played for Rest of the World side in Bicentenary Celebration match at Lord's July 2014; associated with England and Scotland cricket teams as coach and supporting staff, including as mem. Scotland's coaching staff for Cricket World Cup 2015; named as Limited Overs Consultant for England Sept. 2015; writes a fortnightly column for BBC; voted Player of the Year by the Durham mems 2000, Jack Ryder Medal for Best Player in Melbourne Premier League (co-recipient) 2001, Wisden Cricketer of the Year (co-recipient) 2007. *Leisure interests:* playing golf, going to the gym, Sunderland Asscn Football Club. *Address:* c/o Durham County Cricket Club, County Ground, Riverside, Chester-le-Street, DH3 3QR, County Durham, England. *Telephone:* (191) 387-1717. *Fax:* (191) 387-1616. *E-mail:* reception@durhamccc.co.uk. *Website:* www.durhamccc.org.uk.

COLLINS, Sir Alan Stanley, Kt, KCVO, CMG; British diplomatist (retd); m. Ann Collins; two s. one d.; joined FCO 1981, Officer, Western European Dept 1981–83, Desk Officer, Middle East Dept 1983–86, Deputy Head of Mission, Addis Ababa 1986–90, Deputy Head of Mission, Manila 1990–93, Head of Aviation and Maritime Dept, FCO 1993–95, Dir-Gen. British Trade and Cultural Office, Taipei 1995–98, Amb. to the Philippines 1998–2002, on loan to Shell Int. (Vice-Pres. for Int. Relations) 2002, High Commr to Singapore 2003–07, Consul-Gen. in New York, USA 2007–11; Man. Dir Olympic Legacy, UK Trade & Investment 2011–12; Partner, AFEX 2014–; mem. Bd of Dirs JP Morgan American Investment Trust PLC 2012–, Prudential Assurance Co. Singapore 2012–, ICICI Bank UK PLC 2012–, Prudential General Insurance Hong Kong Ltd 2014–, Amlin plc 2011–14; Chair. Advisory Bd, Vitae VR 2015–; Advisor, Powertec Energy Ltd 2011–, National Strategies, LLC 2013–, Etape Suisse 2013–, Ensygnia 2014–; mem. Advisory Bd London Philharmonic Orchestra 2013–.

COLLINS, Billy, AB, PhD; American poet and academic; b. 22 March 1941, New York; m. Diane Collins 1979; ed Holy Cross Coll., Univ. of California, Riverside; Prof. of English, Lehman Coll., CUNY 1969–2001, Distinguished Prof. 2001; Sr Distinguished Fellow, Winter Park Inst., Rollins Coll., mem. Faculty, MFA Program, Stony Brook Southampton; Visiting Writer, Poets House, NI 1993–96, Lenoir-Rhyne Coll. 1994, Ohio State Univ. 1998; Resident Poet, Burren Coll. of Art, Ireland 1996, Sarah Lawrence Coll. 1998–2000; Adjunct Prof., Columbia Univ. 2000–01; conducts summer poetry workshops at Univ. Coll. Galway, Ireland; US Library of Congress's Poet Laureate Consultant in Poetry 2001, US Poet Laureate 2001–03; Poet Laureate of New York State 2004–06; currently Sr Distinguished Fellow Winter Part Inst., Rollins Coll.; mem. American Acad. of Arts and Letters 2016; Fellow, New York Foundation for the Arts, Nat. Endowment for the Arts, Guggenheim Foundation; NEA Fellowship 1993; Guggenheim Fellowship 1995; New York Foundation for the Arts Poetry Fellowship 1986, Nat. Endowment for the Arts Creative Writing Fellowship 1988, Nat. Poetry Series Competition Winner 1990, Bess Hokin Prize 1991, Literary Lion, New York Public Library 1992, Frederick Bock Prize 1992, Guggenheim Fellowship 1993, Levinson Prize 1995, Paterson Poetry Prize 1999, J. Howard and Barbara M. J. Wood Prize 1999, Pushcart Prize 2002, Mark Twain Prize for Humor in Poetry, Poetry Foundation 2004, Donald Hall-Jane Kenyon Prize in American Poetry 2013, Norman Mailer Prize for Poetry 2014, Peggy V. Helmerich Distinguished Author Award 2016. *Recording:* The Best Cigarette 1997. *Publications include:* Pokerface 1977, Video Poems 1980, The Apple that Astonished Paris 1988, Questions About Angels 1991, The Art of Drowning 1995, Picnic, Lightning 1998, Taking Off Emily Dickinson's Clothes 2000, Sailing Alone Around the Room: New and Selected Poems 2001, Nine Horses 2002, The Trouble with Poetry 2005, She Was Just Seventeen 2006, Ballistics 2008, Horoscopes for the Dead 2012, Aimless Love 2013, Voyage 2014, The Rain In Portugal 2016; editor: Poetry 180: A Turning Back to Poetry, 180 More: Extraordinary Poems for Everyday Life; poems in many anthologies, including The Best American Poetry 1992, 1993, 1997 and periodicals, including Poetry, American Poetry, Review, American Scholar, Harper's, Paris Review and The New Yorker. *Address:* Steven Barclay Agency, 12 Western Avenue, Petaluma, CA 94952, USA (office); Winter Park Institute, Rollins College, 1000 Holt Avenue 2770, Winter Park, FL 32789 (office); 185 Route 202, Somers, NY 10589, USA (home). *Website:* www.rollins.edu/rollins-winter-park-institute/about/billy-collins.html (office); www.facebook.com/BillyCollinsPoetry; www.bigsnap.com.

COLLINS, Christopher Douglas, FCA; British business executive; b. 19 Jan. 1940, Welwyn, Herts.; s. of Lt-Cdr Douglas Raymond Collins and Una Patricia Collins (née Blackhouse); m. Susan Lumb Anne 1976; one s. one d.; ed Eton Coll.; articled clerk, Peat Marwick Mitchell 1958–64; Man. Dir Goya Ltd 1968–75, Dir 1975–80; amateur steeplechase jockey 1965–75; rep. of GB in three-day equestrian events 1974–80; Steward, Jockey Club 1980–81; mem. Horse Race Betting Levy Board 1982–84; Chair. Aintree Racecourse Ltd 1983–88, Nat. Stud 1986–88; joined Hanson PLC 1989, Dir 1991, Vice-Chair. 1995, Deputy Chair. 1997, Chair. 1998–2005; Chair. Forth Ports PLC 2000–, Racecourse Holdings Trust 2005–; Dir Old Mutual PLC 1999–2005, Chair. 2005–09; Dir The Go-Ahead Group PLC 1999–, Alfred McAlpine PLC 2000–. *Leisure interests:* riding, skiing. *Address:* c/o Old Mutual plc, 5th Floor, Old Mutual Place, 2 Lambeth Hill, London, EC4V 4GG, England. *Telephone:* (20) 7002-7204. *E-mail:* matthew.gregorowski@omg.co.uk. *Website:* www.oldmutual.com.

COLLINS, Col (retd) Eileen Marie; American pilot and astronaut (retd) and air force officer (retd); b. 19 Nov. 1956, Elmira, New York; m. Pat Youngs 1987; one s. one d.; ed Elmira Free Acad., Corning Community Coll., Syracuse Univ., Stanford Univ., Webster Univ., Air Force Inst. of Tech.; trained as USAF pilot, Vance Air Force Base, Okla 1979–82; C-141 Aircraft Commdr and Instructor Pilot, Travis Air Force Base, Calif. 1983–85; Asst Prof. of Math. and T-41 Instructor Pilot, USAF Acad., Colo 1986–89; attended Air Force Test Pilot School, Edwards Air Force Base, Calif. 1990; selected by NASA to become astronaut 1991, served in various roles including assignment to Orbiter eng support, mem. support team responsible for Orbiter prelaunch checkout, final launch configuration, crew ingress/egress, landing/recovery, worked in NASA Mission Control as spacecraft communicator (CAPCOM), Astronaut Office Spacecraft Systems Br. Chief, Chief Information Officer, Shuttle Br. Chief, Astronaut Safety Br. Chief, pilot on STS-63 mission 1995 (first woman to pilot space shuttle), STS-84 mission 1997, Commdr STS-93 mission 1999 (first woman to command space shuttle mission), Commdr STS-114 2005; retd from USAF 2005; mem. NASA Advisory Council 2006–; mem. Air Force Asscn, Order of Dedalians, Women Mil. Aviators, US Space Foundation, American Inst. of Aeronautics and Astronautics, Ninety-Nines; Hon. DSc (Univ. Coll. Dublin) 2006; Jackie Robinson Empire State Freedom Medal 1999, Soc. of Women Engineers (SWE) Resnik Challenger Medal 2003; Defense Superior Service Medal, Distinguished Flying Cross, Defense Meritorious Service Medal, Air Force Meritorious Service Medal with one oak leaf cluster, Air Force Commendation Medal with one oak leaf cluster, Armed Forces Expeditionary Medal for Service in Grenada (Operation Urgent Fury) 1983, NASA Outstanding Leadership Medal, NASA Space Flight Medals, Women in Space Science Award, Adler Planetarium 2006; Howard Hughes Memorial Award 2006; elected mem. Aviation Hall of Fame 2009; French Legion of Honor. *Leisure Interests:* running, golf, hiking, camping, reading, photography, astronomy. *Address:* c/o Astronaut Office, Mail Code CB, 2101 NASA Road 1, Houston, TX 77058, USA.

COLLINS, Francis Sellers, BS, MD, PhD; American physician, research scientist and institute director; *Director, National Institutes of Health;* b. 14 April 1950, Staunton, Va; m. 1st Mary Lynn Harman; two c.; m. 2nd Diane Baker; ed Univ. of Virginia, Yale Univ., Univ. of North Carolina; residency in internal medicine, Univ. of N Carolina; Fellowship in Human Genetics, Yale Univ.; Asst Prof. of Internal Medicine and Human Genetics, Univ. of Michigan Medical School 1984–88, Asst Investigator, Howard Hughes Medical Inst., Ann Arbor 1987–88, Chief, Div. of Medical Genetics, Dept of Internal Medicine, Univ. of Michigan 1987–91, Assoc. Prof. of Internal Medicine and Human Genetics 1988–91, Assoc. Investigator, Howard Hughes Medical Inst., Ann Arbor 1988–91, Prof. of Internal Medicine and Human Genetics, Univ. of Michigan 1991–93, Investigator, Howard Hughes Medical Inst., Ann Arbor 1991–93, Prof. of Internal Medicine and Human Genetics, Univ. of Michigan 1993–2003; Dir Nat. Human Genome Research Inst., NIH, Bethesda, Md 1993–2008, also Sr Investigator, Genome Tech. Br., Dir NIH 2009–; mem. Inst. of Medicine, NAS, AAAS, American Soc. of Human Genetics, American Soc. for Microbiology, American Soc. for Clinical Investigation, Human Genome Org., Asscn of American Physicians, American Medical Asscn, American Acad. of Arts and Sciences, Molecular Medicine Soc., American Coll. of Medical Genetics; Dr hc (Emory Univ.) 1990, (Yale Univ.) 1992, (Mount Sinai School of Medicine) 1993, (Univ. of North Carolina) 1994, (George Washington Univ.) 1996, (Univ. of Pennsylvania) 1998, (Brown Univ.) 2000, (Baylor Coll. of Medicine) 2004, (Univ. of Miami School of Medicine) 2007; numerous awards, including Paul di Sant'Agnese Award, Cystic Fibrosis Foundation 1989, Gairdner Foundation Int. Award for work on Cystic Fibrosis (jtly) 1990, Nat. Medical Research Award, Nat. Health Council 1991, Richard and Hinda Rosenthal Award, American Coll. of Physicians 1993, Sarstedt Prize for Scientific Research 1993, Jean-Pierre Lecocq Prize 1994, Susan G. Komen Breast Cancer Foundation Nat. Award for Scientific Distinction 1995, Computerworld Smithsonian Institution Award 1999, Arthur S. Flemming Award, George Washington Univ. 1999, Scientist of the Year, Nat. Disease Research Interchange 2000, Prince of Asturias Award for Technical and Scientific Research 2001, Scientific Achievement Medal, House of Delegates, American Medical Asscn 2001, Lifetime Achievement Award, Virginia Biotechnology Asscn 2002, American Coll. of Physicians-American Soc. of Internal Medicine Award 2003, Albert Einstein Award for Outstanding Achievements in the Life Sciences, Jerusalem Fund 2004, William Allan Award, American Soc. of Human Genetics 2005, American Soc. for Clinical Investigation Award 2005, Antonie Marfan Award, 2006, ASCO Science of Oncology Award 2006, Presidential Medal of Freedom 2007, Inamori Ethics Prize 2008, Nat. Medal of Science 2008, Trotter Prize 2008, Albany Medical Center Prize 2010, Pro Bono Humanum Award, Galien Foundation 2012. *Achievements include:* developed technique called 'positional cloning,' with research team identified gene for cystic fibrosis 1989, for neurofibromatosis 1990, for Huntington disease 1993, for a familial endocrine cancer syndrome, for type 2 diabetes and gene that causes Hutchinson-Gilford progeria syndrome. *Publications include:* The Language of God: A Scientist Presents Evidence for Belief 2006, The Language of Life: DNA and the Revolution in Personalized Medicine 2010, Belief: Readings on the Reason for Faith 2010, The Language of Science and Faith: Straight Answers to Genuine Questions (with Karl Giberson) 2011. *Leisure interests:* guitarist and vocalist for The Directors (rock band comprising NIH scientists and execs). *Address:* Office of the Director, National Institutes of Health, 9000 Rockville Pike, Bethesda, MD 20892, USA (office). *Telephone:* (301) 496-4000 (office). *E-mail:* NIHinfo@od.nih.gov (office). *Website:* www.nih.gov (office).

COLLINS, Gerard; Irish fmr politician; b. 16 Oct. 1938, Abbeyfeale, Co. Limerick; s. of James J. Collins and Margaret Collins; m. Hilary Tattan; ed Univ. Coll. Dublin; fmr vocational teacher; mem. Dáil 1967–97; Acting Gen. Sec. Fianna Fáil Party 1964–67; Parl. Sec. to Minister for Industry and Commerce and to Minister for the Gaeltacht 1969–70; Minister for Posts and Telegraphs 1970–73; mem. Consultative Ass. of Council of Europe 1973–75; Limerick Co. Council 1974–77; Minister for Justice 1977–81, 1987–89, for Foreign Affairs March–Dec. 1982, 1989–93; Chair. Parl. Cttee on EEC Affairs 1983–87; mem. European Parl. 1994–2004 (Vice-Pres. 1998–99), Leader Fianna Fáil Group, Vice-Pres. Union for Europe Group, Pres. European Parl. Del. to S. Asia and South Asian Asscn for Regional Co-operation (SAARC); Chair. of the EU-South Africa Interparliamentary Del. *Leisure interests:* golf, sea angling. *Address:* The Hill, Abbeyfeale, Co. Limerick, Ireland (home).

COLLINS, James J., AB, DPhil; American biomedical engineer and academic; *Termeer Professor of Medical Engineering & Science, Massachusetts Institute of Technology;* b. 26 June 1965, New York, NY; ed Coll. of the Holy Cross, Univ. of Oxford, UK (Rhodes Scholar); Prof. of Biomedical Eng, Boston Univ., also William F. Warren Distinguished Prof., Univ. Prof. and Co-Dir Center for BioDynamics –2014; currently Termeer Prof. of Medical Eng & Science, MIT, also Prof. of Biological Eng, mem. Harvard-MIT Health Sciences & Tech. Faculty; Chair. Scientific Advisory Bd, Synlogic, Sample6 Technologies, EnBiotix, Joule Unlimited, enEvolv, Indigo, Agilis Biotherapeutics, Aquinnah Pharmaceuticals; Dir Collins Lab; Founding Faculty mem., Wyss Inst. for Biologically Inspired Eng, Harvard Univ.; Visiting Prof., Dept of Systems Biology, Harvard Medical School; Howard Hughes Medical Inst. Investigator; mem. NAS, Nat. Acad. of Eng, Nat. Acad. of Medicine, American Acad. of Arts & Sciences; Charter Fellow Nat. Acad. of Inventors; MacArthur Fellow, Metcalf Cup and Prize, Boston Univ. 2000, NIH Dir's Pioneer Award 2007, Anthony J. Drexel Exceptional Achievement Award, Drexel Univ. 2009, Lagrange-CRT Foundation Prize 2010, World Technology Award in Biotechnology 2011. *Publications:* numerous papers in professional journals on synthetic biology, systems biology and antibiotics. *Address:* Institute for Medical Engineering and Science, Department of Biological Engineering, Massachusetts Institute of Technology, E25-337, 45 Carleton Street, Cambridge, MA 02139, USA (office). *Telephone:* (617) 324-6607 (office). *Fax:* (617) 253-7498 (office). *E-mail:* jimjc@mit.edu (office). *Website:* www.collinslab.mit.edu (office).

COLLINS, Dame Joan Henrietta, DBE, OBE; British actress, author and philanthropist; b. 23 May 1933, London; d. of Joseph William Collins and Elsa Collins (née Bessant); sister of Jackie Collins; m. 1st Maxwell Reed 1954 (divorced 1957); m. 2nd George Anthony Newley 1963 (divorced 1970); one s. one d.; m. 3rd Ronald S. Kass 1972 (divorced 1983); one d.; m. 4th Peter Holm 1985 (divorced 1987); m. 5th Percy Gibson 2002; ed RADA; actress in numerous stage, film, and TV productions, producer and author; Freedom of the City of London 2014; Best TV Actress, Golden Globe 1982, Hollywood Walk of Fame, Career Achievement 1983, Favourite TV Performer, People's Choice 1984, 1986, Millennium Award of Achievement, Golden Camera Film Council 1999, Golden Nymph, Outstanding Female Actor, Monte Carlo TV Festival 2001, Lifetime Achievement Award, San Diego Int. Film Festival 2005, Legend Award, Los Angeles Italia-Film, Fashion and Arts Festival 2008, New York City Int. Film Festival, Best Actress, Fetish 2010, Beverly Hills Film, TV and New Media Festival, Best Actress, Fetish 2010, Cosmetic Exec. Women (UK) Lifetime Achievement Award 2011, Shorts Awards, Visionary Actress, Fetish 2012, Lifetime Achievement Award, Sedona Int. Film Festival 2013. *Theatre includes:* The Last of Mrs Cheyne, London 1979–80, Private Lives London 1990, Broadway 1991, Love Letters (US tour) 2000, Over the Moon, London 2001, Full Circle (UK tour) 2004, Legends (US tour) 2006–07, An Evening with Joan Collins (UK tours, London, New York) 2006–15. *Films include:* I Believe in You 1952, Our Girl Friday 1953, The Good Die Young 1954, Land of the Pharaohs 1955, The Virgin Queen 1955, The Girl in the Red Velvet Swing 1955, The Opposite Sex 1956, Island in the Sun 1957, Sea Wife 1957, The Bravados 1958, Seven Thieves 1960, Road to Hong Kong 1962, Warning Shot 1966, The Executioner 1969, Quest for Love 1971, Revenge 1971, Alfie Darling 1974, The Big Sleep 1978, The Stud 1979, The Bitch 1980, Neck 1983, Georgy Porgy 1983, Nutcracker 1984, Decadence 1994, In the Bleak Midwinter 1995, Hart to Hart 1995, Annie: A Royal Adventure 1995, The Clandestine Marriage 1998, Joseph and the Amazing Technicolor Dreamcoat 1999, The Flintstones – Viva Rock Vegas 2000, These Old Broads 2000, Clandestine Marriage 2001, Ozzie 2001, Ellis in Glamourland 2004, Valentino: The Last Emperor 2009, Fetish 2010, Saving Santa 2012, Molly Moon: The Incredible Hypnotist 2014. *Television includes:* Tales of the Unexpected 1979–80, Dynasty (series) 1981–89, Cartier Affair 1985, Sins 1986, Monte Carlo 1986, Tonight at 8.30 1991, Pacific Palisades (series) 1997, Will and Grace, USA 2000, Guiding Light 2002, Slavery and the Making of America (series) 2005, Hotel Babylon (series) 2006, Footballers' Wives (series) 2006, Agatha Christie's Marple (series) – They Do It with Mirrors 2009, Verbotene Liebe (series) 2010, Rules of Engagement (series) 2010, Happily Divorced (series) 2012–13, Benidorm (series) 2014–15, The Royals (series) 2015. *Publications include:* Past Imperfect 1978, The Joan Collins Beauty Book 1980, Katy, A Fight for Life 1982, Prime Time 1988, Love and Desire and Hate 1990, My Secrets 1994, Too Damn Famous 1995, Second Act 1996, My Friends' Secrets 1999, Star Quality 2002, Joan's Way 2002, Misfortune's Daughters 2004, The Art of Living Well 2007, The World According to Joan 2011, A Passion For Life 2013. *Telephone:* (20) 7792-4600 (office). *Fax:* (20) 7792-1893 (office). *E-mail:* joanathan@roarglobal.com (office); info@petercharlesworth.co.uk (office); percygibson@aol.com. *Website:* www.joancollins.net.

COLLINS, Joseph Jameson, AB, MBA; American communications industry executive; *Chairman, Aegis LLC;* b. 27 July 1944, Troy, New York; s. of Mark Francis Collins and Olive Elizabeth Collins (née Jameson); m. Maura McManmon 1972; one s. three d.; ed Brown Univ., Harvard Business School; several exec. positions with American TV and Communications Corpn (ATC) 1964–84, Chair. and CEO 1988–90; Pres. Home Box Office, Time Inc. 1984–88; Chair. and CEO Time Warner Cable (after merger with ATC) 1990–2001, CEO Time Warner Interactive Video div. 2001–03 (retd); currently Chair. Aegis LLC; mem. Bd of Dirs Comcast Corpn 2004–; Dir Emer. Cable TV Labs Inc.; Distinguished Vanguard Award for Leadership, Nat. Cable and Telecommunications Asscn, President's Award and Grand TAM Award, Cable and Telecommunications Asscn for Marketing. *Address:* Aegis LLC, 1760 Old Meadow Road, Suite 400, McLean, VA 22102, USA (office). *Telephone:* (571) 482-1260 (office). *E-mail:* info@aegisworld.us (office). *Website:* www.aegisworld.com (office).

COLLINS, Judith Anne, LLB, LLM, MTaxS; New Zealand lawyer and politician; b. 24 Feb. 1959, Hamilton; d. of Percy Collins and Jessie Collins; m. David Wong Tung; one s.; ed Matamata Coll., Univs of Canterbury and Auckland; fmr owner and operator of two restaurants; solicitor, Subritzky Tetley-Jones & Way 1981–84, Simpson Grierson Butler White 1984–86; Pnr, Morton Tee Collins & Co. (law firm) 1986–89; Assoc., Peak Rogers (law firm) 1989–90; Prin., Judith Collins & Assocs 1990–2000; mem. Council Auckland Dist Law Soc. 1993–97, Vice-Pres. 1997, Pres. 1998; mem. Bd New Zealand Law Soc. 1996–98, Vice-Pres. 1999; Chair. Casino Control Authority 1999–2002; Special Counsel, Minter Ellison Rudd Watts 2000–02; mem. National Party; MP (National Party) for Clevedon 2002–08, for Papakura 2008–; Minister of Police 2008–11, 2015–16, of Corrections 2008–11, 2015–16, of Veterans' Affairs 2008–11, of Justice 2011–14, for Accident Compensation Corpn (ACC), for Ethnic Affairs 2011–14, of Ethnic Communities 2016–17, of Energy and Resources 2016–17, of Revenue 2016–17; Assoc. mem. Papakura, Royal New Zealand Returned and Services' Asscn Inc.; fmr mem. Rotary International, Zonta International; Hon. mem. Royal New Zealand Naval Asscn (Counties Br.) 2005; Ex-Vietnam Services Asscn Pin 2004. *Leisure interests:* walking, cinema, reading, spending time with family. *Address:* PO Box 72 646, Level 1, 98 Great South Road, Papakura – Roselands Shopping Centre, Auckland, New Zealand. *Telephone:* (9) 299-7426. *Fax:* (9) 299–7428 (office). *E-mail:* office@judithcollins.co.nz (office). *Website:* www.judithcollins.co.nz.

COLLINS, Kim; Saint Kitts and Nevis professional athlete; b. 5 April 1976, Ogee's, Saint Peter Basseterre Parish, Saint Kitts; ed Texas Christian Univ.; sprinter; personal bests: 50m (indoor) 5.75 (Liévin, France Feb. 2009), 60m (indoor) 6.47 seconds (Pedro Cup, Łódź, Poland Feb. 2015), 100m 9.96 seconds (London, UK July 2014) 200m 20.20 seconds (Edmonton, Alberta, Canada, Aug. 2001), 4×100m relay 38.47, Daegu, South Korea Sept. 2011; gold medal, 100m, CAC Championships, Guatemala City 2001 (also 200m), Commonwealth Games, Manchester 2002, World Championships, Paris 2003, CAC Championships, St George's 2003, 4×100m relay, Continental Cup, Marrakech 2014; silver medal, 60m, World Indoor Championships, Birmingham 2003, Valencia 2008, 100m, CAC Championships, Bridgetown 1999 (also 4×100m relay), IAAF World Cup, Madrid 2002, Pan American Games, Guadalajara 2011; bronze medal, 200m, World Championships, Edmonton 2001, 100m, Helsinki 2005, Daegu 2011 (also 4×100m relay), 4×100m relay, CAC Championships, Mayagüez 2011, 4×400m relay, Marrakech 2014; finalist: Olympic Games 100m 2000, 2004, 200m 2008, World Championships 100m 2001; ranked 1st in 2003; flagbearer for Saint Kitts and Nevis, Summer Olympic Games, Sydney 2000, Athens 2004, London 2012; coach Monte Stratton; 25 Aug. declared Kim Collins Day by Govt of Saint Kitts and Nevis in his honour 2010. *Address:* c/o Saint Kitts and Nevis Olympic Association, Olympic House, 18 Taylor's Range, Bosseterre, Saint Kitts and Nevis. *Telephone:* 465-6601. *Fax:* 465-8321. *Website:* sknoc@caribsurf.com; www.sknoc.org.

COLLINS, Michael; American fmr astronaut and fmr museum director; b. 31 Oct. 1930, Rome, Italy; m. Patricia M. Finnegan 1957; one s. two d.; ed US Mil. Acad., West Point and Harvard Univ.; commissioned by USAF, served as experimental flight test officer, AF Flight Test Center, Edwards AF Base, Calif.; selected by NASA as astronaut Oct. 1963; backup pilot for Gemini VII mission 1965; pilot of Gemini X 1966; command pilot, Apollo XI mission for first moon landing July 1969; Asst Sec. for Public Affairs, Dept of State 1970–71; Dir Nat. Air and Space Museum 1971–78, Under-Sec. Smithsonian Inst. 1978–80; Maj.-Gen. USAF Reserve; Vice-Pres. LTV Aerospace and Defense Co. 1980–85; Pres. Michael Collins Assocs (aerospace consulting firm), Washington, DC 1985–; Fellow, Royal Aeronautical Soc., American Inst. of Aeronautics and Astronautics; mem. Int. Acad. of Astronautics, Int. Astronautical Fed.; Exceptional Service Medal (NASA), DSM (NASA), Presidential Medal of Freedom, DCM (USAF), DFC, F.A.I. Gold Space Medal. *Publications:* Carrying the Fire 1974, Flying to the Moon and Other Strange Places 1976, Liftoff 1988, Mission to Mars 1990.

COLLINS, Pauline, OBE; British actress; b. 3 Sept. 1940, Exmouth, Devon; d. of William Henry Collins and Mary Honora Callanan; m. John Alderton; two s. one d.; ed Convent of the Sacred Heart, Hammersmith, Cen. School of Speech and Drama; Dr hc (Liverpool Polytechnic) 1991. *Stage appearances include:* A Gazelle in Park Lane (stage debut, Windsor 1962), Passion Flower Hotel 1965, The Erpingham Camp 1967, The Happy Apple 1967, 1970, The Importance of Being Earnest 1968, The Night I Chased the Women with an Eel 1969, Come as You Are 1970, Judies 1974, Engaged 1975, Confusions 1976, Rattle of a Simple Man 1980, Romantic Comedy 1983, Woman in Mind, Shirley Valentine (Olivier Award for best actress, London, Tony, Drama Desk and Outer Critics' Circle awards, New York) 1988, 1989, Shades 1992. *Films include:* Shirley Valentine (Evening Standard Film Actress of the Year 1989, BAFTA Best Actress Award 1990) 1989, City of Joy 1992, My Mother's Courage 1997, Paradise Road 1997, One Life Stand 2000, Mrs Caldicott's Cabbage War 2002, From Time to Time 2009, You Will Meet a Tall Dark Stranger 2010, Albert Nobbs 2011, Quartet 2012. *Television includes:* Emergency-Ward 10 (series) 1957, Amerika 1966, The Making of Jericho 1966, Happy 1969, The Liver Birds (series) 1969, Kings Cross 1972, Upstairs Downstairs (series) 1971–73, No, Honestly (series) 1974, Wodehouse Playhouse (series) 1975, Thomas and Sarah (series) 1979, Long Distance Information 1979, Little Miss Trouble and Friends (series, voice) 1983, Knockback 1984, Tropical Moon Over Dorking 1985, The Black Tower (mini-series) 1985, Forever Green (series) 1989–92, The Ambassador (series) 1998, Little Grey Rabbit (series) 2000, Man and Boy 2002, Sparkling Cyanide 2003, Bleak House (series) 2005, Doctor Who (series) 2006, What We Did on Our Holiday (film) 2006, Marple: The Pale Horse (film) 2010, Merlin (series) 2010, Mount Pleasant (series) 2011. *Publications include:* Letter to Louise 1992. *Address:* c/o ICM, Oxford House, 76 Oxford Street, London, W1D 1BS, England.

COLLINS, Philip (Phil), LVO; British singer, songwriter, musician (drums) and producer; b. 30 Jan. 1951, Hounslow, London; s. of Greville Collins and June Collins; m. 1st 1976 (divorced); one s. one d.; m. 2nd Jill Tavelman 1984 (divorced 1995); one d.; m. 3rd Orianne Cevey 1999 (divorced); two s.; ed Barbara Speake Stage School; fmr child actor, appearing as Artful Dodger in London production of Oliver Twist; fmr mem. various music groups, including The Real Thing, The Freehold, Hickory, Flaming Youth 1967–70; mem. rock group, Genesis, as drummer 1970–96, as lead singer 1975–96, 2006–; mem. Brand X 1975–; solo artist 1981–; record producer for various artists including John Martyn, Frida, Eric Clapton, Adam Ant, Philip Bailey, The Four Tops, Stephen Bishop; Trustee Prince of Wales Trust 1983–; f. Little Dreams Foundation 2000; Hon. DFA (Fairleigh Dickinson Univ.) 1987; Hon. DMus (Berklee Coll. of Music) 1991; Hon. DHist (McMurry Univ.) 2012, Grammy Awards (seven), Ivor Novello Awards (six), BRIT Awards (four), Variety Club of Great Britain Awards (two), Silver Clef Awards (two), Elvis Awards, Golden Globe Award for Best Original Song (two, for Two Hearts, from film Buster and You'll Be in My Heart, from film Tarzan), Acad. Award (for You'll be in My Heart, from film Tarzan) 1999, American Music Award for Favorite Adult Contemporary Artist 2000, inducted into Songwriters Hall of Fame 2003, Rock and Roll Hall of Fame (with Genesis) 2010, Modern Drummer Hall of Fame 2012. *Films include:* as actor: Calamity the Cow 1967, Buster 1988, Hook 1991, Frauds 1993, Balto (voice) 1995, The Jungle Book 2 (voice) 2003; as composer and performer: Tarzan 1999. *Recordings include:* albums: Nursery Cryme 1971, Foxtrot 1972, Genesis Live 1973, Selling England By The Pound 1973, The Lamb Lies Down On Broadway 1974, A Trick Of The Tail 1976, Seconds Out 1977, Wind And Wuthering 1977, And Then There Were Three 1978, Duke 1980, Abacab 1981, Three Sides Live 1982, Genesis 1983, Invisible Touch 1986, We Can't Dance 1991, The Way We Walk: The Shorts 1992, The Way We Walk: The Longs 1993, Calling All Stations 1997, Turn It On Again 1999, Archive 1967–75 1999, Archive 1976–92 2001; with Brand X: Unorthodox Behaviour, Moroccan Roll 1977, Livestock 1977, Product 1979, Do They Hurt? 1980, Is There Anything About? 1982, Xtrax 1986, The Plot Thins 1992, Brand X Featuring Phil Collins 1996, Live At The Roxy 1996, Missing Period 1997, A History 1976–80 1997, The X-Files 1999; solo: Face Value 1981, Hello, I Must Be Going! 1982, No Jacket Required 1985, 12"ers 1987, ...But Seriously 1989, Serious Hits... Live! 1990, Both Sides 1993, Dance Into The Light 1996, ...Hits! 1998, A Hot Night In Paris 1999, Tarzan 1999, Testify 2002, Love Songs: A Complication Old And New 2004, The Platinum Collection 2004, Going Back 2010. *Publications include:* Genesis: Chapter and Verse (with other band mems) 2007, The Alamo and Beyond: A Collector's Journey 2012, Not Dead Yet: The Autobiography 2016. *E-mail:* info@genesis-music.com. *Website:* www.philcollins.com; www.genesis-music.com.

COLLINS, Sir Rory Edwards, Kt, PhD, FRCP, FMedSci, FFPM; British epidemiologist and academic; *British Heart Foundation Professor of Medicine and Epidemiology and Head of Nuffield Department of Population Health, University of Oxford;* Co-Dir Clinical Trial Service Unit (CTSU), Nuffield Dept of Clinical Medicine, Univ. of Oxford 1985–, British Heart Foundation Prof. of Medicine and Epidemiology 1996–; Prin. Investigator and Chief Exec. UK Biobank prospective study of 500,000 British men and women aged 40–69 2005–, Head of Nuffield Dept of Population Health 2013–; Adjunctive Prof., Tokai Univ.; Hon. Dir China Oxford Centre for Int. Health Research; CTSU awarded a Queen's Anniversary Prize for Higher and Further Educ. 2006, J. Allyn Taylor Int. Prize in Medicine, Robarts Research Inst. 2007. *Publications:* numerous scientific papers in professional journals on the establishment of large-scale epidemiological studies of the causes, prevention and treatment of heart attacks, other vascular disease, and cancer. *Address:* Nuffield Department of Population Health, University of Oxford, Richard Doll Building, Old Road Campus, Oxford, OX3 7LF, England (office). *Telephone:* (1865) 743743 (office); (1865) 743834 (office). *Fax:* (1865) 743985 (office). *E-mail:* rory.collins@ndph.ox.ac.uk (office); secretary@ctsu.ox.ac.uk (office). *Website:* www.ndph.ox.ac.uk/team/rory-collins (office); www.ctsu.ox.ac.uk (office).

COLLINS, Susan Margaret, BA; American politician; *Senator from Maine;* b. 7 Dec. 1952, Caribou, Me; d. of Donald Collins and Patricia Collins; ed St Lawrence Univ.; Prin. Advisor on Business Affairs to US Senator Bill Cohen 1975–78; Staff Dir Senate Sub-cttee on Oversight Govt Man. 1981–87; Commr Maine Dept of Professional and Financial Regulation 1987–92; Dir New England Operations, US Small Business Admin 1992–93; Exec. Dir Center Family Business, Husson Coll., Bangor 1993–96; Senator from Maine 1997–, mem. Cttee on Health, Educ., Labor and Pensions 1997–2003, Cttee on Homeland Security 2003–07 (Chair.), Cttee on Govt Affairs 1997–2003, Armed Services, Cttee on Appropriations; mem., Special Cttee on Ageing (Chair. 2015–), on Intelligence; Chair. Maine Cabinet Council on Health Care Policy; cand. for Gov. of Maine 1994; Republican; Outstanding Alumni Award, St Lawrence Univ. 1992, named by American Asscn of Port Authorities as Ports Person of the Year, named by Nat. Fed. of Ind. Businesses as Guardian of Small Business, named by American Diabetes Asscn as Legislator of the Year, honours from other groups, including Veterans of Foreign Wars Asscn and Nat. School Bds Asscn. *Address:* 413 Dirksen Senate Office Building, Washington, DC 20510, USA (office). *Telephone:* (202) 224-2523 (office). *Fax:* (202) 224-2693 (office). *Website:* collins.senate.gov (office).

COLLINS, HE Cardinal Thomas Christopher, MA, ThB, SSL, STD; Canadian ecclesiastic and academic; *Archbishop of Toronto;* b. 16 Jan. 1947, Guelph, Ont.; ed Bishop Macdonell High School, St Jerome Coll., Waterloo, Univ. of Western Ontario, St Peter's Seminary, London, Ont., Pontifical Biblical Inst. and Pontifical Gregorian Univ., Rome; ordained deacon, Diocese of Hamilton, Ont. 1972, ordained priest 1973; served as Assoc. Pastor at Holy Rosary Parish, Burlington and at Christ the King Cathedral, as well as teacher and chaplain at Cathedral Boys' High School; Lecturer in English, King's Coll. from 1978; Lecturer in Scripture, St Peter's Seminary 1978–81, Spiritual Dir 1981–85, Assoc. Prof. of Scripture 1985–86, Dean of Theology and Vice-Rector St Peter's Seminary 1992–95, Rector 1995–97; Assoc. Ed. Discover the Bible 1989–92; Coadjutor Bishop of Saint Paul in Alberta May–June 1997, Bishop of Saint Paul in Alberta 1997–99; Coadjutor Archbishop of Edmonton, Alberta Feb.–June 1999, Archbishop of Edmonton 1999–2006, Apostolic Admin. of Saint Paul in Alberta March–Sept. 2001; Archbishop of Toronto, Ont. 2006–; cr. Cardinal (Cardinal-Priest of San Patrizio) 2012; participated in Papal Conclave 2013; mem. Nat. Comm. of Theology, Canadian Conf. of Catholic Bishops 1997, Chair. Nat. Comm. of Theology 1999–2001, mem. Perm. Council 1999–2003, Chair. Nat. Comm. on Christian Unity 2001–03; mem. Organizing Cttee for World Youth Day, Toronto 2002, Congregation for Catholic Education 2012–, Inst. for the Works of Religion 2014–; Pres. Alberta Conf. of Catholic Bishops 1999–2007, Assembly of Catholic Bishop of Ontario 2008–; mem. Pontifical Council for Social Communications 2010–15. *Address:* Office of the Archbishop, Catholic Pastoral Centre, 1155 Yonge Street, Toronto, ON M4T 1W2, Canada (office). *Telephone:* (416) 934-0606 (ext. 609) (office). *Fax:* (416) 934-3452 (office). *E-mail:* archbishop@archtoronto.org (office). *Website:* www.archtoronto.org (office).

COLLINS OF HIGHBURY, Baron (Life Peer), cr. 2011, of Highbury in the London Borough of Islington; **Rt Hon. Ray Edward Harry Collins,** BA; British trade unionist; b. 21 Dec. 1954, Newport, Isle of Wight; ed Univ. of Kent; mem. Labour Party 1970s–, campaigned for party in every Gen. Election since 1970; apptd Cen. Office Man., Transport & Gen. Workers' Union (T&GWU) 1984, redesignated Head of Admin 1990–99, Asst Gen. Sec. T&GWU section of Unite 1999–2008, helped steer T&GWU into merger with Amicus, creating Unite; T&GWU Rep. on Labour Party Nat. Policy Forum; mem. Nat. Constitutional Cttee of Labour Party, Gen. Sec. Labour Party 2008–11; mem. (Labour), House of Lords 2011–, Opposition Whip 2011–, Shadow Spokesperson (Work and Pensions) 2012–13, Shadow Spokesperson (Int. Devt) 2013–, Shadow Spokesperson (Foreign and Commonwealth Affairs) 2015–. *Leisure interests:* swimming, reading, cinema, supporter of Arsenal Football Club. *Address:* House of Lords, Westminster, London, SW1A 0PW, England (office). *Telephone:* (20) 7219-1675 (office). *Fax:* (20) 7219-5979 (office). *E-mail:* collinsr@parliament.uk (office).

COLLIS, Steven H., BCom, BCom (Hons); South African/American chartered accountant and business executive; *Chairman, President and CEO, AmerisourceBergen Corporation;* ed Univ. of the Witwatersrand, Johannesburg; completed articles of clerkship with Price Waterhouse and received Chartered Accountancy licence 1986; fmr mem. Johannesburg Stock Exchange; emigrated to USA; Prin. and Gen. Man. Sterling Medical, Irvine, Calif. –1994; joined AmerisourceBergen Corpn as Gen. Man. of newly formed ASD Specialty Healthcare unit 1994, Exec. Vice-Pres., AmerisourceBergen Corpn and Pres. ABDC (largest subsidiary) –2010, Pres. and COO AmerisourceBergen Corpn 2010–11, mem. Bd of Dirs, Pres. and CEO 2011–, Chair. 2016–. *Address:* AmerisourceBergen Corporation, 1300 Morris Drive, Suite 100, Chesterbrook, PA 19087-5594, USA (office). *Telephone:* (610) 727-7000 (office). *Fax:* (610) 727-3600 (office). *E-mail:* info@amerisourcebergen.com (office). *Website:* www.amerisourcebergen.com (office).

COLLMAN, James Paddock, PhD; American chemist and academic; *George A. and Hilda M. Daubert Professor of Chemistry, Stanford University;* b. 31 Oct. 1932, Beatrice, Neb.; s. of Perry G. Collman and Frances Dorothy Palmer; m. Patricia Tincher 1955; four d.; ed Univs of Nebraska and Illinois; Instructor, Univ. of NC 1958–59, Asst Prof. 1959–62, Assoc. Prof. 1962–66, Prof. of Organic and Inorganic Chem. 1966–67; Prof., Stanford Univ. 1967–, George A. and Hilda M. Daubert Prof. of Chem. 1980–; mem. NAS, American Acad. of Arts and Sciences; Alfred P. Sloan Foundation Fellow 1963–66; Nat. Science Foundation Sr Postdoctoral Fellow 1965–66; Guggenheim Fellow 1977–78, 1985–86; Churchill Fellow (Cambridge) 1977–; Dr. hc (Univ. of Nebraska) 1988, (Univ. de Bourgogne) 1988; American Chemical Soc. (ACS) Award in Inorganic Chem. 1975, Calif. Scientist of the Year Award 1983, Arthur C. Cope Scholar Award (ACS) 1986, Pauling Award 1990, ACS Award for Distinguished Service in the Advancement of Inorganic Chem. 1991, LAS Alumni Achievement Award, Coll. of Liberal Arts and Sciences Univ. of Ill. 1994, Marker Lecturer Medal 1999, Japanese Coordination Chemistry Award 2008, Ronald Breslow Award for Biomimetic Chemistry 2009. *Publications:* Principles and Applications of Organo-transition Metal Chemistry (with Louis S. Hegedus) 1980, 1987, Naturally Dangerous 2001; and 300 scientific papers. *Leisure interest:* fishing. *Address:* Department of Chemistry, Stauffer II, Room 201, Stanford University, Stanford, CA 94305-5080, USA; 794 Tolman Drive, Stanford, CA 94305-5080 USA (home). *Telephone:* (650) 725-0283 (office); (650) 493-0934 (home). *Fax:* (650) 725-0259 (office). *E-mail:* jpc@stanford.edu (office). *Website:* stanford.edu/group/collman (office).

COLLOMB, Bertrand Pierre Charles, PhD; French business executive; *Honorary Chairman, Lafarge;* b. 14 Aug. 1942, Lyon; s. of Charles Collomb and Hélène Traon; m. Marie-Caroline Collomb 1967; two s. one d.; ed Ecole Polytechnique, Paris, Ecole des Mines, Paris and Univ. of Texas, Austin, USA; worked with French Govt, Founder and Man. Centre for Man. Research, Ecole Polytechnique 1972–75; joined Lafarge as Regional Man. 1975, later Pres. and CEO Ciments Lafarge France, CEO Orsan (Biotechnology Co. of the Lafarge Group) 1983, CEO Lafarge Corp. 1987–88, Vice-Chair. and COO Lafarge 1989, Chair. and CEO 1989–2003, Chair. 2003–07, currently Hon. Chair.; mem. Institut de France (Acad. des Sciences, Morales et Politiques); Commdr, Légion d'honneur, Great Officer, Ordre nat. du Mérite; French Manager of the Year (Le Nouvel Economiste) 1997. *Publications include:* Plaidoyer pour l'entreprise 2010, Pour une entreprise humainement responsable 2011, La France dans le monde 2014. *Leisure interests:* horse riding, hunting. *Address:* Lafarge, 61 rue des Belles Feuilles, BP 40, 75782 Paris Cedex 16 (office); 7433 Oakwood Drive, Warrenton, VA 20186, USA (home). *Telephone:* 1-44-34-12-02 (office); (540) 347-0032 (home). *Fax:* 1-44-34-12-07 (office); (540) 347-1134 (home). *E-mail:* bertrand.collomb@lafarge.com (office). *Website:* www.lafarge.com (office).

COLLOMB, Gérard; French public servant and politician; b. 20 June 1947, Chalon-sur-Saône; s. of Marc Collomb and Marcelle Bib; m. 1st Geneviève Bateau 1968 (divorced 1994); two c.; m. 2nd Caroline Rougé 2001; two c.; ed Univ. of Lyons; began career as teacher of literature in various schools including Lycée Jean Perrin, Lyons, Lycée René Cassin, Tarare; Municipal Councillor, Lyons 1977–2017; mem. Nat. Ass. for Rhône (2nd constituency) 1981–88; Regional Councillor, Rhône-Alpes 1992–99; mem. Council, Urban Community of Lyons 1995–2014, Pres. 2001–14; mem. Senate for Rhône 1999–2017; Mayor of Lyons 2001–17; Pres., Lyons metropolitan area 2015–17; Minister of the Interior 2017–18 (resgnd); mem. Parti Socialiste; Officer, Ordre nat. du Québec 2015. *Publication:* Et si la France s'éveillait... 2011. *Address:* c/o Ministry of the Interior, place Beauvau, 75008 Paris, France (office).

COLMAN, Sir Michael Jeremiah, 3rd Bt, cr. 1907; British business executive; b. 7 July 1928, London; s. of Sir Jeremiah Colman, 2nd Bt and Edith Gwendolyn Tritton; m. Judith Jean Wallop (née William-Powlett) 1955; two s. three d.; ed Eton Coll.; Capt. Yorks Yeomanry 1967; Dir Reckitt and Colman PLC 1970–95, Chair. 1986–95; First Church Estates Commr 1993–99; Dir Foreign and Colonial Ventures Advisors Ltd 1988–99; Trade Affairs Bd Chemical Industries Asscn 1978–84, Council 1983–84; Council Mem. Royal Warrant Holders Asscn 1977–, Pres. 1984; mem. Gen. Council and Investment Cttee, King Edward's Hosp. Fund for London 1978–2004; Assoc. of Trinity House, mem. Lighthouse Bd 1985–94, Younger Brother 1994; mem. Bd UK Centre for Econ. and Environmental Devt 1985–99, Chair. 1996–99; mem. of the Court of Skinners' Co. 1985– (Master 1991–92); mem. Council of Scouts Asscn 1985–2000; Assoc. Trustee St Mary's Hosp., London 1988–2000; Archbishop's Cross of St Augustine 1999; Hon. LLD (Hull) 1993. *Leisure interests:* farming, shooting, forestry, golf. *Address:* Malshanger, Basingstoke, Hants., RG23 7EY (home); 40 Chester Square, London, SW1W 9HT, England. *Telephone:* (1256) 781750 (home). *E-mail:* malshanger.farm@farmline.com (office).

COLMAN, Peter Malcolm, AC, PhD, FAA, FRS, FTSE; Australian medical research scientist; *Head, Structural Biology Division, Walter and Eliza Hall*

Institute of Medical Research; b. 3 April 1944, Adelaide, South Australia; s. of Clement Colman and Kathleen Colman; m. Anne Elizabeth Smith 1967; two s.; ed Univ. of Adelaide; Post-Doctoral Fellow, Univ. of Oregon, USA 1969–72, Max Planck Inst., Munich, Germany 1972–75; Queen Elizabeth II Fellow, Univ. of Sydney 1975–77; consultant, Univ. of Utah, USA 1977; Prin. Investigator, Nat. Health and Medical Research Council, Univ. of Sydney 1977–78, Officer, CSIRO 1978–89, Chief Div. of Biomolecular Eng 1989–97, Dir Biomolecular Research Inst. 1991–2000; Professorial Assoc., Univ. of Melbourne 1988–98, Professorial Fellow 1998–2003; Adjunct Prof., La Trobe Univ. 1998–2001; Sr Prin. Research Fellow (NHMRC), Walter and Eliza Hall Inst. of Medical Research 2001–; Dir Biota Holdings Ltd 1985–91; Hon. DSc (Sydney), Hon. DUniv (Adelaide); Royal Soc. Victorian Medal 1986, Lemberg Medallist and Lecturer, Australian Biochemical Soc. 1988, Burnet Medal, Australian Acad. of Sciences 1995, Australia Prize 1996, Mayne-Florey Medal 2004, Victoria Prize 2008. *Achievements include:* co-discoverer of neuraminidase inhibitors as medicines for influenza virus infection. *Publications include:* over 100 scientific articles in professional journals, mainly on structural biology, influenza viruses and apoptosis. *Leisure interest:* music. *Address:* PO Box 321, East Melbourne, Vic. 3002 (home); Walter and Eliza Hall Institute of Medical Research, 1G Royal Parade, Parkville, Vic. 3050, Australia (office). *Website:* www.wehi.edu.au (office).

COLOM CABALLEROS, Álvaro, BEng; Guatemalan industrial engineer, business executive, politician and fmr head of state; b. 15 June 1951, Guatemala City; m. Sandra Torres de Colom 2003 (divorced 2011); ed Univ. de San Carlos; Deputy Minister for the Economy 1991; Founder and Pres. Unidad Nacional de la Esperanza (UNE) from 2001; runner up in primary presidential elections 2003; Pres. of Guatemala 2008–12; Founder and Pres. Grupo Mega; Exec. Dir Dependencia Presidencial de Asistencia Legal y Resolución de Conflictors sobre la Tierra (CONTIERRA); Founder, Partner and Production Man. Roprisma, Intraexsa; Man. Dept Industrial de DINAH SA; Dir Clothing Comm., Chamber of Industry and Commerce 1977–82; Vice-Pres. Asscn of Guatemalan Exporters 1990–; Dir Fundación para el Análisis y Desarollo de Centroamérica (FADES) 1999–; Adviser, Consejo Nacional de Ancianos Mayas (Mayan Council) 1996–; mem. Consultative Bd, AGEXPRONT 1977–82, Dir 1982–90; Founder and Pres. Nat. Comm. for the Clothing Industry 1984; Adviser, Secretaría de la Paz (SEPAZ) 1997; serves as an ordained Mayan minister. *Address:* Unidad Nacional de la Esperanza (UNE), 2A Avenida 5-11, Zona 9, Guatemala City, Guatemala (office). *Telephone:* 232-4685 (office). *E-mail:* ideas@une.org.gt (office). *Website:* www.une.org.gt (office).

COLOMBANI, Jean-Marie; French journalist; b. 7 July 1948, Dakar, Senegal; m. Catherine Sénès 1976; five c.; ed Lycée Hoche, Versailles, Lycée La Pérouse, Nouméa, New Caledonia, Univ. of Paris II-Assas, Univ. of Paris I Panthéon-Sorbonne, Inst. d'Etudes Politiques and Inst. d'Etudes Supérieures de Droit Public; journalist, ORTF, later Office of FR3, Nouméa 1973; Ed. Political Service, Le Monde 1977, Head of Political Service 1983, Ed.-in-Chief 1990, Deputy Editorial Dir 1991; Man. Dir S.A.–Le Monde March–Dec. 1994, Chair. of Bd and Dir of Publs 1994–2007, mem. Bd of Dirs 2007–08; Co-founder online magazine Slate.fr 2009–; Chair. Advisory Council, Midi-Libre Group 2000–; columnist, Direct Matin 2013–. *Publications include:* Contradictions: entretiens avec Anicet Le Pors 1984, L'utopie calédonienne 1985, Portrait du président ou le monarque imaginaire 1985, Le mariage blanc (co-author) 1986, Questions de confiance: entretiens avec Raymond Barre 1987, Les héritiers (co-author), La France sans Mitterrand 1992, La gauche survivra-t-elle aux socialistes? 1994, Le Double Septennat de François Mitterrand, Dernier Inventaire (jtly) 1995, De la France en général et de ses dirigeants en particulier 1996, Le Résident de la République 1998, La Cinquième ou la République des phratries (co-author) 1999, Les infortunes de la Republique 2000, Tous Américains? 2002, France-Amérique: Déliaisons Dangereuses (with Walter Wells) 2004, Au fil du Monde 2007, Un Américain à Paris 2008. *Leisure interest:* cinema. *Address:* 12, rue d' Athènes, 75009, Paris (office); 5 rue Joseph Bara, 75006 Paris, France (home). *Telephone:* 1-79-85-81-14 (office). *E-mail:* infos@slate.fr (office). *Website:* www.slate.fr (office).

COLOMBO, John Robert, CM, BA, DLitt; Canadian editor, author and consultant; b. 24 March 1936, Kitchener, Ont.; m. Ruth F. Brown 1959; two s. one d.; ed Kitchener-Waterloo Collegiate Inst., Waterloo Coll. and Univ. Coll., Univ. of Toronto; editorial asst, University of Toronto Press 1957–59; Asst Ed., The Ryerson Press 1960–63; Instructor, York Univ., Downsview, Ont. 1963–65; Consulting Ed., McClelland & Stewart 1963–70, Ed.-at-Large 1963–; Gen. Ed. The Canadian Global Almanac 1992–2000; Writer-in-Residence, Mohawk Coll., Hamilton, Ont. 1979–80; Consultant, American Man. Asscn/Canadian Man. Centre; Assoc. Northrop Frye Centre, Victoria Coll., Univ. of Toronto; Dir, Colombo & Co.; Order of Cyril and Methodius 1979; Esteemed Kt of Mark Twain 1979; Hon. DLitt (York Univ., Toronto) 1998; Centennial Medal 1967, Harbour Front Literary Prize 1985, Citation, Univ. of Toronto's '300 Graduates of Achievement' 2002, Citation, Univ. Coll.'s '100 Graduates of Influence' 2012. *Television:* presenter: Colombo Quotes (series) (CBC-TV 1978), Unexplained Canada (series), Space Network 2006. *Publications include:* more than 200 books of poetry, prose, reference, science fiction anthologies and translations, including Colombo's Canadian Quotations 1974, Colombo's Canadian References 1976, Colombo's Book of Canada 1978, Canadian Literary Landmarks 1984, 1,001 Questions about Canada 1986, Colombo's New Canadian Quotations 1987, Mysterious Canada 1988, Songs of the Great Land 1989, Mysterious Encounters 1990, The Dictionary of Canadian Quotations 1991, UFOs over Canada 1991, Worlds in Small 1992, The Mystery of the Shaking Tent 1993, Walt Whitman's Canada 1993, Voices of Rama 1994, 1995, Close Encounters of the Canadian Kind 1995, Ghost Stories of Ontario 1995, Haunted Toronto 1996, The New Consciousness 1997, Weird Stories 1999, Ghosts in our Past 2000, 1000 Questions about Canada 2001, The Penguin Book of Canadian Jokes 2002, The Penguin Treasury of Popular Canadian Poems and Songs 2002, The Penguin Book of More Canadian Jokes 2003, O Rare Denis Saurat 2003, True Canadian Ghost Stories 2003, The Midnight Hour 2004, The Denis Saurat Reader 2004, The Monster Book of Canadian Monsters 2004, Early Earth 2006, All the Poems 2006, All the Aphorisms 2006, Autumn in August 2006, Miniatures 2006, The Penguin Dictionary of Popular Canadian Quotations 2006, Terrors of the Night 2007, The Big Book of Canadian Ghost Stories 2008, Whistle While You Work 2008, A Far Cry 2009, The Big Book of Canadian Hauntings 2009, Indifferences 2009, Poems of Space and Time 2010, Tesseracts 14 (co-ed.) 2010, Entresol 2011, Imponderables 2011, Fascinating Canada 2011, Jeepers Creepers 2011, A Quaint and Curious Volume of Forgotten Lore 2012, Less of Light 2011, The Crime Magnet (ed.) 2012, Pipe Dreams 2012, The Big Book of Canadian Jokes 2013, Ghosts over Canada 2014, The Sax Rohmer Miscellany 2014, A World of Differences 2014, Late in the Day 2015. *Leisure interest:* reading. *Address:* 42 Dell Park Avenue, Toronto, ON M6B 2T6, Canada. *Telephone:* (416) 782-6853. *Fax:* (416) 782-0285 (home). *E-mail:* jrc@colombo.ca. *Website:* www.colombo.ca.

COLOMBO, Paolo Andrea, BA (Econ); Italian academic and business executive; *Chairman, Saipem SpA;* b. 12 April 1960, Milan; ed Bocconi Univ., Milan, New York Univ., USA; certified chartered accountant and public accountant 1985–; Prof. of Accounting and Financial Reporting, Bocconi Univ. 1989–2010, Sr Prof. 2010–; Founding Partner, Chair. and CEO Borghesi Colombo & Associati (financial advisory firm) 2006–12; Founding Partner and Chair. Colombo & Associati 2012–; Chair. Enel SpA and Enel Distribuzione 2011–14; fmr mem. Bd of Dirs Saipem SpA, Chair. Bd of Statutory Auditors –2008, Chair. 2015–; fmr Chair. Bd of Statutory Auditors, GE Capital Interbanca; Deputy Chair. Banca Intesa San Paolo 2016–; Founding Partner and Chair. Colombo & Associati (financial advisory firm) 2012–; fmr Chair. Bd of Statutory Auditors, Aviva Vita, Stream and Ansaldo STS; fmr mem. Bd of Statutory Auditors, Gian Marco Moratti S.a.p.a., of Gian Marco Moratti & Massimo Moratti S.a.p.a., of Massimo Moratti, Humanitas Mirasole (health care, Gruppo Techint), GE Capital Interbanca and Sacbo, Winterthur, Credit Suisse Italy, Banca Intesa, Lottomatica, Montedison, Techint Finanziaria, HDPNet, Internazionale FC; fmr mem. Bd of Dirs Telecom Italia Mobile, Pirelli Pneumatici, Publitalia '80 (Mediaset group), RCS Quotidiani, RCS Libri, RCS Broadcast and Fila Holding (RCS Mediagroup), Sias, Interbanca and Aurora (Unipol group), Versace. *Address:* Saipem S.p.A., Via Martiri di Cefalonia, 67, 20097 San Donato Milanese, Milan (office); Colombo & Associati, Piazza Mercanti 11, 20121 Milan, Italy (office). *Telephone:* (02) 44231 (Saipem) (office); (02) 778787201 (office). *Fax:* (02) 44244415 (Saipem) (office); (02) 778787225 (office). *E-mail:* media.relations@saipem.com (office); pcolombo@colombo-associati.it (office). *Website:* www.saipem.com (office); www.colombo-associati.it (office).

COLOMBO SIERRA, Agustín, DJur; Argentine diplomatist, government official and international organization official; *Director, Universidad de Tres de Febrero;* b. 1952, Buenos Aires; ed Univ. of Buenos Aires, Univ. of the Sorbonne-Paris II, France, Univ. of San Andrés; held various positions within several multinational telecommunications cos 1992–2003; Chief of Staff, Secr. of Foreign Relations, Ministry of Foreign Affairs 2003–05, Advisory Group Coordinator and Tech. Policy Del. to World Summit of Information Society Phase I, Geneva 2003, Phase II, Tunis 2005, Chief of Staff, Chancery 2005–06, Under-Sec. for Latin American Policy 2007–10; Exec. Dir Mercosur (Mercado Común del Sur) 2010–11; Dir, Universidad de Tres de Febrero 2012–; mem. Bd of Educ.ar 2005–, Internet Governance Forum 2006–, Advisory Group of UN Sec.-Gen. 2006–. *Address:* Universidad de Tres de Febrero, Avenue San Martín, 2024 Planta Alta, B1678GPW Caseros, Argentina (office). *Telephone:* (11) 4734-4258 (office). *Website:* www.untrefvirtual.edu.ar (office).

COLOMINA, Beatriz, MA, PhD; Spanish architect and academic; *Professor of History and Architecture, Princeton University;* ed Escuela Tecnica Superior de Arquitectura, Universidad de Barcelona; trained as architect, Valencia and Barcelona –1976; Asst Prof., Columbia Univ., New York, USA 1984–88; Asst Prof., Princeton Univ. 1988, later Assoc. Prof. of the History and Theory of Architecture, currently Prof., Dir Graduate Studies (PhD), Dir Program in Media and Modernity; has lectured extensively throughout world including Museum of Modern Art, New York, Architectural Inst. of Japan, Tokyo, Centre for Contemporary Art and Architecture, Stockholm, DIA Art Foundation, New York, Museum of Contemporary Art, Barcelona, Museo de Bellas Artes, Buenos Aires, Harvard and Yale Univs, Architectural Asscn, London, Helsinki Univ., Auckland Univ., Wissenschaftskolleg, Berlin; Titulo de Architecto; recipient of grants and fellowships from Chicago Inst. for Architecture, SOM Foundation, Graham Foundation, Fondation Le Corbusier, Center for Advanced Studies in the Visual Arts, Washington, DC, Canadian Centre for Architecture, Montreal. *Publications include:* Architectureproduction (ed.) 1988, Sexuality and Space (ed.) (AIA Int. Book Award 1993) 1992, Privacy and Publicity: Modern Architecture as Mass Media (AIA Int. Book Award 1995) 1994, The Work of Charles and Ray Eames (co-author) 1997, Frank Gehry Architect (co-author) 2001, Cold War Hothouses (co-ed.) 2004, Doble Exposicion: La Arquitectura a través del Arte 2006, Domesticity at War 2006, Clip/Stamp/Fold: The Radical Architecture of Little Magazines 2010; numerous articles. *Address:* School of Architecture, Princeton University, Princeton, NJ 08544-5264, USA (office). *Telephone:* (609) 258-3741 (office). *Fax:* (609) 258-4740 (office). *E-mail:* colomina@princeton.edu (office). *Website:* www.princeton.edu/~soa (office).

COLTRANE, Robbie, OBE; British actor; b. 31 March 1950, Glasgow, Scotland; m. Rhona Irene Gemmel 2000; one s. one d.; ed Glasgow School of Art; Co-Producer, Young Mental Health (documentary) 1973; Co-writer and Dir Jealousy (BBC) 1992, Brothers Bloom 2007; Peter Sellers Comedy Award, Evening Standard 1990, Best Actor, Royal TV Soc. 1993, Best Actor, Broadcasting Press Guild 1993, Best Actor TV Series, BAFTA 1993, 1994, 1995, Best Actor, Monte Carlo TV Festival 1994, Fipa d'Or for Best Actor, Nice Film and TV Festival 1995, Best Actor in Film or Mini-series, Nat. Cable Ace Awards (USA) 1996, Best Actor in TV Series, Royal TV Soc. 1996, Goldener Gong for Best Actor, German TV 1996. *Stage appearances include:* Waiting for Godot, Endgame, The Bug, Mr Joyce is Leaving, The Slab Boys, The Transfiguration of Benno Blimpie, The Loveliest Night of the Year, Snobs and Yobs, Your Obedient Servant (one-man show) 1987, Mistero Buffo 1990, The Brother's Suit 2005. *Films include:* Mona Lisa, Subway Riders, Britannia Hospital, Defence of the Realm, Caravaggio, Eat The Rich, Absolute Beginners, The Fruit Machine, Slipstream, Nuns On The Run, Huckleberry Finn, Bert Rigby, You're A Fool, Danny, Champion of the World, Henry V, Let It Ride, The Adventures of Huckleberry Finn, Goldeneye, Buddy, Montana, Frogs for Snakes, Message in a Bottle, The World is Not Enough 1999, On the Nose 2000, From Hell 2000, Harry Potter and the Philosopher's Stone 2001, Harry Potter and the Chamber of Secrets 2002, Harry Potter and the Prisoner of Azkaban 2004, Ocean's 12 2004, Harry Potter and the Goblet of Fire 2005, Stormbreaker 2006, Provoked 2006, Harry Potter and the Order of the Phoenix

2007, The Brothers Bloom 2008, Tales of Despereaux 2008, Harry Potter and the Half-Blood Prince 2009, Harry Potter and the Deathly Hallows: Part 1 2010, Part 2 2011, Arthur Christmas (voice) 2011, Brave (voice) 2012, Great Expectations 2012, Effie 2013. *Television includes:* Yes, Prime Minister, The Comic Strip Presents... 1982–2012, Five Go To Rehab, Five Go Mad In Dorset, The Beat Generation, War, Summer School, Five Go Mad on Mescalin, Susie, Gino, Dirty Movie, The Miner's Strike, The Supergrass (feature film), The Ebb-tide, Alice in Wonderland, The Young Ones, Kick Up the Eighties, The Tube, Saturday Night Live, Lenny Henry Show, Blackadder, Tutti Frutti, Coltrane in a Cadillac, Cracker, Boswell and Johnson's Tour of the Western Isles 1990, The Plan Man 2003, Cracker 9/11 2005, Coltrane's B-Road Britain 2007, Murderland (mini-series) 2009, The Gruffalo (voice) 2009, Lead Balloon (series) 2011, The Gruffalo's Child (voice) 2011. *Publications include:* Coltrane in a Cadillac 1992, Coltrane's Planes and Automobiles 1999, B-Road Britain 2008. *Leisure interests:* sailing, film, vintage cars, music, art. *Address:* 125 Gloucester Road, London, SW7 4TE, England (home). *Telephone:* (20) 7373-3323 (home). *E-mail:* cda@cdalondon.com (office).

COLUMBUS, Chris; American film director and screenwriter; b. 10 Sept. 1958, Spangler, Pa; s. of Alex Michael Columbus and Mary Irene Puskar; m. Monica Devereux 1983; two d.; ed New York Univ. Film School; wrote and developed TV cartoon series Galaxy High School; f. 1942 Productions (production co.). *Screenplays include:* Reckless 1983, Gremlins 1984, The Goonies 1985, The Young Sherlock Holmes 1985, Only the Lonely 1991, Little Nemo: Adventures in Slumberland (jtly) 1992, Nine Months 1995, Christmas with the Kranks 2004. *Films include:* Gremlins 1984, Young Sherlock Holmes 1985, Adventures in Babysitting 1987, Heartbreak Hotel 1988, Home Alone 1990, Only the Lonely 1991, Home Alone 2: Lost in New York 1992, Mrs Doubtfire 1993, Nine Months (also producer) 1995, Jingle All the Way (also producer) 1996, Stepmom (also producer) 1998, Monkey Bone 1999, Bicentennial Man (also producer) 1999, Harry Potter and the Philosopher's Stone (also producer) 2001, Harry Potter and the Chamber of Secrets (also producer) 2002, Rent (also producer) 2005, Night at the Museum (producer) 2006, 4: Rise of the Silver Surfer (producer) 2007, Night at the Museum 2 (producer) 2009, I Love You, Beth Cooper 2009, Perry Jackson and the Lightning Thief (also producer) 2010, The Help (producer) 2011, Night at the Museum: Secret of the Tomb (producer) 2014, Pixels 2015, Mediterranea (producer) 2015. *TV directed includes:* Amazing Stories, Twilight Zone, Alfred Hitchcock Presents (series), Applebaum (film) 2012. *Address:* c/o Beth Swofford, CAA, 2000 Avenue of the Stars, Los Angeles, CA 90067, USA.

COLWELL, Rita Rossi, BS, MS, PhD; American marine microbiologist, epidemiologist and academic; *Adjunct Professor, Bloomberg School of Public Health, Johns Hopkins University;* b. 23 Nov. 1934, Mass.; d. of Louis Rossi and Louise DiPalma; m. Jack H. Colwell 1956; two d.; ed Purdue Univ. and Univ. of Wash.; Research Asst, Drosophila Genetics Lab. Purdue Univ. 1956–57; Research Asst, Dept of Microbiology, Univ. of Washington 1957–58, Predoctoral Assoc. 1959–60, Asst Research Prof. 1961–64; Asst Prof. of Biology, Georgetown Univ. 1964–66, Assoc. Prof. 1966–72; Prof. of Microbiology, Univ. of Maryland 1972–98, Vice-Pres. for Academic Affairs 1983–87, Founding Dir Center of Marine Biotechnology 1987–91, Founder and Pres. Biotechnology Inst. 1991–98, Distinguished Univ. Prof. 2004–; Distinguished Univ. Prof., Bloomberg School of Public Health, Johns Hopkins Univ. 2004, now Adjunct Prof.; Dir NSF 1998–2004; Chair., Canon US Life Sciences, Inc. 2004–06, Sr Advisor and Hon. Chair. 2006–; fmr Chair. Bd of Govs American Acad. of Microbiology; fmr Pres. AAAS, American Society for Microbiology, Int Union of Microbiological Societies, Sigma Xi Nat Science Hon. Society; mem. NAS, Royal Swedish Acad. of Sciences, Stockholm, American Acad. of Arts and Sciences, American Philosophical Society; numerous hon. doctorates; Gold Medal, Canterbury, UK 1990, Purkinje Gold Award, Prague 1991, Maryland Pate Civic Award 1991, Barnard Medal, Colorado Univ. 1996, Gold Medal, UCLA 2000, Achievement Award, American Asscn of Univ. Women 2001, Carey Award, AAAS 2001, Nat. Medal of Science 2007, Stockholm Water Prize 2010, Int. Prize for Biology 2017, Lee Kuan Yew Water Prize 2018. *Publications:* 16 books, over 600 articles in journals, book chapters, abstracts. *Leisure interests:* gardening, sailing, jogging. *Address:* Bloomberg School of Public Health, 615 North Wolfe Street, Baltimore, MD 21205 (office); 5010 River Hill Road, Bethesda, MD 20816, USA (home). *Telephone:* (410) 955-3720 (office). *Fax:* (410) 955-0617 (office). *E-mail:* rcolwell@jhsph.edu (office). *Website:* www.jhsph.edu (office).

COLYER, Jeff, BA, MA, MD; American surgeon and politician; b. 3 June 1960, Hays, Kan.; s. of James Daniel Colyer and Lorene Colyer; m. Ruth Gutierrez Colyer 1991; three d.; ed Georgetown Univ., Univ. of Cambridge, England, Univ. of Kansas; Resident, Gen. Surgery, Washington Hosp. Center 1986–88, 1989–91; Resident, Plastic Surgery, Univ. of Missouri 1991–93; Resident, Craniofacial Surgery, Int. Craniofacial Inst., Dallas 1993–94; Chair. Legislative Health Reform Task Force 2007; mem. House of Reps, Kan. 2007–09, Senate 2009–11; Lt-Gov. of Kan. 2010–18, Gov. 2018–19; mem. Advisory Bd, Univ. of Kansas; mem. Chamber of Commerce; Int. Affairs Fellow, Ronald Reagan and George H.W. Bush Presidential Admins, White House; volunteered as a surgeon in war zones of Afghanistan, Iraq, the Balkans, Libya and Africa.

COMANECI, Nadia Elena; American (b. Romanian) fmr gymnast; b. 12 Nov. 1961, Oneşti, Bacău Co.; d. of Gheorghe Comaneci and Stefania-Alexandria Comaneci; m. Bart Connor 1996; one s.; ed Coll. of Physical Educ. and Sports, Bucharest; overall European champion Skien 1975, Prague 1977, Copenhagen 1979; overall Olympic champion, Montreal 1976, first gymnast to be awarded a 10; overall World Univ. Games Champion, Bucharest 1981; gold medals European Championships, Skien 1975 (vault, asymmetric bars, beam), Prague 1977 (bars), Copenhagen 1979 (vault, floor exercises), World Championships, Strasbourg 1978 (beam), Fort Worth 1979 (team title), Olympic Games, Montreal 1976 (bars, beam), Moscow (beam, floor), World Cup, Tokyo 1979 (vault, floor); World Univ. Games, Bucharest 1981 (vault, bars, floor and team title); silver medals European Championships, Skien 1975 (floor), Prague 1977 (vault), World Championships, Strasbourg 1978 (vault), Olympic Games, Montreal 1976 (team title), Moscow 1980 (individual all-round, team title), World Cup, Tokyo 1979 (beam); bronze medal Olympic Games, Montreal 1976 (floor); retd May 1984, jr team coach 1984–89; granted refugee status in USA 1989; currently with Bart Connor Gymnastics Acad., Okla, USA; Contributing Ed. International Gymnast magazine; Prin. (with husband) Perfect 10 Productions, Inc. (TV production co.), Grips, Etc.(gymnastics supply co.), GymDivas, Inc.; UN Spokesperson for Int. Year of Volunteers 2001; f. Nadia Comaneci Children's Clinic, Bucharest 2004; Vice-Chair. Special Olympics Int.; Vice-Pres. Muscular Dystrophy Asscn; mem. Bd of Dirs Laureus Sports For Good Foundation; United Press Int. Athlete of the Year Award 1975, 1976, Hero of Socialist Labour, Associated Press Athlete of the Year, BBC Overseas Sports Personality of the Year 1976, inducted into the Int. Gymnastics Hall of Fame 1996, Flo Hyman Award 1998, Sportswomen of the Century Prize, Athletic Sports Category 1999, Govt Excellence Diploma 2001, The Olympic Order 2004, Great Immigrant Honoree, Carnegie Corpn of New York 2016. *Publication:* Letters to a Young Gymnast 2004. *Address:* c/o Paul Ziert, Paul Ziert and Associates, 3214 Bart Conner Dr., Norman, OK 73072, USA (office); c/o Bart Conner Gymnastics Academy, 3206 Bart Conner Drive, POB 720217, Norman, OK 73070-4166, USA (office). *Telephone:* (405) 364-5344 (office); (405) 447-7500 (office). *Fax:* (405) 321-7229 (office); (405) 447-7600 (office). *E-mail:* paul@intlgymnast.com (office). *Website:* www.bartconnergymnastics.com (office); www.bartandnadia.com.

COMĂNESCU, Lazăr, PhD; Romanian diplomatist and politician; b. 4 June 1949, Horezu (Ursani), Vâlcea Co.; m. Mihaela Comănescu; one d.; ed Acad. of Econ. Studies, Bucharest, Sorbonne, Paris; Jr Diplomat, Ministry of Foreign Affairs (MFA) 1972–82, Counsellor, later Minister-Counsellor, Mission to EU, Brussels 1990–94, Dir EU Directorate, MFA 1994–95, Dir-Gen. and Adviser to Minister of Foreign Affairs, also Head of Minister's office 1995, State Sec., MFA 1995–98, Amb. and Head, Mission to NATO and WEU 1998–2001, Amb. and Head of Mission to EU 2001–07, Perm. Rep., EU, Brussels 2007–08; Minister of Foreign Affairs April–Dec. 2008, 2015–17; Amb. to Germany 2009–15; Foreign Policy Adviser to Pres. Klaus Iohannis 2015–; Prof. of Int. Econs, Acad. of Econ. Studies, Bucharest 1982–90; mem. Scientific Consultative Bd European Inst. in Romania; mem. Scientific Bd Romanian Inst. for Int. Studies; Founding mem. Warsaw Cen. European Forum; Grand Officer, Romanian Nat. Order of Loyal Service 2000, Romanian Nat. Order of Loyal Service with Great Cross 2007. *Publications:* author of several univ. courses and books; numerous articles in journals. *Address:* c/o Ministry of Foreign Affairs, 011822 Bucharest, Al. Alexandru 31, Romania. *E-mail:* opinia_ta@mae.ro.

COMASTRI, HE Cardinal Angelo; Italian ecclesiastic; *President of the Fabric of St Peter;* b. 17 Sept. 1943, Sorano; s. of Fernando Comastri and Beneria Comastri; ed Pontificia Università Lateranense; ordained priest 1967; Bishop of Massa Marittima-Piombino 1990–94; Archbishop (Personal Title) of Loreto 1996–2005 (retd); Pres. Fabric of St Peter 2005–13, 2013–; Coadjutor Archpriest of the Basilica di San Pietro in Vaticano and Coadjutor Papal Vicar for the Vatican City 2005–06, Archpriest of the Basilica di San Pietro in Vaticano and Papal Vicar for the Vatican City 2006–; cr. Cardinal (Cardinal-Deacon of San Salvatore in Lauro) 2007, Cardinal-Priest (San Salvatore in Lauro) 2018–; Dir Italian Bishops' Nat. Vocations Centre 1994; Pres. Nat. Cttee for the Great Jubilee of the Year 2000 1994. *Publication:* The Holy Door of the Vatican Basilica (co-author) 2015. *Address:* Fabbrica di San Pietro, 00120 Vatican City, Rome, Italy (office). *Telephone:* (06) 6988-3367 (office). *Fax:* (06) 6988-5518 (office). *Website:* www.vatican.va/various/basiliche/san_pietro/it/fabbrica/cenni_storici.htm (office).

COMBS, Sean John, (Puff Daddy, Diddy); American rap artist, record producer, fashion designer and business executive; *Chairman and CEO, Bad Boy Worldwide Entertainment Group;* b. 4 Nov. 1969, Harlem, New York; s. of Melvin Combs and Janice Combs; fmr pnr Misa Hylton-Brim; one s.; fmr pnr Kim Porter; two s. twin d.; ed Mount Saint Michael High School, Bronx, Howard Univ.; early positions at Uptown Records (R&B label) 1990–93; talent spotter for artists such as Jodeci and Mary J. Blige; producer for Ma$e, Sting, MC Lyte, Faith Evans, The Lox, Mariah Carey, Aretha Franklin, 112, Notorious BIG, Jennifer Lopez, Britney Spears, Jay-Z, Rick Ross; f. Bad Boy Entertainment record label 1994 (now distributed by Epic Records); remixed and reworked songs by artists including Jackson 5, Sting, Goldie, Trent Reznor and The Police; co-producer (with Jimmy Page) of soundtrack to film Godzilla; soundtrack to approx. 50 films; launched fashion collection under name Sean John 1998, opened flagship store in Manhattan 2002; producer of MTV's Making the Band; launched fragrances Unforgiveable 2006, I Am King 2009; Grammy Award for Best Rap Performance by a Duo or Group for I'll Be Missing You, with Faith Evans 1998, for Shake Ya Tailfeather 2004, Council of Fashion Designers of America menswear designer of the year award 2004. *Play:* A Raisin in the Sun (actor) 2004. *Films:* Bad Boy's 10th Anniversary..., The Hits (video) 2004, The Notorious B.I.G.: Ready to Die – The Remaster (video short) 2004, Notorious 2009, Undefeated (documentary) (Academy Award for Best Documentary Feature 2012) 2011. *Television includes:* Making the Band 2 (series) 2002, Borrow My Crew (documentary) 2005, Making the Band 3 (series) 2005, P. Diddy Presents the Bad Boys of Comedy (series documentary) 2005, Celebrity Cooking Showdown (mini-series) 2006, The Making of 'Press Play' (film) 2006, Diddy Makes an Album (film) 2006, Making the Band 4 (series) 2007, Taquita & Kaui (series) 2007, A Raisin in the Sun (film) 2008, If I Were King: Sean John Internship by Design (documentary) 2008, Daddy's Girls (series) 2009, Run's House (series documentary) 2005–09, Making His Band (series) 2009, StarMaker (series) (exec. producer) 2009, (co-exec. producer) 2009, I Want to Work for Diddy (series) 2008–10, Nicki Minaj: My Time Now (documentary) 2010. *Recordings include:* albums: No Way Out (Grammy Award for Best Rap Album 1998) 1997, Forever 1999, The Saga Continues... 2001, We Invented the Remix 2002, Maximum Puff Daddy 2003, Press Play 2006, Last Train to Paris (with Dirty Money) 2010. *Website:* www.seanjohn.com; puffdaddyandthefamily.com.

COMEY, James Brien, Jr, JD; American lawyer and government official; b. 14 Dec. 1960, Yonkers, NY; m. Patrice Comey; five c.; ed Northern Highlands Regional High School, Coll. of William and Mary, Univ. of Chicago Law School; grew up in Allendale, NY; served as law clerk for then-US Dist Judge John M. Walker, Jr in Manhattan; Assoc., Gibson, Dunn & Crutcher, New York; with US Attorney's Office for Southern Dist of New York 1987–93, served as Deputy Chief of the Criminal Div.; Man. Asst, US Attorney in charge of Richmond Div. of US Attorney for Eastern Dist of Va 1996–2001; Adjunct Prof. of Law, Univ. of Richmond School of Law 1996–2001; US Attorney for Southern Dist of New York 2002–03; US Deputy Attorney Gen. 2003–05; Gen. Counsel and Sr Vice-Pres., Lockheed Martin 2005–10; mem. Sr Man. Cttee, Bridgewater Assocs 2010–13; Sr Research Scholar and Hertog Fellow on Nat. Security Law, Columbia Univ. Law

School 2013–; Dir FBI 2013–17; mem. Bd of Dirs HSBC Holdings, London 2013; mem. Defense Legal Policy Bd 2012–.

COMMENDA, Gen. Othmar; Austrian army officer; *Chief of the Defence Staff;* b. 29 May 1954; m. Sabine Commenda; two c. from previous m.; ed Theresian Mil. Acad., Nat. Defence Acad., Vienna, US Army War Coll., Führungsakademie der Bundeswehr, Germany; joined Austrian army 1975, has held numerous positions including Co. Commdr, 14th Tank Bn, Wels 1979, Co. Commdr with UN Disengagement Observer Force Zone (UNDOF), Golan Heights 1983–84, Tactical Training Officer, Nat. Defence Acad., Vienna 1988–91, Commdr, Army Reconnaissance Bn, Mistelbach, Lower Austria 1992–94, Commdr, 3rd Mechanized Brigade, Senftenberg, Chief of Staff and Deputy Brigade Commdr, 3rd Tank Brigade, Mautern an der Donau 1994, with foreign exercise Cooperative Guard 99 under Partnership for Peace operation, Czech Repub., Commdr, 15th Gen. Staff Training Course 1996–2000, Deputy Head of Mil. Policy, Gen. Troop Inspectorate, Ministry of Defence 2000, Chief of Staff, Dept of Defence in the cabinet 2001–03, Chef de Cabinet of Minister of Defence 2003, Head of Project Man., Armed Forces Reform Comm. 2003–04, Head of Dept responsible for restructuring of Austrian Armed Forces under Minister of Defence 2004–08, Deputy Chief of Defence Staff 2008–11, Acting Chief of Defence Staff 2011–13, Chief of Defence Staff 2013–; Großes Ehrenzeichen für Verdienste um die Republik Österreich 2004, Große Goldene Ehrenzeichen für Verdienste um die Republik Österreich 2013; Mil. Service Award 1st, 2nd and 3rd Class, Mil. Service Medal in bronze. *Address:* Federal Ministry of Defence and Sports, Rossauer Lände 1, 1090 Vienna, Austria (office). *Telephone:* (1) 502-01-0 (office). *Fax:* (1) 502-01-10-17-041 (office). *E-mail:* presse@bmlvs.gv.at (office). *Website:* www.bmlv.gv.at (office).

COMOLLI, Jean-Dominique, MEconSc; French business executive and fmr public servant; b. 25 April 1948, Bougie, Algeria; s. of Yvan Comolli and Jacqueline Courtin; m. Catherine Delmas 1968; two s. one d.; ed Institut d'Etudes Politiques, Paris, Ecole Nat. d'Admin; civil servant, Budget Dept, Ministry of Economy, Finance and Budget 1977–81, Minister of the Budget's Tech. Adviser to Cabinet, then Prime Minister's Tech. Adviser to Cabinet 1981–86, Asst Dir Budget Dept 1986–88, Prin. Pvt. Sec. to Minister of the Budget 1988–89, Dir-Gen. Customs and Indirect Duties, Ministry of the Budget 1989–95; Chair. and CEO Soc. Nat. d'Exploitation Industrielle des Tabacs et Allumettes (Seita) 1993–99; Co-Chair. Bd of Dirs Altadis SA (tobacco co. cr. out of merger of Seita and Tabacalera) 1999–2005, Chair. 2005–08, Deputy Chair. Imperial Tobacco Group PLC (following acquisition of Altadis) 2008–10; CEO Agence des participations de l'État 2010–12; Ind. Dir, Pernod-Ricard SA 1997–2010; Dir, Credit Agricole Corp. and Investment Bank (fmrly Calyon SA) 2005–10, Casino Guichard Perrachon & Cie SA 2009–11, France Telecom 2010–, Air France-KLM 2010–12, 2013–; mem. Supervisory Bd, Areva SA 2011–; Officier, Légion d'honneur; Chevalier, Ordre nat. du Mérite. *Address:* Air France-KLM, AFKL.FI, 95737 Roissy Charles de Gaulle Cedex (office); 23 avenue de l'Observatoire, 75006 Paris, France (home). *E-mail:* info@airfranceklm.com (office). *Website:* www.airfranceklm.com (office).

COMPAGNON, Antoine Marcel Thomas; French academic and writer; *Blanche W. Knopf Professor of French and Comparative Literature, Columbia University;* b. 20 July 1950, Brussels, Belgium; s. of Gen. Jean Compagnon and Jacqueline Terlinden; ed Lycée Condorcet, Paris, The Maret School, Washington, DC, USA, Prytanée Militaire, La Flèche, Ecole Polytechnique, Paris, Ecole Nat. des Ponts et Chaussées, Paris, Univ. of Paris VII; with Fondation Thiers and Research Attaché, CNRS 1975–78; Asst Lecturer, Univ. of Paris VII 1975–80; Asst Lecturer, Ecole des Hautes Etudes en Sciences Sociales, Paris 1977–79; Lecturer, Ecole Polytechnique, Paris 1978–85; teacher at French Inst., London 1980–81; Lecturer, Univ. of Rouen 1981–85; Prof. of French, Columbia Univ., New York 1985–91, Blanche W. Knopf Prof. of French and Comparative Literature 1991–; Visiting Prof., Univ. of Pennsylvania 1986, 1990; Prof., Univ. of Le Mans 1989–90; Prof., Univ. of Paris IV-Sorbonne 1994–2006, Collège de France 2006–; Sec.-Gen. Int. Asscn of French Studies 1998–2008; Guggenheim Fellow 1988; Visiting Fellow, All Souls Coll., Oxford 1994; Fellow, American Acad. of Arts and Sciences 1997, Academia Europaea 2006; Corresp. Fellow, British Acad. 2009; Commdr des Palmes académiques, Officier de l'ordre du Mérite, Chevalier, Légion d'honneur; Dr hc (King's Coll., London) 2010, (Univ. de Liège) 2013, (Univ. of Bucharest) 2017; Prix Claude Lévi-Strauss 2011. *Publications include:* La Seconde Main ou le travail de la citation 1979, Le Deuil antérieur 1979, Nous, Michel de Montaigne 1980, La Troisième République des lettres, de Flaubert à Proust 1983, Ferragosto 1985, critical edn of Marcel Proust, Sodome et Gomorrhe 1988, Proust entre deux siècles 1989, Les Cinq Paradoxes de la modernité 1990, Chat en poche: Montaigne et l'allégorie 1993, Connaissez-vous Brunetière? 1997, Le Démon de la théorie 1998, Baudelaire devant l'innombrable 2003, Les Antimodernes 2005, Le Cas Bernard Faÿ 2009, La Classe de rhéto 2012, Un été avec Montaigne 2013, Une question de discipline 2013, Baudelaire l'irréductible 2014, L'Âge des lettres (memoir) 2015, Petits spleens numériques 2015, Les Chiffonniers de Paris 2017; numerous articles on French literature and culture. *Address:* Columbia University, Department of French and Romance Philology, 513 Philosophy Hall, 1150 Amsterdam Avenue, New York, NY 10027, USA (office); Collège de France, 11 place Marcelin-Berthelot, 75005 Paris, France (office). *Telephone:* (212) 854-2500 (New York) (office); 1-44-27-10-79 (Paris) (office). *Fax:* (212) 854-5863 (New York) (office). *E-mail:* amc6@columbia.edu (office); antoine.compagnon@college-de-france.fr (office). *Website:* www.columbia.edu/cu/french (office).

COMPAORÉ, Blaise; Burkinabè fmr head of state and fmr army officer; b. 3 Feb. 1951, Ouagadougou; m. Chantal K. Terrasson; one d.; trained as soldier in Cameroon and Morocco; fmr second in command to Capt. Thomas Sankara whom he overthrew in a coup in Oct. 1987; Minister of State to the Pres., then Minister for Justice 1983–87; Chair. Popular Front of Burkina Faso and Head of Govt Oct. 1987–, Interim Head of State June–Dec. 1991, Pres. of Burkina Faso 1991–2014 (forced to resign following army-led uprising), Minister of Nat. Defence and War Veterans 2011–14; Assoc. mem. Overseas Acad. of Sciences, France 1995–; in exile in Côte d'Ivoire; Commdr, Ordre Int. des Palmes académiques 2005; Dr hc (Ecole des Hautes Etudes Ints de Paris) 1992, (Soka Univ., Japan) 1995, (Jean-Moulin de Lyon 3 Univ., France) 2004, (Ramkhamaeng Univ., Thailand) 2005.

COMPAORÉ, Jean-Baptiste Marie Pascal, MEconSc, DES; Burkinabè politician, banker and economist; *Vice-Governor, Banque Centrale des États de l'Afrique de l'ouest (BCEAO);* b. 12 April 1954, Ouagadougou; m.; four c.; ed Phillipe Zinda Kabore Coll., Ouagadougou, Univ. of Benin, Nigeria, Lomé, Togo, Centre Ouest Africain de Formation aux Études Bancaires (COFEB); joined Banque Centrale des États de l'Afrique de l'ouest (BCEAO), Dakar 1981, served in Credit and Inspection Divs, Inspector of Banks, Banking Comm. of W Africa Monetary Union 1990–95, Vice-Gov. BCEAO 2008–, Interim Gov. Jan.–Sept. 2011; Counsellor, Dir of Econ. and Social Affairs, Office of the Pres. 1995–96, Sec.-Gen. of Ministry 1996–2000; Minister to the Prime Minister, responsible for Finance and the Budget 2000–02, Minister of Finance and the Budget 2002–07, of the Economy and Finances 2007–08, also Gov. IMF, World Bank Group, African Devt Bank, Econ. Community of West African States (ECOWAS); fmr Lecturer (part-time), Lomé Tech. School, Togo; fmr Chair. Inter-Departmental Cttee to Follow-up Recommendations of Arbitrator of Faso; Officier, Commdr, Ordre Nat. Burkina; Commdr, Ordre Nat. (Côte d'Ivoire). *Address:* Banque Centrale des États de l'Afrique de l'ouest (BCEAO), siège BP 3108, Dakar, Senegal (office). *Telephone:* 33-839-0500 (office). *Website:* www.bceao.int (office).

COMPER, Francis Anthony (Tony), CM, BA; Canadian banker; b. 24 April 1945, Toronto, Ont.; m. Elizabeth Comper 1971 (died 2014); ed Univ. of Toronto; began career with BMO Financial Group 1967, Sr Vice-Pres., Personal Banking 1982, Sr Vice-Pres. and Sr Operations Officer, Treasury Group 1982–84, Man., London, UK Br. 1984–86, Sr Marketing Officer, Corp. and Govt Banking 1986–87, Exec. Vice-Pres., Operation 1987–89, Chief Gen. Man. and COO 1989–90, Pres., COO and Dir 1990–99, Pres. CEO and Dir 1999, Chair., CEO and Dir 1999–2007; Chair. Capital Campaign for the Univ. of Toronto 1997–2002; mem. Bd of Dirs, Spectra Energy Corpn, Canadian Inst. of Advanced Research, Harris Bancorp, Inc., Harris Trust and Savings Bank, Toronto, C.D. Howe Inst., C.D. Howe Memorial Foundation, Canadian Club, BMO Nesbitt Burns Inc., Catalyst, NY; Trustee Canadian Centre for Architecture; mem. Int. Advisory Cttee, Li Ka Shing Knowledge Inst. of St Michael's Hosp.; Hon. Chair. Bd of Govs The Yee Hong Centre for Geriatric Care; Order of Canada 2010; Hon. DHumLitt (Mount Saint Vincent), Hon. LLD (Univ. of Toronto), Hon. DLitt (Univ. of New Brunswick); Human Relations Award, Canadian Council of Christians and Jews 1998, B'nai Brith Order of Merit 2003, Scopus Award (with his wife), Hebrew Univ. of Jerusalem. *Leisure interests:* golf, tennis, theatre, arts, reading. *Address:* c/o BMO Financial Group, First Bank Tower, First Canadian Place, Toronto, ON M5X 1A1, Canada.

COMSTOCK, Beth; American business executive; *Vice-Chair of Business Innovations, General Electric Company;* b. 1960, Va; m.; two d.; ed Coll. of William and Mary, Va; began career working for a TV news service and in local cable programming in Va; held a succession of communications and publicity positions at NBC, Turner Broadcasting and CBS Entertainment from 1986; Vice-Pres. NBC News Communications 1993–96, Sr Vice-Pres. Communications, NBC 1996–98, Vice-Pres. Corp. Communications, General Electric Co. (GE) 1998–2003, Corp. Vice-Pres. and Chief Marketing Officer, GE 2003–05, Pres. NBC Universal Digital Media and Market Devt (now Integrated Media) 2005–08, Chief Marketing Officer and Sr Vice-Pres. GE 2008–15, Vice-Chair. of Business Innovations 2015–; named by Business Week an innovation "transformer" 2005, named by BtoB Magazine Marketing Exec. of the Year, named by PR Week PR Professional of the Year, Matrix Award, New York Women in Communications 2006. *Address:* General Electric Company, 3135 Easton Turnpike, Fairfield, CT 06828, USA (office). *Telephone:* (203) 373-2211 (office). *Website:* www.ge.com (office).

CONANT, Douglas R.; American business executive; *Chairman, Avon Products, Inc.;* b. Chicago, Ill.; m.; three c.; ed Northwestern Univ.; began career in marketing dept, General Mills Inc. 1976; joined Kraft Foods 1986; Pres. Nabisco Foods Co. 1995–2000; Pres. and CEO Campbell Soup Co. 2001–11; Chair. Avon Products, Inc. 2012–; Chair. Kellogg Exec. Leadership Inst., Northwestern Univ. 2013–; Founder and CEO DRC LLC, ConantLeadership 2011–; mem. Bd of Dirs, Applebee's International Inc. 1999–2007, Int. Tennis Hall of Fame and Museum 2006–, Partnership for Public Service 2009–, Nat. Org. on Disability 2010–, Enactus 2010–, AmerisourceBergen 2013–16, Arthur Ashe Learning Center 2013–; Chair. Cttee Encouraging Corp. Philanthropy 2011–; fmr Chair. Bd of Trustees, The Conference Bd; fmr Chair. Grocery Mfrs Asscn/Food Processors of America; Chair.'s Award, Int. Tennis Hall of Fame 2010, Catalyst Award 2010, Work Life Legacy Award, Families and Work Life Inst. 2011, Champions for Children Award, Arthur Ashe Youth Tennis and Educ. Center 2011, Hall of Achievement Award, Grocery Mfrs Asscn 2011, Champion of Workplace Learning and Performance Award, American Soc. of Training and Devt 2011, Corporate Citizen Award, Jonathan M. Tisch Coll. of Citizenship and Public Service, Tufts Univ. 2012, Inspirational Leadership Award, Global Man. Challenge USA 2013. *Address:* Avon Products, Inc., 777 Third Avenue, New York, NY 10017, USA (office). *Telephone:* (212) 282-7000 (office). *Website:* www.avoncompany.com (office); conantleadership.com.

CONDÉ, Alpha, DenD; Guinean professor of law, politician and head of state; *President;* b. 4 March 1938, Boké; ed Univ. Paris IV (Sorbonne), France; fmr Prof., Faculty of Law and Econ. Sciences, Univ. Paris I (Panthéon-Sorbonne); co-f. Mouvement Nat. Démocratique (MND) 1977; unsuccessful cand. in presidential elections 1993, 1998; sentenced to five years' imprisonment 2000, pardoned and released 2001; exiled in France 2001–05; Pres. Repub. of Guinea 2010–; Chair. African Union 2017–18; Leader, Rassemblement du peuple de Guinée. *Publications:* several books including Guinée, Albanie d'Afrique ou néo-colonie américaine 1972, Quel avenir pour la Guinée 1984, Pour que l'espoir ne meure 1985, Un africain engagé: ce que je veux pour la Guinée 2010. *Address:* Office of the President, BP 1000, Boulbinet, Conakry, Guinea (office). *Telephone:* 30-41-10-16 (office). *Fax:* 30-41-16-73 (office).

CONDÉ, Mamadi; Guinean fmr government official; fmr Minister of Information; Minister of Foreign Affairs and Co-operation 2004–05, 2006–07. *Address:* c/o Ministry of Foreign Affairs, face au Port, ex-Primature, BP 2519, Conakry, Guinea.

CONDE DE SARO, Francisco Javier, M.L.; Spanish lawyer, business executive and fmr diplomatist; *President, Sociedad Estatal para Exposiciones Internacionales;* b. 13 March 1946, Madrid; s. of Francisco Javier Conde and María Jesús de Saro; m. Ana Martínez de Irujo; one s. two d.; ed Univ. of Madrid, Diplomatic School, Madrid; Dir-Gen. for Int. Econ. Relations, Ministry of Foreign Affairs 1971;

Asst Dir-Gen. for Int. Relations, Directorate of Maritime Fisheries 1976; Dir of Political Affairs for Africa and Asia, Ministry of Foreign Affairs 1978; counsellor Ministry of Transport, Tourism and Communications 1978; Econ. and Commercial Counsellor, Embassy in Rabat 1979–83, in Buenos Aires 1983–86; Dir-Gen. Juridical and Institutional Co-ordination, Sec. of State for EU, Ministry of Foreign Affairs 1986–90, Sec.-Gen. 1994; Amb. to Algeria 1990–94; Perm. Rep. to NATO, Brussels 1996–2000; Perm. Rep. to EU, Brussels 2000–04; Amb. to Japan 2004–06; currently Pres. Sociedad Estatal para Exposiciones Internacionales (State Co. for Int. Exhibitions); Vice-Pres. Foundation Bd Fundación Arquitectura y Sociedad; Kt Commdr of Civil Merit (Spain), of Isabel la Católica (Spain), of Mayo Order (Argentina), of Order of the Lion (Senegal); Kt of Order of El Ouissam El Mohammadi (Morocco); Grand Cross for Naval Merit (Spain), Grand Cross of Merit (Austria). *Address:* Sociedad Estatal para Exposiciones Internacionales, C/ José Abascal, 4–4° B, 28003 Madrid, Spain (office). *Telephone:* (91) 7004000 (office). *E-mail:* info@expo-int.com (office). *Website:* www.expo-int.com (office).

CONDO, George; American artist; b. 1957, Concord, New Hampshire; m. Anna Condo; ed Univ. of Massachusetts; Visiting Lecturer, Harvard Univ. 2004, Columbia Univ., Yale Univ., Pasadena Art Center, and many prestigious Insts.; Acad. Award in Art, American Acad. of Arts and Letters 1999, Francis J. Greenburger Award 2005, Anderson Ranch Nat. Artist Award 2008.

CONDON, Baron (Life Peer), cr. 2001, of Langton Green in the County of Kent; **Paul Leslie Condon,** QPM, DL, CCMI (CIMgt), FRSA; British fmr police commissioner and international organization official; b. 1 Jan. 1946, Dorset, England; m.; two s. one d.; ed St Peter's Coll. Oxford; joined Metropolitan Police 1967, Insp. 1975–78, Chief Insp. 1978–81, Supt, Bethnal Green 1981–82, Staff Officer to Commr as Supt, then as Chief Supt 1982–84; Asst Chief Constable of Kent 1984–87; Deputy Asst Commr Metropolitan Police 1987–88, Asst Commr 1988–89; Chief Constable of Kent 1989–92; Commr, Metropolitan Police 1993–2000; Dir Anti-Corruption Unit, Int. Cricket Council 2001–; Dir or fmr Dir (non-exec.), Securicor PLC from 2000, G4S 2004–12 (Deputy Chair. 2006–12), Tenix (Holdings) UK Ltd, Vidient Systems Inc.; mem. (Crossbench), House of Lords 2011–, Vice-Chair. Pvt. Security Group 2006–, mem. EU Home Affairs Sub-Cttee 2015–; Pres. British Security Industry Asscn; Life mem. Asscn of Chief Police Officers; CStJ 1994. *Address:* House of Lords, Westminster, London, SW1A 0PW, England (office). *Telephone:* (20) 7219-5353 (office). *Fax:* (20) 7219-5979 (office). *E-mail:* condonp@parliament.uk (office). *Website:* www.parliament.uk/biographies/lords/lord-condon/2171 (office).

CONDOR, Sam Terrence, BA; Saint Kitts and Nevis politician, business executive and diplomatist; *Permanent Representative, United Nations;* b. 4 Nov. 1949; m.; one s. two d.; ed Ruskin Coll., Oxford, Univ. of Sussex, UK; printer, Saint Kitts and Nevis Govt Printery 1967–82; Sr Clerk, Inland Revenue Dept 1980–82; Man. Dir Quality Foods Ltd 1986–95; MP 1989–2015; Deputy Prime Minister 1995–2013, Minister of Trade, Industry, CARICOM Affairs, Youth, Sports and Community Devt 1995–99, Minister of Foreign Affairs, Int. Trade and CARICOM Affairs, Community and Social Devt and Gender Affairs 2000–01, Minister of CARICOM Affairs, Int. Trade, Labour, Social Security, Telecommunications and Tech. 2001–04, Minister for Educ., Youth, Social Devt, Community and Gender Affairs 2004–10, Minister of Foreign Affairs and National Security, Labour, Immigration and Social Security 2010–11, Minister of Foreign Affairs, Homeland Security, Labour and Social Security 2011–13; Vice-Chair. Young Labour 1980–82, Deputy Leader Saint Kitts-Nevis Labour Party 1990–2013; Founder and Deputy Leader People's Labour Party 2013–; Amb. and Perm. Rep. to UN, New York 2015–; mem. Saint Kitts and Nevis Tourist Bd 1975–78; Nat. Football Player 1969–72, Man. and Coach Nat. Football Team 1986–88; Margaret Marsh Prize for Most Outstanding Overseas Student, Ruskin Coll. 1979–80. *Leisure interests:* playing football, jogging, fast walking, drama. *Address:* Permanent Mission of Saint Kitts and Nevis, 414 East 75th Street, 5th Floor, New York, NY 10021, USA (office); North Pelican Drive, Bird Rock, Saint Kitts, Saint Kitts and Nevis (home). *Telephone:* (212) 535-1234 (office); 465-1545 (home). *Fax:* (212) 535-6854 (office). *E-mail:* sknmission@aol.com (office).

CONEWAY, Peter Richard, MBA; American business executive and fmr diplomatist; *Managing Director, Riverstone Holdings LLC;* b. 13 April 1944, Cleveland, Ohio; m. Lynn M. Coneway; two d.; ed Coll. of Business Admin, Univ. of Texas, Stanford Univ.; joined Goldman, Sachs & Co. 1969, later fmr Advisory Dir, f. Houston office for Goldman Sachs 1975, named Gen. Pnr 1978, est. firm's equities sales, trading and research div., Tokyo 1987–88, returned to manage Houston office; Amb. to Switzerland (also accred to Liechtenstein) 2006–08; currently Man. Dir Riverstone Holdings LLC, New York; immediate past Chair. and mem. Bd of Visitors for Univ. of Texas M. D. Anderson Cancer Center; apptd to Univ. of Texas System Bd of Regents 1993; fmr mem. Nat. Bd Smithsonian Inst.; mem. Bd of Dirs Cobalt Int. Energy; fmr Chair. Stanford Business School Trust, Houston/Harris County Sports Facility Public Advisory Cttee; fmr Dir Greater Houston Partnership; Trustee, Texas Heart Inst., Houston Museum of Fine Arts; Outstanding Young Texas Ex Award 1983, named a Distinguished Alumnus 2003, McCombs Business School Hall of Fame Award 2004. *Address:* Riverstone Holdings LLC, 1000 Louisiana Street, Suite 1000, Houston, TX 77002, USA (office). *Telephone:* (713) 357-1400 (office). *Fax:* (713) 357-1399 (office). *E-mail:* pconeway@riverstonellc.com (office). *Website:* www.riverstonellc.com (office).

CONFALONIERI-RICCA, Fedele; Italian media executive; *Chairman, Mediaset SpA;* b. 6 Aug. 1937, Milan; ed State Univ. of Milan; Chair. Mediaset SpA (commercial TV broadcaster), Deputy Chair. Mediaset Espana Comunicacion SA; mem. Bd of Dirs Il Giornale (nat. daily newspaper); mem. Bd of Dirs and Vice-Pres. Gestevision Telecinco SA 2000–; mem. Bd, Italian Confed. of Industry (Confindustria); mem. Exec. Cttee and Bd Lombardy Industrialists Confed. (Assolombarda); Chair. Nat. Television Broadcasters Asscn (part of Nat. Broadcasting Fed.); mem. Man. Council of Assonime (Asscn for Italian limited liability cos); Founding mem. ACT (European Asscn of Commercial Television Broadcasters). *Address:* Mediaset SpA, Viale Europa 46, 6th Floor, 20093 Cologno Monzese, Milan, Italy (office). *Telephone:* (02) 25141 (office). *E-mail:* simone.sole@mediaset.it (office). *Website:* www.mediaset.it/corporate (office).

CONILLE, Garry, MA, PhD; Haitian gynaecologist, UN official and politician; b. 26 Feb. 1966; s. of Serge Conille and Marie Antoinette Darbouze; m. Betty Rousseau; two d.; ed Univ. of Haiti, Univ. of North Carolina, USA; with Haitian Asscn for Nat. Devt 1994–98; Project Officer, UN Population Fund (UNPF), Haiti 1999–2001, Programme Officer 2001–02, Tech. Adviser, Int. Population Services, Haiti 2002–04, Sub-regional Tech. Adviser, Africa/Ethiopia Div., UNPF 2004–06, Chief Tech. Adviser for Africa region 2007, Team Leader, UNDP Millennium Devt Goals Unit 2008–10, Chief Aide, Office Man. for Special Envoy of UN Sec.-Gen. for Haiti (Bill Clinton) 2010, UNDP Resident Rep. and Humanitarian Coordinator in Niger June–Oct. 2011; Prime Minister 2011–12 (resgnd).

CONLON, James Joseph, BMus; American conductor; *Music Director, Los Angeles Opera;* b. 18 March 1950, New York; s. of Joseph Conlon and Angeline Conlon; m. Jennifer Ringo; two d.; ed High School of Music and Art, New York and Juilliard School; since making debut with New York Philharmonic has conducted every major US orchestra and many leading European orchestras; Conductor, New York Philharmonic Orchestra 1974–, debut at Metropolitan Opera 1976, Covent Garden 1979, Paris Opera 1982, Lyric Opera of Chicago 1988, La Scala, Milan 1993, Kirov Opera 1994; Music Dir Cincinnati May Festival 1979–2016, Rotterdam Philharmonic Orchestra 1983–91, Ravinia Festival 2005–15; Prin. Conductor, Paris Opera 1995–2004; Gen. Music Dir, City of Cologne 1989–2002, simultaneously Music Dir Gürzenich Orchestra and Cologne Opera; Music Dir Los Angeles Opera 2006–; Prin. Conductor, RAI National Symphony Orchestra, Turin 2016–; fmr mem. Faculty, Juilliard School of Music, residency 2007–; Commdr, Ordre des Arts et Lettres 1996, Officier, Légion d'honneur 2002; Dr hc (Juilliard School), (Brandeis Univ.), (Chapman Univ.); Premio Galileo Award 2000, Grand Prix du Disque for recording of Poulenc Piano Concertos, Opera News Award 2005, Crystal Globe Award, Anti-Defamation League 2007, Medal of the American Liszt Soc. 2008, Dushkin Award, Inst. of Chicago 2009, Lifetime Achievement Award, Istituto Italiano di Cultura 2010, Sachs Fund Prize, Arts Wave Org. for artistic achievements and outstanding contribution to the cultural life of Cincinnati 2016. *Recordings include:* numerous works by Mozart, Liszt, Poulenc; Rise and Fall of the City of Mahagonny (DVD) (Grammy Awards for Best Classical Album and Best Opera Recording 2009), Beethoven: Triple Concerto 2012, Dett Oratorio The Ordering of Moses 2016, Corigliano: The Ghosts Of Versailles (Grammy Award for Best Classical Engineered Album 2017) 2016. *Address:* c/o Jonathan Brill, Opus 3 Artists, 470 Park Avenue South, 9th Floor North, New York, NY 10016, USA (office). *Telephone:* (212) 584-7500 (office). *Fax:* (646) 300-8200 (office). *E-mail:* info@opus3artists.com (office). *Website:* www.opus3artists.com (office); www.laopera.org; www.jamesconlon.com.

CONN, Iain Cameron, FREng, FRSE, FICE; British business executive; *Chief Executive, Centrica plc;* b. 22 Oct. 1962, Edinburgh, Scotland; ed Imperial Coll., London; joined BP Oil International 1986, various roles in oil trading, commercial refining and exploration before becoming, on merger with Amoco 1999, Vice-Pres. BP Amoco Exploration's mid-continent business unit 1999–2000, returned to London as Group Vice-Pres. and mem. refining and marketing segment's Exec. Cttee 2000–01, responsible for BP's marketing operations in Europe 2001–02, Chief Exec. BP Petrochemicals 2002–04, mem. Bd of Dirs, BP plc 2004–14, Group Exec. Officer, Strategic Resources 2004–07, Chief Exec., Downstream 2007–14; Chief Exec. Centrica plc 2015–, Chair. Exec. Cttee, Disclosure Cttee; Dir (non-exec.), BT Group plc; Dir (non-exec.) and Sr Ind. Dir, Rolls-Royce Holdings plc 2005–14; Chair. Advisory Bd, Imperial Coll. Business School, mem. Council of Imperial Coll.; mem. Advisory Bd, Centre for European Reform, Centre for China in the World Economy, Tsinghua Univ.; Fellow, Royal Acad. of Eng, City and Guilds of London Inst. *Address:* Centrica plc, Millstream, Maidenhead Road, Windsor, Berks., SL4 5GD, England (office). *Telephone:* (1753) 494000 (office). *Fax:* (1753) 494001 (office). *E-mail:* info@centrica.co.uk (office). *Website:* www.centrica.co.uk (office).

CONNEH, Sekou Damate, Jr; Liberian politician; b. 1960, Gbarnga, Bong Co.; s. of Sekou Damate Conneh Sr and Margaret Makay; m. Aisha Keita Conneh; ed William V.C. Tubman Methodist High School; joined Progressive People's Party 1980, served as Sr Co-ordinator, Kokoyah Dist; exiled in Uganda 1980–85; apptd revenue agent, Ministry of Finance 1986; f. and served as Man. Dir Damate Corpn (import/export co.); Pres. Nat. Exec. Cttee, Liberians United for Reconciliation and Democracy (Progressive Democratic Party since 2005) from 2003, later Leader; unsuccessful cand. in presidential election 2005; f. Damate Peace Foundation. *Address:* c/o Progressive Democratic Party, McDonald Street, Monrovia, Liberia. *Telephone:* (6) 521091.

CONNELLY, Deirdre P., BA; American business executive; *President, North American Pharmaceuticals, GlaxoSmithKline plc;* b. San Juan, Puerto Rico; ed Lycoming Coll., Pa, Harvard Univ.'s Advanced Man. Program; joined Lilly as Sales Rep. 1983, Marketing Assoc. in San Juan 1984–89, joined Int. Man. Devt Program at Lilly Corp. Center 1989, Sales Supervisor in Phila, Pa 1989–90, Diabetes Product Man., San Juan 1990–91, Nat. Sales Man. for Puerto Rico affiliate 1991–92, Marketing and Sales Dir for Puerto Rico 1992–93, Dir of Sales and Marketing for Caribbean Basin Region, including Cen. America, Puerto Rico and Caribbean Island countries 1993–95, Gen. Man. Eli Lilly Puerto Rico, SA 1995–97, returned to Indianapolis 1997, held positions of Regional Sales Dir, Exec. Dir Global Marketing for Evista, and Team Leader for Evista Product Team 1997–2001, Leader, Woman's Health Business Unit in US affiliate 2001–03, Exec. Dir Human Resources for US affiliate 2003–04, Vice-Pres. Human Resources for Pharmaceutical Operations 2004–05, Sr Vice-Pres. Human Resources for Lilly and mem. Operations Cttee and Sr Man. Council 2005, Pres. Lilly USA, Eli Lilly & Co. 2005–09 (resgnd); Pres. North American Pharmaceuticals, GlaxoSmithKline (GSK) plc 2009–, CEO and Pres. Human Genome Sciences Inc. (co. acquired by GSK 2012) 2012–; mem. Bd of Dirs Macy's Inc. 2007–; Outstanding Achievement Award, Lycoming Coll. Alumni Asscn 2007. *Address:* GlaxoSmithKline, 5 Moore Drive, PO Box 13398, Research Triangle Park, NC 27709, USA (office). *Telephone:* (919) 483-2100 (office). *Fax:* (919) 549-7459 (office). *Website:* us.gsk.com (office).

CONNELLY, Jennifer; American actress; b. 12 Dec. 1970; d. of Gerard Connelly and Eileen Connelly; one s. with David Dugan; m. Paul Bettany 2002; three c.; ed Saint Ann's School, Brooklyn, Yale Univ. and Stanford Univ.; fmr model. *Films include:* Once Upon A Time in America 1984, Il mondo dell'orrore di Dario Argento 1985, Seven Minutes in Heaven 1985, The Valley 1985, Phenomena 1985, Labyrinth 1986, Inside the Labyrinth 1986, Some Girls 1988, Etoile 1988, The Hot Spot 1990, Career Opportunities 1991, The Rocketeer 1991, Of Love and

Shadows 1994, Higher Learning 1995, Far Harbor 1996, Mulholland Falls 1996, Inventing the Abbotts 1997, Dark City 1998, Requiem for a Dream 2000, Waking the Dead 2000, A Beautiful Mind (Acad. Award, BAFTA Award and Golden Globe Award for Best Supporting Actress 2002) 2001, Pollock 2001, House of Sand and Fog 2003, Hulk 2003, Dark Water 2005, Little Children 2006, Blood Diamond 2006, Reservation Road 2007, The Day the Earth Stood Still 2008, Inheart 2008, He's Just Not That Into You 2009, 9 (voice) 2009, Creation 2009, What's Wrong with Virginia 2010, The Dilemma 2011, Salvation Boulevard 2011, Stuck in Love 2012, Winter's Tale 2014, Aloft 2014, Noah 2014, Shelter 2014, American Pastoral 2016, Only the Brave 2017, Alita: Battle Angel 2019. *TV appearances include:* Tales of the Unexpected 1984, The $treet 2001. *Recording:* Monologue of Love (single, in Japanese). *Leisure interests:* hiking, camping, swimming, bike riding, quantum physics, philosophy. *Address:* c/o CAA, 2000 Avenue of the Stars, Los Angeles, CA 90067, USA (office).

CONNERY, Sir Sean, Kt; British actor; b. (Thomas Sean Connery), 25 Aug. 1930, Fountainbridge, Edinburgh, Scotland; s. of Joseph Connery and Euphamia Connery; m. 1st Diane Cilento 1962 (divorced 1973); one s. one step-d.; m. 2nd Micheline Boglio Roquebrun 1975; served in RN; Dir Tantallon Films Ltd 1972–; Fellow, Royal Scottish Acad. of Music and Drama 1984; mem. Scottish Nat. Party 1992–; Dir Fountainbridge Films (production co.) –2002; Freeman, City of Edinburgh 1991; Commdr des Arts et des Lettres 1987; Chevalier, Légion d'honneur; Hon. DLitt (Heriot-Watt) 1981, (St Andrews) 1988; American Cinematique Award 1991, Rudolph Valentino Award 1992, Nat. Board of Review Award, BAFTA Lifetime Achievement Award 1990, BAFTA Fellowship 1998. *Films include:* No Road Back 1955, Time Lock 1956, Action of the Tiger 1957, Another Time, Another Place, Hell Drivers, 1958, Darby O'Gill and the Little People 1959, Tarzan's Greatest Adventure 1959, On the Fiddle 1961, The Longest Day 1962, The Frightened City 1962, Woman of Straw 1964, Marnie 1964, The Hill 1965, A Fine Madness 1966, Shalako 1968, The Molly Maguires 1968, The Red Tent 1969, The Anderson Tapes 1970, The Offence 1973, Zardoz 1974, Murder on the Orient Express 1974, Ransom 1974, The Wind and the Lion 1975, The Man Who Would Be King 1975, Robin and Marian 1976, A Bridge Too Far 1977, The Great Train Robbery 1978, Meteor 1978, Cuba 1979, Outland 1981, The Man with the Deadly Lens 1982, The Untouchables (Acad. Award, Best Supporting Actor 1987) 1986, The Name of the Rose 1987, The Presidio 1988, Rosencrantz and Guildenstern are Dead, A Small Family Business, Indiana Jones and the Last Crusade 1989, Hunt for Red October 1989, The Russia House (BAFTA Award 1990) 1989, Mutant Ninja Turtles 1990, Highlander 2 1990, Medicine Man 1992, Rising Sun 1993, A Good Man in Africa 1994, First Knight 1994, Just Cause 1994, The Rock 1996, Dragonheart 1996, The Avengers 1998, Entrapment 1999, Playing By Heart 1999, Finding Forrester 2000, The League of Extraordinary Gentlemen 2003, Sir Billi the Vet (short) (voice) 2006, Sir Billi (voice) 2012; as James Bond in Dr. No 1962, From Russia with Love 1963, Goldfinger 1964, Thunderball 1965, You Only Live Twice 1967, Diamonds are Forever 1971, Never Say Never Again 1983. *Publications:* Neither Shaken Nor Stirred 1994, Being a Scot (memoirs) (with Murray Grigor) 2008. *Leisure interests:* golf, tennis, reading. *Address:* c/o Creative Artists Agency, 2000 Avenue of the Stars, Los Angeles, CA 90067, USA (office); Fountainbridge Films, 8428 Melrose Place, Unit C, Los Angeles, CA 90069, USA. *Telephone:* (424) 288-2000 (office); (323) 782-1177. *Fax:* (424) 288-2900 (office). *Website:* www.caa.com (office); www.seanconnery.com.

CONNES, Alain, PhD; French mathematician and academic; *Professor, Collège de France;* b. 1 April 1947, Draguignan (Var); ed Ecole Normale Supérieur, Paris; Research Fellow, CNRS 1970–74, Dir of Research 1981–84; Visiting Research Fellow, Queen's Univ., Kingston, Canada 1975; Assoc. Prof. and Prof., Univ. of Paris VI 1976–80; Long Term Prof. and Léon Motchane Prof., Institut des Hautes Etudes Scientifiques 1979–; Prof., Collège de France (chaire d'Analyse et Géométrie) 1984–; Distinguished Prof., Vanderbilt Univ., Nashville, Tenn., USA 2003–; Ed. Journal of Functional Analysis, Inventiones Mathematicae 1978–98, Communications in Mathematical Physic, Journal of Operator Theory, Ergodic Theory and Dynamical Systems 1981–93, Comptes rendus de l'Académie des sciences, Letters in Mathematical Physics, K-theory, Selecta Mathematica, Publications Mathématiques de l'IHES, Advances in Mathematics; Corresp. mem. Acad. des Sciences 1980, mem. 1983–; Foreign Assoc. mem. Royal Danish Acad. of Sciences 1980, Norwegian Acad. of Science 1993, NAS 1997, Russian Acad. of Sciences 2003; Foreign FRSC 1996; Hon. Foreign mem. American Acad. of Arts and Sciences 1990; Dr hc (Queen's Univ., Kingston) 1979, (Univ. of Rome Tor Vergata) 1997, (Univ. of Oslo) 1999, (Univ. of Southern Denmark) 2009, (Free Univ. of Brussels) 2010; Prix Aimé Berthé, Acad. des Sciences 1975, Prix Peccot-Vimont, Collège de France 1976, Médaille d'argent, CNRS 1977, Prix Ampère, Acad. des Sciences 1980, Fields Medal 1982, Clay Research Award 2000, Crafoord Prize 2001, CNRS Gold Medal 2004. *Publications:* Matière à pensée (co-author) 1989, Géométrie non commutative 1990, Noncommutative geometry 1994, Conversations on Mind, Matter, and Mathematics (co-author) 1995, Triangle de pensées (co-author) 2000, Triangle of Thought (co-author) 2001, Noncommutative Geometry, Quantum Fields and Motives (co-author) 2 2007; more than 150 publs in scientific journals. *Address:* Collège de France, 3 rue d'Ulm, 75231 Paris Cedex 05, France (office). *Telephone:* 1-44-27-17-05 (office). *Fax:* 1-44-27-17-04 (office). *E-mail:* alain@connes.org (office). *Website:* www.college-de-france.fr (office); www.ihes.fr (office); www.alainconnes.org; www.vanderbilt.edu (office).

CONNICK, Harry, Jr; American jazz musician (piano), singer and actor; b. 11 Sept. 1967, New Orleans, La; m. Jill Goodacre 1994; three c.; ed New Orleans Center for the Creative Arts, Hunter Coll. and Manhattan School of Music; studied with Ellis Marsalis. *Films include:* Memphis Belle 1990, Little Man Tate 1991, Copycat 1995, Independence Day 1996, Excess Baggage 1997, Action League Now!! (voice) 1997, Hope Floats 1998, The Iron Giant (voice) 1999, Wayward Son 1999, My Dog Skip (voice) 2000, The Simian Line 2000, Life Without Dick 2001, Basic 2003, Mickey 2004, The Happy Elf (voice) 2005, Bug 2006, P.S. I Love You 2007, New in Town 2009, Dolphin Tale 2011, Angels Sing 2013, Dolphin Tale 2 2014. *Theatre includes:* Thou Shalt Not (composer, Broadway) 2001, The Pajama Game (actor, Broadway) 2005. *Recordings include:* albums: 11 1978, Harry Connick Jr 1987, 20 1988, When Harry Met Sally (Grammy Award for Male Jazz Vocal Performance 1990) 1989, Lofty's Roach Soufflé 1990, We Are In Love 1990, Blue Light, Red Light 1991, 25 1992, When My Heart Finds Christmas 1993, Imagination 1994, She 1994, Whisper Your Name 1995, Star Turtle 1995, All Of Me 1996, To See You 1997, Come By Me 1999, 30 2001, Songs I Heard 2001, Other Hours: Connick On Piano, Vol. I 2003, Harry For The Holidays 2003, Only You 2004, Occasion 2005, Harry on Broadway, Act 1 2006, Oh, My Nola 2007, Chanson de Vieux Carré 2007, What a Night! A Christmas Album 2008, Your Songs 2009, In Concert on Broadway 2011, Music from the Happy Elf 2011, Smokey Mary 2013, That Would Be Me 2015; contrib. music for films Memphis Belle 1990, Little Man Tate 1991. *Television includes:* South Pacific (film) 2001, Will & Grace (series) 2002–06, Living Proof (film) 2008, Law & Order: Special Victims Unit (series) 2012, judge, American Idol 2013–16. *Address:* Wilkins Management Inc., 323 Broadway, Cambridge, MA 02139, USA (office). *Telephone:* (617) 354-2736 (office). *E-mail:* info@wilkinsmanagement.com (office); info@harryconnickjr.com (office). *Website:* www.harryconnickjr.com.

CONNOLLY, Sir Billy, Kt, CBE; British actor, comedian, playwright and presenter; b. 24 Nov. 1942, Anderston, Glasgow, Scotland; m. 1st Iris Pressagh (divorced 1985); one s. one d.; m. 2nd Pamela Stephenson 1990; three d.; worked as apprentice welder; performed originally with Gerry Rafferty and The Humblebums; first play, The Red Runner, staged at Edinburgh Fringe 1979; Patron Nat. Asscn for Bikers with a Disability, The Celtic Foundation; Freedom of the City of Glasgow 2010; Hon. DLitt (Glasgow) 2001, (Nottingham) 2010; Dr hc (Royal Scottish Acad. of Music and Drama, Glasgow) 2006; BAFTA Lifetime Achievement Award 2003, named Number One in Channel 4's 100 Greatest Stand Ups 2007, 2010, BAFTA Scotland Award for Outstanding Achievement in Television and Film 2012, Special Recognition Award, Nat. Television Awards 2016. *Plays written:* An' Me wi' a Bad Leg Tae 1975, When Hair Was Long and Time Was Short 1977, Red Runner 1979. *Theatre:* The Great Northern Welly Boot Show, The Beastly Beatitudes of Balthazar B 1982, What About Dick? 2012. *Films include:* Absolution 1978, Worzel Gummidge: A Cup o' Tea an' a Slice o' Cake 1980, Bullshot 1983, To the North of Katmandu 1986, The Hunting of the Snark 1987, The Return of the Musketeers 1989, The Big Man 1990, Indecent Proposal 1993, Pocahontas (voice) 1995, Treasure Island (Muppet Movie) 1996, Deacon Brodie (BBC Film) 1996, Beverly Hills Ninja 1997, Mrs Brown 1997, Ship of Fools 1997, Middleton's Changeling 1998, The Impostors 1998, Still Crazy 1998, The Debt Collector 1999, The Boondock Saints 1999, Beautiful Joe 2000, An Everlasting Piece 2000, The Man Who Sued God 2001, The Last Samurai 2003, Timeline 2003, Lemony Snicket's A Series of Unfortunate Events 2004, Garfield 2 2006, Open Season (voice) 2006, Fido 2006, The X Files: I Want to Believe 2008, Boondock Saints II 2009, Gulliver's Travels 2010, Open Season 2 2008, Good Sharma 2010, The Ballad of Nessie (voice) 2011, Brave (voice) 2012, Quartet 2012, The Hobbit: The Desolation of Smaug 2013, The Hobbit: There and Back Again 2014, What We Did on Our Holiday 2014, The Hobbit: The Battle of the Five Armies 2014, Wild Oats 2016; numerous video releases of live performances including Bite Your Bum (Music Week and Record Business Award 1982) 1981, An Audience with Billy Connolly 1985, Billy Connolly – Live in New York 2005, Billy Connolly Live – Was It Something I Said?. *Television includes:* Just Another Saturday (play) 1975, The Elephants' Graveyard (play) 1976, Blue Money 1982, Androcles and the Lion 1984, Return to Nose and Beak (Comic Relief), Head of the Class (series) 1990–91, South Bank Show Special (25th Anniversary Commemoration) 1992, Billy (series) 1992, Billy Connolly's World Tour of Scotland (six-part documentary) 1994, The Big Picture 1995, Billy Connolly's World Tour of Australia 1996, Deacon Brodie 1997, Erect for 30 Years 1998, Columbo: Murder with Too Many Notes 2000, Gentlemen's Relish 2001, Prince Charming 2001, Billy Connolly's World Tour of England, Ireland and Wales 2002, Gentleman's Relish, Billy Connolly's World Tour of New Zealand, Journey to the Edge of the World, Billy Connolly's Route 66 2011, House MD 2012, Billy Connolly's Big Send Off 2014, Who Do You Think You Are? (series) 2014. *Albums include:* The Great Northern Welly Boot Show (contains No. 1 hit D.I.V.O.R.C.E.), Pick of Billy Connolly (Gold Disc) 1982. *Publications include:* Gullible's Travels 1982. *Leisure interests:* Lifetime mem. Celtic Football Club. *Address:* c/o Tickety-boo Ltd, 2 Triq il-Barriera, Balzan, BZN 1200, Malta (office). *Telephone:* 21556166 (office). *Fax:* 21557316 (office). *E-mail:* tickety-boo@tickety-boo.com (office). *Website:* www.tickety-boo.com (office); www.billyconnolly.com.

CONNOR, Dean A., HBA; Canadian business executive; *President and CEO, Sun Life Financial Inc.;* ed Richard Ivey School of Business, Univ. of Western Ontario; with Mercer Human Resource Consulting 1978–2006, most recently as Pres. for the Americas –2006; joined Sun Life as Exec. Vice-Pres. with responsibility for UK and Reinsurance operations, strategic int. activities and corp. functions 2006–08, Pres. of Sun Life's Canadian operations 2008–10, COO with responsibility for Canadian and UK operations, MFS, Marketing, Human Resources, Information Tech. and other shared business services 2010–11, mem. Bd of Dirs, Pres. and CEO Sun Life Financial Inc. 2011–; mem. Ivey Advisory Bd; Dir Canadian Life and Health Insurance Asscn; Trustee, Univ. Health Network, Toronto; Fellow, Soc. of Actuaries, Canadian Inst. of Actuaries. *Address:* Sun Life Financial Inc., 150 King Street West, Toronto, ON M5H 1J9, Canada (office). *Telephone:* (416) 979-9966 (office). *Fax:* (416) 597-9108 (office). *E-mail:* boarddirectors@sunlife.com (office). *Website:* www.sunlife.com (office).

CONNORS, James Scott (Jimmy); American tennis player (retd); b. 2 Sept. 1952, East St. Louis, Ill.; s. of James Scott Connors I and Gloria Thompson Connors; m. Patti McGuire 1978; one s. one d.; ed Univ. of California, Los Angeles; amateur player 1970–72, professional 1972–96; Australian Open Champion 1974; Wimbledon Champion 1974, 1982; US Open Champion 1974, 1976, 1978, 1982, 1983; SA Champion 1973, 1974; WCT Champion 1977, 1980; Grand Prix Champion 1978; commentator for NBC; played Davis Cup for USA 1976, 1981; ranked World Number 1 for a record 157 weeks; won 109 tournament titles; joined BBC tennis commentary team for 2005 Wimbledon championships; coached Andy Roddick 2006–08; BBC Overseas Sports Personality 1982; inducted into International Tennis Hall of Fame 1998. *Publication:* The Outsider (autobiography) 2013. *Leisure interest:* golf. *Address:* c/o Electra Star Management, 9229 West Sunset Blvd, Suite 415, West Hollywood, CA 90069, USA (office). *Telephone:* (310) 943-1000 (office). *E-mail:* info@electrastarmgmt.com (office). *Website:* www.electrastarmgmt.com (office); jimmyconnors.net.

CONRAD, (Gaylord) Kent, AB, MBA; American fmr politician; b. 12 March 1948, Bismarck, ND; m. Lucy Calautti 1987; one d.; ed Univ. of Missouri, Stanford Univ. and George Washington Univ.; Asst to Tax Commr, State of ND Tax Dept,

Bismarck 1974–80, Tax Commr 1981–86; Senator from North Dakota 1987–2013 (retd), Chair. Budget Cttee Jan. 2001, June 2001–03, 2007–13; mem. Nat. Comm. on Fiscal Responsibility and Reform (Simpson-Bowles comm.) 2010; mem. Bd of Dirs Genworth Financial Inc. 2013–; Democrat. *Address:* c/o Board of Directors, Genworth Financial Inc., 6620 West Broad Street, Richmond, VA 23230, USA.

CONRAD, Kevin Mark, BS, MBA; Papua New Guinea/American diplomatist and international organization official; *Executive Director, Coalition for Rainforest Nations;* b. 21 June 1968, California; ed Ukarumpa High School, Eastern Highlands Prov., Papua New Guinea, Univ. of Southern California, USA, London Business School, UK, Columbia Univ., New York, USA; grew up in Arapesh tribe nr Wewak, East Sepik Prov., Papua New Guinea; worked in investment banking; serves as Special Envoy and Amb. for Environment and Climate Change for Papua New Guinea, also Special Envoy and Amb. to UN Climate Change Conf., Durban 2011; mem. Faculty, School for Int. and Public Affairs, Columbia Univ.; Exec. Dir Coalition for Rainforest Nations, has been instrumental in establishment of World Bank's Forest Carbon Partnership Facility and UN's UN-REDD (Reducing Emissions from Deforestation and Forest Degradation in developing countries) programme; has advised govts in Africa, Asia, Latin America and the Pacific on sustainable devt, econ. reform and investment incentive programmes; Distinguished Service Award, Columbia Business School 2005, named by Time magazine No. 1 in 'Leaders & Visionaries' category of Heroes of the Environment 2008, named 'Champion of the Earth' by UNEP 2009. *Address:* Coalition for Rainforest Nations, 52 Vanderbilt Avenue, 14th Floor, New York, NY 10017, USA (office). *Telephone:* (212) 535-2000 (office). *Fax:* (212) 504-2622 (office). *E-mail:* Kevin@cfrn.org (office). *Website:* www.rainforestcoalition.org (office).

CONRADO, Dan, MBA, MBA; Brazilian business executive; *Chairman, Vale;* ed Universidade Dom Bosco, Mato Grosso do Sul, COPPEAD/Universidade Fed. do Rio de Janeiro, Instituto de Ensino e Pesquisa em Administração (INEPAD); CEO Previ (pension fund of the employees of Banco do Brasil) 2012–; CEO Valepar 2012–; mem. Bd of Dirs and Chair. Vale 2012–; mem. Bd of Dirs FRAS-LE SA 2010–; Alt. mem. Bd of Dirs BRASILPREV SA Jan.–March 2010, Aliança do Brasil SA 2010–11, Mapfre BBSH2 Participações SA 2011–; Dir for Marketing and Communications, Banco do Brasil SA 2009, also served as Dir of Distribution 2010–11, and Vice-Pres. for Retail, Distribution and Operations 2011–12; mem. Fiscal Council, Centrais Elétricas de Santa Catarina SA 2000–02, WEG SA 2002–05. *Address:* Vale, Av. Graça Aranha, 26, 20030-900 Rio de Janeiro RJ, Brazil (office). *Telephone:* (21) 3814-4477 (office). *Fax:* (21) 3814-4040 (office). *E-mail:* info@vale.com (office). *Website:* www.vale.com (office).

CONRAN, Jasper Alexander Thirlby, OBE; British fashion designer; *Chairman and Chief Creative Director, The Conran Shops;* b. 12 Dec. 1959, London; s. of Sir Terence Conran (q.v.) and Shirley Conran; m. Oisin Byrne 2015; ed Bryanston School, Dorset, Parsons School of Art and Design, New York; launched his first women's wear collection in 1978; founding bd mem. London Designer Collections (renamed London Fashion Week); Fashion Designer, Man. Dir Jasper Conran Ltd 1978–; designer of lines for Debenhams 1997–; designed theatre costumes and sets for various performative arts (more than 13 plays, ballets and operas) including Jean Anouilh's The Rehearsal, Almeida Theatre 1990, My Fair Lady 1992; Sleeping Beauty, Scottish Ballet 1994, The Nutcracker Sweeties, Birmingham Royal Ballet 1996, Edward II 1997, Arthur 2000; launched signature Fragrances Man and Woman 2003, Eyewear Collection with Specsavers 2008; Chair. and Creative Dir, The Conran Shop 2012–15; Chair. Conran Holdings Ltd 2014–15; f. Jasper Conran Foundation 2013; opened L'Hotel Marrakech 2016; Visiting Prof. Univ. of Arts London; collaborated with various brands including Waterford, Wedgewood; Amb. Prince's Foundation; Trustee Wallace Collection; Hon. DLitt (Heriot-Watt Univ.) 2004, Hon. DCL (Univ. of East Anglia) 2006; Fil d'Or (Int. Linen Award) 1982, 1983, British Fashion Council Designer of the Year Award 1986–87, Fashion Group of America Award 1987, Laurence Olivier Award for Costume Designer of the Year 1991, British Collections Award (in British Fashion Awards) 1991, Prince's Medal, Homes & Gardens Classic Design Award 2003, 2006, British Interior Design Association Award for Outstanding Design 2004, 'Object of Desire' Design and Decoration Award 2005, 'Innovation & Design' Conde Nast Traveller Award 2011. *Publication:* Country 2010. *Address:* Jasper Conran Ltd, 1–7 Rostrevor Mews, Fulham, London, SW6 5AZ, England. *Telephone:* (20) 7384-0800. *Fax:* (20) 7384-0801. *E-mail:* info@jasperconran.com. *Website:* www.jasperconran.com.

CONRAN, Sir Terence Orby, Kt, CH, FCSD; British designer, retail executive and writer; b. 4 Oct. 1931, Esher, Surrey, England; s. of Rupert Conran and Christina Halstead; m. 1st Brenda Davison (divorced); m. 2nd Shirley Conran (divorced 1962); two s.; m. 3rd Caroline Herbert 1963 (divorced 1996); two s. one d.; m. 4th Vicki Davis 2000; ed Bryanston School and Cen. School of Art and Design, London; Chair. Conran Holdings Ltd 1965–68; Jt Chair. Ryman Conran Ltd 1968–71; Chair. Habitat Group Ltd 1971–88, Habitat/Mothercare PLC 1982–88; Chair. Habitat France SA 1973–88, Conran Stores Inc. 1977–88, J. Hepworth & Son Ltd 1981–83 (Dir 1979–83), Richard Shops 1983; Chair. Storehouse PLC 1986–90, CEO 1986–88, Dir (non-exec.) 1990; Chair. The Conran Shop Ltd 1976–, Conran Roche 1980–, Jasper Conran 1982–, Butlers Wharf 1984–90, Bibendum Restaurant 1986–, Benchmark Ltd 1989–, Blueprint Café 1989–, Terence Conran Ltd 1990–, Conran Holdings 1990–, The Conran Shop SNC 1990–, Le Pont de la Tour 1991–, Quaglino's Restaurant Ltd 1991–, The Butler's Wharf Chop House Ltd 1992–; CD Partnership 1993–, Conran Restaurants Ltd 1994–, Bluebird Store Ltd 1994–, Mezzo Ltd 1995–, Conran Shop Marylebone 1995–, Conran Shop Germany 1996–, Coq d'Argent Ltd 1997–, Orrery Ltd 1997–; Vice-Pres. FNAC 1985–89; Dir Conran Ink Ltd 1969–, The Neal Street Restaurant 1972–89, Electra Risk Capital 1981–84, Conran Octopus Ltd 1983–, Heal & Son Ltd 1983–87, Savacentre 1986–88, British Home Stores 1986–88, Michelin House Investment Co. Ltd 1989–; f. Conran Foundation, Butler's Wharf; launched Content by Conran range of furniture for Christie Tyler 2003; mem. Royal Comm. on Environmental Pollution 1973–76; mem. Council, RCA 1978–81, 1986–, Provost 2003–11; mem. Advisory Council, Victoria & Albert Museum 1979–83, Trustee 1984–90; Trustee Design Museum 1989–, Chair. 1992–; mem. Creative Leaders' Network; Commdr des Arts et des Lettres 1991; Dr hc (RCA) 1996, Hon. DLitt (Portsmouth) 1996, (London South Bank) 2007; Hon. Dr of Architecture (Univ. of Pretoria) 2012; RSA Bicentenary Medal 1982, Minerva Medal, Chartered Society of Designers, Prince Philip Designers Prize for lifetime achievements in design 2003. *Publications include:* The House Book 1974, The Kitchen Book 1977, The Bedroom & Bathroom Book 1978, The Cook Book (with Caroline Conran) 1980, The New House Book 1985, The Conran Directory of Design 1985, The Soft Furnishings Book 1986, Plants at Home 1986, Terence Conran's France 1987, Terence Conran's D.I.Y. by Design 1989, D.I.Y. in the Garden 1991, Terence Conran's Toys and Children's Furniture 1992, Terence Conran's Kitchen Book 1993, The Essential House Book 1994, Terence Conran on Design 1996, The Essential Garden Book 1998, Easy Living 1999, Chef's Garden 1999, Terence Conran on Restaurants 1999, Terence Conran on London 2000, Q and A: A Sort of Autobiography 2001, Terence Conran on Small Spaces 2001, How to Live in Small Spaces 2006, Outdoors: The Garden Design Book for the Twenty-First Century (with Diarmuid Gavin) 2007, Terence Conran's Inspiration (with Stafford Cliff) 2009, Essential Colour 2011, Eco House Book 2012, Plain, Simple, Useful – The Essence of Conran Style 2014. *Leisure interests:* gardening, cooking. *Address:* 22 Shad Thames, London, SE1 2YU, England. *Telephone:* (20) 7378-1161. *Fax:* (20) 7403-4309. *E-mail:* hello@conran.com. *Website:* www.conran.com.

CONSTANT, Paule, DèsSc; French author; b. 25 Jan. 1944, Gan; d. of Yves Constant and Jeanne Tauzin; m. Auguste Bourgeade 1968; one s. one d.; ed Univ. of Bordeaux and Univ. of Paris (Sorbonne); Asst Lecturer in French Literature, Univ. of Abidjan 1968–75; Maître-assistant, then Maître de Conférences in French Literature and Civilization, Univ. of Aix-Marseille III 1975–90, Inst. of French Studies for Foreign Students 1986–95; Prof., Université Aix–Marseille III 1995–; diarist, Revue des Deux Mondes, Paris 1990–92; Founder and Pres. Centre des Ecrivains du Sud - Jean Giono; mem. Académie Goncourt 2013–; mem. jury, Prix Femina 2009–13; Chevalier, Légion d'honneur, Ordre de l'Educ. Nat. de Côte d'Ivoire. *Television includes:* L'Education des Jeunes Filles de la Légion d'Honneur 1992, Mon héros préféré: La Princesse de Clèves 1996, Les grands fleuves racontés par des écrivains: L'Amazone 1997, Galilée: Paule Constant sur les traces de Jean Giono 2001. *Publications include:* novels: Ouregano 1980 (Prix Valery Larbaud), Propriété privée 1981, Balta 1983, White Spirit 1989 (Prix François Mauriac, Prix Lutèce, Prix du Sud Jean-Baumel, Grand Prix du Roman, Acad. Française), Le Grand Ghâpal 1991, La Fille du Gobernator 1994, Confidence pour confidence 1998 (Prix du roman France-Télévision, Prix Goncourt, Un monde à l'usage des demoiselles (essay) 1987 (Grand Prix de l'Essai, Acad. Française 1987), Sucre et Secret 2003 (Prix du roman, Amnesty international), La Bête à Chagrin 2007. *Leisure interest:* bibliophile (18th and 19th century works on educ.). *Address:* Institut d'études françaises pour étudiants étrangers, 23 rue Gaston de Saporta, 13100 Aix-en-Provence (office); 29 rue Cardinale, 13100 Aix-en-Provence, France. *Telephone:* 4-42-38-45-08 (office). *Fax:* 4-42-23-02-64 (office). *Website:* www.pauleconstant.com.

CONSTANTINE, David John, BA, PhD, FRSL; British poet, writer and translator; b. 4 March 1944, Salford, Lancs.; s. of Bernard Constantine and Bertha Constantine; m. Helen Frances Best 1966; one s. one d.; ed Wadham Coll., Oxford; Lecturer, then Sr Lecturer in German, Durham Univ. 1969–81; Fellow in German, The Queen's Coll., Oxford 1981–2000; Co-Ed. (with Bernard O'Donoghue) Oxford Poets anthologies 2000–11, (with Helen Constantine) Modern Poetry in Translation magazine 2004–12; mem. Poetry Soc., Soc. of Authors; Hon. DLitt (Durham) 2009; Alice Hunt Bartlett Prize 1984, Runciman Prize 1985, Southern Arts Literature Prize 1987, European Poetry Trans. Prize 1998, BBC Nat. Short Story Award 2010, Frank O'Connor Int. Short Story Award 2013. *Publications include:* poetry: A Brightness to Cast Shadows 1980, Watching for Dolphins 1983, Mappi Mundi 1984, Madder 1987, Selected Poems 1991, Caspar Hauser 1994, Sleeper 1995, The Pelt of Wasps 1998, Something for the Ghosts 2002, Collected Poems 2004, A Poetry Primer 2004, Nine Fathom Deep 2009, Elder 2014; fiction: Davies 1985, Back at the Spike 1994, Under the Dam (short stories) 2005, The Shieling (short stories) 2009, Tea at the Midland (short story) (BBC Nat. Short Story Prize 2010), Tea at the Midland and Other Stories 2012, In Another Country (selected stories); non-fiction: The Significance of Locality in the Poetry of Friedrich Hölderlin 1979, Early Greek Travellers and the Hellenic Ideal 1984, Hölderlin 1988, Friedrich Hölderlin 1992, Fields of Fire: A Life of Sir William Hamilton 2001, A Living Language 2004; translator: Hölderlin: Selected Poems 1990, 1996, 2018, Henri Michaux: Spaced, Displaced (with Helen Constantine) 1992, Philippe Jaccottet: Under Clouded Skies/Beauregard (with Mark Treharne) 1994, Goethe: Elective Affinities 1994, Kleist: Selected Writings 1998, Hölderlin's Sophocles 2001, Hans Magnus Enzensberger: Lighter Than Air 2002, Goethe: Faust 2005, 2009; ed.: German Short Stories 2 1972, Goethe: Werther, Brecht: Love Poems (with Tom Kuhn), Brecht Collected Poems (with Tom Kuhn) 2018. *Leisure interest:* walking. *Address:* The Queen's College, Oxford, OX1 4AW (office); 1 Hill Top Road, Oxford, OX4 1PB, England (home). *Telephone:* (1865) 244701 (office). *E-mail:* david.constantine@queens.ox.ac.uk (office).

CONSTANTINE II, King of the Hellenes; Greek; b. 2 June 1940, Athens; s. of King Paul and Queen Frederica of the Hellenes; m. Princess Anne-Marie of Denmark 1964; three s. two d.; ed Anavryta School and Law School, Athens Univ.; mil. training 1956–58, graduated from three mil. acads (army, navy, air force); visited USA 1958, 1959; succeeded to throne March 1964; left Greece Dec. 1967; deposed June 1973; monarchy abolished by Nat. Referendum Dec. 1974; deprived of Greek citizenship, remaining property in Greece nationalized April 1994; won ruling in European Court of Human Rights for compensation; returned to live in Greece 2013; Pres., Round Square, International Dragon Asscn; Gold Medal, Sailing (Dragon Class), Olympic Games, Rome 1960, Beppe Croce Trophy in recognition of outstanding voluntary contrib. to sport of sailing, Int. Sailing Fed. (ISAF) 2010. *Address:* 27 Hill Street, London, W1J 5LP, England (office). *Website:* www.greekroyalfamily.org.

CONSTANTINESCU, Emil, PhD, DSc; Romanian politician, jurist, geologist and fmr head of state; *President, Romanian Foundation for Democracy;* b. 19 Nov. 1939, Tighina (now Repub. of Moldova); s. of Ion Constantinescu and Maria Constantinescu; m. Nadia Ileana Bogorin; one s. one d.; ed Bucharest Univ.; practising lawyer 1960–61; Lecturer and Sr Lecturer, Bucharest Univ. 1966–90, Prof. of Mineralogy 1990–, Vice-Rector 1990–92, Rector 1992–96, Hon. Pres. of Senate 1996–, Prof. of Mineralogy-Crystallography 2001–; Visiting Prof., Duke Univ., NC, USA 1991–92; Chair Nat. Romanian Council of Univ. Rectors 1992–96; mem. Steering Cttee of European Univs Assoc. (CRE) 1992–98, Int. Assoc. of Univ.

Presidents 1994–96, Founder-mem. Univ. Solidarity 1990; Pres. Civic Acad. 1990–92; Acting Chair. Romanian Anti-Totalitarian Forum 1991; Pres. Democratic Convention 1992–96; Pres. of Romania 1996–2000; currently Pres. Romanian Foundation for Democracy, Romanian Academic Forum, Inst. for Advanced Studies in Levant Culture and Civilization; Gen. Sec. Romanian Geological Soc. 1987–93, 1990–93; Co-Chair. World Justice Project (sponsored by ABA, European Bar Asscn, World Bar Asscn) 2007–; mem. A Global Forum on New Democracies, Taipei 2008; mem. Balkan Political Club 2001–, East West Inst., Victims of Communism Memorial Foundation, Washington, DC, High Council Int. Org. of Francophony 2004–; Int. Centre for Democratic Transition, Budapest 2006–; Fellow, World Acad. of Art and Science; Hon. Citizen of Athens, Prague, Budapest, San Francisco and Helsinki; Hon. mem. Geological and Mineralogical Socs of America, UK, Germany, SA, Japan, Greece; Hon. mem. Nat. Geographical Soc. of USA and Geographical Soc. of France; Grand Master, Order of Michael the Brave, Order of the Star of Romania; Emblema de Onoare a Armatei Române 2010; numerous int. decorations, including Grand Croix, Stara Planina with Ribbon (Romania), Great Cross of St Olaf (Norway), Order of the Dannebrog, St Andrew Order, Patriarchy of Constantinople, Orthodox Order of the Holy Grave with Collar, Orthodox Patriarchy in Jerusalem, Collar of Dom Infante Henrique (Portugal), Great Cross of High Order of St Michael and St George (UK), White Rose of Finland with Collar 1998, Order of Merit (Austria) 1999, State Decoration (Turkey) 1999, Kt, Order of the Elephant (Denmark) 2000, Grand Order of King Tomislav (Croatia) 2000, Grand Cross (or First Class), Order of the White Double Cross (Slovakia) 2000; Hon. DSc (Univs of Athens, Liège, Montréal, Delhi, Beijing, Ankara, Chişinău, Astana, Maribor, Bangkok, Sofia, Ecole Nationale Supérieur, Paris); numerous awards including Romanian Acad. Award in Geology 1980, Aristide Calvany Award for Peace, Democracy and Human Devt Paris 1997, Award for Democracy of Democratic Center, Washington, DC 1998, European Coudenhove-Kalergi Award for Contrib. to Devt of Europe and Free Movt of Ideas, Bern 1998; awards and medals from Acad. des Sciences, Inst. de France, Univs of Paris-Sorbonne, Prague, Amsterdam, Bratislava, Szeged, São Paulo. *Publications:* 12 books and more than 60 articles in scientific journals and more than 100 articles, speeches and essays on political, econ., social, educational, cultural and environmental issues; Time of Tearing Down, Time of Building (four vols). *Address:* Romanian Foundation for Democracy, 050093 Bucharest, Splaiul Independenţei 17, bloc 101, parter, sector 5, Romania (office). *Telephone:* (21) 3160397 (office). *Fax:* (21) 3160397 (office). *E-mail:* emil@constantinescu.ro (home); office@frd.org.ro (office). *Website:* frd.org.ro (office); www.constantinescu.ro.

CONSTAS, Dimitri, LLB, PhD; Greek academic, research institute director and fmr government official; *Professor of International Relations, Panteion University;* ed Panteion Univ., Univ. of Thessaloniki, Carleton Univ., Canada, Tufts Univ., USA; Founder and Prof. of Int. Relations, Inst. of Int. Relations, Panteion Univ., Athens 1989–, Rector, Panteion Univ. 1990–95; Interim Minister for Press and Mass Media 1996; Perm. Rep. to Council of Europe, Strasbourg 1997–99; Head of Task Forces on Euro-Mediterranean Co-operation, Middle East Peace Process, Greek role in Int. Conflict Resolution 2000; Pres. Hellenic Soc. of Int. Law and Int. Relations 1989–91; Vice-Pres. Foundation for Hellenic Culture 1994–95; Fellow, Woodrow Wilson Int. Center for Scholars 1998; Int. Relations Scholar, Minda de Gunzburg Center for European Studies, Harvard Univ. 2011; Fulbright Scholar 1976–79, MacJannet Fellow, Institut des Hautes Etudes Internationaux 1978, Robert Schumann Fellow in European Integration 1979, Noted Scholar, Univ. of British Columbia 1996, Sr Fulbright Scholar, Princeton Univ. 1996. *Publications include:* The Greek–Turkish Conflict in the 1990s (ed.) 1991, Modern Diasporas in World Politics: the Greeks in Comparative Perspective (co-ed.) 1993, Greece Prepares for the Twenty-First Century (co-ed.) 1995, Greek and European Foreign Policy (1991–99), Diplomacy and Politics 2003, La revue internationale et stratégique, N° 61, Printemps 2006 (co-author) 2006. *Address:* Institute of International Relations, Panteion University, 3–5 Hill Street, Athens 105 58, Greece (office). *Telephone:* (21) 13312325 (office). *Fax:* (21) 13313575 (office). *E-mail:* constas@idis.gr (office). *Website:* www.idis.gr (office).

CONTAMINE, Philippe, DèsSc; French historian and academic; *Professor Emeritus of Medieval History, Université Paris-Sorbonne;* b. 7 May 1932, Metz; s. of Henry Contamine and Marie-Thérèse Dufays; m. Geneviève Bernard 1956; two s. one d.; ed Lycée Malherbe, Caen, Lycée Louis-le-Grand, Paris, Sorbonne; history and geography teacher, Lycée, Sens 1957–60, Lycée Carnot, Paris 1960–61; Asst Prof. of Medieval History, Sorbonne 1962–65; Asst Lecturer, Lecturer then Prof. of Medieval History, Univ. of Nancy 1965–73; Prof. of Medieval History, Univ. of Paris (Nanterre) 1973–89; Prof. of Medieval History, Univ. of Paris (Sorbonne) 1989–2000, Prof. Emer. 2000–; Dir Dept of History 1976–79; Sec. to Soc. de l'histoire de France 1984–; Pres. Nat. Soc. of Antique Dealers 1999; mem. Institut de France (Acad. des Inscriptions et Belles-Lettres, Pres. 2000) 1990, Academia Europaea 1993; Corresp. Fellow, Royal Historical Soc. 1993; Pres. Soc. Nat. des Antiquaires de France 1999; Chevalier, Légion d'honneur 2000, Officier 2009; Commdr des Palmes académiques; Officier des Arts et des Lettres. *Publications include:* La Guerre de cent ans 1968, Guerre, Etat et Société à la fin du Moyen Age 1972, La Vie quotidienne en France et en Angleterre pendant la guerre de cent ans 1976, La guerre au Moyen Age 1980, La France aux XIVe et XVe siècles 1981, La France de la fin du XVe siècle (co-ed.) 1985, L'Etat et Les Aristocraties (ed.) 1989, L'histoire militaire de la France 1992, Des pouvoirs en France 1300–1500 1992, L'Economie Mediévale 1993, De Jeanne d'Arc aux guerres d'Italie 1994, La Noblesse au royaume de France de Philippe Le Bel à Louis XII 1997, Guerre et concurrence entre les Etats européens du XIVe au XVIIIe siècle (ed.) 1998, Autour de Marguerite d'Ecosse: reines, princesses et dames du XVe siècle (ed.) 1999, Les enceintes urbaines XIIIe-XVIe (co-author) 2002, Histoire de la France politique 2002. *Address:* 11–15 rue de l'Amiral Roussin, 75015 Paris, France.

CONTE, Fernando, BSc, MBA; Spanish airline executive; *Chairman and President, Orizonia Travel Group sl;* b. 28 Feb. 1950, Mérida, Mexico; m.; two d.; ed Instituto Catolico de Artes e Industrias, Instituto de Empresa (pvt. business school); worked for Asea Brown Boveri 1974–2003, positions included Sales Engineer/Product Man., Madrid, Regional Man. for Cen. America/Caribbean, Asea AB, Guatemala City, Industrial Div. Man. for Asea in Venezuela, Cen. Region Man., Asea Eléctrica, Madrid, Man. Power Transmission and Distribution Div., ASEA/ABB Energía, Madrid, Gen. Man. ABB Subestaciones, Madrid, Gen. Man. ABB Trafo, Madrid, Segment Vice-Pres. Asea Brown Boveri, SA, Madrid, Exec. Vice-Pres. and CEO Asea Brown Boveri, SA, Madrid, mem. Bd ABB Portugal, mem. ABB Ltd Group Exec. Team, Zurich; Ind. Bd mem. Iberia 2001–03, Chair. and CEO Iberia Group 2003–13; Chair. and Pres. Orizonia Travel Group sl (formed from Grupo Iberostar) 2013–; Ind. Bd mem. Amadeus 2000–03; Chair. oneworld (airline alliance) 2005–06, Audit Cttee IATA 2005–, Asscn of European Airlines 2007–; Javier Benjumea Prize, Coll. Asscn of Engineers—ICAI 2005. *Address:* Orizonia Travel Group sl, Calle De Rita Levy, 07121 Palma, Spain (office). *Telephone:* (91) 357-13-93 (office). *Fax:* (91) 732-59-64 (office).

CONTE, Giuseppe; Italian academic and politician; *Prime Minister;* b. 8 Aug. 1964, Volturara Appula, Foggia; s. of Nicola Conte and Lillina Roberti; m. Valentina Fico (divorced); one c.; partner Olivia Paladino; ed La Sapienza Univ. of Rome, Duquesne Univ., Int. Culture Inst., Vienna, Sorbonne Univ.; taught at Roma Tre Univ., LUMSA Univ. of Rome, Univ. of Malta, Univ. of Sassari; taught Pvt. Law at Faculty of Econs, Libera Università Internazionale degli Studi Sociali Guido Carli (LUISS) 2007–08, Scientific Man. 2006; Prime Minister 2018–; mem. Bureau of Admin. Justice, Chamber of Deputies 2013; Prof. of Private Law, Univ. of Florence. *Publications include:* Il volontariato: Libertà dei privati e mediazione giuridica dello Stato 1996, Matrimonio civile e teoria della simulazione 1996, La simulazione del matrimonio nella teoria del negozio giuridico 1999, Le regole della solidarità. Iniziative non profit dei privati e mediazione dei pubblici poteri 2001, Il danno non patrimoniale 2018, La formazione del contratto 2018. *Address:* Office of the Prime Minister, Palazzo Chigi, Piazza Colonna 370, 00187 Roma, Italy (office). *Telephone:* (06) 67791 (office). *E-mail:* ufficio_stampa@governo.it (office). *Website:* www.governo.it (office).

CONTEH, Maj. (retd) (Alfred) Palo, LLB (Hons), LLM; Sierra Leonean army officer (retd) and government official; ed Univs of London and East London, UK; served in Sierra Leone army 1976–92, rose to rank of Maj. and CO of the Mil. Police; went to UK on leave to pursue legal studies 1986; Court Liaison Officer and Prosecution Sec., Dept for Work and Pensions for the investigation service in London –2007; Minister of Defence 2007–16, 2017, of Internal Affairs 2016–17; CEO Nat. Ebola Response Centre 2014–16.

CONTI, Fulvio; Italian business executive; b. 28 Oct. 1947, Rome; m.; one s.; ed Univ. of Rome 'La Sapienza'; joined Mobil Group 1969, Chief of Finance for Europe 1989–90; Head, Accounting, Finance and Control Dept Montecatini 1991–93; Head of Finance Montedison-Compart 1993–96; Gen. Man. and Chief Financial Officer Italian Nat. Railways 1996–98; also held important positions in other cos, including Metropolis and Grandi Stazioni; Vice-Chair. Eurofima 1997; Gen. Man. and Chief Financial Officer Telecom Italia 1998–99, also held important positions in other cos of the group, including Finsiel, TIM, Sirti, Italtel, Meie and STET International; Chief Financial Officer Enel SpA 1999–2005, CEO and Gen. Man. 2005–14; Chair. Eurelectric 2011–13; Deputy Chair. Endesa SA 2009–14, Research Dept of Confindustria; Vice-Pres. Eurelectric Aisbl from 2008; mem. Bd of Dirs Barclays plc 2006–14, AON Corpn 2008–, RCS MediaGroup SpA 2012–; Dir, Nat. Acad. of Santa Cecilia, Italian Tech. Inst.; Cavaliere del Lavoro della Repubblica Italiana 2009, Officier, Légion d'honneur 2009. *Address:* RCS MediaGroup, Via Angelo Rizzoli 8, 20132 Milan, Italy (office). *Telephone:* (02) 25841 (office). *E-mail:* ufficiostampa.rcs@rcs.it (office). *Website:* www.rcsmediagroup.it (office).

CONTI, Most Rev. Mario Joseph, PhL, STL, FRSE; British ecclesiastic; *Archbishop Emeritus of Glasgow;* b. 20 March 1934, Elgin, Moray, Scotland; s. of Louis Joseph Conti and Josephine Quintilia Conti (née Panicali); ed Blairs Coll., Aberdeen, Pontifical Scots Coll. and Gregorian Univ., Rome; ordained priest 1958; apptd Curate, St Mary's Cathedral, Aberdeen 1959, apptd Parish Priest, St Joachim's Wick 1962; Bishop of Aberdeen 1977–2002; Archbishop of Glasgow 2002–12, Archbishop Emer. 2012–; Apostolic Admin. Diocese of Paisley 2004–05; Pres.-Treas. Scottish Catholic Int. Aid Fund 1978–84; Pres. Nat. Liturgy Comm. 1981–85, Nat. Comm. for Christian Doctrine and Unity 1985–; Vice-Pres. Comm. for Migrant Workers and Tourism 1978–84, Scottish Catholic Heritage Comm. 1980–; mem. Council for Promotion of Christian Unity (Rome) 1984–, Int. Comm. for English in the Liturgy 1978–87, Pontificial Comm. for Cultural Heritage of the Church, Rome 1994–2004; Convener, Action of Churches Together in Scotland 1990–93; Co-Moderator of Jt Working Group, RC Church and WCC 1995–2008; Prin. Chaplain to British Asscn of the Order of Malta 1995–2000, 2005–, Conventual Chaplain Grand Cross 2001–; mem. Historic Buildings Council of Scotland 1995–2000; Hon. Prof. of Theology, Univ. of Aberdeen 2002; Order of Merit of the Italian Repub. 1982; Kt Commdr of Holy Sepulchre 1989; Kt, Order of St John of Jerusalem Rhodes and Malta 1991; Grande Ufficiale della Stella della Solidarietà Italiana 2007; Hon. DD (Aberdeen) 1989, (Glasgow) 2010. *Publications:* Oh Help! The Making of an Archbishop 2003; occasional articles and letters in nat. and local press. *Leisure interests:* walking, travel, swimming, music and the arts. *Address:* Curial Offices, 196 Clyde Street, Glasgow, G1 4JY (office); 40 Newlands Road, Glasgow G43 2JD, Scotland (home). *Telephone:* (141) 226-5898 (office). *Fax:* (141) 225-2600 (office). *E-mail:* curia@rcag.org.uk (office). *Website:* www.rcag.org.uk (office).

CONTI, Tom; British actor, theatre director and novelist; b. (Thomas Antonio Conti), 22 Nov. 1941, Paisley, Renfrewshire, Scotland; s. of Alfonso Conti and Mary McGoldrick; m. Kara Drummond Wilson 1967; one d.; ed Hamilton Park School and Royal Scottish Acad. of Music and Drama, Glasgow; West End Theatre Mans' Award, Royal Television Soc. Award, Variety Club of Great Britain Award 1978, Tony Award of New York 1979. *Theatre includes:* Savages (Christopher Hampton) 1973, The Devil's Disciple (Shaw) 1976, Whose Life is it Anyway? (Brian Clarke) 1978, They're Playing Our Song (Neil Simon/Marvin Hamlisch) 1980, Romantic Comedy (Bernard Salde), An Italian Straw Hat 1986, Two Into One, Treats 1989, Jeffrey Bernard is Unwell 1990, The Ride Down Mt. Morgan 1991, Present Laughter (also dir) 1993, Chapter Two 1996, Jesus My Boy 1998–99, 2009, Twelve Angry Men 2014, Rough Justice (Terence Frisby) 2015. *Films include:* Flame, Full Circle, Merry Christmas Mr. Lawrence, Reuben, American Dreamer, Saving Grace, Miracles, Heavenly Pursuits, Beyond Therapy, Roman Holiday, Two Brothers Running, White Roses, Shirley Valentine, Someone Else's America, Crush Depth, Something to Believe In 1996, Out of Control 1997, The Enemy 2000, Derailed 2005, Paid 2006, Almost Heaven 2006, Rabbit Fever 2006, O Jerusalem

2006, Dangerous Parking 2007, Deeply Irresponsible 2007, A Closed Book 2009, The Tempest 2010, Rekindle 2011, StreetDance 2 2012, Run for Your Wife 2012, The Dark Knight Rises 2012, City Slacker 2012. *Television includes:* Madame Bovary, Treats, The Glittering Prizes, The Norman Conquests, The Beate Klarsfield Story, Fatal Dosage, The Quick and the Dead, Blade on the Feather, The Wright Verdicts, Deadline, Friends 1998, Deadline (series) 2000–01, I Was a Rat (series) 2001, Andy Pandy (series) 2002, Donovan (series) 2004–06, Deeply Irresponsible 2007, 10 Days to War (series) 2008, Four Seasons (mini-series) 2008–09, Lark Rise to Candleford (series) 2010, Miranda (series) 2010, Atlantis: End of a World, Birth of a Legend (film) 2011, Parents (series) 2012. *Directed:* Last Licks, Broadway 1979, Before the Party 1980, The Housekeeper 1982, Treats 1989, Present Laughter 1993, Last of the Red Hot Lovers 1999. *Publication:* The Doctor (novel) 2004. *Leisure interest:* music. *Address:* c/o Gersh, 9465 Wilshire Boulevard, Sixth Floor, Beverly Hills, CA 90212, USA (office); c/o Artists Independent Network, 32 Tavistock Street, London, WC2E 7PB, England. *Telephone:* (310) 274-6611 (office); (20) 7352-7722. *Fax:* (310) 278-6232 (office). *E-mail:* info@gershla.com (office). *Website:* www.gershagency.com (office); www.tomconti.co.uk.

CONTOGEORGIS, George, MA, PhD; Greek political scientist and professor of political science; *Professor of Political Science, Panteion University of Athens;* b. 14 Feb. 1947, Letkas; s. of Dimitri Contogeorgis and Elia Contogeorgis; m. Catherine Kampourgiannidou 1972; two d.; ed Univ. of Athens, Univ. of Paris II, Ecole Pratique des Hautes Etudes, Ecole des Hautes Etudes en Sciences Sociales; Prof. of Political Science, Panteion Univ. of Athens 1983–, Rector 1984–90; Gen. Dir ERT SA (Hellenic Broadcasting Corpn) 1985, Pres.-Gen. Dir 1989; Minister, Ministry of the Presidency (State Admin., Communication, Media), Govt Spokesman 1993; Founding mem. European Political Science Network (EPSNET); Dir European Masters Programme in Political Science; Founder-mem. and Sec.-Gen. Greek Political Sciences Asscn 1975–80; fmr Dir of Research, CNRS, France; leader writer in Athenian daily newspapers; mem. High Council and Research Council, European Univ., Florence 1986–94; mem. High Council, Univ. of Europe, Paris and Centre of Regional Studies, Montpellier; Visiting Prof., Inst. d'Etudes Politiques, Paris, Univ. Libre de Bruxelles, Univ. Catholique de Louvain, Univs of Montpellier, Tokyo, IEP Bordeaux, Lille etc.; Prof., Franqui Chair., Univ. of Brussels; Prof. of European Studies, Univ. of Siena; mem. Council Pôle Sud, Political Science Review, Revue Internationale de Politique Comparée, Journal of Southern Europe; Corresp. mem. Int. Acad. of Culture (Portugal); mem. French Political Science Asscn, IPSA and other int. asscns; Chevalier des Palmes académiques, titulaire de la chair Francqui. *Publications include:* The Theory of Revolution in Aristotle 1975, The Popular Ideology: Socio-political Study of the Greek Folk Song 1979, Social Process and Political Self-government: The Greek City-State Under the Ottoman Empire 1982, Political System and Politics 1985, History of Greece 1992, Système de communication et système d'échange: La télévision 1993, After Communism (in collaboration) 1993, Greek Society in the 20th Century 1995, Democracy in the Technological Society 1995, Society and Politics 1996, New World Order 1998, Identité cosmosystémique ou identité nationale? Le Paradigme hellénique 1999, Le Citoyen dans la cité (Typology of Citizenship) 2000, Modernity and Progress 2001, Work and Freedom 2003, Citizenship and State, Concept and Typology of Citizenship 2004, The Authoritarian Phenomenon 2004, Nation and Modernity 2006, The Hellenic Cosmosystem: Vol. 1, The Statocentric Period 2006, Democracy as Freedom. Democracy and Representation 2007, Youth, State and Freedom 2009, The 'Hellenic Democracy' of Rhigas Feraios 2009, Economic Systems and Freedom 2010, On the Nation and the Greek Continuity 2010, L'Europe et le Monde. Civilization et Pluralisme Culturel 2011, De l'Europe politique 2011, Partitocracy and Dynastic State 2012. *Leisure interest:* water sports. *Address:* Panteion University of Athens, 136 Sygrou Avenue, Athens 17671 (office); 37 Dafnomili Street, Athens 11471, Greece (home). *Telephone:* (210) 9201743 (office); (210) 6399662 (home); (210) 6081780 (home). *Fax:* (210) 9201743 (office). *E-mail:* gdc14247@gmail.com (office). *Website:* www.panteion.gr (office).

CONWAY, Craig A., BSc; American business executive (retd); b. 17 Oct. 1954, Fort Wayne, Ind.; m. Tina Conway; two c.; ed State Univ. of New York, Brockport; began career working in various positions at Oracle Corpn, including as Exec. Vice-Pres. of Marketing, Sales and Operations; Pres. and CEO TGV Software 1993–96; Pres. and CEO One Touch Systems 1996–99; joined PeopleSoft Inc. May 1999, Pres. and CEO 1999–2004; mem. Bd of Dirs Guidewire Software, Inc. 2010–, Exec. Chair. 2010–14, Chair. 2014–15; mem. Bd of Dirs Salesforce.com 2005–; fmr mem. Bd of Dirs, Kazeon Systems, Inc., Unisys Corpn, Advanced Micro Devices, Inc., eMeter Corpn, Pegasystems Inc. *Address:* 170 Olive Hill Lane, Woodside, CA 94062, USA.

CONWAY, Heather, BA, MA; Canadian media executive; *Executive Vice-President, English Services, Canadian Broadcasting Corporation;* spent six years as Exec. Vice-Pres., Alliance Atlantis, responsible for strategic marketing, publicity and on-air creative plans for 13 Canadian cable speciality channels; also held sr exec. and consulting positions in pvt. sector, working with TD Bank Financial Group, Hill & Knowlton, The Neville Group; Chief Business Officer, Art Gallery of Ontario –2013; Exec. Vice-Pres., English Services, CBC, in charge of TV, radio and online properties, including CBC Radio One, CBC Radio 2, CBC Television, CBC News Network, cbc.ca, documentary and digital operations 2013–; mem. Bd of Dirs, IGM Financial, American Express Canada; named as one of Canada's Top 40 Under 40 2001. *Address:* CBC/Radio, PO Box 3220, Station C, Ottawa, ON K1Y 1E4, Canada (office). *Telephone:* (613) 288-6000 (General) (office). *E-mail:* liaison@cbc.ca (office). *Website:* www.cbc.ca (office); www.cbc.radio-canada.ca (office).

CONWAY, John Horton, BA, PhD, FRS; British mathematician and academic; *Professor Emeritus of Mathematics, Princeton University;* b. 26 Dec. 1937, Liverpool; s. of Cyril Horton Conway and Agnes Boyce; m. Diana Conway; three s. four d.; ed Gonville and Caius Coll., Cambridge; Lecturer in Pure Math., Univ. of Cambridge –1973, Reader in Pure Math. and Math. Statistics 1973–83, Prof. of Math. 1983–87, Fellow, Sidney Sussex Coll. 1964–70, Gonville and Caius Coll. 1970–87; Visiting von Neumann Prof., Princeton Univ., USA 1986–87, John von Neumann Distinguished Prof. of Math. 1987–, now Prof. Emer.; Hon. Fellow, Gonville and Caius Coll. Cambridge 1999; Hon. DSc (Liverpool) 2001; Brown Prize for Pure Math., Gonville and Caius Coll. 1960, Junior Berwick Prize, London Math. Soc. 1975, IEEE Award for outstanding paper of the year 1987, Polya Prize London Math. Soc. 1987, Frederic Esser Nemmers Prize, Northwestern Univ. 1999, Steele Prize, American Math. Soc. 1999, Joseph Priestley Award, Dickinson Coll. 2001. *Publications:* Regular Algebra and Finite Machines 1971, On Numbers and Games 1976, Winning Ways for Your Mathematical Plays (Vol. 2) 1982, 2003, Atlas of Finite Groups 1985, Sphere Packings, Lattices and Groups 1987, The Book of Numbers 1996, The Sensual Quadratic Form 1997, On Numbers and Games 2000, Winning Ways for You Mathematical Plays (Vol. 1) 2001, On Quaternions and Octonions, Winning Ways for Your Mathematical Plays (Vol. 3) 2003, Winning Ways for Your Mathematical Plays (Vol. 4) 2004; more than 140 papers in professional journals. *Leisure interests:* puzzles, games, knots, knowledge. *Address:* Department of Mathematics, 310 Fine Hall, Princeton University, Washington Road, Princeton, NJ 08544 (office); 71 Patton Avenue, Princeton, NJ 08540, USA (home). *Telephone:* (609) 258-6468 (office); (609) 683-0206 (home). *Fax:* (609) 921-0353 (home). *E-mail:* conway@princeton.edu (office). *Website:* math.princeton.edu/directory/john-conway (office).

CONWAY, Kellyanne Elizabeth, BA, JD; American political adviser; *Counselor to the President;* b. (Kellyanne Elizabeth Fitzpatrick), 20 Jan. 1967, Camden, NJ; m. George T. Conway III 2001; four c.; ed Trinity Coll., Washington, DC, George Washington Univ. Law School; began career as clerk for Richard A. Levie, Superior Court, Washington, DC; worked for polling firms Wirthlin Group 1988 and Luntz Research Companies; Owner, Pres. and CEO The Polling Company Inc./Woman Trend 1995–; fmr Adjunct Prof., George Washington Univ. Law Center; Sr Advisor to Newt Gingrich during presidential election campaign 2012; Campaign Man. for Donald Trump Aug.–Nov. 2016; Counselor to the Pres. 2017–; mem. Bd of Trustees Phillips Foundation 2010, Nat. Women's History Museum, Nat. Journalism Center, Clare Boothe Luce Policy Inst. *Television:* To The Contrary (panellist) 1996–. *Publication:* What Women Really Want (with Celinda Lake) 2005. *Address:* The White House Office, 1600 Pennsylvania Avenue, NW, Washington, DC 20500, USA (office). *Telephone:* (202) 456-1414 (office). *Fax:* (202) 456-2461 (office). *Website:* www.whitehouse.gov (office).

COOGAN, Stephen (Steve) John; British actor, comedian, impressionist, producer and writer; b. 14 Oct. 1965, Middleton, Lancs.; m. Caroline Hickman 2002 (divorced 2005); one c.; began career working as a voice artist on satirical puppet show Spitting Image 1987; began creating original comic characters early 1990s; Co-founder and Chair. Baby Cow Productions 1999–; Perrier Award, Edinburgh Festival Fringe 1992. *Films include:* Resurrected 1989, The Indian in the Cupboard 1995, The Wind in the Willows 1996, The Revengers' Comedies 1998, The Parole Officer 2001, 24 Hour Party People 2002, Coffee and Cigarettes (segment 'Cousins?') 2003, Around the World in 80 Days 2004, Happy Endings 2005, A Cock and Bull Story 2005, Lies & Alibis 2006, Marie Antoinette 2006, Night at the Museum 2006, Hamlet 2 2008, Finding Amanda 2008, Tropic Thunder 2008, Tales of the Riverbank 2008, In the Loop 2009, What Goes Up 2009, Night at the Museum 2 2009, Percy Jackson & the Lightning Thief 2010, Marmaduke (voice) 2010, The Other Guys 2010, The Trip 2010, Our Idiot Brother 2011, Darkwood Manor 2011, Ruby Sparks 2012, What Maisie Knew 2012, The Look of Love 2013, Despicable Me 2 (voice) 2013, Alan Partridge: Alpha Papa 2013, Philomena (with Jeff Pope, Best Screenplay, Venice Film Festival, Best Movie About Women, Women Film Critics Circle) 2013, Northern Soul 2013, The Trip to Italy 2014, Minions (voice) 2015, Shepherds and Butchers 2016, Rules Don't Apply 2016, Mindhorn 2016, The Dinner 2017, Despicable Me 3 (voice) 2017, The Trip to Spain 2017, Ideal Home 2018, Irreplaceable You 2018, Hot Air 2018, Holmes and Watson 2018, Stan and Ollie 2018, The Professor and the Madman 2019. *Television includes:* Spitting Image (series) 1987–93, The Day Today (series) 1994, Knowing Me, Knowing You with Alan Partridge (series) (Best Male TV Performer, British Comedy Awards) 1994–95, Coogan's Run (series) 1995, The Tony Ferrino Phenomenon (film) 1997, Introducing Tony Ferrino: Who and Why? A Quest (film) 1997, The Friday Night Armistice (series) 1997, The Fix (film) 1997, I'm Alan Partridge (series) (Best TV Comedy Actor, British Comedy Awards 1998, BAFTA Awards for Best Comedy Performance and Best Comedy (Programme or Series) 1998) 1997–2002, Bob and Margaret (series) 1998, Alice Through the Looking Glass (film) 1998, Live from the Lighthouse (film) 1998, A Small Summer Party (film) 2001, Dr. Terrible's House of Horrible (series) 2001, Cruise of the Gods (film) (Best TV Comedy Actor, British Comedy Awards 2003) 2002, Paul and Pauline Calf's Cheese and Ham Sandwich (short) 2003, Anglian Lives: Alan Partridge (film) 2003, The Private Life of Samuel Pepys (film) 2003, Monkey Trousers (film) 2004, I Am Not an Animal (series) 2004, Monkey Trousers (series) 2005, Little Britain (series) 2006, Saxondale (series) 2006–07, Curb Your Enthusiasm (series) 2007, Sunshine (series) 2008, Neighbors from Hell (series) 2010, Chekhov Comedy Shorts (series) – The Dangers of Tobacco 2010, The Trip (series) (BAFTA for Best Male Comedy Performance 2011) 2010, Mid Morning Matters with Alan Partridge (series) 2010–16, Documental (film) 2011, Alan Partridge on Open Books with Martin Bryce (film) 2012, Moone Boy (series) 2012, Uncle Wormsley's Christmas (film) 2012, Alan Partridge: Welcome to the Places of My Life (BAFTA for Best Male Comedy Performance 2013) 2012, Doubt (film) 2013, Happyish (series) 2015, This Time with Alan Partridge (series) 2019. *Publications:* I, Partridge: We Need To Talk About Alan 2011, Easily Distracted (autobiography) 2015. *Address:* Baby Cow Productions Ltd, 33 Foley Street, London, W1W 7TL, England. *Telephone:* (20) 7612-3370. *Fax:* (20) 7612-3352. *E-mail:* info@babycow.co.uk. *Website:* www.babycow.co.uk.

COOK, Alastair Nathan, CBE, MBE; British professional cricketer; b. 25 Dec. 1984, Gloucester, Glos.; s. of Graham Cook and Stephanie Cook; m. Alice Hunt 2011; two d.; ed Bedford School; opening batsman; left-hand batsman; right-arm slow bowler; played for Bedfordshire 2002, Essex 2003–, MCC 2004–07, England Under-19s and England Lions 2000–06, England 2006–18 (Capt. One-Day Int. (ODI) Team 2011–14, Capt. Test side 2012–17); played for the Essex Acad. aged 15, debut (First-class) for the first XI 2003; Test debut: India v England, Nagpur 1 March 2006; ODI debut: England v Sri Lanka, Old Trafford, Manchester 28 June 2006; T20I debut: England v West Indies, The Oval 28 June 2007; played in 161 Tests and scored 12,472 runs (33 hundreds and 57 fifties), highest score 294, average 45.35, has taken one wicket; ODI career: 92 matches, 3,204 runs (5 hundreds and 19 fifties), highest score 137, average 36.40; mem. England Ashes-winning team against Australia 2009, 2010/11, 2013, 2015 (latter two as Capt.); captained ODI series-winning team against Sri Lanka 2011; youngest Englishman to reach 1,000, 2,000, 3,000, 4,000, 5,000, 6,000 and 12,000 Test runs (second youngest player behind Sachin Tendulkar) and youngest ever player to score 8,000, 9,000, 10,000, 11,000 and 12,000 Test runs, making centuries in his first Test matches against India, Pakistan, West Indies and Bangladesh; only Englishman to score seven Test centuries before his 23rd birthday; set England record partnership in Australia, world record partnership and innings at The Gabba, Brisbane (329 with Jonathan Trott, 235 not out) Nov. 2010; world record time spent batting in a five-Test series, second most series runs by an Englishman (36 hours 11 minutes, 766 runs) Jan. 2011; captained England to first Test series victory on Indian soil since 1984–85 2012, broke record for most Test centuries for England (23) and became the first captain to score a century in each of his first five Tests in charge, England's highest run scorer in India (866 runs) Dec. 2012; became leading run-scorer in Test matches for England, surpassing Graham Gooch May 2015; batted for 836 minutes against Pakistan in first test at Abu Dhabi for score of 263 (third-longest innings by time in Test history and longest ever by an Englishman) Oct. 2015, became only second player ever to bat for more than 12 hours for second occasion in his Test career, after Brian Lara, also overtook record for most Test runs ever scored by an overseas batsman in Asia, beating previous record set by Jacques Kallis; became the youngest player to score 10,000 Test runs, 30 May 2016; retd from int. cricket 2018; columnist, The Daily Telegraph and Metro; Pres. The Young Lord's Taverners (charity); Hon. Life mem. Maldon Cricket Club; Freeman of the City of London 2011; NBC Denis Compton Award 2003, 2004, 2005, 2006, CWC Young Cricketer of the Year 2005, PCA Young Cricketer of the Year 2005, 2006, ICC Test Player of the Year 2011, ICC World Test XI Opening Batsmen 2011, Wisden Cricketer of the Year 2012, ICC World Test XI Opening Batsmen 2012, ICC World ODI XI Opening Batsmen 2012, ICC World Test XI Captain 2013. *Leisure interest:* playing the clarinet, piano and saxophone. *Address:* c/o Essex County Cricket Club, The Ford County Ground, New Writtle Street, Chelmsford, Essex, CM2 0PG, England (office). *Telephone:* (1245) 252420 (office). *Fax:* (1245) 254030 (office). *E-mail:* info@essexcricket.org.uk (office). *Website:* www.essexcricket.org.uk (office).

COOK, Christopher Paul, BA, MA; British artist, poet and academic; *Associate Professor (Reader) in Painting, University of Plymouth;* b. 24 Jan. 1959, Great Ayton, N Yorks., England; s. of E. P. Cook and J. Leyland; m. Jennifer Jane Mellings 1982; two s.; ed Univ. of Exeter, Royal Coll. of Art, Accademia di Belle Arti, Bologna, Italy; Italian Govt Scholar, Accad. di Belle Arti, Bologna 1986–89; Fellow in Painting, Exeter Coll. of Art 1989–90; guest artist, Stadelschule, Frankfurt 1991; Visiting Fellow, Ruskin School, Univ. of Oxford 1992–93; Distinguished Visiting Artist, Calif. State Univ., Long Beach 1994; Visiting Artist to Banaras Hindu Univ., Varanasi, India 1994, 1996; Assoc. Prof. (Reader) in Painting, Univ. of Plymouth 1997–; Artist-in-Residence, Eden Project, Cornwall 2001–03; Resident Artist, Univ. of Memphis 2004; Yokohama Museum residency, Japan 2005; Artist-in-Residence, Savannah Coll. of Art and Design, Atlanta, USA 2009; Resident Artist, Langgeng Foundation, Jogjakarta, Indonesia 2011; Bogliasco Fellowship, Italy 2013; Prizewinner, John Moores Univ., Liverpool XXI 1999, Arts Council of England Award 2000, British Council Award to Artists 2003, Daiwa Award 2005, AHRC Award 2005, British Council Award, Beijing 2006, 2007, Phillips Award, British School at Rome 2009, Bogliasco Scholarship 2013, First Prize, New Light exhibition 2017. *Film:* Journey 2007. *Publications include:* Dust on the Mirror 1997, For and Against Nature 2000, A Thoroughbred Golden Calf 2003, Notes to the Graphites 2009, Falls at Ono on the Kiso Road 2014. *Leisure interest:* the outdoors. *Address:* c/o Ryan Lee Gallery, Inc., 515 West 26th Street, New York, NY 10001, USA (home). *Telephone:* (212) 397-0742 (home). *Fax:* (212) 397-0742 (home). *E-mail:* c1cook@plymouth.ac.uk (home). *Website:* www .cookgraphites.com.

COOK, Gordon Charles, MD, DSc, MRCS, FRCP, FRCPE, FRACP, FLS; British physician specialising in tropical medicine and infectious diseases and medical historian; *Visiting Professor, University College London;* b. 17 Feb. 1932, Wimbledon; s. of Charles F. Cook and Kate Cook (née Kraninger, then Grainger); m. Elizabeth J. Agg-Large 1963; one s. three d.; ed Wellingborough, Kingston-upon-Thames, Raynes Park Grammar Schools and Royal Free Hosp. School of Medicine, Univ. of London; jr appointments, Royal Free Hosp., Brompton Hosp. and Royal Northern Hosp. 1958–60; medical specialist, captain, RAMC and Royal Nigerian Army 1960–62; Lecturer in Medicine, Royal Free Hosp. School of Medicine 1963–65, 1967–69, Makerere Univ. Coll., Uganda 1965–67; Prof. of Medicine, Univ. of Zambia 1969–74, Univ. of Riyadh, Saudi Arabia 1974–75; Visiting Prof. of Medicine, Univs of Basrah and Mosul, Iraq 1976; Sr Lecturer in Clinical Tropical Medicine, London School of Hygiene and Tropical Medicine 1976–97; Consultant Physician, Univ. Coll. London Hosps and Hosp. for Tropical Diseases, London 1976–97; Prof. of Medicine and Chair. Clinical Sciences Dept, Univ. of Papua New Guinea 1978–81; Hon. Sr Lecturer in Medicine, Univ. Coll. London 1981–2002, Visiting Prof. 2002–; Hon. Consultant Physician, St Luke's Hosp. for the Clergy 1988–2009; Visiting Prof. of Medicine, Doha, Qatar 1989; Hon. Lecturer in Clinical Parasitology, Medical Coll. of St Bartholomew's Hosp., London 1992–; Sr Research Fellow, Wellcome Centre for the History of Medicine 1997–2002; Founder and Chair. Erasmus Darwin Foundation, Lichfield 1994–2011, Vice-Pres. 2011–; Vice-Pres. Royal Soc. of Tropical Medicine and Hygiene 1991–93, Pres. 1993–95; Vice-Pres. History of Medicine Section, Royal Soc. of Medicine 1994–96, Pres. 2003–04; Examiner, Royal Coll. of Physicians, Univs of London and Makerere, Uganda; Ed. Journal of Infection 1995–97; mem. Editorial Bd, The Postgraduate Medical Journal; mem. Jt Cttee on Higher Medical Training, Exec. Cttee and Examiner Faculty of History and Philosophy of Medicine and Pharmacy, The Worshipful Soc. of Apothecaries 1997–; mem. of Council, History of Medicine Section, Royal Soc. of Medicine 1999–; mem. Code of Practice Cttee, Asscn of British Pharmaceutical Industry; mem. Asscn of Physicians of GB and Ireland 1973–; mem. numerous other medical and scientific socs; Hon. Research Assoc., Greenwich Maritime Inst. 2003–; Hon. Archivist, Seamen's Hosp. Soc. 2002–, Life Gov. 2008–; Charlotte Brown Prize, Cunning and Legg Awards, Royal Free Hosp. School of Medicine, Frederick Murgatroyd Memorial Prize, Royal Coll. of Physicians, London 1973, Hugh L'Etang Prize, Royal Soc. of Medicine 1999, Monckton Copeman Lecturer, Soc. of Apothecaries 2000, Denny Lecturer, Barbers Co. 2003. *Publications include:* Acute Renal Failure (jtly) 1964, Tropical Gastroenterology 1980, Communicable and Tropical Diseases 1988, Parasitic Disease in Clinical Practice 1990, From the Greenwich Hulks to Old St Pancras: A History of Tropical Disease in London 1992; 100 Clinical Problems in Tropical Medicine (co-ed.) 1987, 1998, Travel-associated Disease (ed.) 1995, Gastroenterological Problems from the Tropics (ed.) 1995, Manson's Tropical Diseases (ed.) (20–22nd edns) 1994–2009, Victorian Incurables: A History of the Royal Hospital for Neuro-Disability, Putney 2004, John MacAlister's Other Vision: A History of the Fellowship of Postgraduate Medicine 2005, The Incurables Movement: An Illustrated History of the British Home 2006, Tropical Medicine: An Illustrated History of the Pioneers 2007, Twenty-Six Portland Place: The Early Years of the Royal Society of Tropical Medicine and Hygiene 2011, Torrid Disease: Memoirs of a Tropical Physician in the Late Twentieth Century 2011, Origin of a Medical Specialty: The Seamen's Hospital Society and Tropical Medicine 2012, The Tropical Disease that Never Existed: a History of 'Sprue' 2013, The Rise and Fall of a Medical Specialty: London's Clinical Tropical Medicine 2014, National Service 50 Years Ago: Life of a medical conscript in West Africa 2014, The Germ Theory: a History of Cause and Management of Infectious Disease Before 1900 2015, The Milk Enzyme: Adventures with the Human Lactose Polymorphism 2015, Disease and Sanitation in Victorian Britain 2015; more than 500 papers on physiology, gastroenterology, tropical medicine, nutrition and medical history. *Leisure interests:* cricket, listening to Baroque and classical music, walking, medical and scientific history, African and Pacific artefacts. *Address:* 11 Old London Road, St Albans, Herts., AL1 1QE, England (home). *Telephone:* (1727) 869000 (home).

COOK, Peter, CBE, BSc (Hons), MSc, PhD, DSc, FTSE; Australian geologist, academic and consultant researcher; *Professorial Fellow, University of Melbourne;* b. 15 Oct. 1938, UK; s. of John Cook and Rose Cook; m. Norma Cook; two s.; ed Durham Univ., UK, Australian Nat. Univ., Univ. of Colorado, USA; Sr Research Fellow, ANU 1976–82; Assoc. Dir, Bureau of Mineral Resources 1982–90; Dir British Geological Survey 1990–98; Exec. Dir Petroleum CRC 1998–2003; Pres. EuroGeoSurveys; Dir PJC International Pty Limited; est. GEODISC programme 1998, and subsequently Co-operative Research Centre for Greenhouse Gas Technologies (CO2CRC), Chief Exec. 2003–11, Prin. Adviser 2011–; Chair. NSW Water Expert Panel 2017–; Professorial Fellow, Univ. of Melbourne 2011–; co-ordinating lead author of Special IPCC volume on CO_2Capture and Storage; Fellow, Australian Acad. of Technological Sciences; Chevalier, Ordre nat. du Mérite; John Coke Medal, Centennial Medal, Lewis G. Weeks Medal, Leopold von Buch Medal, Greenman Award. *Publications include:* Clean Energy Climate and Carbon 2012, Geologically Storing Carbon 2014; numerous books and scientific papers on greenhouse issues, especially carbon capture and storage, sedimentary geology, phosphate deposits, Australian geology and palaeogeography, unconventional gas. *Leisure interests:* skiing, walking, history, small-scale farming. *Address:* 11–15 Argyle Place South, Carlton, Melbourne, Vic. 3053, Australia (office). *Telephone:* (3) 8595-9600 (office); 419-490044 (mobile). *Fax:* (2) 6239-6049 (office). *E-mail:* pjcook@co2crc.com.au (office). *Website:* www.co2crc.com.au (office); www.petercook.unimelb.edu.au (home).

COOK, Sir Peter Frederick Chester, Kt, AADip, RIBA, BDA, FRSA, MEASA; British architect and academic; b. 22 Oct. 1936, Southend-on-Sea, Essex, England; s. of Maj. Frederick William Cook and Ada Alice Cook (née Shaw); m. 1st Hazel Aimée Fennell 1960 (divorced 1990); m. 2nd Yael Reisner 1990; one s.; ed Bournemouth Coll. of Art, Architectural Asscn (AA), London; Architectural Asst, James Cubitt & Partners, London 1960–62; Asst Architect, Taylor Woodrow Design Group, London 1962–64; taught at AA 1964–89; Dir Inst. of Contemporary Arts, London 1970–72; Partner, Archigram Architects 1964–75, Cook and Hawley Architects, London 1976–; Bartlett Prof. of Architecture, Bartlett School of Architecture and Planning, Univ. Coll. London 1990–2005, now Emer., Chair. Bartlett School of Architecture 1990–2006; Prof. of Architecture, Royal Acad. of Arts; Life Prof. of Architecture, Hochschule fur Bildende Kunste (Städelschule), Frankfurt am Main, Germany 1984–; Visiting Prof., Oslo Architecture School 1982–83, RI School of Design 1981, 1984; visiting critic at numerous schools of architecture in USA and abroad; Architect of Plug-in-City 1964–66, Instant City 1969–70, Monte Carlo Entertainments Centre 1971–73, Arcadia City 1979–82, Landstuhl Solar Houses 1984, Layer City 1986, Lutzowplaz Housing, Berlin (with Christine Hawley) 1992, Stadelschule Kantine, Frankfurt 1995, Kunsthaus, Graz (with Colin Fournier) 1998–2004, Social Housing, Madrid 2012, Law Faculty, Vienna Business and Econs Univ. 2013, Abedian School of Architecture, Bond Univ., Gold Coast, Australia 2013; works featured in several books; mem. Hessische Architektenkammer; Sr Fellow, RCA 2008; Fellow, Univ. Coll. London; Commdr des Arts et des Lettres 2003; Hon. DTech (Lund Univ., Sweden) 2010; Graham Foundation Award 1970, Monte Carlo Competition 1st Prize 1970, Landstuhl Housing Competition 1st Prize 1980, LA Prize (AIA) 1988, Int. Competition for Historic Museum 1st Prize, Austria 1995, Jean Tschumi Prize (UIA) 1996, Int. Competition for Kunsthaus, Graz 1st Prize, Austria 2000, Grand Prize of the Buenos Aires Biennale 2001, RIBA Royal Gold Medal 2000 (as mem. of Archigram), Mario Pani Award for Architecture, Mexico City 2010. *Publications include:* Primer 1996, The Power of Contemporary Architecture 1999, The Paradox of Contemporary Architecture 2001, The City as Inspiration 2001, The City, Seen as a Garden of Ideas 2003, Drawing: The Motive Force of Architecture 2008 (second edn 2014). *Leisure interests:* listening to music, talking to young architects, restaurants. *Address:* Crab Studio, 81 Essex Road, London, N1 2SF (office); 54 Compayne Gardens, London, NW6 3RY, England (home). *Telephone:* (20) 7837-4262 (office); (20) 7372-3784 (home). *E-mail:* info@crabstudio.net (office). *Website:* www.crab-studio.com (office).

COOK, R. James, BSc, MSc, PhD; American plant pathologist, soil scientist and academic; *Professor Emeritus of Plant Pathology and Crop and Soil Sciences, Washington State University;* b. 1937, Minn.; m. Beverly Cook; four c.; ed North Dakota State Univ., Univ. of California, Berkeley; Research Plant Pathologist with US Dept of Agric. (USDA) Agricultural Research Service, Washington State Univ. 1965–98, R. James Cook Endowed Chair in Wheat Research 1998–2003, Interim Dean, Coll. of Agricultural, Human and Natural Resource Sciences 2003–05, Prof. Emer. of Plant Pathology and Crop and Soil Sciences 2005–; Chief Scientist, USDA's Nat. Research Initiative Competitive Grants Program 1993–96; Citizen trustee, Board Authority of Washington State's Life Sciences Discovery Fund; Past Pres. Washington State Acad. of Sciences; mem. NAS 1993; Fellow, American Phytopathological Soc., Crop Science Soc. of America, American Soc. of Agronomy, AAAS; Dr hc (North Dakota State Univ.); Superior Service Award, Distinguished Service Award, Agricultural Research Service Distinguished Scientist of the Year,

ARS Science Hall of Fame (all from USDA); Award of Distinction and Ruth Allen Award, American Phytopathological Soc., recognition from grower orgs include Washington Crop Improvement/O.A. Vogel Award, Pioneer Direct Seeder Award, Pacific Northwest Direct Seed Asscn, and No-till Innovator Award for Research and Teaching, Nat. No-till Conf.; Wolf Prize in Agric. (Israel) (co-recipient) 2011. *Publications:* Biological Control of Plant Pathogens (co-author), Wheat Health Management (co-author); more than 200 peer-reviewed papers in professional journals on soil-borne plant diseases. *Address:* Department of Plant Pathology, PO Box 646430, Washington State University, Pullman, WA 99164-6430, USA (office). *Telephone:* (509) 592-0086 (office). *E-mail:* plpath@wsu.edu (office). *Website:* plantpath.wsu.edu/people/faculty/emeritus (office).

COOK, Sarah, PhD; British economist and international organization official; *Director, Innocenti Research Centre, United Nations Children's Fund (UNICEF);* ed Univ. of Oxford, London School of Econs, Harvard Univ., USA; has carried out int. academic research and has taught in field of devt studies; has undertaken policy and advisory work for int. governmental and non-governmental devt agencies; spent more than 12 years living in China, and has also worked in India, East Africa, Cambodia and Mongolia; Research Fellow, Inst. of Devt Studies, Univ. of Sussex, Brighton 1995–2009, Ford Foundation China 2000–05; Dir UN Research Inst. for Social Devt 2009–15; Dir UNICEF Innocenti Research Centre 2015–. *Publications:* numerous articles on social policy, social protection in Asia, social welfare in China, the informalization of employment and the gender impacts of econ. reform. *Address:* UNICEF Innocenti Research Centre, Piazza SS. Annunziata 12, 50122 Florence, Italy (office). *Telephone:* (55) 20330 (office). *E-mail:* info@unicef-irc.org (office). *Website:* www.unicef-irc.org (office).

COOK, Stephen Arthur, OM, PhD, FRS, FRSC; American/Canadian computer scientist and academic; *University Professor Emeritus, Department of Computer Science, University of Toronto;* b. 1939, Buffalo, New York; s. of Gerhard A. Cook and Lura Cook; m. Linda Cook 1968; two s.; ed Univ. of Michigan and Harvard Univ.; Asst Prof. of Math., Univ. of California, Berkeley 1966–70; Assoc. Prof. of Computer Science, Univ. of Toronto 1970–75, Prof. 1975–85, Univ. Prof. 1985–, now Prof. Emer.; E.W.R. Staecie Memorial Fellowship 1977–78; Killam Research Fellow, Canada Council 1982–83; mem. NAS, American Acad. of Arts and Science; Turing Award, Asscn for Computing Machinery 1982, Killam Prize 1997, CRM/Fields Inst. Prize 1999. *Publications:* numerous articles in professional journals on theory of computation. *Leisure interest:* sailing. *Address:* Department of Computer Science, 40 St George Street, Room 7224, University of Toronto, Toronto, ON M5S 2E4, Canada (office). *Telephone:* (416) 978-5183 (office). *E-mail:* sacook@cs.toronto.edu (office). *Website:* www.cs.toronto.edu/~sacook (office).

COOK, Timothy (Tim) Donald, BS, MBA; American computer industry executive; *CEO, Apple Inc.;* b. 1 Nov. 1960, Mobile, Ala; s. of Donald Cook and Geraldine Cook; ed Robertsdale High School, Auburn Univ., Duke Univ. (Fuqua Scholar); spent 12 years with IBM, most recently as Dir of North American Fulfillment; fmr COO Reseller Div., Intelligent Electronics; Vice-Pres. of Corp. Materials, Compaq Computer Corpn 1998; joined Apple Inc. as Sr Vice-Pres. for Worldwide Operations 1998, Sr Vice-Pres., Worldwide Operations, Sales, Service and Support 2000–02, Exec. Vice-Pres., Worldwide Sales and Operations 2002–05, COO 2002–11, served as CEO (during absence on sick leave of CEO Steve Jobs) 2004, 2009, CEO 2011–; Ind. Dir, Nike, Inc., Nat. Football Foundation; inducted into Alabama Acad. of Honor 2015, Financial Times Person of the Year 2014, Ripple of Change Award 2015, World's Greatest Leader, Fortune magazine 2015, Visibility Award, Human Rights Campaign 2015. *Leisure interests:* hiking, cycling, going to the gym. *Address:* Apple Inc., 1 Infinite Loop, Cupertino, CA 95014, USA (office). *Telephone:* (408) 996-1010 (office). *Fax:* (408) 974-2113 (office). *E-mail:* media.help@apple.com (office). *Website:* www.apple.com (office).

COOK-BENNETT, Gail C. A., BA, PhD; Canadian business executive and academic; *Chairman, Institute of Corporate Directors;* b. 1941; ed Carleton Univ., Univ. of Michigan, USA; fmr Exec. Vice-Pres. C.D. Howe Inst., Montreal; fmr Prof., Dept of Political Economy, Univ. of Toronto; mem. Bd of Dirs Manulife Financial Corpn 1978–2013, mem. Man. Resources and Compensation Cttee, Vice-Chair. 2007–08, Chair. (first woman) 2008–13; Chair. Canada Pension Plan Investment Bd 1998–2008, Chair. and mem. Investment Cttee, mem. Governance Cttee; Vice-Chair. Bennecon Ltd –1998; mem. Bd of Dirs Inst. of Corp. Dirs 2009–, Chair. 2014–; mem. Bd of Dirs Petro-Canada 1991– (Chair. Pension Cttee, mem. Audit, Finance and Risk Cttee), Transcontinental Inc. (also known as Groupe Transcontinental GTC Ltée; fmr mem. Audit Cttee) Cadillac Fairview Inc., Enbridge Consumers Gas Co., Mackenzie Financial Corpn, Emera Inc. (mem. Audit Cttee, Nominating and Corp. Governance Cttee), Nova Scotia Power Inc. (mem. Nominating and Corp. Governance Cttee), Bank of Canada, TD Bank, N.A.; Order of Canada 2010; Hon. LLD (Carleton Univ., York Univ.). *Address:* Institute of Corporate Directors, 250 Yonge Street, Toronto, ON M5B 2L7, Canada (office). *Telephone:* (416) 593-774-411 (office). *Fax:* (416) 593-0636 (office). *E-mail:* boardinfo@icd.ca (office). *Website:* www.icd.ca (office).

COOKE, Dominic, CBE; British theatre director and playwright; *Artistic Director, Royal Court Theatre;* b. 1966; partner Alexi Kaye Campbell; Asst Dir RSC 1992–93, Assoc. Dir 2002–06; Assoc. Dir Royal Court Theatre 1999–2002, Artistic Dir 2007–; Hon. DLitt (Warwick) 2013; Int. Theatre Inst. Award for Excellence in Int. Theatre 2013. *Productions include:* Royal Court Theatre: Other People 2000, Fireface 2000, Spinning into Butter 2001, Redundant 2001, Fucking Games 2001, Plasticine, The People are Friendly, This is a Chair (co-dir) 2002, Identical Twins 2002, The Pain and the Itch 2007, Rhinoceros 2007, War & Peace/Fear & Misery 2008, Wig Out! 2008, Now or Later 2008, Seven Jewish Children 2009, The Fever 2009, Aunt Dan & Lemon 2009, Clybourne Park 2010, The Comedy of Errors 2011, Chicken Soup with Barley 2011, In Basildon 2012, Choir Boy 2012, Ding Dong The Wicked 2012, In the Republic of Happiness 2013, The Low Road 2013; RSC: The Malcontent 2002, Cymbeline 2003, Macbeth 2004, As You Like It 2005, Postcards From America 2005, The Winter's Tale, Pericles, The Crucible (Gielgud; Best Dir and Best Revival, Laurence Olivier Awards 2007) 2006; other: Arabian Nights (Old Vic and on tour) (TMA/Equity Award for Best Show for Young People) 1998, Noughts and Crosses 2007, By the Bog of Cats (Wyndham's), The Eccentricities of a Nightingale (Gate, Dublin), The Weavers, Hunting Scenes From Lower Bavaria (Gate), The Bullet (Donmar Warehouse), Afore Night Come, Entertaining Mr Sloane (Clwyd), The Importance of Being Earnest (Atlantic Theatre Festival, Canada), Caravan (Nat. Theatre of Norway), My Mother Said I Never Should (Oxford Stage Co/Young Vic), Kiss of the Spider Woman (Bolton Octagon), Of Mice and Men (Nottingham Playhouse), Autogeddon (Assembly Rooms) (Fringe First Award). *Opera includes:* The Magic Flute (Welsh Nat. Opera), I Capuleti e i Montecchi, La Bohème (Grange Park Opera). *Radio:* adaptations of Plasticine and Arabian Nights for BBC Radio 2002. *Publications:* Arabian Nights (adaptation) 1998, Noughts and Crosses (adaptation) 2007. *Address:* Royal Court Theatre, Sloane Square, London, SW1W 8AS, England (office). *Telephone:* (20) 7565-5050 (office). *Fax:* (20) 7565-5001 (office). *E-mail:* info@royalcourttheatre.com (office). *Website:* www.royalcourttheatre.com (office).

COOKSON, (Michael) Brian, OBE; British sports administrator and fmr cyclist; *President, Union Cycliste Internationale (International Cycling Union);* b. 22 June 1951, Lancs.; m. Sian Cookson; three s.; Exec. Dir (Regeneration), Pendle Borough Council –2013; competed in road racing, track, cyclo-cross and MTB; won Lakeland Division Road Race championship 1971; completed the Pyrenees Coast to Coast ride 2011; Chair. Pendle Cycle Fest which included the Nat. Road Championships, Colne GP circuit race, Pendle Pedal sportive; Div. Road Race Sec., British Cycling Fed. (BCF) 1981–85, Div. Vice-Chair. 1984–87, Div. Chair. 1993–97, mem. Racing and Exec. Cttees 1984–93, mem. Bd Exec. Cttee and Bd, BCF 1996–2013, Pres. British Cycling 1997–2013, qualified as UCI Int. Commissaire (judge/referee) 1986, represented cycling at British Olympic Asscn since 1996; elected to Union Cycliste Internationale (UCI—Int. Cycling Union) Man. Cttee 2009, Pres. UCI Cyclo-Cross Comm. 2009–11, Pres. UCI Road Comm. 2011–13, Pres. UCI 2013–; mem. Exec. Cttee, British Olympic Asscn 2005–; Hon. Fellow, Univ. of Central Lancashire 2009. *Address:* Union Cycliste Internationale (UCI), Ch. de la Mêlée 12, 1860 Aigle, Switzerland (office); c/o British Cycling Federation, Stuart Street, Manchester, M11 4DQ, England. *Telephone:* (24) 4685811 (office). *Fax:* (24) 4685812 (office). *E-mail:* brian.cookson@uci.ch (office). *Website:* www.uci.ch (office); www.briancookson.org.

COOLIDGE, Martha; American film director and producer; b. 17 Aug. 1946, New Haven, Conn.; d. of Robert Tilton Coolidge and Jean McMullen; one s.; ed Rhode Island School of Design, Columbia Univ. and New York Univ. Inst. of Film and TV Grad. School; producer, dir and writer of documentaries including Passing Quietly Through, David: Off and On, Old Fashioned Woman; wrote and produced daily children's TV show Magic Tom, Canada; Pres. Dirs Guild Asscn 2002–03; Blue Ribbon Award, American Film Festival (Not a Pretty Picture), Independent Spirit Award, Best Dir (Rambling Rose), Crystal Award, Women in Film, Breakthrough Award, Method Fest, Robert Aldrich Award, Dirs Guild Award. *Films include:* Valley Girl 1983, City Girl 1984, Joy of Sex 1984, Real Genius 1985, Plain Clothes 1988, Rambling Rose 1991, Lost in Yonkers 1993, Angie 1994, Three Wishes 1995, Out to Sea 1997, The Prince and Me 2004, Material Girls 2006, An American Girl: Chrissa Stands Strong (video) 2007. *Television includes:* Trenchcoat in Paradise (film), Bare Essentials, Crazy in Love, Introducing Dorothy Dandridge 1999, If These Walls Could Talk II 2000, The Ponder Heart 2000, The Flamingo Rising 2001, Leap Years 2001, The Twelve Days of Christmas Eve (film) 2004, Tribute (film) 2009; directed episodes of numerous series. *Leisure interest:* breeding Paso-Fino horses. *Address:* c/o Beverly Magid Guttman Associates, 118 South Beverly Drive, Suite 201, Beverly Hills, CA 90212, USA. *Telephone:* (310) 246-4600 (office). *Website:* www.marthacoolidge.com (office).

COOMARASWAMY, Indrajit, MA, DPhil; Sri Lankan economist, government official and central banker; *Governor, Central Bank of Sri Lanka;* b. 3 April 1950, Colombo; s. of Rajendra Coomaraswamy and Wijeyamani Coomaraswamy; m. Tara de Fonseka; two s.; ed Royal Coll., Colombo, Emmanuel Coll., Cambridge and Univ. of Sussex, UK; joined Cen. Bank of Sri Lanka 1973, served as Staff Officer in Econ. Research, Statistics and Bank Supervision Divs 1973–89, seconded to Ministry of Finance and Planning 1981–89, Gov. Cen. Bank of Sri Lanka 2016–, also Chair. of Monetary Bd; joined Commonwealth Secr. as Chief Officer, Econs, Int. Finance and Markets Section 1990, later Dir Econ. Affairs Div. and Deputy-Dir Office of Sec. –2008, Interim Dir Social Transformation Program Div. Jan.–July 2010; Advisor to Prime Minister Ranil Wickremesinghe and to Minister of Econ. Reforms, Science and Tech. 2001–02; Sr Advisor, Ministry of Devt Strategies and Int. Trade –2016; fmr Special Advisor, Galleon Group; mem. Bd of Dirs Tokyo Cement Co. (Lanka) PLC 2011–16, John Keells Holdings PLC 2011–16, Sarvodaya Devt Finance Ltd, MMBL-Pathfinder; fmr mem. Bd of Study Univ. of Sri Jayewardenepura. *Achievements include;* played first-class cricket for Univ. of Cambridge Cricket Club 1971–72; Capt. Sri Lankan Nat. Rugby Team 1974, also played for Ceylonese Rugby and Football Club. *Address:* Central Bank of Sri Lanka, 30 Janadhipathi Mawatha, POB 590, Colombo 1, Sri Lanka (office). *Telephone:* (11) 2477000 (office). *Fax:* (11) 2346304 (office). *E-mail:* cbslgen@cbsl.lk (office). *Website:* www.cbsl.gov.lk (office).

COOMARASWAMY, Radhika, BA, LLM, JD; Sri Lankan lawyer and UN official; ed Yale, Columbia and Harvard Univs and UN Int. School, New York, USA; Special Rapporteur on Violence Against Women 1994–2003; Chair. Sri Lanka Human Rights Comm. 2003–06; Dir Int. Centre for Ethnic Studies, Colombo; Special Rep. of the Sec.-Gen. for Children and Armed Conflict, UN 2006–12, mem. Sec.-Gen.'s High-Level Advisory Bd on Mediation 2017–; Visiting Fellow, Center for Constitutional Transitions, New York Univ. School of Law 2013, also mem. Global Faculty; teaches a summer course at New Coll., Oxford, UK every July; title of 'Deshamanya' conferred on her by Pres. of Sri Lanka 2005 (only female recipient); Hon. PhD (Amherst Coll.), (Univ. of Edinburgh), (Univ. of Essex); ABA Int. Law Award, Human Rights Award, Int. Human Rights Law Group, Bruno Kreisky Award 2000, Special Jury Prize, Fondation Chirac 2012, Leo Ettinger Human Rights Prize, Univ. of Oslo, Cesar Romero Award, Univ. of Dayton, William J. Butler Award, Univ. of Cincinnati, Robert S. Litvack Award, McGill Univ. *Publications:* two books on constitutional law and numerous articles on ethnic studies and the status of women. *Address:* c/o Office of the Special Representative of the Secretary-General for Children and Armed Conflict, United Nations, Room S-3161, New York, NY 10017, USA.

COOMBER, John R., BSc; British insurance executive; b. 7 Feb. 1949; m.; ed Univ. of Nottingham; began career with Phoenix Insurance Co.; joined Swiss Re 1973, specialized in life reinsurance, Company Actuary 1983–90, Head of Life Div. 1987, Head of UK Operations 1993, apptd mem. Exec. Bd 1995, Head of Life and Health Div. 1995–2000, mem. Exec. Bd Cttee 2000–03, CEO Swiss Reinsurance

Co. (first non-Swiss person in position) 2003–05 (retd), Dir (non-exec.) 2006–14; apptd Dir (non-exec.), Pension Insurance Corpn 2006, Exec. Vice-Chair., CEO 2009–15; Chair. Climate Group, Climatewise, MacTavish; mem. Deutsche Bank Climate Change Advisory Bd; fmr mem. Supervisory Bd Euler Hermes, Bd of Telent plc. *Address:* c/o Pension Insurance Corporation, 14 Cornhill, London, EC3V 3ND, England (office). *Telephone:* (20) 7105-2000 (office). *Fax:* (20) 7105-2001 (office). *Website:* www.pensioncorporation.com (office).

COOMBS, Stephen; British pianist; b. 11 July 1960, Birkenhead, Wirral; s. of Geoffrey Samuel Coombs and Joan Margaret Jones; ed Royal Northern Coll. of Music, RAM; debut at Wigmore Hall 1975; has given concerts and masterclasses in UK, France, Germany, Italy, Hungary, Portugal, Switzerland, Scandinavia, Korea, Thailand, the Philippines, Hong Kong, USA; has appeared in festivals at Cheltenham, Salisbury, Snape Maltings Proms, Henley, the Three Choirs, Radley, Bath, Lichfield, Cardiff, Spoleto, Italy, St Nazaire, France, Sintra, Portugal; Visiting Lecturer, Univ. of Cen. England 1994–96; Founder and Artistic Dir 'Pianoworks' Int. Piano Festival, London 1998–99; joined chamber group Room-Music 2000; Dir of Instrumental Studies, Blackheath Conservatoire of Music and the Arts from 2001; Gold Medal, First Int. Liszt Concourse, Hungary 1977, Worshipful Co. of Musicians/Maisie Lewis Award 1986 and numerous other awards and prizes. *Recordings include:* Two Piano Works of Debussy 1989, Ravel: Music for Two Pianos (with Christopher Scott) 1990, Mendelssohn Two Double Piano Concertos 1992, Arensky Piano Concerto in F Minor and Fantasy on Russian Folk Songs 1992, Bortkiewicz Piano Concerto No. 1 1992, Arensky Suites for Two Pianos 1994, Glazunov Complete Piano Works (first of four vols) 1995, Glazunov Piano Concertos Nos 1 & 2 1996, Goedicke Concertstück 1996, Reynaldo Hahn Piano Concerto 1997, Massenet Piano Concerto 1997, Bortkiewicz Piano Works 1997, Liadov Piano Works 1998, Milhaud Works for Two Pianos 1998, Arensky Piano Works 1998, Scriabin Early Piano Works 2001, Hahn Piano Quintet 2001, Hahn & Verne Piano Quintets 2001, Pierné: The Complete Works for Piano and Orchestra 2003, music by Catoire 2004, solo piano works of Glazunov (Vol. 4) 2006, Sergei Bortkiewicz: Piano Music 2008, Benjamin James Dale: The Romantic Viola 2013. *Leisure interests:* genealogy, pubs, reading. *Address:* c/o Hyperion Records Ltd, 19–20 Chiltonian Industrial Estate, Manor Lane, London, SE12 0TX, England. *Website:* www.hyperion-records.co.uk.

COONS, Christopher Andrew (Chris), BA, MA, JD; American lawyer and politician; *Senator from Delaware;* b. 9 Sept. 1963, Greenwich, Conn.; s. of Ken Coons and Sally Coons; m. Annie Lingenfelter 1996; two s. one d.; ed Tower Hill School, Amherst Coll. (Truman Scholarship), Univ. of Nairobi, Kenya, Yale Univ. Law School and Yale Divinity School; worked for Investor Responsibility Research Center, Washington, DC, wrote a book on S Africa and US divestment movement; then worked as volunteer for S African Council of Churches and as relief worker in Kenya, before returning to USA to work for Coalition for the Homeless, New York; worked as clerk for Judge Jane Richards Roth on US Court of Appeals for the Third Circuit; then worked for Nat. I Have a Dream Foundation, New York; In-house Counsel for W.L. Gore & Assocs, Inc., Newark, Del. (makers of Gore-Tex fabrics and other high-tech materials) 1996–2004; served on New Castle Co. Council, Del. 2001–05, Co. Exec. New Castle Co. 2005–10; Senator from Del. (special election to term ending 3 Jan. 2015, seat previously held by apptd Senator Edward E. Kaufman) 2010–, mem. Budget, Foreign Relations, Judiciary, and Energy and Natural Resources Cttees 2010–; mem. Bd First State Innovation, Bear/Glasgow Boys & Girls Club, Delaware Coll. of Art & Design, Wilmington Riverfront Devt Corpn, Better Business Bureau, First State Innovation, Hearts and Minds Film Org.; Democrat; Hon. Commdr 166th Air Wing of Delaware Air Nat. Guard, Hon. Life mem. Minquadale Fire Co.; Gov.'s Outstanding Volunteer Award for his work with I Have a Dream Foundation, Gov.'s Mentoring Council and United Way of Delaware 1999, Aspen-Rodel Fellow, Aspen Inst. Rodel Fellowships in Public Leadership 2009. *Address:* 127A Russell Senate Office Building, Washington, DC 20510, USA (office). *Telephone:* (202) 224-5042 (office). *Fax:* (202) 228-3075 (office). *Website:* coons.senate.gov (office).

COOPER, Alice; American singer; b. (Vincent Damon Furnier), 4 Feb. 1948, Detroit, Mich.; s. of Mick Furnier and Ella Furnier; m. Sheryl Goddard; one s. two d.; ed Cortez High School, Phoenix, Ariz.; mem. band Alice Cooper, adopted this name after band split; first to stage theatrical rock concert tours; among first to film conceptual rock promotional videos (pre-MTV); considered among originators and greatest hard rock artists; host on Virgin Radio Classic Rock 2005; Owner, Alice Cooper'stown restaurant, Phoenix; mem. BMI, NARAS, SAG, AFTRA, AFofM; Foundations Forum Lifetime Achievement Award 1994, inducted into Rock and Roll Hall of Fame 2011. *Film appearances:* Sextette 1978, Sgt. Pepper's Lonely Hearts Club Band 1978, Leviatán 1984, Prince of Darkness 1987, Freddy's Dead: The Final Nightmare 1991, The Attic Expeditions 2001, Suck 2009, Dark Shadows 2012, Bigfoot 2012, Skum Rocks! 2013. *Recordings include:* with band Alice Cooper: Pretties For You 1969, Live At The Whisky 1969, Easy Action 1970, Love It To Death 1971, Killer 1971, School's Out 1972, Billion Dollar Babies 1973, Muscle of Love 1973, Alice Cooper's Greatest Hits 1974; solo: Welcome To My Nightmare 1975, Alice Cooper Goes To Hell 1976, Lace And Whiskey 1977, Alice Cooper Show (live) 1977, From The Inside 1978, Flush The Fashion 1980, Special Forces 1981, Zipper Catches The Skin 1982, Dada 1982, Constrictor 1986, Raise Your Fist And Yell 1987, Trash 1989, Prince Of Darkness 1989, Hey Stoopid 1991, The Last Temptation 1994, Fistful Of Alice (live) 1997, He's Back 1997, Science Fiction 2000, Brutal Planet 2000, Alice Cooper Live 2001, Take 2 2001, Dragontown 2001, Eyes Of Alice Cooper 2003, Hell Is 2003, Dirty Diamonds 2005, Along Came a Spider 2008, Welcome to My Nightmare 2 2011. *Publication:* Golf Monster (memoir) 2007. *Address:* c/o Shep Gordon, Alive Enterprises, PO Box 5542, Beverly Hills, CA 90211, USA (office). *Website:* www.alicecooper.com.

COOPER, Alison J., BSc, ACA; British business executive; *Chief Executive, Imperial Tobacco Group PLC;* with PricewaterhouseCoopers –1999, worked with Imperial Tobacco in several areas, including acquisitions; joined Imperial Tobacco 1999, Dir of Finance and Planning and mem. Chief Exec.'s Cttee 2001–05, Sales and Marketing Regional Dir for Western Europe 2005–07, mem. Bd of Dirs and Corp. Devt Dir 2007–09, mem. Altadis acquisition team, COO 2009–10, Chief Exec. 2010–; Dir (non-exec.) Inchcape plc 2009–. *Address:* Imperial Tobacco Group PLC, 121 Winterstoke Road, Bristol, BS3 2LL, England (office). *Telephone:* (117) 963-6636 (office). *Fax:* (117) 966-7405 (office). *E-mail:* info@imperial-tobacco.com (office). *Website:* www.imperial-tobacco.com (office).

COOPER, Bradley Charles, BA (Hons), MFA; American actor and producer; b. 5 Jan. 1975, Philadelphia, Pa; s. of Charles J. Cooper and Gloria Cooper (née Campano); m. Jennifer Esposito 2006 (divorced 2007); one c.; ed Germantown Acad., Villanova Univ., Georgetown Univ., spent six months as an exchange student in Aix-en-Provence, France, Actors Studio Drama School at The New School, New York; worked at the Philadelphia Daily News while a student; began his professional acting career on TV Sex and the City 1999; also served as a presenter for Globe Trekker; film debut in Wet Hot American Summer 2001; own production co. 22 & Indiana Pictures; Int. Man of the Year Award, GQ magazine (UK) 2011, named by People magazine as the Sexiest Man Alive 2011. *Films include:* Wet Hot American Summer 2001, My Little Eye 2002, Bending All the Rules 2002, Stella Shorts 1998–2002 (video) 2002, Wedding Crashers 2005, Failure to Launch 2006, The Comebacks 2007, American Evil 2008, The Rocker 2008, The Midnight Meat Train 2008, Bang Blow & Stroke (video short) 2008, Yes Man 2008, New York, I Love You 2009, He's Just Not That Into You 2009, The Hangover 2009, Case 39 2009, All About Steve 2009, Valentine's Day 2010, The A-Team 2010, Limitless 2011, The Hangover Part II 2011, Kaylien (short) 2011, The Words 2012, Hit and Run 2012, The Place Beyond the Pines 2012, Silver Linings Playbook 2012, The Hangover Part III 2013, American Hustle (Screen Actors Guild Award for Outstanding Performance by a Cast in a Motion Picture 2014) 2013, Serena 2013, Guardians of the Galaxy (voice) 2014, American Sniper 2014, Aloha 2015, Burnt 2015, War Dogs 2016, Guardians of the Galaxy Vol 2 (voice) 2017, Avengers: Infinity War 2017, A Star is Born (Nat. Bd of Review Award for Best Dir 2019) 2018, The Mule 2017. *Television includes:* Sex and the City (series) 1999, Treks in a Wild World (series) 2000, Wall to Wall Records (film) 2000, The $treet (series) 2000–01, Alias (series) 2001–06, The Last Cowboy (film) 2003, Miss Match (series) 2003, The Reality of Love (film) 2004, Touching Evil (series) 2004, Jack & Bobby (series) 2004–05, Law & Order: Special Victims Unit (series) 2005, Law & Order: Trial by Jury (series) 2005, Kitchen Confidential (series) 2005–06, Nip/Tuck (series) 2007–09, Cubed (series) 2010, Wet Hot American Summer: First Day of Camp 2015, Limitless 2015–16. *Address:* c/o Dave Bugliari, Creative Artists Agency, 2000 Avenue of the Stars, Los Angeles, CA 90067, USA (office). *Telephone:* (424) 288-2000 (office). *Fax:* (424) 288-2900 (office). *Website:* www.caa.com (office).

COOPER, Chris; American actor; b. 9 July 1951, Kansas City, Mo.; s. of Charles Cooper and Mary Ann Cooper; m. Marianne Leone 1983; one s.; ed Univ. of Missouri; studied ballet at Stephens Coll., Mo.; entered US Coast Guard Reserves following high school graduation; studied theatre acting under Stella Adler and Wynn Handman, NY 1976; first Broadway appearance in Of the Fields Lately 1980; Best Actor Award, Cowboy Hall of Fame 1991, Peter J. Owens Award, San Francisco International Film Festival 2004. *Films include:* Bad Timing 1980, Matewan 1987, Non date da mangiare agli animali 1987, Guilty by Suspicion 1991, Thousand Pieces of Gold 1991, City of Hope 1991, This Boy's Life 1993, Money Train 1995, Pharaoh's Army 1995, Boys 1996, Lone Star 1996, A Time to Kill 1996, Great Expectations 1998, The Horse Whisperer 1998, The 24 Hour Woman 1999, October Sky 1999, American Beauty (Screen Actors Guild Award 2000) 1999, Me, Myself & Irene 2000, The Patriot 2000, Interstate 60 2002, The Bourne Identity 2002, Adaptation (Best Supporting Actor, Acad. Awards 2004, Golden Globe Awards, Nat. Bd of Review, San Francisco Film Critics, Toronto Film Critics, San Diego Film Critics, Broadcast Film Asscn, LA Critics Asscn) 2002, Seabiscuit 2003, Silver City 2004, Syriana 2005, Capote 2005, Jarhead 2005, Breach 2007, The Kingdom 2007, Married Life 2007, The Company Men 2010, Remember Me 2010, Amigo 2010, The Town 2010, The Tempest 2010, The Muppets 2011, The Company You Keep 2012, August: Osage County 2013. *Television includes:* Lonesome Dove (mini-series) 1989, Return to Lonesome Dove (mini-series) 1993, My House in Umbria (film) 2003, The Corrections (film) 2012. *Stage appearances include:* Of the Fields Lately 1980, The Ballad of Soapy Smith 1983, A Different Moon 1983, Cobb, The Grapes of Wrath, Sweet Bird of Youth, Love Letters. *Address:* c/o PMK, 8500 Wilshire Boulevard, Suite 700, Beverly Hills, CA 90211-3105, USA (office).

COOPER, Jilly, CBE, OBE; British writer; b. 21 Feb. 1937, Hornchurch, Essex; d. of Brig. W. B. Sallitt, OBE and Mary Elaine Whincup; m. Leo Cooper 1961 (died 2013); one s. one d.; ed Godolphin School, Salisbury; reporter, Middx Independent 1957–59; account exec.; copy writer; publr's reader; various temporary roles 1959–69; columnist, The Sunday Times 1969–82, Mail on Sunday 1982–87; British Book Awards Lifetime Achievement Award 1998, Variety Club Heart of Yorkshire Award for Services to the Media 2004; Hon. DLitt (Univ. of Gloucester) 2009; Dr hc (Anglia Ruskin Univ.) 2011. *Publications include:* How to Stay Married 1969, How to Survive from Nine to Five 1970, Jolly Super 1971, Men and Super Men 1972, Jolly Super Too 1973, Women and Super Women 1974, Jolly Superlative 1975, Emily 1975, Super Men and Super Women 1976, Bella 1976, Harriet 1976, Octavia 1977, Work and Wedlock 1977, Superjilly 1977, Imogen 1978, Prudence 1978, Class 1979, Intelligent and Loyal 1980, Supercooper 1980, Violets and Vinegar (co-ed with Tom Hartman) 1980, The British in Love (ed) 1980, Love and Other Heartaches 1981, Jolly Marsupial 1982, Animals in War 1983, Leo and Jilly Cooper on Rugby 1984, The Common Years 1984, Riders 1985, Hotfoot to Zabriskie Point 1985, How to Survive Christmas 1986, 1996, Turn Right at the Spotted Dog 1987, Rivals 1988, Angels Rush In 1990, Polo 1991, The Man Who Made Husbands Jealous 1993, Araminta's Wedding 1993, Apassionata 1996, Score! 1999, Pandora 2002, Wicked! 2006, Jump! 2010, Mount 2016. *Leisure interests:* merry-making, mongrels, music, wild flowers, greyhounds. *Address:* c/o Vivienne Schuster, Curtis Brown Ltd, Fourth Floor, Haymarket House, 28–29 Haymarket, London, SW1Y 4SP, England (office). *Telephone:* (20) 7393-4400 (office). *Fax:* (20) 7393-4401 (office). *E-mail:* schusteroffice@curtisbrown.co.uk (office). *Website:* www.curtisbrown.co.uk (office); www.jillycooper.co.uk.

COOPER, Leon N., AB, AM, PhD; American scientist and academic; *Thomas J. Watson, Senior Professor of Physics and Director, Brain and Neural Systems, Brown University;* b. 28 Feb. 1930, New York; s. of Irving Cooper and Anna Zola; m. Kay Anne Allard 1969; two d.; ed Columbia Univ.; mem. Inst. for Advanced Study 1954–55; Research Assoc., Univ. of Ill. 1955–57; Asst Prof., Ohio State Univ. 1957–58; Assoc. Prof., Brown Univ. 1958–62, Prof. 1974–, Thomas J. Watson, Sr Prof. of Physics 1974–, Dir Center for Neural Science 1978–90, Inst. for Brain and Neural Systems 1991–, Brain Science Program 2000–; Visiting Lecturer, Varenna,

Italy 1955; Visiting Prof., Brandeis Summer Inst. 1959, Bergen Int. School of Physics, Norway 1961, Scuola Internazionale Di Fisica, Erice, Italy 1965, L'Ecole Normale Supérieure, Centre Universitaire Int., Paris 1966, Cargèse Summer School 1966, Radiation Lab., Univ. of Calif., Berkeley 1969, Faculty of Sciences, Quai St Bernard, Paris 1970, 1971, Brookhaven Nat. Lab. 1972; consultant for various industrial and educational orgs; Chair. of Math. Models of Nervous System Fondation de France 1977–83; mem. Conseil supérieur de la Recherche Univ. René Descartes, Paris 1981–88; mem. Defence Science Bd 1989–93; NSF Post-doctoral Fellow 1954–55; Alfred P. Sloan Foundation Research Fellow 1959–66; John Simon Guggenheim Memorial Foundation Fellow 1965–66; Fellow, American Physical Soc., American Acad. of Arts and Sciences; Sponsor, American Fed. of Scientists; mem. NAS, American Philosophical Soc., Soc. of Neuroscience, AAAS; Hon. DSc (Columbia, Sussex), 1973, (Illinois, Brown) 1974, (Gustavus Adolphus Coll.) 1975, (Ohio State Univ.) 1976, (Univ. Pierre et Marie Curie, Paris) 1977; Comstock Prize, NAS 1968, Nobel Prize 1972, Award in Excellence, Columbia Univ. 1974, Descartes Medal, Acad. de Paris, Univ. René Descartes 1977, Yrjo Reenpaa Award, Finnish Cultural Foundation 1982, John Jay Award, Columbia Coll. 1985, Alexander Hamilton Award, Columbia Univ. 1995, College de France Medal 2000, Susan Culver Rosenberger Medal, Brown Univ. 2013. *Publications include:* An Introduction to the Meaning and Structure of Physics 1968, Structure and Meaning 1992, How We Learn, How We Remember 1995; numerous scientific papers. *Leisure interests:* skiing, music, theatre. *Address:* Department of Physics and Neuroscience, Box 1843, Barus & Holley, Room 718, Brown University, Providence, RI 02912-1843, USA (office). *Telephone:* (401) 863-2585 (office). *E-mail:* Leon_Cooper@brown.edu (office). *Website:* www.brainscience.brown.edu (office).

COOPER, Richard Newell, PhD; American economist, academic and fmr public official; *Maurits C. Boas Professor of International Economics, Harvard University;* b. 14 June 1934, Seattle, Wash.; s. of Richard W. Cooper and Lucile Newell; m. 1st Carolyn Cahalan 1956 (divorced 1980); m. 2nd Ann Lorraine Hollick 1982 (divorced 1994); m. 3rd Jin Chen 2000; two s. two d.; ed Oberlin Coll., London School of Econs, UK, Harvard Univ.; Sr Staff Economist, Council of Econ. Advisers, The White House 1961–63; Deputy Asst Sec. of State for Monetary Affairs, US State Dept, Washington, DC 1965–66; Prof. of Econs, Yale Univ. 1966–77, Provost 1972–74; Under-Sec. of State for Econ. Affairs, 1977–81; Maurits C. Boas Prof. of Int. Econs, Harvard Univ. 1981–; Chair. Nat. Intelligence Council 1995–97; mem. Bd of Dirs Fed. Reserve Bank of Boston 1987–92, Chair. 1990–92; mem. Bd of Dirs Rockefeller Brothers Fund 1975–77, Schroders Bank and Trust Co. 1975–77, Warburg-Pincus Funds 1986–98, Center for Naval Analysis 1992–95, Phoenix Cos 1983–2005, Circuit City Stores 1983–2004, CNA Corpn 1997–2015, Inst. for Int. Econs 1983–; consultant to US Treasury, Nat. Security Council, World Bank, IMF, USN; Marshall Scholarship (UK) 1956–58; Fellow, American Acad. of Sciences 1974; Hon. LLD (Oberlin Coll.) 1958; Dr hc (Paris II) 2000, (Cyprus Inst.) 2016; Nat. Intelligence Distinguished Service Medal 1996, USN Medal for Superior Public Service 2006. *Publications include:* The Economics of Interdependence 1968, Economic Policy in an Interdependent World 1986, The International Monetary System 1987, Stabilization and Debt in Developing Countries 1992, Boom, Crisis and Adjustment (co-author) 1993, Environment and Resource Policies for the World Economy 1994, Trade Growth in Transition Economies (ed.) 1997, What The Future Holds (ed.) 2002, Rebalancing the Global Economy (co-author) 2010; more than 300 articles. *Address:* Center for International Affairs, Harvard University, 1737 Cambridge Street, Cambridge, MA 02138 (office); 4 Bryant Street, Cambridge, MA 02138, USA (home). *Telephone:* (617) 495-5076 (office). *Fax:* (617) 495-8292 (office). *E-mail:* rcooper@harvard.edu (office). *Website:* www.economics.harvard.edu (office).

COOPER, Sir Robert Francis, Kt, KCMG, CMG, MVO, MA; British diplomatist and academic; *Visiting Senior Fellow, LSE Ideas, London School of Economics;* b. 28 Aug. 1947, Brentwood, Essex; s. of Norman Cooper and Frances Cooper; partner Dame Mitsuko Uchida; ed Delamere School, Nairobi, Worcester Coll., Oxford, Univ. of Pennsylvania, USA; joined FCO 1970, worked at various embassies abroad, including Tokyo and Bonn, Head of Policy Planning Staff, FCO 1989–93, seconded to Bank of England and spent a period in the Cabinet Office as Deputy Sec. for Defence and Overseas Affairs, UK Special Rep. in Afghanistan –2002; Dir-Gen. for External and Politico-Mil. Affairs, Gen. Secr. of the Council of the EU 2002–10, mem. European Council on Foreign Relations 2007, mem. Steering Cttee that drew up proposals for the European External Action Service (EEAS), Counsellor, EEAS 2010–13, Special Adviser, European Comm. 2013–14; fmr Special Adviser to the High Rep. on Burma/Myanmar; fmr Adviser to UK Prime Minister Tony Blair; currently Visiting Senior Fellow, LSE Ideas (think-tank); Thouron Award. *Publications include:* The Post-Modern State and the World Order 2000, The Post-Modern State, in Mark Leonard (ed.) Re-Ordering the World: The Long-Term Implications of September 11 (Foreign Policy Centre: London) 2002, The Breaking of Nations: Order and Chaos in the Twenty-First Century (Orwell Prize for Political Writing) 2003. *Address:* LSE Ideas, 9th floor, Towers 1 & 3, Clement's Inn, London, WC2A 2AZ, England. *E-mail:* ideas@lse.ac.uk. *Website:* www.lse.ac.uk/IDEAS/Home.aspx.

COOPER, Roy Asberry, BA, JD; American lawyer and politician; *Governor of North Carolina;* b. 13 June 1957, Rocky Mount, NC; s. of Roy Asberry Cooper, Jr and Beverly Cooper (née Batchelor); m. Kristin Bernhardt; three d.; ed Univ. of North Carolina; Partner, Fields and Cooper (family law firm) 1982–2001; mem. NC House of Reps 1987–91, Chair. Judicial Cttee 1989–91; mem. NC Senate 1991–2001, Democrat Majority Leader 1997–2001; Attorney-Gen. of North Carolina 2001–17; Gov. of North Carolina Jan. 2017–; mem. Nat. Asscn of Attorneys-Gen. (Pres. 2010–11); Democrat. *Address:* Office of the Governor, 20301 Mail Service Center, Raleigh, NC 27603-0301, USA (office). *Telephone:* (919) 814-2000 (office). *E-mail:* governor.office@nc.gov (office). *Website:* governor.nc.gov (office).

COOPER, Rt Hon. Yvette; British politician; b. 20 March 1969, Inverness, Scotland; d. of Tony Cooper and June Cooper; m. Ed Balls (q.v.) 1998; one s. two d.; ed Balliol Coll., Oxford, Harvard Univ., USA, London School of Econs; fmr Econ. Researcher for John Smith; fmr Policy Adviser, Bill Clinton Presidential Campaign, USA; fmr Policy Adviser to Labour Treasury Team on public spending; econs columnist and leader writer, The Independent (daily newspaper); MP (Labour) for Pontefract and Castleford 1997–2010, for Normanton, Pontefract and Castleford 2010–; Parl. Under-Sec. of State for Public Health 1999–2002, Parl. Sec. at Lord Chancellor's Dept 2002–03, in Office of Deputy Prime Minister 2003–05, Minister of State (Minister for Housing and Planning), Dept for Communities and Local Govt 2005–07, Minister for Housing 2007–08, Chief Sec. to Treasury 2008–09, Sec. of State for Work and Pensions 2009–10 (with Ed Balls, first married couple to serve together in UK cabinet); Shadow Minister for Women and Equalities 2010–13, Shadow Sec. of State for Work and Pensions May–Oct. 2010, Shadow Foreign Sec. 2010–11, Shadow Sec. of State for the Home Dept (Shadow Home Sec.) 2011–15, Chair. Home Affairs Select Cttee 2016–. *Address:* House of Commons, Westminster, London, SW1A 0AA (office); 1 York Street, Castleford, West Yorks., WF10 IJS, England (office). *Telephone:* (20) 7219-5080 (London) (office); (1977) 553388 (Castleford) (office). *Fax:* (20) 7219-0912 (London) (office); (1977) 559753 (Castleford) (office). *E-mail:* coopery@parliament.uk (office). *Website:* www.yvettecooper.com.

COOPER FORT, Claudia María Amelia Teresa, BEcons, MA, PhD; Peruvian economist and politician; b. 13 Sept. 1968, Lima; ed Univ. del Pacífico, New York Univ.; fmr econ. adviser with Andino Investment Holding; fmr external consultant, Inter-American Devt Bank (IDB); worked for Grupo Apoyo Comunicación (consultancy); Head, Market Risk Service, Banco de Crédito del Perú 1997–2001, Prin. Economist and Man., Treasury Dept 2001–08; mem. Advisory Bd, Ministry of Economy and Finance 2008–09; Product Devt Man. for institutional investors, Compass Group Peru 2013–16; Vice Minister of Economy and Finance 2016–17, Minister 2017–18; fmr columnist Diario Gestión (periodical), Perú 21 (daily newspaper); Dir Corporación Financiera de Desarrollo SA (Cofide), Fondo de Seguro de Depósitos (Deposit Insurance Fund), Superintendencia del Mercado de Valores (securities regulator). *Address:* c/o Ministry of Economy and Finance, Jirón Junín 319, 4°, Circado de Lima, Lima 1, Peru (office).

COOR, Lattie Finch, PhD; American academic; *President Emeritus, Arizona State University;* b. 26 Sept. 1936, Phoenix, Ariz.; s. of Lattie F. Coor and Elnora Coor (née Witten); m. Elva Wingfield 1994; three c. from a previous marriage; ed Northern Arizona Univ., Washington Univ., St Louis, American Coll., Greece; Admin. Asst to Gov. of Mich. 1961–62; Asst to Chancellor, Washington Univ., St Louis 1963–67, Asst Dean, Grad. School of Arts and Sciences 1967–69, Dir Int. Studies 1967–69, Asst Prof. of Political Science 1967–76, Vice-Chancellor 1969–74, Univ. Vice-Chancellor 1974–76; Pres., Univ. of Vt, Burlington 1976–89; Pres. Ariz. State Univ. 1990–2002, Pres. Emer. 2002–, Prof. and Ernest W. McFarland Chair in Leadership and Public Policy, School of Public Affairs 2002–; Chair. and CEO Center for the Future of Arizona 2002–; consultant for Dept of Health, Educ. and Welfare; special consultant to US Commr for Educ. 1971–74; Chair., Cttee on governmental relations, American Council on Educ. 1976–80; Dir New England Bd of Higher Educ. 1976–; mem. Pres.'s Comm., Nat. Coll. Athletic Asscn, Nat. Asscn State Univs and Land Grant Colls (Chair. Bd 1991–92). *Address:* Center for the Future of Arizona, 541 East Van Buren, Suite B-5, Phoenix, AZ 85004, USA (office). *Telephone:* (602) 496-1360 (office). *E-mail:* info@arizonafuture.org (office). *Website:* www.arizonafuture.org (office).

COORS, Peter (Pete) H., BEng, MBA; American business executive; *Chairman, Molson Coors Brewing Company; Vice-Chairman, MillerCoors;* b. 20 Sept. 1946, Golden, Colo; great-grand s. of Adolph Coors, Founder of the Golden brewery in 1873; m. Marilyn Coors; six c.; ed Phillips Exeter Acad., NH, Cornell Univ., NY, Univ. of Denver; joined Adolph Coors Co. 1971, held several exec. and man. positions, including Dir Coors and Coors Brewing Co. 1973–2005, Exec. Vice-Pres. and Chair. brewing div. of Coors (before being organized as Coors Brewing Co.) –1993, interim Treas. and Chief Financial Officer Coors 1993–95, Vice-Chair. and CEO Coors Brewing Co. 1993, Chair. Coors Brewing Co. and Pres. and CEO Adolph Coors Co. 2000–02, Chair. Adolph Coors Co. and Coors Brewing Co. 2002–05, Chair. Coors Brewing Co. and Vice-Chair. Molson Coors Brewing Co. 2005–08, Chair. MillerCoors (following merger of Miller Brewing Co. and Coors Brewing Co.) 2008–15, Vice-Chair. 2015–, Chair. Molson Coors Brewing Co. 2008–; Chair. Univ. of Colorado Hosp. Foundation 2006–; unsuccessful cand. (Republican) for Senator from Colo 2004; mem. Bd of Dirs Energy Corporation of America 1996–; mem. Int. Chapter of Young Presidents Org., Denver Univ.'s Daniels School of Business Advisory Bd; mem. Exec. Cttee Nat. Western Stock Show Asscn; fmr Nat. Pres. and Chair. Ducks Unlimited; Trustee and mem. Exec. Bd Denver Area Council of the Boy Scouts of America; Trustee Seeds of Hope Foundation, Johnson & Wales Univ.; Dr hc (Regis Univ.) 1991, (Wilberforce Univ.) 1992, (Johnson & Wales Univ.) 1997. *Leisure interests:* outdoor pursuits, wildlife conservation. *Address:* Molson Coors Brewing Co., 1225 17th Street, Suite 3200, Denver, CO 80202, (office); MillerCoors LLC, 250 South Wacker Drive, Suite 800, Chicago, IL 60606-5888, USA (office). *Telephone:* (312) 496-2700 (Chicago) (office); (303) 927-2337 (Denver) (office). *Fax:* (303) 277-5415 (Denver) (office). *E-mail:* mcbcmedia@molsoncoors.com (office). *Website:* www.molsoncoors.com (office); www.millercoors.com (office).

COPA CONDORI, Nilda; Bolivian trade unionist and politician; b. 4 Oct. 1977, La Quebrada; joined trade union aged 16; Sec. of Women's Affairs, Huayllajara Dist 1998–99; Health and Educ. Sec., Cen. Provincial Ass. 2000–03; Policy Sec., Nat. Confed. of Rural Indian Bolivian Women 'Bartolina Sisa', Sucre 2003–08, Sec.-Gen. 2008–10; mem. Asamblea Legislativa (Parl.) for Tarija 49th Dist 2006–; mem. Bolivian Constituent Ass. 2006–07; Minister of Justice 2010; local Minister for Community Rural Development and Plural Economy, Tarija. *Address:* Ministry of Justice, Avenida 16 de Julio (El Prado) 1769, La Paz, Bolivia (office). *Telephone:* (2) 212-4725 (office). *Fax:* (2) 231-5468 (office). *E-mail:* ministerio@justicia.go.bo (office). *Website:* www.justicia.gob.bo (office).

COPE, George A., BBA, CM; Canadian telecommunications executive; *CEO, Bell Canada Enterprises (BCE) Inc;* b. 1961, Scarborough, Ont.; ed Univ. of Western Ont.; Pres. and CEO Clearnet Communications Inc. 1987–2000 (acquired by TELUS Mobility 2000), Pres. and CEO TELUS Mobility 2000–05; Pres. and CEO Bell Canada 2005–08, CEO Bell Canada Enterprises (BCE) Inc. 2008–; Dir BMO Financial Group, NII Holdings Inc.; mem. Advisory Bd Richard Ivey School of Business, Univ. of Western Ont.; Canada's Top 40 Under 40 Award 1996. *Address:* Bell Canada Enterprises Inc., 1 Carrefour Alexander Graham Bell Building A, 4th Floor, Verdun, Montreal, PQ H3E 3B3, Canada (office). *Telephone:* (1) 888 932-

6666 (office). *Fax:* (514) 766-5735 (office). *E-mail:* bcecomms@bce.ca (office). *Website:* www.bce.ca (office).

COPÉ, Jean François; French politician; *Mayor of Meaux;* b. 5 May 1964, Boulogne-Billancourt (Hauts-de-Seine); s. of Prof. Roland Copé and Monique Ghanassia; m. 1st Valérie Ducuing 1991 (divorced 2007); two s. one d.; m. 2nd Nadia D'Alincourt 2011; one d.; ed École Active Bilingue Jeannine Manuel, Lycée Victor Duruy, Science-Po, École nationale d'Admin; worked at Caisse des dépôts et consignations (financial institution) 1989–91; Head of Cabinet for CEO, Dexia (financial institution) 1991–93; teacher of Local Economy and Finance, Science-Po; mem. Rally for the Republic (RPR) 1993, Deputy Gen. Sec. 2001–02; Assoc. Prof. of Economy and Finance, Univ. of Paris VIII 1997–2002; returned to Caisse des dépôts et consignations 1997–99; mem Supervisory Bd of Dexia 2000–02; Sec. of State for Relationships with Parl. and Govt Spokesman 2002–04; Deputy (Union pour un Mouvement Populaire—UMP), Nat. Ass. for Seine-et-Marne 1995–97, 2002–17, Pres. UMP Group 2007–10 (resgnd); Minister delegated to the Interior and Govt Spokesman March–Nov. 2004; Minister of Budget, Budget Reform and Govt Spokesman 2004–05, of Budget, State Reform and Govt Spokesman 2005–07; Regional Councillor of Île-de-France 1998–2007 (resgnd); Municipal Councillor of Meaux 1995–, Mayor of Meaux 1995–2002 (resgnd), 2005–, Deputy Mayor of Meaux 2002–05; Pres. and mem. Communauté d'agglomération du Pays de Meaux 2003–; Gen. Sec. UMP 2010–12, Pres. 2012–14; Of Counsel, Stehlin & Associés 2017–. *Publications include:* Finances locales – Economica 1990, Ce que je n'ai pas appris à l'ENA. L'aventure d'un maire 1999, Devoir d'inventaire. Le dépôt de bilan de Lionel Jospin 2002, Promis, j'arrête la langue de bois 2006, Manifeste pour une droite décomplexée 2012. *Address:* Maison du Brie de Meaux, Cité épiscopale, 77100 Meaux, France (office); Stehlin & Associés, 48 avenue Victor Hugo, 75016 Paris, France (office). *Telephone:* 1-64-33-02-26 (office); 1-44-17-07-70 (office). *Fax:* 1-44-17-07-77 (office). *E-mail:* jf.cope@stehlin-legal.com (office). *Website:* www.stehlin-legal.com (office); www.jfcope.fr.

COPE, Jonathan, CBE; British ballet dancer (retd) and répétiteur; b. 1963, Crediton, Devon; m. Maria Almeida; one s. one d.; ed Royal Ballet School; joined Royal Ballet 1982, Soloist 1985–86, Prin. 1987–90, 1992–2005 (retd), Répétiteur 2005–; est. property devt business 1990–92; involved in London 2012 Olympic Closing Ceremony, alongside fmr Prin. Dancer and Partner Darcey Bussell 2012; South Bank Show Dance Award 2003, Critics' Circle/Nat. Dance Awards, Best Male Dancer 2004. *Leading roles (with Royal Ballet) include:* Prince in Swan Lake, The Sleeping Beauty and The Nutcracker, Romeo and Juliet (partnering Sylvie Guillem and Darcey Bussell), Solor in La Bayadère, Albrecht in Giselle, Le Baiser de la Fée, The Prince of the Pagodas, Cinderella, Palemon in Ondine, Serenade, Agon, Apollo, Opus 19/The Dreamer, The Sons of Horus, Young Apollo, Galanteries, The Planets, Still Life at the Penguin Café, The Spirit of Fugue, Concerto, Gloria, Requiem, A Broken Set of Rules, Pursuit, Piano, Grand Pas Classique, Monotones, Crown Prince Rudolph in Mayerling, Woyzeck in Different Drummer, Second Friend in The Judas Tree, Beliaev in A Month in the Country, Birthday Offering, La Valise, Air Monotones II, Fox in Renard, Fearful Symmetries, Symphony in C (partnering Sylvie Guillem), Duo Concertant, If This Is Still a Problem, Des Grieux in Manon, Illuminations. *Address:* The Royal Ballet, Royal Opera House, Bow Street, Covent Garden, London, WC2E 9DD, England. *Telephone:* (20) 7240-1200. *Fax:* (20) 7212-9121. *Website:* www.roh.org.uk/people/jonathan-cope.

COPE, Wendy Mary, OBE, MA, FRSL; British author; b. 21 July 1945, Erith, Kent; d. of Fred Stanley Cope and Alice Mary Cope (née Hand); m. Lachlan Mackinnon; ed Farringtons School, St Hilda's Coll., Oxford, Westminster Coll. of Educ., Oxford; primary school teacher, London 1967–86; freelance writer 1986–; mem. Soc. of Authors (mem. Man. Cttee 1992–95); Hon. Fellow, Goldsmiths, Univ. of London 2013; Hon. DLitt (Winchester) 2000, (Oxford Brookes) 2003; Cholmondeley Award for Poetry 1987, Michael Braude Award for Light Verse, American Acad. of Arts and Letters 1995. *Publications include:* Across the City 1980, Hope and the 42 1984, Making Cocoa for Kingsley Amis 1986, Poem from a Colour Chart of House Paints 1986, Men and Their Boring Arguments 1988, Does She Like Wordgames? 1988, Twiddling Your Thumbs 1988, The River Girl 1990, Serious Concerns 1992, If I Don't Know 2001, Two Cures for Love: Selected Poems 2008, Family Values 2011, Life, Love and The Archers 2014, Christmas Poems 2017, Anecdotal Evidence 2018; editor: Is That the New Moon? – Poems by Women Poets 1989, The Orchard Book of Funny Poems 1993, The Funny Side 1998, The Faber Book of Bedtime Stories 2000, Heaven on Earth – 101 Happy Poems 2001, George Herbert: Verse and Prose (a selection) 2002; contribs to newspapers and reviews. *Leisure interests:* playing the piano, gardening. *Address:* c/o Faber & Faber, Bloomsbury House, 74–77 Great Russell Street, London, WC1B 3DA, England (office). *Telephone:* (20) 7927-3800 (office). *Website:* www.faber.co.uk (office).

COPELAND, Misty Danielle; American ballet dancer; *Principal Dancer, American Ballet Theatre;* b. 10 Sept. 1982, Kansas City, Mo.; ed San Pedro City Ballet, Lauridsen Ballet Center; began ballet studies aged 13 with San Pedro City Ballet; joined American Ballet Theatre (ABT) Studio Co. 2000, participated in Summer Intensive Program 1998–2000, mem. Corps de Ballet 2001–07, Soloist 2007–15, Prin. Dancer (first African-American woman) 2015–, Spokesperson, Project Plie (ABT diversity initiative) 2013–; chosen by Prince to star in his Crimson and Clover video, also special guest artist at several concert performances; mem. Pres.'s Council on Fitness, Sports and Nutrition 2014–; winner, ballet category, Los Angeles Music Center Spotlight Awards 1998, Nat. Coca Cola Scholar, ABT 2000, Leonore Annenberg Fellowship in the Arts 2008, Nat. Youth of the Year Amb. for Boys & Girls Clubs of America 2013. *Plays:* Broadway debut in On the Town 2015. *Television includes:* guest judge, So You Think You Can Dance 2014. *Publication:* Life in Motion: An Unlikely Ballerina (autobiography) 2014. *Address:* American Ballet Theatre, 890 Broadway, 3rd Floor, New York, NY 10003, USA (office). *Telephone:* (212) 477-3030 (office). *Fax:* (212) 254-5938 (office). *Website:* www.abt.org (office); www.mistycopeland.com.

COPPENS, Yves; French professor of palaeoanthropology and prehistory; *Professor Emeritus, Collège de France;* b. 9 Aug. 1934, Vannes, Morbihan; s. of René Coppens and Andrée Coppens; m. Françoise Le Guennec 1959; ed Univ. of Rennes, Univ. of Paris (Sorbonne); Research Asst, CNRS, Paris 1956–69; Assoc. Prof., then Prof., Nat. Museum of Natural History 1969–83; Prof. of Palaeoanthropology and Prehistory, Collège de France 1983–2005, Prof. Emer. 2005–; mem. Acad. of Sciences 1985, Nat. Acad. of Medicine 1991, Royal Acad. of Sciences (Belgium) 1992, Pontifical Acad. of Sciences 2014; Hon. Fellow, Royal Anthropological Inst. of GB and Ireland; Chevalier, Légion d'honneur, Grand Officier; Grand Officier, Ordre nat. du Mérite; Commdr des Palmes académiques, des Arts et des Lettres 2010; Officier, Ordre Nat. Tchadien; Commdr, Order of Cultural Merit of Monaco; Dr hc (Bologna) 1988, (Liège) 1992; Prix Edmond Hébert 1963, Prix André C. Bonnet 1969, Médaille d'or de l'Empereur d'Éthiopie 1973, Grand Prix Jaffé, Acad. des Sciences 1974, Grand Prix scientifique, Fondation de France 1975, Médaille Fourmarier, Soc. Géologique de Belgique 1975, Prix Glaxo 1978, Médaille d'argent, CNRS 1982, UNESCO Prix Kalinga 1984, Médaille Vandenbroeck, Soc. belge de géologie, de paléontologie et d'hydrologie 1987, Médaille André Duveyrier, Soc. de Géographie 1989, Médaille d'or de l'encouragement au progrèscience 1991, Prix Nonino (Italy) 2005, asteroid (172850) Coppens named in his honour 2005, Nouveau Prix de Rome 2015. *Documentary film:* Homo sapiens 2005. *Publications include:* Le Singe, l'Afrique et l'homme 1983, Préhistoire de l'art occidental (with Brigitte Delluc, André Leroi-gourhan) 1990, Origines de la bipédie (with Brigitte Senut) 1992, La plus belle histoire du monde 1996, Le genou de Lucy 1999, Pré-ambules : les premiers pas de l'homme 1999, Grand entretien 2001, Aux origines de l'humanité 2001, Les origines de l'homme T 1 et T 2 (with Pascal Picq) 2002, L'Odyssée de l'espèce 2003, Homo sapiens 2004, Origines de l'homme – De la matière à la conscience 2010, Origines de l'Homme, origines d'un homme : Mémoires 2018; over 400 scientific papers. *Address:* Collège de France, 3, rue d'Ulm, 75231 Paris, Cedex 5; Musée de l'Homme, Palais de Chaillot, place du Trocadéro, 75116 Paris (office); 4 rue du Pont-aux-Choux, 75003 Paris, France (home). *Telephone:* 1-44-27-10-23. *E-mail:* yves.coppens@college-of-france.fr. *Website:* www.college-de-france.fr/site/yves-coppens/index.htm.

COPPERFIELD, David; American magician; b. (David Kotkin), 1956, Metuchen, NJ; ed Fordham Univ.; Prof. of Magic, New York Univ. 1974; appeared in musical Magic Man 1974; presenter, The Magic of ABC; performer, dir, producer, writer, The Magic of David Copperfield 1978–; Founder and Chair. Project Magic 1982–; Founder Int. Museum and Library of Conjuring Arts, Nev. 1991; Owner, Musha Cay resort, Bahamas; performs more than 550 shows per year world-wide; Dr hc (Fordham Univ.); Chevalier, Ordre des Arts et des Letters; Golden Rose Award, Montreux Film Festival 1987, Bambi Award 1993, 19 Emmy Awards. *Film:* Terror Train 1980. *Achievements include:* illusions include levitating across Grand Canyon 1984, walking through Great Wall of China 1986, escaping from Alcatraz prison 1987, making Statue of Liberty disappear 1989, going over Niagara Falls 1990, making Orient Express disappear 1991; introduced flying illusion 1992; escaped from burning ropes 13 storeys above ground, Caesar's Palace 1993. *Publication:* Tales of the Impossible 1996. *Website:* www.davidcopperfield.com.

COPPERWHEAT, Lee; British fashion designer; s. of Terence Copperwheat and Diana Frances Brooks; ed Tresham Coll., Northampton, London Coll. of Fashion; fmrly tailor with Aquascutum; est. design room and fmr man. of sampling and production Passenger sportswear; freelance design projects for numerous clients; fmr teacher menswear tailoring Brighton Univ.; fmr Lecturer, St Martin's School of Art, London; est. Copperwheat Blundell with Pamela Blundell; est. menswear label Copperwheat in New York with Ben Copperwheat 2009, now Creative Dir; Young Designer of the Year 1994 (with Pamela Blundell). *E-mail:* info@bencopperwheat.com (office).

COPPOLA, Francis Ford; American film director, film producer and screenwriter; b. 7 April 1939, Detroit, Mich.; s. of Carmine Coppola and Italia Coppola; m. Eleanor Neil; two s. (one deceased) one d. Sofia Coppola (q.v.); ed Hofstra Univ., Univ. of California; theatre direction includes Private Lives, The Visit of the Old Lady, San Francisco Opera Co. 1972; founder and Artistic Dir Zoetrope Studios 1969–; Owner, Niebaum-Coppola Estate (winery), Napa Valley; f. Zoetrope Argentina, Buenos Aires; Commdr, Ordre des Arts et des Lettres; Cannes Film Award for The Conversation 1974; Dir's Guild Award for The Godfather; Acad. Award for Best Screenplay for Patton, Golden Palm (Cannes) 1979 for Apocalypse Now, also awarded Best Screenplay, Best Dir and Best Picture Oscars for The Godfather Part II; US Army Civilian Service Award, Irving G. Thalberg Memorial Award, Acad. of Motion Picture Arts and Sciences 2010; Praemium Imperiale Award, Japan Arts Foundation 2013. *Films directed include:* The Playgirls and the Bellboy 1962, Tonight for Sure 1962, Dementia 13 1963, You're a Big Boy Now 1966, Finian's Rainbow 1968, The Rain People 1969, The Godfather 1972, The Conversation 1974, The Godfather: Part II 1974, Apocalypse Now 1979, One from the Heart 1982, The Outsiders 1983, Rumble Fish 1983, The Cotton Club 1984, Captain EO 1986, Peggy Sue Got Married 1986, Gardens of Stone 1987, Tucker: The Man and His Dream 1988, New York Stories 1989, The Godfather: Part III 1990, Dracula 1992, Jack 1996, The Rainmaker 1997, Youth Without Youth 2007, Tetro 2009, Twixt Now and Sunrise 2011; also numerous screenplays and films produced including American Graffiti. *Address:* Zoetrope Studios, 916 Kearny Street, San Francisco, CA 94133; Niebaum Coppola, POB 208, Rutherford, CA 94573; c/o CAA, 9830 Wilshire Boulevard, Beverly Hills, CA 90212, USA. *Website:* www.zoetrope.com; www.inglenook.com.

COPPOLA, Sofia; American actress, film director, screenwriter, film producer and photographer; b. 14 May 1971, New York; d. of Francis Ford Coppola (q.v.) and Eleanor Coppola; m. Spike Jonze 1999 (divorced 2003); pnr Thomas Mars; two d.; cr. pop-culture magazine show Hi-Octane 1994; fmr designer, Milkfed fashion label; photography has appeared in Interview, Paris Vogue and Allure; mem. Writers Guild of America. *Films include:* Frankenweenie 1984, Peggy Sue Got Married 1986, Anna 1987, The Godfather: Part III 1990, Inside Monkey Zetterland 1992, Ciao L.A. 1994, Lick the Star (dir, producer and writer) 1998, The Virgin Suicides (dir and writer) 1999, Star Wars: Episode I: The Phantom Menace 1999, CQ 2001, Lost in Translation (dir, producer and writer) (Acad. Award for Best Original Screenplay 2004, Golden Globe Awards for Best Picture, Best Screenplay 2004, Independent Spirit Awards for Best Screenplay, Best Dir, Best Picture 2004, Cesar Award for Best Foreign Feature 2005) 2003, Marie-Antoinette (dir, producer and writer) 2006, Somewhere (Golden Lion Award, Venice Film Festival) 2010, The Bling Ring (dir and writer) 2013, A Very Murray Christmas (dir, producer and writer) 2015, The Beguiled (dir, producer and writer) (Best Dir, Cannes Film Festival 2017) 2017. *Opera includes:* as dir: La Traviata (Teatro Costanzi di Roma) 2016. *Address:* c/o Bart Walker, Cinetic Media LLC, 555 West 25th Street, 4th Floor, New York, NY 10001, USA.

COPPS, Sheila Maureen, OC, PC, BA; Canadian consultant and fmr politician; *President, Sheila Copps and Associates;* b. 27 Nov. 1952, Hamilton, Ont.; d. of Victor Kennedy Copps and Geraldine Florence Copps (née Guthro); m. Austin Thorne; one d.; ed Univ. of Western Ontario, Univ. of Rouen, France, McMaster Univ.; journalist, Ottawa Citizen 1974–76, Hamilton Spectator 1977; Constituency Asst to Leader Liberal Party, Ont. 1977–81; mem. Ont. Legis. Ass. for Hamilton Centre 1981–84; mem. House of Commons (Parl.) 1984–2004, Deputy Leader of Opposition, Fed. Liberal Party 1991; Deputy Prime Minister 1993–97, Minister of the Environment 1993–96, Minister of Canadian Heritage 1996–2004; currently Pres. Sheila Copps and Assocs, Ottawa; Hon. DIur (Univ. of Sainte-Anne), (King's Coll. London); Achievement Award, Canadian Council for the Arts 2003, Eurovision Henrik Ingberg Award, Nature Conservancy of Canada, Lifetime Achievement Award, City of Hamilton, Lifetime Achievement Award, Canadian Asscn of Broadcasters. *Publications:* Nobody's Baby 1986, Worth Fighting For 2004. *Address:* Sheila Copps and Associates, Inc., 1103–1480 Riverside Drive, Ottawa, ON K1G 5H2, Canada (office). *Telephone:* (613) 355-0004 (office). *E-mail:* sheila@sheilacopps.ca (office). *Website:* www.sheilacopps.ca (office).

CORBAT, Michael L., BA (Econ); American banking executive; *CEO, Citigroup Inc.;* ed Harvard Univ.; has been at Citigroup and its predecessor cos since graduation in 1983, worked in Fixed Income Sales Dept in Atlanta and worked in New York and London, held several positions at Salomon Brothers (predecessor of Citigroup) including Man. Dir roles in Emerging Markets, High Yield and Derivatives, later Head of Global Emerging Markets Debt, Citigroup, then Head of the Global Corp. Bank and Global Commercial Bank –2008, CEO Global Wealth Man., CEO Citi Holdings, Inc. 2009–11, CEO Europe, Middle East and Africa, Citigroup Jan.–Oct. 2012, CEO Citigroup Inc. Oct. 2012–; Dir British American Business, Inc.; mem. Bd of Dirs, Swedish American Chamber of Commerce; mem. Bd of Trustees, Salisbury School. *Address:* Citigroup Inc., 399 Park Avenue, New York, NY 10043, USA (office). *Telephone:* (212) 559-1000 (office). *Fax:* (212) 793-3946 (office). *E-mail:* info@citigroup.com (office). *Website:* www.citigroup.com (office).

CORBETT, Gerald Michael Nolan, MA, MSc, DL; British business executive; *Non-Executive Chairman, Britvic PLC;* b. 7 Sept. 1951, Hastings, Sussex; s. of John Michael Nolan Corbett and Pamela Muriel Corbett (née Gay); m. Virginia Moore Newsum; one s. three d.; ed Pembroke Coll. Cambridge, London Business School, Harvard Business School, USA; with Boston Consulting Group 1975–82; Group Financial Controller Dixons Group PLC 1982–86, Corp. Finance Dir 1986–87; Group Finance Dir Redland PLC 1987–94, Grand Metropolitan PLC 1994–97; Dir (non-exec.) MEPC PLC 1995–98, Burmah Castrol PLC 1998–2000; CEO Railtrack PLC 1997–2000; Chair. Woolworths Group PLC 2001–07, Health Club Holdings, Holmes Place 2003–, SSL International 2005–10, Britvic PLC 2005–, Moneysupermarket.com Group Ltd 2007–14, Towry 2012–14, Betfair plc 2012–, Numis 2014–; Chair. Bd of Govs, Abbots Hill School 1997–2002; Chair. Royal Nat. Inst. for the Deaf (now called Action on Hearing Loss) 2007–13, Hertfordshire Community Foundation (Bd of Trustees), St Albans Cathedral Music Trust, MCC 2015–; High Sheriff of Hertfordshire 2010–11; mem. Council, Shrieval Asscn 2008–12; DL Herts. 2015; Foundation Scholar, Pembroke Coll., Cambridge 1972–75, William Pitt Prize 1974, London Business School Prize 1979. *Leisure interests:* golf, country pursuits. *Address:* Britvic Group and GB Head Office, Breakspear Park, Breakspear Way, Hemel Hempstead, HP2 4TZ, Herts., England (office). *Telephone:* (121) 711-1102 (office). *E-mail:* info@britvic.com (office). *Website:* www.britvic.com (office).

CORBETT, Roger Campbell, AO, AM, BComm; Australian business executive; *Chairman, ALH Group Proprietary Limited;* b. 1942; m. Rosemary Corbett; one s. two d.; ed Univ. of New South Wales; began career working on dock, Woolworths Store, Chatswood; fmr Dir of Operations and Dir, David Jones (Australia) Pty Ltd; fmr Merchandising and Stores Dir and Dir, Grace Brothers; Man. Dir Big W (gen. merchandise discount stores), Woolworths Ltd (Australia) 1990–97, apptd Exec. Dir Woolworths Ltd (Australia) 1990, Man. Dir of Retail 1997–98, COO 1998–99, CEO, Group Man. Dir 1999–2006 (retd); Dir, Wal-Mart Stores Inc. 2006–, Reserve Bank of Australia, Fairfax Media Ltd, Outback Stores; Chair. ALH Group Pty Ltd; fmr Chair. CIES Food Business Forum, France; Deputy Chair. PrimeAg Australia; mem. Advisory Council, Australian Grad. School of Man., Univ. of New South Wales; mem. Liberal Party of Australia; B'nai B'rith (Australia-NZ) Gold Medal. *Address:* ALH Group Pty Ltd, Locked Bag 4040, South Melbourne, Vic. 3205 (office); ALH Group Pty Ltd, Level 2, 10 Yarra Street, South Yarra, Vic. 3141, Australia (office). *Telephone:* (3) 9829-1000 (office). *Website:* www.alhgroup.com.au (office).

CORBETT, Thomas Wingett (Tom), Jr, BA, JD; American lawyer, business executive, politician and fmr state governor; b. 17 June 1949, Philadelphia, PA; s. of Thomas Wingett Corbett and Mary Bernadine Corbett (née Diskin); m. Susan Jean Manbeck 1972; one s. one d.; ed Lebanon Valley Coll., St Mary's Univ. Law School, San Antonio; teacher; served in 28th Infantry Div., PA Army Nat. Guard 1971–84, attained rank of Capt.; called to the Bar in 1976, US Dist Court (Western Dist), PA 1976, US Court of Mil. Appeals 1979, US Supreme Court 1984; began legal career as Asst Dist Attorney, Allegheny Co., Pittsburgh, PA 1976–80; Asst US Attorney for Western Dist of PA 1980–83; pvt. law practice for several years; Assoc., Rose, Schmidt, Hasley & DiSalle 1983–86, Partner 1986–89, Thorp, Reed & Armstrong, Pittsburgh 1993–95, 1997–98; elected as township commr in Pittsburgh suburb of Shaler Township; apptd to monitor Allegheny Co. jail while under court's supervision 1988; US Attorney for Western Dist of PA 1989–93 (resgnd), mem. US Attorney-Gen.'s Advisory Cttee 1991–93, Chair. 1992–93; adviser to successful gubernatorial campaign of Tom Ridge; served on several state comms, including Pennsylvania Comm. on Crime and Delinquency (Chair.); Attorney-Gen. of Commonwealth of PA 1995–97, 2005–11; Asst Gen. Counsel for Govt Affairs, Waste Management Inc., Pittsburgh 1998–2002; Partner, Thomas Corbett & Assocs 2002–05; Gov. of Pennsylvania 2011–15; del., Republican Nat. Convention 2000; mem. Gov.'s Partnership for Safe Children 1995–2003, Pennsylvania Weed & Seed Program 1995–2003, Pennsylvania Comm. on Crime and Delinquency 1995–2003; Pres. St Mary's Parent-Teacher Guild, Glenshaw; mem. Shaler Township Republican Cttee 1984–89, Allegheny Co. Republican Cttee 1985–89; mem. ABA, Allegheny Co. Bar Asscn, Pennsylvania Bar Asscn, Ancient Order of Hibernians, Nat. Rifle Asscn; Republican. *Leisure interests:* skiing, golf, reading. *Address:* c/o Office of the Governor, 225 Main Capitol Building, Harrisburg, PA 17120, USA (office).

CORBO LIOI, Vittorio, PhD; Chilean economist, academic, business executive and fmr central banker; *Non-Executive Chairman, Banco Santander Chile;* b. 22 March 1943, Iquique; s. of Gerardo Corbo and Maria Lioi; m. Veronica Urzua 1967; one s. one d.; ed Universidad de Chile and Mass Inst. of Tech.; Asst Prof. of Econs, Concordia Univ., Canada 1972–81; Prof., Inst. of Econs, Pontificia Univ. Católica de Chile 1981–84, 1991–2003; Visiting Prof., Georgetown Univ., Washington, DC 1984–91; Sr Adviser, IBRD 1984–87, Div. Chief. 1987–91; Chief, Macroeconomic Devt and Growth Div., World Bank 1984–91, mem. Chief Economist Advisory Council 2004–; Econ. Adviser to Santander Group in Chile 1991–2003, 2008–14, Dir, Banco Santander-Chile 1995–2003, Chair. (non-exec.) 2014–, Dir, Banco Santander 2011–; Chair. Cen. Bank of Chile 2003–07; Chair. (non-exec.), Compañía de Seguros SURA-Chile SA; Pres. ING Seguros de Vida SA (insurance co.), Santiago from 2008; Vice-Chair. Inmobiliaria Simonetti 2008–; Dir, Global Devt Network 1999–2003, Universia-Chile 2000–03, Chilean Pacific Foundation 2000–, Cruz Verde Pharmacies 2008–; Vice-Pres. Int. Econ. Asscn 1998–2002; mem. Man. Council, Global Devt Network 1993–2003, Int. Advisory Council, Center for Social and Econ. Research (CASE), Warsaw, Poland, Advisory Bd, Stanford Center for Int. Devt 1999–; Sr Research Fellow, Research Center for Econ. Devt and Policy Reform, Stanford Univ. 1999; Visiting Sr Scholar, Research Dept, IMF 2000, 2003; mem. Editorial Cttee, Journal of Development Economics, Journal of Applied Economics; Economist of the Year, El Mercurio newspaper 2003. *Publications include:* Inflation in Developing Countries 1974, Monetary Policy in Latin America in the 1990s 2000. *Leisure interest:* skiing. *Address:* Banco Santander Chile, Bandera 140, Santiago, Región Metropolitana, Chile (office). *Telephone:* (2) 23202000 (office). *Fax:* (2) 23201409 (office). *E-mail:* webmaster@santander.cl (office). *Website:* www.santander.cl (office).

CORBYN, Rt Hon Jeremy Bernard, PC; British politician; *Leader, Labour Party;* b. 26 May 1949, Chippenham, Wilts.; s. of David Benjamin Corbyn and Naomi Corbyn (née Josling); m. 1st Jane Chapman 1974 (divorced 1979); m. 2nd Claudia Bracchitta 1987 (divorced 1999), three s.; m. 3rd Laura Álvarez 2013; ed Adams Grammar School, Shropshire; began career as reporter for Newport and Market Drayton Advertiser (newspaper); spent two years with Voluntary Service Overseas in Jamaica; fmr official for Nat. Union of Tailors and Garment Workers and later Nat. Union of Public Employees; mem. Haringey Council 1974–83; MP (Labour) for Islington N 1983–, mem. London Regional Select Cttee 1983–87, 2009–10, Social Security Select Cttee 1992–97, Justice Select Cttee 2010–15, Chair. All-Party Parl. Group (APPG) on Chagos Islands, Chair. APPG on Mexico, Vice-Chair. APPG on Latin America, Vice-Chair. APPG on Human Rights, mem. APPG on Cycling, mem. several Parl. Trade Union Groups, Leader of the Opposition 2015–; Chair. Stop the War Coalition 2011–15; fmr columnist, Morning Star; mem. Socialist Campaign Group 1983–2015; mem. Campaign for Nuclear Disarmament, Vice-Pres. 2015–; fmr mem. Nat. Exec. Anti-Apartheid Movement; mem. Amnesty International; mem. Labour Party, Leader 2015–; Gandhi Int. Peace Award 2013, Seán MacBride Peace Prize (jt recipient) 2017. *Address:* Labour Party, One Brewer's Green, London, SW1H 0RH, England (office). *Telephone:* (845) 092-2299 (office). *E-mail:* leader@labour.org.uk (office). *Website:* www.labour.org.uk (office).

CORCORAN, Timothy J.; American business executive; *Chairman, Nationwide Mutual Insurance Company;* Owner/Partner, Corcoran Farms; mem. Bd of Dirs, Nationwide Mutual Insurance Co. 2001–, Chair. 2014–; mem. Nat. Asscn of Corp. Dirs; fmr Chair. The Ohio State Univ. Alumni Asscn of Ross Co.; mem. Bd of Trustees, Ohio Farm Bureau Fed. 1994–2001, served as Treas. and First Vice-Pres. *Address:* Nationwide Mutual Insurance Co., One Nationwide Plaza, Columbus, OH 43215-2220, USA (office). *Telephone:* (614) 249-7111 (office). *Fax:* (614) 249-7705 (office). *E-mail:* info@nationwide.com (office). *Website:* www.nationwide.com (office).

CORDANI, David M., MBA; American business executive; *President and CEO, CIGNA Corporation;* b. 10 Feb. 1966, Waterbury, CT; ed Texas A&M Univ., Univ. of Hartford; chartered financial consultant; joined CIGNA Corpn 1991, Sr Vice-Pres., Customer Segments and Marketing, CIGNA HealthCare 2004–05, Pres. CIGNA HealthCare 2005–08, Pres. and COO CIGNA Corpn 2008–09, mem. Bd of Dirs Oct. 2009–, Pres. and CEO Dec. 2009–; Chair. US-Korea Business Council 2017–; mem. Bd of Dirs Nat. Asscn of Mfrs, Cigna Foundation. *Publication:* The Courage to Go Forward: The Power of Micro Communities 2018 (co-author). *Address:* CIGNA Corporation, 2 Liberty Place, 1601 Chestnut Street, Philadelphia, PA 19192, USA (office). *Telephone:* (215) 761-1000 (office). *E-mail:* info@cigna.com (office). *Website:* www.cigna.com (office).

CORDEN, James Kimberley, OBE; British actor, comedian, television comedy writer, producer and television host; *Host, The Late Late Show (CBS);* b. 22 Aug. 1978, Hillingdon, London, England; s. of Malcolm Corden and Margaret Corden; m. Julia Carey 2012; two c.; ed Holmer Green Upper School; first stage appearance in musical Martin Guerre aged 18; early TV work included Gareth Jones in series Boyz Unlimited 1999; Co-creator, co-writer and star of sitcom Gavin & Stacey (BBC) 2007–10; co-presented the BRIT Awards 2009, host 2011, 2012; appeared in as the lead in comedy play One Man, Two Guvnors, Nat. Theatre (later transferred to West End and Broadway) 2011; featured on No. 1 single Shout, along with Dizzee Rascal (unofficial anthem of the England football team for FIFA World Cup, South Africa) 2010; host of The Late Late Show (CBS) 2015–, Tony Awards 2016, Grammy Awards 2017, 2018. *Theatre includes:* Martin Guerre (Prince Edward Theatre) 1996, The History Boys (Lyttelton Theatre, London, then touring) 2006, A Respectable Wedding (Young Vic, London) 2007, One Man, Two Guvnors (Lyttelton Theatre, London, Adelphi Theatre, London, Music Box Theatre, New York City) (Tony Award, Leading Role in a Play 2012) 2011–12. *Films include:* Twenty Four Seven 1997, Whatever Happened to Harold Smith? 1999, All or Nothing 2002, Heartlands 2002, Cruise of the Gods 2002, Pierrepoint 2005, Heroes and Villains 2006, The History Boys 2006, Starter for 10 2006, How to Lose Friends & Alienate People 2008, Lesbian Vampire Killers 2009, Telstar 2009, The Boat That Rocked 2009, Planet 51 (voice) 2009, Gulliver's Travels 2010, Animals United (voice) 2010, The Three Musketeers 2011, One Chance 2013, Begin Again 2013, Into the Woods (Satellite Award for Best Cast – Motion Picture 2015) 2014, Kill Your Friends 2015, The Lady in the Van 2015, Ocean's 8 2018. *Radio includes:* The

History Boys (BBC Radio 4). *Television includes:* Out of Tune 1996–98, Renford Rejects 1998, Boyz Unlimited 1999, Hollyoaks 2000, Fat Friends 2000–05, Jack and the Beanstalk: The Real Story (film) 2001, Teachers 2001–03, Cruise of the Gods 2002, Little Britain 2004, Dalziel and Pascoe 2004, Gavin & Stacey (also co-writer) (Best Male Comedy Performer, British Comedy Awards 2007, BAFTA Television Award for Best Male Comedy Performance 2008) 2007–10, Horne & Corden 2009, The Gruffalo 2009, James Corden's World Cup Live (ITV, presenter) 2010, Doctor Who 2010–11, A League of Their Own (game show, Sky 1, host) 2010–14, Little Charley Bear 2011, The Gruffalo's Child 2011, Stella 2012, The Wrong Mans (BBC 2, creator, writer and star) 2013–15, Roald Dahl's Esio Trot (narrator) 2015, The Late Late Show with James Corden (CBS, host) (Emmy Award for Outstanding Interactive Program 2016) 2015–18, Carpool Karaoke: The Series (Emmy Award for Outstanding Variety Special 2017, Producers Guild Award for Outstanding Short Film Program 2018, Emmy Award for Outstanding Short Form Variety Series 2018) 2017–, James Corden's Next James Corden (Emmy Award for Outstanding Actor in a Short Form Comedy or Drama Series, for Outstanding Short Form Comedy or Drama Series 2018) 2018–. *Publications:* May I Have Your Attention, Please?: The Autobiography 2011. *Address:* c/o Ruth Young, United Agents, 12–26 Lexington Street, London, W1F 0LE, England (office). *Telephone:* (20) 3214-0800 (office). *Fax:* (20) 3214-0801 (office). *E-mail:* ztossell@unitedagents.co.uk (office). *Website:* unitedagents.co.uk/james-corden (office).

CORDEN, Warner Max, AC, MComm, MA, PhD, FBA, FASSA; Australian economist and academic; *Professorial Fellow, Department of Economics, University of Melbourne;* b. 13 Aug. 1927, Breslau, Germany (now Wrocław, Poland); s. of Ralph S. Corden; m. Dorothy Martin 1957; one d.; ed Melbourne Boys High School, Univ. of Melbourne and London School of Econs; Lecturer, Dept of Econs, Univ. of Melbourne 1958–61, Professorial Fellow 2002–; Nuffield Reader in Int. Econs and Fellow of Nuffield Coll., Oxford 1967–76; Professorial Fellow, ANU 1962–67, Prof. of Econs 1976–88; Chung Ju Yung Prof. of Int. Econs, Paul H. Nitze School of Advanced Int. Studies, Johns Hopkins Univ., Washington, DC, USA 1989–2002, Prof. Emer. of Int. Econs 2002–; Visiting Prof., Univ. of California, Berkeley 1965, Univ. of Minnesota 1971, Princeton Univ. 1973, Harvard Univ. 1986; Sr Adviser, IMF 1986–88; Pres. Econ. Soc. of Australia and New Zealand 1977–80; mem. Group of Thirty 1982–90; Foreign Hon. mem. American Econ. Asscn 1986, Distinguished Fellow, Econ. Soc. of Australia 1995; Dr hc (Melbourne) 1995; Bernard Harms Prize 1986. *Publications include:* The Theory of Protection 1971, Trade Policy and Economic Welfare 1974, 1997, Inflation, Exchange Rates and the World Economy 1977, 1985, Protection, Growth and Trade 1985, International Trade Theory and Policy 1992, Economic Policy, Exchange Rates and the International System 1994, The Road to Reform 1997, Too Sensational: On the Choice of Exchange Rate Regimes 2002. *Address:* Department of Economics, University of Melbourne, Melbourne, Vic. 3010, Australia (office). *Telephone:* (3) 8344-5296 (office). *Fax:* (3) 8344-6899 (office). *E-mail:* m.corden@unimelb.edu.au (office). *Website:* www.maxcorden.com.

CORDES, Eckhard, MBA, PhD; German business executive; *Founding Partner, Emeram Capital Partners GmbH;* b. 25 Nov. 1950, Neumünster; m. 1st; two s.; m. 2nd; two s.; ed Univ. of Hamburg; joined DaimlerChrysler Group 1976, Asst Plant Man. Sindelfingen Plant 1977–81, Sr Man. Investment Planning, Sindelfingen Plant 1981–83, Head, Product Control, New Commercial Vehicle P 1983–86, Dir Accounting and Control, Mercedes-Benz, Sao Paulo, Brazil 1986–89, Dir Control AEG, Frankfurt 1989–91, Sr Vice-Pres. Control, Corp. Planning and Mergers and Acquisitions 1991–94, Sr Vice-Pres. Corp. Planning and Control, Daimler-Benz AG 1994–95, Sr Vice-Pres. Corp. Devt 1995–96, mem. Man. Bd, Corp. Devt and Directly-Managed Businesses 1997, Corp. Devt and IT Man. and MTU/Diesel Engines and TEMIC DaimlerChrysler AG 1998–2000 (after Daimler-Benz merged with Chrysler Corpn 1998), mem. Man. Bd, Corp. Devt and IT Man. DaimlerChrysler AG 2000–04, Commercial Vehicles Div. 2000–04, Head, Mercedes Car Group 2004–05; CEO and Chair. Man. Bd Franz Haniel & Cie. GmbH 2006–09; Chair. Supervisory Bd Metro AG 2006–07, Chair. Man. Bd 2007–11, Chief Human Resources Officer 2010–11; Founding Partner, Emeram Capital Partners GmbH 2011–; Partner, Cevian Capital 2012–; Chair. Bilfinger SE (construction co.) 2014–; Chair. Fed. of German Industries' Cttee on Eastern European Econ. Relations 2010–15. *Address:* Emeram Capital Partners GmbH, Mühlbaurstr. 1, 81679 Munich (office); Bilfinger SE, Carl-Reiß-Platz 1–5, 68165 Mannheim, Germany (office). *Telephone:* (89) 41999670 (Munich) (office); (621) 459-0 (Mannheim) (office). *Fax:* (89) 419996710 (Munich) (office); (621) 4592366 (Mannheim) (office). *E-mail:* eckhard.cordes@emeram.com (office); eckhard.cordes@bilfinger.com (office). *Website:* emeram.com (office); www.bilfinger.com (office).

CORDES, HE Cardinal Paul Josef; German ecclesiastic; *President Emeritus of the Pontifical Council 'Cor Unum';* b. 5 Sept. 1934, Kirchhundem; ed briefly studied medicine before entering the seminary, doctoral studies at Univ. of Mainz; ordained priest of Paderborn 1961; apptd Titular Bishop of Naissus and Auxiliary Bishop of Paderborn 1975, Titular Archbishop of Naissus 1995; Vice-Pres. Pontifical Council for the Laity 1980; Pres. Pontifical Council 'Cor Unum' 1995–2005, 2005–10, Pres. Emer. 2010–; cr. Cardinal (Cardinal-Deacon of S. Lorenzo in Piscibus) 2007, Cardinal Priest 2018. *Address:* Pontifical Council 'Cor Unum', Piazza S. Calisto 16, 00153 Rome, Italy (office). *Telephone:* (06) 6988-9411 (office). *Fax:* (06) 6988-7301 (office).

CÓRDOBA RUIZ, Piedad Esneda; Colombian lawyer and politician; b. 25 Jan. 1955, Medellín, Antioquia; d. of Zabulón Córdoba and Lía Ruiz; ed Universidad Pontificia Bolivariana, Medellín; began her political career working as community leader in several neighbourhoods in Medellín; Municipal Sub-controller 1984–86; Pvt. Sec. to Mayor William Jaramillo 1986; elected Councilwoman, Medellín 1988–90; cand. for Chamber of Reps of Colombia 1990; elected Deputy of Antioquia Dept Ass. 1990; Deputy, Chamber of Reps 1992–94; Mayor of Medellín 1994; mem. Senate 1994–2010; Senator and mem. Seventh Comm. of Congress 2006, in charge of debating labour topics, previously worked on Third Comm. (Financial affairs), Fifth Comm. (Mining and Energy) and Second Comm. (Foreign Affairs), Pres. Senate's Human Rights Comm. and the Peace Comm.; leading figure of Latin American feminist movt in Colombia, represents minority groups as part of Poder Ciudadano Siglo XXI Movt; participated in Fourth World Conf. on Women, Beijing 1995; kidnapped by leader of paramilitary group United Self-Defense Forces of Colombia (AUC) 1999, eventually freed and exiled with her family in Canada, returned to Colombia in 2000; Pres. Liberal Nat. Directorate (Head of Partido Liberal Colombiano—Colombian Liberal Party) 2003; participated as official Govt mediator, along with Pres. Hugo Chávez of Venezuela, in humanitarian exchange discussions between Colombia Govt and Fuerzas Armadas Revolucionarias de Colombia (FARC) guerrilla group Aug.–Nov. 2007, banned from public office due to alleged ties to FARC 2010. *E-mail:* piedadcordobaruiz@gmail.com. *Website:* www.piedadcordoba.com.

CÓRDOVA, France Anne, BA, PhD; American astrophysicist, academic and university administrator; *Chairman of the Board of Regents, Smithsonian Institution;* b. Paris, France; m. Christian J. Foster; one s. one d.; ed Bishop Amat High School, La Puente, Calif., Stanford Univ., California Inst. of Tech.; early career at Los Angeles Times News Service 1971; Staff Scientist, Earth and Space Science Div., Los Alamos Nat. Lab. (LANL) 1979–89, Deputy Group Leader, Space Astronomy and Astrophysics Group 1989; Prof. of Astronomy and Astrophysics, Pennsylvania State Univ. 1989–96, Dept Head 1989–93; Chief Scientist, NASA 1993–96; Prof. of Physics, Univ. of California, Santa Barbara 1996–2002, Vice-Chancellor Research 1996–2002; Chancellor Univ. of California, Riverside 2002–07; Pres. Purdue Research Foundation 2007–12, Purdue Univ. 2007–12; fmr Chair. numerous NASA bds including Exceptional Scientific Achievement Medal Panel 1993–96, Science Council 1994–96, Search Cttee for Dir Astrobiology Inst. 1998, Science Working Group, Constellation X Mission 1998–2000, Hubble Space Telescope Time Allocation Cttee 2001, Strategic Roadmap Cttee on Educ. (Co-Chair.) 2004; Chair. Research Advisory Council, Earth and Environmental Sciences Div. (LANL) 1985–86, Geosciences Space Science and Astrophysics (GSSA) Category Team (LANL) 1986–88, Science and Eng Advisory Council (SEAC) 1988–89; Co-founder Int. Astronomical Union Working Group on Multi-Frequency and Multi-Facility Astrophysics 1988; Vice-Chair. High Energy Astrophysics Div., American Astronomical Soc. 1989, Chair. 1990, Vice-Pres. American Astronomical Soc. 1993–96; Chair.-Elect Comm. on Human Resources and Social Change, Nat. Asscn State Univs and Land-Grant Colls (NASULGC) 2005–07; mem. of numerous panels and bds including Scientific Program Cttee, AAAS 2000–, NRC Policy and Global Affairs Advisory Cttee 2001–, Univ. of California Mexico Comm. on Educ. Science Tech. 2002–, Univ. of California Pres.'s Council on Nat. Labs 2002–, Calif. Council on Science and Tech. 2003–, Belo 2003–, NAS Roundtable on Scientific Communication and Security 2003–, Edison International 2004–, Nat. Panel of Pres and Chancellors, Models for Flexible Tenure-track Faculty Career Pathways, American Council on Educ. (ACE) 2004–, Univ. California Long-Range Guidance Team 2005–, Nat. Science Bd 2008, Bd of Regents, Smithsonian Inst. 2009– (Chair. 2011–); Fellow, Asscn for Women in Science 1999, AAAS 2007, American Acad. of Arts and Sciences 2008; Hon. Prof., China Agricultural Univ. 2005; Dr hc (Loyola-Marymount Univ.) 1997, (Ben Gurion Univ. of the Negev) 2011, (Purdue Univ.) 2012; NASA Distinguished Service Medal 1996, Hispanic Achievement Award, Hispanic Magazine 1997, NASA Group Achievement Award for Outstanding Teamwork, Swift Midsize Explorer Team 2000, Kilby Prize Laureate, Jack Kilby Int. Awards Foundation 2000, Nat. Assoc. of Nat. Acads 2002, named by Hispanic Business Magazine as one of the 80 Elite Hispanic Women 2002, nominated to Stanford Univ. Multicultural Alumni Hall of Fame 2008. *Publications include:* approx. 140 scientific reports and papers; ed.: Multiwavelength Astrophysics 1988, The Spectroscopic Survey Telescope 1990; contribs. to Mademoiselle magazine; fiction: The Women of Santo Domingo. *Leisure interests:* rock-climbing, canoeing, reading, writing. *Address:* c/o John K. Lapiana, Chief of Staff to the Regents, Office of the Regents, Smithsonian Institution, MRC 050, PO Box 37012, Washington, DC 20013-7012, USA (office). *Telephone:* (202) 633-5230 (office). *E-mail:* lapianaj@si.edu (office). *Website:* www.si.edu/Governance/Members (office).

COREA, Chick; American musician (piano) and composer; b. (Armando Corea), 12 June 1941, Chelsea, Mass; m. Gayle Moran; one s. one d.; ed Juilliard School of Music; pianist with numerous artists, including Mongo Santamaria 1962, Blue Mitchell 1965, Stan Getz 1966–68, Miles Davis 1969–71, Sarah Vaughan 1970; Founder-mem., leader, pianist with group, Return To Forever 1971, The Elektric Band 1986, The Vigil 2013; Dr hc (Norwegian Univ. of Science and Technology) 2010; numerous magazine awards from Downbeat, Keyboard Magazine; Jazz Life Musician of World, Jazz Forum Music Poll 1974, Best Electric Jazz group 1990, Best Acoustic Pianist 1990, Top Jazz Pianist 1990; 22 Frankfurter Musikpreis 1990, Grammy Awards including Best Improvised Jazz Solo (for 500 Miles High) 2012, Best Instrumental Composition (for Mozart Goes Dancing), Best Improvised Jazz Solo (with Gary Burton) (for Hot House) 2013, Best Improvised Jazz Solo (for Fingerprints) 2015, Jazz Journalists' Asscn Award for Keyboard Player of the Year 2015, Downbeat Magazine Jazz Artist of the Year 2015. *Recordings include:* Piano Improvisations 1 and 2, Leprechaun, My Spanish Heart, Mad Hatter, Delphi 1, 2 and 3, Light As A Feather, Romantic Warrior, Hymn of The Seventh Galaxy, Music Magic, Voyage (with Steve Kujala) 1984, The Chick Corea Akoustic Band 1989, Elektric Band Inside Out 1990, Chick Corea Akoustic Band Alive! 1991, Elektric Band Beneath The Mask 1991, Time Warp 1995, Remembering Bud Powell 1997, Native Sense 1997, Standards 2000, Past Present and Futures 2001, Elektric Band: To The Stars 2004, The Ultimate Adventure (Grammy Awards for Best Jazz Instrumental Album, Individual or Group, for Best Instrumental Arrangement 2007) 2006, The Enchantment (with Béla Fleck) (Latin Grammy Award for Best Instrumental Album) 2007, The New Crystal Silence (with Gary Burton) (Grammy Award for Best Jazz Instrumental Album 2009) 2008, Five Peace Band—Live (with John McLaughlin Five Peace Band) (Grammy Award for Best Jazz Instrumental Album 2010) 2009, Forever (with Stanley Clarke and Lenny White) (Grammy Award for Best Jazz Instrumental Album 2012) 2011, Orvieto 2011, Further Explorations 2012, The Continents 2012, Hot House 2012, The Mothership Returns 2012, Mozart Goes Dancing (with Gary Burton) (Grammy Award for Best Instrumental Composition 2013) 2012, The Vigil (with Hadrien Feraud, Marcus Gilmore, Tim Garland and Charles Altura) 2013, Trilogy (Grammy Award for Best Jazz Instrumental Album 2015) 2013, Two 2015. *Address:* Chick Corea Productions Inc., 411 Cleveland Street, No. 215, Clearwater, FL 33755, USA (office). *Telephone:* (727) 446-8100 (office). *E-mail:* bill rooney@chickcorea.com (office). *Website:* www.chickcorea.com.

CORELL, Hans Axel Valdemar, LLB; Swedish lawyer, judge and diplomatist (retd); b. 7 July 1939, Västermo; s. of Alf Corell and Margit Norrman; m. Inger Peijfors 1964; one s. one d.; ed Univ. of Uppsala; court clerk, Eksjö Dist Court and Göta Court of Appeal 1962–67; Asst Judge, Västervik Dist Court 1968–72; Legal Adviser, Ministry of Justice 1972, 1974–79; Assoc. Judge of Appeal, Svea Court of Appeal 1973; Asst Under-Sec. Div. for Constitutional and Admin. Law, Ministry of Justice 1979–81; Judge of Appeal 1980; Under-Sec. for Legal Affairs, Ministry of Justice 1981–84; Amb. and Under-Sec. for Legal and Consular Affairs, Ministry of Foreign Affairs 1984–94; mem. Perm. Court of Arbitration, The Hague 1990–2014; Under-Sec.-Gen. for Legal Affairs, The Legal Counsel of the UN 1994–2004; Sr Counsel, Mannheimer Swartling Advokatbyrå AB (law firm), Stockholm 2005–09; Chair. Bd of Trustees Raoul Wallenberg Inst. of Human Rights and Humanitarian Law 2006–12, Stockholm Centre for Int. Law and Justice 2013–; mem. Advisory Bd Int. Center for Ethics, Justice and Public Life, Brandeis Univ. 2005–; mem. Council Human Rights Inst., Int. Bar Asscn 2005–, Co-Chair. 2015–; Counsellor, American Soc. of Int. Law 2006–09; mem. Int. Law Asscn, ABA; Council mem.-at-large Int. Law Section 2009–15; Hon. LLD (Stockholm) 1997, (Lund) 2007; William J. Butler Human Rights Medal, Univ. of Cincinnati Coll. of Law 2001, Cox Int. Humanitarian Award for Advancing Global Justice, Case Western Reserve Univ. 2005. *Music:* Sec.-Gen. Kofi Annan's Prayer for Peace, Hymn composed for the Great Highland Pipe 2004. *Publications include:* Sekretesslagen (co-author) 1992, Proposal for an International War Crimes Tribunal for the Former Yugoslavia (CSCE Report) (co-author) 1993; various legal publs. *Leisure interests:* art, music (Piper of the Caledonian Pipes and Drums of Stockholm 1975–84), ornithology. *Address:* Norr Mälarstrand 70, 112 35 Stockholm, Sweden. *Website:* www.havc.se.

COREY, Elias James, PhD; American chemist and academic; *Professor Emeritus of Chemistry, Harvard University;* b. 12 July 1928, Methuen, Mass.; s. of Elias J. Corey and Tina Hasham; m. Claire Higham 1961; two s. one d.; ed Mass. Inst. of Tech.; Instructor in Chem., Univ. of Ill. 1951–53, Asst Prof. of Chem. 1953–55, Prof. 1956–59; Prof. of Chem., Harvard Univ. 1959–68, Chair. Dept of Chem. 1965–68, Sheldon Emery Prof. 1968, currently Prof. Emer.; Alfred P. Sloan Foundation Fellow 1955–57, Guggenheim Fellow 1957, 1968–69; mem. American Acad. of Arts and Sciences 1960–68, NAS 1966; Hon. AM, Hon. DSc; Pure Chem. Award of ACS 1960, Fritzsche Award of ACS 1967, Intra-Science Foundation Award 1967, Harrison Howe Award, ACS 1970, Award for Synthetic Organic Chem. 1971, CIBA Foundation Award 1972, Evans Award, Ohio State Univ. 1972, Linus Pauling Award 1973, Dickson Prize in Science, Carnegie Mellon Univ. 1973, George Ledlie Prize, (Harvard) 1973, Remsen Award, Arthur C. Cope Award 1976, Nichols Medal 1977, Buchman Memorial Award (Calif. Inst. of Tech.) 1978, Franklin Medal 1978, Scientific Achievement Award Medal 1979, J. G. Kirkwood Award (Yale) 1980, C. S. Hamilton Award (Univ. of Nebraska) 1980, Chemical Pioneer Award (American Inst. of Chemists) 1981, Rosenstiel Award (Brandeis Univ.) 1982, Paul Karrer Award (Zurich Univ.) 1982, Medal of Excellence (Helsinki Univ.) 1982, Tetrahedron Prize 1983, Gibbs Award (ACS) 1984, Paracelsus Award (Swiss Chem. Soc.) 1984, V. D. Mattia Award (Roche Inst. of Molecular Biology) 1985, Wolf Prize in Chemistry (Wolf Foundation) 1986, Silliman Award (Yale Univ.) 1986, Nat. Medal of Science 1988, Japan Prize 1989, Nobel Prize for Chem. 1990, Priestley Medal of ACS 2004 and numerous other awards and honours. *Publications:* nearly 1,000 scientific publs. *Leisure interests:* outdoor activities and music. *Address:* Department of Chemistry, Harvard University, 12 Oxford Street, Cambridge, MA 02138-2902 (office); 20 Avon Hill Street, Cambridge, MA 02140, USA (home). *Telephone:* (617) 495-4033 (office); (617) 864-0627 (home). *Fax:* (617) 495-0376 (office). *E-mail:* corey@chemistry.harvard.edu (office). *Website:* www.chem.harvard.edu (office).

CORKER, Robert Phillips (Bob), Jr, BS; American business executive and politician; b. 24 Aug. 1952, Orangeburg, SC; s. of Robert Phillips Corker and Jean J. Corker (née Hutto); m. Elizabeth Corker 1987; two d.; ed Univ. of Tennessee, Knoxville; moved to Tenn. aged 11; worked for four years as construction supt then f. own construction co., Bencor, sold in 1990; purchased two largest real estate cos in Chattanooga 1999, sold most of these holdings 2006; cand. for US Senate 1994; Commr of Finance and Admin for State of Tennessee 1995–2001; Mayor of Chattanooga 2001–05; Senator from Tenn. 2007–18 (retd); Republican; inducted into Entrepreneurial Hall of Fame, Univ. of Tennessee at Chattanooga. *Address:* c/o 185 Dirksen Senate Office Building, Washington, DC 20510, USA (office).

CORKUM, Paul Bruce, OC, BSc, MSc, PhD, FRS, FInstP, FRSC; Canadian physicist; *Director of the Attosecond Science Program, National Research Council of Canada;* b. 30 Oct. 1943, Saint John, NB; ed Acadia Univ., Wolfville, NS, Lehigh Univ., Bethlehem, Pa; Post-doctoral Fellow, Nat. Research Council of Canada 1973–, Dir Attosecond Science Program, Canada Research Chair in Attosecond Photonics 2008–; Adjunct Prof. of Chem., Univ. of Toronto; Adjunct Prof. of Physics, McMaster Univ. 1997–2009, Univ. of British Columbia 2001–09, Texas A&M Univ. 2006–; Adjunct Prof. of Physics, Univ. of Ottawa 2003–08, Prof. of Physics 2008–; Adjunct Research Prof., Univ. of New Mexico 2012–14; mem. Int. Advisory Bd Max Planck Inst. for Quantenoptik, Garching, Germany 1996–, Advisory Bd for Advanced Synchronton Sources, Brookhaven Nat. Labs 2001, Networks of Centres of Excellence: Canadian Inst. for Photonics Innovation and Team Leader for Ultrafast Dynamic Imaging Thrust; Program Chair. Conf. on Lasers and Electro-Optics/Int. Quantum Electronics Conf. 1996, Gen. Chair. 1998; Co-Chair. two Canadian workshops on femtosecond X-rays 2001–02; Program Chair. Int. Conf. on Ultrafast Optics 2001, Gen. Chair. 2003; Co-Chair. Gordon Conf. on Control of Light with Matter and Matter with Light 2003 (Chair. 2005), Dynamic Imaging Workshop, Sherbrooke, PQ 2003, Harvard-ITAMP Workshop on Attosecond Science 2003, 10th Int. Conf. on Multiphoton Processes 2005, Ultrafast Phenomena Conf. 2006; Chair. NSERC Jt Prizes Selection Cttee Competition 2013; Deputy Ed., Journal of Physics B: Atomic, Molecular and Optical Physics 2009–11, Ed. 2011–; mem. Editorial Advisory Bd, International Journal of Nonlinear Optics, Journal of Physics B; Foreign mem. NAS 2009, Austrian Acad. of Sciences 2012; Fellow, American Physical Soc., 2007, Optical Soc. of America 2010; Hon. Fellow, Royal Photographic Soc. 2013; Distinguished Research Prof., Univ. of Central Florida 2014; Order of Ont. 2013; Hon. PhD (Acadia) 2006, (Université Laval) 2015, Isaac Newton Medal, Inst. of Physics 2018; Canadian Asscn of Physicists' Gold Medal for Lifetime Achievement in Physics 1996, Einstein Award, Soc. for Optical and Quantum Electronics 1999, LEOS Distinguished Lecturer 2001–03, Queen's Golden Jubilee Medal 2003, RSC Tory Medal 2003, Charles Townes Award, Optical Soc. of America 2005, IEEE Quantum Electronics Award 2005, Killam Prize for Physical Sciences 2006, Arthur Schawlow Award for Quantum Electronics, American Physical Soc. 2006, NSERC Polanyi Award 2008, NSERC Gerhard Herzberg Gold Medal for Science and Eng 2009, King Faisal Int. Prize for Science (co-recipient) 2013, Harvey Prize, Technion (Israel) (co-recipient) 2013, Royal Photographic Society Progress Medal 2013, Frederic Ives Medal/Quinn Prize, Optical Soc. of America 2014, Lomonosov Gold Medal, Russian Acad. of Sciences 2015. *Publications:* more than 280 scientific papers in professional journals. *Address:* Steacie Institute for Molecular Sciences, National Research Council of Canada, 100 Sussex Drive, Room 2063, Ottawa, ON K1A OR6, Canada (office). *Telephone:* (613) 993-7390 (office). *Fax:* (613) 991-3437 (office). *E-mail:* paul.corkum@nrc-cnrc.gc.ca (office). *Website:* www.jaslab.ca/corkum_e.html (office).

CORLĂŢEAN, Titus, PhD; Romanian lawyer and politician; b. 11 Jan. 1968, Medgidia, Constanţa Co.; m. Madalina Corlăţean; one c.; ed Univ. of Bucharest, Nat. Inst. for Public Admin, Paris, Nat. Defence Coll., Bucharest; Research Asst, Romanian Inst. of Int. Studies 1993–94; Co-agent of Romanian Govt before European Court of Human Rights 1997–2001; worked at Ministry of Foreign Affairs 1994–2001; Adviser to Prime Minister on Foreign Policy Issues 2001–03, Sec. of State for Romanian Diaspora 2003–04; mem. Chamber of Deputies for Braşov CUNY 2004–07, mem. European Affairs Cttee, European Integration Cttee; Senator for Braşov 2008–12, Chair. Foreign Policy Cttee; observer to European Parl. 2005–06, mem. 2007–08; Minister of Justice May–Aug. 2012, of Foreign Affairs 2012–14 (resgnd); mem. Social Democratic Party 2002–. *Address:* c/o Ministry of Foreign Affairs, 011822 Bucharest, Sector 1, Al. Alexandru 31, Romania. *Website:* www.tituscorlatean.ro.

CORLEY, Elizabeth Pauline Lucy, CBE, FRSA, FCII; British business executive and author; *CEO, Allianz Global Investors;* b. 19 Oct. 1956, Luton, Beds.; m.; one step-d.; ed Post Grad. Diploma in Man. Studies; worked for several years in life and pensions sector; Partner, Coopers & Lybrand –1994; worked at Merrill Lynch Investment Managers (fmrly Mercury Asset Management) 1993–2004, became Man. Dir and Head of EMEA Asia Pacific Mutual Fund Business as well as mem. of various bds, including MLIM UK Ltd and Merrill Lynch International Investment Funds; joined Allianz 2005, later CEO Allianz Global Investors Europe, currently CEO Allianz Global Investors, mem. Exec. Cttee of Allianz Asset Management AG (financial holding co. for Allianz's asset man. businesses); Chair. Forum of European Asset Managers 2006–07, 2010–; mem. Advisory Council TheCityUK Ltd and its Int. Regulatory Strategy Group; Dir (non-exec.) Financial Reporting Council (UK) 2011–; mem. Crime Writers' Asscn (fmr Cttee mem. and Vice-Chair.), SvB of Euler Hermes, ESMA Stakeholder Group 2014–, Investment Comm. of the British Museum; Fellow, Chartered Insurance Inst.; Europamedaille (State of Bavaria) for special merits for Bavaria in Europe 2011. *Publications:* crime novels: Requiem Mass 1998, Fatal Legacy 2000, Grave Doubts 2006, Innocent Blood 2008, Dead of Winter 2013. *Leisure interests:* travel, gardening, music. *Address:* Allianz Global Investors GmbH, Seidlstrasse 24–24A, 80335 Munich, Germany (office). *Telephone:* (89) 1220-70 (office). *Fax:* (89) 1220-7900 (office). *E-mail:* info@allianzgi.com (office). *Website:* www.allianzglobalinvestors.com (office); www.allianzam.com (office); www.fantasticfiction.co.uk/c/elizabeth-corley.

CORMACK, Baron (Life Peer), cr. 2010, of Enville in the County of Staffordshire; **Patrick Thomas Cormack,** BA, FSA, FRHistS; British politician, historian, journalist and author; *Chairman, Historic Lincoln Trust and History of Parliament Trust;* b. 18 May 1939, Grimsby, Lincs.; m. Kathleen Mary MacDonald 1967; two s.; ed Havelock School, Univ. of Hull; Second Master, St James's Choir School 1961–66; training and educ. officer with Ross Ltd 1966–67; Asst House Master, Wrekin Coll., Wellington 1967–69; Head of History, Brewood Grammar School 1969–70; contested Labour parl. seat of Bolsover in Gen. Election 1964, hometown seat of Grimsby in Gen. Election 1966; mem. Bow Group –1971; MP (Conservative) for Cannock 1970–74, for SW Staffs. 1974–83 (South Staffs. 1983–2010); Parl. Pvt. Sec. to Dept of Health and Social Security 1970–73; mem. Educ. Select Cttee 1979–83, Chair.'s Panel 1983–; Deputy Shadow Leader of House of Commons 1997–2000; unsuccessful cand. for Speaker of House of Commons (following retirement of Betty Boothroyd) 2000, 2010; Chair. NI Select Cttee 2005–10; Chair. Historic Lincoln Trust 2011–, History of Parliament Trust; consultant and adviser to FIRST (int. affairs org.) 1985–; Council mem. British Archaeology 1979–83; Ed., House Magazine 1982–2005, Life Pres. 2005–; mem. Worshipful Co. of Glaziers and Painters of Glass 1979–; Rector's Warden, St Margaret's, Westminster (Parl.'s parish church) 1978–90; Trustee, Churches Preservation Trust 1972–2004, Winston Churchill Memorial Trust 1983–93; Vice-Pres. Nat. Churches Trust 2004–; Vice-Pres. Tennyson Soc. 2009–; Pres. Prayer Book Soc. 2011; Freeman of the City of London 1980; Hon. Fellow, Historical Asscn; Hon. DLitt (Hull), Hon. LLD (Catholic Univ. of America). *Publications:* numerous books on subjects ranging from the history of parliament, British castles, English cathedrals, and a book on William Wilberforce. *Address:* House of Lords, Westminster, London, SW1A 0PW, England (office). *Telephone:* (20) 7219-5353 (office). *Fax:* (20) 7219-5979 (office).

CORMAN, Igor, PhD; Moldovan diplomatist and politician; b. 17 Dec. 1969, Ciulucani; m.; two c.; ed State Univ. of Moldova, Alexandru Ioan Cuza Univ., Romania, Ludwig Maximilian Univ., Germany, George Marshall Coll., Germany; Third, Second, First Sec., Political Analysis and Planning Dept, Ministry of Foreign Affairs 1995–97, Third, Second, First Sec., responsible for Political Affairs, Chargé d'affaires a.i., Embassy in Berlin 1997–2001, Dir of Gen. Dept for Europe and N America, Ministry of Foreign Affairs 2001–03, Amb. to Germany 2004–09; mem. Parl. (Partidul Democrat din Moldova—Democratic Party of Moldova—in Alianţa pentru Integrare Europeană—Alliance for European Integration coalition) 2009–, Chair. Cttee for Foreign Policy and European Integration, Chair. (Speaker) of Parl. 2013–15; Medal for Civil Merit from Pres. of Moldova 2006, Great Cross of Merit of FRG 2009. *Address:* Parlamentul, 2073 Chişinău, bd. Ştefan cel Mare şi Sfânt 105, Moldova (office). *Telephone:* (22) 26-82-44 (office). *Fax:* (22) 23-30-12 (office). *E-mail:* inform@parlament.md (office). *Website:* www.parlament.md (office).

CORMAN, Roger William, AB, AFM; American film director and film producer; *President, New Horizons Picture Corporation;* b. 5 April 1926, Detroit, Mich.; m.

Julie Ann Halloran; two s. two d.; ed Stanford Univ., Univ. of Oxford, UK; Founder and Pres. New World Pictures (fmrly Concorde-New Horizons) 1970–83, New Horizons Picture Corpn 1983–; distributed films including: Cries and Whispers, Amarcord, Fantastic Planet, The Story of Adele H, Small Change, The Tin Drum; mem. Producers Guild of America, Directors Guild of America; Dr hc (American Film Inst.); Lifetime Achievement Award, LA Film Critics 1997, 1st Producers of Century Award, Cannes Film Festival 1998, Award of Venice Film Festival, PGA Lifetime Achievement Award, Acad. Award for Lifetime Achievement 2009. *Films directed include:* Swamp Women 1955, Apache Woman 1955, Five Guns West 1955, Day the World Ended 1956, The Oklahoma Woman 1956, It Conquered the World 1956, Naked Paradise 1957, Carnival Rock 1957, Not of This Earth 1957, Attack of the Crab Monsters 1957, The Undead 1957, Rock All Night 1957, Teenage Doll 1957, Sorority Girl 1957, The Saga of the Viking Women 1957, I Mobster 1958, War of the Satellites 1958, Machine-Gun Kelly 1958, Prehistoric World 1958, She Gods of Shark Reef 1958, A Bucket of Blood 1959, Ski Troop Attack 1960, The Wasp Woman 1960, House of Usher 1960, The Little Shop of Horrors 1960, Last Woman on Earth 1960, Atlas 1961, Creature from the Haunted Sea 1961, Pit and the Pendulum 1961, The Premature Burial 1962, The Intruder 1962, Tales of Terror 1962, Tower of London 1962, The Young Racers 1963, The Raven 1963, The Terror 1963, The Haunted Palace 1963, Man with the X-Ray Eyes 1963, The Masque of the Red Death 1964, The Secret Invasion 1964, The Tomb of Ligeia 1965, The Wild Angels 1966, The St. Valentine's Day Massacre 1967, The Trip 1967, Target: Harry 1969, Bloody Mama 1970, Gas-s-s-s 1971, The Red Baron 1971, Frankenstein Unbound 1990. *Films produced include:* more than 300 films including The Fast and the Furious 1954, Attack of the Crab Monsters 1957, Teenage Cave Man 1958, Attack of the Giant Leeches 1959, The Premature Burial 1962, Queen of Blood 1966, Big Bad Mama 1974, Death Race 2000 1975, I Never Promised You a Rose Garden 1977, Saint Jack 1979, Rage and Discipline 2004, DinoCroc 2004, Scorpius Gigantus 2005. *Film appearances include:* The Silence of the Lambs, The Godfather Part II, Philadelphia, Apollo 13, Scream 3, The Independent, A Galaxy Far Far Away. *Publication:* How I Made 100 Films in Hollywood and Never Lost a Dime (autobiog.) 1990. *Address:* New Horizons Picture Corporation, 11600 San Vicente Blvd., Los Angeles, CA 90049, USA. *Website:* www.newhorizonspictures.com.

CORMANN, Mathias Hubert Paul, LLB; Australian (b. Belgian) politician; *Minister of Finance and thePublic Service;* b. 20 Sept. 1970, Eupen, Belgium; m. Hayley Cormann; two d.; ed Notre Dame Univ., Namur, Catholic Univ. of Leuven; Chief of Staff to Minister for Family and Children's Services (WA) 1997–2000; Sr Adviser to State Premier of WA 2000–01; Adviser to Minister for Justice and Customs 2001–03; Health Services Man., HBF Health Insurance 2003–04, Acting Gen. Man. 2006–07, Gen. Man. Healthguard 2004–06; mem. Senate for W Australia 2007–, Deputy Leader of the Govt in the Senate 2015–17, Leader 2017–; Minister of Finance 2013–18, of Finance and the Public Service 2018–; mem. Liberal Party of Australia; Grand Cross, Order of Merit (Germany) 2018. *Address:* Department of Finance and Deregulation, One Canberra Avenue, Forrest, ACT 2603, Australia (office). *Telephone:* (2) 6215-2222 (office). *Fax:* (2) 6273-3021 (office). *E-mail:* mediaenquiries@finance.gov.au (office). *Website:* www.finance.gov.au (office); www.mathiascormann.com.au.

CORNEJO DÍAZ, René, MBA; Peruvian engineer and politician; b. 1962, Arequipa; ed Universidad Nacional de Ingeniería, Pontificia Universidad Católica del Perú, Escuela de Administración de Negocios para Graduados, Univ. of California, Los Angeles, USA; served as Project Man. on various public-sector and pvt. infrastructure projects; Dir FONAFE (Nat. Fund for Financing State Enterprise Activity) 2000–02; Exec. Sec. MIVIVIENDA (Mortgage Housing Promotion Fund) 2002–04; Exec. Dir PROINVERSION (Agency for the Promotion of Private Investment) 2004–07; Minister of Housing, Construction and Sanitation 2011–14, Pres. Council of Ministers (Prime Minister) Feb.–July 2014 (resgnd); mem. Partido democratico. *Address:* c/o Office of the President of the Council of Ministers, Jirón Carabaya, cuadra 1 s/n, Anexo 1105–1107, Lima, Peru.

CORNELIS, François; Belgian business executive; *Chairman, LBC Tank Terminals;* b. 25 Oct. 1949, Uccle, Brussels; m. Colette Durant 1973; two s. two d.; ed Collège Cardinal Mercier, Universite Catholique de Louvain; joined Petrofina SA as systems engineer, subsequently Co-ordinator of Supply and Refining Operations, Brussels, Supply and Shipping Man., Petrofina UK, London, Vice-Pres., Special Asst to Pres., American Petrofina, Dallas, Tex., USA 1983–84, Gen. Man. and Asst to Pres., Petrofina 1984–86, Exec. Dir, Office of the Chair. 1986–90, CEO and Vice-Chair. 1991–99, after merger with Total Vice-Chair. of Exec. Cttee, Totalfina and Sr Vice-Pres., Petrochemicals, Paints and US Operations (after merger with Total) 1999–2000, Exec. Vice-Pres. Chemicals Div., TotalFinaElf 2000, Vice-Chair. Exec. Cttee and Pres. of Chemicals, Total SA 1999–2011, Chair. Atofina 2000–03; Chair. LBC Tank Terminals 2013–, Bpost 2013–; Chair. European Chemical Industry Council 2006–08, Royal Automobile Club of Belgium 2002–; mem. Bd of Dirs Carmeuse Group 2013–, Equis 2012–; mem. Global Advisory Council of The Conference Board and Chair. European Steering Cttee. *Address:* LBC Tank Terminals, Schaliënhoevedreef 20 E, 2800 Mechelen, Belgium (office). *E-mail:* info@lbctt.com (office). *Website:* www.lbctt.com (office).

CORNELIUS, James M., BA, MBA; American pharmaceutical industry executive; *Chairman, Mead Johnson & Company, LLC;* b. Kalamazoo, Mich.; m.; two c.; ed Michigan State Univ.; Pres. and CEO IVAC Corpn 1980–82; Chief Financial Officer, mem. Bd of Dirs and Exec. Bd Lilly 1983–95; Chair. Guidant Corpn 1994–2000, Chair. (non-exec.) 2000–05, Chair. and Interim CEO 2005–06, Chair. Emer. 2006–; apptd mem. Bd of Dirs Bristol-Myers Squibb 2005, Interim Chief Exec. 2006, CEO 2006–10, Chair. 2010–15; Chair. Mead Johnson & Co., LLC 2009–; mem. Bd of Dirs Arcamed, Inc., YourEncore; Pres. Cornelius Family Charitable Foundation; mem. Scientific Advisory Bd Heron Capital Venture Capital. *Leisure interest:* American football. *Address:* Office of the Chairman, Mead Johnson & Company, LLC, 2701 Patriot Blvd., Fourth Floor, Glenview, IL 60026, USA (office). *Telephone:* (812) 429-5000 (office). *Website:* www.meadjohnson.com (office).

CORNELL, Brian C., BA; American business executive; *Chairman and CEO, Target Corporation;* b. 1960; m. Martha Cornell; one s. one d.; ed Univ. of California, Los Angeles and its Anderson Grad. School of Man.; Chief Marketing Officer and Exec. Vice-Pres., Safeway, Inc. 2004–07; CEO Michaels Stores, Inc. 2007–09; Pres. and CEO Sam's Club (div. of Wal-Mart Stores, Inc.) and Exec. Vice-Pres., Wal-Mart Stores, Inc. 2009–12, Assoc., Sam's West, Inc. 2012; CEO PepsiCo America Foods (div. of PepsiCo, Inc.) 2012–14; Chair. and CEO Target Corpn 2014–; mem. Bd of Dirs, OfficeMax, Inc. 2004–07, The Home Depot, Inc. 2008–09, Centerplate, Inc. 2010–, Polaris Industries, Inc. 2012–15, Yum! Brands 2015–, Catalyst 2016–; mem. Bd of Visitors, Anderson School of Man., UCLA, Retail Industry Leaders Asscn, Smithsonian Inst.'s Nat. Museum of African American History and Culture. *Address:* Target Corporation, 1000 Nicollet Mall, Minneapolis, MN 55403, USA (office). *Telephone:* (612) 304-6073 (office). *Fax:* (612) 696-3731 (office). *E-mail:* info@target.com (office). *Website:* www.target.com (office).

CORNELL, Eric Allin, BS, PhD; American physicist and academic; *Professor Adjoint, Department of Physics, University of Colorado;* b. 1961, Palo Alto, Calif.; s. of Allin Cornell and Elizabeth Cornell (née Greenberg); m. Celeste Landry; two d.; ed Stanford Univ., Massachusetts Inst. of Tech.; Research Asst, Stanford Univ. 1982–85, MIT 1985–90; Teaching Fellow, Harvard Extension School 1989; Post-doctoral research, Jt Inst. for Lab. Astrophysics, Boulder 1990–92, Fellow 1994–; Asst Prof. Adjoint, Dept of Physics, Univ. of Colorado at Boulder 1992–95, Prof. Adjoint 1995–; Sr Scientist, Nat. Inst. of Standards and Tech., Boulder 1992–, Fellow 1994–; Fellow, American Physical Soc. 1997–, Optical Soc. of America 2000–; mem. NAS 2000–; numerous awards including Dept of Commerce Gold Medal 1996, Fritz London Prize in Low Temperature Physics 1996, King Faisal Int. Prize in Science 1997, I. I. Rabi Prize 1997, Lorentz Medal, Royal Netherlands Acad. of Arts and Sciences 1998, Benjamin Franklin Medal in Physics 1999, R. W. Wood Prize, Optical Soc. of America 1999, Nobel Prize in Physics (jt recipient) 2001. *Address:* Joint Institute for Laboratory Astrophysics, University of Colorado, Campus Box 440, Boulder, CO 80309-0440, USA (office). *Telephone:* (303) 492-6281 (office). *Fax:* (303) 492-5235 (office). *E-mail:* cornell@jila.colorado.edu (office). *Website:* jilawww.colorado.edu/bec/CornellGroup (office); jilawww.colorado.edu (office).

CORNILLAC, Clovis; French actor, film director and screenwriter; b. 16 Aug. 1968, Lyon (Rhône); s. of Roger Cornillac and Myriam Boyer; m. 1st Caroline Proust 1994 (divorced 2010); two twin d.; m. 2nd Lilou Fogli 2013; one s.; began theatre studies aged 14; acted in Peter Brooke's Mahabharata 1984–86; Commdr des Arts et des Lettres 2005; César Award for Best Supporting Actor 2005. *Films include:* Hors-la-loi (aka Outlaws) 1985, Il y a maldonne 1988, The Unbearable Lightness of Being 1988, Les années sandwiches 1988, Suivez cet avion 1989, Le trésor des îles chiennes 1990, Trois nuits 1991, Traverser le jardin 1993, Pétain 1993, Les Mickeys 1994, Les amoureux 1994, Bons baisers de Suzanne 1995, Marie-Louise ou la permission 1995, Ouvrez le chien 1997, La mère Christain 1998, Karnaval 1999, Tea Time 2001, Grégoire Moulin contre l'humanité 2001, Bois ta Suze 2002, Une affaire privée 2002, Carnages 2002, Maléfique 2002, Une affaire qui roule (aka A Great Little Business) 2003, À la petite semaine (aka Nickel and Dime) 2003, Après la pluie, le beau temps 2003, Mariées mais pas trop (aka The Very Merry Widows) 2003, Vert paradis (aka Les cadets de Gascogne, TV title) 2003, Je t'aime, je t'adore 2003, Malabar Princess 2004, Doo Wop 2004, Grossesse nerveuse 2004, La femme de Gilles 2004, Mensonges et trahisons et plus si affinités… 2004, Un long dimanche de fiançailles (A Very Long Engagement) 2004, Close-Up 2005, Brice de Nice 2005, Au suivant! 2005, Les chevaliers du ciel (Sky Fighters) 2005, Le cactus 2005, Les brigades du Tigre 2006, Poltergay 2006, Le serpent 2007, Scorpion 2007, Astérix at the Olympic Games 2008, The New Protocol 2008, Ca$h 2008, Paris 36 2008, Inspector Bellamy 2009, Bitter Victory 2009, L'amour, c'est mieux à deux 2010, Protéger & servir 2010, In Gold We Trust 2010, Requiem for a Killer 2011, Monsieur Papa 2011, Une folle envie 2011, Dans la tourmente 2011, Radiostars 2012, Mes héros 2012, Tour de Force 2013, Un peu, beaucoup, aveuglément! 2015. *Television includes:* Le village sur la colline (mini-series) 1982, Tu peux toujours faire tes bagages 1984, Les cadavres exquis de Patricia Highsmith: Légitime défense (episode) 1990, Les dessous de la passion 1991, Bonne chance Frenchie (mini-series) 1992, Van Loc: un grand flic de Marseille – La Grenade (episode) 1993, Le juge est une femme: Aux marches du palais (episode) 1993, Le JAP, juge d'application des peines: Chacun sa gueule (episode) 1993, Navarro: En suivant la caillera (episode) 1994, Un été à l'envers 1994, La bavure 1994, Les cordier, juge et flic: Un si joli témoin (episode) 1995, Billard à l'étage 1996, L'échappée 1998, Les vilains 1999, Sam 1999, L'amour prisonnier 2000, L'île bleue 2001, Orages 2003, Central nuit (aka Night Squad) 2001–09, Mister BOB (film) 2011, Chefs (mini-series) 2015.

CORNILLET, Thierry Pierre Fernand, DèsScPol; French politician and international organization official; *Founder-President, Association Internationale des Régions Francophones;* b. 23 July 1951, Montélimar, Drôme; s. of Col Jean-Baptiste Cornillet and Inès Genoud; m. Marie-France Rossi 1983; one s. one d.; ed Lycée Alain Borne, Montélimar, Univs of Lyon II, Lyon III and Paris I–Panthéon Sorbonne; Head of Dept, Office of Dir of Civil Security at Ministry of Interior 1977–81; Head of Dept, Office of Minister of External Trade, then of Admin. Reform 1980–81; Export Man., Lagarde SA, Montélimar 1981–83; Dir Office of Deputy Mayor of Nancy 1983–85; Legal Adviser to Jr Minister, Ministry of Interior 1985–86, Chef de Cabinet 1986–88; Head of Dept, Cie nationale du Rhône 1988–93; Municipal Councillor, Montélimar 1983, Mayor 1989–99; mem. Gen. Council of Drôme 1985–93, Vice-Chair. 1992–93; mem. and Sec. Regional Council of Rhône-Alpes 1986, Vice-Pres. 1999–2004; mem. Assemblée nationale (UDF) from Drôme 1993–97; Vice-Chair. Parti Radical 1988–97, Chair. 1997–2000, mem. European Parl. 1999–, Vice-Chair. EU Jt Parl. Ass. on Africa, Caribbean, Pacific; Founder-Pres. Association Internationale des Régions Francophones; Chevalier Ordre nat. du Mérite. *Address:* Association Internationale des Régions Francophones, 8 rue Paul Montrochet, 69002 Lyon, France (office). *Telephone:* 4-26-73-54-73 (office). *Fax:* 4-26-73-57-57 (office). *E-mail:* airf@regions-francophones.com (office). *Website:* www.regions-francophones.com (office).

CORNISH, (Robert) Francis, CMG, LVO, FRSA; British business executive and diplomatist (retd); b. 18 May 1942, Bolton; s. of Derrick Cornish and Catherine Cornish; m. Alison Jane Dundas 1964; three d.; ed Charterhouse, Royal Mil. Acad., Sandhurst; commissioned 14th/20th King's Hussars and served in Libya, UK and Germany, becoming Adjutant 1966; joined HM Diplomatic Service 1968, served in Kuala Lumpur and Jakarta before becoming Head of Greek Desk, London; First Sec. (EEC), Bonn 1976–80; apptd Asst Pvt. Sec. to Prince of Wales 1980, also worked for Princess of Wales 1980–83; High Commr to Brunei 1983–86; Dir of Public Diplomacy, Washington, DC and Head of British Information Services, New York 1986–90; Head of News Dept, FCO and Spokesman for Foreign Sec. 1990–93, Sr British Trade Commr, Hong Kong 1993, first Consul-Gen. Hong Kong 1997; Sr Directing Staff, Royal Coll. of Defence Studies 1998; Amb. to Israel 1998–2001; Chair. South West Tourism Ltd 2003–09; Chair. Taunton Town Centre Co. Ltd 2005–13, later Vice Chair.; Dir Grosshill Properties 2002–11, Sydney & London Properties 2003–11. *Leisure interests:* farming, theatre, riding, hill-walking.

CORNISH, William Rodolph, CMG, LLD, BCL, FBA; British/Australian barrister (retd) and academic; *Professor Emeritus of Law, University of Cambridge;* b. 9 Aug. 1937, S Australia; s. of Jack R. Cornish and Elizabeth E. Cornish; m. Lovedy E. Moule 1964; one s. two d.; ed St Peter's Coll., Adelaide and Adelaide Univ., Australia, Univ. of Oxford, UK; Lecturer in Law, LSE 1962–68; Reader in Law, Queen Mary Coll., London 1969–70; Prof. of English Law, LSE 1970–90; Prof. of Law, Univ. of Cambridge 1990–95, Dir Centre for Euro Legal Studies 1991–94, Herchel Smith Prof. of Intellectual Property Law, Univ. of Cambridge 1995–2004, Prof. Emer. 2004–; Fellow, Magdalene Coll., Cambridge 1990–, Pres. 1998–2001; Academic Dir British Law Centre, Warsaw Univ., Poland 1992–2005; External Academic mem. Max Planck Inst., Intellectual Property 1990–; Hon. QC 1997, Bencher Gray's Inn 1998; Hon. LLD (Edinburgh) 2005, (Univ. of Adelaide) 2018, Dr hc (Sofia Univ., Bulgaria) 2018. *Publications:* The Jury 1968, Intellectual Property 1981–2010, Encyclopaedia of UK and European Patent Law (with others) 1978, Law and Society in England 1750–1950 1989, Oxford History of the Laws of England (Vols XI–XIII); numerous articles in legal periodicals. *Leisure interests:* gardening, piano, chamber music. *Address:* Magdalene College, Cambridge, CB3 0AG, England (office). *Telephone:* (1223) 330062 (office). *Fax:* (1223) 330055 (office). *E-mail:* wrc1000@cam.ac.uk (office). *Website:* www.law.cam.ac.uk (office).

CORNWALL, HRH The Duchess of, GCVO; British b. (Camilla Rosemary Shand), 17 July 1947, London; d. of Maj. Bruce Shand and Hon. Rosalind Cubitt; m. 1st Andrew Parker Bowles 1973 (divorced); one s. one d.; m. 2nd HRH The Prince of Wales 2005; ed Dumbrells School, Sussex, Queen's Gate School, South Kensington, Mon Fertile, Switzerland, Institut Britannique, Paris; made debut in London 1965; Patron, Animal Care Trust, Cornwall Community Foundation, Friends of Westonbirt Arboretum, London Chamber Orchestra, New Queen's Hall Orchestra, Public Catalogue Foundation's Cornish Catalogue, Soc. of Chiropodists and Podiatrists, Royal National Hospital For Rheumatic Diseases, St John's Smith Square Charitable Trust, Wicked Young Writers Award, Children's Hospice South West, Emmaus; Pres. Nat. Osteoporosis Soc., Barnardo's, Scotland's Gardens Scheme, Shelterbox. *Address:* Clarence House, St James's Palace, London, SW1A 1BA, England. *Website:* www.princeofwales.gov.uk.

CORNWELL, Andrew, BSc, MSc; British politician and journalist; b. 30 Sept. 1966, London; partner Rachel; ed London School of Econs; financial journalist 1988–98; mem. Bd, London Pensions Fund Authority 2001–06; European Media Officer BOND (British Overseas NGOs for Devt) 2001; Green Party cand. in Gen. Election 2001; Chair. Green Party of England and Wales 2002–03; Vice-Chair. Green Liberal Democrats 2004–; Councillor and Exec. Mem. for Finance, London Borough of Islington 2006–08, Chair. Overview and Scrutiny Cttee. *Achievements:* rode with his partner from Land's End to John O'Groats in a series of seven 200 km day stages 2010; int. tours undertaken include London-Paris-London and London to Amsterdam. *E-mail:* info@cyclingcouncillor.com. *Website:* www.cyclingcouncillor.com.

CORNWELL, Bernard, (Susannah Kells), OBE, BA; British writer; b. 23 Feb. 1944, London; m. Judy Acker 1980; ed Univ. of London. *Publications include:* Redcoat 1987, Wildtrack 1988, Sea Lord (aka Killer's Wake) 1989, Crackdown (aka Murder Cay) 1990, Stormchild 1991, Scoundrel 1992, Stonehenge 2000 BC 1999, The Archer's Tale 2001, The Last Kingdom 2004, The Pale Horseman 2005, Lords of the North Country 2006, Agincourt 2008, The Burning Land 2009, The Fort 2010, The Pagan Lord 2013, The Empty Throne 2014, Waterloo: The History of Four Days, Three Armies and Three Battles 2014, Warriors of the Storm 2015; Starbuck Chronicles series: Rebel 1993, Copperhead 1994, Battle Flag 1995, The Bloody Ground 1996; Arthur series: The Winter King 1995, Enemy of God 1996, Excalibur 1997; Sharpe series: Sharpe's Eagle 1981, Sharpe's Gold 1981, Sharpe's Company 1982, Sharpe's Sword 1983, Sharpe's Enemy 1984, Sharpe's Honour 1985, Sharpe's Regiment 1986, Sharpe's Siege 1987, Sharpe's Rifles 1988, Sharpe's Revenge 1989, Sharpe's Waterloo 1990, Sharpe's Devil 1992, Sharpe's Battle 1995, Sharpe's Tiger 1997, Sharpe's Triumph 1998, Sharpe's Fortress 1999, Sharpe's Trafalgar 2000, Sharpe's Prey 2001, Sharpe's Skirmish (short story) 2002, Sharpe's Havoc 2003, Sharpe's Escape 2004, Sharpe's Fury 2006; Grail Quest series: Harlequin 2000, Vagabond 2002, Heretic 2003, 1356 2012; as Susannah Kells: A Crowning Mercy 1983, The Fallen Angels 1984, Coat of Arms 1986, The Aristocrats 1987. *Address:* Toby Eady Associates Ltd, Third Floor, 9 Orme Court, London, W2 4RL, England (office). *Telephone:* (20) 7792-0092 (office). *Fax:* (20) 7792-0879 (office). *E-mail:* toby@tobyeady.demon.co.uk (office). *Website:* www.tobyeadyassociates.co.uk (office); www.bernardcornwell.net (office).

CORNWELL, David John Moore, (John le Carré), BA; British writer; b. 19 Oct. 1931, Poole, Dorset; s. of Ronald Thomas Archibald Cornwell and Olive Glassy; m. 1st Alison Ann Veronica Sharp 1954 (divorced 1971); three s.; m. 2nd Valerie Jane Eustace 1972; one s.; ed St Andrew's Preparatory School, Pangbourne, Sherborne School, Berne Univ., Switzerland and Lincoln Coll., Oxford; teacher, Eton Coll. 1956–58; in Foreign Service (Second Sec., Bonn, then Political Consul Hamburg) 1959–64; Hon. Fellow, Lincoln Coll., Oxford 1984–; Commdr des Arts et des Lettres 2005; Hon. DLitt (Exeter) 1990, (St Andrews) 1996, (Southampton) 1997, (Bath) 1998, (Berne Univ., Switzerland) 2008, (Oxford) 2012; Somerset Maugham Award 1963, MWA Edgar Allan Poe Award 1965, James Tait Black Award 1977, CWA Gold Dagger 1978, MWA 'Grand Master Award' 1986, Premio Malaparte 1987, CWA Diamond Dagger 1988, Nikos Kazantzakis Prize 1991, CWA 'Dagger of Daggers' 2005, Sunday Times Award for Literary Excellence 2010, Goethe Medal (Germany) 2011. *Films:* as exec. dir: The Tailor of Panama 2001, Tinker Tailor Soldier Spy 2011, A Most Wanted Man 2014, The Night Manager 2016, Our Kind of Traitor 2016. *Screenplays:* End of the Line 1970, A Murder of Quality 1991. *Publications include:* Call for the Dead 1961, Murder of Quality 1962, The Spy Who Came in from the Cold 1963, The Looking Glass War 1965, A Small Town in Germany 1968, The Naive and Sentimental Lover 1971, Tinker, Tailor, Soldier, Spy 1974, The Honourable Schoolboy 1977, Smiley's People 1979, The Quest for Karla (collected edn of previous three titles) 1982, The Little Drummer Girl 1983, A Perfect Spy 1986, The Russia House 1989, The Secret Pilgrim 1991, The Night Manager 1993, Our Game 1995, The Tailor of Panama 1996, Single and Single 1999, The Constant Gardener (British Book Awards Play.com TV & Film Book of the Year 2006) 2000, Absolute Friends 2004, The Mission Song 2006, A Most Wanted Man 2008, Our Kind of Traitor 2010, A Delicate Truth 2013, A Legacy of Spies 2017; non-fiction: The Good Soldier 1991, The United States Has Gone Mad 2003, Afterword 2014, The Pigeon Tunnel: Stories from My Life (memoir) 2016. *Website:* www.johnlecarre.com.

CORNWELL, Patricia Daniels, BA; American writer; b. 9 June 1957, Miami, Fla; ed Davidson Coll.; police reporter, Charlotte Observer, NC 1979–81; computer analyst, Office of the Chief Medical Examiner, Richmond, Va 1985–91; mem. Authors Guild, Int. Asscn of Identification, Int. Crime Writers Asscn, Nat. Asscn of Medical Examiners; Investigative Reporting Award, North Carolina Press Asscn 1980, Gold Medallion Book Award, Evangelical Christian Publishers Asscn 1985, Edgar Award 1990, Prix du Roman d'Aventure 1991, Gold Dagger Award 1993, Sherlock Holmes Award 1999. *Publications include:* non-fiction: A Time of Remembering: The Story of Ruth Bell Graham 1983 (re-issued as Ruth: a Portrait 1997); fiction: Postmortem (John Creasey Award, British Crime Writers' Asscn 1991, Anthony Award, Boucheron Award, World Mystery Convention, MacAvity Award, Mystery Readers Int) 1990, Body of Evidence 1991, All That Remains 1992, Cruel and Unusual 1993, The Body Farm 1994, From Potter's Field 1995, Cause of Death 1996, Hornet's Nest 1996, Unnatural Exposure 1997, Point of Origin 1998, Southern Cross 1999, Black Notice 1999, The Last Precinct 2001, Isle of Dogs 2001, Portrait of a Killer: Jack the Ripper 2002, Blow Fly 2003, Trace 2004, Predator 2005, At Risk 2006, Book of the Dead (British Book Award for Best Crime Thriller 2008) 2007, Scarpetta 2008, The Front 2008, The Scarpetta Factor 2009, Port Mortuary 2010, Red Mist (RBA Int. Thriller Prize) 2011, The Bone Bed 2012, Dust 2013, Flesh and Blood 2014. *Address:* c/o Don Congdon Associates Inc., 156 5th Avenue, Suite 625, New York, NY 10010-7002, USA. *Website:* www.patriciacornwell.com.

CORNYN, John, LLM; American judge and politician; *Senator from Texas;* b. 2 Feb. 1952, Houston, Tex.; s. of John Cornyn and Gale Cornyn; m. Sandy Cornyn; two d.; ed Trinity Univ. and St Mary's School of Law, San Antonio, Univ. of Virginia Law School; Dist Court Judge, San Antonio 1984–90; elected to Tex. Supreme Court 1990, re-elected 1996; Attorney-Gen. of Tex. 1997–2003; Senator from Tex. 2003–, fmr Vice-Chair. Senate Republican Conf., Chair. Nat. Republican Senatorial Cttee 2008–, mem. Finance, Judiciary, Armed Services, and Budget Cttees; mem. Bush-Cheney Transition Advisory Cttee 2000; St Mary's Distinguished Law School Grad. 1994; Trinity Univ. Distinguished Alumnus 2001; Outstanding Texas Leader Award, John Ben Shepperd Foundation of Texas 2000, James Madison Award, Freedom of Information Foundation of Texas 2001, Border Texan of the Year Award 2005, Children's Champion Award, Nat. Child Support Enforcement Asscn, Friend of Farm Bureau Award, American Farm Bureau Fed., Fighter for Free Enterprise Award, Texas Asscn of Business, Guardian of Small Business Award, Nat. Fed. of Ind. Business, Latino Leadership Award, Nat. Coalition of Latino Clergy and Christian Leader (CONLAMIC), Int. Leadership Legis. Award, Texas Asscn of Mexican American Chambers of Commerce, amongst others. *Address:* 517 Hart Senate Office Building, Washington, DC 20510, USA (office). *Telephone:* (202) 224-2934 (office). *Fax:* (202) 228-2856 (office). *Website:* cornyn.senate.gov (office).

CORONEL, Sheila S., BA, MA; Philippine journalist and academic; *Toni Stabile Professor of Professional Practice in Investigative Journalism, Columbia University Graduate School of Journalism;* b. 1958, Manila; ed Univ. of the Philippines, London School of Econs, UK; began as cub reporter for Philippine Panorama 1983; reporter for The Manila Times, Manila Chronicle; Co-founder and Exec. Dir Philippine Center for Investigative Journalism 1989–2006; currently Toni Stabile Prof. of Professional Practice in Investigative Journalism, Columbia Univ. Graduate School of Journalism, also Dir Toni Stabile Center for Investigative Journalism and Dean of Academic Affairs; Ramón Magsaysay Award for Journalism 2003, Presidential Teaching Award, Columbia Univ. 2011. *Publications include:* more than 12 books, including Coups, Cults and Cannibals, The Rulemakers, Pork and Other Perks. *Address:* Columbia University Graduate School of Journalism, Pulitzer Hall, 701E, 2950 Broadway, New York, NY 10027, USA. *Telephone:* (212) 854-5748 (office). *E-mail:* ssc2136@columbia.edu (office). *Website:* www.journalism.columbia.edu (office).

COROPCEAN, Maj. Gen. Ion Stefan; Moldovan army officer (retd); b. 11 March 1960, Livădeni, Donduseni; s. of Ştefan Coropcean; m. Valentina Coropcean; one s. one d.; ed Poltava Mil. Air Defence High School, Mil. Air Defence Acad.; cadet 1977–81, Air Defence Platoon Commdr 1981–84, Air Defence Battery Commdr 1984–87, Air Defence Bn Commdr 1987–88, Air Defence Acad. 1988–91, Chief of Staff and Deputy Commdr Air Defence Regt 1991–92, Deputy Commdr Air Defence Brigade 1992–97, Commdr Mil. Coll. 1997–98, Chief of Gen. Staff Nat. Army and Deputy Minister of Defence 1998–2006, Chief of Gen. Staff and Nat. Army Commdr 2006–13 (retd); Interim Minister of Defence June–July 2007; rank of Maj. Gen. 2008; Advisor to the Prime Minister 2013–; Medal of Courage, Medal of Mil. Merit, Award for Allegiance to the Motherland, Order 'Credinţa Patriei', Class III 2006. *Publication:* The Foreign Policy of the Republic of Moldova in the Context of Integration Processes: Interests and Priorities. *Leisure interests:* books, football, literature. *Address:* Office of the Council of Ministers, 2033 Chişinău, Piaţa Marii Adunări Naţionale 1 (office); 2071 Chişinău, Alba Julia str. 200/1, Apt 100, Moldova (home). *Telephone:* (22) 250101 (office); (2) 514874 (home). *Fax:* (2) 234434 (office). *E-mail:* coropcei@md.pims.org (office); ion.coropcean@army.md (office). *Website:* www.gov.md (office).

CORRALES ÁLVAREZ, Arturo Gerardo, MEng; Honduran politician; b. 27 March 1961; s. of Hernán Padilla Corrales; m. Patricia Corrales Suazo; four s.; ed Univ. Nacional Autónoma de Honduras, Univ. of Florida, USA; f. several agricultural and livestock cos including Empresa Ingeniería Gerencial, Ingeniería Agrícola y Ganadera SA and Exportadora de Vegetales, Comayagua Prov.; mem. Consejo Nacional de Convergencia (est. to seek consensus on political, social and econ. issues) 1995–96; unsuccessful cand. (for Partido Demócrata Cristiano de Honduras) in presidential election 1997; mem. Honduran Nat. Emergency Cttee

1998; Commr, Perm. Contingency Comm. of Honduras (disaster relief coordinating agency) 1999; Sec. (Minister), Tech. and Int. Cooperation Secr. 2000–01, Secr. of Planning and External Cooperation 2010, Sec. (Minister) of Foreign Affairs 2011–13, 2014–16, Sec. (Minister) for Security Affairs 2013–14; mem. Partido Demócrata Cristiano de Honduras (PDCH), Pres. 1998–2002; José Trinidad Cabañas Award, Distinguished Services Cross (Colombia). *Address:* c/o Secretariat of Foreign Affairs, Centro Cívico Gubernamental, Antigua Casa Presidencial, Blvd Kuwait, Contiguo a la Corte Suprema de Justicia, Tegucigalpa, Honduras (office).

CORRÊA ABREU, Alexandre, BBA, MBA; Brazilian business executive; b. 29 Nov. 1965, Aimorés, Minas Gerais; ed Faculdade São Luís, Univ. of São Paulo; joined Banco do Brasil 1986, held positions as Vice-Pres. of Retail Services, Vice-Pres. of Retail, Distribution and Operations, Dir of Insurance, Pension Plans and Capitalization Bonds, Dir of Credit and Debit Cards, Div. Man. and Regional Man. in São Paulo Superintendence, CEO Banco do Brasil 2015–16. *Address:* c/o Banco do Brasil SA, SBS Qd. 01 Bloco C, Edificio Sede III, 24° Andar, 70073-901 Brasília, DF, Brazil. *E-mail:* presidencia@bb.com.br.

CORREA DELGADO, Rafael, MSc, PhD; Ecuadorean economist, politician and fmr head of state; b. 6 April 1963, Guayaquil; ed Universidad Católica de Santiago de Guayaquil, Catholic Univ. of Louvain, Belgium, Univ. of Illinois, USA; teaching asst, Econs Faculty, Universidad Católica de Santiago de Guayaquil 1983–85, Assoc. Prof. 1988–89; Industrial Specialist, Centre of Industrial Devt 1984–87; volunteer in Mission of the Salesian Fathers, Zumbahua, Cotopaxi 1987–88; Admin. Dir in charge of educational projects financed by IDB 1992–93; Head Prof., Dept of Econs, Universidad San Francisco de Quito 1993–2005; Minister of the Economy (following overthrow of Lucio Gutierrez) April–Aug. 2005 (resgnd); Founder, Alianza PAIS (Patria Altiva i Soberana), Chair. 2006–17; Pres. of Ecuador 2007–17. *Publications:* El Reto del Desarrollo: ¿Estamos Preparados para el Futuro? 1996, La Vulnerabilidad de la Economía Ecuatoriana 2004, Ecuador: From Banana Republic to Non Republic 2009; numerous journal contribs. *E-mail:* info@rafaelcorrea.com. *Website:* www.rafaelcorrea.com.

CORREIA, Carlos; Guinea-Bissau politician; b. 6 Nov. 1933; mem. Partido Africano da Independência da Guiné e Cabo Verde (PAIGC) –1999; fmr Minister of State for Rural Devt and Agric.; Prime Minister of Guinea-Bissau 1991–94, 1997–98, Aug.–Dec. 2008, Sept. 2015–May 2016; fmr Perm. Sec. Council of State; fmr Gov. for Guinea Bissau, African Devt Bank. *Address:* c/o Office of the Prime Minister, Av. dos Combatentes da Liberdade da Pátria, CP 137, Bissau, Guinea-Bissau.

CORREIA, Olavo Avelino Garcia; Cabo Verde economist and politician; *Deputy Prime Minister and Minister of Finance;* b. 10 Feb. 1967, Praia; ed Univs in Berlin and Bavaria, Germany; began career in Dept of Markets and Statistics, Banco de Cabo Verde (BCV) 1993, becoming Gov., BCV and Alt Gov. for Cabo Verde at IMF 1999–2004, mem. BCV Advisory Bd 2004–; Adviser to Pres. of the Repub. 1993–; Deputy Sec. of State for Finance and Dir-Gen. of Treasury 1997, Minister of Finance 2016–, also Deputy Prime Minister; Chair. Bd of Dirs, Tecnicil Indústria 2004–, also Dir, Group Tecnicil; Deputy Dir, Banco Montepio Geral Cabo Verde (BMGCV) 2006–; mem. Conselho da República (presidential advisory council) 2011–; mem. Assembleia Nacional (parl.) for Santiago Sul; Visiting Prof. of Econs, Instituto Superior de Ciências Jurídicas e Sociais 2014–; Pres., Fundação Escola de Preparação Integral de Futebol (EPIF, football training org.) 2012–16; mem. Movimento para a Democracia (MpD), Vice-Pres. 2013–. *Address:* Ministry of Finance and Public Administration, 107 Av. Amílcar Cabral, CP 30, Praia, Santiago, Cabo Verde (office). *Telephone:* 2607400 (office). *E-mail:* aliciab@gov1.gov.cv (office). *Website:* www.mf.gov.cv (office).

CORREIA E SILVA, José Ulisse de Pina; Cabo Verde business executive and politician; *Prime Minister;* b. 4 June 1962, Praia; m.; two c.; ed Instituto Superior de Economia, Univ. Técnica de Lisboa, Portugal; Sr Technician, Banco de Cabo Verde 1989–93, Dir, Admin Dept 1993–94; Sec. of State for Finance 1995–98, Minister of Finance 1999–2000; Dean, Univ. Jean Piaget, Praia 2002–07; mem. Assembleia Nacional (parl.) for Santiago Sul 2002–08, 2016–, Leader, MpD Parl. Group 2006–08; Pres. Câmara Municipal da Praia 2008–15; Prime Minister 2016–; Pres. IDC África 2014; Pres., Exec. Cttee, União das Cidades Capitais Luso-Afro-Americo-Asiáticas (UCCLA) 2013–15; mem. Movimento para a Democracia (MpD), Pres. 2013–. *Address:* Gabinete do Primeiro Ministro, Palácio do Governo, Várzea, CP 16, Praia, Cabo Verde (office). *Telephone:* 2610411 (office). *Fax:* 2613099 (office). *E-mail:* gab.imprensa@gpm.gov.cv (office). *Website:* www.primeiroministro.cv (office).

CORRELL, A(lston) D(ayton) (Pete), MS; American paper industry executive; *Chairman Emeritus, Georgia–Pacific Corporation;* b. 28 April 1941, Brunswick, Ga; s. of Alston Dayton Correll and Elizabeth Correll (née Flippo); m. Ada Lee Fulford 1963; one s. one d.; ed Univs of Georgia and Maine; tech. service engineer, Westvaco 1963–64; instructor, Univ. of Maine (Orono) 1964–67; various positions in pulp and paper man., Weyerhaeuser Co. 1967–77; Div. Pres., Paperboard, Mead Corpn 1977–80, Group Vice-Pres. 1980–83, Sr Vice-Pres., Forest Products 1983–88; Sr Vice-Pres., Pulp and Printing Paper, Georgia–Pacific Corpn 1988–89, Exec. Vice-Pres., Pulp and Paper 1989–91, Pres., COO 1991–93, CEO 1993–2005, Chair. 1993–2006, Chair. Emer. 2006–; currently Chair. Atlanta Equity Investors, LLC, Grady Memorial Hospital Corpn; mem. Bd of Dirs Mirant Corpn, Norfolk Southern Corpn, SunTrust Banks, Inc., Georgia Aquarium, Empower Software Solutions, LLC, Consumer Financial Services, LLC, Marshall Physician Services, LLC, The Mother Nature Network, LLC; Nat. Brotherhood Award 1991, Distinguished Alumnus Award, Univ. Georgia Terry Coll. of Business 1994, Salute to Greatness Award, The King Center 1999, Atlanta Urban League Distinguished Community Service Award 2001, Oglethorpe Sword, British American Business Group 2002, Silver Hope Award, Nat. Multiple Sclerosis Soc. 2003, CEO of the Year, Business to Business Magazine 2004, Paperloop CEO of the Year 2005; elected Business Hall of Fame, Georgia State Univ. 2005. *Address:* Atlanta Equity Investors, LLC, 191 Peachtree Street NE, Suite 4050, Atlanta, GA 30303, USA (office). *Telephone:* (404) 478-6770 (office). *Fax:* (404) 478-6771 (office). *Website:* www.atlantaeq.com (office).

CORRIGAN, E(dward) Gerald, BS, MA, PhD; American banker and economist; *Partner and Managing Director, Goldman Sachs & Co.;* b. 3 June 1941, Waterbury, Conn.; m. Cathy Minehan; ed Fairfield and Fordham Univs; Group Vice-Pres. (Man. and Planning) Fed. Reserve Bank of New York 1976–80, Pres. 1985–93; Special Asst to Chair., Bd of Govs Fed. Reserve System, Washington, DC 1979–80; Pres. Fed. Reserve Bank of Minneapolis 1981–84; Chair. Basel Cttee on Banking Supervision 1991–93; Chair. Int. Advisers, Goldman Sachs & Co. 1994–96, Man. Dir 1996–, now Partner and Man. Dir, Chair. GS USA (bank holding co.) 2008–, Co-Chair. firm-wide Risk Man. Cttee, Vice-Chair. firm-wide Business Practices Cttee, mem. firm-wide Commitments Cttee; Chair. Russian-American Enterprise Fund 1993; Chair. Counterparty Risk Man. Policy Group 1999–; Pres. BRI 1991–; mem. Trilateral Comm. 1986–, Group of Thirty Consultative Group on Int. Econ. and Monetary Affairs, Inc. (G-30), Washington, DC; Trustee, Macalester Coll. 1981–, Jt Council for Econ. Educ. 1981–, Fairfield Univ. 1985–; chair., trustee or mem. of several non-profit orgs; Fellow, American Acad. of Arts and Sciences 2005; Alumni Professional Achievement Award, Fairfield Univ. 1981, Risk Man. of the Year, Global Asscn of Risk Professionals 2006. *Address:* Goldman Sachs & Co., 200 West Street, New York, NY 10282, USA (office). *Telephone:* (212) 902-1000 (office). *Website:* www2.goldmansachs.com (office).

CORRIGAN, (Francis) Edward, MA, PhD (Cantab.), FRS; British mathematician and academic; *Professor of Mathematics and Head of Department, University of York;* b. 10 Aug. 1946, Birkenhead, Merseyside, England; s. of Anthony Corrigan and Eileen Corrigan (née Ryan); m. Jane Mary Halton 1970; two s. two d.; ed St Bede's Coll., Manchester, Christ's Coll., Cambridge; Addison Wheeler Fellow, Durham Univ. 1972–74; CERN Fellow, CERN, Geneva 1974–76; Lecturer, Durham Univ. 1976, Reader 1987, Prof. of Math. 1992–99, Visiting Prof. 1999–2007, Prof. of Math. and Prin. of Collingwood Coll. 2008–11; Prof. of Math., Univ. of York 1999–2007, 2011–, Head of Dept 1999–2004, 2005–07, 2011–; Visiting Prof., Centre for Partide Theory, Kyoto Univ. 2005; Visiting Research Assoc., ENS-Lyon 2005, Univ. of Bologna 2005; Life mem. Clare Hall, Cambridge 1992–; Ed.-in-Chief, Journal of Physics A 1999–2003; Adrian-Daiwa Prize 1998. *Publications:* more than 95 articles in learned journals and conf. proceedings. *Leisure interests:* music, squash, walking. *Address:* University of York, Department of Mathematics, Heslington, York, YO10 5DD (office); Panmure Cottage, Gate Helmsley, Yorks., YO41 1NE, England (home). *Telephone:* (1904) 433074 (office). *Fax:* (1904) 323071 (office). *E-mail:* edward.corrigan@york.ac.uk (office). *Website:* maths.york.ac.uk/www/ec9 (office).

CORSEPIUS, Uwe; German economist and international organization official; *Chief Adviser on European Affairs to Federal Chancellor;* b. 9 Aug. 1960, Berlin; m.; two c.; ed Univ. of Erlangen-Nuremberg, Kiel Inst. for World Econs; Research Fellow, Kiel Inst. for World Econs 1985–89; Economist, Int. Econ. Policy Div., Fed. Ministry of Econs 1990; Economist, Policy Dept, IMF, Washington, DC 1992–94; several positions with German Fed. Chancellery including Economist, Directorate for Gen. Econ. Questions 1991–92, Div. for Gen. Econ. Policy 1994–96, Private Sec. to Dir-Gen. 1995, Head of Div. for Econ. Issues relating to European Integration 1997–99, Head of Div. for G8, IMF, WTO and International Financial Market Issues 1999–2003, Head of Group for European Policy Coordination, Econ. Aspects of European Integration 2003–05, Dir-Gen., European Policy Adviser to Fed. Chancellor 2006–11, G8-Sherpa Feb.–June 2011, Chief Adviser on European Affairs to Fed. Chancellor 2015–; Sec.-Gen. Council of the EU, Brussels 2011–15. *Address:* Federal Chancellery, Bundeskanzler-Amt, Willy-Brandt Str. 1, 10557 Berlin, Germany (office). *Telephone:* (30) 40000 (office). *Fax:* (30) 40002357 (office). *E-mail:* internetpost@bpa.bund.de (office). *Website:* www.bundeskanzlerin.de (office).

CORSTENS, Geert J. M., PhD; Dutch judge; b. 1 Feb. 1946, Helvoirt; m. Madeleine Mignot; three d.; ed Radboud Univ., Nijmegen, Univ. of Amsterdam; Asst Public Prosecutor, Amsterdam 1973–75; Law Clerk, Dist Court of Amsterdam 1975–76; lawyer, Goudsmit & Branbergen (law firm), Amsterdam 1976–77; Public Prosecutor, Arnhem 1977–81; Prof. of Criminal Law, Catholic Univ., Nijmegen, 1982–95; Visiting Prof., Univ. of Poitiers 1986; Justice, Supreme Court of the Netherlands 1995–2006, Vice-Pres. 2006–08, Pres. 2008–14; Pres. Advisory Bd Nat. Research Project on Criminal Procedure 1998–2003, on the Quality of Criminal Judgements 2005–; mem. Bd and Pres. Advisory Bd, Dutch Law Asscn 1983–86, Nat. Cttee for the Reform of Criminal Procedure 1989–93; mem. Bd of Int. Advisors, Int. Judicial Acad., Washington, DC 2001–; mem. and Pres. Editorial Bd Nederlands Juristenblad 1995–2005; Pres. Network of Presidents of Highest Judicial Courts in the EU; Appointing Authority, Iran–US Claims Tribunal; Officier, Ordre des Palmes académiques, Chevalier, Légion d'honneur, Commander, Order of Orange-Nassau 2014; Dr hc (Antwerp) 2011. *Publications include:* several books, including European Criminal Law (with Jean Pradel) 2002, Droit pénal européen (third edn) 2009, Het Nederlands strafprocesrecht (seventh edn) 2011, De rechtsstaat moet je leren 2014; more than 350 contribs to nat. and int. and legal journals. *Address:* c/o Hoge Raad der Nederlanden, PO Box 20303, 2500 EH The Hague, Netherlands (office).

CORT, Errol; Antigua and Barbuda politician, economist and lawyer; *Head of Chambers, Cort and Cort Law Firm;* m.; c.; ed trained as economist and attorney; Attorney-Gen. of Antigua and Barbuda and Minister of Justice and Legal Affairs 1999–2001; elected mem. Parl. for St John's E, Leader of Govt Business 2004–14; Minister of Finance, Econ. Devt and Planning 2004–09, of Nat. Security and Labour 2009–14; Head of Chambers, Cort and Cort Law Firm 2014. *Address:* Cort and Cort Law Firm, Church Street, St John's, Antigua (office). *Telephone:* 462-5232 (office).

CORTÉS, Joaquín; Spanish dancer and actor; b. (Joaquín Pedraja Reyes), 22 Feb. 1969, Córdoba, Andalucía; joined Spanish Nat. Ballet 1985, Prin. Dancer 1987–90; f. Joaquín Cortés Flamenco Ballet 1992; now appears in own shows, blending gypsy dancing, jazz blues and classical ballet; appeared in Pedro Almodóvar's film The Flower of My Secret and Carlos Saura's film Flamenco; launched Stop Anti-Gypsyism campaign 2000; apptd Amb. for the Roma people to EU 2007. *Shows include:* Cibayí, Pasión Gitana, Soul, Live, De Amor y Odio, Mi Soledad, Unleashed 2009. *Films include:* Flamenco (de Carlos Saura) 1995, Flor de mi secreto, La 1995, Gitano 2000, Vaniglia e cioccolato 2004. *Television includes:* Sabadabada (series) 1981, Hola Raffaella! (series) 1992. *Address:* C/ Alcalá, 155. E.Izda. 2°C, Madrid, Spain. *Telephone:* (91) 7580350. *Fax:* (91) 5595245. *E-mail:* info@joaquincortes.org. *Website:* www.joaquincortes.org.

CORTEZ MASTO, Catherine Marie, BSc, JD; American lawyer and politician; *Senator from Nevada;* b. 29 March 1964, Las Vegas, Nev.; d. of Manny Cortez and Joanna Cortez (née Musso); m. Paul Masto; ed Univ. of Nevada, Gonzaga Univ. School of Law; joined Nevada State Bar Asscn 1990; apptd mem. staff, US Dist Court, Dist of Nevada 1991 and US Court of Appeals (Ninth Circuit) 1994; Chief of Staff to Gov. of Nevada Bob Miller –2002; Fed. Criminal Prosecutor, Office of US Attorney-Gen. –2002; Asst County Manager for Clark County, Nev. 2002–07; Attorney-Gen. of Nevada 2007–15; Senator from Nevada 2017–; apptd Exec. Vice-Chancellor, Nevada System of Higher Educ. 2014; mem. Nat. Asscn of Attorneys-Gen. (mem. Exec. Cttee 2012–13); Democrat. *Address:* B40A, Dirksen Senate Office Building, Washington, DC 20510, USA (office). *Telephone:* (202) 224-3542 (office). *Website:* www.senate.gov (office); catherinecortezmasto.com.

CORTINA DE ALCOCER, Alfonso, BEng; Spanish business executive; b. 13 March 1944, Madrid; ed Univ. of Madrid; Vice-Pres. Sociedad Hispano Hipotecario 1981–84; Vice-Pres. Cementera Portland Valderrivas 1984–93, Pres. 1993–96; CEO Repsol YPF 1996–2004, Pres. Fundación Repsol from 2004; Chair. Inmobiliaria Colonial 2005–06; Vice Chair. Rothschild Europe and Sr Adviser for Spain and Latin America and mem. European Advisory Council, Rothschild; Sr Adviser Texas Pacific Group, Madrid 2007–; mem. Exec. Cttee Foundation for Technological Innovation; mem. Bd of Dirs, Mutua Madrileña Automovilística Sociedad de Seguros a Prima Fija, Recoletos Grupo de Comunicación SA; mem. Int. Advisory Bd and Jt Advisory Council, Allianz Companies; mem. Advisory Cttee, Altamar Private Equity; mem. Trilateral Comm. *Address:* c/o Fundación Repsol, Velázquez 166, 28002 Madrid, Spain.

CORVALÁN MENDOZA, Jorge Raúl, MSc; Paraguayan economist, academic and central banker; b. 23 April 1969, Asunción; m.; three c.; ed Univ. Nacional de Asunción, Univ. of Illinois, Urbana-Champaign, USA; Prof., Inst. of Devt, Univ. Nacional de Asunción 2002–; Gen. Co-ordinator, devt project financed by Japanese Govt and World Bank, Carapeguá and Ñemby municipalities 2006–08; Dir Gen. Minister's Technical Cabinet, Ministry of Industry and Commerce 2006; Dir, Int. Econs Dept, Banco Central del Paraguay 2001–05, Pres. Banco Central del Paraguay 2008–13. *Leisure interests:* spending time with family, tennis. *Address:* c/o Office of the President, Banco Central del Paraguay, Avda Federación Rusa y Cabo 1° Marecos, Casilla 861, Barrio Santo Domingo, Asunción, Paraguay. *E-mail:* informaciones@bcp.gov.py.

CORY, Suzanne, AC, PhD, FAA, FRS; Australian molecular biologist; b. 11 March 1942, Melbourne; m. Dr Jerry McKee Adams; two d.; ed Canterbury Girls' Secondary School, Univ. High School, Univ. of Melbourne, MRC Laboratory of Molecular Biology, UK; Post-doctoral Fellow, Univ. of Geneva, Switzerland 1969–71; Queen Elizabeth II Fellow, Univ. of Melbourne Walter and Eliza Hall Inst. of Medical Research 1971–74, Roche Fellow 1974–76, Research Fellow 1977, Sr Research Fellow 1978–83, Prin. Research Fellow 1984–88, NHMRC Sr Prin. Research Fellow and Jt Head, Molecular Genetics of Cancer Div. 1988–96, Research Prof. of Molecular Oncology, Univ. of Melbourne 1993–96, Dir Walter and Eliza Hall Inst. 1996–2009, later Research Prof., Molecular Genetics of Cancer Div.; Int. Research Scholar, Howard Hughes Medical Inst. 1992–97; Pres. Australian Acad. of Science 2010–; Pasteur Scientific Advisory Bd 2007–; L'Oreal Australia for Women in Science Fellowships Selection Committee 2007–; Univ. of Auckland Maurice Wilkins Centre Molecular Biodiscovery Scientific Advisory Bd 2008–; Gairdner Foundation Medical Advisory Bd 2010–; KwaZulu-Natal Research Inst. for Tuberculosis and HIV Scientific Advisory Bd 2014–; Australian National Univ. Council; Foreign mem. NAS; Assoc. Foreign mem. Acad. des Sciences; Fellow, Royal Soc. of Victoria 1997, Inaugural Class of the AACR Acad., Inaugural Class American Asscn of Cancer Research, Academician Pontifical Acad. of Science, Australian Acad. of Science; Hon. mem. The Japan Acad., Foreign Hon. mem. American Acad. of Arts and Sciences, Hon. Distinguished Professorial Fellow, Molecular Genetics of Cancer Division, Walter and Eliza Hall Inst. of Medical Research; Chevalier, Légion d'honneur 2009; David Syme Prize, Univ. of Melbourne 1982, Charles S. Mott Prize, General Motors Cancer Research Foundation (jtly) 1988, Avon Australia Spirit of Achievement Award 1992, Lemberg Medal, Australian Soc. for Biochemistry and Molecular Biology 1995, Burnet Lecturer, Australian Acad. of Science 1997, Australia Prize 1998, L'Oreal-UNESCO Women in Science Award 2001, Royal Medal, Royal Soc. 2002, Pearl Meister Greengard Prize 2009, Colin Thomson Medal 2011, Australian Eureka Prize for Leadership in Science 2012. *Publications:* numerous articles in scientific journals. *Leisure interests:* hiking, reading, music, photography. *Address:* The Walter and Eliza Hall Institute of Medical Research, 1G Royal Parade, Parkville, Vic. 3052, Australia (office). *Telephone:* (3) 9345-2492 (office). *Fax:* (3) 9347-0852 (office). *E-mail:* cory@wehi.edu.au (office). *Website:* www.wehi.edu.au (office).

CORYDON, Bjarne Fog; Danish politician; b. 1 March 1973, Kolding; m. Nina Eg Hansen 1998; four c.; ed Univ. of Aarhus; mem. Socialdemokraterne (Social Democrats—SD) 1992–, political and econ. adviser to SD leadership, Christiansborg 2000–05, Chief of Staff to SD Chair. Helle Thorning-Schmidt 2005–11, Leader, SD Analysis and Information Div. 2005; mem. Folketing (Parl.) for S Jutland constituency 2011–; Minister of Finance 2011–15. *Address:* c/o Ministry of Finance, Christiansborg Slotspl. 1, 1218 Copenhagen K, Denmark (office). *Website:* bjarnecorydon.dk.

CORZINE, Jon Stevens, MBA; American business executive and fmr politician; b. 1 Jan. 1947, Taylorville, Ill.; s. of Roy Allen Corzine and Nancy June Corzine (née Hedrick); m. Joanne Dougherty 1968 (divorced 2003); two s. one d.; ed Univs of Chicago and Illinois; bond officer, Continental Illinois Nat. Bank 1970; Asst Vice-Pres. BancOhio Corpn 1974–75; joined Goldman, Sachs & Co. 1975, Vice-Pres. 1977, Pnr 1980–98, man. consultant 1985–94, Co-Head, Fixed Income Div. 1988–94, Sr Pnr and Chair. Man. Cttee, CEO 1994–99; Senator from NJ 2001–05, mem. Foreign Relations Cttee; Gov. of NJ 2005–10; Chair. and CEO MF Global Holdings Ltd, New York 2010–11 (resgnd); Operating Pnr, J.C. Flowers & Co. LLC 2010–11; John L. Weinberg/Goldman Sachs and Co. Visiting Prof., Woodrow Wilson School of Public and Int. Affairs, Princeton Univ. 2010–11; fmr mem. Bd of Dirs New York Philharmonic 1996, Public Securities Asscn (Vice-Chair. 1985, Chair. 1986).

COSBY, William (Bill) H., Jr, MA, EdD; American comedian and actor; b. 12 July 1937, Philadelphia, Pa; s. of William Cosby and Anna Cosby; m. Camille Hanks 1964; five c. (one s. deceased); ed Temple Univ. and Univ. of Massachusetts; served in USNR 1956–60; Pres. Rhythm and Blues Hall of Fame 1968; mem. Bd of Dirs Sickle Cell Anemia Foundation, United Negro Coll. Fund, Operation PUSH; Trustee, Temple Univ. 1982–2014 (resgnd); found guilty of indecent assault April 2018, sentenced to 3 to 10 years' imprisonment Sept. 2018; numerous hon. degrees; recipient of four Emmy Awards and eight Grammy Awards, Bob Hope Humanitarian Award, Presidential Medal of Freedom 2002, Acad. of TV Arts and Sciences 2003; named to Hall of Fame, Acad. of TV Arts and Sciences 1994, to Nat. Asscn for the Advancement of Colored People Image Awards Hall of Fame 2007, Mark Twain Prize for American Humor 2009. *Films include:* Black History: Lost, Stolen or Strayed 1968, Bob & Carol & Ted & Alice 1969, Aesop's Fables 1971, Hickey and Boggs 1972, Uptown Saturday Night 1974, Let's Do It Again 1975, Mother, Jugs and Speed 1976, A Piece of Action 1977, California Suite 1978, The Devil and Max Devlin 1981, Leonard: Part VI 1987, Bill Cosby: 49 1987, Ghost Dad 1990, The Meteor Man 1993, Jack 1996, Baadasssss! 2003, Fat Albert 2004, Far From Finished 2013. *Television includes:* I Spy 1965–68, The Bill Cosby Show 1969–71, Hey, Hey, Hey, It's Fat Albert 1969, Man and Boy 1971, The Electric Company 1971–73, The New Bill Cosby Show 1972, Fat Albert and the Cosby Kids 1972–85, To All My Friends On Shore 1972, Journey Back to Oz 1974, Cos 1976, Pinwheel 1977–90, Top Secret 1978, The Cosby Show 1984–92, A Different World 1987, You Bet Your Life 1992–93, Cosby Mystery Series 1994–95, I Spy Returns 1994, Cosby 1996–2000, Kids Say the Darndest Things 1998–2000, Little Bill 1999–2004, OBKB 2010–12. *Recordings include:* Wonderfulness 1966, Revenge 1967, To Russell, My Brother, Whom I Slept With 1968, 8:15 12:15 1969, When I Was a Kid 1971, For Adults Only 1971, Inside the Mind of Bill Cosby 1972, Fat Albert 1973, At Last Bill Cosby Really Sings 1974, Bill Cosby Is Not Himself These Days 1976, My Father Confused Me... What Must I Do? What Must I Do? 1977, Bill Cosby: Himself 1982, Those of You With or Without Children, You'll Understand 1986, Where You Lay Your Head 1990, Oh, Baby! 1991, Hello Friend: To Ennis, With Love 1997, Quincy Jones & Bill Cosby: The Original Jam Sessions 1969 2004, State of Emergency 2009, Keep Standing 2010. *Publications include:* The Wit and Wisdom of Fat Albert 1973, Bill Cosby's Personal Guide to Power Tennis, Fatherhood 1986, Time Flies 1988, Love and Marriage 1989, Childhood 1991, Little Bill Series 1999, Congratulations! Now What? 1999, Friends of a Feather (juvenile), I Didn't Ask to Be Born (But I'm Glad I Was) 2011.

COSENZA JIMÉNEZ, Luis, BS, PhD; Honduran engineer, development banker, politician and academic; ed Univ. of Notre Dame, USA; worked for Empresa Nacional De Energía Eléctrica (state-owned power utility) becoming CEO 1976; Energy Specialist, IDB 1981–89; Prin. Power Engineer responsible for east Africa and much of central American region, World Bank 1989; campaign man. for Ricardo Maduro (Arriba Honduras cand.) during presidential election in 2000; Minister of the Presidency 2002–05; Exec. Dir for Belize, Costa Rica, El Salvador, Guatemala, Honduras and Nicaragua, IDB 2005–06; Visiting Fellow, Kellogg Inst. for Int. Studies, Univ. of Notre Dame 2006–07, Hewlett Visiting Fellow for Public Policy 2009–10; mem. Bd of Advisors Concern Yourself, Inc.; fmr Exec. Pres. Honduran Foundation for Investment and Promotion of Exports (FIDES). *Address:* Cosenza & Cia, Tegucigalpa, Honduras (office).

COSGROVE, Art, BA, PhD; Irish historian, academic, barrister and fmr university president; b. 1 June 1940, Newry, Co. Down, NI; m. Emer Sweeney 1968; nine c.; ed Abbey Christian Brothers School, Newry, Co. Down, NI and Queen's Univ., Belfast, NI; mem. academic staff, Univ. Coll. Dublin 1963–94, Sr Lecturer, Dept of Medieval History 1976, Assoc. Prof. and Acting Head of Dept 1990, apptd Chair. Combined Depts of History 1991, Pres. Univ. Coll. Dublin 1994–2003; mem. Bd of Dirs, racecaller.com 2008–; Visiting Prof., History Dept, Univ. of Kansas 1974; fmr Pres. Dublin Historical Asscn and Ed. of its publs; Hon. LLD (Queen's Univ., Belfast) 1995. *Publications:* Studies in Irish History presented to R. D. Edwards (co-author) 1979, Late Medieval Ireland 1370–1541 1981, Parliament and Community (co-author) 1981, Marriage in Ireland 1985, A New History of Ireland II: Medieval Ireland 1169–1534 1987, Dublin Through the Ages 1988. *E-mail:* artjcosgrove@hotmail.com.

COSGROVE, Gen. Sir Peter John, Kt, AK, AM, MC; Australian army officer (retd) and government official; b. 28 July 1947; m. Lynne Payne 1976; three s.; ed Waverley Coll., Royal Mil. Coll., Duntroon; joined Australian Army 1965, served with 1st Bn, Royal Australian Regt (RAR) in Malaysia and with 9th Bn, RAR in Viet Nam 1969, Commdr, 1st Bn, RAR 1983–84, 1st Div. 1998–99, led int. forces in East Timor peacekeeping mission (INTERFET) 1999–2000, Chief of Army 2000–02, Chief of Defence Force 2002–05, retd from army 2005; Chancellor, Australian Catholic Univ. 2010–14; Gov.-Gen. of Australia 2014–19; Dir Qantas 2005–14; attained rank of Lt 1968, Col 1989, Lt-Gen. 2000, Gen. 2002; Officier, Légion d'honneur; Commdr, Legion of Merit (USA); numerous awards, including Mil. Cross 1971, Vietnam Medal, Nat. Medal 1980, Australian of the Year 2001. *Publication:* My Story (autobiog.) 2006. *Address:* c/o Government House, Canberra, ACT 2600, Australia (office). *Telephone:* (02) 6283 3533 (office). *Fax:* (02) 6281 3760 (office). *Website:* www.gg.gov.au (office).

COŞKUN, Ali, MSc; Turkish politician and business executive; b. 1939, Başpınar village, Kemaliye, Erzincan; m.; two c.; ed Faculty of Electrical Eng, Yıldız Tech. Univ., Wirtschaft Akad., Hamburg, Germany; fmr Pres. Admin. Bd, Ihlas Finance Inst. and Bisan Bicycle Industry and Commerce; fmr Deputy Pres. Istanbul Chamber of Commerce; fmr Pres. Turkish Union of Chambers and Commodities Exchanges (TOBB); fmr Deputy Pres. Islamic Countries Union of Chambers; mem. Parl. (ANAP) for Istanbul Constituency 1995–2005, Chair. Nat. Defence Comm., mem. Plan and Budget Comm., Industry, Trade, Energy and Tech. Comm.; Minister of Industry and Commerce 2005–07; Hon. Pres. TOBB; Hon. mem. Asscn of Istanbul Chamber Industry, Asscn of Ankara Chamber of Trade, Asscn of Turkish Exporters. *Publication:* Energy Problems of Turkey and Solutions 1986. *Address:* Öğretmenler Cad. Usta Apt. A Blok 1/1, 06140, Çukurambar, Ankara, Turkey. *Telephone:* (312) 2857037. *Fax:* (312) 2857034.

COSPEDAL GARCÍA, María Dolores de; Spanish lawyer and politician; b. 13 Dec. 1965, Madrid; d. of Ricardo de Cospedal Peinado and Maria Luisa García Sánchez; m. Ignacio López del Hierro; one s.; ed CEU San Pablo Univ.; State Attorney, Basque Country 1991–92; worked in Legal Dept, Ministry of Public Works, Transport and Environment 1992–94; Chief State Attorney, Ministry of Social Affairs 1994–96; Adviser to Cabinet of Minister of Labour and Social Affairs

1996–97; Labour and Social Affairs Counsellor, Embassy in Washington, DC 1998–99; Gen. Technical Sec., Ministry of Labour and Social Affairs 1999–2000; Under-Sec. of Public Admin 2000–02; Sec. of State, Ministry of the Interior 2002–04; State Attorney, Court of Human Rights May–Dec. 2004; Minister of Transport and Infrastructure, Community of Madrid 2004–06; mem. Senate 2006–11; mem. Congress of Castilla-La Mancha for Toledo 2007–16, Pres., Regional Govt of Castilla-La Mancha 2011–15; mem. Congress of Deputies for Toledo 2016–; Minister of Defence 2016–18; mem. People's Party (PP), Pres., Castilla-La Mancha PP 2006–, PP Sec.-Gen. 2008–; Grand Cross, Order of Isabella the Catholic 2004.

COSSART, Pascale, MSc, PhD; French bacteriologist and academic; *Head of Bacteria-Cell Interactions, Cell Biology and Infection Department, Institut Pasteur;* b. 21 March 1948, Cambrai; ed Lille Univ., Georgetown Univ., USA, Univ. of Paris VII; Asst, Univ. Inst. Tech., Lille; Fellow, Georgetown Univ. 1970–71; Prof., Royal School of Medicine, Laos 1974–75; joined Institut Pasteur, Paris 1972, Head of Listeria Molecular Genetics Lab. 1991–94, Prof. and Head of Bacterial-Cellular Interactions Unit 1994, apptd Dir Cell Biology and Infection Dept 2006, currently Head of Bacteria-Cell Interactions, Cell Biology and Infection Dept; Int. Research Scholar, Howard Hughes Medical Inst. 2000–; mem. Scientific Advisory Bd at Research Centre for Infectious Diseases, Würzburg Univ., Germany 2000–, at Biozentrum, Univ., Basel, Switzerland 2002–; mem. Scientific Council, Ville de Paris 2003–, Nat. Ethics Consultative Cttee 2003, EMBO Course and Workshop Cttee 1999–2004, Chair. 2001–04; mem. Scientific Council, Institut Pasteur 2002–06, Pres. 2003–05; mem. Scientific Council, CNRS 2005–06, Soc. Francaise de Microbiologie 1977–, American Soc. for Microbiology 1987, American Soc. for Cell Biology 1993–, Soc. Francaise de Biologie Cellulaire 2007–, Soc. Francaise de Biochimie et de Biologie Moléculaire 2007–; mem. Cttee de Pilotage, Agence Nat. pour la Recherche 2006–; mem. editorial bds of several journals; mem. Deutsche Akad. der Naturforscher Leopoldina, Acad. des Sciences 2002–, American Acad. of Microbiology 2009–, European Acad. of Microbiology 2009–; Chevalier, Légion d'honneur 1998, Officier 2007, Officier, Ordre National du Mérite 2002, Commdr 2010; Dr hc (École polytechnique fédérale de Lausanne) 2009, Fellow, Royal Soc. (London) 2010; UNESCO Carlos Finlay Prize 1995, Louis Rapkin Award 1997, Richard Lounsbery Prize, L'Oreal-UNESCO Women in Science Award 1998, Louis Pasteur Gold Medal, Swedish Soc. of Medicine 2000, Nestle Prize 2000, Valade Senior Price, Fondation de France 2003, INSERM Prize of Fundamental Research 2005, Glaxo Smith Kline Int. Mem. of the Year Award 2007, Robert Koch Prize 2007, Descartes Prize 2008, Louis Jeantet Prize for Medicine 2008, Balzan Prize for Infectious Diseases 2013, Ernst Jung Gold Medal for Medicine 2017. *Publications:* numerous publs in scientific journals. *Address:* Cell Biology and Infection Department, Institut Pasteur, 25–28 rue du Dr Roux, 75015 Paris, France (office). *Telephone:* 1-45-68-80-00 (office). *E-mail:* pcossart@pasteur.fr (office). *Website:* www.pasteur.fr (office).

COSSÉ, Steven A., BA, JD; American oil company executive; b. 1948; ed Southeastern Louisiana Univ., Loyola Univ.; Gen. Counsel, Ocean Drilling & Exploration Co. (ODECO, subsidiary of Murphy Oil Corpn) 1983–91, Vice-Pres. Murphy Oil Corpn 1993, Sr Vice-Pres. 1994–2005, also served as Chief Financial Officer, later Vice-Pres. and Gen. Counsel, Murphy Exploration & Production Co. USA (subsidiary of Murphy Oil Corpn), General Counsel 1991–2011, Exec. Vice-Pres. Murphy Oil Corpn 2005–11, mem. Bd of Dirs 2011–, Pres. and CEO 2011–13; Lead Dir Simmons First Nat. Corpn 2004–, Simmons First Nat. Bank, Simmons First Bank of El Dorado, NA, Nat. Assen of Mfrs, SHARE Foundation, Medical Center of South Arkansas; mem. Advisory Bd Union County Rape and Family Violence Center; mem. American Corp. Counsel Asscn, Louisiana Bar Asscn, Union County Bar Asscn; fmr Chair. South Arkansas Chapter of American Red Cross. *Address:* Simmons First National Corporation, 501 Main Street, Pine Bluff, AR 71611-7009, USA (office). *Telephone:* (870) 541-1000 (office). *E-mail:* bankanywhere@simmonsbank.com (office). *Website:* ir.simmonsbank.com (office).

COSSONS, Sir Neil, Kt, OBE, MA, FSA; British foundation executive; b. 15 Jan. 1939, Nottingham, Notts.; s. of Arthur Cossons and Evelyn Cossons (née Bettle); m. Veronica Edwards 1965; two s. one d.; ed Henry Mellish Grammar School, Nottingham, Univ. of Liverpool; Curator of Tech., Bristol City Museum 1964; Deputy Dir, City of Liverpool Museums 1969; Dir Ironbridge Gorge Museum 1971; Dir Nat. Maritime Museum, Greenwich 1983; Dir Science Museum, London 1986–2000; Commr Historic Buildings and Monuments Comm. for England (English Heritage) 1989–95, 1999–2000, Chair. 2000–07; Pres. Royal Geographical Soc. 2003–06; mem. RCA Council 1989–2015, also Sr Fellow, Pro-Provost and Chair of Council 2007–15; mem. Design Council 1990–94, British Waterways Bd 1995–2001; Pres. European Museum Forum 2001–08; Fellow and Past Pres. of the Museums Asscn; mem. Comité Scientifique, Conservatoire Nat. des Arts et Métiers 1991–2000; Trustee, Nat. Heritage Memorial Fund/Heritage Lottery Fund 2016–19; Fellow Int. Inst. for Conservation 2017; Hon. Prof., Univ. of Birmingham 1994, Hon. Companion, Royal Aeronautical Soc. 1996, Hon. mem. Soc. of Chemical Industry 2002, Hon. FRIBA 2002, Sr Fellow, RCA 2015; Hon. DSocSc (Birmingham) 1979, Hon. DUniv (Open Univ.) 1984, (Sheffield Hallam) 1995, (York) 1998, Hon. DLitt (Liverpool) 1989, (Bradford) 1991, (Nottingham Trent) 1994, (Univ. of the West of England) 1995, (Bath) 1997, (Greenwich) 2004, (Chester) 2018, Hon. DSc (Leicester) 1995, (Nottingham) 2000, Hon. DArts (De Montfort) 1997; Norton Medlicott Medal, Historical Asscn 1991, Pres.'s Medal, Royal Acad. of Eng 1993. *Publications include:* Industrial Archaeology of the Bristol Region (with R. A. Buchanan) 1968, Industrial Archaeology 1975, Transactions of the First International Congress on the Conservation of Industrial Monuments (ed.) 1975, Rees's Manufacturing Industry (ed.) 1975, Ironbridge – Landscape of Industry (with H. Sowden) 1977, The Iron Bridge – Symbol of the Industrial Revolution (with B. S. Trinder) 1979, The Management of Change in Museums (ed.) 1985, Making of the Modern World (ed.) 1992, Perspectives on Industrial Archaeology (ed.) 2000, England's Landscape (eight-vol. series, gen. ed.) 2006, Liverpool: Seaport City (with M. Jenkins) 2011. *Leisure interests:* travel, design, industrial archaeology. *Address:* The Old Rectory, Rushbury, Shropshire, SY6 7EB, England (home). *Telephone:* (1694) 771603. *E-mail:* nc@cossons.org.uk (office).

COSTA, Antonio Luís dos Santos da; Portuguese lawyer and politician; *Prime Minister;* b. 17 July 1961, Lisbon; s. of Orlando da Costa and Maria Antónia Palla; m. Fernanda Maria Gonçalves Tadeu 1987; one s. one d.; ed Univ. of Lisbon; mem. Municipal Ass. of Lisbon 1982–93; Deputy Ass. of Repub. 1991–2007, mem. Partido Socialista, Pres. Parl. Group 2002–04; Sec. of State for Parl. Affairs 1995–97; Govt Rep. Expo '98 1997–98; Minister of Justice 1999–2002; mem. European Parl. 2004–05, Vice-Pres. European Parl.; Minister of State and Internal Admin 2005–07; Mayor of Lisbon 2007–15; Leader of the Opposition 2014–15; Prime Minister 2015–; Sec.-Gen. Socialist Party 2014–; numerous decorations including Grand Cross, Ordem do Infante D. Henrique 2006, Commdr, Order of Polónia Restituta (Poland) 2012, Ordem de Rio Branco (Brazil) 2014, Order of the Sacred Treasure (Japan) 2015. *Address:* Office of the Prime Minister, Presidency of the Council of Ministers, Rua da Imprensa à Estrela 4, 1200-888 Lisbon, Portugal (office). *Telephone:* (21) 3923500 (office). *Fax:* (21) 3951616 (office). *E-mail:* pm@pm.gov.pt (office). *Website:* www.portugal.gov.pt (office).

COSTA, Antonio Maria, PhD; Italian economist, editor and fmr UN official; b. 16 June 1941, Mondovi; s. of Francesco Costa and Maria Costa; m. Patricia Agnes Wallace 1971; two s. one d.; ed Acad. of Sciences of the USSR, Univ. of Turin, Univ. of California, Berkeley USA; Visiting Prof. of Econs, Moscow Univ. and Acad. of Sciences of the USSR 1965–67; Instructor of Econs, Univ. of Calif., Berkeley 1968–70; Sr economist UN Dept of Int. Econs and Social Affairs 1969–83; Prof. of Econs, New York Univ. 1976–83; Sr Econ. Adviser to the UN 1970–83; Special Counsellor in Econs to the Sec.-Gen. of OECD 1983–87; Dir Gen. Econ. and Financial Affairs, EC 1987–92; Sec.-Gen. EBRD, London, UK 1992–2001; Exec. Dir UN Office on Drugs and Crime (fmrly UN Office for Drug Control and Crime Prevention), Vienna, Austria 2002–10, also Dir-Gen. UN Office at Vienna (UNOV) 2002–10; currently Ed.-in-Chief, Journal of Policy Modelling. *Publications:* The Checkmate Pendulum (novel) 2014; articles on econs and politics. *Leisure interest:* work. *Website:* www.antoniomariacosta.com/cc/index.php; www.econmodels.com/public/index.php.

COSTA, Enrico, PhD; Italian astrophysicist and research institute director; b. 1944, Sassari, Sardinia; ed Univ. of Rome; family moved to Rome 1954; participated in rocket experiments with X-ray detectors at Istituto di Astrofisica Spaziale (IAS), Rome; joined IAS and worked on balloon experiments 1976, later involved in BeppoSAX (Italian X-ray astronomy satellite); part of team of Livio Scarsi that proposed the construction of the satellite for X-ray detection 1981, Dir of Research, Inst. of Space Astrophysics and Planetology, Nat. Inst. of Astrophysics; Shaw Prize in Astronomy (co-recipient) 2011. *Achievements include:* developed X-ray detector for Italian X-ray/gamma-ray satellites AGILE 1999, which started in 2007; developed X-ray polarimeters. *Publications:* numerous papers in professional journals. *Address:* c/o Instituto di Astrofisica e Planetologia Spaziali, Room 1B04, Via del Fosso del Cavaliere 100, 00133 Rome, Italy (office).

COSTA, Francisco; Brazilian fashion designer; *Creative Director, Calvin Klein Collection for Women, Calvin Klein Inc.;* b. 10 May 1964; s. of Jacy Neves da Costa and Maria-Francisca da Costa; partner John DeStefano Jr; ed Hunter Coll., New York, Fashion Inst. of Tech., USA; fmr designer for Gucci, Balmain and Oscar de la Renta; joined Calvin Klein 2002, Design Dir for Womenswear (following sale of co. to Phillips-Van Heusen and retirement of Calvin Klein as Design Dir) 2003–, debut collection at NY Fashion Week 2003; Award for Womenswear Designer of the Year, Council of Fashion Designers America 2006, 2008, Cooper-Hewitt Nat. Fashion Design Award 2009. *Address:* Calvin Klein Inc., 205 West 39th Street, New York, NY 10018, USA (office). *Website:* explore.calvinklein.com/en_GB/bios (office).

COSTA, Gabriel Arcanjo Ferreira da, BLL; São Tomé and Príncipe politician, lawyer and diplomatist; b. 11 Dec. 1954; lawyer and magistrate; mem. Parl. (Juventude Movimento Libertação de São Tomé e Príncipe) in first Ass. following nat. independence 1975–98; Counsellor for Legal and Political Affairs to Pres. Trovoada 1991–95, Head of Cabinet of Pres. 1996–98; State Minister of Justice, Admin. Reform and Local Admin –1998; Special Rep. of Exec. of CPLP for Guinea-Bissau 1998–2000; Amb. to Portugal, Morocco and Spain 2000–02; Prime Minister of São Tomé e Príncipe March–Oct. 2002, 2012–14; mem. Movimento de Libertação de São Tomé e Príncipe—Partido Social Democrata.

COSTA, Jean-Paul, LLM, PhD; French judge; b. 3 Nov. 1941, Tunis, Tunisia; widower; remarried; five c.; ed Lycée Carnot of Tunis, Lycée Henri IV, Paris, Inst. of Political Studies, Nat. School of Man., Paris; clerk, Council of State 1966, Advisor, Judicial Section 1966–71, 1977–80, 1987–89, Assessor of Sub-section of Judicial Section 1989–93, Pres. of Sub-section of Judicial Section 1993–98; Political Sec. to Minister of Educ. 1981–84; Assoc. Prof., Orléans Univ. 1989–98, Panthéon-Sorbonne Univ. 1992–98; Judge, European Court of Human Rights 1998–2011, Vice-Pres. 2001–06, Pres. 2007–11; Pres. Int. Inst. of Human Rights René Cassin 2012; Hon. Bencher, Inner Temple, London 2002, King's Inn, Dublin 2008; Chevalier des Arts et des Lettres, des Palmes académiques; Commdr, Ordre nat. du Mérite 1999, Légion d'honneur 2005, Ordre de la Couronne de Chêne (Luxembourg) 2011; Cavaliere di Gran Croce dell'Ordine Equestre di Sant'Agata (San Marino) 2007; Grand Decoration of Honour in Gold with Sash (Austria) 2011; Grand-Croix, Ordre du Mérite civil espagnol 2012; Hon. LLD (Univ. of Bucarest) 2003, (Univ. of Košice, Poland) 2008, (Univ. Masaryk, Brno, Czech Repub.) 2009. *Publications include:* Les libertés publiques en France et dans le monde 1986, La déclaration des droits de l'homme et du citoyen (collective work) 1992, Le Conseil d'Etat dans la société contemporaine 1993, Les droits de l'homme et le rôle des administrations publiques (ed.) 1997, Les laïcités à la française (co-author) 1998; numerous articles in professional journals.

COSTA, Pedro; Portuguese film director and writer; b. 3 March 1959, Lisbon; s. of dir and writer Luís Filipe Costa; ed Univ. of Lisbon, Escola Superior de Teatro e Cinema. *Films include:* É Tudo Invenção Nossa (also producer) 1984, Um Adeus Português (asst dir) 1986, Uma Rapariga no Verão (asst dir) 1986, Agosto (August) (asst dir) 1987, O Sangue (The Blood) (also writer) 1989, Casa de Lava (Down to Earth) (also writer) (Special Artistic Achievement, Thessaloniki Film Festival 1994, Grand Prix for Best Foreign Film, Entrevues Film Festival 1994) 1994, Ossos (Bones) (also writer) (Grand Prix for Best Foreign Film, Entrevues Film Festival 1997) 1997, No Quarto da Vanda (In Vanda's Room) (also cinematographer) (Don Quixote Award (Special Mention), Special Mention, and Youth Jury Award, Locarno Int. Film Festival 2000, FIPRESCI Prize (Int. Competition), Yamagata Int. Documentary Festival 2001, France Culture Award for Cineaste of the Year, Cannes Film Festival 2002) 2000, 6 Bagatelas (video) 2001, Ne change rien 2005, Juventude Em Marcha (Colossal Youth) (also writer and cinematographer) (Independent/Experimental Film and Video Award, Los Angeles Film Critics Association Awards 2007) 2006, O Estado do Mundo (State of the World; segment Tarrafal) (also cinematographer) 2007, Memories (segment, The Rabbit Hunters) 2007, Change Nothing (documentary) 2009, O nosso Homem (short) 2010, Centro Histórico (segment, Sweet Exorcism) 2012, Horse Money 2014. *Television includes:* Cinéma, de notre temps (episode Danièle Huillet/Jean-Marie Straub: Où gît votre sourire enfoui?) (also cinematographer) 2001.

COSTA-GAVRAS, Constantin; French (b. Greek) film director and screenwriter; b. (Konstantinos Gavras), 12 Feb. 1933, Loutra Iraias, Arcadia; s. of Panayotis Gavras and Panayota Gavras; m. Michele Ray 1968; three c.; ed Univ. of the Sorbonne and Institut de Hautes Etudes Cinématographiques, Paris; worked as asst to film dirs Yves Allegret, Jacques Demy, René Clair, René Clément; Pres. Soc. des Réalisateurs Français 1973–75, Cinémathèque Française 1982–87, 2007–, Festival Paris-Cinéma 2003–; Chevalier, Légion d'honneur; Commdr des Arts et des Lettres; Officier, Ordre nat. du Mérite; Dr hc (Univ. of Thessaloniki); Prix Acad. française for Life Achievement 1998, Magritte Honorary Award, 3rd Magritte Awards 2013. *Opera directed:* Il Mondo della Luna (Joseph Haydn), Teatro San Carlo, Naples 1994. *Films directed include:* The Sleeping Car Murder (also writer) (MWA Award) 1965, Un Homme de Trop (Moscow Film Festival Prize) 1966, Z (co-writer) (Jury Award, Cannes, Award for Best Foreign-Language Film) 1969, L'Aveu (co-writer) 1970, State of Siege (co-writer) (Louis Delluc Prize) 1973, Section Spéciale (co-writer) (Best Dir, Cannes) 1975, Clair de Femme (writer) 1979, Missing (co-writer) (Palm d'or, Cannes, Academy Award, best screenplay, British Acad. best screenplay) 1982, Hanna K (co-writer) 1983, Family Business (writer) 1985, Betrayed (ACLUF Award) 1988, Music Box (Golden Bear, Berlin) 1989, The Little Apocalypse (co-writer) 1993, Mad City 1996, Amen 2001, Parthenon (short) 2003, Le Couperet 2005, Eden Is West 2009, Capital 2012. *Publication:* Etat de Siège: The Making of the Film. *Leisure interests:* theatre, opera, books, films. *Address:* c/o Bertrand de Labbey, Artmédia, 20 avenue Rapp, 75007, Paris, France (office); 244 rue Saint-Jacques, 75005 Paris, France (office). *Telephone:* 1-43-17-33-00 (office); 1-44-41-13-73 (office). *E-mail:* info@artmedia.fr (office); kgprod@wanadoo.fr (office). *Website:* www.artmedia.fr (office). *Fax:* 1-44-41-13-74 (office).

COSTA PEREIRA, Renato Cláudio; Brazilian aviation official and international organization official; b. 30 Nov. 1936; m.; ed Brazilian Air Force Acad.; Personnel Commdr, Belo Horizonte Air Force Base 1961–67; Officer, Brazilian Air Force Gen. Personnel Command 1967–70, Instructor Officer, Brazilian Air Force Improvement Officer School 1970–74; Pilot Instructor, Brazilian Air Force Acad. 1974–77; Man. and Co-ordinator of Research and Devt project 1978–84; Dir Flight Protection Inst. 1984–85; Logistics Adviser to Minister of Aeronautics 1985–87; Chief, Brazilian Air Comm., London, England 1987–89; Sec. of Planning and Contracting, Secr. of Econ. and Finance, Ministry of Aeronautics 1989–90; Dir Operations Sub-Dept, Civil Aviation Dept 1990–92, Dir Planning Sub-Dept 1990–94; Pres. Latin American Comm. of Civil Aviation 1990–97, responsible for establishing the basis for the enlargement of the Comm. to a Pan-American body in 1997; Pres. Brazilian Govt agency for int. air navigation affairs 1990–97; Sec.-Gen. ICAO 1997–2003. *Address:* c/o International Civil Aviation Organization, 999 University Street, Montreal, PQ H3A 5H7, Canada. *Website:* www.icao.int/secretariat/SecretaryGeneral/Pages/biography-secretary-general-pereira.aspx.

COSTA SANHÁ, Maj.-Gen. Eduardo; Guinea-Bissau politician and fmr judge; *Minister of National Defence;* fmr Presiding Judge, Superior Mil. Tribunal; Minister of Nat. Defence 2015–. *Address:* Ministry of National Defence, Amura, Bissau, Guinea-Bissau (office). *Telephone:* 3223646 (office).

COSTEDOAT, Lt-Gen. Pierre-Jacques; French army officer and business executive; *CEO, Scutum Security First;* b. 27 Jan. 1942, Casablanca, Morocco; s. of René Costedoat and Marguerite Bosc; m. Anne-Marie Delamare 1965; four d.; ed Saint-Cyr-Coëtquidan Mil. Acad.; Second Lt, 74th Artillery Regt 1964, Lt 1966; Capt., 1st Artillery Regt 1972, then Battery CO; Maj., 11th Artillery Regt 1977, Lt-Col 1981, Col 1984; attended as auditeur Centre des hautes études militaires and Institut des hautes études de défense nationale 1987–88; CO 93rd Mountain Artillery Regt, then Staff 1988–89, at Direction Générale de la Sécurité extérieure 1989–95; Brig. 1992; CO Saint-Cyr Coëtquidan Mil. Acad. 1995–98; rank of Maj.-Gen. 1995, later Lt-Gen.; Asst Gen. Sec. of Nat. Defence 1998–2000; Gen. de corps 1998–; Mil. Gov. of Paris, Commdr of Ile-de-France, Officer Gen. Paris Zone of Defence 2000–02; Advisor to Pres. of Sécurité Sans Frontières (risk prevention and man. consultancy) 2003–08; CEO Scutum Security First 2008–; Officier, Légion d'honneur; Commdr, Ordre nat. du Mérite. *Leisure interests:* skiing, tennis, golf, hiking. *Address:* Scutum Security First, 14 rue Magellan, 75008 Paris, France (office). *Telephone:* 1-55-57-16-10 (office). *Fax:* 1-55-57-16-11 (office). *E-mail:* info@securite-sf.com (office). *Website:* www.securite-sf.com (office).

COSTELLO, Elvis; British singer and songwriter; b. (Declan Patrick Aloysius McManus), 25 Aug. 1954, London, England; s. of Ross McManus and Lillian McManus (née Costello); m. 1st Mary Costello 1974; one s.; m. 2nd Cait O'Riordan 1986 (divorced 2003); m. 3rd Diana Krall 2003; twin s.; fmr mem. Flip City; formed Elvis Costello and the Attractions 1977; Dir South Bank Meltdown 1995; Hon. DMus, (New England Conservatory) 2013; BAFTA Award for Best Original Television Music (for G.B.H.) 1992, MTV Video Award for Best Male Video 1989, Rolling Stone Award for Best Songwriter 1990, two Ivor Novello Awards, Nordoff-Robbins Silver Clef Award, ASCAP Founders Award 2003. *Films include:* Americathon 1979, No Surrender 1985, Straight to Hell 1987, Prison Song 2001, De-Lovely 2004. *Television includes:* Scully (Granada TV for Channel 4) 1984, The Juliet Letters 1993, presenter, Spectacle: Elvis Costello With... (Sundance Channel) 2008–10. *Recordings include:* albums: My Aim Is True 1977, This Year's Model 1978, Armed Forces 1979, Get Happy 1980, Trust 1980, Almost Blue 1981, Taking Liberties 1982, Imperial Bedroom 1982, Punch The Clock 1983, Goodbye Cruel World 1984, The Best Of 1985, Blood and Chocolate 1986, King of America 1986, Spike 1989, Mighty Like A Rose 1991, The Juliet Letters (with the Brodsky Quartet) 1993, Brutal Youth (with Steve Nieve, Pete Thomas, Bruce Thomas and Nick Lowe) 1994, The Very Best of Elvis Costello and The Attractions 1995, Kojak Variety 1995, Deep Dead Blue, Live At Meltdown (with Bill Frisell) 1995, All This Useless Beauty 1996, Extreme Honey 1997, Terror and Magnificence 1997, Painted From Memory (Grammy Award 1999) 1998, The Sweetest Punch: The Songs of Costello 1999, Best of Elvis Costello 1999, For The Stars (with Anne-Sofie von Otter) 2001, When I Was Cruel 2002, North 2003, My Flame Burns Blue 2006, The River in Reverse (with Allen Toussaint) 2006, Momofuku 2008, Secret, Profane and Sugarcane 2009, National Ransom 2010, Wise Up Ghost 2013, Look Now 2018. *Publication:* Unfaithful Music & Disappearing Ink (autobiography) 2015. *Address:* c/o Darrell Gilmour, Macklam Feldman Management, Suite 200, 1505 West 2nd Avenue, Vancouver, BC V6H 3Y4, Canada (office). *Telephone:* (604) 630-3199 (office). *E-mail:* gilmour@mfmgt.com (office); info@mfmgt.com (office). *Website:* www.mfmgt.com (office); www.elviscostello.com.

COSTELLO, Hon. Peter Howard, AC, BA, LLB (Hons); Australian politician; b. 14 Aug. 1957, Melbourne, Vic.; s. of R. J. Costello and M. A. Costello; m. Tanya Costello 1982; one s. two d.; ed Carey Grammar School, Monash Univ.; solicitor, Mallesons, Melbourne 1981–84; tutor (part-time), Monash Univ. 1984–86; mem. Victorian Bar 1984–90; MP for Higgins, Vic. 1990–2009; Shadow Minister for Corp. Law Reform and Consumer Affairs 1990–92; Shadow Attorney-Gen. and Shadow Minister for Justice 1992–93, for Finance 1993–94; Deputy Leader of the Opposition and Shadow Treas. 1994–96; Treas., Commonwealth of Australia 1996–2007; mem. Liberal Party, Deputy Leader 1996–2007; Chair. Ind. Advisory Bd to World Bank, Washington, DC; Chair. Future Fund; Hon. LLD (Monash Univ.). *Publications:* Arbitration in Contempt (co-author) 1986, (memoir) 2008; articles for periodicals and journals. *Leisure interests:* swimming, football, reading. *Address:* c/o Liberal Party of Australia, PO Box 6004, Kingston, ACT 2604, Australia. *E-mail:* info@petercostello.com.au. *Website:* www.petercostello.com.au.

COSTELLOE, Paul; Irish fashion designer and artist; b. 23 June 1945, Dublin; m. 1982; six s. one d.; ed Blackrock Coll., Dublin, design coll. in Dublin and Chambre Syndical Paris; Design Asst Jacques Esterel, Paris 1969–71; Designer, Marks & Spencer 1972; Chief House Designer, A. Rinascente, Milan 1972–74; Designer, Anne Fogerty, New York, Pennaco, New York and Trimfit, Philadelphia 1974–79; est. own design house, Paul Costelloe Int. Ltd in conjunction with business pnr Robert Eitel 1979; merchandise sold in UK, Ireland, Europe, Scandinavia and N America under Paul Costelloe Collection and Dressage labels; opened flagship store, Knightsbridge 1994; designer of British Airways uniform 1994; Hon. DLitt (Ulster) 1996; Fil d'Or award, Int. Linen Council, 1987, 1988, 1989; British Designer of the Year 1989 and other awards. *Leisure interests:* rugby, tennis, golf. *Address:* Paul Costelloe Design Ltd, 57 Gloucester Place, London, W1U 8JH, England (office). *Telephone:* (20) 7224-1927 (office). *Website:* www.paulcostelloe.com.

COSTNER, Kevin; American actor and film director; b. 18 Jan. 1955; m. 1st Cindy Silva (divorced); one s. two d.; one s. by Bridget Rooney; m. 2nd Christine Baumgartner 2004; one s.; ed California State Univ., Fullerton; directing debut in Dances with Wolves 1990 (Acad. Award for Best Picture 1991); mem. band, Modern West; f. Tatanka Interpretive Center, Deadwood, SDak; Founder/Partner, TIG Productions/Treehouse Films. *Films include:* Malibu Hot Summer 1981, Chasing Dreams 1982, Night Shift 1982, Table for Five 1983, Stacy's Knights 1983, The Big Chill 1983, Testament 1983, Fandango 1985, Silverado 1985, American Flyers 1985, Shadows Run Black 1986, The Untouchables 1987, No Way Out 1987, Bull Durham 1988, Field of Dreams 1989, The Gunrunner 1989, Revenge (also exec. producer) 1989, Dances with Wolves (also dir and producer) (Golden Globe Award for Best Motion Picture and Best Dir 1991, Acad. Award for Best Picture, Best Dir 1991, BAFTA Award for Best Actor and Best Dir, Outstanding Single Achievement, Berlin Int. Film Festival 1991, Best Foreign Film, Japanese Acad. 1991, Outstanding Directorial Achievement in Motion Pictures, Dirs Guild of America 1991, Best Film and Best Dir, Nat. Board of Review 1991, numerous other awards) 1990, Robin Hood: Prince of Thieves 1991, JFK 1991, The Bodyguard (also producer) 1992, A Perfect World 1993, Wyatt Earp (also producer) 1994, The War 1994, Waterworld (also producer) 1995, Tin Cup 1996, The Postman (also producer) 1997, Message in a Bottle (also producer) 1998, For Love of the Game 1999, Play It to the Bone 1999, Thirteen Days (also producer) 2000, 3000 Miles to Graceland 2001, The Road to Graceland (short) 2001, Dragonfly 2002, Open Range (also producer) 2003, The Upside of Anger 2005, Rumor Has It... 2005, The Guardian 2006, Mr. Brooks (also producer) 2007, Swing Vote 2008, The New Daughter 2009, The Company Men 2010, Man of Steel 2013, Jack Ryan: Shadow Recruit 2014, 3 Days to Kill 2014, Draft Day 2014, Black or White (also producer) 2014, McFarland USA 2015, Criminal 2016, Hidden Figures 2016, Molly's Game 2017, The Highwaymen 2019, The Art of Racing in the Rain 2019; co-producer Rapa Nui, China Moon 1993, exec. producer Rapa Nui 1994. *Television includes:* Amazing Stories (series) 1985, Hatfields & McCoys (mini-series) (Emmy Award for Best Lead Actor in a Miniseries or Movie 2012, Golden Globe Award for Best Performance by an Actor in a Mini-Series or Motion Picture Made for Television 2013) 2012, Yellowstone (series) 2018–. *Recording:* album: with Modern West: Untold Truths 2008. *Publication:* The Explorer's Guild: Volume One (with Jon Baird) 2014. *Leisure interest:* golf. *Address:* William Morris Endeavor Entertainment, LLC, 9601 Wilshire Blvd, Beverly Hills, CA 90210, USA (office); TIG Productions, 4450 Lakeside Drive, Burbank, CA 91505, USA. *Telephone:* (818) 260-8707. *Website:* www.kevincostner.com; kevincostnermodernwest.com.

COSTOLO, Richard (Dick) W., BS; American internet business executive; b. 10 Sept. 1963; m. Lorin Costolo; ed Univ. of Michigan; served eight years as Sr Man., Andersen Consulting; Co-founder Burning Door Networked Media; Co-founder and CEO SpyOnIt.com (internet monitoring co.); Co-founder and CEO FeedBurner (internet man. co.) 2004–07; Group Product Man., Google, Inc. 2007–09; Chief Operating Officer, Twitter, Inc. 2009–10, CEO 2010–15; fmr Sr Man., Eagle Advanced Tech. Group; mem. Nat. Security Telecommunications Advisory Cttee 2011. *Address:* c/o Twitter, Inc., 1355 Market Street, Suite 900, San Francisco, CA 94103, USA.

COT, Jean-Pierre, Docteur en droit; French politician, international organization official and academic; *Judge, International Tribunal for the Law of the Sea;* b. 23 Oct. 1937, Geneva, Switzerland; s. of Pierre Cot and Luisa Phelps; m.; three c.; ed Faculté de Droit, Paris; Prof., then Dean, Faculty of Law, Amiens 1968; Prof. of Int. Law and Political Sociology, Univ. of Paris I (Panthéon-Sorbonne) 1969, Dir Disarmament Research and Study Centre (CEREDE); mem. Steering Cttee, Parti Socialiste (PS) 1970, 1973, mem. Exec. Bureau 1976; Mayor of Coise-Saint-Jean-Pied-Gauthier 1971–95; Deputy (Savoie) to Nat. Ass. 1973–81; Gen. Councillor, Savoie 1973–81; PS Nat. Del. for matters relating to the EC 1976–79; mem. European Parl. 1978–79, 1984–99, Pres. Budget Cttee 1984–87, Chair. Socialist

Group 1989–94, Vice-Pres. 1997–99; Judge, Int. Tribunal for the Law of the Sea 2002–, Pres. Chamber for Marine Environment Disputes 2008–11; Minister-Del. for Co-operation, attached to Minister for External Relations 1981–82; mem. Exec. Council UNESCO 1983–84, Soc. française pour le droit int. (Pres. 2004–12); Chevalier de la Légion d'honneur. *Publications:* La conciliation internationale 1968, A l'épreuve du pouvoir: le tiers-mondisme, pour quoi faire? 1984, La Charte des Nations Unies, commentaire article par article (co-author, third edn) 2005; numerous articles on int. law and political science. *Address:* Coise-Saint-Jean-Pied-Gauthier, 73800 Montmélian, France (home); International Tribunal for the Law of the Sea, Am Internationalen Seegerichtshof 1, 22609 Hamburg, Germany (office). *Telephone:* (40) 35607-0 (office). *E-mail:* cot@itlos.org (office). *Website:* www.itlos.org/index.php?id=83 (office).

COTE, David M., BBA; American business executive; ed Univ. of New Hampshire; various man. positions with General Electric –1996, Corp. Sr Vice-Pres., Pres. and CEO General Electric Appliances 1996–99; Pres., CEO and Chair. TRW, Cleveland 1999–2002; Pres. and CEO Honeywell International Inc. Feb.–July 2002, Chair. and CEO July 2002–17; mem. Bd of Dirs JP Morgan Chase, Federal Reserve Bank of New York 2014–18; adviser to Kohlberg Kravis Roberts & Co.; mem. Nat. Security Telecommunications Advisory Cttee; one of 10 US CEOs invited to serve on US-India CEO Forum est. by Pres. George W. Bush and Indian Prime Minister Manmohan Singh 2005, Co-Chair. 2009; named by Pres. Barack Obama to serve on bipartisan Nat. Comm. on Fiscal Responsibility and Reform 2010; Vice-Chair. Business Roundtable 2011, Chair. Energy and Environment Cttee; one of several CEOs from major global corpns to join USAID Admin. Henrietta Fore on her public pvt. partnership earthquake relief mission to Sichuan Prov., China following the earthquake May 2008; Hon. Prof., Beihang Univ. Aeronautics and Astronautics, Beijing 2009; Hon. LLD (Graziadio School of Business and Man., Pepperdine Univ.) 2001, Hon. DHumLitt (Univ. of New Hampshire) 2011; Corporate Social Responsibility Award, Foreign Policy Asscn 2007, Peter G. Peterson Award for Business Statesmanship, Cttee for Econ. Devt 2011, 2012, Distinguished Achievement Award, B'nai B'rith International 2011, Global Leadership Award, Asia Soc. 2012, named CEO of the Year by Chief Executive magazine 2013, recognized as one of the World's Best CEOs by Barron's magazine 2013.

COTILLARD, Marion; French actress and singer; b. 30 Sept. 1975, Paris; d. of Jean-Claude Cotillard (actor, playwright and dir) and Niseema Theillaud (actress and drama teacher); partner Guillaume Canet 2007; one s.; ed Conservatoire d'Art Dramatique, Orléans; raised in Orléans; made acting debut as child with role in one of her father's plays; cinema debut with film L'Histoire du garçon qui voulait qu'on l'embrasse 1994; second actress (with Sophia Loren) to win Academy Award for Best Actress performing in a language other than English; Chevalier des Arts et des Letters 2010, Chevalier, Legion d'Honneur 2016. *Films include:* L'Histoire du garçon qui voulait qu'on l'embrasse 1994, Snuff Movie 1995, Comment je me suis disputé… (ma vie sexuelle) (aka My Sex Life… or How I Got Into an Argument, USA) 1996, La belle verte 1996, Taxi 1998, La guerre dans le Haut Pays (aka War in the Highlands) 1999, L'Appel de la cave 1999, Du bleu jusqu'en Amérique (aka Blue Away to America) 1999, Quelques jours de trop 2000, Le Marquis 2000, Taxi 2 2000, Heureuse 2001, Boomer 2001, Lisa 2001, Les jolies choses (aka Pretty Things) 2001, Une affaire privée (aka A Private Affair) 2002, Taxi 3 2003, Jeux d'enfants (aka Love Me If You Dare) 2003, Big Fish 2003, Innocence 2004, Un long dimanche de fiançaille (aka A Very Long Engagement) (César Award for Best Supporting Actress) 2004, Edy 2005, Cavalcade 2005, Ma vie en l'air 2005, Mary 2005, Sauf le respect que je vous dois 2005, La boîte noire 2005, Toi et moi 2006, Fair Play 2006, A Good Year 2006, played and sang role of Édith Piaf in La Môme (retitled 'La Vie en Rose' in USA) (Academy Award for Best Actress 2008, César Award for Best Actress 2008, BAFTA Award for Best Actress in a Leading Role 2008, Golden Globe Award 2008, Czech Lion Award for Best Actress 2008, Los Angeles Film Critics' Asscn Award 2008, London Critics' Circle Film Award 2008, Boston Soc. of Film Critics Award 2008, Palm Springs Int. Film Festival Award 2008, Cabourg Romantic Film Festival Award 2008) 2007, Public Enemies 2009, Le Dernier Vol 2009, Nine 2009, Forehead Tittaes (video short) 2010, Lady Blue Shanghai (short) 2010, Inception 2010, Little White Lies 2010, Lady Grey London (short) 2011, Midnight in Paris 2011, Contagion 2011, L.A.dy Dior (short) 2011, Rust & Bone 2012, The Dark Knight Rises 2012, David Bowie: The Next Day (video short) 2013, Blood Ties 2013, The Immigrant 2013, Anchorman 2: The Legend Continues 2013, Two Days, One Night 2014 (New York Film Critics Circle Award for Best Actress 2015), Macbeth 2015, The Little Prince (voice) 2015, From the Land of the Moon 2016, It's Only the End of the World 2016, Allied 2016, Assassin's Creed 2017. *Television includes:* Extrême limite (series) 1994, Chloé 1996, Interdit de vieillir 1998, Les redoutables (series) 2001, Une femme piégée 2001, Vertiges (series) 2001, Jeanne d'Arc au bûcher (film) 2012, Le débarquement (series) 2013, Nature Is Speaking (series) 2015. *Address:* c/o Creative Artists Agency, 4th Floor, Space One, 1 Beadon Road, London, W6 0EA, England (office). *E-mail:* info@cotillard.net. *Website:* www .cotillard.net.

COTLER, Irwin, OC; Canadian lawyer, politician and professor of law; b. 8 May 1940, Montreal; Prof. Emer. of Law, McGill Univ., Dir Human Rights Programme, Chair. InterAmicus Int. Human Rights Advocacy Centre (on leave); fmr Visiting Prof., Harvard Law School; fmr Woodrow Wilson Fellow, Yale Law School; MP for Mount Royal 1999–, mem. Standing Cttee on Foreign Affairs, Sub-cttee on Human Rights and Int. Devt, Cttee on Justice and Human Rights, Liberal Party of Canada's Critic for Rights and Freedoms and Int. Justice; Special Advisor to Minister of Foreign Affairs on Int. Criminal Court 2000–03; Minister of Justice and Attorney-Gen. 2003–06; Chair. Int. Comm. of Inquiry into the Fate and Whereabouts of Raoul Wallenberg, Comm. on Econ. Coercion and Discrimination; 11 hon. doctorates; numerous awards, including President's Award, Canadian Bar Asscn, Centennial Medal, Int. Raoul Wallenberg Foundation, Canadian Parliamentarian of the Year 2014. *Address:* House of Commons, Justice Building, Ottawa, ON K1A 0A6, Canada (office). *Telephone:* (613) 995-0121 (office). *Fax:* (613) 992-6762 (office). *E-mail:* irwin.cotler@parl.gc.ca (office); irwin.cotler.c1@parl.gc.ca (office). *Website:* irwincotler.liberal.ca (office); www.irwincotler.ca.

COTTA, Elena; Italian actress; b. 19 Aug. 1931, Milan; m. Carlo Alighiero; two c.; ed Accad. Nazionale di Arte Drammatica Silvio D'Amico; mem. La compagnia dei giovani stage co.; film debut in Miracolo a Viggiù 1951; co-f. (with husband) own production co. 1975. *Films include:* Miracolo a Viggiù 1951, La leggenda del piave (as Elena Cotta Ramusino) 1952, Arriva la banda 1959, Le tue mani sul mio corpo 1970, La guerra è finita (short) 1997, Looking for Alibrandi 2000, Sotto il vestito niente – L'ultima sfilata 2011, A Street in Palermo (Via Castellana Bandiera) (Volpi Cup for Best Actress, Venice Film Festival) 2013. *Television includes:* Antigone (film) 1958, La pisana (mini-series) 1960, Con rabbia e con dolore (mini-series) 1972, Lungo il fiume e sull'acqua (mini-series) 1973, La traccia verde (mini-series) 1975–76, Diagnosi (mini-series) 1975.

COTTA, Michèle, LèsL; French journalist; *Vice-President, IDF1;* b. 15 June 1937, Nice; d. of Jacques Cotta and Helène Scoffier; m. 1st Claude Tchou (divorced); one s. (deceased) one d.; m. 2nd Phillipe Barret 1992; ed Lycée de Nice, Faculté de Lettres de Nice and Inst. d'études politiques de Paris; journalist with L'Express 1963–69, 1971–76, with Europ I 1970–71, 1986; political diarist, France-Inter 1976–80; Head of political service, Le Point 1977–80, Reporter 1986; Chief Political Ed. RTL 1980–81; Pres. Dir-Gen. Radio France 1981–82; Pres. Haute Autorité de la Communication Audiovisuelle 1982–86; Producer, Faits de Soc. on TF1 1987, Dir of Information 1987–92, Pres. Sofica Images Investissements 1987; producer and presenter, La Revue de presse, France 2 1993–95; political ed., Nouvel Economiste 1993–96; producer and presenter, Polémiques, France 2 1995–99, Dir-Gen. France 2 1999–2002 (retd); editorial writer, RTL 1996–99; apptd Dir-Gen. JLA Groupe 2002; currently Vice-Pres., TV channel IDF1; mem. Conseil économique et social; Officier, Légion d'honneur, Officier, Ordre nat. du mérite. *Publications include:* La collaboration 1940–1944, 1964, Les elections présidentielles 1966, Prague, l'été des Tanks 1968, La Vième République 1974, Les miroirs de Jupiter 1986, La Sixième République 1992, Les Secrets d'une Victoire 1999, Politic Circus 2004, Cahiers secrets de la Ve République (Vol. 1) 1965–1977 2007, Cahiers secrets de la Ve République (Vol. 2) 1977–1986 2008, Cahiers secrets de la Ve République (Vol. 3) 1986–1997 2009, Cahiers secrets de la Ve République (Vol. 4) 1997–2007 2010, Le rose et le gris 2013. *Address:* IDF1, 7 rue des Bretons, 93210 Saint-Denis la Plaine, France (office). *Telephone:* (1) 49-17-27-27 (office). *E-mail:* michele.cotta@groupe-jla.com (office). *Website:* www.idf1.fr (office).

COTTE, Bruno; French judge; b. 10 June 1945, Lyon; s. of André Cotte and Hélène Perol; m. Catherine Mathieu; three d.; ed Univ. of Lyon, Ecole Nationale de la Magistrature, Bordeaux; studies in Paris; Teaching Asst in Criminology, Faculty of Law, Univ. of Paris II 1970; Magistrate in Ministry of Justice and Head, Office of Dir of Criminal Affairs and Pardons 1970–73; Deputy Public Prosecutor, Tribunal de Grande Instance de Lyon (Lyon Dist Court) 1973–75; Head of Prosecution Bureau, Directorate of Criminal Affairs and Pardons, Ministry of Justice with competence in econ., financial and social criminal matters 1975–80; Lecturer, French Nat. School for Judiciary, Bordeaux 1975–80; Special Asst to First Pres. of Supreme Court of Appeal (judicial competence of First Pres.) 1980–81; Special Asst to Attorney-Gen., Paris Court of Appeal, serving as Sec.-Gen. of Public Prosecutor's Dept 1981–84; Deputy Dir of Criminal Justice, Directorate of Criminal Affairs and Pardons, Ministry of Justice 1983–84, Dir for Criminal Affairs and Pardons 1984–90; Attorney-Gen. to Versailles Court of Appeal May–Sept. 1990; Public Prosecutor in Tribunal de Grande Instance de Paris (Paris Dist Court) 1990–95; Counsel for Prosecution to Supreme Court of Appeal (Criminal Chamber) 1995–2000; Lecturer in Criminal Procedure to mems of Prefectural Police, Ministry of the Interior 1995–2000; Pres. of jury that confers rank of judicial police officers to student inspectors of Nat. Police Force, Ministry of the Interior 1996–2000; Pres. Criminal Chamber of Supreme Court of Appeal 2000–08; Lecturer in Criminal Procedure, Nat. School for the Judiciary, Paris 2000–07; Acting First Pres. Cour de Cassation (Supreme Court of Appeal) March–May 2007; Judge, Int. Criminal Court, The Hague 2008–14; mem. Paris Aide aux Victimes, amongst others; Chevalier du Mérite agricole 1979, Commdr, Ordre nat. du Mérite 2001, Commdr, Légion d'honneur 2005; Penitentiary Medal. *E-mail:* bruno.cotte@live.fr; cbcotte@gmail.com.

COTTI, Flavio; Swiss politician; b. 18 Oct. 1939, Prato Sornico, Tessin; m. Renata Naretto; one d.; ed Univ. of Freiburg; barrister and public notary in Locarno 1965–75; mem. Locarno Communal Council 1964–75; mem. of cantonal Parl. of Ticino 1967–75; mem. of Govt, canton of Ticino, Head of Dept of Home Affairs, Econ. Affairs, Justice and Mil. Matters 1975–83; mem. Nat. Council 1983–86; mem. Fed. Council 1987–99; Head of Fed. Dept of Home Affairs 1987–93, Dept of Foreign Affairs 1994–99, Pres. of Swiss Confed. 1991 and 1998, Vice-Pres. 1990, 1997; Pres. Bd of Dirs Ticino Cantonal Tourist Office 1976–84; Pres. Christian Democratic People's Party (CDPP) of Ticino 1981, CDPP of Switzerland 1984; Chair. OSCE 1996; Chair. Int. Advisory Bd Credit Suisse Group –2007; mem. Bd of Dirs, Fiat SpA 2000–05, Jakobs Foundation (and Trustee) 1999–2010, Georg Fischer Ltd 2000–10, Intier Automotive Inc. 2002–04; mem. Foundation Bd, World Econ. Forum 1999–2010; Fischhof Prize 1999. *Address:* c/o Christlichdemokratische Volkspartei der Schweiz—Parti démocrate-chrétien suisse (Christian Democratic People's Party), Klaraweg 6, Postfach 5835, 3001 Bern, Switzerland. *Website:* www.admin.ch/gov/en/start/federal-council/members-of-the-federal -council/flavio-cotti.html.

COTTINGHAM, Robert; American artist; b. 26 Sept. 1935, Brooklyn, New York; s. of James Cottingham and Aurelia Cottingham; m. Jane Weismann 1967; three d.; ed Brooklyn Tech. High School, Pratt Inst.; served in US army 1955–58; Art Dir with Young and Rubicam Advertising Inc., New York 1959–64, Los Angeles 1964–68; left advertising to paint 1968–; taught at Art Centre Coll. of Design, Los Angeles 1969–70; moved to London 1972–76; returned to USA 1976; Nat. Endowment for the Arts 1974–75; numerous solo exhbns; works in many public galleries in USA and also in Hamburg Museum, Tate Gallery, London and Utrecht Museum; MacDowell Colony Residencies 1993, 1994; Walter Gropius Fellowship, Huntington Museum of Art 1992; mem. Nat. Acad. of Design. *Publications:* numerous print publs (lithographs, etchings). *Leisure interests:* travel, music, history. *Address:* PO Box 604, Blackman Road, Newtown, CT 06470; c/o Forum Gallery, 730 5th Avenue, Suite 201, New York, NY 10019, USA.

COTTON, Thomas (Tom) Bryant, BA, JD; American lawyer, politician and fmr army officer; *Senator from Arkansas;* b. 13 May 1977, Russellville, Ark.; s. of Thomas Leonard and Avis (Bryant) Cotton; m. Anna Peckham 2014; ed Harvard Coll., Harvard Law School; Law clerk to Hon. Jerry Edwin Smith, US Court of Appeals (Fifth Circuit) 2002–03; Assoc., Gibson Dunn & Crutcher LLP (law firm)

2003–05; served in Iraq and Afghanistan with 101st Airborne Div., US Army 2005–09; Man. Consultant, McKinsey & Co. 2010–11; mem. US House of Reps from 4th Ark. Dist, Washington, DC 2013–15, mem. House Foreign Services Cttee, House Financial Services Cttee 2013; Senator from Arkansas 2015–; Republican; Army Commendation Medal, Combat Infantryman Badge, Iraq Campaign Medal, Bronze Star Medal. *Address:* B-33 Russell Senate Office Building, Washington, DC 20510, USA (office). *Telephone:* (202) 224-2353 (office). *Website:* www.cotton.senate .gov (office).

COUCEIRO PIZARRO BELEZA, Luís Miguel, PhD; Portuguese economist and banker; b. 28 April 1950, Porto; s. of José Júlio Pizaro Beleza and Maria dos Prazeres Couceiro da Costa Pizarro Beleza; m.; two c.; ed Massachusetts Inst. of Tech., USA; fmr Asst Prof., then Assoc. Prof., Faculty of Econs, Univ. Nova de Lisboa; econ. adviser and consultant Bank of Portugal 1979–87, mem. Bd 1987–90, Gov. 1992–94, mem. Advisory Bd 1994–; adviser, IMF 1984–87; Minister of Finance 1990–91; fmr adviser, Banco Comercial Português; fmr Visiting Prof., Brown Univ., Univ. dos Açores, INSEAD, Fontainebleau; Dir Banco Expresso Atlântico Lisbon, Siemens Portugal; consultant and Ed. Economia journal (Univ. Católica Portuguesa); Grand Cross, Nat. Order, Cross of the South (Brazil), Grand Cross, Order of Merit. *Publications:* numerous articles in journals. *Address:* c/o Advisory Board, Banco de Portugal, R. Francisco Ribeiro 2, 1150-165 Lisbon, Portugal (office). *Telephone:* (21) 3213200 (office). *Fax:* (21) 3128115 (office). *E-mail:* info@bportugal.pt (office). *Website:* www.bportugal.pt (office).

COUCHEPIN, François; Swiss lawyer; b. 19 Jan. 1935, Martigny; s. of Louis Couchepin and Andrée Couchepin; m. Anne Marie Cottier 1957; six c.; ed Univ. of Lausanne; legal practitioner at Rodolphe Tissières 1959–64; own legal practice in Martigny 1964–; elected to Cantonal Council of Canton Valais 1965, re-elected 1969, 1973, 1977; Sec. Radical Group 1965–77, Pres. 1977–79; Head of French Section, Cen. Language Service, Fed. Chancellery 1980; Vice-Chancellor responsible for gen. admin. of Fed. Chancellery 1981; Chancellor of the Swiss Fed. 1991–99; mem. Defence Staff. *Address:* c/o Federal Chancellery, Bundeshaus-West, 3003 Berne; Avenue Ruchonnet 41, 1003 Lausanne, Switzerland (home).

COUCHEPIN, Pascal; Swiss politician and fmr head of state; b. 5 April 1942, Martigny; m.; three c.; ed Lausanne Univ.; elected mem. local council Martigny 1968; Deputy Mayor of Martigny 1976, Mayor 1984–98; elected to the Nat. Council 1979; Chair. Parl. Group, Liberal Democrat Party (LDP) 1989–96; fmr Chair. Nat. Council's Cttee for Science and Research; fmr Chair. Fed. Dept of Justice and Police section of the Control Cttee; elected to Fed. Council 1998 (resgnd 2009); Vice-Pres. of the Swiss Confed. 2002, 2007, Pres. of the Swiss Confed. 2003, 2008; Head of Fed. Dept of Econ. Affairs 1998–2002, of Home Affairs 2003–09 (resgnd); fmr Gov. IBRD, EBRD; mem. Global Leadership Foundation; Officier de la Légion d'honneur 2011; Dr hc (Kaslik, Lebanon 2008). *Address:* Av. du Grand St-Bernard 35, 1920 Martigny, Switzerland (office).

COUCHER, Iain, BSc, MBA; British transport industry executive; *Managing Director, Alvarez & Marsal;* b. 22 Aug. 1961, St Albans, Herts.; s. of Brian Coucher; m. 2nd Tanya Nightingale 1993; one s. one d.; ed Ashville Coll., Harrogate, North Yorks., Imperial Coll., London and Henley Man. Coll. (now Henley Business School and part of Univ. of Reading); air-to-ground missile designer, Huntingloc Engineering 1982–85; worked for EDS (US consultancy group) 1985–99, positions included Head of Mergers and Acquisitions; formed transport consultancy with Victoria Pender, Coucher Pender Ltd 1999; CEO TubeLines 1999–2002, seconded as CEO to TranSys consortium 1996–98; Man. Dir Network Rail 2002, Deputy CEO 2002–07, CEO 2007–10; Interim Chief Exec. LBC Tank Terminals 2010–12; Man. Dir Alvarez & Marsal 2012–. *Leisure interests:* cycling, birdwatching. *Address:* Alvarez & Marsal, One Finsbury Circus, London, EC2M 7EB, England (office). *Telephone:* (20) 7715-5200 (office). *Fax:* (20) 7715-5201 (office). *E-mail:* icoucher@alvarezandmarsal.com (office). *Website:* www.alvarezandmarsal.co.uk/ iain-coucher (office).

COUGHLAN, Mary, B.Soc.Sc; Irish politician; b. 1965, Co. Donegal; d. of Cathal Coughlan; m. David Charlton (died 2012); one s. one d.; ed Ursuline Convent, Sligo, Univ. Coll., Dublin; early career in social work; mem. Co. Donegal Co. Council 1986–2001; mem. North Western Health Bd 1987–2001; mem. Fianna Fáil; mem. Dáil (TD) for Donegal SW 1987–2011; Chair. Oireachtas Jt Cttee on Irish Language 1993–95; Minister of State, Dept of Arts, Heritage, Gaeltacht and the Islands 2000–02, Minister for Social, Community and Family Affairs 2002–04, Minister for Agric. and Food 2004–08, Tánaiste (Deputy Prime Minister) 2008–11, Minister for Enterprise, Trade and Employment 2008–10, Minister for Educ. and Skills 2010–11, also for Health and Children 2011; mem. Co. Donegal Vocational Educ. Cttee 1986–99 (Chair. 1991–92); Chair. Bd of Man. Abbey Vocational School, Donegal Town; mem. Bd of Man. Tourism Coll., Killybegs; fmr mem. Comhchoiste na Gaeilge (Chair. 1993–94); Pres. Killybegs Coast and Cliff Rescue Service; Hon. Sec. Fianna Fáil Party 1995. *Address:* c/o Department of Education and Skills, Marlborough Street, Dublin 1, Ireland (office). *Telephone:* (1) 8896400 (office). *Fax:* (1) 8892367 (office). *Website:* www.education.ie (home).

COUGHLIN, Cathy M., BA, MS; American telecommunications industry executive; *Senior Executive Vice-President and Global Marketing Officer, AT&T Inc.;* b. St Louis, Mo.; ed Northwestern Univ., St Louis Univ.; began communications career at Southwestern Bell Telephone Co., St Louis 1979; has held sr man. roles in sales, marketing, operations and advertising; Pres. and CEO AT&T Midwest –2007, Sr Exec. Vice-Pres. and Global Marketing Officer, AT&T Inc. 2007–; mem. Bd of Dirs Northwestern Univ., Girl Scouts of the USA; mem. Bd of Trustees, American Film Inst. *Address:* AT&T Inc., 175 East Houston, San Antonio, TX 78205-2233, USA (office). *Telephone:* (210) 821-4105 (office). *Fax:* (210) 351-2071 (office). *E-mail:* info@att.com (office). *Website:* www.att.com (office).

COUILLARD, Philippe, MD, PC, MNA; Canadian neurosurgeon and politician; b. 26 June 1957, Montréal; s. of Joseph Alfred Jean Pierre Couillard de Lespinay and Hélène Yvonne Pardé; ed Univ. de Montréal, Coll. des médecins du Québec, Royal Coll. of Physicians and Surgeons of Canada; Chief Surgeon, Dept of Neurosurgery, Hôpital Saint-Luc 1989–92; Co-founder and Neurosurgeon, Dhahran Dept of Neurosurgery, Saudi Arabia 1992–96; Prof., Faculty of Medicine, Univ. de Sherbrooke 1996–2003, Chief Surgeon and Dir, Dept of Surgery, Centre Hospitalier Universitaire de Sherbrooke 2000–03; Dir of Research in Health Law, McGill Univ. 2009, Prof. 2009–11; mem. Nat. Ass. of Québec (Prov. Parl.) for Mount Royal 2003–07, for Jean-Talon 2007–08, for Outremont 2013–14, for Roberval 2014–18; Minister of Health and Social Services, Quebec 2003–08; Premier of Quebec 2014–18, also Minister responsible for Saguenay–Lac-Saint-Jean region 2014–18; Leader, Québec Liberal Party 2013–18; Canadian Rep. on Bd of Dirs, Société de Neurochirurgie de Langue Française 1999–2003; mem. James IV Asscn of Surgery 2002–; Pnr, PCP (Persistence Capital Partners) Investment Fund; Chair. Canadian Health Services Research Foundation, Quebec Network for Personalized Healthcare; Strategic Adviser in Healthcare and Life Sciences, Secor (global asset man. firm) 2011; mem. Int. Advisory Bd, Saudi Arabian Ministry of Health; mem. Security Intelligence Review Cttee; Dir Amorfix Life Sciences, Thallion Pharmaceuticals; mem. Bd, Royal Coll. of Physicians and Surgeons of Canada, mem. Public Affairs and Policy Research Cttee 2000–03; mem. Queen's Privy Council for Canada (QPC) 2010; Culture and Society Prize, Univ. de Montréal Medicine 2006, Jacques Cartier Medal 2007. *Address:* c/o Office of the Premier, Edif. Honoré-Mercier, 3e étage, 835 blvd René-Lévesque est, Québec, PQ G1A 1B4, Canada (office).

COULIBALY, Amadou Gon; Côte d'Ivoirian engineer and politician; *Prime Minister;* b. 19 Feb. 1959; m.; five c.; ed Ecole des Travaux Publics, Paris, Centre des Hautes Etudes de la Construction, Paris; Technical adviser on investment and public enterprise to Prime Minister 1990–93; Deputy Dir-Gen., Direction et Contrôle des Grands Travaux 1994–95; Dir Int. Cabinet, Conseil d'Etudes et de Formation 1996–2000; Mayor of Korhogo 2001; mem. Nat. Ass. (parl.) 1995–99, 2011–; Minister of Agric. 2000–03; Minister of State, Ministry of Agric. (in govt of nat. reconciliation) 2003–05; Sec.-Gen. to the Presidency 2011–12; Minister of State, Sec.-Gen. to the Presidency 2012–17; Prime Minister 2017–; mem. Rassemblement des Républicains (RDR), mem. Cen. Cttee 1995–, Deputy Sec.-Gen. 2006; Grand officier, ordre nat. du Mérite ivoirien. *Address:* Office of the Prime Minister, blvd Angoulvant, 01 BP 1533, Abidjan 01, Côte d'Ivoire (office). *Telephone:* 20-31-50-00 (office). *Fax:* 20-22-18-33 (office). *Website:* www .premierministre.ci (office).

COULIBALY, Tiéman Hubert, DESS; Malian business executive and politician; b. 1967, Bamako; ed Univ. Saint-Étienne, France; fmr Dir-Gen. Radio Klédu Agence nationale de communication; Sec.-Gen. Forum Afrique unie 1991–94; Operations Man., Société malienne de services (hygiène et assainissement) 1994–96; worked for Mali Panafcom (first pvt. man. consultancy in West and Central Africa); f. Stellis Communication (consultancy and advertising agency) 2006; Minister of Foreign Affairs and Int. Cooperation 2012, Minister of State Property, Land Affairs and Heritage 2014–15, of Defence 2015–16, of Territorial Administration May–Dec. 2017, of Foreign Affairs and Int. Co-operation 2017–18; fmr Dir of Cements and Materials, Vicat Group, Mali, also Gen. Man. subsidiary co. Kulubali Industries (mining, quarrying, services); fmr Vice-Pres. Nat. Council of Employers of Mali; mem. Union pour la démocratie et le développement, Sec.-Gen. 2010–. *Address:* c/o Ministry of Foreign Affairs, African Integration and International Co-operation, Koulouba, Bamako, Mali (office).

COULIBALY, Tiéna, BS, MS; Malian economist and politician; b. 1952, Boré, Douentza Dist; m.; four c.; ed Laval Univ., Canada, Purdue Univ., USA; Technical Adviser, Ministry of Livestock 1981–87; Asst Dir-Gen., Libyan-Malian Livestock Devt Co. 1987–88; Minister of Finance and Trade 1988–91; arrested and charged following revolution 1991, later acquitted; Technical Adviser, Mission de restructuration du secteur coton (cotton restructuring body) 2001; CEO Compagnie malienne de développement des textiles (state cotton co.) 2008–12; Minister of the Economy, Finance and the Budget 2012–13, of Commerce and Industry 2013, of Defence and War Veterans 2017–18. *Address:* c/o Ministry of Defence and War Veterans, route de Koulouba, BP 2083, Bamako, Mali (office).

COUMAKOYE, Nouradine Delwa Kassiré, DenD; Chadian politician; *President, VIVA—Rassemblement National pour la Démocratie et le Progrès (VIVA—RNDP);* b. 31 Dec. 1949, Bongor; ed École Nat. d'Admin, Chad, Inst. Int. d'Admin Publique, Paris, Univ. de Paris I and II; Minister of Justice 1981–82, of Public Works, Housing and Town Planning 1987–88, of Justice 1988–89, of Posts and Telecommunications 1989–90, of Higher Educ. and Scientific Research 1989–90, of Communications and Liberties, of Justice June–Nov. 1993; Govt Spokesperson April–June 1993; Gen. Inspector of Admin 1987–; Prime Minister of Chad 1993–95, 2007–08; Pres. Econ., Social and Cultural Council 2008–; mem. and Pres. VIVA—Rassemblement Nat. pour la Démocratie et le Progrès (VIVA—RNDP) 1992–; also Leader, Convention de l'opposition démocratique (alliance of opposition parties); sentenced to three months' imprisonment for possessing illegal weapons 1996; Chevalier, Ordre de Mérite Centrafricain 1976; Commdr, Ordre nat. du Tchad 1994. *Achievements include:* Cen. African champion in 3,000m steeple chase 1965 (record unbroken). *Address:* VIVA—Rassemblement National pour la Démocratie et le Progrès (VIVA—RNDP), N'Djamena, Chad (office).

COUPE, Michael (Mike) Andrew, BA; British retail executive; *CEO, J Sainsbury plc;* b. 1960; m.; two d.; ed The Weald School, Billingshurst, Univ. of Birmingham; held various sr man. positions for both ASDA and Tesco; Bd Dir, Big Food Group plc and Man. Dir Iceland Food Stores –2004; Trading Dir, J Sainsbury plc 2004–07, mem. Operating Bd and Exec. Dir 2007–, Group Commercial Dir responsible for Trading, Marketing, IT and Online 2010–14, CEO J Sainsbury plc 2014–; mem. Bd of Dirs Greene King plc 2011–, Insight 2 Communication 2012–, Inst. of Grocery Distributors, GlobalNetXChange; mem. Supervisory Bd, GS1U 2010–. *Address:* J Sainsbury plc, 33 Holborn, London, EC1N 2HT, England (office). *Telephone:* (20) 7695-6000 (office). *Fax:* (20) 7695-7610 (office). *E-mail:* info@j -sainsbury.co.uk (office). *Website:* www.j-sainsbury.co.uk (office).

COUPLES, Frederick Stephen (Fred); American golfer; b. 3 Oct. 1959, Seattle, Wash.; m. Thais Couples; one s. one d.; ed Univ. of Houston; turned professional 1980; mem. US Ryder Cup Team 1989, 1991, 1993, 1995, 1997, Asst Capt. 2012; mem. President's Cup Team 1994, 1996, 1998, Capt. 2009; won Kemper Open 1984, Tournament Players Championship 1984, Byron Nelson Golf Classic 1987, Nissan Los Angeles Open 1990, Federal Express St Jude Classic BC Open, Johnnie Walker World Championship 1991, Nissan Los Angeles Open, Nestlé Int., Masters 1992, Honda Classic 1993, Buick Open 1994, World Cup 1994, Dubai Desert Classic, Johnnie Walker Classic 1995, The Players' Championship 1996, Bob Hope Chrysler Classic 1998, Memorial Tournament 1998, Shell Houston Open 2003; won maiden sr major at Senior Players Championship 2011; won Senior British

Open Championship 2012; won Chubb Classic PGA Tour Champions 2017, American Family Insurance Championship 2017; mem. Bridgestone Golf Tour Staff 2005–; PGA Tour Player of the Year 1991, 1992, Arnold Palmer Award 1992, inducted into World Golf Hall of Fame 2013. *Leisure interests:* tennis, all sports, antiques, bicycling, vintage cars. *Address:* c/o PGA Tour, 100 Avenue of the Champions, P.O. Box 109601, Palm Beach Gardens, FL 33410, USA. *Website:* www.bridgestonegolf.com/tour/fred-couples.

COURANT, Ernest David, PhD; American (b. German) physicist and academic; *Distinguished Scientist Emeritus, Brookhaven National Laboratory;* b. 26 March 1920, Göttingen, Germany; s. of Richard Courant and Nina Runge; m. Sara Paul 1944; two s.; ed Swarthmore Coll. and Univ. of Rochester, USA; Scientist, Nat. Research Council (Canada), Montreal 1943–46; Research Assoc. in Physics, Cornell Univ. 1946–48; Physicist, Brookhaven Nat. Lab., Upton, NY 1948–60, Sr Physicist 1960–89, Distinguished Scientist Emer. 1990–; Prof. (part-time), Yale Univ. 1961–67, State Univ. of NY, Stony Brook 1967–85; Visiting Prof., Univ. of Mich. 1989–; Hon. Prof., Univ. of Science and Tech. of China, Hefei 1994; mem. NAS 1976; Fellow, AAAS 1981; Hon. DSc (Swarthmore Coll.) 1988; Pregel Prize, New York Acad. of Sciences 1979, Fermi Award 1986, R. R. Wilson Prize 1987. *Achievements include:* co-discoverer of Strong-focusing principle, particle accelerators. *Publications:* various articles; contrib. to Handbuch der Physik 1959, Annual Review of Nuclear Science 1968. *Address:* 40 West 72nd Street, New York, NY 10023, USA (home). *Telephone:* (212) 580-1006 (home). *E-mail:* ecourant@msn.com (home).

COURIC, Katherine (Katie); American broadcast journalist; b. 7 Jan. 1957, Arlington, Va; m. 1st Jay Monahan (deceased); two d.; m. 2nd John Molner 2014; ed Univ. of Virginia; began career as desk asst for ABC news bureau, Washington, DC 1979; Assignment Ed., CNN 1980, later Assoc. Producer, Atlanta, later Producer of Take Two; worked at WTVJ, Miami for three years; joined NBC Network News 1989, later Nat. Corresp., The Today Show, Washington, DC, Co-Anchor 1991–2006, Co-host, Now with Tom Brokaw and Katie Couric 1993–94; Contributing Anchor, Dateline NBC 2005; Anchor and Man. Ed. CBS Evening News 2006–11, also contrib. to 60 Minutes and other CBS News specials; host, Katie (syndicated daytime talk show), ABC 2012–13, also special corresp. for ABC News; Global Anchor, Yahoo News 2013–; six Emmy Awards, named Best in the Business by Washington Journalism Review 1993. *Publication:* The Best Advice I Ever Got: Lessons From Extraordinary Lives 2011. *Address:* Yahoo! Inc., 701 First Avenue, Sunnyvale, CA 94089, USA (office). *Website:* news.yahoo.com (office); katiecouric.com.

COURIER, Jim; American business executive and fmr professional tennis player; b. 17 Aug. 1970, Sanford Fla; m. Susanna Lingman 2010; ed Nick Bollettieri Tennis Acad.; coached by José Higueras; winner, French Open 1991, 1992, Indian Wells (doubles) 1991; runner-up, US Open 1991, ATP World Championship 1991; winner, Australian Open 1992–93, Italian Open 1993; runner-up, French Open 1993, Wimbledon 1993; winner of 23 singles titles and six doubles titles and over US $16 million in prize money at retirement in May 2000; now plays Delta Tour of Champions 2004–; Founding Partner, InsideOut Sports & Entertainment, LLC 2004–; Capt. US Davis Cup team 2010–18; f. Raymond James Courier's Kids (inner-city youth tennis program); mem. Bd of Dirs First Serve, Gullikson Foundation; mem. Advisory Bd Falconhead Capital; elected to Int. Tennis Hall of Fame 2005. *Address:* InsideOut Sports & Entertainment LLC, 401 Lafayette, Suite 600, New York, NY 10003, USA (office). *Telephone:* (646) 367-2770 (office). *Fax:* (646) 367-2780 (office). *E-mail:* info@insideoutse.com (office). *Website:* www.insideoutse.com (office).

COURT, Rev. Margaret, AO, MBE; Australian ecclesiastic and fmr tennis player; *Senior Pastor, Victory Life Centre;* b. 16 July 1942, Albury, New South Wales; d. of Lawrence Smith and Maud Smith; m. Barry Court 1967; one s. three d.; ed St Augustines, Wodonga, Vic.; amateur player 1960–67; professional 1968–77; Australian champion 1960, 1961, 1962, 1963, 1964, 1965, 1966, 1969, 1970, 1971, 1973; French champion 1962, 1964, 1969, 1970, 1973; Wimbledon champion 1963, 1965, 1970; US champion 1962, 1965, 1969, 1970, 1973; held more major titles in singles, doubles and mixed doubles than any other player in history; won two Grand Slams, in mixed doubles 1963 and singles 1970; played Federation Cup for Australia 1963, 1964, 1965, 1966, 1968, 1969, 1971; ordained a Pentecostal minister in 1991, f. the Victory Life Centre, Perth 1996, currently Sr Pastor; elected to Int. Tennis Hall of Fame 1979, Australian Tennis Hall of Fame 1993, Australian Sports Medal 2000, Centenary Medal 2001, Show Court One at Melbourne Park renamed Margaret Court Arena 2003, Western Australia Greatest Ever Tennis Player 2005, Western Australia Greatest Ever Female Sports Star 2005, Philippe Chatrier Award 2006, Golden Racket Award, Italian Tennis Fed. 2007. *Publications include:* The Margaret Smith Story 1964, Court on Court 1974, Winning Faith (with Barbara Oldfield) 1993, Winning Words 1999, Our Winning Position 2003. *Address:* Victory Life Centre, PO Box 20, Osborne Park, WA 6917, Australia (office). *Telephone:* (8) 9202-7111 (office). *Fax:* (8) 9201-1299 (office). *E-mail:* court.margaret@victorylifecentre.com.au (office); reid.marylyn@victorylifecentre.com.au (office). *Website:* www.victorylifecentre.com.au (office).

COURT, Richard, AC; Australian fmr politician and diplomatist; *Ambassador to Japan;* b. 27 Sept. 1947, Nedlands, WA; s. of Sir Charles Court and Rita Steffanoni; brother-in-law of Margaret Court; m. Jo Court; ed Univ. of Western Australia; mem. Liberal Party 1982–, Deputy Leader 1987–92, 1992–2001; mem. WA Parl. (Nedlands) 1982–2001, Opposition Spokesperson for Resources and Industrial Devt, Mines and Aboriginal Affairs 1984, Premier Western Australia 1993–2001; Amb. to Japan 2017–. *Address:* Australian Embassy, 2-1-14, Mita, Minato-ku, Tokyo 108-8361, Japan (office). *Telephone:* (3) 5232-4111 (office). *Fax:* (3) 5232-4149 (office). *Website:* www.australia.or.jp (office).

COURTENAY, Sir Thomas (Tom) Daniel, Kt, KBE; British actor; b. 25 Feb. 1937, Hull, East Riding of Yorks.; s. of Thomas Henry Courtenay and Annie Eliza Quest; m. 1st Cheryl Kennedy 1973 (divorced 1982); m. 2nd Isabel Crossley 1988; ed Kingston High School, Hull, Univ. Coll. London, Royal Acad. of Dramatic Art; started acting professionally 1960; Fellow, Univ. Coll. London; Hon. DLitt (Hull); Best Actor Award, Prague Festival 1968, TV Drama Award (for Oswald in Ghosts) 1968, Golden Globe Award for Best Actor 1983, Drama Critics' Award and Evening Standard Award 1980, 1983, BAFTA Award for Best Actor 1999. *Plays include:* Billy Liar 1961–62, The Cherry Orchard 1966, Macbeth 1966, Hamlet 1968, She Stoops to Conquer 1969, Charley's Aunt 1971, Time and Time Again (Variety Club of GB Stage Actor Award) 1972, Table Manners 1974, The Norman Conquests 1974–75, The Fool 1975, The Rivals 1976, Clouds 1978, Crime and Punishment 1978, The Dresser (Drama Critics Award and Evening Standard Award for Best Actor) 1980, 1983, The Misanthrope 1981, Andy Capp 1982, Jumpers 1984, Rookery Nook 1986, The Hypochondriac 1987, Dealing with Clair 1988, The Miser 1992, Moscow Stations, Edinburgh 1993, London 1994, New York 1995, Poison Pen, Manchester 1993, Uncle Vanya, New York 1995, Art, London 1996, King Lear, Manchester 1999, Uncle Vanya, Royal Exchange, Manchester 2001, Pretending To Be Me (one-man show), West Yorkshire Playhouse, Leeds then on tour 2003. *Films include:* The Loneliness of the Long Distance Runner 1962, Private Potter 1962, Billy Liar 1963, King and Country 1964, Operation Crossbow 1965, King Rat 1965, Doctor Zhivago 1965, The Night of the Generals 1967, The Day the Fish Came Out 1967, A Dandy in Aspic 1968, Otley 1969, One Day in the Life of Ivan Denisovich 1970, Catch Me a Spy 1971, The Dresser 1983, The Last Butterfly 1990, Let Him Have It 1991, The Boy from Mercury 1996, Whatever Happened to Harold Smith 1999, Last Orders 2002, Nicholas Nickleby 2002, Flood 2006, The Golden Compass 2007, The End of an Era (short) 2012, Quartet 2012, Gambit 2012, Night Train to Lisbon 2013, 45 Years (Silver Bear for Best Actor, Berlin Int. Film Festival) 2015, The Legend of Barney Thomson 2015, Dad's Army 2016. *Television includes:* She Stoops to Conquer 1971, I Heard the Owl Call My Name 1973, Me and the Girls 1985, Absent Friends 1985, Redemption (film) 1991, The Adventures of Young Indiana Jones: Treasure of the Peacock's Eye 1995, The Old Curiosity Shop (film) 1995, A Rather English Marriage (film) 1998, Ready When You Are Mr. McGill (film) 2003, Little Dorrit (mini-series) 2008, The Royle Family 2008, Unforgotten (BAFTA for Best Supporting Actor 2016) 2015. *Publication:* Dear Tom: Letters from Home (memoir) 2000. *Leisure interests:* playing the flute, watching sport. *E-mail:* giacomo@independenttalent.com (office).

COURVILLE, Isabelle, BEng, BCL; Canadian engineer, lawyer and business executive; *Chairman, Laurentian Bank;* ed École Polytechnique de Montréal, McGill Univ.; has spent most of her career in the telecommunications industry, with Bell Canada, where she held several exec.-level positions, also led the team responsible for managing Stentor's nat. and int. alliances as Vice-Pres., Alliances and Legal Services at Stentor Resource Centre, later Sr Vice-Pres., Supply Chain and Capital Man., later Pres. and CEO Bell Nordiq Group (Télébec-NorthernTel), later Pres., Enterprise, Bell Canada; Pres. Hydro-Québec Distribution and Hydro-Québec TransenErgie 2007–13; mem. Bd Laurentian Bank 2007– (currently Chair.), Canadian Pacific Railway; mem. Bd of Dirs Sainte-Justine Hosp. Foundation; fmr mem. Conseil des gouverneurs associés de l'Université de Montréal; fmr mem. Bd of Dirs Conf. Bd of Canada, Montréal International; mem. Ordre des ingénieurs du Québec, Barreau du Québec, Canadian Bar Assn; twice awarded Canada's Most Powerful Women: Top 100 Award in the Corp. Execs category, Women's Exec. Network (WXN), Prix Hommage, Ordre des ingénieurs du Québec 2010. *Address:* Laurentian Bank, 1981 McGill College Avenue, 20th floor, Montréal, PQ H2Z 1A4, Canada (office). *Telephone:* (514) 284-4500. *E-mail:* ghislaine.boucher@banquelaurentienne.ca (office). *Website:* www.banquelaurentienne.ca (office).

COUSIN, Ertharin, BA, JD; American diplomatist, government official and UN official; *Executive Director, United Nations World Food Programme;* b. 1957, Chicago, Ill.; d. of Anne Cousin; ed Univ. of Illinois, Chicago, Univ. of Georgia School of Law; fmr Asst Attorney-Gen., State of Illinois, Chicago; Deputy Chief of Staff, Democratic Nat. Cttee, Washington, DC 1993–94; White House liaison, US Dept of State 1994–96; Exec. Dir, Pres. Clinton Re-election Campaign Team for Illinois 1997; Vice-Pres. Govt, Community and Political Affairs, Presidential Inaugural Cttee 1997; Vice-Pres. for Govt and Community Affairs, Jewel Food Stores 1997–99; Vice-Pres. of Public Affairs, Albertsons Foods 1999–2001, Sr Vice-Pres. for Public and Govt Affairs 2001–04, also served as Pres. and Chair. of co.'s corp. foundation; Exec. Vice-Pres. and COO Feeding America (fmrly America's Second Harvest) 2004–06; Founder and Pres. The Polk Street Group (nat. public affairs firm), Chicago 2007–09; Commr Bd for Int. Food and Agricultural Devt, USAID 1997–2001; Amb. and Perm. Rep. to UN Agencies for Food and Agric., Rome 2009–12; Exec. Dir UN World Food Programme, Rome 2012–. *Address:* United Nations World Food Programme, Via C.G.Viola 68, Parco dei Medici, 00148 Rome, Italy (office). *Telephone:* (06) 65131 (office). *Fax:* (06) 6590632 (office). *Website:* www.wfp.org (office).

COUSTEAU, Jean-Michel; French explorer, oceanographer, environmentalist activist, educator and film producer; *Founder and President, Ocean Futures Society;* b. 6 May 1938, Toulon; first s. of ocean explorer Jacques-Yves Cousteau and Simone Melchior; one s. one d.; partner Nancy Marr; Exec. Vice-Pres. The Cousteau Soc. for nearly 20 years; Founder and Pres. Ocean Futures Soc., Santa Barbara, Calif. (non-profit marine conservation and educ. org.) 1999, now offices in France, Brazil and Italy; has served as spokesman on water issues at UN World Summit on Sustainable Devt in Johannesburg, at 3rd World Water Forum in Kyoto, at Dialogues on Water for Life and Security in Barcelona; spokesperson for US Pavilion at Expo '98, Lisbon, Portugal 1998; merged Jean-Michel Cousteau Inst. with Free Willy Keiko Foundation to continue research and care for Keiko (captive killer whale) 1999; mem. Bd of Dirs Athens Environmental Foundation for Athens 2004 Olympic Games; launched Sustainable Reefs Program (package of materials including CD-ROM, cartoon book and video on sustainable man. of coral reef systems) 2004; Hon. DHumLitt (Pepperdine Univ.) 1976; DEMA Reaching Out Award 1994, NOGI Award, Acad. of Underwater Arts and Sciences 1995, SeaKeepers Award, Showboats International 1996, John M. Olguin Marine Environment Award, Cabrillo Marine Aquarium 1996, Environmental Hero Award, White House Nat. Oceans Conf. 1998, first Oceana Ocean Hero Award 2003, inducted into Int. Scuba Diving Hall of Fame 2003, Poseidon/Lifetime Achievement Award, Reef Check 2006, Emmy Award, Peabody Award, 7 d'Or, Cable Ace Award. *Achievements include:* first person to represent the Environment in Opening Ceremony of Olympic Games, Salt Lake City 2002. *Films:* has produced more than 75 films, including Jean-Michel Cousteau's Ocean Adventures (three-year series of HD TV specials on PBS and internationally) (exec. producer), Sharks 3D, Return to the Amazon 2008, Dolphins and Whales 3D: Tribes of the Ocean 2008, Call of the Killer Whale (TV film documentary) 2009, Mon père le commandant: Jacques-Yves Cousteau (TV film documentary) 2011, The Secret Ocean 3D 2015; appears in IMAX documentary film Coral Reef Adventure; also appeared in documentary-type special feature on DVD version of Spongebob Squarepants Movie; did similar feature for DVD of Disney/Pixar movie Finding Nemo. *Publications include:* Water Culture (ed. and contributing author), My Father, the Captain 2004, America's Underwater Treasures (co-author) 2006, My Father, The Captain: My Life with Jacques Cousteau 2012. *Address:* Ocean Futures Society, 513 De La Vina Street, Santa Barbara, CA 93101, USA (office). *Telephone:* (805) 899-8899 (office). *E-mail:* contact@oceanfutures.org (office). *Website:* www.oceanfutures.org (office).

COUTO, Mia; Mozambican biologist, writer and journalist; b. (António Emílio Leite Couto), 5 July 1955, Beira; fmr journalist, daily newspaper Notícias de Maputo; fmr Dir Mozambique Information Agency; columnist, Notícias daily newspaper, Tempo magazine; currently works as environmental biologist at Limpopo Transfrontier Park; Nat. Award for Literature, Mozambican Nat. Journalistic Asscn 1991, Best of 1995 Award, Sao Paulo Art Critics Asscn 1996, Prémio Vergílio Ferreira 1999, Latin Union Prize for Literature 2007, Camões Prize for Literature 2013, Neustadt International Prize for Literature 2014. *Publications include:* poetry: Raiz de'Orvalho 1983, Tradutor de Chuvas 2011; stories: Vozes Anoitecidas (trans. as Voices Made Night) 1986, Cada homem e uma raca 1990 (trans. as Every Man is a Race 1994), Cronicando 1991, Estórias abensonhadas 1994, Contos do nascer da terra 1997, Vinte e Zinco 1999, Na berma de nenhuma estrada 2001, O fio das missangas 2004; novels: Terra Sonambula 1992, Under the Frangipani 2001, Um Rio Chamado Tempo, Uma Casa Chamada Terra 2002, Vozes Anoitecidas 2002, Contos do Nascer da Terra 2002, The Last Flight of the Flamingo 2004, O fio das missangas 2002, A chuva pasmada 2004, Pensatempos 2005, O outro pé da Sereia 2006, Venenos de Deus, Remédios do Diabo 2008, Jesusalém 2009, A Confissão da Leoa 2012, Pensativities: Selected Essays 2015, Mulheres de cinzas 2015, A Espada e a Azagaia 2016, O Bebedor de Horizontes 2017; juvenile: Mar me quer 2000, A chuva pasmada 2004; picture books: O gato e o escuro 2001, O beijo da palavrinha 2008; short prose: Pensatempos 2005, E se Obama fosse africano 2009. *Address:* Literarische Agentur Mertin, Taunusstrasse 38, 60329 Frankfurt, Germany (office). *Telephone:* (69) 27108966 (office). *Fax:* (69) 27108967 (office). *E-mail:* info@mertin-litag.de (office). *Website:* www.mertin-litag.de (office); www.miacouto.org.

COUTURE, Pierre-François; French business executive and civil servant; *Senior Advisor, Lysios Public Affairs;* b. 15 May 1946, Grenoble; s. of André Couture and Françoise Couture (née Dubourguez); m. 2nd Jocelyne Kerjouan; one s.; three c. from previous m.; ed Ecole Nat. d'Admin, Inst. d'Etudes Politiques, Paris, Univ. of Paris II; Dir Industry and Energy Dept, Ministry of the Econ. and Finance 1974–78, mem. Oil Co. Audit Programme 1979; Dir of Budgets Ministries of Finance and Justice and Office of the Prime Minister 1978–79; Gen. Sec. Exploration and Production Div., Cie Française des Pétroles 1979–81; Tech. Adviser Ministry of the Budget 1981–83; Tech. Adviser Ministry of Industry 1983–84, Dir of Gas, Electricity and Coal 1983–90; Adviser to Chair. of La Poste 1996; Special Adviser to Industry Sec. in charge of Postal Services and Telecommunications, Ministry of the Economy, Finance and Industry 1997–99; Chair. Enterprise Minière et Chimique (EMC) 1999–2004; Head of Econ. and Financial Audit Programme, Ministry of Economy, Finance and Industry 2005–; apptd Special Del. for Econ. Devt in Ardennes 2006; currently Sr Advisor, Lysios Public Affairs; mem. Bd of Dirs, Charbonnages de France; Chair. Viet Nam Cttee, Medef International; Officier, Ordre Nat. du Mérite; Chevalier, Légion d'honneur. *Leisure interests:* travel, mountain sports, golf. *Address:* Lysios Public Affairs, 260 boulevard Saint Germain, 75007 Paris, France (office). *Telephone:* 1-71-18-33-60 (office). *E-mail:* pfc@lysios.com (office). *Website:* www.lysios.fr/en/consultants-and-experts (office).

COUVREUR, Philippe; Belgian lawyer and international organization official; *Registrar, International Court of Justice;* b. 29 Nov. 1951, Schaerbeek; ed Collège Jean XXIII, Brussels, Facultés Notre-Dame de la Paix, Namur, Université Catholique de Louvain, King's Coll., London, UK, Universidad Complutense de Madrid, Spain; Intern, Legal Service, Comm. of EC 1978–79 (worked on accessions of Spain and Portugal to join EC); Special Asst in offices Registrar and Deputy-Registrar, Int. Court of Justice, The Hague 1982–86, Sec. 1986–94, First Sec. 1994–95, Prin. Legal Sec. 1995–2000, Registrar Int. Court of Justice, 2000– (re-elected 2007 and 2014); Asst Prof., Centre d'études européennes and in Law Faculty of Université Catholique de Louvain 1976–82; Visiting Prof. in the Law of Int. Orgs, Univ. of Ouagadougou, Burkina Faso 1980–82; Professeur extraordinaire in Law of Nations and Comparative Constitutional Law, Ecole des Hautes études commerciales Saint-Louis, Brussels 1986–96; Sr Guest Lecturer in Public Int. Law, Université Catholique de Louvain 1997–; Corresp. mem. Spanish Royal Acad. of Moral and Political Sciences; mem. Scientific and Pedagogic Council of Institut du Droit de la Paix et du Développement, Nice, France, Scientific and Teaching Council of Int. Law and Int. Relations, Vitoria-Gasteiz, Spain and of various other learned socs; Commdr, Order of Isabella the Catholic (Spain); Commdr, Order of Civil Merit (Spain); Officier, Légion d'honneur; Netherlands Embassy Prize 1969. *Publications:* numerous publs and articles. *Address:* International Court of Justice, Peace Palace, Carnegieplein 2, 2517 KJ The Hague, The Netherlands (office). *Telephone:* (70) 302-23-23 (office). *Fax:* (70) 364-99-28 (office). *E-mail:* sg@icj-cij.org (office). *Website:* www.icj-cij.org (office).

COVENEY, Simon, BSc; Irish politician; *Minister of Foreign Affairs and Trade;* b. 16 June 1972, Cork; s. of Hugh Coveney; m. Ruth Furney; three d.; ed Univ. Coll. Cork, Gurteen Agric. Coll., Royal Agric. Coll., UK; mem. Dáil Éireann (Parl.) for Cork South–Central constituency (Fine Gael) 1998–, fmr Shadow Minister for Drugs and Youth Affairs, Communications, Marine and Natural Resources and Transport; mem. Cork County Council 1999–2003, Southern Health Bd 1999–2003; mem. European Parl. (EPP-ED) 2004–07, mem. Foreign Affairs Cttee, Internal Market and Consumer Protection Cttee; Minister for Agric., Food and the Marine 2011–16, also for Defence 2014–16, Minister for Housing, Planning, Community and Local Govt 2016–17, of Foreign Affairs and Trade 2017–, Deputy Prime Minister 2017–; mem. Fine Gael, Deputy Leader 2017–, Chair. Party Policy Devt Cttee. *Leisure interests:* rugby, sailing. *Address:* Department of Foreign Affairs and Trade, Iveagh House, 80, St Stephen's Green, Dublin 2, Ireland (office). *Telephone:* (1) 4082000 (office). *Fax:* (1) 4082400 (office). *E-mail:* simon.coveney@oireachtas.ie (office). *Website:* www.dfa.ie (office); www.simoncoveney.ie.

ČOVIĆ, Dragan, PhD; Bosnia and Herzegovina politician; b. 20 Aug. 1956, Mostar, Socialist Repub. of Bosnia and Herzegovina, Socialist Fed. Repub. of Yugoslavia; m. Bernardica Čović; two d.; ed Univ. of Mostar, Sarajevo Univ.; with SOKO co., Mostar, holding sr managerial positions 1977–98; Assoc. Prof., then Prof., Univ. of Mostar 1996–; fmr mem. Croat Democratic Union; Deputy Prime Minister and Minister of Finance, Fed. of Bosnia and Herzegovina 1998–2001; elected to Tripartite State Presidency 2002, Leader of Presidency 2003–04, dismissed by High Rep. of the Int. Community in Bosnia and Herzegovina Paddy Ashdown following indictment for financial corruption ahead of trial 29 March 2005 (found guilty of corruption but later cleared on appeal); Vice-Pres. Hrvatska Demokratska Zajednica Bosne i Hercegovine (Croatian Democratic Union of Bosnia and Herzegovina) 1998–2005, Pres. 2005–; mem. House of Peoples 2011–, Chair. 2012–14; Croat mem. of the tripartite State Presidency 2014–18, Chair. July 2015–March 2016, July 2017–March 2018. *Address:* Hrvatska Demokratska Zajednica Bosne i Hercegovine (Croatian Democratic Union of Bosnia and Herzegovina), 88000 Mostar, Mostar-Zapad, Kneza Domagoja b.b, Bosnia and Herzegovina. *Telephone:* (36) 310701. *Fax:* (36) 315024. *E-mail:* hdzbih@hdzbih.org. *Website:* www.hdzbih.org.

ČOVIĆ, Željko, BSc, MSc; Croatian business executive; b. 9 Jan. 1953, Zagreb; ed Zagreb Univ., Int. Inst. of Man. Devt; joined PLIVA, Zagreb 1980, Dir Foodstuffs Div. 1985–86, Head of Sales, Foodstuffs Div. 1986–88, Head of Marketing and Sales 1988–91, Chair. and CEO PLIVA d.d. 1993–95, Pres. Man. Bd and CEO 1995–2008 (resgnd); CEO Genera Pharmaceuticals Ltd, Rakov Potok 2009–12; mem. Exec. City Council and Sec. for Econ. Affairs, City of Zagreb 1991–93, Advisor to Vice-Pres. of the Economy, Croatian Govt 1993; mem. American Chamber of Commerce, Croatian Nat. Council on Competitiveness (Pres. 2002–05), Croatian Employers' Asscn (Pres. 2001–02); Order of the Croatian Star 1995, Order of the Croatian Pleter 1995; Croatian Chamber of Commerce Golden Award 1994, Managers and Entrepreneurs Asscn Manager of the Year 1995, ING Barings and Emerging Markets CEO of the Year Award 1999. *E-mail:* zc9876@gmail.com (office).

COWELL, Simon Phillip; British television personality, television executive and record company executive; b. Lambeth, London; s. of Eric Cowell and Julie Brett (née Josie Dalglish); one s. with Lauren Silverman; ed Dover Coll., Windsor Technical Coll., St Columba's Coll., St Albans; brought up in Elstree, Herts.; worked for EMI Music Publishing 1977–82; Founder Fanfare Records (with Iain Burton) 1982–89; A&R Consultant, BMG Records 1989; screen debut on TV series Sale of the Century 1990; Founder and Co-Owner, S Records 2001; first TV appearance on Pop Idol 2001, then on American Idol 2002; f. Syco record label (subsidiary of Sony BMG) 2002, artists include Westlife, Five, Robson & Jerome, Zig & Zag, Girl Thing, Will Young, Gareth Gates, Six, Il Divo, Steve Brookstein, Shayne Ward, Journey South, Paul Potts, Ray Quinn, Leona Lewis, Olly Murs, Rebecca Ferguson, Cher Lloyd, Susan Boyle, Little Mix, One Direction; Record Exec. of the Year 1998, 1999, A & R Man. of the Year 1999, Variety Club Showbusiness Personality of the Year 2005, BAFTA Special Award 2010. *Films:* as producer: One Chance 2013, Pudsey the Dog: the Movie 2014. *Television includes:* writer, producer and judge, Pop Idol (ITV) 2001–02, American Idol: The Search for a Superstar (Fox TV) 2002–10, Cupid 2003, The X Factor (ITV) 2004–10, 2013–, (producer) 2011–13, The Xtra Factor 2004–16, America's Got Talent 2006–, Celebrity Duets 2006, American Inventor 2006–07, Grease Is the Word (ITV) 2007, Britain's Got Talent (ITV) (BAFTA Award for Best Entertainment Programme 2010) 2007–, Britain's Got More Talent 2007–, Rock Rivals (ITV drama) 2008, Piers Morgan's Life Stories (special episodes) 2010–, Red or Black (ITV) 2011–13, The X Factor USA 2011–13.

COWEN, Brian, BCL; Irish solicitor, politician and business executive; *Managing Director, BTC Consulting;* b. 10 Jan. 1960, Tullamore, Co. Offaly; s. of Bernard Cowen and Mary Cowen; m. Mary Molloy 1990; two d.; ed Univ. Coll. Dublin and Inc. Law Soc. of Ireland; mem. Offaly Co. Council 1984–93; TD (mem. Dáil) for Laois-Offaly 1984–2011; Minister for Labour 1991–92, for Transport, Energy and Communications 1992–94, for Health and Children 1997–2000, for Foreign Affairs 2000–04, Jan.–Feb. 2011, for Finance 2004–08 (also Tánaiste—Deputy Prime Minister 2007–08), Taoiseach (Prime Minister) 2008–11, also Acting Minister of Defence Feb.–March 2010; Leader Fianna Fáil 2008–11 (resgnd), Leader Parl. Party 2008; fmr Opposition Spokesperson on Agric. and Food; Man. Dir BTC Consulting 2013–; Dir (non-exec.), Topaz Energy Group Ltd 2014–. *Leisure interests:* sport, reading, music. *Address:* Grand Canal House, William Street, Tullamore, Co. Offaly, Ireland. *Telephone:* (57) 9321976. *Fax:* (57) 9321910. *Website:* www.fiannafail.ie.

COWLEY, Alan Herbert, BS, MS, PhD, FRS; British chemist and academic; *Robert A. Welch Professor of Chemistry, University of Texas;* b. 29 Jan. 1934, Manchester; s. of Herbert Cowley and Dora Cowley; m. Deborah Elaine Cole 1975; two s. three d.; ed Univ. of Manchester; Postdoctoral Fellow, then Instructor, Univ. of Florida, USA 1958–60; Tech. Officer, Exploratory Group, ICI (Billingham Div.), UK 1960–61; Asst Prof. of Chem., Univ. of Texas at Austin 1962–67, Assoc. Prof. 1967–70, Prof. 1970–84, George W. Watt Centennial Prof. of Chem. 1984–88, Richard J.V. Johnson Regent's Prof. of Chem. 1989–91, Robert A. Welch Prof. of Chem. 1991–; Sir Edward Frankland Prof. of Inorganic Chem., Imperial Coll., London 1988–89; Vice-Chair. Bd of Trustees, Gordon Research Conferences 1993–94 (Chair. 1994–95); mem. Editorial Bd, Inorganic Chemistry 1979–83, Chemical Reviews 1984–88, Polyhedron 1984–2000, Journal of the American Chemical Society 1986–91, Journal of Organometallic Chemistry 1987–, Organometallics 1988–91, Dalton Transactions 1997–2000, Inorganic Syntheses 1983–; Corresp. mem. Mexican Acad. of Sciences 2004; Guggenheim Fellowship 1976–77; Chevalier, Ordre des Palmes académiques 1997; Dr hc (Univ. of Bordeaux) 2003; RSC Award for Main-Group Element Chem. 1980, RSC Centenary Medal and Lectureship 1986, ACS Southwest Regional Award 1986, Stiefvater Memorial Award and Lectureship, Univ. of Nebraska 1987, Chemical Pioneer Award, American Inst. of Chemists 1994, Von Humboldt Prize 1996, Gauss Professorship, Göttingen Acad. of Sciences 2005. *Publications:* more than 450 articles in learned journals. *Leisure interests:* squash, sailing, classical music, literature. *Address:* Room WEL 4.330, Department of Chemistry and Biochemistry, University of

Texas at Austin, 1 University Station A5300, Austin, TX 78712-0165, USA (office). *Telephone:* (512) 471-7484 (office). *Fax:* (512) 471-6822 (office). *E-mail:* cowley@mail.utexas.edu (office). *Website:* www.cm.utexas.edu/alan_cowley (office); cowley.cm.utexas.edu/acowley (office).

COWLEY, Sir; **Steven,** Kt, FRS, FREng, FInstP, BA, PhD; British physicist; *President, Corpus Christi College;* two s.; ed Corpus Christi Coll., Oxford, Princeton Univ.; began career at Culham Centre for Fusion Energy (Culham Lab.), UK Atomic Energy Authority (UKAEA) 1985, becoming Dir, Culham Lab. 1998, CEO, UKAEA 2009–16; Lecturer in Physics, Princeton Univ. 1987–93, UCLA 1993–2008 (becoming Full Prof. 2000), Imperial Coll. 2001–16; Pres., Corpus Christi Coll., Oxford 2016–; mem. Prime Minister's Council of Science and Tech. 2011–; presented TED talk entitled Fusion is Energy's Future 2009; Fellow, American Physical Soc.; Inst. of Physics Glazebrook Medal 2012. *Publications:* over 170 refereed articles. *Address:* Corpus Christi College, Merton Street, Oxford, OX1 4JF, England (office). *Telephone:* (1865) 276700 (office). *Fax:* (1865) 276767 (office). *E-mail:* president@ccc.ox.ac.uk (office). *Website:* www.ccc.ox.ac.uk (office).

COWPER-COLES, Sir Sherard Louis, Kt, KCMG, LVO; British diplomatist; b. 8 Jan. 1955, London; s. of Sherard Hamilton Cowper-Coles and Dorothy Cowper-Coles (née Short); m. 1st Bridget Cowper-Coles (divorced); four s. one d.; m. 2nd Jasmine Zerinini; one d.; ed Tonbridge School, Hertford Coll., Oxford; joined FCO 1977; Third, then Second Sec., Cairo 1980–83; First Sec. Planning Office, FCO 1983–85, Pvt. Sec. to Perm. Under-Sec. of State 1985–87; First Sec., Washington, DC 1987–91; Asst Security Policy Dept, FCO 1991–93, Head Hong Kong Dept 1994–97; Counsellor, Paris 1997–99; Prin. Pvt. Sec. to Sec. of State for Foreign and Commonwealth Affairs 1999–2001; Amb. to Israel 2001–03, to Saudi Arabia 2003–07, to Afghanistan 2007–09; Foreign Sec.'s Special Rep. to Afghanistan and Pakistan 2009–10; Int. Business Devt Dir, BAE Systems 2010–13; Sr Adviser to Group Chair. and Group CEO HSBC Holdings; Hon. Fellow, Hertford Coll. Oxford 2002. *Publications:* From Defence to Security 2004, Ever the Diplomat: Confessions of a Foreign Office Mandarin 2013. *Address:* Foreign and Commonwealth Office, King Charles Street, London, SW1A 2AH, England (office). *Telephone:* (20) 7008-1500 (office). *E-mail:* sherard.cowper-coles@fco.gov.uk (office). *Website:* www.gov.uk/government/organisations/foreign-commonwealth-office (office).

COX, Barry Geoffrey, CBE, BA, FRTS; British journalist and television industry executive (retd); b. 25 May 1942, Guildford, Surrey, England; m. 1st Pamela Doran 1967 (divorced 1977); two s. two d.; m. 2nd Kathryn Kay 1984 (divorced 1992); m. 3rd Fiona Hillary 2001; ed Tiffin School, Kingston, Surrey, Magdalen Coll., Oxford; reporter, The Scotsman 1965–67; feature writer, Sunday Telegraph 1967–70; Producer/Dir World in Action, Granada TV 1970–74; The London Programme, London Weekend TV 1974–77, Head of Current Affairs 1977–81, Controller of Features and Current Affairs 1981–87, Dir of Corp. Affairs 1987–94, Special Adviser to Chief Exec. 1994–95; Dir Independent TV Asscn 1995–98; Deputy Chair. Channel 4 1999–2007; consultant to United Broadcasting and Entertainment 1998–2001, to Independent TV News 1998–2008; Chair. Digital TV Stakeholders Group 2002–04, Digital UK Ltd 2005–12, SwitchCo Ltd 2005, Oval House Theatre 2001–07; News International Visiting Prof. of Broadcast Media, Univ. of Oxford 2003; mem. Council Inst. of Educ. 2000–08; Chair. Digital Radio Working Group 2010. *Television:* Eighteen Months to Balcombe Street (producer) 1977, Weekend World (exec. producer) 1977–81. *Publications:* Civil Liberties in Britain 1975, The Fall of Scotland Yard 1977, Free For All: Public Service Television in the Digital Age 2004. *Leisure interests:* tennis, walking, theatre. *Address:* 72 Wilton Road, Victoria, London, SW1V 1DE, England. *E-mail:* barry.cox3@btopenworld.com.

COX, Brian Denis, CBE; British actor, director and writer; b. 1 June 1946, Dundee, Scotland; s. of Charles Mcardle Campbell Cox and Mary Ann Gillerine (née McCann); m. 1st Caroline Burt 1968 (divorced 1987); one s. one d.; m. 2nd Nicole Ansari 2001; two s.; ed London Acad. of Music and Dramatic Art; Hon. LLD (Dundee) 2006; Hon. Dr of Drama (Royal Scottish Acad. of Music and Drama) 2006; Scottish BAFTA Award for Contrib. to Scottish Broadcasting 2004. *Stage appearances include:* debut at Dundee Repertory 1961; Royal Lyceum, Edinburgh 1965–66, Birmingham Repertory 1966–68, As You Like It, Birmingham and Vaudeville (London debut) 1967, Peer Gynt, Birmingham 1967, When We Dead Awaken, Edinburgh Festival 1968, In Celebration, Royal Court 1969, The Wild Duck, Edinburgh Festival 1969, The Big Romance, Royal Court 1970, Don't Start Without Me, Garrick 1971, Mirandolina, Brighton 1971, Getting On, Queen's 1971, The Creditors, Open Space 1972, Hedda Gabler, Royal Court 1972; Playhouse, Nottingham: Love's Labour's Lost, Brand, What The Butler Saw, The Three Musketeers 1972; Cromwell, Royal Court 1973; Royal Exchange, Manchester: Arms and the Man 1974, The Cocktail Party 1975; Pilgrim's Progress, Prospect Theatre 1975, Emigres, Nat. Theatre Co., Young Vic 1976; Olivier Theatre: Tamburlaine the Great 1976, Julius Caesar 1977; The Changeling, Riverside Studios 1978; Nat. Theatre: Herod, The Putney Debates 1978; On Top, Royal Court 1979, Macbeth, Cambridge Theatre and tour of India 1980, Summer Party, Crucible 1980, Have You Anything to Declare?, Manchester then Round House 1981, Danton's Death, Nat. Theatre Co., Olivier 1982, Strange Interlude, Duke of York (Drama Magazine Best Actor Award 1985) 1984 and Nederlander, New York 1985, Rat in the Skull, Royal Court (Drama Magazine and Olivier Best Actor Awards 1985) 1984 and New York 1985, Fashion, The Danton Affair, Misalliance, Penny for a Song 1986, The Taming of the Shrew, Titus Andronicus 1987, The Three Sisters 1989, RSC and Titus Andronicus on tour, Madrid, Paris, Copenhagen (Olivier Award for Best Actor in a Revival and Drama Magazine Best Actor Award for RSC 1988) 1988, Frankie and Johnny in the Claire-de-Lune, Comedy 1989, Richard III, King Lear, nat. and world tour 1990–91, The Master Builder, Edinburgh 1993, Riverside 1994, St Nicholas, The Bush Theatre 1997, New York (Lucille Lortel Award 1998) 1998, Skylight, Los Angeles 1997, Dublin Carol, Old Vic and Royal Court 2000, Uncle Varrick, Royal Lyceum, Edinburgh 2004, Rock 'n' Roll, Royal Court Theatre, Lolita, National Theatre, That Championship Season, Broadway 2011, The Weir, Donmar/West End 2013, 2014. *Plays directed:* Edinburgh Festival: The Man with a Flower in his Mouth 1973, The Stronger 1973; Orange Tree, Richmond: I Love My Love 1982, Mrs Warren's Profession 1989; The Crucible, Moscow Art Theatre, London and Edinburgh 1989, The Philanderer, Hampstead Theatre Club (world premier of complete version) (Int. Theatre Inst. Award 1990) 1991. *Radio:* McLevy (BBC series). *Films include:* Nicholas and Alexandra 1971, In Celebration 1975, The Privilege (short) 1982, Manhunter 1986, Shoot for the Sun 1986, Hidden Agenda 1990, Deceptions 1992, L'oeil de Vichy (narrator of English version) 1993, Iron Will 1994, Prince of Jutland 1994, The Cutter 1994, I Was Catherine the Great's Stable Boy (short) 1994, Rob Roy 1995, Braveheart 1995, Chain Reaction 1996, The Glimmer Man 1996, The Long Kiss Goodnight 1996, Kiss the Girls 1997, The Boxer 1997, Desperate Measures 1998, Merchants of Venus 1998, Rushmore 1998, The Minus Man 1998, The Corruptor 1998, For Love of the Game 1999, The Invention of Dr. Morel (short) 2000, Complicity 2000, Mad About Mambo 2000, A Shot at Glory 2000, Saltwater 2000, Zulu 9 (short) (voice) 2001, The Legend of Loch Lomond (short) (narrator) 2001, Super Troopers 2001, L.I.E. 2001, Strictly Sinatra 2001, The Affair of the Necklace 2001, Bug 2002, The Rookie 2002, The Bourne Identity 2002, The Ring 2002, Adaptation 2002, 25th Hour 2002, The Reckoning 2003, X2 2003, Sin 2003, Troy 2004, The Bourne Supremacy 2004, Get the Picture (short) 2004, Match Point 2005, Red Eye 2005, The Ringer 2005, A Woman in Winter 2005, The Flying Scotsman 2006, Burns 2006, Running with Scissors 2006, Zodiac 2007, The Martyr's Crown (short) 2007, Battle for Terra (voice) 2007, The Water Horse 2007, Trick 'r Treat 2007, Shoot on Sight 2007, Red 2008, The Escapist 2008, Agent Crush (voice) 2008, Scooby-Doo and the Samurai Sword (video) (voice) 2009, Tell-Tale 2009, The Good Heart 2009, Fantastic Mr. Fox (voice) 2009, As Good as Dead 2010, Wide Blue Yonder 2010, Red 2010, Coriolanus 2011, Ironclad 2011, The Key Man 2011, The Veteran 2011, Rise of the Planet of the Apes 2011, Edwin Boyd 2011, Exit Humanity (narrator) 2011, Blumenthal 2012, Theatre of Dreams (as Matt Busby) 2012, The Campaign 2012, Dog Fight 2012, Blood 2012, Anna 2013, The Anomaly 2014, The Jesuit 2015, Forsaken 2015, Pixels 2015, Killing Thyme (short) 2015, The Carer 2015, The Autopsy of Jane Doe 2015. *Television includes:* The Wednesday Play 1965, Redcap (series) 1966, ITV Playhouse 1967, The Gamblers (series) 1967, Theatre 625 1968, Z Cars (series) 1969, Thirty-Minute Theatre (series) 1969–71, When We Dead Awaken (film) 1970, ITV Sunday Night Theatre 1970, Doomwatch (series) 1970, Manhunt (series) 1970, Stage 2 (series) 1971, Ego Hugo (film) 1973, BBC Play of the Month – The Changeling 1974, Sutherland's Law (series) 1974, Churchill's People – The Wallace 1975, The Master of Ballantrae (short) 1975, Shades of Greene (series) 1975, Play for Today – Clay, Smeddum and Greenden 1976, Crown Court (series) 1976–82, Rooms (series) 1977, Target (series) 1977, Henry II in The Devil's Crown (series) 1978, Out (series) 1978, Thérèse Raquin (mini-series) 1980, BBC 2 Playhouse – Dalhousie's Luck 1980, Hammer House of Horror – The Silent Scream 1980, Bothwell 1980, The House on the Hill (series) 1981, Play for Today – A Cotswold Death 1982, Minder (series) 1982, King Lear (film) 1983, Jemima Shore Investigates (series) 1983, J.S. Bach in The Cantor of St Thomas's (film) 1984, Pope John Paul II 1984, Scotland's Story (series) 1984, Florence Nightingale (film) 1985, The Deliberate Death of a Polish Priest (film) 1986, The Fourth Floor (film) 1986, Shoot for the Sun (film) 1986, Unnatural Causes (series) 1986, The Modern World: Ten Great Writers (mini-series documentary) (voice of Henrik Ibsen) 1988, Beryl Markham: A Shadow in the Sun (film) 1988, Murder on the Moon (film) 1989, Secret Weapon (film) 1990, Perfect Scoundrels – The Milk of Human Kindness 1990, Red Fox (mini-series) 1991, Acting in Tragedy (BBC Masterclass) 1990, The Lost Language of Cranes (film) 1992, The Cloning of Joanna May (film) 1992, Van der Valk (series) 1992, Screen Two – The Lost Language of Cranes 1992, Shakespeare: The Animated Tales (series) (voice of Macbeth) 1992, The Big Battalions (mini-series) 1992, Inspector Morse (series) 1993, Sharpe's Rifles (film) 1993, Sharpe's Eagle (film) 1994, Scene – Pig Boy 1993, Six Characters in Search of an Author (film) 1994, Grushko (series) 1994, The Negotiator (film) 1994, Witness Against Hitler (film) 1995, Blow Your Mind See A Play 1995, Red Dwarf (series) 1997, Superman (series) 1997, Great Performances – Henry V at Shakespeare's Globe (narrator) 1997, Food for Ravens (film) 1997, Family Brood (film) 1998, Poodle Springs (film) 1998, Longitude (film) 2000, Nuremberg (mini-series) (Emmy Award for Best Actor) 2000, Animated Tales of the World (series) (narrator) 2000, Smallpox 2002: Silent Weapon (film) (narrator) 2002, Frasier (series) 2002, The Biographer (film) 2002, Rasputin: The Devil in the Flesh (documentary) (narrator) 2002, French and Saunders (series) 2004, The Court 2002, Blue/Orange (film) 2005, Lost: The Journey (film) (narrator) 2005, The Strange Case of Sherlock Holmes & Arthur Conan Doyle (film) 2005, Danny Phantom (series) (voice) 2005, Deadwood (series) 2006, The Outsiders (film) 2006, Timewatch (series documentary) (narrator) 2007, The Secret of the Nutcracker (film) 2007, The Colour of Magic (film) (narrator) 2008, Lost & Found (film) 2009, Marple: They Do It with Mirrors (film) 2009, The Take (mini-series) 2009, Kings (series) 2009, Doctor Who (series) (voice) 2009, The Day of the Triffids (mini-series) 2009, On Expenses (film) 2010, The Big C (series) 2010, The Sinking of the Laconia (mini-series) 2010–11, The Straits (series) 2012, An Adventure in Space & Time 2013, Bob Servant (two series) 2013, 2015, Shetland 2014, The Slap (series) 2015, War & Peace 2015. *Publications include:* Salem to Moscow: An Actor's Odyssey 1991, The Lear Diaries 1992. *Leisure interests:* keeping fit, tango. *Address:* c/o Nicola van Gelder, Conway van Gelder Grant Ltd, Third Floor, 8–12 Broadwick Street, London, W1F 8HW, England (office). *Website:* www.conwayvangeldergrant.com (office).

COX, Carrie S., BS; American pharmacist and business executive; *CEO, Humacyte, Inc.;* ed Massachusetts Coll. of Pharmacy and Health Sciences; held a variety of positions in market research, sales and product man. during a 10-year career with Sandoz Pharmaceuticals; Vice-Pres. Women's Health Care, Wyeth-Ayerst for seven years; Exec. Vice-Pres. and Pres. Global Prescription Business, Pharmacia Corpn (fmrly Pharmacia & Upjohn) 1997–2003; Exec. Vice-Pres. and Pres. Global Pharmaceuticals, Schering-Plough Corpn 2003–09 (until merger with Merck & Co., Inc.); mem. Bd of Dirs and CEO Humacyte, Inc. 2010–; mem. Bd of Dirs Texas Instruments Inc. 2004–, Cardinal Health, Celgene. *Address:* Humacyte, Inc., PO Box 12695, Durham, NC 27709 (office); Humacyte, Inc., 21 Davis Drive, Suite 140, Research Triangle Pa, NC 27709 (office); Humacyte, Inc., 7020 Kit Creek Road, Morrisville, NC 27560, USA (office). *Telephone:* (919) 806-4599 (office). *E-mail:* info@humacyte.com (office). *Website:* www.humacyte.com (office).

COX, (Charles) Geoffrey, QC, MP; British barrister and politician; *Attorney-General;* b. 30 April 1960, Wiltshire; m. Jeanie Cox; three c.; ed Downing Coll., Cambridge; called to the Bar at Middle Temple 1982; practice as barrister 1992–2018; co-founder Thomas More Chambers 1992, becoming Head of Chambers; Standing Counsel to govt of Mauritius 1996; mem. House of Commons (Conservative) for Torridge and W Devon 2005–; Attorney-Gen. for England and

Wales and Advocate Gen. for N Ireland 2018–; mem. Criminal Bar Asscn, British Inst. of Int. and Comparative Law; mem. Conservative Party. *Address:* Attorney-General's Office, 20 Victoria St, London, SW1H 0NF, England (office). *Telephone:* (20) 7271-2492 (office). *E-mail:* correspondence@attorneygeneral.gsi.gov.uk (office). *Website:* www.gov.uk/government/organisations/attorney-generals-office; www.geoffreycox.co.uk (office).

COX, Christopher, BA, MBA, JD; American lawyer, politician and fmr government official; *Partner, Bingham McCutchen LLP;* b. 16 Oct. 1952; m. Rebecca Gernhardt; three c.; ed Univ. of Southern California, Harvard Business School, Harvard Law School; fmr Ed. Harvard Law Review; Clerk US Court of Appeals 1977–78; Assoc. Latham & Watkins 1978–82, Pnr 1984–86; Lecturer in Business Admin, Harvard Business School 1982–83; Sr Assoc. Counsel to Pres., White House 1986–88; mem. US House of Reps from Calif. 1988–2005, Chair. House Cttee on Homeland Security, House Policy Cttee 1994–2005; Chair. SEC 2005–09 (resgnd); currently Partner, Bingham McCutchen LLP (law firm), Costa Mesa, Calif., also Pres. Bingham Consulting LLC. *Address:* Bingham McCutchen LLP, 600 Anton Boulevard, Suite 1800, Costa Mesa, CA 92626-7653, USA (office). *Telephone:* (714) 830-0606 (office). *Fax:* (714) 830-0700 (office). *E-mail:* chris.cox@bingham.com (office). *Website:* www.bingham.com (office).

COX, Courteney; American actress and film producer; b. 15 June 1964, Birmingham, Ala; d. of Richard Lewis and Courteney Cox (née Bass-Copland); m. David Arquette 1999 (divorced 2013); one d.; partner Johnny McDaid; modelling career in New York; appeared in Bruce Springsteen music video Dancing in the Dark 1984; Co-founder Coquette Productions 2004. *Films include:* Down Twisted 1986, Masters of the Universe 1987, Cocoon: The Return 1988, Mr Destiny 1990, Blue Desert 1990, Shaking the Tree 1992, The Opposite Sex 1993, Ace Ventura, Pet Detective 1994, Scream 1996, Commandments 1996, Scream 2 1997, The Runner 1999, Alien Love Triangle 1999, Scream 3 2000, The Shrink Is In 2000, 3000 Miles to Graceland 2001, Get Well Soon 2001, Alien Love Triangle 2002, November 2004, Alpha Dog 2006, Barnyard (voice) 2006, Zoom 2006, The Tripper (also producer) 2006, The Monday Before Thanksgiving 2008, Bedtime Stories 2008, Web Therapy 2009, Scream 4 2011, Step One 2011. *Television series:* Misfits of Science 1985–86, Family Ties 1987–88, The Trouble with Larry 1993, Friends 1994–2004, Dirt (also exec. producer) 2007–08, Scrubs 2009, Web Therapy (series) 2009, 2011, Cougar Town 2009–15, Private Practice 2011, Go On 2013, Drunk History 2014. *Television films include:* Roxanne: The Prize Pulitzer 1989, Till We Meet Again 1989, Curiosity Kills 1990, Morton and Hays 1991, Topper 1992, Sketch Artist II: Hands That See 1995, Tall Hot Blond 2012. *Address:* c/o WME, 9601 Wilshire Blvd, Beverly Hills, CA 90210, USA.

COX, Sir David Roxbee, Kt, PhD, FRS, FRSC; British statistician; b. 15 July 1924, Birmingham; s. of Sam R. Cox and Lilian Cox (née Braines); m. Joyce Drummond 1948; three s. one d.; ed Handsworth Grammar School, Birmingham and St John's Coll. Cambridge; with Royal Aircraft Establishment 1944–46; Wool Industries Research Asscn 1946–50; Statistical Lab., Univ. of Cambridge 1950–55; with Dept of Biostatistics, Univ. of North Carolina 1955–56, Birkbeck Coll., London 1956–66; Bell Telephone Labs 1965; Prof. of Statistics, Imperial Coll. of Science and Tech., London 1966–88; Warden, Nuffield Coll., Oxford 1988–94, Hon. Fellow 1994–; Science and Eng Research Council Sr Research Fellow 1983–88; Ed. Biometrika 1966–91; Pres. Int. Statistics Inst. 1995–97; Fellow, Imperial Coll., Birkbeck Coll., London; Hon. Fellow, St John's Coll. Cambridge, Inst. of Actuaries, British Acad.; Hon. Foreign mem. US Acad. of Arts and Sciences, Royal Danish Acad., NAS, American Philosophical Soc., Indian Acad. of Sciences, Finnish Statistical Soc.; Hon. mem. Portuguese Statistical Soc.; Hon. DSc (Reading, Bradford, Heriot Watt, Helsinki, Limburg, Queen's, Kingston, Ont., Waterloo, Neuchâtel, Padua, Minnesota, Toronto, Abertay Dundee, Crete, Bordeaux 2, Athens Univ. of Econs, Harvard, Elche, Rio de Janeiro, Leeds, Gothenburg, Glasgow); Guy Medals in silver and gold, Royal Statistical Soc., Weldon Medal, Univ. of Oxford, Deming Medal, ASQC, Kettering Medal and Prize, General Motors Cancer Research Foundation, Max Planck Prize, Copley Medal, Royal Soc. (co-recipient) 2010, Int. Research Prize 2017, BBVA Frontier of Knowledge Award 2017. *Publications:* several books on statistics, articles in Journal of the Royal Statistical Soc., Biometrika etc. *Address:* Nuffield Coll., Oxford, OX1 1NF, England (office). *Telephone:* (1865) 278690 (office). *Fax:* (1865) 278621 (office). *E-mail:* david.cox@nuffield.ox.ac.uk (office). *Website:* www.stats.ox.ac.uk/people/associate_staff/david_cox (office).

COX, Sir George Edwin, Kt, BSc; British business executive; b. 28 May 1940; s. of George Herbert Cox and Beatrice Mary Cox; m. 1st Gillian Mary Mannings (divorced 1996); two s.; m. 2nd Lorna Janet Peach 1996; two d.; ed Quintin School, Queen Mary Coll., Univ. of London; began career in aircraft industry, in factory man. and in precision eng; Man. Dir Butler Cox (IT consultancy and research group) 1977; Chief Exec. then Chair. PE Int.; fmr UK Chief Exec. Unisys UK, Head of Unisys Services Businesses across Europe; Dir-Gen. Inst. of Dirs 1999–2004; Chair. The Design Council 2004–07; fmr Chair. Merlin (Medical Emergency Relief Int.); mem. Bd of Dirs Shorts 2000–; fmr Dir Inland Revenue 1996–99, London Int. Financial Futures and Options Exchange (LIFFE) 1995–2002, Bradford & Bingley PLC; Visiting Prof., Man. School, Royal Holloway, Univ. of London 1995–; Pres. Royal Coll. of Speech Therapists 2004–; mem. Supervisory Bd Euronext 2003–; apptd mem. Advisory Bd Warwick Business School 2003, Chair. 2005, currently Pro-Chancellor and Chair of Council mem. Council Univ. of Warwick; Trustee VSO 2005–; Past Pres. Man. Consultancies Asscn; Past Master of Worshipful Co. of Man. Consultants; carried out Cox Review of Creativity in Business, commissioned by HM Govt 2005; Hon. Fellow, Queen Mary, London; Companion of Chartered Inst. of Man., Royal Aeronautical Soc.; Dr hc (Univ. of Middlesex) 2002, (Univ. of Wolverhampton) 2004, (Northumbria Univ.) 2007, (Univ. of Huddersfield) 2008. *Leisure interest:* rowing, history of aviation, theatre.

COX, Patrick (Pat), BA, MA; Irish academic, journalist, politician and EU official; *President, Jean Monnet Foundation for Europe;* b. 28 Nov. 1952, Dublin; m. Cathy Cox; six c.; ed Ardscoil Rís Christian Brothers School, Limerick, Trinity Coll., Dublin; Economist, Dept of Econs, Inst. of Public Admin, Dublin 1974–76; Lecturer in Econs, Nat. Inst. of Higher Educ. (now Univ. of Limerick), Limerick 1976–82; reporter/presenter, 'Today Tonight' current affairs programme, RTÉ 1982–86; Gen. Sec. Progressive Democrats 1986–89, Deputy Leader 1990–94; MEP for Munster 1989–2004, Deputy Leader European Liberal Democrats (ELDR) 1994–98, Pres. 1998–2002, Pres. European Parl. 2002–04; TD (mem. Irish Parl.) for Cork S Cen. and Progressive Democrats Spokesperson on Finance 1992–94; Pres. European Movement International 2005–11 (Vice-Pres. European Movement, Ireland), Former Members Asscn of the European Parl. 2010–14; Pres. Jean Monnet Foundation for Europe, Lausanne, Switzerland 2015–, Alliance Française, Dublin; mem. Fine Gael 2011–; mem. Supervisory Bd, Michelin (France), European Advisory Council of Liberty Global (Netherlands), Yalta European Strategy (YES), Ukraine; Chair. Public Interest Cttee, KPMG (Ireland); mem. Bd of Trustees, Friends of Europe (Belgium); Leader of Needs Assessment Mission on parliamentary reform for the European Parl. and the Verkhovna Rada, Kiev, Ukraine; European Co-ordinator for the Scandinavian–Mediterranean TEN T Core Network Corridor, EU; mem. Bd, Third Age Foundation (Ireland); Sr Fellow, Inst. for Int. and European Affairs (Ireland); Freeman, City of Limerick; Grand Cross, Order of the Star of Romania; Kt Grand Cross, Order of Merit of the Italian Repub.; decorations from Lithuania and Bulgaria; Dr hc (Nat. Univ. of Ireland, Trinity Coll. Dublin, American Coll. Dublin, Open Univ.); Pres.'s Medal, Univ. of Limerick, MEP of the Year 2001, Campaigner of the Year, Brussels 2003, Special Diploma of Minister of Foreign Affairs (Poland) 2003, Polish Business Oscar 2003, Transatlantic Business Award of the Year, American Chamber of Commerce to the EU 2004, Int. Charlemagne Prize 2004. *Address:* Jean Monnet Foundation for Europe, Ferme de Dorigny, 1015 Lausanne, Switzerland (office); Crawford Hall, Western Road, Cork, Ireland (home). *Telephone:* (21) 6922090 (office). *Fax:* (21) 6922095 (office). *E-mail:* gilles.grin@fjme.unil.ch (office); pcoxmep@eircom.net (office). *Website:* jean-monnet.ch/en/president-of-the-foundation (office).

COX, Hon. Paula Ann, CMG, JP, BA; Bermudian politician and lawyer; d. of C. Eugene Cox CBE, MP, JP and Alinda Cox; m. Germain Nkeuleu; one s.; ed McGill Univ., Canada, Univ. of Manchester, UK; fmr Vice-Pres. and Sr Legal Counsel, Global Funds Bank of Bermuda Ltd; Corp. Counsel, ACE Ltd 1996; MP 1996–2012; Minister of Labour, Home Affairs and Public Safety 1998–2001, of Educ. and Devt 2001–02; Attorney-Gen. and Minister of Educ. 2003–04, Minister of Finance 2004–12, also Deputy Premier 2006–10, Premier of Bermuda 2010–12; Leader Progressive Labour Party 2010–12; Hon. Alumnus, Dalhousie Univ. 2009; Dr hc (Wheelock Coll.) 2004; Most Effective Politician 2001, 2003. *Leisure interests:* reading int. biographies, collecting African antiquities. *Address:* Progressive Labour Party, Alaska Hall, 16 Court Street, Hamilton, HM 17, Bermuda (office). *Telephone:* 292-4623 (office). *E-mail:* pcox@plp.bm (office). *Website:* plp.bm/leadership/mps/14 (office).

COX, Paulus Henriqus Benedictus (Paul); Dutch film director, screenwriter and author; *Chairman, Illumination Films;* b. 16 April 1940, Venlo, Limburg; s. of W. Cox; two s. one d.; ed Univ. of Melbourne, Univ. of Technology, Sydney, Australia; settled in Australia 1965; photographic exhbns in Australia, the Netherlands, Germany, Japan, India and USA; taught photography and cinematography for several years; f. Illumination Films (production co.) with Tony Llewellyn-Jones and Bernard Eddy 1977, currently Chair.; Hon. Dr in Creative Arts; Chauvel Award for distinguished contrib. to Australian Cinema, Brisbane Int. Film Festival 1993, named in Phillip Adams List of 100 Nat. Treasures in April 2015. *Films directed:* feature length: The Journey 1972, Illuminations 1976, Inside Looking Out 1977, Kostas 1978, Lonely Hearts 1981, Man of Flowers (Golden Spike, Vallidolid International Film Festival 1984) 1983, Death and Destiny (A Journey into Ancient Egypt) 1984, My First Wife (AFI Award for Best Dir and Best Screenplay 1984, Golden Spur, Flanders Int. Film Festival 1986) 1984, Cactus 1986, Vincent 1988, Island 1989, Golden Braid 1990, A Woman's Tale (Feature Film Award, Human Rights and Equal Opportunity Comm. 1991, Golden Spur, Flanders Int. Film Festival 1992) 1991, The Nun and the Bandit 1992, Exile 1993, Lust and Revenge 1996, The Hidden Dimension 1997, Molokai 1998, Innocence (FIPRESCI Prize, Taormina Int. Film Festival 2000, Grand Prix des Amériques, Montreal World Film Festival 2000, Best Feature Film, IF Awards 2000) 1998, The Diaries of Vaslav Nijinsky (Jury Prize, Montreal Int. Festival of Films on Art 2003) 2001, Human Touch (Grand Prix des Amériques, Montreal World Film Festival) 2004, Salvation 2008, Force of Destiny 2015; documentaries: Calcutta 1970, All Set Backstage 1974, For A Child Called Michael 1979, The Kingdom of Nek Chand 1980, Underdog 1980, Death and Destiny 1984, Kaluapapa Heaven 2007, The Dinner Party 2012; shorts: Mantuta: An Early Morning Fantasy 1965, Time Past 1966, Skindeep 1968, Marcel 1969, Symphony 1969, Mirka 1970, Phyllis 1971, Island 1975, We are All Alone My Dear 1975, Ways of Seeing 1977, Ritual 1978, Handle with Care 1985. *Television includes:* The Paper Boy 1985, The Secret Life of Trees 1986, The Gift 1988, Touch Me 1993. *Publications:* Home of Man: The People of New Guinea 1971, Human Still Lives of Nepal 1971, Mirka 1980, Vincent: The Life and Death of Vincent van Gough 1987, I Am 1997, Reflections 1998, Three Screenplays 1998, Tales from the Cancer Ward 2011. *Address:* Illumination Films, 1 Victoria Avenue, Albert Park, Vic. 3206, Australia (office). *Telephone:* (3) 9690-5266 (office). *Fax:* (3) 9696-5625 (office).

COX, Philip Sutton, AO, BArch, PhD, RIBA; Australian architect; *Director, Cox Architecture;* b. 1 Oct. 1939, Killara, Sydney; s. of Ronald Albert Cox and Lilian May Cox; m. Virginia Louise Gowing 1972; two d.; ed Sydney Church of England Grammar School, Sydney Univ.; worked in New Guinea 1962; apptd Tutor in Architecture, Univ. of Sydney 1963; est. Ian McKay & Philip Cox pvt. practice with Ian McKay 1963; est. Philip Cox and Assocs (later Cox Richardson Architects & Planners, now Cox Architecture) 1967; Architect Sydney Olympics, Stage I; Tutor in Architecture, Univ. of New South Wales 1971, 1973, 1978, Prof. 1989–; Founding mem. The Australian Acad. of Design 1990–; Life Fellow, Royal Australian Inst. of Architects, Chair. Educ. Bd, Fed. Chapter; Vice-Chair. Architecture and Design Panel, Visual Arts Bd, Australia Council; Fellow, Australian Acad. of Humanities; Hon. FAIA Commonwealth Scholarship 1956; numerous awards and prizes including Royal Australian Inst. of Architects Gold Medal and Merit Awards, Commonwealth Asscn of Architects Sir Robert Matthew Award, Blacket Award, Sir John Sulman Medal. *Major Artistic Works include:* Emirates Univ. Uluru, Doya Stadium, Sydney Football Stadium, Sydney Exhbn Centre 1988, Brisbane Convention and Exhbn Centre 1995, Allphones Arena 1999, Singapore EXPO 2000, James Street Market 2003, Brisbane Magistrate Court 2004, Challenger Inst. of Tech.-Maritime Campus 2005, Nat. Inst. of Circus Arts 2007, Macintosh Island Bridge 2007, Li Ning Corp. Headquarters 2008, North Melbourne Rail Station 2009, Sanctuary Cove Golf Club 2010, The Helix Bridge

2010, Adelaide Studios 2011, West End Ferry Terminal 2012, Sir Samuel Griffith Centre 2013, Kaohsiung Exhbn Centre 2014, Japan Nat. Stadium 2015, Jubilee Bridge 2015, Anna Meares Velodrome 2016, Sir John Monash Centre 2018. *Publications:* several books including The Australian Homestead (with Wesley Stacey) 1972, Historic Towns of Australia (with Wesley Stacey) 1973, Restoring Old Australian Houses and Buildings, an Architectural Guide (with others) 1975, Australian Colonial Architecture (with Clive Lucas), The Functional Tradition (with David Moore) 1987, Cox Architects & Planners 1960–2010 (with others) 2008, Home, Evolution of the Australian Dream (with others) 2011. *Leisure interests:* gardening, swimming, walking, painting. *Address:* Cox Architecture, Level 2, 204 Clarence Street, Sydney, NSW 2000, Australia (office). *Telephone:* (2) 9267-9599 (office). *Fax:* (2) 9264-5844 (office). *E-mail:* sydney@cox.com.au (office); www.coxarchitecture.com.au (office).

COX, Stephen Joseph, RA; British sculptor; b. 16 Sept. 1946, Bristol; s. of Leonard John Cox and Ethel Minnie May McGill; m. Judith Atkins 1970; two d.; ed St Mary Redcliffe, Bristol, West of England Coll. of Art, Bristol and Cen. School of Art and Design, London; lives and practises near Ludlow, England as well as, Italy, India and Egypt; works held in collections of Tate Gallery, Victoria and Albert Museum, British Museum, South Bank Centre, Arts Council of GB, British Council, Walker Art Gallery, Liverpool, Henry Moore Centre for Sculpture, Leeds City Gallery, Southampton Museum, Fogg Museum, USA, Groningen Museum, Netherlands, Peter Ludwig Collection, FRG, Uffizi Gallery, Florence, Fattoria di Celle, Pistoia, Palazzo del Commune, Spoleto, Santa Maria della Scala, Siena, Regione di Aosta and pvt. collections in India, Egypt, USA and Europe; numerous public sculptures in England, including Broadgate, Ludgate and Finsbury Square, London, St Paul's Church, Harringay, St Luke's, Chelsea, St Nicholas, Newcastle upon Tyne, Altar for St Anselm's Chapel, Canterbury Cathedral, Lincoln Coll. Oxford and British govt comms in Delhi, Cairo and Canberra; consultant sculptor, Rajiv Gandhi Samadhi, Delhi; Sr Research Fellow, Wimbledon School of Art 1995–96; Brian Montgomery Visiting Fellow in Sculpture, Lincoln Coll., Oxford 2009; subject of book The Sculpture of Stephen Cox by Stephen Bann 1995; Gold Medal Indian Triennale, Arts Council Major Awards 1978, 1980, British Council Bursaries 1978, 1979, Hakone Open Air Museum Prize, Japan 1985, Goldhill Sculpture Prize, Royal Acad. 1988, Arts & Business Award 1988, ACE (Art and Christianity Enquiry) Award for Art in a Religious Context 2007–08. *Television:* contrib., The Divine Michelangelo (BBC) 2004. *Address:* Lower House Farm, Coreley, nr Ludlow, Salop., SY8 3AS, England (home). *Telephone:* (1584) 891532 (home). *E-mail:* info@stephencox.info; stephen@stephencoxra.com (home). *Website:* stephencox.info.

COX, Vivienne, CBE, BSc, MSc, MBA; British energy industry executive and government adviser; b. 29 May 1959; m.; two d.; ed Univ. of Oxford and Institut européenne d'admin des affaires (INSEAD), Paris, France; joined BP Chemicals 1981, various sales and marketing posts 1981–85, moved to BP Exploration 1985, moved to BP Finance 1987, set up commodity derivatives group within oil trading 1990–93, took over responsibility for BP's share holding in Rotterdam refinery 1993–96, Man. New Business in Cen. and Eastern Europe, Vienna 1996–98, CEO Air BP 1998, Integrated Supply and Trading 2001, Group Vice-Pres. 2004, Exec. Vice-Pres. for Gas, Power and Renewables 2005–09; Adjunct Prof., Imperial Coll. London; Dir (non-exec.), Eurotunnel PLC 2002–04, Rio Tinto plc 2005–14, Climate Change Capital Ltd 2008–12 (Chair. 2009–12), Vallourec SA 2009– (Chair. 2013–), BG Group 2012–, Pearson Group 2012– (Sr Ind. Dir 2013–), St Francis Hospice; Lead Ind. Dir, Dept for Int. Devt, UK Govt 2009–; Commr, Airport Comm., UK Dept for Transport 2012–; mem. Kingfisher plc Net Positive Advisory Council 2013–; Bd mem. INSEAD; Dr hc (Hull) 2009; Harpers and Queen Businesswoman of the Year 2004, Veuve Clicquot Businesswoman of the Year 2006. *Address:* Climate Change Capital Ltd, 3 More London Riverside, London, SE1 2AQ, England (office). *Telephone:* (20) 7939-5000 (office). *Fax:* (20) 7939-5030 (office). *Website:* www.climatechangecapital.com (office).

COX, Warren Jacob, BA, MArch, FAIA; American architect; *Partner Emeritus, Hartman-Cox Architects;* b. 28 Aug. 1935, New York, NY; s. of Oscar Sydney Cox and Louise Bryson Cox (née Black); m. Claire Christie-Miller 1975; one s. one d.; ed The Hill School, Yale Univ., Yale Univ. School of Architecture; Partner, Hartman-Cox Architects, Washington, DC 1965–2011, Partner Emer. 2011–; Visiting Architectural Critic, Yale Univ. 1966, Catholic Univ. of America 1967, Univ. of Virginia 1976; Dir Center for Palladian Studies in America 1982–2013; mem. Editorial Bd Guide to the Architecture of Washington, DC 1965, 1974; fmr mem. Georgetown Review Bd, Comm. of Fine Arts; Dir Acad. Art Museum, Center for Palladian Studies in America; fmr Dir DC Preservation League; Chair. Council of Friends, Alibi Club; fmr Chair. Literary Soc., Cosmos Club; lecturer at numerous architectural schools and insts; juror for design awards programmes; Euram Bldg, Nat. Perm. Bldg, Sumner Square, Market Square, Mount Vernon Coll. Chapel, Folger Shakespeare Library Additions, Concert Hall Redesign, Kennedy Center, Renovation of the Nat. Archives, Patent Office Bldg and Lincoln and Jefferson Memorials, Washington, DC, Winterthur Museum New Exhbn Bldg, Wilmington, Del., Chrysler Museum, Norfolk, Va, John Carter Brown Library Addition, Providence, Rhode Island, Nat. Humanities Center, Raleigh, North Carolina, US Embassy, Kuala Lumpur, Malaysia, Law School, Washington Univ., Law School, Tulane Univ., Library, Addition and Residence Hall, Georgetown Univ. Law Center, Washington, DC, Library, Case Western Reserve Univ., Cleveland, Ohio, Law Library, Univ. of Connecticut, Hartford, Conn., Fed. Courthouse, Corpus Christi, Tex., Divinity School Addition, Duke Univ., Durham, North Carolina, City and County Courthouses, Lexington, Ky, McIntire School of Commerce, Monroe Hall Addition and Special Collections Library, Univ. of Virginia, Charlottesville, Jefferson Library, Charlottesville, Va, Addition and Renovation, Morehead Foundation, Univ. of North Carolina, Addition and New Building, Univ. of Michigan Law School, Rooftop Addition, Hay-Adams Hotel, Washington, DC; AIA Architectural Firm Award 1988, AIA Nat. Honor Awards 1970, 1971, 1981, 1983, 1989, 1994, Louis Sullivan Prize 1972, Arthur Ross Award, Centennial Award, DC AIA, History of Art Prize, Yale Univ. School of Architecture, Henry Adams Prize, AIA Centennial Award D.C. for Service, and more than 120 other architectural design awards. *Publications include:* Hartman-Cox Architects/Master Architects Series 1994, 2009, various books and periodicals. *Leisure interests:* architectural history, automobile racing, fishing, shooting, golden retriever and English springer spaniel dogs, farming, book collecting. *Address:* 3111 N Street NW, Washington, DC 20007; Kennersley, PO Box 1, Church Hill, MD 21623, USA. *Telephone:* (202) 965-0615. *E-mail:* wjcarch@gmail.com.

COX, Winston A., MSc (Econs); Barbadian banker and international organization official; m. Sylvia Potvin; five c.; ed Univ. of the West Indies, Inst. of Social Studies, Netherlands; joined Cen. Bank of Barbados 1974, Adviser to Gov. 1982–87, Gov. 1997; Dir of Finance, Ministry of Finance 1987–91; mem. Exec. Bd IBRD 1994–97; Gov. Cen. Bank of Barbados 1997–99; Deputy Sec.-Gen. (for Devt Co-operation), Commonwealth Secr. 2000–06; Alt. Exec. Dir for the Bahamas, Barbados, Guyana, Jamaica, and Trinidad and Tobago, IDB 2006–08, Exec. Dir 2008–11; Gold Crown of Merit 2009. *Address:* c/o Inter-American Development Bank, 1300 New York Avenue NW, Washington, DC 20577, USA. *E-mail:* info@iadb.org.

COYIUTO, Robert R., Jr, BS; Philippine business executive; *President and Chief Operating Officer, Oriental Petroleum & Minerals Inc.;* b. 1953; s. of Robert Coyiuto; m. Rosie Ty-Coyiuto; ed San Beda Coll., Manila; Dir Oriental Petroleum & Minerals Inc. 1982–, Chair. 1991–93, Pres. and Chief Operating Officer 1994–; Chair. and CEO Coyiuto Group of Cos; Chair. and CEO Prudential Guarantee and Assurance (PGA) Inc.; f. PGA Cars Inc. 1996, currently Chair.; Chair. and Pres. Calaca High Power Corpn; Chair. and CEO PGA Sompo Japan Insurance Inc.; Chair. Manila Stock Exchange, Pioneer Tours Corpn, Coyiuto Foundation, Nissan North Edsa; Vice-Chair. First Guarantee Life Assurance Co. Inc., First Life Financial Co. Inc.; Dir Robinsons Land Corpn 1990–2008, Universal Robina Corpn 2002–, Interport Resources Corpn 2008–, Philippine Stock Exchange Inc., Canon Philippines Inc., Destiny Financial Plan Inc., R. Coyiuto Securities Inc.; fmr owner Manila Chronicle. *Address:* Oriental Petroleum & Minerals Corporation, 40th Floor, Robinsons Equitable Tower, Pasig City 1605, Philippines (office). *Telephone:* (2) 6371670 (office). *Fax:* (2) 3952586 (office). *Website:* www.opmc.com.ph (office).

CRABB, Rt Hon. Stephen, PC, BSc, MBA; British politician and business executive; b. 20 Jan. 1973, Inverness, Scotland; m. Béatrice Monnier; one s. one d.; ed Tasker Milward School, Haverfordwest, Pembrokeshire, Wales, Univ. of Bristol, London Business School, Open Univ.; began career at Nat. Council for Voluntary Youth Services in 1990s; Christian Action Research and Educ. parl. intern 1995–96; Chair. Southwark North and Bermondsey Conservative Asscn 1998–2000, election monitor in Bosnia and Herzegovina 1998; with London Chamber of Commerce and Industry 1998–2002; marketing consultant 2002–04; MP for Preseli, Pembrokeshire 2005–, mem. Welsh Affairs Cttee, Int. Devt Cttee 2007–09, Treasury Select Cttee, chaired Conservative Party's Human Rights Comm. 2006; Opposition Jr Whip 2009–10, Asst Govt Whip 2010; Leader of Project Umubano (Conservative Party's social action project in Rwanda and Sierra Leone) 2010–13; Lord Commr of HM Treasury and Parl. Under-Sec., Wales Office 2012–14, Sec. of State for Wales 2014–16, for Work and Pensions March–July 2016; Patron Pembrokeshire Mencap; Conservative. *Leisure interests:* rugby, mountain biking, tennis, has run London Marathon three times, cooking, playing guitar, learning French. *Address:* House of Commons, Westminster, London, SW1A 0AA, England (office). *Telephone:* (20) 7219-6518 (office). *E-mail:* stephen.crabb.mp@parliament.uk (office). *Website:* www.stephencrabb.com.

CRABTREE, Robert H., MA, DSc, DPhil, FRS; British/American chemist and academic; *Whitehead Professor of Chemistry, Yale University;* b. 17 April 1948, London, England; s. of Arthur Crabtree; m. Holly Darico; ed Brighton Coll. and Univs of Oxford and Sussex, UK; Attaché de Recherche, CNRS, France 1975–77; Asst Prof. of Chem., Yale Univ., USA 1977–82, Assoc. Prof. 1982–85, Prof. 1985–, now Whitehead Prof.; Fellow, American Acad. of Arts and Sciences, NAS; Hon. DSc (Univ. of Bath) 2016; ACS Organometallic Chem. Award 1993, Dow Lecturer, Berkeley 2004, Williams Lecturer, Oxford 2004, Sabatier Lecturer, Toulouse 2006, Osborn Lecturer, Strasbourg 2009, Kosolapoff Award 2010, Stauffer Lecturer, Univ. of Southern California 2010, King Lecturer, Univ. of Georgia 2011, McElvain Lecturer, Univ. of Wisconsin 2013, Yale Postdoctoral Mentoring Award 2013, Siedle Lecturer, Indiana Univ. 2014, RSC Centenary Award 2014, Clarivate Highly Cited List 2014–18, Coates Award 2015. *Publications include:* The Organometallic Chemistry of the Transition Metals 2005 (seventh edn 2019). *Leisure interest:* travel. *Address:* Yale Chemistry Department, PO Box 208107, 225 Prospect Street, New Haven, CT 06520-8107, USA (office). *Telephone:* (203) 432-3925 (office). *Fax:* (203) 432-6144 (office). *E-mail:* robert.crabtree@yale.edu (office). *Website:* www.chem.yale.edu/people/robert-crabtree (office).

CRACE, Jim, BA; British writer and dramatist; b. 1 March 1946, Brocket Hall, Lemsford, Hertfordshire; m. Pamela Ann Turton 1975; one s. one d.; ed Birmingham Coll. of Commerce, Univ. of London; freelance writer and journalist 1976–87; Distinguished Writer-in-Residence, James Michener Center, Univ. of Texas, Austin 2008; Dr hc (Univ. of Central England) 2000; Antico Fattore Prize, Italy 1988, American Acad. of Arts and Letters E. M. Forster Award 1992, Soc. of Authors Travel Award 1992, Windham–Campbell Literature Prize (Fiction) 2014, Dobie Paisano Int. Residency Prize, Univ. of Texas at Austin 2017. *Publications include:* Continent (David Higham Award 1986, Guardian Prize for Fiction 1986, Whitbread Award – First Novel 1986) 1986, The Gift of Stones (GAP Int. Prize for Literature 1989) 1988, Arcadia 1992, Signals of Distress (RSL Winifred Holtby Memorial Prize 1995) 1994, The Slow Digestions of the Night 1995, Quarantine (Whitbread Award – Novel 1997) 1997, Being Dead (Nat. Book Critics' Circle Award, USA 2001) 1999, The Devil's Larder 2001, Genes 2001, Six 2003, Genesis 2003, The Pesthouse 2007, All That Follows 2010, Harvest (James Tait Black Memorial Prize 2014, Int. Dublin Literary Award 2015) 2013, The Melody 2018; short stories: Refugees 1977, Annie, California Plates 1977, Helter Skelter, Hang Sorrow, Care'll Kill a Cat 1977, Seven Ages 1980; other: radio plays. *Address:* 23 Mayfield Road, Moseley, Birmingham, B13 9HJ, England.

CRACKNELL, James Edward, OBE, MBE; British oarsman, journalist and motivational speaker; b. 5 May 1972, Sutton, Surrey, England; m. Beverley Turner 2002; one s. two d.; ed Kingston Grammar School; mem. Leander Club; coached by Jürgen Gröbler; int. debut in coxed pair (finished tenth at Jr World Championships) 1989; won gold medal in Coxless Four, Jr World Championships 1990; sr int. debut in Coxless Four (finished seventh in World Championships) 1991; won silver medal in Eight at World Student Games 1993; part of British Coxless Four team 1997: gold medals at World Championships 1997–99, gold medals, FISA (Fédération Internationale des Socs d'Aviron) World Cup 1997, 1999, 2000, gold medals at Olympic Games, Sydney 2000, Athens 2004; with Matthew Pinsent, won gold medals in the Pair at World Championships 2001, 2002 (also gold medal in Coxed Pair); qualified geography teacher; took a 12-month break from rowing 2004; Co-founder Threshold Sports 2008; currently presenter for Channel 4 and ITV, including The Boat Race with Mark Durden-Smith 2007 (ITV), British Superbike Championship (ITV), Red Bull Air Race World Series (Channel 4), also columnist for The Daily Telegraph; unsuccessful Conservative Party cand. for SW England and Gibraltar in European Parl. election 2014; Vice-Pres. Headway (charity); apptd to lead Policy Exchange work on obesity and physical activity. *Achievements:* ran the London Marathon April 2006; successfully completed the Amundsen Omega3 South Pole Race with Ben Fogle and Dr Ed Coats and The Race Across The Atlantic, also with Ben Fogle. *Television includes:* Toughest Race on Earth with James Cracknell (film documentary) 2011, Shackleton's South with James Cracknell (film documentary) 2011, Coldest Race on Earth with James Cracknell (Documentary) 2012, Who Wants to Be a Millionaire (series) 2012, Britain's Greatest Gold Medallists (film documentary) 2012, Race Across America with James Cracknell (film documentary) 2013, World's Toughest Expeditions with James Cracknell (series documentary) 2013, Sports Life Stories (series documentary) 2013, The London Marathon (series) 2015. *Publications:* The Crossing (with Ben Fogle) 2006, Race to the Pole (with Ben Fogle) 2010. *Address:* c/o M&C Saatchi Merlin, 36 Golden Square, London, W1F 9EE, England (office). *Telephone:* (20) 7259-1460 (office). *E-mail:* enquiries@mcsaatchimerlin.com (office). *Website:* www.mcsaatchimerlin.com/clients/james-cracknell-obe (office); www.jamescracknell.com.

CRADDOCK, Gen. (retd) (Bantz) John, BA, MA; American army officer (retd) and consultant; b. 1950, West Union, Doddridge Co., W Va; m. Linda Craddock; one s. one d.; ed West Virginia Univ., Command and Gen. Staff Coll., US Army War Coll.; commissioned as Armour Officer; Tank Co. Commdr, 3rd Armoured Div.; Systems Analyst then Exec. Officer, Office of Program Man., Abrams Tank System, Warren, Mich. 1981; assumed command of 4th Bn 64th Armour 24th Infantry Div. (Mechanised), Fort Stewart, Ga 1989; Asst Chief of Staff, (Operations) for 24th Div.; assumed command of 194th Separate Armoured Brigade 1993–95, then Asst Chief of Staff (Operations) for III Corps, Fort Hood, Tex.; Asst Deputy Dir (Plans and Policy), Jt Staff at Pentagon 1996–98; Asst Divisional Commdr for Manoeuvre of 1st Infantry Div. (Mechanised), Germany 1998; Commanding Gen. 7th Army Training Command, US Army Europe, then assumed command of 1st Infantry Div. (Mechanised); Sr Mil. Asst to Sec. of Defense; Combatant Commdr US Southern Command –2004, led US Southern Command 2004–06; Supreme Allied Commdr Europe and Commdr US European Command, NATO 2006–09; fmr Pres. MPRI Div., L-3 Communications; fmr Sr Vice-Pres., Engility Corpn, now Global Strategic Advisor; currently Sr Consultant, MBDi; mem. Bd of Dirs Atlantic Council; mem. Council on Foreign Relations; Valorous Unit Award, Defense Distinguished Service Medal, Distinguished Service Medal, Silver Star, Defense Superior Service Medal with 1 Oak Leaf Cluster, Legion of Merit with 2 Oak Leaf Clusters, Bronze Star. *Address:* MBDi, 7422 Carmel Executive Park Drive, Charlotte, NC 28226, USA (office). *Telephone:* (704) 553-0000 (office). *E-mail:* info@mbdi.com (office). *Website:* mbdi.com (office).

CRAFORD, M. George, BA, MS, PhD; American electrical engineer; *Solid State Lighting Fellow, Philips Lumileds Lighting;* b. 29 Dec. 1938, Sioux City, Ia; ed Univs of Iowa and Illinois; mem. staff, Monsanto Chemical Co., St Louis, Mo. 1967–74, Dir of Tech., Monsanto Electronics Div., Palo Alto, Calif. 1974–79, rose to become leader of LED technology group, led devt of improved new GaAsP:N LED technology 1971; Tech. Man., Optoelectronics Div., Hewlett Packard 1979–99; Chief Tech. Officer, Lumileds Lighting (joint venture between Agilent and Philips, later became Philips Lumileds Lighting Co., acquired by consortium led by GO Scale Capital 2015) from 1999, later Solid State Lighting Fellow, Philips Lumileds Lighting Co.; mem. Nat. Acad. of Eng; Fellow, IEEE; IEEE Morris N. Liebmann Award 1995, Nat. Medal of Tech. 2002, Alumni Distinguished Service Award, Univ. of Illinois, IEEE Third Millennium Medal, Nick Holonyak Jr Award, Optical Soc. of America, Welker Award, Int. Symposium on Compound Semiconductors, MRS Medal, Materials Research Soc., Electronic Div. Award, Electrochemical Soc., Economist Innovation Award, Strategies in Light LED Pioneer Award, Global Solid State Lighting Devt Award, Int. SSL Alliance, Charles Stark Draper Prize, Nat. Acad. of Eng (co-recipient) 2015. *Publications:* numerous papers in professional journals. *Address:* Lumileds Lighting LLC, 370 West Trimble Road, San Jose, CA 95131, USA (office). *Telephone:* (408) 964-2900 (office). *E-mail:* info@lumileds.com (office). *Website:* www.lumileds.com (office).

CRAFT, Kelly Knight, BA; American diplomatist; *Ambassador to Canada;* b. 24 Feb. 1962, Glasgow, Ky; d. of Bobby Guilfoil and Sherry Dale Guilfoil; m. 1st David S. Moross; m. 2nd Judson Knight; m. 3rd Joe Craft 2016; two c. from previous m.; ed Univ. of Kentucky; apptd by Pres. George W. Bush as Alt. US Del. to UN 2007; Amb. to Canada 2017–; co-f. Morehead State Univ. Craft Acad. for Excellence in Science and Math.; mem. Bd of Trustees, Univ. of Kentucky; mem. Bd of Dirs Kentucky Arts Council, Lexington Philharmonic, YMCA of Central Kentucky, United Way of The Bluegrass; Republican; Dr hc (Morehead State Univ.). *Address:* Embassy of the USA, 490 Sussex Dr., POB 866, Station B, Ottawa, ON K1P 5T1, Canada (office). *Telephone:* (613) 238-5335 (office). *E-mail:* (613) 688-3082 (office). *Website:* ca.usembassy.gov (office).

CRAGG, Sir Anthony (Tony) Douglas, Kt, CBE, MA, RA; British sculptor and academic; *Rektor, Kunstakademie Düsseldorf;* b. 9 April 1949, Liverpool; s. of Douglas R. Cragg and Audrey M. Rutter; m. 1st Ute Oberste-Lehn 1977; two s.; m. 2nd Tatjana Verhasselt 1987; one s. one d.; ed Gloucester Coll. of Art and Design, Wimbledon School of Art, RCA; lab. technician, Nat. Rubber Producers Research Asscn 1966–68; fmr Prof., Ecole des Beaux Arts de Metz; moved to Wuppertal 1977, first exhbns 1977; teacher, Kunstakademie Düsseldorf 1978–2001, Prof. 2005–, Co-Dir 2008, Rektor 2009–; Prof., Hochschule der Künste (HdK), Berlin 2001–05; Visiting Prof., Univ. of the Arts, London 2005; elected to Akad. der Künste, Berlin 2001, European Acad., Nordrhein-Westfalen Akad. der Wissenschaften und der Künste; over 300 solo exhbns in galleries and museums and numerous group exhbns 1977–; Hon. Prof., Budapest, Kunstakademie Düsseldorf 2015; Hon. Fellow, John Moores Univ. 2001, Univ. of the Arts London 2012; Citizen of Honour, City of Wuppertal 2014; Chevalier des Arts et des Lettres 1992; Order of Merit (First Class) of FRG 2012; Dr hc (Univ. of Surrey) 2001, (RCA) 2009, (Azerbaijan) 2014; Mentione Speciale, Venice Biennale 1988, Von-der-Heydt Prize 1989, Turner Prize 1988, Shakespeare Prize 2001, Peipenbrock Prize for Sculpture 2002, First Prize, Beijing Biennale 2005, Praemium Imperiale 2007, Ehrenring der Stadt Wuppertal 2009, Prize for Non-Chinese-Artists, Beijing 2010, Artist's Medal of Honour of the Hermitage, Russia 2012, Int. Sculpture Centre Lifetime Achievement in Contemporary Sculpture Award (jt recipient) 2017. *Leisure interests:* walking, geology. *Address:* Kunstakademie Düsseldorf, Eiskellerstraße 1, 40213 Düsseldorf (office); Lise-Meitner-Str. 33, 42119 Wuppertal, Germany (home). *Telephone:* (211) 13960 (office); (202) 551350 (home). *Fax:* (211) 1396225 (office); (202) 5513512 (home). *E-mail:* postmaster@kunstakademie-duesseldorf.de (office); jm@tony-cragg.com. *Website:* www.kunstakademie-duesseldorf.de (office); www.tony-cragg.com.

CRAIG, Daniel Wroughton; British actor; b. 2 March 1968, Chester, Cheshire; s. of Timothy John Wroughton Craig and Carol Olivia Craig (née Williams); m. 1st Fiona Loudon 1992 (divorced 1994); one d.; m. 2nd Rachel Weisz 2011; ed Hilbre High School, West Kirby, Merseyside, Calday Grange Grammar School, Nat. Youth Theatre, Guildhall School of Music and Drama, London; played rugby union for Hoylake RFC; began acting in school plays aged six; film debut in the drama The Power of One 1992; best known for being cast as the fictional British secret agent James Bond 007 Oct. 2005, first film in the role, Casino Royale, released 2006; apptd first UN global advocate for the elimination of mines and explosive hazards 2015. *Theatre includes:* A Number, Royal Court 2002, A Steady Rain, Broadway 2009, Betrayal, Broadway 2013, Othello, New York Theatre 2016. *Films include:* The Power of One 1992, A Kid in King Arthur's Court 1995, Obsession 1997, Love and Rage 1998, Elizabeth 1998, Love Is the Devil: Study for a Portrait of Francis Bacon (Edinburgh Int. Film Festival Award for Best British Performance) 1998, The Trench 1999, I Dreamed of Africa 2000, Some Voices (British Ind. Film Award for Best Actor) 2000, Hotel Splendide 2000, Lara Croft: Tomb Raider 2001, Road to Perdition 2002, Ten Minutes Older: The Cello 2002, Occasional, Strong 2002, The Mother 2003, Sylvia 2003, Enduring Love 2004, Layer Cake 2004, The Jacket 2005, Sorstalanság 2005, Fateless 2005, Munich 2005, Renaissance (voice) 2006, Infamous 2006, Casino Royale (Evening Standard British Film Award for Best Actor 2007) 2006, The Invasion 2007, The Golden Compass 2007, Flashbacks of a Fool 2008, Quantum of Solace 2008, Defiance 2008, Cowboys & Aliens 2011, Dream House 2011, The Adventures of Tintin: The Secret of the Unicorn 2011, One Life (narrator) 2011, The Girl with the Dragon Tattoo 2011, Skyfall 2012, Spectre 2015. *Television includes:* Sharpe's Eagle 1993, Zorro 1993, Drop the Dead Donkey 1993, The Young Indiana Jones Chronicles 1993, Between the Lines 1993, Heartbeat 1993, Screen Two 1993, Kiss and Tell (film) 1996, Our Friends in the North 1996, The Fortunes and Misfortunes of Moll Flanders 1996, Tales from the Crypt 1996, The Ice House (film) 1997, The Hunger 1997, Shockers: The Visitor 1999, Sword of Honour 2001, Copenhagen 2002, Archangel 2005, Saturday Night Live 2012, London 2012 Olympic Opening Ceremony: Isles of Wonder (film) 2012, Superheroes Unite for BBC Children in Need (narrator) 2014. *Leisure interests:* rugby union, Liverpool Football Club. *Address:* c/o Creative Artists Agency, 2000 Avenue of the Stars, Los Angeles, CA 90067, USA (office). *Telephone:* (424) 288-2000 (office). *Fax:* (424) 288-2900 (office). *Website:* www.caa.com (office).

CRAIG, Ian Jonathan David, BSc (Hons), PhD; British astrophysicist and academic; *Professor, Department of Mathematics, University of Waikato;* b. 30 Aug. 1950, Sheffield. Yorks., England; s. of Ronald W. Craig and Beatrice I. Craig; m. Fumiko Nishimura; one s. one d.; ed Chesterfield Coll. of Tech. and Westfield Coll. and Univ. Coll., London; Research Fellow, Dept of Astronomy, Univ. of Glasgow 1974–76, 1977–79; Research Assoc., Inst. for Plasma Research, Stanford Univ., USA 1976–77; Lecturer in Math., Univ. of Waikato, NZ 1979–85, Sr Lecturer 1985–93, Assoc. Prof. 1993–2002, Prof. 2002–, Chair. of Dept 2002; Research Astronomer, Inst. for Astronomy, Univ. of Hawaii 1990–91; guest investigator on Skylab 1977; mem. Int. Astronomical Union. *Publications include:* Inverse Problems in Astronomy–A Guide to Inversion Strategies for Remotely Sensed Data (with J. C. Brown) 1986. *Leisure interests:* cycling, swimming, skiing, windsurfing; wood: growing it, working it and burning it. *Address:* Room G3.21, Computing & Mathematical Sciences, University of Waikato, Private Bag, Hamilton (office); 25 Cranwell Place, Hamilton, New Zealand (home). *Telephone:* (7) 838-4466 (ext. 8323) (office). *Fax:* (7) 838-4666 (office). *E-mail:* i.craig@waikato.ac.nz (office). *Website:* www.cms.waikato.ac.nz/people/math0097 (office).

CRAIG, Larry Edwin, BA; American politician; b. 20 July 1945, Council, Ida; s. of Elvin Craig and Dorothy Craig; m. Suzanne Thompson 1983; two s. one d.; ed Univ. of Idaho and George Washington Univ.; farmer and rancher in Midvale, Ida area; mem. Ida Farm Bureau 1965–79; mem. Nat. Rifle Asscn, Future Farmers of America; Pres. Ida Young Republican League 1976–77; mem. Ida Republican Exec. Cttee 1976–78; mem. Ida Senate 1974–80; mem. US House of Reps from 1st Dist of Ida 1981–91; Senator from Idaho 1991–2009 (retd); Republican. *Leisure interest:* gardening.

CRAIG, Mary, MA; British author and broadcaster; b. 2 July 1928, St Helens, Lancs.; d. of William Joseph Clarkson and Anne Mary Clarkson; m. Francis John Craig 1952 (died 1995); four s. (one deceased); ed Notre Dame Convent, St Helens, Liverpool Univ., St Anne's Coll., Oxford; NW Organizer, Sue Ryder Trust 1962–68; TV Critic, Catholic Herald 1971–76; presenter and features writer (freelance) with BBC Radio 1969–77; interviewer, Thames TV, Southern TV (freelance); freelance journalist and book reviewer; Officer's Cross, Order of Polonia Restituta 1987; John Harriott Award 1993 and other awards. *Publications include:* Longford 1978, Woodruff at Random 1978, Blessings (The Christopher Book Award, USA 1979) 1979, Man from a Far Country 1979, Candles in the Dark 1983, The Crystal Spirit 1986, Spark from Heaven 1988, Tears of Blood: A Cry for Tibet 1992, Kundun: The Dalai Lama, His Family and His Times 1997, The Last Freedom: A Journal 1997, Waiting for the Sun: A Peasant Boy in Occupied Tibet 1999, His Holiness the Dalai Lama (anthology, ed.) 2001, Voices from Silence 2010; for children: Pope John Paul II 1982, Mother Teresa 1984, Lech Wałęsa 1989. *Leisure interests:* reading modern history and biography, logic puzzles, listening to music, playing the piano, travel. *Address:* c/o PFD, Drury House, 34–43 Russell Street, London, WC2B 5HA, England (office); 1 Lodge Gardens, Penwood, Burghclere, nr Newbury, Berks., RG20 9EF, England (home). *Telephone:* (20) 7344-1000 (office). *Fax:* (20) 7836-9543 (office). *Website:* www.pfd.co.uk (office).

CRAIG-MARTIN, Sir Michael, Kt, CBE, MFA, RA; Irish/British artist; *Professor Emeritus of Fine Art, Goldsmiths College;* b. 28 Aug. 1941, Dublin, Ireland; s. of

Paul F. Craig-Martin and Rhona Gargan Craig-Martin; m. Janice Hashey 1963 (divorced); one d.; ed The Priory School, Washington DC, Fordham Univ., NY, Yale Univ., Yale Univ. School of Art; family moved to USA 1946, returned to UK 1966; Lecturer, Bath Acad. of Art 1966–69; Artist in Residence, King's Coll., Cambridge 1970–72; Sr Lecturer, Goldsmiths Coll., Univ. of London 1974–88, Millard Prof. of Fine Art 1994–2000, now Prof. Emer.; Trustee, Tate Gallery 1989–99, The Art Fund 2004–14; Hon. Fellow, Goldsmiths Coll.; Dr hc (San Francisco Art Inst.) 2001, (Christ Church Univ., Canterbury) 2012. *Publication:* On Being An Artist 2014. *Address:* c/o Gagosian Gallery, 4–24 Britannia Street, London, WC1X 9JD, England. *Telephone:* (20) 7841-9960. *E-mail:* mcraigmartin@gmail.com (office). *Website:* www.michaelcraig-martin.com.

CRAIG OF RADLEY, Baron (Life Peer), cr. 1991, of Helhoughton in the County of Norfolk; **Marshal of the RAF David Brownrigg Craig,** GCB, OBE, MA, DSc, FRAeS; British fmr air force officer; b. 17 Sept. 1929, Dublin, Ireland; s. of Maj. Francis Brownrigg Craig and Olive Craig; m. Elizabeth June Derenburg 1955; one s. one d.; ed Radley Coll. and Lincoln Coll., Oxford; commissioned in RAF 1951, Commanding Officer RAF Cranwell 1968–70; ADC to The Queen 1969–71; Dir Plans and Operations, HQ Far East Command 1970–71, Commanding Officer RAF Akrotiri 1972–73, ACAS (Ops) Ministry of Defence 1975–78, Air Officer Commanding No. 1 Group RAF Strike Command 1978–80, Vice-Chief of the Air Staff 1980–82, Air Officer, C-in-C, RAF Strike Command and C-in-C UK Air Forces 1982–85, Chief of Air Staff 1985–88, Chief of Defence Staff 1988–91; Air ADC to The Queen 1985–88; Chair. Council of King Edward VII Hosp. (Sister Agnes) 1998–2004; Deputy Chair. RAF Benevolent Fund 1996–2013; mem. (Crossbench), House of Lords 1991–, mem. Select Cttee on Science and Tech. 1993–99, House Cttee 2007–13, Liaison Cttee 2013–, Convenor Crossbench Peers 1999–2004; Pres. RAF Club 2002–12; Hon. Fellow, Lincoln Coll., Oxford 1984; Hon. DSc (Cranfield). *Leisure interests:* fishing, shooting. *Address:* House of Lords, Westminster, London, SW1A 0PW, England (office). *Telephone:* (20) 7219-2200 (office). *E-mail:* craigd@parliament.uk (office). *Website:* www.parliament.uk/biographies/lords/lord-craig-of-radley/3385 (office).

CRAIGG, Wendy M., CBE, MA; Bahamian economist and fmr central banker; *Economic Policy Advisor, Office of the Prime Minister;* m. Anthony Craigg; ed St Augustine's Coll., Coll. of Mount St Vincent and Fordham Univ., USA; began career in Research Dept, Central Bank of the Bahamas 1978, apptd mem. Bd of Dirs 1997, Deputy Gov. 1997–2005, Gov. and Chair. 2005–15; Econ. Policy Advisor, Office of the Prime Minister 2016–; fmr Deputy Chair. Securities Comm. of The Bahamas; fmr mem. Strategic Man. Cttee, Caribbean Centre for Money and Finance, Trinidad and Tobago. *Publications:* numerous papers on econ. issues. *Address:* Office of the Prime Minister, Sir Cecil Wallace-Whitfield Centre, West Bay Street, POB CB-10980, Nassau, Bahamas (office). *Telephone:* 327-5826 (office). *Fax:* 327-5806 (office). *E-mail:* primeminister@bahamas.gov.bs (office).

CRAIK, Fergus Ian Muirden, BSc, PhD, FRSC, FRS; British/Canadian psychologist and academic; *Senior Scientist, Rotman Research Institute;* b. 17 April 1935, Edinburgh, Scotland; s. of George Craik and Frances Crabbe; m. Anne Catherall 1961; one s. one d.; ed George Watson's Boys' Coll., Edinburgh and Univs of Edinburgh and Liverpool; mem. scientific staff, MRC Unit for Research on Occupational Aspects of Ageing, Univ. of Liverpool 1960–65; Lecturer in Psychology, Birkbeck Coll., London 1965–71; Assoc. Prof., then Prof. of Psychology, Univ. of Toronto, Canada 1971–2000, Univ. Prof. Emer. 2000–, Chair. Dept of Psychology 1985–90; Scientist, Rotman Research Inst., Baycrest Centre for Geriatric Care 2000–10, Sr Scientist 2010–; Fellow, Center for Advanced Study in Behavioral Sciences, Stanford Univ. 1982–83, Soc. of Experimental Psychologists, Canadian Psychological Asscn, American Psychological Asscn; Dr hc (Bordeaux) 2006; Killam Research Fellowship 1982–84, Guggenheim Fellowship 1982–83, William James Fellow Award 1993, D.O. Hebb Award 1998, Killam Prize for Science 2000, Anderson Lifetime Achievement Award 2009. *Publications:* Levels of Processing in Human Memory (co-ed.) 1979, Aging and Cognitive Processes (co-ed.) 1982, Varieties of Memory and Consciousness (co-ed.) 1989, The Handbook of Aging and Cognition (co-ed.) 1992, The Oxford Handbook of Memory (co-ed.) 2000, Lifespan Cognition (co-ed.) 2006. *Leisure interests:* reading, walking, tennis, music. *Address:* Rotman Research Institute, Baycrest Centre for Geriatric Care, 3560 Bathurst Street, Toronto, ON M6A 2E1, Canada (office). *Telephone:* (416) 785-2500 (ext. 3526) (office). *Fax:* (416) 785-2862 (office). *E-mail:* fcraik@rotman-baycrest.on.ca (office). *Website:* research.baycrest.org/fcraik (office).

CRAMER, Kevin, BA, MA; American politician; *Senator from North Dakota;* b. 21 Jan. 1961, Rolette, North Dakota; s. of Richard Cramer and Clarice Cramer (née Hjelden); m. Kris Cramer; three s. two d.; ed Concordia Coll., Univ. of Mary; Chair. North Dakota Republican Party 1991–93; Dir of Tourism, State Govt of North Dakota 1993–97, Dir of Economic Devt and Finance 1997–2000; Exec. Dir, Harold Schafer Leadership Center 2000–03; elected to the ND Public Service Comm. 2003, Commr 2004–; Adjunct Instructor, Marketing/Man., Univ. of Mary, also Bd mem. and Exec. Trustee 2006–; mem. US House of Reps 2012–19; Senator from ND 2019–; mem. Cttees on Armed Services, Environment and Public Works, Veterans' Affairs, Banking and Budget; Republican; Dr hc (Univ. of Mary) 2013. *Address:* United States Senate, B40C Dirksen Senate Office Building, Washington, DC 20510, USA (office). *Telephone:* (202) 224-2043 (office). *Website:* www.cramer.senate.gov (office).

CRANBROOK, 5th Earl of (cr. 1892), 5th Viscount (cr. 1878); **Gathorne Gathorne-Hardy,** MA, PhD, CBiol, DL; British biologist (retd); *Adjunct Senior Research Fellow, Monash University;* b. 20 June 1933, London; m. Caroline Jarvis 1967; two s. one d.; ed Eton Coll., Corpus Christi Coll., Cambridge and Univ. of Birmingham; Tech. Asst, Sarawak Museum 1956–58; Lecturer, Sr Lecturer in Zoology, Univ. of Malaya 1961–70; Ed. Ibis (journal of British Ornithologists' Union) 1973–80; mem. Royal Comm. on Environmental Pollution 1981–92; Trustee, Natural History Museum 1982–86; mem. Natural Environment Research Council 1982–88; mem. Nature Conservancy Council 1990–91; Chair. English Nature 1991–98, ENTRUST 1996–2002; Dir (non-exec.) Anglian Water 1989–98; mem. Broads Authority, Harwich Haven Authority 1988–98; mem. Bd Foundation for European Environmental Policy 1987–98, Chair. 1990–98; Vice-Pres. Nat. Soc. for Clean Air and Environmental Protection; also partner in family farming business in Suffolk; Chair. Inst. for European Environmental Policy 1990–98; Chair. Int. Trust for Zoological Nomenclature 2001–08; Adjunct Sr Research Fellow, Monash Univ., Australia 2014; Hon. Johan Bintang Sarawak (JBS) 1997, Hon. Panglima Negara Bintang Sarawak (PNBS) 2005, Hon. Fellow, Linnean Soc. 2006; Hon. DSc (Aberdeen) 1989, (Cranfield) 1996; Royal Geographical Soc. Founder's Gold Medal 1995, WWF Duke of Edinburgh Conservation Medal 2014, Merdeka Award (Malaysia) 2014. *Publications:* Mammals of Borneo 1965, Birds of the Malay Peninsula (co-author) 1974, Riches of the Wild: Mammals of South East Asia 1987, Belalong: A Tropical Rain Forest (co-author) 1994, Wonders of Nature in South East Asia 1997, Ballad of Jerjezang (co-author) 2001, Swiftlets of Borneo (co-author) 2002 (second edn 2014). *Leisure interest:* walking. *Address:* Glemham House, Great Glemham, Saxmundham, Suffolk, IP17 1LP, England (home). *Telephone:* 7775-755825 (mobile) (home). *Fax:* (1728) 663339 (home). *E-mail:* lordcranbook@greatglemhamfarms.co.uk (office).

CRANDALL, Robert Lloyd, BA; American business executive; b. 6 Dec. 1935, Westerly, RI; s. of Lloyd Evans Crandall and Virginia Crandall (née Beard); m. Margaret Jan Schmults 1957; two s. one d.; ed William and Mary Coll., Univ. of Rhode Island, Wharton School, Univ. of Pennsylvania; Dir of Credit and Collections, then Vice-Pres. Data Services TWA 1967–73; COO American Airlines 1973–85, Sr Vice-Pres. (Finance) 1973–74, Sr Vice-Pres. Marketing 1974–80, Dir 1976–, Pres. 1980–95, Chair. and CEO 1985–98 (retd), Pres., Chair. and CEO AMR Corpn 1985–98, now Chair. Emer.; Chair. Celestica Inc. 2004–12; Chair. Pogo Jet Inc.; mem. Bd of Dirs Gogo, Inc; mem. US Fed. Aviation Admin Man. Advisory Cttee; Horatio Alger Award 1997, Wright Brothers Memorial Trophy, Nat. Aeronautic Asscn 2004, Eagle of Aviation Award, Embry-Riddle Aeronautical Univ. 2004. *Leisure interests:* skiing, tennis, running, reading. *Address:* Pogo Jet, Inc., 611 Access Road, Suite 105, Stratford, CT 06615, USA (office). *E-mail:* contact@flypogo.com (office). *Website:* www.flypogo.com (office).

CRANDALL, Roger W., BA, MBA, CFA; American insurance company executive; *Chairman, President and CEO, Massachusetts Mutual Life Insurance Company (MassMutual);* b. 1965; ed Univ. of Vermont, Wharton School of Business, Univ. of Pennsylvania; joined Massachusetts Mutual Life Insurance Co. (MassMutual) 1988, has held positions as Head of Corp. Bond Man., Public Bond Trading and Institutional Fixed Income, Chief Investment Officer, and Chair. Babson Capital (now Barings Corporate Investors) 2005–08, mem. Bd of Trustees Babson Capital Participation 2005–09, Pres. and CEO Babson Capital Man. LLC 2006–08, Pres. and COO MassMutual 2008–09, Pres. and CEO Jan. 2010–, Chair. 2010–; mem. CFA Inst.; mem. Bd of Dirs American Council of Life Insurers. *Address:* Massachusetts Mutual Life Insurance Co. (MassMutual), 1295 State Street, Springfield, MA 01111-0001, USA (office). *Telephone:* (413) 788-8411 (office). *Fax:* (413) 744-6005 (office). *E-mail:* info@massmutual.com (office). *Website:* www.massmutual.com (office).

CRANE, Christopher M.; American business executive; *President and CEO, Exelon Corporation;* b. 1959; ed New Hampshire Tech. Coll., Advanced Man. Program, Harvard Business School; worked in new plant start-up at Comanche Peak Nuclear Plant, Tex. and Palo Verde Nuclear Plant, Ariz.; served as Browns Ferry Nuclear site Vice-Pres. for the Tennessee Valley Authority; joined Exelon Corpn (utility holding co., then ComEd) 1998, Chief Nuclear Officer 2004–07, Pres. and COO Exelon Corpn and Pres. Exelon Generation 2008–12, Pres. and CEO Exelon Corpn 2012–, Chair. Bd of Dirs Pepco Holdings LLC 2016; Vice-Chair. Nuclear Energy Inst. 2012–15, Chair. 2015; Vice-Chair. Bd of Dirs Edison Electric Inst. (EEI) 2018–; mem. Bd of Dirs Inst. of Nuclear Power Operations, Exec. Cttee Nuclear Energy Inst. (also served as Chair. New Plant Oversight Cttee and mem. Nuclear Strategic Issues Advisory Cttee, Nuclear Fuel Supply Cttee, Materials Initiative Group); Vice-Chair. World Nuclear Asscn; mem. Bd Foundation for Nuclear Studies; mem. Bd of Trustees Rush University Medical Center. *Address:* Exelon Corpn, PO Box 805398, 48th Floor, 10 South Dearborn Street, Chicago, IL 60680-5398, USA (office). *Telephone:* (800) 483-3220 (office). *E-mail:* info@exeloncorp.com (office). *Website:* www.exeloncorp.com (office).

CRANE, Sir Peter Robert, Kt, PhD, FRS; British environmentalist, plant scientist and academic; *President, Oak Spring Garden Foundation;* b. 18 July 1954, Kettering, Northants.; s. of Walter Robert Crane and Dorothy Mary Crane (née Mills); m. Elinor Margaret Hamer 1986; one s. one d.; ed Univ. of Reading; Lecturer, Dept of Botany, Univ. of Reading 1978–82; Post-doctoral Research Scholar, Dept of Biology, Indiana Univ. 1981–82; Curator Dept of Geology, The Field Museum, Chicago 1982–92, Vice-Pres. Center for Evolutionary and Environmental Biology 1992–93, Vice-Pres. Academic Affairs and Dir The Field Museum 1994–99; mem. Paleontological Soc. (Pres. 1998–2000); Dir Royal Botanic Gardens, Kew 1999–2005; John and Marion Sullivan Univ. Prof., Dept of Geophysical Sciences, Univ. of Chicago 2006–09; Prof. of Botany and Carl W. Knobloch Jr Dean, School of Forestry and Environmental Studies, Yale Univ. 2009–16; currently Pres. Oak Spring Garden Foundation; Foreign Assoc., NAS 2001; Foreign mem. Royal Swedish Acad. of Sciences 2002, German Acad. Leopoldina 2004; mem. American Acad. of Arts and Sciences 2008; Hon. DSc, (Cambridge) 2009, (Univ. Connecticut) 2011, (Univ. of South, Sewanee); Bicentenary Medal, Linnean Soc. 1984, Schuchert Award, Paleontological Soc. 1993, Int. Prize for Biology, Japan Soc. for the Promotion of Science 2014. *Publications include:* The Origins of Angiosperms and their Biological Consequences (co-ed) 1987, The Evolution, Systematics and Fossil History of the Hamamelidae Vols 1 and 2 (co-ed) 1989, The Origin and Diversification of Land Plants (co-author) 1997, Early Flowers and Angiosperm Evolution (co-author) 2011, Ginkgo: The Tree That Time Forgot 2013. *Address:* 1776, Loughborough Lane, Upperville VA 20184, USA (office). *Telephone:* (540) 592-3159 (office). *E-mail:* peter.crane@yale.edu (office). *Website:* environment.yale.edu/profile/crane (office).

CRANFIELD, Thomas L., BA; Irish banker and civil servant; b. 3 Feb. 1945, Dublin; m.; three d.; ed Faculté catholique de Lyon, Univ. Coll., Dublin, Irish Man. Inst.; religious 1962–68; grad. asst, Fed. of Irish Industry 1968–69; Asst Personnel Officer, then Personnel Officer, then Personnel Admin., Technicon Ltd (US biomedical eng co.), Dublin 1970–73; Head of Div., EIB (Luxembourg) 1973–90; Deputy Registrar, European Court of Justice, Luxembourg 1990–2000; fmr Dir-Gen. Office for Official Publs of the EU (OPOCE) from 2000; fmr mem. Cttee of Experts, Centre Virtuel de la Connaissance sur l'Europe. *Address:* c/o Centre Virtuel de la Connaissance sur l'Europe, Château de Sanem, 4992 Sanem, Luxembourg.

CRANHAM, Kenneth Raymond; British actor; b. 12 Dec. 1944, Dunfermline, Scotland; s. of Ronald Cranham and Margaret McKay Ferguson; m. Fiona Victory; two d.; ed Tulse Hill School, London, Royal Acad. of Dramatic Art (RADA), Nat. Youth Theatre; Bancroft Gold Medal, RADA 1966, Christine Silver Memorial Prize, Herbert Tree Prize. *Plays include:* RSC: School for Scandal, Ivanov, The Iceman Cometh; Nat. Theatre: Flight, An Inspector Calls, Kick for Touch, The Cherry Orchard, Cardiff East, From Kipling to Vietnam, The Caretaker, Strawberry Fields, Love Letters on Blue Paper, The Passion, The Country Wife, Old Movies, Madras House, The UN Inspector; Royal Court: Saved, Ruffian on the Stair, Samuel Beckett's Play, Cascando, The London Cuckolds, Tibetan in Roads, Magnificence, Cheek, Owners, Geography of a Horse Dreamer; West End: Loot, Comedians, Entertaining Mr Sloane, The Novice, Doctor's Dilemma, Paul Bunyan (Royal Opera House), Endgame, Broadway: Loot, An Inspector Calls, Gaslight (Old Vic), The Homecoming, Little Malcolm and his Struggle Against the Eunuchs, Traverse, Edinburgh and European tour, A Month in the Country (Chichester Festival Theatre), The Herd (Bush Theatre) 2014, The Father (Ustinov, Bath) 2014, (Tricycle Theatre, London) (Olivier Award for Best Actor 2016) 2015. *Radio includes:* The Barchester Chronicles, New Grub Street, Sons and Lovers, Hard Times, Answered Prayers, Earthly Powers, Barrack Room Ballads, Gilgamesh, The Complete Smiley, The Pantomine Life of Joseph Grimaldi, Dr Johnson, The Interrogation 2012– (four series). *Films:* Oliver! 1968, Otley 1968, All the Way Up 1970, Fragment of Fear 1970, Up Pompeii 1971, Brother Sun, Sister Moon 1972, Vampira 1975, Peer Gynt 1976, Robin and Marian 1976, Joseph Andrews 1977, Heart of the High Country 1985, Making Waves (short) 1987, Chocolate 1988, Stealing Heaven 1988, Hellbound: Hellraiser II 1988, Prospero's Books 1991, Under Suspicion 1991, Tale of a Vampire 1992, Bed of Roses 1996, Deep in the Heart 1996, The Boxer 1997, RPM 1998, Vigo: A Passion for Life 1998, Women Talking Dirty 1999, The Last Yellow 1999, Kevin & Perry Go Large (as Ken Cranham) 2000, Gangster No. 1 (as Ken Cranham) 2000, Born Romantic 2000, The Most Fertile Man in Ireland 2000, Shiner 2000, Two Men Went to War 2002, Man Dancin' 2003, Blackball 2003, Bible Mysteries – Revelation: The End of the World 2004, Trauma (as Ken Cranham) 2004, Layer Cake 2004, The Rising: Ballad of Mangal Pandey 2005, A Good Year 2006, Hot Fuzz 2007, The Curry Club (short) 2007, Valkyrie 2008, Running in Traffic 2009, Made in Dagenham 2010, Michael Stilton (as Ken Cranham), 5 Days of War 2011, Flying Blind 2012, Suspension of Disbelief 2012, Closed Circuit 2013, Maleficent 2014, Film Stars Don't Die in Liverpool 2017, Mr Jones 2019. *Television includes:* Ways with Words (series) 1967, City '68 – The Shooting War 1967, The Wednesday Play – Death of a Private 1967, – Sling Your Hook 1969, ITV Playhouse – Rogues' Gallery: The Misfortunes of Lucy Hodges 1968, Boy Meets Girl (series) 1969, Thirty-Minute Theatre – Gangster 1969, Z Cars (series) 1970, ITV Playhouse – Private Lillywhite's Dead 1970, Omnibus (series documentary) 1970, Softly Softly: Task Force (series) 1970–72, A Family at War (series) 1971, Hadleigh (series) 1971, From a Bird's Eye View (series) 1971, New Scotland Yard (series) 1972, Budgie (series) 1972, ITV Sunday Night Theatre – The Samaritan 1972, Thirty-Minute Theatre – The Chauffeur and the Lady 1972, Achilles Heel (film) 1973, Crown Court (series) 1973–82, BBC Play of the Month (series) 1974, Village Hall (series) 1975, Against the Crowd (series) 1975, Holding On (series) 1977, Play for Today (series) 1978–81, Danger UXB (series) 1979, Screenplay (series) 1979, Thérèse Raquin (mini-series) 1980, Enemy at the Door (series) 1980, Strangers (series) 1980–82, Tis Pity She's a Whore (film) 1980, Cribb (series) 1980, Brideshead Revisited (mini-series) 1981, The Bell (series) 1982, The Bell (series) 1982, Shine on Harvey Moon (series) 1982–85, La ronde (film) 1982, Reilly: Ace of Spies (mini-series) 1983, Summer Season (series) 1985, Theatre Night (series) 1985–89, Dead Man's Folly (film) 1986, A Sort of Innocence (series) 1986, Inspector Morse (series) 1987, Normal Service (film) 1988, The Play on One (series) 1988–89, Screenplay (series) 1988–92, Just Another Secret (film) 1989, Rules of Engagement (mini-series) 1989, Oranges Are Not the Only Fruit (mini-series) 1989, Boon (series) 1989, Casualty (series) 1990, El C.I.D. (series) 1990–92, Wales Playhouse (series) 1990, Dunrulin (film) 1990, Bergerac (series) 1990, Van der Valk (series) 1991, Chimera (mini-series) 1991, Murder Most Horrid (series) 1991, The Young Indiana Jones Chronicles (series) 1992, Between the Lines (series) 1992, Minder (series) 1993, Lovejoy (series) 1993, Screen One – Royal Celebration 1993, Shooting to Stardom (short) 1993, Requiem Apache (film) 1994, On Dangerous Ground (film) 1996, Heartbeat (series) 1996, The Tenant of Wildfell Hall (mini-series) 1996, Midnight Man (film) 1997, Get Well Soon – Tucker's Gambit 1997, Our Mutual Friend (mini-series) 1998, Kavanagh QC – Dead Reckoning 1998, The Murder of Stephen Lawrence (film) 1999, Without Motive (series) 2000, Justice in Wonderland (film) 2000, Lady Audley's Secret (film) 2000, The Ancients (film) 2000, The Sins (mini-series) 2000, Hannibal: The Man Who Hated Rome (documentary) (narrator) 2001, NCS: Manhunt (film) 2001, Dalziel and Pascoe (series) 2001, Night Flight (film) 2002, Dickens (series) 2002, Believe Nothing (series) 2002, Pollyanna (film) 2003, Killing Hitler (documentary) 2003, Sparkling Cyanide (film) 2003, The Genius of Mozart (mini-series) 2004, M.I.T.: Murder Investigation Team (series) 2005, Genghis Khan (film) (voice of Genghis Khan) 2005, Rome (series) (as Pompey Magnus) 2005, The Lavender List (film) 2006, The Chatterley Affair (film) 2006, Hustle (series) 2006, Hannibal (film) (narrator) 2006, New Tricks (series) 2006, The Line of Beauty (mini-series) 2006, Afterlife (series) 2006, Doc Martin (series) 2006, Lilies – The Tallyman 2007, Lusitania: Murder on the Atlantic (documentary) 2007, The Last Detective – The Man from Montevideo 2007, Heroes and Villains (series documentary) – Napoleon 2007, Tess of the D'Urbervilles (mini-series) 2008, Merlin (series) 2008, Marple: A Pocket Full of Rye (film) 2008, Spanish Flu: The Forgotten Fallen (film) 2009, Midsomer Murders – Blood on the Saddle (film) 2010, The Night Watch (film) 2011, National Theatre Live – The Cherry Orchard 2011, Upstairs Downstairs (series) 2012, War and Peace 2016. *Publication:* 50 Years at the Royal Court Theatre. *Leisure interests:* vernacular music, art, food, travel, some people, thinking on trains. *Address:* c/o Markham, Froggatt & Irwin, 4 Windmill Street, London, W1 2HZ, England (office). *Telephone:* (20) 7636-4412 (office). *Fax:* (20) 7637-5233 (office). *E-mail:* admin@markhamfroggattandirwin .com (office). *Website:* www.markhamfroggattandirwin.com (office).

CRANSTON, Bryan Lee; American actor, screenwriter and director; b. 7 March 1956, Canoga Park, Calif.; s. of Joseph L. (Joe) Cranston and Peggy Sell; m. 1st Mickey Middleton 1977 (divorced 1982); m. 2nd Robin Dearden 1989; one d.; ed Canoga Park High School, Los Angeles Valley Coll.; began acting career in local and regional theatres, started at Granada Theatre, San Fernando Valley; numerous TV commercials; voice acting includes English dubbing of Japanese anime, under the name Lee Stone; original cast mem. ABC soap opera Loving; part-owner of ind. theatre Cinemas Palme d'Or in Palm Desert; Spotlight Award, Actor, Palm Springs Int. Film Festival 2016. *Films include:* Oritsu uchûgun Oneamisu no tsubasa (voice: English version) 1987, Amazon Women on the Moon 1987, The Big Turnaround 1988, Corporate Affairs 1990, Dead Space 1991, Morudaibâ (video short) (voice: English version) 1993, The Super Dimension Century Orguss 02 (video short) (voice: English version) 1993, Erotique 1994, Clean Slate 1994, Macross Plus (video) (voice: English version) (as Lee Stone) 1994, Armitage III (video) (voice: English version) 1995, That Thing You Do! 1996, Street Corner Justice 1996, Strategic Command 1997, Armitage III: Poly Matrix (video) (voice) 1997, Time Under Fire 1997, Saving Private Ryan 1998, Last Chance (also dir) 1999, The Big Thing 2000, The Prince of Light 2000, Terror Tract 2000, Seeing Other People 2004, Illusion 2004, Magnificent Desolation: Walking on the Moon 3D (documentary short) (voice) 2005, Little Miss Sunshine 2006, Intellectual Property 2006, Hard Four 2007, Love Ranch 2010, The Lincoln Lawyer 2011, Detachment 2011, Drive 2011, Leave 2011, Larry Crowne 2011, Contagion 2011, Batman: Year One (video) (voice) 2011, Red Tails 2012, John Carter 2012, Madagascar 3: Europe's Most Wanted (voice) 2012, Rock of Ages 2012, Total Recall 2012, Argo (New York Film Critics Online for Best Ensemble Cast 2012) 2012, Eye of Winter 2013, Cold Comes the Night 2013, Writer's Block (short) 2013, Get a Job 2013, Godzilla 2014, Trumbo 2015, The Infiltrator 2016, Wakefield 2016, The Upside 2019. *Plays include:* All The Way (Tony Award for Best Lead Actor in a Play 2014) 2014, Network (Olivier Award for Best Actor 2018) 2017. *Television includes:* Seinfeld (series) 1994–97, Diagnosis Murder (series) 1996–98, From the Earth to the Moon (mini-series) 1998, Clerks: The Animated Series (series) (voice) 2000–01, Malcolm in the Middle (series) (also dir) 2000–06, 'Twas the Night (film) 2001, The Santa Claus Brothers (film) 2001, Thanksgiving Family Reunion (film) 2003, Lilo & Stitch: The Series (series) (voice) 2003–04, American Dad! (series) (voice) 2005–10, How I Met Your Mother (series) 2006–13, Fallen (mini-series) 2007, The Hollywood Quad (film) 2008, Breaking Bad (series) (also dir) (Primetime Emmy Award for Outstanding Lead Actor in a Drama Series 2008, 2009, 2010, 2014, Satellite Award for Best Actor in a Series (Drama) 2008, 2009, 2010, TV Critics Asscn Award for Individual Achievement in Drama 2009, Critics' Choice TV Award for Best Drama Actor 2012, Saturn Award for Best Actor on TV 2012, 2013, Screen Actors Guild Award for Outstanding Performance by a Male Actor in a Drama Series 2013, 2014, Golden Globe Award for Best Actor in TV Series, Drama 2014) 2008–13, SuperMansion (series) 2015, Sneaky Pete 2015; dir: Special Unit (film) 2006, Big Day (series) 2006, Modern Family (series) 2012, The Office (series) 2012, 30 Rock 2012, The Simpsons 2013, All the Way (SAG Award for Outstanding Performance by a Male Actor in a Mini-series 2017) 2016. *Leisure interests:* collector of baseball memorabilia, fan of the Los Angeles Dodgers. *Address:* c/o United Talent Agency, 9336 Civic Center Drive, Beverly Hills, CA 90210, USA (office). *Telephone:* (310) 273-6700 (office). *Fax:* (310) 247-1111 (office). *Website:* www.unitedtalent.com (office).

CRANSTON, David Alan, CBE; British business executive and fmr army officer; b. 20 Oct. 1945, Windermere, Cumbria; s. of Stanley Cranston and Mary Cranston (née Fitzherbert); m. Pippa Ann Reynolds 1968; three d.; ed Strathallan School, Perthshire, Royal Mil. Acad., Sandhurst; served in army first in artillery and then as aviator 1966–95, retd with rank of Brig.; with Personal Investment Authority 1995–97, Royal Bank of Scotland Group 1997–2000; Dir-Gen. Nat. Asscn of Pension Funds 2000–02; Dir (non-exec.) Voller Energy Group PLC, Scandia UK, Austin Reed Group Pension Fund Ltd, WBB Minerals Pension Fund Ltd; Chair. British Biathlon Union 1996–2011; Chair. MRC Pension Scheme Trustee Bd, Nat. Olympic Cttee, Bank of America Exec. Bd, Diocese of Salisbury Audit & Risk Cttee. *Leisure interests:* gardening, reading, sport, qualified helicopter pilot. *Telephone:* 7833-472878 (mobile) (office).

CRAPO, Michael Dean (Mike), BA, JD; American lawyer and politician; *Senator from Idaho;* b. 20 May 1951, Idaho Falls, Bonneville Co., Ida; s. of George Lavelle Crapo and Melba Crapo (née Olsen); m. Susan Diane Hasleton 1974; two s. three d.; ed Idaho Falls High School, Brigham Young Univ., Univ. of Utah, Harvard Law School; called to Bar in Calif. 1977, in Idaho 1979; law clerk, US Ninth Circuit Court of Appeals, San Diego 1977–78; Assoc., Gibson, Dunn & Crutcher (law firm) 1978–79; attorney, Holden, Kidwell, Hahn & Crapo 1979–92, Pnr 1983–92; mem. Idaho State Senate 1984–93, Asst Majority Leader 1987–88, Pres. Pro Tempore 1989–92; mem. US House of Reps from 2nd Idaho Dist 1992–99; Senator from Idaho 1999–, mem. Banking, Housing, and Urban Affairs Cttee, Budget Cttee, Environment and Public Works Cttee, Finance Cttee, Indian Affairs Cttee, Co-Chair. Canada-US Interparliamentary Group, Chair. Republican Capital Markets Task Force; Republican. *Leisure interests:* back-packing, skiing. *Address:* 239 Dirksen Senate Building, Washington, DC 20510, USA (office). *Telephone:* (202) 224-6142 (office). *Fax:* (202) 228-1375 (office). *Website:* crapo .senate.gov (office).

CRAVEN, Sir John Anthony, Kt, BA; Canadian/British merchant banker; b. 23 Oct. 1940; m. 3rd Ning Ning Chang 2005; three s. from 3rd m.; one s. one d. from 1st m.; ed Michaelhouse, S Africa, Jesus Coll., Cambridge, Queen's Univ., Kingston, Ont.; with Clarkson & Co., Toronto 1961–64, Wood Gundy Bankers 1964–67; Dir S. G. Warburg & Co. 1967–73, Vice-Chair. 1979; Chief Exec. White Weld & Co. Ltd 1973–78; Founder and Chair. Phoenix Securities Ltd 1981–89; CEO Morgan Grenfell Group 1987–89, Chair. 1989–97; mem. Bd of Man. Dirs, Deutsche Bank AG, Frankfurt 1990–96, Supervisory Bd, Société Générale de Surveillance Holding, Geneva 1989–98; Chair. (non-exec.), Tootal Group 1985–91, Lonmin PLC 1997–2009; Dir Securities and Investment Bd 1990–93; Dir Rothmans International PLC 1991–99; Dir (non-exec.), Reuters 1997–2004, Robert Fleming Holdings Ltd 1999–2000; Dir, Gleacher & Co. Ltd 2000–03, Fleming Family & Partners Ltd 2000–03, Chair. 2003–07, Ducati Motor Holdings SpA 1999–2000; mem. Ont. Inst. of Chartered Accountants, Canadian Inst. of Chartered Accountants. *Leisure interests:* hunting, shooting, skiing. *Address:* c/o Lonmin Plc, 4 Grosvenor Place, London, SW1X 7YL, England.

CRAVID, Raul Antonio da Costa; São Tomé and Príncipe politician; fmr Dir, Empresa de Agua e Electricidade (EMAE—electricity and water utility co.); Minister of Planning and Finance Feb.–June 2008, of the Interior, Territorial Admin and Civil Defence 2008–10; fmr Sec.-Gen. Movimento Democrático Força da Mudança. *Address:* c/o Movimento Democrático Força da Mudança (MDFM), São Tomé, São Tomé and Príncipe (office).

CRAWFORD, Cynthia (Cindy) Ann; American model; b. 20 Feb. 1966, DeKalb, Ill.; m. 1st Richard Gere (q.v.) 1991 (divorced); m. 2nd Rande Gerber 1998; one s. one d.; promoted Revlon (cosmetics) and Pepsi Cola; presented own fashion show on MTV (cable and satellite); has appeared on numerous covers for magazines; model for numerous fashion designers; has released several exercise videos; spokesperson for eStyle.com, Omega watches, 24 Hr. Fitness (also Dir), EAS Health and Sports Products; signature fragrance collection launched 2002, Cindy Crawford Feminine launched 2003; f. Cindy Crawford Home collection. *Films include:* Fair Game 1995, 54 1998, The Simian Line 2000. *Publications:* Cindy Crawford's Basic Face 1996, About Face (for children) 2001. *Website:* www.cindy.com.

CRAWFORD, Sir Frederick William, Kt, DL, DEng, DSc, CCIM, FREng, FIEEE, FIET, FInstP, FIMA; British scientist (retd); b. 28 July 1931, Birmingham; s. of William Crawford and Victoria Maud Crawford; m. Béatrice Madeleine Jacqueline Hutter 1963; one s. (deceased) one d.; ed George Dixon Grammar School, Birmingham, Univs of London and Liverpool; Research Trainee, J. Lucas Ltd 1948–52; scientist, Nat. Coal Bd Mining Research Establishment 1956–57; Sr Lecturer in Electrical Eng, Birmingham Coll. of Advanced Tech. 1958–59; Stanford Univ., Calif., USA 1959–82; Prof. (Research), Inst. for Plasma Research 1964–67, Assoc. Prof. 1967–69, Prof. 1969–82, Consulting Prof. 1982–84, Chair. 1974–80; Dir Centre for Interdisciplinary Research 1973–77; Visiting Prof., Math. Inst. 1977–78, Visiting Fellow, St Catherine's Coll., Oxford 1977–78, 1996–97; Vice-Chancellor of Aston Univ. 1980–96; Criminal Cases Review Comm. 1996–2003; Chair. US Nat. Cttee, Union Radio-Scientifique Internationale 1975–81, Int. Comm. 1978–81, UK Rep. 1982–84, Int. Scientific Cttee, Int. Conf. on Phenomena in Ionised Gases 1979–81; mem. US-UK Educ. Comm. 1981–84, British North-American Cttee 1987–2013, Franco-British Council 1987–98; Chair. Birmingham Civic Soc. 1983–88; High Sheriff, W Midlands Co. 1995; Pres. Smeatonian Soc. 2017; Freeman, City of London 1986, Hon. Fellow, Inst. of Linguists 1987, Master, Worshipful Co. of Engineers 1996, Co. of Information Technologists 2000, Hon. Bencher, Inner Temple 1996; Hon. DSc (Buckingham) 1996. *Publications include:* numerous publs on higher educ. and plasma physics. *Address:* 47 Charlbury Road, Oxford, OX2 6UX, England (home). *E-mail:* f.w.crawford@btinternet.com.

CRAWFORD, James Richard, AC, BA, LLB, DPhil, LLD, SC, FBA; Australian judge and academic; *Judge, International Court of Justice;* b. 14 Nov. 1948, Adelaide, SA; s. of James Crawford and Josephine Bond; m. 1st Marisa Luigina Ballini 1971 (divorced 1990); four d.; m. 2nd Patricia Hyndman 1992 (divorced 1998); m. 3rd Joanna Gomula 1998 (divorced 2014); one s.; m. 4th Freya Baetens 2014; one s.; ed Brighton High School and Univ. of Adelaide, Univ. of Oxford, UK; Lecturer, then Sr Lecturer, Reader, Prof. of Law, Univ. of Adelaide 1974–86; mem. Australian Law Reform Comm. 1982–84, part-time 1984–90; Challis Prof. of Int. Law, Univ. of Sydney 1986–92, Dean, Faculty of Law 1990–92; Whewell Prof. of Int. Law, Univ. of Cambridge 1992, Dir Lauterpacht Research Centre for Int. Law 1997–2003, 2006–12, Chair. Faculty Bd of Law 2003–06; fmr Research Prof. of Law, Latrobe Univ.; barrister, SC (NSW, Australia) 1997; Judge, Int. Court of Justice, The Hague 2015–; mem. UN Int. Law Comm. 1992–2001; mem. Matrix Chambers 2014; Hon. LLD (Paris I-Sorbonne), (Amsterdam), (Budapest), (Adelaide), (Neuchatel); Wolfgang Friedmann Memorial Award 2009, Nessim Habif World Prize for Int. Law 2010, Manley Hudson Medal 2012. *Publications include:* The Creation of States in International Law 1979 (second edn 2006), The Rights of Peoples (ed.) 1988, Australian Courts of Law (third edn) 1993, The International Law Commission Articles on State Responsibility 2002, International Law as an Open System 2002, The Law of International Responsibility (co-ed.) 2010, Cambridge Companion to International Law (co-ed.) 2012, Brownlie's Principles of Public International Law (ed.) 2013, International Responsibility: The General Part 2013, Chance, Order, Change: The Course of International Law 2013. *Leisure interests:* reading, cricket. *Address:* International Court of Justice, Peace Palace, 2597 KJ The Hague, The Netherlands (office); 7 Archway Court, Barton Road, Cambridge, CB3 9LW, England (home). *Telephone:* (70) 3022323 (office). *E-mail:* J.Crawford@icj-cij.org (office). *Website:* www.icj-cij.org (office).

CRAWFORD, Lionel, BA, PhD, FRS, FRSE; British virologist and academic; b. 30 April 1932; s. of John Mitchell Crawford and Fanny May Crawford; m. Elizabeth Minnie; one d.; ed Rendcomb Coll., Glos., Emmanuel Coll., Cambridge, Univ. of Cambridge; Nat. Service 1950–52; mem. scientific staff, MRC Inst. of Virology, Glasgow 1960–68; Head of Dept of Molecular Virology, Imperial Cancer Research Fund (ICRF, now Cancer Research UK), London 1968–88 (Chair. Cellular and Molecular Biology Groups 1968–70), Head of ICRF Tumour Virus Group, Pathology Dept, Univ. of Cambridge 1988–95; Visiting Research Fellow (Rockefeller Foundation Travel Fellowship), Virus Lab., Univ. of California, Berkeley 1958, Div. of Biology, California Inst. of Tech. 1959; Co-organizer of first Tumour Virus Workshops, Cold Spring Harbor 1969, European Molecular Biology Org. 1972; Ed. Journal of General Virology 1975–80, Oncogene Research 1986; expert in the field of DNA tumour viruses; Hon. mem. Biochemical Soc. 2004; Royal Soc. Gabor Medal 2005. *Publications include:* numerous scientific papers in professional journals on small DNA tumour viruses. *Address:* 18 Salters Road, Gosforth, Newcastle upon Tyne, NE3 1DJ, England (home).

CRAWFORD, Michael, CBE, OBE; British actor and singer; b. (Michael Dumbell-Smith), 19 Jan. 1942, Salisbury, Wilts.; ed St Michael's Coll., Bexley, Oakfield School, Dulwich; films for Children's Film Foundation; hundreds of radio broadcasts; appeared in original productions of Noyes Fludde and Let's Make an Opera by Benjamin Britten; has toured in UK, USA and Australia; Los Angeles Drama Critics Circle Award for Distinguished Achievement in Theatre (Lead Performance) 1990, named Showbusiness Personality of the Year by the Variety Club of GB. *Stage roles include:* Travelling Light 1965, The Anniversary 1966, No Sex Please, We're British 1971, Billy 1974, Same Time, Next Year 1976, Flowers for Algernon 1979, Barnum (Olivier Award for Best Actor in a Musical) 1981–83, 1984–86, Phantom of the Opera, London (Olivier Award for Best Actor in a Musical) 1986–87, Broadway (Tony Award for Best Actor in a Musical, Drama Desk Award for Outstanding Actor in a Musical, Outer Critics Circle Award for Best Actor in a Musical) 1988, Los Angeles 1989, The Music of Andrew Lloyd Webber (concert tour), USA, Australia, UK 1991–92, EFX, Las Vegas 1995–96, Dance of the Vampires (Broadway) 2002–03, The Woman in White (Outstanding Stage Performance Award, Variety Club of GB, Best Supporting Actor in a Musical, Theatregoers Choice Award voted by on-line readers of WhatsonStage.com) 2004–05, The Wizard of Oz (BroadwayWorld UK Award for Best Featured Actor in a Musical) 2011–12. *Films include:* Soap Box Derby 1950, Blow Your Own Trumpet 1954, Two Living One Dead 1962, The War Lover 1963, Two Left Feet 1963, The Knack 1965, A Funny Thing Happened on the Way to the Forum 1966, The Jokers 1966, How I Won the War 1967, Hello Dolly 1969, The Games 1969, Hello Goodbye 1970, Alice's Adventures in Wonderland 1972, Condorman 1981, Barnum 1986, Once Upon a Forest (voice) 1993, David Foster's Christmas Album 1993, Tony Palmer's Film About The Fantastic World of Michael Crawford 1996, My Favorite Broadway: The Love Songs 2001, The Ghosts of Christmas Eve 2001, WALL-E (archive footage from the film version of Hello Dolly!) 2008. *Television includes:* Sir Francis Drake (series) 1962, Some Mothers Do 'Ave 'Em (series) 1973–78, Chalk and Cheese (series) 1979, Sorry (play) 1979, Barnum (film) 1986, Coronation Street 1998. *Publication:* Parcel Arrived Safely: Tied with String (autobiog.) 2000. *Address:* c/o Knight Ayton Management, 35 Great James Street, London, WC1N 3HB, England (office). *Telephone:* (20) 7831-4400 (office). *Fax:* (20) 7831-4455 (office). *E-mail:* info@knightayton.co.uk (office). *Website:* www.knightayton.co.uk (office).

CRAWFORD, Michael Hewson, BA, MA, FBA; British historian and academic; *Professor Emeritus of Ancient History, University College, London;* b. 7 Dec. 1939, Twickenham, Middx; s. of Brian Hewson Crawford and Margarethe Bettina Crawford (née Nagel); ed St Paul's School, London and Oriel Coll., Oxford; Research Fellow, Christ's Coll., Cambridge 1964–69, Univ. Lecturer, Univ. of Cambridge 1969–86; Jt Dir Excavations of Fregellae 1980–86, Valpolcevera Project 1987–94, Velleia Project 1994–95, S. Martino Project 1996–; Chair. British Epigraphy Soc. 1996–99; Visiting Prof., Pavia Univ. 1983, 1992, Ecole Normale Supérieure, Paris 1984, Univ. of Padua 1986, Sorbonne, Paris 1989, Univ. of San Marino 1989, Univ. of Milan 1990, L'Aquila Univ. 1990, Ecole des Hautes Etudes, Paris 1997, Ecole des Hautes Etudes en Sciences Sociales, Paris 1999; Prof. of Ancient History, Univ. Coll., London 1986, now Prof. Emer.; mem. Academia Europaea; Foreign mem. Istituto Lombardo 1990, Reial Academia de Bones Lletres; Foreign Corresp. mem. Institut de France 2006; Trustee, Entente Cordiale Scholarships 2000; Officier des Palmes académiques 2001; Joseph Crabtree Orator 2000, Archer Huntington Medal, American Numismatic Soc. 2002. *Publications:* Roman Republican Coinage 1974, The Roman Republic 1978, La Moneta in Grecia e a Roma 1981, Sources for Ancient History 1983, Coinage and Money under the Roman Republic 1985, L'Impero romano e la struttura economica e sociale delle province 1986, Medals and Coins from Budé to Mommsen (co-author) 1990, Antonio Agustín between Renaissance and Counter-reform 1993, Roman Statutes (ed.) 1995, Historia Numorum (co-author) 2001, The Customs Law of Asia (co-author) 2008, Imagines Italicae 2012. *Address:* Office B21, 24 Gordon Square, London, WC1H, England (office). *Telephone:* (20) 7679-7363 (office). *E-mail:* imagines.italicae@sas.ac.uk (office). *Website:* www.ucl.ac.uk/history/people/academic-staff/professor_crawford (office).

CRAWFORD, Shawn; American sprinter (retd); b. 14 Jan. 1978, Van Wyck, SC; ed Indian Land High School, Clemson Univ.; fmr 100m and 200m SC State Champion; Goodwill Games Champion 2001; Bronze Medal 200m, World Outdoor Championships 2001; Gold Medal 200m, World Indoor Championships 2001, US Outdoor Championships 2001, 2002, Athens Olympics 2004; Silver Medal 60m, World Indoor Championships 2004; Silver Medal 4×100m, Athens Olympics 2004; Gold Medal 60m, US Indoor Championships 2004; Silver Medal 200m, Beijing Olympics 2008; banned from competition for two years in 2013 for missing out-of-competition drug tests; retd 2013; coach Bob Kersee.

CRAWLEY, Edward F., SB, SM, ScD; American engineer and academic; *Ford Professor of Engineering, Professor of Aeronautics and Astronautics and of Engineering Systems and Executive Director, Bernard M. Gordon-MIT Engineering Leadership Program, Massachusetts Institute of Technology;* ed Massachusetts Inst. of Tech.; Asst Prof., MIT 1980–84, Assoc. Prof. 1984–90, Dir Space Eng Research Center 1986–96, Prof. of Aeronautics and Astronautics 1990–, MacVicar Faculty Fellow 1992–2002, Prof. of Eng Systems 2000–, also Ford Prof. of Eng, Co-Dir Systems Design and Man. Program 1993–96, Dept Head of Aeronautics and Astronautics 1996–2003, Exec. Dir Cambridge MIT Inst. (jt venture with Univ. of Cambridge, UK) 2003–06, Exec. Dir Bernard M. Gordon-MIT Eng Leadership Program 2007–; Pres. Skolkovo Inst. of Science and Tech., Moscow (on leave); mem. Nat. Acad. of Eng, ASME, Soaring Soc. of America; Fellow, AIAA, AAAS, ACS; mem. Editorial Bd, NAS, NIH, NSF, RSC; Regional Soaring Champion 1991, 1995. *Publications:* numerous papers in professional journals. *Address:* Department of Aeronautics and Astronautics, Massachusetts Institute of Technology, Building 33-207, 77 Massachusetts Avenue, Cambridge, MA 02139, USA (office). *Telephone:* (617) 253-7510 (office). *E-mail:* crawley@mit.edu (office). *Website:* esd.mit.edu (office); systemarchitect.mit.edu (office).

CRAWLEY, Phillip, CBE; British/Canadian newspaper executive; *Publisher and CEO, The Globe and Mail;* b. 1944, Northumberland, England; m. Stephanie Crawley; three c., two step-c.; ed Univ. of Manchester; worked in various editorial roles for Thomson Regional Newspapers –1979; Ed. The Journal, Newcastle upon Tyne 1979–87; worked for Conrad Black as Northern Ed. The Daily Telegraph, London 1987–88; worked for Rupert Murdoch (q.v.) 1988–97, first as Ed. The South China Morning Post, Hong Kong 1988–93, then as Man. Dir The Times Supplements in London 1993–97; Man. Dir The New Zealand Herald 1997–98; Pres. and COO The Globe and Mail, Toronto 1998–99, Publr and CEO 1999–; Chair. of The Canadian Press; mem. Bd Audit Bureau of Circulation, Canadian Newspaper Asscn, World Asscn of Newspapers/IFRA; mem. Bd Sunnybrook Health Sciences Centre, Charter for Business (raises funds for the Duke of Edinburgh's Award in Canada), Royal Conservatory of Music, Sir Edmund Hillary Foundation; Hon. Consul for NZ in Toronto. *Address:* The Globe and Mail, 444 Front Street West, Toronto, ON M5V 2S9, Canada (office). *Telephone:* (416) 585-5000 (office). *Fax:* (416) 585-5150 (office). *E-mail:* pcrawley@globeandmail.com (office). *Website:* www.globeandmail.com (office).

CREAN, Hon. Simon Findlay, BEcons, LLB; Australian politician and trade union official; b. 26 Feb. 1949, Melbourne, Vic.; s. of Frank Crean and Mary Crean; m. Carole Lamb 1973; two d.; ed Middle Park Cen. School, Melbourne High School and Monash Univ.; Research Officer, Federated Storemen and Packers' Union of Australia 1970–74, Asst Gen. Sec. 1976–79, Gen. Sec. 1979–85; Jr Vice-Pres. Australian Council of Trade Unions 1981–83, Sr Vice-Pres. 1983–85, Pres. 1985–90; mem. House of Reps (for Hotham, Vic.) 1990–13, Minister of Science and Tech. and Treas. 1990–91, of Primary Industries and Energy 1991–93, of Employment, Educ. and Training 1993–96; Man. Opposition Business, Shadow Minister for Industry and Regional Devt 1996–98, Shadow Treas. and Deputy Leader of the Opposition 1998–2001, Leader of the Opposition 2001–02, Shadow Treas. 2003–04, Shadow Minister for Regional Devt 2005–06, Shadow Minister for Trade and Regional Devt 2006–07, Fed. Minister for Trade 2007–10, Fed. Minister for Educ., Minister for Employment and Workplace Relations, Minister for Social Inclusion 2010; Minister for Regional Australia, Regional Devt and Local Govt 2010–13, for the Arts 2010–13; Deputy Leader of the Australian Labor Party 1998–2001, Leader 2001–02; Pres. Australian Council of Trades Unions 1985–90; mem. Econ. Planning Advisory Council, Nat. Labor Consultative Council, ILO Governing Body, Qantas Bd, Transport Industry Advisory Council, Business Educ. Council. *Leisure interest:* tennis, swimming, cycling, bushwalking. *Address:* 401 Clayton Road, Clayton, Vic. 3168, Australia (office). *Telephone:* (3) 9545-6211 (office). *Fax:* (3) 9545-6299 (office). *Website:* www.simoncrean.net.

CREECH, Rt Hon. Wyatt Beetham, CNZM, BA; New Zealand accountant, vintner, business executive, government official and fmr politician; *Chairman, New Zealand Fire Service Commission;* b. Oct. 1946, Oceanside, Calif., USA; s. of Jesse Wyatt Creech; m. Diana (Danny) Creech; three s.; ed Massey and Victoria Univs; mem. Martinborough Council 1980–86; MP for Wairarapa 1988–99; Minister of Revenue, Customs, in Charge of the Public Trust Office and responsible for Govt Superannuation Fund 1990–91, Minister of Revenue, in Charge of the Public Trust Office and responsible for Govt Superannuation Fund and Sr Citizens, Assoc. Minister of Finance and Social Welfare 1991–93, Minister of Revenue and Employment, Deputy Minister of Finance 1993–96, Minister of Educ., for Courts, for Ministerial Services and Leader of the House 1996–98, Deputy Prime Minister 1998–99; Assoc. Spokesperson for Foreign Affairs and Trade; Deputy Leader Nat. Party 1997–2001; Chair. Cabinet Social Policy Cttee, Cabinet Legislation Cttee; mem. Nat. Party; Chair. Open Country Cheese Co. 2001–08, Kaimai Cheese 2007–13; Dir or fmr Dir, Bluechip 2004–06, NZ Windfarms 2009–13, Seales Ltd, Cognition Education Trust, Healthcare Holdings Ltd (now Deputy Chair.); Deputy Chair. New Zealand Fire Service Comm. 2009–14, Chair. 2014–, Heritage New Zealand Pouhere Taonga; led NZ Election Observer Team for General Election in Solomon Islands 2010; served on Int. Election Observer Team for the Falkland Islands referendum on its future status 2013. *Leisure interests:* gardening, outdoor pursuits, wine tasting. *Address:* New Zealand Fire Service Commission, PO Box 2133, Wellington 6140, New Zealand (office). *Telephone:* (4) 496-3600 (office). *Fax:* (4) 496-3700 (office). *E-mail:* question@fire.org.nz (office). *Website:* www.fire.org.nz (office).

CREED, Martin; British artist and musician; b. 21 Oct. 1968, Wakefield, West Yorks., England; s. of John Creed and Gisela Grosscurth; partner Anouchka Grose; ed Lenzie Academy School, Glasgow, Slade School of Fine Art, London; moved with family to Glasgow aged three; formed band Owada 1994; f. own label, Telephone Records; now works as a solo artist. *Dance:* Work No. 1020 (ballet), Sadler's Wells, London 2009, 2011, Traverse Theatre, Edinburgh as part of Edinburgh Festival Fringe 2010. *Music:* released album Nothing with Owada 1995; singles: Thinking/ Not Thinking 2011, Where You Go 2012, Fuck Off and Die (double AA side single) 2012, You're The One For Me 2012; album: Love To You 2012, Mind Trap 2014, Thoughts Lined Up 2016; music published by Novello & Co.; works with record label Moshi Moshi. *Address:* c/o Hauser & Wirth London, 23 Savile Row, London, W1S 2ET, England. *Telephone:* (20) 7287-2300. *E-mail:* mail@martincreed.com (home). *Website:* www.hauserwirth.com; www.martincreed.com.

CREEL, Michael A.; American business executive; *CEO, Enterprise Products Partners LP;* Certified Public Accountant; Sr Vice-Pres. Enterprise Products GP, LLC (EPGP) (previous gen. partner of EPD) 1999–2001, Chief Financial Officer (CFO) EPGP 2000–07, Exec. Vice-Pres. 2001–07, mem. Bd of Dirs 2006–10, Pres. and CEO EPGP 2007–10, CFO Enterprise Products Co. (EPCO) 2000–07, COO 2005–07, mem. Bd of Dirs EPCO 2007–, Group Vice-Chair. and CFO EPCO 2007–10, Vice-Chair. EPCO 2010–, mem. Bd of Dirs, Pres. and CEO Enterprise GP 2005–07, Exec. Vice-Pres. and CFO DEP GP 2006–07, mem. Bd of Dirs Enterprise GP 2009–10, DEP Holdings, LLC (DEP GP) 2006–10, mem. Bd of Dirs, Pres. and CEO Enterprise Products Holdings LLC (current gen. partner of EPD (Enterprise GP) following merger of EPE with a subsidiary of EPD Nov. 2010–13, CEO 2013–. *Address:* Enterprise Products Partners LP, 1100 Louisiana Street, Houston, TX 77002 (office); Enterprise Products Partners LP, PO Box 4324, Houston, TX 77210-4324, USA. *Telephone:* (713) 381-6500 (office). *E-mail:* info@epplp.com (office). *Website:* www.epplp.com (office).

CREEL MIRANDA, Santiago; Mexican lawyer, politician and business executive; b. 11 Dec. 1954, Mexico City; one d. with Edith González; ed Univ. Nacional Autónoma de México, Univ. of Michigan, USA; lawyer, pvt. law firm, Noriega y Escobedo, later Man. Partner; fmr Sec. Vuelta periodical; f. Este País magazine; fmr Prof., Autonomous Tech. Inst. of Mexico, Head Acad. Dept; Citizen Adviser to Gen. Council, Fed. Electoral Inst. 1994–96, Fed. Deputy 1997–; joined Partido Acción Nacional, cand. for Head of Govt of Fed. Dist 1999; Sec. of the Interior 2000–05; mem. Senado (Senate) 2006–12, Pres. Senate 2007–08; Dir, EZCORP, Inc. 2014–; mem. Mexican Bar, Coll. of Lawyers, Mexican Acad. of Human Rights, Lawyers' Cttee for Human Rights. *Address:* EZCORP, Inc., 2500 Bee Cave Road, Building 1, Suite 200, Rollingwood, TX 78746, USA (office). *Telephone:* (512) 314-3400 (office). *Fax:* (512) 314-3404 (office). *E-mail:* info@ezcorp.com (office). *Website:* www.ezcorp.com (office).

CRENSHAW, William Edwin (Ed), BBA; American retail executive; *Chairman, Publix Super Markets Inc.;* b. 1951, grandson of George Jenkins (founder of Publix); m. Denise Crenshaw; ed Baylor Univ.; joined Publix Super Markets Inc. 1974, becoming Dir of Retail Operations, Lakeland, Fla Div. 1984–90, Vice-Pres. Lakeland Div. 1990–91, Dir Publix Super Markets Inc. 1990–, Vice-Pres. Publix Atlanta Div. 1991–94, Exec. Vice-Pres. of Retailing 1994–96, Pres. 1996–2008, CEO 2008–16, Chair. 2016–; Vice-Chair. Food Marketing Inst.; mem. Advisory Bd Hankamer School of Business. *Address:* Publix Super Markets Corporate Office, 3300 Publix Corporate Parkway, Lakeland, FL 33811, USA (office). *Telephone:* (863) 688-1188 (office). *Fax:* (863) 284-5532 (office). *E-mail:* info@publix.com (office). *Website:* www.publix.com (office).

CRÉPIN, Frédéric R., MA, MA, MPA, LLM; French lawyer and business executive; *General Secretary, Vivendi SA;* b. 1969; ed Univ. of Paris II, Univ. of Paris X, Institut d'études politiques, New York Univ. School of Law, USA; admitted to the Bars of Paris and New York; Attorney at Law and Assoc., Gide, Loyrette, Nouel, Paris –1995, Siméon & Associés, Paris 1995–98, Weil, Gotshal & Manges LP, New York 1999–2000; Special Adviser to Gen. Counsel and at Legal Dept, Vivendi Universal 2000–05, Sr Vice-Pres., Head of Legal Dept, Vivendi SA 2005–, Sec. Supervisory and Man. Bds 2012–14, Gen. Sec. 2014–; Dir, Activision Blizzard, Inc. 2008–13; mem. Bureau of MEDEF Business Law Cttee. *Address:* Vivendi SA, 42 avenue de Friedland, 75008 Paris, France (office). *Telephone:* 1-71-71-10-00 (office). *Fax:* 1-71-71-10-01 (office). *E-mail:* info@vivendi.com (office). *Website:* www.vivendi.com (office).

CRESSON, Édith; French politician; *President, Fondation des écoles de la deuxième chance;* b. (Édith Campion), 27 Jan. 1934, Boulogne-sur-Seine; d. of Gabriel Campion and Jacqueline Campion; m. Jacques Cresson 1959 (died 2001); two d.; ed École de Haut Enseignement Commercial pour les Jeunes Filles (HECJF); Nat. Sec. Parti Socialiste; Youth Organizer, Parti Socialiste 1975; Mayor, Châtellerault 1983–97; Gen. Counsellor Châtellerault-Ouest 1982–97; mem. European Parl. 1979–81; Minister of Agric. 1981–83, of Foreign Trade and Tourism 1983–84, of Industrial Redeployment and Foreign Trade 1984–86, of European Affairs 1988–90; Prime Minister of France 1991–92; Pres. L'Asscn démocratique des français de l'étranger 1986; Pres. SISIE 1992–94; European Commr for Educ., Research, Science and Devt 1995–99; mem. Nat. Ass. for Vienne 1981, 1986–88; mem. Nat. Secr. Parti Socialiste 1974–90; Pres. Fondation des écoles de la deuxième chance 2002–; Pres. Inst. d'Études Européennes Univ. de Seine St Denis 1992; Chevalier, Légion d'honneur, Grand-Croix, Ordre nat. du Mérite; Dr hc (Weizmann Inst., Open Univ., UK, Technion, Israel). *Publications include:* Avec le soleil 1976, L'Europe à votre porte: manuel pratique sur les actions de la CEE intéressant les opérateurs économiques (co-author) 1989, Innover ou subir 1998, Histoires françaises 2006. *Address:* Fondation des écoles de la deuxième chance, 21 boulevard de Grenelle, 75015 Paris, France (office). *Telephone:* 1-45-78-34-15 (office). *E-mail:* edith.cresson@wanadoo.fr (office). *Website:* www.fondatione2c.org (office).

CRESSWELL, Peter, BSc, MSc, PhD, FRS; British/American immunobiologist and academic; *Eugene Higgins Professor of Immunobiology and Professor of Cell Biology and Dermatology, School of Medicine, Yale University;* b. 6 March 1945, Mexborough, S Yorks., England; s. of Maurice Cresswell and Mary Cresswell; m. Ann K. Cooney 1969 (died 2014); two s.; ed Newcastle Univ., Univ. of London, Harvard Univ., USA; fmrly Chief Div. of Immunology, Duke Univ. Medical Center; Prof. of Immunobiology and Biology (now Eugene Higgins Prof. of Immunobiology and Prof. of Cell Biology and Dermatology), Yale Univ. School of Medicine 1991–; also currently Investigator, Howard Hughes Medical Inst., Chevy Chase, Md 1991–2017; The Newton-Abraham Visiting Prof., Univ. of Oxford 2007, Fellow of Lincoln Coll. 2007; mem. Scientific Advisory Bd, The Jane Coffin Childs Memorial Fund 2002–10, Center for HIV/AIDS Vaccine Immunology (CHAVI) 2005–; Assoc. Ed., Immunity 1994–; mem. Editorial Bd Traffic 1999–, PNAS 2001–, Immunological Reviews 2002–08, Tissue Antigens 2002–, Annual Review of Cell and Developmental Biology 2003–; mem. American Asscn of Immunologists 1976, American Soc. for Histocompatibility and Immunogenetics 1980, American Soc. for Cell Biology 1996, New York Acad. of Sciences 2000, NAS 2001, Inst. of Medicine, AAAS; Assoc. mem. European Molecular Biology Org. 1995; ASHI Rose Payne Distinguished Scientist Award 1995, Buchanan Medal, Royal Soc. 2010, AAI Meritorious Career Award 2012. *Publications include:* numerous papers on the mechanisms regulating generation of complexes of peptides with Major Histocompatability Complex (MHC) molecules, essential in the immune response. *Address:* Yale University School of Medicine, PO Box 208011, New Haven, CT 06520, USA (office). *Telephone:* (203) 785-5176 (Yale) (office). *Fax:* (203) 785-4461 (Yale) (office). *E-mail:* peter.cresswell@yale.edu (office). *Website:* medicine.yale .edu (office).

CRETNEY, Stephen Michael, MA, DCL, FBA; British professor of law; *Fellow Emeritus, All Souls College, University of Oxford;* b. 25 Feb. 1936, Witney, Oxon.; s. of Fred Cretney and Winifred Cretney; m. Rev. Antonia L. Vanrenen 1973; two s.; ed Cheadle Hulme School, Magdalen Coll., Oxford; Parter, Macfarlanes (Solicitors), London 1964–65; Lecturer, Kenya School of Law, Nairobi 1966–67, Univ. of Southampton 1968–69; Fellow and Tutor in Law, Exeter Coll., Oxford 1969–78; mem. Law Comm. for England and Wales 1978–83; Prof. of Law, Univ. of Bristol 1984–93, Dean of Law Faculty 1984–88; Fellow, All Souls Coll. Oxford 1993–2001, Fellow Emer. 2001–; Hon. QC; Hon. LLD (Bristol). *Publications include:* Enduring Powers of Attorney (4th edn) 1996, Principles of Family Law (7th edn) 2002, Law, Law Reform and the Family 1998, Family Law (4th edn) 2000, Family Law in the 20th Century: A History 2003, Same Sex Relationships, from 'Odious Crime' to 'Gay Marriage' 2006.

CREȚU, Corina; Romanian economist, journalist, politician and EU official; *Commissioner for Regional Policy, European Commission;* b. 24 June 1967, Bucharest; d. of Prof. Traian Crețu; m. Ovidiu Rogoz 2012; ed Faculty of Planning and Econ. Cybernetics, Bucharest Univ. of Econ. Studies; worked as economist for factories in Blaj and Bucharest until 1990; employed as commentator on current events by Azi, Curierul Național and Cronica Română newspapers from 1990; Adviser and Spokesperson for Pres. Iliescu 1992–96, 2000–04; mem. Partidul Social Democrat (PSD—Social Democratic Party), Head of PSD Image Dept, First Deputy Chair. PSD Women's Org. 1997–2000, Deputy Chair. PSD 2011–, PSD Rep. in Presidency of Party of European Socialists; Presidential Adviser (with rank of Minister), Presidential Spokesperson and Head of Public Communication Dept 2000–04; Senator (PSD), Romanian Parl. 2004–07, mem. Foreign Policy Cttee, Romanian Del. to Parl. Ass. of OSCE; invited to Amman, Jordan and conducted training seminar for appointees to spokesperson positions in Iraq Jan. 2005; OSCE observer to parl. elections in Moldova March 2005, to gen. election in Bosnia and Herzegovina 2006; Observer at European Parl. 2006–07; mem. European Parl.

(Group of the Progressive Alliance of Socialists and Democrats in the European Parl.) 2007–14, Vice-Pres. Parl., mem. Parl. Bureau, mem. Cttee on Employment and Social Affairs, Del. for relations with Israel, Del. to Parl. Ass. of the Union for the Mediterranean, Substitute mem. Cttee on Civil Liberties, Justice and Home Affairs, Del. to EU-Serbia Stabilization and Asscn Parl. Cttee; Commr for Regional Policy, EC, Brussels Nov. 2014–; mem. Bd Romanian Television Co. 2002; Kt, Order of the Star of Romania 2013. *Address:* European Commission, 200 Rue de la Loi/Wetstraat 200, 1049 Brussels, Belgium (office). *Telephone:* (2) 299-11-11 (switchboard) (office). *E-mail:* corina-cretu-contact@ec.europa.eu (home). *Website:* ec.europa.eu/commission/2014-2019/cretu_en (office); www.corina-cretu.ro.

CRIADO-PÉREZ TREFAULT, Carlos; Argentine retail executive; *Executive Chairman, DinoSol Supermercados;* b. 1954, Buenos Aires; m.; three c.; with SHV Makro 1976–90, worked in Portugal, Brazil and Taiwan 1990–97, also Exec. Dir; COO Int. Div., Wal-Mart Inc. 1997–99; COO Safeway PLC 1999, CEO 1999–2004; Exec. Chair. DinoSol Supermercados, Madrid 2004–; mem. Supervisory Bd, X5 Retail Group NV 2007–09; Sr Advisor, UBS Bank 2007–; mem. Advisory Bd, Permira UK; adviser to Marks and Spencer's on int. expansion; Retail Personality of the Year, Retek 2001. *Leisure interests:* opera (Mozart), running marathons. *Address:* DinoSol Supermercados, C / Luis Correa Medina 9, 1ª Miller Bajo, 35013 Las Palmas de Gran Canaria, Spain (office). *Telephone:* (928) 303600 (office). *E-mail:* comunicacion@grupodinosol.es (office). *Website:* dinosol.es (office).

CRISP, Baron (Life Peer), cr. 2006, of Eaglescliffe in the County of Durham; **(Edmund) Nigel (Ramsay) Crisp,** KCB, MA; British civil servant; b. 14 Jan. 1952; s. of Edmund Theodore Crisp and Dorothy Shephard Crisp (née Ramsay); m. Siân Elaine Jenkins 1976; one s. one d.; ed Uppingham School and St John's Coll., Cambridge; Deputy Dir Halewood Community Council 1973; Production Man. Trebor 1978; Dir Cambs. Community Council 1981; Unit Gen. Man. E Berks. Health Authority 1986; Chief Exec. Heatherwood and Wexham Park Hosps 1988; Chief Exec. Oxford Radcliffe Hosps NHS Trust 1993–96; Regional Dir S Thames 1977–98, London 1999–2000; Perm. Sec., Dept of Health and Chief Exec. Nat. Health Service 2000–06 (retd); mem. (Crossbench), House of Lords 2006–, mem. Merits of Statutory Instruments Cttee 2007–09; Dir, Global HDE Ltd; Chair. of Trustees, Sightsavers International 2007–, Advisory Bd, King's Centre for Global Health; Co-Chair. Zambia UK Health Workforce Alliance 2009–, Uganda UK Health Alliance; Trustee, RAND Europe; Global Amb., Global Health Workforce Alliance; Amb., Archbishop Tutu's Global eHealth Ambassador Programme; mem. Advisory Bd, African Centre for Global Health and Social Transformation, Council of Univ. of Reading. *Publications:* Turning the World Upside Down – The Search for Global Health in the 21st Century 2010, 24 Hours to Save the NHS: The Chief Executive's Account of Reform 2000–2006 2011, African Health Leaders: Making Change and Claiming the Future (co-ed.) 2014. *Leisure interest:* the countryside. *Address:* House of Lords, Westminster, London, SW1A 0PW, England (office). *Telephone:* (20) 7219-5353 (office). *E-mail:* crisp@parliament.uk (office). *Website:* www.parliament.uk/biographies/lords/lord-crisp/3783 (office); www.nigelcrisp.com.

CRIST, Charles (Charlie) Joseph, Jr, BA, JD; American lawyer and politician; b. 24 July 1956, Altoona, Pa; s. of Charles Joseph Crist, Sr and Nancy Crist (née Lee); m. 1st Amanda Morrow 1979 (divorced 1980); m. 2nd Carole Rome 2008; ed St Petersburg High School, Fla, Wake Forest Univ., Florida State Univ., Cumberland School of Law, Birmingham, Ala; worked as intern in Fla State Attorney's Office before accepting position as Gen. Counsel for Nat. Asscn of Professional Baseball Leagues 1982–87; cand. for Fla State Senate 1986; began his govt service as State Dir for US Senator Connie Mack, Chair. Baseball Anti-Trust Advisory Cttee, mem. Fed. Judicial Advisory Comm. 1989–92; attorney, Wood & Crist law firm, Tampa 1987–; Fla State Senator 1993–99, Chair. Senate Ethics and Elections Cttee, Appropriations Criminal Justice Sub-cttee; cand. for US Senate 1998; Deputy Sec. Fla Dept of Business and Professional Regulation 1999–2000; Commr of Educ. 2001–03; State Attorney-Gen. 2003–06; Gov. of Fla 2007–11; Partner, Morgan & Morgan, St Petersburg 2011–16; mem. US House of Reps from Fla 13th District 2017–; mem. Domestic Security Oversight Bd, ABA Pres.'s Council, American Lung Asscn, Admin. Bd American Swiss Asscn Center Against Spouse Abuse, First United Methodist Church Ethics Cttee, Fla Bar Asscn, Bd Fla Conservation Asscn, Foundation for Fla's Future, Hillsborough Bar Asscn, Pinellas Park Chamber of Commerce, Rotary, St Petersburg Bar Asscn, St Petersburg Chamber of Commerce, Bd of Dirs Suncoasters Civic Club; Fellow, American Swiss Asscn; Pinellas Co. Fellow; Republican; Hon. Sheriff, Fla Sheriffs' Asscn, Police Benevolent Asscn 1995; Roll Call Award, Florida Chamber of Commerce 1993, Legislator Award, Pinellas School Admins 1993, Florida Asscn School Admins 1993, Florida Sheriffs Asscn 1994, 1996, named Conservationist Legislator of the Year, Florida Wildlife Fed. 1995, Govt Award, Urban League 1995, Senatorial Leadership Award, Florida Prosecuting Attorneys Asscn 1995, Legislator Conservation Award, Florida Conservation Asscn 1996, Distinguished Legislator Award, Florida Police Benevolent Asscn 1996, Phil Piton Award for service to MLB, Leadership St Petersburg. *Leisure interests:* water-skiing, reading, jogging. *Address:* 427 Cannon HOB, Washington, DC 20515, USA (office). *Telephone:* (202) 225-5961 (office). *Website:* crist.house.gov (office).

CRISTAS MACHADO DA GRAÇA, Maria da Assunção de Oliveira, PhD; Portuguese lawyer, academic and politician; b. 28 Sept. 1974, Luanda, Angola; m. Tiago Pereira dos Reis Machado da Graça; three c.; ed Univ. of Lisbon; Monitor, Faculty of Law, Univ. of Lisbon 1995–96, Asst Intern 1997–99; admitted to the Bar 1999; Deputy Minister of Justice April–Oct. 2002; Asst then Assoc. Prof. of Law, Universidade Nova de Lisboa 2005–09; legal consultant, Morais Leitão, Galvão Teles, Soares da Silva & Associados 2010–11; mem. Democratic and Social Centre–People's Party (CDS–PP) 2007–, now Vice-Pres.; mem. Ass. of the Repub. 2009–; Minister of Agric., Sea, Environment and Spatial Planning 2011–13. *Address:* Praça do Comércio, 1149-010 Lisbon (office); c/o Morais Leitão, Galvão Teles, Soares da Silva & Associados, Rua Castilho 165, 1070-050 Lisbon, Portugal (office). *Telephone:* (213) 234600 (Ministry) (office); (213) 234652 (Ministry). *Fax:* (213) 234604 (Ministry) (office). *E-mail:* gabministra@mamaot.gov.pt (office); assuncaocristas@mlgts.pt (office). *Website:* www.min-agricultura.pt (office); www.portugal.gov.pt (office).

CRISTEA, Valerian; Moldovan politician and diplomatist; b. 1 Aug. 1950, Viprova, Orhei Co.; m.; one c.; ed Polytechnic Inst., Chişinău; party instructor, Chisinau 1979–82; Chair. union of the State Enterprise Energoreparaţia 1982–86; Chair. Republican Cttee of Trades Unions 'Sindenergo' 1986–94, Deputy Chairmanship of the Gen. Fed. of Trades Unions of Moldova 1994–98; mem. Parl. (CP of Moldova) 1998–2006, Chair. Perm. Comm. for Social Protection, Health and Family 1998–2001; Deputy Prime Minister 2001–06; Amb. to Czech Repub. 2007–09; Order 'Gloria Muncii' 2000; Merit Prize of the Alliance War Against Trafficking (USA). *Address:* Ministry of Foreign Affairs and European Integration, 2012 Chişinău, str. 31 August 80, Moldova (office). *Telephone:* (22) 57-82-07 (office). *Fax:* (22) 23-23-02 (office). *E-mail:* secdep@mfa.md (office). *Website:* www.mfa.gov.md (office).

CRISTIANI, Mario; Italian gallery director; *Co-Director and Partner, Galleria Continua;* co-f., with Lorenzo Fiaschi and Maurizio Rigillo, Galleria Continua in San Gimignano, Tuscany 1990, other locations include Beijing 2004, Boissy-le-Châtel, France 2007, Les Moulins; represents artists Etel Adnan, Ai Weiwei, Jonathas de Andrade, Juan Araujo, Kader Attia, Daniel Buren, Cai Guo-Qiang, Loris Cecchini, Chen Zhen, Nikhil Chopra, Marcelo Cidade, Berlinde De Bruyckere, Leandro Erlich, Carlos Garaicoa, Kendell Geers, Antony Gormley, Gu Dexin, Shilpa Gupta, Subodh Gupta, Mona Hatoum, Ilya & Emilia Kabakov, Zhanna Kadyrova, Kan Xuan, Anish Kapoor, Andre Komatsu, Jannis Kounellis, Jorge Macchi, Cildo Meireles, Sabrina Mezzaqui, Margherita Morgantin, Moataz Nasr, Hans Op de Beeck, Ornaghi & Prestinari, Giovanni Ozzola, Michelangelo Pistoletto, Qiu Zhijie, Arcangelo Sassolino, Manuela Sedmach, Serse, Kiki Smith, Nedko Solakov, Jose Antonio Suarez Londono, Hiroshi Sugimoto, Sun Yuan & Peng Yu, Pascale Marthine Tayou, Nari Ward, Sophie Whettnall, Sislej Xhafa, José Yaque. *Address:* Galleria Continua, Via del Castello 11, 53037 San Gimignano, Italy (office). *Telephone:* (0577) 943134 (office). *E-mail:* info@galleriacontinua.com (office). *Website:* www.galleriacontinua.com (office).

CRISTOFORETTI, Samantha, OM; Italian astronaut, pilot and engineer; b. 26 April 1977, Milan; ed Liceo Scientifico, Trento, Technical Univ. of Munich, Germany, École nationale supérieure de l'aéronautique et de l'espace, France, Mendeleev Russian Univ. of Chemistry and Tech., Russia, Accademia Aeronautica, Pozzuoli; based at Sheppard Air Force Base, Tex. 2005–06, fighter pilot and Capt. in Italian Air Force, assigned to 132nd Squadron, 51st Bomber Wing, Istrana 2006, served in Plans and Operations Section 2007–08, served with 101st Squadron, 32nd Bomber Wing, Foggia 2008–09; selected as ESA astronaut 2009, completed training 2010, assigned to Italian Space Agency ASI mission, Int. Space Station (ISS) 2012, Flight Engineer for ISS Expedition 42 2014–15, ISS Expedition 43 2015. *Achievements include:* first Italian woman to fly into space, longest uninterrupted space flight by a European astronaut, longest single space flight by a woman (199 days, 16 hours) during ISS Expedition 43 2015. *Address:* European Space Agency Communication Department, ESRIN, Via Galileo Galilei, Casella Postale 64, 00044 Frascati, Italy (office). *Telephone:* (06) 941801 (office). *Website:* www.esa.int (office).

CRISTÓVÃO, Cirilo José Jacob Valadares; Timor-Leste judge and politician; b. 20 March 1966; mem. Conselho Superior da Magistratura Judicial (Superior Council of the Judiciary) 2003, also Judge, Court of Justice; mem. Nat. Parl. 2007–12; Dir-Gen. Serviço Nacional de Inteligência (intelligence agency) 2009; Minister of Defence and Security 2015–17; fmr Co-Chair. Indonesia–Timor-Leste Comm. on Truth and Friendship; mem. Congresso Nacional da Reconstrução de Timor-Leste (CNRT, Nat. Congress for the Reconstruction of Timor-Leste). *Address:* c/o Ministry of Defence and Security, Palácio do Governo, Edif. 2, 1°, Av. Presidente Nicolau Lobato, Dili, Timor-Leste (office).

CRNADAK, Igor; Bosnia and Herzegovina politician and fmr journalist; *Minister of Foreign Affairs;* b. 28 July 1972, Zadar, Socialist Repub. of Croatia, Socialist Fed. Repub. of Yugoslavia; s. of Mihailo Crnadak and Ljubica Crnadak; m. Đurđica Crnadak; two d.; ed Grammar School in Banja Luka, Faculty of Economy, Banja Luka Univ., ongoing postgraduate studies at Dept of Global Markets and European Union; worked as journalist, anchor, producer and radio ed. and wrote for numerous print media 1990s; Corresp., Voice of America from Banja Luka 1996–98; mem. European Integration Cttee, Nat. Ass. of Republika Srpska 2006; Deputy Minister of Defence, responsible for Int. Co-operation and Chair. BiH NATO Co-ordination Team 2007–09; mem. Partija Demokratskog Progresa (PDP—Party of Democratic Progress) 1999–, Head of PDP Caucus, City Ass. of Banja Luka 2000–04, PDP Spokesperson 2001–04, Exec. Dir PDP 2005, Sec. for Int. Relations 2009, Sec.-Gen. PDP 2011–, acted as head of PDP's election HQ during three election cycles; Minister of Foreign Affairs 2015–. *Address:* Ministry of Foreign Affairs, 71000 Sarajevo, Musala 2, Bosnia and Herzegovina (office). *Telephone:* (33) 281100 (office). *Fax:* (33) 227156 (office). *E-mail:* info_mvpbih@mvp.gov.ba (office). *Website:* www.mfa.gov.ba (office).

CROCKER, Chester Arthur, BA, MA, PhD; American academic and fmr government official; *James R. Schlesinger Professor of Strategic Studies, Edmund A. Walsh School of Foreign Service, Georgetown University;* b. 29 Oct. 1941, New York, NY; s. of Arthur Crocker and Clare Crocker; m. Saone Baron 1965; three d.; ed Ohio State Univ., Johns Hopkins Univ.; editorial asst, Africa Report 1965–66, News Ed. 1968–69; Lecturer, American Univ. 1969–70; staff officer, Nat. Security Council 1970–72; Dir Master of Science, Foreign Service Program, Georgetown Univ. 1972–78, James R. Schlesinger Prof. of Strategic Studies, Edmund A. Walsh School of Foreign Service 1989–; Dir African Studies, Center for Strategic and Inst. Studies 1976–81; Asst Sec. of State for African Affairs 1981–89; Chair. African Working Group, Reagan Campaign 1980; Chair. US Inst. of Peace 1992–2004; work as int. consultant; mem. Bd of Dirs Global Leadership Foundation, US Inst. of Peace, Universal Corpn, G3 Good Governance Group Ltd, Ngena Foundation, Int. Peace and Security Inst.; Distinguished Fellow, Centre for Int. Governance Innovation; fmr mem. Ind. Advisory Bd, World Bank; Chevalier, Ordre de merite congolais; Hon. LLD (Rhodes Univ.) 2012; Presidential Citizen's Medal, Sec. of State's Distinguished Service Award, Vicennial Award for Service and John Carroll Medal, Georgetown Univ., Woodrow Wilson Award for Distinguished Public Service, Johns Hopkins Univ., Alumni Distinguished Achievement Award, Ohio State Univ. 2011. *Publications include:* South Africa into the 1980s 1979, South Africa's Defense Posture 1982, High Noon in Southern Africa 1992, African Conflict Resolution 1995, Managing Global Chaos 1996, Herding Cats: Multiparty Mediation in a Complex World 1999, Turbulent Peace: The Challenges of Managing International Conflict 2001, Taming Intractable Conflicts 2004, Grasping the Nettle: Analysing Cases of Intractable Conflict 2005, Leashing the Dogs of War: Conflict Management in a Divided World 2007, Rewiring Regional Security in a Fragmented World 2011, Managing Conflict in a World Adrift 2015; numerous articles. *Leisure interests:* music, tennis, fishing. *Address:* Room 801, Intercultural Center, Edmund A. Walsh School of Foreign Service, Georgetown University, Washington, DC 20057, USA (office). *Telephone:* (202) 687-5074 (office). *Fax:* (202) 687-2315 (office). *E-mail:* crockerc@georgetown.edu (office). *Website:* global.georgetown.edu/people/chester-crocker (office).

CROCKER, Ryan Clark, BA; American academic and diplomatist; b. 19 June 1949, Spokane, Wash.; s. of Carol Crocker; m. Christine Barnes; ed Univ. Coll. Dublin, Ireland, Whitman Coll., Walla Walla, Wash., Princeton Univ.; joined Foreign Service 1971, diplomatic positions in Iran 1972–74, Qatar 1974–76, Iraq 1978–80, Lebanon 1981–84; Deputy Dir Office of Arab-Israeli Affairs 1985–87; Political Counsellor, Embassy in Cairo 1987–90; Dir State Dept's Iraq-Kuwait Task Force 1990; Amb. to Lebanon 1990–93, to Kuwait 1994–97, to Syria 1998–2001, Deputy Asst Sec. of State for Near Eastern Affairs 2001–03, Interim Envoy to new Govt of Afghanistan 2002–04, rank of Career Amb. 2004, Amb. to Pakistan 2004–07, to Iraq 2007–09, to Afghanistan 2011–12; Int. Affairs Adviser, Nat. War Coll., Washington, DC 2003–04; Dean, Bush School of Govt and Public Service, Texas A&M Univ. 2010–11; Hon. Marine, US Marine Corps 2012; Hon. LLD (Whitman Coll.) 2001; Dr hc (Nat. Defense Univ.) 2010, (American Univ. of Afghanistan) 2013; Presidential Distinguished Service Award 1994, Dept of Defense Medal for Distinguished Civilian Service 1997, Presidential Meritorious Service Award 1999, 2003, State Dept Award for Valor, Three Superior Honor Awards, American Foreign Service Asscn Rivkin Award, State Dept Distinguished Honor Award 2004, Sec.'s Distinguished Service Award 2008, Presidential Medal of Freedom 2009. *Address:* Department of State, 2201 C Street NW, Washington, DC 20520, USA (office). *Telephone:* (202) 647-4000 (office). *Website:* www.state.gov (office).

CROCQUEVIEILLE, Hélène; French government official; *Director-General, Customs and Excise;* ed École polytechnique, École nationale de la statistique et de l'admin économique, Institut d'études politiques de Paris (Sciences Po); began career as Head of Surveys, Directorate of Studies and Econ. Analysis, Institut Nat. de la Statistique et des Études Économiques (INSEE) 1992–95, Insp. Gen. INSEE; involved with management of Budget 1995–2003, including monitoring of fiscal policy in context of Econ. and Monetary Union, Deputy Dir of Budget Man. 2003–06, became head of the fourth sub-division in charge of ecology, energy, planning, transport policy, housing, urban policy, the Overseas culture, youth, sports and tourism 2006–09, Dir of Human Resources, Gen. Secr. Dept of Gender Equality and Housing (METL) and Ecology, Sustainable Devt and Energy (MEDDE) 2009–13; Dir-Gen. Customs and Excise 2013–. *Address:* Douanes et Droits Indirects, 139 rue de Bercy, 75572 Paris Cedex 12, France (office). *Telephone:* 1-72-40-78-50 (office). *E-mail:* ids@douane.finances.gouv.fr (office). *Website:* www.douane.gouv.fr (office).

CROFF, Davide; Italian business executive; *Chairman, Permasteelisa Group;* b. 1 Oct. 1947, Venice; ed Università Ca' Foscari di Venezia, Pembroke Coll., Oxford, UK; Asst Prof. of Political Econ., Univ. of Padua 1971–72; Research Dept Officer, Banca d'Italia, Rome 1974–79; Foreign and Financial Affairs Dept, Fiat SpA, Turin 1979–83, in charge of Int. Treasury Dept 1982, Finance Man. 1983–86, Sr Vice-Pres. 1986–89; CEO Finance and Int., Banca Nazionale del Lavoro, Rome 1989–90, Man. Dir 1990–2003; Chair. Permasteelisa Group 2006–; Pres. La Biennale di Venezia from 2004; Chair. BPM 360 Gradi, Fondazione Ugo e Olga Levi, Venice; Sr Adviser to Texas Pacific Group in Italy 2006–13; Ind. Dir, Fiera Milano SpA 2012–; Dir Man. Bd, Banca Popolare Milano; mem. Bd of Dirs, European Inst. of Oncology, Genextra, Gala SpA, Elica SpA; mem. Council for the United States and Italy, Comitato Leonardo, Bd of Assonime; adviser to Roland Berger; Kt Grand Cross, Order of Merit of the Italian Repub. 2000. *Address:* Permasteelisa Group, Viale E. Mattei 21–23, 31029 Vittorio Veneto, Treviso, Italy (office). *Telephone:* (0438) 505000 (office). *Fax:* (0438) 694509 (office). *E-mail:* info@permasteelisagroup.com (office). *Website:* www.permasteelisagroup.com (office).

CROITORU, Lucian, DEcon; Romanian economist and politician; b. 13 Feb. 1957, Otopeni, Ilfov Co.; ed Academiei de Studii Economice (Acad. of Econ. Studies), Bucharest; Economist, Bucharest Well and Water Works 1982–84; Researcher, Inst. of Industrial Economy 1984–98; Expert, Govt Dept for Econ. Reform 1991–95; Consultant, Bucharest Investment Group 1995–96; Research Pnr, EU Phare Investment Programme 1996–97, 2001–02; Lecturer in Int. Macroeconomics, Faculty of Int. Econ. Relations, Academiei de Studii Economice 1998–2003; Chief Adviser to Finance Minister 1998; Adviser to Gov., Nat. Bank of Romania 1998–2003; Chief Adviser, IMF Exec. Directorate 2003–07; nominated by Pres. Traian Băsescu as Prime Minister Oct. 2009, nomination rejected by Parl. Nov. 2009; Commdr, Order of the Star of Romania 2000; Aurelian Prize, Romanian Acad. 1995. *Publications:* several books and over 150 articles on econs. *Address:* c/o Banca Naţională a României, 030031 Bucharest 3, Str. Lipscani 25, Romania.

CROLL, Peter J.; German economist and research institute director; *Associate Researcher, Bonn International Centre for Conversion;* ed Univs of Giessen and Mainz; fmr Head of Dept, Southern Africa Devt Co-ordinating Conf.; fmr Sr Advisor to Development Bank of Zambia, Lusaka; fmr Assoc. Expert for Industrial Devt, ECLA, Mexico City; held several positions with German Technical Cooperation (GTZ, devt org.), including Country Dir in Harare, Zimbabwe 1992–97, in Nairobi, Kenya 1997–2001; Facilitator, UNDP/FAO cross-border ecological programme in South Africa and other programmes in Africa and India; Dir Bonn Int. Centre for Conversion 2001–12, Assoc. Researcher 2012–; Assoc. Lecturer for Conflict Resolution, Univ. of Duisburg-Essen. *Address:* BICC, Pfarrer-Byns-Straße 1, Bonn, 53121, Germany (office). *Telephone:* (228) 911960 (office). *Fax:* (228) 9119622 (office). *E-mail:* bicc@bicc.de (office). *Website:* www.bicc.de (office).

CROMBIE, Sir Alexander (Sandy), Kt, FFA; British insurance executive; *Chairman, Creative Scotland;* b. 1949, Leslie, Fife; joined Standard Life Insurance Co. 1966, various sr and man. positions including CEO Standard Life Investments (SLI) 1998–2004, Dir 2000–06, CEO Standard Life Assurance Co. 2004–06, Group Chief Exec. Standard Life PLC 2006–09; Vice-Chair. Royal Conservatoire of Scotland 2007–; Sr Ind. Dir, Royal Bank of Scotland PLC 2009–; Chair. Creative Scotland 2010–; mem. Chancellor of the Exchequer's high-level business group; mem. Bd Dirs Asscn of British Insurers 2002–09; The Prince's Amb. for Corp. Social Responsibility in Scotland 2007; Fellow, Faculty of Actuaries. *Address:* Creative Scotland, Waverley Gate, 2–4 Waterloo Place, Edinburgh, EH1 3EG, Scotland (office). *Telephone:* (330) 333-2000 (office). *Website:* www.creativescotland.com (office).

CROMME, Gerhard, DJur; German business executive; *Chairman of the Supervisory Board, Siemens AG;* b. 25 Feb. 1943, Vechta/Oldenburg; m.; four d.; ed Münster, Lausanne, Switzerland, Univ. of Paris, France and Harvard Univ., USA; joined Compagnie de Saint-Gobain 1971, later Deputy Del.-Gen. for FRG and Chair. Man. Bd VEGLA/Vereinigte Glaswerke GmbH, Aachen; Chair. Man. Bd Krupp Stahl AG, Bochum 1986; mem. Exec. Bd Fried. Krupp GmbH, Essen 1988 (now Fried. Krupp AG Hoesch-Krupp), CEO 1989–99; CEO ThyssenKrupp AG 1999–2001, Chair. Supervisory Bd 2001–; mem. Supervisory Bd Siemens AG 2003–, Chair. 2007–; mem. or fmr mem. Supervisory Bd Allianz SE, Axel Springer AG, Compagnie de Saint-Gobain (France); Chair. and mem. several supervisory bds and advisory councils; Saarland Amb.; Großes Bundesverdienstkreuz 2004, Order of Merit of North Rhine-Westphalia 2007, Grand Officier, Chevalier, Légion d'honneur 2015. *Address:* Siemens AG, Wittelsbacherplatz 2, 80333 Munich (office); ThyssenKrupp AG, PO Box, 45063 Essen (office); ThyssenKrupp AG, ThyssenKrupp Allee 1, 45143 Essen, Germany (office). *Telephone:* (69) 797-6660 (Munich) (office); (201) 844-536212 (Essen) (office). *Fax:* (201) 844-536000 (Essen) (office). *E-mail:* contact@siemens.com (office). *Website:* www.siemens.com (office); www.thyssenkrupp.com (office).

CRONA, Kristina, BSc, PhD; Swedish mathematician and academic; *Assistant Professor, Department of Mathematics and Statistics, American University;* ed Univ. of Stockholm; Postdoctoral Researcher, Univ. of California, Berkeley, USA Jan.–June 2000, 2001, Osnabrück Univ., Germany July–Dec. 2000; Acting Assoc. Prof., Linköpings Univ. 2002–03, visited MSRI and UCLA; Visiting Scholar, Univ. of California 2004–05; Visiting Researcher, Univ. of Stockholm July–Dec. 2005, part-time parental leave, part-time non-academic work and supervision of undergraduate research projects 2006–07; Lecturer, Univ. of California, Merced 2008–11, Asst Project Scientist 2011–14; Asst Prof., Dept of Math. and Statistics, American Univ., Washington, DC 2014–; World Tech. Award (Health and Medicine) (co-recipient) 2015. *Publications:* numerous papers in professional journals on math. evolutionary biology. *Address:* Gray 208, College of Arts and Sciences, American University, 4400 Massachusetts Avenue, NW, Washington, DC 20016-8050, USA (office). *Telephone:* (202) 885-3182 (office). *Fax:* (202) 885-3155 (office). *E-mail:* kcrona@american.edu (office). *Website:* www.american.edu/cas/mathstat (office).

CRONENBERG, David, OC, FRSC; Canadian film director, actor, producer and screenwriter; b. 15 March 1943, Toronto; s. of Milton Cronenberg and Esther Cronenberg; m. Margaret Hindson (divorced 1979; one d.; m. Carolyn Zeifman; two c.; ed Univ. of Toronto; fmr cinematographer and film editor; has directed fillers and short dramas for TV; mem. Order of Ontario 2014; Hon. Patron, Univ. Philosophical Soc., Trinity Coll., Dublin 2010; Chevalier, Légion d'honneur 2009; Queen Elizabeth II Diamond Jubilee Medal 2012, Cannes Film Festival Lifetime Achievement Award 2006, Member, Order of Ontario 2014, Golden Lion for Lifetime Achievement 2018. *Plays:* Opera version of The Fly, Théâtre du Châtelet, Paris 2008. *Films:* Transfer (writer, dir, producer) 1966, From the Drain (writer, dir) 1967, Stereo (writer, dir, producer) 1969, Crimes of the Future (writer, dir, producer) 1970, The Victim (dir) 1974, Shivers (writer, dir) 1974, Rabid (writer, dir) 1976, Fast Company (writer, dir) 1979, The Brood (writer, dir) 1979, Scanners (writer, dir) 1980, Videodrome (writer, dir) 1982, The Dead Zone (dir) 1983, Into the Night (actor) 1985, The Fly (writer, dir, actor) 1986, Dead Ringers (writer, dir, producer) 1988, Nightbreed (actor) 1990, Naked Lunch (writer, dir) 1991, Blue (actor) 1992, M. Butterfly (dir) 1993, Henry & Verlin (actor) 1994, Boozecan (actor) 1994, Trial by Jury (actor) 1994, To Die For (actor) 1995, Blood & Donuts (actor) 1995, Crash (writer, dir, producer) (Cannes Jury Special Prize 1997) 1996, The Stupids (actor) 1996, Extreme Measures (actor) 1996, I'm Losing You (exec. producer) 1998, Last Night (actor) 1998, Resurrection (actor) 1999, eXistenZ (writer, dir, producer) (Silver Berlin Bear 1999) 1998, Camera (writer, dir) 2000, Jason X (actor) 2001, Spider (dir, producer) 2002, A History of Violence (dir, producer) 2005, Chacun son cinéma (dir, segment) 2007, Eastern Promises (People's Choice Award, Toronto Int. Film Festival 2007) 2007, Drone (producer) 2008, A Dangerous Method (dir) 2011, Cosmopolis 2012, Rewind (actor) 2013, Maps to the Stars 2014. *Television:* Programme X (dir episode: Secret Weapons) 1970, Tourettes (film, dir, writer) 1971, Letter from Michelangelo (film, dir, writer) 1971, Jim Ritchie Sculptor (film dir, writer, prod.) 1971, Winter Garden (film dir, writer) 1972, Scarborough Bluffs (film dir, writer) 1972, Lakeshore (film, dir, writer) 1972, In the Dirt (film, dir, writer) 1972, Fort York (film, dir, writer) 1972, Don Valley (film, dir, writer) 1972, Peep Show (dir episodes: The Lie Chair, The Victim) 1975, Teleplay (writer, dir episode: The Italian Machine) 1976, Friday the 13th (dir episode: Faith Healer) 1987, Scales of Justice (dir episode: Regina vs Horvath) 1990, Moonshine Highway (actor) 1996, The Judge (actor) 2001. *Publications:* Crash 1996, Cronenberg on Cronenberg 1996, Consumed (novel) 2014. *Address:* David Cronenberg Productions Ltd, 217 Avenue Road, Toronto, ON M5R 2J3, Canada (office).

CRONIN, Jeremy, MA; South African poet and politician; *Deputy Minister of Public Works;* b. 12 Sept. 1949, Durban; s. of Denis Cronin and Freda Kemp; m. Gemma Paine; one s. one d.; ed Univ. of Cape Town and Sorbonne, Univ. of Paris; Lecturer in Philosophy and Political Science, Univ. of Cape Town 1974–76; imprisoned for seven years for his involvement with the African Nat. Congress (ANC) 1976; fmr Educ. Officer, United Democratic Front; spent time in exile in England and Zambia; Ed. African Communist, Umsebenzi; mem. cen. cttee South African Communist Party 1989–, Deputy Sec.-Gen. 1995–; mem. Nat. Exec. Cttee, ANC 1991–; mem. Parl. 1999–, Chair. Standing Cttee on Transport; Deputy Minister of Transport 2009–12, of Public Works 2012–. *Publications include:* poetry: Inside (Ingrid Jonker Prize) 1983, Even the Dead 1997, Inside and Out 1999, More Than a Casual Contact 2006; non-fiction: Ideologies of Politics (co-ed.) 1976, 30 Years of the Freedom Charter (with R. Suttner) 1986, 50 Years of Freedom Charter (with R. Suttner) 2006. *Address:* Ministry of Public Works, AVN Bldg, 6th Floor, cnr Skinner and Andries Streets, Pretoria 0002; PO Box 1027,

2000 Johannesburg, South Africa (office). *Telephone:* (12) 3105951 (office). *Website:* www.publicworks.gov.za.

CROSBIE, John Carnell, PC, OC, QC, BA, LLB; Canadian politician and lawyer; b. 30 Jan. 1931, St John's, Newfoundland; s. of Chesley A. Crosbie and Jessie Crosbie (née Carnell); m. Jane Furneaux; two s. one d.; ed St Andrew's Coll., Aurora, Ont., Queen's Univ., Ont., Dalhousie Law School, Univ. of London, LSE; called to Newfoundland Bar 1957; Prov. Minister of Municipal Affairs and Housing 1966, mem. Newfoundland House of Ass. 1966, 1971–76; Minister of Finance, Econ. Devt, Fisheries, Inter-Govt Affairs, Mines and Energy and Pres. of the Treasury Bd, Leader of House of Ass. 1975; mem. House of Commons 1976–93; Minister of Finance 1979, of Justice and Attorney-Gen. of Canada 1984–86, of Transport 1986–89, of Int. Trade 1989–91, of Fisheries and Oceans and the Atlantic Canada Opportunities Agency 1991–93; Counsel to Patterson Palmer Law (now Cox and Palmer) 1994–2008; Chancellor Memorial Univ. of Newfoundland 1994–2008; Lt Gov. Newfoundland and Labrador 2008–13; mem. Progressive Conservative Party. *Publication:* No Holds Barred 1997. *Leisure interests:* reading, tennis, salmon and trout fishing. *Address:* PO Box 23119, St John's, Newfoundland, A1B 4J9, Canada (home). *Telephone:* (709) 895-3308 (home). *E-mail:* jane .crosbie@nf.sympatico.ca (home).

CROSBY, James Robert; British business executive; b. 14 March 1956; m.; four c.; ed Lancaster Royal Grammar School and Brasenose Coll., Oxford; joined Scottish Amicable 1977, Investment Dir, Fund Man. 1983–87, Gen. Man. 1987–94; Man. Dir Halifax Life 1994–96, Financial Services and Insurance Dir Halifax PLC 1996–99, CEO Halifax Group PLC 1999–2001, Group CEO HBOS PLC (after merger of Halifax PLC and Bank of Scotland) 2001–06; Chair. Public Pvt. Forum on Identity Man., HM Treasury 2006; Chair. Misys plc 2009 (acquired by Vista Equity Partners 2012); mem. Bd of Dirs ITV plc 2002–12, Financial Services Authority 2003–09 (Deputy Chair. 2004–09), Moneybarn 2011–14 (acquired by Provident Financial Group 2014); Dir (non-exec.) Compass Group plc 2007–13 (resgnd); Trustee, Cancer Research UK 2008–13; Fellow, Faculty of Actuaries 1980; appeared before the British Parl. Comm. on Banking Standards over his role as CEO during the collapse of HBOS Dec. 2012, formally stripped of his knighthood by the Honours Forfeiture Cttee June 2013.

CROSBY, Sidney Patrick; Canadian professional ice hockey player; b. 7 Aug. 1987, Cole Harbour, Nova Scotia; s. of Troy Crosby and Trina Crosby; ed Shattuck-Saint Mary's Boarding School, Minn., USA; centre; played amateur ice hockey with Dartmouth Subways and Shattuck-Saint Mary's Sabres; leading scorer in Quebec Major Junior Hockey League 2004, 2005; first pick overall in Nat. Hockey League (NHL) Entry Draft 2005 by Pittsburgh Penguins; youngest player in NHL history to be named team capt., to record 100 points in a season, to record 200 career points, to have two consecutive 100 point seasons, to be named to All-Star Team; oungest player to win a World Championship scoring title; youngest team captain to win the Stanley Cup 2008/09; silver medal, World Junior Championships, Finland 2004, gold medal, USA 2005; gold medal (team), Olympic Winter Games, Vancouver 2010, Sochi 2014; Quebec Major Junior Hockey League: Michel Briere Trophy (most valuable player) 2004, 2005, Jean Béliveau Trophy (league leading scorer) 2004, 2005, Mike Bossy Trophy (best professional prospect) 2005, Paul Dumont Trophy (personality of the year) 2004, 2005, Guy Lafleur Trophy (playoff MVP) 2005, Michel Bergeron Trophy (offensive rookie of the year) 2004; Canadian Hockey League: Rookie of the Year 2004, Player of the Year 2004, 2005; NHL: Art Ross Trophy 2007, Lester B. Pearson Award 2007, Hart Memorial Trophy 2007, First Team All-Star 2007, Mark Messier Leadership Award 2007, Maurice Richard Trophy for most goals in a season 2010, Ted Lindsay Award (fmrly the Lester Pearson Award) for the 2012/13 season as the NHL's most outstanding player 2013. *Leisure interest:* watching movies. *Address:* c/o Pittsburgh Penguins, 1 Chatham Center, Suite 400, Pittsburgh, PA 15219-3447, USA. *Telephone:* (412) 642-1300. *Fax:* (412) 642-1859. *Website:* www .pittsburghpenguins.com; www.nhl.com/ice/player.htm?id=8471675; www .crosby87.com.

CROSS, George Alan Martin, PhD, FRS; British scientist and academic; *Professor Emeritus, Rockefeller University;* b. 27 Sept. 1942, Cheshire; s. of George Bernard Cross and Beatrice Mary Cross (née Horton); one s.; ed Cheadle Hulme School, Downing Coll., Cambridge; Scientist, Biochemical Parasitology, MRC 1969–77; Head, Dept of Immunochemistry and Molecular Biology, Wellcome Foundation Research Labs 1977–82; apptd André and Bella Meyer Prof. of Molecular Parasitology, Rockefeller Univ. 1982–, now Prof. Emer., Dean of Grad. and Postgraduate Studies 1995–99; Fleming Prize, Soc. for Gen. Microbiology 1978, Chalmers Medal, Royal Soc. of Tropical Medicine and Hygiene 1983, Paul Ehrlich and Ludwig Darmstaedter Prize 1984, Leeuwenhock Lecturer, The Royal Soc. 1998. *Leisure interests:* sailing, tennis, photography. *E-mail:* george.cross@ rockefeller.edu. *Website:* tryps.rockefeller.edu (office).

CROW, Michael M., BA, PhD; American academic and university administrator; *President, Arizona State University;* b. 11 Oct. 1955, San Diego, Calif.; m. Sybil Francis; one s. two d.; ed Iowa State Univ., Syracuse Univ.; Research Asst, Energy and Mineral Resources, Iowa State Univ. 1974–77, Assoc. Prof. of Man. 1988–91; Research Assoc., Inst. for Energy Research, Syracuse Univ. 1982–83, Sr Research Assoc., Maxwell School of Citizenship and Public Affairs, Syracuse Univ. 1983–87, Research Fellow 1987–89; Asst Prof. of Public Admin, Univ. of Kentucky 1984–85; Prof. of Science and Tech. Policy, School of Int. and Public Affairs, Columbia Univ. 1992–2002, Assoc. Vice Provost 1991–92, Vice-Provost 1992–98, Exec. Vice-Provost 1998–2002; Prof., School of Public Affairs, Arizona State Univ. 2002–, Pres. Arizona State Univ. 2002–; f. Center for Science, Policy and Outcomes, Washington, DC 1998; Fellow, Nat. Acad. of Public Admin 2006–. *Publication:* Designing the New American University (with William B. Dabars) 2015. *Address:* Office of the President, Arizona State University, PO Box 877705, Tempe, AZ 85287-7705, USA (office). *Telephone:* (480) 965-8972 (office). *Fax:* (480) 965-0865 (office). *E-mail:* Michael.Crow@asu.edu (office). *Website:* president.asu.edu (office).

CROW, Sheryl; American singer, songwriter and musician (guitar); b. 11 Feb. 1962, Kennett, Mo.; two adopted s.; ed Univ. of Missouri; trained as classical pianist; worked as music teacher and part-time bar singer; fmr backing singer to Rod Stewart, Eric Clapton, Don Henley, Michael Jackson, Joe Cocker; solo artist mid-1980s–; BRIT Award for Best Int. Female Artist 1997, American Music Awards for Best Female Pop/Rock Artist 2003, 2004. *Film appearance:* De-Lovely 2004. *Recordings include:* albums: Tuesday Night Music Club (three Grammy Awards 1995) 1993, Sheryl Crow 1996, The Globe Sessions 1999, Sheryl Crow and Friends: Live in Central Park 1999, C'mon C'mon 2002, Sheryl Crow: Live At Budokan 2003, Wildflower 2005, Hits and Rarities 2007, Detours 2008, 100 Miles from Memphis 2010, Feels Like Home 2013, Be Myself 2017. *E-mail:* sheryl@ sherylcrow.com. *Website:* www.sherylcrow.com.

CROW, Thomas, BA, MA, PhD; American art historian, critic and academic; *Rosalie Solow Professor of Modern Art, Institute of Fine Arts, New York University;* b. (Thomas Eugene Crow), 3 Jan. 1948, Oak Park, Ill.; m. Catherine Phillips; ed Pomona Coll., Univ. of California, Los Angeles; fmr Instructor, California Inst. of the Arts; Asst Prof. of History of Art, Univ. of Chicago 1978–80; Asst Prof. of Art and Archeology, Princeton Univ. 1980–86; Assoc. Prof. of History of Art, Univ. of Michigan, Ann Arbor 1986–90; Prof. and Chair. in History of Art, Univ. of Sussex, UK 1990–96; Robert Lehman Prof. of History of Art, Yale Univ. 1996–2000; Dir Getty Research Inst. 2000–07; Rosalie Solow Prof. of Modern Art, New York Univ. Inst. of Fine Arts 2007–, Assoc. Provost for the Arts 2007–12; Contributing Ed. Artforum; mem. American Acad. of Arts and Sciences; Hon. DFA (Pomona Coll.) 2006. *Publications include:* Painters and Public Life in Eighteenth Century Paris (Eric Mitchell Prize in Art History, Charles Rufus Morley Book Award) 1985, Emulation: Making Artists for Revolutionary France 1995, The Rise of the Sixties: American and European Art in the Era of Dissent 1996, Modern Art in the Common Culture 1996, The Intelligence of Art 1999, Gordon Matta-Clark 2003, Comprendre Andy Warhol/Comprendre l'art contemporain 2013, The Long March of Pop: Art, Music and Design 1930–1995 2014. *Address:* The James B. Duke House, 1 East 78 Street, New York, NY 10075, USA (office). *Telephone:* (212) 992-5834 (office). *Fax:* (212) 992-5807 (office). *E-mail:* tc59@nyu.edu (office). *Website:* www.nyu.edu/gsas/dept/fineart/faculty/crow.htm (office).

CROWE, Russell; New Zealand actor; b. 7 April 1964; s. of John Alexander Crowe and Jocelyn Yvonne Crowe (née Wemyss); m. Danielle Spencer 2003 (divorced 2018); two s.; singer, 30 Odd Foot of Grunts –2005, The Ordinary Fear of God 2006–; Male Star of the Year, Golden Apple Award 2000, Actor of the Year, Hollywood Film Awards 2000, Global Achievement Award, Australian Film Inst., Male Star of the Year, ShoWest Award, Australian Centenary Medal 2001, Special Award for Actor of our Lifetime, Empire Awards 2009. *Films include:* Proof (Australian Film Inst. Award for Best Actor in a Supporting Role) 1991, Romper Stomper (Seattle Int. Film Festival Award for Best Actor, Australian Film Inst. Award for Best Actor in a Lead Role, Film Critics Circle of Australia Award for Best Actor – Male 1993) 1992, The Crossing 1993, The Quick and the Dead 1995, Rough Magic 1995, Virtuosity 1995, Under the Gun 1995, Heaven's Burning 1997, Breaking Up 1997, LA Confidential (Chlotrudis Award for Best Actor 1998) 1997, Mystery Alaska 1999, The Insider (Best Actor, LA Film Critics Assen, Nat. Bd of Review 1999, Nat. Soc. of Film Critics 1999, Critics Choice Award for Best Actor, Broadcast Film Critics Asscn 2000) 1999, Gladiator (Acad. Award for Best Actor 2000, Blockbuster Entertainment Award for Favourite Actor-Action 2001, Critics Choice Award for Best Actor, Broadcast Film Critics Asscn 2001, Empire Award for Best Actor 2001) 2000, Proof of Life 2000, A Beautiful Mind (Golden Globe, BAFTA Award, Screen Actors' Guild Award, Awards Circuit Community Award, Critics Choice Award, Broadcast Film Critics Asscn and Dallas-Fort Worth Film Critics Asscn Award for Best Actor) 2001, Master and Commander 2003, Cinderella Man (Australian Film Inst. Award for Best Actor 2005) 2005, A Good Year 2006, 3:10 to Yuma 2007, American Gangster 2007, Body of Lies 2008, Tenderness 2008, State of Play (Australian Film Inst. Award for Best Int. Actor) 2009, Robin Hood 2010, The Next Three Days 2010, The Man with the Iron Fists 2011, Les Misérables 2012, Man of Steel 2013, Winter's Tale 2014, Noah 2014, The Water Diviner (Film Critics Circle of Australia Award for Best Actor 2015) 2014, Fathers & Daughters 2015, The Nice Guys 2016, The Mummy 2017, Boy Erased 2018. *Address:* c/o WME, 9560 Wilshire Blvd, Beverly Hills, CA 90210, USA (office); Bedford & Pearce Management Ltd, PO Box 506, Katoomba, NSW 2780, Australia (office). *Telephone:* (310) 285-9000 (USA) (office); 8279-6009 (Australia) (office). *E-mail:* bp@bedfordpearce.com.au (office). *Website:* wmeentertainment .com (office); www.bedfordpearce.com.au (office).

CROZIER, Adam Alexander, BA; British business executive; *Non-Executive Chairman, Vue International;* b. 26 Jan. 1964, Isle of Bute, Scotland; s. of Robert Crozier and Elinor Crozier; m. Annette Edwards 1994; two d.; ed Graeme High School, Heriot-Watt Univ., Edinburgh; with Pedigree Petfoods, Mars (UK) Ltd 1984–86; with Daily Telegraph 1986–88; joined Saatchi & Saatchi 1988, Dir 1990, Media Dir 1992, Vice-Chair. 1994, Jt Chief Exec. 1995–99; Chief Exec. Football Asscn 2000–02; Chair. Group Exec. Team and Chief Exec. Royal Mail Group, Royal Mail Holdings PLC 2003–10; CEO ITV plc 2010–17; Non-Exec. Chair. Vue Int. 2017–; mem. Bd of Dirs, Camelot Group, Debenhams PLC 2006–; mem. Pres.'s Cttee of CBI. *Leisure interests:* football, golf, music. *Address:* Vue International, 10 Chiswick Park, 566 Chiswick High Road, London, W4 5XS, England (office). *Telephone:* (20) 8396-0100 (office). *Website:* www.vue-international.com (office).

CRUICKSHANK, Sir Donald Gordon, Kt, MA, MBA, LLD, CA; British government official, financial administrator and business executive; *Chairman, 7digital Group plc;* b. 17 Sept. 1942; s. of Donald C. Cruickshank and Margaret Morrison; m. Elizabeth B. Taylor 1964; one s. one d.; ed Univ. of Aberdeen and Manchester Business School; consultant, McKinsey & Co. 1972–77; Gen. Man. Sunday Times, Times Newspapers 1977–80; with Pearson PLC 1980–84; Man. Dir Virgin Group 1984–89; Chair. Wandsworth Health Authority 1986–89; CEO Nat. Health Service in Scotland 1989–93; Dir Gen. UK Office of Telecommunications 1993–98; Chair. Action 2000 1997–2000, UK Banking Review 1998–2000, SMG PLC 1999–2004, London Stock Exchange 2000–03; mem. Financial Reporting Council 2002–08; Dir (non-exec.) and Chair. Taylor & Francis PLC 2004, mem. Bd of Dirs, T&F Informa plc (formed by merger of Taylor & Francis and Informa) 2004–05; Chair. (non-exec.) Formscape Group Ltd 2003–06, Clinovia 2004–06, 7digital Group plc 2014–; Ind. Dir, Qualcomm Inc. 2005–16; mem. Bd, Bureau of Investigative Journalism 2016–; mem. Inst. of Chartered Accountants of Scotland; Hon. LLD (Aberdeen). *Leisure interests:* writing, sport, golf, theatre, cinema, opera. *Telephone:* 7802-306492 (mobile) (office). *E-mail:* ddgc_135@live.com (office).

CRUICKSHANK, John D.; Canadian journalist and publisher; *Publisher, Toronto Star;* m.; two c.; ed Richview Collegiate and Trinity Coll. at Univ. of Toronto; began as a writer with Parisian theatre troupe 1976; with Montreal Gazette and Kingston Whig-Standard newspapers 1977, before holding several positions at The Globe and Mail 1981–95, beats included educ. and Queen's Park, then Vancouver bureau chief, editorial writer, Assoc. Ed., Man. Ed. 1992–95; Ed. The Vancouver Sun 1995–2000; Vice-Pres. Editorial and Co-Ed. Chicago Sun-Times 2000–03, Publr 2003–07, also COO Sun-Times Media Group; Publr CBC News, Toronto 2007–08; Publr Toronto Star and Pres. Star Media Group 2008–. *Address:* Toronto Star Newspapers Ltd, 1 Yonge Street, Toronto, ON M5E 1E6, Canada (office). *Telephone:* (416) 367-2000 (office). *E-mail:* jcruickshank@thestar.ca (office). *Website:* www.thestar.com (office).

CRUISE, Tom; American actor and film producer; b. (Thomas Cruise Mapother IV), 3 July 1962, Syracuse, New York; s. of Thomas Cruise Mapother III and Mary Lee (née Pfeiffer); m. 1st Mimi Rogers 1987 (divorced 1990); m. 2nd Nicole Kidman 1990 (divorced 2001); one adopted s. one adopted d.; m. 3rd Katie Noelle Holmes 2006 (divorced 2012); one d.; Exec. Producer, United Artists Corpn 2006–; Bravo Otto Germany Award for Best Actor 1986, 1987, 1989, 1990, 1993, 1996, Special Award for Box Office Star of the Year, ShoWest Convention 1987, People's Choice Award 1990, 1994, Man of the Year, Hasty Pudding Theatricals 1994, American Cinematheque Award 1996, John Huston Award, Artists Rights Foundation 1998, MTV Italian Music Award 2003, David di Donatello Lifetime Achievement Award 2005, Britannia Award for Excellence in Film 2005, Distinguished Achievement in Performing Arts 2005, Broadcast Film Critics Asscn Awards 2005, Simon Wiesenthal Humanitarian Award 2011, Entertainment Icon Award, Friars Club 2012, Legend Award, Empire magazine 2014, Will Rogers Motion Picture Pioneers Award for Pioneer of the Year 2018. *Films include:* Endless Love 1981, Taps 1981, All the Right Moves 1983, Losin' It 1983, The Outsiders 1983, Risky Business 1983, Legend 1985, Top Gun 1986, The Color of Money 1986, Rain Man (Kansas City Film Critics Circle Award for Best Supporting Actor 1988) 1988, Cocktail 1989, Born on the Fourth of July (Golden Globe Award for Best Performance by an Actor in a Motion Picture-Drama, Chicago Film Critics Asscn Award for Best Actor 1990) 1989, Days of Thunder (also writer) 1990, Sure as the Moon 1991, Far and Away 1992, A Few Good Men 1992, The Firm 1993, Interview with the Vampire (Blockbuster Entertainment Award for Favourite Actor-Mystery/Thriller, On Video 1995) 1994, Mission: Impossible (also producer) (Nova Award for Most Promising Producer in Theatrical Motion Pictures 1997) 1996, Jerry Maguire (Nat. Bd of Review for Best Actor 1996, Golden Globe Award for Best Performance by an Actor in a Motion Picture-Comedy or Musica, Blockbuster Entertainment Award for Favourite Actor-Comedy/Romance, MTV Movie Award for Best Male Performance, Online Film & Television Asscn Award for Best Comedy/Musical Actor, Golden Satellite Award for Best Actor in a Motion Picture, Comedy or Musical 1997) 1996, Without Limits (producer) 1998, Eyes Wide Shut 1999, Magnolia (Golden Globe Award for Best Performance by an Actor in a Supporting Role in a Motion Picture, Blockbuster Entertainment Award for Favourite Supporting Actor-Drama, Chicago Film Critics Asscn Award for Best Supporting Actor, Florida Film Critics Circle Award for Best Ensemble Cast, Online Film & Television Asscn Award for Best Supporting Actor 2000) 1999, Mission: Impossible II (also producer) (Special Silver Ribbon, Italian Nat. Syndicate of Film Journalists 2000, MTV Movie Award for Best Male Performance 2001) 2000, Vanilla Sky (also producer) (Saturn Award for Best Actor 2002) 2001, Minority Report (Empire Award for Best Actor 2003) 2002, Narc (exec. producer) 2002, Space Station 3D (voice) 2002, Hitting It Hard (video) (producer) 2002, Shattered Glass (exec. producer) 2003, The Last Samurai (also producer) (Ethnic Multicultural Media Award for Best Film Actor, MTV Movie Award for Funniest American in Japan 2004) 2003, Collateral 2004, Ask the Dust (producer), Elizabethtown (producer) 2005, War of the Worlds 2005, Mission: Impossible III (also producer), Ask the Dust (producer) 2006, Lions for Lambs 2007, Tropic Thunder 2008, Valkyrie (Bambi Award for Courage 2007) 2008, Knight and Day 2010, Mission Impossible: Ghost Protocol 2011, Rock of Ages 2012, Jack Reacher 2012, Oblivion 2013, Edge of Tomorrow 2014, Mission: Impossible-Rogue Nation (also producer) 2015, Jack Reacher: Never Go Back 2016, The Mummy 2017, American Made 2017, Mission: Impossible-Fallout 2018. *Television includes:* Fallen Angels (dir series episode The Frightning Frammis) 1993, hosted Nobel Peace Prize Concert 2004. *Leisure interests:* skydiving, scuba diving and piloting stunt plane. *Address:* United Artists Corporation, 10250 Constellation Boulevard, Los Angeles, CA 90067 (office); c/o Creative Artists Agency, 2000 Avenue of the Stars, Los Angeles, CA 90067, USA (office). *Telephone:* (424) 288-2000 (office). *Fax:* (424) 288-2900 (office). *Website:* www.tomcruise.com.

CRUMB, George, BM, MM, DMA; American composer; b. 24 Oct. 1929, Charleston, W Va; s. of George Henry and Vivian Reed; m. Elizabeth Brown 1949; two s. one d.; ed Mason Coll. of Music, Univ. of Illinois, Univ. of Michigan, Hochschule für Musik, Berlin; Prof., Univ. of Colorado 1959–63; Creative Assoc., State Univ. of New York at Buffalo 1963–64; Prof. of Composition, Univ. of Pa 1971–83, Annenberg Prof. of the Humanities 1983–97, Emer. 1997–; mem. Nat. Inst. of Arts and Letters 1975–; Fulbright Scholarship 1955, Rocke-feller Grant 1964, Guggenheim Grant 1967, 1973, Koussevitsky Int. Recording Award 1971, UNESCO Int. Rostrum of Composers Award 1971, Fromm Grant 1973, Ford Grant 1976, Prince Pierre de Monaco Prize 1989, Edward MacDowell Colony Medal, Peterborough 1995, Grammy Award (for Star Child) 2000. *Compositions include:* Two Duos for flute and clarinet 1944, Four Songs for voice, clarinet and piano 1945, Sonata for piano 1945, Four Pieces for violin and piano 1945, Poem 1946, Three Early Songs for voice and piano 1947, Gethsemane for orchestra 1947, Alleluja for chorus 1948, Sonata for violin and piano 1949, A Cycle of Greek Lyrics 1950, Prelude and Toccata 1951, Three Pastoral Pieces for oboe and piano 1952, String Trio 1952, Sonata for viola and piano 1953, String Quartet 1954, Sonata for cello 1955, Diptych for orchestra 1955, Variazioni for orchestra 1959, Five Pieces for piano 1962, Night Music I for soprano, piano and two percussionists 1963, Four Nocturnes for violin and piano 1964, Eleven Echoes of Autumn 1966, Madrigals, Books 1–4 1965–69, Songs, Drones and Refrains of Death 1968, Echoes of Time and the River (Pulitzer Prize for Music) 1968, Night of the Four Moons 1969, Ancient Voices of Children 1970, Black Angels for electric string quartet 1970, Vox Balaenae for three masked musicians 1971, Lux Aeterna 1971, Makrokosmos vols I–IV 1972–79, Dream Sequence for violin, cello, piano and percussion 1976, Star-Child for soprano, children's chorus and orchestra (Grammy Award for Best Contemporary Composition 2001) 1977, Apparition 1979, A Little Suite for Christmas 1979, Gnomic Variations for piano 1981, Pastoral Drone for organ 1982, Processional for piano 1983, A Haunted Landscape for orchestra 1984, The Sleeper 1984, An Idyll for the Misbegotten 1986, Federico's Little Songs for Children for soprano, flute and percussion 1986, Zeitgeist for two amplified pianos 1988, Easter Dawning for carillon 1991, Quest for guitar and ensemble 1994, Mundus Canis for guitar and percussion 1998, American Songbooks 2001–04, Unto the Hills 2001, A Journey Beyond Time 2002, Eine Kleine Mitternachtmusik 2002, Otherworldly Resonances 2002, River of Life 2003, Winds of Destiny 2004, Voices from a Forgotten World 2006, Voices from the Morning of the Earth 2007, The Ghosts of Alhambra for baritone, guitar and percussion 2009, Sun and Shadow for soprano, piano 2009, Voices from the Heartland 2010, The Yellow Moon of Andalusi, mezzo-soprano, piano 2013, Yester-Year 2013, Xylophony for Percussion Quintet 2014. *Leisure interest:* reading. *Address:* c/o Becky Starobin, Bridge Records, Inc., 200 Clinton Avenue, New Rochelle, NY 10801, USA (office). *Telephone:* (914) 654-9270 (office); (610) 565-2438 (home). *Fax:* (914) 636-1383 (office). *E-mail:* bridgerec@aol.com (office). *Website:* www.bridgerecords.com (office); www.georgecrumb.net.

CRUMPTON, Michael Joseph, CBE, PhD, FRS, FMedSci; British biochemist and immunologist; b. 7 June 1929; s. of Charles E. Crumpton and Edith Crumpton; m. Janet Elizabeth Dean 1960; one s. two d.; ed Poole Grammar School, Univ. Coll., Southampton and Lister Inst. of Preventive Medicine, London; joined scientific staff Microbiological Research Establishment, Porton, Wilts. 1955–60; Deputy Dir Research Labs., Imperial Cancer Research Fund Labs., London 1979–91, Dir 1991–93; Dir Imperial Cancer Research Tech. Ltd 1989–99 (COO 1993–94); Visiting Scientist Fellowship, NIH, Bethesda, Md, USA 1959–60; Research Fellow, Dept of Immunology, St Mary's Hosp. Medical School, London 1960–66; mem. scientific staff, Nat. Inst. for Medical Research, Mill Hill 1966–79, Head of Biochemistry Div. 1976–79; Visiting Fellow, John Curtin School for Medical Research, Australian Nat. Univ., Canberra 1973–74; mem. Cell Bd MRC 1979–83, Science Council, Celltech Ltd 1980–90, EMBO 1982–, WHO Steering Cttee for Encapsulated Bacteria 1984–91 (Chair. 1988–91), Sloan Cttee Gen. Motors Research Foundation 1986–88 (Chair. 1988), Council Royal Inst. 1986–90 (mem. Davy Faraday Lab. Comm. 1985–90, Chair. 1988–90), MRC 1986–90, Royal Soc. 1990–92, Scientific Advisory Comm., Lister Inst. 1986–91, MRC AIDS Directed Prog. Steering Cttee 1987–91, Scientific Cttee Swiss Inst. for Experimental Cancer Research 1989–96; Chair. Scientific Advisory Bd Biomedical Research Centre, Univ. of British Columbia 1987–91, Health and Safety Exec., Dept of Health Advisory Comm. on Dangerous Pathogens 1991–99; Dir (non-exec.) Amersham Int. PLC 1990–97, Amersham Pharmacia Biotech Ltd 1997–2001, Amersham Pharmacia Biotech Inc. 2001–02; mem. Governing Body British Postgraduate Medical Foundation 1987–95, Academia Europea 1996–, Governing Body Imperial Coll. 1994–98; mem. numerous Editorial Bds; Biochemistry Soc. Visiting Lecturer, Australia 1983; Trustee, EMF Biological Research Trust (fmr Chair.) 1995, Breakthrough Breast Cancer 1997–; Hon. FRCPath; Hon. Fellow, Inst. of Cancer Research, Breakthrough Breast Cancer; Hon. mem. American Asscn of Immunology 1995. *Publications:* numerous scientific papers. *Leisure interests:* gardening, reading. *Address:* c/o EMF Biological Research Trust, PO Box 23, South Croydon, CR2 7ZL (office); 8 Ticknell Piece Road, Charlbury, Oxon., OX7 3TW, England (home). *Telephone:* (1608) 811845 (home). *E-mail:* mikcrumpton@googlemail.com (home).

CRUTZEN, Paul Josef; Dutch atmospheric chemist and academic; *Professor Emeritus, Max Planck Institute for Chemistry;* b. 3 Dec. 1933, Amsterdam; s. of Josef Crutzen and Anna Crutzen; m. Terttu Soininen 1958; two d.; ed Stockholm Univ., Sweden; various computer consulting, teaching and research positions at Dept of Meteorology, Stockholm Univ. 1959–74; Post-doctoral Fellow, European Space Research Org., Clarendon Lab., Univ. of Oxford, UK 1969–71; Research Scientist, Upper Atmosphere Project, Nat. Center for Atmospheric Research (NCAR), Boulder, Colo, USA and Consultant at Aeronomy Lab., Environmental Research Labs, Nat. Oceanic and Atmospheric Admin, Boulder 1974–77; Sr Scientist and Dir Air Quality Div., NCAR 1977–80; Adjunct Prof., Atmospheric Sciences Dept, Colorado State Univ. 1976–81; Dir Atmospheric Chem. Div., Max Planck Inst. for Chem., Mainz, Germany 1980–2000, Exec. Dir Max Planck Inst. for Chem. 1983–85, now Prof. Emer.; Prof., Dept of Geophysical Sciences, Univ. of Chicago, USA 1987–91; Prof., Scripps Inst. of Oceanography, Univ. of California, San Diego 1992–2000; Prof., Inst. for Marine and Atmospheric Sciences, Utrecht Univ., Netherlands 1997–2000, Prof. Emer. 2000–; mem. Royal Swedish Acad. of Sciences 1991, Royal Swedish Acad. of Eng 1991, Deutsche Akademie der Naturforscher Leopoldina 1991, Accad. Nazionale dei Lincei 1997; mem. Council of Pontifical Acad. of Sciences 2001; Founding mem. Academia Europaea 1988; Foreign Assoc. NAS 1994; Corresp. mem. Royal Netherlands Acad. of Science 1990; Foreign mem. Russian Acad. of Sciences 1999, Royal Soc. 2006; Fellow, American Geophysical Union 1986; Foreign Hon. mem. American Acad. of Arts and Sciences 1986; Hon. mem. American Meteorological Soc. 1997, European Geophysical Soc. 1997, Comm. on Atmospheric Chem. and Global Pollution 1998, Swedish Meteorological Soc. 2000, World Innovation Foundation 2002; Hon. Prof., Johannes Gutenberg Univ. of Mainz 1993; Hon. Chair. Climate Conference 2001, Utrecht 2001; Dr hc (York Univ., Canada) 1986, (Université Catholique de Louvain) 1992, (Univ. of East Anglia, UK) 1994, (Aristotle Univ., Thessaloniki, Greece) 1996, (Univ. of Liège, Belgium) 1997, (Univ. of San José, Costa Rica) 1997, (Tel-Aviv Univ.) 1997, (Oregon State Univ.) 1997, (Univ. of Chile) 1997, (Université de Bourgogne, Dijon, France) 1997, (Univ. of Athens, Greece) 1998, (Democritus Univ. of Thrace, Greece) 2001, (Nova Gorica Polytechnic, Slovenia) 2002, (Univ. of Hull, UK) 2002; Tyler Environment Prize 1989, Volvo Environmental Prize 1991, German Environmental Prize 1994, Max-Planck Research Prize 1994, Nobel Prize in Chem. 1995 (co-recipient), most cited author in the geosciences world-wide 1991–2001 2002. *Publications include:* Atmospheric Change; An Earth System Perspective (with T. E. Graedel) 1993. *Address:* Max Planck Institute for Chemistry, Joh.-Joachim-Becher-Weg 27, 55128 Mainz, Germany (office). *Fax:* (61) 31-305-511 (office). *E-mail:* paul.crutzen@mpic.de (office). *Website:* www.mpic.de (office).

CRUZ, Alex, MSc; Spanish business executive; *Chairman and CEO, British Airways PLC;* b. 1966, Bilbao; m.; four c.; ed Central Michigan Univ., Ohio State Univ.; Consultant, Man. and Dir, American Airlines 1990–95; Sr Dir, Sabre Corpn

1995–2000; Assoc. Dir, Arthur D. Little (consultancy) 2000–01; Man. Dir, Alnad Ltd (travel industry consultancy) 2001–04; Partner, Aviation Practice, Accenture 2005–06; Founding CEO, clickair 2006 (merged with Vueling 2009), Chair. and CEO, Vueling Airlines 2006–16; Chair. and CEO, British Airways PLC 2016–; Assoc. Prof., IESE Business School 2009–; Visiting Lecturer, ESADE Business & Law School 2010–; Dir (non-exec), Goldcar Rental 2015–16. *Address:* British Airways Plc, Waterside, POB 365, Harmondsworth UB7 0GB, England (office). *Telephone:* (844) 453-0235 (office). *Website:* www.britishairways.com (office).

CRUZ, Avelino J., Jr; Philippine lawyer and government official; *Senior Partner, Cruz Marcelo & Tenefrancia;* ed Univ. of the Philippines Coll. of Law; Chief Presidential Legal Counsel 2000–04; fmr mem. Cabinet Oversight Cttee on Internal Security; Sec. of Nat. Defence 2004–06 (resgnd), fmr mem. Nat. Security Council; adviser to Liberal Party Pres. Manuel Roxas II; Chair. Nat. Disaster Co-ordinating Council 2004–06, ASEAN Defence Ministers Meeting 2006; currently Sr Partner, Cruz Marcelo & Tenefrancia; Pres. Philippine Bar Assen. *Address:* Cruz Marcelo & Tenefrancia, 6th, 7th, 8th & 10th Floors, CVCLAW Center, 11th Avenue cor. 39th Street, Bonifacio Triangle, Bonifacio Global City, 1634 Metro Manila, The Philippines (office). *Telephone:* 8105858 (office). *Fax:* 8103838 (office). *E-mail:* aj.cruz@cruzmarcelo.com (office). *Website:* www.cruzmarcelo.com/our-lawyers/name-partners/3-avelino-j-cruz-jr (office).

CRUZ, Lourdes Jansuy, BS, MS, PhD; Philippine biochemist and academic; ed Univ. of the Philippines, Univ. of Iowa, USA; est. Rural Livelihood Incubator 2001; Outstanding Young Scientist Award, Nat. Acad. of Science and Tech. 1981, NRCP Achievement Award in Chem. 1982, Sven Brohult Award 1994, Outstanding Women in Nation's Services Award (Biochemistry), Laureate for Asia Pacific, L'Oréal-UNESCO Awards for Women in Science 2013. *Publications:* more than 120 papers in professional journals. *Address:* c/o Nat. Acad. of Science and Tech., 3rd Level Philippine Science Heritage Centre, DOST Complex, Bicutan, Taguig, 1631 Metro Manila, The Philippines. *Telephone:* (632) 838-7739. *Fax:* (632) 837-3170. *E-mail:* secretariat@nast.ph.

CRUZ, Penélope; Spanish actress; b. 28 April 1974, Madrid; d. of Eduardo and Encarna Cruz Sánchez; m. Javier Bardem 2010; one s.; ed Nat. Conservatory, Madrid; Chevalier, Ordre des Arts et des Lettres 2006. *Films:* Live Flesh, Belle Epoque 1992, Jamón, Jamón 1992, La Celestina 1996, Open Your Eyes 1997, The Hi-Lo Country 1998, Talk of Angels 1998, The Girl of Your Dreams (Goya Award) 1998, All About My Mother 1999, Woman on Top 1999, All the Pretty Horses 2000, Captain Corelli's Mandolin 2001, Blow 2001, Vanilla Sky 2001, Fanfan La Tulipe 2003, Gothika 2003, Noel 2004, Head in the Clouds 2004, Non ti muovere (Don't Move) 2004, Bandidas 2006, Volver (Goya Award for Best Actress 2007) 2006, The Good Night 2007, Elegy 2007, Vicky Cristina Barcelona (BAFTA Award for Best Supporting Actress 2009, Acad. Award for Best Supporting Actress 2009) 2008, La concejala antropófaga 2009, Los abrazos rotos 2009, Nine 2009, Sex and the City 2 2010, Pirates of the Caribbean: On Stranger Tides 2011, To Rome with Love 2012, Twice Born 2012, I'm So Excited 2013, The Counsellor 2013, Ma Ma 2015, The Queen of Spain 2016. *Address:* c/o Kuranda Management International, 8626 Skyline Drive, Los Angeles, CA 90046, USA (office).

CRUZ, (Rafael Edward) Ted, BA, JD; American lawyer and politician; *Senator from Texas;* b. 22 Dec. 1970, Calgary, Alberta, Canada; s. of Rafael Cruz and Eleanor Darragh; m. Heidi Nelson Cruz; two d.; ed Faith West Acad., Katy, Texas, Second Baptist High School, Houston, Princeton Univ., Harvard Law School; fmr Ed. Harvard Law Review, fmr Exec. Ed. Harvard Journal of Law & Public Policy, Founding Ed. Harvard Latino Law Review; served as law clerk to J. Michael Luttig of the US Court of Appeals for the Fourth Circuit 1995 and William Rehnquist, Chief Justice of the US Supreme Court 1996; with Cooper, Carvin & Rosenthal, (now Cooper & Kirk LLC) 1997–98; fmr Dir Office of Policy Planning, Fed. Trade Comm.; fmr Assoc. Deputy Attorney Gen., US Dept of Justice; Domestic Policy Advisor to Pres. George W. Bush on the 2000 Bush-Cheney campaign 1999–2000; Partner, Morgan, Lewis & Bockius law firm 2008–13 (led the firm's US Supreme Court and national appellate litigation practice); Solicitor Gen. of the State of Texas 2003–08; Adjunct Prof. of Law, Univ. of Texas School of Law, Austin 2004–09; Senator from Texas 2013–, Vice-Chair. Nat. Republican Senatorial Cttee 2012–; announced he would run for Republican Party nomination in 2016 presidential election March 2015; Republican; named by American Parl. Debate Assen as Speaker of the Year and Team of the Year (with his debate partner, David Panton) 1992, Traphagen Distinguished Alumnus, Harvard Law School, named by Newsweek amongst 20 Young Hispanic Americans on the Rise 1999, named by National Law Journal amongst 50 Most Influential Minority Lawyers in America 2008, named by Chambers USA amongst America's Leading Lawyers for Business 2009, 2010, named by Texas Lawyer amongst 25 Greatest Texas Lawyers of the Past Quarter Century 2010. *Address:* United States Senate, Washington, DC 20510, USA (office). *Telephone:* (202) 224-3121 (office). *Website:* www.senate.gov (office).

CRUZ SEQUEIRA, Arturo José, BA, MA, DPhil; Nicaraguan economist, politician, academic and diplomatist; *Professor, Instituto Centroamericano de Administración de Empresas (INCAE) Business School;* b. 1953; s. of Arturo José Cruz Porras and Consuelo Sequeira Ximénez; ed American Univ., Washington, DC and Paul H. Nitze School of Advanced Int. Studies, Johns Hopkins Univ., Univ. of Oxford, UK; supported Edén Pastora (fmr Sandinista commdr starting up rebel Democratic Revolutionary Alliance) 1982, then became involved with United Nicaraguan Opposition (rebel umbrella group) 1985, involved in exile politics of Contra rebels opposing Sandinista (FSLN) Govt 1987; Prof., Instituto Centroamericano de Administración de Empresas (INCAE) Business School, Managua –2007, 2009–; Visiting Prof., Advanced School of Econs and Business, San Salvador, El Salvador 2007; Amb. to USA 2007–09; fmr Bradley Fellow, Hudson Inst., Washington, DC. *Publications:* Memoirs of a Counter-Revolutionary, Nicaragua's Conservative Republic 1853–1893 2002 (translated and published in Spanish 2003), Varieties of Liberalism in Central America: Nation-States as Works in Progress (with Forrest Colburn) 2007; articles on the analysis of social, econ. and political trends in Latin America. *Address:* Instituto Centroamericano de Administración de Empresas (INCAE), Campus Francisco de Sola, Apartado 2485, Managua, Nicaragua (office). *Telephone:* (22) 489700 (office). *Fax:* (22) 658617 (office). *E-mail:* arturo.cruz@incae.edu (office). *Website:* www.incae.edu/es/directorio/arturo-cruz.html (office).

CRVENKOVSKI, Branko; Macedonian politician, engineer and fmr head of state; b. 12 Oct. 1962, Sarajevo, Bosnia and Herzegovina; m. Jasmina Crvenkovska; one s. one d.; ed SS Cyril and Methodius Univ., Skopje; computer engineer, SEMOS Co. 1987–90; mem. Nat. Ass. 1990–2004; Chair. Social Democratic Alliance of Macedonia 1990–92, 2009–13, Pres. 1991–2004; Chair. Cabinet of Ministers (Prime Minister) 1992–98, 2002–04; Pres. of Fmr Yugoslav Repub. of Macedonia 2004–09; Hon. mem. Int. Raoul Wallenberg Foundation, Key of the City of Tirana. *Address:* Social Democratic Alliance of Macedonia (Socijaldemokratski sojuz na Makedonija), 1000 Skopje, Bihakjka 8, North Macedonia (office). *Telephone:* (2) 3293100 (office). *Fax:* (2) 3293109 (office). *E-mail:* web@sdsm.org.mk (office). *Website:* www.sdsm.org.mk (office).

CRYAN, John, BA; British business executive; b. 16 Dec. 1960, Harrogate, North Yorks.; m. Mary Cryan; ed Univ. of Cambridge; began career as trainee chartered accountant at Arthur Andersen, London; worked in corp. finance and client advisory roles at UBS and SG Warburg, London, Munich and Zurich from 1987; Group Chief Financial Officer, UBS AG 2008–11; Pres. for Europe, Temasek Holdings Pte Ltd, Singapore 2012–14; mem. Supervisory Bd, Deutsche Bank 2013–15, Chair. Audit Cttee and mem. Risk Cttee 2013–15, Co-Chair. Man. Bd and Co-CEO Deutsche Bank 2015–16, Chair. Man. Bd and CEO 2016–18. *Address:* c/o Deutsche Bank AG, Taunusanlage 12, 60262 Frankfurt, Germany (office).

CRYSTAL, Billy; American actor and comedian; b. 14 March 1947, Long Beach, NY; s. of Jack Crystal and Helen Crystal; m. Janice Crystal (née Goldfinger); two d.; ed Marshall Univ., Nassau Community Coll., New York Univ.; mem. of the group 3's Company; solo appearances as a stand-up comedian; Emmy Award for Outstanding Writing 1991, Mark Twain Prize for American Humor 2007, World Soundtrack Award for Best Original Song Written Directly for a Film (for If I Didn't Have You, Monster, Inc.) 2002, Grammy Award for Best Spoken Word Album (for Still Foolin' Em 2014). *Television:* Soap (series) 1977–81, The Billy Crystal Hour 1982, Saturday Night Live 1984–2015, The Comedians 2015, The Love Boat, The Tonight Show; TV films include: Breaking up is Hard to do 1979, Enola Gay, The Men, The Mission, The Atomic Bomb 1980, Death Flight. *Stage appearances include:* 700 Sundays (one-man show) (Tony Award for special theatrical event 2005, Drama Desk Award for Outstanding Solo Performance 2005). *Films include:* The Rabbit Test 1978, This is Spinal Tap 1984, Running Scared 1986, The Princess Bride 1987, Throw Momma from the Train 1987, When Harry Met Sally 1989, City Slickers 1991, Mr Saturday Night (also dir producer, co-screen-play writer) 1993, Forget Paris 1995, Hamlet, Father's Day, Deconstructing Harry, My Giant 1998, Analyze This 1998, The Adventures of Rocky & Bullwinkle 2000, Monsters Inc. (voice) 2001, Mike's New Car (voice) 2002, Analyze That 2002, Howl's Moving Castle (voice) 2004, Cars (voice) 2006, Tooth Fairy 2010, Small Apartments 2012, Parental Guidance 2012, Monsters University (voice) 2013, The Comedian 2016, Untogether 2018. *Publications:* Absolutely Mahvelous 1986, I Already Know I Love You (juvenile) 2004, 700 Sundays (autobiog.) 2005. *Address:* c/o CAA, 2000 Avenue of the Stars, Los Angeles, CA 90067, USA.

CSABA, László, PhD, DrSci, DrHab; Hungarian economist and academic; *Professor of Economics and European Studies, Central European University;* b. 27 March 1954, Budapest; s. of Ede Csaba and Márta Biró; m. Gabriella Ónody 1980; one s. one d.; ed Univ. of Budapest, Hungarian Acad. of Sciences; Fellow, Inst. for World Econs, Budapest 1976–87; economist/researcher, then Sr Economist, Kopint-Datorg Econ. Research 1988–2000; Hon. Prof. of Int. Econs, Coll. of Foreign Trade, Budapest Univ. of Econs 1991–97, Prof. 1997–; Prof. of Econs and European Studies, Cen. European Univ. 2000–; Head of Doctoral Programme, Univ. of Debrecen 1999–2004; Vice-Pres. European Assen for Comparative Econs 1990–94, 1996–98, Pres. 1999–2000; mem. Econs Cttee Hungarian Acad. of Sciences 1986–, Co-Chair. 1996–99, 2000–02, Chair. 2003–05; Visiting Prof., Bocconi Univ., Milan 1991, Helsinki Univ. 1993, Europa Univ., Viadrina, Frankfurt 1997, Freie Univ., Berlin 1998–2000, Cen. European Univ. 1998; mem. Bd TIGER Inst., Poland, NORDI Inst., Finland; mem. editorial bd of various journals; mem. Hungarian Acad. of Sciences, Science Europe (Social Science section), Academia Europea 2013; Hon. Prof. of Econs, Szent István Univ., Gödöllő; Cross of the Hungarian Repub. 2012; Ministry of External Econ. Affairs Prize 1994, Bezeredi Prize for European Integration 2003, Nat. Bank of Hungary Prize 2004, Akademia Publishing House Best Economics Book Award 2005, Prof. of the Year, Corvinus Univ. 2011. *Publications:* 12 books and six edited vols, including Eastern Europe in the World Economy 1990, The Capitalist Revolution in Eastern Europe 1995, The New Political Economy of Emerging Europe 2005, Crisis in Economics? 2009; several books chapters and more than 340 articles published in 22 countries. *Leisure interests:* classical music, travel, soccer. *Address:* Department of International Relations and European Studies, Central European University, 1051 Budapest, Nador u. 9 (office); 1074 Budapest, Dohány u. 94, Hungary (home). *Telephone:* (1) 327-30-17 (office); (1) 322-05-19 (home). *Fax:* (1) 327-32-43 (office). *E-mail:* csabal@ceu.hu (office). *Website:* www.ceu.hu (office); www.csabal.com.

CSÁKY, Pál, MSc; Hungarian politician; b. 21 March 1956, Šahy, Czechoslovakia (now Slovakia); m.; four d.; ed Univ. of Pardubice, Czech Repub.; Chief Technologist, Levitex textile factory, Levice 1981–90; mem. Nat. Council of Slovak Repub. 1990–2010, mem. Jt Parl. Cttee Nat. Council of Slovak Repub. and European Parl. 1994–98; Deputy Chair. for Foreign Affairs, Hungarian Christian-Democratic Movt (HCDM) 1991–98, Chair. HCDM Parl. Group 1992–98; mem. Parl. Ass. of Council of Europe 1993–94; Deputy Prime Minister of Slovakia for Human Rights, Minorities, and Regional Devt 1998–2002, for European Affairs, Human Rights and Minorities 2002–06; Chair. Party of the Hungarian Coalition (Strana madarskej koalície/Magyar Koalíció Pártja) 2007–10; mem. European Parl. (Group of the European People's Party (Christian Democrats)) 2014–, Vice-Chair. Cttee on Petitions, mem. Del. for Relations with India; Chair. Govt Council for Minorities and Ethnic Groups, Cttee of Ministers for European Affairs, Govt Council for Regional Policy and Control over Structural Operations, Govt Council for Third Sector, Govt Council for Sustainable Devt, Cttee of Ministers Against Drug Abuse and Drug Dependencies. *Publications include:* in Hungarian: Emlékek könyve (Book of Memoirs) 1992, Csillagok a falu felett (Stars Above the Village) 1993, Úton (On the Way) 1994, Magyarként Szlovákiában (Being a Hungarian in Slovakia) 1994, Két világ között (Between Two Worlds) 1998; more than 1,000 articles, political literature and fiction, mainly in Hungarian. *Leisure interests:* music, piano, literature, theatre, fitness, swimming. *Address:* European Parliament, Altiero Spinelli 09E258, 60 rue Wiertz, 1047 Brussels, Belgium (office). *Telephone:* (2) 284-56-01 (office). *Fax:* (2) 284-96-01 (office). *E-mail:* pal.csaky@europarl.europa.eu (office). *Website:* www.europarl.europa.eu/meps/en/124930/PAL_CSAKY_home.html (office).

CSÁNYI, Sándor, BBA, MSc, PhD; Hungarian economist, banker and auditor; *Chairman and CEO, OTP Bank Plc;* b. 20 March 1953, Jászárokszállás; m.; five c.; ed Coll. of Finance and Accounting, Budapest Univ. of Econs; following graduation became a chartered accountant; first job at Ministry of Finance 1974–83; also worked for Ministry of Food and Agric. 1983–86 and at Hungarian Credit Bank 1986–89; Deputy CEO Commercial and Credit Bank (K&H) 1989–92; Chair. and CEO OTP Bank Plc 1992–; Vice-Pres. Bd Hungarian Oil and Gas Co. (MOL); mem. European Advisory Bd of Mastercard 2006–; Co-Chair. Nat. Asscn of Entrepreneurs and Employers (VOSZ), Chinese-Hungarian Business Council 2012–; mem. Institut Int. d'Études Bancaires; Pres. Hungarian Football Fed. 2010–; mem. Organizing Cttee for FIFA World Cup 2011–14, Financial Cttee 2015–17, FIFA Cttee 2017–18, Vice Pres. 2019–; First Vice-Chair. Nat. Asscns Cttee of UEFA 2013–, mem. UEFA Exec. Cttee 2015–; Hon. Prof., Univ. of Western Hungary 2004, Hon. Citizen, Budapest Corvinus Univ. 2005; Hon. Sign of Pres. of Bulgaria 2011, Grand Cross, Hungarian Order of Merit 2015; Honoris Causa Pro Scientia Gold Medal, Council of Nat. Scientific Students Asscn; Global Leader of Tomorrow, World Econ. Forum, Davos 1996, Entrepreneur of the Year (Hungary) 2000, Ernst & Young Entrepreneur of the Year 2003, Mercur Prize, Bd and Man. Collegium, Hungarian Acad. of Sciences 2006, voted Banker of the Year by banking professionals in Hungary 2006, Báthory Prize 2007, Kálmán Tódor Award 2007. *Leisure interests:* football, tennis, hunting, reading. *Address:* Nádor u. 16, 1051 Budapest, Hungary (office). *Telephone:* (1) 473-5000 (office). *Fax:* (1) 311-0072 (office). *E-mail:* csanyi.sandor@otpbank.hu (office). *Website:* www.otpbank.hu (office).

CSIKSZENTMIHALYI, Mihaly, BA, PhD; American psychologist and academic; *Distinguished Professor of Psychology, Claremont Graduate University;* b. 29 Sept. 1934, Fiume, Italy; s. of Alfred Csikszentmihályi and Edith Csikszentmihályi (née Jankovich de Jessenice); m. Isabella Selega 1961; two s.; ed Univ. of Chicago; emigrated to USA in 1956; Assoc. Prof. and Chair., Dept of Sociology and Anthropology, Lake Forest Coll. 1965–71; Prof. of Human Devt, Univ. of Chicago 1971, Chair. Dept of Behavioral Sciences 1985–87; Davidson Prof. of Man., Drucker School of Man., Claremont Grad. Univ. 1999, now Distinguished Prof. of Psychology, also Dir Quality of Life Research Center; visiting professorships in Canada, NZ, Italy, Finland, UK and Australia; mem. Bd of Advisers, Encyclopaedia Britannica 1985–; Consultant, The JP Getty Museum, Malibu 1985–; Sr Fulbright Scholar, Brazil 1984, New Zealand 1990; Fellow, American Acad. of Arts and Sciences, American Acad. of Political and Social Sciences, Hungarian Acad. of Sciences, Nat. Acad. of Educ., Nat. Acad. of Leisure Sciences, World Econ. Forum, Center for Advanced Study in the Behavioral Sciences; Hon. DSc (Lake Forest Coll.) 1999, (Colorado Coll.) 2002, (Rhode Island School of Design) 2003, doctorates in Science and the Arts from several other univs; Research Awards from Nat. Endowment for the Arts, Nat. Inst. of Mental Health, Spencer Foundation, Templeton Foundation, The Atlantic Philanthropies, Don Clifton Prize, 2005, Szechenyi Prize 2011. *Publications:* Beyond Boredom and Anxiety 1975, The Creative Vision 1976, The Meaning of Things 1981, Being Adolescent 1984, Optimal Experience 1988, Flow–The Psychology of Optimal Experience 1990, Television and the Quality of Life 1990, The Art of Seeing 1990, Talented Teenagers 1993, The Evolving Self 1993, Creativity 1996, Finding Flow in Everyday Life 1997, Flow in Sport 1999, Becoming Adult 2000, Good Work 2001, Good Business 2003; contrib. to several other books. *Leisure interests:* mountain climbing, chess, history. *Address:* School of Behavioral and Organizational Sciences, Claremont Graduate University, 150 East 10th Street, Claremont, CA 91711 (office); 700 East Alamosa Drive, Claremont, CA 91711, USA (home). *Telephone:* (909) 607-3307 (office); (909) 971 3723 (home). *Fax:* (909) 621-8543 (office). *E-mail:* miska@cgu.edu (office). *Website:* www.cgu.edu/pages/154.asp (office).

CUARÓN, Alfonso; Mexican film director and producer; b. 28 Nov. 1961, Mexico City; s. of Alfredo Cuarón; m. 1st Mariana Elizondo 1980 (divorced 1993); one c.; m. 2nd Annalisa Bugliani 2001 (divorced 2008); two c.; ed Centro Universitario de Estudios Cinematográficos, Nat. Autonomous Univ. of Mexico. *Films include:* Quartet for the End of Time (also writer) 1983, Who's He Anyway (also screenplay) 1983, Cita con la muerte 1989, Sólo con tu pareja (also screenplay and producer) 1991, Camino largo a Tijuana (co-producer) 1991, A Little Princess 1995, Sistole Diastole (screenplay) 1997, Great Expectations 1998, Y tu mamá también (also screenplay and producer) 2001, Me la debes (exec. producer) 2001, Harry Potter and the Prisoner of Azkaban 2004, Temporada de patos (exec. producer) 2004, Crónicas (producer) 2004, The Assassination of Richard Nixon (producer) 2004, Black Sun (exec. producer) 2005, Paris, je t'aime (writer segment 'Parc Monceau') 2006, Pan's Labyrinth (producer) (BAFTA Award for Best Film Not in the English Language 2007) 2006, Children of Men (also screenplay) 2006, Rudo y Cursi (producer) 2008, Biutiful (assoc. producer) 2010, Gravity (also producer) (Future Film Digital Award, Venice Film Festival 2013, Golden Globe Award for Best Dir 2014, Outstanding Directorial Achievement in Feature Film, Dirs Guild of America 2014, BAFTA Award for Best Dir 2014, Academy Award for Best Dir, Academy Award for Best Film Editing (with Mark Sanger) 2014, Hugo Award for Best Dramatic Presentation, Long Form 2014) 2013, Desierto (producer) 2015, This Changes Everything (documentary) 2015, Roma (also writer, producer, ed.) (Golden Lion, Venice Film Festival 2018, New York Film Critics Circle Award for Best Dir 2018, Dirs Guild of America 2019, Golden Globe Award for Best Director 2019, BAFTA Award for Best Dir and for Best Cinematography 2019, Academy Award for Directing and for Cinematography 2019) 2018. *Television includes:* Hora Marcada 1988–90, Believe (series) 2013. *Address:* c/o Anonymous Content, 3532 Hayden Avenue, Culver City, CA 90232, USA (office). *Telephone:* (310) 558-6000 (office). *Fax:* (310) 558-2724 (office). *Website:* www.anonymouscontent.com (office).

CUBAS GRAU, Raúl Alberto; Paraguayan business executive, politician and fmr head of state; b. 23 Aug. 1943, Asunción; m. Mirta Gusinsky de Cubas; two d. (one deceased); ed Universidad Nacional de Asunción, Universidade Católica do Rio de Janeiro; worked as engineer for ANDE 1967–73; Commercial Dir, CIE SRL 1977–79; Dir CONCRET-MIX SA 1970–88; Legal Rep. 14 de Julio SA 1980–1993; Dir, COPAC VIAL SA 1987–91; Legal Rep. of consortium OCHO A SACI–14 Julio SA–CONPASA 1992; Exec. Minister of State for Ministry of Econ. and Social Planning and Devt 1994–96; Minister of Finance 1996; Pres. of Paraguay 1998–99; mem. Colorado Party.

CUBITT, Sir Hugh (Guy), Kt, CBE, JP, DL, FRICS, FRSA; British fmr business executive; b. 2 July 1928, London; s. of Col the Hon. Guy Cubitt and Rosamond M. E. Cholmeley; m. Linda I. Campbell 1958; one s. two d.; ed Royal Naval Coll., Dartmouth and Greenwich; served in RN 1949–53; Partner, Rogers, Chapman & Thomas 1958–67, Cubitt & West 1962–79; Chair. The Housing Corpn 1980–90, Lombard North Cen. PLC 1980–91; Commr English Heritage 1988–94; Chair. Anchor Group of Housing Assocs 1991–98; Chair. Rea Brothers Group PLC 1996–98; Dir PSIT PLC 1962–97; Dir National Westminster Bank 1977–90, mem. UK Advisory Bd 1990–91; Gov. Peabody Trust 1991–2003 (Chair. 1998–2003); mem. Westminster City Council 1963–78; Lord Mayor of Westminster 1977–78; Hon. Steward, Westminster Abbey 1978–2002 (Chief Steward 1997–2002); Pres. London Chamber of Commerce 1988–91; High Sheriff of Surrey 1983–84; Hon. FRAM. *Leisure interests:* travel, photography, painting. *Address:* Chapel House, West Humble, Dorking, Surrey, RH5 6AY, England (home). *Telephone:* (1306) 882994 (home). *E-mail:* hughcubitt@btinternet.com (home).

CUCCHIANI, Enrico Tommaso, BA, MBA; Italian business executive; b. 20 Feb. 1950, Milan; ed Bocconi Univ., Milan, Stanford Univ. and Harvard Univ., USA; began career working for a large US bank 1977–79; with McKinsey & Co., worked in Milan, London and New York 1979–85; Gen. Man. Gucci Group 1985–92; f. venture capital firm 1992–96; joined Lloyd Adriatico 1996, later, progressively, Gen. Man., CEO, mem. Exec. Cttee and Chair.; Chair. Allianz SpA and mem. Man. Bd Allianz SE, with responsibility for Italy, Spain, Portugal, Turkey, Greece and South America and of global strategic devt and restructuring programme for the Claims business and distribution system of the insurance group –2011; Man. Dir and CEO Intesa Sanpaolo SpA 2011–13 (resgnd); mem. Gen. Council of Aspen Inst. in Italy, Advisory Council of Stanford Univ., Trilateral Comm. (Italy), Exec. Cttee of US-Italy Council, Bilderberg Group 2013–; Cavaliere del Lavoro 2008; Alumnus of the Year, Asscn of Bocconi Grads 2006. *Address:* c/o Intesa Sanpaolo SpA, Piazza San Carlo 156, 10121 Turin, Italy.

CUEVAS ARGOTE, Javier Gonzalo, MBS; Bolivian government official; b. 1955, La Paz; ed Universidad Mayor de san Andrés, Universidad de Chile, Universidad Privada Boliviana, Florida Int. Univ., USA; dir of numerous public and pvt. finance insts; adviser to Pres. of Cen. Bank; Vice-Minister, Ministry of Finance –2003, Minister of Finance 2003–06. *Address:* c/o Ministry of Economy and Public Finance, Edif. Palacio de Communicaciones, 19°, CP 3744, La Paz, Bolivia. *E-mail:* ministro_web@economiayfinanzas.gob.bo.

ČUFER, Uroš, DrSc; Slovenian banker and politician; b. 1970; ed Université Paris IX – Dauphine, France; began career at Bank of Slovenia 1999, Dir Analysis and Research Dept 1999–2004; Dir Man. Centre for Financial Man., Nova Ljubljanska Banka 2004–13; Minister of Finance 2013–14, also Gov. for Slovenia, EIB; mem. Pozitivna Slovenija (PS—Positive Slovenia). *Address:* c/o Ministry of Finance, 1502 Ljubljana, Župančičeva 3, Slovenia.

CUI, Naifu; Chinese politician (retired); b. 8 Oct. 1928, Beijing; s. of Cui Yu Lian and Chang Wei Fung Cui; m. 1955; one s. one d.; joined CCP 1948; Dir Propaganda Dept and Dean of Studies, Lanzhou Univ.; Vice-Chair. Lanzhou Univ. Revolutionary Cttee; Vice-Minister of Civil Affairs 1981, Minister 1982–93; mem. 12th Cen. Cttee CCP 1982–87, 13th Cen. Cttee CCP 1987–92, 14th Cen. Cttee 1992–97; mem. 8th NPC 1993–98, NPC Deputy Jiangxi Prov.; Deputy Head, Group for Resettlement of Ex-Servicemen and Retired Officers 1983–88, Head 1988–; Research Soc. for Theory of Civil Admin. and Social Welfare 1985; Chair. China Org. Comm. of UN Decade of Disabled Persons 1986; Deputy Dir China Org. Comm. of Int. Decade of Natural Disaster Reduction 1991; apptd Pres. China Charity Fed. 1994, currently Lifetime Hon. Pres.; Hon. Dir China Welfare Fund for the Handicapped 1985–; Hon. Pres. China Asscn for the Blind and Deaf Mutes 1984, China Asscn of Social Workers 1991. *Leisure interest:* calligraphy. *Address:* No. 9, Xi Huang Cheng Gen Street, Beijing 100032, People's Republic of China. *Telephone:* 66017240. *Fax:* 66017240.

CUI, Tiankai; Chinese diplomatist; *Ambassador to USA;* b. Oct. 1952, Shanghai; m.; one d.; ed Shanghai Normal Univ., Johns Hopkins Univ., USA; teacher, Shanghai Normal Univ. 1977–78; interpreter, UN HQ, New York 1981–84; began career at Ministry of Foreign Affairs with Dept of Int. Orgs and Confs, serving successively as Attaché, Third Sec., Deputy Dir, Dir, Counsellor 1984–96, Deputy Dir-Gen. Information Dept 1996–97, Minister Counselor, Perm. Mission to UN, New York 1997–99, Deputy Exec. Dir-Gen. Policy Research Office 1999–2001, Dir-Gen. Policy Research Office 2001–03, Dir-Gen. Dept of Asian Affairs 2003–06, Asst Minister of Foreign Affairs, responsible for Asian Affairs, Int. Orgs and Confs and Arms Control 2006–07, Amb. to Japan 2007–09, Vice-Minister of Foreign Affairs 2009–13, Amb. to USA 2013–. *Address:* Chinese Embassy, 3505 International Place NW, Washington, DC 20522, USA (office). *Telephone:* (202) 495-2000 (office). *Fax:* (202) 495-2138 (office). *E-mail:* chinaembpress_us@mfa.gov.cn (office). *Website:* www.china-embassy.org (office).

CUISIA, José L., Jr, BA, BS, MBA; Philippine business executive, central banker and diplomatist; *Chairman FWD Life Insurance Company Limited, Philippines;* b. 16 July 1944, Manila; s. of Jose Cuisia and Magdalena Cuisia (née Lampe); m. Maria Victoria Jose Cuisia 1973; five d.; ed De la Salle Univ., The Wharton School, Univ. of Pennsylvania (Univ. Scholar), USA; served in several financial insts, including Philippine American Life & General Insurance Co., American International Group, Far East Bank & Trust Co., Insular Bank of Asia and America, Union Bank of the Philippines; CEO Filinvest Credit Corpn Jan.–Aug. 1980, Insular Bank of Asia and America 1980–84, Pres. and CEO 1984–85; Admin. Social Security System 1986–90; Chair. Barcelon Roxas Securities Inc. 1986, Union Bank of the Philippines 1986–90, Monetary Bd; Vice-Chair. Century Bank 1986, Philippine Business for Social Progress; Gov. Central Bank and Chair. Monetary Bd and concurrently Chair. Philippine Deposit Insurance Corpn 1990–93; fmr Pres. and CEO/Admin. Social Security System and Dir Philippine Nat. Bank, Commr (representing the Employer's Group) Sept.–Dec. 2010; Amb. to USA

2011–16; Chair. FWD Life Insurance Public Co. Ltd, Philippines 2018–; Chair. Bd Paraclete Foundation; Gov. Cen. Monetary Authority; fmr mem. Bd of Dirs SM Prime Holdings, Phinma Corpn, Holcim Philippines Corpn, Manila Water Trust Co., San Miguel Corpn, Philippine Long Distance Telephone Trust Co., Philippine Airlines; mem. Bd of Trustees, Asian Man. Inst., Makati Medical Center, Pres. Philippine Financial Exec. Inst. 1984, Philippine Man. Asscn 1984; numerous awards and accolades, including the Ten Outstanding Young Men Award for Domestic Banking, Distinguished La Sallian Award, Raul Locsin CEO of the Year Award 2004, Management Man of the Year, Management Asscn of the Philippines 2007, Joseph Wharton Award for Lifetime Achievement 2011, Manuel L. Quezon Award for Exemplary Governance. *Address:* 626 Adelfa Street, New Ayala Alabang Village, Muntinlupa, Manila, Philippines (home). *Website:* www.fwd.com.ph (office).

CUKJATI, France, MD; Slovenian physician, politician and theologian; b. 15 Feb. 1943, Šentgotard; m.; four c.; ed Jesuit Inst. of Philosophy, Zagreb, Croatia and Univ. of Ljubljana; fmr Jesuit priest; practised medicine at Health Centre of Ljubljana-Šiška; fmr Dir Vrhnika Health Centre, entered pvt. practice 1994; mem. Državni zbor (Nat. Ass.) 2000–, Chair. (Speaker) 2004–08, Vice-Chair. 2008–11; Founding mem. and fmr Sec.-Gen. Slovenian Chamber of Medicine. *Address:* Državni zbor (National Assembly), 1102 Ljubljana, Šubičeva ulica 4, Slovenia (office). *Telephone:* (1) 4789400 (office). *Fax:* (1) 4789845 (office). *E-mail:* gp@dz-rs.si (office). *Website:* www.dz-rs.si (office).

CULHANE, John Leonard, PhD, CPhys, FInstP, FRS; Irish physicist and academic; *Emeritus Professor of Physics, University College London;* b. 14 Oct. 1937, Dublin; s. of John Thomas Culhane and Mary Agnes Culhane (née Durkin); m. Mary Brigid Smith 1961; two s.; ed Univ. Coll., Dublin, Univ. Coll., London; Lecturer in Physics, Univ. Coll. London 1967–69, 1970–76, Reader 1976–81, Prof. 1981–2006, Prof. Emer. 2006–; research scientist, Lockheed Palo Alto Lab. 1969–70; Dir Mullard Space Science Lab., Univ. Coll. London 1983–2003, Head Dept of Space and Climate Physics 1993–2003; UK Del. and Vice-Pres. European Space Agency Science Programme Cttee 1989–94; Chair. British Nat. Space Centre Space Science Programme Bd 1989–92, COSPAR Comm. 1994–2002, European Space Science Cttee, European Science Foundation 1997–2002; mem. Advisory Panel European Space Agency Space Science Dept 1995–2000, UK Particle Physics and Astronomy Research 1996–2000; Foreign mem. Norwegian Acad. of Sciences and Letters 1996; Hon. DSc (Wrocław) 1996; Gold Medal, Royal Astronomical Soc. 2007. *Publications:* X-Ray Astronomy, over 350 papers on Solar and Cosmic X-Ray Astronomy, X-Ray Instrumentation and Plasma Spectroscopy. *Leisure interests:* music, motor racing. *Telephone:* (1483) 204100 (office). *Fax:* (1483) 278312. *E-mail:* j.culhane@ucl.ac.uk (office).

CULKIN, Macaulay; American actor; b. 26 Aug. 1980, New York; s. of Christopher Culkin and Pat Culkin; m. Rachel Milner 1998; ed St Joseph's School of Yorkville, New York, George Balanchine's School of Ballet, New York. *Films include:* Rocket Gibraltar 1988, Uncle Buck 1989, See You In The Morning 1989, Jacob's Ladder 1990, Home Alone 1990, My Girl 1991, Only the Lonely 1991, Home Alone 2: Lost in New York 1992, The Nutcracker, The Good Son 1993, The Pagemaster 1994, Getting Even With Dad 1994, Richie Rich 1995, Body Piercer 1998, Saved! 2004, Jerusalemski sindrom 2004, Sex and Breakfast 2007. *Play:* Madame Melville, Vaudeville Theatre, London 2000. *Television includes:* Foster Hall 2004, Robot Chicken (series) 2005–10, Kings (series) 2009. *Publication:* Junior 2006.

CULLELL MUNIESA, Rosa; Spanish media executive; *CEO, Media Capital (Grupo PRISA);* b. 14 March 1958, Barcelona; m.; two c.; ed Universidad Autónoma de Barcelona, IESE; worked as journalist with Mundo Diario, BBC, TVE-Catalonia and El País; Dir of Communication, La Caixa 1988, later Gen. Man., Exec. Vice-Pres. and Sr Exec. Vice-Pres. –2002, representing La Caixa on the Bds of Panrico, Telesp (Telefónica de Sao Paulo) and Port Aventura 2002–; apptd CEO Grup 62 2002; Dir-Gen., Gran Teatre del Liceu 2005–08; CEO Media Capital (Grupo PRISA) 2011–; mem. Editorial Bd El País 2011–16; Journalist then Dir-Gen. Corporación Catalana de Radio y Televisión. *Address:* Grupo PRISA, Gran Vía 32, 28013 Madrid, Spain (office). *Telephone:* (91) 3301000 (office). *Website:* www.prisa.com (office).

CULLEN, Hon. Sir Michael John, KNZM, MA, PhD; New Zealand fmr politician; *Chairman, New Zealand Post;* b. 5 Feb. 1945, London, England, UK; m. 1st Rowena Joy Knight; two d.; m. 2nd Anne Lowson Collins; ed Christ's Coll. Christchurch, Univ. of Canterbury and Univ. of Edinburgh, UK; Asst Lecturer, Univ. of Canterbury, Tutor Univ. of Stirling, Sr Lecturer in History, Univ. of Otago, Dunedin and Visiting Fellow, ANU 1968–81; MP for St Kilda 1981–96, for Dunedin South 1996–99, for Labour Party List 1999–2009; Sr Govt Whip 1984–87; Minister of Social Welfare 1987–90; Assoc. Minister of Finance 1987–89, of Health 1989–90, of Labour 1989–90; Opposition Spokesperson on Finance 1991, apptd Deputy Leader of Opposition 1996; Acting Minister for Accident Insurance 1999–2001; Minister of Revenue 1999–2005, of Finance 1999–2008; Leader of the House 1999–2008; Deputy Prime Minister 2002–08, Minister of Tertiary Educ. 2005–07, Minister in charge of Treaty of Waitingi Negotiations 2007–08, Attorney Gen. 2005, 2006–08; Shadow Leader of the House and Shadow Minister for Treaty of Waitingi Negotiations 2008; Deputy Chair. New Zealand Post 2009–10, Chair. 2010–; mem. Labour Party 1974–, mem. Party Exec. 1976–81, Party Council 1976. *Leisure interests:* music, reading, house renovation, golf. *Address:* Office of the Chairman, New Zealand Post, New Zealand Post House, 7 Waterloo Quay, Wellington Central, Wellington 6011, New Zealand (office). *Website:* www.nzpost.co.nz (office).

CULLINAN, Edward (Ted) Horder, CBE, RA, RIBA; British architect; *Chairman, Edward Cullinan Architects;* b. 17 July 1931, London; s. of Edward Revil Cullinan and Dorothea Joy Horder; m. Rosalind Sylvia Yeates 1961; one s. two d.; ed Ampleforth Coll., Univ. of Cambridge, Architectural Asscn, Univ. of Calif., Berkeley, USA; with Denys Lasdun 1958–65; est. Edward Cullinan Architects 1965, currently Chair.; numerous professorships include Bannister Fletcher Prof., Univ. of London 1978–79, Graham Willis Prof., Univ. of Sheffield 1985–87, Massachusetts Inst. of Tech. 1985, George Simpson Prof., Univ. of Edinburgh 1987–90; currently Visiting Prof., Univ. of Nottingham; Chair. Urban Vision, N Staffordshire; Trustee, Sir John Soane's Museum, London, Construction Industry for Youth Trust, Building Experiences Trust, Koestler Award Trust; represented at RA Summer Exhbn and many others; Hon. Fellow, Royal Incorporation of Architects in Scotland; Financial Times Architecture at Work Award 1991, Special Commendation at Prince Philip Designers Prize 2005, RIBA Royal Gold Medal 2008, numerous other awards and prizes. *Publications:* Edward Cullinan Architects 1984, 1995, Master Plan for the University of North Carolina at Charlotte 1995, Ends Middles Beginnings 2005; contribs to journals. *Leisure interests:* horticulture, cycling, surfing, Arctic and Sahara travel, history, building, geography. *Address:* Cullinan Studio, Foundry, 5 Baldwin Terrace, London, N1 7RU, England (office). *Telephone:* (20) 7704-1975 (office). *Fax:* (20) 7354-2739 (office). *E-mail:* studio@cullinanstudio.com (office); eca@ecarch.co.uk (office). *Website:* www.edwardcullinanarchitects.com (office); www.cullinanstudio.com (office).

CULP, H. Lawrence, Jr, BA, MBA; American business executive; *Chairman and Chief Executive, General Electric Company;* b. 1964; ed Washington Coll., Harvard Business School; joined Veeder-Root (part of Danahar Corpn) 1990, becoming Pres. 1993, Group Exec. and Corp. Officer, with responsibility for Environmental and Electronic Test and Measurement Divs, Danahar Corpn 1995, also Pres., Fluke and Fluke Networks, Exec. Vice Pres. Danahar Corpn 1999–2001, Chief Operating Officer 2001, Pres. and CEO 2001–14; Lead Dir, Chair. and CEO, General Electric Co. 2018–; Sr Lecturer of Business Admin, Harvard Business School; Sr Adviser, Bain Capital Private Equity; mem. Bd of Dirs T. Rowe Price Group, GlaxoSmithKline; mem. Bd of Visitors and Govs Washington Coll.; mem. Bd of Trustees Wake Forest Univ. *Address:* General Electric Company, 41 Farnsworth Street, Boston, Mass 02210, USA (office). *Telephone:* (617) 443-3000 (office). *Website:* www.ge.com (office).

CULVER, Chester (Chet) John, BA, MA; American teacher, politician and consultant; *Founder, Chet Culver Group LLC;* b. 25 Jan. 1966, Washington, DC; s. of fmr US Senator John Chester Culver and Ann Culver (née Cooper); m. Mariclare Thinnes Culver; one s. one d.; ed Bethesda-Chevy Chase High School, Md, Virginia Polytechnic Inst. and State Univ., Drake Univ.; worked as lobbyist 1989–90, clients included Ia Trial Lawyers' Asscn, Ia Beef Processors, Des Moines Univ.; began public service career as environmental and consumer advocate in Ia Attorney-Gen.'s Office 1991–95; teacher, Roosevelt High School and Hoover High School, Des Moines; Sec. of State for Ia 1999–2007, mem. Exec. Council, Chair. Exec. Council Insurance Advisory Cttee, Chair. State Voter Registration Comm., mem. State Records Man. Cttee; Gov. of Iowa 2007–11; Founder, Chet Culver Group LLC (renewable energy and infrastructure consultancy), Des Moines 2011–; Fed. Liaison for Democratic Govs' Asscn 2008–09; est. Iowa Student Political Awareness Club; mem. Nat. Asscn of Secs of State (mem. Elections and Voter Participation Cttee, Presidential Caucuses and Primaries Cttee, New Millennium Youth Initiative), Elections Task Force, Council of State Govts, Iowa State Educ. Asscn; Democrat; Fulbright Memorial Fund Teacher's Scholarship to Japan, Ia State Educ. Asscn 1997. *Address:* The Chet Culver Group LLC, 2501 Grand Avenue, Suite B, Des Moines, IA 50312, USA. *E-mail:* chet@chetculvergroup.com. *Website:* thechetculvergroup.com.

CUMBERBATCH, Benedict Timothy Carlton, CBE, BA, MA; British actor and film producer; *President, London Academy of Music & Dramatic Art;* b. 19 July 1976, Hammersmith, London; s. of Timothy Carlton (Cumberbatch) and Wanda Ventham; m. Sophie Hunter 2015; two s.; ed Brambletye School, West Sussex, Harrow School (arts scholar), London, Univ. of Manchester, London Acad. of Music and Dramatic Art; took gap year volunteering as an English teacher at a Tibetan monastery in Darjeeling, India; first performed at the Open Air Theatre, Regent's Park, London in productions including Love's Labour's Lost 2001, A Midsummer Night's Dream 2001, Romeo and Juliet 2002; Amb. of The Prince's Trust, Motor Neurone Disease Asscn; Pres. London Acad. of Music & Dramatic Art 2018–; Visiting Fellow, Lady Margaret Hall, Oxford 2016; BAFTA Britannia Award for British Artist of the Year 2013. *Theatre includes:* Royal Nat. Theatre: After the Dance 2010, Frankenstein (Laurence Olivier Award for Best Actor in a Play, Evening Standard Award, Critics' Circle Theatre Award) 2011; Barbican Theatre: Hamlet 2015. *Films include:* Hills Like White Elephants (short) 2002, To Kill a King 2003, Starter for 10 2006, Amazing Grace 2006, Inseparable (short) 2007, Atonement 2007, The Other Boleyn Girl 2008, Burlesque Fairytales 2009, Creation 2009, Four Lions 2010, Third Star 2010, The Whistleblower 2010, Tinker Tailor Soldier Spy 2011, War Horse 2011, Wreckers 2011, Girlfriend in a Coma (documentary) (voice) 2012, The Hobbit: An Unexpected Journey 2012, Electric Cinema: How to Behave (short) 2012, Star Trek: Into Darkness 2013, 12 Years a Slave 2013, The Fifth Estate 2013, August: Osage County 2013, Little Favour (short, also producer) 2013, The Hobbit: The Desolation of Smaug 2013, Cristiano Ronaldo: World at His Feet (voice) 2014, The Imitation Game 2014, Penguins of Madagascar (voice) 2014, The Hobbit: The Battle of Five Armies 2014, Black Mass 2015, Zoolander 2 2016, Dr Strange 2017, Thor Raganarok 2017, Avengers: Infinity War 2018. *Television includes:* Heartbeat (series) 2000, 2004, Fields of Gold (film) 2002, Tipping the Velvet (mini-series) 2002, Cambridge Spies (mini-series) 2003, Hawking (film) 2004, To the Ends of the Earth (mini-series) 2005, Stuart: A Life Backwards (film) 2007, The Last Enemy (mini-series) 2008, Small Island (film) 2009, Van Gogh: Painted with Words (film) 2010, Sherlock (series) (Primetime Emmy Award for Outstanding Lead Actor in a Miniseries or a Movie 2014) 2010–, The Hollow Crown (mini-series) 2012, Parade's End (mini-series) 2012, The Hollow Crown 2016, The Child in Time 2017, Patrick Melrose (series) 2018. *Address:* c/o John Grant, Conway van Gelder Grant Ltd, Third Floor, 8–12 Broadwick Street, London, W1F 8HW, England (office); London Academy of Music & Dramatic Art, 155 Talgarth Road, London, W14 9DA, England (office). *Telephone:* (20) 7287-0077 (office); (20) 8834-0500 (office). *E-mail:* nick@conwayvg.co.uk (office). *Website:* www.conwayvangeldergrant.com (office).

CUMING, Frederick (Fred) George Rees, RA, ARCA; British painter; b. 16 Feb. 1930, London; s. of Harold Cuming and Grace Cuming; m. Audrey Lee Cuming 1962; one s. one d.; ed Univ. School, Bexleyheath, Sidcup Art School, Royal Coll. of Art; travelling scholarship to Italy; exhbns in Redfern, Walker, New Grafton, Thackeray and Fieldborne Galleries; works in collections, including Dept of the Environment, Treasury, Chantrey Bequest, RA, Kendal Museum, Scunthorpe Museum, Bradford, Carlisle, Nat. Museum of Wales, Brighton and Hove Museum, Maidstone Museum, Towner Gallery, Eastbourne, Monte Carlo

Museum, Farringdon Trust, Worcester Coll. Oxford, St John's Coll. Oxford, WH Smith Ltd, Thames TV, Nat. Trust Foundation for Art, Guinness Collection; mem. New English Art Club; Hon. DLitt (Kent) 2004; Grand Prix, Art Contemporaine, Monte Carlo (co-recipient) 1977, Sir Brinsley Ford Award, New English Club 1986, Grand Prix, Art Contemporaries 1988, House and Garden Award 1994. *Publications:* A Figure in the Landscape, A Painter's Progress, Practical Art School. *Leisure interests:* tennis, golf, snooker, reading, music, travelling. *Address:* Gables Art, 21 Angel Hill, Tiverton, Devon, EX16 6PE, England (office). *E-mail:* gablesartfc@gmail.com (office). *Website:* www.fredcuming.com (office).

CUNLIFFE, Sir Jonathan Stephen, Kt, CB, MA; British civil servant, diplomatist and banker; *Deputy Governor, Bank of England;* b. 2 June 1953; s. of Ralph Cunliffe and Cynthia Cunliffe; m. Naomi Brandler 1984; two d.; ed St Marylebone Grammar School, Univs of London and Manchester; joined Civil Service 1980, various posts in Depts of Environment and Transport 1980–90; Head Public Sector Pay Div., HM Treasury 1990–92, Head Int. Financial Insts Div. 1992–94, Treasury Debt and Reserves Man. Div. 1994–96, Deputy Dir Macroeconomic Policy and Prospects and Head of Treasury European Monetary Union team 1996–98, Deputy Dir Macroeconomic Policy and Int. Finance 1998–2001, Man. Dir Finance Regulation and Industry, HM Treasury 2001–02, Man. Dir Macroeconomic Policy and Int. Finance 2002–05, Second Perm. Sec. 2005–07; Head of the European and Global Issues Secr. and Int. Econ. and EU Adviser to the Prime Minister, Cabinet Office 2007–11; Amb. and Perm. Rep. to EU, Brussels 2012–13; Deputy Gov. for Financial Stability, Bank of England 2013–; Alt. Dir EBRD 1992–94; Alt. mem. EU Monetary Cttee responsible for Debt and Reserves Man. 1996–98. *Leisure interests:* tennis, cooking, walking. *Address:* Bank of England, Threadneedle Street, London, EC2R 8AH, England (office). *Telephone:* (20) 7601-4999 (office). *Fax:* (20) 7601-3047 (office). *Website:* www.bankofengland.co.uk (office).

CUNNINGHAM, (Edward) Patrick, MAgrSc, PhD, MRIA; Irish academic, international public servant and scientific adviser; *Professor of Animal Genetics, Trinity College Dublin;* b. 4 Aug. 1934, Dublin; s. of Eugene Cunningham and Kathleen Moran; m. Catherine Dee 1965 (died 1998); four s. two d.; ed Clongowes Wood Coll., Univ. Coll. Dublin, Cornell Univ., USA; Housemaster, Albert Agricultural Coll. Dublin 1956–57; Research and Teaching Asst, Univ. Coll. Dublin 1957–58, Cornell Univ. 1960–62; Research Officer, The Agricultural Inst., Dublin 1962, Head Dept of Animal Breeding and Genetics 1970, Deputy Dir Agricultural Inst. 1980–88; Prof. of Animal Genetics, Trinity Coll., Dublin 1974–; Dir Animal Production and Health Div., FAO, Rome 1990–93, Dir Screwworm Emergency Centre for N Africa 1990–92; Jt Founder and Chair. Identigen Ltd 1997–; Chief Scientific Adviser to Govt of Ireland 2007–12; Visiting Prof., Agricultural Univ. of Norway 1968–69, Econ. Devt Inst., IBRD 1988; Chair. int. panel to review the direct actions of the JRC under FP7 (2007–13) 2014–15; mem. Royal Swedish Acad. of Agriculture and Forestry, Royal Norwegian Acad. of Science and Letters, Russian Acad. of Agricultural Sciences, Acad. d'Agriculture de France; A.M. Leroy Fellowship 1991; Chevalier, Ordre du Mérite agricole; Hon. DAgric (Agric. Univ., Norway) 1997; Hon. DSc (Univ. of Dublin) 1997, (Univ. Coll. Dublin) 2009; Golden Egg Int. Award, Verona 1983, Boyle Medal, Royal Dublin Soc. 1996. *Publications:* Animal Breeding Theory 1969, Development Issues in the Livestock Sector 1992. *Leisure interests:* farming, history. *Address:* Department of Genetics, Trinity College Dublin, College Green, Dublin 2 (office); Vesington House, Dunboyne, Co. Meath, Ireland (home). *Telephone:* (1) 8961000 (switchboard) (office); (1) 8255350 (home). *E-mail:* epcnnghm@tcd.ie (office). *Website:* www.tcd.ie/Genetics/staff/cunningham.php (office).

CUNNINGHAM, Ralph S., BS, MS, PhD; American engineer and business executive; *Chairman, TETRA Technologies Inc.;* ed Ohio State Univ., Auburn Univ.; began career in Exxon's refinery operations; held various exec. positions with Huntsman Corpn (Vice-Chair. 1994–95), Clark Oil and Refining, Tenneco, Inc.; Pres. Texaco Chemical Co. 1990–94; Pres. and CEO CITGO Petroleum Corpn 1995–97 (retd); Dir of Enterprise Products Co. (EPCO) 1987–97, 2006, Group Vice-Chair. 2007–10, Dir, Pres. and CEO EPE Holdings 2007–10, Group Exec. Vice-Pres. and COO EPGP 2005–07, Interim Pres. and Interim CEO June–Aug. 2007, Dir of Enterprise Products GP, LLC (EPGP) 1998–2005, 2006–10, DEP GP 2007–10, COO Enterprise Products GP LLC (gen. partner of Enterprise Products Operating LP) 2005–07, Interim Pres. and CEO June–July 2007, Group Exec. Vice-Pres. Enterprise Products GP LLC (gen. partner of Enterprise Products Partners LP) 2005–07, Vice-Chair. Enterprise Products Holdings LLC 2005–14, Pres. and CEO EPE Holdings, LLC (gen. partner of Enterprise GP Holdings LP) 2007–10, Dir of LE GP, LLC (gen. partner of Energy Transfer Equity, LP) 2009–10, mem. Bd of Dirs Enterprise Products Holdings LLC 2010–, Chair. 2010–13; Dir and Chair. Safety, Health and Responsibility Cttee Cenovus Energy Inc.; Chair. TETRA Technologies Inc. 2006–, Texas Eastern Products Pipeline Co., LLC (gen. partner of Teppco Partners LP) March–Nov. 2005, Dir 2005–06; Advisory Dir Pilko & Assocs; Ind. Dir Agrium Inc. 1996–2013, TETRA Technologies Inc. 1999–, Cenovus Energy Inc. 2009–, Reaction Design, Inc.; Corp. Dir of EnCana Corpn 2003–; mem. Auburn Univ. Chemical Eng Advisory Council, Auburn Univ. Eng Advisory Council, Univ. of Texas at Tyler Eng Advisory Council. *Address:* TETRA Technologies Inc., 24955 Interstate 45 North, The Woodlands, TX 77380, USA (office). *Telephone:* (281) 367-1983 (office). *E-mail:* corpsecretary@tetratec.com (office). *Website:* www.tetratec.com (office).

CUNNINGHAM, William Hughes, BA, MBA, PhD; American marketer, academic and fmr university administrator; *James L. Bayless Chair for Free Enterprise, McCombs School of Business, Department of Marketing, University of Texas;* b. 5 Jan. 1944, Detroit, Mich.; m. Isabella Cunningham; one s.; ed Michigan State Univ.; Asst Prof. of Marketing, Univ. of Texas, Austin 1971–73, Assoc. Prof. 1973–79, Prof. 1979–, Foley's/Sanger Harris Prof. of Retail Merchandising 1982–83, Dean, Coll. of Business Admin/Grad. School of Business 1983–85, Regents Chair in Higher Educ. Leadership 1985–92, James L. Bayless Chair. for Free Enterprise, McCombs School of Business, Dept of Marketing 1988–, Pres. Univ. of Texas at Austin 1985–92, Chancellor Univ. of Texas System 1992–2000, Lee Hage and Joseph D. Jamail Regents Chair in Higher Educ. Leadership 1992–2000, Fellow, IC^2 Inst.; mem. Bd of Dirs Lincoln Nat. Corpn (fmrly Jefferson-Pilot) 1985–, John Hancock Mutual Funds 1986–, Southwest Airlines 2000–, Pinnacle Foods Corpn 2000–03, Introgen Therapeutics 2000–09, Hicks Acquisition Co., Inc. 2007–09, Resolute Energy Corpn 2009–, LIN Television 2009–; mem. Bd of Dirs College Football Asscn 1988–89; mem. Econ. Advisory Cttee of US Dept of Commerce 1983–85; Hon. LLD (Michigan State Univ.) 1993; Outstanding Tex. Leader, John Ben Shepperd Leadership Forum 1987, Jewish Nat. Fund Tree of Life Award 1992, Distinguished Alumnus Award, Michigan State Univ. 1993, Presidential Citation, Univ. of Texas, Austin 2005, inducted into Univ. of Texas, Austin McCombs School of Business Hall of Fame 2011. *Publications:* with others: The Personal Force in Marketing 1977, Consumer Energy Attitudes and Behavior in the Southwest 1977, Effective Selling 1977, Métodos Efectivos de Ventas 1980, Marketing: A Managerial Approach 1987, Grondslagen van het Marketing Management 1984, Introduction to Business 1988, Business in a Changing World 1992 (fourth edn 1995), The Texas Way: Money, Power, Politics and Ambition at The University 2013. *Leisure interests:* golf, tennis, racquetball, horseback riding. *Address:* PO Box E, Austin, TX 78713 (office); 1412 Barton Creek Boulevard, Austin, TX 78735, USA (home). *Telephone:* (512) 232-7540 (office). *Fax:* (512) 232-7541 (office). *E-mail:* whc@po.utexas.edu (office).

CUNNINGHAM OF FELLING, Baron (Life Peer), cr. 2005, of Felling in the County of Tyne and Wear; **John (Jack) Anderson Cunningham,** PC, DL, PhD; British politician; b. 4 Aug. 1939, Newcastle upon Tyne; s. of Andrew Cunningham; m. Maureen Cunningham 1964; one s. two d.; ed Jarrow Grammar School and Bede Coll., Durham Univ.; fmr Research Fellow in Chem., Durham Univ.; fmr school teacher, trades union officer; MP for Whitehaven, Cumbria 1970–83, for Copeland 1983–2005; Parl. Pvt. Sec. to Rt Hon. James Callaghan 1972–76; Parl. Under-Sec. of State, Dept of Energy 1976–79; Opposition Spokesman on Industry 1979–83, on Environment 1983–89, Shadow Leader of the House and Campaigns Co-ordinator 1989–92, Opposition Spokesman on Foreign and Commonwealth Affairs 1992–94, on Trade and Industry 1994–95, on Nat. Heritage 1995–97; Minister of Agric., Fisheries and Food 1997–98, for the Cabinet Office and Chancellor of the Duchy of Lancaster 1998–99; mem. (Labour), House of Lords 2005–, mem. EU Energy and Environment Sub-cttee 2015–; DL, Cumbria 1991. *Leisure interests:* fell walking, fly-fishing, shooting, gardening, theatre, classical and folk music, reading, Newcastle United Football Club, listening to other people's opinions. *Address:* House of Lords, Westminster, London, SW1A 0PW, England (office). *Telephone:* (20) 7219-5353 (office). *Fax:* (20) 7219-5979 (office). *E-mail:* contactholmember@parliament.uk (office). *Website:* www.parliament.uk/biographies/lords/lord-cunningham-of-felling/496 (office).

CUNY, Jean-Pierre, MSc; French business executive; *Chairman and CEO, Bigot Mécanique Sopram;* b. 8 April 1940, Menton; s. of Robert Cuny and Marie-Louise Marchal; m. Anne-Marie Fousse 1968; two d.; ed Ecole Centrale, Paris and Massachusetts Inst. of Tech., USA; engineer, Serete 1968–70; Data Processing Man. Firmin Didot 1970–73; Gen. Man. Dafsa Documentation 1973–76; Project Man. CGA 1976–77; Cost Controller Placoplatre 1977–78, Production Dir 1978–82, Sales and Marketing Dir 1982–85, CEO 1985–86, Chair. and CEO 1986–89, Dir BPB PLC (parent co. of Placoplatre) 1988–89, Deputy Chair. Gypsum Div. 1988–94, CEO BPB PLC 1994–99; Pres. Eurogypsum 1996–99; Chair. and CEO Bigot Mécanique 2002–11, Sopram 2003–11, Bigot Mécanique Sopram 2011–; Chevalier, Légion d'honneur. *Leisure interests:* skiing, theatre, reading, music, film. *Address:* Bigot Mécanique Sopram, 194 Chaussée Jules César, 95250 Beauchamp, France (office). *Telephone:* 1-39-95-60-47 (office). *E-mail:* jean-pierre.cuny@wanadoo.fr (office).

CUOMO, Andrew Mark, BA, JD; American lawyer, state governor and fmr government official; *Governor of New York State;* b. 6 Dec. 1957, Queens, NY; s. of Mario Cuomo and Matilda Cuomo (née Raffa); m. Kerry Kennedy 1992 (divorced 2005); three d.; partner Sandra Lee 2005–; ed Archbishop Molloy High School, Fordham Univ., Albany Law School; Campaign Man., Mario Cuomo Gubernatorial Campaign, New York 1982; Special Asst to Gov. Mario Cuomo, State of NY, Albany 1983; Asst Dist Attorney, Manhattan Dist Attorney's Office, New York City 1984–85; Partner, Blutrich, Falcone & Miller, NY 1985–88; Chair. New York City Comm. on the Homeless 1991–93; Asst Sec. for Community Planning and Devt, Dept of Housing and Urban Devt, Washington, DC 1993–97, Sec. of Housing and Urban Devt 1997–2001; unsuccessful cand. for Gov. 2002; Attorney-Gen. of NY 2007–10; Gov. of New York State 2011–; Vice-Chair.-elect Nat. Govs. Asscn 2018–; f. H.E.L.P. – Housing Enterprise for the Less Privileged (now HELP USA) 1986, Co-Chair. 2001; Visiting Fellow, Harvard Univ. Inst. of Politics; Man of the Year Award, Coalition of Italian American Orgs 1988, Ed Sulzberger Award, Our Town – Manhattan Media LLC 1989, Public Service Award, Council of Jewish Orgs 1989, Distinguished Community Service Award, New York University, 1991, Innovation Award, Harvard University John F. Kennedy School Government, 1998. *Publication:* Crossroads: The Future of American Politics (ed.) 2003. *Address:* Office of the Governor, State Capitol Building, Albany, NY 12224-0341 (office); Washington Office of the Governor, State of New York, 444 North Capitol Street, Suite 301, Washington, DC 20001, USA (office). *Telephone:* (518) 474-7516 (office); (202) 434-7100 (DC) (office). *Fax:* (202) 434-7110 (DC) (office). *Website:* www.governor.ny.gov (office); www.andrewcuomo.com.

CUPITT, Rev. Don, MA; British ecclesiastic and university lecturer; b. 22 May 1934, Oldham, Greater Manchester; s. of Robert Cupitt and Norah Cupitt; m. Susan Marianne Day 1963; one s. two d.; ed Charterhouse, Trinity Hall, Cambridge, Westcott House, Cambridge; ordained 1959; Curate, St Philip's Church, Salford 1959–62; Vice-Prin. Westcott House, Cambridge 1962–65; Fellow, Emmanuel Coll., Cambridge 1965–96, Dean 1966–91, Life Fellow 1996–; Asst Lecturer, Univ. of Cambridge 1968–73, Lecturer in Divinity 1973–96; Fellow of the Jesus Seminar, Westar Inst., Ore., USA 2001; Hon. DLitt (Bristol) 1985. *Television documentaries:* Who Was Jesus? 1977, The Sea of Faith (series) 1984. *Publications include:* Christ and the Hiddenness of God 1971, Crisis of Moral Authority 1972, The Leap of Reason 1976, The Worlds of Science and Religion 1976, Who Was Jesus? (with Peter Armstrong) 1977, The Nature of Man 1979, Explorations in Theology 1979, The Debate about Christ 1979, Jesus and the Gospel of God 1979, Taking Leave of God 1980, The World to Come 1982, The Sea of Faith 1984, Only Human 1985, Life Lines 1986, The Long-Legged Fly 1987, The New Christian Ethics 1988, Radicals and the Future of the Church 1989, Creation out of Nothing 1990, What is a Story? 1991, The Time Being 1992, After All 1994, The Last Philosophy 1995, Solar Ethics 1995, After God: The Future of Religion 1997, Mysticism after Modernity 1997, The Religion of Being 1998, The Revelation of

Being 1998, The New Religion of Life in Everyday Speech 1999, The Meaning of It All in Everyday Speech 1999, Kingdom Come in Everyday Speech 2000, Philosophy's Own Religion 2000, Reforming Christianity 2001, Emptiness and Brightness 2001, Is Nothing Sacred? 2002, Life, Life 2003, The Way to Happiness: A Theory of Religion 2005, The Great Questions of Life 2006, The Old Creed and the New 2006, Radical Theology 2006, Impossible Loves 2007, Above Us It's Only Sky 2008, The Meaning of the West 2008, A New Method of Religious Enquiry 2008, Jesus and Philosophy 2009, Theology's Strange Return 2010, A New Great Story 2010, The Fountain 2010, Turns of Phrase 2011, The Last Testament 2012, Creative Faith 2015, Ethics in the Last Days of Humanity 2016. *Leisure interest:* the arts. *Address:* Emmanuel College, Cambridge, CB2 3AP, England (office). *Telephone:* (1223) 334200 (office). *Fax:* (1223) 334426 (office). *E-mail:* susan .cupitt@gmail.com (home). *Website:* www.doncupitt.com.

CURA, José; Argentine/Spanish singer (tenor), conductor, director and stage designer; b. 5 Dec. 1962, Rosario, Santa Fe; m. Silvia Ibarra; two s. one d.; ed Rosario Univ., School of Arts, Teatro Colon, Buenos Aires; appearances at leading opera houses 1992–; debut at Royal Opera House, Covent Garden in Stiffelio 1995, at Vienna State Opera in Tosca 1996, at La Scala in La Gioconda 1997, at Teatro Colón, Buenos Aires and Metropolitan Opera 1999, Wiener Staatsoper 2003, Semperoper Dresden 2016; Pres. Cuibar Productions; apptd Prof. of Voice, RAM, London 2007; Hon. Prof., CAECE Univ., Argentina 1999, Hon. Citizen of Rosario, Argentina 1999, of Veszprém, Hungary 2004, Hon. Founding mem. Portuguese Asscn against Leukaemia 2007; Chevalier, Ordre du Cèdre (Lebanon) 2000; Premio Abbiati, Italian Critics' Award, Premio Carrara, Cultura Millenaria 1997, XII Premio Internazionale di Arte e Cultura Cilea 1997, Orphée d'Or, Acad. du Disque Lyrique 1998, ECHO Klassik Award: Singer of the Year, Deutsche Phono-Akad. 1999, Ewa Czeszejko Prize, Sochacka Foundation Award 2002, Giovanni Zanatello Prize for Best Artist of the Year, Arena di Verona 2005, Best Argentinian Opera Singer of the Year, Fundación Teatro Colón 2007, One of the Best 100 Argentinian Artists of the Last 10 Years, Fundación Konex 2009, Österreicher Kammersänger, Austrian Ministry of Culture 2010, Sarmiento Honor, Argentinian Senate. *Address:* José Cura Management, Ronda de la Abubilla 30 bis, 28043 Madrid, Spain (office). *Telephone:* (91) 3000134 (office). *E-mail:* management@ josecura.com (office). *Website:* www.josecura.com (office).

CURIGER, Beatrice (Bice) Gabriella Livia; Swiss art historian, critic and curator; *Director, Fondation Vincent van Gogh Arles;* b. 18 July 1948, Zurich; ed Univ. of Zurich; wrote art reviews for Zürich Tages-Anzeiger early 1980s; curated Saus & Braus, Stadtkunst exhbn 1980; co-curated Double Take with Lynne Cooke, Hayward Gallery, London; Co-founder (with Walter Keller, Jacqueline Burckhardt, Dieter von Graffenried and Peter Blum) and Ed.-in-Chief Parkett magazine 1984–2017; Publishing Dir Tate Etc magazine (produced by London's Tate Gallery) 2004–14; Curator Zürich Kunsthaus 1993–2013; Dir Visual Arts Sector, with responsibility for curating the Venice Biennale 54th Int. Art Exhbn 2011; Dir Fondation Vincent van Gogh Arles 2014–; mem. Swiss Fed. Art Comm. 1984–94; mem. Council Univ. of Zurich 1999–2004; Rudolf Arnheim Prof., Humboldt Univ. of Berlin 2006–07; Chevalier des Arts et des Lettres 2013; Heinrich Wolfflin Medal 2007, Art Educator Award, City of Zurich 2009, SI Award, Swiss Inst., New York, ranked by ArtReview magazine amongst the ArtReview Power 100 (sixth) 2010, Kulturpreis des Kantons Zürich 2012, Meret Oppenheim Prize, Swiss Fed. 2012. *Publications include:* Defiance in the Face of Freedom (monograph about Meret Oppenheim) 1982; author of various publs and catalogues of contemporary art. *Address:* Fondation Vincent van Gogh Arles, 20 rue de la Liberté, 13200 Arles, France (office). *Telephone:* (4) 90-93-08-08 (office). *E-mail:* b.curiger@fvvga.org (office); b.curiger@parkettart.com (office). *Website:* www.fondation-vincentvangogh-arles.org (office); www.parkettart.com (office).

CURRAN, Charles E., STD; American academic and ecclesiastic; *Elizabeth Scurlock University Professor of Human Values, Southern Methodist University;* b. 30 March 1934, Rochester, New York; s. of John F. Curran and Gertrude L. Beisner; ed St Bernard's Coll., Rochester, Gregorian Univ., Rome and Accad. Alfonsiana, Rome, Italy; ordained RC priest 1958; Prof. of Moral Theology, St Bernard's Seminary, Rochester, New York 1961–65; Asst Prof., then Assoc. Prof., then Prof. of Moral Theology, Catholic Univ. of America, Washington, DC 1965–89; Sr Research Scholar, Kennedy Center for Bio-Ethics, Georgetown Univ. 1972; External Examiner in Christian Ethics, Univ. of the West Indies 1982–86; Visiting Prof. of Catholic Studies, Cornell Univ. 1987–88; Visiting Brooks and Firestone Prof. of Religion, Univ. of Southern Calif. 1988–90; Visiting Eminent Scholar in Religion, Auburn Univ. 1990–91; Elizabeth Scurlock Univ. Prof. of Human Values, Southern Methodist Univ. 1991–; Pres. Catholic Theological Soc. of America 1969–70, Soc. of Christian Ethics 1971–72, American Theological Soc. 1989–90; mem. American Acad. of Arts and Sciences 2010; Dr hc (Charleston, W Va) 1987, (Concordia Coll., Portland, Ore.) 1992; J.C. Murray Award, Catholic Theological Soc. of America 1972, Building Bridges Award, New Ways Ministry 1992, Presidential Award, Coll. Theology Soc. 2003, Lifetime Achievement Award, Soc. of Christian Ethics 2016. *Publications include:* author, ed. co-ed. of more than 50 books, including Catholic Social Teaching 1891–Present: A Historical, Theological and Ethical Analysis, The Origins of Moral Theology in the United States: Three Different Approaches, The Catholic Moral Tradition Today: A Synthesis, The Moral Theology of Pope John Paul II, Catholic Moral Theology in the United States: A History (American Publr's Award for Professional and Scholarly Excellence in Theology and Religion 2008) 2008, The Social Mission of the U.S. Catholic Church: A Theological Perspective 2011, The Development of Moral Theology: Five Strands 2013, Tradition and Church Reform: Perspectives on Catholic Moral Theology 2016, Diverse Voices in Modern U.S. Moral Theology 2018; numerous articles, lectures and addresses. *Leisure interests:* reading, golf, swimming. *Address:* Southern Methodist University, 317 Dallas Hall, PO Box 750317, Dallas, TX 75275-0317 (office); 4125 Woodcreek, Dallas, TX 75220, USA (home). *Telephone:* (214) 768-4073 (office); (214) 352-8974 (home). *Fax:* (214) 768-4129 (office). *E-mail:* ccurran@mail.smu.edu (office). *Website:* www.smu.edu/ theology (office).

CURRAN, Kevin; British trade union official; b. 1954, Stepney, London; s. of John Curran; m. June Curran; two c.; ed LSE; trained as welder in eng construction industry, Tipton, E Midlands; welding instructor in voluntary sector, London from 1980; joined GMB (fmrly Boilermakers Union) as shop steward 1975, led disputes at Ford Motor Co., Dagenham and W Thurrock Power Station, Essex 1976, elected Br. Sec. Penge Boilermakers Br. 1978, GMB Safety Rep. 1978, elected Chair. London Dist Cttee of Boilermakers Soc. 1982, mem. GMB London Regional Council 1982, Regional Health and Safety Officer, London Region 1988–90, Regional Organiser, Southern Region 1990–96, Sr Organiser, Southern Region 1996–97, Regional Sec., Northern Region 1997–2003, est. North East Maritime Group (NEMG) to revitalize shipbuilding industry in NE 1997, Gen. Sec. GMB 2003–05 (resgnd); apptd to Bd of Regional Devt Agency by Sec. of State 1998; mem. Working Group on productivity and industrial clusters devt policy, Dept of Trade and Industry 2001; mem. Treasury Cttee, TU(C)/CBI. *Leisure interests:* running (marathons), football, history. *Website:* www.gmb.org.uk.

CURRIE, James McGill, MA; British company director, civil servant and EU official; b. 17 Nov. 1941, Kilmarnock, Scotland; s. of David Currie and Mary Currie (née Smith); m. Evelyn Barbara MacIntyre 1968; one s. one d.; ed St Joseph's High School, Kilmarnock, Blairs Coll., Aberdeen, Royal Scots Coll., Valladolid, Univ. of Glasgow; admin. trainee, Scottish Office, Edinburgh 1968–72; Prin. Scottish Educ. and Devt Depts 1972–77; Asst Sec. Scottish Industry Dept 1977–82; Transport and Environment Counsellor, UK Perm. Representation to EC 1982–86; Dir of Programmes Directorate-Gen. XVI Regional Policy 1987–88; Chief of Staff to Competition Policy Commr Sir Leon Brittan 1989–93; Deputy Head of Del., Washington, DC 1993–96; Dir-Gen. (Customs and Indirect Taxation), EC 1996–97, (Environment, Nuclear Safety and Civil Protection) 1997–2001; Visiting Prof. of Law, Georgetown Law Center, Washington, DC, USA 1997–; Dir (non-exec.), Royal Bank of Scotland Group 2001–, British Nuclear Fuels plc 2002–05, Total UK Holdings; Int. Adviser, Eversheds LLP; Hon. DLitt (Glasgow) 2001. *Leisure interests:* golf, guitar, good food, tennis. *Address:* Flat 7, 54 Queen's Gate Terrace, London, SW7 5PJ, England. *E-mail:* jamesmcurrie@hotmail.com.

CURRIE, Lt-Col Nancy Jane, BA, MS, DEng; American astronaut; b. 29 Dec. 1958, Wilmington, Del.; d. of Warren Decker and Shirley Decker; m. David W. Currie (divorced); one d.; ed Ohio State Univ., Univ. of Southern California, Univ. of Houston; Neuropathology Research Asst, Coll. of Medicine, Ohio State Univ.; command 2nd Lt US Army 1981, helicopter instructor pilot, section leader, platoon leader, brigade flight standardization officer, master and aviator; flight simulation engineer, shuttle training aircraft, NASA Johnson Space Center, Houston 1987, astronaut 1991–, flight crew rep. for crew equipment, lead for remote manipulator system, spacecraft communicator; flight engineer mission specialist on STS-57 (Endeavour space shuttle) 1993, STS-70 (Discovery space shuttle) 1995, STS-88 (Endeavour space shuttle) 1998, STS-109 (Columbia space shuttle) 2002; chief astronaut robotics br.; currently Chief Engineer for NASA Eng and Safety Center, Johnson Space Center; mem. Army Aviation Asscn, Ohio State Univ. and ROTC Alumni Asscns, Inst. of Industrial Engineers, Human Factors and Ergonomics Soc.; NASA Flight Simulation Eng Award 1988, Defence Superior Service Medal 1993, Silver Order of St Michael, Army Aviation Award 1997, NASA Space Flight Medal 1993, 1995, 1998, 2002; inducted into Ohio Veterans Hall of Fame 1994, Troy Hall of Fame 1996, Ohio State Univ. Army ROTC Hall of Fame 1996. *Leisure interests:* weightlifting, running, swimming, scuba-diving, skiing. *Address:* NASA Lyndon B. Johnson Space Center, Houston, TX 77058, USA (office). *Website:* www .nasa.gov/centers/johnson/home/index.html.

CURRIE, Richard (Dick) J., OC, BS, MBA, LLD; Canadian business executive; b. St John, New Brunswick; m. Beth Currie; ed Univ. of New Brunswick, Tech. Univ. of Nova Scotia (TUNS), Harvard Business School, USA; began career with Atlantic Sugar Refineries; staff mem. McKinsey & Co., NY –1972; joined Loblaw Cos Ltd, Toronto 1972, Pres. 1976–96; Pres. and Dir George Weston Ltd 1996–2002; Dir Bell Canada Enterprises (BCE) Inc. 1995–2008, Chair. 2002–09; fmr Chair. (non-exec.) Telesat Canada; Chancellor Univ. of New Brunswick 2003–12, Chancellor Emer. 2013–; mem. Bd of Dirs CAE Inc., Staples Inc., Petro-Canada; mem. Int. Advisory Bd RJR Nabisco, Atlanta, USA, Jacobs Suchard, Zürich, Switzerland; fmr Chair. Food Marketing Inst., Washington DC; fmr Chair. Advisory Bd, Richard Ivey Business School, Univ. of Western Ontario; fmr mem. Visiting Cttee, Harvard Business School; Fellow, Inst. of Corp. Dirs 2004; Dr hc (Univ. of New Brunswick), (Univ. of Nova Scotia), (Dalhousie University) 2010; Golden Pencil Award, Rabb Award, Distinguished Retailer of the Year 1997, Canada's Outstanding CEO of the Year 2001, elected to Canadian Business Hall of Fame 2003, McGill Man. Achievement Award 2004, Retail Council of Canada Lifetime Achievement Award 2005, Business Leader of the Year, Richard Ivey School of Business, Univ. of Western Ontario 2009.

CURRIE OF MARYLEBONE, Baron (Life Peer), cr. 1996, of Marylebone, in the City of Westminster; **David Anthony Currie,** MSocSc, PhD, DSc, DLitt; British economist and company director; *Chairman, Competition and Markets Authority;* b. 9 Dec. 1946, London; s. of Kennedy Moir Currie and Marjorie Currie (née Thompson); m. 1st Shaziye Gazioglu 1965 (divorced); two s.; m. 2nd Angela Mary Piers Dumas 1995; ed Battersea Grammar School, Univs of Manchester, Birmingham and London; Economist, Hoare Govett 1971–72, Sr Economist, Econ. Models 1972; Lecturer in Econs, Queen Mary Coll., London 1972–79, Reader 1979–81, Prof. 1981–88; Houblon-Norman Research Fellow, Bank of England 1985–86, Visiting Scholar, IMF 1987; Prof. of Econs, London Business School 1988–2000, Dir Centre for Econ. Forecasting 1988–95, Research Dean 1989–92, Deputy Prin. 1992–95, Deputy Dean External Relations 1999–2000; Dean, City Univ.'s Cass Business School 2001–08; Chair. Office of Communications (Ofcom) 2002–09; mem. (Crossbench) House of Lords 1996–; mem. Advisory Bd to Research Councils 1992–93, Treasury's Panel of Ind. Forecasters 1992–95, OFGEM Man. Bd 1999–2001; Panel mem. Leveson Inquiry 2011–; Chair. Semperian PPP Investment Partners 2008–12; Chair. Independent Audit Ltd 2003–07, Int. Centre for Financial Regulation 2009–12, Council, Univ. of Essex 2011–13, Alacrity Foundation UK 2011–13; Chair. Competition and Markets Authority 2012–; mem. Bd of Dirs Abbey Nat. PLC 2001–02, Dubai Financial Services Authority 2004–, BDO 2008–12, Royal Mail 2009–12, IG Group 2010–12; Dir (non-exec.) London Philharmonic Orchestra 2007–12; Gov. London Business School 1989–95, 1997–2000, Inst. for Govt 2009–; Trustee, Joseph Rowntree Reform Trust 1991–2002. *Publications:* Advances in Monetary Economics 1985, The Operation and Regulation of Financial Markets (co-author) 1986, Macroeconomic Interactions Between North and South (co-author) 1988, Macroeconomic Policies in an Interdependent World (co-author) 1989, Rules, Reputation and Macroeconomic

Policy Co-ordination (co-author) 1993, European Monetary Union: Problems in the Transition to a Single European Currency (co-author) 1995, North-South Linkages and International Macroeconomic Policy (co-author) 1995, The Pros and Cons of EMU 1997, Will the Euro Work? 1998. *Leisure interests:* music, literature, swimming. *Address:* House of Lords, Westminster, London, SW1A 0PW, England (office). *E-mail:* david.currie@cma.gsi.gov.uk (office). *Website:* www.parliament .uk/biographies/lords/lord-currie-of-marylebone/2727 (office).

CURRY, Ann, BA; American broadcast journalist and photographer; b. 19 Nov. 1956, Guam; d. of Robert Paul Curry and Hiroe Nagase; m. Brian Wilson Ross 1987; one s. one d.; ed Ernest J. King School on mil. base in Sasebo, Japan, Ashland High School, Ore., Univ. of Oregon School of Journalism; lived in Japan as a child for several years, later moved to Ashland, Ore.; began broadcasting career as an intern at the then NBC-affiliate KTVL, Medford, Ore. 1978, rose to become station's first female news reporter; reporter and anchor, NBC-affiliate KGW, Portland, Ore. 1980; reporter for KCBS-TV, Los Angeles, Calif. 1984–90; joined NBC News 1990, first as NBC News Chicago Corresp. then as anchor of NBC News at Sunrise 1991–96, also served as substitute anchor and news anchor for NBC news shows Today and Weekend Today, named co-anchor of Dateline NBC with Stone Phillips 2005–07, main anchor 2007–, has been one of the three anchors for Today's third hour 2007–, also substitute anchor for NBC Nightly News, news anchor, The Today Show 1997–2011, anchor, Dateline NBC 2005–11, Co-Anchor (with Matt Lauer) Today 2011–12, Nat. and Int. Corresp. and Anchor at Large, Today 2012–; Hon. Doctorate in Journalism (Southern Oregon Univ.) 2010, Hon. LHD (Wheaton Coll., Norton, Mass) 2010, hon. degree from Providence Coll., Providence, RI 2010; Emmy Award, Acad. of Television Arts and Sciences 1987, 1989, 2007, Golden Mike Award, Radio & Television News Asscn of Southern California 1986, 1987, 1989, Certificate of Excellence, Associated Press 1987, 1988, three Gracie Awards, The Foundation of American Women in Radio and Television, Excellence in Reporting, Nat. Asscn for the Advancement of Colored People (NAACP) 1989, awards from Save the Children, Anti-Defamation League as a Woman of Achievement, inducted into Hall of Achievement, Univ. of Oregon School of Journalism and Communication 2002, Americares Humanitarian Medal Award 2002, Nat. Journalism Award, Asian American Journalists Asscn 2003, Pioneer Award, Univ. of Oregon 2003, Simon Wiesenthal Medal of Valour for her extensive reporting in Darfur 2007, Common Wealth Award of Distinguished Service for outstanding achievements in mass communications, PNC Bank 2008, numerous awards for charity work, primarily for breast cancer research. *Leisure interest:* art history. *Address:* c/o Today Show, 30 Rockefeller Plaza, New York, NY 10112-0002, USA (office). *Telephone:* (212) 664-2555 (office). *Website:* today.msnbc .msn.com/id/4515786 (office).

CURRY, (Wardell Stephen) Steph; American professional basketball player; b. 14 March 1988, Akron, Ohio; s. of Dell Curry; m. Ayesha Alexander 2011; two d.; ed Davidson Coll., N Carolina; point guard; played NCAA basketball for Davidson Coll. 2006–09, NCAA Division I scoring leader 2009, set all-time scoring record for both Davidson and Southern Conference; selected with seventh overall pick in Nat. Basketball Asscn (NBA) draft by Golden State Warriors 2009, (NBA champions 2015); first played for US nat. team at Int. Basketball Fed. (FIBA) Under-19 World Championship 2007, played for Gold Medal winning US Nat. Team at FIBA World Championships 2010, 2014; has set several NBA records for three-point shooting; NBA Sportsmanship Award 2011, NBA All-Star 2014–16, All-NBA First Team 2015, NBA Most Valuable Player 2015, 2016, ESPY Award for Best Male Athlete and Best NBA Player 2015, BET Award for Sportsman of the Year 2015, AP Male Athlete of the Year 2015, BET Award for Sportsman of the Year 2016. *Address:* Golden State Warriors, 1011 Broadway, Oakland, CA 94607, USA (office). *Telephone:* (510) 986-2200 (office). *Website:* www.nba.com/warriors (office).

CURTEIS, Ian Bayley, FSA; British dramatist; b. 1 May 1935, London; m. 1st Dorothy Joan Armstrong 1964; two s.; m. 2nd Joanna Trollope (q.v.) 1985; two step-d.; m. 3rd Deirdre Grantley; two step-s.; ed Univ. of London; dir and actor in theatres throughout UK and BBC TV script reader 1956–63; BBC and ATV staff dir (drama) 1963–67; Chair. Cttee on Censorship, Writers' Guild of Great Britain 1981–85, Pres. of Guild 1998–2001. *Plays for TV:* Beethoven, Sir Alexander Fleming (BBC entry, Prague Festival 1973), Mr Rolls and Mr Royce, Long Voyage Out of War (trilogy), The Folly, The Haunting, Second Time Round, A Distinct Chill, The Portland Millions, Philby, Burgess and Maclean (British entry, Monte Carlo Festival 1978), Hess, The Atom Spies, Churchill and the Generals (Grand Prize for Best Programme of 1981, New York Int. Film and TV Festival), Suez 1956, Miss Morrison's Ghosts (British entry Monte Carlo Festival), BB and Lord D.; writer of numerous TV series; screenplays: La Condition humaine (André Malraux), Lost Empires (adapted from J. B. Priestley), Eureka, Graham Greene's The Man Within (TV) 1983, The Nightmare Years (TV) 1989, The Zimmerman Telegram 1990, The Choir (BBC 1), The Falklands Play 2002, More Love 2003, Yet More Love 2004, Miss Morrison's Ghosts 2004, The Bargain 2007, Boscobel 2008, The Last Tsar 2009; numerous articles and speeches on the ethics and politics of broadcasting. *Plays for radio:* Eroica 2000, Love 2001, After the Break, The Falklands Play 2002. *Publications:* Long Voyage Out of War (trilogy) 1971, Churchill and the Generals 1980, Suez 1956, 1980, The Falklands Play 1987. *Leisure interest:* avoiding television. *Address:* Markenfield Hall, North Yorks., HG4 3AD; 2 Warwick Square, London, SW1V 2AA, England. *Telephone:* (1765) 603411 (office); (20) 7821-8606 (home). *Fax:* (1765) 607195 (office). *E-mail:* info@ markenfield.com (office).

CURTIS, Jamie Lee, Lady Haden-Guest; American actress and author; b. 22 Nov. 1958, Los Angeles, Calif.; d. of Tony Curtis and Janet Leigh; m. Christopher Guest; one s. one d.; ed Choate School, Univ. of the Pacific. *Films include:* Halloween, The Fog, Terror Train, Halloween II, Road Games, Prom Night, Love Letters, Trading Places, The Adventures of Buckaroo Banzai: Across the 8th Dimension, Grandview, USA, Perfect, 8 Million Ways to Die, Mother's Boys, Drowning Mona, Amazing Grace and Chuck, A Man in Love, Dominick and Eugene, A Fish Called Wanda, Blue Steel, My Girl, Forever Young, My Girl 2, True Lies 1994 (Golden Globe Award for Best Actress in a musical or comedy), House Arrest 1996, Fierce Creatures 1996, Halloween H2O 1998, Virus 1999, The Tailor of Panama 2000, Daddy and Them 2001, Halloween: Resurrection 2002, True Lies 2 2003, Freaky Friday 2003, Christmas with the Cranks 2004, Beverly Hills Chihuahua 2008, You Again 2010, Little Engine That Could (voice) 2011, Veronica Mars 2014, Spare Parts 2015, Halloween 2018. *Television includes:* She's In The Army Now, Dorothy Stratten: Death of a Centrefold, Operation Petticoat, The Love Boat, Columbo, Quincy, Charlie's Angels, Anything but Love (dir), Money on the Side, As Summers Die, Anything but Love, Actor, The Heidi Chronicles, Nicholas' Gift, NCIS (series) 2012, New Girl (series) 2012–15, Only Human (film) 2014, Scream Queens (series) 2015. *Publications include:* When I Was Little, A Four-Year-Old's Memoir of her Youth 1993, Tell Me Again About the Night I Was Born 1996, Today I Feel Silly and Other Moods That Make My Day 1999, Where Do Balloons Go? An Uplifting Mystery 2000, I'm Gonna Like Me Letting Off a Little Self-Esteem 2002, It's Hard To Be Five, Learning How To Work My Control Panel 2004, Is There Really a Human Race? 2006, Big Words for Little People 2008. *Leisure interest:* photography.

CURTIS, Penelope, BA, MA, PhD; British art gallery director; *Director, Museu Calouste Gulbenkian;* ed Corpus Christi Coll., Oxford, Courtauld Inst. of Art, Univ. of London; first Exhibitions Curator, Tate Liverpool 1988–94; Head of Henry Moore Centre for Study of Sculpture, Leeds Museums and Galleries 1994–99, led its transformation into Henry Moore Inst., Curator 1999–2010; Dir Tate Britain 2010–15; Dir Museu Calouste Gulbenkian, Lisbon 2015–; mem. Turner Prize Jury 1997; mem. British Council Cttee for Venice Biennale 2008; fmr mem. Advisory Cttee for Govt Art Collection; mem. Advisory Cttee British School at Rome. *Publications:* Sculpture 1900–1945 (in The Oxford History of Art 1999), Patio & Pavilion: The Place of Sculpture in Modern Architecture 2007. *Address:* Museu Calouste Gulbenkian, Avenida Berna 45A, 1067-001 Lisbon, Portugal (office). *Telephone:* (21) 7823000 (office). *Website:* museu.gulbenkian.pt (office).

CURTIS, Richard Whalley Anthony, CBE, BA; British screenwriter, film director and film producer; b. 8 Nov. 1956, New Zealand; s. of Anthony J. Curtis and Glynness S. Curtis; two s. one d. by Emma Vallencey Freud; ed Harrow School, Christ Church, Oxford; Co-founder and Producer Comic Relief 1985–2000; BAFTA Fellowship 2007. *Films include:* Dead On Time 1983, The Tall Guy (writer) 1988, Four Weddings and a Funeral (writer, exec. producer) 1994, Bean (writer, exec. producer) 1997, Notting Hill (writer, exec. producer) 1999, Bridget Jones's Diary (screenplay) 2001, Love Actually (writer, dir) 2003, Bridget Jones: The Edge of Reason (screenplay) 2004, The Boat that Rocked (writer) 2009, War Horse (writer) 2011, About Time (writer, dir) 2013. *Television includes:* Not the Nine O'Clock News (series writer) 1979–82, The Black Adder (series writer) 1983, Spitting Image (series writer) 1984, Blackadder II (series writer) 1986, Blackadder the Third (series writer) 1987, Blackadder's Christmas Carol (writer) 1988, Blackadder: The Cavalier Years (writer) 1988, Blackadder Goes Forth (series writer) 1989, The Robbie Coltrane Special (contrib.) 1989, Mr Bean (series writer) 1989–95, Bernard and the Genie (writer) 1991, Merry Christmas Mr Bean (writer) 1992, Rowan Atkinson Live (contrib.) 1992, The Vicar of Dibley (series writer, exec. producer) 1994–2007, Hooves of Fire (writer) 1999, French & Saunders Live (contrib.) 2000, Legend of the Lost Tribe (exec. producer) 2002, The Girl in the Café (writer and exec. producer) (Humanitas Prize 2006) 2005, The No.1 Ladies' Detective Agency 2008. *Leisure interests:* TV, films, pop music. *Address:* c/o Anthony Jones, United Agents, 12–26 Lexington Street, London, W1F 0LE, England (office); Portobello Studios, 138 Portobello Road, London W11 2DZ, England (office). *Telephone:* (20) 3214-0800 (office). *Fax:* (20) 3214-0801 (office). *E-mail:* dwalker@unitedagents.co.uk (office). *Website:* unitedagents.co.uk (office).

CUSACK, John; American actor; b. 28 June 1966, Evanston, Ill.; s. of Richard Cusack and Nancy Cusack; brother of Joan Cusack; mem. Piven Theatre Workshop, Evanston from age 9–19; f. New Criminals Theatrical Co., Chicago 1988; f. New Crime Productions 1992. *Films include:* Class 1983, Sixteen Candles 1984, Grandview USA 1984, The Sure Thing 1985, Journey of Natty Gann 1985, Better Off Dead 1985, Stand By Me 1985, One Crazy Summer 1986, Broadcast News 1987, Hot Pursuit 1987, Eight Men Out 1988, Tapeheads 1988, Say Anything 1989, Fatman and Little Boy 1989, The Grifters 1990, True Colors 1991, Shadows and Fog 1992, Roadside Prophets 1992, The Player 1992, Map of the Human Heart 1992, Bob Roberts 1992, Money for Nothing 1993, Bullets Over Broadway 1994, The Road to Wellville 1994, City Hall 1995, Anastasia 1997, Con Air 1997, Hellcab 1997, Midnight in the Garden of Good and Evil 1997, Grosse Pointe Blank (also dir, writer) 1997, High Fidelity (also screenwriter) 1997, This is My Father 1998, The Thin Red Line 1999, Pushing Tin 1998, Being John Malkovich 1999, The Cradle Will Rock (also screenwriter) 1999, America's Sweethearts 2001, Life of the Party 2000, Arigo (also producer) 2000, Serendipity 2001, Max 2002, Adaptation 2002, Identity 2003, Runaway Jury 2003, The Ice Harvest 2005, Must Love Dogs 2005, The Contract 2006, Grace Is Gone 2007, 1408 2007, War, Inc. 2007, Martian Child 2007, Igor (voice) 2008, 2012 2009, Shanghai 2010, Hot Tub Time Machine (also producer) 2010, The Factory 2011, The Raven 2012, The Paperboy 2012, The Numbers Station 2013, Adult World 2013, The Frozen Ground 2013, The Butler 2013, Grand Piano 2013, No somos animales 2013, The Carrier 2014, Maps to the Stars 2014, Drive Hard 2014, The Prince 2014, Love & Mercy 2014, Reclaim 2014, Dragon Blade 2015. *Address:* New Crime Productions, 555 Rose Avenue, Venice, CA 90291, USA (office).

CUSACK, Sinéad Moira; Irish actress; b. 18 Feb. 1948, Dalkey, Co. Dublin; d. of Cyril Cusack and Maureen Kiely; m. Jeremy Irons (q.v.) 1977; two s.; acting at the Abbey Theatre in the 1960s; moved to England 1970s, debuted with the RSC at Stratford-on-Avon; numerous appearances in TV drama; played Paulina in The Winter's Tale, directed by Sam Mendes in the Bridge Project shared between the Brooklyn Acad. of Music, New York and the Old Vic, London 2009–12; Hon. DLitt (Univ. Coll. Dublin) 2013. *Theatre includes:* Lady Amaranth in Wild Oats, Lisa in Children of the Sun, Isabella in Measure for Measure, Celia in As You Like It, Evadne in The Maid's Tragedy, Lady Anne in Richard III, Portia in The Merchant of Venice, Ingrid in Peer Gynt, Kate in The Taming of the Shrew, Beatrice in Much Ado About Nothing, Lady Macbeth in Macbeth, Roxanne in Cyrano de Bergerac (all for RSC), Virago in A Lie of the Mind 2001, The Mercy Seat 2003, Oxford Festival, Gate Theatre, Dublin, Royal Court etc. *Films include:* Alfred the Great 1969, The Rise and Rise of Michael Rimmer 1970, The Ballad of Tam Lin 1970, Revenge 1971, Hoffman 1971, A Likely Story 1973, The Last Remake of Beau Geste 1977, Rocket Gibraltar 1988, Venus Peter 1989, Waterland 1992, Bad Behaviour 1993, The Cement Garden 1993, Sparrow 1993, Uncovered 1995, Stealing Beauty 1996, The Nephew 1998, Passion of Mind 2000, My Mother Frank 2000, Dream 2001, I Capture the Castle 2003, Mathilde 2004, V for Vendetta 2005,

The Tiger's Tail 2006, Eastern Promises 2007, Cracks 2009, Wrath of the Titans 2012. *Television includes:* Sanctuary – The Voice of His Calling 1967, ITV Playhouse – Square on the Hypotenuse 1969, David Copperfield (film) 1969, ITV Playhouse – A Sound from the Sea 1970, Armchair Theatre – The Dolly Scene 1970, The Sinners (mini-series) 1971, The Persuaders! (series) 1971, Scoop (series) 1972, Menace (series) 1973, Thriller (series) 1973, The Playboy of the Western World (film) 1974, The Protectors (series) 1974, Affairs of the Heart (series) 1974, Notorious Woman (mini-series) 1974, Quiller (series) 1975, BBC Play of the Month – Love's Labour's Lost 1975, – Trilby 1976, BBC 2 Play of the Week – The Kitchen 1977, Romance – The Black Knight 1977, Supernatural – Ghosts of Venice 1977, Twelfth Night (film) 1980, Cyrano de Bergerac (film) 1985, Screenplay – The Hen House 1989, God on the Rocks (film) 1990, Performance (series) 1992, Oliver's Travels (mini-series) 1995, Mirad (film) 1997, Have Your Cake and Eat It (mini-series) 1997, Food for Ravens (film) 1997, Winter Solstice (film) 2003, North & South (mini-series) 2004, Dad (film) 2005, The Strange Case of Sherlock Holmes & Arthur Conan Doyle (film) 2005, Summer Solstice (film) 2005, Home Again (series) 2006, A Room with a View (film) 2007, The Deep (mini-series) 2010, Camelot (series) 2011, 37 Days 2014, Jekyll and Hyde 2015, Marcella 2016.

CUSHING, Sir Selwyn (John), KNZM, CMG, FCA; New Zealand business executive; *Chairman, Skellerup Holdings Limited;* b. 1 Sept. 1936; s. of Cyril John Cushing and Henrietta Marjory Belle Cushing; m. Kaye Dorothy Anderson 1964; two s.; ed Hastings High School, Univ. of New Zealand; Partner, Esam Cushing & Co., Hastings 1960–86; Dir, Brierly Investments Ltd 1986–93, Chair. and CEO 1999–2001; Deputy Chair. Air New Zealand 1988, Chair. –2001; Chair. Carter Holt Harvey Ltd 1991–93, Electricity Corpn of NZ 1993–97, New Zealand Symphony Orchestra 1996–2005, Skellerup Holdings Ltd 2007–; fmr mem. Securities Comm., NZ Apple and Pear Marketing Bd. *Leisure interests:* cricket, music. *Address:* Skellerup Holdings Ltd, PO Box 74526, Greenlane, Auckland 1546, New Zealand (office). *Telephone:* (9) 523-8240 (office). *E-mail:* ea@skellerupgoup.com (office). *Website:* www.skellerupholdings.co.nz (office).

CUSSLER, Clive Eric, PhD; American novelist; b. 15 July 1931, Aurora, Ill.; s. of Eric Cussler and Amy Hunnewell; m. Barbara Knight 1955 (died 2003); three c.; ed Pasadena City Coll., Orange Coast Coll., California State Univ.; Owner, Bestgen & Cussler Advertising, Newport Beach, Calif. 1961–65; Copy Dir Darcy Advertising, Hollywood, Calif. and Instructor in Advertising Communications, Orange Coast Coll. 1965–67; Advertising Dir Aquatic Marine Corpn, Newport Beach, Calif. 1967–79; Vice-Pres. and Creative Dir of Broadcast, Meffon, Wolff and Weir Advertising, Denver, Colo 1970–73; Founder and Chair. Nat. Underwater and Marine Agency (NUMA) (non-profit org.); Fellow, New York Explorers Club, Royal Geographical Soc.; Lowel Thomas Award, New York Explorers Club. *Publications include:* The Mediterranean Caper 1973, Iceberg 1975, Raise the Titanic 1976, Vixen O-Three 1978, Night Probe 1981, Pacific Vortex 1982, Deep Six 1984, Cyclops 1986, Treasure 1988, Dragon 1990, Sahara 1992, Inca Gold 1994, Shock Wave 1995, Sea Hunters 1996, Flood Tide 1997, Clive Cussler and Dirk Pitt Revealed 1997, Serpent 1998, Atlantis Found 1999, Blue Gold 2000, Valhalla Rising 2001, Fire Ice (with Paul Kemprecos) 2002, Sea Hunters II 2002, The Golden Buddha (with Craig Dirgo) 2003, White Death 2003, Trojan Odyssey 2003, Black Wind (with Dirk Cussler) 2004, Sacred Stone 2005, Lost City (with Paul Kemprecos) 2006, Skeleton Coast 2006, Treasure of Khan (with Dirk Cussler) 2006, Dark Watch (with Jack Du Brul) 2007, The Chase 2007, Polar Shift 2007, Plague Ship 2008, Arctic Drift 2008, Corsair (with Jack du Brul) 2009, Medusa (with Paul Kemprecos) 2009, Spartan Gold (with Grant Blackwood) 2009, The Wrecker (with Justin Scott) 2009, The Silent Sea (with Jack du Brul) 2010, The Adventures of Hotsy Totsy 2010, The Spy (with Justin Scott) 2010, Lost Empire (with Grant Blackwood) 2010, Crescent Dawn (with Dirk Cussler) 2010, The Race (with Justin Scott) 2011, Devil's Gate (with Graham Brown) 2011, The Kingdom (with Grant Blackwood) 2011, The Jungle (with Jack Du Brul) 2011, Serpent (with Paul Kemprecos) 2011, Poseidon's Arrow 2012, The Striker 2013, The Mayan Secrets 2013, Mirage 2013, The Bootlegger 2014, Ghost Ship 2014, Eye of Heaven 2014, Havana Storm 2014, The Pharaoh's Secret 2015, Odessa Sea 2016, Nighthawk 2017, Celtic Empire 2018, The Rising Sea 2018, Shadow Tyrants 2018. *Leisure interests:* discovering shipwrecks, collecting classic cars. *Address:* c/o Penguin Group (USA) Inc., G.P. Putnam's Sons, 375 Hudson Street, New York, NY 10014, USA. *Fax:* (212) 366-2636. *E-mail:* putnampublicity@us.penguingroup.com. *Website:* www.penguin.com/publishers/gpputnamssons; www.cusslerbooks.com; www.clive-cussler-books.com; www.numa.net.

CUTIFANI, Mark, BSc (Eng); Australian business executive; *Chief Executive, Anglo American plc;* ed Wollongong Univ.; held sr exec. positions with Normandy Group, Sons of Gwalia, Western Mining Corpn, Kalgoorlie Consolidated Gold Mines and CRA (Rio Tinto); COO Vale Inco, responsible for global nickel business –2007; CEO AngloGold Ashanti Ltd 2007–13; Chief Exec. Anglo American plc 2013–; mem. Bd of Dirs and Group Man. Cttee and Chair. De Beers 2013–; Pres. South African Chamber of Mines; mem. Int. Advisory Cttee, Kellogg Innovation Network (USA); mem. Exec. Cttee and Treas. Int. Council on Mining and Metals; mem. Mining & Metals Steering Bd and Gov., Mining and Metals Industry Programme, World Econ. Forum. *Address:* Anglo American plc, 20 Carlton House Terrace, London, SW1Y 5AN, England (office). *Telephone:* (20) 7968-8888 (office). *Fax:* (20) 7968-8500 (office). *E-mail:* info@angloamerican.com (office). *Website:* www.angloamerican.com (office).

CUTTAREE, Hon. Jaya Krishna (Jayen), BSc, MSc, PhD; Mauritian lawyer and politician; *Deputy Leader, Mouvement Militant Mauricien;* b. 22 June 1941; m.; two c.; ed Univ. of Edinburgh, UK, Uppsala Univ., Sweden, Univ. of Cambridge, UK; called to the Bar, Lincoln's Inn, London, UK; fmr Asst Conservator of Forests, Ministry of Agric. and Natural Resources; fmr Gen. Man. Sugar Planters' Mechanical Pool Corpn; fmr Chief of Natural Resources Div., OAU, Addis Ababa, Ethiopia; fmr Programme Specialist (Research and Devt in Natural Resources), UNESCO, Paris, France; mem. Legis. Ass. for Stanley and Rose Hill 1982–; Minister of Labour and Industrial Relations 1982–83, Attorney-Gen. and Minister of Housing, Lands, Town and Country Planning 1991, of Industry, Industrial Tech., Scientific Research and Handicraft 1996, of Industry and Commerce 1996–97, of Industry, Commerce and Int. Trade 2000–03, of Foreign Affairs, Int. Trade and Regional Co-operation 2003–05; Deputy Leader, Mouvement Militant Mauricien 1993–; Spokesman, Pacific Common Market, Indian Ocean Comm. and Pacific Forum at WTO meeting, Doha, Qatar 2001; led negotiations between EU and African Pacific Caribbean countries under Cotonou Agreement 2002; Spokesman of African Union at WTO meeting, Cancun, Mexico 2003; Head of Mauritian Del. and Spokesman of the African Union at Africa Growth and Opportunity Act (AGOA) Conf., Washington, DC, 2003; unsuccessful (African Union) cand. for post of Dir Gen. of WTO 2005. *Publication:* Behind The Purple Curtain: A Political Autobiography 2011. *Address:* c/o Mouvement Militant Mauricien, 21 Poudrière Street, Port Louis; Parliament House, Place d'Armes, Port Louis, Mauritius. *Telephone:* 212-6553 (MMM). *Fax:* 208-9939 (MMM). *Website:* www.mmm.mu; mauritiusassembly.govmu.org/English/Pages/MembersElection2000/Hon--Jaya-Krishna-Cuttaree.aspx.

CUTTS, Simon; British artist, poet and publisher; *Director, Coracle Press;* b. 30 Dec. 1944, Derby; s. of George Tom Cutts and Elizabeth Purdy; m. 1st Annira Uusi-Illikainen (divorced 1973); one s.; m. 2nd Margot Hapgood (died 1985); m. 3rd Erica Van Horn 1989; ed Herbert Strutt Grammar School, Belper, Derbyshire, Nottingham Coll. of Art, Trent Polytechnic; travel and miscellaneous employment including The Trent Bookshop, Nottingham 1962–69; Jt Ed. Tarasque Press 1964–72; publishing, lecturing and writing 1972–74; Dir and Co-Partner Coracle Press Books (now Coracle Press) 1975–87, 1996–, Dir, Coracle Press Gallery 1983–86; Dir Victoria Miro Gallery 1985–; org. of exhbns in Europe and New York. *Publications:* Quelques Pianos 1976, Pianostool Footnotes 1983, Petits-Airs for Margot 1986, Seepages 1988, The Rubber Stamp Mini Printer 1993, 1995, After Frank O'Hara and Morton Feldman (with Erica van Horn) 1996, The A. Goldsworthy Questionnaires 1997, A Smell of Printing 2000, Eclogues 2004, A English Dictionary of French Place Names 2004, Ceillets des Poètes 2005, Some Forms of Availability 2006, As If It Is At All 2007, Some More Notes on Writing & Drinking 2010, The Manifestation of the Poem 2011, 8 Old Irish Potatoes 2011, Six Jugs (co-author) 2011, Affinity 2011. *Leisure interests:* walking, running, cooking, eating, drinking and the nostalgia of innocence. *E-mail:* books@coracle.ie (office); coraclepress@eircom.net (office). *Website:* www.coracle.ie (office).

CVETKOVIĆ, Mirko, MA, PhD; Serbian economist and politician; b. 16 Aug. 1950, Zaječar; s. of Srboljub Cvetković and Stana Cvetković; m. Zorica Cvetković; two c.; ed Faculty of Econs, Univ. of Belgrade; began career as economist at Inst. of Mining and Inst. of Econs; consultant, CES MECON (advisory and research firm); fmr foreign consultant on World Bank projects in Pakistan, India and Turkey; Econ. Adviser, Inst. of Mining 1998–2001; Deputy Minister of Economy and Privatization 2001–04; Dir Privatization Agency 2003–04; apptd Special Adviser to CEO Intercom Consulting/CES MECON 2005; Minister of Finance 2007–08, 2011–12; Prime Minister 2008–12. *Publications:* several papers and articles on privatization published in Serbia and abroad. *Leisure interests:* playing piano, saxophone and clarinet.

CVIJANOVIČ, Željka, MA; Bosnia and Herzegovina academic and politician; *President, Republika Srpska;* b. (Željka Grabovac), 1967, Teslić, Socialist Repub. of Bosnia and Herzegovina, Socialist Fed. Repub. of Yugoslavia; m.; two c.; ed Faculty of Philosophy, Sarajevo, Faculties of Philosophy and of Law, Banja Luka; Prof. of English Language and Literature; worked as Sr Interpreter and later an Asst to EU Mission in Bosnia and Herzegovina, as an Adviser to Prime Minister of Republika Srpska for European Integration and Co-operation with Int. Orgs, as Head of Republika Srpska Co-ordination and European Integration Unit in Office of the Prime Minister, and as Chief of Staff to the Prime Minister of Republika Srpska; mem. Savez Nezavishnih Socijaldemokrata (SNSD—Alliance of Ind. Social Democrats); mem. Nat. Ass. of Republika Srpska, mem. Expert Group to Cttee for European Integration and Regional Co-operation; Minister of Econ. Relations and Regional Co-operation –2013; Prime Minister of Republika Srpska 2013–18, Pres. 2018–. *Address:* Office of the President of Republika Srpska, 78000 Banja Luka, Bana Milosavljevića 4, Bosnia and Herzegovina (office). *Telephone:* (51) 248100 (office). *Fax:* (51) 248161 (office). *E-mail:* info@predsjednikrs.net (office). *Website:* www.predsjednikrs.net (office).

CYPRIANO, Márcio Artur Laurelli, JD; Brazilian banker and farmer; b. 20 Nov. 1943; ed Mackenzie Presbyterian Univ.; began career with Banco da Bahia SA 1967; joined Banco Bradesco SA 1973, Dept Dir 1984–86, Asst Dir 1986–88, Man. Dir 1988–95, Dir and Vice-Pres. 1995–99, Pres. and CEO 1999–2009, mem. Exec. Cttee 2002–10; Dir Fed. of Brazilian Banking Asscn (FEBRABAN) from 2001, Pres. of the Bd 2002–09; Dir, Bradespar SA from 2002; Dir Serasa SA 1984–86, Empresas BCN 1998–99. *Address:* c/o Banco Bradesco SA, Cidade de Deus, Predio Novo 4 andar, Sao Paulo 06029-900, Brazil. *E-mail:* info@bradesco.com.br.

CYRULNIK, Boris; French doctor, ethologist, neurologist and psychiatrist; *Director of Teaching, Faculty of Arts and Social Sciences, Université du Sud – Toulon-Var;* b. 26 July 1937, Bordeaux; s. of Aaron Cyrulnik and Nadia Cyrulnik, orphaned and raised by a foster family; m. Florence Cyrulnik; one s. one d.; ed Univ. of Paris; escaped capture by Nazis in Bordeaux during World War II, then worked as a farm labourer until the end of the war; studied medicine; now Dir of Teaching, Faculty of Arts and Social Sciences, Univ. of the South, Toulon-Var; Prix Renaudot de l'essai 2008, Prix des Droits de l'Homme 2013. *Publications include:* author of several books on popular psychology, including La Naissance du sens 1992 (translated as The Dawn of Meaning 1998), Le Murmure des fantômes 2003 (translated as The Whispering of Ghosts: Trauma and Resilience 2005), Parler d'amour au bord du gouffre 2004 (translated as Talking of Love on the Edge of a Precipice 2007), Resilience: How Your Inner Strength Can Set You Free from the Past 2011. *Address:* UFR de Lettres et Sciences Humaines, Université du Sud – Toulon-Var, Campus de La Garde – Bâtiment Y, Avenue de l'Université, BP 20132, 83957 La Garde Cedex, France (office). *Telephone:* (4) 94-14-20-26 (office). *Fax:* (4) 94-14-20-90 (office). *E-mail:* info@univ-tln.fr (office); cyrulnik.boris@orange.fr (home). *Website:* www.univ-tln.fr (office).

CYWIŃSKA, Izabella, MA; Polish theatre producer and director; *Artistic Director, Athenaeum Theatre, Warsaw;* b. 22 March 1935, Kamień; d. of Andrzej Cywiński and Elżbieta Łuszczewska; m. Janusz Michałowski 1968; ed Warsaw Univ., State Acad. of Drama, Warsaw; Asst, Rural Architecture Faculty, Warsaw Univ. of Tech. 1956–58; Stage Dir, Theatre in Cracow-Nowa Huta 1966–68, Polski Theatre, Poznań 1966–68; Dir and Artistic Man. Wojciech Bogusławski Theatre, Kalisz 1969–73, Nowy Theatre, Poznań 1973–88; Vice-Pres. Understanding Cttee of Creative Circles, Poznań 1980–81; Minister of Culture and Art 1989–91; Founder and Vice-Pres. Culture Foundation 1991–93; Artistic Dir 50th Anniversary of the Revolt in the Warsaw Ghetto; currently Artistic Dir, Athenaeum Theatre, Warsaw; mem. Polish Stage Artists' Asscn, Presidential Council for Culture 1992–95, Gen. Ass. European Cooperation Foundation, Brussels; Minister of Culture and Art Award (Second class) 1977, Kt's Cross, Order of Polonia Restituta, Gloria Artis Gold Medal 2005, Officer's Cross of Merit (Lithuania) 2006; All-Poland Drama Festivals, Kalisz 1970, 1973, 1980, Opole 1976, Wrocław 1976, Medal Kalos Kagathos, Gold Cross of Merit, Nat. Educ. Comm. Medal, Nat. Broadcasting Council of Poland Award 1999, Special Prix Europa Award 2000, Willy Brandt Award, Prix Europa Int. TV Festival, Berlin 2000 (Lithuania) 2000, Star of Polish Television Award 2002. *Plays directed include:* Iphigenie auf Tauris 1968, The Morals of Mrs Dulska 1970, The Death of Tarelkin 1973, I giganti della montagna 1973, Lower Depths 1974, They 1975, Wijuny 1976, Bath-house 1978, Judas from Karioth 1980, The Accused: June '56 1981, Enemy of the People 1982, Dawn 1986, Virginity 1986, Cementeries 1988, Tartuffe 1989, Antygona in New York 1993, Hanemann 2002, Your Excellency 2006; also Dir in USA and USSR, I Leave You 2003. *TV films:* Frédéric's Enchantment (about Chopin) 1998, Purym's Miracle 1999. *Television productions include:* God's Lining (series) 1997, Beauty (TV theatre) (First Prize, Int. TV Festival, Plovdiv, Bulgaria 1997) 1998, Second Mother 1999, Touch (TV theatre) 2001, Marilyn Mongol (TV theatre) 2002, Bar World (TV theatre) 2003, God's Lining II (series) 2004, Lovers from Marona (feature film) 2004. *Publication:* Nagłe zastępstwo 1992. *Leisure interests:* foreign travel, politics. *Address:* ul. Jaracza 2, Warsaw (office); ul. Piwna 7A m. 5, 00-265 Warsaw, Poland (home). *Telephone:* (22) 635-32-33 (office). *Fax:* (22) 625-22-421; (22) 635-32-33 (home). *E-mail:* cywinska@hoga.pl (home); koordynacja@teatrateneum.pl.

CZAPUTOWICZ, Jacek Krzysztof, PhD; Polish public servant and politician; *Minister of Foreign Affairs;* b. 30 May 1956, Warsaw; widower; five d.; ed Warsaw Central School of Planning and Statistics, Polish Acad. of Sciences Inst. of Political Studies, Univ. of Warsaw; fmr political activist during communist era (imprisoned several times 1981–92, 1986); mem. Civic Cttee to Chair. Solidarność (trade union) 1988–90; joined Ministry of Foreign Affairs (MFA) 1990, Deputy Dir, later Dir, Consular and Emigration Dept 1990–92, Dir, Dept of Strategy and Foreign Policy Planning 2006–08, Dir MFA Diplomatic Acad. Jan.–Sept. 2017, Under-Sec. of State, MFA 2017–18, Minister of Foreign Affairs 2018–; Deputy Head of Civil Service 1998–2006; Dir, Nat. School of Public Admin 2008–12; Researcher, Inst. of European Studies, Faculty of Political Science and Int. Studies, Univ. of Warsaw, also Head, Dept of European Research Methodology; mem. Prawo i Sprawiedliwość (PiS—Law and Justice); Officer's Cross, Order of Polonia Restituta 2007, Cross of Freedom and Solidarity 2017. *Publications:* over 100 articles and academic monographs. *Address:* Ministry of Foreign Affairs, 00-580 Warsaw, Al. Szucha 23, Poland (office). *Telephone:* (22) 5239000 (office). *E-mail:* dabw.sekretariat@msz.gov.pl (office). *Website:* www.msz.gov.pl (office).

CZERWIŃSKA, Teresa; Polish economist and politician; *Minister of Finance;* b. 7 Sept. 1974, Daugavpils, Latvian SSR, USSR; d. of Bronisław Tumanovsky and Ludmiła Tumanovska; m.; one d.; ed Univ. of Gdańsk; began career as Assoc. Prof., Dept of Investment and Real Estate, Faculty of Man., Univ. of Gdańsk; worked at Comm. of Insurance and Pension Fund Supervision 2005; Assoc. Prof., later Prof., Dept of Financial Systems, Faculty of Man., Univ. of Warsaw 2011–; mem. Scientific Advisory Cttee, Office of the Financial Ombudsman 2014–15; Sec. Finance Cttee, Polish Acad. of Sciences 2015–18; Under-Sec. of State, Ministry of Science and Higher Educ. 2015–17; Under-Sec. of State, Ministry of Finance 2017–18, Minister of Finance 2018–. *Publications:* author or co-author of several scientific publications and textbooks on macroeconomics, insurance and investment management. *Address:* Ministry of Finance, 00-916 Warsaw, ul. Świętokrzyska 12, Poland (office). *Telephone:* (22) 6945555 (office). *E-mail:* kancelaria@mf.gov.pl (office). *Website:* www.mf.gov.pl (office).

CZIBERE, Tibor, Dr Ing; Hungarian engineer, politician and academic; *Professor Emeritus of Mechanical Engineering, University of Miskolc;* b. 16 Oct. 1930, Tapolca; s. of Jozsef Czibere and Maria Loppert; m. Gabriella Nagy 1956; two d.; ed Tech. Univ. of Heavy Industry, Miskolc; devt engineer at Ganz-MÁVAG Machine Works 1956; lecturer, Univ. of Miskolc 1963, Prof., Dept of Mechanical Eng 1968–88, Prof. Emer. 1989–, Dean of Mechanical Eng Faculty 1968–74, Rector 1978–86; Minister of Culture 1988–89; mem. Parl. 1983–85, 1988–90; Vice-Pres. Nat. Council of Patriotic People's Front 1985–89; mem. Local Editorial Council, Journal of Computational and Applied Mechanics; Corresp. mem. Hungarian Acad. of Sciences 1976, mem. 1985; Labour Order of Merit 1971, Star, Order of Merit, People's Repub. of Hungary 1986; Kossuth Prize 1962, Szetgyörgyi Albert Prize 1996, Szénchenyi Prize 2006. *Address:* Department of Fluid and Heat Engineering, University of Miskolc, 3515 Miskolc-Egyetemváros, Hungary (office). *Telephone:* (46) 365111 (office). *E-mail:* aramczt@gold.uni-miskolc.hu (office). *Website:* www.uni-miskolc.hu (office).

D

DA CÂMARA PESTANA, Carlos; Brazilian business executive; ed Universidade Clássica de Lisboa, Portugal; mem. Bd of Dirs Itaú Unibanco SA 1986–2003, Exec. Vice-Pres. 1986–90, CEO 1990–94, mem. Bd of Dirs Itaú Unibanco Holding SA 2003–08, Chair. Sept.–Nov. 2008, mem. Int. Advisory Bd 2003–09, Pres. Audit Cttee 2004–08, mem. Appointments and Compensation Cttee 2005–09, Pres. 2008–09, Vice-Chair. Itaúsa-Investimentos Itaú SA (now Itaú Unibanco Holding SA) 2008–11, Chair. 2011–14. *Address:* c/o Itaú Unibanco Holding SA, Praça Alfredo Egydio de Souza Aranha 100, Torre Olavo Setubal, Parque Jabaquara, São Paulo 04344-902, Brazil. *E-mail:* info@itau.com.

DA COSTA, Zacarias; Timor-Leste politician; m. Milena Pires; served as Conselho Nacional da Resistência Timorense (CNRT) rep. to EU in Brussels, UN in Geneva –1999; fmr Vice-Pres. União Democrática Timorense; Co-founder Partido Social Democrata (PSD) 2000, held several posts including Gen. Sec., Pres. Nat. Congress and Nat. Chair.; consultant for Asian Bank of Devt; Minister of Foreign Affairs 2007–12. *Address:* c/o Ministry of Foreign Affairs and Cooperation, GPA Building 1, Ground Floor, Rua Avenida Presidente Nicolau Lobato, PO Box 6, Dili, Timor-Leste (office).

DA COSTA FLORES, Ricardo José, BA, MBA; Brazilian economist and business executive; b. Pernambuco; ed Escola de Administração de Empresas, Fundação Getulio Vargas, EBAP-FGV; mem. Bd, Banco do Brasil SA 2009–, Vice-Pres. Credit, Accounting & Global Risk 2009–, served as its Vice-Pres. of Credit Controlling and Risk Man. and Dir of Insurance, Pensions and Capitalization, CEO Previ (pension fund of the employees) 2010–12; Chair. and CEO Valepar 2010–; Chair. Vale SA 2010–12; CEO Brasilprev Seguros e Previdencia SA 2012–13; Pres. Federação Nacional de Capitalização (Fenacap) 2008–11; Vice-Pres. Confederação Nacional das Empresas de Seguros Gerais, Previdência Privada e Vida, Saúde Suplementar e Capitalização (CNSeg) 2008–11; Head of Industry Rep. Group – FenaCap, Banco Bradesco SA; fmr mem. Bd of Exec. Officers, Federação Brasileira de Bancos (Febraban); fmr Exec. Man. Assets Restructuring Unit and Dir of Operational Assets Restructuring of Ativos SA–Financial Credit Security; fmr Pres. Chair. Brasilcap Capitalização SA; fmr Chair. Banco Nossa Caixa. *Address:* c/o Brasilprev Seguros e Previdencia SA, Rua Alexandre Dumas, nº 1671, Térreo Bloco C, Chácara Santo Antônio, São Paulo, SP 04717-004, Brazil. *E-mail:* info@brasilprev.com.

DA CRUZ VILAÇA, José Luís, LLM, PhD; Portuguese judge, lawyer and professor of law; *Judge, Court of Justice of the European Union;* b. 20 Sept. 1944, Braga; s. of Fernando da Costa Vilaça and Maria das Dores G. Cruz Vilaça; m. Marie-Charlotte Opitz 1995; two s. two d. (three c. from previous m.); ed Univ. of Coimbra, Univ. of Paris I, France, Univ. of Oxford, UK, Fordham Univ., New York, USA; Asst Faculty of Law, Univ. of Coimbra 1966, Prof. of Fiscal Law and Community Law 1979; mil. service, Naval Legal Dept 1969–72; mem. Parl. 1980–86; Sec. of State for Home Affairs 1980, for Presidency of Council of Ministers 1981, for European Affairs 1982; Advocate-Gen. Court of Justice of EC 1986–89; Full Prof. and Dir Inst. for European Studies, Lusiada Univ. Lisbon 1988–2000; Pres. Court of First Instance of EC 1989–95; Partner and Head of Competition Practice, PLMJ – A.M. Pereira, Sáragga Leal, Oliveira Martins, Júdice e Associados (law firm), Lisbon 1996–; Judge, Court of Justice of the EU 2012–; Visiting Prof. Univ. Nova de Lisboa 2001–; Chair. Disciplinary Bd of EC 2003–07; Prof., Portuguese Catholic Univ., Lisbon 2004–; Pres. Portuguese Asscn of European Law (APDE) 1999–; Gran Croce, Ordine di Merito (Italy), Grand-Croix, Couronne de Chêne (Luxembourg), Officier, Légion d'honneur, Grã-Cruz, Ordem do Infante (Portugal). *Publications include:* A empresa cooperativa 1969, L'économie portugaise face à l'intégration économique européenne 1978, Introdução ao estudo da Economia 1979, Modelo económico da CEE e modelo económico português 1984, Y a-t-il des limites matérielles à la révision des traités? 1993, The Development of the Community Judicial System before and after Maastricht 1994, La procédure en référé comme instrument de protection juridictionnelle des particuliers en droit communautaire 1998, Código da União Europeia 2001, On the Application of Keck in the Field of Free Provision of Services 2002, Código da Concorrência 2004, The Precautionary Principle in EC Law 2004, How Far Should National Courts Go in Drawing All the Necessary Inferences from the Last Sentence of Article 88(3) EC? 2005, Regional Selectivity and State Aid: The Azores Case 2006, Competition Law – Portuguese Law: An Overview 2007, Material and Geographical Selectivity in State Aid – Recent Developments: A Personal View 2009. *Leisure interests:* tennis, gardening, literature. *Address:* Court of Justice of the European Union, Palais de la Cour de Justice, Boulevard Konrad Adenauer, Kirchberg, 2925 Luxembourg Ville, Luxembourg (office); PLMJ – A.M. Pereira, Sáragga Leal, Oliveira Martins, Júdice e Associados, Avenida da Liberdade 224, 1250-148 Lisbon, Portugal (office). *Telephone:* 4303-1 (Luxembourg) (office); (213) 197321 (Lisbon) (office). *Fax:* 4303-2600 (Luxembourg) (office); (213) 197319 (Lisbon) (office). *E-mail:* jcv@plmj.pt (office). *Website:* curia.europa.eu/jcms/jcms/Jo2_7026 (office); www.plmj.com (office).

DA GRAÇA VERÍSSIMO E COSTA, Desidério; Angolan politician; b. 4 April 1934, Luanda; s. of Fernando Pascoal da Costa; m.; five c.; ed Montanuniversität Leoben, Austria, studies in Petroleum Man. in Cambridge, Mass, USA; went to school in Portugal and later sought refuge in FRG from prosecution by Polícia Internacional e de Defesa do Estado secret police, prepared to study medicine, then served for several years as pres. of asscn of students from Portuguese colonies with seat in Morocco, before turning to study of petroleum eng; mem. Angolan Nat. Comm. for Restructuring the Petroleum Industry 1976–77; Gen. Deputy Dir Sonangol 1977–79; Nat. Dir of Petroleum 1982–84; Vice-Minister of Petroleum 1984–2002, Minister of Petroleum 2002–08; Chair. African Petroleum Producers Asscn 2005–06. *Address:* c/o Ministry of Petroleum, Av. 4 de Fevereiro 105, CP 1279, Luanda, Angola. *E-mail:* geral@minpet.gov.ao.

DA GRAÇA VIEGAS SANTIAGO, Ângela Maria, MSc; São Tomé and Príncipe economist and politician; b. 14 Oct. 1961; ed Donetsk Univ., Ukraine, Bricham Int. Univ.; economist, Ministry of Econ. and Financial Affairs 1988–93; Dir Dept of Statistics and Econ. Studies, Banco Central de São Tomé e Príncipe 1997–98; Prin. Adviser to Minister of Planning and Finance 1999–2001; mem. Nat. Ass. 2002–10, Adviser to Prime Minister 2002–04; Minister of Finance and Planning 2008–10; mem. Movimento de Libertação de São Tomé e Príncipe–Partido Social Democrata (MLSTP-PSD).

DA SILVA, Luis Inácio (Lula) (see LULA DA SILVA, Inácio).

DA SILVA, Valter Filipe Duarte, BPhil, LLM; Angolan lawyer and central banker; b. 4 June 1974; ed Sacred Heart Seminary, Luanda, Portuguese Catholic Univ.; fmr teacher, Catholic Univ. of Angola, Gregório Semedo e Lusíadas de Angola; Legal Adviser, Banco de Fomento Angola 2005–08; Vice-Pres. Instituto Angolano e Sistemas Eleitorais e Democracia 2008–13; Legal Adviser, Vice-Pres. of Angola 2010–13; Gov. Banco Nacional de Angola (cen. bank) 2016–17; fmr Curator, Fundação Eduardo dos Santos (FESA). *Publication:* O Banco Nacional de Angola e a Crise Financeira 2012.

DA SILVA COSTA, Carlos; Portuguese economist and central banker; *Governor, Banco de Portugal;* b. 3 Nov. 1949; ed Oporto Univ., Univ. Paris I (Sorbonne) and Institut Européen d'Admin des Affaires (INSEAD), France; Lecturer, Faculty of Econs, Oporto Univ. 1973–86; joined Banco Português do Atlântico (now Banco Comercial Português) 1978, Head of Dept for Research on Portuguese Economy 1981–85; Coordinator, Econ. and Financial Affairs Dept, Perm. Mission to EU, Brussels, also mem. EU Econ. Policy Cttee 1986–92; Prof., European Studies Centre, Portuguese Catholic Univ. of Oporto 1986–2000; mem. Portuguese Higher Council for Reform of Financial System 1988–92; Head of Cabinet of European Commr João de Deus Pinheiro 1993–99, with responsibility for Communication, Culture and Audiovisual Policies 1993–94, for EU cooperation policy with Africa, the Caribbean and the Pacific 1995–99; Exec. Dir, Caixa Geral de Depósitos 2004–06, also Chair. Caixa Geral de Aposentações, Banco Nacional Ultramarino SA, Macao; Pres. Banco Caixa Geral (Spain) 2004–06; Vice-Pres. EIB 2006–10 (now Hon. Vice-Pres.); Gov. Banco de Portugal 2010–; Chair. Nat. Council of Financial Supervisors; Vice-Pres. European MANUFUTURE High Level Group 2005–06; Visiting Full Prof., Portuguese Catholic Univ. of Oporto, Univ. of Aveiro; mem. Governing Council and Gen. Council, European Central Bank; mem. Gen. Bd European Systemic Risk Bd; mem. Financial Stability Bd, Regional Consultative Group for Europe; mem. Bd of Dirs Unibanco Holdings SA, Brazil Jan.–Aug. 2005; Dir (non-exec.) Nat. Statistical Inst. 1990–92; Grand Officer, Order of Prince Henry the Navigator. *Address:* Office of the Governor, Banco de Portugal, Rua do Comércio, 148, 1100-150 Lisbon, Portugal (office). *Telephone:* (21) 3213200 (office). *Fax:* (21) 3215407 (office). *E-mail:* governador@bportugal.pt (office). *Website:* www.bportugal.pt (office).

DABBAGH, Amr Abdullah al-, BA; Saudi Arabian business executive; b. 1966; ed King Abdulaziz Univ., Jeddah, John F. Kennedy School of Govt, Harvard Univ. and Wharton School, Univ. of Pennsylvania, USA; CEO and Pres. Dabbagh Group 1991–2004; Gov. and Chair. Saudi Arabian Gen. Investment Authority 2004–12; Founding Chair. Global Competitiveness Forum, Stars Foundation 2001–; mem. World Econ. Forum, London Business School Middle East Regional Advisory Bd; fmr Chair. Jeddah Econ. Forum, Jeddah Marketing Bd; fmr mem. Bd Harvard Inst. for Social and Econ. Policy in the Middle East, Kennedy School of Govt; World Econ. Forum Global Leader of Tomorrow, 12th Arab Econ. Forum Leadership Award. *Address:* c/o Stars Foundation, 11 Belgrave Road, London, SW1V 1RB, England.

DABDOUB, Ibrahim Shukri; Palestinian banking executive; b. 1938, Jerusalem; m. Hilda Dabdoub; one s. (deceased) one d.; ed Collège des Frères, Bethlehem, Middle East Tech. Univ. Ankara, Turkey, Stanford Univ., USA; joined Nat. Bank of Kuwait (NBK) 1961, Head of Credit 1969, Deputy CEO 1981, CEO 1983–2014, Group CEO 2008–14; Chair. Nat. Bank of Kuwait Investment Management, London, Nat. Bank of Kuwait (Banque Privée Suisse) SA, Geneva, Nat. Bank of Kuwait (Lebanon) SAL, Beirut; Vice-Chair. Nat. Bank of Kuwait (International) PLC, London; Dir, Jordan Mobile Telephone Services Co., Centre for Contemporary Arab Studies, Georgetown Univ., Washington DC; mem. Int. Advisory Bd Council on Foreign Relations, Arab Thought Forum, Jordan; mem. Bd of Trustees, Kuwait Maastricht Business School, America Univ. of Beirut 2004–15 (then Trustee Emer.); mem. Arab Business Council, World Econ. Forum, Geneva; fmr Dir Inst. of Int. Finance, Washington, DC; Banker of the Year, Arab Bankers Asscn of N America 1995, Arab Banker of the Year, Union of Arab Banks 1997, Euromoney Award for Outstanding Contrib. to Devt of Financial Services in the Middle East 2005, The Banker (magazine) Lifetime Achievement Award 2009. *Leisure interests:* fishing, reading. *Address:* c/o National Bank of Kuwait SAK, PO Box 95, 13001 Safat, Abdullah al-Ahmad Street, Kuwait City, Kuwait (office). *Telephone:* 22422011 (office). *Fax:* 22462469 (office). *E-mail:* webmaster@nbk.com (office). *Website:* www.nbk.com (office).

DABOUB, Juan José, PhD; Salvadorean politician and international organization official; *Chairman and CEO, The Daboub Partnership;* ed North Carolina State Univ., USA; led family-owned businesses for nearly a decade before joining Bd of CEL (electricity utility); fmr Pres. ANTEL (state-owned telecommunications co. which he privatized); served three different govts for 12 years and then returned to pvt. sector; fmr Chief of Staff to Pres. of El Salvador, co-ordinated donors and oversaw reconstruction of El Salvador after two earthquakes of 2001; Minister of Finance and Chief of Staff to the Pres. 1999–2004; Co-founder and Dir America Libre Inst. 2004–06; Man. Dir World Bank Group 2006–10; Chair. World Econ. Forum Council on Climate Change 2012–14; selected by UN Framework Convention on Climate Change (UNFCCC) to serve on the Momentum for Change Advisory Panel 2013; currently Chair. and CEO The Daboub Partnership; Founding CEO Global Adaptation Inst. *E-mail:* ctobar1@gmail.com. *Website:* daboubpartnership.com.

DĄBROWSKI, Waldemar; Polish arts administrator and fmr government official; *General Director, Teatr Wielki – Polish National Opera;* b. 23 Aug. 1951, Radzymin; ed Electronics Faculty, Warsaw Polytechnic, Exec. Programme for Leaders in Devt, Harvard Univ., USA; Founder and Dir, Riwiera-Remont student club 1973–78; Deputy Dir, Cultural Dept, City of Warsaw 1979–81; Co-Man., Warsaw Studio Art Centre 1982, produced more than 70 plays, co-f. Sinfonia

Varsovia with Jerzy Maksymiuk and Yehudi Menuhin; Deputy Minister of Culture and Art and Head, Cttee of Cinematography 1990–94, Minister of Culture 2002–05; Pres. State Foreign Investment Agency 1994–98, conceived and created Vacation Festival of Stars in Miedzyzdroje (West Pomerania voivodship); Gen. Dir, Teatr Wielki – Polish Nat. Opera 1998–2002, 2008–; fmr Pres. Soc. for Encouragement of Fine Arts; fmr Vice-Pres. American-Polish-Israeli Foundation 'Shalom'; fmr Hon. Pres. Polish Golfing Asscn; Hon. Citizen of Opole Prov. 2006; Hon. KBE 2004; Chevalier, Ordre des Arts et Lettres, Orderem Świętego Stanisława Pierwszej Klasy 2005; Kt's Cross, Order of Polonia Restituta 2011, Officer's Cross 2014, Commdr's Cross 2015; scholarships from British Council, Goethe Inst., US Dept of State; Merited for Warsaw Distinction, Warsaw City Council 2001, Special Felix Warsaw for the devt of the modern opera stage 2010, Gold Medal Gloria Artis 2011. *Address:* Teatr Wielki—Opera Narodowa, Plac Teatralny 1, 00-950 Warsaw, Poland (office). *Telephone:* (22) 6920200 (office). *Fax:* (22) 8260423 (office). *E-mail:* office@teatrwielki.pl (office). *Website:* www.teatrwielki.pl (office).

DABWIDO, Sprent Jared; Nauruan politician and fmr head of state; b. 16 Sept. 1972; MP for Meneng constituency 2004–; Minister of Transport and Telecommunications 2007–11; Pres. of Nauru and Minister for Public Service, Police & Emergency Services, Home Affairs and Climate Changes 2011–13. *Address:* Parliament of Nauru, Parliament House, Yaren, Nauru (office).

DACCORD, Yves, BA; Swiss international organization official and fmr journalist; *Director-General, International Committee of the Red Cross;* b. 1964, Zurich; m.; three c.; ed Univ. of Geneva, Ashridge Business School, UK; broadcast journalist, Radio Television Suisse (RTS) 1987–89, Exec. Producer and journalist, RTS 1990–91; joined Int. Cttee of the Red Cross (ICRC) 1992, Head of ICRC Del., Sanaa, Yemen 1994–95, Head of ICRC Mission, Grozhny Jan.–July 1995, Head of ICRC Del., Tbilisi 1996–97, Head of Communications, ICRC 1998–2002, Dir of Communications and mem. Directorate 2002–10, Dir-Gen., ICRC 2010–, Chair., Steering Cttee for Humanitarian Response 2014–; Vice-Chair. Advisory Bd, The Performance Theatre (non-profit org.) 2015–; mem. Bd, Musée international de la Croix-Rouge et du Croissant-Rouge 2007–. *Address:* Office of the Director-General, International Committee of the Red Cross (ICRC), 19 avenue de la Paix, 1202 Geneva, Switzerland (office). *Telephone:* 227346001 (office). *Fax:* 227332057 (office). *E-mail:* press.gva@icrc.org (office). *Website:* www.icrc.org (office).

DACI, Nexhat, MA, PhD; Kosovo politician and academic; *President, Kosovo Academy of Sciences and Arts;* b. 26 July 1944, Tërnoc, Serbia and Montenegro (now in Kosovo); m. Zineta Daci; one s. two d.; ed Univs of Belgrade and Zagreb, also educated in UK and Belgium; Univ. Prof., Univ. of Priština 1983–; Pres. and Sec., Kosovo Acad. of Sciences and Arts 1995–2002, 2017–; Pres. of Kosovo Ass. 2001–06; Acting Pres. of Kosovo Jan.–Feb. 2006; mem. Democratic League of Kosovo, European Acad. for the Environment, American Chem. Asscn, European Acad. of Arts and Sciences 2014–. *Publications:* four text books, ten scientific projects and more than 100 scientific publs. *Address:* Kosovo Academy of Sciences and Arts, Rruga Agim Ramadani 305, Priština (office); Velania 18/IV, Priština, Kosovo (home). *Telephone:* (38) 249303 (office); (38) 229964 (office). *Fax:* (38) 244636 (office). *E-mail:* ashak@ashak.org (office). *Website:* www.ashak.org (office).

DAČIĆ, Ivica; Serbian politician; *First Deputy Prime Minister and Minister of Foreign Affairs;* b. 1 Jan. 1966, Prizren, Autonomous Province of Kosovo and Metohija, Socialist Repub. of Serbia, Socialist Fed. Repub. of Yugoslavia; m. Sonja Dačić; one s. one d.; ed Faculty of Political Science, Univ. of Belgrade; Pres. Socialist Youth Brigade, Belgrade 1990; Deputy, Fed. Ass. of Yugoslavia 1992–2004; mem. Socijalistička Partija Srbije (SPS—Socialist Party of Serbia), Party Spokesman 1992–2000, Vice-Chair. 2000–03, Pres. 2006–; mem. Nat. Ass. of Serbia 2007–; mem. Parl. Ass., Council of Europe, Brussels 2003–04, 2006–, mem. Cttee on Culture, Science and Educ., on Equal Opportunities for Women, on Migration, Refugees and Population; unsuccessful cand. in Serbian presidential election 2004; Minister of Finance 2007–08; First Deputy Prime Minister 2008–12, 2014–17, 2017– Acting Prime Minister May–June 2017; Minister of Internal Affairs 2008–14; Prime Minister 2012–14; Minister of Foreign Affairs 2014–; Chair.-in-Office OSCE 2015. *Address:* Ministry of Foreign Affairs, 11000 Belgrade, Kneza Miloša 24–26, Serbia (office). *Telephone:* (11) 3616333 (office). *Fax:* (11) 3618366 (office). *E-mail:* mfa@mfa.rs (office). *Website:* www.mfa.gov.rs (office).

DACRE, Paul Michael, BA, FRSA; British newspaper editor; *Editor-in-Chief, Associated Newspapers;* b. 14 Nov. 1948, London, England; s. of Peter Dacre and Joan Dacre (née Hill); m. Kathleen Thomson 1973; two s.; ed Univ. Coll. School, London, Univ. of Leeds; reporter, feature writer, Assoc. Features Ed., Daily Express 1970–76, Washington and New York Corresp. 1976–79; New York Bureau Chief, Daily Mail 1980, News Ed., London 1981–85, Asst Ed. (News and Foreign) 1986, Asst Ed. (Features) 1987, Exec. Ed. 1988, Assoc. Ed. 1989–91, Ed. Daily Mail 1992–2018, Ed.-in-Chief Assoc. Newspapers 1998–, also Chair. 2018–; Ed. Evening Standard 1991–92; Dir Associated Newspaper Holdings 1991–, Daily Mail & General Trust PLC 1998–, Teletext Holdings Ltd 2000–02; Chair. Editors' Code of Practice Cttee 2008–16; mem. Press Complaints Comm. 1998–2008, Press Bd of Finance 2004–, Govt Review into 30 Year Rule 2008; Amb. for Alzheimer's Soc. 2007; Hon. mem. Nat. Soc. for the Prevention of Cruelty to Children 2009; Cudlipp Lecturer, London Coll. of Commerce 2007. *Address:* Daily Mail, Northcliffe House, 2 Derry Street, London, W8 5TT, England (office). *Telephone:* (20) 7938-6000 (office). *Fax:* (20) 7937-7977 (office). *E-mail:* news@dailymail.co.uk (office). *Website:* www.dailymail.co.uk (office).

DADAE, Hon. Bob, BCom, MBA; Papua New Guinea politician; *Governor-General;* ed Bugandi High School, Univ. of Papua New Guinea, Griffith Univ., Australia; fmr Deputy Speaker of Parl.; Minister of Defence 2007–11; Accountant, Evangelical Lutheran Church of Papua New Guinea 2011–12; MP for Kabwum Open 2012–, Chair. Public Works Perm. Cttee; Leader, United Party 2007, now mem. People's National Congress; Gov.-Gen. 2017–; mem. Bd, Christian Press Inc., Bumayong Lutheran High School; Church Elder in his local parish. *Address:* Office of the Governor-General, Waigani, NCD, Papua New Guinea (office).

DADNADJI, Djimrangar Joseph, DEA; Chadian politician and fmr public servant; b. 1 Jan. 1954, Bebo-Pen, Mandoul Region; s. of Assingar Dadnadji and Lakoussal Sambaye; m.; 15 c.; ed Ecole Normale Supérieure d'Afrique Centrale, Fort-Lamy (now N'Djamena), Ecole Nat. d'Admin, N'Djamena, Univ. of N'Djamena, Univ. of Poitiers, France; joined civil service 1975, Head, Dept of Materials, Research and Legislation, Ministry of Interior and Security 1976–77, Acting Deputy Prefect, city of Kélo, Tandjilé Region 1977–79; Sec.-Gen. of Council, Koumra Town Hall 1980–82; Dir of Admin., Financial and Material Affairs, Ministry of Nat. Educ. 1988–91, Project Coordinator, Teacher Training Programme 1993–96, Dir-Gen., Ministry of Nat. Educ. 1996–2002; Minister of Planning, Devt and Cooperation 2002–03, of the Environment and Water 2003–04; Technical Adviser to Pres. for Legal and Admin. Affairs and Human Rights 2004–05; Sec.-Gen. of the Presidency 2005–08, 2009–10, Dir, Civil Cabinet of the Presidency 2008–09, 2012–13; Minister of Spatial Planning, Urban Planning and Housing 2010–11; Prime Minister Jan.–Nov. 2013; cand. in presidential election 2016; Founder mem. Nat. Union Party 1992; fmr univ. prof.; mem. Patriotic Salvation, mem. Nat. Political Bureau 2003–08, 2011–; Commdr, Ordre Nat. du Tchad, Chevalier des Palmes Académiques Françaises. *Address:* c/o Office of the Prime Minister, BP 463, N'Djamena, Chad.

DADOO, J. K., BA, MBA, LLB; Indian government official and civil servant; b. 10 Dec. 1957; ed St Stephen's Coll., Univ. of Delhi, Indian Inst. of Man., Ahmedabad, Indian Inst. of Foreign Trade, New Delhi; man. trainee, Procter & Gamble 1980–81; Br. Man., Core Parentals 1981–82; Sr Marketing Officer, Associated Cement Cos Ltd, Bombay 1983; joined Indian Admin. Service, AGMUT Cadre 1983, Sub-divisional Magistrate, Delhi 1985–87, also functioned as Deputy Dir (Panchayat) and Admin. of Agricultural Produce Marketing Cttee of Najafgarh and Narela; Jt Sec., Planning and Devt, Govt of Arunachal Pradesh 1987–88; Deputy Commr in Lower Subansiri Dist 1988–89, Chair. Dist Rural Devt Agency, also Dist and Sessions Judge; Sec., Gen. Admin, Personal Labour and Press, Arunachal 1990; Jt Sec. (Health), Delhi Admin 1990–91; Additional Commr, Sales Tax, Delhi 1991–94; Additional Dir and Jt Sec. (Educ.), Govt of Delhi 1994–95; Sec. to Gov. of Goa with additional charge as Sec., Industry and Mines and Sec. (Power) (initiated process of privatization of power in Goa) 1995–96; Dir (Air Force), Dir (Resettlement) and Dir (Int. Co-operation), Ministry of Defence 1997–2000; Counsellor (Co-ordination), Embassy in Moscow 2000–04; Devt Commr for Daman Diu and Dadra Nagar Haveli; Devt Commr of Goa 2005–06, Acting Chief Sec. of Goa on several occasions; Prin. Sec., Environment, Forests and Wildlife, Govt of Nat. Capital Territory of Delhi and also Chair. Delhi Pollution Control Cttee; Admin. of Union Territory of Lakshadweep 2009–11; Jt Sec., Dept of Commerce, Ministry of Commerce 2011–15, Additional Sec. 2015–17; mem. various bds and insts, including High Court Cttee on Plastic Waste Man., Advisory Bd of The Energy Research Inst., Fed. of Indian Chambers of Commerce and Industry Task Force on Climate Change, Bd of Dirs of Bombay Suburban Electric Supply; mem. Bd, Delhi State Civil Supplies Corpn Ltd, Indian Inst. of Packaging, Indian Inst. of Foreign Trade, Nat. Centre for Trade Information.

DAERR, Hans-Joachim; German diplomatist; b. 22 Dec. 1943, Frankenstein, Schleswig; m. Alexa Daerr; two s.; ed Baccalauréat in Paris, France; nat. service in German Navy 1962–64, law studies in Tübingen, Bonn and Berlin 1964–68, Japanese studies, Tübingen 1969, joined Foreign Service 1970, Rep. to EC, Brussels 1970–71, posted to Consulate Gen., Osaka-Kobe 1973–76, NATO Dept, Foreign Office, Bonn 1976–79, Embassy in Tokyo 1979–83, Planning Staff, Foreign Office 1983–86, Head of Strategic Issues Operations Staff 1986–87, Perm. Rep., Embassy in Lagos 1988–91, Head of S Africa Dept, Foreign Office 1991–95, Head of Subdivision 20 (NATO, WEU, OSCE, GASP, N America) and Deputy Political Dir 1995–98, Amb. to Pakistan 1998–2001, Rep. of Fed. Govt for Issues on Disarmament and Arms Control, Berlin 2001–02, Amb.-at-Large for Afghanistan 2001–02, Head of Dept for Global Issues, UN, Human Rights and Humanitarian Aid, Foreign Office, Berlin 2003–06, Amb. to Japan 2006–09, then Sr Adviser on Sustainable Devt, Perm. Rep. (acting) to UN in Geneva 2016–17. *Address:* Federal Ministry of Foreign Affairs, 11013 Berlin, Germany (office). *Telephone:* (30) 5000-0 (office). *Fax:* (30) 18173402 (office). *E-mail:* poststelle@auswaertiges-amt.de (office). *Website:* www.auswaertiges-amt.de (office).

DAFA, Bader Omar ad-, MA; Qatari diplomatist and UN official; *Executive Director, Global Dry Land Alliance;* b. 2 Oct. 1950; m. Awatef Mohamed Al-Dafa; one s. two d.; ed Kalamazoo Community Coll., Western Michigan Univ., School of Advanced Int. Studies, Johns Hopkins Univ., USA; diplomatic attaché, Ministry of Foreign Affairs 1976–77, 1981–82; First Sec., Qatar Embassy, Washington, DC 1977–81; Amb. to Spain 1982–88, to Egypt (also Perm. Rep. to Arab League) 1988–93, to France 1993–95, to Russia 1995–98; Dir of European and American Affairs, Ministry of Foreign Affairs 1998–2000; Amb. to USA and Perm. Observer to OAS 2000–05, 2002–07; Exec. Sec. UN Econ. and Social Comm. for Western Asia (ESCWA) 2007–10; currently Amb.-at-Large and Exec. Dir Global Dry Land Alliance 2012–; mem. Selection Cttee, Takreem Arab Achievement Awards 2011–; Ordre nat. du Mérite. *Leisure interests:* reading, painting, music. *Address:* Global Dry Land Alliance, Onaiza, Zone 66, Street 826 Villa No. 50, PO Box 22043, Doha, Qatar (office). *Telephone:* 40377200 (office). *Fax:* 40377202 (office). *E-mail:* info@globaldrylandalliance.com (office). *Website:* globaldrylandalliance.org (office).

DAFFA, Ali Abdullah ad-, BS, MS, PhD; Saudi Arabian mathematician and academic; *Professor, King Fahd University of Petroleum and Minerals;* b. 1940, Unaizah; m.; four c.; ed Ohio Univ., Stephen F. Austin State Univ., Vanderbilt Univ., USA; Asst Prof. of Math., King Fahd Univ. of Petroleum and Minerals, Dhahran 1973–74, Chair. Dept of Math. 1974–77, Dean Coll. of Sciences 1977–84, Prof. of Math. and History of Pure Science 1980–; Visiting Prof., King Saud Univ., Riyadh 1979–82, Harvard Univ. 1981, Princeton Univ. 1991; Pres. Union of Arab Mathematicians and Physicists 1974–81, 1986–88, Supreme Council of Union of Arab Physicists and Mathematicians; mem. editorial Bd Encyclopedia of Islamic Civilization; mem. Int. Comm. on the History Science, Nat. Library Bd, Islamic Foundation for Science, Tech. and Devt, Bd of King Faisal for Islamic Research, Asscn of Muslim Scientist and Engineers, Asscn of Arab Scientists, The Arabic Acad. (Jordan), Islamic World Acad. of Science, Arabic Scientific Soc., American Math. Soc., British Soc. for History of Science; Founding Fellow, Islamic Acad. of Sciences 1986; Hon. mem. Acad. of Arabic Language. *Publications:* 48 books and more than 250 articles on math. and history of science. *Address:* King Fahd University of Petroleum and Minerals, Dhahran 31261, Saudi Arabia (office). *Telephone:* (3) 860-0000 (office). *Fax:* (3) 860-3306 (office). *E-mail:* aldaffa@kfupm.edu.sa (office). *Website:* www.kfupm.edu.sa (office).

DAFOE, Willem; American actor; b. 22 July 1955, Appleton, Wis.; s. of William Dafoe; ed Univ. of Wisconsin; Lifetime Achievement Award, San Sebastian Film Festival 2005. *Films include:* The Loveless 1981, New York Nights 1981, The Hunger 1982, Communists are Comfortable (and three other stories) 1984, Roadhouse 66 1984, Streets of Fire 1984, To Live and Die in LA 1985, Platoon 1986, The Last Temptation of Christ 1988, Saigon 1988, Mississippi Burning 1989, Triumph of the Spirit 1989, Born on the 4th of July 1990, Flight of the Intruder 1990, Wild at Heart 1990, The Light Sleeper 1991, Body of Evidence 1992, Far Away, So Close 1994, Tom and Viv 1994, The Night and the Moment 1994, Clear and Present Danger 1994, The English Patient 1996, Basquiat 1996, Speed 2: Cruise Control 1997, Affliction 1997, Lulu on the Bridge 1998, eXistenZ 1998, American Psycho 1999, Shadow of the Vampire 2000, Bullfighter 2000, The Animal Factory 2000, Edges of the Lord 2001, Spider-Man 2002, Auto Focus 2002, Once Upon a Time in Mexico 2003, The Clearing 2004, The Reckoning 2004, The Life Aquatic with Steve Zissou 2004, The Aviator 2004, xXx: State of the Union 2005, Ripley Under Ground 2005, Manderlay 2005, Inside Man 2006, American Dreamz 2006, Paris, je t'aime 2006, The Walker 2007, Mr. Bean's Holiday 2007, Spider-Man 3 2007, Go Go Tales 2007, Anamorph 2007, Fireflies in the Garden 2008, Adam Resurrected 2008, I skoni tou hronou (The Dust of Time) 2008, Antichrist 2009, L'affaire Farewell 2009, My Son, My Son, What Have Ye Done 2010, The Hunter 2011, John Carter 2012, Tomorrow You're Gone 2012, Odd Thomas 2013, Out of the Furnace 2013, Nymphomaniac: Vol. II 2013, A Most Wanted Man 2014, The Grand Budapest Hotel 2014, Bad Country 2014, The Fault in Our Stars 2014, Pasolini 2014, John Wick 2014, My Hindu Friend 2015, Dog Cat Dog 2016, Sculpt 2016, A Family Man 2016, Padre 2016, The Florida Project 2017, What Happened to Monday 2017, Murder on the Orient Express 2017, Opus Zero 2017. *Address:* c/o Widescreen Management, 270 Lafayette Street, Suite 402, New York, NY 10012; WME, 9601 Wilshire Blvd., Beverly Hills, CA 90210, USA.

DAFT, Douglas (Doug) Neville, AC, BA; Australian business executive; b. 20 March 1943, Cessnock, NSW; m. Delphine Daft; one s. one d.; ed Univ. of New England, Armidale, Univ. of New South Wales; taught science at Vaucluse Boys' High School, Sydney 1960s; joined Coca-Cola Co., Australia 1969, Pres. Cen. Pacific Div. 1984, N Pacific Div. 1988, Pres. Coca-Cola (Japan) Co. 1988, Pres. Pacific Group, Atlanta 1991, Head of Middle and Far East and Africa Groups, Head of Schweppes Div. 1999, Chair. and CEO 2000–04 (retd); mem. Bd of Dirs, McGraw-Hill Ryerson Ltd 2003–12, Wal-Mart Stores Inc. 2005–15, Sistema-Hals 2006–, Green Mountain Coffee Roasters 2009–12, Graff Diamonds Corpn 2012–, Tisbury Fund Ltd; Chair. Advisory Bd, Churchill Archives Center, Churchill Coll., Cambridge; mem. Advisory Bd Longreach, Inc., Tisbury Capital, Thomas H. Lee Partners; mem. European Advisory Council, N.M. Rothschild & Sons Ltd; mem. Bd of Overseers, Int. Business School, Brandeis Univ.; Trustee, Thunderbird School of Global Man., Cambridge Foundation; Patron American Australian Asscn; Dr hc (Thunderbird Univ., Glendale, Ariz.). *Address:* Board of Directors, Graff Diamonds Corporation, 28–29 Albermarle Street, London, W1S 4JA, England (office). *Telephone:* (20) 7584-8571 (office). *Fax:* (20) 7581-3415 (office). *E-mail:* info@graffdiamonds.com (office). *Website:* www.graffdiamonds.com (office).

DAGHR, Ahmad Obaid bin; Yemeni politician; b. 2 Dec. 1952; ed Univ. of Aden; began work in agricultural sector and cooperative movement 1973, becoming Pres., Farmers Union 1976; mem. Supreme People's Council (fmr Parl. of S Yemen) for Shibam Dist 1986, also mem. Supreme People's Council Presidium 1986; mem. House of Reps (Parl. following unification of Yemen 1990), Chair. Agric. and Fisheries Cttee; Minister of Communications and Information Tech. in govt of nat. reconciliation 2011; Adviser to Pres. Abd al-Rabbuh Mansur al-Hadi 2015; Deputy Prime Minister 2015–16, Prime Minister 2016–18; mem. Yemen Socialist Party –2006; mem. Gen. People's Congress 2006–, fmr Sec.-Gen.; Nov. 30 (Independence Day) Medal. *Address:* c/o Office of the Prime Minister, San'aa, Yemen (office).

DAGWORTHY PREW, Wendy Ann, OBE, BA; British fashion designer and academic; b. (Wendy Ann Dagworthy), 4 March 1950, Gravesend, Kent; d. of Arthur S. Dagworthy and Jean A. Stubbs; m. Jonathan W. Prew 1973; two s.; ed Medway Coll. of Design and Hornsey Coll. of Art; Founder, Designer and Dir Wendy Dagworthy Ltd (design co.) 1972–; Dir London Designer Collections 1982; consultant to CNAA Fashion/Textiles Bd 1982–; Course Dir Fashion BA Hons Degree, Central St Martin's Coll. of Art and Design 1989–, Prof. of Fashion 1998–2014; Prof. of Fashion and Head of Fashion Programmes, RCA 1998–, Dean of the School of Material 2011–14, Prof. Emer. 2014–; Judge, Royal Soc. of Arts Bd; judge of art and design projects for various mfrs; participating designer in Fashion Aid and many charity shows; exhibited seasonally in London, Milan, New York and Paris; Lecturer and External Assessor at numerous polytechnics and colls of art and design; frequent TV appearances; Hon. Fellow, Kent Inst. of Design, Univ. of the Creative Arts 2005; Fil d'Or Int. Linen Award 1986. *Leisure interests:* dining out, cooking, reading, painting, drawing. *Address:* Royal College of Art, Kensington Gore, London, SW7 3EU (office); 18 Melrose Terrace, London, W6 7RL, England (home). *Telephone:* (20) 7590-4444 (office); (20) 7602-6676 (home). *Fax:* (20) 7590-4360 (office). *E-mail:* wendy.dagworthy@rca.ac.uk (office). *Website:* www.rca.ac.uk (office).

DAHABI, Nader al-, MSc, MPA; Jordanian politician; b. 7 Oct. 1946, Amman; m.; two s. one d.; ed Al Hussein Coll., Amman, Hellenic Air Force Acad., Tatoi, Greece, Cranfield Inst. of Tech., UK, Auburn Univ., USA; cadet in Royal Jordanian Air Force 1964, served for 30 years becoming Asst Commdr for Logistics 1992–94; CEO Royal Jordanian Airlines 1994–2001; Minister of Transport 2001–03; Chief Commr Aqaba Special Econ. Zone Authority 2004–07; Prime Minister and Minister of Defence 2007–09 (resgnd); mem. Exec. Cttee Arab Air Carriers Org., Chair. 1994–95; Chair. Royal Jordanian Air Falcons 1994–; Pres. IATA 1996–97, mem. Bd of Govs 1995–98; Dir Royal Jordanian Acad.; mem. Higher Cttee Jerash Festival for Culture and Arts, Higher Council of Tourism. *Leisure interest:* AEK Athens Football Club. *Address:* c/o Office of the Prime Minister, PO Box 80, Amman 11180, Jordan. *E-mail:* info@pm.gov.jo.

DAHAL, Pushpa Kamal, (Prachanda), BSc (Agric.); Nepalese politician and fmr guerrilla leader; b. (Chhabilal Dahal), 11 Dec. 1954, Dhikure Pokhari, Kaski Dist; ed Inst. of Agric. and Animal Science, Rampur, Chitwan; once employed at rural devt project in Jajarkot sponsored by USAID; joined CP of Nepal (Fourth Convention) 1981, becoming Gen. Sec. (Leader) CP of Nepal (Mashal) 1989, party later renamed CP of Nepal (Maoist); lived underground after restoration of democracy in 1990, controlled clandestine wing of party, became internationally known (as Prachanda) as Leader of CPN (M), presiding over mil. and political wings 1996–, leader of Maoist insurgency 1996–2006, Chair. CPN (M) 2001–; negotiated with seven-party alliance, signed comprehensive peace agreement with Govt Nov. 2006, CPN (M) entered Parl. and Govt 2007, party merged with CPN (Unity Centre-Masal) to become Unified CP of Nepal (Maoist) (UCPN—M) 2009, now CP of Nepal (Maoist Centre), Leader Parl. Party 2018–; Prime Minister 2008–09 (resgnd), 2016–17 (resgnd). *Address:* Communist Party of Nepal (Maoist Centre) (CPN—MC), Central Office, Perishdanda, Koteshwor, Kathmandu, Nepal (office). *Telephone:* (1) 4602290 (office). *Fax:* (1) 4602289 (office). *E-mail:* ucpnminfo69@gmail.com (office). *Website:* www.ucpnmaoist.org (office).

DAHAN, René; Dutch business executive; b. 26 Aug. 1941; began career as process technician in refinery, Exxon Corpn, Rotterdam 1963, Man. Supply and Planning Dept, Esso Nederland 1973–74, Man. Refining Dept 1974–77, Head Corp. Planning Div., Esso Europe, London 1977–79, Man. Natural Gas Dept 1979–81, Deputy Man. Petroleum Products Dept, Exxon Corpn HQ, USA 1981–83, Exec. Vice-Pres. Esso BV, Breda 1983–85, Pres. and CEO Esso BV 1985–91, Exec. Vice-Pres. ECI 1991–92, Vice-Pres. Exxon Corpn 1992–95, Sr Vice-Pres. 1995–2001, Dir 1998–2001, Exec. Vice-Pres. Exxon Mobil Corpn 2001–04; Acting Chair. Supervisory Bd Royal Ahold NV 2004–05, Chair. 2005–13, Chair. Selection and Appointment Cttees; mem. Supervisory Bd Nielsen Holdings NV (also known as VNU NV) 2003–06, PostNL NV 2003–08, TPG NV 2003–, Aegon NV; Institutional Outside Dir, Repsol, SA 2013–; mem. Int. Advisory Bd, CVC Capital Partners, Inst. de Empresa; mem. Bd of Dirs, Jr Achievement Int.; mem. Bd Trustees, US Council for Int. Business. *Address:* Shareholder Information Office, Repsol, SA, 900 100 100, C/ Méndez Álvaro 44, 28045 Madrid, Spain (office). *E-mail:* infoaccionistas@repsol.com (office). *Website:* www.repsol.com (office).

DAHL, Birgitta, BA; Swedish politician; b. 20 Sept. 1937, Råda, Härryda Municipality, Västra Götaland Co.; d. of Sven Dahl and Anna-Brita Axelsson; m. Enn Kokk; one s. two d.; ed Univ. of Uppsala; teacher, clerical officer, Scandinavian Inst. of African Studies, Uppsala 1960–65; Sr Admin. Officer, Dag Hammarskjöld Foundation 1965–68, Swedish Int. Devt Authority 1965–82; mem. Parl. 1968–2002; mem. Advisory Council of Foreign Affairs; del. to UN Gen. Ass.; mem. Exec. Cttee Social Democratic Party 1975–96; Minister with special responsibility for Energy Issues, Ministry of Energy 1982–86, for the Environment and Energy 1987–90, for the Environment 1990–91; Spokesperson on Social Welfare; Chair. Environment Cttee of Socialist International 1986–93, Confed. of Socialist Parties of EC 1990–94, High Level Advisory Bd on Sustainable Devt to Sec.-Gen. 1996–97; Speaker of the Riksdag (Swedish Parl.) 1994–2002; Chair. Swedish Coral Asscn 2002–05, Nat. Museum of Cultural History, Centre for Gender Research, Uppsala Univ.; Pres. UNICEF Sweden World Infections Foundation; Sr Adviser Global Environment Facility 1998–; mem. Panel of Eminent Persons on United Nations-Civil Society; mem. Bd Stockholm Environment Inst., Int. Inst. for Industrial Environment Econs, Lund Univ.; fmr mem. Bd of Dirs Nat. Housing Bd; Gran Condecoración de Honor del Senado (Chile) 2000, Grand Cross Order of the White Rose (Finland) 2002; Cross of Terra Mariana (Estonia) 2002, Das Grosse Goldene Ehrenzeichens am Bande für Verdienste (Austria) 2002, Illis Quorum Meruere Labores (Sweden) 2003, Medal of Merit (Algeria) 2006. *Publications:* contrib. numerous articles and chapters to magazines and books on democracy and human rights, peace and int. cooperation, sexual equality, children's rights, education and science, the environment and sustainable devt. *Address:* Idrottsgatan 12, 753 35 Uppsala, Sweden (home). *Telephone:* (18) 211793 (home). *Fax:* (18) 211793 (home). *E-mail:* 34dahl@telia.com (home).

DAHL, Lawrence F., BS, PhD; American chemist and academic; *Professor Emeritus, Department of Chemistry, University of Wisconsin;* b. 1929; ed Univ. of Louisville, Iowa State Univ.; R.E. Rundle Prof. of Chemistry, Univ. of Wisconsin 1978, Hilldale Chair Prof. 1991, now Prof. Emer.; fmr Visiting Lecturer, Technische Universität, Germany 1965, Univ. of Louisville 1969, Univ. of Notre Dame 1987, Univ. of Illinois 1990, Texas A&M Univ. 1996, Bristol Univ., UK 1997, Tulane Univ. 1998; mem. NAS 1988–; Guggenheim Fellow 1969–70; Fellow, NY Acad. of Sciences, 1975–, AAAS 1980–, American Acad. of Arts and Sciences 1992–; Hon. DSc (Univ. of Louisville) 1991; ACS Award in Inorganic Chemistry 1974, Alexander von-Humboldt-Stiftung Sr US Scientist Humboldt Award 1985, Hilldale Award in the Physical Sciences, Univ. of Wisconsin 1994, Amoco Distinguished Lecturer, Ind. Univ. 1996, ACS Willard Gibbs Medal 1999, American Inst. of Chemists Pioneer Award 2000, F. Albert Cotton Award in Synthetic Inorganic Chemistry 2010. *Address:* University of Wisconsin, Department of Chemistry, Room 8121, Chemistry Building, 1101 University Avenue, Madison, WI 53706, USA (office). *Telephone:* (608) 262-5859 (office). *Fax:* (608) 262-6143 (office). *E-mail:* dahl@chem.wisc.edu (office). *Website:* www.chem.wisc.edu/users/dahl (office).

DAHL, Sophie; British fmr model and author; b. 1978, granddaughter of Patricia Neal and Roald Dahl; m. Jamie Cullum 2010; began career as a model, gave up modelling to concentrate on writing career 2007; fmr long-term Contributing Ed. at Men's Vogue, currently regular contrib. to both US and UK edns of Vogue, and to Waitrose Food Illustrated magazine; has also contributed to, amongst others, The Observer, The Guardian, The Saturday Times Magazine; wrote book chronicling her misadventures with food, Miss Dahl's Voluptuous Delights 2009; wrote and presented BBC 2 TV cookery programme, The Delicious Miss Dahl 2010; designed and modelled a capsule collection for British heritage cashmere brand Brora 2013. *Television:* wrote and presented BBC2 documentary The Marvellous Mrs Beeton 2011. *Publications:* The Man with the Dancing Eyes (illustrated novella) (Times bestselling book) 2003, Playing with the Grown Ups 2007, Miss Dahl's Voluptuous Delights 2009, From Season to Season 2011. *Address:* Tavistock Wood, 45 Conduit Street, London, W1S 2YN, England (office). *E-mail:* info@tavistockwood.com (office). *Website:* www.sophiedahl.com.

DAHLAN, Mohammed, (Abu Fadi), BA; Palestinian politician; b. 29 Sept. 1961, Khan Yunis Refugee Camp, Khan Yunis, Gaza Strip; m. Jaleela Dahlan; four c.; ed Islamic Univ. of Gaza; brought up in refugee camp in Gaza after fleeing 1948 war; become politically active as a teenager 1981; grassroots organizer of Youth Br. of Fatah; arrested for subversive pro-Palestinian activities (ten times) 1981–86, deported to Jordan during intifada 1987; mem. Palestinian Liberation Org. (PLO) 1988–; involved in secret negotiations with Israel, leading to Oslo Peace Accords and creation of Palestinian Authority (PA) 1993–94; apptd Head of PA Preventative Security Force by Yasser Arafat 1994, resgnd June 2002; Minister of State for Security Affairs, PA April–Oct. 2003; visited UK to study English, returned to Gaza June 2004; Minister for Civil Affairs 2005–06; Nat. Security Adviser to Pres. Abbas 2006–07; mem. Fatah Party, mem. Fatah Cen. Cttee 2009–; gained Montenegrin citizenship 2012, Serbian citizenship 2013. *Address:* c/o Fatah, PO Box 1965, Ramallah, Palestinian Territories. *Telephone:* (2) 2986892. *Fax:* (2) 2987947. *E-mail:* m.dhaln.office@gmail.com. *Website:* www.fateh.ps; dahlan.ps.

DAHLBÄCK, Claes, MSc (Econs), PhD; Swedish business executive; b. 1947; ed Stockholm School of Econs; analyst, Investor AB, New York, USA 1973–78, Pres. and CEO 1978–99, Exec. Vice-Chair. 1999–2001, Chair. 2002–05, Sr Adviser 2005–; Dir, Stora 1990–98, Chair. 1997–98, Chair. Stora Enso Oyj (following merger of Stora and Enso 1998) 1998–2010; Vice-Chair. Skandinaviska Enskilda Banken 1997–2002, also Chair. Vin & Spirit AB 1991–2007, Gambro AB, EQT Funds; Dir (non-exec.), Goldman Sachs 2003–15; Sr Advisor, Foundation Asset Management AB 2007–; mem. Bd of Dirs, ABB, Zurich, Switzerland 1991–97, Ericsson 1993–96, Stockholm School of Econs, (Chair. Stockholm School of Econs Foundation); mem. Bilderberg Group; Pres. Int. Wine and Spirit Competition 2003; mem. Royal Swedish Acad. of Eng Sciences, Royal Swedish Soc. of Naval Sciences; Commdr, Order of the White Rose of Finland; King's Medal of the Twelfth Night with the Seraphim Ribbon. *Address:* c/o Investor AB, Arsenalsgatan 8, 111 47 Stockholm, Sweden.

DAHLFORS, John Ragnar, MCE; Swedish civil engineer; *Management Consultant, JD Management AB;* b. 31 Dec. 1934, Stockholm; s. of Mats Dahlfors and Astrid Dahlfors; m. 1st Anita Roger 1962 (divorced); one s. two d.; m. 2nd Ing-Britt Schlyter 1998; ed Royal Inst. of Tech., Stockholm; engineer with Gränges AB Liberia project 1962–66, Sales Man. Gränges Hedlund AB 1967–68, Pres. 1970–74, Tech. Man. Gränges Construction AB 1969, Pres. Gränges Aluminium AB 1974–78; Pres. Boliden AB 1978–86; fmr man. consultant Sevenco, currently consultant JD Man. AB. *Leisure interests:* sailing, golf, tennis, hunting. *Address:* Karlaplan 12, 115 20 Stockholm, Sweden (home). *Telephone:* (70) 889-85-77 (mobile); (8) 660-24-04 (home). *Fax:* (8) 660-24-04 (home). *E-mail:* john.dahlfors@telia.com (home).

DAHLIE, Bjorn; Norwegian fmr Olympic skier; b. 19 June 1967, Elverum; pnr Vilde; two s.; winner of a record total of 29 medals (gold, silver and bronze) 1991–99, including eight Gold Olympic medals, nine Gold World Championship medals; Hon. Pres. Cross Country World Championships 2005; retd 2001; introduced Nordic skiwear collection 1996; majority stockholder Bj Sport AS. *Publication:* Gulljakten (autobiog.) 1997. *Leisure interest:* hunting. *Address:* Bj Sport AS, Adminbygget Hellerudsletta, 2013 Skjetten, Norway (office). *E-mail:* info@bjsport.no (office). *Website:* www.dahlie.com (office).

DAHOUL, Safwan, DFA; Syrian artist; b. 1961, Hama; ed Faculty of Fine Arts, Damascus Univ., Ecole Supérieure des Arts Plastiques et Visuels, Mons, Belgium; instructor, Faculty of Fine Arts, Damascus Univ.; regular participant in int. art fairs and solo and group exhbns throughout the Middle East, Europe and USA; best known works are oil/acrylic paintings in Hulum (Rêve/Dream) series. *Address:* c/o Ayyam Gallery, Mezzeh West Villas 30, Chile Street, Samawi Building, Damascus, Syria. *Telephone:* (11) 6131088. *Fax:* (11) 6131087. *E-mail:* info@ayyamgallery.com. *Website:* www.ayyamgallery.com/artists/safwan-dahoul; safwandahoul.com.

DAI, Bingguo; Chinese politician and diplomatist; *Chairman, Jinan University;* b. March 1941, Yinjiang Co., Guizhou Prov.; ed Foreign Affairs Coll., Sichuan Univ.; joined CCP 1973; Deputy Div. Chief, later Div. Chief, Dept of USSR and Eastern European Affairs, Ministry of Foreign Affairs 1973–85, Deputy Dir 1985–86, Dir 1986–89, Amb. to Hungary 1989–91, Asst Minister of Foreign Affairs 1991–93, Deputy Minister of Foreign Affairs 1993–95, 2003–07; Deputy Head Int. Liaison Dept of CCP Cen. Cttee 1995–97, Head 1997–2003; mem. 15th CCP Cen. Cttee 1997–2002, 16th CCP Cen. Cttee 2002–07, 17th CCP Cen. Cttee 2007–12; mem. State Council 2008–13; Chair. Jinan Univ. 2013–. *Address:* Office of the Chairman, Jinan University, 601 Huangpu W Ave, Tianhe, Guangzhou, Guangdong, People's Republic of China (office). *Website:* welcome.jnu.edu.cn/en2014/ (office).

DAI, Hongjie, MS, PhD; American (b. Chinese) chemist and academic; *J.G. Jackson and C.J. Wood Professor in Chemistry, Stanford University;* b. 1966; ed Tsing Hua Univ., People's Repub. of China, Columbia Univ., Harvard Univ.; Postdoctoral Fellow, Harvard Univ. 1995–97; Postdoctoral Fellow, Rice Univ. 1997; Terman Fellow, Stanford Univ. 1998, Packard Fellow for Science and Eng 1999, Alfred P. Sloan Research Fellow 2001, Asst Prof. of Chem. 1997–2002, Assoc. Prof. 2002–05, Prof. of Chem. 2005–07, J.G. Jackson and C.J. Wood Prof. in Chem. 2007–; Founder, Molecular Nanosystems Inc. 2001; Changjian Visiting Professorship, Tsinghua Univ. 2005–08; Fellow, American Acad. of Arts and Sciences 2009–, AAAS 2011; mem. Editorial Bd several journals including Nano Letters, Chemical Physics Letters, International Journal of Nanoscience; Camille Dreyfus Teacher-Scholar Award 2002, ACS Pure Chem. Award 2002, Julius Springer Prize for Applied Physics 2004, American Physical Soc. James McGroddy Prize for New Materials 2006, Ramabrahmam and Balamani Guthikonda Award, Columbia Univ. 2009. *Publications:* more than 150 articles in profesional journals. *Address:* Stanford University, Department of Chemistry, Keck Chemistry Building, Room 125A, Stanford, CA 94305-5080, USA (office). *Telephone:* (650) 725-9156 (office). *Fax:* (650) 725-0259 (office). *E-mail:* hdai1@stanford.edu (office). *Website:* www.stanford.edu/dept/chemistry/faculty/dai/group (office).

DAI, Gen. (retd) Tobias Joaquim; Mozambican politician and fmr army officer; b. 25 Nov. 1950, Manica City; s. of Joaquin Dai and Beatriz Mucudo Dai; m.; two c.; ed João XXII and Pêro de Anaia Secondary Schools; joined Mozambique Armed Forces 1971; Instructor and Commdr, Nachingweia 1971–76; Weapons Commdr, Vestrel de Moscovo Mil. Acad., USSR 1976–78; Commdr Mil. Garrison, City of Maputo 1978–80; several sr mil. positions, including Vice-Commdt and Head of Mil. House of Pres. of the Repub., Prov. Mil. Commdr in Manica, Head of Directorate of Operations, and C-in-C of Armed Forces 1980–95; Sec.-Gen., Ministry of Nat. Defence 1995–2000; Minister of Nat. Defence 2000–08; participated in Peace Negotiations 1993–94; elected to House of Reps 1987–94; mem. Frelimo Party; Veteran of the Struggle for Nat. Independence of Mozambique Medal. *Leisure interests:* sports, reading. *Address:* c/o Ministry of National Defence, Avenida Mártires de Mueda 280, CP 3216, Maputo, Mozambique. *E-mail:* mdn@mdn.gov.mz.

DAI, Weili, BA; American (b. Chinese) business executive; *Co-founder, Marvell Technology Group;* b. Shanghai, China; m. Sehat Sutardja; two c.; ed Univ. of California, Berkeley; involved in software devt and project man. at Canon Research Center America, Inc. –1995; Co-founder (with husband) Marvell Technology Group 1995, has served as Gen. Man., Exec. Vice-Pres., Pres. 2013–16 and COO Communications Business Group, also served as mem. Bd of Dirs Marvell Technology Group Ltd and Corp. Sec. of the Bd; mem. Bd Give2Asia; mem. Committee of 100; Silicon Valley Entrepreneur of the Year Award 2013, California-Asia Business Council New Silk Road Award 2013. *Address:* Marvell Semiconductor, Inc., 5488 Marvell Lane, Santa Clara, CA 95054, USA (office). *Telephone:* (408) 222-2500 (office). *Fax:* (408) 988-8279 (office). *E-mail:* info@marvell.com (office). *Website:* www.marvell.com (office).

DAI, Xianglong; Chinese politician, banking executive, economist and fmr central banker; b. 1 Oct. 1944, Yizheng City, Jiangsu Prov.; ed Cen. Inst. of Finance and Banking; mem. CCP 1973–; Deputy Section Chief, People's Bank of China (PBC), Jiangsu Prov. Br. 1978; Deputy Section Chief and Deputy Head of Dept Agricultural Bank of China (ABC), Jiangsu Br., Vice-Gov. 1983; Sec. CCP Group, Communications Bank of China (CBC), also Gen. Man. and Vice-Chair. Bd CBC 1989; Chair. Bd China Pacific Insurance Co. Ltd 1990–93; Vice-Gov. People's Bank of China 1993–95, Gov. 1995–2003; Alt. mem. 14th CCP Cen. Cttee 1992–97, 15th CCP Cen. Cttee 1997–2002, 16th CCP Cen. Cttee 2002–07, 17th CCP Cen. Cttee 2007–12; Acting Mayor Tianjin Municipality 2002–03, Vice-Mayor 2002–03, Mayor 2003–07, Deputy Sec. CCP Municipal Cttee 2003–07; Chair. Nat. Council for Social Security Fund 2008–13. *Address:* National Council for Social Security Fund, Mailbox No.2, South Tower, Fortune Time, Building 11, Fenghuiyuan, Xicheng District, Beijing 100032, People's Republic of China (office). *Website:* www.ssf.gov.cn (office).

DĂIANU, Daniel, PhD; Romanian economist, academic and politician; b. 30 Aug. 1952, Bucharest; ed Acad. of Econ. Studies, Bucharest, Acad. of Sciences, Bucharest and Harvard Business School, USA; Visiting Scholar, Russian Research Center, Harvard Univ. 1990–92; Deputy Minister of Finance Feb.–Aug. 1992; Chief Economist, Nat. Bank of Romania 1992–97; Minister of Finance 1997–98; fmr Prof. of Econs, Acad. of Econ. Studies, Bucharest; Prof. of Econs, Nat. School of Political Studies and Public Admin (SNSPA, Bucharest; Pres. Supervisory Bd Banca Comercială Română 2005–07; mem. European Parl. (Nat. Liberal Party) 2007–09; Visiting Scholar, Woodrow Wilson Center, Washington, DC 1992, IMF, Washington, DC 1993, UN/ECE; Visiting Sr Fellow, NATO Defense Coll., Rome 1995; Visiting Prof., Univ. of California, Berkeley 1999, Anderson School of Man., UCLA 2000–02, Univ. of Bologna 2000–02; Chair. Romanian Econ. Soc.; Pres. European Asscn for Comparative Econ. Studies 2002–04, OSCE Econ. Forum 2001; First Deputy Pres. Romanian Financial Supervision Authority 2013–14; mem. High Level Group on Own Resources of the EU, European Council for Foreign Relations 2012–, Bd CEC Bank 2012–13, Bd Nat. Bank of Romania 2014–; Pres. Junior Achievement Romania; mem. Aspen Inst. Romania; Corresp. mem. Romanian Acad. 2001, Full mem. 2013; Fellow, William Davidson Inst., Univ. of Michigan Business School, Centre for Social and Econ. Research, Warsaw 2010; Hon. Pres. Romanian Acad. of European Studies; Acad. of Sciences Highest Award for Econs 1994. *Publications include:* Funcţionarea economiei şi echilibrul extern 1992, Economic Vitality and Viability – A Dual Challenge for European Security 1996, Transformation of Economies as a Real Process – An Insider's Perspective 1998, Romania – Winners and Losers: The Impact of Reform of Intergovernmental Transfers (research report, co-author) 1999, Balkan Reconstruction (co-ed.) 2001, Ethical Boundaries of Capitalism (co-author) 2005, Pariul României. Economia noastră: reformă şi integrare 2006, Ce vom fi în Uniune 2006, South East Europe and The World We Live In 2008, The Macroeconomics of EU Integration: The Case of Romania 2008, Which Way Goes Capitalism? 2009, Lupta cu criza financiară. Eforturile unui membru român al PE/Combating the Financial Crisis: A Romanian MEPs Struggle, Bucharest 2009, Whither Economic Growth in Central and Eastern Europe (co-author) 2010, EU Economic Governance Reform: Are We at a Turning Point?, RCEP Policy Brief No. 17 2010, The Crisis of the Eurozone: The Future of Europe (co-ed.) 2014; columns have appeared in Ziarul Financiar, Piaţa Financiară, Bursa, Southeast European Times European Voice, Les Echos, Europe's World, World Commerce Review. *Leisure interests:* reading, football, basketball. *Address:* Centre for Social and Economic Research, al. Jana Pawla II 61/212 01-031 Warsaw, Poland (office). *Telephone:* (22) 206-29-00 (office). *Fax:* (22) 206-29-01 (office). *E-mail:* case@case-research.eu (office). *Website:* www.case-research.eu (office).

DAIBER, Hans Joachim, DPhil Habil.; German philologist and academic; *Professor Emeritus of Oriental Philology and Islam, University of Frankfurt am Main;* b. 1 April 1942, Stuttgart; s. of Otto Daiber and Martha Daiber; m. Helga Brosamler 1971; one s. one d.; ed Theological Seminaries of Maulbronn and Blaubeuren, Univs of Tübingen and Saarbrücken; Research Fellow, German Oriental Inst., Beirut, Lebanon 1973–75; Lecturer in Arabic, Univ. of Heidelberg 1975–77; Prof. of Arabic, Free Univ., Amsterdam 1977–95; Prof. of Oriental Philology and Islam, Univ. of Frankfurt am Main 1995–2010, Prof. Emer. 2010–; Special Visiting Prof., Univ. of Tokyo 1992; Visiting Prof., Int. Inst. of Islamic Thought and Civilization, Kuala Lumpur 2001; mem. Royal Netherlands Acad. of Arts and Sciences, German Oriental Inst., Beirut 1973–75; Ed. Aristoteles Semitico-Latinus, Islamic Philosophy, Theology and Science; Best Doctoral Thesis of the Year, Univ. of Saarbrücken 1967, Islamic Thought in the Middle Ages. Studies in Text, Transmission and Translation, in honour of Hans Daiber 2008. *Publications include:* Die arabische Übersetzung der Placita philosophorum 1968, Das theologisch-philosophische System des Muammar Ibn Abbad as-Sulami 1975, Gott, Natur und menschlicher Wille im frühen islamischen Denken 1978, Aetius Arabus 1980, The Ruler as Philosopher: A New interpretation of al-Farabi's View 1986, Wasil Ibn Ata' als Prediger und Theologe 1988, Catalogue of Arabic Manuscripts in the Daiber Collection (Vol. I) 1988, (Vol. II) 1996, Neuplatonische Pythagorica in arabischem Gewande 1995, The Islamic Concept of Belief in the 4th/10th Century 1995, Bibliography of Islamic Philosophy (two vols) 1999, (Supplement) 2006, The Struggle for Knowledge in Islam: Some Historical Aspects

2004, Islamic Thought in the Dialogue of Cultures: A Historical and Bibliographical Survey 2012; numerous articles in journals on Islamic philosophy, theology, history of sciences, Greek heritage in Islam. *Address:* Am Hüttenhof 10, 40489 Düsseldorf, Germany (home). *Telephone:* 17-24908395 (mobile). *E-mail:* daiber@em.uni-frankfurt.de (office).

DAILY, Gretchen C., BS, MS, PhD; American ecologist and academic; *Bing Professor of Environmental Science, Department of Biology, Stanford University;* b. 1964; ed Stanford Univ.; Research Asst, Worldwatch Inst., Washington, DC 1985–87; Research Asst, Ludwig Maximillian Univ., Munich, FRG 1988; Winslow/Heinz Postdoctoral Fellow, Energy and Resources Group, Univ. of California, Berkeley 1992–95; Bing Interdisciplinary Research Scientist, Dept of Biological Sciences, Stanford Univ. 1995–2002, Assoc. Prof. (Research), Dept of Biology and Sr Fellow, Inst. for Int. Studies 2002–05, Bing Prof. of Environmental Science 2005–, currently Dir Center for Conservation Biology, Dir Interdisciplinary Program in Environment and Resources; Sr Fellow, Woods Inst. for the Environment; Co-founder and Chair. Natural Capital Project; mem. or fmr mem. Bd of Eds Ecological Applications, Ecological Economics, Ecosystems, Encyclopedia of Biodiversity; Fellow, American Acad. of Arts and Sciences 2003, NAS 2005, California Acad. of Sciences 2010; Einstein Professorship, Chinese Acad. of Sciences 2010; Frances Lou Kallman Award for Excellence in Science and Grad. Study 1992, Pew Fellow in Conservation and the Environment 1994, Fellow, Aldo Leopold Leadership Program 1999, 21st Century Scientist Award 2000, Smith Sr Scholar of The Nature Conservancy 2003, Sophie Prize 2008, Int. Cosmos Prize, The Expo '90 Foundation, Japan 2009, Environment and Energy Award for Thought Leadership, Aspen Inst. 2010, Heinz Award, The Heinz Family Philanthropies 2010, Midori Prize for Biodiversity, AEON Environmental Foundation, Ministry of the Environment, Japan, Secr. of the Convention on Biological Diversity and United Nations Univ. 2010, Volvo Environment Prize 2012, Blue Planet Prize 2017. *Achievements include:* has developed concepts of countryside biogeography, ecosystem services and conservation finance; works extensively with economists, lawyers, business people and govt agencies to incorporate environmental issues into business practice and govt policy. *Publications:* The Stork and the Plow: The Equity Solution to the Human Dilemma (co-author) 1995, Nature's Services: Societal Dependence on Natural Ecosystems (ed.) 1997, The Encyclopedia of Biodiversity (co-ed.) 2001, The New Economy of Nature: The Quest to Make Conservation Profitable (with Katherine Ellison) 2002, Natural Capital: Theory & Practice of Mapping Ecosystem Services (co-ed.) 2011; more than 150 scientific papers and popular articles. *Address:* Department of Biology, Stanford University, 371 Serra Mall, Stanford, CA 94305-5020, USA (office). *Telephone:* (650) 723-9452 (office). *Fax:* (650) 725-1992 (office). *E-mail:* gdaily@stanford.edu (office). *Website:* www.stanford.edu/group/CCB/cgi-bin/ccb/content/gretchen-daily (office).

DAINBA, Gyaincan; Chinese government official; b. 1940, Lhasa, Tibet; joined CCP 1964; Mayor of Lhasa Municipality 1980–87. *Address:* Government of Xizang Autonomous Region, Lhasa City, People's Republic of China.

DAINES, Steven (Steve) Daly, BS; American business executive and politician; *Senator from Montana;* b. 20 Aug. 1962, Van Nuys, Calif.; m. Cindy Daines; two s. two d.; ed Montana State Univ.; held various man. roles with Procter & Gamble Co. 1984–91, later with Procter & Gamble Co., Hong Kong 1991–97; with pvt. construction business, Bozeman, Mont. 1997–2000; various positions with Right-Now Technologies, Bozeman, Mont. 2000–12, including Vice-Pres., Customer Service, Vice-Pres., Asia-Pacific, Vice-Pres., N American Sales; mem. US House of Reps from Montana 1st Congressional Dist 2013–15, mem. House Transportation and Infrastructure Cttee, House Natural Resources Cttee, House Homeland Security Cttee; Senator from Montana 2015–; Republican. *Address:* 1 Russell Senate Courtyard, Washington, DC 20510, USA (office). *Telephone:* (202) 224-2651 (office). *Website:* www.daines.senate.gov (office).

DAINTITH, Terence Charles, MA; British legal scholar and academic; *Professor Emeritus of Law, University of London;* b. 8 May 1942, Coulsdon, Greater London, England; s. of Edward Daintith and Irene M. Parsons; m. Christine Bulport 1965; one s. one d.; ed Wimbledon Coll. and St Edmund Hall, Oxford, Univ. of Nancy, France (Leverhulme Euro Scholar); called to Bar, Lincoln's Inn 1966; Assoc. in Law, Univ. of California, Berkeley 1963–64; Lecturer in Constitutional and Admin. Law, Univ. of Edin. 1964–72; Prof. of Public Law, Univ. of Dundee 1972–83, Dir Centre for Petroleum and Mineral Law Studies 1977–83; Prof. of Law, European Univ. Inst., Florence, Italy 1981–87; Prof. of Law, Univ. of London 1988–2002, Prof. Emer. 2002–, Dir Inst. of Advanced Legal Studies 1988–95, Dean School of Advanced Study 1994–2001; Prof. of Law, Univ. of Western Australia 2002–; Visiting Prof. of Law, Univ. of Melbourne, Australia 2004–; Bencher, Lincoln's Inn 2000; Ed. Journal of Energy and Natural Resources Law 1983–92; mem. Academia Europaea (Chair. Law Cttee 1993–96, Social Sciences Section 1996–98); Hon. LLD (De Montfort) 2001, (Aberdeen) 2013; Kuntz Memorial Award, Univ. of Oklahoma 2010. *Publications:* The Economic Law of the United Kingdom 1974, United Kingdom Oil and Gas Law (with G. D. M. Willoughby) 1977 (third edn 2000), Energy Strategy in Europe (with L. Hancher) 1986, The Legal Integration of Energy Markets (with S. Williams) 1987, Law as an Instrument of Economic Policy 1988, Harmonization and Hazard (with G. R. Baldwin) 1992, Implementation of EC Law in the United Kingdom 1995, The Executive in the Constitution (with A. C. Page) 1999, Discretion in the Administration of Offshore Oil and Gas: A Comparative Study 2006, Finders Keepers? How the Rule of Capture Shaped the World Oil Industry 2010. *Address:* Institute of Advanced Legal Studies, 17 Russell Square, London, WC1B 5DR, England (office); Law School, University of Western Australia, Crawley, WA 6009, Australia (office). *Telephone:* (20) 7862-5800 (London) (office).

DAIRI, Mohammed al-, BA, MA; Libyan diplomatist and government official; *Minister of Foreign Affairs and of International Co-operation;* b. 7 March 1952, Tripoli; ed Univ. of Grenoble, France; Amb. and UNHCR Regional Rep. in Egypt, to the Arab League and the Palestinian Authority –2014; Minister of Foreign Affairs and of Int. Co-operation (in al-Thani govt) 2014–; Ind. *Address:* Ministry of Foreign Affairs and of International Co-operation, Tripoli, Libya (office). *Telephone:* (21) 3402121 (office). *E-mail:* info@foreign.gov.ly (office). *Website:* www.foreign.gov.ly (office).

DALAI LAMA, The, former temporal and spiritual head of Tibet; Fourteenth Incarnation (Tenzin Gyatso); Tibetan; b. 6 July 1935, Taktser, Amdo Prov., NE Tibet; s. of Chujon Tsering and Tsering Dekyi; born of Tibetan peasant family in Amdo Prov.; enthroned at Lhasa 1940; rights exercised by regency 1934–50; assumed political power 1950; fled to Chumbi in S Tibet after abortive resistance to Chinese State 1950; negotiated agreement with China 1951; Vice-Chair. Standing Cttee CPPCC, mem. Nat. Cttee 1951–59; Hon. Chair. Chinese Buddhist Asscn 1953–59; Del. to Nat. People's Congress 1954–59; Chair. Preparatory Cttee for the 'Autonomous Region of Tibet' 1955–59; fled Tibet to India after suppression of Tibetan national uprising 1959; Dr of Buddhist Philosophy (Monasteries of Sera, Drepung and Gaden, Lhasa) 1959; Supreme Head of all Buddhist sects in Tibet (Xizang); announced his retirement from active participation in Tibetan political affairs March 2011; Presidential Distinguished Prof., Emory Univ., USA 2007–; Hon. Citizen of Paris 2008; Memory Prize 1989, Congressional Human Rights Award 1989, Nobel Peace Prize 1989, Freedom Award (USA) 1991, Presidential Congressional Gold Medal (USA) 2007, Templeton Prize 2012. *Publications include:* My Land and People 1962, The Opening of the Wisdom Eye 1963, The Buddhism of Tibet and the Key to the Middle Way 1975, Universal Responsibility and the Good Heart 1977, Deity Yoga (with Jeffrey Hopkins) 1981, Four Essential Buddhist Commentaries 1982, Collected Statements, Interviews & Articles 1982, Advice from Buddha Shakyamuni 1982, Kindness, Clarity and Insight 1984, A Human Approach to World Peace 1984, Opening the Mind and Generating a Good Heart 1985, Opening of the Eye of New Awareness (translated by Donald S. Lopez with Jeffrey Hopkins) 1985, Kalachakra Tantra – Rite of Initiation (with Jeffrey Hopkins) 1985, Tantra in Tibet (with Jeffrey Hopkins) 1987, The Union of Bliss & Emptiness (translated by Dr Thupten Jinpa) 1988, Transcendent Wisdom (translated, edited and annotated by B. Alan Wallace) 1988, The Dalai Lama at Harvard (translated and edited by Jeffrey Hopkins) 1988, The Bodhgaya Interviews (edited by Jose Ignacio Cabezon) 1988, Ocean of Wisdom 1989, Policy of Kindness (compiled and edited by Sidney Piburn) 1990, The Nobel Peace Prize and the Dalai Lama (compiled and edited by Sidney Piburn) 1990, My Tibet (with Galen Rowell) 1990, The Global Community & the Need for Universal Responsibility 1990, Freedom in Exile (autobiog.) 1991, Path to Bliss 1991, Mind Science – An East-West Dialogue (with Herbert Benson, Robert A. Thurman, Howard E. Gardner and Daniel Goleman) 1991, Cultivating a Daily Meditation 1991, Gentle Bridges – Conversations with the Dalai Lama on the Sciences of the Mind (with Jeremy Hayward and Francisco Verela) 1992, Worlds in Harmony (with conf. participants) 1992, Generous Wisdom – Commentaries on the Jatakamala 1993, Words of Truth 1993, A Flash of Lightning in the Dark of Night 1994, The World of Tibetan Buddhism (translated, edited and annotated by Dr Thupten Jinpa) 1995, The Way to Freedom (edited by John Avedon and Donald S. Lopez) 1995, The Spirit of Tibet: Universal Heritage – Selected Speeches and Writings (edited by A. A. Shiromany) 1995, The Power of Compassion 1995, The Path to Enlightenment (translated and edited by Glenn H. Mullin) 1995, His Holiness the Dalai Lama Speeches Statements Articles Interviews from 1987 to June 1995 1995, Dimensions of Spirituality 1995, Dialogues on Universal Responsibility and Education 1995, Commentary on the Thirty Seven Practices of a Bodhisattva (translated by Acharya Nyima Tsering, edited by Vyvyan Cayley and Mike Gilmore) 1995, Awakening the Mind, Lightening the Heart (edited by John Avedon and Donald S. Lopez) 1995, The Good Heart – A Buddhist Perspective on the Teachings of Jesus 1996, Beyond Dogma 1996, Buddha Nature 1997, Sleeping, Dreaming and Dying (edited and narrated by Francisco Varela) 1997, Love, Kindness and Universal Responsibility 1997, The Joy of Living and Dying in Peace (edited by John Avedon & Donald S. Lopez) 1997, The Heart of Compassion 1997, Healing Anger – The Power of Patience from a Buddhist Perspective (translated by Dr Thupten Jinpa) 1997, The Gelug/Kagyu Tradition of Mahamudra (with Alexander Berzin) 1997, Spiritual Advice for Buddhists and Christians 1998, The Political Philosophy of His Holiness the Dalai Lama – Selected Speeches and Writings (edited by A. A. Shiromany) 1998, The Path to Tranquillity – Daily Meditations (compiled and edited by Renuka Singh) 1998, The Four Noble Truths (translated by Dr Thupten Jinpa, edited by Dominique Side and Dr Thupten Jinpa) 1998, The Art of Happiness (with Howard C. Cutler) 1998, Ethics for the New Millennium 1998, Violence and Compassion 1998, The Power of Buddhism (with Jean-Claude Carriere) 1999, Imagine All the People – The Dalai Lama on Money, Politics and Life as It Could Be (with Fabian Quaki) 1999, Introduction to Buddhism 1999, Training the Mind 1999, The Little Book of Buddhism (compiled and edited by Renuka Singh) 1999, The Heart of the Buddha's Path (translated by Dr Thupten Jinpa, edited by Dominique Side and Dr Thupten Jinpa) 1999, Consciousness at the Crossroads – Conversations with the Dalai Lama on Brain Science and Buddhism 1999, Ancient Wisdom, Modern World – Ethics for a New Millennium 1999, Essential Teachings 1999, The Path to Tranquility: Daily Wisdom 1999, Buddha Heart, Buddha Mind – Living the Four Noble Truths 2000, Dalai Lama's Book of Wisdom (edited by Matthew Bunson) 2000, Transforming the Mind: Eight Verses on Generating Compassion and Transforming Your Life (translated by Dr Thupten Jinpa, edited by Dominique Side and Dr Thupten Jinpa) 2000, The Little Book of Wisdom 2000, A Simple Path: Basic Buddhist Teachings by His Holiness the Dalai Lama 2000, The Meaning of Life – Buddhist Perspectives on Cause and Effect (translated and edited by Jeffrey Hopkins) 2000, The Art of Living: A Guide to Contentment, Joy and Fulfillment 2001, The Transformed Mind – Reflections on Truth, Love and Happiness 2001, Stages of Meditation: Training the Mind for Wisdom (translated by Geshe Lobsang Jordhen, Lobsang Choephel Ganchenpa and Jeremy Russell) 2001, An Open Heart (edited by Nicholas Vreeland) 2001, Pocket Dalai Lama (compiled and edited by Mary Craig) 2002, Compassionate Life 2001, His Holiness the Dalai Lama: In My Own Words 2001, Illuminating the Path to Enlightenment 2002, Essence of the Heart Sutra 2002, How to Practise (translated and edited by Jeffrey Hopkins) 2002, The Spirit of Peace 2002, Advice on Dying (translated and edited by Jeffrey Hopkins) 2002, Healing Emotions – Conversation with the Dalai Lama on Emotions and Health 2003, Heart of Compassion 2003, 365 – Dalai Lama Daily Advice from the Heart (edited by Mathieu Ricard) 2003, Warm Heart Open Mind 2003, The Compassionate Life 2003, Destructive Emotions (with Daniel Goleman) 2004, Practicing Wisdom – The Perfection of Shantideva's Bodhisattva Way (translated by Geshe Tubten Jinpa) 2004, New Physics and Cosmology – Dialogues with the Dalai Lama (with Arthur Zajonc and Zara Houshmand) 2004, Dzogchen: Heart Essence of the Great Perfection 2004, The Wisdom of Forgiveness (with Victor Chan) 2004, Many Ways to Nirvana 2004, Path of Wisdom, Path of Peace – A Personal Conversation (with

Felizitas Von Schoenborn) 2005, Lighting the Path, Teachings on Wisdom and Compassion (translated by Geshe Tubten Jinpa) 2005, Art of Happiness at Work (with and Howard C. Cutler) 2005, Widening the Circle of Love (translated and edited by Jeffrey Hopkins) 2005, The Universe in a Single Atom – The Convergence of Science and Spirituality 2005, Yoga Tantra – Paths to Magical Seats (with Dzong-ka-ba and Jeffrey Hopkins) 2005, Teachings on Je Tsong Khapa's Three Principal Aspects of the Path (translated by Ven. Lhakdor and edited by Jeremy Russell) 2006, Activating Bodhichitta and a Meditation on Compassion 2006, Mind in Comfort and Ease – The Vision of Enlightenment in the Great Perfection 2007, How to See Yourself as You Really Are 2007, Dalai Lama at MIT (edited by Anne Harrington and Arthur Zajonc) 2008, In My Own Words – An Introduction to My Teachings and Philosophy (edited by Rajiv Mehrotra) 2008, Becoming Enlightened (translated and edited by Jeffrey Hopkins) 2009, Emotional Awareness (with Paul Ekman) 2009, Art of Happiness in a Troubled World (with Howard C. Cutler) 2009, All You Ever Wanted to Know about Happiness, Life and Living (compiled by Rajiv Mehrotra) 2009, Leaders's Way – Business, Buddhism and Happiness in an Interconnected World (with Laurens van den Muyzenberg) 2009, The Middle Way – Faith Grounded in Reason (translated by Thubten Jinpa) 2009, Toward a True Kinship of Faiths 2010, My Spiritual Journey (with Sofia Stril-Rever) 2010. *Leisure interests:* gardening, mechanics. *Address:* The Office of His Holiness the Dalai Lama Thekchen Choeling, PO McLeod Ganj, Dharamsala 176219, Himachal Pradesh, India (office). *Telephone:* (1892) 221343 (office); (1892) 221879 (office). *Fax:* (1892) 221813 (office). *E-mail:* ohhdl@dalailama.com (office). *Website:* www.dalailama.com (office).

DALBERTO, Michel; French pianist; b. 2 June 1955, Paris; s. of Jean Dalberto and Paulette Girard-Dalberto; ed Lycée Claude Bernard, Lycée Racine, Conservatoire Nat. Supérieur de Musique, Paris with Vlado Perlemuter and Jean Hubeau; started professional career 1975; concerts in major musical centres and at int. festivals including Lucerne, Maggio Musicale Florence, Aix-en-Provence, Vienna, Edinburgh, Schleswig-Holstein, Roque d'Anthéron; has worked with conductors including Leinsdorf, Sawallisch, Dutoit, Masur, Davis and Dausgaard and with orchestras including Orchestre de Paris, Orchestre Nat. de France, Amsterdam Concertgebouw, Philharmonia, Santa Cecilia in Rome, Oslo Philharmonic, BBC Philharmonic, Orchestras of Beijing, Shanghai and Guangzhou, St Petersburg Philharmonic, Ensemble Orchestral de Paris, Orchestre Philharmonique de Liège; Artistic Dir, Acad.-Festival des Arcs 1991–; as chamber musician, has collaborated with artists including Henryk Szeryng, Lynn Harrell, Renaud and Gautier Capuçon, Dmitri Sitkovetsky, Boris Belkin, Vadim Repin, Yuri Bashmet and Truls Mørk; Pres. Jury, Clara Haskil Competition 1991–; Chevalier, Ordre nat. du Mérite; Clara Haskil Prize 1975; First Prize, Mozart Piano Competition, Salzburg 1975, Leeds Int. Pianoforte Competition 1978; Acad. Charles Cros Award 1980 and Acad. du Disque Français Award 1984 for recordings; Diapason d'Or Award for Best Concerto Recording 1991. *Recordings include:* albums: Grieg/Strauss 1992, French Melodies (with Barbara Hendricks); Debussy Preludes, Mozart Concerti 2000, Un Piano à l'Opéra (Gramophone Award, Classic FM Award, Diapason d'Or) 2004, Schubert Piano Music (complete recordings) 2006, Brahms Sonatas for cello and piano 2008, Fauré: Complete Chamber Music for Strings and Piano (ECHO Klassik Award for Chamber Music Recording of the Year 2012) 2011. *Leisure interests:* skiing, scuba diving, vintage cars. *Address:* c/o Agence Artistique Jacques Thélen, 15 Avenue Montaigne, 75008 Paris, France (office). *Telephone:* (1) 56-89-32-00 (office). *Fax:* (1) 56-89-32-01 (office). *E-mail:* thelen@wanadoo.fr (office). *Website:* www.jacquesthelen.com (office); www.micheldalberto.com.

DALBORG, Hans Folkeson, MBA, PhD; Swedish banker; *Honorary Chairman, Nordea Bank AB;* b. 21 May 1941, Säter, Dalarna; m. Anna Ljungqvist 1965; one s. two d.; ed Univ. of Uppsala and Stockholm School of Econs; teacher and admin., Stockholm School of Econs 1967–72; joined Skandia 1972, Deputy Man. Dir responsible for int. business 1981–83, Pres. and COO Skandia Int. Insurance Corpn 1983–89, Sr Exec., Vice-Pres., COO Skandia Group and CEO Skandia Int. Insurance Corpn 1989–91; Pres. and CEO Nordbanken AB 1991–97, Pres., Group CEO MeritaNordbanken PLC 1998–99, Pres. and CEO Nordea Bank AB 2000–04, Chair. 2004–11, Hon. Chair. 2011–; Chair. Royal Swedish Opera 1997–2005, Royal Swedish Acad. of Eng Sciences (IVA) 2005–08, Swedish Code of Corp. Governance, Uppsala Univ.; mem. Bd of Dirs Axel Johnson AB, Stockholm Inst. of Transition Econs and East European Economies (SITE), Stockholm Inst. for Financial Research; mem. European Round Table of Financial Services (EFR); HM The King's Medal, 12th Class of the Seraphim Ribbon 2000; Golden Gavel 2005. *Address:* c/o Nordea Bank AB, Smålandsgatan 17, 105 71 Stockholm, Sweden. *E-mail:* info@nordea.com.

DALDRY, Stephen David, CBE, BA; British theatre and film director; b. 2 May 1960, Dorset; s. of Patrick Daldry and Cherry Daldry (née Thompson); m. Lucy Daldry 2001; one c.; ed Huish Grammar School, Taunton, Univs of Sheffield and Essex; trained with Il Circo di Nando Orfei, Italy; f. Metro Theatre Co., Artistic Dir 1984–86; Assoc. Artist, Crucible Theatre, Sheffield 1986–88; Artistic Dir Gate Theatre, London 1989–92; Artistic Dir English Stage Co., Royal Court Theatre, London 1992–99, Assoc. Dir 1999–; Dir Stephen Daldry Pictures 1998–; Cameron Mackintosh Visiting Prof. of Contemporary Theatre, Oxford Univ. 2002; Creative Dir of Ceremonies, London Olympic Games 2012; Int. Filmmaker Award, Palm Springs Int. Film Festival 2003. *Theatre includes:* Billy Elliot (Dir, musical) (Tony Award for Best Direction of a Musical 2009) 2004. *Films include:* Eight 1998, Via Dolorosa 1999, Dancer (Dir) 2000, Billy Elliot (Dir) (BAFTA Award for Best British Film 2000) 2000, The Hours (Vancouver Film Critics Circle Award for Best Dir 2003) 2002, The Reader (Evening Standard British Film Award for Best Dir 2009) 2008, Extremely Loud & Incredibly Close 2011, Billy Elliot the Musical Live 2014, Trash (People's Choice Gala Award, Rome Film Festival 2015) 2014. *Television includes:* Games of the XXX Olympiad Opening and Closing Ceremonies 2012, The Crown 2016– (Emmy Award for Outstanding Directing for a Drama Series 2018, Golden Globe Award for Best Television Series Drama 2018). *Producer:* Six Degrees of Separation, Oleanna, Damned for Despair (Gate) 1991, An Inspector Calls (Royal Nat. Theatre) 1992, (Aldwych) 1994, (Garrick) 1995, (NY) 1995, (Playhouse) 2001, Machinal (Royal Nat. Theatre) 1993, The Kitchen (Royal Court) 1995, Via Dolorosa (Royal Court) 1998, (NY) 1999, Far Away (Royal Court) 2000, (Albery) 2001, then New York Theatre Workshop 2002–03, A Number, Jerwood Theatre Downstairs, Royal Court Theatre 2002, then New York Theatre Workshop 2002–03, Judgement Day, Ingoldstadt, Figaro Gets Divorced, Rat in the Skull. *Address:* c/o Creative Artists Agency, 2000 Avenue of the Stars, Los Angeles, CA 90067, USA. *Telephone:* (424) 288-2000. *Fax:* (424) 288-2900. *Website:* www.caa.com.

DALE, Jim; British actor; b. (James Smith), 15 Aug. 1935; m.; three s. one d.; ed Kettering Grammar School; music hall comedian 1951; singing, compering, directing 1951–61; first film appearance 1965; appeared in nine Carry On films; later appeared with Nat. Theatre and Young Vic; appeared in London's West End in The Card 1973; host, Sunday Night at the London Palladium (TV show) 1973–74; with Young Vic appeared on Broadway in The Taming of the Shrew and Scapino 1974; Broadway appearances: Barnum (Tony Award) 1980, Joe Egg 1985, Me and My Girl 1987–88, Candide 1997; other stage appearances include: Privates on Parade (New York), Travels With My Aunt (off-Broadway) 1995, Fagin in Oliver! (London Palladium) 1995–97; lyricist for film Georgy Girl; Grammy Award for Best Spoken Word Album for Children (for Harry Potter and the Deathly Hallows) 2008. *Films include:* Lock Up Your Daughters, The Winter's Tale, The Biggest Dog in the World, National Health, Adolf Hitler—My Part in his Downfall, Joseph Andrews, Pete's Dragon, Hot Lead Cold Feet, Bloodshy, The Spaceman and King Arthur, Scandalous, Carry On Cabby, Carry On Cleo, Carry On Jack, Carry On Cowboy, Carry On Screaming, Carry On Spying, Carry On Constable, Carry On Doctor, Carry On Don't Lose Your Head, Carry On Follow That Camel, Carry On Columbus 1992, Hunchback of Notre Dame 1997. *Address:* c/o Sharon Bierut, CED, 257 Park Avenue South, New York, NY 10010, USA; c/o Janet Glass, 28 Berkeley Square, London, W1X 6HD, England.

D'ALEMA, Massimo; Italian politician and journalist; *President, Fondazione Italianieuropei;* b. 20 April 1949, Rome; m. Linda Giuva; two c.; ed Univ. of Pisa; mem. Camera dei Deputati 1987–2004, 2006–13, Chair. Parl. Cttee on Institutional Reform 1997; Dir L'Unità 1988–90; Sec. Partito Democratico della Sinistra, renamed Democratici di Sinistra (DS) 1998, Pres. 2000–07, mem. Partito Democratico (formed by merger of Democratici di Sinistra and Democrazia è Libertà) 2007–; Prime Minister of Italy 1998–2000; mem. European Parl. 2004–06; Deputy Prime Minister and Minister of Foreign Affairs 2006–08; Pres. Fondazione Italianieuropei 2000–, Foundation for European Progressive Studies 2010–; Chair. Parl. Cttee for the Intelligence and Security Services (COPASIR) 2010–13; Vice-Pres. Socialist International 2003–12. *Publications include:* Dialogo su Berlinguer (co-author) 1994, Un paese Normale: La Sinistra e il Futuro dell'Italia 1995, Progettare il Futuro 1996, La Sinistra nell'Italia che Cambia 1997, La Grande Occasione. L'Italia verso le Riforme 1997, Parole a Vista (co-author) 1998, Kosovo: Gli italiani e la Guerra (co-author) 1999, Oltre la Paura 2002, La Politica ai Tempi della Globalizzazione 2003, A Mosca l'Ultima Volta 2004, Il Mondo Nuovo 2009, Controcorrente 2013, Non solo euro 2014. *Telephone:* (06) 45508600 (office). *Fax:* (06) 45508698 (office). *E-mail:* segreteria@italianieuropei.it (office). *Website:* www.massimodalema.it.

DALES, Sir Richard Nigel, Kt, KCVO, CMG, MA; British diplomatist (retd); b. 26 Aug. 1942, Woodford, Essex; s. of Maj. K. Dales and O. M. Dales; m. Elizabeth M. Martin 1966; one s. one d.; ed Chigwell School, Essex and St Catharine's Coll., Cambridge; joined Foreign Office 1964, Third Sec., Embassy in Yaoundé, Cameroon 1965–67, with FCO, London 1968–70, Second Sec., later First Sec., Embassy in Copenhagen 1970–73, Asst Pvt. Sec. to Sec. of State for Foreign and Commonwealth Affairs 1974–77, Head of Chancery, Sofia 1977–81, FCO, London 1981–82, Head of Chancery, Copenhagen 1982–86, Deputy High Commr in Zimbabwe 1986–89, Head of Southern Africa Dept, FCO 1989–91; seconded to Civil Service Comm. 1991–92; High Commr to Zimbabwe 1992–95, Dir (Africa and Commonwealth), FCO 1995–98, Amb. to Norway 1998–2002; Chair. Anglo-Norse Soc. 2003–; mem. Bd Norfolk and Norwich Festival 2003–06; mem. Council of Univ. of East Anglia 2004–13; Chair. International Alert 2005–10. *Leisure interests:* music and the arts, walking, life in retirement.

D'ALESSANDRO, Dominic, OC, BSc; Italian chartered accountant and financial services executive; b. 18 Jan. 1947, Molise; m. Pearl D'Alessandro; two s. one d.; ed Loyola Coll., Montreal, Canada; accountant, Coopers & Lybrand 1968–75; with Genstar Ltd 1975–81, Dir of Finance, Dhahran, Saudi Arabia, subsequently Gen. Man., Dhahran, later Vice-Pres. Materials and Construction Group, San Francisco; with Royal Bank of Canada 1981–88, Vice-Pres. and Controller, then Exec. Vice-Pres. for Finance –1988; Pres. and CEO Laurentian Bank of Canada 1988–94; mem. Bd Dirs, Pres. and CEO Manulife Financial Corpn 1994–2009; Dir, American Council of Life Insurance, The Hudson's Bay Co., TransCanada PipeLines, Suncor Energy Inc. 2009–; mem. Business Council on Nat. Issues; fmr Chair. Bd Canadian Life and Health Insurance Asscn; mem. Advisory Cttee on the Public Service of Canada 2006–, North American Competitiveness Council of North American Free Trade Agreement (NAFTA) 2006–; Co-Chair. Corp. Fund for Breast Cancer Research Campaign 1996; Campaign Chair. for the Salvation Army, Ont. Cen. Div., for Greater Toronto United Way Campaign 1998; Fellow, Inst. Chartered Accountants 1993; Commendatore, Order of the Star of Italy 2008; Dr hc (Concordia Univ.) 1998, (York Univ.) 2006; Bronze Medal, Inst. of Chartered Accountants 1971, Man. Achievement Award, McGill Univ. 1999, Arbour Award, Univ. of Toronto 1999, CEO Award of Excellence in Public Relations, Canadian Public Relations Soc. 2001, named Canada's Outstanding CEO for 2002, voted Canada's Most Respected CEO 2004, Loyola Medal, Concordia Univ. 2004, honoured with Int. Horatio Alger Award 2005, Special Lifetime Man. Achievement Award, McGill Univ. 2005, Int. Distinguished Entrepreneur Award, Univ. of Manitoba 2007, Canadian Business Leader Award, Univ. of Alberta School of Business 2007, inducted into Insurance Hall of Fame 2008. *Address:* Suncor Energy Inc., PO Box 2844, 150 – 6 Avenue SW, Calgary, Alberta, T2P 3E3, Canada (office). *Telephone:* (403) 296-8000 (office). *Fax:* (403) 296-3030 (office). *E-mail:* media@suncor.com (office). *Website:* www.suncor.com (office).

DALEY, Richard Michael, BA, JD; American lawyer and fmr politician; *Of Counsel, Katten Muchin Rosemann LLP;* b. 24 April 1942, Chicago, Ill.; s. of Richard J. Daley and Eleanor Guilfoyle; brother of William M. Daley; m. Margaret Corbett 1972; one s. (and one s. deceased) two d.; ed De La Salle High School, Providence Coll., DePaul Univ.; mem., US Marine Corps Reserve 1961–67; Asst Corpn Counsel, City of Chicago 1969; Del., Ill. Constitutional Convention 1970; Partner, Simon and Daley (law firm) 1970–72, Daley, Riley & Daley 1972–80; mem. Ill. State Senate 1973–80; State's Attorney, Cook Co., Ill. 1980–89; Mayor of

Chicago 1989–2011; currently Of Counsel, Katten Muchin Rosemann LLP, Chicago; Man. Prin., Tur Partners LLC, Chicago, Ill. 2011–; Sr Advisor, JP Morgan Chase & Co. 2011–; Distinguished Sr Fellow, Univ. Chicago Harris School Public Policy 2011–; mem. Bd of Dirs Coca-Cola Company 2013–, Diamond Resorts International, Inc.; Special Advisor, Wuhan, China; mem. Chicago Bar Asscn, Ill. State Bar Asscn, ABA, Catholic Lawyers Guild; Democrat; Hon. Chair. Corp. Bd, Boys And Girls Clubs, Chicago; numerous awards including Outstanding Leader, Ill. Asscn of Social Workers 1978, Public Official of Year, Governing magazine 1997, Politician of Year, Library Journal 1997, J. Sterling Morton Award, Nat. Arbor Day Foundation 1999, Nat. Trust for Historic Preservation Nat. Preservation Award, 2000, 2002, Lifetime Achievement Award, US Conference Mayors 2005, Kevin Lynch Award, MIT 2005, Official of Year, Alliance for Great Lakes 2006. *Leisure interests:* cinema, reading. *Address:* Katten Muchin Rosemann LLP, 525 West Monroe Street, Chicago, IL 60661-3693, USA (office). *Telephone:* (312) 902-5288 (office). *Fax:* (312) 577-4888 (office). *E-mail:* richard.daley@kattenlaw.com (office). *Website:* www.kattenlaw.com/Richard-Daley (office).

DALEY, Thomas Robert (Tom); British diver and television personality; b. 21 May 1994, Plymouth, Devon; s. of Robert Daley and Debbie Daley (née Selvester); m. Dustin Lance Black 2016; ed Eggbuckland Community Coll., Plymouth Coll.; began diving aged seven; won individual 10m platform event at British Championships 2008, 2009, 2012, 2013, 2015, European Championships, Eindhoven 2008, 2012, London 2016; represented GB at Junior World Championships, Aachen (silver medal in 3m springboard, silver in 10m platform), at Olympics Games, Beijing 2008 where he was Britain's youngest competitor, the youngest competitor of any nationality outside the sport of swimming, and the youngest to participate in a final; participated in FINA Jr World Championships 2008, finished second in category 'B' platform competition (for 14- and 15-year-old boys), finished second in 3m springboard competition in same category; won individual 10m platform event at FINA World Championships, Rome 2009; ranked No. 1 for the 10m platform in FINA World Diving Rankings; won two gold medals in 10m synchro springboard (with Max Brick) and 10m Individual Platform competition at Commonwealth Games, New Delhi 2010; gold medals, synchro 3m springboard and 10m platform, Junior World Championships, Adelaide 2012; bronze medal, 10m platform, Olympics Games, London 2012; silver medal, 10m synchro diving (with James Denny) and gold in 10m Individual Platform at Commonwealth Games, Glasgow 2014; gold medal, mixed 3m springboard synchro (with Grace Reid), European Championships, London 2016; silver medal, 10m synchro diving (with Daniel Goodfellow), European Championships, London 2016; silver medal, 10m platform, European Championships, Berlin 2014; gold medal, team event and bronze medal, 10m platform, World Championships, Kazan 2015; mem. Plymouth Diving Club; celebrity supporter of ChildLine 2007–; coach, Andy Banks –2014, Jane Figueredo 2014–; named BBC South West Sports Personality of the Year, and Young Sports Personality of the Year 2009, named BBC Young Sports Personality of the Year 2007, 2009, 2010 (only person ever to win this award more than once), Sports Personality of the Year, The Herald Awards 2007, 2009, 2012, LEN Magazine's Athlete of the Year Award for mens' divers, on behalf of European Swimming Fed. 2009, ranked third on World Pride Power list 2014. *Television includes:* The Xtra Factor (series) 2010–12, The Big Fat Quiz of the Year 2012, 2014, The BRIT Awards (presenter) 2013, 2014, mentor to the celebrity competitors, Splash! (ITV) 2013–14, National Television Awards (presenter) 2014, Tom Daley Goes Global (host, ITV 2) 2014, TFI Friday (series) 2015, Aegon Championships (series) 2015. *Address:* c/o London Aquatics Centre, Queen Elizabeth Olympic Park, Stratford, London, E20 2ZQ, England. *Telephone:* (20) 8536-3150. *E-mail:* info@londonaquaticscentre.org. *Website:* londonaquaticscentre.org.

DALEY, William M., BA, JD; American lawyer, business executive and fmr government official; *Managing Partner, Argentière Capital LP;* b. 9 Aug. 1948, Chicago, Ill.; s. of Richard J. Daley and Eleanor Guilfoyle; brother of Richard Michael Daley; m. Loretta Daley; three c.; ed Loyola Univ., John Marshall Law School; called to Ill. Bar 1975; fmrly with Daley and George, Chicago; Pnr, Mayer, Brown and Platt; Vice-Chair. Amalgamated Bank, Chicago 1989, Pres., COO 1990–93; US Sec. of Commerce, Washington, DC 1997–2000; Chair. of Vice-Pres. Albert Gore's presidential election campaign 2000; Vice-Chair. Evercore Capital Pnrs LP Jan.–Nov. 2001; Pres. SBC Communications 2001–04; Chair. Midwest Operations, JPMorgan Chase, Chicago 2004–11, also mem. Exec. Cttee, Operating Cttee and Int. Advisory Council; Chief of Staff to Pres. Barack Obama, The White House, Washington, DC 2011–12 (resgnd); Co-Chair. Pres. Obama's 2012 re-election campaign team, Chicago; Man. Partner and head of US operations, Argentière Capital LP (hedge fund), Chicago 2014–; fmr mem. Bd of Dirs Boeing Co., Abbott Laboratories, Boston Properties Inc., Art Inst. of Chicago, Joffrey Ballet of Chicago, Loyola Univ. of Chicago, Northwestern Memorial Hosp., Northwestern Univ.; fmr Special Counsel to Pres. for North American Free Trade Agreement; mem. Council on Foreign Relations; Trustee Emer., John F. Kennedy Center for the Performing Arts; St Ignatius Award for Excellence in the Practice of Law, World Trade Award, World Trade Center, Chicago 1994, Making History Award for Distinction in Civic Leadership, Chicago History Museum 2010. *Address:* Argentière Capital LP, 71 South Wacker Drive, Suite 2120, Chicago, IL 60606, USA (office). *Telephone:* (312) 212-3996 (office). *Website:* www.argentiere.ch (office).

DALGLISH, Sir Kenneth (Kenny) Mathieson, Kt, MBE; British professional football manager and fmr professional footballer; b. 4 March 1951, Glasgow, Scotland; m. Marina Dalglish; four c.; deep-lying forward; played for Celtic 1969–77 (made 204 appearances and scored 112 goals), Scottish League champions 1972, 1973, 1974, 1977, Scottish Cup Winners 1972, 1974, 1975, 1977, Scottish League Cup winners 1975; played for Liverpool 1977–90 (made 355 appearances and scored 118 goals), European Cup winners 1978, 1981, 1984, European Super Cup 1984, FA Cup winners 1986, 1989, League Cup winners 1981, 1982, 1983, 1984, Charity Shield 1980, 1981, 1983, shared 1978, 1987, Man. 1985–91, Acad. Amb. (Int. Recruitment and Devt) 2009–11, Man. 2011–12, Football League Cup 2012, Dir (non-exec.) 2013–; Man. Blackburn Rovers 1991–95, Newcastle United 1997–98; Dir of Football Operations, Celtic Feb.–June 2000; 102 full caps for Scotland, scoring 30 goals (both nat. records); Co-founder (with wife) The Marina Dalglish Appeal 2004; Freeman of the City of Glasgow 1986; Football Writers' Asscn Player of the Year 1979, 1983, PFA Players' Player of the Year 1983, Manager of the Year 1986, 1988, 1990, 1995, elected to Scottish Sports Hall of Fame 2001, Inaugural Inductee to English Football Hall of Fame 2002, Scottish Football Hall of Fame 2004, FIFA 100. *Publication:* My Liverpool Home (autobiog.) 2010. *Address:* Liverpool Football Club, Anfield Road, Liverpool, L4 0TH; The Marina Dalglish Appeal, 78 Seel Street, Liverpool, L1 4BH, England. *Telephone:* (151) 709-7079 (charity). *E-mail:* info@liverpoolfc.tv; dianne@marinadalglishappeal.org. *Website:* www.marinadalglishappeal.org; www.liverpoolfc.com/history/past-players/kenny-dalglish.

DALIBARD, Barbara, MA; French telecommunications executive; *Director General, SNCF Voyages;* b. (Barbara Ploux), 23 May 1958, Suresnes, Paris; m.; three c.; ed École Normale Supérieure, École Nationale Supérieure des Télécommunications; began career with France Télécom SA in 1982, various man. positions in sales, Corp. Services Dir Orange France and Vice-Pres. Orange Business 2001–02, Exec. Vice-Pres. Corp. Solutions 2003–04, Exec. Vice-Pres. Enterprise Communications Services 2004–, Chair. Supervisory Bd Equant (now Orange Business Services—subsidiary of France Télécom) 2003–05 (mem. Strategy and Compensation Cttees), Pres. and CEO Equant SA 2005–10; Dir-Gen. SNCF Voyages and mem. Man. Cttee SNCF (Soc. Nationale des Chemins de Fer Français) 2010–; Pres. Alcanet International SAS 1998, Sales Man. for New Operators, Alcatel CIT 1999, later Sales Man. for France; mem. Bd Eurostar; mem. Supervisory Bd Michelin SA (France), Supervisory Bd Wolters Kluwer (Netherlands); Chevalier, Légion d'honneur, Officier, Ordre nat. du Mérite. *Address:* SNCF Voyages, 2 place de la Défense, Cnit 1, 92053 Paris la Défense Cedex, France (office). *Telephone:* 1-74-54-01-02 (office). *E-mail:* barbara.dalibard@sncf.fr (office). *Website:* www.sncf.com (office).

DALIĆ, Martina, MSc, PhD; Croatian economist and politician; b. (Martina Štimac), 12 Nov. 1967, Velika Gorica, Socialist Repub. of Croatia, Socialist Fed. Repub. of Yugoslavia; m.; two c.; ed Univ. of Zagreb, Univ. of Split; Asst, Faculty of Econs, Univ. of Zagreb 1991–95; joined Ministry of Finance 1995, Head of Macroeconomic Forecasting Dept 1995–97, Deputy Minister of Finance 1997–2000, Head of Cen. State Strategy Office 2004–05 (led Croatia-EU accession negotiations), Minister of Finance 2010–11; Chief Economist, Privredna banka dd, Zagreb 2000–04; Chair. Partner banka dd, Zagreb 2008; fmr mem. Hrvatska Demokratska Zajednica (HDZ) (Croatian Democratic Union), Ind. 2014–; mem. Ass. (Sabor) 2011–15; Deputy Prime Minister, Minister of the Economy, Small and Medium-sized Enterprises and Crafts 2016–18. *Publications:* numerous papers and reports on economic issues.

DALLARA, Charles H., BA, MA, PhD, MALD; American international organization official and fmr government official; b. 1948, Spartanburg, NC; m. 1st Carolyn Gault; one s. one d.; m. 2nd Peixin Li; ed Univ. of South Carolina and Fletcher School of Law and Diplomacy; int. economist, US Treasury Dept 1976–79; Special Asst to Under-Sec. for Monetary Affairs 1979–80; Guest Scholar, Brookings Inst. 1980–81; Special Asst to Asst Sec. for Int. Affairs 1981–82; Alt. Exec. Dir IMF 1982–83; Deputy Asst Sec. for Int. Monetary Affairs, US Treasury Dept 1983–85; Exec. Dir IMF 1984–89; Asst Sec. for Policy Devt and Sr Adviser for Policy 1988–89; Asst Sec. for Internal Affairs 1989–93; Man. Dir JP Morgan 1991–93; Man. Dir Inst. of Int. Finance 1993–2013. *Address:* 12196 Goldenchair Court, Oak Hill, VA 20171, USA (home).

D'ALLEST, Frédéric Jean Pierre; French engineer; b. 1 Sept. 1940, Marseille; s. of Pierre d'Allest and Luce d'Allest; m. Anne-Marie Morel 1963; three s.; ed Ecole St Joseph and Lycée Thiers, Marseilles, Ecole Polytechnique and Ecole Nat. Supérieure d'Aéronautique; with Centre Nat. d'Etudes Spatiales (CNES) 1966–70, Head of Ariane Project 1973–76, Dir Ariane Programme 1976–82, Dir-Gen. CNES 1982–89; with Europa III project, European Launcher Devt Org. 1970–72; Pres. Soc. Arianespace 1980–90 (Hon. Pres. 1990–), Matra Transport 1992–, Matra Hachette 1993–; Dir-Gen. Groupe Matra 1990–93, Groupe Lagardère 1996–2000; f. Marseille Provence 1988; Officier, Légion d'honneur, Ordre nat. du Mérite; Prix de l'Aéronautique, IMechE James Watt Prize 1993. *Leisure interests:* sport, mountaineering. *Address:* 6 rue Marcel Allegot, 92190 Meudon, France. *E-mail:* frederic.dallest@orange.fr.

DALLI, Hon. John, FCCA, CPA, CIM; Maltese accountant, politician and consultant; b. 5 Oct. 1948, Qormi; s. of Carmelo Dalli and Emma Bonnici; m. Josette Callus; two d.; ed Malta Coll. of Arts, Science and Tech.; posts in financial admin and gen. man., Malta and Brussels; Man. Consultant; MP, Nationalist Party 1987–2010; Parl. Sec. for Industry 1987–90; Minister for Econ. Affairs 1990–92, of Finance 1992–96, 1998–2003, of Finance and Econ. Affairs 2003–04, of Foreign Affairs and Investment Promotion 2004 (resgnd); Shadow Minister and Opposition Spokesman for Finance 1996–98; Co-Chair. Malta-Libya Joint Commission 1987–2004; Commr for Health and Consumer Policy, EC, Brussels 2010–14; Exec. Chair. Tabor Consult Ltd; mem. Inst. of Man., USA. *Address:* 2461 Blk 24, Portomaso, St Julians PTM01, Malta (home).

D'ALMEIDA, Armindo Vaz; São Tomé and Príncipe politician; b. 1953; Prime Minister 1995–96; mem. Movimento de Libertação de São Tomé e Príncipe/Partido Social Democrata (MLSTP-PSD—Movt for the Liberation of São Tomé and Príncipe/Social Democratic Party). *Address:* c/o Movimento de Libertação de São Tomé e Príncipe/Partido Social Democrata, Estrada Riboque, Edif. Sede do MLSTP, São Tomé, São Tomé e Príncipe (office). *Telephone:* 2222253 (office). *Fax:* 223341 (office). *E-mail:* mlstppsd@cstome.net (office).

D'ALOISIO, Tony, BA, LLB (Hons); Australian barrister and business executive; *Chairman, Australian Securities and Investments Commission;* b. 6 Nov. 1946; ed Monash Univ.; admitted to practice as a barrister and solicitor in Vic., WA, Queensland and the ACT, and as a solicitor in NSW; Prin. legal officer with Commonwealth Attorney-Gen.'s Dept in Business and Consumer Affairs Div., Canberra –1977; joined Mallesons Stephen Jaques in 1977, practised as commercial lawyer 1977–92, Chief Exec. 1992, Chief Exec. Pnr, Mallesons 1992–2004; Man. Dir and CEO Australian Securities Exchange (ASX) 2004–06; Commr Australian Securities and Investments Comm. (ASIC) 2006–07, Chair. ASIC 2007–; mem. Business Council of Australia 1994–2006 (mem. Bd of Dirs 2003–06), Int. Legal Services Advisory Council 1998–2004 (Chair. Globalisation of Legal Services Cttee), Bd of Taxation 2002–04; mem. Bd of Dirs Australian Charities Fund 2001–, World Fed. of Stock Exchanges 2002–04, Boral Ltd 2003–04; Australian Law Awards Man. Pnr of the Year 2001, 2002, Australian Govt Centenary Medal for services to law and taxation 2000. *Address:* Australian

Securities and Investments Commission, GPO Box 9827, Sydney, NSW 2001, Australia (office). *Telephone:* (2) 9911-2200 (office). *Fax:* (2) 9911-2333 (office). *Website:* www.asic.gov.au (office).

DALRYMPLE, Frederick Rawdon, AO; Australian diplomatist; b. 6 Nov. 1930, Sydney, NSW; s. of Frederick Dalrymple and Evelyn Dalrymple; m. Ross E. Williams 1957; one s. one d.; ed Sydney Church of England Grammar School, Univ. of Sydney, Univ. of Oxford, UK; Lecturer in Philosophy, Univ. of Sydney 1955–57; joined Dept of External Affairs 1957, served in Bonn, London 1959–64; Alt. Dir Asian Devt Bank, Manila 1967–69; Minister, Djakarta 1969–71; Amb. to Israel 1972–75, to Indonesia 1981–85, to USA 1985–89, to Japan 1989–93; Chair. ASEAN Focus Group Pty Ltd 1994–2001; Visiting Prof., Univ. of Sydney 1994–2002; Hon. Fellow, Univ. of Sydney 2003; Hon. DSc (Econ) (Sydney); New South Wales Rhodes Scholar, Univ. of Sydney 1952. *Publications include:* Looking East and West from Down Under 1992, Continental Drift: Australia's Search for a Regional Identity 2003. *Leisure interests:* reading, golf. *Address:* 13/8 Young Street, Paddington, NSW 2021, Australia (home). *Telephone:* (2) 9331-7738. *E-mail:* rdalrymp@ozemail.com.au.

DALRYMPLE, John (Jack), BS; American politician and business executive; b. 16 Oct. 1948, Minneapolis, Minn.; m. Betsy Wood 1971; four d.; ed Yale Univ.; early career working on family farm, Casselton, North Dakota; worked with Casselton Jobs Devt Comm.; co-f. Share House, Inc. (welfare programme); mem. North Dakota House of Reps for Cass Co. 1985–2000, fmr Chair. House Appropriations Cttee; Lt-Gov. of North Dakota 2000–10, Gov. of North Dakota 2010–16; Chair. Dakota Growers Pasta Co., Casselton; fmr Chair. Prairie Public Television; Republican; Outstanding Young Farmer, USA 1983, Ernst and Young Midwest Master Entrepreneur of the Year Award 2007. *Address:* c/o Office of the Governor, 600 East Blvd Avenue, Bismarck, ND 58505-0001, USA (office).

DALRYMPLE, William Benedict Hamilton, MA, DLit, FRSL, FRGS, FRAS; British writer and historian; b. 20 March 1965, Edinburgh, Scotland; s. of Sir Hew Hamilton-Dalrymple and Lady Anne-Louise Hamilton-Dalrymple; m. Olivia Fraser; two s. one d.; ed Ampleforth Coll., Trinity Coll., Cambridge; Founder and Co-Dir Jaipur Literature Festival; Dr hc (Univ. of Lucknow) 2007, (Aberdeen) 2008, (Bradford) 2012, (Edinburgh) 2016; Royal Scottish Geographical Soc. Mungo Park Medal, 2002, Stanford St Martin Religious Broadcasting Prize 2002, RSAA Percy Sykes Award 2005, FPA Media Award for Print Artist of the Year 2005, James Todd Memorial Prize 2008, Media Citizen Puraskar 2010,. *Radio includes:* Three Miles an Hour 2002, The Long Quest 2002. *Television:* Stones of the Raj 1997, Indian Journeys (BAFTA Grierson Award for Best Documentary 2002) 1998, Sufi Soul 2005. *Publications include:* In Xanadu (Yorkshire Post Best First Work Award 1990, Scottish Arts Council Award 1990) 1989, City of Djinns (Thomas Cook Travel Book Award 1994, Sunday Times Young British Writer of the Year 1994) 1993, From the Holy Mountain (Scottish Arts Council Autumn Book Award 1997) 1997, The Age of Kali (Prix de l'Astrobale-Etonnants voyageurs, France 2005) 1998, White Mughals: Love and Betrayal in Eighteenth-Century India (Wolfson Prize for History 2001, Scottish Book of the Year 2003) 2002, Begums, Thugs and White Moghuls 2003, The Last Mughal (Duff Cooper Prize 2007, Vodafone Crossword Book Award 2007) 2006, Nine Lives: In Search of the Sacred in Modern India (Asia House Award 2010) 2009, Return of a King: the Battle for Afghanistan 1839–42 (Kapuściński Prize 2015) 2013, The Writer's Eye 2016, Kohinoor: The Story of the World's Most Infamous Diamond 2016; contrib. to TLS, Guardian, New York Times, New York Review of Books, New Statesman. *Leisure interests:* reading, walking, travelling, listening to music. *Address:* c/o David Godwin Associates, 55 Monmouth Street, London, WC2H 9DG, England (office); 1 Pages' Yard, Church Street, London, W4 2PA, England (home). *Telephone:* (20) 7240-9992 (office). *Fax:* (20) 7395-6110 (office). *E-mail:* sophie@davidgodwinassociates.co.uk (office); wdalrymple1@aol.com. *Website:* www.davidgodwinassociates.co.uk (office); www.williamdalrymple.com.

DALTON, Grant Stanley, OBE; New Zealand yachtsman; *Managing Director, Emirates Team New Zealand;* b. 1 July 1957, Auckland; m. Nicki Dalton; one s. one d.; fmr accountant; trainee sailmaker 1977; first participation in Whitbread round the world race (now the Volvo Ocean Race) on board Dutch Flyer II 1981–82, Lion New Zealand 1985–86; skipper, Fischer & Peykel 1989–90, New Zealand Endeavour 1993–94 (race winner), Wor 60 1997–98 (Merit Cup), Club Med Catamaran, The Race (winner) March 2001, Nautor Challenge Team, Volvo Ocean Race 2001; other races include Sydney-Hobart race (four times), Fastnet Race (five times), Admiral's Cup 1985, Americas Cup, Fremantle, Australia 1987; Man. Dir Emirates Team New Zealand 2003–, won Louis Vuitton ACC Championship 2004, 2006; entered Manx GP and F1 Classic TT 2014; New Zealand Yachtsman of the Year 2001. *Address:* Emirates Team New Zealand, 135 Halsey Street, Freemans Bay, Auckland 1010, New Zealand (office). *Telephone:* (9) 355-0900 (office). *Fax:* (9) 355-0901 (office). *E-mail:* info@emiratesteamnz.com (office). *Website:* emirates-team-new-zealand.americascup.com (office).

DALTON, Timothy Peter; British actor; b. 21 March 1946, Colwyn Bay, Denbighshire, North Wales; partner Vanessa Redgrave 1971–86; one s. with Oksana Grigorieva; ed Herbert Strutt Grammar School, Derbyshire, Royal Acad. of Dramatic Art, London; joined Nat. Youth Theatre; first London appearance at Royal Court Theatre; toured with Prospect Theatre Co.; guest artist with RSC. *Stage appearances include:* King Lear, Love's Labour's Lost, Henry IV, Henry V (all with Prospect Theatre Co.), Romeo and Juliet (RSC), The Samaritan, Black Comedy and White Liars, The Vortex, The Lunatic, The Lover and the Poet 1980, The Romans 1980, Henry IV, Part I (RSC) 1981, Antony and Cleopatra 1986, The Taming of the Shrew 1986, A Touch of the Poet 1988, His Dark Materials (Royal Nat. Theatre) 2003–04. *Films include:* The Lion in Winter 1968, Wuthering Heights 1970, Cromwell 1970, The Voyeur 1970, Mary, Queen of Scots 1971, Permission to Kill 1975, Sextette 1978, The Man Who Knew Love 1978, Agatha 1979, Flash Gordon 1980, Chanel Solitaire 1981, The Doctor and the Devils 1985, role of Ian Fleming's James Bond in The Living Daylights 1987 and Licence to Kill 1989, Hawks 1988, Brenda Starr 1989, The King's Whore 1990, Rocketeer 1991, Naked in New York 1993, Salt Water Moose 1996, The Beautician and the Beast 1997, The Informant 1997, Made Men 1999, The Reef 1999, Bitter Suite 2000, American Outlaws 2001, Looney Tunes: Back in Action 2003, Tales from Earthsea (voice: English version) 2006, Hot Fuzz 2007, Toy Story 3 (voice) 2010, The Tourist 2010, Hawaiian Vacation (short) (voice) 2011, Small Fry (short) (voice) 2011, Tinker Bell: Secret of the Wings (video) (voice) 2012, Toy Story Toons: Partysaurus Rex (short) 2012. *Television includes:* Sat'day While Sunday (series) 1967, The Three Princes (film) 1968, Judge Dee (series) 1969, BBC Play of the Month (series) – Five Finger Exercise 1970, – Candida 1971, Centennial (mini-series) 1978–79, Charlie's Angels (series) 1979, The Flame Is Love (film) 1979, Antony and Cleopatra (film) 1983, Jane Eyre (mini-series) 1983, The Master of Ballantrae (film) 1984, Mistral's Daughter (mini-series) 1984, Florence Nightingale (film) 1985, Faerie Tale Theatre (series) – The Emperor's New Clothes (narrator) 1985, Sins (mini-series) 1986, Tales from the Crypt (series) – Werewolf Concerto 1992, Framed (series) 1992, Lie Down with Lions (film) 1994, Scarlett (mini-series) 1994, Stories from My Childhood (series) – The Prince and the Swan (voice) 1998, Cleopatra (mini-series) 1999, Possessed (film) 2000, Dunkirk (documentary) (narrator) 2004, Hercules (film) 2005, Agatha Christie Marple: The Sittaford Mystery (film) 2006, Unknown Sender (series) 2008, Doctor Who (series) 2009–10, Chuck (series) 2010–11, Toy Story of Terror (short) 2013, Toy Story That Time Forgot (short) 2014, Penny Dreadful (series) 2014–16. *Leisure interest:* Manchester City Football Club. *Address:* c/o Independent Talent Group Ltd, Oxford House, 76 Oxford Street, London, W1D 1BS, England. *Telephone:* (20) 7636-6565. *Fax:* (20) 7323-0101 (office). *E-mail:* info@independenttalent.com. *Website:* www.independenttalent.com.

DALTREY, Roger Harry, CBE; British singer and actor; b. 1 March 1944, Hammersmith, London, England; m. Heather Daltrey; two d. two s. (one by previous m.); mem. rock group, The Detours, renamed The Who 1964–84 (various reunion tours and recordings); numerous festival appearances and tours; solo artist 1984–; Gold Ticket Madison Square Garden 1979, Ivor Novello Award for Outstanding Contribution to British Music 1982, BRIT Award for Outstanding Contribution to British Music 1988, Q Legend Award 2006, South Bank Show Award for Lifetime Achievement 2007, Kennedy Center Honor 2008, co-recipient (with Pete Townshend), George and Ira Gershwin Award for Lifetime Musical Achievement, UCLA 2016, Music Industry Trusts Award 2016. *Films include:* Tommy 1974, Lisztomania 1975, The Legacy 1979, McVicar 1980, Threepenny Opera 1989. *Recordings include:* albums: with The Who: My Generation 1965, A Quick One 1966, Happy Jack 1967, The Who Sell Out 1967, Magic Bus 1968, Tommy 1969, Live At Leeds 1970, Who's Next 1971, Meaty Beefy Big And Bouncy 1971, Quadrophenia 1973, The Who By Numbers 1975, The Story Of The Who 1976, Who Are You 1978, The Kids Are Alright (live) 1979, Face Dances 1981, Hooligans 1982, It's Hard 1982, Once Upon A Time 1983, Who's Last (live) 1984, Two's Missing 1987, Joined Together (live) 1990, Live At The Isle Of Wight Festival 1970 1996, The BBC Sessions 2000, Moonlighting 2005, Endless Wire 2006; solo: Daltrey 1973, Ride A Rock Horse 1975, One Of The Boys 1977, If Parting Should Be Painless 1984, Under A Raging Moon 1985, I Can't Wait To See The Movie 1987, Rocks In The Head 1992, McVicar 1996, Martyrs And Madmen 1997, Anthology 2002, As Long as I See You 2018; with Wilko Johnson: Going Back Home 2014. *Publications:* Thanks A Lot Mr Kibblewhite: My Story 2018. *Website:* www.thewho.com.

DALY, Brendan; Irish fmr politician; b. 2 Feb. 1940, Cooraclare, Co. Clare; m. Patricia Carmody (died 2014); two s. one d.; ed Kilrush Co. Boys' School; mem. Dáil 1973–89, 1997–2002; Minister of State, Dept of Labour 1980–81; Minister for Fisheries and Forestry March–Dec. 1982, for the Marine 1987–89, for Defence Feb.–Nov. 1991, for Social Welfare 1991–92; Minister of State, Dept of Foreign Affairs 1992–93; mem. Seanad Éireann 1993–97, 2002–07; mem. NI Peace Forum 1994; mem. Irish Parl. Foreign Affairs Cttee 1993–; mem. Fianna Fáil. *Address:* Cooraclare, Kilrush, Co. Clare, Ireland (home). *Telephone:* (65) 9059040 (home).

DALY, John Patrick; American professional golfer; b. 28 April 1966, Carmichael, Calif.; s. of Jim Daly and Lou Daly; m. Cherie Daly; two c.; ed Univ. of Arkansas; turned professional 1987; won Missouri Open 1987, Ben Hogan Utah Classic 1990, PGA Championship, Crooked Stick 1991, BC Open 1992, BellSouth Classic 1994, British Open 1995, Dunhill Cup 1993, 1998, BMW Int. Open 2001; f. John Daly Enterprises LLC 2000; Partner, Loudmouth Golf; inducted into Arkansas Sports Hall of Fame. *Recording includes:* My Life 2002 (album), I Only Know One Way 2010 (album). *Publication* My Life In and Out of the Rough 2009 (autobiography). *Leisure interests:* sports, writing lyrics, playing the guitar. *E-mail:* john@johndaly.com. *Website:* www.johndaly.com.

DALY, Robert (Bob) Anthony; American business executive; *President, Rulemaker Inc.;* b. 8 Dec. 1936, Brooklyn, New York; s. of James Daly and Eleanor Daly; m. Carole Bayer Sager; two s. one d.; one step-s.; ed Brooklyn Coll.; Dir Business Affairs, then Vice-Pres. Business Affairs, then Exec. Vice-Pres. CBS TV Network 1955–80; Pres. CBS Entertainment Co. 1977–80; Chair. and Co-CEO Warner Bros, Burbank, Calif. 1980, Chair., CEO 1982–99, Chair. and Co-CEO 1994; Chair. and Co-CEO Warner Music Group 1995–99 (resgnd); Man. Gen. Pnr, Chair. and CEO LA Dodgers professional baseball team 1999–2004; currently Pres. Rulemaker Inc. (investment consultancy), LA; Chair. Bd of Dirs American Film Inst. 2009–; mem. Bd of Dirs Museum of TV and Radio; mem. Acad. of Motion Picture Arts and Sciences, Nat. Acad. of TV Arts and Sciences; Chair. Save the Children Bd of Trustees 2005–10; Hon. DFA (American Film Inst.) 1999, Hon. DHumLitt (Trinity Coll.) 2001; Steven J. Ross/Time Warner Award from Univ. of Southern Calif. School of Cinema-TV 2004. *Address:* Rulemaker Inc., 10877 Wilshire Boulevard, Suite 610, Los Angeles, CA 90024, USA (office). *Telephone:* (310) 208-1555 (office). *E-mail:* bdaly@rulemakerinc.com (office).

DAM, Kenneth Willard, JD; American lawyer, academic and fmr government official; *Max Pam Professor Emeritus and Senior Lecturer, Law School, University of Chicago;* b. 10 Aug. 1932, Marysville, Kan.; s. of Oliver W. Dam and Ida L. Dam; m. Marcia Wachs 1962; one s. one d.; ed Univs of Kansas and Chicago; law clerk for Mr Justice Whittaker, US Supreme Court 1957–58; Assoc., Cravath, Swaine & Moore, New York 1958–60; Asst Prof., Univ. of Chicago Law School 1960–61, Assoc. Prof. 1961–64, Prof. 1964–71, 1974–76, Harold J. & Marion F. Green Prof. of Int. Legal Studies 1976–85, Max Pam Prof. of American and Foreign Law 1992–2001, Prof. Emer. 2001–, also Sr Lecturer 2003–; Provost, Univ. of Chicago 1980–82; Consultant, Kirkland & Ellis, Chicago 1961–71, 1974–80, 1993–; Exec. Dir Council on Econ. Policy 1973; Asst Dir for Nat. Security and Int. Affairs, Office of Man. and Budget 1971–73; Deputy Sec. of State 1982–85; Deputy Sec., US Treasury 2001–03; Vice-Pres., Law and External Relations, IBM Corpn 1985–92; Pres., CEO United Way America 1992; mem. Bd of Dirs Alcoa 1987–2001; Chair.

German-American Academic Council 1999–2001; mem. American Acad. of Arts and Sciences, American Acad. of Diplomacy; mem. Bd Council on Foreign Relations 1992–2001, Chicago Council on Foreign Relations 1992–2001. *Publications include:* Federal Tax Treatment of Foreign Income (with L. Krause) 1964, The GATT: Law and International Economic Organization 1970, Oil Resources: Who Gets What How? 1976, Economic Policy Beyond the Headlines (with George P. Shultz) 1978, The Rules of the Game: Reform and Evolution in the International Monetary System 1982, Cryptography's Role in Securing the Information Society (co-ed.) 1996, The Rules of the Global Game: A New Look at US International Economic Policy 2001, The Law–Growth Nexus: The Rule of Law and Economic Development 2006, Technology, Policy, Law and Ethics Regarding US Acquisition and Use of Cyberattack Capabilities (co-ed.) 2009; numerous articles on legal and economic issues. *Address:* 5609 South Kenwood Avenue, Chicago, IL 60637, USA (home). *Telephone:* (773) 255-2428 (office). *E-mail:* kdam@law.uchicago.edu (office). *Website:* www.law.uchicago.edu (office).

DAMADIAN, Raymond V., BS, MD; American physician and business executive; *Chairman, Fonar Corporation;* b. 16 March 1936, Forest Hills, New York; s. of Vahan Damadian and Odette Damadian (née Yazedjian); m. Donna Terry 1960; two s. one d.; ed Juilliard School of Music, Univ. of Wisconsin, Albert Einstein School of Medicine, Yeshiva Univ., Israel; est. Fonar Corpn 1978, now Chair.; Prof., State Univ. of New York Health Science Center, Brooklyn, New York; Hon. Fellow, American Inst. for Medical and Biological Engineering 2009; Nat. Medal of Tech. 1988, inducted into Nat. Inventors Hall of Fame, US Patent Office 1989, Lemelson-MIT Lifetime Achievement Award 2001, Inventor of the Year (for Upright MRI technology), Intellectual Property Owners Educ. Foundation 2007. *Achievements include:* developed first Magnetic Resonance scanning machine named Indomitable 1977, introduced first commercial MRI (Magnetic Resonance Imaging) scanner 1980. *Address:* Fonar Corporation, 110 Marcus Drive, Melville, NY 11747, USA (office). *Telephone:* (631) 694-2929 (office). *Fax:* (631) 753-5150 (office). *E-mail:* info@fonar.com (office). *Website:* www.fonar.com (office).

DAMANAKI, Maria, MSc; Greek chemical engineer, politician, international organization official and fmr EU official; *Global Managing Director for Oceans, The Nature Conservancy;* b. 31 May 1952, Aghios Nikolaos, Crete; d. of Theodore Damanaki and Eleftheria Damanaki; m. Dimitris Danikas (divorced); one s. two d.; ed Nat. Tech. Univ. of Athens, Lancaster Univ., UK; mem. Communist Youth of Greece (KNE); active in underground student opposition to the dictatorship in Greece 1970–74; took part in Athens Polytechnic Uprising Nov. 1973, voice of 'This is the Polytechnic' radio broadcast, calling on Greek citizens to support uprising; arrested, tortured and imprisoned by the dictatorship 1973–74; engineer, Pechiney Aluminum Industries 1974; Admin., Dept of Import-Export Planning, Ministry of Finance 1975–76; elected to Vouli (Parl.), Athens 1977–93, Vice-Pres. Vouli (first woman) 1986–90; mem. Communist Party of Greece (KKE), Tech. Chamber of Greece; Pres. Coalition of the Left (Synaspismos) 1991–93, resgnd from party 2003; cand. Mayor of Athens 1994, 1998, Head of Opposition in City Council; mem. Parl. (Panhellenic Socialist Movt—PASOK) 2000–09, Chair. Select Cttee on Foreign Affairs and Defence 2009, mem. Cttee on Culture, Science and Educ., Sub-cttee on Youth and Sport, Alt. mem. Cttee on Equal Opportunities for Women and Men, Sub-cttee on Equal Participation of Women and Men in Decision-making, Sub-cttee on Science and Ethics, PASOK Co-ordinator of Educ. and Culture Issues; Commr of Maritime Affairs and Fisheries, EC, Brussels 2010–14; Global Man. Dir for Oceans, The Nature Conservancy 2014–; mem. Political Council of PASOK, responsible for Educ. 2004–06, Social Affairs 2006–07, and Culture 2008–09; mem. Group of the Unified European Left; Section Man., Dept of Energy and Waste Man., Helector SA 2003–04. *Publications include:* The Female Face of Power 1995, The Return of Politics 2001, Associative Democracy 2004, The University in Transition 2006. *Leisure interests:* cinema, reading. *Address:* The Nature Conservancy, Outer Circle, Regent's Park, London, NW1 4RY, England (office); Filothei 24, Thisseos Street, Athens, Greece (home). *Telephone:* (210) 3707000 (home). *Fax:* (210) 3692170 (home). *E-mail:* office@damanaki.net; info@nature.org (office). *Website:* www.nature.org (office); www.damanaki.gr.

DAMASCENO ASSIS, HE Cardinal Raymundo; Brazilian ecclesiastic; b. 15 Feb. 1937, Capela Nova, Minas Gerais; ordained priest, Diocese of Brasília, DF 1968; Auxiliary Bishop of Brasília 1986–2004; Titular Bishop of Nova Petra 1986–2004; Archbishop of Aparecida, São Paulo 2004–16; cr. Cardinal (Cardinal-Priest of Immacolata al Tiburtino) 2010; Pres. Nat. Conference of Bishops of Brazil 2011–15; participated in Papal Conclave 2013. *Address:* c/o Curia Metropolitana, Rua Barao do Rio Branco 412, C.P. 82, 12570-000 Aparecida, São Paulo, Brazil (office).

D'AMATO, Alfonse M., BA, LLB; American lawyer, business executive and fmr politician; *Founder and Managing Director, Park Strategies LLC;* b. 1 Aug. 1937, Brooklyn, New York; s. of Armand D'Amato and Antoinette D'Amato (née Ciofarri); m. 1st Penelope Ann Collenburg 1960 (divorced); two s. two d. m. 2nd Katuria Elizabeth Smith 2004; one s. one d.; ed Syracuse Univ.; Receiver of Taxes, Town of Hempstead 1971–72, Supervisor, Hempstead 1972–78, Presiding Supervisor 1978–81; Vice-Chair. Nassau County Bd of Supervisors 1977–80; Senator from New York 1981–98, mem. Banking, Housing and Urban Affairs Cttee (Chair. 1995), Finance Cttee, Appropriations Cttee; Founder and Man. Dir Park Strategies LLC (business devt consultancy), New York 1999–; mem. Bd of Dirs Computer Associates Int. Inc. 1999–; commentator, Fox News Channel, Bloomberg Radio. *Publication:* Power, Pasta and Politics (autobiography) 1995. *Address:* Park Strategies LLC, 101 Park Avenue, Suite 2506, New York, NY 10178, USA (office). *Telephone:* (212) 883-5608 (office). *Website:* www.parkstrategies.com (office).

DAMAZER, Mark David, CBE, BA; British university administrator and fmr broadcasting executive; *Master, St Peter's College, Oxford;* b. 15 April 1955; s. of Stanislaw Damazer and Suzanne Damazer; m. Rosemary Jane Morgan 1981; one s. one d.; ed Gonville and Caius Coll., Cambridge, Harvard Univ., USA; trainee with ITN 1979–81; Producer BBC World Service 1981–83, TV-AM 1983–84, BBC Six O'Clock News 1984–86, Output Ed. Newsnight 1986–88, Deputy Ed., Nine O'Clock Main Evening News 1988–89, Ed. 1989–94, Ed. TV News 1994–96, Head of Current Affairs 1996–98, Head of Political Programmes 1998–2000, Asst Dir BBC News 1999–2001, Deputy Dir 2001–04, Controller BBC Radio 4 and BBC Radio 7 2004–10; Master, St Peter's Coll., Oxford 2010–; mem. Bd Inst. of Contemporary British History; Fellow, American Political Soc. 1978–79; Vice-Chair. and mem., Int. Press Inst.; Fellow, Radio Acad. 2008; Harkness Fellowship. *Television:* mem. winning team for Gonville and Caius Coll. on Christmas University Challenge (BBC) 2013. *Publications:* articles in various newspapers and magazines. *Leisure interests:* opera, Tottenham Hotspur Football Club, Boston Red Sox, gardening, coarse tennis, Italian painting. *Address:* St Peter's College, New Inn Hall Street, Oxford, OX1 2DL, England (office). *Telephone:* (1865) 278900 (home). *Fax:* (1865) 278855 (office). *E-mail:* masters.pa@spc.ox.ac.uk (office). *Website:* www.spc.ox.ac.uk/whos-here/academic/mark-damazer (office).

D'AMBROSIO, Louis J., BS, MBA; American business executive; ed Pennsylvania State Univ. (Valedictorian), Harvard Business School; with IBM Corpn 1986–2002, held several exec. posts and was mem. Worldwide Man. Cttee, roles included leading strategy for Global Services, Sales and Marketing for Software, and Industry Operations for Asia Pacific; Group Vice-Pres., Avaya Global Services, Avaya Inc. 2002–03, Group Vice-Pres., Global Sales, Channels and Marketing 2004–05, Sr Vice-Pres. and Pres. Global Sales and Marketing 2005–06, mem. Bd of Dirs, Pres. and CEO Avaya Inc. 2006–08; Pres. and CEO Sears Holdings Corpn 2011–13; mem. Bd of Dirs Sensus 2010–, Chair. 2013–; fmr Chair. (non-exec.) Sensus (clean technology co.); Trustee, Jackson Laboratory, Walnut Street Theatre.

D'AMICO DE CARVALHO, Caterina; Italian film industry executive, screenwriter and academic; *CEO, RAI Cinema SpA;* b. Rome; d. of Fedele d'Amico and Suso Cecchi d'Amico; began career working as a theatre company dir, Rome 1972–76; Dean of Centro Sperimentale di Cinematografia (nat. film school) 1999–2007; CEO RAI Cinema SpA (film production and distribution arm of govt-run Italian broadcaster RAI) 2007–; Founding mem. and Pres. Théatre des Italiens Foundation 1998–2003. *Films:* Luchino Visconti (consultant) 1999, My Voyage to Italy (assoc. producer) 2001. *Address:* RAI Cinema SpA, Piazza Adriana 12, 00193 Rome, Italy (office). *Telephone:* (06) 684701 (office). *E-mail:* info@raicinema.it (office). *Website:* www.raicinema.it (office).

DAMON, Matt; American actor; b. 8 Oct. 1970, Cambridge, Mass.; m. Luciana Barroso 2005; three d.; Chairman's Award, Palm Springs Int. Film Festival 2016. *Films include:* Mystic Pizza 1988, Rising Son (TV) 1990, School Ties 1992, Geronimo: An American Legend 1993, The Good Old Boys (TV) 1995, Courage Under Fire 1996, Glory Daze 1996, Chasing Amy 1997, The Rainmaker 1997, Good Will Hunting (also co-writer) (Acad. Award for Best Writing, Screenplay written directly for Screen, Silver Berlin Bear Award for Outstanding Single Achievement 1997) 1997, Saving Private Ryan 1998, Rounders 1998, Dogma 1999, The Talented Mr Ripley 1999, Titan A.E. (voice) 1999, All the Pretty Horses 1999, The Legend of Baggar Vance 2000, Finding Forrester 2000, Ocean's Eleven 2001, The Majestic (voice) 2001, Gerry (also writer) 2002, Spirit: Stallion of the Cimarron (voice) 2002, The Third Wheel 2002, The Bourne Identity 2002, Confessions of a Dangerous Mind 2003, Stuck on You 2003, Eurotrip 2004, Jersey Girl 2004, The Bourne Supremacy (Empire Film Award for Best Actor 2005) 2004, Ocean's Twelve 2004, The Brothers Grimm 2005, Syriana 2005, The Departed 2006, The Good Shepherd 2006, Ocean's Thirteen 2007, The Bourne Ultimatum 2007, The Informant! 2009, Invictus 2009, Green Zone 2010, 30 Rock 2010, Hereafter 2010, True Grit 2010, The Adjustment Bureau 2011, Contagion 2011, Margaret 2011, Happy Feet Two (voice) 2011, We Bought a Zoo 2011, Promised Land 2012, Behind the Candelabra 2013, Elysium 2013, The Monuments Men 2014, Interstellar 2014, The Martian (Golden Globe Award for Best Performance in Motion Picture – Musical or Comedy 2016) 2015. *Address:* WME, 9601 Wilshire Blvd, Beverly Hills, CA 90210, USA (office).

DAMRAU, Diana; German singer (soprano); b. 1971, Günzburg an der Donau; m. Nicolas Testé; two s.; ed Musikhochschule Würzburg, studied with Carmen Hanganu in Würzburg and Hanna Ludwig in Salzburg; began her career with performances in Würzburg, Mannheim and Frankfurt; particularly associated with roles from Mozart, Strauss and the Italian bel canto repertory; debuts at Royal Opera Covent Garden as Queen of the Night in Mozart's Die Zauberflöte 2003 and at Metropolitan Opera as Zerbinetta in Strauss's Ariadne auf Naxos 2005; has performed with leading conductors, including Zubin Mehta, Lorin Maazel, Sir Colin Davis, Christoph von Dohnányi, Adam Fischer, Ivor Bolton, Nikolaus Harnoncourt, Pierre Boulez, Placido Domingo, Gianandrea Noseda, Yannick Nézet-Séguin, Sir Antonio Pappano, Peter Schneider, among others; regular appearances at the world's leading opera houses, including Teatro alla Scala, Milan, Opéra de Paris, Bayerische Staatsoper, Deutsche Oper Berlin, Opernhaus Zürich, Wienerstaatsoper, LA Opera, Teatro Real de Madrid, and many others; regular appearances at Salzburg Festival, Kissinger Sommer, Munich and Schubertiade Schwarzenberg Festivals; numerous Lied-duo song concerts with Argentinian baritone, Iván Paley; Artist-in-Residence, Barbican Centre, London 2018/19; Bayerischer Maximiliansorden für Wissenschaft und Kunst 2010, Bayerischer Verdienstorden 2016, Kammersängerin of the Bavarian State Opera; Bavarian Culture Prize 2007, Bayerische Europa-Medaille 2008, Int. Opera Awards Best Female Singer 2014, Echo Klassik ohne Grenzen Prize 2014, Österreichischer Musiktheaterpreis 2016. *Operatic roles include:* Marzelline in Beethoven's Fidelio, title role in Donizetti's Lucia di Lammermoor, title role in Donizetti's Maria Stuarda, Small Woman in Cerhas' Der Riese vom Steinfeld, title role in Massenet's Manon, Queen of the Night in Mozart's Die Zauberflöte, Contessa in Mozart's Nozze di Figaro, Konstanze in Mozart's Die Entführung aus dem Serail, Zerbinetta in Strauss's Ariadne auf Naxos, Fiakermilli and Zdenka in Strauss's Arabella, Adele in Strauss's Die Fledermaus, Aithra in Strauss's Die Ägyptische Helena, Sophie in Strauss's Der Rosenkavalier, Violetta in Verdi's La traviata, Gilda in Verdi's Rigoletto. *Recordings include:* Des Knaben Wunderhorn, Schumann's Myrten, Der Riese vom Steinfeld, Mozart's Zaide, Salzburger Liederabend 2005, Schubertiade 2006, Arie di Bravura by Mozart, Salieri and Righini 2007, Mozart's Donna 2008, Liszt Lieder 2011, Forever 2013, Mozart: Die Entführung aus dem Serail (with Chamber Orchestra of Europe) 2015, Fiamma del Belcanto 2015, Meyerbeer Grand Opera 2017, Wolf: Italienisches Liederbuch (with Jonas Kaufmann) 2019. *Address:* c/o Christina Sienel, Hilbert Artists Management, Maximilianstrasse 22, 80539 Munich, Germany (office). *Telephone:* (89) 29074750 (office). *Fax:* (89) 29074790 (office). *E-mail:* sienel@hilbert.de (office). *Website:* www.hilbert.de (office); www.diana-damrau.com.

DAMSTÉ, Jaap S. Sinninghe, PhD; Dutch geochemist and academic; *Professor of Organic Geochemistry, Utrecht University;* b. 1959, Baarn; ed Tech. Univ. of

Delft; Researcher, Royal Netherlands Inst. for Sea Research (NIOZ), currently Head of Dept; Prof. of Organic Geochemistry, Utrecht Univ.; also Dir Netherlands Earth System Science Centre; mem. Royal Netherlands Acad. of Arts and Sciences; Spinoza Grant, Netherlands Org. for Scientific Research (NWO) 2004, Advanced Grant, European Research Council 2008, Dr A.H. Heineken Prize for Environmental Sciences, Royal Netherlands Acad. of Arts and Sciences 2014. *Publications:* author or co-author of more than 600 published papers. *Address:* Department of Earth Sciences, Faculty of Geosciences, Utrecht University, PO Box 80.021, 3508 TA Utrecht (office); Aardwetenschappen, Budapestlaan 4, Room NIOZ, 3584 CD Utrecht, The Netherlands (office). *Telephone:* (30) 2535105 (office); (30) 2535005 (office); (222) 369550 (NIOZ) (office). *Fax:* (30) 2535302 (office). *E-mail:* j.s .sinninghedamste@uu.nl (office); jaap.damste@nioz.nl (office); damste@nioz.nl (office). *Website:* www.uu.nl (office); www.nioz.nl (office).

DAN, Carmen Daniela, MA; Romanian politician; *Minister of Internal Affairs;* b. 9 Oct. 1970, Bucharest; ed Ziua Kosmodemianskaia High School of Philology and History, Bucharest, Ecological Univ. of Bucharest, Acad. of Econ. Studies; Sec. Provisional Council of Nat. Unity March–Sept. 1990; Sec.-Gen. School No. 3, Videle 1990–96; Adviser to Bank Agricola, Videle 1996–2001; Front Office Teller, Raiffeisen Bank, Videle 2001–02; Legal Adviser to Teleorman Co. Council Legal Service 2002–10; Exec. Dir Public Community Service, Teleorman Co. Council 2010–12; Sub-prefect of Teleorman Co. 2012–14, Prefect 2014–16; elected Senator and named Pres., Senate Legal Cttee for Appointments, Discipline, Immunities and Validations Dec. 2016; mem. Partidul Social Democrat (PSD—Social Democratic Party); Minister of Internal Affairs 2017–. *Address:* Ministry of Internal Affairs, 010086 Bucharest 1, Piaţa Revoluţiei 1A, Romania (office). *Telephone:* (21) 2648526 (office). *Fax:* (21) 2648677 (office). *E-mail:* petitii@mai.gov.ro (office). *Website:* www.mai.gov.ro (office).

DAN, Nicuşor Daniel, PhD; Romanian mathematician and political activist; *Leader, Uniunea Salvaţi România (Save Romania Union);* b. 20 Dec. 1969, Făgăraş; ed Univ. of Bucharest, École Normale Supérieure, Univ. Paris-XIII; won gold medals at Int. Mathematics Olympiad 1987, 1988; f. Asociaţia Tinerii pentru Acţiune Civică (Young People for Civic Action Asscn) 1998; co-f. Şcoala Normală Superioară Bucureşti 2000, Exec. Dir 2006, currently Prof. of Math.; Researcher, Simion Stoilow Mathematical Inst. of the Romanian Acad.; cand. for Mayor of Bucharest 2011, 2016; Gen. Counsel of Bucharest July–Dec. 2016; mem. Chamber of Deputies for Bucharest 42 constituency 2016–; f. Asociaţia Salvaţi Bucureştiul (Save Bucharest Asscn) 2006 (renamed Uniunea Salvaţi România—Save Romania Union 2016). *Address:* Uniunea Salvaţi România, Str. Carol Davila 91, Bucharest, Romania (office). *E-mail:* nicusor.dan@cdep.ro (office). *Website:* usr.ro (office); nicusordan.ro.

DAN-ALI, Brig.-Gen. (retd) Mansur, MPPA; Nigerian government official and fmr military commander; *Minister of Defence;* b. 25 Aug. 1959, Birnin Magaji, Zamfara State; m.; c.; ed Kaduna Polytechnic, Bayero Univ., Kano, Nigeria Defence Acad., Kaduna; commissioned as Lt Dec. 1984, served in different capacities in both command and staff including as Capt., 311 Artillery, Epe Area, Battery Capt., Adjutant and Battery Commdr 1985–88, Co. Commdr/Instructor, Nigeria Defence Acad. (NDA) 1994–96, Gen. Officer Training, HQ Nigerian Army Corps of Artillery 1996–98, Gen. Staff Officer (Examination), Army HQ Operations 1998–2000, Directing Staff, Armed Forces Command and Staff Coll. 2003–05, Col (Courses), Army HQ, Abuja 2005–06, Commdr, 301 Artillery Regt (Gen. Support), Gombe 2006–08; fmr Commdr, Nigerian Bn, UN–African Union Mission in Darfur (UNAMID); Chief Instructor, NDA 2010; Commdr, 32 Artillery Brigade, Akure 2012–13; retd from Nigerian Army 30 Aug. 2013; Minister of Defence 2015–; Forces Meritorious and Distinguished Service Stars, Pass Staff Course (Dagger) Command Medal, Field Command Medal, Silver and Golden Jubilee Medals, Sarkin Yakin Zamfara, Zamfara State Council. *Leisure interests:* horse riding (polo), jogging. *Address:* Ministry of Defence, Ship House, Central Area, Area 10, Garki, Abuja, Nigeria (office). *Telephone:* (9) 2340534 (office). *Fax:* (9) 2340714 (office). *E-mail:* mamed@nigeria.gov.ng (office). *Website:* www.defence.gov.ng (office).

DANA, Thierry; French diplomatist and business consultant; b. 23 Aug. 1956; two c.; ed Ecole nat. d'admin, Institut d'etudes politiques; first posting to Algiers 1984–86, Dept of North Africa and the Middle East, Ministry of Foreign Affairs (MFA) 1987–88, assigned to Sub-Directorate of Strategic Affairs 1988, Deputy Dir 1990–93, Deputy Diplomatic Advisor to the Prime Minister 1993–95, Sec.-Gen. Summit of Industrialized Countries (Lyon summit) 1995, Consul-Gen. in Hong Kong 1996–98, joined Office of Pres. of the Repub., in charge of Asian and Strategic Issues 1998–2002, Dir, Dept of Asia and Oceania, MFA 2002–05; est. consulting firm providing services to groups, French SMEs and foreign investors in France 2005–14; Amb. to Japan 2014–17; Chevalier, Ordre nat. du Mérite.

DANAILOV, Stefan, MA; Bulgarian actor and politician; b. 12 Sept. 1942, Sofia; ed Krastyo Sarafov Nat. Acad. for Theatre and Film Arts; currently Prof., Nat. Acad. of Theatre and Film Arts; mem. Nat. Ass. 2001–, (mem. Parl. Cttee on Culture 2001–); Minister of Culture 2005–09; mem. Bulgarian Socialist Party; Order of Stara Planina, Commdr, l'Ordre des Arts et des Lettres 2006; Paisiy Hilendarsky (Ministry of Culture) 2002. *Plays:* prominent roles include Camille Demolen, The Danton Case (Psibishevska), Stylo, Banzy is Dead (Ethole Fewgard), Edmond, Long Day's Journey into the Night (Eugene O'Neill), Chadski, Blame His Misfortunes on His Wits (Griboedov), Hamlet (Shakespeare), Stavrogin, The Possessed (Dostoyevsky), Peer Gynt (Ibsen), Shylock, The Price (Arthur Miller), Alessandro Medici, Lorenzaccio (Alfreу de Musset), Danton, Danton's Death (Buchner), Trigorin, The Seagull (Chekhov). *Films:* The Traces Remain 1956, The Inspector and the Night 1963, Quiet Paths 1967, The Sea 1967, Taste of Almonds 1967, The First Courier 1968, The Prince 1970, The Black Angels 1970, There Is Nothing Finer Than Bad Weather 1971, Affection 1972, Ivan Kondarev 1974, Houses Without Fences 1974, Glow Over the Drava River 1974, Life or Death 1974, The Weddings of King Ioan Assen 1975, A Real Man 1975, Beginning of the Day 1975, The Soldier of the Supply Column 1976, Guilt 1976, Amendment to the Defense-of-State Act 1976, RMS Five 1977, A Year of Mondays 1977, Warmth 1978, Moments in a Matchbox 1979, Something Out of Nothing 1979, The Porcupines' War 1979, The Blood Remains 1980, Ladies Choice 1980, The Queen of Turnovo 1981, Autumn Sun 1982, Crystals 1982, Twenty-Four Hours Raining 1982, The Odyssey in the Deliorman 1983, Balance 1983, Blood That Had to Be Shed 1985, The Conversion to Christianity & Discourse of Letters 1985, Manoeuvres on the Fifth Floor 1985, Misty Shores 1986, Transports of Death 1986, Three Marias and Ivan 1986, Ballad 1986, Dreamers 1987, A Sky for All 1987, The Mooncalf 1987, Protect the Small Animals 1988, Monday Morning 1988, The Carnival 1990, I Want Amerika 1991, The Berlin Conspiracy 1992, Crisis in the Kremlin 1992, Don Quixote Returns 1996, A Spanish Fly 1998, After the End of the World 1998, Vercingétorix 2001, The Lark Farm 2007, St. George Shoots the Dragon 2008. *Television:* At Each Kilometer (series) 1969–71, Dying in the Worst 1978, Oncoming Traffic 1978, Time for Travelling 1987, Home for Our Children 1987, Big Game 1988, People Who Never Disappear 1988, The Black Frames 1989, Live Dangerously 1990, Fathers and Sons 1990, In fondo al cuore 1997, Racket 1997, Fine secolo 1999, Aleph 2000, Forgive Us 2003. *Address:* National Assembly, 1169 Sofia, pl. Narodno Sobranie 2, Bulgaria. *Fax:* (2) 981-31-31. *E-mail:* prof.st .danailov@parliament.bg. *Website:* www.parliament.bg.

DANCE, Charles, OBE; British actor, writer and film director; b. 10 Oct. 1946, Rednal, Worcs., England; s. of Walter Dance and Eleanor Perks; m. Joanna Haythorn 1970; one s. one d.; worked in industry; with RSC 1975–80, 1981–92; Best Actor, Paris Film Festival 1996. *Theatre includes:* Coriolanus (title role) (RSC) 1989, Irma La Douce, Turning Over, Henry V, Three Sisters 1998, Good 1999, Long Day's Journey Into Night 2001, The Play What I Wrote 2002, Eh Joe (Sydney Theatre Festival), Shadowlands 2007–08 (London Theatre Critics Circle Best Actor Award 2008). *Films include:* For Your Eyes Only 1981, Plenty 1985, The Golden Child 1986, White Mischief 1987, Good Morning, Babylon 1987, Hidden City 1987, Pascali's Island 1988, La valle di pietra 1992, Alien 3 1992, Last Action Hero 1993, Century 1993, China Moon 1994, Kabloonak 1994, Desvío al paraíso 1994, Exquisite Tenderness 1995, Potemkin: The Runner's Cut (short) 1996, Space Truckers 1996, Michael Collins 1996, The Blood Oranges 1997, What Rats Won't Do 1998, Hilary and Jackie 1998, Chrono-Perambulator (short) 1999, Don't Go Breaking My Heart 1999, Jurij 2001, Dark Blue World 2001, Gosford Park 2001, Ali G Indahouse 2002, Black and White 2002, City and Crimes 2003, Swimming Pool 2003, Labyrinth 2003, Ladies in Lavender (writer and dir) 2004, Dolls (short) (narrator) 2006, Scoop 2006, Starter for 10 2006, Désaccord parfait 2006, Twice Upon a Time 2006, The Contractor (video) 2007, Intervention 2007, The Clerk's Tale (short) 2010, Paris Connections 2010, The Commuter (short) 2010, The Mapmaker (short) 2011, Ironclad 2011, There Be Dragons 2011, Your Highness 2011, The Door (short) 2011, Winds of Change 2011, Underworld: Awakening 2012, St George's Day 2012, Midnight's Children 2012, Viy. Vozvrashchenie 2013. *Radio:* The Heart of the Matter 2001, The Charge of the Light Brigade 2001. *Television appearances include:* Father Brown (series) 1974, Edward the Seventh (series) 1975, Raffles (series) 1977, Tales of the Unexpected (film) 1979, BBC2 Playhouse (series) – Fatal Spring (as Siegfried Sassoon) 1980, Nancy Astor (mini-series) 1982, Frost in May (mini-series) 1982, BBC Play of the Month (series) – Little Eyolf 1982, The Last Day (film) 1983, The Professionals (series) 1983, The Jewel in the Crown (mini-series) 1984, Play for Today (series) – Dreams of Leaving 1980, – Rainy Day Women 1984, The Secret Servant (series) 1984, Thunder Rock (film) 1985, This Lightning Always Strikes Twice (film) 1985, Screen Two (series) 1986, Out on a Limb (film) 1987, Tales of the Unexpected (series) 1987, Out of the Shadows (film) 1988, First Born (mini-series) 1988, Goldeneye (film) 1989, The Lancaster Miller Affair (mini-series) 1990, The Phantom of the Opera (film) 1990, Undertow (film) 1996, Rebecca (film) 1997, In the Presence of Mine Enemies (film) 1997, Murder Rooms: Mysteries of the Real Sherlock Holmes (series) 2000, Justice in Wonderland (film) 2000, Randall & Hopkirk (Deceased) (series) 2000, The Life and Adventures of Nicholas Nickleby (film) 2001, Foyle's War (series) 2002, Trial & Retribution (series) 2003, Henry VIII (film) 2003, Looking for Victoria (film) 2003, When Hitler Invaded Britain (documentary) (narrator) 2004, Don Bosco (film) 2004, Last Rights (mini-series) 2005, Fingersmith (series) 2005, Titanic: Birth of a Legend (documentary) (narrator) 2005, To the Ends of the Earth (mini-series) 2005, Bleak House (mini-series) 2005, Marple: By the Pricking of My Thumbs (film) 2006, Fallen Angel (mini-series) 2007, Consenting Adults (film) 2007, Jam & Jerusalem (series) 2009, Merlin (series) 2009, Trinity (series) 2009, Going Postal (film) 2010, This September (series) 2010, Neverland (mini-series) 2011, Game of Thrones (series) 2011–12, Strikeback (series) 2012, Coup (series) 2012. *Address:* Angharad Wood, Tavistock Wood, 45 Conduit Street, London, W1S 2YN, England (office). *Telephone:* (20) 7494-4767 (office).

DĂNCILĂ, Vasilica Viorica; Romanian engineer and politician; *Prime Minister;* b. 16 Dec. 1963, Roşiorii Vede; m. Cristinel Dăncilă; one c.; ed Faculty of Hydrocarbon Drilling and Exploitation, Ploiesti, Nat. School of Political and Admin. Studies, Bucharest; Engineer, OMV Petrom SA Oil and Gas Production Monitoring Service, Videle Br. 1988–2009; Teacher, Industrial High School, Videle 1989–97; mem. Videle Local Council (Partidul Social Democrat—PSD—Social Democratic Party) 2004–08; mem. Teleorman County Council (PSD) 2008–09; MEP 2009–18, Vice-Chair., European Parl. Agric. and Rural Devt Cttee 2014–18; Prime Minister of Romania (first female) 2018–; Pres. Org. of Social Democratic Women 2015–; mem. PSD 1996–, Pres. Videle Municipality PSD Org. 2003–11, mem. PSD Nat. Standing Bureau 2015–. *Address:* Office of the Prime Minister, 011791 Bucharest 1, Piaţa Victoriei, Romania (office). *Telephone:* (21) 3143400 (office). *Fax:* (21) 3139846 (office). *E-mail:* drp@gov.ro (office). *Website:* www.gov.ro (office).

D'ANCONA, Matthew, BA, FRSA; British journalist, writer and editor; b. 1968, London; m. Sarah Schaefer; two s.; ed St Dunstan's Coll., Magdalen Coll., Oxford; fmrly worked for human rights magazine, Index on Censorship; trainee, news reporter, education correspondent The Times 1991–94, Asst Ed. 1994–95; Deputy Ed. comment section and political columnist The Sunday Telegraph 1996–98, Deputy Ed. 1998–2006, now political columnist; Ed. The Spectator 2006–09; political columnist, GQ magazine 2006–09, now Contributing Ed.; columnist, Evening Standard 2009–, The Guardian; mem. Bd of Dirs Centre for Policy Studies 1998–2006; Prize Fellow, All Souls Coll., Oxford 1989–96, now Quondam Fellow; mem. Advisory Council, Demos 1998–2006, Millennium Comm. 2001–06, Policy Advisory Bd, Social Market Foundation 2002–06, Puttnam Comm. on Parliament in the Public Eye 2004–05; Charles Douglas-Home Memorial Trust Prize 1995, British Press Award for Political Journalist of the Year 2004, Editor of the Year (Current Affairs), British Soc. of Magazine Editors 2007. *Publications include:* The Jesus Papyrus (non-fiction, with Carsten Peter Thiede) 1997, The Quest for the True Cross (non-fiction, with Carsten Peter Thiede) 2002, Going East (novel) 2004,

Tabatha's Code (novel) 2006, Nothing to Fear 2008. *Address:* Evening Standard, Northcliffe House, 2 Derry Street, London, W8 5EE, England. *Website:* www.standard.co.uk/biography/matthew-d-ancona; www.theguardian.com/profile/matthew-dancona.

DANDA, Mahamadou; Niger politician; b. 25 July 1951, Tahoua; m.; six c.; ed Ecole Nat. d'Admin, Niamey; also studied in Bordeaux, France, Burkina Faso and Canada; Sub-Prefect of Niamey 1979–80, of Filingué 1983–87; Minister of Animal Resources and Hydraulics 1987–88; fmr Admin. Sec., Nat. Exec. Bureau, Mouvement nat. pour la société de développement; Chief Tech. Adviser for Institutional Issues to the Prime Minister 1997–99; Minister of Communication, Culture, Youth and Sports, also Govt Spokesman April–Dec. 1999; Political Counsellor, Canadian Embassy, Niamey 2009–10; Prime Minister of Niger 2010–11. *Address:* c/o Office of the Prime Minister, BP 893, Niamey, Niger.

DANELIUS, Hans Carl Yngve; Swedish judge and diplomatist; b. 2 April 1934, Stockholm; s. of Sven Danelius and Inga Danelius (née Svensson); m. Hannah Schadee 1961; three s. one d.; ed Dept of Legal Studies, Stockholm Univ.; law practice in Swedish courts 1957–64; mem. Secr., European Comm. of Human Rights (ECHR), Strasbourg 1964–67, mem. ECHR 1983–99; Asst Judge, Svea Court of Appeal 1967–68; Adviser, Ministry of Justice 1968–71; Deputy Head, Legal Dept, Ministry for Foreign Affairs 1971–75, Head 1975–84, rank of Amb. 1977–84; Amb. to the Netherlands 1984–88; Judge, Supreme Court of Sweden 1988–2001; Pres. Council on Legislation 2001–03; Arbitrator, ICSID 1999–2013; mem. Perm. Court of Arbitration at The Hague 1982–2012; mem. Court of Conciliation and Arbitration, OSCE 1995–2007; mem. Constitutional Court of Bosnia and Herzegovina 1996–2002; Chief Ed. Svensk Juristtidning (Swedish Law Journal) 1973–84; numerous Swedish and foreign decorations; Dr hc (Stockholm) 1988. *Publications include:* The United Nations Convention against Torture 1988, Mänskliga Rättigheter (Human Rights) (fifth edn) 1993, Mänskliga Rättigheter i Europeisk Praxis (Human Rights in European Practice) (fifth edn) 2015; numerous articles in Swedish and foreign journals. *Address:* Roslinvägen 33, 16851 Bromma, Sweden (home). *Telephone:* (8) 37-34-91 (home). *Fax:* (8) 37-34-91 (home). *E-mail:* hans.danelius@telia.com.

DANES, Claire Catherine; American actress; b. 12 April 1979, New York, NY; d. of Chris Danes and Carla Danes; m. Hugh Dancy 2009; ed performing arts school, NY and Lee Strasberg Studio; first acting roles in off-Broadway theatre productions: Happiness, Punk Ballet and Kids on Stage. *Plays include:* The Vagina Monologues (Westside Theatre) 2000, Christina Olson: American Model (Performance Space 122) 2005, Edith and Jenny (Performance Space 122) 2007, Pygmalion (American Airlines Theatre) 2007. *Films include:* Dreams of Love (debut) 1992, Thirty (short) 1993, The Pesky Suitor (short), Little Women 1994, Romeo and Juliet (London Film Critics Circle Award for Actress of the Year 1996, MTV Movie Award for Best Female Performance 1996) 1996, To Gillian on Her 37th Birthday 1996, Polish Wedding, U-Turn 1997, The Rainmaker 1997, Les Misérables 1998, The Mod Squad 1999, Brokedown Place 1999, Monterey Pop 2000, Dr T and the Women 2000, Flora Plum 2000, The Cherry Orchard 2002, Igby Goes Down 2002, The Hours 2002, Terminator 3: Rise of the Machines 2003, Stage Beauty 2004, Shopgirl 2005, The Family Stone 2005, Evening 2007, The Flock 2007, Stardust 2007, Me and Orson Welles 2008, As Cool as I Am 2013. *Television includes:* My So-Called Life (series) (Golden Globe Award for Best Actress – Television Series Drama 1994), No Room for Opal (film), The Coming Out of Heidi Leiter, Temple Grandin (film) (Primetime Emmy Award for Outstanding Lead Actress in a Miniseries or a Movie 2011, Golden Globe Award for Best Performance by an Actress in a Mini-series or Motion Picture Made for TV 2011, Screen Actors Guild Award for Outstanding Performance by a Female Actor in a Miniseries or Television Movie 2011) 2010, A Child's Garden of Poetry (film, voice) 2011, Homeland (series) (Golden Globe Award for Best Performance by an Actress in a Television Series – Drama 2012, 2013, Emmy Award for Best Lead Actress in a Drama 2012, 2013) 2011–. *Address:* c/o ICM, Constellation Boulevard, Los Angeles, CA 90067, USA (office). *Telephone:* (310) 550-4000 (office). *Website:* www.icmtalent.com (office).

DANESH JAFARI, Davoud, PhD; Iranian government official; b. 1954, Tehran; ed Regional Eng Coll., Srinagar (affiliated to Indian Univ. of Kashmir), Allameh Tabatabaei Univ., Tehran; expert Construction Jihad, Tehran Prov. 1979, later Commdr Eng Section, with Cen. HQ for Reconstruction 1983, Head, Logistics and Eng HQ, Construction Jihad 1984, mem. Cen. Council 1988; Man. Dir Inst. for Devt Jihad 1988; Deputy Minister of Construction Jihad for Reconstruction of Gilan and Zanjan Provs 1989, for Reconstruction of Palm Groves 1990, for Planning 1992; mem. Parl.; Minister of Econ. Affairs and Finance 2005–08; Gov., Islamic Development Bank; mem. High Monetary and Credit Council, High Council on Banks; Medal of Honour. *Address:* c/o Ministry of Economic Affairs and Finance, Bab Homayoon Street, Imam Khomeini Square, Tehran, Iran. *E-mail:* media@mefa.gov.ir.

DANEV, Bojidar, MSc, PhD; Bulgarian economist and business executive; *Executive President, Bulgarian Industrial Association;* b. 5 Nov. 1939, Sofia; ed Tech. Univ., Sofia; began career at Inst. of Cybernetics, Bulgarian Acad. of Sciences, attained rank of Sr Research Assoc.; worked for two years at Univ. of Hanover, Germany; returned to Bulgaria 1980 to work as expert in Econ. Analysis Dept, Bulgarian Industrial Econ. Asscn (now Bulgarian Industrial Asscn) 1980–87, Vice-Pres. 1989–91, Chair. and Exec. Pres. 1993–; Vice-Chair. on financial issues, Cen. Cooperative Union 1987–89; Man. Sofia Stock Exchange 1991–97; Co-Chair. EU-Bulgaria Jt Consultative Cttee 1999–2004; Vice-Pres. Econ. and Social Council of Repub. of Bulgaria and of Nat. Council of Tripartite Cooperation 2006–, mem. European Econ. and Social Cttee 2007–, Head of working group on Lisbon Strategy; mem. Man. Cttee Bulgarian Acad. of Sciences; Vice-Pres. New Bulgarian Univ. Bd; Exec. Dir and mem. Man. Bd, Interlease AD 1995–; mem. Man. Bd Solvay-Sodi AD, Industrial Holding Bulgaria, Doverie Insurance Co.; and Chair., Industrial Holding Bulgaria AD; Exec. Chair. Bulgarian Industrial Asscn 2011–. *Publications:* three monographs and more than 150 articles in scientific publs. *Address:* Bulgarian Industrial Association, 1000 Sofia, 16–20 Alabin Str., Bulgaria (office). *Telephone:* (2) 9800303 (office). *Fax:* (2) 9872604 (office). *E-mail:* danev@bia-bg.com (office). *Website:* www.bia-bg.com (office).

DANFORTH, John Claggett, AB, BD, LLB; American politician, lawyer, diplomatist and ecclesiastic; *Partner, Dowd Bennett LLP;* b. 5 Sept. 1936, St Louis, Mo.; s. of Donald Danforth and Dorothy Danforth (née Claggett); m. Sally B. Dobson 1957; one s. four d.; ed St Louis County Day (High) School, Princeton Univ., Yale Univ. Law School and Yale Divinity School; admitted to New York Bar 1963, Mo. Bar 1966; with Davis Polk (law firm) 1963–66; Pnr, Bryan Cave LLP (law firm) 1966–68, 1995–2004, 2005–15; Attorney-Gen. of Mo. 1969–76; Senator from Missouri 1976–95; Head of Special Envoy to Sudan 2001–04; US Perm. Rep. to UN, New York 2004 (resgnd); Partner, Dowd Bennett LLP, St Louis 2015–; ordained priest, Episcopal Church 1964, Asst or Assoc. Rector of churches in New York City, St Louis, Jefferson City; Assoc. Rector, Church of the Holy Communion, University City, Mo. 1995–; Chair. Mo. Law Enforcement Assistance Council 1973–74; Asst Chaplain, Memorial Sloan-Kettering Cancer Center, New York; Asst Rector, Church of Epiphany, New York; Sr Fellow, Bipartisan Policy Center; Hon. Assoc., St Alban's Church, Washington, DC; Hon. Board mem. Wings of Hope; numerous awards including Presidential World Without Hunger Award, Legislative Leadership Award of Nat. Comm. against Drunk Driving, Brotherhood and Distinguished Missourian awards of Nat. Conf. of Christians and Jews. *Film appearance:* The Devil Came on Horseback 2006. *Publications include:* Resurrection: The Confirmation of Clarence Thomas 1994, Faith and Politics: How the Moral Values Debate Divides America and How to Move Forward Together 2006, The Relevance of Religion 2015. *Address:* Dowd Bennett LLP, 7733 Forsyth Blvd, Suite 1900, St. Louis, MO 63105, USA (office). *Telephone:* (314) 889-7342 (office). *E-mail:* jdanforth@dowdbennett.com (office). *Website:* www.dowdbennett.com (office).

DANG, Thi Ngoc Thinh; Vietnamese party official and politician; *Acting President;* b. 25 Dec. 1959, Quang Nam Prov.; m.; two s.; mem. Dang Cong San Viet Nam (Communist Party of Viet Nam) 1979–, becoming Vice-Head, Office of the Party Cen. Cttee; mem. 11th Nat. Ass. (Parl.) 2002–07, 13th Nat. Ass. 2011–16, mem. Foreign Relations Cttee; mem. Exec. Cttee, Provincial Standing Cttee and Deputy Sec. of Provincial Party Cttee, Vinh Long 2009, Sec. 2010–15; Vice-Pres., Viet Nam Women's Union 2007–12; Vice-Pres. of Viet Nam 2016–, Acting Pres. (following death of Tran Dai Quang) Sept. 2018–. *Address:* Office of the Vice-President, No. 2 Hung Vuong Street, Ba Dinh District, Hanoi, Viet Nam (office). *Telephone:* 08043176 (office). *Fax:* 0437335256 (office). *Website:* chinhphu.vn (office); vpctn.gov.vn/Pages/trangchu.aspx.

DANGOTE, Aliko; Nigerian business executive; *Group President and CEO, Dangote Group;* b. 10 April 1957, Kano; s. of Mohammed Dangote and Mariya Sanusi Dantata; m.; two c.; ed Al-Azhar Univ., Egypt; began career trading in commodities including flour, sugar, rice and cement; Founder, Group Pres. and CEO Dangote Group (manufacturing conglomerate active in numerous fields including cement plants, sugar refineries, salt processing facilities, beverage manufacture) 1977–; Officer, Order of Niger 2000, Commdr, Order of Niger 2005; ZIK Award 1992, Int. Award of Sir Ahmadu Bello, Cross River State Roll of Honour Award 2002, Thisday Newspapers Award for CEO of the Year 2005. *Address:* Dangote Group, Union Marble House, 1 Alfred Rewane Road, PMB 40032, Falomo, Ikoyi, Lagos, Nigeria (office). *Telephone:* (1) 4480815 (office); (1) 4480816 (office). *Fax:* (1) 2702893 (office); (1) 2712231 (office). *E-mail:* communications@dangote-group.com (office). *Website:* www.dangote-group.com (office).

DANIEL, Sir John Sagar, Kt, OC, MA, MAEdTech, ATh, DèsSc; British/Canadian academic, university administrator and international organization official; *Chancellor, Acsenda School of Management;* b. 31 May 1942, Banstead, Surrey, England; s. of John Edward Daniel Sagar and Winifred Sagar; m. Kristin Anne Swanson 1966 (died 2011); one s. two d.; ed Christ's Hosp., Sussex and St Edmund Hall, Oxford, UK, Univ. of Paris, France, Concordia Univ., Canada; Assoc. Prof., Ecole Polytechnique, Université de Montréal 1969–73; Dir des Etudes, Télé-Univ., Université de Québec 1973–77; Vice-Pres. Athabasca Univ., Alberta 1977–80; Academic Vice-Rector Concordia Univ. 1980–84; Pres. Laurentian Univ., Sudbury 1984–90; Vice-Chancellor Open Univ., UK 1990–2001; Pres. Open Univ., USA 1999–2001; Asst Dir-Gen. for Educ., UNESCO 2001–04; Pres. and CEO Commonwealth of Learning 2004–12; mem. Council of Foundation, Int. Baccalaureate 1992– (Vice-Pres. 1996–99), British North American Cttee 1995–2001; Chair. Int. Bd United World Colls (UWC) 2012–18; Chancellor, Acsenda School of Man. 2018–; mem. Council, Open Univ., Hong Kong 1996–2001, CBI 1996–98; mem. Bd Canadian Council on Learning 2005–12; Trustee, Carnegie Foundation for the Advancement of Teaching 1993–99; Forum Fellow, World Econ. Forum, Switzerland 1998; Fellow, Open Univ. (UK); Sr Fellow, European Distance Educ. Network 2007; Hon. Fellow, St Edmund Hall, Oxford; Officier, Ordre des Palmes académiques; 32 hon. degrees, including Hon. DLitt (Indira Gandhi Nat. Open, India) 2003, (Thompson Rivers, Canada) 2005, (Netaji Subhas Open, India) 2005, (McGill Univ., Canada), (Univ. of South Africa) 2010, (Univ. of Ghana) 2013; Hon. DSc (Coll. Mil. Royal, Saint-Jean) 1988, (Open Univ. of Sri Lanka) 1994, (Univ. of Paris VI) 2001 (Univ. of Winneba, Ghana) 2006; Hon. DEd (Open Univ. Malaysia) 2009, (Empire State Coll., State Univ. of NY) 2011; Hon. LLD (Waterloo, Canada) 1993, (Univ. of Wales) 2002, (Laurentian Univ. Canada) 2006, (Univ. Canada West) 2008; Hon. DUniv (Univs of Athabasca, Portugal, Humberside, Anadolu Univ., Turkey, Sukhothai Thammathirat Open Univ., Thailand, Télé-université, Université du Québec, Canada, Univ. of Derby, Open Univ., Hong Kong, New Bulgarian Univ., Univ. of Montréal); Individual Award of Excellence, Commonwealth of Learning 1995, Morris T. Keeton Award, Council for Adult and Experiential Learning (USA) 1999, Queen's Jubilee Medal (Canada), Symons Medal, Asscn of Commonwealth Univs 2008, Frank H. Klassen Award of the Int. Council for Education for Teaching 2009, Educ. Master, Beijing DeTao Masters Acad. 2011. *Publications:* more than 350 articles and books, including Learning at a Distance: A World Perspective 1982, Developing Distance Education (co-author) 1988, Mega-universities and Knowledge Media: Technology Strategies for Higher Education 1996, Mega-Schools, Technology and Teachers: Achieving Education for All 2010. *Leisure interests:* walking, reading, swimming. *E-mail:* odlsirjohn@gmail.com. *Website:* www.sirjohn.ca; www.acsenda.com (office).

DANIEL, Patrick, BA (Hons), MPA; Singaporean journalist and newspaper executive; *Editor-in-Chief, English and Malay Newspapers Division, Singapore Press Holdings Ltd;* ed Univ. Coll., Oxford, UK, Kennedy School of Govt, Harvard Univ., USA; with Singapore Govt's Admin. Service, including post of Dir in Ministry of Trade and Industry –1986; Sr Leader/Feature Writer, The Straits

Times Press Ltd 1975, Econs Ed., The Straits Times 1989, Man. Ed. 1990–92, Ed. The Business Times 1992–2002, Man. Ed. English and Malay Newspapers Div., Singapore Press Holdings Ltd 2002–06, Ed.-in-Chief 2006–. *Address:* Singapore Press Holdings Ltd, SPH News Centre, P2M, 1000 Toa Payoh North, Singapore City, 318994, Singapore (office). *Telephone:* 6319-5111 (office). *Fax:* 6319-8282 (office). *E-mail:* pdaniel@sph.com.sg (office). *Website:* www.sph.com.sg (office); www.straitstimes.com (office).

DANIEL, Hon. Wilmoth; Antigua and Barbuda politician and auctioneer; b. 18 Aug. 1948, Bolans; m.; one s. one d.; ed Hill Secondary School; fmr Man. Brysons Wholesale Dept, Bottling Plant and Building Supplies Dept; United Nat. Democratic Party cand. in St Phillip's South Constituency 1984; Senator in Upper House 1989–94; mem. Parl. for St Phillip's South 1994–99, 2004–; Deputy Prime Minister and Minister of Works, Transportation and the Environment 2004, later Minister of Health, Social Transformation and Consumer Affairs; Co-founding mem. and currently Deputy Leader of United Progressive Party. *Address:* United Progressive Party (UPP), UPP Headquarters Bldg, Upper Nevis St, POB 2379, St John's, Antigua (office). *Website:* www.uppantigua.com/leadership/daniel (office).

DANIELS, J(ohn) Eric, BA, MSc; American banker; b. 14 Aug. 1951, Mont.; ed Cornell Univ., Massachusetts Inst. of Tech.; joined Citibank 1975, Corp. Banking, Panama City 1975–80, Chief Financial Officer and Br. Man. of 15 brs in Argentina 1980–82, Business Man. Citibank, Chile 1982–85, Country Head, Citibank, Argentina 1985–88, Divisional Exec. Citibank Private Bank, London 1988–91, Head, Citibank Corp. Taskforce (charged with restoring bank's profitability) NY 1992, Pres. FSB Calif. (Citibank consumer franchise) San Francisco 1992–96, Regional Head, Citibank Consumer Bank Europe, Brussels 1996–97, COO Citigroup Consumer Bank NY 1998, Chair. and CEO Travelers Life & Annuity, Hartford, Conn. 1998–2000; Founder, Chair. and CEO Zona Financiera 2000–01; Group Exec. Dir UK Retail Banking Lloyds TSB 2001–03, Group Chief Exec. Lloyds TSB Group plc (renamed Lloyds Banking Group plc following acquisition of HBOS plc 2009) 2003–11; Dir (non-exec.) BT Group. *Address:* c/o Lloyds Banking Group plc, 25 Gresham Street, London, EC2V 7HN, England.

DANIELS, Jeff; American actor; *Executive Director, Purple Rose Theatre;* b. 19 Feb. 1955, Athens, Ga; m. Kathleen Treado; 3 c.; ed Cen. Mich. Univ.; apprentice Circle Repertory Theatre, New York; f. Purple Rose Theatre Co., Chelsea, Mich. *Theatre:* The Farm 1976, Brontosaurus 1977, My Life 1977, Feedlot 1977, Lulu 1978, Slugger 1978, The Fifth of July 1978, Johnny Got His Gun 1982 (Obie Award), The Three Sisters 1982–83, The Golden Age 1984, Lemon Sky, Redwood Curtain 1993, Short-Changed Review 1993, Blackbird 2007, 2016, God of Carnage 2009–10, To Kill a Mockingbird 2018. *Films include:* Ragtime 1981, Terms of Endearment 1983, The Purple Rose of Cairo 1985, Marie 1985, Heartburn 1986, Something Wild 1986, Radio Days 1987, The House on Carroll Street 1988, Sweet Hearts Dance 1988, Grand Tour 1989, Checking Out 1989, Arachnophobia 1990, Welcome Home, Roxy Carmichael 1990, Love Hurts 1990, The Butcher's Wife 1992, Gettysburg 1993, Speed 1994, Dumb and Dumber 1994, Fly Away Home 1996, Two Days in the Valley 1996, 101 Dalmatians 1996, Trial and Error 1997, Pleasantville 1998, All the Rage 1999, My Favorite Martian 1999, Chasing Sleep 2000, Escanaba in da Moonlight 2000, Super Sucker 2002, Blood Work 2002, The Hours 2002, Gods and Generals 2002, I Witness 2003, Imaginary Heroes 2004, Because of Winn-Dixie 2005, The Squid and the Whale 2005, Good Night and Good Luck 2005, RV 2006, Infamous 2006, The Lookout 2007, Space Chimp (voice) 2008, Traitor 2008, Arlen Faber 2009, State of Play 2009, Away We Go 2009, Paper Man 2009, Howl 2010, Quad 2011, Looper 2012, Quad 2013, Dumb and Dumber To 2014, Steve Jobs 2015, The Martian 2015, The Divergent Series: Allegiant 2016, The Catcher was a Spy 2018. *Television includes:* A Rumor of War 1980, Fifth of July 1982, Invasion of Privacy 1983, The Caine Mutiny Court Martial 1988, No Place Like Home 1989, Disaster in Time 1992, Redwood Curtain 1995, Teamster Boss: The Jackie Presser Story, The Goodbye Girl 2004, The Five People You Meet in Heaven 2004, Sweet Nothing in My Ear (film) 2008, The Newsroom (series) (Emmy Award for Best Actor in a Drama 2013) 2012–14, Godless (Emmy Award for Outstanding Supporting Actor in a Limited Series or Movie 2018) 2017, The Looming Tower 2018. *Plays (author):* Shoeman 1991, The Tropical Pickle 1992, The Vast Difference 1993, Thy Kingdom's Coming 1994, Escanaba in da Moonlight 1995, Guest Artists 2005. *Address:* Purple Rose Theatre, 137 Park Street, Chelsea, MI 48118, USA (office). *Telephone:* (734) 433-7782 (office). *Fax:* (734) 475-0802 (office). *Website:* www.purplerosetheatre.org (office).

DANIELS, Mitchell (Mitch) Elias, Jr; American business executive, politician, fmr state governor and university administrator; *President, Purdue University;* b. 7 April 1949, Monongahela, Pa; s. of Mitchell Elias Daniels, Sr and Dorothy Mae Daniels (née Wilkes); m. Cheri Lynn Herman 1978 (divorced 1993, re-m. 1997); four d.; ed North Central High School, Indianapolis, Woodrow Wilson School of Public and Int. Affairs at Princeton Univ., Indiana Univ. School of Law, Georgetown Univ. Law Center; Chief of Staff to Richard Luger, Mayor of Indianapolis 1971–82; Exec. Dir Nat. Republican Senatorial Cttee 1983–84; political adviser and asst to Pres. Ronald Reagan and liaison with state and local officials, Washington, DC 1985–87; Exec. Vice-Pres. and COO Hudson Inst. 1987–90; also Pnr, Baker & Daniels (law firm); Vice-Pres. Corp. Affairs Eli Lilly and Co. 1990–93, Pres. N American Pharmaceutical Operations 1993–97, Sr Vice-Pres. of Corp. Strategy and Policy 1997–2001; Dir Office of Man. and Budget, Washington, DC 2001–03; Gov. of Indiana 2005–13; Pres. Purdue Univ. 2013–; Co-Chair. Nat. Research Council cttee to review and make recommendations on the future of the US human spaceflight programme 2013–14; mem. Bd of Dirs Energy Systems Network 2013–; Republican; eight hon. degrees, including Butler Univ., Rose-Hulman Inst. of Tech. and Wabash Coll.; Inaugural Medal for Distinguished Service to Educ., Woodrow Wilson Nat. Fellowship Foundation 2010, one of three recipients of the first Fiscy Award, Fiscy Awards Cttee, Real Leader Award, State Budget Solutions 2010, Friend of the Family Award Indiana Family Inst. 2011, Wetland Conservation Achievement Award, Ducks Unlimited 2011, Najeeb Halaby Award for Public Service, Arab-American Inst. 2011, Chancellor Award for Conservation and Wildlife Protection, Weatherby Foundation 2012, Theodore Roosevelt Award, Indiana Wildlife Fed. 2012, Woodrow Wilson Award, Princeton Univ. 2013, Bradley Prize, Lynde and Harry Bradley Foundation 2013, Excellence in Innovation Award, Centric's Indiana Innovation Network 2013. *Publications:* Notes from the Road 2004, Keeping the Republic: Saving America by Trusting Americans 2011. *Address:* Office of the President, Purdue University, Hovde Hall, Room 200, 610 Purdue Mall, West Lafayette, IN 47907-2040, USA (office). *Telephone:* (765) 494-4600 (office). *E-mail:* president@purdue.edu (office). *Website:* www.purdue.edu/president (office).

DANIELS, Ronald J., CM, BA, LLM, JD; Canadian professor of law and university administrator; *President, Johns Hopkins University;* b. 16 Aug. 1959; m. Joanne Rosen; four c.; ed Univ. of Toronto, Yale Univ. Law School; Asst Prof., Faculty of Law, Univ. of Toronto 1988–93, Assoc. Prof. 1993–99, Dean and James M. Tory Prof. of Law 1995–2002; John M. Olin Visiting Fellow, Cornell Univ. Law School 1993; Visiting Prof. and Coca-Cola World Fellow, Yale Univ. Law School 2003–04; Prof., Univ. of Pennsylvania Law School 2005–08, Provost 2005–08; Pres. Johns Hopkins Univ. 2009–; mem. Bd of Dirs, Moore Wallace Inc. 2001–, Rockwater Capital Corpn 2003–06, Brookfield Renewable Power 2004–08, Canwest Global Communications Corpn 2004–10; mem. American Philosophical Soc. 2018–, Mutual Fund Dealers Assen of Canada, Computershare Investor Services; Fellow, American Acad. of Arts and Sciences 2009–; Trustee Johns Hopkins Hospital, ACS Media Income Fund; mem. American Philosophical Soc. 2018; Carnegie Corporation Academic Leadership Award 2015. *Publications include:* Rethinking the Welfare State 2005, Rule of Law Reform and Development: Charting the Fragile Path of Progress (with Michael J. Treblicock) 2008; contrib. to various books, journals, articles. *Address:* Office of the President, Johns Hopkins University, 242 Garland Hall, 3400 N Charles Street, Baltimore, MD 21218, USA (office). *Telephone:* (410) 516-8068 (office). *Fax:* (410) 516-6097 (office). *E-mail:* rjdaniels@jhu.edu (office); president@jhu.edu (office). *Website:* www.president.jhu.edu (office).

DANIELS, William Burton, MS, PhD; American physicist and academic; *Unidel Professor Emeritus of Physics and Astronomy, University of Delaware;* b. 21 Dec. 1930, Buffalo, NY; s. of William C. Daniels and Sophia P. Daniels; m. Adriana A. Braakman 1958; two s. one d.; ed Univ. of Buffalo, Case Inst. (now Case-Western Reserve Univ.); Asst Prof. of Physics, Case Tech. 1957–59; Research Scientist, Union Carbide Corpn 1959–61; Asst Prof., Princeton Univ. 1961–63, Assoc. Prof. 1963–66, Prof. of Mechanical Eng 1966–72; Unidel Prof. of Physics, also of Astronomy, Univ. of Delaware 1972–2000, Unidel Prof. Emer. of Physics and Astronomy 2001–, Chair. Physics Dept 1977–80; Fellow, American Physical Soc.; John Simon Guggenheim Memorial Fellow 1976–77; Humboldt Sr Award 1982, 1992. *Publications:* more than 100 articles on the physics of solids at high pressures. *Leisure interests:* sailing, hiking. *Address:* Park Plaza Condos, Unit 1208, 1100 Lovering Avenue, Wilmington, DE 19806, USA (home). *Fax:* (302) 384-8720 (home). *E-mail:* family_daniels@hotmail.com (home).

DANILOV, Yuri Mikhailovich; Russian judge; *Constitutional Court Judge;* b. 1 Aug. 1950, Mukachevo, Ukraine; m.; two s. one d.; ed Voronezh State Univ.; fmr metalworker in Lugansk; People's Judge, Povorinsk Dist Court, Voronezh Region 1971–80; mem. Voronezh Regional Court 1980–83, Chair. 1985–89; instructor, Voronezh Regional CP Cttee 1983–85; First Deputy Head of Dept of Gen. Courts, USSR Ministry of Justice 1989–91, Deputy Minister of Justice 1991–92; Chief Jurist, Vice-Pres. Int. Food Exchange 1992–93; Deputy Chair. State Cttee on Anti-Monopoly Policy and Support of New Econ. Structures; Chair. Comm. on Stock Exchanges 1993–94; Judge Sec. Constitutional Court of Russian Fed. 1994–, mem. Second Chamber 1995–; Merited Jurist of Russian Fed.; Distinguished Jurist of the Russian Fed. *Address:* Constitutional Court of Justice of the Russian Federation, 103132 Moscow, Ilyinka str. 21, Russia (office). *Telephone:* (495) 206-16-29 (office). *Website:* www.ksrf.ru (office).

DANILOV-DANILYAN, Victor Ivanovich, DEcon; Russian politician; *Director, Institute of Aquatic Studies, Russian Academy of Sciences;* b. 9 May 1938, Moscow; m.; three s.; ed Moscow State Univ.; jr researcher, engineer, sr engineer, Computation Cen., Moscow State Univ. 1960–64; researcher, leading engineer, Head of Lab., Cen. Inst. of Math. and Econs, USSR Acad. of Sciences 1964–76; Head of Lab., Prof., All-Union Research Inst. of System Studies, USSR Acad. of Sciences 1976–80; Head of lab., Chair. Acad. of Nat. Econ., USSR Council of Ministers 1980–91; Deputy Minister of Nature Man. and Environmental Control of USSR Aug.–Nov. 1991, Minister of Ecology and Natural Resources, Russian Fed. 1991–92, of Environmental Control and Natural Resources 1992–96; Chair. Governmental Flood Control Comm. 1992–94, Governmental Comm. for Lake Baikal 1993–2000, Governmental Comm. for the Caspian Sea 1994–2000, State Cttee for Environmental Control 1996–; Pres.-Rector Int. Industrial Ecology and Political Univ. (MNEPU) 1991–; mem. State Duma (parl.) 1993–96; Founder and author, ecological programme of Kedr (Cedar) Movt 1994; Dir Inst. of Aquatic Studies and Corresp. mem. Russian Acad. of Sciences 2003–; Head of Dept of Industry and Natural Resources Man. and mem. Academic Council, Lomonosov Moscow State Univ. 2009–; Ed.-in-Chief, Encyclopedia Publishing House LLC 2007–; mem. Russian Acad. of Natural Sciences; Prize of the Govt of the Russian Fed. 1996. *Publications include:* author or co-author of more than 350 scientific publs, including 24 monographs, Ecological Problems in Russia (co-author) 1993, Ecological Problems on the Way to Integration of Russia and Europe (co-author) 1997, Ecological Challenge and Sustainable Development (co-author) 2000, Ecological Safety: The General Principles and Russian Aspect (co-author) 2001, Strategy and Problems of Sustainable Development in Russia in the 21st Century (co-author) 2002. *Address:* Institute of Aquatic Studies, Russian Academy of Sciences, 119333 Moscow, 3 Gubkina Street (office); MNEPU, 111250 Moscow, Krasnokazarmennaya str. 14, Russia (office). *Telephone:* (499) 135-54-56 (office); (495) 273-55-48 (office). *Fax:* (499) 135-54-15 (office). *E-mail:* tina@aqua.laser.ru (office). *Website:* www.iwp.ru (office).

DANILOVIĆ, Goran; Montenegrin journalist and politician; b. 1971, Podgorica; ed Faculty of Philosophy, Nikšić; Co-founder Radio Svetigore; fmr Ed. Glasa Crnogorca; mem. Nova Srpska Demokratija (NOVA—New Serbian Democracy), part of the Demokratski Front (DF—Democratic Front) coalition; mem. (DF) Parl.; Minister of Internal Affairs May–Nov. 2016. *Publication:* Riječi i reči (Words and Words; poetry collection) 2012. *Address:* c/o Ministry of Internal Affairs, 81000 Podgorica, bul. Svetog Petra Cetinjskog 22, Montenegro. *E-mail:* kabinet@mup.gov.me.

DANILOVICH, John Joseph, BA, MA; American business executive, international organization official, fmr diplomatist and fmr government official; b. 25

June 1950, California; m. Irene Forte; three c.; ed Choate School, Conn., Stanford Univ.; mem. Exec. Man. Bd, Atlas Interocean Shipping Group 1977–90; Partner and Consultant, Eisenhower Group 1987–90; Amb. to Costa Rica 2001–04, to Brazil 2004–05; CEO Millennium Challenge Corpn 2005–09; Sec.-Gen., ICC 2014–16; Chair. Asgaard Navigation LLP; mem. Bd of Dirs d'Amico International Shipping, Panama Canal Comm. 1991–96; mem. European Advisory Council, Trilantic Capital Partners LLP; fmr mem. Bd of Dirs Stanford Univ. Trust, US–UK Fulbright Comm.; mem. Advisory Bd Pelham Bell Pottinger; fmr Trustee American Museum in Britain; Life mem. Council on Foreign Relations, New York; mem. North American Advisory Council, Chatham House, UK; mem. American Acad. of Diplomacy; Orden Nacional Juan Mora Fernandez (Costa Rica), Companion, Order of Volta (Ghana), Grand Cordon du Ouissan Alaouite (Morocco).

DANIÑO ZAPATA, Roberto Enrique; Peruvian lawyer, politician and business executive; *Deputy Chairman, Hochschild Mining PLC;* b. 2 March 1951, Lima; ed Catholic Univ. of Peru, Harvard Univ., USA; fmr Sec.-Gen. Ministry of Economy, Finance and Trade; fmr Pres. Foreign Investment and Tech. Agency, Chair. Foreign Public Debt Comm.; Founding Gen. Counsel Inter-American Investment Corpn, Washington, DC, Chair. Inter-American Devt Bank's External Review Group for Pvt. Sector Operations; Pnr, Wilmer, Cutler & Pickering, Head of Latin American Practice Group 1996–2001; Pres. Council of Ministers (Prime Minister) of Peru 2001–02; Sec.-Gen. Int. Centre for Settlement of Investment Disputes 2003–06 (resgnd); currently Deputy Chair. Hochschild Mining PLC; fmr mem. Bd Newbridge Andean Partners, Royal & Sun Alliance/Fenix, Cementos Pacasmayo, Sindicato Pesquero, Violy, Byorum & Partners, The Mountain Inst., The Infant Nutrition Fund; fmr mem. The Coca-Cola Co. Latin American Advisory Bd, Americas Soc. Chair.'s Council, Carnegie Endowment's G-50 Bd. *Address:* Hochschild Mining PLC, Calle La Colonia No. 180, Urb. El Vivero Santiago de Surco, Lima 33, Peru (office).

DANISH, Mohammad Sarwar; Afghan politician; *Second Vice-President;* b. 1961, Daikundi Prov.; ed studied law and Islamic education in Qom, Iran, and in Iraq and Syria; worked in publishing 1982–2001; mem. Emergency Loya Jirga 2002, also mem. Constitutional Drafting Comm., Constitutional Loya Jirga; Gov. Daikundi Prov. 2004; Minister of Justice 2004–10, of Higher Educ. 2010–14; Second Vice-Pres. of Afghanistan 2014–. *Publications:* numerous books and essays. *Address:* c/o Office of the President, Gul Khana Palace, Presidential Palace, Kabul, Afghanistan (office). *Telephone:* (20) 2141135 (office). *E-mail:* aimal.faizi@arg.gov.af (office). *Website:* www.president.gov.af (office).

DANISHEFSKY, Samuel J., BS, PhD; American chemist and academic; *Professor, Department of Chemistry, Columbia University;* b. 10 March 1936, Bayonne, New Jersey; ed Yeshiva and Columbia Univs, Harvard Univ.; NIH postdoctoral fellowship, Columbia Univ. 1962; Asst Prof., Univ. of Pittsburgh 1964–68, Assoc. Prof. 1968–71, Prof. 1971–79, Univ. Prof. 1978–79; Prof., Yale Univ. 1979–93, Eugene Higgins Prof. 1983–89, Sterling Prof. 1989–93; Dir Sloan-Kettering Inst. for Cancer Research, Lab. for Bioorganic Chem. 1991–, Kettering Chair 1993–; Prof., Dept of Chem., Columbia Univ. 1993–; mem. NAS 1986, Connecticut Acad. of Sciences 1987; Fellow, Japanese Soc. for the Promotion of Science 1980, AAAS 1985; Hon. DSc (Yeshiva Univ.) 1987; ACS Guenther Award 1980, Arthur C. Cope Scholar 1986, ACS Aldrich Award for Creative Work in Synthetic Organic Chem. 1986, Edgar Fahs Smith Award, Philadelphia Section, ACS 1988, Pfizer Grad. Training Award 1991, Cliff Hamilton Award Univ. of Nebraska 1994, Max Tishler Prize Lecturer, Harvard Univ. 1995, Wolf Prize in Chem. (jtly) 1996, Tetrahedron Prize 1996, ACS Claude S. Hudson Award in Carbohydrate Chem. 1996, Allan Day Medal, Univ. of Pennsylvania 1997, ACS Cope Medal 1998, Paul Ehrlich Lecture Prize 1998, ACS Nichols Medal 1999, Nagoya Gold Medal 1999, ACS H.C. Brown Medal 2000, F.A. Cotton Medal 2001, New York City (Mayor's) Award for Science and Tech. 2003, Remsen Prize for Maryland Section, Johns Hopkins Univ. 2004, Benjamin Franklin Award in Chem. 2006, Bristol Myers Squibb Lifetime Achievement Award 2006, NAS Award in the Chemical Sciences 2006, ACS North Jersey Section Award for Creativity in Molecular Design and Synthesis 2006, ACS Roger Adams Award in Organic Chem. 2007, Inaugural Award for Chem. in Cancer Research, American Asscn for Cancer Research 2007. *Publications include:* numerous articles and research papers. *Address:* Department of Chemistry, Columbia University, 3000 Broadway, MC 3106, New York, NY 10027; Department of Bioorganic Chemistry, Sloan-Kettering Institute, 1275 York Avenue, New York, NY 10021, USA (office). *Telephone:* (212) 854-6195 (Columbia); (212) 639-5502 (office). *Fax:* (212) 854-7142 (Columbia) (office); (212) 772-8691 (home). *E-mail:* sjd15@columbia.edu (office); s-danishefsky@ski.mskcc.org (office). *Website:* www.columbia.edu/cu/chemistry (office); www.ski.edu/lab (office).

DANJUMA, Lt-Gen. (retd) Theophilus Yakubu; Nigerian business executive and fmr army official; *Chairman, South Atlantic Petroleum Ltd;* b. 9 Dec. 1938, Takum, Taraba State; s. of Kuru Danjuma and Rufkatu Asibi; m.; ed Benue Provincial Secondary School; commissioned into Army as Second Lt and Platoon Commdr in the Congo, later joined UN peacekeeping force in Sante, Kataga Province in Congo; promoted to Capt. 1966, Lt Col 1967, Col 1971, Brig. and GOC 1975, Chief of Army Staff 1975–79 (retd); rep. to International Court Martial, Trinidad and Tobago 1970; f. NAL-Comet Group 1979; Minister of Dfence 1999–2003; Founder-Chair. South Atlantic Petroleum Ltd 1995–, TY Danjuma Foundation 2008–; fmr Chair. Presidential Advisory Council; Grand Commdr, Order of Niger; Leadership Person of the Year 2011. *Address:* South Atlantic Petroleum Ltd, 11th and 12th Floor, South Atlantic Petroleum Towers, 1, Adeola Odeku Street, PO Box 73152, Victoria Island, Lagos, Nigeria (office). *Telephone:* (1) 2701906 (office). *Fax:* (1) 2701907 (office). *E-mail:* info@sapetro.com (office). *Website:* www.sapetro.com (office).

DANKO, Andrej, JUDr; Slovak lawyer and politician; *Speaker, National Council of the Slovak Republic (Národná Rada Slovenskej Republiky);* b. 12 Aug. 1974, Revúca, Slovak Socialist Repub., Czechoslovak Socialist Repub.; ed Comenius Univ., Bratislava; following compulsory mil. service, est. several commercial cos and worked as an ind. lawyer 1998–2003; attorney at law 2003–12, pvt. law practice 2012–16; Asst to MPs from Slovenská Národná Strana (SNS—Slovak Nat. Party), Nat. Council of Slovakia 2006–10, mem. several parl. comms, Speaker of Nat. Council 2016–; first Vice-Pres. SNS 2010–12, Chair. 2012–; promoted by eight ranks to Capt. in Slovak Army Reserve 2016. *Address:* Cabinet of the Speaker, Národná Rada Slovenskej Republiky (National Council of the Slovak Republic), nám. Alexandra Dubčeka 1, 812 80 Bratislava, Slovakia (office). *Telephone:* (2) 5972-1111 (office). *Fax:* (2) 5441-9529 (office). *E-mail:* andrej_danko@nrsr.sk (office); info@nrsr.sk (office). *Website:* www.nrsr.sk (office).

DANNATT, Baron (Life Peer), cr. 2011, of Keswick in the County of Norfolk; **(Francis) Richard Dannatt,** Kt, GCB, KCB, CBE, MC, BA, DL; British fmr army officer; *Constable of the Tower of London;* b. 23 Dec. 1950, Chelmsford, Essex, England; m. Philippa Margaret Gurney 1977; three s. one d.; ed Felsted School, Essex, St Lawrence Coll., Ramsgate, Hatfield Coll., Durham Univ.; fmr Pres. Durham Union Soc.; commissioned into The Green Howards 1971; has served with 1st Battalion in NI, Cyprus and Germany, Commdr in Airmobile role 1989–91; Commdr 4th Armoured Brigade in Germany and Bosnia 1994–96; Commdr 3rd (UK) Div. and Commdr British Forces in Kosovo 1999, Deputy Commdr, Operations of the Stabilisation Force (SFOR) 2000; Asst Chief of Gen. Staff, Ministry of Defence 2001–02; Commdr NATO Allied Rapid Reaction Corps 2002–05; C-in-C Land Command 2005–06; Chief of the Gen. Staff 2006–09; adviser on defence issues to Conservative Party 2009–10; Constable of the Tower of London 2009–; Sr Adviser, Control Risks PLC (specialist risk consultancy) 2010–, Ricardo PLC (technology, product innovation and strategic consulting) 2010–; writer, Telegraph Media Group; speaker, Celebrity Speakers Agency; Chair. Royal United Services Inst. 2009, Strategic Devt Bd Durham Global Security Inst.; Pres. Army Rifle Asscn, Army Rugby Union, Army Winter Sports Asscn, Soldiers' and Airmen's Scripture Readers Asscn, Norfolk Churches Trust 2011–; Vice-Pres. Armed Forces Christian Union, The Western Front Association 2013–; church-warden, Keswick and Intwood, Norfolk; Trustee, Historic Royal Palaces, Royal Armouries, Windsor Leadership Trust; mem. (Crossbench) House of Lords 2011–; Queen's Commendation for Valuable Service 1999; Hon. DCL (Univ. of Kent at Medway) 2009. *Publication:* Leading from the Front: The Autobiography 2010. *Leisure interests:* cricket, rugby, tennis, skiing, shooting, fishing, reading. *Address:* The Tower of London, London, EC3N 4AB (office); House of Lords, Westminster, London, SW1A 0PW, England (office). *Telephone:* (844) 482-7777 (from UK) (office); (20) 3166-6200 (from outside UK) (office); (20) 7219-5353 (House of Lords) (office). *E-mail:* dannattr@parliament.com (office); richarddannatt8@hotmail.com (home). *Website:* www.hrp.org.uk/TowerOfLondon (office); www.parliament.uk/biographies/lords/lord-dannatt/4220 (office).

DANON, Danny, MA; Israeli politician and diplomatist; *Permanent Representative to UN;* b. 8 May 1971, Ramat Gan; s. of Yosef Danon and Yoheved Danon; m.; three c.; ed Florida Int. Univ., Hebrew Univ. of Jerusalem; worked for Israel Defense Forces 1994–96; joined Likud-Nat. Liberal Movement 1996, Chair. Likud Party Cen. Cttee 2013; Chair. of Likud Faction, World Zionist Org. 2004–09; Chair. World Likud Org. 2006–15; mem. of Knesset 2009–15, Deputy Speaker 2009–12, also Chair., Cttee on the Rights of the Child, Cttee for Immigration, Absorption and Diaspora Affairs, mem. Foreign Affairs and Defence, Econ. Affairs, Educ., Constitution and Women's Rights Cttees; Deputy Minister of Defence 2013–14, Minister of Science, Tech. and Space 2014–15; Amb. and Perm. Rep. to UN 2015–; mem. Bd of Dirs Jewish Agency for Israel 2004–09. *Publication:* Israel: the Will to Prevail 2012. *Address:* Permanent Mission of Israel, 800 Second Avenue, New York, NY 10017, USA (office). *Telephone:* (212) 499-5510 (office). *Fax:* (212) 499-5515 (office). *E-mail:* UNInfo@newyork.mfa.gov.il (office).

DANON, Laurence; French business executive; *Chairman, Leonardo & Co. France;* m. Pierre Danon; two c.; ed Ecole Normale Superieur and Corps des Mines; started career at Ministry of Industry; joined Elf group 1989, Gen. Man. Bostik (Ato Findley) 1996, merged with Total in 1999; joined Printemps in 2001, Chair. Man. Bd and CEO France Printemps 2002–07 (led buyout of Printemps from PPR); mem. Exec. Bd Edmond de Rothschild Corp. Finance 2007–13, Chair. 2009–13; Co-Pres. Exec. Bd Leonardo & Co. France 2012–13, apptd Co-CEO 2013, currently Chair.; mem. Bd of Dirs Plastic Omnium 2003–10, Diageo PLC 2006–, Experian Group Ltd 2007–10, Rhodia SA 2008–11; Officier, Légion d'honneur, ordre du Mérite. *Address:* Leonardo & Co. SAS, 32, rue de Lisbonne, 75008 Paris, France (office). *Telephone:* 1-73-44-44-00 (office). *Fax:* 1-73-44-44-01 (office). *E-mail:* mailto.fr@leonardo-co.com (office). *Website:* www.leonardo-co.com (office).

DANSON, Ted; American actor; b. 29 Dec. 1947, San Diego, Calif.; s. of Edward Danson and Jessica McMaster; m. 1st Randall L. Gosch 1970 (divorced 1977); m. 2nd Cassandra Coates 1977 (divorced); two d.; m. 3rd Mary Steenburgen 1995; ed The Kent School, Connecticut and Stanford and Carnegie-Mellon Univs; teacher, The Actor's Inst. Los Angeles 1978; CEO Anasazi Productions (fmrly Danson/Fauci Productions). *Theatre includes:* The Real Inspector Hound 1972, Comedy of Errors. *Films include:* The Onion Field 1979, Body Heat 1981, Creepshow (segment Something To Tide You Over) 1982, Little Treasure 1985, Just Between Friends 1986, A Fine Mess 1986, 3 Men and a Baby 1987, Cousins 1989, Dad 1989, 3 Men and a Little Lady 1990, Made in America 1993, Getting Even with Dad 1994, Pontiac Moon 1994, Loch Ness 1996, Jerry and Tom 1998, Homegrown 1998, Saving Private Ryan 1998, Mumford 1999, Mrs. Pilgrim Goes to Hollywood 2002, Fronterz 2004, The Moguls 2005, Nobel Son 2007, Mad Money 2008, The Human Contract 2008, The Open Road 2009, Fight for Your Right Revisited (short) 2011, Jock (voice) 2011, Big Miracle 2012. *Television includes:* Somerset (series) 1975–76, The Doctors (series) 1977, The Amazing Spider-Man (series) 1979, Mrs. Columbo (series) 1979, The French Atlantic Affair (mini-series) (uncredited) 1979, B.J. and the Bear (series) 1979, Laverne & Shirley (series) 1980, Family (series) 1980, The Women's Room (film) 1980, Once Upon a Spy (film) 1980, Benson (series) 1981, Magnum, P.I. (series) 1981, Dear Teacher (film) 1981, Our Family Business (film) 1981, Taxi (series) 1982, Tucker's Witch (series) 1982, Cheers (series) 1982–93, Allison Sydney Harrison (film) 1983, Cowboy (film) 1983, Something About Amelia (film) 1984, When the Bough Breaks (film) 1986, We Are the Children (film) 1987, Mickey's 60th Birthday (film) 1988, The Simpsons (series) (voice) 1994, Frasier (series) 1995, Gulliver's Travels (film) 1996, Ink (series) (also producer) 1996–97, Pearl (series) 1997, Veronica's Closet (series) 1998, Becker (series) 1998–2004, Thanks of a Grateful Nation (film) 1998, Grosse Pointe (series) (voice) 2000, Curb Your Enthusiasm (series) 2000–09, Living with the Dead (film) 2002, Electric Playground (series) 2002, Gary the Rat (series) (voice) 2003, Surviving Love (film) 2004, Our Fathers (film) 2005, Knights of the South Bronx (film) 2005, Guy Walks Into a Bar (film) 2006, Bye Bye Benjamin (short) 2006, Heist (series) 2006, Help Me Help You (series) 2006–07, Damages (series) 2007–10, King of the Hill (series) 2008, Bored to Death (series) 2009–11, The Magic 7 (film) (voice) 2009, Tim and Eric Awesome Show, Great Job! (series) 2010, CSI: Crime Scene Investigation (series) 2011–12. *Address:* 10345 North Olympic Blvd, Suite 200, Los Angeles, CA 90054-2524, USA; c/o Josh Liberman, Creative Artists Agency, 2000 Avenue of the Stars, Los Angeles, CA 90067, USA (office). *Telephone:* (424) 288-2000 (office). *Fax:* (424) 288-2900 (office). *Website:* www.caa.com (office).

DANYLYSHYN, Bohdan Myhaylovich, DEcon; Ukrainian economist, academic and government official; b. 6 June 1965, Tserkivna, Dolyn dist, Ivano-Frankivsk Oblast; ed Ternopol State Pedagogical Inst.; Prof. of Econs 2003–; fmr Head of Council on Productive Forces Research, Nat. Acad. of Sciences of Ukraine; Minister of the Economy 2007–10; granted political asylum by Czech Repub. following charges of misusing public funds 2011; Corresp. mem. Nat. Acad. of Sciences of Ukraine 2004; State Prize of Ukraine in Science and Tech. *Publications include:* more than 150 scientific papers on regional policy, econs and exploration of nature resources.

DANYLYUK, Oleksandr Oleksandrovych, MBA; Ukrainian lawyer and politician; b. 22 July 1975, Grygoriopil, Moldova; ed Nat. Tech. Univ., Kyiv Polytechnical Inst., Kyiv Inst. for Investment Man., Indiana Univ. Kelly School of Business, USA; Man., TEKT (investment co.) 1995–96; Head of Dept, CJSC Alfa-Capital 1996–97; Deputy Investment Man., Western NIS Enterprise Fund Jan.–Aug. 1998; Vice-Pres., Avechurs Co. 2001–02; Sr Consultant, McKinsey and Co., London 2002–05; Adviser to Prime Minister of Ukraine 2005–06; CEO Rurik Investment (investment co.), London 2006–10; Head, Coordination Centre for the Implementation of Economic Reforms, Kyiv 2010–15; rep. of Pres. in Cabinet of Ministers 2014–16; Deputy Head, Admin of Pres. 2015–16; Minister of Finance 2016–18. *Address:* c/o Ministry of Finance, 01008 Kyiv, vul. M. Hrushevskoho 12/2, Ukraine (office).

DANYSZ, Magda; French art dealer and gallery director; *Owner/Director, Gallery Magda Danysz;* ed École Supérieure des Sciences Économiques et Commerciale (ESSEC); began in the art business early 1990s, opened first art space 1991; pursued a consulting career with Arthur Andersen 1997–2004, consultant for French retail group Carrefour; various posts with Ministry of Culture, Christie's, Theatre Marigny, Nantes Museum, the Louvre, others; Owner/Dir Gallery Magda Danysz, Paris 1999–, opened branch in Shanghai; has participated in numerous art fairs world-wide; has taught cultural policies and economics at Sciences Po, Paris 2001–; mem. Bd multimedia cultural art centre Le Cube, Issy-les-Moulineaux; Co-founder contemporary art fair ShowOff, Paris 2006; apptd to direct Bund 18 gallery in Shanghai, China 2009; Vice-Pres. Fashion Group International of Paris 2009–; mem. Comité Professionnel des Galeries d'Art 2002–, French Art Dealers Cttee, Friends of the Palais de Tokyo 2005–; Young Leader, French American Foundation 2009–; mem. Compagnie Nat. des Experts, apptd expert in Chinese contemporary art and street art 2010–; Chevalier des Arts et des Lettres 2007; ESSEC Alumni 1998. *Publications include:* has published an extensive anthology about street art entitled From Style Writing to Art. *Address:* Gallery Magda Danysz, 78 rue Amelot, 75011 Paris, France (office); Gallery Magda Danysz, 188 Linqing Road, Shanghai, People's Republic of China (office). *Telephone:* 1-45-83-38-51 (Paris) (office). *E-mail:* info@magda-gallery.com (office). *Website:* www.magda-gallery.com (office).

DAOUDA, Idrissou L.; Benin economist and politician; ed Univ. de Paris IX Dauphine, France; fmr Econ. Adviser to Govt of Benin; Prin. Economist and Head of Treasury Div., Banque Centrale des Etats de l'Afrique de l'Ouest (BCEAO), Dakar, Senegal 1977–91, Deputy Dir of Issue and Financial Operations 1991–96, Head of Cotonou Br. 1996–98, Nat. Dir for Benin, BCEAO 1998–2006; Adviser to Provisional Authority, Regulation des Postes et Télécommunications de Benin 2007–10; Minister of Economy and Finance 2010. *Address:* c/o Ministry of the Economy and Finance, BP 302, Cotonou, Benin. *E-mail:* sgm@finance.gouv.bj.

DAOUDI, Riad Rashad ad-, PhD; Syrian lawyer, professor of law, international arbitrator and university administrator; *President, Syrian Virtual University;* b. 22 July 1942, Damascus; s. of Rashad Daoudi and Adallat Fares; m. Viviane Collin 1978; two s. one d.; ed Institut des Hautes Etudes Internationales, Paris; Prof. of Int. Law, Damascus Law School 1978–91; Asst Dean for Academic Affairs, Faculty of Law, Univ. of Damascus 1980–82; lawyer, mem. Syrian Bar 1982–; Registrar, Judicial Tribunal OAPEC 1983, now lawyer and legal adviser, Registrar Judicial Tribunal OAPEC; Legal Adviser to Ministry of Foreign Affairs 1991–; mem. UN Int. Law Comm. 2001–06; currently Pres. Syrian Virtual Univ., Damascus; Lauréat, best doctoral thesis, Univ. of Paris 1977–78. *Publications:* Parliamentary Immunities: Comparative Study in Arab Constitutions (in Arabic) 1982, Peace Negotiations: Treaty of Versailles (textbook for law students, in Arabic) 1983, Arab Commission for Human Rights, An Encyclopedia of Public International Law (in English) 1985; articles and contribs to books on int. affairs and int. law. *Leisure interests:* tennis, reading. *Address:* Syrian Virtual University, Ministry of Higher Education, BP 9251, place Mezzeh Gamarik, Damascus (office); Dam Zoukak Al Sakhar Salim Al Sharah Street, Hadjar Building, 3rd Floor, Damascus, Syria (home). *Telephone:* (11) 2149-9531 (office). *Fax:* (11) 2149-9534 (office). *E-mail:* rdaoudi@svuonline.org (office). *Website:* www.svuonline.org (office).

DAR, Muhammad Ishaq, BCom; Pakistani economist and politician; b. 13 May 1950; ed Hailey Coll. of Commerce, Univ. of Punjab, Lahore, Inst. of Chartered Accountants in England and Wales (ICAEW); Dir of Finance British Textiles Group, London 1974–76; Sr Auditor, Auditor Gen. Dept 1976–77; returned to Pakistan 1977; apptd Nat. Pnr in a Charted Accounting Firm 1977, Financial Adviser to multinational construction Co. 1980; acted Chair./CEO of non-banking financial Inst. 1989–97; Chief Exec. Pakistan Investment Bd 1992–93; elected to National Assembly of Pakistan 1993–99; Minister of Commerce 1997–99, of Finance 1998–99, of Finance and for Econ. Affairs and Statistics March–May 2008, of Finance, Revenue, Econ. Affairs and Statistics and Privatization 2013–17, Minister of Finance, Revenue and Economic Affairs 2017–18; Chair. Bd of Govs Islamic Devt Bank 1998–99; Senator (Pakistan Muslim League—Nawaz) (PML—N) 2003–18, also PML—N Parl. Leader 2012–13; Pres. Int. Affairs, PML—N; Chair. Special Parliamentary Cttee on Election Reforms 2014–, Economic Coordination Cttee 2014–17, Standing Cttee Industries and Production, mem. Senate Finance Cttee, Exec. Cttee of Senate Employees Welfare Fund; Vice-Chair. Bd of Govs, Asian Dept Bank –2017, Univ. of Health Sciences, Punjab; Pres. Lahore Chamber of Commerce and Industry 1993; Fellow, ICAEW 1980 (life mem.) 2012–, Inst. of Chartered Accountants of Pakistan 1984, Inst. of Public Finance Accountants of Pakistan; mem. Bd of Govs Pakistan Inst. of Parl. Services; Nishan-e-Imtiaz 2011. *Address:* Apartment No.18, Minister's Enclave, Islamabad (home); 7-H, Gulberg-III, Lahore, Pakistan. *Telephone:* (42) 35881594 (office). *Fax:* (42) 35881521 (office). *E-mail:* minister@finance.gov.pk (office); mohammad.ishaq.dar@senate.gov.pk (office). *Website:* www.finance.gov.pk (office); www.senate.gov.pk (office).

DARABOS, Norbert, MA; Austrian politician; b. 31 May 1964, Vienna; m.; one s. one d.; ed Univ. of Vienna; Chief Exec. Dr.-Karl-Renner-Inst., Burgenland 1988–91; mem. Municipal Council of Nikitsch/Burgenland 1987–2003; Press Speaker for Gov. of Prov. of Burgenland Karl Stix 1991–98; mem. Diet of Burgenland 1999–2004, Pres. SPÖ Club 2000–03; Leader of Burgenland Prov. Social-Democratic Party of Austria—SPÖ 1998–2003, Sec.-Gen. Social Democratic Party of Austria 2003, Federal Man. 2013–; mem. Austrian Parl. for Burgenland Süd 2004–; Minister of Defence 2007–13, also of Sports 2008–13; Grosses Goldenes Ehrenzeichen am Bande für die Verdienste um die Republik Österreich 2010, National Order of Merit 2012. *Address:* Social Democratic Party of Austria, Löwelstraße 18, 1090 Vienna, Austria (office). *Telephone:* (1) 534-27 (office). *Fax:* (1) 535-96-83 (office). *E-mail:* norbert.darabos@spoe.at; direkt@spoe.at. *Website:* www.spoe.at (office).

DARAR HOUFFANEH, Hassan; Djibouti politician; b. 15 Oct. 1962, Wê'a, Arta Region; ed Ecole Nat. d'Admin, Paris, France; several years working in Ministry of Interior; fmr Second Deputy to Mayor of Djibouti, becoming First Deputy to Mayor of Djibouti; fmr Dir Population Office; Gov. Arta Region 1994; Minister of the Interior –2013, of Defence 2013–16. *Address:* c/o Ministry of Defence, BP 42, Djibouti, Djibouti (office).

DARBINYAN, Armen Razmikovich, DEcon; Armenian politician, university rector and scientist; *Rector and President, Russian-Armenian (Slavonic) University;* b. 23 Jan. 1965, Gyumri, Armenia; m.; one d.; ed Moscow State Univ.; Lecturer, Moscow State Univ. 1986–89; Sr Expert, Head of Dept, Perm. Mission of Armenia to Russian Fed., Plenipotentiary Rep., Intergovt Comm. on Debts of Vnesheconombank 1989–92; Dir-Gen. Armenian Foreign Trade Co. Armenintorg 1992–94; First Deputy Chair. Cen. Bank of Armenia 1994–97; Minister of Finance 1997, of Finance and Econs 1997–98; Prime Minister of Armenia 1998–99; Minister of Nat. Economy 1999–2000; Chair. Fund for Devt, Yerevan 2000–; Chair. Bd of Trustees, Int. Centre for Human Devt 2000–; Rector and Pres., Russian-Armenian (Slavonic) Univ. 2001–; mem. Russian Acad. of Natural Sciences 2002; Corresp. mem. Armenian Nat. Acad. of Sciences 2006; Commdr, World Order of Science, Educ. and Culture 2002, Order Mihailo Lomonosov, Russian Cttee for Public Awards 2006, Order of Friendship of the Russian Fed. 2010, Badge of Honour, Ministry of Foreign Affairs of the Russian Fed. and Rossotrudnichestvo 2014; recognized by the World Economic Forum as a Young World Leader 2006, Int. Socrates Award (Oxford) 2006, Commemorative Medal, Ministry of Educ. and Science 2006. *Publications:* over 60 publs, including Role of the State in Countries with Transition Economies, Economic Development: Prospects and Role of the Diaspora, from Stability to Economic Growth. *Leisure interests:* music and composing songs. *Address:* Russian-Armenian (Slavonic) University, ul. Hovsep Emin 123, Yerevan 0051, Armenia (office). *Telephone:* (10) 23-05-27 (RAU) (office). *Fax:* (10) 22-14-63 (ICHD) (office). *E-mail:* armen.darbinyan@rau.am (office). *Website:* rau.am/rector (office).

DARBOE, Ousainou N., LLB, BL, LLM; Gambian lawyer and politician; b. 8 Aug. 1948; ed Univ. of Ottawa, Canada, Fed. Law School, Lagos, Univ. of Lagos; State Counsel, Attorney Gen.'s Chambers, Banjul, Chief Prosecutor and Legal Adviser to Govt 1973–76, Acting Registrar-Gen. 1976–77; legal draftsman 1979–80; represented two-thirds of people detained under Govt's emergency powers regulations after 1981 abortive coup 1981–82, successfully defended leader of opposition Nat. Convention Party against charges of treason; est. pvt. legal practice, Banjul 1991; mem. Bd of Dirs Gambia Public Transport Corpn 1987–92; apptd mem. Nat. Advisory Cttee for nomination of judges to Int. Court of Justice 1992, OAU Observer team in Eritrean referendum 1993; apptd Vice-Pres. Gambian Bar Asscn 1991; apptd Deputy Chair. Gambia Law Reform Comm. 1992; Chair. Gambian Wrestling Fed. 1985–95, Bansang Yeriwa Kafo (charity) 1990; apptd First Vice-Pres. The Gambia Nat. Olympic and Sports Cttee 1989; Sec.-Gen. and Leader, United Democratic Party (UDP); unsuccessful cand. in presidential elections 1996, 2001, 2006, 2011; Minister of Foreign Affairs 2017–18; Vice-Pres. of the Gambia 2018–19. *Publications:* numerous articles in professional journals. *Address:* c/o Office of the Vice-President, State House, Banju, The Gambia (office).

D'ARCEVIA, Bruno; Italian painter and sculptor; b. 21 Oct. 1946, Arcevia, Ancona; s. of Benedetto Bruni and Amelia Filippini; m. Maria Falconetti 1972; one s. one d.; worked in France and Venezuela 1975–78; co-f. Nuova Maniera Italiana Movt 1982–83; one of 20 Italian artists included in ArToday review, London 1996; Commendatore, Ordine della Repubblica Italiana; Gold San Valentino Award, named Marchigiano dell'Anno 1998. *Leisure interests:* underwater fishing. *Address:* Vicolo del Monastero, 60011 Arcevia, Italy (office). *Telephone:* (07) 319050 (office); 333-7415883 (mobile). *E-mail:* info@brunodarcevia.com. *Website:* www.brunodarcevia.com; arakhnos.wix.com/brunodarcevia.

DARCHIEV, Alexander N.; Russian diplomatist; *Ambassador to Canada;* b. 1960; m.; one d.; ed Moscow State Univ.; postgraduate student, Jr, then Sr Research Fellow, Inst. of the US and Canada Studies, Russian Acad. of Sciences; joined Ministry of Foreign Affairs (MFA), Dept of North America 1992, First Sec., Head of Section, Dept of North America 1992–97, Counsellor, Embassy in Washington, DC 1997–2002, Deputy Dir, Dept of North America, MFA 2003–05, Deputy Chief of Mission, Embassy in Washington, DC 2005–10, Dir, Dept of North America, MFA 2010–14, Amb. to Canada 2014–; numerous decorations and awards. *Address:* Embassy of the Russian Federation, 285 Charlotte Street, Ottawa, ON K1N 8L5, Canada (office). *Telephone:* (613) 235-4341 (office). *Fax:* (613) 236-6342 (office). *E-mail:* info@rusembassy.ca (office). *Website:* www.rusembassy.ca (office).

DARCOS, Xavier, DèsL; French politician, scholar and civil servant; *Chancellor, Institut de France;* b. 14 Aug. 1947, Limoges (Haute-Vienne); s. of Jean-Gabriel Darcos and Anne-Marie Banvillet; m. 1st Marie-Lys Beaudry (deceased); one s. one d.; m. 2nd Laure Driant 1999; one s.; began career as teacher, Périgueux, at Lycée Montaigne, Bordeaux 1982–87, at Lycée Louis-le-Grand, Paris 1987–92; Insp.-Gen. of Educ. 1992–98; Assoc. Prof., Univ. de Paris-Sorbonne 1996; Counsellor, Ministry of Educ. 1993–94, 1995–97, Vice-Minister for School Educ. 2002–04, for Co-operation, Devt and Francophony 2004–05, Minister of Nat. Educ. 2007–09, of Labour, Social Relations, the Family and Solidarity 2009–10; Mayor of Périgueux 1997–2008; Senator for Dordogne 1998–2002, Vice-Pres. Senate Cultural Comm. 2001; Perm. Rep. to OECD 2005–07; mem. Acad. des sciences morales et politiques 2006 (Perpetual-Sec. 2010–16), Acad. française 2013, Acad. of Sciences 2017, Chancellor, Institut de France 2018–; Amb. for the foreign cultural policy of France 2010–15, for the influence of French abroad 2015–17; Exec.-Pres. l'Institut Français 2010–15; Pres. Défense de la langue française, DLF; mem. UNESCO Comm. for Educ., Science and Culture; Hon. mem. l'Observatoire du patrimoine religieux, Académie nationale des sciences, belles-lettres et arts de Bordeaux; Commdr, Légion d'honneur 2011, L'ordre des Arts et des Lettres 2014, L'ordre du Mérite de la République Italienne 2015, Officier de l'ordre national du Mérite, Grand Officier de l'ordre du Ouissam Alaouite, Morocco, Commdr des Palmes académiques. *Publications:* Histoire de la littérature française 1992, Approches ovidiennes de la mort 1995, Mérimée 1998, Robert des grands écrivains de langue française (co-author), L'Art d'apprendre à ignorer 2000, Dictionnaire des mythes féminins (co-author) 2002, Lettre à tous ceux qui aiment l'école (co-author) 2003, Deux voix pour une école (co-author) 2004, L'École de Jules Ferry (Prix Louis Pauwels 2006) 2005, L'État et les Églises, 1905–2005 2005, L'État et les Églises, la question laïque 2006, Tacite, ses vérités sont les nôtres 2007, La escuela republicana en Francia 2008, Peut-on améliorer l'école sans dépenser plus ? (with Vincent Peillon) 2009, Une anthologie historique de la poésie française 2010, Dictionnaire amoureux de la Rome antique 2011, La Poésie française 2012, Histoire de la littérature française 2013, Auguste et son siècle 2014, Jean-Pierre Angrémy, dit Pierre-Jean Remy 2015, Dictionnaire amoureux de l'École 2016, Dictionnaire amoureux de la Rome antique 2018. *Address:* Institut de France, 23 quai de Conti, 75006 Paris, France. *Website:* www.institut-de-france.fr.

DARCY LILO, Gordon; Solomon Islands politician; b. 28 Aug. 1965; ed Univ. of Papua New Guinea, Australian Nat. Univ.; fmr Perm. Sec. for Ministry of Finance, for Ministry of Forestry, Environment and Conservation; mem. Parl. (Peoples Alliance Party) for Gizo, Kolombangara 2001–14, Leader Ind. Group in Parl. 2001–06; Minister for Nat. Planning and Aid Co-ordination –2006, of Finance and Treasury 2006–07, 2010–11, for Justice and Legal Affairs Nov. 2007, for Environment and Conservation Dec. 2007–10, Prime Minister 2011–14; Chair. Forum Econ. Ministers Meeting 2006. *Address:* c/o Office of the Prime Minister, PO G1, Honiara, Solomon Islands (office).

DARDARI, Abdullah Abdel Razzaq ad-, BA, MA; Syrian politician, UN official and fmr journalist; *Senior Advisor on Reconstruction, Middle East and North Africa Division, World Bank;* b. 1963, Damascus; m.; three c.; ed Richmond American Int. Univ. of London, UK, Univ. of Southern California, USA, London School of Econs, UK; fmr head of bureau of Alhayat pan-Arab daily in Syria; later local deputy of UN Resident Rep.; fmr Chair. State Planning Comm.; Deputy Prime Minister, responsible for Econ. Affairs 2005–11 (resgnd with rest of cabinet at Pres.'s request following popular protests); Chief Economist and Dir of Econ. Devt and Globalization Div., UN Econ. and Social Comm. for Western Asia (ESCWA) 2011–14, Deputy Exec. Sec. ESCWA 2014–17; Sr Advisor on Reconstruction, Middle East and N Africa Div., World Bank 2017–; Dr hc (Yalova Univ., Istanbul). *Address:* World Bank (MENA Division), 1818 Street, Washington, DC 20433, USA (office). *E-mail:* mnateam@worldbank.org (office). *Website:* www.worldbank.org/en/region/mena (office).

DARDENNE, Jean-Pierre; Belgian film producer, director and screenwriter; b. (Carl Higgans), 21 April 1951, Liège; brother of Luc Dardenne; ed Arts Inst.; made several videos with his brother Luc about rough life in blue-collar small towns in the Wallonie 1970s; Pres. Jury Cannes Film Festival, Short Films 2000, Caméra d'Or 2006, Cinéfondation Jury 2012. *Films produced include:* Je pense à vous 1992, Faute de soleil (co-producer) 1995, L'héritier (exec. producer) 1999, Rosetta 1999, La devinière (documentary) (line producer) 2000, Le lait de la tendresse humaine (The Milk of Human Kindness) (co-producer) 2001, Le fils (The Son) 2002, Premier amour (First Love) 2002, Romances de terre et d'eau (documentary) 2002, Stormy Weather 2003, Le monde vivant (The Living World) (co-producer) 2003, Le soleil assassiné (The Assassinated Sun) 2003, Le couperet (The Ax) (co-producer) 2005, L'enfant (The Child) 2005, Mon colonel (The Colonel) 2006, Vous êtes de la police? (co-producer) 2007, Why We Can't See Each Other Outside When the Sun is Shining (documentary) 2007, Premier Jour (short) 2008, The Silence of Lorna 2008, The Front Line 2009, K.O.R. (documentary) 2010, The Kid with a Bike 2011, Beyond the Hills (co-producer) 2012, Two Days, One Night 2014, Vie sauvage (co-producer) 2014, Diary of a Chambermaid (co-producer) 2015, Long Live the Bride (co-producer) 2015, Inhebek Hedi (co-producer) 2016. *Films directed include:* Le chant du rossignol (documentary) 1978, Lorsque le bateau de Léon M. descendit la Meuse pour la première fois (documentary short) 1979, Pour que la guerre s'achève, les murs devaient s'écrouter (documentary) 1980, R… ne répond plus (documentary) 1982, Leçons d'une université volante 1982, Regard Jonathan/Jean Louvet, son oeuvre (documentary) 1983, Il court, il court, le monde (short) 1987, Falsch 1987, Je pense à vous (I Think of You) 1992, La promesse (The Promise) (numerous awards in many festivals) 1996, Gigi, Monica… et Bianca (documentary) 1997, Rosetta (Palme d'Or, Cannes Festival 1999) 1999, Le fils (The Son) (Ecumenical Jury Prize, Cannes Festival 2002) 2002, L'enfant (The Child) (Palme d'Or, Cannes Festival 2005, Best Foreign Film and co-winner Best Dir, Toronto Film Critics Asscn 2006) 2005, Le Silence de Lorna (Best Screenplay, Cannes Festival) 2008, The Kid with a Bike (Grand Prix, Cannes Festival) 2011, The Unknown Girl 2016. *Television includes:* Brook by Brook (documentary) (co-producer) 2002. *Address:* Cinéfondation, 3 rue Amélie, 75007 Paris, France. *Telephone:* 1-53-59-61-00. *Fax:* 1-53-59-61-10. *E-mail:* cinefondation@festival-cannes.fr. *Website:* www.cinefondation.com; www.festival-cannes.fr.

DARDENNE, Luc; Belgian film producer, director and screenwriter; b. (Eric Higgans), 10 March 1954, Liège; brother of Jean-Pierre Dardenne; ed Arts Inst.; made several videos with brother Jean-Pierre about rough life in blue-collar small towns in Wallonie 1970s. *Films produced include:* Nous étions tous des noms d'arbres 1982, Je pense à vous 1992, Faute de soleil (co-producer) 1995, Rosetta 1999, Les siestes Grenadine 1999, Le lait de la tendresse humaine (The Milk of Human Kindness) (co-producer) 2001, Le fils (The Son) 2002, Premier amour (First Love) 2002, Romances de terre et d'eau (documentary) 2002, Stormy Weather 2003, Le monde vivant (The Living World) (co-producer) 2003, Le soleil assassiné (The Assassinated Sun) 2003, Le couperet (The Ax) (co-producer) 2005, L'enfant (The Child) 2005, Mon colonel (The Colonel) 2006, Vous êtes de la police? (co-producer) 2007, Why We Can't See Each Other Outside When the Sun is Shining (documentary) 2007, Premier Jour (short) 2008, The Silence of Lorna 2008, The Front Line 2009, K.O.R. (documentary) 2010, The Kid with a Bike 2011, Beyond the Hills (co-producer) 2012, Two Days, One Night 2014, Vie sauvage (co-producer) 2014, Diary of a Chambermaid (co-producer) 2015, Long Live the Bride (co-producer) 2015, Inhebek Hedi (co-producer) 2016. *Films directed include:* Le chant du rossignol 1978, Lorsque le bateau de Léon M. descendit la Meuse pour la première fois 1979, Pour que la guerre s'achève, les murs devaient s'écrouter 1980, R… ne répond plus 1982, Leçons d'une université volante 1982, Regard Jonathan/Jean Louvet, son oeuvre 1983, Il court… il court le monde 1987, Falsch 1987, Je pense à vous (I Think of You) 1992, La promesse (The Promise) (numerous awards in many festivals) 1996, Rosetta (Palme d'Or, Cannes Festival 1999) 1999, Le fils (The Son) (Ecumenical Jury Prize, Cannes Festival 2002) 2002, L'enfant (The Child) (Palme d'Or, Cannes Festival 2005, Best Foreign Film and co-winner Best Dir Toronto Film Critics Asscn 2006) 2005, To Each His Own Cinema (segment Dans l'Obscurité) 2007, Le Silence de Lorna (Best Screenplay, Cannes Festival) 2008, The Kid with a Bike (Grand Prix, Cannes Festival) 2011, The Unknown Girl 2016. *Television includes:* Brook by Brook (co-producer) 2002. *Address:* Cinéfondation, 3 rue Amélie, 75007 Paris, France. *Telephone:* 1-53-59-61-00. *Fax:* 1-53-59-61-10. *E-mail:* cinefondation@festival-cannes.fr. *Website:* www.cinefondation.com; www.festival-cannes.fr.

DARLING OF ROULANISH, Baron (Life Peer), cr. 2015, of Great Bernara in the County of Ross and Cromarty; **Rt Hon Alistair Maclean Darling,** LLB; British lawyer and politician; b. 28 Nov. 1953, London; s. of Thomas Darling MP and Anna Darling; m. 2nd Margaret McQueen Vaughan 1986; one s. one d.; ed Loretto School, Musselburgh, East Lothian, Univ. of Aberdeen; Pres. Aberdeen Univ. Students Union; advocate 1978–82; mem. Faculty of Advocates 1984–2010 (resgnd); mem. Lothian Regional Council 1982–87 (Chair. Transport Cttee 1986–87), Lothian and Borders Police Bd 1982–86; Gov. Napier Coll., Edinburgh 1982–87; MP (Labour) for Edinburgh Cen. 1987–2005, for Edinburgh SW 2005–15; Opposition Spokesman on Home Affairs 1988–92, on Treasury Affairs 1992–96; Shadow Chief Sec. to HM Treasury 1996–97; Chief Sec. to HM Treasury 1997–98; Sec. of State for Social Security 1998–2001, for Work and Pensions 2001–02, for Transport 2002–06, and for Scotland 2005–06, for Trade and Industry 2006–07; Chancellor of the Exchequer 2007–10; mem. Econ. Affairs Cttee, House of Lords 2016–; Chair. Better Together Campaign 2012–14; Pres. Royal Inst. of Int. Affairs; mem. Bd of Dirs Morgan Stanley 2016–. *Publications:* Back from the Brink 2011. *Leisure interests:* listening to Pink Floyd, Coldplay, Leonard Cohen and US rock band The Killers. *Address:* House of Lords, London, SW1A 0PW, England (office). *Telephone:* (20) 7219-4584 (office). *E-mail:* alistair.darling.mp@parliament.uk (office). *Website:* www.alistairdarlingmp.org.uk.

DARMAATMADJA, HE Cardinal Julius Riyadi, SJ, BPhil; Indonesian ecclesiastic; *Archbishop Emeritus of Jakarta;* b. 20 Dec. 1934, Muntilan, Magelang, Cen. Java; s. of Joachim Djasman Darmaatmadja and Maria Soepartimah; ed Canisius Secondary School, Muntilan, St Peter Canisius Minor Seminary Nertoyudan, Magelang, St Stanislaus Coll., De Nobili Coll., Pontifical Athenaeum, Poona, India, St Ignatius Coll., Yogyakarta; entered St Stanislaus Novitiate of Soc. of Jesus, Giri Sonta-Klepu, Semarang 1957, took first vows 1959; teacher, St Peter Canisius Minor Seminary 1964–66, Vice-Prefect 1971–83, Rector 1977–81; ordained priest of Soc. of Jesus by Cardinal Justinus Darmojuwono, Archbishop of Semerang 1969; parish priest, Kalasan Parish, Yogyakarta 1971, Giri Sonta-Klepu 1971–73; Socius Magistri and House Minister, St Stanislaus Novitiate 1971–73; Socius Provincialis in Karangpanas 1973–77; Provincial of Indonesian Prov. of Soc. of Jesus 1981–83; Archbishop of Semarang 1983–96; Mil. Ordinary for Catholic Mems of Indonesian Armed Forces 1984–2006; Pres. Nat. Bishops' Conf. of Indonesia 1988–97, 2001; cr. Cardinal (Cardinal Priest of Sacro Cuore di Maria) 1994; Archbishop of Jakarta 1996–2010; participated in Papal Conclave 2005; Pres.-Del. Special Ass. for Asia, World Synod of Bishops 1998; del. to Ordinary Ass., World Synod of Bishops, Vatican 2001. *Address:* Archdiocese of Jakarta, Keuskupan Agung, Jl. Katedral 7, Jakarta 10710, Indonesia (office). *Telephone:* (21) 3813345 (office). *Fax:* (21) 3855681 (office).

DARNTON, Robert Choate, BA, DPhil; American historian and academic; *Carl H. Pforzheimer Professor and Director of the University Library, Harvard University;* b. 10 May 1939, New York; s. of Byron Darnton and Eleanor Darnton; m. Susan Lee Glover 1963; one s. two d.; ed Phillips Acad., Harvard Univ., Univ. of Oxford, UK; reporter, The New York Times 1964–65; Jr Fellow, Harvard Univ., 1965–68; Asst Prof., subsequently Assoc. Prof., Prof., Princeton Univ. 1968–2007, Shelby Cullom Davis Prof. of European History 1984–2007, Dir Program in European Cultural Studies 1987–95; Carl H. Pforzheimer Prof. and Dir of Univ. Library, Harvard Univ. 2007–15, then Emer.; fellowships and visiting professorships include Ecole des Hautes Etudes en Sciences Sociales, Paris 1971, 1981, 1985, Netherlands Inst. for Advanced Study 1976–77, Inst. for Advanced Study, Princeton 1977–81, Oxford Univ. (George Eastman Visiting Prof.) 1986–87, Collège de France, Wissenschafts-Kolleg zu Berlin 1989–90, 1993–94; Pres. Int. Soc. for Eighteenth-Century Studies 1987–91, American Historical Asscn 1999–2000; mem. Bd of Dirs, Voltaire Foundation, Oxford, Social Science Research Council 1988–91; mem. Bd of Trustees Center for Advanced Study in the Behavioral Sciences 1992–96, Oxford Univ. Press, USA 1993–, The New York Public Library 1994–; mem. various editorial bds; Fellow, American Acad. of Arts and Sciences, American Philosophical Soc., American Antiquarian Soc.; Adviser, Wissenschafts-Kolleg zu Berlin 1994–; Foreign mem. Academia Europaea, Acad. Royale de Langue et de Littérature Françaises de Belgique; Guggenheim Fellow 1970; Corresp. Fellow, British Acad. 2001; Officier, Ordre des Arts et des Lettres 1995, Chevalier, Légion d'Honneur 2000; Dr hc (Neuchâtel) 1986, (Lafayette Coll.) 1989, (Univ. of Bristol) 1991, (Univ. of Warwick) 2001, (Univ. of Bordeaux) 2005,

(Yvelines-Saint Quentin) 2006, (Univ. of Paris IV-Sorbonne) 2006, (Univ. of St Andrews) 2010; Leo Gershoy Prize, American Historical Asscn 1979, MacArthur Prize 1982, Los Angeles Times Book Prize 1984, Prix Médicis 1991, Prix Chateaubriand 1991, Nat. Book Critics Circle Award 1996, Gutenberg Prize 2004, Lifetime Achievement Award, American Printing History Asscn 2005, Prix France-Amériques 2011, National Humanities Medal 2012. *Television series:* Démocratie (co-ed.), France 1999. *Publications include:* Mesmerism and the End of the Enlightenment in France 1968, The Business of Enlightenment 1979, The Literary Underground of the Old Regime 1982, The Great Cat Massacre 1984, The Kiss of Lamourette 1989, Revolution in Print (co-ed.) 1989, Edition et sédition 1991, Berlin Journal, 1989–1990 1991, Gens de lettres, gens du livre 1992, The Forbidden Best-Sellers of Pre-Revolutionary France 1995, The Corpus of Clandestine Literature 1769–1789 1995, Démocratie (co-ed.) 1998, J.-P. Brissot: His Career and Correspondence 1779–1787 2001, Poesie und Polizei 2002, Pour les Lumières 2002, George Washington's False Teeth: An Unconventional Guide to the 18th Century 2003, The Case for Books: Past, Present, and Future 2009, The Devil in the Holy Water, or the Art of Slander from Louis XIV to Napoleon 2009, Poetry and the Police: Communication Networks in Eighteenth-Century Paris 2010, Censors at Work: How States Shaped Literature 2014. *Leisure interests:* squash, travel. *Address:* Robinson Hall, 35 Quiney Street, Cambridge, MA 02138, USA (office). *Telephone:* (617) 495-3551 (office). *E-mail:* robert_darnton@harvard.edu (office). *Website:* www.robertdarnton.org (office).

DARROCH, Sir (Nigel) Kim, Kt, KCMG, CMG, BSc; British diplomatist; *Ambassador to USA;* b. 30 April 1954, South Stanley, Co. Durham; m.; one s. one d.; ed Durham Univ.; joined FCO 1976, served in Protocol Dept, Planning Staff and News Dept 1976–80, Desk Officer Channel Tunnel Project and Law of the Sea, Maritime, Aviation and Environment Dept 1985–86, Pvt. Sec. to Minister of State dealing with Middle East, Arms Control, Eastern Europe 1987–89, Asst then Deputy Head of EU Dept 1993–95, Head of Eastern Adriatic Dept 1995–97, Head of News Dept 1998, Dir EU Affairs 2000, Dir-Gen. EU Affairs 2003; EU Adviser to Prime Minister and Head of Cabinet Office European Secr. 2004; overseas postings include Third, then Second, then First Sec., Embassy in Tokyo 1980–84, First Sec., Embassy in Rome 1989–92, Counsellor, Perm. Mission to EU, Brussels 1997–98, Perm. Rep. to EU 2007–11; Nat. Security Adviser to HM Govt 2012–15; Amb. to USA 2016–. *Address:* British Embassy, 3100 Massachusetts Avenue NW, Washington, DC 20008, USA (office). *Telephone:* (202) 588-6699 (office). *Fax:* (202) 588-7850 (office). *E-mail:* britishembassyenquiries@gmail.com (office). *Website:* www.gov.uk/government/world/organisations/british-embassy-washington (office).

DAS, Jatin, Dip. in Fine Art; Indian artist and sculptor; *Chairman, JD Centre of Art;* b. 2 Dec. 1941, Mayurbhanj, Orissa; three c.; ed Sir JJ School of Art, Bombay; Prof. Emer., Jamia Millia Islamia Univ. 2008–, Visiting Prof., Faculty of Fine Arts 2009–; Visiting Prof., Coll. of Art, Nat. School of Drama, Nat. Inst. of Design and School of Planning and Architecture; Founder Chair. JD Centre of Art, Bhubaneshwar; Founder Pres. Odissa Forum, Delhi, Mayurbhanj Cultural Devt Foundation; Founder mem. Poetry Soc. of India; Art Adviser, Housing and Urban Devt Corpn; Trustee, Delhi Blue Pottery Trust; Life Fellow, Royal Soc. of Arts, London; Cultural Amb. to Cabinet, UK; Life mem. Indian Nat. Trust for Art and Cultural Heritage; mem. Governing Bd Royal Soc. of Arts India; mem. Advisory Cttee Nat. Natural History Museum, Bhubaneshwar, Delhi Urban Art Comm., Rural India Complex 1972 (now Nat. Crafts Museum), Republic Day Parade Cttees; mem. India Int. Centre, Delhi, British Library, Chelsea Arts Club, London, Ghalib Memorial Movt, Delhi, Fan Circle Int., London, Soc. to Save Rocks, Hyderabad; mem. Jury, Nat. War Memorial 2017; Order of the Star of Italian Solidarity (Italy); Padma Bhushan; Hon. DLitt (Utkal Univ. of Culture, Bhubaneswar) 2007; Utkala Award 2006, Bharat Nirman Award 2007, Distinguished Artist Award 2016. *Publication:* Poems by Jatin Das 1972. *Leisure interests:* interested in everything in life. *Telephone:* (11) 26642430 (office). *Fax:* (11) 26492449 (home). *E-mail:* jatin@jatindas.com. *Website:* www.jdcentreofart.org (office); www.jatindas.com.

DAS, Maarten; Dutch lawyer and business executive; *Non-Executive Chairman, Heineken Holding NV;* b. 19 June 1948, Amsterdam; m.; three c.; ed Free Univ., Amsterdam, Parker School of Comparative Law, Columbia Univ., USA; attorney, Loyens & Loeff 1975–, Pnr 1980–; mem. Supervisory Bd Heineken NV 1994–95, Del. mem. Supervisory Bd 1995–, mem. Bd of Dirs Heineken Holding NV 1994–, Chair. (non-exec.) 2002–. *Address:* Heineken NV, PO Box 28, 1000 AA Amsterdam (office); Heineken NV, Tweede Weteringplantsoen 21, 1017 ZD Amsterdam, The Netherlands (office). *Telephone:* (20) 523-92-39 (office). *Fax:* (20) 626-35-03 (office). *E-mail:* info@heinekeninternational.com (office). *Website:* www.heinekeninternational.com (office).

DAS, Nandita, BA, MA; Indian actress and director; *Chairperson, Children's Film Society;* b. 7 Nov. 1969, New Delhi; d. of Jatin Das and Varsha Das; m. Saumya Sen 2002 (divorced 2009); m. 2nd Subodh Maskara 2010; one s.; ed Univ. of Delhi; started career with theatre group Jannatya Manch; teacher, Rishi Valley School; Chair. Children's Film Soc. 2009–; mem. main jury Cannes Film Festival 2005, Karlovy Vary Int. Film Festival 2007, Marrakech Int. Film Festival 2009; mem. South Asians for Human Rights; mem. Advisory Bd Alliance for a New Humanity; Chevalier, Ordre des Arts et des Lettres; Fédération Internationale des Associations de Producteurs de Films Award 2018. *Films include:* Parinati 1989, Fire 1996, Earth 1996, Hazaar Chaurasi Ki Maa (Nat. Award 1997) 1998, Rockford 1999, Punaradhivasam (Best Foreign Feature Film, Atlantic Film Festival) 1999, Hari-Bhari (Nat. Award 1999) 1999, Bawandar (Best Actress, Santa Monica Film Festival 2001) 2000, Aks 2001, Aamaar Bhuvan (Best Actress, Cairo Film Festival 2002) 2002, Pitaah 2002, Lal Salaam 2002, Supari 2003, Bas Yun Hi 2003, Vishwa Thulasi (Golden Special Jury Award, World Fest Houston Int. Film Festival 2005) 2004, Fleeting Beauty 2005, Maati Maay (Best Actress, Madrid Int. Film Festival 2007) 2005, Podokkhep 2006, Before the Rains 2007, Provoked 2007, Ramchand Pakistani 2008, Firaaq (dir) (Best Film, Best Screenplay and Foreign Critics Award, Asian Festival of First Films, Singapore, Special Award Thessaloniki Int. Film Festival, Greece, Best Editor Dubai Int. Film Festival 2008, Best Film Kara Int. Film Festival 2009, Best Film, The Maverick Spirit Award, Cinequest Film Festival, San Jose, Special Jury Prize, Istanbul Film Festival 2009) 2008, I Am 2010; short films: Saanjh 1999, Fleeting Beauty 2003, Indo-Pak Music Film 2004, Saayey 2005, Rainwater Harvesting (dir), Education for All (dir), Learning is Child's Play (dir), Imprint in Clay (documentary) (dir). *Plays include:* Heads Ya Tails, The Spirit of Anne Frank, Moteram Ka Satyagrah, Mother, Equus. *Address:* Children's Film Society, Films Division Complex, 24, Dr G. Deshmukh Marg, Mumbai 400 026, India (office). *Telephone:* (22) 23517148 (office). *Fax:* (22) 23522610 (office). *E-mail:* chairperson@cfsindia.org (office); contact@nanditadas.com. *Website:* www.cfsindia.org (office); www.nanditadas.com.

DAS, Raghubar, BSc, LLB; Indian politician; *Chief Minister of Jharkhand;* b. 3 May 1955, Jamshedpur; s. of Chavan Das and Sonbatti Ram; m. Rukmani Devi 1978; one s. one d.; ed Jamshedpur Cooperative Coll.; early job as labourer with Tata Steel; participated in 'Total Revolution' movt, Jharkhand, arrested and imprisoned, Gaya 1974 and during state of emergency 1975; joined Janata Party 1977, then founding mem. Bharatiya Janata Party (BJP) 1980, apptd chief of Sitaramdera Unit in Jamshedpur, Chief of BJP in Jharkhand 2004, Vice-Pres. BJP Nat. Cttee 2014–, mem. Jharkhand Legis. Ass. for Jamshedpur E 1995–; Jharkhand State Minister of Labour and Employment 2000, of Finance, Urban Devt and Commercial Tax 2005–06; Deputy Chief Minister of Jharkhand Shibu Soren 2009–10, Chief Minister of Jharkhand 2014–. *Address:* Office of the Chief Minister, Government of Jharkhand, Secretariat, Ranchi 834 001, India (office). *Telephone:* (651) 2403233 (office). *Fax:* (651) 2440061 (office). *Website:* jharkhand.gov.in (office).

DAS NEVES CEITA BAPTISTA DE SOUSA, Maria; São Tomé and Príncipe economist and politician; b. 1958; two c.; ed Univ. of the East, Santiago de Cuba, Cuba; fmr economist at World Bank and UNICEF; mem. Movimento de Libertação de São Tomé e Príncipe—Partido Social Democrata; Minister of Trade, Industry and Tourism and Minister of the Economy –2002; Prime Minister of São Tomé e Príncipe (first woman premier in W Africa) 2002–04; cand. in presidential election 2016. *Address:* c/o Movimento de Libertação de São Tomé e Príncipe—Partido Social Democrata, Estrada Riboque, Edif. Sede do MLSTP, São Tomé, São Tomé e Príncipe (office).

DASCHLE, Thomas (Tom) Andrew, BA; American lawyer, government official and fmr politician; *Founder and Chairman, Daschle Group;* b. 9 Dec. 1947, Aberdeen, SDak; s. of Sebastian C. Daschle and Elizabeth B. Daschle (née Meier); m. Linda Hall Daschle; one s. two d.; ed South Dakota State Univ.; served as 1st Lt, USAF 1969–72; Chief Legis. Aide and then Field Co-ordinator to US Senator 1973–77; mem. US House of Reps from 1st SDak Dist 1977–87; Senator from SDak 1987–2005, Senate Minority Leader 1995–2001, 2002–05, Majority Leader 2001–02; Special Policy Advisor, Alston & Bird LLP, Washington, DC 2005–08; worked for DLA Piper –2014; Founder and Chair. Daschle Group (subsidiary of Baker Donelson law firm) 2014–; Distinguished Sr Fellow, Center for American Progress 2005–08; Visiting Prof., Public Policy Inst., Georgetown Univ. 2005–08; Co-founder Bipartisan Policy Center, Washington, DC 2007; Richard von Weizsäcker Distinguished Visitor, American Acad. in Berlin, Germany 2008; Democrat; numerous awards including Distinguished Service Award, Nat. Rural Electric Cooperation Asscn 2000. *Publications include:* Critical: What We Can Do About the Health Care Crisis 2008, Getting It Done: How Obama and Congress Finally Broke the Stalemate to Make Way for Health Care Reform 2010. *Address:* Daschle Group, 901 K Street, NW, #900, Washington, DC 20001, USA (office). *Telephone:* (202) 508-3400 (office). *E-mail:* info@daschlegroup.com (office). *Website:* www.daschlegroup.com (office); www.bakerdonelson.com/the-daschle-group (office).

D'ASCOLI, Bernard Jacques-Henri Marc; French concert pianist; *Artistic Director, Piano Cantabile;* b. 18 Nov. 1958, Aubagne; one s.; ed Marseille Conservatoire; became blind 1962; took up music 1970; youngest Baccalauréat matriculate of France 1974; first public appearances on both piano and organ 1974; began int. professional career 1982, following debuts at major London concert halls with Royal Philharmonic Orchestra and first recording; toured Australia with Chamber Orchestra of Europe 1983; debuts: Amsterdam Concertgebouw 1984, Houston Symphony 1985, Musikverein, Vienna 1986, Tokyo Casals Hall and Bunka Kaikan Hall 1988, Boston Symphony Orchestra 1992, Dresden Philharmonic 1998, Montréal Symphony 1999, English Chamber Orchestra 2004; festival appearances: BBC Proms, Sintra, Besançon, Oviedo, La Roque d'Anthéron, Sydney Olympics cultural festivities; Founder and Artistic Dir Piano Cantabile; named best young French talent of the year (Megève) 1976, First Prize, Int. Maria Canals Competition, Barcelona 1979, Prizewinner, Marguerite Long, Paris, Leipzig Bach Competition, Warsaw Chopin Competition 1980, Chopin Prize, Santander, Third Prize, Leeds Int. Piano Competition 1981. *Radio:* numerous BBC Radio broadcasts in recital and as soloist with orchestra. *Television:* South Bank Show, Face the Music. *Recordings include:* Liszt Sonata, Franck Prelude Chorale and Fugue 1982, Schumann and Chopin recordings 1988, 1989, Schumann Quintet with Schidlof Quartet 1999, Chopin Complete Nocturnes, Scherzi and Impromptus 2005, 2006. *Leisure interests:* reading, swimming, humane sciences. *Address:* c/o Eleanor Harris, Piano Cantabile, 350 Impasse du Baou, 13400 Aubagne, France (office). *Telephone:* (4) 42-84-02-36 (office). *E-mail:* eleaharr@orange.fr (office). *Website:* www.bernard-dascoli.com.

DASGUPTA, Sir Partha Sarathi, Kt, BSc, BA, PhD, FRS, FBA; Indian/British economist and academic; *Frank Ramsey Professor Emeritus of Economics, University of Cambridge;* b. 17 Nov. 1942, Dhaka, then in India, now in Bangladesh; s. of Prof. Amiya Dasgupta and Shanti Dasgupta; m. Carol M. Meade 1968; one s. two d.; ed Univs of Delhi and Cambridge; Lecturer in Econs, LSE 1971–75, Reader 1975–78, Prof. of Econs 1978–85; Prof. of Econs, Univ. of Cambridge 1985–2010, Frank Ramsey Prof. of Econs 1994–2010, Prof. Emer. 2010–, Fellow, St John's Coll. 1985–; Prof. of Econs and Prof. of Philosophy and Dir of Program on Ethics in Society, Stanford Univ., Calif., USA 1989–92; Andrew D. White Prof.-at-Large, Cornell Univ. 2007–13; Chair. Beijer Int. Inst. of Ecological Econs, Stockholm; Pres. European Econ. Asscn 1999, Royal Econ. Soc. 1998–2001, European Asscn of Environmental and Resource Economists 2008–09; Founder-mem. Man. and Advisory Cttee South Asian Network for Devt and Environmental Econs 1999–; mem. Pontifical Acad. of Social Sciences 1997, Academia Europaea 2009; Foreign mem. Royal Swedish Acad. of Sciences 1991, American Acad. of Arts and Sciences 1991, American Philosophical Soc. 2005, Istituto Veneto di Scienze, Lettere ed Arti 2009; Foreign Assoc. NAS 2001; Fellow, Econometric Soc. 1975, Third World Acad. of Sciences 2001; Hon. Prof. of Environmental and Climate

Econs, Univ. of Copenhagen 2008–10; Hon. Fellow, LSE 1994, Trinity Coll. Cambridge 2010; Distinguished Fellow CES, Univ. of Munich 2011; Dr hc (Wageningen) 2000, (Catholic Univ. of Louvain) 2007, (Faculté Universitaire Saint-Louis) 2009, (Bologna) 2010, (Tilberg) 2012, (Harvard) 2013; Stevenson Prize, Univ. of Cambridge 1967, Volvo Environment Prize 2002, John Kenneth Galbraith Award, American Agricultural Econs Asscn 2007, Erik Kempe Award in Environmental and Resource Econs, Kempe Foundation and the European Asscn of Environmental and Resource Economists (co-recipient) 2007, Zayed Int. Prize for the Environment (Category 2) 2011, European Lifetime Achievement Award in Environmental Econs, European Asscn of Environmental and Resource Economists 2014, Blue Planet Prize 2015, Tyler Prize for Environmental Achievement 2016. *Publications include:* Guidelines for Project Evaluation (co-author) 1972, Economic Theory and Exhaustible Resources (co-author) 1979, The Control of Resources 1983, An Inquiry into Well-Being and Destitution 1993, Social Capital: A Multifaceted Perspective (co-ed.) 2000, Human Well-Being and the Natural Environment 2001, Economic Theory for the Environment: Essays in Honour of Karl-Göran Mäler (co-ed.) 2002, The Economics of Non-Convex Ecosystems (co-ed.) 2003, Ecosystems and Human Well-Being: Synthesis (co-author) (synthesised the findings of the Millennium Ecosystem Assessment, which has been awarded the Zayed International Prize 2005) 2005, Economics: A Very Short Introduction 2007 (translated into Arabic, Chinese, Japanese, Portugese, Spanish, Italian and German), Poverta, Ambiente e Societa (collected papers on poverty, environment and society, translated and edited by Elena Podrecca and Maurizio Zenezini) 2007, Selected Papers of Partha Dasgupta, Vols I & II, Vol. 1: Institutions, Innovations, and Human Values, Vol. 2: Poverty, Population, and Natural Resources 2010, Green National Accounts in India: A Framework (Report of an Expert Group convened by the Prime Minister of India. Issued by the Government of India) (co-author) 2013, Sustainable Humanity, Sustainable Nature: Our Responsibility (co-ed.) 2015, Discounting: the 2011 Arrow Lecture at Columbia University 2016; books and articles on econs of environmental and natural resources, technological change, normative population theory, political philosophy, devt planning and the political economy of destitution. *Leisure interests:* cinema, theatre, reading. *Address:* Faculty of Economics and Politics, University of Cambridge, Sidgwick Avenue, Cambridge, CB3 9DD (office); 1 Dean Drive, Holbrook Road, Cambridge, CB1 7SW, England (home). *Telephone:* (1223) 335227 (office). *E-mail:* partha.dasgupta@econ.cam.ac.uk (office). *Website:* www.econ.cam.ac.uk/faculty/dasgupta (office).

DASH-YONDON, Büdragchaagiin, PhD; Mongolian politician and diplomatist; b. 17 Feb. 1946, Tsetserleg soum, Khövsgöl Prov.; s. of Jugnaa Budragchaa and Sengee Chogjmoo; m. Choijamtsyn Batjargal 1979; one s. three d. (one adopted); ed Mongolian State Univ., State Univ. of Kiev, USSR; Prof., Mongolian State Univ. 1968–74; officer at Scientific and Educational Dept, Mongolian People's Revolutionary Party (MPRP) Cen. Cttee 1978–79; Vice-Chancellor, Higher Party School, MPRP Cen. Cttee 1979–85; Deputy Head and Head of Dept, MPRP Cen. Cttee 1985–90; First Sec.-Gen., MPRP Ulan Bator City Party Cttee 1990–91; MPRP Sec.-Gen. 1991–96; apptd Political Adviser to Pres. 1997; Amb. to Bulgaria 2001–05. *Leisure interests:* reading, chess. *Address:* c/o Mongolian People's Revolutionary Party, Baga Toiruu 37/1, Ulan Bator, Mongolia. *Website:* www.maxn.mn.

DASKALOPOULOS, Dimitris, BA, MBA; Greek business executive and art collector; *Founder, NEON;* b. 1957, Athens; ed Athens School of Man., Northwestern Univ., USA; Chair. and CEO Delta Holding SA 1983–2007 (merged with Mechelany International SA, Goody's, Flocafé and several other cos to form Vivartia SA 2006), fmr Chair. Delta Dairy SA, Delta Ice Cream SA; Chair. Hellenic Federation of Enterprises (SEV) 2006–14, now Hon. Pres.; Vice-Pres. BUSINESSEUROPE 2013–15; f. NEON 2013; Chair. diaNEOsis 2015; founder and currently Chair. DAMMA Holdings SA; fmr Vice-Chair. General Frozen Foods SA; mem. Bd of Dirs Nat. Bank of Greece, several cos listed on Athens Stock Exchange; Chair. Fed. of Hellenic Food Industries, Hellenic Fed. of Enterprises; mem. Bd Fed. of Greek Industries, American-Hellenic Chamber of Commerce; mem. Nat. Agricultural Policy Council, Asscn of Young Entrepreneurs of Greece, Greek Man. Asscn, Greek Inst. of Man., Euroglaces (European Ice Cream Asscn), Fed. of Greek Food Industries to CIAA (Confed. of the Food and Drink Industries of the EU), European Round Table of Industrialists, and many others; mem. Leadership Council of the New Museum, Tate's Int. Council; Trustee, Solomon R. Guggenheim Foundation; collection of modern art includes around 400 works, ranging from what is believed to be the last Marcel Duchamp urinal in pvt. hands to Christoph Büchel's 450m installation Unplugged (Simply Botiful) 2006–07; Leo Award 2014. *Leisure interests:* adventure trips, mountain climbing, photography, collecting modern art. *Telephone:* (213) 018-7700 (office). *E-mail:* contact@neon.org.gr (office). *Website:* www.neon.org.gr (office).

DASSAULT, Olivier, BA, MA, PhD; French politician, business executive and fmr air force pilot; b. 1 June 1951, Boulogne-Billancourt (Hauts-de-Seine); s. of Serge Dassault and Nicole Dassault (née Raffel); grandson of Marcel Dassault; ed École de l'Air; qualified as professional IFR pilot 1975; Pres. Dassault Communications; Chair. Valmonde (publr); mem. Bd Journal des Finances financial newspaper; Admin. of Dassault subsidiary Socpresse; mem. Nat. Ass. (Union pour un Mouvement Populaire) for the first circonscription of Oise 2002–, mem. Comm. des finances; composer and musician and contributed several scores for well-known French films. *Achievements include:* set several world speed records: New York to Paris in Dassault Falcon 50 1977, New Orleans to Paris in Dassault Falcon 900 (both with Hervé Le Prince-Ringuet) 1987, Paris to Abu Dhabi in Falcon 900 EX 1996, Paris to Abu Dhabi in Falcon 900 EX (both with Guy Mitaux-Maurouard and Patrick Experton) 1996. *Publications:* has published several books of photos. *Leisure interest:* photography. *Address:* Assemblée Nationale, 126 rue de l'Université, 75355 Paris 07 SP, France (office). *E-mail:* odassault@assemblee-nationale.fr (office). *Website:* www.assemblee-nationale.fr (office); www.olivierdassault.fr.

DASSONVILLE, Yves, MEcon; French civil servant and government official; b. 1948, Paris; ed Ecole Nat. d'Admin, Paris; apptd Civil Admin. (2nd Class), Ministry of the Interior and Decentralization 1983; apptd Chief of Staff to Commr of Eure-et-Loire 1983; Deputy Sec.-Gen. of French Polynesia, Overseas Secr. 1984–86; Chief of Staff to Sec. of State to Minister in charge of South Pacific issues 1986; Sec.-Gen. Landes Pref. 1986–88; Civil Admin. (1st Class) and Deputy Prefect of Saint-Dizier 1988–92; Civil Admin. (unclassified), Sec.-Gen. for Regional Affairs of Languedoc and Sr Deputy Prefect 1992–95; Sec.-Gen. Pref. of Réunion 1995–98; Deputy Prefect of Lorient 1998–2001; Prefect Del. for Security and Defence to Prefect of the Southern Defence Zone 2001–02; Prefect of Jura 2002–04; Prefect (Commr) of Martinique 2004; Chief of Staff to Sec. of State for Overseas Territories 2004–07; High Commr of New Caledonia 2007–10; Prefect, region of Limousin 2010–11, region of Poitou Charentes 2011–13, region honoraire 2013–; mem. Mission d'écoute et de conseil sur l'avenir institutionnel de la Nouvelle Calédonie 2014–; Chevalier, Légion d'honneur 2000, Officier 2010; Chevalier, Ordre nat. du Mérite. *Address:* Ministry of the Interior, place Beauvau, 75008 Paris (office). *Telephone:* 1-49-27-49-27 (office). *Fax:* 1-43-59-89-50 (office). *E-mail:* sirp@interieur.gouv.fr (office). *Website:* www.interieur.gouv.fr (office).

DASTIS QUECEDO, Alfonso Maria; Spanish diplomatist; b. 5 Oct. 1955, Jerez de la Frontera, Cadiz; m.; two c.; entered diplomatic service 1983, Judge's clerk, European Court of Justice 1987–89, fmr Exec. Adviser in Cabinet of Minister of Foreign Affairs, Counsellor at Perm. Mission to UN, New York 1989–94, adviser in Prime Minister's Office 1996–2000, mem. convention on the future of Europe 2001–03, Dir of support unit of Organizing Cttee of Spanish Presidency of EU 2002, Sec.-Gen. of European Affairs, Ministry of Foreign Affairs 2000–04, Amb. to the Netherlands 2004–07, Co-ordinator, Cttee of Perm. Reps of the EU (COREPER) 2007–11, Amb. and Perm. Rep. to EU, Brussels 2011–16; Minister of Foreign Affairs and Co-operation 2016–18. *Leisure interest:* golf.

DATTU, Handyala L.; Indian lawyer and judge; *Chairperson, National Human Rights Commission;* b. 3 Dec. 1950, Chikkapattanagere village, Chikmagalur dist, Karnataka; m. Gayathri Dattu; enrolled as advocate 1975, practised in civil, criminal, constitutional and taxation cases, Bangalore; worked as High Court Govt Pleader for Sales Tax Dept 1983–90, Govt Advocate 1990–93, Standing Counsel, Income Tax Dept 1992–93, Sr Standing Counsel 1993–95; Judge, High Court of Karnataka 1995–97, Chief Justice, High Court of Chattisgarh 2007; transferred to High Court of Kerala and assumed charge 2007; Justice, Supreme Court 2008–15, Chief Justice 2014–15; Chair. Nat. Human Rights Comm. 2016–. *Address:* National Human Rights Commission, Manav Adhikar Bhawan Block-C, GPO Complex, INA, New Delhi 110 023, India (office). *Telephone:* (11) 24651330 (office). *Fax:* (11) 24651329 (office). *E-mail:* covdnhrc@nic.in (office). *Website:* www.nhrc.nic.in (office).

DAUDZAI, Mohammad Umar, MSc; Afghan diplomatist and government official; b. 12 Oct. 1957, Qarabagh Dist; ed Univ. of Manchester, UK; involved in mujahidin struggle against Soviet occupation 1980–84; community mobilization team leader, Save the Children Fund (UK), Peshawar 1984–86, Man. Primary Health Care Programme 1986–88, Deputy Project Dir and Head Training Unit 1988–90, adviser to Field Dir 1992–93; Regional Dir Swedish Cttee for Afghanistan 1993–96; Programme Officer UNDP, Afghanistan 1996–99; Asst Resident Rep., UNDP, Islamabad 1999–2002; Area-based Devt Specialist, Switzerland 2000–03; Chief of Staff to Pres. Hamid Karzai 2003–05; Amb. to Iran and Perm. Rep. to Secr. of ECO 2005–07; Chief of Staff, Office of the Pres. 2007–11; Amb. to Pakistan 2011–13; Minister of Interior Affairs 2013–14.

DAUDZE, Gundars; Latvian physician and politician; b. 9 May 1965, Ventspils; m. Marcus Daudze; two d.; ed Riga Medicine Inst.; mem. Saeima (Parl.) (Union of Greens and Farmers—ZZS list) for Kurzeme constituency 2006–11, 2014–, Chair. (Speaker) Saeima 2007–10, Deputy Speaker 2010–11, 2014–; Head of the Chancery of the Pres. of Latvia 2011–14; Chair. Nat. Security Cttee, mem. Foreign Affairs Cttee 2007–10, Public Health Sub-cttee and Social Security Sub-cttee of Social and Employment Matters Cttee 2007–11, 2014–, Legal Affairs Cttee 2007–11, 2014–. *Leisure interests:* sailing, sport. *Address:* Saeima, Jēkaba iela 11 Riga 1811, Latvia (office). *Telephone:* 6708-7321 (office). *Fax:* 6708-7100 (office). *E-mail:* info@saeima.lv (office). *Website:* www.saeima.lv (office); www.daudze.lv.

DAUGAARD, Dennis M., BS, JD; American lawyer, politician and fmr state governor; b. 11 June 1953, Garretson, SDak; m. Linda Schmidt 1981; one s. two d.; ed Dell Rapids High School, Univ. of South Dakota, Northwestern Univ. School of Law, Chicago, Ill.; raised on family farm nr Garretson, SDak; called to Bar of South Dakota; attorney, Supena & Nyman 1978–79, Shand Morahan & Co. 1980–81; Vice-Pres. and Trust Officer, First Bank of South Dakota 1981–90; Devt Dir, Children's Home Soc., SDak 1990–2002, Exec. Dir 2003–09; mem. for Dist 9, SDak State Senate 1997–2003, Pres. SDak Senate, Chair. Workers' Compensation Advisory Council, served as mem. comm. that dealt with amendments to legislative article of SDak's Constitution, as chair. of state task force examining ways to reduce number of South Dakotans without health insurance; Lt-Gov. of South Dakota 2003–11, Gov. of South Dakota 2011–18; Chair. Western Governors' Asscn 2017–18; mem. South Dakota Planned Giving Council, Sioux Falls Estate Planning Council, South Dakota Bar Asscn, Nat. Soc. of Fund Raising Execs, Rotary; Republican. *Address:* c/o Office of the Governor, 500 East Capitol Avenue, Pierre, SD 57501, USA (office).

DAUKORU, Edmund Maduabebe, CON, PhD; Nigerian geologist, politician, international organization official and ruler; *Amayanabo of Nembe;* b. 13 Oct. 1943; ed Imperial Coll. of Science and Tech., London, UK; Special Studies Geologist, Shell Int. Petroleum Co. 1978, held various positions in co. both in Nigeria and internationally, including Chief Geologist, apptd Div. Man. SPDC 1984; Group Man. Dir and CEO Nigerian Nat. Petroleum Corpn 1992–2003, Alt. Chair. 2003–; Special Adviser on Petroleum and Energy to Pres. of Nigeria 2003–05; Minister of State for Petroleum Resources 2005–06; Minister of Energy 2006–07; Sec.-Gen. OPEC and Pres. OPEC Conf. 2006–07; Amayanabo (traditional ruler) of Nembe Kingdom (took the name Mingi XIII) 2008–; Chair. Solid Mineral Cttee for Bayelsa State; mem. Niger Delta Peace Forum, Ijaw Elder's Forum (Bayelsa State); Trustee, Bayelsa State Devt Fund. *Address:* c/o Royal Palace, Nembe Kingdom, Bayelsa State, Nigeria.

DAUKŠYS, Kęstutis; Lithuanian politician; b. 31 Jan. 1960, Alytus; m.; two s.; ed Univ. of Vilnius and G. Plechanov Russian Acad. of Econs, Moscow; Asst, Political Economy Dept, Univ. of Vilnius 1983–85; Deputy Head of Planning Div., Furniture Design Construction Bureau 1985–87, Specialist of Foreign Trade Div. 1989–90; mil. service 1987–89; Dir UAB Balticum 1990–95, UAB Balticum grupė 1995–98, 2004; Dir-Gen. AB Kilimai 1998–2003, Chair. 1999–2004; mem. Seimas (Parl.) 2004–, mem. Cttee on Foreign Affairs 2008–, Nuclear Energy Comm. 2008–;

Minister of the Economy 2005–06; mem. Darbo Partija (Labour Party). *Leisure interests:* music, fishing. *Address:* Seimas, Room I-438, Gedimino pr. 53, Vilnius 01109, Lithuania (office). *Telephone:* (5) 239-6958 (office). *E-mail:* Kestutis .Dauksys@lrs.lt (office). *Website:* www.lrs.lt (office).

DAUMAN, Philippe P., BA, JD; American lawyer and media executive; b. 1 March 1954, New York; s. of Henri Dauman; m. Deborah Ross 1970; two c.; ed Yale Univ., Columbia Univ. Law School; Partner, Shearman & Sterling (law firm), New York 1978–93, prin. outside counsel to Viacom, Sr mem. Mergers and Acquisitions Practice Group; mem. Bd of Dirs Viacom Inc. (predecessor of Viacom) 1987–, Gen. Counsel and Sec. 1993–98, Deputy Chair. 1996–2000, mem. Exec. Cttee and Exec. Vice-Pres. in charge of strategic transactions, legal and govt affairs, human resources and admin, supervising Paramount Entertainment, Showtime Networks and Simon & Schuster 1994–2000, mem. Bd of Dirs Viacom Jan. 2006–, Pres. and CEO Viacom Sept. 2006–16, Exec. Chair. Feb.–Sept. 2016; Co-founder, Co-Chair. and CEO DND Capital Partners LLC (pvt. equity firm) 2000–06; mem. Bd of Dirs National Amusements, Inc., Lafarge North America Inc., CBS Corpn; mem. Bd Trustees, Museum of the City of New York; mem. Bd Visitors, Columbia Law School; mem. Bd of Trustees, Paley Center for Media, North Shore-Long Island Jewish Health System Foundation; mem. Exec. Cttee, Lenox Hill Hospital.

DAUNT, Sir Timothy Lewis Achilles, Kt, KCMG; British diplomatist; b. 11 Oct. 1935, Brecon, Powys, Wales; s. of L. H. G. Daunt and Margery Daunt (née Lewis Jones); m. Patricia Susan Knight 1962; one s. two d.; ed Sherborne School, St Catharine's Coll., Cambridge; mil. service with King's Royal Irish Hussars 1954–56; entered FCO 1959, Ankara 1960, Foreign Office 1964, Nicosia 1967, Pvt. Sec. to Perm. Under-Sec. of State, FCO 1970; with Bank of England 1973; mem. UK Mission, New York 1973; Counsellor OECD, Paris 1975; Head of S European Dept, FCO 1978–81; Assoc. Centre d'études et de recherches internationales, Paris 1982; Minister and Deputy Perm. Rep. to NATO, Brussels 1982–85; Asst Under-Sec. of State (Defence), FCO 1985–86; Amb. to Turkey 1986–92; Deputy Under-Sec. of State (Defence), FCO 1992–95; Lt-Gov. Isle of Man 1995–2000; Chair. British Inst., Ankara 1995–2006, Anglo-Turkish Soc. 2001–09, The Ottoman Fund Ltd 2005–10. *Address:* 20 Ripplevale Grove, London, N1 1HU, England. *Telephone:* (20) 7607-1612. *E-mail:* t.daunt@btinternet.com.

DAUTRY-VARSAT, Alice, DSci; French cell biologist and academic; b. 1950, Paris; ed Paris-Sud Univ., State Univ. of New York at Stony Brook, USA; training in solid-state physics and molecular biology, France and USA; joined Institut Pasteur, Paris 1977, currently Prof. and Dir Biology of Cell Interaction Unit, Pres. 2005–13; mem. Scientific Council, Life Sciences Dept, CNRS; Prof., École Polytechnique; fmr Visiting Scientist, MIT; mem. External Reference Group for Health Research Strategy, WHO; Trustee, Ecole Polytechnique, ISTA (Austria), DNDi (Switzerland); Chevalier, Légion d'honneur. *Publications:* over 130 publs on receptors and infections by intracellular bacteria. *Address:* c/o Institut Pasteur, 25–28 rue du Dr Roux, 75724 Paris Cedex 15, France.

DAVENPORT, Lindsay; American fmr professional tennis player; b. (Lindsay Ann Davenport Leach), 8 June 1976, Palos Verdes, Calif.; d. of Wink Davenport and Ann Davenport; m. Jon Leach 2003; one s. three d.; ed Murriela Valley High School; turned professional 1993; has won 51 singles titles including Lucerne 1993, 1994, Brisbane 1994, singles and doubles (with Jana Novotna) Bausch & Lomb Championships 1997, Bank of the West 1998, Toshiba Classic 1998, Acura Invitational 1998, US Open 1998, European Championships 1998, Tokyo Pan Pacific 1998, 2001, 2003, Sydney Int. 1999, Wimbledon 1999 (singles and doubles), Advanta Championships, Philadelphia 1999, Chase Championships, New York 1999, Australian Open 2000, Indian Wells 2000; mem. Olympic Team 1996, gold medallist singles 2000; mem. US Fed. Cup Team 1993–2000, 2002, 2005, 2008; 93 career professional titles in total (39 doubles titles); singles champion, ASB Classic, Auckland 2008; Women's single champion Cellular Couth Cup, Memphis 2008; retd 2010; Analyst, Tennis Channel 2008; Coach, Madison Keys 2014–15, 2017–; mem. Bd Oracle US Tennis Awards Cttee 2018–; inducted into the Int. Tennis Hall of Fame 2014. *Leisure interests:* watching hockey, sports in general, music, crosswords, going to the beach. *Address:* Tennis Channel, 250 Park Avenue, Suite 825, New York, NY 10177, USA (office). *Telephone:* (646) 402-5031 (office). *Website:* www.oracle.com.

DAVENPORT, Paul Theodore, OC, BA, MA, PhD; Canadian economist, academic and university administrator; *President Emeritus, University of Western Ontario;* b. 24 Dec. 1946, Summit; s. of Theodore Davenport and Charlotte Lomax Paul; m. Josette Brotons 1969; one s. two d.; ed Stanford Univ. and Univ. of Toronto; Prof., Dept of Econs McGill Univ. 1973–89, Assoc. Dean, Faculty of Grad. Studies and Research, 1982–86, Vice-Prin. (Planning and Computer Services) 1986–89; Pres. and Vice-Chancellor Univ. of Alberta 1989–94; Pres. Univ. of Western Ontario 1994–2009, Pres. Emer. 2009–; Chair. Asscn of Univs and Colls of Canada 1997–99, Council of Ont. Univs 1999–2001; Chevalier Légion d'Honneur 2001; Hon. LLD (Alta) 1994, (Toronto) 2000, (Int. Univ. of Moscow) 2002. *Publications include:* Reshaping Confederation: The 1982 Reform of the Canadian Constitution (ed. with R. Leach) 1984, Universities and the Knowledge Economy in Renovating the Ivory Tower (ed. David Laidler) 2002. *Leisure interests:* biking, Impressionist painting, modern jazz, photography. *Address:* c/o Office of the President, University of Western Ontario, Natural Sciences Centre, Stevenson Hall, Suite 2107, London, ON N6A 5B8; 1836 Richmond Street, London, ON N5X 4B9, Canada (home).

DAVEY, Rt Hon. Sir Edward (Ed) Jonathan, Kt, BA, MSc (Econ), FRSA; British politician; b. 25 Dec. 1965, Nottingham; m. Emily Gasson 2005; one s.; ed Nottingham High School, Jesus Coll., Oxford, Birkbeck Coll., London; worked in the Commons as economics researcher for Liberal Democrats 1989–93, later party's Sr Econs Adviser; left Parl. to work for Omega Partners 1993–97, specialized in consultancy in postal services sector; MP for Kingston and Surbiton 1997–2010, for Kingston and Surbiton (revised boundary) 2010–15, 2017–; Liberal Democrat: London Whip 1997–2000; Spokesperson for the Treasury (Public Spending and Taxation) 1997–99, for the Economy 1999–2001, for London 2000–03; Shadow Chief Sec. to the Treasury 2001–02; Spokesperson for Office of the Deputy Prime Minister 2002–05; Shadow Sec. of State for Educ. and Skills 2005–06, for Trade and Industry 2006; Chief of Staff to Sir Menzies Campbell as Leader of the Liberal Democrats 2006–07; Shadow Sec. of State for Foreign and Commonwealth Affairs 2007–10; Parl. Under-Sec. of State (Minister for Employment Relations, Consumer and Postal Affairs), Dept for Business, Innovation and Skills 2010–12; Sec. of State for Energy and Climate Change 2012–15; Spokesperson for Home Affairs 2017–; mem. Fed. Policy Cttee 1994–95, Liberal Democrat Policy Group (Econs, Tax and Benefits and Transport), Asscn of Liberal Democrat Councillors; Chair. Campaigns and Communications Cttee 2006–09; Liberal Democrat; Royal Humane Soc. Bravery Award 1995. *Publications:* Making MPs Work For Our Money: Reforming Parliament's Role In Budget Scrutiny 2000, contrib. to The Orange Book 2004. *Address:* Constituency Office, Liberal Democrats, 21 Berrylands Road, Surbiton, KT5 8QX, England (office). *E-mail:* edward@edwarddavey.co.uk. *Website:* www.edwarddavey.co.uk.

DAVEY, Grenville, BA; British sculptor, artist and academic; *Senior Lecturer, School of Arts and Digital Industries, University of East London;* b. 28 April 1961, Launceston, Cornwall; ed Exeter Coll., Goldsmiths Coll., London; Visiting Prof., Univ. of the Arts, London; Artist-in-Residence, Dept of Theoretical Physics, Queen Mary Univ. of London 2010–12, Isaac Newton Inst. of Math. Sciences, Cambridge 2012; currently Sr Lecturer, School of Arts and Digital Industries, Univ. of East London; Turner Prize, Tate Gallery 1992, Art and Architecture Award, Royal Soc. of Arts 1995. *Leisure interests:* work, walking. *Address:* Room G.50, School of Arts and Digital Industries, University of East London, Docklands Campus, 4–6 University Way, London, E16 2RD, England (office). *Telephone:* (20) 8223-7603 (office). *E-mail:* g.c.davey@uel.ac.uk (office). *Website:* www.uel.ac.uk/research/profiles/adi/grenvilledavey (office).

DAVEY, Kenneth George, OC, PhD, FRSC, FESC; Canadian academic and scientist; *Distinguished Research Professor Emeritus of Biology, York University;* b. 20 April 1932, Chatham, Ontario; s. of William Davey and Marguerite Davey (née Clark); m. Jeannette Isabel Evans 1959 (separated 1989); one s. two d. (one deceased); ed McKeough Public School, Chatham, Chatham Collegiate Inst., Univ. of Western Ontario, Univ. of Cambridge, UK; NRC Fellow (Zoology), Univ. of Toronto 1958–59; Drosier Fellow, Gonville and Caius Coll., Cambridge 1959–63; Assoc. Prof. of Parasitology, McGill Univ., Montreal 1963–66, Dir Inst. of Parasitology 1964–74, Prof. of Parasitology and Biology 1966–74; Prof. of Biology, York Univ., Toronto 1974–84, Chair. of Biology 1974–81, Dean of Science 1982–85, Distinguished Research Prof. of Biology 1984–2000, Prof. Emer. 2000–, Vice-Pres. (Academic Affairs) 1986–91; Ed. International Journal of Invertebrate Reproduction and Development 1979–85, Canadian Journal of Zoology 1995–2004; Assoc. Ed. Encyclopedia of Reproduction 1996–; Vice-Chair. Canadian Science Publishing 2011–; mem. Bd of Dirs Huntsman Marine Lab. 1978–80, 1982–85, Pres. and Chair. of Bd 1977–80; Pres. Biological Council of Canada 1979–82, Canadian Soc. of Zoologists 1981–82; Sec. Acad. of Science, Royal Soc. of Canada 1979–85; mem. Council, Royal Canadian Inst. 1996– (Pres. 2000–02), mem. Nat. Council on Ethics in Human Research (Pres. 2002–03); Fellow, Entomological Soc. of Canada 1997; Hon. Fellow, Royal Entomological Soc. 2004; Queen's Jubilee Medal 1977, 2002, 2012; Hon. DSc (Western Ontario) 2002; Gold Medal, Entomological Soc. of Canada 1981, Fry Medal, Canadian Soc. of Zoologists 1987, Gold Medal, Biological Council of Canada 1987, Distinguished Biologist Award, Canadian Council of Univ. Biology Chairs 1992, Hitschfeld Award, Canadian Asscn Univ. Research Admins 1997, Wigglesworth Medal, Royal Entomological Soc., London 2004. *Publications include:* Reproduction in Insects 1964, Biology: Exploring the Diversity of Life (co-author) 2010; 200 articles on endocrinology of invertebrate animals. *Leisure interests:* handweaving, food and wine. *Address:* 96 Holm Crescent, Thornhill, ON L3T 5J3, Canada (home). *Telephone:* (905) 882-5077 (home). *E-mail:* davey@yorku.ca (office).

DAVID, Cristian, PhD; Romanian politician; b. (Cristian Troacă), 26 Dec. 1967, Bucharest; m. 1st 2001 (divorced); m. 2nd Vanda Vlasov 2005; ed Univ. of Bucharest and Romanian Nat. Defence Coll.; with TMUCB Bucharest (eng co.) 1986–90, Designer 1990–91; Co-ordinator Nat. Liberal Univ. Youth Org. 1990–93, Sec.-Gen. 1993–97; Adviser, Ministry of Youth and Sport 1997–98; mem. Standing Cttee, Nat. Liberal Party—Partidul Național Liberal 1991–93, Dir Foreign Relations Dept 1997–2004, mem. Nat. Rep. Del. 2002–04, Chair. Foreign Affairs Comm. 2004–05, mem. Cen. Standing Cttee 2005–06, mem. Cen. Political Bureau 2006–; Dir Van Soestbergen Import Export SRL 1992–94, Team Int. Import Export SRL 1995–96, Team Int. Consult SRL 1999–2004; Assoc. Lecturer, Dept of Statistics and Econ. Forecasting, Acad. of Econ. Studies 2001–04; mem. Senate 2004–12, mem. Senate Human Rights, Cults and Minorities Comm.; Minister-Del. responsible for internationally financed projects 2004–07; Minister of the Interior and Admin. Reform 2007–08; Minister for the Diaspora 2012–14; mem. Romanian Asscn for Liberty and Devt 1997–2000; Founding mem. Liberal Studies Inst. 2006. *Publications include:* various articles on econs and statistics. *Address:* c/o Partidul Național Liberal (National Liberal Party), 011866, Bucharest, Boulevard Aviatorilor 86, Romania (office). *Telephone:* (21) 2310795 (office). *Fax:* (21) 2310796 (office). *E-mail:* dre@pnl.ro (office). *Website:* www.pnl.ro (office).

DAVID, François Paul; French civil servant; *Chairman, Coface;* b. 5 Dec. 1941, Clermont-Ferrand; s. of Jean David and Rose David (née Cabane); m. Monique Courtois 1967; two s.; ed French Lycée, London, Faculté de Lettres, Paris, Ecole nat. d'admin.; mem. staff Dept of Foreign Econ. Relations, Ministry of Finance 1969–73, Head Agric. Policy Office 1976–78; Commercial Counsellor, Embassy in the UK 1974–76; Tech. Adviser Office of Minister of Foreign Trade 1978–80; Asst Dir Ministry of Economy, Finance and Budget 1981–84, Deputy Dir 1984–86, Dir Office of Jr Minister in charge of Foreign Trade at Ministry of Economy, Finance and Privatization 1986–87, Dir Dept of Foreign Econ. Relations 1987–89; Dir-Gen. Int. Affairs, Aérospatiale 1990–94; Chair. Compagnie française d'assurance pour le commerce extérieur (Coface) 1994–; mem. Bd Dirs European Aeronautic Defence and Space Co. (EADS NV), Vinci; Censor of Rexel; Commdr, Légion d'honneur 1999, Grand Officier 2015; Chevalier, Ordre nat. du Mérite; Officier du Mérite agricole; Officier, Ordre de Saint-Charles (Monaco). *Publications:* Le Mythe de l'exportation 1971, Autopsie de la Grande-Bretagne 1976, Le Commerce international à la dérive 1982, La Guerre de l'export 1987, Relations économiques internationales: La politique commerciale des grandes puissances face à la crise 1989, Jacques Cœur, l'aventure de l'argent 1990. *Leisure interests:* tennis, karate. *Address:* Coface, 12 cours Michelet, La Défense 10, 92065 Paris -la-Défense Cedex (office). *Telephone:* 1-49-02-13-00 (office). *Fax:* 1-49-02-14-21 (office). *E-mail:* francois_david@coface.com (office). *Website:* www.coface.com (office).

DAVID, George Alfred Lawrence, BA, MBA; American business executive; b. 7 April 1942, Bryn Mawr, Pa; s. of Charles Wendell David and Margaret Simpson; m. 1st Barbara Osborn 1965 (divorced 1997); one s.; m. 2nd 2003 (divorced 2009); two d.; m. 3rd Wendy Ann David 2012; ed Harvard Univ. and Univ. of Virginia; Asst Prof., Univ. of Va, Charlottesville 1967–68; Vice-Pres. Boston Consulting group 1968–75; Sr Vice-Pres. (Corp. Planning and Devt) Otis Elevator Co., New York 1975–77, Sr Vice-Pres. and Gen. Man. Latin American Operations, West Palm Beach, Fla 1977–81, Pres. N American Operations, Farmington, Conn. 1981–85, Pres. and CEO Otis Elevator Co. 1985–89; Exec. Vice-Pres. and Pres. (Commercial/Industrial) United Technologies Corpn (parent co.) 1989–92, Pres. and COO 1992–94, CEO 1994–2008, Chair. 1997–2009 (retd); mem. Bd of Dirs Citigroup Inc., Nat. Acad. Foundation, Inst. Int. Econs, Washington 1996–; mem. The Business Council, The Business Roundtable; Trustee, Carnegie Hall Corpn, Inc., Nat. Minority Supplier Devt Council, US-ASEAN Council, Transatlantic Business Dialogue; Order of Friendship (Russia) 1999, Légion d'honneur 2002; John R. Alison Award, Air Force Asscn, CEO of the Year, Chief Executive Magazine 2005.

DAVID, Jacques-Henri; French business executive; *Chairman, Acxior Corporate Finance;* b. 17 Oct. 1943, Ygrande (Allier); s. of André David and Suzanne Dupeyrat; m. Isabelle Lamy 1967; one d.; ed Lycée Louis-le-Grand, Paris, Ecole Polytechnique, Inst. d'Etudes Politiques, Paris and Ecole Nat. Supérieure de la Statistique et des Études Économiques (Insee), Paris; Admin. Insee 1967–68; Head, econometric studies service, Banque de France 1969–75; Deputy Sec.-Gen. Conseil Nat. du Crédit 1973–75; Prof. Inst. d'Etudes Politiques 1975; Insp. des Finances, Ministry of Econ. and Finance 1975–79; Adviser, Office of Minister of Econ. 1979, Deputy Dir 1980, Dir 1980–81; Sec.-Gen. Conseil Nat. du Crédit 1981–84; Finance Dir Cie Saint-Gobain 1984–86, Dir-Gen. 1986–89; Pres. Banque Stern 1989–92; Pres. Centre de Recherche pour l'expansion de l'économie (Rexecode) 1989–96; Dir-Gen. Compagnie Gen. des Eaux 1993–95; Pres. CEPME 1995–99, Sofaris 1996–99, Bank for Devt of Small and Medium-Sized Businesses (BDPME) 1997–99; mem. Deutsche Bank Group Social and Econ. Council 1996–99; Chair. Deutsche Bank in France 1999–2009; Chair. Acxior Corporate Finance 2010–; Chair. Comm. de contrôle des activités financières de Monaco 2011–13; Vice-Chair. Global Corporate Finance; Officier, Légion d'honneur; Commdr, Ordre nat. du Mérite. *Publications:* La Politique monétaire 1974, Réévaluation et verité des bilans 1977, La Monnaie et la politique monétaire 1983, Crise financière et relations monétaires internationales 1985, Le Financement des opérations à risque dans les PME 1997. *Leisure interests:* skiing, yachting, golf. *Address:* Acxior Corporate Finance, 69 boulevard Malesherbes, 75008 Paris, France (office). *Telephone:* 1-53-04-31-30 (office). *Fax:* 1-53-04-98-39 (office). *E-mail:* info@acxior.com (office). *Website:* www.acxior.com (office).

DAVID, Peter; Grenadian/Canadian politician; *Minister of Foreign Affairs;* mem. House of Reps for St George 2003–; Gen. Sec., Nat. Democratic Congress Party; Minister of Foreign Affairs 2008–10, 2018–. of Tourism and Civil Aviation 2010–12; Asst Gen. Sec., New Nat. Party 2017–. *Address:* Ministry of Foreign Affairs and International Business, Ministerial Complex, 4th Floor, Botanical Gardens, Tanteen, St George's, Grenada (office). *Telephone:* 440-2640 (office). *Fax:* 440-4184 (office). *E-mail:* foreignaffairs@gov.gd (office).

DAVID SANTIAGO, Adelino Castelo; São Tomé and Príncipe economist, fmr central banker and government official; Gov. Banco Central de São Tomé e Príncipe 1992–94; Minister of Planning and Finance 1999–2001, 2004–05, Co-ordinator, Centre for Research and Analysis of Policies for Devt of São Tomé and Príncipe, Ministry of Planning and Finance 2007–. *Address:* Ministry of Finance and Public Administration, Largo Alfândega, BP 168, São Tomé, São Tomé e Príncipe (office). *Telephone:* 2221083 (office). *Fax:* 2222683 (office). *E-mail:* adelinocd@yahoo.com (home); mpfc@cstome.net (office). *Website:* www.min-financas.st (office).

DAVID-WEILL, Michel; French business executive; *Chairman of the Supervisory Board, EURAZEO;* b. 23 Nov. 1932, Paris; s. of Pierre David-Weill and Berthe Haardt; m. Hélène Lehideux 1956; four d.; ed Lycée français, New York and Inst. d'études politiques, Paris; Lazard Frères & Co. LLC, NY 1961–65, Chair. and Sr Pnr 1977–2005; Gen. Pnr Lazard Frères & Cie, Paris 1965, Maison Lazard & Cie 1976–2005; Gen. Pnr and Chair. Lazard Pnrs Ltd Partnership 1984–2005; Chair. Lazard Brothers & Co. Ltd, London 1990–92, Deputy Chair. 1992, Chair. Lazard LLC (after merger of Lazard Bros. Paris, London and NY offices) 2000–05; mem. Bd of Dirs EURAZEO 1972, now Chair. of Supervisory Bd; mem. Man. Bd, Sovac 1972–, Chair. 1982–95; mem. Bd of Dirs, Danone, later Vice-Chair.; mem. Man. Bd Publicis; Dir La France IARD, La France-Vie, La France Participations et Gestion, SA de la Rue Impériale de Lyon, Fonds Partenaires-Gestion (FPG), Fiat SpA, Euralux, Exor Group, ITT Corp., The Dannon Co. Inc.; fmr Dir Pearson PLC, NY Stock Exchange; Chair. Artistic Council, Réunion des Musées Nationaux, Paris, Metropolitan Museum Council, New York, New York Hosp. Morgan Library; mem. Inst. (Acad. des Beaux Arts, Paris); Grand Officier, Légion d'honneur 2007, Grand Croix 2011; Officier, Ordre nat. du Mérite; Commdr des Arts et des Lettres. *Publication:* L'esprit en fête 2007. *Address:* Institut de France, 23 quai Conti, 75006 Paris, France (office). *Telephone:* 1-44-15-89-34 (office). *Fax:* 1-47-66-43-72 (office). *E-mail:* staff@md-w.com (office). *Website:* www.eurazeo.com (office).

DAVIDE, Hilario Gelbolingo, Jr, BSc, BL; Philippine chief justice and diplomatist; b. 20 Dec. 1935, Barangay Colawin, Argao, Cebu; s. of Hilario P. Davide, Sr and Josefa L. Gelbolingo; m. Virginia (Gigi) Jimenea Perez; three s. two d.; ed Abellana Vocational High School, Univ. of the Philippines; Pvt. Sec. to Vice-Gov. then to Gov. of Cebu 1959–63; Faculty mem. Coll. of Law, Southwestern Univ., Cebu City 1962–68; Del. to Constitutional Convention 1971, Chair. Cttee on Duties and Obligations of Citizens and Ethics of Public Officials; Minority Floor Leader 1978–79; mem. interim Batasang Pambansa Ass. representing Region VII 1978–84; Chair. Comm. on Elections 1988–90, Presidential Fact Finding Comm. 1990–91; Assoc. Justice of the Supreme Court 1991–98, Sr Assoc. Justice Oct.–Nov. 1998, Chief Justice 1998–2005; Amb. and Perm. Rep. to UN, New York 2007–10, Vice-Chair. ECOSOC; Chair. Philippine Truth Comm. 2010–11; mem. Advisory Council of Eminent Jurists, UNEP, Regional Office for Asia and the Pacific; Hon. Pres. World Jurist Asscn of the World Peace Through Law Centre; Kt Grand Cross of the Pontifical Order of St Sylvester 2011; Hon. LLD (Southwestern Univ.) 1999, (Far Eastern Univ.) 2001, (Univ. of the Philippines) 2001, (Angeles Univ. Foundation) 2001, (De La Salle Univ.) 2001; Hon. DH (Univ. of Cebu) 2000, (Ateneo de Manila Univ.) 2001, (Univ. of the Visayas) 2001; Service to the Nation Award 1987, Outstanding Kts of Columbus Award 1995, Nat. Maagap Award, Organized Response for the Advancement of Soc. (ORAS) 1998, The Outstanding Filipino Award in Environmental Law 1999, Millennium Medal of Merit, Order of the Kts of Rizal 2000, Filipino of the Year Award, Philippine Daily Inquirer 2000, Rajah Humabon Award 2001, Grand Perlas Award, Philippine Foundation Inc. 2001, Chief Justice Techankee Foundation 2001, Chino Roces Foundation Freedom Award 2001, Rizal Peace Award, Univ. of S Philippines 2001, Rule of Law Award 2001, Ramon Magsaysay Award for Govt Service 2002, Man of the Year Award, Philippine Free Press 2003, Chief Justice Roberto Concepcion Award for Legal Aid, Integrated Bar of the Philippines 2003, Most Distinguished Alumnus Award, Univ. of the Philippines Alumni Asscn 2005, ABA Int. Rule of Law Award 2006. *Address:* c/o Department of Foreign Affairs, DFA Building, 2330 Roxas Blvd, Pasay City, 1330 Metro Manila, The Philippines (office). *Telephone:* (2) 8344000 (office). *Fax:* (2) 8321597 (office). *E-mail:* webmaster@dfa.gov.ph (office). *Website:* www.dfa.gov.ph (office).

DAVIDS, Willibrord Jacob Maria, LLM; Dutch judge; b. 17 Oct. 1938, Rotterdam; m. Marianne Baan; ed Roman Catholic Univ. of Nijmegen; worked at civil law notary office in Hilversum, Curaçao (Netherlands Antilles) and Groningen 1965; lectured in civil law, Groningen Univ. 1975–80; apptd judge, dist court, Assen 1980, Vice-Pres. 1984; apptd Justice, Supreme Court of the Netherlands 1986, Vice-Pres. 1998–2004, Pres. 2004–08; Pres. Benelux Court, Court of Appeal for Supervision of Standards of Certified Architects, Asscn of Dutch Architects; Chair. Advisory Cttee on assessment of Restitutions Applications for items of cultural value and the Second World War 2009; Chair. Cttee of Iraq Inquiry, The Netherlands 2009; mem. Coll. of Appeal, Benelux Asscn of Trade Mark Lawyers and Counsellors; Kt of the Order of the Dutch Lion 1995, Commdr, Order of Oranje Nassau, Grand Officier, Ordre Grand-Ducal de la Couronne de Chêne (Luxembourg) 2008, Grand Officier, Crown Order (Belgium) 2009. *Publications:* several books and articles on real estate law, corpn law and criminal law. *Address:* c/o De Hoge Raad der Nederlanden, PO Box 20303, 2500 EH The Hague, Netherlands (office). *E-mail:* kabinetpresident@HogeRaad.nl (office).

DAVIDSON, Janet Marjorie, ONZM, FRSNZ, MA, DSc; New Zealand archaeologist and ethnologist (retd); b. 23 Aug. 1941, Lower Hutt, Wellington, North Island; d. of Albert Dick Davidson and Christine Mary Davidson (née Browne); m. Bryan Foss Leach 1979; one d.; ed Hutt Valley High School, Univ. of Auckland; Field Assoc., Bernice P. Bishop Museum, Honolulu 1964–66; E. Earle Vaile Archaeologist, Auckland Inst. and Museum 1966–79; Rhodes Visiting Fellow, Lady Margaret Hall, Oxford, UK 1974–76; Hon. Lecturer in Anthropology, Univ. of Otago 1980–86; ethnologist, Nat. Museum of New Zealand 1987–91; Curator (Pacific Collections), Museum of New Zealand Te Papa Tongarewa 1991–2002, Hon. Research Assoc. 2002–; extensive archaeological field work in New Zealand and the Pacific; Hon. Research Assoc., Museum of New Zealand Te Papa Tongarewa. *Publications include:* Archaeology on Nukuaro Atoll 1971, The Prehistory of New Zealand 1984, Archaeology on Taumako: a Polynesian Outlier in the Eastern Solomon Islands (with B. F. Leach) 2008, numerous articles on the archaeology and prehistory of New Zealand and various Pacific Islands. *Leisure interests:* music, theatre, opera, ballet, cooking.

DAVIDSON, John Macdonald, AM, BArch, LFRAIA; Australian architect; b. 21 Oct. 1926, Sydney, NSW; s. of John H. Davidson and Daisy Macdonald; m. Helen M. King 1954; two s. one d.; ed Geelong Coll. and Univ. of Melbourne; Assoc. Godfrey and Spowers (architects) 1954–61, Pnr, later Dir 1961, Chair. Godfrey and Spowers Australia Pty Ltd 1979–91; Co-founder (with son Hugo Davidson) and Dir, Catalyst Design Group 1991–2004, Prin., Catalyst Architecture 2004–14; Pres. Royal Australian Inst. of Architects 1978–79; mem. Expert Panel in Architecture (COPQ) 1978–; mem. Int. Council, Int. Union of Architects (UIA) 1981–85, Vice-Pres. UIA 1985–87; Chair. Metropolitan Strategy Consultative Cttee 1984–89, South Yarra Collaborative Pty Ltd 1983–89; Hon. FAIA 1985. *Publication:* The Awarding and Administration of Architectural Contracts 1961. *Leisure interests:* music, art, writing. *Address:* 502/633 Church Street, Richmond, Vic. 3121, Australia (home). *Telephone:* (3) 9421-1378 (office). *E-mail:* jmd425@gmail.com (office).

DAVIDSON, Sir Martin Stuart, Kt, KCMG, CMG, MA, FRSA; British organization official; *Chairman, Great Britain China Centre;* b. 14 Oct. 1955, Lowestoft, Suffolk; m.; three c.; ed St Andrew's Univ.; Admin. Officer, Hong Kong Govt 1979–83; with British Council, Peking 1984–87, Regional Officer, China 1987–89, Dir S China 1989–93, Asst Regional Dir E and S Europe 1993–95, Cultural Counsellor and Dir China 1995–2000, Regional Dir E Asia and the Americas 2000–03, Regional Dir Europe 2003–06, Deputy Dir-Gen. 2006–07, CEO British Council 2007–14; Chair. Adam Smith Int. 2017; mem. Exec. Cttee GB China Centre, Chair. 2015–; Trustee, Leonard Cheshire Disability; Gov., Goodenough Coll. *Leisure interests:* hill walking, flying. *Address:* Great Britain China Centre, 5 Belgrave Square, London, SW1X 8PS, England (office). *Telephone:* (20) 7235-6696 (office). *E-mail:* contact@gbcc.org.uk (office). *Website:* www.gbcc.org.uk (office).

DAVIDSON, Ogunlade R., BEng, PEng, CEng; Sierra Leonean engineer, academic and international organization official; ed Univ. of Sierra Leone, UMIST (now Univ. of Manchester) and Univ. of Salford, UK; chartered engineer 1993; Lecturer, Univ. of Sierra Leone 1978–83, Sr Lecturer 1983–93, first Dir of Research 1985–92, Head of Dept of Mechanical and Maintenance Eng 1993–2000, Prof. of Mechanical Eng 1993–, Dean of Faculty of Eng 1996–2000, 2003–05, currently Dean of Post-Grad. Studies; Prof. and Dir Energy and Devt Research Centre, Univ. of Cape Town, South Africa 2000–03; Minister of Energy and Water Resources 2010–12; Sr Fulbright Scholar, Univ. of California, Berkeley, USA 1987; MacArthur Scholar, Princeton Univ. and Lawrence Berkeley Lab., USA 1990–92; Visiting Prof., Univ. of Gothenburg, Sweden, ENDA-TM, Senegal, Riso Nat. Lab., Denmark; Co-Chair. Working Group III, Intergovernmental Panel on Climate Change (IPCC) 1997–2008, Vice-Chair. IPCC 2008–09; Co-Chair. Steering Cttee of Global Network on Energy for Sustainable Devt; has worked as consultant in energy, tech., climate change and environment for several nat. and int. bodies, including UNESCO, UNIDO, ILO, UN Econ. Comm. for Africa, UNDP, UNEP, Global Environment Facility, UN Framework Convention on Climate Change, New Partnership for Africa's Devt (NEPAD), Arab Devt Bank, World Bank,

Batelle Labs and Carnegie Corpn, New York; Corp. mem. Sierra Leone Inst. of Engineers 1979, Nigerian Soc. of Engineers 1985, Inst. of Energy (UK) 1993; Fellow, Univ. Research Council 1987, African Acad. of Sciences 1991, Sierra Leone Inst. of Engineers 2001. *Publications:* more than 300 publs, including books, book chapters, journal articles and conf. papers on African energy systems and policies, power sector reform, renewable energy policy, climate change-greenhouse gas mitigation and nat. climate change strategy.

DAVIDSON, Richard K., BS; American business executive (retd); b. 1942, Allen, Kan.; m. Trish Davidson; three c.; ed Washburn Univ., Harvard Univ.; Conductor, Missouri Pacific Railroad 1960, Asst Trainmaster, Shreveport, LA 1966, later various operating positions in Fort Worth, Kansas City and N Little Rock, becoming Asst to Vice-Pres., Operations, St Louis 1975, Vice-Pres., Operations, 1976; joined Union Pacific Railroad (following merger with Missouri Pacific and Western Pacific) 1982, Vice-Pres., Operations 1986, Exec. Vice-Pres. 1989–91, Pres. and CEO 1991–2006, Chair. 1991–2006 (retd), Chair. Union Pacific Corpn 1997–2007; fmr Chair. Pres.'s Nat. Infrastructure Advisory Cttee; mem. Bd of Dirs Chesapeake Energy Corpn 2006–; Trustee and Dir Malcolm Baldrige Nat. Quality Award Foundation; fmr mem. US Strategic Command Consultation Cttee; mem. Horatio Alger Asscn; mem. Bd of Advisors Thayer Capital Pnrs; fmr Trustee, Boy Scouts of America, Washburn Univ. Endowment Asscn, Strategic Air and Space Museum, Omaha; Dr hc (Washburn Univ.) 1984, (Bellevue Univ.) 2003, (Univ. of Nebraska, Kearney) 2003; Kan. Business Hall of Fame 2001, Horatio Alger Asscn of Distinguished Americans 2002, Light of Wellness Award 2003, Railway Age Railroader of the Year 2003, Neb. Business Hall of Fame 2004, Omaha Business Hall of Fame 2006.

DAVIES, A. Michael, MA, FCA; British business executive; b. 23 June 1934; s. of Angelo Henry Davies and Clarice Mildred Davies; m. Jane Priscilla Davies 1962; one s. (deceased) one d.; ed Shrewsbury School, Queens' Coll., Cambridge; Chair. Tozer Kemsley & Millbourne 1982–86, Bredero Properties 1986–94, Worth Investment Trust 1987–95, Calor Group 1989–97 (Dir 1987–97), Perkins Foods 1987–2001, Berk 1988–95, Wiltshier 1988–95, Nat. Express Group PLC 1991–2004, Simon Group 1993–2003, Corporate Services Group 1999–2002; Deputy Chair. T.I. Group 1990–93 (Dir 1984–93), Manpower 1987–91, AerFi 1993–2000; Dir Imperial Group 1972–82, Littlewoods Org. 1982–88, TV-am 1982–88, British Airways 1983–2002, Worcester Group 1991–92. *Address:* Little Woolpit, Ewhurst, Cranleigh, Surrey, GU6 7NP, England. *Telephone:* (1483) 277344. *Fax:* (1483) 277899. *E-mail:* amdavies@btinternet.com.

DAVIES, Sir David Evan Naunton (Den), Kt, CBE, PhD, DSc, FRS, FREng; British electrical engineer and academic; *Non-Parliamentary Board Member, Parliamentary Office of Science and Technology;* b. 28 Oct. 1935, Cardiff, Wales; s. of D. E. Davies and Sarah Samuel; m. 1st Enid Patilla 1962 (died 1990); two s.; m. 2nd Jennifer E. Rayner 1992; ed Univ. of Birmingham; Lecturer, then Sr Lecturer in Electrical Eng, Univ. of Birmingham 1961–67; Asst Dir Research Dept, British Railways Bd 1967–71; Visiting Industrial Prof. of Electrical Eng, Univ. of Loughborough 1969–71; Prof. of Electrical Eng, Univ. Coll. London 1971–88, Pender Prof. of Electrical Eng 1985–88, Vice-Provost Univ. Coll. 1986–88; Vice-Chancellor Loughborough Univ. of Tech. 1988–93; Chief Scientific Adviser, Ministry of Defence 1993–99; Chair. Defence Scientific Advisory Council 1992–93; Pres. IEE 1994–95; Vice-Pres. Royal Acad. of Eng 1995–96, Pres. 1996–2001; Chair. Railway Safety 2000–03; Chair. Hazards Forum 2002–10; Dir Strategy Ltd 1974–79, Gaydon Tech. 1986–88, Loughborough Consultants 1988–93, Inst. Consumer Ergonomics 1988–93, ERA Tech. 1997–, Lattice PLC 2000–02; Adviser to Bd, Nat. Grid PLC 2003–08; mem. Defence Acad. Advisory Bd, Bd ERA Foundation 2002–07; Non-Parl. Bd mem. Parl. Office of Science and Tech. 2010–; Foreign mem. Russian Acad. of Sciences 2004; Fellow, Learned Soc. of Wales 2010; Hon. Fellow, Univ. of Wales, Coll. of Cardiff 2001, Univ. Coll. London 2006; Hon. FIMechE; Hon. Fellow Inst. of Eng and Tech.; Hon. DSc (Birmingham) 1994, (Loughborough) 1994, (South Bank) 1994, (Bradford) 1995, (Surrey) 1996, (Warwick) 1997, (Bath) 1997, (Heriot-Watt) 1999, (UMIST) 2000, (Wales) 2002; Rank Prize for Optoelectronics 1984, IEEE Centennial Medal 1984, IEE Faraday Medal 1987, Royal Acad. of Eng Pres.'s Medal 2007. *Publications:* about 120 publs on antennas, radar and fibre optics. *Address:* Parliamentary Office of Science and Technology, 14 Tothill Street, London, SW1H 9NB, England. *E-mail:* den@easonestates.freeserve.co.uk (office); post@parliament.uk. *Website:* www.parliament.uk/post; www.raeng.org.uk/about-us/people-council-committees/the-president/past-presidents/davies.

DAVIES, Edward Brian, BA, DPhil, FRS; British mathematician and academic; *Professor Emeritus in Analysis, King's College London;* b. 13 June 1944, Cardiff, Wales; m. Jane Christine Phillips 1968; one s. one d.; ed St John's Coll., Oxford; Lecturer in Math., Univ. of Oxford 1970–81; Prof. of Math., King's Coll., London 1981–2010, Head of Dept 1990–93, Prof. Emer. in Analysis 2010–, Fellow, King's Coll. 1996; Founding Ed. London Math. Soc. Student Texts 1983–90, Journal of Spectral Theory 2010–; Pres. London Math. Soc. 2008–09; Senior Berwick Prize, London Math. Soc. 1998, Pólya Prize 2011. *Publications:* Quantum Theory of Open Systems 1976, One-Parameter Semigroups 1980, Heat Kernels and Spectral Theory 1989, Spectral Theory and Differential Operators 1995, Spectral Theory and Geometry 1999, Science in the Looking Glass: What do Scientists Really Know 2003, Linear Operators and their Spectra 2007, Why Beliefs Matter 2010; more than 200 research papers. *Leisure interests:* philosophy, science. *Address:* Room S4.20, Strand Building, Department of Mathematics, King's College, Strand, London, WC2R 2LS, England (office). *Telephone:* (20) 7848-2698 (office). *Fax:* (20) 7848-2017 (office). *E-mail:* e.brian.davies@kcl.ac.uk (office). *Website:* www.kcl.ac.uk/nms/depts/mathematics/people/atoz/daviesb.aspx (office); www.mth.kcl.ac.uk/~davies (office).

DAVIES, Gavyn, OBE, BS; British economist and business executive; *Founding Partner, Active Private Equity Advisory LLP;* b. 27 Nov. 1950; s. of W. J. F. Davies and M. G. Davies; m. Susan Jane Nye 1989; two s. one d.; ed St John's Coll., Cambridge and Balliol Coll., Oxford; Econ. Adviser, Policy Unit, 10 Downing Street 1974–79; economist, Phillips and Drew 1979–81; Chief UK Economist, Simon & Coates 1981–86; Chief UK Economist, Goldman Sachs 1986–93, Partner 1988–2001, Head of Investment Research (London) 1991–93, Chief Int. Economist and Head of European Investment Research 1993–97, Chair. Investment Research Dept 1999–2001, Advisory Dir 2001–; Vice-Chair. BBC 2001, Chair. 2001–04 (resgnd); Founding Partner, Active Private Equity Advisory LLP; Founder and Advisory Partner, Prisma Capital Partners; Chair. Fulcrum Asset Management; writes a blog on macroeconomics for the Financial Times 2010–; Visiting Prof. of Econs, LSE 1988–98; Prin. Econs Commentator, The Independent 1991–99; mem. HM Treasury's Ind. Forecasting Panel 1993–97; Chair. Govt Inquiry into the Future Funding of the BBC 1999; Hon. Fellow, Aberystwyth Univ. 2002; Hon. DScS (Southampton) 1998; Hon. LLD (Nottingham) 2002; Dr hc (Middlesex). *Leisure interest:* Southampton Football Club. *Address:* Active Private Equity Advisory LLP, 2nd Floor, 6 Burnsall Street, London, SW3 3ST, England (office). *Telephone:* (20) 7042-8200 (office). *Fax:* (20) 7351-9169 (office). *E-mail:* enquiries@apeq.co.uk (office). *Website:* apeq.co.uk (office); www.prismapartners.com.

DAVIES, Gideon John, BSc, PhD, DSc, FRS, FRSC, FMedSci; British chemist and academic; *Professor of Chemistry, University of York;* b. 6 July 1964, Great Sutton, Cheshire; m. Valérie Marie-Andrée Ducros 1999; two d.; ed Univ. of Bristol; post-doctoral research at European Molecular Biology Lab., Hamburg Outstation on the use of synchrotron radiation in protein crystallography 1990; moved to York to work on the structure of DNA gyrase, then continued there working on carbohydrate-active enzymes, study periods at CERMAV Grenoble and in Uppsala, Prof. of Chem., Univ. of York 2001–, apptd 40th Anniversary Prof. 2004; Peter Wall Catalytic Visitor, Univ. of British Columbia 2000; Fellow, Acad. of Medical Sciences 2014–; mem. European Molecular Biology Org. 2010–; Royal Society Ken Murray Research Professorship 2017–; numerous awards, including Royal Soc. Univ. Research Fellowship 1996, Gabor Medal, Royal Soc. 2010, Khorana Prize, Royal Soc. of Chemistry 2014, Davy Medal, Royal Soc. 2015, iCHEME Global Energy Award 2016. *Publications:* more than 300 papers in professional journals. *Address:* York Structural Biology Laboratory, Department of Chemistry, University of York, Heslington, York, YO10 5DD, England (office). *Telephone:* (1904) 328260 (office). *Fax:* (1904) 328266 (office). *E-mail:* gideon.davies@york.ac.uk (office). *Website:* www.york.ac.uk/chemistry/staff/academic/d-g/gdavies (office).

DAVIES, Sir Graeme John, Kt, BE, MA, PhD, ScD, FRSE, FREng; British (b. New Zealand) university vice-chancellor; *Vice-Chancellor Emeritus, University of London;* b. 7 April 1937, Auckland; s. of Harry J. Davies and Gladys E. Davies; m. Florence I. Martin 1959 (deceased 2014); one s. one d.; ed Univ. of Auckland, Univ. of Cambridge; Lecturer, Univ. of Cambridge 1962–77, Fellow, St Catharine's Coll. 1967–76; Prof., Dept of Metallurgy, Univ. of Sheffield 1977–86; Vice-Chancellor Univ. of Liverpool 1986–91; Chief Exec. Univs' Funding Council 1991–93, Polytechnics' and Colls' Funding Council 1992–93, Higher Educ. Funding Council for England 1992–95; Prin. and Vice-Chancellor Univ. of Glasgow 1995–2003; Vice-Chancellor Univ. of London 2003–10, Vice-Chancellor Emer. 2010–; Freeman, City of London, Freeman and Burgess Holder, City of Glasgow, Hon. FRSNZ, Hon. Fellow, Trinity Coll. of Music 1995, School of Pharmacy 2012, Royal Veterinary Coll. 2012; Hon. DSc (Nottingham) 1995, (Edin.) 2003, (Ulster) 2004, (London South Bank) 2006, Hon. DMet (Sheffield) 1995; Hon. LLD (Liverpool) 1991, (Strathclyde) 2000, (London) 2012, Hon. DEng (Manchester Metropolitan) 1996, (Auckland) 2003, Hon. DUniv (Glasgow, Paisley) 2004, Hon. DLitt (Bath Spa) 2010. *Publications include:* Solidification and Casting 1973, Textures and Properties of Materials 1976, Hot Working and Forming Processes 1980, Superplasticity 1981, Essential Metallurgy for Engineers 1985. *Leisure interests:* cricket, bird-watching, The Times crossword. *Address:* The Coach House, Fosse Road, Farndon, Newark, NG24 3SF, England (home). *Telephone:* (1636) 673117 (home). *E-mail:* graeme.davies@lon.ac.uk (office).

DAVIES, Sir Howard John, Kt, MA, MSc; British academic administrator and business executive; *Chairman, Royal Bank of Scotland;* b. 12 Feb. 1951, Prestbury; s. of Leslie Davies and Marjorie Davies; m. Prudence Keely 1984; two s.; ed Manchester Grammar School, Merton Coll., Oxford and Stanford Grad. School of Business; Foreign Office 1973–74, Pvt. Sec. to British Amb. in Paris 1974–76; HM Treasury 1976–82; McKinsey & Co. Inc. 1982–87; Controller, Audit Comm. 1987–92; Dir GKN PLC 1990–95; Dir-Gen. Confed. of British Industry (CBI) 1992–95; Deputy Gov., Bank of England 1995–97, Dir (non-exec.) 1998–2003; Chair. Financial Services Authority (fmrly Securities and Investments Bd) 1997–2003; Dir LSE 2003–11; Dir Nat. Theatre 2011–15; Prof. of Practice, Inst. of Political Studies (Sciences Po), Paris 2011–; mem. NatWest Int. Advisory Bd 1992–95; Chair. Advisory Bd, China Securities Regulatory Comm. 2012–; Chair. Phoenix Group 2012–15; Chair. Royal Bank of Scotland 2015–; mem. Bd Morgan Stanley 2004–15, Paternoster UK Ltd 2006–10, Prudential PLC 2010–; mem. Advisory Bd, China Banking Regulatory Comm. 2003–, Int. Advisory Bd, Govt Investment Corpn of Singapore 2011–12; Chair. Airports Comm. 2012–15; Deputy Chair. Rowntree Cttee Enquiry 1993; Dir (non-exec.), Prudential PLC 2011– (Chair. Risk Cttee); mem. Bd, Royal Nat. Theatre 2011–15, Advisory Bd, SWIFT Inst. 2012–14, Advisory Bd, Asian Bureau for Financial and Econ. Research (Singapore) 2013–; Pres. Age Concern England 1994–98; Chair. Employers' Forum on Age 1996–2004; Chair. panel of judges Man Booker Prize 2007; Trustee, Tate Gallery 2002–10; Gov. RAM 2004–13; Chair. of Trustees, London Library 2015–. *Publications:* Chancellors Tales 2006, Global Financial Regulation: The Essential Guide (with David Green) 2008, Banking on the Future (with David Green) 2010, The Financial Crisis: Who's to Blame 2010, Can Financial Markets Be Controlled 2015; writes regularly for The Financial Times, Times Higher Education, Project Syndicate, Times Literary Supplement. *Leisure interests:* cricket, writing for publication. *Address:* Royal Bank of Scotland, 280 Bishopsgate, London, EC2M 4RB, England (office). *Telephone:* (131) 523-2672 (Edinburgh) (office). *Website:* www.rbs.com (office).

DAVIES, Jonathan, OBE, MBE; British sports commentator and fmr rugby player (rugby union and rugby league); b. 24 Oct. 1962, Trimsaran, Carmarthenshire, Wales; s. of Leonard Davies and Diana Davies (née Rees); m. 1st Karen Marie Davies 1984 (died 1997); two s. one d.; m. 2nd Helen Jones 2002; ed Gwendraeth Grammar School; rugby union outside-half; played for the following rugby union clubs: Trimsaran, Neath 1982–88, Llanelli 1988–89; turned professional in 1989; with Cardiff 1995–97; played for Welsh nat. team 1985–97, (v. England) 1985, World Cup Squad (6 appearances) 1987, Triple Crown winning team 1988, tour NZ (2 test appearances) 1988, 29 caps, sometime Capt.; also played for Barbarians Rugby Football Club; rugby league career: played at three-quarters; Widnes (world record transfer fee) 1989, Warrington 1993–95 (free transfer); for Welsh nat. team 1993–95; British nat. team 1989–94, tour NZ 1990, six caps, fmr Capt.; reverted to rugby union 1995; retd 1997; commentator on rugby union and league for Channel 4 Wales; TV pundit for BBC covering both rugby codes, in both English and Welsh; Pres. Super League side Crusaders –2009. *Television:* hosts own rugby-themed chatshow, Jonathan (S4C) 2004–. *Publication:* Jonathan (autobiog.) 1989. *Leisure interest:* all sports. *Address:* c/o S4C, Parc Tŷ Glas, Llanishen, Cardiff, CF14 5DU, Wales. *Website:* www.bbc.co.uk/programmes/p02b52d4.

DAVIES, Dame Kay Elizabeth, DBE, CBE, MA, DPhil, FRS, FRCPath, MRCP, FMedSci; British geneticist and academic; *Associate Director (Development, Impact and Equality), Medical Sciences Division, University of Oxford;* b. 1 April 1951, Stourbridge, West Midlands; d. of Harry Partridge and Florence Partridge; m. Stephen Graham Davies 1973 (divorced); one s.; ed Somerville and Wolfson Colls, Oxford; Guy Newton Jr Research Fellow, Wolfson Coll., Oxford 1976–78; Royal Soc. European Postdoctoral Fellow, Service de Biochimie, Centre d'études nucléaires de Saclay, Gif-sur-Yvette, France 1978–80; Cystic Fibrosis Research Fellow, Biochemistry Dept, St Mary's Hosp. Medical School, London 1980–82, MRC Sr Research Fellow, 1982–84; MRC Sr Research Fellow, Nuffield Dept of Clinical Medicine, John Radcliffe Hosp., Oxford 1984–86, MRC External Staff 1986–89, Molecular Genetics Group, Inst. of Molecular Medicine 1989–92, MRC Research Dir, Royal Postgraduate Medical School 1992–94, Head of Molecular Genetics Group, Inst. of Molecular Medicine 1994–95; Prof. of Molecular Genetics, Univ. of London 1992–94; Prof. of Genetics, Dept of Biochemistry, Univ. of Oxford 1995–97, Dr Lee's Prof. of Anatomy 1998–2018, currently Assoc. Dir (Devt, Impact and Equality), Medical Sciences Div.; Hon. Dir MRC Functional Genetics Unit, Oxford 1999–2017; Co-Dir Oxford Centre for Gene Function 2001–; Univ. Research Lecturer, Nuffield Dept of Clinical Medicine, John Radcliffe Hosp. 1989–92; Fellow, Green Coll., Oxford 1989–92, 1994–95, Keble Coll., Oxford 1995–, Hertford Coll., Oxford 1997–; Gov., Wellcome Trust 2008–17; Wellcome Trust Award 1996, SCI Medal 1999, Feldberg Foundation Prize 1999, Gaetano Conte Prize in Basic Myology 2002, Huxley Lecturer, Univ. of Birmingham 2007, SET Award for Science and Tech. 2008, Award for Excellence in Molecular Diagnostics, AMP, Orlando, USA 2009, Harveian Oration, Royal Coll. of Physicians 2013, WISE Lifetime Achievement Award 2014, BNA Award for Outstanding Contrib. to British Neuroscience 2014, Outstanding Scientist Award for William Harvey 2015, William Allan Award, American Soc. of Human Genetics 2015, Muscular Dystrophy Award for Scientist of the Year 2015, Vallee Visiting Professor (VVPs) Award 2017, Croonian Medal and Lecture, Royal Soc. of London 2018. *Publications:* more than 350 papers in scientific journals. *Leisure interests:* walking, music, gardening. *Address:* Department of Physiology, Anatomy and Genetics, University of Oxford, Parks Road, Oxford, OX1 3PT, England (office). *Telephone:* (1865) 285880 (office). *Fax:* (1865) 285878 (office). *E-mail:* kay.davies@dpag.ox.ac.uk (office). *Website:* www.dpag.ox.ac.uk (office).

DAVIES, Dame Laura Jane, DBE, CBE, MBE; British professional golfer; b. 5 Oct. 1963, Coventry, Warwicks., England; d. of David Thomas Davies and Rita Ann Davies (née Foskett); turned professional 1985; has won four major tournaments, including 1987 US Open 1987, LPGA Championship 1994, Du Maurier 1996, LPGA Championship 2006; other victories include Ladies' British Open 1986, La Manga Spanish Open 1986, Italian Ladies' Open 1987, 1988, European Ladies' Open 1992, Ladies' English Open 1992, 1993, BMW Italian Ladies' Open 1992, Sara Lee Classic 1994, Irish Open 1994, 1995, Evian Masters 1995, 1996, Wilkinson Sword Ladies' English Open 1995, 1996, McDonald's WPGA Championship 1999, TSN Ladies World Cup of Golf (Individual) 2000, WPGA Int. Matchplay 2001, AAMI Women's Australian Open 2004, 2009, SAS Masters 2006, UNIQA Ladies' Golf Open 2007, 2008, 2010, Pegasus New Zealand Women's Open 2010, UniCredit Ladies' German Open 2010, Open De España Femenino 2010, Hero Honda Women's Indian Open 2010, ISPS Handa Legends Tour Open Championship (Legends Tour event) 2012; rep. England in World Team Championship, Taiwan 1992, 2005, 2006, 2007, Europe in Solheim Cup 1990, 1992 (winners), 1994, 1996, 1998, 2000 (winners), 2002, 2003 (winners), 2005, 2007, 2009, 2011 (winners), International team in Lexus Cup 2006, World team in Handa Cup 2013 (winners); mem. BBC Sport commentary team for The Open Championship and other major golfing events 2001–; Capt. of Rest of the World team in annual Rest of the World v. Australia cricket match held during ANZ Ladies Masters; Ladies European Tour (LET) Rookie of the Year 1985, LET Order of Merit 1985, 1986, 1992, 1996, 1999, 2004, 2006, Rolex Player of the Year 1996, LET Player of the Year 1996, 1999, LPGA Tour Money Winner 1994, LPGA Tour Player of the Year 1996, GWAA Female Player of the Year 1994, 1996, Best Female Golfer ESPY Award 1995, 2000, ASAPSports/Jim Murray Award, Golf Writers Asscn of America 2013. *Publication:* Carefree Golf 1991. *Leisure interests:* fast cars, all sports (follows Liverpool Football Club), shopping. *Website:* www.lauradaviesgolf.com.

DAVIES, Nicholas Barry, BA, DPhil, FRS; British biologist and academic; *Professor of Behavioural Ecology, Department of Zoology, University of Cambridge;* b. 23 May 1952, Liverpool; s. of Anthony Barry Davies and Joyce Margaret Davies; m. Jan Parr 1979; two d.; ed Merchant Taylors' School, Crosby, Pembroke Coll., Cambridge, Wolfson Coll., Oxford; Demonstrator in Zoology, Edward Grey Inst., Univ. of Oxford 1976–79; Jr Research Fellow, Wolfson Coll., Oxford 1977–79; Demonstrator, Dept of Zoology, Univ. of Cambridge 1979–84, Lecturer 1984–92, Reader 1992–95, Prof. of Behavioural Ecology 1995–, Fellow, Pembroke Coll. Cambridge 1979–; Pres. Int. Soc. for Behavioural Ecology 2000–02; Corresp. mem. German Ornithological Soc. 2000; Corresp. Fellow, American Ornithologists' Union 1999, Hon. Fellow 2004; Hon. mem. Spanish Ornithological Soc. 2004; Dr hc (Bielefeld) 2011; Scientific Medal, Zoological Soc. of London 1987, Cambridge Univ. Teaching Prize 1995, William Bate Hardy Prize, Cambridge Philosophical Soc. 1995, Medal of Asscn for Study of Animal Behaviour 1996, Frink Medal, Zoological Soc. of London 2001, Elliott Coues Award, American Ornithologists' Union 2005, Hamilton Prize Lecturer, Int. Soc. for Behavioural Ecology 2010, Royal Soc. Croonian Medal and Lecture 2015. *Publications include:* Behavioural Ecology: an Evolutionary Approach (co-ed.) 1978 (fourth edn 1997), An Introduction to Behavioural Ecology (co-author) 1981 (fourth edn 2012), Dunnock Behaviour and Social Evolution 1992, Cuckoos, Cowbirds and Other Cheats (Best Book of the Year Award, British Trust for Ornithology 2000) 2000, Cuckoo: Cheating by Nature 2015. *Leisure interests:* birdwatching, mountains, music. *Address:* Department of Zoology, University of Cambridge, Downing Street, Cambridge, CB2 3EJ, England (office). *Telephone:* (1223) 334405 (office). *Fax:* (1223) 336676 (office). *E-mail:* nbd1000@cam.ac.uk (office); n.b.davies@zoo.cam.ac.uk (office). *Website:* www.zoo.cam.ac.uk (office).

DAVIES, Omar, DEcon; Jamaican economist, academic and politician; b. 28 May 1947, Clarendon; m.; three c.; ed Univ. of the West Indies, Northwestern Univ., USA; Asst Prof., Stanford Univ. 1973–76; Sr Lecturer, Univ. of the West Indies 1981–89; Dir-Gen. Planning Inst. of Jamaica 1989–93; mem. People's Nat. Party; with Office of the Prime Minister April–Aug. 1993; Minister without Portfolio responsible for Planning Devt Project Implementation Aug.–Nov. 1993; mem. Parl. 1993–2017, apptd Chair. Public Accounts Cttee 2007; Minister of Finance and Planning 1993–2007, of Transport, Works and Housing 2012–16.

DAVIES, Rt Hon. Ron(ald), PC; British politician; b. 6 Aug. 1946; s. of Ronald Davies; m. 1st Anne Williams; m. 2nd Christina Elizabeth Rees 1981; one d.; m. 3rd Lynne Hughes 2002; ed Bassaleg Grammar School, Portsmouth Polytechnic, Univ. Coll. of Wales, Cardiff; schoolteacher 1968–70; Workers' Educ. Asscn Tutor/Organizer 1970–74; Further Educ. Adviser, Mid-Glamorgan Local Educ. Authority 1974–83; mem. Rhymney Valley Dist Council 1969–84 (fmr Vice-Chair.); MP (Labour) for Caerphilly 1983–2001, Opposition Whip 1985–87, Labour Spokesman on Agric. and Rural Affairs 1987–92, on Wales 1992–97, Sec. of State for Wales 1997–98; elected leader of Labour Group in Nat. Ass. for Wales Sept. 1998, resgnd Oct. 1998; mem. Nat. Ass. for Wales for Caerphilly 1999–2003 (resgnd), Chair. Econ. Devt Cttee 1999–2003; mem. Labour Party –2004, Forward Wales party 2004–09, Policy Dir; Ind. 2009–10; mem. Plaid Cymru 2010–, unsuccessful cand. for Caerphilly in Welsh Ass. elections 2011, for Bedwas 2012; Highest Order, Gorsedd of the Bards 1998. *Publications:* pamphlets on Welsh devolution. *Leisure interests:* walking, gardening, sport. *Address:* c/o Plaid Cymru—Party of Wales, Tŷ Gwynfor, Anson Court, Atlantic Wharf, Cardiff, CF10 4AL, Wales (office). *Telephone:* (29) 2047-2272 (office). *E-mail:* post@plaid.cymru (office). *Website:* www.plaid.cymru (office).

DAVIES, Dame Sally Claire, DBE, FRS, FMedSci, MB, ChB, MSc; British civil servant and fmr physician; *Chief Medical Officer of England;* b. 24 Nov. 1949, Birmingham; d. of John Davies; m. 3rd Willem Ouwehand 1989; two d.; ed Manchester Medical School, Univ. of Manchester, Univ. of London; early career as jr doctor in clinical practice; Consultant Haematologist, Central Middlesex Hosp. 1985, Prof. of Haemoglobinopathies 1997, Emer. Prof., Imperial Coll. London 2011–; joined Civil Service to take up research position in London 2004, becoming Dir-Gen. of Research and Devt and later Chief Scientific Adviser to Dept of Health; apptd Chief Medical Officer of England (first female) 2010–; Chair. UK Clinical Research Collaboration; mem. World Health Org. (WHO) Exec. Bd, WHO Advisory Cttee on Health Research 2000–12; mem. Bd, Office for Strategic Co-ordination of Health Research, Medical Research Council, Int. Advisory Cttee for A*STAR, Singapore, Caribbean Health Research Council; 24 hon. degrees including (Lancaster) 2011, (Leeds) 2011, (Manchester) 2012, (Newcastle) 2013, (Surrey) 2014, (Leicester) 2014, (Loughborough) 2014, (Univ. Coll. London) 2016. *Address:* Room 114, Department of Health, Richmond House, 79 Whitehall, London, SW1A 2NS, England (office). *Telephone:* (20) 7210-4850 (office). *Fax:* (115) 902-3202 (office). *E-mail:* CMOweb@dh.gsi.gov.uk (office). *Website:* www.gov.uk/government/people/sally-davies (office).

DAVIES, Stephen (Steve) Graham, BA, MA, DPhil, DSc, CChem, MRSC; British chemist and academic; *Waynflete Professor of Chemistry, University of Oxford;* b. 24 Feb. 1950, Birmingham; s. of Gordon W. J. Davies and June M. Murphy; one s. from previous m.; partner Anne Tennant-Eyles; ed Univ. of Oxford; ICI Postdoctoral Fellow, Oxford 1975–77; NATO Postdoctoral Fellow, Oxford 1977–78; Attaché de Recherche, CNRS, Paris 1978–80; Fellow, New Coll., Oxford 1980–; Univ. Lecturer in Chem., Univ. of Oxford 1980–, Prof. 1996–2004, Waynflete Prof. of Chem. 2006–, Chair. of Chem. Dept 2006–11; Founder and Dir Oxford Asymmetry International PLC 1991–2000, Summit Therapeutics Ltd and Inc. 2003–, Oxstem Ltd 2011–; mem. of various cttees, editorial bds; Hickinbottom Fellowship 1984; Dr. hc (Univ. of Salamanca, Spain) Pfizer Award for Chem. 1985, 1988, Corday Morgan Medal 1984, RSC Award for Organometallic Chem. 1989, RSC Bader Award 1989, Tilden Lecture Award 1996, RSC Award in Stereochemistry 1997, Prize Lectureship, Soc. of Synthetic Organic Chemistry, Japan 1998, RSC Perkin Medal 2011. *Publications:* Organometallic Chemistry: Applications to Organic Chemistry 1982; more than 570 papers in learned journals. *Leisure interests:* chemistry, wine, food. *Address:* Chemistry Research Laboratory, University of Oxford, Mansfield Road, Oxford, OX1 3TA, England (office). *Telephone:* (1865) 275695 (office). *E-mail:* steve.davies@chem.ox.ac.uk (office). *Website:* research.chem.ox.ac.uk/steve-davies.aspx (office).

DAVIES, Terence; British film director and screenwriter; b. 10 Nov. 1945, Liverpool, England; ed Sacred Heart RC Boys' School, Coventry Drama School and Nat. Film School; articled clerk in shipping office 1960–61; worked in accountancy practice 1961–73; professorship, Univ. of Liverpool 2010; hon. degree from Univ. of Liverpool 2010; British Film Inst. Fellowship 2007, Maverick Spirit Award, Cinequest Film Festival 2012. *Films:* Children 1977, Madonna and Child (short) 1980, Death and Transfiguration (short) 1983, Distant Voices, Still Lives (Int. Critics Prize, Cannes Film Festival) 1988, Movie Masterclass 1990, The Long Day Closes (Evening Standard British Film Award for Best Screenplay) 1992, The Neon Bible 1995, The House of Mirth 2000, Of Time and the City (documentary) (New York Film Critics Circle Award for Best Non-Fiction Film 2009, Australian Film Critics Asscn Award for Best Documentary 2009) 2008, The Deep Blue Sea 2011, Sunset Song 2015, A Quiet Passion 2015. *Radio:* Travels in Celluloid (BBC Radio 4 Book of the Week) 2000, The Walk to the Paradise Garden (BBC Radio 3) 2001, Virginia Woolf's The Waves (adaptation), Intensive Care (BBC Radio 3) 2010. *Publications:* Hallelujah Now (novel) 1983, A Modest Pageant 1992; subject of Terence Davies: A Critical Study (by Wendy Everett). *Leisure interests:* reading, listening to music, dining, humour. *E-mail:* info@terencedavies.com. *Website:* www.terencedavies.com.

DAVIES OF ABERSOCH, Baron (Life Peer), cr. 2009, of Abersoch in the County of Gwynedd; **E(van) Mervyn,** CBE, JP, FCIB; British banking executive and government official; *Vice-Chairman, Corsair Capital LLC;* b. 1952; s. of Richard Aled Davies and Margaret Davies; m. Jeanne Marie Gammie 1979; one s. one d.; ed

Rydal School, North Wales, Harvard Business School; Man. Dir UK Banking and Sr Credit Officer, Citibank 1983–93; joined Standard Chartered Bank PLC with responsibility for Global Account Man. 1993, Head of Corp. and Investment Banking, Singapore –1997, mem. Bd Dirs 1997–2009, Group Exec. Dir responsible for Group-wide Tech. and Operations in Hong Kong, China and NE Asia 1997–2001, Group Chief Exec., London 2001–06, Chair. 2006–09 (resgnd); Minister for Trade Promotion and Investment 2009–10, also Labour Whip in House of Lords 2009–; Chair. Fleming Family & Partners, Nordic Windpower Ltd; Vice-Chair. Corsair Capital LLC 2010–14, Chair. 2014–; Dir (non-exec.) Tesco PLC 2003–08, Breakingviews Ltd, Tottenham Hotspur Football Club, Trinity Ltd; mem. Advisory Cttee Corsair Capital LLC, UK India Business Council; Chair. Interim Exec. Cttee of Int. Centre for Financial Regulation 2007–, Business Council for Britain 2007–; Chair. Garden Bridge Trust 2013–; mem. Mayor of London's Int. Business Advisory Council, London; JP Hong Kong 2000; mem. Hong Kong Exchange Fund Cttee, Singapore British Business Council, UK-India Forum; mem. Exec. Cttee Hong Kong Community Chest –2001; fmr Chair. Hong Kong Youth Arts Festival, Hong Kong Asscn of Banks, Asia Youth Orchestra; Chair. Council of the Univ. of Wales; Dir Visa Int. Asia Pacific Regional Bd –2001; Chair. British Chamber of Commerce, Hong Kong 2000–01 (also fmr Chair.), The Roundhouse's Major Projects Bd, Corp. Bd of Royal Acad. of Arts; mem. Bd of Dirs Hong Kong Asscn 2007–; Gov. LSE; Trustee, Royal Acad. Trust, Sir Kyffin Williams Trust; Fellow, Inst. of Bankers. *Leisure interests:* sport, Welsh art, antiques, opera, music, reading. *Address:* Corsair Capital LLC, 53 Davies Street, London, W1K 5JH, England (office). *Telephone:* (20) 7152-6535 (office). *E-mail:* corsair@corsair-capital.com (office). *Website:* www.corsair-capital.com (office).

DAVIGNON, Viscount Etienne, LLD; Belgian diplomatist and business executive; b. 4 Oct. 1932, Budapest, Hungary; m. Françoise de Cumont 1959; one s. two d.; joined Ministry of Foreign Affairs 1959, Attaché then Head of Office of Minister of Foreign Affairs Paul-Henri Spaak 1961–65; Political Dir 1969–76; Chair. Governing Bd, Int. Energy Agency 1974–77; Commr for Industry and Int. Markets, Comm. of European Communities 1977–81, Vice-Pres. for Industry, Energy and Research Policies 1981–85; joined Société Générale de Belgique 1985, 1988–2001, Exec. Chair. 1989–2001, Vice-Chair. 2001–03, Vice-Chair. Suez-Tractebel SA (subsidiary) 2003–10; Dir CMB NV 1985– (Vice-Chair. 2014–), Gilead Palo Alto, Inc. 1990–, Recticel NV 1992–2015, Umicore 1989–2005; Co-founder Brussels Airlines 2006–, currently Chair.; Chair. Palais des Beaux-Arts, Brussels, Compagnie Maritime Belge, Institut Catholique des Hautes Etudes Commerciales, Spaak Foundation; Pres. Friends of Europe (think-tank), Brussels, CSR Europe, Brussels; Hon. DHumLitt (American Coll. in Paris) 1988. *Leisure interests:* golf, skiing, tennis. *Address:* Brusssels Airlines, 100–102 Avenue des Saisons, Box 30, 1050 Brussels (office); 12 Avenue des Fleurs, 1150 Brussels, Belgium (home). *Website:* www.brusselsairlines.com (office).

DAVIS, Adrian Derek; British economist and diplomatist; m. Sujue Davis; two c.; economist with Official Devt Assistance (ODA) 1974–77, First Sec. and Econ. Adviser, British High Comm. in Dhaka 1977–79, Econ. Adviser, South-East Asia Devt Div., Dept for Int. Devt (DFID)/ODA, Bangkok 1980–83, First Sec. (Aid/Econ.), Embassy at Cairo 1984–87, Head UK 'Know-How-Fund' for Poland, Hungary, Czechoslovakia and Bulgaria, ODA 1989–91, UK Rep. Asian Devt Bank, Manila 1991–94, Head of East Asia and Pacific Dept, DFID London 1994–96, Head of Information Systems and Services Dept, DFID London and East Kilbride 1996–99, Head of Environmental Policy Dept, DFID London 1999–2003, DFID Country Dir for China, Beijing 2003–07, DFID Country Dir North and East Asia, Beijing 2007, Gov. of Montserrat 2011–15. *Address:* c/o Office of the Governor, 8 Farara Plaza, Brades, Montserrat (office).

DAVIS, Sir Andrew, Kt, CBE; British conductor; *Musical Director, Lyric Opera of Chicago;* b. 2 Feb. 1944; m. Gianna Rolandi 1989; one s.; ed Royal Coll. of Music, King's Coll., Cambridge, studied conducting with Franco Ferrara, Rome; continuo player with Acad. of St Martin-in-the-Fields and English Chamber Orchestra; Festival Hall debut conducting BBC Symphony Orchestra 1970; Asst Conductor, Philharmonia Orchestra 1973–77; Prin. Guest Conductor, Royal Liverpool Philharmonic Orchestra 1974–77; Music Dir, Toronto Symphony 1975–88, Conductor Laureate 1988–; Musical Dir, Glyndebourne Festival Opera 1988–2002; Chief Conductor, BBC Symphony Orchestra 1989–2000, Conductor Laureate 2000–, tours with orchestra to Far East 1990, Europe 1992, Japan 1993, 1997, USA 1995, 1998, South America 2001, Far East and Australia 2002; Prin. Guest Conductor, Royal Stockholm Philharmonic 1995–99; Musical Dir, Chicago Lyric Opera 2000–; Chief Conductor and Artistic Dir, Melbourne Symphony Orchestra 2013–(19); has conducted London Philharmonic, London Symphony, Royal Philharmonic, Boston, Chicago, Cleveland, Los Angeles Philharmonic, New York Philharmonic, Pittsburg Symphony, Orchestre Nat. de France, Frankfurt Radio Orchestra, Royal Concertgebouw Orchestra, Tonhalle Orchestra, Stockholm Philharmonic Orchestra, Israel Philharmonic, Bavarian Radio Symphony and Berlin Philharmonic orchestras, London Sinfonietta, Dallas Symphony and Dresden Staatskapelle orchestras; has conducted at Glyndebourne Festival Opera, Covent Garden Opera, Metropolitan Opera, Washington, DC, Chicago Lyric Opera, Bavarian State Opera, Paris Opéra, La Scala, Milan, Sir Henry Wood Promenade Concerts, maj. British and European music festivals; tours of People's Republic of China 1978, Europe 1983 with Toronto Symphony Orchestra. *Recordings include:* Duruflé's Requiem (Grand Prix du Disque 1978), cycle of Dvořák symphonies, Tippett's The Mask of Time (Gramophone Record of the Year Award 1987, Grand Prix du Disque 1988), Vaughan Williams symphony cycle, Elgar The Dream of Gerontius/Sea Pictures (Gramophone Award for Best Choral Recording 2015) 2014. *Leisure interest:* medieval stained glass. *Address:* Columbia Artist Management Inc., 1790 Broadway, New York, NY 10019-1412, USA (office). *Telephone:* (212) 841-9500 (office). *Fax:* (212) 841-9744 (office). *E-mail:* cami@cami.com (office); office@sirandrewdavis.com. *Website:* www.cami.com (office); www.lyricopera.org; sirandrewdavis.com.

DAVIS, Clive; American music company executive and producer; *Chief Creative Officer, Sony BMG Worldwide;* b. 4 April 1932, New York; ed New York Univ., Harvard Law School; lawyer CBS 1960, Vice-Pres. and Gen. Man. 1966; with Columbia Records –1973, joined Bell Records 1974, founder Arista Records 1975, later Pres.; Founder, Chair. and CEO J Records (jt project with RCA Music Group) 2000–08; Chair. and CEO RCA Music Group 2000–08; Chair. and CEO BMG North America 2000–08; Chief Creative Officer Sony BMG Worldwide 2008–; producer for Dido, Aretha Franklin, Sarah McLachlan, Whitney Houston, Billy Joel, Janis Joplin, Alicia Keys, Carlos Santana, Patti Smith and Bruce Springsteen; Grammy Trustees Award 2000, Grammy President's Merit Award 2009. *Publications:* Clive – Inside the Record Business (autobiography) 1974, The Soundtrack of My Life (autobiography) 2013. *Address:* Sony BMG, 550 Madison Avenue, New York, NY 10022-3211, USA (office). *Telephone:* (212) 833-8000 (office). *Website:* www.clivedavis.com.

DAVIS, Sir Crispin Henry Lamert, Kt, MA; British business executive; b. 19 March 1949; s. of Walter Patrick Davis and Jane Davis (née Lamert); m. Anne Richardson 1970; three d.; ed Charterhouse, Oriel Coll., Oxford; joined Procter & Gamble 1970, Man. Dir Procter & Gamble Co., Germany 1981–84, Vice-Pres. Food Div., Procter & Gamble USA 1984–90; European Man. Dir United Distillers 1990–92, Group Man. Dir 1992–94; CEO Aegis PLC 1994–99; Chief Exec. Reed Elsevier 1999–2009; mem. Finance Cttee, National Trust 2000–. *Leisure interests:* sport, gardening, art. *Address:* Hills End, Titlarks Hill, Sunningdale, Berks., SL5 0JD, England (home). *Telephone:* (1344) 291233 (home).

DAVIS, D. Scott, BSc, CPA; American business executive; b. 1952, Medford, Ore.; s. of Darrell Davis and Rose Davis; ed Portland State Univ., Univ. of Pennsylvania Wharton School; began career with Arthur Andersen Accountants; fmr Chief Financial Officer and later CEO II Morrow Inc., Oregon –1986, joined UPS Inc. (following UPS purchase of II Morrow) 1986, Chief Financial Officer and mem. Man. Cttee from 2001, Dir 2006–16, Vice-Chair. 2006–07, Chair. and CEO 2008–14, Chair. (non-exec.) 2014–16 (retd); CEO Overseas Partners Ltd, Bermuda 1998–2000; Deputy Chair. Fed. Reserve Bank of Atlanta 2007, Chair. 2007–09; mem. Bd Dirs, Honeywell International Inc.; Chair. Georgia Council on Econ. Educ.; mem. Pres.'s Export Council 2010–, The Business Council, The Carter Center Bd of Councilors; Trustee, Annie E. Casey Foundation. *Address:* c/o UPS Inc., 55 Glenlake Parkway NE, Atlanta GA 30328, USA. *E-mail:* info@ups.com.

DAVIS, Rt Hon. David Michael, PC, MSc; British politician and business executive; b. 23 Dec. 1948, York; s. of Ronald Davis and Elizabeth Davis; m. Doreen Margery Cook 1973; one s. two d.; ed Warwick Univ., London Business School and Harvard Univ.; joined Tate & Lyle Transport 1974, Man. Dir Tate and Lyle 1980–82, Strategic Planning Dir Tate and Lyle PLC 1984–87, Dir (non-exec.) 1987–90; MP (Conservative) for Boothferry 1987–97, for Haltemprice and Howden 1997–, Asst Govt Whip 1990–93, Parl. Sec. Office of Public Service and Science, Cabinet Office 1993–94, Minister of State, FCO 1994–97, Chair. House of Commons Public Accounts Cttee 1997–2001, Shadow Sec. of State for the Office of the Deputy Prime Minister 2002–03, Shadow Sec. of State for Home, Constitutional and Legal Affairs, Shadow Home Sec. 2003–08, Sec. of State for Exiting the EU 2016–18; Chair. Conservative Party 2001–02; Chair. Fed. of Conservative Students 1973–74; Chair. Financial Policy Cttee, Confed. of British Industry 1977–79. *Publications:* BBC Guide to Parliament, How to Turn Round a Business; numerous articles on business and politics. *Leisure interests:* writing, mountaineering. *Address:* c/o House of Commons, Westminster, London, SW1A 0AA (office); Constituency Office, Spaldington Court, Spaldington, Howden, DN14 7NG, England (office).

DAVIS, Don H., Jr., BS, MBA; American business executive (retd); b. 1939; m. Sallie Oxford 1960; ed Texas A&M Univ.; joined Allen-Bradley Co. 1963, Pres. 1989; fmrly Exec. Vice-Pres., COO Rockwell Automation and Semiconductor Systems, Pres. Automation, Rockwell Int. Corpn (later Rockwell Automation) 1993, Sr Vice-Pres. 1993, Pres., COO 1995–97, Pres. and CEO 1997–98, Chair. and CEO 1998–2004, Chair. 2004–05 (retd); CEO and Pres. MicroTouch Systems Inc. 1996; mem. Bd of Dirs Apogent Technologies Inc. 1992–, Illinois Tool Works, Inc. 2000–15, Ciena Corpn 2002–06, Teledyne Scientific & Imaging LLC, Journal Communications Inc. 2003–08; Regent, Milwaukee School of Eng; mem. Bd of Govs, Boys and Girls Club of America, now Gov. Emer. *Address:* 1600 East St Andrew Place, Santa Ana, CA 92705, USA (office). *Telephone:* (714) 566-1000 (office).

DAVIS, Gareth, BA; British business executive; *Chairman, Ferguson PLC;* b. 13 May 1950, Bolton, Lancs., England; m. Andrea Davis 1973; one d.; ed Beal Grammar School, Ilford, Essex, Univ. of Sheffield; joined Imperial Tobacco as man. trainee 1972, managed factory producing cigarettes in Newcastle upon Tyne 1973–79, Production Control Man., Bristol 1979–88, Man. Dir Int. Operations 1988–96, Chief Exec. Imperial Tobacco Group on demerger from Hanson 1996–2010, mem. Chief Exec.'s Cttee; Dir (non-exec.), Wolseley (now Ferguson) PLC 2003–04, Sr Ind. Dir 2004–11, Chair. 2011–; Chair. William Hill PLC 2010–18; Dir (non-exec.), DS Smith PLC 2010–, Chair. 2012–. *Leisure interests:* cricket, golf, snooker, Bolton Wanderers Football Club. *Address:* Ferguson PLC, Corporate Headquarters, Grafenauweg 10, 6301 Zug, Switzerland (office); Ferguson plc, Group Services Office, Parkview 1220, Arlington Business Park, Theale, Berks., RG7 4GA (office); DS Smith PLC, 7th Floor, 350 Euston Road, Regent's Place, London, NW1 3AX, England (office). *Telephone:* (41) 7232230 (Zug) (office); (118) 929-8700 (Theale) (office); (20) 7756-1800 (London, DS Smith) (office). *Fax:* (118) 929-8701 (Theale) (office); (41) 7232231 (Zug) (office). *Website:* www.fergusonplc.com (office).

DAVIS, Geena, BFA; American actress; b. 21 Jan. 1957, Wareham, Mass.; m. 1st Richard Emmolo 1981 (divorced 1983); m. 2nd Jeff Goldblum (q.v.) (divorced 1990); m. 3rd Renny Harlin 1993 (divorced); m. 4th Reza Jarrahy 2001; one d. two s.; ed Boston Univ.; mem. Mount Washington Repertory Theatre Co.; worked as a model; f. Dads and Daughters - See Jane program; Chair. Calif. Comm. on the Status of Women and Girls; Dr hc (Bates Coll.) 2009. *Films include:* Tootsie 1982, Fletch 1984, Transylvania 6-5000 1985, The Fly 1986, Beetlejuice 1988, The Accidental Tourist 1988 (Acad. Award for Best Supporting Actress), Earth Girls are Easy 1989, Quick Change 1990, The Grifters, Thelma and Louise 1991, A League of Their Own 1992, Hero 1992, Angie 1994, Speechless (also producer) 1994, Cutthroat Island 1995, The Long Kiss Goodnight 1996, Stuart Little 1999, Stuart Little 2 2002, Stuart Little 3: Call of the Wild (voice) 2005, Accidents Happen 2009, In a World 2013, Me Him Her 2016, Marjorie Prime 2017. *TV appearances include:* Buffalo Bill (series) 1983, Sara (series) 1985, Secret Weapons 1985, The Geena Davis Show (series) 2000, Commander-in-Chief (series) 2005–06 (Golden Globe Award for Best Actress in a Drama TV Series 2006), Exit 19 (film) 2009, Coma (mini-series) 2012, Grey's Anatomy (series) 2014–15, The Exorcist (series) 2016. *Address:* California Commission on the Status of Women and Girls, 901 P Street, Suite 142-A, Sacramento, CA 95814; 2401 Main Street, Santa Monica, CA 90405-3515; c/o Dads & Daughters - See Jane, 2 West 1st Street, Suite 101, Duluth, MN 55802, USA. *Website:* women.ca.gov.

DAVIS, (Alexander) Giles, BSc, PhD; British electrical engineer and academic; *Professor of Electronic and Photonic Engineering and ProDean for Research, University of Leeds;* ed Univs of Bristol and Cambridge; Rouse Ball Fellowship, Trinity Coll., Cambridge 1990–91; Australian Research Council Postdoctoral Research Fellow, School of Physics, Univ. of New South Wales 1991–95; Royal Soc. Univ. Research Fellow, Cavendish Lab., Univ. of Cambridge 1995–2002; Trevelyan Fellow, Coll. Lecturer, Dir of Studies, Dean, Selwyn Coll., Cambridge 1995–2002; Prof. of Electronic and Photonic Eng, Univ. of Leeds 2002–, Admissions Tutor, Dir Inst. of Microwaves and Photonics, Dir of Research, Deputy Head of School, School of Electronic and Electrical Eng 2002–, currently Chair. of Electronic and Photonic Eng and ProDean for Research; Exec. mem. Biomedical Health Research Centre; Faraday Medal, Inst. of Physics (co-recipient) 2014. *Publications:* numerous papers in professional journals on the devt of terahertz science and tech. and the use of biological processes for nanotechnology. *Address:* Room 457, School of Electronic and Electrical Engineering, University of Leeds, Leeds, LS2 9JT, England (office). *Telephone:* (113) 343-7075 (office). *Fax:* (113) 343-7265 (office). *E-mail:* g.davies@leeds.ac.uk (office). *Website:* www.engineering.leeds.ac.uk (office).

DAVIS, Glyn, AC, BA, PhD, DUniv, FASSA, FIPAA; Australian university administrator; *Vice-Chancellor and Principal, University of Melbourne;* ed Univ. of New South Wales, Australian Nat. Univ.; Lecturer in Politics and Public Policy, Griffith Univ., Queensland 1985, Australian Research Council QE II Research Fellow 1988, Prof. 1998–2005, Vice-Chancellor 2002–04; Commr for Public Sector Equity in Queensland Public Sector Man. Comm. 1990–93, Dir-Gen. Office of Cabinet 1995–96, Queensland Dept of Premier and Cabinet 1998–2002; Vice-Chancellor and Prin. Univ. of Melbourne 2005–(18); Foundation Chair. Australia and New Zealand School of Govt (ANZSOG) 2002–05; Dir Australia 21; fmr Chair. Universitas 21; Dir Menzies Centre for Australian Studies, King's Coll. London; mem. Sesquicentenary Cttee for Queensland; Dir, Melbourne Theatre Co., Grattan Inst., LH Martin Inst., Asialink; Harkness Fellowship, Univ. of California, Berkeley, Brookings Inst., Washington, DC and John F. Kennedy School of Govt, Harvard Univ. 1987–88, Boyer Lecturer 2010. *Publications include:* The Future of Australian Governance: Policy Choices (co-ed.) 2000, Are You Being Served? State, Citizens and Governance (co-ed.) 2001, The Australian Policy Handbook (fourth edn, with Catherine Althaus and Peter Bridgman) 2007, The Republic of Learning: Higher Education Transforms Australia (lecture) 2010. *Address:* Office of the Vice-Chancellor, The University of Melbourne, 9th Floor, Raymond Priestley Building, Melbourne, Vic. 3010, Australia (office). *Telephone:* (3) 8344-6134 (office). *E-mail:* vc@unimelb.edu.au (office). *Website:* www.unimelb.edu.au (office).

DAVIS, Gray, BA, JD; American lawyer and fmr politician; *Of Counsel, Loeb & Loeb LLC;* b. 26 Dec. 1942; s. of Joseph Graham Davis, Sr and Doris Meyer Morell; m. Sharon Ryer 1983; ed Stanford Univ. and Columbia Univ. Law School; Capt., US Army 1968–69; Chief of Staff to Gov. of California 1974–81, State Rep. 1982–86, State Controller 1986–94, Lt Gov. 1994–99, Gov. of California 1999–2003 (recalled); Of Counsel, Loeb & Loeb LLC, Los Angeles 2004–; mem. Southern Calif. Leadership Council; Distinguished Policy Fellow, UCLA School of Public Policy; mem. Bd of Dirs DiC Entertainment; f. Calif. Foundation for the Protection of Children. *Address:* Loeb & Loeb LLC, 10100 Santa Monica Boulevard, Suite 2200, Los Angeles, CA 90067-4120, USA (office). *Telephone:* (310) 282-2206 (office). *Fax:* (310) 510-6727 (office). *E-mail:* gdavis@loeb.com (office). *Website:* www.loeb.com/gdavis (office); www.gray-davis.com.

DAVIS, Ian, MA; British business executive; *Senior Partner Emeritus, McKinsey & Company;* b. 10 March 1951, Kent, England; brother of Crispin Davis; m. Penny Davis; one s. one d.; ed Charterhouse, Balliol Coll., Oxford; began career with Bowater (paper manufacturing co.) 1972–79; joined McKinsey & Co. 1979, variety of positions in several countries with focus on consumer-related and retail industries, Head of London Office (with responsibility for Ireland and the Middle East) 1996–2003, Worldwide Man. Dir 2003–09, Sr Partner Emer. 2010–; Chair. (non-exec.) Rolls-Royce PLC 2013–; Dir (non-exec.) BP PLC 2010–, Johnson & Johnson Inc. 2010–; Sr Adviser, Apax LLP 2010–; mem. (non-exec.) UK Cabinet Office 2011–; Trustee, Teach For All; Dir, Big Society Trust. *Leisure activities:* tennis, cricket, the Alps. *Address:* McKinsey & Co., 1 Jermyn Street, London, SW1Y 4UH, England (office). *Telephone:* (20) 7961-7085 (office). *Fax:* (20) 7961-5349 (office). *Website:* www.mckinsey.com (office).

DAVIS, Judy; Australian actress; b. 23 April 1956, Perth; m. Colin Friels; one s. one d. *Films include:* My Brilliant Career, High Tide, Kangaroo, A Woman Called Golda, A Passage to India, Impromptu, Alice, Barton Fink, Where Angels Fear To Tread, Naked Lunch, Husbands and Wives, The Ref, The New Age, Children of the Revolution, Blood and Wine, Absolute Power, Deconstructing Harry, Celebrity, Gaudi Afternoon, The Man Who Sued God 2001, Swimming Upstream 2003, Marie Antoinette 2006, The Break-Up 2006 The Eye of the Storm 2011, To Rome with Love 2012, The Dressmaker 2015. *Television includes:* Life with Judy Garland: Me and My Shadows (Golden Globe Award) 2001, The Reagans 2003, Coast to Coast 2004, The Starter Wife (Emmy Award for Best Supporting Actress in a Mini-series 2007) 2007–08, Diamonds (mini-series) 2008, Page Eight 2011, Salting the Battlefield 2014, Feud: Bette and Joan 2017. *Address:* c/o Shanahan Management Pty Ltd, PO Box 478, King's Cross, NSW 2011, Australia.

DAVIS, Karen, BA, PhD; American economist and academic; *Director, Roger C. Lipitz Center for Integrated Health Care;* b. 14 Nov. 1942, Okla; ed Rice Univ., Houston; Asst Prof. of Econs, Rice Univ. 1968–70; Research Assoc., Brookings Inst., Washington, DC 1970–74, Sr Fellow 1974–77; Visiting Lecturer on Econs, Harvard Univ. 1974–75; Deputy Asst Sec. of Planning and Evaluation/Health, Office of the Sec., US Dept of Health and Human Services, Washington, DC 1977–80; Admin., Health Resources Admin, Public Health Service, Hyattsville, Md 1980–81; Prof. of Econs, Johns Hopkins Univ. 1981–92, Chair. Dept of Health Policy and Man., School of Hygiene and Public Health 1983–92, Eugene and Mildred Lipitz Prof., Dept of Health, Policy and Man. 2013–, Dir, Roger C. Lipitz Center for Integrated Health Care 2013–; Exec. Vice-Pres. Commonwealth Fund 1992–94, Pres. 1994–2012; mem. Kaiser Comm. on Medicaid and the Uninsured 1991–, Pres.'s Council, Health Policy Forum, United Hosp. Fund 1992–, New York Acad. of Medicine 1992–, Health Care Exec. Forum 1993–, Council on the Econ. Impact of Health Care Reform 1993–; mem. Bd of Dirs Geisinger Health System Foundation 2004–; mem. Panel of Health Advisors, Congressional Budget Office 2007–; mem. Bd of Trustees, Maumee Valley Country Day School; mem. NAS, Inst. of Medicine 1975, Nat. Acad. of Social Insurance 1991, American Acad. of Arts and Sciences 2009; Adam Yarmolinsky Medal, Inst. of Medicine 2007; Dr hc (Johns Hopkins Univ.) 2001, (Univ. of Maryland, Baltimore) 2009, (Newcastle Univ., UK) 2009; Health Achievement Award 1980, Distinguished Alumna Award, Rice Univ. 1991, Baxter-Allegiance Foundation Prize for Health Services Research 2000, AcademyHealth Distinguished Investigator Award 2006, Picker Award for Excellence in Advancement of Patient Centered Care 2006, Julio Palmaz Award for Innovation in Healthcare and the Biosciences, BioMed San Antonio 2007, Healthcare Financial Man. Asscn Bd of Dirs Award 2009. *Publications include:* Net Income of Hospitals 1961–1969 1970, Community Hospitals: Inflation in the Pre-Medicare Period (co-author) 1972, National Health Insurance: Benefits, Costs and Consequences 1975, Health and the War on Poverty: A Ten Year Appraisal (co-author) 1978, Medicare Policy: New Directions for Health and Long-Term Care (co-author) 1986, Health Care Cost Containment (co-author) 1990; numerous articles in professional jounals. *Address:* Roger C. Lipitz Center for Integrated Health Care, John Hopkins Bloombery School of Public Health, 615 N Wolfe Street, Baltimore, MD 21205, USA (office). *Telephone:* (410) 614-1932 (office). *E-mail:* karen.davis@jhu.edu (office). *Website:* www.jhsph.edu (office).

DAVIS, Leonard (Leon) Andrew, AO; Australian engineer and business executive; b. 3 April 1939, Port Pirie, South Australia; s. of Leonard Harold Davis and Gladys Davis; m. Annette Brakenridge 1963; two d.; ed S Australian Inst. of Tech.; Man. Dir Pacific Coal 1984–89; Group Exec. CRA Ltd 1989–91; Mining Dir RTZ Corpn 1991–94; Man. Dir, Chief Exec. CRA Ltd 1994–95; Deputy Chief Exec., COO RTZ–CRA 1996; CEO Rio Tinto 1996–2000, Deputy Chair. 2000–05; Chair. Westpac Banking Corpn 2000–07 (retd); Pres. Walter and Eliza Hall Inst. of Medical Research –2013; mem. Bd of Dirs, Huysmans Pty Ltd, Trouin Pty Ltd; Gov., Ian Potter Foundation; Hon. DSc (Curtin) 1998, (Queensland) 2004, (South Australia) 2005; Centenary Medal (Australia) 2004. *Address:* Walter and Eliza Hall Institute of Medical Research, Royal Parade, Parkville, Vic. 3052, Australia (office). *Telephone:* (3) 9345-2555 (office). *E-mail:* information@wehi.edu.au (office). *Website:* www.wehi.edu.au (office).

DAVIS, Marc, SB, MS, PhD; American astronomer, physicist and academic; *Professor Emeritus of Astronomy and of Physics, University of California, Berkeley;* b. 8 Sept. 1947, Canton, Ohio; ed Massachusetts Inst. of Tech., Princeton Univ.; Instructor of Physics, Dept of Physics, Princeton Univ. 1973–74; Asst Prof., Dept of Astronomy, Harvard Univ. 1975–80, Assoc. Prof. 1980–81; Prof., Depts of Astronomy and Physics, Univ. of California, Berkeley 1981, then Prof. Emer.; Chair. Dept of Astronomy 1988–92; mem. NAS 1991, American Acad. of Arts and Sciences 1992, American Astronomical Soc., Int. Astronomical Union; Fellow, AAAS 1988, American Physical Soc. 1989; Hon. PhD (Chicago) 2008; Alfred P. Sloan Foundation Fellowship 1975–79, Newton Lacy Pierce Prize, American Astronomical Soc. 1982, Miller Research Prof. 1986–87, 1999, Dannie Heineman Prize for Astrophysics, American Inst. of Physics and American Astronomical Soc. 2006, Cosmology Prize, The Gruber Foundation (co-recipient) 2011, among numerous other prizes and awards. *Achievements include:* collaborated with George Efstathiou, Carlos Frenk and Simon White (DEFW) to establish the validity of the 'cold dark matter' theory for the formation of galaxies and other cosmic structures during 1980s; led CfA (Harvard-Smithsonian Center for Astrophysics) galaxy survey that inspired the DEFW collaboration; helped organize and run an all-sky model of dust distribution in the Milky Way galaxy as well as the DEEP (Deep Extragalactic Evolutionary Probe) survey of 50,000 distant galaxies, conducted on the two ten-meter Keck telescopes in Hawaii. *Publications:* numerous papers in professional journals. *Leisure interest:* skiing. *Address:* Department of Astronomy, University of California, 517 Campbell Hall, MC 3411, Berkeley, CA 94720-3411, USA (office). *Telephone:* (510) 642-5156 (office). *Fax:* (510) 642-3411 (office). *E-mail:* mdavis@berkeley.edu (office). *Website:* astro.berkeley.edu/~marc (office); deep.ps.uci.edu (office).

DAVIS, Natalie Zemon, CC, BA, MA, PhD; Canadian/American historian and academic; *Professor Emerita of History, University of Toronto;* b. (Natalie Zemon), 8 Nov. 1928, Detroit, Mich., USA; d. of Julian Zemon and Helen Lamport; m. Chandler Davis 1948; three c.; ed Kingswood School, Cranbrook, Smith Coll., Radcliffe Coll., Harvard Univ., Univ. of Michigan; taught at Brown Univ. 1959–63; mem. Faculty, Univ. of Toronto, Canada 1963–71; mem. Faculty, Univ. of Calif., Berkeley 1971–77; mem. Faculty, Princeton Univ. 1978–96, Henry Charles Lea Prof. of History 1981–96, Henry Charles Lea Prof. Emer. of History 1996–, Dir Shelby Cullom Davis Center for Historical Studies –1996, Northrop Frye Prof. of Literary Theory 1996; Adjunct Prof. of History and Anthropology, Sr Fellow in Comparative Literature and Prof. of Medieval Studies, Univ. of Toronto 1996, now Prof. Emer.; Pres. American Historical Asscn 1987; numerous hon. degrees; Holberg Int. Memorial Prize (Norway) 2010, Nat. Humanities Medal 2012, Gold Medal, American Acad. of Arts and Letters 2014. *Publications include:* Society and Culture in Early Modern France: Eight Essays 1975, The Return of Martin Guerre 1983, Fiction in the Archives: Pardon Tales and their Tellers in Sixteenth Century France 1987, Women on the Margins: Three Seventeenth-Century Lives 1995, Remaking Imposters: From Martin Guerre to Sommersby 1997, The Gift in Sixteenth-Century France 2000, Slaves on Screen: Film and Historical Vision 2002, Trickster Travels 2006; numerous articles. *Address:* History Department, University of Toronto, Sidney Smith Hall, 100 St George Street, Room 2074, Toronto, ON M5S 3G3, Canada (office). *Telephone:* (416) 978-3363 (office). *E-mail:* nz.davis@utoronto.ca (office). *Website:* www.history.utoronto.ca (office).

DAVIS, Hon. Paul, MHA; Canadian police officer and politician; b. 1961, Conception Bay South, Newfoundland and Labrador; m. Cheryl Davis; one s.; ed Holland Coll.; joined Royal Newfoundland Constabulary (RNC) 1985, worked with Corner Brook Div. of Constabulary 1987–92, re-assigned to Criminal Investigation Div. in St John's, also assigned to Property Crimes, Major Crimes and Child Abuse

Sexual Assault Units, RNC Media Relations Officer 2006–10; Town Councillor, Conception Bay South, St John's 2001–10, Deputy Mayor 2005–10; mem. (Progressive Conservative), Newfoundland and Labrador (NL) House of Ass. for Topsail 2010–15, for Topsail-Paradise 2015–; Minister of Service NL and Minister Responsible for Govt Purchasing Agency, Office of the Chief Information Officer, and Workplace Health, Safety and Compensation Comm., NL 2011–12, Minister of Transportation and Works 2012–13, Minister of Child, Youth and Family Services 2013–14, of Health and Community Services May–July 2014; mem. Progressive Conservative Party of Newfoundland and Labrador, Leader 2014–; Premier of Newfoundland and Labrador 2014–15; Leader of the Opposition, NL 2015–. *Address:* Progressive Conservative Party of Newfoundland and Labrador, 20 Hallett Crescent, St John's, NL A1B 3P2, Canada (office). *Telephone:* (709) 753-6043 (office). *E-mail:* info@pcpartynl.ca (office). *Website:* www.pcpartynl.ca (office).

DAVIS, Sir Peter (John), Kt, FRSA; British business executive and fmr university administrator; b. 23 Dec. 1941, Heswall, Cheshire; s. of John Stephen Davis and Adriaantje Davis (née de Baat); m. Susan J. Hillman 1968; two s. one d.; ed Shrewsbury School, Inst. of Marketing; man. trainee, The Ditchburn Org., Lytham, Lancs. 1959–65; Gen. Foods Ltd, Banbury, Oxon. 1965–72; Marketing Dir Key Markets 1973; Man. Dir David Grieg and Group Man. Dir Key Markets, David Grieg 1975–76; Departmental Dir (non-foods) J. Sainsbury PLC 1976, mem. Bd responsible for marketing 1977, Asst Man. Dir Buying and Marketing 1979–86; Dir then Deputy Chair. Homebase Ltd 1983–86; Group CEO J. Sainsbury PLC 2000–04, Chair. 2004; Dir Shaws Supermarkets, USA 1984–86, Chair. 2000–03; Deputy Chief Exec. Reed Int. PLC 1986, Chief Exec. 1986–94, Chair. 1990–94, CEO and Deputy Chair. of Reed Elsevier 1993 (following merger Jan. 1993), Co-Chair. 1993–94; Vice-Pres. Chartered Inst. of Marketing 1991–2006; Chair. Nat. Advisory Council for Educ. and Training Targets 1993–97, Basic Skills Agency 1991–97, Welfare to Work New Deal Task Force 1997–2000, Govt's Employer Task on Pensions 2004–05; mem. Bd Business in the Community 1991–2005, Deputy Chair. 1991–97, Chair. 1997–2001; Founder and Bd mem. Marketing Council 1994–2002; apptd mem. Curry Comm. on the Future of Farming and Food 2001, Implementation Group for Food and Farming Strategy 2002; Sr Adviser and mem. Advisory Bd Permira Advisers (pvt. equity co.) 2006–09; Dir (non-exec.) Granada Group 1987–91, British Satellite Broadcasting (BSB) 1988–90, Boots Co. 1991–2000, Prudential Corpn 1994–95 (Group Chief Exec. 1995–2000), UBS AG 2001–07; Partner, Vestra Wealth Man. LLP 2009–16; fmr mem. Supervisory Bd Aegon, Elsevier; mem. Bd of Dirs Royal Opera House 1999–2005, Trustee 1994–2005, also Chair. Royal Opera House Foundation -2005; Pro-Chancellor Univ. of Bangor 2007–11, Deputy Chair. of Govs 2012–16; Chair. Int. Advisory Bd, Welsh Nat. Opera 2011–15, mem. Bd WNO 2013–16; Trustee, Victoria and Albert Museum 1994–96, Marie Curie Cancer Care Jan.–Sept. 2006 (Chair. 2006–11, Life Vice-Pres. 2011–); Fellow, Marketing Soc., City & Guilds 2004; Hon. LLD (Exeter) 2000; Gold Medal, Chartered Man. Inst. 2003. *Leisure interests:* sailing, opera, reading, wine.

DAVIS, Richard K., BA; American banking executive; b. 1958, Los Angeles, Calif.; m.; three c.; ed California State Univ., Fullerton, Univ. of Washington, Cornell Univ.; has held man. positions with U.S. Bancorp since joining Star Banc Corpn (a predecessor) as Exec. Vice-Pres. 1993, Vice-Chair. U.S. Bancorp (following merger of Firstar Corpn and U.S. Bancorp 2001) 2001–04, responsible for Consumer Banking, including Retail Payment Solutions (card services), assumed additional responsibility for Commercial Banking 2003–04, Pres. U.S. Bancorp 2004–16, COO 2004–06, mem. Bd of Dirs and CEO 2006–17, Chair. 2007–17, Exec. Chair. 2017–18; mem. Bd of Dirs Xcel Energy Inc. 2006–,Dow Chemical Co. 2015–; mem. of Bd Nat. American Red Cross, Minn. Orchestra, Twin Cities, YMCA, Minneapolis Art Inst., Univ. of San Diego, Business Council, Univ. of Minnesota Foundation; fmr Chair. Financial Services Roundtable; fmr Rep. for Ninth Dist of Fed. Reserve serving on its Financial Advisory Cttee; Dr hc (Univ. of St Thomas), (Coll. of Mount. St Joseph); Banker of the Year, American Banker 2010, Exec. of the Year, Twin Cities Business Journal 2010, Henrickson Ethical Leadership Medal, St Mary's Univ., Minnesota 2011, President's Lifetime Volunteer Service Award.

DAVIS, Roger J., MA, MPhil, PhD, FRS; British biologist, biochemist and academic; *H. Arthur Smith Chair and Professor, Program in Molecular Medicine, University of Massachusetts Medical School and Howard Hughes Medical Institute;* b. 26 March 1958; ed Queens' Coll., Cambridge; Research Fellow, Univ. of Cambridge 1983; Damon Runyon-Walter Winchill Cancer Fund Fellow, Dept of Biochemistry and Molecular Biology, Univ. of Massachusetts Medical School, Worcester, MA, USA 1984–85, Asst Prof. 1985–90, Assoc. Prof., Program in Molecular Medicine 1990–93, Prof. 1993–, H. Arthur Smith Chair, Molecular Medicine 2002–; Asst Investigator, Howard Hughes Medical Inst., Chevy Chase, MD 1990–93, Assoc. Investigator 1993–97, Investigator 1997–; Established Investigator, American Heart Assen 1990–95; mem. AAAS 1990, Soc. for Microbiology 1990; Open Entrance Scholarship Queens' Coll. 1976–78, Foundation Scholarship 1978–81, Science and Eng Research Council Scholarship 1979–82, Munro Studentship 1981–82, ranked 1st by Citation Index Inst. for Scientific Information 1996. *Publications:* more than 180 publs in scientific journals. *Address:* Program in Molecular Medicine, University of Massachusetts Medical School, Biotech II-Suite 309, 373 Plantation Street, Worcester, MA 01605, USA (office). *Telephone:* (508) 856-6054 (office). *Fax:* (508) 856-3210 (office). *E-mail:* roger.davis@umassmed.edu (office). *Website:* www.umassmed.edu (office); www .hhmi.org (office).

DAVIS, Steve, OBE; British professional snooker player (retd); b. 22 Aug. 1957, Plumstead, London; s. of Harry George Davis and Jean Catherine Davis; m. Judith Lyn Greig 1990 (divorced 2005); two s.; ed Alexander McLeod Primary School, Abbey Wood School, London; began playing at Lucania Snooker Club, Romford, Essex; won English Under-19 Billiards Championship 1976; turned professional 1978; professional TV debut on Pot Black (BBC) playing against Fred Davis; has won 80 titles (28 ranking, 52 non-ranking) from 115 finals; in list of top 16 players for record 22 seasons; major titles include: UK Professional Champion 1980, 1981, 1984, 1985, 1986, 1987; Masters Champion 1981, 1982, 1988, 1997; Int. Champion 1981, 1983, 1984; World Professional Champion 1981, 1983, 1984, 1987, 1988, 1989; winner, Asian Open 1992, European Open 1993, Welsh Open 1994; 325 century breaks; mem. Bd World Professional Billiards and Snooker Asscn 1993–, Leyton Orient Football Club; regular snooker presenter on BBC TV; retd 2016; Hon. Pres. Snooker Writers' Asscn; BBC Sports Personality of the Year 1988, BBC TV Snooker Personality of the Year 1997, inducted into World Snooker Hall of Fame 2011. *Radio includes:* presents show on progressive rock and Canterbury scene on local radio station Phoenix FM 1996–. *Television includes:* Steve Davis and Friends (chat show), They Think It's All Over (guest team capt.) 2003–06. *Music includes:* joined musical duo Chas & Dave and other snooker stars, calling themselves The Matchroom Mob, on novelty record Snooker Loopy (UK Top 10 hit) 1986, follow-up single, Romford Rap 1987. *Publications include:* Steve Davis, World Champion 1981, Frame and Fortune 1982, Successful Snooker 1982, Steve Davis: Snooker Champion 1983, Matchroom Snooker 1988, The Official Matchroom 1990, Simply Fix – The Steve Davis Interesting Cookbook No. 1 – Interesting Things to Do with Meat 1994, Simply Fix – The Steve Davis Interesting Cookbook No. 2 – Interesting Things to Make with Poultry 1994, Simply Fix – The Steve Davis Interesting Cookbook No. 3 – Interesting Things to Make Using Vegetables 1994, Steve Davis Plays Chess (with David Norwood) 1995, Grandmaster Meets Chess Amateur (with David Norwood) 1995. *Leisure interests:* collecting R & B and soul records, chess, Tom Sharpe books, Charlton Athletic Football Club. *Address:* 10 Western Road, Romford, Essex, RM1 3JT; Matchroom Sport Ltd, Mascalls, Mascalls Lane, Brentwood, CM14 5LJ, England. *Telephone:* (1277) 3599-11 (office). *Fax:* (1277) 3599-35 (office). *E-mail:* nick.teale@matchroom.com (office). *Website:* www.matchroomsport.com (office).

DAVIS, Rt Hon. Terence (Terry) Anthony Gordon, CMG, PC, LLB, MBA; British politician and international organization official; b. 5 Jan. 1938, Stourbridge, West Midlands; s. of Charles Gordon Davis and Gladys Rose Davis; m. Anne Cooper 1963; one s. one d.; ed Univ. Coll., London, Univ. of Michigan, USA; Internal Auditor, Esso Oil Co. 1962–65; Man. Clarks Shoes 1965–68; Man. Chrysler Parts UK 1968–71; Sr Man. Leyland Cars 1974–79; joined Labour Party 1965; fmr local govt councillor; MP for Bromsgrove 1971–74, for Birmingham Stechford 1979–83, for Birmingham Hodge Hill 1983–2004, Opposition Whip 1979–80, Opposition Spokesman for Health, Finance and Economic Affairs, then for Trade and Industry 1980–87, mem. Public Accounts Cttee 1987–94, Public Records Advisory Cttee, Special Cttee of PCs; mem. WEU Ass. 1992–2004, Leader, British Del. 1997–2002, Vice-Pres. 1997–2001; mem. Parl. Ass. of Council of Europe 1992–2004, Leader, British Del. 1997–2002, Vice-Pres. Ass., mem. Bureau, Pres. Socialist Group 2002–04, Sec.-Gen. Council of Europe 2004–09; fmr Rapporteur, EBRD, North South Centre, OECD, Georgia's admission to Council of Europe; fmr Leader and mem. UK Del. to WEU Ass., fmr Vice-Pres. Ass., fmr Pres. Socialist Group, Rapporteur for several reports on defence and security issues; fmr mem. UK Del. to OSCE Ass., Leader of UK Del. to Parl. Ass.; fmr mem. Exec. Cttee of UK Br., IPU; fmr mem. UK Del. to UN Gen. Ass.; fmr Visiting Lecturer, Civil Service Coll.; Chair. Ind. Comm. of Inquiry into the Treatment of Elderly People in Birmingham 2001–02; attended two Parl. Confs for South East Europe Stability Pact; observed elections in Albania, Georgia, Latvia and Ukraine; mem. Amnesty International. *Address:* Hermitage, The Green, Adderbury, Oxon., OX17 3ND, England (home). *Telephone:* (1295) 810813 (home). *E-mail:* rthonterrydavis@gmail.com (home).

DAVIS, Viola; American actress; b. 11 Aug. 1955, St Matthews, South Carolina; d. of Dan Davis and Mary Alice Davis; m. Julius Tennon 2003; one d., two step-s.; ed Cen. Falls High School, Rhode Island Coll., Juilliard School; Dr hc (Rhode Island Coll.) 2002. *Stage credits include:* Seven Guitars, Broadway 1996, God's Heart 1997, Pericles 1998, Everybody's Ruby 1999, The Vagina Monologues 1999, King Hedley II, Broadway (Tony Award for Best Featured Actress in a Play 2001, Drama Desk Award for Outstanding Featured Actress in a Play 2001) 2001, Intimate Apparel (Drama Desk Award for Outstanding Actress in a Play 2004) 2004, Fences (Tony Award for Best Actress in a Play 2010, Drama Desk Award for Outstanding Featured Actress in a Play 2010) 2010. *Television includes:* NYPD Blue 1996, New York Undercover 1996, The Pentagon Wars 1998, Judging Amy 2000, Providence 2001, The Guardian 2001, Third Watch 2001, Law & Order: Criminal Intent 2002, The Division 2002, CSI: Crime Scene Investigation 2002, Hack 2003, The Practice 2003, Jesse Stone 2005–06, Threshold 2005, Without a Trace 2006, Brothers and Sisters 2008, The Andromeda Strain 2008, United States of Tara 2009, How to Get Away with Murder 2014 (SAG Outstanding Performance by a Female Actor in a Drama Series 2015); recurring roles in: City of Angels 2000, Law & Order: Special Victims Unit 2003–08, Century City 2004, Traveler 2007, Brothers & Sisters 2008, The Andromeda Strain 2008, Law & Order: Special Victims Unit 2003–08, United States of Tara 2009, How to Get Away with Murder (Primetime Emmy Award for Outstanding Lead Actress in a Drama Series 2015, SAG Award for Outstanding Performance by a Female Actor in a Drama Series 2016) 2014–. *Films include:* The Substance of Fire 1996, Out of Sight 1998, Traffic 2000, The Shrink is In 2001, Kate & Leopold 2001, Far from Heaven 2002, Antwone Fisher 2002, Solaris 2002, Get Rich or Die Tryin' 2005, World Trade Center 2006, The Architect 2006, Disturbia 2007, Nights in Rodanthe 2008, Doubt (Black Reel Award for Best Supporting Actress 2008, Nat. Bd of Review of Motion Pictures Award for Breakthrough Performance by an Actress 2008) 2008, Madea Goes to Jail 2009, State of Play 2009, Law Abiding Citizen 2009, Knight and Day 2010, Eat Pray Love 2010, It's Kind of a Funny Story 2010, Trust 2010, The Help (Black Reel Award for Best Actress 2011, NAACP Image Award for Outstanding Actress in a Motion Picture 2011, SAG Award for Outstanding Performance by a Female Actor in a Motion Picture 2011) 2011, Extremely Loud and Incredibly Close 2011, Beautiful Creatures 2012, Won't Back Down 2012, Beautiful Creatures 2013, Ender's Game 2013, Get On Up 2014, Blackhat 2015, Lila & Eve 2015, Custody 2015, Fences (SAG Award for Outstanding Performance by a Female Actor in a Supporting Role 2017, Golden Globe Award for Best Performance by an Actress in Supporting Role 2017, BAFTA Award for Best Supporting Actress 2017, Acad. Award for Best Supporting Actress 2017) 2016. *Address:* c/o Principal Entertainment New York, 130 West 42nd Street, Suite 614, New York, NY 10036, USA (office). *Telephone:* (212) 997-9191 (office). *Fax:* (212) 997-9280 (office). *Website:* www.principalentertainment.com (office).

DAVIS-BLAKE, Alison, BS, MOB, PhD; American professor of management and university dean; *President-elect, Bentley University;* d. of Prof. Gordon Davis; m.; two s.; ed Brigham Young Univ., Stanford Univ.; worked as an auditor in New York City office of Touche Ross & Co. 1979–80; Asst Prof. of Industrial Admin, Carnegie Mellon Univ. 1986–90; Asst Prof., later Assoc. Prof., later Prof., Univ. of Texas

1990–2006, Eleanor T. Mosle Fellow 1995, Co-Dir Exec. Master's Degree in Human Resource Devt Leadership 1995–2001, Chair. Dept of Man. 2002–03, Eddy C. Scurlock Centennial Prof. of Man. and Sr Assoc. Dean for Academic Affairs, McCombs School of Business 2003–06; Investors in Leadership Distinguished Chair in Organizational Behavior and Dean, Carlson School of Man., Univ. of Minnesota 2006–11; Leon Festinger Collegiate Prof. of Man., Univ. of Michigan 2011–18, Edward J. Frey Dean, Stephen M. Ross School of Business 2011–16; Pres.-elect Bentley Univ. 2018–; mem. Editorial Bd Journal of Management, Academy of Management Review, Administrative Science Quarterly; mem. Bd Asscn to Advance Collegiate Schools of Business. *Publications:* numerous papers in professional journals on the effects of outsourcing on organizations and employees, organizational promotion systems, and determinants and consequences of contingent worker use and organizational wage structures. *Leisure interests:* musical theatre, global travel, spending time with her family. *Address:* Bentley University, 175 Forest Street, Waltham, MA 02452, USA (office). *Telephone:* (781) 891-2000 (office). *Website:* www.bentley.edu (office).

DAVISON, Edward Joseph, BASc, MA, PhD, ScD, FIEEE, FRSC, ARCT, FCAE, P.Eng; Canadian electrical engineer and academic; *University Professor Emeritus, Department of Electrical Engineering, University of Toronto;* b. 12 Sept. 1938, Toronto, Ont.; s. of Maurice J. Davison and Agnes E. Quinlan; m. Zofia M. Perz 1966; four c.; ed Royal Conservatory of Music, Toronto, Univ. of Toronto, Univ. of Cambridge, UK; Asst Prof., Dept of Electrical Eng, Univ. of Toronto 1964–66, 1967–68, Assoc. Prof. 1968–74, Prof. 1974–2001, Univ. Prof. Emer. 2001–; Asst Prof., Univ. of California, Berkeley 1966–67; Pres. IEEE Control Systems Soc. 1983 (Distinguished mem. 1984–); Chair. Int. Fed. of Automatic Control (IFAC) Theory Cttee 1987–90, mem. IFAC Council 1991–93, 1993–96, Vice-Chair. IFAC Tech. Bd 1991–93, Vice-Chair. IFAC Policy Cttee 1996–99, Fellow, IFAC 2005; Dir Electrical Eng Assocs Ltd, Toronto 1977–, Pres. 1997–; Consulting Engineer, Asscn of Professional Engineers of Prov. of Ont. 1979–; mem. Russian Acad. of Nonlinear Sciences 1998–; Foreign mem. Nat. Acad. of Eng (USA) 2010; Hon. Prof., Beijing Inst. of Aeronautics and Astronautics 1986; Athlone Fellowship 1961, E.W.R. Steacie Research Fellowship 1974, Killam Research Fellowship 1979, 1981, IEEE Centennial Medal 1984, IFAC Quazza Medal 1993, IFAC Outstanding Service Award 1996, Hendrik W. Bode Lecture Prize, IEEE Control Systems Soc. 1997, Killam Prize in Eng, Canada Council 2003, inducted into Univ. of Toronto Eng Alumni Hall of Fame 2003, Canada Outstanding Engineer Award, IEEE (Canada) 2010. *Publications:* more than 500 research papers in numerous journals. *Leisure interests:* backpacking, skiing. *Address:* Department of Electrical Engineering, University of Toronto, Toronto, ON M5S 1A4, Canada (office). *Telephone:* (416) 978-6342 (office). *Fax:* (416) 978-0804 (office). *E-mail:* ted@control.utoronto.ca (office). *Website:* www.control.utoronto.ca/people/profs/ted/ted.html (office).

DAVISON, Ian Frederic Hay, CBE, BSc (Econ), FCA; British business executive and accountant (retd) and financial services regulator; b. 30 June 1931, Hillingdon, Middx; s. of Eric Hay Davison and Inez Davison; m. Maureen Patricia Blacker 1955; one s. two d.; ed Dulwich Coll., LSE and Univ. of Michigan, USA; mem. Inst. of Chartered Accountants (mem. Council 1975–99); Man. Partner Arthur Andersen & Co., Chartered Accountants 1966–82; Ind. mem. NEDC for Bldg Industry 1971–77; mem. Price Comm. 1977–79; Chair. Review Bd for Govt Contracts 1981; Chief Exec. and Deputy Chair. Lloyd's 1983–86; Dept of Trade Insp., London Capital Securities 1975–77; Insp. Grays Bldg Soc. 1978–79; Chair. Accounting Standards Cttee 1982–84; Chair. The Nat. Mortgage Bank PLC 1992–2000, Roland Berger Ltd 1996–98; Chair. Dubai Financial Services Authority 2002–04; Chair. Ruffer LLP 2002–11; Chair. (non-exec.) Northgate PLC (fmrly McDonnell Information Systems) 1993–99, Newspaper Publrs 1993–94 (Dir 1986–94); Chair. Monteverdi Trust 1979–84 (Pres. 2014–), Sadler's Wells Foundation 1995–2003, Pro Provost RCA 1996–2007, Crédit Lyonnais Capital Markets 1988–91, Charterail 1991–92; Pres. Nat. Council for One-Parent Families 1991–2004; Dir Morgan Grenfell Asset Man. 1986–88, Midland Bank PLC 1986–88, Storehouse PLC 1988–96 (Chair. 1990–96), Chloride PLC 1988–98, Cadbury Schweppes PLC 1990–2000, CIBA PLC 1991–96; Dir and Trustee, Royal Opera House, Covent Garden 1984–86; Trustee, Victoria and Albert Museum 1984–93, SANE 1996–2015 (Chair. 2000–02); Gov. LSE 1982–2006; Chair. Railway Heritage Cttee 1999–2004, Council of Exeter Cathedral 2002–08, Museum of East Asian Art, Bath 2012–13; Fellow, Dulwich Coll. 2015; Hon. Fellow, LSE 2004, Hon. Sr Fellow, Royal Coll. of Art 2011; Hon. DSc (Aston) 1985, Hon. LLD (Bath) 1998. *Publication:* Lloyd's: A View of the Room 1987. *Leisure interests:* music, theatre, bell-ringing. *Address:* 13 Catharine Place, Bath, BA1 2PR, England (home). *Telephone:* (1225) 445000 (home); 7932-160482 (mobile). *E-mail:* ihdavison@aol.com (home).

DAVUTOĞLU, Ahmet, PhD; Turkish academic and politician; b. 26 Feb. 1959, Taşkent; m. Sare Davutoğlu 1984; four c.; ed Boğaziçi Univ.; fmr Chair. Dept of Int. Relations, Beykent Univ., Istanbul; began working at Marmara Univ. 1993, Prof. 1999–2003; Foreign Policy Adviser to the Prime Minister 2003–09; Minister of Foreign Affairs 2009–14; mem. Grand Nat. Ass. 2011–; Prime Minister of Turkey 2014–16 (resgnd); Leader, Justice and Devt Party (AKP) 2014–16 (resgnd). *Publications include:* Alternative Paradigms: The Impact of Islamic and Western Weltanschauungs on Political Theory 1993, Civilizational Transformation and the Muslim World 1994, Stratejik derinlik: Türkiye'nin uluslararası konumu 2001, Küresel Bunalım 2002, Osmanlı Medeniyeti: Siyaset İktisat Sanat 2005. *Address:* Grand National Assembly, TBMM 06543, Bakanlıklar, Ankara, Turkey (office). *Telephone:* (312) 4205000 (office). *Fax:* (312) 4206756 (office). *E-mail:* assembly@tbmm.gov.tr (office). *Website:* www.tbmm.gov.tr (office).

DAVYDOV, Mikhail Ivanovich, DrMed; Russian clinical oncologist; *Regional Co-ordinator for Russia and CIS, N.N. Blokhin Russian Cancer Research Centre, Russian Academy of Medical Sciences;* b. 11 Oct. 1947, Konotop, Sumy region, Ukraine; s. of Ivan Ivanovich Davydov and Asmar Tamrazovna Davydova; m. Irina Borisovna Zborovskaya; one s.; ed Moscow 1st Sechenov Inst. of Medicine; Researcher, Sr Researcher, Head of Lab., Head of Div., Deputy Dir Moscow Blokhin Oncological Scientific Centre (now N.N. Blokhin Russian Cancer Research Centre), Russian Acad. of Medical Sciences, Dir Research Inst. of Clinical Oncology 1980, Prof. 1986, now Regional Co-ordinator for Russia and CIS; mem. Int. Soc. of Surgeons, American and European Soc. of Surgeons, New York Acad. of Sciences; mem. Russian Acad. of Sciences 2003, Russian Acad. of Medical Sciences 2004; numerous decorations including Merited Worker of Science of Russia 1996; State Prize Laureate in Science and Tech. 2002. *Publications:* more than 300 scientific publs on oncological surgery, including three monographs and six methodical films. *Leisure interests:* boxing, sports, hunting, classical and retro music. *Address:* N.N. Blokhin Russian Cancer Research Centre, Russian Academy of Medical Sciences, 115478 Moscow, Kashirskoye Shosse 24, Russian Federation (office). *Telephone:* (495) 324-11-14 (office). *Fax:* (495) 323-57-77 (office). *E-mail:* davydov@eso.ru (office). *Website:* www.ronc.ru (office).

DAWE, Donald Bruce, AO, MLitt, PhD; Australian writer and academic; b. 15 Feb. 1930, Geelong; s. of Alfred James Dawe and Mary Ann Matilda Dawe; m. Gloria Desley Dawe (née Blain) 1964 (died 1997); two s. two d.; ed Northcote High School, Univs of Melbourne, New England and Queensland; Educ. Section, RAAF 1959–68; teacher, Downlands Sacred Heart Coll., Toowoomba, Queensland 1969–71; Lecturer, Sr Lecturer, Assoc. Prof., Faculty of Arts, Univ. of Southern Queensland 1971–93; Hon. Prof., Univ. of Southern Queensland 1995; Hon. DLitt (Univ. of Southern Queensland) 1995, (Univ. of NSW) 1997; Myer Poetry Prize 1965, 1968, Patrick White Award 1980, Christopher Brennan Award 1984, Paul Harris Fellowship, Rotary Int. 1990, Philip Hodgins Memorial Medal for Literary Excellence 1997, Australia Council for the Arts Emer. Writers Award 2001, Centenary Medal 2003. *Publications include:* poetry: No Fixed Address 1962, A Need of a Similar Name (Ampol Arts Award 1966) 1964, An Eye for a Tooth 1968, Beyond the Subdivisions 1969, Condolences of the Season: Selected Poems 1971, Over Here, Hark! and Other Stories 1983, Speaking in Parables 1987, The Side of Silence: Poems 1987–90 1990, Mortal Instruments: Poems 1990–95 1995, Sometimes Gladness: Collected Poems 1954–97 1997, A Poet's People 1999, Towards a War 2003, Sometimes Gladness 2006, Blind Spots 2013, Kevin Almighty 2013, Border Security 2016; non-fiction: Essays and Opinions 1990; children's fiction: No Cat – and That's That 2002, The Chewing Gum Kid 2002, Luke and Lulu 2004, Smarty-Cat 2007. *Leisure interests:* gardening, watching Australian Rules football. *Address:* Authors, c/o Penguin Group (Australia), PO Box 701, Hawthorn 3122, Vic., Australia (office). *Website:* www.penguin.com.au (office).

DAWES, Kwame Senu Neville, BA, PhD; American/Ghanaian/Jamaican poet, playwright, critic and novelist; *Chancellor's Professor of English, University of Nebraska-Lincoln;* b. 28 July 1962, Accra, Ghana; s. of Neville Agustus Dawes and Sophia Dawes (née Tevi); m. Lorna Marie; three c.; ed Univ. of the West Indies, Univ. of New Brunswick; moved to Jamaica 1971; Chair. of the Division of Arts and Letters 1993–96; Asst Prof. in English, Univ. of S Carolina (USC) at Sumter 1992–96, Guest Lecturer, USC at Columbia 1994, Assoc. Prof. of English, USC 1996–2001, Prof. of English 2002–12, Distinguished Poet-in-Residence and Louise Frye Scudder Prof. of Humanities –2012, Dir MFA/Creative Writing program 2001–03, Dir USC English Dept Spring Writers Festival 2002–03, f. S Carolina Poetry Initiative 2003, Exec. Dir USC Arts Inst. 2005–12; currently Chancellor's Prof. of English and Glenna Luschei Ed. of Prairie Schooner, Univ. of Nebraska-Lincoln; Series Ed. Caribbean Play Series, Peepal Tree Books, UK 1999–, Assoc. Poetry Ed. Peepal Tree Books 2006–; Criticism Ed. Obsidian II literary journal, Raleigh, NC 2000–05; programmer of annual Calabash Int. Literary Festival, Jamaica 2000–; Chancellor Acad. of American Poets 2018–; Faculty Mem., Pacific Univ. MFA program; mem. Nat. Book Critics' Circle, S Carolina Humanities Council (Bd mem.) 2000–07, S Carolina Book Festival (mem. Advisory Bd); Assoc. Fellow, Univ. of Warwick 1996; Hon. Fellow, Univ. of Iowa Int. Writing Program 1986; S Carolina Arts Comm. Individual Artist Fellowship 1996, Winner Poetry Business Chapbook Competition 2000, Ohio Univ. Press Hollis Summers Poetry Prize 2000, Pushcart Prize 2001, Musgrave Silver Medal 2004, Elizabeth O'Neill Verner Governor's Award 2008, Emmy Award 2009, People's Voice Webby Award 2009, Barnes and Noble Writers for Writers Award 2011, Guggenheim Fellowship 2012, Windham Campbell Literature Prize in Poetry 2019. *Plays:* In the Warmth of the Cold, And the Gods Fell, In Chains of Freedom, The System, The Martyr, It Burns and it Stings, Charity's Come, Even Unto Death, Friends and Almost Lovers, Dear Pastor, Confessions, Brown Leaf, Coming in from the Cold, Song of an Injured Stone (musical), In My Garden, Charades, Passages, A Celebration of Struggle, Stump of the Terebinth, Valley Prince, One Love 2001. *Writing for radio:* Salut Haiti (poem/drama), Samaritans (play), New World A-Comin' (play). *Publications include:* poetry: Progeny of Air (Forward Poetry Prize for Best First Collection 1994) 1994, Resisting the Anomie 1995, Prophets 1995, Jacko Jacobus 1996, Requiem 1996, Shook Foil 1998, Wheel and Come Again: Reggae Anthology (ed.) 1998, Midland 2001, Selected Poems 2002, Bruised Totems 2004, Wisteria: Twilight Songs from The Swamp Country 2005, Brimming 2006, Gomer's Song 2007, Impossible Flying 2007, Back of Mount Peace 2009, Wheels 2010, Duppy Conqueror 2013, Speak from Here to There: Two Poem Cycles (with John Kinsella) 2016, City of Bones: A Testament 2017; fiction: A Place to Hide (short stories) 2002, She's Gone (novel) (Hurston/Wright Legacy Award for Fiction 2008) 2007, Bivouac 2010; non-fiction: Natural Mysticism: Towards a New Reggae Aesthetic (literary criticism) 1998, Talk Yuh Talk: Interviews with Caribbean Poets 2000, Bob Marley: Lyrical Genius 2002, A Far Cry from Plymouth Rock (memoir) 2007, Fugue and Other Writings 2012; contrib. to numerous journals and periodicals, including Beat Magazine, Black Issues, Black Warrior Review, Bristol Evening Post, Calabash, Caribbean Writer, Dagens Nyheter (Sweden), Globe and Mail, Impact, Library Journal, Lines, Morning Star, Poetry London Newsletter, Poetry Review, Publishers Weekly, The Atlanta Journal/Constitution, The Brunswickan, The Courier, The Daily Gleaner, The Daily News, The English Review, The Guardian, The Herald, The London Times, The Observer, The State, The Sumter Item, The Telegraph Journal, The Voice, Time Out London, Venue, Wasafiri, Western Daily Press, World Literature Today, World Literature Written in English, Granta. *Address:* Department of English, University of Nebraska, 110 C Andrews Hall, Lincoln, NE 68588-0333, USA (office). *Telephone:* (402) 472-1812 (office). *E-mail:* kdawes4@unl.edu (office); kwamedaw@kwamedawes.com. *Website:* www.unl.edu/english/faculty/profs/kdawes.html (office); www.kwamedawes.com.

DAWKINS, Hon. John Sydney (Joe), AO, BEc, RDA; Australian politician, economist and business consultant; *Co-Chairman, GRACosway;* b. 2 March 1947, Perth, Western Australia; m. 1st (divorced); one s. one d.; m. 2nd Maggie Dawkins 1987; one d. one step-s.; ed Scotch Coll., Roseworthy Agricultural Coll., Univ. of W Australia; fmr mem. Senate, Univ. of Western Australia; worked for Bureau of

Agricultural Econs and Dept of Trade and Industry 1971–72; MP, House of Reps, Seat of Tangney, WA 1974–75, Seat of Fremantle, WA 1977–94; Minister for Finance and Minister Assisting the Prime Minister for Public Service Matters 1983–84, Minister for Trade and Minister Assisting the Prime Minister for Youth Affairs 1984–87, for Employment, Educ. and Training 1987–91, Treas. 1991–93; Chair. Cairns Group of Agricultural Exporting Countries 1985–87, OECD Ministerial Council 1993, John Dawkins and Co. 1994–, Medical Corpn of Australasia 1997–2000, Elders Rural Bank Ltd 1998–2006; fmr mem. Bd, Sealcorp Holdings, Fred Hollows Foundation, Indian Ocean Centre; mem. Nat. Exec., Australian Labor Party, Party Vice-Pres. 1982–83; Australian Govt Special Investment Rep. 1994–95; Press Officer, WA Trades and Labor Council 1976–77; Chair. Australian Qualification Framework Council; Dir, Government Relations Australia (lobbying firm, merged with Cosway Australia to become GRACosway 2014), currently Co-Chair.; Hon. DUniv (Univ. of South Australia, Queensland Univ. of Tech.) 1997, (Ballarat); Australia Centenary Medal. *Leisure interests:* farming, viticulture, travel. *Address:* GRACosway, Level 1, 8 Leigh Street, Adelaide, SA 5000, Australia (office). *Telephone:* (8) 7202-1300 (office). *E-mail:* jdawkins@gracosway.com.au (office). *Website:* gracosway.com.au (office).

DAWKINS, (Clinton) Richard, MA, DSc, FRS, FRSL; British biologist, academic and author; *Emeritus Fellow, New College, University of Oxford;* b. 26 March 1941, Nairobi, Kenya; s. of Clinton John Dawkins and Jean Mary Vyvyan Dawkins (née Ladner); m. 1st Marian Stamp 1967 (divorced 1984); m. 2nd Eve Barham 1984 (died 1999); one d.; m. 3rd Hon. Lalla Ward 1992; ed Balliol Coll., Oxford; Asst Prof. of Zoology, Univ. of California, Berkeley, USA 1967–69; Lecturer, Univ. of Oxford 1970–89, Reader in Zoology 1989–96, Charles Simonyi Reader in the Public Understanding of Science 1995–96, Charles Simonyi Prof. 1996–2008 (retd), Professorial Fellow, New Coll., Oxford 1970, now Emer. Fellow; Ed. Animal Behaviour 1974–78, Oxford Surveys in Evolutionary Biology 1983–86; Gifford Lecturer, Univ. of Glasgow 1988, Sidgwick Memorial Lecturer, Newnham Coll., Cambridge 1988; Kovler Visiting Fellow, Univ. of Chicago 1990; Nelson Lecturer, Univ. of California, Davis 1990; f. Richard Dawkins Foundation for Reason and Science 2006; Hon. Fellow, Regent's Coll., London 1988, Balliol Coll. 2004, Hon. Patron, Philosophical Soc., Trinity Coll. Dublin 2004, mem. Freedom From Religion Foundation's Hon. Bd of distinguished achievers 2010; Hon. DLitt (St Andrews) 1995, (ANU Canberra) 1996; Hon. DSc (Westminster) 1997, (Hull) 2001, (Sussex) 2005, (Durham) 2005, (Brussels) 2005; Hon. DUniv (Open Univ.) 2003; numerous awards including Silver Medal, Zoological Soc. 1989, Michael Faraday Award, Royal Soc. 1990, Nakayama Prize 1994, Int. Cosmos Prize 1997, Kistler Prize 2001, Bicentennial Kelvin Medal, Royal Soc. of Glasgow 2002, Richard Dawkins Award given annually by Atheist Alliance International to the atheist whose work has done most to raise public awareness of atheism 2003–, Shakespeare Prize for contribution to British Culture, Hamburg 2005, British Book Award for Author of the Year 2007, Nierenberg Prize for Science in the Public Interest 2009. *Television includes:* Nice Guys Finish First (BBC) 1985, The Blind Watchmaker (BBC) 1986, Break the Science Barrier (Channel 4) 1994, Royal Institution Christmas Lectures (BBC) 1992, Big Ideas in Science (Channel 5) 2004, The Root of All Evil? (Channel 4) 2006, The Enemies of Reason (Channel 4) 2007, The Genius of Charles Darwin (Channel 4) (Best TV Documentary Series, British Broadcast Awards 2008) 2008, Doctor Who: The Stolen Earth (as himself) 2008, Expelled: No Intelligence Allowed (as himself) 2008, The Purpose of Purpose – Lecture tour among American universities 2009, Faith School Menace? (More4) 2010, Beautiful Minds (BBC 4 documentary) 2012. *Publications include:* The Selfish Gene 1976, The Extended Phenotype 1982, The Blind Watchmaker (RSL Prize 1987, LA Times Literature Prize 1987) 1986, The Tinbergen Legacy (ed with M. Dawkins and T. R. Halliday) 1991, River Out of Eden 1995, Climbing Mount Improbable 1996, Unweaving the Rainbow: Science, Delusion and the Appetite for Wonder 1998, A Devil's Chaplain (essays) 2003, The Ancestor's Tale: A Pilgrimage to the Dawn of Life 2004, The God Delusion 2006, The Oxford Book of Modern Science Writing (ed) 2008, The Greatest Show on Earth: The Evidence for Evolution 2009, The Magic of Reality: How We Know What's Really True 2011, An Appetitite for Wonder: the Making of a Scientist 2013, Brief Candle in the Dark: My Life in Science 2015, Science in the Soul: Selected Writings of a Passionate Rationalist 2017; numerous articles in scientific journals. *Leisure interest:* human intercourse. *Address:* Richard Dawkins Foundation for Reason and Science, 1012 14th Street, NW, Suite 209, Washington, DC 20005, USA; New College, Holywell Street, Oxford, OX1 3BN, England (office). *E-mail:* contact@richarddawkins.net (office). *Website:* richarddawkins.net.

DAWOOD, Mohammad Hussain, BMet, MBA; Pakistani business executive; *Chairman, Dawood Hercules Corporation Limited;* s. of Ahmad Dawood; ed Salford Tech. Coll. and Sheffield Hallam Univ., UK, Northwestern Univ.– Kellogg School of Man., USA; Owner and Chair. Dawood Hercules Corpn Ltd, Chair. and CEO Dawood Hercules Chemicals Ltd, Dawood Cotton Mills and other cos within group; Chair. Engro Corpn Ltd, Hub Power Co. Ltd, Pakistan Poverty Alleviation Fund, The Dawood Foundation; mem. Bd of Dirs Dawood Bank Ltd; Chair. Int. Advisory Council of the Cradle to Cradle Inst., San Francisco, Karachi Educ. Initiative's Karachi School for Business & Leadership; mem. Govt of Pakistan Educ. Task Force; Dir, Pakistan Business Council, Pakistan Centre for Philanthropy, Beaconhouse Nat. Univ.; Global Charter mem. The Indus Entrepreneurs (TiE); Hon. Consul of Italy in Lahore 2002; Ufficiale Ordine Al merito della Repubblica Italiana. *Address:* Dawood Centre, M.T. Khan Road, Karachi, Pakistan (office). *Telephone:* (21) 35686001 (office). *Fax:* (21) 35693416 (office). *E-mail:* info@dawoodhercules.com (office). *Website:* www.dawoodhercules.com (office).

DAWSON, Sir Daryl Michael, Kt, AC, KBE, CB, LLM, QC; Australian judge; *Professorial Fellow, University of Melbourne;* b. 12 Dec. 1933, Melbourne, Vic.; s. of Claude Charles Dawson and Elizabeth May Dawson; m. Mary Louise Thomas 1971; ed Canberra High School and Melbourne Univ. and Yale Univ., USA; admitted to Bar, Vic. 1957; Lecturer, Council of Legal Educ. 1962–74; mem. Ormond Coll. Council 1965–73 (Chair. 1992–93); QC 1971; mem. Victoria Bar Council 1971–74; admitted to Tasmania Bar 1972; Solicitor-Gen. State of Vic. 1974–82; mem. Australian Motor Sport Appeal Court 1974–86 (Chair. 1982–86); Judge, High Court of Australia 1982–97; Judge, Hong Kong Court of Final Appeal 1997–2003; Chair. Longford Royal Comm. 1998–99, Trade Practices Act Review Cttee 2002–03; Adjunct Prof., Monash Univ. 1998–2006; Professorial Fellow, Univ. of Melbourne 1998–; mem. Council Menzies Foundation (fmr Chair.); Fulbright Scholar 1955; Hon. LLD (Monash) 2006, (Melbourne) 2008. *Leisure interest:* gardening. *Address:* PO Box 147, East Melbourne, Vic. 8002, Australia (office). *E-mail:* dawson.dl@dawsd.com.au.

DAWSON, Jill Dianne, BA, MA; British novelist, poet, editor and teacher; b. 1962, Durham; partner Meredith Bowles; two s.; ed Univ. of Nottingham, Sheffield Hallam Univ., Anglia Ruskin Univ.; Royal Literary Fund (RLF) Fellow, RLF Advisory Fellow; mem. Bd, Writers Centre, Norwich; tutor at Univ. of East Anglia; Dir, Gold Dust Mentoring Ltd; mem. Nat. Asscn of Writers in Educ., Soc. of Authors; Hon. DLitt (Anglia Ruskin); Eric Gregory Award 1992, second prize, London Writers Short Story Competition 1994, Blue Nose Poet of the Year 1995, London Arts Board New Writers 1998, Fiction Uncovered Award 2011, Jt First Prize, Harpers Bazaar Short Story Competition 2014, East Anglia Book of the Year 2016. *Publications include:* School Tales (ed) 1990, How Do I Look? (non-fiction) 1991, Virago Book of Wicked Verse (ed) 1992, Virago Book of Love Letters (ed) 1994, Wild Ways (co-ed with Margo Daly), White Fish with Painted Nails (poems) 1994, Trick of the Light (novel) 1996, Magpie (novel) 1998, Fred and Edie (novel) 2001, Gas & Air (co-ed with Margo Daly), Wild Boy (novel) 2003, Watch Me Disappear 2006, The Great Lover 2009, Lucky Bunny (Fiction Uncovered Award 2012) 2011, The Tell-Tale Heart (Spectator Book of the Year) 2014, Crime Writer 2016; contrib. to anthologies and periodicals. *Leisure interests:* swimming, yoga, bird-watching, travel. *Address:* c/o United Agents, 12–26 Lexington Street, London, W1F 0LE, England (office). *Telephone:* (20) 3214-0800 (office). *Fax:* (20) 3214-0801 (office). *E-mail:* cdawnay@unitedagents.co.uk (office). *Website:* www.jilldawson.co.uk.

DAWSON, Dame Sandra June Noble, DBE, BA, MA, FIPH, FCGI, CIMgt; British college principal and professor of management studies; *KPMG Professor Emeritus of Management, Judge Business School, University of Cambridge;* b. 4 June 1946, Bucks.; d. of Wilfred Denyer and Joy Denyer (née Noble); m. Henry R. C. Dawson 1969; one s. two d.; ed Dr Challoner's Grammar School, Amersham, Univ. of Keele; research officer, Govt Social Survey 1968–69; research officer, then Lecturer, Sr Lecturer, Industrial Sociology Unit, Dept of Social and Econ. Studies, Imperial Coll. of Science, Tech. and Medicine 1969–90, Deputy Dir Man. School 1987–94, Prof. of Organizational Behaviour, Man. School 1990–95; KPMG Prof. of Man. Studies, Univ. of Cambridge 1995–2013, Emer. 2013–, Dir Judge Business School, 1995–2006, Fellow, Jesus Coll., Cambridge 1995–99; Master, Sidney Sussex Coll., Cambridge 1999–2009, now Fellow; Chair. Riverside Mental Health Trust 1992–95, Exec. Steering Cttee, Advanced Inst. of Man. 2007–12; mem. Bd of Dirs (non-exec.) Riverside Health Authority 1990–92, Cambridge Econometrics 1996–2006, Fleming Claverhouse Investment Trust 1996–2003, Rand Europe (UK) 2002–03, Barclays PLC 2003–09, Oxfam 2006–12, Social Science Research Council (USA) 2009– (Chair. Exec. Cttee 2014–), Inst. for Govt 2012–, Data Research Services 2012–, Winton Capital Group 2013–, TSB (Sr Ind. Dir) 2014–; mem. Research Strategy Bd, Offshore Safety Div., Health and Safety Exec. 1991–95, Strategic Review Group, Public Health Lab. Service 1994–99, Sr Salaries Review Body 1997–2003, Econ. and Social Research Council Research Priorities Bd 2000–03, UK-India Round Table; Fellow, City & Guilds of London Inst. 1999; Trustee, American Univ. of Sharjah 2014–; Hon. Fellow, Jesus Coll. Cambridge; Hon. DSc (Keele Univ.), Hon. DLitt (Keele) 2000; Anglian Businesswoman of the Year 2000. *Publications include:* Analysing Organisations 1986, Safety at Work: The Limits of Self Regulation 1988, Managing the NHS 1995, Policy Futures for UK Health 2000, Future Health Organisations and Systems 2005, Engaging with Care (jtly) 2007, Future Public Health: Burdens, Challenges and Opportunities (co-author) 2009; papers on man. in learned journals. *Leisure interests:* music, walking, family. *Address:* c/o Judge Business School, University of Cambridge, Trumpington Street, Cambridge, CB2 1AG (office); Sidney Sussex College, Sidney Street, Cambridge, CB2 3HU, England. *Telephone:* (1223) 766331 (office); (1223) 338800 (office). *Fax:* (1223) 766332 (office). *E-mail:* s.dawson@jbs.cam.ac.uk (office). *Website:* www.jbs.cam.ac.uk (office); www.sid.cam.ac.uk.

DAWSON, Thomas C., II, AB (Econs), MBA; American economist; b. 9 March 1948, Washington, DC; s. of Allan Duval Dawson and Jane Dodge Dawson; m. Moira Jane Haley 1974; two s. one d.; ed Stanford Univ., Woodrow Wilson School of Public and Int. Affairs, Princeton Univ.; Financial Economist, Office of Investment Affairs, US Dept of State 1971–72, Staff Asst to Asst Sec. for Econ. Affairs 1972–73, Staff Asst to Under-Sec. for Econ. Affairs 1973–74, Economist, US Consulate Gen., Rio de Janeiro 1974–78; Consultant, McKinsey and Co. 1978–80; Deputy Asst Sec. for Developing Nations, US Treasury Dept 1981–84, Asst Sec. for Business and Consumer Affairs 1984–85; Deputy Asst to the Pres. and Exec. Asst to Chief of Staff, White House 1985–87; Exec. Vice-Pres. Regdon Associates 1987–89; Special Asst to Asst Sec. for Int. Affairs, US Treasury Dept 1989; US Exec. Dir IMF 1989–93, Dir External Relations Dept 1999–2006; First Vice-Pres. Merrill Lynch and Co. 1993–94, Dir Financial Insts Group 1993–99. *Television:* Global Protest (film documentary) 2000. *Address:* 50 Portland Road, Summit, NJ 07901, USA (home).

DAWUNI, Rocky; Ghanaian singer; b. 1969; s. of Koyatu Dawuni and Asibi Dawuni; m. Carry Dawuni; ed Univ. of Ghana; f. Rocky Dawuni Independence Splash (annual music festival); apptd Goodwill Amb. for Tourism, Ministry of Tourism 2011; mem. Bd of Advisors Jammin Java Corpn 2011–; often referred to as 'Ghana's Bob Marley'; Best African Artist, Int. Reggae and World Music Awards 2011, Kwame Nkrumah Award (Artist of the Year), Bass Awards 2016. *Recordings include:* The Movement 1996, Crusade 1998, In Ghana (Reggae Song of the Year, Ghana Music Awards 2000) 1999, Awakening 2001, Book of Changes 2005, Hymns for the Rebel Soul 2010, Sun is Shining 2010, Branches of the Same Tree 2015. *Address:* c/o Cary Sullivan, PO Box 1510, Pacific Palisades, CA 90272, USA (office). *Telephone:* (310) 663-7227 (office). *E-mail:* afrofunke@yahoo.com (office). *Website:* www.rockydawuni.com.

DAY, Catherine, MA; Irish fmr EU official; b. 16 June 1954, Mount Merrion, Dublin; ed Univ. Coll., Dublin; loan officer, Investment Bank of Ireland 1974–75; EC Information Officer, Confed. of Irish Industry 1975–79; Admin., Directorate Gen. (DG) III 1979–82, mem. Cabinet of Richard Burke, in charge of Personnel and Admin 1982–84, Cabinet of Peter Sutherland, in charge of Competition 1985–89, Cabinet of Sir Leon Brittan, in charge of Competition and External Relations 1989–95, Deputy Chef de Cabinet to Sir Leon Brittan, in charge of External Relations 1995–96, Dir DG IA (External Relations) responsible for relations with the Balkans, Turkey and Cyprus 1996–97, Dir DG IA, subsequently DG Enlargement, responsible for relations with cand. countries of Cen. and Eastern Europe 1997–2000, Deputy Dir-Gen. DG for External Relations, responsible for relations with the Western Balkans, New Ind. States (NIS), Mediterranean including the Middle East 2000–02, Dir-Gen. DG Environment 2002–05, Sec.-Gen. EC 2005–15; Hon. LLD (Nat. Univ. of Ireland) 2003. *Address:* Secretariat-General, European Commission, rue de la Loi 200, 1049 Brussels, Belgium (office). *Telephone:* (2) 2958312 (office). *Fax:* (2) 2993229 (office). *E-mail:* catherine.day@ec.europa.eu (office). *Website:* ec.europa.eu/dgs/secretariat_general (office).

DAY, Christine, BA; Canadian business executive; *CEO, Luvo;* m.; three c.; ed Central Washington Univ., Advanced Man. Program, Harvard Business School; spent 20 years at Starbucks in various capacities, including as Vice-Pres., Sales and Operations for Business Alliances and Sr Vice-Pres., North American Finance and Admin, sr man. positions, included Pres. of the Pacific Group of Starbucks Coffee International; joined Lululemon Athletica as Exec. Vice-Pres., Retail Operations 2008, oversaw Retail Operations in North America and internationally, as well as the Community Relations, Real Estate Devt, Guest Educ. Centre and Wholesale businesses, CEO Lululemon Athletica 2008–13; CEO Luvo 2014–; mem. Bd of Dirs Rick Hansen Foundation, Vancouver. *Leisure interests:* yoga, hiking the local mountains, biking on the seawall paths with her family. *Address:* Luvo, 410–1580 West Broadway, Vancouver, BC V6J 5K8, Canada (office). *Website:* luvoinc.com (office).

DAY, Doris; American actress and singer; b. (Doris Mary Anne von Kappelhoff), 3 April 1924, Cincinnati, Ohio; d. of Frederick Wilhelm and Alma Sophia von Kappelhoff; m. 1st Al Jorden 1941 (divorced 1943); one s. (deceased 2004); m. 2nd George Weilder 1946 (divorced 1949); m. 3rd Marty Melcher 1951 (died 1968); m. 4th Barry Comden 1976 (divorced 1981); professional dancing appearances, Doherty and Kappelhoff, Glendale, Calif.; singer, Karlin's Karnival, radio station WCPO; singer with bands, Barney Rapp, Bob Crosby, Fred Waring, Les Brown; singer and leading lady, Bob Hope radio show (NBC) 1948–50; f. Doris Day Animal Foundation 1998; Founder and Pres. Doris Day Animal League; Laurel Award, Leading New Female Personality in Motion Picture Industry 1950, Top Audience Attractor 1962, American Comedy Lifetime Achievement Award 1991, Grammy Award for Lifetime Achievement 2008. *Achievements include:* oldest artist to achieve a UK Top 10 hit album featuring new material (My Heart), entering at No. 9 Sept. 2011. *Recordings:* albums: You're My Thrill 1949, Tea for Two 1950, Lullaby of Broadway 1951, On Moonlight Bay 1951, I'll See You in My Dreams 1951, By the Light of the Silvery Moon 1953, Young Man with a Horn 1954, Day Dreams 1955, Day in Hollywood 1955, Young at Heart 1955, Love Me or Leave Me 1955, Most Happy Fella 1956, Day by Day 1957, Hooray for Hollywood Vols I and II 1959, Cuttin' Capers 1959, Day by Night 1959, Boys and Girls Together 1959, Hot Canaries 1959, Lights Cameras Action 1959, Listen to Day 1960, Show Time 1960, What Every Girl Should Know 1960, I Have Dreamed 1961, Bright and Shiny 1961, You'll Never Walk Alone 1962, Duet 1962, The Best of Doris Day 2002, My Heart (compilation of previously unreleased recordings produced by her son, Terry Melcher, prior to his death in 2004) 2011; singles: Day by Day 1949, Sugarbush 1952, Secret Love 1954, The Black Hills of Dakota 1954, If I Give My Heart to You 1954, Ready Willing and Able 1955, Whatever Will Be Will Be (Que Sera Sera) 1956, Move Over Darling 1964. *Films include:* Romance on the High Seas 1948, My Dream is Yours 1949, Young Man with a Horn 1950, Tea for Two 1950, West Point Story 1950, Lullaby of Broadway 1951, On Moonlight Bay 1951, I'll See You in My Dreams 1951, April in Paris 1952, By the Light of the Silvery Moon 1953, Calamity Jane 1953, Lucky Me 1954, Yankee Doodle Girl 1954, Love Me or Leave Me 1955, The Pajama Game 1957, Teacher's Pet 1958, The Tunnel of Love 1958, It Happened to Jane 1959, Pillow Talk 1959, Please Don't Eat the Daisies 1960, Midnight Lace 1960, Lover Come Back 1962, That Touch of Mink 1962, Jumbo 1962, The Thrill of It All 1963, Send Me No Flowers 1964, Do Not Disturb 1965, The Glass Bottom Boat 1966, Caprice 1967, The Ballad of Josie 1968, Where Were You When the Lights Went Out? 1968, With Six You Get Egg Roll 1968, Sleeping Dogs, Hearts and Souls 1993, That's Entertainment III 1994. *Television includes:* Doris Day Show (CBS) 1952–53, 1968–72, The Governor & J.J. (series) 1970, The Pet Set 1972, Doris Day and Friends 1985–86, Doris Day's Best 1985–86. *Publication:* Doris Day: Her Own Story (autobiog., with A. E. Hotchner) 1975. *Address:* c/o Doris Day Animal Foundation, 8033 Sunset Boulevard, Suite 845, Los Angeles, CA 90046, USA. *Website:* www.dorisday.com.

DAY, Sir (Judson) Graham, Kt, OC, ONS, CD, QC, JD; Canadian/British lawyer and business executive; *Of Counsel, Stewart McKelvey;* b. 3 May 1933, Halifax, NS, Canada; s. of Frank C. Day and Edythe G. Day (née Baker); m. L. Ann Creighton 1958; one s. two d.; ed Queen Elizabeth High School, Halifax, NS and Dalhousie Univ., Halifax; called to Bar of NS 1956, Ont. 1967; pvt. law practice, Windsor, NS 1956–64; Canadian Pacific Ltd, Montreal and Toronto 1964–71; Deputy Chair. Org. Cttee for British Shipbuilders and Deputy Chair. and Chief Exec. desig., British Shipbuilders 1975–76; Prof. of Business Studies and Dir Canadian Marine Transportation Centre, Dalhousie Univ. 1977–81; Vice-Pres. Shipyards and Marine Devt, Dome Petroleum Ltd 1981–83; Chair. and CEO British Shipbuilders 1983–86; Chair. and CEO The Rover Group (fmrly BL) PLC 1986–91, CEO 1986–88; Dir Cadbury Schweppes PLC 1988–93, Chair. 1989–93 (retd); Deputy Chair. MAI 1989–93; Chair. British Aerospace 1991–92, PowerGen 1990–93 (retd), Sobeys Inc. 2001–04; currently Of Counsel, Stewart McKelvey LLP (law firm); Herbert Lamb Chair in Business Educ., Dalhousie Univ. Graduate Business School; Special Consultant to Ashurst Morris Crisp 1994–96; mem. Bd of Dirs Jacques Whitford, Extendicare Canada Inc., The Laird Group PLC 1985–98, NOVA Corpn of Alberta 1990–2000; Chair. Exec. Cttee Bank of NS (Canada) 1989–2004; Pres. Inc. Soc. of British Advertisers 1991–93; Dir (non-exec.) Ugland Int. Holdings (Deputy Chair. 1997–2000); Lead Dir, DHX Media Ltd 2006; Dir (non-exec.) Scotia Investments Ltd 2004–11 (Chair. 2008–11), The CSL Group Inc. 2000–11; QC 2011; Hon. Fellow, Cardiff Univ. 1990; Hon. Col West Nova Scotia Regt 2005–11, Canadian Forces Legal Br. (JAG) 2011–; Order of Nova Scotia 2011; Dr hc (Humberside) 1992, (City Univ., London, CNAA, Cranfield Inst., Univs of Aston, Warwick, South Bank). *Television:* mem. original cast, later Musical Dir, Singalong Jubilee (CBC). *Leisure interests:* reading, lakeside chalet in Canada. *Address:* Stewart McKelvey, Suite 900, Purdy's Wharf Tower One, 1959 Upper Water Street, PO Box 997, Halifax, NS, B3J 3N2, Canada (office). *Telephone:* (902) 420-3376 (office). *Fax:* (902) 420-1417 (office). *E-mail:* sirgraham@win.eastlink.ca (office). *Website:* www.stewartmckelvey.com (office).

DAY, Julian C., MA, MBA; British retail executive; b. 14 May 1952; m.; two s.; ed Univ. of Oxford, London Business School; began career providing man. services for a variety of cos, including Kohlberg, Kravis and Roberts; fmr Dir, European Devt Chase Manhattan Bank; Pres. and CEO Bradley Printing Co. –1992; Exec. Vice-Pres. and Chief Financial Officer, Safeway Inc. 1992–98; Exec. Vice-Pres. and Chief Financial Officer, Sears, Roebuck & Co. 1999–2000, Exec. Vice-Pres. and COO 2000; Pres. and COO Kmart Holding Co. 2002–03, Pres. and CEO 2003–04, mem. Bd of Dirs, Sears Holding Corpn (after merger of Kmart and Sears, Roebuck & Co.) 2004–06; Chair. and CEO RadioShack Corpn 2006–11 (retd). *Leisure interests:* running, surfing, fitness. *Address:* c/o RadioShack Corporation, 300 RadioShack Circle, Fort Worth, TX 76102, USA.

DAY, Peter, MA, DPhil, FRS, FRSC, FInstP; British chemist and academic; *Professor Emeritus of Chemistry, University College London;* b. 20 Aug. 1938, Wrotham, Kent; s. of Edgar Day and Ethel Hilda Day (née Russell); m. Frances Mary Elizabeth Anderson 1964; one s. one d.; ed Maidstone Grammar School, Wadham Coll., Oxford; Cyanamid European Research Inst., Geneva 1962; Jr Research Fellow, St John's Coll., Oxford 1963–65, Tutor 1965–91; Departmental Demonstrator Univ. of Oxford 1965–67, Lecturer in Inorganic Chem. 1967–89; Oxford Univ. Prof. Associé de Paris-Sud 1975; Guest Prof., Univ. of Copenhagen 1978, Visiting Fellow, ANU 1980; Du Pont Lecturer, Indiana Univ. 1988; Sr Research Fellow, SRC 1977–82; mem. Neutron Beam Research Cttee Science and Eng Research Council 1983–88, Chem. Cttee 1985–88, Molecular Electronics Cttee 1987–88, Nat. Cttee on Superconductivity 1987–88, Materials Comm. 1988–90, Medicines Comm. 1998–2005; Vice-Pres. Dalton Div., Royal Soc. of Chem. 1986–88; Dir Inst. Laue-Langevin, Grenoble 1988–91; Dir Royal Inst. and Davy Faraday Research Lab. 1991–98, Fullerian Prof. of Chem. 1994–2008, Prof. Emer. 2008–; Visiting Prof., Univ. Coll., London 1991, Royal Inst. Research Fellow 1995–2008, Prof. Emer. of Chem. 2008–; mem. Academia Europaea, Treas. 2000–09; Fellow, IUPAC 2009; Hon. Foreign mem. Indian Acad. of Science, Materials Research Soc. of India, Hon. Fellow, Wadham Coll., Oxford 1991, St John's Coll., Oxford 1996, Univ. Coll. London 2002; Hon. DSc (Newcastle) 1994, (Kent) 1999; Royal Soc. of Chem. Corday-Morgan Medal 1971, Solid State Chem. Award 1986, Royal Soc. Blackett Memorial Lecturer 1994, Daiwa Adrian Prize 1999, Bakerian Lecturer 1999, Humphry Davy Lecturer 2002. *Publications include:* Physical Methods in Advanced Inorganic Chemistry (co-author) 1968, Electronic States of Inorganic Compounds 1974, Emission and Scattering Techniques 1980, Electronic Structure and Magnetism of Inorganic Compounds (Vols 1–7) 1972–82, The Philosopher's Tree 1999, Nature Not Mocked 2005, Molecules Into Materials 2007, On The Cucumber Tree 2012; numerous papers on inorganic chem. in learned journals. *Leisure interest:* driving slowly through rural France. *Address:* Chemistry Department, University College London, 20 Gordon Street, London, WC1H 0AJ (office); Field House, Marsh Baldon, Oxford, OX44 9LL, England (home). *Telephone:* (20) 7679-7466 (office); (20) 7679-0072 (office). *Fax:* (20) 7670-2958 (office). *E-mail:* p.day@ucl.ac.uk (office); pday@ri.ac.uk (office). *Website:* www.ucl.ac.uk/chemistry/staff/emeritus/peter_day (office).

DAY, Peter Rodney, PhD; American (b. British) agricultural scientist (retd); b. 27 Dec. 1928, Chingford, Essex, England; s. of Roland Percy Day and Florence Kate (née Dixon); m. Lois Elizabeth Rhodes 1950; two s. one d.; ed Chingford County High School and Birkbeck Coll., Univ. of London; John Innes Inst. 1946–63; Assoc. Prof., Ohio State Univ., Columbus, USA 1963–64; Chief, Genetics Dept, Conn. Agricultural Experiment Station, New Haven 1964–79; Dir Plant Breeding Inst., Cambridge, UK 1979–87; Prof. of Genetics and Dir Biotechnology Center for Agric. and the Environment, Rutgers Univ. 1987–2001; Special Professorship, Univ. of Nottingham 1981–87; Sec. Int. Genetics Fed. 1984–93; Pres. British Soc. for Plant Pathology 1985; Chair. Cttee on Managing Global Genetic Resources, NAS, USA 1986–94; mem. Exec. Cttee, Norfolk Agricultural Station 1980–87, Cttee on Genetic Experimentation, Int. Council of Scientific Unions 1984–93, Bd of Trustees, Int. Centre for Maize and Wheat Improvement, 1986–92, panel mem. Int. Food Biotechnology Council 1988–90; Fellow, American Phytopathological Soc.; Commonwealth Fund Fellow, Univ. of Wisconsin 1954–56; John Simon Guggenheim Memorial Fellow, Univ. of Queensland 1972; non-resident Fellow, Noble Foundation, Ardmore, Okla 1991–97; Visiting Fellow, Japan Soc. for the Promotion of Science 1998; Frank Newton Prize, Birkbeck Coll., Univ. of London 1950. *Publications:* Fungal Genetics (co-author) 1963, Genetics of Host-Parasite Interactions 1974, Plant-Fungal Pathogen Interaction: A Classical and Molecular View (co-author) 2001; more than 100 scientific papers. *Leisure interests:* music, Scottish country dancing, birdwatching. *Address:* 8200 Tarsier Avenue, New Port Richey, FL 34653-6559, USA. *Telephone:* (727) 372-6382. *E-mail:* p1rd@verizon.net.

DAY, Hon. Stockwell Burt; Canadian consultant and fmr politician; *CEO, Stockwell Day Connex Ltd;* b. 16 Aug. 1950, Barrie, Ont.; s. of Stockwell Day and Gwendolyn Day (née Gilbert); m. Valorie Martin 1971; three s.; auctioneer, Alberta 1972–74; Dir Teen Challenge Outreach Ministries, Edmonton, Alberta 1974–75; contractor, Commercial Interiors, Alberta 1976–78; School Admin., Asst Pastor, Bentley (Alberta) Christian Centre 1978–85; mem. Legis. Ass. Alberta, Edmonton 1986–2000; MP for Okanagan—Coquihalla 2000–11; Minister of Labour 1992–96, of Family and Social Services 1996–97; Prov. Treas., Ministry of Finance, Acting Premier 1997–2000; Leader, Official Opposition of Canada, Canadian Alliance 2000–02 (merged with Progressive Conservative Party of Canada to become Conservative Party of Canada 2003); Minister for Public Safety and Emergency Preparedness Canada 2006–08, for Int. Trade 2008–10, of Asia Pacific (Chair. Cabinet Cttee on Afghanistan), Pres. of the Treasury Bd 2010–11; Founder Stockwell Day Connex Ltd (consultancy); Sr Strategic Advisor, McMillan LLP; mem. Bd of Dirs Telus, RCI Capital, WesternOne Equity, Baylin Technologies, Canada-India Business Council; Vice-Chair. Canada-China Business Council; Distinguished Fellow, Asia Pacific Foundation; commentator, CBC Television; Hon. PhD (Trinity Western Univ.), (Univ. of St Petersburg). *Leisure interests:* marathon running, ocean kayaking, back-packing, reading, chess. *Address:* Stockwell Day Connex Ltd, 142–757 West Hastings Street, Vancouver, BC V6C 3M2, Canada (office). *Telephone:* (604) 800-9227 (office); (778) 214-0577 (office).

Fax: (604) 685-7084 (office). *E-mail:* stockwellday@stockwellday.com (office). *Website:* stockwellday.com (office).

DAY-LEWIS, Sir Daniel Michael Blake, Kt; British/Irish actor; b. 29 April 1957, London, England; s. of Cecil Day-Lewis and Jill Balcon; m. Rebecca Miller 1996; two s.; one s. with Isabelle Adjani; ed Sevenoaks School, Sherington, SE London, Bedales and Bristol Old Vic Theatre School; Hon. DLit (Bristol) 2010; Berlinale Camera Award, Berlin Film Festival 2005. *Plays include:* Class Enemy, Funny Peculiar, Bristol Old Vic; Look Back in Anger, Dracula, Little Theatre, Bristol and Half Moon Theatre, London; Another Country, Queen's Theatre; Futurists, Nat. Theatre; Romeo, Thisbe, RSC, Hamlet 1989. *Films include:* Sunday Bloody Sunday (uncredited) 1971, Gandhi 1982, The Bounty 1984, My Beautiful Laundrette 1985, A Room with a View 1985, Nanou 1986, The Unbearable Lightness of Being 1988, Stars and Bars 1988, Eversmile, New Jersey 1989, My Left Foot (Acad. Award for Best Actor, BAFTA Award, Best Actor) 1989, The Last of the Mohicans 1992, The Age of Innocence 1993, In the Name of the Father 1993, The Crucible 1996, The Boxer 1997, Gangs of New York (Screen Actors Guild Award for Best Actor 2003, BAFTA Award for Best Actor in a Leading Role 2003) 2002, The Ballad of Jack and Rose 2005, There Will Be Blood (numerous awards, including Acad. Award for Best Actor 2008, Golden Globe for Best Actor in a Drama 2008, Outstanding Performance by a Male Actor in a Leading Role, Screen Actors Guild 2008) 2007, Nine 2009, Lincoln (Golden Globe Award for Best Actor in a Motion Picture – Drama 2013, BAFTA Award for Best Actor in a Leading Role 2013, Acad. Award for Best Actor 2013) 2012, Phantom Thread 2017. *Television includes:* Shoestring (series) 1980, Thank You, P.G. Wodehouse (film) 1981, Artemis 81 (film) 1981, How Many Miles to Babylon? (film) 1982, Frost in May (mini-series) – Beyond the Glass 1982, BBC Play of the Month (series) – Dangerous Corner 1983, My Brother Jonathan (film) 1985, Screen Two (series) – The Insurance Man 1986. *Address:* c/o Victoria Belfrage, Julian Belfrage Associates, 3rd Floor, 9 Argyll Street, London, W1F 7TG, England (office). *E-mail:* email@julianbelfrage.co.uk (office). *Website:* www.julianbelfrage.com (office).

DAYAN, Edouard; French international organization official; Head of Air Transport Bureau 1984–86; held positions successively as Head Int. Mail Man. Dept, Int. Accounting Dept and Int. Partnership Strategy Dept, La Poste 1986–92, Deputy Dir of European and Int. Affairs 1993–97, Dir 1998–2005; Postal Expert, European Comm. 1992–93; Dir-Gen. UPU 2005–13; apptd Chair. European Social Dialogue Cttee 1994; Chair. Tech. Cooperation Action Group, UPU 2001, also Chair. Quality of Service Fund Cttee and Bd of Trustees; fmr mem. Bd of Man. PostEurop; Chevalier, Légion d'honneur, Ordre nat. du Mérite. *Address:* c/o Universal Postal Union, International Bureau, CP 312, 3000 Berne 15, Switzerland. *Telephone:* 313503111.

DAYAN, Peter, BA, PhD; British neuroscientist; *Professor of Computational Neuroscience and Director, Gatsby Unit, University College London;* ed Cambridge Univ., Edinburgh Univ.; postdoctoral fellowships with MRC Research Centre in Brain and Behaviour at Oxford, Computational Neurobiology Lab., Salk Inst. for Biological Studies, San Diego and Dept of Computer Science, Univ. of Toronto; Asst Prof., MIT 1996–98; co-f. Gatsby Computational Neuroscience Unit, Univ. Coll. London 1998, Dir 2002–, also Prof. of Computational Neuroscience; David E. Rumelhart Prize 2012, Lundbeck Foundation Brain Prize (jt winner) 2017. *Publications:* approximately 200 publications. *Address:* Gatsby Computational Neuroscience Unit, University College London, Room 241, 25 Howland Street, London, W1T 4JG, England (office). *Telephone:* (20) 3108-8101 (office). *E-mail:* dayan@gatsby.ucl.ac.uk (office). *Website:* www.gatsby.ucl.ac.uk/~dayan/ (office).

DAYANANDA, Mahendra; Sri Lankan business executive; *Chairman, Total Tea Concepts (Pvt) Limited;* Exec. Dir 1872 Clipper Tea Co. Ltd, B.P. De Silva Holdings Ltd; Dir Capital Suisse Asia, Risis Ltd, De Silva (Ceylon) Ltd; Chair. Tea Tang Ltd 1992–2006; Chair. Total Tea Concepts (Pvt.) Ltd, Indo Asia Teas (Pvt.) Ltd; fmr Chair. B.P. de Silva Investments Ltd, Lewis Brown & Co. Ltd; Vice-Chair., then Chair. Colombo Tea Traders' Asscn; fmr Chair. and Deputy Chair. Ceylon Chamber of Commerce; Vice-Pres. Sri Lanka Japan Business Cttee; mem. Nat. Bd of Arbitrators; Ind. Dir (non-exec.) Nestlé Lanka PLC, Chair. Remuneration Cttee 2009–; mem. Bd of Dirs So Others May See Inc.; Hon. Consul for Benin. *Address:* c/o Sri Lanka Tea Board, 574, Galle Road, PO Box 1750, Colombo 03, Sri Lanka. *E-mail:* teaboard@pureceylontea.com.

DAYTON, Mark Brandt; American politician and fmr state governor; b. 26 Jan. 1947, Minneapolis, Minn.; s. of Bruce Bliss Dayton and Gwendolen May Dayton (née Brandt); m. 1st Alida Rockefeller (divorced); two s.; m. 2nd Janice Haarstick (divorced); ed The Blake School, Minneapolis, Yale Univ.; science teacher, New York City Public Schools 1969–71; counsellor and admin. for social service agency, Boston 1971–75; legis. asst to Walter Mondale, Senator from Minn. 1975–77; mem. staff, Office of Minn. Gov. Rudy Perpich 1977–78; Commr of Econ. Devt, State of Minn. 1978–82, Commr of Energy and Econ. Devt 1982–86; cand. for Senate 1982; elected Minn. State Auditor 1990–94; held key positions in election campaign of Senator Paul Wellstone 1995–96; Senator from Minn. 2001–07, mem. Agric. Cttee, Armed Services Cttee, Rules Cttee, Governmental Affairs Cttee; Gov. of Minnesota 2011–19 (retd); mem. Exec. Cttee Nat. Govs Asscn; mem. Minnesota Democratic–Farmer–Labor Party, affiliates with the nat. Democratic Party; Pres.'s Award, Nat. Asscn for the Advancement of Colored People (NAACP), Minnesota chapter 1995, Distinguished Citizen Award, Minnesota Veterans of Foreign Wars 1995, Golden Triangle, Minnesota Nat. Farmers Union 2002, 2003, Legislator of the Year, American Ambulance Asscn 2003, Public Service award, Minnesota State Fed. Council for Exceptional Children 2003. *Address:* c/o Office of the Governor, 130 State Capitol Building, 75 Rev. Dr Martin Luther King Jr Blvd, St Paul, MN 55155, USA (office). *Website:* www.markdayton.org.

DE ALVEAR, Helga; Spanish art collector and gallery curator; *Director, Galería Helga de Alvear;* b. 1936, Kirn/Nahe, Germany; m. Jaime de Alvear 1959; three d.; f. Galería Helga de Alvear, located in 900m space nr the Reina Sofia Nat. Museum Art Centre, Madrid, focuses on photography, video and installations, as well as other media used by conceptual and minimalist artists, artists represented include Helena Almeida, Slater Bradley, Angela Bulloch, James Casebere, José Pedro Croft, Angela de la Cruz, Michael Elmgreen & Ingar Dragset, Alicia Framis, Katharina Grosse, Axel Hütte, Prudencio Irazabal, Isaac Julien, Jürgen Klauke, Imi Knoebel, Ester Partegás, Dan Perjovschi, Jorge Queiroz, Santiago Sierra, D.J. Simpson, Frank Thiel, Jane & Louise Wilson; endowed foundation in Cáceres with 2,500-strong collection of works by Flavin, Judd, Smithson and numerous contemporary int. and Spanish artists; Medal of Extremadura 2007, Gold Medal for Merit in Fine Arts, Spanish Ministry of Culture 2008, Medal of Cáceres 2011. *Address:* Galería Helga de Alvear, Doctor Fourquet 12, 28012 Madrid, Spain (office). *Telephone:* (91) 468-05-06 (office). *Fax:* (91) 467-51-34 (office). *E-mail:* galeria@helgadealvear.com (office). *Website:* www.helgadealvear.com (office).

DE BEAUCÉ, Thierry Martin; French fmr government official and writer; b. 14 Feb. 1943, Lyon; s. of Bertrand Martin de Beaucé and Simone de la Verpillère; two d.; ed Univ. of Paris and Ecole Nat. d'Admin; civil admin., Ministry of Cultural Affairs 1968–69; seconded to Office of Prime Minister 1969–73; Tech. Adviser, Pvt. Office of Pres. of Nat. Ass. 1974; seconded to Econ. Affairs Directorate, Ministry of Foreign Affairs 1974–76; Cultural Counsellor, Japan 1976–78; Second Counsellor, Morocco 1978–80; Vice-Pres. for Int. Affairs Société Elf Aquitaine 1981–86; Dir-Gen. of Cultural, Scientific and Tech. Relations, Ministry of Foreign Affairs 1986–87; State Sec. attached to Minister of Foreign Affairs 1988–91; Adviser to Pres. on African Affairs 1991–94; Vice-Pres. Conf. on Yugoslavia 1992; Amb. to Indonesia 1995–97; Dir of Int. Affairs, Vivendi 1997–2000; Chevalier, Légion d'honneur. *Publications:* Les raisons dangéreuses (essay) 1975, Un homme ordinaire (novel) 1978, L'Ile absolue (essay) 1979, Le désir de guerre 1980, La chute de Tanger (novel) 1984, Nouveau discours sur l'universalité de la langue française 1988, Le livre d'Esther 1989, La République de France 1991, La Nonchalance de Dieu 1995, L'absent de Marrakech 2006. *Address:* 45 rue de Richelieu, 75001 Paris, France.

DE BELOT, Jean Marie Louis, MA; French journalist and editor; b. 15 Dec. 1958, Neuilly-sur-Seine; s. of Philippe de Belot and Claude de Belot (née Vimal-Dessaignes); m. Frédérique Brunet 1983; two s. three d.; ed Univ. of Paris II-Panthéon Assas; journalist, La Tribune de l'economie 1984; journalist then Chief Econ. Reporter, Le Figaro 1985, Chief Reporter, Expansion Group 1987, Chief of Financial Services 1990, Editorial Dir 2000–04; Jt Chief Ed. Les Echos 1992, Chief Econ. Ed. 1998; Vice-Pres. and Partner Euro RSCG 2005–07; f. Aria Partners (public relations co.) 2007. *Publications:* La chute d'un agent de change: L'affaire Baudouin 1989. *Address:* Aria Partners, 3, Avenue Hoche, 75008 Paris, France. *Website:* www.aria-partners.com; www.wmaker.net/jeanbelot.

DE BENEDETTI, Carlo; Italian/Swiss business executive; *Chairman, Gruppo Editoriale L'Espresso SpA;* b. 14 Nov. 1934, Turin; m. Margherita Crosetti 1960; three s.; ed Turin Polytechnic; with Compagnia Italiana Tubi Metallici Flessibili 1959; Chair. and CEO Gilardini 1972–76; Dir Euromobiliare Finance Co. 1973–, Vice-Chair. 1977–; f. Compagnia Industriali Riunite (CIR) 1976, Vice-Chair. and CEO 1976–95, Chair. 1995–2009, Hon. Chair. 2009–; f. Finco 1976 (renamed Cofide–Compagnia Finanziaria De Benedetti 1985), Vice-Chair. and CEO 1976–91, Chair. 1991–; Vice-Chair. and CEO Olivetti & Co. SpA 1978–83, Chair. and CEO 1983–96, Hon. Chair. 1996–99; Dir SMI SpA 1983–; Chair. Cerus (Paris) 1986–; Chair. Sogefi; f. CDB Web Tech 2000, Exec. Chair. 2000–; f. Rodolfo Debenedetti Foundation 1998, Chair. 1998–; Vice-Chair. European Round Table of Industrialists, Brussels –2004; Vice-Pres. Confindustria 1984–; mem. Int. Council, Morgan Guaranty Trust 1980–; Chair. Fondiara 1989–; controlled Editore Arnoldo Mondadori 1990, half-share 1991–; f. Management & Capitali (investment firm) 2005; Chair. Gruppo Editoriale L'Espresso SpA 2006–; Co-Chair. Council for USA and Italy; mem. Supervisory Bd, Compagnie Financière Edmond de Rothschild Banque, Paris 2008–; mem. European Advisory Cttee, NY Stock Exchange 1985–2005; fmr mem. Int. Council, Centre for Strategic and Int. Studies, Int. Advisory Council, China Int. Trust and Investment Corpn, Beijing, Royal Swedish Acad. of Eng Science, Italian Council, European Inst. of Business Admin; Cavaliere del Lavoro 1983, Officier, Légion d'honneur 1987; Hon. LLD (Wesleyan Univ.) 1986. *Publications:* L'Avventura della Nuova Economia 2000, lectures and articles in business journals. *Address:* Gruppo Editoriale L'Espresso SpA, Via Cristoforo Colombo n. 98, 00147 Rome, Italy (office). *Website:* www.gruppoespresso.it (office).

DE BERNARDIS, Paolo, BSc, PhD; Italian astrophysicist and academic; *Full Professor, Università di Roma 'La Sapienza';* b. 1 Feb. 1959, Florence; m.; one s.; ed Università di Roma 'La Sapienza'; Researcher, Università di Roma 'La Sapienza' 1984–92, Assoc. Prof. 1992–2001, Prof. 2001–04, Full Prof. 2004–; Co-investigator, int. experiments Archeops, MAXIMA and BOOMERanG on the Cosmic Microwave Background; Co-investigator, High Frequency Instrument, ESA Planck Satellite, in charge of cryogenic pre-amplifiers of all Planck-HFI detectors; mem. ESA Astronomy Working Group 2002–04; Co-investigator High Frequency Instrument of Planck Satellite of ESA, launched 2009; led int. proposals B-Pol for ESA Cosmic Vision Call 2008, COrE for 2010 call, PRISM for Large Missions Science call 2013; fmr referee, Astrophysical Journal, Astronomy and Astrophysics, Nature; Ed. Journal of Cosmology and Astroparticle Physics, Memorie della Società Astronomica Italiana; Corresp. mem. Accad. Nazionale dei Lincei; mem. Italian Acad. of Science 'Accad. Nazionale delle Scienze detta dei XV'; Premio Feltrinelli, Accad. dei Lincei 2001, Balzan Prize for Observational Astronomy and Astrophysics 2006, Dan David Prize (co-recipient) 2009, Giuseppe and Vanna Cocconi Prize for Particle Astrophysics and Cosmology, European Physical Soc. (co-recipient) 2011, Van Duzer Prize, IEEE Council on Superconductivity 2011. *Publications:* Osservare l'Universo 2010; more than 200 papers in scientific journals on experimental astrophysics and cosmology, especially the Cosmic Microwave Background. *Address:* Dipartimento di Fisica, Edificio Marconi, Stanza 148, Università degli Studi di Roma 'La Sapienza', Piazzale Aldo Moro 2, 00185 Rome, Italy (office). *Telephone:* (06) 49914271 (office). *Fax:* (06) 4957697 (office). *E-mail:* paolo.debernardis@roma1.infn.it (office). *Website:* www.uniroma1.it (office); oberon.roma1.infn.it/pdb (office); oberon.roma1.infn.it/boomerang/b2k (office).

DE BERNIÈRES, Louis, BA, MA, PGCE; British writer; b. (Louis Henry Piers de Bernière-Smart), 8 Dec. 1954, London; s. of Maj. Reginald Piers Alexander de Bernière-Smart; ed Bradfield Coll., Univ. of Manchester, Leicester Polytechnic, Inst. of Educ., Univ. of London; landscape gardener 1972–73; teacher and rancher, Colombia 1974; philosophy tutor 1977–79; car mechanic 1980; English teacher 1981–84; bookshop asst 1985–86; supply teacher 1986–93; mem. Antonius Players 2003–; mem. PEN; Hon. Fellow, Trinity Coll. of Music; Dr hc (Univ. of East Anglia, Deree Univ. of Athens, Univ. of Aberdeen, Inst. of Educ., London); Granta Best of Young British Novelists 1994, Author of the Year Award 1997, Whittaker

Platinum Award, Millepages Prize for Best Foreign Novel (France) 2006. *Plays:* Sunday Morning at the Centre of the World 2001, Mr Handel 2010. *Publications include:* novels: (trilogy) The War of Don Emmanuel's Nether Parts 1990, Señor Vivo and the Coca Lord 1991, The Troublesome Offspring of Cardinal Guzman 1992, Captain Corelli's Mandolin (Commonwealth Writers' Prize, Eurasia region 1991) 1994, Red Dog 2001, Birds Without Wings 2004, A Partisan's Daughter 2008, The Dust That Falls from Dreams: A Novel 2015; short stories: Labels 1997, A Day Out for Mehmet Erbil 1999, Gunter Weber's Confession 2001; other: The Book of Job 1999, Notwithstanding 2009, Imagining Alexandria (poems) 2013, Of Love And Desire (poems) 2016; contrib. to Second Thoughts, Granta. *Leisure interests:* music, literature, golf, fishing, carpentry, gardening, cats. *Address:* Felicity Bryan Literary Agency, 2a North Parade Avenue, Oxford, OX2 6LX, England (office). *E-mail:* agency@felicitybryan.com (office). *Website:* www.louisdebernieres.co.uk.

DE BLASIO, Bill, BA, MA; American politician; *Mayor of New York City;* b. (Warren Wilhelm, Jr), 8 May 1961, New York City; s. of Warren Wilhelm, Sr and Maria (De Blasio) Wilhelm; m. Chirlane McCray 1994; one s. one d.; ed New York Univ., Columbia Univ.; Political Organizer, Quixote Center (social justice org.) 1987; worked for non-profit org. aiming to improve healthcare in Central America; Aide to Deputy Mayor Bill Lynch, New York City 1989; Campaign Man., Hillary Clinton's successful Senate campaign 2000; Regional Dir, US Dept of Housing and Urban Devt 1996–99; City Councilman for Dist 39, New York City Council 2001–09, Chair. Gen. Welfare Cttee; Public Advocate, New York City 2010–13; Mayor of New York City 2014–; Democrat. *Address:* Office of the Mayor, City Hall, New York, NY 10007, USA (office). *Website:* www1.nyc.gov/office-of-the-mayor (office).

DE BODINAT, Henri, MSc, PhD; French business executive; *President, TIME Equity Partners;* b. 15 July 1948, Paris; m. Clèmence de Lasteyrie 1989; two s. two d.; ed Institut d'études politiques de Paris, Harvard Business School, USA; CEO Sony Music, France 1985–93; Exec. Vice-Pres. Sony Software Europe 1993–94; fmr Man. Dir Saatchi & Saatchi PLC; Man. Dir Club Mediterrannée 1994–98; Founder and Man. Dir Cantos Music 1999–2002; Vice-Pres. Arthur D Little 2003–08; Pres. TIME Equity Partners 2009–; mem. Bd of Dirs CCM Benchmark, Thema TV, iConcerts, Catering International & Services CIS 2007–, Mobile Network Group 2014–, Zound Industries 2015–, Oh BiBi 2016; Co-founder, Actuel magazine; mem. Supervisory Bd LaBoutiqueOfficielle.com 2016–. *Publications include:* Influence in the Multinational Corporation 1977, The State: A Parenthesis in History? 1996. *Address:* TIME Equity Partners, 18 rue Bayard, 75008 Paris, France (office). *Telephone:* 1-40-73-87-30 (office). *Fax:* 1-40-73-78-00 (office). *E-mail:* hdebodinat@time-ep.com (office); contact@time-ep.com (office). *Website:* www.time-ep.com (office).

DE BOECK, Karel, MEcon, MMechEng; Belgian business executive; ed Catholic Univ. of Leuven; worked at Generale Bank 1976–93, Gen. Man. Retail Marketing 1990–93; joined ASLK-CGER Bank 1993, Gen. Man. Marketing & Retail; apptd Man. Dir Fortis Bank 1999, CEO Commercial & Private Banking, Fortis AG and Fortis (B) SA 2005–06, Chair. Fortis Bank AŞ (fmrly Turk Dis Ticaret Bankasi AŞ) 2005–06, Man. Dir Fortis (a holding of Fortis Bank A.S.), Chief Risk Officer, Ageas SA/NV (fmrly Fortis SA/NV) –2007, CEO Fortis Holdings (UK) Ltd, ABN AMRO Holdings (UK) Ltd, Chief Risk Officer and Regional Co-ordinator of Europe Region of Fortis (B) SA, Regional Co-ordinator of Europe, Fortis AG, CEO Fortis Holding NV –2008, CEO Ageas NV (also called Fortis NV) 2008–09, Exec. Dir Fortis NV 2008–09; Vice-Chair. Man. Bd RBS Holdings NV (fmrly ABN AMRO Holding NV) 2007–08, mem. Man. Bd 2007–08; Chair. Man. Bd and CEO Dexia SA 2012–16, CEO Dexia Crédit Local 2012–; Chair. European Financial Man. and Marketing Asscn 2003–06, Belgian Banking Asscn 1999–; Dir, ASLK-CGER Bank 1993–, Fortis Bank AŞ 2005–, Banca Intermobiliare di Investimenti e Gestioni SpA.

DE BOER, Yvo; Dutch fmr UN official and international organization official; b. 12 June 1954, Vienna, Austria; s. of a Dutch diplomatist; m.; three c.; ed boarding school in UK, tech. degree in social work in the Netherlands; involved in climate change policies since 1994; worked for UN Centre for Human Settlements (UN-HABITAT); served as Deputy Dir-Gen. for Environmental Protection, Ministry of Housing, Spatial Planning and Environment, as Head of Climate Change Dept; Dir for Int. Affairs, Ministry of Housing, Spatial Planning and Environment –2006; apptd by UN Sec.-Gen. as Exec. Sec. UN Framework Convention on Climate Change (UNFCCC) 2006–10 (resgnd); Global Chair. Climate Change & Sustainability Services, KPMG 2010–14; apptd to chair World Econ. Forum's Global Agenda Council on Climate Change 2011; Dir-Gen. Global Green Growth Inst. 2014–16; helped prepare EU position in lead-up to negotiations on Kyoto Protocol, assisted in design of internal burden sharing of EU and led dels to UNFCCC negotiations; fmr Vice-Pres. Conf. of Parties to UNFCCC; fmr Vice-Chair. Comm. on Sustainable Devt; fmr mem. China Council for Int. Cooperation on Environment and Devt, Bureau of the Environment Policy Cttee of OECD, Advisory Group of the Community Devt Carbon Fund of the World Bank; fmr mem. Bd of Dirs, Centre for Clean Air Policy; Fellow, Int. Centre for Integrated Assessment and Sustainable Devt, Univ. of Maastricht 2010.

DE BOER-BUQUICCHIO, Maud, LLD; Dutch lawyer and international organization official; b. 28 Dec. 1944, Hoensbroek; m. Gianni Buquicchio; two s.; ed Leiden Univ.; mem. Legal Secr., Applications Div., European Comm. on Human Rights (ECHR) 1969–71; mem. Pvt. Office of Sec.-Gen. of Council of Europe 1972–77; Prin. Legal Officer, Case Law and Research Div., ECHR Secr. 1977–90, Head of Div. 1990–92; Sec. to First Chamber of ECHR 1992–98; Deputy Registrar, European Court of Human Rights 1998–2002; Deputy Sec.-Gen. Council of Europe 2002–12 (retd); Pres. Missing Children Europe 2013–; mem. Exec. Bd and Man. Bd, Vienna 2012–; Cavaliere Grand'Ufficiale, Ordine Equestre di Sant'Agata (San Marino) 2007; Gold Medal of the Pres. of the Italian Repub. 2007. *Publications include:* Informationsfreiheit und die audio-visuelle Revolution (co-author) 1989, The Impact of the European Convention on Human Rights and the Rights of Children 1996, Council of Europe Convention to protect women against violence 2008; articles in professional journals and chapters in books on human rights and EU orgs. *Address:* European Union Agency for Fundamental Rights, Schwarzenbergplatz 11, 1040 Vienna, Austria (office). *E-mail:* information@fra.europa.eu (office). *Website:* fra.europa.eu (office).

DE BOGRÁN, María Antonieta Guillén; Honduran politician; b. 13 July 1955, Tegucigalpa; m. Roberto Bográn Idiáquez; three c.; Dir Instituto Hondureño de Turismo 1990–94; fmr Univ. Prof.; fmr Consultant, Ricardo Ernesto Maduro Andreu Educ. Foundation; fmr Minister of the Presidency; First Vice-Pres. of Honduras 2010–14; mem. Partido Nacional.

DE BOISSIEU, Pierre; French economist, diplomatist and international organization official; b. 14 June 1945, Paris; grand-nephew of fmr French pres. Charles de Gaulle; ed École nationale d'Admin, Paris; fmr Amb. to EU; Deputy Sec.-Gen. Council of the EU 1999–2009, Sec.-Gen. 2009–11; Officier, Légion d'honneur 2002, Commdr 2010.

DE BONO, Edward Francis Charles Publius, DPhil, PhD; British author and academic; b. 19 May 1933; s. of Prof. Joseph de Bono and Josephine de Bono (née O'Byrne); m. Josephine Hall-White 1971; two s.; ed St Edward's Coll., Malta, Royal Univ. of Malta, Christ Church, Oxford; Research Asst, Univ. of Oxford 1958–60, Jr Lecturer in Medicine 1960–61; Asst Dir of Research, Dept of Investigative Medicine, Univ. of Cambridge 1963–76, Lecturer in Medicine 1976–83; Dir Cognitive Research Trust, Cambridge 1971–; Sec.-Gen. Supranational Independent Thinking Org. 1983–; f. Edward de Bono Nonprofit Foundation; Chair. Council, Young Enterprise Europe 1998–; creator of two TV series: The Greatest Thinkers 1981, de Bono's Thinking Course 1982; apptd EU Amb. for Thinking for the Year of Creativity 2009; Hon. Registrar, St Thomas' Hosp. Medical School, Harvard Medical School; Hon. Consultant, Boston City Hosp. 1965–66; planet DE73 named edebono after him. *Publications include:* The Use of Lateral Thinking 1967, The Five-Day Course in Thinking 1968, The Mechanism of Mind 1969, Lateral Thinking: A Textbook of Creativity 1970, The Dog Exercising Machine 1970, Technology Today 1971, Practical Thinking 1971, Lateral Thinking for Management 1971, Children Solve Problems 1972, Po: Beyond Yes and No 1972, Think Tank 1973, Eureka: A History of Inventions 1974, Teaching Thinking 1976, The Greatest Thinkers 1976, Wordpower 1977, The Happiness Purpose 1977, The Case of the Disappearing Elephant 1977, Opportunities: A Handbook of Business Opportunity Search 1978, Future Positive 1979, Atlas of Management Thinking 1981, de Bono's Thinking Course 1982, Conflicts: A Better Way to Resolve Them 1985, Six Thinking Hats 1985, Letter to Thinkers 1987, I Am Right You Are Wrong 1990, Positive Revolution for Brazil 1990, Six Action Shoes 1991, Serious Creativity 1992, Teach Your Child to Think 1992, Water Logic 1993, Parallel Thinking 1994, Teach Yourself to Think 1995, Mind Pack 1995, Edward de Bono's Textbook of Wisdom 1996, How to be More Interesting 1997, Simplicity 1998, New Thinking for the New Millennium 1999, Why I Want to be King of Australia 1999, The Book of Wisdom 2000, The de Bono Code 2000, H+ (Plus) A New Religion 2006, Tactics: The Art and Science of Success 2007, How to Have Creative Ideas 2007, Six Frames for Looking at Information, Think–Before it is too late 2009, Reversed Quotations; numerous publs in Nature, Lancet, Clinical Science, American Journal of Physiology. *Leisure interests:* travel, toys, thinking. *Address:* Cranmer Hall, Fakenham, Norfolk, NR21 9HX, England (home). *Website:* edwdebono.com.

DE BORTOLI, Ferruccio, LLB; Italian journalist; *President, Longanesi;* b. 20 May 1953, Milan; s. of Giovanni De Bortoli and Giancarla Soresini; m. Elisabetta Cordani 1982; one s. one d.; ed Univ. of Milan; journalist 1973–; mem. editorial staff, Corriere d'Informazione 1975–78; Econs Corresp. Corriere della Sera, RCS MediaGroup 1978–85, Dir 1997–2003, 2009–15, Ed.-in-Chief, Econs Section 1987–93, Deputy Ed. 1993–96, Ed. 1997–2003, Ed.-in-Chief 2009–15; Ed.-in-Chief, L'Europeo (magazine) 1985–86; apptd CEO RCS Libri 2003; apptd Pres. Flammarion 2003; Dir Il Sole 24 Ore 2005–09, currently Pres. Longanesi, Pres. Vidas milan 2015–; Renato Fabrizi Benedict Award 2012. *Leisure interests:* reading, music, skiing. *Address:* Vidas Milan, Corso Italy 17, 20122 Milan (office); Longanesi, Via Gherardini 10, 20145 Milan (office); Via Donatello 36, 20131 Milan, Italy (home).

DE BOTTON, Alain; Swiss writer; b. 20 Dec. 1969, Zürich; ed Gonville and Caius Coll., Cambridge; Chevalier, Ordre des Arts et des Lettres 2003. *Publications include:* Essays in Love (US edn On Love) 1993, The Romantic Movement: Sex, Shopping, and the Novel 1994, Kiss and Tell 1995, How Proust Can Change Your Life: Not a Novel 1997, The Consolations of Philosophy 2000, The Art of Travel (Charles Veillon European Essay Prize, Switzerland 2003) 2002, Status Anxiety 2004; The Architecture of Happiness 2006, The Pleasures and Sorrows of Work 2009, A Week at the Airport: A Heathrow Diary 2009, Religion for Atheists 2012, Art as Therapy (co-author) 2013, The News: a User's Manual 2014, The Course of Love 2016; contrib. articles, book and television reviews to various periodicals. *Address:* c/o Caroline Dawnay, United Agents, 12–26 Lexington Street, London, W1F 0LE, England (office). *Telephone:* (20) 3214-0800 (office). *Fax:* (20) 3214-0801 (office). *E-mail:* ohunt@unitedagents.co.uk (office). *Website:* www.alaindebotton.com.

DE BRICHAMBAUT, Marc Perrin; French judge, diplomatist and international organization official; b. 29 Oct. 1948, Rabat, Morocco; m.; two c.; ed Ecole Normale Supérieur de Saint-Cloud, Institut d'Etudes Politiques and Ecole Nationale d'Admin, Paris; began career at Conseil d'Etat, first as admin. judge, later as Conseiller d'Etat; posted to New York as Special Asst to UN Under-Sec.-Gen. for Int. Econ. and Social Affairs 1978; adviser to French Foreign Minister 1981–83; Chief of Staff, Ministry of European Affairs 1983–86, Ministry of Foreign Affairs 1984–86; Counsellor, Embassy in Washington, DC 1986–88; Prin. Adviser to Minister of Defence 1988–91; Head of French Del., CSCE (later became OSCE), Vienna 1991–94; Head, Legal Div., Ministry of Foreign Affairs 1994–98; Dir for Strategic Affairs, Ministry of Defence 1998–2005; Sec.-Gen. OSCE 2005–11; mem. Vienna Advisory Council, International Peace Inst. *Address:* Conseil d'Etat, 1 place du Palais-Royal, 75100 Paris 01 SP, France (office). *E-mail:* lise.ardhuin@conseil-etat.fr (office). *Website:* www.conseil-etat.fr (office).

DE BROGLIE, Prince Gabriel Marie Joseph Anselme; French administrator; *Honorary Chancellor, Institut de France;* b. 21 April 1931, Versailles; s. of Prince Edouard de Broglie and Princess Hélène Le Bas de Courmont; m. Diane de Bryas 1953; one s. one d.; Tech. Adviser, Ministry of Social Affairs 1966–68, to Prime Minister 1968–69, Minister of State for Cultural Affairs 1970; Sec.-Gen. Office de Radiodiffusion-Télévision Française 1971, Asst Dir-Gen. 1973; Dir Radio-France 1975–77, Dir-Gen. 1977–79; Pres. Inst. nat. de l'audiovisuel 1979–81; mem. Haut Conseil de l'Audiovisuel 1972; Pres. TV Historical Cttee, Haute Autorité de l'Audiovisuel 1981–86; Pres. Comm. Nat. de la Communication et des Libertés 1986–89; Pres. Soc. des Bibliophiles François, Soc. d'histoire diplomatique; Chancellor, Institut de France 2006–17, Hon. Chancellor 2018–; foreign correspondent, Acad. of Moral and Political Sciences of Argentina; foreign mem., Royal Acad. of literature, history and antiquities of Sweden; mem. Acad. des Sciences Morales et Politiques 1997, Acad. française 2001–, Roxburghe Club of London; Hon. mem., Romanian Acad.; Grand Croix de la Légion d'honneur; Chevalier, Ordre nat. du Mérite; Commdr des Arts et des Lettres, des Palmes académiques. *Publications include:* Le Général de Valence ou l'insouciance et la gloire 1972, Ségur sans cérémonie, ou la gaieté libertine 1977, L'histoire politique de la Revue des Deux Mondes 1979, L'Orléanisme, la ressource libérale de la France 1981, Une image vaut dix mille mots 1982, Madame de Genlis (Gobert Prize) 1985, Le français, pour qu'il vive 1986, Guizot (Amb.'s Prize) 1990, Le XIXesiècle, l'éclat et le déclin de la France 1995, Mac Mahon 2000, Monarchy of July 2011, Impardonnable XXème siècle 2017. *Leisure interest:* books. *Address:* Institut de France, 23 quai Conti, 75006 Paris (office); 96 rue de Grenelle, 75007 Paris, France (home). *Telephone:* 01-47-66-01-21 (office). *E-mail:* fondation-del-duca@institut-de-france.fr (office).

DE CARLO, Massimo; Italian gallery owner; f. Galleria Massimo De Carlo in Milan 1987, opened in Via Panfilo Castaldi with exhbn of Olivier Mosset, moved to new space in Via Bocconi 1992, and to Viale Corsica 1998, moved to space in Via Ventura 2003, opened Carlson Gallery in London 2009, moved to a second major venue in London in South Audley Street 2012 (renamed Massimo De Carlo, London), focuses on introducing Italian artists to European and US audiences and US and European artists to Italy; represents artists including John Armleder, Massimo Bartolini, Chris Burden, Maurizio Cattelan, Paul Chan, Spartacus Chetwynd, Steven Claydon, Dan Colen, George Condo, Roberto Cuoghi, Elmgreen & Dragset, Roland Flexner, Gelitin, Thomas Grünfeld, Carsten Höller, Christian Holstad, Rashid Johnson, Elad Lassry, Sol LeWitt, Nate Lowman, Matthew Monahan, Olivier Mosset, Matt Mullican, Steven Parrino, Diego Perrone, Paola Pivi, Jim Shaw, Josh Smith, Ettore Spalletti, Rudolf Stingel, Piotr Uklanski, Kelley Walker, Pei-Ming Yan and Andrea Zittel. *Address:* Galleria Massimo De Carlo Mdc SRL, Via Giovanni Ventura 5, 20134 Milan, Italy (office); Gallery Massimo De Carlo, London, 55 South Audley Street, London, W1K 2QH, England (office). *Telephone:* (02) 70003987 (Milan) (office); (20) 7287-2005 (London) (office). *Fax:* (02) 7492135 (Milan) (office). *E-mail:* milano@massimodecarlo.com (office); london@massimodecarlo.com (office). *Website:* www.massimodecarlo.com (office).

DE CAROLIS, Patrick; French broadcasting executive, journalist, television producer and museum director; *Director, Musée Marmottan Monet;* b. 19 Nov. 1953, Arles; s. of Dominique de Carolis and Lucette-Mary Mounier; m. Carol-Anne Hartpence 1980; four c.; ed École Supérieure de Journalisme de Paris; positions with several TV channels, including TFI, M6, France 5; joined France 3 1974, presenter, Des racines et des ailes programme 1997–2005, 2013–14, Le Grand Tour 2012–14; Gen. Dir Figaro magazine 2001–04; CEO France Télévisions 2005–10; fmr Chair. Supervisory Bd France 24; f. own film production co., Anaprod 2010; Dir, Musée Marmottan Monet 2013–; mem. Acad. des beaux-arts 2010–, Vice-Pres. 2017; Chevalier, Légion d'honneur, Ordre nat. du Mérite; Officier des Palmes académiques, Ordre des Arts et des Lettres; Commdr avec plaque, Ordre de Saint-Grégoire-le-Grand. *Publications include:* Conversation (co-author) 2001, Les demoiselles de Provence 2005, Refuge pour temps d'orage 2009, La Dame du Palatin 2011, Les Ailes intérieures 2016. *Address:* Musée Marmottan Monet, 2, Rue Louis-Boilly, 75016 Paris, France (office). *Website:* www.marmottan.fr (office).

DE CARVALHO, Col Celestino; Guinea-Bissau air force officer and politician; b. 14 June 1955; s. of Domingos de Carvalho and Josefa Cabral; trained as mil. pilot; fmr Chief of Staff of Air Force; Adviser on Air Force Matters to Armed Forces Chief of Staff 2004; Dir Instituto Nacional de Defesa (Nat. Defence Inst.) –2012; mem. mil. command group that led coup d'état April 2012; Minister of Nat. Defence and Fighters for the Country's Freedom 2012–14.

DE CARVALHO, Mário Costa Martins; Portuguese writer, lawyer and academic; b. 25 Sept. 1944, Lisbon; s. of Domingos Martins Carvalho and Maria Luísa Costa Carvalho; m. Maria Helena Taborda Duarte 1969; two d.; ed Univ. of Lisbon Law School; involved in student resistance to dictatorship; received conviction for political activities; served with army; in exile in Paris and Lund, Sweden 1973–74; returned to Portugal after revolution of 1974; involved in politics 1974–77; f. law practice 1981; Prof. of Scriptwriting, Cinema School 1999–2001; mem. Bd Portuguese Asscn of Writers; Prof. of Playwriting, Univ. of Lisbon 2000–02; Dir of Creative Writing, Instituto Português do Livro e das Bibliotecas, Sociedade Portuguesa de Autores 2003–; Grande Oficial, Ordem Militar de Sant'Iago da Espada 2014; Prémio Vergílio Ferreira (for body of work) 2009. *Plays include:* Água em Pena de Pato 1991, Se Perguntarem por Mim, Não Estou, Haja Harmonia (Grande Prémio APE) 1999. *Publications:* Contos da Sétima Esfera (short stories) 1981, Casos do Beco das Sardinheiras (short stories) 1982, O Livro Grande de Terras, Navio e Mariana (Prémio Município de Lisboa) 1982, A inaudita guerra da Avenida Gago Coutinho (short stories) 1983, Fabulário (short stories) 1984, Contos Soltos (short stories) 1986, A Paixão do Conde de Fróis (Prémio D. Dinis) 1986, E se Tivesse a Bondade de Me Dizer Porquê? (with Clara Pinto Correia) 1986, Os Alferes (Prémio Int. Città di Cassino) 1989, Quatrocentos Mil Sestércios, O Conde Jano (novella) (Grande Prémio de Conto Camilo Castelo Branco) 1991, Um Deus Passeando Pela Brisa da Tarde (Pegasus Prize 1996, Prémio Literário Giuseppe Acerbi, Prémio Fernando Namora, Grande Prémio de Romance e Novela APE/IPLB) 1995, Era Bom que Trocássemos umas Ideias sobre o Assunto 1995, Apuros de um Pessimista em Fuga (novella) 1999, Contos Vagabundos (short stories) 2000, Fantasia para dois coronéis e uma piscina (Prémio PEN Clube Português de Ficção, Grande Prémio de Literatura ITF/DST) 2003, O Homem que Engoliu a Lua (for children) 2003, A Sala Magenta (Prémio Fernando Namora) 2008, A Arte de Morrer Longe 2010, O Homem do Turbante Verde 2011, Quando o Diabo Reza 2011, A Liberdade de Pátio (short stories, Grande Prémio De Conto e Novela APE) 2013, Quem disser o contrário é porque tem razão 2014, Novelas Extravagantes 2015. *Address:* R. António Pereira Carrilho 27 R/C, 1000-046 Lisbon (home); Sociedade Portuguesa de Autores, a/c ALA – Edição Av. Duque de Loulé 31, 1069-153 Lisbon, Portugal (office). *Telephone:* (21) 3594462 (office); (21) 8460576 (home). *Fax:* (21) 3530257 (office); (21) 8464227 (home). *E-mail:* edicao@spautores.pt (office). *Website:* www.spautores.pt (office); www.mariodecarvalho.com.

DE CASTELLA, (François) Robert, (Deek), MBE, BSc, AO; Australian company director and fmr athlete; *Managing Director, The Indigenous Marathon Foundation;* b. 27 Feb. 1957, Melbourne; s. of Rolet François de Castella and Ann M. Hall; m. Gayelene J. Clews 1980 (divorced 1998); two s. one d.; m. Theresa de Castella 2003; one d.; ed Xavier Coll., Kew, Monash Univ. and Swinburne Inst. of Tech.; winner, Fukuoka Marathon (world's fastest for out-and-back course) 1981; Marathon Champion, Commonwealth Games, Brisbane 1982; winner Rotterdam Marathon 1983; World Marathon Champion, Helsinki 1983; winner Boston Marathon 1986; winner Commonwealth Games 1986; Dir Australian Inst. of Sport 1990–95; Chair. Health Promotions Bd ACT (Healthpact) 1996–2003; Man. Dir SmartStart (Australia) Pty Ltd 1997–; Chair. Leisure Australia Foundation 1999–2009; Founder Rob de Castella's SmartStart for Kids 2004–; Founder and Man. Dir The Indigenous Marathon Foundation 2010–; mem. Bd of Dirs Decorp Pty Ltd 1995–, Action Potential 1996–98, RWM Publs 1996–2000, Your Bread Co. Pty Ltd 2003–, Deeks Food; mem. Bd Australian Sports Comm. –1999, Bd Sports Australian Hall of Fame 1997–; Dr hc (Univ. of Sunshine Coast) 2008, (Univ. of Canberra) 2008; Australian of the Year 1983, Sports Australia Hall of Fame, Athletics Australia Hall of Fame 2008. *Publications include:* de Castella on Running 1984, Deek, Australia's World Champion 1984, Smart Sport 1996. *Leisure interests:* motorcycling, scuba diving, traditional Okinawian Goju karate. *Address:* IMG, Level 3/480, St Kilda Road, Melbourne, Vic., 3004, Australia (office); The Indigenous Marathon Project, PO Box 6127, Mawson, ACT 2607, Australia (office). *Telephone:* (3) 9864-1111 (office); (2) 6260-5750 (office). *Website:* www.imgworld.com (office); www.imf.org.au (office). *Fax:* (2) 6260-5799 (office). *E-mail:* robert.d@imf.org.au (office).

DE CASTRO, Manuel (Noli) Leuterio, Jr, BCom; Philippine politician and broadcaster; b. 6 July 1949, Pola, Oriental Mindoro; s. of Inay Nene; ed Pola Cen. School, Pola Catholic High School, Univ. of the East (UE), Manila; began career in broadcasting as field reporter for Johnny de Leon 1976; radio anchorman, DWW 1982–86; joined ABS-CBN 1986, hosted TV programmes Good Morning, Philippines, At Your Service 1986, Magandang Umaga 1987–98, Overseas Limited 1988, TV Patrol, Magandang Gabi... Bayan (Good Evening... Nation) 1998; hosted radio programme Kabayan, My Fellow Filipinos, DZMM (radio station of ABS-CBN); apptd Vice-Pres. DZMM and Head of Production TV Patrol 1999–2001; elected to Senate 2001; Vice-Pres. of the Philippines 2004–10, also Chair. Housing and Urban Devt Coordinating Council. *Address:* c/o Office of the Vice-President, 7th Floor, PNB Financial Center, President Diosdado Macapagal Boulevard, Pasay City 1300, Metro Manila, Philippines (office).

DE CESARE, Vittorio; Italian accountant and business executive; b. 31 Aug. 1935, Naples; ed Univ. of Naples; substitute teacher of accounting and bookkeeping, Instituto Tecnico professionale alberghiero di Napoli 1965; employee with Naples shipping co. 1965; employee at major Italian chemical group with responsibility for Admin. Office (man. of corp. issues and tax) 1973–79; practised as Chartered Accountant in Milan 1980; Tech. Consultant for Judge, Civil Court of Milan; has acted as auditor to Supervisory Bd Napoletana Gas SpA; fmr Auditor, Premafin Finanziaria SpA, Chair. Supervisory Bd 2008–13 (merged with Unipol Assicurazioni and Milano Assicurazioni in Fondiaria-Sai to form UnipolSai Assicurazioni SpA 2013). *Address:* c/o UnipolSai Assicurazioni SpA, Via Stalingrado 45, 40128 Bologna, Italy. *E-mail:* unipolsaiassicurazioni@pec.unipol.it.

DE CHALENDAR, Pierre-André; French business executive; *Chairman and CEO, Compagnie de Saint-Gobain;* b. April 1958; ed École supérieure des sciences économiques et commerciales, École nat. d'admin, Strasbourg; Finance Insp., later Deputy Dir-Gen. of Energy and Raw Materials, Ministry of Industry and Regional Devt –1989; Vice-Pres., Corp. Planning, Cie de Saint-Gobain 1989–92, Head of European Abrasives Div. 1992–96, also CEO Norton Abrasifs Europe (subsidiary co.) 1992–96, Pres. Worldwide Abrasives Div., N America 1996–2000, Gen. Del. for Saint-Gobain UK and Ireland 2000–02, CEO Meyer International (following acquisition by Saint-Gobain) 2000, Pres. Building Distribution Sector 2003–05, COO Compagnie de Saint-Gobain 2005–07, mem. Bd 2006–, CEO 2007–, Chair. 2010–, supervisor of Innovative Materials Sector 2015–; mem. Bd of Dirs, Veolia Environnement, BNP Paribas; Chair. Entreprises pour l'Environnement 2012–15. *Address:* Compagnie de Saint-Gobain, Les Miroirs, 18 avenue d'Alsace, 92400 Courbevoie, France (office). *Telephone:* 1-47-62-30-00 (office). *Fax:* 1-47-62-50-62 (office). *E-mail:* info@saint-gobain.com (office). *Website:* www.saint-gobain.com (office).

DE CHARETTE DE LA CONTRIE, Hervé Marie Joseph; French politician; b. 30 July 1938, Paris; s. of Hélion de Charette de la Contrie and Jeanne de Nolhac; m. 2nd Michèle Delor; one c. and three c. by previous m.; ed Ecole des Hautes Etudes Commerciales, Inst. d'Etudes Politiques, Paris and Ecole Nat. d'Admin.; Deputy Sec.-Gen. Council of State 1969–72, Maître des requêtes 1973; Ministry of Labour 1973–78; Pres. Admin. Council, Nat. Immigration Office 1977; Dir Office of Minister of Educ. 1978; Pres. Sonacotra 1980–81; Deputy Sec.-Gen. Parti Républicain 1979; returned to Council of State 1981; Deputy for 6th Dist of Maine-et-Loire to Nat. Ass. 1986, 1988–93, 1997–2012; Asst Minister, Office of Prime Minister 1986–88; Mayor of St-Florent-le-Vieil 1989–2014; mem. Union pour la Démocratie Française (UDF) 1986–2002, Vice-Pres. 1991; Vice-Pres. Conseil Régional, Pays de la Loire 1992–; Minister of Housing 1993–95, of Foreign Affairs 1995–97; Pres. Parti populaire pour la démocratie française 1995, convention démocratie 2002; mem. Union pour un mouvement populaire (now Les Républicains) 2002–10, Nouveau Centre 2010–12, Union des démocrates et indépendants 2012–; Pres. Chambre du Commerce Franco-Arabe 2008–16; Chair. Institut français de finance islamique 2009–. *Publications:* Ouragon sur la République 1995, Lyautey 1997, Pour un nouveau partenariat euro-méditerranéen 2006.

DE CHASSEY, Éric, PhD; French art historian, art critic and professor of art history; *Professor of Art History, École Normale Supérieure de Lyon;* b. (Éric de Buretel de Chassey), 1965, Pittsburgh, Pa, USA; ed École Normale Supérieure and Université Paris IV-Sorbonne, Paris; specialist on 20th and 21st century abstract art, on photography and on American art; Asst Prof. of Contemporary Art History, Université Paris IV-Sorbonne 1996–99; Prof. of Contemporary Art History,

Université François-Rabelais, Tours 1999–2012; Dir Acad. de France à Rome, Villa Medici 2009–15; Prof. of Art History, École Normale Supérieure de Lyon 2012–; mem. Institut Universitaire de France 2004–09. *Publications include:* La peinture efficace, Une histoire de l'abstraction aux États-Unis 1910–1960 2001, Platitudes, Une histoire de la photographie plate 2006, Repartir à zéro, comme si la peinture n'avait jamais existé 1945-1949 2008, Europunk The visual culture of punk in Europe 1976–1980, Pour l'histoire de l'art 2011. *Address:* 6 rue Oudinot, 75007 Paris, France (office). *Telephone:* 6-12-30-37-86 (mobile) (office). *E-mail:* eric.dechassey@ens-lyon.fr (office).

DE CHASTELAIN, Gen. (retd) (Alfred) John Gardyne Drummond, CC, CMM, CH, CD, BA; Canadian (b. British) army officer and diplomatist; b. 30 July 1937, Bucharest, Romania; s. of Alfred George Gardyne de Chastelain and Marion Elizabeth de Chastelain (née Walsh); m. Mary Ann Laverty 1961; one s. one d.; ed Fettes Coll., Edin., UK, Mount Royal Coll., Calgary, Royal Mil. Coll. of Canada, Kingston, British Army Staff Coll., Camberley, Surrey, UK; emigrated to Canada 1955, naturalized 1962; commissioned 2nd Lt, 2nd Bn, Princess Patricia's Canadian Light Infantry (PPCLI) 1960, Capt., ADC to Chief of Gen. Staff, Army HQ 1962–64, Co. Commdr, 1st Bn, PPCLI, FRG 1964–65, Co. Commdr, Edmonton, rank of Maj., later with 1st Bn, UN Force, Cyprus 1968; Brigade Maj., 1st Combat Group, Calgary 1968–70, Commdg Officer, 2nd Bn, PPCLI, Winnipeg 1970–72, rank of Lt-Col, Stagiare, Fed. Bicultural Program, Laval Univ., Quebec 1972–73, Sr Staff Officer, Quartier Gen. Dist, Quebec 1973–74, rank of Col, Commdr Canadian Forces Base, Montreal 1974–76, Deputy Chief of Staff, HQ UN Forces, Cyprus and Commdr Canadian Contingent 1976–77, rank of Brig.-Gen. and apptd Commdt, Royal Mil. Coll. of Canada, Kingston 1977–80, command of 4th Canadian Mechanized Brigade Group, FRG 1980–82, Dir-Gen. Land Doctrine and Operations, Nat. Defence HQ, Ottawa 1982–83, rank of Maj.-Gen. 1983, Deputy Commdr Mobile Command, St Hubert, Quebec 1983–86, rank of Lt-Gen. and apptd Asst Deputy Minister (Personnel) Nat. Defence HQ, Ottawa 1986–88, Vice-Chief, Defence Staff 1988–89, rank of Gen. and Chief of the Defence Staff 1989–93; Amb. to USA 1993; re-apptd Chief of the Defence Staff 1994–95; mem. Int. Body on Decommissioning of Arms in Northern Ireland 1995–96, Chair. Business Cttee and Co-Chair. Strand Two Talks, Northern Ireland Peace Process (leading to the Good Friday Agreement) 1996–98, Chair. Ind. Int. Comm. on Decommissioning (Northern Ireland) 1997–2011; Col of the Regt, PPCLI 2000–03; Pres. Dominion of Canada Rifle Asscn 1986–93; fmr mem. Royal Canadian Legion; Past First Nat. Vice-Pres., Boy Scouts of Canada; mem. St Andrews Soc. of Montreal; Hon. Fellow, Lady Margaret Hall, Oxford 2006; Canadian Forces Decoration 1968, Commdr, Order of Mil. Merit 1985, Commdr, Order of St John of Jerusalem (Kts of Malta) 1991, Commendation Medal of Merit and Honour (Greece) 1991, Officer of the Order of Canada 1993, Commdr, US Legion of Merit 1995, Companion of Honour, UK 1998; Hon. DMilSc (Royal Mil. Coll. of Canada) 1996, Hon. LLD (Royal Roads Univ.) 2002, (Nipissing) 2006, (Carleton) 2006, (Queen's Univ., Kingston) 2007, (St Mary's, Halifax, Nova Scotia) 2008, (Brock Univ.) 2011, (Concordia Univ.) 2012, (Mount Alison Univ.) 2014, (Edinburgh Univ.) 2014; Vimy Award 1992, Birchall Leadership Award, Royal Mil. Coll. Club of Canada 2006, inducted to Wall of Honour at Royal Mil. Coll. of Canada 2010, Presidential Distinguished Service Award for the Irish Abroad 2017. *Publications include:* articles on mil. affairs and int. diplomacy. *Leisure interests:* bagpipes, Scottish country dancing, fishing, painting. *Address:* 1008–111 Wurtemburg Street, Ottawa, ON K1M 8M1, Canada (home).

DE CHATEAUVIEUX, Jacques d'Armand; French business executive; *Chairman, Bourbon;* b. 13 Feb. 1951, Saint-Denis-de-la-Reunion; ed Institut Supérieur de Gestion, Paris, Columbia Univ., New York, USA; man. auditor, Union des Transports Aériens 1975–77; consultant, Boston Consulting Group (BCG) 1977–79; Chair. and CEO Bourbon 1979–2010, Chair. 2011–; mem. Supervisory Bd, AXA Group 2005–, Chair. 2008–10, mem. Bd 2010–; Chair. and CEO JACCAR; Chair. Sapmer SA, SAGES SAS, Cana Tera SAS; mem. Bd of Dirs or Supervisory Bd, Sinopacific Shipbuilding Group (China), Piriou SAS; Non-Man. Partner, Michelin 2011; Dir, Greenships Holdings (Singapore) Advisor to CBo Territoria SA. *Address:* Bourbon, 33 rue du Louvre, 75002 Paris, France (office). *Telephone:* 1-40-13-86-16 (office). *Fax:* 1-40-28-40-31 (office). *E-mail:* bourbon@bourbonoffshore.com (office). *Website:* www.bourbonoffshore.com (office).

DE CLERCK, Stefaan Maria Joris Yolanda; Belgian politician; *Chairman, Proximus Group;* b. 12 Dec. 1951, Kortryk; m.; two s. three d.; ed Katholieke Universiteit Leuven; mem. Parl. (Flemish) 1990–95, (Chamber) 1998–2001; mem. Senate (Flemish) 2003–04, 2004–07, (Chamber) 2007–08; Minister of Justice 1995–98, 2008–11; Congressman 2010–13; Nat. Chair. Christelijke Volkspartij (CVP, renamed Christen-Democratisch en Vlaams—CD&V 2001) 1999–2003; Councillor, Kortrijk 2001–, Mayor 2001–12; Chair. Belgacom (now Proximus) 2013–. *Publications:* Het bos en de bomen, justitie hervormen (The wood and the trees, reforming justice) 1997, Het open boek: Een boeiend verslag van wat leeft in de regio (The open book: a thrilling report on what lives in the region) (with Luc Martens) 1998–99, Hartslagen Christen-Democratische verkenningen (The heartbeats of Christian-Democrat observations) (co-author) 2000, Voor mensen en waarden (For people and values) 2003. *Address:* Proximus Group, Koning Albert II-laan 27, 1030 Brussels, Belgium (office). *Telephone:* (2) 202-82-41 (office). *E-mail:* stefaan.de.clerck@skynet.be (home); info@proximus.com (office). *Website:* www.proximus.com (office).

DE CLERCQ, Peter; Dutch UN official; *Deputy Special Representative, United Nations Assistance Mission in Somalia (UNSOM);* b. 1959; m.; five c.; ed Clingendael, The Hague, Univ. of Tilburg; worked with UNHCR 1985–, held various positions in Geneva, Budapest, covered field assignments in Sudan, Zimbabwe, Angola, Pakistan, Special Adviser on Disarmament, Demobilization and Reintegration, UN Org. Mission in Democratic Republic of the Congo (MONUC), Kinshasa, Democratic Republic of the Congo 2001–04, UNDP Senior Return, Reintegration and Recovery Adviser, S Sudan 2004–06, Head of Supply Man., UNHCR 2006–09, Resident Coordinator and Humanitarian Coordinator ad interim, Sudan –2012, Deputy Special Rep. of Sec.-Gen. for Somalia ad interim, UN Political Office for Somalia (UNPOS) 2012–13, Deputy Special Rep. of Sec.-Gen. and UN Resident Coordinator and Humanitarian Coordinator, United Nations Stabilization Mission in Haiti (MINUSTAH) 2013–15, Deputy Special Rep., UN Assistance Mission in Somalia (UNSOM) 2015–, also UN Resident Coordinator, Humanitarian Coordinator and UNDP Resident Rep. 2015–. *Address:* United Nations Assistance Mission in Somalia (UNSOM), Department of Political Affairs, United Nations, New York, NY 10017, USA (office). *Telephone:* (212) 963-1234 (office). *Fax:* (212) 963-4879 (office). *E-mail:* admin@unsom.org (office). *Website:* www.unsom.org (office).

DE CONCINI, Dennis, LLB; American lawyer and fmr politician; *Vice-President and Partner, Parry, Romani, De Concini & Symms Associates;* b. 8 May 1937, Tucson, Ariz.; s. of Evo and Ora De Concini; one s. two d.; ed Univ. of Arizona and Univ. of Arizona Coll. of Law; Committeeman, Pima Co. 1958–76; worked with family law practice 1963–65; special counsel to Gov. of Ariz. 1965, Admin. Asst to Gov. 1965–67; Pnr, DeConcini & McDonald, law firm 1968–73; Pima Co. Attorney 1972–76; Admin., Ariz. Drug Control Dist 1975–76; fmr mem. Ariz. Democratic Exec. Cttee, Vice-Chair. 1964, 1970; Senator from Arizona 1977–95, mem. Judiciary Cttee, Appropriations Cttee, Rules Cttee, Special Select Cttee on Indian Affairs, Veterans' Affairs Cttee; mem. Select Cttee on Intelligence, Senate Caucus on Int. Narcotics Control; Vice-Pres. and Partner, Parry, Romani, De Concini & Symms Associates, Washington, DC 1995–, DeConcini, McDonald, Yetwin & Lacy, Tucson 1995–; Dir Nat. Center for Missing and Exploited Children 1995–, Federal Home Loan Mortgage Corporation (Freddie Mac) 1995–2000, Saf T Lok Inc. 1997–2001, Protective Products of America Inc. 2007–09; mem. Académie Française 1993–; Chair. Comm. on Security and Co-operation in Europe; served US Army 1959–60, Judge Advocate Gen. Corps. 1964–67; mem. Arizona Board of Regents 2006–; mem. or fmr mem. Pima Co. Bar Asscn, Ariz. Bar Asscn, ABA, American Judicature Soc., American Arbitration Asscn, Nat. District Attorneys' Asscn; mem. Ariz. County Attorneys' and Sheriffs' Asscn, Sec.-Treas. 1975, Pres. 1976. *Publication:* Senator Dennis DeConcini: From the Center of the Aisle 2007. *Leisure interests:* golf, boating, jogging. *Address:* Parry, Romani, De Concini & Symms Associates, 517 C Street, NE, Washington, DC 20002 (office); 2525 E Broadway, Suite 111, Tucson, AZ 85716, USA. *Telephone:* (202) 547-4000 (Washington) (office); (520) 325-9600 (Tucson) (office); (858) 459-5460 (LaJolla) (office). *Fax:* (202) 543-5044 (Washington) (office); (520) 327-9744 (Tucson) (office); (858) 459-5471 (LaJolla) (office). *E-mail:* prdands@aol.com (office); d.deconcini@atl.net (office). *Website:* www.lobbycongress.com (office).

DE CORTE, Frans, DrChemSci; Belgian physicist and academic; ed Univ. of Ghent; Prof., Dept of Analytical Chem., Inst. for Nuclear Sciences, Univ. of Ghent 1964–2007 (retd); mem. Int. Advisory Bd, Radiochemical Conf. (RadChem), Mariánské Lázně, Czech Repub. 2002; mem. IUPAC; Hevesy Medal 2000.

DE CREM, Pieter Frans Norbert Jozef Raymond; Belgian politician; *Minister of Security and of the Interior;* b. 22 July 1962, Aalter; m. Caroline Bergez; three c.; ed Univ. Catholique de Louvain, Univ. Libre de Bruxelles; worked for Roularta Media Group 1987–89; Pres. of youth section of CVP (Christelijke Volkspartij), Gand-Eeklo 1989–95; Attaché, Cabinet of Prime Minister Wilfried Martens 1989–92, Cabinet of Minister of Defence 1992–93; Adviser to De fabrieken van de Gebroeders De Beukelaar 1993–94; elected Mayor of Aalter 1995, re-elected 2000, 2006; elected to Chamber of Reps for Gand-Eeklo (CVP) 1995, re-elected 1999, elected to Chamber of Reps for Flanders East (party renamed Christen-Democratisch en Vlaams—CD&V) 2003, re-elected 2007, Head, CD&V parl. group 2003–07, Pres. Interior Comm. 2007, mem. OSCE parl. cttee; Minister of Defence 2007–14; Deputy Prime Minister 2013–14; Sec. of State for Foreign Trade 2014–18; Minister of Security and of the Interior 2018–; Officier, Ordre de Léopold. *Address:* Federal Public Service of the Interior, 2 Rue de la Loi, 1000 Brussels (office). *Telephone:* (2) 504-85-13 (office). *Fax:* (2) 504-85-25 (office). *E-mail:* info@ibz.fgov.be (office). *Website:* www.ibz.be (office); www.pieterdecrem.be.

DE CUENCA Y CUENCA, Luis Alberto; Spanish philologist, poet, translator and writer; b. 1950, Madrid; ed Universidad Autónoma de Madrid; Prof. of Philology Inst. of Council for Scientific Research, then Publs Dir; literary critic for several publs including El País; Dir Biblioteca Nacional (Nat. Library) 1996–2000; Sec. of State for Culture 2000–04; Academician, Academia de Buenas Letras de Granada 2009–, Real Academia de la Historia 2010–; Gran Cruz de Isabel la Católica 2004; Premio de Cultura (Literatura), Madrid 2007. *Publications include:* Los Retratos 1971, Elsinore 1972, Scholia 1978, Necrofilia 1983, Breviora 1984, La Caja de Plata 1985, Seis poemas por amor 1986, El otro sueño 1987, Poesía 1970–89 1990, Nausícaa 1991, El héroe y sus máscaras 1991, 77 Poemas 1992, Willendorf 1992, El hacha y la rosa 1993, El desayuno y otros poemas 1993, Los gigantes de hielo 1994, Animales domésticos 1995, Tres poemas 1996, Por fuertes y fronteras 1996, El bosque y otros poemas 1997, En el país de las maravillas 1997, Los mundos y los días 1998, Alicia 1999, Insomnios 2000, Mitologías 2001, Vamos a ser felices y otros poemas de humor y deshumor 2003, El enemigo oculto 2003, El puente de la espada: poemas inéditos 2003, Diez poemas y cinco prosas 2004, Ahora y siempre 2004, Su nombre era el de todas las mujeres y otros poemas de amor y desamor 2005, La vida en llamas 2006, Poesía 1979–1996 2006, A quemarropa 2006, Manantial 2007, Los mundos y los días: poesía 1970–2002 2007, Héroes y villanos del cómic 2007, En la cama con la muerte 25 poemas fúnebres 2011, Nombres propios 2011, Los mundos y los días 2012, Cuaderno de vacaciones 2014.

DE FONBLANQUE, John, CMG, MA, MSc; British diplomatist; b. 20 Dec. 1943, Fleet, Hants; s. of Maj.-Gen. E. B. De Fonblanque and Elizabeth De Fonblanque; m. Margaret Prest 1984; one s.; ed Ampleforth School, King's Coll., Cambridge, London School of Econs; joined FCO 1968, Second Sec. Jakarta 1969–72, Second, later First Sec. to EC, Brussels 1972–77; Prin. HM Treasury 1977–80; FCO 1980–83; Asst Sec. Cabinet Office 1983–86; Head of Chancery, New Delhi 1986, Counsellor (Political and Institutional) Mission to EC, Brussels 1988, Asst Under-Sec. of State Int. Orgs, then Dir Global Issues 1994–98, Dir (Europe) FCO 1998–99, Head of Del. to OSCE with rank of Amb. 1999–2003; Dir Office of OSCE High Commr on Nat. Minorities 2004–06. *Leisure interest:* mountain walking.

DE GEUS, Aart; Dutch lawyer and international organization executive; *Chairman and CEO, Bertelsmann Foundation;* m.; three c.; ed Erasmus Univ., Rotterdam, Nijmegen Univ.; worked as lawyer in industry sector of Christian Trade Union –1988; mem. Exec. Bd Nat. Fed. of Christian Trade Unions 1988–98, Vice-Chair. Exec. Bd 1993–98; pnr in Amsterdam-based co. for strategy and man. 1998–2002; Minister of Social Affairs and Employment 2002–07; Chair. OECD Social Policy Ministerial Meeting 2005, has served in various functions at local, nat. and int. level, Deputy Sec.-Gen. OECD 2007–11, in charge of Political

Economy of Reform, and preparations for Ministerial Council Meeting and Exec. Cttee in Special Session; mem. Bd Bertelsmann Foundation 2011–12, Chair. and CEO 2012–. *Address:* Office of the Chairman, Bertelsmann Foundation, Carl-Bertelsmann-Str. 256, 33311 Gütersloh, Germany (office). *Website:* www.bertelsmann-stiftung.de (office).

DE GIORGI, HE Cardinal Salvatore; Italian ecclesiastic; *Archbishop Emeritus of Palermo;* b. 6 Sept. 1930, Vernole, Apulia; ordained priest of Lecce 1953; consecrated Auxiliary Bishop of Oria and Titular Bishop of Tulana 1973, Coadjutor Bishop of Oria 1975–78, Bishop of Oria 1978–81, Archbishop of Foggia, Bishop of Bovino and Bishop of Troia 1981–86, Archbishop of Foggia-Bovino 1986–87, Archbishop of Taranto 1987–90, Archbishop of Palermo 1996–2006 (retd), Archbishop Emer. 2006–; cr. Cardinal (Cardinal-Priest of Santa Maria in Ara Coeli) 1998; apptd to a comm. to investigate leaks of reserved and confidential documents on TV, in newspapers and in other media 2012; Special Envoy to concluding celebration of fifth centenary of creation of Diocese of Lanciano, Italy (now the Archdiocese of Lanciano-Ortona) 2015. *Address:* Curia Arcivescovile, Corso Vittorio Emanuele 461, 90134 Palermo, Italy (office). *Telephone:* (091) 6077111 (office). *Fax:* (091) 6113642 (office). *E-mail:* arcivescovo@diocesipa.it (office). *Website:* www.diocesipa.it (office).

DE GLINIASTY, Jean; French diplomatist; b. 27 Sept. 1948; m.; three c.; ed Institut d'Etudes Politiques, Paris, Ecole Nationale d'Admin, Paris; with Cen. Admin (N Africa and Near East), Ministry of Foreign 1975–78, Econ. and Financial Affairs 1978–81, Asst to Chief of Centre of Analysis and Forecast 1981–82, Second Adviser with Perm. Representation of France to European Communities, Brussels 1982–85, with Cen. Admin (Econ. and Financial Affairs), delegated with functions of Deputy Man. 1985–86, N Africa and Middle East, delegated with functions of Deputy Man., N Africa 1986–89, Cultural, Scientific and Tech. Relations, Dir of Devt and Scientific, Tech. and Educational Co-operation 1989–91, Consul-Gen. in Jerusalem 1991–95, with Cen. Admin (Political and Security Affairs), Dir UN and Int. Orgs 1995–99, Amb. to Senegal (also accred to The Gambia) 1999–2003, to Brazil 2003–06, with Cen. Admin, Dir of Africa and the Indian Ocean 2003–06, Amb. to the Russian Fed. 2009–13. *Address:* Ministry of Foreign Affairs, 37 quai d'Orsay, 75351 Paris Cedex 07, France (office). *Telephone:* 1-43-17-53-53 (office). *Fax:* 1-43-17-52-03 (office). *Website:* www.diplomatie.gouv.fr (office).

DE GRAAF, Thomas (Thom) Carolus, LLM; Dutch jurist, politician and fmr civil servant; *President, Netherlands Association of Universities of Applied Sciences (HBO-raad);* b. 11 June 1957, Amsterdam; m.; two c.; ed Catholic Univ. of Nijmegen; fmr Lecturer in Constitutional Law, Catholic Univ. of Nijmegen; civil servant, Ministry of Interior 1985–94; Deputy Dir for Police Affairs 1991–94; fmr Municipal Councillor, Leiden; mem. De Koning Cttee on Constitutional Reform 1992–93; joined Democraten 66 (D66) 1977, Sec. Nat. Bd 1986–90, Chair. D66 Parl. Group 1997; mem. House of Reps 1994–2003; Deputy Prime Minister 2003–05, Minister of Govt Reform and Kingdom Relations 2003–05; Mayor of Nijmegen 2007–12; Senator for D66 (Chair. of Group) 2015–, Eerste Kamer, States-General 2011–; Pres. Netherlands Asscn of Univs of Applied Sciences (HBO-raad) 2012–. *Leisure interests:* history, poetry, tennis, ice skating. *Address:* Eerste Kamer, Binnenhof 22, PO Box 20017, 2500 AA The Hague (office); Vereniging Hogescholen, Netherlands Association of Universities of Applied Sciences, PO Box 123, 2501 CC The Hague, The Netherlands. *Telephone:* (70) 3129200 (office); (70) 3122121. *Fax:* (70) 3129390 (office); (70) 3122100. *E-mail:* postbus@eerstekamer.nl (office). *Website:* www.eerstekamer.nl/persoon/mr_th_c_de_graaf_d66 (office); www.vereniginghogescholen.nl.

DE GRASSE TYSON, Neil, BA, MPhil, PhD; American astrophysicist, museum administrator and writer; *Frederick P. Rose Director, Hayden Planetarium, American Museum of Natural History;* b. 5 Oct. 1958, New York, NY; m.; two c.; ed Bronx High School of Science, Harvard Univ., Columbia Univ.; Lecturer, Dept of Astronomy, Univ. of Maryland 1987; Postdoctoral Research Assoc., Dept of Astrophysical Sciences, Princeton Univ. 1991–94, Visiting Research Scientist and Lecturer 1994–2003; Staff Scientist, Hayden Planetarium, American Museum of Natural History 1994–95, Acting Dir 1995–96, Frederick P. Rose Dir 1996–, Founder and Chair. Dept of Astrophysics 1997–99, Research Assoc., Dept of Astrophysics 2003–; essayist for Natural History magazine 1995–2005; mem. cttee studying the future of the US Aerospace Industry 2001, and Implementation of US Space Exploration Policy 2004; Dr hc (York Coll., Univ. of New York) 1997, (Ramapo Coll.) 2000, (Pace Univ.) 2006, (Univ. of Pennsylvania) 2008, (Univ. of Alabama) 2010, (Gettysburg Coll.) 2011; Hon. DS (Western New England Coll.) 2012, (Mount Holyoke Coll.) 2012, (Amherst Coll.) 2015; Medal of Excellence, Columbia Univ., New York City, NASA Distinguished Public Service Medal, Klopsteg Memorial Award 2007, Douglas S. Morrow Public Outreach Award 2009, Isaac Asimov Award 2009, Critics Choice Award: Best Host of Reality Series (for Cosmos: A Spacetime Odyssey) 2014, Public Welfare Medal, NAS 2015, Cosmos Award, Planetary Soc. 2015, Knight Innovation Award, CUNY School of Journalism 2015. *Television includes:* host, NOVA Science Now 2006–11, Star Talk 2009, Cosmos: A Spacetime Odyssey 2014. *Publications include:* Merlin's Tour of the Universe 1989, Universe Down to Earth 1994, Just Visiting This Planet 1998, The Sky is Not the Limit: Adventures of an Urban Astrophysicist 2000, One Universe: at Home in the Cosmos 2000, Cosmic Horizons: Astronomy at the Cutting Edge (ed.) 2001, City of Stars 2002, My Favorite Universe 2003, Origins: Fourteen Billion Years of Cosmic Evolution (with Donald Goldsmith) 2005, Death by Black Hole 2007, The Pluto Files 2009, Space Chronicles: Facing the Ultimate Frontier 2012, Welcome to the Universe: An Astrophysical Tour 2016, StarTalk: The Book 2016. *Address:* Hayden Planetarium, American Museum of Natural History, Central Park West at 79th Street, New York, NY 10024, USA (office). *Telephone:* (212) 769-5913 (office). *Fax:* (212) 769-5007 (office). *E-mail:* tyson@amnh.org (office). *Website:* www.haydenplanetarium.org/tyson (office).

DE GRAVE, Franciscus (Frank) Hendrikus Gerardus, DJur; Dutch politician and organization official; b. 27 June 1955, Amsterdam; m. 1983; one s. one d.; ed Univ. of Groningen; Int. Sec. JOVD youth org. 1977–78, Nat. Pres. 1978–80; mem. Volkspartij voor Vrihoid en Democratie (VVD) Parl. group 1977–81; Asst Sec. to Man. Bd AMRO bank 1980–82; Amsterdam City Councillor 1982–86; mem. First Chamber of Parl. 1982–90; Councillor for Finances and Deputy Mayor, Amsterdam City Council 1990–94, Acting Mayor Jan.–June 1994; Sec. of State for Social Security and Employment 1996–98; Minister of Defence 1998–2002; Chief Financial Officer DSB Bank March–May 2009; Chair. Artis Zoo, Amsterdam 2008–13; Senator, Eerste Kamer, States-General 2011–, Chair. Standing Cttee on Finance 2015–; mem. Vaste Comm. for Defence 1982–86, Bd Vereniging Nederlandse Gemeenten; fmr Commr RAI, Bank Nederlandse Gemeenten and Amsterdam Arena; Vice-Chair. Supervisory Bd, NTR (educational and cultural broadcasting) 2011–14; mem. Advisory Bd PA International, Brussels 2013–; Officer, Order of Orange-Nassau 2002. *Address:* Eerste Kamer, Binnenhof 22, PO Box 20017, 2500 AA The Hague, The Netherlands (office). *Telephone:* (70) 3129200 (office). *Fax:* (70) 3129390 (office). *E-mail:* postbus@eerstekamer.nl (office). *Website:* www.eerstekamer.nl/persoon/mr_f_h_g_de_grave_vvd (office).

DE GUCHT, Karel; Belgian politician and fmr EU official; b. 27 Jan. 1954, Overmere; m. Mireille Schreurs; two s.; ed Koninlijk Atheneum Aalst, Free Univ. of Brussels; Chair. Liberal Students' Union Brussels 1974–75, Nat. Chair. 1975–77; mem. European Parl. 1980–94; Vice-Chair. PVV party 1985–88; Senator 1994–95; Nat. Chair. Flemish Liberals and Democrats–Citizens' Party 1999; Minister of State 2002–04, of Foreign Affairs 2004–07 (resgnd), 2007–09; Commr for Devt and Humanitarian Aid, EC, Brussels 2009–10, for Trade 2010–14. *Publications:* De Tijd Wacht op Niemand (co-author; trans. Time and Tide Wait for No Man) 1990, Er Zijn Geen Eilanden Meer: Over Democratie, Vrijheid en Mensenrechten (co-author) 1999, Het Einde der Pilaren: Een Toscaans Gesprek (co-author) 2001, De Toekomst is Vrij 2002, Vrijheid: Liberalisme in tijden van Cholera 2012. *Address:* c/o European Commission, 200 rue de la Loi/Wetstraat 200, 1049 Brussels, Belgium (office).

DE GUILLENCHMIDT, Jacqueline, MLaw; French lawyer; *Member, Constitutional Council;* b. 25 Sept. 1943, Beijing, China; d. of Robert Barbara de Labelotterie and France Pasquet du Bousquet de Lauriere; m. Michel de Guillenchmidt 1966; ed Institut d'études politiques de Paris; barrister, Paris 1972–82; Magistrate High Court of Pontoise 1982–85; Judge, Dept of Justice 1985; Bureau Chief of the Commercial Law 1989–92, then in regulation in the conduct of civil affairs and Seal of the Dept of Justice 1992–93; Tech. Advisor to Minister of Justice 1993–94, Deputy Dir of cabinet of Minister of Justice 1994–95; State Councillor 1995; Chair. Comm. for Supervision and Control of Publications for Children and Adolescents 1995–99; Chair. Comm. for Support Fund for Expression Radio 1995–99; mem. Conseil supérieur de l'audiovisuel 1999–2004, Conseil Constitutionnel 2004–; Officier, Légion d'honneur, Ordre nat. du Mérite; Chevalier, Ordre des Palmes académiques, Ordre du Mérite agricole. *Address:* Conseil Constitutionnel, 2 rue de Montpensier, 75001 Paris, France (office). *Telephone:* 1-40-15-30-00 (office). *Fax:* 1-40-20-93-27 (office). *E-mail:* jacqueline.guillenchmidt@gmail.com (office). *Website:* www.conseil-constitutionnel.fr (office).

DE GUINDOS JURADO, Luis Jáuregui, BSc (Econs), PhD; Spanish economist, academic, business executive and government official; *Vice President, European Central Bank;* b. 16 Jan. 1960, Madrid; m.; two c.; ed Universidad Complutense de Madrid; Counsellor, Ministry of Economy and Planning 1986, Asst Dir-Gen., Secr.-Gen. of Commerce 1987; Partner and Dir AB Asesores 1988–96; Dir-Gen. for Econ. Policy and Defence of Competition, Ministry of Economy and Finance 1996–2000, Sec.-Gen. 2000–02, Sec. of State for Econ. Affairs 2002–04, Minister of Econ. Affairs and Competitiveness 2011–18, also of Industry 2016–18; Visiting Prof., Faculty of Econs, Univ. of Navarra 2005; CEO for Spain and Portugal, Lehman Brothers 2006–08; CEO Nomura Securities, Spain 2008; Sr Partner, PricewaterhouseCoopers Spain 2008–10; Dir IE Business School 2010–11; Pres. Jury, III Jaime Fernández de Araoz Prize for Corp. Finance 2011; Vice-Pres. European Cen. Bank 2018–. *Address:* European Central Bank, 60640 Frankfurt am Main, Germany (office). *Telephone:* (49) 6913440 (office). *E-mail:* info@ecb.europa.eu (office). *Website:* www.ecb.europa.eu (office).

DE HAVILLAND, Olivia Mary; American (b. British) actress; b. 1 July 1916, Tokyo, Japan; d. of Walter Augustus de Havilland and Lilian Augusta Ruse (stage name Lilian Fontaine); m. 1st Marcus Aurelius Goodrich 1946 (divorced 1953); one s.; m. 2nd Pierre Paul Galante 1955 (divorced 1979); one d.; ed Notre Dame Convent, Los Gatos Union High School; stage debut in A Midsummer Night's Dream 1934, film debut in screen version 1935; Pres. Cannes Film Festival 1965 (first woman); on lecture tours in USA 1971–80; Acad. of Motion Picture Arts and Sciences tribute to her career, Los Angeles 2006; mem. Bd of Trustees of American Coll. in Paris 1970–71, of American Library in Paris 1974–81; mem. Altar Guild, Lay Reader, American Cathedral in Paris 1971–81; Hon. Bd mem. American Library in Paris; Chevalier, Légion d'Honneur 2010; DHumLitt (American Univ. of Paris) 1994; Hon. DLitt (Univ. of Hertfordshire) 1998; numerous awards include Acad. Award 1946, 1949, New York Critics Award 1948, 1949, Look Magazine Award 1942, 1948, 1949, Exhibitor Laurel Award 1948, Winged Victory Award 1950, Women's Nat. Press Club Achievement Award for Outstanding Accomplishment in the Theatre 1950, Prix Femina Belge du Cinéma 1957, American Legion Humanitarian Medal 1967, Filmex Tribute 1978, American Acad. of Achievement Award 1978, American Exemplar Medal 1980, American Acad. of Achievement 25th Anniversary Salute to Excellence Statuette 1986, Golden Globe 1988, Birmingham Southern Coll. Gala XIV Women of Achievement Award 1999, John F. Kennedy Center for the Performing Arts Gold Medal 2005, Los Angeles County Museum Tribute 2006, Viennale: Vienna Int. Film Festival Tribute 2006, Nat. Medal of Arts 2008. *Films include:* A Midsummer Night's Dream 1935, Captain Blood 1935, Anthony Adverse 1936, The Adventures of Robin Hood 1938, Gone with the Wind 1939, Hold Back the Dawn 1941, Princess O'Rourke 1942, To Each His Own (Acad. Award, Ciné-Revue Award, Belgium) 1946, The Dark Mirror 1946, The Snake Pit 1947 (Nat. Bd of Review of Motion Pictures Best Actress Award 1948, Brazilian Film Critics' Award 1948, New York Film Critics' Award 1948, Box Office Blue Ribbon Award 1948, San Francisco Film Critics' Award 1948, Silver Mask, Italian Film Critics' Award 1950), The Heiress (Acad. Award 1949, Golden Globe Award 1949, Venice Film Festival Award 1949, New York Film Critics' Award 1949, San Francisco Film Critics' Award 1949, Cité-Revue Award 1950) 1949, My Cousin Rachel 1952, Not as a Stranger 1954, The Proud Rebel 1957, The Light in the Piazza 1961, Lady in a Cage 1963, Hush Hush Sweet Charlotte 1964, The Adventurers 1968, Airport '77 1976, The Swarm 1978, The Fifth Musketeer 1979. *Plays include:* Romeo and Juliet 1951, Candida 1951–52, A Gift of Time 1962. *Television includes:* Noon Wine 1966, Screaming Woman 1972, Roots, The Next Generations 1979, Murder is Easy 1981, Charles and Diana: A Royal

Romance 1982, North and South II (mini-series) 1986, Anastasia (Golden Globe Award) 1986, The Woman He Loved 1988. *Publications:* Every Frenchman Has One 1962, Mother and Child (contrib.) 1975. *Leisure interests:* crossword puzzles, reading tales of mystery and imagination, painting on Sunday. *Address:* BP 156-16, 75764 Paris Cedex 16, France.

DE HOOP, Adrianus Teunis, PhD; Dutch professor of electromagnetic theory and applied mathematics; *Lorentz Chair Professor Emeritus, Delft University of Technology;* b. 24 Dec. 1927, Rotterdam; m. J. C. E. M. (Annelies) van Dijk; ed Delft Univ. of Tech.; Research Asst, Delft Univ. of Tech. 1950–52, Asst Prof. 1953–56, Assoc. Prof. 1957–60, Prof. 1960–96, Lorentz Chair Prof. Emer. 1996–; Reserve Officer, Royal Netherlands Navy 1952–53; Research Asst, UCLA, USA 1956–57; Visiting Research Scientist, Philips Research Labs, Eindhoven 1976–77, Consultant 1977–89; mem. Royal Netherlands Acad. of Arts and Sciences 1989, Royal Flemish Acad. of Arts and Sciences of Belgium 1998; Hon. PhD (Ghent) 1982, (Vaxjo) 2008; Kt, Order of the Netherlands Lion 2003; awards from Stichting Fund for Science, Tech. and Research 1986, 1989, 1990, 1993, 1994, Gold Research Medal, Royal Inst. of Eng 1989, Heinrich Hertz Medal, IEEE 2001, URSI Balthasar van der Pol Gold Research Medal 2002. *Publications:* Handbook of Radiation and Scattering of Waves 1995; numerous articles in journals. *Leisure interest:* playing the piano. *Address:* Faculty of Electrical Engineering, Mathematics and Computer Science, Delft University of Technology, Mekelweg 4, 2628 CD Delft (office); Korenmolen 17, 2661 LE Bergschenhoek, The Netherlands (home). *Telephone:* (10) 5220049 (home). *E-mail:* a.t.dehoop@tudelft.nl (office). *Website:* www.atdehoop.com.

DE HOOP SCHEFFER, Jakob Gijsbert (Jaap); Dutch politician and international organization official; b. 3 April 1948, Amsterdam; s. of Jakob Gijsbert Nicholas de Hoop Scheffer and Mariëtta van der Meulen; m. Jeannine de Hoop Scheffer-van Oorschot 1974; two d.; ed St Ignatius Coll., Amsterdam, Leiden Univ.; fmr Reserve Officer in Air Force; fmr Sec. Del. of Netherlands to NATO, Brussels; mem. Parl. (Christen-Democratisch Appèl—Christian Democrats) 1986–2009, Deputy Parl. Leader 1995–97, Leader 1997–2001; Minister of Foreign Affairs 2002–03; Sec.-Gen. NATO 2004–09; Pieter Kooijmans Chair. for Peace, Law and Security, Leiden Univ. 2009–14, Lecturer 2014–; Chair. Supervisory Bd, Rijksmuseum, Amsterdam 2012–18, Advisory Council on Int. Affairs 2014–, Advisory Comm. for the Civil Honours 2014–; mem. Supervisory Bd, Air France/KLM 2011–; Kt, Order of Orange-Nassau 2002, Officer 2003, Kt Grand Cross 2009; Grand Cross, Order of the Star of Romania 2004; Grand Officer, Order of the Three Stars (Latvia) 2004; Kt Grand Cross, Grand Order of King Tomislav (Croatia) 2009; Order of Stara Planina, First Class (Bulgaria) 2009; Grand Cross, Order of the Cross of Terra Mariana (Estonia) 2009; Grand Cross, Order of Vytautas the Great (Lithuania) 2009; Grand Cross, Order of Merit of the Repub. of Poland 2009; Grand Cross, Order of Merit of the Italian Repub. 2009; Grand Cross (or First Class), Order of the White Double Cross (Slovakia) 2009; Hon. KCMG 2010. *Leisure interests:* running, playing tennis and squash, singing, Dutch, French and English literature, French films. *Address:* Room 4.14, Universiteit Leiden, Campus Den Haag, Lange Voorhout 86, 2514 EJ The Hague, The Netherlands (office). *Telephone:* (71) 5272727 (The Hague) (office). *Fax:* (71) 5273118 (The Hague) (office). *E-mail:* j.g.de.hoop.scheffer@cdh.leidenuniv.nl (office). *Website:* www.leiden.edu (office).

DE JAGER, Cornelis (Kees), PhD; Dutch astrophysicist and academic (retd); b. 29 April 1921, Den Burg, Texel; s. of Jan de Jager and Cornelia Kuyper; m. Duotje Rienks 1947; two s. two d.; ed Univ. of Utrecht; Asst in Theoretical Physics, Univ. of Utrecht 1946; Asst in Astronomy, Univ. of Leiden; Asst Astronomy Inst., Utrecht; Assoc. Prof. of Stellar Astrophysics, Univ. of Utrecht 1957, Ordinary Prof. in Gen. Astrophysics 1960–86; Extraordinary Prof., Univ. of Brussels and Founder, Space Research Lab., Utrecht Astronomy Inst., Brussels 1961; Man. Dir Utrecht Astronomy Inst. 1963–78, Chair. Inst. Council 1978–83; Asst Gen. Sec. Int. Astronomical Union 1967–70, Gen. Sec. 1970–73; Pres. Netherlands Astronomy Comm. 1975–83; mem. Exec. Council Cttee on Space Research (COSPAR) 1970–72, Pres. 1972–78, 1982–86; mem. Exec. Council, ICSU 1970–82, Vice-Pres. 1976–78, Pres. 1978–80; Chair. Skepsis (for critical evaluation of the paranormal) 1987–97, European Council of Sceptical Orgs 1995–2001, Council of Chancellors of Global Foundation 2001–; Aggregate Prof., Univ. of Brussels 1970–86, currently Prof. Emer. of Space Research; mem. Royal Netherlands Acad. of Art and Sciences (Foreign Sec. 1985–90), Royal Belgium Acad. of Art and Sciences, Academia Europaea (Paris and London); Assoc. mem. Royal Astronomical Soc. (London); Corresp. mem. Soc. Royale de Science, Liège; mem. Int. Acad. Astronautics, Chair. Basic Sciences Section 1984–92; Foreign mem. Deutsche Akad. Leopoldina, Halle; Foreign Fellow, Indian Nat. Scientific Acad.; voluntary co-worker, Royal Netherlands Inst. for Sea Research; Hon. mem. Netherlands Soc. of Astronomy and Meteorology 1996; Hon. Citizen, Texel 2006; Kt, Order of the Dutch Lion 1983; Dr hc (Univ. of Wrocław, Poland) 1975, (Observatoire de Paris) 1976; Karl Schwarzschild Medal 1974, Yuri Gagarin Medal (USSR) 1984, J. Janssen Medal (France) 1984, Ziolkowski Medal, USSR Acad. of Sciences, Gold Medal, Royal Astronomical Soc., London 1988, Hale Medal, American Astronomical Soc. 1988, COSPAR Medal for Int. Co-operation in Space Science 1988, Silver Medal, Royal Netherlands Acad. Arts and Sciences, Gold Medal, Netherlands Soc. Astronomy and Meteorology, In Praise of Reason Award CSICOP, Buffalo, NY 1990, Von Karman Award, Int. Acad. of Astronautics 1993, Hon. Silver Medal, City of Utrecht 2003. *Publications:* about 550 publs including: The Hydrogen Spectrum of the Sun 1952, Structure and Dynamics of the Solar Atmosphere 1959, The Solar Spectrum 1965, Solar Flares and Space Research (with Z. Svestka) 1969, Sterrenkunde 1969, Reports on Astronomy 1970, 1973, Highlights in Astronomy 1970, Ontstaan en Levensloop van Sterren (with E. van den Heuvel) 1973 (second edn), Image Processing Techniques in Astronomy (with H. Nieuwenhuyzen) 1975, The Brightest Stars 1980, Instabilities in Evolved Super- and Hyper-Giants 1992, Bolwerk van de Sterren 1993, Tien Opmerkelijke Sterrekundige Ontdekkingen 1995, Kannibalen bij de grenzen van het heelal 1996, Solar Flares and Collisions Between Current-carrying Loops (co-author) 1996, Van het Clijf tot Den Hoorn (co-author) 1998, Terugblik 2014. *Leisure interests:* birds, plants, jogging, history. *Address:* Molenstraat 22, 1791 DL Den Burg, Texel, Netherlands (home). *Telephone:* (620) 420611 (office); (222) 320816 (home). *E-mail:* info@cdejager.nl (office). *Website:* www.nioz.nl (office); www.cdejager.com.

DE JAGER, Jan Cornelis (Jan Kees), BBA, LLM; Dutch business executive and politician; *Chief Financial Officer, KPN;* b. 10 Feb. 1969, Kapelle; ed Nyenrode Univ., Erasmus Univ., Rotterdam; Co-founder Spectra Vision BV 1992, Dir and Man. Dir 1992–2010, Dir ISM BV 1997–2010 (renamed ISM eCompany 2004); State Sec. for Finance 2007–10, Minister of Finance 2010–12; mem. Christen Democratisch Appèl (CDA), mem. Bd CDA policy inst.; Chief Financial Officer KPN 2014–; mem. Advisory Bd Centres for Work and Income, ICT-Office (IT org.). *Address:* Koninklijke KPN N.V. Maanplein 55, 2516 CK The Hague, Netherlands.

DE JESUS CASTELHANO MAURÍCIO, Amadeu; Angolan fmr central banker; fmr Chair. Unipetrol; Gov. Banco Nacional de Angola 2006–09; Alt. Gov., IMF 2006. *Address:* c/o Banco Nacional de Angola, CP 1243, Avenida 4 de Fevereiro 151, Luanda 1243, Angola.

DE JONGH, Eduard S.; Dutch art historian and academic; *Professor Emeritus of Art History, University of Utrecht;* b. 7 June 1931, Amsterdam; m. Lammijna Oosterbaan 1977; two s. one d.; ed Baarns Lyceum and Univ. of Utrecht; journalist and art critic, Het Parool and Vrij Nederland 1954–74; Librarian, Inst. for Art History, Univ. of Utrecht 1963–66; Ed. Openbaar Kunstbezit (radio course) 1963–73; Ed. Simiolus (art history quarterly) 1966–77; mem. staff, Centrum Voortgezet Kunsthistorisch Onderzoek, Univ. of Utrecht 1966–73; Asst Prof., Inst. for Art History, Univ. of Utrecht 1973–76, Prof. of Art History 1976–89, Prof. Emer. 1989–; Ed. Kunstschrift 1990–; Visiting Scholar, Getty Center for History of Art and Humanities 1987; mem. Royal Netherlands Acad.; Foreign mem. Royal Belgian Acad.; Dr hc (Amsterdam) 2002; Karel van Mander Award 1987, De Gijselaar-Hintzenfondsprijs 2011. *Publications include:* Zinne- en minnebeelden in de schilderkunst van de zeventiende eeuw 1967, Tot Lering en Vermaak: Betekenissen van Hollandse genrevoorstellingen uit de zeventiende eeuw 1976, Still Life in the Age of Rembrandt 1982, Portretten van echt en trouw: Huwelijk en gezin in de Nederlandse kunst van de zeventiende eeuw 1986, Kunst en het vruchtbare misverstand 1993, Faces of the Golden Age: Seventeenth-Century Dutch Portraits 1994, Kwesties van betekenis: Thema en motief in de Nederlandse schilderkunst van de zeventiende eeuw 1995, Mirror of Everyday Life: Genre Prints in The Netherlands 1550–1700 (with Ger Luijten) 1997, Questions of Meaning: Theme and Motif in Dutch Seventeenth-Century Painting 2000, Dankzij de tiende muze: 33 Opstellen uit Kunstschrift 2000, Charles Donker, etser (with Peter Schatborn) 2002, Muziek aan de muur: Muzikale voorstellingen in de Nederlanden 1500–1700 2008, Peter Vos en Charles Donker (with J. P. Filedt Kok) 2010, Peter Vos, Metamorfosen (with J. P. Filedt Kok) 2013; numerous articles on iconological and art theoretical subjects. *Address:* Frederik Hendrikstraat 29, 3583 VG Utrecht, Netherlands (home).

DE JONGH, John Percy, Jr, BA; American politician, state governor and business executive; b. 13 Nov. 1957, Brooklyn, New York; m. Cecile René Galiber 1986; two s. one d.; ed Catholic Central High School, Detroit, Mich., Antioch Coll., Yellow Spring, Ohio; fmr mem. Tri-Island Econ. Devt Council; then hired by Chase Manhattan Bank for six years, became first Country Consumer Man. responsible for all consumer banking products in the US Virgin Islands, British Virgin Islands and St Maarten; mem. Industrial Devt Comm. 1984–87; apptd Commr of Finance 1987; also served as Chair. Governing Bd Virgin Islands Water and Power Authority and Exec. Dir Virgin Islands Public Finance Authority; re-entered pvt. sector as Sr Man. Consultant for Public Financial Man., Inc. 1993; served as Pres., COO and Dir, Lockhart Companies Inc.; fmr Pres. St Thomas-St John Chamber of Commerce, Community Foundation of the Virgin Islands; unsuccessful cand. for Gov. 2002; Gov. of the US Virgin Islands 2007–15; Democrat. *Address:* Democratic National Committee, 430 South Capitol Street SE, Washington, DC 20003, USA (office). *Telephone:* (202) 863-8000 (office). *Fax:* (202) 863-8174 (office). *Website:* www.democrats.org (office).

DE JONGH-ELHAGE, Emily Saïdy; Curaçao politician; b. 7 Dec. 1946; Commr of Public Works and Public Housing of Curaçao 1998–99, Commr of Educ., Sport and Cultural Affairs 1999–2002; Minister of Educ. and Culture, Netherlands Antilles 2002–03; Commr of Public Enterprises and Public Housing of Curaçao 2004–05; Prime Minister and Minister of Gen. Affairs and Foreign Relations 2006–10 (last Prime Minister before dissolution of Netherlands Antilles); Leader, Partido Antia Restrukturá (Party for the Restructured Antilles—PAR) 2005–12. *Address:* c/o Partido Antía Restrukturá (PAR), Fokkerweg 26, Unit 3, Willemstad, Curaçao (office).

DE JUNIAC, Alexandre; French business executive; *Director-General, International Air Transport Association;* b. 10 Nov. 1962; ed École Polytechnique de Paris, École Nationale d'Admin; Auditor, then Master of Petitions and Deputy Sec.-Gen. of the Conseil d'Etat (Council of State) 1988–93; Tech. Adviser, then Asst Dir, responsible for issues related to communication in the cabinet of Nicolas Sarkozy, Dept of Budget 1993–95; Dir of Planning and Devt, Thomson SA 1995–97; Sales Dir, Sextant Avionics 1997–98, Dir of Econ. Interest Grouping, CNS Avionics (jt venture between Sextant Avionics and Dassault Electronics) 1998–99; Sec.-Gen. Thomson-CSF (became Thales 2000) 1999–2004, Sr Vice-Pres. in charge of Aviation Systems Div. 2004–08, Gen. Man. for Asia, Africa, the Middle East and Latin America 2008–09; Pvt. Sec. to Christine Lagarde, Minister for the Economy, Industry and Employment 2009–11; Chair. and CEO Air France 2011–13, mem. Bd of Dirs Air France-KLM 2012–16, Chair. and CEO 2013–16; Dir-Gen. IATA 2016–; mem. Supervisory Bd Vivendi 2013–. *Address:* IATA, PO Box 113, Montreal, QC H4Z 1M1, Canada (office). *Telephone:* (514) 874-0202 (office). *Fax:* (514) 874-2662 (office). *E-mail:* corpcomms@iata.org (office). *Website:* www.iata.org (office).

DE KEERSMAEKER, Baroness; **Anne Teresa;** Belgian choreographer; *Founder and Artistic Director, Rosas Dance Company;* b. 11 June 1960, Wemmel; one s. one d.; ed Mudra, School of Maurice Béjart, Brussels and Tisch School of the Arts, New York Univ., USA; presented first work, Asch, in Brussels 1980; Founder and Artistic Dir Rosas Dance Co. 1983–; Rosas became co.-in-residence, Théâtre de la Monnaie, Brussels with herself as resident choreographer 1992–2007; directed opera Bluebeard (Bartók) 1997; Founder and Artistic Dir, Performing Arts Research and Training Studios (PARTS), Brussels 1995–; Stage Dir Paris Opera 2016–17; has also directed work for video; Officier, Ordre des Arts et des Lettres 2000, Commdr, Ordre des Arts et des Lettres 2008, Golden Order of Merit 2011, Prize for General Cultural Merit (Belgium) 2012, Golden Medal of the city of

Lisbon 2012, Austrian Decoration for Science and Arts 2015; Dr hc (Flemish Univ. of Brussels) 1995; Eugène Baie Prize 1996, City of Paris Médaille de Vermeil 2002, Gabriella Moortgat Stichting Award 2002, Flemish Govt Erepenning Medal 2002, Oost Vlaanderen Keizer Karelprijs 2004. *Choreographic works include:* Asch 1981, Fase: four movements to music of Steve Reich 1982, Rosas danst Rosas (Bessie Award 1988) 1983, Elena's Aria 1984, Bartók/Aantekeningen 1986, Verkommenes Ufer/Medeamaterial/Landschaft mit Argonauten 1987, Mikrokosmos-Monument/ Selbstporträt mit Reich und Riley (und Chopin ist auch dabei)/Im zart fliessender Bewegung-Quatuor Nr. 4 (Japanese Dance Award for Best Foreign Production 1989) 1987, Ottone, Ottone 1988, Stella (London Dance and Performances Award 1989) 1989, Achterland 1990, Erts 1992, Mozart/Concert Arias, un moto di gioia 1992, Toccata 1993, Kinok 1994, Amor Constante más allá de la muerte 1994, Erwartung/Verklärte Nacht 1995, Woud 1996, Just Before 1997, Three Solos for Vincent Dunoyer 1997, Duke Bluebeard's Castle 1998, Drumming (Golden Laurel Wreath, Sarajevo 1998) 1998, Quartett 1999, I Said I 1999, In Real Time 2000, Rain 2001, Small Hands (out of the lie of no) 2001, (but if a look should) April Me 2002, Repertory Evening 2002, Once 2002, Bitches' Brew/Tacoma Narrows 2003, Kassandra – Speaking in Twelve Voices 2004, Desh 2005, Raga for the Rainy Season/A Love Supreme 2005, D'un soir un jour 2006, Bartók/Beethoven/ Schönberg Repertory Evening 2006, Steve Reich Evening 2007, Keeping Still 2007, The Song 2008, En atendant 2010, Partita 2 2013, Vortex Temporum 2013, Twice 2014, Golden Hours 2015, My Breathing Is My Dancing 2015, Mitten wir im Leben sind (with Jean-Guihen Queryas) 2017, Così fan tutte 2017, Six Brandenburg Concertos 2018. *Films:* Hoppla! 1989, Achterland 1994, Rosas danst Rosas 1997, Tippeke 1996, Fase, Four Movements to the Music of Steve Reich 2002, Rain 2012, Work/Travail/Arbeid 2017. *Address:* Rosas VZW, Van Volxemlaan 164, 1190 Brussels, Belgium (office). *Telephone:* (2) 344-55-98 (office). *Fax:* (2) 343-53-52 (office). *E-mail:* mail@rosas.be (office). *Website:* www.rosas.be (office).

DE KEPPER, Christophe; Belgian lawyer and international organization official; *Director-General, International Olympic Committee;* b. 1963, Uccle; ed Univ. of Louvain, Univ. of Brussels; fmr Asst to Legal Dir Belgian Olympic Cttee; Chief of Staff, Exec. Office of Pres., IOC 2002–11, Dir-Gen. IOC 2011–; fmr Dir European Olympic Cttee's liaison office with EU. *Address:* International Olympic Committee (IOC), Château de Vidy, 1007 Lausanne, Switzerland (office). *Telephone:* 216216111 (office). *Fax:* 216216216 (office). *Website:* www.olympic.org (office).

DE KERCHOVE D'EXAERDE, François, MSc, Lic.en science; Belgian diplomatist; *Ambassador to France;* b. 22 May 1960, Rhode Saint Genèse, Brabant; not m.; ed London School of Econs and Political Science, UK, Université Libre de Bruxelles; joined Dept of Diplomatic Traineeship, Ministry of Foreign Affairs (MFA) 1989, Second Sec., Embassy in Kuwait, Qatar and Bahrain 1991–93, Head of commercial section, Embassy in Tokyo 1993–97, Consul-Gen., Osaka 1997–2007, Desk Officer (Afghanistan and Pakistan), MFA 2001–02, Dir-Gen., Royal Inst. for Int. Relations (now Egmont Inst.), Brussels 2002–04, Minister-Counsellor, Embassy in Berlin 2004–08, Deputy Dir of Security Policy, MFA 2008–09, Dir of Security Policy 2009–11, Amb. to EU Political and Security Cttee, Brussels June–Dec. 2011, Dir, Cabinet of Foreign Affairs, Ministry of Foreign Trade and European Affairs 2011–14, Perm. Rep. to NATO 2014–18, Amb. to France (also accred to Monaco) 2018–; Officer (Infantry), Reserve Comm. *Address:* Embassy of Belgium, 9 rue de Tilsitt, 75840 Paris Cedex 17, France (office). *Telephone:* 1-44-09-39-39 (office). *Fax:* 1-47-54-07-64 (office). *E-mail:* paris@ diplobel.fed.be (office). *Website:* france.diplomatie.belgium.be (office).

DE KLERK, F(rederik) W(illem), LLB; South African politician, lawyer and fmr head of state; b. 18 March 1936, Johannesburg; s. of J. de Klerk; m. 1st Marike Willemse 1959 (divorced 1998); two s. one d.; m. 2nd Elita Georgiadis 1998; ed Monument High School, Krugersdorp, Potchefstroom Univ.; in law practice 1961–72; mem. House of Ass. 1972; Information Officer Nat. Party, Transvaal 1975; Minister of Posts and Telecommunications and of Social Welfare and Pensions 1978, subsequently Minister of Posts and Telecommunications and of Sport and Recreation 1978–79, of Mines, Energy and Environmental Planning 1979–80, of Mineral and Energy Affairs 1980–82, of Internal Affairs 1982–85, of Nat. Educ. and Planning 1984–89; Acting State Pres. of South Africa Aug.–Sept. 1989, State Pres. of South Africa 1989–94; Exec. Deputy Pres., Govt of Nat. Unity 1994–96; Leader of the Official Opposition 1996–97; mem. Nat. Party, Transvaal Leader 1982–89, Leader 1989–97; also fmr Chair. of the Cabinet and C-in-C of the Armed Forces; fmr Chair. Minister's Council and Leader of the House of Ass.; one Hon. Fellowship; South African Decoration for Meritorious Service; nine hon. doctorates; shared Nobel Prize for Peace with Nelson Mandela 1993, jt winner Houphouet Boigny Prize (UNESCO) 1991, Asturias Prize 1992, Prix du Courage Politique Internationale 1992, Philadelphia Liberty Medal 1993, Order of Mapungubwe Gold Medal 2002. *Publications:* The Last Trek: A New Beginning (autobiog.) 1999; various articles and brochures. *Leisure interests:* golf, reading. *Address:* PO Box 15785, 7506 Panorama, Cape Town, South Africa (office). *Telephone:* (21) 9200966 (office). *Fax:* (21) 9300995 (office). *E-mail:* fw@fwdeklerk .org (home). *Website:* www.fwdeklerk.org (office).

DE KLOET, E. R. (Ron), MSc, PhD; Dutch endocrinologist, pharmacologist and academic; *Academy Professor, Royal Netherlands Academy of Arts and Sciences;* b. 19 Aug. 1944, Maarssen; ed Univ. of Utrecht; Research Fellow, Organon International BV, Oss, The Netherlands 1969–73; Postdoctoral Fellow, The Rockefeller Univ., New York, USA 1973–75; Assoc. Prof., Rudolf Magnus Inst., Univ. of Utrecht 1975–90; Prof. and Head of Dept of Medical Pharmacology, Leiden Univ. 1990–2009, Prof. Emer. 2009–; Acad. Prof., Royal Netherlands Acad. of Arts and Sciences 2004–; Chair. Scientific Advisory Bd, Max Planck Inst. for Psychiatry, Munich 2003–14, Int. Conf. on Psychoneuroendocrinology, Leiden 2006; Co-Chair. Biannual Meeting of Int. Soc. of Investigation of Stress 2010; Receiving Ed., Journal of Neuroendocrinology 1989–98; Co-founder and Ed.-in-Chief, Stress 1996–2000; mem. Editorial Bd, Neuroendocrinology 1989–94, Hormones & Behavior 1995–2001, Endocrinology 1998–2003, Journal of Neuroscience Research 1993–99, Psychoneuroendocrinology, Journal of Psychiatric Research, European Archives of Psychiatry and Clinical Neuroscience, Journal of Steroid Biochemistry & Molecular Biology, Frontiers in Neuroendocrinology; mem. Scientific Advisory Bd, Corcept Therapeutics 2001–, Scientific Advisory Cttee, Pharmaseed 2012–; Chief Scientific Officer, Dynacorts Therapeutics 2011–; Prof. of Honour, China Medical Univ., Shenyang City 2014; Order of the Dutch Lion 2010; Dutch Pharmacology Prize 1987, Emile Kraepelin Guest Prof., Max Planck Inst. for Psychiatry, Munich 1998, European Medal, British Endocrine Soc. 1998, Allan Munck Guest Prof., Dartmouth Coll., USA 2003, Geoffrey Harris Prize, European Fed. of Endocrine Socs 2005, ECNP Neuropsychopharmacology Award, European Coll. of Neuropsychopharmacology 2007, Promotor of Dr hc Florian Holsboer, Leiden Univ. 2008, Lifetime Achievement Award, Int. Soc. for Psychoneuroendocrinology 2008, NIEHS Distinguished Lecturer 2011, Laqueur Lecturer, Dutch Endocrine Soc. 2014, Golden Kraepelin Medal, Max-Planck-Gesellschaft (co-recipient) 2014. *Publications:* Stress, the Brain and Depression (co-author) 2004; six edited books and more than 600 papers in professional journals; several patents. *Address:* Room HB-902, Gorlaeus Laboratories, Einsteinweg 55, 2333 CC Leiden (office); Leiden Academic Centre of Drug Research, Gorlaeus Laboratories, Leiden University, PO Box 9502, 2300 RA Leiden, The Netherlands (office). *Telephone:* (71) 527-6210 (office). *E-mail:* e.kloet@lacdr.leidenuniv.nl (office); erdekloet@gmail.com; erdekloet@live.com. *Website:* medicalpharmacology .leidenuniv.nl/people/de-kloet (office); www.rondekloet.nl.

DE KORTE, Rudolf Willem, Dr rer. nat; Dutch politician and business executive; b. 8 July 1936, The Hague; s. of Bartel de Korte and Käthe Paula Schönfelder; m. Karin Laetitia Munk 1966; one s. one d.; ed Maerlant Gymnasium, The Hague, Univ. of Leiden, Harvard Business School, USA; in various positions in Hong Kong 1964–66, in Ethiopia 1967–68; Gen. Sales Man. Unilever-Emery NV 1969–71, Dir 1972–77; Sec. People's Party for Freedom and Democracy (VVD) 1971–78; mem. Parl. 1977–86, 1989–95; Minister for Home Affairs March–July 1986, Deputy Prime Minister and Minister for Econ. Affairs 1986–89; mem. (VVD) Lower House of Parl. 1989; mem. Wassenaar Municipal Council 1978–82; Vice-Pres. EIB 1995–2001; mem. Bd, Klachteninstituut Financiële Dienstverlening (Financial Services Complaints Inst.) 2007–; Commdr, Order of Orange-Nassau 1989. *Publications include:* Naar een vrije samenleving. Een nieuw-liberale toekomstvisie 1979. *Leisure interests:* tennis, windsurfing, painting. *Address:* c/o Volkspartij voor Vrijheid en Democratie (People's Party for Freedom and Democracy), Laan Copes van Cattenburch 52, PO Box 30836, 2500 GV The Hague, The Netherlands. *E-mail:* info@vvd.nl.

DE LA BILLIÈRE, Gen. Sir Peter (Edgar de la Cour), Kt, KCB, KBE, DSO, MC, DL; British army officer (retd) and banker (retd); b. 29 April 1934, Plymouth; s. of Surgeon Lt-Commdr Claude Dennis Delacour de Labillière and Frances Christing Wright Lawley; m. Bridget Constance Muriel Goode 1965; one s. two d.; ed Harrow School, Staff Coll., Royal Coll. of Defence Studies; joined King's Shropshire Light Infantry 1952; commissioned, Durham Light Infantry; served Japan, Korea, Malaya (despatches 1959), Jordan, Borneo, Egypt, Aden, Gulf States, Sudan, Oman, Falkland Islands; Commdg Officer, 22 Special Air Service (SAS) Regt 1972–74; Gen. Staff Officer 1 (Directing Staff), Staff Coll. 1974–77; Commdr British Army Training Team, Sudan 1977–78; Dir SAS and Commdr SAS Group 1978–83; Commdr British Forces, Falkland Islands and Mil. Commr 1984–85; Gen. Officer Commdg Wales 1985–87; Col Comdt. Light Div. 1986–90; Lt-Gen. Officer commanding SE Dist 1987–90; Commdr British Forces in Middle East Oct. 1990–91; rank of Gen. 1991 after Gulf War, Ministry of Defence Adviser on Middle East 1991–92; retd from army June 1992; Pres. SAS Asscn 1991–96, Army Cadet Force 1992–99; mem. Council Royal United Services Inst. 1975–77; Chair. Jt Services Hang Gliding 1986–88; Cdre Army Sailing Asscn 1989–90; Commr Duke of York's School 1988–90; Freeman City of London 1991; Hon. Freeman Fishmongers' Co. 1991; Pres. Harrow School Asscn 2002–; Trustee Imperial War Museum 1992–99; Dir (non-exec.), Middle East and Defence Adviser, Robert Fleming Holdings 1992–99; Chair. Meadowland Meats 1994–2002; Jt Chair. Dirs FARM Africa 1995–2001 (mem. Bd 1992–2001); DL Hereford and Worcester 1993; Trustee Naval and Mil. Club 1999–2003, mem. Bd 1999–2003; Pres. Friends of Imperial War Museum 2003; Pres. Harrow Asscn 2002–; Meritorious Service Cross (Canada) 1991, Legion of Merit Chief Commdr (USA) 1993, Order of Abdul Aziz 2nd Class (Saudi Arabia) 1993, Kuwait Decoration of the First Class, Order of Qatar Sash of Merit; Hon. DSc (Cranfield) 1992; Hon. DCL (Durham) 1993. *Television:* Discovery: Clash of the Generals 2004. *Publications include:* Storm Command: A Personal Story of the Gulf War 1992, Looking for Trouble (autobiog.) 1994, Supreme Courage: Heroic Stories from 150 Years of the Victoria Cross 2004. *Leisure interests:* family, squash, apiculture, farming, sailing.

DE LA CROIX DE CASTRIES, Henri René Marie Augustin; French insurance business executive and fmr civil servant; b. 15 Aug. 1954, Bayonne (Basses-Pyrénées); s. of François de La Croix de Castries and Gisèle de La Croix de Castries (née de Chevigné); m. Anne Millin de Grandmaison 1984; one s. two d.; ed Ecole Saint-Jean-de-Passy, Coll. Stanislas, Faculté de droit, Paris, École des Hautes Études Commerciales, Ecole Nat. d'Admin; Deputy Insp., then Insp. of Finance, 2nd Class, Treasury 1984, Deputy Sec.-Gen. Interministerial Cttee on Industrial Restructuring 1984–85, Head, Office of Capital Goods 1985–88, of Foreign Exchange and Balance of Payments 1988–89; Man. Finance Dept, AXA (insurance group) 1989–90, Corp. Sec. 1991–93, Sr Exec. Vice-Pres. for Group's asset man., financial and real-estate businesses 1993–97, Chair. The Equitable Cos Inc. (now AXA Financial, Inc.) 1997–2000, mem. Exec. Cttee and Chair. Man. Bd AXA 2000–10, CEO 2000–, Chair. 2010–, Chair. AXA Assurances IARD Mutuelle, AXA Assurances Vie Mutuelle, AXA Financial, Inc. (USA); mem. Bd of Dirs AXA SA, AXA France IARD, AXA UK PLC (UK), AllianceBernstein Corpn (USA), AXA Equitable Life Insurance Co. (USA), AXA America Holdings, Inc. (USA), MONY Life Insurance Co. (USA), MONY Life Insurance Co. of America (USA); Chair. of Europe and Special Advisor, Gen. Atlantic LLC 2017–; mem. Bd of Dirs Nestlé; mem. Bd Asscn pour l'Aide aux Jeunes Infirmes, Musée du Louvre, Fondation Nationale des Sciences Politiques; Officier, Légion d'honneur 2009, Ordre nat. du Mérite; Commdr 2009, Ordre des Arts et des Lettres 2012. *Address:* General Atlantic LLC, 23 Savile Row, London, W1S 2ET, England (office); 17 rue du Cherche-Midi, 75006 Paris (home); Château de Gastines, 49150 Fougeré, France (home). *Telephone:* (20) 7484-3200 (office). *Fax:* (20) 7484-3290 (office). *Website:* www.generalatlantic.com (office).

DE LA DEHESA ROMERO, Guillermo; Spanish lawyer, economist, business executive and government official; *International Advisor, Goldman Sachs Europe Limited;* b. 19 July 1941, Madrid; m. Michèle Barbé; two d.; ed Universidad Complutense de Madrid; govt economist 1968, served at Ministries of Trade,

Industry and Energy and Economy and Finance, apptd Dir-Gen. of Trade, Sec.-Gen. of Industry and Energy 1978–80, Sec.-Gen. of Trade, Deputy Sec. of Commerce at Ministry of Economy and Finance 1982–86, Sec. of State of Economy and Finance 1986–88 and Sec. of the Comm. for Econ. Affairs of Council of Ministers 1978–88; also worked at Bank of Spain as Man. Dir of Foreign Currency Assets Man. and Int. Relations 1980–82; participated in negotiations for accession of Spain to EU; later, mem. 113 Cttee and of ECOFIN; also served as mem. OECD ministerial meetings, Deputy Gov. IMF and World Bank and Gov. of Inter American, Asian and African Devt Banks for several years; CEO Banco Pastor 1988–95; Chair. Gas Madrid 1988–91, Plus Ultra, Pastor-Aliance 1989–93, Fondos Galicia 1990–2000, Plus Ultra 1999–2002; Vice-Chair. Hullas de Coto Cortes 1990–2000, Santander Group 2002– (mem. Exec. Cttee), Amadeus IT Holding (IT) 2010–; Dir, Cubiertas y MZOV 1988–90, Ibersuizas 1990–93, Telepizza 1999–2006; Ind. Dir (non-exec.), Campofrío Food Group SA, Madrid 1994–2014, Aviva PLC, London, UK 1999–2008 (Chair. (non-exec.) Aviva Grupo Corporativo, SL and Aviva Vida y Pensiones, SA de Seguros y Reaseguros 2002–), Unión Fenosa 1988–2007, Madrid, Amadeus IT Holding SA, Grupo San José 2012–14; apptd Vice-Chair. Goldman Sachs Europe Ltd 1988, Int. Advisor 1988–; Spanish Advisor to Taconic Capital (Investment Fund) 2012–, Centene Corpn 2013–; mem. European Advisory Bd, Eli Lilly 2000–, Coca Cola 2004–06; Chair. Centre for Econ. Policy Research, London, European Cen. Bank Observatory, Madrid, Bd Instituto de Empresa, Madrid, Steering Cttee of Advisory Bd of ESCP-EAP (École Supérieure de Commerce de Paris merged with EAP-Ecole Européenne des Affaires to form ESCP-EAP European School of Man.), Paris, France, Governing Bd of Instituto de Empresa Business School, Madrid; Chair., later Hon. Chair. High Council of Chambers of Commerce, Industry and Navigation of Spain 1991–2005; Chair. of Trustees, Reina Sofia Museum of Contemporary Art 2010–, Financieros sin Fronteras 2012–; mem. Euro 50 Group, Brussels, Belgium, Advisory Bd of CREI at Univ. Pompeu Fabra, Barcelona, Scientific Advisory Bd of Instituto de Estudios Europeos and of Instituto Elcano, Madrid; monetary expert, Econ. and Monetary Cttee of European Parl.; mem. Group of Thirty Consultative Group on Int. Econ. and Monetary Affairs, Inc. (G-30), Washington, DC; regular columnist for El País, Madrid, La Nación, Buenos Aires, Gazeta Mercantil, São Paulo and Reforma, Mexico; Trustee, Germán Sanchez Ruipérez Foundation –2013, Círculo de Bellas Artes 2005–, Eli Lilly Foundation in Spain 2007–, Prado Museum 2008–, Empresa y Crecimiento Foundation 2008–, Foundation Alcohol y Sociedad 2012–. *Publications:* author of eight books in Spanish and four books in English and co-author of 20 books in Spanish and 14 books in English on econs; more than 100 papers in econ. journals and more than 300 articles in newspapers and magazines. *Address:* Goldman Sachs Group Holdings (UK), 133 Fleet Street, London, EC4A 2BB, England (office). *Telephone:* (20) 7774-1000 (office). *E-mail:* info@guillermodeladehesa.com (office). *Website:* www.goldmansachs.com (office); www.guillermodeladehesa.com.

DE LA GUARDIA, Dulcidio, MPA, CFA; Panamanian politician and fmr investment banker; b. 28 March 1964; ed Florida State Univ., Loyola Univ., USA; Devt Man., Panama Stock Exchange 1990–95; Vice-Pres. of Private Banking and Investments, Banco Continental de Panama, SA 1999–2002; Vice-Pres. of Investment Banking, Primer Banco del Istmo (Banistmo) 2002, Exec. Vice-Pres. 2005, Head of Corp. Investment Banking and Markets (following merger between HSBC Banks (Panama) and Banistmo) 2006–07, Head of Private Banking 2007–08; Dir of Wealth Man., MMG Bank 2008–09; Vice-Minister of Finance 2009–11; Chief Operating Officer, Morgan & Morgan Group, Panama 2011–14; Minister of Economy and Finance 2014–18; fmr mem. Bd of Dirs Panama Stock Exchange, Inc., Elektra Noreste, Progreso AFP, Profuturo AFP, Primer Banco del Istmo, SA, HSBC Bank (Panama), SA, Central Latinoamericana de Valores (Latinclear), Corporacion Andina de Fomento (CAF), Panamanian Chamber of Capital Markets; mem. Bd of Dirs Helados La Italiana, SA, City Sightseeing Panama, SA. *Address:* c/o Ministry of the Economy and Finance, Edif. Ogawa, Vía España y Calle 52 Este, Calle del Santuario Nacional, Apdo 5245, Panamá 5, Panama (office). *Telephone:* 507-7000 (office). *E-mail:* uabrmercadeo@mef.gob.pa (office). *Website:* www.mef.gob.pa (office).

DE LA HOYA, Oscar; American boxer; b. 4 Feb. 1973, Los Angeles, Calif.; s. of Joel De La Hoya and Cecilia De La Hoya; m. Millie Corretjer; three s. two d.; ed James A. Garfield High School, Los Angeles, Calif.; fmr amateur boxer, 223 victories (163 knockouts), only 5 losses; turned professional after winning gold medal lightweight Barcelona Olympics 1992; Int. Boxing Fed. (IBF) lightweight title 1995; World Boxing Council (WBC) super lightweight title (over Julio César Chávez) 1996; WBC welterweight title (over Pernell Whitaker) 1997; lost WBC welterweight belt to Felix Trinidad in a majority decision in 1999; lost to Sugar Shane Mosley in 2000 in his 2nd career defeat; has won major titles in six weight divisions: 130, 135, 140, 147, 154 and 160 pounds; lost super welterweight title to Mosley 2003; won World Boxing Org. middleweight title June 2004 defeating Felix Sturm, lost it when defeated by Bernard Hopkins Sept. 2004; defeated WBC jr middleweight champion Ricardo Mayorga 2006, lost title to Floyd Mayweather, Jr. 2007; lost to Manny Pacquiao 2008; retd from boxing 2009; f. Oscar de la Hoya Foundation; Owner, Golden Boy Promotions LLC; Boxer of the Year, USA Boxing 1991, Fighter of the Year 1995, Best Fighter, Pound for Pound 1997, Ring magazine, WBC Boxer of the Decade 2001, mem. United States Olympic Hall of Fame 2008. *Album:* Oscar (topped Billboard's Latin Dance charts for several weeks). *Publication:* American Son (autobiography) 2008. *Address:* c/o Golden Boy Promotions, 626 Wilshire Blvd, Suite 350, Los Angeles, CA 90017, USA (office). *Telephone:* (213) 489-5631 (office). *Fax:* (213) 489-9048 (office). *E-mail:* info@goldenboyllc.com (office). *Website:* www.goldenboypromotions.com (office); www.oscardelahoya.com.

DE LA MARNIÈRE, Caroline; French business executive; *President, Capitalcom;* four c.; f. Ecocom 1994, acquired by Publicis Groupe 2001, CEO Publicis Consultants Ecocom 2001–05; Founder and Pres. Capitalcom communications agency 2005–; Prix du Jury de'Assemblée Générale du CAC 40 2010. *Leisure interests:* trekking, yoga, skiing, 70s music, travel. *Address:* Capitalcom, 10 boulevard Malesherbes, 75008 Paris, France (office). *Telephone:* 1-45-49-93-37 (office). *Fax:* 1-45-51-33-72 (office). *E-mail:* info@capitalcom.fr (office). *Website:* www.capitalcom.fr (office).

DE LA NUEZ RAMÍREZ, Raúl; Cuban politician; fmr Vice-Minister, Basic Industry Ministry; Minister of Foreign Trade 2000–09 (ministry merged with Ministry of Foreign Investment). *Address:* c/o Ministry of Foreign Trade and Investment, Infanta y 23, Plaza de la Revolución, Mirama, Havana, Cuba (office). *E-mail:* secretariataller@mincex.cu.

DE LA PEÑA NAVARRETE, Alejandro; Mexican diplomatist and international organization executive; *Secretary-General, Latin American Integration Association (ALADI);* b. 27 Sept. 1951, Chihuahua; m.; two s.; ed Institut des Hautes Études Internationales, Geneva; Deputy Econ. Counsellor, Mission of Mexico in Geneva 1977–79, Econ. Counsellor, Embassy in Washington, DC 1981–83, Econ. Counsellor, Perm. Mission to EU, Brussels 1985–86, Deputy Perm. Rep. to GATT, Geneva 1987–92, Minister of Trade and Industry Promotion's Rep. to EC 1992–93, Perm. Rep. to WTO, Geneva 1995–2001; Deputy Exec. Dir, APEC May–Dec. 2001, Exec. Dir 2002–03; Dir-Gen. Comm. for Social Research Foundation, AC 2008–09; Amb. to Brazil 2010–12; Sec.-Gen. Latin American Integration Asscn (ALADI) 2017–. *Address:* Latin American Integration Association, Calle Cebollatí 1461, Barrio Palermo, Casilla de Correo n° 20.005, 11200 Montevideo, Uruguay (office); Secretariat of State for Foreign Affairs, Plaza Juárez 20, Col. Centro, Del. Cuauhtémoc, 06010 Mexico City, DF, Mexico (office). *Telephone:* (2) 4101121 (ALADI) (office); (55) 3686-5100 (office). *Fax:* (2) 4190649 (ALADI) (office); (55) 3686-5582 (office). *E-mail:* sgaladi@aladi.org (office); atencionciudadanasre@sre.gob.mx (office). *Website:* www.aladi.org (office); www.sre.gob.mx (office).

DE LA QUADRA-SALCEDO FERNÁNDEZ DEL CASTILLO, Tomás, PhD; Spanish lawyer, politician and academic; *Professor of Administrative Law, Carlos III University of Madrid;* b. 1946, Madrid; m.; two c.; ed Univ. Complutense of Madrid; Asst Lecturer in Admin. Law, Faculty of Law, Univ. Complutense of Madrid 1977–81 (Temporary Lecturer 1968), in Audiovisual Media, Information Sciences Faculty 1981–; mem. Lawyers' Asscn of Madrid 1968–; Minister of Territorial Admin. 1982–85; Pres. Council of State 1985–91; Minister of Justice 1991–93; lawyer of Bar Asscn of Madrid 1995–; currently Prof. of Admin. Law, Universidad Carlos III de Madrid, Dir Doctorate in Law and Rector 1997–, Master of Law, Telecommunications and Information Tech. 2001–, Research Master in Law –2009, Master in Public Law 2009–; Visiting Prof. at several foreign universities, including Paris X Nanterre, Cardozo School of Law, New York, University of El Salvador, Buenos Aires, Argentina Grad. Studies; mem. Int. Acad. of Comparative Law, Spanish Asscn of Admin. Law, Italo-Spanish Asscn of Profs of Public Law; Gran Cruz de Carlos III; Gran Cruz de San Raimundo de Peñafort; Medalla al Mérito Constitucional. *Publications:* El régimen jurídico de la Comunicación Local 2002, Comentarios a la Ley General de Telecomunicaciones 2004; several book chapters and various articles. *Address:* Room 11.1.15, Department of Public State Law, Faculty of Social Sciences and Law, Carlos III University of Madrid, C/Madrid 126, 28903 Getafe Madrid, Spain (office). *Telephone:* (91) 6249840 (office). *Fax:* (91) 6249877 (office). *E-mail:* tsalcedo@der-pu.uc3m.es (office). *Website:* www.uc3m.es (office).

DE LA RÚA, Fernando; Argentine politician; b. 15 Sept. 1937, Córdoba; s. of Antonio de la Rúa and Eleonora Bruno de la Rúa; m. Inés Pertiné; two s. one d.; ed Liceo General Paz, Córdoba, Universidad Nacional de Córdoba; joined Unión Cívica Radical (UCR) as a student; mem. staff Ministry of Interior 1963–66; cand. for Vice-Pres. 1973, Senator for Fed. Capital 1973–76, 1983–96; visiting lecturer univs in USA, Mexico and Venezuela during mil. dictatorship; f. Centro de Estudios Para la República (now Fundación de estudios sobre temas políticos), Buenos Aires 1982; Mayor of Buenos Aires 1996–99; Leader ALIANZA coalition; Pres. of Argentina 1999–2001 (resgnd), put on trial accused of bribing senators for votes during his time in office 2012–13; Prof. of Criminal Law, Univ. of Buenos Aires; Founder-mem. Consejo Argentino para las Relaciones Internacionales. *Leisure interests:* gardening, birds, nature, reading. *Address:* c/o Casa de Goberniero, Balcarce 50, 1064 Buenos Aires, Argentina (office).

DE LA TORRE MUÑOZ, Carlos Alberto, MEcon; Ecuadorean economist and politician; b. 3 March 1971, Quito; m.; ed Colegio Americano de Quito, Inst. Tecnológico Autónomo de México, Univ. San Francisco de Quito; Economist, Banco Central del Ecuador 1994–2004, Adviser to Man. Bd 2016–17; Prof., Faculty of Econs, Pontificia Univ. Católica del Ecuador 1996–, Asst Dean, Faculty of Econs 2010–16, Dir, Inst. de Investigaciones Económicas 2016–17; Consultant to Gen. Secr., Andean Community and Inter-American Devt Bank (IDB) Sept.–Dec. 2004; Consultant, UN Conference for Trade and Devt (UNCTAD) and World Bank 2005–06; Consultant, Org. of American States (OAS) 2005–06; Consultant, Latin American Integration Asscn (ALADI) May–July 2008; Minister of Finance 2017–18.

DE LA TOUR, Frances; British actress; b. 30 July 1944, Bovingdon, Herts.; d. of Charles de la Tour and Moyra de la Tour (née Fessas); m. Tom Kempinski 1972 (divorced 1982); one s. one d.; ed Lycée français de Londres, Drama Centre, London; Hon. Fellow, Goldsmiths Coll., Univ. of London 1999. *Stage appearances include:* with RSC: As You Like It 1967, The Relapse 1969, A Midsummer Night's Dream 1971, The Man of Mode 1971, Antony and Cleopatra 1999; Small Craft Warnings (Best Supporting Actress, Plays and Players Award) 1973, The Banana Box 1973, As You Like It (Oxford Playhouse) 1974, The White Devil 1976, Hamlet (title role) 1979, Duet for One (Best Actress, New Standard Award, Best Actress, Critics Award, Best Actress, Soc. of West End Theatres—SWET Award) 1980, Skirmishes 1981, Uncle Vanya 1982, Moon for the Misbegotten (Best Actress, SWET Award) 1983, St Joan (Royal Nat. Theatre) 1984, Dance of Death (Riverside Studios) 1985, Brighton Beach Memoirs (Royal Nat. Theatre) 1986, Lillian 1986, Façades 1988, King Lear 1989, Chekhov's Women (Moscow Arts Theatre) 1990, When She Danced (Olivier Award) 1991, The Pope and the Witch 1992, Greasepaint 1993, Les Parents Terribles (Royal Nat. Theatre) 1994, Three Tall Women 1994–95, Blinded by the Sun (Royal Nat. Theatre) 1996, The Play About the Baby (Almeida Theatre) 1998, The Forest (Royal Nat. Theatre) 1998–99, Fallen Angels (Apollo) (Best Actress, Royal Variety Club) 2000–01, The Good Hope and Sketches by Harold Pinter (Royal Nat. Theatre) 2001–02, Dance of Death (Lyric) 2003, The History Boys (Nat. Theatre) 2004–05, (Broadway) (Tony Award for Best Supporting Actress) 2006, The Habit of Art (Nat. Theatre) 2009. *Films include:* Rising Damp (Best Actress, Standard Film Award) 1980, The Cherry Orchard 1998, Harry Potter and the Goblet of Fire 2005, The History Boys 2006, Alice in Wonderland 2018, Nutcracker: The Untold Story 2010, The Book of Eli

2010, Harry Potter and the Deathly Hallows: Part 1 2010, Hugo 2011. *Television appearances include:* Rising Damp 1974, 1976, Flickers 1980, Skirmishes 1982, Duet for One 1985, Clem 1986, A Kind of Living (series) 1987–88, Cold Lazarus 1996, Tom Jones 1997, The Egg 2002, Waking the Dead 2004, Poirot: Death on the Nile 2004, Sensitive Skin 2005, Agatha Christie: The Moving Finger 2005, 3 lbs 2006, Vicious (series) 2013–16, Big School (series) 2013–14, Outlander 2016–. *Address:* c/o Claire Maroussas, ICM, Oxford House, 76 Oxford Street, London, W1N 0AX, England (office).

DE LABOULAYE, Stanislas François Jean Lefebvre; French diplomatist (retd) and business executive; *Senior Vice-President, Sovereign Global Solutions;* b. 12 Dec. 1946, Beirut, Lebanon; m.; four c.; ed Collège Stanislas, Lycée Henri-IV, Univ. of Paris, Sorbonne, Vincennes Univ., Agrégé de l'Université, Ecole Nationale d'Admin; held teaching posts at Lycée de Garçons de Sfax, Tunisia 1970–72, Univ. of Manchester, UK 1972–76; joined Foreign Service 1980, served in several positions including Sec., Asia Div., Ministry of Foreign Affairs 1980–81, Econ. Div. 1981–84, Communications Dir 1991–95, Asst Sec.-Gen. and Political Dir 2002; First Sec., then Second Counsellor, Perm. Mission to EU, Brussels 1984–87, Second Counsellor, Embassy in Madrid 1987–91, Consul-Gen. in Jerusalem 1996–99, Amb. to Madagascar 2000–02, Asst Sec.-Gen. and Dir-Gen. for Political Affairs and Security 2002–06, Amb. to Russia 2006–09, to the Holy See (Vatican City) 2009–12; Diplomatic Adviser to the Govt 2012; Sr Vice-Pres., Sovereign Global Solutions 2013–; Officier, Légion d'honneur 2008; Commdr, Ordre nat. du Mérite 2011. *Address:* Sovereign Global Solutions, 129 rue de l'Université, 75007 Paris, France (office). *Telephone:* 6-79-58-26-99 (mobile) (office). *E-mail:* sdelaboulaye@so-global.com (office). *Website:* www.so-global.com (office).

DE LADOUCETTE, Philippe, MA, DScS, DrSc (Econ); French business executive and government official; *Chairman, Commission de régulation de l'énergie;* b. 15 March 1948, Paris; s. of Charles de Ladoucette; ed Ecole Nationale des Ponts et Chaussées; fmr civil engineer with Ministry of Equipment (responsible for state contracts with medium-sized towns) 1974–77; Commr for Industrialization, Ardennes 1977–83; responsible for industrial devt, DATAR 1983–86; tech. adviser, Ministry of Industry, Posts and Telecommunications and Tourism 1986–88; responsible for industrial matters, Secr.-Gen. of Channel Tunnel 1988–93; Asst Dir Office of Minister of Enterprise and Econ. Devt 1993–94; Chair. Houillères du Bassin du Centre et du Midi 1994–; CEO SNET 1996–2000; CEO Charbonnages de France 1996–2006; apptd Pres. Commission de régulation de l'énergie 2006, Chair. 2011–; Chevalier, Légion d'honneur, Officier Ordre Nat. du Mérite. *Leisure interests:* swimming, jogging, cycling. *Address:* Commission de régulation de l'énergie, 2 rue du Quatre-Septembre, 75084 Paris Cedex 02 (office); 40 avenue Marceau, 75008 Paris, France (home). *Website:* www.cre.fr (office).

DE LANGE, Titia, PhD; Dutch cell biologist, geneticist and academic; *Leon Hess Professor, Laboratory of Cell Biology and Genetics, The Rockefeller University;* b. 11 Nov. 1955, Rotterdam; ed Univ. of Amsterdam and Netherlands Cancer Inst.; Grad. Teaching Asst, Dept of Biochemistry, Univ. of Amsterdam 1981–85; Postdoctoral Fellow, Univ. of California, San Francisco 1985–90; Asst Prof., The Rockefeller Univ. 1990–94, Assoc. Prof. 1994–97, Prof. 1997–, Leon Hess Prof. 1999–, Assoc. Dir Anderson Center for Cancer Research 2006–11, Dir 2011–; American Cancer Soc. Research Prof. 2010–; Pres. Harvey Soc. 2000–01; mem. Editorial Bd, Molecular and Cellular Biology 1997–, Trends in Biological Science 2000–, PLoS Biology 2004–07, Genes and Development 2008–, Nucleus 2009–, Journal of Cell Biology 2010–, Current Opinion in Genetics and Development 2011–; mem. and Corresp., Royal Netherlands Acad. of Sciences 2000, Inst. of Medicine 2010; Foreign mem. European Molecular Biology Org. 2001; Foreign Assoc., NAS 2006; Fellow, New York Acad. of Sciences 2005, American Soc. for Microbiology 2006, American Acad. for Arts and Sciences 2007, AAAS 2007, American Acad. for Cancer Research 2014; Dr hc (Utrecht) 2003; Dr Catharine van Tussenbroek Award 1980, Christiaan and Constantijn Huygens Award 1985–87, Lucille P. Markey Trust Scholar Award 1987–95, Irma T. Hirschl-Monique Weill-Caulier Trust Award 1993–98, Rita Allen Award 1995–2000, Burroughs Wellcome Toxicology Scholar Award 1997–2002, New York Community Trust Cancer Research Award 1997–99, Ellison Medical Foundation Sr Scholar Award 2000–04, first Paul Marks Prize for Cancer Research (co-recipient) 2001, Charlotte Friend Memorial Award, American Asscn for Cancer Research (AACR) 2004, NIH MERIT Award (GM) 2005, NIH Dir's Pioneer Award 2005, Award for Excellence in Teaching, The Rockefeller Univ. 2007, Massachusetts Gen. Hosp. Cancer Center Prize 2008, AACR G.H.A. Clowes Memorial Award 2010, Vilcek Prize in Biomedical Sciences 2011, Rosalind E. Franklin Award, Nat. Cancer Inst. 2012, Vanderbilt Prize in Biomedical Science 2012, Dr H.P. Heineken Prize for Biochemistry and Biophysics 2012, Breakthrough Prize in Life Sciences (co-recipient) 2013, Jill Rose Award, Breast Cancer Research Foundation 2013, Canada Gairdner Int. Award 2014. *Achievements include:* one of the first to isolate the telomeres of human chromosomes. *Publications:* more than 130 papers in professional journals. *Address:* Laboratory for Cell Biology and Genetics, The Rockefeller University, 1230 York Avenue, New York, NY 10065, USA (office). *Telephone:* (212) 327-8146 (office). *Fax:* (212) 327-7147 (office). *E-mail:* titia.de .lange@rockefeller.edu (office); delange@mail.rockefeller.edu (office). *Website:* www.rockefeller.edu/research/faculty/labheads/TitiadeLange (office); delangelab .rockefeller.edu (office).

DE LAROSIÈRE DE CHAMPFEU, Jacques Martin Henri Marie; French international civil servant; *Senior Adviser, BNP Paribas;* b. 12 Nov. 1929, Paris; s. of Robert de Larosière and Hugayte de Larosière (née de Champfeu); m. France du Bos 1960; one s. one d.; ed Lycée Louis-le-Grand, Paris Univ. and Ecole nat. d'Admin; Insp. adjoint 1958, Insp. des Finances 1960; Chargé de Mission in Inspectorate-Gen. of Finance 1961, External Finance Office 1963, Treasury 1965; Asst Dir Treasury 1967; Deputy Dir then Head of Dept, Ministry of Econs and Finance 1971; Prin. Pvt. Sec. to Valéry Giscard d'Estaing (then Minister of Econs and Finance) 1974; Under-Sec. of Treas. 1974–78; Pres. Group of Ten 1976–78; Dir-Gen. IMF 1978–87; Gov. Banque de France 1987–93, Hon. Gov. 1993–; Chair. Cttee of Govs, Group of Ten 1990–93; Pres. EBRD 1993–98; Sr Adviser BNP Paribas 1998–; Chair. Strategic Cttee of French Treasury 2000–; Insp. Gen. des Finances 1981; mem. Bd of Dirs Renault 1971–74, Banque nat. de Paris 1973–78, Air France and Soc. nat. de chemins de fer français (SNCF) 1974–78, Soc. nat. industrielle aérospatiale 1976–78, Power Corpn 1998–2001; Alstom 1998–2001, France Télécom 1998–2009, Stichting NYSE Euronext (the Dutch Foundation) 2007–; mem. AIG International Advisory Bd; Trustee Reuters 1999–2004; Censeur Banque de France 1974–78, Crédit nat. 1974–78, Comptoir des Entrepreneurs 1973–75, Crédit foncier de France 1975–78; Vice-Pres. Caisse nat. des Télécommunications 1974–78; mem. Acad. of Moral and Political Sciences 1993; Hon. mem. Soc. des Cincinnati de France; Commdr, Légion d'honneur; Chevalier, Ordre nat. du Mérite; Hon. KBE; numerous awards. *Address:* BNP Paribas, 3 rue d'Antin, 75078 Paris Cedex 02 (office); 10 bis, rue Paul Baudry, 75008 Paris, France (home). *Telephone:* 1-42-98-24-28 (office); 1-42-98-72-74 (office). *Fax:* 1-42-98-22-37 (office). *E-mail:* jacques.delarosiere@bnpparibas.com (office). *Website:* www.bnpparibas.net (office).

DE LIMA, Leila Norma Eulalia Josefa, AB, LLB; Philippine lawyer, human rights activist and politician; b. 27 Aug. 1959, Iriga City, Camarines Sur; d. of Vicente B. De Lima and Norma E. Magistrado; divorced; two s.; ed San Beda Coll., De La Salle Univ.; began career as mem. legal staff for Supreme Court Assoc. Justice Isagani A. Cruz 1986–89; Jr Assoc., Jardeleza Sobreviñas Diaz Hayudini and Bodegon Law Offices 1989–91, Jardeleza Law Offices 1991–93; Jr Partner, Roco, Buñag, Kapunan and Migallos (law firm) 1995–98; Founding and Man. Partner, De Lima & Meñez Law Offices 1998–2007; Man. Partner, The De Lima Law Firm 2007–08; Prof. of Law, San Beda Coll. 1986–94, 2006–07; Law Clerk and Sec., House of Reps Electoral Tribunal 1993–95; Chair. Philippine Comm. on Human Rights 2008–10; Sec. (Minister), Dept of Justice 2010–15; Chair., Inter-Agency Council Against Trafficking; mem. Senate 2016–, Chair. Senate Justice and Human Rights Cttee 2016, Senate Electoral Reforms and People's Participation Cttee 2016–; mem. Philippine Asscn of Law Profs 1988–; mem. Liberal Party 2015–; MetroBank Foundation Professorial Chair for Public Service and Governance 2010, Excellent Public Servant Award, Defender of People's Rights, Agent of Change Award 2010, Prize of Freedom 2018. *Address:* Room 502 & 16 (New Wing 5/F), GSIS Bldg, Financial Center, Diokno Blvd, Pasay City, Manila, Philippines (office). *Telephone:* 807-8489 (office). *E-mail:* senleilamdelima@gmail.com (office). *Website:* www.senate.gov.ph (office).

DE LIMA GERCICH, Frank Georges, BBA; Panamanian economist and politician; ed Boston Univ., Georgetown Univ., Washington DC, Ciudad del Saber, Panamá; consultant specializing in issues of competitiveness, int. trade, strategic planning and public policy reform; led Panama team in negotiations with World Bank and UN, and at taxation agreements with several OECD countries; represented Govt of Panama at Meso-American Council on Competitiveness; campaign spokesman and head of finance cttee, presidential campaign of Ricardo Martinelli 2009; Deputy Minister of Economy and Finance 2009–11, Minister of Economy and Finance 2011–14; mem. Cambio Democrático. *Publications include:* articles on econ. issues and int. competitiveness in publs including La Prensa, Capital Finance, El Panama America. *Address:* Ministry of the Economy and Finance, Edif. Ogawa, Vía España, Calle del Santuario Nacional, Apdo 5245, Panamá 5, Panama (office). *Telephone:* 507-7000 (office). *E-mail:* prensa@mef.gob .pa (office). *Website:* www.mef.gob.pa (office).

DE LIMA MASSANO, José; Angolan accountant and fmr central banker; *Governor, Banco Nacional de Angola;* b. 1971; ed City Univ., London, UK, Salford Univ., Manchester; Head of Tech. Support Office and Accounting, Sonangol EP (state-owned oil firm) 1997–2000; Exec. Dir Banco Comercial Português 2000–05; Exec. Dir Banco Angolano de Investimentos (BAI) 2005–06, CEO 2006–10, 2015–17; Gov. Banco Nacional de Angola (central bank) 2010–15, 2017–; Pres. SADC Banking Asscn 2004–05, Angolan Asscn of Banks (ABANC) 2006–09. *Address:* Office of the Governor, Banco Nacional de Angola, Avenue 4 de Fevereiro 151, CP 1243, Luanda, Angola (office). *Telephone:* 222679200 (office). *Fax:* 222679200 (office). *E-mail:* bna.cri@ebonet.net (office). *Website:* www.bna.ao (office).

DE LIMA NETO, Antônio Francisco, BEcons, MBA; Brazilian banker; b. 13 June 1965; ed Univ. Fed. de Pernambucom, Fundacão Dom Cabral, Pontificia Universidade Catolica; joined Banco do Brasil SA as apprentice 1979, becoming Dir of Int. and Wholesale Business 2004–05, Man. Dir BB Leasing SA and BB Securities, Vice-Pres., Retail Div. 2006–07, Interim CEO 2006–07, Vice-Chair., Pres. and CEO Banco do Brasil SA 2007–09, also Counsellor, BB Securities Ltd; Regional Dir Associação Brasileira das Empresas de Leasing; Pres. Banco Fibra 2009–13; mem. Audit Cttee, Banco Itáu Unibanco Holding SA 2015–; Embassy of Brazil and Brazilian Chamber of Commerce in GB Personality of the Year 2007. *Address:* Banco Itáu Unibanco Holding SA, Praca Alfredo Egydio de Souza Aranha 100, T. Olavo Setubal, Parque Jabaquara, Sao Paulo 04344-902, Brazil (office). *Telephone:* (11) 2794-3547. *Fax:* (11) 2794-3933. *E-mail:* investor.relations@itau -unibanco.com.br (office). *Website:* www.itauunibanco.com.br (office).

DE LUCCHI, Michele; Italian designer; b. 8 Nov. 1951, Ferrara; s. of Alberto De Lucchi and Giuliana Zannini; ed Liceo Scientifico Enrico Fermi, Padua, Faculty of Architecture, Univ. of Florence; Founder-mem. Cavart (avant-garde design and architecture group) 1973–76; Asst Prof., Univ. of Florence 1976–77; worked with Gaetano Pesce, Superstudio, Andrea Branzi, Ettore Sottsass 1977–80; consultant, Centrokappa Noviglio, Milan 1978, Olivetti Synthesis, Massa 1979–, Olivetti SpA, Ivrea 1984–; freelance designer, several furniture mfrs 1979–; Founder-mem. Int. Designer Group Memphis 1981. *Publication:* Architetture Verticali 1978. *Leisure interest:* travel photography. *Address:* Architetto Michele De Lucchi Srl, 15 Via Varese, 20121 Milan, Italy (office). *Telephone:* (02) 63786817 (office). *Fax:* (02) 63786814 (office). *E-mail:* amdl@amdl.it (office); info@produzioneprivata.it (office). *Website:* www.produzioneprivata.it (office); www.micheledelucchi.com; www .micheledelucchiartworks.it.

DE MAESENEIRE, Baron Patrick; Belgian engineer and business executive; *CEO, Jacobs Holding AG;* b. 1957; ed Solvay Brussels School of Econs and Man. (SBS-EM), Ghent Univ. London Business School, UK, Institut Européen d'Admin des Affaires (INSEAD), Fontainebleau, France; held exec. positions at Belgian TV station VTM, Sun International, Apple Computer, as well as sr positions at Wang in Belgium and Arthur Andersen Consulting 1986–97; held leading positions within Adecco Group, starting out as Country Man. for Benelux region then led Adecco Group's worldwide professional staffing business from New York 1998–2002, CEO Adecco 2009–15; CEO, Barry Callebaut (cocoa and chocolate products) 2002–09, Jacobs Holding AG 2015–; title of Baron granted by King

Albert II 2007. *Address:* Jacobs Holding AG, Seefeldquai 17, PO Box, 8034 Zürich, Switzerland (office). *Telephone:* (44) 388-61-61 (office). *Fax:* (44) 388-61-55 (office). *E-mail:* info@jacobsag.ch (office). *Website:* www.jacobsag.ch (office).

DE MAGISTRIS, HE Cardinal Luigi; Italian ecclesiastic; *Pro-Major Penitentiary Emeritus of the Apostolic Penitentiary;* b. 23 Feb. 1926, Cagliari; ordained priest, Archdiocese of Cagliari 1952; apptd Regent of Apostolic Penitentiary 1979; consecrated Titular Bishop of Nova 1996–2001, Titular Archbishop of Nova 2001–; Pro-Major Penitentiary of Apostolic Penitentiary 2001–03, Emer. 2003–; cr. Cardinal (Cardinal-Deacon of Santissimi Nome di Gesù e Maria in Via Lata) 2015. *Address:* Palazzo della Cancelleria, Piazza della Cancelleria 1, 00186 Rome, Italy (office). *Telephone:* (06) 69887526 (office). *Fax:* (06) 69887557 (office). *Website:* www.vatican.va/roman_curia/tribunals/apost_penit/index_it.htm (office).

DE MAIZIÈRE, Lothar; German lawyer and politician; b. 2 March 1940, Nordhausen; m.; three d.; mem. Christian Democratic Union, Leader 1989–90; Deputy Prime Minister and Spokesman on Church Affairs 1989–90; Prime Minister of GDR and Minister of Foreign Affairs March–Oct. 1990; Minister without Portfolio 1990–91, Deputy Chair. CDU, Chair Brandenburg CDU Oct.-Dec. 1990, 1991; Leader Lutheran Church Council; resgnd as CDU Deputy 1991; Hon. Citizen of Nordhausen 2010; Order of Friendship (Russia) 2010; Quadriga Prize 2010. *Publication:* Anwalt der Einheit 1996. *Address:* Am Kupfergraben 6/6A, 10117 Berlin, Germany.

DE MAIZIÈRE, Thomas, DrJur; German lawyer and politician; b. 21 Jan. 1954, Bonn; s. of Ulrich de Maizière and Eva Werner; m. Martina de Maizière; three c.; ed Wilhelms-Univ. Münster, Univ. Freiburg; began career in office of Mayor of Berlin 1983–85; Leader, Grundsatzreferat (Basic Issues Div.), Senate Chancellery for Land of Berlin 1985–89; mem. W German del. to negotiations on German reunification 1990; Sec. of State in Ministry of Culture, Land of Mecklenburg-W Pomerania 1990–94, Chief of Staff of Chancellery, Mecklenburg-W Pomerania 1994–98; Adviser and Minister, later Chief of Chancellery, Land of Saxony 1999–2001, Minister of Finance, Saxony 2001–02, Prov. Minister of Justice 2002–04, of the Interior 2004–05, mem. Saxony Landtag (Prov. Ass.) 2004–05; Chief of Staff at Fed. Chancellor's Office and Fed. Minister for Special Affairs 2005–09, Fed. Minister of the Interior 2009–11, 2013–18, of Defence 2011–13; mem. CDU 1971–; Cavaliere di Gran Croce (Italy) 2006. *Address:* c/o Federal Ministry of the Interior, Alt-Moabit 101, 10559 Berlin, Germany (office). *Website:* www.thomasdemaiziere.de.

DE MARIA Y CAMPOS, Mauricio, MA; Mexican economist, diplomatist and academic; *Director, Instituto de Investigaciones sobre Desarrollo Sustentable y Equidad Social, Universidad Iberoamericana;* b. 13 Oct. 1943, Mexico DF; s. of Mauricio de María y Campos and Teresa Castello; m. Patricia Meade 1981; two s. one d.; ed Nat. Univ. of Mexico, Univ. of Sussex, UK; Head of Planning and Policy Unit, Mexican Nat. Science and Tech. Council 1971–72; Deputy Dir Evaluation Dept Tech. Transfer Ministry of Trade and Industry 1973–74, Dir-Gen. Foreign Investment 1974–77, Vice-Minister Industrial Devt 1982–89; Dir-Gen. Tax Incentives and Fiscal Promotion Ministry of Finance 1977–82; Exec. Vice-Pres. Banco Mexicano SOMEX 1989–92; Deputy Dir-Gen. UNIDO 1992–93, Dir-Gen. 1993–97; Amb. at Large and Special Adviser on UN Affairs, Ministry of Foreign Affairs 1998–2001; Amb. to South Africa 2002–07; currently Dir Instituto de Investigaciones sobre Desarrollo Sustentable y Equidad Social (Research Inst. for Sustainable Devt and Social Equity), Universidad Iberoamericana; mem. Int. Club of Rome 1998– (Pres. of Mexican Chapter 1998–), Mexican Council on Foreign Relations (COMEXI); Grand Commendateur Ordre nat. du Mérite, Order of Francisco de Miranda (Venezuela); Great Decoration in Gold on the Sash (Austria); Grand Ordre du Mono (Togo). *Publications:* Challenges and Opportunities for Scientific and Technological Collaboration between the EEC and Mexico 1990, The Transformation of the Mexican Automobile Industry during the 1980s 1992; various publs on industrial and technological policy and on regional devt. *Leisure interests:* classical music, writing, reading, swimming, jogging, dancing, journalism. *Address:* Instituto de Investigaciones sobre Desarrollo Sustentable y Equidad Social (Research Institute for Sustainable Development and Social Equity), Edificio Q, 3er. piso, Universidad Iberoamericana Ciudad de México, Prolongación Paseo de la Reforma 880, Lomas de Santa Fe, México, C.P. 01219, Distrito Federal 01219 México, DF, Mexico (office). *Telephone:* (55) 5950-4339 (office). *Fax:* (55) 5950-4195 (office). *E-mail:* mauricio.demaria@uia.mx (office). *Website:* www.uia.mx (office).

DE MELLO BRANDÃO, Lázaro; Brazilian economist and banking executive; b. 15 June 1926, Itápolis, São Paulo; joined Casa Bancária Almeida & Cie (renamed Banco Brasileiro de Descontos SA, then Banco Bradesco SA) 1942, various positions including Exec. Officer 1963–77, Deputy CEO 1977–81, Pres. 1981–99, Deputy Chair. 1982–90, Chair. 1990–2017; Chair. Companhia Brasileira de Securitação (CIBRASEC) 1997–99, Bradespar SA 2004–; Chair. Man. Body and CEO Fundação Bradesco; mem. Bd of Dirs Banco Espírito Santo SA, Lisbon, Portugal, Nat. Housing Bank 1984–85; Chair. Credit Guarantor Fund (FGC) 1999–2001; Exec. Officer, Bank Trade Asscn in States of São Paulo, Paraná, Mato Grosso, Mato Grosso do Sul, Acre, Amazonas, Pará, Amapá, Rondônia and Roraima 1966–74, CEO 1974–83; Vice-Pres. Bd of Exec. Officers, Nat. Fed. of Banks (FENABAN) 1971–76, 1980–83, mem. Bd of Dirs 1983–91, 1994–2001; mem. Bd of Dirs Brazilian Fed. of Bank Asscns (FEBRABAN), Advisory Bd VBC Participações SA; Chair. and CEO Foundation Inst. for Digestive System and Nutrition Diseases (FIMADEN); Hon. Citizen of Joinville.

DE MELLO PAZ, Bernardo; Brazilian mining industry executive and art collector; b. 11 July 1950, Belo Horizonte, Minas Gerais; s. of Achilles Paz and Mercês Paz; m. 5th Adriana Varejão (divorced); seven c.; began by buying land and setting up mining cos; sold Itaminas (Itaminas Comércio de Minérios SA) (pig iron producer) to East China Mineral Exploration and Development Bureau, Nanjing (Chinese state-owned co.) 2010; Founder and mem. Bd of Dirs Centro de Arte Contemporânea Inhotim (or Instituto Inhotim) 2006–, botanical garden and contemporary art museum located on one of his properties. *Address:* Inhotim, Rua B 20, Brumadinho, Minas Gerais, 35460-000, Brazil (office). *Telephone:* (31) 32270001 (office). *E-mail:* info@inhotim.org.br (office). *Website:* www.inhotim.org.br (office).

DE MENEZES, Fradique Bandeira Melo; São Tomé and Príncipe business executive, diplomatist and fmr head of state; b. 21 March 1942, São Tomé; m. (deceased); ed Instituto Superior de Psicologia Aplicada, Portugal and Univ. of Brussels, Belgium; fmr Minister for Foreign Trade; fmr Amb. to Belgium and Netherlands; Pres. of São Tomé and Príncipe 2001–11, also C-in-C of Armed Forces; fmr mem. Acção Democrática Independente Party, now Pres. Movimento Democrático Força da Mudança.

DE METZ, Robert; French business executive; *Chairman, Dexia SA;* ed Inst. of Political Studies, Paris, École Nat. d'Admin, Strasbourg; began career in Gen. Finance Inspectorate; joined Banque Indosuez 1983, held posts in Hong Kong and France before joining Demachy Worms & Cie; joined Paribas 1991, held numerous posts before being apptd to the Bd of Dirs, responsible from London for fixed income, forex and derivatives markets; Dir Cobepa 1993–99; Deputy Dir-Gen. Vivendi Group in charge of mergers-acquisitions and strategy 2002–07; Chair. Dexia SA 2012–; Exec. Dir and mem. Accounts Cttee La Fayette Management Ltd; mem. Supervisory Bd Canal+ France; Dir, Média-Participations (Paris-Brussels), L.A. Finances (Paris); CEO Bee2Bees SA (Brussels); mem. Exec. Cttee Fondation Demeure Historique pour l'avenir du patrimoine. *Address:* Dexia SA, Square de Meeûs 1, 1000 Brussels, Belgium (office). *Telephone:* (2) 213-57-00 (office). *Fax:* (2) 213-57-01 (office). *E-mail:* webmaster@dexia.com (office). *Website:* www.dexia.com (office).

DE MEURON, Pierre, DipArch; Swiss architect; b. 1950, Basel; ed Fed. Tech. Univ. (ETH), Zurich; Asst to Prof. Dolf Schnebli, ETH, Zurich 1977; f. architectural practice Herzog & De Meuron (with Jacques Herzog q.v.) 1978; Prof. of Architecture and Design, ETH 1999–; Visiting Prof., Harvard Univ., Cambridge, Mass. 1989, Tulane Univ., New Orleans 1991; (all jtly with Jacques Herzog) Architecture Prize, Berlin Acad. of Arts 1987, Andrea Palladio Int. Prize for Architecture, Vicenza, Italy 1988, Pritzker Architecture Prize 2001, Praemium Imperiale 2007. *Principal works include:* Blue House, Oberwil 1979–80, Photostudio Frei, Weil am Rhein 1981–82, Sperrholz Haus, Bottmingen 1984–85, Apartment Bldg, Hebelstr. 11, Basel 1984–88, Wohn- und Geschäftshaus Schwitter, Basel 1985–98, Goetz Art Gallery, Munich 1989–92, Wohn- und Geschäftshaus Schützenmattstr., Basel 1992–93, Dominus Winery, Napa Valley, Yountville, Calif. 1995–97, Tate Gallery Extension (Tate Modern), Bankside, London (RIBA Gold Medal 2007) 1995–99, Cultural Centre and Theatre, Zurich 1996, Ricola Marketing Bldg, Laufen 1998, Laban Centre for Contemporary Dance (Stirling Prize) 2003, M. H. de Young Memorial Museum, San Francisco 2005, Walker Art Center expansion, Minneapolis, Minnesota 2005, Beijing Nat. Stadium, China ('The Bird's Nest', Lubetkin Prize 2009) 2008, Pérez Art Museum Miami 2013, Messe Basel 2014, Blavatnik School of Govt, Univ. of Oxford, UK 2015, Tate Modern Switch House, London 2016, Elbe Philharmonic Hall, Hamburg 2017. *Works in progress include:* Prada Headquarters, New York, São Paulo Companhia de Dança Brazil, Kolkata Museum of Modern Art, India, National Library of Israel, as well as projects in UK, France, Germany, Italy, Spain and Japan. *Address:* Herzog & De Meuron Architekten, Rheinschanze 6, Basel, 4056, Switzerland (office). *Telephone:* (61) 3855758 (office). *Fax:* (61) 3855757 (office). *E-mail:* info@herzogdemeuron.com (office).

DE MEY, Jozef; Belgian actuary and insurance industry executive; *Chairman, Ageas;* b. 1943; ed Univs of Gent and Louvain; began career at Insurance Control Authorities, Ministry of Econ. Affairs 1967; worked at Kredietbank Belgium 1969–71; joined John Hancock (financial services provider) 1971, held various positions –1990; joined Fortis 1990, served as Gen. Man. Fortis International, CEO Fortis AG, apptd mem. Exec. Cttee 2000, Chief Investment Officer within Exec. Cttee 2007, continued to hold several non-exec. bd memberships in Fortis operating cos, Chair. (non-exec.) Fortis (renamed Ageas April 2010) 2009–; Chair. Bd of Dirs Ageas, AG Insurance, Vice-Chair. Muang Thai Fortis Holding (Thailand), Muang Thai Life Insurance Co., De Eik NV, Credimo NV, Credimo Holding NV, Zinner NV, Festival van Vlaanderen Gent. *Address:* Ageas SA/NV, rue du Marquis 1, 1000 Brussels, Belgium (office). *Telephone:* (2) 557-57-11 (office). *Fax:* (2) 557-57-51 (office). *E-mail:* info@ageas.com (office). *Website:* www.ageas.com (office).

DE MEZA, Mike Eric; Aruban business executive and politician; *Minister of Tourism, Transport, Energy and Environment;* b. 13 May 1963, Curaçao; m.; three c.; owner of an eng co.; mem. Arubaanse Volkspartij (AVP—Aruba People's Party); currently mem. Staten (Parl.); Minister of Finance, Transportation and Utilities 2009–14, of Econ. Affairs, Communications, Energy and the Environment 2014, currently Minister of Tourism, Transport, Energy and Environment. *Address:* Ministry of Tourism, Transport, Energy and Environment, L. G. Smith Boulevard 76, Oranjestad, Aruba (office). *Telephone:* 5284986 (office). *Fax:* 5827556 (office). *Website:* www.mikedemeza.com.

DE MICHELIS, Gianni; Italian chemist, academic and politician; b. 26 Nov. 1940, Venice; Prof. of Chem., Univ. of Padua; Lecturer in Chem., Univ. of Venice; Nat. Chair. Unione Goliardica Italiana 1962–64; Councillor, Venice 1964–76; mem. Cen. Cttee Italian Socialist Party (PSI) 1969–76, mem. Nat. Exec. 1976–; mem. Parl. for Venice 1976–; fmr Minister for State-owned Industries; Minister of Labour and Social Security 1986–87; Deputy Prime Minister 1988–89; Minister of Foreign Affairs 1989–92; Deputy Leader PSI 1992; charged with fraud May 1995; sentenced to two years' imprisonment for corruption; Founder and Sec. Partito Socialista 1996, merged to become Nuovo Partito Socialista Italiano 2001, Sec. 2001–07; mem. new Partito Socialista Italiano; mem. European Parl. 2004–09; Chair. Inst. for Relations between Italy and Africa, Latin America and the Middle East and Far East (IPALMO) 2002–; joined party of Stefania Craxi called Riformisti Italiani 2011; Hon. Pres. Aspen Inst. 2015. *Publications:* several books, including Dialogo a Nordest. Sul futuro dell'Italia tra Europa e Mediterraneo 2010. *Address:* c/o Riformisti Italiani, Via Montevideo 2/A, 00198 Rome, Italy. *E-mail:* info@riformistitaliani.it. *Website:* www.riformistitaliani.it.

DE MIRANDA, João Bernardo; Angolan politician; b. 18 July 1952, Bengo; m.; Dir of Information, Rádio Nacional de Angola 1977–80; Ed.-in-Chief Jornal de Angola newspaper 1980–84; Sec., Movimento Popular de Libertação de Angola (MPLA) Ideological Area (Prov. of Luanda); Head of Political and Legal Affairs Div., MPLA Cen. Cttee 1985–89, Head of Information and Propaganda Dept 1989–91; Vice-Minister of Information 1991, of Foreign Relations 1991–99,

Minister of Foreign Affairs 1999–2008; African Union Envoy to Guinea-Bissau 2009. *Publications include:* Nambuangongo. *Address:* Movimento Popular de Libertação de Angola, Av. Ho Chi Minh 34, Luanda, Angola (office). *Fax:* 222322545 (office). *E-mail:* sede@mpla-angola.org (office). *Website:* www.mpla.ao (office).

DE MISTURA, Staffan Domingo; Italian/Swedish government official and fmr UN official; b. 25 Jan. 1947, Stockholm, Sweden; m.; two d.; ed Univ. La Sapienza, Rome; joined UN 1970, intern for UN WFP in Cyprus early 1970s, WFP project officer in Sudan 1971, led food aid and relief operations in Ethiopia, the Balkans and Rwanda, emergency relief officer in Chad 1973; Deputy Chef de Cabinet, FAO 1976–85; Dir WFP Operations in Sudan 1987; Dir of Fund-Raising and External Relations, UN Office of the Co-ordinator for Afghanistan 1988–91; Special Envoy of UN Sec.-Gen. to Albania 1990; UN Humanitarian Co-ordinator for Iraq March–Aug. 1997; Special Adviser to High Commr for Refugees on Kosovo April–June 1999; Dir UN Information Centre, Rome –2000; Personal Rep. of UN Sec.-Gen. in S Lebanon 2001–05; Deputy Special Rep. of UN Sec.-Gen. in Iraq 2005–06, Special Rep. 2007–09; Dir UN Systems Staff Coll., Turin, Italy 2006–07; Deputy Exec. Dir for External Relations, UN WFP, Rome, Italy 2009–10; Special Rep. of UN Sec.-Gen. and Head of UN Assistance Mission in Afghanistan (UNAMA) 2010–11; Under-Sec. of Foreign Affairs in Italy's technocratic cabinet headed by Mario Monti 2011–13; Special Envoy of the Prime Minister to resolve the case of two Italian Navy marines, held in India since Feb. 2012 following shooting and killing of two Indian fishermen 2013; UN and Arab League Special Envoy tasked with seeking a peaceful resolution of the conflict in Syria 2014–18. *Address:* c/o Office of the Secretary-General, United Nations, New York, NY 10017, USA.

DE MOLINA, Alvaro G., BA, MBA; Cuban/American business executive; *Chairman, Regional Management Corporation;* b. 13 July 1957, Cuba; ed Bergen Catholic High School, Oradell, NJ, Fairleigh Dickinson Univ., Rutgers Business School, Duke Univ. Advanced Man. Program; began career with PriceWaterhouse 1979; later served in lead financial role for emerging markets at J.P. Morgan; spent 17 years at Bank of America, served as Chief Financial Officer, also served as CEO Bank of America Securities, Pres. Global Corp. and Investment Banking, and Corp. Treas.; with Cerberus Capital Management June–Aug. 2007; COO GMAC Financial Services (renamed Ally Financial Inc. 2010) Aug. 2007–08, CEO 2008–09 (resgnd); Dir, Regional Management Corpn 2012– (Chair. 2014–), Walter Investment Management Corpn 2012–, Tenex Health, Inc. 2014–; mem. Bd, Duke Univ. Fuqua School of Business, Foundation for the Carolinas, Florida International Univ., Financial Services Volunteer Corps. *Address:* Regional Management Corpn, 509 West Butler Road, Greenville, SC 29607, USA (office). *E-mail:* info@regionalmanagement.com (office). *Website:* www.regionalmanagement.com (office).

DE MONTEBELLO, Comte Philippe, BA, MA; French art historian and museum director; *Fiske Kimball Professor in the History and Culture of Museums, Institute of Fine Arts, New York University;* b. 16 May 1936, Paris; m. Edith Bradford Myles 1961; ed Harvard Univ., Inst. of Fine Arts, New York Univ., USA; Curatorial Asst, later Asst Curator, Assoc. Curator, Dept of European Paintings, Metropolitan Museum of Art, New York 1963–69, Vice-Dir for Curatorial and Educational Affairs 1974–77, Acting Dir 1977–78, Dir 1978–99, Dir and CEO 1999–2008 (retd); first Fiske Kimball Prof. in the History and Culture of Museums, Institute of Fine Arts, New York Univ. 2009–, Special Advisor for the visual arts at NYU's Abu Dhabi Campus; first Scholar in Residence, Prado Museum, Madrid 2009–; Humanitas Visiting Prof. in the History of Art, Univ. of Cambridge, UK 2012; Chair. Bd of Overseers, Hispanic Soc. of America 2015–; Dir Museum of Fine Arts, Houston, Tex. 1969–74, Acquavella Galleries, New York 2017–; mem. Bd of Trustees, Musée d'Orsay 2015–; Gallatin Fellow, New York Univ. 1981; Kt Commdr, Pontifical Order of St Gregory the Great 1984; Commendatore, Order of Merit (Italy) 1988; Chevalier, Légion d'honneur 1991, Officier 2007; Orden de Isabel la Catolica (Spain) 1992; Officier, Ordre de Léopold (Belgium) 1994; Commdr, des Arts et des Lettres 2001; Order of the Rising Sun, Gold and Silver Star (Japan) 2007; Hon. LLD (Lafayette Coll.) 1979, (Dartmouth Coll.) 2004, Hon. DHumLitt (Bard Coll., New York) 1981, Hon. DFA (Iona Coll., New Rochelle) 1982, (Harvard) 2006, (New York) 2007; Award of Excellence, Int. Center, New York, Nat. Inst. of Social Sciences Gold Medal 1989, Spanish Inst. Gold Medal Award 1992, National Council of Jewish Women, Rebekah Kohut Award 1993, Distinguished Alumnus Award, New York Univ. 1998, Mayoral Proclamation 2002, Blerancourt Prize 2002, Celebration of twenty-five years as Dir of the Metropolitan Museum of Art, Nat. Endowment for the Arts, Nat. Medal of Arts 2003, Amigos del Museo del Prado Prize 2004, Conféd. Int. des Négociants en Oeuvres d'Art Prize 2005, Mayor's Arts Award 2007, Nat. Humanities Medal 2010, and other awards. *Publications:* Peter Paul Rubens (monograph) 1968, articles in the Metropolitan Museum of Art Bulletin and the Bulletin, Museum of Fine Arts, Houston on topics from the Renaissance to the contemporary, more than 200 entries in the McGraw Hill Dictionary of Art 1967, including those on Velasquez, Murillo and Goya; The High Cost of Quality Museum News August 1984, The Met and the New Millennium: A Chronicle of the Past and a Blueprint for the Future 1994, introductions to numerous exhibition catalogues published by the Metropolitan Museum of Art. *Leisure interests:* chess, tennis, music. *Address:* Institute of Fine Arts, 1 East 78th Street, Floor 1, New York, NY 10021, USA (office); 25 East 86th Street, 3E, New York, NY 10028, USA (home). *Telephone:* (212) 992-5840 (office); (212) 289-4475 (home). *Fax:* (212) 992-5807 (office). *E-mail:* philippe.demontebello@nyu.edu (office). *Website:* www.nyu.edu/gsas/dept/fineart/people/faculty/de-montebello.htm (office).

DE MONTFERRAND, Bernard de Faubournet, LLB; French diplomatist and arts foundation executive; *President, Platform, Regroupement des Fonds régionaux d'art contemporain;* b. 6 Aug. 1945, Caudéran, Gironde; m. Catherine de Tavernost; three c.; ed Faculty of Law, Paris, Inst. of Political Studies, Paris, Ecole Nat. d'Admin; Sec. of Foreign Affairs, Econ. and Financial Affairs Div., Ministry of Foreign Affairs 1974–79; Lecturer, then Dir of Studies, Inst. of Political Studies, Paris 1975–79; Counsellor for Econ., Financial and Admin. Affairs, French Mil. Govt in Berlin 1979–82; Deputy Dir and Jt Head of Personnel and Gen. Admin, Ministry of Foreign Affairs 1982–85; Consul-Gen. in San Francisco, USA 1985–86; Dir of Cabinet for Minister of Co-operation Michel Aurillac 1986–88; Amb. to Singapore 1989–93, to the Netherlands 1995–2000, to India 2000–02, to Japan 2002–06, to Germany 2007–11; Diplomatic Adviser to Prime Minister Edouard Balladur 1993–95; Founder and Pres. Centre int. de recherches préhistoriques de la vallée de la Couze; Pres. Platform, Regroupement des Fonds régionaux d'art contemporain 2007–; Commdr, Légion d'honneur; Chevalier, Ordre nat. du Mérite. *Publications:* La France et l'Etranger 1987, La vertu des Nations 1993, Défendre l'Europe: la tentation suisse 1999, Diplomatie, des volontés françaises 2006, France-Allemagne: l'heure de vérité, Le choc des modèles 2011. *Address:* Platform, Regroupement des Fonds régionaux d'art contemporain, 32 rue Yves Toudic, 75010 Paris, France (office). *Telephone:* 1-42-39-48-52 (office). *E-mail:* info@frac-platform.com (office). *Website:* www.frac-platform.com (office).

DE MORNAY, Rebecca; American actress; b. (Rebecca Jane Pearch), 29 Aug. 1959, Los Angeles, Calif.; d. of Wally George and Julie Eagar; m. Bruce Wagner 1989 (divorced 1991); ed in Austria and at Lee Strasberg Inst. in Los Angeles; apprenticed at Zoetrope Studios. *Theatre includes:* Born Yesterday 1988, Marat/Sade 1990. *Films include:* One from the Heart 1982, Risky Business 1983, Testament 1983, The Slugger's Wife 1985, Runaway Train 1985, The Trip to Bountiful 1985, Beauty and The Beast 1987, And God Created Woman 1988, Feds 1988, Dealers 1989, Backdraft 1991, The Hand that Rocks the Cradle (Best Actress, Cognac Crime Film Festival 1992), Guilty as Sin 1993, The Three Musketeers 1993, Never Talk to Strangers 1995, The Winner 1996, Thick as Thieves 1998, Table for One 1998, The Right Temptation 2000, Identity 2003, Raise Your Voice 2004, Lords of Dogtown 2005, Wedding Crashers 2005, Music Within 2007, American Venus 2007, Flipped 2010, Mother's Day 2010, Collar 2011, Apartment 1303 3D 2012, Collar 2015, I Am Wrath 2016, Periphery 2018. *Television appearances include:* The Murders in the Rue Morgue 1986, By Dawn's Early Light 1990, An Inconvenient Woman 1992, Blind Side 1993, Getting Out 1994, The Shining 1996, The Con 1997, Night Ride Home 1999, The Conversion (Dir) 1996, ER 1999, Night Ride Home 1999, Range of Motion 2000, A Girl Thing 2001, Salem Witch Trials 2002, Law and Order 2006, John from Cincinnati (series) 2007–09, Hatfields & McCoys (film) 2013, Hatfields & McCoys (film) 2013, Jessica Jones (series) 2015–18. *Address:* c/o The Gersh Agency, 232 North Canon Drive, Beverly Hills, CA 90210, USA. *Telephone:* (310) 274-6611.

DE NARVÁEZ, Francisco; Argentine (b. Colombian) business executive and politician; b. 22 Sept. 1953, Bogotá, Colombia; s. of Juan de Narváez and Doris Steur; m. 1st; three c.; m. 2nd Agustina Ayllón (fmr model); three c.; ed attended mil. acad. in Toronto, Canada; family moved to Buenos Aires, Argentina 1959; entered maternal grandfather's supermarket chain, Casa Tía 1970, took over man. of Casa Tía chain, along with brother Carlos 1980, attained Argentine citizenship 1983, apptd sole Man. Dir 1989, sold Casa Tía chain for US $638 million 1999; owner or main shareholder of: La Rural SA (exhbn and conf. centre in Buenos Aires), broadcaster América TV, Buenos Aires financial newspaper Ámbito Financiero, radio station La Red; Co-founder Fundación Unidos del Sud (political think-tank) 2001; mem. Partido Justicialista (PJ, Peronists) 2002–; Nat. Deputy for Buenos Aires Prov. (first foreigner to be elected to Congress in Argentina) 2005–, mem. 'El General' (anti-Kirchnerista Peronist group of PJ deputies and senators) 2006–; unsuccessful cand. for Gov. of Buenos Aires 2007; defeated fmr Pres. Nestór Kirchner in legis. mid-term elections in prov. of Buenos Aires June 2009. *Address:* Cámara de Diputados, Congreso de la Nación, Av. Rivadavia 1864, C. P. C1033AAU, Ciudad Autónoma de Buenos Aires, Argentina (office). *Telephone:* (11) 6310-7100 (ext. 3117) (office); (800) 4444336. *Fax:* (11) 6313-6048 (office). *E-mail:* fdenarvaez@diputados.gov.ar (office); info@franciscodenarvaez.com. *Website:* www.diputados.gov.ar (office); www.franciscodenarvaez.com.

DE NIRO, Robert; American actor; b. 1943, New York; s. of Robert De Niro and Virginia Admiral; m. 1st Diahnne Abbott 1976; one s. one d.; two s. by Toukie Smith; m. 2nd Grace Hightower 1997; one s.; Founder and Pres. TriBeCa Productions 1989–; co-cr. We Will Rock You (musical) 2002; Co-owner Nobu restaurants; Pres. Jury, Cannes Film Festival 2011; Commdr, Ordre des Arts et des Lettres; Chevalier, Légion d'honneur; Lifetime Achievement Award, Gotham Awards 2001, American Film Inst. Lifetime Achievement Award 2003, Kennedy Center Honor 2009, Cecil B DeMille Award for Lifetime Achievement, Hollywood Foreign Press Asscn 2011, Presidential Medal of Freedom 2016, Hon. Heart of Sarajevo–Lifetime Achievement Award, Sarajevo Film Festival 2017. *Films include:* The Wedding Party 1969, Jennifer On My Mind 1971, Bloody Mama, Born to Win 1971, The Gang That Couldn't Shoot Straight 1971, Bang the Drum Slowly 1973, Mean Streets 1973, The Godfather, Part II 1974 (Acad. Award for Best Supporting Actor), The Last Tycoon, Taxi Driver 1976, 1900 1976, New York, New York 1977, The Deer Hunter 1978, Raging Bull (Acad. Award Best Actor) 1980, True Confessions 1981, The King of Comedy 1982, Once Upon a Time in America 1984, Falling in Love 1984, Brazil 1984, The Mission 1985, Angel Heart 1986, The Untouchables 1987, Letters Home from Vietnam, Midnight Run 1988, We're No Angels 1989, Stanley and Iris 1989, Goodfellas 1989, Jacknife 1989, Awakenings 1990, Fear No Evil 1990, Backdraft 1990, Cape Fear 1990, Guilty of Suspicion 1991, Mistress 1992, Night and the City 1992, Mad Dog and Glory 1992, This Boy's Life 1993, Mary Shelley's Frankenstein 1993, A Bronx Tale (also dir, co-producer) 1993, Sleepers 1996, The Fan 1996, Marvin's Room 1996, Great Expectations 1997, Jackie Brown 1998, Ronin 1998, Analyze This 1999, Flawless 1999 (also producer), The Adventures of Rocky and Bullwinkle (also producer) 1999, Meet the Parents (also producer) 2000, Men of Honor 2000, 15 Minutes 2001, The Score 2001, Showtime 2002, City By the Sea 2002, Analyze That 2002, Godsend 2004, Shark Tale (voice) 2004, Meet the Fockers (also producer) 2004, The Bridge of San Luis Rey 2004, Hide and Seek 2005, Arthur and the Invisibles (voice) 2006, The Good Shepherd (also dir) 2006, Stardust 2007, What Just Happened? (also producer) 2008, Righteous Kill 2008, Everybody's Fine 2009, Machete 2010, Stone 2010, Little Fockers (also producer) 2010, Manuale d'amore 3 2011, The Ages of Love 2011, Limitless 2011, Killer Elite 2011, New Year's Eve 2011, Red Lights 2012, Being Flynn 2012, Crossfire 2012, Silver Linings Playbook 2012, The Big Wedding 2013, Killing Season 2013, The Family 2013, Last Vegas 2013, Grudge Match 2013, The Carrier 2014, The Intern 2015, Heist 2015, Joy 2015, Dirty Grandpa 2016, Hands of Stone 2016. *Television:* exec. producer: NYC 22 (series) 2012. *Address:* Tribeca Productions, 375 Greenwich Street, 8th Floor, New York, NY 10013 (office). *Telephone:* (212) 941-2000 (office). *Fax:* (212) 941-2012 (office). *E-mail:* contactus@tribecafilm.com (office). *Website:* www.tribecafilm.com (office).

DE NOINVILLE, Guillaume, LLM, MEcons, MBA; French business executive; *President-Director General, Electrolux France SAS;* b. 8 May 1960, Paris; s. of Christian Durey de Noinville and Béatrice Gallimard; m. Claire de Laguiche; three s. one d.; ed Inst. d'Etudes Politiques, Paris; Finance and Control Dept, Bull Group, Paris 1984–86; Treas. Electrolux France, Senlis 1986–92, Man. Dir Electrolux Financement (leasing co.), Senlis 1992–96, Chief Finance Officer Electrolux France 1994–2002, Electrolux Belgium 1998–2002, Pres.-Dir-Gen. Electrolux France SA 2001–, Chief Admin. Officer, Western Europe, Electrolux Group 2003–12; Head of Holding EMEA, Electrolux Group 2012–. *Address:* Electrolux France SAS, BP 20139, 43 avenue Félix Louat, 60307 Senlis Cedex (office); 29 avenue de la Grande Armée, 75116 Paris, France (home). *Telephone:* (3) 44-62-26-39 (office). *Fax:* (3) 44-62-21-89 (office). *E-mail:* guillaume.de-noinville@electrolux.com (office). *Website:* www.electrolux.com (office).

DE OLIVEIRA, Constantino, Jr; Brazilian business executive; *Chairman, Gol Linhas Aéreas Inteligentes SA;* b. 1969, Patrocínio, Minas Gerais; s. of Nenê Constantino de Oliveira; ed Univ. of the Fed. Dist, Brasília; mem. Exec. Bd Grupo Áurea 1994–2000; mem. Admin. Council, GOL 2001–, CEO 2001–12, Pres. and CEO Gol Linhas Aéreas Inteligentes SA (airline) 2004–12, Chair. 2012–; Admin. Emer., Regional Admin. Council of São Paulo 2006–; Exec. of Value, Valor Econômico 2001, 2002, Exec. Leader, Gazeta Mercantil 2003, Federico Bloch Prize, Int. Asscn of Latin-American Air Transport 2005, Business Leader of the Year, Latin Trade Awards 2006. *Address:* Gol Linhas Aéreas Inteligentes SA, Rua Gomes de Carvalho, 1629, Vila Olímpia, 05457-006 São Paulo, Brazil (office). *Telephone:* (11) 3169-6800 (office). *Fax:* (11) 3169-6570 (office). *Website:* www.voegol.com.br (office).

DE OLIVEIRA CAMPOS, Paulo Cesar; Brazilian diplomatist; *Ambassador to France;* b. 25 July 1952, Rio de Janeiro; son of Jayme de Almeida Campos and Laurentina de Oliveira Campos; m. Adriana Rafael Campos; one s. one d.; ed Univ. of Brasilia, Instituto Rio Branco; joined diplomatic service as Third Sec. 1976, Second Sec. 1979, First Sec. 1983, Adviser 1989, Minister Second Class 1996, Minister First Class 2003, with Int. Orgs Div. 1977–80, assigned to Embassy in Washington, DC 1980–83, Cultural Service and Press Relations Dept and Congress, Embassy in Tokyo 1983–87, Deputy Dir Commodities Div. 1987–88, Deputy Dir Visits Div. 1988–89, Dir 1989–90, 1995–96, Head of Trade Promotion Dept, Embassy in Bonn 1991–93, Head of Trade Promotion Dept, Embassy in Tokyo 1993–95, Deputy Dir of Protocol, Head of Political Dept and Head of Consular Section 1996–99, Consul Gen. in London 1999–2002, Dir of Protocol of the Presidency of the Repub. 2003–09, Amb. to Spain 2009–15, to France 2015–; Officer, Order of Rio Branco 1986, Commdr 1994, Grand Officer 1998, Grand Cross 2003; Commdr, Order of Naval Merit 1998, Grand Officer 2004; Kt, Order of Mil. Merit 1988, Grand Officer 2010, Officer, Order of Aeronautical Merit 1989, Grand Officer 2004; Grand Officer, Order of Merit of Defence 2006; Grand Officer, Order of Merit of Brasilia 1999; decorations from other countries: Grand Cross, Order of Civil Merit (Spain) 2003, Grand Cross, Order of Prince Henry (Portugal) 2003, Grand Cross, Order of the Sun (Peru) 2004, Grand Cross, May Order of Merit (Argentina) 2006, Grand Cross, Order of Merit of the Italian Repub. (Italy) 2008, Grand Cross, Order of Isabella the Catholic (Spain) 2015; Medal 'Mérito Tamandaré' 1996, Medal 'Mérito Santos-Dumont' 1997, Peacemaker Medal 2004, Commemorative Medal for 20 years of the Superior Court of Justice 2009. *Address:* Embassy of Brazil, 34 cours Albert 1er, 75008 Paris, France (office). *Telephone:* 1-45-61-63-00 (office). *Fax:* 1-42-89-03-45 (office). *E-mail:* ambassade@bresil.org (office). *Website:* www.bresil.org (office).

DE OLIVEIRA MACIEL, Marco Antônio, LLB, MA; Brazilian lawyer, politician and professor of law; b. 21 July 1940, Recife; s. of José do Rego Maciel and Carmen Sylvia Cavalcanti de Oliveira Maciel; m. Anna Maria Ferreira; one s. two d.; ed Catholic Univ. of Pernambuco, Pernambuco Univ.; adviser to Pernambuco State Govt 1964–66; Prof. of Public and Int. Law, Catholic Univ. of Pernambuco 1966–; State Deputy, Pernambuco Legis. Ass., Govt Leader 1967–71; Regional Sec. ARENA Party 1969–70, Second Nat. Sec. 1972, First Sec. 1974–75; Fed. Deputy 1971–79, Pres. Chamber of Deputies 1977–79; Gov. Pernambuco State 1979–82; Fed. Senator for PDS Party 1982; Minister for Educ. 1985–86; Minister Chief of Staff of Pres. 1986; mem. Partido da Frente Liberal (PFL) 1984–2007, Pres. Provisional Nat. Comm. 1984–85, Nat. Pres. 1987, mem. Nat. Council; Fed. Senator 1983–94, 2003–11, Minority Leader 1990, Govt Leader 1991–92; Vice-Pres. of Brazil 1995–2003; mem. Democratas (Democrats) 2007–; mem. Pernambuco Section Brazilian Bar Asscn, Brazilian Acad. of Political and Moral Sciences 1993–, Argentinian Law Asscn, Academia Brasileira de Letras 2003–; numerous honours including Grand Cross, Order of Rio Branco, Brasilia Order of Merit, Légion d'honneur (France), Grand Cross, Order of Infante Dom Henrique (Portugal), Grand Cross, Order of May (Argentina) 1979, Cross of Merit (FRG), Ordre nat. du Mérite (France), City of Recife Medal of Merit. *Publications:* numerous publs on politics and educ. *Address:* Democratas, Senado Federal (Federal Senate), Anexo I, 5° andar, salas 1 a 6, Palácio do Congresso Nacional, Praça dos Três Poderes, 70165-900 Brasília, DF, Brazil (office). *Telephone:* (61) 3311-4305 (office). *Fax:* (61) 3224-1912 (office). *E-mail:* democratas25@democratas.org.br (office). *Website:* www.dem.org.br (office).

DE PADT, Guido, LenD; Belgian politician; *Mayor of Geraardsbergen;* b. 23 May 1954, Geraardsbergen; mem. Vlaamse Liberalen en Demokraten (VLD); Prov. Counsellor for E Flanders 1982–2003; Deputy Mayor of Geraardsbergen 1982–94, 2007–08, Mayor of Geraardsbergen 2001–06, 2011–; Deputy for E Flanders 1994–2000; mem. Chamber of Reps 2003–; Minister of the Interior 2008–09, Govt Commr 2009–10; Senator, Open Flemish Liberals and Democrats 2010–14; Chair. Centre-Publique-d'Aide-Sociale for Geraardsbergen 2007–08. *Address:* Karmelietenstraat 51, 9500 Geraardsbergen, Belgium (office). *Telephone:* (5) 441-55-62 (office). *E-mail:* guido.de.padt@pandora.be (office). *Website:* www.guidodepadt.be (office).

DE PALMA, Brian, BA, MA; American film director; b. 11 Sept. 1940, Newark, New Jersey; s. of Anthony Federico De Palma and Vivienne De Palma (née Muti); m. 1st Nancy Allen 1979 (divorced 1983); m. 2nd Gale Ann Hurd 1991 (divorced 1993); one d.; m. 3rd Darnell Gregorio-De Palma 1997 (divorced) one c.; ed Sarah Lawrence Coll., Bronxville and Columbia Univ. *Films include:* (short films) Icarus 1960, 660124: The Story of an IBM Card 1961, Wotan's Wake 1962; (feature length) The Wedding Party 1964, The Responsive Eye (documentary) 1966, (films) Murder à la Mode 1967, Greetings 1968, Dionysus in '69 (co-Dir) 1969, Hi Mom! 1970, Get to Know Your Rabbit 1970, Sisters 1972, Phantom of the Paradise 1974, Obsession 1975, Carrie 1976, The Fury 1978, Home Movies 1979, Dressed to Kill 1980, Blow Out 1981, Scarface 1983, Body Double 1984, Wise Guys 1985, The Untouchables 1987, Casualties of War 1989, Bonfire of the Vanities 1990, Raising Cain 1992, Carlito's Way 1993, Mission Impossible 1996, Snake Eyes 1998, Mission to Mars 2000, Femme Fatale 2002, The Black Dahlia 2006, Redacted (Silver Lion, Venice Film Festival 2007) 2007, Passion 2012, Domino 2019. *Address:* c/o Jeff Berg, International Creative Management, 10250 Constellation Blvd, Los Angeles, CA 90067, USA (office).

DE PERETTI, Jean-Jacques; French politician; *Conseiller, Conseil d'Etat;* b. 21 Sept. 1946, Clermont-Ferrand; three c.; ed Inst. des Hautes Etudes Internationales; Asst Lecturer, St-Maur Faculty of Law and Univs of Orléans and Paris I 1969–84; Chargé de Mission, Cabinet of Pierre Messmer 1972; Dir de Cabinet to Pres. of Paris Region 1974; Chargé de Mission to André Bord, Sec.-Gen. of Union des Démocrates pour la République (UDR) 1976; Chargé de Mission, Cabinet of Antoine Rufenacht, Sec. of State to Prime Minister; Sec. of State to Minister for Industry, Trade and Craft Trades; Man. Exec. IBM –1986; Adviser to Prime Minister Jacques Chirac 1986; Mayor of Sarlat 1989–; fmr mem. Regional Council and Deputy to Nat. Ass. for Dordogne Dept's 4th constituency; Departmental Councillor for Dordogne 1992–; Nat. Sec. Rassemblement pour la République (RPR) 1990–93, Deputy Sec.-Gen. 1994–95; Minister for Overseas France May–Nov. 1995; Minister-Del. to Prime Minister with responsibility for Overseas France 1995–97; mem. Regional Council of Aquitaine; Conseiller, Conseil d'Etat; mem. Hudson Inst. 1969–; Legion d'Honneur. *Publications:* L'envol de la France dan les anées 80 (with Herman Khan and the Hudson Inst.) 1979, Gagner les Municipales 1988. *Address:* Hôtel de ville, 24200 Sarlat-la-Canéda, France (home). *Telephone:* (5) 53-31-53-30 (office); 1-47-53-80-53 (office). *Fax:* (5) 53-31-08-04 (office); 1-47-53-80-53 (office). *E-mail:* jjpc@wanadoo.fr (office). *Website:* jean-jacques.de-peretti@conseil-etat.fr (office).

DE PURY, Baron Simon; Swiss auctioneer, curator and art dealer; *Partner, de Pury de Pury;* b. 1951, Basel; m. 1st (divorced); four c.; m. 2nd Michaela Neumeister; one c.; ed Acad. of Fine Arts, Tokyo, Japan; worked at Kornfeld & Klipstein auctioneers, Bern and subsequently studied at Sotheby's Inst. before joining Sotheby's, working in London, Geneva and Monte Carlo; Curator, Thyssen-Bornemisza collection, Lugano 1979–86; returned to Sotheby's first as Chair. Sotheby's Switzerland and then as Chair. of Sotheby's Europe and the co's Prin. Auctioneer 1986; co-f. (with Daniella Luxembourg) de Pury & Luxembourg Art (art advisory co.), Geneva 1997, merged with Phillips Auctioneers to become Phillips, de Pury and Luxembourg 2001, Chair. and majority shareholder, Phillips de Pury & Company 2004–12; Co-founder (with wife) and Partner, de Pury de Pury 2013–, opened office in Zurich, Switzerland 2015. *Telephone:* (20) 7409-3085 (office). *E-mail:* simon@depurydepury.com (office). *Website:* depurydepury.com (office).

DE QUEIROZ DUARTE, Sergio, BA, BL; Brazilian fmr diplomatist and fmr UN official; b. Rio de Janeiro; m.; two c.; ed Fed. Fluminense Univ., Rio de Janeiro, Brazilian School of Public Admin (Getúlio Vargas Foundation), Rio de Janeiro, Brazilian Diplomatic Acad. (Instituto Rio Branco), Rio de Janeiro; joined Foreign Service, apptd Third Sec. 1957, diplomatic appointments included Embassies in Rome 1961–63, in Buenos Aires 1963–66, in Washington, DC 1970–74, Perm. Mission to UN, Geneva 1966–68 (mem. Brazilian del. to 18-nation Disarmament Cttee); Alt. Rep., Office of Special Rep. of Brazil for Disarmament Affairs, Geneva 1979–86, Amb. to Nicaragua 1986–91, to Canada 1993–96, to People's Repub. of China 1996–99, to Austria 1999–2002 (also accred to Slovakia, Slovenia and Croatia and as Rep. to Int. Orgs, Vienna); Gov. for Brazil at Bd of Govs, IAEA, Chair. Bd Govs 1999–2000; Head of Personnel, Ministry of Foreign Affairs 1975–79, apptd Sec.-Gen. for Budget Control and Insp.-Gen. 1991, Exec. Sec.-Gen. 1991–92, Under-Sec.-Gen. for Foreign Service 1992–93, Amb.-at-Large for Disarmament and Non-Proliferation 2003–04; UN Under-Sec.-Gen. and High Rep. for Disarmament Affairs 2007–12; elected Pres. Review Conf. of Parties to Treaty Prohibiting the Emplacement of Nuclear Weapons on the Seabed and the Subsoil Thereof, Geneva 1988, VII Review Conf. of Parties to Treaty on the Non-proliferation of Nuclear Weapons, New York 2005.

DE QUERCIZE, Stanislas; French business executive; extensive career within Richemont Group since 1989, worked with Montblanc, Alfred Dunhill, Cartier (Pres. Cartier North America Inc.), Pres. and CEO Van Cleef & Arpels SA 2005–12, CEO Cartier SA 2012–15, mem. Man. Cttee Compagnie Financière Richemont SA.

DE RAAD, Ad, MSc; Dutch UN official; b. 7 Dec. 1952; ed Delft Univ. of Tech.; sr positions with UNDP Country Offices in Bangladesh 1980–84, Tanzania 1984–87, various posts, Bureau for Finance and Admin, UNDP, New York 1987–93, Dir of Budget, UNDP, New York 1993–98; Deputy Exec. Coordinator, UN Volunteers (UNV) programme, Bonn, Germany 1998–2003, Acting Exec. Coordinator 2003–04, Exec. Coordinator 2004–08. *Address:* Le Pla, Ariege, Frankrijk 09460, France.

DE RIBEROLLES, Dominique, BEcons, MBA; Spanish business executive; ed Ecole Polytechnique, Paris, France, Univ. of Washington, USA; began career as Admin. and Financial Man. of Lubricants Area, ELF Group, in charge of coordinating relations in Madrid between ELF and Compañía Española de Petróleos SA (CEPSA) 1990–96, Vice-Pres. CEPSA's Corp. Planning and Control Div. 1996–98, Sr Vice-Pres. 1998–2003, Exec. Dir 2003–06, CEO CEPSA 2006–11; mem. Bd of Dirs Compania Logistica De Hidrocarburos CLH SA 2007–11, Tecnocom Telecomunicaciones y Energia SA 2011–.

DE RIVAZ, Vincent; French business executive; ed École Nationale Supérieure d'Hydraulique, Grenoble; joined Electricité de France (EDF) SA's Centre for External Eng within Int. Affairs Dept 1977, Exec. Vice-Pres. of Far East 1985–92, Exec. Vice-Pres., Nat. Hydraulic Equipment Centre, Equipment Div. 1992–95, Asst Dir, Int. Div. 1995–96, Project Man. 1996–99, Operating Vice-Pres., Finance Div. 1999–2000, Exec. Vice-Pres. of Finance Strategy and Operations 2000–02, CEO, Exec. Dir and Chair. Exec. Cttee, EDF Energy (UK) Ltd 2002–17, Dir, EDF Energy Networks (EPN) PLC and EDF Energy Networks (LPN) PLC; Dir, British Energy Group PLC 2009–, South Eastern Power Networks PLC; Hon. FIMechE 2009; Chevalier, Légion d'honneur; Hon. CBE 2012; 71st Melchett Award, The Energy Inst. 2006.

DE ROBIEN, Gilles, LenD; French politician; b. 10 April 1941, Cocquerel, Somme; began career as gen. insurance agent, Amiens 1965; Deputy in Nat. Ass. for 2nd Somme constituency 1986–, mem. Finance Cttee, Cttee of Enquiry into Causes, Consequences and Prevention of Floods, Vice Pres. Nat. Ass. 1993–98, architect of Robien Act on reform of working hours 1996; Mayor of Amiens 1989–2008; Minister for Capital Works, Transportation, Housing, Tourism and Maritime Affairs 2002, for Nat. Educ., Higher Educ. and Research 2005–07; Chair. Communauté d'Agglomération Amiens-Métropole; mem. Picardie Regional Council 1992; mem. Exec. Bureau and Steering Cttee, Republican Party 1990–; mem. Nat. Council and Political Cttee, Union pour la démocratie française (UDF) 1991, Chair. UDF Group in Nat. Ass. 1995–97, mem. Political Bureau and Vice-Chair. UDF 1998; mem. Bd of Dirs and French Govt Delegate, ILO 2007– (Chair. 2012–13); Hon. KBE; Chevalier, Légion d'honneur, Commandeur, Order of Palmes académiques, Grand Officer, Ordem Nacional do Cruzeiro do Sul, Grand Cross, Orden al Mérito de Chile, Grand Cross, Orden del Mérito Civil, Knight Grand Cross, Ordine al merito (Italy), Grand Officer, Order of Ouissam Alaouite. *Address:* International Labour Organization, 4 route des Morillons, 1211 Geneva 22, Switzerland. *Website:* www.ilo.org.

DE ROMANET DE BEAUNE, Augustin; French business executive; *Chairman and CEO, Aéroports de Paris SA;* b. 2 April 1961, Boulogne-Billancourt; s. of Luc de Romanet de Beaune and Anne-Marie de Romanet de Beaune (née Lafont); m. Florence Burin des Roziers 1986; three c.; ed Inst. of Political Studies, Paris, Ecole Nationale d'Administration; began career in Budget Dept, Ministry of the Economy and Finance; Financial Attaché, Perm. Mission of France to EC, Brussels 1990–93, Head, Budget Office 1993–95; Chief of Staff to State Sec. for Budget and Special Adviser to Minister of Economy, Finance and Planning 1995–2002; Chief of Staff to the Minister responsible for Budget and Budget Reform and Deputy Chief of Staff to Minister of Economy, Finance and Industry 2002–04; Chief of Staff to the Minister of Employment, Work and Social Cohesion and Deputy Chief of Staff to Prime Minister 2004–05; Deputy Sec.-Gen. to the Presidency 2005; Deputy Dir for Finance and Strategy and mem. Exec. Cttee, Crédit Agricole SA 2006; Chair. and CEO Caisse des Dépôts 2007–12; Chair. and CEO Aéroports de Paris SA 2012–, Vice-Pres. TAV Airports Holding (after acquisition by Aéroports de Paris) 2013–; Vice-Chair. InfraMed; mem. Bd of Dirs Oddo et Compagnie 1999–, Man. Pnr, Oddo Pinatton Corp. 2000–; mem. Bd of Dirs Dexia SA 2007, Soc. Nat. Immobilière (SNI), Accor, Veolia, Icade, CNP Assurance 2007–; Chair. Bd, Fonds stratégique d'investissement 2008; Prof., Inst. of Political Studies, Paris 1986–90, Ecole Nationale d'Administration 1990–93; Chevalier, Légion d'honneur; Nat. Defence Medal. *Address:* Aéroports de Paris SA, 291 Boulevard Raspail, 75014 Paris, France (office). *Telephone:* 1-70-36-39-50 (office). *Website:* www.aeroportsdeparis.fr (office).

DE ROSNAY, Joël, DèsSc; French biologist and consultant; b. 12 June 1937, Mauritius; s. of Gaëtan de Rosnay and Natacha Koltchine; m. Stella Jebb 1959; one s. two d.; ed MIT; fmr Research Assoc., MIT; fmr Scientific Attaché, Embassy in Washington, DC; Scientific Dir European Enterprises Devt Co. (venture capital group) 1971–75; Dir of Applied Research, Inst. Pasteur 1975–84; Dir of Devt and Int. Relations, Cité des sciences et de l'industrie de La Villette 1988–97, Dir of Strategy 1997–99, Dir of Evaluation 1999–2002, Special Advisor to the Pres. 2002–18; CEO Biotics International (consulting firm) 2004–18; columnist, Europe 1 1987–95; Officier, Légion d'honneur, Officier, Ordre nat. du Mérite; Prix de l'Information Scientifique, Acad. des Sciences 1990. *Publications:* Les origines de la vie 1965, Le macroscope 1975, La révolution biologique 1982, Branchez-vous 1985, L'avenir du vivant 1988, L'avenir en direct 1989, Les rendez-vous du futur 1991, L'homme symbiotique 1995, La plus belle histoire du monde (contrib.) 1996. *Leisure interests:* skiing, surfing. *Telephone:* (1) 45-50-38-03 (office). *Fax:* (1) 78-76-82-61 (office). *E-mail:* contact@biotics.fr (office). *Website:* www.biotics.fr; www.carrefour-du-futur.com.

DE ROUSIERS, Gen. Patrick; French air force officer; b. 11 May 1955, Dijon; m. Bénédicte de Rousiers; five c.; ed Canadian Forces Coll., Toronto, Canada, Defence Staff Coll., Paris; 'Capitaine Duthoit' entry at Air Force Acad. 1975; awarded fighter pilot's wings, Tours 1979; began service at Strasbourg Air Force Base 1979; head of a Mirage F1 CR detachment in Chad May–July 1986; Deputy Commdr, then Commdr 02.004 'La Fayette' fighter Squadron, Luxeuil Air Base 1986–89; Chief of Operations, Deputy Commdr, then Commdr 33rd Recce Wing, Strasbourg Air Base 1990–93; Deputy then Chief of Planning, Plans and Budget Dept, Air Force Staff, Paris 1994–97; Chief of Planning Dept, Defence Staff, Paris 1997–99; Base Commdr, Nancy Air Base 1999–2002; Deputy to Vice-Chief of Defence Staff and Chief of Studies and Overall Mil. Strategy, Defence Staff, Paris 2002–04, Chief of Defence Euro-Atlantic Dept 2004–06; C-in-C Air Defence and Air Operations Command, Paris 2006–08; rank of Gen. 2006; Mil. Rep. to EU Mil. Cttee, Brussels 2008–10; Mil. Rep. to NATO, Brussels 2009–10; Insp. Gen. of the Armed Forces 2010–12; rank of Général d'armée aérienne 2010; Chair. EU Mil. Cttee 2012–15; Commdr, Légion d'honneur, Ordre nat. du Mérite; Medal of Aeronautics, Ehrenkreuz der Bundeswehr in Gold. *Address:* European Union Military Committee, European External Action Service, 1046 Brussels, Belgium (office). *Telephone:* (2) 584-11-11 (office). *Website:* www.eeas.europa.eu/index_en.htm (office).

DE RUITER, Hendrikus (Henny); Dutch business executive; b. 3 March 1934, The Hague; m. Theodora O. van der Jagt 1957; one s. two d.; ed Technological Univ. of Delft; Research Chemist, Koninklijke/Shell Laboratorium Amsterdam (KSLA) 1956; Chief Technologist, Berre Refinery, Compagnie de Raffinage Shell-Berre 1965–67; returned to KSLA 1967; joined Shell Int. Petroleum Co. Ltd (SIPC), London 1969; Man. Dir Shell Co. of Thailand and Pres. Société Shell du Laos 1972; Coal Production and Trading Co-ordinator, SIPC 1975; Pres. Shell Int. Trading Co. 1979; Dir Shell Internationale Petroleum Maatschappij BV 1981; Man. Dir NV Koninklijke Nederlandsche Petroleum Maatschappij; mem. Presidium, Bd of Dirs Shell Petroleum NV and Man. Dir The Shell Petroleum Co. Ltd 1983–94; mem. Supervisory Bd AEGON NV (Vice-Chair. 1993–2004, Heineken NV 1993–2004, Koninklijke Ahold NV (Chair.) 1994–2003, Wolters Kluwer NV (Chair.) 1994–2006, Royal Dutch Petroleum Co. 1994–2004, Beers NV (Chair) 1995–2002, Coris Group PLC (fmrly Hoogovens Group BV) (Vice-Chair.) 1995–2002, Koninklijke Vopak NV (fmrly Koninklijke Pakhoed NV) 1995–2002; Dir Shell Petroleum NV 1994–2004, The Shell Petroleum Co. Ltd 1994–2004, Chair. Univar NV (fmrly part of Koninklijke Vopak) 2002–04; Kt Order of the Netherlands Lion 1987. *Address:* c/o Royal Dutch Petroleum Company, Carel van Bylandtlaan 30, PO Box 162, 2501 AN The Hague, The Netherlands.

De SANCTIS, Roman William, MD; American cardiologist; b. 30 Oct. 1930, Cambridge Springs, Pa; s. of Vincent De Sanctis and Marguerita De Sanctis; m. Ruth A. Foley 1955; four d.; ed Univ. of Arizona, Harvard Medical School; Resident in Medicine, Mass. Gen. Hosp. 1958–60, Fellow in Cardiology 1960–62, Dir Coronary Care Unit 1967–80, Dir Clinical Cardiology 1980–98, Dir Emer. 1998–; Physician 1970–; mem. Faculty of Medicine, Harvard Medical School 1964–, Prof. 1973–98, James and Evelyn Jenks and Paul Dudley White Prof. of Medicine 1998–; Consultant to USN and Asst to Attending Physician to US Congress 1956–58; Master, American Coll. of Physicians 1995; Fellow, American Coll. of Cardiology, Inst. of Medicine; Hon. DSc (Wilkes Coll., Univ. of Ariz.); Distinguished Clinical Teaching Award, Harvard Medical School 1980; Gifted Teacher Award (American Coll. of Cardiologists), Glozny-Reisbeck Award, NY Acad. of Medicine 2003. *Publications:* author and co-ed. of over 130 scientific papers. *Leisure interests:* travel, music, golf. *Address:* Yawkey Building, Suite 5700, 55 Fruit Street, Boston, MA 02114 (office); 5 Thoreau Circle, Winchester, MA 01890, USA (home). *Telephone:* (781) 726-2889 (office); (617) 729-1453 (home). *Fax:* (617) 643-1615.

DE SAVARY, Peter John; British entrepreneur; *Ambassador for Inward Investment, Government of Grenada;* b. 11 July 1944, Essex; m. 3rd Lucille Lana Paton; three d. (and two d. from previous m.); ed Charterhouse, Godalming, Surrey; commercial activities in finance, energy, leisure and property; British challenger for The Americas Cup 1983, 1987; Chair. The Carnegie Club, Scotland 1994–; Chair. Carnegie Abbey, Rhode Island; Chair. Cherokee Plantation, SC; Owner and Chair. Millwall Football Club 2005–06; currently Amb. for Inward Investment, Govt of Grenada; Tourism Personality of the Year, English Tourist Bd 1988. *Leisure interests:* sailing, carriage driving, riding. *Address:* Azzurra Castle, Seaview Lane, L'Ance aux Epines, St Georges, Grenada (home). *E-mail:* info@desavary.com. *Website:* www.desavary.com.

DE SÈZE, Amaury; French business executive; ed Centre de Perfectionnement dans l'Admin des Affaires, Stanford Grad. School of Business, USA; began career with Bull General Electric; fmr consultant, Towers Perrin Inc., Forster & Crosby; fmr Man. of Industrial Relations, Videocolor (Jt Venture Thomson-RCA); worked in Volvo Group holding various positions 1978–93, including Exec. Vice-Pres., Pres. and CEO Volvo France, Sr Vice-Pres. AB Volvo, Pres. Volvo European Corp. Office, one of four mems Group Exec. Cttee AB Volvo; mem. Man. Bd Compagnie Financière 1993, Bank Paribas 1998, Group Exec. Cttee BNP Paribas 1998, 2003; joined Paribas as Head of PAI 1993, Chair. and CEO PAI Partners 1998–2007; Vice-Chair. Power Corpn of Canada 2008–; mem. Supervisory Bd Carrefour SA 2005–08, Vice-Chair. 2006–08, Chair. Carrefour Group 2009–11, Lead Dir 2011–; mem. Bd of Dirs Power Corpn of Canada 2001–, Vice-Chair. 2008–; mem. Bd of Dirs Elis SA, Groupe Bruxelles Lambert SA 1994–, Suez Environnement SA, Atos Origin SA, French Postal Service, Fives-Lille, Schneider, Groupe Industriel Marcel Dassault SA, Poliet, Clemessy, Compagnie de Fives Lille, La Poste (France), Sema Group, IMS Int. Metal Service SA 1988–, Pargesa Holding SA (Switzerland) 2001–, Thales 2009–, GIB SA, United Biscuits Holding Ltd (UK), Imerys SA, PAI Partners srl (I), PAI Europe III General Partner Ltd (GG), PAI Europe IV UK General Partner Ltd (GB) (fmrly PAI Europe III UK General Partner Ltd), PAI Europe IV General Partner NC (GG), Vivarte SA (F), Paribas Santé SA (F), Sema PLC (GB), Erbe SA (B), Gepeco SA, Novasaur SAS (F) 2005–, Bergesen Worldwide Ltd 2007–, Saeco Int. Group SpA, United Biscuits (Equity) Ltd; Rep. and Dir, NHG SAS; mem. Supervisory Bd Publicis Groupe SA (fmrly Saatchi & Saatchi PLC) 1998–, Gras Savoye SA; mem. Bd of Supervisors Publicis SA; mem. Strategic Cttee Imerys SA; fmr mem. Bd of Dirs SAS, UGC SA, United Biscuits Ltd, Corparex Int. SA (F), IMS SA (F), Eiffage SA 1993–2008, UGC SA (France), Cobepa SA, Novalis SAS (France); fmr mem. Supervisory Bd Gras Savoye SCA (France); fmr mem. Exec. Cttee BNP Paribas (France). *Address:* Groupe Carrefour, 33 avenue Émile Zola, ZAC Ile Seguin, TSA 55555, 92649 Boulogne-Billancourt Cedex, France (office). *Telephone:* 1-41-04-26-00 (office). *Fax:* 1-41-04-26-01 (office). *E-mail:* info@carrefour.com (office). *Website:* www.carrefour.com (office).

DE SILGUY, Count Yves-Thibault Christian Marie; French construction industry executive and fmr diplomatist; *Vice-Chairman and Senior Director, Vinci;* b. 22 July 1948, Rennes; s. of Raymond de Silguy and Claude de Pompery; m. Jacqueline de Montillet de Grenaud (deceased); one s. one d.; ed Inst. Saint-Martin, Faculté de Droit et des Sciences Economiques, Rennes, Univ. de Paris I, Inst. d'Etudes Politiques de Paris and Ecole Nat. d'Admin; worked at Ministry of Foreign Affairs 1976–81, Deputy Chef de Cabinet to François-Xavier Ortoli, Vice-Pres. of EC Comm. 1981–85, Second Counsellor, Embassy in Washington, DC 1985–86; Adviser on European Questions and Int. Econs, Office of Prime Minister Chirac 1986–88; Dir, Int. Affairs Dept, Usinor-Sacilor 1988–90, Dir for Int. Affairs 1990–93; Sec.-Gen. Interdepartmental Cttee for Questions of Econ. Cooperation in Europe and Adviser for European Affairs to Prime Minister Balladur 1993–95; Commr for Econ. and Monetary Union, EC 1995–99; currently Man. Dir YTSeuropaconsultants; mem. Exec. Bd Suez Group 2000–, CEO 2001–03, Exec. Vice-Pres. 2003–06; Vice-Chair. Mouvement des entreprises de France (MEDEF) International 2000–, Chair. France-Qatar Cttee of Medef International; Chair. Vinci 2006–10, Vice-Chair. and Sr Dir 2010–; Dir and Chair. Performance Audit Cttee, LVMH (France); Dir and Chair. Nominations and Compensation Cttee, Solvay (Belgium); Commdr, Légion d'honneur, Officier du Mérite nat., Commdr des Arts et des Lettres. *Publications include:* Le syndrome du diplodocus 1996, L'euro 1998, L'economie, fil d'Ariane de l'Europe 2000. *Leisure interests:* sailing, hunting. *Address:* Vinci, 1 cours Ferdinand-de-Lesseps, 92851 Rueil-Malmaison Cedex, France (office). *Telephone:* 1-47-16-35-00 (office). *Fax:* 1-47-51-91-02 (office). *E-mail:* yves-thibault.desilguy@vinci.com (office). *Website:* www.vinci.com (office).

DE SILVA, Asoka N.; Sri Lankan judge (retd); *Senior Legal Adviser to the President;* ed St Antony's Coll., Kandy, Univ. of Ceylon; enrolled as advocate of Supreme Court 1972; joined Attorney-Gen.'s Dept as State Counsel 1974, rose to position of Sr Deputy Solicitor-Gen. 1987; Judge, Court of Appeal 1995–2001, Pres. Feb.–Aug. 2001; Judge of Supreme Court Aug. 2001–, Chief Justice of Sri Lanka 2009–11; Sr Legal Adviser to the Pres. 2011–; served as a perm. judge of Int. Criminal Tribunal for Rwanda. *Address:* President's Secretariat, Republic Square,

Colombo 1, Sri Lanka (office). *Telephone:* (11) 2324801 (office). *Fax:* (11) 2331246 (office). *E-mail:* priu@presidentsoffice.lk (office). *Website:* www.president.gov.lk (office).

DE SILVA, Gen. Crisanthe; Sri Lankan army officer and diplomatist; m. Nayana De Silva; two s.; ed Royal Coll., Colombo, Army Command and Staff Coll., Camberley, UK, Higher Command Coll. Nanjing, China; enlisted in Sri Lanka Army 1980, commissioned as Second-Lt with 1 Field Engineer Regiment of the Corps of Sri Lanka Engineers 1981, promoted to Capt. 1985, Major 1989, Lt-Col 1994, Col 1997, Brig. 2003, Major-Gen. 2009, command positions included Commdr, 562 Infantry Brigade, Engineer Brigade of the Sri Lanka Army, 6 Field Engineer Regiment of the Corps of Sri Lanka Engineers, and Security Force Headquarters Commdr, Kilinochchi, staff positions included Military Sec., Dir of Operations, Commdt and Chief Instructor of Army Command and Staff Coll. and Sri Lanka Military Acad., Diyatalawa, Additional Military Sec., Brigadier Gen. Staff at Security Forces HQ, Dir of Plans, Col (Admin) at Directorate of Personnel Admin, Commdr, Sri Lanka Army Volunteer Force –2013, Chief of Staff of the Army 2013–14, Deputy Chief of Mission, Embassy in Moscow 2014–15, Commdr of the Army 2015–17, simultaneously promoted to rank of Lt-Gen., Chief of Defence Staff June–Aug. 2017, simultaneously promoted to rank of Gen.; Rana Wickrama Padakkama, Uttama Seva Padakkama, Vishista Seva Vibhushanaya.

DE SMET, Bart; Belgian insurance executive; *CEO, Ageas;* b. 1957; ed Catholic Univ. of Louvain, diplomas in Math., Actuarial Sciences and Managerial Sciences; began career with Argenta 1982; Exec. Vice-Pres., Life Div., Nationale Suisse insurance co. 1985–93; joined ING Insurance Belgium 1994, mem. Exec. Cttee, responsible for individual and group life insurance, health insurance and banking activities; joined Fortis 1998, mem. Man. Cttee Fortis AG, responsible for Fortis Employee Benefits, took charge of Broker Channel at Fortis Insurance Belgium 2005–07, CEO Fortis Insurance Belgium 2007–09, CEO Ageas (renamed from Fortis Holding) 2009–; mem. Bd of Dirs Ageas, Ageas Insurance International, AG Insurance, Ageas UK, Tai Ping Life, Maybank Ageas Holding, IDBI Federal, Credimo. *Address:* Ageas SA/NV, rue du Marquis 1, 1000 Brussels, Belgium (office). *Telephone:* (2) 557-57-11 (office). *Fax:* (2) 557-57-50 (office). *E-mail:* info@ageas.com (office). *Website:* www.ageas.com (office).

DE SOTO, Alvaro; Peruvian diplomatist; b. 16 March 1943, Argentina; s. of Alberto Soto de la Jara and Rosa Polar; divorced; two s. one d.; ed Int. School, Geneva, Catholic Univ. Lima, San Marcos Univ. Lima, Diplomatic Acad. Lima and Inst. of Int. Studies, Geneva; Acting Dir Maritime Sovereignty Div. Ministry of Foreign Affairs 1975–78; Deputy Perm. Rep. of Peru at UN, Geneva 1978–82; Special Asst to UN Sec.-Gen. 1982–86; Asst Sec.-Gen. and Exec. Asst to UN Sec.-Gen. 1987–91; Personal Rep. of UN Sec.-Gen. in El Salvador Peace Negotiations 1990–91; Asst Sec.-Gen. UN Office for Research and Collection of Information 1991; Sr Political Adviser to UN Sec.-Gen. 1992–94; Asst Sec.-Gen. for Political Affairs 1995–99, Under-Sec.-Gen., Special Adviser to Sec.-Gen. on Cyprus 1999–2004; UN Special Envoy for Myanmar 1995–99; Special Rep. of the Sec.-Gen. for Western Sahara and Chief of the UN Mission for the Referendum in Western Sahara (MINURSO) 2003–05; UN Special Coordinator for the Middle East Peace Process, Personal Rep. of the Sec.-Gen. to the Palestine Liberation Org. and the Palestinian Authority and Sec.-Gen.'s Envoy to the Middle East Quartet 2005–07; Invited Prof., Paris School of Int. Affairs, Sciences Po, Paris; mem. Global Leadership Foundation; mem. various advisory bds in New York and in Europe; mem. Bd of Advisors and Host, 'Conversations with Alvaro de Soto' series, Center for International Conflict Resolution, Columbia Univ.; Hon. LLD (St Joseph's Univ., Philadelphia) 1992; Orden de José Simeón Cañas, Libertador de los Esclavos, Gran Cruz (El Salvador) 2007. *Address:* Center for International Conflict Resolution, 1325 International Affairs Building, 420 West 118th Street, MC 3369, New York, NY 10027, USA. *Website:* www.cicr-columbia.org.

DE SOTO, Hernando; Peruvian economist; *President, Institute for Liberty and Democracy;* b. 2 June 1941, Arequipa; ed Institut Universitaire de Hautes Etudes Internationales, Geneva, Switzerland; fmr economist for GATT; fmr Pres. Exec. Cttee, Copper Exporting Countries Org. (CIPEC); fmr Man. Dir Universal Eng Corpn; fmr Prin. Swiss Bank Corpn Consultant Group; fmr Gov. Cen. Reserve Bank, Peru; Personal Rep. and Chief Adviser to Pres. Alberto Fujimori; currently Pres. Inst. for Liberty and Democracy, Lima; apptd rep. of Pres. to USA on free trade agreement 2006; Co-Chair. UN High Level Comm. on Legal Empowerment for the Poor; Downey Fellow, Yale Univ., USA 2003; Most Admirable Order of the Direkgunabhorn (Fifth Class), Thailand 2004; Hon. mem. Univ. Philosophical Soc., Trinity Coll. Dublin (Ireland) 2009; Hon. DLitt (Buckingham, UK) 2005; Sir Antony Fisher Int. Memorial Award – Atlas 1990, 2001, The Freedom Prize (Switzerland), Goldwater Award (USA) 2002, Adam Smith Award, Asscn of Pvt. Enterprise Educ. (USA) 2002, CARE Canada Award for Outstanding Devt Thinking 2002, inducted into Democracy Hall of Fame Int., Nat. Grad. Univ. 2003, Templeton Freedom Prize (USA) 2004, Milton Friedman Prize for Advancing Liberty (USA) 2004, Deutsche Stiftung Eigentum prize for Property Rights Theory 2004, IPAE Award, Peruvian Inst. of Business Admin 2004, Forbes' Compass Award for Strategic Direction 2004, Americas Award 2005, Acad. of Achievement Golden Plate Award, USA 2005, Innovation Award, The Economist Magazine 2005, Bradley Prize, Bradley Foundation 2006, Humanitarian Award, Project Concern International 2007, Poder-BCG Business Award 2007, Hernando de Soto Award for Democracy, Center of Int. Private Enterprise 2009, Hayek Medal, Friedrich A. von Hayek-Gesellschaft 2010, Medal of the Presidency of the Italian Cabinet (Council of Ministers), Int. Scientific Committee of the Pio Manzu Centre (Italy) 2010, Latin American Innovative American's Award 2011. *Television documentaries:* The Power of the Poor with Hernando de Soto 2009, Globalization at the Crossroads with Hernando de Soto 2011, Unlikely Heroes of the Arab Spring 2013. *Publications:* The Other Path 1986, The Mystery of Capital: Why Capitalism Triumphs in the West and Fails Everywhere Else (translated into 30 languages and received 25 prizes in Europe and North America) 2000. *Address:* Instituto Libertad y Democracia, Avenida Las Begonias 441, Oficina 901, San Isidro, Lima 27, Peru (office). *Telephone:* (1) 616-6100 (office). *Fax:* (1) 616-6190 (office). *E-mail:* hds@ild.org.pe (office). *Website:* www.ild.org.pe (office).

DE SOUSA MANGUEIRA, Augusto Archer, PhD; Angolan economist and government official; *Minister of Finance;* b. 26 Sept. 1962, Luanda; s. of Augusto de Sousa Mangueira and Mariana Manuel Gouveia; m.; ed Bruno Leuschner Higher School of Econs, Germany, Complutense Univ. Madrid; fmr Lecturer, Faculty of Econs, Univ. Agostinho Neto, Luanda; fmr Sr Technician, Study and Planning Office, Empresa de Electricidade de Luanda (EDEL, state-owned electricity co.); Trade Rep. of Angola in Spain 2005–07; fmr Dir, Clinica Multiperfil; fmr Econ. Adviser to Pres. of Repub.; fmr Coordinator, Technical Group of Council of Ministers; fmr Sec. of State for Trade; Deputy Minister of Commerce 2010–12; Chair. Angolan Capital Market Comm. 2012–16; Minister of Finance 2016–; Pres. Angolan Handball Fed.; Vice-Pres. Angolan Olympic Cttee; mem. Nat. Comm. for Rural Devt and Combating Poverty. *Address:* Ministry of Finance, Largo da Mutamba, Luanda, Angola (office). *Telephone:* 222338548 (office). *Fax:* 222338548 (office). *E-mail:* geral@minfin.gov.ao (office). *Website:* www.minfin.gv.ao (office).

DE SOUZA, Marcel Alain, MEconSc; Benin economist, politician and international organization official; b. 20 Oct. 1953, Pobè; m.; seven c.; ed Univ. of Dakar, West African Training Centre for Banking Studies, IMF Inst., Washington, DC, USA; long career with Banque Centrale des Etats de l'Afrique de l'Ouest (BCEAO), including as Internal Auditor, Cotonou, later Nat. Dir for Benin, becoming Dir of Admin, BCEAO HQ, Dakar; Minister of Devt, Econ. Analysis and Forecast 2011; mem. Nat. Ass. (FCBE) 2015–16; ind. cand. in 2016 presidential election; Pres., Econ. Community of West African States (ECOWAS) Comm. 2016–18; mem. Forces Cauris pour un Bénin Emergent (FCBE).

DE SWAAN, Tom; Dutch banking executive; *Chairman, Zurich Insurance Group Limited;* b. 1946; joined De Nederlandsche Bank NV 1972, mem. Governing Bd 1986–98; mem. Man. Bd and Chief Financial Officer ABN AMRO Bank 1999–2006, Adviser to Man. Bd 2006–07; mem. Bd of Dirs Zurich Insurance Group Ltd and Zurich Insurance Co. Ltd 2006–, Vice-Chair. 2012–13, Acting Chair. Aug.–Sept. 2013, Chair. Sept. 2013–, CEO a.i. Dec. 2015–March 2016; Chair. Amsterdam Financial Centre 1987–88, Banking Supervisory Sub-cttee of European Monetary Inst. 1995–97; mem. Basel Cttee on Banking Supervision 1991–96, Chair. 1997–98; Dir (non-exec.), Financial Services Authority (UK) 2001–06, GlaxoSmithKline plc 2006–15; mem. Supervisory Bd, Van Lanschot NV (holding co. of F. van Lanschot Bankiers) 2008–16, Chair. –2015. *Address:* Zurich Insurance Group Ltd, Austrasse 46, 8045 Zurich, Switzerland (office). *Telephone:* (44) 625-25-25 (office). *Fax:* (44) 625-02-99 (office). *E-mail:* info@zurich.com (office). *Website:* www.zurich.com (office).

DE TAVERNOST, Nicolas Bellet; French television executive, company director and fmr civil servant; *CEO and Chairman of the Executive Board, Métropole Télévision SA;* b. 22 Aug. 1950, Villefranche-sur-Saône; ed Collège Notre-Dame de Mongré, Lycée Saint-Joseph de Tivoli, Sciences-Po, Bordeaux; served at French Ministry of Int. Commerce 1974–76; Gen. Sec. French Chamber of Commerce, Zurich, Switzerland 1976–78; Head of Information and Public Relations, Ministry of Posts, Telegraphs and Telephones 1978–84, Head of Public Services Div., Video Communications Dept 1984–86; Dir of Audiovisual Business, Lyonnaise des Eaux 1986–87; Deputy Dir-Gen. M6 (Métropole Télévision SA) channel 1987–90, Dir-Gen. 1990–2000, CEO, Chair. Exec. Bd and mem. Exec. Cttee 2000–; Dir, Série Club, Nexans Hellas SA, TF6, Paris Premiere SA, SND, Extension TV SA, TF6 Gestion SA, Soc. Nouvelle de Distribution SA, Home Shopping Service SA, Tecipress, Antena 3, FRA Business Interactif, GL Events 2008–; Ind. Dir, Nexans SA 2007–, Nexans Maroc SA; mem. Supervisory Bd Édiradio RTL SA; Pres. Asscn of European Commercial Television; Admin. Girondins de Bordeaux club 1999–; Chevalier, Ordre nat. du Mérite 1994, Légion d'honneur 2003. *Address:* Métropole Télévision SA, 89 avenue Charles-de-Gaulle, 92575 Neuilly-sur-Seine, Île-de-France, France (office). *Telephone:* 1-41-92-66-66 (office). *Fax:* 1-41-92-66-10 (office). *E-mail:* marie-clotilde.perre@m6.fr (office). *Website:* www.m6.fr (office).

DE THUIN, Aude; French psychologist and business executive; *President, Thuin et Associés Consulting;* b. (Aude Le Roux), 18 Sept. 1950, Ploudaniel, Brittany; m. Hubert Zieseniss 1989; six c.; cr. and managed Promotion Bourgogne (free newspaper in Burgundy) 1972; has f. several cos since 1981, including ADT Consultants sarl to edit La Semaine Internationale du Marketing Direct 1981 (acquired by CEP Exposium 1993), Compagnie Scheffer to organize two events, L'Art du Jardin flower show 1993–2003 and Créations et Savoir Faire (DIY fair) 1995–2003 (Compagnie Scheffer acquired by Hachette Filipacchi/Comexpo 2003), La Belle Ecole (first int. school devoted to the French art de vivre) 2003, PV Concept sarl (through its subsidiary Wefcos) to launched first edn of Women's Forum for the Economy and Society, Deauville 2005 (acquired by Publicis 2011); Founder and Pres. Thuin et Associés Consulting 2011–, publr of forum Dare France (to highlight French talent in all areas of industry, business science, research, education and the arts); Founder and Chair. Women in Africa Initiative 2016–; Chevalier, Légion d'honneur, Officier, Ordre nat. du Mérite, Chevalier du Mérite agricole; EDC Ethique et Gouvernance Award 2012, Femme Entrepreneur Award, World Entrepreneurship Forum 2012. *Publications:* Le Livre Blanc du Marketing Direct 1985, En Direct 1993, Jardins Ephémères 1999, Femmes, si vous osiez (Women, If You Dare) 2012, Forcer le destin (Forcing Fate) 2016. *Address:* Thuin et Associés Consulting, 7 rue Scheffer, 75116 Paris, France (office). *Telephone:* 1-45-05-23-63 (office); 1-47-04-36-00 (office).

DE VABRES, Renaud Donnedieu; French politician and organization official; *Founder and President, RDDV Partner;* b. 13 March 1954, Neuilly-sur-Seine, Haut de Seine; grandson of Prof. Henri Donnedieu de Vabres; ed Institut d'Etudes Politiques, Paris and Ecole Nationale d'Admin; nat. service in navy on board patrol ship La Paimpolaise; Prin. Pvt. Sec. to Préfet of Indre-et-Loire; Sec.-Gen. Centre Region Police Admin 1980–81, Alpes de Hautes Provence 1981–82; Sous-Préfet Château-Thierry 1982–85; Sr Lecturer, Institut d'Etudes Politiques, Paris 1984; mem. Conseil d'Etat 1985; Deputy to Assemblé Nationale for Indre-et-Loire 1997, Vice-Pres. Comm. for Foreign Affairs; mem. Tours Municipal Council 2001; mem. Centre Regional Council 1986–2001, Chair. Union pour la démocratie française (UDF) Group and Gen. Rapporteur on the Budget and Planning 1986–93, Vice-Chair. and Gen. Rapporteur on the Budget 1993–98; Delegate-Gen. of Parti Républicain (PR) as mem. Political Bureau 1986–96; Special Asst to François Léotard, Minister of State, Minister of Defence 1993–95; Delegate-Gen. of UDF 1996–98, of Nouvelle UDF 1998–2002, and concurrently Prin. Pvt. Sec. to François Léotard (PR) 1986 and UDF 1996–98; fmr Minister Del. for European Affairs; Minister of Culture and Communication 2003–07; Vice-Pres. Indre-et-Loire Union pour un Mouvement Populaire (UMP) 2002–09, Spokesman for nat. Union pour un

Mouvement Populaire 2003–04, Nat. Sec. in charge of cultural and artistic affairs 2009; Adviser, Group Allard (consulting firm) 2009–; Pres. Atout France (tourism agency) 2009–12; Adviser, Groupe Allard 2009–11; Founder and Pres. RDDV Partner, Paris 2011–; Hon. mem., Observatory of the Religious Heritage; Chevalier, Legion d'Honneur 2009. *Television includes:* Les 4 vérités 1997–2007, La fête de la chanson française 2005, La nuit des Césars (documentary) 2006–07, L'aventure du Rond-Point: Audace joyeuse et rire de résistance (documentary) 2010. *Address:* RDDV Partner, 50, rue de Bourgogne, 75007 Paris, France (office). *Telephone:* 6-82-73-91-49 (office). *E-mail:* contact@rddvpartner.fr (office). *Website:* www.rddvpartner.fr (office).

DE VASCONCELOS, Álvaro; Portuguese research institute director; *Associate Senior Researcher and Director of Projects, Arab Reform Initiative;* m. 1st Brigitte Courot; one d.; m. 2nd Maria do Rosário de Moraes Vaz (deceased); two d.; Co-founder and Head of Inst. of Strategic and Int. Studies (IEEI), Lisbon 1981–2007, launched several networks, including Euro-Latin American Forum and Euro-MeSCo; Dir EU Inst. for Security Studies, Paris 2007–12; Assoc. Sr Researcher and Dir of Projects, Arab Reform Initiative (consortium of 20 think tanks in the Arab world and the West) and Steering Cttee Co-ordinator, Global Governance Group (GG10) 2012–; regular columnist in Portuguese and int. press; Chevalier, Légion d'honneur; Comendador do Ordem do Rio Branco (Brazil). *Publications:* author or co-ed. numerous books, articles and reports, notably in areas of EU Common Foreign and Security Policy, Euro-Mediterranean relations and on theme of world order, including Portugal: A European Story, La PESC: Ouvrir l'Europe au Monde, The European Union, Mercosul and the New World Order, and A European Strategy for the Mediterranean, What Ambitions for European Defence in 2020? 2009, The Obama Moment – European and American Perspectives 2009, Listening to Unfamiliar Voices – The Arab Democratic Wave 2012, Global Trends 2030 – Citizens in an Interconnected and Polycentric World (ed. and contrib.) 2013, The Challenges of Inclusive Multilateralism (report of the GG10) (ed. and contrib.) 2013, La vague démocratique arabe: L'Europe et la question islamiste 2014. *Address:* Arab Reform Initiative, Paris, France (office). *Telephone:* (9) 51-34-05-28 (office). *Fax:* (9) 56-34-05-28 (office). *E-mail:* contact@arab-reform.net (office). *Website:* www.arab-reform.net/alvaro-vasconcelos (office).

DE VASCONCELOS LIMA, José Jorge, MS; Brazilian politician; b. 18 Nov. 1944, Recife, Pernambuco; m.; two d.; ed Universidade Federal de Pernambuco, Univesidade Católica de Pernambuco, Univesidade Fed. do Rio de Janeiro, Universidad de Madrid, Spain; Prof., Universidade Fed. de Pernambuco in 1970s; Educ. Sec., Pernambuco 1975–79, Housing Sec. 1979–82; joined Partido da Frente Liberal—PFL (now Democratas) 1982, Pres. PFL 1989–90, 1993–94; mem. Câmara dos Deputados 1982–98; mem. Senado Fed. for Pernambuco 1999–2007, Minority Leader 2005–06; Minister of Mines and Energy 2001–02, Federal Audit Court 2009–14; unsuccessful PFL cand. for Vice-Pres. 2006; CEO Brasilia Energy Co. 2007–09; mem. Bd of Dirs Centrais Elétricas do Pára SA 2014–, Companhia Energética de Brasília 2015–.

DE VASCONSELOS, Abraão F.; Timor-Leste economist and central banker; *Governor, Banco Central de Timor-Leste;* fmr Dir-Gen. Autoridade Bancária e de Pagamentos de Timor Leste; Chair. Investment Advisory Bd 2006–08; fmr Gen. Man. Banco Central de Timor-Leste, now Gov. *Address:* Office of the Governor, Banco Central de Timor-Leste, Avenida Xavier Do Amaral, POB 59, Dili, Timor-Leste (office). *Telephone:* 3313712 (office). *Fax:* 3313713 (office). *E-mail:* info@bancocentral.tl (office). *Website:* www.bancocentral.tl (office).

DE VAUCLEROY, Baron Gui, LLD, MEconSc; Belgian business executive; b. 28 Sept. 1933, Dendermonde; ed Univ. of Louvain; Research Asst Centre for Social Studies 1957–59; joined Delhaize Le Lion (later Delhaize Group) 1960, mem. Exec. Cttee 1967, Vice-Pres. Exec. Cttee 1984, CEO and Pres. Exec. Cttee 1990–98, Chair. 1999–2004, now Hon. Chair. and Hon. CEO; Chair. Fed. of Enterprises in Belgium 1999–2002; Vice-Pres. Union of Industrial Employers Europe 2000–02; Commdr, Ordre de Léopold, Grand Officier, Ordre de Léopold II. *Address:* Avenue Baron Albert d'Huart 137, 1950 Kraainem, Belgium (home).

DE VIDO, Julio Miguel; Argentine politician; b. 26 Dec. 1949, Buenos Aires; ed Universidad de Buenos Aires; qualified architect; Dir-Gen. of Public Works, Inst. of Urban Devt, Santa Cruz 1988–90; Minister of Economy and Public Works of Santa Cruz 1991–99, Minister of Govt 1999–2003; elected Prov. Deputy, Santa Cruz 1997; adviser to presidential cand. Néstor Kirchner during election campaign 2003; Minister of Federal Planning, Public Investment and Services 2003–15. *Address:* c/o Ministry of Federal Planning, Public Investment and Services, Hipólito Yrigoyen 250, 11°, Of. 1112, C1086AAB, Buenos Aires, Argentina (office).

DE VILLIERS, A(braham) B(enjamin); South African professional cricketer; b. 17 Feb. 1984, Pretoria, Transvaal; s. of Dr Abraham Benjamin de Villiers and Millie de Villiers; m. Danielle Swart; two s.; ed Afrikaans Hoër Seunsskool, Pretoria; right-handed batsman; right-arm medium pace bowler; occasional wicketkeeper; played for Carrickfergus Cricket Club in NI as youngster; plays for Northerns 2003–04, Titans 2004–, S Africa 2004–18, Delhi Daredevils 2008–10, Royal Challengers Bangalore 2011–, Africa XI; First-class debut: 2003/04; Test debut: S Africa v England, Port Elizabeth 17–21 Dec. 2004; One-Day Int. (ODI) debut: S Africa v England, Bloemfontein 2 Feb. 2005; T20I debut: S Africa v Australia, Johannesburg 24 Feb. 2006; Capt. South African ODI and T20I teams 2011–17, Test team 2011–16; played 114 Tests (to March 2018), scored 8,765 runs (average 50.66) with 22 centuries and 46 fifties, highest score 278 not out against Pakistan, Abu Dhabi 2010; played 228 ODIs (to Feb. 2018), scored 9,577 runs (average 53.50) with 25 centuries and 53 fifties, highest score 176 against Bangladesh, Paarl 2017, played 78 T20Is (to Oct. 2017), scored 1672 runs (average 26.12) with 10 fifties, highest score 79 against Scotland, The Oval 2009; played 141 First-class matches, scored 10,689 runs (average 49.71) with 25 centuries and 60 fifties, highest score 278 not out; retd from int. cricket 2018. *Achievements include:* became second youngest and second fastest S African to reach 1,000 Test runs after Graeme Pollock; holds the record for the fastest 50 (16 balls), 100 (31 balls, eventually scoring 149 runs off 44 balls Jan. 2015) and 150 (64 balls) in ODIs; holds record for most Test innings (78) before getting out for a duck. *Leisure interest:* playing guitar. *Address:* c/o Titans Cricket, SuperSport Park, Centurion, Gauteng Province, South Africa. *Telephone:* (12) 663-1005. *Fax:* (12) 663-3329. *E-mail:* info@titans.co.za. *Website:* www.titans.co.za; www.abdevilliers.com.

DE VRIES, Gijs, MA; Dutch politician and international civil servant; b. 22 Feb. 1956, New York City, USA; m.; two c.; ed Univ. of Leiden; Lecturer in Int. Relations, Faculty of Law, Univ. of Leiden 1981–84; mem. Leiden City Council 1981–84; mem. European Parl. 1984–98, Leader, Liberal and Democratic Group 1994–98; Deputy Minister of Interior Affairs 1998–2002; Rep. of Netherlands at Convention of Future of EU, Brussels 2002–03; mem. Expert Cttee for Council of Europe's European Charter for Regional or Minority Languages 2003–04; Counter-Terrorism Co-ordinator, EU 2004–07; Chair. European Security Research and Innovation Forum 2007–08; Sr Fellow, Clingendael, Netherlands Inst. for Int. Relations 2008; mem. Bd Algemene Rekenkamer (Netherlands Court of Audit) 2008–10; mem. European Court of Auditors 2011–13; Visiting Sr Fellow, European Inst., LSE; Commdr, Hellenic Order of Merit 1996. *Address:* London School of Economics and Political Science, Houghton Street, London, WC2A 2AE, England (office). *E-mail:* g.de-vries@lse.ac.uk (office); gijs.devries@outlook.com (office). *Website:* www.lse.ac.uk (office).

DE VRIES, Jan Egbert, PhD; Dutch immunologist and institute director; *CEO, AIMM Therapeutics BV;* ed Univs of Utrecht and Amsterdam; Visiting Scientist, John Mendelsohn Lab., Univ. of California, San Diego 1977–79; Chair. Dept of Immunology, Nat. Cancer Research Inst., Amsterdam 1979–85; Dir of a biotechnology enterprise in Lyon, France (subsidiary of US pharmaceutical co. Schering Plough) 1985–88; moved with his research team to biotechnology enterprise DNAX, Palo Alto, Calif., USA (cr. by Nobel Laureates Paul Berg and Arthur Kornberg) 1988–97; joined Novartis as Global Head of Dermatology Disease Area, Novartis Research Inst., Vienna 1997, apptd Global Head of Auto-Immunity and Transplantation Disease Area with research activities in Vienna and Basel 2003, fmr Head of Novartis Insts for BioMedical Research, Basel; CEO AIMM Therapeutics BV 2012–; Chair. Artax Inc.; mem. of Bd of Dirs Cassiopea 2015–; mem. Scientific Advisory Bd Anaptys Inc.; Wilhelm Exner Medal, Austrian Asscn for SME (Oesterreichischer Gewerbeverein—OGV) (jtly) 2005. *Publications:* more than 300 scientific publs and reviews in professional journals; 20 patents. *Address:* AIMM Therapeutics, Meibergdreef 59, 1105 BA Amsterdam, Netherlands (office). *Telephone:* (20) 5662145 (office). *Fax:* (20) 5669081 (office). *E-mail:* info@aimmtherapeutics.com (office). *Website:* www.aimmtherapeutics.com (office).

DE WAART, Edo; Dutch conductor; *Music Director, New Zealand Symphony Orchestra;* b. 1 June 1941, Amsterdam; s. of M. de Waart and J. Rose; one s. one d.; ed Amsterdam Music Lyceum with Haakon Stotijn, Hilversum with Franco Ferrara; Co-Prin. Oboe, Amsterdam Philharmonic 1961, Concertgebouw Orchestra 1963; Asst Conductor, New York Philharmonic 1965–66, Concertgebouw Orchestra, Amsterdam 1966; Musical Dir Netherlands Wind Ensemble 1966; Conductor Rotterdam Philharmonic 1967, Musical Dir and Prin. Conductor 1973–79; Prin. Guest Conductor, San Francisco Symphony Orchestra 1975–77, Music Dir 1977–85; Music Dir Minnesota Orchestra 1986–95; Artistic Dir Nederlandse Omroep Stichtung (Dutch radio org.); apptd Chief Conductor, Netherlands Radio Philharmonic Orchestra 1989, later Conductor Laureate; Prin. Guest Conductor, Santa Fe Opera 1991–92; Artistic Dir and Chief Conductor, Sydney Symphony Orchestra 1993–2003; Artistic Dir and Chief Conductor, Hong Kong Philharmonic Orchestra 2004–12; Chief Conductor, Santa Fe Opera 2007–09; Music Dir Milwaukee Symphony Orchestra 2009–17, then Conductor Laureate; apptd Artistic Partner, St Paul Chamber Orchestra 2010; Music Dir Royal Flemish Philharmonic Orchestra 2012–16; Music Dir New Zealand Symphony Orchestra 2016–; Prin. Guest Conductor San Diego Symphony Orchestra 2019–; guest conductor with leading orchestras at venues in USA and Europe and at festivals including Spoleto, Bayreuth and Holland; Hon. AO 2005, Hon. Fellow, Hong Kong Acad. for Performing Arts; Kt, Order of the Dutch Lion; First Prize, Dimitri Mitropoulos Competition, New York 1964. *Address:* Harrison Parrott, The Ark, 201 Talgarth Road, London, W6 8BJ, England (office); New Zealand Symphony Orchestra, Level 8, Crowe Horwath House, 57 Willis Street, Wellington 6011, New Zealand (office). *Telephone:* (20) 7229-9166 (office); (4) 801-2034 (office). *Fax:* (20) 7221-5042 (office). *E-mail:* info@harrisonparrott.com (office); info@nzso.co.uk (office). *Website:* www.harrisonparrott.com (office); www.nzso.co.nz (office).

DE ZOYSA, Tilak; Sri Lankan business executive; *Chairman, Carson Cumberbatch PLC;* Deputy Chair. and Man. Dir Associated Motorways Ltd 1993–; Chair. Carson Cumberbatch & Co. Ltd (now Carson Cumberbatch PLC) 2001–; fmr Pres. Nat. Chamber of Commerce; fmr Chair. HelpAge Int., Ceylon Chamber of Commerce; Dir Bukit Darah Co. Ltd 2004–09; Vice-Pres. Sri Lanka–France Business Council 2004–; mem. Monetary Bd of Sri Lanka 2003–09; mem. Bd of Dirs Taj Lanka Hotels Ltd Bansei Royal Resorts Hikkaduwa Plc 2014–; mem. Tariff Advisory Council; Hon. Consul for Croatia 1999–; Order of the Rising Sun, Gold Rays with Neck Ribbon, Japan. *Address:* Carson Cumberbatch PLC, 61 Janadhipathi Mawatha, Colombo 1, Sri Lanka (office). *Telephone:* (11) 2039200 (office). *Fax:* (11) 2039300 (office). *E-mail:* carsons@carcumb.com (office). *Website:* www.carsoncumberbatch.com (office).

DEACON, Richard, CBE, RA, MA; British sculptor; b. 15 Aug. 1949, Bangor, Wales; s. of Group Capt. Edward William Deacon and Joan Bullivant Winstanley; m. Jacqueline Poncelet 1977 (divorced 2001); one s. one d.; ed Somerset Coll. of Art, St Martin's School of Art, RCA, Chelsea School of Art; Prof., Ecole Nat. Supérieure des Beaux-Arts, Paris 1998–2009; Vice-Chair. Baltic Centre for Contemporary Art Trust 1999–2005; mem. British Council, Arts Council of England Architecture Advisory Group 1996–99; Visiting Prof., Chelsea School of Art 1992–; Prof., Kunstakademie Düsseldorf 2009–15; Trustee, Tate Gallery 1992–97, Art Fund 2015–; Chevalier, Ordre des Arts et des Lettres 1997; Hon. DLitt (Leicester) 2005, Hon. Fellow, Plymouth Coll. of Art 2017; Turner Prize 1987, Robert Jacobsen Prize 1995, Ernst Vogelmann Prize 2017. *Works include:* What Could Make Me Feel This Way?, Struck Dumb, Doubletalk, Body of Thought No 2, The Back of My Hand, Distance No Object No 2, Dummy, Under My Skin, Breed, Skirt, Laocoon, After, Moor, Let's Not Be Stupid, No Stone Unturned, Building From the Inside, Can't See the Wood for the Trees, Out of Order, The Same But Different, Mountain, Another Mountain, Dead Leg, Nosotros Tres, Water Under The Bridge, Strut, Upper Strut, Piccadilly, Rain Or Shine, Grove, From There To Here. *Leisure interests:* swimming, walking. *Address:* c/o Lisson Gallery, 67 Lisson Street, London, NW1 5DA, England. *E-mail:* contact@richarddeacon.net (office). *Website:* www.richarddeacon.net.

DEAL, (John) Nathan, BA, JD; American lawyer, politician and fmr state governor; b. 25 Aug. 1942; m. Sandra Dunagan; one s. three d.; ed Mercer Univ., Macon, Ga, Walter F. George School of Law; Capt., Judge Advocate Gen. Corps, US Army 1966–68; pvt. law practice 1979–82; Asst Dist Attorney, Northeast Circuit, Hall Co., Ga 1970–71, Judge, Juvenile Court 1971–72, attorney 1977–79; mem. from Dist 10, Georgia State Senate 1981–93, Pres. Pro Tempore 1991–93; originally a Democrat, elected to US House of Reps for 9th Congressional Dist of Ga 1993–2003 (switched to Republican Party 1995), 2007–10, for 10th Congressional Dist of Ga 2003–07 (resgnd from Congress to run in Ga gubernatorial election March 2010), mem. House Energy and Commerce Cttee 2007–10; Gov. of Georgia 2011–19; mem. Congressional Boating Caucus, Congressional Caucus on Unfunded Mandates, Congressional Travel and Tourism Caucus, Congressional Vietnam-Era Veterans Caucus, Rural Health Care Coalition, Speaker's Immigration Task Force; mem. Bd of Trustees, Mercer Univ., Advisory Bd Honors Programs, North Georgia Coll. and Univ.; Republican. *Address:* c/o Office of the Governor, 203 State Capitol, Atlanta, GA 30334, USA (office).

DEAN, Dame Caroline, DBE, OBE, BA, DPhil, FRS; British plant scientist and molecular biologist; *Project Leader, Cell and Developmental Biology, John Innes Centre;* b. 2 April 1957; m. Jonathan D. G. Jones 1991; one s. one d.; ed Univ. of York; currently Project Leader, Cell and Developmental Biology, John Innes Centre, Norwich; mem. Faculty (non-resident), Salk Inst., USA 2012–; mem. German Leopoldina Acad. 2008; Foreign mem. NAS 2008; Fellow, European Molecular Biology Org. (EMBO) 1999; Genetics Soc. Medal 2002, BBSRC Anniversary Award for Excellence in Bioscience, 2014, FEBS/EMBO Women in Science Award 2015, Darwin Medal, Royal Soc. 2016. *Publications:* numerous papers in professional journals on the molecular control of timing of flowering in plants. *Address:* John Innes Centre, Norwich Research Park, Norwich, NR4 7UH, England (office). *Telephone:* (1603) 450000 (switchboard) (office). *E-mail:* caroline .dean@jic.ac.uk (office). *Website:* www.jic.ac.uk (office).

DEAN, Christopher, OBE; British fmr ice skater; b. 27 July 1958, Nottingham; s. of Colin Dean and Mavis (née Pearson) Dean; m. 1st Isabelle Duchesnay 1991 (divorced 1993); m. 2nd Jill Ann Trenary 1994; two s.; police constable 1974–80; British Ice Dance Champion (with Jayne Torvill q.v., 1978–83, 1994; European Ice Dance Champion (with Jayne Torvill) 1981, 1982, 1984, 1994; World Ice Dance Champion (with Jayne Torvill) 1981–84, World Professional Champions 1984–85, 1990, 1995–96; Olympic Ice Dance gold medal (with Jayne Torvill) 1984, Olympic Ice Dance bronze medal (with Jayne Torvill) 1994; choreographed Encounters for English Nat. Ballet 1996, Stars on Ice in USA 1998–99, 1999–2000; Hon. MA (Nottingham Trent) 1994, BBC Sports Personality of the Year (with Jayne Torvill) 1984, Figure Skating Hall of Fame (with Jayne Torvill) 1989. *Ice Dance:* World tours with own and int. companies of skaters 1985, 1988, 1994, 1997, also tours of Australia and New Zealand 1984, 1991, UK 1992, 1997–98, Japan 1996, USA and Canada 1997–98. *Television:* Path to Perfection (ITV video) 1984, Fire & Ice (also video) 1986, Bladerunners (BBC documentary), The Artistry of Torvill & Dean (ABC TV) 1994, Face the Music 1995, Torvill & Dean, The Story So Far (biographical video) 1996, Bach Sixth Cello Suite (with Yo-Yo Ma) 1996, Dancing on Ice 2007–14 (followed by nat. tours). *Publications:* Torvill and Dean's Face the Music and Dance (with Jayne Torvill) 1993, Torvill and Dean: An Autobiography (with Jayne Torvill) 1994, Facing the Music (with Jayne Torvill) 1995. *Leisure interests:* theatre, ballet, fast cars. *Address:* c/o Sue Young, PO Box 32, Heathfield, East Sussex, TN21 0BW, England (office). *Telephone:* (1435) 867825 (office); (1273) 330798.

DEAN, Graham, BA; British artist; b. 5 Dec. 1951, Birkenhead; s. of Leslie Dean and Dorothy Dean; m. Denise Warr 1989; one s. one d.; ed Laird School of Art, Birkenhead, Bristol Polytechnic Faculty of Art and Design; artist since 1974 with over 100 solo exhbns and numerous mixed exhbns world-wide; Abbey Award in Painting, British School, Rome 1992, ICCD Studio Residency, Trivandrum, India 2000, Int. Fellowship, Vermont Studio Center, USA 2003. *Dance:* collaborations with Darshan Singh Bhuller, including No Go Zone, White Picket Fence. *Radio:* Painting by Radio (series), BBC Radio 4, 1984. *Films:* several ind. shorts and videos, including Solsbury Hill (with Peter Gabriel). *Leisure interests:* tennis, supporting Liverpool football club. *Address:* 17 Norfolk Road, Brighton, East Sussex, BN1 3AA (home); Waterhouse and Dodd, 26 Cork Street, London, W1S 3ND, England; Voc Palombaro, 32/37 San Vito, 05010 San Venanzo Terne, Umbria, Italy. *Telephone:* (20) 7734-7800 (office). *E-mail:* graham.dean1@virgin .net (home); jamie@waterhousedodd.com (office). *Website:* www.modbritart.com; www.grahamdean.com.

DEAN, Howard, BA, MD; American politician and physician; *Senior Advisor, Public Policy and Regulation Practice, Dentons US LLP;* b. 17 Nov. 1948, East Hampton, NY; s. of Howard Brush Dean and Andrea Maitland; m. Judith Steinberg; one s. one d.; ed Yale Univ., Albert Einstein Coll. of Medicine, Yeshiva Univ.; Intern, then resident in internal medicine, Medical Center Hosp. Vermont 1978–82; internal medicine specialist medical practice in Shelburne, Vt; mem. Vermont House of Reps 1983–86, Asst minority leader 1985–86; Lt Gov. State of Vermont 1986–91; Gov. of Vermont 1991–2003; sought Democratic Party presidential candidacy 2004; Chair. Democratic Nat. Cttee 2005–09, now Chair. Emer.; Sr Advisor, Public Policy and Regulation Practice, Dentons US LLP 2009–; mem. Advisory Bd Mobile Corpn 2014; mem. Int. Advisory Bd Tilray, Inc. 2018–. *Publications:* Winning Back America 2003, You Have the Power: How to Take Back our Country and Restore Democracy in America 2004, Howard Dean's Prescription for Real Healthcare Reform 2009. *Address:* Dentons US LLP, 1900 K Street, NW, Suite 600, East Tower, Washington, DC 20006, USA (office). *Telephone:* (202) 496-7500 (office). *Fax:* (202) 496-7756 (office). *E-mail:* Howard .Dean@dentons.com (office). *Website:* www.dentons.com (office).

DEAN, Hon. John Gunther, PhD; American diplomatist; b. 24 Feb. 1926, Germany; s. of Dr Joseph Dean and Lucy Dean (née Aschkenazy); m. Martine Duphénieux 1952; two s. one d.; ed Harvard Coll., Harvard Univ. Graduate School and Univ. of Paris Law School, France; entered govt service 1950, diplomatic posts in France, Belgium, Viet Nam, Laos, Togo, Mali and in US Dept of State; Dir Pacification Program in Mil. Region 1, Viet Nam 1970–72; Deputy Chief Mission, Embassy in Laos 1972–74; Amb. to Khmer Repub. 1974–75, to Denmark 1975–78, to Lebanon 1978–81, to Thailand 1981–85, to India 1985–88; Personal Rep. of Dir-Gen. of UNESCO for Cambodia 1989–90; mem. bd Petroleum Inst. of Thailand 1991, Inst. Supérieur de Gestion 1991, General Mediterranean Holdings 1992, Maersk Line Shipping 1992–2007; numerous US and foreign decorations. *Publications:* The Oral History of John Gunther Dean, The Donation of Documents by Ambassador John Gunther Dean to the National Archives 2004, 2005, Danger Zones: A Diplomat's Fight for America's Interests 2009. *Address:* 29 boulevard Jules Sandeau, 75116 Paris, France (office); BP 1318, Chalet Crettaz-Cô, 1936 Verbier, Valais, Switzerland (home). *Telephone:* 1-45-04-71-84 (office); 277712917 (home). *Fax:* 1-45-04-78-57 (office). *E-mail:* johnmartinedean@aol.com (home).

DEAN, Tacita Charlotte, CBE, RA; British visual artist and filmmaker; b. 1965, Canterbury, Kent; ed Kent Coll., Canterbury, Falmouth School of Art, Slade School of Art; comms include Millennium Dome, London, Sadler's Wells Theatre, European City of Culture celebrations, Cork, Ireland; Deutscher Akademischer Austausch Dienst Scholarship, Berlin, Germany 2000; Aachen Art Prize 2002, Fondazione Sandretto Re Rebaudengo, Turin, Italy 2004, 51st Venice Biennale Sixth Benesse Prize 2005, Solomon R. Guggenheim Museum Hugo Boss Prize, New York 2006, Kurt Schwitters Prize 2009. *Films include:* The Story of Beard 1992, The Martyrdom of St Agatha (in several parts) 1994, Girl Stowaway 1994, How to Put a Boat in a Bottle 1995, A Bag of Air 1995, Disappearance at Sea 1996, Delft Hydraulics 1996, Foley Artist 1996, Disappearance at Sea II 1997, The Structure of Ice 1997, Gellért 1998, Bubble House 1999, Sound Mirrors 1999, From Columbus, Ohio, to the Partially Buried Woodshed 1999, Banewl 1999, Teignmouth Electron 2000, Totality 2000, Fernsehturm 2001, The Green Ray 2001, Baobab 2002, Ztrata 2002, Section Cinema (Homage to Marcel Broodthaers) 2002, Diamond Ring 2002, Mario Merz 2002, Boots 2003, Pie 2003, Palast 2004, The Uncles 2004, Presentation Sisters 2005, Kodak 2006, Noir et Blanc 2006, Human Treasure 2006, Michael Hamburger 2007, Darmstädter Werkblock, 2007, Merce Cunningham Performs Stillness 2008, Amadeus 2008, Prisoner Pair 2008, Still Life 2009, Day for Night 2009, Craneway Event 2009, Manhattan Mouse Museum 2011, Edwin Parker 2011, JG 2013. *Publications include:* Teignmouth Electron 1999, Floh 2001, Seven Books 2003, Berlin Works 2005, Analogue 2006, Tacita Dean 2006, Die Regimentstochter 2006, Tacita Dean 2009, Film Works with Merce Cunningham 2009. *Address:* c/o Marian Goodman Gallery, 24 West 57th Street, New York, NY 10019, USA.

DEANE, Derek, OBE; British ballet dancer and choreographer; b. (Derek Shepherd), 18 June 1953, Redruth, Cornwall, England; s. of William Gordon Shepherd and Margaret Shepherd; ed Royal Ballet School; with Royal Ballet Co. 1972–89, reaching rank of Premier Dancer; Asst Dir Rome Opera 1990–92; Artistic Dir English Nat. Ballet 1993–2001; has also created work for Royal Ballet, Birmingham Royal Ballet, Teatro alla Scala, Shanghai Ballet and others; directed Strictly Gershwin at Royal Albert Hall, London 2011. *Television:* Swan Lake (film) 1982, Agatha Christie's Miss Marple: 4.50 from Paddington (film, dancer) 1987, Trial & Retribution (series, choreographer) 2005, Concert for Diana (special documentary, as himself) 2007, Agony and Ectasy: A Year at the English National Ballet (BBC 4 documentary) 2011. *Leisure interests:* tennis, gardening, reading, dinner parties, theatre, performing arts, travel. *Address:* c/o English National Ballet, Markova House, 39 Jay Mews, London, SW7 2ES, England.

DEANE, Seamus Francis, BA, MA, PhD, MRIA; Irish academic, poet and novelist; *Donald and Marilyn Keough Professor Emeritus of Irish Studies, University of Notre Dame;* b. 9 Feb. 1940, Derry City, NI; s. of Winifred Deane and Frank Deane; m. 1st Marion Treacy 1963; three s. one d.; m. 2nd Emer Nolan; one d.; ed Queen's Univ., Belfast, Univ. of Cambridge; Fulbright and Woodrow Wilson Scholar, Visiting Lecturer, Reed Coll., Portland, Ore. 1966–67; Visiting Lecturer, Univ. of California, Berkeley 1967–68, Visiting Prof. 1978; Lecturer, Univ. Coll., Dublin 1968–77, Sr Lecturer 1978–80, Prof. of English and American Literature 1980–93; Visiting Prof., Univ. of Notre Dame, Indiana, USA 1977, Donald and Marilyn Keough Prof. of Irish Studies 1993–2005, Prof. Emer. 2005–; Walker Ames Prof., Univ. of Washington, Seattle 1987, Jules Benedict Distinguished Visiting Prof., Carleton Coll., Minn. 1988; Dir Field Day Theatre Co. 1980–; Ed. Field Day Review 2005–; Hon. DLitt (Ulster) 1999; Ireland/America Fund Literary Award 1988, South Bank Award for Literature 1997, Guardian Fiction Prize 1997. *Publications include:* Gradual Wars (AE Memorial Award for Literature 1972) 1972, Celtic Revivals 1985, Short History of Irish Literature 1986, Selected Poems 1988, The French Revolution and Enlightenment in England 1789–1832 1988, Field Day Anthology of Irish Writing 550–1990 1991, Reading in the Dark (Irish Times Int. Fiction Prize 1997, Irish Times Irish Literature Prize 1997, Ruffino Antico Fattore Int. Literary Award 1998) 1996, Strange Country 1997, Foreign Affections: Essays on Edmund Burke 2005. *Address:* Field Day Publications, c/o O'Connell House, 58 Merrion Square, Dublin 2, Ireland (office). *E-mail:* deane.4@nd.edu (office).

DEANE, Hon. Sir William Patrick, AC, KStJ, KBE, BA, LLB, QC; Australian judge and fmr Governor-General; b. 4 Jan. 1931, St Kilda; s. of C.A. Deane, MC and Lillian Hussey; m. Helen Russell 1965; one s. one d.; ed St Joseph's Coll. Sydney, Sydney Univ. and Trinity Coll. Dublin, Ireland; Teaching Fellow in Equity, Univ. of Sydney 1956–61; barrister 1957; Justice, Supreme Court, New South Wales 1977, Fed. Court of Australia 1977–82; Pres. Australian Trade Practices Tribunal 1977–82; Justice, High Court of Australia 1982–95; Gov.-Gen. of Australia 1996–2001; Hon. LLD (Sydney, Griffith, Notre Dame, Trinity Coll., Univ. of New South Wales, Univ. of Tech. of Sydney, Univ. of Queensland), Hon. DUniv (Southern Cross, Australian Catholic Univ., Queensland Univ. of Tech., Univ. of W Sydney), Hon. DSacredTheol (Melbourne Coll. of Divinity). *Address:* PO Box 4168, Manuka, ACT 2603, Australia (home). *Telephone:* (2) 6239-4716 (office). *Fax:* (2) 6239-4916 (office). *E-mail:* deaneoffice@pmc.gov.au (office).

DEARLOVE, Sir Richard (Billing), Kt, KCMG, OBE, MA; British diplomatist and college principal; b. 23 Jan. 1945, Gorran Haven; m. Rosalind McKenzie 1968; two s. one d.; ed Monkton Combe School, Kent School, Conn., USA, Queens' Coll., Cambridge; joined the Foreign Office 1966, postings to Nairobi 1968–71, Prague 1973–76, FCO, London 1971–73, 1976–80, 1984–87, First Sec., Embassy in Paris 1980–84, Counsellor, UK Mission to the UN (UKMIS), Geneva 1987–91, Embassy in Washington, DC 1991–93; Dir of Personnel and Admin., Secret Intelligence Service 1993–94, Dir of Operations 1994–99, Asst Chief 1998–99, Chief 1999–2004; Master of Pembroke Coll., Cambridge 2004–15; mem. Int. Advisory Bd AIG 2005–11; Sr Adviser, Monitor Group 2004–11; Chair. Ascot Underwriting 2006–; Chair. of Trustees, Cambridge Union Soc. 2007–15; Dir Kosmos Energy 2013–;

Gov. English Speaking Union 2008–10; Hon. Fellow, Queens' Coll., Cambridge 2004; Hon. LLD (Exeter Univ.) 2007. *Leisure interests:* painting, fly-fishing, the future of Cornwall. *Address:* The Master's Lodge, Pembroke College, Cambridge, CB2 1RF, England (office). *Telephone:* (1223) 338129 (office). *Fax:* (1223) 766395 (office).

DEATON, Sir Angus Stewart, Kt, OBE, BA, MA, PhD; British/American economist and academic; *Dwight D. Eisenhower Professor Emeritus of International Affairs, Woodrow Wilson School, Princeton University;* b. 19 Oct. 1945, Edinburgh, Scotland, UK; two c.; ed Fettes Coll. (Foundation Scholar), Fitzwilliam Coll., Cambridge; Economist, Econ. Intelligence Dept, Bank of England 1967–68; Jr Research Officer, Dept of Applied Econs, Univ. of Cambridge 1969, Fellow and Dir of Studies in Econs, Fitzwilliam Coll. and Research Officer, Dept of Applied Econs 1972; Prof. of Econometrics, Univ. of Bristol 1976–83; Visiting Prof., Princeton Univ., USA 1979–80; Overseas Fellow, Churchill Coll., Cambridge 1990–91; fmr William Church Osborn Prof. of Public Affairs, Princeton Univ., now Dwight D. Eisenhower Prof. Emer. of Int. Affairs, Prof. Emer. of Econs and Int. Affairs and Sr Scholar, Woodrow Wilson School; Asst Ed., Review of Economic Studies 1975–80; Programme Chair., Econometric Soc. European Meeting, Athens 1979; Co-Ed., Econometric Society Monographs 1980–84; Assoc. Ed., Econometrica 1978–80, Co-Ed. 1980–84, Ed. 1984–88; Assoc. Ed., Pakistan Development Review 1990–97; mem. Editorial Bd, World Bank Research Observer 1991–2007; mem. Chief Economist's Advisory Council, World Bank 2001–; Sr Research Scientist, Gallup Organization 2007–; Pres., Section F, British Asscn 2001–02; mem. Exec. Cttee, American Econ. Asscn 1997–2000, Vice-Pres. 2004–05, Pres. 2009, Distinguished Fellow 2010; Commr, President Sarkozy's Comm. on the Measurement of Econ. Performance and Social Progress 2007–09; mem. American Philosophical Soc. 2014; Fellow, Econometric Soc. 1979 (mem. Council 1981–), American Acad. of Arts and Sciences 1992; Corresp. Fellow, British Acad. 2001, Royal Soc. of Edinburgh 2010; Hon. Fellow, Fitzwilliam Coll., Cambridge 2009, Univ. of Bristol 2016; Hon. FRSE 2016; Laurea hc, (Univ. of Rome, Tor Vergata) 2007; Hon. DSc (Econ) (Univ. Coll., London) 2007; Hon. DLitt (St Andrews) 2008; Hon. DSc in Social Science (Edinburgh) 2011; Hon. DEcon (Univ. of Cyprus) 2012; Hon. DHumLitt (Brown Univ.) 2016; Stevenson Prize for Research in Econs, Univ. of Cambridge 1971, first recipient of Frisch Medal, Econometric Soc. 1978, Medal of the University of Helsinki 1981, First Simon Kuznets Memorial Lecturer, Yale Univ. 1987, I.W. Arthur Memorial Lecturer, Univ. of Iowa 1989, Fisher-Schultz Lecturer, Econometric Soc. European Meetings, Munich 1989, Marshall Lecturer, Univ. of Cambridge 1993, Jacob Marshak Lecturer, Latin American Meetings of the Econometric Soc., Caracas 1994, Review of Econ. Statistics Lecturer, Harvard Univ. 2003, Terence Gorman Memorial Lecturer, Univ. Coll. London 2005, D. Gale Johnson Memorial Lecturer, Chicago 2005, WIDER Annual Lecturer, Helsinki 2006, David Kinley Memorial Lecturer, Univ. of Illinois, Urbana-Champaign 2007, Keynes Lecturer, British Acad., London 2007, John Kenneth Galbraith Award, Agricultural and Applied Econs Asscn Foundation 2009, Foundation Lecturer, Fitzwilliam Coll., Cambridge 2010, Stone Lecturer, Dept of Econs, Univ. of Cambridge 2010, Hicks Lecturer, Dept of Econs, Univ. of Oxford 2011, BBVA Foundation Frontiers of Knowledge Award in Econs, Finance, and Man. 2012, Leontief Prize for Advancing the Frontiers of Econ. Thought 2014, Lionel Robbins Memorial Lecturer, LSE 2014, Sveriges Riksbank Prize in Econ. Sciences in Memory of Alfred Nobel 2015, Royal Medal, Royal Soc. of Edinburgh 2016. *Publications include:* Economics and Consumer Behavior (co-author) 1980, Understanding Consumption 1992, The Analysis of Household Surveys: A Microeconometric Approach to Development Policy 1997, The Great Indian Poverty Debate (co-ed.) 2005, The Great Escape: Health, Wealth, and the Origins of Inequality 2013; numerous papers in professional journals. *Address:* 127 Julis Romo Rabinowitz Building, Woodrow Wilson School, Princeton University, Princeton, NJ 08544, USA (office). *E-mail:* deaton@princeton.edu (office). *Website:* scholar.princeton.edu/deaton (office).

DEB, Biplab Kumar; Indian politician; *Chief Minister of Tripura;* b. 25 Nov. 1971, Gomoti Dist, Tripura; s. of Hirudhan Deb and Mina Rani Deb; m. Niti Deb; one s. one d.; ed Udaipur Coll., Tripura Univ., Delhi Univ.; spent 15 years in New Delhi, various jobs including as professional gym instructor, later Asst to Ganesh Singh, BJP mem. Lok Sabha (lower house of parl.) and Private Sec. to fmr BJP leader K. N. Govindacharya; mem. Tripura Legis. Ass. for Banamalipur 2018–; Chief Minister of Tripura 2018–; fmr mem. Rashtriya Swayamsevak Sangh (RSS); mem. Bharatiya Janata Party (BJP) (also BJP-in-charge for state of Tripura) 2014–, Pres. Tripura BJP Div. 2016–. *Address:* Office of the Chief Minister, Government of Tripura, Agartala 799 001, India (office). *Telephone:* (381) 2324000 (office). *Fax:* (381) 2223201 (office). *E-mail:* cs-tripura@nic.in (office). *Website:* tripura.gov.in (office).

DEBBASCH, Charles, DenD; French legal scholar and academic; *Professor of Law, Université d'Aix-Marseille III;* b. 22 Oct. 1937, Tunis, Tunisia; s. of Max Debbasch; m. 2nd Ivonne Chawki-Kamel; three s. three d.; tutorial asst 1957; Jr Lecturer, Law Faculty, Université d'Aix-Marseille III 1959–62; Prof. of Law, Grenoble Univ. 1962–63; Prof. of Law, Université d'Aix-Marseille II 1963–67, Chair of Public Law, Faculty of Law and Econ. Sciences 1967, Dir Centre of Research into Legal Admin. 1966–, Centre of Research and Study on Mediterranean Societies 1969–71; Head of Research Comm., Ministry of Educ. 1968–69; Dir Teaching and Research Unit attached to Faculty of Law and Political Sciences, Aix-Marseille Univ. 1966, Dean, Faculty of Law and Political Sciences 1971–73; Pres. Nat. Asscn of Pres. of Univs Specializing in Law and Politics and Deans of Law Faculties 1971–78; Prof., Coll. of Europe, Bruges 1975–81; Pres. Consultative Cttee, Public Law Univs 1978; tech. adviser, Gen. Secr., French presidency 1978–81; Pres. Fondation Vasarely 1981–91; Dir and Dir-Gen. of Press Group, Dauphiné Libéré 1984–89; Pres. Agence générale d'information 1985–89, Supervisory Council of Dauphiné Libéré 1989–94, Observatoire int. de la démocratie 1994–; Dir Inst. Int. du droit des médias 1989–; Minister and Special Adviser to Pres. of Togo 2005–; Officier, Ordre nat. du Mérite, Chevalier, Légion d'honneur, Chevalier des Palmes académiques, Grand Officer of the Aztec Eagle (Mexico), Commdr, Order of Tunisian Repub., Officer of Merit, Senegal. *Publications include:* Procédure administrative contentieuse et procédure civile 1962, La République tunisienne 1962, Le Droit de la radio et de la télévision 1970, L'Administration au pouvoir 1970, L'Université désorientée 1971, Droit administratif 1973, La France de Pompidou 1974, Institutions administratives 1975, Les Chats de l'émirat 1976, Institutions et droit administratifs (three vols) 1980–99, Introduction à la politique 1982, L'Elysée dévoilé 1982, Les constitutions de la France 1983, Lexique de politique 1984, Contentieux administratif 1985, Les Associations 1985, La Ve République 1985, La Disgrace du socialisme 1985, Droit constitutionnel 1986, La Cohabitation froide 1988, Le Droit de l'audiovisuel 1988, La société française 1989, Les grands arrêts du droit de l'audiovisuel 1991, Mémoires du Doyen d'Aix-en-Provence 1996, Droit des médias 1999, Droit administratif des biens 1999, La Constitution de la Ve République 2000, Un amour de Love 2001, Contes de nos animaux favoris 2004, La succession d'Eyadema 2006, L'entrée en Sarkozy 2008; contrib. to numerous other works. *Address:* 25 avenue Mozart, 75116 Paris, France (office). *Telephone:* 1-45-20-45-72 (home); 9-0042316 (Togo) (mobile) (office). *E-mail:* debbasch.charles@wanadoo.fr (home). *Website:* www.charlesarthur.space-blogs.com (office); www.charlesdebbasch.com.

DEBEN, Baron (Life Peer), cr. 2010, of Winston in the County of Suffolk; **Rt Hon. John Selwyn Gummer,** PC, MA; British politician; *Chairman, Sancroft International Ltd;* b. 26 Nov. 1939, Stockport, Greater Manchester, England; s. of Canon Selwyn Gummer and Sybille Gummer (née Mason); brother of Peter Selwyn Gummer, now Lord Chadlington (q.v.); m. Penelope J. Gardner 1977; two s. two d.; ed King's School, Rochester and Selwyn Coll., Cambridge; Ed., Business Publs 1962–64; Ed.-in-Chief, Max Parrish and Oldbourne Press 1964–66; Editorial Controller, BPC Publishing 1967–73; Dir Shandwick Publishing Co. 1966–81; Dir Siemssen Hunter Ltd 1973–80, Chair. 1979–80; Man. Dir EP Group of Cos 1975–81; Chair. Selwyn Sancroft Int. 1976–81; MP for Lewisham W 1970–74, Eye, Suffolk (now Suffolk Coastal) 1979–2010; Parl. Pvt. Sec. to Minister of Agric. 1972; Vice-Chair. Conservative Party 1972–74, Chair. 1983–85; Asst Govt Whip 1981, Lord Commr Treasury (Whip) 1982; Under-Sec. of State for Employment Jan.–Oct. 1983, Minister of State for Employment 1983–84, Paymaster-Gen. 1984–85; Minister of State at Ministry of Agric., Fisheries and Food 1985–88; Minister for Local Govt, Dept of Environment 1988–89; Minister of Agric. 1989–93; Sec. of State for the Environment 1993–97; Chair. Conservative Group for Europe 1997–2000, Sancroft International Ltd 1997–, Marine Stewardship Council 1998–2005, Valpak Ltd 1998–, Asscn of Professional Financial Advisers 2003–, Veolia Water UK 2004–13, Quality of Life Challenge 2006–07, Forewind (offshore wind co.) 2010–12, Corlan Hafren (energy co.) 2011–12, Cttee on Climate Change 2012–; mem. Gen. Synod of Church of England 1979–92 (resgnd); mem. Bd of Dirs Prince Albert II of Monaco Foundation; Dir (non-exec.), Catholic Herald newspaper; Trustee, Blue Marine Foundation; joined Roman Catholic Church 1994; The Ordre Saint-Charles 2012; Medal of Honour, Royal Soc. for the Protection of Birds 1998. *Publications include:* When the Coloured People Come 1966, To Church with Enthusiasm 1969, The Permissive Society 1970, The Christian Calendar (with L. W. Cowie) 1971, Faith in Politics (with Alan Beith and Eric Heffer) 1987, Christianity and Conservatism 1990. *Leisure interests:* gardening, Victorian buildings. *Address:* Sancroft International Ltd, 46 Queen Anne's Gate, London, SW1H 9AP, England (office); House of Lords, Westminster, London, SW1A 0PW, England (office). *Telephone:* (20) 7960-7900 (office). *E-mail:* office@sancroft.com (office). *Website:* www.sancroft.com (office).

DEBONO, Giovanna, BA; Maltese politician; b. (Giovanna Attard), 25 Nov. 1956, Gozo; d. of Coronato Attard and Anna Attard (née Tabone); m. Anthony Debono; one s. one d.; ed Univ. of Malta; teacher, Educ. Dept 1981–87; MP (Nationalist Party) 1987–; Parl. Sec. Ministry for Social Devt 1995–96; Minister for Gozo 1998–2013. *Address:* Nationalist Party, Herbert Ganado Street, Pietà PTA 1541, Malta (office). *Telephone:* 21243641 (office). *Fax:* 21243641 (office). *E-mail:* admin@pn.org.mt (office). *Website:* www.pn.org.mt (office).

DEBRAY, (Jules) Régis; French writer and government official; b. 2 Sept. 1940, Paris; s. of Georges Debray and Janine Alexandre; m. Elisabeth Burgos 1968; one d.; ed Ecole normale supérieure de la rue d'Ulm; colleague of Che Guevara, imprisoned in Bolivia 1967–70; Co-ed. Comité d'études sur les libertés 1975; adviser on foreign affairs to François Mitterrand; responsible for Third World Affairs, Secr.-Gen. of Presidency of Repub. 1981–84, with Office of Pres. of Repub. 1984–85, 1987–88; Maître des requêtes, Conseil d'Etat 1985–93; Sec.-Gen. Conseil du Pacifique Sud 1984–85; Pres. Conseil scientifique de l'École nationale supérieure des sciences de l'information 1998–2002, Institut Européen en Sciences en Religions 2002–04; elected mem. Académie Goncourt (seventh seat) 2011. *Publications:* Entretiens avec Allende 1971, La Critique des armes 1973, La Guerilla du Che 1974, Les Epreuves du fer 1974, L'Indésirable 1975, La Neige brûle (Prix Fémina) 1977, Lettre aux communistes français et á quelques autres 1978, Le Pouvoir intellectuel en France 1979, Le Scribe 1980, Critique de la raison politique 1981, La Puissance et les rêves 1984, Les Empires contre l'Europe 1985, Comète, ma comète 1986, Eloges 1986, Les Masques, une éducation amoreuse 1988, Que vive la République 1988, A demain de Gaulle 1990, Cours de médiologie générale 1991, Christophe Colomb, le visiteur de l'aube: les traités de Tordesillas 1992, Vie et mort de l'image: une histoire du regard en Occident 1992, Contretemps: Eloge des idéaux perdus 1992, Ledannois 1992, L'Etat séducteur 1993, L'Oeil naïf 1994, Manifestes médiologiques 1994, Loués soient les seigneurs 1996, Par amour de l'art 1998, L'Abus monumental 1999, Croire, voir, faire 1999, L'Emprise 2000, i.f. suite et fin 2000, Introduction à la médiologie 2000, L'Enseignement du fait religieux dans l'école laïque 2002, L'Edit de Caracalla ou plaidoyer pour les Etats-Unis d'occident 2002, L'Ancien Testament à travers 100 chefs-d'œuvre de la peinture 2003, Le Nouveau Testament à travers 100 chefs-d'œuvre de la peinture 2003, Dieu, un itinéraire 2003, Haïti et la France: Rapport à Dominique de Villepin, ministre des Affaires étrangères 2004, Le siecle et la règle 2004, Ce que nous voile le voile 2004, La Mythologie gréco-latine à travers 100 chefs-d'oeuvres de la peinture 2004, L'Histoire ancienne à travers 100 chefs-d'oeuvres de la peinture 2004, Chroniques de l'idiotie triomphante 2004, Journal D'Un Petit Bourgeois Entre Deux Feux Et Quatre Murs 2004, Le Plan Vermeil 2004, Le Feu Sacré 2005, Julien Le Fidèle Ou Le Banquet Des Démons 2005, Sur le pont d'Avignon 2005, Aveuglantes Lumières 2006, Supplique Aux Nouveaux Progressistes Du XXie Siècle 2006, Eloge des frontières 2010. *Address:* c/o Editions Gallimard, 5 rue Sébastien Bottin, 75007 Paris, France (office). *Website:* www.regisdebray.com.

DEBRÉ, Bernard André Charles Robert, DenM; French politician and surgeon; b. 30 Sept. 1944, Toulouse; s. of Michel Debré and Anne-Marie Lemaresquier; m. Véronique Duron 1971; three s. one d.; ed Lycée Janson de

Sailly and Faculté de Médecine, Paris; hosp. doctor 1965–80; hosp. surgeon 1980; Prof., Faculté de Médecine, Paris 1985; Head of Urology, Hôpital Cochin 1990; Deputy (RPR) to Nat. Assembly 1986–94, 2004– (joined UMP 2007); Mayor of Amboise 1992–2001; Minister of Cooperation 1994–95; Councillor, Paris XVI arrondissement 2008–; mem. of French Cttee of Ethics 1986–88; f. Pour Paris Asscn (cr. to oppose policies of incumbent Mayor of Paris, Betrand Delanoë) 2005; Chevalier, Légion d'Honneur and numerous foreign decorations. *Publications:* La France malade de sa santé 1983, Un traité d'urologie (4 vols) 1985, Le voleur de vie (la bataille du Sida) 1989, L'illusion humanitaire 1997, Le retour de Mwami 1998, La grande transgression 2000 (Prix Louis Pauwels 2001), Le suicide de France (jtly) 2002, Avertissement aux Malades, aux Médicins et aux Elus (ed.) 2002, De la mauvaise conscience en général et de l'Afrique en particulier 2003, Tant que nous t'aimerons (L'Euthanasie la loi impossible) 2004, Le Roman de Shangai 2005, La revanche du serpent ou la fin de l'homo sapiens 2005, La Véritable Histoire des génocides rwandais 2006, Et si l'on parlait d'elle? 2007, articles in French and foreign journals. *Leisure interests:* travel, collecting antique plates, sports. *Address:* Assemblée nationale, 126 rue de l'Université, 75355 Paris 07 SP (office); 30 rue Jacob, 75006 Paris, France (home). *Telephone:* 1-43-25-51-41 (home); 6-85-30-45-73. *Fax:* 1-58-41-27-55 (office). *E-mail:* bdebre@assemblee-nationale.fr (office); bdebre@yahoo.fr. *Website:* www.assemblee-nationale.fr (office).

DEBRÉ, Jean-Louis, DenD; French magistrate and politician; *President, Conseil supérieur des Archives;* b. 30 Sept. 1944, Toulouse; s. of Michel Debré (fmr Prime Minister of France) and Anne-Marie Lemaresquier; m. Ann-Marie Engel 1971; two s. one d.; ed Lycée Janson-de-Sailly, Inst. d'Etudes Politiques, Faculté de Droit, Paris and Ecole Nat. de la Magistrature; Asst Faculté de Droit, Paris 1972–75; Adviser, Office of Jacques Chirac 1974–76; Deputy Public Prosecutor, Tribunal de Grande Instance, Evry 1976–78; Magistrate, Cen. Admin. of Ministry of Justice 1978; Chef de Cabinet to Minister of Budget 1978; Examining Magistrate, Tribunal de Grande Instance, Paris 1979; RPR Deputy to Nat. Ass. 1986–95, 1997–2002, Pres. RPR Group 1997–2002; Town Councillor, Evreux 1989; Conseiller Général, Canton de Nonancourt 1992–2001; Deputy Sec.-Gen. and Spokesman for Gaullist Party 1993; Minister of the Interior 1995–97; Vice-Pres. Gen. Council of the Euro 1998–; Mayor of Evreux 2001–07; Pres. Nat. Ass. 2002–07; Pres. Conseil Constitutionnel 2007–16; Pres., Conseil supérieur des Archives 2016–; Chevalier du Mérite agricole, Grand-Croix, Ordre d'Isabelle la catholique (Spain); Prix du Trombinoscope 2003, Marianne d'Or 2004. *Publications include:* Les idées constitutionnelles du Général de Gaulle 1974, La constitution de la Ve République 1974, Le pouvoir politique 1977, Le Gaullisme 1978, La justice au XIXe 1981, Les républiques des avocats 1984, Le curieux 1986, En mon for intérieur 1997, Pièges 1998, Le Gaulisme n'est pas une nostalgie 1999, Qu'est-ce que l'Assemblée nationale? 2006, Jeux de haine 2011, Le Monde selon Chirac 2015, Ce que je ne pouvais pas dire 2016. *Leisure interests:* riding, tennis. *Address:* Conseil supérieur des Archives, Ministry of Culture and Communication, 3 rue de Valois, 75001 Paris (office); 126 rue de l'Université, 75007 Paris, France (home). *Website:* www.archivesdefrance.culture.gouv.fr/archives-publiques/organisation-du-reseau-des-archives-en-france/conseil-superieur-des-archives/ (office).

DEBS, Richard A., BA, MA, PhD, JD; American lawyer and business executive; *Advisory Director and Member of the International Advisory Board, Morgan Stanley & Company;* m. Barbara Knowles Debs 1958; one d.; ed Colgate Coll., Harvard Law School and Advanced Man. Program at Harvard Business School, Princeton Univ. (Ford Foundation Fellow); fmr Fulbright Scholar in Egypt, subsequently held a jt Harvard-Princeton research fellowship; mem. NY Bar; served as COO Fed. Reserve Bank of New York, also Alt. mem. Fed. Open Market Cttee –1976; joined Morgan Stanley as Founding Pres. Morgan Stanley International 1976, currently Advisory Dir, Morgan Stanley and mem. Int. Advisory Bd; Chair. Bd of American Univ. of Beirut; Chair. Emer. Carnegie Hall; mem. Fulbright Asscn; mem. Emer. Group of Thirty Consultative Group on Int. Econ. and Monetary Affairs, Inc. (G-30), Washington, DC; Trustee, Carnegie Endowment for Int. Peace, Inst. of Int. Educ. 2001–; mem. Bd of Dirs Malaysia Fund, Industrial Bank of Japan, Gulf Int. Bank, UK, Mizuho Corporate Bank, Bank Julius Baer, United Gulf Group; f. R.A. Debs Consulting; Hon. DLit (American Univ. of Beirut) 2005; first recipient of Lifetime Achievement Award, Fulbright Asscn, King Abdul Aziz Medal. *Address:* Morgan Stanley & Co. Inc., 1585 Broadway, New York, NY 10036, USA (office). *Telephone:* (212) 761-4000 (office). *Fax:* (212) 761-0086 (office). *E-mail:* info@morganstanley.com (office). *Website:* www.morganstanley.com (office).

DÉBY ITNO, Gen. Idriss; Chadian army officer and head of state; *President;* b. (Idriss Déby), 1952, Berdoba; m. 1st Amani Musa Hilal; two s. (one deceased); m. 2nd Hinda Déby 2005; ed École Française à Fada; served in Army, trained as helicoptor pilot; fmr C-in-C of Armed Forces; fmr mil. adviser to Pres. Hissène Habré, overthrew him in coup Dec. 1990; Chair. Interim Council of State, Head of State 1990–91, Pres. of Chad 1991–, also C-in-C of Armed Forces; Chair. African Union 2016–17; mem. Mouvement patriotique du salut (MPS); Grand Croix, Ordre nat. de la République centrafricaine 2012, Grand-croix, Ordre int. des Palmes Académiques du Conseil Africain et Malgache pour l'Enseignement Supérieur 2013. *Address:* Office of the President, Palais rose, BP 74, N'Djamena, Chad (office). *Telephone:* 22-51-44-37 (office). *Fax:* 22-52-45-01 (office). *Website:* www.presidencetchad.org (office).

DÉCEMBRE, Ronald Grey; Haitian civil servant and politician; *Minister of the Economy and Finance;* more than 25 years with Ministry of the Economy and Finance, becoming Sec. of State for Tax Reform 2012, for Finance 2017–18, Minister of the Economy and Finance 2018–. *Address:* Ministry of the Economy and Finance, Palais des Ministères, rue Mgr Guilloux, Port-au-Prince, Haiti (office). *Telephone:* 2223-7113 (office). *Fax:* 2223-1247 (office). *E-mail:* mef@mefhaiti.gouv.ht (office). *Website:* www.mefhaiti.gouv.ht (office).

DECKER, Susan L., BSc, MBA; American business executive and accountant; ed Tufts Univ. and Harvard Business School; Chartered Financial Analyst; Publishing & Advertising Equity Securities Analyst, Donaldson, Lufkin & Jenrette 1986–98, Global Dir Equity Research 1998–2000; Chief Financial Officer, Yahoo! Inc. 2000–, Sr Vice-Pres. Finance and Admin 2000–02, Exec. Vice-Pres. Finance and Admin 2002–07, Pres. 2007–09; Entrepreneur-in-Residence, Harvard Business School 2009; mem. Bd of Dirs Costco Wholesale 2004–, Pixar Animation Studios 2004–06, Stanford Inst. for Econ. Policy Research 2005–07, Berkshire Hathaway, Intel Corpn; mem. Financial Accounting Standards Advisory Council 2000–04.

DECQ, Odile; French architect; *Partner, Studio Odile Decq;* b. 1955; ed School of Architecture, Rennes, Univ. of Paris School of Architecture at La Villette, Inst. of Political Studies, Paris; Founding Partner (with Benoit Cornette), Odile Decq Benoit Cornette Architects (now Studio Odile Decq) 1985–; teacher, Ecole d'Architecture de Paris—La Villette 1984–86; Guest Prof., Univ. of Montréal, Canada 1992, Univ. of Kansas 1997, 2000, Technische Universität, Vienna 1998, University Coll., London, UK 1998–2000; Prof. of Architecture and Head of Dept, Ecole Spéciale d'Architecture, Paris 1992–99, Dir 2007–; taught at Columbia Univ., New York 2001–03, Akademie Künst, Vienna 2003, Kunst Akademie, Dusseldorf, Germany 2004, Southern California Inst. of Architecture, Los Angeles 2006; jury mem. Westminster Univ. and Bartlett School, London, UK; elected mem. Acad. d'Architecture; Int. Fellow, RIBA 2007–; Prof., l'Ecole Spéciale d'Architecture, Paris 1992–2007, Dir 2007–12; Founder of CONFLUENCE: Institute for Innovation and Creative Strategies in Architecture, Lyon, France 2014; Hon. mem. Nat. Soc. of Architects, Czech Repub. 2007–; Commdr, Ordre des Arts et Lettres, Chevalier, légion d'Honneur 2003, Officier de l'Ordre du Mérite 2012, Médaille de Vermeil et d'Honneur, Académie d'architecture 2014; The Golden Lion Award, Architecture Biennale, Venice, Oscar du Design, Le Nouvel Economiste, Paris, Prix Plus Beaux Ouvrages de Construction Metallique, USINOR, Paris, Premier Award, Ninth Int. Prize for Architecture, London, DuPont Benedictus Commercial Award for Innovation in Architectural Laminated Glass, Premio Il Principe e l'Architetto, Museum of Contemporary Art, Rome 2003, Int. Architecture Award 2006, 2008, 2010, World Architecture Community Award 2008, MIPIM Future Project Award 2009, ECOLA Award 2012, Designer of the Year, Maison & Objet 2013, Women Architect of the year 2013, ARVHA prize. *Architectural works include:* Banque Populaire de L'Ouest, Rennes (received ten nat. and int. awards) 1990, Parc d'activités aéroportuaires, St Jacques de la Lande, Rennes 1994, Métafort, Aubervilliers 1995, Cité des Arts de Fort d'Aubervilliers 1995, Viaduct of Highway A14 and Highway Man. Centre, Nanterre 1996, French Pavilion, Venice Biennale 1996, A Third Bridge City, Rotterdam 1998, School of Econ. Sciences and Law Library, Univ. of Nantes 1998, Port de Gennevilliers 1999, Multiplex, Cambridge 1999, Collective Housing Project, Clichy 1999, Social Housing Complex, Paris 1999, Banque de France Office HQ, Montpellier, Vanishing black holes, (installation) Venice, Italy, 2000, Ice skating rink, Bordeaux 2000, 2001, Renovation of the Conf. Hall, UNESCO, Paris 2001, Client Centre, Dunkerque, France 2001, Flat unlimited (installation), Beijing, China 2004, Lillle Italy (restaurant), Paris 2004, Il Tre (restaurant), Paris 2005, Boat Wally 141, Fano, Italy 2006 (Int. Show Boats Award 2007), social housing, Paris 2006, MACRO contemporary art museum in Rome 2010, Phantom restaurant, Opera Garnier, Paris, France 2011, FRAC Bretagne, Rennes, France 2012, LG Headquarters, Lyon, France 2014, Foundation of CONFLUENCE: Institute for Innovation and Creative Strategies in Architecture, Lyon, France 2014, Great site of Homo Erectus Fossils Museum, Nanjing, China 2015. *Publications include:* The Architect's Journal 1997, 100 Red Candles for Reading 2007; articles in professional journals, exhibition catalogues, monologues. *Address:* Studio Odile Decq, 11 rue des Arquebusiers, 75003 Paris, France (office). *Telephone:* 1-42-71-27-41 (office). *Fax:* 1-42-71-27-42 (office). *E-mail:* office@odiledecq.com (office). *Website:* www.odiledecq.com (office).

DeCRANE, Alfred C., Jr; American lawyer and business executive; b. 11 June 1931, Cleveland, Ohio; s. of Alfred Charles DeCrane and Verona DeCrane (née Marquard); m. Joan Elizabeth Hoffman 1954; one s. five d.; ed Notre Dame and Georgetown Univs; attorney, Texaco Inc., Houston and New York 1959, Asst to Vice-Chair. 1965, to Chair. 1967, Gen. Man. Producing Dept, Eastern Hemisphere 1968, Vice-Pres. 1970, Sr Vice-Pres. and Gen. Counsel 1976, mem. Bd of Dirs 1977–96, Exec. Vice-Pres. 1978–83, Pres. 1983–86, Chair. of Bd 1987–96, CEO 1993–96; Hon. Dir American Petroleum Inst.; mem. Bd of Dirs, Corn Products Int., Harris Corpn; mem. Advisory Bd Morgan Stanley Int.; mem. Bd of Trustees Univ. of Notre Dame; Hon. DHL (Manhattanville Coll.) 1990; Hon. JD (Univ. of Notre Dame) 2002. *Address:* 600 Steamboat Road, Suite 107, Greenwich, CT 06830-7181, USA (office). *Telephone:* (203) 863-6582 (office).

DEE, Elizabeth; American gallery owner and art dealer; est. Elizabeth Dee Gallery, New York; represents artists including Alex Bag, Mark Barrow, Eric Baudelaire, Philippe Decrauzat, Harry Dodge & Stanya Kahn, Lizzie Fitch & Ryan Trecartin, Renée Green, Gareth James, Kevin Landers, Miranda Lichtenstein, Virgil Marti, Ryan McNamarra, Josephine Meckseper, Amir Mogharabi, Carl Ostendarp, Adrian Piper, Meredyth Sparks, Mika Tajima/New Humans and Ryan Trecartin; Founder and mem. Advisory Bd X-Initiative (non-profit consortium of global art community to present exhbns and programming responding to the major philosophical and econ. shifts in contemporary art) 2009–; presented, with Darren Flook of London's Hotel gallery, Independent, an art fair that attracted participation from int. array of commercial galleries 2010. *Films:* has produced many of Trecartin's movies, including I-BE AREA 2007, K-Corea INC. K (Section A) 2009, Sibling Topics (Section A) 2009, P.opular S.ky (section ish) 2009. *Address:* Elizabeth Dee Gallery, 545 West 20th Street, New York, NY 10011, USA (office). *Telephone:* (212) 924-7545 (office). *Fax:* (212) 924-7671 (office). *E-mail:* edee@elizabethdeegallery.com (office). *Website:* www.elizabethdeegallery.com (office); www.x-initiative.org.

DEECH, Baroness (Life Peer), cr. 2005, of Cumnor in the County of Oxfordshire; **Ruth Lynn Deech,** DBE, MA; British regulator and lawyer; b. (Ruth Fraenkel), 29 April 1943, London, England; d. of Josef Fraenkel and Dora Rosenfeld; m. John Deech 1967; one d.; ed St Anne's Coll., Oxford and Brandeis Univ. USA; called to Bar, Inner Temple 1967, Bencher; Legal Asst, Law Comm. 1966–67; Asst Prof., Univ. of Windsor Law School, Canada 1968–70; Fellow and Tutor in Law, St Anne's Coll., Oxford 1970–91, Vice-Prin. 1988–91, Prin. 1991–2004; mem. Univ. of Oxford Hebdomadal Council 1986–2000; Chair. Univ. of Oxford Admissions Cttee 1993–97, 2000–03; Gov. Oxford Centre for Hebrew and Jewish Studies 1994–2000; Chair. Human Fertilization and Embryology Authority 1994–2002; Pro-Vice-Chancellor Univ. of Oxford 2001–04; Gresham Prof. of Law 2008–12; Chair. Bar Standards Bd 2009–14; mem. Human Genetics Comm. 2000–02; Rhodes Trustee 1997–2006; Visiting Prof., Osgoode Hall Law School, Canada 1978; Gov. BBC

2002–06; Ind. Adjudicator for Higher Educ. 2004–08; Freeman of the Drapers' Co. 2003, of the City of London 2003; Hon. Fellow, Soc. for Advanced Legal Studies 1997; Hon. Bencher, Inner Temple 1996–; Hon. QC 2013; Hon. LLD (Richmond American Int. Univ.) 2000, (Strathclyde) 2003; Hon. PhD (Ben Gurion Univ., Israel). *Publications:* Divorce Dissent 1994, From IVF to Immortality 1997; articles on family law, property law, autobiog. etc. *Leisure interests:* music, after-dinner speaking. *Address:* House of Lords, Westminster, London, SW1A 0PW, England. *Telephone:* (20) 7219-3562. *E-mail:* deechr@parliament.uk. *Website:* www.law.ox.ac.uk/people/baroness-ruth-deech-dbe-qchon.

DEEN, Mohamed Waheed; Maldivian business executive and government official; b. 3 March 1947, Malé; m. Aisha Sayed Mohamed; four s. eight d.; ed attended coll. in Sri Lanka; Vice-Pres. Maldives Chamber of Commerce and Industries; mem. Human Rights Comm. of the Maldives; Minister of Atolls Devt 2005–07, of Youth and Sports 2007–08; Vice-Pres. of the Maldives 2012–13; exec. mem. Maldives Tourism Advisory Bd; Exec. mem. Maldives Tourism Promotion Bd, Sports Tourism Cttee; Exec. Vice-Pres. Commonwealth Bodybuilding Fed.; Exec. Vice-Pres. Asian Bodybuilding Fed.; Founder-mem. and Chair. Diabetes and Cancer Soc., Project Hope; mem. Exec. Bd Maldives Asscn of Tourism Industry; Founder Maldives Bodybuilding Fed.; Founder and Pres. Maldives Surfing Asscn; Man. Dir Orchid Holdings; Dir Thulhagiri Development, HPL Resorts; CEO Orchid Resorts Management Pvt. Ltd; Man. Dir Deens Orchid Agency; Chair. Bandos Island Resort; Presidential Commemoration for Nat. Service in recognition of service to the nation during terrorist attack of November 1988, Nat. Award in recognition of service to tourism industry 1993, Nat. Award in recognition of service to community devt 1997, Hon. Award from Ministry of Tourism in recognition of 25 years of distinguished service towards sustainable devt of tourism. *Leisure interests:* football, cricket, squash, badminton, health and fitness. *Address:* Orchid Resorts Management Pvt. Ltd, H. Deens Villa, Mihelli Goathé, Henveinu, Malé, The Maldives (office).

DEFAR, Meseret; Ethiopian athlete; b. 19 Nov. 1983, Addis Ababa; silver medal, 3,000m, World Youth Championships 1999; gold medal, 5,000m, African Championships, Bambous 2006, silver medal, 5,000m, Algiers 2000, Addis Ababa 2008, Nairobi 2010; silver medal, 5,000m, World Jr Championships 2000, gold medal, 3,000m, 5,000m. 2002; gold medal, 5,000m All-African Games 2003, 2007, Afro-Asian Games 2003; gold medal, 5,000m, Athens Olympics 2004, bronze medal, 5,000m, Beijing Olympics 2008, gold medal, 5,000m, London Olympics 2012; gold medal, 3,000m, World Indoor Championships, Budapest 2004, Moscow 2006, Valencia 2008, Doha 2010, silver medal, 3,000m, Istanbul 2012, bronze medal, 3,000m, Birmingham 2003; silver medal, 5,000m, World Championships, Helsinki 2005; gold medal, 5,000m, World Championships, Osaka 2007, bronze medal Berlin, 5,000m, Berlin 2009, Daegu 2011; gold medal, 5,000m, World Championships, Moscow 2013; Women's 5,000m Best Year Performance 2005–07, Women's 3,000m Best Year Performance 2006–07, Women's Track & Field Athlete of the Year 2007. *Address:* c/o Ethiopian Athletics Federation, PO Box 3241, Addis Ababa, Ethiopia. *Website:* www.ethiosports.com.

DeGENERES, Ellen; American comedienne, actress and television presenter; b. 26 Jan. 1958, Metairie, La; d. of Elliott DeGeneres and Betty Jane DeGeneres (née Pfeffer); m. Portia DeGeneres (b. Amanda Lee Rogers) 2008; ed Grace King High School, Metairie, Atlanta High School, Univ. of New Orleans; began performing stand-up comedy at small clubs and coffee houses; emcee at Clyde's Comedy Club, New Orleans by 1981; began touring nationally early 1980s; appeared for first time on the Tonight Show with Johnny Carson 1986; Special Envoy for Global AIDS Awareness 2011; named Showtime's Funniest Person in America 1982, Emmy Award for Outstanding Writing in a Comedy Series (Ellen: The Puppy Episode) 1997, Favorite Voice from an Animated Movie, Kids' Choice Awards 2004, People's Choice Awards: Favorite Funny Female Star 2005, 2006, 2007, 2008, Favorite Talk Show Host 2005, 2006, 2007, 2008, 2009, 2010, Favorite Yes I Chose This Star 2008; Pres.'s Medal, Tulane Univ. 2009, Mark Twain Prize for American Humor 2012, Daytime Emmy Award for Outstanding Talk Show Entertainment 2013, 2014, 2015, Daytime Emmy Award for Outstanding Special Class Writing 2014, Presidential Medal of Freedom 2016, People's Choice Award for Favorite Daytime TV Host, Favorite Animated Movie Voice, and Favorite Comedic Collaboration 2017. *Films include:* Wisecracks 1991, Coneheads 1993, Mr Wrong 1996, Doctor Doolittle (voice) 1998, Goodbye Lover 1999, EdTV 1999, The Love Letter 1999, Reaching Normal 1999, Finding Nemo (voice) 2003, My Short Film 2005, Unity 2014. *Television includes:* Women of the Night (as herself) 1988, Duet (series) 1988–89, Open House 1989, Laurie Hill 1992, Ellen 1994–98 (also producer), Roseanne 1995, Mad About You 1998, If These Walls Could Talk 2 (also exec. producer) 2000, On the Edge 2001, The Ellen Show (18 episodes) 2001–02, host Emmy Awards 2001, 2005, Ellen DeGeneres: Here and Now 2003, MADtv 2003, Ellen: The Ellen DeGeneres Show (Daytime Emmy Awards for Outstanding Talk Show 2004, 2005, 2006, 2007, Outstanding Talk Show Host 2005, 2006, 2007, 2008, Outstanding Special Class Writing 2005, 2006, 2007) 2003–, E! True Hollywood Story 2004, Six Feet Under 2004, Joey 2005, host Acad. Awards ceremony 2007, Ellen's Really Big Show 2007, Sesame Street (uncredited) 2007, Forbes 20 Richest Women in Entertainment 2007, The Bachelorette 2007, American Idol 2007–08 (Co-Judge 2009–10), Ellen's Even Bigger Really Big Show 2008, Ellen's Bigger, Longer & Wider Show 2009, So You Think You Can Dance (Guest Judge) 2009, The Simpsons (as herself in episode 'Judge Me Tender') 2010, Acad. Awards 2014. *Recording includes:* Ellen DeGeneres: Taste This (stand-up comedy, live CD) 1996. *Publications include:* My Point… And I Do Have One 1995, The Funny Thing Is… 2003, Seriously…I'm Kidding 2011. *Address:* Ellen DeGeneres Show, PO Box 7788, Burbank, CA 91523, USA. *Website:* www.ellentv.com.

DEGENHART, Elmar, Dipl-Ing, PhD; German business executive; *Chairman of the Executive Board, Continental AG;* b. 29 Jan. 1959, Dossenheim; ed Univ. of Stuttgart; fmr scientific employee, Fraunhofer Inst. for Manufacturing Eng and Automation IPA, Head of Dept of Handling and Industrial Robot Systems 1987–93; Dir of Operations, Brake Systems North America, ITT Automotive Europe GmbH 1993–98; Exec. Vice-Pres., Electronic Brake Systems, Continental AG and mem. Man. Bd Continental Teves AG & Co. oHG 1998–2003, Chair. Exec. Bd Continental AG, additionally responsible for Corp. Communications, Corp. Quality and Environment, Continental Business System, Continental Automotive Functions 2009–, additionally temporary responsibility for Div. Chassis & Safety Aug. 2013–; Pres. Chassis Systems, Robert Bosch GmbH 2004–05; CEO Keiper Recaro Group 2005–08; Pres. Schaeffler Group Automotive 2008–09. *Address:* Continental AG, Vahrenwalder Straße 9, 30165 Hanover, Germany (office). *Telephone:* (511) 938-01 (office). *E-mail:* info@conti-online.com (office). *Website:* www.conti-online.com (office).

DEGHATI, Reza; French (b. Iranian) photojournalist; *Founder, Webistan Photo Agency;* b. 26 July 1952, Tabriz, Iran; ed Univs of Tabriz and Tehran; photographer with Agence France Presse during Iranian revolution 1978; corresp. with Newsweek, Iran 1978–81, with Time Magazine 1983–88; consultant to UN Humanitarian Programme, Afghanistan 1989–91; Reporter for UNICEF 1989–95, for National Geographic Magazine 1990–; f. Webistan Photo Agency 1991–; photographs have appeared in numerous int. magazines, including Der Spiegel, Paris-Match, Le Nouvel Observateur, The Observer, El País, Oggi, Newsweek, Life, etc.; regular corresp. for BBC Radio Persia and Radio France Int. Persia; Founder and Pres. Aïna (non-profit org.); Lecturer, George Washington Univ., Washington, DC, Stanford Univ., Beijing Univ., Sorbonne, Paris; mem. Advisory Bd National Geographic All Roads Film Project; mem. Exec. Cttee HSBC Bank Foundation; Sr Fellow, Ashoka Foundation 2008; Fellow, National Geographic; Chevalier, Ordre nat. du Mérite 2005; Dr hc (American Univ. of Paris) 2009; UNICEF Hope Prize for 'Portraits of Lost Children in Rwanda' 1996, Prince of Asturias Humanitarian Medal (Spain) 2006, Honor Medal, Univ. of Missouri (Columbia School of Journalism) 2006, Award of Recognition, Chicago Univ. 2006, Pictet Prize, Paris 2008, Lucie Award for Achievement in Documentary, Lucie Foundation 2009, Int. Center of Photography Infinity Award 2010, Human Right Awards (Special Mention) 2010, Hamdan bin Mohammed bin Rashid Al Maktoum Int. Photography Award (HIPA) 2013. *Films:* National Geographic films: Into Forbidden Zone (Emmy Award 2002), Inside Mecca 2003, Reza: Shooting Back 2008, Afghan Warrior 2010, Parvaz 2010. *Publications:* Paix en Galilee 1983, Bayan Ko! 1986, Paris-Pekin-Paris '87 1987, Around the World 1992, Kurdes: Les Chants Brules 1995, Massoud, des Russes aux Talibans 2001, Plus loin sur la Terre 2002, Le pinceau de Bouddha 2002, Eternités Afghanes 2002, Crossing Destinies 2003, Insouciances 2004, The Silk Road 2007, War Peace 2008, Reporters without Borders 2008, Sindbad 2009, Chemins parallèles 2009, Derrière l'Objectif 2010, Les âmes rebelles (Rebellious souls) 2010, L'Envol, La Conférence des Oiseaux (Soaring: The Conference of the Birds) 2010, Algérie (Algeria) 2012, Learning a Living 2012, Soul of Coffee (in seven languages) 2013, The Elegance of Fire 2014, The Massacre of the Innocents 2014, Kurdistan Renaissance 2017. *Address:* Webistan Photo Agency, 122 rue Haxo, 75019 Paris, France (office). *Telephone:* 1-53-19-83-83 (office). *E-mail:* reza@rezaphoto.org (office). *Website:* www.rezaphoto.org (office); www.webistan.com (office).

DEGUARA, Louis, MD; Maltese physician and politician; b. 18 Sept. 1947, Naxxar; m. Maria Fatima Mallia; one s. one d.; ed St Aloysius Coll., Birkikara, Univ. of Malta; medical practitioner 1973; fmrly houseman, St Luke's, Sir Paul Boffa and Gozo Gen. Hosps, Prin. Medical Officer of Health, Northern Region; Gen. Practitioner 1977–; MP (Nationalist Party) 1981–2011; Parl. Sec., Ministry for Social Devt 1995–96; Shadow Minister and Opposition Spokesman for Health 1996–98; Minister of Health 1998–2008. *Address:* c/o Partit Nazzjonalista (Nationalist Party), Herbert Ganado Street, Pietà PTA 1541, Malta. *E-mail:* admin@pn.org.mt.

DEGUTIENĖ, Irena; Lithuanian politician; *Vice-Chairman (Deputy Speaker), Seimas (Parliament);* b. 1 June 1949, Šiauliai; m. Gedminias Degutis; one s. one d.; ed Vilnius Univ.; worked in Vilnius Red Cross Hosp. 1975–94; Deputy Minister of Health Care 1994–96; Minister for Social Security and Labour 1996–2000; mem. conservative Homeland Union—Lithuanian Christian Democrats; mem. Seimas (Parl.) 1996–, Deputy Chair. Cttee on Social Affairs and Labour 2000–04, Chair. (Speaker) Seimas (first woman) 2009–12, Vice-Chair. (Deputy Speaker) 2012–, mem. Cttee on Budget and Finance 2012–16, Comm. of the Seimas of the Repub. of Lithuania and the Lithuanian World Community 2013–; mem. Cttee on Health Affairs 2016–; Acting Prime Minister of Lithuania 4–18 May 1999, 27 Oct.–3 Nov. 1999. *Address:* Seimas (Parliament), Gedimino pr. 53, Vilnius 01109, Lithuania (office). *Telephone:* (5) 239-6651 (office). *E-mail:* irena.degutiene@lrs.lt (office); irdegu@lrs.lt (office). *Website:* www.lrs.lt (office).

DEHAENE, Stanislas, PhD; French mathematician, neuroscientist, academic and author; *Director, INSERM-CEA Cognitive Neuroimaging Unit, Collège de France;* b. 12 May 1965, Roubaix; m. Ghislaine Dehaene-Lambertz; three s.; ed École Normale Supérieure, Paris, Univ. of Paris VI, École des Hautes Études en Sciences Sociales, Paris; Research Scientist, Cognitive Sciences and Psycholinguistics Lab., Institut Nat. de la Santé et de la Recherche Médicale (INSERM) 1989–99, Research Dir, INSERM 1997–2005, Dir INSERM-CEA Cognitive Neuroimaging Unit 2002–; Postdoctoral Fellow, Inst. of Cognitive and Decision Sciences, Univ. of Oregon, USA 1992–94; Prof. of Experimental Psychology, Collège de France 2005–; Assoc. Ed. Cognition 1999–2005, Frontiers in Neurosciences 2008–; mem. Editorial Bd, Mathematical Cognition 1991–97, Neuroimage 2001–, PLOS Biology 2003–, Mind Brain and Education 2006–, Trends in Cognitive Science 2011; mem. Bd of Reviewing Editors, Science 2008–; Editorial Advisor, Editions Odile Jacob, Paris 1996–; Action Ed., Cognitive Neuropsychology 1998–2003; mem. Acad. des sciences 2005, Pontifical Acad. of Sciences 2008, American Philosophical Soc. 2010, NAS 2010; Corresp. FBA 2010; Hon. Prof., East China Normal Univ., Shanghai 2010; Chevalier, Ordre nat. du Mérite 2008, Légion d'honneur 2011; Dr hc (Lisbon) 2011; Fanny Emden Prize, Acad. des sciences 1996, James S. McDonnell Foundation Centennial Fellowship (co-recipient) 1999, Villemot Prize, Acad. des sciences 2000, Jean-Louis Signoret Prize, IPSEN Foundation 2001, Pius XI Medal, Pontifical Acad. of Sciences 2002, Louis D. Prize (co-recipient), Institut de France 2003, Gold Medal, Asscn Arts-Sciences-Lettres 2007, Dr A.H. Heineken Prize for Cognitive Science 2008. *Films:* La bosse des maths (documentary, ARTE/Transeurope Film) 2000, Dans le secret de nos émotions (documentary, ARTE/Transeurope Film) (Primé au festival int. Telecienca de Vila Real, Portugal 2003, Premier Prix, Festival Int. du Film de Santé de Liège, Belgique 2004, Prix de la réalisation, 17ème Festival Int. du Film Scientifique d'Orsay 2004) 2004. *Publications:* Numerical Cognition (ed.) 1993, Le Cerveau en action: l'imagerie cérébrale en psychologie cognitive (ed.) 1997, La Bosse des Maths (Jean Rostand Award) 1997, The Number Sense 1997 (second edn 2011), The Cognitive Neuroscience of Consciousness (ed.) 2001, From Monkey

Brain to Human Brain (co-ed.) 2005, Vers une science de la vie mentale 2007, Les neurones de la lecture (Grand Prix RTL-Lire) 2007, Reading in the Brain 2009, Parole et musique: aux origines du dialogue humain (co-ed.) 2009, Space, Time and Number in the Brain: Searching for the Foundations of Mathematical Thought (co-author) 2011, Characterizing Consciousness: From Cognition to the Clinic? (co-ed.) 2011, Apprendre à lire. Des sciences cognitives à la salle de classe 2011; 39 book chapters and more than 220 papers in professional journals. *Address:* Inserm-CEA Cognitive Neuroimaging Unit, CEA/SAC/DSV/DRM/NeuroSpin, Bât 145, Point Courrier 156, 3, 91191 Gif-sur-Yvette, France (office). *Telephone:* 1-69-08-79-32 (office). *Fax:* 1-69-08-79-73 (office). *E-mail:* stanislas.dehaene@cea.fr (office). *Website:* www.college-de-france.fr/site/en-stanislas-dehaene (office); www.unicog.org/pm/pmwiki.php/Main/StanislasDehaene (office).

DEHECQ, Jean-François; French pharmaceuticals industry executive; *Honorary Chairman, Sanofi SA;* b. 1 Jan. 1940, Nantes; ed Ecole Nat. Supériere des Arts et Métiers, Lille; began career as math. teacher, Lycée catholique Saint-Vincent de Senlis, Oise 1964; Man. Dir Sanofi (subsidiary of Elf-Aquitaine Group) 1973–98, Chair. and Man. Dir Sanofi-Synthélabo (following merger of Sanofi and Synthélabo 1998) 1999–2004, Chair. Sanofi-Aventis (following merger of Sanofi-Synthélabo and Aventis) 2004–10, Hon. Chair. 2010– (co. name changed to Sanofi 2011); Pres. European Fed. of Pharmaceutical Industries and Asscns (EFPIA) 2001–02; Vice-Pres. Conseil national de l'industrie; Commdr du Mérite de l'Ordre souverain de Malte 1995; Officier, Ordre nat. du Mérite agricole 1996; Commdr, Légion d'honneur, Grand Officier 2010; Commdr, Ordre nat. du Mérite 2002; Chevalier, Confrérie Internationale 'La Toison d'Or' 2002; Commdr des Palmes académiques 2008; Nessim Habif Prize 2003, Congrès des Ingénieurs Arts et Métiers 2003. *Address:* Sanofi SA, 174 avenue de France, 75013 Paris, France (office). *Telephone:* 1-53-77-42-23 (office). *Fax:* 1-53-77-42-65 (office). *E-mail:* info@sanofi.com (office). *Website:* www.sanofi.com (office).

DEHGAN, Brig.-Gen. Hossein; Iranian politician and fmr air force officer; b. 1957, Shahreza, Isfahan Prov.; ed Tehran Univ.; joined Iranian Revolution Guards Corps (IRGC) 1979, becoming Commdr, IRGC Tehran Div. 1980–82, Commdr Isfahan (Dist 2), Commdr IRGC in Syria and Lebanon 1982–83, Deputy Commdr, IRGC Air Force 1986–90, Commdr 1990–92, Gen. Man. IRGC Cooperatives Foundation 1996, Deputy Minister of Defence 1997–2003, Acting Minister of Defence 2003, Minister of Defence 2013–17; Defence Industries Adviser to Chief Commdr of Iranian Armed Forces 2017–; Deputy Pres. Bonyad Shadid (martyrs' foundation charitable trust) 2005, Pres. 2005–09; Deputy Head, Armed Forces Strategic Studies Centre 2009–10; Sec., Expediency Council Political, Defence and Security Cttee 2010–13; mem. Moderation and Devt Party.

DEIGHTON, Len; British writer; b. 1929, London. *Publications include:* The Ipcress File 1962 (also film), Horse under Water 1963, Funeral in Berlin 1964 (also film), Où est le Garlic 1965, Action Cook Book 1965, Cookstrip Cook Book (USA) 1966, Billion Dollar Brain 1966 (also film), An Expensive Place to Die 1967, Len Deighton's London Dossier (guide book) 1967, The Assassination of President Kennedy (co-author) 1967, Only When I Larf 1968 (also film), Bomber 1970 (also radio dramatization), Declarations of War (short stories) 1971, Close-Up 1972, Spy Story 1974 (also film), Yesterday's Spy 1975, Twinkle, Twinkle, Little Spy 1976, Fighter: The True Story of the Battle of Britain 1977, SS-GB 1978, Airshipwreck (co-author) 1978, Blitzkrieg 1979, Battle of Britain (co-author) 1980, XPD 1981, Goodbye Mickey Mouse 1982, Berlin Game 1983, Mexico Set 1984, London Match 1985, Winter: A Berlin Family 1899–1945 1987, Spy Hook 1988, ABC of French Food 1989, Spy Line 1989, Spy Sinker 1990, Basic French Cookery Course 1990, Mamista 1991, City of Gold 1992, Violent Ward 1993, Blood, Tears and Folly 1993, Faith 1994, Hope 1995, Charity 1996, Sherlock Holmes and the Titanic Swindle (short story) 2006, James Bond: My Long and Eventful Search for His Father (non-fiction) 2012. *Address:* c/o Jonathan Clowes Ltd, 10 Iron Bridge House, Bridge Approach, London, NW1 8BD, England (office). *Telephone:* (20) 7722-7674 (office). *Fax:* 871-528-3647 (office). *E-mail:* admin@jonathanclowes.co.uk (office). *Website:* www.jonathanclowes.co.uk (office).

DEISS, Joseph, PhD; Swiss economist, politician, UN official and business executive; *Chairman, Alstom Switzerland;* b. 18 Jan. 1946, Fribourg; m. Elizabeth Mueller; three s.; ed Coll. Saint-Michel, Fribourg, Univ. of Fribourg, King's Coll., Cambridge, UK; Lecturer (part-time) in Political Economy, Univ. of Fribourg 1973–83, Prof. Extraordinary 1984–99, Sr Faculty mem. Dept of Social and Econ. Science 1996–98, Prof. of Political Economy 2007–; Deputy, Great Council of Fribourg 1981–91, Pres. 1991, Nat. Adviser 1991–99; Vice-Pres. Comm. on Foreign Policy, Nat. Council 1995–96; Pres. Comm. on Revision of Fed. Constitution 1996; Head of Fed. Dept of Foreign Affairs 1999–2002; mem. Swiss Fed. Council 1999–2006, Pres. of the Swiss Confed. 2004; Head of Fed. Dept of Econ. Affairs 2003–06 (resgnd); Pres. 65th Session of the Gen. Ass., UN, New York 2010–11; Pres. Banque Raiffaisen du Haut-Lac 1996–99; Chair. Schuhmacher AG, Schmitten 1996–99; Chair. Alstom Switzerland 2012–; Vice-Chair. Advisory Council, Zurich Financial Services Int.; Bd mem. Emmi Group, Switzerland, Zurich Insurance Co., Ireland and South Africa; mem. Bd of Govs World Bank, EBRD; mem. Christlichdemokratische Volkspartei der Schweiz—Parti démocrate-chrétien suisse (Christian Democratic People's Party), Strategic Council, Saint Joseph Univ., Beirut; Hon. mem. Int. Raoul Wallenberg Foundation; Officier, Légion d'honneur 2007; Grand Cordon, Order of the Rising Sun (Japan) 2008; Dr hc (Univ. of Sofia, Bulgaria) 2001, (Univ. of Neuchâtel, Switzerland) 2007, (Business School of Lausanne, Switzerland) 2009. *Publications:* The Regional Adjustment Process and Regional Monetary Policy 1978, Economie politique et politique économique de la Suisse 1979, Initiation à l'économie politique: Analyse économique de la Suisse 1982, Manuel d'économie politique (co-author) 1994. *Address:* Alstom Switzerland, Brown Boveri Strasse 7, 5401 Baden, Switzerland (office). *Telephone:* (58) 5057733 (office). *Website:* www.alstom.com (office).

DEISSEROTH, Karl, AB, MD, PhD; American neuroscientist, physician and academic; *D.H. Chen Professor of Bioengineering and of Psychiatry and Behavioral Sciences, Stanford University;* b. 18 Nov. 1971, Boston, Mass; m. Michelle Leigh Monje; ed Harvard and Stanford Univs; MD internship/licensure, Stanford Univ. 2000–01, Psychiatry Residency 2000–04; Diplomate, American Bd of Neurology and Psychiatry 2006; Prin. Investigator and Clinical Educator, Dept of Psychiatry, Stanford Univ. School of Medicine 2004–05, Asst Prof. of Bioengineering and Psychiatry 2005–08, Assoc. Prof. of Bioengineering and Psychiatry 2009–12, HHMI Early Career Investigator 2009–13, Prof. of Bioengineering and Psychiatry, Stanford Univ. 2012–, D.H. Chen Professorship and Chair 2012–; Foreign Adjunct Prof., Karolinska Institutet, Sweden 2013–; Investigator, Howard Hughes Medical Inst. 2014–; Scientific Advisor, Kinetics Foundation for Parkinson's Research 2007–; mem. NARSAD Council (Brain and Behavior Research Foundation) 2009–; mem. Inst. of Medicine 2010, NAS 2011; John Harvard Scholarship: Academic Achievement of the Highest Distinction, Harvard Univ. 1990–92, Stanford Yanofsky Grad. Research Award 1997, NIMH Outstanding Resident Award 2002, American Psychiatric Asscn Resident Research Award 2004, Charles E. Culpeper Scholarship in Medical Science Award 2004, Klingenstein Fellowship Award and Robert H. Ebert Clinical Scholar Award 2005, Whitehall Foundation Award 2005, NARSAD Young Investigator Award 2005, American Psychiatric Inst. for Research and Educ. Young Faculty Award 2005, McKnight Foundation Technological Innovations in Neuroscience Award 2005, Coulter Foundation Early Career Translational Research Award in Biomedical Eng 2005, NIH Dir's Pioneer Award 2005, Presidential Early Career Award in Science and Eng 2006, McKnight Foundation Scholar Award 2007, World Econ. Forum Lecturer, Davos, Switzerland 2008, William M. Keck Foundation Medical Research Award 2008, Lawrence C. Katz Prize, Duke Univ. 2008, Schuetze Prize, Columbia Univ. 2008, Soc. for Neuroscience YIA Award 2009, Soc. for Neuroscience Special Lecture: Optogenetics: Development and Application 2009, Gill YIA Award, Indiana Univ. 2010, Koetser Prize, Zurich, Switzerland 2010, Nakasone Prize, Int. Human Frontier Science Program/HFSP 2010, Alden Spencer Prize, Columbia Univ. 2011, Perl/UNC Prize 2012, Record Prize, Baylor Univ. 2012, Zuelch Prize, Max Planck Soc. 2012, NAS Richard Lounsbery Prize 2013, Dickson Prize in Science 2014, Keio Medical Science Prize 2014, Lurie Prize in Biomedical Sciences 2015, NIH Pioneer Award 2015, Albany Medical Center Prize 2015, Breakthrough Prize in Fundamental Physics (co-recipient) 2016, Kyoto Prize in Advanced Tech. 2018, Berthold Leibinger Zukunftspreis 2018, Rumford Prize, American Acad. of Arts and Sciences (co-recipient) 2019. *Publications:* more than 140 papers in professional journals. *Leisure interest:* fly-fishing. *Address:* 318 Campus Drive West, Clark Center W083, Department of Bioengineering, Stanford University, Stanford, CA 94305, USA (office). *Telephone:* (650) 725-8524 (office). *E-mail:* deissero@stanford.edu (office). *Website:* web.stanford.edu/group/dlab/about_pi.html (office); www.hhmi.org/scientists/karl-deisseroth (office).

DEITCH, Jeffrey, MBA; American art dealer, art critic and exhibition organizer; b. 1952; ed Wesleyan Univ., Harvard Business School; art critic and exhbn curator since mid-1970s; fmr Asst Dir John Weber Gallery, New York; fmr Curator De Cordova Museum, Lincoln, Mass; Vice-Pres. Citibank, responsible for developing and managing the bank's art advisory and art finance businesses 1979–88; f. own art advisory firm 1988; first American Ed. Flash Art; first important curatorial project was Lives, a 1975 exhbn about artists who used their own lives as an art medium, presented in vacant office bldg in Tribeca, lower Manhattan; opened a public gallery, Deitch Projects 1996–2010; Dir, Museum of Contemporary Art, Los Angeles 2010–13; mem. Art Dealers Asscn of America; mem. Bd Trustees Wesleyan Univ. 1982–85; Art Critic's Fellowship, Nat. Endowment for the Arts 1979. *Publications include:* numerous catalogue essays, including projects for the Museum of Modern Art, Paris, Stedelijk Museum, Amsterdam, Whitney Museum, New York; essay The Art Industry was included in catalogue for the Metropolis exhbn, Martin-Gropius-Bau, Berlin 1991; contrib. to Arts, Art in America, Artforum, and numerous other publs. *Address:* The Gallery, Deitch Projects, 76 Grand Street, New York, NY 10012, USA (office). *Telephone:* (212) 343-7300 (office). *Fax:* (212) 343-2954 (office). *E-mail:* info@deitch.com (office). *Website:* www.deitch.com (office).

DEJEAN-ASSÉMAT, Anne, PhD; French molecular biologist and academic; *Permanent Scientist and Director, Laboratory of Nuclear Organization and Oncogenesis, Pasteur Institute;* ed Université Pierre et Marie Curie, Paris; Researcher, INSERM (French Nat. Inst. for Health and Medical Research) 1985–91, Research Dir 1991–2003, Perm. Scientist and Dir Lab. of Nuclear Organization and Oncogenesis, Pasteur Inst. and of INSERM Research Unit of Molecular and Cellular Biology of Tumors 2003–; Corresp., Acad. des sciences 1999, mem. 2004; mem. European Molecular Biology Org. 2004; Hamdan Medicine Award 2000, Gagna & Van Heck Award 2003, Laureate for Europe, L'Oréal-UNESCO Awards for Women in Science 2010. *Publications:* numerous papers in professional journals on the molecular and cellular mechanisms involved in the development of human cancers. *Address:* Nuclear Organization and Oncogenesis Unit, Pasteur Institute, 28 rue du Docteur Roux, 75724 Paris Cedex 15, France (office). *Telephone:* 1-45-68-80-00 (office). *Fax:* 1-43-06-98-35 (office). *E-mail:* anne.dejean@pasteur.fr (office). *Website:* www.pasteur.fr (office).

DEKA, Ramesh C., MD; Indian physician and academic; *Distinguished Chair Professor, Medical Education and Research, Amity University;* b. 1 Oct. 1948, Assam; ed Gauhati Medical Coll. and Hosp., All India Inst. of Medical Sciences; Reader and Head, Dept of Otorhinolaryngology, Kasturba Medical Coll., Manipal 1976–79; with Jawaharlal Inst. of Postgraduate Medical Educ. and Research, Pondicherry 1979–81; joined faculty at All India Inst. of Medical Sciences 1981, Head of Dept of Otorhinolaryngology 1995–, Dean 2006–09, Dir All India Inst. of Medical Sciences 2009–13; Pres. Asscn of Otolaryngologists, Delhi 1988–89, mem. Governing Body 1993–94; Treasurer Neuro-otological and Equilibriometric Soc. 1981–82, Gen. Sec. 1982–90, Vice-Pres. 1991–92, Pres. 1993–94; Pres. All India Rhinology Soc. 2001–02, Asscn of Otolaryngologists 2002–03; Chair. Indian Acad. of Otolaryngology, Head and Neck Surgery 2002–10; Chair. Organizing Cttee Int. Asian Research Symposium in Rhinology, Mumbai 2004, Regional Consultation Meeting of WHO for SEA regional countries on Colombo for Prevention and Control of Deafness 2004; currently Distinguished Chair Prof., Medical Education and Research, Amity Univ.; Fellow, American Acad. of Otolaryngology 2004–, Int. Medical Sciences Acad. 2007–; mem. Int. Advisory Cttee Asian Research Symposium in Rhinology 2004–08; Chair. Editorial Bd Indian Journal of Otolaryngology, Head and Neck Surgery 1994–96; Editorial Chief Vertigo View Point; mem. Editorial Bd Indian Journal of Otolaryngology, Acta Otolaryngologica (Sweden), Otology and Neuro-otology (USA), Otolaryngology & HN Surgery, USA, Pakistan Journal of Otolaryngology (Pakistan); Hon. Sec., Asscn of Otolaryngologists, Delhi 1985–86; Dr R.A.F Copper (Gold Medal) Award, Asscn of Otolaryngologists 1975, NES India Research Award (Gold Medal), Neurotological Soc. of India 1984, G.D Birla Oration Award, Kashmir Univ. 1991, Rashtriya Ratan Award 1999, Best

ENT Services Award, Jammu ENT Soc. 2000, Bharat Gaurav Award, Best Citizen Of India, Int. Publishing House 2007, Lifetime Achievement Award 2010. *Address:* Amity University, Sector 125, Noida, 201 303, India (office). *Telephone:* (12) 04713600 (office). *Website:* www.amity.edu (office); www.rameshcdeka.com.

DEKHEL, Turki ibn Abdullah al-, MSc; Saudi Arabian broadcaster and journalist; *General Manager, Al Arabiya News Channel;* b. 2 July 1973, Riyadh; three c.; ed Imam Muhammad ibn Saud Islamic Univ., Riyadh, Makased Univ., Beirut, Lebanon; began career as mosque imam; fmr columnist with Al Hayat (daily newspaper) from 1989, also fmr contrib. to most major Saudi newspapers, including Al Riyadh, Al Sharq Al Awsat, Al Majala magazine; Political Corresp., Radio MBC FM, Dubai 1999, Radio Monte Carlo, Saudi Arabia 1997–98; daily columnist, Al Watan newspaper; hosts own TV programme on Al Arabiya News Network and radio show on Panorama radio channel since 2003; contributed to establishment of UK-based Elaph Arabic-language news portal as well as Al-Arabiya channel and its website, Gen. Site Admin. –2007; Gen. Man. Al Arabiya News Channel 2015–; Owner Al Mesbar Studies and Research Centre, Madarek Publishing House, Dubai; Annual Award, America Abroad Media 2014. *Publications:* Memoirs of a Previously Obese Man (in Arabic). *Address:* Al Arabiya News Channel, PO Box 72627, Dubai Media City, United Arab Emirates (office). *Telephone:* (4) 3919999 (office). *Fax:* (4) 3919900 (office). *E-mail:* english.contact@alarabiya.net (office). *Website:* english.alarabiya.net (office).

DEKKER, Cornelis (Cees), MSc, PhD; Dutch physicist and academic; *Distinguished University Professor, Department of Bionanoscience, Delft University of Technology;* b. 7 April 1959, Haren, Groningen; m.; three c.; ed Univ. of Utrecht; Research Asst, Univ. of Utrecht 1984–88, Asst Prof. 1988–93; Visiting Researcher, IBM Research, Yorktown Heights, USA 1990–91, Technion, Israel Inst. of Tech., Haifa 2000; Assoc. Prof., Delft Univ. of Tech. 1993–99, Antoni van Leeuwenhoek Prof. 1999–, Prof. of Molecular Biophysics 2000–, Group Leader of Molecular Biophysics Group 2001–10, Distinguished Univ. Prof. 2006–, Founding Chair. Dept of Bionanoscience 2010–13, Scientific Dir 3TU Centre of Excellence 'Bionanoapplications' 2010–, Dir Kavli Inst. of Nanoscience Delft 2010–; mem. Royal Netherlands Acad. of Arts and Sciences 2003, New York Acad. of Sciences 2005, Bataafsch Genootschap der Proefondervindelijke Wijsbegeerte 2013; Fellow, Inst. of Physics 2004, American Physical Soc. 2006; Kt Order of Netherlands Lion 2014; Discover Award for Emerging Future Technologies 1999, Netherlands Org. for Scientific Research Pioneer Award 2000, European Physical Soc. Agilent Technologies Europhysics Prize 2001 (co-recipient), Julius Springer Prize for Applied Physics 2002, Netherlands Org. for Scientific Research Spinoza Prize 2003, Int. Montefiore Award 2005, Innovation in Nano Research Prize (Repub. of Korea) 2006, inaugural Reijer Hooykaas Prize 2011, Nanoscience Prize, Int. Soc. for Nanoscale Science, Computation and Eng 2012, Physica Prize, Dutch Physical Soc. 2012, Royal Acad. Professor Prize, Royal Netherlands Acad. of Arts and Sciences 2015. *Publications:* more than 240 papers in scientific journals on carbon nanotubes, single-molecule biophysics and nanobiology; five patents. *Address:* Kavli Institute of NanoScience, Delft University of Technology, Lorentzweg 1, 2628 CJ Delft, The Netherlands (office). *Telephone:* (15) 2786094 (office). *Fax:* (15) 2781202 (office). *E-mail:* c.dekker@tudelft.nl (office). *Website:* ceesdekkerlab.tudelft.nl (office).

DEKKER, Wout; Dutch business executive; *Chairman of the Supervisory Board, Randstad NV;* b. 10 Nov. 1956; CEO and Chair., Nutreco 2000–12; mem. Supervisory Bd, Randstad NV (Chair. 2012–), Macintosh Retail Group NV 2007–14, Rabobank Group 2010–, Chair. 2013–16, Royal FrieslandCampina NV 2017– (also Chair. Remuneration and Appointment Cttee), SHV Holdings 2017–; Chair., Princess Máxima Center 2013–; mem. Taskforce Biodiversity and Natural Resources; mem. Advisory Council for Issuers, NYSE Euronext. *Address:* Randstad NV, PO Box 12600, 1112 TC Diemen, Netherlands (office). *Telephone:* (20) 569-59-11 (office). *Website:* www.randstad.com (office).

DEKKERS, Marijn, PhD; Dutch/American business executive; *Chairman, Unilever NV and Unilever PLC;* b. 22 Sept. 1957, Tilburg, The Netherlands; m.; three d.; ed Radboud Univ., Nijmegen, Univ. of Eindhoven; began career in research with General Electric in USA; moved to Honeywell 1995–2000; COO Thermo Electron Corpn (renamed Thermo Fisher Scientific, Inc. following acquisition of Fisher Scientific) 2000–02, Pres. and CEO 2002–10; mem. Bd of Man., Bayer AG Jan. 2010–16, Chair. Oct. 2010–16; Chair. Unilever NV and Unilever PLC 2016–; Ind. Dir, General Electric 2012–; Pres. German Chemical Industry Asscn 2014–16; Vice-Pres. Fed. of German Industry. *Address:* Unilever PLC, Unilever House, 100 Victoria Embankment, London, EC4Y 0DY, England (office). *Telephone:* (20) 7822-5252 (office). *Fax:* (20) 7822-5511 (office). *E-mail:* press-office.london@unilever.com (office). *Website:* www.unilever.com (office).

DEL CASTILLO GÁLVES, Jorge Alfonso Alejandro; Peruvian lawyer and politician; b. 2 July 1950, Lima; ed Nat. Univ. of San Marcos, Lima, Pontifical Catholic Univ. of Peru; District Councillor of Barranco 1981–83; Mayor of Barranco Ward, Lima 1984–86, apptd Prefect of Lima 1985; mem. Partido Aprista Peruano—PAP, Sec.-Gen. PAP 1999–2006, 2010–14, Rep. of PAP before OAS; Mayor of Metropolitan Lima Co. 1987–89; mem. Chamber of Deputies 1990–92; elected to Peruvian Congress of the Repub. for Lima 1995–, re-elected 2000, 2001, 2006; Pres. Council of Ministers (Prime Minister of Peru) 2006–08 (resgnd). *Address:* Partido Aprista Peruano, Avenida Alfonso Ugarte 1012, Breña, Lima 5, Peru (office). *Telephone:* (1) 4250218 (office). *E-mail:* ofisistemapap@apra.pe (office). *Website:* www.apra.org.pe (office).

DEL CID DE BONILLA, María Antonieta; Guatemalan fmr central banker and government official; Exec. Dir for Guatemala, IDB 1998; Minister of Public Finance 2004–08; fmr Vice-Pres. Banco de Guatemala (cen. bank), Pres. 2008–10; Pres. Distribuidoras de Electricidad de Occidente y Oriente (Deocsa-Deorsa) 2011–. *Address:* c/o Banco de Guatemala, 7A Avda 22-01, Zona 1, Apdo 365, Guatemala City, Guatemala.

DEL GENIO, Anthony D., BS, MS, PhD; American atmospheric scientist and academic; *Physical Scientist, Goddard Institute for Space Studies, National Aeronautics and Space Administration;* b. 21 Feb. 1952, New York, NY; m.; one c.; ed Cornell Univ., Univ. of California, Los Angeles; Scientific Programmer/Analyst, Climate Group, GTE Information Systems, NASA/Goddard Inst. for Space Studies (GISS), New York June–Sept. 1976, Consultant 1976–77, Nat. Research Council (NRC) RRA 1978–80, Man. Planetary Group, Sigma Data Services 1980–85, Physical Scientist, NASA/GISS 1985–; Grad. Research Asst, Dept of Earth and Space Sciences, UCLA 1973–76, 1976–78; Coordinator, Columbia Univ. Grad. Program in Atmospheric and Planetary Science 1984–; Lecturer, GISS/Columbia Univ. Summer Inst. on Planets and Climate 1980–85; Adjunct Asst Prof., Dept of Physics, Queensborough Community Coll., CUNY 1982–85; Adjunct Assoc. Prof., Dept of Environmental Science, Barnard Coll. 1993–99; Lecturer, Dept of Earth and Environmental Sciences, Columbia Univ. 1983–89, Adjunct Asst Prof. 1989–92, Adjunct Assoc. Prof. 1992–, Adjunct Prof. 1997–, Adjunct Prof., Dept of Applied Physics 1995–; Invited Lecturer, NATO ASI, Energy and Water Cycles in the Climate System, Glücksburg, Germany 1991, Int. Research Inst. for Climate Prediction, Applications and Training Pilot Project 1993, NCAR Summer School on Clouds and Climate 1993, NATO ASI, Remote Sensing of Energy and Water Cycles, Plon, Germany 1995, Goddard Earth Science and Tech. Summer Program 2003–04; Co-Investigator, Pioneer Venus Orbiter Cloud Photopolarimeter Experiment 1978–92; Pioneer Venus Dynamics and Structure Working Group 1979–80; Organizer, GISS/Columbia Univ. Summer Inst. on Planets and Climate 1983, 1985, 1987; Science Advisory Group, NASA Lidar Atmospheric Sensing Experiment 1988–97; Co-Investigator/Interdisciplinary, Earth Observing System 1989–99; Science Steering Group, GEWEX Water Vapor Project 1990; Prin. Investigator, Atmospheric Radiation Measurement Program 1993–; Team mem. Cassini Saturn Orbiter Imaging Science Subsystem 1990–; Cassini/Huygens Atmospheric Working Group 1991–; mem. NASA/Goddard Space Flight Center (GSFC) Dir's Discretionary Fund Review Panel 1991–93; Science Team mem. NASA TRMM/GPM 1991–97, 1998–2001, 2003–; Prin. Investigator, First ISCCP Regional Experiment III 1995–98, Cttee 1995–98; mem. Science Team Exec. Cttee, Dept of Energy ARM Program 1996–2000, 2002–05, SGP Site Advisory Cttee 1995–98, Cloud Modeling Working Group Steering Cttee 2000–; Assoc. Ed. Journal of Climate 1996–2004, Ed. 2004–; mem. Drafting Panel, FIRE-IV: CRYSTAL Research Plan 1998–99; Prin. Investigator, Global Aerosol Climatology Project 1998–2002; Reviewer, NAS/NRC Report 'Understanding Climate Change Feedbacks'; Science Team mem. NASA Aqua AMSR-E 2003–07, CloudSat/CALIPSO 2007–; mem. Writing Panel, American Meteorological Soc. Statement on Climate Change 2007; mem. American Geophysical Union 1978, American Astronomical Soc. (Div. for Planetary Sciences) 1981, American Meteorological Soc. 1987 (Fellow 2007); NASA GISS Peer Award 1986, NASA Certificate of Outstanding Performance 1987, 1988, 1989, 1990, 1992, 1994, 1995, 1998, 2007, 2009, 2010, 2011, 2012, 2013, 2014, NASA GISS Best Publication Award 1989, 1990, 1993, 1994, 1997, 2000, 2002, 2003, 2006, 2007, 2009, Citation for Excellence in Reviewing, Icarus 1992, 1998, Outstanding Teacher Award, Columbia Univ. Dept of Earth and Environmental Sciences 1994, 2001, 2006, NASA Group Achievement Award, Cassini Imaging Science Subsystem 1998, NASA GSFC Earth Sciences Directorate Special Act Award 2004, 2005, 2006, NASA Exceptional Scientific Achievement Medal 2008, NASA Group Achievement Award, Cassini Saturn and Cross-Discipline Target Working Teams 2009. *Publications:* more than 100 scientific papers in professional journals on stratiform and cumulus cloud parameterization in general circulation models, hydrologic cycle feedbacks on climate, comparative dynamics of planetary atmospheres. *Address:* NASA Goddard Institute for Space Studies, 2880 Broadway, New York, NY 10025, USA (office). *Telephone:* (212) 678-5588 (office). *Fax:* (212) 678-5552 (office). *E-mail:* adelgenio@giss.nasa.gov (office); anthony.d.delgenio@nasa.gov (office). *Website:* www.giss.nasa.gov (office).

DEL NINNO, Giulio, BEng; Italian business executive; b. 12 June 1940, Milan; ed Politecnico di Milano; plant designer, Termosystem 1968–69; Researcher, Snia Viscose SpA 1969–73; Production Dir, Garzanti SpA 1973–76; Tech. and Research Dir, Montefibre (Montedison Group) 1976–79, Total Quality Dir 1986–88, Dir of Electrical Energy Sector, Edison SpA (Montedison Group) 1988–96, CEO Montedison SpA (now Edison) 2001–05, CEO Edipower SpA (subsidiary of Edison) 2003–08, currently Pres. and CEO Edison Gas SpA; Chair. Due Palme SpA 1979–86; Ind. Dir, Prysmian SpA 2012–. *Address:* Edison Gas SpA, Foro Buonaparte 31, 20121 Milan, Italy (office). *Telephone:* (02) 62221 (office). *Fax:* (02) 62227379 (office). *Website:* www.edison.it (office).

DEL PINO DIAZ, Eulogio Antonio, MS; Venezuelan geophysical engineer and business executive; *Chairman and President, Petróleos de Venezuela SA (PDVSA);* ed Universidad Central de Venezuela, Stanford Univ., USA; began career at INTEVEP (Tech. and Research Centre for PDVSA), held several tech. and supervisory positions; Pres. Corporación Venezolana del Petróleo 1979; Tech. Man. for Latin America, Western Atlas Co. 1990–91; joined Petróleos de Venezuela SA (PDVSA) 1991, held several man. positions at Corpoven (PDVSA affiliate), Exploration and Delineation Man. PDVSA Exploration and Production 1997–2003, responsible for co-ordinating PDVSA's restart Offshore Exploration Campaign in the Plataforma Deltana 2001, Gen. Man. Strategic Asscns from de Corporación Venezolana de Petróleo (PDVSA affiliate), in charge of representation at Strategic Asscn of Orinoco Oil Belt 2003–05, Dir, PDVSA and Pres. PDVSA CVP 2005–14, fmr Vice-Pres. of Exploration and Production, Chair. and Pres. PDVSA 2014–; Chair. Nynas AB 2012–; Vice-Pres. and Pres. Venezuelan Soc. of Geophysical Engineers 1990–94; Vice-Pres. Soc. of Exploration Geophysicists (USA) 1996–97; Founder and Co-ordinator Latin American Geophysical Union; fmr Dir, CITGO Petroleum Corpn; fmr Prof., Universidad Central de Venezuela, Universidad Simón Bolívar, Caracas. *Address:* PDVSA, Edificio Petróleos de Venezuela, Caracas, Distrito Federal 1050, Venezuela (office). *Telephone:* (212) 708-4111 (office). *Fax:* (212) 708-4661 (office). *E-mail:* info@pdvsa.com (office). *Website:* www.pdvsa.com (office).

DEL PINO VEINTIMILLA, Eugenia Maria, PhD; Ecuadorean biologist and academic; *Professor of Biology, Pontifical Catholic University of Ecuador;* b. 19 April 1945, Quito; ed Pontifical Catholic Univ. of Ecuador, Quito, Vassar Coll., Emory Univ., Atlanta, Ga, USA; Pontifical Catholic Univ. of Ecuador 1972–, currently Prof. of Biology; Vice-Pres. for Ecuador, Darwin Foundation 1992–96, Vice-Pres. Gen. Ass. 1998–2001; Alexander von Humboldt Foundation Fellowship, Cancer Research Centre, Heidelberg, Germany 1984–85; Dept of Embryology, Fulbright Comm., Carnegie Inst., Washington, DC 1990; mem. Latin American Acad. of Sciences, Third World Acad. of Sciences (TWAS), American Acad. of Arts and Sciences (hon. foreign mem.), NAS; L'Oreal-UNESCO Award for Women in Science 2000, Sheth Distinguished Int. Alumni Award, Emory Univ. 2003, Medal of the Acad. of Science for the Developing World, TWAS 2005, Eugenio Espejo

Medal, City of Quito 2005, Eugenio Espejo Nat. Prize 2012. *Publications:* numerous publs in scientific journals. *Address:* School of Biological Sciences, Pontificia Universidad Católica del Ecuador, 12 de Octubre entre Patria y Veintimilla, Apartado 17-01-2184 Quito, Ecuador (office). *Telephone:* (2) 299-1700 (office). *Fax:* (2) 299-1687 (office). *E-mail:* edelpino@puce.edu.ec (office). *Website:* www.puce.edu.ec (office).

DEL PONTE, Carla, LLM; Swiss lawyer, international organization official and diplomatist (retd); *Commissioner, Independent International Commission of Inquiry for Syria;* b. 9 Feb. 1947, Lugano; one s.; ed Univs of Berne and Geneva; in pvt. practice, Lugano 1975–81; Investigating Magistrate, then Public Prosecutor, Lugano 1981–94; Attorney-Gen. and Chief Prosecutor of Switzerland 1994–2000, mem. Fed. Comm. on White-Collar Crime 1994–99; Chief Prosecutor, Int. Criminal Tribunals of Rwanda 1999–2003, of the Fmr Yugoslavia 1999–2007; Amb. to Argentina 2008–11; Commr, Independent Int. Comm. of Inquiry for Syria 2012–; Dr hc (Liège) 2002, (Wales, Bangor) 2003, Hon. Dottore in Giurisprudenza (Genoa) 2004; 22nd Peace Prize, UNA (Spain) 2002, Goler T. Butcher Prize 2004. *Publications:* Madame Prosecutor (memoir) 2009. *Address:* c/o Office of the United Nations High Commissioner for Human Rights (OHCHR), Palais des Nations, 1211 Geneva 10, Switzerland. *E-mail:* www.ohchr.org (office).

DEL REY, Lana; American singer and songwriter; b. (Elizabeth Woolridge Grant), 21 June 1985, New York, NY; d. of Robert Grant; ed Kent School, Conn., Fordham Univ.; early releases issued under name of Lizzy Grant; signed to Stranger Records 2011; signed to Next Model Management 2012; Q Awards Next Big Thing 2011, BRIT Award for Best Int. Breakthrough Act 2012, MTV Europe Music Award for Best Alternative 2012, 2015. *Recordings include:* albums: Lana Del Rey AKA Lizzy Grant 2010, Born to Die 2012, Ultraviolence 2014, Honeymoon 2015, Lust for Life 2017. *Address:* c/o Next Model Management, 15 Watts Street, 6th Floor, New York, NY 10013, USA (office). *Telephone:* (212) 925-5100 (office). *Fax:* (212) 925-5931 (office). *Website:* www.nextmodels.com (office); www.lanadelrey.com (office).

DEL SOLAR LABARTHE, Salvador, MA; Peruvian actor and politician; *President of the Council of Ministers;* b. 1 May 1970, Lima; s. of Salvador del Solar Figuerola and Labarthe Elvira Flores; m. Ximena Bellido Denegri; two c.; ed Pontifical Catholic Univ. of Peru, Syracuse Univ., New York; early career as theatre actor; Dir of Content, Pendulo Films 2012–; Minister of Culture 2016–17; Pres., Council of Ministers (Prime Minister) 2019–; Visiting Scholar, David Rockefeller Center for Latin American Studies, Harvard Univ. 2018–19; mem. jury, 16th Lima Film Festival 2012. *Theatre includes* Presas del salón 1993, The Laws of Hospitality 1994, Seventh Heaven 1995, Pretty Eyes, Ugly Pictures 1996, Enrique V 2005, The Merchant of Venice 2005, The Lieutenant of Inishmore 2010. *Films include:* as actor: Courage 1998, El bien esquivo 2001, The Robbery 2004, Pirates in the Callao 2005, Greetings to the Devil 2011, The Vanished Elephant 2014, Double 2017; as Dir and screenwriter: Magallanes 2015. *Address:* Office of the President of the Council of Ministers, Jirón Carabaya, cuadra 1 s/n, Anexo 1105-1107, Lima, Peru (office). *Telephone:* (1) 2197000 (office). *Fax:* (1) 4449168 (office). *E-mail:* atencionciudadana@pcm.gob.pe (office). *Website:* www.pcm.gob.pe (office).

DEL TORO, Benicio; Puerto Rican/Spanish actor, director and writer; b. (Benicio Monserrate Rafael Del Toro Sánchez), 19 Feb. 1967, Santurce, Puerto Rico; s. of Gustavo Del Toro and Fausta Sanchez Del Toro; one d.; ed Univ. of California, San Diego, Circle in the Square Acting School, Stella Adler Conservatory; began with small TV parts during late 1980s; breakthrough role in The Usual Suspects 1995; gained Spanish citizenship 2011; hon. degree from Inter-American Univ. of Puerto Rico 2012. *Films include:* Big Top Pee-wee 1988, Christopher Columbus: The Discovery 1992, Fearless 1993, Money for Nothing 1993, China Moon 1994, The Usual Suspects 1995, Swimming With Sharks 1995, Cannes Man 1996, The Funeral 1996, Basquiat 1996, The Fan 1996, Joyride 1997, Excess Baggage 1997, Fear and Loathing in Las Vegas 1998, Snatch 2000, Traffic (Acad. Award for Best Supporting Actor) 2000, The Way of the Gun 2000, The Pledge 2001, Bread and Roses 2001, The Hunted 2002, 21 Grams 2003, Sin City 2005, Things We Lost in the Fire 2007, Che (Cannes Film Festival Best Actor Prize) 2008, The Wolfman 2010, Somewhere 2010, The Upsetter (documentary, narrator) 2011, Savages 2012, 7 Days in Havana (dir segment El Yuma) 2012, Jimmy Picard 2013, Guardians of the Galaxy 2014, Inherent Vice 2014, Escobar: Paradise Lost 2014, A Perfect Day 2015, Sicario (Hollywood Film Award for Best Supporting Actor) 2015, The Little Prince (voice) 2015. *Television includes:* Shell Game 1987, Miami Vice 1987, Private Eye 1987, Drug Wars: The Camarena Story (mini-series) 1990, Tales from the Crypt 1994, Fallen Angels 1995, Todos Contra Juan 2008. *Address:* c/o Ilene Feldman, IFA Talent Agency, 8730 Sunset Boulevard, Suite 490, Los Angeles, CA 90069, USA (office). *Telephone:* (310) 659-5522 (office).

DEL TORO, Guillermo; Mexican film director, producer, screenwriter and novelist; b. 9 Oct. 1964, Guadalajara, Jalisco; m. Lorenza Newton; two d.; ed Centro de Investigación y Estudios Cinematográficos, Guadalajara; first got involved in film-making aged eight; spent ten years as make-up supervisor; f. The Tequila Gang (production co.). *Films include:* Doña Lupe 1985, Doña Herlinda y su hijo (exec. producer) 1985, Geometria 1987, Un Embrujo (producer) 1988, Cronos (also writer) 1993, Mimic (also screenplay) 1997, Bullfighter (actor) 2000, El Espinazo del diablo (also writer and producer) 2001, Asesino en serio (exec. producer) 2002, Blade II 2002, Hellboy (also screenplay) 2004, Crónicas (producer) 2004, Caleuche: El llamado del mar (exec. producer) 2006, Pan's Labyrinth (also screenplay and producer, Best Film Nat. Soc. of Film Critics 2007, Goya Award for Best Original Screenplay 2007, BAFTA Award for Best Film not in the English Language 2007) 2006, The Orphanage (producer) 2008, Hellboy II: The Golden Army (also screenplay) 2008, Splice 2009, Biutiful (assoc. producer) 2010, Julia's Eyes (producer) 2010, Don't Be Afraid of the Dark (producer) 2010, Kung Fu Panda 2 (exec. producer) 2011, Puss in Boots (exec. producer) 2011, The Captured Bird (short) (exec. producer) 2012, Rise of the Guardians (exec. producer) 2012, The Hobbit: An Unexpected Journey (screenplay) 2012, Mama (exec. producer) 2013, Pacific Rim (dir) 2013, The Hobbit: The Battle of the Five Armies (screenplay) 2014, Crimson Peak 2015, The Shape of Water (dir, Golden Lion for Best Film 2017, Golden Globe Award for Best Director 2018, Academy Award for Best Director 2018) 2017. *Television includes:* Hora Marcada 1988, The Strain 2014–17, Trollhunters 2016. *Publications:* The Strain (with Chuck Hogan) 2009, The Fall (with Chuck Hogan) 2010, The Night Eternal 2011. *Address:* c/o Robert Newman, WME Entertainment, 9601 Wilshire Boulevard, Beverly Hills, CA 90210-5213, USA (office). *Telephone:* (310) 285-9000 (office). *Fax:* (310) 285-9010 (office). *Website:* www.wma.com (office).

DEL VECCHIO, Leonardo; Italian business executive; *Chairman, Luxottica Group SpA;* b. 22 May 1935, Milan; m.; six c.; sent to orphanage aged seven; apprentice at factory that made moulds for automobile parts; opened own moulding shop 1958; Founder and Chair. Luxottica (world's largest designer and manufacturer of high-quality eyeglass frames and sunglasses) 1961–, owns Sunglass Hut, LensCrafters, Ray-Ban and Oakley; Deputy Chair. Foncière des Régions SA; Dir, Beni Stabili SpA, SIIQ, GiVi Holding SpA, Gianni Versace SpA, Kairos Julius Baer SIM, Delfin Sàrl, Aterno Sàrl; est. museum for one of world's oldest collection of spectacles, Agordo, Italy; Cavaliere dell'Ordine al Merito del Lavoro 1986; hon. degree in Business Admin (Venice Cà Foscari Univ.) 1995; Master hc in Int. Business (MIB Man. School, Trieste) 1999; hon. degree in Managerial Eng (Univ. of Udine) 2002; hon. degree in Materials Eng (Politecnico of Milan) 2006; Hon. MBA (CUOA) 2012. *Leisure interests:* Medieval European antiques and paintings. *Address:* Luxottica Group SpA, Piazzale Cadorna 3, 20123 Milan, Italy (office). *Telephone:* (02) 863341 (office). *Fax:* (0437) 63223 (office). *Website:* www.luxottica.com (office).

DELACÔTE, Jacques; French conductor; s. of Pierre Delacôte and Renée Wagner Delacôte; m. Maria Lucia Alvares-Machado 1975; ed Music Conservatoire, Acad. of Music, with Prof. Hans Swarowsky, Austria; fmrly Asst to Darius Milhaud and Leonard Bernstein; orchestras conducted include Orchestre de Paris, Orchestre Nat. de France, New York Philharmonic, Vienna Philharmonic, Vienna Symphony, Israel Philharmonic, Orchestre Nat. de Belgique, London Symphony, San Francisco, Cleveland, Scottish Chamber, Scottish Nat. Opera, RIAS Berlin, WDR Cologne, SF Stuttgart, SWF Baden-Baden, Bavarian Radio, Munich, English Chamber, BBC, London, London Philharmonic, Royal Philharmonic, London, Japan Philharmonic, Yomiuri Symphony, Dresdner Staatskapelle, Royal Opera House, Covent Garden (including Far East tour, Korea and Japan), English Nat. Opera, Opernhaus Zürich, Teatro Real, Madrid, Teatro Liceo, Barcelona, La Fenice, Venice, Vienna State Opera, Deutsche Oper, Berlin, Pittsburgh Opera, Welsh Nat. Opera, Opéra de Paris, Teatro Colón, Buenos Aires, Canadian Opera Co., Royal State Opera, Copenhagen, State Opera, Hamburg, State Opera, Munich, Chicago Lyric Opera, Semper Oper, Dresden; also recordings with EMI, Philips London and Tring London; First Prize and Gold Medal, Mitropoulos Competition, New York 1971. *Festivals include:* Flandernfestival, Macerata Festival, Klangbogen Vienna, Dresden Musiktage. *Leisure interest:* chess. *Address:* Agentur Klein, Hanselmannstr. 11, 80809 Munich, Germany (office). *E-mail:* aklein@agenturklein.de (office). *Website:* www.jacques-delacote.com.

DeLANEY, William (Bill) J., BBA, MBA; American business executive; *President and CEO, Sysco Corporation;* ed Univ. of Notre Dame, Wharton Grad. Div., Univ. of Pennsylvania; Asst Treas., Sysco Corpn 1987–91, Treas. 1991–93, Vice-Pres. 1993–94, Chief Financial Officer (CFO), Sysco Food Services, Syracuse 1996–98, Sr Vice-Pres. 1998–2002, Exec. Vice-Pres. 2002–04, Pres. and CEO Sysco Food Services, Charlotte 2004–06, Sr Vice-Pres. of Financial Reporting 2006–07, Exec. Vice-Pres. and CFO 2007–09, Pres. and CEO 2010–, Chair. Employee Benefits Cttee, mem. Finance Cttee, Exec. Cttee; mem. Bd of Dirs, Express Scripts, Inc., The Center for Houston's Future, Greater Houston Partnership. *Address:* Sysco Corporation, 1390 Enclave Parkway, Houston, TX 77077-2099, USA (office). *Telephone:* (281) 584-1390 (office). *E-mail:* info@sysco.com (office). *Website:* www.sysco.com (office).

DELANOË, Bertrand Jacques Marie; French politician; b. 30 May 1950, Tunis, Tunisia; s. of Auguste Delanoë and Yvonne Delanoë (née Delord); ed Inst. Sainte-Marie, Rodez, Univ. of Toulouse; mem. Conseil de Paris (18th arrondissement) 1977–83, 1986–2014, Socialist Deputy 1981–86, Senator 1995–2001, Mayor of Paris 2001–14; Pres. of Paris Socialist Group 1993–2001; mem. Cttee of Dirs, Parti Socialiste 1979–, Party Spokesman 1981–83, mem. Exec. Bureau 1983–87; Pres. France-Egypt Friendship Group 1981–86, Int. Asscn of French-speaking Mayors (AIMF) 2001–, World Org. of United Cities and Local Govts 2004–10, Founding Pres. of Honour 2010–; Hon. Citizen of Ouagadougou (Burkina Faso) 2012; Dr hc (Univ. of Quebec, Canada) 2006; Officier, Ordre nat. du Québec 2012. *Publications:* Pour l'honneur de Paris 1999, La Vie, passionnément (autobiog.) 2004, De l'audace (with Laurent Joffrin) 2008. *Address:* Hôtel de Ville, 75196 Paris RP, France (office). *Fax:* 1-42-76-53-43 (office). *Website:* www.paris.fr (office); bertranddelanoe.net.

DELATTRE, François Marie; French diplomatist; *Permanent Representative, Security Council, United Nations;* b. 15 Nov. 1963, Saint-Marcellin, Isère; ed Paris Inst. of Political Studies, École nationale d'administration; posted to Embassy in Bonn, in charge of environmental issues and econ. consequences of Germany's re-unification –1991, with Strategic, Security and Disarmament Dept, Ministry of Foreign Affairs 1991–93, adviser to Foreign Minister Alain Juppé 1993–95, mem. Pres. Jacques Chirac's Foreign Policy Team 1995–98, Press and Communications Dir, Embassy in Washington, DC 1998–2002, Deputy Dir Foreign Minister's Office 2002–04, Consul Gen. in New York 2004–08, Amb. to Canada 2008–11, to USA 2011–14, Amb. and Perm. Rep. to UN Security Council and Head of Perm. Mission to UN, New York 2014–; mem. Advisory Bd, European Inst.; Hon. Trustee, UN Int. School. *Address:* Permanent Mission of France to the United Nations, One Dag Hammarskjöld Plaza, 245 East 47th Street, 44th Floor, New York, NY 10017, USA (office). *Telephone:* (212) 702-4900 (office). *Fax:* (212) 421-6889 (office). *E-mail:* france@franceonu.org (office). *Website:* www.franceonu.org (office).

DELAY, Florence; French writer, actress and university lecturer; b. 19 March 1941, Paris; d. of Jean Delay and Marie Madeleine Delay (née Carrez); ed Lycée Jean de la Fontaine, Paris, Univ. of Paris (Sorbonne); Lecturer in Gen. and Comparative Literature, Univ. of Paris III 1972–; Theatre Critic, Nouvelle Revue française 1978–85; mem. Editorial Bd Critique magazine 1978–96, Reading Cttee Gallimard publrs 1979–86; mem. Acad. française 2000–; Commdr des Arts et des Lettres, Officier Légion d'honneur, Officier Ordre nat. du Mérite; Grand prix du roman de la Ville de Paris 1999. *Films:* Procès de Jeanne d'Arc 1962, Le Jouet criminel 1969, Mort de Raymond Roussel 1975, Écoute voir 1979. *Publications:* Minuit sur les jeux 1973, Le Aïe aïe de la corne de brume 1975, L'Insuccès de la fête

1980, Riche et légère (Prix Femina) 1983, Course d'amour pendant le deuil 1986, Petites formes en prose après Edison (essays) 1987, Partition rouge 1989 (jtly), Hexaméron 1989, Etxemendi (Prix François Mauriac) 1990, Semaines de Suzanne 1991, Catalina 1994, La Fin des temps ordinaires 1996, La Séduction brève (essays) 1997, Dit Nerval 1999, L'Evangile de Jean (trans. of Gospel of John) 2001, Trois désobéissances 2004, Graal Theatre 2005, Mon Espagne or et ciel (essays) 2008, Mes Cendriers 2010, Il me semble, mesdames 2012; several trans of Spanish dramatists including Fernando de Rojas, Pedro Calderón, Lope de Vega. *Address:* c/o Gallimard, 5 rue Sébastien Bottin, 75007 Paris, France (office).

DELAY, Tom, BS; American fmr politician; b. 8 April 1947, Laredo, Tex.; s. of Charles Ray DeLay and Maxine Evelyn DeLay; m. Christine DeLay; one d.; ed Baylor Univ., Univ. of Houston; owned and operated small business in Tex. 1970s; elected to Texas House of Reps 1978; mem. US Congress from 22nd Dist, Texas, held various positions in House of Reps including Republican Conf. Sec., Deputy Whip, Chair. Republican Study Cttee, Majority Whip 1995–2003, Majority Leader 2003–05 (resgnd after indictment by Tex. grand jury for money laundering, convicted 2010), mem. Appropriations Cttee; mem. Advisory Bd Child Advocates of Fort Bend Co.; Founder Grassroots Action and Information Network (GAIN) 2006–; f. First Principles, LLC, Delay Foundation; columnist, The Washington Times; Taxpayers Friend Award, Nat. Taxpayers Union; Golden Bulldog Award, Watchdog of the Treasury; Nat. Security Leadership Award, Peace Through Strength Coalition. *Publication:* No Retreat, No Surrender: One American's Flight (with Stephen Mansfield) 2007. *Website:* www.tomdelay.com.

DELCOURT, Guy; French editor and publisher; *Publisher, Editions Delcourt;* b. 27 March 1958, Versailles; ed ESSEC Business School; fmr Ed. Pilote magazine; Founder of Delcourt publishing house through merger of Charlie Mensuel and Pilote magazines 1986, now one of the largest publrs of comics and manga in France, produces some 480 comics annually, became majority shareholder in Soleil Productions 2011; Chevalier, Ordre nat. du Mérite 2006. *Publications include:* Les Aventures de Sarkozix, Et ils coulèrent des jours heureux... 2010, N'en jetez plus! 2011, Zodiac (with Guy Delcourt and Eric Corbeyran) 2012–13. *Address:* Editions Delcourt, 8 rue Léon Jouhaux, 75010 Paris, France (office). *Telephone:* 1-56-03-92-20 (office). *Fax:* 1-56-03-92-30 (office). *E-mail:* info@editions-delcourt.fr (office). *Website:* www.editions-delcourt.fr (office).

DELEBARRE, Michel Stéphane Henry Joseph; French politician; *Mayor of Dunkirk;* b. 27 April 1946, Bailleul (Nord); s. of Stéphane Delebarre and Georgette Deroo; m. Janine Debeyre 1969; one d.; Asst Sec.-Gen. Cttee for the Expansion of the Nord-Pas de Calais area 1968–71, Sec.-Gen. 1971–74; Cabinet Dir for Pres. of Nord-Pas de Calais Regional Council 1974–78; Gen. Del. for Devt for City of Lille 1977–80; Sec.-Gen. City of Lille 1980; Pres. regional fund for contemporary art 1982; mem. of Cabinet of Prime Minister 1981–82; Cabinet Dir 1982–84; unassigned prefect 1983; Minister of Labour, Employment and Professional Training 1984–86; Socialist mem. of Parl. for Nord 1986–88, 1997–98, 2002–11; mem. Senate for Nord 2001–; mem. Exec. Bd Socialist Party 1987; Minister of Transport and Marine Affairs 1989; Minister of State, Minister of Town and Physical Planning 1990–91; Minister of State, Minister of Civil Service and Public Admin. Enhancement 1991–92; Adviser for Urban and Regional Planning; Chair. Cttee of Experts advising Lionel Jospin, Leader Socialist Party 1995; First Deputy Pres., Regional Council for Nord-Pas de Calais 1986–97, Pres. 1998–2001, regional counsellor 2001–02; Mayor of Dunkirk 1989–; Pres. Urban Community of Dunkirk 1995–, L'Union nationale des fédérations d'organismes d'HLM 1999–; mem. Nat. Council of Evaluation 1999–; Pres., Cttee of the Regions, EU 2006–08, First Vice-Pres. 2008–10. *Address:* Hôtel de Ville, place Charles Valentin, 59386 Dunkirk cedex 1, France (office). *Telephone:* 3-28-59-12-34 (office). *E-mail:* maire@ville-dunkerque.fr (office). *Website:* www.michel-delebarre.fr.

DELFIM DA SILVA, Fernando; Guinea-Bissau academic, public servant, diplomatist and politician; *Permanent Representative to UN;* b. 13 May 1956, Bissau; ed St Petersburg State Univ., Russia, Lusíada Univ., Portugal; fmr Prof., Portuguese School of Bissau; Deputy Minister of Educ., Bafatá Region, also Dir Bafatá Secondary School 1974–81; Dir-Gen., Presidency of the Council of State 1980; with Technical Office of Studies and Planning, Ministry of Nat. Educ. 1986–87; apptd Minister of Nat. Educ. 1993, Sec. of State for Transport and Communications 1994, concurrently Sec. of State for Youth Culture and Sports (position first held in 1991); Minister of Foreign Affairs, Int. Co-operation and Communities 1998, 2013–14; Advisor to Pres. on Political and Diplomatic Affairs 2002–05; Philosophy and History Lecturer, Portuguese School of Bissau and Liceu João XXIII 2015–17; Perm. Rep. to UN 2017–. *Address:* Permanent Mission of Guinea Bissau, 336 E 45th Street, 13th Floor, New York, NY 10017, USA (office). *Telephone:* (212) 896-8311 (office). *Fax:* (212) 896-8313 (office). *E-mail:* guinea-bissau@un.int (office).

DELGADO CAMPAÑA, Pedro Miguel; Ecuadorean economist and fmr central banker; b. 10 Nov. 1962; ed INCAE Business School, Costa Rica; fmr Risk Man., Corporación Financiera Nacional; fmr Dir Intendente Nacional de Instituciones Financieras (financial supervisory body); Pres. Fideicomiso 'AGD CFN No Más Impunidad' (anti-corruption body); Dir Unidad de Gestión y Ejecución de Derecho Público (deposit insurance co.); Pres. Banco Central del Ecuador 2011–12 (resgnd).

DELGADO DURÁN, Norberto; Panamanian politician and organization official; ed Univ. of Panamá; Exec. Dir Multi Credit Bank 1990–98, fmr Vice-Pres. Commercial; Prof. Instituto de Microfinanzas 1998–; Vice-Minister of Finance 1999–2000, Minister of Finance and the Treasury 2000–04; Gov. for Panama, Inter-American Devt Bank 2000–04; mem. Bd of Dirs, Panama Canal Authority (ACP) from 2004; Pres. Instituto Panameño Autónomo Cooperativo (IPACOOP) 1999; Pres. Bd of Dirs, Fondo de Inversión Social 1999. *Address:* c/o Panama Canal Authority, PO Box 526725, Miami, FL 33152-6725, USA.

ĐELIĆ, Božidar, MA, MBA, MPA; Serbian economist, politician and investment banker; *Managing Director, Sovereign Advisory Group, Lazard Limited, Paris;* b. 1 April 1965, Belgrade; m. Marie-Laure Đelić (divorced 2003); two d.; ed Institut d'Etudes Politiques de Paris, Ecole des Hautes Etudes Commerciales, Paris, Ecole des Hautes Etudes en Sciences Sociales, Harvard Business School and Kennedy School of Govt, Harvard Univ., USA; worked as expert adviser to several East European transition govts on issues of privatization, banking reform and macro-econ. reform, adviser to Leszek Balcerowicz in Poland (also helped establish Warsaw Stock Exchange) 1991–92, to Anatolii Chubais in Russia 1992–93, in Romania 1996; Partner, McKinsey & Co. (consulting firm) 1991, returned on unpaid leave to Belgrade Nov. 2000; served as main negotiator with IMF, Paris Club and other financial insts; mem. Democratic Party; Minister of Finance 2001–04; withdrew from politics 2004–06; Man. for Southeastern Europe, Crédit Agricole 2005–06; returned to politics and became active in Democratic Party's election campaign late 2006, cand. for Prime Minister; Deputy Prime Minister, in charge of European Integration 2007–11, Minister of Science and Technological Devt 2008–11; mem. Parl. 2012–13; Man. Dir Sovereign Advisory Group, Lazard Ltd, Paris 2014–; Ind. Dir (non-exec.), Bank of Georgia Holdings PLC; mem. Supervisory Bd, JSC Bank of Georgia 2013–. *Address:* Lazard Frères SAS, 121 boulevard Haussmann, 75382 Paris Cedex 08, France (office). *Telephone:* 1-44-13-01-11 (office). *E-mail:* office@djelic.net. *Website:* www.lazard.com (office); www.djelic.net.

DELIENNE, Pierrot, LLB, MBA; Haitian lawyer, academic and politician; b. 13 Dec. 1954; m.; ed Univ. d'État d'Haïti, Univ. du Québec, Canada, Univ. de Genève, Switzerland; began career with Accounting Dept, American Express, Haiti 1975–80, with Planning, Customer Services and Credit Card Dept, American Express, Montreal 1981–82; Prof. of Accounting and Business, École de Commerce Julien Craan, Port-au-Prince 1979–82, 1983–85; Head of Documentation Service, Promotion Dept, Nat. Technical Information Service (NTIS) 1980–81; Tenured Prof., Centre Univ. Int. d'Haïti 1983–2004; mem. Bd of Dirs, Fonds d'assistance économique et sociale (FAES) 1990–91; pvt. legal practice as Assoc. with Cabinet Duplan-Sanon, Port au Prince 1991–; Prin. Consultant in Tourism Marketing, Ministry of Trade and Industry 1991–92; Dir-Gen., Office Nat. du Tourisme Haïti 1992–94; Vice-Dean, Programme Coordinator and Tenured Prof., Univ. Quisqueya 1995–2006; Adviser to Minister of Justice March–Nov. 2004; Minister-Counsellor, Mission of Haiti to WTO in Geneva 2006–16; Minister of Foreign Affairs and Religion and Acting Minister of Interior and Territorial Collectivities 2016–17; mem. Agence française de Marketing, American Management Asscn, American Marketing Asscn.

DELIGNE, Vicomte Pierre René, PhD; Belgian mathematician and academic; *Professor Emeritus, School of Mathematics, Institute for Advanced Study;* b. 3 Oct. 1944, Etterbeek; ed Athénée Adolphe Max, Brussels, Univ. of Brussels, Université Libre de Bruxelles, Ecole Normale Supérieure, Paris, France; Jr Scientist, Fond Nat. de la Recherche Scientifique (FNRS), Brussels 1967–68; Guest Scientist, Institut des Hautes Etudes Scientifiques, Bures-sur-Yvette, France 1967–68, Visiting mem. 1968–70, Perm. mem. 1970–84; Prof., Inst. for Advanced Study, Princeton, NJ, USA 1984–2007, Prof. Emer. 2008–; mem. American Philosophical Soc. 2009; Foreign Assoc. mem. Acad. des Sciences, Paris 1978; Assoc. mem. Acad. Royale de Belgique 1994; Foreign mem. Accad. Nazionale dei Lincei 2003, Royal Swedish Acad. of Sciences 2009; Foreign Assoc. NAS 2007; Foreign mem. Russian Acad. of Sciences 2016–; Foreign Hon. mem. American Acad. of Arts and Sciences 1978; Dr hc (Flemish Univ. of Brussels) 1989, (Ecole Normale Supérieure) 1995; Francois Deruyts Prize, Acad. Royale de Belgique 1974, Henri Poincaré Medal, Acad. des Sciences (Paris) 1974, Quinquennal Prize 'Doctor A. De Leeuw-Damry-Bourlart', FNRS 1975, Fields Medal, Int. Congress of Mathematicians (Helsinki) 1978, Crafoord Prize (Stockholm) (co-recipient) 1988, Balzan Prize 2004, Wolf Prize in Math. (co-recipient) 2008, Abel Prize, Norwegian Acad. of Science and Letters 2013. *Publications:* Commensurabilities among Lattices in PU(1,n) 1993; more than 80 publs in math. journals. *Address:* Fuld Hall 210, School of Mathematics, Institute for Advanced Study, Einstein Drive, Princeton, NJ 08540, USA (office). *Telephone:* (609) 734-8370 (office). *E-mail:* deligne@math.ias.edu (office). *Website:* www.math.ias.edu (office).

DeLILLO, Don, BA; American writer; b. 20 Nov. 1936, New York; m. Barbara Bennett 1975; ed Cardinal Hayes High School, New York, Fordham Coll.; fmr advertising copywriter, Ogilvy, Benson & Mather; Guggenheim Fellowship 1978; American Acad. of Arts and Letters Award in Literature 1984, Jerusalem Prize for the Freedom of the Individual in Soc. 1999, William Dean Howells Medal 2000, PEN/Saul Bellow Award for Achievement in American Fiction 2010, St Louis Literary Award 2012, Carl Sandberg Literary Award 2012, Library of Congress Prize for American Fiction 2013, Norman Mailer Prize for Lifetime Achievement 2014, Distinguished Contribution to American Letters Medal, National Book Awards 2015. *Plays:* The Engineer of Moonlight 1979, The Day Room 1987, Valparaiso 1999, Love-Lies-Bleeding 2005, The Word for Snow 2007. *Publications include:* Americana 1971, End Zone 1972, Great Jones Street 1973, Ratner's Star 1976, Players 1977, Running Dog 1978, The Names 1982, White Noise (Nat. Book Award 1985) 1985, Libra (Irish Times Fiction Prize 1989) 1988, Mao II (PEN/Faulkner Award 1992) 1991, Underworld (William Dean Howells Medal 2000, Riccardo Bacchelli Int. Award 2000) 1997, The Body Artist 2000, Cosmopolis 2003, Falling Man 2007, Point Omega 2010, Zero K 2016; short stories: The River Jordan 1960, Take the "A" Train 1962, The Uniforms 1970, Total Loss Weekend 1972, Human Moments in World War III 1983, The Runner 1988, The Angel Esmeralda 1995, Still Life 2007, The Border of Fallen Bodies 2009, Hammer and Sickle 2010, The Angel Esmeralda: Nine Stories 2011, The Itch 2017. *Address:* c/o Wallace Literary Agency, 229 East 79th Street, Suite 5A, New York, NY 10075, USA (office). *Telephone:* (212) 570-9090 (office). *Fax:* (212) 772-8979 (office). *Website:* authors.simonandschuster.com/Don-DeLillo/1098974.

DELL, Anne, CBE, PhD, FRS, FRSC, FMedSci; Australian biochemist and academic; *Professor of Carbohydrate Biochemistry, Imperial College London;* b. 11 Sept. 1950, Perth; ed Univ. of Western Australia, Univ. of Cambridge, UK; Prof. of Carbohydrate Biochemistry, Imperial Coll., London 1991–, Head of Dept of Life Sciences 1999–2001, Head of Dept of Life Sciences 2002–07, Head of GlycoTRIC Centre 2004–, Wellcome Sr Research Investigator 2014–17; Chair. Biotechnology and Biological Sciences Research Council (BBSRC) Tools and Resources Strategy Panel 2002–07 (mem. BBSRC Strategy Bd, BBSRC Council), Royal Soc./Wolfson Lab. Refurbishment Grants Cttee, Royal Soc. Mercer Cttee; Pres. Soc. of Glycobiology 2011; mem. Steering Cttee NIH Consortium for Functional Glycomics, 1851 Science Scholarships Cttee, Advisory Cttee Nat. Physical Lab., British Library Advisory Council; Advisory mem. Human Disease Glycomics Proteome Initiative; Chair. Glycobiology Gordon Conf., Ventura, Calif., USA 2001; mem. European Acad. of Science 2004; Hon. DSc (Univ. of Western Australia) 2010, (Univ. of Waterloo, Canada) 2011; Tate & Lyle Medal, Royal Soc. of Chem.

1986, Whistler Award, Int. Carbohydrate Org. 2000, Haworth Memorial Medal and Lecture, Royal Soc. of Chem. 2003, Int. Glycoconjugate Award, Int. Glycoconjugate Org. 2005, Karl Meyer Lectureship Award, Soc. for Glycobiology 2016. *Publications:* numerous papers in professional journals. *Address:* Room 101B, Sir Ernst Chain Building, Imperial College London, South Kensington Campus, London, SW7 2AZ, England (office). *Telephone:* (20) 7594-5219 (office). *Fax:* (20) 7225-0458 (office). *E-mail:* a.dell@imperial.ac.uk (office). *Website:* www.imperial.ac.uk (office).

DELL, Michael S.; American computer industry executive; *Chairman and CEO, Dell Inc.;* b. 23 Feb. 1965, Houston, Tex.; s. of Alexander Dell and Lorraine Dell; m. Susan Lieberman 1989; four c.; ed Univ. of Texas; Founder, Chair. and CEO Dell Computer Corpn (fmrly PCs Ltd, now Dell Inc.), Austin, Tex. 1984–2004, Chair. 2004–, CEO 2007–; f. MSD Capital 1998; co-f., with his wife, The Michael & Susan Dell Foundation 1999; Vice-Chair. US Business Council; mem. Exec. Cttee of Int. Business Council, US Business Council, US Pres.'s Council of Advisors on Science and Tech., Tech. CEO Council, Governing Bd of Indian School of Business, Hyderabad; mem. Pres. Trump's American Manufacturing Council Jan.–Aug. 2017; mem. Bd of Dirs Catalyst; Hon. mem. Foundation Bd of World Econ. Forum; Bower Award for Business Leadership 2013. *Publication:* Direct from Dell: Strategies that Revolutionized an Industry 1999. *Address:* Dell Inc., 1 Dell Way, Round Rock, TX 78682-0001 (office); MSD Capital, LP 645 Fifth Avenue, 21st Floor, New York, NY 10022-5910; Michael & Susan Dell Foundation, PO Box 163867, Austin, TX 78716, USA. *Telephone:* (512) 338-4400 (Round Rock) (office); (212) 303-1650 (New York). *Fax:* (512) 728-3653 (Round Rock) (office); (212) 303-1634 (New York); (512) 600-5501 (Austin). *E-mail:* webmaster@dell.com (office); info@msdf.org. *Website:* www.dell.com (office); www.msdcapital.com; www.msdf.org.

DELLA VALLE, Diego; Italian fashion designer and art collector; *Chairman and CEO, Tod's SpA;* b. 30 Dec. 1953, Sant'elpidio a Mare, Ascoli Piceno; s. of Dorino della Valle, founder of the original Della Valle shoemakers 1940s; m. 1st; one s.; m. 2nd Barbara Pistilli; one s.; studied law in Bologna; brief work experience in USA 1975; joined his father in family business, leading role in definition of co. strategies and brand creation, Chair. and CEO Tod's SpA 2000–; mem. Bd of Dirs, IRI SpA, Banca Commerciale Italiana SpA, Assicurazioni Generali, Banca Nazionale del Lavoro, LVMH, Ferrari, Maserati, Compagnia Immobiliare Azionaria, Confindustria; mem. Fundraising Cttee, Umberto Veronesi Cancer Research; Chair. Della Valle Onlus Foundation; bought football club ACF Fiorentina 2002, now Hon. Pres.; hon. degree in Business and Econs (Univ. of Ancona) 2000; Cavaliere del Lavoro 1996. *Address:* Tod's SpA, Via Filippo Della Valle 1, Sant'elpidio a Mare, Ascoli Piceno, Italy (office). *Telephone:* (0734) 871671 (office). *Website:* www.todsgroup.com (office).

DELLER, Jeremy, MA; British artist; b. 1966, London; ed Courtauld Inst. of Art; acts as curator, producer or dir of broad range of projects, including orchestrated events, films and publs; Trustee Tate Gallery 2007–11; Albert Medal, RSA 2010. *Works include:* Acid Brass (ongoing project and collaboration with The Williams Fairey Brass Band) 1997–, Fig. 1 2000, Folk Archive (ongoing project with Alan Kane investigating UK folk and vernacular art) 2000–, The Battle of Orgreave: The English Civil War Part II (co-production by Artangel/Channel 4, film by Mike Figgis) 2001, Social Parade (video), Five Memorials, This is US (CD produced in asscn with Bard Coll., Red Hook, USA) 2003, Memory Bucket (video documentary about Crawford, Texas—home town of George W. Bush—and Branch Davidian siege in nearby Waco) (Turner Prize 2004) 2003, Speak To The Earth And It Will Tell You 2007, It Is What It Is 2009, Sacrilege 2012, English Magic 2013, All That Is Solid Melts Into Air 2014, Do Touch 2015, We're Here Because We're Here 2016, This Place 2018. *Address:* c/o Gavin Brown's Enterprise, 620 Greenwich Street, New York, NY 10014, USA (office). *E-mail:* gallery@gavinbrown.biz (office).

DELL'OLIO, Louis; American fashion designer; b. 23 July 1948, New York, NY; ed Parsons School of Design, New York; intern for Norman Norell 1965; asst designer to Dominic Rompello of Teal Traina, New York 1969–71; Chief Designer, Georgini div. of Originala, New York 1971–74; design collaborator with Donna Karan, Anne Klein & Co. 1974–79, Chief Designer following Karan's departure 1984–93; spent time working with Council of Fashion Designers of America's Fashion Targets Breast Cancer initiative 1993–96; cr. Dei Tre collection for Bergdorf Goodman, Neiman Marcus and Holt Renfrew 1996; launched outer-wear collection 1997; introduced exclusive collection for QVC 2000; mem. Fashion Designers of America; Parsons Gold Thimble Award 1969, Coty American Fashion Critics Awards (all with Donna Karan) 1977, 1982, 1984. *Address:* Louis Dell'Olio Co. Ltd, 435 Ocean Drive West, Stamford, CT 06902, USA.

DELON, Alain; French actor; b. 8 Nov. 1935, Sceaux; m. Nathalie Delon (divorced); one s.; one s. one d. by Rosalie Van Breemen; with French Marine Corps 1952–55; ind. actor-producer under Delbeau (Delon-Beaume) Productions 1964–; Pres. and Dir-Gen. Adel Productions 1968–87, Leda Productions 1987–; cr. Alain Delon Diffusion SA (specializing in luxury goods) 1978; Commdr des Arts et des Lettres, Officier, Ordre nat. du Mérite 1995, Officier, Légion d'honneur 2005. *Films include:* Christine 1958, Faibles femmes 1959, Le chemin des écoliers 1959, Purple Noon 1959, Rocco and His Brothers 1960, Eclipse 1961, The Leopard 1962, Any Number Can Win 1962, The Black Tulip 1963, The Love Cage 1963, L'insoumis 1964, The Yellow Rolls Royce 1964, Once a Thief 1964, Les centurions 1965, Paris brûle-t-il? 1965, Texas Across the River 1966, Les adventuriers 1966, Le samourai 1967, Histoires extraordinaires 1967, Diaboliquement votre 1967, Adieu l'ami 1968, Girl on a motorcycle 1968, La piscine 1968, Jeff 1968, Die Boss, Die Quietly 1969, Borsalino 1970, Madly 1970, Doucement les basses 1970, Le cercle rouge 1971, L'assassinat de Trotsky 1971, La veuve Couderc 1971, Un flic 1972, Le professeur 1972, Scorpio 1972, Traitement de choc 1972, Les granges brûlées 1973, Deux hommes dans la ville 1973, Borsalino & Co. 1973, Les seins de glace 1974, Creezy 1975, Zorro 1975, Le gitan 1975, Mr Klein 1975, Le gang 1977, Mort d'un pourri 1977, Armageddon 1977, L'homme pressé 1977, Attention, les enfants regardent 1978, Le toubib 1979, Trois hommes à abattre 1980, Pour la peau d'un flic 1981 (dir), Le choc 1982 (dir), Le battant 1983 (dir), Un Amour de Swann 1984, Notre Histoire (César, Best Actor 1985) 1984, Parole de flic 1985, Le passage 1986, Ne réveillez pas un flic qui dort, Nouvelle Vague 1989, Dancing Machine 1990, Le Retour de Casanova 1992, Un Crime 1993, L'Ours en peluche 1994, Le Jour et La Nuit 1996, Une Chance sur deux 1998, Les Acteurs 2000, Les Nouveaux refus 2004, Astérix at the Olympic Games 2008. *Stage performances:* 'Tis Pity She's a Whore 1961, 1962, Les yeux crevés 1967, Variations énigmatiques 1996. *Television:* Comme au Cinéma (series) 1988, Fabio Montale (series) 2001, Le Lion 2003, Frank Riva (series) 2003–04. *Leisure interests:* swimming, riding, boxing. *Address:* Alain Delon International Diffusion SA, 7 rue des Battoirs, 1205 Geneva, Switzerland (office). *Telephone:* 227021108 (office). *E-mail:* info@alaindelon.com (office). *Website:* www.alaindelon.com.

DeLONG, Mahlon R., BA, MD; American neurologist and academic; *William Patterson Timmie Professor of Neurology, Emory University;* b. 17 March 1938, Des Moines, Ia; ed Free Univ. of Berlin, Germany, Harvard Medical School; Research Assoc., Nat. Inst. of Mental Health (NIMH) Clinical Sciences Lab., Bethesda, Md 1969–70, Sr Staff Fellow 1970–71, Sr Staff Fellow, NIMH Neurophysiology Lab. 1971–73; Resident in Neurology, Johns Hopkins Univ., Baltimore, Md 1973–76, Asst Prof. of Neurology and Physiology 1975–80; Chief of Neurology Service, Columbia Medical Plan, Columbia, Md 1976–80; Chief Dept of Neurology, Baltimore City Hospitals 1980–85; Assoc. Prof. of Neurology and Neuroscience, Johns Hopkins School of Medicine 1980–85, Prof. of Neurology and Neuroscience 1986–89; Chair. Dept of Neurology, Emory Univ. School of Medicine, Atlanta, Ga 1989–2003, William Patterson Timmie Prof. of Neurology 1993–, Interim Dir Comprehensive Neuroscience Center 2003–06, Founder and Co-Dir eNTICE (Emory Neuromodulation and Technology Innovation Center); mem. Dana Alliance for Brain Initiative; mem. AAAS, American Neurological Asscn, Nat. Inst. of Mental Health, Nat. Inst. of Neurological Disorders and Stroke, Soc. for Neuroscience/Govt & Public Affairs; Arnold Carmichael Lecturer, Nat. Hosp. for Neurology and Neurosurgery, London, UK, Johns Hopkins Univ. Soc. of Scholars 1998, Schneider Lecturer, American Asscn of Neurological Surgeons 1999, Special Lecturer, Soc. for Neuroscience 2000, Fred Springer Award, American Parkinson's Disease Foundation, Edward B. Henderson Lecture Award, American Geriatrics Soc. 2001, Distinguished Lecturer, Northwestern Univ. Neuroscience, American Top Doctors Distinguished Leadership Award, Breakthrough Prize in Life Sciences 2014, Lasker–DeBakey Clinical Medical (co-recipient) 2014. *Publications:* numerous papers in professional journals. *Address:* Emory Clinic, Building A, 1365 Clifton Road NE, Atlanta, GA 30322, USA (office). *Telephone:* (404) 778-3444 (office). *Website:* www.emoryhealthcare.org (office).

DELORS, Jacques Lucien Jean; French politician and economist; b. 20 July 1925, Paris; s. of Louis Delors and Jeanne Rigal; m. Marie Lephaille 1948; one s. (deceased) one d. (Martine Aubry (q.v.)); ed Lycée Voltaire, Paris, Lycée Blaise-Pascal, Clermont-Ferrand, Univ. of Paris, Centre d'Etudes Supérieur de Banque (IEP); Head of Dept, Banque de France 1945–62, attached to staff of Dir-Gen. of Securities and Financial Market 1950–62, mem. Gen. Council 1973–79; mem. Planning and Investments Section, Econ. and Social Council 1959–61; Head of Social Affairs Section, Commissariat général du Plan 1962–69; Sec.-Gen. Interministerial Cttee for Vocational Training and Social Promotion 1969–72; Adviser to Jacques Chaban-Delmas 1969, Chargé de mission 1971–72; Assoc. Prof. of Co. Man., Univ. of Paris IX 1973–79; f. Club Echange et Projets 1974; Dir Labour and Soc. Research Centre 1975–79; Parti Socialiste Nat. Del. for int. econ. relations 1976–81; elected mem. European Parl. 1979, Chair. Econ. and Monetary Cttee 1979–81; Minister for the Economy and Finance 1981–84, for the Economy, Finance and Budget 1983–84; Mayor of Clichy 1983–84; Pres. Comm. of the European Communities (now European Commission) 1985–94; Pres. EMU Comm. 1988–89, Int. Comm. on Educ. for the Twenty-First Century, UNESCO 1992–99; Pres. Conseil d'admin. Collège d'Europe, Bruges 1995–99, Conseil de l'emploi, des revenus et de la cohésion sociale (CERC) 2000–08; Founding Pres. Notre Europe/Jacques Delors Inst. 1996–2004; Officier, Légion d'honneur; hon. degrees from 30 univs in Europe, USA and Canada; Prix Jean Monnet 1988, Prix Louis Weiss 1989, Prix Prince des Asturies 1989, Prix Charlemagne 1992, Prix Carlos V 1995, Prix Erasme 1997, Prix de l'économie mondiale 2006, Nijmegen Medal of Peace 2010, Leonardo European Corporate Learning Award (first recipient) 2010. *Publications include:* Les indicateurs sociaux 1971, Changer 1975, En sortir ou pas (jtly) 1985, La France par l'Europe (jtly) 1988, Le Nouveau concert Européen 1992, Our Europe 1993, L'Unité d'un homme 1994, Combats pour l'Europe 1996, Mémoires 2004, Europe tragique et magnifique 2006, Investir dans le social 2009. *Address:* Notre Europe, Institut Jacques Delors, 19 rue de Milan, 75009 Paris, France (office). *Telephone:* 1-44-58-97-95 (office). *Fax:* 1-44-58-97-99 (office). *E-mail:* jdelors@notre-europe.eu (office). *Website:* www.delorsinstitute.eu (office).

DELPY, Julie; American (b. French) actress; b. 21 Dec. 1969, Paris; d. of Albert Delpy and Marie Pillet; m. Marc Streitenfeld 2007 (divorced 2012); one s.; ed New York Univ. Film School; European Achievement in World Cinema Award 2017. *Films include:* Detective 1985, Mauvais Sang 1986, La Passion Béatrice 1987, L'Autre Nuit 1988, La Noche Oscura 1989, Europa Europa 1991, Voyager 1991, Warszawa 1992, Young and Younger 1993, The Three Musketeers 1993, When Pigs Fly 1993, The Myth of the White Wolf 1994, Killing Zoe 1994, Mesmer 1994, Trois Couleurs Blanc 1994, Trois Couleurs Rouge 1994, Before Sunrise 1995, An American Werewolf in Paris 1997, The Treat 1998, LA Without a Map 1998, Blah, Blah, Blah (Dir), The Passion of Ayn Rand 1999, But I'm A Cheerleader 1999, Tell Me 2000, Sand 2000, Beginner's Luck 1999, Waking Life 2001, MacArthur Park 2001, Looking for Jimmy 2002, Cinemagique 2002, Notting Hill Anxiety Festival 2003, Before Sunset (Empire Film Award for Best Actress 2005) 2004, Frankenstein (TV) 2004, Broken Flowers 2005, 3 & 3 2005, The Legend of Lucy Keyes 2006, The Hoax 2006, The Air I Breathe 2007, Deux jours à Paris (Two Days in Paris) 2007, The Countess 2009, Les passages 2010, Le Skylab 2011, Les passages 2012, 2 Days in New York 2012, Before Midnight 2013, Lolo (also writer and Dir) 2015, Wiener-Dog 2016, The Bachelors 2017. *Television includes:* ER 2001. *Address:* c/o Glenn Rigberg, Gina Rugolo-Judd, Rigberg-Rugolo Entertainment, 1180 South Beverly Drive, Suite 601, Los Angeles, CA 90035-1153, USA. *Telephone:* (310) 712-0712.

DELYAGIN, Mikhail Gennadyevich, DEcon; Russian economist, politician and author; b. 18 March 1968, Moscow; ed Moscow State Univ.; served in Soviet Army 1986–88; mem. govt analytical expert group 1990–93; Head of Analytical Centre Kominvest, then Chief Analyst, Analytical Dept of the Presidency of Russian Fed. 1994–97; adviser to Deputy Chair. of the Govt 1997–99; adviser and Head of Motherland All-Russia 1997–99; Founder and Dir Inst. of Globalization Studies 1998–2002, Scientific Dir and Chair. Presidium 2002–06, Dir 2006–07; adviser to

Prime Minister of Russian Fed. 2002–03; mem. Presidium Ideological Council of Rodina party 2004–06, Presidium Congress of Russian Communities, Political Conf., Drugaia Rossiya, Council on Foreign and Defence Policy 1999, Russian Soc. of Oxford 2011, Social and Scientific Council of the Fed. Migration Service in Moscow 2011, Public Council under Rosoboronzakaz 2013; Deputy Chair. Russian Union of Taxpayers 2003; Research Prof., Moscow State Inst. of Int. Relations 2003, Acad. of Natural Sciences 2004; mem. Russian Acad. of Natural Sciences; Hon. Prof., Jilin Univ., China 2000; Leontief Medal 2011. *Publications include:* 15 monographs, including Economics of Nonpayments 1997, Ideology of Renaissance 2000, The Practice of Globalization: The Game and the Rules of a New Era (co-author) 2000, The World Crisis: General Globalization Theory 2003, Russia after Putin: Is the 'Orange Revolution' Really Inevitable in Russia? 2005, Drive Humanity 2008, The Crisis of Mankind: Will Russia Survive in the Non-Russian Discord? 2010, New Oprichnina, or Why Not to Blame Russia Right Now, 2011, Time to Win: Conversations about the Main Thing 2014, Overcoming Liberal Plague: Why and How We Will Win! 2015; more than 1,000 articles in Russia and abroad. *Leisure interests:* travel, scuba diving, skiing, sleeping. *Telephone:* (495) 510-57-71. *E-mail:* info@iprog.ru. *Website:* delyagin.ru.

DEMARCO, Richard, CBE, OBE, FRSA; British artist and academic; *Professor Emeritus of European Cultural Studies, Kingston University;* b. 9 July 1930, Edinburgh, Scotland; s. of Carmine Demarco and Elizabeth Valentine Fusco; m. Anne C. Muckle 1957; ed Holy Cross Acad., Edin. Coll. of Art, Moray House Coll. and Royal Army Educ. Corps; art master, Duns Scotus Acad., Edin. 1956–67; Vice-Chair. Founding Cttee and Vice-Chair. Bd of Dirs, Traverse Theatre, Edin. 1963–67; Dir Sean Connery's Scottish Int. Educ. Trust (SIET) 1972–74; Dir Richard Demarco Gallery 1966–, European Youth Parl. 1993– (Artistic Adviser 1992–); Trustee, Kingston-Demarco European Cultural Foundation 1993–95; Dir Demarco European Art Foundation, Edinburgh 1993–; Prof. of European Cultural Studies, Kingston Univ. 1993–2000, Prof. Emer. 2001–; consultant to Ministries of the Environment and Culture, Malta 1999; mem. Royal Scottish Soc. of Painters in Watercolours; Hon. Fellow, Royal Incorporation of Architects; Cavaliere della Repubblica Italiana 1986; Chevalier des Arts et des Lettres; Hon. LLD (Dundee); Dr hc from univs in Europe and North America; Gold Medal from Polish Govt 1976, Gold Medals from Germany, Poland and Romania 2012, European Citizen's Medal 2013, engraved Loving Cup from Edinburgh City Council presented by the Lord Provost in the City Chambers 2014. *Publications:* The Artist as Explorer 1978, The Road to Meikle Seggie 1978, A Life in Pictures 1994, Art = Wealth 1995. *Leisure interests:* exploring the road to Meikle Seggie in the footsteps of Roman legionnaires, Celtic saints and scholars, respectful of the Rule of St Benedict. *Address:* Demarco European Art Foundation, 1 Milkhall Cottages, Howgate, Penicuik, Midlothian, EH26 8PX (office); 23A Lennox Street, Edinburgh, EH4 1PY, Scotland (home). *Telephone:* 7748-961315 (mobile) (office); (131) 343-2124 (home). *Fax:* (131) 343-3124 (home). *Website:* www.richarddemarco.org.

DEMBY, Albert Joe, PhD; Sierra Leonean politician; b. 1934, Gerihun, Kenema Dist; Vice-Pres. of Sierra Leone 1996–97, 1998–99, 2000–02; Deputy Leader, Sierra Leone People's Party. *Address:* c/o Sierra Leone People's Party, 15 Wallace Johnson Street, Freetown, Sierra Leone. *E-mail:* info@slpp.ws.

DEMEKSA, Kuma; Ethiopian politician; *Ambassador to Germany;* b. Gore; s. of Wodajo Tokon and Muluye; ed Menelik II Primary School, Bore; fmr Minister of Internal Affairs; officially removed from presidency of Oromia State after he was dismissed from Oromo People's Democratic Org. for "abuse of power, corruption and anti-democratic practices"; absent from political scene until apptd State Minister of Capacity Building; Minister of Nat. Defence 2005–08; Mayor of Addis Ababa 2008–13; Amb. to Germany 2014–. *Address:* Embassy of Ethiopia, Boothstr. 20a, 12207, Berlin, Germany. *Telephone:* (30) 772060 (office). *Fax:* (30) 7720626 (office). *E-mail:* emb.ethiopia@t-online.de (office). *Website:* www.aethiopien-botschaft.de (office).

DEMEL, Herbert H., PhD; Austrian business executive; *CEO, M+W Group GmbH;* b. 14 Oct. 1953, Vienna; ed Vienna Tech. Univ.; with Robert Bosch GmbH, Stuttgart as Co-ordinator of Anti-Lock Braking Systems 1984–90, also responsible for gearbox control units 1989–90; joined Audi AG, Ingolstadt as Sr Man. 1990, mem. Man. Bd in charge of Research and Devt 1993, Speaker of Man. Bd and CEO responsible for Research and Devt and Sales and Marketing 1994, Chair. Man. Bd 1995–97; Pres. Volkswagen do Brasil 1997–2001; Pres. and CEO Magna Steyr AG, Oberwaltersdorf, Austria 2002–03; CEO Fiat Auto 2003–05; Pres. Magna Powertrain, Canada 2005–07, COO, Vehicles and Powertrain, Magna International Inc. 2007–10, Exec. Vice-Pres. Magna International Inc. 2010–13, Chief Strategy Officer 2012–13, Strategic Advisor 2013–; COO M+W Group GmbH, Stuttgart Jan. 2014–, CEO Nov. 2014–; Hon. Prof., Vienna Tech. Univ. 2012–. *Address:* M+W Group GmbH, Lotterbergstraße 30, 70499 Stuttgart, Germany (office). *Telephone:* (711) 8804-0 (office). *E-mail:* info@mwgroup.net (office). *Website:* www.mwgroup.net (office).

DEMETRIADES, Panicos O., BA, MA, PhD; Cypriot economist, academic and fmr central banker; b. 9 Jan. 1959, Limassol; ed Univ. of Essex, Univ. of Cambridge, UK; Officer, Econ. Research Dept, Central Bank of Cyprus 1985–90, Gov. Central Bank of Cyprus 2012–14; Lecturer in Econs, Univ. of Keele, UK 1990–95, Sr Lecturer 1995–96, Reader in Econs 1996–97; Prof. of Financial Econs, South Bank Univ., London 1997–2000; Prof. of Financial Econs, Univ. of Leicester 2000–12, Head of Econs Dept 2002–05; with Research Dept, IMF 1994; Consultant, Co-operative Central Bank of Cyprus 1996–98; Gen. Ed. Cyprus Journal of Economics 1989–96; Ed. Ekonomia 1997–2007; mem. Governing Bd Cyprus Univ. of Tech. 2009–10. *Publications include:* numerous articles in academic journals.

DEMETRIOU, Andreas Panteli, BA, PhD; Cypriot psychologist, academic and politician; b. 15 Aug. 1950, Strongylo, Famagusta; m. Julia Tsakalea; two s.; ed Aristotelian Univ. of Thessaloniki, Univ. of New South Wales, Australia; Research and Teaching Asst, Dept of Psychology and Educ., Aristotelian Univ. of Thessaloniki 1975–83, Lecturer in Developmental Psychology 1983–86, Asst Prof. of Developmental Psychology 1986–92, Prof. 1992–96, mem. Univ. Senate 1990–91, Head of Dept of Psychology 1991–92, Pres. School of Psychology 1993–95, mem. Research Cttee 1995–96; Visiting Asst Prof. of Psychology, Dept of Educ., Univ. of Thessaly 1988–90; Prof. of Psychology, Univ. of Cyprus 1996–, Head of Dept of Educational Science 1996–98, Vice-Rector 1999–2002, Acting Rector 2003, Dean of School of Humanities and Social Sciences 2004–06; Visiting Scholar, Univ. of New South Wales, Australia 1978, Stanford Univ., USA 1991; Consultant Visitor at Harvard, Yale, and Pittsburgh Univs, USA 1985; Visiting Research Fellow, Univ. of Melbourne, Australia 1988; Visiting Prof., Univ. of Ljubljana, Slovenia 1995, Univ. of Porto, Portugal 1998, Univ. of Marribor, Slovenia 2003; Pres. First Conf. for Psychological Research 1989, Greek Psychological Soc. 1989–91, Sec.-Gen. 1991–93; Pres. Seventh Conf., Hellenic Psychological Soc. 1998, Interim Governing Bd, Technological Univ. of Cyprus 2004–08, Conf. of Rectors of the Univs of Cyprus 2007–08; Pres. Univ. of Nicosia Research Foundation 2011–, Pancyprian Asscn of Psychologists 2012–; Founding Ed. Psychology: The Journal of Greek Psychological Society 1992–96, mem. Editorial Bd 1997–; mem. Editorial Bd, The European Journal of the Psychology of Education 1985–, Newsletter of the European Association for Research on Learning and Instruction 1987–91, Adult Development Series 1989–, Bulletin of the Didactics of Mathematics 1990–96, Developmental Science 1998–, The Child and the Adolescent: A Journal of Mental Health and Psychopathology 1999–, The Child and the Adolescent: The Journal of the Greek Association of Psychoanalytic Psychotherapy of Children 2001, MountainRise: An Electronic Journal Dedicated to Scholarship of Teaching and Learning 2004–; mem. Int. Programme Cttee, Third Conf. of European Asscn for Research on Learning and Instruction 1989, mem. Exec. Cttee 1989–93, Cttee for Oeuvre Award 2001, Conf. Pres. 2003–05; mem. Psychology Cttee, Inter-Univ. Center for Recognition of Foreign Degrees (Diapanepistimiako Kentro Anagnorisis Titlon Spoudon Allodapis—DIKATSA) 1989–92; mem. Psychological Practice Licencing Cttee, Ministry of Health and Social Services 1994–95; mem. Ad Hoc Cttee for Evaluation of Integrated Lyceum, Ministry of Educ.; mem. Governing Bd, Research Promotion Foundation 2000–03; Rep. to European Science Foundation 2001–03; Minister of Educ. and Culture 2008–11; Fellow, Int. Acad. of Educ. 2004, Academia Europaea 2012; Distinguished Visiting Prof., Univ. of Fribourg, Switzerland 2001; Hon. Visiting Prof., Northeastern Normal Univ., China 2009; Hon. DUniv (Middlesex Univ., UK) 2010; Initiative Founder Award, Eduvision 2020 Conference 2011. *Publications:* The Neo-Piagetian Theories of Cognitive Development: Toward an Integration 1988; numerous contribs to academic journals. *Address:* c/o Ministry of Education and Culture, Kimonos and Thoukydidou, 1434 Nicosia, Cyprus. *E-mail:* moec@moec.gov.cy.

DEMIAN, Hani Qadri, BA, MIA; Egyptian economist and politician; ed Helwan Univ., School of Int. and Public Affairs, Columbia Univ., USA; joined Ministry of Finance 2004 as Sr Adviser and Dir, Macro-Fiscal Unit, Office of the Minister of Finance, becoming Deputy Minister of Finance 2007, First Deputy Minister 2012–13 (resgnd), Minister of Finance 2014–16; Chair of Deputies, IMF Int. Monetary and Financial Cttee 2008; fmr dir several govt and non-govt insts including Egyptian Competition Authority, Nat. Telecommunication Regulatory Authority, Post Authority, Bd of Trustees, Egyptian Radio and TV Union, Misr-Bank Europe, Frankfurt. *Address:* c/o Ministry of Finance, Ministry of Finance Towers, Cairo (Nasr City), Egypt (office).

DEMING, Claiborne P., BA, JD; American lawyer and business executive; *Chairman, Murphy Oil Corporation;* b. 1955; m. Elaine Deming; four c.; ed Tulane Univ.; joined Murphy Oil Corpn as staff attorney 1979, held numerous exec. positions, including Pres. Murphy Oil USA, Inc. 1989–93, Exec. Vice-Pres. and COO 1993–94, mem. Bd of Dirs 1993–, Pres. and CEO 1994–2008, Chair. Exec. Cttee 2009–, Chair. of the Bd 2012–; mem. Bd of Dirs Entergy Corpn 2002–06; mem. Ark. State Bd of Educ. 1999–2002; Vice-Chair. Nat. Petroleum Council; Pres. El Dorado Educ. Foundation; Past Pres. 25 Year Club of the Oil and Gas Industry, South Ark. Symphony, United Way of Union Co.; mem. Tulane Law School Bd of Advisors, A.B. Freeman School of Business of Tulane Univ. Bd of Advisors; mem. Bd of Dirs, American Petroleum Inst., Jefferson Scholars Foundation, Univ. of Virginia; mem. Bd of Trustees Vanderbilt Univ.; mem. ABA, Ark. Bar Asscn, La Bar Asscn. *Address:* Murphy Oil Corporation, PO Box 7000, El Dorado, AR 71731-7000 (office); Murphy Oil Corpn, 200 Peach Street, El Dorado, AR 71730, USA (office). *Telephone:* (870) 862-6411 (office). *E-mail:* webmaster@murphyoilcorp.com (office). *Website:* www.murphyoilcorp.com (office).

DeMINT, James (Jim) Warren, AB, MBA; American research foundation executive and fmr politician; b. 2 Sept. 1951; m. Debbie DeMint; four c.; ed Univ. of Tennessee, Clemson Univ.; est. marketing co.; mem. US House of Reps from S Carolina, 4th Dist 1998–2004, served as mem. House Educ. and Workforce Cttee, Transportation and Infrastructure Cttee, Small Business Cttee, Vice-Chair. Sub-Cttee on Employer and Employee Relations; Senator from S Carolina 2005–13 (resgnd), mem. Cttee on Commerce, Science and Transportation, Cttee on Banking, Housing and Urban Affairs, Cttee on Foreign Relations, Jt Econ. Cttee; Pres. The Heritage Foundation 2013–17; Friend of the Taxpayer Award, American for Tax Reform, Spirit of Enterprise Award, US Chamber of Commerce, 'A' Rating, Nat. Rifle Asscn, ranked by National Journal as the Senate's most conservative mem. 2012, ranked by Nat. Taxpayers Union as the No. 1 senator voting for responsible tax and spending policies 2012. *Publications:* Why We Whisper: Restoring Our Right to Say It's Wrong (co-author) 2007, Saving Freedom: We Can Stop America's Slide Into Socialism 2009, The Great American Awakening: Two Years that Changed America, Washington, and Me 2011, Now or Never: Saving America from Economic Collapse 2012, Falling in Love with America Again 2014.

DEMIRAJ, Col Dritan; Albanian army officer and government official; m.; three c.; ed Mil. Skenderbej Acad., Public Order Acad., Faculty of Law; postgraduate studies in int. security policy; sr mil. officer; Lecturer, Mil. Acad. and Univ. of Sports; Commdr of Special Forces of the Army and of the Regt Command of Special Forces 2007–13; has run the first Albanian mil. missions in Afghanistan within framework of Int. Security Assistance Force; Minister of Internal Affairs May–Aug. 2017; Honour of the Nation for special contribs to nat. security and enhancement of the image of the Albanian state through missions abroad. *Publications:* several books, manuals and academic articles in the fields of security and counter-terrorism. *Leisure interests:* sports (holds title of Meritorious Master in karate and kick-boxing). *Address:* c/o Ministry of Internal Affairs, Sheshi Skënderbej 3, 1001 Tirana, Albania (office). *Telephone:* (4) 2247155 (office).

DEMIRALP, Mustafa Oğuz; Turkish diplomatist; b. 22 Jan. 1952, Istanbul; m.; two c.; ed Middle East Tech. Univ.; mil. service 1977–78; Second Sec., Gen. Directorate of Int. Political Affairs, Ministry of Foreign Affairs (MFA) 1978–83,

Consul, Consulate Gen. in Munich 1980–83, First Sec., Embassy in Tehran 1983–85, Head of Section, Dept for Policy Planning 1985–87, Counsellor, Perm. Mission to UN, Geneva 1987–91, Head of Section, Gen. Directorate of Multilateral Political Affairs, MFA 1991–92, Head of Dept, Dept for OSCE Affairs 1992–93, Deputy Perm. Rep., Perm. Mission to Council of Europe 1993–97, Special Advisor to Minister of Foreign Affairs 1997–2000, Amb. and Perm. Rep. to WTO, Geneva 2000–02, Amb. and Perm. Rep. to EU, Brussels 2002–05, Amb. and Gen. Sec. for EU Affairs, Gen. Secr. for EU Affairs, MFA 2006–09, Amb. to Switzerland 2009–10, Amb. and Perm. Rep. to UN, Geneva 2010–13, Amb. to Mexico 2013–17.

DEMIRCHIAN, Stepan; Armenian politician; *Chairman, People's Party of Armenia;* b. 7 June 1959, Yerevan; s. of Karen Demirchian (died 1999); m.; three d.; ed Yerevan Polytechnic Inst.; began career working at electrical eng plant; fmr dir of industrial machinery co.; elected Chair. People's Party of Armenia 1999, confirmed in post 2001–; cand. in presidential election 2003; Head of Justice (Artarutiun) bloc (alliance of opposition parties) to contest legis. elections 2003. *Address:* People's Party of Armenia (Hayastani Zhoghovrdakan Kusaktsutyun—HzhK), 0002 Yerevan, Parpetsi Street, Armenia (office). *Telephone:* (10) 53-15-01 (office). *Fax:* (10) 53-77-01 (office). *E-mail:* npa_armenia@yahoo.com (office). *Website:* www.ppa.am (office).

DEMOLLI, Haki, LLM, SJD; Kosovo lawyer, professor of law and politician; b. 17 Feb. 1963, Prishtina; m.; three c.; ed Faculty of Law, Univ. of Pristina; Judicial Intern, Prishtina Dist Court 1986–87; Asst Lecturer in Criminology, Faculty of Law, Univ. of Prishtina 1987, Univ. Co-operator, Lecturer, Asst Prof., Assoc. Prof. and Full Prof., Faculty of Law 2002, 2008, 2012, mem. Steering Cttee, Univ. of Prishtina 2005–08; Lecturer in Legal Affairs, Kosovo Police Service School, Vushtrri 1999–2003; Dir Kosovo Law Centre 2003–10; mem. Experts Team for Reforming the Kosovo Judicial System 2003–04; expert engaged in drafting the Law on The Prevention of Money Laundering, Law on Sport etc. 2007; Minister of Justice March–Oct. 2010; mem. Lidhja Demokratike e Kosovës (LDK—Democratic League of Kosovo), Kosovo Ass. 2011–, Chair. Cttee for Electoral Reform, mem. Oversight Cttee for the Kosovo Intelligence Agency 2011–; Minister of the Kosovo Security Force 2014–17; Vice-Pres. Kosovo Football Fed. 2000–08. *Publications include:* Terrorism 2002, Murders in Post-war Kosovo 2006, Economic Crime in Kosovo in the Eighties 2009. *Address:* c/o Faculty of Law, 10000 Prishtina, Str. Agim Ramadani no 60, Kosovo (office). *Telephone:* (38) 229063 (office). *E-mail:* hakidemolli@yahoo.com.

DEMPSEY, Gen. Martin E., BS, MA, MS; American army officer; b. 14 March 1952; m. Deanie Dempsey; one s. two d.; ed John S. Burke Catholic High School, Goshen, NY, US Mil. Acad., Duke Univ., Nat. War Coll.; commissioned as an Armor officer 1974; first duty assignment in 2nd Armored Cavalry Regt, served as a Scout and Support Platoon Leader and Squadron Adjutant; completed Armor Officer Advanced Course, apptd Motor Officer for 1st Squadron, 10th Cavalry, Fort Carson, Colo 1979; later commanded Alpha and HQ Troops, 1st Squadron, 10th Cavalry, as well as serving as Squadron Operations Officer; assigned to English Dept, West Point 1984, performed duties as an instructor, Asst Prof. –1987; assigned to Command and Gen. Staff Coll., Fort Leavenworth, Kan.; reported to 3rd Armored Div., Friedberg, Germany 1988, served as Exec. Officer of 4th Bn, 67th Armor Regt, then as Operations Officer and later Exec. Officer for 3rd Brigade, 3rd Armored Div., deploying in support of Operations Desert Shield and Desert Storm; assumed command of 4th Bn, 67th Armored Regt, 1st Armored Div. 1991; assigned as Chief of Armor Br., US Total Army Personnel Command 1993; returned to Fort Carson to take command of 3rd Armored Cavalry Regt 1996; Asst Deputy Dir for Politico-Mil. Affairs Europe and Africa J5 and Special Asst to Chair. of Jt Chiefs of Staff, Washington, DC 1998–2001; Program Man., Saudi Arabian Nat. Guard Modernization Program, Saudi Arabia 2001–03; commanded 1st Armored Div. and deployed to Iraq in support of Operation Iraqi Freedom 2003–04; redeployed the div. to Germany and completed his command tour July 2005; returned to Iraq and assumed command of Multi-Nat. Security Transition Command-Iraq Aug. 2005–07; Deputy Commdr US Cen. Command 2007–08, Acting Commdr March–Oct. 2008; Commdr US Army Training and Doctrine Command 2008–11; Chief of Staff of the US Army April–Oct. 2011; Chair. Jt Chiefs of Staff Oct. 2011–15; rank of 2nd Lt 1974, 1st Lt 1976, Capt. 1978, Maj. 1985, Lt Col 1991, Col 1995, Brig. Gen. 2001, Maj. Gen. 2004, Lt Gen. 2005, Gen. 2008; Defense Distinguished Service Medal (with one bronze Oak Leaf Cluster), Army Distinguished Service Medal (with two Oak Leaf Clusters), Defense Superior Service Medal, Legion of Merit (with two Oak Leaf Clusters), Bronze Star Medal with Oak Leaf Cluster and 'V' Device, Meritorious Service Medal (with two Oak Leaf Clusters), Joint Service Commendation Medal, Army Commendation Medal, Army Achievement Medal (with Oak Leaf Cluster), Joint Meritorious Unit Award (with Oak Leaf Cluster), Valorous Unit Award (with Oak Leaf Cluster), Army Superior Unit Award (with Oak Leaf Cluster), Nat. Defense Service Medal (with two bronze Service Stars), Southwest Asia Service Medal with three bronze Service Stars, Iraq Campaign Medal, Global War on Terrorism Expeditionary Medal, Global War on Terrorism Service Medal, Army Service Ribbon, Army Overseas Service Ribbon (with award numeral '4'), NATO Medal for Service with ISAF, Kuwait Liberation Medal (Saudi Arabia), Kuwait Liberation Medal (Kuwait), Combat Action Badge, Basic Parachutist Badge, Office of the Jt Chiefs of Staff Identification Badge, Army Staff Identification Badge, 7 Overseas Service Bars, 3rd Armored Cavalry Regt Distinctive Unit Insignia, 1st Armored Div. Combat Service Identification Badge. *Address:* c/o Office of the Chairman of the Joint Chiefs of Staff, 9999 Joint Staff Pentagon, Washington, DC 20318-9999, USA.

DEMPSEY, Noel, BA, HDip in Ed; Irish politician and fmr teacher guidance counsellor; *Public Affairs Adviser, Noel Dempsey Consulting ULC;* b. 6 Jan. 1953, Trim, Co. Meath; s. of Michael Dempsey and Maureen Dempsey (née Byrne); m. Bernadette Rattigan; two s. two d.; ed St Michael's Christian Brothers' School, Trim, Univ. Coll., Dublin, St Patrick's Coll., Maynooth (Diploma in Career Guidance, Diploma in Youth Leadership); fmr career guidance counsellor; Nat. Sec. Local Authority Members Asscn 1984–89; Chair. Meath Co. Council 1986–87; fmr mem. and Chair. Co. Meath Vocational Educ. Cttee; fmr Dir Midland East Regional Tourism Org.; fmr mem. numerous local govt cttees; mem. Dáil Eireann (Irish Parl.) 1987–2011, mem. Dáil Public Accounts Cttee 1987–89, 1990–92; fmr Opposition Spokesperson on Environment; Fianna Fáil Co-ordinator on Forum for Peace and Reconciliation; Nat. Treasurer Fianna Fáil; fmr Minister of State at Depts of the Taoiseach, Defence, and Finance; Govt Chief Whip 1992–94; Minister for the Environment and Local Govt 1997–2002, for Educ. and Science 2002–04, for Communications, Marine and Natural Resources 2004–07, for Transport 2007–11; Public Affairs Adviser, Noel Dempsey Consulting ULC 2011–; currently also Chair. Temple Bar Co.; European Road Safety Pin Award. *Leisure interests:* Gaelic football and hurling, reading, golf. *Address:* Newtown, Trim, Co. Meath, Ireland (home). *E-mail:* noeldempseyconsulting@gmail.com (office).

DEMSZKY, Gábor, DrIur; Hungarian politician, journalist, editor and sociologist; b. 4 Aug. 1952, Budapest; s. of Rudolf Demszky and Irén Király; m. Vera Révai (divorced); m. Anikó Németh; four c.; ed Eötvös Loránd Univ.; contrib. to periodical Világosság (Lucidity) 1977; Founding mem. SZETA (fund to support poor) 1979; Founder AB Független Kiadó (ind. publr) 1981; Ed. illegal Hirmondó (Courier) 1983; Founding mem. Network of Free Initiative and SZDSZ 1988; Founding mem. Alliance of Free Democrats, mem. Exec. Bd 1989, Pres. 2000–01; mem. Parl. 1990 (resgnd), 1998; Chair. Cttee of Nat. Security 1990; mem. Exec. Bd, Alliance of Free Democrats 1994–, Pres. of Alliance 2000–01; Founder Children's Rescue Soc.; negotiator in Moscow talks on Soviet troops withdrawal and on Hungary's leaving the Warsaw Pact; Mayor of Budapest 1990–2010; Global Fellow, Global Europe Program, Global Sustainability and Resilience Program 2014–16; Vice-Pres. Standing Conf. of Local and Regional Authorities, Council of Europe 1992–94, Congress of Local and Regional Authorities 1994–96; mem., European Parl. 2004 (resgnd due to conflict of interest); Founding mem. and Dir Asscn to Save the Children; Co-Pres. Budapest Bank for Budapest Foundation; Pres. Budapest Sports Asscn; Freedom to Publish Prize, Int. Asscn of Publishers, Vienna 1984. *Publications:* Underground Lines (co-author) 2000, Reconquest of Freedom 2001, The Eastern Eden 2008. *Leisure interests:* jogging, sailing, riding, water-skiing, fishing. *Address:* Woodrow Wilson International Center for Scholars, Ronald Reagan Building and International Trade Center, One Woodrow Wilson Plaza, 1300 Pennsylvania Avenue NW, Washington, DC 20004-3027, USA (office). *Telephone:* (202) 691-4000 (office). *E-mail:* gabor.demszky@wilsoncenter.org (office). *Website:* www.wilsoncenter.org/person/gabor-demszky (office).

DENAJ, Anila; Albanian politician and banker; *Minister of Finance and Economy;* b. 18 Sept. 1973, Tirana; m.; one s.; ed Univ. of Tirana; consultant, IPC GmbH 2001–07; held numerous senior positions at ProCredit Group bank branches in Salvador, Bolivia, Ecuador, Romania and Mozambique, later becoming Deputy CEO ProCredit Bank 2007–13; Gen. Dir, Ministry of Finance and Economy 2013–15; Deputy Team Leader, GFA Consulting Group GmbH 2017–18; Gen. Dir Albanian Compulsory Health Care Security Fund (FSDKSH) 2018–; Minister of Finance and Economy 2018–; part-time lecturer, Albanian School of Public Admin (ASPA) 2014–; mem. Bd of Dirs Electronic and Postal Communications Authority (AKEP) 2015–18; mem. Bd of Supervisors, INSIG SH.A. *Address:* Ministry of Finance and Economy, Bulevardi Dëshmorët e Kombit, 3, 1010 Tirana, Albania (office). *Telephone:* (4) 2230803 (office). *Fax:* (4) 2228405 (office). *E-mail:* info@financa.gov.al (office). *Website:* financa.gov.al (office).

DENCH, Dame Judith (Judi) Olivia, CH, DBE, FRSA; British actress; b. 9 Dec. 1934, York; d. of Reginald Arthur Dench and Eleanora Olave Dench (née Jones); m. Michael Williams 1971 (died 2001); one d.; ed The Mount School, York, Central School of Speech and Drama, London; performed in Old Vic seasons 1957–61, appearing in parts including Ophelia (Hamlet), Katherine (Henry V), Cecily (The Importance of Being Earnest), Juliet (Romeo and Juliet), appeared with Old Vic Co. at two Edin. Festivals, Venice, on tour to Paris, Belgium and Yugoslavia and on tour to USA and Canada; appearances with RSC 1961–62, including parts as Anya (The Cherry Orchard), Titania (A Midsummer Night's Dream), Dorcas Bellboys (A Penny for a Song), Isabella (Measure for Measure); on tour to W Africa with Nottingham Playhouse 1963; mem. Bd Nat. Theatre 1988–91; subsequent roles include Irina (The Three Sisters) and Doll Common (Alchemist), Oxford Playhouse 1964–65, title-role in Saint Joan and Barbara (The Astrakhan Coat), Nottingham Playhouse 1965, Amanda (Private Lives), Lika (The Promise) 1967, Sally Bowles (Cabaret) 1968, Grace Harkaway (London Assurance) 1970, 1972, Barbara Undershaft (Major Barbara) 1970; Assoc. mem. RSC 1969–, appearing as Bianca (Women Beware Women), Viola (Twelfth Night), Hermione and Perdita (Winter's Tale), Portia (Merchant of Venice), Duchess (Duchess of Malfi), Beatrice (Much Ado About Nothing), Lady Macbeth (Macbeth), Adriana (Comedy of Errors), also on tour with RSC to Japan and Australia 1970, Japan 1972; other performances include Vilma (The Wolf), Oxford and London 1973, Miss Trant (The Good Companions), 1974, Sophie Fullgarney (The Gay Lord Quex) 1975, Nurse (Too True to be Good) 1975, 1976, Millament (Way of the World) 1978, Cymbeline 1979, Juno and the Paycock 1980–81, Lady Bracknell (The Importance of Being Earnest) 1982, Deborah (A Kind of Alaska) 1982, Pack of Lies 1983, Mother Courage 1984, Waste 1985, Mr and Mrs Nobody 1986, Antony and Cleopatra 1987, Entertaining Strangers 1987, Hamlet 1989, The Cherry Orchard 1989, The Sea 1991, The Plough and the Stars 1991, Coriolanus 1992, The Gift of the Gorgon 1993, The Seagull (Royal Nat. Theatre) 1994, The Convent 1995, Absolute Hell (Royal Nat. Theatre) 1995, A Little Night Music (Royal Nat. Theatre) 1995, Amy's View (Royal Nat. Theatre) 1997, (New York) 1999, Filumena 1998, The Royal Family 2001, The Breath of Life (Theatre Royal, Haymarket) 2002, All's Well that Ends Well (Theatregoers' Award for Best Supporting Actress 2005) 2003–04, Madame de Sade (Donmar Warehouse) 2009, A Midsummer Night's Dream (Rose Theatre, Kingston) 2010, Peter and Alice (Noel Coward Theatre) 2013; Dir Much Ado About Nothing 1988, Look Back in Anger 1989, The Boys from Syracuse 1991; mem. Bd, Nat. Theatre 1988–; Hon. Fellow, Royal Holloway Coll., London, Lucy Cavendish Coll., Cambridge; Foreign Hon. Fellow, American Acad. of Arts and Sciences 2009; Freedom of the City of London 2011, Hon. Pres. Brontë Soc.; Hon. DLitt (Warwick) 1978, (York) 1983, (Keele) 1989, (Birmingham) 1989, (Loughborough) 1991, (Open Univ.) 1994, (London) 1994, (Oxford) 2000; Dr hc (Surrey) 1996, (Mary Baldwin Coll., Va) 2004, (Juilliard Acad., New York) 2004, (Royal Acad. of Music and Drama, Glasgow), (Queen Margaret Univ. Coll., Edinburgh), (Univ. of East Anglia), (Univ. of Wales), (Leeds), (Hull), (St Andrews), (Nottingham Trent); numerous awards, including Paladino d'Argentino (Venice Festival Award for Juliet) 1961, Best Actress of Year (Variety London Critics for Lika in The Promise) 1967, Most Promising Newcomer (British Film Acad. for Four in the Morning) 1965, Best Actress of the Year (Guild of Directors for Talking to a Stranger) 1967, Soc. West End Theatre Award (for Lady Macbeth) 1977, Best Actress New

Standard Drama Awards (for Juno and the Paycock) 1980, (for Lady Bracknell in The Importance of Being Earnest and Deborah in A Kind of Alaska) 1983, (for Cleopatra in Antony and Cleopatra) 1987, Olivier Award for Best Actress in Antony and Cleopatra 1987; BAFTA Award for Best Television Actress 1981, for Best Supporting Actress (for A Room with a View) 1987 and (for A Handful of Dust) 1988, Golden Globe and BAFTA Best Actress Award for Mrs Brown, Olivier Award for Outstanding Contrib. to Theatre 2004, Evening Standard Special Award for Outstanding Contrib. to British Theatre 2004, European Film Acad. Lifetime Achievement Award 2008, BFI Fellowship 2011, Sky Arts Award for Outstanding Achievement 2011, Crystal Globe for Outstanding Artistic Contrib. to World Cinema, 46th Int. Film Festival, Karlovy Vary, West Bohemia 2011, Praemium Imperiale Award, Japan Art Asscn 2011, Golden Seagull Award, Moscow Arts Theatre 2012, London Film Critics' Circle Awards British Actress of the Year 2012, Olivier Award for Best Actress in a Supporting Role (for A Winter's Tale) 2016, Richard Harris Award, British Ind. Film Awards 2018. *Films include:* The Third Secret 1964, Four in the Morning 1965, A Study in Terror 1965, He Who Rides a Tiger 1965, A Midsummer Night's Dream (RSC Production) 1968, Luther 1974, Dead Cert 1974, Spaceship Earth (short) (4th edition narrator) 1982, Wetherby 1985, A Room with a View 1985, The Angelic Conversation (narrator) 1987, 84 Charing Cross Road 1987, A Handful of Dust 1988, Henry V 1989, Jack & Sarah 1995, GoldenEye 1995, Hamlet 1996, Mrs Brown 1997, Tomorrow Never Dies 1997, Shakespeare in Love (Acad. Award for Best Supporting Actress) 1998, The Bear (short) (narrator American version) 1998, Tea with Mussolini 1999, The World Is Not Enough 1999, Chocolat 2000, Iris (BAFTA Award for Best Actress 2002) 2001, The Shipping News 2001, The Importance of Being Earnest 2002, Die Another Day 2002, Home on the Range (voice) 2004, Disney Sing Along Songs: Home on the Range – Little Patch of Heaven (video short) 2004, The Chronicles of Riddick 2004, Ladies in Lavender 2004, A Dairy Tale (video short) (voice) 2004, Pride & Prejudice 2005, Angelina Ballerina: Angelina's Princess Dance (video) (voice) 2005, Mrs Henderson Presents 2205, Doogal (narrator) 2006, Angelina Ballerina: Angelina Sets Sail (voice) 2006, Casino Royale 2006, Notes on a Scandal 2006, Quantum of Solace 2008, Rage 2009, Nine 2009, James Bond Supports International Women's Day (short) (voice) 2011, Run for Your Wife (cameo) 2011, Jane Eyre 2011, Pirates of the Caribbean: On Stranger Tides 2011, My Week with Marilyn 2011, Friend Request Pending (short) 2011, J. Edgar 2011, The Best Exotic Marigold Hotel 2011, Skyfall 2012, Philomena 2013, The Second Best Exotic Marigold Hotel 2014, Spectre 2015, Tulip Fever 2016, Victoria & Abdul 2017, Murder on the Orient Express 2017, Red Joan 2018, All is True 2019. *Television includes:* Hilda Lessways (series) 1959, The Terrible Choice (series) 1960, Armchair Theatre (series) – Pink String and Sealing Wax 1960, An Age of Kings (series) 1960, The Four Just Men (series) 1960, The Cherry Orchard (film) 1962, Z Cars (series) 1963, Festival (series) – August for the People 1964, Detective (series) 1964, The Troubleshooters (series) 1965, ITV Play of the Week (series) 1959–66, Court Martial (series) 1966, Talking to a Stranger (mini-series) 1966, Theatre 625 (series) 1964–66, BBC Play of the Month (series) – Days to Come 1966, Confession (series) 1970, Ooh La La! (series) 1973, 2nd House (series) – Frank's for the Memory 1974, Jackanory (series) (storyteller) 1968–78, The Comedy of Errors (film) 1978, A Performance of Macbeth (film) 1979, BBC 2 Play of the Week (series) – On Giant's Shoulders 1979, – Langrishe Go Down 1978, ITV Playhouse (series) – On Approval 1968, – Village Wooing 1979, Love in a Cold Climate (mini-series) 1980, BBC 2 Playhouse (series) – Going Gently 1981, The Cherry Orchard (film) 1981, Saigon: Year of the Cat (film) 1983, A Fine Romance (series) 1981–84, The Browning Version (film) 1985, Star Quality: Mr. and Mrs. Edgehill (film) 1985, Theatre Night (series) 1987, Behaving Badly (mini-series) 1989, Screen One (series) 1990, Absolute Hell (film) 1991, The Torch (mini-series) 1992, As Time Goes By (series) 1992–2005, Middlemarch (mini-series) 1994, 1914–1918 (series) – Total War (narrator as Dame Judi Dench) 1996, The Last of the Blonde Bombshells (film) 2000, Angelina Ballerina (series) 2001–07, Angelina Ballerina: The Show Must Go On (film) (voice) 2002, Cranford (mini-series) 2007–09, National Theatre Live (series) – 50 Years on Stage 2013, Roald Dahl's Esio Trot 2014, The Hollow Crown 2016. *Publications include:* Judi Dench: A Great Deal of Laughter (biog.), Judi Dench: With a Crack in Her Voice 1998, Scenes from My Life 2005, And Furthermore 2010. *Leisure interests:* painting, drawing, swimming, sewing, catching up with letters. *Address:* c/o Julian Belfrage Associates, 3rd Floor, 9 Argyll Street, London, W1F 7TG, England (office). *E-mail:* email@julianbelfrage.com (office).

DENCKER, Nils Jonas, BSc, PhD (Habil.); Swedish mathematician and academic; *Professor of Mathematics, Lund University;* b. 14 Dec. 1953, Lund; s. of Sven Jonas Dencker and Solveig Dencker; m. Anna Dencker; two s. two d.; ed Lund Univ.; Teaching Asst and Student Counsellor, Lund Univ. 1976–81, Asst Prof. 1983–88, Assoc. Prof. 1988–2006, Dir of Studies, Dept of Math. 2001–03, Prof. of Math. 2006–; C.L.E. Moore Instructor, MIT, USA 1981–83; Chair. Swedish Math. Soc. 2007–09; Visiting Researcher, Univ. of California, Berkeley, USA 2002, 2006, 2014; Swedish Del. to EMS Gen. Council, Turin, Italy 2006, to IMU Gen. Ass., Santiago de Compostela, Spain 2006, Bangalore, India 2010, Gyeongju, Korea 2014; Chair. Meetings Cttee, European Math. Soc. 2013–16; mem. Scientific Council for Natural and Eng Sciences, Swedish Research Council 2016–; mem. Royal Swedish Acad. of Sciences 2008 (Chair. Class for Math. 2013–), Royal Physiographic Soc., Lund 2009 (Pres. 2015), Swedish Nat. Cttee for Math. 2009–14, 2018–; Fellow, American Math. Soc. 2012; VR (Swedish Research Council) grant 2001–17, Gaarding Prize, Royal Physiographic Soc., Lund 2003, Clay Research Award, Clay Math. Inst. (co-recipient) 2005, Invited Speaker, 5th ECM, Amsterdam, The Netherlands 2008, Invited Speaker, ICM2010, Hyderabad, India 2010. *Achievement:* complete resolution of a conjecture made by F. Treves and L. Nirenberg in 1970. *Publications:* numerous papers in professional journals on micro-local analysis of partial differential equations and calculus of pseudo-differential operators. *Address:* Room 507, Center for Mathematical Sciences, Faculty of Science, Lund University, Box 118, 221 00 Lund, Sweden (office). *Telephone:* (46) 222-44-62 (office). *Fax:* (46) 222-42-13 (office). *E-mail:* nils.dencker@gmail.com (office). *Website:* www.maths.lth.se/matematiklu/personal/dencker/homepage.html (office).

DENDIAS, Nikolaos, LLM; Greek lawyer and politician; b. 7 Oct. 1959, Corfu; m. Dafni Lala; two s.; ed Univ. of Athens, Univ. Coll. London, London School of Econs; called to Corfu Bar 1986; mem. Nea Dimokratia 1978–, mem. Parl. Group for the Control of Tourism 2002, Cttee for the Revision of the Constitution 2006; mem. Parl. for Corfu 2004–, mem. Perm. Cttee on Finance, Special Perm. Cttee on Nat. Budget and Cttee of Deontology 2007–, Vice-Pres. fact-finding Cttee for the Vatopedi Case 2008; apptd Minister of Justice 2009, of Public Order and Citizen Protection 2012–14, of Nat. Defence 2014–15; mem. Centre for Political Research and Educ. 2006–; mem. Hellenic Cancer Soc. 2006–; currently Pres. Eptanission Politia Cultural Asscn. *Address:* c/o Ministry of National Defence, Odos Mesogeion 227–231, Holargos, 154 51 Athens, Greece. *Website:* dendias.gr/en.

DENEUVE, Catherine; French actress; b. (Catherine Dorléac), 22 Oct. 1943, Paris; d. of Maurice Dorléac and Renée Deneuve; m. David Bailey (q.v.) 1965 (divorced); one s. by Roger Vadim; one d. by Marcello Mastroianni; ed Lycée La Fontaine, Paris; film début in Les petits chats 1959; Pres., Dir-Gen. Films de la Citrouille 1971–79; f. Société Cardeva 1983; UNESCO Goodwill Amb. for the Safeguarding of Film Heritage 1994–2003; Hon. Golden Bear, Berlin Film Festival, Arts de l'Alliance française de New York Trophy 1998, Bangkok Film Festival Lifetime Achievement Award 2006, Lifetime Achievement Prize, European Film Awards, Berlin 2014, Praemium Imperiale 2018. *Films include:* Les portes claquent 1960, L'homme à femmes 1960, Le vice et la vertu 1962, Et Satan conduit le bal 1962, Vacances portugaises 1963, Les parapluies de Cherbourg 1963 (Palme d'Or, Festival de Cannes 1964), Les plus belles escroqueries du monde 1963, La chasse à l'homme 1964, Un monsieur de compagnie 1964, La Costanza della Ragione 1964, Repulsion 1964, Le chant du monde 1965, La vie de château 1965, Liebes Karusell 1965, Les créatures 1965, Les demoiselles de Rochefort 1966, Belle de jour 1967 (Golden Lion at Venice Festival 1967), Benjamin 1967, Manon 70 1967, Mayerling 1968, La chamade 1966, Folies d'avril 1969, Belles d'un soir 1969, La sirène du Mississippi 1969, Tristana 1970, Peau d'âne 1971, Ça n'arrive qu'aux autres 1971, Liza 1971, Un flic 1972, L'évènement le plus important depuis que l'homme a marché sur la lune 1973, Touche pas la femme blanche 1974, La femme aux bottes rouges 1975, La grande bourgeoisie 1975, Hustle 1976, March or Die 1977, Coup de foudre 1977, Ecoute, voir… 1978, L'argent des autres 1978, A nous deux 1979, Ils sont grands ces petits 1979, Le dernier métro 1980, Je vous aime 1980, Le choix des armes 1981, Hôtel des Amériques 1981, Le choc 1982, L'Africain 1983, The Hunger 1983, Le bon plaisir 1984, Paroles et musiques 1984, Le lieu du crime 1986, Pourvu que ce soit une fille 1986, Drôle d'endroit pour une rencontre 1989, La reine blanche 1991, Indochine 1992 (César award for Best Actress 1993), Ma saison préférée 1993, La Partie d'Échecs 1994, The Convent 1995, Les Cent et une nuits 1995, Les Voleurs 1995, Genéalogie d'un crime 1997, Place Vendôme 1998, Le Vent de la nuit 1999, Belle-Maman 1999, Pola x 1999, Time Regained 1999, Dancer in the Dark 2000, Je centre à la maison 2001, Absolument fabuleux 2001, 8 Femmes 2002, Au plus près du paradis 2002, Un film parlé 2003, Palais Royal! 2006, Le Concile de Pierre 2006, Le Héros de la famille 2006, Persepolis (voice) 2007, Un conte de Noël 2008, Je veuz voir 2008, Mes stars et moi 2008, La fille dud RER 2009, Cyprien 2009, Bancs publics 2009, Mères et filles 2009, Potiche 2010, The Big Picture 2010, Les yeux de sa mère 2011, Beloved 2011, Lines of Wellington 2012, God Loves Caviar 2012, Astérix and Obélix: God Save Britannia 2012, On My Way 2013, In the Courtyard 2014, In the Name of My Daughter 2014, 3 Hearts 2014, The Midwife 2017. *Television:* As Linhas de Torres Vedras (mini-series) 2012. *Publication:* Close Up and Personal (autobiog.) 2005. *Address:* c/o Artmédia, 20 avenue Rapp, 75007 Paris, France.

DENG, Nan; Chinese politician; *Vice-Chairman, China Association for Science and Technology;* b. Oct. 1945, Guang'an, Sichuan Prov.; d. of Deng Xiaoping (fmr Gen. Sec. CCP and fmr Chair. Gen. Mil. Comm., CCP) and Zhuo Lin; ed Beijing Univ.; worker, Semiconductor Research Inst., Chinese Acad. of Sciences 1973; fmr Deputy Div. Chief, Policy Dept, State Science and Tech. Comm., later Deputy Dir, later Deputy Dir Science and Tech. Policy Dept, Dir 1989–91, Vice-Minister in charge of State Science and Tech. Comm. 1991–98; Vice-Minister of Science and Tech. 1998–2005; fmr Deputy Dir Environmental Protection Cttee of the State Council; joined CCP 1978; Del., CCP Nat. Congress 1992–97; mem. 17th CCP Cen. Cttee 2007–12; Vice-Chair. China Asscn for Science and Tech. 2005–; fmr Deputy Dir China Cttee of the Int. Decade for Natural Disaster Reduction; fmr mem. Exec. Cttee, All-China Women's Fed.; UN Boutros Boutros-Ghali Special Research Prize. *Address:* China Association for Science and Technology, 3 Fuxing Lu, Beijing 100032, People's Republic of China (office). *Website:* english.cast.org.cn (office).

DENG, Pufang; Chinese politician; b. 16 April 1944; s. of Deng Xiaoping (fmr Gen. Sec. CCP and fmr Chair. Gen. Mil. Comm., CCP) and Zhuo Lin; ed Beijing Univ.; joined CCP 1965; fmr staff mem. Service Dept, Cen. Mil. Comm. of People's Repub. of China; Vice-Pres. Welfare Fund for Handicapped 1984–85, Pres. 1985–; Ed.-in-Chief Spring Breeze (Journal) 1984–; Vice-Chair. China Organizing Comm. of UN's Decade of Disabled Persons 1986–90, Chair. 1990–; Vice-Chair. Cttee for Coordination of Work for the Disabled; Chair. China Disabled Persons' Fed. 1988–; Adviser, China Asscn for Int. Friendly Contacts 1991–; Del., 14th CCP Nat. Congress 1992–97; Alt. mem. 15th CCP Cen. Cttee 1997–2002, 16th CCP Cen. Cttee 2002–07; mem. Standing Cttee, 9th CPPCC Nat. Cttee 1998–2003, Vice-Chair. 11th CPPCC Nat. Cttee 2008–13; Exec. Pres. Chinese Olympic Cttee 2003–; Rehabilitation International (RI) Presidential Awards, 15th RI World Ass. 1990, 17th RI World Ass. 1992, recipient of Testimonial from UN Sec.-Gen. 1998, UN Human Rights Award 2003, Paralympic Order 2005, UN Peace Messenger, Special Award of Asian and Pacific Decade of Disabled Persons, Lions Clubs International Award, Paul Harris Award of Rotary Int. *Address:* China Welfare Fund for Handicapped, Beijing, People's Republic of China.

DENG, Qilin, MA; Chinese steel industry executive; *President, Wuhan Iron and Steel (Group) Corporation (WISCO);* ed Wuhan Iron and Steel Inst.; joined Wuhan Iron and Steel (Group) Corpn (WISCO) 1970, served as Dir WISCO No. 2 Smelting Plant, Chief of WISCO Production Dept and Asst to the Gen. Man., apptd Deputy Man. WISCO 1995, Gen. Man. 1995–2013, Pres., Chair. and CEO 2013–15; fmr Chair. China Iron and Steel Asscn; mem. Communist Party of China 1978–2016 (expelled); sentenced to 15 years' imprisonment for bribery 2017.

DENG, Yaping, MA, PhD; Chinese media executive and table tennis player (retd); *President, Jike.com;* b. 5 Feb. 1973, Zhengzhou, He'nan Prov.; m. Lin Zhigang 2007; one s.; ed Tsinghua Univ., Beijing, Univ. of Nottingham, UK; mem. Chinese women's table tennis team 1988; won over 20 gold medals in various world championships, including Barcelona Olympics 1992, Atlanta Olympics 1996; top-ranked female table tennis player 1991–98; retd 1997; mem. Sports Cttee of IOC;

has co-chaired Chinese Olympic Cttee and Sports Asscn of China; mem. CPPCC; elected Deputy Sec. China Communist Youth League Beijing Cttee 2009; Deputy Sec. People's Daily (official newspaper of the CP of China), also Pres. Goso.cn (now jike.com) People's Daily news search engine 2010; Chinese Sports Personality of the Century 1999, mem. Laureus World Sports Acad. *Address:* Jike.com East Third Ring Road, Chaoyang District, One World Financial Center, 100020 Beijing, People's Republic of China (office). *Telephone:* (10) 57699999 (office). *Fax:* (10) 57699998 (office). *E-mail:* service@jike.com (office). *Website:* www.jike.com (office).

DENG, Youmei; Chinese writer; *Deputy Chairman, Chinese Writers' Association;* b. 1931, Tianjin; messenger in CCP-led New 4th Army 1945; entered Cen. Research Inst. of Literature 1952; in political disgrace 1957–77; Sec. Chinese Writers' Asscn 1985–96, Deputy Chair. 1996–. *Publications:* On the Precipice, Our Army Commander, Han the Forger, Tales of Taoranting Park, Snuff Bottles, Na Wu, Moon Over Liangshan Mountain. *Address:* Chinese Writers' Association, 25 Dongtucheng Road, Beijing 100013, People's Republic of China. *Telephone:* (10) 64261554.

DENG ATHORBEI, David; South Sudanese politician; ed Univ. of Khartoum; Minister of Transport and Roads in regional semi-autonomous Govt of South Sudan 2007, also fmr Minister of Finance; first Minister of Finance and Econ. Planning of South Sudan following independence 2011, Minister of Electricity and Dams –2013, of Finance, Commerce and Econ. Planning 2015–18; mem. Sudan People's Liberation Movt. *Address:* c/o Ministry of Finance, Commerce and Economic Planning, PO Box 80, Juba, South Sudan.

DENG NHIAL, Nhial; South Sudanese lawyer and politician; *Minister of Foreign Affairs and International Co-operation;* ed Univ. of Khartoum; Minister of Regional Cooperation in regional semi-autonomous Govt of South Sudan 2007, also fmr Minister of Defence; mem. Sudan People's Liberation Movt (SPLM) Leadership Council and Political Bureau; led SPLM del. to Naivasha peace talks, Kenya 2002–05; first Minister of Sudan People's Liberation Army (SPLA) and Veteran Affairs of South Sudan following independence July–Aug. 2011, Minister of Foreign Affairs and Int. Co-operation 2011–13, 2018–. *Address:* Ministry of Foreign Affairs and International Co-operation, Juba, South Sudan.

DENHAM, John Yorke, BSc; British politician; b. 15 July 1953, Seaton, Devon, England; m. Ruth Eleanor Dixon (divorced); three c.; ed Univ. of Southampton; Head of Youth Affairs, British Youth Council 1979–83; responsible for public educ. and advocacy for War on Want (charity) 1984–88; Hants. Co. Councillor 1981–89; Southampton City Councillor 1989–93, Chair. Southampton City Housing Cttee 1989–93; MP (Labour) for Southampton Itchen 1992–2015; Minister of State at Home Office 2001–03, Chair. Home Affairs Select Cttee 2003–07, Sec. of State for Innovation, Univs and Skills 2007–09, for Communities and Local Govt 2009–10; Shadow Sec. of State for Communities and Local Government May–Oct. 2010, for Business, Innovation and Skills Oct. 2010–11; Parl. Pvt. Sec. to Ed Miliband 2011–13; Vice-Pres. Local Govt Asscn 2010–; mem. AMICUS/MSF (trade union). *Leisure interests:* cookery, walking, music, Southampton Football Club. *Address:* c/o Southampton Itchen Parliamentary Office, 20–22 Southampton Street, Southampton, SO15 2ED, England. *E-mail:* john@johndenham.org.uk. *Website:* www.johndenham.org.uk.

DENHAM, Susan, BA, LLB, LLM, SC, MRIA; Irish judge; *Chief Justice, Supreme Court of Ireland;* b. 22 Aug. 1945, Dublin; d. of Douglas Gageby and Dorothy Mary Gageby (née Lester); m. Brian Denham 1970; three s. one d. (and one s. deceased); ed Alexandra Coll. Dublin, Trinity Coll. Dublin, King's Inns, Dublin and Columbia Univ. New York; called to Irish Bar 1971; mem. Midland Circuit 1971–91; called to Inner Bar 1987; Bencher, King's Inns 1991–; Judge, High Court 1991–92, Supreme Court 1992–2017, Chief Justice 2011–17; Chair. Working Group on a Courts Comm. 1995–98, Chair. Courts Service 2001–04; Chair. Family Law Devt Cttee 1999–2001, Finance Cttee 2001–04; mem. Courts Service Bd 2004–08; Chair. Irish Sentencing Information System 2006–17; Chair. Comm. on Court Practice and Procedures 2000, Cttee on Videoconferencing, Working Group on Court of Appeal 2006–09; Chair. Courts Service 2011–17, Finance Cttee 2011–17, Cttee for Judicial Studies 2011–17, Judicial Appointments Advisory Bd 2011–17, Superior Court Rules Cttee 2011–17, Working Group for Renewal 2013–17, Cttee on Judicial Induction and Mentoring 2012–17, Courts Centenary Commemoration Cttee 2013–, Interim Judicial Council 2011–17; Gov. of Marsh's Library, Dublin 2011–17; Vice-Pres. Network of Presidents of Supreme Judicial Courts of EU 2011–15, Pres. 2015–16; Pro-Chancellor, Univ. of Dublin 1996–2010; Founding mem. European Network of Councils for the Judiciary 2004; mem. ENCJ Steering Comm. 2004–07, Presidential Comm. of Ireland 2011–17, Council of State of Ireland 2011–17; Hon. Bencher, Middle Temple 2005; Hon. LLD (Queen's Univ., Belfast) 2002, (Univ. of Ulster) 2013, (Univ. College, Dublin) 2014, Hon. DPhil (Dublin City Univ.) 2014; Distinguished Fellowship Award, Griffith Coll., Dublin 2013. *Leisure interests:* Connemara ponies, gardens, reading. *Address:* Supreme Court of Ireland, Four Courts, Inns Quay, Dublin 7, Ireland (office). *Telephone:* (1) 8886540 (office). *E-mail:* supremecourt@courts.ie (office). *Website:* www.supremecourt.ie (office).

DENHARDT, David (Dave) Tilton, PhD, FRSC; American biologist and academic (retd); *Professor Emeritus of Cell Biology, Rutgers University;* b. 25 Feb. 1939, Sacramento, Calif.; s. of David B. Denhardt and Edith E. Tilton; m. Georgetta Louise Harrar 1961; one s. two d.; ed Swarthmore Coll., Pa and California Inst. of Tech., Pasadena; Instructor, Biology Dept, Harvard Univ. 1964–66, Asst Prof. 1966–70; Assoc. Prof. of Biochemistry Dept, McGill Univ., Montreal 1970–76, Prof. 1976–80; Dir Cancer Research Lab. and Prof. of Biochemistry, Microbiology and Immunology, Univ. of Western Ontario 1980–88; Chair. Biological Sciences, Rutgers Univ., NJ 1988–95, Dir Bureau of Biological Research 1988–95, Prof. of Biological Sciences 1988–2010, Prof. Emer. of Cell Biology 2010–, Chair. Biology Dept 1988–95; Ed. Journal of Virology 1977–87, GENE 1985–93, Experimental Cell Research 1994–2004; Assoc. Ed. Journal of Cell Biochemistry 1994–; mem. numerous bds; Fellow, American Acad. of Microbiology 1993. *Leisure interests:* travel, reading, canoeing, skiing, camping. *Address:* A301A Nelson Labs, Rutgers University, 604 Allison Road, Piscataway, NJ 08854-6999, USA (office). *Telephone:* (732) 445-4569 (office); (908) 704-0279 (home). *Fax:* (908) 704-0279 (home). *E-mail:* denhardt@dls.rutgers.edu (office). *Website:* lifesci.rutgers.edu (office).

DENIS, Claire; French film director, writer and academic; *Professor of Film, European Graduate School;* b. 21 April 1948, Paris; ed Institut des Hautes Études Cinématographiques (now École Nationale Supérieure des Métiers de l'Image et du Son); raised in colonial Africa (Burkina Faso, Somalia, Senegal and Cameroon), where her father was a French colonial administrator; following graduation, worked as an asst dir to Dušan Makavejev, Costa Gavras, Jacques Rivette, Jim Jarmusch and Wim Wenders; film debut with Chocolat 1988, a non-biographical account of post-colonialism; Prof. of Film, European Grad. School, Saas-Fee, Switzerland 2002–, also conducts an Intensive Summer Seminar; mem. jury, Venice Film Festival 2005; Lifetime Achievement Award, Stockholm Film Festival 2013. *Films include:* acted in: Mais où et donc Ornicar 1979, En avoir (ou pas) 1995, Le jour de Noël (short) 1998, Venus Beauty Salon 1999; directed: Chocolat (also writer) 1988, Man No Run (documentary) 1989, S'en fout la mort (also writer) 1990, Keep It for Yourself (short) (also writer) 1991, Contre l'oubli (segment 'Pour Ushari Ahmed Mahmoud, Soudan') 1991, Boom-Boom 1994, J'ai pas sommeil (also screenplay) 1994, A propos de Nice, la suite (segment 'Nice, Very Nice') 1995, Nénette et Boni (also writer) 1996, Beau travail (also writer) 1999, Trouble Every Day (also writer) 2001, Friday Night (also writer) 2002, Ten Minutes Older: The Cello (segment 'Vers Nancy') (also writer) 2002, The Intruder (also writer) 2004, Vers Mathilde (documentary) 2005, 35 Shots of Rum (also scenario) 2008, White Material (also scenario) 2009, To the Devil (short) 2011, Bastards 2013, Venice 70: Future Reloaded (documentary) 2013, Voilà l'enchainement 2014; writer: El Medina 1999. *Television includes:* Cinéma, de notre temps (documentary series) (Jacques Rivette – Le veilleur) 1990, Monologues (short series) (also writer; La robe à cerceau) 1993, Tous les garçons et les filles de leur âge... (series) (also writer) (US Go Home) 1994. *Address:* Media and Communication Division, European Graduate School, Alter Kehr 20, 3953 Leuk-Stadt, Switzerland (office). *Telephone:* (27) 4749917 (office). *Fax:* (27) 4749969 (office). *Website:* www.egs.edu/faculty/claire-denis/biography (office).

DENIS, Hervé, MPolSci; Haitian business executive, diplomatist and politician; b. 29 July 1945; m.; three c.; ed Univ. of Bordeaux, Univ. Laval, Québec; Auditor, Superior Court of Auditors 1969; Deputy Gen. Inspector of Mixed and State Enterprises 1976; 18 years in diplomatic service, including as Vice-Consul of Haiti in Montréal, Amb. at large, Amb. to UN, Geneva, Amb. to Dominican Repub., Amb. to Canada, Minister Counselor, Embassy in Berlin, Chargé d'Affaires, Embassy in Santiago; Minister of Labour and Social Affairs 1985; worked in Haitian business sector in fields of import-export and hotel and tourism management from 1992; fmr Pres. Deba Plastics Inc., Canada; Adviser, RPM Inc., Québec; nine years as Advisor, Chambre de Commerce et d'Industrie d'Haïti (CCIH), Pres. 2010–12; Minister of Nat. Defence 2017–18; co-founder and fmr Chair. Haiti–Canada Chamber of Commerce and Industry; shareholder and consultant, Hotel Visa Lodge, CAB SA, Gonâve 2000 SA, Gestion Avenir SA; Ordre Nat. d'Honneur et Mérite d'Haïti, Order of Malta, Order of St John of Jerusalem. *Address:* c/o Ministry of National Defence, 2 rue Bazelais, Delmas 60, BP 1106, Pétion-Ville, Port-au-Prince, Haiti (office).

DENIS, Paul; Haitian politician; fmr mem. Democratic Convergence of Haiti; mem. Sénat 1995–99; mem. Tripartite Council (apptd following coup) 2004; Head, comm. of inquiry into misuse of public funds 2005; Leader, Organisation du Peuple en Lutte (OPL), unsuccessful OPL cand. for Pres. of Haiti 2006; Adviser to Pres. René Préval 2009; Minister of Justice and Public Security 2009–11 (resgnd). *Address:* c/o Ministry of Justice and Public Security, avenue Charles Sumner 19, Port-au-Prince, Haiti.

DENISOV, Andrei Ivanovich; Russian politician and diplomatist; *Ambassador to People's Republic of China;* b. 3 Oct. 1952, Kharkov, Ukraine; m. Natalya Denisova; one d.; ed Moscow Inst. of Int. Relations; joined Ministry of Foreign Affairs 1992, various diplomatic posts in ministry and abroad, Dir Dept of Econ. Co-operation 1997–2000, Deputy Minister of Foreign Affairs responsible for Int. Econ. Co-operation 2001–04, Amb. to Egypt 2000–01, Amb. and Perm. Rep. to UN, New York and Rep. of Russian Fed. to UN Security Council 2004–06, First Deputy Minister of Foreign Affairs 2006–13, Amb. to People's Repub. of China 2013–. *Address:* Embassy of the Russian Federation, 4 Dong Zhi Men Nei, Bei Zhong Jie, Beijing 100600, People's Republic of China (office). *Telephone:* (10) 65321381 (office). *Fax:* (10) 65324851 (office). *E-mail:* embassy@russia.org.cn (office). *Website:* www.russia.org.cn (office).

DENKTAŞ, Serdar; Turkish-Cypriot politician; *Deputy Prime Minister and Minister of Finance;* b. 1959, Lefkoşa; s. of Rauf Denktaş (fmr Pres. of 'Turkish Repub. of Northern Cyprus'); m.; three c.; ed Cardiff Coll., UK; est. Turkish Students Asscn of Cardiff Coll., Northern Cyprus Cultural Asscn 1986, Young Businessman Asscn 1989; Dir-Gen. Cyprus Credit Bank –1990; elected mem. 'Turkish Repub. of Northern Cyprus' Parl. for Lefkoşa 1990; Minister of Interior, Rural Affairs and Environment 1990–92; Dist Chair. for Lefkoşa, then Sec.-Gen. Demokrat Parti (fmrly Nine Movt) 1992–93, Leader 1996–2000, 2002–; elected mem. Parl. for Lefkoşa 1993; Minister of Youth and Sports 1994–95, of Tourism and Environment 2001–03; Deputy Prime Minister and Minister of Foreign Affairs 2003–06; Deputy Prime Minister and Minister of Econs, Tourism, Culture and Sport 2013–15; Deputy Prime Minister and Minister of Finance 2016–. *Address:* Ministry of Finance, Lefkoşa (Nicosia), Mersin 10, (office); Demokrat Parti, Hasane Ilgaz Sok. 13a, Lefkoşa (Nicosia), Mersin 10, Turkey. *Telephone:* 2283116 (Ministry) (office); 2283795 (Demokrat Parti) (office). *Fax:* 2278230 (Ministry) (office); 2287130 (Demokrat Parti) (office). *E-mail:* kktcmaliyebasin@gmail.com (Ministry) (office); yenidem@kktc.net (Demokrat Parti) (office). *Website:* www.kktcmaliye.com (Ministry) (office); www.demokratparti.net (home).

DENNARD, Robert (Bob) Heath, BS, MS, PhD; American electronic engineer; *IBM Fellow Emeritus, IBM Research Division;* b. 5 Sept. 1932, Terrell, Tex.; s. of Buford Dennard and Loma Dennard; m. Jane Bridges; ed Southern Methodist Univ., Carnegie Inst. of Tech. (now Carnegie Mellon Univ.); began career with IBM 1958, mem. research team on six-transistor memory cell, invented one-transistor dynamic random access memory (DRAM) 1967 and contrib. to MOS transistor scaling theory 1972, currently IBM Fellow Emer., IBM Research Div., Yorktown Heights, New York; mem. Nat. Acad. of Eng, American Philosophical Soc.; Life Fellow, IEEE; Dr hc (Carnegie Mellon Univ.) 2010; Nat. Medal of Tech. 1988, Industrial Research Inst. Achievement Award 1989, Harvey Prize, Technion, Israel 1990, inducted into Nat. Inventors Hall of Fame 1997, IEEE Edison Medal

2001, Aachener and Münchener Award for Tech. and Applied Natural Sciences 2001, Lifetime Achievement Award, Lemelson-MIT 2005, C&C Prize 2006, Benjamin Franklin Medal in Electrical Eng, The Franklin Inst. 2007, Charles Stark Draper Prize, Nat. Acad. of Eng 2009, IEEE Medal of Honor 2009, Kyoto Prize 2013. *Achievements:* invention of the DRAM (Dynamic Random Access Memory) cell and contribs to MOSFET scaling principles. *Publications include:* Design of Ion-Implanted MOSFETs with Very Small Physical Dimensions 1974; more than 100 scientific papers; 64 US patents in semiconductors and microelectronics since 1965. *Leisure interests:* choral singing, Scottish country dancing. *Address:* Thomas J. Watson Research Center, PO Box 218, Yorktown Heights, NY 10598, USA (office). *Telephone:* (914) 945-1371 (office). *E-mail:* dennard@us.ibm.com (office). *Website:* researcher.ibm.com/researcher/view.php?person=us-dennard (office).

DENNEHY, Brian; American actor, producer and director; b. (Brian Manion Dennehy), 9 July 1938, Bridgeport, Conn.; m. 1st Judith Scheff; m. 2nd Jennifer Dennehy; three c. from previous m.; ed Chaminade High School, Columbia and Yale Univs; served with US Marine Corps for five years; numerous stage appearances. *Films include:* Looking for Mr. Goodbar 1977, Semi-Tough 1977, F.I.S.T 1978, Foul Play 1978, Butch and Sundance: The Early Days 1979, 10 1979, Little Miss Marker 1980, Split Image 1982, First Blood 1982, Never Cry Wolf 1983, Gorky Park 1983, Finders Keepers 1984, The River Rat 1984, Cocoon 1985, Silverado 1985, Twice in a Lifetime 1985, F/X 1986, The Cheque Is in the Post 1986, Legal Eagles 1986, The Belly of an Architect 1987, Best Seller 1987, The Man from Snowy River II 1988, Miles from Home 1988, Cocoon: The Return (uncredited) 1988, Indio 1989, Seven Minutes 1989, Blue Heat 1990, Presumed Innocent 1990, F/X2 1991, Gladiator 1992, Tommy Boy 1995, The Stars Fell on Henrietta 1995, Romeo + Juliet 1996, Out of the Cold 1999, Silicon Towers 1999, Dish Dogs (video) 2000, Summer Catch 2001, Stolen Summer 2002, She Hate Me 2004, Assault on Precinct 13 2005, 10th & Wolf 2006, Everyone's Hero (voice) 2006, Ratatouille (voice) 2007, Welcome to Paradise 2007, War Eagle, Arkansas 2007, Cat City 2008, Righteous Kill 2008, Alleged 2010, Every Day 2010, Meet Monica Velour 2010, The Next Three Days 2010, The Big Year 2011, Twelfth Night 2012. *Television includes:* Kojak (series) 1977, Serpico (series) 1977, Johnny, We Hardly Knew Ye (film) 1977, Lanigan's Rabbi (series) 1977, M*A*S*H (series) 1977, Lucan (series) 1977, The Fitzpatricks (series) 1977, Lou Grant (series) 1977, It Happened at Lakewood Manor (film) 1977, The Tony Randall Show (series) 1978, Ruby and Oswald (film) 1978, A Death in Canaan (film) 1978, Dallas (series) 1978, Pearl (mini-series) 1978, A Real American Hero (film) 1978, Silent Victory: The Kitty O'Neil Story (film) 1979, The Jericho Mile (film) 1979, Dummy (film) 1979, Big Shamus, Little Shamus (series) 1979, The Seduction of Miss Leona (film) 1980, A Rumor of War (film) 1980, Knots Landing (series) 1980, Fly Away Home Dynasty (series) 1981, Once They Marched Through a Thousand Towns (film) 1981, Darkroom (series) 1981, Star of the Family (series) 1982, I Take These Men (film) 1983, Blood Feud (film) 1983, Cagney & Lacey (series) 1984, Pigs vs. Freaks (film) 1984, Hunter (series) 1984, The Ferret (film) 1985, The Last Place on Earth (mini-series) 1985, Evergreen (mini-series) 1985, Tall Tales & Legends (series) – Annie Oakley 1985, Acceptable Risks (film) 1986, Faerie Tale Theatre (series) – The Little Mermaid (narrator) 1987, Miami Vice (series) 1987, The Lion of Africa (film) 1988, Das Rattennest (film) 1988, Day One (film) 1989, Perfect Witness (film) 1989, Pride and Extreme Prejudice (film) 1990, Evidence of Love (film) 1990, Rising Son (film) 1990, In Broad Daylight (film) 1991, The Burden of Proof (film) 1992, To Catch a Killer (film) 1992, The Diamond Fleece (film) 1992, Teamster Boss: The Jackie Presser Story (film) 1992, Deadly Matrimony (film) 1992, Foreign Affairs (film) 1993, Murder in the Heartland (film) 1993, Prophet of Evil: The Ervil LeBaron Story (film) 1993, Final Appeal (film) 1993, Jack Reed: Badge of Honor (film) 1993, Birdland (series) 1994, Leave of Absence (film) 1994, Jack Reed: A Search for Justice (film) 1994, Midnight Movie (film) 1994, Deadly Justice (film) 1995, Shadow of a Doubt (film) 1995, Jack Reed: A Killer Among Us (film) 1996, A Season in Purgatory (film) 1996, Dead Man's Walk (mini-series) 1996, Undue Influence (film) 1996, Jack Reed: Death and Vengeance (film) 1996, Nostromo (mini-series) 1997, Indefensible: The Truth About Edward Brannigan (film) 1997, Thanks of a Grateful Nation (film) 1998, Voyage of Terror (film) 1998, NetForce (film) 1999, Too Rich: The Secret Life of Doris Duke (film) 1999, Sirens (film) 1999, Death of a Salesman (film) (Tony Award for Best Actor in a Drama) 2000, The American Experience (series documentary) – The Duel (voice) 2000, Fail Safe (film) 2000, Warden of Red Rock (film) 2001, The Fighting Fitzgeralds (series) 2001, Night Visions (series) 2001, Three Blind Mice (film) 2001, Great Performances (series) – Making 'The Misfits' (narrator) 2002, – The Girls in Their Summer Dresses and Other Stories 1981, A Season on the Brink (film) 2002, The Crooked E: The Unshredded Truth About Enron (film) 2003, The Agency (series) 2003, The Roman Spring of Mrs. Stone (film) 2003, Just Shoot Me! (series) 1998–2003, Behind the Camera: The Unauthorized Story of 'Three's Company' (film) 2003, Category 6: Day of Destruction (film) 2004, The Exonerated (film) 2005, The West Wing (series) 2005, Our Fathers (film) 2005, The 4400 (series) 2006, Law & Order: Special Victims Unit (series) – Scheherazade 2007, The Ultimate Gift 2006, Marco Polo (film) 2007, Masters of Science Fiction (mini-series) – The Discarded 2007, 30 Rock (series) 2008, Bunker Hill (film) 2009, Rules of Engagement (series) 2009, Rizzoli & Isles (series) 2010, The Good Wife 2012, The Challenger 2013, The Big C 2013.

DENNER, Volkmar, Dr rer. nat; German business executive; *Chairman of the Board of Management, Robert Bosch GmbH;* b. 30 Nov. 1956, Uhingen; m.; three c.; ed Univ. of Stuttgart; has held several positions in Bosch Group including in Semiconductors and Electronic Control Units Div. 1986–89, Dept Head in Power Semiconductor Tech. Devt 1989–91, Dept Head in Integrated Circuit Devt 1991–94, Dir of Sales, ECU Devt, and Systems Application, Gasoline Engine Man. Div. 1994–98, Dir Engine ECU Devt 1998–2003, Product Man. for Engine ECUs 2000–03, Exec. Vice-Pres., Sales and Devt, Pres. Semiconductors and Electronic Control Units Div., Automotive Electronics Div. 2003–12, mem. Bd of Man., Robert Bosch GmbH 2006–, Chair. Bd of Man. 2012–. *Address:* Robert Bosch GmbH, Postfach 106050, 70049 Stuttgart, Germany (office). *Telephone:* (711) 811-0 (office). *Fax:* (711) 8116630 (office). *E-mail:* kontakt@bosch.com (office). *Website:* www.bosch.com (office).

DENNETT, Daniel Clement, BA, DPhil; American philosopher, academic and author; *University Professor, Austin B. Fletcher Professor of Philosophy and Co-Director, Center for Cognitive Studies, Tufts University;* b. 28 March 1942, Boston, Mass; s. of Daniel C. Dennett, Jr and Ruth M. Leck; m. Susan Bell 1962; one s. one d.; ed Phillips Exeter Acad., Wesleyan Univ., Harvard Univ., Univ. of Oxford, UK; Asst Prof. of Philosophy, Univ. of California, Irvine 1965–70, Assoc. Prof. 1971; Assoc. Prof., Tufts Univ. 1971–75, Prof. 1975–85, Distinguished Arts and Sciences Prof. 1985–2000, Co-Dir Center for Cognitive Studies 1985–, Univ. Prof. 2000–, also Austin B. Fletcher Prof. of Philosophy; Visiting Prof., Harvard 1973–74, Pittsburgh 1975, Oxford 1979, Ecole Normale Supérieure, Paris 1985, Dept of Philosophy, Auburn Univ. 2011; Visiting Fellow, All Souls Coll., Oxford 1979; Writer-in-Residence, Bellagio Study and Conf. Centre, Italy 1990, 2001; Fellow, Center for Advanced Study in Behavioral Sciences 1979, American Acad. of Arts and Sciences 1987, Zentrum für Interdisziplinäre Forschung, Bielefeld, Germany 1990; Visiting Erskine Fellow, Univ. of Canterbury, Christchurch, NZ 1995; Distinguished Fellow, Centre for the Mind, Inst. for Advanced Study, ANU, Canberra 1998, Collegium Budapest, Hungary 2002; Fellow, SAGE Center, Univ. of California, Santa Barbara 2008; William Miller Fellow, Santa Fe Inst., NM 2010; Fellow, AAAS 2009; Hon. DHumLitt (Connecticut) 2003; Hon. DLitt (Edinburgh) 2007; Hon. DSc (McGill) 2007, (Bucharest) 2007; Dr hc (Amsterdam) 2012; Woodrow Wilson Fellow 1963, Guggenheim Fellow 1973, 1986, Santayana Fellowship, Harvard Univ. (hon.) 1974, Nat. Endowment for the Humanities Younger Humanist Fellowship 1974, Fulbright Fellow 1978, John Locke Lecturer, Oxford 1983, Gavin David Young Lecturer, Adelaide, Australia 1984, Jean Nicod Lecturer, Institut Nicod, Paris 2001, Daewoo Lecturer, Seoul, S Korea 2002, American Humanist Asscn Humanist of the Year 2004, Petrus Hispanus Lecturer, Faculdade de Letras de Lisboa, Lisbon 2004, Patten Lecturer, Indiana Univ. 2006, Distinguished Fellow Award, Cognitive Science Soc. 2009, Erasmus Prize 2012. *Publications include:* Content and Consciousness 1969, Brainstorms 1978, The Mind's I (with Douglas Hofstadter) 1981, Elbow Room 1984, The Intentional Stance 1987, Consciousness Explained 1991, Darwin's Dangerous Idea 1995, Kinds of Minds 1996, Brainchildren 1998, Freedom Evolves 2003, Breaking the Spell: Religion as a Natural Phenomenon 2006, Dove nascono le idée (translated by Francesca Garofoli) 2006, Science and Religion: Are They Compatible? (with Alvin Plantinga) 2011, Inside Jokes: Using Humor to Reverse-Engineer the Mind (with Matthew Hurley and Reginald B. Adams, Jr) 2011, From Bacteria to Bach and Back: The Evolution of Minds 2017; numerous articles in professional journals. *Leisure interests:* sculpture, farming, cider-making, sailing, choral singing. *Address:* Center for Cognitive Studies, 115 Miner Hall, Tufts University, Medford, MA 02155-7059, USA (office). *Telephone:* (617) 627-3297 (office). *Fax:* (617) 627-3952 (office). *E-mail:* daniel.dennett@tufts.edu (office). *Website:* ase.tufts.edu/cogstud (office).

DENNIS, Bengt, MA; Swedish banker; *Managing Director, Bengt Dennis Consulting AB;* b. 5 Jan. 1930, Grengesberg; m. Turid Stroem 1962; one s. one d.; ed Columbia Univ., New York, USA; econ. journalist 1959–67; Head of Dept, Ministry of Finance 1967–70; Under-Sec. of State, Ministry of Commerce 1970–76; Amb., Ministry of Foreign Affairs 1977–80; Ed.-in-Chief, Dagens Nyheter 1981–82; Gov. Cen. Bank of Sweden 1982–92; Chair. BIS 1990–93; Sr Adviser, Skandinaviska Enskilda Banken 1994–2001; Man. Dir Bengt Dennis Consulting AB 2002–; mem. Bd of Dirs Nordic Credit Partners AB 2015–. *Publication:* 500% 1998. *Leisure interests:* sailing, skiing, skating. *Address:* Maria Sandels gränd 3, 112 69 Stockholm, Sweden (home). *Telephone:* 70-258-10-20 (mobile) (office); (8) 651-04-32 (home). *E-mail:* bengt.dennis@bdco.biz (office).

DENNISON, Lisa, MA; American auction house executive and fmr art museum director; *Chairman, North and South America, Sotheby's;* m. Roderick Waywell 1983; two s.; ed Wellesley Coll., Brown Univ.; curatorial internships at Guggenheim Museum 1973, Fogg Art Museum, Harvard Univ. 1974–76, Museum of Fine Arts, Boston 1977–78; Exhbn Coordinator, Solomon R. Guggenheim Museum, New York 1978–81, Asst Curator 1981–90, Assoc. Curator 1990–91, Collections Curator 1991–94, Curator of Collections and Exhbns 1994–96, Deputy Dir and Chief Curator 1996–2005, Dir and Chief Curator 2005–07, played key role in building Museum's perm. collections in New York and Bilbao, Spain; Chair. North and South America, Sotheby's, New York 2007–; fmr mem. Bd of Dirs American Asscn of Museum Curators, Byrd-Hoffman Foundation; Founding mem. Creative Arts Advisory Bd, Brown Univ.; mem. New York Cttee, Wellesley Coll. Friends of Art, Nat. Advisory Council, Visual Arts, Wake Forest Univ., Int. Advisory Bd Louise T. Blouin Foundation; mem. ArtTable. *Publications:* numerous essays in exhbn catalogues. *Address:* Sotheby's, 1334 York Avenue at 72nd Street, New York, NY 10021, USA (office). *Telephone:* (212) 894-1424 (office). *Fax:* (212) 606-7105 (office). *E-mail:* lisa.dennison@sothebys.com (office). *Website:* www.sothebys.com (office).

DENNISS, Tom, PhD; Australian athlete, oceanographer, mathematician, business executive and musician; *Executive Director and Chief Technology Officer, Oceanlinx Limited;* b. 24 Feb. 1961, Wollongong, NSW; ed Lake Illawarra High School, Univ. of Wollongong, Univ. of New South Wales; played to audiences in eight different countries as a professional musician; taught at Newtown High School, Sydney 1984–90; Assoc. Lecturer in Math. and Oceanography, Univ. of New South Wales 1990–94; with Macquarie Bank (investment bank) 1994–99; Founder and CEO Energetech Australia Pty Ltd (now called Oceanlinx Ltd) 1997–2006, Exec. Dir and Chief Tech. Officer 2006–; mem. Global Roundtable on Climate Change 2005–09; Australian Govt's Rep. on IEA's Ocean Energy Systems Cttee 2007–11; mem. Australian Govt's Advisory Bd for the Clean Energy Innovation Centre 2010–11; contrib. to marine tech. industry over many years through both academia and industry confs and cttees worldwide; wave energy technology he invented named by Int. Acad. of Science as one of Ten Most Outstanding Technologies in the World 2006, inducted into Int. Ocean Energy Hall of Fame 2007, technology he invented ranked third by UNIDO in its annual list of the Top Ten Renewable Energy Investment Opportunities in the World 2009. *Achievement:* set a new world record for the fastest circumnavigation of the Earth on foot 2013. *Address:* Oceanlinx Ltd, PO Box 116, Botany, NSW 1455, Australia (office). *Telephone:* (2) 9549-6300 (office). *Fax:* (2) 9549-6399 (office). *E-mail:* tom.denniss@oceanlinx.com (office). *Website:* www.oceanlinx.com (office).

DENOIX DE SAINT MARC, Renaud; French lawyer and civil servant; b. 24 Sept. 1938, Boulogne-sur-Seine; s. of Henri Denoix de Saint Marc and Marie du Cheyron du Pavilion; m. Marie-Christine de Buchère de l'Epinois 1964; two c.; ed

Ecole nationale d'admin, Institut d'études politiques de Paris; Second Class Auditor, Conseil d'État 1964–65, First Class Auditor 1975–72, Maître des requêtes 1972–86, Govt Comm. Ass. of Conseil d'État 1974–78, 1983–86; Head, Legal Advisory Mission, Ministry of Agriculture 1968–69, Legal Mission of Directorate Gen. 1970–73; apptd Legal Advisor to Directorate of Land Transport, Ministry of Transport 1973; Deputy Comm. of Govt l'Office national de la chasse 1972–75; Vice-Pres. Higher Council for Classified Installations, Ministry of Quality of Life 1977–80; Deputy Dir of Cabinet, Minister of Justice Alain Peyrefitte 1978–79; Dir of Civil Affairs and Seal 1979–82; Prof. l'Institut d'études politiques de Paris 1983–87; Prof. l'École nationale d'administration 1985–87, Vice-Pres. History Cttee 2000–06; Deputy Rapporteur, Conseil constitutionnel 1983–86; State Councillor 1985–95; Alt. Comm. of Govt Dispute Tribunal 1985–86; Secrétaire général du Gouvernement 1986–95; Pres. of Bd l'Office national de la chasse (now Office national de la chasse et de la faune sauvage) 1999–2004; apptd Pres. jury de l'Association Claude Erignac 2000; Vice-Pres. Conseil d'État 2005–06 (retd); mem. Conseil cynégétique, forestier et scientifique de Chambord 1997; mem. Acad. des sciences morales et politiques 2005, Conseil Constitutionnel 2007–16, Acad. Nationale de Medecine 2009; Grand Croix de la Légion d'honneur 2008; Chevalier, Ordre nat. du Mérite, du Mérite agricole, des Palmes académiques; Croix de la Valeur militaire; Prix Edouard Bonnefous 2001. *Publications:* Leçons de droit public 1989, Le service public 1996, L'Etat 2004, Histoire de la loi 2008. *Address:* c/o Conseil Constitutionnel, 2 rue de Montpensier, 75001 Paris (office); 1 rue du Capitaine Scott, 75015 Paris, France (home). *Telephone:* 1-40-15-30-00 (office); 1-45-48-75-67 (home). *Fax:* 1-40-20-93-27 (office). *E-mail:* relations-exterieures@conseil-constitutionnel.fr (office). *Website:* www.conseil-constitutionnel.fr (office).

DENT ZELEDÓN, Alberto; Costa Rican politician and banker; *President, Dent Consultores;* b. 11 Dec. 1945; m.; four c.; ed California State Polytech. Univ., USA; Gen. Man. Dent and Sons Ltd 1973–84; Pres. Banex Bank Ltd 1980–84; Exec. Pres. BFA Financial Group 1984–96; Dir Costa Rican Bankers' Asscn 1985–96, Pres. 1986–90; Adviser to Pres. of Costa Rica 1998–2000; Vice-Pres. Cen. Bank of Costa Rica 1998–2000; Minister of Agric. and Livestock 2000–01; Minister of Finance 2001–02, 2003–04 (resgnd); currently Pres. Dent Consultores; Pres., Consejo Nacional de Supervisión del Sistema Financiero (CONASSIF, financial system supervision council) April–July 2003, 2006–08. *Address:* Dent Consultores, 25 meters west of Farolito Barrio Escalante, San José, Costa Rica (office). *Telephone:* 2255-3352 (office). *Fax:* 2221-3578 (office). *Website:* dentconsultores.com (office).

DENTON, Charles Henry, BA, FRSA, FRTS; British television executive; b. 20 Dec. 1937; s. of Alan Charles Denton and Mary Frances Royle; m. Eleanor Mary Player 1961; one s. two d.; ed Reading School and Univ. of Bristol; worked as deckhand 1960; trainee advertising 1961–63; with BBC 1963–68; freelance TV producer Granada, ATV and Yorkshire TV cos 1969–70; Dir Tempest Films Ltd 1969–71; Man. Dir Black Lion Films 1979–81; Head of Documentaries ATV 1974–77, Controller of Programmes 1977–81; Dir of Programmes Cen. Ind. TV 1981–84; Dir Cen. Ind. Television PLC 1981–87; Founder and Chief Exec. Zenith Productions 1984–93, Chair. Zenith North Ltd 1988–93; Head of Drama BBC 1993–96; Chair. Action Time Ltd 1988–93, Producers' Alliance for Cinema and TV (PACT) 1991–1993, Cornwall Film 2001; Gov. BFI 1992–99; mem. Arts Council of England 1996–98; mem. Bd Film Council 1999–2002. *Leisure interests:* walking, music.

DENTON, Derek Ashworth, AC, MB, BS, FRS, FAA, FRACP, FRCP; Australian research physiologist; *Honorary Professor of Physiology, University of Melbourne;* b. 27 May 1924, Launceston, Tasmania; s. of A. A. Denton; m. Dame Margaret Scott 1953; two s.; ed Launceston Grammar School and Univ. of Melbourne; Haley Research Fellow, Walter & Eliza Hall Inst. of Medical Research 1948; Overseas Nat. Health and Medical Research Council (New Hampshire & MRC) Fellow, Cambridge 1952–53; Medical Research Fellow, later Sr Medical Research Fellow, Nat. Health and Medical Research Council 1949–63, Prin. Research Fellow, Admin. Head and Chief Scientist 1964–70; Dir and originating Bd mem. Howard Florey Inst. of Experimental Physiology and Medicine 1971–89, Emer. Dir 1990–; Visiting Prof., British Heart Foundation and Balliol Coll., Oxford, UK; Adjunct Scientist, Southwest Foundation for Biomedical Research, San Antonio, Tex., USA; Dir The David Syme Co. Ltd 1984–, Australian Ballet Foundation 1983–, Sydney Dance Co. 1994–; First Vice-Pres. Int. Union of Physiological Sciences 1983–89, Chair. Nominating Cttee of Council 1986–89, Chair. Cttee to Review Comms 1986–95; Consultant Scientist, Baker IDI Heart and Diabetes Inst. 2004; mem. Jury of Basic and Clinical Medical Awards, Albert and Mary Lasker Foundation 1979–89; OECD Examiner of Science and Tech. Policy of Govt of Sweden; Foreign Medical mem. Royal Swedish Acad. of Sciences; Foreign Assoc. NAS 1995, Acad. des Sciences 2000, Inst. of France 2000; Hon. Foreign Fellow, American Acad. of Arts and Sciences 1986, Hon. Foreign mem. American Physiology Soc. 1987, Hon. Prof. of Physiology, Florey Neuroscience and Mental Health Insts, Univ. of Melbourne 2010; Centenary Medal 2001; Hon. LLD (Melbourne) 2006. *Publications include:* The Hunger for Salt 1982, The Pinnacle of Life 1993, Primordial Emotions: The Dawning of Consciousness 2006; 400 articles and reviews. *Leisure interests:* tennis, fishing, ballet, music, wine. *Address:* Office of the Dean, Faculty of Medicine, Dentistry and Health Sciences, University of Melbourne, 766 Elizabeth Street, Melbourne, Vic. 3010 (office); 816 Orrong Road, Toorak, Vic. 3142, Australia (home). *Telephone:* (3) 8344-5639 (office); (3) 9827-2640 (home). *Fax:* (3) 9347-0846 (office); (3) 9826-5457 (home). *E-mail:* ddenton@unimelb.edu.au.

DENTON, Frank Trevor, BA, MA, LLD, FRSC; Canadian economist and academic; *Professor Emeritus of Economics, McMaster University;* b. 27 Oct. 1930, Toronto, Ont.; s. of Frank W. Denton and Kathleen M. Davies; m. 1st Marilyn J. Shipp 1953 (died 2002); three s. one d.; m. 2nd Helen R. Evans 2003; ed Univ. of Toronto; Economist, Prov. Govt of Ont. 1953–54, Fed. Govt of Canada 1954–59, 1961–64, Philips Electronics Industries Ltd 1959–60, Senate of Canada Cttee staff 1960–61; Dir of Econometrics, Dominion Bureau of Statistics 1964–68; Consultant, Econ. Council of Canada 1964–68; Prof. of Econs, McMaster Univ. 1968–96, Prof. Emer. 1996–; Dir McMaster Program for Quantitative Studies in Econs and Population 1981–96; various other consulting appointments; Fellow, American Statistical Asscn, Royal Soc. of Canada; Hon. LLD (McMaster Univ.) 2008. *Publications include:* Growth of Manpower in Canada 1970; co-author: Historical Estimates of the Canadian Labour Force 1967, Working-Life Tables for Canadian Males 1969, Population and the Economy 1975, The Short-Run Dynamics of the Canadian Labour Market 1976, Unemployment and Labour Force Behaviour of Young People: Evidence from Canada and Ontario 1980, Pensions and the Economic Security of the Elderly 1981, Independence and Economic Security in Old Age (co-ed.) 2000; numerous monographs, articles, technical papers in economics, statistics, demography. *Address:* Department of Economics, KTH 413, McMaster University, Hamilton, ON L8S 4M4 (office); 23 Pelham Drive, Ancaster, ON L9K 1L4, Canada (home). *Telephone:* (905) 525-9140 (ext. 23820) (office); (905) 304-9395 (home). *E-mail:* dentonf@mcmaster.ca (office). *Website:* www.economics.mcmaster.ca (office).

DENTON, John W.H., BA, AO; Australian fmr diplomatist, business executive and international organizations official; *Secretary-General, International Chamber of Commerce;* m. Jane Turner; three c.; ed Univ. of Melbourne, Harvard Business School; worked for Dept of Foreign Affairs and Trade 1983–92; joined Corrs Chambers Westgarth as Articled Clerk 1993, Man. Partner, Melbourne Office 1997–, CEO 2001–; Founding Chair. of Australia for UNHCR 2002–; First Vice-Chair. ICC 2016–18, Sec.-Gen. 2018–; Chair. Global Engagement Taskforce, Business Council of Australia; mem. Business Council of Australia 2003–13, Asialink 2010–, Human Rights Watch 2012–; mem. Bd of Dirs The Australian Ballet 2017–, IFM Investors 2018–. *Address:* International Chamber of Commerce, 33-43 avenue du Président Wilson, 75116 Paris, France (office). *Telephone:* 1-49-53-28-28 (office). *Fax:* 1-49-53-28-59 (office). *E-mail:* icc@iccwbo.org (office). *Website:* www.iccwbo.org (office).

DENTON, Richard Michael, MA, PhD, DSc, FMedSci, FRS; British biochemist and academic; *Professor Emeritus of Biochemistry, University of Bristol;* b. 16 Oct. 1941, Sutton Coldfield, Birmingham; s. of Arthur Benjamin Denton and Eileen Mary Denton (née Evans); m. Janet Mary Jones 1965; one s. two d.; ed Wycliffe Coll., Stonehouse, Glos., Christ's Coll., Cambridge; Lecturer in Biochemistry, Univ. of Bristol 1973–78, Reader 1978–87, Prof. (Personal Chair) 1987–2010, Prof. Emer. 2010–, Head of Biochemistry Dept 1995–2000, Chair. Medical Sciences 2000–04, Dean of Medical and Veterinary Sciences 2003–04; MRC Research Fellowship 1984–88, mem. Council of MRC 1999–2004, Chair. MRC Training and Career Devt Bd 2002–04; Founder-Fellow, Acad. of Medical Sciences 1998. *Publications:* Hormones and Cell Metabolism (co-author) 1974, Metabolic Regulation 1976; more than 240 research papers in various int. research journals, with maj. topics the molecular basis of the control of metabolism by insulin and other hormones, and the role of calcium ions within mitochondria. *Leisure interests:* family, fell walking, keeping fit, cooking. *Address:* School of Biochemistry, Medical Sciences Building, University of Bristol, University Walk, Bristol, BS8 1TD, England (office). *E-mail:* r.denton@bristol.ac.uk (office). *Website:* www.bristol.ac.uk/biochemistry (office).

DEOL, Abhay; Indian actor; b. 15 March 1976, Mumbai; s. of Ajit Deol and Usha Deol; f. Forbidden Films (production co.). *Films:* Socha Na Tha 2005, Ahista Ahista 2006, Honeymoon Travels Pvt Ltd 2007, Ek Chalis Ki Last Local 2007, Manorama Six Feet Under 2007 (Best Actor, MIAAC Festival, New York), Oye Lucky! Lucky Oye! 2008, Dev D 2009, Aisha 2010, Zindagi Na Milegi Dobara 2011, Shanghai 2012, Chakravyuh 2012, Raanjhanaa 2013. *Address:* Forbidden Films, B-31, Pandurang Wadi, near Juhu Post Office, Juhu, Mumbai 400 049, India (office). *Telephone:* (22) 26184189 (office). *E-mail:* fqfilms@yahoo.com (office).

DEP, Priyasad; Sri Lankan lawyer; *Chief Justice of Supreme Court;* s. of Arthur C. Dep; ed Univ. of Colombo, Int. Inst. of Social Studies, The Hague, Netherlands; Solicitor-Gen. 2007–11; apptd Justice Supreme Court 2011, Chief Justice 2017–. *Publications:* numerous books in Sinhala and English. *Address:* Supreme Court Complex, Hultsdorf, Colombo 12, Sri Lanka (office). *Telephone:* (1) 328651 (office). *Fax:* (1) 435446 (office).

DEPARDIEU, Gérard; French actor and vintner; b. (Gérard Xavier Marcel Depardieu), 27 Dec. 1948, Châteauroux (Indre); s. of René Depardieu and Alice Depardieu (née Marillier); m. Elisabeth Guignot 1970; one s. (deceased) one d.; ed Ecole communale, Cours d'art dramatique de Charles Dullin and Ecole d'art dramatique de Jean Laurent Cochet; Pres. Jury, 45th Cannes Int. Film Festival 1992; Cultural Amb. of Montenegro 2013; Chevalier, Ordre nat. du Mérite 1985, Légion d'honneur 1996, des Arts et des Lettres, Ordre Nat. du Québec 2002; Grand Prix Gérard Philippe, Jury des Grands Prix de la ville de Paris 1973, Prix ACIC (Asscn des Cadres de l'Industrie Cinématographique) for lifetime achievement 1983, Fellowship, British Film Inst. 1989, named Meilleur Acteur Etranger des années 1980–90, critique cinématographique américaine 1990, Piper-Heidseick Award, San Francisco Int. Film Festival 1994, Grand Prix Spécial des Amériques for his exceptional contrib. to cinema, Montréal World Film Festival 1995, Golden Camera (Germany) 1996, Prix Rudolph Valentino 1997, Lion d'Or for lifetime achievement, 54ème Mostra de Venise XXIV 1997, Stanislavsky Prize, Moscow Int. Film Festival 2006, Jules Verne Award 2009, Prix Lumière 2011, Int. Classical Music Award for Choral 2011. *Plays include:* Boudu sauvé des eaux 1968, Les Garçons de la bande 1969, Une fille dans ma soupe 1970, Galapagos 1971, Saved 1972, Home 1972, Ismé 1973, Isaac 1973, La Chevauchée sur le lac de Constance 1974, Les Gens déraisonnables sont en voie de disparition 1977, Tartuffe (also dir) 1983, Lily Passion 1986, Les portes du ciel 1999, Œdipus Rex 2001, Le Carnaval des animaux 2001, La bête dans la jungle 2004, Love Letters 2013, La musica deuxiéme 2014. *Films include:* Le beatnik et le minet (short) 1967, Cry of the Cormoran 1970, Nathalie Granger (short) 1971, La vie sentimentale de Georges Le Tueur (short) 1971, Sunlight on Cold Water 1971, The Annuity 1972, Killer 1972, Nathalie Granger 1972, Hit Man 1972, At the Meeting with Joyous Death 1973, The Year 01 1973, The Dominici Affair 1973, Deux hommes dans la ville 1973, Rude journée pour la reine 1973, Les gaspards 1973, Les valseuses 1974, La femme du Gange 1974, Stavisky… 1974, Vincent, François, Paul… et les autres 1974, Maîtresse 1975, Pas si méchant que ça 1975, 7 morts sur ordonnance 1975, I Love You, I Don't 1976, The Last Woman 1976, 1900 1976, Barocco 1976, Rene the Cane 1977, The Lorry 1977, Baxter, Vera Baxter 1977, Dites-lui que je l'aime 1977, At Night All Cats Are Crazy 1977, Préparez vos mouchoirs 1978, Ciao maschio 1978, Violanta 1978, Die linkshändige Frau 1978, Le sucre 1978, L'ingorgo – Una storia impossibile 1979, Les chiens 1979, Buffet Froid 1979, Temporale Rosy 1980, My American Uncle 1980, Loulou 1980, The Last Metro 1980, Inspector Blunder 1980, Je vous aime 1980, Le choix des armes 1981, The Woman Next Door 1981, La chèvre 1981, The Return of Martin Guerre 1982, Le grand frère 1982, Danton

1983, The Moon in the Gutter 1983, Les compères 1983, Fort Saganne 1984, Le tartuffe (also dir) 1984, Rive droite, rive gauche 1984, Police 1985, A Woman or Two 1985, Tenue de soirée 1986, Jean de Florette 1986, Je hais les acteurs (uncredited) 1986, The Way Out 1986, Les fugitifs 1986, Under the Sun of Satan 1987, Strange Place for an Encounter 1988, Camille Claudel 1988, Deux 1989, Too Beautiful for You 1989, I Want to Go Home 1989, Cyrano de Bergerac 1990, Uranus 1990, Green Card 1990, 'Merci la vie' 1991, Mon père, ce héros 1991, Tous les Matins du Monde 1991, From Time to Time (short) 1992, 1492: Conquest of Paradise 1992, Oh, Woe Is Me 1993, Germinal 1993, My Father the Hero 1994, A Pure Formality 1994, Le colonel Chabert 1994, La machine 1994, Les cent et une nuits de Simon Cinéma 1995, Élisa 1995, The Horseman on the Roof (uncredited) 1995, Guardian Angels 1995, Le garçu 1995, Unhook the Stars 1996, Bogus 1996, The Secret Agent 1996, The Best Job in the World 1996, Hamlet 1996, XXL 1997, The Man in the Iron Mask, La parola amore esiste 1998, Bimboland 1998, Asterix and Obelix Take on Caesar 1999, Un pont entre deux rives (also dir) 1999, Mirka 2000, Tutto l'amore che c'è 2000, Vatel 2000, 102 Dalmatians 2000, The Envy of Gods 2000, The Closet 2001, Unfair Competition 2001, CQ 2001, Vidocq 2001, Witches to the North 2001, Asterix & Obelix: Mission Cleopatra 2002, I Am Dina 2002, A Loving Father 2002, Between Strangers 2002, City of Ghosts 2002, Blanche 2002, Le pacte du silence 2003, Crime Spree 2003, Bon voyage 2003, Nathalie... 2003, Shut Up! 2003, The Car Keys 2003, RRRrrrr!!! 2004, San Antonio 2004, New France 2004, 36 2004, Les temps qui changent 2004, La vie de Michel Muller est plus belle que la vôtre 2005, Je préfère qu'on reste amis 2005, Boudu 2005, How Much Do You Love Me? 2005, Olé! 2005, Last Holiday 2006, Paris, je t'aime (segment "Quartier Latin") 2006, Quand j'étais chanteur 2006, La vie en rose 2007, Michou d'Auber 2007, Asterix at the Olympic Games 2008, Vsyo mogut koroli 2008, Disco 2008, The Easy Way 2008, Babylon A.D. 2008, Mesrine: Killer Instinct 2008, Mesrine: Killer Instinct 2008, Bouquet final 2008, Hello, Goodbye 2008, Les enfants de Timpelbach 2008, Diamond 13 2009, In the Beginning 2009, Inspector Bellamy 2009, Coco 2009, Dumas 2010, Mammuth 2010, Glenn, the Flying Robot 2010, My Afternoons with Margueritte 2010, Potiche 2010, Pozdnyaya lyubov 2010, Je n'ai rien oublié 2010, Grenouille d'hiver (short) 2011, A Butterfly Kiss 2011, My Sinful Angel 2012, Le grand soir 2012, The Death of Ipu 2012, Life of Pi 2012, L'homme qui rit 2012, Astérix and Obélix: God Save Britannia 2012, Turf 2013, La marque des anges 2013, A Farewell to Fools 2013, Les invincibles 2013, Welcome to New York 2014, La voix des steppes 2014, Valley of Love 2015, Saint Amour 2016, Stalin's Couch 2016, Let the Sunshine In 2017, Bonne pomme 2017, Amoureux de ma femme 2018, Saving My Pig 2018, Alad'2 2018. *Television includes:* Nausicaa (film) 1970, Tango (film) 1970, Le cyborg ou Le voyage vertical (film) 1970, La pomme de son oeil (film) 1970, Rendez-vous à Badenberg (series) 1970, Les aventures de Zadig (film) 1970, Les enquêtes du commissaire Maigret (series) 1973, Un monsieur bien rangé (mini-series) 1973, Les gaspards 1974, L'inconnu (film) 1973, The Count of Monte Cristo (mini-series) 1999, Balzac (film) 1999, Les Misérables (mini-series) 2000, Bérénice (film) 2000, Napoléon (mini-series) 2002, Ruy Blas (film) 2002, Uboynaya sila (series) 2003, Volpone (film) 2003, The Lady Musketeer (film) 2004, A Cursed Monarchy (mini-series) 2005, L'abolition (film) 2008, Groland magzine (series) 2009, Le grand restaurant (film) 2010, Raspoutine (film) 2011, Marseille (series) 2016–18. *Publications:* Lettres volées 1988, Ca s'est fait comme ça 2014, Innocent 2015. *Address:* c/o Bertrand De Labbey and Claire Blondel, Voyez mon agent, 20 avenue Rapp, 75007 Paris, France (office). *Telephone:* 1-43-17-37-00 (office). *Website:* www.vma.fr (office).

DEPARDON, Raymond; French photographer; b. 6 July 1942, Villefranche-sur-Saône; s. of Antoine Depardon and Marthe Bernard; m. Claudine Nougaret 1987; two s.; ed primary school in Villefranche; apprentice to Louis Foucherand, Paris 1958, Asst 1959; copy then photographic reporter, Dalmas agency 1960; Co-founder Gamma agency 1967; mem. Magnum Agency, Paris and New York 1978; Artistic Dir Rencontres Int. d'Arles 2006; solo exhbn Correspondance new yorkaise, San Clemente, Paris 1984, Lausanne 1985; Dragon of Dragons, Kraków Film Festival 2000. *Films include:* Jan Pallach, Tibesti Tou (short) 1974, Numéros zéro 1977, Reporters 1981, Faits divers: les Années déclic 1983, Empty Quarter 1985, Urgences 1987, La Captive du désert 1990, La Colline des Anges 1993, Délits flagrants 1994, Sida propos 1995, Afriques: Comment ça va avec la douleur 1995, Paris 1998, Muriel Leferle 1999, Profils paysans l'approche 2001, Un homme sans l'Occident 2002, Quoi de neuf au Garet? 2004, Dixieme chambre – Instants d'audiences (Gold Plaque) 2004, Profils paysans: le quotidien 2005, Profils paysans: la vie moderne 2007, Le tour du monde en 14 jours 2008, Donner la parole 2008, Journal de France 2012. *Publications include:* photographic albums: Tchad 1978, Notes 1979, Correspondance new yorkaise 1981, Le Désert américain 1983, San Clemente 1984, Les Fiancées de Saigon 1986, Hivers 1987, Depardon cinéma 1993, Return to Vietnam (with Jean-Claude Guillebaud) 1994, La Ferme du Garet 1995, La Porte des Larmes (with Jean-Claude Guillebaud) 1995, En Afrique 1995, Voyages 1998, Silence rompu 1998, Corse 2000, Détours (Nadar Prize) 2000, Errances 2000, Rêves de déserts 2000, A Tombeau Ouvert 2000, Désert: un Homme sans l'Occident 2002, Piemonte: Una Definizione Fotografica 2003, 06 Alpes Maritimes 2003, Paroles Prisonnières 2004, Jeux Olympiques 2004, Images politiques 2004, Paris Journal 2004, Afriques 2005, Photographies de Personnalités Politiques 2006, La Solitude Heureuse du Voyageur 2006, Depardon-New York 2006. *Address:* 18 bis rue Henri Barbusse, 75005 Paris, France (home).

DEPP, John (Johnny) Christopher; American actor; b. 9 June 1963, Owensboro, Ky; m. Lori Anne Allison 1983 (divorced 1985); partner Vanessa Paradis 1998–2012; one s. one d.; m. Amber Heard 2015 (divorced 2017); fmr rock musician; Co-founder and CEO Infinitum Nihil (production co.) 2004–; Actor of the Year, Hollywood Film Festival 2003, People's Choice Award for Favorite Male Movie Star 2005–08, La Grande médaille de Vermeil (France) 2006, Favorite Male Action Star 2007, Favorite Movie Actor 2010–12. *Films include:* A Nightmare on Elm Street 1984, Private Resort 1985, Platoon 1986, Cry Baby 1990, Edward Scissorhands 1990, Freddy's Dead: The Final Nightmare 1991, Benny and Joon 1993, What's Eating Gilbert Grape 1993, Arizona Dream 1993, Ed Wood 1994, Don Juan de Marco 1994, Dead Man 1995, Nick of Time 1995, The Brave 1997 (also writer and dir), Donnie Brasco 1997, Fear and Loathing in Las Vegas 1998, The Astronaut's Wife 1999, The Source 1999, The Ninth Gate 1999, Sleepy Hollow 1999, The Man Who Cried 2000, Before Night Falls 2000, Chocolat 2000, Blow 2001, From Hell 2001, Pirates of the Caribbean: The Curse of the Black Pearl (Screen Actors Guild Award Best Actor 2004) 2003, Once Upon a Time in Mexico 2003, Secret Window 2004, Finding Neverland 2004, The Libertine 2004, And They Lived Happily Ever After 2004, Charlie and the Chocolate Factory 2005, Corpse Bride (voice) 2005, Pirates of the Caribbean: Dead Man's Chest 2006, Pirates of the Caribbean: At World's End 2007, Sweeney Todd: The Demon Barber of Fleet Street (Golden Globe for Best Actor in a Musical or Comedy 2008) 2007, The Imaginarium of Doctor Parnassus 2009, Public Enemies 2009, Alice in Wonderland 2010, The Rum Diary 2010, The Tourist 2010, Rango (voice) 2011, Pirates of the Caribbean: On Stranger Tides 2011, Dark Shadows 2012, 21 The Lone Ranger 2013, Transcendence 2014, Into the Woods 2014, Mortdecai 2015, Yoga Hosers 2015, Black Mass (Desert Palm Achievement Award – Actor, Palm Springs Int. Film Festival 2016) 2015. *Television includes:* Slow Burn 1986, 21 Jump Street (series) 1987–90, United States of Poetry (series) 1995, King of the Hill (episode, Hank's Back; voice) 2004, SpongeBob SquarePants (aka SpongeBob vs. the Big One) (episode) 2009. *Address:* c/o United Talent Agency, 9560 Wilshire Blvd, Suite 500, Beverly Hills, CA 90212-2401, USA (office); Infinitum Nihil, 9100 Wilshire Blvd, #275W, Beverly Hills, CA 90212, USA. *Telephone:* (310) 273-6700 (office). *Fax:* (310) 247-1111 (office). *Website:* www.unitedtalent.com (office).

DERANT LAKOUÉ, Enoch; Central African Republic politician; b. 5 Oct. 1944, Fort Lamy (now N'Djamena, Chad); fmr mem. Mouvement pour la Libération du Peuple Centrafricain (MLPC—Liberation Movt of the Cen. African People's Party); Founder and Pres. Parti social-démocrate (PSD) early 1990s; Prime Minister of Cen. African Repub. March–Oct. 1993; presidential cand. 1993, 1999; Minister of State in charge of the Economy, Planning and Int. Co-operation 2013; Founder Co-ordination of Opposition Political Parties; Dir BERETEC/CENTRAFRIQUE, Bangui; Order of Industrial and Crafts Merit 1972.

DERBEZ BAUTISTA, Luis Ernesto, BA, PhD; Mexican economist, politician and university administrator; *Rector, Universidad de las Américas Puebla;* b. 1 April 1947, Mexico City; m.; two d.; ed San Luis Potosí Autonomous Univ., Univ. of Oregon and Iowa State Univ., USA; economist for IBRD, responsible for regional areas including Chile 1983–86, Cen. America 1986–89, Africa 1989–92, Western and Cen. Africa 1992–94, India, Nepal and Bhutan 1994–97 (also dir multilateral econ. assistance and structural adjustment programmes in Chile, Costa Rica, Honduras and Guatemala); ind. consultant, World Bank Group, Mexico City office and IDB, Washington, DC 1997–2000; Econ. Adviser and Co-ordinator of Econ. Affairs to Pres.-Elect of Mexico 2000; fmr Sec. for Economy; Sec. of State for Foreign Affairs 2003–06; Dir-Gen. Centre for Globalization, Competitiveness and Democracy, Instituto Tecnológico de Monterrey 2007–; Sec. for Int. Affairs, Partido Acción Nacional 2007–08; Rector, Universidad de las Américas Puebla 2008–; fmr Prof., Grad. School of Business Man., Instituto Tecnológico y de Estudios Superiores de Monterrey (also Dir Econometric Studies Unit and Econs Dept); fmr Vice-Rector Univ. of the Americas, Cholula, Mexico; fmr Visiting Prof., Johns Hopkins Univ. School of Int. Studies, USA; mem. Advisory Bd Bombardier, Metropolitan Council of Grupo Financiero Banorte, Council of Mexican Inst. of Water Tech.; mem. Tech. Investment Bd, Ve por Más; Distinguished Achievement Alumni Award, Iowa State Univ. 2006, Distinguished Alumni Award, Univ. of Oregon 2007. *Address:* Office of the Rector, Universidad de las Américas Puebla, Sta Catarina Mártir, Apdo Postal 100, 72820 Cholula, Puebla, Mexico (office). *Telephone:* (222) 229-2000 (office). *Fax:* (222) 229-2009 (office). *E-mail:* luisernesto.derbez@udlap.mx (office). *Website:* www.udlap.mx/rector (office).

DERCON, Chris; Belgian art historian, curator and theatre director; b. 1958, Lier; ed Univ. of Leiden; fmr art critic, De Standaard (daily newspaper); Program Dir, Inst. for Contemporary Art, P.S.1, New York 1988–89; Dir, Witte de With centre for contemporary art, Rotterdam 1990–95; Dir, Museum Boijmans Van Beuningen, Rotterdam 1996–2003; Dir, Haus der Kunst, Munich 2003–11; Dir, Tate Modern, London 2011–17; Artistic Dir, Volksbühne theatre, Berlin 2017–18; extensive collaboration with cultural producers in Brazil, N and W Africa, Japan, China, India, The Gulf and Saudi Arabia; mem. Artistic Advisory Cttee, Wiels Contemporary Art Centre, Brussels. *Publications include:* contributor and ed. of numerous catalogues, art publications, lectures and interviews worldwide. *Address:* c/o Volksbühne Berlin, Linienstraße 227, London, 10178 Berlin, Germany (office).

DEREVYANKO, Anatoly Panteleyevich, DrHist; Russian scientist, archaeologist and academic; *Scientific Director, Institute of Archaeology and Ethnography, Siberian Branch, Russian Academy of Sciences;* b. 9 Jan. 1943, Kozmo-Demyanovka village, Amurskaya Oblast; m.; two c.; ed Blagoveshchensk Pedagogical Inst.; Jr Researcher, Head of Museum, Deputy Dir, Inst. of History, Dialectics and Philosophy, Siberian br. of Russian Acad. of Sciences 1965–76; Sec. Cen. Cttee of Comsomol 1976–79; Prof. and Rector, Novosibirsk Univ. 1980–83; Scientific Dir Inst. of Archaeology and Ethnography, Siberian br. of Russian Acad. of Sciences 1983–, currently also Chair. United Academic Council of Humanitarian Studies; specialist in the archaeology and ancient history of Siberia and the Far East; Corresp. mem. USSR (now Russian) Acad. of Sciences 1979–87, Academician 1987; State Prize of the Russian Fed. 2001, 2012, Demidov Prize 2004, Lomonosov Gold Medal, Russian Acad. of Sciences (co-recipient) 2015. *Publications include:* monographs include Palaeolithic of the Far East and Korea 1983, Palaeolithic of Japan 1984, Foreign Archaeology 1986; more than 400 scientific publs on general history. *Address:* Institute of Archaeology and Ethnography, Siberian branch of Russian Academy of Sciences, Academika Lavretyeva prosp. 17, Novosibirsk 630090, Russian Federation (office). *Telephone:* (383) 330-05-37 (office). *Fax:* (383) 330-11-91 (office). *E-mail:* derev@archaeology.nsc.ru (office). *Website:* www.sati.archaeology.nsc.ru (office).

DER'I, Aryeh Machluf; Israeli politician; *Minister of the Interior;* b. 17 Feb. 1959, Meknes, Morocco; m.; nine c.; ed Porat Yosef Yeshiva, Jerusalem, Hebron Talmudic Coll.; mem. Gush Etzion Settlement Regional Council 1981–83; Sr Adviser to Minister of the Interior 1985; Minister of Internal Affairs 1988–92, June–Sept. 1993, Minister without Portfolio May–June 1993, Minister of the Economy May–Nov. 2015, also Minister for Devt of Negev and Galilee May–Nov. 2015, Minister of Interior 2016–; mem. Knesset 1992–99, 2013–, mem. Foreign Affairs and Defense Cttee, Jt Cttee for Defense Budget; convicted of taking bribes, served two years in prison 2000–02; Founding mem. Shas (Sephardic Torah Guardians), Leader 1984–99, Chair. 2013–. *Address:* Ministry of Interior, POB

6158, Kiryat Ben-Gurion, Jerusalem 91061, Israel (office). *Telephone:* 2-6701400 (office). *Fax:* 2-566376 (office). *E-mail:* meda@moin.gov.il (office). *Website:* www.moin.gov.il (office).

DERIPASKA, Oleg Vladimirovich; Russian/Cypriot business executive; b. 2 Jan. 1968, Dzerzhinsk, Gorkii (now Nizhnii Novgorod) Oblast, Russian SFSR, USSR; m. Polina Yumasheva; two c.; ed Moscow State Univ., Plekhanov Acad. of Nat. Econs; Financial Dir Jt Stock Mil. Investment and Trade Co. 1990–92; Dir-Gen. Rosaluminproduct 1992–93; Dir Krasnoyarskaluminprodukt 1993; Dir-Gen. Aluminprodukt 1993–94, Chief Financial Officer 1994–96; Dir Sayany Aluminium Plant 1996–2000; Pres. Sibirskii Aluminium Group 1997–2000; Dir-Gen. Russian Aluminium Corpn (RUSAL, formed from merger of aluminium smelters and alumina refineries of Sibirskii Aluminium Group and Sibneft oil co.) 2000–03, mem. Bd of Dirs 2006–, CEO United Company RUSAL (formed from merger of RUSAL, SUAL Group and alumina assets of Glencore International AG 2007) 2009–14, Chair. Man. Bd 2009–18; Founder and Chair. Supervisory Bd Basic Element LLC (holding group for RUSAL) 2001–, GAZ (automobile mfrs), Aviacor (aircraft mfrs), Ingosstrakh (insurance co.); Chair. Bd Russian Nat. Cttee of Int. Chamber of Commerce; mem. Entrepreneurship Council of Govt of Russian Fed.; mem. Business Advisory Council APEC 2004–, Chair. Russian section 2007–; Vice-Pres. Russian Union of Businessmen and Entrepreneurs 1999–; Trustee, Nat. Science Support Foundation, Bolshoi Theatre, Schools of Business Admin of Moscow State Univ. and St Petersburg State Univ.; Order of Friendship 1999, Order of Alexander Nevsky; named by Vedomosti (business daily) Businessman of the Year 1999, 2006, 2007. *Website:* www.deripaska.com.

DERMER, Ron, MA; Israeli diplomatist; *Ambassador to USA;* b. 1971, Miami Beach, Fla, USA; s. of Jay Dermer and Yaffa Rosenthal; m. Rhoda Pagano; five c.; ed Wharton School of Business, Univ. of Pennsylvania, Univ. of Oxford, UK; spent three years as columnist for Jerusalem Post; Econ. Affairs Minister, Embassy in Washington, DC 2005–08; Sr Adviser to Prime Minister Benjamin Netanyahu 2009–13; Amb. to USA 2013–. *Publication:* The Case For Democracy: The Power of Freedom to Overcome Tyranny and Terror (with Natan Sharansky) 2004. *Address:* Israeli Embassy, 3514 International Drive NW, Washington, DC 20008, USA (office). *Telephone:* (202) 364-5500 (office). *Fax:* (202) 364-5566 (office). *E-mail:* info@washington.mfa.gov.il (office). *Website:* www.israelemb.org (office).

DERN, Bruce MacLeish; American actor; b. 4 June 1936, Chicago, Ill.; s. of John Dern and Jean Dern (née MacLeish); ed The Choate School (now Choate Rosemary Hall) and Univ. of Pennsylvania. *Films include:* Marnie 1964, Hush…Hush, Sweet Charlotte 1964, The Wild Angels 1966, The War Wagon 1967, The St. Valentine's Day Massacre 1967, The Trip 1967, Waterhole Three 1967, Will Penny 1968, Psych-Out 1968, Hang 'Em High 1968, Support Your Local Sheriff! 1969, Castle Keep 1969, Number One 1969, The Cycle Savages 1969, They Shoot Horses, Don't They? 1969, Bloody Mama 1970, The Rebel Rousers 1970, The Incredible 2-Headed Transplant 1971, Drive, He Said (Nat. Soc. of Film Critics Award for Best Supporting Actor) 1971, The Cowboys (Bronze Wrangler for Best Theatrical Motion Picture) 1972, Silent Running 1972, The King of Marvin Gardens 1972, Thumb Tripping 1972, An Investigation of Murder 1973, The Great Gatsby 1974, Posse 1975, Smile 1975, Family Plot 1976, Won Ton Ton: The Dog Who Saved Hollywood 1976, The Twist 1976, Black Sunday 1977, Coming Home 1978, The Driver 1978, Middle Age Crazy 1980, Tattoo 1981, That Championship Season (Silver Bear for Best Actor) 1982, Harry Tracy: Dead or Alive 1982, On the Edge 1986, The Big Town 1987, World Gone Wild 1988, 1969 1988, The 'Burbs 1989, After Dark, My Sweet 1990, Diggstown 1992, Mrs. Munck 1995, Wild Bill 1995, Down Periscope 1996, Last Man Standing 1996, Small Soldiers (voice) 1998, The Haunting 1999, If… Dog… Rabbit 1999, All the Pretty Horses 2000, The Glass House 2001, Masked and Anonymous 2003, Milwaukee, Minnesota 2003, Monster 2003, Madison 2005, Down in the Valley 2005, Believe in Me 2006, Walker Payne 2006, The Astronaut Farmer 2006, The Hard Easy 2006, The Cake Eaters 2007, Swamp Devil (Philadelphia Film Festival Jury Prize) 2008, The Golden Boys 2008, American Cowslip 2009, The Hole 2009, The Lightkeepers 2009, Choose 2010, Trim 2010, From Up on Poppy Hill (English version, voice) 2011, Inside Out 2011, Twixt 2011, Hitting the Cycle 2012, Django Unchained 2012, Coffin Baby 2013, Northern Borders 2013, Nebraska (Award for Best Cast, Boston Soc. of Film Critics, Best Actor Award, Cannes Film Festival, Award for Best Actor, Dublin Film Critics' Circle, Award for Best Actor, Los Angeles Film Critics' Asscn, Award for Best Actor, Nat. Bd of Review) 2013, Fighting for Freedom 2013, Cut Bank 2014, The Hateful Eight 2015. *Television includes:* Stoney Burke (series) 1962–63, The Dick Powell Theatre (series) 1962–63, Wagon Train (series) 1963–65, The Fugitive (series) 1963–66, The Virginian (series) 1964–65, 12 O'Clock High (series) 1964–65, F.B.I. (series) 1965–68, Gunsmoke (series) 1965–69, The Long Hunt of April Savage (film) 1966, Run for Your Life (series) 1966–67, The Big Valley (series) 1966–68, Lancer (series) 1968–69, Who Killed the Mysterious Mr. Foster? (film) 1971, Toughlove (film) 1985, Roses Are for the Rich (film) 1987, Uncle Tom's Cabin (film) 1987, Trenchcoat in Paradise (film) 1989, The Court-Martial of Jackie Robinson (film) 1990, Into the Badlands (film) 1991, Carolina Skeletons (film) 1991, It's Nothing Personal (film) 1993, Dead Man's Revenge (film) 1994, Amelia Earhart: The Final Flight (film) 1994, A Mother's Prayer (film) 1995, Comfort, Texas (film) 1997, When the Bough Breaks II: Perfect Prey (film) 1998, Hard Time: The Premonition (film) 1999, Hard Ground (film) 2003, Big Love (series) 2006–11, Unicorn Plan-It (series) 2012–13, Pete's Christmas (film) 2013. *Address:* c/o Creative Artists Agency, 2000 Avenue of the Stars, Los Angeles, CA 90067, USA (office). *Telephone:* (424) 288-2000 (office). *Fax:* (424) 288-2900 (office). *Website:* www.caa.com (office).

DERN, Laura Elizabeth; American actress, director and producer; b. 10 Feb. 1967, Los Angeles, Calif.; d. of Bruce Dern and Diane Ladd; m. Ben Harper 2005 (divorced 2013); one s. one d.; ed Lee Strasberg Inst., Royal Acad. of Dramatic Art, London, UK. *Films include:* Foxes 1980, Ladies and Gentlemen, The Fabulous Stains 1981, Teachers 1984, Mask 1985, Smooth Talk 1985, Blue Velvet 1986, Predator: The Concert 1987, Haunted Summer 1988, Fat Man and Little Boy 1989, Wild at Heart 1990, Rambling Rose 1991, Jurassic Park 1993, A Perfect World 1993, Devil Inside, Citizen Ruth 1996, Bastard Out of Carolina 1996, October Sky 1999, Dr T and the Women 2000, Daddy and Them 2001, Focus 2001, Novocaine 2001, Jurassic Park III 2001, I Am Sam 2001, Novocaine 2001, We Don't Live Here Anymore 2004, Happy Endings 2005, The Prize Winner of Defiance, Ohio 2005, Lonely Hearts 2006, Inland Empire 2006, Year of the Dog 2007, The Monday Before Thanksgiving (short) 2008, Tenderness 2009, Everything Must Go 2010, Little Fockers 2010, The Master 2012, The Fault in our Stars 2014, Wild 2014, Bravetown 2015, Certain Women 2016, The Founder 2016, Wilson 2017. *Television includes:* Happy Endings 1983, The Three Wishes of Billy Greer 1984, Afterburn (film) 1992, Fallen Angels (series) 1993, Down Came a Blackbird (film) 1995, Frasier (series) 1995, The Siege at Ruby Ridge (film) 1996, Ellen (series) 1997, The Baby Dance 1998, Hallmark Hall of Fame (series) 1999, A Season for Miracles 1999, Within These Walls (film) 2001, The West Wing (episode) 2002, Damaged Care (film) 2002, King of the Hill (series) 2002–03, Recount (Golden Globe Award for Best Supporting Actress in a Series 2009) 2008, Enlightened (series) (Golden Globe Award for Best Performance by an Actress in a Television Series – Comedy or Musical 2012) 2011–13, F is for Family (voice) 2015–, Big Little Lies (Emmy Award for Outstanding Supporting Actress in a Limited Series or Movie 2017, Golden Globe Award for Best Performance by an Actress in a Supporting Role in a Series, Limited Series or Motion Picture Made for Television 2018) 2017, Twin Peaks 2017; Dir The Gift 1994. *Address:* c/o Fred Specktor, Creative Artists Agency, 2000 Avenue of the Stars, Los Angeles, CA 90067, USA (office); c/o Wolf-Kasteler, 9350 Wilshire Blvd, Suite 450, Beverly Hills, CA 90212, USA (office). *Telephone:* (424) 288-2000 (office); (310) 205-0618 (office). *Fax:* (424) 288-2900 (office). *Website:* www.caa.com (office); www.wktpr.com (office).

DERR, Kenneth T., MBA; American business executive; b. 1936; m. Donna Mettler 1959; three c.; ed Cornell Univ.; with Chevron Corpn (fmrly Standard Oil Co. of Calif.) 1960–99, Vice-Pres. 1972–85, Pres. Chevron USA Inc. 1978–84, Head Merger Program, Chevron Corpn and Gulf Oil Corpn 1984–85, Vice-Chair. Chevron Corpn 1985–88, Chair. 1989–99, CEO 1989–99; Dir Calpine Corpn 2001–05, Chair. and Acting CEO 2005, Chair. 2005–08 (retd); mem. Bd of Dirs Citigroup Inc. 1987–2009, AT&T 1995–2005, Halliburton 2001–09; Dir American Petroleum Inst. (fmr Chair.), American Productivity. *Address:* 345 California Street, Floor 3D, San Francisco, CA 94104-2638, USA (office).

DERSHOWITZ, Alan Morton, LLB; American lawyer, writer and academic; *Felix Frankfurter Professor of Law Emeritus, Harvard University;* b. 1 Sept. 1938, New York; s. of Harry Dershowitz and Claire Ringel; m. Carolyn Cohen; two s. one d.; ed Brooklyn Coll. and Yale Univ.; admitted to DC Bar 1963, Mass Bar 1968, US Supreme Court 1968; law clerk to Chief Judge David Bazelon, US Court of Appeal 1962–63, to Justice Arthur Goldberg, US Supreme Court 1963–64; joined Faculty, Harvard Coll. 1964, apptd Prof. of Law 1967, now Prof. Emer., apptd Felix Frankfurter Prof. of Law 1993, now Felix Frankfurter Prof. of Law Emer.; Fellow, Center for Advanced Study of Behavioral Sciences 1971–72; consultant to Dir Nat. Inst. for Mental Health 1967–69, President's Comm. on Civil Disorders 1967, President's Comm. on Causes of Violence 1968, Nat. Asscn for Advancement of Colored People Legal Defense Fund 1967–68, President's Comm. on Marijuana and Drug Abuse 1972–73, Ford Foundation Study on Law and Justice 1973–76; rapporteur, Twentieth Century Fund Study on Sentencing 1975–76; Guggenheim Fellow 1978–79; mem. Comm. on Law and Social Action, American Jewish Congress 1978; Dir American Civil Liberties Union 1968–71, 1972–75, Asscn of Behavioral and Social Sciences, NAS 1973–76; Chair. Civil Rights Comm. New England Region, Anti-Defamation League, B'nai B'rith 1980; Hon. MA (Harvard Coll.) 1967, Hon. LLD (Yeshiva) 1989. *Publications:* Psychoanalysis, Psychiatry and the Law (with others) 1967, Criminal Law: Theory and Process 1974, The Best Defense 1982, Reversal of Fortune: Inside the von Bülow Case 1986, Taking Liberties: A Decade of Hard Cases, Bad Laws and Bum Raps 1988, Chutzpah 1991, Contrary to Popular Opinion 1992, The Abuse Excuse 1994, The Advocate's Devil 1994, Reasonable Doubt 1996, The Vanishing American Jew 1997, Sexual McCarthyism 1998, Just Revenge 1999, The Genesis of Justice 2000, Letters to a Young Lawyer 2001, Shouting Fire: Civil Liberties in a Turbulent Age 2002, Why Terrorism Works 2002, Supreme Injustice: How the High Court Hijacked Election 2000 2002, America Declares Independence 2003, America on Trial 2004, Letters to a Young Lawyer 2005, The Case for Israel 2005, Rights from Wrongs: A Secular Theory of the Origins of Rights 2005, The Case for Peace: How the Arab-Israeli Conflict Can be Resolved 2006, Preemption: A Knife That Cuts Both Ways 2007, What Israel Means to Me 2007, Blasphemy 2008, The Case against Israel's Enemies 2008, Finding, Framing, and Hanging Jefferson 2009, The Case for Moral Clarity 2009, The Trials of Zion 2010, Israel on Trial 2011, Taking the Stand: My Life in the Law 2013; contrib. of articles to legal journals. *Address:* Harvard University Law School, Hauser Hall 520, 1575 Massachusetts Avenue, Cambridge, MA 02138-2801, USA (office). *Telephone:* (617) 495-4617 (office). *Fax:* (617) 495-7855 (office). *E-mail:* dersh@law.harvard.edu (office). *Website:* www.law.harvard.edu (office); www.alandershowitz.com.

DERVAN, Peter B, BS, PhD; American chemist and academic; *Bren Professor of Chemistry, California Institute of Technology;* b. 28 June 1945, Boston, Mass; ed Boston Coll., Yale Univ.; Postdoctoral Fellow, Stanford Univ. 1973; Asst Prof. of Chem., Calif. Inst. of Tech. 1973–79, Assoc. Prof. 1979–82, Prof. 1982–88, Bren Prof. of Chem. 1988–, also Chair., Div. of Chem. and Chemical Eng 1994–99; Visiting Prof. at several int. univs including Eidgenössische Technische Hochschule Zürich, Switzerland 1983, MIT 1987, Univ. of Cambridge, England 1989, Johann Wolfgang Goethe Univ., Frankfurt, Germany 1993, Univ. Catholique de Louvain, Belgium 1994; Co-founder Gilead Sciences 1987, Gensoft; mem. Scientific Advisory Bd Robert A. Welch Foundation and several other biotechnology cos including Xencor Inc., Fluidigm; mem. Editorial Bd several journals including Chemical Reviews 1984–89, Journal of the American Chemical Society 1986–92, Journal of Medicinal Chemistry 1991–93, Bioorganic and Medicinal Chemistry 1993–; mem. Bd of Scientific Govs., Scripps Research Inst.; Trustee, Yale Univ. 2008– (Alumni Fellow 2008–14); mem. NAS 1986–, American Acad. of Arts and Sciences 1987–, NAS Inst. of Medicine, American Philosophical Soc. 2002–; mem. several NSF Advisory Cttees; Foreign mem. French Acad. of Sciences 2000–, German Acad. of Sciences 2004–; Hon. DrSci (Boston Coll.) 1997 numerous awards including Willard Gibbs Medal 1993, Nichols Medal 1994, Kirkwood Medal 1998, Richard C. Tolman Medal 1999, Linus Pauling Award 1999, Tetrahedron Prize 2000, Harvey Prize 2002, Nat. Medal of Science 2006. *Address:* 351 Crellin, California Institute of Technology, Pasadena, CA 91125, USA (office). *Telephone:* (626) 395-6002 (office). *Fax:* (626) 5568-87443 (office). *E-mail:* dervan@caltech.edu (office). *Website:* chemistry.caltech.edu (office).

DERVIŞ, Kemal, BA, MA, PhD; Turkish economist, politician and UN official; *Vice-President and Director, Global Economy and Development, Brookings Institution;* b. 10 Jan. 1949, Istanbul; m. Catherine Anne Derviş; ed London School of Econs, UK, Princeton Univ., USA; Lecturer in Econs, Middle Eastern Tech. Univ. 1973; adviser on issues of econ. and int. relations to Prime Minister Bülent Ecevit 1973–76; Lecturer in Int. Relations and Econs, Princeton Univ. 1977; mem. Research Dept, World Bank 1978–82, Head of Industrial Strategy and Policy, Global Industry Dept 1982–86, Sr Economist for Europe, Middle East and N African Affairs 1986–87, Head of Cen. Europe Div. 1987–96, Vice-Pres. in charge of Middle East and N Africa Region 1996–2000, Vice-Pres. in charge of Poverty Reduction and Econ. Man. 2000–01; returned to Turkey 2001; Minister of Econ. Affairs and the Treasury (without party affiliation) 2001–02 (resgnd); mem. Cumhuriyet Halk Partisi (CHP—Republican People's Party—centre-left) 2002–; mem. Parl. for Istanbul 2002–05, represented Turkish Parl. in Constitutional Convention on the Future of Europe, mem. Jt Comm. of Turkish and European Parls; Admin. UNDP and Chair. UN Devt Group 2005–09; Vice-Pres. and Dir Global Economy and Devt program, Brookings Inst., Washington, DC 2009–17, Sr Fellow; Sr Advisor, Istanbul Policy Center, Sabanci Univ.; Adjunct Prof., Columbia Univ. 2009–15; has taught economics at Princeton Univ., Bilkent Univ., Middle East Univ.; mem. Comm. on Growth and Devt (sponsored by World Bank and others), Comm. on the Measurement of Econ. Performance and Social Progress, Advisory Cttee Centre for Econ. and Foreign Policy Studies (EDAM), Advisory Cttee Turkish Econ. and Social Studies Foundation (TESEV); fmr mem. Int. Task Force on Global Public Goods, Special Comm. on the Balkans; mem. Advisory Bd Institut de Prospective Economique du Monde Méditerranéen, Institut du Bosphore (also Co-Chair.), Center for Global Devt, La Caixa Bank, Office Chérifien des Phosphates. *Publications include:* General Equilibrium Models for Development Policy (co-author) 1982, A Better Globalization 2005, Recovery from the Crisis and Contemporary Social Democracy 2006; numerous papers in academic journals as well as current affairs publs on topics ranging from math. models of growth and social mobility and quantitative models of trade, to European enlargement and transatlantic relations (in English, Turkish, French and German). *Address:* The Brookings Institution, 1775 Massachusetts Avenue, NW, Washington, DC 20036, USA (office); Türkiye Büyük Millet Meclisi, 06543 Ankara, Turkey (home). *Telephone:* (202) 797-6000 (office). *E-mail:* communications@brookings.edu (office); kdervis@chp.org.tr (home). *Website:* www.brookings.edu (office).

DERWENT, Henry, CB; British civil servant and international organization official; *Senior Adviser, Climate Strategies;* ed Berkhamsted School, Worcester Coll., Oxford; held several positions in Depts of Transport and Environment, covering roads, transport industries, vehicle licensing, finance, local government and other fields, also acted as Corp. Finance Exec. on loan to major int. investment bank; Dir Int. Climate Change, Energy and Environmental Risk, Dept for Environment, Food and Rural Affairs –2008, acted as Special Rep. to Prime Minister on Climate Change during UK Presidency of EU 2005; Pres. and CEO Int. Emissions Trading Asscn 2008–13, now Hon. Vice-Pres.; currently Sr Adviser, Climate Strategies. *Address:* Climate Strategies, 40 Bermondsey Street, London, SE1 3UD, England. *Telephone:* (20) 3102-1526. *E-mail:* info@climatestrategies.org. *Website:* climatestrategies.org.

DERYCKE, Erik, LLM; Belgian politician and lawyer; *Judge, Constitutional Court of Belgium;* b. 28 Oct. 1949, Waregem; m.; two c.; ed Rijksuniversiteit, Gent; barrister in Kortrijk 1972–; Provincial Councillor for W Flanders 1975–84; Rep. for Kortrijk, Belgian Chamber of Reps 1984; Municipal Councillor for Waregem 1989; Sec. of State for Science Policy 1990–91; Minister for Devt Aid and Deputy Minister for Science Policy 1991–92; Sec. of State for Devt Aid 1992–95; Minister for Foreign Affairs and Devt Co-operation March–June 1995; Minister for Foreign Affairs 1995–99; Judge, Constitutional Court of Belgium 2007–; Hon. Pres. Socialist Party of Waregem; mem. Socialist Party Bureau. *Address:* Constitutional Court of Belgium, 7 place Royale, 1000 Brussels, Belgium (office). *Website:* www.const-court.be (office).

DESAI, Anita, BA, FRSL; Indian writer and academic; *John E. Burchard Professor Emerita of Humanities, Massachusetts Institute of Technology;* b. 24 June 1937, Mussoorie; d. of D. N. Mazumdar and Toni Nimé; m. Ashvin Desai 1958; two s. two d.; ed Queen Mary's School, Delhi and Miranda House, Univ. of Delhi; Elizabeth Drew Visiting Prof., Smith Coll., Mass, USA 1987–88; Purington Prof. of English, Mount Holyoke Coll. 1988–92; John E. Burchard Prof. of Humanities, MIT, Cambridge, Mass 1993–2002, now Prof. Emer.; Gildersleeves Prof., Barnard Coll.; Visiting Scholar, Rockefeller Foundation, Bellagio, Italy; Sidney Harman Visiting Prof. and Writer-in-Residence, Baruch Coll. 2003; mem. RSL, American Acad. of Arts and Letters, PEN, Sahitya Akademi, India; Hon. Fellow, Girton Coll., Cambridge 1988, Clare Hall, Cambridge 1991, Hon. mem. American Acad. of Arts and Letters; Royal Soc. of Literature Winifred Holtby Prize 1978, Sahitya Acad. Prize 1978, Fed. of Indian Publishers Award 1978, Guardian Prize for Children's Fiction 1983, Hadassah Prize, New York 1988, Padma Sri 1989, Literary Lion, New York Public Library 1993, Scottish Arts Council Neil Gunn Award for Int. Writing 1994, Alberto Moravia Prize for Literature, Italy 1999, Benson Medal for lifetime achievement, RSL 2003, Giuseppe de Lampedusa Award, Italy 2006, Padma Bhushan 2014. *Film screenplay:* In Custody 1994. *Television includes:* The Village By The Sea (BBC) 1994. *Publications include:* Cry, The Peacock 1963, Voices in the City 1965, Bye-Bye, Blackbird 1971, Where Shall We Go This Summer? 1973, Fire on the Mountain 1978, Games at Twilight 1979, Clear Light of Day 1980, The Village by the Sea 1983, In Custody 1984, Baumgartner's Bombay 1988, Journey to Ithaca 1995, Fasting, Feasting 1999, Diamond Dust and Other Stories 2000, The Zigzag Way 2004, The Artist of Disappearance 2011; children's books: The Peacock Garden 1974, Cat on a Houseboat 1976, The Village by the Sea 1982. *Address:* c/o Rogers, Coleridge & White Ltd., 20 Powis Mews, London, W11 1JN, England (office). *Telephone:* (20) 7221-3717 (office). *Fax:* (20) 7229-9084 (office). *E-mail:* info@rcwlitagency.com (office). *Website:* www.rcwlitagency.com (office).

DESAI, Baron (Life Peer), cr. 1991, of St Clement Danes in the City of Westminster; **Meghnad Jagdishchandra Desai,** PhD; British economist and academic; *Professor Emeritus of Economics, London School of Economics;* b. 10 July 1940, Baroda, India; s. of Jagdishchandra Desai and Mandakini Desai (née Majmundar); m. 1st Gail Wilson 1970 (divorced 2004); one s. two d.; m. 2nd Kishwar Rosha 2004; ed Univ. of Bombay, Univ. of Pennsylvania, USA; Assoc. Specialist, Dept of Agricultural Econs, Univ. of Calif., Berkeley, USA 1963–65; Lecturer, LSE 1965–77, Sr Lecturer 1977–80, Reader 1980–83, Prof. of Econs 1983–, now Prof. Emer., Head Devt Studies Inst. 1990–95, Dir Centre for the Study of Global Governance 1992–2003, Chair. Econ. Research Div. 1983–95; consultant at various times to FAO, UNCTAD, Int. Coffee Org., World Bank, UNIDO, UNDP, Ministries of Industrial Devt and Educ., Algeria, British Airports Authority and other bodies; Co-Ed. Journal of Applied Econometrics 1984–; mem. Editorial Bds Int. Review of Applied Econs and several other journals; mem. Council, Royal Econ. Soc. 1988; mem. Exec. Cttee Asscn of Univ. Teachers in Econs 1987– (Pres. 1987–90); mem. Univ. of London Senate representing LSE 1981–89; mem. Nat. Exec. of Council for Academic Freedom and Democracy 1972–83, Speaker's Comm. on Citizenship 1989–, Berndt Carlson Trust; mem. or fmr mem. Governing Body of Courtauld Inst., British Inst. in Paris, Cen. School of Arts, Polytechnic of N London; Chair. Holloway Ward (Islington Cen.) Labour Party 1977–80; Chair. Islington S and Finsbury Labour Party 1986–92, Pres. 1992–; Dr hc (Kingston Univ.) 1992; Hon. DSc (Econs) (E London) 1994; Hon. DPhil (London Guildhall) 1996; Hon. LLD (Monash Univ.) 2005; Pravasi Puraskar (Distinguished Diaspora Indian Award) 2004, Distinguished Alumnus Award, Wharton School of Finance 2004, Padma Bhushan 2008. *Film:* Life Goes On (cameo) 2009. *Publications include:* Marxian Economic Theory 1974 (trans. in several languages), Applied Econometrics 1976, Marxian Economics 1979, Testing Monetarism 1981, Marx's Revenge 2001, Global Governance and Financial Crises 2003, Nehru's Hero: Dilip Kumar in the Life of India 2004, Development and Nationhood 2005, The Route to All Evil: Political Economy of Ezra Pound 2006, Rethinking Islamism 2006, Dead on Time (novel) 2009, The Rediscovery of India 2009; ed. several books; numerous papers and contribs to books and journals. *Leisure interests:* reading, politics. *Address:* House of Lords, Westminster, London, SW1A 0AA (office); 3 Deepdene Road, London, SE5 8EG, England (home). *Telephone:* (20) 7219-5066 (office); (20) 7274-5561 (home). *Fax:* (20) 7219-5979 (office). *E-mail:* desaim@parliament.uk (office); lord.mdesai@gmail.com (home). *Website:* www.parliament.uk/biographies/lords/lord-desai/2699 (office); www.lse.ac.uk/Depts/global (office).

DESAI, Nitin Dayalji, BA, MA; Indian economist, civil servant and UN official; b. 5 July 1941, Bombay (now Mumbai); s. of Dayalji M. Desai and Shantaben Desai; m. Aditi Gupta 1979; two s.; ed St Xavier's High School and Elphinstone Coll., Mumbai, Univ. of Bombay, London School of Econs, UK; Lecturer in Econs, Univ. of Liverpool, UK 1965–67, Univ. of Southampton, UK 1967–70; consultant, Tata (India) Econ. Consultancy Services 1970–73; consultant/adviser, Planning Comm. Govt of India 1973–85; Sr Adviser, Brundtland Comm. 1985–87; Special Sec. Planning Comm. India 1987–88; Sec./Chief Econ. Adviser, Ministry of Finance 1988–90; Deputy Under-Sec.-Gen. UNCED, Geneva 1990–92, Under-Sec.-Gen. for Econ. and Social Affairs, UN 1992–2003, Under-Sec.-Gen. of Dept for Policy Co-ordination and Sustainable Devt 1993–97, Sec.-Gen. of Johannesburg Summit 2002, Special Adviser to the Sec.-Gen. for the World Summit on the Information Soc. 2003–05, Special Adviser to Sec.-Gen. for Internet Governance, Internet Governance Forum, UN 2003–10; Chair. Bd of Trustees, Oxfam Int. 2013; mem. Advisory Bd IDEAcarbon; Chair. Cttee on Tech. Innovation and Venture Capital set up by Planning Comm., Govt of India 2006, Int. Working Group on Internet Governance; Co-Chair. (with Lord Chris Patten) India-UK Round Table; Finance Chair. The Poona Club Ltd; associated with Helsinki Process on Globalisation and Democracy; Distinguished Visiting Fellow, Centre for the Study of Global Governance, LSE 2003–04, Energy and Resources Inst.; Trustee WWF International; fmr mem. Commonwealth Secretariat Expert Group on Climate Change; Hon. Fellow, LSE 2004. *Publications include:* several articles and papers on devt planning, regional econs, industry, energy and int. econ. relations; writes a monthly column for Business Standard (economic daily published from Delhi).

DESAILLY, Marcel David; French (b. Ghanaian) fmr professional footballer; b. (Odenke Abbey), 7 Sept. 1968, Nima-Accra, Ghana; m. Virginie Desailly; three s. one d.; defender/midfielder with Nantes Atlantique 1986–92, with Olympique de Marseille 1992–93 (won Champions League 1993), with AC Milan 1993–98 (won UEFA Champions League 1994, UEFA Super Cup 1994, Serie A 1994, 1996, Supercoppa Italiana 1994), with Chelsea 1998–2004 (Capt. 2000–04, won UEFA Super Cup 1998, FA Cup 2000, FA Charity Shield 2000), with Al-Gharafa, Qatar 2004–05 (won Qatari League 2005), with Qatar SC 2005–06; played for French nat. team 1993–2004 (made 116 appearances and scored three goals, Capt. 2000–04), winner World Cup 1998, European Football Championship 2000, Confederations Cup 2001, 2003; retd from int. football 2004; apptd UNICEF Nat. Goodwill Amb. for Ghana; Lifetime Goodwill Amb., OrphanAid Africa; mem. Laureus Sports for Good Foundation; Chevalier, Légion d'honneur; Overall Team of the Decade – Premier League 10 Seasons Awards (1992/93–2001/02), ranked by FIFA amongst 100 greatest living players 2004. *E-mail:* contact_desailly@athleteline.com. *Website:* www.marcel-desailly.com.

DESALEGN, Hailemariam, BSc, MSc; Ethiopian civil engineer and politician; b. 19 July 1965, Hombareka, Wolaita; ed Addis Ababa Univ.; began career as civil engineer, Arba Minch Water Tech. Inst. (renamed Arba Minch Univ. 2004) 1990, various positions including Registrar, Deputy Dean and Dean; Vice-Pres. Southern Nations, Nationalities and Peoples' Region 2003, Pres. 2004; Adviser on Social Affairs and Civic Orgs and Partnerships, Prime Minister's Office, Addis Ababa 2005–07; apptd Govt Whip, Fed. Parl. 2008; Chair. Privatization and Public Enterprises Supervisory Agency 2007; mem. and fmr Chair. Southern Ethiopian Peoples' Democratic Movt; Deputy Chair. Ethiopian People's Revolutionary Democratic Front 2010–12, Chair. 2012–18; Minister of Foreign Affairs 2010–12, Deputy Prime Minister 2010–12, Acting Prime Minister (following death of Meles Zenawi) Aug.–Sept. 2012, Prime Minister 2012–18; Chair. African Union Ass. 2013–14; mem. Advisory Bd Brenthurst Foundation 2018–. *Website:* www.eprdf.org.et.

DeSANTIS, Ronald (Ron) Dion, BA, JD; American lawyer, politician and fmr naval officer; *Governor of Florida;* b. 14 Sept. 1978, Jacksonville, Fla; s. of Ronald DeSantis and Karen DeSantis (née Rogers); m. Casey DeSantis (née Black) 2010; one s. one d.; ed Yale Univ., Harvard Law School; apptd to Judge Advocate-Gen.'s Corps (JAG), USNR Center, Dallas 2004, JAG Prosecutor, USN 2005, sworked at Guantanamo Bay, Cuba, then Advisor, USN Sea, Air and Land Teams (SEALS),

Iraq 2007, apptd Lt, USNR 2010; Federal Prosecutor, United States Dept of Justice 2008–10; mem. US House of Reps 2013–18; also founder mem. Freedom Caucus 2015–; Gov. of Florida 2019–; mem. American Legion, Veterans of Foreign Wars; Iraq Campaign Medal, Bronze Star Medal, Navy and Marine Corps Commendation Medal, Achievement Medal. *Publications:* Dreams From Our Founding Fathers: First Principles in the Age of Obama 2011; contrib. articles to National Review, The Washington Times, The American Spectator, Human Events, American Thinker. *Address:* Office of the Governor, State of Florida, The Capitol, 400 S Monroe Street, Tallahassee, FL 32399-0001, USA (office). *Telephone:* (850) 717-9337 (office). *Website:* www.flgov.com (office).

DESARIO, Vincenzo, BA; Italian banker; b. 11 June 1933, Barletta; m. Luciana Modonesi; three c.; ed Univ. of Bari; joined Banca d'Italia (Bank of Italy), Foggia br. 1960, Banking Supervision Inspectorate, Bank of Italy head office, Rome 1968, Cen. Man. for Banking and Financial Supervision 1983, Bank of Italy Del. to Interbank Deposit Protection Fund 1991, Deputy Dir-Gen. Bank of Italy 1993–94, Dir-Gen. 1994–2006, now Hon. Dir-Gen.

DESCALZI, Claudio; Italian oil industry executive; *CEO, Eni SpA;* b. 1955, Milan; ed Univ. of Milan; joined Eni SpA as oil and gas field petroleum engineering and project man. for devt of North Sea, Libya, Nigeria and Congo 1981, Head of Reservoir and Operating Activities for Italy 1990–94, Man. Dir Eni subsidiary in the Congo 1994–98, Vice-Chair. and Man. Dir Naoc (Eni subsidiary in Nigeria) 1998–2000, Exec. Vice-Pres. for Africa, Middle East and China 2000–01, Exec. Vice-Pres. for Italy, Africa, Middle East 2002–05, Deputy COO Eni SpA Exploration & Production Div. 2005–08, COO 2008–10, Chair. Eni UK 2010–14, CEO Eni SpA 2014–; Pres. Assomineraria 2006–14; Vice-Pres. Confindustria Energia; Charles F. Rand Memorial Gold Medal, Soc. of Petroleum Engineers and American Inst. of Mining Engineers 2012, named Man of the Year by Staffetta quotidiana magazine 2014. *Address:* Eni SpA, Piazzale Enrico Mattei 1, 00144 Rome, Italy (office). *Telephone:* (06) 59821 (office). *Fax:* (06) 59822141 (office). *E-mail:* segreteriasocietaria.azionisti@eni.it (office); ufficio.stampa@eni.it (office). *Website:* www.eni.com (office).

DESCHAMPS, Didier Claude; French football manager and fmr professional footballer; *Manager, French National Football Team;* b. 15 Oct. 1968, Bayonne (Pyrénées-Atlantiques); m. Claude Deschamps; one s.; ed St Bernard pvt. school, Bayonne, Nantes Football Acad.; amateur player, Aviron Bayonnais; played for FC Nantes 1985–89, Olympique de Marseille (OM) 1989–90, FC des Girondins de Bordeaux 1990–91, OM 1989–94 (won Ligue 1 1990, 1992), Juventus, Turin, Italy 1994–99 (won UEFA Champions League 1993, 1996, Intercontinental Cup 1996, European Super Cup 1996, Italian Cup 1995, Italian Super Cup 1995, 1997, Serie A 1995, 1997, 1998), Chelsea, UK 1999–2000 (won FA Cup 2000), Valencia, Spain 2000–01; played for French nat. team 1989–2000 (made 103 appearances (nat. record) and scored four goals), Capt. and player, Euro 92, Tournoi de France 1997, Capt. of winning team of FIFA World Cup 1998 and UEFA European Football Championship 2000; fmr Man. Club de Football de Concarneau; Sports Dir and Coach AS Monaco 2001–05, won Coupe de la Ligue 2003, reached Champions' League final 2004; Head Coach Juventus, Italy 2006–07 (won Serie B 2007); Head Coach and Man. Olympique de Marseille 2009–12, won Ligue 1 2009–10, runner-up 2010–11, won Coupe de la Ligue 2010, 2011, 2012, Trophée des Champions 2010, 2011; Man. France French nat. team 2012–, winners of FIFA World Cup 2018; consultant, Canal+ 2007–09; Chevalier, Légion d'honneur 1998, Officier 2018; French Footballer of the Year 1996, UEFA Euro Team of the Tournament 1996, Médaille de la ville de Bayonne 1998, ranked by FIFA amongst top 100 greatest living footballers 2004; Ligue 1 Manager of the Year 2004, Best Men's Coach, FIFA Football Awards 2018. *Website:* www.fff.fr/equipes-de-france/tous-les-selectionneurs/fiche-selectionneur/313-didier-deschamps.

DESCHANEL, Zooey Claire; American actress, musician and singer-songwriter; b. 17 Jan. 1980, Los Angeles, Calif.; d. of Caleb Deschanel and Mary Jo Deschanel (née Weir); m. 1st Ben Gibbard 2009 (divorced 2012); m. 2nd Jacob Pechenik 2015; one d.; ed French Woods Festival of the Performing Arts, attended Northwestern Univ.; guest role on TV series Veronica's Closet 1998; film debut in Mumford 1999; breakthrough role as Anita in Almost Famous 2000; performed in jazz cabaret act If All the Stars Were Pretty Babies with Samantha Shelton from 2001; released debut album Volume One (recorded with M. Ward as She & Him) 2008; follow-up albums: Volume Two 2010, Volume 3 2013, Classics 2014; often sings in her films. *Films include:* Mumford 1999, Almost Famous 2000, Manic 2001, The Good Girl 2002, Abandon 2002, Big Trouble 2002, The New Guy 2002, All the Real Girls 2003, It's Better to Be Wanted for Murder Than Not to Be Wanted at All 2003, Elf 2003, Eulogy 2004, The Hitchhiker's Guide to the Galaxy 2005, Winter Passing 2005, Failure to Launch 2006, Live Free or Die 2006, The Good Life 2007, The Go-Getter 2007, Bridge to Terabithia 2007, Flakes 2007, Surf's Up (voice) 2007, The Assassination of Jesse James by the Coward Robert Ford 2007, The Happening 2008, Gigantic 2008, Yes Man 2008, 500 Days of Summer 2009, Havin' a Summah (video short) 2010, Our Idiot Brother 2011, Your Highness 2011, The Driftless Area 2015, Rock the Kasbah 2015, Trolls (voice) 2016. *Television includes:* American Dad! (series) (voice) 2005–13, Once Upon a Mattress (film) 2005, Weeds (series) 2006–07, Tin Man (mini-series) 2007, The Simpsons (series) (voice) 2008–13, Bones (series) 2009, Drunk History (series) 2010, New Girl (series) 2011–18. *Address:* c/o Christian Carino, Creative Artists Agency, 2000 Avenue of the Stars, Los Angeles, CA 90067, USA (office). *Telephone:* (424) 288-2000 (office). *Fax:* (424) 288-2900 (office). *Website:* www.caa.com (office).

DESCÔTES, Anne-Marie, BA, MA; French diplomatist; *Ambassador to Germany;* b. 5 Dec. 1959, Lyon; m.; one d.; ed Ecole normale supérieure, Ecole nationale d'administration; fmr German Language Teacher; Cultural Attaché French Embassy, Bonn, Germany 1987–90, Head, External Relations, EU 1994–97, Head, European Co-operation Dept 1997, Tech. Adviser, Personal Advisory Bd, Minister of European Affairs 1997–2001, Consultant, EU Enlargement, Perm. Representation to EU, Brussels 2001–05, USSR, Washington 2005–08, Head, Dept for Globalization, Culture, Educ. and Int. Devt, Ministry of Foreign Affairs 2013–17, Amb. to Germany 2017–; Dir Agency for French Educ. Abroad (AEFE) 2008–13; Chevalier, Ordre national du mérite 2009, Chevalier, Legion d'honneur 2014. *Address:* French Embassy, Pariser Pl. 5, 10117 Berlin, Germany (office). *Telephone:* (30) 590039100 (office). *Fax:* (30) 590039110 (office). *E-mail:* cad.berlin-amba@diplomatie.gouv.fr (office). *Website:* www.ambafrance-de.org (office).

DESHAPRIYA, Mahinda; Sri Lankan government official; *Chairman, Election Commission;* ed Peradeniya Univ.; Class 1 Officer, Sri Lankan Admin. Service; Asst Commr of Elections 1983–2006, Deputy Commr 2006–10, Additional Commr 2010–11, apptd Commr 2011, Chair. Election Comm. 2015–. *Address:* Elections Secretariat, PO Box 02, Sarana Mawatha, Rajagiriya 10107, Sri Lanka (office). *Telephone:* (11) 2868441 (office). *E-mail:* election@slt.lk (office). *Website:* www.slelections.gov.lk (office).

DESHCHYTSYA, Andriy, BA, MA, PhD; Ukrainian diplomatist and politician; b. 22 Sept. 1965, Pervyatychi, Lviv region; ed Ivan Franko Lviv Nat. Univ., Univ. of Alberta, Canada; Press Sec., First Sec., Embassy in Warsaw 1996–99; Sr Co-ordinator, Polish-American-Ukrainian Co-operation Initiative 1999–2001; Counsellor, Embassy in Helsinki 2001–04, Counsellor, Minister-Counsellor, Embassy in Warsaw 2004–06, Spokesperson, Ministry of Foreign Affairs 2006–08, Amb. to Finland 2008–12, Amb.-at-Large 2012–, Special Rep. of OSCE Chairperson-in-Office for Conflict Resolution 2013–14; Acting Minister of Foreign Affairs Feb.–June 2014. *Address:* c/o Ministry of Foreign Affairs, 01018 Kyiv, pl. Mykhailivska 1, Ukraine.

DESHPANDE, Shashi, BA, MA, BL; Indian writer; b. 19 Aug. 1938, Dharwad, Karnataka; d. of Adya Rangacharya and Sharada Adya; m. D. H. Deshpande 1962; two s.; ed Univs of Mumbai and Bangalore; fmrly worked for a law journal and magazine; full-time writer 1970; mem. Sahitya Akademi Bd for English 1989–94; Thirumathi Rangammal Prize 1984, Sahitya Akademi Award 1991, Padma Shri 2009. *Film script:* Drishti 1990. *Publications include:* The Dark Holds No Terrors (Nanjangud Thirumalamba Award) 1980, If I Die Today 1982, Come Up and Be Dead 1982, Roots and Shadows 1983, That Long Silence (Sahitya Akademi Award 1990) 1988, The Binding Vine 1993, A Matter of Time 1999, Small Remedies 2000, Moving On 2004, In the Country of Deceit 2008, Shadow Play 2013, Strangers to Ourselves 2015; short stories: The Legacy and Other Stories 1978, It Was Dark 1986, The Miracle and Other Stories 1986, It Was the Nightingale 1986, The Intrusion and Other Stories 1994, The Stone Women 2000, Collected Stories, Vol. I 2003, Vol. II 2004; non-fiction: Writing from the Margin and other essays 2003, Opening Scenes (trans. from Kannada of memoirs and a play), Deliverance (novel translated from Marathi). *Leisure interests:* reading, music. *Address:* c/o Alison M. Bond Agency, 155 West 72nd Street, New York, NY 10023, USA (office); Apt 401, Vaishnavi Paradise, 47th Cross, Jayanagar 8th Block, Bangalore 560070, India (home). *Telephone:* (80) 26636228 (home). *Fax:* (80) 26641137 (home). *E-mail:* shashideshpande04@gmail.com (home).

DESJOYEAUX, Michel; French yachtsman; b. 16 July 1965; three c.; began racing at age 18; set fastest time ever and became first man to achieve a solo, non-stop navigation of the world in less than 100 days (93 days 4 hours approx.); Whitbread 1985–86, winner Triangle du Soleil 1986, Twostar (with Jean Maurel) 1992, Solitaire du Figaro 1992, 1998, 2007, Leg 2 of Mini Transat 1991, Transat AG2R 1992, Figaro French Championships 1996, 1998, Multihull Trophy 1994, Spi Ouest 1997, Leg 1 of Transat AG2R (with Frank Cammas) 1998, Grand Prix de Fécamp (with Alain Gautier) 1999, Grand Prix de la Trinité (with Alain Gautier) 2000, Vendée Globe 2001, 2009, transatlantic sprint Route du Rhum 2002, Transat 2004 and others; pioneered the swing keel early 1990s. *Publication:* L'enfant de la vallée des fous 2001, Coureur des océans, Vues de mer 2009. *Address:* Mer Agitée SARL, Port La Forêt, 29940 La Forêt Fouesnant, France (office). *Telephone:* 2-98-56-82-85 (office). *Fax:* 2-98-56-81-69 (office). *E-mail:* micheldesjoyeaux@meragitee.com (office). *Website:* www.meragitee.com (office).

DESLONGCHAMPS, Pierre, OC, OQ, BSc, PhD, DSc, FRS, FRSC, FCIC; Canadian chemist and academic; *Professeur-Associé of Chemistry, Laval University;* b. 8 May 1938, St-Lin, Québec; s. of Rodolphe Deslongchamps and Madeleine Magnan; m. 1st Micheline Renaud 1960 (divorced 1975); two s.; m. 2nd Shirley E. Thomas 1976 (divorced 1983); m. 3rd Marie-Marthe Leroux 1987; ed Univ. of Montréal, Univ. of New Brunswick; Post-doctoral Fellow, Harvard Univ. 1965–66; Asst Prof., Univ. of Montréal 1966–67; Asst Prof., Sherbrooke Univ. 1967–68, Assoc. Prof. 1968–72, Prof. of Chem. 1972–2005, Prof. Emer. 2006–; Professeur-Associé of Chem., Laval Univ. 2008–; Exec. Scientific Advisor, OmegaChem Inc.; mem. Canadian Cttee of Scientists and Scholars 1993–, Soc. française de Chimie 1995; Foreign Assoc. mem. Acad. des Sciences de Paris 1995; Fellow, AAAS and numerous other academic socs; Fellow, Guggenheim Foundation 1979, World Innovation Foundation (WIF), UK 2002; Dr hc (Université Pierre et Marie Curie, Paris VI) 1983, (Bishop's Univ., Lennoxville, Québec) 1984, (Univ. of Montreal) 1984, (Laval Univ.) 1984, (Univ. of New Brunswick) 1985, (Univ. of Moncton) 1995; A.P. Sloan Fellowship 1970–72, Scientific Prize of Québec 1971, E.W.R. Steacie Fellowship and Prize 1971–74, Médaille Vincent, Asscn francophone pour le savoir (ACFAS) 1975, Izaak Walton Killam Memorial Scholarships in Science 1976–77, Merck, Sharp and Dohme Lectures Award, Chemical Inst. of Canada 1976, ACFAS Médaille Pariseau 1979, Marie-Victorin Prize, Prov. of Québec 1987, Alfred Bader Award in Organic Chem., Canadian Soc. for Chem. (CSC) 1991, Canada Gold Medal for Science and Eng, Natural Sciences and Eng Research Council of Canada 1993, R.U. Lemieux Award for Organic Chem., CSC 1994, CSC Bernard Belleau Award 2011. *Publications:* Stereoelectronic Effects in Organic Chemistry 1983; more than 230 publs in the area of organic synthesis and devt of concept of stereoelectronic effects in organic chem. *Leisure interests:* reading, fishing, hunting. *Address:* Département de chimie, Faculté des sciences et de génie, Université Laval, 1045 avenue de la Médecine, Pavillon Alexandre-Vachon, Québec, QC G1V 0A6 (office); 5607, St Louis Street, Apt 403, Lévis, QC G6V 4G2, Canada (home). *Telephone:* (418) 603-3753 (home). *E-mail:* pierre.deslongchamps@chm.ulaval.ca (office). *Website:* www.chm.ulaval.ca (office).

DESMARAIS, André, OC, OQ; Canadian business executive; *Deputy Chairman, President and Co-CEO, Power Corporation of Canada;* b. 26 Oct. 1959; s. of Paul Desmarais, Sr; brother of Paul Desmarais, Jr (q.v.); m. France Chrétien; four c.; joined Power Corpn of Canada 1983, Deputy Chair., Pres. and Co-CEO 1996–; Co-Chair. Power Financial Corpn 1996–; mem. Hong Kong Chief Exec.'s Council of Int. Advisers 1998–2007; Chair. Foundation Baxter & Alma Ricard; mem. Int. Council J.P. Morgan Chase & Co. Inc. 2003–10; Dir Great West Life Co. Inc., Investors Group Inc.; Dr hc (Concordia Univ.), (Université de Montréal), (McGill

Univ.). *Address:* Power Corporation of Canada, 751 Victoria Square, Montreal, PQ H2Y 2J3, Canada (office). *Telephone:* (514) 286-7425 (office). *Fax:* (514) 286-7484 (office). *E-mail:* info@powercorporation.com (office). *Website:* www.powercorporation.com (office).

DESMARAIS, Paul, Jr, OC, BComm, MBA; Canadian business executive; *Chairman and Co-CEO, Power Corporation of Canada;* b. 3 July 1957; s. of Paul Desmarais, Sr (q.v.); brother of André Desmarais (q.v.); m. Hélène Desmarais; four c.; ed McGill Univ., Institut Européen d'Admin des Affaires (INSEAD), France; with S.G. Warburg & Co. Ltd, London 1979–80; Planning Man. Standard Brands Inc., NY 1980–81; Dir of Planning Power Corpn of Canada (financial services and communications co.) 1981–82, Vice-Pres. 1982–91, Vice-Chair. 1991–96, Chair. and Co-CEO 1996–; Vice-Pres. Power Financial Corpn 1984–86, Pres. and COO 1986–90, Vice-Chair. 1989–90, Chair. 1990–2005, Chair. Exec. Cttee 2005–08, Co-Chair. 2008–; Exec. Vice-Chair., then Exec. Chair. Man. Cttee Pargesa Holding SA 1991–2003, Co-CEO 2003–13, Chair. 2013; Chair. and CEO Parfinance, France 1993–98 (co. dissolved 1998); Dir and mem. Exec. Cttee IGM Financial Inc., Investors Group Inc., Mackenzie Inc., Great-West Lifeco Inc., The Great-West Life Assurance Co., Great-West Life & Annuity Insurance Co., London Insurance Group Inc., London Life Insurance Co., Pargesa Holding SA, Groupe Bruxelles Lambert SA; Dir Gesca Ltd, La Presse Ltd, Les Journaux Trans-Canada Inc. 1996, Suez, Total, Lafarge; mem. Strategic Cttee Imerys, then Vice-Chair. of the Bd; Chair. Advisory Bd SAGARD Private Equity Partners; Chair. HEC Int. Advisory Bd; mem. Bd of Dirs and Int. Council INSEAD; mem. Global Advisory Council Merrill Lynch; Hon. Chair. Faculty of Man., Int. Advisory Bd McGill Univ.; Canada 125 Medal 1992, Insigne d'Officier de l'Ordre de la Couronne (Belgium) 1994, Queen's Golden Jubilee Medal 2002, Officer of the Nat. Order of Québec 2009. *Leisure interests:* golf, skiing, hunting, fishing. *Address:* Power Corporation of Canada, 751 Victoria Square, Montreal, PQ H2Y 2J3, Canada (office). *Telephone:* (514) 286-7424 (office). *Fax:* (514) 286-7484 (office). *E-mail:* info@powercorporation.com (office). *Website:* www.powercorporation.com (office).

DESMAREST, Thierry Jean Jacques; French mining engineer and business executive; *Honorary Chairman, Total SA;* b. 18 Dec. 1945, Paris; s. of Jacques Desmarest and Edith Desmarest (née Barbe); m. Annick Geraux 1972; one s. two d.; ed École Polytechnique, Ecole Nat. Supérieure des Mines de Paris; qualified mining engineer; worked as engineer with Mines Directorate, New Caledonia 1971–73, Dir of Mines and Geology 1973–75; Tech. Adviser, Ministry of Industry 1975–78, of Econ. 1978–80; mem. Bd Dirs, Total Algeria 1981–83, Dir for Latin America and W Africa 1983–87, for the Americas, France, Far East and Dir Man. and Econ. Div. 1988–89, CEO Total Exploration Production 1989–95, mem. Exec. Cttee 1989–95, Chair. and CEO Total 1995–99, Chair. and CEO TotalFina 1999–2000, Chair. and CEO TotalFinaElf 2000–03, Chair. and CEO Total SA 2003–07, Chair. 2007–10, 2014–15, Hon. Chair. 2010–14, 2015–; Chair. Total Foundation; Dir Sanofi-Aventis, Air Liquide, Renault SA, Renault SAS, Bombardier; mem. Supervisory Bd Aveva; Pres. Fondation de l'École polytechnique –2014; Officier, Légion d'honneur 2004; Man. of the Year 1999, Nouvel Economiste. *Leisure interest:* skiing. *Address:* Total SA, 2 place Jean Millier, La Défense 6, 92078 Paris La Défense Cedex, France (office). *Telephone:* 1-47-44-22-44 (office); 1-47-44-22-33 (office). *Fax:* 1-47-44-49-53 (office). *E-mail:* thierry.desmarest@total.com (office). *Website:* www.total.com (office).

DESMAZIÈRES, Érik; French cartoonist and writer; b. 1948, Rabat, Morocco; ed Institut d'Etudes Politiques de Paris; spent childhood in Morocco before coming to France to study 1967, graduated 1971; studied engraving with Jean Delpech, with the encouragement of Philippe Mohlitz; work includes drawings and etchings in collections worldwide; mem. Editorial Bd Nouvelles de l'estampe magazine; Pres. Soc. des peintres-graveurs français 2006–; elected to Acad. des beaux-arts 2008; Grand Prix des arts de la ville de Paris 1978. *Works include:* La Tentation de saint Antoine (the Caprices series), L'Atelier René Tazé, La Rue de Marignan, La Rue Charles-Nodier, Le Quai de Montebello, as well as views of Amsterdam (performed on the occasion of his exhbn at the Rembrandhuis), Voyage au centre de la bibliothèque 2012. *Publications include:* illustrated books: Benito Cereno of Herman Melville for Les Bibliophiles de France 1980, Le tremblement de terre du Chili, Heinrich von Kleist (translated by G. La Flize) for Les Bibliophiles d'Automobile Club de France 1986, Une invitation au voyage by Olivier Rolin (work commissioned by Nat. Library of France on the occasion of the restoration of the Globes de Coronelli) 2005, Le Prince Pluie by Maxime Préaud (illustrated with engravings in mezzotint) 2009. *E-mail:* info@erikdesmazieres.fr. *Website:* erikdesmazieres.fr.

DESMOND-HELLMANN, Susan, MD, MPH; American oncologist, academic, business executive and university administrator; *CEO, Bill & Melinda Gates Foundation;* b. Reno, Nev.; ed Univ. of Nevada, Reno and Univ. of California, Berkeley School of Public Health; Adjunct Assoc. Prof. of Epidemiology and Biostatistics, Univ. of Calif., San Francisco, fmr Asst Prof. of Hematology-Oncology; Assoc. Dir Clinical Cancer Research, Pharmaceutical Research Inst., Bristol-Myers Squibb –1995; Clinical Scientist, Genentech Inc. 1995, Chief Medical Officer 1996, Exec. Vice-Pres. Devt and Product Operations and mem. Exec. Cttee 1999–2004, Pres. Product Devt and mem. Exec. Cttee 2004–09; Chancellor, Univ. of Calif., San Francisco 2009–13, also Arthur and Toni Rembe Rock Distinguished Prof.; CEO Bill & Melinda Gates Foundation 2014–; mem. US Dept of Health and Human Services Advisory Cttee on Regulatory Reform 2002; mem. Bd of Dirs Affymetrix 2004–, Biotechnology Industry Org. 2001–09, American Asscn for Cancer Research 2005–08; spent two years as visiting faculty mem., Uganda Cancer Inst. studying AIDS and cancer; also spent two years in pvt. practice; numerous honours and awards for work in oncology and AIDS research. *Address:* Bill & Melinda Gates Foundation, 500 5th Avenue North, Seattle, WA 98102, USA (office). *Telephone:* (206) 709-3100 (office). *Website:* www.gatesfoundation.org (office).

DESRAS, Simon Dieuseul; Haitian lawyer and politician; b. 18 Dec. 1967, Saut-d'Eau; s. of Guito Saint-Eloi and Yvonne Benicia Desras; m. Bianca Emmanuela Shinn 2000; ed Univ. d'État d'Haïti, Inst. Nat. d'Admin, de gestion et des hautes études internationales (INAGHEI), Norwalk Community Coll., Connecticut, USA; fmr mem. Int. Secr., Fédération nationale des étudiants haïtiens (Feneh); Prof. of Statistics, INAGHEI 1994, also Prof. of Physics, Lycée Jean Jacques Dessalines; Prof. of Math., Ecole de commerce Julien Craan, Port-au-Prince 1997; mem. Senate (upper house of parl.) for Centre 2000–01, 2011–16, Pres. of Senate 2012–15; Minister of Nat. Defence 2016, of the Environment 2016–17; mem. Fanmi Lavalas (political party); mem. Bar, Port-au-Prince 1999–.

DESSENS, C. W. M.; Dutch business executive; *Chairman of the Supervisory Board, GasTerra BV;* b. 30 Oct. 1947, Vlaardingen; ed Leiden Univ.; joined Directorate-Gen. for Industry and for Energy, Ministry of Econ. Affairs 1974, Dir-Gen. for Energy 1988–99; Dir-Gen. for Law Enforcement, Ministry of Justice 1999–2005; self-employed 2005–; mem. Supervisory Bd GasTerra BV (fmrly NV Nederlandse Gasunie) 2006–, Chair. 2007–, Chair. Cttee of Del. Mems; Chair. Stichting Aanpak Voertuigcriminaliteit (Foundation for Tacking Vehicle Crime); mem. Bd Meld Misdaad Anoniem; Chair. Exec. Bd CATO (CO2 Capture, Transport and Storage) project. *Address:* GasTerra BV, PO Box 477, 9700 AL Groningen (office); GasTerra BV, Rozenburglaan 11, 9727 DL Groningen, Netherlands (office). *Telephone:* (50) 364-86-48 (office). *Fax:* (50) 364-86-00 (office). *E-mail:* communicatie@gasterra.nl (office). *Website:* www.gasterra.com (office).

DESSERTINE, Philippe, PhD; French economist and academic; *Professor of Management Sciences, Institut d'administration des entreprises, Paris;* b. 12 Oct. 1963, Rouen; ed Lycée Saint-Joseph-de-Tivoli, Institut d'admin des entreprises, Bordeaux; Dir Inst. of Finance 2004–; Dir, Master of Financial Sciences degree, Univ. Paris Ouest-Nanterre La Défense 2009–; currently Prof. of Man. Sciences, Institut d'admin des entreprises, Univ. Paris 1 Panthéon-Sorbonne; mem. Haut Conseil des Finances Publiques 2013–. *Publications:* numerous papers in professional journals. *Address:* IAE de Paris, Centre Broca, 21 rue Broca, 75240 Paris Cedex 05, France (office). *Telephone:* 1-53-55-27-50 (office). *Fax:* 1-53-55-27-01 (office). *E-mail:* dessertine.iae@univ-paris1.fr (office). *Website:* www.iae-paris.com (office).

DESVIGNE, Michel; French landscape architect and author; *President, École nationale supérieure du paysage;* b. 1958, Montbéliard (Doubs), Franche-Comté; m. Christine Dalnoky 1988; ed Univ. of Lyon-II, École Nationale Supérieure du Paysage, Versailles; led various projects, alone or in collaboration with Christine Dalnoky, Michel Corajoud and Alexandre Chemetoff 1983–86; resident in Villa Medici, Rome 1986–87; co-f. agency Desvigne & Dalnoky 1988; works with architects including Renzo Piano, Richard Rogers and Norman Foster; with Christine Dalnoky developed projects in Paris, Lyon, Avignon, Montpellier, Rome and Antwerp; collaborated on Greenwich Peninsula Masterplan, London with Richard Rogers; worked on gardens of Walker Art Center, Minneapolis with Herzog and De Meuron; central square of Almere, Belgium with Rem Koolhaas, Millau viaduct with Norman Foster; participated in Lyon Confluence 2004; has taught at École Nationale Supérieure du Paysage, Versailles 1985–95; Visiting Prof., École Polytechnique Federale de Lausanne, Switzerland 1993, Architectural Inst., Geneva, Switzerland 1994–98, Harvard Univ., USA 1999, Architectural Asscn School of Architecture, London 2000; Perm. Prof., Accademia di Architettura di Mendrisio, Switzerland 2006–12; Pres. École nationale supérieure du paysage 2009–; Chevalier des Arts et des Lettres 2003; numerous prizes, including Lauréat du concours de l'Acad. de France à Rome (Architecture) 1986, 'Diploma com a Finalista', jury int. du prix européen du paysage Rosa Barba 2002, Civic Trust Award 2002, Medal of the Acad. of Architecture 2000, Grand Prix de l'urbanisme 2003, Lauréat du Grand Prix de l'urbanisme 2011, prix de l'aménagement urbain 2013. *Publications:* The Return of the Landscape (with Christine Dalnoky) 1997; several articles in L'architecture d'aujourd'hui. *Address:* École nationale supérieure du paysage, 10 rue du Maréchal Joffre, 78000 Versailles, France (office). *Telephone:* 1-39-24-62-00 (office). *Fax:* 1-39-24-62-01 (office). *Website:* www.ecole-paysage.fr (office).

DESYATNIKOV, Leonid Arkadievich; Russian composer; b. 1955, Kharkov, Ukraine; ed Leningrad State Conservatory, studied with Boris Arapov and Boris Tishchenko; Music Dir, Bolshoi Theatre 2009–10; mem. Composers' Union 1979–; State Prize of Russia 2003. *Films include:* as composer: Sunset 1990, Lost in Siberia 1991, Capital Punishment 1992, Touch 1992, Moscow Nights 1994, Katia Izmailova 1994, Hammer and Sickle 1994, Giselle's Mania 1995, The Prisoner of the Mountains 1996, The One Who is More Tender 1996, Moscow (Grand Prix, Int. Cinema Music Festival, Golden Ram Prize) 2000, His Wife's Diary 2000, Tycoon: A New Russian 2002, Captive 2008, Target 2011. *Works include:* opera: Poor Lisa, The Children of Rosenthal; ballet: Love Song in Minor, The Children of Rosenthal (special jury prize, Golden Mask National Theatre Prize 2006), Lost Illusions (Golden Mask Prize as Best Composer 2012); tango-operetta: Astor Piazzola's Maria de Buenos Aires; instrumental: The Right of Winter 1949, Sketches for Sunset 1992, Russian Seasons; vocal: The Gift 1981, Love and Death of a Poet 1989, The Leaden Echo 1990.

DETTORI, (Lanfranco) Frankie; Italian professional flat race jockey; b. 15 Dec. 1970, Milan; s. of 13-times Italian champion jockey Gianfranco Dettori and Iris Maria Niemen; m. Catherine Allen 1997; two s. three d.; has ridden races in England, France, Germany, Italy, USA, Dubai, Australia, Hong Kong and other countries in the Far East 1992–; 1,000 rides and 215 wins in UK 1995; horses ridden include Lamtarra, Barathea, Vettori, Mark of Distinction, Balanchine, Moonshell, Lochsong, Classic Cliché, Dubai Millennium, Daylami, Sakhee, Opinion Poll, Colour Vision; major race victories include St Leger (twice), The Oaks (twice), The Breeders Cup Mile, Arc de Triomphe (twice), French 2,000 Guineas (twice), English 1,000 Guineas, Queen Elizabeth II Stakes, Prix L'Abbaye, The Japan Cup (twice), The Dubai World Cup, Royal Ascot 2012, Canadian Int. Stakes 2012, Asian Trader, Sandown 2013, Breeders' Cup Juvenile Turf 2014, Emir's Trophy 2014, 2015, Caribbean Champion Stakes 2014, Lockinge Stakes 2014, Prix Jean Romanet 2014, Diamond Jubilee Stakes 2015, Derby 2015, Middle Park Stakes 2015, The Crown Prince Cup 2015, 2016, Prix de l'Arc de Triomphe 2015, Prix de Diane 2015, Irish Champion Stakes 2015; rode winners of all seven races at Ascot 1996; launched signature range of food 2001; associated with Godolphin team 1994–2012; Hon. MBE, Commendatore, Italy 2005; Jockey of the Year 1994, 1995, 2004, BBC Sports Personality of the Year 1996, Int. Sports Personality of the Year, Variety Club 2000, World's Best Jockey 2015. *Television includes:* Team Capt., A Question of Sport, BBC TV 2002–04. *Publications include:* A Year in the Life of Frankie Dettori 1996, Frankie: The Autobiography 2004, Frankie's: Recipes from an Italian Family (with Marco Pierre White) 2007. *Leisure interests:* golf, wine, cooking. *Address:* c/o Ray Cochrane, 10 Rectory Farm Road, Little Wilbraham, Cambridge, CB21 5LB, England (office).

DEUBA, Sher Bahadur, MA; Nepalese politician; b. 12 June 1946, Angra, Dadeldhura Dist; m. Dr Arju Rana Deuba; one s.; ed Tribhuvan Univ.; Chair. Far Western Students Cttee, Kathmandu 1965–68; served a total of nine years' imprisonment for political activities 1966–85; Founder-mem. and Pres. Nepal Students' Union 1971–80; active in Popular Movt for Restoration of Democracy in Nepal 1980; Research Fellow, LSE, UK 1988–90; mem. Parl. 1991–; Minister of Home Affairs; Leader Parl. Party, Nepali Congress 1994; Prime Minister 1995–97, 2001–02, 2004–05, 2017–18; Minister of Foreign Affairs and Defence 2001–02, also Minister of Agric. Devt, of Commerce, of Cooperatives and Poverty Alleviation, of Culture, Tourism and Civil Aviation, of Defence, of Energy, of Forest and Soil Conservation, of General Admin, of Health, of Information and Communication, of Industry, of Irrigation, of Land Reform and Man., of Livestock Devt, of Peace and Reconstruction, of Population and Environment, of Physical Infrastructure and Transportation, of Science and Tech., of Supplies, of Water Supply and Sanitation, of Women, Children and Social Welfare Devt and of Youth and Sports 2017–18; sentenced to two-year jail term for corruption July 2005, released Feb. 2006; Pres. Nepali Congress Party (Democratic) (merged again with Nepali Congress under Girja Prasad Koirala as Nepali Congress 2007) 2002–06, May–Sept. 2006; Pres. Nepali Congress Party 2016–; Vice-Pres. Socialist International 2008; Dr hc (Jawaharlal Nehru Univ.) 2016. *Address:* Nepali Congress (NC) Central Office, B.P. Smriti Bhawan, B.P.Nagar, Sanepa, Lalitpur, Nepal (office). *Telephone:* (1) 5183263 (office); (1) 4375376 (home). *Fax:* (1) 5183266 (office); (1) 4377307 (home). *E-mail:* info@nepal.gov.np (office); ncparty@wlink.com.np (office); piyushrl26@gmail.com. *Website:* www.nepalicongress.org (office).

DEUBET, Kalzeubé Pahimi; Chadian economist and politician; m. Neldjikingar Madjimta; fmr teacher; fmr Gov. Chari-Baguirmi and Bahr el-Ghazal regions; fmr Minister of the Civil Service and of Communication; fmr Chef de cabinet to Pres.; Dir-Gen. Société Cotonnière du Tchad –2013; Prime Minister 2013–16 (resgnd); fmr mem. Rassemblement pour la Démocratie et le Progrès; mem. Mouvement patriotique du Salut. *Address:* c/o Office of the Prime Minister, BP 463, N'Djamena, Chad (office).

DEUTCH, John M., BA, BS, PhD; American chemist, academic and fmr government official; *Institute Professor, Department of Chemistry, Massachusetts Institute of Technology;* b. 27 July 1938, Brussels, Belgium; s. of Michael J. Deutch and Rachel Fischer Deutch; m. Pat Lyons; three s.; ed Amherst Coll., Massachusetts Inst. of Tech.; Systems Analyst, Office of US Sec. of Defense 1961–65; Fellow, NAS/NRC, Nat. Bureau of Standards 1966–67; Asst Prof., Princeton Univ. 1967–70; mem. Faculty, MIT 1970–, Prof. of Chem. 1971–; Chair. Dept of Chem. 1976–77, Dean, School of Science 1982–85, Provost 1985–90, Inst. Prof. 1990–; Dir of Energy Research, Dept of Energy 1977–79, Acting Asst Sec. 1979, Under-Sec. 1979–80; Under-Sec. for Acquisition and Tech., Dept of Defense 1993–94, Deputy Sec. 1994–95, President's Foreign Intelligence Advisory Cttee 1990–94; Dir CIA 1995–96; Sec., Energy Advisory Bd 2010; mem. White House Science Council 1985–89; mem. Bd of Dirs Citigroup Inc. 1987–93, 1996–, Citibank NA 1987–93, 1996–98, Cummins Engine Co. 1997–, Raytheon Co. 1998–, Cheniere Energy Inc. 2007–; mem. Nat. Petroleum Council 2008, ACS, American Physical Soc., American Acad. of Arts and Sciences, Council on Foreign Relations, Trilateral Comm. 1991; Research Fellow, Alfred P. Sloan Foundation 1967–69; Guggenheim Fellow 1974; Fellow, American Acad. of Arts and Sciences 1978; Trustee, Center for American Progress, Mass Hospital Physician Org., Museum of Fine Arts, Boston; Hon. DSc (Amherst Coll.) 1978; Hon. DPhil (Lowell) 1986; recipient of awards from Dept of State 1980, Dept of Energy 1980, Dept of Defense 1994, 1995, Dept of Army 1995, Dept of Navy 1995, Dept of Air Force 1995, Coast Guard 1995, Central Intelligence Distinguished Intelligence Medal 1996, Intelligence Community Distinguished Intelligence Medal 1996, Speaker Thomas P. O'Neill Award, Greater Boston Federal Exec. Bd 2002, Aspen Strategy Group Leadership Award 2004. *Publications:* research articles. *Address:* Department of Chemistry, Massachusetts Institute of Technology, 77 Massachusetts Avenue, Room 6-215, Cambridge, MA 02139, USA (office). *Telephone:* (617) 253-1479 (office). *Fax:* (617) 258-5700 (office). *E-mail:* jmd@mit.edu (office). *Website:* web.mit.edu/chemistry/deutch (office).

DEUTSCH, David Elieser, MA, DPhil, FRS; British physicist, academic and author; *Non-stipendiary Visiting Professor, Centre for Quantum Computation, University of Oxford;* b. 1953, Haifa, Israel; with Centre for Quantum Computation, Clarendon Lab., Univ. of Oxford 1990–, becoming Non-stipendiary Visiting Prof.; Hon. Fellow, Wolfson Coll. Oxford; Distinguished Fellow, British Computer Soc. 1998, Paul Dirac Prize and Medal, Inst. of Physics 1998, Fourth Int. Award on Quantum Communication for "theoretical work on Quantum Computer Science" 2002, Edge of Computation Science Prize, Edge Foundation, Inc. 2005, Dirac Prize 2018. *Achievements include:* pioneered the field of quantum computers by being the first person to formulate a specifically quantum computational algorithm 1985; proponent of the many-worlds interpretation of quantum mechanics and of the multiverse hypothesis. *Publications include:* The Fabric of Reality 1997 (translated into German, Italian, Spanish, Japanese, Finnish, Brazilian Portuguese, Russian, Chinese, French and Polish), The Beginning of Infinity 2011; several scientific papers in professional journals on quantum computing, quantum theory and parallel universes. *Address:* Centre for Quantum Computation, The Clarendon Laboratory, Parks Road, Oxford, OX1 3PU, England (office). *E-mail:* david.deutsch@qubit.org (office). *Website:* daviddeutsch.physics.ox.ac.uk (office); daviddeutsch.org.uk.

DEUTSCH, Tamás; Hungarian politician; b. 27 July 1966, Budapest; s. of György Deutsch and Julianna Takács; m. Ágnes Sarolta Für (divorced); four s. two d.; ed Eötvös Loránd Univ., Budapest; Co-founder Alliance of Young Democrats (FIDESZ) 1988, mem. Nat. Steering Cttee 1988–90, campaign chief during 1990 local elections and 1998 parl. elections, party Vice-Pres. 1993–2003, Head of FIDESZ Budapest org. 2001–04, Leader Budapest FIDESZ-Hungarian Christian Democratic Alliance jt faction 2002–04, Head of President's Office 2006–09; mem. Budapest Municipal Ass. 2002–04; mem. Nat. Ass. (Parl.) 1990–2009, Deputy Speaker 2004–06, Deputy Leader FIDESZ Parl. Group 1990–2009; Minister for Youth and Sport 1999–2002; MEP 2009–, Vice-Chair. Cttee on Budgetary Control; 2012–14; lawyer in pvt. practice 2012–14; Vice-Chair. Hungarian Olympic Cttee 1999–2001, Deputy Chair. 2012–14; Pres. MTK Sports Asscn 2010–14; mem. Budapest Municipal Ass. 2002–03; Hon. Citizen, Csongrád County 2013. *Publications:* contributing author to Gyermekek a Jognak Asztalánál (Children at the Table of the Law) 1991. *Leisure interests:* film, football. *Address:* European Parliament, rue Wiertz, Altiero Spinelli 09E169, 1047 Brussels, Belgium (office). *Website:* deutsch.fidesz-eu.hu.

DEV, Kapil (see KAPIL DEV).

DEV SEN, Nabaneeta, BA, MA, AM, PhD; Indian writer and academic; b. 13 Jan. 1938, Calcutta (now Kolkata); d. of Narendra Dev and Radharani Devi; m. Amartya Sen (divorced); three d.; ed Calcutta (now Kolkata) Univ., Jadavpur Univ., Harvard Univ., Indiana Univ., USA; Bengali writer; Researcher, Newnham Coll., Cambridge 1961–64; Asst Prof. of Comparative Literature, Jadavpur Univ. 1970–72, Assoc. Prof. 1972–83, Prof. 1983–2002, Chair., Dept of Comparative Literature 1987–89; Maytag Prof. of Comparative Literature, Univ. of Colorado, USA 1988–89; Visiting Fellow, St Antony's Coll., Oxford 1997; Radhakrishnan Memorial Lecturer, Oxford Univ. 1996–97; Founder and Pres. West Bengal Women Writers Asscn; Vice-Pres. Indian Nat. Comparative Literature Asscn; mem. Bharatiya Jnanpith Award Language Advisory Cttee 1975–90, Advisory Bd Bengali, Sahitya Akademi 1978–82; Kavi Prize for Poetry 1976, Pratisuti Award for Literary Criticism 1979, Prasad Prize for Poetry 1985, Sisir Kumar Prize 1986, Kalkut Prize 1988, Celli Award 1993, Sanskritiki Award 1994, Saratchandra Award 1994, Archana Choudhury Memorial Prize 1998, Marwari Mitra Samsad Samman for Literature 1998, Harmony Award 1998, Shatabir Kanya Award 1999, Sahitya Akademi Award 1999, Bishwa Banga Sammelan Award 2000, Rajiv Gandhi Memorial Millennium Gold Medal 2000, Bharat Nirman Award 2000, Padma Shri 2000, Bimal Mitra Memorial Award 2001, Mahadevi Verma Memorial Award 2001, Shreyasi Samman for Literature 2001, Lifetime Achievement Award, Bangla Acad. 2003, Pratima Mitra Memorial Prize 2004, Narayan Gangopadhyay Smarak Puraskar 2006, Saratchandra Smriti Puraskar 2007, Mystic Kalinga Literary Award 2017, Bharatiya Bhasha Parishad Award, Gouridevi Memorial Award, Prasad Puraskar. *Publications include:* fiction: Ami Anupan 1978, Prabaase Doibera Bashe 1985, Swabhumi 1986, Sheet Saahasik Hemanta lok 1988, Ekti Dupur 1996, Baamaa Bodhini 1997, Deshaantar 1998, Thhikaanaa 1999, Maayaa Roye Gelo 2000, Shani-Rabi 2001, Paari 2002, Ural 2003, Dashti Upanyas 2003, Titli 2004, Albatross 2004, Ekati Iitibachak Premkahini 2005, Dwiragaman 2006, Ramdhan Mittir Lane 2006; juvenile fiction: Samudrer Sannyasini 1979, Icchamati 1995, Kayak 1996, Palachpurer Picnic 1997, Buddhi Bechaar Saudagar 1999, Chakum-chukum 2000, Saat Kanyer Desh 2000, Monkemoner Galpa 2002, Chhotoder Galpasangra 2005, Rankineer Rajyapat 2005, Sandesher Galpa 2006, Ek Dazan Roopkatha 2006; non-fiction: Karuna tomaar Kon Path Diye 1978, Ishwarer Pratidwandwi o Anyanya Prabandha 1978, Truckbahoney MacMahoney 1983, Hey Purna Taba Charaner Kachhe 1984, Birashaiba Santakabi ebang Birashaiba Sadhana 1987, Tin Bhubaner Parey 1990, Bhraamer Nabaneeta 2006; poetry: Pratham Pratyay 1959, Swaagata Debdut 1974, Shreshthha Kabita 1989. *Address:* 72 Hindustan Park, Kolkata 700 029, India (home). *Telephone:* (33) 24641603 (home).

DEV VRAT, Acharya, BEd; Indian social worker, educationalist and state official; *Governor of Himachal Pradesh;* b. 18 Jan. 1959; ed Punjab and Kurukshetra Univs, All India Council of Naturopathy; Prin., Samprati Gurukul (residential school), Kurukshetra 1981–2015; Gov., Himachal Pradesh 2015–. *Publications include:* Swasthya ka Anmol Marg – Prakritik Chikitsa, Gurukul Kurukshetra ka Gauravshali Itihaas. *Address:* Governor's Secretariat, Raj Bhavan, Shimla 171 002, Himachal Pradesh, India (office). *Telephone:* (177) 2624152 (office). *Fax:* (177) 2624814 (office). *E-mail:* governorsecy-hp@nic.in (office). *Website:* himachalrajbhavan.nic.in (office).

DEVA, Prabhu; Indian actor, choreographer and director; b. 3 April 1973, Mysore; s. of Mugur Sundar; m. Ramlath 1995 (divorced 2011); three c. (one died 2008); currently Chair. and Dir Prabhudeva's Dance Acad., Singapore; launched dance school in Dubai 2009; Life mem. Int. Film and TV Research Centre, Asian Acad. of Film and TV; Padma Shri Award 2019. *Films include:* choreographer: Agni Nakshatram 1988, Vetri Vizha 1989, Raja Vikramarka 1990, Idhayam 1991, Kshana Kshanam 1991, Gharaana Mogudu 1992, Mechanic Alludu 1993, Rakshana 1993, Kadhalan 1994, Bombay 1995, Minsaara Kanavu (Nat. Award) 1997, Pukar 2000, Tappu Chesi Pappu Koodu 2002, Khushi 2003, Samba 2004, Lakshya (Nat. Award, Star Screen Award, Filmfare Award) 2004, Nuvvostanante Nenoddantana (also directed) (Filmfare Award) 2005, Jillunu Oru Kaadhal 2006, Sivaji 2007, Aegan 2008, Endhiran 2010, Dhoni 2012, Rowdy Rathore (also dir) 2012, Oh My God 2012, Ramaiya Vastavaiya (also dir) 2013, Boss 2013, R... Rajkumar (also dir) 2013, Happy New Year 2014, Action Jackson (also dir) 2014; directed: Paurnami (also writer) 2006, Pokkiri (also writer) (Vijay Award, Mathubhumi Award) 2007, Shankardada Zindabad 2007, Villu 2009, Wanted 2009, Engeyum Kadhal 2010, Singh is Bling 2015. *Films include:* actor: Indhu 1994, Kaadhalan 1994, Mr. Romeo 1996, VIP 1997, Love Story 1999 1998, Ninaivirukkum Varai 1999, Time 1999, Eazhaiyin Sirippil 2000, Ullam Kollai Poguthae 2001, Charlie Chaplin 2002, One Two Three 2002, Kalyana Ramudu 2003, Engal Anna 2004, Style 2006, Michael Madana Kamaraju 2008, Urumi 2011, ABCD 2013, ABCD 2 2015.

DEVAKULA, Pridiyathorn, Mom Rajawongse, BA (Econ), MBA; Thai fmr government official and fmr central banker; b. 15 July 1947, Bangkok; s. of Prince Prididebyabongs Devakula and Mom Taengthai Devakula; m. Prapapan Devakula Na Ayudhya; two s. one d.; ed Wharton School, Univ. of Pennsylvania, USA, Thammasat Univ., Bangkok; joined Thai Farmers Bank 1971, Dir and Sr Exec. Vice-Pres. –1990; Govt Spokesperson for Prime Minister Gen. Chatichai Choonhavan 1990–91; Deputy Minister of Commerce 1991–92; Pres. Export-Import Bank of Thailand 1993–2001; Gov. Bank of Thailand 2001–06; Deputy Prime Minister and Minister of Finance 2006–07 (resgnd); Deputy Prime Minister 2014–15; mem. Wharton School Exec. Bd for Asia; Kt, Order of The Crown of Thailand; Kt Grand Cross, Order of The White Elephant; Grand Companion, Order of Chula Chom Klao; Hon. DBA (Chulalongkorn Univ.) 2002, (Mahasarakam Univ.) 2003, (Chiang Rai Rajabhat Univ.) 2008, Hon. DEcons (Sripatum Univ.) 2003, (Univ. Thai Chamber of Commerce) 2006, (Thammasat Univ.) 2008, Dr hc (Rangsit Univ.) 2013, (Kasembundit Univ.) 2017. *Leisure interest:* golf. *Address:* 33 Serivilla, Soi 7, Srinakarin Road 55, Nongborn, Praves, Bangkok 10250, Thailand (home). *Telephone:* (2) 399-1599 (home). *Fax:* (2) 399-1745 (home). *E-mail:* prideva@gmail.com.

DEVANEY, John Francis, CEng, FIEE, FIMechE; British business executive; *Chairman, Tersus Energy Ltd;* b. 25 June 1946; s. of George Devaney and Alice Ann Devaney; two s. one d.; ed St Mary's Coll., Blackburn and Univ. of Sheffield; worked for Perkins Engines 1968–69, mfg positions in Peterborough 1968–76, Project Man., Ohio, USA 1976–77, Pres. 1983–88, Group Vice-Pres. European Components Group, Peterborough 1988, Group Vice-Pres. Enterprises Group, Toronto, Canada 1988–89; Chair., CEO and Group Vice-Pres. Kelsey-Hayes Corpn, Detroit, Mich., USA 1989–92; Man. Dir Eastern Electricity PLC (later Eastern Group PLC) 1992, CEO 1993, Exec. Chair. 1995–98; Dir EXEL Logistics (formed from merger of Nat. Freight Corpn with Ocean Group) 1996, Chair. 2000–02; Chair. Marconi PLC (later Telent PLC) 2002–07; Founder and Chair. British Energy; Chair. Liberata –2002; Chair. Nat. Air Traffic Services (NATS) 2005–14; Chair. Tersus Energy Ltd 2005–, Cobham PLC 2010–; fmr Chair. EA Technology; Pres. Electricity Asscn 1994–95, Inst. for Customer Services 1998; mem. Bd of Dirs Northern Rock 2007–10; fmr mem. Bd of Dirs HSBC Bank PLC, British Steel PLC. *Leisure interests:* skiing, golf, tennis, sailing. *Address:* Tersus Energy Ltd, 44 Kensington Park Gardens, London, W11 2QT, England (office). *Telephone:* (20) 3174-2270 (office). *Fax:* (20) 7221-5410 (office). *E-mail:* power@tersusenergy.com (office). *Website:* www.tersusenergy.com (office).

DEVE GOWDA, Haradanahalli Dodde Gowda; Indian politician; *President, Janata Dal—Secular;* b. 18 May 1933, Haradanahalli; s. of Dodde Gowda and Devamma Gowda; m. Chennamma; four s. two d.; ed govt polytechnic inst.; trained as civil engineer; ran contracting business; mem. Congress Party 1953–62 (resigned 1962); mem. Karnataka State Legis. Ass. 1962–89, Leader of Opposition 1972–77; imprisoned during state of emergency in 1970s; Minister of Public Works and Irrigation, Karnataka –1980; Pres. Janata Dal 1994, currently Pres. Janata Dal—Secular; Chief Minister of Karnataka 1994–96; fmr mem. Lok Sabha; Leader of multiparty United Front 1996; Prime Minister 1996–97, Minister of Home and Agric., Science and Tech., Personnel and Atomic Energy 1996–97. *Address:* Janata Dal—Secular, 5 Safdarjung Lane, New Delhi 110 003, India (office). *Telephone:* (11) 23794499 (office); (11) 3794747 (home). *E-mail:* jdsecular2013@gmail.com (office). *Website:* www.jds.ind.in (office); hddevegowda.in.

DEVEDJIAN, Patrick; French lawyer and politician; b. 26 Aug. 1944, Fontainebleau (Seine-et-Marne); m. Sophie Vanbremeersch 1969; four c.; ed Université Panthéon-Assas Paris II; fmr mem. Occident group; admitted to Paris Bar 1970; joined Gaullist movt 1971; helped establish RPR party 1976; Mayor of Antony (Hauts-de-Seine) 1983–2001; mem. Assemblée Nat. for Hauts-de-Seine 1986, re-elected 1988, 1993, 1997, 2002, 2005; Vice-Pres. Mouvement européen (France) 2002; Minister for Local Liberties 2002–04, for Industry 2004–05, Minister in the Office of the Prime Minister, in charge of Implementation of the Econ. Stimulus Plan 2008–10; adviser to Nicolas Sarkozy during presidential bid 2007; Exec. Sec.-Gen. Union pour un Mouvement Populaire (UMP) 2007–08; Pres. Conseil général des Hauts-de-Seine 2007–15, Conseil départemental des Hauts-de-Seine 2015–; Chair. Paris Métropole 2014–15. *Website:* www.patrickdevedjian.fr.

DEVERS, Gail, BA; American athlete; b. 19 Nov. 1966, Seattle, Wash.; m. 1st Ron Roberts 1988 (divorced 1992); m. 2nd Mike Phillips; three d.; ed Univ. of California, Los Angeles; holds record for most World Championship gold medals won by a woman (five): 100m. 1993, 100m. hurdles 1993, 1995, 1999, 4x100m. relay 1997; Olympic champion 100m. 1992, 1996; Olympic gold medal 4x100m. relay 1996; won IAAF Grand Prix final 100m. hurdles 2000, 2002; won World Cup 100m. hurdles 2002; US champion 100m. hurdles (seven times); est. Gail Devers Foundation; inducted into Nat. Track & Field Hall of Fame 2011, United States Olympic Hall of Fame 2012; NCAA Silver Anniversary Award 2013. *Address:* c/o Gail Devers Foundation, 6555 Sugarloaf Parkway, Suite 307-137, Duluth, GA 30097, USA.

DEVESHWAR, Yogesh Chander; Indian business executive; *Chairman, ITC Ltd;* b. 4 Feb. 1947, Lahore, British India; ed Indian Inst. of Tech., Delhi, Harvard Business School, USA, Cornell Univ., USA; joined ITC Ltd 1968, man. buyout adviser to corp. HQ, Kolkata 1974, Gen. Man. packaging and printing plant, Chennai 1978, mem. Bd of Dirs 1984–, Chair. Tobacco Div. 1991–94, Chair. ITC Ltd 1996–17, Chair. (non-Exec.) 2017–; Chair. and Man. Dir Air India 1991–94; apptd Pres. Confed. of Indian Industry 2005 (also mem. Bd of Dirs); Chair. Woodlands Hospital and Medical Research Centre Ltd (also mem. Bd of Dirs), Surya Nepal Pvt. Ltd (also mem. Bd of Dirs); Dir (non-exec.) HT Media Ltd –2011; mem. Bd of Dirs, West Bengal Industrial Devt Corpn Ltd, Reserve Bank of India; mem. Bd of Govs Indian School of Business; fmr Chair. Bd of Govs Indian Inst. of Man.; Man. Entrepreneur of the Year, Ernst & Young 2001, Business Person of the Year Award, UK Trade and Investment 2006, Hall of Pride, Indian Science Congress 2006, Sustainable Asset Management/Sustainable Performance Group Sustainability Leadership Award 2007, Global Leadership Award, US-India Business Council, US Chamber of Commerce 2010, Padma Bhushan 2011, Banga Vibhushan 2017. *Address:* ITC Ltd, 37 J. L. Nehru Road, Kolkata 700 071, India (office). *Telephone:* (33) 22889371 (office). *Website:* www.itcportal.com (office).

DEVGN, Ajay; Indian actor, film director and film producer; b. (Vishal Veeru Devgan), 2 April 1969, New Delhi; s. of Veeru Devgan and Veena Devgan; m. Kajol Devgan 1999; one s. one d.; ed Bappu School, Juhu, Mithibai Coll.; Padma Shri 2016. *Films include:* Phool Aur Kaante (Filmfare Award) 1991, Jigar, Dil Hai Betaab 1992, Sangram 1993, Dhanwaan 1993, Dilwale 1994, Vijaypath 1994, Suhaag 1994, Hulchul 1995, Haqeeqat 1995, Diljale 1996, Jaan 1996, Itihaas 1997, Ishq 1997, Zakhm (Nat. Film Award) 1998, Major Saab 1998, Pyar To Hona Hi Tha 1998, Dil Kya Kare 1999, Kachche Dhaage 1999, Hum Dil De Chuke Sanam 1999, Lajja 2001, Deewane 2000, Raju Chacha (producer) 2000, Lajja 2001, Yeh Raaste Hain Pyaar Ke 2001, Company 2002, The Legend of Bhagat Singh (Nat. Film Award, Filmfare Critics Award) 2002, Deewangee (Filmfare Award) 2002, Bhoot 2003, Gangaajal 2003, LOC Kargil 2003, Khakee 2004, Raincoat 2004, Yuva 2004, Blackmail 2005, Apaharan 2005, Golmaal 2006, Omkara 2006, Cash 2007, Sunday 2008, U, Me aur Hum (producer, dir) 2008, Golmaal Returns 2008, London Dreams 2009, All the Best (Aprasara Award, Stardust Award) 2009, Rajneeti 2010, Once Upon a Time in Mumbai 2010, Aakrosh 2010, Golmaal 3 2010, Toonpur Ka Superrhero 2010, Dil Toh Baccha Hai Ji 2011, Singham 2011, Bol Bachchan 2012, Satyagraha 2013, Action Jackson 2014, Singham Returns 2014, Drishyam 2015. *Address:* Sea Cliff, 1st Floor, Gandhigram Road, Juhu, Mumbai (home); 5/6, Sheetal Apartments, Ground Floor, Opposite Chandan Cinema, Juhu, 400 049, India (home). *Telephone:* (22) 6200253 (home); (22) 6201977 (home). *Website:* www.ajaydevgn.com.

DEVINSKY, Ferdinand, DSc; Slovak medicinal chemist, academic and politician; b. 17 Aug. 1947, Bratislava; m.; two c.; ed Slovak Univ. of Tech., Bratislava; researcher, Slovakofoarma 1970–72; Lecturer, Comenius Univ., Bratislava 1972–2002, Rector 1997–2003, now Rector Emer., Head of Dept, Faculty of Pharmacy 1990; research studies in UK 1986–87, 1991–2007, Belgium, USA, Germany 1991; elected mem. Parl. (Slovak Democratic and Christian Union) 2002, Chair. Cttee for Educ., Science, Sport, Youth, Culture and Media 2002–06; mem. Steering Cttee European Univ. Asscn 2006; mem. Governing Bd Slovak Academic Ranking and Rating Agency; Hon. Sr Research Fellow, King's Coll. London, UK; Stella Della Solidarieta Italiana (Commendatore) 2004; Jubilee Medal, Charles Univ., Prague 1998. *Publications include:* numerous scientific papers and textbooks. *Leisure interests:* tennis, any creative work.

DeVITO, Danny; American actor and director; b. 17 Nov. 1944, New Jersey; m. Rhea Perlman 1982; two s. two d.; ed American Acad. of Dramatic Arts, Wilfred Acad. of Hair and Beauty Culture; Co-founder and Co-Chair. Jersey Films (production co.); Golden Globe Award for Taxi 1979, Emmy Award 1981. *Stage appearances include:* The Man with a Flower in His Mouth, Down the Morning Line, The Line of Least Existence, The Shrinking Bride, Call Me Charlie, Comedy of Errors, Merry Wives of Windsor, Three by Pirandello, One Flew over the Cuckoo's Nest. *Films include:* Dreams of Glass 1970, Lady Liberty 1971, Hot Dogs for Gauguin 1972, Scalawag 1973, Hurry Up or I'll Be 30 1973, One Flew over the Cuckoo's Nest 1975, Deadly Hero 1976, The Money 1976, Car Wash 1976, The Van 1977, The World's Greatest Lover 1977, Goin' South 1978, Swap Meet 1979, Going Ape 1981, Terms of Endearment 1983, Romancing the Stone 1984, Johnny Dangerously 1984, Head Office 1985, Jewel of the Nile 1985, Wiseguys 1986, Ruthless People 1986, My Little Pony (voice) 1986, Tin Men 1987, Throw Momma from the Train (also dir) 1987, Twins 1988, War of the Roses (also dir) 1989, Other People's Money 1991, Batman Returns 1992, Hoffa (also producer, dir) 1992, Jack the Bear 1993, Look Who's Talking Now (voice) 1993, Renaissance Man 1994, Junior 1994, Get Shorty (also co-producer) 1995, Matilda (also dir, co-producer) 1996, Space Jam (voice) 1996, Mars Attacks 1996, The Rainmaker 1997, LA Confidential 1997, Living Out Loud (also producer) 1998, Man on the Moon (also producer) 1999, The Virgin Suicides 1999, The Big Kahuna 1999, Drowning Mona (also producer) 2000, Screwed 2000, Heist 2001, What's the Worst That Could Happen? 2001, Death to Smoochy (also dir) 2002, Duplex (voice, also dir) 2003, Anything Else 2003, Big Fish 2003, Family of the Year 2004, Catching Kringle (voice) 2004, Christmas in Love 2004, Marilyn Hotchkiss' Ballroom Dancing and Charm School 2005, Be Cool (also producer) 2005, The OH in Ohio 2006, Bye Bye Benjamin (exec. producer) 2006, Even Money 2006, Relative Strangers (also producer) 2006, Deck the Halls 2006, The Good Night 2007, Reno 911!: Miami 2007, Nobel Son 2007, Just Add Water 2008, House Broken, Solitary Man 2009, When in Rome 2010, Girl Walks Into a Bar 2011, The Lorax (voice) 2012, Hotel Noir 2010, All the Wilderness 2014, Wiener-Dog 2016. *Television includes:* Taxi (series, also dir), Mary (dir), Valentine, The Rating Game (dir), All the Kids Do It, A Very Special Christmas Party, Two Daddies? (voice), The Selling of Vince DeAngelo (dir), Amazing Stories (also dir), The Simpsons (voice), It's Always Sunny in Philadelphia (series) 2006–. *Address:* Jersey Films, 10351 Santa Monica Blvd., Suite 200, Los Angeles, CA 90025, USA. *Telephone:* (310) 203-1000.

DEVLIN, Dean; American actor, screenwriter and producer; b. 27 Aug. 1962; George Pal Memorial Award 1998. *Film produced:* The Patriot 2000, Eight Legged Freaks 2002, Cellular 2004, Who Killed the Electric Car? 2006, Flyboys 2006. *Films written and produced:* Stargate 1994 (Best Picture, Acad. of Science Fiction, Fantasy and Horror Films, Readers' Choice Award, Sci-Fi Universe magazine), Independence Day 1996 (Best Picture, Acad. of Science Fiction, Fantasy and Horror Films, People's Choice Best Picture), Godzilla 1998. *Film screenplay:* Universal Soldier 1992. *Films acted in:* My Bodyguard 1980, The Wild Life 1984, Real Genius 1985, City Limits 1985, Martians Go Home 1990, Moon 44 1990, Total Exposure 1991. *TV series:* The Visitor (creator, exec. producer) 1997, Leverage (series) 2008–09. *TV appearances in:* North Beach 1985, Rawhide 1985, Hard Copy 1987, Generations 1989; guest appearances in: LA Law, Happy Days, Misfits of Science. *Address:* 11601 Wilshire Boulevard, Suite 2150, Los Angeles, CA 90025-0509, USA.

DEVONSHIRE, 12th Duke of, cr. 1694, Baron Cavendish, Earl of Devonshire, Marquess of Hartington, Earl of Burlington, Baron Cavendish (UK); **Peregrine Andrew Morny Cavendish,** Kt, KCVO, CBE, DL; British horse racing executive and landowner; b. 27 April 1944; s. of 11th Duke of Devonshire and Hon. Deborah Vivian Freeman Mitford; m. Amanda Carmen Heywood-Lonsdale 1967; one s. two d.; ed Eton Coll. and Exeter Coll., Oxford; Sr Steward, Jockey Club 1989–94; Chair. British Horseracing Bd 1993–96; Dir Sotheby's Holdings Inc. 1994–, Deputy Chair. 1996–; Chair. Devonshire Arms Hotel Group; HM's Rep. at Ascot 1997–2011; succeeded to the title of Duke of Devonshire 2004; Trustee, Yorkshire Dales Nat. Park Millennium Trust, Sheffield Galleries and Museums Trust, Wallace Collection 2007–; Chancellor Univ. of Derby 2008–. *Address:* Chatsworth, Bakewell, Derbyshire DE45 1PP, England (home). *Telephone:* (1246) 565300 (office). *Website:* www.chatsworth.org (office).

DEVOS, Elizabeth (Betsy), BSc; American business executive, philanthropist and government official; *Secretary of Education;* b. 8 Jan. 1958, Holland, Mich.; d. of Edgar Prince and Elsa Prince (née Zwiep); m. Richard M. DeVos, Jr; four c.; ed Calvin Coll.; Market Research Analyst, Amway Corpn 1979–81; Co-Chair., Kent County Republican Finance Cttee 1983–84, Chair. 1985–88, 1996–; Republican Nat. Committeewoman, State of Mich. 1992–97, Chair., Mich. State Republican Party 1996–2000; mem. Nat. Republican Cttee 1996–, Republican Congressional Leadership Council; Pres. Windquest Group (investment firm); Co-Founder Dick and Betsy DeVos Family Foundation; mem. Bd of Dirs Blodgett Memorial Medical Center 1986–, Ada Christian School 1992–; US Sec. of Educ. 2017–. *Address:* Department of Education, 400 Maryland Avenue, SW, 7E-247, Washington, DC 20202, USA (office). *Telephone:* (202) 401-2000 (office). *Fax:* (202) 401-0596 (office). *Website:* www.ed.gov (office).

DEVRIES, William Castle, MD; American surgeon; b. 19 Dec. 1943, Brooklyn, New York; s. of Henry Devries and Cathryn L. Castle; m. Ane Karen; seven c.; ed Univ. of Utah, Army Medical Dept Basic Officer program; Intern, Duke Univ. Medical Center 1970–71, Resident in Cardiovascular and Thoracic Surgery 1971–79; Asst Prof. of Surgery, Univ. of Utah 1979–84; Chief of Thoracic Surgery, Salt Lake Hosp. –1984; Pres. De Vries & Assocs 1988–99; Surgeon, Hardin Memorial Hosp., Elizabethtown, Ky 1999–; joined US Defense Department as medical contractor Walter Reed Army Medical Center, Washington, DC, joined US Army Reserve as Lt Col 2000–; Fellow, American Coll. of Surgeons, American Coll. of Cardiology, American Coll. of Chest Physicians; mem. American Medical Asscn, Soc. of Thoracic Surgeons. *Achievements include:* implanted first permanent artificial heart 1982. *Publications include:* published several papers and case reports in various journals. *Leisure interest:* sports.

DEVROYE, Luc, BEng, PhD; Belgian/Canadian computer scientist and academic; *Professor of Computer Science, McGill University;* b. Tienen, Belgium; m. Bea Van Nuffel; ed Univ. of Leuven, Osaka Univ., Japan, Univ. of Texas at Austin, USA; Asst Prof., McGill Univ. 1977–81, Assoc. Prof. 1981–87, Prof. of Computer Science and Assoc. mem. Dept of Math. and Statistics 1987–, James McGill Prof. 2003–; working at Computational Geometry Lab., Carleton Univ., Ottawa 2006; fmr mem. editorial bds of numerous Canadian and int. math. and computer science journals; Hon. mem. Belgian Statistical Soc. 1997; Dr hc (Catholic Univ. of Louvain) 2002, (Universiteit Antwerpen) 2012; E.W.R. Steacie Memorial Fellowship 1987, Research Award, Alexander von Humboldt Foundation (Germany) 2004, Killam Prize, Canada Council for the Arts 2005, Gold Medal, Statistical Soc. of Canada 2008. *Address:* School of Computer Science, McGill University, Office MC300N, 3480 University Street, Montreal, PQ H3A 0E9 (office); 3425 Redpath, Montreal, PQ H3G 2G2, Canada (home). *Telephone:* (514) 398-3738 (office); (514) 849-1564 (home). *E-mail:* lucdevroye@gmail.com (office). *Website:* www.cs.mcgill.ca (office); luc.devroye.org.

DEW, John Anthony; British diplomatist and artist; b. 3 May 1952; m. Marion Bewley Kirkwood 1975; three d.; ed Univ. of Oxford; began print making at Ruskin School of Drawing, Oxford 1973, his drawings have been used for various book covers by Editorial StockCero; joined FCO 1973, Second Sec., British Embassy, Caracas 1975–78, worked in Perm. Under-Sec.'s Dept and EC Dept, FCO early 1980s, Falkland Islands Dept 1982–83, 1988–90, UK Perm. Del. to OECD, Paris 1983–87, Repub. of Ireland Dept, FCO 1987–88, British Embassy, Dublin 1992–96, Minister and Deputy Head of Mission, Madrid 1996–2000, Head of Latin America and Caribbean Dept 2000–03, secondment to Lehman Brothers investment bank, London 2003–04, Amb. to Cuba 2004–08, to Colombia 2008–12. *Website:* www.johndew.co.uk.

DEW, HE Cardinal John Atcherley; New Zealand ecclesiastic; *Archbishop of Wellington;* b. 5 May 1948, Waipawa; s. of George Dew and Joan Dew; ed St Joseph's Coll., Marist Brothers Juniorate, Tuakau, Holy Name Seminary, Holy Cross Coll., Inst. of St Anselm, UK; spent year working at Bank of New Zealand, Waipukurau, Anderson's Nurseries, Napier and studying horticulture; ordained priest, Archdiocese of Wellington 1976; Asst Priest, St Joseph's Parish, Upper Hutt 1976–79; served in Cook Islands in Diocese of Rarotonga 1980–82; returned to Wellington 1982; responsible for Archdiocesan Youth Ministry and Cook Islands Māori Community 1983–87; mem. staff, Holy Cross Coll., Mosgiel, NZ nat. Seminary 1988–91; Parish Priest, St Anne's Parish, Newtown 1993–95; Auxiliary Bishop of Wellington 1995–2004, consecrated Titular Bishop of Privata 1995, Coadjutor Archbishop of Wellington 2004–05, Archbishop of Wellington 2005–; fmr Sec., NZ Catholic Bishops' Conf., Conf. Deputy for Nat. Cttee for Professional Standards and for Finance and Conf. Rep. on Nat. Council for Young Catholics, currently Pres. NZ Catholic Bishops' Conf.; fmr Moderator of Tribunal; Bishop of Mil. Ordinariate of NZ 2005–; apptd by Pope Benedict XVI to serve as a Synod father for Synod of Bishops on The New Evangelization for Transmission of Christian Faith 2012; 'relator' for one of large English-speaking groups in Third Extraordinary Gen. Ass. of Synod of Bishops on Pastoral Challenges of Family in Context of Evangelization 2014; Pres. Fed. of Catholic Bishops' Confs of Oceania –2015; cr. Cardinal (Cardinal-Priest of Sant'Ippolito) 2015. *Address:* Archdiocese of Wellington, 22–30 Hill Street, Wellington 6015 (office); PO 1937, Thorndon, Wellington 6140, New Zealand (office). *Telephone:* (4) 496-1737 (office). *Fax:* (4) 496-1754 (office). *E-mail:* info@wn.catholic.org.nz (office). *Website:* www.wn.catholic.org.nz (office).

DEWAEL, Patrick; Belgian politician; b. 13 Oct. 1955, Lier; m. Marleen Van Doren; three c.; ed Vrije Universiteit Brussel; solicitor 1977–85; Sec., House of Reps 1985; mem. Parl. (Vlaamse Liberalen en Demokraten—VLD) for Tongeren-Maaseik Dist 1985–95, for Hasselt-Tongeren-Maaseik Constituency 1995, Leader, Liberal Party Group (VLD) 1992–99; Community Minister for Culture 1985–92; Mayor of Tongeren 1995–; Minister-Pres. of Govt of Flanders 1999–2001, Minister of Govt of Flanders for Finance, Budget, Foreign Policy and European Affairs, Minister-Pres. of Govt of Flanders 2001–03; Deputy Prime Minister and Minister of the Interior 2003–07 (resgnd), reappointed Minister of Interior Dec. 2007, resgnd March 2008; Pres. Chamber of Reps 2008–10, June–Oct. 2014; Kt, Grand Cross Order of Merit (Italy) 2002, Kt, Grand Cross in the Order of Leopold II 2014. *Publications include:* De warme hand 1991, Wederzijds respect. De gevaren van het Blok 2001, Vooruitzien 2001, Het Vlaams Manifest. Meer ruimte voor de regio's 2002, Eelt op mijn ziel 2007. *Address:* Office of the Mayor, Maastrichterstraat 10, 3700 Tongeren, Belgium. *E-mail:* steven.coenegrachts@stadtongeren.be. *Website:* www.dewael.com/NL.

DEWAR, Robert (Bob) Scott, CMG; British diplomatist (retd); b. 10 June 1949; m. Jennifer Dewar; one s. one d.; joined FCO 1973, Near East/N Africa Dept 1973–74, Third Sec., Chancery (Information), Colombo 1974–78, Rhodesia Dept, FCO 1978, Commonwealth Co-ordination Dept 1978–79, West African Dept 1980–81, First Sec. (Commercial) and Head of Chancery, Luanda 1981–84, South Asian Dept, FCO 1984–87, Deputy Head of Mission, Dakar 1988–92, Deputy High Commr, Harare 1992–96, Amb. to Madagascar 1996–99, High Commr to Mozambique 2000–03, Amb. to Ethiopia and Perm. Rep. to the African Union 2003–07, High Commr to Nigeria (also accred as Perm. Rep. to Econ. Community of West African States—ECOWAS) 2007–11 (retd); mem. Bd of Trustees, British Red Cross.

DEWEY, John Frederick, MA, PhD, DSc, ScD, FRS, FGS; British professor of geology; *Distinguished Emeritus Professor, University of California, Davis and University College, Oxford;* b. 22 May 1937, London; s. of John Edward Dewey and Florence Nellie Mary Dewey; m. Frances Mary Blackhurst 1961; one s. one d.; ed Bancroft's School, Univ. of London; lecturer, Univ. of Manchester 1960–64, Univ. of Cambridge 1964–70; Prof. Univ. of Albany, NY 1970–82; Prof. Univ. of Durham 1982–86; Prof. of Geology, Univ. of Oxford 1986–2000, Fellow Univ. Coll. 1986–, Sr Research Fellow 2001–07, Emer. Fellow 2007–; Prof. of Geology, Univ. of Calif., Davis 2000–07, Distinguished Prof. 2001, Distinguished Emer. Prof. 2007–; mem. Academia Europaea 1990, Australian Acad. of Science; Foreign mem. NAS 1997; Hon. MRIA; T.N. George Medal, Univ. of Glasgow 1983, Lyell Medal, Geological Soc. of London 1984, Penrose Medal, Geological Soc. of America 1992, Arthur Holmes Medal, European Union of Geosciences 1993, Wollaston Medal, Geological Soc. of London 1999, Fourmarier Medal, Belgian Acad. of Sciences 2000. *Publications:* 138 papers in scientific journals. *Leisure interests:* skiing, tennis, cricket, model railways, watercolour painting, British, Irish and American music 1850–1950. *Address:* Department of Geology, One Shields Avenue, University of California, Davis, CA 95616-8605, USA (office); University College, Oxford, OX1 4BH (office); Sherwood Lodge, 93 Bagley Wood Road, Kennington, OX1 5NA, England (home). *Telephone:* (1865) 735525 (home). *E-mail:* jfdewey@ucdavis.edu (office). *Website:* www.geology.ucdavis.edu (office).

DeWINE, R. Michael (Mike), BS, JD; American lawyer, academic and politician; *Governor of Ohio;* b. 5 Jan. 1947, Springfield, Ohio; s. of Richard DeWine and Jean DeWine; m. Frances Struewing 1967; four s. four d.; ed Miami Univ., Ohio Northern Univ.; admitted to Bar, Ohio 1972, US Supreme Court 1977; Asst Prosecuting Attorney, Green Co., Xenia, Ohio 1973–75, Prosecuting Attorney 1977–81; mem. Ohio State Senate 1981–82; mem. US House of Reps, Washington, DC 1983–90; Lt-Gov. of Ohio 1991–94; Senator from Ohio 1995–2007; Visiting Scholar, Center for Political Studies, Cedarville Univ. 2007; Co-Chair. Corp. Investigations Group, Keating Muething & Klekamp, Cincinnati 2007–; Attorney-Gen. of State of Ohio 2010–; Gov. of Ohio 2019–; Republican. *Address:* Office of the Attorney-General, 30 East Broad Street, 14th Floor, Columbus, OH 43215 (office); Office of the Governor, Riffe Center, 30th Floor, 77 South High Street, Columbus, OH 43215-6117; 2587 Conley Road, Cedarville, OH 45314-9525, USA (home). *Telephone:* (614) 466-4986 (office); (614) 752-9777 (office). *Website:* www.ohioattorneygeneral.gov (office); governor.ohio.gov (office).

DeWOLFE, Richard B., BAS; American business executive; *Chairman, Manulife Financial Corporation;* ed Boston Univ., American Coll. of Corp. Dirs; Man. Partner, DeWolfe & Co. LLC; fmr Chair. and CEO The DeWolfe Companies, Inc. (acquired by Cendant Corpn 2002); Founder and fmr Chair. Reliance Relocations Services, Inc.; mem. Bd of Dirs Manulife Financial Corpn 2004–, Vice-Chair. 2012–13, Chair. 2013–; mem. Bd of Dirs Avantair, Inc.; Trustee, Boston Univ. (fmr Chair. Bd of Trustees); Hon. Dir The Boston Center for Community and Justice. *Address:* Manulife Financial Corpn, 200 Bloor Street East, NT 11, Toronto, ON M4W 1E5, Canada (office). *Telephone:* (416) 926-3000 (office). *Fax:* (416) 926-5410 (office). *E-mail:* info@manulife.com (office). *Website:* www.manulife.com (office).

DEXTER, Hon. Darrell, BEd, LLB, MLA; Canadian politician; b. 10 Sept. 1957, Halifax, NS; s. of Elvin Dexter and Florence Dexter; m. Kelly Wilson; one s.; ed Dalhousie Univ., Univ. of King's Coll., Halifax; served in Canadian Navy, attained rank of Sub-Lt; worked as lawyer in pvt. practice in Halifax; fmr Chair. Dartmouth Downtown Devt Corpn; elected Dartmouth City Councillor 1994; mem. Legis. Ass. (regional parl.) for Cole Harbour 1998–2013; mem. New Democratic Party, Leader 2001–13; Premier of Nova Scotia 2009–13, also Pres. Exec. Council, Minister of Policy and Priorities, Minister of Intergovernmental Affairs, Minister of Aboriginal Affairs and Minister responsible for Mil. Relations. *Address:* c/o Nova Scotia New Democratic Party, 1660 Hollis Street, Halifax, NS B3J 1V7, Canada (office). *Website:* www.ns.ndp.ca (office).

DHALIWAL, Daljit, MA; British journalist; b. 8 Sept. 1962, London; m. Lee Patrick Sullivan (divorced); ed Univ. of East London, Univ. of London; reporter for BBC, London 1990, NI Corresp. and Anchor, BBC World –1995; reporter ITN, London 1995, Anchor, World News for Public TV, Channel 4 News and World Focus 1996–2001; Anchor, Your World Today and World Report CNN (Cable Network News) Int., Atlanta, Ga USA 2002–04; Anchor, Wide Angle (Public Broadcasting System), New York, 2002, 2006–07, Anchor, Global Watch 2008, host, Foreign Exchange with Daljit Dhaliwal 2008–09; Anchor and Correspondent, Al-Jazeera 2010–; moderator and host, UN confs in New York and The Hague; Judge, Amnesty Int. Media Awards, BAFTA Awards; Dr hc (Univ. of East London). *Address:* HD Reps, Suite 2800, 800 3rd Ave, New York, NY 10022, USA (office). *Telephone:* (212) 292-3800 (office). *E-mail:* david@hdreps.com (office). *Website:* www.hdreps.com (office).

DHANABALAN, Suppiah, BA; Singaporean company director and fmr government official; b. 8 Aug. 1937; m. Tan Khoon Hiap; one s. one d.; ed Victoria School and Univ. of Malaya; Sr Industrial Economist, Deputy Dir (Operations and Finance) Econ. Devt Bd 1961–68; Vice-Pres., Exec. Vice-Pres. Devt Bank of Singapore (now DBS Group Holdings Ltd) 1968–78, Chair. 1998–2005; mem. Parl. 1976–96; Sr Minister of State 1978–80; Minister of Foreign Affairs 1980–88, Culture 1981–84, Community Devt 1984–86, Nat. Devt 1987–92, of Trade and Industry 1992–93; Chair. Parameswara Holdings 1994–2012; Sr Adviser, Nuri Holdings (S) Pte. Ltd 1994–99; Chair. Singapore Airlines Ltd 1996–98; Chair. Temasek Holdings (Pte.) Ltd (govt-owned investment co.) 1996–2013. *Leisure interests:* reading, golf. *Address:* c/o Temasek Holdings (Pte.) Ltd, 60B Orchard Road, #06-18, Tower 2, The Atrium@Orchard, Singapore 238891, Singapore (office).

DHANAPALA, Jayantha, BA, MA; Sri Lankan diplomatist and consultant; *President, Pugwash Conferences on Science and World Affairs;* b. 30 Dec. 1938, Colombo; s. of James Angus and Kumarihamy Dhanapala Ratemahatmaya; m. Maureen Elhart; one s. one d.; ed Univ. of Peradeniya, Univ. of London, UK, American Univ., Washington, DC, USA; corp. exec. in pvt. sector 1962–65; joined Foreign Service 1965, diplomatic appointments in People's Repub. of China, UK and USA 1965–77; Dir Non-Aligned Movt Div., Ministry of Foreign Affairs 1978–80, Dir-Gen. and Additional Sec., Ministry of Foreign Affairs 1992–94; Deputy High Commr to India 1981–83; Amb. and Perm. Rep. to UN, Geneva,

Switzerland 1984–87, Dir UN Inst. for Disarmament Research 1987–92; Amb. to USA (also accred to Mexico) 1995–97; apptd Pres. Review and Extension Conf. of Treaty on the Non-Proliferation of Nuclear Weapons 1995; UN Under-Sec.-Gen. for Disarmament Affairs 1998–2003; Sec.-Gen. Secr. for Co-ordinating the Peace Process 2004–05 (resgnd); Chief Negotiator in talks with LTTE 2004–05, Sr Adviser to Pres. 2005–07; Visiting Simons Prof., Simon Fraser Univ., Vancouver, Canada Jan.–April 2008; Overseas Visiting Scholar, St Johns Coll., Cambridge Univ. Oct.–Dec. 2009; Sr Visiting Scholar, US Inst. of Peace March–June 2010; Chair. UN Univ. Council 2006–08; Pres. Pugwash Confs on Science and World Affairs 2007–; Deputy Chair. Stockholm Int. Peace Research Inst. 2012–; Dir (non-exec.) Dialog Telekom 2007–, Cargils (Ceylon) Ltd 2008–; mem. Canberra Comm., Australia 1995–96; Diplomat-in-Residence, Center for Non-Proliferation Studies, Monterey Inst. of Int. Studies, Calif., USA 1997–98; mem. Advisory Bd, Geneva Centre for Democratic Control of Armed Forces 2003–12, Advisory Bd of Stanford Inst. for Int. Studies 2003–, Int. Advisory Bd of Bonn Int. Center for Conversion 2003–, Weapons of Mass Destruction Comm. 2004–06, Int. Advisory Group, ICRC 2004–07, Int. Advisory Bd, Center for Nonproliferation Studies, Monterey Inst. of Int. Studies 2006–; Dr hc (Univ. of Peradeniya) 2000, (Univ. of Sabaragamuwa) 2003, Dubna Int. Univ. of Nature, Society and Man, Russia 2009, Hon. DHumLitt (Monterey Inst. of Int. Studies) 2001, Hon. DSc in Social Sciences (Univ. of Southampton) 2003; Winner, Herald Tribune Essay Competition 1957, Jit Trainor Award for Distinction in the Conduct of Diplomacy, Georgetown Univ., USA 1995, Lifetime Achievement Award, Monterey Inst. for Int. Studies, USA 1998, Leadership in Crisis Award, Ploughshares Fund and Fourth Freedom Forum 2000, Pax Christi Ireland Peace Award 2002, Alan Cranston Peace Award, Global Security Inst., USA 2002, Mohamed Sahabdeen Award 2005, Mohamed Sahabdeen Award for Peace and Int. Understanding 2005, Sri Lankan of the Year, Lanka Monthly Digest 2006, Sean MacBride Peace Prize 2007, Simons Foundation Award for Distinguished Global Leadership in the service of Peace and Disarmament 2008, Sarvodaya Trust Fund Annual Nat. Award 2008. *Publications include:* China and the Third World 1984, Nuclear War, Nuclear Proliferation and their Consequences (co-author) 1985, Multilateral Diplomacy and the NPT: An Insider's Account 2005. *Leisure interests:* reading, watching sports, theatre and film. *Address:* 25/6 Pepiliyana Road, Nugegoda, Sri Lanka (home). *Telephone:* (11) 2856297 (home). *E-mail:* jdhanapala@yahoo.co.uk (office). *Website:* www.jayanthadhanapala.com (home).

DHANARAJAN, Tan Sri Dato' Gajaraj (Raj), BSc, MSc, PhD; Malaysian educationalist; *Chairman, Board of Governors, Wawasan Open University;* ed Univ. of Madras, India, Univ. of London and Aston Univ., UK; Research Officer and Lecturer, School of Biological Sciences, Univ. of Science, Malaysia, Assoc. Prof. of Distance Educ. and Deputy Dir Centre for Off-Campus Studies; Assoc. Dir (Academic) Open Learning Inst. of Hong Kong (now Open Univ. of Hong Kong) 1989–91, Dir 1991–95, Prof. 1992–95, Prof. Emer. 1995–; Pres. and CEO The Commonwealth of Learning, Vancouver 1995–2004; Council Mem., United Nations Univ. 2010–16; fmr Sec.-Gen. Asian Asscn of Open Univs; fmr Vice-Chancellor and CEO Wawasan Open Univ., now Chair. Bd of Govs; fmr educational adviser, Int. Union for the Conservation of Nature; has served as consultant for World Bank, Asian Development Bank, African Development Bank, Inter-American Bank, Caribbean Development Bank; Hon. Fellow, Coll. of Preceptors, London 1996–; Order of Chivalry, State of Penang 1994; 10 hon. degrees; Asian Asscn of Open Univs Meritorious Service Award 1997, Lifelong Contribution to Open Education, Int. Council for Distance Educ. 2013. *Address:* Board of Governors, Wawasan Open University, 54 Jalan Sultan Ahmad Shah, 10050 Penang, Malaysia (office). *Website:* www.wou.edu.my/board-of-governors (office).

DHANOA, Air Chief Marshal Birender Singh; Indian air chief officer; *Chief of the Air Staff, Indian Air Force;* b. 7 Sept. 1957, SAS Nagar, Punjab; s. of Sarayan Singh Dhanoa; m. Kamalpreet Dhanoa; one s.; ed Rashtriya Indian Military Coll., Nat. Defence Acad., Defence Services Staff Coll.; commissioned in the Indian Air Force as a fighter pilot 1978; qualified flying instructor and has flown various types of fighter aircraft including HJT-16 Kiran, MiG-21, SEPECAT Jaguar, MiG-29 and Su-30MKI; fmr Sr Air Instructor and Chief Air Instructor, Defence Services Staff Coll.; also worked as leader of Indian Air Force Training Team abroad; squadron leader, Kargil War 1999; held several key appointmens including Dir Targeting Cell Air Headquarters, Dir Fighter Operations and War Planning Headquarters Western Air Command, Asst Chief of Air Staff (Intelligence), Air Headquarters, Sr Air Staff Officer of Eastern and Western Air Command, Air Officer Commanding-in-Chief of South-Western Air Command; Vice-Chief of the Air Staff 2015–16; Chief of the Air Staff 2016–; Hon. ADC to the President 2015; Vayu Sena Medal 1999, Yudh Seva Medal 1999, Ati Vishisht Seva Medal 2015, Param Vishisht Seva Medal 2016. *Address:* Indian Air Force, Directorate of Public Relations, Ministry of Defence, Room Number 91, South Block, New Delhi 110011, India (office). *Telephone:* (11) 23019745 (office). *Fax:* (11) 23010231 (office). *E-mail:* proiaf.dprmod@nic.in. *Website:* indianairforce.nic.in (office).

DHAWAN, Neelam, MBA; Indian computer industry executive; *Managing Director, Hewlett Packard India;* m. Atul Dhawan; two c.; ed St Stephen's Coll., Delhi, Faculty of Man. Studies, Delhi Univ.; began career working for HCL Computers Technologies 1980s; Vice-Pres. Sales and Marketing, IBM India 1995–99; joined Compaq 1999, Vice-Pres. Customer Solutions Group, Hewlett Packard India (following HP and Compaq merger) –2005, Man. Dir Hewlett Packard India 2008–, also responsible for Tech. Solutions Group; Man. Dir Microsoft India 2005–08. *Leisure interests:* puzzles and crosswords, cooking Sunday meals. *Address:* Hewlett-Packard India Sales Pvt. Ltd, 24 Salarpuria Arena, Adugodi Hosur Road, Bangalore 560 030, India (office). *Telephone:* (80) 2563-3555 (office). *Fax:* (80) 2563-3222 (office). *Website:* www.hp.com/country/in/en (office).

DHIEU DAU, Stephen, BCom; South Sudanese banker and politician; b. Melut County, Upper Nile State; ed Univ. of Manchester, UK, Univ. of Cairo, Egypt, Higher Inst. of Financial Banking Studies, Khartoum, Sudan Univ. of Science and Tech.; joined Central Bank of Sudan 1991, undertook professional courses in various banking operations in the Gulf and UK; provided technical support to Sudan People's Liberation Movt (SPLM) negotiating team on wealth-sharing at peace talks in Naivasha, Kenya during negotiation of Comprehensive Peace Agreement (CPA) 2005, mem. CPA wealth-sharing Cttee; Minister of Trade and Industry, Govt of Autonomous region of S Sudan 2005–10; Minister of Petroleum and Mining 2014–16, of Trade and Industry April–July 2016, of Finance and Econ. Planning 2016–18. *Address:* c/o Ministry of Finance and Economic Planning, Juba, South Sudan (office). *Telephone:* 122249178 (office). *E-mail:* kitoundo@hotmail.com (office).

DHOININE, Ikililou, PhD; Comoran pharmacist, politician and head of state; b. 14 Aug. 1962, Djoiezi; m. Hadidja Aboubacar Boinariziki; two c.; ed univ. Gamal Abdel Nasser, Conakry, Guinea; trained as pharmacist, owner of pharmacy, Moheli; leader of several dels on funding, vaccination, etc to WHO; worked for several years in Ministry of Finance; Interim Pres. Nzwani island March 2008; Vice-Pres. of the Comoros 2008–11, responsible for Finance, Budget and Promotion of Women Entrepreneurs 2008–10, for Land Settlement, Infrastructure, Town Planning and Housing 2010–11, Pres. of the Comoros 2011–16. *Address:* Office of the Head of State, Palais de Beit Salam, BP 521, Moroni, Comoros (office). *Telephone:* 7744808 (office). *Fax:* 7744829 (office). *E-mail:* presidence@comorestelecom.km (office). *Website:* www.beit-salam.km (office).

DHOLAKIA, Baron (Life Peer), cr. 1997, of Waltham Brooks in the Co. of West Sussex; **Rt Hon. Navnit Dholakia,** PC, OBE, DL, BSc; British politician; *Deputy Leader, Liberal Democrats Peers;* b. 4 March 1937, Tabora, Tanganyika (now Tanzania); m.; two d.; ed P.P. Inst., Bhavnagar, Gujerat, India, Brighton Tech. Coll.; fmr magistrate; fmr mem. Bd of Visitors, HM Prison Lewes; mem. (Liberal Democrat), House of Lords 1997–, Asst Whip 1997–2002, Deputy Leader, Liberal Democrat Peers 2004–; Pres. Liberal Democrat party 1999, 2002, Spokesperson on Home Affairs; Pres. Nat. Asscn for the Care and Resettlement of Offenders (NACRO); mem. Council, Howard League for Penal Reform; mem. Man. Bd, Policy Research Inst. on Ageing and Ethnicity; mem. Advisory Cttee on Business Appointments; Vice-Pres. Mental Health Foundation, Pallant House Gallery, Chichester; DL W Sussex 1999; Melvin Jones Fellowship, Lions Clubs International; Hon. DIur (Univ. of Hertfordshire) 2009, (York) 2010, (East London) 2010; Asian of the Year 2000, Bhartiya Samman Award (India) 2003. *Publications:* various articles on criminal justice matters. *Leisure interests:* photography, cooking, gardening, walking. *Address:* House of Lords, Westminster, London, SW1A 0PW, England (office). *Telephone:* (20) 7219-5203 (office). *Fax:* (20) 7219-3423 (office). *E-mail:* dholakian@parliament.uk (office). *Website:* www.parliament.uk/biographies/lords/lord-dholakia/2685 (office).

DHONI, Mahendra Singh; Indian professional cricketer; b. 7 July 1981, Ranchi, Bihar (now in Jharkhand); s. of Pan Singh and Devaki Devi; m. Sakshi Singh Rawat 2010; one d.; wicketkeeper; right-handed batsman; right-arm medium pace bowler; plays for Bihar 1999–2004, Jharkhand 2004–, India Capt. One-Day Int. (ODI) side 2007–16, Test side 2008–14, Chennai Super Kings 2008–15, 2018–, Rising Pune Super Giants 2016–17, Asia XI; First-class debut: 1999/2000; Test debut: India v Sri Lanka, Chennai 2–6 Dec. 2005; ODI debut: Bangladesh v India, Chittagong (MAA) 23 Dec. 2004; T20I debut: S Africa v India, Johannesburg 1 Dec. 2006; played in 90 Tests, scored 4,876 runs (average 38.09) with six centuries, 33 fifties, highest score 224 against Australia, Chennai 2013; played in 327 ODIs, scored 10,123 runs (average 50.61) with 10 centuries and 67 fifties, highest score 183 not out against Sri Lanka, Jaipur 2005, took one wicket, average 14.00; First-class: 131 matches, 7,038 runs, average 36.84, highest score 224; played in 93 T20Is, scored 1,170 runs (average 37.17), highest score 56 against England, Bangalore 2017; mem. winning Indian team in ICC (Int. Cricket Council) World Twenty20 2007; Capt. winning Indian team of ICC Cricket World Cup 2011; maiden century against Pakistan in Faisalabad (148) is the fastest century scored by an Indian wicketkeeper; announced retirement from Test Cricket Dec. 2014; co-partnered Akkineni Nagarjuna in buying bike racing team Mahi Racing Team India; co-owner, Indian Super League team Chennaiyin FC; Vice-Pres. India Cements Ltd, Air India; launched SEVEN (lifestyle brand) 2016; Hon. Lt-Col, Indian Territorial Army; Dr hc (De Montfort Univ.) 2011; MTV Youth Icon of the Year 2006, Idea NDTV Youth Icon 2006, MTV Most Stylish Person in Sports 2006, Rajiv Gandhi Khel Ratna Award 2007–08, ICC ODI Player of the Year 2008 (first Indian player) 2009, ICC World ODI XI 2008, 2009, 2010, 2011, 2012, 2013, ICC World Test XI 2009, 2010, 2013, Padma Shri 2009, ICC Spirit of Cricket Award 2011, LG People's Choice Award 2013, Padma Bhushan 2018. *Leisure interests:* music, long drives, spending time with friends. *Address:* Board of Control for Cricket in India, 4th Floor, Cricket Centre, Wankhede Stadium, 'D' Road, Churchgate, Mumbai 400020, Maharashtra, India (office). *Telephone:* (22) 22898800 (office). *Fax:* (22) 22898801 (office). *E-mail:* office@bcci.tv (office).

DHOWAN, Adm. (retd) Robin K.; Indian naval officer; m. Minu Dhowan; two s. one d.; ed Nat. Defence Acad., Defence Services Staff Coll., Naval War Coll., USA, Royal Naval Air Station, UK; served on INS Delhi 1974; commissioned into Navy 1975, Chief Staff Officer (Operations), Western Naval Command 2004–05, Deputy Chief of Naval Staff, Integrated HQs, Ministry of Defence (Navy) 2009–11, Vice-Chief of Naval Staff 2011–14, Chief of Naval Staff 2014–16 (retd), also Prin. Hon. Naval Aide-de-camp to Pres., ships commanded include INS Khukri, INS Ranjit, INS Delhi, other positions included Deputy Dir Naval Operations, Jt Dir Naval Plans, Asst Chief of Naval Staff (Policy and Plans), New Delhi, Flag Officer, Commanding Eastern Fleet, Chief of Staff HQs, Eastern Naval Command, Visakhapatnam; Indian Naval Adviser, High Comm. of India, London 2000–03; Sr Instructor, Defence Service Staff Coll., Wellington; Commdt Nat. Defence Acad., Khadakvasla –2009; Param Vishisht Seva Medal (PVSM), Ati Vishisht Seva Medal (AVSM), Yudh Seva Medal (YSM). *Leisure interests:* golf, yachting.

DHUMAL, Prem Kumar, LLB, MA; Indian politician and government official; b. 10 April 1944, Samirpur, Hamirpur; s. of Capt. Mahant Ram and Phulmu Devi; m. Sheela Devi 1972; two s.; ed Punjab Univ., Chandigarh, Guru Nanak Dev Univ., Amritsar; lectured at pvt. coll. in Punjab; Sec., Bhartiya Janata Yuva Morcha (BJYM) 1980–82, Vice-Pres. 1982–85; associated with many social orgs, including Bharat Vikas Parishad, Vivekanand Memorial Soc. and Himachal Hitkarini Sabha; State Sec. BJYM 1980, Vice-Pres. 1982–85; Gen. Sec. Bharatiya Janata Party (BJP) 1985–93, Pres. BJP 1993–98; contested parl. election 1984, elected MP to Lok Sabha (BJP) for Hamirpur constituency 1989, 1991, 2007, mem. Consultative Cttee Union Ministry of Communications 1989–96, Standing Cttee for Transport and Tourism and Railway Convention Cttee 1991–96, Nat. Council for Teachers' Educ. 1993–96, Alt. Chair. Estimates Cttee of Lok Sabha 1989–91; fmr

Indian Rep. in Int. Parl. Union; Leader of Opposition in Himachal Pradesh State Legis. Ass. 2003–07; Chief Minister of Himachal Pradesh 1998–2003, 2007–12; Golden Peacock Award for Environmental Leadership 2008. *Leisure interests:* reading, writing short stories and articles for newspapers and magazines, listening to music. *Address:* Village and PO Samirpur, Teh. Bhoranj, Hamirpur Dist, 177 601, Himachal Pradesh, India (home). *Telephone:* (177) 2621384 (home); 98-68180104 (mobile).

DI MAIO, Luigi; Italian journalist and politician; *Deputy Prime Minister and Minister of Economic Development, Labour and Social Policies;* b. 6 July 1986, Avellino; s. of Antonio di Maio and Paola Esposito; ed Univ. of Naples Federico II; early career as journalist from 2007; co-f. Friends of Beppe Grillo (political group) 2007; mem. Chamber of Deputies (Camera dei Deputati, lower house of parl.) for Campania 2013–, Vice-Pres. (youngest ever) 2013–18; mem. MoVimento 5 Stelle (M5S, Five Star Movt), Leader 2017–; Minister of Econ. Devt, Labour and Social Policies 2018–, Deputy Prime Minister 2018–. *Address:* Ministry of Economic Development, Via Molise 2, 00187 Roma, Italy (office). *Telephone:* (06) 47051 (office). *Fax:* (06) 47887770 (office). *Website:* www.movimento5stelle.it (office); www.luigidimaio.it.

DI MONTEZEMOLO, Luca Cordero, LLM; Italian automotive industry executive; b. 31 Aug. 1947, Bologna; s. of Massimo and Clotilde Cordero Lanza dei Marchese di Montezemolo; m. 1st Sandra Monteleoni (divorced); one s.; one d. (with Barbara Parodi); m. 2nd Ludovica Andreoni 2000; two d.; ed Univ. of Rome, Columbia Univ., New York, USA; began career working with the Chiomenti law firm, Rome, later joined Bergreen & Bergreen, New York; Team Man., Ferrari Formula One Racing Team and Asst to Chair. Enzo Ferrari 1973–77; Dir Public Affairs Dept, Fiat Group 1977–81, CEO ITEDI SpA (holding co. for Fiat Group's publishing interests) 1981–83, Chair. Fiat SpA 2004–10, Chair. and CEO Ferrari SpA 1991–2006, Chair. 2006–14; CEO Cinzano International SpA 1984–86; Gen. Man. Italia '90 Football World Cup Organising Cttee 1986–90; CEO RCS Video and Chair. RCS Home Video 1990–91; Chair. and CEO Maserati SpA 1997–2005; Pres. Confindustria (Italian Employers' Asscn) 2004–08; mem. Bd of Dirs Pinault-Printemps-Redoute, La Stampa, Tod's, Poltrona Frau; Chair. Italian Asscn of Newspaper Publrs 2001–, Confindustria 2004–08; Pres. Modena Business and Industry Asscn 1996–2002, Bologna Int. Fair Org.; Pres. LUISS (Libera Università Internazionale degli Studi Sociali—Ind. Int. Univ. of Social Sciences), NTV (Nuovo Trasporto Viaggiatori), Industrialists of the Prov. of Modena 1996–2002, FIEG (Federazione Italiana Editori Giornali—Italian Newspaper Publrs Asscn) –2004; Vice-Pres. UNICE; mem. Gen. Council and Exec. Cttee Assonime; mem. Int. Advisory Bd Citi Inc.; Founder Charme (financial-entrepreneurial fund); Cavaliere del Lavoro; Chevalier, Légion d'honneur 2005; Hon. BEng (Modena) 2001; hon. degree in Business Man. (Genoa) 2001; hon. degree in Industrial Design (Politecnico of Milan) 2001. *Address:* c/o Ferrari SpA, Via Abetone Inferiore 4, 41053 Maranello, Italy. *E-mail:* info@ferrari.com.

DI PAOLA, Adm. Giampaolo; Italian naval officer and government official; b. 15 Aug. 1944, Torre Annunziata, Naples; m. Roberta di Paola; two d.; ed Naval Acad., Submarine School, NATO Defence Coll., Rome; served aboard conventional submarines Gazzana and Piomarta 1968–74; Commdr submarines Cappellini 1974–75, Sauro 1980–81; served as ASW and Undersea Warfare Programme Officer, Long Term Planning Br., SACLANT, Norfolk, Virginia, USA 1981–84; CO frigate Grecale 1984–86; Plans and Programmes Br. Chief, Gen. and Financial Planning Div., Navy Staff, Rome 1986–89; Capt. CO aircraft carrier Garibaldi 1989–90; Exec. Asst to Deputy Chief of Staff 1990–91; Chief of Naval Plans and Policy Br., Plans and Operations Div. 1991–92; Asst Chief of Staff for Plans and Operations 1993–94; Chief of Mil. Policy Div. 1994–98; Chief of the Cabinet, Ministry of Defence 1998–2001; Sec.-Gen. of Defence and Nat. Armaments Dir 2001–04; Chief of Defence Staff 2004–08; Chair. NATO Mil. Cttee, Brussels 2008–11; Minister of Defence (in Mario Monti's 'govt of technocrats') 2011–13; rank of Rear Adm. 1997, Adm. 2004; numerous decorations including Kt Grand Cross, Order of Merit, Commdr, Ordre nat. du Mérite, Grand Cross with Swords, Grand Officer, Order of Infante Dom Enrique (Portugal), Commdr, Legion of Merit (USA), Commdr, Légion d'honneur, Distinguished Award for Submariners, Sr Service Gold Cross, Bronze Medal for Sea-Duty Service in the Navy, Commemorative Medal of Sovereign Mil. Hospitaller Order of St John of Jerusalem, UN Medal for UN Peacekeeping Mission in Kosovo, NATO Afghanistan Medal. *Leisure interests:* arts, music, mountain climbing. *Address:* c/o Ministry of Defence, Palazzo Baracchini, Via XX Settembre 8, 00187 Rome, Italy.

DI PIETRO, Antonio; Italian lawyer and politician; b. 2 Oct. 1950, Montenero di Bisaccia; m. 1st Isabella Ferrara; one s.; m. 2nd Susanna Mazzoleni 1995; two c.; ed Statale Univ. Milan, Pavia Univ.; studied law at evening classes; fmr factory hand, Germany; fmr police officer; fmr magistrate, Bergamo; Prosecutor, Milan 1984–94; uncovered bribery of officials in Milan 1992, led Operation Clean Hands exposing high levels of political corruption in Italy 1992–94; Chair. Penal Rights in Economy, Libero Istituto Universitario di Castellanza 1995–96; consultant, Parl. Comm. on Slaughter, on Co-operation with Developing Countries 1995–96; Minister of Public Works 1996–97; mem. Senate 1997–2011; mem. European Parl. 1999–2006, Chair. Euro Parl. Del. for relations with S America, Cen. Asia and SA; Minister of Infrastructure 2006–08; Founder and Exec. Pres. Italia dei Valori party 2000–14; Dr hc (Thrace Univ., Greece) 1995. *Publications:* Costituzione italiana: Diritti e doveri 1994, Costruire il futuro. Testo di educazione civica per le scuole medie superiori 1995, Memoria 1999, Intervista su Tangentopoli 2000, Mani Pulite–La Vera Storia 2002, Il guastafeste: La storia, le idee, le battaglie di un ex magistrato entrato in politica senza chiedere permesso 2008, Ad ogni costo: Battaglie e proposte per un'altra Italia 2010, Politici: Da Craxi a Berlusconi, da Bossi a Fini, da Prodi a Grillo a Monti, quattordici ritratti insoliti 2012. *E-mail:* dipietro@antoniodipietro.it. *Website:* www.antoniodipietro.it.

DI RUPO, Elio, DSc; Belgian politician; b. 18 July 1951, Morlanwelz; ed Université de Mons; Researcher, Chef de Cabinet, Budget and Energy Minister, Walloon Region 1982–85; Communal Councillor, Mons 1982–2000; mem. Parl. 1987–89, mem. European Parl. 1989–91; Pres. Energy Comm.; Senator 1991–95; Minister of Educ. 1992–94; Deputy Prime Minister and Minister of Communications and Public Enterprises 1994–95, Deputy Prime Minister and Minister for Economy and Telecommunications 1995–99; Prime Minister 2011–14 (resgnd); Minister-Pres. of Wallonia 1999–2000, 2005–07; Mayor of Mons 2001–; Pres. Socialist Party 2000–11. *Address:* c/o Cabinet of the Prime Minister, 16 rue de la Loi, 1000 Brussels (office).

DIÃ DE SOUSA, Rui; Guinea-Bissau lawyer and politician; mem. Assembleia Nacional Popular (Parl.), PAIGC Parl. Leader –2014, mem. Constitutional Reform Cttee; Minister of Foreign Affairs and Int. Co-operation 2015; mem. Partido Africano da Independência da Guiné e Cabo Verde (PAIGC).

DIAB, Rashid, MFA, PhD; Sudanese artist and gallery director; b. 1 Jan. 1957, Wad Medani, Gezira Prov.; s. of Mubarak and Daralnaeem Diab; m. Mercedes Diab (divorced); one s. one d.; ed School of Fine and Applied Arts, Khartoum, Complutense Univ., Madrid, Spain; Teacher, Faculty of Fine Art, Complutense Univ., Madrid 1991–99; currently Owner and Dir, Medani Galería, Madrid; f. Rashid Diab Art Centre, Khartoum 2006; toured northern deserts of Sudan 2000; artistic adviser for presidential palace and govt offices, Sudan; works held in numerous public collections including OFID (OPEC Fund for Int. Devt) Collection, Vienna, Wifredo Lam Centre of Contemporary Art, Havana, Museum of Fine Arts, Alexandria, Modern Museum of Etching, Cairo, Arab World Inst., Paris, UNESCO, Paris. *Address:* Dara Art Gallery, PO Box 6554, Altakamul, Khartoum, Sudan. *E-mail:* daragallery@hotmail.com. *Website:* www.rashiddiabartscentre.net.

DIABRÉ, Zéphirin, MBA, PhD; Burkinabè international civil servant and business executive; b. 26 Aug. 1959, Ouagadougou; ed Ecole Supérieure de Commerce, Bordeaux, France, Univ. of Bordeaux; Prof. of Business Admin. 1987–89; Man. Dir Burkina Brewery 1989–92; Minister for Trade, Industry and Mining 1992–94, for Economy, Finance and Planning 1994–96; Chair. Council of Econ. and Social Affairs 1996–97; Visiting Scholar, Harvard Inst. for Int. Devt, Fellow, Weatherhead Center for Int. Affairs, USA 1997–98; Assoc. Admin. UNDP, New York 1999–2006; Chair. Africa and Middle East Regions, Int. and Marketing Dept AREVA (Société des Participations du Commissariat à l'Energie Atomique) 2006–11, also adviser to Chair.; cand. in presidential election Dec. 2015; Officier, Ordre nat. du Mérite, Burkina Faso, Chevalier, Légion d'honneur. *Address:* c/o AREVA SA, 3 rue La Fayette, 75442 Paris Cedex 9, France (office).

DIACK, Lamine; Senegalese international sports official and politician; b. 7 June 1933, Dakar; m.; 15 c.; long jump record holder, France and W Africa 1957–60; football coach, Foyer France Senegal football team 1963–64; Pres. African Amateur Athletic Confed. (AAAC) 1963–64, 1973–2003; Technical Dir Senegal Nat. Football Team 1964–68; Gen. Commr for State Sport 1969–70, Sec. of State for Youth and Sport 1970–73; mem. Exec. Cttee Supreme Council for Sport in Africa (SCSA) 1973–87; Pres. ASC DIARAAF football team 1974–78, 1994–; apptd mem. Nat. Olympic Cttee of Senegal 1974, Pres. 1985; Gen. Sec. Senegalese Athletic Fed. 1974–78, Pres. 1974–78, Hon. Pres. 1978–; mem. Int. Olympic Cttee 1999–2013, Hon. mem. 2013–15; Vice-Pres. Int. Asscn of Athletics Feds (IAAF) 1976–91, Sr Vice-Pres. 1991–99, Pres. 1999–2015, Pres. Int. Athletics Foundation 1999–2015 (resgnd); Chair. City Council (Mayor) of Dakar 1978–80; mem. Nat. Ass. of Senegal (Parl.) 1988–93, Sr Vice-Pres. (Deputy Speaker) 1988–93; Chief Insp. of Taxes and State Property 1995–2001; Chair. Bd Soc. Nat. des Eaux (SONES) 1995–2001; numerous honours, including Grand Cordon of the Order of the Rising Sun (Japan), Grand Officier de l'Etoile Equatoriale (Gabon), Commdr Order of Good Hope (S. Africa), Chevalier, Légion d'honneur, Chevalier de l'Ordre Nat. du Lion (Senegal), Officiale di Grancroce (Italy), Officier de la Médaille de la Reconnaissance Centrafricaine, Médaille de l'Ordre du Nil de la République Arabe d'Egypte, Bernardo O'Higgins Medal, 1st Degree (Chile), Order of the Officer Cross Budapest (Hungary), Olympic Order, IAAF Order of Merit, ACNO Order of Merit, SCSA Order of Merit, CAF Order of Merit; Dr hc (Donetsk Nat. Univ.), (Beijing Sport Univ.). *Address:* c/o Office of the President, International Association of Athletics Federations, 17 rue Princesse Florestine, BP 359, MC 98007, Monaco (office).

DIACONESCU, Cristian, LLB; Romanian judge and politician; *Presidential Adviser and Head of the Presidential Chancellery;* b. 2 July 1959, Bucharest; m. Mariana Diaconescu; one d.; ed Univ. of Bucharest; mil. service, attained rank of 2nd Lt; judge, Court of Ilfov Agricultural Sector 1983–85, Court of Bucharest Fourth Dist and Tribunal of Bucharest 1985–89; Inspector Ministry of Justice 1989–90; mem. Perm. Mission to OSCE, then Perm. Mission to Int. Orgs, Vienna 1990–96; mem. OSCE Directorate, Ministry of Foreign Affairs 1996–97, Dir 1997, Gen. Dir, Gen. Directorate for Judicial and Consular Affairs 1998; Deputy Sec. Black Sea Org. for Econ. Cooperation 2000; Sec. of State for Bilateral Affairs, Ministry of Foreign Affairs 2000–04; mem. Senate for Constanţa County 2004–08, for Constituency No. 42, Bucharest 2008–12 (Vice-Pres. 2010–12); Minister of Justice March–Dec. 2004, of Foreign Affairs 2008–09, Jan.–May 2012; Presidential Adviser and Head of the Presidential Chancellery 2012–; Assoc. Prof., Chair of Int. Public Law, Hyperion Univ. 1993; mem. Nat. Defence Coll. Foundation 1995–, Prof. 1997–; Prof., Human Rights Inst. 1998–2000; mem. Partidul Social Democrat (PSD—Social Democratic Party) –2010; Ind. 2010–14, 2014–; mem. Partidul Mişcarea Populară (PMP—People's Movt Party) May–Aug. 2014; unsuccessful cand. for president Aug. 2014. *Address:* Office of the President, 060116 Bucharest 5, Palatul Cotroceni, Str. Geniului 1–3, Romania (office). *Telephone:* (21) 4100581 (office). *Fax:* (21) 4103858 (office). *E-mail:* procetatean@presidency.ro (office). *Website:* www.presidency.ro (office); www.cristiandiaconescu.eu.

DIACONESCU, Dan Cristian; Romanian journalist, politician and TV presenter; b. 9 Dec. 1967, Caracal, Olt Co.; ed Faculty of Mechanical Eng, Univ. of Bucharest; Chief of Section, Curierul Naţional newspaper 1990–92; Dir-Gen. Jurnalal Naţional newspaper 1992–95; presenter, TV Supernova 1997–98; Dir, Cotidianul newspaper 1998–2000; presenter, Tele 7abc 1998–2000; f. Ocram Television (OTV) 2000, Owner 2000–13; f. DDTV 2009; Co-founder, with other OTV show presenters, and first Pres. Partidul Poporului—Dan Diaconescu (PP—DD—People's Party—Dan Diaconescu) 2011; cand. in presidential election 2014; sentenced to three years' imprisonment for blackmail by First Dist Court Dec. 2013, sentence increased to five years and six months and forbidden election to public office for three years following sentence by Court of Appeal March 2015; Dan Voiculescu Humanist Foundation Prize 1992, Panfil Şeicara Award 1998, various awards for TV talk shows. *Address:* Partidul Poporului—Dan Diaconescu (People's Party—Dan Diaconescu), Bucharest, Romania (office). *Telephone:* (21) 3114199 (office). *Fax:* (21) 3114199 (office). *E-mail:* mansimona@partidul.poporului.ro (office). *Website:* www.partidul.poporului.ro (office).

DIALLO, Abdoulaye Daouda; Senegalese public servant and politician; *Minister of Finance and the Budget;* ed Univ. Cheikh Anta Diop, Dakar, Nat. School of Admin and Magistracy; several roles within Ministry of Finance, including Head of Inspection, Centre of Tax Services 1993–94, Head of Combined M & E Inspection Dept, assigned to Large Company Dept 1996–2000; Admin. and Financial Dir, Dakar Dem Dick (nat. transportation co.) 2000; Dir Gen., Senegalese Nat. Lottery 2001–03; Head, Office of Legislation 1 (Taxes and Direct), Directorate Gen. of Taxes 2004–05; Sec. Gen., Council of the Repub. for Econ. and Social Affairs 2005–07; Sec. Gen., Inst. de Prévoyance Retraite du Sénégal (IPRES, pension agency) 2008; Asst to Head of DP1 Centre and Head of Liberal Professions Recovery Office 2009–12; Minister-del. to Minister of Economy and Finance, in charge of the Budget 2012–13; Minister of the Interior 2013, of Infrastructure and Transport –2019, of Finance and the Budget 2019–. *Address:* Ministry of Finance, rue René Ndiaye, BP 4017, Dakar, Senegal (office). *Telephone:* 33-889-2100 (office). *Fax:* 33-822-4195 (office). *E-mail:* infos@minfinances.sn (office). *Website:* www.finances.gouv.sn (office).

DIALLO, Cellou Dalein; Guinean economist and politician; *President, Union des forces démocratiques de Guinée;* b. 3 Feb. 1952, Labé; ed Faculty of Economics, Univ. of Conakry; worked at Cen. Bank of Guinea 1985–95; joined ministerial cabinet of Pres. Lansan Conté 1995; Minister of Transport, Communications, Tourism and Public Works 1997–99, of Public Works and Transport 1999–2004, of Fisheries 2004; Prime Minister of Guinea 2004–06; Pres. Union des forces démocratiques de Guinée 2007–; unsuccessful cand. in presidential election 2010, 2015. *Address:* Union des forces démocratiques de Guinée, BP 3036, Conakry, Guinea (office). *E-mail:* baggelmalal@yahoo.fr (office). *Website:* www.ufdg.org (office).

DIAMOND, Abel J. (Jack), OC, BArch, MArch, DEng, FRAIC, ARIBA, RCA, MCIP, MAIP; Canadian architect; *Principal and Founding Partner, Diamond and Schmitt Architects Inc.;* b. S. Africa; s. of Jacob Diamond and Rachel Zipporah Diamond (née Werner); m. Gillian Mary Huggins 1959; one s. one d.; ed Univ. of Cape Town, South Africa, Univ. of Oxford, UK, Univ. of Pennsylvania, USA; Asst Prof. of Architecture and Architectural Asst to Louis Kahn, Philadelphia 1963–64; Assoc. Prof., Univ. of Toronto 1964–69; Prof., Univ. of York 1969–72; Adjunct Prof., Univ. of Texas at Arlington 1980–81; Sr Pnr, A. J. Diamond, Donald Schmitt and Co. (now Diamond and Schmitt Architects Inc.) 1975–; Chair. Nat. Capital Comm., Design Advisory Comm., Ottawa; mem. Advisory Bd, School of Architecture, Univ. of Toronto 1987; Commr Ont. Human Rights Comm. 1986–89; mem. Bd of Govs, Mount Sinai Hosp., Toronto 1987; Graham Prof. of Architecture, Univ. of Pa 1996; mem. Royal Acad. of Arts, Canada, RIBA, Canadian Inst. of Planners, American Inst. of Planners; Sr Fellow, Design Futures Council; Hon. FAIA; Hon. DEng (Dalhousie) 1996, Hon. LLD; numerous design prizes including Toronto Arts Award 1990, Royal Architectural Inst. Gold Medal 2001; Order of Ont. 1998. *Works include:* Ontario Medical Asscn HQ 1970, Univ. of Alberta Long Range Plan 1970, Alcan HQ Office, Toronto 1972, Montreal 1978, Cleveland 1982, Queen's Univ. Housing, Kingston, Ont. 1976, Citadel Theatre, Edmonton, Alberta 1976 (with B. Myers and R. L. Wilkin), Nat. Ballet School Stage Training Facility, Toronto 1983, Burns Bldg Renovation, Calgary 1983, Berkeley Castle Renovation, Toronto 1983, Metro Toronto Central YMCA 1984, Ont. Arts Council HQ Offices, Toronto 1985, Four Seasons HQ Offices, Toronto 1985, Imperial Theatre, St John, NB 1988, Earth and Sciences Center, Univ. of Toronto 1988, Curtiss Hall, Toronto 1988, Sunny Brook Hosp., Newcastle Town Hall 1989, York Univ. Student Centre 1991, Lois Hancsey Aquatic Center 1991, Jerusalem City Hall 1992, Richmond Hill Cen. Library 1992, HQ Toronto Historic Bd 1993, Israeli Foreign Ministry, Jerusalem 1996, 'Alumbrera', Mustique 2000, Garland House, Toronto, Jewish Community Center, Manhattan 2001, Harman Center for the Arts, Washington DC 2007, Women's Coll. Hosp. Hospital 2009, Montreal Symphony House, Montreal 2011, Li Ka Shing Knowledge Inst., Toronto 2011, Osgoode Hall Law School, Toronto 2012, The Mariinsky Theatre, Russia 2013. *Publications include:* Works: The Architecture of A.J. Diamond, Donald Schmitt and Company, 1968–1994 1996, Insight and On Site: The Architecture of Diamond and Schmitt 2008, Sketches from Here and There 2010. *Leisure interest:* watercolour painting. *Address:* Diamond and Schmitt Architects Inc., 384 Adelaide Street West, Suite 300, Toronto, ON M5V 1R7, Canada (office). *Telephone:* (416) 862-8800 (office). *E-mail:* ajd@dsai.ca (office). *Website:* www.dsai.ca (office).

DIAMOND, Douglas, AB, MA, MPhil, PhD; American economist and academic; *Merton H. Miller Distinguished Service Professor of Finance and Richard N. Rosett Faculty Fellow, Graduate School of Business, University of Chicago;* b. Oct. 1953; m.; two c.; ed Brown Univ., Yale Univ.; Summer Research Assoc., Bd of Govs, US Fed. Reserve System, summers of 1976–78; Teaching Fellow, Dept of Econs, Yale Univ. 1977–78, Prof. of Finance, Yale School of Org. and Man. 1987–88; Instructor, Univ. of Chicago 1979, Asst Prof. 1980–83, Assoc. Prof. 1983–86, Prof. of Finance 1988–93, 1986–87, Theodore O. Yntema Prof. of Finance 1993–2000, Merton H. Miller Distinguished Service Prof. of Finance and Richard N. Rosett Faculty Fellow, Grad. School of Business 2000–; Research Assoc., Nat. Bureau of Econ. Research; Visiting Scholar, Fed. Reserve Bank of Richmond; Assoc. Ed. Journal of Finance 1988–96, 2000–03, Journal of Financial Services Research 1993–, Journal of Banking and Finance 1995–; mem. Bd of Dirs, Center for Research in Security Prices 1994–; Fellow, Econometric Soc. 1990–, American Acad. of Arts and Sciences 2001–, American Finance Asscn 2004– (Pres. 2003), Financial Man. Asscn 2004–; Dr hc (Univ. of Zurich, Switzerland) 2013; Morgan Stanley-American Finance Asscn Award for Excellence in Finance 2012, Onassis Prize in Finance 2018. *Publications include:* articles in numerous journals. *Address:* University of Chicago Booth School of Business, 5807 South Woodlawn Avenue, Chicago, IL 60637-1610, USA (office). *Telephone:* (773) 702-7283 (office). *E-mail:* douglas.diamondchicagobooth.edu (office). *Website:* faculty.chicagobooth.edu/douglas.diamond (office).

DIAMOND, Jared Mason, BA, PhD; American biologist, physiologist, academic and writer; *Professor of Geography and Physiology, David Geffen School of Medicine, University of California, Los Angeles;* b. 10 Sept. 1937, Boston, Mass; s. of Louis K. Diamond and Flora K. Diamond; m. Marie Nabel Cohen 1982; twin s.; ed Harvard Coll., Univ. of Cambridge, UK; Fellow, Trinity Coll., Cambridge 1961–65, Jr Fellow, Soc. of Fellows, Harvard Univ. 1962–65; Assoc. in Biophysics, Harvard Medical School 1965–66; Assoc. Prof. of Physiology, David Geffen School of Medicine, Univ. of California Medical School, Los Angeles 1966–68, Prof. of Geography, UCLA 1968–; Research Assoc., Dept of Ornithology, American Museum of Natural History 1973–; US Regional Dir World Wide Fund for Nature; mem. Editorial Bd Skeptic Magazine; mem. NAS; Fellow, American Acad. of Arts and Sciences, American Physiological Soc., Biophysics Soc., American Philosophical Soc., American Soc. of Naturalists, American Ornithologists Union 1978; Hon. DLitt (Sejong Univ., S Korea) 1995; Dr hc (Katholieke Universiteit Leuven, Belgium) 2008; Prize Fellowship in Physiology, Trinity Coll., Cambridge 1961–65, Lederle Medical Faculty Award 1968–71, Distinguished Teaching Award, UCLA Medical Class 1972, 1973, Distinguished Achievement Award, American Gastroenterological Asscn 1975, Kaiser Permanente/Golden Apple Teaching Award 1976, Nathaniel Bowditch Prize, American Physiological Soc. 1976, Franklin L. Burr Award, Nat. Geographic Soc. 1979, MacArthur Foundation 'Genius' Grant 1985, Archie Carr Medal 1989, MacArthur Foundation Fellow 1990, Tanner Lecturer, Univ. of Utah (and many other endowed lectureships) 1992, Royal Soc. Prizes for Science Books (Rhone-Poulenc Prize) 1992, 1998, Science Book Prize, New Scientist London 1992, Los Angeles Times Science Book Prize 1992, Zoological Soc. of San Diego Conservation Medal 1993, Randi Award, Skeptics Soc. 1994, Faculty Research Lecturer, UCLA 1996, Phi Beta Kappa Science Book Prize 1997, Elliott Coues Award, American Ornithologists' Union 1998, Gold Medal in nonfiction, California Book Awards 1998, Nat. Medal of Sciences 1999, Lannan Literary Award for Nonfiction 1999, Tyler Prize for Environmental Achievement 2001, Lewis Thomas Prize for Writing about Science 2002, Dickson Prize in Science 2006, Wolf Prize in Agric. 2013. *Television:* Guns, Germs and Steel (three-part PBS documentary) 2005. *Publications include:* The Avifauna of the Eastern Highlands of New Guinea 1972, Ecology and Evolution of Communities (co-ed.) 1975, Birds of Karkar and Bagabab Islands, New Guinea (co-author) 1979, The Avifaunas of Rennell and Bellona Islands. The Natural History of Rennell Islands, British Solomon Islands 1984, Community Ecology (co-author) 1985, Birds of New Guinea (co-author) 1986, The Third Chimpanzee: The Evolution and Future of the Human Animal 1992, 2006, Why is Sex Fun? – The Evolution of Human Sexuality 1997, Guns, Germs, and Steel: The Fates of Human Societies (Pulitzer Prize 1998, Cosmos Prize 1998) 1998, The Birds of Northern Melanesia: Speciation, Ecology, & Biogeography (co-author) 2001, Guns, Germs, and Steel Reader's Companion 2003, Collapse: How Societies Choose to Fail or Succeed 2004, Natural Experiments of History (with James A. Robinson) 2010, The World until Yesterday: What Can We Learn from Traditional Societies? 2012; several hundred research papers on physiology, ecology and ornithology; contribs to Discover, Natural History, Nature. *Address:* 1255 Bunche Hall, University of California, Los Angeles, CA 90095-1524, USA (office). *Telephone:* (310) 825-6177 (office). *Fax:* (310) 206-5976 (office). *E-mail:* jdiamond@geog.ucla.edu (office). *Website:* healthsciences.ucla.edu/dgsom (office); www.geog.ucla.edu (office); www.jareddiamond.org.

DIAMOND, Neil Leslie; American singer and composer; b. 24 Jan. 1941, Brooklyn, New York; m. 2nd Marcia Murphey 1975; two c. (and two c. from previous m.); m. 3rd Katie McNeil 2012; ed New York Univ.; fmr songwriter for publishing co.; numerous tours worldwide, television and radio broadcasts; mem. SESAC; inducted into Songwriters Hall of Fame 1984, Rock and Roll Hall of Fame 2011, Honoree, Annual Kennedy Center Honors 2011, Billboard Icon Award 2011, Billboard Legend of Live Award 2012. *Film scores:* Jonathan Livingston Seagull (Grammy Award) 1973, Every Which Way But Loose 1978, The Jazz Singer 1980; songs for numerous other films. *Film appearance:* The Jazz Singer 1980. *Recordings include:* albums: The Feel of Neil Diamond 1966, Just For You 1967, Velvet Gloves and Spit 1968, Brother Love's Travelling Salvation Show 1969, Touching You Touching Me 1969, Tap Root Manuscript 1970, Shilo 1970, Gold (live) 1970, Stones 1971, Hot August Night (live) 1972, Moods 1972, Serenade 1974, Beautiful Noise 1976, Love At The Greek (live) 1977, I'm Glad You're Here With Me Tonight 1977, Carmelita's Eyes 1978, You Don't Bring Me Flowers 1978, September Morn 1979, Voices Of Vista: Show # 200 1979, On The Way To The Sky 1981, Heartlight 1982, Song Sung Blue 1982, Primitive 1984, Headed For The Future 1986, Hot August Night II (live) 1987, The Best Years Of Our Lives 1989, Lovescape 1991, The Christmas Album 1992, Up On the Roof: Songs From The Brill Building 1993, The Christmas Album Vol. II 1994, Live In America 1994, Tennessee Moon 1996, Live In Concert 1997, The Movie Album: As Time Goes By 1998, Three Chord Opera 2001, 12 Songs 2005, Home Before Dark 2008, A Cherry Cherry Christmas 2009, Dreams 2010, Melody Road 2014, Acoustic Christmas 2016. *Website:* www.neildiamond.com.

DIAMOND, Robert (Bob) Edward, Jr, BA, MBA; American business executive; *Founding Partner and CEO, Atlas Merchant Capital LLC;* b. 27 July 1951, Springfield, Mass; m. Jennifer Diamond; two s. one d.; ed Colby Coll., Univ. of Connecticut Business School; began career as Lecturer at School of Business, Univ. of Connecticut 1976; held sr leadership roles at Credit Suisse First Boston in Tokyo and New York 1992–96, Morgan Stanley International; joined Barclays 1996, mem. Group Exec. Cttee 1997, Exec. Dir 2005–12, Pres. Barclays PLC and Chief Exec. of Corp. and Investment Banking, Barclays Wealth, comprising Barclays Capital, Barclays Corporate and Barclays Wealth, Pres. and Deputy Chief Exec. 2010–11, Chief Exec. 2011–12 (resgnd), mem. Bd BlackRock (following integration of Barclays Global Investors) –2012; Founding Partner and CEO Atlas Merchant Capital LLC 2013–, Co-founder and Dir (non-exec.) Atlas Mara Co-Nvest Ltd 2013– (Chair. 2013–19); Pres. New York Chapter of Invest Africa; mem. Bd of Dirs Diamond Family Foundation, Old Vic Productions PLC, Paperless Receipts Ltd, BlackRock, Inc.; Life mem. Council on Foreign Relations; mem. Atlantic Council; Chair. Bd of Trustees, Colby Coll.; Trustee, Mayor's Fund for London, American Foundation of the Imperial War Museum Inc.; Hon. DHumLitt (Univ. of Connecticut) 2006, Hon. LLD (Colby Coll.) 2008. *Leisure interests:* supports Boston Red Sox in baseball, Chelsea in UK football, New England Patriots in American football, Boston Celtics in basketball. *Address:* Atlas Merchant Capital LLC, 375 Park Avenue, 21st Floor, New York, NY 10152, USA (office). *Telephone:* (212) 883-4330 (office). *E-mail:* info@atlasmerchantcapital.com (office). *Website:* www.atlasmerchantcapital.com (office).

DIAMOND, Shelley; American advertising executive; *Chief Client Officer, Young & Rubicam;* m. Richard Diamond; three c.; ed State Univ. of NY at Buffalo; began advertising career at Foote Cone & Belding; subsequently worked at Grey Advertising and Ted Bates Advertising; Man. Dir of New York office of Young & Rubicam 2007–10, Worldwide Man. Partner on the Dell, Campbell's Soup and

Xerox accounts 2010–14, Global Chief Client Officer 2014–, also serves as a Dir on the global Young & Rubicam Bd; mem. Bd Students In Free Enterprise, Acad. of Urban Planning; mem. Bd of Dirs PAETEC Holding 2009–; mem. W.O.M.E.N in America, Fortune/State Dept's Vital Voice initiatives; named by YWCA as Woman of the Year 1995, Advertising Women of New York 2005, Advertising Working Mothers of the Year Award, recognized by Working Mother magazine as a trailblazer in the industry. *Address:* Young & Rubicam, 3 Columbus Circle, New York, NY 10019, USA (office). *E-mail:* info@yr.com (office); info@yrnyc.com (office). *Website:* www.yr.com (office); yrnorthamerica.com (office).

DIANÉ, Elhadj Madifing; Guinean government official and fmr diplomatist; b. 1946, Kita, Mali; m.; ten c.; ed Acad. of Cairo, Egypt; Official, Directorate of State Security 1971–72; Foreign Auditor, Acad. of Algiers 1972–73; several years with Office of the Pres. including as Head, Central Bureau of Revenue 1973–78, First Counsellor, responsible for Middle East and W Europe 1978–81, Dir of Safety Man. 1981–83; Head of Security, Labé City (attached to Office of the Pres.) 1983–84; Deputy Dir-Gen., Police Services 1984–85; Deputy Dir-Gen., Intelligence 1985–87; Adviser to Sec. of State for Security, responsible for external relations 1987–90; Dir, Office for Supervision of Police and Republican Guard 1990–93; Dir of Security, Kindia Region (responsible for security of presidential elections in Maritime Guinea) 1993–94; Dir of Security, Labé City (responsible for legislative and community elections in that region) 1994–96; Inspector-Gen. of Security Services 1996–2007; Technical Adviser, responsible for cooperation 2007–08; Minister of Security and Civil Protection Sept.–Dec. 2008, 2013–14; Amb. to Senegal (also accred to The Gambia, Mauritania and Cabo Verde) 2011–13; helped to open peace negotiations between Iraq and Iran under the auspices of Comité Islamique de Paix 1978–80; Vice-Pres. Asscn of Guinea–Arab Security 1981; Hero of the Liberation Struggle in Guinea-Bissau and Cape Verde 1972, White Cross Medal, Order of Merit of the Spanish Police Force. *Leisure interests:* reading, classical music. *Address:* c/o Ministry of Security, Civil Protection and the Reform of Security Services, Coléah-Domino, Conakry, Guinea.

DIARÉ, Mohamed; Guinean politician; b. Kissidougou; ed Univ. de Conakry, IMF Inst., École nat. d'admin, France; Minister-Del. for the Budget 2011–14; Minister of the Economy and Finance 2014–15. *Address:* c/o Ministry of the Economy and Finance, Boulbinet, BP 221, Conakry, Guinea.

DIARRA, Cheick Modibo, PhD; Malian astrophysicist and politician; *President, Rassemblement pour le Développement du Mali (RpDM);* b. 1952, Nioro du Sahel; son-in-law of Moussa Traoré (fmr Pres. of Mali); three c.; ed Université Pierre et Marie Curie, France, Howard Univ., USA; worked as interplanetary navigator at NASA Jet Propulsion Lab., collaborated in numerous space programmes including Magellan probe to Venus, Ulysses probe to the sun, Galileo spacecraft to Jupiter, Mars Observer and Mars Pathfinder, also worked on Mars Exploration Program Educ. and NASA Public Outreach Program; Pres. Microsoft Africa 2006; est. solar energy research lab., Bamako 2002; Founder-Pres. Rassemblement pour le Développement du Mali (RpDM) 2011–; Prime Minister April–Dec. 2012; cand. in presidential election 2013, 2018; Pres. Africal Virtual Univ., Kenya –2005; Co-founder Université Numérique Francophone Mondiale 2005; Founder-Pres. African Science and New Tech. Summit; f. Fondation Pathfinder (educ. programme), Bamako 1999; Vice-Pres. UN World Comm. for the Ethics of Scientific Knowledge and Tech.; mem. Ind. Comm. on Africa and the Challenges of the Third Millennium; UNESCO Goodwill Amb. 2000–01; African Lifetime Achievement Award 1998. *Publication:* Navigateur interplanétaire (autobiography). *Address:* Rassemblement pour le Développement du Mali (RpDM), rue 303, Porte 330, ACI 2000, Hamdallaye, Bamako, Mali (office). *Telephone:* 7619-3352 (office). *E-mail:* rpdm@rpdm.com (office). *Website:* www.rpdm-mali.com (office); www.cheickmodibodiarra.com.

DIARRA, Cheick Sidi; Malian diplomatist and UN official; *President, Commission d'Organisation du Sommet Afrique-France;* b. 31 May 1957, Kayes; m.; two c.; ed Dakar Univ., Senegal; joined civil service in 1981, assigned to Ministry of Foreign Affairs and Int. Co-operation, Legal Adviser 1987–88; First Counsellor, Perm. Mission to UN, New York 1989–93, Perm. Rep. to UN, New York 1993–2007; UN Under-Sec.-Gen. and High Rep. for the Least Developed Countries, Landlocked Developing Countries and Small Island Developing States 2007–08, Special Adviser on Africa and Under-Sec.-Gen. and High Rep. for the Least Developed Countries, Landlocked Developing Countries and Small Island Developing States 2008–12; Pres. Comm. d'Organisation du Sommet Afrique-France 2014–; fmr Commr, ITU Broadband Comm. for Digital Devt; Chevalier, Ordre Nat. du Mali. *Address:* c/o Ministry of Foreign Affairs, African Integration and International Co-operation, Koulouba, Bamako, Mali. *Website:* sommetafrique-france2016.com (office).

DIARRA, Djeneba, LLM; Malian lawyer and international organization official; *Secretary-General, African Union Commission;* d. of Mamadou Diarra; ed Lycée Franco-Ethiopian Guebre Mariam, Addis Ababa, Univ. of Bordeaux III, Talence; joined Office of the Legal Counsel, Org. of African Unity (OAU), as Legal Officer 1996, (OAU replaced by African Union 2002), becoming Deputy Legal Counsel, African Union (AU) 2004–14, Acting Legal Counsel 2012–13, Acting Exec. Sec., AU Advisory Bd on the Fight against Corruption 2014–15, Sec.-Gen., AU Comm. (first female) 2015–; Acting Sec.-Gen., Pan African Parl. 2004; Acting Registrar, African Court on Human and Peoples' Rights, Arusha, 2006. *Address:* Commission of the African Union, Roosevelt St, Old Airport Area, POB 3243, Addis Ababa, Ethiopia (office). *Telephone:* (11) 5517700 (office). *Fax:* (11) 5517844 (office). *E-mail:* webmaster@africa-union.org (office). *Website:* au.int (office).

DIARRA, Fatoumata Dembele, LLB; Malian judge and professor of law; *Judge, Constitutional Court of Mali;* b. 15 Feb. 1949, Koulikoro; m.; six c.; ed Ecole Nat. de la Magistrature, Paris, France, Ecole Nat. d'Admin, Bamako, Dakar Univ., Senegal; Investigative Judge, Jr Admin. Office, First Instance Tribunal of Bamako 1977–80; Trial Attorney, Office of the Prosecutor, Tribunal of Bamako 1980–81; Vice-Pres. Labour Court of Bamako 1981–82; Investigative Judge, Sr Investigation Office, Bamako 1984–86; Legis. Councillor Nat. Ass. of Mali 1986–91; Legal Adviser to Transition Cttee for the Reinstallation of Republican Inst., Office of the Head of State 1991; Gen. Dir Malian Office for Intellectual Property and Copyright 1991–93; Official Rep. of Office of the Comm. for the Promotion of Women 1993–94; Appeal Court Adviser, Criminal Chamber 1994–96; Pres. Criminal Chamber, Bamako Appeal Court 1996–99; Nat. Dir Justice Admin 1999–2001; elected Judge ad litem Int. Criminal Tribunal for the Fmr Yugoslavia (ICTY) 2001; Judge, Int. Criminal Court 2003–, Judge, Pre-Trial Chamber II 2004–08, Pres., Pre-Trial Chamber III, Judge, Trial Chamber II Oct. 2008, First Vice-Pres. 2009–12; Judge, Constitutional Court of Mali 2013–; Prof. of Constitutional Law, Civil Law and Criminal Law, Cen. School for Industry, Trade and Admin (ECICA) 1986–91; Gen. Sec. Asscn of Malian Women Lawyers 1986–88, Pres. 1988–95; Founding Pres. Legal Clinic for Women and Children Without Means 1993; Pres. Support Group for Legal Reform 1994, Observatory for the Rights of Women and Children (ODEF) 1995–, Legal Br. of Int. Council for French-speaking Women (CIFF) 1996–, Malian Electoral Support Network 1997–; Vice-Pres. Int. Fed. of Women with Legal Careers (FIFCJ) 1994–97, Fed. of African Women Lawyers (FJA) 1995–; mem. numerous working groups and parl. cttee on legal reform; frequent participant in UN Comm. on the Status of Women; Chevalier, Ordre nat. du Mali 2001, Chevalier, Légion d'honneur (France) 2009; Outstanding Achievement Award, Arizona State Univ., title of Pionnière, Fed. des Juristes Africaines. *Publications include:* numerous articles in professional journals on women's rights and int. law; special contribs on ICC-related issues, such as war crimes, crimes against humanity and genocide in particular in relation to women; other examples of individual criminal responsibility as foreseen in the Rome Statute, article 25. *Address:* Constitutional Court, Hamdallaye ACI 2000, Commune IV, BP E 213, Bamako, Mali (office). *Telephone:* 2022-5609 (office). *Fax:* 2023-4241 (office). *E-mail:* tawatybouba@yahoo.fr (office). *Website:* www.cc.insti.ml (office).

DIARRA, Mamadou Igor, BEng; Malian politician and fmr banking executive; b. 26 Dec. 1966, Krivoi Rog, Ukraine; m.; six c.; ed HEC Man. School, Univ. of Liège, Belgium; joined Banque de Développement du Mali SA 1991, various positions including Deputy Head of Operations 1991, Head of Paris office 1995, Operations Dir, Credit Analyst 1998, Deputy Dir of Network 1999, Project Man. for cards and ATMs, Adviser to CEO 2000, Dir of Network 2001, Operations Dir of Bamako Br. 2002, Asst Sec. of Man. Cttee –2004; Gen. Man., Banco da Uniao, Guinea Bissau 2005; CEO, Banque Internationale pour le Mali 2006–08; fmr Chair. Office malien de l'habitat (housing agency); Minister of Mining and Water 2008–11, fmr Acting Minister of Economy and Finance, Housing and Land Tenure Affairs, Environment and Sanitation, Minister of Finance 2015–16; fmr Dir-Gen. Bank of Africa Mali; fmr Sec.-Gen., APBEF Mali (Professional Asscn of Banks and Financial Institutions). *Leisure interests:* reading, football, tennis, cinema. *Address:* c/o Ministry of the Economy and Finance, Bamako, Mali.

DIARRA, Seydou Elimane; Côte d'Ivoirian agronomist, diplomatist, politician and banker; b. 23 Nov. 1933, Katiola; m.; ed Lycée Fénelon, La Rochelle, France; won scholarship to study agric. in France; researcher, Office de la recherche scientifique et technique d'outre-mer (Orstom) 1961; apptd Dir Centre national de la mutualité agricole 1962; Commercial Dir Caisse de stabilisation du café et du cacao (Caistab) 1965, Rep. of Caistab in London; fmr head of state-run agric. co-operation and insurance body, Abidjan; Pres., Dir-Gen. Saco et Chocodi 1985; fmr head of govt org. in charge of cocoa; fmr African Rep. to Int. Coffee Org.; fmr Amb. to Brazil, EU and UK; Chair. Chamber of Commerce and Industry, Côte d'Ivoire 1992; Minister of State, responsible for Governmental Co-ordination and the Planning of Devt Jan.–May 2000; Prime Minister of Côte d'Ivoire May–Oct. 2000 (resgnd), 2003–05; Pres. Bd of Dirs Banque Internationale pour l'Afrique Occidentale, Cote d'Ivoire 2002; Chair. Banque Internationale pour le Commerce et l'Industrie de Cote d'Ivoire SA (BICICI) 2009; Chevalier, Nat. Order of Madagascar, Officer, Merit of Nat. Educ. of Côte d'Ivoire, Commdr, Agricultural Merit of Côte d'Ivoire, Officer then Commdr, Ordre national de la Légion d'honneur, Grand Officer, Order of Rio Branco (Brazil), Grand Officer, Order of Cruzeiro do Sul (Brazil), Grand Officer, Nat. Order of Côte d'Ivoire, Grand Officer, Order of the Crown (Belgium), Grand Officer, Merit of Luxembourg, Grand Cross, Order of Merit Ivorian. *Address:* 6 BP 2452, Abidjan 06, Côte d'Ivoire. *Telephone:* 22-40-45-90. *Fax:* 22-40-45-92. *E-mail:* bureaudiarra@afnet.net. *Website:* www.seydouelimanediarra.net.

DIAS DIOGO, Luisa, MEconSc; Mozambican economist, politician and international organization official; b. 11 April 1958, Dist of Mágoè, Tete; d. of Luís João Diogo and Laura Atanásia Dias; m. António Albana Silva; two s. one d.; ed Univ. Eduardo Mondlane, Univ. of London, UK; joined Ministry of Planning and Finance 1980, with Dept of Econs and Investment 1980–84, Assoc. Head of Dept 1984–86, Programme Officer Study Dept 1986–89, Head, Dept of Budget 1989–92, Nat. Dir of Budget 1993–94; Programme Officer IBRD, Maputo 1994; Vice-Minister of Planning and Finance 1994–2000; Minister of Planning and Finance 2000–05; Prime Minister of Mozambique 2004–10; Chair. Nat. Council of the Fight against HIV/AIDS 2005–09; Co-Chair. High-level Panel on UN System-wide Coherence in the Areas of Development, Humanitarian Assistance and the Environment 2006; Chair. Bd of Dirs Barclays Bank Mozambique SA 2012–; apptd Chair. Devt Assistance Cttee 2016; fmr Vice-Chair. Advisory Bd Harvard Ministerial Leadership Forum of Health And Educ. Ministers; apptd mem. Africa Comm. 2008; mem. UN High-level Panel on Global Sustainability 2010; mem. Advisory Bd Brenthurst Foundation 2010, Universidade Nova de Lisboa; mem. Advisory Council for Peace and Security, African Comm. 2010; mem. Council on Women World Leaders; mem. Council African Union Foundation; mem. Club de Madrid; Global Women's Leadership Award 2008, Eduardo Mondlane Medal 2010. *Leisure interests:* reading, listening to music, spending time with family and friends. *Address:* Barclays Bank Mozambique S.A., Av. 25 de Setembro, Andar 1184-15°, POB 757, Maputo, Mozambique (office). *Website:* www.barclays.co.mz (office).

DIAS FERREIRA LEITE, Maria Manuela, BEcons; Portuguese economist and politician; b. 3 Dec. 1940, Lisbon; d. of Carlos Eugénio Dias Ferreira and Julieta de Carvalho; ed Instituto Superior de Ciências Económicas e Financeiras, Tech. Univ. of Lisbon; researcher, Calouste Gulbenkian Foundation 1964–73; asst, Public Finance and Econs, Instituto Superior de Economia e Gestão 1966–79; Dir Dept of Statistics, Inst. of State Holdings 1975–77; Co-ordinator Finance Group, Research Bureau, Banco de Portugal 1977–86; Dir-Gen. Public Accounting, Ministry of Finance 1986–90; Sec. of State of Budget 1990–91; Sec. of State attached to Minister of Budget 1991–93; with Ministry of Educ. 1993–95; mem. Parl. 1991–95, 1995–2000; Vice-Pres. of Parl. Group, Social Democratic Party 1996–2001, Pres. Sept. 2001, Pres. Leader of the Opposition 2008–10; Minister of State and of Finance 2002–04; mem. Council of State 2006–08; consultant to Banco de Portugal

2004; mem. Admin. Council, Banco Santander Totta 2006. *Address:* c/o Banco de Portugal, Rua do Ouro 27, 1100-150 Lisbon; c/o Administrative Council, Banco Santander Totta, Rua de Ouro 88, 1100-061 Lisbon, Portugal. *E-mail:* info@bportugal.pt. *Website:* www.bportugal.pt; www.santandertotta.pt.

DIAZ, Cameron Michelle; American actress and fmr model; b. 30 Aug. 1972, San Diego, Calif.; d. of Emilio Diaz and Billie Diaz (née Early); m. Benji Madden 2015; model with Elite Model Management 1988–93; rose to prominence during 1990s with roles in films including The Mask, My Best Friend's Wedding and There's Something About Mary. *Films include:* She's No Angel: Cameron Diaz (video short) 1992, The Mask 1994, The Last Supper 1995, Feeling Minnesota 1996, She's the One 1996, Head Above Water 1996, Keys to Tulsa 1997, My Best Friend's Wedding 1997, A Life Less Ordinary 1997, Fear and Loathing in Las Vegas 1997, There's Something About Mary 1998, Very Bad Things 1998, Being John Malkovich 1999, Invisible Circus 1999, Any Given Sunday 1999, Charlie's Angels 2000, Things You Can Tell Just by Looking at Her 2000, Shrek (voice) 2001, Vanilla Sky (Boston Soc. of Film Critics Best Supporting Actress 2001, Chicago Film Critics Best Supporting Actress 2002) 2001, The Sweetest Thing 2002, Gangs of New York 2002, Charlie's Angels: Full Throttle 2003, Shrek II (voice) 2004, In Her Shoes 2005, The Holiday 2006, Shrek the Third (voice) 2007, What Happens in Vegas 2008, My Sister's Keeper 2009, The Box 2009, Shrek Forever After (voice) 2010, Knight and Day 2010, The Green Hornet 2011, Bad Teacher 2011, What to Expect When You're Expecting 2012, Gambit 2013, The Counselor 2013, The Other Woman 2014, Sex Tape 2014, Annie 2014. *Television includes:* Trippin (documentary) 2005, Shrek the Halls (voice) 2007, Saturday Night Live 2008–09, Sesame Street 2009, Top Gear 2010, Scared Shrekless (short) (voice) 2010, The X Factor (French edn, guest judge) 2011. *Address:* c/o Creative Artists Agency, 2000 Avenue of the Stars, Los Angeles, CA 90067, USA (office). *Telephone:* (424) 288-2000 (office). *Fax:* (424) 288-2900 (office). *Website:* www.caa.com (office).

DIAZ, Illac Angelo, BA, MA, MBA; Philippine social entrepreneur and environmental campaigner; *Founder and Executive Director, MyShelter Inc.;* b. 1971; ed Ateneo de Manila Univ., De La Salle Univ., Manila, Asian Inst. of Man., Manila, Kennedy School of Govt, Harvard Univ., USA; Research Fellow, Special Program for Urban and Regional Studies, MIT, USA 2006; Co-founder USAP-KAMAY Program (support for deaf-mute students), Ateneo de Manila Univ. 1988–95; Founding Pres. Good Guys Inc. (support for law students) 1998–2003; Exec. Dir CentroMigrante (self-help housing community) 2003; Founder and Exec. Dir MyShelter Inc. 2005–; Founder and Exec. Dir Pier One Seafarers' Dormitories (sustainable shelter systems), Manila; Lead Convenor, Walk For Light Movement, Boston; Mason Fellow, Harvard Kennedy School of Govt; Ernst & Young Entrepreneur of the Year 2006, named one of the 10 Outstanding Young Persons of the World by Jaycees Int. 2006, Harvard's Green Carpet Award. *Address:* Corte Real, Real cor. Solana Streets, Intramuros, Manila (office); 210 Loring Street, Pasay City, Philippines. *Telephone:* (2) 301-0600 (office).

DIAZ, Miguel Humberto, BA, MA, PhD; American theologian, academic and diplomatist; *University Professor of Faith and Culture, University of Dayton;* b. 29 Sept. 1963, Havana, Cuba; m. Marian K Díaz 1993; four c.; ed St Thomas Univ., Univ. of Notre Dame, Ind.; Theology Instructor, Dept of Theology, Univ. of Notre Dame 1995–96; Asst Prof., Dept of Religious Studies, Univ. of Dayton, Ohio 1996–98; Asst Prof. in Systematic/Philosophical Theology, St Vincent de Paul Regional Seminary, Fla 1998–2001; Academic Dean, Vincent de Paul Seminary, Fla 2001–03; Assoc. Prof., Barry Univ., Fla 2003–04, Dept of Theology, Coll. of St Benedict/St John Univ., St John's School of Theology Seminary, St Joseph and Collegeville, Minnesota 2004–09, Prof. 2009; Amb. to the Holy See (Vatican City) 2009–12; Univ. Prof. of Faith and Culture, Univ. of Dayton 2012–; Chair. Multi-Cultural Cttee, St John's School of Theology Seminary 2007, Co-Chair. Intercultural Directions Council 2006; mem. Bd Voices for the Common Good, Catholic Theological Soc. of America 2008, Acad. of Catholic Hispanic Theologians, USA (Vice-Pres. 2005, Pres. 2006–08) 2001–08; mem. Steering Cttee Karl Rahner Soc. 2004–08; mem. Assessment Cttee, Dept of Theology 2006–07, Grad. Theological Studies Cttee 2005–06, Cttee of Latin American/Latino Studies Program at CSB/SJU 2004; Educational Trailblazer Theologian of the Year Award 2007. *Publications include:* From the Heart of Our People: Latino/a Explorations in Catholic Systematic Theology (co-ed) 1999, On Being Human: US Hispanic and Rahnerian Perspectives (Hispanic Theological Initiative Book of the Year Award, Princeton Theological Seminary 2002) 2002. *Address:* University of Dayton, HM 254, 300 College Park, Dayton, OH 45469, USA (office). *Telephone:* (937) 229-2105 (office). *Website:* www.udayton.edu (office).

DÍAZ-CANEL BERMUDEZ, Miguel Mario; Cuban politician and head of state; *President, Council of State and Council of Ministers;* b. 20 April 1960, Santa Clara; mil. service with Fuerzas Armadas Revolucionarias 1982–85; early career as electrical engineer; Prof., Central Univ. of Las Villas 1985; various roles with Unión de Jóvenes Comunistas (communist youth league) from 1987; mem. Partido Comunista de Cuba (PCC—Communist Party of Cuba), PCC Rep. in Nicaragua –1989, elected to PCC Central Cttee 1991, PCC First Sec., Villa Clara Prov. 1994–2003, First Sec., Holguin Prov. 2003–08, elected to Political Bureau (youngest-ever mem.) 2003; Minister of Higher Educ. 2009–12; Vice-Pres., Council of Ministers, with responsibility for educ. issues 2012–13; First Vice-Pres., Council of State and Council of Ministers 2013–18, Pres., Council of State and Council of Ministers 2018–. *Address:* Consejo de Estado, Havana, Cuba (office).

DÍAZ RUEDA, Ruth Marina, LLD; Colombian lawyer and judge; *President, Supreme Court of Justice;* b. Socorro, Santander Dist; ed Univ. Santo Tomás de Aquino, Bucaramanga; started career as judge, Barichara, Santander 1978, later becoming judge, civil law court, Sorocco and municipal criminal, juvenile and circuit courts, San Gil (first woman); fmr Judge, Civil Court of the Circuit of Bogotá; Judge (first woman), Civil Appeal Chamber, Supreme Court of Justice 2006, Pres. 2007, 2010, Vice-Pres. Supreme Court of Justice 2012–13, Pres. (first woman) 2013–; fmr Prof. of law, Univ. Santo Tomás de Aquino, Bucaramanga, Univ. Libre, Bogotá, Fundación Universitaria de San Gil. *Address:* Supreme Court of Justice, Edif. de Palacio de Justicia, Calle 12, No 7-65, Bogotá, DC, Colombia (office). *Telephone:* (1) 562-2000 (office). *Website:* www.cortesuprema.gov.co (office).

DIBABA, Tirunesh; Ethiopian athlete; b. 1 June 1985, Bekoji, Arsi; d. of Dibaba Keneni and Gutu Tola; m. Sileshi Sihine; long-distance track athlete; began athletics running aged 14; moved to Addis Ababa 2000; finished 5th, aged 15, in women's jr race at Int. Asscn of Athletics Feds (IAAF) World Cross Country Championships 2001; gold medal, 5,000m, World Championships, Paris 2003, 5,000m and 10,000m, Helsinki 2005, 10,000m, Osaka 2007, 10,000m, Moscow 2013; gold medal, Jr Race, World Cross Country Championships, Lausanne 2003, Short Course, Saint-Galmier 2005, Long Course, Saint-Galmier 2005, Long Course, Fukuoka 2006, Sr Race, Edinburgh 2008; silver medal, Jr Race, World Cross Country Championships, Dublin 2002, Short Race, Brussels 2004, Sr Race, Mombasa 2007; silver medal, 5,000m, World Jr Championships, Kingston 2002; bronze medal, 5,000m, Olympic Games, Athens 2004, gold medal, 5,000m and 10,000m (Olympic record), Beijing Olympics 2008, gold medal, 10,000m and bronze medal, 5,000m, London Olympics 2012; gold medal, 10,000m, African Championships, Addis Ababa 2008, Nairobi 2010, silver medal, 5,000m, Bambous 2006; first woman to win 10,000m/5,000m double at same championships, Helsinki 2005; won five out of six Golden League events (5,000m) in same season 2006; set a new 5,000m world record of 14 minutes 11.15 seconds at Oslo Golden League 2008; first ever woman to win both 5,000m and 10,000m at same Olympics 2008; Int. Asscn of Athletics Fed. Award 2005, 2008, Women's Track & Field Athlete of the Year 2008, Women's 5,000m Best Year Performance 2008–09, rank of Chief Supt conferred on her by her club The Prisons Police 2008, hosp. outside Addis Ababa named after her. *Address:* c/o Ethiopian Athletics Federation, PO Box 3241, Addis Ababa, Ethiopia. *Website:* www.ethiosports.com; www.tiruneshdibaba.net.

DIBANGO, Manu; Cameroonian musician (saxophone, piano); b. 12 Dec. 1934, Douala; ed piano lessons; moved to Paris 1949, then Brussels, Belgium 1956; residency at Black Angels Club, Brussels; joined band led by Joseph Kabsele, African Jazz 1960, played with African Jazz in Zaire –1963; returned to Cameroon to form own band 1963–65; studio musician, Paris 1965; backed musicians, including Peter Gabriel, Sinead O'Connor, Angélique Kidjo, Geoffrey Oryema, Ray Lema, Touré Kunda; solo artist 1968–; Pres., Francophone Diffusion; apptd UNESCO Artist for Peace 2004; Chevalier, Ordre et de la Valeur (Cameroon) 1988, Commdr des Arts et des Lettres 2001, Chevalier, Legion d'honneur 2010; Grammy Award for Best R&B Instrumental Performance of the Year 1973, Grand Prix de Académie Charles Cros 2003, Ronnie Scott Award for Services to Jazz 2007, Grande Medaille de Vermeil de la Ville de Paris 2013. *Compositions include:* commissioned by President Ahidjo to write song for Africa Cup football match 1971. *Recordings include:* albums: Manu Dibango 1968, Saxy-Party 1969, O Boso 1971, Soma Loba 1971, Soul Makossa 1972, African Voodoo 1972, Africadelic 1973, Blue Elephant 1973, Makossa Man 1974, African Funk 1974, Makossa Music 1975, African Rhythm Machine 1975, Super Kumba 1976, Manu 76 1976, Afrovision 1976, Big Blow 1978, A L'Olympia 1978, Ceddo 1978, Gone Clear 1979, Ambassador 1981, Waka Juju 1982, Deliverence 1983, Sweet and Soft 1983, Melodies Africaines vols 1 and 2 1983, Deadline 1984, Electric Africa 1985, Afrijazzy 1986, Negropolitains Vol. 1 1989, Polysonik 1991, Bao Bao 1992, Negropolitains Vol. 2 1992, Wakafrika 1994, Lamastabastani 1996, Sax & Spirituals 1996, Manu Safari 1998, Mboa' Su 1999, From Africa 2003, Voyage Anthologique 2004, Essential Recordings 2006, Lion of Africa 2007, Anthology 2009, Soft and Sweet 2010, Choc'n'Soul 2010, Past Present Future 2011, Ballad Emotion 2011, Africa Boogie 2013, Akoko Party 2013, Lagos Go Slow 2013, Balade en Saxo 2013. *Publications:* Trois Kilos de Café (autobiography) 1990. *Address:* c/o Global Mix Media Limited, PO Box 4702, Henley on Thames, RG9 9AA, England (office). *E-mail:* claire@manudibango.net (office). *Website:* www.manudibango.net (office).

DIBBITS, Taco; Dutch art historian and museum director; *General Director, Rijksmuseum;* b. 7 Sept. 1968, Amsterdam; m. Rhiannon Pickles; three s.; ed Vrije Univ. Amsterdam, Univ. of Cambridge; Dir, Old Masters Dept, Christie's, London 1997–2002; Curator of 17th-century painting, Rijksmuseum 2002–06, Head of Fine and Decorative Arts 2006–08, Dir of Collections 2008–16, Gen. Dir 2016–; mem. Cttee on Museum Acquisitions from 1933; mem. Bd of Dirs De Pont Museum of Contemporary Art, Duivenvoorde Foundation; mem. Recommendations Cttee, Young in Prison (int. NGO). *Address:* Rijksmuseum, Postbus 74888, 1070 DN Amsterdam, Netherlands (office). *Telephone:* (20) 6747000 (office). *E-mail:* info@rijksmuseum.nl (home). *Website:* www.rijksmuseum.nl/en/taco-dibbits (office).

DIBIAGGIO, John A., DDS, MA; American dentist and university administrator; *President Emeritus, Tufts University;* b. 11 Sept. 1932, San Antonio, Tex.; s. of Ciro DiBiaggio and Acidalia DiBiaggio; m. Nancy Cronemiller 1989; one s. two d. (from previous marriage); ed Eastern Michigan Univ., Univ. of Detroit, Univ. of Michigan; gen. dentistry practice, New Baltimore, Mich. 1958–65; Asst Prof., School of Dentistry, Univ. of Detroit 1965–67; Asst Dean of Student Affairs, Univ. of Kentucky 1967–70; Prof., Dean School of Dentistry, Va Commonwealth Univ., Richmond 1970–76; Vice-Pres. for Health Affairs and Exec. Dir of the Health Center, Univ. of Conn., Farmington 1976–79, Pres. Univ. of Conn., Storrs 1979–85; Pres. Mich. State Univ., East Lansing 1985–92; Pres. Tufts Univ., Medford, Mass. 1992–2001, Pres. Emer. 2001–; mem. Bd American Automobile Asscn 1994–2002, Kaman Corpn 1984–2008; Trustee, American Cancer Soc. Foundation 1993– (Pres. 1999), Univ. of Massachusetts 2003–; 11 hon. degrees; Order of Merit (Italy); Man of the Year, City of Detroit 1985, Pierre Fauchard Gold Medal Award 1989. *Publications:* Applied Practice Management: A Strategy for Stress Control (with others) 1979; articles in professional journals. *Leisure interest:* tennis. *Address:* c/o President's Office, Tufts University, Medford, MA 02155 (office); PO Box 5346, Snowmass Village, CO 81615-5346, USA (home). *Telephone:* (617) 628-5000 (office). *E-mail:* john.dibiaggio@tufts.edu (office). *Website:* www.tufts.edu (office).

DIBY, Charles Koffi, BA, MA; Côte d'Ivoirian economist and politician; *Chairman of Economic and Social Council;* b. 7 Sept. 1957, Bouaké; s. of Mathurin Yao Kra; m.; five c.; ed Nat. School of Man. and Int. Inst. of Public Admin, Paris; began career at Treasury 1984, responsible for Nat. Inst. for the Youth and Sports 1985–90, for Nat. Inst. for Professional Training 1990–91, Rep. for Cen. Agency for Public Spending 1991–93, Treas. for Bondoukou Prov. 1993–94, Treas. for Daoukro Prov. 1994–97, Accountant, Cen. Agency for Public Spending 1997–98, Paymaster-Gen. 1998–99, Deputy Dir-Gen. of the Treasury 1999–2000, Dir-Gen. 2001–07; Counsellor to Minister of the Economy and Finance 2000–01; Minister Del. of the Economy and Finance 2006–07; Minister of the Economy and Finance

2007–12; Minister of State, Minister of Foreign Affairs 2012–16; Vice-Pres. Democratic Party of Ivory Coast (PDCI) 2016–; Chair. Econ. and Social Council 2016–; Chevalier, Ordre Nat. de la République de Côte d'Ivoire, Officier, Commdr; Commdr, Légion d'honneur; Dr hc (Univ. of Montesquieu, Abidjan); named by The Financial Times and Emerging Markets as the Best Minister of Finance for Africa 2010, 2013. *Publication includes:* Management des services publics en Afrique 2007. *Address:* Economic and Social Council, 04 BP 301, Abidjan 04, Côte d'Ivoire. *E-mail:* ces@ces.ci. *Website:* www.ces.ci.

DiCAPRIO, Leonardo Wilhelm; American actor and film producer; b. 11 Nov. 1974, Los Angeles, Calif.; s. of George DiCaprio and Irmelin DiCaprio; f. Appian Way production co.; Commdr des Arts et des Lettres; Platinum Award, Santa Barbara Int. Film Festival 2005. *Films include:* Critters 3 1991, Poison Ivy 1992, This Boy's Life 1993, What's Eating Gilbert Grape 1993, The Foot Shooting Party (short) 1994, Les cent et une nuits de Simon Cinéma (uncredited) 1995, The Quick and the Dead 1995, The Basketball Diaries 1995, Total Eclipse 1995, Marvin's Room 1996, William Shakespeare's Romeo + Juliet 1996, Titanic 1997, The Man in the Iron Mask 1998, Celebrity 1998, The Beach 2000, Don's Plum 2001, Gangs of New York 2002, Catch Me If You Can 2002, The Aviator 2004, The Departed (Best Int. Actor, Irish Film and TV Awards 2007) 2006, Blood Diamond 2006, The 11th Hour (voice, producer) 2007, Body of Lies 2008, Revolutionary Road 2009, Shutter Island 2010, Inception 2010, J. Edgar 2011, Django Unchained 2012, The Great Gatsby 2013, The Wolf of Wall Street (Golden Globe Award for Best Actor in a Motion Picture, Comedy or Musical 2014) 2013, The Revenant (Golden Globe Award for Best Performance in Motion Picture - Drama 2016, Screen Actors Guild Award for Outstanding Performance by a Male Actor in a Leading Role 2016, BAFTA Best Performance by an Actor in a Leading Role 2016, Acad. Award for Best Actor 2016) 2015. *Television includes:* The New Lassie (series) 1989, The Outsiders (series) 1990, Santa Barbara (series) 1990, Parenthood (series) 1990–91, Roseanne (series) 1991, Growing Pains (series) 1991–92. *Address:* c/o Special Artists Agency, 9465 Wilshire Blvd, Suite 890, Beverly Hills, CA 90212, USA (office); Appian Way, 9255 Sunset Blvd, Suite 615, West Hollywood, CA 90069; c/o Birken Productions Inc., PO Box 291958, Los Angeles, CA 90029, USA (office). *Telephone:* (310) 300-1390 (Appian Way). *Website:* www.leonardodicaprio.com (office).

DiCARLO, Rosemary Anne, MA, PhD; American diplomatist and UN official; *Under-Secretary-General for Political Affairs;* b. 1947; m. Thomas Graham; ed Brown Univ.; joined Foreign Service, overseas assignments in Moscow and Oslo, Dir Democratic Initiatives for New Ind. States, Dept of State, US Coordinator for Stability Pact Implementation, Deputy Asst Sec. of State European and Eurasian Affairs, Dept of State, Dir UN Affairs, Nat. Security Council; Alt. Rep. for Special Political Affairs, UN, Deputy Perm. Rep. to UN; mem. Secr. of UNESCO, Under-Sec.-Gen. for Political Affairs 2018–; Pres. Nat. Cttee on American Foreign Policy 2015–18; apptd Lecturer and Sr Fellow Jackson Inst. for Global Affairs, Yale Univ. 2015. *Address:* Department of Political Affairs, United Nations Headquarters, 405 E 42nd Street, New York, NY 10017, USA (office). *Telephone:* (212) 963-1234 (office). *Fax:* (212) 963-4879 (office). *Website:* www.un.org (office).

DiCHRISTINA, Mariette, BS; American editor; *Editor-in-Chief, Scientific American;* b. 16 April 1964, North Tarrytown, NY; m. Carl John Gerosa 1989; two d.; ed Boston Univ.; reporter, Gannett-Westchester newspapers 1986–87; joined Popular Science magazine as copy ed., later becoming Assoc. Ed., Sr Ed. and Exec. Ed. 1987–2001; Exec. Ed. Scientific American 2001–09, Ed.-in-Chief 2009–; Adjunct Prof. in Science Writing, New York Univ.; Pres. Nat. Asscn of Science Writers 2009–10; adviser, Citizen Science Alliance, Origins Inst. at Arizona State Univ., Bulletin of Atomic Scientists; Fellow, AAAS 2011; Douglas S. Morrow Public Outreach Award 2001, Scientific American Nat. Magazine Award for General Excellence 2011. *Address:* Scientific American, Nature America, 75 Varick Street, 9th Floor, New York, NY 10013-1917, USA (office). *Telephone:* (212) 451-8200 (office). *E-mail:* mdichristina@sciam.com (office). *Website:* www.scientificamerican.com (office).

DICK, Cressida Rose, CBE, MPhil; British civil servant and police officer; *Commissioner, Metropolitan Police;* b. 1960, Oxford; d. of Marcus William Dick and Cecilia Dick (née Buxton); ed Dragon School, Oxford High School, Balliol Coll., Oxford and Fitzwilliam Coll., Cambridge, Bramshill Police Coll.; began career working in large accountancy firm; joined Metropolitan Police, London as constable 1983; transferred to Thames Valley Police as superintendent 1995–2000, rising to chief superintendent and Area Commdr for Oxford; returned to Metropolitan Police as Commdr 2001–06, becoming Head of Operation Trident, Specialist Crime Directorate 2003, Deputy Asst Commr, Specialist Operations 2006, Asst Commr 2009, Asst Commr for Specialist Operations 2011–15, Acting Deputy Commr 2011–13, Commr, Metropolitan Police (first woman) 2017–; Queen's Police Medal. *Address:* Metropolitan Police, Victoria Embankment, Westminster, London, SW1A 2JL, England (office). *Telephone:* (20) 7230-1212 (office). *Website:* www.met.police.uk (office).

DICKERSON, Vivian M., MD; American physician and professor of obstetrics and gynaecology; one s.; ed Univ. of California, Santa Barbara, Univ. of California, San Diego School of Medicine; joined Peace Corps and worked in Togo, West Africa 1970s; completed residency training at UCLA Cedars-Sinai Medical Center; fmr Sr Research Analyst, Susan Samueli Center for Complementary and Alternative Medicine, Irvine, Clinical Prof. of Obstetrics and Gynecology, Univ. of California, Irvine (UCI) Medical Center –2006, now Assoc.; apptd Exec. Medical Dir of Women's Health Programs and Care, Hoag Memorial Hosp. Presbyterian, Newport Beach, Calif. 2006; held numerous positions with American Coll. of Obstetricians and Gynecologists (ACOG), including Chair. Dist IX (Calif.), Council of Dist Chairs, Cttee on Int. Relations, Grievance Cttee and Admin. Comm. 1984–2004, Pres. ACOG 2004–05; Chair. California Family Health Council 2000–04; Ed. in Chief The Female Patient (journal); mem. Advisory Bd Esprit Pharma Inc., Mirabel Medical Systems Ltd, Neomatrix LLC Inc.; ACOG Outstanding Dist Service Award, American Medical Women's Asscn Gender Equity Award 2000, UCI Coll. of Medicine, Golden Apple Award 2002. *Leisure interests:* hiking, skiing, scuba diving. *Address:* 615D E West View Drive, Orange, CA 92869, USA.

DICKIE, Brian James; British opera director (retd) and consultant; *Artistic Adviser, Bertelsmann Stiftung;* b. 23 July 1941, Newark, Notts.; s. of Robert Kelso Dickie and Harriet Elizabeth Dickie (née Riddell); m. 1st Victoria Teresa Sheldon (née Price) 1968; two s. one d.; m. 2nd Nancy Gustafson 1989; m. 3rd Elinor Rhys Williams 2002; one d.; ed Trinity Coll., Dublin; Admin. Asst, Glyndebourne Opera 1962–66; Admin. Glyndebourne Touring Opera 1967–81; Opera Man., Glyndebourne Festival Opera 1970–81, Gen. Admin. 1981–89; Artistic Dir Wexford Festival 1967–73; Artistic Adviser, Théâtre Musical de Paris 1981–87, Bertelsmann Stiftung; Gen. Dir Canadian Opera Co. 1989–93; Artistic Counsellor, Opéra de Nice 1994–97; Gen. Dir EU Opera 1997–99, Chicago Opera Theater 1999–2012; Chair. London Choral Soc. 1978–85, Theatres Nat. Cttee Opera Cttee 1976–85; Vice-Chair. Theatres Nat. Cttee 1980–85; Vice-Pres. Theatrical Man. Asscn 1983–85; mem. Bd Opera America 1991–93; Chicagoan of the Year, Chicago Tribune 2000, 2002, Annual Cultural Award, Univ. Club of Chicago 2010. *Leisure interests:* cricket, photography, wine and food, travel, my blog. *Address:* 4 Bancroft Court, 35 Ackmar Road, London, SW6 4UR, England. *Telephone:* (20) 7736-1031; 7966-467512 (mobile). *E-mail:* briandickie@mac.com. *Website:* www.briandickie.com.

DICKIE, Lloyd Merlin, PhD, FRSC; Canadian ecologist and academic; *Research Scientist Emeritus, Department of Fisheries and Oceans;* b. 6 March 1926, Kingsport, Nova Scotia; s. of Ebenezer Cox Dickie and Pearl (née Sellars) Dickie; m. Marjorie C. Bowman 1952; one s. two d.; ed Acadia Univ., Yale Univ., Univ. of Toronto; research scientist, Fisheries Research Bd, NB 1951–62, Great Lakes Inst., Toronto 1962–65; Dir Marine Ecology Lab., Bedford Inst. Oceanography, Dartmouth, NS 1965–74; Chair. and Prof. of Oceanography, Dalhousie Univ., Halifax 1974–77, Dir Inst. of Environmental Studies, Dalhousie Univ. 1974–76; Research Scientist, Marine Ecology Lab. and Marine Fish Div., Bedford Inst. of Oceanography, Dartmouth, NS 1976–87; Sr Research Scientist, Biological Sciences Br., Dept of Fisheries and Oceans 1987–93, Research Scientist Emer. 1994–; participant in Ocean Production Enhancement Network 1991–92; mem. SPICES (Sr People of Int. Council for the Exploration of the Sea) Network; Oscar-Sette Memorial Award, American Fish Soc. 1991. *Publications:* Ad Mare: Canada Looks to the Sea (with R. W. Stewart) 1971, The Biomass Spectrum: A Predator-Prey Theory of Aquatic Production (co-author) 2001; more than 80 scientific papers. *Address:* 7 Lakewood Court, Dartmouth, NS B2X 2R6, Canada. *Telephone:* (902) 435-1545. *E-mail:* lloyd.dickie@eastlink.ca.

DICKINSON, Angie; American actress; b. (Angeline Brown), 30 Sept. 1931, Kulm, ND; d. of Fredericka (née Hehr) and Leo Henry Brown; m. 1st Gene Dickinson (divorced 1960); m. 2nd Burt Bacharach (divorced 1981); one d. (deceased); ed Immaculate Heart Coll., Glendale Coll. *Films include:* Lucky Me 1954, Man With the Gun, The Return of Jack Slade, Tennessee's Partner, The Black Whip, Hidden Guns, Tension at Table Rock, Gun the Man Down, Calypso Joe, China Gate, Shoot Out at Medicine Bend, Cry Terror, I Married a Woman, Rio Bravo, The Bramble Bush, A Fever in the Blood, The Sins of Rachel Cade, Jessica, Rome Adventure, Captain Newman MD, The Killers, The Art of Love, Cast a Giant Shadow, The Chase, The Poppy is Also a Flower, Last Challenge, Point Blank, Sam Whiskey, Some Kind of a Nut, Young Billy Young, Pretty Maids All in a Row, The Resurrection of Zachary Wheeler, The Outside Man, Big Bad Mama, Klondike Fever, Dressed to Kill, Charlie Chan and the Curse of the Dragon Queen, Death Hunt, Big Bad Mama II, Even Cowgirls Get the Blues, The Maddening, Sabrina, The Sun, The Moon and The Stars, Pay It Forward, Sealed with a Kiss 1999, The Last Producer 2000, Duets 2000, Pay it Forward 2000, Big Bad Love 2001, Elvis Has Left the Building 2004. *Television series:* Police Woman, Cassie & Co. *Television films:* The Love War, Thief, See the Man Run, The Norliss Tapes, Pray for the Wildcats, A Sensitive Passionate Man, Overboard, The Suicide's Wife, Dial M for Murder, One Shoe Makes it Murder, Jealousy, A Touch of Scandal, Stillwatch, Police Story: The Freeway Killings, Once Upon a Texas Train, Prime Target, Treacherous Crossing, Danielle Steel's Remembrance, Mending Fences 2009; mini-series: Pearl, Hollywood Wives, Wild Palms. *Address:* 1715 Carla Ridge, Beverly Hills, CA 90210-1911, USA.

DICKSON, William Andrew; British diplomatist and business executive; *CEO, Independent (UK) Exports Limited;* b. 17 Dec. 1950, Glasgow, Scotland; s. of William Paul McBean Dickson and Isabella Dickson (née Goodwin); m. Patricia Ann Dickson (née Daniels) 2007; ed Univ. of Stirling, Northumbria Univ.; Training Dept, FCO 1969, on special unpaid leave (univ./Royal Marines) 1969–76, Vice-Consul, Embassy in Cairo 1976–79, Third Sec. (Commercial), High Comm. in Nairobi 1980–82, Second Sec. (Commercial), Embassy in Budapest 1982–85, Foreign Office Spokesman, News Dept 1985–89, First Sec., IAEA, Vienna 1989–93, British Govt Spokesman, Hong Kong 1994–98, Head of Atlantic and Oceans, Overseas Territories Dept, FCO 1998–2001, Admin. and Magistrate, Ascension Island 2000, Consul-Gen., Admin. and Magistrate, Tristan da Cunha 2001–04, Deputy Head of Information Man. Group 2005–07, Consul-Gen., Embassy in Erbil 2007–08, Amb. to Mongolia 2009–11; Dir of UK Operations, MongoliaNation; Dir, Orgill-Dickson Assocs 2011–15, International Export Partners Ltd; CEO Independent (UK) Exports Ltd 2012–; mem. Bd Broads Authority 2015– (Vice Chair. 2018–), Marine Man. Org. 2019–. *Leisure interests:* boating, allotment gardening. *Address:* 12 Trail Quay Cottages, Marsh Road, Hoveton, NR12 8UH, Norfolk, England (home). *E-mail:* shipwreckbt@hotmail.com (office).

DICTUS, Richard; Dutch UN official; *United Nations Resident Coordinator and UNDP Resident Representative in Arab Republic of Egypt;* m.; three c.; ed Technical Univ. of Twente; Jr Professional Officer, UNIDO, South Yemen 1987; Asst Resident Rep. (Programme), UNDP, Sudan 1990–92, Lesotho 1992–94, Bangladesh 1994–98, Deputy Resident Rep., UNDP, Pakistan 1998–2000, Man. Adviser (Deputy Chief), Admin. Services Div., Bureau of Man., UNDP, New York 2000–01, Deputy Dir of Human Resources, Bureau of Man. 2001–05, UN Resident Coordinator and UNDP Resident Rep. in Fiji 2005–09, UN Resident Coordinator and UNDP Resident Rep. in Malawi 2009–12, Exec. Coordinator UN Volunteers 2013–16, UN Resident Coordinator and UNDP Resident Rep. and Designated Official for Security in Arab Repub. of Egypt 2017–. *Address:* United Nations Development Programme, Egypt Country Office, World Trade Center, 1191 Corniche El Nil Street, Boulac, Cairo, Egypt. *Telephone:* (2) 24564811. *Fax:* (2) 22561647. *E-mail:* fatma.yassin@undp.org. *Website:* www.eg.undp.org/content/egypt/en/home/operations/leadership.html.

DIDDY (see COMBS, Sean).

DIDI, Ahmed Abdulla, PhD; Maldivian lawyer and judge; *Chief Justice of Supreme Court;* b. 11 Oct. 1966, S Hithadhoo; ed Faculty of Shari'a and Law, Al Azhar Univ., Cairo; worked as consultant in Maldives and Egypt 1996; Deputy Attorney-Gen., Office of Attorney-Gen. 2008–09; Sr Lecturer, Faculty of Shari'a and Law, Maldives Nat. Univ. Feb.–June 2010; Counsel-Gen., People's Ass. July–Aug. 2010; Justice, Supreme of Maldives 2010–18, Chief Justice 2018–; participated in Convention on the Rights of the Child, Geneva 2009, 23rd Law Asia Conf., India 2010, World Congress on Justice Governance and Law for Environmental Sustainability, Brazil 2012. *Address:* Supreme Court of the Maldives, Theemuge, Orchid Magu, Malé, Maldives (office). *Telephone:* 3009990 (office). *Fax:* 3008554 (office). *E-mail:* info@supremecourt.gov.mv (office). *Website:* www.supremecourt.gov.mv (office).

DIDI, Ali Hussain; Maldivian civil servant and diplomatist; joined civil service 1983, Dir Passport Office 2001–03, Controller of Immigration and Emigration March–Dec. 2003, Dir-Gen. Dept of Penitentiary and Rehabilitation, Ministry of Home Affairs and Environment 2004; Chair. Malé Municipality 2004–07; CEO Maldives Airports Co. 2007–08; High Commr to Sri Lanka 2008–11; Perm. Rep. to EU and Amb. to Belgium 2011–12.

DIDI, Mariya Ahmed; Maldivian politician, women's rights activist and lawyer; *Minister of Defence and National Security* first qualified female lawyer in Maldives; fmr state prosecutor and Asst Exec. Dir, Attorney-Gen.'s Office; one of six women mems of People's Majlis (Parl.), non-aligned MP, then mem. Maldivian Democratic Party 2005– (Chair. 2008–11), for Kaafu Atoll 2005–09, one of only two elected women (other four apptd by Pres.); MP for North Machangolhi, Malé City 2010–; Minister of Defence and National Security 2018–; organized first-ever women's rights rally in Maldives in 2006; co-recipient, first Int. Women of Courage Award, US Dept of State 2007. *Address:* Ministry of Defence and National Security, Ameer Ahmed Magu, Malé 20-126 (office); Maldivian Democratic Party, H. Sharasha, 2nd Floor, Sosun Magu, Malé 20-059, Maldives (office). *Telephone:* 3322601 (office); 3340044 (office). *Fax:* 3325525 (office); 3322960 (office). *E-mail:* admin@defence.gov.mv (office); secretariat@mdp.org.mv (office). *Website:* www.defence.gov.mv; www.mdp.org.mv (office).

DIDION, Joan, BA; American writer; b. 5 Dec. 1934, Sacramento, Calif.; d. of Frank Reese Didion and Eduene Didion (née Jerrett); m. John Gregory Dunne 1964 (died 2003); one d. (died 2005); ed Univ. of Calif., Berkeley; Assoc. Features Ed. Vogue magazine 1956–63; fmr columnist, Esquire, Life, Saturday Evening Post, fmr contributor Nat. Review; freelance writer 1963–; mem. American Acad. of Arts and Letters, American Acad. of Arts and Sciences, Council on Foreign Relations; Dr hc (Harvard Univ.) 2009, (Yale Univ.) 2011; First Prize Vogue's Prix de Paris 1956, American Acad. of Arts and Letters Morton Dauwen Zabel Prize 1978, Edward McDowell Medal 1996, George Polk Award 2001, American Acad. of Arts and Letter Gold Medal for Belles Lettres 2005, Medal for Distinguished Contrib. to American Letters, Nat. Book Foundation 2007, Nat. Humanities Medal 2012. *Screenplays include:* Panic in Needle Park 1971, Play It as It Lays 1972, A Star is Born 1976, True Confessions 1981, Hills Like White Elephants 1991, Broken Trust 1995, Up Close and Personal 1996, As it Happens 2012. *Publications include:* novels: Run River 1963, Play It as It Lays 1970, A Book of Common Prayer 1977, Telling Stories 1978, Democracy 1984, The Last Thing He Wanted 1996; essays: Slouching Towards Bethlehem 1969, The White Album 1978, After Henry 1992; non-fiction: Salvador 1983, Miami 1987, After Henry 1992, Political Fictions 2001, Where I Was From: A Memoir 2003, The Year of Magical Thinking (Nat. Book Award for Non-fiction; also screenplay) 2005, Blue Nights 2011, South and West: From a Notebook 2017. *Address:* Janklow & Nesbit, 445 Park Avenue, New York, NY 10022-2606, USA (office). *Website:* www.facebook.com/JoanDidionAuthor (office).

DIDO; British singer, musician (piano, violin) and songwriter; b. (Dido Florian Cloud de Bounevialle Armstrong), 25 Dec. 1971, London; sister of Rollo Armstrong; m. Rohan Gavin 2010; one s.; ed Guildhall School of Music, London; toured UK with classical music ensemble before joining pop groups aged 16; toured with brother Rollo's band, Faithless; signed solo deal with Arista Records, New York; BRIT Award for Best Female Solo Artist 2002, 2004, Ivor Novello Award for Songwriter of the Year 2002, BAMBI Award for Best Int. Pop Act 2003, ASCAP Award for Songwriter of the Year 2008. *Recordings include:* albums: No Angel (BRIT Award for Best British Album 2002) 1999, Life for Rent 2003, Safe Trip Home 2008, Girl Who Got Away 2013, Still on My Mind 2019; singles: The Highbury Fields (EP) 1999, Here With Me 2001, Thank You 2001, Hunter 2001, All You Want 2002, Life for Rent 2003, White Flag (BRIT Award for Best British Single 2004) 2003. *Website:* www.didomusic.com.

DIEDERICHSEN, Diedrich; German cultural critic and academic; *Professor of Theory, Practice and Communication of Contemporary Art, Academy of Fine Arts, Vienna;* b. 1957, Hamburg; ed Univ. of Hamburg; Ed. Sounds (magazine) 1979–83; Ed. Spex (magazine) 1985–90; Prof. of Theory, Practice and Communication of Contemporary Art, Acad. of Fine Arts, Vienna, Austria 2008–; Prof. of Aesthetic Theory and Cultural Studies, Merz Acad., Stuttgart 1998–2007; Visiting Prof., Art Center Coll. of Design, Los Angeles, USA, Akad. der Bildenden Künste, Munich, Hochschule für Gestaltung, Offenbach, Bremen Univ., Bauhaus-Univ., Weimar, Justus-Liebig-Univ., Giessen, Univ. of Vienna; regular contrib. to Artforum, Texte Zur Kunst, Theater heute, tageszeitung; mem. Jury, Fed. Cultural Foundation of Germany 2002–05; mem. Advisory Bd, Zentrum für Medien und Interaktivität 2002, Arsenal der Freunde der Deutschen Kinemathek (cinema) 2005, Grey Room. *Publications include:* Sexbeat: 1972 bis heute 1985, Elektra 1986, Herr Dietrichsen 1987, 1500 Schallplatten 1989, Freiheit macht arm: Das Leben nach Rock'n'Roll 1990–93 1993, Politische Korrekturen 1996, Der lange Weg nach Mitte 1999, 2000 Schallplatten 1979–1999 2000, Musikzimmer: Avantgarde und Alltag 2005, Eigenblutdoping (Doping with Your Own Blood) 2008, On (Surplus) Value of Art 2008, Kritik des Auges 2008, Stein, Schere, Papier – Rock, Scissors, Paper (co-ed.) 2009, Utopia of Sound (co-ed.) 2010, Psicodelia y ready-made 2011, The Sopranos 2012, The Whole Earth (co-ed.) 2013, Über Pop-Musik 2014, Körpertreffer 2016, (Over-)Production and Value 2017. *Address:* Academy of Fine Arts, Augasse 2–6, 1090 Vienna, Austria (office). *Telephone:* (1) 588-16-8200 (office). *Fax:* (1) 588-16-1898 (office). *E-mail:* d.diederichsen@akbild.ac.at (office). *Website:* www.akbild.ac.at (office); diedrich-diederichsen.de.

DIEKMANN, Kai; German newspaper executive; *Editorial Director and Editor-in-Chief, Bild Group;* b. 27 June 1964, Ravensburg; Parl. Corresp., Bild and Bild am Sonntag, Bonn 1987; Chief Reporter Bunte magazine, Munich 1989–91; Deputy Ed. B.Z., Berlin 1991–92, Deputy Ed. and Chief Political Corresp. Bild, Hamburg 1992–97; Chief Ed. Welt am Sonntag, Berlin 1998–2000, Ed.-in-Chief Bild and Publr Bild and Bild am Sonntag, Hamburg 2001–, Content Exec. bild.de 2007–; Editorial Dir Bild Group 2007–; Head, Bild hilft e.V. – Ein Herz für Kinder (charity org.) 2001–; External Bd mem. Hürriyet 2004–; non-Exec. Bd mem. Times Newspaper Holdings Ltd 2011–; Goldene Feder 2000, 2005, World Media Award 2002, German Media Exec. of the Year 2009. *Publications include:* Rita Süssmuth im Gespräch (co-author) 1994, Die neue Bundespräsident im Gespräch (co-author) 1994, Helmut Kohl. Ich wollte Deutschlands Einheit (co-author) 1996, Der große Selbstbetrug 2007, The Wall – Photographs 1961–1992 2009, Helmut Kohl – On the Path and in Past and Present 2010, Das BILD-Buch 2012. *Address:* Bild, Axel Springer AG, Axel-Springer-Straße 65, 10888 Berlin, Germany (office). *Telephone:* (30) 2591-0 (office). *Fax:* (30) 2591-76009 (office). *Website:* www.bild.de (office).

DIEKMANN, Michael; German business executive; *Chairman of the Board of Management (CEO), Allianz SE;* b. 23 Dec. 1954, Bielefeld; m.; three c.; ed Göttingen Univ.; Financial Dir Diekmann/Thieme GBR 1983–86, Pres. 1987–88; Exec. Asst to Head of Hamburg Regional Office, Allianz Versicherungs-AG 1988–89, Head of Sales, Hamburg Harburg Office 1990, Head of Hanover Office 1991–92, Head of Customer Relationship Man. for pvt. customers, Munich 1993, mem. Exec. Bd of Man. of regional office for N Rhine-Westphalia as Head of Sales 1994–95, Dir Allianz Insurance Man. Asia Pacific Pte Ltd, Singapore 1996–97, mem. Bd of Man. Allianz AG, Munich responsible for Asia-Pacific region 1998, responsible for Asia-Pacific, Cen. and Eastern Europe, Middle East, Africa and Group Man. Devt 2000, responsible for the Americas and Group Human Resources 2002–03, Chair. Bd of Man. (CEO) Allianz AG (renamed Allianz SE 2006) 2003–, also Chair. Allianz Asset Management AG, Vice-Chair. Allianz France SA; Vice-Chair. BASF SE, Linde AG; mem. Bd of Dirs Siemens AG, Allianz Deutschland AG, Allianz SpA; mem. European Financial Services Round Table, EVIAN (Franco-German Roundtable), Geneva Asscn (Vice-Chair.), Int. Business Leaders Advisory Council for the Mayor of Shanghai, Monetary Authority of Singapore Advisory Panel, Pan-European Insurance Forum, Bd of Stifterverband für die Deutsche Wissenschaft. *Address:* Allianz SE, Königinstrasse 28, 80802 Munich, Germany (office). *Telephone:* (89) 3800-0 (office). *Fax:* (89) 3800-3810 (office). *E-mail:* michael.diekmann@allianz.com (office). *Website:* www.allianz.com (office).

DIEMU, (Ghislain) Chikez; Democratic Republic of the Congo politician; mem. Parl. 1997–; Sec. for Strategic Planning 1997–99; Vice-Pres. in charge of organization of Govt 1999–2001; Vice-Minister of Interior 2001–04; Gen. Sec. People's Party for Reconstruction and Democracy 2001–05; Vice-Gov. Katanga Prov. 2004–07; Minister of Defence, Demobilization and War Veterans' Affairs 2007–08; freelance 2008–. *Address:* c/o Ministry of National Defence and War Veterans, BP 4111, Kinshasa-Gombe, Democratic Republic of the Congo.

DIENER, Theodor Otto, DrSc; American (b. Swiss) plant virologist and academic; *Distinguished University Professor Emeritus, Center for Biosystems Research, University of Maryland;* b. 28 Feb. 1921, Zurich, Switzerland; s. of Theodor E. Diener and Hedwig R. Baumann; m. Sybil Mary Fox 1968 (died 2012); three s. (from previous m.); ed Swiss Fed. Inst. of Tech. (ETH), Zurich; Plant Pathologist, Swiss Fed. Agricultural Research Station, Waedenswil 1948–49; Asst Prof. of Plant Pathology, Rhode Island State Univ., Kingston, USA 1950; Asst-Assoc. Plant Pathologist, Washington State Univ., Prosser 1950–59; Research Plant Pathologist, Plant Virology Lab., Agricultural Research Service, US Dept of Agric., Beltsville, Md 1959–88; Collaborator, Agricultural Research Service, US Dept of Agric., Beltsville, Md 1988–97; Prof., Center for Agric. Biotech. and Dept of Botany, Univ. of Md, College Park 1988–, Acting Dir Center for Agric. Biotech. 1991–92, Distinguished Univ. Prof. 1994–; Distinguished Prof., Univ. of Md Biotech. Inst. 1998–99, Distinguished Univ. Prof. Emer., Center for Biosystems Research 1999–; discovered and named viroids, smallest known agents of infectious disease; mem. NAS, American Acad. of Arts and Sciences, Leopoldina (German Acad. of Natural Scientists); Fellow, New York Acad. of Sciences, American Phytopathological Soc.; Campbell Award, American Inst. of Biological Sciences 1968, Superior Service Award, US Dept of Agric. 1969, Distinguished Service Award, US Dept of Agric. 1977, Alexander von Humboldt Award (FRG) 1975, Wolf Prize (Israel) 1987, E. C. Stakman Award, Univ. of Minn. 1988, Nat. Medal of Science (USA) 1987, Science Hall of Fame, Agricultural Research Service, US Dept of Agric. 1989, Circle of Discovery, Coll. of Chemical and Life Sciences, Univ. of Maryland 2007. *Publications:* Viroids and Viroid Diseases 1979, The Viroids (ed.) 1987; ed. numerous chapters in scientific books and more than 200 scientific papers. *Leisure interest:* private pilot. *Address:* PO Box 272, Beltsville, MD 20705, USA. *E-mail:* tod26@juno.com.

DIENG, Adama; Senegalese registrar, lecturer and UN official; *Special Adviser to the Secretary-General on the Prevention of Genocide, United Nations;* b. 22 May 1950, Dakar; m. Aissatou Dieng; two one c.; ed Training Inst. in Law and Admin, Centre de Formation et de Perfectionnement Administratifs, Dakar, Research Centre of The Hague Acad. of Int. Law, Netherlands; Registrar, Regional and Labour Courts of Senegal 1973; Registrar of the Supreme Court 1974–80; Legal Officer, Int. Comm. of Jurists 1982–89, Exec. Sec. 1989–90, Sec.-Gen. 1990–2000; apptd UN Ind. Expert for Haiti 1985; Asst Sec.-Gen. and Registrar for International Criminal Tribunal for Rwanda (ICTR) 2001–12, Special Adviser to the Sec.-Gen. on the Prevention of Genocide, UN 2012–; mem. Bd of Dirs International Inst. for Human Rights (Institut René Cassin); mem. Exec. Bd Africa Leadership Forum; Pres. International Jury, UNESCO Human Rights Educ. Prize; lecturer on international law at various univs and insts; consultant for numerous orgs., including UNESCO, UNITAR, Ford Foundation, UN Comm. on Human Rights (UNCHR), OAU; Hon. Chair. African Centre for Human Rights and Democratic Studies. *Publications include:* more than 60 pubs on human rights, democracy in Africa, int. law, the judicial system etc. *Leisure interest:* reading. *Address:* Office of the Special Adviser on the Prevention of Genocide, United Nations, New York, NY 10017, USA (office). *Website:* www.un.org/en/preventgenocide/adviser/genocide_prevention.shtml (office).

DIEPGEN, Eberhard; German lawyer and politician; b. 13 Nov. 1941, Berlin; m. Monika Adler 1975; one s. one d.; ed Free Univ. of Berlin; joined CDU 1962, later Chair., W Berlin CDU, Hon. Chair. 2004; mem. Berlin Chamber of Deputies 1971–81; mem. Bundestag (Parl.) as W Berlin Rep. 1980–81; Mayor of Berlin 1984–89, 1991–2001; Senator for Justice 1999–2001; Chair. Supervisory Bd Berlin Brandenburg Flughafen Holding GmbH 1996; attorney, Thümmel, Schütze & Partner, Berlin; Hon. KBE 1994; Grosses Goldenes Ehrenzeichen am Bande für Verdienste (Austria) 1993, Grosses Bundesverdienstkreuz mit Stern 1994, Orden für Verdienst 1998, Orden des Marienland-Kreuzes 2000, Verdienstorden des Landes Berlin 2007, Commdr, Merit of the Repub. of Hungary 2011. *Leisure interests:* soccer, European history.

DIESS, Herbert, PhD; Austrian business executive; *Chairman of Managing Board and CEO, Volkswagen AG;* b. 24 Oct. 1958, Munich; ed Munich Univ. of Applied Science; Scientific Asst for automation projects Munich Tech. Univ. 1984–88, Dir Assembly Automation Dept, Inst. for Tool Machines and Plant Man. 1988–89; Tech. Dir Planning, Robert-Bosch 1990–93, Gen. Man. 1993–96; Dir Long-Term and Structural Planning, BMW AG 1996–97, Dir Process Consulting, Production Div. 1997–98, Dir Process Consulting, Eng and Tech. 1998–99, Dir Birmingham Plant 1999–2000, Dir Oxford Plant 2000–03, Dir BMW Motorcyles 2003–07, mem. Bd of Man. Purchasing and Supplier Network 2007–14, Chair. Man. Board Passenger Cars 2015–18, Chair. Sociedad Española de Automóviles de Turismo (SEAT) 2018–, Chair. Audi AG 2018–, Chair. Man. Board and CEO Volkswagen AG 2018–; mem. bd Infineon Technologies AG 2015–, Saic Volkswagen Automotive Co. Ltd 2015–, Faw Volkswagen Automobile Co. Ltd 2015–, Porsche Holding GmbH 2015–, Porsche Retail GmbH 2015–, Porsche Austria AG 2015–; Autocar Editor's Award 2018. *Address:* Berliner Ring 2, 38440 Wolfsburg, Germany (office). *Telephone:* 49536190 (office). *Fax:* 5361928282 (office). *E-mail:* vw@volkswagen.de (office). *Website:* www.volkswagenag.com (office).

DIETRICH, Siegfried, PhD; German chemist and academic; *Director, Max-Planck-Institut für Metallforschung;* b. 27 Jan. 1954, Singen; ed Univ. of Konstanz, Univ. of Munich; Research Assoc., Univ. of Washington, Seattle, USA 1982–83; Research Assoc., Ludwig-Maximilians-Universität, Munich 1983–86; Assoc. Prof., Univ. of Würzburg 1987–88, also Univ. of Mainz 1988; Full Prof., Univ. of Wuppertal 1989–2000, Univ. of Stuttgart 2000–; Scientific mem. and Dir Max-Planck-Institut für Metallforschung 2000–; Chair. for Theoretical Solid State Physics, Univ. of Stuttgart; Fellow, Japan Soc. for the Promotion of Science 1997; mem. Int. Union of Pure and Applied Chem.; German Physical Soc. Walter-Schottky-Preis 1985, Max Born Medal and Prize 2002. *Address:* Max-Planck-Institut fur Metallforschung, Heisenbergstr. 3, 70569 Stuttgart, Germany (office). *Telephone:* (711) 689-1921 (office). *Fax:* (711) 689-1922 (office). *E-mail:* dietrich@mf.mpg.de (office). *Website:* www.mf.mpg.de/de (office).

DIEWERT, Walter Erwin, BA, MA, PhD, FRSC; Canadian economist and academic; *Professor of Economics, Vancouver School of Economics, University of British Columbia;* b. 4 Dec. 1941, Vancouver, BC; s. of Ewald Diewert and Linda Diewert; m. Virginia Diewert; ed Univ. of British Columbia, Univ. of California, Berkeley; mem. Faculty of Econs, Univ. of Chicago 1968–70; Prof. of Econs, Vancouver School of Econs, Univ. of British Columbia 1970–; Research Assoc., Nat. Bureau of Econ. Research; Chair. Statistics Canada Advisory Cttee on Prices, mem. Statistics Canada Services Advisory Cttee, Statistics Canada Advisory Group on Science and Tech.; Vice-Pres. Soc. for Econ. Measurement; Adjunct Prof., School of Business, Univ. of Alberta; mem. NAS Panel on Conceptual, Measurement and Other Statistical Issues in Developing Cost of Living Indexes, Washington, DC 1999–2000; Assoc. Ed. Macroeconomic Dynamics; Fellow, Econometric Soc., World Acad. of Productivity Science, Journal of Econometrics 2014, Acad. of Social Sciences in Australia 2015, American Econ. Asscn; Distinguished Fellow, Canadian Econs Asscn; mem. UN Canberra Group on Capital Measurement, UN Ottawa Group on Price Measurement; consultant for OECD, ILO, IMF, World Bank, US Bureau of Econ. Analysis, US Bureau of Labor Statistics, NZ Treasury, Australian Bureau of Statistics; Killam Prize, Canada Council for the Arts 2003, Doug Purvis Memorial Prize, Canadian Econs Asscn 2005, Julius Shiskin Memorial Award for Econ. Statistics 2005. *Publications:* more than 260 publs in econ journals and books; numerous reports, including the report to NZ Business Roundtable, major contributor to 2004 Consumer Price Index Manual, 2004 Producer Price Index Manual and 2009 Export Import Price Index Manual. *Leisure interest:* tennis. *Address:* Faculty of Arts, Vancouver School of Economics, 6000 Iona Drive, Vancouver, BC V6T 1L4, Canada (office). *Telephone:* (604) 822-2876 (office). *Fax:* (604) 822-5915 (office). *E-mail:* Erwin.Diewert@ubc.ca (office). *Website:* economics.ubc.ca (office).

DIFFIE, (Bailey) Whitfield (Whit), BS; American cryptographer; *Consulting Scholar, Center for International Security and Cooperation, Freeman Spogli Institute for International Studies, Stanford University;* b. 5 June 1944, Washington, DC; s. of Justine Louise Whitfield; m. Mary Fischer; ed Jamaica High School, Queens, New York, Massachusetts Inst. of Tech. Univ.; Research Asst, MITRE Corpn 1965–69, helped develop Mathlab (early symbolic manipulation system); Research Programmer, Stanford Artificial Intelligence Lab., worked on LISP 1.6 programming language 1969–73; pursued ind. research in cryptography from 1973; Research Asst, Stanford Univ. 1975–78; Man. Secure Systems Research, Northern Telecom, designed key man. architecture for PDSO security system for X.25 networks 1978–91; apptd Distinguished Engineer, Sun Microsystems Labs, Menlo Park, Calif. 1991, later Chief Security Officer, later Vice-Pres. –2009, later a Sun Fellow; Vice-Pres. for Information Security and Cryptography, Internet Corpn for Assigned Names and Numbers (ICANN) 2010–12; Visiting Scholar, Center for Int. Security and Cooperation, Freeman Spogli Inst. for Int. Studies, Stanford Univ. 2009–10, Affiliate 2010–12, currently Consulting Scholar; Visiting Prof., Information Security Group, Royal Holloway, Univ. of London 2008; mem. Tech. Advisory Bd, Cryptomathic; Fellow, Marconi Foundation, Computer History Museum 2011; Visiting Fellow, Isaac Newton Inst.; Dr hc (Swiss Fed. Inst. of Tech.) 1992; Hon. DSc (Royal Holloway, Univ. of London) 2008; IEEE Donald G. Fink Prize Paper Award (with Martin Hellman) 1981, Kanellakis Award, Asscn for Computing Machinery (ACM) 1996, Louis E. Levy Medal, The Franklin Inst. 1997, Golden Jubilee Award for Technological Innovation, IEEE Information Theory Soc. 1998, Marconi Prize 2000, IEEE Richard W. Hamming Medal 2010, ACM A.M. Turing Award (with Martin Hellman) 2015. *Achievements include:* while at Stanford collaborated on research paper that introduced radically new method of distributing cryptographic keys (Diffie–Hellman key exchange) 1976. *Publications:* New Directions in Cryptography (paper, with Martin Hellman) 1976, Privacy on the Line with Susan Landau 1998 (revised edn 2007). *Address:* c/o Center for International Security and Cooperation, Freeman Spogli Institute for International Studies, 616 Serra Street C100, Stanford University, Stanford, CA 94305-6055, USA (office). *E-mail:* whitfielddiffie@gmail.com (office). *Website:* cisac.fsi.stanford.edu (office).

DIFORIO, Robert George, BA; American publishing executive; *Principal, D4EO Literary Agency* and *Mandevilla Press;* b. 19 March 1940, Mamaroneck, NY; s. of Richard John Diforio, Sr and Mildred Kuntz; m. Birgit Rasmussen 1983; one s. one d.; ed Williams Coll., Harvard Business School's Advanced Man. Program; Vice-Pres. Kable News Co. 1970; Vice-Pres. and Sales Man. New American Library 1972, Sr Vice-Pres. and Marketing Dir 1976, Pres. and Publr 1980–82, CEO and Chair. Bd New American Library/E. P. Dutton 1983–89; Prin. D4EO Literary Agency 1991–, Mandevilla Press 2012–. *Leisure interest:* golf. *Address:* 7 Indian Valley Road, Weston, CT 06883, USA (office). *Telephone:* (203) 544-7180 (office); (203) 544-7182 (home). *Fax:* (203) 544-7160 (office). *E-mail:* bob@d4eo.com (office). *Website:* www.d4eoliteraryagency.com (office); mandevillapress.com.

DIGUIMBAYE, Christian Georges; Chadian economist and politician; b. 3 July 1963, N'Djamena; s. of Georges Diguimbaye; m.; five c.; with Banque des Etats de l'Afrique Centrale 1987–2000; worked in Disbursements Dept, African Devt Bank (ADB) 2000–08; Dir-Gen. Banque Agricole et Commerciale 2009–11; Minister of Finance and the Budget 2011–13, Feb.–Nov. 2017; Coordinator, Office of Support to Jt Secr. of ADB, African Union and UN Econ. Comm. for Africa, Addis Ababa 2013–17.

DIJKGRAAF, Henk G.; Dutch energy industry executive; b. 1946; ed Univ. of Delft, Massachusetts Inst. of Tech., USA; began career with Royal Dutch/Shell 1972, held various positions in Borneo, Kuala Lumpur, Gabon, Syria, London and The Hague; Dir Nederlandse Aardolie Maatschappij (NAM) 1992–95; CEO Shell Int. Gas and Shell Coal Int. 1995–99; Pres. Shell Nederland BV 1999–2003; Group CEO NV Nederlandse Gasunie 2004–05, CEO Gasunie Trade and Supply BV (after restructuring) 2005–06; mem. Bd of Dirs Eneco Holding, Royal Tropical Institute KIT, Sasol LTD ADR 2006–; Deputy Chair. Netherlands Inst. for the Near East. *Address:* c/o Board of Governors, Netherlands Institute for the Near East, PO Box 9515, 2300 RA Leiden, Netherlands.

DIJKHOFF, Klaas Henricus Dominicus Maria, LLM, MPhil, PhD; Dutch lawyer and politician; b. 13 Jan. 1981, Soltau; s. of Henricus Dijkhoff and Petronella Thijssen; m.; one d.; ed Tilburg Univ.; Prof., Tilburg Univ. 2005–09, Inholland Univ. of Applied Sciences 2009–10; pnr Dijkhoff Advies Groep (legal consultancy) 2008–10; mem. Volkspartij voor Vrijheid en Democratie (VVD) (People's Party for Freedom and Democracy) 1998–, Sec. 2007–08, Deputy Chair. 2008–09, mem. VVD Defence Cttee 2007–10, mem. VVD Party Council 2008–10; mem. Breda city council 2010–13; mem. States Gen. Second Chamber (lower house of parl.) 2010–15, 2017–, VVD Leader in Second Chamber 2017–; State Sec. for Security and Justice 2015–17; Minister of Defence 4–26 Oct. 2017. *Address:* Volkspartij voor Vrijheid en Democratie, Laan Copes van Cattenburch 52, POB 30836, 2500 GV The Hague, Netherlands (office). *Telephone:* (70) 3613061 (office). *Fax:* (70) 3608276 (office). *E-mail:* info@vvd.nl (office); k.dijkhoff@tweedekamer.nl (office). *Website:* www.vvd.nl (office); www.klaasdijkhoff.nl/.

DIJOUD, Paul Charles Louis; French politician and fmr diplomatist; b. 25 July 1938, Neuilly-sur-Seine; s. of Jules-Raoul Dijoud and Andrée Claquin; m. Catherine Cochaux 1968 (divorced 1983); one s. one d.; m. 2nd Maryse Dolivot 1988; ed Lycée Condorcet, Faculté de Droit de Paris, École Nat. d'Admin, Inst. d'Etudes politiques de Paris; Commercial Attaché, Dept of External Econ. Relations in Ministry of Econ. and Finance; elected to Nat. Ass. 1967, 1968, 1973, 1978; Asst Sec.-Gen. Ind. Republican Party 1967–69; Conseiller Général for Canton of Embrun 1968–88; Pres. Ind. Republican Exec. Cttee for Provence-Côte d'Azur 1968–88; Mayor of Briançon 1971–83; Sec. of State attached to Prime Minister's Office 1973–74, later to Minister of Cultural Affairs and the Environment, to Minister of Employment with Responsibility for Immigrant Workers 1974, Secretary of State for Sport 1977, for Overseas Depts and Territories 1978; Commercial Adviser to Cen. Admin., Ministry of Economy and Finance 1981; Man. Dir Cie Commerciale Sucres et Denrées 1982–84; Pres. Comidex 1984; Pres. Conseil d'admin du parc nat. des Ecrins 1973; Plenipotentiary Minister 1988; Amb. to Colombia 1988–91, to Mexico 1992–94; Minister of State with responsibility for the principality of Monaco 1994–97; Amb. to Argentina 1997–2003; Mayor of Les Orres, Hautes Alpes 2006–14; Officier, Légion d'honneur.

DIJSSELBLOEM, Jeroen René Victor Anton, BEcons; Dutch politician; b. 29 March 1966, Eindhoven; two c.; ed Wageningen Univ., Univ. Coll. Cork, Ireland; began career as Asst to Partij van de Arbeid (PvdA—Labour Party) MEPs, Brussels 1992; joined staff of parl. PvdA, The Hague 1993, three years as policy officer in area of spatial planning (including environment, agric. and nature); mem. Wageningen municipal council 1994–97; Political-Admin. Adviser to Minister of Agric., Nature Man. and Fisheries 1996–98, Deputy Head, Ministry Advisory Section 1998–2000; mem. House of Reps (lower house of Parl.) 2000–02, 2002–12, 2017–; Chair. Parl. investigation Cttee on educational reform 2007–08; Minister of Finance 2012–17; Pres. Eurogroup 2013–, Bd of Govs European Stability Mechanism 2013–; mem. PvdA 1985–, Deputy Leader of Parl. party 2008–, mem. Electoral Programme Cttee 2010, 2012. *Address:* European Council, Rue de la Loi/Wetstraat 175, B-1048, Brussels, Belgium (office). *Telephone:* (2) 281-61-11 (office). *Fax:* (2) 281-69-34 (office).

ĐIKIĆ, Ivan, MD, PhD; Croatian physician, medical scientist, academic and research institute director; *Director, Institute of Biochemistry II, Goethe University Medical School;* b. 28 May 1966, Zagreb; ed Univ. of Zagreb, New York Univ. School of Medicine, USA; Medical Doctor, Univ. of Zagreb 1986–91; worked at Inst. for Health Care of Mother and Child, New York 1991–92; Postdoctoral Fellow, New York Univ. School of Medicine 1995–97; Group Leader, Ludwig Inst. for Cancer Research, Uppsala, Sweden 1997–2002; Prof., Faculty of Medicine, Univ. of Split 2002–03, now Guest Prof.; Prof. C3, Inst. of Biochemistry II, Goethe Univ., Frankfurt, Germany 2002–08, Dir of Inst. 2009–; Scientific Dir, Buchmann Inst. for Molecular Life Sciences 2009–13; mem. AAAS, New York Acad. of Sciences,

World Asscn of Croatian Physicians, American Asscn for Cancer Research, European Molecular Biology Org., American Soc. for Biochemistry and Molecular Biology, Int. Union Against Cancer, German Soc. for Biochemistry and Molecular Biology; Order of Duke Branimir; D. Perović Award for the Best Graduates in Medicine 1991, Chancellor's Award 1991, Award for Young Explorers 1997, Award for Young Leaders in Science 2002, AACR Award for Outstanding Achievements in Cancer Research 2006, Binder Award 2006, EACR Award for Cancer Research 2006, Ernst Jung Prize (co-recipient) 2013, Gottfried Wilhelm Leibniz Prize 2013, William C. Rose Award 2013. *Publications:* numerous papers in professional journals. *Address:* Institute of Biochemistry II, Goethe University, Hessen, 60590 Frankfurt am Main, Germany (office). *Telephone:* (69) 63015964 (office). *Fax:* (69) 63015577 (office). *E-mail:* ivan.dikic@biochem2.de (office). *Website:* www.biochem2.com (office).

DIKSHIT, Sheila, MA; Indian politician; b. 31 March 1938, Kapurthala, Punjab; m. Vinod Dikshit (deceased); one s. one d.; ed Convent of Jesus and Mary School, Univ. of Delhi; mem. Parl. 1984–89; Minister of Parl. Affairs, Minister of State in the Prime Minister's Office 1986–89; Pres. Delhi Pradesh Congress Cttee 1998; mem. New Delhi Legis. Ass. 1998–2008; Chief Minister, Govt of Nat. Capital Territory of Delhi 1998–2013; Gov. of Kerala March–Aug. 2014 (resgnd); Indian Nat. Congress cand. for Chief Minister of UP 2016; Sec. Indira Gandhi Memorial Trust; fmr Chair. Young Women's Asscn; represented India at UN Comm. on Status of Women 1984–89; Dr hc (Delhi); Best Chief Minister of India, Journalist Asscn of India 2008, Politician of the Year, NDTV (news channel) 2009. *Address:* Uttar Pradesh Congress Committee, Nehru Bhawan, 10, Mall Avenue, Lucknow, Uttar Pradesh, India (office). *Telephone:* (22) 2238858 (office). *E-mail:* upcclko@hotmail.com (office). *Website:* uttarpradeshcongress.com (office).

ĐILAS, Dragan; Serbian politician and business executive; b. 22 Feb. 1967, Belgrade; m. 1st Milica Delević 1994 (divorced 2007); two d.; m. 2nd Iva Đilas 2009; one s. one d.; ed Faculty of Mechanical Eng, Univ. of Belgrade; worked as journalist at Radio Index, merged with Ritam Srca radio programme to form Radio B92 (Founder) 1989, later news ed.; student leader/activist against rule of Slobodan Milošević, led student protests 1991, 1992; continued to participate in various anti-Milošević rallies 1996–2000; active in Serbian media market mid-1990s–; holds stake in limited-liability co. Multikom Group; Co-owner (through Multikom Group) Direct Media (closed jt stock media co.) 2001–; Dir People's Office of the Pres. 2004–07; Minister without Portfolio in charge of Nat. Investment Plan 2007–08; Mayor of Belgrade 2008–13; Pres. Democratic Party (Demokratska Stranka—DS) 2012–14; Pres. Basketball Fed. of Serbia 2009–16; Founder and Vice-Pres. Naša Srbija (humanitarian org. for Serbian children).

DILAWARI, Noorullah, BS; Afghan economist, international organization official and fmr central banker; ed Univ. of California, Los Angeles, USA; Vice-Pres., Multinational Div., Lloyds Bank of California, LA, USA 1986–2002; Sr Adviser to Minister of Finance 2002; Founding Pres. and CEO Afghan Investment Support Agency 2003–04, 2008–11; Gov. Da Afghanistan Bank (Cen. Bank of Afghanistan) 2004–08, 2011–14; currently Chair. Economic Development for Peace; mem. Bd of Dirs Afghan American Chamber of Commerce 2015–, Chair. Access to Capital Working Group. *E-mail:* info@ed4p.com (office). *Website:* www.ed4p.com (office).

DILEITA, Dileita Mohamed; Djibouti politician and diplomatist; *African Union Special Envoy for Libya;* b. 12 March 1958, Tadjourah; ed Centre for Vocational Training (CFA), Médéa, Algeria; with Embassy in Paris 1990; Amb. to Ethiopia 1990, to Uganda 2000–01; Prime Minister of Djibouti 2001–13; mem. African Union (AU) High-Level Panel for Egypt, AU Special Envoy for Libya 2014–; Vice-Pres. Rassemblement populaire pour le progrès (RPP) 2003–. *Address:* c/o Commission of the African Union, POB 3243, Roosevelt Street (Old Airport Area), W21K19 Addis Ababa, Ethiopia (office).

DILENSCHNEIDER, Robert, BA, MA; American business executive; *Founder and Principal, The Dilenschneider Group;* b. 21 Oct. 1943, New York; s. of Sigmund J. Dilenschneider and Martha Witucki; m. Janet Hennessey 1969; two s.; ed Univ. of Notre Dame, Ohio State Univ.; Account Supervisor, Hill and Knowlton Inc., New York 1967–70, Vice-Pres. 1970–73, Sr Vice-Pres. 1973–80, Exec. Vice-Pres., Chicago 1980–84, Pres. and COO, Chicago 1984–86, Pres. and CEO Hill and Knowlton, New York 1986–91; Chair. and Prin. The Dilenschneider Group Inc., New York 1991–; mem. US-Japan Business Council, Public Relations Soc. of America, Int. Public Relations Asscn, Bretton Woods Cttee, Econ. Clubs of New York and Chicago; mem. Bd of Govs., New York Chapter of Nat. Acad. of TV Arts and Sciences; mem. Advisory Bd Center for Strategic and Int. Studies, New York Hosp., Cornell Medical Center, Coll. of Business Admin. at Univ. of Notre Dame; Fellow, Int. Asscn of Business Communications; Dr hc (Muskingum Coll., now Muskingum Univ.); New York's Big Apple Award. *Publications include:* Power and Influence: A Briefing for Leaders 1991, On Power 1993, Power and Influence: The Rules have Changed 2007, The AMA Handbook of Public Relations 2010, 50 Plus!: Critical Career Decisions for the Rest of Your Life. *Address:* The Dilenschneider Group Inc., 405 Lexington Avenue, 57th Floor, New York, NY 10174, USA (office). *Telephone:* (212) 922-0900 (office). *Fax:* (212) 922-0971 (office). *E-mail:* jma@dgi-nyc.com (office). *Website:* www.dilenschneider.com (office).

DILIBERTO, Oliviero; Italian politician and academic; *Professor of Roman and Levantine Law, University of Rome 'La Sapienza';* b. 13 Oct. 1956, Cagliari; s. of Marco Diliberto and Mariadonella Reale; m. Gabriella Serrenti 1997; ed in Cagliari, Rome, Frankfurt and Paris; Prov. Sec., Juvenile Fed. of Italian CP 1978, mem. Prov. Sec.'s Office, Italian CP 1982, mem. Nat. Sec.'s Office, Reconstructed CP 1994, Dir Liberazione (party journal) 1994, Gen. Sec., Partito dei Comunisti Italiani (Party of Italian Communists) 2000–13, mem. Partito Comunista d'Italia (Communist Party of Italy) 2014–; mem. Parl. 1994–2008, Leader Partito dei Comunisti Italiani Parl. Group 1995, Pres. Progressive Parl. Group; Minister of Justice 1998–2001; fmr Prof. of Roman Law, Univ. of Cagliari; currently Prof. of Roman and Levantine Law, Univ. of Rome 'La Sapienza'. *Address:* Department of Law, University of Rome 'La Sapienza', Piazzale Aldo Moro 5, 00185 Rome, Italy (office). *Telephone:* (06) 49690311 (office). *Fax:* (06) 49690267 (office). *Website:* www.scienzegiuridiche.uniroma1.it (office).

DILKS, David Neville, BA, FRSL, FCGI; British historian, academic and university administrator; b. 17 March 1938, Coventry; s. of Neville Ernest and Phyllis Dilks; m. Jill Medlicott 1963; one s.; ed Royal Grammar School, Worcester, Hertford Coll. and St Antony's Coll., Oxford; Asst Lecturer, then Lecturer LSE 1962–70; Prof. of Int. History, Univ. of Leeds 1970–91, Chair. School of History 1974–79, Dean Faculty of Arts 1975–77; Vice-Chancellor Univ. of Hull 1991–99; Visiting Fellow, All Souls Coll., Oxford 1973; Chair. and Founder Commonwealth Youth Exchange Council 1968–73; mem. Advisory Council on Public Records 1977–85, Univs Funding Council 1988–91; Trustee Edward Boyle Memorial Trust 1982–96, Imperial War Museum 1983–91, Lennox-Boyd Trust 1984–91, Royal Commonwealth Soc. Library Trust 1987–91; Pres. Int. Cttee for the History of the Second World War 1992–2000; Freeman, Goldsmiths' Co. 1979, Liveryman 1984; Fellow, City and Guilds of London Inst.; Dr hc (Russian Acad. of Sciences) 1996; Curzon Prize, Univ. of Oxford 1960, Prix du rayonnement de la langue française 1994, Médaille de Vermeil, Acad. Française 1994. *Television:* historical adviser, The Gathering Storm (HBO/BBC) 2002, Winston Churchill at War (HBO/BBC) 2009. *Publications:* Curzon in India (Vols 1 & 2) 1969, 1970, The Diaries of Sir Alexander Cadogan (ed.) 1971, Retreat from Power (two vols, ed.) 1981, The Missing Dimension: Government and Intelligence Communities in the Twentieth Century (ed.) 1984, Neville Chamberlain: Pioneering & Reform, 1869–1929 1984, Barbarossa 1941, The Axis, The Allies and World War: Retrospect, Recollection, Revision (co-ed.) 1994, Grossbritannien und der deutsche Widerstand (co-ed.) 1994, The Great Dominion: Winston Churchill in Canada 1900–1954 2005, Churchill and Company 2012; numerous articles in learned journals. *Leisure interests:* ornithology, steam railways, organ music, Bentley cars. *Address:* Wits End, Long Causeway, Leeds, LS16 8EX, West Yorks., England (home). *Telephone:* (113) 267-3466 (home).

DILLANE, Stephen; British actor; b. 1957, London; s. of John Dillane and Bridget Dilla; partner Naomi Wirthner; one c.; ed Univ. of Exeter, Bristol Old Vic Drama School; early career as journalist for Croydon Advertiser newspaper; attended drama school, then worked in repertory in Coventry, Manchester and Chester; Tony Award for Best Leading Actor (The Real Thing) 2000. *Films include:* Business as Usual 1987, La Chance 1994, Two If by Sea 1996, Welcome to Sarajevo 1997, Firelight 1997, Déjà Vu 1997, Love and Rage 1998, The Darkest Light 1999, Ordinary Decent Criminal 2000, The Parole Officer 2001, Spy Game 2001, The Gathering 2002, The Truth About Charlie 2002, The Hours (Gold Derby Film Award for Best Ensemble Cast 2003) 2002, King Arthur 2004, Haven 2004, Nine Lives 2005, Goal! 2005, The Greatest Game Ever Played 2005, Klimt 2005, Goal II: Living the Dream 2006, Savage Grace 2007, Fugitive Pieces 2007, Freakdog 2008, Storm 2009, 44 Inch Chest 2009, Perfect Sense 2011, Papadopoulos & Sons 2012, Twenty8k 2012, Zero Dark Thirty 2012. *Television includes:* Comeback 1987, The Secret Garden 1987, The One Game 1988, An Affair in Mind 1988, Christabel 1988, The Yellow Wallpaper 1989, Heading Home 1991, Achilles Heel 1991, Frankie's House 1992, Hostages 1993, You Me + It 1993, The Rector's Wife 1994, The Widowing of Mrs. Holroyd 1995, Anna Karenina (mini-series) 2000, The Cazalets (series) 2001, John Adams (series) 2008, God on Trial 2008, The Shooting of Thomas Hurndall (British Acad. TV Award for Best Actor 2009) 2008, Hunted 2012, Secret State 2012, Murder: Joint Enterprise 2012, Game of Thrones 2012–15, A Touch of Cloth 2013, The Tunnel (Int. Emmy Award for Best Actor 2014) 2013–16. *Plays:* (Royal Nat. Theatre) The Beaux's Strategem, Dancing at Lughnasa, Long Day's Journey into Night, Angels in America, Millennium Approaches, Perestroika; Hush (Royal Court); Endgame (Donmar Warehouse); Hamlet (Gielgud Theatre).

DILLARD, Annie, MA; American author; b. 30 April 1945, Pittsburgh, Pa; d. of Frank Doak and Gloria Lambert; m. 1st R. H. W. Dillard 1965 (divorced 1975); m. 2nd Gary Clevidence 1979 (divorced); m. 3rd Robert D. Richardson, Jr 1988; one d. two step-d.; ed Hollins Coll.; Contributing Ed. Harper's Magazine 1974–85; Scholar-in-Residence, Western Washington Univ. 1975–79; Distinguished Visiting Prof., Wesleyan Univ. 1979–83, Adjunct Prof. 1983, Writer-in-Residence 1987, now Prof. Emer., mem. Bd of Dirs Wesleyan Writers Conf. 1984–2001 (Chair. 1991–2001); Contributing Ed. Harper's magazine 1974–81, 1983–85; mem. Nat. Cttee on US–China Relations 1982–; Nat. Endowment for the Arts (Literature) Grant 1981, John Simon Guggenheim Memorial Grant 1985, Gov. of Connecticut's Award 1993, Campion Award 1994, Milton Prize 1994, American Arts and Letters Award in Literature 1998, Nat. Humanities Medal 2015. *Publications include:* Tickets for a Prayer Wheel (poetry) 1974, Pilgrim at Tinker Creek (Pulitzer Prize 1975) 1974, Holy the Firm 1978, Living by Fiction 1982, Teaching a Stone to Talk 1982, Encounters with Chinese Writers 1984, An American Childhood 1987, The Writing Life 1989, The Living (novel) 1992, The Annie Dillard Reader 1994, Mornings Like This (poetry) 1995, For the Time Being 1999, The Maytrees (prose) 2007, The Abundance: New & Selected Essays 2015. *Leisure interests:* soup kitchens in Key West, Fla and Chapel Hill, NC. *Address:* c/o Rob McQuilkin, Lippincott Massie McQuilkin, 27 West 20th Street, Suite 305, New York, NY 10011, USA (office). *Telephone:* (212) 352-2055 (office). *E-mail:* rob@lmqlit.com (office). *Website:* www.anniedillard.com (office).

DILLER, Barry; American entertainment executive; *Chairman, IAC/InterActive Corporation;* b. 2 Feb. 1942, San Francisco; s. of Michael Diller and Reva (née Addison) Diller; Asst to Vice-Pres. in charge of programming ABC-TV 1966–68, Exec. Asst to Vice-Pres. in programming and dir of feature films, ABC, 1968, Vice-Pres. Feature Films and Program Devt 1969–71, Vice-Pres. Feature Films Circle Entertainment, div. of ABC) 1971–73, created TV movies of the week and miniseries, Vice-Pres. of prime-time TV, ABC network 1973; Chair. Bd and CEO Paramount Pictures Corpn 1974–84 (resgnd); Chair. and CEO 20th Century Fox Inc. 1984, Chair. and CEO Fox Inc. 1985–92 (resgnd); Chair. and CEO QVC Network 1992–95; Chair. and CEO Silver King Communications 1995–98, Chair. Home Shopping Network (HSN) 1995–98, Chair. and CEO USA Interactive (later IAC/InterActive Corpn) including USA Networks Inc., New York 1998–2001, Chair. 2001–, including Expedia, Inc. and Live Nation Entertainment 2010; Chair. and CEO Vivendi Universal Entertainment (VUE) 2002–03; mem. Bd of Dirs Washington Post Co., Coca-Cola Co., Conservation Int., Channel 13/WNET, Museum of TV and Radio; fmr mem. Bd of Dirs News Corpn Ltd; Trustee, New York Univ.; mem. Bd of Councilors Univ. of Southern Calif. School of Cinema-TV, Dean's Council Tisch School of the Arts, Exec. Bd for Medical Sciences UCLA, American Film Inst., Variety Clubs Int., Hollywood Radio and TV Soc., Acad. of Motion Picture Arts and Sciences. *Address:* IAC/InterActive Corporation, 152

West 57th Street, 42nd Floor, New York, NY 10019, USA (office). *Telephone:* (212) 314-7300 (office). *Fax:* (212) 314-7379 (office). *Website:* www.iac.com (office).

DILLER, Elizabeth, BArch; American architect and academic; *Co-Founder, Diller Scofidio + Renfro;* b. 17 June 1954, Łodz, Poland; m. Ricardo Scofidio; ed The Cooper Union School of Architecture; co-f. (with Ricardo Scofidio q.v.), Diller & Scofidio (now Diller Scofidio + Renfro 2004), New York 1979, cr. installations and electronic media projects; known for High Line park, New York; taught at The Cooper Union School of Architecture 1981–90; Assoc. Prof. of Architectural Design, Princeton Univ. 1990, apptd Dir Grad. Studies 1993, currently Prof. of Architectural Design; jt recipient (with Ricardo Scofidio) fellowships from Graham Foundation for Advanced Study in the Fine Arts 1986, New York Foundation for the Arts 1986, 1987, 1989, Chicago Inst. for Architecture and Urbanism 1989, Tiffany Foundation Award for Emerging Artists 1990, Progressive Architecture Award (for Slow House) 1991, Chrysler Award for Achievement and Design 1997, James Beard Foundation Design Award for Outstanding Restaurant Design 2000, National Design Award in Architecture, Smithsonian 2005, chosen (with Ricardo Scofidio) by Time magazine amongst 100 Most Influential People in the World 2009, Royal Acad. Architecture Prize 2019. *Publications:* (with Ricardo Scofidio) Flesh 1995, Back to the Front: Tourisms of War 1996, Flesh: Architectural Probes 1998, Blur: The Making of Nothing 2002. *Address:* 601 West 26th Street, Suite 1815, New York, NY 10001 (office); S-11, Princeton University School of Architecture, Princeton, NJ 08544-5264, USA (office). *Telephone:* (212) 260-7971 (New York) (home); (609) 258-3753 (Princeton) (office). *Fax:* (609) 258-4740 (Princeton) (office). *E-mail:* ediller@dsrny.com (office); soa@princeton.edu (office). *Website:* dsrny.com (office); soa.princeton.edu (office).

DILLMAN, Linda M.; American retail executive; b. Fort Wayne, Ind.; ed Univ. of Indianapolis; with Hewlett-Packard 1987–92; joined Wal-Mart in 1992, served in several key information services man. positions including Applications Devt Man. for SAM'S CLUB and Applications Devt Man. for Wal-Mart Store Systems, Dir Applications Devt 1997–98, Vice-Pres. Applications Devt 1998, later Vice-Pres. Int. Systems, Sr Vice-Pres. Information Systems Div. 2002, Exec. Vice-Pres. and Chief Information Officer Wal-Mart Stores Inc. 2002–06, Exec. Vice-Pres. Risk Man. and Benefits Admin 2006–09; Sr Vice-Pres. 2009–12; Chief Information Officer, QVC Inc. 2012–, mem. Bd of Dirs 2010–; mem. Bd Network of Exec. Women, GS1 Global, Nat. Center for Women and Information Tech.; mem. Advisory Bd Univ. of Indianapolis; Univ. of Indianapolis Distinguished Alumni Award 2003, David D. Lattanze Center at Loyola Coll. Information Systems Exec. of the Year 2004, Univ. of Michigan Stephen M. Ross School of Business Women in Leadership Award 2005, EMC Information Leadership Award, Computerworld 2006. *Leisure interests:* skiing, watching Formula 1 racing, travelling with college friends. *Address:* QVC Inc, 1200 Wilson Drive, West Chester, PA 19380, USA (office). *Telephone:* (484) 701-1000 (office). *Website:* www.qvc.com (office).

DILLON, David Brian, BA, LLB; American retail executive; b. 30 March 1951, Hutchinson, Kan.; m. Dee A. Ehling 1973; one s. two d.; ed Hutchinson High School, Univ. of Kansas, Southern Methodist Univ.; various positions with family-owned business Dillon Cos including Head of Supermarket, Convenience Store and Mfg Operations, Vice-Pres. 1983–86, Pres. 1986–90; Exec. Vice-Pres. The Kroger Co. 1990–95, mem. Bd of Dirs 1995–2014, Pres. 1995–2000, Pres. and COO 2000–03, CEO 2003–04, Chair. and CEO 2004–13, Chair. 2013–14; mem. Bd of Dirs, Convergys Corpn 2000–02. *Address:* c/o The Kroger Co., 1014 Vine Street, Cincinnati, OH 45202-1100, USA. *E-mail:* kroger.investors@kroger.com.

DILLON, Maj.-Gen. (retd) Edmund Ernest, MSc; Trinidad and Tobago politician and fmr military commander; *Minister of Housing and Urban Development;* b. 1955, Cochrane Village; s. of Edwin Dillon and Evadne Dillon; m. Ava Dillon; three c.; ed Univ. of the West Indies, US Army Command and Gen. Staff Coll., Fort Leavenworth, Inter-American Defence Coll., Royal Mil. Acad., Sandhurst, UK, Canadian Forces Staff School, Canadian Land Forces Command and Staff Coll.; enlisted in Trinidad and Tobago Coast Guard, transferred to Army as Commissioned Officer, 36 years' service in Trinidad and Tobago Defence Force, roles include Bn Adjutant, Company Commdr, Staff Officer Finance, Second in Command of CARICOM Bn (part of multinational force operating alongside US forces in Operation Restore Democracy, Haiti 1994), CO of Trinidad and Tobago Regt 2004, Chief of Defence Staff, Trinidad and Tobago Defence Force –2005; Dir of Corp. Security, Atlantic LNG Trinidad and Tobago –2015; mem. House of Reps for Point Fortin (People's Nat. Movt) 2015–; Minister of Nat. Security 2015–18, of Housing and Urban Devt 2018–; Fellow, Inst. of Leadership and Man., UK; Gold Medal of Merit, Mil. Long Service Medal, Naval Order of Merit Medal, US Army Commendation Mil. Medal of Merit, Delaware Distinguished Service Medal. *Address:* Ministry of Housing and Urban Development, NHA Bldg, 44–46 South Quay, Port of Spain, Trinidad and Tobago (office). *Telephone:* 623-4663 (office). *Fax:* 625-2793 (office). *E-mail:* info@housing.gov.tt (office). *Website:* www.mphe.gov.tt (office).

DILLON, Matt; American actor; b. 18 Feb. 1964, New Rochelle, NY; s. of Paul Dillon and Mary Ellen Dillon. *Films include:* Over the Edge 1979, Little Darlings 1980, My Bodyguard 1980, Liar's Moon 1982, Tex 1982, The Outsiders 1983, Rumble Fish 1983, The Flamingo Kid 1984, Target 1985, Rebel 1985, Native Son 1986, The Big Town (The Arm) 1987, Kansas 1988, Drugstore Cowboy 1989, A Kiss Before Dying 1991, Singles 1992, The Saint of Fort Washington, Mr. Wonderful 1993, Golden Gate 1994, To Die For 1995, Frankie Starlight 1995, Beautiful Girls 1996, Grace of My Heart 1996, Albino Alligator 1996, In and Out 1997, Wild Things 1998, There's Something About Mary 1998, One Night at McCool's 2000, Deuces Wild 2000, City of Ghosts (also Dir) 2002, Employee of the Month 2004, Loverboy 2004, Crash 2005, Factotum 2005, Herbie Fully Loaded 2005, You, Me and Dupree 2006, Nothing But the Truth 2008, Old Dogs 2009, Armoured 2009, Takers 2010, Girl Most Likely 2012, Sunlight Jr. 2013, Hustlers 2013, The Art of the Steal 2013, Bad Country 2014. *Television includes:* Wayward Pines (series) 2016.

DILNOT, Sir Andrew William, Kt, CBE, BA; British economist, broadcaster and fmr university administrator; *Chair, Geospatial Commission;* b. 19 June 1960; ed Olchfa Comprehensive School, Swansea, St John's Coll., Oxford; joined Inst. of Fiscal Studies 1981, Dir 1991–2002; Prin. St Hugh's Coll., Oxford 2002–12; Pro Vice-Chancellor, Univ. of Oxford 2005–12; Warden of Nuffield College, Oxford 2012–; visiting lecturer at numerous univs in UK and abroad; Chair. Statistics User Forum 2009–12, Comm. on Funding of Care and Support (Dilnot Comm.) 2010–11, UK Statistics Authority 2012–17; Chief Exec. Ordnance Survey 2015–18; Chair Geospatial Comm. 2018–; regular contrib. to broadcast and printed media, including BBC Radio 4 programmes Analysis and More or Less; mem. Social Security Advisory Cttee, Govt Evidence-Based Policy Panel, National Consumer Council; mem. Council, Royal Econ. Soc., Queen Mary and Westfield Coll.; fmr Trustee, Nuffield Foundation; Hon. Fellow, St John's Coll., Oxford, Queen Mary, Univ. of London, Swansea Inst. of Higher Educ., Inst. of Actuaries; Dr hc (City Univ., London). *Publication:* The Tiger That Isn't: Seeing Through a World of Numbers (with Michael Blastland) 2007. *Address:* Cabinet Office, 70 Whitehall, London, SW1A 2AS (office); Office of the Warden, Nuffield College, New Road, Oxford, OX1 1NF, England (office). *Telephone:* (20) 7276-1234 (Cabinet Office). *E-mail:* publiccorrespondence@cabinetoffice.gov.uk; authority.enquiries@statistics.gsi.gov.uk (office). *Website:* www.nuffield.ox.ac.uk (office); www.gov.uk/government/organisations/geospatial-commission.

DILSHAN, Tillakaratne Mudiyanselage, (Tuwan Mohammad Dilshan); Sri Lankan professional cricketer; b. 14 Oct. 1976, Kalutara; m. 2nd Manjula Thilini 2008; two s. two d.; one s. from previous m.; wicketkeeper; right-handed batsman; right-arm off-break bowler; plays for Kalutara Town Club 1996–97, Singha Sports Club 1997–98, Sebastianites Cricket and Athletic Club 1998–2000, Sri Lanka 1999–2016 (Capt. 2011–12), Bloomfield Cricket and Athletic Club 2000, Basnahira South 2007–, Delhi Daredevils 2008–10, Royal Challengers Bangalore 2011–13, Asia XI, Dhaka Gladiators 2013, Sydney Thunder 2014, Guyana Amazon Warriors 2015–, Chittagong Warriors 2015, Peshawar Zalmi 2017–; First-class debut: 1993/94; Test debut: Zimbabwe v Sri Lanka, Bulawayo 18–22 Nov. 1999 (retd 2016); One-Day Int. (ODI) debut: Zimbabwe v Sri Lanka, Bulawayo 11 Dec. 1999; T20I debut: England v Sri Lanka, Southampton 15 June 2006; played 87 Tests, scored 5,492 runs (average 40.98) and took 39 wickets (average 43.87) with 16 centuries and 23 fifties, highest score 193 against England, Lord's 2011, best bowling 4/10 against Bangladesh, Chittagong 2009; played 330 ODIs, scored 10,290 runs (average 39.27) and took 106 wickets (average 45.07) with 22 centuries and 47 fifties, highest score 161 not out against Bangladesh, Melbourne 2015, best bowling 4/4 against Zimbabwe, Pallekele 2011; played 80 T20Is, scored 1,889 runs (average 28.19) and took 9 wickets (average 34.77) with one century and 13 fifties, highest score 104 not out against Australia, Pallekele 2011, best bowling 2/4 against Kenya, Johannesburg 2007; played 223 First-class matches (till Aug. 2015), scored 13, 979 runs (average 38.83) and took 90 wickets (average 36.16) with 38 centuries and 59 fifties, highest score 200 not out, best bowling 5/49; developed batting stroke now called the Dilscoop after him during the ICC World Twenty20 held in England June 2009; retd from Test Cricket 2013; Founder, Hotel D Pavilion Inn 2014; retd from One-Day Int. Cricket and Twenty20 Int. 2016; Twenty20 Int. Performance of the Year, ICC Awards 2009. *Television:* Kopi Kade 2017, Mithuu 2018. *Address:* D Pavilion Inn, 82 Stratford Avenue, Colombo, Sri Lanka.

DIMAS, Pyrros; Greek weightlifter (retd) and politician; b. (Pirro Ohima), 13 Oct. 1971, Himarra, Albania; m. Anastasia Sdougkou; two s. two d.; ed Univ. of Athens; light-heavyweight lifter; emigrated to Greece 1991; gold medal Barcelona Olympic Games 1992, Atlanta Olympic Games 1996, Sydney Olympic Games 2000; World Championship title 1993, 1995, 1998; European Championship title 1995; world record in the snatch (85kg category); bronze medal, Athens Olympic Games 2004 (retd); Pres. Hellenic Weightlifting Fed. 2008–; mem. Parl. (PASOK) 2012–15; serves as Major in Greek army; Greek Athlete of the Year 1992, 1993, 1995, 1996; Top Athlete in the 1995 World Championship, Weightlifter of the Century Award, Int. Weightlifting Fed. 2005. *Leisure interests include:* video games, backgammon, cinema. *Address:* c/o The Hellenic Weightlifting Federation, 43 Sygrou Avenue, 117 43 Athens, Greece (office). *Telephone:* (210) 9231780 (office); (210) 92311683 (office). *Fax:* (210) 9243875 (office). *E-mail:* info@weightlifting.gr (office). *Website:* www.weightlifting.gr (office); www.hellenicparliament.gr.

DIMAS, Stavros, LLM; Greek lawyer and politician; *Vice-President, Nea Demokratia (New Democracy);* b. 30 April 1941, Athens; ed Univ. of Athens, New York Univ., USA; lawyer, Sullivan & Cromwell law firm, New York 1969–70; lawyer for legal dept of Int. Finance Corpn, World Bank 1970–75; Deputy Gov. Hellenic Industrial Devt Bank 1975–77; mem. Parl. (New Democracy party) 1977–2004, Parl. Spokesman 1985–89; Deputy Minister of Econ. Co-ordination 1977–80; Minister of Trade 1980–81, of Agric. 1989–90, of Industry, Energy and Tech. 1990–91, of Foreign Affairs 2011–12; Sec.-Gen. Nea Demokratia (New Democracy) 1995–2000, Sr mem. Political Analysis Steering Cttee 2000–03, Head of Del. to Council of Europe 2000–04, Vice-Pres. 2010–; EU Commr for Employment and Social Affairs March–Oct. 2004, for Environment 2004–09; mem. negotiating cttee for accession of Greece to EEC 1977. *Address:* Nea Demokratia, Leoforos Syngrou 340, 176 73 Kallithea, Athens, Greece (office). *Telephone:* (210) 9444000 (office). *Fax:* (210) 7251491 (office). *E-mail:* ndpress@nd.gr (office). *Website:* www.nd.gr (office).

DIMBLEBY, David, MA; British broadcaster and journalist; b. 28 Oct. 1938, Surrey; s. of Richard Dimbleby and Dilys Thomas; m. 1st Josceline Gaskell 1967 (divorced 2000); one s. two d.; m. 2nd Belinda Giles 2000; one s.; ed Univs of Oxford, Paris and Perugia; presenter and interviewer, BBC Bristol 1960–61; Chair. Dimbleby and Sons Ltd 1986–2001, apptd Man. Dir 1967; currently commentator and presenter BBC; Pres. Dimbleby Cancer Care; Dr hc (Univ. of Essex) 2005; Richard Dimbleby Award, BAFTA 1998. *Television:* Quest (religious programme), What's New? (children's science), People and Power 1982–83, General Election Results Programmes 1979, 1983, 1987, 2001, various programmes for the Budget, by-elections, local elections etc.; Presenter, Question Time (BBC) 1994–2018, A Picture of Britain (BBC) 2005, How We Built Britain (also writer) 2007, Seven Ages of Britain (BBC 1) 2010. *Films:* documentaries: Ku-Klux-Klan, The Forgotten Million, Cyprus: The Thin Blue Line 1964–65, South Africa: The White Tribe (Royal TV Soc. Supreme Documentary Award) 1979, US–UK Relations: An Ocean Apart 1988, The Struggle for South Africa (US Emmy Award, Monte Carlo Golden Nymph) 1990, David Dimbleby's India 1997; live commentary on many public occasions including: State Opening of Parliament, Trooping the Colour, Wedding of HRH Prince Andrew and Sarah Ferguson, HM The Queen Mother's 90th Birthday Parade (Royal TV Soc. Outstanding Documentary Award), Funeral of Diana, Princess of Wales 1997, memorial services including Lord Olivier (Royal TV Soc. Outstanding Documentary Award). *Publications:* An Ocean Apart (with

David Reynolds) 1988, A Picture of Britain 2005, How We Built Britain 2007, Seven Ages of Britain 2010. *Address:* c/o Rosemary Scoular, United Agents, 12–26 Lexington Street, London, W1F 0LE, England (office). *Telephone:* (20) 3214-0894 (office). *Fax:* (20) 3214-0801 (office). *E-mail:* wmillyard@unitedagents.co.uk (office). *Website:* www.unitedagents.co.uk (office).

DIMBLEBY, Jonathan, BA; British broadcaster, journalist and writer; b. 31 July 1944, Aylesbury, Bucks.; s. of Richard Dimbleby and Dilys Thomas; m. 1st Bel Mooney 1968 (divorced); one s. one d.; m. 2nd Jessica Ray 2007; two d.; ed Univ. Coll. London; reporter, BBC Bristol 1969–70, World at One (BBC Radio) 1970–71, This Week (Thames TV) 1972–78, 1986–88, TV Eye 1979, Jonathan Dimbleby in Evidence series (Yorkshire TV) 1980–84; Assoc. Ed./Presenter First Tuesday 1982–86; Presenter/Ed. Jonathan Dimbleby on Sunday (TV-am) 1985–86, On the Record (BBC TV) 1988–93, Charles: The Private Man, The Public Role (Central TV) 1994, weekly political programme Jonathan Dimbleby (ITV) 1995–2006; presenter, Any Questions? (BBC Radio 4) 1987–; main presenter of Gen. Election coverage, ITV; Chair. Index on Censorship 2009–; Pres. Voluntary Service Overseas 1999–, Soil Asscn 1997–2009, Royal Soc. for Protection of Birds 2001–04, Bath Festivals Trust 2003–06; Vice-Pres. Campaign for Protection of Rural England 1997–; Trustee Dimbleby Cancer Care; Hon. Fellow, Univ. Coll. London 1990–2015 (resgnd); Richard Dimbleby Award 1974. *Publications include:* Richard Dimbleby 1975, The Palestinians 1979, The Prince of Wales: A Biography 1994, The Last Governor 1997, Russia: A Journey to the Heart of a Land and its People 2008. *Leisure interests:* tennis, riding, music, rural life. *Address:* c/o David Higham Associates Ltd, 5 Lower John Street, Golden Square, London, W1R 4HA, England (office). *Telephone:* (20) 7437-7888 (office). *Website:* www.davidhigham.co.uk/clients/Jonathan_Dimbleby.htm (office).

DiMICCO, Daniel R.; American business executive; ed Brown Univ., Univ. of Pennsylvania; joined Nucor Corpn as Plant Metallurgist and Man. of Quality Control for Nucor Steel, Plymouth, Utah 1982, Gen. Man. Nucor-Yamato joint venture in Blytheville, Ark. 1991, Vice-Pres. Nucor Corpn 1992–99, Exec. Vice-Pres. 1999–2000, mem. Bd of Dirs, Pres. 2000–10, CEO 2000–12, Vice-Chair. 2001–06, Chair. 2006–12, Exec. Chair. Jan.–Dec. 2013, Chair. Emer. 2013–; Chair. American Iron and Steel Inst. –2011, Vice-Chair. 2011–13; fmr Chair. American Iron and Steel Inst.; mem. Bd of Dirs Duke Energy Corpn 2007–; mem. United States Manufacturing Council 2008–11; inducted into IndustryWeek magazine's Manufacturing Hall of Fame 2011, North Carolina Business Hall of Fame 2015. *Address:* c/o Nucor Corporate Office, 1915 Rexford Road, Charlotte, NC 28211, USA (office). *Website:* www.dandimicco.com.

DIMITRIEV, Emil; Macedonian sociologist and politician; *Secretary-General, Vnatrešno-Makedonska Revolucionerna Organizacija-Demokratska Partija za Makedonsko Nacionalno Edinstvo;* b. 19 March 1979, Probištip; ed Philosophy Faculty and Inst. of Sociology, Univ. of Skopje, School for Reserve Officers, Mil. Acad., Skopje; worked at Zletovica Hydro System; Co-ordinator of Vnatrešno-Makedonska Revolucionerna Organizacija-Demokratska Partija za Makedonsko Nacionalno Edinstvo (VMRO-DPMNE—Internal Macedonian Revolutionary Org.-Democratic Party for Macedonian Nat. Unity) group of councillors at Probištip Municipality, Sec.-Gen. VMRO-DPMNE; Deputy Minister of Defence 2008, 2011; mem. Sobranie (Ass.) 2011–; Prime Minister 2016–17. *Address:* Vnatrešno-Makedonska Revolucionern Organizacija-Demokratska Partija za Makedonsko Nacionalno Edinstvo (Internal Macedonian Revolutionary Organization-Democratic Party for Macedonian National Unity), 1000 Skopje, Ploshtad VMRO 1, North Macedonia (office). *Telephone:* (2) 3215550 (office). *Fax:* (2) 3215551 (office). *E-mail:* contact@vmro-dpmne.org.mk (office). *Website:* vmro-dpmne.org.mk (office).

DIMITROV, Aleksander; Macedonian lawyer, politician and editor; b. 29 Nov. 1949, Skopje; ed Skopje Univ.; mem. Man. Bd Air Service Skopje, Sec., Forum for Int. Relations; ed. Forum (newspaper) 1969–72, Mlad Borac (newspaper) 1972–78; Sec., Council for Foreign Relations 1979–82; Under-Sec., Cttee for Int. Relations 1982–92; Dir for Int. Affairs, Dir Office of Palair 1993–96; Minister of Foreign Affairs 1998–2000; joined New Alternative party 2007; Diplomatic Ed., Fokus (periodical) 2011–. *Address:* Fokus, Skopje, Železnička 53, North Macedonia (office). *Telephone:* (2) 3111327 (office). *Fax:* (2) 3111685 (office).

DIMITROV, Martin; Bulgarian economist and politician; b. 13 April 1977, Sofia; m.; Analyst, Inst. for Market Economics, Sofia 2000–03, Chief Economist 2003–05; elected mem. Parl. 2005, Vice-Chair. Cttee on the Budget and Finance; mem. European Parl. (Group of the European People's Party–Christian Democrats and European Democrats) Jan.–June 2007, mem. Cttee on Budgets, Cttee on Internal Market and Consumer Protection, Del. for Relations with Mashreq Countries; Leader, Union of Democratic Forces (UDF) 2008–12; mem. Parl. for 24-Sofiya 2 constituency (Parl. Group of The Blue Coalition – UDF, DSB, The United Agrarians, BSDP, RDP) 2009–13, Chair. Econ. Policy, Energy and Tourism Cttee, Friendship Group Bulgaria–Estonia, Deputy Chair. Friendship Group Bulgaria–Australia, Bulgaria–UK; Co-founder Bulgarian Soc. for Individual Liberty.

DIMITROV, Nikola, LLM; Macedonian diplomatist and politician; *Minister of Foreign Affairs;* b. 30 Sept. 1972, Skopje, Socialist Repub. of Macedonia, Socialist Fed. Repub. of Yugoslavia; s. of Dimitar Dimitrov and Ratka Dimitrova; m. Natasha Dimitrova; three c.; ed SS Cyril and Methodius Univ., Skopje, King's Coll., Cambridge, UK; Human Rights Officer, Ministry of Foreign Affairs 1996–2000, Deputy Minister of Foreign Affairs 2000; Nat. Security Adviser to Pres. 2000–01; Amb. to USA 2001–06; Chief Negotiator in talks with Greece about use of name Macedonia 2003–08; Nat. Coordinator for NATO Integration 2006–09; Nat. Security Adviser to the Prime Minister 2007–08; Special Envoy of the Govt for European and Euro-Atlantic Integration in Brussels 2007–08; Co-Agent before Int. Court of Justice, The Hague 2008–11; Amb. to The Netherlands 2009–13; with Inst. for Global Justice, The Hague 2014; Minister of Foreign Affairs 2017–. *Publication:* The Framework Convention for the Protection of National Minorities: Historical Background and Theoretical Implications. *Address:* Ministry of Foreign Affairs, 1000 Skopje, Filip II Makedonski 7, North Macedonia (office). *Telephone:* (2) 3115266 (office). *Fax:* (2) 3115790 (office). *E-mail:* mailmnr@mfa.gov.mk (office). *Website:* www.mfa.gov.mk (office).

DIMITROV, Petar, DEcon; Bulgarian politician; b. 27 Jan. 1949, Klisura; ed Moscow Inst. of Econs and Statistics, Nottingham Trent Univ., UK 1994; Lecturer, Varna Univ. of Econs 1976–93, Deputy Rector 1989–93, Assoc. Prof. in Social Man. 1988, Head of Higher School of Man. 1990; mem. Nat. Ass. 1994–2009, Chair. Parl. Comm on Budget and Finance 2005–07, mem. Comm on Educ. and Science, on Econ. Policy, Budget and Finance; Minister of Economy and Energy 2007–09. *Address:* c/o Ministry of the Economy and Energy, 1000 Sofia, ul. Slavyanska 8, Bulgaria.

DIMITROV, Philip, JD; Bulgarian lawyer, politician, diplomatist, academic and author; *Member, Constitutional Court;* b. 31 March 1955, Sofia; s. of Dimitar Vassilev Dimitrov and Katherine Philipova Dimitrova; m. Elena Valentinova Gueorgieva-Dimitrova 1988; ed St Kliment Ohridsky Univ., Sofia; attorney 1979–91, 2002–05; Vice-Pres. Union of Democratic Forces 1990, Pres. 1990–94; Prime Minister of Bulgaria 1991–92; mem. Parl. 1991–97; Vice-Chair. Jt Parl. Cttee, EU–Bulgaria 1995–97; Perm. Rep. to UN, New York 1997–98; Amb. to USA 1998–2002; Special Envoy of OSCE Pres. for Armenia and Azerbaijan 2004; Deputy Speaker, Nat. Ass. (Parl.) 2005–07; MEP 2007; Head, EU Delegation, Georgia 2010–14; mem. Constitutional Court 2015–; Woodrow Wilson Center Public Policy Scholar, Washington, DC 2003; Adjunct Prof., American Univ. in Bulgaria 2003–; mem. Sofia Bar Asscn; Truman-Reagan Freedom Award for contrib. to overcoming communism 1999; Dimitrov Scholarships and Lectures, American Univ. in Bulgaria, Sofia inaugurated 2002. *Publications include:* The Myths of the Bulgarian Transition 2003, The New Democracies and the Trans-atlantic Link 2003; three historical novels, For They Lived, O Lord 1991, The True Story of the Round Table Knights 1996, Light of Men 2003. *Leisure interest:* history. *Address:* Constitutional Court of Bulgaria, 1 bul. Dondukov, Sofia 1594, Bulgaria (office). *Telephone:* (2) 9402337 (office). *E-mail:* secretariat@constcourt.bg (office). *Website:* www.constcourt.bg (office).

DIMMELER, Stefanie, BSc, PhD, Dr rer. nat; German biologist, biochemist and academic; *Professor of Experimental Medicine and Director, Institute of Cardiovascular Regeneration, University of Frankfurt;* b. 18 July 1967, Ravensburg; ed Univ. of Konstanz; completed a fellowship in Experimental Surgery at Univ. of Cologne; completed a fellowship in Molecular Cardiology at Univ. of Frankfurt, Head of Div. of Molecular Cardiology 1997–, Prof. of Experimental Medicine 2001–, Dir Inst. of Cardiovascular Regeneration 2008–; Visiting Prof., Baylor Coll. of Medicine Houston, USA 2005, New York Medical Coll. 2006–08, Stanford Univ. 2009, Robert L. Krakoff International Lectureship in Cardiovascular Medicine, Harvard Medical School, Boston, USA 2012; Edmond Hustinx Chair (Visiting Prof.), CARIM, Univ. of Maastricht 2007–08; Chief Ed. EMBO Molecular Medicine 2010–; mem. Editorial Bd Circulation 2001–, Circulation Research 2000– (Assoc. Ed. 2008–), Basic Research in Cardiology 2001–, Journal of Molecular and Cellular Cardiology 2005–; mem. German Ethical Cttee (Deutscher Ethikrat) 2008–12; mem. Advisory Bd Lifeboat Foundation; Preis des Stifterverbandes für die Deutsche Wissenschaft 1991, Fritz Külz Prize, Deutschen Gesellschaft für Pharmakologie und Toxikologie 1994, Research Prize, Deutschen Stiftung für Herzforschung 1998, Herbert and Hedwig Eckelmann Foundation Prize 1999, Fraenkel Prize, Deutschen Gesellschaft für Kardiologie 2000, Alfried-Krupp-Förderpreis für junge Hochschullehrer 2002, Forßmann Prize, Ruhr-Universität Bochum 2004, Leibniz Prize 2005, Ernst Jung Prize, Jung-Stiftung für Wissenschaft und Forschung (co-recipient) 2007, Science4Life Energy Award 2008, Research Award, GlaxoSmithKline Foundation 2010, Life Achievement Award, Dutch-German Molecular Cardiology Working Groups 2010, Madrid Award for Cell therapy and Cardiovascular Regeneration 2014. *Achievements include:* responsible, together with Dr Zeiher, for scientific discoveries culminating in current clinical trial of human progenitor cells for cardiac repair. *Publications:* more than 270 scientific papers in professional journals on endothelial biology, including signal transduction, apoptosis, and renewal by circulating endothelial progenitor cells in health and disease. *Address:* Institute of Cardiovascular Regeneration, Centre for Molecular Medicine, Goethe-University Frankfurt, Theodor Stern Kai 7, 60590 Frankfurt am Main, Germany (office). *Telephone:* (69) 6301-7440 (office). *E-mail:* Dimmeler@em.uni-frankfurt.de (office). *Website:* www.cardiovascular-regeneration.com (office).

DIMON, James (Jamie) L., MBA; American financial services industry executive; *Chairman and CEO, JPMorgan Chase & Company;* b. 13 March 1956, New York, NY; m. Judith Kent; three d.; ed The Browning School, New York, Tufts Univ., Harvard Univ.; Asst to Pres., American Express 1982–85; Pres. and COO Travelers Group 1991–98, also COO Smith Barney Inc. (subsidiary co.) –1996, Chair. and CEO 1996–97, Chair. and Co-CEO, Salomon Smith Barney Holdings Inc. (following merger) 1997–98; Pres. Citigroup 1998–2000; Chair. and CEO Bank One Corpn March 2000–04, Pres., COO and Dir JPMorgan Chase & Co. (after merger between Bank One Corpn and JPMorgan Chase & Co.) 2004–05, CEO and Pres. 2005–, Chair. 2006–; mem. Pres.'s Strategic and Policy Forum Jan.–Aug. 2017; Vice-Chair. NYU School of Medicine Foundation Bd; Dir Tricon Global Restaurants Inc., Center on Addiction and Substance Abuse; Trustee, Mount Sinai-NYU Medical Center; mem. Council on Foreign Relations. *Address:* JPMorgan Chase & Co., 270 Park Avenue, New York, NY 10017-2070, USA (office). *Telephone:* (212) 270-6000 (office). *Fax:* (212) 270-1648 (office). *E-mail:* joseph.evangelisti@jpmchase.com (office). *Website:* www.jpmorganchase.com (office).

DINARDO, HE Cardinal Daniel Nicholas, BA, MA, LicTheol; American ecclesiastic; *Archbishop of Galveston-Houston;* b. 23 May 1949, Steubenville, Ohio; ed Catholic Univ. of America, Washington, DC, Pontifical Gregorian Univ. and the Augustinianum, Rome; ordained priest in Pittsburgh 1977; staff mem. Vatican Congregation for Bishops 1984–90; also served as Dir of Villa Stritch (residence for American priests working at the Vatican); taught a theology seminar in methodology at Gregorian Univ.; held pastoral posts in Pittsburgh Diocese, where he taught in the ongoing formation programme for priests and was Asst Spiritual Dir at St Paul Seminary 1990–97; Coadjutor Bishop of Sioux City, Ia 1997–98, Bishop of Sioux City 1998–2004; Coadjutor Bishop of Galveston-Houston, Tex. Jan.–Dec. 2004, Coadjutor Archbishop of Galveston-Houston Dec. 2004–06, Archbishop of Galveston-Houston 2006–; cr. Cardinal (Cardinal-Priest of Sant'Eusebio) 2007; participated in Papal Conclave 2013; Vice-Pres. US Conf. of Catholic Bishops 2013–; mem. Secr. for the Economy 2014–; mem. Bd Trustees, Catholic Univ. of America. *Address:* Chancery Office, Archdiocese of Galveston-Houston, PO Box 907, 1700 San Jacinto Street, Houston, TX 77001-0907, USA (office).

Telephone: (713) 659-5461 (office). *Fax:* (713) 759-9151 (office). *E-mail:* info@diogh.org (office). *Website:* www.diogh.org (office).

DINARELLO, Charles A., MD; American professor of medicine; *Professor of Medicine and Immunology, School of Medicine, University of Colorado, Denver;* b. 22 April 1943, Boston, Mass; ed Yale Univ., Massachusetts Gen. Hosp.; Investigator, NIH, Bethesda, Md 1971–77; Prof. of Medicine and Immunology, School of Medicine, Univ. of Colorado, Denver 1996–; Prof. of Experimental Medicine, Radboud Univ., Nijmegen, The Netherlands; mem. Bd of Govs Weizmann Inst. of Science, Israel, Ben Gurion Univ., Israel; fmr Vice-Pres. American Soc. of Clinical Investigation; fmr Pres. International Cytokine Soc.; f. Interleukin Foundation (charity) 2009; mem. editorial bds of several scientific journals; mem. NAS 1998; Foreign mem. Royal Netherlands Acad. of Arts and Sciences 2011; hon. degrees from Univ. of Marseille (France), Weizmann Inst. of Science, Univ. of Frankfurt (Germany), Roosevelt Univ., Albany Medical Coll., Radboud Univ. (Netherlands), Trinity Coll. (Ireland); Squibb Award, Ernst Jung Prize in Medicine (Germany) 1993, Chirone Prize, Italian Nat. Acad. of Medicine, Carol Nachman Prize (Germany), Sheikh Hamdan bin Rashdid al Madktoum Award (UAE), Beering Prize, Bonfils-Stanton Prize, Bonazinga Award, Albany Prize in Medical Research (co-recipient) 2009, Crafoord Prize, Royal Swedish Acad. of Sciences (co-recipient) 2009, Paul Ehrlich and Ludwig Darmstaedter Prize (Germany) 2010, Novartiz Prize in Clinical Immunology (Switzerland) (co-recipient) 2010. *Publications:* more than 600 original research articles and 250 reviews and book chapters on cytokines, particularly on Interleukin-1, Interleukin-18 and related cytokines. *Address:* Division of Infectious Diseases, 12700 East 19th Avenue, Box B168, Aurora, CO 80045, USA (office). *Telephone:* (303) 724-4922 (office). *E-mail:* charles.dinarello@ucdenver.edu (office). *Website:* www.ucdenver.edu/academics/colleges/medicalschool (office).

DÎNCU, Vasile Sebastian, PhD; Romanian sociologist, academic and politician; b. 25 Nov. 1961, Năsăud; m. Maria Dîncu; one s. one d.; ed Univ. of Cluj; Prof. of Sociology, Univ. of Bucharest; Prof. of Sociology, Faculty of Sociology and Faculty of Political, Admin. and Communication Sciences, Babeş-Bolyai Univ., Cluj-Napoca; mem. Partidul Social Democrat (PSD—Social Democratic Party); mem. European Parl. (Group of European Socialists) Jan.–May 2007; Senator 2004–08; fmr Minister, Ministry of Public Information; Deputy Prime Minister and Minister of Regional Devt and Public Admin 2015–17; Pres. Romanian Inst. for Evaluation and Strategy 2009–15; mem. Cttee of Sociology, Political Science and Public Admin, Nat. Council for Attesting Titles, Diplomas and Certificates 2012; Founder of regional weekly magazines, Reporter and Sinteza; mem. European Soc. for Opinion and Marketing Research, Soc. of Sociologists from Romania, Asscn of Sociologists from Romania, Writers' Union of Romania 2014. *Publications include:* Audienţa radio în România 1998, Societatea civilă şi administraţia locală 1999, Comunicarea simbolică. Arhitectura discursului publicitar 1999, 2009, Comunicarea în managementul instituţional 1999, Ţara telespectatorilor fericiţi. Contra-ideologii 2000, Politica inutilă 2007, Patrie de unică folosinţă 2010, Mitologii, fantasme şi idolatrie 2011, Poveştile, viaţa şi moartea 2011, O Românie interioară 2013, Triburile. O patologie a politicii româneşti de la Revoluţie la Generaţia Facebook 2015. *Leisure interests:* football, literature, music. *Address:* 3400 Cluj-Napoca, Nic. Titulescu nr. 20/37, Cluj, jud., Romania (home). *Telephone:* (723) 300120 (home). *E-mail:* vasile.dancu@gmail.com (home). *Website:* vasiledancu.blogspot.co.uk.

DINDAR, Mohammad Naim, BS, Ing.Agric.; Afghan banker; *Secretary-General, Afghan Red Crescent Society;* b. 29 Sept. 1947, Khwabgah, Kabul City; s. of Mohammad Yasin and Zohra Begum; ed American Univ. of Beirut, Lebanon; Exchange Student, American Field Service 1964–65; Pres. Afghan Students' Asscn 1968–69; Sr Agricultural Expert, Office of Admin. Affairs, Pres. of Afghanistan 1991–95; Chief of Staff, Ministry of Finance 2003–05, Dir Gen. of Internal Audit 2009; fmr Pres., Int. Relations, Antinarcotic Comm.; Sr Agriculture Analyst, Office of Agricultural Affairs; Pres. and CEO Banke Millie Afghan 2005–09; Vice-Chair. Afghan Banking Asscn; Sec.-Gen. Afghan Red Crescent Soc. 2011–; mem. Bd Afghan Telecom 2005–11, Ariana 2005–09. *Publications:* Afghan Marketing (co-author) 1975, Design of Earth Channels; contribs to Journal of Agriculture; several translations. *Address:* Afghan Red Crescent Society, Shahid Ostad Rabani Road District No. 5, Kabul, Afghanistan (office). *Telephone:* (77) 7767101 (office). *E-mail:* alavi.arcs@gmail.com (office). *Website:* www.redcrescent.af (office).

DINE, James, BFA; American artist; b. 16 June 1935, Cincinnati, Ohio; m. Nancy Minto 1957; three s.; ed Cincinnati Art Acad., Univ. of Cincinnati; first solo exhbn at Reuben Gallery, New York 1960; Guest Lecturer, Yale Univ. 1965; Artist-in-Residence, Oberlin Coll. 1965, Williams Coll.; mem. American Acad. of Arts and Letters 1980–; work appears in numerous public collections including Guggenheim Museum, Moderna Museet, Stockholm, Museum of Modern Art, New York, Dallas Museum of Fine Arts, Tate Gallery and Whitney Museum of Modern American Art; Pyramid Atlantic Award of Distinction 1992. *Publications:* Welcome Home, Lovebirds 1969 (also illustrator); co-author and illustrator The Adventures of Mr. and Mrs. Jim & Ron 1970; illustrator, The Poet Assassinated 1968, Drawing from the Glypothek 1993. *Address:* c/o Jonathan Novak Contemporary Art, 1880 Century Park East, Los Angeles, CA 90067, USA.

DING, Fengying; Chinese party official; *Vice-Chairman, Hubei Provincial Committee, Chinese People's Political Consultative Conference;* b. 1943, Luotian Co., Hubei Prov.; ed Huazhong Teachers Coll., Cen. China Teachers' Coll.; Sec. CCP CYLC and Chair. Women's Fed., Beifeng Commune, Luotian Co. 1960–69; Deputy Sec. and Sec. CCP Party Cttee, Beifeng Commune Fourth Brigade, Luotian Co. 1960–69; joined CCP 1961; Deputy Dir CCP Revolutionary Cttee, Luotian Co. 1969–71, Deputy Sec. CCP Co. Cttee 1969–71; Chair. Hubei Branch, Chinese Women's Fed. 1973; Vice-Chair. Revolutionary Cttee, Hubei Prov. 1973–79; Alt. mem. 12th CCP Cen. Cttee 1982–87; First Sec. CCP Cttee, Huangguang Pref. 1983–; Deputy Sec. CCP Cttee, Hubei Prov. 1986, mem. CCP 5th Hubei Prov. Cttee 1988–, Sec. Comm. for Discipline Inspection, Hubei Prov. 1988–; mem. CCP Cen. Discipline Inspection Comm. 1992–, 9th CPPCC Nat. Cttee 1998–2003; Vice-Chairman CPPCC Hubei Prov. Cttee 2003–. *Address:* Hubei Dangwei, 1 Beihuanlu Road, Shuiguohu, Wuchang City, Hubei Province, People's Republic of China. *Telephone:* 813351.

DING, Gen. Henggao; Chinese politician and scientist; b. 3 Feb. 1931, Nanjing Co., Jiangsu Prov.; m. Nie Lili (d. of Marshal Nie Rongzhen); ed Nanjing Univ., Leningrad Inst. of Precision Machinery and Optical Instruments, USSR; Asst Researcher, Chinese Acad. of Sciences 1952–57; joined CCP 1953; held posts of Section Chief, Worker, Ministry of Defence 1961–62, Deputy Dir 1962–63, Dir 1963–65, Research Fellow 1977–82; joined PLA 1962, Lieutenant-Gen. 1988–94, Gen. 1994–; Deputy Dir State Comm. of Science, Tech. and Industry for Nat. Defence 1982–85, Dir 1985–96, Party Cttee Sec. 1989–; Alt. mem. 12th CCP Cen. Cttee 1982–87, mem. 13th CCP Cen. Cttee 1989–92, 14th CCP Cen. Cttee 1992–97; mem. State Leading Group for Science and Tech.; mem. Standing Cttee, 9th CPPCC Nat. Cttee 1998–2003; Pres. Chinese Soc. of Inertial Tech. 1995–; Prof. Tsinghua Univ.; mem. Chinese Acad. of Eng 1994–; Hon. Pres. Chinese Astronautics Soc.; State Special Class Award for scientific and technological achievements for nat. defence 1994, Holeung Ho Lee Technological Science Prize 2006. *Address:* 1 South Building, Aimin Street, Xicheng District, Beijing 100034, People's Republic of China. *Telephone:* (10) 66056357. *Fax:* (10) 66738111. *E-mail:* engach@mail.cae.ac.cn (office).

DING, Shisun; Chinese university administrator and mathematician; b. 5 Sept. 1927, Shanghai; s. of Ding Rounong and Liu Huixian; m. Gui Linlin 1956; two s.; ed Tsinghua Univ.; Asst Tsinghua Univ. 1950–52; joined China Democratic League 1952; joined staff Beijing Univ. 1952, promoted to Lecturer then Prof. of Math. 1979, Vice-Chair. Math. Dept 1978–80, Chair. 1981–82, Pres. Beijing Univ. 1984–89; Pres. Math. Soc. of Beijing 1986–88; Vice-Pres. Chinese Math. Soc. 1988–91; fmr Chair. Jiang Zehan Scholarship Fund Cttee; fmr Vice-Chair. Zhou Peiyuan Fund Cttee; fmr Vice-Pres. Chinese Educ. Asscn for Int. Exchanges; fmr Deputy Head, Math. Examination and Appraisal Group, Nat. Natural Science Foundation of China; fmr mem. 2nd Panel of Judges of State Academic Degrees Cttee, Exec. Council of China Overseas Exchanges Asscn, Exec. Council of China Soc. of Higher Educ., Council of Chinese People's Inst. of Foreign Affairs; visited Math. Dept, Harvard Univ., USA 1983; Exec. Vice-Chair. China Democratic League Cen. Cttee 1988–96, Chair. 1996–2005, Hon. Chair. 2005–; mem. 7th CPPCC Nat. Cttee 1988–93, Standing Cttee of 8th CPPCC Nat. Cttee 1993–98; Vice-Chair. Educ. and Culture Cttee; Vice-Chair. Standing Cttee of 9th NPC 1998–2003, Standing Cttee of 10th NPC 2003; Chair. Advisory Cttee American Studies Center, Peking Univ.; Pres. Western Returned Students' Asscn 1999; mem. Macao Special Admin. Region Preparatory Cttee, Govt Del., Macao Hand-Over Ceremony 1999; Dr hc (Soka, Japan) 1985; Hon. DSc (Nebraska) 1988. *Publications:* Concise Textbook of Higher Algebra, Analytic Geometry and Orders of Linear Displacement Register; numerous math. papers on algebra and number theory. *Leisure interest:* classical music.

DING, Gen. Wenchang; Chinese party official and army officer; b. Oct. 1933, Suxian Co., Anhui Prov.; ed PLA High Infantry School, Air Force Aviation School; joined CCP 1956; Chief, Political Dept, Air Force, PLA Services and Arms, Dir 1988, Political Commissar 1992–99, Party Cttee Sec.; rank of Maj.-Gen. 1988–90, Lt-Gen. of Air Force 1990–96, Gen. 1996–; Deputy, 7th NPC 1988–93; mem. 14th CCP Cen. Cttee 1992–97, 15th CCP Cen. Cttee 1997–2002. *Address:* Political Department of Air Force, Beijing, People's Republic of China.

DING, William, BSc; Chinese internet executive; *CEO, NetEase.com Inc.;* b. (Ding Lei), Oct. 1971, Ningbo City, Zhejiang Prov.; ed China Electronic Science and Tech. Univ., Chengdu; tech. engineer, Ningbo Telecom 1993–95; tech. support engineer, Sybase Guangzhou Co. 1995–96, Guangzhou Feijie Co. 1996–97; Founder and CEO NetEase.com Inc. (introduced first free e-mail service, online community and personalized information service in China) 1997–2000, Chief Tech. Officer 2000–01, Acting CEO and COO June–Sept. 2001, Chair. and Chief Tech. Officer 2001–, CEO 2005–; named one of the 10 most influential Internet celebrities in China 1999, named one of China's Top Ten IT Figures 2001, 2002. *Address:* NetEase.com, SP Tower D, 26th Floor, Tsinghua Science Park, Building 8, No. 1 Zhongguancun East Road, Haidian District, Beijing 100084 (office); 2nd Floor, Tower B, Keeven International R&D Centre, Beijing 100086, People's Republic of China. *Telephone:* (10) 82558163 (office). *Fax:* (10) 82618163 (office). *E-mail:* ir@service.netease.com (office). *Website:* ir.netease.com (office).

DING, Xiaqi; Chinese mathematician and research professor; b. 25 May 1928, Yiyang Co., Hunan Prov.; m. Luo Peizhu 1957; three d.; ed Dept of Math., Wuhan Univ.; Research Asst, Assoc., Assoc. Prof., Prof., Inst. of Math., Acad. Sinica 1951–79; Research Prof., Inst. of Systems Sciences, Acad. Sinica 1979–91; Research Prof., Inst. of Applied Math., Academia Sinica 1991–; Prof. and Dir Wuhan Inst. of Math., Acad. Sinica 1985–94, Dr Wuhan Inst. of Math. Physics; Academician, Chinese Acad. of Sciences 1991–; fmr Prof. Center of Mathematical Sciences, Zhejiang Univ. Hangzhou; mem. Cttee Math. Soc. of China; Standing mem. Cttee of Chinese Soc. of Systems Eng; Prize Award, Nat. Science Conf., Beijing 1978, Prize of Chinese Acad. of Sciences 1978, 1st Class Prize, Chinese Acad. of Science 1988, 2nd Class Prize Natural Science Prize of People's Repub. of China 1989, Holeung Ho Lee Mathematics Prize 2006. *Publications:* more than 80 papers on PDE, functions spaces, number theory and numerical analysis; 4 monographs. *Leisure interest:* mathematics. *Address:* c/o Center of Mathematical Sciences, Zhejiang University, Hangzhou 310027, People's Republic of China (office). *Telephone:* (571) 87953030 (office). *Fax:* (571) 87953035 (office). *E-mail:* xqding@public.bta.net.cn (office). *Website:* www.cms.zju.edu.cn (office).

DING, Xuedong; Chinese government official; *Chairman and CEO, China Investment Corporation;* b. 1960, Jiangsu Prov.; ed Research Inst. for Fiscal Science, Ministry of Finance; fmr Dir-Gen., Dept of Property Rights; fmr Dir-Gen., Dept of Human Resources and Head of Gen. Office, State-owned Asset Admin Bureau; Dir, Agric. Dept, Ministry of Finance 2000–05, Dir, Educ., Science and Culture Dept 2005–06, Asst Minister of Finance 2006–08, Vice-Minister of Finance 2008–10; Deputy Sec.-Gen., State Council 2010–13; Chair. and CEO, China Investment Corpn (sovereign wealth fund) 2013–; Deputy Dir, Nat. Cttee for Disaster Reduction 2013; Deputy Dir, State Council Leading Group for Poverty Alleviation and Devt 2013–; mem. CCP 1984–, mem. Ministry of Finance CCP Leading Party Group 2006–10. *Address:* China Investment Corporation, New Poly Plaza, No.1 Chaoyangmen Beidajie, Dongcheng District, Beijing 100010, People's Republic of China (office). *Telephone:* (10) 8409 6277 (office). *Fax:* (10) 6408 6908 (office). *E-mail:* pr@china-inv.cn (office). *Website:* www.china-inv.cn/cicen (office).

DINGWALL, Bruce; British petroleum industry executive; *Chairman, Trinity Exploration and Production PLC;* b. 1959; began career as geophysicist with Exxon working in North Sea; Business Devt Man. for Asia, Vice-Pres. of Exploration for Indonesia and Exploration Man. for Pakistan, LASMO PLC –1997; Founder and CEO Venture Production (petroleum co.) 1997–2004; f. Ten Degrees North Energy Ltd (oil exploration co.), Trinidad 2005; Chair. MTEM 2005–07; Pres. UKOOA (UK Offshore Petroleum Operators Asscn) 2002; currently Chair. Trinity Exploration and Production PLC; mem. Bd of Dirs Tullibardine Ltd (distiller) 2005. *Address:* Trinity Exploration and Production PLC, 3rd Floor, Southern Supplies Limited Building, 40–44 Sutton Street, POB 3519 La Romain, San Fernando, Trinidad and Tobago. *Telephone:* 653-7651. *E-mail:* info@trinioil.com. *Website:* trinityexploration.com.

DINH, Tien Dung, MBA; Vietnamese accountant; *Minister of Finance;* b. 10 May 1961; ed Ninh Binh; apptd Deputy Chief Accountant, Song Da Construction Corpn 1987, Deputy, Finance Dept, Song Da Materials Supply Co. 1988, Chief Accountant 1989, Chief Accountant, Song Da 1 Construction Co. 1991; Chief Accountant of Glass and Ceramic Corpn, Ministry of Construction 1993, Dir of Finance, Accounting Dept 1997, mem. Staff Cttee of Deputy Minister of Construction 2003; Deputy Sec. Dien Bien Prov. Party Cttee 2008, Chair. 2008; Sec. Ninh Binh Prov. Party Cttee 2010; Gen. State Auditor 2011; Minister of Finance 2013–. *Address:* Ministry of Finance, 28 Tran Hung Dao, Hoan Kiem District, Hanoi, Viet Nam (office). *Telephone:* (24) 22202828 (office). *Fax:* (24) 22208091 (office). *E-mail:* support@mof.gov.vn (office). *Website:* www.mof.gov.vn (office).

DINI, Abdulkadir Sheikh; Somali army officer and politician; ed Odessa Mil. Acad., Ukraine, John F. Kennedy Special Warfare Center and Army Command War Coll., USA; began mil. career as cadet in Somali Army 1971, becoming Major Commdr of Mil. Police Forces, Bn level 1979, joined Commando Brigade, Baledogle 1980, Commdr 1982, called to assist in developing security policy for Transitional Fed. Govt 2010, Chief of Army (under both Transitional Fed. Govt and succeeding Fed. Govt of Somalia) 2011–13; Minister of Defence 2015–17.

DINI, Lamberto; Italian economist, banker and politician; b. 1 March 1931, Florence; m.; one d.; ed Univ. of Florence, Univs of Minnesota and Michigan, USA; economist, IMF, Washington, DC, then various posts to Deputy Dir Africa Dept 1959–76, mem. Bd Exec. Dirs 1976–78, now Alt. Gov. for Italy; joined Banca d'Italia (cen. bank) as Asst Gen. Man. 1979, later Gen. Man.; mem. Monetary Cttee of EU, Bd Dirs BIS; Minister of the Treasury 1994–95; Prime Minister of Italy 1995–96; Minister of Foreign Affairs 1996–2001; mem. Senate for Lazio 2001–13, Deputy Speaker of Senate 2001–06, Pres. Foreign Affairs Comm. 2006–13; Pres. Liberal Democratici Riformisti (Liberal Democrats) 2007–08; joined Popolo della Libertà (People of Freedom) 2008; Fulbright Scholar; Commander, Ordine al merito della Repubblica Italiana 1977, Grand Officer, Ordine al merito della Repubblica Italiana 1982, Kt Grand Cross, Ordine al merito della Repubblica Italiana 1991, Cross of Commander, Order of Merit (Poland) 1997, Grand Cross, Order of Isabella the Catholic (Spain) 1998, Grand Cross, Order of Merit (Poland) 2000, Hon. Kt Grand Cross, Order of St Michael and St George (UK) 2000, Order of the Rising Sun (Japan) 2009.

DINKIĆ, Mlađan, BA, MSc; Serbian economist, academic, government official and fmr central banker; b. 20 Dec. 1964, Belgrade; s. of Dušan Dinkić and Milosinka Dinkić; m. Tatjana Dinkić; ed Univ. of Belgrade; research asst, Faculty of Econs, Univ. of Belgrade 1990–93, Assoc. Prof. 1994–; f. G17 (political party, later G17 Plus), Co-ordinator 1997–2001, Vice-Pres. 2001–06, Pres. 2006–, affiliated to United Regions of Serbia (Ujedinjeni regioni Srbije—URS) 2010–; Gov. Nat. Bank of Yugoslavia 2000–03, Gov. Nat. Bank of Serbia 2003–04; fmr econ. adviser to govt; Minister of Finance 2004–06, of the Economy and Regional Devt 2007–11, Deputy Prime Minister 2008–11; Minister of Finance and the Economy 2012–13; Int. Consultant (Montenegro) UNDP 2014–16; Man. Pnr MD Solution 2014–; Adviser (econ. issues) to Pres. of Montenegro 2018–; mem. Bd Dirs Sberbank Srbija, Belgrade 2014–; Euromoney Finance Minister of the Year, Euromoney Magazine 2007, Reformer of 2009 Award. *Publications:* Measuring Economic Efficiency 1994, The Economy of Destruction 1995, Final Account: Economic Consequences of NATO Bombing 1999. *Leisure interests:* music (has own rock band called Monetary Coup), guitar, piano. *Address:* Office of the President, 81000 Podgorica, Sveti Petra Cetinjskog 12, Montenegro (office). *Telephone:* (20) 241410 (office). *Fax:* (20) 245849 (office). *E-mail:* info@predsjednik.me (office). *Website:* www.predsjednik.me (office).

DINKINS, David, BA, LLB; American lawyer, academic and fmr politician; *Professor in the Practice of Public Affairs and Senior Fellow, Center for Urban Research and Policy, School of International and Public Affairs, Columbia University;* b. 10 July 1927, Trenton, NJ; m. Joyce Burrows 1953; one s. one d.; ed Howard Univ., Washington, DC and Brooklyn Law School; served in US Marine Corps 1945–46; in pvt. law practice, New York 1956–75; mem. New York State Ass. 1966; Pres. Bd of Elections, New York City 1972–73; City Clerk, New York City 1975–85; Manhattan Borough Pres. 1986–89; Mayor of New York 1990–94; Prof. in Practice of Public Affairs and Sr Fellow, Center for Urban Research and Policy, Columbia Univ.'s School of Int. and Public Affairs 1993–; host, Dialogue with Dinkins radio public affairs program; mem. Council on Foreign Relations; mem. Bd of Govs American Stock Exchange; Democrat. *Leisure interest:* tennis. *Address:* School of International and Public Affairs, Columbia University, 420 West 118th Street, New York, NY 10027, USA. *Telephone:* (212) 854-4253. *E-mail:* dd98@columbia.edu. *Website:* www.sipa.columbia.edu.

DINKLAGE, Peter Hayden; American actor; b. 11 June 1969, Morristown, NJ; m. Erica Schmidt 2005; one d.; ed Bennington Coll.; Satellite Awards Special Achievement Award 2004, named by New York Times magazine as one of the Eight Actors Who Turn Television into Art Sept. 2011. *Theatre includes:* The Killing Act, Imperfect Love, Richard III, Hope Leaves the Theatre, Things We Want, A Month in the Country, Cyrano. *Films include:* Living in Oblivion 1995, Safe Men 1998, Pigeonholed 1999, Never Again 2001, Human Nature 2001, 13 Moons 2002, Just a Kiss 2002, The Station Agent (Best Actor Award, Ourense Ind. Film Festival 2003) 2003, Tiptoes 2003, Elf 2003, Surviving Eden 2004, The Baxter 2005, Escape Artists 2005, Lassie 2005, Fortunes 2005, The Limbo Room 2006, Find Me Guilty 2006, Little Fugitive 2006, Penelope 2006, Death at a Funeral 2007, Ascension Day 2007, Underdog 2007, The Chronicles of Narnia: Prince Caspian 2008, Saint John of Las Vegas 2009, Death at a Funeral 2010, I Love You Too 2010, The Last Rites of Ransom Pride 2010, Pete Smalls Is Dead 2010, A Little Bit of Heaven 2011, Ice Age: Continental Drift (voice) 2012, A Case of You 2013, Knights of Badassdom 2013, Low Down 2014, X-Men: Days of Future Past 2014, The Angriest Man in Brooklyn 2014, Taxi 2015, Pixels 2015, The Boss 2016, Rememory 2017, Three Billboards Outside Ebbing, Missouri (Critic's Choice Award for Best Acting Ensemble 2017, Georgia Film Critics Asscn Award for Best Ensemble 2017) 2017, Three Christs 2017, I Think We're Alone Now 2018, Avengers: Infinity War 2018. *Television includes:* The $treet (series) 2001, Third Watch (series) 2002, I'm with Her (series) 2004, Life As We Know It (series) 2005, Testing Bob (film) 2005, Ultra (film) 2006, Threshold (series) 2005-06, Nip/Tuck (series) 2006, 30 Rock (series) 2009, Game of Thrones (series) (Emmy Award for Best Supporting Actor in a Dramatic Series 2011, Golden Globe Award for Best Supporting Actor in a Series for Television 2012, Primetime Emmy Award for Outstanding Supporting Actor in a Drama Series 2015, Emmy Award for Outstanding Supporting Actor in a Drama Series 2018) 2011–17. *Address:* c/o Insight Entertainment, 1134 South Cloverdale Avenue, Los Angeles, CA 90019-6737, USA (office).

DINNAGE, Susanna; British business executive; *Global President, Animal Planet, Inc.;* b. 1966, London; fmr audience insight specialist, MTV Networks; part of team that launched Channel Five in 1997; joined Discovery Communications, Inc. 2009, held a series of senior roles, Global Pres. Animal Planet, Inc. (peripheral of Discovery) 2017–, mem. Exec. Bd Discovery Women's Network; Chair Commercial Broadcasters Asscn (COBA) 2015–19; mem. Bd of Dirs All4Media Productions BV, Liberty Global BV. *Address:* Animal Planet, Inc., Discovery Communications, Inc., One Discovery Place, Silver Spring, MD 29010, USA (office). *Telephone:* (240) 662–0000 (office). *Website:* www.animalplanet.com (office).

DINOPOULOS, Argyris, LLM; Greek lawyer, journalist, war correspondent and politician; ed French Lyceum of Athens, Athens Law School, Univ. of Paris, France, Univ. Coll., London, UK; worked as a lawyer until 1980s, then a reporter for ERT (state TV network); worked for Antenna network 1989–2002; one of first foreign corresps to reach northern Afghanistan 2001; covered US mil. invasion of Baghdad 2003; producer of a documentary series shot in various locations in the Mediterranean and the Balkans 2006; mem. Nea Democratia (New Democracy); Mayor of Vrilissia, north Athens 2002; mem. Vouli (Parl.) for Athens 2007–14; Minister of the Interior 2014–15. *Publication:* A War Video-Tape (novel) 2001. *Address:* c/o Ministry of the Interior, Odos Stadiou 27, 101 83 Athens. *E-mail:* adin@otenet.gr. *Website:* ww.dinopoulos.gr.

DIOMBAR, Thiam; Mauritanian government official and politician; b. 31 Dec. 1959, Wothie, Brakna Region; m.; five c.; ed École Nat. d'Admin, Nouakchott, École Nat. des Services du Trésor, France; long career in Treasury Dept, including as Head of Litigation Div. 1982–86, Regional Treas., Assaba 1986–87, Head of Studies at Dept of Budget and Accounts 1989–96, Deputy Dir of Budget in charge of Research 1997–2007, Dir of Lands, Registration and Stamps 2007–08, Dir-Gen. of Budget Feb.–Oct. 2008, Dir-Gen. of Taxation 2008–10, State Inspector Gen. 2010–11, Minister of Finance 2011–15; mem. numerous Mauritanian dels to IMF and World Bank; mem. Union pour la République (UPR). *Address:* c/o Ministry of Finance, BP 181, Nouakchott, Mauritania.

DION, Céline, CC, OQ; Canadian singer; b. (Marie Claudette Céline Dion), 30 March 1968, Charlemagne, Québec; d. of Adhémar Dion and Thérèse Tanguay; m. René Angélil 1994 (died 2016); three s.; recording artist 1981–; winner, Eurovision song contest, Dublin 1988; performed anthem The Power of the Dream at opening ceremony of Olympic Games, Atlanta 1996; Las Vegas show, A New Day 2002–07, Celine 2011–14; Taking Chances World Tour 2008–09; apptd FAO Goodwill Amb. 2010; Medal of Arts (France) 1996, Légion d'honneur 2008; Dr hc (Laval Univ.) 2008; numerous awards including Gala de L'ADISQ Awards (Quebec) for Pop Album of the Year 1983, for Best Selling Record 1984, 1985, for Best Selling Single 1985, for Pop Song of the Year 1985, 1988, for Female Artist of Year 1983–85, 1988, for Discovery of the Year 1983, for Best Québec Artist Outside Québec 1983, 1988, Journal de Québec Trophy 1985, Spectrel Video Award for Best Stage Performance 1988, Juno Awards for Female Vocalist of the Year 1991–94, 1997, 1999, for Album of the Year 1991, 1995, 1999, for Single of the Year 1993, Acad. Award for Best Song Written for a Motion Picture or TV (for Beauty and The Beast duet with Peabo Bryson) 1992, Grammy Award (for Beauty and the Beast) 1993, (for My Heart Will Go On, from film Titanic) 1999, American Music Award for Best Adult Contemporary Artist 2003, World Music Diamond Award 2004, Billboard Icon Award 2016. *Recordings include:* albums: Tellement J'ai d'Amour, Incognito, Unison 1990, Dion chante Plamondon 1991, Céline Dion 1991, The Colour of My Love 1993, Les Premières Années 1994, Des Mots Qui Sonnent 1995, Power of Love 1995, The French Album 1995, D'Eux 1995, Falling into You 1996, Live à Paris 1996, Let's Talk About Love 1997, A l'Olympia 1998, Chansons en Or 1998, Céline Dion Vol. 2 1998, S'il Suffisait d'Aimer 1998, These Are Special Times (Grammy and Juno Awards 1999) 1998, Amour 1998, Au Coeur du Stade 1999, Tout en Amour 2002, All The Way – A Decade of Song 1999, A New Day Has Come 2002, One Heart 2003, 1 Fille & 4 Types 2003, Miracle 2004, Taking Chances 2007, My Love: Essential collection 2008, Taking Chances World Tour – The Concert 2010, Tournée mondiale Taking Chances: Le spectacle 2010, Sans attendre 2012, Loved Me Back to Life 2013, Encore un soir 2016. *Publications include:* Celine 1997, My Story, My Dreams 2001, Miracle (with Anne Geddes) 2004, For Keeps 2006. *Leisure interests:* architecture, fashion, philanthropy, photography, looking after sons, golf. *Address:* Les Productions Feeling, 2540 blvd Daniel-Johnson, Bureau 755, Laval, PQ H7T 2S3, Canada (office). *Telephone:* (450) 978-9555 (office). *Fax:* (450) 978-1055 (office). *E-mail:* info@feelingprod.com (office). *Website:* www.celinedion.com.

DION, Hon. Stéphane, PC, BA, MA, PhD; Canadian diplomatist, politician and academic; *Ambassador to Germany;* b. 28 Sept. 1955, Quebec City; s. of Léon Dion and Denyse Kormann; m. Janine Krieber; one d.; ed Laval Univ., Inst. d'études politiques de Paris, France; Asst Prof. of Political Science, Univ. of Moncton Jan.–May 1984; Asst Prof. of Political Science, Univ. of Montreal 1984–89, Assoc. Prof. 1989–95, Prof. 1995; MP (Liberal Party of Canada) for St-Laurent/Cartierville 1996–2015, for St-Laurent 2015–; Minister of Intergovernmental Affairs and Pres. Queen's Privy Council for Canada 1996–2003, Minister of Environment 2004–06, Leader Liberal Party of Canada 2006–08 (resgnd), also Leader of the Opposition

2006–08, Minister of Foreign Affairs 2015–17; Special Envoy to EU 2017–, Ambassador to Germany 2017–; Pres. UN Climate Change Conference, Montreal 2005; Guest Scholar, Brookings Inst., Washington, DC 1990–91, Laboratoire d'économie publique de Paris 1994–95; Research Fellow, Canadian Centre for Man. Devt 1990–91; Co-Ed. Canadian Journal of Political Science 1990–93; mem. Aid to Scholarly Publs Cttee of Social Sciences Fed. of Canada, Advisory Council of Inst. of Intergovernmental Relations, Queen's Univ.; Dr hc (Carlos III Univ. of Madrid) 2002. *Address:* Embassy of Canada, Leipziger Platz 17, 10117 Berlin, Germany (office). *Telephone:* (30) 203120 (office). *Fax:* (30) 20312121 (office). *E-mail:* brlin-pa@international.gc.ca (office). *Website:* www.canadainternational .gc.ca/germany-allemagne (office).

DION NGUTE, Joseph, Lic.en droit, LLM, PhD; Cameroonian politician; *Prime Minister;* b. 12 March 1954, Bongong Barombi, Southwest Region; ed Univ. of Yaoundé, Univ. of Warwick, Univ. of London; Prof. of Law, Univ. of Yaoundé II during 1980s; Deputy Dir Nat. School of Admin and Magistracy 1986–91, Dir-Gen. 1991–97; Minister-Del. to Minister of External Relations 1997–2018, Special Advisor to the Presidency 2018–19; Prime Minister of Cameroon 2019–; mem. Cameroon People's Democratic Movt, mem. Cen. Cttee. *Address:* Office of the Prime Minister, Yaoundé, Cameroon (office). *Telephone:* 222-23-80-05 (office). *Fax:* 222-23-57-35 (home). *E-mail:* spm@spm.gov.cm (office). *Website:* www.spm.gov.cm (office).

DIONNE, Mohamed Boun Abdallah; Senegalese computer scientist, UN official and politician; *Prime Minister;* b. 1959, Gossas; ed Conservatoire Nat. des Arts et Métiers (CNAM-IIE), France, Univ. Grenoble 2-Pierre Mendès-France; began career as Tech. Engineer, External Operations Div., Compagnie IBM France 1983–86; Authorized Officer, later Deputy Dir and Dir, Banque Centrale des Etats de l'Afrique de l'Ouest 1986–97; seconded to Govt of Senegal 1997, becoming Dir of Industry in Ministry of Industry 1997–2003, Head of Senegal Econ. Bureau, Paris (rank of Minister-Counsellor) 2003–05, Chef de Cabinet to Prime Minister Macky Sall 2005–07, Chef de Cabinet to Pres. of Nat. Ass. (Parl.) 2007–08; UNIDO Rep. in Algeria 2008–10, Sr UNIDO Coordinator for South-South Industrial Cooperation, Vienna, Head of UNIDO programme for Africa and Less Advanced Countries 2011–14; Minister-Counsellor at the Presidency, responsible for monitoring Plan Sénégal Emergent (econ. and social devt plan) March–Aug. 2014; Prime Minister 2014–. *Address:* Office of the Prime Minister, Bldg Administratif, 9e étage, avenue Léopold Sédar Senghor, BP 4029, Dakar, Senegal (office). *Telephone:* 33-889-6969 (office). *Fax:* 33-823-4479 (office). *Website:* www.gouv.sn (office).

DIOP, Abdoulaye; Senegalese politician; ed Lycée El Hadj Malick Sy de Thiès, Univ. of Dakar and Ecole Nat. d'Admin et de Magistrature; asst to Prin. Paymaster, Thiès 1980–81; rate collector, Commune de Fatick 1981–84, Commune de Mbour 1984–87, Commune de Pikine 1987–90; tax collector, Dakar Centre 1990–93; tax and rate collector, Ville de Dakar 1993–95, Dakar Urban Community 1993–95; Sr Banking Exec., Treasurer-Gen. and Dir of Treasury and Public Finance 1995–98; Minister Del., Ministry of Economy and Finance 2000; Minister of State, Minister of Economy and Finance 2001–12; mem. Observatoire des finances locales de Cotonou 1996, Comm. de réforme des textes de la décentralisation; Pres. Tech. Cttee responsible for Reform of Local Finance in Senegal; Chevalier, Ordre nat. du Lion de la République du Sénégal 1996.

DIOP, Abdoulaye, BA, MA; Malian politician and fmr diplomatist; b. 17 Sept. 1965, Brazzaville, Repub. of Congo; m.; five c.; ed École Nat. d'Admin d'Alger, Algeria, Int. Inst. of Public Admin, Paris, France, Paris-Sud 11 Univ.; several years' diplomatic service including positions as Head of multilateral cooperation issues, Embassy in Belgium 1998–99, Adviser to Minister of Foreign Affairs in charge of political and diplomatic issues 1999–2000; oversaw Mali's participation in UN Security Council 2000–01; mem. Steering Cttee, New Partnership for Africa's Devt (NEPAD) 2000–01; Sr Diplomatic Adviser, Office of the Pres. 2000–03; Amb. to USA 2003–09; Country Dir for WFP, Malawi 2009–12, Dir, WFP Liaison Office and Rep. to African Union and UN Econ. Comm. for Africa, Addis Ababa 2013–14; Minister of Foreign Affairs, African Integration and Int. Cooperation 2014–17; mem. Bd of Dirs Partnership to Cut Hunger and Poverty in Africa; Dr hc (Chatham Univ., USA).

DIOP, Bécaye; Senegalese politician; b. 1945; m.; six c.; Minister Del. to Minister of Educ. for Tech. Educ., Vocational Training, Adult Literacy and Nat. Languages 2000–01; Minister of the Armed Forces 2002–09, 2010–11, of the Interior, Local Communities and Decentralization 2009–10, Minister of State, Minister of Town Planning and Sanitation 2012; mem. Parti Démocratique Sénégalais (PDS).

DIOP, Bineta; Senegalese peace campaigner; *Founder and Executive Director, Femmes Africa Solidarité;* b. 1950; d. of Marèma Lô; m.; ed Coll. in Addis Ababa, Centre d'études stratégiques, Paris; Programme Coordinator, Int. Comm. of Jurists, Geneva 1981–96; Founder and Exec. Dir Femmes Africa Solidarité 1996–; campaigns for women's rights and social issues; mem. various dels to observe elections in post-conflict areas including Burundi, Congo and Liberia; Chair. UN Working Group on Peace, Geneva; Co-Chair. Civil Soc. Advisory Group on UN Security Council Resolution 1325 on Women, Peace and Security 2010–; Chair. African Union Comm. as Special Envoy on Women, Peace and Security 2014–; Co-Chair. World Econ. Forum 2014; Vice-Pres. African Union Women's Cttee, mem. African Union Women's Cttee for Peace and Devt; mem. Group of Int. Advisers to Int. Cttee of Red Cross; Chevalier, Légion d'honneur 2012; West African Women Asscn Award 2005, Int. Women Fed. for World Peace Leadership and Good Governance Award. *Address:* Femmes Africa Solidarité, PO Box 45077, Dakar Fann, Senegal (office). *Telephone:* 33-869-8106 (office). *Fax:* 33-860-2047 (office). *E-mail:* infodk@fasngo.org (office). *Website:* www.fasngo.org (office).

DIOP, Mamadou; Niger international banker and politician; *Minister of Finance;* b. 15 Sept. 1949, Garagoumsa, Zinder Region; m.; seven c.; ed Univ. of Poitiers, IMF Training Inst.; began career with Banque Int. pour l'Afrique de l'Ouest (BIAO), Niger; long career with Banque Centrale des Etats de l'Afrique de l'Ouest (BCEAO), including 14 years as Nat. Dir for Niger, later Head of Dept, BCEAO HQ, Dakar, becoming Special Adviser to Gov., Sec. Gen., West African Monetary Union (WAMU) Banking Comm., Abidjan, Vice-Gov., BCEAO 2011–18; Minister of Finance 2019–. *Address:* Ministry of Finance, BP 389, Niamey, Niger (office). *Telephone:* 20-72-23-74 (office). *Fax:* 20-73-59-34 (office). *Website:* www.finances .gouv.ne (office).

DIOUF, Abdou, LenD, LèsL; Senegalese fmr head of state and international organization official; b. 7 Sept. 1935, Louga; m. Elizabeth Diouf 1963; ed Lycée Faidherbe, St Louis, Dakar and Paris Univs; Dir of Tech. Co-operation and Minister of Planning Sept.–Nov. 1960; Asst Sec.-Gen. to Govt 1960–61; Sec.-Gen. Ministry of Defence June–Dec. 1961; Gov. Sine-Saloum Region 1961–62; Dir de Cabinet of Minister of Foreign Affairs 1962–63, of Pres. of Repub. 1963–65; Sec.-Gen. to Pres.'s Office 1964–68; Minister of Planning and Industry 1968–70; Prime Minister 1970–80; Pres. of Senegal 1981–2000, of Confed. of Senegambia 1982–89; Chair. OAU 1985–86; mem. Nat. Ass. for Longa Département 1973–; mem. Senegalese Progressive Union (UPS) 1961–, later Asst Sec.-Gen.; fmr Asst Sec.-Gen. Parti socialiste sénégalais (PS), currently Chair.; Sec.-Gen. Organisation internationale de la Francophonie, Paris 2003–14; Eminent Mem. Sergio Vieira de Mello Foundation; mem. Honour Cttee of Fondation Chirac 2008–, Int. Advisory Bd, Int. Multilateral Partnership Against Cyber Threats (IMPACT); Nat. Order of the Lion, Nat. Order of Merit, Legion of Honour (France), Nat. Order of Québec (Canada), Nat. Order of the Leopard (Democratic Repub. of Congo), Order of La Pléiade (Org. internationale de la Francophonie), Hon. OBE, Order of Good Hope (South Africa), Decoration of Honour for Services to the Repub. of Austria, Mil. Order of Saint James of the Sword (Portugal), Order of the Grand Conqueror (Libya); Jt Winner Africa Prize for Leadership 1987, King Faisal Int. Prize for Service to Islam.

DIOUF, Jacques, BSc, PhD; Senegalese international civil servant and agronomist; b. 1 Aug. 1938, Saint-Louis; m. Aïssatou Seye 1963; one s. four d.; ed Lycée Faidherbe, Saint-Louis, Ecole Nat. d'Agric., Paris/Grignon, Ecole Nat. d'Application d'Agronomie Tropicale, Paris/Nogent and Sorbonne, Paris; Dir European Office and Agricultural Programme of Marketing Bd, Paris and Dakar 1963–64; Exec. Sec. African Groundnut Council, Lagos 1965–71; Exec. Sec. West African Rice Devt Asscn, Monrovia 1971–77; Sec. of State for Science and Tech., Govt of Senegal, Dakar 1978–83; mem. Nat. Ass. 1983–84, Chair. Foreign Relations Cttee and elected Sec., Dakar 1983–84; Adviser to the Pres. and Regional Dir of International Development Research Centre, Ottawa 1984–85; Sec.-Gen. Banque centrale des états de l'Afrique de l'ouest, Dakar 1985–90; Special Adviser to the Governor, Banque centrale des états de l'Afrique de l'ouest, Dakar 1990–91; Perm. Rep. of Senegal to UN 1991–93; Dir-Gen. FAO 1994–2011; led Senegalese dels to UN Confs on Science and Tech., Vienna 1979 (Chair. of 1st Comm.), Industrial Devt, New Delhi 1980, New and Renewable Energy Sources, Nairobi (Vice-Chair.) 1981, Peaceful Use of Space, Vienna 1982; African Rep., Consultative Group on Int. Agricultural Research, Washington; mem. Bd of Dirs ISNAR, The Hague, IITA Lagos, IIRSDA Abidjan, ICRAF, Nairobi, Int. Foundation for Science, Stockholm, African Capacity Building Foundation, Harare, World Inst. for Devt Econs Research, Helsinki, Council of African Advisers of the World Bank, Washington DC; Chair. SINAES, Dakar; mem. Consultative Cttee on Medical Research, WHO, Geneva; Grand Commdr, Order of the Star of Africa (Liberia) 1977, Commdr, Order of Agricultural Merit (Canada) 1995, Grand Cross, Order of Merit in Agric., Fisheries and Food (Spain) 1996, Order of Solidarity (Cuba) 1998, Commdr, Légion d'honneur 1998, Grand Cross, Order of May for Merit (Argentina) 1998, Two Niles Decoration (Sudan), 2000, Nat. Order of Merit for Co-Operation and Devt (Guinea Bissau) 2001, Distinguished Cross, Order of the Quetzal (Guatemala) 2001, Commdr, Order of St Charles (Monaco) 2002, Distinguished Cross (Peru) 2002, Kt Grand Cross (First Class) of the Most Exalted Order of the White Elephant (Thailand) 2003, Order of the Golden Fleece (Georgia) 2003, Golden Fortune Saint George Award 'Honour, Eminence, Labour' (First Grade) (Ukraine) 2003, Medal of Commdr, Nat. Order of Merit (Mauritania) 2003, Congressional Medal of Achievement (Philippines) 2004, Order of Vasco Nuñez de Balboa (Panama) 2004, Order of Ulises Rojas (Guatemala) 2004, Order of the Golden Heart, Rank of Grand Cross (Philippines) 2004, Grand Master Nat. Order (Madagascar) 2005, Order of Malta 2006, Commdr Grand Cross, Order of Merit of Repub. of Hungary 2007, Kt of Grand Cross of Equestrian Order of St Agatha (San Marino) 2009, Commdr, Nat. Order of Benin 2010, Grand Cross, Order of Independence (Equatorial Guinea) 2011, Grand Cordon, Order of the Rising Sun (Japan) 2012; numerous hon. doctorates; Award for Services to Educ. (France) 1979, Hilal Award (Pakistan) 2005, European Football Leagues Asscn Special Award 2010, Action Against Hunger Humanitarian Award 2010, Khalifa Int. Date Palm Award 2011. *Publications include:* La détérioration du pouvoir d'achat de l'Arachide 1972, Les fondements du dialogue scientifique entre les civilisations Euro-occidentale et Négro-Africaine 1979, The Challenge of Agricultural Development in Africa 1989. *Leisure interests:* reading, music, sports. *Address:* c/o Food and Agriculture Organization of the United Nations, Viale delle Terme di Caracalla, 00153 Rome, Italy. *E-mail:* fao-hq@fao.org.

DIPICO, Manne Emsley, BA; South African civil servant and trade union official; *Regional Chairman, African National Congress, Northern Cape;* b. 21 April 1959, Kimberley; ed St Boniface High School, Kimberley, Univ. of Fort Hare, Wharton Business School at Univ. of Pennsylvania, USA; joined African Nat. Congress (ANC) 1982; Nat. Educ. Co-ordinator Nat. Union of Mineworkers; Azanian Students' Org. (AZASO) rep. for United Democratic Front (UDF) Exec. Border Region, AZASO Treas. Univ. of Fort Hare; mem. UDF, Northern Cape 1985–86; detained, Ciskei 1984, detained under state of emergency, Kimberley 1986, arrested and sentenced to five years for furthering the aims of a banned org. through terrorist activities 1987–90, released before end of sentence; Regional Sec. ANC 1991–92, Regional Chair. Northern Cape 1992–; Regional Elections Co-ordinator 1993–94; Premier of Northern Cape Prov. 1994–2004; Chair. South African Nuclear Energy Corpn SOC Ltd (Necsa) 2006–12; Chair. Ponahalo Holdings (De Beers Group), Deputy Chair. De Beers Consolidated Mines Ltd; first Pres. SA-China People's Friendship Asscn; Hon. Pres. Kimberley Children's Choir. *Address:* c/o Private Bag X5016, Kimberley 8301 (office); 5248 Magashula Street, PO Mankurwane, Galeshawe-Kimberley 8345, South Africa (home). *Telephone:* (53) 8309300 (home). *Fax:* (53) 8332122 (office). *E-mail:* cmatlhacko@pancmail .ncape.gov.za (office).

DIPPENAAR, Lauritz (Laurie), MCom, CA; South African business executive; b. 25 Oct. 1948; m.; three c.; ed Univ. of Pretoria; Investigating Accountant, Industrial Devt Corpn of South Africa Ltd 1973–76; Co-founder Rand Consolidated

Investments (RCI) 1977, mem. Bd of Dirs 1977–84, Man. Dir Rand Merchant Bank (acquired by RCI 1985) 1988–92, Chair. 1992–98, fmr Dir (non-exec.) RMB Holdings Ltd; est. FirstRand Ltd 1998, CEO 1998–2005, Chair. (non-exec.) 2008–17; Chair. MMI Holdings 2010–11; Chair. (non-exec.) Discovery Holdings Ltd, OUTsurance, Momentum Group Ltd; mem. Business Trust. *Leisure interests:* cycling, canoeing, watching rugby.

DIRCEU DE OLIVEIRA E SILVA, José; Brazilian lawyer and fmr politician; b. 16 March 1946, Passa Quatro; m. 1st Clara Becker (divorced); m. 2nd Maria Rita Garcia de Andrade; one s. two d.; ed Pontifical Catholic Univ. of São Paulo; fmr student leader, organized protest of 100,000 people against Brazilian mil. dictatorship 1967, jailed 1968, released 1969 in exchange for kidnapped US Amb. Charles Elbrick, went into exile in Cuba where he underwent plastic surgery to change his appearance and received guerrilla training, returned permanently to Brazil 1975, assumed false identity (Carlos Henrique Gouveia de Melo) in Cruzeiro do Oeste, Paraná, became a shopkeeper; amnestied 1979; Co-founder (with Luiz Inácio Lula da Silva) Workers' Party (PT), later Gen. Sec., Leader 1994, apptd Pres. 1995; Deputy Fed. Parl. 1991–95, 1999–2003; Gov. State of São Paulo 1994; Chief Adviser to Pres.-elect Luiz Inácio Lula da Silva, Chief of Cabinet 2003–05 (resgnd); charged with conspiracy and corruption 2007 and sentenced to seven years in prison.

DIRIÖZ, Hüseyin Lazip, BA, MA; Turkish diplomatist; *Ambassador to Russia;* b. 1956, Istanbul; m.; two c.; ed Tarsus American Coll., Univ. of Ankara, Univ. of Virginia, USA; entered diplomatic service 1978, First Sec. and Second Clerk, Embassy in Kabul 1982–84, First Sec., Perm. Mission to Council of Europe 1984–87, NATO Defence Coll. course, Rome 1987–88, with NATO Directorate of Mil. Works 1988–89, Embassy Undersecretary and Perm. Rep. to NATO, Brussels 1989–93, Int. Officer, NATO Secr. 1993–96, Undersecretary to the Special Counsel 1996–97, Head of Perm. Mission to NATO 1997–98, Amb.-Counsellor, Embassy in Washington, DC 1998–2000, Spokesperson, Information Dept, Ministry of Foreign Affairs (MFA) 2000–04, Amb. to Jordan 2004–08, with Dept of the Middle East, Gen. Directorate, MFA 2008, Foreign Affairs Advisor to Pres. Abdullah Gul 2009–10, Defence Policy and Planning Officer to Deputy Sec.-Gen. of NATO 2010–13, Amb. to Brazil 2013–16, to Russia 2016–. *Address:* Embassy of Turkey, 119121 Moscow, 7-i Rostovskii per. 12, Russian Federation (office). *Telephone:* (495) 246-14-89 (office). *Fax:* (495) 246-49-89 (office). *E-mail:* dtmos@dtmos.ru (office). *Website:* moscow.emb.mfa.gov.tr (office).

DIRKS, Nicholas, BA, MA, PhD; American historian, anthropologist, academic and university administrator; ed Wesleyan Univ., Conn., Univ. of Chicago; part-time Instructor in Cultural Anthropology, George Williams Coll. 1973; Instructor in Asian History, California Inst. of Tech., Pasadena 1978–80, Asst Prof. of History 1980–85, Assoc. Prof. of History, Div. of Humanities and Social Sciences 1986–87; Academic Visitor, Dept of Anthropology, LSE, UK Jan.–Dec. 1986; Assoc. Prof. of History, Univ. of Michigan 1987–90, Prof. of History and Anthropology 1990–97, Co-founder and Dir Interdepartmental Program in Anthropology and History, Univ. of Michigan 1988–97, Dir Center for South and Southeast Asian Studies 1992–95, Dir Advanced Study Center, Int. Inst. 1995–97; Directeur d'Études Associé, École des Hautes Études en Sciences Sociales, Paris Jan.–April 1992; Prof. of Anthropology and History, Columbia Univ., New York 1997–2000, Franz Boas Prof. of Anthropology and History 2000–12, Chair. Dept of Anthropology 1997–2003; Vice-Pres. Arts and Sciences and Dean of the Faculty, Univ. of California, Berkeley 2004–09, Exec. Vice-Pres. and Dean of the Faculty of the Arts and Sciences 2009–12, Chancellor Univ. of California, Berkeley 2013–16 (resgnd); Sr Fellow, Council on Foreign Relations 2005–; Sr Research Fellow, American Inst. of Indian Studies, Smithsonian Inst. 1980; John D. and Catherine T. MacArthur Residential Fellow, Inst. for Advanced Study, Princeton 1989–90; Sr Fellow, Michigan Soc. of Fellows 1995–97; Old Dominion Fellow, Humanities Council and Dept of History, Princeton Univ. 2005; Trustee, Columbia University Press 2003–12, Series Ed., Cultures of History 2002–, Chair. Faculty Publs Bd 2003–05, mem. Faculty Bd 2001–03; Honours in Social Studies, Wesleyan Univ., Cum Laude in Gen. Scholarship, Wesleyan Univ., NDEA Title VI, 1972–73, 1973–74, Kent Fellow, The Danforth Foundation 1974–78, Fulbright-Hays Doctoral Dissertation Research Abroad Fellow 1975–76, Guggenheim Fellow 1989–91, Univ. of Michigan Faculty Recognition Award 1994, Julia Lockwood Certain Award, Univ. of Michigan 1995, Mellon Foundation, Sawyer Seminar Co-Convener (Michigan) 1996–97, Invited Mem., Center for Advanced Study in the Behavioral Sciences, Stanford, Calif. 1996, Mellon Foundation, Sawyer Seminar Convener (Columbia) 1999–2002. *Publications include:* Colonialism and Culture (ed.) 1992, Culture/Power/History: A Reader in Contemporary Social Theory (co-ed.) 1993, The Hollow Crown: Ethnohistory of an Indian Kingdom (second edn) 1993, In Near Ruins: Cultural Theory at the End of the Century (ed.) 1998, Castes of Mind: Colonialism and the Making of Modern India (Lionel Trilling Award for Best Book 2002) 2001, The Scandal of Empire: India and the Creation of Imperial Britain 2006; numerous papers in professional journals. *Address:* c/o Office of the Chancellor, University of California, 200 California Hall #1500, Berkeley, CA 94720-1500, USA (office).

DISKIN, Yuval, BA, MA; Israeli security consultant and fmr state security official; b. 1956; m. 1st; four c.; m. 2nd; one d.; ed Bar Ilan Univ., Haifa Univ.; joined Shin Bet (Israel Security Agency) 1978, Co-ordinator Nablus Dist 1979–84, Dist Co-ordinator Nablus, Jenin, Tulkarm 1984–89, Dir Dept for Counter-terrorism, Arab Affairs Br. 1990, Deputy Dir Arab Affairs Br., Dir 1994, Dir Jerusalem, Judea and Samaria Region 1997–2000, Deputy Dir Shin Bet 2000–03, Dir 2005–11; Co-founder Diskin Advanced Technologies Ltd (security consultancy), Herzliya 2011–. *E-mail:* info@diskinat.com. *Website:* www.diskinat.com.

DISNEY, Anthea; British media executive; b. 13 Oct. 1946, Dunstable, Beds.; d. of Alfred Leslie and Elsie Wale; m. Peter Robert Howe 1984; ed Queen's Coll.; New York corresp., London Daily Mail 1973–75, Features Ed. 1975–77, New York Bureau Chief 1977–79; columnist, London Daily Express, New York 1979–84; Managing Ed. New York Daily News 1984–87; Ed. Sunday Daily News 1984–87; Ed. US magazine 1987–88; Ed.-in-Chief Self magazine 1988–89; magazine developer, Murdoch magazines 1989–90; Exec. Producer, A Current Affair, Fox TV 1990–91; Ed.-in-Chief TV Guide magazine 1991–95; Editorial Dir Murdoch Magazines 1994–95; Pres. and CEO HarperCollins Publrs 1996–97; Chair. and CEO News America Publishing 1997–99; Exec. Vice-Pres. of Content, News Corpn 1999–2009; Founding Partner, Women's Enterprise Initiative; mem. Litchfield County Women's Network. *Address:* 50 East 89th Street, New York, NY 10128-1225; Women's Enterprise Initiative, PO Box 264, Litchfield, CT 06759-0264, USA (office).

DISSANAYAKE, Anura Kumara, BSc; Sri Lankan politician; *Leader, Janatha Vimukthi Peramuna (People's Liberation Front);* b. 24 Nov. 1968; ed Thambuththegama Central School, Univ. of Peradeniya, Univ. of Kelaniya; participated in student political activities with Janatha Vimukthi Peramuna (JVP) 1988, associated with launch of Samajavadi Shishya Sangamaya (Socialist Students Soc.), functioned as nat. organizer 1994, elected to JVP Central Cttee 1996, mem. Political Bureau 1998, Finance Sec. 2008–14, Leader JVP 2014–; mem. Parl. (JVP) as rep. from Kurunegala Dist) 2004–, Parl. Group Leader 2008–; Cabinet Minister of Agric., Livestock, Lands and Irrigation 2004–05. *Address:* Janatha Vimukthi Peramuna, 464/20, Pannipitiya Road, Pelawatta, Battaramulla, Colombo, Sri Lanka (office). *Telephone:* (11) 2785612 (office); (11) 2785545 (office). *Fax:* (11) 2786050 (office). *E-mail:* anura@jvpsrilanka.com (office); dissanayaka_a@parliament.lk (office). *Website:* www.jvpsrilanka.com (office).

DISSANAYAKE, Ariyawansa; Sri Lankan politician; *Leader, New Democratic Front;* unsuccessful cand. for Pres. (Democratic United Nat. Front) 1999; Leader, New Democratic Front.

DISSANAYAKE, Dayananda; Sri Lankan government official (retd); ed Univ. of Kelaniya, Univ. of Ceylon Peradeniya; apptd Asst Commr Dept of Elections 1983, Deputy Commr 2006, Additional Commr 2010, Commr 1995–2011; acted as Commonwealth Observer during elections in Guyana Aug. 2006.

DITTUS, Peter, DEcon; German economist; m.; three c.; ed Saarbrücken Univ., Univ. of Michigan, USA; worked as economist at World Bank and OECD; joined BIS as economist 1992, apptd Deputy Sec.-Gen. 2000, Sec.-Gen. 2005–16, mem. Exec. Cttee. *Publications include:* Die Wahl der Geldverfassung 1987, A Macroeconomic Model for Debt Analysis of the Latin America Region and Debt Accounting Models for the Highly Indebted Countries (co-author) 1991, Trade and Employment: Can We Afford Better Market Access for Eastern Europe? (co-author) 1994, Corporate Governance in Central Europe: The Role of Banks 1994, Corporate Control in Central Europe and Russia: Should Banks Own Shares? (co-author) 1995, numerous papers on int. econs.

DITZ, Johannes, DScS; Austrian business executive and politician; b. 22 June 1951, Kirchberg; m.; three c.; ed Vienna Univ. of Econs; employed at Industriellenvereinigung (Industrial Asscn) 1978–79; worked in Dept of Econ. Affairs, ÖVP (Österreichische Volkspartei—Austrian People's Party) fed. party leadership 1979–87; Sec. of State for Finance 1987–88, 1991–95; Deputy to Nat. Council 1988–93; took over leadership of Austrian People's Business Fed. in Econ. Chamber Austria, Exec. Sec. 1989–93; mem. Parl. Nov.–Dec. 1994, Jan.–March 1996; Fed. Minister for Econ. Affairs 1995–96 (resgnd); Chief Financial Officer Holding Post and Telekom Austria and Deputy Gen. Dir Post und Telekom AG 1996–99; apptd to Bd of Österreichische Industrieholding AG (govt holding co.) 1999; mem. Supervisory Bd ESTAG 2003–05, Chair. 2004–05; CEO A-Tec Industries AG Feb. 2006; apptd Chair. Supervisory Bd Austrian Airlines 2001; fmr Chair. Supervisory Bd OMV (oil and gas co.); fmr Vice-Chair. Supervisory Bd Böhler-Uddeholm AG; returned to politics Sept. 2006; supported Chancellor Wolfgang Schüssel in election campaign 2006; Chair. Hypo Alpe Adria Bank Int. AG 2010–13; mem. Univ. Council, Univ. of Vienna 2010.

DIVUNGUI-DI-N'DINGE, Didjob; Gabonese engineer and politician; b. 5 May 1946, Alombié; m.; six c.; ed Ecole Nat. Supérieure des Arts et Métiers, Paris, France, Institut Nat. Polytechnique, Grenoble, France; fmr employers' rep. and Vice-Chair. Perm. Comm. to the Econ. and Social Council; Dir-Gen. Soc. d'Energie et d'Eau du Gabon 1974; Adviser to Pres. of Gabon for Electrical Energy and Water Resources 1975; Minister of Energy and Water Resources 1983; presidential cand. 1993; Vice-Pres. of Gabon 1997–2009; Sec.-Gen. Alliance Democratique et Républicaine 1993–; Grand Croix, Ordre Nat. de l'Etoile Equatoriale, Grand Croix, Ordre Nat. du Mérite Gabonais, Grand Officer, Ordre Nat. du Mérite Français, Commandeur, Ordre Nat. de Côte d'Ivoire.

DIXIT, Avinash Kamalakar, BSc, BA, PhD; American (b. Indian) economist and academic; *John J. F. Sherrerd '52 Professor Emeritus of Economics, Princeton University;* b. 8 June 1944, Bombay (now Mumbai), India; s. of Kamalakar Ramachandra Dixit and Kusum Dixit; ed Bombay Univ., Univ. of Cambridge, UK, Massachusetts Inst. of Tech.; Research Asst, MIT 1965–67; Acting Asst Prof., Univ. of California, Berkeley 1968–69; Lord Thomson of Fleet Fellow and Lecturer in Econs, Balliol Coll., Oxford 1970–74; Prof. of Econs, Univ. of Warwick 1974–80; Prof. of Econs and Int. Affairs, Princeton Univ. 1981–85, Prof. of Econs 1985–89, John J.F. Sherrerd '52 Prof. of Econs 1989–2010, now Prof. Emer.; Visiting Research Assoc., MIT 1972, Visiting Prof. 1977, 1994; Visiting Scholar, IMF 1990, 2000; Visiting Scholar, Russell Sage Foundation 2002–03; Vice-Pres. American Econ. Asscn 2002, Pres. 2008; Fellow, Econometric Soc. 1977, Vice-Pres. 2000, Pres. 2001; Guggenheim Fellowship 1992; Fellow, American Acad. of Arts and Sciences 1992; mem. NAS; Padma Vibhushan 2016. *Publications include:* Theory of International Trade (co-author) 1980, Thinking Strategically (co-author) 1991, Investment under Uncertainty (co-author) 1994, Lawlessness and Economics 2004, The Art of Strategy (co-author) 2008. *Address:* Department of Economics, Fisher Hall, Princeton University, Princeton, NJ 08544, USA (office). *Fax:* (609) 258-6419 (office). *E-mail:* dixitak@princeton.edu (office). *Website:* www.princeton.edu/~dixitak/home (office).

DIXON, Sir (David) Jeremy, Kt, AA Dip. (Hons), RIBA; British architect; *Principal, Dixon Jones Ltd;* b. 31 May 1939; s. of Joseph L. Dixon and Beryl M. Braund; m. Fenella Dixon (née Clemens) 1964 (separated 1990); one s. two d.; partner Julia Somerville; ed Merchant Taylors' School, Architectural Asscn School of Architecture, London; Tutor, Architectural Asscn 1974–83, RCA 1979–81; Prin., Jeremy Dixon (with Fenella Dixon) 1975–90, Jeremy Dixon BDP 1983–90; Chair. RIBA Regional Awards Group 1991; Trustee, Midsummer Music and London Chamber Music Soc. 2012. *Works include:* int. competitions, First Prize: Northampton Co. Offices 1973, Royal Opera House 1983, Piazzale Roma, Venice 1990, Chelsea Barracks 2009; other competitions won: Tate Gallery Coffee Shop and Restaurant 1984, Study Centre Darwin Coll., Cambridge 1988, Robert Gordon Univ. Residence, Aberdeen 1991, Univ. of Portsmouth Science Bldg 1993, Nat.

Portrait Gallery extension 1994, Saïd Business School, Oxford 1996, Magna Carta Building, Salisbury Cathedral 2001, Panopticon, Univ. Coll., London 2001, St Peter's Arcade, Liverpool 2001, Kings Place devt 2002, Exhibition Road Project 2004; other works: reconstruction of Tatlin Tower at RA 1971, 2012, London housing, St Mark's Road 1975, Compass Point, Docklands 1989, Henry Moore Sculpture Inst., Leeds 1988, Sainsbury's superstore, Plymouth 1991, Regent Palace devt 2005. *Leisure interests:* walking in English landscape, contemporary sculpture and painting, music. *Address:* Dixon Jones Ltd, 2–3 Hanover Yard, Noel Road, London, N1 8YA, England (office). *Telephone:* (20) 7483-8888 (office). *Fax:* (20) 7483-8899 (office). *E-mail:* mail@dixonjones.co.uk (office). *Website:* www.dixonjones.co.uk (office).

DIXON, Kenneth Herbert Morley, CBE, DL, BA (Econs), FRSA; British business executive; b. 19 Aug. 1929, Stockport; s. of Arnold Morley Dixon and Mary Jolly; m. Patricia Oldbury Whalley 1955; two s.; ed Cranbrook School, Sydney, Univ. of Manchester, Harvard Business School, USA; joined Rowntree & Co. Ltd 1956, Dir 1970, Chair. UK Confectionery Div. 1973–78, Deputy Chair. Rowntree Mackintosh Ltd 1978–81, Group Chair. Rowntree Mackintosh PLC (now Rowntree PLC) 1981–89; Vice-Chair. Legal and General Group 1986–94; Deputy Chair. Bass PLC 1990–96; mem. Council Inc. Soc. of British Advertisers 1971–79, Council Cocoa, Chocolate and Confectionery Alliance 1972–79, Council Advertising Asscn 1976–79, CBI Cos Cttee 1979–84, Council CBI 1981–90, BIM Econ. and Soc. Affairs Cttee 1980–84, Food and Drink Fed. Exec. Cttee 1986–89 (mem. Council 1986–87); mem. Council York Univ. 1983–2001, Pro-Chancellor 1987–2001, Chair. 1990–2001; Trustee, Joseph Rowntree Foundation 1996–, Deputy Chair. 1998–2001, Chair. 2001–04; Morrell Fellow, Univ. of York 2007; Hon. DUniv (York) 1993, (Open) 1997. *Leisure interests:* reading, music, fell walking. *Address:* Low Hall, Askham Bryan, York, YO23 3QU, England.

DIXON, Richard Newland, PhD, ScD, FRS, CChem, FRSC; British chemist and academic; *Professor Emeritus of Chemistry and Senior Research Fellow, University of Bristol;* b. 25 Dec. 1930, Borough Green, Sevenoaks, Kent, England; s. of Robert T. Dixon and Lilian Dixon; m. Alison M. Birks 1954; one s. two d.; ed Judd School, Tonbridge, King's Coll. London and St Catharine's Coll. Cambridge; Scientific Officer, UKAEA, Aldermaston 1954–56; Postdoctoral Fellow, Univ. of Western Ont., Canada 1956–57, Nat. Research Council, Ottawa 1957–59; ICI Fellow, Univ. of Sheffield 1959–60, Lecturer in Chem. 1960–69; Prof. of Chem., Univ. of Bristol 1969–96, Alfred Capper Pass Prof. of Chem. 1990–96, Prof. Emer. 1996–, Leverhulme Fellow Emer. 1996–99, Univ. Sr Research Fellow 1996–, Dean, Faculty of Science 1979–82, Pro-Vice Chancellor 1989–92; Dir (non-exec.) United Bristol Healthcare NHS Trust 1994–2003, Vice-Chair. 1995–2003; Chair. Univ. of Bristol Alumni Foundation 1996–2009; Trustee, Charitable Trusts for United Bristol Hosps 2003–11, Chair. 2006–11; Sorby Research Fellow, Royal Soc. 1964–69; mem. Council, Faraday Div. Royal Soc. of Chem. 1985–98 (Vice-Pres. 1989–98), Cttees of Science and Eng Research Council 1980–83, 1987–90; Corday Morgan Medal, Royal Soc. of Chem. 1968, Spectroscopy Medal, Royal Soc. of Chem. 1985; Hallam Lecturer, Univ. of Wales 1988, Liversidge Lecturer, Royal Soc. of Chem. 1993, Harkins Lecturer, Univ. of Chicago, USA 1993, Rumford Medal, Royal Soc. 2004. *Publications include:* Spectroscopy and Structure 1965, Theoretical Chemistry, Vol. I 1972, Vol. II 1974, Vol. III 1977; 220 research articles in scientific journals. *Leisure interests:* mountain walking, photography, gardening, theatre-going. *Address:* School of Chemistry, University of Bristol, Cantock's Close, Bristol, BS8 1TS (office); 22 Westbury Lane, Coombe Dingle, Bristol, BS9 2PE, England (home). *Telephone:* (117) 928-7661 (office); (117) 968-1691 (home). *Fax:* (117) 925-1295 (office). *E-mail:* r.n.dixon@bris.ac.uk (office). *Website:* www.chm.bris.ac.uk/staff/rdixon.htm (office).

DJÁ, Baciro; Guinea-Bissau politician; b. 1 Jan. 1973; ed Instituto Superior de Psicologia Aplicada, Lisbon, Univ. of Havana; Pres. Instituto de Defesa Nacional 2006–08; Minister of Youth and Sport 2009, of Nat. Defence 2011–12, of the Presidency of the Council of Ministers and Parl. Affairs 2012–15, Prime Minister Aug.–Sept. 2015 (resgnd), May–Nov. 2016; Vice-Pres. Nat. Comm. for UNESCO; mem. Partido Africano da Independência da Guiné e Cabo Verde. *Address:* c/o Office of the Prime Minister, Avenida dos Combatentes da Liberdade da Pátria, CP 137, Bissau, Guinea-Bissau (office).

DJAFFAR, Ahmed Ben Saïd; Comoran politician; fmr head of local devt charity funded by EU; Minister of External Relations and Co-operation, with responsibility for the Diaspora and Francophone and Arab Relations 2006–10. *Address:* c/o Ministry of External Relations and Co-operation, BP 428, Moroni, The Comoros. *E-mail:* mirex@snpt.km.

DJALÓ PIRES, Mamadu Saliu; Guinea-Bissau lawyer and politician; Pres. Supreme Court –1999; Minister of Justice –2011, of Foreign Affairs, Int. Co-operation and Communities 2011–12. *Address:* c/o Ministry of Foreign Affairs, International Co-operation and Communities, Avenida dos Combatentes da Liberdade da Pátria, Bissau, Guinea-Bissau.

DJANGONÉ-BI, Djessan Philippe, MA, PhD; Côte d'Ivoirian academic and diplomatist; b. 1 Jan. 1946; m. Martine Djangoné-Bi; two c.; ed Brandeis Univ., USA, Univ. of Abidjan, Sorbonne Univ., Paris, Univ. of Paris III, France; Second Asst to Dean of Faculty of Arts and Humanities, Nat. Univ. of Côte d'Ivoire 1979–82, Dir of English Dept 1980–82; Sr Lecturer, Dept of English, Univ. of Cocody, Abidjan; Head of Int. Co-operation Div., Ministry of Higher Educ. and Scientific Research 2000–01; Amb. and Perm. Rep. to UN, New York 2001–06, Amb. to UK 2007–11; Chevalier de l'Ordre Nat. 2002. *Address:* Ministry of Foreign Affairs and African Integration, Bloc Ministériel, boulevard Angoulvand, BP V109, Abidjan, Côte d'Ivoire (office). *Telephone:* 20-22-71-50 (office). *Fax:* 20-33-23-08 (office). *E-mail:* infos@mae.ci (office). *Website:* www.mae.ci (office).

DJELLAB, Muhammad; Algerian banker and politician; b. 7 March 1951, Biskra; Asst Dir, Algerian Development Bank 1976–81; joined Crédit Populaire d'Algérie (CPA) 1981, becoming Deputy Gen. Man. 1999–2005, CEO 2005–13; Minister of Finance 2014–15; Chair. Algerian-Libyan BAMIC-Bank 2005–13; Chair. SATIM (Interbank Electronic Banking Corpn) 2005–13; mem. Bd of Dirs El Khalifa Bank March–June 2003, ARESBANK, Madrid 2005–13, Credit Guarantee Fund for SMEs 2006–13, Air Algeria 2006–13. *Address:* c/o Ministry of Finance, Immeuble Ahmed Francis, Ben Aknoun, Algiers, Algeria (office).

DJEREJIAN, Edward P.; American business executive and fmr diplomatist; *Managing Partner, Djerejian Global Consultancies, LLP;* b. 6 March 1939, New York; m. Françoise Andree Liliane Marie Djerejian (née Haelters); two c.; ed Georgetown Univ.; served in US Foreign Service 1962–94, including as Special Asst to Pres. Ronald Reagan and Deputy Press Sec. for Foreign Affairs, White House 1985–86, Amb. to Syria 1988–91, Asst Sec. of State for Near Eastern Affairs 1991–93, Amb. to Israel 1993–94; Founding Dir Baker Inst. for Public Policy, Rice Univ.; Dir Occidental Petroleum Corpn 1996–15, Ind. Chair. 2013–15, mem. Corp. Governance, Nominating and Social Responsibility Cttee; currently Man. Partner Djerejian Global Consultancies, LLP; mem. Bd of Trustees, Carnegie Corpn of New York 2011, Vice-Chair. 2018–; fmr mem. Bd of Dirs Global Industries, Ltd and Chair. Governance Cttee; Fellow, American Acad. of Arts and Sciences 2011; Presidential Distinguished Service Award, Dept of State's Distinguished Honor Award and numerous other honours, including the Ellis Island Medal of Honor, Anti-Defamation League's Moral Statesman Award; Asscn of Rice Alumni's Gold Medal. *Publication:* Danger and Opportunity: An American Ambassador's Journey through the Middle East 2008. *Address:* Djerejian Global Consultancies, LLP, 2027 Sunset Boulevard, Houston, TX 77005, USA (office). *Telephone:* (713) 522-7824 (office). *Fax:* (713) 524-6154 (office). *E-mail:* djerejian@globalconsultancies.com (office). *Website:* www.globalconsultancies.com (office).

DJINNIT, Said; Algerian politician, diplomatist and UN official; *Special Envoy of the Secretary-General for the Great Lakes Region of Africa, United Nations;* b. 7 June 1954, Ziama; ed Ecole Nationale d'Admin, Algiers, Centre for Int. Relations Studies, Univ. of Brussels, Inst. of Political Affairs, Univ. of Algiers; served on various diplomatic missions, including as Chargé d'affaires, Embassy in Brussels and Deputy Head of Mission in Addis Ababa; also served in various capacities in OAU (now African Union), including as OAU Asst Sec.-Gen. for Political Affairs, also served as Chair. OAU Secr. Task Force on drafting of Constitutive Act of African Union 1999–2000; Commr for Peace and Security at African Union, with responsibility for issues including Darfur conflict –2008; Special Rep. of UN Sec.-Gen. and Head of UN Office for West Africa (UNOWA) 2008–14, Special Envoy of UN Sec.-Gen. for the Great Lakes Region of Africa 2014–. *Address:* Office of the Secretary-General, United Nations, New York, NY 10017, USA (office). *Telephone:* (212) 963-1234 (office). *Fax:* (212) 963-4879 (office). *E-mail:* djinnitsaid@yahoo.com (home). *Website:* www.un.org/sg (office).

DJOJOHADIKUSUMO, Hashim, BA; Indonesian business executive; *Chairman, Asari Group;* s. of Sumitro Djojohadikusumo and Dora Sigar; ed Pomona Coll., Calif., USA; grew up in exile in London; began career as mergers and acquisitions trainee, Lazard Frères & Co., Paris 1976; returned to Indonesia 1978; fmr Chair. and Pres. Nations Energy Ltd, Calgary, Canada; fmr Chair. and CEO Tirtamas Group, Pres. Tirtamas Comexindo (holding co.), Tirtamas Majutama, PT Kiani Kertas (pulp and paper co.), PT Semen Cibinong (cement co.); Founder Arsari Group (conglomerate); Founder Arsari Djojohadikusumo Foundation; fmr Propr PT Bank Niaga; Chair. Percasi, the Indonesian chess federation; Chair. Supervisory Bd Ragunan Zoo, Jakarta; Chair. Bd of Trustees, Indonesian Heritage Trust; fmr Chair. Indonesia Polo Asscn. *Address:* Asari Group, MidPlaza 2, 6th Floor, Jl. Jend. Sudirman Kav. 10–11, Jakarta 10220, Indonesia (office). *Telephone:* (21) 5732988 (office). *Website:* www.arsari.co.id (office).

DJOJONEGORO, Husain; Indonesian business executive; *Commissioner, ABC Group;* b. 1949; s. of Chandra Djojonegoro; m.; four c.; apptd Pres. ABC Group (family-owned co., conglomerate with diverse interests including batteries, sanitary products, toothpaste, consumer brand distribution) 1968, now Commr; fmr Commr PT Istana Pualam Kristal (PTIPK). *Address:* ABC Group, Jl. Rasak No. 7, Medan 20113, North Sumatra, Indonesia (office). *Telephone:* (61) 4566468 (office). *Fax:* (61) 4573124 (office). *E-mail:* hartini@abc-drycell.co.id (office). *Website:* www.abc-drycell.co.id (office).

DJOKOVIC, Novak; Serbian professional tennis player; b. (Novak Nikhil Đoković), 22 May 1987, Belgrade, SFR Yugoslavia (now Serbia); s. of Srđan Djokovic and Dijana Djokovic; m. Jelena Djokovic 2014; one s.; ed trained at Nikola Pilić's tennis acad., Munich, Germany; right-handed; two-handed backhand; turned professional 2003; winner, Dutch Open, Amersfoort 2006, Open de Moselle, Metz 2006, Next Generation Adelaide Int., Asscn of Tennis Professionals (ATP) Tour, Adelaide 2007, ATP Masters Series, Miami 2007, Estoril Open 2007, Masters Series Rogers Cup, Montreal 2007, 2011, BA-CA Tennis Trophy, Vienna 2007, Masters Series Pacific Life Open, Indian Wells, Calif. 2008, BNP Paribas Open, Indian Wells 2011, 2014, 2015, 2016, Masters Series singles title, Internazionali d'Italia, Rome 2008, 2011, 2014, 2015, Tennis Masters Cup, Shanghai 2008, ATP World Tour Masters 1000 Paris 2009, 2013, 2014, 2015, Basel 2009, Beijing 2009, 2010, Dubai 2009, 2011, 2013, Belgrade 2009, 2010, 2011, ATP World Tour Masters 1000, Indian Wells 2011, ATP World Tour Masters 1000, Miami 2011, 2012, 2014, 2015, 2016, ATP World Tour Masters 1000, Madrid 2011, 2016, Shanghai Masters 2012, 2013, 2015, ATP World Tour Finals, London 2012, 2013, 2014, 2015, Monte Carlo Masters 2013, 2015, China Open 2013, 2014, 2015, Qatar ExxonMobil Open, Doha 2016, 2017, Rogers Cup, Toronto 2016, Eastbourne 2017; Grand Slam results: winner, Australian Open 2008, 2011, 2012, 2013, 2015, 2016, 2019, Wimbledon 2011, 2014, 2015, 2018, US Open 2011, 2015, French Open 2016, finalist, US Open 2007, 2010, 2012, 2013, 2018, French Open 2012, 2014, semifinalist, French Open 2007, 2008, 2011, 2013, Wimbledon 2007, 2010, 2012; bronze medal, Olympic Games, Beijing 2008; led Serbia to win Davis Cup 2010; coached by Riccardo Piatti 2005–06, Marián Vajda 2006–, Mark Woodforde 2007, Todd Martin 2009–10, Boris Becker (Head Coach, along with Marian Vajda, Miljan Amanovic and Gebhard Phil-Gritsch) 2013–; became eighth player in history to achieve a Career Grand Slam and third man to hold all four major titles at the same time (first since Rod Laver in 1969) and the first on three different surfaces (hardcourt, clay and grass) June 2016; apptd Goodwill Amb. UNICEF 2015; f. Novak Djokovic Foundation (previously Novak Fund) 2007; mem. Player Council, Asscn of Tennis Professionals 2016–; Key to the City of Andrićgrad; Order of Republika Srpska, Order of St Sava of I Class, Patriarch Irinej of Serbia 2011, Order of the Karađorđe's Star (First Degree) 2012; ATP Most Improved Player of the Year 2006, 2007, The Best Sportperson of Serbia Award 2007, 2010, DSL Sport Golden Badge 2007, 2010, 2011, Award for The Best Sportsman, Olympic Cttee of Serbia, Serbian Oscar Of Popularity Sportsman of the Year 2007, 2010, 2011, 2013, BBC Overseas Sports Personality of the Year 2011, ITF World Champion 2011,

2012, Golden Bagel Award 2011, 2012, 2013, US Sports Acad. Male Athlete of the Year 2011, GQ ACE of the Year 2011, Best Grand Slam/Davis Cup/Olympic Match of the Year 2011, 2012, 2013, Laureus World Sportsman of the Year 2012, Best Male Tennis Player ESPY Award 2012, 2013, US Open Series Champion 2012, Arthur Ashe Humanitarian of the Year 2012, Pride of the Nation Award, Serbia Tennis Fed. 2012, The Centrepoint GB Youth Inspiration Award from HRH Prince William, Duke of Cambridge, Vermillion Medal for Physical Educ. and Sports from Albert II, Prince of Monaco 2012, Laureus World Sportsman of the Year Award 2016, 2019. *Leisure interests:* golf, Internet, music, movies. *E-mail:* contact@novak-djokovic.com. *Website:* novakdjokovic.com.

DJOTODIA, Michel Am Nondroko; Central African Republic politician, fmr rebel leader and fmr head of state; b. 1949, Vakaga, Oubangui-Chari (now part of Central African Repub.); m. 1st; two d.; m. 2nd; ed studied in USSR; fmr Consul, Nyala, Sudan; fmr Pres. Union of Democratic Forces for Unity and Patriotic Action Group for the Liberation of the Central African Repub.; lived in exile in Cotonou, Benin; imprisoned 2006–08; leader of Séléka rebel coalition during Dec. 2012 rebellion; First Deputy Prime Minister and Minister of Nat. Defence, Restructuring of the Armed Forces, War Veterans and War Victims Feb.–March 2013; Pres. (self-declared, 24 March 2013, following overthrow of François Bozizé, confirmed by Nat. Transitional Council 13 April, re-designated Interim Pres. 18 July 2013, sworn in 18 Aug. 2013) and Minister of Defence 2013–14.

DJOUDI, Karim, BSc, MSc; Algerian banker and government official; b. 13 July 1958, Montpellier, France; ed Louis Pasteur Univ., Strasbourg and Univ. of Paris, Sorbonne, France; joined Central Bank of Algeria 1988, Central Dir 1990; Dir-Gen. of the Treasury, Ministry of Finance 1999–2003; Minister Del. responsible for Promotion of Investment 2003–05, responsible for Financial Reform 2005–07; Minister of Finance 2007–14. *Address:* c/o Ministry of Finance, Immeuble Maurétania, place du Pérou, Algiers, Algeria.

DJUROVIC, Gordana, MA, DEconSci; Montenegrin (b. Serbian) economist, academic and politician; *Professor of Economic Development, International Economic Relations and EU Enlargement Policy, University of Montenegro;* b. 2 March 1964, Novi Knezevac, Serbia; m.; two s.; ed Herceg-Novi Secondary School of Econs, Faculty of Econs, Univ. of Belgrade and Univ. of Montenegro, Podgorica; Devt Strategy and Poverty Reduction in Montenegro 2003; Minister for Int. Econ. Relations and European Integration, Govt of Montenegro 2004–06; Deputy Prime Minister with responsibility for European Integration 2006–09, Minister for European Integration 2009–10; Full Prof. of Econ. Devt, Int. Econ. Relations and EU Enlargement Policy, Faculty of Econs 2010–; Jean Monnet Prof. and Head of EU project-JM Chair 2012–; Pres. Montenegrin Pan European Union 2016–; nat. and regional consultant for various projects (Income and Asset Declaration in Practice, Transposition of Service Directive, Nat. Strategy for Sustainable Devt 2015–2030, Action Plan for Montenegro-SEE 2020, etc.). *Publications include:* Economic Development (co-author) 1996, Alternative Development Concepts of the Economy of Montenegro (co-author) 2002, Integration in the European and Euro-Atlantic structures (ed.) 2010, The EU and Montenegro: Goals of Economic, Social and Territorial Cohesion 2012, The EU and Montenegro: Enlargement Policy 2012, The EU and Montenegro 2016, The EU and Montenegro: The Accession Process 2017. *Leisure interests:* walking, Pilates. *Address:* Faculty of Economics, University of Montenegro, 81000 Podgorica, Jovana Tomaševića 37, Montenegro (office). *Telephone:* (20) 241138 (office); 69-070452 (mobile) (home). *Fax:* (20) 241757 (office). *E-mail:* gordana@t-com.me (office). *Website:* www.ekonomija.ac.me (office); www.panevropa.me.

DLADLA, Thuli; Swazi politician; *Minister of Foreign Affairs and International Cooperation;* fmr teacher; Dir, SEBENTA Nat. Inst. (non-profit literacy org.) –2008; apptd to House of Ass. (lower house of parl.) 2013, fmr Chair. Public Accounts Cttee; apptd to Senate (upper house of parl.) 2018; Minister of Foreign Affairs and Int. Cooperation (first female) 2018–; fmr Deputy Chair. SADC Parl. Women's Caucus. *Address:* Ministry of Foreign Affairs and International Co-operation, Interministerial Bldg, Block 8, Level 3, Mhlambanyatsi Rd, POB 518, Mbabane, Eswatini (office). *Telephone:* 24042661 (office). *Fax:* 24042669 (home). *E-mail:* psforeignaffairs@realnet.co.sz (office).

DLAMINI, Absalom Themba, MBA; Swazi politician and business executive; *Chairman, Royal Swaziland Sugar Corporation;* b. 1 Dec. 1950; ed Univ. of Botswana, Univ. of Swaziland, Univ. of Nairobi; served in various positions with Cen. Bank of Swaziland, Swazi Nat. Provident Fund, Swaziland Industrial Devt Co.; Prime Minister of Swaziland 2003–08; currently Chair. Royal Swaziland Sugar Corpn; apptd CEO and Dir Tibiyo TakaNgwane (nat. devt co. owned by royal family) 1991, Man. Dir 2009–; mem. Bd of Dirs Commonwealth Partnership for Tech. Man. Ltd 2003–, Ubombo Sugar Co., Managa Sugar Packers, Royal Villas. *Address:* Office of the Chairman, Royal Swaziland Sugar Corporation, Simunye Sugar Estate, POB 1, Simunye L301, Eswatini. *Telephone:* 23134000. *Fax:* 23838171. *E-mail:* info@rssc.co.sz. *Website:* www.rssc.co.sz.

DLAMINI, Lutfo Ephraim; Swazi politician and business executive; b. 7 July 1960; m. Thelma Ncane Smith-Dlamini; four c.; Marketing Man. Swaziland Brewers Ltd 1990–95; mem. House of Ass. (Parl.) for Ndzingeni 2003–13; Minister of Enterprise and Employment 1998–2008, of Foreign Affairs 2008–11, of Labour and Social Security 2011–13; Chair. World Cup Facilitation Cttee; Dir of Marketing, Bosscon Construction Co. 2014–15; Dir and Co-owner Umnotfo Fertilizer 2012–; Dir and Co-owner House Call Doctor, Swaziland (renamed Eswatini 2018) 2014–; Exec. Chair. TSD & Associates Group; marketing consultant with Coca Cola and SAB. *Address:* TSD & Associates Group, Mbabane, Eswatini (office). *Website:* www.tsdandassociates.com.

DLAMINI, Mabili David, BA; Swazi politician and diplomatist; b. 10 April 1957, Mankayane; m.; three s.; ed Univ. of Botswana and Swaziland; fmr Amb. to Malaysia and Singapore; Minister of Foreign Affairs and Trade 2003–06, of Housing and Urban Devt 2006; Senator 2003–08; Vice-Chair. Border Restoration Cttee 2013. *Leisure interests:* golf, soccer.

DLAMINI, Mandvulu Ambrose, BCom, MBA; Swazi business executive and politician; *Prime Minister;* b. 5 March 1968; m. Dumile Portia Dlamini 1997; three d.; ed Univ. of Eswatini, Hampton Univ., USA; Finance Officer, Swaziland Development & Savings Bank 1992–97; Franchise Finance Man., Absa (bank), Johannesburg 1997–98; Business Man. Consultant, Standard Bank South Africa 1999–2000; Man. Dir, Nedbank (Swaziland) Ltd 2003–10; CEO, MTN Eswatini (telecoms co.) 2010—18; Prime Minister (apptd by King Mswati III) 2018–; fmr Pres. Eswatini Fed. of Employers; fmr Chair. Eswatini Revenue Authority, Esicojeni Foundation (charity); Inst. of People Man. CEO of the Year 2016, 2018. *Address:* Office of the Prime Minister, Cabinet Offices, Hospital Hill, POB 395, Swazi Plaza, Mbabane, Eswatini (office). *Telephone:* 24042251 (office). *Fax:* 24043943 (home). *Website:* www.gov.sz (office).

DLAMINI, Martin Gobizandla; Swazi economist, government official and fmr central banker; m. Victoria Dlamini; two s. two d.; Man. Ed. Times of Swaziland group of newspapers –2009; Dir Smart Partnership Secretariat (based in Office of the Prime Minister) 2009–12; Gov. Central Bank of Eswatini –2013; Minister of Finance 2013–18; apptd to Senate 2013. *Address:* c/o Ministry of Finance, Mhlambanyatsi Road, POB 443, Mbabane, Eswatini (office).

DLAMINI, Moses Mathendele; Swazi politician and diplomatist; b. 2 Dec. 1947; s. of Gombolo Dlamini; m. Maria Buyile Dlamini; two s. four d.; fmr Amb. to Taiwan; fmr Pres. of the Senate; fmr Chair. Parl. Del. to UN; Minister of Foreign Affairs and Trade 2006–08; mem. Advisory Council (Liqoqo) to King Mswati III 2009–11, Chair. SADC Troika, apptd by King Mswati III 2009; Order of Brilliant Star with Grand Cordon (Taiwan).

DLAMINI-ZUMA, Nkosazana Clarice, BSc, MB ChB; South African politician, medical doctor and international organization official; *Minister in the Presidency, responsible for Planning, Monitoring and Evaluation;* b. 27 Jan. 1949, Pietermaritzburg; d. of Willibrod Gweva Dlamini and Rose Dlamini; m. Jacob Zuma (divorced); four c.; ed Amanzintoti Training Coll., Univ. of Zululand, Univ. of Natal, Univs of Bristol and Liverpool, UK; Research Technician Medical School, Univ. of Natal 1972; Vice-Pres. South African Students Org. 1975–76; Chair. African Nat. Congress (ANC) Youth Section, Great Britain 1977–78; House Officer Frenchay Hosp., Bristol, England 1978–79; House Officer Canadian Red Cross Memorial Hosp., Berks., England 1979–80; Medical Officer (Pediatrics) Mbabane Govt Hosp., Swaziland (renamed Eswatini 2018) 1980–85; Pediatric attachment Whittington Hosp. 1987–89; Vice-Chair. Regional Political Cttee of ANC Great Britain 1978–88, Chair. 1988–89; ANC Health Dept Lusaka, Zambia 1989–90; Research Scientist Medical Research Council, Durban 1991–94; Minister of Health 1994–99, of Foreign Affairs 1999–2009, of Home Affairs 2009–12; Chair. African Union Comm. 2012–17; mem. Nat. Ass. (Parl.) (ANC) 2009–12, 2017–; Minister in the Presidency, responsible for Planning, Monitoring and Evaluation 2018–; Chair. S Natal Region Health Cttee of ANC 1990–92; Chair. S Natal Region ANC Women's League 1991–93; mem. ANC Nat. Exec. Cttee 1994–; apptd Pres. World Conf. Against Racism 2001; mem. Exec. Cttee S Natal Region of ANC 1990–93; mem. Steering Cttee Nat. AIDS Co-ordinating Cttee 1992–; Bd mem. Centre for Social Devt Studies Univ. of Natal, Durban 1992–; Trustee, Health Systems Trust 1992–; Chancellor ML Sultan Technikon 1996; Hon. Prof., Belarusian State Univ., Fellow, Royal Coll. of Obstetricians and Gynaecologists 2017; Maitre de L'Ordre Nat. (Mali) 2002, Nat. Order of Luthuli in Gold (South Africa) 2013, Platinum Order of Merit, Confed. of African Football 2015; Dr hc (Univ. of Natal) 1995, (Univ. of Bristol) 1996, (Univ. of Transkei) 1997, (Univ. of Rome) 2013, (Univ. of Fort Hare) 2014, (Jomo Kenyatta Univ. of Agriculture and Technology) 2014; Tobacco Free World Award, WHO 1999, Women Who Make a Difference Award, Women In Film 2002, States Women of the Year Award, BBQ 2004, Int. Renaissance Women of the Year Award 2012, UN S-S Award for Global Leadership 2012, Chair.'s Award, Black Business Exec. Circle 2013, UN Women African Women's Pioneers Award 2013, Africa America Inst. Institutional Legacy Award 2013, Gulen Peace Awards 2015, eThekwini Living Legends Awards 2015, WIP Award for Lifetime Achievement in Female Political Empowerment 2016, Jerusalem Medal 2016, Lifetime Achievement Award, World Political Leader Global Forum 2017. *Telephone:* (11) 5182804/5 (office); (11) 5182919/2914 (office); (12) 3005200 (office). *E-mail:* kotannoul@africa-union.org (office). *Address:* The Presidency, Union Bldgs, West Wing, Government Ave, Pretoria 0001 (office); 602 Stretten Bay, St Andrews Street, Durban 4001, South Africa (home). *Fax:* (12) 3238246 (office). *Website:* www.thepresidency.gov.za (office); www.nkosazana.com.

DLOUHÝ, Vladimír, CSc, MBA; Czech economist and politician; *European Deputy Chairman, Trilateral Commisssion;* b. 31 July 1953, Prague; m. 1st (divorced 1999); m. 2nd Eliška Břízoá 2001; one s. one d.; ed Prague School of Econs, Charles Univ., Prague and Catholic Univ., Louvain; fmr teacher, Prague School of Econs; researcher, Inst. of Econ. Forecasting, Czechoslovak Acad. of Sciences 1983–89, latterly Deputy Dir; Deputy Prime Minister and Chair. State Planning Comm. 1989–90; Minister of the Economy 1990–92; Minister of Trade and Industry of Czech Repub. 1992–97; Int. Advisor for Cen. and Eastern Europe, Goldman Sachs 1997–; Adviser to Exec. Man., ABB 1997–2010; currently Assoc. Prof. of Macroeconomics and Econ. Policy, Charles Univ., Prague; mem. Civic Democratic Alliance 1991–98, Vice-Pres. March–Oct. 1992, Deputy Chair. 1993–97; mem. State Defence Council 1993; Chair. Council of Customs Union 1994–97, Bd of Supervisors Stock Co. Unipetrol 1996–97; Deputy Chair. Bd of Supervisors, Volkswagen-Skoda Group, Mladá Boleslav 1994–95; Chair. Advisory Bd, Chayton Capital, London, Meridiam Infrastructure, Paris; European Deputy Chair., Trilateral Comm. 2010–; mem. Parl. 1996–98; mem. Bd of Overseers, Illinois Inst. of Tech., Chicago; mem. Exec. Cttee Trilateral Comm.; mem. Bd of Supervisors, Foundation Bohemiae 1992–2001; mem. Bd of Dirs Cofinec 1997–2000, KSK Power Ventur, Hyderabad; mem. Scientific Bd Faculty of Econs and Public Admin, School of Econs, Prague; Grand-Croix, Ordre de Léopold II (Belgium). *Publications:* Ekonometrický model čs. obchodní bilance 1985, Models of Disequilibrium and Shortage in Centrally Planned Economies 1989; articles in Czechoslovak and int. econ. journals. *Leisure interest:* music. *Address:* The European Group, 5, rue de Téhéran, 75008 Paris, France (office). *Telephone:* 1-45-61-42-80 (office). *Website:* trilateral.org (office).

DMITRIEV, Alexander Sergeevich; Russian conductor; *Artistic Director and Chief Conductor, St Petersburg Symphony Orchestra;* b. 19 Jan. 1935, Leningrad; m.; one s.; ed Leningrad Choir School, Leningrad State Conservatory, Vienna Akad. für Musik und darstellende Kunst, Austria; Conductor, Karelian Radio and TV Symphony Orchestra 1961, Prin. Conductor 1962–71; Prin. Conductor, Maly Opera and Ballet Theatre, Leningrad (now St Petersburg) 1971–77, Chief Conductor and Artistic Dir St Petersburg Symphony Orchestra 1977–; Prin.

Conductor, Stavanger Symphony Orchestra, Norway 1990–98; Prof., Rimsky-Korsakov St Petersburg State Conservatory; Order of Honour of Cultural and Art Merit; Merited Worker of Arts of Karelian ASSR 1967, People's Artist of USSR 1976, USSR People's Artist, Prize 2nd USSR Competition for Conductors 1966, State Prize of the Russian Fed., Prize of the St Petersburg Govt in Literature, Art and Architecture 2009. *Recordings include:* Handel's Messiah, Haydn's Creation, Schubert's Symphony Nos. 1–9, Tchaikovsky's Symphonies 4, 5, 6, Rachmaninov's Symphony No. 2, Debussy's 3 Nocturnes, Ravel's Valses nobles et sentimentales, Ma Mère l'Oye, Saeverud's Peer Gynt, Symphony dolorosa, Balakirev's Piano Concerto, Medtner's Piano Concerto No. 1, Rachmaninov's Piano Concerto No. 3, Britten's Violin concerto, Sibelius Violin Concerto, Shostakovich and Tchaikovsky Violin Concertos, Shostakovich Symphony No. 7, Scriabin Symphony No. 3. *Address:* St Petersburg Symphony Orchestra, St Petersburg 191186, Mikhailovskaya str. 2, Russia (office). *E-mail:* dmitriev@mail.spbnit.ru (office). *Website:* www.philharmonia.spb.ru (office).

DMITRIYEVSKY, Anatoly Nikolayevich; Russian engineer; b. 6 May 1937; m.; one s. one d.; ed Gubkin Moscow Inst. of Oil and Gas; Sr Teacher, Gubkin Moscow Univ. of Oil and Gas; Pro-rector and Chair. Algerian Nat. Inst. of Oil, Gas and Chem.; apptd Dir Oil and Gas Research Inst., Russian Acad. of Sciences 1987; Pres. Union of Scientific and Eng Orgs of Russia; mem. of Bd Int. Gas Union; mem. Russian Acad. of Sciences 1991; Adviser to Russian Ministry of Fuel and Energy, to Pres. of Rosneft, to Chair. of Gazprom; mem. Advisory Bd Russian Resources Energy, Inc.; USSR State Prize 1986, State Prize of Russia 1998. *Publications include:* Lithological System and Genetic Analysis of Oil and Gas Sedimentary Basins 1982, Fundamental Basis of Oil and Gas Geology 1991. *Leisure interests:* tennis, mountain skiing, photography.

DO NASCIMENTO, Edson Arantes (see PELÉ).

DOBBINS, James Francis, BA; American diplomatist; *Senior Fellow and Distinguished Chair in Diplomacy and Security, RAND Corporation;* b. 31 May 1942, New York; m. Toril Kleivdal; two s.; ed Georgetown Univ. School of Foreign Service; US naval officer; mem. US Mission to OECD 1967–68, US Del. to Viet Nam Peace Talks 1968; Political Officer, US Embassy, Paris 1969; mem. Policy Planning Staff, State Dept, Washington, DC 1969–71, Deputy Asst Sec. 1982–85, Prin. Deputy Asst Sec. 1989–90, Acting Asst Sec. for European and Canadian Affairs 1991, Special Asst to Pres., Nat. Security Council Staff 1996–99, Special Adviser to Pres. for Kosovo and Dayton Implementation 1999–2000, Asst Sec. of State for European Affairs 2000–01; mem. US Mission to UN 1973–75, Political-Mil. Officer, US Embassy, London 1978–81; Deputy Chief of Mission, Bonn, FRG 1985–89; Amb. to the EC 1991–93; Special Envoy to Afghanistan 2001–03; Special Rep. for Afghanistan and Pakistan 2013–14; Sr Fellow, RAND Corpn 1993, Dir Int. Security and Defense Policy Center 2003–, Distinguished Chair in Diplomacy and Security; mem. Council on Foreign Relations 1995–96; two Superior Honor Awards, three Presidential Awards, six Sr Performance Awards, Dept of the Army Decoration for Dist Civilian Service, Armed Forces Expeditionary Medal, Nat. Defense Service Medal, Expeditionary Medal, Repub. of Viet Nam. *Publications include:* America's Role in Nation-Building: From Germany to Iraq (co-author) 2003, The UN's Role in Nation-Building: From the Congo to Iraq (co-author) 2005, The Beginner's Guide to Nation-Building (co-author) 2007, Europe's Role in Nation-Building: From the Balkans to the Congo (co-author) 2008, After the War: Nation-Building from FDR to George W. Bush (co-author) 2008, After the Taliban: Nation-Building in Afghanistan 2008, Occupying Iraq: A History of the Coalition Provisional Authority (co-author) 2009. *Address:* International Security and Defense Policy Center, RAND Corporation, 1200 South Hayes Street, Arlington, VA 22202, USA (office). *Telephone:* (703) 413-1100 (office). *Fax:* (703) 414-4732 (office). *E-mail:* James_Dobbins@rand.org (office). *Website:* www.rand.org (office).

DOBBS, Baron (Life Peer), cr. 2010, of Wylye in the County of Wiltshire; **Michael John Dobbs,** PhD, MALD, MA; British author, politician and broadcaster; b. Nov. 1948, Herts., England; m. Rachel Dobbs; four s.; ed Christ Church, Oxford and Fletcher School of Law and Diplomacy, USA; UK Govt Special Adviser 1981–87; Chief of Staff, UK Conservative Party 1986–87, Jt Deputy Chair. 1994–95; Deputy Chair. Saatchi & Saatchi 1983–91; BBC TV and radio presenter 1999–2009; mem. (Conservative), House of Lords 2010–; Dir (non-exec.), M&C Saatchi PLC 2016–; Visting Prof., Fletcher School of Law & Diplomacy 2017; UK Lifetime Political Book Award 2013, Lifetime Achievement Award, Tufts Univ. 2014, P.T. Barnum Award for Excellence in Entertainment 2014, ICS Blenheim Award 2017. *Play:* The Turning Point 2009. *Television includes:* House of Cards (UK) 1990, House of Cards (USA) 2013–18. *Publications include:* House of Cards 1989, Last Man to Die 1991, To Play the King 1992, The Touch of Innocents 1994, The Final Cut 1995, Goodfellowe MP 1997, The Buddha of Brewer Street 1998, Whispers of Betrayal 2000, Winston's War 2002, Never Surrender 2003, Churchill's Hour 2004, Churchill's Triumph 2005, First Lady 2006, The Lords' Day 2007, The Edge of Madness 2008, The Reluctant Hero 2010, A Sentimental Traitor 2011, A Ghost at the Door 2013. *Address:* House of Lords, Westminster, London, SW1A 0PW, England (office). *E-mail:* michael@michaeldobbs.com (office); dobbsm@parliament.uk (office). *Website:* www.parliament.uk/biographies/lords/lord-dobbs/4192 (office); www.michaeldobbs.com.

DOBESCH, Gerhard, DPhil; Austrian historian and academic; *Professor of Roman History, Archaeology and Epigraphy, University of Vienna;* b. 15 Sept. 1939, Vienna; s. of Dr Carl Dobesch and Gustave Dobesch; ed Univ. of Vienna; Lecturer in Ancient History 1967–73; Prof. of Greek and Roman History, Univ. of Graz 1973–76; Prof. of Roman History, Archaeology and Epigraphy, Univ. of Vienna 1976–; Corresp. mem. Austrian Archaeological Inst. 1972–98 (mem. 1998–), Austrian Acad. of Sciences 1980–84 (mem. 1984–). *Publications include:* Caesars Apotheose zu Lebzeiten und sein Ringen um den Königstitel 1966, Der Panhellen: Gedanke und der Philippos des Isokrates 1968, Wurde Caesar zu Lebzeiten in Rom als Staatsgott anerkannt? 1971, Nikolaos von Damaskus und die Selbstbiographie des Augustus 1978, Die Kelten in Österreich nach den ältest 1980, Die Kimbern in den Ostalpen und die Schlacht bei Noreia 1982, Zu Caesars Sitzenbleiben vor dem Senat 1988, Zur Einwanderung die Kelten in Oberitalien 1989, Caesar als Ethnograph 1989, Autonomie des Menschen und Werthaftigkeit in der Antike 1990, Die Kelten als Nachbarn der Etrusker 1992, Principis dignationem 1993, Vom äusseren Proletariat zum Kulturträger 1994, Phokion und der Korinthische Bund 1994, Aus der Vor-und Nachgeschichte der Markomannenkriege 1994, Das europäische 'Barbaricum' und die Zone der Mediterrankultur 1995, Würdigung Fritz Schachermeyr 1996, Die römische Kaiserzeit–eine Fortsetzung des Hellenismus? 1996, Ende und Metamorphose des Etruskertums 1998, Der Weltreichsgedanke bei Caesar 1998, Einige merkwürdige Überlieferungen über Caesar 2000, Urgeschichtliches Eisen in der Sicht des Althistorikers 2000, Caesars monarchische Ideologie 2000, Ausgewählte Schriften (two vols) 2001, Caesars Volcae Tectosages in Mitteleuropa 2001, Caesar und der Hellenismus 2004, Zentrum, Peripherie und 'Barbaren' in der Urgeschichte und der Alten Geschichte 2004, Einige Beobachtungen zu Politik und Tod des Haeduers Diviciacus und seines Bruders Dumnorix 2005, Das 'regnum Noricum' und die römische Okkupation 2006, Kleine Überlegungen zur gallo-römischen Kultur 2006, Varro Atacinus und sein 'Bellum Sequanicum' 2006, Aussenpolitische Strukturen der antiken Keltenstämme: Ein Überblick 2007, Die Römer in Niederösterreich 2008, Zwei Fragmente des Ephoros – Zwei Gedanken zur keltischen Religion 2007, Augustus, Tiberius, Caligula und Britannien 2007, Caesar as Ethnographer 2007, Politik zwischen Marbod und Rom 2009, Die Arverner in den Commentarii Caesars 2010, Zweierlei ferrum Noricum? 2011; numerous specialist articles. *Leisure interests:* literature, art history. *Address:* Universität Wien, Institut für Alte Geschichte, Universitätsring 1, 1010 Vienna (office); Spitalgasse 29/10, 1090 Vienna, Austria (home). *Telephone:* 4277-40520 (office); 407-9522 (home). *Fax:* 4277-9405 (office). *E-mail:* gerhard.dobesch@univie.ac.at (office); gerhard.dobesch@oeaw.ac.at (office).

DOBRETSOV, Nikolai Leontyevich, DGeol; Russian geologist; *Chairman Siberian Branch, Russian Academy of Sciences;* b. 15 Jan. 1936, Leningrad (now St Petersburg); m.; five c.; ed Leningrad Inst. of Mines; chief of Altai Mining expedition, Jr then Sr Researcher; Head of Lab. Inst. of Geology and Geophysics, Siberian br. of USSR (now Russian) Acad. of Sciences in Novosibirsk 1960–71; Head of Lab. Inst. of Tectonics and Geophysics, USSR Acad. of Sciences in Khabarovsk 1971–72; Dir Buryat Inst. of Geology 1980–88, Chair. Presidium of Buryat Research Cen. Siberian br. of USSR Acad. of Sciences 1987, Dir-Gen. United Inst. of Geology, Geophysics and Mineralogy 1990, Dir Inst. of Geology, Siberian br. of Russian Acad. of Sciences 1990, Chair. Siberian br. of Russian Acad. of Sciences 1997–, Vice-Pres. Russian Acad. of Sciences 1997–, Science Advisor, Inst. of Geology and Mineralogy, Siberian br. of Russian Acad. of Sciences –2011, Chief Research Scientist, Trofimuk Inst. of Petroleum Geology and Geophysics, Siberian br. of RAS 2011; Vice-Pres. Asscn of Asian Acads of Sciences 1997–2008; Corresp. mem. USSR (now Russian) Acad. of Sciences 1984, mem. 1987, mem. Presidium 1991, Pres. of Siberian br. 1997–2008, Vice-Pres. RAS; Pres. Asscn of Acads of Sciences in Asia (AASA) 2008–11; Order of Red Banner of Labour 1986, Order of Friendship 2006; Dr hc (St Petersburg Mining Technical Univ.) 2000; Lenin Prize 1976, Labourer of the Red Banner 1986, State Prize of the Russian Fed. 1997, Demidov Prize 1999, A.N. Kossygin Prize 2003, Medal of Mongolian Acad. of Science 2006, Lavrentiev Prize 2007, Order of Merit for Fath 2007. *Publications include:* Introduction to Global Petrology 1980, Global Petrological Processes 1981, Deep-level Geodynamics 1994; papers on tectonics and petrography. *Leisure interests:* books, fishing. *Address:* Trofimuk Institute of Petroleum Geology and Geophysics, Siberian Branch of Russian Academy of Sciences, 630090 Novosibirsk, Prospect Acad. Koptyuga 3, Russia (office). *Telephone:* (383) 330-89-81 (office). *Fax:* (383) 333-23-01 (office). *E-mail:* dobr@igm.nsc.ru (office). *Website:* www.sbras.ru (office); www.ipgg.nsc.ru (office).

DOBRIANSKY, Paula J., MA, PhD, BSFS; American diplomatist; *Senior Fellow, The Future of Diplomacy Project, JFK Belfer Center for Science and International Affairs, Harvard University;* b. 14 Sept. 1955, Alexandria, Va; ed Harvard Univ., Georgetown Univ. School of Foreign Service; early career positions include Dir European and Soviet Affairs, Nat. Security Council, The White House; Deputy Asst Sec. of State, Human Rights and Humanitarian Affairs; fmr Assoc. Dir Policy and Programs, US Information Agency; fmr Co-Chair Int. TV Council, Corpn for Public Broadcasting; fmr Sr Int. Affairs and Trade Advisor, Hunton and Williams (law firm); fmr Sr Int. Affairs and Trade Advisor, Baker Hostetler (law firm); fmr Sr Vice-Pres. and Dir, George F. Kennan Sr Fellow for Russian and Eurasian Studies, Washington Office, Council of Foreign Relations; Under-Sec. for Democracy and Global Affairs, US State Dept 2001–09, apptd Special Envoy for NI 2007; Sr Vice-Pres. and Global Head of Govt and Regulatory Affairs, Thomson Reuters 2010–12; also Distinguished Nat. Security Chair, US Naval Acad. 2010–12; currently Sr Fellow, The Future of Diplomacy Project, John F. Kennedy Belfer Center for Science and Int. Affairs, Harvard Univ.; mem. Bd Western NIS Enterprise Fund, Nat. Endowment for Democracy (NED) (also Vice-Chair.), Freedom House, American Council of Young Political Leaders, ABA Cen. and E European Law Initiative, US Advisory Comm. on Public Diplomacy; mem. Bd of Advisors, Center on Sanctions and Illicit Finance at Foundation for Defense of Democracies; Host, Freedom's Challenge (three years); Co-host Worldwise (Nat. Empowerment TV); Ford and Rotary Foundation Fellow; Poland's Highest Medal of Merit, Grand Cross, Commdr of Order of Lithuanian Grand Duke Gediminas; Dr hc (Fairleigh Dickinson Univ., Flagler Coll., Roger Williams Univ.); US State Dept Superior Honor Award, Dialogue on Diversity's Int. Award 2001, NED Service Medal, Georgetown Univ. Annual Alumni Achievement Award. *Address:* Belfer Center for Science and International Affairs, 79 John F. Kennedy Street, Cambridge, MA 02138, USA (office). *Telephone:* (617) 495-1400 (office). *Website:* belfercenter.ksg.harvard.edu (office).

DOBRIŢOIU, Lt-Gen. (retd) Corneliu; Romanian army officer and politician; b. 18 Sept. 1955, Bucharest; ed Balcescu Army Acad., Sibiu, Acad. of Mil. Studies, Bucharest, NATO Coll., Rome, Italy, Naval Postgraduate School, Monterey, USA; officer in 1st Mechanized Regt, Bucharest platoon 1977–78, infantry co. commdr 1978–80, Deputy Chief of Research Bureau 1980–83; Bn Commdr, Inst. of Mil. Medicine, Bucharest 1983–87; apptd expert on human resource mobilization within a Territorial Command of Bucharest 1987; transferred to 3rd Mechanized Regt, Bucharest 1991; Head of Research Office, 2nd Mechanized Regt 1993; Deputy Chief of Bureau Research, 57th Tank Div., Bucharest 1993–94; expert on political-military analysis, Dept of Political-Mil. Analysis and International Mil. Relations, Ministry of Defence 1994–95; participated in defence training courses organized by Centre for European Security Studies, George C. Marshall Coll. of Strategic Studies and Defence Econs 1995; Chief of Mil. Liaison Team in Romanian-American cooperation programme; Head of International Office Contact Point, International Mil. Relations Directorate, Ministry of Defence 1995–96,

Head of Dept of Evaluation International Mil. Relations, Directorate of International Mil. Relations 1996–98; Officer of the Directorate Staff, Regional Security Cooperation and the International Mil. Staff, NATO HQ, Brussels 1998–2000; attained rank of Brig. Gen. (one star) 2002, Maj. Gen. (two stars) 2004; Head of Euro-Atlantic Integration and International Relations, Ministry of Nat. Defence 2000–04, Deputy State Sec., Ministry of Nat. Defence and Head of Euro-Atlantic Integration Dept and Defence Policy 2004–06; attained rank of Lt-Gen. 2006 (retd); Minister of Nat. Defence Sept.–Oct. 2006, May–Dec. 2012; mem. Partidul Național Liberal (PNL) 2006–; Kt, Nat. Order 'Star of Romania' 2000. *Address:* Partidul Național Liberal (PNL), 011866 Bucharest, Bd. Aviatorilor 86, Sector 1, Romania (office). *Telephone:* (21) 2310795 (office). *Fax:* (21) 2310796 (office). *E-mail:* dre@pnl.ro (office). *Website:* www.pnl.ro (office).

DOBRODEYEV, Oleg Borisovich, CandHistSc; Russian television producer; *Chairman, All-Russian State Television-Radio Company (VGTRK);* b. 28 Nov. 1959, Moscow; m.; one s.; ed Moscow State Univ.; mem. of staff Inst. of USA and Canada 1982–83; Ed. TV programme Vremya, USSR Cen. TV, later Deputy Ed.-in-Chief 1983–90; Ed.-in-Chief news programme Vesti; Ed.-in-Chief Information TV Agency (ITA) 1990–91, Ostankino Co. 1991–93; Ed.-in-Chief Information Service, NTV Co., later Vice-Pres. 1993–2000, Dir-Gen. NTV Co. 1997–2000; Chair. All-Russian State TV-Radio Co. (VGTRK) 2000–; Order of Honour 1999. *Leisure interest:* reading people's memoirs. *Address:* All-Russian State TV-Radio Co., Yamskogo Polya 5th str. 19/21, 125124 Moscow, Russia (office). *Telephone:* (495) 250-0511 (office); (495) 213-7170 (office). *Fax:* (495) 214-2347 (office). *E-mail:* info@rfn.ru (office); vgtrk2@space/ru (office). *Website:* www.vgtrk.com (office).

DOBRZAŃSKI, Stanisław; Polish business executive and government official; b. 22 March 1949, Hrubieszów; m.; two c.; ed Maria Skłodowska-Curie Univ., Lublin; Deputy Dir Polish Nat. Library, Warsaw 1982–85; Dept Dir Ministry of Culture and Art; Dir Wschodni Bank Cukrownictwa; Under-Sec. of State, Office of the Council of Ministers 1993–96; Minister of Nat. Defence 1996–98; Pres. of Man. Bd Polskie Sieci Elektroenergetyczne SA (Polish Power Grid Co.) 2001–06; mem. Polskie Stronnictwo Ludowe (Polish People's Party); Order of the Rebirth of Polish 1998.

DOBSON, Sir; **Christopher (Chris) Martin,** Kt, BA, DPhil, FRS, FMedSci; British chemist, academic and college principal; *Master, St John's College, Cambridge;* b. 8 Oct. 1949; ed Keble Coll. and Merton Coll., Oxford; held research fellowships at Merton Coll. and Linacre Coll. before working at Harvard Univ., USA; returned to Oxford as Fellow of Lady Margaret Hall and Univ. Lecturer in Chem. 1980, later Reader, then Prof. in Chem.; John Humphrey Plummer Prof. of Chemical and Structural Biology, Univ. of Cambridge 2001–, Master of St John's Coll. 2007–; Presidential Visiting Scholar, Univ. of California, San Francisco 2001; Sammet Guest Prof., Johann Wolfgang Goethe Univ., Frankfurt, Germany 2007; mem. European Molecular Biology Org. 1999; Foreign Assoc., NAS 2013; Fellow, Int. Soc. of Magnetic Resonance 2008; Hon. mem. Nat. Magnetic Resonance Soc. of India 2004; Foreign Hon. mem. American Acad. of Arts and Sciences 2007; Hon. Fellow, Linacre Coll., Oxford 2008, Lady Margaret Hall, Oxford 2008, Merton Coll., 2009, Keble Coll., Oxford 2009, Chemical Council of India 2010, Darwin Coll. Cambridge 2014; Hon. MD (Umeå Univ., Sweden) 2005, (Univ. of Florence, Italy) 2006; Dr hc (Univ. of Leuven, Belgium) 2001, (Univ. of Liège, Belgium) 2007; Hon. DSc (King's Coll. London) 2012; RSC Corday-Morgan Medal and Prize 1981, Howard Hughes Int. Research Scholar 1992, Brunauer Award, American Ceramic Soc. 1996, Dewey and Kelly Award, Univ. of Nebraska 1997, Nat. Lecturer, American Biophysical Soc. 1998, RSC Interdisciplinary Award 1999, Bijvoet Medal, Univ. of Utrecht, The Netherlands 2002, Silver Medal, Italian Soc. of Biochemistry 2002, Bakerian Lecturer, Royal Soc. 2003, Stein and Moore Award, The Protein Soc. 2003, Davy Medal, Royal Soc. 2005, Hans Neurath Award, The Protein Soc. 2006, Royal Medal, Royal Soc. 2009, RSC Khorana Award 2010, Dr H.P. Heineken Prize for Biochemistry and Biophysics 2014, Accademia Nazionale dei Lincei Feltrinelli Int. Prize for Medicine 2014. *Publications:* more than 700 papers in professional journals. *Address:* Department of Chemistry, University of Cambridge, Lensfield Road, Cambridge, CB2 1EW, England (office). *Telephone:* (1223) 763070 (office). *Fax:* (1223) 336362 (office). *E-mail:* cmd44@cam.ac.uk (office). *Website:* www.ch.cam.ac.uk (office).

DOBSON, Frank (Gordon), BSc (Econs); British politician; b. 15 March 1940; s. of James William Dobson and Irene Shortland Dobson; m. Janet Mary Alker 1967; two s. one d.; ed Archbishop Holgate Grammar School, York, LSE; admin. appointments with Cen. Electricity Generating Bd 1962–70, Electricity Council 1970–75; mem. Camden Borough Council 1971–76, Leader 1973–75; Asst Sec. Comm. for Local Admin. 1975–79; MP for Holborn and St Pancras South 1979–83, for Holborn and St Pancras 1983–2015; Opposition Spokesman on Educ. 1981–83, on Health 1983–87, on Energy 1989–92, on Employment 1992–93, on Transport and London 1993–94, on Environment and London 1994–97; Sec. of State for Health 1997–99; Labour candidate for Mayoralty of London 2000; Shadow Leader of the House of Commons 1987–89; Gov. LSE 1986–2003, Inst. of Child Health 1987–92; Gov. Royal Veterinary Coll. 2004–; mem. of Court, Univ. of York 2004–; mem. of Court, London School of Hygiene and Tropical Medicine 2009–. *Address:* 22 Great Russell Mansions, Great Russell Street, London, WC1B 3BE, England. *Telephone:* (20) 7242-5760.

DOBSON, Michael William Romsey, MA; British banking and finance executive; *Chairman, Schroders PLC;* b. 13 May 1952, London; s. of Sir Denis (William) Dobson; m. Frances de Salis 1998; two d.; ed Eton Coll., Trinity Coll. Cambridge; joined Morgan Grenfell 1973, with Morgan Grenfell New York 1978–80, Man. Dir 1984–85, Chief Exec. Morgan Grenfell Asset Management 1987–88, Deputy CEO Morgan Grenfell Group (now Deutsche Morgan Grenfell) 1988–89, CEO 1989–96; mem. Bd of Man. Dirs Deutsche Bank AG 1996–2000 (responsible for investment banking 1996–98, for asset man. 1998–2000), mem. Advisory Bd; f. Beaumont Capital Man. Ltd 2000 (acquired by Schroders PLC 2001); Dir (non-exec.) Schroders PLC April–Nov. 2001–, CEO 2001–16, Chair. 2016–; Chair. Investment Bd, Cambridge Univ. Endowment Fund 2005–11; mem. Advisory Cttee (staff retirement plan), IMF 2004–13. *Leisure interests:* tennis, golf, skiing, watching Chelsea play football. *Address:* Schroders PLC, 1 London Wall Place, London, EC2Y 5AU, England (office). *Telephone:* (20) 7658-6000 (office). *E-mail:* michael.dobson@schroders.com (office). *Website:* www.schroders.com (office).

DOCDJENGAR LEOPOLD, Ngarlenan; Chadian politician; b. 14 Dec. 1964; ed Univ. of Paris Dauphine; various roles in Ministry of Finance and the Budget, including Dir-Gen. of Taxation, Ministry Sec.-Gen., Minister of Finance and Budget 2015–16; Chair. Tech. Cttee for HIPC Initiative negotiations with World Bank and IMF; mem. African Tax Admin Forum. *Address:* c/o Ministry of Finance and the Budget, BP 816, N'Djamena, Chad (office).

DOCHANASHVILI, Guram; Georgian writer and film industry executive; b. 1939, Tbilisi; s. of Petre Dochanashvili and Gulnara Emukhvari; m. Natela Sepiashvili; one d.; ed Tbilisi State Univ.; worked in Dept of Archaeology, Inst. of History, Georgian Acad. of Sciences 1962–75; Head of Div. of Prose Mnatobi (magazine) 1975–85; Deputy Dir Gruzia Film Studio (now J.S.C. Georgian Film) 1985–; St George's Order for Establishing Moral Values, Patriarchate of Georgia 2013; Ivane Dzhavakhishvili Medal, Tbilisi State Univ. 1984, State Prize of Georgia 1994, Literary Award Saba for Contribution in the Devt of Literature 2003, 2010. *Publications include:* There, Behind the Mountain 1966, The First Garment 1975 (Book 2 1978) (Book 3 1980) (Book 4 1990), The Best Grand-Father: A Fairy Tale for School Children 1976, Platform 1988, Besame 1989, Havaiuri valsi 1990, A Man Who Loved Literature 2001, Waterloo or Reconstruction Works 2002, Only One Man 2002, Difficult: Short Stories 2002, Boulder on Which Once There was a Church 2002, Khorumi is a Georgian Dance 2003, Western Omara and Givia and Planet Hollywood 2005, The Kezheradzes 2005, What I Remember and Recollect More Often 2010.

DOCHERTY, David, BA, PhD; British broadcasting executive and writer; *CEO, National Centre for Universities & Business;* b. 10 Dec. 1956, Scotland; s. of David Docherty and Anna Docherty; m. Kate Stuart-Smith 1992; two d.; ed Univ. of Strathclyde, London School of Econs; Research Fellow, Broadcasting Research Unit, London 1984–88; Dir of Research Broadcasting Standards Council 1988–89; Head of Broadcasting Analysis, BBC TV 1990–92, Head of TV Planning and Strategy, BBC Network TV 1992–96, Dir of Strategy and Channel Devt, BBC Broadcast 1996–97, Deputy Dir of TV BBC Broadcasting 1997–2000, Dir New Media, BBC Bd of Man. 1997–2000; Man. Dir of Broadband Content, Telewest Communications 2000–02; CEO iPublic div., YooMedia PLC's 2003–04, Group Chief Exec. YooMedia PLC 2003–05; CEO CSC Media Group 2006–08; CEO Nat. Centre for Universities and Business 2009–; Chair. Digital Television Group 2009–; Chair. Bd of Govs and Pro Vice-Chancellor, Univ. of Luton 2001–06; fmr mem. Bd BBC America UKTV; columnist, The Guardian; Hon. Fellow, Leeds Univ. *Publications:* The Last Picture Show?: Britain's Changing Film Audience 1987, Keeping Faith?: Channel 4 and Its Audience 1988, Running the Show: 21 Years of London Weekend Television 1990, Violence in Television Fiction 1991, The Spirit Death 2000, The Killing Jar 2002, The Fifth Season 2003, Fear Less 2005, Digital Messiah 2007. *Leisure interest:* writing. *Address:* National Centre for Universities & Business, Studio 11, Tiger House, Burton Street, London, WC1H 9BY (office); Serge Hill, Abbots Langley, Herts., WD5 0RY, England (home). *E-mail:* david.docherty_ceo@ncub.co.uk (office). *Website:* www.ncub.co.uk (office).

DODD, Christopher (Chris) John, BA, JD; American lawyer, association executive and fmr politician; *Chairman and CEO, Motion Picture Association of America;* b. 27 May 1944, Willimantic, Conn.; s. of Thomas J. Dodd and Grace Mary Dodd (née Murphy); m. 1st Susan Mooney 1970 (divorced 1982); m. 2nd Jackie Clegg 1999; two d.; ed Providence Coll. and Univ. of Louisville School of Law, Ky; volunteer with US Peace Corps, Dominican Repub. 1966–68; admitted to Conn. Bar 1973; mem. US House of Reps, Washington, DC from 2nd Dist of Conn. 1975–81; Senator from Conn. 1980–2011 (retd), fmr Chair. Banking, Housing and Urban Affairs Cttee, Sr mem. Senate Foreign Relations Cttee; Chair. and CEO Motion Picture Asscn of America 2011–; Democrat; numerous awards. *Address:* Motion Picture Association of America, 15301 Ventura Blvd, Sherman Oaks, CA 91403, USA (office). *Telephone:* (818) 995-6600 (office). *Fax:* (818) 285-4403 (office). *E-mail:* info@mpaa.org (office). *Website:* www.mpaa.org (office).

DODD, Lois; American artist; b. 22 April 1927, Montclair, NJ; d. of Lawrence Dodd and Margaret Vanderhoff; one s.; ed Montclair High School, Cooper Union Art School; Co-founder, Tanager Gallery 1952–62; mem. Bd of Govs Skowhegan School of Painting and Sculpture 1980– (Chair. 1986–88); mem. Nat. Acad. of Design 1988–, American Acad. of Arts and Letters 1998–; Hon. degree (Old Lyme Acad., Conn.); American Acad. and Inst. of Arts and Letters Award 1986, Hassam, Speicher, Betts and Symons Purchase Prize 1991, Nat. Acad. of Design Leonilda S. Gervas Award 1987, Henry Ward Ranger Purchase Award 1990, 2005, Augustus St Gaudens Award for Achievement from Cooper Union 2005. *Publications:* Lois Dodd: Catching the Light 2012. *Address:* 30 East 2nd Street, New York, NY 10003, USA (home). *Telephone:* (212) 254-7159 (home).

DODGE, David A., OC, BA, PhD, FRSC; Canadian economist, academic, consultant, university administrator and fmr central banker and fmr politician; *Senior Advisor, Bennett Jones LLP;* b. 8 June 1943, Toronto, Ont.; m. Christiane Dodge; ed Queen's Univ., Princeton Univ., USA; fmr Asst Prof. of Econs, Queen's Univ.; Assoc. Prof. of Canadian Studies and Int. Econs, School of Advanced Int. Studies, Johns Hopkins Univ., USA; Dir Int. Econs Programme, Inst. for Research on Public Policy 1979–80; fmr fed. public servant, sr positions in Cen. Mortgage and Housing Corpn, Anti-Inflation Bd, Dept of Employment and Immigration, Dept of Finance; Deputy Minister of Health 1998–2001; fmr Deputy Minister of Finance; mem. Bd of Dirs Bank of Canada 1992–97, Gov. and Chair. 2001–08; currently Sr Advisor, Bennett Jones LLP; Dir, Scotiabank, Atco/CU Ltd. *Address:* Bennett Jones LLP, Suite 1900, World Exchange Plaza, 45 O'Connor Street, Ottawa, ON K1P 1A4, Canada (office). *Telephone:* (613) 683-2304 (office). *Fax:* (613) 683-2323 (office). *E-mail:* dodged@bennettjones.com (office). *Website:* www.bennettjones.com (office).

DODGE, Toby, BA, MSc, PhD; British research institute director and academic; *Professor, Department of International Relations and Director, Middle East Centre, London School of Economics;* ed SOAS, Univ. of London; fmr Lecturer on Int. Relations and Middle Eastern Politics, Dept of Political Studies, SOAS; Researcher, Middle East Programme, Royal Inst. of Int. Affairs (RIIA); fmr Sr Research Fellow, Centre for the Study of Globalisation and Regionalisation, Univ. of Warwick; fmr Dir of Gulf States Programme, IISS, London Consulting Sr Fellow for Middle East, 2003–; fmr Reader in Int. Politics, Dept of Politics, Queen Mary, Univ. of London; currently Prof., Dept of Int. Relations and Dir, Middle East

Centre, London School of Econs and Political Science. *Publications include:* Globalisation and the Middle East, Islam, Economics, Culture and Politics (co-Ed.) 2002, Inventing Iraq: The Failure of Nation Building and a History Denied 2003, Iraq's Future: The Aftermath of Regime Change 2005, Iraq: From War to a New Authoritarianism 2013; numerous research papers and scholarly articles. *Address:* Department of International Relations, London School of Economics and Political Science, Houghton Street, London, WC2A 2AE, England (office). *Telephone:* (20) 7955-6176 (office). *E-mail:* b.t.dodge@lse.ac.uk (office). *Website:* www.lse.ac.uk/middleEastCentre/people/TobyDodge.aspx (office).

DODIG, Victor George, BCom, MBA; Canadian banking executive; *President and CEO, Canadian Imperial Bank of Commerce;* b. May 1965; s. of Veselko Dodig and Janja Dodig; m. Maureen Dodig; three s. one d.; ed St Michael's Coll., Univ. of Toronto, Institut d'études politiques, France, Harvard Univ., USA; Man. Consultant, McKinsey & Co. 1994–97; five years as Man. Dir in Canada, USA and UK for Merrill Lynch & Co.; Man. Dir and CEO in Canada for UBS Global Asset Management –2005; Exec. Vice-Pres., Wealth Management, Canadian Imperial Bank of Commerce (CIBC) 2005–07, Exec. Vice-Pres., Retail Distribution 2007–11, Group Head, Wealth Management 2011–14, Pres. and CEO and mem., Bd of Dirs 2014–; mem. Bd of Dirs Bank of N.T. Butterfield & Son Ltd 2011–. *Address:* Canadian Imperial Bank of Commerce, Commerce Court, Toronto, ON M5L 1A2, Canada (office). *Telephone:* (416) 980–2211 (office). *Website:* www.cibc.com (office).

DODIK, Milorad; Bosnia and Herzegovina politician; *Chairman of the Presidency;* b. 12 March 1959, Banja Luka, Socialist Repub. of Bosnia and Herzegovina, Socialist Fed. Repub. of Yugoslavia; m.; two c.; ed Univ. of Belgrade; Pres. Exec. Bd Municipal Ass. of Laktaši 1986–90; mem. Parl. Socialist Repub. of Bosnia and Herzegovina 1990; Rep. Republika Srpska People's Ass. (Narodna Skupština Republike Srpske); Prime Minister of Republika Srpska 1998–2001, 2006–10; Pres. of Republika Srpska 2010–18; mem. Tripartite State Presidency 2018–, Chair. 2018–; Founder and Chair. Savez Nezavisnih Socijaldemokrata (Alliance of Ind. Social Democrats); Hon. Pres. Partizan Belgrade Basketball Club; Order of Republika Srpska, Order of Peter the Great (Russia), Order of St Sava (Serbian Orthodox Church), Holy Cross of the Guard of the Tomb of Christ (Patriarch of Jerusalem). *Address:* Office of the President of Republika Srpska, 78000 Banja Luka, Bana Milosavljevića 4, Bosnia and Herzegovina (office). *Telephone:* (51) 248100 (office). *Fax:* (51) 248161 (office). *E-mail:* info@predsjednikrs.net (office). *Website:* www.predsjednikrs.net (office).

DODIN, Lev Abramovich; Russian theatre director; *Artistic Director and General Manager, Maly Drama Theatre;* b. 14 May 1944, Leningrad; m. Tatyana Borisovna Shestakova (q.v.) 1972; ed Leningrad Theatre Inst.; lecturer in drama, Leningrad Theatre Inst. 1963–83; with Leningrad Youth Theatre 1967– (now Chief Dir), Artistic Dir and Gen. Man. Leningrad Maly Drama Theatre 1983–; Prof., St Petersburg Acad. of Dramatic Art; mem. Gen. Ass. of the Union of Theatres of Europe; USSR State Prize 1986, State Prize of Russia 1992, Triumph Prize 1992, Ubu Prize, Italy 1993, 1995, Stanislavsky Prize 1996, RSFSR Merited Artist 1986, People's Artist of Russian Fed., Golden Sofit Saint Petersburg Theatre Award 1996, Golden Mask National Theatre Award 1997, 1999, 2004, Abbiati Italian Critics' Award "for best opera staging" 1998, European Theatre Award 2000, Russian Presidential Award "for excellent service" in 2001, Tovstonogov's Award "for outstanding achievements in the art of theatre" 2002, Russian State Prize 2003, Chayka Moskow Theatre Award 2003, Pro Cultura Hungarica Hugary State Prize 2005; Order of Literature and Arts, France 1994. *Productions include:* The Robber (K. Čapek) 1974, The Gentle One (Dostoyevsky) 1980, The House (F. Abramov) 1980, Brothers and Sisters (F. Abramov) 1985, Lord of the Flies 1986, Stars in the Morning Sky (A. Galin) 1988, Gaudeamus 1990, The Demons (Dostoyevsky) 1992, Claustrophobia (V. Yerofeev) 1994, The Cherry Orchard (A. Chekhov) 1994, Play With No Title (A. Chekhov) 1966, Chevengur (A. Platonov) 1999, Molly Sweeney (Brian Friel) 2000. *Operas include:* Elektra (R. Strauss) 1995, Lady Macbeth of Mtsensk (Franco Abbiati Prize for best musical performance, Italy 1998) (D. Shostakovich) 1998, Mazeppa (Tchaikovsky) 1999, The Queen of Spades (Tchaikovsky) 1998–2001. *Address:* Maly Drama Theatre, Rubinstein Str. 18, St Petersburg, Russia. *Telephone:* (812) 113-21-08. *Fax:* (812) 113-33-66 (office). *E-mail:* levdodin@mdt.sp.ru (office). *Website:* www.mdt-dodin.ru (office).

DODON, Igor, DEcon; Moldovan economist, academic, politician and head of state; *President;* b. 18 Feb. 1975, Sadova, Străşeni Dist, Moldovan SSR, USSR; m.; two c.; ed Agrarian Univ. of Moldova, Acad. of Econ. Studies, Int. Inst. of Man.; worked at Moldovan Stock Exchange 1997–2005, positions included Sr Specialist in Clearing and Listing Depts, Man. of Electronic Systems of Negotiation, Dir of Marketing, Listing and Quotations Dept; Chair. Nat. Securities Depository 2001–05; Chair. Moldovan Commodity Exchange 2003–05; Deputy Minister of Economy and Trade 2005–06, Minister of Economy and Trade 2006–08, First Deputy Prime Minister and Minister of Economy and Trade 2008–09; mem. Parl. (Parlamentul) 2009–16; unsuccessful cand. for Mayor of Chişinău 2011; mem. Partidul Comuniştilor din Republica Moldova (Party of Communists of the Repub. of Moldova) –2011; mem. and Chair. Partidul Socialiştilor din Republica Moldova (PSRM—Party of Socialists of the Repub. of Moldova) 2011–16; Ind. 2016–; Pres. of Moldova 2016–; fmr Prof., Acad. of Econ. Studies, Free Int. Univ. of Moldova, Int. Inst. of Man., State Univ. of Moldova. *Address:* Office of the President, 2073 Chişinău, bd. Ştefan cel Mare şi Sfânt 154, Moldova (office). *Telephone:* (22) 25-10-16 (office). *E-mail:* petitii@prm.md (office). *Website:* www.prezident.md (office).

DOER, Hon. Gary Albert, OM; Canadian diplomatist and politician; b. 31 March 1948, Winnipeg, Man.; m. Ginny Devine; two d.; first elected to Manitoba Legis. Ass. as MP for Concordia 1986, Minister of Urban Affairs 1986–88, of Crown Investments 1987–88, of Man. Telephone Systems 1987–88, also Minister responsible for Man. Liquor Control Comm.; Leader New Democrats 1988–2009, Leader of the Opposition 1988–99, Premier of Man. 1999–2009, Pres. Exec. Council and Minister of Fed.–Prov. Relations 1999–2009 (resgnd); Amb. to USA 2009–16; Pres. Man. Govt Employees' Asscn 1979–86; fmr Deputy Supt, Vaughan Street Detention Centre; Vice-Pres. Man. Special Olympics, Pres. Boys' and Girls' Club of Winnipeg; mem. Bd Winnipeg Blue Bombers, Prairie Theatre Exchange, Niagara Inst., Univ. of Manitoba. *Leisure interest:* water skiing. *Address:* c/o Canadian Embassy, 501 Pennsylvania Avenue NW, Washington, DC 20001, USA.

DOERR, Anthony, MFA; American writer; b. 17 Oct. 1973, Cleveland, Ohio; m. Shauna Doerr; two s.; ed Bowling Green State Univ., Bowdoin Coll.; Writer-in-Residence for the state of Idaho 2007–10; fmr teacher, Warren Wilson Coll.; columnist, Boston Globe; contributor, The Morning News (online magazine); Guggenheim Fellowship 2010; American Acad. of Arts and Letters Rome Prize in Literature 2004–05. *Publications include:* short stories: The Shell Collector (New York Public Library Young Lions Fiction Award 2003, Barnes & Noble Discover Prize) 2002, Memory Wall (Ohioana Book Award 2011, The Story Prize 2011) 2010; novels: About Grace (Ohioana Book Award 2005) 2004, All the Light We Cannot See (Pulitzer Prize for Fiction 2015) 2014; memoir: Four Seasons in Rome: On Twins, Insomnia and the Biggest Funeral in the History of the World 2007. *Address:* c/o Amanda Urban, International Creative Management, 730 Fifth Avenue, New York, NY 10019, USA (office). *Telephone:* (212) 556-5600 (office). *E-mail:* aurban@icmpartners.com (office). *Website:* www.icmtalent.com (office); www.anthonydoerr.com (office).

DOERR, L. John, BS, MS, MBA; American inventor and investment company executive; *Partner, Kleiner Perkins Caufield & Byers;* b. 29 June 1951, St Louis, Mo.; m. Ann Howland Doerr; two c.; ed Rice Univ., Harvard Univ.; joined Intel Corpn as salesman 1974; Pnr, Kleiner Perkins Caufield & Byers, Menlo Park, Calif. 1980–, has directed venture capital funding to several tech. cos, including Compaq, Netscape, Symantec, Sun Microsystems, drugstore.com, Amazon.com, Intuit, Google, Friendster, Go.com, myCFO; Co-founder Erly, Inc. 2011–; fmr Founding CEO Silicon Compiler Systems Corp.; mem. American Acad. of Arts and Sciences; currently mem. Bd of Dirs Alphabet Inc., Amazon.com, Intuit, Homestore, Sun Microsystems, Dir, Zynga, Inc. 2013–, Zazzle, Good Technology, Miasole, Purkinje, Segway Inc., Spatial Photonics; mem. Advisory Bd Generation Investment Man. LLP, Upromise, Inc.; helped found TechNet (lobbying org.); has also invested heavily in 'carbon trading'; Fellow, American Acad. of Arts and Sciences 2009–. *Achievements include:* holds patents for computer memory devices. *Leisure interests:* kids' stuff (trampolines and rock concerts), cycling, hiking, skiing, photography, surfing (the web), travelling, reading, music, messing around with computers/technology. *Address:* Kleiner Perkins Caufield & Byers, 2750 Sand Hill Road, Menlo Park, CA 94025, USA (office). *Telephone:* (650) 233-2750 (office). *Fax:* (650) 233-0300 (office). *E-mail:* johnd@kpcb.com (office). *Website:* www.kpcb.com (office).

DOGAN, Akhmed Demir, PhD; Bulgarian politician; b. 29 March 1954, Drundar, Varna Dist; two c.; ed Univ. of Sofia, Bulgarian Acad. of Sciences; f. underground resistance org. against so-called revival process (forcible re-naming of ethnic Turks in Bulgaria) 1985; arrested and sentenced for being leader of an anti-state org. (amnestied 1989); f. Movt for Rights and Freedoms party 1990, Chair. 1990–2013, Hon. Chair. 2013–; elected Deputy, 7th Grand Nat. Ass. 1990, Chair. MRF Parl. Group; Deputy to 36th Nat. Ass. 1991–94, 37th Nat. Ass. 1994–97, Chair. Nat. Salvation Alliance (coalition) Parl. Group in 38th Nat. Ass. 1997–2001, 39th Nat. Ass. 2001–04, also Chair. MRF Parl. Group, Deputy to 40th Nat. Ass. 2005–09, 41st Nat. Ass. 2009–; Chair. Liberal Democratic Union 1998–99; Chair. Inst. for Integration Studies 1999; acquitted by Supreme Admin. Court of corruption charges brought by Parl. Comm. Oct. 2010. *Address:* Movement for Rights and Freedoms, 1301 Sofia, bul. A. Stamboliyski 45A, Bulgaria (office). *Telephone:* (2) 811-44-52 (office). *Fax:* (2) 811-44-53 (office). *E-mail:* press@dps.bg (office). *Website:* www.dps.bg (office).

DOĞAN, Aydın; Turkish media executive; *Chairman, Doğan Şirketler Grubu Holding A.Ş.;* b. 1936, Kelkit; m.; four c.; ed Istanbul High Economy and Commerce Acad.; started business operations while still at school, f. his first industrial co. 1974; currently Chair. Doğan Şirketler Grubu Holding A.Ş.; owner of eight newspapers including Hürriyet and Milliyet and two TV stations; fmr mem. Ass. and Admin. Bd Istanbul Chamber of Commerce; fmr Bd mem. Union of Chambers and Stock Markets; Chair. Newspaper Owners' Union 1986–96; Deputy Chair. World Asscn of Newspapers 2004–; f. Aydın Doğan Foundation 1996; Hon. DHumLitt (Girne American Univ.) 1999, Dr hc (Aegean Univ.) 2000; State Superior Services Medal 1999. *Address:* Doğan Şirketler Grubu Holding A.Ş., Oymacı Sok. No:15/1 Altunizade 34662, Üsküdar, İstanbul (office); Aydın Doğan Vakfi, Hürriyet Medya Towers, 34544, Güneşli, Istanbul, Turkey (office). *Telephone:* (212) 677-0760 (office). *Fax:* (212) 677-0762 (office). *E-mail:* advakfi@hurriyet.com.tr (office). *Website:* www.doganholding.com.tr (office).

DOGAR, Hon. Abdul Hameed, BSc, LLB; Pakistani judge; b. 22 March 1944, Gaarhi Mori, Khairpur Dist, Sindh Prov.; ed Punjab Univ., Int. Islamic Univ. Islamabad, Al-Azhar Univ., Cairo, Egypt, Macca and Madina Univ., Saudi Arabia; Sec., Dist Bar Asscn, Khairpur 1973–74, Pres. 1987–88, 1989–90, 1991–92, 1993–94, 1994–95; Vice-Chair. Dist Council, Khairpur 1979–83; Jt Sec., High Court Bar Asscn, Sukkur Bench 1984–85; Justice of Sindh High Court 1995–2000, Justice of Supreme Court 2000–09 (retd), Chief Justice of Pakistan 2007–09 (took oath on Prov. Constitution Order (PCO) which replaced the Constitution 3 Nov. 2007, later took fresh oath according to Article 178 of the Constitution 15 Nov. 2007, Supreme Court Pakistan later declared that taking oath on PCO was not legal and held that Justice Dogar was never a Constitutional Chief Justice of Pakistan as office of Chief Justice of Pakistan was never vacant by *de jure* Chief Justice, hence treated him the *de facto* Chief Justice of Pakistan by protecting all his admin., financial acts and any oath made before him in ordinary course of affairs of office of Chief Justice of Pakistan 31 July 2009); Chair. Bd Govs IBA March–April 2000; mem. Sindh Madresah Bd, Karachi 1980–83, Syndicate, Shah Abdul Latif Univ., Khairpur 1996–2000; mem. Bd Govs, Bd of Intermediate and Secondary Educ., Sukkur 1988–90, Nat. Univ. of Modern Languages, Islamabad 2003; Judge-in-Charge, Supreme Court Employees' Co-operative Housing Soc., Islamabad 2004; Acting Chief Election Commr July–Aug. 2004, Nov.–Dec. 2004, 2005–06; Chair. Supreme Judicial Council, Law and Justice Comm., Fed. Judicial Acad., Nat. Judicial Policy-making Cttee, Governing Body, Access to Justice Devt Fund; Hon. Sec., Dist Red Crescent Soc., Khairpur 1980–85.

DOHERTY, Peter Charles, AC, MVSc, PhD, FRS; Australian immunologist and academic; *Laureate Professor, Department of Microbiology and Immunology, University of Melbourne;* b. 15 Oct. 1940, Oxley; s. of Eric Doherty and Linda Doherty; m. Penelope Stephens 1965; two s.; ed Indooroopilly High School, Univ. of Queensland and Univ. of Edinburgh, UK; following graduation, worked as rural veterinary officer in Queensland Dept of Agric. and Stock, later worked in Animal

Research Inst., Yeerongpilly; worked in CSIRO and Serum Labs; Sr Scientific Officer, Dept of Experimental Pathology, Moredun Research Inst., Edinburgh 1967–71; Assoc. Prof., then Prof. Wistar Inst., Philadelphia, USA 1975–82; Head of Dept of Experimental Pathology, John Curtin School of Medical Research, Canberra, 1982–88; Michael F. Tamer Endowed Chair for Immunology Biomedical Research, Co-Leader of Infection and Host Defense Program and Chair. Dept of Immunology, St Jude Children's Research Hosp., Memphis, Tenn., USA 1988–2002, mem. Dept of Immunology 2002–; Adjunct Prof. of Pediatrics and Pathology, Univ. of Tennessee, Memphis 1992–2002; Laureate Prof., Dept of Microbiology and Immunology, Univ. of Melbourne 2002–; mem. Bd Int. Lab. for Research in Animal Diseases, Nairobi, Kenya 1987–92; mem. Scientific Review Bd, Howard Hughes Medical Inst. 1997–; Patron, Peter Doherty Inst. for Infection and Immunity 2014–; Hon. Fellow, Acad. of Medical Sciences 2015; Hon. DVSc (Queensland), Hon. DSc (Australian Nat. Univ., Edin., Tufts, Warsaw, Latrobe, Imperial Coll. London, Autonomous Univ. Barcelona, North Carolina State, Guelph, Pennsylvania, Michigan State, Illinois, of Technology, Sydney), Hon. DMSc (Rhodes), Hon. DPh (Kyorin); Paul Ehrlich Prize for Medicine, Germany 1983, Gairdner Int. Award for Medical Science, Canada 1986, Albert Lasker Basic Medical Research Award 1995, Nobel Prize in Medicine (jt recipient) 1996, Australian of the Year 1997, Nat. Trust Australian Living Treasure. *Publications:* The Beginner's Guide to Winning the Nobel Prize 2005, A Light History of Hot Air 2007, Sentinel Chickens 2012, The Knowledge Wars; numerous publs in scientific journals, chapters in books and review articles. *Leisure interests:* walking, reading. *Address:* Department of Microbiology and Immunology, Peter Doherty Institute for Infection and Immunity, University of Melbourne, 792 Elizabeth Street, Melbourne, Victoria 3010, Australia (office). *Telephone:* (3) 8344-7968 (office). *E-mail:* pcd@unimelb.edu.au (office). *Website:* www.microbiol.unimelb.edu.au/people/doherty (office).

DOIG, Anne Frances, MD, LMCC, CCFP, FCFP; Canadian physician and organization official; m. Robert J. Cowan; five s. one d.; ed Coll. of Medicine, Univ. of Saskatchewan; in full-time family practice, City Centre Family Physicians PC Inc., Saskatoon 1978–; Clinical Assoc., Dept of Obstetrics and Gynecology, Univ. of Saskatchewan; mem. Active Staff, Saskatoon Regional Health Authority Practitioner Staff; mem. Bd of Dirs Saskatchewan Blue Cross 1995–; Pres. Canadian Medical Asscn 2009–10; mem. Saskatoon Regional Medical Staff Asscn, Saskatchewan Medical Asscn, Coll. of Physicians and Surgeons of Saskatchewan, Coll. of Family Physicians of Canada, Soc. of Obstetricians and Gynecologists of Canada, Univ. of Saskatchewan Coll. of Medicine Alumni Asscn (Founding mem. and fmr Pres.), Univ. of Alberta Health Law Inst., Canadian Asscn of Medical Educ.; Pres. Swim Saskatchewan Inc.; represents Saskatchewan on Bd of Dirs Swimming/Natation Canada; mem. Bd of Dirs Canada Health Infoway Inc. 2010–, Third Avenue Centre 2012–, STARS Air Ambulance 2012–; fmr Pres. Saskatoon Goldfin Swim Club; Clinical Teacher of the Year in Family Medicine, Saskatoon City Hospital 1990, Excellence in Teaching Award, Asscn of Profs of Obstetrics and Gynecology 1996, Saskatchewan Centennial Leadership Award 2005. *Address:* City Centre Family Physicians, 514 Queen Street, Saskatoon, SK S7K 0M5, Canada (office). *Telephone:* (306) 244-3016 (office).

DOIG, Peter, MA; British painter and academic; b. 1959, Edinburgh; ed Chelsea School of Art, Wimbledon School of Art, St Martin's School of Art; grew up in Canada; moved to Trinidad 2002; Trustee, Tate Gallery 1995–2000; Prof., Düsseldorf State Acad. of Art 2005–. *Works include:* Architect's Home in the Ravine 1991, Blotter 1993, Olin MKIV Part II 1995–96, Daytime Astronomy 1997–98, 100 Years Ago 2001, Almost Grown 2001, Country Rock 2001, Black Orpheus 2003, Curious 2005. *Address:* c/o Victoria Miro Gallery, 16 Wharf Road, London, N1 7RW, England (office). *Telephone:* (20) 7336-8109 (office). *E-mail:* info@victoria-miro.com (office). *Website:* www.victoria-miro.com (office).

DOJE, Cedain; Chinese government official; b. 1924; m. Gesang Zhuoga; ed Beijing Normal Univ.; Gov. of Xizang (Tibet) Autonomous Region 1983–85; Researcher, Inst. of Research on World Religions, Chinese Acad. of Social Sciences 1985–; adviser, United Front Work Dept under CCP Cen. Cttee 1986–; mem. Standing Cttee 6th NPC 1986–88, Standing Cttee 7th NPC 1988–93, 8th NPC 1993–97; Vice-Chair. Educ., Science, Culture and Public Health Cttee under the NPC 1986; Deputy Head China-Spain Friendship Group 1986; Gen. Sec. China Nat. Center for Tibetan Studies; Chair. Tibetan Folk Arts Asscn. *Publications:* Education in Tibet 1995, Tibet's Feudal Serfdom Society 2005. *Address:* c/o China National Center for Tibetan Studies, 3/F A2 Building (Rongfeng 2008), Blk 8, 305 Guang An Men Wai Street, Xuanwu District, Beijing, People's Republic of China.

DOJE, Cering; Chinese government official; b. 1939, Xiahe Co., Gansu Prov.; worked as clerk in Tibet 1959; joined CCP 1960; magistrate, Co. (Dist) People's Court, Nagarze Co. and Gyaca Co., Tibet 1962; mem. Tibet Autonomous Region CCP 1974–90; mem. Standing Cttee Tibet CCP 1977–90; First Sec. Xigaze Municipality CCP 1979–82; Vice-Chair. Tibet Autonomous Region 1983–85, Acting Admin. Head 1986–88, Chair. 1988–90; Deputy for Tibet Autonomous Region, 7th NPC 1988–; Vice-Minister of Civil Affairs 1990–93, Minister 1993–2003; Chair. 10th NPC Ethnic Affairs Cttee 2003–08; Vice-Chair. China Cttee Int. Decade for Nat. Disaster Reduction 1998–; mem. 8th NPC 1993–97; mem. 14th CCP Cen. Cttee 1992–97, 15th CCP Cen. Cttee 1997–2002, 16th CCP Cen. Cttee 2002–07. *Address:* c/o Ministry of Civil Affairs, 147 Beiheyan Dajie, Dongcheng Qu, Beijing 100721, People's Republic of China (office).

DOKLE, Namik; Albanian journalist and politician; b. 11 March 1946, Durres; ed Univ. of Agric., Univ. of Tirana; journalist, Puna newspaper 1970–83; Ed. journal Puna 1983–89; Ed.-in-Chief Zeri Popullit (Albanian Socialist Party newspaper) 1991; mem. Parl. 1991–, Deputy Chair. of Parl. 1997–2001, Speaker of Parl. 2001–02, Deputy Prime Minister 2003–05; mem. Albanian Socialist Party (SP). *Publications include:* Storybooks: Kur erdhi pranvera 1971, Shokët e babait tim 1973, Kripë mbi dëborë 1976; Drama: Era e lartësive 1974, Të pamposhtur në shtrëngatë 1975, Buka e pathyer 1978, Mungojnë dy fishekë 1980, Koha në gjunjë s'na ka parë 1981, Mjegulla e dimrit të largët 2003, Kthimi i të munduarve 2003, Ura midis jetës dhe vdekjes 2003, Anija fantazmë 2004, Dënimi i dyte i Homerit 2008; over 700 articles, essays and interviews. *Address:* People's Assembly (Kuvendi Popullor), Bulevardi Dëshmorët e Kombit 4, 1010 Tirana, Albania (office). *Telephone:* (4) 2278261 (office). *E-mail:* albana.shtylla@parlament.al (office). *Website:* www.parlament.al (office).

DOKTOR, Martin, PhDr; Czech canoeist and sports coach; *Director of Sport, Czech Olympic Committee;* b. 21 May 1974, Polička; s. of Josef Doktor and Zuzana Doktorová; m. Kateřina Svobodová 2000; one s. one d.; ed Charles Univ., Prague; silver medals 500m and 1000m Canoeing World Championships, Duisburg, Germany; gold medals 500m and 1000m Olympic Games, Atlanta, USA 1996; silver medals 200m and 1000m, gold medal 500m Canoeing World Championships, Dartmouth, Canada 1997; silver medal 500m, gold medal 1000m European Championships, Plovdiv, Bulgaria 1997; World Cup winner 1998; gold medal 200m World Championships, Szeged, Hungary 1998, silver medal 1000m; World Cup winner 1999; silver medals 200m, 500m and 1000m European Championships, Zagreb, Croatia 1999; silver medal 200m and 500m, bronze medal 1000m Canoeing World Championships, Milan, Italy 1999; gold medal 1000m, bronze medal 200m European Championships 2000; World Cup winner 2000; bronze medal 1000m European Championships, Italy 2001; silver medal 1000m World Championships, Poland 2001; World Cup winner 2002, silver medal C1 200m and bronze medal C1 500m, World Championships, Gainesville, USA 2003; World Cup winner 2003, 2004, silver medal C1 200m European Championships, Račice, Czech Repub. 2006; Head Coach of Czech nat. team 2008–; Coach in CS MV-ČR; Dir of Sport, Czech Olympic Cttee 2013–; mem. Council, Czech TV 2017–; mem. Bd, Czech Fair Play Club, Czech Olympians; Best Czech Sportsman of the Year 1996, Gut Jarkovský Prize 1996. *Publications:* Story of the Defeated Champion 2000, Technique and Tactics of Paddling in Flat Water Canoes 2001. *Leisure interests:* skiing, music, cycling, golf. *Address:* Czech Olympic Committee, Benešovská 6, 101 00 Prague 10 (office); Slunečni 627, 533 04 Sezemice (home); Račice 64, 411 08 Štětí, Czech Republic (home). *E-mail:* doktor@olympic.cz (home). *Website:* www.olympic.cz (office).

DOLAN, Charles F.; American media executive; *Chairman, Cablevision Systems Corporation;* b. 16 Oct. 1926, Cleveland, Ohio; m. Helen Burgess; three s. three d.; ed John Carroll Univ.; served in USAF; with wife est. co. producing and distributing sports and industrial films; subsequently f. Teleguide Inc. (providing information services via cable to New York hotels) and Sterling Manhattan Cable (first urban cable TV co. in USA), Home Box Office Inc.; Founder and Chair. Cablevision Systems Corp. 1985–; Co-owner Madison Square Garden Properties 1995–; Dir Cold Spring Harbor Lab., St Francis Hosp., Long Island; Chair. Nat. Acad. of TV Arts and Sciences; a Man. Dir of Metropolitan Opera, New York; Trustee, Fairfield Univ.; mem. Bd of Govs Nat. Hockey League. *Address:* Cablevision Systems Corporation, 1111 Stewart Avenue, Bethpage, NY 11714-3533, USA. *Telephone:* (516) 803-2300. *Fax:* (516) 803-2273. *Website:* www.cablevision.com.

DOLAN, James L.; American business executive; *President and CEO, Cablevision Systems Corporation;* s. of Charles F. Dolan and Helen Ann Dolan (née Burgess); m. Kristin Dolan; five c.; fmrly Asst Gen. Man., Cablevision Chicago, Vice-Pres. for Advertising Sales; fmr Man. WKNR-AM radio station, Cleveland; Corpn Dir, Advertising, Rainbow Programming Holdings, CEO 1992–95; CEO and Pres. Cablevision Systems Corpn 1995–; Exec. Chair., Madison Square Garden Co. (MSG), New York 1999–, MSG Networks Inc., also mem. Bd of Dirs; Co-founder and mem. Bd of Dirs Lustgarten Foundation; mem. Bd of Dirs AMC Networks Inc., Weinstein Co. *Leisure interests:* yachting, music. *Address:* Cablevision Systems Corporation, 1111 Stewart Avenue, Bethpage, NY 11714, USA (office). *Telephone:* (516) 803-2300 (office). *Fax:* (516) 803-2273 (office). *Website:* www.cablevision.com (office); www.themadisonsquaregardencompany.com (office).

DOLAN, Peter Robert, BA, MBA; American business executive; b. 6 Jan. 1956, Salem, Mass; m. Katherine Lange 1981; two s.; ed Tufts Univ., Tuck School of Business, Dartmouth Coll.; with Gen. Foods 1980–88; Vice-Pres. of Marketing, Bristol-Myers Products Div. 1988–90, Sr Vice-Pres. of Marketing and Sales 1990–91, Sr Vice-Pres. of Marketing, Sales and Operations 1991–92, Exec. Vice-Pres. 1992, Pres. 1993–94, Group Pres. Nutritionals and Medical Devices, Bristol-Myers Squibb Co. 1997–98, Pres. Europe and Worldwide Medicines 1998, Sr Vice-Pres. of Strategy 1998–2000, Pres. 2000–05, Chair. 2001–05, CEO 2001–06 (resgnd); Chair. (non-exec.) Allied Minds; mem. Bd of Trustees, Tufts Univ. 2001–, Chair. 2013–; mem. Bd of Dirs New York Botanical Garden, Nat. Center on Addiction and Substance Abuse, Columbia Univ., American Express, Nat. Center on Addiction and Substance Abuse. *Address:* Office of the Trustees, Tufts University, Ballou Hall, 4th Floor, Medford, MA 02155, USA (office). *Telephone:* (617) 627-3320 (office). *Fax:* (617) 627-3867 (office). *Website:* trustees.tufts.edu (office).

DOLAN, Ray, FRS, FRCP, FMedSci, MB, BCh, MD; Irish neuroscientist; *Mary Kinross Professor of Neuropsychiatry and Director, Wellcome Trust Centre for Neuroimaging, University College London;* b. 21 Jan. 1954; s. of John Dolan and Julia Coppenger; ed Nat. Univ. of Ireland; specialist training in psychiatry in UK 1979–86; Consultant Neuropsychiatrist, Nat. Hosp. for Neurology and Neurosurgery, London 1987–; co-f. Wellcome Trust Functional Imaging Lab., Inst. of Neurology, Univ. Coll. London 1994, Mary Kinross Prof. of Neuropsychiatry 1999–, Founding Dir, Wellcome Trust Centre for Neuroimaging 2006–, Prof. and Dir, Max Planck Centre for Computational Psychiatry & Ageing, UCL 2014–; Visiting Einstein Fellow, Humboldt Univ., Berlin 2010–14; mem. Royal Irish Acad., Royal Coll. of Psychiatrists; Hon. Prof., Humboldt Univ., Berlin; External mem. Max Planck Soc.; Minerva Foundation Golden Brain Award 2006, Int. Max Planck Research Award 2007, Santiago-Grisolia Award 2012, Klaus Joachim Zülch Prize 2013, Lundbeck Foundation Brain Prize (jt winner) 2017. *Publications:* over 650 peer review papers. *Leisureinterests:* Hiking, literature, music. *Address:* Wellcome Trust Centre for Neuroimaging, University College London, 12 Queen Square, London, WC1N 3BG, England (office). *Telephone:* (20) 3448-4362 (office). *E-mail:* r.dolan@ucl.ac.uk (office). *Website:* www.fil.ion.ucl.ac.uk/Dolan/ (office).

DOLAN, HE Cardinal Timothy Michael, BA, LicSacredTheol; American ecclesiastic and academic; *Archbishop of New York;* b. 6 Feb. 1950, St Louis, Mo.; s. of Robert Dolan and Shirley Dolan (née Radcliffe); ed St Louis Preparatory Seminary South, Shrewsbury, Cardinal Glennon Coll., Catholic Univ. of America, Pontifical North American Coll. and the Angelicum, Rome; ordained priest, Archdiocese of St Louis 1976; served as Assoc. Pastor at Immacolata Roman Catholic Parish, Richmond Heights –1979; doctoral studies at Catholic Univ. of America, Washington, DC; performed pastoral work in Mo. 1983–87; collaborated with Archbishop John May in reforming the archdiocesan seminary; Sec., Apostolic Nunciature, Washington, DC; appointed Vice-Rector Kenrick-Glennon Seminary 1992, also served as Spiritual Dir and taught Church history; fmr Adjunct Prof. of Theology, St Louis Univ.; rank of Mgr 1994; Rector, Pontifical North American Coll., Rome 1994–2001; taught at Pontifical Gregorian Univ. and the Angelicum; Auxiliary Bishop of St Louis and Titular Bishop of Natchesium 2001–02; Archbishop of Milwaukee, Wis. 2002–09; Apostolic Admin. of Green Bay, Wis. 2007–08; Archbishop of New York 2009–; cr. Cardinal (Cardinal-Priest of Nostra Signora di Guadalupe a Monte Mario) 2012; participated in Papal Conclave 2013; Chair. Catholic Relief Services –2010; Pres. US Conf. of Catholic Bishops 2010–, Chair. Priestly Life and Ministry Cttee, mem. Sub-cttee on the Church in Africa; mem. Bd of Trustees Catholic Univ. of America; Apostolic Visitor to Irish seminaries as part of Apostolic visitation to Ireland following publication of Ryan and Murphy Reports 2009; mem. Pontifical Council for Promotion of New Evangelisation 2011–, Pontifical Council for Social Communications 2011–. *Television:* co-hosted a programme with his brother called Living Our Faith. *Publications:* Called to Be Holy 2005, To Whom Shall We Go? Lessons from the Apostle Peter 2008, Priests for the Third Millennium 2009. *Address:* Archdiocese of New York, 1011 First Avenue, New York, NY 10022-4134, USA (office). *Telephone:* (212) 371-1000 (office). *Fax:* (212) 826-6020 (office); (212) 826-8379 (office). *E-mail:* communications@archny.org (office). *Website:* www.ny-archdiocese.org (office).

DOLCE, Domenico; Italian fashion designer; *CEO, Dolce & Gabbana;* b. 13 Aug. 1958, Polizzi Generosa, nr Palermo, Sicily; s. of Saverio Dolce; designer, father's atelier, then Asst in a Milan atelier; with Stefano Gabbana opened fashion consulting studio 1982, selected to take part in New Talents show, Milano Collezioni 1985; co-f. Dolce & Gabbana 1985, first maj. women's collection 1985, knitwear 1987, beachwear, underwear 1989, men's wear 1990, women's fragrance 1992, D&G line, men's fragrance 1994, eyewear 1995; est. Dolce and Gabbana Industria production units 1999–2000; acquired and renovated Cinema Metropol in Milan for fashion shows and exhibitions 2005; opened boutiques in major cities in Europe, America and Asia; with Stefano Gabbana, Woolmark Award 1991, Perfume Acad. Int. Prize for Best Feminine Fragrance of Year 1993, Best Masculine Fragrance of Year 1995, French "Oscar des Parfums", UK FHM Designers of the Year 1996, Footwear News Designers of the Year 1997, Russian Harper's Bizarre Style Award 1999, T de Telva Award for Best Designers of the Year 2002, US GQ Best Designers of the Year 2003, UK Elle Best Int. Designers 2004, Premio Resultati 2004, Russian GQ Best Int. Designers 2005. *Publications:* with Stefano Gabbana, 10 Years Dolce and Gabbana 1996, Wildness 1997, Dolce and Gabbana Mémoires de la Mode 1998, Hollywood 2003, Calcio 2004, Music 2004, 20 years Dolce and Gabbana 2005. *Leisure interests:* gym, travel, modern art. *Address:* Dolce & Gabbana, Via San Damiano 7, 20122 Milan, Italy (office). *Telephone:* (02) 774271 (office). *Fax:* (02) 76020600 (office). *Website:* www.dolcegabbana.it (office).

DOLE, Elizabeth Hanford, MA, JD; American fmr politician; b. 29 July 1936, Salisbury, N Carolina; d. of John Van Hanford and Mary E. Cathey; m. Robert J. Dole (q.v.) 1975; ed Duke and Harvard Univs, Univ. of Oxford, UK; called to DC Bar 1966; Staff Asst to Asst Sec. for Educ., US Dept of Health, Educ. and Welfare, Washington, DC 1966–67; practising lawyer, Washington, DC 1967–68; Assoc. Dir Legis. Affairs, then Exec. Dir Pres.'s Comm. for Consumer Interests 1968–71; Deputy Asst Office of Consumer Affairs, The White House, Washington, DC 1971–73; Commr Fed. Trade Comm. 1973–79; Asst to Pres. for Public Liaison 1981–83; Sec. of Transportation 1983–87; Sec. of Labor 1989–90; Pres. American Red Cross 1991–98; cand. for Republican presidential nomination 1999; Senator from N Carolina 2003–09; Trustee, Duke Univ. 1974–88; mem. Visiting Comm., John F. Kennedy School of Govt 1988–; mem. Comm. Harvard School of Public Health 1992–, Bd of Overseers, Harvard Univ. 1989–95; hon. doctorates from 40 colls and univs; Radcliffe Coll. Medal, Distinguished Service Award, Nat. Safety Council 1989, N Carolina Award 1991, Lifetime Achievement Award, Women Execs in State Govt 1993, named N Carolinian of the Year by NC Press Asscn 1993, Leadership Award, League of Women Voters 1994, Raoul Wallenberg Award for Humanitarian Service 1995, Churchwoman of the Year, Religious Heritage of America 1995, named one of the world's three most admired women in Gallup Poll 1998, inducted into Safety and Health Hall of Fame International 1998, Humanitarian Award, Nat. Comm. Against Drunk Driving 1998, Nat. Religious Broadcasters' Bd of Dirs Award 1999, Foreign Policy Asscn Medal. *Website:* www.elizabethdole.net.

DOLE, Robert Joseph (Bob); American lawyer and fmr politician; *Special Counsel, Alston & Bird LLP;* b. 22 July 1923, Russell, Kan.; s. of Doran R. Dole and Bina Dole; m. 1st Phyllis Holden 1948 (divorced 1972, died 2008); one d.; m. 2nd Elizabeth Hanford Dole (q.v.) 1975; ed Univ. of Kansas and Washbourn Municipal Univ.; mem. Kansas State Legislature 1951–53; Russell Co. Attorney 1953–61; mem. US House of Reps, Washington, DC 1960–68; Senator from Kansas 1969–96, Senate Majority Leader 1995–96, Senate Republican Leader 1987–96, Chair. Senate Finance Cttee 1981–84; Chair. Republican Nat. Cttee 1971–72; unsuccessful cand. for Vice-Pres. 1976, for Pres. 1996; mem. of Counsel, Verner, Liipfert, Bernhard, McPherson and Hand; Special Counsel, Alston and Bird LLP, Washington, DC 2003–; Pres. Bob Dole Enterprises, Inc.; Pres. Dole Foundation 1983–99; Dir Mainstream Inc.; Adviser, US Del. to FAO Conf., Rome 1965, 1974, 1977; mem. Congressional del. to India 1966, to Middle East 1967; mem. US Helsinki Comm., del. to Belgrade Conf. 1977; Chair. Int. Comm. on Missing Persons 1997–; Trustee, William Allen White Foundation, Univ. of Kan; mem. Nat. Advisory Cttee, The John Wesley Colls; mem. Nat. Advisory Cttee on Scouting for the Handicapped, Kan. Asscn for Retarded Children, Advisory Bd of United Cerebral Palsy, Kan.; mem. ABA; Republican; Hon. mem. Advisory Bd of Kidney Patients Inc.; Presidential Medal of Freedom 1997, Distinguished Service Award 1997, World Food Prize (shared with George McGovern) 2008. *Publications:* Great Political Wit (co-ed.) 1999, Great Presidential Wits 2001, One Soldier's Story 2005. *Leisure interests:* politics, watching the news. *Address:* Alston & Bird LLP, The Atlantic Building, 950 F Street NW, Washington, DC 20004-1404, USA (office). *Telephone:* (202) 756-3300 (office). *Fax:* (202) 756-3333 (office). *E-mail:* bdole@alston.com (office). *Website:* www.alston.com (office); www.bobdole.org.

DOLGEN, Jonathan L., BS, JD; American film industry executive; *Principal, Wood River Ventures, LLC;* b. 27 April 1945, New York; ed Cornell Univ., New York. Univ. Law School; lawyer, Fried, Frank, Harris, Shriver & Jacobson 1969–76; Asst Gen. Counsel then Deputy Gen. Counsel, Columbia Pictures Industries 1976–85, Sr Vice-Pres. World Business Affairs 1979, Exec. Vice-Pres. 1980, Pres. Columbia's Pay Cable & Home Entertainment Group 1983; Sr Exec. Vice-Pres. Fox Inc. 1985–90; Pres. TV Div., Twentieth Century Fox Inc. 1985–88, Pres. 1988–93, Chair. Twentieth TV 1988–90; Pres. Columbia Pictures 1990–94, Pres. Columbia Pictures, Culver City 1991–94; Chair. and CEO Viacom Entertainment Group 1994–2004; Prin., Wood River Ventures, LLC 2004–; Sr Consultant, ARTISTdirect Inc. 2006–08; f. Friends of Cornell Univ. Arts Center, Founder-mem. Educ. First; mem. Alumni Council, New York Univ. Law School; mem. City of Los Angeles Advisory Council, Los Angeles County Homeland Security Advisory Council, Cornell Univ. Major Gifts Cttee; mem. Bd Dirs Sony Pictures, Charter Communications Inc. 2004–08, Expedia Inc. 2005–, Nation Entertainment, Inc. 2010–, Simon Wiesenthal Center; mem. Bd of Trustees, Claremont Graduate School; Fellow, Claremont Univ. Center and Grad. School. *Address:* Wood River Ventures, LLC, 301 North Canon Drive, Suite 206, Beverly Hills, CA 90210, USA (office). *Telephone:* (310) 858-6970 (office).

D'OLIVEIRA DOS RAMOS, Américo; São Tomé and Príncipe economist and politician; Minister of Finance and Int. Co-operation 2010–12, 2014–18; fmr mem. Bd of Govs, African Devt Bank. *Address:* c/o Ministry of Planning and Finance, Largo Alfândega, CP 168, São Tomé, São Tomé and Príncipe (office).

DOLLÉ, Guy; French steel industry executive; b. 1942; ed Ecole Polytechnique; began career with IRSID Steel Research Centre, Metz; Head of Plates and Tubes Div., Usinor 1980, Chair. GTS (subsidiary co.) 1985, Exec. Vice-Pres. Usinor Aciers 1986, Head of Production, Sollac N Region (following merger wih Usinor), Vice-Pres. Industrial Affairs 1987, Chair. and CEO Unimétal 1993–95, Exec. Vice-Pres. for Strategy, Usinor 1995–97, Head of Stainless Steel and Alloys Div. 1997–99, Sr Exec. Vice-Pres., Usinor 1999–2002, Chair. and CEO Arcelor SA (following merger of Aceralia, Arbed and Usinor groups) 2002–06; mem. Bd of Dirs Gaz de France 2004–06. *Address:* c/o Gaz de France, 23 rue Philibert-Delorme, 75840 Paris, France (office).

DOLLERY, Sir Colin (Terence), Kt, BS, MB, ChB, FRCP, FMedSci; British physician; b. 14 March 1931; s. of Cyril Robert Dollery and Thelma Mary Dollery; m. Diana Myra Stedman 1958; one s. one d.; ed Lincoln School and Univ. of Birmingham; House Officer, Queen Elizabeth Hosp. Birmingham, Hammersmith Hosp. and Brompton Hosp. 1956–58; Medical Registrar, Hammersmith Hosp. 1958–60, Sr Registrar and Tutor in Medicine 1960–62; Consultant Physician 1962–2000; Lecturer in Medicine, Royal Postgraduate Medical School, Univ. of London 1962–65, Prof. of Clinical Pharmacology 1965–87, Prof. of Medicine 1987–91, Dean 1991–96, Pro-Vice-Chancellor for Medicine 1992–96; Sr Consultant Research and Devt, SmithKline Beecham PLC 1996–2000, GlaxoSmithKline 2001–; Dir (non-exec.) Larson-Davis, Inc. 1998–99, Discovery Partners, Inc. 2001–, Predict, Inc. 2001–; Distinguished Visitor, Nat. Physical Laboratory 2016–; mem. MRC 1982–84, Univ. Funding Council (fmrly Univ. Grants Cttee) 1984–91; Fellow Imperial Coll. London 2003; fmr Pres. Int. Union of Pharmacology; Hon. mem. Asscn of American Physicians; Chevalier, Ordre Nat. du Mérite; British Pharmacological Soc. Wellcome Gold Medal. *Publications:* The Retinal Circulation 1971, Therapeutic Drugs 1991; papers in scientific journals. *Leisure interests:* travel, amateur radio, work. *Address:* c/o GlaxoSmithKline PLC, 3rd Avenue, Harlow CM19 5AW (office); 101 Corringham Road, London, NW11 7DL, England (home). *Telephone:* (1279) 646154 (office). *E-mail:* colin-dollery-1@gsk.com (office).

DOLOGUÉLÉ, Anicet G.; Central African Republic politician; b. 17 April 1957, Bozoum; m.; three c.; ed Univ. de Bangui, Bordeaux Univ., France; fmr Finance and Budget Minister; Prime Minister, Minister of the Economy, Finance, Planning and Int. Co-operation 1999–2001; Chair. Banque de Développement des Etats de l'Afrique Centrale 2001–10; unsuccessful cand. (Union pour le renouveau centrafricain) in presidential election Feb. 2016; Grand Officier Ordre du Mérite Centrafricain, Commdr Ordre du Mérite Centrafricain, Médaille d'or Ordre du Mérite Centrafricain. *Address:* Union pour le renouveau centrafricain, Bangui, Central African Republic (office).

DOMARKAS, Juozas; Lithuanian conductor; *Honorary Conductor, Lithuanian National Symphony Orchestra;* b. 28 July 1936, Plunge; m.; two s.; ed Klaipeda Simkus Coll. of Music, Lithuanian Acad. of Music, St Petersburg State Conservatory (conducting Symphony Orchestra and Opera, with Prof. Ilja Musin); Asst Conductor, Vilnius Band 1957–60; Artistic Dir and Chief Conductor, Lithuanian Nat. Symphony Orchestra 1964–2015, Hon. Conductor 2015–; participated in numerous nat. and int. festivals; teacher, sr teacher, Assoc. Prof., Lithuanian Acad. of Music and Theatre 1968–93, Chair. and Prof. 1993–; mem. of jury for numerous int. competitions for symphony conducting in Russia, Poland and Finland; Grand Cross, Order of the Lithuanian Grand Duke Gediminas 1998, Chevalier Cross, Order Zasługi Rzeczypospolitej Polskiej 2006; People's Artist of the USSR 1986, Award of Govt of Lithuania for Merit to Lithuanian Culture 1997, Nat. Prize of Lithuanian Repub. 2000. *Address:* Lietuvos Nacionaline Filharmonija, Ausros Vartu 5, 01129 Vilnius (office); Zydu 4–15, 01131 Vilnius, Lithuania (home). *Telephone:* (5) 266-5210 (office); (5) 262-8461 (home). *Fax:* (5) 266-5266 (office); (5) 262-8461 (home). *E-mail:* juozas.domarkas.1@gmail.com (home); info@filharmonija.lt (office). *Website:* www.filharmonija.lt (office).

DOMBROVSKIS, Valdis; Latvian economist, politician and EU official; *Commissioner for the Euro and Social Dialogue and for Financial Stability, Financial Services and the Capital Markets Union and Vice-President, European Commission;* b. 5 Aug. 1971, Rīga, Latvian SSR, USSR; m.; ed Univ. of Latvia, Rīga Tech. Univ., Univ. of Mainz, Germany, Univ. of Maryland, USA; lab. asst, Inst. of Solid State Physics, Univ. of Latvia 1991–93 (Asst 1997), Dept of Semiconductor Physics 1993–95, Inst. of Physics, Univ. of Mainz, Germany 1995–96; Research Asst, A. James Clark School of Eng, Univ. of Maryland, USA 1998; Macroeconomic Analyst, Monetary Policy Dept, Bank of Latvia 1998–99, Sr Economist 1999–2001, Chief Economist 2001–02; Founder-mem. Jaunais Laiks (New Era) party 2002–11, mem. Bd 2002–04; mem. Parl. 2002–04, 2010–14; Observer, Council of the EU 2003–04; Minister of Finance 2002–04; mem. European Parl. (Group of the European People's Party) 2004–09; Minister for Children, Family and Integration Affairs March–July 2009; Prime Minister of Latvia 2009–13 (resgnd), also Minister for Regional Devt and Local Govt 2010–11; Founder and mem. Bd,

Vienutība (Unity) party 2011–; Commr for the Euro and Social Dialogue, EC Nov. 2014–, also for Financial Stability, Financial Services and the Capital Markets Union 2016–, Vice-Pres. EC; Order of Three Stars 2014; Int. Award from Friedrich August von Hayek Stiftung 2011, The Vašek and Anna Maria Polák Visiting Lecturer's Award 2012. *Publications:* How Latvia Came through the Financial Crisis (with A. Åslund) 2011; numerous publs on economics and politics in various periodicals, journals and electronic media. *Address:* European Commission, rue de la Loi/Wetstraat 200, 1049 Brussels, Belgium (office). *Telephone:* (2) 299-11-11 (switchboard) (office). *E-mail:* cab-dombrovskis-contact@ec.europa.eu (office); birojs@valdisdombrovskis.lv; birojs@vienotiba.lv. *Website:* ec.europa.eu/commission/2014-2019/dombrovskis_en (office); www.vienotiba.lv; valdisdombrovskis.lv.

DOMBROVSKIS, Vjačeslavs, BA, PhD; Russian/Latvian politician and economist; b. 27 Dec. 1977, Rīga, Latvian SSR, USSR; ed Rīga High School No. 88, Univ. of Latvia, Clarke Univ., Iowa, USA; gained Latvian citizenship through naturalization process 1997; fmr researcher, Baltic Int. Econ. Policy Research Centre; fmr Assoc. Prof., Stockholm School of Econs; joined newly founded Zatlers' Reform Party 2011; mem. Parl. 2011–, Leader of Zatlers' Reform Party Parl. Group 2011–13, Chair. Econ., Agricultural, Environmental and Regional Policy Cttee; Minister for Educ. and Science 2013–14, of the Economy Jan.–Nov. 2014. *Address:* c/o Ministry of the Economy, Brīvības iela 55, Rīga 1519, Latvia. *E-mail:* pasts@em.gov.lv.

DOMINGO, Eugene; Philippine theatre, film and television actress and comedienne; b. 23 July 1971; began career by enrolling in Theatre Arts Programme, Univ. of the Philippines, apprenticed as an actress, production and stage management staff under univ.'s theatre co. Dulaang UP; appeared in several sitcoms, tele-series and drama anthologies on ABS-CBN and GMA Network; Filipino voice of Tagalog dubbed Cinderella of ABS-CBN as Fairy Godmother or Bb. Polette; best known for playing the role of Rowena in the Ang Tanging Ina series; Comedy Actress of the Year, Guillermo Mendoza Memorial Scholarship Foundation 43rd Box-Office Entertainment Awards 2012, Tokyo International Film Festival Award for Best Actress 2013, Golden Screen TV Award for Outstanding Game or Talent Program Host 2014, 2015. *Films include:* Maricris Sioson: Japayuki 1993, Sa ngalan ng pag-ibig 1995, Ikaw pa rin ang iibigin 1998, Pagdating ng panahon 1998, Ms. Kristina Moran: Babaeng palaban 1999, Bullet 1999, Dito sa puso ko 1999, Mahal kita, walang iwanan 2000, Demons 2000, Laro sa baga 2000, Kung ikaw ay isang panaginip 2002, Pakisabi na lang... Mahal ko siya 2002, Lastikman 2003, Ang tanging ina 2003, Malikmata 2003, Volta 2004, Can This Be Love 2005, Bikini Open 2005, Tuli 2005, Kutob 2005, D' Lucky Ones! 2006, Kapag tumibok ang puso: Not Once, But Twice 2006, You Are the One 2006, Txt 2006, Reyna: Ang makulay na pakikipagsapalaran ng mga achucherva, achuchuva, achechenes... 2006, Shake Rattle and Roll 8 (segment 'LRT') 2006, The Promise 2007, Ang cute ng ina mo! 2007, Foster Child 2007, Paano kita iibigin 2007, Philippine Science 2007, Four in One 2007, Pasukob 2007, Shake, Rattle & Roll 9 (segment 'Bangungot') 2007, Katas ng Saudi 2007, Bahay kubo: A pinoy mano po! (Best Supporting Actress, Metro Manila Film Festival Philippines 2007) 2007, Pisay (Best Supporting Actress, Gawad Tanglaw Awards 2008) 2008, Foster Child (Best Supporting Actress, Gawad Tanglaw Awards 2008) 2008, Ploning 2008, Ikaw pa rin: Bongga ka boy! 2008, My Monster Mom 2008, 100 (Best Supporting Actress, Cinemalaya Ind. Film Festival 2008) 2008, I.T.A.L.Y. (I Trust and Love You) 2008, Ang tanging ina n'yong lahat 2008, Comedians (Bert Marcelo Award, Guillermo Mendoza Foundation Awards 2009) 2009, Kimmy Dora: Kambal sa kiyeme (Movie Actress of the Year, PMPC Star Awards for Movies 2010, Best Actress in a Comedy or Musical, Golden Screen Awards 2010) 2009, Soliloquy 2009, Nobody Nobody But Juan 2009, Shake Rattle & Roll XI (segment 'Diablo') (voice) 2009, Working Girls 2010, Here Comes the Bride 2010, Mamarazzi 2010, Petrang Kabayo 2010, Ang tanging ina mo: Last na 'to! (Best Supporting Actress, Metro Manila Film Festival 2010) 2010, RPG Metanoia (voice) 2010, My Valentine Girls (segment 'Gunaw') 2011, Who's That Girl? 2011, The Howl & the Fussyket (short) 2011, Ang babae sa septic tank (Best Actress, Cinemalaya 2011, People's Choice Award for Best Actress, Asian Film Awards 2012, Best Actress, Gawad Tanglaw for Films 2012) 2011, Zombadings 1: Patayin sa shokot si Remington 2011, Anatomiya ng Korupsiyon 2011 Wedding tayo, Wedding hindi! 2011, My Househusband: Ikaw na! (Best Supporting Actress, Metro Manila Film Festival 2011) 2011, Enteng ng Ina mo 2011, Shake Rattle Roll 13 (segment 'Rain Rain Go Away') 2011, Barber's Tales 2014, La Amigas 2015. *Television includes:* Kokey (series) 2001–07, Sa Dulo Ng Walang Hanggan (series) 2001, Buttercup (series) 2003, Tanging Ina (series) 2003, Marina (series) 2004, Kampanerang Kuba (series) 2005, Komiks (series) 2006, SineSerye (series) 2007, Love Spell (series) 2006–07, Volta (mini-series) 2008, Everybody Hapi (series) 2008, Ako si Kim Samsoon (series) 2008, Obra (series) 2008–10, Ang babaeng hinugot sa aking tadyang (series) 2009, Cool Center: Hello It's Me! (series) 2009, Adik sa'yo (series) 2009, First Time (series) 2010, Jejemom (series) 2010, Inday Wanda (series) 2010–11, Sa ngalan ng ina (series) 2011, Celebrity Bluff 2012–16, Dear Uge 2016–. *Address:* c/o ABS-CBN Corporation, Quezon City, The Philippines. *E-mail:* info@abs-cbn.com. *Website:* www.abs-cbn.com.

DOMINGO, Plácido, FRCM, FRNCM; Spanish singer (tenor) and conductor; *General Director, Los Angeles Opera;* b. 21 Jan. 1941, Madrid; s. of Plácido Domingo and Pepita Domingo (née Embil); m. Marta Ornelas; three s.; ed Nat. Conservatory of Music, Mexico City; operatic debut at Monterrey, Mexico 1961; with Israel Nat. Opera for over two years; debut at Metropolitan Opera, New York 1968; British debut in Verdi's Requiem at Royal Festival Hall 1969; Covent Garden debut in Tosca 1971, returned to sing in Aïda, Carmen 1973, La Bohème 1974, Un Ballo in Maschera 1975, La Fanciulla del West; has taken leading roles in about 120 operas; with New York City Opera 1965–; Artistic Dir Washington Nat. Opera 1994–2003, Gen. Dir 2003–11; Artistic Dir Los Angeles Opera 2000–03, Gen. Dir 2003–; engagements include Tosca (conducting), Romeo and Juliet at Metropolitan Opera, New York, Aïda, Il Trovatore in Hamburg, Don Carlos in Salzburg, I vespri siciliani and La forza del destino in Paris, Turandot in Barcelona, Otello in Paris, London, Hamburg and Milan, Carmen in Edinburgh, Turandot at the Metropolitan Opera; New York stage debut in My Fair Lady 1988 (213 performances by 2000); Luigi in Il Tabarro at the Metropolitan Opera 1989; Otello at Covent Garden 1990, Lohengrin at Vienna Staatsoper, Don José at Rio de Janeiro, Otello at the Metropolitan Opera and Barcelona; Don Carlos at Los Angeles, Dick Johnson at Chicago, Riccardo in Un Ballo in Maschera at the 1990 Salzburg Festival; debut as Parsifal at the Metropolitan Opera 1991 and 2001, Otello at Covent Garden 1992, Siegmund in Die Walküre at the Vienna Staatsoper 1992; 1997 season included Don José and Siegmund at the Metropolitan Opera and Gabriele Adorno in Simon Boccanegra at Covent Garden; 1999 season Herman in the Queen of Spades at the Metropolitan Opera, and at Covent Garden 2002; concert performance of Verdi's Battaglia di Legnano with the Royal Opera 2000; Canio in Pagliacci at Covent Garden 2003; Nero in premiere of Monteverdi's Poppea in Los Angeles 2003; Rasputin in premiere of Deborah Drattell's Nicholas and Alexandra, Los Angeles 2003; opened 2002/03 Los Angeles Opera season in Puccini's Fanciulla del West; Maurizio in Adriana Lecouvreur, Metropolitan Opera 2009; sang first baritone title role in Verdi's Simon Boccanegra at Berlin Staatsoper 2009, Covent Garden 2010, the Metropolitan Opera 2010; cr. and performed at inaugural Plácido Domingo Festival, Spain 2012; 2015 season included debut in the title role of Verdi's Macbeth, Berlin, Don Carlo in Ernani in New York and title role of Gianni Schicchi in Los Angeles; Commdr, Légion d'honneur, Hon. KBE 2002, Medal of Freedom, Star of the Order of Merit (Hungary) 2005; Dr hc (Royal Coll. of Music) 1982, (Univ. Complutense de Madrid) 1989, Hon. DMus (Univ. of Oxford) 2003, (California State Univ.) 2010, (Harvard) 2013, (Salamanca) 2015; 12 Grammy Awards, European Culture Foundation Culture Prize 2003, Classic FM Gramophone Listeners' Choice Award 2005, Opera News Award 2005, Classic BRIT Award for Lifetime Achievement 2006, Birgit Nilsson Prize 2009, Person of the Year, Latin Recording Acad. 2010, Wolf Foundation Prize in Music (shared with Sir Simon Rattle) 2012, Praemium Imperiale Award, Japan Art Foundation 2013. *Films include:* Madama Butterfly with von Karajan, La Traviata 1982, Carmen 1984, Otello 1986. *Recordings include:* has made well over 100 recordings, including Aïda, Un Ballo in Maschera, Tosca, Tannhäuser 1989, Die Frau ohne Schatten 1993, Gounod's Roméo et Juliette 1996, Merlin by Albeniz 2000, Tristan and Isolde (Critics' Choice Award, Classical Brit Awards 2006), Pasión Española (Latin Grammy Award for Best Classical Album) 2008; has made more than 50 videos. *Publications include:* My First Forty Years (autobiog.) 1983, My Operatic Roles 2000. *Address:* c/o Nancy Seltzer and Associates, 6220 Del Valle Drive, Los Angeles, CA 90048, USA (office). *Telephone:* (323) 938-3562 (office). *E-mail:* nseltzer@nsapr.com (office). *Website:* www.laopera.org; www.placidodomingo.com.

DOMINGUEZ, Carlos 'Sonny' Garcia, III, BA, MBA; Philippine business executive and politician; *Secretary of Finance;* b. 16 Sept. 1945, Zamboanga; s. of Carlos Dominguez, II and Virginia Garcia-Dominguez Anderson; m. Cynthia Andrews; four c.; ed Ateneo de Davao Univ.; Lecturer, Ateneo de Davao Univ. School of Business 1973, also mem. Bd of Trustees 1973–95 (Chair. 1982–95); Exec. Vice-Pres., AMS Farming Corpn and Soriano Fruits Corpn 1973–76; Exec. Vice-Pres. and COO, JVA Management Corpn, Davao Fruits Corpn, Hijo Plantation, Inc., Twin Rivers Plantation, Inc. 1976–83; Vice-Pres., Bank of The Philippine Islands 1984–86; Pres., Agricultural Development Bank 1984–86; Sec. (Minister) of Natural Resources 1986–87; Sec. (Minister), Dept of Agric., Quezon City 1987–89; Dir, Land Bank of the Philippines 1987–89; Chair., Republic Planters Bank, Makati 1988–92; Chair. and Pres., Philippine Airlines 1993–95; Pres., C.G. Dominguez and Associates Inc. 1993; Sec. (Minister) of Finance 2016–; owns several businesses in Davao City including Marco Polo Hotel and other real estate developments; Chair. and Pres. Baesa Redevelopment Corpn, Huntly Corpn, The Linden Suites Inc. 1997, Halifax Capital Resources Inc.; Chair. RCBC Capital Corpn, Alip River Development and Export Corpn, Intelligent Agro-Technical Resources Inc.; Pres., Philippine Tobacco Flue-Curing 1992–, Philippine Associated Smelting and Refining Corpn 1999–2002; CEO and Pres., Lafayette Philippines Inc. 2006; Chair. Asian Devt Bank 2017–; mem. Bd of Dirs Alsons Consolidated Resources Inc., United Paragon Mining Corpn, Central Azucarera Don Pedro, Northern Mindanao Power Corpn, Shangri-La Plaza Corpn 1994, Mindanao Power Corpn 1994, Sports Specialists Worldwide Inc., Hervey Asia Corpn, Halifax Davao Hotel and Transnational Diversified Group, Inc., Manila Electric Company 2001–05, Easycall Communications Philippines Inc. 2002–06; Chair. Banana Growers Asscn 1977–83; Trustee, Benigno Aquino, Jr Foundation; mem. Philippine Eagle Foundation, Foundation of Development Through Education, Philippine Business for Social Progress, Philippine Dairy Foundation; Hon. DPhil (Ateneo de Davao) 1997. *Address:* Department of Finance, DOF Bldg, BSP Complex, Roxas Blvd, 1004 Metro Manila, Philippines (office). *Telephone:* (2) 5236051 (office). *Fax:* (2) 5268474 (office). *E-mail:* helpdesk@dof.gov.ph (office). *Website:* www.dof.gov.ph (office).

DOMINI, Amy, BA; American mutual fund company executive; *CEO and President, Domini Social Investments LLC;* b. 25 Jan. 1950, New York, NY; d. of Enzo Vice Domini and Margaret Cabot Domini (née Colt); m. Peter D. Kinder 1980 (divorced); two s.; ed Boston Univ.; stockbroker, Tucker Anthony & RL Day, Cambridge, Mass 1975–80, Moseley Securities, Cambridge 1980–85; portfolio man., Franklin R & D Corpn, Boston 1985–87; pvt. trustee, Loring, Wolcott & Coolidge 1987–; Chair. Bd Linder, Lydenberg, Domini & Co., Cambridge 1991–; f. Domino Social Equity Fund 1991; Founder, CEO and Pres. Domini Social Investments LLC, Boston 1996–; Chair. Pension Fund Episcopal Church, New York 1994–; mem. Governing Bd, Interfaith Center on Corp. Responsibility, New York 1985–95, Bd of Dirs, Social Investment Forum, Washington, DC 1994–, Bd Progressive Govt Inst. 2003–; mem. Nat. Community Capital Asscn, Boston Security Analysis Soc.; Hon. DHumLitt (Berkeley Divinity School at Yale) 2007, Hon. DBA (Northeastern Univ. Law School) 2007; Accioniste Award, Accion International 1992, SRI (Socially Responsible Investing) Service Award 1996, Best Mutual Funds Award, Money Magazine 1998, Theodore M. Hesburgh Award for Business Ethics, Notre Dame Univ. 2005, citation from Pres. Bill Clinton for work with UN Foundation 2005. *Publications include:* Ethical Investing 1984, Challenges of Wealth 1988, The Social Investment Almanac 1992, Investing for Good 1993, Socially Responsible Investing: Making a Difference and Making Money 2001; several articles on ethical investment in professional journals. *Leisure interests:* day-sailing, gardening. *Address:* Loring, Wolcott & Coolidge, 230 Congress Street, Floor 12, Boston, MA 02110-2437 (office); 7 Dana Street, Cambridge, MA 02138, USA (home). *Telephone:* (617) 622-2240 (home); (617) 547-3236 (home). *Fax:* (617) 523-6531 (office). *E-mail:* adomini@domini.com (office). *Website:* domini.com (office).

DOMLJAN, Zarko, PhD; Croatian editor and politician (retd); b. 14 Sept. 1932, Imotski; m. Iva Marjanovic; one d.; ed Zagreb Univ., Music Coll.; mem. Croatian

Nat. Theatre Orchestra 1955–57; Ed.-in-Chief and Deputy Dir Editorial Dept, Lexicographical Inst. 1968–86; Ed.-in-Chief Yugoslav Encyclopedia of Art and Encyclopedia of Croatian Art 1985–96, Life of Art Journal 1967–73; research adviser, Inst. of Art History 1987–90; mem. and Pres. Sabor (Parl. of Croatian Repub.) 1990–92, Vice-Pres. 1992–2000; Chair. Foreign Policy Bd; mem. State Council of Defence and Nat. Security and of Presidential Council; Grand Order of King Petar Krešimir IV 1992. *Publications include:* Architect Hugo Ehrlich 1979, Modern Architecture in Yugoslavia 1986, Umjetnička topografija Hrvatske, Krievci – grad i okolica (Art Topography of Croatia, Krievci – The Town and its Environs) (co-ed.) 1993, Visoko podignimo zastavu (Let's Raise High the Flag) (autobiog.) 2010. *Leisure interests:* tennis, mountain trekking. *Address:* Kukuljevićeva 32, 10000 Zagreb, Croatia (home). *Telephone:* (1) 4822775 (home). *E-mail:* zarko.domljan@zg.t-com.hr (office).

DOMMISSE, Ebbe, MA, PhD; South African newspaper editor and author; b. 14 July 1940, Riversdal; s. of Jan Dommisse and Anna Dommisse; m. Daléne Laubscher 1963; two s. one d.; ed Univ. of Stellenbosch, Grad. School of Journalism, Columbia Univ., USA; reporter, Die Burger, Cape Town 1961, Chief Sub-Ed. 1968, News Ed. 1971; Asst Ed. and Political Commentator, Beeld, Johannesburg (Founder-mem. of new Johannesburg daily) 1974; Asst Ed. Die Burger 1979, Sr Asst Ed. 1984, Ed. 1990–2000; Dir Helpmekaarfonds; mem. Akad. vir Wetenskap en Kuns. *Publications:* with Alf Ries: Broedertwis 1982, Leierstryd 1990; Anton Rupert 2005, Sir David Graaff 2012. *Leisure interests:* reading, the arts, ecology, tennis. *Address:* 25 Chesterfield Road, Oranjezicht, Cape Town 8001, South Africa (home). *Telephone:* (21) 4651237 (home). *E-mail:* edommisse@mweb.co.za.

DON MALAVO, Estanislao; Equatorial Guinean politician; *Presidential Counsellor for Financial Institutions and Communauté Économique et Monétaire de l'Afrique Centrale (CEMAC);* ed San Diego State Univ., USA; Deputy Minister of Finance and the Budget 2006–08, Minister of Finance and the Budget 2008, of Labour and Social Security 2010–13; Presidential Counsellor for Financial Inst. and Communauté Économique et Monétaire de l'Afrique Centrale (CEMAC) 2014–; Chair. Organizing Cttee for the Emerging Equatorial Guinea Symposium. *Address:* c/o Office of the President, Malabo, Equatorial Guinea. *Website:* www.guineaecuatorialpress.com.

DONAGHY, Baroness (Life Peer), cr. 2010, of Peckham in the London Borough of Southwark; **Rita Margaret Donaghy,** CBE, OBE, BA, FRSA; British public servant; b. (Rita Margaret Willis), 9 Oct. 1944, Bristol, England; d. of William Scott Willis and Margaret Brenda Howard; m. 1st James Columba Donaghy 1968 (divorced 1985); m. 2nd Ted (Edward) Easen-Thomas; ed Durham Univ.; Asst Registrar, then Perm. Sec. of Students' Union, Univ. of London Inst. of Educ. 1968–2000; Pres. Nat. and Local Govt Officers' Asscn (NALGO) 1989–90, TUC 2000; mem. Low Pay Comm. 1997–2000; Chair. Advisory, Conciliation and Arbitration Service (ACAS) 2000–07; Dir (non-exec.) King's Coll. Hosp. 2005–09; mem. Cttee on Standards in Public Life (Kelly Cttee) 2000–07, Acting Chair. 2007; Chair., Dept of Work & Pensions Inquiry on Fatal Accidents in Construction; conducted Review of Women's Nat. Comm. for Dept of Communities & Local Govt 2007; mem. (Labour), House of Lords 2010–, Chair. House of Lords Information Cttee, mem. House of Lords Select Cttee on Personal Services 2014–15, House of Lords EU Sub-cttee on Internal Markets 2015–; ind. consultant on human resources and employment relations; Fellow, Chartered Inst. of Personnel and Devt 2002; Hon. DUniv (Open Univ.) 2002, (Keele Univ.) 2004; Hon. DBA (Greenwich) 2005. *Publication:* One Death is Too Many: Inquiry into the Underlying Causes of Construction Fatal Accidents (report to Sec. of State for Work and Pensions) 2009. *Leisure interests:* theatre, gardening, reading. *Address:* House of Lords, Westminster, London, SW1A 0PW, England (office). *Telephone:* (20) 7703-4573 (home). *Fax:* (20) 7703-4573 (home). *E-mail:* donaghyr@parliament.uk (office). *Website:* www.parliament.uk/biographies/lords/baroness-donaghy/4166 (office).

DONAHOE, Patrick R., BS (Econs), MS; American business executive; b. Pittsburgh, Pa; m.; two c.; ed Univ. of Pittsburgh, Massachusetts Inst. of Tech. (Sloan Fellow); entered US Postal Service as a clerk in Pittsburgh, Pa, positions included Vice-Pres. of Allegheny Area Operations, Sr Vice-Pres. of Human Resources, Sr Vice-Pres. of Operations, Exec. Vice-Pres., Deputy Postmaster Gen. and COO –2010, Postmaster Gen. of USA and CEO US Postal Service 2010–15 (retd).

DONAHUE, Timothy M., BA; American telecommunications industry executive (retd); ed John Carroll Univ.; Pres. Paging Div., McCaw Cellular Communications (now AT&T Wireless) 1986–89, Pres. US Cen. Region 1989–91, Pres. Northeast Region and Gen. Man. AT&T Wireless 1991–96; Pres. and COO Nextel Communications Inc. 1996–99, Pres. and CEO 1999–2005, Exec. Chair. Sprint Nextel Corpn 2005–06 (retd); Dir, Eastman Kodak Co., NVR Inc., John Carroll Univ., Covidien, Tyco Healthcare from 2007.

DONALD, Dame Athene Margaret, DBE, PhD, FRS; British physicist and academic; *Master, Churchill College Cambridge;* b. (Athene Margaret Griffith), 15 May 1953, London, England; d. of Walter Griffith and Annette Marian Tylor; m. Matthew J. Donald 1976; one s. one d.; ed Camden School for Girls, London and Girton Coll., Cambridge; postdoctoral researcher, Cornell Univ., USA 1977–81; Fellow, Robinson Coll., Cambridge 1981–2014, Science and Eng Research Council Research Fellow, Univ. of Cambridge 1981–83, Royal Soc. Research Fellow 1983–85, Lecturer 1985–95, Reader 1985–98, Prof. of Experimental Physics 1998–, Deputy Vice-Chancellor 2009–, mem. Council Univ. of Cambridge 2009–14, Gender Equality Champion, Master of Churchill Coll. 2014–; Pres. British Science Asscn 2015–16; Chair. Steering Advisory Council of Dept Culture, Media and Sports 2015–17; mem. Governing Council, Inst. of Food Research 1999–2003; mem. Biotechnology and Biological Sciences Research Council Strategy Bd 2003–04; mem. Royal Soc. Council 2004–06, 2012–15, Chair. Royal Soc. Educ. Cttee 2010–14; Chair. Interdisciplinary Panel for REF21 2017–; mem. Research Assessment Exercise panel E19 (2008 exercise), Scientific Council of the European Research Council 2013–18; Trustee, Science Museum Group 2011–16; mem. Academia Europaea 2009; Hon. FInstP 2013; Hon. ScD (East Anglia) 2012, (Exeter) 2012, (Sheffield) 2013, (Univ. Coll. London) 2014, (Swansea) 2014, (Heriot Watt) 2015, (Manchester) 2015, (Liverpool) 2015, (Leeds) 2016, (Bath) 2017, (Open Univ.) 2017, (Brunel) 2018, (York) 2018; Samuel Locker Award in Physics, Univ. of Birmingham 1989, Charles Vernon Boys Prize, Inst. of Physics 1989, Rosenhain Medal and Prize, Inst. of Materials 1995, William Hopkins Prize, Cambridge Philosophical Soc. 2003, Mott Prize, Inst. of Physics 2005, Bakerian Lecturer, Royal Soc. 2006, L'Oréal-UNESCO Award For Women in Science (Europe) 2009, Faraday Medal, Inst. of Physics 2010, Lifetime Achievement Award, UKRC Women of Outstanding Achievement 2011. *Publications:* Liquid Crystalline Polymers (co-author) 1992 (second edition 2006), Starch: Structure and Function (co-author) 1997, Starch: Advances in Structure and Function (co-author) 2001; numerous articles in scientific journals. *Leisure interests:* music, walking, ornithology. *Address:* Department of Physics, Cavendish Laboratory, University of Cambridge, JJ Thomson Avenue, Cambridge, CB3 0HE (office); Churchill College, Storey's Way, Cambridge, CB3 0DS, England (office). *Telephone:* (1223) 337382 (office); (1223) 336142 (office). *Fax:* (1223) 337000 (office). *E-mail:* amd3@cam.ac.uk (office). *Website:* www.phy.cam.ac.uk/people/donalda.php (office); www.bss.phy.cam.ac.uk/~amd3 (office).

DONALD, Luke Campbell, MBE; British professional golfer; b. 7 Dec. 1977, Hemel Hempstead, Herts., England; s. of Colin Donald; m. Diane Antonopoulos 2007; three d.; ed Royal Grammar School, High Wycombe, Bucks., Northwestern Univ., USA; played junior golf at Hazlemere Golf Club and Beaconsfield Golf Club (club champion twice); joined College Prospects of America and took golf scholarship at Northwestern Univ. 1997; won individual NCAA Div. I Men's Golf Championships men's title 1999; turned professional 2001; plays mainly on US-based PGA (Professional Golfers Asscn) Tour 2001–, also mem. of European Tour 2003–; winner Southern Farm Bureau Classic 2002, Scandinavian Masters by Carlsberg 2004, Omega European Masters 2004, Honda Classic 2006, Madrid Masters 2010, WGC-Accenture Match Play Championship 2011, BMW PGA Championship 2011, 2012, Barclays Scottish Open 2011, Children's Miracle Network Hospitals Classic 2011, Race to Dubai 2011, Transitions Championship 2012; other wins include Target World Challenge (unofficial money-list event) 2005, Gary Player Invitational (with Sally Little) 2007; results in major championships: tied for third at US Masters 2005, tied for fourth 2011, tied for third at PGA Championship 2006, tied for fifth at British Open 2009, 2012; mem. winning Ryder Cup teams representing Europe 2004, 2006, 2010, 2012, WGC-World Cup team representing England 2004 (winners), 2005; reached top ten in Official World Golf Rankings for first time 2006; briefly highest ranked European golfer Jan. 2007; first became No. 1 in World Rankings after winning BMW PGA Championship May 2011; first man to win both US and European money lists in one year after finishing third at Dubai World Championship Dec. 2011; Hon. Life mem. European Tour 2012; Fred Haskins Award 1999, PGA Tour leading money winner 2011, Vardon Trophy 2011, Byron Nelson Award 2011, PGA Player of the Year 2011, PGA Tour Player of the Year 2011, European Tour Race to Dubai winner 2011, European Tour Golfer of the Year 2011. *Leisure interests:* painting and drawing, collecting contemporary art, Tottenham Hotspur Football Club. *Address:* c/o IMG, Building 6, Chiswick Park, 566 Chiswick High Road, London, W4 5HR, England.

DONALDSON, Roger; New Zealand (b. Australian) film director; b. 15 Nov. 1945, Ballarat, Australia; emigrated to New Zealand aged 19; established still photography business, then started making documentary films. *Television:* Winners and Losers (series of short dramas). *Films include:* Sleeping Dogs (also producer) 1977, Nutcase 1980, Smash Palace (also producer and writer) 1981, The Bounty 1984, Marie 1985, No Way Out 1987, Cocktail 1988, Cadillac Man (also producer) 1990, White Sands 1992, The Getaway 1994, Species 1995, Dante's Peak 1997, Thirteen Days 2000, The Recruit 2003, The World's Fastest Indian (also producer and writer) 2005, The Bank Job 2007, Seeking Justice 2011. *Address:* c/o CAA, 2000 Avenue of the Stars, Los Angeles, CA 90067, USA.

DONALDSON, Samuel (Sam) Andrew, BA; American broadcast journalist; b. 11 March 1934, El Paso, Tex.; s. of Samuel A. Donaldson and Chloe Hampson; m. 1st Billie K. Butler 1963; three s. one d.; m. 2nd Janice C. Smith 1983; ed Univ. of Texas, El Paso and Univ. of Southern California; radio and TV news reporter, anchorman, WTOP, Washington, DC 1961–67; Capitol Hill Corresp., ABC News, Washington, DC 1967–77, White House Corresp. 1977–89, Chief White House Corresp. 1998–99, News Contributor and Analyst 2010–; Pres. Advisory Board, Woodrow Wilson Int. Center for Scholars; Bd mem. Library of American Broadcasting, American Acad. of Achievement; Chair. Emer., Advisory Bd, H. Lee Moffett Cancer Center, Fla.; Broadcaster of the Year Award, Nat. Press Foundation 1998 and numerous other awards. *Television:* Anchor: World News Sunday 1979–89, Prime Time Live 1989–98, SamDonaldson@abcnews.com 1999–2001, The Sam Donaldson Show (ABC Radio Network) 2001–04, Politics Live 2004–10; Co-anchor: 20/20 Live (ABC Network) 1998–2000, This Week With Sam Donaldson and Cokie Roberts (ABC Network) 1996–2002, Politics Live (ABC News Now); panelist, This Week 1981–96, 2002–. *Publication:* Hold on Mr President 1987. *Address:* ABC News, 7 West 66th Street, New York, NY 10023, USA (office). *E-mail:* samdonaldson@abcnews.com (office). *Website:* www.abcnews.go.com (office).

DONALDSON, Sir Simon Kirwan, Kt, DPhil, FRS; British mathematician and academic; *Royal Society Research Professor, Imperial College London;* b. 20 Aug. 1957, Cambridge, England; s. of Peter Donaldson and Jane Stirland; m. Ana Nora Hurtado 1986; two s. one d.; ed Sevenoaks School, Kent, Pembroke Coll., Cambridge, Worcester Coll., Oxford; Jr Research Fellow, All Souls Coll., Oxford 1983–85; Wallis Prof. of Math., Univ. of Oxford 1985–98; Fellow, St Anne's Coll., Oxford 1985–98; Prof. of Pure Math., Imperial Coll., London 1998–, currently Royal Soc. Research Prof., Pres. Inst. of Math. Sciences 2003–; Perm. mem. Simons Center for Geometry and Physics, Stony Brook Univ., New York 2014–; Foreign mem. Royal Swedish Acad. of Sciences 2010; Fellow, American Math. Soc. 2012; Hon. Fellow, Pembroke Coll., Cambridge 1992, St Anne's Coll., Oxford 1999; Junior Whitehead Prize, London Math. Soc. 1985, Fields Medal 1986, Crafoord Prize (with S-T Yau) 1994, King Faisal Int. Prize (with M. S. Narasimhan) 2006, Nemmers Prize, Northwestern Univ. 2008, Shaw Prize (with C. H. Taubes) 2009, Breakthrough Prize in Mathematics 2015. *Publications:* The Geometry of Four-manifolds (with P. B. Kronheimer) 1990, Floer Homology Groups in Yang-Mills Theory 2002; numerous papers in math. journals. *Leisure interest:* sailing. *Address:* Room 674, Huxley Building, Department of Mathematics, Imperial

College, 180 Queen's Gate, London, SW7 2BT, England (office). *Telephone:* (20) 7594-8559 (office). *Fax:* (20) 7594-8517 (office). *E-mail:* s.donaldson@imperial.ac (office). *Website:* www3.imperial.ac.uk/people/s.donaldson (office); www2.imperial .ac.uk/~skdona (office).

DONALDSON, William H., BA, MA, MBA, CFA; American business executive and fmr government official; m. Jane Donaldson; three c.; ed Yale Univ., Harvard Business School; rifle platoon Commdr and later aide-de-camp to Commanding Gen. 1st Provisional Marine Air Ground Task Force, US Marine Corps 1953–55; Co-Founder Donaldson, Lufkin & Jenrette, New York 1959, Chair. and CEO 1959–73, Sr Advisor 1996–2000; Under-Sec., US State Dept, Washington, DC 1973–75; Counsel to Vice-Pres. 1975; Dean and William S. Beinecke Prof. of Man., Grad. School of Man., Yale Univ. 1975–80; Chair. and CEO Donaldson Enterprises Inc. (investment co.); New York Chair. 1980–90, 2001–; Chair. and CEO New York Stock Exchange 1990–95; Chair., Pres. and CEO Aetna Inc. 2000–02; Chair. SEC, New York 2003–05; Chair. Carnegie Endowment for International Peace 1999–2003; mem. Pres.'s Econ. Recovery Advisory Bd 2009–; mem. Advisory Bd, Tokarz Group Advisers LLC; Founding Dean, Yale School of Man., Yale Univ. 1975, Chair. Bd of Advisors 1995–2003; Trustee, Ford Foundation 1968–80, Yale Univ. 1970–75.

DONCHEV, Tomislav, MA, MBA; Bulgarian politician and lecturer; b. 6 Aug. 1973, Gabrovo; ed SS Cyril & Methodius Univ. of Veliko Tarnovo, Int. Summer School of Political Science and Int. Relations, Poland, Inst. in Negev, Israel, Acad. of Business Mentoring, Oxford, UK; volunteer, mem. of man. and staff of various non-governmental orgs in educ. and science and also collaborated with a sociological research agency 1995–2000; taught Psychology, Logic, Ethics and Philosophy at SS Cyril & Methodius High School of Humanities, Veliko Tarnovo 1997–99; Ed., Radio Gabrovo 1999–2000; Exec. Dir High-Tech. Business Incubator, Gabrovo 2000–04; a Program Dir, Open Society Inst. 2004–07; Mayor of Gabrovo 2007–10; Minister for Management of EU Funds 2010–13; mem. Grazhdani za Evropeysko Razvitie na Balgariya (GERB—Citizens for European Devt of Bulgaria); mem. Nat. Ass. (GERB) 2013–14; mem. European Parl. (EPP Group) May–Nov. 2014; Deputy Prime Minister for EU Funds and Econ. Policy Nov. 2014–17. *Address:* Grazhdani za Evropeysko Razvitie na Balgariya (Citizens for European Development of Bulgaria), 1463 Sofia, pl. Balgariya 1, NDK Administration Buillding 17, Bulgaria (office). *Telephone:* (2) 490-13-13 (office). *Fax:* (2) 490-09-51 (office). *E-mail:* pr@gerb.bg (office). *Website:* www.gerb.bg (office).

DONDRA, Henri Marie; Central African Republic politician and fmr international organization official; *Minister of Finance and the Budget;* b. 14 Aug. 1966, Kinshasa, Democratic Repub. of the Congo; m.; five c.; Head Cen. Agency, Banque Populaire Maroco Centrafricaine (BPMC), Bangui 1992–93, mem. Man. and Credit Cttee 1992–93, Head Int. Dept of Cen. Services 1993–96; joined Fonds Africain de Garantie et de Coopération Économique (FAGACE, trade promotion agency and guarantee fund), Cotonou 1997, Accountant and Dir of Finance 2002–05, Int. Trade Promotion Dir 2006–07, FAGACE Regional Rep. in Central African Repub. 2008–09, Dir-Gen. 2009–16; Pres. Professional Asscn of Guarantee Insts. of Africa (APIGA) 2014–; Minister of Finance and the Budget 2016–; Commdr, Cen. African Order of Merit 2014, Kt, Cen. African Order of Merit 2014, Grand Officer, Order of Community Merit of CEMAC 2017. *Leisure interests:* traveling, reading, music. *Address:* Ministry of Finance and the Budget, Avenue Abdel Gamal Nasser, BP 912, Bangui, Central African Republic (office). *Telephone:* 21-61-38-28 (office). *Fax:* 21-61-41-87 (office). *E-mail:* contact@finances.cf (office). *Website:* www.minfb.cf (office).

DONDUKOV, Alexander Nikolayevich, DTechSc; Russian engineer and politician; b. 29 March 1954, Kuybyshev (now Samara); engineer, then sr engineer, then leading constructor, Moscow Machine Construction Bureau (designers' office), Moscow 1977–85, Deputy Chief Constructor, Moscow Machine Construction factory Skorost 1985–91, Chief Constructor 1991, Head, Gen. Constructor 1991–93; Chair. Bd of Dirs Gen. Constructor A. S. Yakovlev Machine Designers' Office 1993–2000, 2001; mem. Govt Council for Industrial Policy 1994; mem. Congress of Russian Intelligentsia 1994; Minister of Industry, Science and Tech., Russian Fed. 2000–02; mem. Fed. Council (representing Belgorod) 2002–03.

DONE, Kenneth Stephen, AM; Australian artist; b. 29 June 1940, Sydney, NSW; s. of Clifford Wade Done and Lillian Maureen Done; m. Judith Ann Walker; one s. one d.; ed Katoomba and Mosman High Schools, Nat. Art School, Sydney; Creative Dir Advertising Samuelson Talbot, Sydney, J. Walter Thompson 1960–78; Chair. Ken Done Group of Cos 1979–; Goodwill Amb. for UNICEF Australia; Paul Harris Fellow, Rotary International; Hon. Fellow, Design Inst. of Australia 1999; Hon. Bachelor of Design (Sydney Graphics Coll.) 2002; NSW Tourism Award 1986, Rotary Award for Excellence 1993, Spirit of Australia Award 1993, Cannes Gold Lion Award, Export Hero Award, Westpac Banking Corpn 1999, Life Fellow, Medal Powerhouse Museum 2002, Japanese Foreign Minister's Award 2007. *Publications:* Ken Done: Paintings and Drawings 1975–87, Craftsman House 1992, Ken Done Paintings (1990–94) 1994, Ken Done: The Art of Design 1994, Ken Done's Sydney, 20 Years of Painting 1999, The Art of Ken Done, Craftsman House 2002. *Leisure interests:* golf, swimming, diving, travelling. *Address:* 1 Hickson Road, The Rocks, NSW 2000, Australia (office). *Telephone:* (2) 8274-4599 (office). *Fax:* (2) 8274-4545 (office). *E-mail:* gallery@done.com.au (office). *Website:* kendone.com.au (office).

DONG, Kejun; Chinese woodcut artist; b. 18 Feb. 1939, Chongqing, Sichuan; s. of Dong Xueyuan and Gue Ximing; m. Lü Hengfen 1969; one s.; Dir of Chinese Artistic Asscn; Standing Dir Chinese Woodcut Asscn; Vice-Chair., Guizhow Artistic Asscn, Guizhou Provincial Artists Asscn, Visiting Prof., Guizhou Folk Univ.; Chair. Guiyang Artistic Asscn; Vice-Pres. Acad. of Painting and Calligraphy; mem. Standing Cttee of Guizhou Br. of CPPCC; Vice-Chair. Guizhou Prov. Br. Artists' Assoc. 1988; Chair. Artists' Assoc. Guiyang Br. 1988; Council mem. Artists' Assoc. 1988; Hon. Dean, Guizhou Provincial Art Acad.; Prizewinner, 9th Nat. Woodcut Exhbn 1986, Prize for Outstanding Work at the Ninth China Exhbn of Printmaking, Lu Xun Prize for Printmaking, Guizhou Cultural and Arts Awards; First Grade Nat. Artist. *Works include:* Spring Returns to the Miao Mountain 1979, A Close Ball 1979, An Illustration of the Continuation of Feng Xuefeng's Fables (a hundred pieces) 1980, Company 1981, Go Back Drunkenly 1982, Lively Spring 1983, The Miao Nat Sisters in Their Splendid Costume 1985, Contemporary Totem-1 1986, Mountain Breath 1986, A White Cottage 1987, Sunny Rain 1988, A Hundred Pieces of Coloured Inkwash Drawings 1991–92, The Big Sleep 1993, The Bird Market 1993, Illusion 1993, Eagle 1994, Man and Horse 1995, Going to Market 1995. *Publications:* Dong Kejun Woodcut Works, Selected Paintings of Dong Kejun 1992, Selected Chinese Coloured Inkwash Paintings 1995. *Leisure interests:* literature, music, film and dance. *Address:* Guiyang Artistic Asscn, 27 Road Shizi, Guiyang, Guizhou Prov., People's Republic of China.

DONG, Mingzhu; Chinese business executive; *Chairman and President, Gree Electric Appliances Inc.;* joined Gree Electric Appliances Inc. (then called Haili), Zhuhai 1990, later Business Man., later Departmental Man. of Business Dept, later Vice-Gen. Man., Gen. Man. 2001, Pres. 2001–12, Chair. and Pres. 2012–; Chair. Female Asscn of Entrepreneurs, Zhuhai City 2002–; Deputy Dir Chinese Household Appliances Asscn; mem. Female Asscn of Entrepreneurs, Guangdong, currently Vice-Chair.; mem. Standing Cttee Zhuhai Political Consultative Conf.; Del., 10th NPC 2003–; Nat. Excellent Woman Worker 1998, Guangdong Prov. Excellent Female Man. 1999, Nat. May 1 Labour Medal, received title of Excellent Woman in Guangdong Prov. 2000, Chinese Outstanding Woman 2001, elected one of Female Entrepreneurs of All Time in China 2002. *Publication:* Lay Out in the World (autobiog., adapted for TV by China-Central TV Station). *Address:* Gree Electric Appliances Inc., 6 West Jinji Road, Qianshan, Zhuhai 519070, Guangdong Province, People's Republic of China (office). *Telephone:* (756) 8614883 (office). *Fax:* (756) 8614998 (office). *E-mail:* gree@gree.com (office). *Website:* www.gree.com.cn (office).

DONG, Wenbiao; Chinese economist and business executive; b. 1957; fmr Sec. CCP Cttee, Vice-Pres. and Pres. China Minsheng Banking Corpn Ltd, Chair. –2015; Vice-Chair. All China Fed. of Industry and Commerce, China Civilian Chamber of Commerce; fmr Chair. and Pres. Haitong Securities Co. Ltd; fmr Man. Dir Zhengzhou Br. of Bank of Communications; fmr Dir, Bank of Communications; fmr Deputy Dean Henan Inst. of Financial Man.; mem. Standing Cttee 12th CPPCC Nat. Cttee; fmr Deputy Dir CPPCC Econ. Cttee, mem. CPPCC Nat. Cttee. *Address:* c/o China Minsheng Banking Corporation Ltd, 2 Fuxingmennei Avenue, Beijing 100873, People's Republic of China. *E-mail:* webmaster@cmbc.com.cn.

DONG, Zigang, MD, MS, DrPH; American biologist and academic; *Hormel-Knowlton Professor and Executive Director, Hormel Institute, University of Minnesota;* ed Henan Medical Univ., Columbia Univ.; Guest Prof., The First Mil. Medical Univ., Guangzhou, China 2000–06; Hon. Prof., The Fourth Mil. Univ., Xian, Shanxi, China 2000; Hormel-Knowlton Prof. and Exec. Dir Hormel Inst., Univ. of Minn. 2001–, also McKnight Presidential Prof. in Cancer Prevention 2006–, Prof., Dept of Biochemistry, Molecular Biology and Biophysics 2009–, I.J. Holton Prof., Hormel Inst. 2013–, Dir China-US Hormel Cancer Inst. 2014–; Assoc. Ed. Molecular Carcinogenesis 2005–; mem. American Asscn for Cancer Research 1988–, American Soc. for Biochemistry and Molecular Biology 1995–, NIH Reviewer Reserve 1997–, Study Section of Cancer Centers for NIH 2000, Grant Review Panel of American Inst. for Cancer Research 2000, Working Group for RAPID (Rapid Access for Preventive Intervention Devt) programme of Nat. Cancer Inst. 2002, Special Emphasis Study Section of NIH 2002, Chemical/Dietary Prevention Study Section of NIH 2014–, Cancer Prevention Review Cttee of Cancer Prevention Research Inst. of Texas 2014–; mem. Editorial Bd Biofactors 2003–, Journal of Biological Chemistry 2011–; Hon. Prof., The Fourth Mil. Univ., Xian, China 2000–; NIH Merit Award 2008–14, Oh Dang Award, Pharmaceutical Soc. of Korea 2011, Stars in Nutrition and Cancer Lecturer Award, Division of Cancer Prevention, Nat. Cancer Inst. 2012, Int. Science and Tech. Collaboration Award, Hunan, China 2013, Yellow River Friendship Award, China 2014. *Publications:* numerous articles in scientific journals. *Address:* Hormel Institute, University of Minnesota, 801 16th Avenue, NE, Austin, MN 55912, USA (office). *Telephone:* (507) 437-9600 (office). *Fax:* (507) 437-9606 (office). *E-mail:* dongx004@umn.edu (office); zgdong@hi.umn.edu (office). *Website:* www.cancer.umn.edu/research/profiles/dong.html (office); www.hi.umn.edu (office).

DONNELLAN, Declan; British theatre and opera director; b. 4 Aug. 1953, Manchester; ed Univ. of Cambridge; called to Bar (Middle Temple) 1978; freelance theatre productions include Don Giovanni (Scottish Opera Go Round), A Masked Ball (Opera 80), Rise and Fall of the City of Mahagonny (Wexford Festival), Macbeth and Philoctetes (Nat. Theatre of Finland); co-f. Cheek By Jowl (production co.) 1981, Artistic Dir 1981–; productions with Cheek By Jowl include Racine's Andromache, Corneille's The Cid, Twelfth Night, A Midsummer Night's Dream, Hamlet, As You Like It, Measure for Measure, Much Ado About Nothing 1998 and his own trans. of Musset's Don't Fool With Love and The Blind Men; also wrote and directed Lady Betty and Sara Sampson; Assoc. Dir Nat. Theatre (NT) 1989–97; work for NT includes Fuente Ovejuna 1989, Peer Gynt, Sweeney Todd 1993, Angels in America, Perestroika 1993, School for Scandal 1998; Dir Falstaff, Salzburg Festival 2001; Dir Le Cid by Corneille, Avignon Festival; Dir Boris Godunov and Twelfth Night, Russian Theatre Confed.; recipient of six Olivier Awards, Time Out Award (with Nick Ormerod) for Angels in America 1992, Observer Award for Outstanding Achievement, as well as awards in Paris, New York and Moscow. *Film:* Bel Ami 2012. *Publications:* The Actor and The Target. *Address:* Cheek by Jowl Theatre Company, The Barbican Centre, Silk Street, London, EC2Y 8DS, England. *Telephone:* (20) 7382-2391 (office). *Website:* www .cheekbyjowl.com (office).

DONNELLY, Christopher Nigel, CMG, TD, BA; British defence, security and foreign affairs specialist; *Director, Institute for Statecraft;* b. 10 Nov. 1946, Rochdale, Lancs.; s. of Anthony Donnelly and Dorothy M. Morris; m. Jill Norris 1971; one s. one d.; ed Cardinal Langley School, Middleton, Lancs., Univ. of Manchester; Instructor, Royal Mil. Acad. Sandhurst (RMAS) 1969–72; Sr Lecturer, Soviet Studies Research Centre, RMAS 1972–79, Dir 1979–89; TA (Int. Corps) 1970–93; Adjunct Prof., Carnegie Mellon Univ. 1985–89, Georgia Tech. Univ. 1989–93; Special Adviser for Cen. and E European Affairs to Sec.-Gen. of NATO 1989–2003; Founder and Head of Advanced Research and Assessment Group, Defence Acad. of the UK 2003–07, Sr Fellow 2007–10; currently Dir Inst. for Statecraft, London; Hon. Col, Specialist Group Mil. Intelligence; Commdr (Grand Cross), Order of the Grand Duke Gediminas (Lithuania) 2002. *Publications:* Red Banner 1989, War and the Soviet Union 1990, Gorbachev's Revolution 1991, Nations, Alliances and Security 2004; numerous articles on Russian and

Eastern European defence and security issues. *Leisure interest:* field sports. *Address:* The Institute for Statecraft, 2 Temple Place, London, WC2R 3BD, England (office). *E-mail:* cdonnelly@statecraft.org.uk (office). *Website:* www.statecraft.org.uk (office).

DONNELLY, Joseph (Joe) Simon, Sr, BA, JD; American lawyer, politician and business executive; b. 29 Sept. 1955, Massapequa, NY; m. Jill Donnelly; two c.; ed Univ. of Notre Dame and Notre Dame Law School, Washington and Lee Univ.; practised law –1996; ran campaign for Indiana Attorney Gen. 1988, lost at Democratic state convention; served on Indiana State Election Bd 1988–89; also ran unsuccessful campaign for Indiana State Senate 1990; opened Marking Solutions (printing and rubber stamp co.) 1996; served on local school bd 1997–2001, Pres. 2000–01; mem. US House of Reps for 2nd Congressional Dist of Indiana 2007–13, mem. Cttee on Financial Services, Cttee on Veterans' Affairs; Senator from Indiana 2013–19; Democrat. *Address:* c/o 720 Hart Senate Office Building, Washington, DC 20510, USA (office).

DONNER, Jörn Johan, BA; Finnish film director, writer, producer, politician and diplomatist; b. 5 Feb. 1933, Helsinki; s. of Dr Kai Donner and Greta von Bonsdorff; m. 1st Inga-Britt Wik 1954 (divorced 1962); m. 2nd Jeanette Bonnier 1974 (divorced 1988); m. 3rd Bitte Westerlund 1995; five s. one d.; ed Univ. of Helsinki; worked as writer and film dir in Finland and Sweden, writing own film scripts; contrib. and critic to various Scandinavian and int. journals; CEO Jörn Donner Productions 1966–; mem. Helsinki City Council 1969–72, 1984–92; Dir Swedish Film Inst., Stockholm 1972–75, Exec. Producer 1975–78, Man. Dir 1978–82; Chair. Bd Finnish Film Foundation 1981–83, 1986–89, 1992–95; mem. Bd Marimekko Textiles and other cos; mem. Parl. 1987–95, Vice-Chair. Foreign Affairs Cttee 1991–95, Chair. Finnish EFTA Parliamentarians 1991–95; Consul-Gen. of Finland, Los Angeles, USA 1995–96; mem. European Parl. 1996–99; mem. Municipal Council of Ekenäs 1999–2003, Municipal Council of Helsinki 2004–07, 2017–; mem. Parl. 2003, 2013–15; several literary awards. *Films include:* as dir: A Sunday in September (Venice Film Festival Best First Film 1963) 1963, To Love 1964, Adventure Starts Here 1965, Rooftree 1967, Black on White 1968, Sixty-nine 1969, Portraits of Women 1970, Anna 1970, Images of Finland 1971, Tenderness 1972, Three Scenes with Ingmar Bergman 1976, The Bergman File 1975–77, Men Can't Be Raped 1978, Dirty Story 1984, Letters from Sweden 1987, Ingmar Bergman, a Conversation 1998, The President 2000, The Interrogation 2009; numerous films as producer including: Fanny och Alexander (Fanny and Alexander) (Academy Award for Producer of Best Foreign Language Film 1984) 1982, The Faceless Man 1995, Abandoned Houses, Empty Homes 2000, Armi Alive 2005, Raja 1918 2007, Armi Alive! 2014, Memory of Ingmar Bergman 2018. *Television:* host of talk shows (Sweden and Finland) 1974–95. *Publications include:* 65 books, including Father and Son (Finlandia Prize 1985), Report from Berlin 1958, The Personal Vision of Ingmar Bergman 1962, Bergman: PM 2010, Notes on Marshal Mannerheim 2011, Mammutti 2013. *Leisure interest:* fishing. *Address:* PO Box 214, 00171 Helsinki (office); Rauhankatu 3F11, 00170 Helsinki, Finland (home). *Telephone:* 400-205606 (mobile) (office). *E-mail:* j.donner@surfnet.fi (home).

DONNER, Richard; American director and producer; b. (Richard D. Schwartzberg), 24 April 1930, New York; m. Lauren Shuler Donner 1986; actor off-Broadway; collaborated with dir Martin Ritt on TV adaptation of Somerset Maugham's Of Human Bondage; moved to Calif. and began directing commercials, industrial films and documentaries. *Films include:* X-15 1961, Salt and Pepper 1968, Twinky 1969, The Omen 1976, Superman 1978, Superman II 1980, Inside Moves 1981, The Toy 1982, Ladyhawke 1985, The Goonies 1985, Lethal Weapon 1987, Scrooged 1988, Lethal Weapon 2 1989, Radio Flyer 1991, The Final Conflict (exec. producer) 1991, The Lost Boys (exec. producer) 1991, Delirious (exec. producer) 1991, Lethal Weapon 3 1992, Free Willy (co-exec. producer) 1993, Maverick 1994, Assassins 1995, Free Willy 3: The Rescue, Conspiracy Theory 1997, Double Tap (producer) 1997, Lethal Weapon 4 1998 (also producer), Made Men (producer) 1999, Any Given Sunday (producer) 1999, X-Men (producer) 2000, Blackheart (producer) 1999, Timeline (also producer) 2003, 16 Blocks 2006, X-Men Origins: Wolverine (exec. producer), Black & White in Colors (assoc. producer) 2012. *Television includes:* (films) Portrait of a Teenage Alcoholic, Senior Year, A Shadow in the Streets, Tales from the Crypt presents Demon Knight (co-exec. producer), Any Given Sunday 1999, X-Men 2000 (exec. producer); (series episodes) Have Gun Will Travel, Perry Mason, Cannon, Get Smart, The Fugitive, Kojak, Bronk, Lucas Tanner, Gilligan's Island, Man From U.N.C.L.E., Wild Wild West, Twilight Zone, The Banana Splits, Combat, Two Fisted Tales, Conspiracy Theory. *Address:* The Donner Company, 9350 Wilshire Blvd, Suite 302, Beverly Hills, CA 90212-3204, USA.

DONNET, Philippe; French business executive; *Group CEO, Managing Director and General Manager, Assicurazioni Generali SpA;* b. 26 July 1960; began career with AXA in France 1985, served as CEO of AXA RE for two years and of AXA Assicurazioni for three years, CEO AXA for Southern Europe, the Middle East, Canada and Latin America 2001–03, CEO AXA Japan 2003–06, CEO Asia-Pacific region for AXA Group 2006–13; Country Man. of Italy and CEO Generali Italia, Assicurazioni Generali SpA 2013–16, Group CEO, Man. Dir and Gen. Man. Assicurazioni Generali SpA 2016–, mem. Group Man. Cttee; mem. Bd of Dirs Vivendi Group; Co-founder and Partner, HLD Private Equity; certified mem. Institut des Actuaires Français. *Address:* Assicurazioni Generali SpA, Piazza Duca degli Abruzzi 2, 34132 Trieste, Italy (office). *Telephone:* (40) 6711 (office). *Fax:* (40) 671600 (office). *E-mail:* info@generali.com (office). *Website:* www.generali.com (office).

DONOGHUE, Denis, PhD; Irish literary critic and academic; *Professor Emeritus, Department of English, New York University;* b. 1 Dec. 1928, Tullow, Co. Carlow; m. Frances Donoghue; three s. five d.; m. 2nd Melissa Malouf; ed Univ. Coll., Dublin, Univ. of Cambridge; Admin. Office, Irish Dept of Finance 1951–54; Asst Lecturer, Univ. Coll., Dublin 1954–57, Coll. Lecturer 1957–62, 1963–64, Prof. of Modern English and American Literature 1965–79; Visiting Scholar, Univ. of Pennsylvania 1962–63; Univ. Lecturer, Univ. of Cambridge and Fellow, King's Coll. 1964–65; Henry James Prof. of English and American Letters, New York Univ., USA 1979, now Prof. Emer.; mem. Int. Cttee of Asscn of Univ. Profs of English; Hon. DLitt (Nat. Univ. of Ireland) 1989; BBC Reith Lecturer 1982. *Publications include:* The Third Voice 1959, Connoisseurs of Chaos 1965, The Ordinary Universe 1968, Emily Dickinson 1968, Jonathan Swift 1969, Yeats 1971, Thieves of Fire 1974, Sovereign Ghost: Studies in Imagination 1978, Ferocious Alphabets 1981, The Arts Without Mystery 1983, We Irish: Essays on Irish Literature and Society 1987, Walter Pater: Lover of Strange Souls 1995, The Practice of Reading 1998, Words Alone: The Poet T. S. Eliot 2000, Adam's Curse: Reflections on Literature and Religion 2001, Speaking of Beauty 2003, The American Classics: A Personal Essay 2005, On Eloquence 2008, Irish Essays 2011, Warrenpoint 2013, Metaphor 2014; contribs to reviews and journals and ed. of three vols. *Address:* English Department, New York University, 726 Broadway (7th Floor), New York, NY 10003, USA (office); Gaybrook, North Avenue, Mount Merrion, Dublin, Ireland (home). *Telephone:* (212) 998-3950 (office). *E-mail:* dd1@nyu.edu (office). *Website:* as.nyu.edu (office).

DONOHO, David Leigh, BS, PhD; American professor of statistics; *Professor of Statistics and Anne T. and Robert M. Bass Professor in the Humanities and Sciences, Stanford University;* b. 5 March 1957, Los Angeles, Calif.; ed Princeton and Harvard Univs; mem. Faculty, Univ. of California, Berkeley 1984–90; Prof. of Statistics, Stanford Univ. 1990–, Anne T. and Robert M. Bass Prof. in the Humanities and Sciences 2002–; mem. NAS; Foreign Assoc., Acad. des sciences 2009; Fellow, American Acad. of Arts and Sciences 1992, Soc. for Industrial and Applied Math. (SIAM) 2009, American Math. Soc. 2012; Hon. DSc (Univ. of Chicago) 2009, (Univ. of Waterloo) 2016, (Technion) 2017, Dr hc École Polytechnique Fédérale de Lausanne 2012; MacArthur Fellow 1990, COPSS Presidents' Award 1994, John von Neumann Prize, SIAM 2001, Norbert Wiener Prize in Applied Math., SIAM and American Math. Soc. 2010, Shaw Prize in Math. Sciences 2013, Carl Friedrich Gauss Prize 2018. *Publications:* numerous papers in professional journals. *Address:* Statistics Department, Stanford University, Sequoia Hall 390, Serra Mall, Stanford, CA 94305, USA (office). *Telephone:* (650) 723-3350 (office). *Fax:* (650) 725-8977 (office). *E-mail:* donoho@stat.stanford.edu (office). *Website:* statweb.stanford.edu/~donoho (office).

DONOHOE, Amanda; British actress; b. (Joanna M. Donohoe), 29 June 1962, London; d. of Ted Donohoe and Joanna Donohoe; ed Francis Holland School for Girls, London, Cen. School of Speech & Drama, London; mem. Royal Exchange Theatre, Manchester; Broadway debut, Uncle Vanya 1995; Hon. DLit (Univ. of East Anglia) 2007. *Films include:* Foreign Body 1986, Castaway 1986, The Lair of the White Worm 1988, Tank Malling 1989, Diamond Skulls 1989, The Rainbow 1989, The Laughter of God 1990, Paper Mask 1990, The Madness of King George 1994, Liar Liar 1997, One Night Stand 1997, Stardust 1998, The Real Howard Spitz 1998, I'm Losing You 1998, Glory Glory 2000, Circus 2000, Wild About Harry 2000, Phoenix Blue 2001, Starship Troopers 3: Marauder 2008, The Calling 2009, Trafficker 2013, Blue Iguana 2018. *Television includes:* Star Quality 1985, Frankie and Johnnie 1985, An Affair in Mind 1988, Game, Set, and Match (series) 1988, L.A. Law (series) (Golden Globe Award for Best Performance by an Actress in a Supporting Role in a Series, Miniseries or Motion Picture Made for Television 1992) 1990–92, Shame 1992, It's Nothing Personal 1993, Briefest Encounter 1993, The Substitute 1993, A Woman's Guide to Adultery 1993, Shame II: The Secret 1995, Deep Secrets 1996, The Thorn Birds: The Missing Years 1996, A Knight in Camelot 1998, Batman Beyond: The Movie 1999, Rock the Boat 2000, In the Beginning 2000, Lucky Day 2002, Murder City (series) 2004, Bad Girls (series) 2006, Love Trap (series) 2007, Emmerdale (series) 2009, Toast of London (series) 2013–14, Air Force One Is Down (mini-series) 2013, Pramface (series) 2014. *Plays include:* Cymbeline 1984, Great Expectations 1984, The Admirable Crichton 1984, Uncle Vanya 1996, Miss Julie 1996, The Graduate 2001, Hedda Gabler 2001, Teeth 'n' Smiles 2002, Star Quality 2011. *Address:* c/o Artists Rights Group, 4A Exmoor Street, London, W10 6BD, England (office). *Telephone:* (20) 7436-6400 (office). *Fax:* (20) 7436-6700 (office). *E-mail:* argall@argtalent.com (office). *Website:* argtalent.com (office).

DONOHOE, Paschal; Irish politician; *Minister for Finance, and for Public Expenditure and Reform;* b. 19 Sept. 1974, Phibsborough, Dublin; s. of Jimmy Donohoe and Caitlín Donohoe; m. Justine Davey; one s. one d.; ed Univ. of Dublin, Trinity Coll.; worked with Procter & Gamble in England 1997–2003, becoming Dir of Sales and Marketing; worked at Diageo Ireland 2003; mem. Dublin City Council 2004–07; mem. Seanad Éireann (senate) 2007–11; mem. Dáil Éireann (parl.) for Dublin Central 2011–; Minister for European Affairs 2013–14, Minister for Transport, Tourism and Sport 2014–15, Minister for Public Expenditure & Reform 2015–, also Minister for Finance 2017–; mem. Fine Gael. *Address:* Department of Finance, Government Bldgs, Upper Merrion St, Dublin 2, D02 R583, Ireland (office). *Telephone:* (1) 6767571 (office). *Fax:* (1) 6789936 (office). *E-mail:* webmaster@finance.gov.ie (office). *Website:* www.finance.gov.ie (office); paschaldonohoe.ie.

DONOHOE, Peter Howard, CBE, BMus, ARCM, FRNCM; British pianist; b. 18 June 1953, Manchester; s. of Harold Donohoe and Marjorie Donohoe (née Travis); m. Elaine Margaret Burns 1980; one d.; ed Chetham's School of Music, Royal Manchester Coll. of Music, Univ. of Leeds, studied with Derek Wyndham and Yvonne Loriod, Paris; professional solo pianist 1974–; appears several times each season with major symphony orchestras in London and rest of UK and has performed regularly at Promenade Concerts 1979–; performances with LA Philharmonic, Chicago, Boston, Pittsburgh, Cincinnati, Dallas, Detroit and Cleveland orchestras and in Europe with Berlin Philharmonic and Symphony, Leipzig Gewandhaus, Dresden Philharmonic, Vienna Symphony, Czech Philharmonic, Swedish Radio and Radio France Philharmonic orchestras and Maggio Musicale Fiorentino; has also performed at Edin. Festival, Schleswig-Holstein Music Festival, La Roque d'Anthéron, France, and Festival of the Ruhr; Founder and Artistic Dir British Piano Concerto Foundation; Vice-Pres. Birmingham Conservatoire of Music; mem. jury, International Tchaikovsky Competition 2011, 2015; Hon. DMus (Birmingham) 1992, (Univ. of Cen. England), (East Anglia), (Leicester), (Open Univ.); Hon. DLitt (Warwick) 1996; Moscow Int. Tchaikovsky Competition (jt winner) 1982, Grand Prix Int. du Disque (Liszt), Gramophone Concerto Award (Tchaikovsky). *Recordings include:* Messiaen's Turangalila Symphony 1986, Dominic Muldowney's Piano Concerto 1986, Tchaikovsky's Piano Concerto No. 2 (Gramophone magazine's Concerto of the Year 1988) 1986, Brahms Piano Concerto No. 1, Liszt, Berg and Bartók Sonatas, Beethoven, Diabelli Variations and Sonata Opus 101, Rachmaninov Preludes, Four British Concertos with Northern Sinfonia, Foulds' Dynamic Triptych, pieces by Rawsthorne, Bliss,

Darnton, Rowley, Ferguson, Gerhard, Alwyn, Pitfield and Harty. *Leisure interests:* golf, helping young musicians, jazz. *Address:* Ikon Arts Management Ltd, 2–6 Baches Street, London, N1 6DN, England (office). *Telephone:* (20) 7354-9199 (office). *E-mail:* costa@ikonarts.com (office). *Website:* www.peter-donohoe.com.

DONOHUE, Craig S., BA, LLM, JD; American lawyer and business executive; *Executive Chairman, Options Clearing Corporation;* b. 9 Oct. 1961; m.; three c.; ed Drake Univ., Illinois Inst. of Tech., John Marshall Law School, Northwestern Univ.; Assoc., McBride, Baker & Coles, Chicago; attorney, Chicago Mercantile Exchange (CME) 1989–95, Vice-Pres. and Assoc. Gen. Counsel CME Holdings 1995–97, Vice-Pres. Div. of Market Regulation 1997–98, Sr Vice-Pres. and Gen. Counsel CME 1998–2000, Man. Dir Business Devt and Corp./Legal Affairs, CME 2000–01, Man. Dir and Chief Admin. Officer CME 2001–, CME Holdings Aug. 2001, Exec. Vice-Pres. and Chief Admin. Officer, Office of the CEO, CME Holdings and of CME 2002–03, mem. Bd of Dirs and CEO CME Holdings and of CME 2004–06, CEO CME Group Inc. (following merger with Chicago Bd of Trade) 2006–12; Exec. Chair. and CEO Options Clearing Corpn 2014–18, Exec. Chair. 2014–; fmr Vice-Chair. and Chair. Nat. Council on Econ. Educ.; fmr mem. Bd of Dirs Execs' Club of Chicago, Chicagoland Chamber of Commerce; mem. Global Markets Advisory Cttee, Commodity Futures Trading Comm., Advisory Council, Youth Services of Glenview/Northbrook. *Address:* Options Clearing Corpn (OCC), 125 S Franklin Street, Suite 1200, Chicago, IL 60606, USA (office). *Telephone:* (312) 322-6200 (office). *Fax:* (312) 977-0611 (office). *E-mail:* investorservices@theocc.com (office). *Website:* www.theocc.com (office).

DONOVAN, Shaun L., BA, MA, MPA; American architect and government official; b. 24 Jan. 1966, New York City; m. Liza Donovan (née Gilbert); two s.; ed Harvard Univ.; worked as an architect in New York and Italy; Asst Dir Community Preservation Corpn, New York City; Special Asst US Dept of Housing and Urban Devt, Washington, DC 1998–2000, Deputy Asst Sec. for Multifamily Housing 2000–01; acting Fed. Housing Admin Commr during the presidential transition 2000–01; Visiting Scholar, New York Univ.; consultant to Millennial Housing Comm., Washington, DC 2001–02; Man. Dir of FHA lending and affordable housing investments, Prudential Mortgage Capital Co. 2002–04; Commr New York City Dept of Housing Preservation and Devt 2004–08; US Sec. of Housing and Urban Devt, Washington, DC 2009–14; Dir, Office of Man. and Budget 2014–17.

DONSKOI, Sergei; Russian politician and government official; b. 13 Oct. 1968, Elektrostal, Moscow Oblast; ed Gubkin State Acad. of Oil and Gas; microprocessor-based systems lab engineer at Gazpriboravtomatika design bureau 1992–93; worked at financial cos Your Securities and SINT 1993–96; worked at Prema-Invest as dealer and analyst in Financial Instruments Dept, later Head of Information Analysis Section, leading analyst at Analysis and Marketing Dept 1996–98; adviser at Fuel and Energy Ministry, Deputy Head of Dept, then Head of Production Sharing Agreements Dept 1999–2000; worked at LUKoil's Main Dept for Investment and Finance and Main Dept for Corp. Financing and Investment 2000–01; Head of Dept at Zarubezhneft 2001–05; Head of Econs and Finance Dept, Ministry of Natural Resources 2005–08, Deputy Minister for Natural Resources and Environmental Protection 2008–11, Minister of Natural Resources and Ecology 2012–18; Chief Exec. Rosgeologia (state geology holding co.) 2011–12; Deputy Chair. State Comm. for Arctic Devt 2015–; mem. Bd of Dirs Rosgeologiya. *Address:* c/o Ministry of Natural Resources and Ecology, 123993 Moscow, ul. B. Gruzinskaya 4/6, Russia.

DOOCEY, Baroness (Life Peer), cr. 2010, of Hampton in the London Borough of Richmond upon Thames; **Elizabeth (Dee) Doocey,** OBE; British politician and business executive; Dir of Finance and Admin, Liberal Party HQ late 1970s–early 1980s; fmr Group Man. Dir of an int. fashion co. with operations in London, Hong Kong and China; set up own co. DD Enterprises Management Consultancy; Councillor, London Borough of Richmond upon Thames 1986–94; Finance Dir of the Liberal Party for ten years; Financial Advisor to the Liberal Parl. Party for eight years; unsuccessful cand. for SW London constituency in London Ass. Elections 2004, elected as a London-wide mem. of London Ass. 2004–12, Chair. Economy, Culture and Sport Cttee 2004–10, 2011–12, Chair. London Ass. 2010–11, Deputy Chair. 2011–12; mem. Metropolitan Police Authority 2006–, Chair. Finance and Olympics Cttees 2005–12; mem. House of Lords, mem. Olympic and Paralympic Legacy Cttee 2013, Draft Modern Slavery Bill 2014, Leader's Group on Governance 2015–; mem. Home Office Olympic Security Bd, HM's Inspectorate of Constabulary External Reference Group, Advisory Bd, Asscn for Consultancy & Eng; Mayor's Rep., Bd of London Youth Games. *Address:* GLA, City Hall, The Queen's Walk, London, SE1 2AA (office); House of Lords, Westminster, London, SW1A 0PW, England. *Telephone:* (20) 7983-4797 (office); (20) 7219-5353. *E-mail:* dee.doocey@london.gov.uk (office). *Website:* www.london.gov.uk/profile/dee-doocey (office); deedoocey.co.uk.

DOODY, Margaret Anne, BA, MA, PhD; Canadian academic and writer; *John and Barbara Glynn Family Professor of Literature, University of Notre Dame;* b. 21 Sept. 1939, St John, NB; d. of Rev. Hubert Doody and Anne Ruth Cornwall; ed Centreville Regional High School, NB, Dalhousie Univ., Lady Margaret Hall, Oxford, UK; Instructor in English 1962–64; Asst Prof., English Dept, Univ. of Victoria, British Columbia 1968–69; Lecturer, Univ. Coll. of Swansea, UK 1969–77; Visiting Assoc. Prof. of English, Univ. of California, Berkeley 1976–77, Assoc. Prof. 1977–80; Prof. of English, Princeton Univ. 1980–89, Stanley Kelley Jr Visiting Prof. for Distinguished Teaching 2008–09; Andrew W. Mellon Prof. of Humanities and Prof. of English, Vanderbilt Univ. 1989–99, Dir Comparative Literature 1992–99; John and Barbara Glynn Family Prof. of Literature, Univ. of Notre Dame 2000–, Dir PhD Program in Literature 2001–07; Commonwealth Fellowship 1960–62, Canada Council Fellowship 1964–65, Imperial Oil Fellowship 1965–68, Guggenheim Foundation Fellowship 1978, Nat. Endowment for the Humanities Fellowship 2007; Hon. LLD (Dalhousie) 1985; Rose Mary Crawshay Prize 1986. *Play:* Clarissa (co-writer), New York 1984. *Publications include:* non-fiction: A Natural Passion: A Study of the Novels of Samuel Richardson 1974, The Daring Muse 1985, Frances Burney: The Life in the Works 1988, Samuel Richardson: Tercentenary Essays (ed. with Peter Sabor) 1989, The True Story of the Novel 1996, Anne of Green Gables (co-ed. with Wendy Barry and Mary Doody Jones) 1997, Tropic of Venice 2007, Jane Austen's Names: Riddles, Persons, Places 2015; Aristotle detective series: Aristotle Detective 1978, Aristotle and the Fatal Javelin (short story) 1980, Aristotle and Poetic Justice 2002, Aristotle and the Secrets of Life 2003, Poison in Athens (novel) 2004, Mysteries of Eleusis (novel) 2005, Aristotle and the Egyptian Murders 2010, A cloudy day in Babylon 2013, also novella Annello di Bronzo; other fiction: The Alchemists (novel) 1980. *Leisure interests:* travel, looking at ancient buildings, paintings and mosaics, reading detective fiction, visiting Venice, swimming in the sea, music (Mozart, bluegrass). *Address:* c/o Donald Maass Literary Agency, Suite 801, 121 West 27th Street, New York, NY 10001, USA (office); English Department, 356 O'Shaughnessy Hall, University of Notre Dame, Notre Dame, IN 46556 (office); 435 Edgewater Drive, Mishawaka, IN 46545, USA (home). *Telephone:* (212) 727-8383 (office); (574) 257-7927 (home). *Fax:* (212) 727-3271 (office). *E-mail:* info@maassagency.com (office); margaret.doody.1@nd.edu (office). *Website:* www.maassagency.com (office); english.nd.edu (office).

DOOKERAN, Winston, BA, MSc; Trinidad and Tobago economist and politician; b. 24 June 1943, Trinidad and Tobago; m. Shirley Dookeran; one s.; ed Univ. of Manitoba, Canada, London School of Econs; Lecturer in Econs, Univ. of the West Indies 1971–81, 1981–86; MP for Chaguanas constituency 1981–91, MP for St Augustine 2002–; Minister of Planning and Mobilization, Vice-Chair. Nat. Planning Comm. 1986–91; Dir Price-Waterhouse Man. Consultants and to the Caribbean Govs 1992–95; Fellow, Center for Int. Affairs, Harvard Univ. 1993–95; Sr Economist UN ECLAC 1995–97; Gov. Cen. Bank of Trinidad and Tobago 1997–2002; Minister of Finance 2010–12, of Foreign Affairs 2012–15; Visiting Scholar, Weatherhead Center for Int. Affairs Harvard Univ. 2002–03; Leader, United Nat. Congress 2005–06, Congress of the People 2006–11; Hon. LLD (Univ. of Manitoba) 1991. *Publications include:* Choices and Change: Reflections on the Caribbean (ed.) 1996, The Caribbean Quest: Directions for Structural Reforms in a Global Economy (co-ed.) 1999, Uncertainty, Stability and Challenges 2006. *E-mail:* wdookeran@tstt.net.tt. *Website:* www.winstondookeran.com (home).

DOOKUN-LUCHOOMUN, Hon. Leela Devi, BSc, PGCE, PG Dip Educ.; Mauritian lecturer and politician; *Minister of Education and Human Resources, Tertiary Education and Scientific Research;* m. Mahesswarnath Luchoomun; two c.; ed Univ. of Delhi, India, Mauritius Inst. of Educ., Univ. of Brighton, UK; part-time Lecturer, Mauritius Inst. of Educ.; mem. Parl. 2000–, for Constituency No. 8 Moka/Quartier Militaire 2005–10, 2014–, Parl. Pvt. Sec. 2000–04; Minister of Arts and Culture 2004–05, of Social Security, Nat. Solidarity and Reform Insts 2010–11, of Educ. and Human Resources, Tertiary Educ. and Scientific Research 2014–; Founder-mem. Soc. of Biology Teachers, fmr Sec. of Soc.; Vice-Pres. Mouvement Socialiste Militant (MSM) party, Pres. Women's Wing of MSM. *Address:* Ministry of Education and Human Resources, MITD House, Pont Fer, Phoenix, Port Louis, Mauritius (office). *Telephone:* 601-5200 (office). *Fax:* 698-9627 (office). *E-mail:* moeministeroffice@govmu.org (office). *Website:* ministry-education.govmu.org (office).

DOOLITTLE, W. Ford, BA, PhD, FRSC; Canadian microbiologist, geneticist and academic; *Professor Emeritus, Dalhousie University;* ed Harvard Coll., Stanford Univ., USA; USPH Postdoctoral trainee in Microbiology, Univ. of Illinois 1968–69; US Nat. Cancer Inst. Postdoctoral Fellow and Research Assoc., Nat. Jewish Hosp. and Research Center, Denver, Colo 1969–71; Asst Prof. (and MRC Scholar), Dept of Biochemistry, Dalhousie Univ. 1971–76, Assoc. Prof. 1976–82, Prof. 1982–2008, Prof. Emer. 2008–; Sabbatical Prof., Harvard Univ. 1977–78; Sabbatical Prof., Stanford Univ. 1985–86; Dir Canadian Inst. for Advanced Research Program in Evolutionary Biology 1986–2007; Canada Research Chair in Comparative Microbia Genomics 2001–08; mem. Editorial Bd Journal of Molecular Evolution 1984– (Assoc. Ed. 1992–), Molecular Biology and Evolution 1987–95, Environmental Microbiology 2000–, Archaea 2001–, Proceedings of the US National Academy of Sciences 2002–; mem. Advisory Bd Genome Biology 2000–; mem. Advisory Editorial Bd Trends in Microbiology 2000–; mem. Bd of Reviewing Eds Science 2006–; mem. NAS 2002; Fellow, AAAS 1985, Canadian Inst. for Advanced Research 1986, American Acad. of Microbiology 1999; Richard Ivey Fellow 2000; Hon. DSc (Ottawa) 2000; Nat. Merit Scholarship, Harvard Coll. 1959–63, NSF Predoctoral Fellowship, Stanford Univ. 1963–68 (declined), Young Scientist of the Year Award, Atlantic Provs Inter-Univ. Council on the Sciences 1978, Ayerst Award, Canadian Biochemical Soc. 1981, Max Forman Sr Faculty Award, Dalhousie Univ. 1982, Guggenheim Fellowship, Stanford Univ. 1985, Award of Excellence, Genetics Soc. of Canada 1991, Henry Friesen Award, Canadian Soc. for Clinical Investigation and Royal Coll. of Physicians and Surgeons of Canada 1996, Roche Diagnostics Prize for Biomolecular and Cellular Research, Canadian Soc. of Biochemistry and Molecular and Cellular Biology 2001, Herzberg Gold Medal 2014, Killam Prize in the Natural Sciences, Canada Council for the Arts 2017. *Publications:* 17 book chapters and more than 250 papers in professional journals on the evolution of genes and genomes. *Address:* Department of Biochemistry and Molecular Biology, Sir Charles Tupper Building, Room 8C, 5850 College Street, Halifax, NS B3H 1X5, Canada (office). *Telephone:* (902) 494-3569 (office). *Fax:* (902) 494-1355 (office). *E-mail:* w.ford.doolittle@dal.ca (office); ford@dal.ca (office). *Website:* www.biochem.dal.ca (office).

DÖPFNER, Mathias, MA, PhD; German publishing executive; *Chairman and CEO, Axel Springer AG;* b. 15 Jan. 1963, Bonn; m.; journalist, Frankfurter Allgemeine Zeitung 1982; dir public relations agency 1988–90; fmr Asst to CEO, Gruner & Jahr, Hamburg; Ed.-in-Chief Wochenpost, Berlin 1994–96, Hamburger Morgenpost 1996–98; joined Axel Springer AG 1998, Ed.-in-Chief Die Welt 1998–2000, mem. Man. Bd, Multimedia Div. 2000–, Head of Newspapers Div. 2000–02, Chair. and CEO 2002–; Visiting Prof. in Media, Univ. of Cambridge 2010, also mem. St John's Coll.; mem. Bd of Dirs Time Warner 2006–, RHJ Int. 2008–; mem. Int. Advisory Bd Blavatnik School of Govt, Univ. of Oxford; Axel Springer Prize for Young Journalists 1992, Golden Pen Award, Bauer Verlagsgruppe 2000, Journalism Award of German medium-sized businesses 2000, World Econ. Forum Global Leader of Tomorrow 2001, Berlin Order of Merit 2007, Leo Baeck Medal 2007, Jerusalem Award 2008, Global Leadership Award, American Inst. for Contemporary German Studies, New York 2008. *Publications:* Neue Deutsche Welle: Kunst oder Mode 1983, Erotik in der Musik 1986, Musikkritik in Deutschland seit 1945 1991, Brüssel: das Insider-Lexikon 1992, Axel Springer: Neue Blicke auf den Verleger (ed.) 2005, Ernst Cramer: Ich habe es erlebt (ed.) 2008. *Address:* Office of the Chairman, Axel Springer AG, Axel-Springer-Straße

65, 10888 Berlin, Germany (office). *Telephone:* (30) 2591-0 (office). *Website:* www.axelspringer.com (office).

DORDAIN, Jean-Jacques; French professor of fluid mechanics and international organization official; b. 14 April 1946; ed Ecole Centrale; researcher, Office nat. d'études et de recherches aérospatiales (ONERA) 1970–76, Co-ordinator of Space Activities 1976–86, Dir of Fundamental Physics 1983–86; Prof., Ecole Nationale Supérieure de l'Aéronautique et de l'Espace 1973–87; Sr Lecturer in Mechanical Eng, Ecole Polytechnique 1977–93; joined ESA 1986, Head of Space Station and Platforms Promotion and Utilisation Dept 1986, later Head of Microgravity and Columbus Utilization Dept, Assoc. Dir for Strategy, Planning and Int. Policy 1993–99, Dir Directorate of Strategy and Tech. Assessment 1999–2001, Dir of Launchers 2001–03, Dir-Gen. ESA 2003–15; Exec. Sec. Evaluation Cttee of Japanese Space Agency 1997; mem. Académie des Technologies, Académie de l'Air et de l'Espace; Legion d'Honneur, Ordre National du Mérite. *Address:* c/o European Space Agency, 8–10 rue Mario Nikis, 75738 Paris Cedex 15, France.

ĐORĐEVIĆ, Zoran, MEcons; Serbian business executive and politician; *Minister of Labour, Employment, Veterans' Affairs and Social Policy;* b. 11 Feb. 1970, Belgrade; m.; one s. one d.; ed Panteion Univ. of Social and Political Sciences, Greece, Faculty of Int. Econs, Belgrade, School of Nat. Defence, Univ. Business Acad., Novi Sad; several positions in areas of financial and exec. management with nat. and int. cos, including Comtrade (IT co.) and Kabel-X (broadband cable co.); Sec. of State, Ministry of Defence 2012–16, Minister of Defence 2016–17, Minister of Labour, Employment, Veterans' Affairs and Social Policy 2017–; fmr Chair., Govt Political Council for Sexual Equality; fmr Nat. Dir for Weapons, Govt of Serbia; mem. Srpska Napredna Stranka (SNS, Serbian Progressive Party), mem. SNS main bd. *Publications:* several papers in leading nat. and int. scientific and professional journals in the field of econs and finance. *Address:* Ministry of Labour, Employment, Veterans' Affairs and Social Policy, 11000 Belgrade, Nemanjina 22–26, Serbia (office). *Telephone:* (11) 3038661 (office). *Fax:* (11) 3617587 (office). *E-mail:* upravazabzr@minrzs.gov.rs (office). *Website:* www.minrzs.gov.rs (office).

DORÉ, Ousmane; Guinean economist and politician; ed John F. Kennedy School of Govt, Harvard Univ.; fmr Sr Economist, IMF Africa Dept, fmr IMF Rep. to Senegal and Guinea-Bissau; Minister of the Economy, Finance and Planning 2007–08; living abroad for several years when tried, convicted and sentenced in absentia to five years in prison for complicity in embezzlement of US $1.5m. of public funds Feb.–March 2014, court issued arrest warrant against him and ordered confiscation of his property.

DORFF, Stephen; American actor; b. (Stephen Dorff Jr), 29 July 1973, Atlanta, Ga; s. of Steve Dorff and Nancy Dorff; began acting aged nine. *Films:* The Gate 1986, The Power of One 1992, Rescue Me 1992, An Ambush of Ghosts 1993, Judgment Night 1993, Backbeat 1994, S.F.W. 1994, Les cent et une nuits de Simon Cinéma 1995, Innocent Lies 1995, Reckless 1995, I Shot Andy Warhol 1996, Space Truckers 1996, Blood and Wine 1996, City of Industry 1997, Blade 1998, Entropy 1999, Quantum Project (short) 2000, Cecil B. DeMented 2000, Deuces Wild 2002, Riders 2002, FeardotCom 2002, Cold Creek Manor 2003, Britney Spears: Greatest Hits – My Prerogative (video) (segment Everytime) 2004, Alone in the Dark 2005, Tennis, Anyone...? 2005, Shadowboxer 2005, World Trade Center 2006, .45 2006, Botched 2007, The Passage 2007, Felon 2008, Black Water Transit 2009, Public Enemies 2009, Somewhere 2010, Rites of Passage 2011, Bucky Larson: Born to Be a Star 2011, Immortals 2011, Carjacked 2011, Boot Tracks 2011, Brake 2012, The Motel Life 2012, Officer Down 2012, The Iceman 2013. *Television films:* In Love and War 1987, Mutts 1988, Hiroshima Maiden 1988, Quiet Victory: The Charlie Wedemeyer Story 1988, I Know My First Name Is Steven 1989, Do You Know the Muffin Man? 1989, A Son's Promise 1990, Always Remember I Love You 1990, Earthly Possessions 1999, Skip Tracer 2008. *Television series:* Still the Beaver 1985, Diff'rent Strokes 1985, Disneyland – The Absent-Minded Professor 1988, Empty Nest 1989, Married with Children 1989, Roseanne 1989, Father Dowling Investigates 1990, The Outsiders 1990, Blossom 1991, What a Dummy 1990–91, Covert One: The Hades Factor 2006, XIII: The Conspiracy (mini-series) 2008. *Address:* c/o ICM, 10250 Constellation Boulevard, Los Angeles, CA 90067, USA (office). *Telephone:* (310) 550-4000 (office). *Website:* www.icmtalent.com (office).

DORFMAN, (Vladimiro) Ariel; Chilean/American writer and academic; *Walter Hines Page Distinguished Professor of Literature and Latin American Studies, Duke University;* b. 6 May 1942, Buenos Aires, Argentina; s. of Adolfo Dorfman; m. Angélica Dorfman 1966; two s.; ed Univ. of Chile; Teaching Asst, Univ. of Chile 1963–65, Asst Prof. of Spanish Literature and Journalism 1965–68, Assoc. Prof. 1968–70, Prof. 1970–73; exiled after Chilean coup 1973; Maître des Conférences Spanish-American Literature, Sorbonne Paris IV 1975–76; Head Scientific Research, Spanns Seminarium, Univ. of Amsterdam 1976–80; Visiting Prof., Univ. of Maryland 1983; Post-Doctoral Fellow and Consultant Latin American Council, Duke Univ. 1984, Visiting Prof. of Literature and Latin American Studies 1985–89, Research Prof. of Literature and Latin American Studies, 1989–96, Walter Hines Page Distinguished Prof. of Literature and Latin American Studies, Center for Int. Studies and Romance Studies 1996–; Research Scholar, Univ. of Calif., Berkeley 1968–69; Friedrich Ebert Stiftung Research Fellow 1974–76; Fellowship at Woodrow Wilson Int. Center for Scholars 1980–81; Visiting Fellow, Inst. for Policy Studies 1981–84; Fellow, American Acad. of Arts and Sciences; Dr hc (Ill. Wesleyan Univ.) 1989, (Wooster Coll.) 1991, (Bradford Coll.) 1993, (American Univ.) 2001; Time Out Award 1991, New York Public Library Literary Lion 1992, Dora Mavor Award 1994, Int. Poetry Forum Charity Randall Citation 1995, Writers' Guild of Great Britain Best Film for Television 1995, ALOA Prize, Denmark 2002, Lowell Thomas Silver Award for Travel Book 2004, O. Henry Award 2006, North American Congress on Latin America (NACLA) Award for Peace and Justice 2008. *Plays:* Widows (Kennedy Center New American Plays Award) 1988, Death and the Maiden (Olivier Award for Best Play, London 1992) 1991, Reader (Kennedy Center Roger L. Stevens Award) 1992, Who's Who (with Rodrigo Dorfman) 1998, Speak Truth to Power: Voices from Beyond the Dark 2000, Manifesto from Another World: Voices from Beyond the Dark 2004, Purgatorio 2005, Picasso's Closet 2006, The Other Side 2006, Dancing Shadows (with Eric Woolfson) 2007. *Film screenplays:* Death and the Maiden 1994, Prisoners in Time 1995, My House is on Fire 1997, A Promise to the Dead: The Exile Journey of Ariel Dorfman (Insight Award for Excellence in Writing, Nat. Asscn of Film and Digital Media Artists 2008) 2007. *Publications include:* fiction: Hard Rain 1973, My House is On Fire 1979, Widows 1983, Dorando la pildora 1985, Travesía 1986, The Last Song of Manuel Sendero 1987, Máscara 1988, Konfidenz 1995, The Nanny and the Iceberg 1999, Blake's Therapy 2001, The Rabbit's Rebellion 2001, The Burning City (with Joaquin Dorfman) 2003, Americanos: Los Pasos de Murieta 2009; poetry: Missing 1982, Last Waltz in Santiago and Other Poems of Exile and Disappearance 1988, In Case of Fire in a Foreign Land: New and Collected Poems from Two Languages 2002; non-fiction: How to Read Donald Duck (with Armand Mattelart) 1971, The Empire's Old Clothes 1983, Some Write to the Future 1991, Heading South, Looking North: A Bilingual Journey 1998, Exorcising Terror: The Incredible Ongoing Trial of General Augusto Pinochet 2002, Desert Memories: Journeys Through the Chilean North 2004, Other Septembers, Many Americas: Selected Provocations, 1980–2004 2004, Feeding on Dreams: Confessions of an Unrepentant Exile 2011. *Address:* c/o Center for International Studies, Duke University, PO Box 90404, Durham, NC 27708, USA. *Fax:* (919) 684-8749 (office). *E-mail:* adorfman@duke.edu (office). *Website:* www.adorfman.duke.edu (office).

DORGAN, Byron Leslie, BS, MBA; American politician; *Senior Policy Advisor, Arent Fox LLP;* b. 14 May 1942, Dickinson, N Dakota; s. of Emmett Patrick Dorgan and Dorothy Dorgan (née Bach); m. 1st; one s. one d. (deceased); m. 2nd Kimberly Olson; one s. one d.; ed Regent High School, Univ. of North Dakota, Univ. of Denver; Exec. Devt trainee, Martin Marietta Corpn, Denver 1966–67; Deputy Tax Commr, then Tax Commr, State of N Dakota 1967–80; mem. US House of Reps., Washington, DC 1981–93, mem. Ways and Means Cttee 1981–93; Senator from N Dakota 1993–2011 (retd), Asst Democratic Floor Leader 1996–99, Chair. Democratic Policy Cttee 1999, mem. Cttee on Commerce, Science and Transportation, Cttee on Indian Affairs (Chair. 2007–11); Sr Policy Advisor and Co-Chair., Govt Relations Practice, Arent Fox LLP (law firm), Washington, DC 2011–; Founder and Chair. Center for Native American Youth, Aspen Inst.; Adjunct Visiting Prof., Georgetown Univ.; Sr Fellow, Bipartisan Policy Center; Democrat; mem. Bd of Govs Argonne National Laboratory. *Publications include:* Electric Transmission Infrastructure and Investment Needs: Hearing Before the Committee on Energy and Natural Resources (ed.) 2003, Take This Job and Ship It: How Corporate Greed and Brain-Dead Politics Are Selling Out America 2006, Reckless! How Debt, Deregulation and Dark Money Nearly Bankrupted America (And How We Can Fix It!) 2009, Gridlock 2013. *Address:* Arent Fox LLP, 1717 K Street, NW, Washington, DC 20006, USA (office). *Telephone:* (202) 857-6334 (office). *Fax:* (202) 857-6395 (office). *E-mail:* byron.dorgan@arentfox.com (office); info@byrondorgan.com. *Website:* www.arentfox.com (office); www.byrondorgan.com.

DORIA, João Agripino da Costa, Jr; Brazilian journalist, business executive, broadcaster and politician; *Governor of São Paulo;* b. 16 Dec. 1957, São Paulo; s. of João Agripino da Costa Doria Neto and Maria Sylvia Vieira de Morais Dias Doria; m. Bia Doria; three c.; ed Escola Estadual Professora Marina Cintra; Communications Dir, Bandeirantes TV Network 1979–82; Prof. of Marketing, Fundação Armando Alvares Penteado, São Paulo 1981–83; Sec. of Tourism, City of São Paulo 1983–86, also Pres. PAULISTUR (travel agency) 1983–86; Pres. Embratur (Brazilian Tourist Bd) 1986–88; Chair. Nat. Council of Tourism 1986–88; Founder and Chair. Doria Group (communications and marketing group) 1995–2016; Founder and Pres. Exec. Cttee, LIDE (Grupo de Líderes Empresariais) 2003–16; Chair., Casa Cor 2007–11; columnist, Isto É Dinheiro Magazine 2008–11; Mayor of São Paulo 2017–18; Gov. of São Paulo 2018–; Founder and Chair. ISO Council-Solidarity Inst. 1997–99; mem. Partido da Social Democracia Brasileira (PSDB) 2001–. *Television includes:* as presenter: Success 1990–92, Show Business 1992–2016, The Apprentice 2010–11, Face to Face 2015–16. *Address:* Prefeitura Municipal de São Paulo, Viaduto do Cha 15, Centro, São Paulo 01002-020, Brazil (office). *Website:* www.capital.sp.gov.br; www.grupodoria.com.br (office).

DÖRIG, Rolf, Dr iur; Swiss business executive; *Chairman, Adecco Management & Consulting SA;* b. 19 May 1957; m.; three s.; ed Univ. of Zurich, Harvard Business School, USA; called to the Bar, Zurich; joined Credit Suisse 1986, several exec. positions and in different geographical markets, Chief of Staff and Chief Communications Officer, Credit Suisse Group 1997–2000, mem. Exec. Bd responsible for Swiss corp. and retail banking 2000–02, also Chair. Switzerland, Credit Suisse Group 2002; Exec. Vice-Pres. Swiss Life Group (fmrly Swiss Life/Rentenanstalt), CEO 2002–08, Chair. 2009–, Chair. Swiss Life Holding 2009–; Chair. Danzer AG, Baar 2002–, Zurich Chamber of Commerce, Swiss Insurance Asscn 2017–; mem. Bd of Dirs Adecco Management & Consulting SA 2007–, Chair. 2009–, mem. Nomination and Compensation Cttee 2007–08, Corp. Governance Cttee –2008; mem. Bd of Dirs Swiss Insurance Asscn, Kaba Holding AG (Vice-Chair. 2004–), economiesuisse, Zurich 2003–, Grasshopper-Club Zurich. *Address:* Adecco Management & Consulting SA, Sägereistrasse 10, 8152 Glattbrugg (office); Swiss Life, General Guisan-Quai 40, 8022 Zurich, Switzerland (office). *Telephone:* (44) 878-88-88 (Glattbrugg) (office); (43) 284-33-11 (Zurich) (office). *Fax:* (44) 829-88-88 (Glattbrugg) (office); (43) 281-20-80 (Zurich) (office). *E-mail:* info@adecco.com (office); info.com@swisslife.ch (office). *Website:* www.adecco.com (office); www.swisslife.com (office).

DORIS, Ennio; Italian business executive; *Founder and Chairman, Banca Mediolanum SpA;* b. 3 July 1940, Tombolo; began career as salesman for Fideuram 1969; worked for Dival SpA 1971–82; started own fund man. co. Programma Italia 1982, expanded operations into banking and insurance, renamed co. Mediolanum SpA 1996, currently Chair. Banca Mediolanum SpA; mem. Bd of Dirs Mediobanca, Fondazione S. Raffaele del Monte Tabor, Safilo SpA. *Address:* Mediolanum SpA, Palazzo Meucci, Via Francesco Sforza 15, 20080 Basiglio Milan 3, Italy (office). *Telephone:* (02) 90491 (office). *Fax:* (02) 90493434 (office). *E-mail:* info@mediolanum.it (office). *Website:* www.bancamediolanum.it (office).

DORJI, Lyonpo Damcho, BA, LLB, LLM; Bhutanese lawyer and politician; b. 23 June 1965, Chholing village, Gasa; m.; four c.; ed Sherubtse Coll., Univ. of Bombay, India, Georgetown Univ. Law Center, USA, Inst. of Social Studies, The Hague, Netherlands; began career as Deputy Registrar Gen. in High Court 1991–2007; Chief Judge (Drangpon) in dist courts in Gelephu, Mongar, Wangduephodrang and Punakh 2000–06; Dir Office of Legal Affairs May–Aug. 2006, Attorney-Gen. Aug. 2006–07; mem. Nat. Ass. (Parl.) for Khatoed Laya constituency 2008–; apptd Minister for Home and Cultural Affairs 2013, Minister of Foreign Affairs 2015–18; mem. People's Democratic Party; Druk Thuksey (Heart Son) Award. *Address:* c/o Ministry of Foreign Affairs, Gyalyong Tshokhang, POB 103, Thimphu, Bhutan (office). *Telephone:* (2) 326952 (office). *Fax:* (2) 331465 (office). *E-mail:* ddorji@mfa.gov.bt (office). *Website:* www.mfa.gov.bt (office).

DORJI, Lt-Gen. Goongloen Gongma Lam; Bhutanese military officer (retd); b. 23 Oct. 1933, Haa; ed Indian Mil. Acad., Dehra Dun, India; Inspector-Gen. Royal Bhutan Police; Chief of Operations Royal Bhutan Army 1964–2005 (retd); Gen. Sec. Nat. Sports Asscn of Bhutan 1974–78; Royal Order of Bhutan 2010; Druk Zhung Thugsay Medal 1969, Druk Yugyel Medal 1991, Drakpoi Wangyel Medal 2001. *Address:* c/o Royal Bhutan Army Headquarters, Lungtenphu, Bhutan.

DORJI, Dasho Karma; Bhutanese civil servant; ed St Joseph's Coll., Darjeeling, India, State Univ. of New York, USA; joined Ministry of Foreign Affairs 1974, various posts at missions to UN, USA and India, Amb. to Bangladesh (also accred to Maldives, Thailand and Repub. of Korea) 1989–93; Dir Dept of Power 1993–96, Jt Sec. for Power 1996–2000, Sec., Ministry of Trade, Industry and Power (now Ministry of Econ. Affairs) 2000–07; fmr Chair. State Trading Corpn of Bhutan; Man. Dir Karma Group Org.; mem. Bd Bank of Bhutan, Bhutan Devt Finance Corpn, Bhutan Board Products Ltd; Pres. Bhutan Table Tennis Fed.; Nyekemship with Red Scarf and Sword of Honour 1998. *Address:* c/o Ministry of Economic Affairs, Tashichhodzong, PO Box 141, Thimphu, Bhutan. *Telephone:* (2) 322211. *E-mail:* kdorjee@druknet.bt. *Website:* www.moea.gov.bt.

DORJI, Lyonpo Kinzang, BA; Bhutanese politician, government official and fmr central banker; b. 1951, Chali, Mongar Dist; ed Kolkata, India; Zonal Admin. for Sarpang, Zhemgang, Trongsa and Bumthang 1989–91; Dir-Gen. Ministry of Agric. 1991–93, Jt Sec. 1993–94, Sec. 1994–98, Deputy Minister 1998, Minister 1998–2003; elected Speaker Nat. Ass. 1997; Prime Minister, Chair. 2002–03; Minister of Works and Human Settlements 2003–07; Prime Minister 2007–08; Chair. Royal Monetary Authority (cen. bank) 2008–10, Dept of Planning, Tourism Council of Bhutan 2008–; Coronation Medal 1999. *Address:* Tourism Council of Bhutan, PO Box 126, Thimphu, Bhutan (office). *Telephone:* (2) 323251 (office). *Fax:* (2) 323695 (office). *E-mail:* dot@tourism.gov.bt (office). *Website:* www.tourism.gov.bt (office).

DORJI, Lyonpo Leki, BA; Bhutanese government official and diplomatist; b. 31 Dec. 1944, Rukubji, Wangduephodrang; ed Nanital Public School, India, Coll. of Mil. Eng, India, Victoria Univ. of Wellington, NZ; Third Sec., New York mission 1973–74, Second Sec., New Delhi mission 1974–75; Officer on Special Duty, Royal Secr. 1975–77; Head, Registration Dept 1978–80; Sec., Royal Secr. and to Ministry of Agric. 1980; Deputy Minister, Ministry of Agric. 1991–94; Deputy Minister, Ministry of Communications 1994, Minister of Information and Communications 2003–08; Red Scarf 1983, Orange Scarf 1991. *Address:* c/o Ministry of Information and Communications, POB 278, Thimphu, Bhutan.

DORJI, Lyonpo Namgay, BCom (Hons), LLB, BCom; Bhutanese politician; b. 23 Feb. 1968, Ngada village, Draagteng-Langthil, Trongsa; m.; three c.; ed Sherubtse Coll., Bombay Univ., India; Chief Legal Officer, Bhutan Devt Finance Corpn 1992–2008; cand. for People's Democratic Party 2008–13, Treas. 2008–13; Minister of Finance 2013–18; Orange Scarf Award 2013. *Address:* c/o Ministry of Finance, Tashichhodzong, PO Box 117, Thimphu, Bhutan (office). *Telephone:* (2) 324867 (office). *Fax:* (2) 333976 (office). *E-mail:* wnorbu@mof.gov.bt (office). *Website:* www.mof.gov.bt (office).

DORJI, Lyonpo Rinzin, MA; Bhutanese politician; b. 26 June 1964, Shingkhar, Zhemgang; m.; two c.; ed Sherubtse Coll., Inst. of Social Studies, The Hague, Netherlands; joined civil service 1988, Asst Planning Officer, Monggar Dist 1989–99, Asst Planning Officer, Samtse Dist 1990–91, Planning Officer, Chhukha Dist 1992, Personnel Officer, Ministry of Home and Cultural Affairs 1994–95, Admin. Officer, Trashigang Dist 1997–99, Planning Officer, Zhemgang Dist 2000–02, Head, Programme Service Divison, Planning Comm./Gross Nat. Happiness Secretariat 2003–09, Samtse Dist 2009–10, Haa Dist 2011–13, Minister of Foreign Affairs 2013–15; mem. People's Democratic Party 2013–.

DORJI, Lyonpo Sangay Ngedup, BA; Bhutanese politician and fmr diplomatist; b. 1953, Nobgang, Punakha Dist; m.; four c.; ed Dr Graham's Homes School, Kalimpong, St Stephen's Coll., New Delhi, India; joined Bhutanese Foreign Service 1976, served at Perm. Mission to UN, New York 1977, First Sec., New Delhi 1986, Amb. to Kuwait 1986–89; Dir of Trade and Industry, Ministry of Commerce and Industry 1989–92; Jt Sec., Planning Comm. 1991; Sec. of Health 1994–95, of Health and Educ. 1995–98, Deputy Minister of Health and Educ. 1998–99, Minister of Health and Educ. 1999–2003; Chair. Council of Ministers 1999–2000; Minister of Agric. 2001–05; Prime Minister 2005–06; Chair. People's Democratic Party 2007–09, then Pres.; Chair. Exec. Cttee WHO 1996–99; mem. Bd of Dirs Global Alliance for Vaccines and Immunization (GAVI); responsible for establishing Health Trust Fund, Nat. Tech. Training Authority, Nat. Employment Bd, Royal Univ. of Bhutan, Inst. for Zorig Chusum, Trashiyangtse, Be Somebody movt, Educ. Staff Welfare Fund, Youth Counselling, Scouts Programme, Land Man. Campaign; Hon. Pres. Bhutan Scouts Asscn; Red Scarf 1987, Orange Scarf 1998, Druk Thuksay Medal (Heart Son of Bhutan) 1999, Coronation Medal 1999, numerous int. honours and awards.

DORJI, Tandi, MBBS, MD, MBA; Bhutanese physician and politician; *Minister of Foreign Affairs;* b. 2 Sept. 1968; m. Karma Choden; two d.; ed Mymensingh Medical Coll., Dhaka Univ., Armed Forces Medical Coll., Pune Univ., School of Public Health, Univ. of Sydney, Univ. of Canberra; Consultant Paediatrician, Jigme Dorji Wangchuk Nat. Referral Hosp. Thimphu 2001–07; fmr volunteer project asst, AUSTCARE (Australian Caring for Refugees), Sydney; fmr Lecturer and Clinical Instructor, Royal Inst. of Health Sciences, Thimphu; mem. Council, Bhutan Medical and Health Council; Prof., Khesar Gyalpo Univ. of Medical Sciences, Thimphu; fmr Man. Dir and Researcher, Centre for Research Initiative, Bhutan; Chair. Nat. Certification Comm. on Polio Elimination 2013–, Nat. Certification Cttee for measles elimination and rubella/CRS control 2015–18; mem. Nat. Ass. (lower house of parl.) 2018–; Minister of Foreign Affairs 2018–; Founding mem. Druk Nyamrup Tshogpa (DNT, Solidarity, Justice and Freedom) 2012–. *Address:* Ministry of Foreign Affairs, Gyalyong Tshokhang, POB 103, Thimphu, Bhutan (office). *Telephone:* (2) 322459 (office). *Fax:* (2) 331465 (home). *E-mail:* ugyen@mofa.gov.bt (office). *Website:* www.mfa.gov.bt (office).

DORJI, Dasho Topgyal; Bhutanese business executive; *Co-Chairman, Tashi Group of Companies;* s. of Dasho Ugen Dorji; ed St Joseph's School, Darjeeling, India, New Hampshire Coll.; Co-Chair. Tashi Group of Cos 2006–; Chair., Bhutan Carbide & Chemicals Ltd, Bhutan Eco Ventures Private Ltd, Tashi Beverages Ltd and Bhutan Silicon Metal Pvt. Ltd; Pres. Bhutan Chamber of Commerce and Industry 2009–, Tashi Metals & Alloys Ltd; Chair. and Man. Dir Bhutan Ferro Alloys Ltd; mem. Bd Dirs Tai Industries Ltd, JAMIPOL Ltd, Tai Projects Pvt. Ltd, Royal Insurance Corpn of Bhutan Ltd, Bhutan Fruit Products Pvt. Ltd, Bhutan Brewery Pvt. Ltd, Tashi Infocomm Ltd, Rijal Tashi Industries Pvt. Ltd. *Address:* Tashi Group of Companies, Corporate Head Office, Phuntsholing, Bhutan (office). *Telephone:* (5) 252109 (office). *Fax:* (5) 252110 (office). *E-mail:* tashi@tashigroup.bt (office). *Website:* www.tashigroup.bt (office).

DORJI, Dasho Tshering; Bhutanese government official and diplomatist; *Secretary of Ministry of Home and Cultural Affairs;* began career as a trainee officer 1984, fmr Dzongda of Pemagatshel and Chief of Protocol, Ministry of Foreign Affairs; fmr Sec.-Gen. Bhutan Chamber of Commerce and Industry; fmr Sec., Ministry of Works and Human Settlements; Amb. to Bangladesh (also accred to Sri Lanka) 2008–10, to Thailand (also accred to Australia, Singapore) 2010–12; Sec., Ministry of Home and Cultural Affairs 2012–. *Address:* Ministry of Home and Cultural Affairs, Tashichhodzong, POB 133, Thimphu, Bhutan (office). *Telephone:* (2) 322301 (office). *Fax:* (2) 324320 (office). *E-mail:* lmd@mohca.gov.bt (office). *Website:* www.mohca.gov.bt.

DORJI, Dasho Ugen; Bhutanese politician and business executive; *Chairman, Lhaki Group of Companies;* served in Royal Court of HM the Third King of Bhutan –1972; laid foundation of Lhaki Group of Cos, pioneered dolomite mining industry in Bhutan, business concerns include cement, polymers, mining, polytex, steel, export, construction, ferro-alloys, in-bound travel services and hotels, IT, newspaper and media and real estate, currently Chair. Lhaki Group of Cos, Lhaki Cement, Lhaki Steels & Rolling Pvt. Ltd, Lhaki Construction, Jigme Polytex Pvt. Ltd, Jigme Mining Corpn Ltd, Jigme Industries Pvt. Ltd, Druk Ferro Alloys Ltd, Druk Mines & Mineral Ltd, Bhutan Polymers Corpn Ltd; mem. Bhutan Chamber of Commerce and Industry 1980, Pres. 1992–2009; Chair. Bhutan Tourism Corpn Ltd, Bhutan Times Ltd, New Edge Technologies Pvt. Ltd, Citizens Initiative for Coronation and Centenary Celebrations; mem. or fmr mem. Bd Bank of Bhutan Ltd, Bhutan Nat. Bank Ltd, Bhutan Finance Devt Corpn Ltd, Royal Insurance Corpn Ltd, State Trading Corpn of Bhutan Ltd, Penden Cement Authority Ltd, and bds of cos under and co-promoted by the Lhaki Group; represented the business community in the Tshogdu Chenmo (Nat. Ass.) 1998, Deputy Speaker 1998–2001, Speaker 2001–07; mem. Drafting Cttee of first draft constitution of Bhutan upon command of HM the Fourth King 2001–03. *Address:* Lhaki Group of Companies, Corporate Head Office, Lhaki Shopping Complex, Blocks 3 & 4, PO Box 179, Thimphu, Bhutan (office). *Website:* www.lhakibhutan.com (office).

DORJI, Dasho Wangchuk; Bhutanese business executive; *Co-Chairman, Tashi Group of Companies;* s. of Dasho Ugen Dorji; ed St Augustine's School, Kalimpong, India, New Hampshire Coll., USA; currently Chair., Man. Dir –2014, CEO Tai Industries Ltd, Kolkata, India 2005, mem. Bd of Dir 2014–; Co-Chair. Tashi Group of Cos 2006–; Man. Dir Bhutan Carbide Chemical Ltd; mem. Bhutan Mountain Biking Club. *Address:* Tashi Group of Companies, Corporate Head Office, Phuntsholing, Bhutan (office). *Telephone:* (5) 252109 (office). *Fax:* (5) 252110 (office). *E-mail:* tashi@tashigroup.bt (office). *Website:* www.tashigroup.bt (office).

DORJI, Yeshey; Bhutanese diplomatist and politician; ed Univ. of Delhi, India, Royal Inst. of Man., Asian Inst. of Man., Columbia Univ. School of Int. and Public Affairs, USA; Policy Analyst and Programme Co-ordinator, Ministry of Econ. Affairs 2000–08; Diplomat and Sr Desk Officer, Regional Econ. Integration, Ministry of Foreign Affairs 2008–10, First Sec., Perm. Mission to the UN, New York 2010–12, Counsellor 2012–13; Minister of Agriculture and Forests 2013–18. *Address:* c/o Ministry of Agriculture and Forests, POB 252, Thimphu, Bhutan (office). *Telephone:* (2) 323765 (office). *Fax:* (2) 324520 (office). *E-mail:* pgyamtsho@moa.gov.bt (office). *Website:* www.moaf.gov.bt (office).

DORMAN, David W., BS; American business executive; *Chairman (non-executive), CVS Health;* b. 1954, Ga; m. Susan Dorman; three c.; ed Georgia Inst. of Tech.; began career in software devt, sales and marketing; joined Sprint Business 1981, Pres. 1990–94; CEO Pacific Bell 1994–96, later becoming Exec. Vice-Pres. SBC Communications; Chair., Pres. and CEO PointCast Network 1996–99; CEO Concert (global jt venture between AT&T Corpn and British Telecom) 1999–2000; Pres. AT&T Corpn 2000–02, mem. Bd of Dirs Feb. 2002–, Chair. and CEO July 2002–05 (after acquisition of AT&T by SBC Communications, now AT&T Inc.), now consultant; Man. Dir and Sr Advisor, Warburg Pincus pvt. equity firm –2008; Chair. (non-exec.) Motorola, Inc. 2008–11, Lead Ind. Dir, Motorola Solutions, Inc. 2011–15; Chair. (non-exec.), CVS Caremark Corpn (now called CVS Health) 2011–; Founding Partner, Centerview Capital Technology Fund 2013–; mem. Bd of Dirs, 3Com Corpn, ETEK Dynamics Ltd, Sabre, Science Applications Int. Corpn, Scientific-Atlanta Inc., Yum! Brands, Inc., Atlanta Symphony Orchestra; mem. Int. Advisory Bd British American Business Council; mem. Pres. Clinton's Advisory Cttee on High Performance Computing and Communications, Information Tech. and Next Generation Internet. *Address:* CVS Health, 1 CVS Drive, Woonsocket, RI 02895, USA (office). *Telephone:* (401) 765-1500 (office). *Fax:* (401) 766-2917 (office). *E-mail:* info@cvshealth.com (office). *Website:* www.cvshealth.com (office); www.cvs.com (office).

DORMANDY, John Adam, MD, DSc, FRCS, FRCSE; British surgeon; *Consultant Vascular Surgeon, St. George's Hospital;* b. 5 May 1937, Hungary; s. of Paul Szeben and Clara Szeben; m. Klara Dormandy 1982; one s. one d.; ed St Paul's School, London and Univ. of London; Resident in Surgery, St George's Hosp. Medical School 1963–65, Lecturer in Applied Physiology 1970–74, Sr Lecturer in Surgery 1975–80, Prof. of Vascular Sciences 1995–; Consultant Vascular Surgeon, St James' and St George's Hosp. 1973–; Pres. of Section of Clinical Medicine, Royal Soc. of Medicine 1978; Pres. Venous Forum 1984; Chair. Int. Soc. of Haemorheology 1982; Examiner in Physiology, Royal Coll. of Surgeons 1984, Hunterian Prof. 1970; Hamilton Bailey Prize in Surgery 1973, Fahreus Medal 1983. *Publications:* numerous articles in books and scientific journals. *Leisure interests:* tennis, skiing. *Address:* St James' Wing, St George's Hospital, Blackshaw Road, London, SW17 0QT (office); 82 East Hill, London, SW18 2HG, England (home). *Telephone:* (20) 8767-8346 (office). *Fax:* (20) 8682-2550 (office). *E-mail:* dormandyjohn@aol.com (home).

DORMANN, Jürgen; German business executive; b. 12 Jan. 1940; ed Univ. of Heidelberg; began career with Hoechst AG 1963, Finance and Accounting Dir 1987–94, Chair. Man. Bd 1994–2002, apptd Chair. 1999, oversaw merger of Hoechst AG with Rhône-Poulenc SA to create Aventis SA, CEO Aventis SA 1994–99, Chair. Man. Bd 1999–2002, Chair. Group Supervisory Bd 2002–04, Vice-Chair. Sanofi-Aventis 2004; mem. Bd of Dirs ABB (fmrly Asea Brown Boveri) Ltd 1998, Chair. 2001–07, CEO 2002–04; mem. Bd of Dirs Adecco Management & Consulting SA 2004–08, Chair. 2007–08; Chair. Sulzer AG 2009–13; Chair. V-ZUG AG, Metall Zug AG 2008–13; mem. Bd of Dirs IBM 1996–2003, 2005–08, BG Group PLC (UK) 2005–10, Entrepreneur Partners AG; mem. Supervisory Bd Allianz AG 1999–; mem. European Chemical Industry Council 2000; mem. Int. Advisory Bd Blackstone Group; Pres. Bd of Trustees, ETH Zurich Foundation; Hon. councillor, ETH 2015.

DORMENT, Richard, CBE, MA, MPhil, PhD, FSA; British (b. American) art critic (retd); b. 15 Nov. 1946, Glen Ridge, NJ; s. of James Dorment and Marguerite Dorment (née O'Callaghan); m. 1st Kate S. Ganz 1970 (divorced 1981); one s. one d.; m. 2nd Harriet Mary Waugh 1985; ed Georgetown Prep. School, Princeton and Columbia Univs; Asst Curator European Painting Phila Museum of Art 1973–76; Curator Alfred Gilbert: Sculptor and Goldsmith Exhbn, London 1985–86; art critic Country Life 1986; Co-Curator James McNeill Whistler Exhbn, Tate Gallery 1994–95; Chief Art Critic, Daily Telegraph 1987–2015 (retd); reviewer for New York Review of Books; contrib. to Burlington Magazine, Times Literary Supplement, Literary Review; Trustee, Watts Gallery 1996–, Wallace Collection, London 2004–14, Wallace Foundation 2014–; mem. British Council Advisory Cttee 1997–2007, Govt Art Collection Advisory Cttee 1996–2005; mem. Reviewing Cttee on Export of Works of Art 1996–2002; mem. Judging Panel, Turner Prize 1989; Hawthornden Prize for Art Criticism in Britain 1992, Critic of the Year, British Press Awards 2000. *Publications include:* Victorian High Renaissance (exhbn catalogue contrib.) 1976, Alfred Gilbert 1985, British Painting 1750–1900: A Catalogue of British Paintings in the Philadelphia Museum of Art 1986, Alfred Gilbert: Sculptor and Goldsmith 1986, James McNeill Whistler (with Margaret MacDonald) 1994, Manet and the Sea (exhbn catalogue contrib.) 2003, Pre-Raphaelite and Other Masters: The Andrew Lloyd Webber Collection (exhbn catalogue contrib.) 2003, Exhibitionist: Writing About Art for a Daily Newspaper 2016. *Address:* Flat 1, 63 Montagu Square, London, W1H 2LU, England (home). *Website:* www.telegraph.co.uk/journalists/richard-dorment.

DORN, Ludwik, MA; Polish politician; b. 5 June 1954, Warsaw; m.; three c.; ed Warsaw Univ.; involved in anti-communist opposition, participated in ind. meetings of 1st Warsaw Scout's Czarna Jedynka, activist in Workers' Defence Cttee; mem. editorial team underground newspaper Głos, Solidarity, KSR; f. Documentation and Analysis Centre; Ed. Wiadomości underground newspaper; mem., then Deputy Chair., Centre Accord party; Head of Analysis Team, Chancellery of Pres. of Repub. of Poland 1991; co-f. Law and Justice party, fmr Deputy Chair.; Deputy, Sejm (Parl.) 1997–2015; Deputy Prime Minister 2005–07; Minister of Interior and Admin 2005–07 (resgnd); Marshal, Sejm 2007; Chair. Parl. Club of Law and Justice 2002–05; Chair. Poland Plus 2009; joined Solidarna Polska 2011. *Publications:* translated novels by John Le Carré and Len Deighton; O śpiochu tłuściochu i psie Sabie (About the Fat Sleepyhead and Saba the Dog), Zdruzgotki (rows) 2008, Rozrachunki i wyzwania (Settlements and challenges) 2009, Anatomia słabości (Anatomy of weakness) 2013; numerous literary essays. *Leisure interests:* roller blading, connoisseur of fine wines and cuisine.

DORNY, Serge; Belgian music administrator; *General Director, Opéra de Lyon;* b. 4 Feb. 1962; ed l'université de Gand; musical playwright Théâtre de la Monnaie 1983; Artistic Dir Flanders Festival 1987; apptd Gen. and Artistic Dir, London Philharmonic Orchestra 1996; Gen. Dir, Opéra de Lyon 2003–; Lecturer, Univ. of Zurich 2008–14, l'Accademia dell Teatro alla Scala de Milan 2016–; mem. Bd of Dirs Queen Elizabeth Int. Music Competition Brussels, French Youth Orchestra, Nat. Conservatory Music, Music and Dance Lyon; Légion d'honneur France 2012, l'Ordre de la Couronne 2013; Dr hc (Univ. of Montreal) 2008. *Publications:* Opera-De toekomst van een verleden (with Johan Thieleman) 1991. *Address:* Opéra de Lyon, 1 Place de la Comedie, 69001, Lyon, France (office). *Telephone:* 4-72-00-45-00 (office). *E-mail:* contact@opera-lyon.com. *Website:* www.opera-lyon.com.

DORONINA, Tatyana Vasiliyevna; Russian actress; *Artistic Director, Moscow Gorky Arts Theatre;* b. 12 Sept. 1933, Leningrad; d. of Vasiliy Ivanovich Doronin and Anna Ivanovna Doronina; m. Robert Dimitrievich Takhnenko; ed Studio School of Moscow Art Theatre; Leningrad Lenin Komsomol State Theatre 1956–59; Leningrad Maxim Gorky State Bolshoi Drama Theatre 1959–66; Moscow Art Theatre 1966–71; Moscow Mayakovski Theatre 1971–83; Moscow Arts Theatre 1983–, Artistic Dir Moscow Gorky Arts Theatre 1987–; works as actress and stage dir; Order of Friendship of Peoples 1994, Order of Merit for the Fatherland, 4th Class 1998, 3rd Class 2003, Order of Honour 2008; People's Artist of the USSR 1981, Tsarskoselskaya Art Prize 2011. *Theatre roles include:* Zhenka Shulzhenko (Factory Girl by Volodin), Lenochka (In Search of Happiness by Rozov), Sophia (Wit Works Woe by Griboyedov), Nadya Rozoyeva (My Elder Sister by Volodin), Nadezhda Polikarpovna (The Barbarians by Gorky), Lushka (Virgin Soil Upturned by Sholokov), Nastasya Filippovna (The Idiot by Dostoyevsky), Valka (Irkutsk Story by Arbuzov), Oxana (Loss of the Squadron by Korneichuk), Masha (Three Sisters by Chekhov), Grushenka (Brothers Karamazov by Dostoyevsky), Arkadina (The Seagull by Chekhov). *Films include:* Pereklichka 1965, Starshaya Sestra 1966, Yeshche Raz Pro Lyubov 1968, Tri Topolya Na Plyushchikhe 1969, Chudnyy Kharakter 1970, Machekha 1973, Kakaya U Vas Ulybka 1974, Na Yasnyy Ogon 1975, Kapel 1981, Valentin I Valentina 1985. *Address:* Moscow Gorky Arts Theatre, 119146 Moscow, 22 Tverskoi Blvd, Russia. *Telephone:* (495) 203-74-66.

DORR, Noel, MA, BComm, HDipEd; Irish fmr diplomatist; b. 1 Nov. 1933, Limerick; s. of John Dorr and Bridget Clancy; m. Caitríona Doran 1983; ed St Nathy's Coll., Ballaghaderreen, Nat. Univ. of Ireland, Georgetown Univ., Washington, DC, USA; Third Sec., Dept of Foreign Affairs, Dublin 1960–62, Embassy in Brussels 1962–64, First Sec., Embassy in Washington, DC 1964–70, Dept of Foreign Affairs, Dublin 1970–72, Counsellor (Press and Information) 1972–74, Asst Sec. and Political Dir 1974–77, Deputy Sec. and Political Dir 1977–80, Amb. and Perm. Rep. to UN 1980–83, Amb. to UK 1983–87, Sec.-Gen. Dept of Foreign Affairs 1987–95 (retd), Personal Rep. of Minister for Foreign Affairs, EU Intergovernmental Conf. 1996–97, 2000; Chair. Údarás na hOllscoile (Governing Authority), Nat. Univ. of Ireland, Galway 2005–12; mem. Royal Irish Acad.; Dr hc (Nat. Univ. of Ireland, Galway) 2001. *Publications include:* Ireland and the United Nations: Memories of the Early Years 2010, A Small State at the Top Table: Memories of Ireland on the UN Security Council, 1981–82 2011, Sunningdale: The search for peace in Northern Ireland 2017. *Leisure interests:* reading, swimming. *Address:* 19 Whitebeam Avenue, Clonskeagh, Dublin 14, Ireland. *Telephone:* (1) 2694086. *E-mail:* ndorr@eircom.net.

DORRELL, Stephen James, BA; British business executive and fmr politician; *Senior Adviser, Healthcare and Public Sector Practice, KPMG UK;* b. 25 March 1952, Worcester, England; s. of Philip Dorrell; m. Penelope Anne Wears Taylor 1980; three s. one d.; ed Uppingham School, Brasenose Coll. Oxford; MP (Conservative) for Loughborough 1979–97, for Charnwood 1997–2015, Chair. Health Cttee 2010–14; Parl. Pvt. Sec. to Sec. of State for Energy 1983–87, Asst Govt Whip 1987–88, a Lord Commr of Treasury 1988–90, Parl. Under-Sec. of State, Dept of Health 1990–92, Financial Sec. to Treasury 1992–94; Sec. of State for Nat. Heritage 1994–95, for Health 1995–97; Shadow Sec. for Educ. and Employment 1997–98; Sr Adviser, Healthcare and Public Sector practice, KPMG UK 2014–; Gov., Loughborough Endowed Schools; Trustee, Uppingham School. *Leisure interests:* walking, reading. *Address:* c/o KPMG UK, 15 Canada Square, London, E14 5GL, England (office). *Telephone:* (20) 7311-1000 (office). *E-mail:* info@kpmg.com (office). *Website:* www.kpmg.com/uk (office).

DORSAINVIL, Daniel, PhD; Haitian economist and government official; b. 25 Aug. 1959, Port-au-Prince; ed Univ. of Pennsylvania, USA; fmr official, USAID; Econ. Adviser to Pres. Préval –2006; Minister of the Economy and Finance 2006–09; Vice-Pres. Societe Haitienne De Promotion Immobilier SA 2010–; CEO Phareview SA 2010–.

DORSEY, Jack; American internet industry executive; *Chairman, CEO and Co-founder, Twitter Inc.;* b. 19 Nov. 1976, St Louis, Mo.; s. of Tim Dorsey and Marcia Dorsey; ed Missouri Univ. of Science and Tech., New York Univ., Univ. of California, Berkeley; began career with dispatch co., Manhattan, New York 1999–2000; f. co. to dispatch couriers, taxis and emergency services using internet, Oakland 2000; Co-founder (with Isaac 'Biz' Stone) Obvious Corpn 2006 (spun off Twitter Inc. 2006); creator, Twitter.com 2006, Co-founder Twitter Inc., San Francisco 2007, CEO 2007–08, Chair. 2008–, Interim CEO then CEO 2015–; Co-founder and CEO Square (iPhone-based payment system); mem. Advisory Bd Ustream.tv 2009–; named one of The World's Most Influential People, TIME magazine 2009, Technology's Best & Brightest Young Entrepreneurs, Business Week magazine; named to TR35, an outstanding innovator under the age of 35, MIT Technical Review. *Address:* Twitter Inc., 539 Bryant Street, Suite 402, San Francisco, CA 94107, USA (office). *Telephone:* (415) 896-2008 (office). *Website:* twitter.com (office); squareup.com (office).

DOS ANJOS, Carlos Gustavo; São Tomé and Príncipe government official and diplomatist; *Ambassador to Angola;* b. 1956; fmr foreign affairs adviser to the Pres.; Minister of Foreign Affairs, Co-operation and Communities 2006–07; Amb. to Belgium 2010–14, to Angola 2017–. *Address:* Embassy of São Tomé and Príncipe, Rua Armindo de Andrade 173–175, Luanda, Angola (office). *Telephone:* 222345677 (office).

DOS RAMOS, Manuel Salvador; São Tomé and Príncipe journalist and politician; b. 25 June 1956, Conceiçao; ed Int. Inst. for Journalism, Germany, Moscow State Univ., USSR, Agostino Neto Univ., Luanda, Angola; Ed., later Sr Ed., Radio Nationale de São Tomé and Príncipe 1977–83, Head of Programming 1983–84; joined Ministry of Foreign Affairs 1986, held numerous positions including Head of Political Affairs Dept 1985–91, Head of Int. Politics Dept 1986–87, Head of Press Office 1991–92, Head of Bilateral Affairs Dept, Political Affairs and Int. Legal Div. 1991–92, Adviser to Pres. on Diplomatic Affairs 1993–95, on Diplomatic and Political Affairs 1995–97, Amb. to Angola 1997, fmr Amb. to Gabon, Minister of Foreign Affairs and Communities 2010–12, 2014–16; Pres., Nat. Cttee for Celebration of 40th Anniversary of UN 1985. *Address:* c/o Ministry of Foreign Affairs and Communities, Av. 12 de Julho, CP 111, São Tomé, São Tomé and Príncipe (office).

DOS SANTOS, Carlos, BA, MSc; Mozambican diplomatist; *Ambassador to USA;* b. 8 July 1961, Manhica, Maputo Prov.; m. Maria Isabel dos Santos; three c.; ed Univ. of Zimbabwe; joined Ministry of Foreign Affairs 1980, Protocol Officer 1980–82; Attaché, Perm. Mission to UN, New York 1982–84; Third Sec., Embassy in Harare, Zimbabwe 1985; Head of Political Dept, Africa and Middle East Div. 1990–91; Chef du Cabinet 1991–92; Counsellor and Pvt. Sec. to Pres. of Mozambique 1992–95; Perm. Rep. to UN, New York 1996–2002; High Commr to UK 2011–15, Amb. to USA 2016–; Del. to UN, OAU, Non-Aligned Movt and other int. orgs; mem. African Assn of Political Scientists. *Address:* Embassy of Mozambique, 1525 New Hampshire Avenue, NW, Washington, DC 20036, USA (office). *Telephone:* (202) 293-7146 (office). *Fax:* (202) 835-0245 (office). *E-mail:* embamoc@aol.com (office). *Website:* www.embamoc-usa.org (office).

DOS SANTOS, Eduardo; Brazilian diplomatist; *Ambassador to UK;* b. 29 Dec. 1952, Rio de Janeiro; ed Fed. Univ. of Rio de Janeiro; career diplomat since 1975, has held various high-level positions at Ministry of External Relations and other govt agencies, served at Embassies in Moscow, Buenos Aires and London, and subsequently as Amb. to Uruguay, to Switzerland and to Paraguay, Advisor to Office of Minister of Foreign Affairs 1986–89, 1992–93, Special Advisor to Office of Minister of Finance 1993, Diplomatic Advisor to the Pres. 1999–2002, Sec.-Gen., Ministry of External Relations 2013–15, Amb. to UK 2015–; Hon. CVO 1997. *Address:* Embassy of Brazil, 14–16 Cockspur Street, London, SW1Y 5BL, England (office). *Telephone:* (20) 7747-4500 (office). *Fax:* (20) 7747-4555 (office). *E-mail:* info .london@itamaraty.gov.br (office). *Website:* londres.itamaraty.gov.br (office).

DOS SANTOS, Fernando (Nandó) da Piedade Dias; Angolan politician; *President, National Assembly;* b. 5 March 1950, Luanda, Overseas Prov. of Angola, Portugal; ed Instituto Industrial de Luanda; involved with Grupo Boa Esperança from 1970 (pro-independence); nat. service, Portuguese colonial army 1973–74, deserted to join guerilla forces of Movimento Popular de Libertação de Angola (MPLA); mem. staff FAPLA (Armed Forces of MPLA), rank of Maj. 1984, Col 1986, Maj.-Gen. 1992; Insp., Corpo do Polícia Popular de Angola (CPPA—People's Police

Force of Angola) 1976–78, Head of 1st Command Div. 1978–79, Head of Political Dept and Personnel Section in Nat. Directorate 1979–81, Nat. Dir of People's Police 1984–86; Deputy Head of Nat. Political Directorate, Ministry of the Interior 1981–84, Nat. Dir of Personnel 1982–84, Deputy Minister of State Security 1984, of the Interior 1984, also Head of Information Services 1990, Deputy Minister of the Interior responsible for Internal Order 1995–99, Minister of the Interior 1999–2002; Deputy to Nat. Ass. 1986–, Pres. (Speaker) 2008–10, 2012–; Commdr-Gen. and Gen. Commr of Nat. Police (Polícia Nacional) 1995–; Co-ordinator Exec. Cttee of Inter-Ministerial Comm. of Process of Peace and Reconciliation 2001, Nat. Comm. for Social and Productive Reintegration of Demobilized Troops and Displaced Persons 2002; Prime Minister of Angola 2002–08; Vice-Pres. of Angola 2010–12. *Address:* Assembleia Nacional, Rua do 1° Congresso do MPLA, C.P. n° 1204, Luanda, Angola (office). *Telephone:* (222) 339591 (office). *Fax:* (222) 339591 (office). *E-mail:* assembleianacional@parlamento.ao (office). *Website:* www.parlamento.ao (office).

DOS SANTOS, Isabel; Angolan business executive; b. 1973, Baku, Azerbaijan; d. of José Eduardo dos Santos (fmr Pres. of Angola) and Tatiana Kukanova; m. Sindika Dokolo 2003; three c.; ed King's Coll., London; f. Urbana 2000; f. Miami Beach Club (night club), Luanda 2006; worked for Ascorp diamond trading co.; Owner, Kento Holding Ltd; holds stakes in telecoms, diamonds and banking in Angola, also Portuguese media conglomerate Zon Multimedia, Banco Espírito Santo, Banco Português de Investimento, and energy co. Energias de Portugal; Pres. Sociedade Nacional de Combustíveis de Angola (SONANGOL) (Angolan state oil co.) 2016–17; Pres. Angola Red Cross.

DOS SANTOS, José Eduardo; Angolan politician and fmr head of state; b. 28 Aug. 1942, Luanda; s. of Eduardo Avelino dos Santos and Jacinta José Paulino; m. three times; seven c.; ed Liceu Salvador Correia; joined Movimento Popular de Libertação de Angola (MPLA) 1961; went into exile 1961 and was a founder mem. and Vice-Pres. of MPLA Youth based in Léopoldville, Congo (now Kinshasa, The Democratic Repub. of the Congo); first Rep., MPLA, Brazzaville 1961; sent with group of students for training in Moscow 1963; graduated as Petroleum Engineer, Inst. of Oil and Gas, Baku 1969; then mil. course in telecommunications; returned to Angola and participated in war against Portuguese 1970–74; Second-in-Command of Telecommunications Services, MPLA Second Politico-Military Region, Cabinda; mem. Provisional Readjustment Cttee, Northern Front 1974; mem. MPLA Cen. Cttee and Political Bureau 1974–, Chair. of MPLA 1979–2018; Minister of Foreign Affairs, Angola 1975; Co-ordinator, MPLA Foreign Relations Dept 1975; Sec. Cen. Cttee for Educ., Culture and Sport, then for Nat. Reconstruction, then Economic Devt and Planning 1977–79; First Deputy Prime Minister, Minister of Planning and Head of Nat. Planning Comm. 1978–79; Pres. of Angola 1979–2017 and Chair. of Council of Ministers 1979–2017, also Prime Minister 1999–2002; C-in-C of FAPLA (Armed Forces of MPLA).

DOS SANTOS DINIZ, Abílio; Brazilian retail executive; *Chairman, BRF Brasil;* b. 28 Dec. 1936, São Paulo; s. of Valentim Diniz; m. 1st Auriluce Falleiros; two s. two d.; m. 2nd Geyze Marchesi two c.; ed Getúlio Vargas Business Foundation, Columbia Univ., Ohio Univ., USA; joined Companhia Brasileira de Distribuição – Pão de Açúcar 1956, Vice-Pres. 1989–96, CEO 1996–2002, Pres. Admin. Council 2000, Chair. Grupo Pao de Acucar –2013; Chair. Brasil Foods SA (now BRF Brasil) 2013–; Pres. Peninsula Holdings (family investment holding co.); f. São Paulo Supemarket Asscn; Admin. Emer., Regional Admin. Council of São Paulo 1983; mem. Nat. Monetary Council 1979–89; mem. Superior Council Portuguese-Brazilian Community of São Paulo 2006, Brazilian Govt's Bd of Policy and Man., Performance and Competitiveness; mem. Bd of Dirs Viavarejo SA 2009–; Personality of the Year, Brazilian Asscn of Retail Mans 1971. *Address:* BRF Brasil, Av. Escola Politécnica, 760, 2nd floor, 05350-901 São Paulo, Brazil (office). *E-mail:* www.brf-global.com (office).

DOSBOL, Nur uulu, PhD; Kyrgyzstani politician; b. 26 April 1948; ed Kyrgyz State Univ.; Jr Research Asst, History Inst. of Kyrgyz SSR Acad. of Sciences 1972–81, Intern-Researcher 1981–83, Sr Research Asst 1983–89, doctorate degree study 1989–92, Head of Dept, History Inst. 1993–95; Deputy of Zhogorku Kenesh (Parl.) 1995–2000; Minister of Educ., Science and Youth Policy 2005–07; Deputy Prime Minister 2007–08; apptd State Sec. of Kyrgyzstan 2008; Chair. Jany Kyrgyzstan (New Kyrgyzstan) party; fmr mem. Agrarian-Labor Party.

DOSS, Alan Claude, CMG; British UN official; *Executive Director, Kofi Annan Foundation;* b. 7 Jan. 1945, Cardiff, Wales; m. Soheir Doss; three d.; ed London School of Econs; held posts with UN in China, Kenya, Niger, Zaïre and Benin; fmr UN Resident Co-ordinator Regional Rep. of UNDP in Bangkok, Thailand; fmr Dir UN Border Relief Operation (Thai-Cambodia border); fmr Dir UNDP European Office, Geneva, Switzerland; Rep. of UNDP to Devt Assistance Cttee and OECD; Dir UN Devt Group (UNDG) –2001; Deputy Special Rep. of Sec.-Gen., UN Mission in Sierra Leone (UNAMSIL) 2001–04, Prin. Deputy Special Rep. of Sec.-Gen. for Côte d'Ivoire 2004–05, Special Rep. of Sec.-Gen. in Liberia 2005–07, in Democratic Repub. of the Congo (DRC) and Head of UN Org. Mission in DRC (MONUC, now MONUSCO), with rank of Under-Sec.-Gen. 2007–10 (retd); Visiting, then Assoc. Fellow, Geneva Centre for Security Policy 2010; Sr Political Advisor, then Exec. Dir Kofi Annan Foundation 2011–; Nelson Mandela Africa Lecturer, Royal United Services Inst. 2009. *Address:* Kofi Annan Foundation, PO Box 157, 1211 Geneva 20, Switzerland (office). *Telephone:* (22) 9197520 (office). *Fax:* (22) 9197529 (office). *E-mail:* info@kofiannanfoundation.org (office). *Website:* kofiannanfoundation.org (office).

DOSSAEV, Erbolat Askarbekovich; Kazakhstani politician; *Governor, National Bank of Kazakhstan;* b. 1970; m. Gulnara Dosayeva; ed Almaty Energy Inst., Bauman Moscow State Technical Univ.; Deputy Chair. of Bd, Bank TuranAlem 1997; Chair. of Bd, ATF Bank 1997; Chair. Agency on Regulation of Natural Monopolies, Protection of Competition and Support of Small Business 2001–03; Chair. and CEO, Baiterek Nat. Holding Co. 2016–17; Chair. Bd of Dirs, KazInvestBank 2006–12; Adviser to the Prime Minister 1998, Deputy Minister of Energy, Industry and Trade 1998–2000, of Finance 2003–04, of Healthcare 2004–06, of Econ. Devt and Trade 2012–16, of Economy and Budget Planning 2012–16, of Nat. Economy 2012–16, Deputy Prime Minister 2017–18; Gov. Nat. Bank of Kazakhstan 2019–; co-f. Public Fizmat Endowment Fund 2017; co-founder and bd mem. of Alumni Fund, Republican Physics and Mathematics School; Order of Kurmet 2013, Jubilee Medal on 20 years of the Constitution of the Repub. of Kazakhstan. *Address:* National Bank of Kazakhstan, 050040 Almaty, Koktem-3 21, Kazakhstan (office). *Telephone:* (727) 270-45-91 (office). *Fax:* (727) 270-47-03 (office). *E-mail:* hq@nationalbank.kz (office). *Website:* www.nationalbank.kz (office).

DOSSAR, Col Mohamed Bacar; Comoran politician and fmr agronomist; fmr Dir, Nat. Dept of Environment; fmr Minister of Defence, fmr Chief of Staff to Presidency, with Minister of Finance 2006–11, Minister of External Relations and Int. Co-operation, with responsibility for Comorans Abroad 2016–17; mem. Juwa (Sun) party.

DOSTUM, Gen. Abdul Rashid; Afghan politician and military leader; *Vice-President;* b. 1954, Khowaja Dukoh, Jowzjan Prov.; fmr plumber; with Oil and Gas Exploration Enterprise 1979; undertook mil. training in USSR 1980; Commdr pro-Soviet Jozjani Dostum Militia, North Afghanistan 1980–92; Defence Minister in Pres. Najibullah's Govt 1986–92; allied with Gulbuddin Hekmatyar's Pashtun warriors and Shi'a guerrillas following transition of power 1992; est. Itehad Shamal/Northern Unity org. which controlled most North Afghanistan provs 1993–97; fled to Turkey when Taliban occupied Mazar-i-Sharif 1997; returned to fight with Northern Alliance (NA) against Taliban 2001; Deputy Minister of Defence 2001–04; presidential cand. 2004; apptd Chief of Staff to C-in-C of Armed Forces 2005, temporarily suspended 2008; Vice-Pres., Islamic Republic of Afghanistan 2014–; Leader, Junbesh-i Melli-i Islami (Nat. Islamic Movt), Uzbek mil. wing of NA –2005; mem. Jabhe-ye-Motahed-e-Milli (United Nat. Front) 2007–; f. Balkh Air (airline); awarded Hero of the Repub. of Afghanistan Medal by Pres. Najibullah. *Address:* c/o Office of the President, Gul Khana Palace, Presidential Palace, Kabul, Afghanistan. *Telephone:* (20) 2141135. *Website:* www.president.gov.af.

DOTÉ, Elie, PhD; Central African Republic politician and government official; b. Bangui; m.; six c.; with Ministry of Agric. and Animal Husbandry 1974–80; fmr mem. staff, African Devt Bank (ADB), Chief of Agric. and Rural Devt 2001; Prime Minister and Head of Govt of Central African Repub. 2005–08 (resgnd), Minister of Finance 2006–08 (resgnd).

DOUBANE, Charles-Armel, BS, MS; Central African Republic diplomatist and politician; b. 12 Nov. 1966, Zemio; m.; ed Univ. of Paris XI, France, Univ. of Bangui; Minister for Relations with Parl. 1997–99; mem. Nat. Ass. (Alliance for Democracy and Progress, ADP) for Zemio constituency 1998–2000; joined Public Service Cen. 2000; fmr Diplomatic Adviser to Pres. François Bozizé –2006; Minister of Educ., Literacy, Higher Educ. and Research 2006–08; Dir-Guarantor, CAP Chimie SARL 2008–11; Amb. and Perm. Rep. to UN, New York 2011–16; apptd Minister of Foreign Affairs 2013 but did not take up post; unsuccessful cand. in presidential election Oct. 2015; Minister of Foreign Affairs, African Integration and Central Africans Abroad 2016–18.

DOUDNA, Jennifer Anne, BA, PhD; American chemist, molecular biologist and academic; *Professor of Biochemistry and Molecular Biology, University of California, Berkeley;* b. 1964, Washington, DC; m. Jamie Cate; one s.; ed Pomona Coll., Harvard Univ. Medical School; Postdoctoral Research Fellow in Molecular Biology, Massachusetts Gen. Hosp./Harvard Medical School 1989–91; Postdoctoral Research Fellow in Biomedical Science, Univ. of Colorado 1991–94; Asst Prof., then Assoc. Prof., Yale Univ. 1994–98, Henry Ford II Prof. of Molecular Biophysics and Biochemistry 1999–2002; R.B. Woodward Visiting Prof., Harvard Univ. 2000–01; Prof. of Biochemistry and Molecular Biology, Univ. of California, Berkeley 2003–, Head of Div. of Biochemistry, Biophysics and Structural Biology, holds Li Ka Shing Chancellor's Chair in Biomedical Sciences, also Faculty Scientist, Physical Biosciences Div., Lawrence Berkeley Nat. Lab. 2003–; Investigator, Howard Hughes Medical Inst. 1997–; Co-founder Caribou Biosciences, Inc. 2011, currently mem. Scientific Bd; mem. NAS 2002, Inst. of Medicine 2010; Fellow, American Acad. of Arts and Sciences 2003; Foreign mem. Royal Soc. 2016; Nat. Research Service Award in Biomedical Science 1986, Lucille P. Markey Scholar Award in Biomedical Science 1991, Searle Scholar Award 1996, Johnson Foundation Prize for innovative research 1996, Arnold & Mabel Beckman Foundation Beckman Young Investigator Award 1996, David & Lucile Packard Foundation Fellow Award 1996, Nat. Science Foundation Alan T. Waterman Award 2000, ACS Eli Lilly Award 2001, Foundation for Nat. Inst. of Health Lurie Prize in Biomedical Sciences 2014, Dr Paul Janssen Award for Biomedical Research (co-recipient) 2014, Jacob Heskel Gabbay Award (co-recipient) 2014, Princess of Asturias Award for Tech. and Scientific Research (co-recipient) 2015, Int. Soc. for Transgenic Technologies Prize (co-recipient) 2015, Genetics Prize, Gruber Foundation 2015, Breakthrough Prize in Life Sciences (co-recipient) 2015, World Technology Awards (Biotechnology) (co-recipient) 2015, Canada Gairdner Int. Award (co-recipient) 2016, Dr H.P. Heineken Prize for Biochemistry and Biophysics 2016, L'Oréal-UNESCO Award for Women in Science (N America) 2016, Tang Prize 2016, Japan Prize (co-recipient) 2017, Albany Medical Center Prize (co-recipient) 2017, Kavli Prize in Nanoscience 2018, Award in Chemical Sciences, NAS 2018, Pearl Meister Greengard Prize, Rockefeller Univ. 2018. *Achievements include:* research in the molecular structures of Ribonucleic acid (RNA) molecules and devt of gene-editing tech. allowing the modification of genetic material (Crispr-Cas9 genome editing technique). *Address:* UC Berkeley Doudna Lab, 708A Stanley Hall, Berkeley, CA 94720-3206, USA (office). *Telephone:* (510) 643-0225 (office). *Fax:* (510) 643-0080 (office). *E-mail:* doudna@berkeley.edu (office). *Website:* rna.berkeley.edu (office).

DOUGAN, Brady W., BA (Econs), MBA; American banking executive; b. 1959; ed Univ. of Chicago, Ill.; began career in derivatives group of Bankers Trust; with Credit Suisse First Boston 1990–, fmr Co-Head, Global Debt Capital Markets Group and of Credit Suisse Financial Products marketing effort in the Americas, Head of Equities Div. 1996–2001, Global Head, Securities Div. 2001–02, Co-Pres. Institutional Securities 2002–04, mem. Exec. Bd, Chair. Man. Council and CEO, mem. Exec. Bd Credit Suisse Group AG 2004–07, CEO Credit Suisse Investment Bank 2004–07, CEO Credit Suisse Group AG 2007–15; mem. Bd of Dirs, Humacyte Inc. 2005–; mem. Bd of Trustees, Univ. of Chicago 2013–. *Address:* c/o Credit Suisse Group AG, PO Box 1, 8070 Zurich, Switzerland. *E-mail:* info@credit-suisse.com.

DOUGHERTY, Michele Karen, CBE, BSc, PhD, FRS, FRAS; British (b. South African) astrophysicist; *Professor of Space Physics, Imperial College London;* b. 1962, South Africa; ed Univ. of Natal; Particle Physics and Astronomy Research Council (PPARC) Advanced Fellow in Space Physics, Imperial Coll. London 2000, currently Prof. and Chair of Space Physics; fmr Guest Investigator, NASA Jupiter System Data Analysis Program (part of Galileo unmanned spacecraft project); Prin. Investigator for J-MAG (magnetometer) for ESA JUICE spacecraft (due for launch June 2022); Prin. Investigator for NASA-ESA-ASI Cassini-Huygens mission to Saturn; Assoc. Ed. JGR (Space Physics) 1997–2001; Ed. Physics Departmental Annual Review 1998–99; Fellow American Geophysical Union; awarded Royal Soc. Research Professorship 2014; Royal Soc. Hughes Medal 2008, Royal Astronomical Soc. Gold Medal in Geophysics 2017, Richard Glazebrook Medal and Prize 2018. *Address:* Department of Physics, Faculty of Natural Sciences, Imperial College, London, SW7 2AZ, England (office). *Telephone:* (20) 7594-7757 (office). *E-mail:* m.dougherty@imperial.ac.uk (office). *Website:* www.imperial.ac.uk/people/m.dougherty (office).

DOUGLAS, Rt Hon. Denzil Llewellyn, PC, BSc, MD; Saint Kitts and Nevis politician; b. 14 Jan. 1953; ed Univ. of the West Indies; fmr high school teacher; community service, including leadership of the 4H movt; opened pvt./family medical practice 1986; first Young Labour Rep. to sit on Nat. Exec. of Saint Kitts-Nevis Labour Party, Deputy Chair. 1987–89, Chair. 1989–; MP for St Christopher #6 1989–; Prime Minister of Saint Kitts and Nevis 1995–2015, also Minister of Finance, of Nat. Security, of Information, of Planning and of Foreign Affairs 1995–2001, Minister of Finance, Devt Planning and Nat. Security 2001–04, Minister of Finance, Sustainable Devt, Information and Tech. and Minister of Tourism, Sports and Culture 2004–10, Minister of Finance, Sustainable Devt, Human Resource Devt, Constituency Empowerment and Social Security 2010–15; Chair. Bd Caribbean Devt Bank 2002–03, 2014–15; Pres. Saint Kitts and Nevis Medical Asscn; Order of Brilliant Star with Special Grand Cordon (Taiwan), Order of the Liberator (First Class) (Bolivia); Gandhi-King-Ikeda Peace Award, honoured as an outstanding graduate of Univ. of the West Indies, Legacy Award, American Foundation of the UWI, New York, Special Global Award, Trumpet Awards, Las Vegas, USA 2007, South South News Award 2013. *Address:* St Kitts-Nevis Labour Party, Masses House, Church Street, PO Box 239, Basseterre, Saint Kitts and Nevis (office). *Telephone:* 465-5347. *Fax:* 465-8328. *E-mail:* wanda.connor@sknlabourparty.com. *Website:* www.sknlabourparty.com.

DOUGLAS, Gabrielle (Gabby) Christina Victoria; American gymnast; b. 31 Dec. 1995, Virginia; d. of Timothy Douglas and Natalie Hawkins; started formal gymnastics training at Gymstrada at the age of six in 2002; Virginia State Champion 2004; begain training with coach Liang Chow in Ia; competed in Covergirl Classic, Chicago (ninth all-around in jr div.) 2010, Nastia Liukin Supergirl Cup (fourth all-around) 2010; silver medal, balance beam, Jr Nat. Championship 2010; won uneven bars title, gold medal (team), fifth, all-around, Pan American Championships 2010; made sr debut in 2011; seventh, all-around, Nat. Championship, Minn. 2011; gold medal (team), World Championships, Tokyo 2011; winner, AT&T American Cup 2012 (highest total all-around score); gold medal, uneven bars, silver medal, all-round, bronze medal, uneven bars, floor exercise Visa Championships 2012; gold medal, uneven bars, gold medal (team), Pacific Rim Championships 2012; gold medal, individual all-around, gold medal (team all-around), (first African-American woman to win the event), Olympic Games, London 2012; first American gymnast ever to win both team and individual all-around gold at same Olympics; mem. Chow's Gymnastics and Dance Inst. *Address:* c/o Chow's Gymnastics and Dance Institute, 2210 Park Drive, West Des Moines, IA 50265-5767, USA. *Website:* gabrielledouglas.com.

DOUGLAS, James (Jim) Henry, AB; American politician, fmr state governor and academic; *Executive-in-Residence, Middlebury College;* b. 21 June 1951, Springfield, Mass; s. of Robert James Douglas and Cora Elizabeth Douglas (née Holley); m. Dorothy Foster 1975; two s.; ed East Longmeadow High School, Mass, Middlebury Coll., Vt; Gen. Man. Credit Bureau of Middlebury 1972–76; Exec. Dir United Way of Addison Co. 1976–79; mem. Vt House of Reps 1972–79, Majority Whip 1975–77, Majority Leader 1977–79; Exec. Asst to Gov. Richard A. Snelling of Vt 1979–80; Vt Sec. of State, Montpelier 1981–93; State Treas. 1994–2002; Gov. of Vt 2003–11; Exec.-in-Residence, Middlebury Coll. 2011–, also teaches course, Vermont Govt and Politics; Chair. Nat. Govs Asscn 2009–10; mem. Govs Council, Bipartisan Policy Center, Washington, DC 2010–; mem. and fmr Pres. Nat. Asscn of Secs of State; fmr Pres. Addison Co. Chamber of Commerce, Porter Medical Center; mem. Republican Town Cttee; Nat. Order of Quebec (Canada) 2010. *Address:* Middlebury College, MiddCORE House, 20 Old Chapel Road., Middlebury, VT 05753, USA (office). *Telephone:* (802) 443-5000 (office). *E-mail:* middcore@middlebury.edu (office). *Website:* www.middcore.middlebury.edu (office).

DOUGLAS, Kirk, AB; American actor; b. 9 Dec. 1916, Amsterdam, NY; s. of Harry Danielovitch and Bryna Danielovitch (née Sanglel); m. 1st Diana Dill (divorced 1950); two s. including Michael Kirk Douglas; m. 2nd Anne Buydens 1954; two s. (one deceased); ed St Lawrence Univ. and American Acad. of Dramatic Arts; Pres. Bryna Productions 1955–; Dir Los Angeles Chapter, UN Asscn; Acad. Awards 1948, 1952, 1956; Commdr des Arts et Lettres 1979, Légion d'honneur 1985, Presidential Medal of Freedom 1981; New York Film Critics' Award, Hollywood Foreign Press Award, American Film Inst.'s Lifetime Achievement Award 1991, Kennedy Center Honors 1994, Hon. Acad. Award 1996, Lifetime Achievement Award Screen Actors' Guild 1999, Golden Bear, Berlin Film Festival 2000, Nat. Medal of Arts 2002. *Stage appearances include:* Spring Again, Three Sisters, Kiss and Tell, The Wind is Ninety, Alice in Arms, Man Bites Dog, The Boys of Autumn, Before I Forget. *Films include:* The Strange Love of Martha Ivers 1946, Out of the Past (aka Build My Gallows High) 1947, Mourning Becomes Electra 1947, I Walk Alone 1948, The Walls of Jericho 1948, My Dear Secretary 1949, A Letter to Three Wives 1949, Champion 1949, Young Man With a Horn 1950, The Glass Menagerie 1950, Along the Great Divide 1951, Ace in the Hole 1951, Detective Story 1951, The Big Trees 1952, The Big Sky 1952, The Bad and the Beautiful 1952, The Story of Three Loves 1953, The Juggler 1953, Un acte d'amour (Act of Love) 1953, 20,000 Leagues Under the Sea 1954, The Racers 1955, Ulisse (Ulysses) 1955, Man Without a Star 1955, The Indian Fighter 1955, Lust for Life 1956, Top Secret Affair 1957, Gunfight at the O.K. Corral 1957, Paths of Glory (also producer) 1957, The Vikings 1958, Last Train from Gun Hill 1959, The Devil's Disciple 1959, Spartacus (also exec. producer) 1960, Town Without Pity 1961, The Last Sunset 1961, Lonely Are the Brave 1962, Two Weeks in Another Town 1962, The Hook 1963, The List of Adrian Messenger 1963, For Love or Money 1963, Strangers When We Meet, Seven Days in May 1964, In Harms Way 1965, Cast a Giant Shadow 1966, Paris brûle-t-il? (Is Paris Burning?) 1966, Grand Prix (producer) 1966, The Way West 1967, The War Waggon 1967, A Lovely Way to Die 1968, The Brotherhood (also producer) 1968, The Arrangement 1969, There Was a Crooked Man 1970, To Catch a Spy 1971, The Light at the Edge of the World (also producer) 1971, Gunfight 1971, Summertree (producer) 1971, The Special London Bridge Project 1972, Un uomo da rispettare (A Man to Respect) 1972, Cat and Mouse, Scalawag (also dir) 1973, Once Is Not Enough 1975, Posse (also dir and producer) 1975, Holocaust 2000 1977, The Fury 1978, The Villain 1979, Home Movies 1979, Saturn 3 1980, The Final Countdown 1980, The Man from Snowy River 1982, Eddie Macon's Run 1983, Tough Guys 1986, Oscar 1991, Welcome to Veraz 1991, Greedy 1994, Diamonds 1999, Family Jewels 2002, It Runs in the Family 2003, Illusion 2004. *Television work includes:* Tales of the Vikings (series, producer) 1960, Dr. Jekyll and Mr. Hyde 1973, Mousey 1974, The Moneychangers (mini-series) 1976, Victory at Entebbe 1976, Remembrance of Love 1982, Draw! 1984, Amos 1985, Queenie (mini-series) 1987, Inherit the Wind 1988, Two-Fisted Tales 1991, The Secret 1992, Take Me Home Again 1994, Touched by an Angel (series) 2000. *Publications:* The Ragman's Son: An Autobiography 1988, Dance with the Devil (novel) 1990, The Secret (novel) 1992, The Gift (novel) 1992, Last Tango in Brooklyn (novel) 1994, Climbing the Mountain: My Search for Meaning 1997, The Broken Mirror (novel) 1997, My Stroke of Luck 2002, Let's Face It 2007. *Address:* Warren Cowan Associates, 8899 Beverly Boulevard, Suite 412, Beverly Hills, CA 90048-2427 (office); The Bryna Company, 141 S El Camino Drive, Beverly Hills, CA 90212, USA (office). *Telephone:* (310) 274-5294 (office). *Fax:* (310) 274-2537 (office).

DOUGLAS, Michael Kirk, BA; American actor and film producer; b. 25 Sept. 1944, New Brunswick, New Jersey; s. of Kirk Douglas (q.v.) and Diana Douglas; m. 1st Diandra Mornell Luker 1977 (divorced); one s.; m. 2nd Catherine Zeta-Jones (q.v.) 2000; one s. one d.; appeared in TV series Streets of San Francisco; f. Further Films (production co.); Hon. DLit (Univ. of St Andrews, Scotland) 2006; Spencer Tracy Award 1999, UN Messenger of Peace 2000, Golden Globe Cecil B. DeMille Award 2004, Career Achievement Award, Nat. Bd of Review 2007, Lifetime Achievement Award, American Film Inst. 2009, David O. Selznick Achievement Award, Producers Guild of America 2009, Danny Kaye Humanitarian Peace Award 2014. *Film appearances include:* It's My Turn, Hail Hero! 1969, Summertime 1971, Napoleon and Samantha 1972, Coma 1978, Running 1979, Star Chamber 1983, Romancing the Stone (also producer) 1984, A Chorus Line 1985, Jewel of the Nile 1985, Fatal Attraction 1987, Wall Street (Acad. Award for Best Actor 1988) 1987, Heidi 1989, Black Rain 1989, The War of the Roses 1990, Shining Through 1990, Basic Instinct 1992, Falling Down 1993, Disclosure 1994, The American President 1995, The Ghost and the Darkness (also exec. producer) 1996, The Game 1997, A Perfect Murder 1998, One Day in September (voice) 1999, Traffic 2000, Wonder Boys 2000, One Night at McCool's (also producer) 2000, Don't Say a Word 2001, A Few Good Years 2002, It Runs in the Family 2003, Monkeyface 2003, The In-Laws 2003, The Sentinel (also producer) 2006, You, Me and Dupree 2006, King of California 2007, Beyond a Reasonable Doubt 2009, Ghosts of Girlfriends Past 2009, Solitary Man 2009, Wall Street: Money Never Sleeps 2010, Behind the Candelabra (Emmy Award for Best Actor in a Mini-series/Movie, Golden Globe Award for Best Actor in TV Mini-series or Movie, Screen Actors Guild Award for Outstanding Performance by a Male Actor in a TV Movie or Mini-series 2014) 2013, Beyond the Reach (also producer) 2014, Ant-Man 2015, Flatliners 2017, Animal World 2018, Ant-Man and the Wasp 2018. *Films produced include:* One Flew Over the Cuckoo's Nest (Academy Award for Best Film 1975), The China Syndrome, Starman (exec. producer), Flatliners 1990, Stone Cold 1991, Eyes of an Angel (exec. producer) 1991, Radio Flyer 1992, Made in America (co-exec. producer) 1993, Face/Off (exec. producer) 1997, The Rainmaker 1997, Godspeed, Lawrence Mann 2002. *Television appearances include:* The Kominsky Method (Golden Globe Award for Best Actor in a TV Series Musical or Comedy 2019) 2018–. *Address:* c/o Allen Burry, Further Films, 62 W 45th Street, Suite# 901, New York, NY 10036, USA.

DOUGLAS, Hon. Sir Roger Owen, Kt; New Zealand politician and accountant; b. 5 Dec. 1937, Auckland, North Island; s. of Norman V. Douglas and Jennie Douglas; m. Glennis June Anderson 1961; one s. one d.; ed Auckland Grammar School, Auckland Univ.; entered House of Reps as Labour mem. for Manukau 1969 (now Manurewa); Minister of Broadcasting 1973–75, of the Post Office 1973–74, of Housing (with State Advances, Housing Corpn) 1974–75; Minister of Finance and Minister in Charge of the Inland Revenue Dept and of Friendly Socs 1984–87, of Finance 1988, of Police and Immigration 1989–90; MP for ACT Party List 2008–11; Dir Brierley Investments 1990–98 (Chair. (interim) 1998), John Fairfax Ltd 1997–99, Aetna Health (New Zealand) Ltd 1997–99, Tasman Inst. 1997–; fmr Pres. Auckland Labour Regional Council, Manukau Labour Cttee; Finance Minister of the Year, Euromoney Magazine 1985, Max Schmidheiny Freedom Prize, Switzerland 1995, Ludwig Erhard Foundation Prize, Germany 1997, Friedrich von Hayek Medal, Austria 2002, Turgot Freedom Prize, Paris 2008. *Publications include:* There's Got to Be a Better Way 1980, Toward Prosperity 1987, Unfinished Business 1993, Completing the Circle 1996, Welfare: Savings not Taxation (co-author) 2016; several papers on int. and econ. affairs. *Leisure interests:* cricket, rugby, rugby league, reading, grandchildren. *Address:* 411 Redoubt Road, Totara Park, Auckland 2019, New Zealand (home). *Telephone:* (9) 2639596 (home). *E-mail:* rdouglas@xtra.co.nz (office).

DOUSTE-BLAZY, Philippe Jean Georges Marie, DenM; French physician, politician and UN official; *Special Adviser to the Secretary-General on Innovative Financing for Development, United Nations;* b. 1 Jan. 1953, Lourdes; s. of Louis Douste-Blazy and Geneviève Béguère; m. Marie-Yvonne Calazel 1977; ed Lycée Pierre de Caousou, Toulouse and Univ. Paul Sabatier, Toulouse; Intern, Toulouse hosps 1976–82; Head of Cardiology Clinics and Asst to Toulouse hosps 1982–86; Univ. Prof. 1988–; Dir Arcol 1988–; Mayor of Lourdes 1989–2000, of Toulouse 2001–04; mem. European Parl. 1989–93; Regional Councillor for Midi-Pyrénées 1992; Deputy to Nat. Ass. (Union pour la démocratie française) 1993, 1997–2001; Minister of Social Affairs, of Health and the City 1993–95, of Culture 1995–97, of

Health and Social Protection 2004–05, of Foreign Affairs 2005–07; Adviser to Pres. Nicolas Sarkozy 2007–08; Special Adviser to the Sec.-Gen. on Innovative Financing for Devt, UN 2008–; Pres. Union pour la démocratie française group, Nat. Ass. 1998–2004; mem. New York Acad. of Sciences and numerous medical orgs. *Leisure interests:* classical music, golf. *Address:* Office of the Secretary-General, United Nations, New York, NY 10017, USA (office); 1 rue de Bagnères, 65100 Lourdes, France (home). *Telephone:* (212) 963-1234 (office). *Fax:* (212) 963-4879 (office). *Website:* www.un.org/sg (office).

DOUVILLE, Jean; Canadian lawyer and business executive; b. Bedford, Quebec; ed Univ. of Ottawa; called to Québec Bar 1968; joined UAP Inc. 1971, Pres. 1981, CEO 1982, Chair. 1994–; mem. Bd of Dirs Nat. Bank of Canada 1991–, Chair. 2004–14, fmr Chair. Audit and Risk Man. Cttee, Conduct Review and Corp. Governance Cttee; mem. Bd of Dirs Genuine Parts Co. 1990–, Richelieu's Hardware Ltd 2005–; Dir Leroux Steel Inc. 1999–2003, Van Houtte Inc. 1999–2003.

DOVAL, Ajit Kumar, MEcon; Indian intelligence officer and government official; *National Security Advisor to Prime Minister;* b. 20 Jan. 1945, Pauri Garhwal; m. Anu Doval; two s.; ed Univ. of Agra; joined Indian Police Service 1968, involved in numerous counter-terrorism, counter-intelligence and counter-insurgency operations, including diplomatic assignments at Indian High Comms in Pakistan and UK, Head of Operations Dept, Intelligence Bureau (IB) 1994–2004, Founding Chair. IB Multi Agency Centre (MAC) and Jt Task Force on Intelligence (JTFI) 2001, Dir IB 2004–05; Founding Dir Vivekananda Int. Foundation (public policy think tank) 2009; Security Advisor to Govt of Karnataka 2009; Nat. Security Advisor to Prime Minister 2014–; guest lecturer on strategic issues at IISS, London, Capitol Hill, Washington DC, Australia-India Inst., Univ. of Melbourne, Nat. Defence Coll., New Delhi, Lal Bahadur Shastri Nat. Acad. of Admin, Mussoorie; Police Medal for meritorious service, Pres.'s Police Medal, Kirti Chakra (gallantry award) 1988. *Address:* Prime Minister's Office, South Block, Raisina Hill, New Delhi 110 011, India (office). *E-mail:* pmindia@pmindia.nic.in (office). *Website:* www.pmindia.nic.in (office).

DOVE, Rita Frances, BA, MFA; American writer, poet and academic; *Commonwealth Professor of English, University of Virginia;* b. 28 Aug. 1952, Akron, Ohio; d. of Ray Dove and Elvira Dove (née Hord); m. Fred Viebahn 1979; one d.; ed Miami Univ., Ohio, Univ. of Tübingen, Germany and Univ. of Iowa; Asst Prof., Ariz. State Univ., Tempe 1981–84, Assoc. Prof. 1984–87, Prof. of English 1987–89; Prof., Univ. of Virginia, Charlottesville 1989–93, Commonwealth Prof. of English 1993–; Poet Laureate of the USA 1993–95, of the Commonwealth of Virginia 2004–06; Consultant in Poetry, Library of Congress 1993–95; Special Consultant in Poetry, Library of Congress Bicentennial 1999–2000; Assoc. Ed., Callaloo 1986–98, adviser and Contributing Ed. 1998–; adviser and Contributing Ed. Gettysburg Review 1987–, TriQuarterly 1988–, Meridian 1989–, Ploughshares 1992–, Georgia Review 1994–, Bellingham Review 1996–, Poetry Int. 1996–, Int. Quarterly 1997–, Mid-American Review 1998–, Hunger Mountain 2003–, American Poetry Review 2005–; Writer-in-Residence, Tuskegee Inst., Ala 1982; poetry panellist, Nat. Endowment for Arts, Washington, DC 1984–86 (Chair. 1985); judge, Pulitzer Prize in Poetry 1991 (Chair. of Jury 1997); mem. Bd of Dirs Associated Writing Programs 1985–88, Pres. 1986–87; mem. Jury, Anisfield-Wolf Book Awards; Chancellor Acad. of American Poets 2006–12; mem. Acad. of American Poets, Associated Writing Programs, Poetry Soc. of America, Poets and Writers, American Acad. of Arts and Sciences, American Acad. of Arts and Letters, American Philosophical Soc.; 28 hon. doctorates; Fulbright Fellow 1974–75, Nat. Endowment for the Arts grants 1978, 1989, Portia Pittman Fellow, Tuskegee Inst. 1982, Guggenheim Fellowship 1984, Rockefeller Foundation Residency in Bellagio, Italy 1988, Mellon Fellow, Nat. Humanities Center 1989, Fellow, Center for Advanced Studies, Univ. of Virginia 1989–92, Chubb Fellowship, Yale Univ. 2007; numerous awards, including Acad. of American Poets Peter I. B. Lavan Younger Poets Award 1986, Callaloo Award 1986, Gen. Electric Foundation Award for Younger Writers 1987, Ohio Gov.'s Award 1988, Ohioana Library Book Awards 1990, 2000, NY Public Library Literary Lion Awards 1990, 1996, 2000, Nat. Book Award in Poetry 1991, NAACP Great American Artist Award 1993, American Acad. of Achievement Golden Plate Award 1994, Folger Shakespeare Library Renaissance Forum Award 1994, Carl Sandburg Award 1994, Charles Frankel Prize/Nat. Humanities Medal 1996, Heinz Award in the Arts and Humanities 1996, Barnes and Noble Writers Award 1997, Sara Lou Frontrunner Award 1997, Levinson Prize 1998, John Frederick Nims Translation Award (co-recipient with Fred Viebahn) 1999, Duke Ellington Lifetime Achievement Award in the Literary Arts, Ellington Fund in Washington, DC 2001, Emily Couric Leadership Award 2003, Commonwealth Award of Distinguished Service 2006, Library of Virginia Lifetime Achievement Award 2008, Fulbright Asscn Lifetime Achievement Medal 2009, Hurston/Wright Foundation Award for Poetry 2010, Amb.'s Award from Oklahoma Center for Poets and Writers 2010, Ohioana Book Award for Poetry 2010, Nat. Medal of Arts for 2011, Busboys and Poets Award 2012, Nat. Endowment for the Art Works Grant 2013, Furious Flower Poetry Lifetime Achievement Award 2014, Carole Weinstein Prize for Library of Virginia 2014, China's 10th Poetry & People Int. Prize for Poetry 2015, Birmingham Literature Festival (UK) 2015, The UK Poetry Soc. Annual Lecture (London, Liverpool, Newcastle, Edinburgh) 2015, Stone Award for Lifetime Achievement 2016, Harold Washington Literary Award 2017, US Presidential Scholars Award 2017, Callaloo Lifetime Achievement Award 2017, Library of Virginia Award in Poetry 2017, 50 for 50 Arts Inspiration Award, Virginia Comm. for the Arts 2018. *Films include:* Rita Dove: An American Poet (documentary) 2014. *Plays include:* The Darker Face of the Earth (Oregon Shakespeare Festival, Kennedy Center) 1997, (Royal Nat. Theatre, London) 1999, (Guthrie Theater, Fountain Theatre, Los Angeles) 2000. *Publications:* poetry: Ten Poems 1977, The Only Dark Spot in the Sky 1980, The Yellow House on the Corner 1980, Mandolin 1982, Museum 1983, Thomas and Beulah (Pulitzer Prize in Poetry 1987) 1986, The Other Side of the House 1988, Grace Notes 1989, Selected Poems 1993, Lady Freedom Among Us 1994, Mother Love 1995, Evening Primrose 1998, On the Bus with Rosa Parks 1999, Best American Poetry (ed.) 2000, American Smooth 2004, Sonata Mulattica 2009, The Penguin Anthology of Twentieth-Century American Poetry (ed.) 2011, Collected Poems 1974–2004, 2016; prose: Fifth Sunday (short stories) 1985, Through the Ivory Gate (novel) 1992, The Darker Face of Earth (verse play) 1994, The Poet's World (essays) 1995. *Leisure interests:* playing the viola da gamba, classical voice training, ballroom dancing. *Address:* 219 Bryan Hall, University of Virginia, PO Box 400121, Charlottesville, VA 22904-4121, USA (office). *Telephone:* (434) 924-6618 (office). *Fax:* (434) 924-1478 (office). *E-mail:* rfd4b@virginia.edu (office). *Website:* www.people.virginia.edu/~rfd4b (office).

DOVO, Eloi Maxime Alphonse; Malagasy diplomatist and politician; m.; two c.; Asst Higher School of Law, Econs and Man., Univ. of Antananarivo 1986–87; Head Europe Div., Office of Bilateral Relations, Ministry of Foreign Affairs (MFA) 1987–88, Head Div. of America and the Caribbean 1989, Insp. Cabinet Ministers of Foreign Affairs 1990–91, Authorized Rep. 1991–94, Dir Documentation and Support of Int. Dels of Madagascar 1997; Minister of Foreign Affairs 2018–19; Non-Perm. Rep. to Cabinet of Seal Protection, Ministry of Justice 1997; fmr Amb. to Russia. *Address:* c/o Ministry of Foreign Affairs, rue Andriamifidy, Anosy, BP 836, 101 Antananarivo, Madagascar (office).

DOWDESWELL, Elizabeth, OC, OOnt, BSc, MSc; Canadian environmentalist and international organization official; *Lieutenant Governor of Ontario;* b. Belfast, Northern Ireland; ed Univ. of Saskatchewan and Utah State Univ., USA; moved with her family to Saskatchewan 1947; fmr univ. lecturer and high school teacher; fmr Deputy Minister of Culture and Youth, Prov. Govt of Saskatchewan; Man. Consultant, Govt of Canada; fmr Perm. Rep. of Canada to WMO, fmr mem. Exec. Council; Asst Deputy Minister, Environment Canada and Head, Atmospheric Environment Service –1993; Exec. Dir UNEP 1993–98; fmr UN Under-Sec.-Gen.; Visiting Prof. in Public Health Sciences, Jt Centre for Bioethics, Univ. of Toronto, Ont. 2006; fmr Assoc. Fellow, European Centre for Public Affairs; f. own man. consulting business; Jt Chair. Great Lakes Water Quality Bd, Canada-USA Int. Jt Comm.; Canadian Prin. Del. Intergovernmental Panel on Climate Change, Earth Summit, Rio de Janeiro, Brazil 1992, Jt Chair, Working Group on the Framework Convention on Climate Change 1992; Pres. Nuclear Waste Man. Org. 2002–06; Pres. and CEO Council of Canadian Acads; Lt Gov. of Ont. 2014–; several hon. degrees, including six Hon. LLD degrees from various univs and Hon. LHD degree from Mount Saint Vincent Univ., Halifax; Memorial Gold Medal, Charles Univ., Prague, Pierre Elliot Trudeau Mentor 2004. *Publications include:* numerous publs in professional journals and the popular press. *Address:* Office of the Lieutenant Governor of Ontario, Queen's Park, Toronto, ON M7A 1A1, Canada (office). *Telephone:* (416) 325-7780 (office). *Fax:* (416) 325-7787 (office). *E-mail:* lt.gov@ontario.ca (office). *Website:* www.lgontario.ca (office).

DOWELL, Sir Anthony James, Kt, CBE; British director, producer and fmr ballet dancer; b. 16 Feb. 1943, London; s. of Arthur H. Dowell and Catherine E. Dowell; ed Hampshire School, Royal Ballet School; Prin. Dancer, The Royal Ballet 1966, Sr Prin. Dancer 1967–84, Asst to the Dir 1984, Assoc. Dir 1985–86, Dir 1986–2001 (retd); joined American Ballet Theatre 1978; cr. roles in the following ballets: The Dream 1964, Romeo and Juliet 1965, Shadow Play 1967, Monotones 1969, Triad 1972, Manon 1974, A Month in the Country 1976; narrator in Oedipus Rex, Metropolitan Opera House, New York 1981; cr. role of Prospero in Nureyev's The Tempest, Royal Opera House, London 1982; dir new productions of Swan Lake and The Sleeping Beauty for Royal Ballet; designed costumes for Thaïs pas de deux (Frederick Ashton), In the Night (Jerome Robbins) and Symphony in C (George Balanchine) for Royal Ballet; Queen Elizabeth II Coronation Award, Royal Acad. of Dancing 1994, Critics' Circle Award 2001, De Valois Award for Outstanding Achievement in Dance 2002. *Address:* c/o The Royal Ballet, Covent Garden, London, WC2E 7QA, England.

DOWELL, John Derek, PhD, FRS, CPhys, FInstP; British physicist and academic; *Professor Emeritus of Physics, University of Birmingham;* b. 6 Jan. 1935, Ashby-de-la-Zouch, Leics., England; s. of William E. Dowell and Elsie D. Dowell; m. Patricia Clarkson 1959; one s. one d.; ed Coalville Grammar School, Leics. and Univ. of Birmingham; Research Fellow, Univ. of Birmingham 1958–60; Research Assoc., CERN, Geneva 1960–62, Scientific Assoc. 1973–74, 1985–87, mem. Scientific Policy Cttee 1982–90, 1993–96, Research Bd 1993–96, Chair. LEP Cttee 1993–96; Lecturer, Univ. of Birmingham 1962–70, Sr Lecturer 1970–74, Reader 1974–80, Prof. of Elementary Particle Physics 1980–97, Poynting Prof. of Physics 1997–2002, Prof. Emer. 2002–; Visiting Scientist, Argonne Nat. Lab., USA 1968–69; Chair. Science and Eng Research Council (SERC) Particle Physics Cttee 1981–85; mem. European Cttee for Future Accelerators 1989–93, BBC Science Consultative Group 1992–94, DESY Extended Scientific Council 1992–98; Chair. ATLAS Collaboration Bd 1996–98; Lay Chair. Birmingham Children's Hosp. NHS Trust 2002–; mem. UK Particle Physics and Astronomy Research Council 1994–97; mem. Court of Univ. of Warwick 1993–2001, Council, Royal Soc. 1997–98 (also Vice-Pres.); mem. RAE Physics Panel, Higher Educ. Funding Council 2001; Fellow, American Physical Soc.; Rutherford Medal and Prize, Inst. of Physics 1988. *Publications:* numerous papers in physics journals. *Leisure interests:* piano, amateur theatre, golf. *Address:* School of Physics and Astronomy, University of Birmingham, Birmingham, B15 2TT (office); 57 Oxford Road, Moseley, Birmingham, B13 9ES, England (home). *Telephone:* (121) 414-4658 (office); (121) 449-3332 (home). *Fax:* (121) 414-6709 (office). *E-mail:* jdd@hep.ph.bham.ac.uk (office).

DOWLING, John Elliott, AB, PhD; American neuroscientist, neurobiologist and academic; *Gordon and Llura Gund Professor of Neurosciences, Harvard University;* b. 31 Aug. 1935, Rhode Island; s. of Joseph Leo Dowling and Ruth W. (Tappan) Dowling; m. 1st Susan Kinney (divorced 1974); two s.; m. 2nd Judith Falco 1975; one d.; ed Harvard Univ.; Instructor, Harvard Univ. 1961, Asst Prof. 1961–64, Prof. of Biology 1971–87, Chair. of Biology 1975–78, Assoc. Dean 1980–84, Master, Leverett House 1981–98, Prof. of Ophthalmology, Harvard Medical School 1986–, Maria Moors Cabot Prof. of Natural Science 1987–2001, Harvard Coll. Prof. 1999–2001, Pres., Corp. Marine Biological Lab. 1998–2007, Gordon and Llura Gund Prof. of Neurosciences 2001–, Head Tutor, Neurobiology, Harvard Univ. 2006–10; Assoc. Prof., Johns Hopkins Univ. 1964–71; Eldridge Green Lecturer, Royal Coll. of Surgeons of England 1971 mem. NAS, American Acad. of Arts and Sciences, American Philosophical Soc.; Guggenheim Fellow; Hon. MD (Lund, Sweden) 1982; Hon. LLD Laws (Dalhousie, Canada) 2012; Friedenwald Medal 1970, Retinal Research Award 1981, Alcon Research Institute Inst. 1986, Prentice Medal 1991, Von Sallman Prize 1992, Helen Keller Prize 2000, Llura Liggett Gund Award 2001, Paul Kayser Int. Eye Research Award 2008, Glenn A. Fry Medal in Physiological Optics 2009. *Publications:* The Retina: An Approachable Part of the Brain 1987 (revised edn 2012), Neurons and Networks 1992, Creating Mind: How the Brain Works 1998, The Great Brain Debate: Nature or Nurture? 2004; more than 250 publs in professional journals and ed. of five vols. *Leisure interests:* reading, golf and music. *Address:* The Biological Laboratories, Harvard University, 16 Divinity Avenue, Cambridge, MA 02138 (office); 135 Charles Street, Boston, MA 02114, USA (home). *Telephone:* (617) 495-2245 (office); (617) 720-4522 (home). *Fax:* (617) 496-3321 (office). *E-mail:* dowling@mcb.harvard.edu (office). *Website:* www.mcb.harvard.edu (office).

DOWLING, Patrick Joseph, CBE, DL, BE, PhD, FICE, FCGI, FREng, FRS; Irish engineer, academic and university administrator; b. 23 March 1939, Dublin; s. of John Dowling and Margaret McKittrick; m. Grace Lobo 1966; one s. one d.; ed Christian Bros. School, Dublin, Univ. Coll. Dublin and Imperial Coll. London; Sr Demonstrator in Civil Eng, Univ. Coll. Dublin 1960–61; Bursar in Structural Steelwork, Imperial Coll. London 1961–62, research on Steel Bridge Decks 1962–65, Research Fellow 1968–74, Reader in Structural Steelwork 1974–79, Prof. of Steel Structures 1979–94, British Steel Prof. and Head, Dept of Civil Eng 1985–94, currently Prof. Emer. of Steel Structures; bridge engineer, British Constructional Steelwork Asscn 1965–68; Vice-Chancellor and Chief Exec., Univ. of Surrey 1994–2005 (retd), now Prof. Emer.; Pnr, Chapman and Dowling Consulting Engineers 1981–94; Chair. Surrey Satellite Tech. Ltd 1994–2005; Chair. British Science Asscn 2005–09; fmr Chair. Eng Council, Steel Construction Inst., Daphne Jackson Trust, Surrey Research Park Exec.; Pres. Inst. of Structural Engineers 1994–95; fmr Pres. Asscn for Science Educ., City and Guilds Coll. Asscn; fmr Vice-Pres. Royal Acad. of Eng; Fellow, Imperial Coll., London 1997; DL Surrey 1999; Hon. LLD (Nat. Univ. of Ireland) 1995; Dr hc (Vilnius Tech. Univ., Lithuania) 1996, (Ulster) 1998; Telford Premium, ICE 1976, Gustave Trasenster Medal, Asscn des Ingénieurs Sortis de l'Univ. de Liège 1984; several awards from Inst. of Structural Engineers. *Publications:* Steel Plated Structures 1977, Buckling Shells in Offshore Structures 1982, Structural Steel Design 1988, Constructional Steel Design 1992; over 250 refereed papers. *Leisure interests:* travelling, sailing, reading, good company, modern art, theatre. *Address:* c/o British Science Association, Wellcome Wolfson Building, 165 Queen's Gate, London, SW7 5HD, England (office).

DOWNE, William (Bill) A., BA, MBA; Canadian banking executive; b. 1952, Montreal; m. Robin Downe; three s.; ed Wilfrid Laurier Univ., Univ. of Toronto; joined Bank of Montreal (BMO) 1983 as credit analyst, has held numerous sr man. positions in Corp. and Govt Banking, Houston and Denver, Sr Vice-Pres. US Corp. Banking 1992–96, Exec. Vice-Pres. North American Corp. Banking 1996–98, Head of Global Fixed Income Treasury 1998–99, Vice-Chair. Bank of Montreal 1999–2001, Deputy Chair. BMO Financial Group and CEO BMO Nesbitt Burns 2001–06, COO BMO Financial Group 2006–07, Pres. and CEO 2007–17; Chair. Bd of Dirs St Michael's Hosp., Toronto; Rotman Distinguished Business Alumni Award, Joseph L. Rotman School of Man. 2003, Arbor Award, Univ. of Toronto 2005.

DOWNER, Hon. Alexander John Gosse, AC, BA; Australian politician, diplomatist and UN official; b. 9 Sept. 1951; s. of Sir Alexander Downer; m. Nicola Robinson 1978; one s. three d.; ed Geelong Grammar School, Victoria, Radley Coll. and Newcastle Univ., UK; mem. Australian Diplomatic Service 1976–81, Australian Mission to European Communities, Embassy in Belgium and Luxembourg 1977–80; Sr Foreign Affairs Rep., S Australia 1981; Political Adviser to Prime Minister 1982–83; Dir Australian Chamber of Commerce 1983–84; mem. House of Reps (Liberal) for Mayo, S Australia 1984–; Shadow Minister for Arts, Heritage and Environment 1987, for Housing, Small Business and Customs 1988–89, for Trade and Trade Negotiations 1990–92, for Defence 1992–93; Fed. Shadow Treas. 1993–94; Leader Liberal Party 1994–95; Shadow Minister for Foreign Affairs 1995–96; Minister for Foreign Affairs 1996–2007; Special Adviser to UN Sec.-Gen. on Cyprus 2008–14; High Commr to UK 2014–18; Exec. Chair. Int. School of Govt, King's Coll. London 2018–; Dir (non-exec.) CQS, Yellow Cake PLC; mem. Int. Advisory Bd Tilray, Inc. 2018–; Centenary Medal 2001; Hon. DCL (Univ. of South Australia) 2013. *Leisure interests:* reading, music, tennis, golf, car racing. *Address:* c/o Australian High Commission, Australia House, Strand, London, WC2B 4LA, England (office).

DOWNES, Sir (Charles) Peter (Pete), Kt, OBE, PhD, FRS, FRSE, FMedSci; British biochemist, academic and university administrator; *Principal and Vice-Chancellor, University of Dundee;* ed Univ. of Birmingham; spent 11 years working in pharmaceutical industry; mem. staff, Univ. of Dundee 1989–, Head of Dept of Biochemistry and of School of Life Sciences 1994–2003, Vice-Prin. and Head, Coll. of Life Sciences 2003–09, Prin. and Vice-Chancellor 2009–, Co-founder Div. of Signal Transduction Therapy (partnership between Univ. of Dundee and several pharmaceutical cos); Convener, Research and Knowledge Exchange Cttee, Universities Scotland –2012, Convener, Universities Scotland 2012–16; Chair. Advisory Bd, Interface –2017; Pres. Biochemical Soc. 2018–; mem. Council of Soc. of Biology, Council of Royal Soc. of Edinburgh, Nat. Centre for Univs and Business, Scottish Council for Devt and Industry; mem. Bd, Design Dundee Ltd; Trustee, Saltire Foundation; Colworth Medal, British Biochemical Soc. 1987. *Achievements include:* identified the mechanism of action of lithium used to treat manic depression; played role in identifying chemical mediator for insulin in the body. *Publications:* numerous papers in professional journals. *Address:* Principal's Office, University of Dundee Nethergate, Dundee, DD1 4HN, Scotland (office). *Telephone:* (1382) 385562 (office). *E-mail:* principal@dundee.ac.uk (office). *Website:* www.dundee.ac.uk/about/principals-office (office).

DOWNEY, James, OC, PhD; Canadian academic, university administrator and writer; b. 20 April 1939; s. of Ernest Downey and Mimy Ann Downey (née Andrews); m. Laura Ann Parsons 1964; one s. one d.; ed Memorial Univ. of Newfoundland, Univ. of London, UK; Asst Prof. of English, Carleton Univ. 1966–69, Assoc. Prof. 1969–75, Prof. 1975–80, Chair. Dept of English 1972–75, Acting Dean, Faculty of Arts 1975, Dean 1976–78, Vice-Pres. (Acad.) 1978–80, Pres. pro tempore 1979; Pres. and Vice-Chancellor Univ. of New Brunswick 1980–90, Prof. of English 1980; Pres. and Vice-Chancellor Univ. of Waterloo 1993–99, then Prof. of English, Founding Dir Centre for the Advancement of Co-operative Educ. 2002–05, now Pres. Emer.; Chair. Royal Mil. Coll. of Ontario 2005; Founding Pres. and CEO Higher Educ. Quality Council of Ontario 2005–09; Co-Chair. Comm. on Excellence in Educ. in NB 1991–92; Fellow, Univ. of Georgia 1985; Hon. DHumLitt (Maine) 1987, Hon. DLitt (Newfoundland) 1991, Hon. LLD (New Brunswick) 1991, Hon. LLD (Toronto) 1998, (McMaster) 1999, (Carleton) 2000; Symons Medal 2001, David Smith Award 2003. *Publications include:* The Eighteenth Century Pulpit 1969, Fearful Joy 1974 (co-ed.), Schools for a New Century 1993, Innovation: Essays by Leading Canadian Researchers 2002 (co-ed.), Lord Beaverbrook and the Kennedys 2012.

DOWNEY, Robert, Jr; American actor and singer; b. 4 April 1965, New York, NY; s. of Robert Downey and Elsie Ford; m. 1st Deborah Falconer (divorced 2004); one s.; m. 2nd Susan Levin 2005; one s. one d.; first movie role in his father's film Pound 1970; joined cast of tv show Saturday Night Live for one season 1985–86; f. Team Downey (production co.) 2010–. *Films include:* Pound (debut) 1970, Up the Academy (uncredited) 1980, Baby It's You 1983, Firstborn 1984, Deadwait 1985, Tuff Turf 1985, Weird Science 1985, To Live and Die in LA, America 1986, Back to School 1986, The Pick-up Artist 1987, Less Than Zero 1987, Johnny Be Good 1988, Rented Lips 1988, 1969 1988, That's Adequate 1989, True Believer 1989, Chances Are 1989, Air America 1990, Too Much Sun 1991, Soapdish 1991, Chaplin (BAFTA Award) 1992, Heart and Souls 1993, Short Cuts 1993, Hail Caesar 1994, Back to School, Soapdish, The Last Party (also writer) 1993, Natural Born Killers 1994, Only You 1994, Richard III 1995, Restoration 1995, Home for the Holidays 1995, Danger Zone 1996, One Night Stand 1997, Bliss Vision 1997, Two Girls and a Guy (also composed song 'Snakes') 1997, Hugo Pool (aka Pool Girl) 1997, The Gingerbread Man 1998, U.S. Marshals 1998, In Dreams 1999, Friends & Lovers (also composed song 'Carla') 1999, Bowfinger 1999, Black and White 1999, Wonder Boys 2000, Auto Motives 2000, Lethargy 2002, Whatever We Do 2003, The Singing Detective (also singer of 'In My Dreams') 2003, Gothika 2003, Eros 2004, Game 6 2005, Kiss, Kiss, Bang, Bang 2005, The Shaggy Dog 2006, A Scanner Darkly 2006, Goodnight, and Good Luck 2006, Fur: An Imaginary Portrait of Diane Arbus 2006, A Guide to Recognizing Your Saints 2006, Zodiac 2007, Lucky You 2007, Charlie Bartlett 2007, Iron Man 2008, Tropic Thunder 2008, The Soloist 2009, Sherlock Holmes (Golden Globe for best performance by an actor in a motion picture—comedy or musical 2010) 2009, Iron Man 2 2010, Due Date 2010, Sherlock Holmes: A Game of Shadows 2011, Avengers Assemble 2012, Iron Man 3 2013. *Television includes:* Mussolini: The Untold Story (mini-series) 1985, Mr. Willowby's Christmas Tree 1995, as Larry Paul in Ally McBeal (series) 2000–01. *Recording:* album: The Futurist 2005. *Address:* CAA, 2000 Avenue of the Stars, Los Angeles, CA 90067, USA.

DOWNIE, Leonard, Jr, MA; American newspaper executive and academic; *Weil Family Professor of Journalism, Walter Cronkite School of Journalism and Mass Communication, Arizona State University;* b. 1 May 1942, Cleveland, Ohio; s. of Leonard Downie, Sr and Pearl Evenheimer; m. 1st Barbara Lindsey 1960 (divorced 1971); two s.; m. 2nd Geraldine Rebach 1971 (divorced 1997); one s. one d.; m. 3rd Janice Galin 1997; ed Ohio State Univ.; joined The Washington Post 1964, became investigative reporter in Washington, specializing in crime, housing and urban affairs, helped to supervise coverage of Watergate affair, Asst Man. Ed. Metropolitan News 1974–79, London Corresp. 1979–82, Nat. Ed. 1982–84, Man. Ed. 1984–91, Exec. Ed. 1991–2008, Vice-Pres. at Large, The Washington Post Co. 2008–14, Dir Los Angeles Times–Washington Post News Service 1991–2008, International Herald Tribune 1996–2002; Weil Family Prof. of Journalism, Walter Cronkite School of Journalism and Mass Communication, Arizona State Univ. 2009–; Founder and Bd mem. Investigative Reporters and Editors Inc.; Chair. Bd of Advisors, Kaiser Health News 2009–; mem. Bd of Dirs Investigative Reporters and Editors, Inc. Missouri School of Journalism 2009–15, Center for Investigative Reporting 2009–14; Fellow, Alicia Patterson Foundation 1971–72; Hon. LLD, Ohio State Univ.; two Washington-Baltimore Newspaper Guild Front Page Awards, American Bar Asscn Gavel Award for legal reporting, John Hancock Award for business and financial writing, Ben Bradlee Editor of the Year Award, National Press Foundation 2008, Award for Editorial Leadership, American Society of News Editors 2009. *Publications:* Justice Denied 1971, Mortgage on America 1974, The New Muckrakers 1976, The News About the News (with Robert G. Kaiser) 2002, The Rules of the Game (novel) 2009, The News Media (with Michael Schudson and C.W. Anderson). *Leisure interests:* ballet, classical music, travel, sports. *Address:* Room 389, Walter Cronkite School of Journalism, Arizona State University, 555 North Central Avenue, Phoenix, AZ 85004, USA. *Telephone:* (602) 496-7973 (office). *E-mail:* leonard.downie@asu.edu (office). *Website:* cronkite.asu.edu (office).

DOWNIE, Robert Silcock, MA, BPhil, FRSE, FRSA; British philosopher, academic and composer; *Professor Emeritus of Moral Philosophy, University of Glasgow;* b. 19 April 1933, Glasgow, Scotland; s. of Robert M. Downie and Margaret M. Brown; m. Eileen Dorothea Flynn 1958; three d.; ed Univ. of Glasgow, Queen's Coll., Oxford; Tutor, Worcester Coll., Oxford 1958–59; Lecturer in Moral Philosophy, Univ. of Glasgow 1959–68, Sr Lecturer 1968–69, Prof. 1969, currently Prof. Emer. and Hon. Professorial Research Fellow; Visiting Prof., Syracuse Univ., USA 1963–64, Dalhousie Univ., Nova Scotia, Canada 1976, Durham Univ. 2000. *Music:* choral music and songs composed, published and performed; chamber and piano music composed and performed. *Publications include:* Government Action and Morality 1964, Respect for Persons 1969, Roles and Values 1971, Education and Personal Relationships 1974, Caring and Curing 1980, Healthy Respect 1987, Health Promotion: Models and Values 1990, The Making of a Doctor 1992, The Healing Arts 1994, Francis Hutcheson: Selected Writings 1994, Palliative Care Ethics 1996, Medical Ethics 1996, Clinical Judgement 2000, The Philosophy of Palliative Care 2006, End of Life Choices 2009. *Leisure interest:* music. *Address:* Department of Philosophy, University of Glasgow, Glasgow, G12 8QQ, Scotland (office). *E-mail:* robert.downie@glasgow.ac.uk (office). *Website:* www.gla.ac.uk/schools/humanities/philosophy (office).

DOWSON, Duncan, CBE, BSc, PhD, DrSc, FRS, FRSE, FREng, FRSA, FCGI; British mechanical engineer and academic; *Professor Emeritus, School of Mechanical Engineering, University of Leeds;* b. 31 Aug. 1928, Kirkbymoorside N Yorks., England; s. of Wilfrid Dowson and Hannah Dowson; m. Mabel Strickland 1951; one s. (and one s. deceased); ed Lady Lumley's Grammar School, Pickering and Univ. of Leeds; Research Eng, Sir W.G. Armstrong Whitworth Aircraft Co. 1953–54; Lecturer in Mechanical Eng, Univ. of Leeds 1954, Sr Lecturer 1963–65, Reader 1965–66, Prof. of Eng Fluid Mechanics and Tribology 1966–93, Prof. Emer. 1993–, Hon. Fellow and Research Prof. 1998–2001; External Prof., Univ. of Loughborough 2001–, Dir Inst. of Tribology, Dept of Mechanical Eng 1967–87, Head, Dept of Mechanical Eng 1987–93, Pro-Vice-Chancellor 1983–85, Dean for

Int. Relations 1987–93; Pres. IMechE 1992–93; Chair. Yorks. Region, Royal Soc. of Arts 1992–97; Foreign mem. Royal Swedish Acad. of Eng Sciences; Life Fellow, ASME; Hon. Prof., Univ. of Hong Kong 1992–, Univ. of Bradford 1996–; Hon. Fellow, American Soc. of Lubrication Engineers; Hon. FIMechE; Hon. DTech (Chalmers Univ. of Tech., Göteborg) 1979; Hon. DSc (Inst. Nat. des Sciences Appliquées, Lyon) 1991, (Liège) 1996; Hon. DEng (Waterloo, Canada) 2001, (Bradford) 2002, (Leeds) 2003, (Loughborough) 2005; James Clayton Fund Prize, Thomas Hawksley Gold Medal, Tribology Gold Medal 1979, James Alfred Medal 1988, Sarton Medal (Belgium) 1998, James Clayton Memorial Lecturer, IMechE 2000 and numerous other awards. *Publications:* Elastohydrodynamic Lubrication: the fundamentals of roller and gear lubrication (co-author) 1966, History of Tribology 1979, An Introduction to the Biomechanics of Joints and Joint Replacement (co-author) 1981, Ball Bearing Lubrication: The Elastohydrodynamics of Elliptical Contacts (co-author) 1981; numerous papers in professional journals. *Leisure interest:* genealogy. *Address:* Institute of Engineering Thermofluids, Surfaces and Interfaces, School of Mechanical Engineering, University of Leeds, Leeds, LS2 9JT (office); Ryedale, 23 Church Lane, Adel, Leeds, LS16 8DQ, England. *Telephone:* (113) 233-2153 (office); (113) 267-8933 (home). *Fax:* (133) 242-4611 (office); (113) 281-7039 (home). *E-mail:* d.dowson@leeds.ac.uk (office); DDRyedale@aol.com (home). *Website:* www.engineering.leeds.ac.uk/ietsi (office).

DOYLE, James Edward (Jim), Jr, AB, JD; American lawyer and politician; *Of Counsel, Foley & Lardner LLP;* b. 23 Nov. 1945, Washington, DC; s. of James E. Doyle, Sr and Ruth Doyle (née Bachhuber); m. Jessica Laird 1966; two adopted s.; ed Madison West High School, Stanford Univ., Calif., Univ. of Wisconsin-Madison, Harvard Univ. Law School; worked as volunteer teacher, with his wife, in Tunisia, as part of US Peace Corps 1967–69; called to Bar: Ariz. 1973, Wis. 1975, US Dist Court, NM 1973, US Dist Court, Ariz. 1973, US Dist Court, Utah 1973, US Court of Appeals (10th Circuit) 1974, US Dist Court (Western Dist), Wis. 1975, Eastern Dist, Wis. 1976, US Court of Appeals (7th Circuit) 1985, US Supreme Court 1989; Attorney, DNA Legal Services, Navajo Indian Reservation, Chinle, Ariz. 1972–75; Partner, Jacobs & Doyle, Madison, Wis. 1975–77; Dist Attorney, Dane Co. 1977–82; Partner, Doyle & Ritz, Madison 1983–90; Of Counsel, Lawton & Cates, Madison 1990–91; Attorney-Gen. State of Wis. 1991–2002; Gov. of Wis. 2003–11; Of Counsel, Foley & Lardner LLP, Milwaukee 2011–; Pres. Nat. Asscn of Attorneys-Gen. 1997–98; mem. ABA, Wis. Bar Asscn (mem. Bd of Dirs Criminal Law section 1988), 7th Circuit Bar Asscn (Chair. Criminal Law section 1988–89); Democrat. *Address:* Foley & Lardner LLP, Verex Plaza, 150 East Gilman Street, Madison, WI 53703, USA (office). *Telephone:* (608) 258-4301 (office). *Fax:* (608) 258-4258 (office). *E-mail:* jdoyle@foley.com (office). *Website:* www.foley.com (office).

DOYLE, Noreen, BA, MBA; American/Irish banker and international finance official; b. 1949; ed Coll. of Mount St Vincent, Tuck School of Business, Dartmouth Coll.; began career with Morgan Guaranty Trust; joined Bankers Trust 1974, Client Man., New York and Houston, Div. Man. for multinational cos, New York, Man. Dir for distribution of structured financings, New York, responsible for European affairs, London 1990–92; joined EBRD and set up syndication business 1992, responsible for credit and market risks 1997–2001, First Vice-Pres. and Head of Banking 2001–05 (retd), fmr mem. Exec. Cttee; mem. Bd of Dirs Credit Suisse 2004– (Vice-Chair.), Newmont Mining Corpn 2005–, QinetiQ 2005–, Rexam PLC 2005–; Patron Women in Banking and Finance, London; Dame, American Asscn of the Order of Malta. *Address:* c/o Board of Directors, Credit Suisse Group, Paradeplatz 8, 8070 Zurich, Switzerland.

DOYLE, Roddy, BA; Irish writer and playwright; b. 8 May 1958, Dublin; s. of Rory Doyle and Ita Bolger Doyle; m. Belinda Doyle; two s.; ed Univ. Coll. Dublin; Hon. LLD (Univ. of Dundee) 2015. *Play:* Brown Bread 1992, USA 1992. *Publications:* The Commitments (also screenplay with Dick Clement and Ian La Frenais 1991) 1987, The Snapper (screenplay 1992) (French Literary Award 2011) 1990, The Van 1991, Paddy Clarke Ha Ha Ha (Booker Prize) 1993, The Woman Who Walked into Doors 1996, A Star Called Henry 1999, The Giggler Treatment 2000, Rory and Ita 2002, Oh, Play That Thing 2004, Paula Spencer 2006, Wilderness 2007, The Deportees (short stories) 2007, The Dead Republic 2010, A Greyhound of a Girl (children's book) 2012, Two Pints 2012, The Guts (Novel of the Year, Irish Book Awards 2013) 2013, Two More Pints 2014, Dead Man Talking 2014, Roy Keane: The Second Half 2014. *Address:* c/o John Sutton Management, Building Three, Kilmainham Square, Dublin 8, Ireland (office). *E-mail:* john@johnsutton.ie (office). *Website:* www.roddydoyle.ie.

DRABBLE, Dame Margaret, DBE, CBE, BA, FRSL; British author; b. 5 June 1939, Sheffield, Yorks.; d. of J. F. Drabble and Kathleen Drabble (née Bloor); sister of A. S. Byatt; m. 1st Clive Swift 1960 (divorced 1975); two s. one d. (deceased); m. 2nd Michael Holroyd (q.v.) 1982; ed Newnham Coll., Cambridge; Ed. The Oxford Companion to English Literature 1979–2000; Chair. Nat. Book League 1980–82, Soc. of Authors 2008–09; Hon. Foreign mem., American Acad. of Arts and Letters 2002; Hon. Fellow, Sheffield City Polytechnic 1989; Hon. DLitt (Sheffield) 1976, (Bradford) 1988, (Hull) 1992; Dr hc (Manchester) 1987, (Keele) 1988, (East Anglia) 1994, (York) 1995, (Cambridge) 2006; James Tait Black Memorial Prize 1968, Book of the Year Award, Yorkshire Post 1972, E. M. Forster Award, American Acad. of Arts and Letters 1973, St Louis Literary Award 2003, Golden PEN Award 2011. *Publications include:* fiction: A Summer Bird-Cage 1963, The Garrick Year 1964, The Millstone (John Llewelyn Rhys Memorial Prize 1966) 1965, Jerusalem the Golden 1967, The Waterfall 1969, The Needle's Eye 1972, The Realms of Gold 1975, The Ice Age 1977, The Middle Ground 1980, The Radiant Way 1987, A Natural Curiosity 1989, The Gates of Ivory 1991, The Witch of Exmoor 1996, The Peppered Moth 2001, The Seven Sisters 2002, The Red Queen 2004, The Sea Lady 2006, A Day in the Life of a Smiling Woman: Complete Short Stories 2011, The Pure Gold Baby 2013, The Dark Flood Rises 2016; plays: Laura 1964, Isadora 1968, Thank You All Very Much 1969, Bird of Paradise 1969; non-fiction: Wordsworth 1966, Arnold Bennett: A Biography 1974, The Genius of Thomas Hardy (ed.) 1976, For Queen and Country: Britain in the Victorian Age 1978, A Writer's Britain 1979, The Oxford Companion to English Literature (co-ed.) 1985, 2000, The Concise Oxford Companion to English Literature (co-ed. with Jenny Stringer) 1987, Angus Wilson: A Biography 1995, The Pattern in the Carpet: A Personal History with Jigsaws (memoirs) 2009. *Leisure interests:* walking and talking. *Address:* c/o James Gill, United Agents, 12–26 Lexington Street, London, W1F 0LE, England (office). *Telephone:* (20) 3214-0800 (office). *Fax:* (20) 3214-0801 (office). *E-mail:* jgill@unitedagents.co.uk (office). *Website:* www.unitedagents.co.uk/dame-margaret-drabble-cbe (office).

DRAGANOV, Petko, MA; Bulgarian politician, UN official and diplomatist; b. 25 Jan. 1958, Cairo, Egypt; m.; one s. one d.; ed Moscow Inst. for Int. Relations, Russia; Amb. to South Africa 1993–98, Perm. Rep. to UN Office and other Int. Orgs in Geneva 1998–2001, 2005–09, First Deputy Minister of Foreign Affairs 2001–05; Deputy Sec.-Gen., UNCTAD 2009–15; Sec.-Gen.'s Special Rep. for Central Asia and Head, UN Regional Centre for Preventive Diplomacy for Central Asia (UNRCCA) 2015–17.

DRAGHI, Mario, PhD; Italian economist, civil servant, central banker and EU official; *President, European Central Bank;* b. 3 Sept. 1947, Rome; s. of Carlo Draghi and Gilda Mancini; ed La Sapienza Univ. of Rome, Massachusetts Inst. of Tech., USA; Prof. of Econs, Florence Univ., Italy 1981–91; Exec. Dir IBRD (World Bank), Washington, DC, USA 1984–90; Adviser to Bank of Italy 1990; Dir-Gen. Ministry of the Treasury and of the Budget 1991–2001; apptd mem. Econ. and Financial Cttee EEC (now EU) 1991 (Chair. 2000–01); Chair. Italian Cttee for Privatizations 1993; Dir ENI –2001; Vice-Chair. and Man. Dir Goldman Sachs Int., London, UK 2002–06; Gov. Banca d'Italia 2006–11; Pres. European Central Bank 2011–; Gov. for Italy, IBRD, Asian Devt Bank; Chair. Financial Stability Forum 2006–11 (renamed Financial Stability Bd 2009); mem. Group of Seven deputies 1991; mem. Group of Thirty Consultative Group on Int. Econ. and Monetary Affairs, Inc. (G-30), Washington, DC 2007; IOP Fellow, Kennedy School of Govt, Harvard Univ., USA; Trustee, Inst. for Advanced Study, Princeton, NJ, The Brookings Inst., Washington, DC 2003–; Chair. cttee that drafted legislation governing Italian financial markets ('Draghi Law'); Kt Grand Cross, Order of Merit of the Italian Repub. 2000; Dr hc (Padua) 2009; Hon. MBA (Centro Universitario di Organizzazione Aziendale Foundation, Vicenza) 2010. *Publications include:* several articles on int. and European monetary and financial issues. *Address:* European Central Bank, Eurotower, Kaiserstrasse 29, 60311 Frankfurt am Main, Germany (office). *Telephone:* (69) 13447455 (office). *Fax:* (69) 13447404 (office). *E-mail:* info@ecb.europa.eu (office). *Website:* www.ecb.europa.eu (office).

DRAGNEA, Nicolae-Liviu; Romanian engineer and politician; *Chairman, Chamber of Deputies (Camera Deputaţilor);* b. 28 Oct. 1962, Gratia, Teleorman Co.; m. Bombonica Dragnea; two c.; ed Faculty of Transport, Polytechnic Inst. of Bucharest, Intensive Course, School of Admin. Studies, Ministry of the Interior, Italy, Course in Man. of Local Public Admin, Bucharest Univ. of Econ. Sciences (ASE), Defence Coll., Univ. of Nat. Defence; Councillor, Turnu Magurele Local Council June–Dec. 1996; Prefect, Pref. of Teleorman Co. 1996–2000, Pres. Teleorman Co. Council 2000–12; mem. Congress of Local and Regional Authorities of Europe (CLRAE) 2001, Rapporteur of CLRAE for Water Resources Man. in River Basin project 2003, Rapporteur of CLRAE for Young People and Sustainable Devt project 2004; Chair. Nat. Union of Co. Councils of Romania 2004–12; mem./Alt. mem. Cttee of Regions 2007–13; mem. Partidul Social Democrat (Social Democratic Party), Pres. 2015–; fmr mem. Partidul Democrat (Democratic Party); Minister of Admin and Interior Jan.–Feb. 2009; mem. for Teleorman Co., Chamber of Deputies (Camera Deputaţilor) 2012–, Chair. 2016–; Deputy Prime Minister 2012–14, also Minister of Regional Devt and Public Admin 2012–15 (resgnd); convicted of electoral fraud, given one-year suspended jail sentence and banned from holding public office May 2015; Hon. Citizen of Leon Co., Fla, USA 2001; Oscar for Excellence, Teleorman County 2003, Diploma of Excellence, Fed. of Local Authorities from Romania 2004, Compass of Jerusalem 2016. *Address:* Office of the Chairman, Camera Deputaţilor, 050563 Bucharest, Palatul Parlamentului, Street.Izvor nr. 2–4, Sector 5 (office); Partidul Social Democrat, 011346 Bucharest 1, Şoş Kiseleff 10, Romania (office). *Telephone:* (21) 4141111 (Chamber of Deputies) (office); (31) 4135155 (office). *Fax:* (21) 4141417 (Chamber of Deputies) (office); (21) 2223171 (office). *E-mail:* presedinte@psd.ro (office); dragnea.liviu@gmail.com; psd@psd.ro (office); presa@cdep.ro (office). *Website:* www.cdep.ro (office); www.psd.ro (office).

DRĂGOI, Bogdan Alexandru; Romanian politician; b. 27 May 1980; s. of Dan Dragoi; ed Fletcher School of Law and Diplomacy, Tufts Univ., USA; Business Analyst, Inquam Ltd, UK 2002–03, Assoc. 2003–04; Vice-Pres. and Shareholder, FocusSat SA, Bucharest 2004–06; Adviser to Minister, Ministry of European Integration 2006; Sec. of State, Ministry of Finance 2006–07, 2009; Dir-Gen., Econ. Dept, Bucharest City Hall 2007–08; Minister of Public Finance 2012–14; fmr Chair. Bd of Nominees, Fondul Proprietatea (govt compensation agency); mem. Democratic Liberal Party. *Address:* c/o Ministry of Public Finance, 050741 Bucharest 5, Str. Apolodor 17, Romania. *E-mail:* presa.mfp@mfinante.gov.ro.

DRAGU, Anca Dana, PhD; Romanian economist and government official; b. (Anca Dana Paliu), 3 May 1972; m.; one c.; ed Acad. of Econ. Studies, Bucharest, Joint Vienna Inst., Austria, CERGE-EI, Prague, Czech Repub., Georgetown Univ. Scholarship Program for Cen. and Eastern Europe and George Washington Univ., USA, Nat. School of Political Science and Public Admin, IMF Inst.; with Dept of Refinancing and Market Operations, Nat. Bank of Romania 1996–99, Economist, Dept of Regulation and Authorization 2000–01; Economist, Romania and Bulgaria Regional Office, IMF, Bucharest 2001–13; Econ. Analyst, Directorate-Gen. for Econ. and Financial Affairs, European Comm., Brussels, Belgium 2013–15; Minister of Public Finance 2015–17; mem. East Cen. European Scholarship Program, George Washington Alumni Asscn. *Address:* c/o Ministry of Public Finance, 050741 Bucharest 5, Str. Apolodor 17, Romania (office).

DRĂGUŢANU, Dorin; Moldovan economist and central banker; b. 19 March 1974, Chişinău; m. Otilia Dragutanu; two c.; ed Alexandru Ioan Cuza Univ., Iaşi, Romania; with Dept of Int. Relations of commercial bank Bankcoop SA, Chisinau 1996–97; joined PricewaterhouseCoopers (PwC Moldova) as Audit Asst 1998, then apptd Sr Man. in Audit Dept, Office Man. 2003–05, transferred to PwC Serbia 2005, apptd Dir Audit Dept Audit 2008, Dir responsible for risk management, Assurance Dept, PwC Serbia 2008–09; Chair. Council of Admin and Gov. Nat. Bank of Moldova 2009–15 (resgnd); mem. Ministry of Finance working group for developing National Standards on Auditing 2004–05.

DRAGUTINOVIĆ, Diana, MSc, PhD; Serbian economist, central banker and government official; *Vice-Governor, National Bank of Serbia;* b. 6 May 1958, Belgrade; m.; two c.; ed Univ. of Belgrade; Lecturer in Econs, Univ. of Belgrade 1999–; Special Adviser to Ministry of Finance and Economy 2001–02, to IMF

2002–04; Vice-Gov. Nat. Bank of Serbia 2004–08, 2011–; Minister of Finance 2008–11; fmr Co-Ed. Economic Thought (journal); fmr mem. Int. Editorial Bd Economic Annals. *Publications include:* numerous textbooks, 10 monographs and more than 50 studies, articles and journal contribs. *Address:* National Bank of Serbia, 11000 Belgrade, Kralja Petra 12, POB 1010, Serbia (office). *Telephone:* (11) 3027100 (office). *Fax:* (11) 3282285 (office). *E-mail:* informativni.centar@nbs.rs (office). *Website:* www.nbs.rs (office).

DRAHOŠ, Jiří, DrSc; Czech scientist and politician; b. 20 Feb. 1949, Český Těšín, Czechoslovak Repub. (now Czech Repub.); s. of Jiří Drahoš and Anna Drahošová; m. Eva Drahošová; two d.; ed Univ. of Chemistry and Tech., Prague (UCTP); Assoc. Prof. in Chemical Eng, UCTP 1994–2003, Prof. of Chemical Processes 2003–; various positions with Inst. of Chemical Process Fundamentals of Czechoslovak Acad. of Sciences (now Czech Acad. of Sciences) from 1973, including Research Scientist, Sr Research Scientist, Dept Head, Deputy Dir 1992–95, Dir 1996–2003; Deputy Pres., Czech Acad. of Sciences 2005–09, Pres. 2009–17; Alexander von Humboldt Fellow, Univ. of Hanover 1985–86; Pres. Czech Soc. of Chemical Eng; mem. Exec. Bd European Fed. of Chemical Eng (Pres. 2006–09); Fellow, Learned Soc. of the Czech Repub., Eng Acad. of the Czech Repub.; Senator, Academia Scientiarum et Artium Europaea; Hon. Fellow UK Inst. of Chemical Engineers; mem. Bd of Dirs Czech Asscn of Chemical Industry; ind. cand. in presidential election for Společně pro Česko (Together for Czechia) organization 2018; Medal of Merit in the field of science 2012. *Address:* Czech Academy of Sciences, Narodni 3, 117 20 Prague 1, Czech Republic (office); Společně pro Česko (Together for Czechia), Whenever, s.r.o., Karla Engliše 3221/2, 150 00 Prague 5, Czech Republic (office). *Telephone:* 221403111 (office). *E-mail:* drahos@kav.cas.cz (office); media@jiridrahos.cz. *Website:* www.avcr.cz (office); www.jiridrahos.cz (office).

DRAKE, Frank Donald, BEng (Phys), MA, PhD; American astronomer; *Director, Center for the Study of Life in the Universe, Search for Extraterrestrial Intelligence (SETI) Institute;* b. 28 May 1930, Chicago; s. of Richard C. Drake and Winifred Thompson Drake; m. 1st Elizabeth B. Bell 1953 (divorced 1977); three s.; m. 2nd Amahl Shakhashiri 1978; two d.; ed Cornell and Harvard Univs; served as Lt in USN 1947–55; with Harvard Radio Astronomy Project 1955–58; Ewen-Knight Corpn 1957–58; scientist, Head Scientific Services and Telescope Operations on Nat. Radio Astronomy Observatory 1958–63; Chief, Lunar and Planetary Science Section, Jet Propulsion Lab., Pasadena, Calif. 1963–64; Prof. of Astronomy, Cornell Univ. 1964–85, Dir Arecibo Ionospheric Observatory 1966–68, Goldwin Smith Prof. of Astronomy 1976–85, Assoc. Dir Center for Radiophysics and Space Research 1967–75, Chair. Dept of Astronomy 1968–71; Dir Nat. Astronomy and Ionosphere Center 1971–81; Prof. of Astronomy, Univ. of Calif., Santa Cruz 1984–95, Prof. Emer. 1995–, Dean Div. of Natural Sciences 1984–88; Pres. SETI (Search for Extraterrestrial Intelligence) Inst. 1984–2000, Chair. Bd of Trustees 2000–02, Chair. Emer. 2002–, Dir Center for the Study of Life in the Universe 2005–; Pres. Astronomical Soc. of the Pacific 1988–90; mem. AAAS, NAS 1972, The Explorers Club, Advisory Bd The World Book Encyclopedia, Int. Astronomical Union, Int. Scientific Radio Union, American Astronomical Soc.; Fellow, American Acad. of Arts and Sciences; Education Prize, American Astronomical Soc. 2001. *Publications include:* Intelligent Life in Space 1962, Murmurs of Earth 1979, (with Dava Sobel) Is Anyone Out There? 1992; and over 135 papers and articles. *Leisure interests:* snorkelling, horticulture, lapidary. *Address:* Center for the Study of Life in the Universe, SETI Institute, 189 Bernardo Avenue, Suite 200, Mountain View, CA 94043, USA (office). *Telephone:* (650) 961-6633 (office). *Fax:* (650) 961-7099 (office). *E-mail:* fdrake@seti.org (office). *Website:* www.seti.org (office).

DRAKE, Howard Ronald, CMG, OBE; British diplomatist; b. 13 Aug. 1956; m. Gillian Drake; one s. one d.; Vice-Consul (Commercial), Los Angeles, USA 1981–83; Second Sec. (Political), Santiago, Chile 1985–88; Head of Chancery, Singapore early 1990s; Deputy Consul-Gen. and Dir of Inward Investment, New York 1997–2002; worked on EU Affairs, Cyprus, Counter-proliferation, Human Resources, FCO, London 2002–05; Amb. to Chile 2005–09; High Commr to Jamaica 2010–13, to Canada 2013–17.

DRAKE, Michael V., AB, MD; American ophthalmologist, academic and university administrator; *President, Ohio State University;* b. 9 July 1950, New York, NY; m. Brenda Drake; two s.; ed Stanford Univ., Univ. of California, San Francisco; grew up in Englewood, NJ, until moving with family to Sacramento, Calif.; mem. Faculty, Univ. of California, San Francisco (UCSF) School of Medicine from late 1970s, ultimately becoming Steven P. Shearing Prof. of Ophthalmology and Sr Assoc. Dean; Vice-Pres. for Health Affairs, Univ. of California 2000–05; Distinguished Prof. of Ophthalmology (School of Medicine) and of Educ. (School of Education), Chancellor Univ. of California, Irvine 2005–14; Pres. Ohio State Univ. 2014–; mem. Exec. Cttee and Div. I Bd Nat. Collegiate Athletic Asscn, Exec. and Membership Cttees of Asscn of American Univs; Trustee and Pres. Alpha Omega Alpha Honor Medical Soc.; Chair. Bd of Trustees, Asscn of Academic Health Centers; Fellow, Inst. of Medicine (Nat. Acads), American Acad. of Arts and Sciences; numerous honours and awards, including Burbridge Award for Public Service, Asbury Award (Clinical Science), Michael J. Hogan Award (Laboratory Science), UCSF School of Medicine Clinical Teaching Award, S.J. Kimura Teaching Award, UCSF School of Medicine Alumnus of the Year Award, Gold-Headed Cane Soc. Speaker's Cane, Asscn of American Medical Colls Herbert W. Nickens Award for promoting social justice, California Wellness Foundation's Champion of Diversity Award, inaugural Binational Health Pioneer Award, 18th Int. HIV/AIDS Conf., inducted into Stanford Univ. Multicultural Hall of Fame 2009. *Publications:* five textbooks; several book chapters and numerous articles in professional journals. *Address:* Office of the President, 205 Bricker Hall, 190 North Oval Mall, Columbus, OH 43210, USA (office). *Telephone:* (614) 292-2424 (office). *E-mail:* president@osu.edu (office). *Website:* president.osu.edu (office).

DRAKEFORD, Mark, PC, PhD; Welsh politician; *First Minister of Wales;* b. 19 Sept. 1954, Carmarthen; m.; three c.; ed Univ. of Kent at Canterbury, Univ. of Exeter; mem. South Glamorgan County Council 1985–93; fmr probation officer and youth justice worker, Cardiff; Lecturer in applied social studies, Univ. Coll. of Swansea (now Swansea Univ.) 1991–95; Prof. of Social Policy and Applied Social Sciences, Cardiff Univ. 2003–13; advisor to Welsh Govt on health and social policy 2000–10; mem. Welsh Ass. for Cardiff West 2011–; Minister for Health and Social Services, Welsh Govt 2013–16, Cabinet Sec. for Finance 2016–18, Minister for Exiting the EU 2017–18; First Minister of Wales 2018–; mem. Welsh Labour Party, Leader 2018–. *Address:* National Assembly for Wales, Cardiff Bay, Cardiff, CF99 1NA, Wales (office). *Telephone:* (800) 010-5500 (office). *E-mail:* Mark.Drakeford@assembly.wales (office). *Website:* www.assembly.wales (office).

DRAPER, Kenneth, MA, RA; British painter and sculptor; b. 19 Feb. 1944, Killamarsh, Sheffield; s. of Albert Draper and Dorothy Rosa Anne Lamb; m. 1st Heather Lieven Beste 1965 (divorced); one s.; m. 2nd Nadiya Jinnah 1972 (divorced); m. 3rd Jean Macalpine; ed Chesterfield Coll. of Art, Kingston School of Art, RCA; solo exhbns include Redfern Gallery, London 1969, Warwick Arts Trust, London 1981, Galerie Nouvelles Images, Den Haag, Holland 1984, Austin Desmond, London 1991, Adelson Gallery, New York 1993, Friends Room, RA 1993, 2005, Hart Gallery, London 1994, 1996, 1998, Peter Bartlow Gallery, Chicago 1995; group exhbns include: British Sculptors 1972, RA 1972, Silver Jubilee Exhbn Contemporary British Sculpture, Battersea Park 1977, The British Art Show, Mappin, Sheffield 1980, British Sculpture in the Twentieth Century, Whitechapel Art Gallery 1981; work in public collections of Arts Council of GB, Contemporary Arts Soc., Courtauld Inst., London, Ashmolean Museum, Oxford, Usher Gallery, Lincoln; mem., Faculty, British School in Rome 1979; mem. Royal Acad. of Arts 1991–; Mark Rothko Memorial Award 1971. *Leisure interests:* reading, chess, sport, travel. *Address:* Carrer Gran 55A, 07720 Es Castell, Minorca, Balearic Islands, Spain (home). *Telephone:* (971) 353457 (home). *Fax:* (971) 353457 (home). *E-mail:* drapermacalpine@gmail.com (office). *Website:* www.kennethdraper.com (home).

DRAPER, William Henry, III, BA, MBA; American fmr government official; *General Partner, Draper Richards L.P.;* b. 1 Jan. 1928, White Plains, NY; s. of William Henry Draper and Katherine Baum; m. Phyllis Culbertson 1953; one s. two d.; ed Yale and Harvard Univs; with Inland Steel Co., Chicago 1954–59; Draper, Gaither & Anderson, Palo Alto, Calif. 1959–62; Pres. Draper & Johnson Investment Co. Palo Alto 1962–65; Founder and Gen. Pnr, Sutter Hill Capital Co., Palo Alto 1965–70, Sutter Hill Ventures, Palo Alto 1970–81; Pres. and Chair. Export-Import Bank US, Washington, DC 1981–86; Admin., CEO UNDP 1986–93; Man. Dir Draper Int., San Francisco 1994; currently Gen. Pnr Draper Richards L.P.; Trustee Yale Univ. 1991–98, George Bush Library Foundation 1993–; Chair. World Affairs Council, N Calif. 2000–02; Republican; Hon. LLD (Southeastern Univ.); SD Forum Vision Award, Dow Jones VC Hall of Fame 2005, Silicon Valley Fast 50 Lifetime Achievement Award 2006, IIE Distinguished Service Award, IBF Lifetime Achievement Award 2009, Commonwealth Club Lifetime Achievement Award 2009. *Address:* Draper Richards L.P., 50 California Street, Suite 2925, San Francisco, CA 94111 (office); 91 Tallwood Court, Atherton, CA 94027-6431, USA (home). *Telephone:* (415) 616-4050 (office). *Fax:* (415) 616-4060 (office). *E-mail:* bill@draperrichards.com (office). *Website:* www.draperrichards.com (office).

DRAŠKOVIĆ, Vuk; Serbian politician, journalist and writer; *President, Serbian Renewal Movement;* b. 29 Nov. 1946, Međa, Žitište municipality, Central Banat Region, Vojvodina; s. of Vidak Drašković and Stoja Drašković; m. Danica Bošković 1974; ed Univ. of Belgrade; moved to Herzegovina; as student took part in demonstrations 1968; mem. staff Telegraph Agency of Yugoslavia TANJUG 1969–78, worked in Lusaka, Zambia; dismissed from post of corresp. for disinformation 1978; Adviser Council of Trade Unions of Yugoslavia 1978–80; Ed. Rad (newspaper) 1980–85; freelance journalist and writer 1985–; Founder and Pres. Serbian Renewal Movt 1990–; cand. for presidency of SFR Yugoslavia 1990, 1992, of Serbia 1997; mem. Nat. Ass.; detained, released from detention July 1993; leader of mass protests against Pres. Milošević from Nov. 1996; Deputy Prime Minister of Yugoslavia 1998–99 (resgnd); Minister of Foreign Affairs of Serbia and Montenegro 2004–06. *Publications include:* novels: Judge, Knife, Prayer 1, Prayer 2, Russian Consul, Night of the General, Target, Polemics, Answers; numerous articles and collections of articles. *Address:* Serbian Renewal Movement (Srpski pokret obnove), 11000 Belgrade, Kneza Mihailova 48, Serbia (office). *Telephone:* (11) 3283620 (office). *Fax:* (11) 2628170 (office). *E-mail:* vuk@spo.rs (office). *Website:* www.spo.rs (office).

DRASKOVICS, Tibor, LLB; Hungarian banking executive and government official; b. 26 June 1955, Budapest; ed Eötvös Lóránd Univ. of Budapest; started career as legal expert in Ministry of Finance 1979–84, Sec. to Minister 1984–86, Head of Legal Dept 1986, Head of Legal Div. 1988, Deputy State Sec. 1990–91, Admin. State Sec. 1994–98; Man. Dir Concordia Biztosítási (insurance brokers) 1991–93; tax consulting man., Arthur Andersen Ltd 1993–94; mem. Monetary Council, Nat. Bank of Hungary 1995–98; Deputy CEO ABN-AMRO Bank 1999–2000; Deputy CEO K&H Bank 2000–02; Chief of Cabinet of the Prime Minister 2002–04; Minister of Finance 2004–05; Chair. Hungarian Power Works Ltd 2005–07; Minister without Portfolio 2007–08, Minister of Justice and Law Enforcement 2008–09; Partner, PricewaterhouseCoopers 2010–12; Team Leader, Reforming Policy Coordination and the Centre of the Govt in Serbia (EU-funded project) 2013–15; Sr Policy Advisor to govt of Montenegro 2015–, also advises govt of Albania on financial issues of regional devt; Vice-Pres., State Reform Comm. 2006; Order of Merit of the Hungarian Republic's Middle Cross.

DRAVID, Rahul Sharad, BCom; Indian fmr professional cricketer; b. 11 Jan. 1973, Indore, MP; s. of Sharad Dravid and Pushpa Dravid; m. Vijeta Pendharkar; two s.; ed St Joseph's Boys' High School, Bangalore, St Joseph's Coll. of Commerce; right-handed batsman; right-arm off-break bowler; occasional wicketkeeper; plays for Karnataka 1990–, India 1996–2012 (Capt. 2005–07), Kent 2000, Scotland 2003, Royal Challengers Bangalore 2008–10, Canterbury, New Zealand 2009, Rajasthan Royals 2011–13, Asia XI, ICC (Int. Cricket Council) World XI; First-class debut: 1990/91; Test debut: England v India, Lord's 20–24 June 1996; One-Day International (ODI) debut: India v Sri Lanka, Singapore 3 April 1996; has played in 164 Tests, taken 1 wicket and scored 13,288 runs (36 centuries and 63 half centuries), highest score 270, average 52.31, best bowling 1/18; played in 344 ODIs, took 4 wickets and scored 10,889 runs (12 centuries and 83 half centuries), highest score 153, average 39.16, best bowling 2/43; second Indian batsman, after Sachin Tendulkar, and fifth international player to have scored more than 11,000 runs in Test cricket; became sixth player in history of world cricket and third Indian, after Sachin Tendulkar and Sourav Ganguly, to score 10,000 runs in ODI cricket 14 Feb. 2007; first and only batsman to score a century in all ten Test-playing nations; currently holds world record for highest number of catches (more than 200) in Test cricket; has also been involved in more than 75 century partnerships with 18 different partners (world record); retd from international cricket 2012; Goodwill

Amb. Children's Movement for Civic Awareness; Brand Amb. Nat. Tobacco Control Campaign, Ministry of Health; commentator and analyst with several sports channels in India and abroad; mem. Bd of Advisors, GoSports Foundation 2014–; mem. Karnataka Knowledge Comm.; Arjuna Award 1998, Ceat Cricketer of the 1999 World Cup 1999, one of five Wisden Cricketers of the Year 2000, inaugural ICC Player of the Year (Sir Garfield Sobers Trophy) and ICC Test Player of the Year 2004, Padma Shri 2004, MTV Youth Icon of the Year 2004, Capt. of ICC's Test Team 2006, Lifetime Achievement Award, NDTV Indian of the Year 2011, Don Bradman Award 2012, Padma Bhushan 2013, inducted into ICC Cricket Hall of Fame 2018. *Website:* rahuldravid.com.

DRAVINS, Dainis, PhD; Swedish astronomer and academic; *Professor of Astronomy, Lund University;* b. 10 Sept. 1949, Lund; s. of Karlis Dravins and Velta Ruke-Dravina; m. Christina Dravins (née Hedqvist) 1982; one s.; ed Lund and Uppsala Univs and Calif. Inst. of Tech., USA; Prof. of Astronomy, Lund Univ. 1984–; mem. Royal Swedish Acad. of Sciences 1987; Foreign mem. Latvian Acad. of Sciences 1992. *Publications:* numerous articles on astronomy. *Address:* Lund Observatory, Box 43, 22100 Lund, Sweden (office). *Telephone:* (46) 2227297 (office); (46) 2227000 (office). *Fax:* (46) 2224614 (office). *E-mail:* dainis@astro.lu.se (office). *Website:* www.astro.lu.se/~dainis (office).

DRAZEN, Jeffrey M., BS, MD; American physician, academic and editor; *Editor-in-Chief, New England Journal of Medicine;* b. 19 May 1946, St Louis, Mo.; m.; two s.; ed Tufts Univ., Harvard Medical School; currently Distinguished Parker B. Francis Prof. of Medicine, Harvard Medical School, also Prof. of Physiology, Harvard School of Public Health and Prof., Dept of Environmental Health; currently also Sr Physician Brigham and Women's Hospital; Ed.-in-Chief, New England Journal of Medicine 2000–; Co-Chair. Inst. of Medicine Forum on Drug Discovery, Development, and Translation; mem. Inst. of Medicine 2003–, Global Initiative for Asthma Science Cttee, WHO Scientific Advisory Group on Clinical Trials Registration; fmr Assoc. Ed. Journal of Clinical Investigation, American Review of Respiratory Disease; Dr hc (Univ. of Ferrara, Italy), (Nat. and Kapodistrian Univ. of Athens, Greece); Amberson Lecturer, American Thoracic Soc. 1999, Chadwick Medal, Massachusetts Thoracic Soc. 2000. *Publications include:* Five Lipoxygenase Products in Asthma (ed.) 1998; contribs to Genomic Medicine: Articles from the New England Journal of Medicine 2001. *Address:* Department of Environmental Health, 10 Shattuck Street, Boston, MA 02115-6094, USA (office). *Telephone:* (617) 734-9800 (office). *Fax:* (617) 739-9864 (office). *E-mail:* jdrazen@nejm.org (office). *Website:* www.hsph.harvard.edu/jeffrey-drazen (office); www.nejm.org (office).

DRENNAN, Peter Thomas; Australian police officer and UN official; *Under-Secretary-General for Safety and Security, United Nations;* b. 1957; m.; two c.; ed Australian Inst. of Police Man., Australian Grad. School of Man., FBI Nat. Exec. Inst., USA; began police career 1979, Deputy Commr for Nat. Security, Australian Federal Police 2009–14, also served as Asst Commr for Counter-Terrorism, Econ. and Special Operations, Border and Int. Network, Federal Police Dir of Operations for the Eastern Region and Regional Liaison Coordinator for East and South East Asia, Hong Kong; Under-Sec.-Gen. for Safety and Security, UN 2014–; represented Australia at nat. and int. policing forums with Int. Criminal Police Org. (INTERPOL) and ASEAN Asscn of Heads of Police (ASEANPOL); Australian Police Medal 2009. *Address:* Department of Safety and Security, United Nations, New York, NY 10017, USA (office). *Telephone:* (212) 963-1234 (office). *Fax:* (212) 963-4879 (office). *E-mail:* dsshelp@un.org (office). *Website:* www.un.org/undss/ (office).

DRENTH, Pieter Johan Diederik, PhD; Dutch academic; *Honorary President, European Network of Academies of Science (ALLEA);* b. 8 March 1935, Appelscha; s. of Gerrit Drenth and Froukje Wouda; m. Maria Annetta Elizabeth de Boer 1959; three s.; ed Vrije Univ., Amsterdam, New York Univ., USA; served in Royal Dutch Navy 1955–60; Research Fellow, Social Science Research Div., Standard Oil Co., New York 1960–61; Sr Lecturer in Psychometrics and Industrial Psychology, VU Univ., Amsterdam 1962–67, Prof. of Work and Organizational Psychology and Psychodiagnostics 1967–2000, Prof. Emer. 2000–, Rector Magnificus 1983–87, Dean Faculty of Psychology and Educ. 1998–2000; Visiting Prof., Washington Univ., St Louis 1966, Univ. of Washington, Seattle 1977; mem. Royal Netherlands Acad. of Arts and Sciences 1980–, Pres. 1990–96; Pres. ALLEA (European Network of Acads of Science) 2000–06, Hon. Pres. 2006–; mem. Supervisory Bd Shell-Nederland BV 1991–2011; Kt, Order of the Dutch Lion 1991, Commdr, Order of Oranje-Nassau 1996; Dr hc (Ghent) 1980, (Paris V) 1996; Heymans Award for Outstanding Contrib. to Psychology 1986, Aristotle Award for Outstanding Contribs to European Psychology 1995, IAAP Award for Distinguished Scientific Contribs to the Int. Advancement of Applied Psychology 2006. *Publications include:* Mental Tests and Cultural Adaptation (ed.) 1972, Inleiding in de testtheorie 1976, Decisions in Organizations 1988, Advances in Organizational Psychology (ed.) 1988, New Handbook Work and Organizational Psychology (ed.) 1989, Testtheorie 1990 (revised edn 2006), Gardening in Science 1996, Walks in the Garden of Science 2006; numerous scientific papers and psychological tests. *Leisure interests:* cycling, music, literature. *Address:* Pekkendam 6, 1081 HR Amsterdam, Netherlands. *Telephone:* (20) 6449109. *E-mail:* pjdd@xs4all.nl.

DREW, John Sydney Neville, MA, AM, MBA; British academic, business executive and fmr diplomatist; *Chancellor, Regent's University, London;* b. 7 Oct. 1936, Hornchurch, Essex, England; s. of John Drew and Kathleen Wright; m. Rebecca Usher 1962; two s. one d.; ed King Edward's School, Birmingham, St John's Coll., Oxford, Tufts Univ., USA, London Business School; 2nd Lt Somerset Light Infantry 1955–57; HM Diplomatic Service in Paris, Middle East Center for Arabic Studies, Kuwait, First Sec. Bucharest 1960–73; Dir of Marketing and Exec. Programmes, London Business School 1973–79; Dir of Corp. Affairs, Rank Xerox 1979–84; Dir of European Affairs, Touche Ross International 1984–86; Head, UK Offices, Comm. of EC 1987–93; Dir Durham Inst., Visiting Prof. of European Business, Durham Univ. 1995–2003; Jean Monnet Prof. of European Business and Man., European Business School, London 2007–; Dir Inst. of Contemporary European Studies, Regent's Univ., London 2011–, Chancellor 2013–; Deputy Chair. Enterprise Support Group 1993–94; Dir, Europa Times 1993–94, Change Group International 1996–2003; Pres. Inst. of Linguists 1993–99, EUROTAS 1998–2003; Trustee, Thomson Foundation 1993–2007; Assoc. Fellow, Templeton Coll., Oxford 1982–86; Visiting Prof., Imperial Coll. London 1987–91, Open Univ. 1992–2001; Hon. Ed. European Business Journal 1987–2002; Hon. MBA (Northumbria) 1991. *Publications include:* Doing Business in the European Community 1979, Networking in Organizations 1986, Developing an Active Company Approach to the European Market 1988, Readings in International Enterprise (ed.) 1995, Ways Through the Wall (ed.) 2005, The UK and Europe: Costs, Benefits, Options (ed.) 2013; articles on European integration and personal devt. *Leisure interests:* travel, golf, personal development. *Address:* 49 The Ridgeway, London, NW11 8QP, England (home). *Telephone:* (20) 8455-5054 (office). *E-mail:* profdrew@eurotas.org (office).

DREWS, Juergen, MD, PhD; German physician and business executive; b. 16 Aug. 1933, Berlin; s. of Walter Drew and Lotte Grohnert; m. Dr Helga Eberlein 1963; three d.; ed Univs of Berlin, Innsbruck, Austria, Heidelberg and Yale Univ., USA; Prof. of Medicine, Univ. of Heidelberg 1973–; Head of Chemotherapy Section, Sandoz Research Inst., Vienna 1976–79, Head of Sandoz Research Inst. 1979–82, Int. Pharmaceutical R&D, Sandoz, Basel 1982–85; Dir Pharmaceutical Research, F. Hoffmann-La Roche Ltd, Basel 1985–86, Chair. Research Bd and mem. Exec. Cttee 1986–90, Pres. Int. R&D and mem. Exec. Cttee Roche Group, Hoffmann-La Roche Inc., Nutley, NJ 1991–95, Pres. Global Research, mem. Exec. Cttee 1996–97; Chair. Int. Biomedicine Man. Partners, Basel 1997–2001; Man. Partner, Bear Stearns Health Innoventures Man. LLC, New York 2001–04; fmr Chair. Genomics Pharmaceutical Company, Munich; Chair. Genaissance Pharmaceuticals Inc –2005; fmr Chair. Supervisory Bd Tegenero Immuno Therapeutics AG; mem. Supervisory Board, MorphoSys AG (fmr Deputy Chair.) 1998–2012, Agennix AG 1998–2011; mem. Dean's Council, Yale Univ. School of Medicine 1993; fmr mem. Bd of Dirs Human Genome Sciences, Inc., Cogenics, Inc., Coelacanth Chemical Corpn, PDL BioPharma, Inc., BIOMEDICINE. *Publications:* Chemotherapie 1979, Immunpharmakologie, Grundlagen und Perspektiven 1986, Immunopharmacology 1990, Die verspielte Zukunft 1998, In Quest of Tomorrow's Medicines 1999; more than 200 scientific papers. *Leisure interests:* skiing, climbing, literature, piano.

DREXLER, Millard (Mickey) S., MBA; American business executive; *Chairman, Outdoor Voices;* b. 17 Aug. 1944, Bronx, New York; m. Peggy Drexler; two c.; Pres. and CEO Ann Taylor Co. 1980–83; Exec. Vice-Pres. of Merchandising and Pres. Gap Stores Div. Gap Inc., San Bruno, Calif. 1983–87; Pres. The Gap Inc. 1987–95, Pres. and CEO The Gap Inc., San Francisco 1995–2002; Chair. and CEO J. Crew Group Inc., New York 2003–17, Chair. 2017–19; Chair. Outdoor Voices 2017–; f. Drexler Ventures, LLC 2017; mem. Bd of Dirs Apple Inc. 1999–2015. *Leisure interest:* novels by John Grisham. *Address:* Outdoor Voices, 407 Broome Street, Second Floor, New York, NY 10013, USA (office). *E-mail:* hello@outdoorvoices.com (office). *Website:* www.outdoorvoices.com (office).

DREYFUS, George, AM; Australian composer; b. 22 July 1928, Wuppertal, Germany; two s. one d.; ed Vienna Acad. of Music, Austria; Composer-in-Residence, Tianjin, China 1983, Shanghai 1987, Nanjing 1991; Grosses Bundesverdienstkreuz (Germany); Henry Lawson Award 1972, Prix de Rome 1976, 2004, Mishkenot Sha'ananim, Jerusalem 1980, APRA/AMC Distinguished Services to Australian Music Award 2013. *Compositions include:* Garni Sands, The Gilt-Edged Kid (operas); Symphonies Nos 1, 2 and 3; Symphonie Concertante 1977; Jingles . . . & More Jingles; Reflections in a Glasshouse; The Illusionist; The Grand Aurora Australis Now Show; Galgenlieder; Songs Comic & Curious; Music in the Air; From within Looking out; The Seasons; Ned Kelly Ballads; Quintet after the Notebook of J.-G. Noverre; Sextet for Didjeridoo & Wind Instruments; Old Melbourne; several pieces for young people; The Sentimental Bloke (musical) 1985, Lifestyle 1988, Song of Brother Sun 1988 (choral pieces), Rathenau (opera) 1993, Die Marx Sisters (opera) 1994; more than 100 scores for film and TV including The Adventures of Sebastian the Fox 1963, Rush 1974, Great Expectations 1986. *Television includes:* The Gilt-Edged Kid (Australian Broadcasting Corpn/ABC) 1975, Didjeridu in Deutschland (SBS) 1988, Bicycles and Bassoons (SBS) 1989, Life is Too Serious (ABC) 2000. *Publications include:* The Last Frivolous Book (autobiog.) 1984, Being George – And Liking It! 1998, Don't Ever Let Them Get You 2009, Brush Off! 2011; numerous commercial CDs on the Move label. *Leisure interests:* swimming, gardening. *Address:* 3 Grace Street, Camberwell, Vic. 3124, Australia (home). *Telephone:* (3) 9809-2671 (home). *E-mail:* gdreyfus@bigpond.net.au.

DREYFUS, Gilles D., MD; French cardio-thoracic surgeon and academic; *Medical Director, Monaco Cardio-Thoracic Center;* b. 24 May 1951, Paris; ed Paris V Universite, Rene Descartes Medical School; intern at Paris Hospitals 1978; Chef de Clinique, assistant des hopitaux 1982–86; univ. prof. 1989; Chief of Cardiothoracic Unit, Foch Hospital, Paris 1996–2001; Consultant and Prof. of Cardiac Surgery, Dept of Cardiac Surgery, Royal Brompton & Harefield NHS Trust 2001–09; Prof., Imperial Coll. London; Medical Dir Cardio-Thoracic Centre Monaco 2010–; mem. European Asscn for Cardio-Thoracic Surgery, French Soc. for Thoracic and Cardiovascular Surgery, French Soc. for Cardiology, Soc. for Heart Valve Disease, American Asscn for Thoracic Surgery, Soc. of Thoracic Surgeons, Int. Soc. for Heart and Lung Transplantation, British Cardiac Soc.; Chevalier de la Légion d'honneur. *Leisure interests:* skiing, golf. *Address:* Monaco Cardio-Thoracic Center, 11 bis, avenue d'Ostende, BP 223, 98004 Monaco cedex (office). *Telephone:* 7-92-16-80-00 (office). *Fax:* 7-92-16-82-99 (office). *Website:* www.monaco-cardio.com (office).

DREYFUS, Louis; French newspaper executive; *CEO, Le Monde Group;* b. 19 Dec. 1970, Paris; s. of Tony Dreyfus and Françoise Fabre-Luce; ed HEC Paris, London School of Econs; started career as International Controller at Hachette Filipacchi Media US; Dir Les Inrockuptibles magazine and adviser to Owner and Pres., Matthieu Pigasse –2010, currently Gen. Man.; Chief Financial Officer Libération 2001, Gen. Man. 2005–06; Deputy Gen. Man. Le Nouvel Observateur (now L'Obs) 2006, Gen. Man. 2007–08; Chair. Man. Bd and CEO Le Monde Group 2010–, launched Le Huffington Post in collaboration with Les Nouvelles Editions Indépendantes and The Huffington Post Media Group 2012; fmr Chief Financial Officer La Provence; Chair. Bd of Dirs École supérieure de journalisme de Lille 2013, Sciences Po Lille. *Address:* Le Monde Group, 80 boulevard Auguste-Blanqui, 75707 Paris Cedex 13, France (office). *Telephone:* 1-42-17-20-00 (office). *Fax:* 1-42-17-21-21 (office). *E-mail:* lemonde@lemonde.fr (office). *Website:* www.lemonde.fr (office).

DREYFUSS, Richard Stephan; American actor; b. 29 Oct. 1947, New York; s. of Norman Dreyfuss and Gerry D. Student; m. Jeramie Dreyfuss 1983; two s. one d.; ed San Fernando Valley State Coll.; alternative mil. service Los Angeles County Gen. Hosp. 1969–71; mem. American Civil Liberties Union Screen Actors Guild, Equity Asscn, American Fed. of TV and Radio Artists, Motion Picture Acad. Arts and Sciences; Golden Globe Award 1978, Acad. Award for Best Actor in The Goodbye Girl 1978. *Stage appearances include:* Julius Caesar 1978, The Big Fix (also producer) 1978, Othello 1979, Death and the Maiden 1992, The Prisoner of Second Avenue 1999, Complicit 2008. *Films include:* American Graffiti 1972, Dillinger 1973, The Apprenticeship of Duddy Kravitz 1974, Jaws 1975, Inserts 1975, Close Encounters of the Third Kind 1976, The Goodbye Girl 1977, The Competition 1980, Whose Life Is It Anyway? 1981, Down and Out in Beverly Hills 1986, Stakeout 1988, Moon over Parador 1989, Let it Ride, Always 1989, Rosencrantz and Guildernstern are Dead, Postcards from the Edge 1990, Once Around 1990, Randall and Juliet 1990, Prisoners of Honor 1991, What About Bob? 1991, Lost in Yonkers 1993, Another Stakeout 1993, The American President, Mr Holland's Opus 1995, Mad Dog Time 1996, James and the Giant Peach (voice) 1996, Night Falls on Manhattan 1997, The Call of the Wild 1997, Krippendorf's Tribe 1998, A Fine and Private Place 1998, The Crew 2000, The Old Man Who Read Love Stories 2000, Who is Cletis Tout? 2001, Silver City 2004, Poseidon 2006, Signs of the Time 2008, W 2008, My Life in Ruins 2009. *Television includes:* Nuts 1987 (dir, producer) Oliver Twist 1997, Fail Safe 2000, Education of Max Bickford 2001–02, Day Reagan Was Shot 2001, Coast to Coast 2003, Copshop 2004, Ocean of Fear 2007, Tin Man 2007. *Publication:* The Two Georges (with Harry Turtledove) 1996. *Address:* William Morris Agency, 1 William Morris Place, Beverly Hills, CA 90212, USA (office). *Telephone:* (310) 859-4000 (office). *Fax:* (310) 859-4462 (office). *Website:* www.wma.com (office).

DRÈZE, Jacques H., PhD; Belgian economist and academic; *Professor Emeritus, Center for Operations Research and Econometrics (CORE);* b. 5 Aug. 1929, Verviers; m.; five s.; ed Univ. de Liège, Columbia Univ., USA; Research Fellow, Carnegie Inst. of Tech. 1954, Visiting Asst Prof. 1957–58; Lecturer, Université Catholique de Louvain 1958–62, Prof. 1962–89; Visiting Assoc. Prof., Northwestern Univ., USA 1962; Ford Foundation Prof., Univ. of Chicago, USA 1963–64, Prof. 1964–68; Titulaire de la Chaire Francqui Belge, Univ. de Bruxelles 1970–71, Katholieke Univ. Leuven 1982–83; Andrew D. White Prof.-at-Large, Cornell Univ. 1971–77; Chargé de recherche Univ. Libre de Bruxelles 1958–60; Research Assoc., Purdue Univ. 1957, Northwestern Univ. 1962, 1963, Univ. of Wisconsin 1964, MIT 1966, Stanford Univ. 1979; Research Dir Center for Operations Research and Econometrics (CORE), Louvain 1966–71, Pres. 1971–83, currently Prof. Emer.; mem. CEPS Macroeconomic Policy Group 1984–85, Chair. 1986–87; Chair. Inst. of Man. Science 1961; Dir Int. Centre for Man. Science, Louvain 1966–71; Assoc. Ed. Econometrica 1963–64, Co-Ed. 1964–69; Vice-Pres. Econometric Soc. 1969, Pres. 1970; Pres. European Econ. Asscn 1985–86, Int. Econ. Asscn 1996–99; Co-ordinator European Unemployment Programme 1985–88; Corresp. FBA 1990; Foreign Assoc., NAS 1993; Corresp. mem. Acad. Royale des Sciences, des Letters et de Beaux-Arts de Belgique 2000; mem. Academica Europaea 1989; Hon. mem. American Econ. Asscn 1976, Asociacion Argentina di Economica Politica 1998, Latin American and Caribbean Econ. Asscn 1999; Foreign Hon. mem. American Acad. of Arts and Science 1978, Royal Netherlands Acad. of Arts and Science 1980; Dr hc (Essex) 1980, (Sorbonne) 1980, (Montréal) 1982, (Liège) 1983, (Antwerp) 1985, (Norges Handelshoyskole, Bergen) 1986, (Bologna) 1988, (Geneva) 1988, (Basel) 1988, (Chicago) 1991, (Aix-Marseille) 1992, (Cergy-Pontoise) 1999, (Bolzano) 2000, (European Univ. Inst.) 2002, (Universidade Catolica Portuguesa) 2003, (Maastricht) 2005, (Universitat Autònoma de Barcelona) 2008, (Sciences P) 2014, (Hebrew Univ. of Jerusalem) 2015; Prix des Alumni, Fondation Universitaire, Brussels 1964, Prix Emile De Laveleye, Acad. Royale des Sciences, des Lettres et des Beaux-Arts de Belgique 1993, Prix, Accad. dei Lincei, Rome 1999. *Publications include:* numerous books and articles on econ. theory and policy, including Allocation under Uncertainty 1974, Essays on Economic Decisions under Uncertainty 1987, Labour Management, Contracts and Capital Markets 1989, Underemployment Equilibria 1991, Advances in Macroeconomics 2001. *Leisure interest:* sailing around the world with wife Monique. *Address:* Centre for Operations Research and Econometrics (CORE), Université Catholique de Louvain, Voie du Roman Pays, 34, 1348 Louvain-la-Neuve, Belgium (office). *Telephone:* (10) 474347 (office). *Fax:* (10) 474301 (office). *E-mail:* jacques.dreze@uclouvain.be (office). *Website:* www.core.ucl.ac.be (office).

DRINFELD, Vladimir Gershonovich, PhD; Ukrainian mathematician and academic; *Harry Pratt Judson Distinguished Service Professor, Department of Mathematics, University of Chicago;* b. 14 Feb. 1954, Kharkov (now Kharkiv); ed Moscow Univ., Steklov Inst., Moscow; B. Verkin Inst. for Low Temperature Physics and Eng, Nat. Acad. of Sciences of the Ukraine 1981–98; Prof., Dept of Math., Univ. of Chicago 1999–2001, Harry Pratt Judson Distinguished Service Prof. 2001–; mem. Nat. Acad. of Sciences of the Ukraine 1992–, American Acad. of Arts and Sciences, NAS 2016; Fields Medal, Int. Congress of Mathematicians, (Kyoto, Japan) 1990, Wolf Prize for Mathematics 2018. *Publications:* Chiral Algebras (co-author) 2004 and numerous publs on quantum groups and number theory.

DRIVER, Adam Douglas; American actor; b. 19 Nov. 1983, San Diego, Calif.; s. of Joe Douglas Driver and Nancy (Needham) Wright; m. Joanne Tucker 2013; ed Mishawaka High School, Univ. of Indianapolis, Juilliard School; moved to Mishawaka, Ind. aged seven; served in US Marine Corps 2001–04; mem. Group 38, Drama Div., Juilliard School 2005–09; appeared in several Broadway and off-Broadway productions; runs non-profit org. Arts in the Armed Forces which stages performances for mil. personnel. *Films include:* J. Edgar 2011, Gayby 2012, Not Waving but Drowning 2012, Frances Ha 2012, Lincoln 2012, Bluebird 2013, Inside Llewyn Davis 2013, Tracks 2013, What If 2013, Hungry Hearts (Volpi Cup for Best Actor, Venice Film Festival) 2014, While We're Young 2014, This is Where I Leave You 2014, Midnight Special 2015, Star Wars: Episode VII – The Force Awakens 2015. *Television includes:* You Don't Know Jack (film) 2010, The Wonderful Maladys (film) 2010, Girls (series) 2012–15. *Address:* Randi Goldstein, Gersh, 9465 Wilshire Boulevard, Sixth Floor, Beverly Hills, CA 90212, USA (office). *Telephone:* (310) 274-6611 (office). *Fax:* (310) 278-6232 (office). *E-mail:* info@gershla.com (office). *Website:* www.gershagency.com (office).

DRIVER, Minnie (Amelia); British actress; b. 31 Jan. 1970, London; d. of Charles Driver and Gaynor Churchward (née Millington); one s.; ed Bedales School, Hants.; Best Newcomer, London Circle of Film Critics 1997, Best Actress, London Circle of Film Critics 1998. *Plays include:* Sexual Perversity in Chicago, Comedy Theatre, London 2003. *Films include:* Circle of Friends 1995, Goldeneye 1995, Baggage 1996, Big Night 1996, Sleepers 1996, Grosse Pointe Blank 1997, Good Will Hunting 1997, The Governess 1998, Hard Rain 1998, At Sachem Farm 1998, Trespasser (voice) 1998, An Ideal Husband 1999, Tarzan (voice) 1999, South Park: Bigger, Longer and Uncut 1999, Slow Burn 2000, Beautiful 2000, Return to Me 2000, The Upgrade 2000, High Heels and Lowlifes 2001, D.C. Smalls 2001, Owning Mahoney 2003, Hope Springs 2003, Ella Enchanted 2004, Portrait 2004, The Phantom of the Opera 2004, The Virgin of Juarez 2006, Ripple Effect 2007, Motherhood 2009, Conviction 2010, Barney's Version 2010, Hunky Dory 2011, I Give It a Year 2013, Return to Zero 2014, Stage Fright 2014, Beyond the Lights 2014, The Crash 2017. *Television includes:* God on the Rocks 1990, Mr Wroe's Virgins 1993, The Politician's Wife 1995, The Riches (series) 2007–08, Modern Family 2010, The Deep (mini-series) 2010, Hail Mary (film) 2011, Lady Friends (film) 2012, About a Boy 2014–15, Speechless 2016–. *Recordings:* albums: Everything I've Got in My Pocket 2004, Seastories 2008, Ask Me to Dance 2014. *Address:* c/o Lou Coulson, First Floor, 37 Berwick Street, London, W1V 3LF, England.

DROGBA TÉBILY, Didier Yves; Côte d'Ivoirian professional footballer; b. 11 March 1978, Abidjan; m. Diakité Lalla; three c.; striker (centre forward); began career as youth player with French clubs Levallois 1996–97, Le Mans 1997–98 (professional debut aged 18); with Le Mans (64 appearances, 12 goals) 1998–2002, Guincamp (45 appearances, 20 goals) 2002–03, Olympique de Marseille (35 appearances, 35 goals) 2003–04, Chelsea FC (226 appearances, 157 goals) 2004–12 (won FA Premier League 2004–05, 2005–06, 2009–10, FA Cup 2006–07, 2008–09, 2009–10, 2011–12, Football League Cup 2004–05, 2006–07, 2014–15, FA Community Shield 2005, 2009, UEFA Champions League 2012) 2014–15, Shanghai Shenhua 2012–13, Galatasaray 2013–14, Montreal Impact 2015–16, Phoenix Rising (co-owner) 2017–; mem. Côte d'Ivoire nat. football team (84 appearances, 54 goals) 2002–, team capt. during African Cup of Nations 2006; UNDP Goodwill Amb. 2007–; first player to score in four different FA Cup Finals, scoring the winner in Chelsea's 2–1 victory over Liverpool FC 5 May 2012; f. Didier Drogba Foundation (charity) 2009; Onze d'Or 2004, UEFA Cup Top Scorer 2004, Ligue 1 Goal of the Year 2004, Ligue 1 Team of the Year 2004, Ligue 1 Player of the Year 2004, Ivorian Footballer of the Year 2006, 2007, African Footballer of the Year 2006, 2009, Chelsea Players' Player of the Year 2007, Premier League Golden Boot 2007, 2010, PFA Team of the Year 2007, 2010, UEFA Team of the Year 2007, ESM Team of the Year 2007, FIFPro World XI 2007, BBC African Footballer of the Year 2009, West African Footballer of the Year 2010, Chelsea Player of the Year 2010, Time Top 100 2010, Côte d'Ivoire all-time Top Scorer, Levallois Sporting Club named its stadium after him 2010, Africa Cup Top Scorer 2012, Africa Cup Team of the Tournament 2006, 2008, 2012, UEFA Champions League Final Man of the Match 2012. *Website:* www.didierdrogba.com.

DRONKE, (Ernst) Peter (Michael), MA, FBA; British medieval Latin scholar and author; *Professor Emeritus of Medieval Latin Literature, University of Cambridge;* b. 30 May 1934; s. of A. H. R. Dronke and M. M. Dronke (née Kronfeld); m. Ursula Miriam Brown 1960 (died 2012); one d.; ed Victoria Univ., NZ and Magdalen Coll., Oxford; Research Fellow, Merton Coll., Oxford 1958–61; Lecturer in Medieval Latin, Univ. of Cambridge 1961–79, Reader in Medieval Latin Literature 1979–89, Prof. 1989–2001, Prof. Emer. 2001–, Fellow, Clare Hall 1964–2001; Visiting Prof. of Medieval Studies, Westfield Coll. London 1981–86; Carl Newell Jackson Lecturer, Harvard Univ., USA 1992; Corresp. Fellow, Real Academia de Buenas Letras, Royal Dutch Acad., Medieval Acad. of America, Austrian Acad. of Sciences, Fondazione Lorenzo Valla, Istituto Lombardo Acad. of Sciences and Letters; Co-ed. Mittellateinisches Jahrbuch 1977–2002; Hon. Pres., Int. Courtly Literature Soc.; Premio Internazionale Ascoli Piceno 1988, Premio Bettarini 2014. *Publications:* Medieval Latin and the Rise of European Love-Lyric (2 Vols) 1965–66, The Medieval Lyric 1968, Poetic Individuality in the Middle Ages 1970, Fabula 1974, Abelard and Heloïse in Medieval Testimonies 1976, Barbara et antiquissima carmina (with Ursula Dronke) 1977, Bernardus Silvestris, Cosmographia (ed.) 1978, Introduction to Francesco Colonna, Hypnerotomachia 1981, Women Writers of the Middle Ages 1984, The Medieval Poet and his World 1984, Dante and Medieval Latin Traditions 1986, Introduction to Rosvita, Dialoghi Drammatici 1986, A History of Twelfth-Century Western Philosophy (ed.) 1988, Hermes and the Sibyls 1990, Latin and Vernacular Poets of the Middle Ages 1991, Intellectuals and Poets in Medieval Europe 1992, Verse with Prose: From Petronius to Dante 1994, Nine Medieval Latin Plays 1994, Hildegard of Bingen, Liber divinorum operum (co-ed.) 1996, Sources of Inspiration 1997, Dante's Second Love (lectures) 1997, Introduction to Alessandro nel medioevo occidentale 1997, Growth of Literature: the Sea and the God of the Sea (with Ursula Dronke) 1998, Etienne Gilson's Letters to Bruno Nardi (ed.) 1998, Hildegard of Bingen: The Context of Her Thought and Art (co-ed.) 1998, Imagination in the Late Pagan and Early Christian World 2003, Forms and Imaginings 2007, The Spell of Calcidius 2008, Giovanni Scoto Eriugena, Periphyseon I (ed) 2012, II (ed) 2013, III (ed) 2014; essays in learned journals and symposia. *Leisure interests:* music, film and Brittany. *Address:* 6 Parker Street, Cambridge, CB1 1JL, England (home).

DROSDICK, John G. (Jack), BS, MS; American business executive; b. 9 Aug. 1943, West Hazelton, Pa; m. Gloria J. Shenosky; four c.; ed Villanova Univ., Univ. of Massachusetts; joined Exxon Corpn 1968, held various man. positions in New Jersey, Tex. and La; Pres. Tosco Corpn 1987–92; Pres. Ultramar Corpn 1992–96; Pres. and COO Sunoco Inc. 1996–2000, Chair., CEO and Pres. 2000–08, Chair. (non-exec.) July–Dec. 2008 (retd), also retd as Chair. Sunoco Partners, LLC, and as Gen. Partner, Sunoco Logistics Partners, LP; mem. Bd of Dirs United States Steel Corpn 2003–, HJ Heinz Co., Lincoln Nat. Corpn; Chair. Bd of Trustees, Villanova Univ.; Trustee, Kimmel Center for the Performing Arts, Philadelphia Museum of Art (also Chair. Exec. Bd).

DROSOS, Gina, BA, MBA; American business executive; *Group President, Global Beauty, Skin, Cosmetics, and Personal Care, Procter & Gamble Company;* ed Wharton School, Univ. of Pennsylvania; summer intern at Procter & Gamble's Spic and Span business, joined co. full time in 1987, began working on Olay skin care business 1992, promoted to positions of increasing responsibility until current position of Group Pres. Global Beauty, Skin, Cosmetics, and Personal Care, responsible for brands including Pantene, Head and Shoulders, Wella, Olay and Old Spice, additional responsibility for antiperspirants and deodorants 2011–. *Address:* Proctor & Gamble Company, 1 Procter & Gamble Plaza, Cincinnati, OH 43202-3315, USA (office). *Telephone:* (513) 983-1100 (office). *Fax:* (513) 983-9369 (office). *E-mail:* info@pg.com (office). *Website:* www.pg.com (office).

DROZDOVA, Margarita Sergeyevna; Russian ballerina; b. 7 May 1948, Moscow; ed Moscow Choreographic School, State Inst. of Theatre Art (GITIS); danced with Stanislavsky Musical Theatre Ballet Co., Moscow 1967–87, apptd teacher/repetiteur and balletmaster 1987; mem. CPSU 1980–91; Int. Competitions for Ballet Dancers in Varna 1972, in Moscow 1973, Anna Pavlova Award, Paris 1968; RSFSR State Prize 1980, People's Artist of USSR 1986. *Roles include:* Odette-Odile, Gayané, The Commissar (M. Bronner's 'Optimistic Tragedy'), Medora (A. Adam's 'Corsaire'), Swanilda (Delibes' 'Coppélia'), Cinderella (Prokofiev). *Address:* c/o Stanislavsky and Nemirovich Danchenko Musical Theatre, Bolshaya Dmitrovka 17, Moscow, Russia. *Telephone:* (495) 629-83-88; (495) 299-31-36 (home).

DRUBICH, Tatyana Lusienovna; Russian actress; b. 7 June 1960, Moscow; m. Sergey Soloviev (divorced); one d.; ed Third Moscow Medical Inst.; worked as a nurse then as a physician; actress 1972–. *Films include:* 15th Spring (debut) 1972, 100 Days after Childhood 1975, Disarray 1978, Particularly Dangerous 1978, The Rescuer 1979, The Direct Heiress 1982, Selected 1983, Tester 1984, Black Monk 1986, Keep Me, My Talisman 1986, Assa 1987, Black Rose – An Emblem of Sorrow, White Rose – An Emblem of Love 1989, Hey, Fools 1996, Moscow 2000, O lyubvi (About Love) 2003, Gololed (Slippery Ice), Anna Karenina 2007, 2-Assa-2, ili vtoraya smert' Anny Kareninoy (2-Assa-2, or The Second Death of Anna Karenina) 2007, Dobrovolets 2009, Posledniaya Skazka Riti (Nadya) 2011. *Address:* Seleznevskaya str. 30, korp. 3, Apt 77, 103473 Moscow, Russia. *Telephone:* (495) 281-60-82.

DRUCKER, Michel; French broadcast journalist and television producer; b. 12 Sept. 1942, Vire (Calvados); s. of Abraham Drucker and Lola Schafler; m. Danielle Savalle (Dany Saval) 1973; ed Lycée Emile-Maupas, Vire; sports reporter for ORTF 1964, presenter of variety programmes 1966, producer and presenter Sport en Fête, football commentator 1969; commentator, World Cup Football Championships 1970, 1974, 1978; presenter, (Radio-Télé-Luxembourg – RTL) C'est vous 1974–76, Les Rendez-vous du dimanche 1975–1981, Stars 1981, Champs-Elysées 1982–85, (Europe 1) Studio 1 1983, (Antenne 2) Champs-Elysées, 1987–90, (TF1) Stars 90 1990–94, Ciné Stars 1991–94, (France 2) Studio Gabriel 1994–97, Faites la fête 1994–98, Drucker & Co., Stars & Co. 1997–98, Vivement dimanche, Vivement dimanche prochain, Tapis rouge 1998–2001, Tenue de soirée 2006–; acquired Production DMD from Canal+ 1998; Host, Tenue de soirée 2006–08, Champs Élysées 2010–13, Le Grand Show 2012–16, L'Été indien 2014–; Chevalier Légion d'honneur, des Arts et Lettres 1984, Officier de la Légion d'honneur 2004, Officier de l'ordre national du Québec 2010; Sports Journalist of the Year, Télémagazine 1971, 1972, 1973, Prix Triomphe de la télévision à la Nuit du cinéma 1973, 1987, 7 d'Or Award for Best Variety Programme Presenter, Prix Gémeaux de la francophonie, Quebec, Canada 2000. *Films include:* L'aventure c'est l'aventure de Claude Lelouch 1972, Un fil à la patte 2005, Trois jeunes filles nues 2006, La Grande Boucle 2013, Avis de mistral 2014, Elle l'adore de Jeanne Herry 2014. *Publications:* La Balle au bond (autobiog.) 1973, La Coupe du monde de football 1974, La Chaîne (novel) 1979, Novembre des amours 1984, Hors antenne, conversation avec Maurice Achard 1987, Les Numéros 1. Tous les grands du football français 1987, Stars 90 2000, Mais Qu'est-ce qu'on va faire de toi? 2007. *Leisure interests:* tennis, cycling, football, skiing, flying. *Address:* Production DMD, 21 rue Jean Mermoz, 75008 Paris (office); Pavillon Gabriel, 9 avenue Gabriel, 75008 Paris, France (home). *Telephone:* 1-40-76-00-89 (office). *Fax:* 1-45-63-61-42 (office).

DRUKER, Brian J., MD; American medical scientist and academic; *JELD-WEN Chair of Leukemia Research and Director, OHSU Knight Cancer Institute, Oregon Health and Science University;* b. 30 April 1955, Minn.; m. 1st Barbara Rodriguez (divorced); m. Alexandra Hardy; three c.; ed School of Medicine, Univ. of California, San Diego; residency in internal medicine at Barnes Hospital, Washington Univ., St Louis, Mo. 1981–84; held Oncology Fellowship at Dana-Farber Cancer Inst., Harvard Medical School; currently JELD-WEN Chair of Leukemia Research, Oregon Health and Science Univ., Dir OHSU Knight Cancer Inst. 2007–; named a Howard Hughes Medical Investigator 2002; mem. Inst. of Medicine of the Nat. Academies 2003, American Asscn of Physicians 2006, NAS 2007; Pres.'s Undergraduate Research Award, Univ. of California, San Diego, Lifetime Achievement Award, Leukemia and Lymphoma Soc., Medal of Honor, American Cancer Soc., Lasker-DeBakey Clinical Medical Research Award (co-recipient) 2009, Meyenburg Cancer Research Prize 2009, Hope Funds Award of Excellence for Clinical Research 2009, Japan Prize (co-recipient) 2012, Tang Prize in Biopharmaceutical Science (co–recipient) 2018, Sjöberg Prize (co–recipient) 2019 and numerous other awards. *Achievements include:* developed, with Nicholas B. Lydon, imatinib (or Gleevec) and other targeted treatments for chronic myeloid leukemia. *Publications:* numerous papers in professional journals. *Address:* OHSU Knight Cancer Institute, Mail Code CR145, 3181 SW Sam Jackson Park Road, Portland, OR 97239-3098, USA (office). *Telephone:* (503) 494-5058 (office). *E-mail:* drukerb@ohsu.edu (office). *Website:* www.ohsu.edu/xd/health/services/cancer/about-us/druker (office).

DRUMMOND, David Carl, BA, JD; American lawyer and technology industry executive; *Senior Vice-President, Corporate Development and Chief Legal Officer, Google, Inc.;* b. 6 March 1963, Carmel, Calif.; m.; ed Santa Clara Univ., Stanford Univ. Law School; fmr Partner, Wilson Sonsini Goodrich and Rosati (law firm); served as first outside law counsel, Google Inc. 1998; Chief Financial Officer and Exec. Vice-Pres. of Finance, SSI Investments II Ltd 1999–2002 (Dir 2000–); Chief Financial Officer and Exec. Vice-Pres. of Finance, SmartForce PLC 1999–2002; Vice-Pres. of Corp. Devt and Gen. Counsel, Google Inc. (now Alphabet Inc.) 2002–06, Sr Vice-Pres. of Corp. Devt 2006–, Chief Legal Officer 2006–, apptd to served as Chair. Google Ventures and Google Capital, Alphabet Inc. (newly formed holding co.) 2015; mem. Bd of Dirs Rocket Lawyer Inc. 2008–, Next Autoworks Co. 2009–, Uber Technologies Inc. 2013–, V-Vehicle Company, KKR Man. LLC 2014–. *Address:* Google Inc., 1600 Amphitheatre Parkway, Mountain View, CA 94043, USA (office). *Telephone:* (650) 253-0000 (office). *Website:* www.google.com (office); abc.xyz (office).

DRURY, Very Rev. John Henry, MA, DD; British ecclesiastic and university administrator; *Chaplain and Fellow, All Souls College, Oxford;* b. 23 May 1936, Clacton; s. of Henry Drury and Barbara Drury; m. Clare Nineham 1972 (died 2004); two d.; ed Bradfield Coll. and Trinity Hall, Cambridge; Curate, St John's Wood Church, London 1963; Chaplain, Downing Coll. Cambridge 1966; Chaplain and Fellow, Exeter Coll. Oxford 1969; Canon of Norwich Cathedral 1973; lecturer, Univ. of Sussex 1979; Dean, King's Coll. Cambridge 1981; Dean, Christ Church, Oxford 1991–2003; Hussey Lecturer Univ. of Oxford 1997; Chaplain and Fellow, All Souls Coll., Oxford 2003–; Hon. Fellow, Exeter Coll., Oxford 1992, Trinity Hall, Cambridge 1997, Hon. Student of Christ Church, Oxford 2003. *Television:* Painting the Word, Channel 5 (UK), 2002. *Publications:* Angels and Dirt 1972, Luke 1973, Tradition and Design in Luke's Gospel 1976, Parables in the Gospels 1985, Critics of the Bible 1724–1873 1989, The Burning Bush 1990, Painting the Word 1999, Music at Midnight: The Life and Poetry of George Herbert 2013. *Leisure interests:* drawing, walking, carpentry. *Address:* All Souls College, Oxford, OX1 4AL, England. *Telephone:* (1865) 279368. *Fax:* (1865) 279299. *E-mail:* john.drury@all-souls.ac.uk.

DRUT, Guy Jacques; French politician and fmr athlete; b. 6 Dec. 1950, Oignies (Pas de Calais); s. of Jacques Drut and Jacqueline Wigley; m. 2nd Véronique Hardy 1984; one d. and one d. by first m.; ed Lycée de Douai, Lycée d'Henin-Liétard, Lycée Roubaix, Ecole Normale Supérieure d'Educ. Physique et Sportive and Inst. Nat. des Sports; French Jr record-holder, 110m hurdles, pole vault and decathlon; French 110m hurdles champion 1970–76, 1981; European 100m hurdles champion, Rome 1974; European 110m hurdles record, Rome 1974, world record, Berlin 1975; silver medal, 110m hurdles, Munich Olympics 1972, gold medal, Montreal Olympics 1976; bronze medal, 50m hurdles, European Championships 1981; retd from competition 1981; Chief of Staff to Prime Minister Jacques Chirac 1975–76; mem. Nat. Council UDR, Cen. Cttee RPR; Deputy Mayor of Paris responsible for Youth and Sport 1985–89; Deputy (RPR) from Seine-et-Marne to Nat. Ass. 1986–95; Town Councillor, Meaux 1989–92; Mayor of Coulommiers 1992–; Minister of Youth and Sport May–Nov. 1995, Minister del. 1995–97; elected Deputy for Seine-et-Marne (Groupe du Rassemblement pour la République) 1997, re-elected (Groupe Union pour un Mouvement Populaire) 2002–07; mem. IOC 1996–2005 (resgnd); Chevalier, Ordre Nat. du Mérite. *Publications:* L'or et l'argent 1976, Jacques Chirac: la victoire du sport (co-author) 1988, J'ai deux mots à vous dire 1997. *Leisure interests:* golf, hunting. *Address:* Mairie, 77120 Coulommiers, France.

D'SOUZA, Baroness (Life Peer), cr. 2004, of Wychwood in the County of Oxfordshire; **Frances D'Souza,** CMG, PC, BSc (Hons), DPhil; British anthropologist and parliamentarian; b. 18 April 1944, North Wales; d. of Robert Anthony O'Brien Russell; m. Dr Stanislaus D'Souza (died 2011); two d.; ed Univ. Coll., London, Lady Margaret Hall, Oxford; worked for Nuffield Inst. of Comparative Medicine 1973–77, for Oxford Polytechnic (now Oxford Brookes Univ.) 1977–80; taught at LSE and Oxford Brookes Univ.; ind. research consultant for UN 1985–88; fmr consultant to REDRESS Trust; Exec. Dir ARTICLE 19 (human rights org.) for nine years; Convenor of the Crossbench Peers, House of Lords 2007–11, Lord Speaker of the House of Lords 2011–16; Jt Pres. Commonwealth Parl. Asscn (UK Br.) 2011–16, British-American Parl. Group, Industry and Parl. Trust; Chair. David Nott Foundation 2016–19; Vice-Chair. British Group, Inter-Parl. Union 2016–; Pres. Police Service Parl. Scheme; Co-Pres. Hansard Soc.; Trustee of several orgs; Dr hc (Hull) 2016. *Publications include:* numerous scientific papers in professional journals. *Leisure interests:* Music (opera, chamber music, flamenco, Indian classical), gardening, travel. *Address:* House of Lords, Westminster, London, SW1A 0PW, England (office). *Telephone:* (20) 7219-3670 (office). *Fax:* (20) 7219-2075 (office). *E-mail:* dsouzaf@parliament.uk (office). *Website:* www.parliament.uk/biographies/lords/baroness-d'souza/3709 (office).

DU, Daozheng; Chinese journalist; b. Nov. 1923, Dingxiang Co., Shanxi Prov.; s. of Du Xixiang and Qi Luaying; m. Xu Zhixian 1950; one s. four d.; ed Middle School, Dingxiang, Shanxi and Beijing Marx-Lenin Coll.; joined CCP 1937; Chief of Hebei and Guangdong Bureau, Xinhua News Agency 1949–56; Ed.-in-Chief Yangchen Wanbao 1956–69; Dir Home News Dept, Xinhua News Agency 1977–82; Ed.-in-Chief Guangming Daily 1982; Dir Media and Publs Office 1987–88; Deputy 7th NPC 1988–92; Dir State Press and Publs Admin. 1988–89; Founder and Publisher, Yanhuang Chunqiu (journal) 1991–2016; Hon. Pres. Newspaper Operation and Man. Asscn 1988; Nat. News Prize 1979. *Publications include:* Explore Japan (co-author), Interviews with Famous Chinese Journalists. *Leisure interest:* photography.

DU, Ming-xin; Chinese composer and music editor; b. 19 Aug. 1928, Qianjiang Co., Hubei Prov.; m. 1966; one s. one d.; ed Yu Cai Music School and Tchaikovsky State Conservatoire, USSR; debut solo piano concert, Shanghai 1948; Prof. of Composition, Cen. Conservatory of Music 1978–, also Doctoral Adviser; participated in Asian Composers' Conf. and Music Festival, Hong Kong 1981; travelled to USA for performance of Violin Concerto No. 1, John F. Kennedy Center 1986, and gave lectures in music insts; Exec. Dir Chinese Musicians' Asscn; mem. 11th CPPCC 1997–2002. *Compositions include:* Violin Concerto No. 1, Violin Concerto No. 2, Piano Concerto No. 1, Piano Concerto No. 2, Great Wall Symphony, Luoshen Symphony, Youth Symphony, The South Sea of My Mother Land (symphonic picture), The Goddess of the River Luo (symphonic fantasia), Flapping! the Flags of Army, The Mermaid (ballet suite), The Red Detachment of Women (ballet suite), Wonderful China (film soundtrack) 1982, piano trio, string quartet. *Address:* Central Conservatory of Music, 43 Baojia Street, Beijing 100031, People's Republic of China. *Website:* en.ccom.edu.cn.

DU, Qinglin, MA; Chinese politician; *Chairman, China Economic Social Council;* b. Nov. 1946, Panshi Co., Jilin Prov.; ed Northeast China Teachers' Univ., Jilin Univ.; joined CCP 1966; mem. Young Cadres Class, CCP Jilin City Cttee 1964–66; mem. and Deputy Group Leader Socialist Educ. Work Team, CCP Liuhe Co. Cttee, Jilin Prov., Yongji Co. Cttee, Jilin Prov., Shulan Co. Cttee, Jilin Prov. 1964–66; clerical worker, Publicity Dept, CCP Jilin City Cttee 1967–68; Sec. CCP Communist Youth League and Head of Workshop, No. 1 Automobile Works

1968–74, Deputy Chair. CCP Revolutionary Cttee 1974–78, Deputy Dir No. 1 Automobile Works 1974–78, Deputy Sec. CCP Party Br. 1974–78; Sec. CCP Communist Youth League, Jilin City Cttee 1978–79; Deputy Sec. Communist Youth League Jilin Prov. Cttee, mem. Communist Youth League Cen. Cttee 1979–84; Deputy Sec. CCP Changchun City Cttee 1984–85; Deputy Sec. CCP Jilin Prov. Cttee 1988–92; Deputy Sec. CCP Hainan Prov. Cttee 1992–98, Sec. 1998–2001; Alt. mem. 14th CCP Cen. Cttee 1992–97, mem. 15th CCP Cen. Cttee 1997–2002, 16th CCP Cen. Cttee 2002–07, 17th CCP Cen. Cttee 2007–12, 18th CCP Cen. Cttee 2012–17, also 18th CCP Cen. Cttee Politburo Secr. 2012–17, mem. CCP Cen. Cttee Cen. LSG for Xinjiang Work 2017–, LSG for Comprehensively Deepening Reform 2017–, LSG for Taiwan Affairs 2017–; Chair. Standing Cttee, Hainan Prov. People's Congress 1993–2001; Minister of Agric. 2001–06; Sec. Sichuan CCP Prov. Cttee 2006–07; Head CCP Cen. Cttee United Front Work Dept 2007–12; Vice-Chair. 11th CPPCC Nat. Cttee 2008–13, 12th CPPCC Nat. Cttee 2013–18; Vice-Pres. China Council for the Promotion of Peaceful Reunification 2008–; Chair. China Econ. and Social Council 2014–. *Address:* China Economic Social Council, No. 23, Taipingqiao Street, Beijing 100811, People's Republic of China (office). *Telephone:* (10) 66192656 (office). *Fax:* (10) 66192665 (office). *E-mail:* cesc@cppcc.gov.cn (office). *Website:* www.china-esc.org.cn (office).

DU, Shuanghua; Chinese business executive; *Chairman, Rizhao Steel Holding Group Co., Ltd.;* b. Hebei Prov.; m. Song Yahong (divorced); two s.; Man. Hengshui Jinghua Steel Pipe Co. Ltd; currently Chair. Rizhao Steel Holding Group Co. Ltd. *Address:* Rizhao Steel Holding Group Co., Ltd, 600, Bin Hai Lu, Rizhao, Shandong Province, People's Republic of China (office). *Telephone:* (633) 6188060 (office). *Fax:* (633) 6180000 (office). *E-mail:* rzgtzb01@163.com (office). *Website:* www.rizhaosteel.com (office).

DU, Gen. Tiehuan; Chinese army officer; b. 1938, Anshan City, Liaoning Prov.; ed PLA Mil. Acad.; Asst Dir PLA Gen. Political Dept 1993–94; Political Commissar Ji'nan Mil. Region 1994–96; Political Commissar, Beijing Mil. Area Command 1996–97; mem. 15th CCP Cen. Cttee 1997–2002; rank of Lt Gen. 1997, Gen. 2000. *Address:* c/o Political Commissar's Office, Beijing Military Area Command, Beijing, People's Republic of China.

DU, Yuzhou; Chinese textile engineer and government official; *Honorary President, China National Textile and Apparel Council;* b. 1942, Qiqihar, Heilongjiang; ed Tsinghua Univ.; joined CCP 1965; technician, Changde Textile Machinery Plant, Hunan 1968–70, Deputy Workshop Head, then Deputy Section Chief 1970–73; engineer, Deputy Dir then Dir Design Inst. of Ministry of Textile Industry 1978–85; Vice-Minister of Textiles 1985–93; Vice-Chair., Chair. Chinese Gen. Asscn of Textile Industry, Dir State Admin. for the Textile Industry 1993–; Pres. China Nat. Garment Asscn; Chair. of China Nat. Fed. of Textile Manufacturers; Hon. Pres. China Nat. Textile and Apparel Council. *Address:* c/o State Administration for the Textile Industry, Huaye Internaional Center, No.39 Dongsihuan Zhonglu, Chaoyang, Beijing 100025, People's Republic of China (office).

DU PLESSIS, Jan, BCom, LLB, CA (SA); South African chartered accountant and business executive; *Chairman, Rio Tinto Group;* b. Cape Town; m.; two s. one d.; ed Univ. of Stellenbosch; qualified as chartered accountant; joined Rembrandt Group 1981, moved to UK 1982, held various positions before co-founding Compagnie Financière Richemont SA (Swiss public co. formed following demerger of Rembrandt's non-South African interests 1988), Group Finance Dir 1988–2004; Finance Dir Rothmans International 1990–96; Dir (non-exec.) British American Tobacco (BAT) PLC 1999–2009, mem. Audit, Nominations and Remuneration Cttees, Chair. (non-exec.) BAT 2004–09 (resgnd), also Chair. Nominations Cttee; mem. Bd of Dirs Rio Tinto Group 2008–, Chair. 2009–; Chair. (non-exec.) RHM PLC 2005–07; Dir (non-exec.) Lloyds TSB Group PLC 2005–09 (Chair. Audit Cttee 2008–09), Marks & Spencer Group PLC 2008–15 (Sr Ind. Dir (non-exec.) 2012–15); Dir (non-exec.) SABMiller PLC 2014–, Chair. 2015–. *Address:* Rio Tinto PLC, 2 Eastbourne Terrace, London, W2 6LG, England (office); Rio Tinto Ltd, 120 Collins Street, Melbourne, Vic. 3000, Australia (office). *Telephone:* (20) 7781-2000 (London) (office); (3) 9283-3333 (Melbourne) (office). *Fax:* (20) 7781-1800 (London) (office); (3) 9283-3707 (Melbourne) (office). *E-mail:* info@riotinto.com (office). *Website:* www.riotinto.com (office).

DU SAUTOY, Marcus Peter Francis, OBE, FRS, BA (Hons), DPhil; British mathematician and academic; *Charles Simonyi Professor for the Public Understanding of Science and Professor of Mathematics, University of Oxford;* b. 26 Aug. 1965, London; m. Shani Ram; one s. twin d.; ed Gillotts School, King James's Coll. (VI Form, now Henley Coll.), Wadham Coll., Oxford; postdoctoral researcher, Hebrew Univ.; then EPSRC Sr Media Fellow and a Royal Soc. Univ. Research Fellow; Charles Simonyi Prof. for the Public Understanding of Science and Prof. of Math., Univ. of Oxford 2008–, fmrly Fellow of All Souls Coll. and of Wadham Coll., now Fellow of New Coll.; Pres. Math. Asscn 2012–13; mem. Gen. Purposes Cttee, All Souls Coll. 1996–, Royal Soc. Cttee Science and Society 1999–; Judge for Crighton Medal, London Math. Soc. 2003; mem. Dialogue in Medical Science and Society, Asscn of Medical Research Charities 2003–; Reviews Ed., LMS newsletter 2002–; Fellow, American Math. Soc.; Senior Math. Prize 1989, Dr Johnson Prize for DPhil thesis 1989, Berwick Prize, London Math. Soc. 2001, Michael Faraday Prize, Royal Soc. of London 2009. *Television includes* numerous episodes of Horizon series; The Code (BBC 2) (documentary series) 2011, Faster Than the Speed of Light? (BBC 2) 2011, Precision: The Measure of All Things (BBC 4) 2013. *Publications:* The Music of the Primes 2003, Finding Moonshine 2007, Symmetry: A Journey into the Patterns of Nature 2008, The Num8er My5teries: A Mathematical Odyssey Through Everyday Life 2010, What We Cannot Know 2016; numerous papers in professional journals on group theory and number theory. *Leisure interests:* Arsenal Football Club, playing football, playing the trumpet. *Address:* Mathematical Institute, University of Oxford, Andrew Wiles Building, Radcliffe Observatory Quarter, Woodstock Road, Oxford, OX2 6GG, England (office). *Telephone:* (1865) 273525 (office). *Fax:* (1865) 273583 (office). *E-mail:* simonyi.professor@maths.ox.ac.uk (office). *Website:* www.simonyi.ox.ac.uk (office).

DUAN, Qingshan, MBA; Chinese auditor and business executive; *Chairman of the Board of Supervisors, China Minsheng Banking Corporation Limited;* b. 1957; fmr Div. Dir Audit Div., Taiyuan Br., People's Bank of China; fmr Chief Financial Officer and Gen. Man. Human Resources Dept, China Minsheng Banking Corpn Ltd, fmr Man. Dir Taiyuan Br., fmr Deputy Head, then Head of Taiyuan Sub-br., currently Chair. Bd of Supervisors. *Address:* China Minsheng Banking Corporation Ltd, 2 Fuxingmennei Avenue, Beijing 100873, People's Republic of China (office). *Telephone:* (10) 68946790 (office). *E-mail:* webmaster@cmbc.com.cn (office). *Website:* www.cmbc.com.cn (office).

DUARTE, Cristina Isabel Lopes da Silva Monteiro, MBA; Cabo Verde politician, economist and international banker; b. 1962, Lisbon, Portugal; d. of Manuel Duarte; m.; one d.; ed Univ. Técnica de Lisboa, Portugal, Univ. of Arizona, USA; Dir of Studies and Planning, Ministry of Rural Devt 1986–91; consultant to FAO, UNDP and World Bank 1992–93; economist with Citibank in Kenya and Angola 1997–2003; Co-ordinator, World Bank Growth and Competitiveness Project 2005–06; Minister of Finance and Planning 2006–16; has worked in several African countries including South Africa, Angola, Cabo Verde, Guinea-Bissau, Kenya and Mozambique. *Address:* Ministry of Finances and Planning, 107 Av. Amílcar Cabral, CP 30, Praia, Santiago, Cabo Verde (office). *Telephone:* (260) 7400 (office). *E-mail:* aliciab@gov1.gov.cv (office). *Website:* www.minfin.cv (office).

DUARTE FRUTOS, Oscar Nicanor, LicenFil, PhD; Paraguayan politician, diplomatist and fmr head of state; b. 11 Oct. 1956, Coronel Oviedo; m. María Gloria Penayo; six c.; ed Nat. Univ. of Asunción, Catholic Univ. of Asunción; journalist, Ultima Hora newspaper 1981–91; Minister of Educ. and Culture 1993–97, 1999–2001; Leader, Partido Colorado 2001; Pres. of Paraguay 2003–08; fmr Prof. of Sociology and Ethics, Faculty of Philosophy, Nat. Univ. of Asunción; Amb. to Argentina 2013–16 (resgnd).

DUARTE LANGA, HE Cardinal Júlio; Mozambican ecclesiastic; *Bishop Emeritus of Xai-Xai;* b. 27 Oct. 1927, Mangunze; ordained priest, Diocese of João Belo 1957; consecrated Bishop of João Belo May–Oct. 1976; Bishop of Xai-Xai Oct. 1976–2004, Bishop Emer. 2004–; cr. Cardinal (Cardinal-Priest of San Gabriele dell'Addolorata) 2015. *Address:* Bispado, Avenida 1 de Majo 39, CP 174, Xai-Xai, Mozambique (office). *Telephone:* (282) 22163 (office). *Fax:* (282) 22298 (office).

DUATO, Nacho; Spanish choreographer; *Artistic Director, Mikhailovsky Theatre;* b. (Juan Ignacio Duato Barcia), 8 Jan. 1957, Valencia; ed Maurice Bejart's Mudra School, Brussels, Belgium; began career by signing professional contract with Cullberg Ballet, Stockholm 1980–81; brought by Jirí Kylián to Nederlands Dans Theater 1981, a resident choreographer 1988–90; Artistic Dir, Compania Nacional de Danza, Madrid 1990–2010, Mikhailovsky Theatre, St Petersburg 2011–, Staatsballet Berlin 2014–; works have been featured in repertoires of major dance cos worldwide, including Paris Opera Ballet, American Ballet Theater, Deutsche Oper Ballet, Stuttgart Ballet, Les Grands Ballets Canadiens, Australian Ballet and Finnish Opera Ballet; Chevalier dans l'Ordre des Arts et des Lettres 1995; Golden Medal for Merit in the Fine Arts 1998, Benois de la Danse at the Stuttgart Opera 2000, Spain's Nat. Dance Award 2003, Chile Arts Critics Circle Prize 2010, Prize of the city of Alcalá for arts and literature 2015. *Address:* Mikhailovsky Theatre, 191186 St Petersburg, Arts Square 1, Russian Federation (office). *Telephone:* (812) 595-43-05 (office). *Fax:* (812) 595-43-19 (office). *E-mail:* info@mikhailovsky.ru (office). *Website:* www.mikhailovsky.ru (office); www.staatsballett-berlin.de (office).

DUBCOVSKY, Jorge, BS, PhD; American (b. Argentine) agronomist and academic; *Professor, University of California, Davis;* b. 18 Jan. 1957, Buenos Aires, Argentina; m. Laura Kuperman; two c.; ed Univ. of Buenos Aires, Molecular Biology Inst. and Univ. of California, Davis, USA; Elementary teacher, Tertiary School Mariano Acosta 1977; Nat. Research Council from Argentina (CONICET) Fellow 1985–91; Visiting Scientist, Dept of Agronomy and Range Science, Univ. of California, Davis 1992–93, Postgraduate Researcher 1994, Asst Prof. 1996–99, Assoc. Prof. 1999–2002, Full Prof. 2003–, Leader of Wheat Breeding Program and Wheat Molecular Genetics Lab., Int. Curator of Catalogue of Gene Symbols for Wheat; Howard Hughes Medical Inst. (HHMI) and the Gordon and Betty Moore Foundation (GBMF) Investigator 2011–; Ed. Crop Science Section C7 2003–06; Assoc. Ed. Theoretical and Applied Genetics 2006–, Proceedings of the National Academy of Sciences of the USA; mem. Editorial Bd, Functional and Integrative Genomics 2008–; mem. NAS 2013, American Soc. of Agronomy 2013, Crop Science Soc. of America 2013; Argentine Nat. Acad. of Agric. & Vetinary Award for Best Research in Bread-making Quality 1996, Award for Excellence in Research, Nat. Asscn of Wheat Growers 2001, Discovery Award, US Dept of Agric. 2007, Hoagland Award, American Soc. of Plant Biologists 2009, Sec.'s Honor Award, US Dept of Agric. 2011, Platinum Konex Award (Argentina) for Best Researcher in Genetics and Genomics 2003–13 2013, Wolf Prize in Agric. (co-recipient) 2014. *Publications:* more than 180 papers in professional journals. *Address:* Department of Plant Sciences, One Shields Avenue, University of California, Davis, CA 95616-8515, USA (office). *Fax:* (530) 752-4361 (office). *E-mail:* jdubcovsky@ucdavis.edu (office). *Website:* www.plantsciences.ucdavis.edu (office); dubcovskylab.ucdavis.edu/home (office).

DUBENETSKY, Yakov Nikolayevich; Russian banker and economist; b. 26 Oct. 1938, Stayki, Belarus; m.; one s.; ed Moscow State Univ.; Deputy Chair. Stroybank of the USSR 1985–87; First Deputy Chair. Bank for Industry and Construction of the USSR (Pomstroybank of the USSR) 1987–91; Chair. Bd Russian Jt Stock Investment and Commercial Bank for Industry and Construction (Pomstroybank of Russia) 1991–99; apptd Chair. Bank Asscn of Russia 1995; currently Head of Centre of Investments, Inst. of Nat. Econ. Forecasting, Russian Acad. of Sciences; Vice-Pres. Asscn of Russian Banks 1995; Co-Chair. Round Table of Russian Business 2000; mem. Political Consultative Council of Pres. of Russian Fed. 1996, Nat. Banking Council 1996, Int. Acad. of Man. 1997, Bd for finance and economy, Rosneftegazstroi 2001; Chair. Revision Comm., Free Economic Society of Russia (VEO); Chair. Revision Comm., Int. Union of Economists; Academician, Int. Acad. of Man.; Corresp. mem., International Informatization Acad.

DUBININ, Sergey Konstantinovich, DEcon; Russian business executive; *Chairman of the Supervisory Council, VTB Group;* b. 10 Dec. 1950, Moscow; m.; two c.; ed Moscow State Univ.; Docent, Researcher and Prof., Moscow State Univ. 1974–91; mem. Pres. Mikhail Gorbachev's admin 1991; Deputy Chair. Russian State Cttee for co-operation with CIS 1992–93; First Deputy Minister of Finance, Acting Minister of Finance 1993–94; First Deputy Chair. Exec. Bd Commercial Bank Imperial 1994–95; mem. Exec. Bd Jt Stock co. Gazprom 1995, Deputy Chair.

Bd Gazprom Co. 1998–2001; Deputy CEO Unified Power Grids of Russia (RAO ES) 2001–04, mem. Man. Bd and Financial Dir 2005–08; currently Chair. Supervisory Council, VTB Group, mem. Bd of Dirs CJSC VTB Capital 2008–; Chair. Cen. Bank of Russia 1995–98; Russian Rep. to IBRD 1996–98; Chair. Interstate Monetary Cttee CIS 1996–98, Supervisory Bd Sberbank and Vneshtorgbank; 850th Anniversary of Moscow Govt Award 1998, Best Independent Dir of the Year, Aristos Award 2013. *Publications:* books on public, int. and corp. finance and finance markets; numerous articles on scientific research. *Leisure interests:* art, classical music, theatre, sports. *Address:* VTB Group, 123100 Moscow, 12 Presnenskaya Embankment, Russia (office). *E-mail:* info@vtb.ru (office). *Website:* www.vtb.com (office).

DUBOCHET, Jacques, PhD; Swiss biophysicist and academic; *Professor Emeritus of Biophysics, Université de Lausanne;* b. 8 June 1942, Agile; m.; two c.; ed Univ. de Lausanne, Univ. of Geneva, Univ. of Basel; worked at Biocentre, Univ. of Basel; mem. Faculty, European Molecular Biology Lab. (EMBL), later Head, Electron Microscopy Applications Lab. 1987–87; Prof. of Biophysics, Univ. de Lausanne 1987–2007, Dir Center for Electron Microscopy 1998–2002, Prof. Emer. 2007–; Lennart Philipson Award, EMBL 2015, Nobel Prize in Chemistry (co-recipient with Joachim Frank and Richard Henderson) 2017. *Address:* Université de Lausanne, Amphimax building, CH- 1015 Lausanne, Switzerland (office). *Telephone:* 216924389 (office). *E-mail:* info.dubochet@unil.ch (office). *Website:* www.unil.ch.

DUBOIS, Jean Baden, BSc, MSc; Haitian economist, banking executive and central banker; *Governor, Banque de la République d'Haïti;* ed Univ. of Haiti, Univ. of Illinois at Chicago, USA; Consultant, Estee Bedding Co. 1989–90; Asst Man. Citibank, Port-au-Prince, Haiti 1990–95; Dir Administratif, Banque de la République d'Haïti 1995–99, Dir Information et Technologie 1999–2001, 2001–11, Expert Del. to Office of Minister of Economy and Finance 2001–02, Dir-Gen. 2011–15, Gov. Banque de la République d'Haïti 2015–, also mem. Bd of Govs, mem. Bd of Dirs IMF; Prof., Universite Notre Dame 2009–11. *Address:* Banque de la République d'Haïti, angle rues du Pavée et du Quai, BP 1570, Port-au-Prince, Haiti (office). *Telephone:* 2299-1202 (office). *Fax:* 2299-1145 (office). *E-mail:* webmaster@brh.net (office). *Website:* www.brh.net (office).

DUBOS, Jean-François, BA; French lawyer, academic and business executive; b. 2 Sept. 1945, Cabourg; ed Univ. of Paris, Acad. of Int. Law, The Hague; fmr Lecturer, École Nationale d'Admin, Univ. of Paris I (Sorbonne), Paris X (Nanterre), Paris V (René Descartes), Institut d'Études Politiques, Aix-en-Provence; Co-head, Cabinet of Ministry of Defence 1981–84; full-time mem. Conseil d'Etat 1984–91; joined Compagnie Générale des Eaux (predecessor of Vivendi) as Deputy to the CEO 1991–94, Gen. Counsel 1994–99, CEO Carrousel du Louvre 1993–99, Exec. Vice-Pres., Gen. Counsel and Sec. of Man. and Supervisory Bds of Vivendi, Chair. Man. Bd 2012–14, Hon. Chair. 2014; mem. Bd of Dirs Société des Eaux de Melun, CMESE, SGH Capital SA; mem. Supervisory Bd Itissalat Al-Maghrib (IAM) SA 2012, Canal+, Groupe Canal+; Vivendi's Perm. Rep. on Bd of SFR; Gen. Sec. Aix-en-Provence Int. Opera Festival; Chair. Maison Européenne de la Photo, Centre de Musique Baroque de Versailles; Vice-Chair. Arles Int. Photography Festival; Senior Advisor LFPI Gestion; mem. Bd American Friends; Dir Amis de Mozart; Dir and Treas. Théâtre du Châtelet; Hon. mem. Maître des Requêtes au Conseil d'Etat; Chevalier, Légion d'honneur, Ordre nat. du Mérite; Officier, Ordre des Arts et des Lettres, several other decorations.

DUBOWITZ, Victor, MD, PhD, FRCP, FRCPCH, DCH; British paediatrician and academic; *Professor Emeritus of Paediatrics, University of London;* b. 6 Aug. 1931, Beaufort West, S Africa; s. of Charley Dubowitz and Olga Schattel; m. Lilly M. S. Sebok 1960 (died 2016); four s.; ed Cen. High School, Beaufort West and Univs of Cape Town and Sheffield; intern, Groote Schuur Hospital, Cape Town 1955; Sr House Officer, Queen Mary's Hosp. for Children 1957–59; Research Assoc., Royal Postgraduate Medical School, Univ. of London 1958–59, Prof. of Paediatrics 1972–96, Prof. Emer. 1996–, Dir Jerry Lewis Muscle Research Centre 1975–96; Lecturer in Clinical Pathology, Nat. Hosp. for Nervous Diseases, London 1960; Lecturer in Child Health, Univ. of Sheffield 1961–65, Sr Lecturer 1965–67, Reader 1967–72; Research Assoc., Inst. for Muscle Disease and Asst Paediatrician, Cornell Medical Coll., New York 1965–66; Consultant Paediatrician, Hammersmith Hosp. 1972–96; Pres. European Paediatric Neurology Soc. 1994–97, World Muscle Soc. 1995–, Medical Art Soc. 1996–2000; Curator of Art, Royal Coll. of Paediatrics and Child Health; Dir of Therapeutic Studies, European Neuromuscular Centre, Netherlands 2000–03; Ed.-in-Chief Neuromuscular Disorders 1990–, European Journal of Paediatric Neurology 1996–2003; several awards. *Publications:* The Floppy Infant 1969, Muscle Biopsy: A Modern Approach (with M. Brooke) 1973, 1985, Gestational Age of the Newborn (with L. M. S. Dubowitz) 1977, Muscle Disorders in Childhood 1978, The Neurological Assessment of the Pre-term and Full-term Newborn Infant (with L. M. S. Dubowitz) 1981, 1999, A Colour Atlas of Muscle Disorders in Childhood 1989, A Colour Atlas of Brain Disorders in the Newborn (with L. de Vries, L. Dubowitz and J. Penock) 1990, Ramblings of a Peripatetic Paediatrician 2005, Muscle Biopsy: A Practical Approach (with Caroline Sewry) 2006, (new edition, with Caroline Sewry and Anders Oldfors) 2012. *Leisure interests:* sculpting, hiking, photography, antique glass. *Address:* 25 Middleton Road, Golders Green, London, NW11 7NR, England (home). *Telephone:* (20) 8455-9352 (home). *Fax:* (20) 8905-5922 (home). *E-mail:* v.dubowitz@imperial .ac.uk (home).

DUBRULLE, Christophe Maurice Paule Marie Joseph; French retail executive; joined Auchan 1965, mem. Bd of Dirs, Groupe Auchan 1999–, Chair. Exec. Bd 1999–2010, also Man. Dir Hypermarkets –2010, Chair. E-Drive 2010–; Man. Dir Leroy Merlin 1982, later Chair. Bd of Admin.; Dir La Rinascente SpA; Dir (non-exec.), Sun Art Retail Group Ltd 2001–12. *Address:* Groupe Auchan, 200 rue de la Recherche, 59650 Villeneuve d'Ascq, France (office). *Telephone:* (3) 28-37-67-00 (office). *Fax:* (3) 20-67-55-20 (office). *E-mail:* info@auchan.com (office). *Website:* www.groupe-auchan.com (office).

DUBUC, Nancy; American media executive; *CEO, Vice Media LLC;* began career at A+E Networks as Dir, Historical Programming for HISTORY, Sr Vice-Pres., Programming –2007, Pres. and Gen. Man. HISTORY and Lifetime Networks 2007–12, Pres. of Entertainment and Media, A+E Networks 2012–18, CEO 2012–18, oversees all content creation, brand development and marketing for the entire A+E Networks' portfolio including A+E Network, Lifetime and HISTORY and their affiliated brands, also oversees A+E Networks' Int. and Digital divs; CEO Vice Media LLC 2018–; named by Multichannel News and WICT as Wonder Woman 2007, Preserve America Presidential Award 2007. *E-mail:* vice@vice.com (office). *Website:* www.vice.com (office).

DUBY, Jean Jacques, PhD; French mathematician and scientist; b. 5 Nov. 1940, Paris; s. of Jean Duby and Lucienne Duby (née Lacomme); m. Camille Poli 1963; one d.; ed Ecole Normale Supérieure, Paris; research staff mem., Thomas J. Watson Research Center, USA 1963–64; Systems Engineer, IBM France 1965–66, Man. Application Systems, IBM Mohansic Lab. 1974–75, Exec. Asst to Vice-Chair. IBM Corpn 1975–76, Br. Office Man. IBM France 1977–78, special assignment, IBM Communications Div. 1979, Dir Switching Systems IBM Europe 1980–82, Dir Science and Tech., IBM France 1986–88, Group Dir Science and Tech., IBM Europe 1988–91; Man. Grenoble Scientific Centre 1967–69; Assoc. Prof., European Systems Research Inst. and Univ. of Geneva 1970–71; Project Man., Paris Stock Exchange 1972–73; Scientific Dir CNRS 1982–86; Scientific Dir Union d'assurances de Paris 1991–97; Pres. Inst. Nat. de recherche sur les transports et leur securité 1992–96; Chair. Ecole Normale Supérieure de Cachan 1994–2000; Dir-Gen. Ecole Supérieure d'Electricité 1995–2005; Professeur des universités 1999; Chair. Scientific Council of Bouygues Telecom 2001; apptd Pres. Observatoire des Sciences et des Techniques 2002; mem. Scientific Council, Schneider Electric 2004; Officier, Ordre nat. du Mérite, Chevalier, Ordre Nat. de la Côte d'Ivoire. *Leisure interests:* skiing, mountaineering.

DUBYNA, Oleh; Ukrainian politician, engineer and business executive; b. 20 March 1959, Elizavetovka, Dniepropetrovsk region; m.; one s. one d.; ed Dnieprodzerzhinsk Industrial Inst., Dnieprodzerzhinsk State Tech. Univ.; employee Dniepr Metallurgic plant 1976, master, Sr master, then engineer 1986–93, Head of Bureau, Deputy Head of Div., First Deputy Dir-Gen. 1996–98; teacher Dnieprodzerzhinsk Polytechnical Higher School 1985–86; Asst to Dir, then Deputy Dir-Gen. Dniepr br. of Intermontage Kam – Soviet-Swiss Joint Venture DEMOS 1993–96; Deputy Head, Chair. Bd of Dirs, Dir-Gen. Alchevsk Metallurgic plant 1998–99; Dir-Gen. Kryvoy Rog State Ore-Metallurgic plant, Krivorozhstal 1999–; Deputy Prime Minister for Econ. Policy 2000–01; First Deputy Prime Minister 2001–02; Adviser to Pres. Leonid Kuchma 2002–04; Pres. Ukrainian Nat. Energy Co. (Ukrenergo) 2004; CEO Dniprodzerzhynsk metallurgical complex 2005–07; Chair. Naftohaz Ukrainy (Oil and Gas of Ukraine) 2007–10 (resgnd). *Address:* c/o Naftogaz Ukrainy, 01001 Kyiv, vul. B. Khmelnytskoho 6B, Ukraine. *E-mail:* ngu@naftogaz.net.

DUCA, Gheorghe, DSci; Moldovan academic; *President, Academy of Sciences of Moldova;* b. 29 Feb. 1952, Sîngerei; ed State Univ. of Moldova, Inst. of Chemical Physics, Russian Acad. of Sciences, Univ. of Odessa; Head of Physical Chem. Dept, State Univ. of Moldova 1988–92, Dir Research Centre of Ecological and Applied Chem. 1991–98, Head of Industrial and Ecological Chem. Dept 1992–98, Dean of Faculty of Ecology 1992–95; Pres. Republican Cttee for awarding prizes to young researchers in science and tech. 1992–2006, Scientific Specialised Council for nomination of DrSci degree 1994–2006; Chair. Parl. Comm. for Culture, Science, Educ., and Mass Media 1998–2001; Pres. Moldovan Research and Devt Asscn 2000–06; Minister of Ecology, Construction and Territory Devt 2001–04; Pres. Acad. of Sciences of Moldova 2004–; Ed.-in-Chief Environment Journal 2002–04; Head of Editorial Bd Chemistry Journal of Moldova 2005–06; mem. Int. Editorial Bd Chemistry and Technology of Water Journal 2001–06, Editorial Advisory Bd Environmental Engineering and Management Journal 2002–06; Co-Pres. Moldo-Polish Intergovernmental Mixed Comm. for Commercial, Econ., Scientific and Tech. Co-operation 2001–05, 2011–, Danube Convention 2003–04; Pres. Admin. Council of Concession Agreement of Redeco 2005–06, Admin. Council of Nat. Science Foundation of Moldova 2005–06; Pres. Asscn of Chemists of Moldova 2011–; mem. ACS 1997–, Cen. European Acad. of Sciences and Arts 1999–, Int. Acad. of Informatics 1999–, Pedagogical Acad. of Russia 1999–; Hon. Consul of Greece in Moldova 2001–, Hon. Pres. Moldovan Research and Devt Asscn, Hon. mem. Romanian Acad. 2007; Order of St Sergius Radonezh of Holy Synod of Russian Orthodox Church 2003, Commdr, Cross of Honour (Poland) 2004, Gloria Muncii Order 2007, Order of the Repub. of Moldova 2011, Commdr, Order of the Crown of Romania 2015; Dr hc (Free Int. Univ., Moldova) 1993, (Gh. Asachi Univ., Romania) 2000, (Real-Humanist Univ. of Cahul) 2001, (Balkan Acad. of Sciences) 2004, (West Univ. V.Goldiş, Romania, State Univ. of Bălţi, Acad. of Economic Study, Moldova) 2006, (State Univ. of Tiraspol, State Univ. of Physical Educ. and Sport, Moldova, Russian Acad. of Sciences) 2011, (State Univ. Comrat) 2015; State Prize for Youth in Science and Tech. 1983, State Prize for Science, Tech. and Production 1995, 2000, Om Emerit Medal, Repub. of Moldova 1996, Scientist of the Year, Acad. of Sciences of Moldova 2005, Medail d'Or 2005, Int. Socrates Prize, Oxford 2007, Silver Medal, Asscn of Innovators of China 2010, Nat. GALEX Prize for best founder of a library 2011. *Address:* Academy of Sciences of Moldova, 2001 Chisinau, 1 Bd. Stefan cel Mare, Moldova (office). *Telephone:* (22) 27-14-78 (office). *Fax:* (22) 27-60-14 (office). *E-mail:* duca@mrda.md (office); duca@asm.md (office). *Website:* www.duca.md (office).

DUCEPPE, Gilles, BA; Canadian politician; b. 22 July 1947, Montréal, Québec; s. of Jean Duceppe and Hélène Rowley; m. Yolande Brunelle; two c.; ed Collège Mont-Saint-Louis, Université de Montréal; Vice-Pres. Union générale des étudiants et étudiantes du Québec (UGEQ) 1968–69; Dir Quartier Latin journal 1970–71; with Company of Young Canadians –1977; Union Negotiator, Confed. of Nat. Trade Unions 1977; MP for Montreal's Laurier-Sainte-Marie riding (Bloc Québécois) 1990–2011, Interim Leader Bloc Québécois Jan.–Feb. 1996, Leader 1997–2011 (resgnd) 2015; Leader of the Opposition 1997.

DUCEY, Doug, BS; American business executive and politician; *Governor of Arizona;* b. 9 April 1964, Toledo, Ohio; m. Angela Ducey; three s.; ed Arizona State Univ.; began career with sales and marketing dept, Proctor & Gamble; co-f. Cold Stone Creamery, Tempe, Ariz., CEO –2007; State Treas., State of Arizona 2011–15; Gov. of Arizona 2015–; Chair. State Bd of Investment, Ariz. Loan Comm.; mem. State Land Election Bd; mem. Arizona Chapter, Young Entrepreneur's Org. (fmr Pres.), Greater Phoenix Economic Club; Republican. *Address:* Office of the Governor, Executive Tower, 1700 West Washington Street, Phoenix, AZ 85007, USA (office). *Telephone:* (602) 542-4331 (office). *Fax:* (602) 542-1381 (office). *Website:* www.azgovernor.gov (office).

DUCH-PEDERSEN, Alf, BSc, MSc; Danish banking executive; b. 15 Aug. 1946; began career with Danish Turnkey Dairies A/S 1973–84; various positions with APV Anhydro A/S 1984–87, APV Pasilac A/S 1987–91, APV PLC, London 1989–91; with Tryg-Baltica Forsikring, Skadesforsikringsselskab A/S 1991–97; mem. Bd Dirs Danisco 1994–97, CEO and Pres. Exec. Bd 1997–2006; mem. Bd Dirs Danske Bank Group 1999–11, Chair. 2003–11; Deputy Chair. Group 4 Securicor PLC (G4S) 2004–06, Chair. 2006–12; mem. Bd Dirs Tech. Univ. of Denmark, Denmark-America Foundation; mem. Cen. Bd Confed. of Danish Industries.

DUCHAUFOUR-LAWRANCE, Noé; French architect and interior designer; b. 25 July 1974, Mende (Lozère); ed École Nationale Supérieure des Arts Appliqués et des Métiers d'Art, Arts Décoratifs, Paris; began career designing Sketch Restaurant in London 2002; f. own studio; collaborates with publrs including Ceccotti Collezioni, Zanotta, Cinna, Baccarat, Tacchini, La Chance, Bernhardt Design, Maison Hermès; projects for Senderens, Air France (in partnership with Brandimage), Ciel de Paris, Transhumance Chalet, #Cloud.paris Lounge, Montblanc, and for brands Paco Rabanne, Yves Saint Laurent, Perrier-Jouët; exhbns at Pierre Berger Gallery, Brussels and BSL, Paris; Tatler Restaurant Award Best Design: The Gallery for Restaurant Sketch, London 2002, Best Design, Theme Magazine for Restaurant Sketch, London 2003, Hotel and Restaurant Magazine Best Design Award for Restaurant Sketch, London 2003, Time Out magazine Eating and Drinking Award: Best Design for Restaurant Sketch, London 2003, Restaurant Senderens – Prix Fooding 2005, Meilleur restaurant avant l'amour 2005, Designer of the Year, Scènes d'intérieur, Maison & Objet, Paris 2007, Wallpaper Design Awards for the bed Buonanotte Valentina, CECCOTTI Collezioni 2009, Prix Elle Déco Int. Design Awards 2009, Lauréat de L'Empreinte de l'Année des Talents du luxe et de la création 2010, Gold Award for the Best of Neocon for the chair Corvo, Bernhardt Design 2010, Red Dot Award Product Design for the chair Corvo, Bernhardt Design 2011, GQ Men of the Year Best Designer 2012, Janus du commerce Air France Award for the CDG Business Lounge 2014, Via Labels for the armchair 'Ciel' edited by Tabisso and desk 'Inside World' edited by Cinna 2015, NeoCon Silver Award for the Bernhardt Design Clue/Chance table 2016, NeoCon Silver Award for the Bernhardt Design lounge furniture collection 'Modern Family' 2016. *Address:* Noé Duchaufour Lawrance, 8 passage de la bonne graine, 75011 Paris, France (office). *Telephone:* 1-43-14-99-59 (office). *E-mail:* contact@neonata.fr (office). *Website:* www.noeduchaufourlawrance.com (office).

DUCHESNEAU, François, Docteur d'état ès-lettres et sciences humaines; Canadian philosopher and academic; *Professor of Philosophy Emeritus, University of Montréal;* ed Univ. of Paris-I, France; taught at Univ. of Ottawa; Prof. of Philosophy, Univ. of Montréal 1979, currently Prof. Emer.; Visiting Prof., Catholic Univ. of Louvain, Belgium (Pulpit Draper) 1995, Univ. of Alberta 1997, École des Hautes Études en sciences sociales, Paris 1999; mem. RSC 1984–; Prix des sciences humaines, Asscn canadienne française pour l'avancement des sciences 1992, Killam Research Fellowship 1995–97, Killam Prize for Humanities, Canada Council for the Arts 2003. *Publications:* L'Empirisme de Locke 1973, La physiologie des lumières – Empirisme, modèles et théories 1982, Genèse de la théorie cellulaire 1987, Leibniz et la méthode de la science 1993, La dynamique de Leibniz 1994, Philosophie de la biologie 1997, Les modèles du vivant de Descartes à Leibniz 1998; more than 160 articles on the history of modern philosophy, the history and philosophy of science, empiricist theories of knowledge and the philosophy and scientific work of Leibniz. *Address:* Département de philosophie, Université de Montréal, CP 6128, succ. Centre-ville, Montréal, PQ H3C 3J7, Canada (office). *Telephone:* (514) 343-7373 (office). *Fax:* (514) 343-2098 (office). *E-mail:* francois.duchesneau@umontreal.ca (office). *Website:* philo.umontreal.ca/repertoire-departement/vue/duchesneau-francois/ (office).

DUCHOVNY, David; American actor; b. 7 Aug. 1960, New York; s. of Amram Duchovny and Meg Duchovny; m. Tea Leoni (q.v.) 1997 (divorced); ed Yale and Princeton Univs; stage appearances include off-Broadway plays, The Copulating Machine of Venice, California and Green Cockatoo; writer and dir of various episodes of The X-Files; Golden Globe for Best Actor in Drama Series 1996. *Films include:* Working Girl 1988, New Year's Day 1989, Bad Influence 1990, Julia Has Two Lovers 1990, The Rapture 1991, Don't Tell Mom the Babysitter's Dead 1991, Denial 1991, Beethoven 1992, Chaplin 1992, Red Shoe Diaries 1992, Ruby 1992, Venice, Venice 1992, Kalifornia 1993, Apartment Zero, Close Enemy, Loan, Independence Day, Playing God 1997, The X-Files 1998, Return To Me 2000, Evolution 2001, Zoolander 2001, Red Shoe Diaries 15: Forbidden Zone (video) 2002, Full Frontal 2002, XIII (voice) 2003, Connie and Carla 2004, House of D (also dir and writer) 2004, The X Files: Resist or Serve (voice) 2004, Area 51 (voice) 2005, Trust the Man 2005, The TV Set 2006, Queer Duck: The Movie (voice) 2006, Things We Lost in the Fire 2007, The X Files: I Want to Believe 2008, The Joneses 2009, Goats 2012, Phantom 2013, Louder Than Words 2013. *Television includes:* Twin Peaks 1990, The X-Files 1993–2002, The X-Files: The Truth 2002, Life With Bonnie 2002, The TV Set 2006, Californication (series) 2007–14, Aquarius (series) 2015–16, The X-Files (series) 2015–16. *Recordings:* albums: Hell or Highwater 2015, Every Third Thought 2018. *Publications:* Holy Cow 2015 Bucky F*king Dent 2016, Miss Subways 2018.

DUCKWORTH, Marilyn, OBE; New Zealand writer; b. (Marilyn Rose Adcock), 10 Nov. 1935, Auckland; d. of Cyril John Adcock and Irene Robinson; sister of Fleur Adcock (q.v.); m. 1st Harry Duckworth 1955 (divorced 1964); m. 2nd Ian Macfarlane 1964 (divorced 1972); m. 3rd Daniel Donovan 1974 (died 1978); m. 4th John Batstone 1985; four d.; ed Queen Margaret Coll., Victoria Univ. of Wellington; ten writing fellowships 1961–96 including Katherine Mansfield Fellowship, Menton 1980, Fulbright Visiting Writer's Fellowship, USA 1987, Victoria Univ. Writing Fellowship 1990, Hawthornden Writing Fellowship, Scotland 1994, 2001, Sargeson Writing Fellowship, Auckland 1995, Auckland Univ. Literary Fellowship 1996; Fellow, Acad. of NZ Literature; Pres. of Honour, NZ Soc. of Authors 2011–12; New Zealand Literary Fund Award for Achievement 1963, New Zealand Book Award for Fiction 1985, Prime Minister's Award for Literary Achievement: Fiction 2016. *Radio:* Home to Mother, Feet First, A Gap in the Spectrum, A Barbarous Tongue. *Television:* Close to Home (series). *Publications include:* 15 novels, including A Gap in the Spectrum 1959, The Matchbox House 1960, A Barbarous Tongue 1963, Over the Fence Is Out 1969, Disorderly Conduct 1984, Married Alive 1985, Pulling Faces 1987, A Message from Harpo 1989, Unlawful Entry 1992, Seeing Red 1993, Leather Wings 1995, Studmuffin 1997, Swallowing Diamonds 2003, Playing Friends 2007; short stories: Explosions on the Sun 1989; poems: Other Lovers' Children 1975, The Chiming Blue 2017; memoir: Camping on the Faultline 2000. *Leisure interest:* playing the violin. *Address:* 41 Queen Street, Mt Victoria, Wellington 6011, New Zealand (home). *Telephone:* (4) 384-9990 (home). *E-mail:* wazilyn@gmail.com (home).

DUCKWORTH, (Ladda) Tammy, BA, MA, PhD; American politician and fmr military officer; *Senator from Illinois;* b. 12 March 1968, Bangkok, Thailand; d. of Franklin Duckworth and Lamai Duckworth (née Sompornpairin); m. Bryan Bowlsbey 1994; one d.; ed Univ. of Hawaii, George Washington Univ., Capella Univ.; joined US Army Reserve 1992, Officer, Illinois Nat. Guard 1996, served as Army helicopter pilot during Iraq war 2004, including as Battle Capt., Asst Operations Officer, Commdr, Company B/1-106th Aviation Regt, fmr Logistics Officer, Chicago Midway Airport; Dir, Illinois Dept of Veterans Affairs 2006–09; Asst Sec. for Public and Intergovernmental Affairs, US Dept of Veterans Affairs, Washington, DC 2009–11; retd from Army Oct. 2014 (rank of Lt-Col); elected mem. US House of Reps from 8th Illinois Dist 2013, mem. House Oversight and Government Reform Cttee, House Armed Services Cttee; Senator from Illinois 2017–; Democrat; Purple Heart 2004, Air Medal, Army Commendation Medal with oak leaf cluster 2004, Meritorious Service medal, Army Reserve Components Achievement medal, Combat Action Badge, Sr Army Aviator Badge, Veterans Leadership Award, Iraq & Afghanistan Veterans of America 2007. *Address:* G12, Dirksen Senate Office Building, Washington, DC 20510, USA (office). *Telephone:* (202) 224-2854 (office). *Website:* www.senate.gov (office).

DUCLOS, Jean-Yves, PC, MP, MEcon, DEcon, FRSC; Canadian economist and politician; *Minister of Families, Children and Social Development;* b. 1965, Quebec City; m.; three c.; ed Univ. of Alberta, London School of Econs, UK; apptd Prof., Laval Univ. 1999, Dir, Dept of Econs 2012–15; Research Coordinator, Partnership for Econ. Policy (int. research network) 2002; Dir Centre interuniversitaire sur le risque, les politiques économiques et l'emploi, Montréal 2005–08; Research Fellow, Instituto de Análisis Económico, Barcelona 2008–09; Coordinator, Econ. and Social Policy Program, Simul Corpn 2010–14; mem. House of Commons (Parl.) for Québec 2015–; Minister of Families, Children and Social Devt 2015–; Pres. Soc. canadienne de science économique 2006–07; Vice-Pres. Canadian Econ. Asscn 2014–, CIRANO (research centre) 2014–; Fellow, C. D. Howe Inst. 2009–, Fondation pour les Études et Recherches sur le Développement Int. 2012–; mem. Liberal Party of Canada; Chair. Petits Chanteurs de Charlesbourg. *Address:* Employment and Social Development Canada, Phase IV, 140 promenade du Portage, Gatineau, PQ K1A 0J9, Canada (office). *Telephone:* (819) 994-5559 (office). *Fax:* (819) 953-7260 (office). *E-mail:* media@hrsdc-rhdcc.gc.ca (office). *Website:* www.esdc.gc.ca (office); jeanyvesduclos.liberal.ca (office).

DUCORNET, Erica (Rikki) Lynn, BA; American/French writer, artist and teacher; b. 19 April 1943, New York; d. of Gerard De Gré and Muriel Harris; m. Jonathan Cohen; one s.; apptd Novelist-in-Residence, Univ. of Denver 1988; has taught writing at Writers at Work, Bard Coll., Brown Univ., Naropa Univ., Vermont Studio Center, Centrum Writer's Workshop, Univ. of Trento; Writer-in-Residence Univ. of Louisiana, Lafayette 2007–09; Lannan Residency, Marfa 2013; Artist-in-Residence, Vermont Studio Center 2016; mem. PEN; Critics Choice Award 1995, Charles Flint Kellogg Award in Arts and Letters 1998, Lannon Literary Fellowship 1993, 1998, Lannan Literary Award for Fiction 2004, Prix Guerlain 2007, Academy Award, American Acad. of Arts and Letters 2008. *Publications:* novels: The Stain 1984, Entering Fire 1986, The Fountains of Neptune 1989, Eben Demarst 1990, The Jade Cabinet 1993, The Butcher's Tales 1994, Phosphor in Dreamland 1995, The Word 'Desire' 1997, The Fan Maker's Inquisition (Los Angeles Times Book of the Year) 2000, Gazelle 2004, Netsuke 2011, Brightfellow 2016; short fiction: The Butcher's Tales 1980, The Complete Butcher's Tales 1994, The Word 'Desire' 1997, The One Marvelous Thing 2008; poetry: From The Star Chamber 1974, Wild Geraniums 1975, Bouche a Bouche 1975, Weird Sisters 1976, Knife Notebook 1977, The Illustrated Universe 1979, The Cult of Seizure 1989; essay: The Monstrous and the Marvelous 1999, The Deep Zoo 2015; children's books: The Blue Bird 1970, Shazira Shazam and the Devil 1972. *Address:* c/o Coffee House Press, 79 Thirteenth Avenue NE, Suite 110, Minneapolis, MN 55413, USA (office). *Telephone:* (612) 338-0125 (office). *E-mail:* info@coffeehousepress.org (office); rikkiducornet@gmail.com. *Website:* coffeehousepress.org (office); www.rikkiducornet.com.

DUCZMAL JAROSZEWSKA, Agnieszka; Polish conductor; *Artistic Director and Conductor, Amadeus Chamber Orchestra of Polish Radio;* b. 7 Jan. 1946, Krotoszyn; d. of Henryk Duczmal and Leokadia Surdyk Duczmal; m.; one s. two d.; ed Acad. of Music, Poznań; Founder, Artistic Dir and Conductor, Amadeus Chamber Orchestra of Polish Radio 1968–; Asst Conductor Poznań Nat. Philharmonic 1971–72, Conductor Poznań Opera 1972–81; performs in Europe, N and S America, Africa and Asia; first female conductor to perform at La Scala, Milan; mem. jury, Eurovision Young Musicians 2012; Commdr's Cross, Order of Polonia Restituta 1998; won award at first Nat. Competition for Conductors, Katowice 1970, distinction, 4th Int. Herbert von Karajan Competition 1975, Silver Medal of Herbert von Karajan at the Meeting of Young Orchestras, West Berlin 1976, La Donna del Mondo Award of St Vincent Int. Culture Centre, Rome 1982. *Recordings:* J.S. Bach/Józef Koffler: Goldberg Variations (world premiere recording), Britten: A Midsummer Night's Dream (Polish premiere), Knittel: The Passion of Our Lord according to St Matthew, Op. 20 (world premiere recording), Alexandre Tansman: Chamber Music (world premiere recording); numerous other world premieres of Polish compositions. *Arrangements:* arrangements for string orchestra of Mussorgsky's Pictures at an Exhibition, and compositions by Chopin, Szymanowski, Brahms, Debussy, Paderewski. *Radio:* archive recordings for Polish Radio, BBC and NDR. *Television:* recordings for Polish, Japanese and French TV. *Leisure interests:* dogs, literary classics, gardening, mountaineering. *Telephone:* (61) 851-66-86 (office). *Fax:* (61) 851-66-87 (office). *E-mail:* agnieszka.duczmal@amadeus.pl (office). *Website:* www.amadeus.pl (office).

DUDA, Andrzej Sebastian, PhD; Polish lawyer, politician and head of state; *President;* b. 16 May 1972, Kraków; s. of Jan Tadeusz Duda and Janina Milewska; m. Agata Kornhauser 1994; one d.; ed Jan III Sobieski High School, Kraków, Jagiellonian Univ.; Asst Prof., Admin. Law Dept, Jagiellonian Univ. 2001–06, on leave of absence 2006–10, 2011–; mem. Unia Wolności (Freedom Union) party 2001–02, Prawo i Sprawiedliwość (Law and Justice) party 2005–15; Undersecretary of State, Ministry of Justice 2006–07; mem. Polish State Tribunal 2007–08; Undersecretary of State, Chancellery of Pres. 2008–10; unsuccessful PiS cand. for Mayor of Kraków 2010; envoy to Sejm 2011–14; mem. European Parl. for Małopolskie and Świętokrzyskie 2014–15; Pres. of Poland 2015–; Grand Cross, Order of Polonia Restituta; Order of the White Eagle; Grand Cross, Order of Merit (Portugal) 2008; Order of Leopold (Belgium) 2015); Order of Stara Planina (Bulgaria) 2016; Order of the White Lion (Czech Repub.) 2016; Grand Cross, Royal Norwegian Order of St Olav 2016. *Leisure interest:* skiing (participated in Polish Academic Championships in Alpine skiing category). *Address:* Chancellery of the President, 00-902 Warsaw, ul. Wiejska 10, Poland (office). *Telephone:* (22) 6252900 (office). *Fax:* (22) 6952238 (office). *E-mail:* listy@prezydent.pl (office). *Website:* www.prezydent.pl (office); andrzejduda.pl.

DUDAMEL, Gustavo; Venezuelan/Spanish conductor, composer and violinist; *Music Director, Orquesta Sinfónica Simón Bolívar; Music Director, Los Angeles Philharmonic Orchestra;* b. 1981, Barquisimento; m. 1st Eloísa Maturén (divorced 2015); one s.; m. 2nd Maria Valverde 2017; ed Jacinto Lara Conservatory, Latin American Acad. of Violin; began as young violinist with El Sistema music educ. programme, later becoming conductor; Musical Dir Amadeus Chamber Orchestra 1996–99; Musical Dir, Orquesta Sinfónica Simón Bolívar (Simón Bolívar Symphony Orchestra), Venezuela 1999–; Music Dir Youth Orchestra of the Andean Countries; attended Int. Conductors' Acad. of the Allianz Cultural Foundation, London 2004–05; Prin. Conductor Gothenburg Symphony Orchestra 2007–11, Hon. Conductor 2013–; Music Dir Los Angeles Philharmonic Orchestra 2009–; has conducted Bamberger Symphoniker, Israel Philharmonic Orchestra, NDR Radio Orchestra Hannover, Royal Stockholm Philharmonic, City of Birmingham Symphony Orchestra, Orchestre Philharmonique de Radio France, Royal Liverpool Philharmonic, Frankfurt Radio Symphony Orchestra, Sächsische Staatskapelle Dresden, Gothenburg Symphony Orchestra at BBC Proms, Los Angeles Philharmonic at Hollywood Bowl (US debut), Philharmonia Orchestra, Boston Symphony Orchestra, Orchestra del Maggio Musicale Fiorentino, Czech Philharmonic Orchestra, Chicago Symphony Orchestra, Vienna Symphony Orchestra 2006–07, Vienna Philharmonic (including New Year's Concert 2017), New York Philharmonic, Berlin Philharmonic, Berlin Staatskapelle, Leipzig Gewandhaus Orchestra, Orchestre Philharmonique de Radio France, San Francisco Symphony, Bavarian Radio Symphony Orchestra; Artist-in-Residence, Princeton Univ. Concerts 2018–(19); citizen of Spain 2018; Winner Bamberger Symphoniker Gustav Mahler Conducting Competition 2004, ECHO Klassik Award for Best New Artist 2007, Premio de la Latinidad, Union Latina 2007, Royal Philharmonic Soc. Award for Best Young Artist 2008, Classical BRIT Award for Male Artist of the Year 2009, Eugene McDermott Award in the Arts, MIT 2010, Gramophone Award for Artist of the Year 2011, Musical America's Musician of the Year 2013, Americas Society Cultural Achievement Award 2016. *Recordings include:* Beethoven Symphonies No. 5 and No. 7 2006, Brahm's Symphony No. 4 (Grammy Award for Best Orchestral Performance 2012) 2011, Mahler: Symphony No. 9 2013, Mahler: Symphony No. 7 2014, Wagner (with Orquesta Sinfónica Simón Bolívar) 2015. *Address:* c/o Mark Newbanks, Fidelio Arts Ltd, 103 Whitecross Street, No. 5, London, EC1Y 8JD, England (office). *E-mail:* mark@fidelioarts.com (office). *Website:* www.fidelioarts.com (office); www.gustavodudamel.com.

DUDAU, Nicolae; Moldovan politician and diplomatist; b. 19 Dec. 1945, Grineuts; m. Galina Dudau; one d.; ed Higher CPSU School, Moscow, Chişinău Tech. Univ.; worked at Chişinău tractor mfg factory 1963–75; army service 1964–67; various admin. posts in orgs in Chişinău 1975–90; Deputy Chair. Chişinău City Planning Cttee 1990–91; First Sec. Chişinău City CP Cttee 1990–91; Exec. Dir Int. Charity Foundation 1991–93; Minister-Counsellor, Embassy in Moscow 1993–94, Amb. to Uzbekistan, Tajikistan and Kyrgyzstan 1994–97, First Deputy Minister of Foreign Affairs 1997–98, Amb. to Belarus 1998–2001, Minister of Foreign Affairs 2001–04, Amb. to Italy 2004–07. *Address:* c/o Ministry of Foreign Affairs and European Integration, 2012 Chişinău, str. 31 August 80, Moldova. *E-mail:* secdep@mfa.md.

DUDERSTADT, James (Jim) Johnson, BEng, MS, PhD; American scientist, academic and fmr university administrator; *President Emeritus and University Professor of Science and Engineering, University of Michigan;* b. 5 Dec. 1942, Madison, Iowa; s. of Mack Henry Duderstadt and Katharine Sydney Johnson Duderstadt; m. Anne Marie Lock 1964; two d.; ed Yale Univ., California Inst. of Tech.; US Atomic Energy Comm. Postdoctoral Fellow, California Inst. of Tech. 1968; Asst Prof. of Nuclear Eng, Univ. of Michigan 1969, Assoc. Prof. 1972, Prof. 1976–81, Dean Coll. of Eng 1981, Provost and Vice-Pres. for Academic Affairs 1986, Pres. 1988–96, Pres. Emer. and Prof. of Science and Eng 1996–, Dir Millennium Project 1996–; mem. US Nat. Science Bd 1985–96 (Chair. 1991–94), Nat. Acad. of Eng Council 1997–2002, Advisory Councils of US Dept of Energy, Dept of Educ., NSF, Nat. Acads, MIT, Caltech, Georgia Tech; Co-Chair. Glion Colloquium; Dir Unisys; numerous hon. degrees and lectureships; Compton Award, American Nuclear Soc. 1985, E.O. Lawrence Award, US Dept of Energy 1986, Reginald Wilson Award, Nat. Medal of Tech., Nat. Acad. of Eng, American Acad. of Arts & Sciences, Duderstadt Center at Univ. of Michigan. *Publications:* Nuclear Reactor Analysis (with L. J. Hamilton) 1976, Transport Theory (with W. R. Martin) 1979, Inertial Confinement Fusion (with G. A. Moses) 1982, Intercollegiate Athletics and the American University 2000, A University for the 21st Century 2000, Higher Education in the Digital Age (co-author) 2003, Beyond the Crossroads: The Future of the Public University in America (co-author) 2003, Engineering Research and America's Future 2005, View from the Helm 2006, Globalization of Higher Education (co-author) 2008, Engineering for a Changing World 2008; numerous tech. publs on nuclear reactor theory, radiation transport, statistical mechanics and kinetic theory, plasma physics and computer simulation. *Address:* Millennium Project, 2001 Duderstadt Center, University of Michigan, 2281 Bonisteel Boulevard, Ann Arbor, MI 48109-2094, USA (office). *Telephone:* (734) 647-7300 (office). *Fax:* (734) 647-6814 (office). *E-mail:* jjd@umich.edu (office). *Website:* milproj.ummu.umich.edu/home/biography.html (office).

DUDLEY, Robert (Bob) Warren, BS, MIM, MBA; American oil company executive; *Group Chief Executive, BP PLC;* b. 14 Sept. 1955, Queens, NY; m. Mary Dudley; two c.; ed Hinsdale Cen. High School, Chicago, Univ. of Illinois, Thunderbird School of Global Man., Southern Methodist Univ., Dallas, Tex.; joined Amoco Corpn 1979 (merged with BP 1998), held a variety of eng and commercial posts in USA and UK, worked on negotiation and devt of projects in South China Sea from 1987, later involved in restructuring of oil and gas research and devt activities in USA, based in Moscow working on corp. devt for both upstream and downstream businesses in Russia 1994–97, Gen. Man. for Strategy 1997–98, Gen. Man. for Strategy, BP PLC 1999–2000, Exec. Asst to Group CEO 1999–2000, apptd Group Vice-Pres. for BP's renewables and alternative energy activities 2000, later Group Vice-Pres. responsible for BP's upstream businesses in Russia, the Caspian Region, Angola, Algeria and Egypt –2003, Pres. and CEO TNK-BP (jt venture between BP and Alfa, Access/Renova Group) 2003–08, Exec. Vice-Pres. and mem. Bd of Dirs BP PLC 2009–, given oversight of co.'s activities in the Americas and Asia, assigned as Pres. and CEO in charge of Gulf Coast Restoration Org. responding to Deepwater Horizon oil spill June–Sept. 2010, mem. BP Exec. Man. Team, Group Chief Exec. 2010–; Dir, Rosneft (following BP's acquisition of a stake in Rosneft) 2013–; mem. Bd of Fellows, Thunderbird School of Global Man.; mem. Soc. of Petroleum Engineers; Hon. CBE 2009. *Address:* BP PLC, International Headquarters, 1 St James's Square, London, SW1Y 4PD, England (office). *Telephone:* (20) 7496-4000 (office). *Fax:* (20) 7496-4630 (office). *E-mail:* info@bp.com (office). *Website:* www.bp.com (office).

DUDLEY, William C., BA, PhD; American banker, financier and economist; *President and CEO, Federal Reserve Bank of New York;* b. 1952; m. Ann E. Darby; ed New Coll., Sarasota, Fla, Univ. of California, Berkeley; Economist, Fed. Reserve Bd, Washington, DC 1981–83; Vice-Pres. Morgan Guaranty Trust Co. 1983–86; joined Goldman Sachs and Co. 1986, Chief US Economist 1995–2005, Partner and Man. Dir 1996–2006, Advisory Dir 2006; Exec. Vice-Pres. and Head of Markets Group, Fed. Reserve Bank of New York 2007–09, Pres. and CEO 2009–; Chair. Cttee on Payment and Settlement Systems of Cen. Banks of G-10 Countries hosted at BIS; Vice-Chair. and Perm. mem. Fed. Open Market Cttee 2009–; mem. Tech. Consultants Group to Congressional Budget Office 1999–2005. *Address:* Federal Reserve Bank of New York, 33 Liberty Street, New York, NY 10045, USA (office). *Telephone:* (212) 720-5000 (office); (646) 720-5000 (office). *E-mail:* general.info@ny.frb.org (office). *Website:* www.newyorkfed.org (office).

DUEA, Bradford (Brad) D., BA, MBA, JD; American business executive; *Managing Director and General Manager, Americas-Pacific, Sonos, Inc.;* ed Univ. of California, Santa Barbara, Univ. of Southern California, Univ. of San Diego; Corp. Assoc., O'Melveny and Myers LLP 1996–2000; Vice-Pres. Corp. Devt, PeopleSupport 2000–01; Vice-Pres. Business Devt, Vice-Pres. Worldwide OEM Sales 2001–04, Pres. Napster Div., Roxio Inc. 2004–10; Sr Vice-Pres., Value Added Services, T-Mobile USA, Inc. 2010–13; Pres. Shoutz 2013–14, now mem. Bd of Dirs; Man. Dir and Gen. Man., Americas-Pacific, Sonos, Inc. 2014–; Ind. Dir, DTS, Inc. 2010–15; mem. State Bar of California 1996–. *Address:* Sonos, Inc., 1501 East Madison Street, Suite 400, Seattle, WA 98122, USA (office). *Website:* www.sonos.com (office).

DUEÑAS, F. Tomás, BBA; Costa Rican business executive, politician and diplomatist; m. Diana Chavarría; ed Univ. of Miami, Columbia Univ., Stanford Univ., Univ. of Pennsylvania, USA; fmr CEO ESCO InterAmerica; fmr Chair. Bd of Dirs and Exec. Cttee Costa Rica Investment and Devt Bank; fmr Chair. Procomer; Minister of Econs 2000, of Foreign Trade 2000–02; Amb. to USA 2004–09; apptd Pres. Harsco Infrastructure Latin America 2009; Amb. to EU 2010–13; fmr Chair. Bd of Trustees Costa Rican Cen. Bank Museums; Vice-Chair. WTO Ministerial Meeting, Doha 2001; fmr Chief Negotiating Minister for a Free Trade Agreement of the Americas, as well as various other free trade agreements; mem. Bd of Dirs (non-exec.) La Nación newspaper and publishing group, Premium Group Holdings 2013–; mem. Chair.'s Int. Advisory Council of the America's Soc./Council of the Americas 2010; fmr Fellow, Aspen Inst. Leadership Program. *Achievements include:* credited with initiating process that led to Cen. American Free Trade Agreement with USA.

DUESBERG, Peter Heinz Hermann, PhD; American (b. German) molecular biologist and academic; *Professor of Molecular and Cell Biology, University of California, Berkeley;* b. 2 Dec. 1936, Münster, Germany; s. of Richard Duesberg and Hilde Saettele; m. Sigrid Duesberg; one s. three d.; ed Univ. of Würzburg, Univ. of Basel, Switzerland, Univ. of Munich, Univ. of Frankfurt; Postdoctoral Fellow, Dept of Molecular Biology and Virus Lab., Max Planck Inst. for Virus Research, Tübingen, Germany 1963; Postdoctoral Fellow and Asst Research Virologist, Univ. of California, Berkeley 1964–68, Asst Prof. in Residence 1968–70, Asst Prof. 1970–71, Assoc. Prof. 1971–73, Prof. 1973–, Prof. of Molecular and Cell Biology 1989–; Fisher Distinguished Prof., Univ. of North Texas, Denton 1992; Guest Prof., Univ. of Heidelberg at the Medical School, Mannheim 1997, Aug.–Dec. 1998, July–Dec. 2000; mem. NAS 1986; mem. Int. Panel of Scientists invited by Pres. Thabo Mbeki and South African Govt to discuss the AIDS crisis, Pretoria 6–7 May 2000, Johannesburg 3–4 July 2000; Fogarty Scholar-in-Residence, NIH, Bethesda, Md 1986–87, Lichtfield Lecturer, Univ. of Oxford, UK 1988, C. J. Watson Lecturer, Abbott Northwestern Hosp., Minneapolis, Minn. 1990, Shaffer Alumni Lecturer, Tulane Univ., New Orleans, La 1992, Constance Ledward Rollins Lecturer, Univ. of New Hampshire, Durham, Distinguished Speaker, Dept of Biology, Univ. of Louisville, Ky; Merck Award 1969, Calif. Scientist of the Year Award 1971, First Annual American Medical Center Oncology Award 1981, NIH Outstanding Investigator Grant 1985–92, Wissenschaftspreis, Hanover, Germany 1988. *Achievements:* isolated the first cancer gene through work on retroviruses in 1970, and mapped the genetic structure of these viruses; came to public attention with claim that HIV is not the cause of AIDS 1987; based on experience with retroviruses, challenged virus-AIDS hypothesis in numerous medical and scientific journals and instead proposed hypothesis that various AIDS diseases are brought on by long-term consumption of recreational drugs and anti-HIV drugs; developed theory that cancers originate from normal cells with individual karyotypes, much like new species. *Publications include:* AIDS: The Good News Is... (with John Yiamouyiannis) 1995, Infectious AIDS: Have We Been Misled? (collection of 13 articles published in scientific journals 1987–96) 1995, AIDS: Virus or Drug Induced? (collection of 27 articles by scientists, independent scholars and investigative journalists from Australia, Europe and USA) 1996, Inventing the AIDS Virus 1996; numerous scientific papers in professional journals on genetic structure of retroviruses and aneuploidy of cancers. *Address:* Department of Molecular and Cell Biology, 353 Donner Lab #3206, University of California at Berkeley, 16 Barker Hall, Berkeley CA 94720-3206, USA (office). *Telephone:* (510) 642-6549 (office). *Fax:* (510) 643-6455 (office). *E-mail:* duesberg@berkeley.edu (office). *Website:* mcb.berkeley.edu/labs/duesberg (office); mcb.berkeley.edu/faculty/BMB/duesbergp.html (office); www.duesberg.com (office).

DUFF, Michael James, BSc, PhD, DIC, FRS, FInstP; British physicist and academic; *Professor Emeritus of Theoretical Physics and Senior Research Investigator, Imperial College London;* b. 28 Jan. 1949, Manchester, England; s. of Edward Duff and Elizabeth Duff (née Kaylor); m. Lesley Yearling 1984; one s. one d.; ed De La Salle Coll., Salford, Queen Mary Coll. and Imperial Coll., London; Post-doctoral fellowships in Theoretical Physics, Int. Centre for Theoretical Physics, Trieste, Italy, Univ. of Oxford, King's Coll. and Queen Mary Coll., London Univ., Brandeis Univ., USA 1972–79; Faculty mem. Imperial Coll. London 1979–88, Prin. of Physical Sciences 2005–06, Abdus Salam Prof. of Theoretical Physics 2006–15, Prof. Emer. of Theoretical Physics and Sr Research Investigator 2015–, Leverhulme Emer. Fellowship 2016–18; Sr Physicist, CERN, Geneva 1984–87; Prof. of Physics, Texas A&M Univ., USA 1988–92, Distinguished Prof. of Physics 1992–99; Oskar Klein Prof. of Physics, Univ. of Michigan 1999–2005, Dir Michigan Center for Theoretical Physics 2000–05; Visiting Prof. of Mathematics, Univ. of Oxford 2017–; Fellow, Hagler Inst. for Advanced Study 2018–19; Fellow, American Physical Soc.; Meeting Gold Medal, El Colegio Nacional, Mexico City 2004, Paul Dirac Gold Medal, Inst. of Physics 2017, Trotter Prize 2018. *Publications include:* Observations on Conformal Anomalies 1977, Kaluza-Klein Supergravity 1986, Strings Solitons 1994, The World in Eleven Dimensions 1999; numerous articles on unified theories of the elementary particles. *Leisure interests:* soccer, watercolours. *Address:* Blackett Laboratory, Imperial College London, Prince Consort Road, London, SW7 2AZ (office); Yew Tree House, Church Lane, Milton, Oxon., OX14 4BL, England (home). *Telephone:* (20) 7594-8571 (office); (1235) 833511 (home). *Fax:* (20) 7594-7844 (office). *E-mail:* m.duff@imperial.ac.uk (office). *Website:* www.imperial.ac.uk/people/m.duff (office).

DUFFEY, Joseph Daniel, PhD; American academic administrator and fmr government official; b. 1 July 1932, Huntington, W Va; s. of Joseph I. Duffey and Ruth Wilson Duffey; m. Anne Wexler 1974 (died 2009); four s.; ed Marshall Univ., Andover Newton Theological School, Yale Univ. and Hartford Seminary Foundation; Assoc. Prof. and Acting Dean, Hartford Seminary Foundation 1960–70; Adjunct Prof. and Fellow, Calhoun Coll. 1970–74; Gen. Sec. and Spokesman, American Assen of Univ. Profs, Washington, DC 1974–76; Asst Sec. of State, US State Dept 1977; Chair. Nat. Endowment for the Humanities 1977–82; US del. to UNESCO 1978–80; Chancellor Univ. of Mass. at Amherst 1982–91, also Pres. Univ. of Mass. System 1990–91; Pres. American Univ., Washington, DC 1991–93; Head of US Information Agency 1993–98; apptd Sr Exec. Chair., Int. Univ. Project, Sylvan Learning Systems (now Laureate Education Inc.), Washington, DC 1999, then Sr Vice-Pres.; Public Policy Scholar, Woodrow Wilson Int. Center for Scholars 2003–04; mem. Bd of Visitors, Univ. of Maryland Univ. Coll.; mem. Council on Foreign Relations 1979–; Order of Leopold II (Belgium) 1979; 15 hon. degrees; Tree of Life Award, American Jewish Congress 1984. *Publications include:* Lewis Mumford's Quest 1979, US Global Competitiveness 1988, Looking Back and Looking Forward: The US and the World Economy 1989. *Address:* 2700 F Street, NW, Washington, DC 20566, USA. *Telephone:* (202) 467-4600. *Fax:* (202) 416-8676. *E-mail:* jduffey@earthlink.net.

DUFFIELD, Dame Vivien Louise, DBE, CBE, MA; British philanthropist; *Campaign Chair, University of Oxford;* b. 26 March 1946; d. of Sir Charles Clore and Francine Halphen; m. John Duffield 1969 (divorced 1976); one s. one d.; ed Cours Victor Hugo, Paris, Lycée Français de Londres, Heathfield School, Lady Margaret Hall, Oxford; Dir Royal Opera House Trust 1985–2001, Royal Opera House 1990–2001; Vice-Chair. Great Ormond Street Hosp. Wishing Well Appeal 1987, Royal Marsden Hosp. Cancer Appeal 1990; currently Campaign Chair., Univ. of Oxford; mem. NSPCC Centenary Appeal Cttee 1983, Financial Devt Cttee 1985; mem. Royal Ballet Bd 1990–, Gov. Royal Ballet 2002–; Chair. Clore Duffield Foundation (after merger with Clore Foundation); Trustee, Dulwich Collection Picture Gallery 1993–2002; Gov. South Bank Bd 2002–; Hon. Mem. Royal Coll. of Music 1987, Hon. FRAM 2003; Hon. DLitt (Buckingham) 1990, Hon. DPhil (Weizmann Inst.) 1985, (Hebrew Univ.) 1998; Beacon Fellowship Prize 2006, Medal for Arts Philanthropy 2008. *Leisure interests:* skiing, opera, ballet, shooting. *Address:* c/o Clore Duffield Foundation, Studio 3, Chelsea Manor Studios, Flood Street, London, SW3 5SR, England. *Telephone:* (20) 7351-6061. *Fax:* (20) 7351-5308. *Website:* www.cloreduffield.org.uk.

DUFFUOR, Kwabena, BSc, MBA, MA, PhD; Ghanaian banking executive and politician; m. Nana Akosua Fosuah; five c.; ed Univ. of Ghana, Syracuse Univ., USA; with Ghana Commercial Bank 1969–95, positions included Special Asst to Man. Dir, Chief Economist and Head of Research Dept; Deputy Gov. Bank of Ghana 1995–97, Gov. 1997–2001; Lecturer in Econs, Finance and Banking, Univ. Ghana 1982–91, mem. Advisory Bd Inst. of Social Statistical and Econ. Research; Minister of Finance and Econ. Planning 2009–12; fmr Chair. Bd of Dirs, UniBank Ghana Ltd; mem. Bd of Dirs, Accra Brewery Ltd 1983–94, State Gold Mining Corpn 1984–91, Shell Ghana Ltd 1986–91, Ecobank, Côte d'Ivoire 1989–95, Ashanti Goldfields Co. Ltd 2000–01; Founder and Sr Advisor, HODA Holdings; mem. Econs Soc.; Chair. Ghana Heart Foundation, Kumawuman Rural Bank; Fellow, Akuafo Hall, Univ. of Ghana; Hon. Fellow, Chartered Inst. of Bankers (Ghana) 1997; voted by Independent Newspaper as Personality of the Year 1999, Int. Distinguished Merit Award, West African Insurance Institute 2010, named by The Banker (Financial Times publ.) Africa's Finance Minister of the Year 2011. *Address:* c/o Ministry of Finance and Economic Planning, PO Box M40, Accra, Ghana. *E-mail:* minister2009@mofep.gov.gh.

DUFFY, Dame Carol Ann, DBE, BA, FRSL; Scottish poet, playwright and academic; *Poet Laureate;* b. 23 Dec. 1955, Glasgow, Scotland; d. of Frank Duffy and Mary Black; one d. with Peter Benson; ed St Joseph's Convent, Stafford and Univ. of Liverpool; Poetry Ed., Ambit 1983–; Lecturer in Creative Writing, then Prof. of Contemporary Poetry, Manchester Metropolitan Univ. 1996–, Creative Dir Manchester Writing School; Poet Laureate 2009–; Head Judge, Manchester Poetry Prize; Judge, Arts Council Awards; mem. Poetry Soc. (Vice-Pres.); Panel mem. Soc. of Authors; Hon. Fellow, British Acad. 2015, Royal Soc. of Edinburgh 2015, Homerton Coll., Cambridge; Dr hc (Dundee), (Hull), (St Andrews), (Warwick); C. Day-Lewis Fellowships 1982–84, Eric Gregory Award 1984, Cholmondeley Award 1992, Lannan Award (USA) 1995, Signal Children's Poetry Award 1999, Nat. Endowment for Science, Tech. and the Arts Award 2001, PEN/Pinter Prize 2012, rated by Woman's Hour (BBC Radio 4) as one of the 100 most powerful women in the UK 2013. *Plays include:* Take My Husband 1982, Cavern of Dreams 1984, Loss 1986, Little Women, Big Boys 1986, Grimm Tales 1994, More Grimm Tales 1997, Casanova, produced at Lyric Theatre, Hammersmith 2007. *Opera:* English translation of The Magic Flute revived by Opera North in a touring production 2007. *Collaboration:* The Manchester Carols (with composer Sasha Johnson Manning, performed at Royal Northern Coll. of Music 2007, 2008, also broadcast on BBC Radio 3). *Poetry commission:* poem 'Leda' commissioned by Barbican Education for exhbn Seduced: Art and Sex from Antiquity to Now, at Barbican Art Gallery, London 2007. *Publications include:* poetry: Fleshweathercock and Other Poems 1973, Standing Female Nude (Scottish Arts Council Award 1986) 1985, Selling Manhattan (Scottish Arts Council Award, Somerset Maugham Award 1988) 1987, Home and Away 1988, The Other Country (Dylan Thomas Prize 1989, Scottish Arts Council Book Award 1990) 1990, Mean Time (Whitbread Poetry Award, Forward Poetry Prize, Scottish Arts Council Book Award) 1993, Selected Poems 1994, The Pamphlet 1998, The World's Wife 1999, Time's Tidings 1999, Feminine Gospels 2001, Underwater Farmyard 2002, Out of Fashion (ed.) 2004, Rapture (T.S. Eliot Prize) 2005, Another Night Before Christmas 2005, Selected Poems 2006, The Lost Happy Endings (with Jane Ray) 2006, The Hat (for children) 2007, Answering Back (ed.) 2008, Mrs Scrooge: A Christmas Poem 2009, New and Collected Poems for Children 2009, The Princess's Blankets 2009, The Twelve Poems of Christmas (ed.) 2009, To The Moon: An Anthology of Lunar Poetry (ed.) 2009, Love Poems 2009, Another Night Before Christmas 2010, The Bees (Costa Book Award for Poetry) 2011, The Christmas Truce 2011, Wenceslas: A Christmas Poem 2012, 1914 – Poetry Remembers (ed.) 2013, Dorothy Wordsworth's Christmas Birthday 2014, Sincerity 2018. *Leisure interest:* holidays. *Address:* c/o Peter Straus, Rogers, Coleridge & White Ltd., 20 Powis Mews, London, W11 1JN, England (office); 219 Geoffrey Manton Building, Manchester Metropolitan University, Rosamond Street West, off Oxford Road, Manchester, M15 6LL, England (office). *Telephone:* (20) 7221-3717 (office); (161) 247-1731 (switchboard) (office). *Fax:* (20) 7229-9084 (office); (161) 247-6769 (office). *E-mail:* info@rcwlitagency.com (office); writingschool@mmu.ac.uk (office). *Website:* www.rcwlitagency.com (office); www2.mmu.ac.uk/english (office).

DUFFY, Francis (Frank) Cuthbert, CBE, PhD, MArch, AADipl (Hons); British architect; b. 3 Sept. 1940, Berwick-upon-Tweed; s. of John Austin Duffy and Annie Margaret Duffy (née Reed); m. Jessica Duffy (née Bear); three d.; ed Architectural Assen School, London, Univ. of California, Berkeley and Princeton Univ., USA; Asst Architect, Nat. Bldg Agency 1964–67; consultant to JFN Assocs, New York 1968–70, est. JFN Assocs in London 1971–74; co-f. DEGW PLC 1974, Partner 1974–89, Chair. 1989–99, Sr Consultant with title of Founder 1999–2014; Independent Consultant 2014–; Harkness Fellow 1967–71; Visiting Prof., MIT 2001–04, Univ. Coll. London, Univ. of Reading, Lancaster Univ.; Pres. RIBA 1993–95, Architects' Council of Europe 1994; est. DEGW's combination of major interior design and architectural work (e.g. Boots the Chemists, Nottingham, Apicorp, Saudi Arabia) and strategic workplace consultancy to int. corp. clients (e.g. BBC, BP, Google, GSK, Microsoft, Lloyds Bank, NM Rothschild) as well as govt clients (e.g. UN, GSA, UK Treasury, Ministry of Defence, Home Office) and cultural insts (e.g. British Museum, Design Museum, Somerset House Trust, South Bank Centre, Nat. Gallery); f. The Edge 1995; mem. Advisory Cttee on Restoration of Windsor Castle; Chair. Stratford City Design Review Panel, including Olympic Village, coordinated with the Design Review of Olympic venues and park, London 2006–11; Pres.'s Award for Lifetime Achievement from British Council of Offices 2004, British Inst. of Facilities Man. Lifetime Achievement Award 2013. *Publications include:* Office Landscaping 1965, Planning Office Space 1966, The ORBIT Studies 1981–85, The Changing Workplace 1982, The Changing City 1989, RIBA Strategic Study 1992–95, The New Office 1997, Design for Change 1998, New Environments for Working 1998, Architectural Knowledge 1998, Work and the City 2008; as Ed.: Architectural Association Journal 1965–67; numerous articles and papers in professional journals, predominantly on workplace design. *Leisure interests:* reading, writing, talking, drawing. *Address:* Threeways, The Street, Walberswick, nr Southwold, Suffolk, IP18 6UE, England (home). *Telephone:* (1502) 723814 (home). *E-mail:* fduffy@degw.com (office); frank@duffydesign.com. *Website:* www.degw.com (office).

DUFFY, Maureen Patricia, (D. M. Cayer), BA, FRSL, FKC, FEA; British writer, poet and copyright consultant; b. 21 Oct. 1933, Worthing, Sussex; d. of Grace Rose Wright; ed Trowbridge High School for Girls, Sarah Bonnell High School for Girls, King's Coll., London; staged pop art exhbn with Brigid Brophy 1969; Chair. Greater London Arts Literature Panel 1979–81, Authors Lending and Copyright Soc. 1982–94, Copyright Licensing Agency 1996–99 (Vice-Chair. 1994–96); Pres. Writers' Guild of GB 1985–88 (Jt Chair. 1977–78); Co-founder Writers' Action Group 1972–79; Vice-Pres. European Writers Congress 1992–2003 (Pres. 2003–05), Beauty without Cruelty 1975–, British Copyright Council 1998–2003 (Vice-Chair. 1981–86, Chair. 1989–98, Hon. Pres. 2003); Fellow, King's Coll., London 2002, Royal Soc. of Literature 1985 (Vice-Pres. 2013–); Hon. Pres. Authors Lending and Copyright Soc. 2002, British Copyright Council; Hon. DLitt (Loughborough), (Kent); CISAC Gold Medal for Literature 2002, Benson Medal RSL 2004. *Plays include:* Pearson (London Playwrights' Award), Rites (Nat. Theatre) 1969, A Nightingale in Bloomsbury Square (Hampstead Theatre) 1974, The Masque of Henry Purcell (Southwark Theatre) 1995, Sappho Singing 2009, The Choice 2018. *Radio:* The Passionate Shepherdess, Only Goodnight. *Television:* Upstairs Downstairs (Episode 11), Josie, Sanctuary. *Publications:* That's How It Was 1962, The Single Eye 1964, The Microcosm 1966, The Paradox Players 1967, Lyrics for the Dog Hour (poems) 1968, Wounds 1969, Love Child 1971, The Venus Touch 1971, The Erotic World of Faery 1972, I Want to Go to Moscow 1973, Capital 1975, Evesong (poems) 1975, The Passionate Shepherdess 1977, Housespy 1978, Memorials of the Quick and the Dead (poems) 1979, Inherit the Earth 1980, Gorsaga 1981, Londoners: An Elegy 1983, Men and Beasts 1984, Collected Poems 1949–84 1985, Change 1987, A Thousand Capricious Chances: Methuen 1889–1989 1989, Illuminations 1991, Occam's Razor 1992, Henry Purcell (biog.) 1994, Restitution 1998, England: The Making of a Myth from Stonehenge to Albert Square 2001, Alchemy 2004, Family Values 2008, The Orpheus Trail 2009, Environmental Studies 2013, In Times Like These 2013, Pictures From An Exhibition 2016, Past Present 2017, Hilda and Virginia 2018. *Leisure interests:* gardening, art. *Address:* c/o Jonathan Clowes Ltd, 10 Ironbridge House, Bridge

Approach, London, NW1 8BD, England (office); 18 Fabian Road, London, SW6 7TZ, England (office). *Telephone:* (20) 7722-7674 (office); (20) 7385-3598 (office). *Fax:* (871) 528-3647 (office). *E-mail:* ann.evans@jonathanclowes.co.uk (office); 113714.1610@compuserve.com (office). *Website:* www.jonathanclowes.co.uk (office); www.maureenduffy.co.uk.

DUFFY, Terrence A.; American business executive; *Executive Chairman and President, CME Group Inc. (Chicago Mercantile Exchange);* b. 15 Aug. 1958, Chicago, Ill.; m. Jennifer Duffy; two s.; ed Univ. of Wisconsin-Whitewater; Pres. TDA Trading, Inc. 1981–2002; mem. Chicago Mercantile Exchange Inc. (CME) 1981–, mem. Bd of Dirs CME 1995–, Vice-Chair. CME 1998–2002, Chair. 2002–06, Vice-Chair. Chicago Mercantile Exchange Holdings Inc. (CME Holdings) 2001–02, Chair. 2002–06, Exec. Chair. CME Group Inc. (following merger with Chicago Bd of Trade) 2006–, Pres. 2012–; mem. Nat. Saver Summit on Retirement Savings 2002–, Fed. Retirement Thrift Investment Bd 2003–13; mem. Bd of Dirs World Business Chicago, Ill. Agricultural Leadership Foundation; mem. Bd of Regents, Mercy Home for Boys and Girls; Co-Chair. Mayo Clinic Greater Chicago Leadership Council; mem. Econ. Club of Chicago, Execs Club of Chicago, Pres.'s Circle of Chicago Council on Global Affairs; Trustee Saint Xavier Univ.; Hon. DLitt (DePaul Univ.) 2007. *Address:* CME, 20 South Wacker Drive, Chicago, IL 60606, USA (office). *Telephone:* (312) 930-1000 (office). *E-mail:* info@cme.com (office). *Website:* www.cme.com (office).

DUFLO, Esther, MA, PhD; French/American economist and academic; *Abdul Latif Jameel Professor of Poverty Alleviation and Development Economics and Director, Abdul Latif Jameel Poverty Action Lab, Massachusetts Institute of Technology;* b. 25 Oct. 1972; ed Ecole Normale Supérieure, Ecole Polytechnique and ENSAE, Paris, Massachusetts Inst. of Tech., USA; Asst Prof. of Econs, MIT 1999–2001, Castle Krob Career Devt Asst Prof. of Econs, on leave at Princeton Univ. 2001–02, Castle Krob Career Devt Asst Prof. of Econs, MIT 2002–04, Prof. of Econs and Dir Poverty Action Lab. 2004–05, Abdul Latif Jameel Prof. of Poverty Alleviation and Devt Econs and Dir Abdul Latif Jameel Poverty Action Lab 2005–, on leave at the Paris School of Econs Jan.–June 2007; Dir Devt Program, Center for Econ. Policy Research; Research Assoc., Nat. Bureau of Econ. Research; Ed. American Econ. Review 2017–; mem. Bd Bureau for Research and Econ. Analysis of Devt, Global Investment Fund 2014–17; Assoc. Ed. Journal of the European Economic Association 2002–06, Review of Economics and Statistics 2002–06, Journal of Economic Perspectives 2004–07; Co-Ed. Journal of Development Economics 2004–06, Review of Economics and Statistics 2005–07; Founding Ed. The American Economic Journal: Applied Economics 2007–16; mem. Bd of Eds Annual Review of Economics 2007–14; mem. Program Cttee European Econ. Asscn Annual Meeting 2003, Econometric Soc. Annual Meeting 2004, Econometric Soc. Ninth World Congress 2004, European Econ. Asscn Meetings 2007, American Econ. Asscn Meetings 2007; Review of Econ. Studies Tour 1999; mem. John D. and Catherine MacArthur Network on the Costs of Inequality 2001–06, President's Global Devt Council 2012–17, NAS 2017; mem. Advisory Bd UBS Centre 2018–; Fellow, American Acad. of Arts and Sciences 2009, Econometric Soc. 2011, American Acad. of Political and Social Science 2016, Distinguished Fellow Centre for Econ. Studies 2012; Corresp. Fellow, British Acad. 2016; Dr hc (Yale Univ.) 2013; Professeur hc (Hautes études commerciales des Paris) 2015; Hon. DHumLitt (Amherst Coll.) 2017; Alfred P. Sloan Doctoral Dissertation Fellowship 1998, John M. Olin Faculty Fellowship, Nat. Asscn of Scholars 2001–02, Alfred P. Sloan Research Fellowship 2002, Elaine Bennett Prize for Research 2003, Best Young French Economist Prize, Le Monde, Cercle des économistes 2005, CNRS Bronze Medal 2005, Best Advisor, Grad. Econs Asscn, MIT 2007–09, Inaugural holder of the chair 'Knowledge Against Poverty', Collège de France, Paris 2008, Prix Luc Durand-Reville, Acad. des Sciences Morale et Politiques (France) 2008, BBVA Foundation Frontiers of Knowledge Award for Devt Cooperation 2009, First recipient, Calvó Armengol Int. Prize, Barcelona Grad. School of Econs 2009, MacArthur Fellowship 2009, John Bates Clark Medal 2010, Dan David Prize 2013, John Von Neumann Award, Hungary 2014, A.SK Social Science Award 2015, Princess of Asturias Award for Social Sciences 2015. *Publications:* Expérience, science et lutte contre la pauvreté 2009, Le Développment Humain (vol. 1) 2010, La polique de l'autonomie (vol. 2) 2010, Poor Economics: A Radical Rethinking of the Way to Fight Global Poverty (with Abhijit Vinayak Banerjee) 2011, Handbook of Field Experiments, Vol. . 1 and 2 (with Abhijit Vinayak Banerjee) 2017; book chapters, reviews and numerous papers in professional journals. *Address:* Room 544G, Building E52, The Morris and Sophie Chang Building, Department of Economics, Massachusetts Institute of Technology, 50 Memorial Drive, Cambridge, MA 02139, USA (office). *Telephone:* (617) 258-7013 (office). *Fax:* (617) 253-6915. *E-mail:* eduflo@mit.edu (office). *Website:* economics.mit.edu/faculty/eduflo (office).

DUFOIX, Georgina, DèsSc Econ; French politician; b. (Georgina Nègre), 16 Feb. 1943, Paris; d. of Alain Nègre and Antoinette Pallier; m. Antoine Dufoix 1963; two s. two d.; ed Lycée de Nîmes and Univs of Montpellier and Paris-Sorbonne; mem. Man. Cttee Parti Socialiste 1979; Sec. of State for Family Affairs 1981–83, for Family Affairs, Population and Immigrant Workers 1983–84; Govt Spokeswoman and Minister for Social Affairs and Nat. Solidarity 1984–86; Conseiller-gén. for Gard 1982, Socialist Deputy 1986–88; Sec. of State for Family Affairs, for Women's Rights and for Repatriates May–June 1988; Chargée de mission auprès du Président 1988–92; Pres. Admin. Council, French Red Cross 1989–92; Del. Fight against Drugs 1989–93; mem. Governing Bd UN Research Inst. for Social Devt, Geneva 1990–2000, Communications Co. Vera, Governing Bd War-torn Soc. Project, Geneva 1998–2008, Governing Bd InterPeace International, Geneva; Woman of the Year (France) 1989. *Leisure interest:* her vineyard. *Address:* Domaine de Montroche, route de Saint Gilles, 30900 Nîmes, France (home). *Telephone:* (4) 66-29-80-00 (office). *E-mail:* gdufoix@free.fr (home).

DUFOUR, Bernard, MSc; French fmr aviation official; b. 14 Feb. 1933; s. of Jean Dufour and Denise Dufour (née Penot); m. Bernadette de Villepin 1956; five c.; ed Ecole Ozanam, Limoges, Lycée Janson de Sailly, Paris, Ecole Ste Geneviève, Ecole Polytechnique, Calif. Inst. of Tech., USA; engineer, Sud Aviation 1956–61, Dir helicopter production 1961–64, St Nazaire 1964–65, Toulouse 1965–76, Usine Belfort Alsthom 1977–89, GEC Alsthom (Electromechanical Div.) 1989–94; Dir-Gen. ALSTOM Electromécanique 1989–94; Pres. and CEO SNECMA 1994–96; Phare (EU pre-accession programme) expert in Romania 1997–98; Chevalier, Ordre nat. du Mérite, Légion d'honneur; Tudor Vladiminescu (Romania); Médaille Aéronautique. *Leisure interests:* cycling, riding, sailing, skiing. *Address:* 4 rue Henri Heine, 75016 Paris, France (home). *Telephone:* 1-45-25-22-78 (home). *Fax:* 1-45-25-22-78 (home). *E-mail:* dufourbern@wanadoo.fr.

DUFOUR, Jean-Marie, BSc, MSc, MA, PhD, FRSC; Canadian economist and academic; *Professor of Economics, University of Montreal;* ed McGill Univ., Univ. of Montreal, Concordia Univ., Univ. of Chicago; Lecturer in Statistics, Univ. of Québec at Trois-Rivières 1972–73; Prof. of Math., Collège Édouard-Montpetit, Longueuil, Montréal 1973–75; Research Assoc., Inst. of Applied Econ. Research, Concordia Univ. 1978–79; Lecturer in Econs (full-time), Dept of Econ. Sciences, Univ. of Montreal 1978–79, Asst Prof. of Econs 1979–83, Assoc. Prof. of Econs 1983–88, Prof. of Econs 1988–, Chair. Dept of Econ. Sciences 1995–97, Holder of Canada Research Chair in Econometrics, Research Fellow, CIREQ (Centre interuniversitaire de recherche en economie quantitative, mem. research staff, Centre for Research in Econ. Devt 1979–85, Sr mem. research staff ('Chercheur régulier') and Dir research programme in econometrics and macroeconomics 1985–90, Dir Centre 1988–95, 1997–99; Lecturer in Econometrics, Univ. of Sherbrooke 1979, 1981; Lecturer in Quantitative Methods (Time Series), École des Hautes Études Commerciales, Montréal 1980, 1981; Fellow, CIRANO (Centre for Interuniversity Research and Analysis on Orgs, Montreal); Dir Canadian Econometrics Study Group; Project Leader Math. and Statistical Methods for Financial Modelling and Risk Man., MITACS (Math. of Information Tech. and Complex Systems) (Canadian network of centres of excellence); Consultant in Econs, Econ. Council of Canada 1981, Office de Planification et de Développement économique du Québec 1982, Royal Comm. on the Econ. Union and Devt Prospects for Canada (McDonald Comm.), Ottawa 1983–84; Research Fellow, CORE (Centre for Operations Research and Econometrics), Université Catholique de Louvain, Belgium 1985–86; Invited Prof. of Econs, Université de Toulouse I, France 1983; Visiting Prof. of Econs, Univ. of Pennsylvania 1992, Stanford Univ. 1999, Univ. of Toronto 2000; Visiting Prof. of Econometrics, Univ. of Lausanne, Switzerland 1995, Institut d'Économie Industrielle, Université des sciences sociales de Toulouse, France 2002, École Nationale de la Statistique et de l'Admin Économique, Paris, France 2004; Visiting Prof. of Econometrics and Statistics, Institut Supérieur de Gestion, Université de Tunis III, Tunisia 1998; Visiting Scholar, Center for Computational Research in Econs and Man. Science, MIT 1980, Queen's Univ. 1986, CEPREMAP, Paris 1986, Université Libre de Bruxelles (Institut de statistique), Belgium 1988, 1989, 1990, 1993, Institut d'Économie Industrielle, Université des Sciences Sociales de Toulouse, France 1992, 1994, Institut für Statistik und Ökonometrie, Humboldt-Universität zu Berlin, Germany 1994, Institut Nat. de Statistique et d'Économie Appliquée, Rabat, Morocco 1997, École Nationale de la Statistique et de l'Admin Économique, Centre de Recherche en Économie et Statistique, Paris 1990, 1991, 1993, 1995, 1997, 2000, 2001, Centre for Econ. Research, Kaltholieke Universiteit Tilburg, Netherlands 2000, Faculty of Econs, Technische Universität Dresden, Germany 2000, Tinbergen Inst. and Dept of Actuarial Science and Econometrics, Universiteit van Amsterdam, Netherlands 1996, 1997, 1999, 2001, 2003, 2004, Deutsche Bundesbank, Frankfurt, Germany 2001, 2004, Institut für Wirtschaftsforschung, Halle, Germany 2005, 2006, 2007; mem. Bd Dirs Soc. canadienne de science économique 1984–87, Pres.-Elect 1998–99, Pres. 1999–2000; Vice-Pres. Canadian Econs Asscn 2000–01, Pres.-Elect 2001–02, Pres. 2002–03; mem. Int. Statistical Inst. 1990–; Assoc. Ed. Canadian Journal of Economics 1984–88, Cahiers du Centre d'Études de Recherche Opérationnelle 1989–, Econometric Theory 1991–93, Annales d'Économie et de Statistique 1990–, Econometric Reviews 1991–96, 1998–2003, Journal of Econometrics 1994–, Econometrica 1996–2002; Guest Ed. Empirical Economics 1993–94; mem. Editorial Bd Empirical Economics 1994–2003; Fellow, Centre for Operations Research and Econometrics, Université Catholique de Louvain, Belgium 1985–86; Benjamin Meaker Visiting Prof. of Econs, Univ. of Bristol, UK 1993, 1999; Killam Research Fellow, Canada Council for the Arts 1998–2000; Netherlands Org. for Scientific Research (Nederlandse Organisatie voor Wetenschappelijk Onderzoek, NWO) Visitor's Fellowship 2003–04; mem. American Econ. Asscn, Canadian Econs Asscn, Inst. of Math. Statistics, Int. Statistical Inst., Soc. Canadienne de Science Économique, Statistical Soc. of Canada; Fellow, Journal of Econometrics 1996–, Econometric Soc. 1998–, American Statistical Asscn 2005–; Officier, Ordre nat. du Québec 2006; Govt of Québec Doctoral Fellowship 1975–78, Canada Council Doctoral Fellowship 1975–78, Leave Fellowship from Social Sciences and Humanities Research Council of Canada 1985–86, Prize for Excellence in Research, Soc. Canadienne de Science Économique 1988, John Rae Prize for Outstanding Research, Canadian Econs Asscn 1994, Marcel Dagenais Prize for Excellence in Research, Soc. Canadienne de Science Économique 2000, Marcel-Vincent Prize pour les sciences sociales, Asscn francophone pour le savoir 2005, Konrad Adenauer Research Award, Alexander von Humboldt Foundation (Germany) 2005, Radio-Canada Personality of the week, La Presse/Radio-Canada 2006, Killam Prize for Social Sciences, Killam Trust and Canada Council for the Arts 2006, Guggenheim Fellow 2006–07. *Publications:* L'aide publique au financement des exportations (co-author) 1983, Government Assistance to Export Financing (English trans. of previous title) 1983, New Developments in Time Series Econometrics (co-ed.) 1993, Recent Developments in the Econometrics of Structural Change (co-ed.) 1996, Resampling Methods in Econometrics (co-ed.) 2006, Heavy Tails and Stable Paretian Distributions in Econometrics (co-ed.) 2007; more than 110 articles in professional journals on econometrics and statistics, macroeconomics, finance and public finance. *Address:* Université de Montréal, Département de sciences économiques 3150, rue Jean-Brillant, Room C-6030, bureau G6088 CP 6128, succursale Centre-ville, Montréal, PQ H3C 3J7 (office); 1060 Bernard Ouest, Apt. 5, Outremont, Montréal, PQ H2V 1V2, Canada (home). *Telephone:* (514) 343-2400 (office); (514) 273-0497 (home). *Fax:* (514) 343-5831 (office). *E-mail:* jean.marie.dufounr@umontreal.ca (office). *Website:* www.fas.umontreal.ca/SCECO/Dufour (office).

DUFOURCQ, Bertrand Charles Albert, LenD; French fmr diplomatist; b. 5 July 1933, Paris; s. of Norbert Dufourcq and Marguerite-Odette Latron; m. Elisabeth Lefort des Ylouses 1961; two s. two d.; ed Lycées Montaigne and Louis-le-Grand, Paris, Faculté de Droit, Paris, Inst. d'Etudes Politiques, Paris and Ecole Nat. d'Admin; joined Sec. for Foreign Affairs 1961, Chef de Cabinet to Prefect/Admin.-Gen. of City of Algiers 1961, Ministry of Foreign Affairs 1962, Cultural Counsellor, embassy in Tokyo 1964, Counsellor for Foreign Affairs 1967; various posts at Ministry of Foreign Affairs and Ministry of Industrial and Scientific Devt 1967–69; Head of Cultural, Scientific and Tech. Service, Embassy in Moscow 1969–72, Ministry of Foreign Affairs 1972–76, 1978–79, Amb. to People's Repub. of Congo 1976–78, European Dir Ministry of External Relations 1979–84; Dir Office of M. Claude Cheysson 1984; special attachment to Minister of External Relations 1984–85; Admin. Ecole Nat. d'Admin. 1980–83; Amb. to Vatican 1985–88, Dir of Political Affairs, Ministry of Foreign Affairs 1988–91, Amb. to USSR 1991, to Russia 1992 (also accred to Mongolia 1991–92), to Germany 1992–93; Sec.-Gen. Ministry of Foreign Affairs 1993–98; Pres. Fondation de France 2000–07; Pres. Centre de Musique Baroque de Versailles 1998/2009; Commdr Légion d'honneur, Ordre nat. du Mérite, Amb. de France. *Address:* 48 rue Madame, 75006 Paris, France (home).

DUGAS, Richard J., Jr., BSc; American construction industry executive; *Chairman, President and CEO, Pulte Homes Inc.;* b. 8 April 1965; m. Susan O. Dugas; three d.; ed Louisiana State Univ.; held marketing and customer service postions with Exxon Co. 1986–89; worked in process improvement and plant operational efficiency, PepsiCo 1990–94; joined Pulte Homes Inc., Bloomfield Hills, Mich. 1994, has held numerous exec. positions including Vice-Pres. Process Improvement, City Pres. and Market Man., Atlanta Div., Coastal Region Pres., Exec. Vice-Pres. and COO 2002–03, Pres. and CEO 2003–, Chair. 2009–; mem. Bd of Dirs Builder Homesite Inc. *Address:* Pulte Homes Inc., 100 Bloomfield Hills Parkway, Suite 300, Bloomfield Hills, MI 48304-2946, USA (office). *Telephone:* (248) 647-2750 (office). *Fax:* (248) 433-4598 (office). *Website:* www.pulte.com (office).

DUGDALE, Kezia, LLB, MSc, MSP; British politician; b. 28 Aug. 1981, Aberdeen; ed Harris Acad., Dundee, Univ. of Aberdeen, Univ. of Edinburgh; worked in public affairs within higher educ. as Campaigns and Welfare Adviser, Edinburgh Univ. Students' Asscn 2004–06; Public Affairs Officer, Nat. Union of Students 2006–07; entered Scottish politics as Office Man. and Political Adviser to Rt Hon Lord George Foulkes MSP 2007–11; mem. Scottish Parl. for Lothian 2011–, mem. Local Govt and Regeneration Cttee, Subordinate Legislation Cttee, Shadow Cabinet Sec. for Educ. and Lifelong Learning 2013–; writes weekly column in the Daily Record; mem. UNITE (trade union); mem. Scottish Labour Party, Deputy Leader 2014–15, Leader 2015–17. *Leisure interests:* theatre, reading Scottish crime novels, enjoying Edinburgh. *Address:* The Scottish Parliament, M1 07, Edinburgh, EH99 1SP, Scotland (office); c/o Scottish Labour Party, 290 Bath Street, Glasgow, G2 4RE, Scotland (office). *Telephone:* (131) 348-6894 (office). *E-mail:* Kezia.Dugdale.msp@parliament.scot (office). *Website:* www.parliament.scot (office); www.keziadugdale.com.

DUGGAL, Vinod Kumar; Indian civil servant; b. 26 Nov. 1944, Sialkot, Pakistan; ed Nat. Defence Acad.; joined Indian Admin. Service 1968, served in various capacities including Municipal Commr of Delhi 1996–2000, Special Sec., Ministry of Environment and Forests, Sec., Water Resources Ministry, Home Sec. 2005–07; Gov. of Manipur 2013–14 (resgnd), also of Mizoram Aug. 2014 (resgnd); mem. numerous Comms and Cttees with rank of Minister of State, including mem., Nat. Disaster Man. Authority. *Address:* c/o Office of the Chief Minister, Government of Manipur, Chief Minister's Secretariat, Imphal 795 001, India. *E-mail:* cmmani@hub.nic.in.

DUGGER, John Scott; American artist and designer; b. 18 July 1948, Los Angeles, Calif.; s. of Dr James Attwood Dugger and Julian Marie Riddle; ed Loy Norrix High School, Kalamazoo, Mich., Gilmore Inst. of Art, School of the Art Inst. of Chicago; created Perennial (first Ergonic Sculpture), Paris 1970; Leader, Soc. for Anglo-Chinese understanding Del. to China 1972; Founder-Dir Banner Arts, London 1976; mem. Exec. Cttee Art Services Grants Ltd (Artists' Housing Charity) 1980–85; Chair. Asscn of Space Artists, London 1984, 1985; Vice-Chair. Int. Artists Asscn, UK Cttee 1986–87; major works include Documenta 5, People's ParticipatioStn Pavilion, Kassel, FRG 1972, Monumental Strip-Banner Installation, Trafalgar Square, London 1974, Sports Banner Exhbn, Inst. of Contemporary Arts, London 1980; Original Art Banners commissioned for HM the Queen's 60th Birthday, Buckingham Palace 1986, Tibet Mountainscape Banner for His Holiness the XIV Dalai Lama—International Year of Tibet 1991; Int. Certified Master Fabric Craftsman, IFAI (Industrial Fabric Asscn) 1992; works on display at Arts Council of GB, Tate Gallery, London; Major Award, Arts Council of GB 1978, Calouste Gulbenkian Foundation Awards 1979, 1980, Int. Achievement Award 1993. *Leisure interests:* oriental art, mountaineering, martial arts. *Address:* 15 Railroad Street, Andover, MA 01810-3516, USA.

DUHALDE MALDONADO, Eduardo Alberto; Argentine lawyer, politician and fmr head of state; *Honorary President, Movimiento Productivo Argentino;* b. 5 Oct. 1941, Lomas de Zamora, Prov. of Buenos Aires; s. of Tomás Duhalde and María Esther Maldonado; m. Hilda Beatriz González 1971; one s. four d.; ed Univ. of Buenos Aires; fmr mem. staff, Legal Dept, Lomas de Zamora Town Council; Pres. Exec. Cttee Partido Justicialista of Lomas de Zamora 1973; Mayor of Lomas de Zamora 1974–76, removed from post following mil. coup, re-elected 1983; Nat. Deputy for Prov. of Buenos Aires 1987–89, First Vice-Pres. Chamber of Deputies 1987–89; Vice-Pres. of Argentina, Pres. Senate 1989–91; Gov. Prov. of Buenos Aires 1991–99; unsuccessful cand. (Partido Justicialista) in presidential elections 1999; Pres. of Argentina 2002–03; Pres. Comisión de Representantes Permanentes del MERCOSUR 2003–05; Hon. Pres., Movimiento Productivo Argentino 2001–; fmr Pres. Congreso Nacional del Partido Justicialista; unsuccessful cand. (Unión Popular) in presidential elections 2011; Orden de Boyacá (Colombia), Orden Cruceiro do Sul (Brazil), Orden del Quetzal (Guatemala), Orden de Bernardo O'Higgins (Chile); Dr hc (Genoa) 1992, (Universidad Hebrea, Argentina) 1999, (Universidad del Salvador) 1999. *Publications:* La revolución productiva (with Carlos Saúl Menem q.v.) 1987, Los políticos y las drogas 1988, Hacía un mundo sin drogas 1994, Política, familia, sociedad y drogas 1997, Comunidad sudamericana: logros y desafíos de la integración 2006, Memorias del incendio 2007, Es hora de que me escuchen. El peligro de los narcoestados 2010, De Tomás Moro al hambre cero 2011. *Leisure interests:* fishing, chess, folk music, reading, watching football. *Address:* Movimiento Productivo Argentino, Hipolito Yrigoyen 1628, Piso 11, Buenos Aires, Argentina (office). *Website:* www.mpargentino.com.ar (office).

DUHAMEL, Olivier, LLD; French academic; *Emeritus Professor of Law and Political Science, University of Paris (Sciences Po);* b. 2 May 1950, Neuilly-sur-Seine; m. Évelyne Pisier; one s. one d.; ed Inst. of Political Studies, Paris; Founder and Ed. Pouvoirs magazine 1977–; Ed. TNS Sofres 1984–; fmr Prof., Univ. de Besançon, Univ. Paris X-Nanterre, Univ. Paris 1 Panthéon-Sorbonne; taught Law and Political Science for 25 years, Univ. of Paris (Sciences Po), currently Prof. Emer.; Adviser to Pres. of Constitutional Council 1983–95; mem. Consultative Comm. for the Revision of the Constitution 1992–93; Founder and Pres. REVE (Réflexion-Engagement-Vision pour l'Europe) 1994; founder mem. AGIR 1995–, SOS Europe (inter-parliamentary group) 1997–; Pres. Europartenaires 1997–2000; mem. European Parl. (Socialist Party) 1997–2004, mem. Cttee on Constitutional Affairs, Cttee on Citizens' Freedoms and Rights 1994–2001, on Justice and Home Affairs; mem. Convention on Future of Europe 2002–03; fmr Visiting Prof., Univ. of Washington, New York Univ.; contrib. Europe 1 (radio), LCI (TV). *Television:* series: Les grandes batailles de la République (France 5), Democratie, democracy (France 5), Présidentielle, les surprises de l'Histoire (France 2), Petite histoire de la constitution européenne (Arte). *Publications:* Chili ou la tentative révolution 1974, Changer le PC? 1979, La Gauche et la 5ème République 1980, Histoire des idées politiques (co-author) 1982, Le nouveau Président (co-author) 1987, Le pouvoir politique en France 1991, Droit constitutionnel et politique 1994, Les Démocraties 1993, Histoire constitutionnelle de la France 1995, Petit Dictionnaire de l'Euro (co-author) 1998, Le Quinquennat 2000, La 5ème République (1958–2001) (co-author) 2001, Présidentielles: les surprises de l'historique (1965–95) 2001, Vive la VIème République 2002, Pour l'Europe 2003, La Constitution européenne 2004, Pour Europe: Le texte intégral de la constitution expliqué et commenté 2005, Des raisons du Non 2005, Matins d'un Européen 2005, Histoire des Présidentielles 2007, La Vie République (1985–2009) 2009, Droit constitutionnel et institutions politiques 2009. *Address:* Sciences Po, 27 rue Saint-Guillaume, 75007 Paris (office); 6 rue de Bièvre, 75005 Paris, France (home). *Telephone:* (6) 31-18-56-28 (home). *E-mail:* lolivier.d@wanadoo.fr (home). *Website:* www.sciences-po.fr (office).

DUIGAN, John, MA; Australian film director, screenwriter and author; b. 19 June 1949, Hartley Wintney, Hampshire, England; ed Univ. of Melbourne; fmr Lecturer, Univ. of Melbourne and Latrobe Univ.; Co-Dir Vietnam (TV mini-series); wrote and directed TV documentaries: Fragments of War: The Story of Damien Parer 1988, Bitter Rice 1989. *Films include:* The Firm Man 1975, Trespassers 1976, Mouth to Mouth 1978, Dimboola 1979, Winter of Our Dreams 1981, Far East 1982, One Night Stand 1984, The Year My Voice Broke 1987 (Australian Acad. Award for Best Dir), Romero 1989, Flirting 1991, Wide Sargasso Sea 1993, Sirens 1994, The Journey of August King 1995, The Leading Man 1996, Lawn Dogs 1997, Molly 1999, Paranoid 2000, The Parole Officer 2001, Head in the Clouds 2004. *Publications:* novels: Badge, Players, Room to Move. *Address:* c/o Creative Artists Management (CAA), 9830 Wilshire Blvd., Beverly Hills, CA 90212-1825, USA.

DUJARDIN, Jean; French actor, comedian, writer and director; b. 19 June 1972, Rueil-Malmaison, Paris; m. Alexandra Lamy 2009; two c.; cabaret performer during mid-1990s; fmr mem. cabaret group Nous C Nous. *Television includes:* Carré Blanc / Nous C Nous 1996–99, Farce Attaque (also writer) 1997–98, Un gars, une fille 1999–2003, Palizzi (also director) 2007. *Films include:* If I Were a Rich Man 2002, Toutes les filles sont folles 2003, Bienvenue chez les Rozes 2003, Le Convoyeur 2004, Les Dalton 2004, Brice de Nice 2005, L'Amour aux trousses 2005, Il ne faut jurer de rien! 2005, OSS 117: Cairo, Nest of Spies (Etoile D'Or Award 2006) 2006, OSS 117: Lost in Rio, Hellphone 2006, 99 francs (Raimu Award for Comedy 2007) 2007, Contre-enquête 2007, Ca$h 2008, A Man and His Dog 2009, OSS 117: Lost in Rio 2009, Lucky Luke 2009, Little White Lies 2010, Un balcon sur la mer (Swann d'Or for Best Actor) 2010, The Clink of Ice 2010, The Artist (Best Actor, Cannes Film Festival 2011, Golden Globe Award for Best Actor – Motion Picture Musical or Comedy 2012, Screen Actors Guild Best Actor Award 2012, BAFTA Best Actor Award 2012, Academy Award for Best Actor 2012) 2011, Les Infidèles (also co-writer and co-dir) 2012, The Wolf of Wall Street 2013, The Monuments Men 2014. *Address:* c/o WME, 9601 Wilshire Boulevard, Beverly Hills, CA 90210, USA (office). *Telephone:* (310) 285-9000 (office). *Fax:* (310) 285-9010 (office). *Website:* www.wmeentertainment.com (office).

DUJOVNE, Nicolás; Argentine economist and government official; *Minister of Public Finance;* b. 18 May 1967, Buenos Aires; s. of Berardo Dujovne; ed Univ. of Buenos Aires, Univ. Torcuato Di Tella, Univ. of California, USA; Chief Advisor to Sec. of the Treasury 1997–98; fmr Prof., Univ. of Buenos Aires; fmr dvisor to Ministry of Finance and Rep. of Minister of Economy to Bd of Dirs of Central Bank; fmr economist, Macroeconomics, Alpha and Citibank (consultancies); Chief Economist, Banco Galicia 2001–11; Econ. Advisor to presidential campaign of Ricardo Alfonsín 2010; Advisor to Radical Civic Union Bloc, Senate 2012–16; Minister of Public Finance 2017–; f. Nicolás Dujovne y Asociados (econ. consultancy) 2014; fmr econ. consultant to World Bank, Buenos Aires and Washington, DC; columnist, La Nación (daily newspaper); co-host, Todo Noticias (cable news channel), Grupo Clarin; fmr Adviser to Fundacion Pensar (econ. think tank). *Address:* Ministry of Public Finance, Hipólito Yrigoyen 250, C1086AAB Buenos Aires, Argentina (office). *Telephone:* (11) 4349-5000 (office). *E-mail:* ciudadano@mecon.gob.ar (office). *Website:* www.mecon.gov.ar (office); nicolasdujovne.com.

DUKA, HE Cardinal Dominik Jaroslav, OP; Czech ecclesiastic and academic; *Archbishop of Prague;* b. 26 April 1943, Hradec Králové, Protectorate of Bohemia and Moravia (now Hradec Králové, Czech Repub.); ed Theological Faculty of Litoměřice, Theological Faculty of St John the Baptist, Warsaw, Poland; professed mem. Order of Friars Preachers (Dominicans) 1969, ordained priest 1970; worked in various parishes of Archdiocese of Prague for five years; deprived of state authorization for the sacred ministry, worked as designer in factories of Škoda Plzeň until collapse of Communism 1989; worked in secret in the Order as novice master and teacher of theology; jailed in Plzeň 1981–82; Provincial of the Dominicans in Bohemia and Moravia 1986–98; elected Fed. Pres. Conf. of Major Superiors 1989; Vice-Pres. Union of European Confs of Major Superiors 1992–96; Lecturer, Faculty of Theology, Palacký Univ., Olomouc 1990–99; Bishop of Hradec Králové 1998–2004; Apostolic Admin. of Litoměřice 2004–10; Archbishop of Prague 2010–; cr. Cardinal (Cardinal-Priest of Santi Marcellino e Pietro) 2012; participated in Papal Conclave 2013. *Address:* Archdiocese of Prague, Hradcanske nam. 16, 119 02 Prague 1, Czech Republic (office). *Telephone:* (2) 20392123 (office). *Fax:* (2) 20514647 (office). *E-mail:* info@apha.cz (office). *Website:* www.apha.cz (office).

DUKAKIS, Michael Stanley, BA, LLB, JD; American academic and fmr politician; *Distinguished Professor, Department of Political Science, Northeastern University;* b. 3 Nov. 1933, Brookline, Mass.; s. of Dr. Panos Dukakis and Euterpe Dukakis; m. Katharine Dickson; one s. two d.; ed Brookline High School, Swarthmore Coll., Harvard Law School; Army service in Korea 1955–57; mem. Town Meeting, Brookline 1959, Chair. Town Cttee 1960–62; Attorney Hill & Barlow, Boston 1960–74; alt. Del. Democratic Nat. Convention 1968; mem. Mass. House of Reps for Brookline 1962–70, later Chair. Cttee on Public Service and mem. Special Comm. on Low Income Housing; f. a research group for public information 1970; moderator of TV public affairs debate programme The Advocates; Gov. of Massachusetts 1975–79, 1983–91; teacher, Fla Atlantic Univ., Boca Raton 1992; Democratic Party cand. for US Pres. 1988; Lecturer and Dir of Inter-Governmental Studies, John F. Kennedy School of Govt, Harvard Univ. 1979–82; Distinguished Prof., Northeastern Univ., Boston; Visiting Prof., Luskin School of Public Affairs, UCLA; Vice-Chair. AmTrack Reform Bd 1998–2003; mem. Bd of Dirs Massachusetts Budget and Policy Center, Free for All Fund, New England Center for Children; Gold Medal, City of Athens, Greece 1996. *Publications include:* Creating the Future: Massachusetts comeback and its promise for America (with Rosabeth Moss Kanter) 1988, How to Get Into Politics and Why: A Reader (with Senator Paul Simon) 2000, Leader-Managers in the Public Sector: Managing for Results (with John Portz) 2010. *Address:* Department of Political Science, Northeastern University, 921 Renaissance Park, 360 Huntington Avenue, Boston, MA 02115 (office); 650 Kelton Avenue, Apartment 302, Los Angeles, CA 90024, USA (home). *Telephone:* (617) 373-4396 (office). *Fax:* (617) 373-5311 (office). *E-mail:* m.dukakis@neu.edu (office). *Website:* www.northeastern.edu/cssh/faculty/michael-dukakis (office).

DUKAKIS, Olympia, MA; American actress, director, producer, teacher and activist and author; b. 20 June 1931, Lowell, Mass; m. Louis Zorich; two s. one d.; ed Arlington High School, Mass, Boston Univ.; London debut at Royal Nat. Theatre in Martin Sherman's one-woman play Rose 1999, followed by world premiere of Timberlake Wertenbaker's Credible Witness at Royal Court Theatre; appeared on BBC TV in film A Life for a Life and on BBC Radio starring in Hecuba; on Broadway, starred in Rose; starred as Clytemnestra in Agamemnon 2004; also performed at A.C.T. in The Mother (world premiere) by Gorky adapted by Constance Congdon; Founding mem. and Producing Artistic Dir of Whole Theatre, Montclair, NJ 1971–90, directed and appeared in many productions; Founding mem. The Actor's Company, Boston, Charles Playhouse, Boston; has appeared in more than 130 productions Off-Broadway and regionally, at venues including A.C.T., Shakespeare in the Park, Studio Arena in Albany, American Place Theatre, APA Phoenix, Circle Rep and Williamstown Summer Theatre Festival, where she also served as Assoc. Dir; taught acting at graduate school, New York Univ. for 15 years, currently teaches master classes at various colls and univs throughout USA; inducted into Arlington High School Hall of Fame, NJ Gov.'s Walt Whitman Creative Arts Award 1992. *Theatre includes:* A Man's A Man (Bertolt Brecht) (Obie Award), The Marriage of Bette and Boo (Christopher Durang), Joseph Papp's Public Theatre (Obie Award), Curse of the Starving Class (Sam Shepard), Titus Andronicus, Electra, and Peer Gynt. *Films include:* Twice a Man 1964, Stiletto 1969, John and Mary 1969, Made for Each Other 1971, The Rehearsal 1974, Death Wish 1974, The Wanderers 1979, Rich Kids 1979, The Idolmaker 1980, National Lampoon's Movie Madness 1982, Walls of Glass 1985, Moonstruck (Academy Award for Best Supporting Actress 1988, New York Film Critics Award, the Los Angeles Film Critics Award, Golden Globe Award) 1987, Working Girl 1988, Dad 1989, Look Who's Talking 1989, Steel Magnolias 1989, In the Spirit 1990, Look Who's Talking Too 1990, Over the Hill 1992, The Cemetery Club 1993, Digger 1993, Look Who's Talking Now 1993, I Love Trouble 1994, Mother (video) 1995, Jeffrey 1995, Mighty Aphrodite 1995, Mr Holland's Opus 1995, Jerusalem 1996, Milk & Money 1996, Never Too Late 1997, Balkan Island: The Last Story of the Century 1997, Picture Perfect 1997, Jane Austen's Mafia! 1998, Better Living 1998, Dead Badge 1999, Brooklyn Sonnet 2000, My Beautiful Son 2001, Ladies and The Champ 2001, And Never Let Her Go 2001, The Intended 2002, The Event 2003, Charlie's War 2003, The Great New Wonderful 2005, The Thing About My Folks 2005, 3 Needles 2005, Whiskey School 2005, Upside Out 2006, Jesus, Mary and Joey 2006, Away from Her 2006, Day on Fire 2006, In the Land of Women 2007, Hove (The Wind) (short) 2009, Dottie's Thanksgiving Pickle (short) 2010, Montana Amazon 2011, Birds of a Feather 2011, Cloudburst 2011, The Last Keepers 2012, Outliving Emily (short) 2012, The Misadventures of the Dunderheads 2012, A Little Game 2014, 7 Chinese Brothers 2015. *Television includes:* The Nurses (series) 1962, Dr. Kildare (series) 1962, Nicky's World (film) 1974, Great Performances (series) 1975, The Seagull 1975, The Andros Targets (series) 1977, F.D.R.: The Last Year (movie) 1980, Breaking Away (series) 1980, American Playhouse (series) – King of America 1982, One of the Boys (series) – His Cheatin' Heart 1982, The Neighborhood (movie) 1982, Search for Tomorrow (series) 1983, The Equalizer (series) – Shades of Darkness 1986, Lucky Day (film) 1991, The General Motors Playwrights Theater (series) – The Last Act Is a Solo (ACE Award) 1991, Fire in the Dark (film) 1991, Sinatra (film) 1992, Tales of the City (mini-series) – Episode 1.1 1993, Young at Heart (movie) 1995, Touched by an Angel (series) – A Joyful Noise 1996, Heaven Will Wait (film) 1997, A Match Made in Heaven (film) 1997, A Life for a Life (film) 1998, Scattering Dad (film) 1998, The Pentagon Wars (film) 1998, More Tales of the City (mini-series) 1998, Joan of Arc (film) 1999, The Last of the Blonde Bombshells (film) 2000, And Never Let Her Go (film) 2001, Ladies and the Champ (film) 2001, My Beautiful Son (film) 2001, Further Tales of the City (mini-series) 2001, Guilty Hearts (film) 2002, The Simpsons (series) 2002, Frasier (series) (voice) 2002, Mafia Doctor (film) 2003, It's All Relative (series) – Thanks, But No Thanks 2003, The Librarian: Quest for the Spear (film) 2004, Center of the Universe (series) 2004–05, Numb3rs (series) – Hot Shot 2006, The Librarian: Return to King Solomon's Mines (film) 2006, Worst Week (series) 2008, Bored to Death (series) 2010–11, Law & Order: Special Victims Unit (series) – Pop 2011, The Christmas Spirit (film) 2013, Forgive Me (series, several episodes) 2013, Sex & Violence (mini-series) 2013–15, Big Driver (film) 2014, F to 7th (series short) 2014. *Publication:* Ask Me Again Tomorrow (memoir). *Telephone:* (212) 777-7786 (ext. 4) (office). *Address:* c/o Parseghian Planco LLP, 322 Eighth Avenue, Suite 601, New York, NY 10001; 684 Broadway #6E, New York, NY 10012, USA (home).

ĐUKANOVIĆ, Milo; Montenegrin politician, economist and head of state; *President;* b. 15 Feb. 1962, Nikšić, Socialist Repub. of Montenegro, Socialist Fed. Repub. of Yugoslavia; s. of Radovan Đukanović and Stana Đukanović; m. Lidija Kuč; one s.; ed Faculty of Econs, Univ. of Montenegro, Podgorica; joined Savez Komunista Jugoslavije (League of Communists of Yugoslavia) 1979 (mem. Cen. Cttee 1986–89), later renamed Demokratska Partija Socialista Crne Gore (Democratic Party of Socialists of Montenegro), Deputy Chair. 1994–98, Chair. 1998–; Chair. of the Govt (Prime Minister) 1991–98, 2003–06, 2008–10, 2012–16 (resgnd); Pres. of Montenegro 1998–2002, 2018–; Acting Minister of Defence June–Nov. 2006; mem. Skupština Crne Gore (Ass. of Montenegro) 2006–; Hon. mem. The Int. Raoul Wallenberg Foundation. *Address:* Office of the President, 81000 Podgorica, Sveti Petar Cetinjski 3, Montenegro (office). *Telephone:* (20) 241410 (office). *Fax:* (20) 245849 (office). *E-mail:* filip.vujanovic@predsjednik.me (office); predsjednik@predsjednik.me (office). *Website:* www.predsjednik.me (office).

DUKE, Elizabeth Ashburn, BA, MBA; American banking executive; *Chair, Wells Fargo & Co.;* b. 23 July 1952, Portsmouth, Va; ed N Carolina State Univ., Univ. of N Carolina at Chapel Hill, Old Dominion Univ.; Vice Pres. and Chief Financial Officer, Bank of Virginia Beach 1978–85; Vice-Pres. and CFO, Bank of Tidewater 1985–87, Pres. 1987–2001, also CEO 1991–2001, (Tidewater acquired by SouthTrust Bank 2001), Exec. Vice-Pres. SouthTrust Bank 2001–04, (SouthTrust acquired by Wachovia Bank 2004), Exec. Vice-Pres. Wachovia Bank NA 2004–05; COO, TowneBank 2005–08; mem. Bd of Govs, Fed. Reserve System 2008–13, Chair. Cttee on Consumer and Community Affairs, mem. Cttee on Bank Supervision and Regulation, Cttee on Bank Affairs, Cttee on Bd Affairs; Exec.-in-Residence, Old Dominion Univ. 2014–15; mem. Bd of Dirs Wells Fargo & Co. 2015–, mem. Credit Cttee, Finance Cttee, Risk Cttee, Vice Chair. Wells Fargo & Co. 2016–12 Chair. (first woman) 2018–mem. Bd of Dirs American Bankers Asscn 1999–2006, Chair. (first woman) 2004–05; mem. Bd of Dirs Fed. Reserve Bank of Richmond; mem. Virginia Bankers Asscn (Pres. 1999). *Address:* Wells Fargo & Co., 420 Montgomery Street, San Francisco, CA 94104, USA (office). *Telephone:* (800) 869-3557 (office). *Website:* www.wellsfargo.com (office).

DUKE, Michael (Mike) Terry, BEng; American business executive; b. 1949; m. Susan Duke; one s. two d.; ed Georgia Inst. of Tech.; spent 23 years working for various retailers including Federated Dept Stores and May Dept Stores; joined Wal-Mart Inc. 1995, Sr Vice-Pres. of Logistics 1995–2000, Sr Vice-Pres. of Distribution and Exec. Vice-Pres. of Logistics 2000, Exec. Vice-Pres. of Admin 2000–03, Pres. Wal-Mart Stores USA 2003–05, Vice-Chair. and Head of Walmart International 2005–09, mem. Bd of Dirs Wal-Mart Stores, Inc. (now called Walmart) 2008–, Pres. and CEO 2009–14, Chair. Exec. Cttee of Bd of Dirs 2014–16; mem. Bd of Dirs The Consumer Goods Forum; mem. Exec. Bd Conservation International's Center for Environmental Leadership in Business, Exec. Cttee of Business Roundtable; mem. Bd of Advisors, Univ. of Arkansas, Advisory Bd Tsinghua Univ. School of Econs and Man., Beijing; mem. Nat. Acad. of Eng.

DUKES, Alan Martin, MA; Irish banker, consultant and fmr politician; b. 22 April 1945, Dublin; s. of James Dukes and Margaret Moran; m. Fionnuala Corcoran 1968; two d.; ed Scoil Colmcille and Colaiste Mhuire, Dublin and Univ. Coll., Dublin; Chief Econ., Irish Farmers Asscn 1967–72; Dir Irish Farmers Asscn, Brussels 1973–76; Personal Adviser to Commr of EEC 1977–80; TD (Fine Gael) for Kildare 1981–2002; Opposition Spokesperson on Agric. March–Dec. 1982; Minister of Agric. 1981–82, for Finance 1982–86, for Justice 1986–87; Leader and Pres. Fine Gael 1987–90; mem. Council of State 1987–90; Minister for Transport, Energy and Communications 1996–97; Opposition Spokesperson on Environment and Local Govt; Pres. Irish Council of the European Movt 1987–91, Chair. 1997–2000; Vice-Pres. Int. European Movt 1991–96; Adjunct Prof. of Public Admin, Man. Univ. of Limerick 1991; Dir-Gen. Inst. of European Affairs 2003–07; mem. Bd of Dirs Anglo Irish Bank 2008–, Chair. 2009–13; Chair. Irish Bank Resolution Corpn –2013; fmr Public Affairs Consultant, WHPR, Dublin; Vice-Pres. European People's Party 1987–96; Chair. Jt Oireachtas Cttee on Foreign Affairs 1995–96; judge, TG4 reality TV show Feirm Factor 2008–10; Officier, Légion d'honneur 2004; Commdr's Cross, Order of Merit (Poland) 2004. *Leisure interests:* reading, music, walking, horse riding, motor sport. *Address:* Tully West, Kildare, Co. Kildare, Ireland. *Telephone:* 87-6846274 (mobile). *E-mail:* alandukes@eircom.net.

ĐUKIĆ-DEJANOVIĆ, Slavica, MA, PhD; Serbian psychiatrist and politician; *Minister without Portfolio;* b. 4 July 1951, Rača Kragujevačka; ed Medical Faculty, Univ. of Belgrade; joined Medical Faculty, Univ. of Kragujevac 1982, currently Prof. and Assoc. Dean for Int. Collaboration; Dir KBC Kragujevac Hosp. 1995–2001; Dir Centrum Neuropsychiatrii, Kragujevac; Minister for the Family 2000–01; mem. Socijalistička partija Srbije (Socialist Party of Serbia) 1990–, Vice-Pres. 1996–97, 2002–; mem. Narodna skupština Republike Srbije (Nat. Ass.), Pres. 2008–12; Acting Pres. of Serbia 5 April–31 May 2012; Minister of Health 2012–14, Minister without Portfolio (with responsibility for Demography and Population Policy) 2016–; Vice-Pres. Asscn of Psychiatrists of Serbia. *Publications:* more than 160 articles published in medical journals. *Address:* Ministry without Portfolio for Demography and Population Policy, 11070 Belgrade, Bulevan Mijhala Pupina 2a, Serbia (office). *Telephone:* (11) 214038 (office). *Fax:* (11) 2145738 (office). *E-mail:* kabinet@mdpp.gov.rs (office); slavica1@eunet.rs (office). *Website:* www.mdpp.gov.rs (office).

DULAIMI, Saadoun ad-, PhD; Iraqi government official, psychologist and statistician; b. 1954, Ramadi; ed Univ. of Keele, UK; fmr army reserve officer; emigrated 1980s; has taught in Jordan and USA; returned to Iraq 2003; est. Centre for Research and Strategic Studies (polling firm) 2003; Minister of Defence 2005–06, Minister of Culture 2010–14, also Acting Minister of Defence 2011. *Address:* c/o Ministry of Culture, POB 624, Qaba bin Nafi Sq., Sadoun St, Baghdad, Iraq (office).

DULIĆ, Oliver, MD; Serbian physician and politician; b. 21 Jan. 1975, Belgrade; m. Andrea Dulić; ed Univ. of Belgrade; trained as orthopaedic surgeon, Belgrade; mem. Democratic Party (Demokratska Stranka) 1997–, Pres. Subotica br. 1997–2000, Vice-Pres. Vojvodina Prov. br. 2000–06, now mem. Exec. Cttee; mem. Narodna skupština Republike Srbije (Parl.) 2003–12 (resgnd), Speaker 2007–08; Minister of the Environment and Spatial Planning 2008–12; cleared of charges of abuse of office 2012; currently with Dept of Orthopaedic Surgery, Clinical Center of Vojvodina.

DULLOO, Madan Murlidhar, LLB, DCL, SC, HSC; Mauritian lawyer and politician; b. 20 Sept. 1949, Port Louis; s. of Balram Bholanath Dulloo and Belwantee Lutchmee Gangaram; m. Indira Priyadarshani Dookun; three c.; ed Univ. of London and Inns of Court School of Law, Middle Temple, London, UK, Univ. of Paris (Sorbonne), France; teacher 1970–71; lawyer 1976–86, 1994–2005; mem. Parl. 1976–2010; between 1986–94 served as Minister of Foreign Affairs and Emigration, Minister of Agric., Minister of Fisheries and Natural Resources, Minister of Justice and Attorney-Gen.; Minister of Foreign Affairs, Int. Trade and Co-operation 2005–08; fmr Leader, Mouvement Militant Socialiste Mauricien. *Leisure interests:* sports, yoga, religion, sun, sea, nature, anthropology. *Address:* Madan Dulloo Chambers, 211, Chancery House, Lislet Geoffroy Street, Port Louis, Mauritius (office).

DUMAS, Axel, BPhil, LLM; French business executive; *CEO, Hermès International SA;* b. 3 July 1970, Neuilly-sur-Seine; s. of Olivier Dumas and Michele Dumas; m. Elisabeth Franck; ed Sciences Po, Paris and Harvard Univ.; banking career with Paribas, now part of BNP Paribas, in Beijing and New York –1993; joined Hermès 1993, Commercial Dir for France, Head of Jewellery Dept before running leather goods div., Man. Dir of Operations, COO and Head of Operations & Sales, Hermès Int. SA 2011–13, Co-CEO June–Dec. 2013, CEO 2014–, CEO Hermes Logistik Gruppe Deutschland GmbH. *Address:* Hermès International SA, 24 rue du Faubourg Saint-Honoré, 75008 Paris, France (office). *Telephone:* 1-49-92-38-92 (office). *E-mail:* service.nl@hermes.com (office). *Website:* www.hermes.com (office).

DUMAS, Marlene, BA; Dutch (b. South African) artist; b. 1953, Cape Town, South Africa; ed Univ. of Cape Town; with Atelier '63, Haarlem, Netherlands 1976–78, Psychological Inst., Univ. of Amsterdam 1979–80; Dr hc (Rhodes Univ., South Africa) 2010, (Faculty of Humanities) 2011, (Univ. of Antwerp) Hon. DPhil (Univ. of Stellenbosch) 2012, Hon. DFA (Univ. of Cape Town) 2015; Sandberg Prize 1989, Thérèse van Duyl-Schwartze Prijs, Netherlands 1989, Coutts Contemporary Art Foundation Coutts Award 1998, David Roell Prize/Prince Bernhard Cultural Prize for Visual Arts 1998, Kunstpreis der Landeshauptstadt Düsseldorf 2007, Rolf Shock Prize in the Visual Arts 2011, Johannes Vermeer Award 2012, Hans Theo Richter Prize, Acad. of Saxon Arts, Dresden 2017. *Publication:* Marlene Dumas 1999, Forsaken 2012, The Image as Burden 2014, Sweet Nothings: Notes and Texts 2015. *Address:* c/o Frith Street Gallery, 17–18 Golden Square, London, W1F 9JJ, England (office). *E-mail:* info@frithstreetgallery.com (office). *Website:* www.frithstreetgallery.com (office); www.marlenedumas.nl.

DUMASY, Lise, DèsL; French academic; *President, University Grenoble-Alpes;* b. (Lise Queffélec), 18 June 1954, Taza, Morocco; d. of Marcel Queffélec and Paulette Haran; m. J.P. Dumasy; two s.; ed Ecole Normale Supérieure, Sèvres, Université Paris-Sorbonne-Paris IV; Visiting Asst, Princeton Univ., USA 1977–78; schoolteacher 1978–80; Research Engineer, CNRS 1980, seconded to Inst. de France 1984; teacher and researcher (Humboldt Foundation, Mannheim Univ. 1987–88; Sr Lecturer, Univ. Stendhal (Grenoble-III) then Prof. 1992–, Head of Dept of French Language, Literature and Civilization 1992–95, mem. Scientific Council 1997, Prin., Univ. Stendhal (Grenoble-III) 1999–2004, Pres. 2008–16, Pres. Univ. Grenoble-Alpes (following merger) 2016–; mem. Nat. Council for Higher Education and Research (CNESER) 2002–09, Nat. Council for Scientific Research (SNESUP) 2008–16; Officier, Ordre des Palmes académiques, Chevalier, Ordre nat, du Mérite. *Publications:* La querelle du roman-feuilleton 1999, Pamphlet, Utopie, Manifeste, XIX-XX (with C. Massol) 2001, Tocqueville, de la démocratie en Amérique, étude littéraire 2004, Stendhal, Balzac, Dumas: un récit romantique? (with C. Massol) 2007, Médecine, sciences de la vie et littérature en France et en Europe, de la Révolution à nos jours (three vols) 2012. *Leisure Interests:* music, reading, travel. *Address:* Office of the President, Université Grenoble-Alpes, 38040 Grenoble Cedex 9, France (office). *Telephone:* (4) 76-82-43-01 (office). *E-mail:* presidence@grenoble-alpes.fr (office). *Website:* www.univ-grenoble-alpes.fr (office).

DUNAWAY, (Dorothy) Faye; American actress; b. 14 Jan. 1941, Bascom, Fla; d. of John Dunaway and Grace Dunaway; m. 1st Peter Wolf 1974; m. 2nd Terry O'Neill 1981; one s.; ed Univ. of Florida and Boston Univ.; spent three years with Lincoln Center Repertory Co. in New York, appearing in A Man For All Seasons, After the Fall and Tartuffe; Off-Broadway in Hogan's Goat 1965; appeared at the Mark Taper Forum, LA in Old Times, as Blanche du Bois in A Streetcar Named Desire 1973, The Curse of an Aching Heart 1982. *Films include:* Hurry Sundown 1967, The Happening 1967, Bonnie and Clyde 1967, The Thomas Crown Affair 1968, A Place For Lovers 1969, The Arrangement 1969, Little Big Man 1970, Doc 1971, The Getaway 1972, Oklahoma Crude 1973, The Three Musketeers 1973, Chinatown 1974, Three Days of the Condor 1975, The Towering Inferno 1976, Voyage of the Damned 1976, Network (Acad. Award Best Actress) 1976, The Eyes of Laura Mars 1978, The Champ 1979, The First Deadly Sin 1981, Mommie Dearest 1981, The Wicked Lady 1982, Supergirl 1984, Barfly 1987, Burning Secret 1988, The Handmaid's Tale 1989, On a Moonlit Night 1989, Up to Date 1989, Scorchers 1991, Faithful 1991, Three Weeks in Jerusalem, The Arrowtooth Waltz 1991, Double Edge, Arizona Dream, The Temp, Dun Juan DeMarco 1995, Drunks, Dunston Checks In, Albino Alligator, The Chamber, Fanny Hill 1998, Love Lies Bleeding 1999, Joan of Arc 1999, The Thomas Crown Affair 1999, The Yards 2000, Stanley's Gig 2000, Yellow Bird 2001, Changing Hearts 2002, The Rules of Attraction 2002, Mid-Century 2002, The Calling 2002, Blind Horizon 2003, Last Goodbye 2004, El Padrino 2004, Jennifer's Shadow 2004, Ghosts Never Sleep 2005, Cut Off 2006, Love Hollywood Style 2006, Rain 2006, Cougar Club 2007, Say It in Russian 2007, The Gene Generation 2007, Flick 2008, La Rabbia 2008, The Seduction of Dr. Fugazzi 2009, The Bait 2009, 21 and a Wake-Up 2009, The Magic Stone 2009, The Bye Bye Man 2017, Inconceivable 2017, The American Connection 2017. *Television includes:* After the Fall 1974, The Disappearance of Aimee 1976, Hogan's Goat, Mommie Dearest 1981, Evita! – First Lady 1981, 13 at Dinner 1985, Beverly Hills Madame 1986, The Country Girl, Casanova, The Raspberry Ripple, Cold Sassy Tree, Silhouette, Rebecca, Gia 1998, Running Mates 2000, The Biographer 2002, Anonymous Rex 2004, Back When We Were Grownups 2004, Midnight Bayou (film) 2009, A Family Thanksgiving (film) 2010. *Publication:* Looking For Gatsby (autobiog., with Betsy Sharkey) 1995. *Address:* ICM Partners, 10250 Constellation Blvd, Los Angeles, CA 90067, USA. *Telephone:* (310) 550-4000. *Website:* www.icmpartners.com.

DUNAYEV, Arman G., PhD; Kazakhstani economist, banking executive and fmr government official; *Chairman, JSC Altyn Bank;* b. 1966; ed Kazakh State Univ., Moscow State Lomonosov Univ.; worked as consultant at NTO Service Centre, then as Sr Specialist and Head of Dept at office of Mayor of South Kazakhstan region; held exec. positions at KHK Astana Holdings and OJSC Bank Turan Alem; joined Ministry of Finance 2000, Vice-Minister of Finance 2001–04, Minister of Finance 2004–06; Chair. Regulation and Supervision of Financial Market and Financial Organizations Agency (FMSA) 2006–08, JSC Sustainable Development Fund Kazyna 2008; Chair. JSC Altyn Bank 2008–; Deputy Chair. of Man. Bd JSC Samruk-Kazyna National Welfare Fund 2008–11; Advisor to Chair. of JSC National Welfare Fund Samruk-Kazyna 2010–11; mem. Bd of Dirs JSC Halyk Bank 2013–; mem. Advisory Bd Tele2 LLP 2012–. *Address:* JSC Altyn Bank, 43, Dostyk Avenue, 050010 Almaty, Kazakhstan (office). *Telephone:* (727) 259-69-00 (office). *Website:* altynbank.kz (office).

DUNBAR, Adrian; British actor; b. 1 Aug. 1958, Enniskillen, Northern Ireland; m. Anna Nygh 1986; one d., one step s.; ed Guildhall School of Music and Drama, London; Hon. DLit (Ulster) 2009. *Films include:* Sky Bandits 1986, Unusual Ground Floor Conversion 1987, The Dawning 1988, A World Apart 1988, My Left Foot 1989, Dealers 1989, Hear My Song 1991 (also writer), Force of Duty 1992, The Playboys 1992, The Crying Game 1992, Pleasure 1994, Widows' Peak 1994, Innocent Lies 1995, Richard III 1995, The Near Room 1995, The General 1998, The Wedding Tackle 2000, Wild About Harry 2000, How Harry Became a Tree 2001, Shooters 2002, Triggerman 2002, The Measure of My Days 2003, Mickybo and Me 2004, Monkey's Blood (dir) 2004, Against Nature 2005, Eye of the Dolphin 2006, The Last Confession of Alexander Pearce 2008, The Act of God II 2009. *Stage appearances include:* Ourselves Alone (Royal Court Theatre) 1985, King Lear (Royal Court), Girl with a Pearl Earring (Theatre Royal Haymarket) 2008. *Television appearances include:* After You've Gone 1984, The Englishman's Wife 1990, Drowning in the Shallow End 1990, Children of the North 1991, Force of Duty 1992, A Statement of Affairs (mini-series) 1993, A Woman's Guide to Adultery 1993, Pleasure 1994, The Blue Boy 1994, Cruel Train 1995, Melissa (mini-series) 1997, The Jump 1998, The Officer from France 1998, Relative Strangers (mini-series) 1999, Tough Love (series) 2000, Murphy's Law: Manic Munday 2003, Suspicion 2003, The Quatermass Experiment 2005, Child of Mine 2005, Ashes to Ashes (series) 2009, Mo 2010, A Touch of Frost 2010, Line of Duty (series) 2012, 2014, 2016, 2017, A Touch of Cloth 2014, The Hollow Crown (mini-series) 2016.

DUNCAN, Andy, BSc; British broadcasting industry executive and business executive; *CEO, Camelot UK Lotteries Ltd;* b. 31 July 1962; ed Univ. of Manchester Inst. of Science and Tech.; joined Unilever in 1984, Chair. Van Den Bergh Foods Business Unit 1995–97, Van Den Bergh Foods Marketing Dir 1997–99, European Category Dir for Food and Beverages Div. and mem. Global Category Bd 1999–2001; Dir of Marketing and Communications, BBC 2001–03, Dir of Marketing, Communications and Audiences 2003–04, mem. Exec. Cttee BBC, Bd of Dirs BBC Commercial Holdings Ltd; CEO Channel 4 2004–09 (resgnd); CEO H.R. Owen PLC 2010; Man. Dir Camelot UK Lotteries Ltd 2011, CEO 2014–; Chair. Media Trust (charity) 2006–14, now Trustee; mem. Exec. Cttee World Lottery Asscn (WLA) and European Lotteries, Chair. WLA Corp. Social Responsibility Cttee; mem. Bd of Dirs HMV Group PLC 2009–13; Chair. Tea Council 1999; Grocer Magazine Overall Grand Prix Advertising Prize 1998, 1999, Marketer of the Year, Marketing Week Effectiveness Awards 2003, numerous IPA Effectiveness and other industry awards. *Address:* Camelot Group, Tolpits Lane, Watford, Herts., WD18 9RN, England (office). *Telephone:* (19) 2342-5000 (office). *Website:* www.camelotgroup.co.uk (office).

DUNCAN, Arne, BA; American school administrator and government official; b. 6 Nov. 1964, Chicago, Ill.; s. of Starkey Duncan and Sue Duncan (née Morton); m. Karen Duncan; two c.; ed Harvard Univ.; professional basketball player in Australia 1987–91; Dir Ariel Educ. Initiative, Chicago 1991–98; dir of magnet schools and Deputy Chief of Staff to CEO of Chicago Public Schools 1998–2001, CEO Chicago Public Schools 2001–08; US Sec. of Educ., Washington, DC 2009–15 (resgnd); mem. Bd of Dirs Ariel Educ. Initiative, Chicago Cares, The Children's Center, Golden Apple Foundation, Illinois Council Against Handgun Violence, Jobs for America's Graduates, Junior Achievement, Nat. Asscn of Basketball Coaches' Foundation, Renaissance Schools Fund, Scholarship Chicago, South Side YMCA; mem. Bd of Overseers, Harvard Univ.; mem. Visiting Cttee Harvard Univ. Grad. School of Educ., Univ. of Chicago School of Social Service Admin; Fellow, Leadership Greater Chicago 1995; mem. Aspen Inst. Henry Crown Fellowship Program 2002; Dr hc (Illinois Inst. of Tech.), (National-Louis Univ.); Hon. LLD (Lake Forest Coll.) 2003; Citizen of the Year, City Club of Chicago 2006. *Achievements include:* was Co-captain of Harvard Univ. basketball team and was named first team Academic All-American. *Address:* c/o Department of Education, 400 Maryland Avenue, SW, Washington, DC 20202, USA.

DUNCAN, Daniel Kablan; Côte d'Ivoirian politician; *Vice-President;* b. 1943, Ouelle; ed Inst. Commercial, Nancy and Inst. de Commerce Int. Paris; Ministry of Economy and Finance 1970; in-house training at IMF, Washington, DC 1973; joined Cen. Bank of W African States (BCEAO); with Caisse Nat. de Prévoyance Sociale; returned to BCEAO HQ, Dakar 1989; Minister Del. responsible for Econ., Finance and Planning, Office of Prime Minister 1990–93; Prime Minister 1993–99, also Minister of Economy, Finance and Planning, Minister of Planning and Industrial Devt; left country for Paris after 1999 coup led by Gen. Robert Guéï, returned to Côte d'Ivoire 2000; Minister of Foreign Affairs 2011–12; Prime Minister and Minister of the Economy, Finance and the Budget 2012–17; Vice-Pres. 2017–; mem. Parti démocratique de la Côte d'Ivoire—Rassemblement démocratique africain. *Address:* Office of the Vice President, 01 BP 1354, Abidjan 01, Côte d'Ivoire (office). *Telephone:* 20-22-02-22 (office). *Fax:* 20-21-14-25 (office). *Website:* www.presidence.ci (office).

DUNCAN, John Morris, BSc, PC; Canadian forester and politician; b. 19 Dec. 1948, Winnipeg; ed Univ. of British Columbia; worked in coastal forest industry, BC 1972–93; MP for Vancouver Island N 1993–2006, 2008–; Pacific Region Adviser to Minister of Fisheries and Oceans 2006–07, Parl. Sec. to Minister of Indian

Affairs and Northern Devt 2008–10, Minister of Indian Affairs (renamed Aboriginal Affairs May 2011) and Northern Devt, Federal Interlocutor for Métis and Non-Status Indians, and Minister of the Canadian Northern Econ. Devt Agency 2010–13, Minister of State and Chief Govt Whip 2013–15; mem. Reform Party 1993–2000, Canadian Reform Conservative Alliance 2000–03, Conservative Party of Canada 2003–. *Address:* Conservative Party of Canada, 130 Albert Street, Suite 1204, Ottawa, ON K1P 5G4, Canada (office). *Telephone:* (613) 755-2000 (office). *Fax:* (613) 755-2001 (office). *Website:* www.conservative.ca (office).

DUNCAN, John Stewart, OBE; British diplomatist; *Chairman, Falkland Island Association;* b. 17 April 1958; m. Anne Marie Duncan; one s. one d.; ed Wycliffe Coll., Keele Univ., Univ. of Paris (Sorbonne), France, NATO Defence Coll., Italy; joined FCO 1980, Scandinavia and Switzerland Desk 1980–82, Third Sec. (Chancery), Embassy in Paris 1982–84, Third Sec. (Aid, Famine Relief and Infrastructure Devt), Embassy in Khartoum 1985–88, Head of Section, Defence Sales, Export Licensing and Out of Area Defence Policy, FCO 1988, Head of Section, Missile Tech. Control Regime 1988–90, Asst Private Sec. to Minister for Africa and Overseas Devt, Overseas Devt Admin 1990–91, Chargé d'affaires, Embassy in Tirana 1992, Head of Section, UK Del. to NATO and WEU, Brussels 1993–96, Deputy Head, S Atlantic Dependant Territories and Antarctic Dept, FCO 1996–98, Deputy Head, Security Policy Dept 1998, UK Int. Affairs Adviser to Supreme Allied Commdr Europe (SACEUR) 1998–2001, Dir, UK Trade and Investment, Paris 2001–06, Amb. for Multilateral Arms Control and Disarmament and Perm. Rep. to Conf. on Disarmament, Geneva and New York 2006–11, Special Rep. to London Conference on Cyberspace 2011, Dir of Engagement and Communications, FCO 2012–13, Gov. British Virgin Islands 2014–17; Chair. Falkland Islands Asscn 2018–; Trustee, Nat. Army Museum 2017–; Distinguished Fellow, New Westminster Coll., British Columbia, Canada. *Address:* Falkland Island Association, Falkland House, 14 Broadway, London, SW1H 0BH, England (office). *Telephone:* (20) 3764-0824 (office). *Website:* www.fiassociation.com (office).

DUNCAN, Kirsty Ellen, PC, BA, PhD; Canadian medical geographer and politician; *Minister of Science;* b. 31 Oct. 1966; ed Univ. of Toronto, Univ. of Edinburgh, Scotland; taught meteorology, climatology and climate change, Univ. of Windsor 1993–2000; Assoc. Prof. of Health Studies, Univ. of Toronto, also fmr Research Dir, AIC Inst. of Corporate Citizenship, Rotman School of Man.; int. scientific expedition to Longyearbyen, Spitsbergen, to investigate the cause of the 1918 Spanish flu virus 1998; mem. House of Commons (Parl.) for Etobicoke North 2008–; Minister of Science 2015–; mem. Intergovernmental Panel on Climate Change (org.; mem. Advisory Bd for Pandemic Flu for Conf. Bd of Canada and Univ. of Toronto; mem. Liberal Party of Canada. *Publications:* Hunting the 1918 Flu: One Scientist's Search for a Killer Virus 2003, Environment and Health: Protecting our Common Future 2008. *Address:* Industry Canada, C. D. Howe Bldg, 11th Floor, East Tower, 235 Queen Street, Ottawa, ON K1A 0H5, Canada (office). *Telephone:* (613) 954-5031 (office). *Fax:* (613) 954-2340 (office). *E-mail:* info@ic.gc.ca (office). *Website:* www.ic.gc.ca (office); kirstyduncan.liberal.ca.

DUNCAN, Lindsay Vere, CBE; British actress; b. 7 Nov. 1950, Edinburgh, Scotland; m. Hilton McRae; one s.; ed King Edwards VI High School for Girls, Birmingham, Cen. School of Speech and Drama, London; worked in theatre before TV productions during 1980s; created role of La Marquise de Merteuil in RSC production of Les Liaisons Dangereuses in Stratford, London and New York. *Theatre includes:* Don Juan (Hampstead Theatre Club) 1976, The Script (Hampstead Theatre Club) 1976, The Ordeal of Gilbert Pinfold (Royal Exchange Theatre, Manchester) 1977 (then Round House Theatre, London 1979), Plenty (Nat. Theatre, London), Comings and Goings (Hampstead Theatre Club) 1978, Julius Caesar (Riverside Studios, London) 1980, Top Girls (Royal Court Theatre, London, then New York Shakespeare Festival, Public Theatre) 1982, Les liaisons dangereuses (RSC, Ambassadors' Theatre, London) 1986 (then Music Box Theatre, New York) 1987, Cat on a Hot Tin Roof (Nat. Theatre, London) 1988, The Cryptogram (Ambassadors' Theatre, London) 1994, A Midsummer Night's Dream (Royal Court Theatre, then Lunt-Fontanne Theatre, New York) 1996, Ashes to Ashes (Royal Court Theatre, then Roundabout Theatre Company, Gramercy Theatre, New York) 1999, The Celebration, and Rose, The Room (double-bill) (Almeida Theatre, London then Laguardia Drama Theatre, New York) 2000, Private Lives (Olivier Award, Tony Award) 2001, Mouth to Mouth (RSC Jerwood Theatre Downstairs, Royal Court Theatre, then Albery Theatre, London) 2001; appeared as Daphne, Present Laughter, as Geraldine, What the Butler Saw, as Gladys, The Skin of Our Teeth, as Lucy, The Rivals, as Sally, Zack, and as Viola, Twelfth Night, all at Royal Exchange Theatre; appeared in title role, Berenice, as Natalie, The Prince of Homburg, and as Ruth, The Homecoming, all at Royal Nat. Theatre, London; appeared as Helen of Troy, Troilus and Cressida, and as Mistress Ford, The Merry Wives of Windsor, both with RSC; appeared as title role, Hedda Gabler, and in Don Juan and Incidents at Tulse Hill, all at Hampstead Theatre Club; also appeared as Anne, The Deep Blue Sea, Cambridge Theatre Co., Cambridge, as Barbara Boyle, Three Hotels, Tricycle Theatre, London, as Belinda, The Provok'd Wife, Nat. Theatre, as Ronnie, Progress, Bush Theatre, London, and as Sylvia, The Recruiting Officer, Bristol Old Vic Theatre and Edinburgh Festival; also appeared in productions at Southwold and Crewe; appeared in Ibsen's John Gabriel Borkman, Abbey Theatre, Dublin 2010. *Films include:* Loose Connections 1983, Samson and Delilah 1985, Prick Up Your Ears 1987, Manifesto (aka A Night of Love) 1988, The Child Eater 1989, Body Parts 1991, City Hall 1996, A Midsummer Night's Dream 1996, An Ideal Husband 1999, Star Wars: Episode I – The Phantom Menace (voice) 1999, Expelling the Demon (voice) 1999, Mansfield Park 1999, AfterLife 2003, Under the Tuscan Sun 2003, The Queen of Sheba's Pearls 2004, Starter for 10 2006, Burlesque Fairytales 2008, Alice in Wonderland 2010, Le Week-End (British Independent Film Award for Best Actress) 2013. *Television includes:* Further Up Pompeii! 1975, The New Avengers 1977, ITV Playhouse – The Winkler 1979, Dick Turpin 1980, BBC 2 Playhouse – Grown-Ups 1980, Muck and Brass (two episodes) 1982, BBC Play of the Month – On Approval 1982, Reilly: Ace of Spies – After Moscow 1983, Play for Today – Rainy Day Women 1984, Travelling Man (six episodes) 1984, Dead Head (three episodes) 1986, Kit Curran (six episodes) 1986, Colin's Sandwich (two episodes) 1988–90, Traffik (five episodes) 1989, The Reflecting Skin (aka L'enfant miroir) 1990, TECX – Getting Personnel 1990, Redemption 1991, G.B.H. (six episodes) 1991, The Storyteller: Greek Myths – Theseus & the Minotaur 1991, A Year in Provence (12 episodes) 1993, The Rector's Wife 1994, Just William 1995, Jake's Progress (six episodes) 1995, The History of Tom Jones, a Foundling (three episodes) 1997, Get Real (seven episodes) 1998, Letters to a Street Child 1999, Shooting the Past 1999, Oliver Twist (four episodes) 1999, Dirty Tricks 2000, Hamilton Mattress (voice) 2001, Perfect Strangers (aka Almost Strangers, USA) 2001, Witness of Truth: The Railway Murders (narrator) 2001, Agatha Christie: Poirot – The Mystery of the Blue Train 2005, Spooks (aka MI-5, USA) (two episodes) 2005–06, Rome (18 episodes) 2005–07, Longford 2006, Frankenstein 2007, Criminal Justice 2008, Lost in Austen (two episodes) 2008, Margaret 2009, Doctor Who – The Waters of Mars 2009, Marple: The Mirror Crack'd from Side to Side 2009, Come Fly with Me (series narrator) 2010–11, The Sinking of the Laconia (mini-series) 2011, Christopher and His Kind (film) 2011, White Heat (series) 2012, Richard II 2012, Spy 2012, Wallander 2012, Count Arthur Strong 2013, Sherlock 2014, 2017, The Honourable Women 2014, Close to the Enemy 2016, Carnage 2017.

DUNCAN, Sam K.; American retail executive; b. 1951, Blytheville, Ark.; m. Sylvia Duncan; three d.; joined Albertson's Inc. 1969, positions including courtesy clerk, store man., Dir of Operations; Vice-Pres. Grocery Dept, Fred Meyer Inc. 1992–97, Exec. Vice-Pres. Food Div. 1997–98, Pres. 2001–02, Pres. Ralph's Supermarkets Div. 1998–2001, Pres. Fred Meyer Inc. 2001; Pres. and CEO Shopko Stores Inc. 2002–05; Chair. and CEO OfficeMax Inc. 2005–11; Pres. and CEO Supervalu Inc. 2013–16 (retd); mem. Bd of Dirs Nash-Finch Co.; Trustee, North Central Coll.

DUNCAN, Tim, BA; American professional basketball player (retd); b. 25 April 1976, St Croix, US Virgin Islands; s. of William Duncan and Ione Duncan; m. Amy Duncan 2001 (divorced 2013); two c.; ed Wake Forest Univ.; as a youth trained as swimmer; began playing organized basketball age 14; played college basketball at Wake Forest Univ. where he was selected All-American; selected by San Antonio Spurs in first round (first pick overall) in 1997 Nat. Basketball Asscn (NBA) draft, named NBA Finals Most Valuable Player 1999, 2003, 2005, 2014 as Spurs won NBA championship in those seasons, retd 2016; chosen for Team USA Team 1999, played 2004 Olympics (Athens) winning Bronze Medal; Founder and Pres. The Tim Duncan Foundation (educational charity) 2001–; Trustee, Children's Bereavement Center, Children's Center of San Antonio, Cancer Therapy and Research Center; John Wooden Award 1997, Naismith Coll. Player of the Year Award 1997, NBA Rookie of the Year 1998; NBA Most Valuable Player 2002, 2003; named to NBA All-Star Team 1997–98, 1999–2009, named to NBA All-Defensive Team 1997–2009, co-MVP NBA All-Star Game 2000; Home Team Community Service Award, Fannie Mae Foundation 2001, Sportsman of Year, Sports Illustrated 2003. *Leisure interests:* video games, swimming, collecting knives and swords. *Website:* www.slamduncan.com.

DUNCAN SMITH, Rt Hon. (George) Iain, PC; British politician; b. 9 April 1954, Edinburgh, Scotland; s. of W. G. G. Duncan Smith and Pamela Mary Duncan Smith (née Summers); m. Elizabeth Wynne Fremantle; two s. two d.; ed HMS Conway (Cadet School), Royal Mil. Acad. Sandhurst; served in Scots Guards 1975–81; Dir GEC (later Marconi) 1981–88, Bellwinch PLC 1988–89; Marketing and Devt Dir Jane's Defence Weekly, Jane's Fighting Ships 1989–92; Conservative Party cand. for Bradford W, gen. election 1987; Vice-Chair. Fulham Conservative Asscn 1991; MP for Chingford 1992–97, for Chingford and Woodford Green 1997–; mem. Select Cttee on Health 1994–95, on Standards and Privileges 1996–97; Vice-Chair. Conservative European Affairs Cttee 1996–97; Shadow Sec. of State for Social Security 1997–99, for Defence 1999–2001; Leader Conservative Party and Leader of the Opposition 2001–03; Sec. of State for Work and Pensions 2010–16 (resgnd); Founder and Chair. Centre for Social Justice 2004–10, Patron 2010–; mem. Bd of Dirs Alyte Ltd 2007–; Freeman of the City of London. *Publications:* The Devil's Tune 2003, pamphlets on social security, European and defence issues. *Leisure interests:* family, painting, fishing, cricket, tennis, shooting, opera, reading. *Address:* House of Commons, Westminster, London, SW1A 0AA; Parliamentary Association Office, 64A Station Road, Chingford, London, E4 7BE, England. *Telephone:* (20) 7219-2667 (Westminster); (20) 8524-4344 (Chingford). *Fax:* (20) 7219-4867 (Westminster); (20) 8523-9697 (Chingford). *E-mail:* alambridesl@parliament.uk (office). *Website:* www.iainduncansmith.org.

DUNDERDALE, Kathy; Canadian politician; b. Burin, Newfoundland; ed Memorial Univ. of Newfoundland; started public service career as town councillor, becoming Deputy Mayor of Burin; fmr Pres. Newfoundland and Labrador Fed. of Municipalities; fmr Dir Canadian Fed. of Municipalities; mem. House of Ass. (Prov. Parl.) for Virginia Waters 2003–, becoming Minister of Innovation, Trade and Rural Devt, also Minister Responsible for the Rural Secretariat 2003–06, Minister of Natural Resources and Minister Responsible for the Forestry and Agrifoods Agency 2006–10, also Minister Responsible for the Status of Women 2008–10, Deputy Premier 2008–10, Acting Premier Feb.–March 2010, Premier of Newfoundland and Labrador Dec. 2010–14; mem. Progressive Conservative Party (fmr Pres. Progressive Conservative Party of Newfoundland and Labrador). *Address:* House of Assembly, PO Box 8700, Saint John's, Newfoundland and Labrador, A1B 4J6, Canada (office). *E-mail:* ClerkHOA@gov.nl.ca (office). *Website:* www.assembly.nl.ca (office).

DUNFORD, Gen. Joseph F., Jr, MA; American army officer; *Chairman, Joint Chiefs of Staff;* b. 8 Dec. 1955, Boston, Mass; m. Ellen Dunford; one c.; ed St Michael's Coll., US Army War Coll., Ranger School, Amphibious Warfare School, Georgetown Univ., Fletcher School of Law and Diplomacy, Tufts Univ.; commissioned into US Marine Corps 1976, rank of 2nd Lt 1977; Platoon and Co. Commdr, 3rd Bn, 1st Marines 1978–81, Co. Commdr, 1st Bn, 9th Marines 1978–81, with Officer Assignment Br., US Marine Corps, Washington, DC 1982, Co. Commdr, L Co., 3rd Bn, 6th Marines 1985–87; Marine Officer Instructor, Coll. of Holy Cross, Mass 1988–91; mem. Commdt's Staff Group, later Sr Aide to Commdt, US Marine Corps, Washington, DC 1992–95; Regimental Exec. Officer, 6th Marines 1995–96, CO, 2nd Bn 6th Marines 1996–98; Exec. Asst to Vice-Chair., Global and Multilateral Affairs Div., Jt Staff, US Dept of Defense 1999–2001, CO, 5th Marine Regt, Div. Chief of Staff and Asst Div. Commdr, 1st Marine Div. 2001–05 (led 5th Marine Regt during 2003 invasion of Iraq); Dir, Operations Div., US Marine Corps 2005–07, Vice-Dir of Operations (J-3) 2007–08; rank of Lt-Gen. 2007; Deputy Commdt, Plans, Policies & Operations 2008–09; rank of Four-Star Gen. 2009; Commdg Gen., I Marine Expeditionary Force and Marine Forces Cen. Command 2009–10; Asst Commdt, US Marine Corps 2010–13; Commdr, US Forces Afghanistan (USFOR-A), Kabul, Afghanistan 2013–14, also Commdr, Int. Security

Assistance Force (ISAF), NATO, Kabul 2013–14, Commdt, US Marine Corps 2014–; Chair. Jt Chiefs of Staff 2015–; numerous mil. awards including Defense Superior Service Medal, Legion of Merit, Navy Sea Service Deployment Ribbon, Global War on Terrorism Service Medal. *Address:* Headquarters, US Marine Corps, 3000 Marine Corps, Pentagon, Washington, DC 20350-3000, USA (office). *Telephone:* (703) 614-2500 (office). *Website:* www.hqmc.marines.mil (office).

DUNHAM, Archie W., BEng, MBA; American business executive (retd); b. 1938; m. Linda Dunham; three c.; ed Univ. of Oklahoma; served in US Marine Corps 1960–64; Pres. and CEO Conoco Inc. 1996–2002, Chair. 1999–2002, Chair. ConocoPhillips (following merger between Conoco and Phillips) 2002–04 (retd); Chair. Chesapeake Energy Corpn 2012–15, Chair. Emer. 2015–; fmr Chair. Nat. Asscn of Mfrs, United States Energy Asscn, National Petroleum Council; mem. Bd of Dirs Union Pacific Corpn 2000–14, Louisiana-Pacific Corpn 1996–2014, Phelps Dodge Corpn 1998–2007; fmr mem. Bd of Dirs American Petroleum Inst., Energy Inst. of the Americas, Nat. Bd, Smithsonian Inst., US–Russia Business Council, Greater Houston Partnership, Memorial Hermann Healthcare System; Chair. and fmr Pres. Houston Grand Opera; mem. Bretton Woods Cttee, Business Round Table, The Business Council; Gov. The Houston Forum; mem. Bd of Visitors M.D. Anderson Cancer Center; mem. Texas Gov.'s Business Council, Comm. on Nat. Energy Policy, Nat. Infrastructure Advisory Council, Marine Corps Heritage Foundation; Trustee, George Bush Presidential Library Foundation, Houston Symphony, United Way of the Texas Gulf Coast; mem. Americas Advisory Bd, DeutscheBank Trust Co.; Dr hc (Oklahoma) 1999; B'nai B'rith Int. Achievement Award 2000, Ellis Island Medal of Honor 2001, Horatio Alger Award 2001, John Rogers Award 2005, Spirit of Excellence Award, Houston Baptist Univ. 2011. *Address:* c/o Chesapeake Energy Corporation, PO Box 18496, Oklahoma City, OK 73154-0496, USA.

DUNKEL, Gunter; German economist and banker; b. 1953, Waiblingen; ed Vienna Univ. of Econs and Business, Univ. of Vienna; Credit Division Man. Asst, GiroCredit, Vienna 1978; fmrly with McKinsey; joined Bayerische Hypotheken- und Wechselbank, Munich 1983 as Head of Retail Banking Planning Dept and Project Man. for implementation of a strategic restructuring, head of branch area Munich-Pasing 1987–90, Exec. Vice-Pres. Gen. Man. of New York branch 1990–95, returned to Germany 1995 as Head of Corp. Customers and Banks; apptd mem. Bd of Man. Norddeutsche Landesbank (NORD/LB) 1997, Deputy Chair. 2007–09, Chair. and CEO 2009–16; Chair. Supervisory Bd Deutsche Hypothekenbank AG, NORD/LB Luxembourg SA, Covered Bond Bank, Luxemburg, NORD/LB Vermögensmanagement Luxembourg SA; mem. Supervisory Bd Continental AG, Bremer Landesbank Kreditanstalt Oldenburg Girozentrale; mem. Bd of Dirs German Savings Banks Asscn (Deutscher Sparkassen- und Giroverband, DSGV), Lower Saxony Savings Bank Asscn (SVN); Pres. Bundesverband Öffentlicher Banken Deutschlands (Asscn of German Public Sector); Chair. NORD/LB Culture Foundation; Vice-Pres. Lower Saxony Foundation; British Hon. Consul 2010–.

DUNKLEY, Michael H., JP, BA; Bermudian business executive and politician; b. 18 June 1958; s. of Henry 'Bill' Dunkley and Marye Lee Dunkley; m. Pamela Dunkley; two d.; ed Trinity Coll. School, George Washington Univ., Univ. of Richmond, USA; mem. numerous govt bds including Hosp. Insurance Comm., Bd of Agric., Immigration Bd –1997; mem. House of Ass. for Devonshire East 1997–2011, Senator 2011–14, several shadow ministerial portfolios including fmr Shadow Minister of Health, Shadow Minister for Public Safety, fmr Opposition Leader in Senate; Minister of Public Safety 2012–13, of Nat. Security 2013–14; Deputy Premier 2012–14, Premier 2014–17; Vice-Pres. and CEO Dunkley's Dairy (milk processing plant); Vice-Pres. Island Properties Ltd (property man. co.), Pres. Dunkley's Management Holdings Ltd (man. consultant co.); Pres. Mid Ocean Club 1999–2005, 2008–11, currently hon. mem.; mem. One Bermuda Alliance, Deputy Leader –2014, Leader 2014–17. *Address:* Dunkley's Ltd, PO Box DV 295, Devonshire, DV BX, Bermuda (office). *Website:* www.dunkleysdairy.com (office).

DUNLEAVY, Michael (Mike) J., BA, MEd; American politician; *Governor of Alaska;* b. 5 May 1961, Scranton, Pa; m. Rose Dunleavy; three c.; ed Misericordia Univ., Univ. of Alaska Fairbanks; fmr mem. Bd Matanuska-Susitna Borough, later Pres. of the Bd; mem. Senate, Alaska 2013–18; Gov. of Alaska 2018–; Republican. *Address:* Office of the Governor, 3rd Floor, State Capitol, Juneau, AK 99811 (office); Governor's Mansion, 716 Calhoun Avenue, Juneau, AK 99801, USA (home). *Telephone:* (907) 465-3500 (office). *Fax:* (907) 465-3532 (office). *Website:* gov .alaska.gov (office); alaska.gov (office).

DUNLOP, Frank, CBE, BA; British theatre director and festival director; b. 15 Feb. 1927, Leeds, Yorks., England; s. of Charles Norman Dunlop and Mary Aaron; ed Kibworth Beauchamp Grammar School, Univ. Coll. London, Old Vic School, London; served in RAF 1946–49; Founder and Dir Piccolo Theatre Co. 1954–2016; Assoc. Dir Bristol Old Vic 1955–59; theatre dir, West End of London and Mermaid Theatre 1959–; theatre dir, Brussels, including Theatre Nat. Belge 1959–; Dir Nottingham Playhouse 1961–64; Founding Dir Pop Theatre 1966–; Assoc. Dir and Admin. Nat. Theatre, London 1967–71; Founder and Dir Young Vic Theatre 1970–78, 1980–83; theatre dir in New York and Los Angeles 1974–; Dir Edinburgh Festival 1983–91; Fellow, Univ. Coll., London 1979; Hon. DUniv (Heriot-Watt) 1989, (Edin.) 1990. *Publication:* Scapino 1975. *Leisure interests:* work and doing nothing. *Address:* Piccolo Theatre Co., 13 Choumert Square, London, SE15 4RE, England (office); c/o Miracle Management, 250 West 57th Street, Suite 1332, New York, NY 10107, USA (office). *Telephone:* (212) 265-8787 (office). *Fax:* (212) 265-8873 (office). *E-mail:* mirmgt@aol.com (office).

DUNN, Brian J.; American business executive; *Chairman, Upsie LLC;* joined Best Buy Co. Inc. 1985, held positions as Store Man., Dist Man., Regional Man., Regional Vice-Pres. and Sr Vice-Pres., Exec. Vice-Pres. of Retail Sales 2002–04, Pres. of Retail Sales for N America 2004–06, Pres. and COO Best Buy Co. Inc. 2006–09, CEO 2009–12 (resgnd); Prin. The Dunn Group 2013–; Chair. Upsie LLC 2015–; mem. Bd of Dirs Grey Cloak Tech 2015–; fmr mem. Bd of Dirs Dick's Sporting Goods Inc., Rock and Roll Hall of Fame. *Address:* Upsie LLC, Suite 5500, 90 South 7th Street, Minneapolis, MN 55402, USA (office). *Telephone:* (612) 294-2754 (office). *E-mail:* media@upsie.com (office). *Website:* www.upsie.com (office).

DUNN, Douglas Eaglesham, OBE, BA, FRSL; Scottish poet and academic; *Honorary Professor, University of St Andrews;* b. 23 Oct. 1942, Inchinnan; s. of William D. Dunn and Margaret McGowan; m. 1st Lesley B. Wallace 1964 (died 1981); m. 2nd Lesley Jane Bathgate 1985; one s. one d.; ed Univ. of Hull; full-time writer 1971–91; Writer-in-Residence, Duncan of Jordanstone Coll. of Art and Dundee Dist Libraries 1986–88; Fellow in Creative Writing, Univ. of St Andrews 1989–91, Prof. 1991–2008, Head School of English 1994–99, Dir St Andrews Scottish Studies Inst. 1992, now Hon. Prof.; Hon. Visiting Prof., Dundee Univ. 1987–89; mem. Scottish PEN; Hon. Fellow, Humberside Coll. 1987; Hon. LLD (Dundee) 1987; Hon. DLitt (Hull) 1995, (St Andrews); Cholmondeley Award 1989. *Publications include:* Terry Street (Somerset Maugham Award 1972) 1969, The Happier Life 1972, New Poems 1972–73 (ed.) 1973, Love or Nothing (Faber Memorial Prize 1976) 1974, A Choice of Byron's Verse (ed.) 1974, Two Decades of Irish Writing (criticism) 1975, The Poetry of Scotland (ed.) 1979, Barbarians 1979, St Kilda's Parliament (Hawthornden Prize 1982) 1981, Europa's Lover 1982, A Rumoured City: New Poets from Hull (ed.) 1982, To Build a Bridge: A Celebration of Humberside in Verse (ed.) 1982, Elegies (Whitbread Poetry Award and Whitbread Book of the Year 1986) 1985, Secret Villages (short stories) 1985, Selected Poems 1986, Northlight 1988, New and Selected Poems 1989, Poll Tax: The Fiscal Fake 1990, Andromache 1990, The Essential Browning (ed.) 1990, Scotland. An Anthology (ed.) 1991, Faber Book of Twentieth Century Scottish Poetry (ed.) 1992, Dante's Drum-Kit 1993, Boyfriends and Girlfriends (short stories) 1995, Oxford Book of Scottish Short Stories (ed.) 1995, The Donkey's Ears, The Year's Afternoon 2000, 20th Century Scottish Poems (ed.) 2000, The Faber Browning 2004, The Noise of a Fly 2017. *Leisure interests:* playing the clarinet and saxophone, listening to jazz, gardening, philately. *Address:* School of English, Castle House, The University of St Andrews, St Andrews, Fife, KY16 9AL, Scotland (office). *Telephone:* (1334) 462666 (office). *Fax:* (1334) 462655 (office). *E-mail:* ded@st-andrews.ac.uk (office). *Website:* www.st-andrews.ac.uk/~www_se (office).

DUNN, John Montfort, BA, FBA, FSA, AcSS; British political theorist and academic; *Professor Emeritus of Political Theory, University of Cambridge;* b. 9 Sept. 1940, Fulmer; s. of Brig. Henry G. M. Dunn and Catherine M. Kinloch; m. 1st Susan D. Fyvel 1965; m. 2nd Judith F. Bernal 1971; m. 3rd Ruth Ginette Scurr 1997; two s. (one deceased) two d.; ed Winchester Coll., Millfield School, King's Coll., Cambridge and Harvard Univ., USA; Official Fellow in History, Jesus Coll., Cambridge 1965–66; Fellow, King's Coll., Cambridge 1966–, Coll. Lecturer, Dir of Studies in History 1966–72; Lecturer in Political Science, Univ. of Cambridge 1972–77, Reader in Politics 1977–87, Prof. of Political Theory 1987–2007, Prof. Emer. 2007–; Visiting Lecturer, Univ. of Ghana 1968–69; Chair. Section P. (Political Studies), British Acad. 1994–97, Bd of Consultants, Kim Dae-Jung Peace Foundation for the Asia-Pacific Region 1994–; Distinguished Visiting Prof., Tulane Univ., Univ. of Minnesota, Yale Univ.; mem. Council of British Acad. 2004–07; Hon. Foreign mem. American Acad. of Arts and Sciences 1991. *Publications include:* The Political Thought of John Locke 1969, Modern Revolutions 1972, Dependence and Opportunity (with A. F. Robertson) 1973, Western Political Theory in the Face of the Future 1979, Political Obligation in its Historical Context 1980, Locke 1984, The Politics of Socialism 1984, Rethinking Modern Political Theory 1985, The Economic Limits to Modern Politics (ed.) 1990, Interpreting Political Responsibility 1990, Storia delle dottrine politiche 1992, Democracy: The Unfinished Journey (ed.) 1992, Contemporary Crisis of the Nation State? (ed.) 1994, The History of Political Theory 1995, Great Political Thinkers (21 vols, co-ed.) 1997, The Cunning of Unreason 2000, Pensare la Politica 2002, Locke: A Very Short Introduction 2003, Setting the People Free: The Story of Democracy 2005, Exploring Utopian Futures of Politics (with Inwon Choue and John Ikenberry) 2008. *Leisure interests:* watching birds and animals, opera, travel. *Address:* The Merchant's House, 31 Station Road, Swavesey, Cambridge, CB4 5QJ, England (home). *Telephone:* (1954) 231451 (home).

DUNN, Baroness (Life Peer), cr. 1990, of Hong Kong Island in Hong Kong and of Knightsbridge in the Royal Borough of Kensington and Chelsea; **Lydia Selina Dunn;** British business executive; *Executive Director, John Swire & Sons Ltd;* b. 29 Feb. 1940; d. of Yenchuen Yeh Dunn and Chen Yin Chu; m. Michael David Thomas, CMG, QC 1988; ed St Paul's Convent School, Coll. of Holy Names, Oakland, Calif., USA and Univ. of California, Berkeley; Exec. Dir John Swire & Sons Ltd 1996–; Dir John Swire & Sons (HK) Ltd 1978–2003, Swire Pacific Ltd 1981–, Cathay Pacific Airways Ltd 1985–97 (Adviser to Bd 1997–2002), Volvo 1991–93 (mem. Int. Advisory Bd 1985–91), Christie's Int. PLC 1996–98, Christie's Fine Art 1998–2000, Marconi PLC (fmrly GEC) 1997–2002; Deputy Chair. Hong Kong & Shanghai Banking Corpn 1992–96 (Dir 1981–96), HSBC Holdings PLC (fmrly Hong Kong and Shanghai Banking Corpn) 1992–2008 (Dir 1990–2008); mem. Hong Kong Legis. Council 1976–88 (Sr mem. 1985–88); mem. Hong Kong Exec. Council 1982–95 (Sr mem. 1988–95); Chair. Lord Wilson Heritage Trust 1993–95; mem. Hong Kong/Japan Business Co-operation Cttee 1983–95, Chair. 1988–95; mem. Hong Kong/US Econ. Co-operation Cttee 1984–93; Chair. Hong Kong Trade Devt Council 1983–91; Pres. The Hong Kong LEP Trust 1993–; mem. Hong Kong Asscn (Chair. 2001–), Confucius Inst. for Business, London 2006–, Asia Task Force 2007–10, Advisory Bd Christie's Greater China 2009–; Hon. Fellow, London Business School 2000; Hon. LLD (Chinese Univ. of Hong Kong) 1984, (Univ. of Hong Kong) 1991, (Univ. of BC, Canada) 1991, (Leeds) 1994; Hon. DSc (Buckingham) 1995; Prime Minister of Japan's Trade Award 1987, US Sec. of Commerce's Award to Peace and Commerce 1988. *Publication:* In the Kingdom of the Blind 1983. *Leisure interests:* study of antiques, theatre, music, opera, ballet. *Address:* John Swire & Sons Ltd, Swire House, 59 Buckingham Gate, London, SW1E 6AJ, England (office). *Telephone:* (20) 7834-7717 (office). *Fax:* (20) 7630-0380 (office). *Website:* www.swire.com (office).

DUNNING, Thom H. Jr, BS, PhD; American chemist and academic; *Affiliate Professor of Chemistry, University of Washington, Seattle;* b. 3 Aug. 1943, Jeffersonville, Ind.; ed Univ. of Missouri, California Inst. of Tech.; Research Fellow, Battelle Memorial Inst., Columbus, Ohio 1970–71; Scientist III, Jet Propulsion Lab. 1971; Research Fellow, Calif. Inst. of Tech. 1971–73; Staff Mem., Laser Theory Group, Los Alamos Nat. Lab. 1973–78, Assoc. Group Leader 1975–76; Sr Scientist, Argonne Nat. Lab. 1978–89, Group Leader, Theoretical and Computational Chemistry Group 1978–79; Visiting Prof., Univ. of Colo 1989; Assoc. Dir Pacific Northwest Nat. Lab. 1989–94, Dir 1994–97, Battelle Fellow 1997–2001; Adjunct Prof., Washington State Univ. 1990–2001; Winslow Fellow, Univ. of Melbourne, Australia 1996; Asst Dir for Scientific Simulation, Office of Science, Washington, DC 1999–2001; Prof. of Chem., Univ. of North Carolina

2001–02; Vice-Pres., High Performance Computing and Communications Div., MCNC Research 2001–02; Distinguished Scientist, Oak Ridge Nat. Lab., Computer Science and Math. Div. 2002–; Distinguished Prof. of Chem., Univ. of Tenn. 2002–04, Dir Univ. of Tenn.–Oak Ridge Nat. Lab. Jt Inst. for Computational Sciences 2002–04; joined Faculty, Univ. of Illinois 2005, Distinguished Chair. for Research Excellence in Chem., Dir National Center for Super Computing Applications, now Prof. Emer.; currently Affiliate Prof. of Chem., Univ. of Washington, Seattle, Co-Dir Northwest Inst. for Advanced Computing; mem. Editorial Bd Journal of Chemical Physics 1998–2001; mem. numerous advisory cttees; mem. American Physical Soc. (Fellow 1992–), AAAS (Fellow 1992–), ACS, Int. Acad. of Quantum Molecular Science; E. O. Lawrence Award in Chem. 1996, Distinguished Assoc. Award, Office of Science, US Dept of Energy 2001, ACS Award for Computers in Chemical and Pharmaceutical Research 2011. *Address:* Department of Chemistry, University of Washington, Box 351700, Bagley Hall 461, Seattle, WA 98195-1700, USA (office). *Telephone:* (206) 616-1439 (office). *E-mail:* thdjr@uw.edu (office). *Website:* www.depts.washington.edu/chem (office).

DUNST, Kirsten Caroline; American actress; b. 30 April 1982, Point Pleasant, New Jersey; d. of Klaus Dunst and Inez Dunst; ed Notre Dame High School; began career aged four as model, Elite agency; first roles in TV commercials; has appeared in more than 40 films and 10 TV guest appearances; Best Female Performance (MTV Movie Awards) 2003, Best Int. Actress (British Empire Awards) 2003, Female Star of the Year (Show West Awards) 2007. *Television includes:* Sisters 1993, ER 1996–97, Tower of Terror 1997, Stories from my Childhood 1998, The Devil's Arithmetic 1999, Fargo 2015. *Films include:* The Bonfire of the Vanities 1990, High Strung 1991, Interview with the Vampire 1994 (MTV Award for Best Breakthrough Performance, Saturn Award for Best Young Actress), Little Women 1994, Jumanji 1995, Mother Night 1996, Wag the Dog 1997, Small Soldiers 1998, Strike! 1998, The Virgin Suicides 1999, Drop Dead Gorgeous 1999, Luckytown Blues 2000, Bring It On 2000, Crazy/Beautiful 2001, The Cat's Meow 2001, Spider-Man 2002, Mona Lisa Smile 2003, Levity 2003, Eternal Sunshine of the Spotless Mind 2004, Spider-Man 2 2004, Wimbledon 2004, Elizabethstown 2005, Marie Antoinette 2006, Spider-Man 3 2007, How to Lose Friends & Alienate People 2008, All Good Things 2010, Melancholia (Best Actress, Cannes Film Festival 2011, National Society of Film Critics Award for Best Actress) 2011, Bachelorette 2012, On the Road 2012, Upside Down 2012, Random Acts of Violence 2013, Anchorman 2: The Legend Continues 2013, The Two Faces of January 2014. *TV appearances include:* Sisters 1991, Star Trek: The Next Generation 1993, ER (several episodes) 1996, The Outer Limits 1997, Stories From My Childhood 1998, Portlandia 2014, Cosmos: A SpaceTime Odyssey (documentary) 2014. *Address:* c/o United Talent Agency, 9336 Civic Center Drive, Beverly Hills, CA 90210, USA (office). *Website:* www.unitedtalent.com (office).

DUNWOODY, (Thomas) Richard, MBE; British business executive and fmr professional jockey; b. 18 Jan. 1964, Belfast, Northern Ireland; s. of George Dunwoody and Gillian Dunwoody (née Thrale); m. (divorced); ed Rendcomb Coll.; rode winner of Grand Nat. (West Tip) 1986, (Minnehoma) 1994, Cheltenham Gold Cup (Charter Party) 1988, Champion Hurdle (Kribensis) 1990; Champion Nat. Hunt Jockey 1992–93, 1993–94, 1994–95; at retirement in 1999 held record for most wins (1,699, record later broken); Group Man. Partner, Dunwoody Sports Marketing 2002; Founder Richard Dunwoody Racing Assocs Ltd 2004; Nat. Hunt Jockey of the Year 1990, 1992–95, Champion of Champions 2001. *Achievements include:* finished second in team race to magnetic North Pole; with Doug Stoup, the first to reach South Pole via route originally attempted by Sir Ernest Henry Shackleton. *Publications include:* Hell For Leather (with Marcus Armytage) 1993, Dual (with Sean Magee) 1994, Hands and Heels (with Marcus Armytage) 1997, Obsessed 2000, Method in My Madness 2009. *Leisure interests:* motor sport, rugby, football, running. *Address:* c/o Tipster Platforms, PO Box 327, Hereford, HR1 9LF, England. *E-mail:* richard.d@du-mc.co.uk. *Website:* www.richarddunwoody.co.uk.

DUPLAT, Jean-Louis; Belgian lawyer, judge and business executive; *Chairman, Portolani NV;* b. 30 May 1937; ed Univ. of Namur, Catholic Univ. of Louvain; practised law in Brussels; apptd First Deputy Prosecutor 1974; Pres. Tribunal de Commerce 1978–89; Chair. Belgian Banking and Finance Comm. 1989–2000, Hon. Chair. 2000–; Sr Adviser, Ernst & Young Special Business Services 2001–; Chair. Aedifica NV –2014, Portolani NV; Chair. Vooruitzicht SA –2005; mem. Bd of Dirs Omega Pharma, Brantano NV; mem. Industry Expert Cttee Bencis Capital Pnrs; Pres. Child Focus 2007–; apptd Prof., Faculty of Law, Univ. of Namur 2000, now Prof. Emer.; Hon. Pres., Banque Bruxelles Lambert, Hon. Chair. Banking, Finance and Insurance Comm. (CBFA). *Address:* Portolani NV, Burburestraat 6, 2000 Antwerp, Belgium (office). *Website:* www.portolani.be (office).

DUPONT, Philippe, MBA; French business executive; b. 18 April 1951, Versailles; ed Lycée Hoche, Versailles, School Vendôme, Paris, Univ. of Paris-Dauphine; Head of Max Smith & Co. 1981–99; Chair. Advisory Cttee for Trade in Cereals and Feed (COCERAL) 1988–91, mem. Advisory Cttee for Cereals, Brussels 1988–94; mem. Bd of Dirs Banque populaire de la région Ouest de Paris 1983, Chair. (non-exec.) 1988–91, Vice-Pres. 1995–99, Vice-Pres. Caisse Centrale des Banques Populaires 1995–99, apptd Chair. Groupe Banque Populaire 1999, mem. Supervisory Bd Groupe BPCE (Banque Populaire Caisse d'Epargne, following merger of Banque Fédérale des Banques Populaires and Caisse Nationale des Caisses d'Epargne) 2008–11, Chair. 2008–11; Pres. Fédération bancaire française (French Banking Fed.) 2003–04; Sr Vice-Pres. French Asscn of Credit Insts and Investment Firms (Asscn française des établissements de crédit et des entreprises d'investissement—AFECEI); fmr mem. Supervisory Bd Fonds de garantie des dépôts (Fund Deposit Guarantee Bd), Conseil nat. du crédit et du titre (Nat. Council of Credit and Securities); Chevalier, Légion d'honneur. *Address:* c/o Groupe BPCE, 50 avenue Pierre Mendès France, 75201 Paris Cedex 13, France. *E-mail:* info@bpce.fr.

DUPUIS, Russell Dean, BS, MS, PhD; American electrical engineer and academic; *Steve W. Chaddick Endowed Chair in Electro-optics, Georgia Institute of Technology;* b. 1947; ed Univ. of Illinois, Urbana-Champaign; worked at Texas Instruments 1973–75; at Rockwell International 1975–79; at AT&T Bell Laboratories 1979–89; Chaired Prof., Univ. of Texas, Austin 1989–2003; Steve W. Chaddick Endowed Chair in Electro-optics, School of Electrical and Computer Eng, Georgia Inst. of Tech. 2003–, also Georgia Research Alliance Eminent Scholar; mem. Nat. Acad. of Eng 1989; Fellow, IEEE 1986, Optical Soc. of America 2000; IEEE Morris N. Liebmann Memorial Award 1985, Distinguished Mem. of the Tech. Staff, AT&T Bell Labs 1986, Young Scientist Award, Gallium Arsenide and Related Compounds Conf. 1986, Distinguished Alumnus Award, Dept of Electrical and Computer Eng, Univ. of Illinois, Urbana-Champaign 1987, IEEE/LEOS Award for Eng Achievement 1995, Alumni Loyalty Award, Univ. of Illinois, Urbana-Champaign 1997, Licensed Professional Engineer, The State of Texas 2001, Nat. Medal of Tech. Laureate 2002, Distinguished Alumnus Award, Coll. of Eng, Univ. of Illinois, Urbana-Champaign 2004, John Bardeen Award, The Minerals, Metals and Materials Soc. 2004, IEEE Edison Medal 2007, Charles Stark Draper Prize, Nat. Acad. of Eng (co-recipient) 2015. *Publications:* numerous papers in professional journals. *Address:* Room BH 201, School of Electrical and Computer Engineering, Van Leer Electrical Engineering Building, Georgia Institute of Technology, 777 Atlantic Drive NW, Atlanta, GA 30332-0250, USA (office). *Telephone:* (404) 385-6094 (office). *Fax:* (404) 385-6096 (office). *E-mail:* dupuis@gatech.edu (office). *Website:* www.mse.gatech.edu/faculty/dupuis (office).

DUPUY, Albert, LenD; French diplomatist and government official (retd); b. 1 Feb. 1947, Alicante, Spain; began career as academic inspector 1972–73; various civil service positions, including Préfecture Attaché 1973, Sr Attaché 1981, Head of Cabinet, Regional Commr, Nièvre Département 1982–83, Deputy Commr, Lesparre–Médoc 1983–84, Head of Cabinet, Minister of Foreign Affairs 1984–85, Sec.-Gen., Haute–Corse Département 1985–86, Lot Préfecture 1986–87; Councillor, Admin. Tribunal, Montpellier 1989–91; Sub-Prefect, Dreux 1991–94; Sec.-Gen., Haute–Savoie Préfecture 1994–95; Prefect, Pointe-à-Pitre, Guadeloupe 1998–2000; Sec.-Gen., Gironde Préfecture 2000–05; Prefect, St Pierre and Miquelon 2005–06, Vosges Département 2007–08, Isère Département 2008–10; High Commr, New Caledonia 2010–13; Chevalier, Légion d'honneur, Chevalier, Ordre Nat. du Mérite. *Address:* c/o Haut-commissariat de la République en Nouvelle-Calédonie, 1 ave du Maréchal Foch, BP C5, 98844 Nouméa Cedex, New Caledonia (office). *Telephone:* 266300 (office). *Fax:* 272828 (office).

DUQUE MÁRQUEZ, Iván, LLM; Colombian lawyer and politician; *President;* b. 1 Aug. 1976, Bogotá; s. of Iván Duque Escobar and Juliana Márquez Tono; m. María Juliana Ruiz; three c.; ed Sergio Arboleda Univ., American Univ., Georgetown Univ.; Consultant, Andean Devt Corpn (CAF) 1999; Sr Advisor to Exec. Directorate for Colombia, Peru and Ecuador, IDB 2001–13; fmr Advisor, Ministry of Finance; Advisor to UN for resolution of Gaza Flotilla Incident 2010–11; mem. Senate (upper house of parl.) (Centro Democrático) 2014–18; Centro Democrático (CD) cand. in 2018 presidential election; Pres. 2018–. *Publications include:* Pecados Monetarios 2007, Machiavelli in Colombia 2010, La Economía Naranja (co–author) 2013, Efecto Naranja 2015, IndignAcción (co-author) 2017, The Future is in the Centre 2018. *Address:* Office of the President, Palacio de Nariño, Carrera 8, No 7-26, Bogotá DC, Colombia (office). *Telephone:* (1) 562-9300 (office); (1) 094-8952. *Fax:* (1) 596-0631 (office). *Website:* www.presidencia.gov.co (office); www.ivanduque.com. *E-mail:* prensa@ivanduque.com.

DUQUESNE, Jacques Henri Louis, LenD; French journalist and writer; b. 18 March 1930, Dunkerque; s. of Louis Duquesne and Madeleine Chevalier; m. Edith Dubois 1954; one s. one d.; ed Coll. Jean-Bart, Dunkerque, Faculté de Droit, Paris, Institut d'Études Politiques, Paris; reporter, La Croix 1957–64; Deputy Dir Panorama Chrétien 1964–70, head of investigations 1967; Asst Ed.-in-Chief, L'Express 1970–71; Co-founder and Asst Ed.-in-Chief, Le Point 1972–74, Ed.-in-Chief 1974–77, Pres.-Dir-Gen. 1985–90; Dir-Gen. La Vie Catholique group of publs 1977–79; news reporter, Europe No. 1 1969–97, La Croix 1983–, Midi Libre 1997–; Pres. Le Bateau Feu-Scène Nationale Dunkerque 1991–2016; Chair. Bd L'Express 1997–2005; mem. Jury, Prix Interallié 1986–; Chevalier, Légion d'honneur. *Publications:* L'Algérie ou la guerre des mythes 1959, Les 16–24 ans 1964, Les prêtres 1965, Les catholiques français sous l'occupation 1966, Demain une Eglise sans prêtres 1968, Dieu pour l'homme d'aujourd'hui 1970, La gauche du Christ 1972, Les 13–62 ans 1974, La grande triche 1977, Une voix, la nuit 1979, La rumeur de la ville 1981, Maria Vadamme 1983, Alice Van Meulen 1985, Saint-Eloi 1986, Au début d'un bel été 1988, les Vents du Nord m'ont dit 1989, Catherine Courage 1990, Jean Bart 1992, Laura C. 1994, Jésus 1994, Théo et Marie 1996, les Années Jean-Paul II 1996 (jtly), Le Dieu de Jésus 1997, Le Bonheur en 36 vertus, Romans du Nord 1999, Les Héritières 2000, Pour comprendre la guerre d'Algérie 2001, Et pourtant nous étions heureux 2003, Marie 2004, Dieu malgré tout 2005, Judas, le deuxieme jour 2007, Le mal d'Algérie 2011, François d'Assise 2014, Dunkerque 1940, une tragédie française 2017. *Address:* 13 rue de Poissy, 75005 Paris, France (home). *Telephone:* 1-43-54-32-41 (home).

DURACK, David Tulloch, MD, DPhil, FRCP, FRACP, FACP; American medical scientist and academic; *Consulting Professor of Medicine, Duke University;* b. 18 Dec. 1944, W Australia; s. of Reginald W. Durack and Grace E. Tulloch; m. Carmen E. Prosser 1970; three s. one d.; ed Scotch Coll., Perth, Univ. of Western Australia, Univ. of Oxford, UK (Rhodes Scholar); intern, Radcliffe Infirmary, Oxford, UK, further training at Royal Postgradaduate Medical School, London; Chief Resident and Instructor, Dept of Medicine, Univ. of Washington 1974–77, fmr Chief Div. of Infectious Diseases and International Health; Assoc. Prof., then Prof., Duke Univ. 1977–95, Consulting Prof. 1995–; Worldwide Medical Dir, Becton Dickinson Microbiology Systems, Baltimore 1995–99, Vice-Pres. Corp. Medical Affairs 1999–2005, Sr Vice-Pres. Corp. Medical Affairs and Chief Medical Officer 2005–12; fmr Chair. ASM Resources Inc.; mem. Bd of Dirs PixelEXX; Fellow, American Coll. of Physicians, Royal Australasian Coll. of Physicians, American Infectious Diseases Soc., American Soc. for Clinical Investigation, American Fed. for Clinical Research; Chair. Scientific Bd of Advisors, Magnolia Medical Technologies, Inc.; mem. Advisory Bd Arbor Vita Corpn. *Publications include:* co-ed. of medical textbooks; more than 200 articles and 30 textbook chapters. *Leisure interest:* flying (multi-engine, instrument-rated pilot). *Address:* Box 3230, DUMC, Durham, NC 27710, USA (office). *Telephone:* (919) 597-6492 (office). *Website:* medicine.duke.edu (office).

DURAK, Osman Turgay, MSc; Turkish mechanical engineer and business executive; *CEO, Koç Holding AŞ;* b. 1952, Istanbul; ed Robert Coll., Istanbul, Northwestern Univ., USA; Design Engineer, Product Devt, Ford Otomotiv Sanayi AŞ 1976–77, Process Engineer, Manufacturing Eng 1977–78, Supervisor, Inönü Plant 1979–81, Project Coordination Man., Inönü Plant New Investment 1982–84, Project Coordination Group Man., New Investments 1984–86, Asst Gen. Man., Marketing 1986–87, Asst Gen. Man., Purchasing 1987–99, Deputy Gen. Man. Ford

Otomotiv Sanayi AŞ 2000–01, Gen. Man. 2002–07, Automotive Group Cos Ford Otosan, Koç Holding AŞ 2006–07, Pres. Automotive Group 2007–09, Deputy CEO Koç Holding AŞ 2009–10, mem. Bd of Dirs and CEO Koç Holding AŞ 2010–. *Address:* Koç Holding AŞ, Nakkastepe, Azizbey Sok. No. 1, Kuzguncuk, 34674 Istanbul, Turkey (office). *Telephone:* (216) 5310272 (office). *Fax:* (216) 3414519 (office). *E-mail:* stephenk@koc.com.tr (office). *Website:* www.koc.com.tr (office).

DURÁN, José-Luis; Spanish business executive; b. 1965; ed Instituto Católico de Administración y Dirección de Empresas; Auditor, Arthur Andersen 1987–90; Man. Auditor, Pryca (subsidiary of Carrefour) 1991–94, Man. Auditor, Southern Europe 1994–96, Americas 1996–97, Chief Financial Officer (CFO) Pryca 1997–99, CFO Carrefour Spain 1999–2001, CFO and Man. Dir of Org. and Systems, Carrefour SA 2001–05, mem. Exec. Cttee, Group Man. Dir 2005, Chair. Bd of Man. 2005–08, CEO 2008; joined Maus Frères International Group 2009, Chair. Gant 2009–15, CEO Lacoste SA 2013–15, Dir Aigle International SA; mem. Bd of Dirs HSBC Holdings PLC 2008–10, Orange 2008–, Inditex 2015–; mem. Supervisory Bd Unibail-Rodamco SE 2011–.

DURÁN, Roberto; Panamanian professional boxer (retd); b. (Roberto Duran Samaniego), 16 June 1951, Chorrillo; m. Felicidad Durán; four c.; professional boxer March 1967–2002; first fighter to win world titles at four different weights; won world lightweight title from Ken Buchanan June 1972; equalled the record number of championship defences (12) before relinquishing title to box as welterweight from Feb. 1979; won World Boxing Council version of world welterweight title from Ray Leonard, Montreal June 1980: lost it to Leonard, New Orleans Nov. 1980, retained it 1989; won WBC version of world middleweight title against Ian Barkley, Atlantic City Feb. 1989, relinquished it to challenge Ray Leonard to WBC super-middleweight title: lost to Leonard, Las Vegas Dec. 1989; announced retirement after losing to World Boxing Asscn Middleweight Champion William Joppy 1998, came back to win Nat. Boxing Asscn Super Middleweight Championship 2000 beating Pat Lawlor, then beating Patrick Goossen, lost title to Héctor Camacho 2001; retd 2002; 119 fights, 103 wins, 70 knockouts; Ring Magazine Comeback of the Year 1983, 1989, ranked by Ring Magazine greatest lightweight of all-time 2001, as fifth best fighter of the past 80 years 2002, inducted into World Boxing Hall of Fame 2006, into Int. Boxing Hall of Fame 2007. *Leisure interest:* cars. *Address:* c/o CMG Worldwide, 9229 West Sunset Blvd, Suite 820, West Hollywood, CA 90069, USA. *Website:* www.cmgww.com/sports/duran.

DURANTE, Nicandro; Brazilian/Italian business executive; *Chief Executive, British American Tobacco PLC;* ed degrees in finance, econs and business admin; spent three years working in finance in two Brazilian cos; joined Souza Cruz (Brazilian subsidiary of British American Tobacco) 1981, seconded to UK head office as Marketing Finance Controller 1996–98, Finance Dir Hong Kong 1998–2002, Finance Dir Souza Cruz 2002, Pres. Souza Cruz April 2002–06, Regional Dir for Africa and the Middle East, British American Tobacco PLC 2006–08, mem. Bd of Dirs and COO 2008–10, Chief Exec. Designate Sept.–March 2010, Chief Exec. March 2011–. *Address:* British American Tobacco PLC, Globe House, 4 Temple Place, London, WC2R 2PG, England (office). *Telephone:* (20) 7845-1936 (office). *Fax:* (20) 7845-2184 (office). *E-mail:* info@bat.com (office). *Website:* www.bat.com (office).

DURANTE, Viviana Paola; Italian ballerina; b. 8 May 1967, Rome; m. Nigel Cliff; one s.; worked at Royal Ballet Co., London 1984–2001, became soloist 1987, Prin. Dancer 1989, left co. 2001; Prin. Dancer, American Ballet Theater 1999–2000; Prin. Guest Artist, La Scala, Milan 2001–03; Prin. Guest Artist, K-Ballet, Japan 2001–; juror, Prix de Lausanne, Beijing Int. Ballet Competition; judge, Royal Ballet School's Ursula Moreton Choreographic Competition 2011, 2016, ENB Emerging Dancer 2016, Hong Kong Ballet Group Stars Award 2016, 2017, MacMillan Choreographic Competition 2017; f. Viviana Durante Company 2018; acted in Italian film Ogni 27 Agosto; choreographer and dir, Dance Base, Edinburgh, Nat. Theatre Studio, Barbican Centre; Assoc. Artist, Wilton's Music Hall; mem. of devt bd, One Dance UK; Patron, Hammond School, New English Ballet Theatre; Prix de Lausanne 1985, Evening Standard Award 1989, Time Out Award 1989, Premio Positano Award (Italy) 1991, Olivier Award 1997, Premio Internazionale Gino Tani 1997, Premio Vignale Danza 2003, Premio Bucchi 2006, Premio Apulia 2007, Dancer of the Year in the UK, Japan, Italy, Chile. *Principal parts include:* Ondine, Juliet, Nikiya (La Bayadère), Odette-Odile (Swan Lake), Aurore (Sleeping Beauty), Cinderella, Princess Rose (Prince of Pagodas), Anastasia, Marie Vetsera (Mayerling), Excelsior 2001; also roles in My Brother and My Sisters, Requiem, Don Quixote, Manon, Nutcracker, Rhapsody, Capriccio, Anna Karenina, Carmen, Symphonic Variations. *Leisure interests:* yoga, reading, life. *Website:* www.viviana-durante.com.

DURBIN, Richard (Dick) Joseph, BS, JD; American lawyer and politician; *Senator from Illinois;* b. 21 Nov. 1944, East St Louis, Ill.; s. of William Durbin and Ann Durbin; m. Loretta Schaefer 1967; one s. two d. (one deceased); ed Georgetown Univ.; called to the Bar, Ill. 1969; Chief Legal Counsel to Lt-Gov. Paul Simon of Ill. 1969–72; parliamentarian, Ill. State Senate 1969–77, staff minority leader, 1972–77; Partner, Durbin & Lestikow, Springfield, Ill. 1979–82; mem. US House of Reps for 20th Ill. Dist, Washington, DC 1983–97; Senator from Illinois 1997–, Asst Minority Whip 2005–07, Majority Whip 2007–15, Minority Whip 2015–, Chair. Defense Appropriations Subcommittee 2013–; Chair. Democratic Nat. Cttee 2004; Assoc. Prof. of Medical Humanities, Southern Illinois Univ. 1978–; Democrat; Friend of Agric. Award, Illinois Farm Bureau 2000, Excellence in Immunization Award, Nat. Partnership for Immunization 2001, Ground Water Protector Award, Nat. Ground Water Asscn 2005, Leadership Award, Nat. Org. on Fetal Alcohol Syndrome 2005, Public Service Award, ACS 2005, Lifetime Achievement Award, American Lung Asscn. *Address:* 711 Hart Senate Office Building, Washington, DC 20510-0001, USA (office). *Telephone:* (202) 224-2152 (office). *Fax:* (202) 228-0400 (office). *E-mail:* dick@durbin.senate.gov (office). *Website:* www.durbin.senate.gov (office).

DURDYLEV, Shamuhammet; Turkmenistani engineer and politician; *Mayor of Ashgabat;* b. 1963, Baharly, Ahal Velayat, Turkmen SSR, USSR; ed Turkmen Polytechnic Inst.; worked as occupational safety and construction technician at Baharden Mobile Mechanical Div. No. 3; construction engineer 1990–92; Head of Baharden self-financed construction field of AshgabatRemBytStroi, responsible for renovation of public amenity centres in Aşgabat 1992–93; briefly Head of Ahal Velayat Gas Production Asscn 1993; Construction Man., Baharly Dist Specialized Mobile Mechanical Div. No. 17 1993–94; Deputy Head of Baharly township 1994–95; worked for Baharly Water Man. Production Admin 1995–2002; Deputy Hakim (Gov.) then Hakim of Ahal Velayat 2002–07; Minister of Construction and Construction Materials Industry 2007–10; Hakim City of Aşgabat 2010–13; Deputy Chair. of the Govt and Chief of the Govt and Presidential Staff 2014–15, responsible for Energy, Construction and Municipal Services, Exec. Sec. Office of the Pres. and the Council of Ministers 2016–17; Mayor of Ashgabat 2017–; 20 Years of Independence of Turkmenistan Medal. *Address:* Mayor's Office, 744000 Aşgabat, Bitarap Türkmenistan köç. 21, Turkmenistan (office). *Telephone:* (12) 35-00-78 (office). *Fax:* (12) 35-44-42 (office). *Website:* ashgabat.gov.tm (office).

DURDYNETS, Gen. Vasyl Vasylyevich; Ukrainian lawyer and army officer; b. 27 Sept. 1937, Romochevytsya; m.; one d.; ed Lvov State Univ.; Sec., then First Sec., Lvov Regional Comsomol Cttee, Deputy Head of Section, Cen. Comsomol Cttee, Moscow, Head of Section, Cen. Cttee of Lviv Regional CP 1960–73; Deputy Head of Dept of Admin., CP Cen. Cttee 1973–78; Deputy Minister of Internal Affairs 1978–82, First Deputy Minister of Internal Affairs 1982–91; People's Deputy of Ukraine 1991–94, Head, Cttee of Defence and Nat. Safety 1991–92, mem. 1997, First Deputy Speaker of Parl. 1992–94; First Deputy Head of Co-ordination Cttee for Fighting Corruption and Organized Crime 1994–95, Head 1995–99; Vice-Prime Minister of Ukraine 1995–96, First Vice-Prime Minister 1996–99, Acting Prime Minister June–July 1997; Dir Nat. Bureau of Investigations 1997–99; Minister for Emergency Situations and Protection of the Population from the Consequences of the Chernobyl Catastrophe 1999–2002; Amb. to Hungary 2002–03; mem. Supreme Econ. Council 1997; Hon. Prof. Acad. of Internal Affairs 1997; Order of Prince Yaroslav the Wise (IV and V class), Order of Merit, Order of the Red Banner of Labour, Order of the Badge of Honour, Order for Personal Courage; ICDO Medal, Int. Civil Defence Org. (Switzerland) 2000, 14 nat. awards, Distinguished Juror of Ukraine 2011.

DURIE, Sir David Robert Campbell, KCMG, KStJ, KCFO, MA, CCMI, FRSA; British public affairs consultant, diplomatist, lecturer and fmr public servant; b. 21 Aug. 1944, Glasgow, Scotland; s. of F. R. E. Durie; m. Susan Frances Weller; three d.; ed Univ. of Oxford; served in various British Govt depts 1966–91; Minister and Deputy UK Perm. Rep. to EU 1991–95; Dir-Gen. for Enterprise and Regions, Dept Trade and Industry 1995–2000; Gov. and C-in-C Gibraltar 2000–03; Ind. Chair. Responsibility in Gambling Trust (fmrly Gambling Industry Charitable Trust) 2004–07; mem. Lord Chancellor's Advisory Council on Nat. Records and Archives 2006–15; Gov. and co-Chair. Queen's Church of England School, Kew 2009–; Ind. mem. GLA Standards Cttee 2008–12. *Leisure interests:* exercise, culture, family.

DURKAN, Mark; Irish politician; b. 26 June 1960, Derry, Northern Ireland; s. of Brendan Durkan and Isobel Durkan (née Tinney); m. Jackie Durkan; one d.; ed St Columb's Coll., Derry, Queen's Univ., Belfast, Magee Coll., Derry; Deputy Pres. Union of Students in Ireland 1982–84; Asst to John Hume, MP 1984–98; Chair. Social Democratic and Labour Party (SDLP) 1990–95, Leader 2001–10; Derry City Council 1993–2002; mem. Northern Ireland Housing Council 1993–95, Western Health and Social Services Council 1993–2000; mem. Forum for Peace and Reconciliation, Dublin 1994–96; SDLP Negotiator in inter-party discussions 1996–98; mem. Northern Ireland Ass. 1998–2010; Minister of Finance 1999–2001, Deputy First Minister 2001–02; MP for Foyle 2005–. *Address:* Constituency Office, 1st Floor, 23 Bishop Street, Derry, BT48 6PR, Northern Ireland (office); House of Commons, Westminster, London, SW1A 0AA, England (office). *Telephone:* (28) 7136-0700 (Derry) (office); (20) 7219-5096 (London) (office). *Fax:* (28) 7136-0808 (Derry) (office); (20) 7219-2694 (London) (office). *E-mail:* m.durkan@sdlp.ie (office); mark.durkan.mp@parliament.uk (office). *Website:* www.parliament.uk/biographies/commons/mark-durkan/1594 (office); www.markdurkan.net.

DURLACHER, Nicholas (Nick) John, CBE, BA (Cantab); British business executive; *Chairman, Xoserve Ltd;* b. 20 March 1946, Plaxtol, Kent; s. of John Sidney Durlacher and Alma Gabriel Adams; m. Mary McLaren 1971; one s.; ed Stowe School, Buckingham, Magdalene Coll., Cambridge; fmrly Chair. London Int. Financial Futures and Options Exchange; Chair. Securities and Futures Authority 1995–2001; Ennismore European Smaller Companies Fund 1998–; Chair. FFastFill PLC 2000–02; Chair. Elexon Ltd 2000–10, Quilter Global Enhanced Income Trust PLC 2000–05, Xoserve Ltd 2011–; Dir UFJ Int. PLC 2002–04; Chair. Allied Schools 2007–; Trustee Brain and Spine Foundation 2000–. *Leisure interests:* skiing, golf, tennis. *Address:* Xoserve Limited, 31 Homer Road, Solihull, West Midlands, B91 3LT (office); 10 Rutland Street, London, SW7 1EH, England (home). *Website:* www.xoserve.com (office).

DURLEŞTEANU, Mariana; Moldovan economist and diplomatist; *Chief Financial Officer, KazMunayGas;* b. 5 Sept. 1971; m.; two c.; ed Babeş-Bolyai Univ., Cluj-Napoca, Romania; fmr nat. gymnast; economist, later leading economist, Foreign Financing and External Debt Dept, Ministry of Finance 1995–96, Chief of External Debt Service Div. 1996–97, Head of Foreign Financing and External Debt Directorate 1997–2001, Deputy Minister of Finance 2001–02, First Deputy Minister of Finance 2002–05, Minister of Finance 2008–09; Gov. for Moldova, Black Sea Trade and Devt Bank (BSTDB) 2001–04; Alt. Gov. for Moldova, IMF 2001–04; Deputy Chair. Moldovagaz (jt venture) 2004–05; Chair. Savings Bank (Banca de Economii) 2004–05; Amb. to UK 2004–08; Sr Banker, European Bank for Reconstruction & Devt (EBRD) 2009–11; Chief Financial Officer KazMunay-Gas, state-owned oil and gas co., Kazakhstan 2011–; Labour Glory Decoration. *Address:* KazMunayGas, 19, Kabanbay-batyrave, 010000 Nur-Sultan, Kazakhstan (office).

DURON, Willy, MSc; Belgian business executive; *Chairman, Van Lanschot;* b. 1945; ed Univ. of Groningen, Netherlands, Catholic Univ. of Louvain; joined ABB-Insurance (Assurantie van de Belgische Boerenbond) as actuary 1970, Chair. Exec. Cttee KBC Insurance (after merger of Kredietbank, CERA Bank and ABB Insurance) 2000–03, Pres. Exec. Cttee KBC Bank and Insurance Holding Co. 2003–05, CEO KBC Group NV 2005–06 (retd), now Hon. Chair.; mem. Supervisory Bd Van Lanschot 2007–, Chair. 2015–; mem. Bd of Dirs TiGenix 2007– (Chair. 2007–12), Agfa-Gevaert NV 2008–, Ravago NV, Vanbreda Risk & Benefits NV, Universitaire Ziekenhuizen Leuven, Z.org KU Leuven. *Address:* Van Lanschot,

Postbus 1021, 5200 HC 's-Hertogenbosch, Netherlands (office). *Telephone:* (20) 3544585 (office). *Website:* corporate.vanlanschot.nl (office).

ĐUROVIĆ, Dragan; Montenegrin politician; b. 31 Oct. 1959, Danilovgrad; m.; three c.; Legal Adviser and Sec., Agro-Econ. Inst. 1982–92; Dir Directorate for Regional Agricultural Devt 1992–93; Chair. Exec. Bd, Danilovgrad Municipality Ass. 1993–95; Dir Pobjeda publishing co. 1995–2001; Deputy Prime Minister of Montenegro with Responsibility for Political System and Internal Policy 2001–06, Minister of Interior Affairs 2003–06; acting Minister of Foreign Affairs 2002–03; acting Prime Minister 2002–03; Deputy, Parl. of Repub. of Montenegro, apptd Deputy, House of Citizens of Fed. Parl. twice, Deputy, Parl. of Repub. of Montenegro three times; Dir Civil Aviation Agency of Montenegro 2009–; fmr mem. Presidency of Democratic Party of Socialists; Chief Deputy, Democratic Party of Socialists Club; Pres. Danilovgrad basketball club. *Television:* Bjelopavlici (co-writer). *Address:* Democratic Party of Montenegrin Socialists (Demokratska Partija Socijalista Crne Gore), 81000 Podgorica, Jovana Tomaševića 33 (office); 104/20 Bulevar Sv. Petar Cetinjski, 81000 Podgorica, Montenegro (home). *Telephone:* (82) 243735 (office); (82) 202060 (home). *Fax:* (82) 242101 (office). *E-mail:* webmaster@dps.cg.yu (office); dragandj@cg.yu (office). *Website:* www.dps.cg.yu (office).

DÜRR, Heinz; German business executive; b. 16 July 1933, Stuttgart; s. of Otto Dürr; m. Heide Dürr; three d.; ed Tech. Hochschule, Stuttgart; Man. and Man. Dir Dürr AG (fmrly Otto Dürr GmbH), Stuttgart 1957–80, Chair. Supervisory Bd 1990–2013, Hon. Chair. 2013–; Chair. Exec. Bd AEG AG, Berlin and Frankfurt 1980–90; mem. Exec. Bd Daimler-Benz AG, Stuttgart 1986–90; Chair. Exec. Bd Deutsche Bundesbahn, Deutsche Reichsbahn 1991–94, Deutsche Bahn AG 1994–97, Supervisory Bd Deutsche Bahn AG 1997–99, Carl-Zeiss-Stiftung (Commr) 1999–2003, Krone GmbH 1999; Chair. Fed. of Metal Working Industries in Baden-Württemberg and mem. Presidium Fed. of Metal and Electrical Industry Employers' Asscns 1975–80; mem. European Advisory Bd, Schroder, Salomon, Smith Barney 2001 and seven supervisory bds; Hon. DrIng (Rhine-Westphalian Tech. Univ., Aachen) 1996; Verdienstorden des Landes Berlin 2002, Verdienstmedaille des Landes Baden-Württemberg 2009. *Leisure interests:* tennis, golf, theatre, jazz, cross-country skiing. *Address:* Dürr AG, Otto-Dürr-Strasse 8, 70435 Stuttgart (office); Charlottenstrasse 57, 10117 Berlin, Germany. *Telephone:* (711) 1360 (office). *Fax:* (711) 1361455 (office). *Website:* www.durr.com (office).

DURR, Hon. Kent D. Skelton; South African business executive, fmr politician and fmr diplomatist; b. 28 March 1941, Cape Town; s. of Dr John M. Durr and Diana Skelton; m. Suzanne Wiese 1966 (deceased); one s. two d.; ed SA Coll. School, Cape Town Univ.; dir of family publishing co. 1966–68; Founder and later Man. Dir Durr Estates 1968–84; Chair. Clean Diesel Technologies Inc. 1995–97, Fuel-Tech NV 1995–97; Exec. Chair. Commonwealth Investment Guarantee Agency Ltd 1997; elected to Prov. Council of Cape 1974, MP for Maitland 1977–91, Deputy Minister (Trade and Industry) 1984–86, (Finance) 1984–88; Minister of Budget and Public Works 1988–89; Cabinet Minister of Trade and Industry and Tourism 1989–91; Amb. to UK 1991–94, High Commr in UK 1994–95; Chair. Commonwealth Investment Guarantee Agency 1995–99, Nasdaq Listed Cos, USA 1995–99; mem. Parl. and Senate (African Christian Democratic Party) 1999–2005 (resgnd); Spokesman, African Christian Democratic Party 2004–05; Chair. Darling Wildlife (Cattle and Game) 1999–2004; Freeman City of London 1995; Spectamur Agendo Award, South African College School 2015. *Leisure interests:* field sports, mountaineering, conservation, game farming. *Address:* Sonquasfontein Private Nature Reserve, Darling, Western Cape 7345, South Africa (home). *Telephone:* (21) 6853908 (home). *Website:* kentdurr.co.za.

DURRANI, Akram Khan, BA, LLB; Pakistani politician; *Minister for Housing and Works;* b. 2 March 1960, Bannu Dist; s. of Ghulam Qadir Khan Durrani and Kalam Bibi; three s. one d.; ed Govt Coll., Nowshera; mem. NW Frontier Prov. (NWFP) Prov. (now Khyber Pakhtunkhwa) Ass. 1990–93, 1997–99, 2002–; Chief Minister of NWFP 2002–07; Fed. Minister for Housing and Works 2014–; mem. Nat. Security Council; mem. Jamiat-e-Ulema-e-Islam. *Address:* Ministry of Housing and Works, Ground Floor, Blue Area, Shaheed-e-Milat Secretariat, Islamabad, Pakistan (office). *Telephone:* (51) 9206036 (office). *Fax:* (51) 9201230 (office). *E-mail:* minister@housing.gov.pk (office). *Website:* www.pha.gov.pk (office).

DURRANT, Jennifer Ann; British artist; b. 17 June 1942, Brighton; d. of Caleb John Durrant and Winifred May Durrant (née Wright); m. William A.H. Henderson 1964 (divorced 1976); m. 2nd Richard Alban Howard Oxby 2000; ed Varndean Grammar School for Girls, Brighton, Brighton Coll. of Art and Crafts, Slade School of Fine Art, Univ. Coll., London; part-time art teacher various colls 1965–74 including St Martin's School of Art, London 1974–87, Chelsea School of Art 1987–89; part-time Lecturer on Painting, RCA 1979–2000, Royal Acad. Schools 1991–98; external assessor at various colls; Exhbn Selector, Northern Young Contemporaries, Whitworth Gallery, Manchester, TV SW Arts; Painting Faculty mem. The British School at Rome 1979–83; Artist-in-Residence, Somerville Coll., Oxford 1979–80; works in collections of Arts Council of GB, British Council, Contemporary Art Soc., Tate Gallery, Museum of Fine Arts, Boston, USA, Neue Galerie, Aachen and in pvt. collections; Abbey Minor Travelling Scholarship British School at Rome 1964, Arts Council Award 1976, Arts Council Major Award 1977, Greater London Arts Asscn Award 1980, Athena Art Award 1988, Independent on Sunday Artist of the Year 1996. *Leisure interests:* classical music, including opera, archaeology, visiting museums, looking at paintings and sculpture, the natural world. *Address:* La Vigna, Via Bondi 14, 06069 Tuoro sul Trasimeno, Italy. *Telephone:* 75829010.

DURRANT, (Mignonette) Patricia, CD, OJ, BA; Jamaican diplomatist and UN official; b. 30 May 1943; ed Univ. of the West Indies, Univ. of Cambridge, UK; Admin. Officer, Ministry of Agric. 1964–70; First Sec. Ministry of Foreign Affairs 1971–72, Prin. Asst Sec. 1972–74; Minister-Counsellor, Mission to OAS, Washington, DC 1974–77; Asst Dir Political Div., Ministry of Foreign Affairs 1977–81, Deputy Dir 1981–83; Deputy Perm. Rep. to UN, New York 1983–87, Amb. and Perm. Rep. 1995–2002, Pres. UN High-Level Cttee on Tech. Co-operation among Developing Countries 1999–2001, Rep. of Jamaica to UN Security Council 2000–01, UN Ombudsman 2002–07; Chair. UN Preparatory Cttee for the Special Session on Children, Chair. Consultative Cttee for the UN UNIFEM, Vice-Chair. Preparatory Cttee for Special Session on Population and Devt 1999 and Vice-Chair. Open-Ended Working Group on the Reform of the UN Security Council; Amb. to FRG (also accred to Israel, the Netherlands, Switzerland and the Holy See) 1987–92; Dir-Gen. Ministry of Foreign Affairs and Foreign Trade 1992–95; Distinguished Grad. Award, Univ. of the West Indies 1998, Distinguished Achievement Award, World Asscn of Fmr UN Interns and Fellows. *Address:* Ministry of Foreign Affairs and Foreign Trade, 21 Dominica Drive, PO Box 624, Kingston 5, Jamaica (office). *Telephone:* 926-4220 (office). *Fax:* 929-5112 (office). *E-mail:* mfaftjam@cwjamaica.com (office). *Website:* www.mfaft.gov.jm (office).

DUŞA, Mircea; Romanian politician; b. 1 April 1955, Topliţa, Harghita Co.; m.; two c.; ed Lucian Blaga Univ., Sibiu; mem. City Council, Topliţa 1976–86, Vice-Pres. 1986–90; Sr Vice-Pres. Asscn of Towns in Romania 1996–2001; Prefect of Harghita City 2001–04; mem. Chamber of Deputies (Parl.) for Harghita 2004–08, Partidul Social Democrat (PSD—Social Democratic Party) Parl. group leader 2010–12; Minister for Relations with Parl. May–Aug. 2012, Minister of Admin and the Interior Aug.–Dec. 2012, of Nat. Defence 2012–15. *Address:* c/o Ministry of National Defence, 050561 Bucharest 5, Str. Izvor 3–5, Romania.

DUSAUTOIR, Thierry; French professional rugby union player; b. 18 Nov. 1981, Abidjan, Côte d'Ivoire; ed graduate chemical engineer; began with judo as his sport; played rugby from age 16; plays as a flanker; played for Bordeaux-Bègles 2001–03, US Colomiers 2003–04, Biarritz 2004–06 (played in final of Heineken Cup losing to Munster 23–19 at Millennium Stadium, Cardiff 2006, won final of Top 14 40–13 against Toulouse 2006), Toulouse 2006–, France 2006–15 (Capt.); Test debut against Romania (62–14), Cotroceni Stadium, Bucharest 2006; played in subsequent Test against the Springboks at Newlands Stadium, Cape Town with France winning 36–26; captained France to a 27–22 win over New Zealand in Dunedin 2009; captained France through to final of Rugby World Cup, losing 7–8 to New Zealand, Eden Park, Auckland 2011; 80 Test caps, six tries; retd from int. rugby Dec. 2015; Man of the Match Award, Rugby World Cup Final 2011, Int. Rugby Bd (IRB) Int. Player of the Year 2011. *Achievements include:* well-known for his try against New Zealand in quarterfinal of World Cup in Cardiff in which he made 38 tackles, two more than the entire All Blacks side 2007. *Address:* Stade Toulousain, BP 42354, 31022 Toulouse Cedex 2, France (office). *Telephone:* (8) 92-69-31-15 (office). *Fax:* (5) 34-42-24-21 (office). *E-mail:* info@stadetoulousain.fr (office). *Website:* www.stadetoulousain.fr (office).

DUSSAULT, René, BA, LLL, PhD, FRSC; Canadian lawyer and judge; *Counsel, Heenan Blaikie LLP;* b. 23 Nov. 1939, Québec City; s. of Daniel Dussault and Madeleine Pelletier; m. Marielle Godbout 1967; two s.; ed Petit Séminaire de Québec, Laval Univ. and London School of Econs and Political Science; called to Bar, Québec 1963; Lecturer in Law, Laval Univ. 1966–70; Legal Counsel, Québec Health and Welfare Inquiry Comm.; Special Adviser to Minister of Social Affairs of Québec 1970–73; Chair. Québec Professions Bd 1973–77; Deputy Minister of Justice, Québec 1977–80; Prof., École nationale d'administration publique 1981–89; Laskin Chair in Public Law, Osgoode Hall Law School 1983–84; fmr legal consultant, Kronström, McNicoll & Assocs, Québec City; Judge, Québec Court of Appeal 1989–2008; Counsel, Heenan Blaikie LLP, Québec City 2008–; Assoc. Ed. Canadian Public Administration journal 1982–89; Co-Chair. Royal Comm. on Aboriginal Peoples 1991–96; Hon. LLD (York) 1992, (Dalhousie) 1997; Québec Bar Asscn Medal 1987, Québec Interprofessional Council Prize 1991, Vanier Medal, Inst. of Public Admin. of Canada 1998, Bertha Wilson Touchstone Award, Canadian Bar Asscn 2001, Council of Canadian Admin. Tribunals Medal 2006, Gloire de l'Escolle Medal, Alumni Asscn of Université Laval 2009. *Publications:* Le contrôle judiciaire de l'administration au Québec 1969, Traité de droit administratif, Vols I & II 1974 (also co-author of subsequent vols), Administrative Law: A Treatise, Vols I–V 1985–90 (Walter Owen Award, Canadian Bar Asscn's Foundation for Legal Research, prix du Concours juridique, Québec Bar Foundation 1988). *Address:* Heenan Blaikie LLP, 900, boul. René-Lévesque Est, Bureau 600, Québec City, PQ G1R 2B5 (office); 1332 James-LeMoine Avenue, Sillery, PQ G1S 1A3, Canada (home). *Telephone:* (418) 649-5053 (office); (418) 527-6332 (home). *Fax:* (418) 524-1717 (office). *E-mail:* rdussault@heenan.ca (office). *Website:* www.heenanblaikie.com (office).

DUSSEY, Robert, PhD; Togolese politician; *Minister of Foreign Affairs, Co-operation and African Integration;* b. 4 Jan. 1971, Bangui, Central African Repub.; early career as theologian, Lion de Juda monastic community (later renamed Communauté des Béatitudes), Congo; fmr teacher, Lomé Univ.; mem. Africa Bureau, Sant'Egidio Community, Rome 2004; Diplomatic Adviser to Pres. of Togo 2005; Minister of Foreign Affairs, Co-operation and African Integration 2013–; mem. Union pour la République (UNIR); Chevalier de la Legion d'Honneur 2012. *Publications include:* several books including La vie sans vie 2000, Pour une paix durable en Afrique 2002, Penser la réconciliation au Togo 2003, L'Afrique malade de ses hommes politiques 2011. *Address:* Ministry of Foreign Affairs, Co-operation and African Integration, pl. du Monument aux Morts, ave Georges Pompidou, BP 900, Lomé, Togo (office). *Telephone:* 22-21-29-10 (office). *Fax:* 22-21-39-74 (office). *E-mail:* maeirtgce@yahoo.fr (office). *Website:* www.diplomatie.gouv.tg (office); www.robertdussey.com.

DUTERTE, Rodrigo (Rody) Roa, (Digong), BA, LLB; Philippine lawyer, politician and head of state; *President;* b. 28 March 1945, Maasin, Southern Leyte Prov.; s. of Vicente G. Duterte and Soledad Roa; m. Elizabeth Zimmerman (divorced); three c.; partner Cieleto Avanceña; one d.; ed Lyceum of the Philippines Univ., San Beda Coll. of Law; Special Counsel, Davao City Prosecution Office 1977–79, Fourth Asst City Prosecutor 1979–81, Third Asst City Prosecutor 1981–83, Second Asst City Prosecutor 1983–86; Deputy Mayor of Davao City 1986–87, 2010–13, Mayor of Davao City Feb.–March 1998, 2001–10, 2013–16; mem. House of Reps (Partido Demokratiko Pilipino-Lakas Ng Bayan—PDP-Laban) from Davao City 1st Dist 1998–2001; Pres. of the Philippines 2016–. *Address:* Office of the President, New Executive Building, Malacañang Palace Compound, J. P. Laurel St, San Miguel, Metro Manila, Philippines (office). *Telephone:* (2) 7356201 (office). *Fax:* (2) 9293968 (office). *E-mail:* op@president.gov.ph (office). *Website:* www.president.gov.ph (office).

DUTHEILLET DE LAMOTHE, Olivier; French lawyer; *Partner, CMS Bureau Francis Lefebvre;* b. 10 Nov. 1949, Neuilly; s. of Alain Dutheillet de Lamothe and

Suzanne Garnier; m. Marie-Caroline Sainsaulieu 1981; one s. one d.; ed Institut d'Etudes Politiques de Paris, Ecole Nationale d'Administration; held several posts at Council d'Etat, including Auditor 1975, Rapporteur Litigation Section 1975–77, Head Documentation Centre and Coordination 1977–79, Maitre des requetes 1979, Advocate General, Ass. of Litigation and other judicial panels 1981–86; Tech. Adviser to Minister of Health and Social Security 1979–81; Legal Adviser to Directorate Gen. of Civil Aviation 1985–86; Adviser to Minister of Social Affairs and Employment 1986–87; Dir of Labour Relations Ministry of Labour, Employment and Vocational Training 1987–95; State Councillor 1992; Social Adviser Presidency of the Repub. 1995–97, Deputy Sec.-Gen. of the Presidency 1997–2000; Rapporteur Litigation Section 2000–01; Prof., Institut d'Etudes Politiques de Paris 2001–10; mem. Conseil Constitutionnel 2001–10; Pres. Section Sociale du Conseil d'Etat 2011–14; Of Counsel, CMS Bureau Francis Lefebvre, 2014–15, Partner 2015–, head of employment and pensions intelligence dept; Pres. Jefferson Circle 2002–08; mem. EC Democracy through Law (Venice Comm.) of Council of Europe 2002–10; Global Distinguished Fellow, Hauser Global Law School Program, New York Univ. School of Law 2005; mem. American Law Inst. 2012–; Chevalier, Légion d'Honneur, Ordre national du Mérite. *Publications include:* Politique de l'emploi et dynamique des entreprises 2005. *Leisure interests:* cinema, skiing. *Address:* CMS Bureau Francis Lefebvre, 2 rue Ancelle, 92522 Neuilly-sur-Seine Cedex, France (office). *Telephone:* 1-47-38-55-00 (office). *E-mail:* olivier.dutheilletdelamothe@cms-bfl.com (office). *Website:* www.cms-bfl.com (office).

DUTKOWSKY, Robert M., BS; American computer industry executive; *CEO and Chairman, Tech Data Corporation;* b. 2 Jan. 1955, Endicott, NY; m. Lorraine Dutkowsky; two c.; ed Cornell Univ., Ithaca, NY; worked at IBM 1977–97, served in sr man. positions including Exec. Asst to fmr CEO Lou Gerstner, Vice-Pres. for Distribution, Asia/Pacific; Exec. Vice-Pres. Sales and Marketing EMC Corpn 1997–2000; Chair., Pres. and CEO GenRad Inc. 2000–02; Pres. Assembly Test Div. Teradyne Inc. 2001–02; Chair., Pres. and CEO JD Edwards Inc. 2002–03; Chair., Pres. and CEO Egenera Inc. 2004–06; mem. Bd of Dirs and CEO Tech Data Corpn 2006–, Chair. 2017–; mem. Bd of Dirs Sepaton, Inc. *Address:* Tech Data Corpn, 5350 Tech Data Drive, Clearwater, FL 33760-3122, USA (office). *Telephone:* (727) 539-7429 (office). *Fax:* (727) 538-7803 (office). *E-mail:* info@techdata.com (office). *Website:* www.techdata.com (office).

DUTOIT, Charles Édouard, OC; Swiss conductor and music director; b. 7 Oct. 1936, Lausanne; s. of Edmond Dutoit and Berthe Dutoit (née Laederman); one s. one d.; ed Conservatoires of Lausanne and Geneva, Accademia Musicale Chigiana, Siena, Italy, Conservatorio Benedetto Marcello, Venice, Italy and Berkshire Music Center, Tanglewood, USA; Assoc. Conductor, Berne Symphony Orchestra 1964, Prin. and Artistic Dir 1966–78; Assoc. Conductor, Tonhalle Orchestra, Zurich 1966; Conductor and Artistic Dir, Zurich Radio Orchestra 1964; Artistic Dir, Nat. Symphony Orchestra of Mexico and Göteborg Symphony Orchestra 1977–2002; Artistic Dir, Montreal Symphony Orchestra 1977–2002; operatic debut at Covent Garden (conducting Faust) 1983; Prin. Guest Conductor, Minnesota Orchestra 1983–84, 1985–86; Artistic Dir and Prin. Conductor, Philadelphia Orchestra summer season, Mann Music Center 1991–2001, Saratoga Springs 1991–2010; Music Dir, Orchestre Nat. de France 1990–2001; Prin. Conductor, NHK Symphony Orchestra, Tokyo 1996–98, Music Dir 1998–2003, Music Dir Emer. 2003–; Chief Conductor and Artistic Advisor, Philadelphia Orchestra 2007–12; Artistic Dir and Prin. Conductor, Royal Philharmonic Orchestra, London 2009–18; Artistic Advisor, Shanghai Symphony Orchestra 2009; Co-Dir MISA Festival, Shanghai 2010; guest conductor of major orchestras in USA, Europe, South America, Asia, Australia and Israel; Hon. Citizen, City of Philadelphia 1991; Hon. Artistic Advisor, Guangzhou Opera House, China 2012; Hon. mem. Igor Stravinsky Foundation, Geneva 2015; Hon. Cttee mem. Maurice Ravel Foundation, Paris 2016; Lifetime Hon. Prof., Nanjing Univ. of the Arts, China 2016; Officier des Arts et des Lettres 1988, Commdr 1996; Grand Officier, Ordre Nat. du Québec 1995; Hon. OC 2002; Commdr, Ordre de Montréal 2016; Dr hc (Montreal) 1984, (Laval) 1985; Hon. DMus (McGill Univ.) 1996, (Curtis Inst., Philadelphia) 2011; two Grammy Awards, Grand Prix de l'Acad. du disque français, High Fidelity Int. Record Critics' Award, Montreux Record Award, Japan Record Acad. Award, Musician of the Year, Canada Music Council 1982, Grand Prix du Président de la République (France), Great Montrealer 1982, Canadian Music Council Medal 1988, Diploma of Honour, Canadian Conf. of the Arts 1994, Prize for the Best Foreign Conductor 2003, Music Critics' Award, Asscn of Argentina 2002, Médaille d'Or de la Ville de Lausanne 2007, Tribute of The Musical Fund Soc. of Philadelphia 2012, Lifetime Achievement Award, Int. Classic Music Awards, Warsaw 2014, Special Contrib. Award, 18th Shanghai Int. Arts Festival 2016, Lauréat, Fondation Vaudoise pour la Culture, Lausanne 2016, Royal Philharmonic Soc. Gold Medal 2017. *Recordings include:* numerous recordings with various orchestras since 1980, winning over 65 int. awards and including Falla's Three Cornered Hat and El amor Brujo, The Planets, Tchaikovsky's 1st Piano Concerto, Saint-Saëns 3rd Symphony, Bizet's L'Arlésienne and Carmen Suites, Gubaidulina Offertorium with Boston Symphony, Symphonies by Honegger, Roussel's Symphonies with French Nat. Orchestra, Saint-Saëns Piano Concertos, Suppé Overtures, Berlioz's Les Troyens. *E-mail:* admin@cdoffice.net (office).

DUTREIL, Renaud, MA, DEA; French business executive and fmr politician; *Chairman, Brasil Beauté;* b. 12 June 1960, Chambéry; ed École Normale Supérieure, Institut d'Études Politiques de Paris, École des Hautes Études en Sciences Sociales, École Nationale d'Admin; Maître des Requêtes, Council of State 1989–, later Govt Commr; elected Deputy, Assemblée Nationale 1993, 1997, 2002; mem. Council Castle-Thierry (Aisne) 1995–2001, Charly-on-Marne, (Aisne) 2001–08; Sec. of State 2002–04; Minister for the Civil Service and Reform of the State 2004–05; Minister of Small and Medium-sized Enterprises, Trade, Crafts and the Liberal Professions 2005–07; Founder and first Pres. Union pour un Mouvement Populaire 2000–02, Union pour la Majorité Présidentielle 2002; Founder Entreprise du Patrimoine Vivant 2004–08; Chair. LVMH Moët Hennessy Louis Vuitton Inc. 2008–12; Chair. Brasil Beauté (develops int. beauty brands in Brazil) 2012–; Founder and Chair. Duplo T 2012–; mem. Bd of Dirs LCapital 2008–13, AHAlife 2012–; mem. Bd New School, Parsons School of Design, Maison Française, Columbia Univ.; mem. Partnership for New York; Pres. Friends of Institut des Hautes Études Scientifiques 2010–; Trustee, Museum of Art and Design, New York; Chevalier, Légion d'honneur. *Publications:* Le coq sur la paille 1993, La République des Ames mortes 2001. *Address:* Duplo T, 45 Rockefeller Plaza, Suite 2000, New York, NY 10111, USA (office). *E-mail:* contact@duplo-T.com (office). *Website:* www.duplot-t.com (office).

DUTT, Barkha, BA; Indian TV journalist; *Group Editor, English News, New Delhi Television;* b. 18 Dec. 1971, New Delhi; d. of S.P. Dutt and Prabha Dutt; ed St Stephen's Coll., Delhi Jamia Millia Islamia, Columbia Univ., USA; started journalism career with New Delhi TV, currently Group Ed., English News; Fellow, Asia Soc. 2006; writes column Third Eye for The Hindustan Times; Global Leader of Tomorrow Award, World Econ. Forum 2001, 2008, Commonwealth Broadcasters Award 2002, Broadcast Journalist of the Year, Indian Express 2005, Padma Shri 2008, Indian News Broadcasting Award for the Most Intelligent News Show Host 2008, Society's Young Achievers Award. *Address:* NDTV Convergence Limited, 207, Okhla Industrial Estate, Phase 3, New Delhi 110 020, India (office). *Telephone:* (11) 26446666 (office). *Website:* www.barkhadutt.tv.

DUTT, Shekhar; Indian government official; ed Univ. of S Wales, Swansea, UK; fmr Indian Army officer; Prin. Sec., Depts of School Educ., Sports & Youth Welfare 1996–98; Prin. Sec., Dept of Tribal Welfare 1998–2001; Dir-Gen. Sports Authority of India 2001–03; Sec., Ministry of Health 2003–04; Defence Sec. 2005–07; Deputy Nat. Security Adviser 2007–09; Gov. of Chhattisgarh 2010–14; mem. Bd of Trustees, DeSales Univ. 2009–; Sena Medal (mil. decoration) 1971. *Address:* c/o Office of the Governor, Raj Bhavan, Raipur 492 001, India (office).

DUTT, Vikram Dev, B.Tech.; Indian civil servant; b. 17 Sept. 1969; held several early positions with Land Revenue Man. and District Admin, including Asst Commr 1995–97, Collector 1997–99, Sec. to Gov., Personnel and Gen. Admin Jan.–Dec. 1999, Man. Dir, State Tourism Devt Corpn March–Dec. 1999, Sec. to Chief Minister, Personnel and Gen. Admin 1999–2002, Deputy Sec., Ministry of Home Affairs 2002–06, Labour Commr and Dir, Labour and Employment 2006–07, Sec., New Delhi Municipal Council 2007–09, Pvt. Sec., Ministry of Home Affairs 2009–11, Personal Sec. to Minister of Sports Feb.–Sept. 2011, Dir Ministry of Textiles 2011–13, Jt Sec., Ministry of Defence 2013–15, held charge of Sec. urban planning, transport and public relation, Chandigarh Admin 2015; Admin., Daman and Diu and Dadra and Nagar Haveli March–Aug. 2016.

DUTTON, Peter Craig, BBus; Australian politician; *Minister for Home Affairs;* b. 18 Nov. 1970, Brisbane; s. of Bruce Dutton and Ailsa Leitch; m. 1st (divorced); one d.; m. 2nd Kirilly Brumby; two s.; ed Queensland Police Acad., Queensland Univ. of Tech.; apptd Policy Vice-Chair., Bayside Young Liberals 1989, Chair. 1990; worked as police officer, Drugs and Sex Offenders' Squad, Queensland Police 1990–99; Sec. Liberal Party, Brisbane Central Branch 2000; co-f. Dutton Holdings 2000; elected to House of Reps. for Dickson, Queensland 2001, 2004, 2007, 2010, 2013, 2016, mem. Standing Cttee, Employment and Workplace Relations 2002–04, Family and Community Services 2002–04, Economics March – Sept. 2008, Nat. Crime Authority 2002–03, Australian Crime Comm. 2003–04; Minister for Workforce Participation 2004–06, for Revenue and Asst Treasurer 2006–07, for Health 2013–14, for Sport 2013–14, for Immigration and Border Protection 2014–18, for Home Affairs 2017–; mem. Opposition Shadow Ministry 2007–13, Shadow Minister for Finance, Competition Policy and Deregulation Dec. 2007 – Sept. 2008, for Health and Ageing 2008–13. *Address:* 3/199 Gympie Road, Strathpine, QLD, 4500, Australia (office); Minister for Home Affairs, PO Box 6022, House of Representatives, Parliament House, Canberra, ACT 2600, Australia (office). *Telephone:* (7) 3205-9977 (office); (2) 6277-7860 (office). *Fax:* (7) 3205-5111 (office). *E-mail:* minister@homeaffairs.gov.au (office); peter.dutton.mp@aph.gov.au (office). *Website:* www.peterdutton.com.au.

DUVAL, Charles Gaëtan Xavier Luc, BA, FCA; Mauritian chartered accountant and politician; b. 28 Jan. 1958; m.; three c.; ed Univ. of Leeds, UK; Audit Man., Casson Beckman, UK 1980–86; Founding Partner, Coopers & Lybrand (Mauritius); fmr Partner and Business Consultant, De Chazal Du Mée (Chartered Accountants); Sr Partner, Nexia, Baker & Arenson 2000–05; Minister of Industry and Tourism 1994–95; Founder and Leader Parti Mauricien Social Démocrate (PMSD) 1989–; mem. Nat. Ass. 1999–; Minister of Industry, Commerce, Corp. Affairs and Financial Services 1999–2000, of Tourism, Leisure and External Communications 2005–10, Deputy Prime Minister 2005–10, Deputy Prime Minister and Minister of Social Integration and Econ. Empowerment 2010–14, Minister of Finance and Econ. Devt 2011–14. *Address:* c/o Parti Mauricien Social Démocrate (PMSD), Melville, Grand Gaube, Mauritius.

DUVAL, David Robert; American professional golfer; b. 9 Nov. 1971, Jacksonville, Fla; s. of sr PGA Tour golfer Bob Duval; m. Susan Persichitte 2004; five c.; ed Georgia Tech. Univ.; turned professional 1993; mem. Walker Cup team 1991, Pres.'s Cup team, 1996, 1998, Ryder Cup team 1999; winner Nike Wichita Open 1993, Nike Tour Championship 1993, Michelob Championship at Kingsmill 1997, 1998, Walt Disney World/Oldsmobile Classic 1997, the Tour Championship 1997, Tucson Chrysler Classic 1998, Shell Houston Open 1998, NEC World Series of Golf 1998, Mercedes Championship 1999, Bob Hope Chrysler Classic 1999, the Players Championship 1999, BellSouth Classic 1999, Ryder Cup 1999, Open Championship, Royal Lytham, UK 2001; f. Duval Designs (golf design and architectural firm) 2005; commentator, The Golf Channel; Collegiate Player of the Year 1993, Dave Williams Award 1993, Jasper Award 1996. *Leisure interests:* reading, fly fishing, surfing, skiing, baseball. *Website:* davidduval.org.

DUVALL, Robert; American actor; b. 5 Jan. 1931, San Diego, Calif.; s. of William H. Duvall; m. 1st Barbara Benjamin 1964 (divorced); m. 2nd Gail Youngs (divorced) 1982; m. 3rd Sharon Brophy 1991; m. 4th Luciana Pedraza 2005; ed Principia Coll. Ill.; student, Neighborhood Playhouse, New York; f. Butchers Run Films (production co.) 1992. *Films include:* To Kill a Mockingbird 1963, Captain Newman, MD 1964, The Chase 1965, Countdown 1968, The Detective 1968, Bullitt 1968, True Grit 1969, The Rain People 1969, M*A*S*H 1970, The Revolutionary 1970, The Godfather 1972, Tomorrow 1972, The Great Northfield, Minnesota Raid 1972, Joe Kidd 1972, Lady Ice 1973, The Outfit 1974, The Conversation 1974, The Godfather Part II 1974, Breakout 1975, The Killer Elite 1975, Network 1976, The Eagle Has Landed 1977, The Greatest 1977, The Betsy 1978, Apocalypse Now 1979, The Great Santini 1980, True Confessions 1981, Angelo My Love (actor and dir) 1983, Tender Mercies (Acad. Award for Best Actor 1984) 1983, The Stone Boy 1984, The Natural 1984, The Lightship 1986, Let's Get Harry 1986, Belizaire the Cajun 1986, Colors 1988, Convicts, Roots in a Parched Ground, The Handmaid's Tale 1990, A Show of Force 1990, Days of Thunder 1990, Rambling Rose 1991,

Newsies 1992, The New Boys 1992, Stalin 1992, The Plague, Geronimo, Falling Down 1993, The Paper 1994, Wrestling Ernest Hemingway 1994, Something To Talk About, The Stars Fell on Henrietta, The Scarlet Letter, A Family Thing (also co-producer), Phenomenon 1996, The Apostle 1997, Gingerbread Man 1997, Deep Impact, A Civil Action 1999, Gone In Sixty Seconds 2000, A Shot at Glory (also producer) 2000, The 6th Day 2000, Apocalypse Now: Redux 2001, John Q 2002, Assassination Tango (also producer and dir) 2002, Secondhand Lions 2003, Gods and Generals 2003, Open Range 2003, Kicking & Screaming 2005, Thank You for Smoking 2005, Lucky You 2007, We Own the Night 2007, Four Christmases 2008, The Road 2009, Get Low 2009, Crazy Heart 2009, Seven Days in Utopia 2011, Jayne Mansfield's Car 2012, Jack Reacher 2012, The Judge 2014. *Television includes:* Lonesome Dove (mini-series) 1989, Broken Trail (mini-series; Emmy Award for Best Actor in a Mini-series 2007) 2006. *Stage appearances include:* A View from the Bridge 1965 (Obie Award), Wait Until Dark 1966, American Buffalo. *Address:* c/o ICM Partners, 10250 Constellation Boulevard, Los Angeles, CA 90067; Butchers Run Films, 100 Universal City Plaza Building 507, Suite 2D, Universal City, CA 91608, USA.

DUVALL, Shelley; American actress and producer; b. 7 July 1949, Houston, Tex.; f. TV production co. Think Entertainment. *Films include:* (actress): Brewster McCloud 1970, McCabe and Mrs. Miller 1971, Thieves Like Us 1974, Nashville 1975, Buffalo Bill and the Indians 1976, Three Women (Cannes Festival Prize 1977) 1977, Annie Hall 1977, The Shining 1980, Popeye 1980, Time Bandits 1981, Frankenweenie 1984, Roxanne 1987, Suburban Commando 1991, Underneath 1995, Portrait of a Lady 1996, Twilight of the Ice Nymphs 1997, Changing Habits 1997, Tale of the Mummy 1998, Home Fries 1998, The 4th Floor 1999, Dreams in the Attic 2000, Big Monster on Campus 2000, Manna From Heaven 2002. *Television includes:* (actress): Bernice Bobs Her Hair, Lily, Twilight Zone, Mother Goose Rock 'n' Rhyme, Faerie Tale Theatre (Rumpelstiltskin, Rapunzel), Tall Tales and Legends (Darlin' Clementine); (exec. producer): Faerie Tale Theatre, Tall Tales and Legends, Nightmare Classics, Dinner at Eight (film), Mother Goose Rock 'n' Rhyme, Stories from Growing Up, Backfield in Motion (film), Bedtime Stories, Mrs. Piggle-Wiggle. *Address:* POB 1660 Blanco, TX 78606, USA.

DUWAISAN, Khalid Abdulaziz al-, BA (Comm); Kuwaiti diplomatist; *Ambassador to UK;* b. 15 Aug. 1947; s. of Abdulaziz Saud al-Duwaisan and Sabeka Abdullah al-Duwaisan; m. Dalal al-Humaizi 1980; one s. one d.; ed Cairo Univ., Univ. of Kuwait; joined Ministry of Foreign Affairs 1970, Diplomatic Attaché 1974, Embassy, Washington, DC 1975; Amb. to Netherlands 1984 (also accred to Romania 1988); Chair. Kuwaiti del. for supervision of demilitarized zone between Iraq and Kuwait and Chief Co-ordinator Comm. for Return of Stolen Property 1991; Amb. to UK 1993–, also Dean of the Diplomatic Corps; mem. Advisory Bd, Centre of Near and Middle East Studies, SOAS 1998–; participant, Workshop on Int. Diplomacy in the New Century, Kuwait Foundation for the Advancement of Sciences and John F. Kennedy School of Govt, Univ. of Harvard, USA 2007; Hon. GCVO (UK) 1995; Freedom of the City of London 2001; Hon. Certificate (Harvard Univ.) 2005; Dr hc (Univ. of East Anglia) 2012; Award of Excellence for Services to Anglo-Kuwaiti Relations, British Business Forum and British Amb. to Kuwait 2009, Diplomat Magazine Lifetime Contrib. to Diplomacy in London Award 2009, Three Faiths Forum Gold Medallion 2010, UN Asscn's Annual Award for Exceptional Service to the Int. Community 2011, Ben TV Diplomatic Award in recognition of Lifetime Achievement as a Diplomat 2011, Diplomat of the Year for the Middle East 2014. *Leisure interests:* tennis, swimming. *Address:* Kuwaiti Embassy, 2 Albert Gate, London, SW1X 7JU (office); 22 Kensington Palace Gardens, London, W8 4QQ, England (home). *Telephone:* (20) 7590-3400 (office); (20) 7221-7374 (home). *Fax:* (20) 7823-1712 (office). *E-mail:* kuwait@dircon.co.uk (office); widad@btconnect.com (office); enquiries@kuwaitinfo.org.uk (office).

DVORAK, Harold Fisher, AB, MD; American pathologist; *Founding Director, Center for Vascular Biology Research, Beth Israel Deaconess Medical Center;* b. 20 June 1937, Milwaukee, Wis.; s. of Harold J. Dvorak and Laura Dvorak (née Fisher); m. Ann Marie Tompkins; one s. two d.; ed Princeton Univ., Harvard Univ.; Asst Pathologist, Massachusetts Gen. Hosp. 1969–75, Assoc. Pathologist 1975–78, Head, Immunopathology Unit 1976–80; Chief, Dept of Pathology, Beth Israel Hosp., Boston, Mass 1979–96, Founding Dir, Center for Vascular Biology Research, Chief, Dept of Pathology, Beth Israel Deaconess Medical Center 1996–2005 (retd); Mallinckrodt Prof. of Pathology, Harvard Medical School 1979–; Fellow, AAAS 1999; mem. American Asscn of Immunologists, American Soc. of Investigative Pathology (Vice-Pres. 1996); ASIP Rous-Whipple Award 2002, Nat. Foundation for Cancer Research Albert Szent-Gyorgyi Prize for Progress in Cancer Research 2006, Canada Gairdner Int. Award 2014. *Address:* Beth Israel Deaconess Medical Center, Department of Pathology, 330 Brookline Avenue, RN-227C, Boston, MA 02215, USA (office). *Telephone:* (617) 667-8529 (office). *Fax:* (617) 667-2913 (office). *E-mail:* hdvorak@bidmc.harvard.edu (office). *Website:* cvbr.hms.harvard.edu (office).

DVORKIN, Maj.-Gen. Vladimir, PhD; Russian naval officer (retd), defence and foreign affairs specialist and academic; *Principal Researcher, Institute of World Economy and International Relations, Russian Academy of Sciences;* b. 12 Jan. 1936, Leningrad (now St Petersburg); ed High Mil. Naval Coll.; worked at State Cen. Naval Testing Site; took part in first Soviet tests of nuclear-powered ballistic missile submarines and in first underwater test launches; worked in 4th Cen. Research Inst., Russian Defence Ministry 1962–2001, Head of Inst. 1993–2001; Sr Advisor at PIR Center and Carnegie Moscow Center; currently Prin. Researcher, Inst. of World Economy and Int. Relations, Russian Acad. of Sciences; Chair. Organizing Cttee, Int. Luxembourg Forum; Prof. and Full mem. Russian Acad. of Missile and Artillery Sciences, Acad. of the Mil. Sciences, Russian Eng Acad., Int. Eng Acad., Acad. of Astronautics; made significant contrib. to formulating Soviet and Russia's position at negotiations on strategic offensive arms control and reduction; participating for many years as an expert in preparing SALT II, the INF Treaty, START I and START II; Merits marked with orders: 'For Merits to the Fatherland' (Fourth Degree), 'For Military Merits', 'Labor Red Banner', 'Red Star'; numerous medals; Honoured Worker of Science and Tech. of Russian Fed. *Publications:* co-author of all major documents related to Strategic Nuclear Forces and Strategic Missile Forces; more than 350 publs. *Address:* Institute of World Economy and International Relations (IMEMO), Profsoyushaya Str. 23, Moscow, B-71, GSP-7, 117997 (office); PIR Center, Na Trekhprudnom, Trekhprudny Per. 9, Bldg 1B, Moscow 103001, Russia. *Telephone:* (495) 120-52-36 (office); (495) 234-05-25. *Fax:* (495) 234-95-58. *E-mail:* imemoran@imemo.ru (office); info@pircenter.org. *Website:* www.imemo.ru (office); www.pircenter.org.

DVORKOVICH, Arkadii Vladimirovich, MA; Russian economist and politician; *President, Fédération Internationale des Échecs (FIDE—World Chess Foundation);* b. 26 March 1972, Moscow, Russian SFSR, USSR; m. Zumrud Rustamova; two s.; ed Moscow State Univ., New Econ. School, Moscow, Duke Univ., Durham, NC, USA; worked for Econ. Expert Group, Ministry of Finance 1994–2000, Head of Economic Expert Group 1997–2000; Adviser to Minister of Econ. Devt and Trade 2000–, Expert of the Strategic Research Centre 2000–01; Deputy Minister of Econ. Devt and Trade 2001–04; Head of Presidential Experts Directorate, Admin of the Pres. of Russian Fed. 2004–08, Aide to the Pres. 2008–12; Deputy Chair. of the Govt 2012–18; Chair. Russian Railways (RZD) 2015–; Pres. Fédération Internationale des Échecs (FIDE—World Chess Foundation) 2018–; Pres. Russian Investment and Finance Analysts' Guild; mem. Nat. Banking Council; First Vice-Pres. Russian Chess Fed. 2007–; Order of Merit for the Fatherland (Fourth Class), Order of Honour, Medal (Second Class) of the Order of Merit for the Fatherland, Medal 'In Commemoration of the 1,000th Anniversary of Kazan', Officer of the Order of Merit of the Italian Repub. *Publications:* various articles on econs. *E-mail:* fidepresident@fide.com (office). *Website:* www.fide.com (office).

DVORSKÝ, Peter; Slovak singer (tenor); *Director, Slovak Institute, Rome;* b. 25 Sept. 1951, Partizánske, Topoľčany Dist; s. of Vendelín Dvorský and Anna Dvorská; m. Marta Varšová 1975; two d.; ed State Conservatoire, Bratislava; studied with R. Carossi and M. di Luggo, Milan 1975–76; opera soloist, Slovak Nat. Theatre, Bratislava 1972–96, 1999; sang at Metropolitan Opera, New York 1977, Covent Garden, London 1978, Bolshoi Theatre, Moscow 1978, La Scala, Milan 1979; performs regularly at Bratislava, Vienna State Opera, Covent Garden, La Scala, New York Metropolitan Opera, Munich, Berlin, Prague, Geneva, Paris, Buenos Aires, Tokyo and in many other cities throughout the world; numerous radio and TV performances; Chair. Council of Slovak Music Union 1991–; Pres. Harmony Foundation 1991–; Dir of Opera, State Theatre, Košice 2006–10, Slovak Nat. Theatre, Bratislava 2010–12; Dir, Slovak Inst., Rome 2013–; performed charity concerts after floods in Czech Repub. 2002; Pres. Dvořak Competition, Karlovy Vary, Czech Repub.; awards include Tchaikovsky Competition, Geneva (5th Prize 1974, 1st Prize 1975), Leoš Janáček Memorial Medal 1978, Giuseppe Verdi Medal 1979, Artist of Merit 1981, Nat. Artist 1984, Kammersänger, Vienna 1986, Francisco Cilea Prize 1991, Wilhelm Furtwängler Prize 1992, Association Museum Enrico Caruso Premio Caruso Award, Milan 2013, Citta di Villafranca Giuseppe di Stefano Award 2013. *Leisure interests:* hunting, music, piano, family. *Address:* J. Hronca 1A, 841 02 Bratislava, Slovakia. *Fax:* (2) 64287626.

DWAN, Renata, M.Phil, PhD; Irish UN Official; *Director, United Nations Institute for Disarmament Research (UNIDIR);* b. 1969; ed Univ. of Oxford; Deputy Dir European Security Programme, EastWest Inst., Budapest 1997–99; Head Programme on Armed Conflict and Conflict Man., Stockholm Int. Peace Research Inst. 1999–2005; Special Adviser to EU Council Secr. 2002–03; Head on Peace Operations, Exec. Office of Sec.-Gen., UN 2015–16, Dir UN Inst. for Disarmament Research (UNIDIR) 2018–, fmr Team Leader Integrated Operational Teams for Afghanistan, Democratic Repub. of Congo, Haiti, Syria and Mali, Dept of Peacekeeping Operations, Special Asst and Chief of Staff, UN Supervision Mission in Syria (UNSMIS), Chief of Policy and Best Practices, Dept of Peacekeeping Operations and Field Support; mem. Task Force on Human Security Doctrine for Europe 2004; mem. Advisory Council, Luc Hoffmann Inst. *Publications:* Ed.: Building Security in Europe's New Borderlands 1999, Building Security in the New States of Eurasia: Subregional Cooperation in the Former Soviet Space 2000, Executive Policing: Enforcing the Law in Peace Operations 2002. *Address:* United Nations Institute for Disarmament Research (UNIDIR), Palais des Nations, 1211 Geneva 10, Switzerland (office). *Telephone:* 229171141 (office). *Fax:* 229170176 (office). *E-mail:* unidir@un.org (office). *Website:* www.unidir.org (office).

DWEK, Raymond Allen, CBE, DPhil, DSc, FRS, FRSC, FRSB, FRCP, CBiol, CChem; British biochemist and academic; *Director, Glycobiology Institute, University of Oxford;* b. 10 Nov. 1941, Manchester; s. of Victor Joe Dwek and Alice Liniado; m. Sandra Livingstone 1964; two s. two d.; ed Carmel Coll., Univ. of Manchester, Lincoln Coll., Oxford, Exeter Coll., Oxford; Research Lecturer in Physical Chem., Christ Church, Oxford 1966–68, in Biochemistry 1975–76; Lecturer in Inorganic Chem., Christ Church, Oxford 1968–75, in Biochemistry, Trinity Coll., Oxford 1976–84; Fellow, Exeter Coll., Oxford 1974–88, Professorial Fellow 1988–2011, Emer. Fellow 2007–; Dir Glycobiology Inst., Univ. of Oxford 1988–, Prof. of Glycobiology 1988–, Head of Dept of Biochemistry 2000–06; Dir for Grad. Training 1998–2000; mem. Oxford Enzyme Group 1971–88; Founder-mem. Oxford Oligosaccharide Group 1983; Univ. of Oxford Dir (non-exec.) and Founder Glycosciences Ltd (fmrly Glycosystems Ltd); Dir and Founding Scientist, IgX, Oxford 1998; Dir United Therapeutics 2002–; Visiting Royal Society Research Fellow, Weizmann Inst., Rehovot, Israel 1969; Royal Society Locke Research Fellow 1974–76; Visiting Prof., Duke Univ., NC; Hon. Life/Founder-mem. Swedish Biophysical Soc. 1979–; Kluge Chair of Tech. and Soc., Kluge Center of the Library of Congress, Washington, DC 2007; Biomedical Research Council Distinguished Visitor, Singapore 2005; mem. European Molecular Biological Org. (EMBO) 1988–, Scientific Advisory Bd, Hepatitis Foundation USA 1994–, Scientific Advisory Bd, Nat. Inst. for Biotechnology in the Negev, Ben-Gurion Univ. of the Negev, Israel (Chair.) 2001–17, Commonwealth Project for Hepatitis Outreach, USA 2002, Bd of Scientific Govs Scripps Research Inst., La Jolla, USA 2003–13 (Inst. Prof. 2008–), European Lipidonics Initiative 2004, Bd of Govs Exec. Cttee, Ben-Gurion Univ., Israel 2005–, Int. Advisory Bd of NIBN, Israel 2005–17; Pres. Inst. of Biology, London 2008–09; Judge, Millennium Fund Competition, The Daily Telegraph 1994; Scientific Adviser to the Pres., Ben Gurion Univ., Negev, Israel; Foreign mem. American Philosophical Soc. 2006, 2010; mem. Chancellors Court of Benefactors, Oxford, UK/Israel Life Sciences Council; Hon. mem. Inst. of Biochemistry, Bucharest 2000–; Hon. Fellow, Lincoln Coll., Oxford 2004; Hon. Fellow, Royal Soc. of Physicians 2007; Commdr, Nat. Romanian Order for Merit 2000; Dr hc (Catholic Univ. of Louvain) 1996, (Cluj, Romania) 2006; Hon. PhD (Ben-Gurion Univ., Israel) 2001; Hon. DSc (Scripps Research Inst., La Jolla, Calif.)

2004, (Univ. Coll. Dublin) 2010; The Wellcome Trust Award for Research in Biochemistry Related to Medicine 1994, Scientific Leadership Award, Hepatitis B Foundation, Philadelphia, Delaware Valley Coll. Centennial Award 1997, Boyce Thompson Distinguished Lecturer, Cornell Univ., USA 1997, Lemieux Lecturer, Univ. of Alberta, Canada 2003, Huxley Medal 2007, K.T. Wang Biooinorganic Prize and Lecture (Taiwan) 2010. *Publications include:* Nuclear Magnetic Resonance (NMR) in Biochemstry 1973, Physical Chemistry Principles and Problems for Biochemists (co-author) 2002, NMR in Biology (co-author) 1977, Biological Spectrosocopy (co-author) 1984; numerous scientific articles and patents. *Leisure interests:* family, patent law, sport, listening to music. *Address:* Glycobiology Institute, Department of Biochemistry, South Parks Road, Oxford, OX1 3QU (office); Exeter College, Oxford, OX1 3DP, England (home). *Telephone:* (1865) 275344 (office). *E-mail:* raymond.dwek@exeter.ox.ac.uk (office). *Website:* www.bioch.ox.ac.uk/research/dwek (office).

DWYER, Deanna (see KOONTZ, Dean Ray).

DWYER, K. R. (see KOONTZ, Dean Ray).

DYADKOVA, Larissa; Russian singer; b. 9 March 1952, Zelenodolsk; m. Alexandre Kogan 1985; one d.; ed Leningrad Conservatory class of J. Levando; joined Kirov Opera Co., making debut as Valvya in Glinka's Ivan Susanin; soloist, Mariinsky Theatre 1978–; guest soloist, Metropolitan Opera 1996–, La Scala, Communale Theatre, Florence, Deutsche Oper Berlin, Arena di Verona, San Francisco Opera, New Israeli Opera, Chicago Lyric Opera; Honoured Artist of Russia 1996, Order of Friendship of Peoples 2010, People's Artist of Russia; 2nd prize winner of Glinka Competition 1984, Golden Sofit prize 1998, Baltika prize 2000, Casta Diva 2001. *Concert appearances:* performs Verdi's Requiem in concerts, vocal series by Mussorgsky and Mahler, cantatas by Prokofiev; works with conductors Levine, Rostropovich, Mehta, Abbado, Temirkanov, Gergiev. *Address:* c/o IMG Artists, Carnegie Hall Tower, 152 West 57th Street, 5th Floor, New York, NY 10019, USA (office). *Telephone:* (212) 994-3500 (office). *Fax:* (212) 994-3550 (office). *E-mail:* atreuhaft@imgartists.com (office). *Website:* www .imgartists.com (office).

DYAKOV, Dumitru; Moldovan politician and journalist; b. 10 Feb. 1952, Kargopole, Kurgan Region, Russia; m.; two d.; ed Belarus State Univ.; Sec. Comsomol Cttee, Moldovan State TV and Radio; corresp., Komsomolskaya Pravda in Moldova –1976; on Comsomol Cen. Cttee, on Moldovan CP Cen. Cttee; Head TASS Bureau in Romania 1989–93; Sec. Moldovan Embassy, Moscow 1993–94; mem. Parl. 1994–; Chair. Parl. Comm. on Foreign Policy 1994–95; Deputy Speaker 1995–97, Speaker 1998–2000; f. Alliance for Democratic and Flourishing Moldova 1998; Founder-Chair. Democratic Party of Moldova 2000–09, Hon. Pres. 2009–. *Address:* Democratic Party of Moldova (Partidul Democrat din Moldova), 2001 Chişinău, str. Tighina 32, Moldova (office). *Telephone:* (22) 27-82-29 (office). *Fax:* (22) 27-82-30 (office). *E-mail:* pdm@mtc.md (office). *Website:* www.pdm.md (office).

DYANKOV, Simeon, MA, PhD; Bulgarian economist and politician; *Professor of Economics and Rector, New Economic School, Moscow;* b. 13 July 1970, Sofia; m. Caroline Freund; two c.; ed Language High School, Lovech, Karl Marx Inst. of Econs (now Univ. of Nat. and World Economy), Univ. of Michigan, USA; Chief Economist on Finance and Pvt. Sector Affairs, World Bank 1995–2009, Prin. Author of annual review of the World Bank – World Development Report 2002; Assoc. Ed. Journal of Comparative Economics 2004–09; Deputy Prime Minister and Minister of Finance 2009–13; Prof. of Econs and Rector, New Economic School, Moscow 2013–; jtly est. Ideas42 think tank (Harvard Univ.-Int. Finance Corpn venture). *Publications:* more than 70 specialized articles in int. econ. journals, including Quarterly Journal of Economics, American Economic Review, Journal of Finance, Journal of Financial Economics, Journal of Public Economics; creator of the annual Doing Business report, World Bank Group 2003. *Address:* Office of the Rector, New Economic School, Office #2.02, 100 Novaya Street, Skolkovo, 143025 Moscow, Russia (office). *Telephone:* (495) 956-95-08 (office). *E-mail:* sdjankov@ nes .ru (office). *Website:* www.nes.ru/ (office).

DYBKJAER, Lone, MChemEng; Danish politician and fmr EU official; b. (Lone Vincents), 23 May 1940, Copenhagen; m. Poul Nyrup Rasmussen (q.v.); two d.; ed Rungsted Statsskole, Tech. Univ. of Denmark; Sec., Acad. of Tech. Sciences 1964–66, Medico-Tech. Cttee 1966–70; Head Information Secr., Tech. Univ. of Denmark 1970–77; Adviser, Geotechnical Inst. 1978–79; mem. Folketing (Parl.) 1973–77, 1979–94; Chair. Parl. Energy Cttee, 1984–87, Tech. Cttee 1984–88, Parl. nine-mem. Cttee on Tech. Bd 1986–88; Social Liberal Party Spokesperson on Energy, Labour Market and Environmental Questions 1979–87, 1990–94, on Foreign Affairs 1987–88; Minister of the Environment 1988–90; mem. European Parl. 1994–2004, First Vice-Chair. Cttee on Devt and Co-operation (responsible for human rights) 1999–2002, mem. Cttee on Women's Rights and Equal Opportunities 1999–2004, Cttee on Constitutional Affairs 2002–04, ACP-EU Ass. 2002–04; Bird Life Prize 1993, Cyclist of the Year 1989, Gold Medal for Conservation of Bldgs 1991. *Publications include:* Tête à tête with a Modern Politician 1998, Peculiar Parliament 1999, Digital Denmark 1999. *Leisure interests:* tennis, reading, family life. *Address:* Christiansborg, 1240 KBHK, Denmark (office); Allégade 6A, 2000 Frederiksberg, Denmark (home). *Telephone:* 33212585 (office). *Fax:* 33253960 (office). *E-mail:* rvlody@ft.dk (office). *Website:* www.lonedybkjaer .dk (office).

DYDUCH, Marek; Polish politician and lawyer; b. 27 Aug. 1957, Świdnica; s. of Hipolit Dyduch and Krystyna Dyduch; m. Dorota Dyduch; one d. one s.; ed Wrocław Univ.; Chair. Local Council 1982–83; Chair. City-Communal Exec. Bd Union of Polish Socialist Youth (ZSMP), Żarów 1982–83, Vice-Chair. Prov. Exec. Bd, Wałbrzych 1983–86, Chair. 1986–91; joined Polish United Workers' Party (PZPR) 1982; mem. Prov. Nat. Council, Wałbrzych 1984–88; Deputy to Sejm (Parl.) 1993–2005, Vice-Chair. Comm. of Justice, Co-Pres. Comm. of Codification for Penal Codes, mem. Social Policy Comm., Comm. for Health Insurance, Comm. for Social Insurance, Justice and Human Rights Comm., Extraordinary Comm. for the Reform of Public Admin, Extraordinary Comm. for Social Insurance; mem. Social Democracy of the Repub. of Poland (SdRP) 1990–99, Democratic Left Alliance (SLD, after party reorganization) 1999–, Chair. Lower-Silesian Prov. Bd, SLD, Wrocław 1999–2002, Sec.-Gen. SLD 2002–05, fmr mem. SLD Nat. Exec. Bd; Sec. of State, Ministry of the Treasury 2001–02; Founder Ferdinand Lassal Foundation, Wrocław; joined Polish People's Party (Polskie Stronnictwo Ludowe) 2008; Bronze Cross of Merit 1989. *Leisure interests:* tennis, skiing, local and global social phenomena, history, science-fiction.

DYER, Alexander Patrick, BS, MBA; American business executive (retd); b. 30 Aug. 1932, Santa Rosa, Calif.; s. of John Dyer and Amie M. Moore; m. Shirley Shine 1954; one s. (and one s. deceased); ed US Mil. Acad., West Point and Harvard Business School; Exec. Vice-Pres. Air Products and Chemicals, BOC Group PLC 1987–89, Man. Dir Gases and CEO 1989–93, Deputy Chair. 1993–96, CEO 1993–96 (retd); Chair. Bunzl PLC 1993–96, Deputy Chair. Bunzl 1996–2005; mem. Bd of Dirs BWAY Corpn 1995–2002. *Publication:* Hardball in the Boardroom (memoir) 2011. *Leisure interests:* golf, skeet, antique collecting, photography. *Address:* 2117 Kirkland Village Circle, Bethlehem, PA 18017, USA (home). *Telephone:* (610) 691-4618 (home). *E-mail:* apdyer1954@aol.com (home).

DYKE, Gregory (Greg), BA; British fmr media executive and organization executive; *Vice-President for Television, British Academy of Film and Television Arts;* b. 20 May 1947; s. of David Dyke and Denise Dyke; m. Sue Howes; one s. one d.; one step-s. one step-d.; ed Hayes Grammar School, Univ. of York and Harvard Business School, USA; reporter on local paper; researcher, London Weekend Television (LWT) 1977, later founding producer, The Six O'Clock Show; joined TV-AM 1983; Dir of Programmes, TVS 1984–87; Dir of Programmes, LWT 1987–90, Man. Dir 1990; Group Chief Exec. LWT (Holdings) PLC 1991–94; Chair. Ind. TV Assen 1992–94; Chair. GMTV 1993–94; Chair. CEO Pearson TV 1995–99; Chair. Channel 5 Broadcasting 1997–99; Dir-Gen. BBC 2000–04 (resgnd); Dir BSkyB 1995, Phoenix Pictures Inc., New York, Pearson PLC 1996–99 and others; Dir (non-exec.) Manchester United Football Club 1997–99; mem. Supervisory Bd ProSiebenSat.1 Media 2004–; adviser, Apax Partners Inc. 2004–, Chair. Sunshine Acquisition Ltd (acquisition vehicle formed by Apax) 2005–, Chair. HiT Entertainment (acquired by Sunshine Acquisition) 2005–; Chair. BFI 2008–16, FC 2006–13, Football Assen 2013–16; Chancellor Univ. of York 2004–15; Vice-Pres. for Television, BAFTA 2015–; Trustee, Science Museum 1996–, English Nat. Stadium Trust 1997–99; Royal TV Soc. Lifetime Achievement Award, Broadcasting Press Guild Award 2004. *Publication:* Memoirs 2004. *Leisure interests:* tennis, theatre, football, cinema. *Address:* BAFTA, Piccadilly, St James's, London, W1J 9LN, England (office). *Telephone:* (20) 7292-5800 (home). *E-mail:* info@bafta.org (office). *Website:* www.bafta.org (office).

DYLAN, Bob; American composer, musician (guitar, piano, harmonica, autoharp) and singer; b. (Robert Allen Zimmerman), 24 May 1941, Duluth, Minn.; m. Sara Lowndes (divorced 1978); four c. one adopted d.; ed Univ. of Minnesota; best known for composition and interpretation of pop, country and folk music; performer, numerous tours and concerts; devised and popularized folk-rock 1965; performed with The Band; f. new group The Traveling Wilburys 1988; host, Theme Time Radio Hour with Your Host Bob Dylan (XM Satellite Radio) 2006–; mem. American Acad. of Arts and Letters 2013–; Commdr, Ordre des Arts et des Lettres 1990, Chevalier, Legion d'honneur 2013; Hon. DMus (Princeton Univ.) 1970, (Univ. of St Andrews) 2004; Tom Paine Award 1963, Dorothy and Lillian Gish Prize 1997, Polar Music Prize 2000, Acad. Award for Best Theme Song (for Things Have Changed, from The Wonder Boys) 2002, Grammy Award for Best Solo Rock Vocal Performance (for Someday Baby) 2007, Premio Príncipe de Asturias 2007, Pulitzer Prize Special Citation 2008, Nat. Medal of Arts 2009, Presidential Medal of Freedom 2012, MusiCare Person of the Year 2015, Nobel Prize for Literature 2016. *Films appearances:* Eat the Document, Pat Garrett and Billy the Kid, Renaldo and Clara (also directed), Hearts of Fire 1986, Concert for Bangladesh, Masked and Anonymous 2003. *Radio:* presenter weekly music programme (Deep Tracks Channel, XM) 2006–. *Recordings include:* albums: The Freewheelin' Bob Dylan 1964, Bringing It All Back Home 1965, Highway 61 Revisited 1965, Blonde On Blonde 1966, John Wesley Harding 1968, Nashville Skyline 1969, Self Portrait 1970, New Morning 1970, Planet Waves (with The Band) 1974, Before The Flood 1974, Blood On The Tracks (with The Band) 1975, Hard Rain 1976, Desire 1976, Street Legal 1978, Slow Train Coming 1979, Infidels 1983, Empire Burlesque 1985, Knocked out Loaded 1986, Down in the Groove 1988, Traveling Wilburys (with Traveling Wilburys) 1988, Dylan and the Dead (with Grateful Dead) 1989, Oh Mercy 1989, Under The Red Sky 1990 (Vol. 3) (with Traveling Wilburys) 1990, The Bootleg Series 1990, Good as I Been to You 1992, World Gone Wrong 1993, Unplugged 1995, Time Out of Mind (Grammy Award 1998) 1997, Love and Theft 2001, Modern Times (Grammy Award for Best Contemporary Folk/Americana Album 2007) 2006, Together Through Life 2009, Christmas in the Heart 2009, Tempest 2012, The Bootleg Series (Vol. 10): Another Self Portrait 2013, Bootleg Series Vol. 11): The Basement Tapes Complete 2014, Shadows in the Night 2015, Fallen Angels 2016. *Publications include:* Tarantula 1966, Writings and Drawings 1973, The Songs of Bob Dylan 1966–1975 1976, Lyrics 1962–1985 1986, Drawn Blank 1994, Highway 61 Revisited (interactive CD-ROM), Chronicles: Volume One (memoir) (Quill Book Award for Best Biography or Memoir 2005) 2004, Lyrics 1962–2001 2005, Dylan's Inspirations 2006. *Address:* c/o Jeff Rosen, PO Box 870, Cooper Station, New York, NY 10276, USA (office). *Website:* www.bobdylan.com.

DYMOCK, Vice-Adm. Sir Anthony Knox, KBE, CB, FRSA; British fmr naval officer; b. 18 July 1949, Liverpool, England; m. Lizzie Frewer; one s. one d.; ed Brighton Hove and Sussex Grammar School, Univ. of East Anglia, Britannia Royal Naval Coll., Dartmouth, Greenwich Naval Coll., Harvard Univ. Kennedy School Sr Exec. Security Program, USA; joined the Royal Navy 1969, served on HMS Antrim during Falklands War 1981–83, promoted to Commdr 1985, Commodore, Rear-Adm. 2000, Vice-Adm. 2006–08; has served as Commdr HMS Plymouth 1985–88, HMS Campbeltown 1992–93, HMS Cornwall 1996–98, HMS Invincible, served on USS Midway during Gulf War 1991, commanded a battle force during Operation Southern Watch, Iraq 1992 and operations in the Adriatic during Kosovo air campaign; NATO experience includes SNFL tour as Flag Captain, NATO course dir, Maritime Tactical School 1992, Deputy Commdr UK Maritime Task Group 1991–92, ASWSTRIKFOR role, apptd Deputy Commdr Strike Force South 2000–02, conducted NATO amphibious exercises around Mediterranean and Black Seas onboard USS Lasalle, Mil. Rep., NATO, Brussels 2006–08; posts with Ministry of Defence include Commdr on Cen. Jt Staff, Capt. First Sea Lord's staff, Defence Attaché in Naples, Italy and Washington, DC 2002–05; retd 2008; has lectured on security at Nat. Defense Univ., Washington, DC, MIT; mem. Nautical Inst.; Freeman, City of London. *Leisure interests:* sailing.

DYNKIN, Alexander A., DrSc (Econs); Russian economist, political scientist and academic; *President, Institute of World Economy and International Relations (IMEMO), Russian Academy of Sciences;* b. 30 July 1948, Moscow; ed Moscow Aviation Inst., Inst. of World Economy and Int. Relations, Russian Acad. of Sciences; Research Fellow, then Sr Research Fellow and Dept Head, Inst. of World Economy and Int. Relations, Russian Acad. of Sciences 1975–89, Deputy Dir 1989–91, First Deputy Dir 1991–2006, Dir 2006–16, Pres. 2017–, Prof. of Econs, Russian Acad. of Sciences 1989–, Academician Sec., Div. for Global and Int. Relations 2010–, Corresp. mem. Russian Acad. of Sciences 2000–06, Full mem. 2006–, Presidium mem. 2010–; Econ. Advisor to Russian Fed. Prime Minister 1998–99; Chair. School of Econs, Moscow Int. Univ. 2001–; Chair. Scientific Council of Russian Council on Foreign Affairs; First Deputy Chair., Pugwash Continuing Cttee; mem. Bd of Dirs Russian Union of Industrialists and Entrepreneurs 2003–07, Acron 2008– (Advisor to CEO 2009–, currently Chair. Strategic Planning and Corp. Governance Cttee); mem. Bd of Trustees, Inst. of Contemporary Devt Foundation 2009–; mem. Council on Competitiveness and Entrepreneurship to Russian Govt 2004–08, High Scientific Attestation Comm. 2007–, Russian Presidential Council on Science, Tech. and Educ. 2008–, Econ. Council under Pres. of Russian Fed., Scientific Expert Council under Chairman of Fed. Council of Russian Fed. Ass., 'International Position of Russia: Economic Guidelines' Expert Group, Council on Grants of Russian Govt Tender Comm. on Selection of Programs for Devt of Univs, Scientific Council of Russian Fed. Security Council, Scientific Council to Minister of Foreign Affairs, Comm. attached to Pres. of Russian Fed. on devt strategy of fuel and energy complex and environmental safety; Order of the Badge of Honour 1986, Order of Friendship 2006, Order of Honour 2012, Order of the Rising Sun, Third Class (Japan) 2017, Order of Alexander Nevsky 2018; Int. Security Acitivities Medal 2016, Primakov Gold Medal 2017. *Publications include:* New Stage of Technological Revolution 1991, Innovation Economy 2001, Business Groups and Modernisation of Russian Economy 2001, The World at the Turn of the Millennium: The Forecast for the World Economy until 2015 2001, World Economy: Forecast Towards 2020 2008, Global Strategic Outlook 2030 2011. *Address:* Primakov National Research, Institute of World Economy and International Relations, Russian Academy of Sciences, Moscow 117997, 23 Profsoyuznaya Street, Russia (office). *Telephone:* (499) 128-0514 (office). *Fax:* (495) 913-6575 (office). *E-mail:* dynkin@imemo.ru (office). *Website:* www.imemo.ru (office).

DYSON, Freeman John, FRS; American physicist and academic; *Professor Emeritus of Physics, Institute for Advanced Study;* b. 15 Dec. 1923, Crowthorne, England; s. of Sir George Dyson and Lady Mildred Dyson (Atkey); m. 1st Verena Huber 1950 (divorced 1958); one s. one d.; m. 2nd Imme Jung 1958; four d.; ed Univ. of Cambridge, UK, Cornell Univ.; worked as civilian scientist for RAF during World War II; Fellow, Trinity Coll., Cambridge 1946; Warren Research Fellow, Birmingham Univ. 1949; Prof. of Physics, Cornell Univ. 1951–53; Prof., Inst. for Advanced Study, Princeton 1953–94, Prof. Emer. 1994–; Chair. Fed. of American Scientists 1962; mem. NAS 1964–; Foreign Assoc., Acad. des Sciences, Paris 1989; Hon. DSc (City Univ., UK) 1981, (Oxford) 1997; Gifford Lecturer, Aberdeen 1985, Heineman Prize, American Inst. of Physics 1965, Lorentz Medal, Royal Netherlands Acad. 1966, Hughes Medal, Royal Soc. 1968, Max Planck Medal, German Physical Soc. 1969, Harvey Prize, Israel Inst. of Tech. 1977, Wolf Prize (Israel) 1981, Matteucci Medal, Rome 1990, Fermi Award (USA) 1994, Templeton Prize 2000, Henri Poincaré Prize 2012. *Publications include:* Disturbing the Universe 1979, Weapons and Hope 1984, Origins of Life 1986, Infinite in All Directions 1988, From Eros to Gaia 1992, Imagined Worlds 1997, The Sun, The Genome and the Internet 1999, The Scientist as Rebel 2006, A Many-Colored Glass 2007; papers in The Physical Review, Journal of Mathematical Physics, etc. *Address:* Institute for Advanced Study, School of Natural Sciences, Einstein Drive, Princeton, NJ 08540 (office); 105 Battle Road Circle, Princeton, NJ 08540, USA (home). *Telephone:* (609) 734-8055 (office). *Fax:* (609) 951-4489 (office). *E-mail:* dyson@ias.edu (office). *Website:* www.sns.ias.edu/dyson (office).

DYSON, Sir James, Kt, OM, CBE, FCSD, MDes; British designer and inventor; *Founder and Chief Engineer, Dyson Appliances Ltd;* b. 2 May 1947; s. of Alec Dyson and Mary Dyson (née Bolton); m. Deirdre Hindmarsh 1967; two s. one d.; ed Gresham's School, Royal Coll. of Art; Dir Rotork Marine 1970–74; Man. Dir Kirk Dyson 1974–79; developed and designed Dyson Dual Cyclone vacuum cleaner 1979–93; Founder and Chair. Prototypes Ltd (now Dyson Research) 1979–; Founder and Chief Engineer, Dyson Appliances Ltd 1992–; Chair. Bath Coll. of Higher Educ. 1990–92, Design Museum 1999–2004; mem. Design Council 1997–; mem. Council RCA 1998–, Provost, RCA 2011–; Founder and Pres. James Dyson Foundation 2002–; Founder Dyson Inst. of Eng and Tech. 2017; mem. Prime Minister's Business Advisory Group 2010–; Fellow, Royal Acad. of Eng 2005; Patron, Design and Technology Asscn 2010–, RUH Bath Cancer Care Campaign 2013–; Trustee, Roundhouse Theatre, London; Hon. Fellow, Liverpool John Moores Univ., MEID (Inst. of Eng Designers) 1997; Hon. Mem. IEEE 2017; numerous hon. doctorates including Hon. DSc (Oxford Brookes) 1997, (Brunel Univ.) 1999, (Bath, Imperial Coll. London, RCA) 2000; numerous design awards and trophies; Royal Designer for Industry Royal Soc. of Arts 2005, Lifetime Achievement Award, Plus X Awards, 2007. *Publications include:* Doing a Dyson 1996, Against the Odds (autobiog.) 1997, History of Great Inventions 2001. *Leisure interests:* running, garden design, tennis, opera, bassoon. *Address:* Dyson Ltd, Tetbury Mill, Malmesbury, Wilts., SN16 0RP, England (office). *Telephone:* (1666) 827200 (office). *Fax:* (1666) 827321 (office). *E-mail:* helen.williams@dyson.com (office). *Website:* www.dyson.com (office).

DYVIK, Helge Julius Jakhelln, DPhil; Norwegian academic; *Professor of General Linguistics, University of Bergen;* b. 23 Dec. 1947, Bodø; s. of Einar Dyvik and Harriet Dyvik (née Jakhelln); m. 1st Eva Sætre 1973 (divorced 1994); one s. one d.; m. 2nd Martha Thunes 2001; one s.; ed Univ. of Bergen, Univ. of Durham, UK; Research Asst (Old Norse), Univ. of Bergen 1974–75, Lecturer 1976, Project Asst (Old Norwegian syntax) 1976–81, Research Fellow (Vietnamese syntax project) 1981–83, Prof. of Gen. Linguistics 1983–; Pres. Nordic Asscn of Linguists 1993–98; mem. Norwegian Language Council 2000–, Programme Cttee for Nordic Council of Ministers' Research Programme on Language Tech. 2000–05 (Chair. 2002–); Chair. Expert Cttee for Standardisation and Language Observation under the Norwegian Language Council 2007–; Fridtjof Nansen Award for Eminent Research, Norwegian Acad. of Letters and Science 1987. *Publications:* Grammatikk og Empiri 1981, Categories and Functions in Vietnamese Classifier Constructions 1983, Semantic Mirrors 1998. *Leisure interests:* play reading, choral singing. *Address:* Department of Linguistic, Literary and Aesthetic Studies, Linguistic Studies Section, University of Bergen, Sydnespl. 7, 5007 Bergen (office); Straumevn. 3A, 5151 Straumsgrend, Bergen, Norway (home). *Telephone:* 55-58-22-61 (office). *E-mail:* helge.dyvik@lili.uib.no (office). *Website:* www.hg.uib.no/i/lili/slf/ans/Dyvik (office).

DŽAFEROVIĆ, Šefik; Bosnia and Herzegovina lawyer, politician and fmr judge; *Member, State Presidency;* b. 9 Sept. 1957, Zavidovići; s. of Salih and Hatka Džaferović; m. Vildana Džaferović; two c.; ed Univ. of Sarajevo; judge, Zavidovići Municipal Court 1979–86; judge, Zenica Higher Court 1986–92; worked as lawyer 1992–93; worked in admin. affairs, Zenica Dist 1993–94; Chief of Zenica Security Services Centre, Ministry of Internal Affairs 1994–96; Chair. Zenica-Doboj Canton Ass. 1996–2000; mem. House of Peoples, Parl. of Fed. of Bosnia and Herzegovina 1998–2000, 2000–02; mem. House of Reps, Parl. Ass. of Bosnia and Herzegovina 2002–14, Chair./Vice-Chair., House of Reps 2014–18; mem. State Presidency of Bosnia and Herzegovina 2018–; mem. Stranka Demokratske Akcije (SDA, Party of Democratic Action) 1990–, Gen. Sec. 2001–05, currently Vice-Chair. *Address:* Office of the State Presidency, 71000 Sarajevo, Maršala Tita 16, Bosnia and Herzegovina (office). *Telephone:* (33) 567510 (office). *Fax:* (33) 555620 (home). *E-mail:* press@predsjednistvobih.ba (office). *Website:* www.predsjednistvobih.ba (office).

DZAIDDIN BIN HAJI ABDULLAH, Tun Mohamed; Malaysian judge; *Chairman, Bursa Malaysia Berhad;* b. 16 Sept. 1937, Arau, Perlis; m. Puan Noriah Binti Tengku Ismael; two c.; ed Sultan Abdul Hamid Coll., Alor Setar; journalist, Malay Mail 1956; joined police service as Insp.; called to Bar, Middle Temple, London, UK 1966; admitted as advocate and solicitor in Kota Bharu and Kuala Lumpur 1967; juridical commr (part-time) 1979–82; High Court Judge, Criminal Div. of Kuala Lumpur High Court 1982–84, Penang High Court 1984–92; Supreme Court Judge (renamed Fed. Court Judge) 1992–2000, Chief Justice of the Fed. Court 2000–03; Chair. Bursa Malaysia Berhad (fmrly Kuala Lumpur Stock Exchange) 2004–; Chair. Deutsche Bank (Malaysia) Berhad, Tun Mohamed Suffian Foundation; apptd Dir (non-exec.) and Public Interest Dir by Minister of Finance 2004; fmr Chair. Royal Comm. to Enhance the Operation and Man. of the Royal Police Force, Kelantan Bar Cttee; Vice-Pres. Malaysian Bar Asscn 1981–82; Life mem. ASEAN Law Asscn of Malaysia, Pres. 1994–97, Pres. ASEAN Law Asscn 1997; Hon. LLD (San Beda Coll.) 2002; several awards, including Seri Paduka Baginda Yang DiPertuan Agong of the Most Esteemed Order of Seri Setia Mahkota Malaysia. *Leisure interest:* golf. *Address:* Office of the Chairman, Bursa Malaysia Berhad, Exchange Square, Bukit Kewangan, 50200 Kuala Lumpur, Malaysia (office). *Telephone:* (603) 2034-7000 (office). *Fax:* (603) 2732-5258 (office). *E-mail:* publicrelations@bursamalaysia.com (office). *Website:* www.bursamalaysia.com (office).

DZASOKHOV, Aleksandr Sergeyevich, CandHistSc, Dr rer. pol, PhD; Russian politician; b. 3 April 1934, Ordzhonikidze, North Ossetian ASSR; m. Farisa Borissovna 1959; two s.; ed North Caucasian Mining-Metallurgical Inst. and CPSU Higher Party School; mem. CPSU 1957–91; First Sec. Ordzhonikidze Komsomol City Cttee 1957–61; Sec. of USSR Cttee of Youth Orgs 1961–64; leader of young Soviet specialists to Cuba 1964–65; First Sec., Pres. of USSR Youth Orgs 1965–67; Deputy Chair., Chair. of Soviet Cttee for Solidarity with Countries of Asia and Africa 1965–86; USSR Amb. to Syria 1986–88; First Sec. of North Ossetian CPSU Dist Cttee (Obkom) 1988–90; USSR People's Deputy 1989–91; Chair. Cttee of USSR Supreme Soviet on Int. Affairs 1990–91; mem., Sec. of Cen. Cttee CPSU, mem. of CPSU Politburo 1990–91; People's Deputy of Russia, mem. Supreme Soviet of Russian Fed. 1992–93; Chair. Sub-Cttee on Asia and the Pacific; mem. State Duma (Parl.) 1993–98; elected Pres. of Repub. of North Ossetia-Alania 1998–2005; Deputy Chair. Inter-Parl. Group of Russian Fed. 1993, Chair. 1996–2001; mem. Acad. of Creative Endeavours; mem. Bd Dirs Pervyi Kanal; Hon. Mem., Russian Acad. of Arts; Order of the Red Banner of Labour 1971, Order of the October Revolution 1981, Order of Friendship of Peoples 1984, Order of Merit for the Fatherland (III class) 2001, (II class) 2004, (IV class) 2009, Order of St Prince Daniel of Moscow; Medal In Commemoration of the 850th Anniversary of Moscow 1997, Medal In Commemoration of the 1000th Anniversary of Kazan 2005; state awards from of Afghanistan, Hungary, Viet Nam and several other states. *Publications:* several books on problems of post-colonialism in third-world countries, including Formation and Evolution of the Post-colonial World 1999.

DZHEMILEV, Mustafa (Abdul-Dzhemil); Ukrainian activist; b. 14 Nov. 1943, Ayserez, Crimea; m. Safinar Dzhemileva; two s. one d.; imprisoned or exiled for dissident activity 1966–67, 1969–72, 1974–75, 1975–77, 1979–82, 1983–86; continued to organize Crimean Tatar protest actions in Cen. Asia and Moscow; returned to Crimea 1989; Chair. Crimean Tatar Majlis 1991; Pres. Crimea Foundation 1991; elected mem. Verkhovna Rada (Supreme Council) 1998, Chair. Council of Reps 1999; political observer, Business magazine; Order of the Republic (Turkey) 2014; Dr hc (Seljuk Univ., Higher Tech. Inst. Gebze, Turkey); Nansen Medal UNHCR 1998, Pylyp Orlyk Int. Award 2000, Yaroslav Mudryi Medal 2001, Hon. Prize of Parliament of Ukraine 2002, Lech Walesa-Prize of Solidarity 2014. *Leisure interest:* studying informative websites. *Address:* 6th Microrayon 100, Bakhchesaray, Crimea, Ukraine (home). *Telephone:* (652) 5443758 (home).

DZHIGARKHANIAN, Armen Borisovich; Armenian/Russian actor; b. 3 Oct. 1935, Yerevan; m. Tatiana Vlasova 1967 (divorced); one s.; ed Yerevan Theatre Inst.; actor with Stanislavsky Russian Drama Theatre in Yerevan 1955–67; with Moscow Lenin Komsomol Theatre 1967–69, with Mayakovsky Theatre 1969–96, with Dzhigarkhanian Theatre 1996–; Hon. Citizen, Yerevan 2001; Order For Merit to the Fatherland, III Class 1995, Order For Merit to the Fatherland, IV Class 2005, Order of Alexander Nevsky 2006, Order For Merit to the Fatherland, II Class 2010, Order of Honour of Armenia 2010; Armenian SSR State Prize 1975, 1979, RSFSR People's Artist 1973, USSR People's Artist 1985, Stanislavsky Award 2001. *Films include:* The New Adventures of the Elusive Avengers 1968, The Crown of the Russian Empire, or Once Again the Elusive Avengers 1971, The Meeting Place Cannot Be Changed 1979, Vanished Empire 2008, O, Luckyman! 2009, Ispoved dyavola 2009, The Edge 2010, Zolotaya rybka v gorode N 2011, 12 mesyatsev 2013, The House in the Heart 2014, A Warrior's Tail (voice) 2015. *Television includes:* Koroleva Margo 1996, Banditskiy Peterburg: Advokat (mini-series) 2000, Chasy bez strelok (film) 2001, Banditskiy Peterburg: Arestant (mini-series) 2003, Zvezda epokhi (mini-series) 2005, Artisty (film) 2007, Yarik (film) 2008, Nemets 2011. *Roles include:* Levinson in Fadeev's Thunder, Stanley in Tennessee Williams' Streetcar Named Desire, Socrates and Nero in Radzinsky's Chats with Socrates and the Theatre in the time of Nero and Seneca, Big Daddy in Tennessee Williams' Cat on a Hot Tin Roof, Max in Pinter's Homecoming, Krapp in Beckett's Krapp's Last Tape, Domenic in E. D. Phillippo's Philoumena Marturano. *Leisure interests:* reading, listening to classical music, playing with pet Siamese cat. *Address:* 121002 Moscow, 37 Starokonysheny per., Apt. 9, Russia. *Telephone:* (495) 930-23-07 (office); (495) 203-30-79 (home). *Fax:* (495) 930-03-47 (office).

DZINTARS, Raivis; Latvian politician and journalist; *Co-Chairman, Nacionālā apvienība (National Alliance);* b. 25 Nov. 1982, Rīga; m. Marta Dzintare; two c.; elected as one of two For Fatherland and Freedom Union/Latvian Nat. Conservative Party reps on joint Nat. Alliance list the party shared with All For Latvia! 2010, Co-Chair. (with Gaidis Bērziņš) when Nat. Alliance became a unitary party 2010–, party formed a centre-right coalition with Zatlers' Reform Party, and Unity; Nat. Alliance cand. for Prime Minister at 2011 election. *Address:* Nacionālā apvienība (National Alliance), Kaļķu iela 11, Rīga 1050, Latvia (office). *Telephone:* 2775-5997 (office). *E-mail:* info@nacionalaapvieniba.lv (office). *Website:* www.nacionalaapvieniba.lv (office).

DZIUBA, Andrzej Franciszek, (Franciszek Wieczyński), DD; Polish ecclesiastic and academic; *Bishop of Łowicz;* b. 10 Oct. 1950, Pleszew; s. of Stanisław Dziuba and Ludwika Ślachciak; ed Primatial Priests' Seminary, Gniezno, Pontifical Theological Faculty, Poznań, Catholic Univ. Lublin, Acad. Alfonsiana, Rome and Univ. Italiana per Stranieri, Perugia; ordained priest, Gniezno 1975; Asst Parish Priest and Catechist, Łobżenica 1975–76; studies in Lublin 1976–79, Rome 1979–81; Sec. to Primate of Poland 1981–98, Dir Secr. 1984–98; Asst Parish Priest, St Martin's Church, Warsaw 1981–98, St Barbara's Church, Warsaw 1998, Bishop of Łowicz 2004–; Prof., Catholic Univ. Lublin 1989–, Acad. of Catholic Theology, Warsaw 1995–99, Primatial Priest's Seminary, Gniezno 1998–, Cardinal S. Wyszyński Univ. 1999–; Hon. Chaplain to the late Pope John Paul II 1990, Prelate 1996; Primate of Poland Foundation in GB 1991; Canon Metropolitan Chapter of Warsaw 1998; Theological Counsellor to Primate of Poland 1998–; Chair. Scientific Council of EPP, Higher Education Team of Church Concordat Cttee; KEP Delegate to Int. Eucharistic Congresses; Chief Chaplain Polish Asscn of Knights of Malta; mem. Church Concordat Cttee; Hon. Citizen of Łowicz 2009; Hon. Conventual Chaplain of Order of Malta 1998, Grand Cross 2005; Kt Commdr of Equestrian Order of Holy Sepulchre of Jerusalem 1996, Cross with Gold Star of Merit of Holy Sepulchre of Jerusalem 1996, Kt Ecclesiastical Grace of Sacred Mil. Constantinian Order 1999; Dr hc (Polish Univ. Abroad) 2009. *Publications include:* Mikołaj z Mościsk, teolog moralista XVII w. 1985, Jan Azor, teolog-moralista 1988, Informator Katolicki 89/90 1990, Droga Krzyżowa 1991, Różaniec święty 1992, Kościół katolicki w Polsce. Informator 1993, Jezus nam przebacza. Przygotowanie do sakramentu pojednania 1994, Matka Boża z Guadalupe 1995, Kościół katolicki w Polsce. Informator 1995, Orędzie moralne Jezusa Chrystusa 1996, Kościół katolicki w Polsce. Informator 1997, Droga krzyżowa 1998, Biography of Cardinal Józef Glemp 1998, Cardinal Stefan Wyszyński Primate of Poland. A Life-Sketch 2000, Spowiedź małżeńska. Życie małżeńskie a sakramentalna posługa pokuty i pojednania 2002, Prestamé spoteczne karolynats Stefana Wyczyniskiego, Prymosa Polski 2004; numerous articles on moral theology, church history, Catholic social sciences. *Address:* Diocese of Łowicz, Stary Rynek 20, 99-400 Łowicz, Poland (office). *Telephone:* (46) 8376615 (office). *Fax:* (46) 8374349 (office). *E-mail:* kuria@diecezja.lowicz.pl (office). *Website:* www.diecezja.lowicz.pl (office).

DZIUBA, Ivan Mykhailovych; Ukrainian literary critic and academic; b. 26 July 1931, Mykolaivka; s. of Mykhailo Dzyuba and Olga Dzyuba; m. Marta Lenets 1963; one d.; ed Donetsk Pedagogical Inst.; ed. of various journals and publs published by Ukrainian State Publishing House; published An Ordinary Man or a Petit Bourgeois as well as numerous samizdat articles in 1960s; expelled from Writers' Union 1972 after publication of Internationalism or Russification? (numerous edns); arrested 1972, sentenced to 5 years' imprisonment 1973; recanted and released Nov. 1973; Writers' Union membership restored 1980s; co-f. People's Movement of Ukraine 1989; Academician, Nat. Acad. of Sciences of Ukraine 1992–, mem. Presidium 1997–; Academician-Sec. Dept of Literature, Language and Arts 1996–2004; Minister of Culture 1992–94; Sr Researcher, T. Shevchenko Inst. of Literature 1994–2001; Ed.-in-Chief Suchasnist (magazine) 1991–2003, Encyclopaedia of Modern Ukraine 1998; Head of Cttee Tazas Shevchenko Nat. Ukrainian Award 1999–2005; Hon. Pres. PEN Ukraine; Order of Rising Sun (Japan) 2006, Kt, Order of Freedom 2009; O. Biletski Prize 1987, Laureate, Shevchenko's Award 1991, Int. Antonovich Prize 1992, V. Zhabotinsky Prize 1996, Vernadsky Prize 2001. *Publications include:* 25 books including Between Politics and Literature 1998, Thirst 2001, Trap 2003; numerous articles on history and devt of Ukrainian literature and writers of former USSR. *Leisure interests:* gardening, mushrooming. *Address:* Presidium of the National Academy of Sciences of Ukraine, 01030 Kiev, Volodymyrska, 54 (office); Antonova str. 7, Apt 60, Kiev 03186, Ukraine (home). *Telephone:* (44) 248-41-77 (home). *Website:* www.nas.gov.ua (office).

DZIWISZ, Cardinal Stanisław, ThD; Polish ecclesiastic; *Archbishop Emeritus of Kraków;* b. 27 April 1939, Raba Wyżna; ed Primatial Priest Seminary, Kraków, Metropolitan Ecclesiastic Seminary, Kraków, Pontifical Acad. of Theology, Kraków; ordained priest, Kraków 1963; Asst Parish Priest, Maków Podhalański 1963–65; Chaplain to Archbishop of Kraków Karol Wojtyła (later Pope John Paul II) 1966–78; Lecturer, Higher Inst. of Catechism, Kraków 1966–78; Ed. Kraków Curie Notificationes e Curia Metropolitana Cracoviensi 1966–78; Personal Sec. to Pope John Paul II 1978–2005, Prelate 1985, Apostolic Protonotary, Canon of Cathedral Chapter, Lviv and Metropolitan Chapter, Kraków 1997; Titular Bishop of San Leone and Prefetto aggiunto (Prefecture of the Sacred Household) 1998–2005; Titulare Archbishop of San Leone 2003–05; Archbishop of Kraków 2005–16, Archbishop Emer. 2016–; cr. Cardinal (Cardinal-Priest of Santa Maria del Popolo) 2006; participated in Papal Conclave 2013; Vice-Chair. John Paul II Foundation 1985; Order of the White Eagle 2017; Cardinal Bea Interfaith Award 2010. *Publications include:* Kult św. Stanisława biskupa w Krakowie do Soboru Trydenckiego (Cult of Saint Stanislaus, Bishop of Kraków until Council of Trent) 1978, Swiadectwo (Testimony) 2007, A Life with Karol 2008. *Address:* Archdiocese of Kraków, ul. Franciszkanska 3, 31 004 Kraków, Poland (office). *Telephone:* (12) 6288100 (office). *Fax:* (12) 4294617 (office). *E-mail:* kuria@diecezja.krakow.pl (office). *Website:* www.diecezja.pl (office).

DŽOMBIĆ, Aleksandar; Bosnia and Herzegovina banking executive and government official; b. 1968, Banja Luka; m.; one c.; ed Univ. of Banja Luka, Belgrade Univ.; worked in Banja Luka City Admin; Head, Dept and Project Man., Kristal Bank, Banja Luka; Dir Agroprom Bank, Banja Luka; Exec. Dir Nova Banka, Bijeljina; Minister of Finance of Republika Srpska 2006–10, Prime Minister of Republika Srpska 2010–13; Alt. Gov. EBRD. *Address:* c/o Office of the Prime Minister, 78000 Banja Luka, trg Republike Srpske 1, Bosnia and Herzegovina. *E-mail:* kabinet@vladars.net.

DZUMAGULOV, Apas Dzumagulovich; Kyrgyzstani engineer, diplomatist and fmr politician; b. 19 Sept. 1934, Arashan, Kyrgyz SSR; m.; three s.; ed Moscow Gubkin Inst. of Oil; mem. CPSU 1962–91; worked at Complex S., Geological Expedition USSR Acad. of Sciences 1958–59; sr geologist, oil field Changar-Tash, Head of Cen. Research Lab., Chief Geologist Drilling Div., Chief Engineer, Oil Co. Kyrghizneft Osh Dist 1959–73; Head of Industrial-Transport Div. Cen. Cttee CP of Kyrgyz SSR 1973–79; Sec., Cen. Cttee CP of Kirgyzia 1979–85; First Sec., Issyk-Kul Dist Cttee 1985–86; Chair. Council of Ministers Kyrgyz SSR 1986–91; Chair. Org. Cttee, then Chair. Regional Soviet of Deputies, Head of Admin. Chuysk Region 1991–93; Deputy to USSR Supreme Soviet 1984–89; USSR People's Deputy 1989–91; People's Deputy of Kyrgyzstan; mem. Revision Comm. CPSU 1986–91; Prime Minister of Kyrgyz Repub. 1993–97; Amb. to Germany, Scandinavian countries and the Holy See 1998–2003.

DZURINDA, Mikuláš, PhD; Slovak politician; b. 4 Feb. 1955, Spišský Štvrtok; m. Eva Dzurindová; two d.; ed Univ. of Transport and Communications, Žilina; econ. researcher, Transport Research Inst., Žilina 1979–80; information tech. officer, Czechoslovak Railways Regional Directorate, Bratislava 1980–88, Head of Automated Control Systems Dept 1988–91; Deputy Minister of Transport and Postal Service of Slovak Repub. 1991–92, 1994; mem. Nat. Council of Slovak Repub. 1992–94, 1994–98, 2006–10; Vice-Chair. for Econ. Christian Democratic Movt 1993–2000; spokesman of Slovak Democratic Coalition 1997–98, Chair. 1998–; Jt Acting Pres. of Slovakia 1998–99; Prime Minister 1998–2002, 2002–06; Minister of Foreign Affairs 2010–12; f. Slovak Democratic and Christian Union (SDKU, merged with Democratic Party 2006) 2000, Chair. 2000–12; has lectured at N American and European univs; Hon. mem. The Int. Raoul Wallenberg Foundation; Vittorino Colombo Award (Italy) 2000. *Publication:* Where There's a Will There's a Way. *Leisure interests:* family, sport, marathon running. *Address:* Slovak Democratic and Christian Union-Democratic Party (Slovenská demokratická a kresčanská únia-Demokratická strana), Ružinovská 28, 827 35 Bratislava, Slovakia (office). *Telephone:* (2) 4341-4102 (office). *Fax:* (2) 4341-4106 (office). *E-mail:* sdku@sdkuonline.sk (office). *Website:* www.sdku-ds.sk (office).

E

EAGLETON, Terence (Terry) Francis, PhD, FBA; British academic and writer; *Distinguished Professor of English Literature, Lancaster University;* b. 22 Feb. 1943, Salford, Lancs.; s. of Francis Paul Eagleton and Rosaleen Riley; m. 1st Elizabeth Rosemary Galpin 1966 (divorced 1976); two s.; m. 2nd Willa Murphy 1996; one s. one d.; ed Trinity Coll., Cambridge; Fellow in English, Jesus Coll., Cambridge 1964–69; Tutorial Fellow, Wadham Coll., Oxford 1969–89; Lecturer in Critical Theory and Fellow of Linacre Coll., Oxford 1989–92; Thomas Warton Prof. of English Literature and Fellow of St Catherine's Coll., Oxford 1992–2001; fmr Prof. of Cultural Theory, Univ. of Manchester, John Edward Taylor Prof. of English Literature 2001–08; Distinguished Prof. of English Literature, Lancaster Univ. 2008–; Hon. DLitt (Salford) 1994, (Durham), (E Anglia), (Univ. of Cen. Lancashire), (Nova Scotia, Canada), (Sacred Heart Univ., USA); Dr hc (Nat. Univ. of Ireland) 1995, (Santiago di Compostela) 1997; Irish Sunday Tribune Arts Award 1990. *Film:* screenplay for Wittgenstein. *Plays:* St Oscar 1989, Disappearances 1998. *Publications include:* Criticism and Ideology 1976, Marxism and Literary Criticism 1976, Literary Theory: An Introduction 1983, The Function of Criticism 1984, The Rape of Clarissa 1985, Against the Grain 1986, William Shakespeare 1986, The Ideology of the Aesthetic 1990, Ideology: An Introduction 1993, The Crisis of Contemporary Culture 1993, Heathcliff and the Great Hunger 1995, The Illusions of Postmodernism 1996, Literary Theory 1996, Crazy John and the Bishop and Other Essays on Irish Culture 1998, Scholars and Rebels in Ireland 1999, The Idea of Culture 2000, The Gatekeeper (autobiog.) 2001, Sweet Violence: The Idea of the Tragic 2002, Figures of Dissent (essays) 2003, After Theory 2003, The English Novel: An Introduction 2004, Holy Terror 2005, The Meaning of Life 2007, Trouble with Strangers: A Study of Ethics 2008, How to Read a Poem 2008, Reason, Faith and Revolution: Reflections on the God Debate 2009, On Evil 2010, Why Marx Was Right 2011; contribs to periodicals incl. London Review of Books. *Leisure interest:* Irish music. *Address:* Department of English and Creative Writing, County College, Lancaster University, Lancaster, LA1 4YD, England (office). *Website:* www.lancs.ac.uk/fass/english (office).

EAGLING, Wayne John; Canadian ballet dancer, choreographer and artistic director; s. of Eddie Eagling and Thelma Eagling; ed P. Ramsey Studio of Dance Arts, Royal Ballet School; Sr Prin., Royal Ballet 1975–91; Artistic Dir Dutch Nat. Ballet 1991–2003; Artistic Dir English Nat. Ballet, London 2005–12. *Ballet roles include:* danced lead roles in Sleeping Beauty, Swan Lake, Cinderella and other major classics; created roles include: Young Boy in Triad, Solo Boy in Gloria, Ariel in The Tempest, Woyzeck in Different Drummer; choreographed The Hunting of the Snark and Frankenstein, The Modern Prometheus, Ruins of Time 1993, Symphony in Waves 1994, Alma Mahler (for La Scala, Milan) 1994, Duet 1995, Lost Touch 1995, Nutcracker and Mouseking (with Toer van Schayk) 1996, The Last Emperor (for Hong Kong Ballet) 1998, Magic Flute (with Toer van Schayk) 1999, Le Sacré du Printemps 2000, Mary Stuart (Rome Opera) 2004. *Publication:* The Company We Keep (with Ross MacGibbon and Robert Jude) 1981. *Leisure interests:* golf, scuba diving.

EALET, Isabelle; French business executive; m.; two c.; ed Institut d'Études Politiques de Paris (SciencesPo); began career trading barrels of crude oil for Total, Paris; joined Goldman Sachs & Co. 1991, ran oil products group, Man. Dir 1999, Partner 2000–, Head of European Trading 2002–07, led team that bought European energy plants once owned by Enron, Global Head of Commodities, Goldman Sachs, London, UK 2007–12, Global Co-Head of Securities 2012–18, mem. Man. Cttee, Client and Business Standards Cttee, Risk Cttee, Principal Investments Cttee and Securities Div. Exec. Cttee; mem. Bd of Dirs Int. Petroleum Exchange, London 1999. *Address:* c/o Goldman Sachs International, Peterborough Court, 133 Fleet Street, London, EC4A 2BB, England.

EAMES, Baron (Life Peer), cr. 1995, of Armagh in the County of Armagh; **Most Rev. Robert Henry Alexander Eames,** LLD, PhD, OM, DD; British ecclesiastic; b. 27 April 1937; s. of William E. Eames and Mary E. T. Eames; m. Ann C. Daly 1966; two s.; ed Methodist Coll., Belfast, Queen's Univ., Belfast and Trinity Coll., Dublin; Research Scholar and Tutor, Faculty of Laws, Queen's Univ., Belfast 1960–63; Asst Curate, Bangor Parish Church 1963–66; Rector, St Dorothea's, Belfast 1966–74; Examining Chaplain to Bishop of Down 1973; Rector, St Mark's, Dunelda 1974–75; Bishop of Derry and Raphoe 1975–80; Bishop of Down and Dromore 1980–86; Archbishop of Armagh and Primate of All Ireland 1986–2006 (retd); Select Preacher, Oxford Univ. 1986–87, Cambridge Univ. 1989; Irish Rep., Anglican Consultative Council 1984, mem. Standing Cttee 1985; Chair. Archbishop of Canterbury's Comm. on Communion and Women in the Episcopate 1988–, Comm. on Inter-Anglican Relations 1988–, Anglican Int. Doctrinal Comm. (USA) 1991; Chair. Consultative Group on the Past (NI) 2007–08; Gov. Church Army 1985–; Hon. LLD (Queen's Univ. Belfast) 1989, (Trinity Coll. Dublin) 1992, (Lancaster) 1994, (Univ. of the South, Sewannee) 2010; Dr hc (Cambridge) 1994, (Open Univ.) 2008; Hon. DD (Exeter) 1999. *Publications:* A Form of Worship for Teenagers 1965, The Quiet Revolution: Irish Disestablishment 1970, Through Suffering 1973, Thinking through Lent 1978, Through Lent 1984, Chains to be Broken 1992; contribs to New Divinity, Irish Legal Quarterly, Criminal Law Review, Northern Ireland Legal Quarterly, Univ. Review and The Furrow. *Leisure interests:* sailing, rugby, football, reading. *Address:* House of Lords, London, SW1A 0PW, England (office); 3 Downshire Crescent, Hillsborough, Co. Down, BT26 6DD, Ireland (home). *Telephone:* (28) 9268-9913 (home).

EANES, Gen. António dos Santos Ramalho; Portuguese politician and army officer; b. 25 Jan. 1935, Alcains; s. of Manuel dos Santos Eanes and Maria do Rosario Ramalho; m. Maria Manuela Duarte Neto Portugal 1970; two s.; ed High School, Castelo Branco, Higher Inst. of Applied Psychology, Lisbon Faculty of Law; enlisted in Army School 1953; commissioned to Portuguese India 1958–60, Macao 1960–62, Mozambique 1962–64, Operations Officer of Light Infantry Battalion, Mozambique 1966–67, Information Officer, Portuguese Guinea (Guinea-Bissau) 1969–73, Angola 1973–74; Physical Education Instructor, Mil. Acad. 1968; Dir of Dept of Cultural and Recreational Affairs 1973; rank of Second Lt 1957, Lt 1959, Capt. 1961, Maj. 1970, Col 1976, Gen. 1978; involved in leadership of mil. movts finally contesting mil. apparatus and colonial wars 1968–74; after April Revolution named to first 'Ad-hoc' Cttee for mass media June 1974; Dir of Programmes of Portuguese TV June–Sept. 1974, Chair. of Bd of Dirs of TV co., resigned after accusation of 'probable implication' in abortive counter-coup March 1975, cleared after inquiry; attained rank of Lt-Col; mem. Cttee restructuring 5th Div., Gen. Staff Armed Forces; Army Chief of Staff (with temporary rank of Gen.) 1975–76; mem. of Mil. Cttee of Council of Revolution; responsible for Constitutional Law approved Dec. 1975; Pres. of Portugal 1976–86; Chair. of Council of Revolution; C-in-C of Armed Forces 1976–80, 1980–81; Leader, Portuguese Democratic Renewal Party 1986–87; mem. Conselho de Estado (Council of State); Kt, Mil. Order of Avis 1972, Grand Collar of the Order of the Tower and Sword 1986, Grand Cross of the Order of Liberty 2004, Grand Collar of the Order of Timor-Leste 2012, Grand Collar of the Order of Liberty 2015; Dr hc (Univ. of Lisbon) 2010; War Cross 2nd class, Silver Medal for Distinguished Services with Palm, Silver Medal for Exemplary Behaviour, Commemorative Medal of the Portuguese Armed Forces. *Leisure interest:* playing bridge.

EARL, Robert I.; British business executive; *Chairman and CEO, Planet Hollywood International Inc.;* b. 1952; f. President Entertainment (theme restaurants) 1977, sold co. to Pleasurama PLC, joined Pleasurama man. team, Man. Hard Rock Cafe PLC 1987–93; Co-founder, CEO and Dir Planet Hollywood Int. 1993–2000, now Chair. and CEO; Co-Chair. BHM Gaming Opportunities (owner of fmr Aladdin Casino hotel now Planet Hollywood, Las Vegas); became shareholder in Everton FC 2006, Dir 2007–. *Address:* Planet Hollywood International Inc., 7598 West Sand Lake Road, Orlando, FL 32819, USA (office). *Telephone:* (407) 903-5500 (office). *Fax:* (407) 352-7310 (office). *E-mail:* general_information@planethollywood.com (office). *Website:* www.planethollywood.com (office).

EARLE, Steve; American singer, songwriter and musician (guitar); b. 17 Jan. 1955, Fort Monroe, Va; s. of Jack Earle and Barbara Earle; m. 1st Sandy Earle; m. 2nd Cynthia Earle; m. 3rd Carol-Ann Earle; m. 4th and 6th Lou-Anne Earle; m. 5th Teresa Ensenat; m. 7th Allison Moorer; moved to Nashville, where became bar room musician, staff writer for the publisher, Sunbury Dunbar, and songwriter; solo artist with own backing band, The Dukes 1982–; BBC Radio 2 Folk Award for Lifetime Achievement 2004. *Film and television appearances include:* Nashville 1975, The Wire (TV series) 2002, Slacker Uprising 2008, Leaves of Grass 2009, Treme (TV series) 2010. *Recordings include:* albums: Pink and Black (EP) 1982, Guitar Town 1986, Early Tracks 1987, Exit O 1987, Copperhead Road 1988, The Hard Way 1990, Shut Up And Die Like An Aviator 1991, Train A Comin' 1995, Fearless Heart 1996, I Feel Alright 1996, Angry Young Man 1996, El Corazón 1997, The Mountain 1999, Transcendental Blues 2000, Together At The Bluebird Cafe 2001, Sidetracks 2002, Jerusalem 2002, Just An American Boy 2003, The Revolution Starts... Now 2004, Live From Austin TX 2004, Washington Square Serenade (Grammy Award for Best Contemporary Folk/Americana Album 2008) 2007, Townes (Grammy Award for Best Contemporary Folk Album 2010) 2009, I'll Never Get Out of This World Alive 2011, The Low Highway 2013, Colvin & Earle (with Shawn Colvin) 2016. *Publications:* Doghouse Roses (short stories) 2001, I'll Never Get Out Of This World Alive (novel) 2011. *Address:* c/o GoldVE Entertainment, 72 Madison Avenue, 8th Floor, New York, NY 10016, USA (office). *Telephone:* (212) 741-2400 (office). *Fax:* (212) 741-4871 (office). *E-mail:* info@goldve.com (office). *Website:* goldve.wordpress.com (office); www.steveearle.com.

EARNHARDT, Dale, Jr; American racing driver; b. 10 Oct. 1974, Kannapolis, NC; s. of Dale Earnhardt and Brenda Gee; grandson of Ralph Earnhardt; began driving career aged 17; competed in street stock div., Concord (NC) Speedway; drives Budweiser No. 8 Chevrolet; winner of two Championships and 13 races in Busch Series 1998–2000; became first third-generation NASCAR Champion after winning Busch Series Title 1998, 1999; moved into NASCAR Nextel Cup Circuit 2000; raced Winston Cup circuit with father 2000; opened Daytona Speedweeks with father as mems of same team 2001; 15 victories in 183 Cup starts 2000–04; winner Atlanta, Bristol, Daytona and Tex. NASCAR Nextel Cups 2004, Budweiser Shootout 2004, 2008, The Winston 2004, USG Sheetrock 400 2005, Quicken Loans 400 2012, Budweiser Duel 2015; Co-owner Chance2 Team, winning Busch Series Championships 2004; Founder and Owner, JR Motorsports LLC 2002–, Hammerhead Entertainment (TV and film production co.) 2006–. *Films include:* Talladega Nights: The Ballad of Ricky Bobby 2006, Transformers: Dark of the Moon 2011. *Television includes:* host, Back in the Day, Speed Channel 2007. *Publication:* Driver No. 8 2002. *Leisure interests:* collecting street cars and race cars, computer games, music. *Address:* JR Motorsports LLC, Mooresville, NC 28115, USA (office). *Telephone:* (704) 799-4800 (office). *Fax:* (704) 799-4801 (office). *E-mail:* Info@jrmotorsport.com (office). *Website:* www.jrmotorsport.com (office); www.hammerheadent.com.

EASLEY, Michael F., JD, BA; American lawyer and politician; b. 23 March 1950, Rocky Mount, NC; s. of Alexander Easley; m. Mary Pipines; one s.; ed Univ. of North Carolina, North Carolina Cen. Univ. School of Law; Dist Attorney, 13th Dist, North Carolina 1982–91; pvt. practice, Southport, North Carolina 1991–92; North Carolina Attorney-Gen. 1993–2000; Gov. of North Carolina 2000–09; fmr Pres. North Carolina Conf. of Dist Attorneys; fmr mem. North Carolina Dist Attorneys Asscn, Nat. Govs Asscn, Southern Govs Asscn, Democratic Govs Asscn; Democrat; Public Services Award, US Dept of Justice 1984, America's Greatest Educ. Gov., Nat. Educ. Asscn 2008. *Publication:* Look Out, College, Here I Come! 2007. *Leisure interests:* hunting, sailing, woodwork.

EAST, Rt Hon. Paul Clayton, CNZM, PC, QC, LLM; New Zealand politician, lawyer and diplomatist; b. 4 Aug. 1946, Opotiki; s. of Edwin Cuthbert East and Edith Pauline Addison East; m. Marilyn Therese Kottmann 1972; three d.; ed Univ. of Virginia School of Law, USA, Univ. of Auckland School of Law, King's Coll.; law clerk, Morpeth Gould & Co., Auckland 1968–70; Partner, East Brewster Solicitors, Rotorua 1974–78; fmr Rotorua City Councillor and Deputy Mayor; MP for Rotorua (National Party) 1978–96; Attorney-Gen., Minister responsible for Serious Fraud Office and Audit Dept 1990–97, Leader of the House 1990–93, Minister of Crown Health Enterprises 1991–96, for State Services 1993–97, for Defence and War Pensions 1996–97, for Corrections 1996–97; High Commr in UK (also accred to Nigeria and Ireland) 1999–2002; Chair. Bd of Trustees Antarctic Heritage Trust (NZ). *Leisure interests:* fishing, skiing, golf. *E-mail:* pauleastnz@hotmail.com.

EASTMAN, John L., BA, JD; American lawyer and business executive; *CEO, MPL Communications, Inc.;* b. 1940, New York; s. of Lee Eastman; brother of Linda McCartney (died 1998); m. Jodie Eastman; three c.; ed Stanford Univ. and New York Univ.; worked for US Senate Commerce Cttee 1963; Office of US Attorney, New York; took part in Robert Kennedy's 1968 presidential election campaign; with father founded Eastman & Eastman (law firm) specializing in contract and copyright law; currently CEO MPL Communications (McCartney Productions Ltd), also lawyer-man. of Paul McCartney; mem. Bd of Dirs, United TV Inc. 1985–2001, BHC Communications Inc. 1989–2001; fmr Dir Apple Corps Ltd Linda McCartney Foods; Trustee, American Museum of Natural History; Trustee, Smith Coll. 1989–99. *Leisure interests:* collecting pictures, 19th-century English literature. *Address:* MPL Communications, Inc., 41 West 54th Street, New York, NY 10019, USA (office). *Telephone:* (212) 246-5881 (office). *Fax:* (212) 246-7852 (office). *E-mail:* contact@mplcommunications.com (office). *Website:* www.mplcommunications.com (office).

EASTON, Sheena; British singer and actress; b. (Sheena Shirley Orr), 27 April 1959, Bellshill, Scotland; m. 1st Rob Light 1985; m. 2nd Tim Delarm 1997; two c.; ed Royal Scottish Acad. of Music and Drama; singer in Glasgow club circuit 1979; career launched by appearance on TV show, The Big Time (BBC 1) 1980; solo recording artist 1980–; numerous concerts and worldwide tours, TV appearances; Grammy Award for Best New Artist 1981, for Best Mexican/American Performance (with Luis Miguel) 1985, Emmy Award (for Sheena Easton… Act 1) 1983. *Stage appearances include:* Man of La Mancha (Chicago, then Broadway) 1991–92, The Colors of Christmas 2001, 42nd Street (London) 2017. *Television appearances include:* Miami Vice (series) 1987–88, Body Bags 1993, The Highlander 1993, The Adventure of Brisco County Jr 1993, TekWar 1995, Gargoyles 1995–96, Outer Limits 1996, Road Rovers 1996, All Dogs go to Heaven 1996–97, Duckman 1997, Chicken Soup for the Soul 1999, The Legend of Tarzan 2001, Young Blades 2005, Phineas and Ferb (series) 2009. *Recordings include:* albums: Take My Time 1981, You Could Have Been With Me 1981, Madness, Money And Music 1982, Best Kept Secret 1983, A Private Heaven 1985, Do You 1985, The Lover In Me 1989, The Collection 1989, What Comes Naturally 1991, No Strings 1993, My Cherie 1995, Body And Soul 1997, Freedom 2000, Fabulous 2000. *Address:* c/o Susan Holder, 21255 Burbank Blvd, #320, Woodland Hills, CA 91367, USA (office). *Telephone:* (323) 229-5209 (office). *E-mail:* sholder@isp.com (office). *Website:* www.sheenaeaston.com.

EASTWOOD, Clint; American actor and film director; b. 31 May 1930, San Francisco, Calif.; s. of Clinton Eastwood and Ruth Eastwood; m. 1st Maggie Johnson 1953 (divorced); one s. one d.; one d. by Frances Fisher 1993; m. 2nd Dina Ruiz 1996; one d.; ed Los Angeles City Coll.; worked as lumberjack in Ore.; served in US Army; appeared in TV series Rawhide 1959–65; Owner, Malpaso Productions 1969–; Owner, Mission Ranch Resort, Carmel, Calif.; Co-Chair. UNESCO Campaign to protect the world's film heritage; mem. Nat. Arts Council 1973; Mayor of Carmel, Calif. 1986–88; Co-founder and Pnr, Tehama Inc. (sportswear co.) 1997–; Vice-Chair. Calif. State Parks and Recreation Comm.; Fellow, BFI 1993; Légion d'honneur, Commdr des Arts et des Lettres; Hon. DFA (Wesleyan) 2000, Hon. DLit (Univ. of Southern California) 2007; numerous awards including Irving G. Thalberg Award 1995, Lifetime Achievement Award, American Film Inst. 1996, Kennedy Center Honors, John F. Kennedy Center Performing Arts 2000, Lifetime Achievement Award, Screen Actors Guild 2003, Broadcast Film Critics Asscn 2004, Lifetime Achievement Award, Dirs Guild of America 2006, Jack Valenti Humanitarian Award, Motion Picture Asscn of America 2007, Nat. Medal of Arts 2009. *Films include:* Revenge of the Creature 1955, Francis in the Navy 1955, Lady Godiva 1955, Tarantula 1955, Never Say Goodbye 1956, The First Travelling Saleslady 1956, Star in the Dust 1956, Escapade in Japan 1957, Ambush at Cimarron Pass 1958, Lafayette Escadrille 1958, A Fistful of Dollars 1964, For a Few Dollars More 1965, The Good, the Bad and the Ugly 1966, The Witches 1967, Hang 'Em High 1968, Coogan's Bluff 1968, Where Eagles Dare 1969, Paint Your Wagon 1969, Kelly's Heroes 1970, Two Mules for Sister Sara 1970, The Beguiled 1971, Play Misty for Me (also dir) 1971, Dirty Harry 1971, Joe Kidd 1972, High Plains Drifter (also dir) 1973, Magnum Force 1973, Breezy (dir) 1973, Thunderbolt and Lightfoot 1974, The Eiger Sanction (also dir) 1975, The Outlaw Josey Wales (also dir) 1976, The Enforcer 1976, The Gauntlet (also dir) 1978, Every Which Way But Loose (also producer) 1978, Escape from Alcatraz 1979, Bronco Billy (also dir) 1980, Any Which Way You Can 1980, Firefox (also dir and producer) 1982, Honky Tonk Man (also dir and producer) 1982, Sudden Impact (also dir and producer) 1983, Tightrope (also producer) 1984, City Heat 1984, Pale Rider 1985 (also dir and producer), Heartbreak Ridge 1986 (also dir and producer), Bird 1988 (dir and producer) (Golden Globe Award for Best Dir 1989), The Dead Pool 1988, Pink Cadillac 1989, White Hunter, Black Heart (also dir and producer) 1989, The Rookie (also dir) 1990, Unforgiven (also dir and producer) (Acad. Awards for Best Film and Best Dir 1993) 1992, In the Line of Fire 1993, A Perfect World (also dir) 1993, The Bridges of Madison County (also dir, producer) 1995, The Stars Fell on Henrietta (co-producer), Absolute Power (also dir and producer) 1997, True Crime 1998, Midnight in the Garden of Good and Evil (dir and producer) 1997, Space Cowboys (dir and producer) 2000, Bloodwork (also dir and producer) 2002, Mystic River (dir and producer) 2003, Million Dollar Baby (also dir and producer) (Special Filmmaking Achievement Award, Nat. Bd of Review of Motion Pictures, Best Dir, Golden Globe Awards, Dirs Guild of America Awards 2005, Best Film, Best Dir, Acad. Awards 2005) 2004, Flags of Our Fathers (dir and producer) 2006, Letters from Iwo Jima (also dir and producer) (Nat. Bd of Review of Motion Pictures Best Film 2006, Los Angeles Film Critics Asscn Best Film 2006) 2006, Changeling (dir and producer) 2008, Gran Torino (also dir and producer) 2008, Invictus (dir and producer) 2009, Hereafter (dir) 2010, J. Edgar (dir and producer) 2011, Trouble with the Curve (also producer) 2012, Jersey Boys (dir and producer) 2014, Indian Horse (dir and producer) 2017, The 15:17 to Paris (dir and producer) 2018. *Address:* Malpaso Productions, c/o Warner Bros, 4000 Warner Blvd., Bldg 81, Burbank CA 91522, USA (office). *Telephone:* (818) 954-3367 (office).

EASTWOOD, Sir David Stephen, Kt, PhD, FRHistS; British historian, academic and university administrator; *Vice-Chancellor and Principal, University of Birmingham;* ed St Peter's Coll., Oxford; Research Fellow, Keble Coll. Oxford 1983–87; Fellow and Sr Tutor, Pembroke Coll. 1988–95, Hon. Fellow, St Peter's Coll., Oxford, Keble Coll., Oxford; Prof. of Modern History, Univ. of Wales, Swansea, also a Head of Dept, Dean and Pro-Vice-Chancellor, co-f. Nat. Centre for Public Policy; Chief Exec. Arts and Humanities Research Bd; Vice-Chancellor Univ. of East Anglia; Chief Exec. Higher Educ. Funding Council for England 2006–09; Vice-Chancellor and Prin. Univ. of Birmingham 2009–; Chair. Russell Group; Dir, Universities Superannuation Scheme; mem. Bd Universities UK (fmr Chair. Longer Term Strategy Group), Arts and Humanities Research Council, Advisory Bd of Higher Educ. Policy Inst., Marketing Birmingham; fmr Chair. Asscn of Univs of East of England, Supporting Professionalism in Admissions, Westminster Educ. Comm. 2009; Fellow, Royal Historical Soc. 1991, Literary Dir 1994–2000, Chair. Studies in History Bd 2000–04; mem. Research Support Libraries Group 2002–03, Roberts Review of Research Assessment Exercise, Tomlinson Group on 14–19 Educ. 2003–04, Council of John Innes Centre, Council of Sainsbury Lab., Bd of Quality Assurance Agency; Chair. Group of Universities 1994; Int. mem. Hong Kong Univ. Grants Cttee; fmr mem. UK Govt's Ind. Review Panel looking at Higher Educ. Funding and Student Finance; DL, West Midlands 2012–; Hon. Fellow, Swansea Univ. *Publications:* numerous articles on the history of the British state, the history of ideas and on electoral politics. *Leisure interests:* music, politics, walking, sport, good wine, writing on football. *Address:* Vice-Chancellor's Office, Aston Webb Building, University of Birmingham, Edgbaston, Birmingham, B15 2TT, England (office). *Telephone:* (121) 414-4536 (office). *E-mail:* l.wilden@bham.ac.uk (office). *Website:* www.birmingham.ac.uk (office).

EASTWOOD, Trevor R., AM, BEng; Australian business executive (retd); ed Univ. of Western Australia, Advanced Man. Program at Harvard Business School, USA; began career with Westralian Farmers Co-operative Ltd 1963, held several man. positions until retirement in 1992, including Man. Dir Wesfarmers Ltd 1984–92, mem. Bd of Dirs 1994–2008, Chair. (non-exec.) 2002–08; mem. Bd of Dirs The WCM Group Ltd; fmr Chair. West Australian Newspapers Holdings Ltd; mem. Bd of Dirs Qantas Airways Ltd 1995–2005. *Publication:* The CEO, the Chairman and the Board: Trevor Eastwood 2009.

EATON, Ashton James, BA; American decathlete (retd); b. 21 Jan. 1988, Portland, Ore.; s. of Roslyn Eaton and Terrance Wilson; m. Brianne Theisen-Eaton 2013; ed Univ. of Oregon; won state high school 400m championship 2006; winner in decathlon, Nat. Collegiate Athletic Asscn (NCAA) Men's Outdoor Track and Field Championship 2008, 2009, 2010; winner in heptathlon, NCAA Indoor Championships 2009, 2010; second in decathlon, Outdoor Track and Field Championships 2009; silver medal in decathlon, IAAF World Championships in Athletics 2011; gold medal in heptathlon, IAAF World Indoor Championships 2012 (set world record of 6,645 points); gold medal in decathlon, Olympic Games, London 2012, Rio de Janeiro, Brazil 2016; winner, World Championships 2013, 2015 (set world record of 9,045 points), IAAF World Indoor Championships 2014; mem. Oregon Track Club Elite team 2010; retd from sports 2017; Div. I Field Athlete of the Year Award 2009, Bowerman Award, Track and Field and Cross Country Coaches Asscn 2010, Fair Play Award 2012.

EATON, Fredrik Stefan, OC, BA, LLD; Canadian business executive and fmr diplomatist; *Chairman, White Raven Capital Corporation;* b. 26 June 1938, Toronto; s. of John David Eaton and Signy Hildur Stephenson; m. Catherine Martin 1962; one s. one d.; ed New Brunswick Univ.; joined The T. Eaton Co. Ltd and held various positions in Victoria, London, Toronto 1962–67, Dir 1967–69, Chair., Pres., CEO 1977–88, Chair. 1988–91; Pres., Dir Eaton's of Canada (parent co. of the other Eaton cos) 1969–77, Chair. Exec. Cttee 1994–97; High Commr in UK 1991–94; Chancellor Univ. of New Brunswick 1993–2003; currently Chair. White Raven Capital Corpn; Chair. Bd of Trustees, Canadian Museum of Civilization Corpn 2007–11; Order of Ontario 2001, Queen Elizabeth II Diamond Jubilee Medal 2012; Hon. LLD (New Brunswick) 1983; Man. Award, McGill Univ. 1987. *Leisure interests:* art, music, reading, shooting, yachting. *Address:* White Raven Capital Corporation, 55 St Clair Avenue West, Suite 260, Toronto, ON M4V 2Y7, Canada (office). *Telephone:* (416) 929-3942 (office). *Fax:* (416) 925-4339 (office).

EATON, George, FCCA; Irish chartered accountant; *Consultant, Eaton Neary;* b. 11 Jan. 1942, Cork; s. of Thomas J. V. Eaton and Catherine Hannon; m. Ellen Patricia O'Grady 1966; one d.; ed Christian Brothers Coll., Cork, Inst. of Chartered Accountants, Ireland; with Touche Ross, Chartered Accountants, Cork 1960–66; Chief Accountant, Seafield Fabrics, Youghal 1966–67; Deputy Man. Dir General Textiles 1967–75; Sr Partner, Eaton Dowd (later Eaton Neary) 1976–2012, Consultant 2012–; Chair. Portuguese Irish Chamber of Commerce 1987–89; Pres. Chambers of Commerce of Ireland 1985–87; Hon. Consul of Hungary 1990–2010. *Publication:* Introducing Ireland 1989. *Leisure interests:* history, genealogy, reading, book collecting. *Address:* Custume Place, Athlone, Ireland (office). *Telephone:* (9064) 78531 (office). *Fax:* (9064) 74691 (office). *E-mail:* companies@eatonneary.ie (office). *Website:* eatonneary.ie (office).

EATON, Robert J., BS; American engineer and automobile industry executive (retd); b. 13 Feb. 1940, Buena Vista, Colo; s. of Gene Eaton and Mildred Eaton; m. Connie Drake 1964; two s.; ed Univ. of Kansas; joined Chevrolet Motor Div., Gen. Motors 1963, transferred to eng staff 1971, Exec. Engineer 1974, Chief Engineer, Corp. Car Programs 1976, Asst Chief Engineer and Dir of Reliability at Oldsmobile 1979, Vice-Pres. in charge of Tech. Staffs 1986, Pres. Gen. Motors Europe 1988–92; COO Chrysler Motors Corpn 1992–93, Chair., CEO 1993–1998 (now Chair. Emer.), Co.-Chair., Co.-CEO Daimler Chrysler 1998–2000 (after 1998 merger of Chrysler with Daimler Benz); mem. Bd of Dirs Group Lotus 1986–, ChevronTexaco Corpn 2000–12, Int. Paper Co., GDI Infotech Inc.; mem. Industrial Advisory Bd Stanford Univ.; mem. Nat. Acad. of Eng; Fellow, Soc. of Automotive Engineers, Eng Soc. of Detroit; Chevalier du Tastevin 1989; Distinguished Service Citation, Univ. of Kansas Alumni Asscn 1994, Distinguished Eng Service Award, Univ. of Kansas 1995, Contemporary Honors Award, Kansas Business Hall of Fame 2005. *Leisure interests:* skiing, golf, hunting.

EATWELL, Baron (Life Peer), cr. 1992, of Stratton St Margaret in the County of Wiltshire; **John Leonard Eatwell,** PhD; British economist and academic; *President, Queens' College, Cambridge;* b. 2 Feb. 1945; s. of Harold Jack Eatwell and Mary Eatwell; m. 1st Hélène Seppain 1970 (divorced); two s. one d.; m. 2nd

Susan Elizabeth Digby 2006; ed Headlands Grammar School, Swindon, Queens' Coll., Cambridge, Harvard Univ., USA; Teaching Fellow, Grad. School of Arts and Sciences, Harvard Univ. 1968–69; Research Fellow, Queens' Coll. Cambridge 1969–70; Fellow, Trinity Coll., Cambridge 1970–96, Asst Lecturer, Faculty of Econs and Politics, Univ. of Cambridge 1975–77, Lecturer 1977, Prof. of Financial Policy (now Prof. Emer.), Pres. Queens' Coll. 1997–; Visiting Prof. of Econs, New School for Social Research, New York 1982–96; Econ. Adviser to Neil Kinnock, Leader of Labour Party 1985–92; Opposition Spokesman on Treasury Affairs and on Trade and Industry, House of Lords 1992–93, Prin. Opposition Spokesman on Treasury and Econ. Affairs 1993–97; Trustee, Inst. for Public Policy Research 1988–95, Sec. 1988–97, Chair. 1997; Chair. Royal Ballet 1998–2001, Commercial Radio Cos Asscn 2000–04, British Library Bd 2001–06, Royal Opera House Pension Scheme 2007, Consumer Panel, Classic FM 2007–; currently Econ. Adviser, EM Warburg Pincus & Co International Ltd, Palamon Capital Partners LLP; Commr, Jersey Financial Services Comm.; mem. Regulatory Decisions Cttee, FSA 2001–05, Econ. Affairs Cttee, House of Lords 2009–; Dir Cambridge Endowment for Research in Finance 2002–; Gov. Royal Ballet School 2003–06, Artsworks Ltd 2007–, SAV Credit Ltd 2008–; Chair. Advisory Bd, Inst. for Policy Research, Univ. of Bath 2014–. *Publications include:* An Introduction to Modern Economics (with Joan Robinson) 1973, Whatever Happened to Britain? 1982, Keynes's Economics and the Theory of Value and Distribution (ed. with Murray Milgate) 1983, The New Palgrave: A Dictionary of Economics, 4 Vols 1987, The New Palgrave Dictionary of Money and Finance, 3 Vols 1992 (both with Murray Milgate and Peter Newman), Transformation and Integration: Shaping the Future of Central and Eastern Europe (jtly) 1995, Global Unemployment: Loss of Jobs in the '90s (ed.) 1996, Not "Just Another Accession": The Political Economy of EU Enlargement to the East (jtly) 1997, Global Finance at Risk: The Case for International Regulation (with L. Taylor) 2000, Hard Budgets, Soft States 2000, Social Policy Choices in Central and Eastern Europe 2002, International Capital Markets (with L. Taylor) 2002, Global Governance of Financial Systems: The International Regulation of Systemic Risk 2006, The Fall and Rise of Keynesian Economics 2011; numerous articles in scientific journals. *Leisure interests:* classical and contemporary dance, Rugby Union football. *Address:* The President's Lodge, Queens' College, Cambridge, CB3 9ET, England (home). *Telephone:* (1223) 335556 (office). *Fax:* (1223) 335555 (home). *E-mail:* pres.sec@queens.cam.ac.uk (office). *Website:* www.queens.cam.ac.uk.

EBADI, Shirin, JD; Iranian lawyer, human rights activist and academic; b. 1947, Hamadan; d. of Mohammad Ali Ebadi; m.; two d.; ed Univ. of Tehran; apptd Judge (first woman) and Pres. Tehran City Court 1974, forced to step down from bench after 1979 revolution, retd 1984; currently runs own law practice specializing in human rights; mem. Cttee for the Defence of Rights of the Victims of Serial Murders; Founder Soc. for Protecting the Rights of the Child, Centre for Defence of Human Rights; Lecturer in Law, Univ. of Tehran; Founding mem. Nobel Women's Initiative 2006; Hon. LLD (Brown Univ.) 2004, (Univ. of British Columbia) 2004; Dr hc (Univ. of Maryland, College Park) 2004, (Univ. of Toronto) 2004, (Simon Fraser Univ.) 2004, (Univ. of Akureyri) 2004, (Australian Catholic Univ.) 2005, (Univ. of San Francisco) 2005, (Concordia Univ.) 2005, (Univ. of York) 2005, (Université Jean Moulin, Lyon) 2005, (Loyola Univ., Chicago) 2007, (New School Univ.) 2007; Human Rights Watch Award 1996, Rafto Prize 2001, Nobel Peace Prize (first Iranian and first Muslim woman) 2003, Bonn Int. Democracy Prize 2004, Lawyer of the Year Award 2004, UCI Citizen Peacebuilding Award 2005, The Golden Plate Award, Acad. of Achievement 2005. *Publications include:* The Rights of the Child: A Study of Legal Aspects of Children's Rights in Iran 1994, History and Documentation of Human Rights in Iran 2000, Iran Awakening 2006, Refugee Rights in Iran 2008, The Golden Cage 2009; numerous other books and journal articles. *Address:* Society for Protecting the Rights of the Child, 26 Tenth Street, Nobakht Street, Tehran, Iran (office). *E-mail:* info@irsprc.org (office). *Website:* www.irsprc.org (office).

EBANKS, Donovan W. F., MBE, JP; Cayman Islands politician and public servant (retd); joined Public Works Dept 1975, Chief Engineer 1983; Deputy Chief Sec. of Cayman Islands 1994–2009, First Official Mem., Legis. Ass. (parl.) 2009–, Chief Sec. and Head of Civil Service 2009–12, also Minister of Internal and External Affairs 2009, Acting Gov. Dec. 2009–12; Chair. Civil Service Appeals Comm. 2013–19; fmr Chair. Nat. Hurricane Cttee. *Address:* c/o Civil Service Appeals Commission, 2nd Floor Artemis House, 67 Fort Street, George Town, Cayman Islands.

EBDANE, Hermogenes, Jr., MSc, PhD; Philippine politician; b. 30 Dec. 1948, Candelaria, Zambales; m. Alma Cabanayan; three c.; ed Philippine Mil. Acad.; fmr Nat. Security Adviser and Dir-Gen., Nat. Security Council; fmr Vice-Chair. Anti-Terrorism Task Force; fmr Nat. Anti-Terrorism Coordinator; fmr Dir Human Resources, Philippine Nat. Police, fmr Deputy Chief of Admin, Chief 2002–04; Sec. of Public Works and Highways 2004–07, 2008–10, of Nat. Defense (acting) 2007; Gov. of Zambales Prov. 2010–16; Philippine Legion of Honor, Distinguished Conduct Star, Bronze Cross Medal, Master Parachutist Badge, numerous military honours. *Address:* Sulong Zambales Party, Iba, Zambales Province, Philippines.

EBERHARTER, Stephan; Austrian skier (retd); b. 24 March 1969, Brixlegg, Tirol; Gold Medal, Super-G and Combined, World Championships, Saalbach 1991, Super-G, St Moritz, Switzerland 2003; Silver Medal, Super-G, World Championships, St Anton 2001; Silver Medal, Giant Slalom, Olympic Games, Nagano, Japan 1998; Gold Medal, Giant Slalom, Olympics Games, Salt Lake City, USA 2002, Silver Medal, Super-G, Bronze Medal, Downhill; World Cup ranking (Gen.): Third 1998, Fourth 1999, Sixth 2000, Second 2001, First 2002, 2003, Second 2004. *Leisure interests:* music, golf. *Address:* Dorfstrasse 21, 6272 Stumm Tirol, Austria. *Fax:* info@eberharter-zillertal.at. *Website:* www.eberharter-zillertal.at; www.steff .at.

EBIHARA, Shin; Japanese diplomatist (retd); b. 16 Feb. 1948, Tokyo; m. Haruko Ebihara; joined Ministry of Foreign Affairs 1971, served as Deputy Dir-Gen. Bureau of Middle Eastern and African Affairs, Exec. Sec. to Prime Minister Keizo Obuchi 1998–2000, Dir-Gen. Treaties Bureau 2001, Dir-Gen. N American Affairs Bureau 2002, Asst Deputy Chief Cabinet Sec. 2005, Amb. to Indonesia 2006–08, to UK 2008–11 (retd); Fellow, Weatherhead Center for Int. Affairs, Harvard Univ. 2000–01; mem. Bd of Dirs Mitsubishi Estate Co. Ltd 2015–.

EBOE-OSUJI, Chile, LLB, LLM, PhD; Nigerian lawyer and international organisation executive; *President, International Criminal Court;* b. 2 Sept. 1962, Añara, Isiala Mbano; ed Univ. of Calabar, McGill Univ., Canada, Univ. of Amsterdam, Netherlands; worked with Nigerian Bar from 1996; worked as Barrister in Canada 1993, 2005–07; Prosecution Counsel and Sr Legal Officer, Int. Criminal Tribunal for Rwanda (ICTR) 1997–2005, Head of Chambers 2008–10; Adjunct Prof. Faculty of Law, Univ. of Ottawa 2005–07; Prin. Appeals Counsel, Special Court of Sierra Leone 2007–08; Legal Adviser to UN High Commr for Human Rights 2010; Judge Int. Criminal Court (ICC) 2012–, Pres. 2018–. *Address:* International Criminal Court (ICC), Oude Waalsdorperweg 10, 2597 AK The Hague, Netherlands (office). *Telephone:* (70) 5158515 (office). *Fax:* (70) 5158555 (office). *E-mail:* otp.informationdesk@icc-cpi.int (office). *Website:* www.icc-cpi.int (office).

EBRAHIM, Al-Hajj Murad; Philippine politician; *Interim Chief Minister of Bangsamoro;* b. (Ahod Balawag Ebrahim), 2 May 1948, Maguindanao; m. Hadja Lupia Ebrahim; two c.; mem. Moro National Liberation Front 1968; Vice-Chair., Military Affairs and Chief of Staff, Bangsamoro Islamic Armed Forces; Chair. Moro Islamic Liberation Front 2003–; Interim Chief Minister Bangsamoro Autonomous Region and Minister of Public Works and Highways 2019–. *Telephone:* (064) 552-0235 (office). *Website:* bangsamoro.gov.ph (office); www .luwaran.net (office).

EBRAHIM, Fakhruddin G., LLM; Pakistani lawyer, government official and fmr judge; b. 12 Feb. 1928, Gujarat, India; ed Sindh Muslim Coll.; fmr Lecturer, Sindh Law Coll.; est. Fakhruddin G Ebrahim and Co. (law firm); Attorney-Gen. 1971–77; Gov. of Sindh 1989–90; fmr Judge and Sr Advocate Supreme Court; Interim Minister of Law July–Oct. 1993, Interim Minister of Justice 1996–97; Chief Election Commr 2012–13; apptd Chair. Anti-Doping Appeals Cttee 2006; Hon. JD (Sindh Law Coll.) 1960. *Address:* 3rd Floor, Ebrahim Estates, D/1 Union Commercial Area Block 7 & 8, Shahrae Faisal, Karachi 75350, Pakistan (office). *Telephone:* (21) 4537772 (office). *Fax:* (21) 4555845 (office).

EBRARD CASAUBÓN, Marcelo Luis, BA; Mexican politician; *Secretary of Foreign Affairs;* b. 10 Oct. 1959, Mexico City; s. of Marcelo Ebrard Maure and Marcela Casaubón; m. 1st Francesca Ramos Morgan (divorced); one s. two d.; m. 2nd Mariagna Pratts 2006 (divorced); m. 3rd Rosalinda Bueso 2011; ed El Colegio de México, École nat. d'admin, Paris; Sec. of Social Devt, Govt of Mexico City 2005–07, Head of Govt of Mexico City 2006–12, Sec. of Public Security 2002–04; mem. Fed. Chamber of Deputies (lower house of parl.) 1997–2000; Sec. (Minister) of Foreign Affairs 2018–; mem. Partido Revolucionario Institucional 1978–95, Partido de Centro Democrático 1995–2000, Partido de la Revolución Democrática 2004–15, Movimiento Ciudadano 2015–18, Movimiento Regeneración Nacional (Morena) 2018–; Pres. UN Global Network on Safer Cities 2012–14. *Address:* Secretariat of State for Foreign Affairs, Plaza Juárez 20, Col. Centro, Del. Cuauhtémoc, 06010 México, DF, Mexico (office). *Telephone:* (55) 3686-5100 (office). *E-mail:* atencionciudadanasre@sre.gob.mx (office). *Website:* www.gob.mx/sre (office).

EBTEKAR, Massoumeh, MSc, PhD, DSc; Iranian scientist, academic and politician; *Vice-President for Women and Family Affairs;* b. 21 Sept. 1960, Tehran; d. of (Prof.) Taghi Ebtekar and Fatima Barzegar; m. Mohammad Hashemi 1978; two c.; ed Shahid Beheshti Univ. and Tarbiat Modares Univ., Tehran; Ed.-in-Chief Keyhan Int. (English daily newspaper) 1981–83; Editorial Dir Farzaneh Journal of Women's Studies and Research; Founding mem. Centre for Women's Studies and Research 1986–; Dir Women's NGO Co-ordination Office, Tehran 1994–; Pres. Network of Women's NGOs in the Islamic Repub. of Iran 1995–; Faculty mem. School of Medical Science, Tarbiat Modares Univ. 1989–95, Asst Prof. of Immunology 1995–2006, apptd Assoc. Prof. 2006; Vice-Pres. of Iran and Head of Dept of the Environment (first female Vice-Pres.) 1997–2005, 2013–17, for Women and Family Affairs 2017–; Founder and Head, Centre for Peace and the Environment, Tehran 2005–; mem. Tehran City Council 2007–, est. and Head of Environment Cttee, currently runs 20 working groups on environmental issues; del., vice-chair. or chair. numerous int. confs on women; Champion of the Earth Award, UNEP 2006, Distinguished Researcher 2007. *Publications include:* book: Natural Peace and Ethics; The Grapes of Shahrivar (Farsi), Memoirs of the First Vice President of Iran 2009; contribs to Farzaneh Journal of Women's Studies and numerous int. journals. *Leisure interests:* swimming, reading, blogging. *Address:* POB 1423-13185, Pasteur Ave, Tehran 13168-43311, Iran. *Telephone:* (21) 55893613 (home). *E-mail:* webmaster@president.ir (office).

ECARMA, Maj.-Gen. (retd) Natalio C., III; Philippine UN official, politician and fmr army officer; b. 3 June 1955, Manila; m. Dr Beverly Antonio; two s.; ed Philippines Mil. Acad., Marine Corp Univ., Nat. Defense Coll. of Philippines; joined Philippine Marine Corps 1977, held several posts including Commdr of the Presidential Guards Bn, Presidential Security Group, 3rd Marine Brigade, Combat and Service Support Brigade; numerous staff appointments including Asst Chief of Staff for Intelligence, Philippine Marine Corps, Asst Supt, Marine Corps Training Center, Chief of Staff, Philippine Marine Corps, Deputy Commdt; Concurrent Commdr, Marine Forces; retd from mil. service 2011; Head of Mission and Force Commdr, UN Disengagement Observer Force (UNDOF) 2010–12; Undersec. of Nat. Defense for Defense Operations 2013–16; Deputy Dir Gen. for Security, APEC Manila 2015; Fellow, AIM TeaM Energy Center for Bridging Leadership; Distinguished Service Stars, Bronze Cross Medals, Military Merit Medal, Military Commendation Medal, Anti-Dissidence Campaign Medal, Luzon Campaign Medal, Visayan Campaign Medal, Military Civic Action Medal, Mindanao-Sulu Campaign Medal; two distinguished service stars, two bronze cross medals 2001, 17 mil. merit medals, six mil. commendation medals. *Leisure interests:* shooting, skydiving, soccer, basketball, tennis, badminton, bowling, swimming, scuba diving, martial arts.

ECCLESTON, Christopher; British actor; b. 16 Feb. 1964, Salford; s. of Joseph Ronald Eccleston and Elsie Lavinia Eccleston; m. Mischka Eccleston (divorced 2015); two c. *Films include:* Let Him Have It 1991, Shallow Grave 1995, Jude 1996, Elizabeth 1998, A Price Above Rubies 1998, Heart 1999, Old New Borrowed Blue 1999, Existenz 1999, Gone in 60 Seconds 2000, The Invisible Circus 2001, The Others 2001, I am Dina 2002, 28 Days Later 2002, The Seeker: The Dark Is Rising 2007, New Orleans, Mon Amour 2008, Unfinished Song 2012, Thor: The Dark

World 2013, Legend 2015. *Theatre includes:* Miss June 2000, Hamlet 2002, Electricity 2004, A Doll's House 2009, Antigone 2012. *Television appearances:* Cracker 1993–94, Hearts and Minds 1995, Our Friends in the North 1996, Hillsborough 1996, Strumpet 2001, Flesh and Blood (Best Actor, Royal TV Soc. Awards 2003) 2002, The Second Coming (TV film) 2003, Doctor Who (BBC) 2005, Perfect Parents 2006, Heroes 2007, Accused (Best Actor, Int. Emmy Awards 2011) 2010, Lucan 2013, The Leftovers 2014–15, Fortitude 2015, The A Word 2016. *Leisure interest:* supporting Manchester United Football Club. *Address:* c/o Claire Maroussas, Talent & Literary Department, Independent Talent Group Ltd, 40 Whitfield Street, London, W1T 2RH, England (office). *Telephone:* (20) 7636-6565 (office). *Fax:* (20) 7323-0101 (office). *Website:* www.independenttalent.com (office).

ECCLESTONE, Bernard (Bernie) Charles, BSc; British business executive; *Chairman Emeritus, Formula One Group;* b. 28 Oct. 1930, Ipswich, Suffolk, England; m. 1st Ivy Ecclestone; one d.; m. 2nd Slavica Radić 1985 (divorced 2009); two d.; m. 3rd Fabiana Flosi 2012; ed Woolwich Polytechnic, London; est. car and motorcycle dealership, Midweek Car Auctions, Bexley, Kent; racing-car driver for short period (Formula 3); Owner Connaught racing team 1957; Man. Jochen Rindt; purchased Brabham racing team 1970 (sold 1990); CEO Formula One Admin. Ltd, Formula One Management Ltd (acquired by Liberty Media Corpn) –2017, Chair. Emer. and Adviser to the Bd 2017–, mem. Bd of Dirs, Delta Topco Ltd (holding co.) –2014; Vice-Pres. Fed. Int. de l'Automobile (FIA) (racing's int. governing body); tried on bribery charges in Germany Jan. 2014, court later ruled he could pay a £60m settlement, without admitting guilt, to end the trial Aug. 2014; Grand Decoration of Honour (Austria) 2000, Medal of the First Degree (Bahrain), Keys to the Cities of São Paulo and Rio de Janeiro, Order of Merit of the Medium Cross (Hungary), Grand Officer, Order of Merit (Italy), Grand Officer, Equestrian Order of St Agatha (San Marino), Commdr of the Order of Saint-Charles (Monaco) 2006; Dr hc (Imperial Coll. London) 2008; Bandeirante Medal (São Paulo), Silver Gilt and Silver grade medals (Monaco), Motorsport Industry Assсn Business Achievement Award, British Racing Driver's Club inaugural Gold Medal. *Address:* Formula One Management Ltd, 6 Prince's Gate, London, SW7 1QJ, England. *Telephone:* (20) 7584-6668. *Fax:* (20) 7589-0311. *E-mail:* ckai@fomltd.com. *Website:* www.formula1.com.

ECHÁVARRI, Luis Enrique, MSc; Spanish business executive and international organization official; b. 17 April 1949, Bilbao; m.; two c.; ed Univ. of Basque Country, Univ. of Madrid; Project Man. for Lemóniz, Sayago and Almaraz nuclear power plants, Westinghouse Electric, Madrid; Tech. Dir and Commr, Consejo de Seguridad Nuclear (Spanish nuclear regulatory comm.); Dir-Gen. OECD Nuclear Energy Agency (NEA) 1997–2014; rep. of Spain at int. fora on nuclear energy, including Int. Atomic Energy Agency and EU; mem. INSAG-IAEA; represents NEA at Int. Energy Agency Governing bd; Order of the Rising Sun (Japan) 2014, Order of Isabella the Catholic (Spain) 2014.

ECHENOZ, Jean Maurice Emmanuel; French writer; b. 26 Dec. 1947, Orange, Vaucluse; s. of Marc Echenoz and Annie Languin; one s.; ed Univ. of Aix-en-Provence, Sorbonne and Univ. of Paris; professional writer 1979–; Grand Prix du roman de la Ville de Paris 1997, Grand Prix de littérature Paul Morand de l'Acad. française 2007, Prix de la Bibliothèque nationale de France 2016, Prix Marguerite Yourcenar 2018. *Film:* Le Rose et le blanc (dir Robert Pansard-Besson) (co-scriptwriter) (Prix Georges Sadoul) 1979. *Publications:* Le Méridien de Greenwich (Prix Fénéon 1980) 1979, Cherokee (Prix Médicis) 1983, L'Equipée malaise (trans. as Double Jeopardy) 1986, L'Occupation des sols 1988 (trans. as Plan of Occupancy), Lac (Grand Prix du Roman de la Société des Gens de Lettres 1990, European Literature Prize, Glasgow 1990) 1989, Nous trois 1992, Les Grandes blondes (trans. as Big Blondes) (Prix Novembre) 1995, Un An 1997, Je m'en vais (trans. as I'm Gone) (Prix Goncourt) 1999, Jérôme Lindon 2001, Josué, Samuel, Daniel, Maccabées (trans. of Bible, jtly) 2001, Au piano (trans. as Piano) 2003, Ravel 2006, Courir (trans. as Running) 2008, Des éclairs (trans. as Lightning) 2010, 14 (trans. as 1914) 2012, Caprice de la reine (trans. as The Queen's Caprice) 2014, Envoyée spéciale 2016. *Address:* c/o Editions de Minuit, 7 rue Bernard-Palissy, 75006 Paris, France (home). *Website:* www.leseditionsdeminuit.com (home).

ECHEVERRY GARZÓN, Juan Carlos, BA, PhD; Colombian economist, academic, politician and business executive; b. 12 Sept. 1962, Ibagué, Tolima; m. Verónica Navas Ospina; two s. one d.; ed Univ. de los Andes, Bogotá, New York Univ., USA, Kiel Inst. for the World Economy, Germany, Univ. Complutense de Madrid, Spain; fmr Dir Departamento Nacional de Planeación; consultant to Banco Interamericano de Desarrollo; Minister of Econ. Planning 2000–02; Dean of Econs, Univ. de los Andes 2002–06, now Assoc. Prof.; Pres. Econcept (financial consulting firm) 2002–10; served as adviser to Govt of Kazakhstan on issues of public investment and budget; fmr rep. in Colombia of Latin Source-Global Source (consultancy based in New York); Minister of Finance and Public Credit 2010–12; CEO Ecopetrol SA (oil and gas co.) 2015–17; writes weekly column for CNN en Español (news channel); columnist, El Tiempo. *Publications:* Las Claves del Futuro. Economía y conflicto en Colombia 2002, ¿Quién Manda sobre las Cuentas Públicas? Inflexibilidad presupuestal en Colombia, Argentina, México y Perú (co-author) 2008, El transporte como soporte al desarrollo de Colombia Una visión al 2040 (co-author) 2009, La Historia Repetida: Economía, Política y Burocracia en Colombia durante el siglo XIX (co-author) 2012. *Address:* c/o Ecopetrol SA, Carrera 13, #36–24, Edificio Principal, Bogotá, Distrito Capital, Colombia.

ECKEL, Keith W.; American business executive; b. Scranton, Pa; ed Newton-Ransom High School, Clarks Summit, Pa, Keystone Junior Coll., Dickinson Coll., Pennsylvania State Univ.; fmr Dir, Nationwide Financial Services, Inc., mem. Bd of Dirs Nationwide 1996–2014, Chair. Nationwide Mutual Insurance Co. (parent co.) 2008–14; fmr Chair. Gartmore Global Asset Man. Trust, Allied Group, Inc.; Owner Fred W. Eckel Sons, Pres. Eckel Farms, Inc.; Ind. Dir, First National Community Bancorp, Inc. and First National Community Bank 2014–; mem. Bd, Int. Food and Agricultural Devt, Pennsylvania Vegetable Growers Assсn; fmr mem. Bd, Pennsylvania Agricultural Land Preservation; Pres. Pennsylvania Farm Bureau for 15 years; fmr Pres. Lackawanna Co. Co-operative Extension Assсn; fmr Vice-Pres. Pennsylvania Council of Cooperative Extension Asscns; fmr mem. Bd and Exec. Cttee, American Farm Bureau Fed.; fmr Trustee, Pennsylvania State Univ., now Emer.; Master Farmer Award, Pennsylvania State Univ. 1982, Distinguished Service Award, American Farm Bureau Fed. 2009. *Address:* First National Community Bancorp, Inc., 102 East Drinker Street, Dunmore, PA 18512, USA (office). *Telephone:* (570) 346-7667 (office). *E-mail:* info@fncb.com (office). *Website:* www.fncb.com (office).

ECKRODT, Rolf, DipEng; German automotive industry executive (retd); b. 25 Feb. 1942, Gronau, Westphalia; ed Univ. of Bochum; Quality Assurance Passenger Cars Dept, Daimler Benz AG 1966–68, Man., Passenger Cars 1968, Project Leader, Production Components 1981–83, Vice-Pres. Axle Production 1983–86, Exec. Asst to Head of Mercedes-Benz Passenger Car Div. 1986–87, Dir Planning and Production, Passenger Cars and Components 1987–90, Dir Worldwide Planning and Production 1990–92, Pres. Mercedes Benz do Brasil 1992–96, Exec. Vice-Pres. and Deputy CEO, Adtranz 1996–98, Pres. and CEO 1998–2001; Exec. Vice-Pres. and COO Mitsubishi Motors Corpn 2001–02, Pres. and CEO 2002–04 (retd); Vice-Pres. German-Brazil Chamber of Commerce, São Paulo 1993–96; Chair. Union of European Railway Industries (UNIFE) 1999–2000; Hon. Consul of Brazil, Potsdam 1999–2001; mem. Exec. Cttee Asien-Pazifik-Forum Berlin e.V. *Address:* c/o Executive Committee, Asien-Pazifik-Forum Berlin e.V, c/o Berlin Partner GmbH, Fasanenstr. 85, 10623 Berlin, Germany.

EDANO, Yukio; Japanese lawyer and politician; *Leader, Constitutional Democratic Party of Japan;* b. 31 May 1964, Utsunomiya City, Tochigi Pref.; m.; two s.; ed Univ. of Tohoku; passed Nat. Bar Examination 1988, registered as attorney 1991; mem. House of Reps for Saitama No 5 Dist (New Japan Party) 1993–96, for Proportional Kitakanto Block (Democratic Party of Japan, DPJ) 1996–2000, for Saitama No 5 Dist 2000–17; Founder mem. DPJ 1996, Chair. DPJ Policy Research Council 2000, Research Comm. on the Constitution 2004, DPJ Sec.-Gen. March–Sept. 2010, 2014–17; Founder-Leader Constitutional Democratic Party of Japan 2017–; Minister of State for Govt Revitalization 2010, Chief Cabinet Sec. and Minister of State for Okinawa and N Territories Affairs Jan.–Sept. 2011, Minister of Economy, Trade and Industry 2011–12, also Minister for Nuclear Incident Economic Countermeasures and Minister of State for the Corpn in Support of Compensation for Nuclear Damage 2011–12. *Address:* Constitutional Democratic Party of Japan, Fuji Building, 3F 2-12-4, Hirakawacho, Chiyoda-ku, Tokyo 102-0093, Japan (office). *Telephone:* (3) 6811-2301 (office). *Fax:* (3) 6811-2302 (office). *Website:* cdp-japan.jp (office).

EDBERG, Stefan; Swedish fmr professional tennis player; b. 19 Jan. 1966, Vastervik; m. Annette Edberg (née Olsen); one s. one d.; won Jr Grand Slam 1983, Milan Open 1984, San Francisco, Basle and Memphis Opens 1985, Gstaad, Basle and Stockholm Opens 1986, Australian Open 1986, 1987, Wimbledon 1988, 1990, finalist 1989, US Open 1991, Masters 1989, German Open 1992, US Open 1992; winner (with Anders Jarryd) Masters and French Open 1986, Australian and US Opens 1987; semi-finalist in numerous tournaments; mem. Swedish Davis Cup Team 1984, 1987; retd in 1996 having won 60 professional titles; joined ATP Champions Tour 2008; coached Roger Federer 2014–15; Co-owner and mem. Bd of Dirs Case Asset Management AB (pvt. investment co.), Stockholm 2004–; f. Stefan Edberg Foundation to assist young Swedish tennis players; Adidas Sportsmanship Award (four times), inducted into Int. Tennis Hall of Fame 2004. *Leisure interest:* golf. *Address:* Case Asset Management AB, PO Box 5352, 102 49 Stockholm, Sweden (office). *E-mail:* info@case.nu (office). *Website:* casefonder.se (office).

EDDINGTON, Sir Roderick (Rod) Ian, Kt, AO, BEng, DPhil; Australian business executive; b. 2 Jan. 1950, Perth, Western Australia; s. of Gilbert Maxwell Eddington and April Mary Eddington; m. Young Sook Park 1994; one s. one d.; ed Christ Church Grammar School, WA, Univ. of Western Australia, Univ. of Oxford, UK; taught at Univ. of Oxford, UK for two years; joined Cathay Pacific Airways Ltd 1979, various positions in Hong Kong, Korea and Japan, Deputy Man. Dir 1990–92, Man. Dir and CEO 1992–96; Dir News Ltd (Australian arm of News Corpn) 1997–2000, Deputy Chair. 1998–2000; Exec. Chair. Ansett Australia 1997–2000; CEO British Airways (BA) 2000–05, also mem. Bd of Dirs; Chair. Victorian Major Events Co. 2006–14, Infrastructure Australia (govt body) 2008–14; Chair. for Australia and New Zealand, JPMorgan 2006–17; mem. Bd of Dirs, John Swire & Sons Pty Ltd 1997–, News Corpn 1999–2013, 21st Century Fox 2013–, Rio Tinto plc 2005–11, Lion Pty Ltd 2011– (Chair. 2012–); apptd by UK Treasury and Dept for Transport to write report on the future of Britain's transport system 2006; mem. Bd of Man. Fremantle Dockers Football Club 1998–2000; business adviser to Labor Party of Australia 2007–; Deputy Chair. Growing Victoria Together Summit 2000; mem. Victoria Govt's Innovation Economy Advisory Bd 2002–07, APEC Business Advisory Council 2014; President Australia-Japan Business Cooperation Committee; Grand Cordon, Order of the Rising Sun (Japan) 2015; Rhodes Scholar 1974. *Leisure interests:* cricket, bridge, football. *Address:* c/o JPMorgan Australia & New Zealand, Level 31, 101 Collins Street, Melbourne, Vic. 3000, Australia.

EDDY, Don, BFA, MFA; American artist; b. 4 Nov. 1944, Long Beach, Calif.; m. Leigh Behnke 1995; one d.; ed Fullerton Jr Coll., Univ. of Hawaii, Univ. of California, Santa Barbara. *Address:* c/o Nancy Hoffman Gallery, 520 West 27th Street, New York, NY 10001, USA (office). *E-mail:* doneddyart@aol.com (office). *Website:* www.nancyhoffmangallery.com (office).

EDELSTEIN, Victor Arnold; British couturier and artist; b. 10 July 1945, London; m. Anna Maria Succi 1973; ed studied painting with David Cranswick in London, with Charles Cecil in Florence, Italy; trainee designer, Alexon 1962, Asst Designer and Pattern Cutter to Biba 1967, designer, Salvador 1971, Christian Dior 1975; f. Victor Edelstein Ltd 1978–93; designed ballet of Rhapsody in Blue for Rambert Dance Co. 1989; pantomime Cinderella, Richmond Theatre 1991, black pas de deux, Swan Lake, Covent Garden 1991. *Leisure interests:* opera, gardening, collecting old master drawings, skiing. *E-mail:* enquiries@victoredelstein.com. *Website:* www.victoredelstein.com.

EDELSTEIN, Yuli-Yoel; Israeli (b. Ukrainian) politician; *Speaker of the Knesset;* b. 5 Aug. 1958, Chernovitz, Ukraine; m.; two c.; ed Moscow Inst. for Teacher Training; fmr Hebrew teacher, Moscow; emigrated to Israel 1987; fmr teacher Melitz Centre for Jewish-Zionist Educ., School for Educational Inst., Jerusalem; Adviser to Opposition Leader Benjamin Netanyahu 1993–94; a founder of Yisrael Ba-Aliya Party 1996; headed party's election campaign; mem. Knesset (Parl.) 1996–, Deputy Speaker, Knesset 1999–2001, Speaker 2013–; Minister of Immigrant Absorption 1996–99, Deputy Minister 2001–03; Minister of Public Diplomacy and the Diaspora 2009–13. *Address:* Office of the Speaker, Knesset, Kiryat

Ben-Gurion, Jerusalem 91006 (office); Alon Shvut, Israel (home). *Telephone:* 2-6753444 (office). *Fax:* 2-6496193 (office). *E-mail:* Yedelstein@knesset.gov.il (office). *Website:* www.knesset.gov.il/main/eng/home.asp (office).

EDELSTENNE, Charles; French aviation industry executive; *Chairman, Dassault Systèmes;* b. 9 Jan. 1938, Paris; s. of Simon Edelstenne and Ida Edelstenne (née Brutman); m. Adèle Edelhertz 1963; one s. one d.; Chief Financial Officer Avions Marcel Dassault-Bréguet Aviation 1960–71, Deputy Sec.-Gen. 1971–75, Sec.-Gen. 1975–86, Vice-Pres. 1986–89, Dir 1989–2000, Chair. and CEO Dassault Aviation 2000–13, f. Dassault Systèmes 1981, Man. Dir 1981–93, Chair. and CEO 1993–2002, Chair. 2002–, Pres. Dassault Systèmes America 1992–2002, Chair. Dassault Falcon Jet Corpn from 1978, Pres. Dassault International USA 2001; Dir Société Anonyme Belge de Constructions Aéronautiques, Belgium, Groupe Industriel Marcel Dassault, Paris, Sogitec Industries, Thales Systems Aéroportes, Dassault Réassurance; Pres. Groupement des Industries Françaises Aéronautiques et Spatiales (GIFAS) 2005–09; Dir French Aircraft Mfrs Asscn (Chair. Econ. Cttee 1981–87); fmr Vice-Pres. Foundation for Defence Studies; Chair. French Defence Industries Council 2006–; Pres. AeroSpace and Defence Industries Asscn Europe 2006–07; Commdr, Légion d'honneur. *Address:* Dassault Systèmes, 10 rue Marcel Dassault, CS 40501, 78946 Vélizy-Villacoublay Cedex, France (office). *Telephone:* 1-61-62-61-62 (office). *E-mail:* info@3ds.com (office). *Website:* www.3ds.com (office).

EDGAR, David Burman, BA; British writer; b. 26 Feb. 1948, Birmingham, England; s. of Barrie Edgar and Joan Edgar (née Burman); m. 1st Eve Brook 1979 (died 1998); two step-s.; m. 2nd Stephanie Dale 2012; ed Oundle School, Univ. of Manchester; Fellow in Creative Writing, Leeds Polytechnic 1972–74; Resident Playwright, Birmingham Repertory Theatre 1974–75, Bd mem. 1985–; Lecturer in Playwriting, Univ. of Birmingham 1975–78, Dir of Playwriting Studies 1989–99, Prof. 1995–99; Founder Theatre Writers' Union 1970s; UK/US Bicentennial Arts Fellow resident in USA 1978–79; Literary Consultant, RSC 1984–88; Fellow, Birmingham Polytechnic 1991, Judith E. Wilson Fellow, Clare Hall, Cambridge 1996; Pres. Writers' Guild of GB 2007–13; Humanitas Visiting Prof. of Drama Studies, Univ. of Oxford 2015; Fellowship, Birmingham Polytechnic; Hon. Sr Research Fellow, Univ. of Birmingham 1988–92, Hon. Prof. 1992–; Hon. MA (Bradford) 1986, Hon. DUniv (Surrey) 1993, Hon. DLitt (Birmingham, Warwick, Worcester); Soc. of West End Theatres Best Play Award 1980, Tony Award for Best Play 1981, Plays and Players Award for Best Play 1983, Evening Standard Award for Best Play 1995. *Plays include:* Two Kinds of Angel 1970, Rent or Caught in the Act 1972, State of Emergency 1972, The Dunkirk Spirit 1974, Dick Deterred 1974, O Fair Jerusalem 1975, Saigon Rose 1976, Blood Sports 1976, Destiny (for RSC) 1976, Wreckers 1977, The Jail Diary of Albie Sachs (for RSC) 1978, Mary Barnes 1978–79, Teendreams 1979, The Adventures of Nicholas Nickleby (adaptation for RSC) 1980, Maydays (for RSC) 1983, Entertaining Strangers 1985, That Summer 1987, The Shape of the Table 1990, Dr Jekyll and Mr Hyde (adaptation for RSC) 1991, Pentecost 1994, Other Place 1994, Young Vic 1995, Albert Speer (adaptation for Nat. Theatre) 2000, The Prisoner's Dilemma 2001, Continental Divide 2003, Playing with Fire (Nat. Theatre, London) 2005, A Time to Keep 2007, Testing the Echo 2008, Arthur and George (adaptation for Birmingham Repertory Theatre) 2010, The Master Builder 2010, Written on the Heart (adaptation for Royal Shakespeare Company) 2011, If Only 2013. *Film:* Lady Jane 1986. *Radio:* Ecclesiastes 1977, A Movie Starring Me 1991. *Television includes:* plays: I Know What I Meant 1974, Baby Love 1974, Vote for Them 1989, Buying a Landslide 1992, Citizen Locke 1994. *Publications include:* Destiny 1976, Wreckers 1977, Teendreams 1979, Maydays 1983, Plays One 1987, The Second Time as Farce 1988, Heartlanders 1989, Plays Two 1990, Plays Three 1991, Pentecost 1995, State of Play (ed.) 1999, Albert Speer 2000, The Prisoner's Dilemma 2001, Continental Divide 2004, Playing With Fire 2005, A Time to Keep 2007, Testing the Echo 2008, How Plays Work 2009, Arthur and George 2010, The Master Builder 2010, Written on the Heart 2011, If Only 2013. *Leisure interests:* fine art, cookery. *Address:* c/o Alan Brodie Representation, Paddock Suite, The Courtyard, 55 Charterhouse Street, London, EC1M 6HA, England (office). *E-mail:* alan@alanbrodie.com (office). *Website:* www.alanbrodie.com (office).

EDGAR, James (Jim); American academic and fmr politician; *Distinguished Fellow, Institute of Government and Public Affairs, University of Illinois;* b. 22 July 1946, Vinita, Okla; m. Brenda Smith; one s. one d.; ed Eastern Ill. Univ., Univ. of Ill. and Sangamon State Univ.; key Asst to Speaker, Ill. House of Reps 1972–73; aide to Pres. Ill. Senate 1974, to House Minority Leader 1976; mem. Ill. House of Reps 1977–91; Dir Legis. Affairs, Gov. of Ill. 1979–80; Sec. of State of Ill. 1981–91; Gov. of Ill. 1991–99; Chair. Nat. Govt's Asscn Comm. Econ. Devt and Tech. Innovation 1991, Strategic Planning Review Task Force 1991; Distinguished Fellow, Inst. of Govt and Public Affairs, Univ. of Ill. 1999–; Pres. Abraham Lincoln Presidential Library Foundation 2004–, Chair. Illinois Financing Partners 2016–; mem. Bd of Dirs The Chicago Council on Global Affairs; Order of Lincoln 1999. *Address:* Institute of Government and Public Affairs, University of Illinois, 1007 W Nevada Street, Apartment MC-037, Urbana, IL 61801, USA (office). *Telephone:* (217) 244-5871 (office). *Fax:* (217) 244-5872 (office). *E-mail:* jedgar@uillinois.edu (office). *Website:* www.igpa.uiuc.edu (office).

THE EDGE; Irish musician (guitar) and songwriter; b. (David Howell Evans), 8 Aug. 1961, Barking, Essex, England; ed Mount Temple School; founder mem. and guitarist, the Feedback 1976, renamed the Hype, finally renamed U2 1978–; major concerts include Live Aid Wembley 1985, Self Aid Dublin, A Conspiracy of Hope (Amnesty Int. Tour) 1986, Smile Jamaica (hurricane relief fundraiser) 1988, Very Special Arts Festival, White House, Washington, DC 1988; numerous tours worldwide; Order of Liberty (Portugal) 2005; U2 have won 22 Grammy awards including Album of the Year and Best Rock Performance by a Duo or Group with Vocal (for The Joshua Tree) 1987, Grammy awards for Best Rock Performance by a Duo or Group with Vocal (for Desire) and Best Performance Video, short form (for Where the Streets Have No Name) 1988, BRIT Awards for Best Int. Act 1988–90, 1992, 1998, 2001, Best Live Act 1993, Outstanding Contribution to the British Music Industry 2001, JUNO Award 1992, World Music Award 1992, Grammy Award for Best Rock Vocal by a Duo or Group (for Achtung Baby) 1992, Grammy Award for Best Alternative Music Album (for Zooropa) 1993, Grammy Award for Best Music Video, long form (for Zoo TV Live from Sydney) 1994, Grammy Award for Song of the Year, Record of the Year, Best Rock Performance by a Duo or Group with Vocal (all for Beautiful Day) 2000, Grammy Awards for Best Pop Performance by a Duo or Group with Vocal (for Stuck In A Moment You Can't Get Out Of), for Record of the Year (for Walk On), for Best Rock Performance by a Duo or Group with Vocal (for Elevation), for Rock Album of the Year (All That You Can't Leave Behind) 2001, American Music Award for Favorite Internet Artist of the Year 2002, Ivor Novello Award for Best Song Musically and Lyrically (for Walk On) 2002, Golden Globe for Best Original Song (for The Hands That Built America, from film Gangs of New York) 2003, Grammy Awards for Best Rock Performance by a Duo or Group with Vocal, Best Rock Song, Best Short Form Music Video (all for Vertigo) 2004, TED Prize 2004, Nordoff-Robbins Silver Clef Award for lifetime achievement 2005, Q Awards for Best Live Act 2005, 2016, Digital Music Award for Favourite Download Single (for Vertigo) 2005, Meteor Ireland Music Award for Best Irish Band, Best Live Performance 2006, Grammy Awards for Song of the Year, for Best Rock Performance by a Duo or Group with Vocal (both for Sometimes You Can't Make it on Your Own), for Best Rock Song (for City of Blinding Lights), for Album of the Year and Best Rock Album of the Year (both for How to Dismantle an Atomic Bomb) 2006, Golden Globe Award for Best Original Song (Ordinary Love in Mandela: Long Walk to Freedom) 2014, Ambs of Conscience Award, Amnesty International 2006, Palm Springs Film Festival Sonny Bono Visionary Award 2014, MTV Europe Music Award for Global Icons 2017. *Plays include:* Spider-Man: Turn Off The Dark (music and lyrics by Bono and The Edge), Broadway, New York 2011–14. *Films include:* Rattle and Hum 1988. *Recordings include:* albums: Boy 1980, October 1981, War 1983, Under a Blood Red Sky 1983, The Unforgettable Fire 1984, Wide Awake In America 1985, The Joshua Tree (Grammy Award for Album of the Year, Best Rock Performance by a Duo or Group with Vocal) 1987, Rattle and Hum 1988, Achtung Baby (Grammy Award for Best Rock Performance by a Duo or Group with Vocal 1992) 1991, Zooropa (Grammy Award for Best Alternative Music Album) 1993, Passengers (film soundtrack with Brian Eno) 1995, Pop 1997, The Best Of 1980–90 1998, All That You Can't Leave Behind (Grammy Award for Best Rock Album 2001) 2000, The Best Of 1990–2000 2002, How To Dismantle An Atomic Bomb (Meteor Ireland Music Award for Best Irish Album 2006, Grammy Awards for Album of the Year, for Best Rock Album 2006) 2004, No Line on the Horizon 2009, Songs of Innocence 2014, Songs of Experience 2017; solo: Captive 1987. *Address:* c/o Principle Management, 30–32 Sir John Rogersons Quay, Dublin 2, Ireland (office). *E-mail:* nadine@numb.ie (office). *Website:* www.u2.com.

EDGLEY, Michael Christopher, MBE; Australian business executive; *Chairman, Edgley Ventures Pty Ltd.;* b. 17 Dec. 1943, Melbourne; s. of Eric Edgley and Edna Edgley (née Luscombe); m. 1st Erica Chamberlain 1962 (divorced); m. 2nd Jennifer Gedge 1972; two s. three d.; ed Trinity Coll., Perth; Chair. Edgley Ventures Pty Ltd 1962–, promoting a wide range of events throughout Australia, NZ, UK, Asia and S Africa; WA Citizen of the Year Award 1976. *Leisure interests:* jogging, tennis. *Address:* Edgley International, 2 Chapel Street, Richmond, Vic. 2121, Australia (office). *Telephone:* (3) 9428-7711 (office). *Fax:* (3) 9428-7712 (office). *E-mail:* headoffice@edgley.com.au (office). *Website:* www.edgley.com.au (office).

EDINBURGH, HRH The Duke of; (Prince Philip), (Prince of the United Kingdom of Great Britain and Northern Ireland, Earl of Merioneth, Baron Greenwich), KG, KT, OM, GBE; b. 10 June 1921, Corfu, Greece; s. of Prince Andrew of Greece and Denmark and Princess Alice of Battenberg; m. 20 Nov. 1947 HRH Princess Elizabeth (HM Queen Elizabeth II q.v.); children: Prince Charles Philip Arthur George, Prince of Wales (q.v.), b. 14 Nov. 1948, Princess Anne Elizabeth Alice Louise, The Princess Royal (q.v.), b. 15 Aug. 1950, Prince Andrew Albert Christian Edward, Duke of York (q.v.), b. 19 Feb. 1960, Prince Edward Antony Richard Louis, Earl of Wessex (q.v.), b. 10 March 1964; ed Cheam, Salem and Gordonstoun Schools, Royal Naval Coll., Dartmouth; renounced right of succession to thrones of Greece and Denmark, naturalized British subject 1947, adopting surname Mountbatten; served Royal Navy 1939–51, served in Indian Ocean, Mediterranean, North Sea, Pacific Ocean during Second World War; Personal ADC to King George VI 1948–52; PC 1951–; ranks of Adm. of the Fleet, Field Marshal, Marshal of the Royal Air Force, Captain-Gen. Royal Marines 1953–2017; Lord High Adm. of the Royal Navy 2011–; Chancellor, Univs of Wales 1948–76, Edinburgh 1952–2010, Salford 1967–91, Cambridge 1977–2011; apptd Pres., Patron or Trustee of numerous orgs including Nat. Playing Fields Asscn 1948, Nat. Maritime Museum 1948, London Fed. of Clubs for Young People (now called London Youth) 1948, City & Guilds of London Inst. 1951–2010, Cen. Council of Physical Recreation 1951, Design Council 1952, RSA 1952, English-Speaking Union of the Commonwealth 1952, Outward Bound Trust 1952, Trinity House 1952, Guild of Air Pilots and Air Navigators 1952, RCA 1955, Commonwealth Games Fed. 1955–90, Duke of Edinburgh's Award Scheme 1956, Duke of Edinburgh's Commonwealth Study Confs 1956, Royal Agric. Soc. of the Commonwealth 1958–2010, Voluntary Service Overseas 1961, World Wildlife Fund UK 1961–82, Int. Equestrian Fed. 1964–86, Maritime Trust 1969–, Royal Commonwealth Ex-Services League 1974, Royal Acad. of Eng 1976, British Trust for Ornithology 1987; Pres. World Wide Fund for Nature 1981–96, Pres. Emer. 1997; Freemason; numerous decorations, hon. degrees and awards worldwide. *Publications:* 14 publs 1957–2004. *Address:* Buckingham Palace, London, SW1A 1AA, England. *Website:* www.royal.gov.uk.

EDLEY, Christopher, Jr, BA, MMP, JD; American professor of law and university administrator; *Honorable William H. Orrick Jr. Distinguished Professor, University of California, Berkeley;* b. 13 Jan. 1953, Boston, Mass; s. of Christopher F. Edley, Sr and Zaida Coles Edley; m. Maria Echaveste; ed Swarthmore Coll., John F. Kennedy School of Government, Harvard Univ., Harvard Law School; called to the Bar, Washington, DC 1980; Asst Dir White House Domestic Policy Staff (Carter Admin), Washington, DC 1978–79; Special Asst to Sec., US Dept of Health, Educ. and Welfare 1979–80; Assoc. Asst to Pres., The White House 1980; Asst Prof., Harvard Law School 1981–87, Prof. 1987–2004; Assoc. Dir Office of Man. and Budget, Washington, DC 1993–95; Special Counsel to Pres., The White House 1995, also Dir White House Review of Affirmative Action, Sr Advisor to Pres. for Race Initiative 1997–99; Honorable William H. Orrick Jr. Distinguished Chair, Univ. of Calif., Berkeley 2004–, Dean, Boalt Hall School of Law 2004–13; Founding Co-Dir The Civil Rights Project; served in Dukakis presidential campaign as Nat. Issues Dir; Sr Advisor on Econ. Policy for Clinton–Gore Presidential Transition 1992; Sr Policy Advisor to Al Gore and mem.

Democratic Platform Drafting Cttee during presidential campaign 2000; mem. US Comm. on Civil Rights 1999–2005, Comm. Task Force on the Future of the Common School (Century Foundation), Nat. Comm. on Fed. Electoral Reform, Council on Foreign Relations, Nat. Acad. of Public Admin; mem. Bd Nat. Immigration Forum, NAS, Assessment Comm. on No Child Left Behind 2006–07, Nat. Research Council, Nat. Assoc. and service on Cttee including Bd on Testing; Founding mem. Advisory Bd for the Madison Soc.; mem. Exec. Cttee of Bd of People for the American Way; Adjunct Scholar, Urban Inst.; Fellow, Nat. Acad. of Public Admin, Council on Foreign Relations, American Law Inst., American Acad. of Arts and Sciences 2007–; Co-Chair., Nat. Comm. on Educ. Equity and Excellence 2011–13; Co-founder and Pres. Opportunity Inst. 2015–; Trustee, Russell Sage Foundation, The Century Foundation; fmr Vice-Chair. Congressional Black Caucus Foundation; fmr Ed. Harvard Review; fmr mem. Editorial Bd Washington Post; mem. American Acad. of Arts and Sciences, Academy of Public Admin, Council on Foreign Relations, Gates Foundation Nat. Programs Advisory Panel, American Law Inst. *Publications include:* Administrative Law: Rethinking Judicial Control of Bureaucracy, Not All Black and White: Affirmative Action, Race and American Values. *Address:* University of California, School of Law, Berkeley, CA 4720-7200, USA (office). *E-mail:* edley@law.berkeley.edu (office). *Website:* www.law.berkeley.edu (office); www.theopportunityinstitute.org.

EDMISTON, Baron (Life Peer), cr. 2011, of Lapworth in the County of Warwickshire; **Robert Norman Edmiston,** FCMA; British automotive industry executive and philanthropist; *Chairman, I.M. Group;* b. 6 Oct. 1946; m.; three c.; began career as a bank clerk; Finance Dir at sports car manufacturer Jensen Motors –1974; est. International Motors 1976, acquired UK franchise for Subaru and Isuzu cars, later branched out into property and vehicle finance, est. I.M. Group (car importer) and I.M. Properties; f. Christian Vision (int. evangelical charity), Coleshill, Warwicks. 1988; sponsor of three secondary schools within English acad. programme, Grace Acad., Coventry, Grace Acad., Solihull, Grace Acad., Darlaston, Chair. Bd Govs of all three acads; apptd mem. House of Lords (Conservative) 2011, retd 2015. *Address:* I.M. Group Ltd, I.M. House, South Drive, Coleshill, B46 1DF, England (office). *Telephone:* (121) 747-4000 (Coleshill) (office). *E-mail:* info@imgroup.co.uk (office). *Website:* www.imgroup.co.uk (office); www.christianvision.com.

EDMOND, Bocchit; Haitian diplomatist and politician; *Minister of Foreign Affairs and Worship;* m.; c.; ed Univ. Latinoamericana de Comercio Exterior, Panama, Oxford Univ.; joined Haitian Foreign Service as Jr Officer 1991, becoming mem., Presidential Comm. to negotiate Haiti's accession to CARICOM 1997–2001, Counsellor, Perm. Mission of Haiti to UN, New York 1999–2000, Counsellor, Embassy in Jamaica 2001–03, Chief of State Protocol (rank of Amb.) 2003–04, Chargé d'affaires, Embassy in Panama 2004–10, Perm. Rep. to OAS, Washington, DC 2012–16, Chargé d'affaires, Embassy in London 2016–18; Minister of Foreign Affairs and Worship 2018–. *Address:* Ministry of Foreign Affairs and Worship, blvd Harry S Truman, Cité de l'Exposition, Port-au-Prince, Haiti (office). *Telephone:* 2222-8482 (office). *Fax:* 2223-1668 (office).

EDMONDS, David, CBE, BA; British company director and fmr business executive; *Chairman, Phone-paid Services Authority;* b. 6 March 1944, Grapenhall, Warrington, Cheshire, England; s. of Albert Edmonds and Gladys Edmonds; m. Ruth Edmonds (née Beech) 1964; two s. two d.; ed Helsby Co. Grammar School, Univ. of Keele; with Ministry of Housing 1966–70, with Dept of the Environment 1970–84; Chief Exec. The Housing Corpn 1984–91; Man. Dir Group Services NatWest Group 1991–98; Dir-Gen. Oftel (Office of Telecommunications) 1998–2004; Chair. NHSDirect 2004–08; mem. Bd, Office of Communications (Ofcom) 2004–06, London Legacy Devt Corpn 2011–15 (Chair. 2015–16); mem. Bd of Dirs Wincanton PLC 2004–11 (Deputy Chair. 2007–08, Chair. 2008–11), Hammerson plc 2003–11, William Hill plc 2005–14, English Partnerships 2000–04 (Chair. Property, Planning and Projects Cttee 2000), Barchester Healthcare 2012–18; Chair. Phone-paid Services Authority 2015–; Chair. Legal Services Bd 2008–14; mem. Council and Treas., Keele Univ. 1997–; Chair. Bd of Kingston Univ. 2012–; Hon. DLitt (Keele) 2004. *Leisure interests:* opera, golf, art, walking. *Address:* Phone-paid Services Authority, 25th Floor, 40 Bank Street, London, E14 5NR, England (office). *Telephone:* (20) 7940-7474 (office). *E-mail:* chairman@psauthority.org.uk (office). *Website:* www.psauthority.org.uk (office).

EDMONDS, John Walter, MA; British fmr trade union official; *Visiting Senior Research Fellow, King's College London;* b. 28 Jan. 1944, London; s. of Maude Rose Edmonds and Walter Edgar Edmonds; m. Janet Linden 1967; two d.; ed Oriel Coll., Oxford; Research Asst, GMB (fmrly Gen., Municipal and Boilermakers' Union) Trade Union 1965, Deputy Research Officer 1967, Regional Organizer 1968, Nat. Officer 1972, Gen. Sec. 1986–2003; fmr mem. Royal Comm. on Environmental Pollution, Council Advisory, Conciliation and Arbitration Service (ACAS), Forestry Comm.; mem. Nat. Employment Panel (fmrly New Deal Task Force) –2002; Visiting Prof., Business School, Durham Univ.; Visiting Sr Research Fellow, King's Coll. London 2003–; Chair. Inland Waterways Advisory Council 2006–12, River Thames Alliance; Dir (non-exec.) Carbon Trust 2002–, Environment Agency 2003–, Salix Finance 2005; Hon. Trustee, Nat. Soc. for the Prevention of Cruelty to Children; Hon. Fellow, Soc. for the Environment 2006; Hon. DIur (Sussex) 1993. *Leisure interests:* cricket, carpentry. *Address:* 50 Graham Road, Mitcham, Surrey, CR4 2HA, England (home). *Telephone:* (20) 8648-9991 (home). *E-mail:* johnedmonds1@hotmail.com (home).

EDWARD, Sir David Alexander Ogilvy, Kt, KCMG, PC, QC, MA, LLD, FRSE; British advocate, judge and professor of European institutions; *Professor Emeritus, University of Edinburgh;* b. 14 Nov. 1934, Perth, Scotland; s. of John O. C. Edward and Margaret I. MacArthur; m. Elizabeth Young McSherry 1962; two s. two d.; ed Sedbergh School, Univ. Coll., Oxford and Univ. of Edinburgh; advocate 1962–, Clerk Faculty of Advocates 1967–70, Treas. 1970–77; Pres. Consultative Cttee, Bars and Law Socs of the EEC 1978–80; Salvesen Prof. of European Insts and Dir Europa Inst., Univ. of Edinburgh 1985–89, Prof. Emer. 1989–; Judge of the Court of First Instance of the European Communities 1989–92, Judge, Court of Justice of the EC 1992–2003; Hon. Pres. Scottish Arbitration Centre; fmr Specialist Adviser to House of Lords Select Cttee on the EEC; fmr Chair. Continental Assets Trust PLC; fmr Dir Adam & Co. PLC, Harris Tweed Asscn Ltd; mem. Scottish Advisory Cttee, British Council, Panel of Arbitrators, Int. Centre for Settlement of Investment Disputes, Comm. on a Bill of Rights; fmr mem. Law Advisory Cttee; fmr mem. Gründungssenat, Europa-Univ. Viadrina, Frankfurt/Oder; Trustee, Trier Acad. of European Law, Industry and Parl. Trust, Carnegie Trust for the Univs of Scotland; fmr Trustee, Nat. Library of Scotland; Hon. Bencher, Gray's Inn; Hon. Fellow, Univ. Coll., Oxford; Hon. LLD (Edinburgh) 1993, (Aberdeen) 1997, (Napier) 1998, (Glasgow) 2003; Hon. DIur (Saarland) 2001, (Münster) 2001; Hon. DUniv (Surrey) 2003, (St Andrews) 2015; Officier, Legion d'Honneur, Chevalier, Ordre des Arts et des Lettres 2012. *Publications:* The Professional Secret: Confidentiality and Legal Professional Privilege in the EEC 1976, European Community Law: an introduction (with R. C. Lane) 1995; articles in legal journals. *Address:* 32 Heriot Row, Edinburgh, EH3 6ES, Scotland (home).

EDWARDES, Sir Michael (Owen), Kt, BA, FBIM; British business executive; b. 11 Oct. 1930, South Africa; s. of Denys Owen Edwardes and Audrey Noel Edwardes (née Copeland); m. 1st Mary Margaret Finlay 1958 (divorced, died 1999); three d.; m. 2nd Sheila Ann Guy 1988; ed St Andrew's Coll., SA, Rhodes Univ., SA; joined Chloride Group in SA as man. trainee 1951, mem. Man. Bd 1969, Chief Exec. 1972, Exec. Chair. 1974–77, Deputy Chair. (non-exec.) 1977–82, Chair. (non-exec.) 1982–88 (acting Chief Exec. 1985–87); Chair. and Chief Exec. British Leyland Ltd. 1977–82; Dir (non-exec.) Hill Samuel Group PLC 1980–87, Standard Securities 1984–87, Minerals and Resources Corpn 1984–, Flying Pictures Ltd 1987–; Chair. Mercury Communications Ltd 1982–83, ICL PLC 1984; Chair. and Chief Exec. Dunlop Holdings 1984–85; Chair. Charter Consolidated PLC 1988–96, Tryhorn Investments Ltd 1987–, Porth Group PLC 1991–95, ARC Int. Ltd 1991–93; Exec. Dir Minorco 1984, Syndicated Services Co. Inc. 1995–; Group Deputy Chair. R. K. Carvill Int. Holdings Ltd (now Carvill Group) 1988, now Dir; Dir (non-exec.) Int. Man. Devt Inst., Washington, DC 1978–94, Hi-Tec Sports 1993–, Strand Partners Ltd 1994–; Pres. Comité des Constructeurs d'Automobiles du Marché Commun 1979–80; Trustee, Thrombosis Research Inst. 1991–; mem. Nat. Enterprise Bd 1975–77, CBI Council 1974 (mem. Pres.'s Cttee 1981–), Review Cttee for Queen's Award for Industry; Hon. Fellow, Inst. of Mechanical Engineers; Hon. DIur (Rhodes Univ., SA) 1980; Young Businessman of the Year 1975. *Publication:* Back From the Brink 1983. *Leisure interests:* water skiing, sailing, squash, tennis.

EDWARDS, Anthony; American actor and director; b. 19 July 1962, Santa Barbara, Calif.; ed Royal Acad. of Dramatic Art, London; joined Santa Barbara Youth Theatre, in 30 productions aged 12–17; working in commercials aged 16; stage appearance in Ten Below, New York 1993; Screen Actors Guild Award 1996, 1998, 1999, Golden Globe 1998. *Films include:* Fast Times at Ridgemont High 1982, Heart Like a Wheel 1982, Revenge of the Nerds 1984, The Sure Thing 1985, Gotcha! 1985, Top Gun 1985, Summer Heat 1987, Revenge of the Nerds II 1987, Mr. North 1988, Miracle Mile 1989, How I Got into College 1989, Hawks 1989, Downtown 1990, Delta Heat, The Client 1994, Us Begins with You 1998, Don't Go Breaking My Heart 1999, Jackpot 2001, Northfork 2003, Thunderbirds 2004, The Forgotten 2004, Zodiac 2007, Motherhood 2009, Flipped 2010, Big Sur 2012, Planes 2013, Experimenter 2015. *Television includes:* series: It Takes Two 1982–83, Northern Exposure 1992–93, ER 1994–2008 (Golden Globe Award for Best Actor 1998, Screen Actors Guild Award for Outstanding Performance by a Male Actor in a Drama Series 1996, 1998), Soul Man, Rock Story 2000; films: The Killing of Randy Webster 1981, High School USA 1983, Going for the Gold: The Bill Johnson Story 1985, El Diablo 1990, Hometown Boy Makes Good 1990, In Cold Blood 1996; specials: Unpublished Letters, Sexual Healing, Zero Hour 2013. *Address:* c/o United Talent Agency, 9336 Civic Center Drive, Beverly Hills, CA 90210, USA.

EDWARDS, Charlotte Marie, CBE, MBE; British professional cricketer (retd); b. 17 Dec. 1979, Huntingdon; right-handed batswoman; right-arm legbreak bowler; teams: East Anglia Women 1994–99, Northern Districts Women 2000–03, Kent Women 2000–16, Western Fury 2014–, Perth Scorchers 2015–16, Southern Vipers 2016–, Adelaide Strikers 2016–, Hampshire Women 2017–; Test debut: England vs New Zealand, Guildford 12 July 1996; ODI debut: England vs South Africa, Bristol 15 Aug. 1997; T20I debut: England vs New Zealand, Hove 5 Aug. 2004; played 23 Tests (to Aug. 2015), scored 1,676 runs (average 44.10) with four centuries and nine fifties, best score of 117 against New Zealand in Scarborough 2004; played 191 ODIs (to 14 Feb. 2016), scored 5,992 runs (average 38.16) with nine centuries and 46 fifties, best score of 173 against Ireland in Pune 1997; played 95 T20Is (to 30 March 2016), scored 2,605 runs (average 32.97) with 12 fifties, best score of 92; apptd Dir Women's Cricket 2018; named ICC Women's Cricketer of the Year 2008, Wisden Cricketers of the Year 2017, ECB Cricketer of the Year 2013–14, 2014–15. *Address:* England and Wales Cricket Board, Lord's Cricket Ground, London, NW8 8QZ, England (office). *Telephone:* (20) 7432-1200 (office). *Fax:* (20) 7286-5583 (office). *Website:* www.ecb.co.uk (office).

EDWARDS, Sir Christopher Richard Watkin, Kt, MD, FRCP, FRCPE, FMedSci, FRSE; British physician and university vice-chancellor; b. 12 Feb. 1942; s. of Thomas Archibald Watkin Edwards and Beatrice Elizabeth Ruby Watkin Edwards; m. Sally Amanda Kidd 1968; two s. one d.; ed Marlborough Coll., Christ's Coll. Cambridge; Lecturer in Medicine, St Bartholomew's Hosp., London 1969–75, Sr Lecturer and MRC Sr Research Fellow 1975–80, Hon. Consultant Physician 1975–80; Moncrieff Arnott Prof. of Clinical Medicine, Univ. of Edinburgh 1980–95, Dean Faculty of Medicine 1991–95, Provost Faculty Group of Medicine and Veterinary Medicine 1992–95; Prin. and Prof. of Medicine Imperial Coll. of Science and Medicine, Univ. of London 1995–2000; Vice-Chancellor Univ. of Newcastle 2001–07; Dir (non-exec.) Chelsea and Westminster Hosp. 2007–; Vice-Chair. (non-exec.), Cluff Geothermal Ltd (now Hotspur Geothermal); mem. MRC 1991–95; Fellow, Imperial Coll. London 2003; Gov. Wellcome Trust 1994–; Co-founder FMedSci 1998; Chair. ICAPPIC Ltd 2015–; Trustee, Planet Earth Inst. 2012–; Patron, Tom's Trust 2013–, Rye Acad. 2013–; Hon. DSc (Aberdeen) 2000. *Publications include:* Clinical Physiology (ed.) 1984, Essential Hypertension as an Endocrine Disease 1985, Endocrinology 1986, Recent Advances in Endocrinology and Metabolism, Vol. 3 (ed.) 1989, Davidson's Principles and Practice of Medicine (ed.) 1995; over 400 scientific papers and communications. *Leisure interests:* running, reading, golf, skiing, painting. *Address:* Hotspur Geothermal Ltd, Charter House, 13–15 Carteret Street, St James, SW1H 9DJ, England (office). *Telephone:* (1303) 261564 (home). *E-mail:* c.edwards@ncl.ac.uk (office). *Website:* www.hotspurgeothermal.com (office).

EDWARDS, Sir Gareth Owen, Kt, MBE, CBE; British business executive and fmr rugby union player; b. 12 July 1947, Gwaun-Cae-Gurwen, Wales; s. of Thomas Granville Edwards and Annie-Mary Edwards; m. Maureen Edwards 1972; two s.; ed Pontardawe Tech. School, Millfield School, Cardiff Coll. of Educ.; scrum half; Welsh Secondary Schools Rugby int. 1965–66; English Schools 200 yards hurdles champion 1966 (UK under-19 record-holder); Welsh nat. team: 53 caps 1967–78, Capt. 13 times, youngest captain (aged 20) 1968; played with Cardiff RFC 1966–78, Barbarians 1967–78, British Lions 1968, 1971, 1974; Jt Dir Euro-Commercials (South Wales) Ltd 1982–, Players (UK) Ltd 1983–88; Chair. Hamdden Ltd 1991–; Chair. Regional Fisheries Advisory Cttee, Welsh Water Authority 1983–89; Patron The Richard Hunt Foundation, Jaguar Acad. of Sport 2010. *Publications:* Gareth – An Autobiography 1978, Rugby Skills 1979, Rugby Skills for Forwards 1980, Gareth Edwards on Fishing 1984, Gareth Edwards on Rugby 1986, Gareth Edwards' 100 Great Rugby Players 1987. *Leisure interests:* fishing, golf. *Address:* 211 West Road, Nottage, Porthcawl, Mid-Glamorgan, CF36 3RT, Wales. *Telephone:* (1656) 785669.

EDWARDS, Huw, BA; British broadcaster, journalist and author; *Presenter, BBC News at Ten;* b. 18 Aug. 1961, Bridgend, Wales; s. of (Prof.) Hywel Teifi Edwards and Aerona Protheroe; m.; five c.; ed Univ. Coll. of Wales, Cardiff; began career as a reporter with local radio station Swansea Sound; joined BBC training scheme 1984, becoming parl. reporter, Political Corresp. BBC News, London 1988, Chief Political Corresp., London 1997–99, BBC News 24, Presenter BBC One O'Clock, Six O'Clock and Breakfast News 1994–99, Six O'Clock News 1999–2003, BBC News at Ten 2003–, BBC News at Five 2006–, shares election night coverage with David Dimbleby 2014–; Pres. London Welsh Assen 2008–; Vice-Pres. National Churches Trust 2013; Pro-Chancellor, Cardiff Univ. 2009–; Hon. Fellow, Univ. of Wales, Cardiff 2003, Lampeter 2006, Swansea 2007, Newport 2007, Swansea Metropolitan 2007, Bangor 2013; Hon. Prof. of Journalism, Cardiff Univ. 2006; Dr hc (Univ. of Glamorgan) 2007; BAFTA Award for News Coverage (for Madrid Bombing) 2004, BAFTA Award for News Coverage (for London Bombings) 2005, BAFTA Award for Best Coverage of a Live Event (for Royal Wedding) 2012, Royal TV Soc. Award 2005, 2008, 2009, BAFTA Award for Best Coverage of a Live Event (for First World War Centenary) 2015, Royal TV Soc. Award for Best Live Programme (for D-Day 70) 2015, Paul Harris Fellow, Rotary International, BAFTA Wales Presenter of the Year 2001, 2002, 2003, 2004, 2009, 2012. *Other television and radio work includes:* Newsnight, Panorama, Songs of Praise, classical music programmes on BBC Two, BBC Radio 3 and Radio 4, The Story of Welsh (BBC Wales) 2002, Bread of Heaven (BBC Wales) 2004, Lloyd George the People's Champion (BBC Wales) 2007, The Prince and the Plotter (BBC Wales) 2009, Beijing Olympics Opening and Closing Ceremonies 2008, Commonwealth Games Opening and Closing Ceremonies, Delhi 2010, The Story of Wales (BBC Wales) 2012, State Opening of Parliament, Trooping the Colour, Festival of Remembrance (all for BBC 1), The Royal Wedding (BAFTA Award for Best Sport & Live Event 2012) 2011, The Queen's Diamond Jubilee 2012, London Olympics Opening and Closing Ceremonies 2012, Commonwealth Games Opening and Closing Ceremonies, Glasgow 2014, Scotland Decides (referendum) Sept. 2014. *Publications:* Capeli Llanelli: A History of Nonconformist Worship in Carmarthenshire 2009, City Mission: The Story Of London's Welsh Chapels 2014. *Address:* c/o Jeremy Lee, JLA, 80 Great Portland Street, London, W1W 7NW, England (office); BBC News, New Broadcasting House, London, W1A 1AA, England (office). *Telephone:* (20) 7907-2800 (office); (20) 7580-4468 (office). *E-mail:* jeremylee@jla.co.uk (office). *Website:* www.jla.co.uk (office); www.bbc.co.uk (office).

EDWARDS, John Bel, BS, JD; American lawyer and politician; *Governor of Louisiana;* b. 16 Sept. 1966, New Orleans, La; s. of Frank M. Edwards, Jr; m. Donna Hutto Edwards; one s. two d.; ed US Mil. Acad., West Point, Louisiana State Univ. Law School; served in US Army as Infantry Officer 1988–96, including as Platoon Leader, later Aide-de-Camp to Asst Div. Commdr (Operations), Adjutant 1993, Rifle Co. Commdr, 82nd Airborne Div., Fort Bragg 1994–96; Law Clerk, US Court of Appeals, New Orleans 1999–2000; Founding Partner and Attorney, Edwards & Stevens LLC 2000–; mem. Louisiana House of Reps for Dist 72 2008–15, Chair. Democratic Caucus, Chair. Special Cttee on Mil. and Veterans Affairs, Minority Leader 2012–15; Gov. of Louisiana 2016–; Democrat. *Address:* Office of the Governor, POB 94004, Baton Rouge, LA 70804, USA (office). *Telephone:* (225) 342-7015 (office). *Fax:* (225) 342-7099 (office). *Website:* gov.louisiana.gov (office).

EDWARDS, John Coates, MA, CMG; British diplomatist; b. 25 Nov. 1934, Tunbridge Wells, Kent; s. of Herbert J. Edwards and Doris M. Edwards (née Starzacher); m. Mary Harris 1959 (died 2006); one s. one d.; ed Skinners' Co. School, Tunbridge Wells and Brasenose Coll. Oxford; Lt, RA 1953–55; Asst Prin., Ministry of Supply 1958; with Colonial Office 1960–62, Pvt. Sec. to UnderSec. of State for the Colonies 1961; Nature Conservancy Council 1962–64; Ministry of Overseas Devt 1965–68, 1976–78; First Sec., Embassy in Bangkok and Perm. Rep. to ECAFE 1968–71, Head, E Africa Devt Div. British High Comm., Nairobi 1972–75, Head, British Devt Div. in the Caribbean, Barbados and UK; Dir Caribbean Devt Bank 1978–81; Head, W Indian and Atlantic Dept, FCO 1981–84, Deputy High Commr in Kenya 1984–88, High Commr in Lesotho 1988–91, in Botswana 1991–94; Head UK Del., EC Monitoring Mission in fmr Yugoslavia 1995–99; Dir Amref Health Africa 1995–2007; JP, Kent 2000–04; fmr Chair. Kenya Soc.; mem. council Royal Overseas League. *Leisure interests:* birdwatching, fishing, visual arts, walking, local history. *Address:* Fairways, Back Lane, Ightham, Sevenoaks, TN15 9AU, England (home). *Telephone:* (1732) 883556 (home). *E-mail:* johncoatesedward@aol.com.

EDWARDS, John Reid, BS, JD; American lawyer and fmr politician; *Partner, Edwards Kirby Law Firm;* b. 10 June 1953; s. of Wallace R. Edwards and Catherine Edwards; m. Mary Elizabeth Anania (died 2010); two s. (one deceased) two d.; one d. with Rielle Hunter; ed Univ. of North Carolina at Chapel Hill; called to Bar, North Carolina 1977, Tenn. 1978; Assoc., Dearborn and Ewing, Nashville 1978–81; trial lawyer, Wade Smith 1981; Assoc., Tharrington Smith and Hargrove, Raleigh 1981–83, Partner 1984–92; Partner, Edwards and Kirby, Raleigh 1993–99; Senator from North Carolina 1999–2005; f. One America Cttee (political action cttee) 2001; unsuccessful pursuit of Democratic nomination for US presidency 2004, Democratic cand. for Vice-Pres. 2004; Dir Center on Poverty, Work and Opportunity, Univ. of North Carolina School of Law 2005–06; Sr Advisor, Fortress Investment Group LLC 2005; unsuccessful cand. for Democratic nomination for Pres. of US 2007–08; Dir Urban Ministries, Raleigh 1996–97; mem. North Carolina Acad. of Trial Lawyers (Vice-Pres. Bd of Govs), North Carolina Bar Assen, Banking, Housing and Urban Affairs, Governmental Affairs, Small Business and Y2K Cttees; Fellow, American Coll. of Trial Lawyers; Co-Founder and Partner, Edwards Kirby Law Firm 2013–. *Publications include:* Four Trials 2003, Home: The Blueprints of Our Lives 2006, Ending Poverty in America 2007. *Address:* Edwards Kirby, LLP, 3201 Glenwood Avenue, Suite, 100, Raleigh, NC 27619, USA (office). *Telephone:* (919) 780-5400 (office). *E-mail:* contact@edwardskirby.com (office). *Website:* edwardskirby.com (office).

EDWARDS, Jonathan, CBE; British fmr athlete; b. 10 May 1966, Windsor, Berks.; s. of Andrew David Edwards and Jill Caulfield; m. Alison Joy Briggs 1990; two s.; ed West Buckland, Devon, Van Mildert Coll., Durham Univ.; bronze medal, World Championships 1993; gold medal, Fifth Athletics World Championships, Gothenburg 1995 (twice breaking own world record for triple jump, clearing 18.29m), Edmonton 2001; silver medal, Olympic Games, Atlanta 1996, World Championships 1997, 1999; gold medal European Championships 1998, European Indoor Championships 1998, Goodwill Games 1998, Olympic Games 2000, World Championships 2001, Commonwealth Games 2002; retd after World Championships 2003; athletics commentator, BBC 2003–16, Eurosport 2017–; Sports Fellowship, Univ. of Durham 1999; Dr hc (Univ. of Exeter) 2006, Hon. DUniv (Univ. of Ulster) 2006; British Sportsman of the Year 1995, IAAF Athlete of the Year 1995, BBC Sports Personality of the Year 1995, British Male Athlete of the Year 1995, 2000, 2001. *Publication:* A Time to Jump 2000. *Address:* c/o Jonathan Marks, MTC, 71 Gloucester Place, London, W1U 8JW, England. *Telephone:* (20) 7935-8000. *Fax:* (20) 7935-8066. *E-mail:* office@mtc-uk.com (office). *Website:* www.mtc-uk.com (office).

EDWARDS, Jorge; Chilean writer and diplomatist; b. 29 July 1931, Santiago; m. Pilar de Castro Vergara; two c.; ed Univ. of Chile, Princeton Univ., USA; joined diplomatic service 1954, First Sec., Embassy in Paris 1962–67, Head of Eastern Europe Div. 1967, Counselor, Embassy in Lima 1970, Chargé d'affaires, Embassy in Havana 1970–71, Minister-Counselor, Embassy in Paris 1971–73, Amb. to UNESCO, Paris 1994–96, Amb. to France 2010–14; mem. Academia Chilena de la Lengua; mem. Council, Instituto Atlántico de Gobierno; Grand Cross, Orden Civil de Alfonso X el Sabio (Spain) 2016; Literary Prize of the City of Santiago 1961, 1991, Atenea Prize of Univ. of Concepción (Chile), Essay Prize of the City of Santiago 1991, Cervantes Prize 1999. *Publications include:* (novels) El patio 1952, Gente de la ciudad 1962, El peso de la noche 1965, Las máscaras 1967, Temas y variaciones 1969, Persona non grata 1973, Desde la cola del dragón 1977, Los convidados de piedra 1978, El museo de cera 1981, La mujer imaginaria 1985, El anfitrión 1988, Cuentos completos 1990, Adiós poeta 1990, El regalo 1991, Fantasmas de carne y hueso 1992, El whisky de los poetas 1994, El origen del mundo 1996, El sueño de la Historia 2000, Diálogos en un tejado 2003, El inútil de la familia 2005, La casa de Dostoievsky (Premio Iberoamericano Planeta–Casa de América de Narrativa) 2008, La muerte de Montaigne 2011.

EDWARDS, Kenneth John Richard, PhD; British university vice-chancellor (retd); b. 12 Feb. 1934; s. of John Edwards and Elizabeth M. Edwards; m. Janet M. Gray 1958; two s. one d.; ed Market Drayton Grammar School, Univ. of Reading and Univ. Coll. of Wales, Aberystwyth; Fellow, Univ. of Calif. 1961–62; ARC Fellow, Welsh Plant Breeding Station, Aberystwyth 1962–63, Sr Scientific Officer 1963–66; Lecturer in Genetics, Univ. of Cambridge 1966–84, Head, Dept of Genetics 1981–84; Lecturer, St John's Coll. Cambridge 1971–84, Fellow 1971–87, Tutor 1981–84; Sec.-Gen. of Faculties, Univ. of Cambridge 1984–87; Vice-Chancellor, Univ. of Leicester 1987–99; Chair. Cttee of Vice-Chancellors and Prins 1993–95; Dir CRAC Ltd 1993–2008, CVCP Properties PLC 1999–2010; mem. Marshall Aid Commemoration Comm. 1991–98, Council ACU 1994–99; Chair. Governing Body, Inst. of Grassland and Environmental Research 1994–99; Pres. Assen of European Univs 1998–2001; Visiting Lecturer, Birmingham 1965; Visiting Prof., Buenos Aires 1973; Leverhulme Research Fellow, Univ. of Calif. 1973; Hon. LLD (Belfast) 1994, (Leicester) 1999; Hon. DSc (Reading) 1995, (Loughborough) 1995, (Warwick) 2000; Dr hc (Cluj, Romania) 1997, (Maribor, Slovenia) 1999, (Olomouc, Czech Repub.) 2002. *Publications include:* Evolution in Modern Biology 1977; articles on genetics in scientific journals. *Leisure interests:* music, gardening. *Address:* 10 Sedley Taylor Road, Cambridge, England. *Telephone:* (1223) 245680 (home). *E-mail:* kenneth.edwards@ntlworld.com (home).

EDWARDS, N. Murray, BComm, LLB (Hons), JD; Canadian lawyer and business executive; *President, Edco Financial Holdings Ltd;* b. 10 Dec. 1959, Regina, Sask.; m. Heather Bala; one s.; ed Univs of Saskatchewan and Toronto; moved to Calgary in 1983 and became lawyer and later Partner, Burnet, Duckworth & Palmer; Owner and Pres. Edco Financial Holdings Ltd (merchant bankers) 1988–; leading investor in and Man. Dir and Exec. Chair. of numerous publicly traded cos, including Canadian Natural Resources Ltd (CNRL), Ensign Resource Service Group Inc., Magellan Aerospace Corpn, Penn West Petroleum Ltd and Resorts of the Canadian Rockies Inc.; Dir and Co-owner of Nat. Hockey League's Calgary Flames; fmr Dir of Business Devt, Bank of Canada; mem. Bd Govs Canadian Unity Council; mem. Council of Champions, Calgary Children's Initiatives, Banff Centre; mem. Bd of Dirs Canadian Council of Chief Execs, Canada West Foundation; Hon. DrIur (Univ. of Toronto) 2013. *Address:* Edco Financial Holdings Ltd, 255 5 Avenue SW, Calgary, AB T2P 3G6, Canada (office). *Telephone:* (403) 221-8155 (office).

EDWARDS, Peter Philip, PhD, FRS, FRSC; British scientist and academic; *Professor and Head of Inorganic Chemistry, University of Oxford;* b. 30 June 1949; s. of Ronald Goodlass and Ethel Mary Edwards; m. Patricia Anne Clancy 1970; two s. one d.; ed Univ. of Salford; Fulbright Scholar and NSF Fellow, Baker Lab. of Chem., Cornell Univ., USA 1975–77; Science and Eng Research Council/NATO Fellow and Ramsay Memorial Fellow, Inorganic Chem. Lab., Univ. of Oxford 1977–79; demonstrator in Inorganic Chem., Jesus Coll., Cambridge 1979–81, Dir of Studies in Chem. 1979–91, Lecturer, Univ. Chem. Labs 1981–91; Visiting Prof., Cornell Univ. 1983–86; Nuffield Science Research Fellow 1986–87; Co-Founder and Co-Dir Interdisciplinary Research Centre in Superconductivity 1988; BP Venture Research Fellow 1988–90; Prof. of Inorganic Chem., Univ. of Birmingham 1991–2003, of Chem. and of Materials 1999–2003, Head of School of Chemistry 1996–99; Prof. and Head of Inorganic Chem., Univ. of Oxford 2003–; Royal Soc.

Leverhulme Trust Sr Research Fellow 1996–97; Vice-Pres. Dalton Div. Royal Soc. of Chem. 1995; Corday Medal 1985, Tilden Medal 1992, Liversidge Medal 1999, Hughes Medal 2003, Bakerian Lecturer 2012. *Publications include:* The Metallic and Non-Metallic States of Matter (jtly) 1985, Metal-Insulator Transitions Revisited 1995. *Leisure interests:* exercise, sports. *Address:* Inorganic Chemistry Laboratory, University of Oxford, South Parks Road, Oxford, OX1 3QR, England (office). *Telephone:* (1865) 272646 (office). *Fax:* (1865) 272656 (office). *E-mail:* peter.edwards@chem.ox.ac.u (office). *Website:* www.chem.ox.ac.uk/icl (office).

EDWARDS, Robert L., BS, MBA; American business executive; ed Brigham Young Univ.; fmr sr exec. at Maxtor Corpn, Imation Corpn and Santa Fe Pacific Corpn; joined Safeway in 2004, Exec. Vice-Pres. and Chief Financial Officer 2004–12, Pres. and CEO Safeway Inc. 2012–13, Pres. and CEO AB Acquisition LLC (acquired by Safeway Inc.) Jan.–April 2015; mem. Bd of Dirs Target Corpn 2015–, KKR Financial Holdings, LLC, Blackhawk Network Holdings, Inc. (subsidiary of Safeway Inc.). *Address:* c/o Target Corporation, 1000 Nicollet Mall, Minneapolis, MN 55403, USA. *Telephone:* (800) 775-3110. *E-mail:* investorrelations@target.com. *Website:* www.target.com.

EFI, HH Tuiatua Tupua Tamasese; fmr head of state; b. 1 March 1938; s. of Tupua Tamasese Mea'ole and Noue Irene Gustava Ta'isi Nelson; m. HH Masiofo Filifilia Imo; ed St Joseph's Coll., Apia, Western Samoa and Victoria Univ., Wellington, NZ; mem. Fono (Western Samoan Parl.) for Anoama'a East constituency 1965–2004; Minister of Works 1973–75; Prime Minister (as the Hon. Ta'isi Tupuola Tufuga Efi) 1976–82, Deputy Prime Minister 1985–88; Leader of the Opposition 1988–2004; Jt Leader Samoa Nat. Devt Party; mem. Council of Deputies 2004–07; Head of State (O le Ao o le Malo) of Samoa 2007–17; Chancellor, Nat. Univ. of Samoa 2008–13. *Address:* Government House, Vailima, Apia, Samoa (office). *Website:* www.govt.ws (office).

EFSTATHIOU, George Petros, BA, PhD, FRS; British astrophysicist; *Professor of Astrophysics and Director, Kavli Institute for Cosmology, University of Cambridge;* b. 2 Sept. 1955, London, England; s. of Petros Efstathiou and Christina Parperi; m. 1st Helena Jane Smart 1976 (divorced 1997); m. 2nd Yvonne Nobis 1998; three s. one d.; ed Somerset Comprehensive School, London, Keble Coll., Oxford, Univ. of Durham; Research Asst, Univ. of Calif., Berkeley 1979–80; Research Asst, Univ. of Cambridge 1980–84, Jr Research Fellow, King's Coll., Cambridge 1980–84, Sr Research Fellow 1984–88, Asst Dir of Research, Inst. of Astronomy, Cambridge 1984–88, Savilian Prof. of Astronomy and Fellow, New Coll., Oxford 1988–97; Prof. of Astrophysics and Fellow, King's Coll. Cambridge 1997–, Dir Inst. of Astronomy 2004–08; Dir Kavli Inst. for Cosmology, Cambridge 2008–; Vainu Bappu Prize, Astronomical Soc. of India 1990, Maxwell Medal and Prize, Inst. of Physics 1990, Bodossaki Foundation Prize for Astrophysics 1994, Robinson Prize in Cosmology, Royal Soc. 1997, Heineman Prize for Astrophysics (co-recipient), American Inst. of Physics 2005, Group Award (2dF Galaxy Survey), Royal Astronomical Soc. 2008, Gruber Cosmology Prize (co-recipient), Peter and Patricia Gruber Foundation 2011, Nemitsas Prize in Physics 2013, Hughes Medal, Royal Soc. 2015. *Publications:* articles in astronomical journals. *Leisure interests:* running, playing guitar, football. *Address:* Kavli Institute for Cosmology, University of Cambridge, c/o Institute of Astronomy, Madingley Road, Cambridge, CB3 0HA, England (office). *Telephone:* (1223) 337530 (office). *Fax:* (1223) 337523 (office). *E-mail:* gpe@ast.cam.ac.uk (office). *Website:* www.ast.cam.ac.uk/~gpe (office); www.kicc.cam.ac.uk/directory/ge12 (office).

EFUMAN, Santiago Nsobeya; Equatorial Guinean politician and business executive; *President, Parliament of the Economic and Monetary Community of Central Africa (CEMAC);* Minister of Foreign Affairs, Int. Co-operation and Francophone Affairs 2001–03; Govt Spokesman, Ministry of Information, Culture and Tourism 2006; fmr CEO Ceiba Intercontinental Airlines (national airline); apptd Second Vice-Pres. of Chamber of Deputies 2013, Vice-Pres. Chamber of Deputies 2014–15; Special Adviser to Sec.-Gen., Democratic Party 2014; Pres. Parl. of Economic and Monetary Community of Central Africa (CEMAC) 2015–. *Address:* Committee on Economic and Monetary Community of Central Africa, Building CEMAC, Avenue des Martyrs, BP 969, Bangui, Equatorial Guinea (office). *Telephone:* (61) 47-81 (office). *Fax:* (14) 15-66 (office). *Website:* www.cemac.int (office).

EGAN, Christopher F., BS, MPA; American business executive and diplomatist; *President, Carruth Capital LLC;* b. Boston, Mass; m. Jean Egan; three c.; ed Univ. of Massachusetts, Amherst, Kennedy School of Govt at Harvard Univ.; Pres. and Founding mem. Carruth Capital, LLC (commercial real estate investment and devt firm); Co-founder and Dir 'Break the Cycle of Poverty'; mem. Bd of Dirs Fallon Community Health Plan (fmr Chair. Finance Cttee); fmr mem. Bd of Dirs MassDevelopment; fmr mem. Cen. Mass Regional Competitiveness Council; fmr Dir Corridor Nine Chamber of Commerce; Co-founder and mem. Bd Arc of Innovation/I-495 Initiative; TV commentator for numerous networks; op-ed. contrib. and documentary maker; Amb. to OECD 2007–09; mem. Advisory Bd, Boston Private Bank & Trust Co.; Chair. The Home For Little Wanderers Inc. 2015–; fmr Trustee, Univ. of Massachusetts Memorial Health Care; Trustee, Egan Family Foundation. *Television:* Eclipsed by the Sun (documentary) 2004. *Address:* Carruth Capital LLC, 116 Flanders Road, Suite 2000, Westborough, MA 01581, USA (office). *Telephone:* (508) 898-3800 (office). *E-mail:* info@carruthcapital.com (office). *Website:* www.carruthcapital.com (office).

EGAN, Sir John Leopold, Kt, MSc Econ, DL, FRAeS, FIC, FIMI, FCIT, FCIPS; British business executive; b. 7 Nov. 1939, Rawtenstall, Lancs.; s. of James Edward Egan; m. Julia Emily Treble 1963; two d.; ed Bablake School, Coventry, Imperial Coll., London, London Business School; petroleum engineer, Shell Int. 1962–66; Gen. Man. AC-Delco Replacement Parts Operation, Gen. Motors Ltd 1968–71; Man. Dir Unipart, Parts and Service Dir, Leyland Cars 1971–76; Corp. Parts Dir Massey Ferguson 1976–80; Chair. Jaguar Cars Ltd 1980–84, Chair and Chief Exec., Chief Exec. and Man. Dir Jaguar PLC 1984–85, Chair. and Chief Exec. Jaguar PLC 1985–90; Chief Exec. BAA PLC 1990–99, Dir 1990; Dir Legal & Gen. Group 1987–97, Vice-Chair. 1993–97, Pres. 1998; Chair. MEPC PLC 1998–2000, Inchcape PLC 2000–05, Harrison Lovegrove Ltd 2000–05, Qinetiq 2001–02, Asite 2001–05, Severn Trent PLC 2005–10; Deputy Pres. CBI 2001–02, Pres. 2002–04; mem. Bd of Dirs Warwick Castle Park Trust Ltd; fmr mem. Bd of Dirs Foreign and Colonial Investment Trust, British Tourist Authority, Owners Group LLP, Borwick Group Ltd; Bd Mentor Criticaleye; Pres. Inst. of Man. 2000–01; Chancellor, Coventry Univ. 2007–; Sr Fellow, RCA; Hon. Prof., Dept of Eng, Univ. of Warwick 1990; Dr hc (Cranfield Inst.) 1986, Hon. DTech (Loughborough) 1987, Hon. LLD (Bath) 1988; Castrol Gold Medal, Inst. of Motor Industry Award 1982, Int. Gold Medal, Inst. of Production Engineers, City and Guilds of London Hon. Insignia Award for Tech. 1987 and several other awards. *Leisure interests:* skiing, squash, walking, music.

EGASHIRA, Toshiaki; Japanese insurance industry executive; fmr Dir in Pres.'s Office, fmr Chief Dir of China, Chief Dir of Kanagawa & Shizuoka, later Man. Exec. Officer and CEO Mitsui Sumitomo Insurance Co. Ltd, later Pres., Exec. Pres. and Rep. Dir, Rep. Dir, Pres. and CEO Mitsui Sumitomo Insurance Group Holdings, Inc. 2008–10, Rep. Dir, Pres. and CEO MS&AD Insurance Group Holdings, Inc. (following merger of Mitsui Sumitomo Insurance Group Holdings, Inc., Aioi Insurance Co. Ltd and Nissay Dowa General Insurance Co. Ltd April 2010) 2010–14, Rep. Dir and Exec. 2014–16.

EGEDE, Aqqaluaq Biilmann; Greenlandic politician; b. 1981, Narsaq; partner; three c.; trained as carpenter; Municipal Commr Narsaq Municipality 2005–08, Kujalleq Muncipality 2008–12; mem. Inatsisartut (legislature) 2009–16, 2018–; Minister for Finance and Taxes 2016–18; mem. Inuit Ataqatigiit (Inuit Brotherhood). *Address:* Inatsisartut, Imaneq 2, POB 1060, 3900 Nuuk, Greenland (office). *Telephone:* 345000 (office). *Fax:* 324606 (office). *E-mail:* aqqe@inatsisartut.gl (office). *Website:* ina.gl (office).

EGELAND, Jan, Mag.Art; Norwegian international organization official and fmr UN official; *Secretary-General, Norwegian Refugee Council;* b. 12 Sept. 1957; m.; two d.; ed Univ. of Oslo, Univ. of California, Berkeley, USA; State Sec., Ministry of Foreign Affairs 1990–97; Special Adviser to UN Sec.-Gen. on Colombia 1999–2002; fmr Dir Int. Dept, Norwegian Red Cross, Sec.-Gen. 2002–03; UN Under-Sec.-Gen. for Humanitarian Affairs and Humanitarian Relief Co-ordinator 2003–06, then Special Adviser to Sec.-Gen. 2007; Dir Norwegian Inst. of Int. Affairs (NUPI) 2007–11; Europe Dir and Deputy Exec. Dir, Human Rights Watch; Sec.-Gen. Norwegian Refugee Council 2013–; Prof., Univ. of Stavanger; Chair. Bd of Dirs Crisis Action; interim Chair. Bd of Dirs, Humanitarian Leadership Acad.; Vice-Chair., World Economic Forum (WEF) Global Agenda Council for Humanitarian Response; fmr Chair. Amnesty International (AI) Norway and Vice-Chair. AI Int. Exec. Cttee; fmr Head of Devt Studies, Henry Dunant Inst., Geneva; fmr Fellow, Int. Peace Research Inst., Oslo and Truman Inst. for the Advancement of Peace, Jerusalem; fmr radio and TV int. news reporter, Norwegian Broadcasting Corpn (NRK). *Achievements include:* co-organized Norwegian channel between Israel and Palestinian Liberation Organisation leading to Oslo Accord 1993; directed Norwegian facilitation of UN-led peace talks leading to ceasefire agreement between Guatemalan govt and Unidad Revolucionaria Nacional Guatemalteca guerrillas 1996. *Publications include:* A Billion Lives: An Eyewitness Report from the Frontlines of Humanity 2008; reports, studies and articles on conflict resolution, humanitarian affairs and human rights. *Address:* Norwegian Refugee Council, Postboks 148, Sentrum, 0102 Oslo, Norway (office). *Telephone:* 23-10-98-00 (switchboard) (office); 90-56-23-29 (office). *E-mail:* sg-office@nrc.no (office). *Website:* www.nrc.no (office).

EGGERS, Dave; American writer and publisher; b. 12 March 1970, Boston, Mass; m. Vendela Vida 2003; two c.; Ed. Might magazine 1994–97; Founder Timothy McSweeney's Quarterly Concern, or 'McSweeney's', journal and publrs 1998–; Founder The Believer magazine 2003; f. 826 Valencia (non-profit writing workshop) 2002; f. ScholarMatch 2010; LA Times Book Prize Innovators Award 2009, Albatross Award, Gunter Grass Foundation 2012, PEN Center USA Award of Honor 2012, Commonwealth Club Inforum's 21st Century Award 2012. *Publications include:* A Heartbreaking Work of Staggering Genius (memoir) 2000, You Shall Know Our Velocity (novel) 2003, The Future Dictionary of America (with Jonathan Safran Foer and Nicole Krauss) 2004, The Best of McSweeney's: Volume 1 (ed.) 2004, Volume 2 (ed.) 2005, How We Are Hungry 2005, What is the What: The Autobiography of Valentino Achak Deng: A Novel (Prix Médicis Étranger 2009) 2006, Zeitoun (LA Times Book Prize, Dayton Literary Peace Prize for Non-Fiction 2010) 2009, The Wild Things 2009, A Hologram for the King 2012, The Circle 2013, Your Fathers, Where Are They? And the Prophets, Do They Live Forever? 2014, Heroes of the Frontier 2016, The Parade 2019; contrib. to numerous periodicals and journals. *Address:* McSweeney's, 849 Valencia Street, San Francisco, CA 94110, USA (office). *E-mail:* letters@mcsweeneys.net (office). *Website:* www.mcsweeneys.net (office); www.believermag.com (office).

EGGLESTON, William; American photographer and academic; b. 27 July 1939, Memphis, Tenn.; Lecturer in Visual and Environmental Studies, Carpenter Center, Harvard Univ. 1974; Researcher in Color Video, MIT 1978; Guggenheim Fellow 1974; Fellow, American Acad. of Arts and Sciences 2009–; Photographic Soc. of Japan Master Photographers of 1960–1979 Award 1989, Univ. of Memphis Distinguished Achievement Award 1996, Hasselblad Award 1998, Nat. Arts Club Gold Medal for Photography, New York 2003, Getty Images Lifetime Achievement Award 2004, Photoespana Award 2004. *Address:* Eggleston Artistic Trust, 3251 Poplar Avenue #110, Memphis, TN 38111, USA (office). *Telephone:* (901) 323-7575 (office). *Fax:* (901) 323-7557 (office). *E-mail:* info@egglestontrust.com (office). *Website:* www.egglestontrust.com (office).

EGGLETON, Hon. Arthur C. (Art), PC; Canadian politician; b. 29 Sept. 1943, Toronto; m. Camille Bacchus; one d.; fmr accountant; mem. Toronto City Council and Metropolitan Toronto Council 1969–93; Mayor of Toronto 1980–91; MP for York Centre 1993–2004; Pres. Treas. Bd and Minister responsible for Infrastructure 1993–96; Minister for Int. Trade 1996–97, of Nat. Defence 1997–2002; mem. Bd of Dirs Luxell Technologies Inc. 2005–, Skylink Group; mem. Senate 2005–18; Voluntary Chair. Rebuilding Lives Campaign, St John's Rehabilitation Hosp.; Co-Founder and Co-Chair. All Party Anti-Poverty Caucus 2012–; Chair. Mayor's Task Force on Toronto Community Housing 2015–16, Global City Indicators Facility 2012–; Vice-Pres. Liberal International 2012–14; Civic Award of Merit, Toronto 1992. *Publication includes:* Toronto: The Heart of the City 1988.

EGILSSON, Ólafur; Icelandic diplomatist and lawyer; b. 20 Aug. 1936, Reykjavik; s. of Egill Kristjánsson and Anna Margrjet Thurídur Ólafsdóttir Briem; m. Ragna Sverrisdóttir Ragnars 1960; one s. one d.; ed Commercial Coll. of Iceland and Iceland Univ.; journalist with newspapers Vísir 1956–58, Morgunbladid 1959–62; Publishing Exec. 1963–64; Head, NATO Regional Information Office, Reykjavik 1964–66; Gen. Sec. Icelandic Assen for Western Co-operation 1964–66; Political Div., Icelandic Foreign Ministry 1966–69; First Sec., then Counsellor, Icelandic Embassy, Paris 1969–71; Deputy Perm. Rep. OECD, UNESCO and Council of Europe 1969–71; Deputy Perm. Rep. N Atlantic Council, Deputy Head, Icelandic Del. to EEC, Counsellor, Embassy in Brussels 1971–74; Counsellor, then Minister Counsellor, Political Div. of Foreign Ministry 1974–80; Chief of Protocol (with rank of Amb.) 1980–83; Acting Prin. Pvt. Sec. to Pres. of Iceland 1981–82; Deputy Perm. Under-Sec. and Dir-Gen. for Political Affairs, Foreign Ministry 1983–87; Amb. to UK 1986–89; Amb. to USSR, later Russia 1990–94; Amb. to Denmark 1994–96; in charge of Arctic co-operation 1996–98; Amb. to China 1998–2002; Chair. Bd of Govs Icelandic Int. Devt Agency 1982–87; Exec. mem. Bible Soc. of Iceland 1977–87, History Soc. 1982–88; currently lawyer, Egill Kristjansson ehf; Commdr Icelandic Order of the Falcon 1981 and decorations from Finland, France, Norway, Spain, Sweden and Luxembourg. *Publications:* Co-author: Iceland and Jan Mayen 1980, NATO's Anxious Birth – The Prophetic Vision of the 1940s 1985; Ed. Bjarni Benediktsson 1983. *Leisure interests:* history, walking, music (classical, opera). *Address:* Valhúsabraut 35, 170 Saltjarnarnes, Iceland (home). *Telephone:* (354) 5515411 (home). *Fax:* (354) 5515411 (home). *E-mail:* olegice@simnet.is (home).

EGOROV, Mikhail P., PhD; Russian chemist and academic; *Director, N.D. Zelinsky Institute of Organic Chemistry, Russian Academy of Sciences;* Dir N.D. Zelinsky Inst. of Organic Chem., Russian Acad. of Sciences; Corresp. mem. Russian Acad. of Sciences, now Full mem. *Publications include:* numerous papers in professional journals. *Address:* N.D. Zelinsky Institute of Organic Chemistry, Russian Academy of Sciences, 117913 Moscow, Leninsky Prospekt 47, Russia (office). *Telephone:* (095) 137-2944 (office). *Fax:* (095) 135-5328 (office). *E-mail:* secretary@ioc.ac.ru (office); mpe@cacr.ioc.ac.ru (office). *Website:* www.ioc.ac.ru (office).

EGOYAN, Atom, OC, BA; Canadian film director; b. 19 July 1960, Cairo, Egypt; s. of Joseph Egoyan and Shushan Devletian; m. Arsinée Khanjian; one c.; ed Univ. of Toronto; Dir Ego Film Arts, Toronto 1982–; Chevalier, Ordre des Arts et des Lettres; Dr hc (Trinity Coll., Univ. of Toronto, Univ. of Victoria, Brock Univ., Ont., Coll. of Art and Design, Univ. of British Columbia); Best Dir, Irish Times 2007, Dan David Prize for Creative Rendering of the Past 2008. *Exhibitions:* Return to the Flock, Irish Museum of Modern Art 1996, Early Development, Le Fresnoy, USA 1997, Notorious, Museum of Modern Art, Oxford 1999, Venice Biennale, Close, Venice Biennale 2001, Steenbeckett, Museum of Mankind, London 2002, Hors d'Usage, Musée d'Art Contemporain de Montréal 2002. *Films:* writer, dir and producer feature films: Next of Kin (Gold Ducat award, Mannheim Int. Film Week 1984) 1984, Family Viewing (Int. Critics Award 1988, Best Feature Film Award, Uppsala, Prix Alcan, Festival du Nouveau Cinéma, Montreal) 1987, Speaking Parts (Best Screenplay Prize, Vancouver Int. Film Festival) 1989, The Adjuster (Special Jury Prize, Moscow Film Festival, Golden Spike Award, Valladolid Film Festival) 1991, Calendar (prize at Berlin Int. Film Festival) 1993, Exotica (Int. Film Critics Award, Cannes Film Festival 1994, Prix de la Critique award for Best Foreign Film 1994) 1994, The Sweet Hereafter (Grand Prix, Int. Critics Prize, Cannes Film Festival 1997) 1997, Elsewhereless 1998, Dr Ox's Experiment 1998, Felicia's Journey 1999, Krapp's Last Tape 2000, Ararat 2002, Where the Truth Lies 2005, Adoration 2008, Chloe 2009, Devil's Knot 2013. *Operas:* Salome, Canadian Opera Co. 1996, Houston Grand Opera 1997, Elsewhereless 1998, Dr Ox's Experiment 1998, Salome (new production), Canadian Opera Co. 2002, 2013, Die Walküre, Canadian Opera Co. 2004, 2006, Così fan tutte, Canadian Opera Co. 2014. *Play:* Eh Joe (interpretation of Samuel Beckett's teleplay for the stage, Dublin and London) 2006, Cruel and Tender (Canadian Stage Co., Toronto) 2012. *Leisure interest:* classical guitar. *Address:* Ego Film Arts, 80 Niagara Street, Toronto, ON M5V 1C5, Canada. *Telephone:* (416) 703-2137 (office). *Fax:* (416) 504-7161 (office). *E-mail:* questions@egofilmarts.com (office). *Website:* www.egofilmarts.com (office).

EGUIAGARAY UCELAY, Juan Manuel, BA, PhD; Spanish economist, academic, politician and think tank director; *Chairman of the Advisory Board of the Laboratory, Fundación Alternativas;* b. 25 Dec. 1945, Bilbao; m.; one s.; ed Univ. of Deusto, Univ. of Nancy, France; Prof. of Econs, Univ. de Deusto 1970–82; joined PSE-PSOE (Workers' Socialist Party of Spain) 1977, mem. Exec. Cttee 1979, Fed. Sec. for the Economy (34th Fed. Congress of PSOE), fmrly PSOE Nat. Parl. Spokesman and PSOE Nat. Parl. Spokesman for Econ. Affairs, Sec. PSOE Fed. Exec. Comm. 1990; Councillor, Town Council, Bilbao 1979, Prov. Deputy, Vizcaya 1979–81, mem. Juntas Generales Vizcaya 1979–83, Deputy and Spokesman for Socialist Party of Basque Parl. 1980–88, Vice-Sec.-Gen. Basque Socialists 1985–88, Govt Del. for Autonomous Community of Murcia, then for Autonomous Community of the Basque Country 1988–89; Minister for Public Admin 1991–93, of Industry and Energy 1993–96; Nat. Deputy for Murcia 1996–2001; Assoc. Prof., Carlos III Univ., Madrid –2006; currently Chair. Advisory Bd of the Laboratory, Fundación Alternativas (think tank), Madrid; Pres. Solidaridad Internacional (NGO); mem. Bd of Dirs European Aeronautic Defence and Space Co. (EADS NV) –2013; mem. Advisory Bd Cap Gemini Spain, FoundationGroup EP. *Address:* Fundación Alternativas, Zurbano 29, 3° Izq., 28010 Madrid, Spain (office). *Telephone:* (91) 3199860 (office). *Fax:* (91) 3192298 (office). *Website:* www.falternativas.org (office).

EHLE, Jennifer; British/American actress; b. 29 Dec. 1969, Winston-Salem, N Carolina, USA; d. of John Ehle and Rosemary Harris; m. Michael Ryan 2001; one s. one d.; ed North Carolina School of the Arts, Cen. School of Speech and Drama, London, UK; stage debut as a toddler in a Broadway revival of A Streetcar Named Desire 1973; spent her childhood between the UK and USA, attending 18 different schools including the Interlochen Arts Acad. *Plays include:* Summerfolk (Royal Nat. Theatre), The Relapse (RSC), The Painter of Dishonour (RSC), Richard III (RSC) 1996, Tartuffe (Playhouse) (Ian Charleson Award) 1991, The Real Thing (Albery) (Tony Award for Best Lead Actress in a Play 2000, Variety Club Award 2000) 1999, (Broadway) 2000 (Tony Award for Best Actress 2000), The Philadelphia Story (Old Vic, London) 2005, The Coast of Utopia (Lincoln Centre, New York) (Tony Award for Best Performance by a Featured Actress in a Play 2007) 2006, The Coast of Utopia: Shipwrecked (Lincoln Centre, New York) 2007, Mr. and Mrs. Fitch (Second Stage Theatre, New York) 2010, Oslo (Lincoln Centre, New York) 2017. *Films include:* Backbeat 1994, Paradise Road 1997, Wilde 1997, Bedrooms and Hallways 1998, This Year's Love 1999, Sunshine (Golden Satellite Award for Best Supporting Actress in a Motion Picture Drama 2001) 1999, Possession 2002, The River King 2005, Alpha Male 2006, Michael Clayton 2006, Before the Rains 2007, Pride and Glory 2008, The Greatest 2009, The King's Speech (Screen Actors Guild Award for Outstanding Performance by a Cast in a Motion Picture 2010, Jury Award for Best Motion Picture Ensemble of the Year 2011) 2010, The Adjustment Bureau 2011, The Ides of March 2011, Zero Dark Thirty 2012, RoboCop 2014, Black or White 2014, The Forger 2014, A Little Chaos 2014, Advantageous 2015, Fifty Shades of Grey 2015, Spooks: The Greater Good 2015, Little Men 2016, The Fundamentals of Caring 2016, A Quiet Passion 2016, Fifty Shades Darker 2017, Detroit 2017, I Kill Giants 2017, The Miseducation of Cameron Post 2018, Monster 2018, Fifty Shades Freed 2018, Vox Lux 2018. *Television includes:* The Camomile Lawn (mini-series) (Radio Times Award for Best Newcomer 1992) 1992, Micky Love (film) 1993, The Maitlands (film) 1993, Self Catering (film) 1994, Pleasure (film) 1994, Beyond Reason (film) 1995, Pride and Prejudice (mini-series) (BAFTA Award for Best Actress 1996) 1995, Melissa (mini-series) 1997, The Russell Girl (film) 2008, A Gifted Man (series) 2011–12. *Address:* c/o Independent Talent Group, 40 Whitfield Street, London, W1T 2RH, England. *Telephone:* (20) 7636-6565. *Fax:* (20) 7323-0101. *Website:* www.independenttalent.com.

EHLERMANN, Claus-Dieter, DrIur; German lawyer and international organization official; *Senior Counsel, Wilmer Cutler Pickering Hale and Dorr LLP;* b. 15 June 1931, Scheessel; s. of Kurt Ehlermann and Hilde Ehlermann (née Justus); m. Carola Grumbach 1959; two d.; ed Univs of Marburg/Lahn and Heidelberg, Univ. of Michigan Law School; Research Asst Fed. Constitutional Court, Karlsruhe 1959–61; Legal Adviser, Legal Service of the Comm. of European Communities 1961–73, Dir and Deputy Financial Controller 1973–77, Dir-Gen. of the Legal Service 1977–87; Spokesman of the Comm. of the European Communities and of its fmr Pres. Jacques Delors (q.v.) 1987–90, Dir-Gen. of Directorate-Gen. for Competition 1990–95; fmr Prof. of Econ. Law, European Univ. Inst., Florence; fmr mem. Appellate Body of WTO, Geneva 1995–2001, Chair. 2001; Sr Counsel, Wilmer, Cutler & Pickering (law firm), Brussels 2002–, Co-Chair. Antitrust and Competition Dept 2005–08; Hon. Prof., Univ. of Hamburg; Hon. Bencher, Gray's Inn, London; Hon. DrIur 1999. *Publications:* numerous documents on the European Community and its legal order. *Leisure interests:* reading, skiing. *Address:* Wilmer Cutler Pickering Hale and Dorr LLP, Bastion Tower, Place du Champ de Mars, Marsveldplein 5, 1050 Brussels, Belgium (office). *Telephone:* (2) 285-49-02 (office). *Fax:* (2) 285-49-49 (office). *E-mail:* claus-dieter.ehlermann@wilmerhale.com (office). *Website:* www.wilmerhale.com/claus-dieter_ehlermann (office).

EHLERS ZURITA, Freddy; Ecuadorean journalist, politician and international organization official; *State Secretary for the Presidential Initiative for the Construction of a Society of Good Life;* b. 30 Nov. 1945, Quito; ed Cen. Univ. of Ecuador; fmr host, TV programme La Televisión; Dir Bd of Cartagena Agreement's Andean TV Program 1980–88; unsuccessful cand. for Pres. of Ecuador 1996, 1998; mem. Andean Parl. for Ecuador 2002–06, Vice-Pres. 2003–04, mem. Cttee on Educ., Culture, Science, Tech. and Communication; Sec.-Gen. Andean Community of Nations (Comunidad Andina de Naciones) 2007–10; Minister of Tourism 2010–13; State Sec. for the Presidential Initiative for the Construction of a Soc. of Good Life 2013–; Global 500 Roll of Honour, UNEP 1993. *Address:* National Secretariat of Planning and Development, Juan León Mera No. 130 and Av Patria, 170517, Quito, Ecuador (office). *Telephone:* (2) 397-8900 (office). *E-mail:* buenvivir@senplades.gob.ec (office). *Website:* www.buenvivir.gob.ec (office).

EHLINGER, Claude; French business executive; *CEO, Oranje-Nassau Développement and Associate Director, Wendel;* ed Ecole des hautes études commerciales de Paris; began career at Thomson Group, Paris 1986; subsequently Group Man. Dir Finacor (European financial broking group); Group Chief Financial Officer, CCMX (French accounting, payroll and human resources software publishing firm for SMEs and chartered accounting firms) 1999–2003; Finance Dir, Cap Gemini France and subsequently also Chief Financial Officer, Cap Gemini's Cen. and Southern European operations 2003–04; Financial Dir, Eutelsat SA from 2004; fmr Man. Dir Louis Dreyfus Commodities Holdings BV, fmr Chief Financial Officer, Louis Dreyfus Commodities BV, Chair. (non-exec.), Biosev at Louis Dreyfus Commodities BV, mem. Man. Bd, Chief Financial Officer and Interim CEO Louis Dreyfus Commodities Holdings BV 2014–15; CEO, Oranje-Nassau Développement and Man. Dir Wendel (investment firm) 2016–. *Address:* Oranje-Nassau Groep BV, Rembrandt Tower, 22nd Floor, Amstelplein 1, 1096 HA Amsterdam, The Netherlands (office). *Telephone:* (20) 5677102 (office). *E-mail:* info@wendelgroup.com (office). *Website:* www.wendelgroup.com (office).

EHRLICH, Paul Ralph, MA, PhD, FRS; American entomologist, population biologist and academic; *Bing Professor of Population Studies and President, Center for Conservation Biology, Stanford University;* b. 29 May 1932, Philadelphia, Pa; s. of William Ehrlich and Ruth Ehrlich (née Rosenberg); m. Anne Fitzhugh Howland 1954; one d.; ed Univs of Pennsylvania and Kansas; Field Officer, Northern Insect Survey (Canadian Arctic and Sub-arctic) summers of 1951 and 1952; Research Asst, DDT Resistance Project, Dept of Entomology, Univ. of Kansas 1952–54, Kansas Univ. Fellow 1954–66, NSF Pre-Doctoral Fellow 1955–57, Assoc. Investigator, USAF research project, Alaska and Univ. of Kansas 1956–57, Research Assoc., Chicago Acad. of Sciences and Univ. of Kansas Dept of Entomology 1957–59; Asst Prof. of Biological Sciences, Stanford Univ. 1959–62, Assoc. Prof. of Biological Sciences 1962–66, Prof. of Biological Studies 1966–, Dir Grad. Studies, Dept of Biological Sciences 1966–69, 1974–76, Bing Prof. of Population Studies 1977–, Pres. Center for Conservation Biology 1988–; NSF Sr Post-Doctoral Fellow, Univ. of Sydney 1965–66; Assoc., Center for the Study of Democratic Insts, Santa Barbara, Calif. 1969–72; Sec. Lepidopterists' Soc. 1957–63, mem. Exec. Council 1968; Corresp. NBC News 1989–92; Pres. Zero Population Growth 1969–70 (Hon. Pres. 1970–), Zero Population Growth Fund 1972–73, The Conservation Soc. 1972–73, American Inst. of Biological Sciences 1989, Assen for Tropical Lepidoptera 2001; Vice-Pres. Soc. for the Study of Evolution 1970; Co-Chair. Research Cttee, Rocky Mountain Biological Lab. 1973–75, Trustee 1971–86; Mem.-at-Large, Governing Bd American Inst. of Biological Sciences 1969–70; mem. Advisory Council, Friends of the Earth 1970–, Scientific Advisory Cttee, Sierra

Club 1972–, Council, Soc. for the Study of Evolution 1974–76; mem. and Active Cttee mem., Int. Asscn for the Study of Ecology 1969–70; mem. Bd Dirs Common Cause 1972; mem. Bd of Consultants, Lizard Island Research Station 1975–78; mem. Bd of Govs Soc. for Conservation Biology 1986–88; mem. Editorial Bd Systematic Zoology 1964–67, International Journal of Environmental Sciences 1969–71, American Naturalist 1974–76, Oecologia 1981–85, 1991–, Revista de Biologia Tropical, Universidad de Costa Rica 1996–; Sr Assoc. Ed. American Naturalist 1984; Advisory Ed. Human Nature 1977–79; mem. NAS 1985, American Philosophical Soc. 1990, European Acad. of Sciences and Arts 1992; Elective mem. American Ornithologists' Union 1989; Foreign mem. Russian Acad. of Natural Sciences 1997–, Royal Soc. (UK) 2012–; Fellow, California Acad. of Sciences 1961, AAAS 1978, American Acad. of Arts and Sciences 1982, Entomological Soc. of America 1987; Hon. Life mem. American Humanist Asscn 1989, British Ecological Soc. 1989, Int. Soc. for Philosophical Enquiry 1991; Sigma Xi-Resa Grant-in-Aid of Research done in Alaska and NW Canada 1955, First Prize, Mitchell Foundation 1979, John Muir Award, Sierra Club 1980, Humanist Distinguished Service Award, American Humanist Asscn 1985, First Distinguished Achievement Award, Soc. for Conservation Biology 1987, Gold Medal, World Wildlife Fund Int. 1987, AAAS/Scientific American Gerard Piel Award for Service to Science in the Cause of Humankind 1989, UN Global 500 Roll of Honour 1989, Crafoord Prize in Population Biology and the Conservation of Biological Diversity, Royal Swedish Acad. of Sciences 1990, Distinguished Service Citation, Univ. of Kansas 1991, MacArthur Prize Fellowship 1990–95, Major Achievement Award, New York City Audubon Soc. 1991, Volvo Environment Prize 1993, World Ecology Medal, Int. Center for Tropical Ecology 1993, UNEP Sasakawa Environment Prize 1994, Heinz Award for the Environment 1995, Distinguished Peace Leader, Nuclear Age Peace Foundation 1996, Tyler Prize for Environmental Achievement 1998, Dr A.H. Heineken Prize for Environmental Sciences 1998, Nat. Audubon Soc., One Hundred Champions of Conservation 1998, Blue Planet Prize, Asahi Glass Foundation (Japan) 1999, Distinguished Scientist Award, American Inst. of Biological Sciences 2001, Eminent Ecologist Award, Ecological Soc. of America 2001, Ramon Margalef Prize in Ecology 2009, BBVA Foundation Frontiers of Knowledge Award (Ecology and Conservation Biology) 2013. *Publications include:* How to Know the Butterflies 1960, Process of Evolution 1963, The Population Bomb 1968, 1971, Population Resources, Environment: Issues in Human Ecology (with A. H. Ehrlich) 1970, 1972, How to Be a Survivor (with R. L. Harriman) 1971, The Race Bomb (with S. Feldman) 1977, Extinction: The Causes and Consequences of the Disappearance of Species (with A. H. Ehrlich) 1981, The Golden Door: International Migration, Mexico and the United States (with D. L. Bilderback and A. H. Ehrlich) 1981, The Cold and the Dark: The World After Nuclear War (with Carl Sagan, Donald Kennedy and Walter Orr Roberts) 1984, Earth (with A. H. Ehrlich) 1987, Science of Ecology (with Joan Roughgarden) 1987, New World, New Mind (with R. Ornstein) 1988, The Birder's Handbook: A Field Guide to the Natural History of North American Birds (with David S. Dobkin and Darryl Wheye) 1988, The Cassandra Conference: Resources and the Human Predicament 1988, The Population Explosion (with A. H. Ehrlich) 1990, Healing the Planet: Strategies for Resolving the Environmental Crisis (with A. H. Ehrlich) 1991, Birds in Jeopardy: The Imperiled and Extinct Birds of the United States and Canada, Including Hawaii and Puerto Rico (with David S. Dobkin and Darryl Wheye) 1992, The Stork and the Plow (with A. H. Ehrlich and G. C. Daily) 1995, A World of Wounds: Ecologists and the Human Dilemma 1997, Betrayal of Science and Reason: How Anti-Environment Rhetoric Threatens Our Future (with A. H. Ehrlich) 1998, Human Natures: Genes, Cultures, and the Human Prospect 2002, One With Nineveh: Politics, Consumption and the Human Future (with A. H. Ehrlich) 2004, The Dominant Animal: Human Evolution and the Environment (with A. H. Ehrlich) 2008; co-ed.: Man and the Ecosphere: Readings from Scientific American (with J. P. Holdren and R. W. Holm) 1971, Global Ecology (with J. P. Holdren) 1971, Human Ecology: Problems and Solutions (with A. H. Ehrlich and J. P. Holdren) 1973, Introductory Biology 1973, Ark II (with D. Pirages) 1974, The Process of Evolution (with R. W. Holm and D. R. Parnell) 1974, The End of Affluence (with A. H. Ehrlich) 1974, Biology and Society (with R. W. Holm and I. Brown) 1976, Ecoscience: Population, Resources, Environment (with A. H. Ehrlich and J. P. Holdren) 1977, Introduction to Insect Biology and Diversity (with H. V. Daly and J. T. Doyen) 1978, Machinery of Nature 1986, Wild Solutions 2001, Butterflies: Ecology and Evolution taking Flight (with Carol Boggs and Ward Watt) 2003, On the Wings of Checkerspots: A Model System for Population Biology (with Ilkka Hanski) 2004, Humanity on a Tightrope (with Robert E. Ornstein) 2010; numerous scientific and popular articles. *Leisure interest:* collecting primitive art. *Address:* Stanford University, Department of Biology, 371 Serra Mall, Room 409, Herrin Labs, Stanford, CA 94305-5020, USA (office). *Telephone:* (650) 723-3171 (office). *Fax:* (650) 723-5920 (office). *Website:* ccb.stanford.edu (office).

EHRLICH, Robert L., Jr, BA, JD; American lawyer and fmr politician; *Senior Counsel, King & Spalding LLP;* b. 25 Nov. 1957, Arbutus, Md; s. of Bob Ehrlich and Nancy Ehrlich; m. Kendel Sibiski; two s.; ed Gilman School, Princeton Univ., Wake Forest Univ. Law School; Assoc., Ober, Kaler, Grimes and Shriver (law firm) 1982–92, Of Counsel 1992–94; mem. Md House of Dels 1987–95; mem. US House of Reps, Washington, DC 1995–2003; Gov. of Md 2003–07; Attorney at Law, Womble Carlyle Sandridge & Rice PLLC, Baltimore 2007–11; Sr Counsel, King & Spalding, LLP, Washington, DC 2011–; co-host (with wife) talk show on WBAL radio; unsuccessful cand. for Gov. of Md 2010; Republican; Outstanding Young Marylander, Md Jaycees 1995, Legislator of the Year, Biotechnology Industry Org., Spirit of Enterprise Award, US Chamber of Commerce, Guardian of Small Business, Nat. Fed. of Ind. Business 1987–90, Fed. Official of the Year, Nat. Industries for the Blind, Man of the Year Award, Better Business Bureau of Greater Md 2004, Gov. of the Year, Nat. Multiple Sclerosis Soc. 2005, Highest Recognition Award, US Sec. of Health and Human Services 2005. *Publications include:* Turn This Car Around: The Road Trip to Restoring America 2011. *Address:* King & Spalding LLP, 1700 Pennsylvania Avenue, NW, Suite 200, Washington, DC 20006, USA (office). *Telephone:* (202) 737-0500 (office). *Fax:* (202) 626-3737 (office). *E-mail:* rehrlich@kslaw.com (office). *Website:* www.kslaw.com (office).

EHRLICH, Thomas, BA, LLB; American lawyer, academic and fmr university president; b. 4 March 1934, Cambridge, Mass; s. of William Ehrlich and Evelyn Seltzer; m. Ellen Rome Ehrlich 1957; two s. one d.; ed Harvard Coll. and Harvard Law School, Cambridge, Mass; law clerk, US Court of Appeals, New York 1959–60; Assoc., Foley, Sammond & Lardner (law firm), Milwaukee, Wis. 1960–62; Special Asst to Legal Adviser, US Dept of State, Washington, DC 1962–65, to Under-Sec. of State George W. Ball 1964–65; Prof., Stanford Univ. Law School, Stanford, Calif. 1965–71, Dean and Richard E. Lang Prof. 1971–75; Pres. Legal Services Corpn, Washington, DC 1976–79; Dir Int. Devt Co-operating Agency, Washington, DC 1979–80; Guest Scholar, The Brookings Inst. 1981; Provost and Prof. of Law, Univ. of Pa, Phila 1982–87; Pres. Ind. Univ. 1987–94; Distinguished Univ. Scholar, Calif. State Univ., San Francisco 1995–2000; Sr Scholar, Carnegie Foundation for the Advancement of Teaching 1997–2010; Visiting Prof., Stanford Univ. Grad. School of Educ. 2009–, also consulting Prof.; fmr Dir, Public Welfare Foundation; fmr Trustee, Univ. of Pennsylvania, Bennett Coll., Mills Coll. and many other orgs; mem. American Acad. of Arts and Sciences; Hon. LLD (Villanova) 1979, (Notre Dame) 1980, (Univ. of Pennsylvania) 1987, (Univ. of the Pacific) 2003, (Indiana). *Publications include:* The International Legal Process (with Abram Chayes and Andreas F. Lowenfeld), (three vols) 1968, Supplement 1974, New Directions in Legal Education (with Herbert L. Packer) 1972, International Crises and the Role of Law, Cyprus 1958–67 1974, International Law and the Use of Force (with Mary Ellen O'Connell) 1993, The Courage to Inquire 1995, The Future of Philanthropy and the Nonprofit Sector in a Changing America (co-ed. with Charles T. Clotfelter) 1999, Higher Education and Civic Responsibility 2000, Educating Citizens (with Anne Colby, Elizabeth Beaumont and Jason Stephens) 2003, Reconnecting Education and Foundations: Turning Good Intentions into Educational Capital 2007, Educating for Democracy (with Anne Colby, Elizabeth Beaumont and Josh Corngold) 2007, Rethinking Undergraduate Business Education: Liberal Learning for the Profession (with Anne Colby, William Sullivan and Jonathan Dolle) 2011, Civic Work, Civic Lessons (with Ernestine Fu) 2013; numerous articles, reviews and other publs. *Address:* Stanford University, Graduate School of Education, CERAS, Room 226, 520 Galvez Mall, Stanford, CA 94305, USA (office). *Telephone:* (650) 721-2500 (office). *Fax:* (650) 723-7578 (office). *E-mail:* tehrlich@stanford.edu (office). *Website:* www.stanford.edu (office).

EHRLING, Marie, BSc (Econs); Swedish business executive; *Chairman, Telia Company AB;* b. 5 May 1955; m.; one s.; ed Stockholm School of Econs; Financial Analyst 4th Swedish Nat. Pension Fund 1977–79, Information Officer Ministry of Education 1979–80, Ministry of Finance 1980–82; Deputy CEO, SAS Group, also COO SAS Airlines and other exec. positions within SAS Group 1982–2002; Pres. TeliaSonera Sweden 2003–06, Chair. Telia Company AB 2013–; mem. Bd of Dirs, Securitas AB 2006– (Chair. 2016–), Axel Johnson Group 2012– (Vice-Chair. 2016–), Axel Johnson Int. AB 2017–; Chair. Corporate Advisory Bd, Stockholm School of Econs; mem. Royal Swedish Acad. of Eng Sciences; Dr hc (Stockholm School of Econs) 2014. *Address:* Telia Company AB, Stjärntorget 1, 169 56 Stockholm, Sweden (office). *Website:* www.teliacompany.com (office).

EHRMAN, Sir William Geoffrey, KCMG; British diplomatist; b. 28 Aug. 1950; m. Penelope Anne Le Patourel; one s. three d.; ed Eton Coll., Trinity Coll., Cambridge; joined FCO 1973; language study, Hong Kong 1973–76; Third Sec., later Second Sec. Beijing 1976–78; First Sec. Perm. Mission to UN, New York 1979–83; First Sec. Beijing 1983–84; Hong Kong and Security Policy Depts, FCO 1985–89, Political Adviser Hong Kong 1989–93, Head Near East and North Africa Dept, FCO 1993–94; mem. Bosnia Contact Group 1994–95; Prin. Pvt. Sec. to Foreign Sec. 1995–97; with Unilever China 1997–98; Amb. to Luxembourg 1998–2000; Dir of Int. Security, FCO 2000–02, Dir-Gen. of Defence and Intelligence 2002–04; Chair. Jt Intelligence Cttee, Cabinet Office 2004–05; Amb. to People's Repub. of China 2006–10; mem. Locarno Group (supports devt and implementation of FCO foreign policy) 2012.

EIBLING, Viktor; German diplomatist; *Ambassador to Mexico;* b. 4 April 1959, Karachi, Pakistan; m.; four c.; ed German School, Bilbao, Spain, Univ. of Bonn; legal training 1984–87, first state examination 1984, second state examination 1987; preparatory service for Higher Foreign Service 1988–89, Fed. Foreign Office, Bonn 1989–90, Sec. for Policy, Embassy in Seoul 1990–93, Speaker of Minister's Office, then Personal Asst to the Fed. Minister, Fed. Foreign Office 1993–98, Deputy Head of Minister's Office 1998–99, Head of Econ. Service, Embassy in Madrid 1999–2003, Head of Int. Econ. and Financial Policies, Dept of State 2003–06, responsible for Globalization, Energy and Climate Policy, Fed. Foreign Office 2006–10, Head of Dept of Economy and Sustainable Devt 2010–14, Amb. to Mexico 2014–. *Address:* Embassy of Germany, Horacio 1506, Col. Los Morales, Del. Miguel Hidalgo, 11530 Mexico City, DF, Mexico (office). *Telephone:* (55) 5283-2200 (office). *Fax:* (55) 5281-2588 (office). *E-mail:* info@mexi.diplo.de (office). *Website:* www.mexiko.diplo.de (office).

EICHEL, Hans; German politician; b. 24 Dec. 1941, Kassel; m. 1st; two c.; m. 2nd Gabriela Wolff Acorn; ed Univs of Marburg and Berlin; fmr schoolmaster; mem. Kassel City Council 1968–75, Chair. Social Democratic Party (SDP) Group 1970–75; mem. Nat. Exec. of Young Socialists 1969–72; Chief Mayor of Kassel 1975–91; mem. SDP Nat. Exec. and Spokesman on Local Govt 1984; Chair. SDP Asscn Hesse 1989; Minister-Pres. of Hesse 1991–99; Federal Minister of Finance 1999–2005; Chair. G7 1999, then Co-founder Chair. G20 2004; currently Spokesman on Sustainable Structural Devt, Friedrich Ebert Foundation; Chair. Advisory Bd FÖS-Beirats (Green Budget Germany) 2016; mem. Council (Germany), European Council on Foreign Relations. *Address:* Friedrich-Ebert-Stiftung, Hiroshimastraße 17, 10785 Berlin (office); Pappenheimstraße 10, 34119 Kassel, Germany (office). *Telephone:* (561) 9885091 (home). *Fax:* (561) 9885092 (home). *E-mail:* hans.eichel@t-online.de. *Website:* www.fes.de (office); www.hans-eichel-kassel.de.

EICHHORN, Lisa; American actress; b. 2 April 1952, Glen Falls, NY; ed Queen's Univ. Ontario, St Peter's Coll., Oxford and Royal Acad. of Dramatic Art, UK. *Films include:* Yanks 1979, The Europeans 1979, Why Would I Lie? 1980, Cutter and Bone (Cutter's Way) 1981, The Weather in the Streets 1983, Wildrose 1984, Opposing Force (Hell Camp) 1986, Grim Prairie Tales 1990, Moon 44 1990, Grim Prairie Tales 1990, King of the Hill 1993, The Vanishing 1993, Mr 247 1994, A Modern Affair 1995, Sticks and Stones 1996, First Kid 1996, Judas Kiss 1998, The Talented Mr Ripley 1999, Goodbye Lover 1999, Boys and Girls 2000, Things Left Unsaid 2000, Things I Don't Understand 2012, About Time 2013. *Television includes:* Diana: A Tribute to the People's Princess 1998, My Neighbor's Daughter

1998, Kenneth Tynan: In Praise of Hardcore 2005, Cracker 2006. *Stage appearances include:* roles in British Shakespearean productions, A Doll's House, A Golden Boy, The Speed of Darkness, The Summer Winds, The Common Pursuit, The Hasty Heart, Pass/Fail, Arms and the Man, Misfits 1996.

EICHLER, Ralph, PhD; Swiss physicist, academic and research institute director; *President Emeritus, Swiss Federal Institute of Technology (ETH Zurich);* b. 31 Dec. 1947, Guildford, Surrey, England; m.; three c.; ed Swiss Fed. Inst. of Tech. (ETH Zurich); Postdoctoral Fellow, Stanford Univ., USA 1977–79; Scientist, Deutsches Elektronen Synchrotron (DESY), Hamburg 1979–82; Scientist, Inst. for Medium-Energy Physics, ETH Zurich 1982–86, Project Leader 1988–90, Assoc. Prof. of Physics 1989–91, Prof. 1993–, Pres. ETH Zurich 2007–14, now Pres. Emer.; Deputy Dir Paul Scherrer Inst. 1998–2002, Dir 2002–07. *Address:* ETH Zürich, Rämistrasse 101, 8092 Zürich, Switzerland (office). *Telephone:* 446332036 (office). *Fax:* 446331104 (office). *E-mail:* ralph.eichler@ethz.ch (office). *Website:* www.ethz.ch (office).

EICK, Karl-Gerhard, PhD; German business executive; b. 1954; ed Univ. of Augsburg; worked in various positions for BMW AG, Munich, including as Head of Controlling in Chair.'s Div. –1988; Head of Controlling, WMF AG 1989–91; Head of Controlling, Planning and IT Div., Carl Zeiss Group 1991–93; worked with Franz Haniel & Cie GmbH, Duisburg 1993–99, mem. Bd of Man. Haniel Group co. Gehe AG, Stuttgart 1993–98, mem. Man. Bd Franz Haniel & Cie GmbH 1998–99; mem. Bd of Man. Deutsche Telekom AG from 2000, Head of Finance Div., Deputy Chair. 2004–; Chair. Man. Bd and CEO Arcandor AG March–Sept. 2009 (acquired by US investor Nicolas Berggruen to save it from insolvency 2010). *Address:* c/o Arcandor AG, Theodor-Althoff-Strasse 2, 45133 Essen, Germany.

EIDE, Espen Barth, CandPolit; Norwegian politician; b. 1 May 1964; m.; three s.; ed Univ. of Oslo, Autonomous Univ. of Barcelona; Sr Researcher, Norwegian Inst. of Int. Affairs 1993–99, Dir, Dept of Int. Politics 2002–05; Sec. of State, Ministry of Foreign Affairs 2000–01, Deputy Minister 2010–11; Sec. of State, Ministry of Defence 2005–10, Minister of Defence 2011–12, Minister of Foreign Affairs 2012–13; several assignments for UN, including expert adviser to High-Level Panel on UN Reform 2005, Special Adviser to Sec.-Gen. on Cyprus 2014–17; Man. Dir World Economic Forum 2014–16; mem. Presidency, Party of European Socialists 2001; mem. Storting (parl.) 2017–; mem. Det norske Arbeiderparti. *Address:* Arbeiderpartiet, PO Box 8743, Youngstorget, 0028 Oslo, Norway (office). *Telephone:* 24-14-40-00 (office). *E-mail:* post@arbeiderpartiet.no (office).

EIFMAN, Boris Yakovlevich; Russian choreographer; *Artistic Director, St Petersburg Eifman Ballet;* b. 22 July 1946, Rubtsovsk, Altai Region; s. of Yankel Borisovich Eifman and Klara Markovna Kuris; m. Valentina Nikolayevna Morozova; one s.; ed Kishinev School of Choreography, Leningrad State Conservatory; Balletmaster, Leningrad School of Choreography 1970–77; concurrently ballet productions in professional theatres including Firebird (Kirov Theatre 1975); Founder and Artistic Dir Leningrad Ensemble of Ballet (now St Petersburg Eifman Ballet) 1977; Chevalier des Arts et des Lettres 1999, Commdr Order of Merit of the Repub. of Poland 2003, Order of Merit for the Fatherland, 2nd Class 2012; People's Artist of Russia 1995, Golden Baton Prize 1995, 1996, 1997, 2001, 2005, Triumph Prize 1996, Golden Mask Prize 1996, 1999, Russian State Prize 1999, Best Choreographer, Benois de la Dance 2006. *Ballets include:* Before Firebird – Gayaney 1972, Idiot (Tchaikovsky's 6th Symphony) 1980, Marriage of Figaro 1982, The Legend 1982, Twelfth Night 1984, The Duel (after Kuprin) 1986, Master and Margarita (after Bulgakov) 1987, Thérèse Raquin 1991, Requiem (Mozart) 1991, Tchaikovsky 1993, Don Quixote or Madman's Fantasy (Minkus) 1994, Brothers Karamazov (after Dostoyevsky) 1995, Red Giselle 1997, 2015, My Jerusalem 1998, Russian Hamlet 1999, Don Juan 2001, Who is Who? 2003, Musagete 2004, Anna Karenina 2005, The Seagull 2007, Rodin 2011, Up & Down 2015. *Address:* St Petersburg Eifman Ballet, 191028 St Petersburg, 32V Gagarinskaya Str, Russia (office). *Telephone:* (812) 579-11-20 (office). *Fax:* (812) 579-11-20 (office). *E-mail:* eifman@inbox.ru (home). *Website:* eifmanballet.ru (office).

EIJK, HE Cardinal Willem Jacobus, MD, PhD, SDL; Dutch ecclesiastic and academic; *Archbishop of Utrecht;* b. 22 June 1953, Duivendrecht, North Holland; ed Coll., Univ. of Amsterdam, Seminary of Rolduc, Kerkrade, Univ. of Leiden, Pontifical Univ. of St Thomas Aquinas (Angelicum) and Pontifical Lateran Univ., Rome; ordained priest, Diocese of Roermond 1985; worked as a curate in Parish of St Anthony of Padua, Venlo Blerick; taught moral theology at seminary of Rolduc; Prof. of Moral Theology, Pontifical Faculty of Theology, Lugano, Switzerland 1997–99; mem. Int. Theological Comm. 1997–2002; Bishop of Groningen-Leeuwarden 1999–2007; Archbishop of Utrecht 2008–; cr. Cardinal (Cardinal-Priest of San Callisto) 2012–; participated in Papal Conclave 2013; mem. Congregation of Catholic Educ., Pontifical Acad. for Life. *Publications:* De zelfgekozen dood naar aanleiding van een dodelijke en ongeneeslijke ziekte 1987, The Ethical Problems of Genetic Engineering of Human Beings 1990, Handboek katholieke medische ethiek (co-ed.) 2010 (translated as Manuals of Catholic Medical Ethics 2014); contrib. of articles in books, periodicals and newspapers. *Leisure interest:* organ-playing. *Address:* Aartsbisdom, PO Box 14019, 3508 SB Utrecht (office); Aartsbisdom, Maliebaan 40, 3581 CR Utrecht, The Netherlands (office). *Telephone:* (30) 233-15-70 (office). *Fax:* (30) 231-19-62 (office). *E-mail:* aartsbisschop@aartsbisdom.nl (office). *Website:* www.aartsbisdom.nl (office).

EILA, Mohamed Taher; Sudanese politician; *Prime Minister;* Dir Sudan Seaports Corpn 1989; Minister for Roads and Bridges 2005; Gov. Red Sea State 2005, Gezira State 2015–19; Prime Minister of Sudan 2019–. *Address:* Ministry of Cabinet Affairs, POB 931, Khartoum, Sudan (office). *Telephone:* (183) 784205 (office). *Fax:* (183) 771331 (office). *E-mail:* info@sudan.gov.sd (office). *Website:* www.sudan.gov.sd (office).

EINARSSON, Sveinn, PhD; Icelandic theatre director and author; b. 18 Sept. 1934, Reykjavik; s. of Einar Ól Sveinsson and Kristjana Thorsteinsdóttir; m. Thora Kristjánsdóttir 1964; one d.; ed Univ. of Stockholm, Univ. of Paris, Sorbonne, Univ. of Iceland; Artistic Dir Reykjavik Theatre Co. 1963–72 (Hon. mem. 1991); Prin. Reykjavik Theatre School 1963–70; Gen. Man. and Artistic Dir Nat. Theatre of Iceland 1972–83; Head of Programme Production, Icelandic State TV 1989–93; Counsellor, Ministry of Culture 1983–89, 1993–2004; Chair. Icelandic Nat. Comm. for UNESCO 1995–2006; Artistic Dir Reykjavik Arts Festival 1998–2001; Vice-Pres. Int. Theatre Inst. 1979–81; mem. (part-time) Faculty, Univ. of Iceland 1970–90; now freelance dir and author; has directed over 90 productions (including opera) on stage and TV in Iceland, the Nordic countries, UK and Germany; productions also presented in Venezuela, Canada, the Baltic States and Korea (Theatre of Nations); several appointments with the Council of Europe: Chair. several cultural cttees; Vice-Pres. Nordic Theatre Union 1975–82; mem. Exec. Bd UNESCO 2001–05; hon. mem. of several socs etc.; Paul Harris Fellow Rotary Club of Reykjavik 2004, Hon. mem. The Nordic Theatre Union 2008; Officer, Order of White Rose of Finland, Order of Merit (Norway), Commdr, Swedish Nordstjärnan, Commdr, Ordre des Arts et Lettres (France) 2004; Children's Book of Year Award 1986, Clara Lachmann Prize 1990, First Prize, Short Story Competition, 50th Anniversary of Repub. of Iceland 1994, Jón Sigurdsson Prize 1997, Best Theatre Production Award 2003, Hon. Award for Lifetime Achievement in the Theatre 2003, The Letterstedt Prize 2010. *Plays include:* Egg of Life 1983, I'm Gold and Treasures 1984, Bukolla 1991, Bandamannasaga 1992, The Amlodi Saga 1996, The Daughter of the Poet 1998, Edda 2000. *Television includes:* (plays) A Stop on My Way 1971, Time is in No Harmony with Me 1993. *Publications include:* on theatre: Theatre By the Lake 1972, My Nine Years Down There 1987, Íslensk Leiklist (History of Icelandic Theatre) Vol. I 1991, Vol. II 1996, My Eleven Years Up There 2000, A People's Theatre Comes of Age 2007, Leiklisten i veröldinni (The Theatre in the World) 2007; novel: The Electricity Man 1998; children's books: Gabriella in Portugal 1985, Dordingull 1994. *Leisure interests:* music, skiing, forestry. *E-mail:* sveinn.einarsson@mrn.stjr.is. *Website:* sveinneinarsson.weebly.com.

EINASTO, Jaan, CandSci, PhD, DSc; Estonian astrophysicist and academic; *Senior Research Fellow, Tartu Observatory;* b. 23 Feb. 1929, Tartu; ed Univ. of Tartu; joined staff of Tartu Observatory as Research Assoc. 1952, Head of Astrophysics Group 1963–68, of Dept of Physics of Galaxies 1976–92, of Dept of Cosmology 1992–97, Sr Research Fellow 1998–, Sr Researcher 2014–; Head of Dept of Astronomy and Physics, Estonian Acad. of Sciences 1983–95; mem. Estonian Academy of Sciences, Academia Europaea 1991, Royal British Soc. of Astronomy 1994; Estonian Science Prize four times, Viktor Ambartsumian Int. Prize, Cosmology Prize, asteroid 11577 Einasto, discovered in 1994, named in his honour, Marcel Grossmann Award 2009, Peter Gruber Foundation (co-recipient) 2014. *Achievements include:* pioneer of the branch of astronomy now called Near Field Cosmology. *Publications:* numerous papers in professional journals. *Address:* Tartu Observatory, 61602 Tõravere, Tartumaa, Estonia (office). *Telephone:* 6962538 (office). *Fax:* 6962555 (office). *E-mail:* jaan.einasto@to.ee (office). *Website:* www.to.ee/eng (office); www.aai.ee/~einasto (office).

EINHORN, Jessica P., BA, MA, PhD; American academic and fmr government official; *Resident Senior Advisor, The Rock Creek Group;* b. 1948; ed Barnard Coll., Columbia Univ., Paul H. Nitze School of Advanced Int. Studies (SAIS), Princeton Univ., London School of Econs, UK, Brookings Inst., Harvard Univ.; various roles with US Treasury, US State Dept and Int. Devt Co-operation Agency of USA –1992; Vice-Pres. and Treas., World Bank, Washington, DC 1992–96, Man. Dir 1996–98; Visiting Fellow, IMF 1998–99; Consultant, Clark & Weinstock, Washington 1999–2002; Dean, Paul H. Nitze School of Advanced Int. Studies (SAIS), Johns Hopkins Univ. 2001–12; Dir, Center for Global Devt, Peterson Inst. for Int. Econs, Nat. Bureau of Econ. Research; Resident Sr Advisor and mem. Advisory Bd, The Rock Creek Group; fmr Dir, Council on Foreign Relations; Chair. Global Advisory Bd J.E. Robert Cos; Dir, Pitney Bowes Inc. 1999–, Time Warner, Inc.; mem. Exec. Cttee Trilateral Comm.; Trustee, Rockefeller Brothers Fund; fmr Trustee, German Marshall Fund. *Publications:* Expropriation Politics 1974; various articles. *Address:* The Rock Creek Group, 1133 Connecticut Avenue NW, Washington, DC 20036, USA (office). *Telephone:* (202) 331-3400 (office). *E-mail:* information@therockcreekgroup.com (office). *Website:* www.therockcreekgroup.com (office).

EINIK, M. Michael, BBA, MBA; American organization official and fmr diplomatist; *Deputy Executive Director, Partnering and Sustainability Department, International Science and Technology Center;* b. 1949, New York; ed Univ. of Miami, George Washington Univ.; joined US Dept of State 1972, Econ./Commercial Officer, Embassy in Brasilia, then Embassy in San Salvador, with Bureau of Econ. and Business Affairs, Dept of State, staff Asst to Asst Sec. of State, worked in Office of Fuels and Energy during 1970s oil crisis, Petroleum Officer, Embassy, Nigeria 1981, served in Econ. Section, Embassy in Moscow, Prin. Officer, Consulate-Gen., Zagreb representing US in both Croatia and Slovenia 1988–92, Chief of Personnel, European Bureau 1992–94, Deputy Chief of Mission, Embassy in Bucharest, Amb. to Macedonia 1999–2002; Chair. AMGAZ SA 2002–07; Pres. Netcare Healthcare Central Europe (Netcare CE) 2004; Exec. Dir Project on Ethnic Relations (PER) Regional Center for Cen., Eastern and Southeastern Europe, Bucharest, Romania 2005–07; Chair. and Pnr, Ratz De Nagylak (ecologically friendly hotel village in Transylvania) 2006; Pnr, Cube Consulting, Romania 2007–; Deputy Exec. Dir, Partnering and Sustainability Dept, International Science and Technology Center, Moscow, Russia 2009–; mem. Bd of Dirs Bulgarian American Business Center, Ratsiu Democracy Foundation. *Address:* International Science and Technology Center, 127473 Moscow, Krasnoproletarskaya 32-34, Russia (office). *Telephone:* (495) 982-3200 (office). *Fax:* (499) 982-3201 (office). *E-mail:* istcinfo@istc.ru (office). *Website:* www.istc.int (office).

EISELE, Maj.-Gen. (retd) Manfred S.; German army officer; b. 17 March 1938, Wilhelmshaven; s. of Wilhelm Eisele and Gertrud Eisele-Meyer; m. Elke Krümpelmann 1962; two d.; ed Blankenese High School, Mil. Acad., Gen. Staff Acad., Hamburg, USA Command and Gen. Staff Coll. and Royal Coll. of Defence Studies; Commdg Officer, Artillery-Bn 125, Bayreuth 1977–78; Chef de Cabinet/Chief of Gen. Staff, Bonn 1978–80; Head of Public Information, Ministry of Defence 1980–81; Commdg Officer, Mechanized Infantry Brigade 17, Hamburg 1984–88; Chief, Combat Requirements Brigade, Supreme HQ Allied Forces Europe (SHAPE), Mons, Belgium 1988–91; Dir Politico-Military Affairs, Ministry of Defence, Bonn 1991–92; Commdg Officer, 12th Panzer Div. Würzburg 1992–94, Armed Forces Office, Bonn 1994; Asst Sec.-Gen. UN Dept of Peace-Keeping Operations 1994–98 (retd); head of UN Comm. on UNAMSIL activities in Sierra Leone (Eisele Mission) 2000–02, then served on mission in Guinea, Liberia, Democratic Repub. of Congo, Rwanda 2002; Lecturer in Int. Politics, Univ. of Applied Sciences Würzburg-Schweinfurt, mem. Advisory Bd NMUN –Nat. Model

United Nations; consultant to UN Dept of Peace-Keeping Operations; Bundesverdienstkreuz, Legion of Merit, USA, Grand Cross, Rider of Vadar, Bulgaria; Dag Hammarskjöld Medal 1998. *Publications include:* Die Vereinten Nationen und das Internationale Krisenmanagement (preface by Kofi Annan) 2000. *Leisure interests:* international politics, history, music, sport. *Address:* Ravensburgstrasse 2B, 97209 Veitshöchheim, Germany. *Telephone:* (931) 9500055. *Fax:* (931) 9500042. *E-mail:* E.u.M.Eisele@t-online.de. *Website:* www.nmun.uni-wuerzburg.de/nmun.

EISEN, Norman L., BA, JD; American lawyer and diplomatist; m. Lindsay Kaplan; one d.; ed Brown Univ., Harvard Law School; Asst Dir Los Angeles office of the Anti-Defamation League 1985–88; Partner, Zuckerman Spaeder law firm, Washington, DC for almost two decades; Co-founder and Chair. Citizens for Responsibility and Ethics in Washington (govt watchdog group) 2003; Deputy Gen. Counsel to the Obama-Biden Presidential Transition 2007–09; Special Counsel to the Pres. for Ethics and Govt Reform, White House 2009–11; Amb. to Czech Repub. 2011–14; Visiting Fellow, Brooking Inst. 2014, now Sr Fellow, Governance Studies Program; political commentator, CNN. *Address:* The Brookings Institution, 1775 Massachusetts Avenue, NW, Washington, DC 20036, USA. *Telephone:* (202) 797-6090 (office). *E-mail:* communications@brookings.edu (office). *Website:* www.brookings.edu (office).

EISENBERG, David S., AB, DPhil; American biochemist, biophysicist and academic; *Professor, University of California, Los Angeles;* b. 15 March 1939, Chicago, Ill.; ed Harvard Univ., Univ. of Oxford, UK (Rhodes Scholar); Postdoctoral Researcher, Princeton Univ. 1964–66, California Inst. of Tech. 1966–69; Prof., Dept of Chem. and Biochemistry, UCLA 1969–, Prof., Dept of Biological Chem., UCLA Medical School, Dir UCLA-DOE Inst. for Genomics and Proteomics 1993–, mem. California NanoSystems Inst.; Investigator, Howard Hughes Medical Inst. 2001–; Pres. Protein Soc. 1987–89; Ed. Advances in Protein Chemistry 1988–; mem. NAS 1989, American Acad. of Arts and Sciences 1991; Fellow, AAAS 2001; Hon. Fellow, The Queen's Coll., Oxford 2010; L.J. Henderson Prize 1961, Harvard Coll. Hon. Scholarships 1958–60, Career Devt Award, US Public Health Service 1972–77, UCLA Distinguished Teaching Award 1975, McCoy Award, UCLA Dept of Chem. and Biochemistry 1982, Pierce Award, Immunotoxin Soc. 1992, Stein & Moore Award, Protein Soc. 1996, ACS Repligen Corpn Award in Chem. of Biological Processes 1998, Amgen Award, Protein Soc. 2000, Seaborg Medal, UCLA 2004, Westheimer Medal, Harvard Univ. 2005, Harvey Prize (Human Health) (co-recipient) 2008, ACS Nobel Laureate Signature Award for Grad. Educ. in Chem. 2008, Emily Gray Award, Biophysical Soc. 2009, Sr Scientist Award, Int. Soc. for Computational Biology 2013, Bert and Natalie Vallee Award in Biomedical Science, American Soc. for Biochemistry and Molecular Biology 2015. *Publications include:* The Structure and Properties of Water 1969, Physical Chemistry: with Applications to the Life Sciences 1979; numerous papers in professional journals. *Address:* Department of Chemistry and Biochemistry, University of California, 201A Boyer Hall, 611 Charles Young Drive East, Los Angeles, CA 90095-1569, USA (office). *Telephone:* (310) 825-3754 (office). *Fax:* (310) 206-3914 (office). *E-mail:* david@mbi.ucla.edu (office). *Website:* www.doe-mbi.ucla.edu (office).

EISENBERG, Jesse Adam; American actor; b. 5 Oct. 1983, New York; s. of Barry Eisenberg and Amy Eisenberg; m. Anna Strout 2017; one s.; ed The New School, New York. *Television includes:* Get Real 1999, Lightning: Fire from the Sky 2001. *Films include:* Roger Dodger (San Diego Film Festival Award for Most Promising New Actor) 2002, The Squid and the Whale 2005, The Hunting Party 2007, Adventureland 2009, Zombieland 2009, Solitary Man 2010, Camp Hope 2010, The Social Network (Boston Soc. of Film Critics Award for Best Actor, Nat. Bd of Review Best Actor, Toronto Film Critics Asscn Award for Best Actor, Nat. Soc. of Film Critics Award for Best Actor) 2010, To Rome With Love 2012, Now You See Me 2013, The Double 2013, The End of the Tour 2015, Batman v Superman: Dawn of Justice 2016, Now You See Me 2 2016, The Hummingbird Project 2018, Zombieland: Double Tap 2019. *Publication:* Bream Gives Me Hiccups 2015. *Address:* c/o Creative Artists Agency, 2000 Avenue of the Stars, Los Angeles, CA 90067, USA (office). *Telephone:* (424) 288-2000 (office). *Fax:* (424) 288-2900 (office). *Website:* www.caa.com (office).

EISENBERG, Lewis M., BA, MBA; American financier and diplomatist; *Ambassador to Italy;* b. 1942, Illinois; m. Judith Ann Eisenberg; three d.; ed Dartmouth Coll., Cornell Univ. Johnson School of Business; worked for Goldman Sachs, New York 1966–89, becoming Partner and co-Head of Equity Div.; co-f. and co-Chair. Granite Capital International Group LP (investment management co.) 1990; co-f. Granum Communications; Sr Advisor, Kohlberg Kravis Roberts (KKR) 2009–; Commr, Port Authority of New York and New Jersey 1994–95, Chair. 1995–2001; Amb. to Italy 2017–; Chair. New Jersey Comm. on Privatization and Competitive Contracting 1994, Victory 2000 campaign 2000; Dir Lower Manhattan Devt Corpn 2002; Life Mem. Cornell Univ. Council; Founder and fmr Chair. Republican Leadership Council, Chair. of Finance Cttee, Republican Nat. Cttee 2002–04; Republican; Hon. LLD (Monmouth Univ.) 2001, Hon. DHumLitt (Rabbinical Coll. of America) 2002; New Jersey Alliance for Action Eagle Award 1995, Monmouth Univ. New Jersey Businessman of the Year 2000. *Address:* Embassy of the USA, Palazzo Margherita, Via Vittorio Veneto 121, 00187 Rome, Italy (office). *Telephone:* (06) 46741 (office). *Fax:* (06) 46742217 (office). *Website:* it.usembassy.gov (office).

EISENMAN, Peter David, BArch, MS, MA, PhD, FAIA; American architect and academic; *Charles Gwathmey Professor in Practice, Yale School of Architecture;* b. 11 Aug. 1932, Newark, NJ; s. of Herschel I. Eisenman and Sylvia H. Heller; m. 1st Elizabeth Henderson 1963 (divorced 1990); one s. one d.; m. 2nd Cynthia Davidson 1990; one s.; ed Cornell Univ., Columbia Univ., Univ. of Cambridge, UK; Founder Inst. of Architecture and Urban Studies, New York 1967, Dir 1967–82; Architect-in-Residence, American Acad., Rome 1976; with Eisenman/Robertson Architects, New York 1980–88; Eisenman Architects 1988–; commissioned to design Berlin Holocaust Memorial; Kea Prof., Univ. of Maryland 1978; apptd Charlotte Davenport Prof., Yale Univ. 1980, Louis I. Kahn Prof. of Architecture 2001, currently Charles Gwathmey Prof. in Practice, Yale School of Architecture; Arthur Rotch Prof., Harvard Univ. 1982–85; apptd Irwin S. Chanin Distinguished Prof. 1986; Louis H. Sullivan Research Prof. of Architecture, Univ. of Illinois 1987–93; John Williams Prof. of Architecture, Univ. of Arkansas 1997; Frank H.T. Rhodes Class of '56 Prof., Cornell Univ. 2008–; mem. American Acad. of Arts and Sciences, American Acad. of Arts and Letters; Hon. DFA (Univ. of Illinois, Pratt Inst., New York, Syracuse Univ.), (Accad. delle Belle Arti di Brera, Milan) 2012, Hon. DArch (Università La Sapienza, Rome) 2003; Arnold W. Brunner Memorial Prize in Architecture, American Acad. and Inst. of Arts and Letters 1984, Medal of Honor, New York Chapter of AIA 2001, Cooper-Hewitt Nat. Design Award in Architecture, Smithsonian Inst. 2001, Golden Lion for Lifetime Achievement, Venice Biennale 2004, Wolf Foundation Prize in the Arts (Architecture) (jtly) 2010. *Principal works include:* Pvt. Residences Princeton, NJ, Hardwick, Vt, Lakeville and Cornwall, Conn. 1968–76, Housing, Koch-Friedrichstrasse, Berlin 1980–86, Wexner Center for Visual Arts, Columbus, Ohio 1983–89, Columbus Convention Centre 1988–93, Univ. of Cincinnati Coll. of Design, Art, Architecture and Planning 1988–96, Koizumi Sangyo Bldg, Tokyo 1989–90, Emory Univ. Art Centre 1991–95, Rebstock Park, Frankfurt, Germany 1991–95, Max Reinhardt Haus, Berlin 1992–, Haus Immendorff, Düsseldorf, Germany 1993–94, Jewish Museum, San Francisco 1996–, Library UN Complex, Geneva 1996–, Staten Island Inst. of Arts and Sciences 1997–2001, Holocaust Memorial, Berlin 1998–2005, City of Culture, Santiago de Compostela, Spain 1999–, Spree Dreieck Tower, Berlin 2000–, Deportivo La Coruña, Spain 2001–, Il Giardino dei Passi Perduti, Verona, Italy 2003, New Hamburg Library, Germany 2005, Univ. of Phoenix Stadium for the Arizona Cardinals (named by Popular Science magazine one of the top five innovators of 2006), Pompei Stazione Santuario, Pompei, Italy 2006–, Sheikh Zayed Nat. Museum, Abu Dhabi, UAE 2007, Pozzuoli Waterfront Masterplan, Pozzuoli, Italy 2009–. *Publications include:* Barefoot on White-Hot Walls 2005, Written Into the Void: Selected Writings 1990–2004 2007, Ten Canonical Buildings, 1950–2000 2008. *Address:* Eisenman Architects, 41 West 25th Street, New York, NY 10010-2043, USA (office). *Telephone:* (212) 645-1400 (office). *Fax:* (212) 645-0726 (office). *E-mail:* info@eisenmanarchitects.com (office). *Website:* www.eisenmanarchitects.com (office).

EISENSTEIN, Daniel, BS, PhD; American (b. Israeli) astronomer, cosmologist and academic; *Professor of Astronomy, Harvard University;* b. 1970; ed Princeton and Harvard Univs; held postdoctoral positions at Inst. for Advanced Study, Princeton, NJ and Univ. of Chicago; mem. Astronomy Faculty, Univ. of Arizona 2001–10; Prof. of Astronomy, Harvard Univ. 2010–, active in the Sloan Digital Sky Survey (SDSS), currently Dir of SDSS III; Shaw Prize in Astronomy (co-recipient) 2014. *Publications include:* numerous papers in professional journals on precision cosmological constraints from the measurement of the large-scale structure of the Universe and the evolution of galaxies and their relation to their environment. *Address:* Perkin Lab, P-326 Harvard-Smithsonian Center for Astrophysics, 60 Garden Street, MS-20, Cambridge, MA 02138, USA (office). *Telephone:* (617) 495-7530 (office). *E-mail:* deisenstein@cfa.harvard.edu (office). *Website:* astronomy.fas.harvard.edu (office); scholar.harvard.edu/deisenstein/book/research (office).

EISGRUBER, Christopher Ludwig, AB, MLitt, JD; American lawyer, constitutional scholar, academic and university administrator; *President, Princeton University;* b. 24 Sept. 1961, Corvallis, Ore.; m. Lori A. Martin; one s.; ed Princeton Univ., Univ. of Oxford (Rhodes Scholar), UK, Univ. of Chicago Law School; Ed.-in-Chief of the law review, Univ. of Chicago Law School; clerked for US Court of Appeals Judge Patrick Higginbotham and US Supreme Court Justice John Paul Stevens; taught at New York Univ. School of Law 1990–2001; joined Princeton Faculty as Dir Program in Law and Public Affairs and Laurance S. Rockefeller Prof. of Public Affairs, Woodrow Wilson School of Public and Int. Affairs and Univ. Center for Human Values 2001, directed Princeton's Program in Law and Public Affairs 2001–04, acting Dir Program in Ethics and Public Affairs 2002–03, Provost 2004–13, Gen. Deputy to Pres. and Chair. Academic Planning Group, Priorities Cttee, Exec. Cttee of Council of Princeton Univ. Community, Pres. Princeton Univ. 2013–; Moderator, Aspen-Rodel Seminars 2010–13; mem. American Law Inst. 2002, American Bar Asscn 2008, Yale Law School 2011, American Council for Education Task Force on Institutional Accreditation 2011–12, American Acad. of Arts and Sciences 2014–, Global Univ. Leaders Forum, World Economic Forum, American Soc. for Political and Legal Philosophy, American Political Science Asscn; mem. Bd of Dirs Liulishuo; fmr mem. Advisory Bd, Coursera, Inc.; Trustee Educational Testing Service 2010, ITHAKA, Artstor; Hon. Fellow, Univ. Coll., Oxford 2017; Dr hc (Univ. of Edinburgh) 2015. *Publications include:* Constitutional Self-Government 2001, Global Justice and the Bulwarks of Localism: Human Rights in Context (co-ed.) 2005, Religious Freedom and the Constitution (with Lawrence G. Sager) 2007, The Next Justice: Repairing the Supreme Court Appointments Process 2007. *Leisure interest:* supports Chicago Cubs baseball team. *Address:* Office of the President, 1 Nassau Hall, Princeton University, Princeton, NJ 08544, USA (office). *Telephone:* (609) 258-6100 (office). *Fax:* (609) 258-1615 (office). *Website:* www.princeton.edu/president/eisgruber (office).

EISNER, Michael Dammann, BA; American business executive; *Founder, Tomante Company LLC;* b. 7 March 1942, Mount Kisco, NY; s. of Lester Dammann and Margaret Dammann; m. Jane Breckenridge 1967; three s.; ed Lawrenceville School, Denison Univ.; Sr Vice-Pres. Prime-Time Production and Devt, ABC Entertainment Corpn 1973–76; Pres. and COO Paramount Pictures Corpn 1976–84; Chair. and CEO The Walt Disney Co. 1984–2004, CEO 2004–05, mem. Bd of Dirs 2005–06; mem. Bd of Dirs Veoh Networks Inc. 2006–; fmr mem. Bd of Dirs Calif. Inst. of the Arts, Denison Univ., American Hosp. of Paris Foundation, UCLA Exec. Bd for Medical Sciences, Nat. Hockey League (ice hockey); mem. Business Steering Cttee of the Global Business Dialogue on Electronic Commerce, The Business Council; est. Eisner Foundation; host, Conversations with Michael Eisner (CNBC) 2006; Founder Tomante LLC 2005–; Chevalier, Légion d'honneur; Advertising Exec. of the Year Award, Advertising Age 1988, IRTS Gold Medal Award 1992, James A. Doolittle Award for Leadership in Theatre, Los Angeles Ovation Awards 2000, inducted in TV Acad. Hall of Fame 2012. *Publications include:* Work in Progress (with Tony Schwartz) 1988, Camp 2005, Working Together: Why Great Partnerships Succeed 2010. *Address:* Tornante LLC, 233 South Beverly Drive, Beverly Hills, CA 90212-3896, USA (office). *Telephone:* (310) 274-2550 (office). *E-mail:* admin@tornante.com (office). *Website:* www.tornante.com (office).

EITEL, Bernhard, Dr rer. nat habil.; German professor of geography and university administrator; *Rector, University of Heidelberg;* b. 1959, Karlsruhe; ed Univs of Karlsruhe and Stuttgart; Lecturer, Dept of Geography, Univ. of Stuttgart 1989–95; Prof. of Physical Geography, Univ. of Passau 1995–2001; Prof. of Physical

Geography, Univ. of Heidelberg 2001–, also Head of Geography Dept, Rector, Univ. of Heidelberg 2007–; mem. Exec. Comm. of the Int. Asscn of Geomorphologists 2002–; mem. German Acad. of Science and Eng (acatech) 2008, German Acad. of Sciences Leopoldina 2010; Corresp. mem. German Archaeological Inst. 2009; Chevalier, Ordre des Palmes académiques 2011. *Publications:* numerous scientific papers in professional journals. *Address:* Office of the Rector, University of Heidelberg, Grabengasse 1, 69117 Heidelberg, Germany (office). *Telephone:* (6221) 542315 (office); (6221) 542316 (office). *Fax:* (6221) 542147 (office). *E-mail:* rektor@rektorat.uni-heidelberg.de (office). *Website:* www.uni-heidelberg.de/institutions/rectorate/bernhard_eitel.html (office).

EJETA, Gebisa, BSc, MS, PhD; Ethiopian/American plant breeder, geneticist and academic; *Distinguished Professor of Plant Breeding and Genetics, Purdue University;* b. west central Ethiopia; ed Alemaya Coll. of Agric., Ethiopia, Purdue Univ., USA; Prin. Plant Breeder, Sorghum at ICRISAT 1979–83; Asst Prof. of Plant Breeding and Genetics, Purdue Univ. 1984–88, Assoc. Prof. of Plant Breeding and Genetics 1988–92, Prof. of Plant Breeding and Genetics 1992–2007, Distinguished Prof., Plant Breeding and Genetics 2007–; mem. Science Council of CGIAR (fmrly Consultative Group on Int. Agricultural Research) 2008–10, mem. CGIAR Consortium Bd 2010–; mem. Bd Sasakawa Africa 2010–; mem. Advisory Bd Chicago Council for Global Affairs; apptd by Pres. Barack Obama to Bd for Int. Food and Agricultural Devt 2011; Fellow, Crop Science Soc. of America 1994, American Soc. of Agronomy 1995, AAAS 2005; Chair. Laureate Selection Cttee, World Food Prize Foundation 2018–; silver plaque for Outstanding Contrib. to Agric. of the Sudan, Sudan Agricultural Research Corpn 1983, Int. Service in Crop Science Award, Crop Science Soc. of America 1994, Int. Service in Agronomy Award, American Soc. of Agronomy 1997, Distinguished Scientific Career Award, African Crop Science Congress 1997, Purdue School of Agric. Dean's Interdisciplinary Team Mem. Award 1998, Distinguished Career Achievement Award, INTSORMIL 2002, Outstanding Research Paper of the Year on Plant Genetic Resources, Crop Science Soc. of America 2005, Certificate of Recognition from Govt of Ethiopia 2007, World Food Prize (co-recipient) 2009, Nat. Hero Award, Govt of Ethiopia 2009, P.E. Nelson Prize for Innovation, State of Indiana 2009, Commemoration by Indiana Gen. Ass. 2009, Dow Agro-Sciences Award for Outstanding Contrib. to Global Agric. 2009, Presidential Award, Crop Science Soc. of America 2009, Indiana Hero Award, Indiana Pacers 2010, Henry Bennett Fellow, School of Int. Studies, Oklahoma State Univ. 2010, Outstanding Scientific Achievement Award, Soc. of Ethiopians in Diaspora 2010, Special Advisor to USAID Admin. 2010, US Govt Presidential Science Envoy 2010. *Publications:* Integrating New Technologies for Striga Control: Towards Ending the Witch-hunt (co-ed.) 2007; numerous papers in professional journals. *Address:* Department of Agronomy, Purdue University, Lilly Hall of Life Sciences 2-363, 915 West State Street, West Lafayette, IN 47907-2054, USA (office). *Telephone:* (765) 494-4320 (office). *Fax:* (765) 496-2926 (office). *E-mail:* gejeta@purdue.edu (office). *Website:* ag.purdue.edu/agry/Pages/gejeta.aspx (office).

EJIOFOR, Chiwetel, CBE, OBE; British actor; b. 10 July 1977, Forest Gate, London, England; s. of Arinze Ejiofor and Obiajulu Ejiofor; ed Dulwich Coll., Nat. Youth Theatre; stage debut in Othello (title role), Bloomsbury Theatre, London 1995; film debut in Deadly Voyage (TV film) 1996. *Theatre includes:* Macbeth 1997, Sparkleshark 1999, Blue/Orange (Jack Tinker Award for Most Promising Newcomer, Critics' Circle Theatre Awards 2000, London Evening Standard Theatre Award for Outstanding Newcomer 2000) 2000, Romeo and Juliet 2000, Peer Gynt 2000, The Vortex (Donmar Warehouse, London) 2002, The Seagull 2007, Othello (Laurence Olivier Award for Best Actor) 2007. *Films include:* Amistad 1997, G:MT Greenwich Mean Time 1999, It Was an Accident 2000, My Friend Soweto 2001, Dirty Pretty Things (British Ind. Film Award for Best Actor, San Diego Film Critics Soc. Award for Best Actor, Evening Standard British Film Award for Best Actor) 2002, 3 Blind Mice 2003, Love Actually 2003, She Hate Me 2004, Red Dust 2004, Melinda and Melinda 2004, Four Brothers 2005, Serenity 2005, Slow Burn 2005, Kinky Boots 2005, Inside Man 2006, Children of Men 2006, Talk to Me 2007, American Gangster (Screen Actors Guild Award) 2007, Redbelt 2008, Slapper (short, writer and dir) 2008, Endgame 2009, 2012 2009, Salt 2010, Columbite Tantalite (short, writer and dir) 2013, Savannah 2013, 12 Years a Slave (BAFTA Award for Best Actor in a Leading Role 2014) 2013, Half of a Yellow Sun 2013, Making a Scene (short) 2013, Z for Zachariah 2015, The Martian 2015, Secret in Their Eyes 2015. *Television includes:* Deadly Voyage (film) 1996, Mind Games (film) 2001, Murder in Mind (series) 2001, Trust (series) 2003, Twelfth Night, or What You Will (film) 2003, Canterbury Tales (mini-series) 2003, Tsunami: The Aftermath (film) 2006, Masterpiece Contemporary (series) 2009, The Shadow Line (mini-series) 2011, Dancing on the Edge (mini-series) 2013, Phil Spector (film) 2013. *Address:* c/o Markham, Froggatt & Irwin, 4 Windmill Street, London, W1T 2HZ, England (office). *Telephone:* (20) 7636-4412 (office). *Fax:* (20) 7637-5233 (office). *E-mail:* admin@markhamfroggattirwin.com (office). *Website:* www.markhamfroggattirwin.com (office).

EK, Daniel; Swedish technologist and music industry executive; *Co-founder and CEO, Spotify AB;* b. 21 Feb. 1983, Stockholm; held sr roles at Tradera (auction co. subsequently acquired by Ebay); f. Advertigo (online advertising co.) 2004, subsequently acquired by TradeDoubler 2006; Chief Tech. Officer, Stardoll (fashion and entertainment community for tweens) 2005–06; Co-founder and CEO uTorrent 2006; Co–founder (with Martin Lorentzon) and CEO Spotify AB, Stockholm 2006, launched music streaming service Spotify 2008. *Leisure interests:* football, playing the guitar. *Address:* Spotify USA Inc., 45 West 18th Street, 7th Floor, New York, NY 10011, USA (office); Spotify AB, 4, Birger Jarlsgatan 61, 113 56 Stockholm, Sweden (office). *Telephone:* (347) 485-6083 (NY) (office). *E-mail:* office@spotify.com (office). *Website:* www.spotify.com (office).

EKE, 'Aisake Valu, BA, MBA, CPA; Tongan politician and fmr civil servant; m.; ed Univ. of South Queensland, Australia; civil servant 1986–2010, positions included Sec. for Finance 1994, Acting Commr of Revenue, posted to World Bank 2002, Acting Minister of Finance 2006; mem. Bd of Dirs Nat. Reserve Bank 2009; Chair. Tonga Devt Bank 2009; mem. Legis. Ass. (parl.) for Tongatapu No. 5 2010–; Minister of Finance and Nat. Planning 2014–17 (resgnd); mem. Tupou High School Advisory Cttee 2001; fmr mem. Democratic Party, currently ind.

EKÉUS, Carl Rolf; Swedish diplomatist; *Commissioner, International Commission on Missing Persons;* b. 7 July 1935, Kristinehamn; m. Christina C. Oldfelt 1970; three s. three d.; ed Univ. of Stockholm; law practice, Karlstad 1959–62; Legal Div. Ministry of Foreign Affairs 1962–63; Sec. Swedish Embassy, Bonn 1963–65; First Sec. Nairobi 1965–67; Special Asst to Minister of Foreign Affairs 1967–73; First Sec., Counsellor, Perm. Mission to UN, New York 1974–78; Counsellor, The Hague 1978–83; Amb. and Perm. Rep. to Conf. on Disarmament, Geneva 1983–89, Chair. Cttee on Chemical Weapons 1984, 1987; Amb. and Head of Swedish Del. to CSCE, Vienna 1989–93; Chair. Cttee on Principles Chapter of Charter of Paris 1991; Exec. Chair. UN Special Comm. on Iraq 1991–97; Amb. to USA 1997–2000; Chair. Stockholm Int. Peace Research Inst. 2000–10; OSCE High Commr on Nat. Minorities 2001–07; Commr of the International Comm. on Missing Persons (ICMP) 2005–; mem. Supervisory Council Int. Luxembourg Forum on Preventing Nuclear Catastrophe, Canberra Comm. on the Elimination of Nuclear Weapons, Advisory Bd Centre for Non-Proliferation, Monetary Inst., Tokyo Forum on Non-Proliferation and Disarmament; mem. Exec. Bd, European Leadership Network 2011–; mem. Advisory Bd UN Sec.-Gen. on Disarmament Matters 1999–2004, Bd of Dirs Nuclear Threat Initiative 2001, Bd Axel and Margaret Ax:son Johnson Foundation 2001–11; mem. Royal Acad. of War Science, Stockholm 2001–, European Council for Foreign Relations 2011–; Hon. LLD (California Lutheran Univ.) 1999; Wateler Peace Prize, Carnegie Foundation 1997. *Publications include:* several articles and reports on foreign policy, int. economy, nuclear non-proliferation, disarmament and arms control, chemical weapons, European security, Iraq and weapons of mass destruction. *Leisure interests:* piano playing, tennis. *Address:* International Commission on Missing Persons, Alipašina 45A, 71000 Sarajevo, Bosnia and Herzegovina (office); Rådmansgatan 57, 113 60 Stockholm, Sweden (home). *Telephone:* (33) 280800 (office); (8) 312653 (home). *Fax:* (33) 280900 (office). *E-mail:* rekeus@gmail.com (home); icmp@ic-mp.org (office). *Website:* www.ic-mp.org (office).

EKREN, Nazim, PhD; Turkish politician, academic and university administrator; *Rector and Professor of Economics, School of Commercial Sciences, Istanbul Commerce University (Istanbul Ticaret Üniversitesi);* b. 4 Dec. 1956, Istanbul; m.; two c.; ed Uludağ and Marmara Univs, Manchester Business School, UK; fmr Dir Türkiye Vakiflar Bankasi; fmr Dir Banking and Insurance Inst., Univ. of Marmara; mem. of Grand Nat. Ass., representing Istanbul 2002–11; Deputy Prime Minister and State Minister for Economy 2007–09; Co-founder and Deputy Chair. (Econ. Affairs), Adalet ve Kalkinma Partisi/Justice and Devt Party (AKP); currently Rector and Prof. of Econs, School of Commercial Sciences, Istanbul Ticaret Üniversitesi (Istanbul Commerce Univ.). *Publications include:* Uluslararası Bankacılık ve Türkiye Örneği 1987, Para ve Finans Ansklopedisi, Finansal Hizmetler Sektörü 1996, 75 Yılda Para'nın Serüveni, Özel Finans Kurumları 1998, Uluslararası İktisat 2013, Bugünkü Makroekonomi 2014, Uygulamalı İktisat 2015, Örnek Olaylarla Mikro İktisat 2015, İktisadi Araştırma El Kitabı 2015; contribs to int. and nat. journals. *Address:* Office of the Rector, Istanbul Ticaret Üniversitesi (Istanbul Commerce University), Ragıp Gümüşpala Caddesi 84, 34378 Eminönü, Istanbul, Turkey (office). *E-mail:* nekren@ticaret.edu.tr (office). *Website:* www.tubis.ticaret.edu.tr (office).

EL-BAZ, Farouk, BS, MS, PhD; Egyptian/American scientist and academic; *Director, Center for Remote Sensing, Boston University;* b. 2 Jan. 1938, Zagazig, Egypt; s. of El-Sayed El-Baz and Zahia Hammouda; m. Catherine Patricia O'Leary 1963; four d.; ed Ain Shams Univ., Cairo, Asyut Univ., Missouri School of Mines and Metallurgy, Univ. of Missouri, Massachusetts Inst. of Tech., Heidelberg Univ., Germany; Demonstrator, Geology Dept, Asyut Univ. 1958–60; Lecturer, Mineralogy-Petrography Inst., Univ. of Heidelberg 1964–65; exploration geologist, Pan-American UAR Oil Co., Cairo 1966; Supervisor, Lunar Science Planning and Operations, BellComm, Bell Telephone Labs., Washington, DC for Apollo Program, NASA HQ 1967–72; Research Dir, Center for Earth and Planetary Studies, Nat. Air and Space Museum, Smithsonian Inst., Washington, DC 1973–82; Science Adviser to Pres. Anwar Sadat of Egypt 1978–81; Vice-Pres. for Science and Tech. and for Int. Devt, Itek Optical Systems, Lexington, Mass. 1982–86; Dir Center for Remote Sensing, Boston Univ. 1986–; Research Prof., Depts of Archeology and Electronic and Computer Eng, Boston Univ.; Adjunct Prof., Faculty of Science, Ain Shams Univ., Cairo, Egypt; pioneering work in the applications of space photography to understanding of arid terrain; Pres. Arab Soc. of Desert Research; mem. Bd of Dirs, USA Civilian R&D Foundation, Mantor Arabia; mem. Advisory Bd, EXPEC-ARC, Aramco, Saudi Arabia; numerous radio interviews, especially on NPR, TV interviews on Al-Jazeerah and other Arab stations; mem. US Nat. Acad. of Eng, Academia Bibliotheca Alexandrina, the African, Arab, Islamic, Palestine, Hassan II (Moroccan) Acad. of Science, TWAS (Acad. of Science for the Developing World); Order of Merit, First Class (Arab Repub. of Egypt); Hon. DSc (New England Coll., NH) 1989, Hon. PhD (Mansoura Univ.), Hon. LLD (American Univ. of Cairo), Hon. DEng (Univ. of Missouri-Rolla), (American Univ. of Beirut); numerous honours and awards, including from NASA: Apollo Achievement Award, Certificate of Merit for contribs to Manned Space Flight, Exceptional Scientific Achievement Medal and Special Recognition Award; from AAAS: Award for Public Understanding of Science and Tech. 1992, Apollo-Soyuz Test Project Experiment Team Award 1992; Golden Door Award, Int. Inst. of Boston, Nevada Medal, Arab Thought Foundation Pioneer Award, Texas Dawa Award; World Water Masters Award 2009. *Publications:* Say It in Arabic 1968, Astronaut Observations from the Apollo-Soyuz Mission 1977, Egypt as Seen by Landsat 1979, Desert Landforms of Southwest Egypt 1982, Deserts and Arid Lands 1984, The Geology of Egypt 1984, Physics of Desertification 1986, The Gulf War and the Environment 1994, Atlas of Kuwait from Satellite Images 2000, Wadis of Oman: Satellite Image Atlas 2002, Development Corridor: Securing a Better Future for Egypt 2007, Remote Sensing in Archaeology 2007. *Leisure interests:* reading history, travel, swimming. *Address:* Center for Remote Sensing, Boston University, 725 Commonwealth Avenue, Boston, MA 02215-1401, USA (office). *Telephone:* (617) 353-9709 (office). *Fax:* (617) 353-3200 (office). *E-mail:* farouk@bu.edu (office). *Website:* www.bu.edu/remotesensing/faculty/el-baz (office).

ELACHI, Charles, MS, MBA, PhD, FIEEE; American (b. Lebanese) electrical engineer and academic; *Professor Emeritus of Electrical Engineering and Planetary Science, California Institute of Technology (Caltech);* b. (Charles Asshur Al-Wadad Elachi), 18 April 1947, Rayak, Lebanon; m. Valerie Gifford; two d.; ed Collège des Apôtres, Jounieh, École Orientale, Zahlé, Joseph Fourier Univ., Grenoble and Grenoble Inst. of Tech., France, California Inst. of Tech. (Caltech), Pasadena, Univ. of Southern California, Univ. of California, Los Angeles; joined

Jet Propulsion Lab. 1970; taught The Physics of Remote Sensing at Caltech 1982–2000, Prof. of Electrical Eng and Planetary Science 2002–16, Prof. Emer. 2016–, Vice-Pres. Caltech 2001–16; Dir Space and Earth Science, Jet Propulsion Lab. late 1980s–90s, Dir Jet Propulsion Lab. 2001–16; Prin. Investigator or Co-Investigator on numerous research and devt studies and flight projects sponsored by NASA including Shuttle Imaging Radar series (SIR-A 1981, SIR-B 1984, SIR-C 1994), Magellan Imaging Radar, Rosetta Comet Nucleus Sounder Experiment; Team Leader Cassini Titan Radar Experiment; participated in several archeological expeditions in Egyptian Desert, Arabian Peninsula and Western Chinese Desert in search of old trading routes and buried cities using satellite data; lecturer and keynote speaker at numerous nat. and int. confs and univs in China, Japan, Australia, France, UK, Netherlands, Denmark, Austria, Switzerland, Norway, Germany, Italy, Greece, Egypt, Kenya, India, Morocco, and Brazil; mem. Univ. of Arizona Eng School Advisory Cttee, Boston Univ. Center of Remote Sensing Advisory Council, UCLA Science Bd of Visitors; fmr Chair. several nat. and int. cttees that developed NASA road-maps for exploration of neighbouring solar systems 1995, our solar system 1997, Mars 1998; mem. Univ. Advisory Bd King Fahd Univ. of Petroleum and Minerals, Saudi Arabia, 2010–, Bd King Abdullah Univ. of Science and Tech., Saudi Arabia; Chair. Bd of Trustees, Lebanese American Univ., Beirut; mem. Nat. Acad. of Eng (NAE) 1989–, NAE 4th Decadal Cttee 1993–95, NAE Membership Cttee 1995; mem. Int. Acad. of Astronautics; Fellow, AIAA; Order of Cedars (Lebanon) 2006, Chevalier, Légion d'honneur 2010; numerous awards including ASP Autometric Award 1980, 1982, NASA Exceptional Scientific Medal 1982, W.T. Pecora Award 1985, IEEE Geoscience and Remote Sensing Distinguished Achievement Award 1987, Asteroid 1982 SU was renamed 4116 Elachi in recognition of his contrib. to planetary exploration 1989, IEEE Medal of Eng Excellence 1992, NASA Outstanding Leadership Medal 1994, Nevada Medal 1995, COSPAR Nordberg Medal 1996, NASA Distinguished Service Medal 1999, Dryden Award 2000, UCLA Dept of Earth and Space Science Distinguished Alumni Award 2002, Wernher Von Braun Award 2002, NASA Outstanding Leadership Medal 2002, Takeda Award 2002, Space Flight Award, American Astronautical Soc. 2005, Bob Hope Distinguished Citizen Award, Nat. Defense Industrial Asscn 2005, NASA Exceptional Service Medal 2005, Massey Award, Royal Soc. of London 2006, Philip Habib Award for Distinguished Public Service, American Task Force for Lebanon 2006, Nat. Acad. of Eng Arthur M. Bueche Award 2011, Gen. James E. Hill Lifetime Space Achievement Award, Space Foundation 2011. *Publications include:* three textbooks and more than 230 publs and patents in the fields of remote sensing, planetary exploration, Earth observation from space, electromagnetic theory and integrated optics. *Leisure interests:* skiing, woodworking, history, travel. *Address:* California Institute of Technology, Division of Engineering and Applied Science, 1200 E California Blvd, Pasadena, CA 91109, USA (office). *Telephone:* (626) 395-4101 (office). *Fax:* (626) 395-2134 (office). *Website:* eas.caltech.edu (office).

ELAHI, Chaudhry Pervez; Pakistani politician; b. 1 Nov. 1945; s. of Chaudhry Manzoor Elahi; ed Forman Christian Coll., Univ. of London, UK; mem. Punjab Prov. Ass. 1985–, Deputy Leader, then Leader of the Opposition 1993–96, Speaker 1997–99; Minister of Local Govt and Rural Devt, Punjab 1985–86, 1988–90, 1990–93; Chief Minister of Punjab 2002–07; Deputy Prime Minister and Minister Responsible for Defence Production and for Industries 2012–13; Pres. Pakistan Muslim League (Q) party in Punjab; mem. Nat. Security Council. *Address:* 30C, Ch. Zahur Elahi Rd, Gulberg-II, Lahore, Pakistan (home). *E-mail:* info@pml.org.pk (office). *Website:* www.pml.org.pk (office).

ELALAMY, Moulay Hafid; Moroccan business executive; *President and Director-General, Saham Group;* b. 1960, Marrakech; ed Univ. of Sherbrooke, Canada; began career as Sr Adviser to Ministry of Finance of Quebec, Canada 1980; served as Gen. Sec. and Dir-Gen. of insurance subsidiary of ONA Group; Head of Information Systems, Saint-Maurice (Canadian insurance co.); Man. Dir Compagnie Africaine d'Assurance 1988; f. Saham Group 1995, currently Pres. and Dir-Gen., also Chair. and Man. Dir CNIA SAADA Assurance; Pres. Gen. Confed. of Enterprises of Morocco 2006–09; Vice-Pres. Moroccan Fed. of Insurance Cos and Reinsurance; Minister of Industry, Investment, Trade and Digital Economy 2017–; Dir Investment Cttee, Caisse Interprofessionnelle Marocaine de Retraite (also mem.); Dir and Treas., Lalla Salma Asscn; mem. Bd of Dirs Colina Holdings Ltd. *Telephone:* (53) 7765227 (Ministry of Industry, Investment, Trade and Digital Economy) (office). *Fax:* (53) 7739302 (Ministry of Industry, Investment, Trade and Digital Economy) (office). *E-mail:* contact@saham.ma (office). *Website:* www.sahamgroup.com (office).

ELBA, Idris, OBE; British actor and hip-hop artist; b. (Idrissa Akuna Elba), 6 Sept. 1972, London; s. of Winston Elba and Eve Elba; m. 1st Kim Nørgaard 1999 (divorced 2003); one d.; m. 2nd Sonya Nicole Hamlin 2006 (divorced 2006); one s. with Naiyana Garth; ed Nat. Youth Music Theatre; started own DJ co. 1987; night shift at Ford factory in Dagenham 1989–90; worked in nightclubs under DJ nickname Big Driis 1991; worked at Nat. Youth Music Theatre; best known for playing Russell 'Stringer' Bell in The Wire (HBO) and title role of Detective John Luther in Luther (BBC 1); Anti-Crime Amb. 2009–; opened for Madonna during her Rebel Heart Tour in Berlin, Germany 2015; collaboration with British fashion label Superdry 2015; Best Actor, BET Awards 2010, 2011, MOBO Inspiration Award 2014. *Films include:* Belle maman 1999, Sorted 2000, Buffalo Soldiers 2001, One Love 2003, The Gospel 2005, Daddy's Little Girls 2007, The Reaping 2007, 28 Weeks Later 2007, American Gangster 2007, This Christmas 2007, Prom Night 2008, RocknRolla 2008, The Human Contract 2008, The Unborn 2009, Obsessed (BET Award for Best Actor 2010) 2009, Legacy: Black Ops (also exec. producer) 2010, The Losers 2010, Takers (BET Award for Best Actor 2011) 2010, Thor 2011, Ghost Rider: Spirit of Vengeance 2011, Demons Never Die (exec. producer) 2011, Prometheus 2012, Pacific Rim 2013, Second Coming 2013, Thor: The Dark World 2013, Mandela: Long Walk to Freedom 2013, No Good Deed 2014, The Gunman 2015, Avengers: Age of Ultron 2015, Beasts of No Nation (Screen Actors Guild Award for Outstanding Performance by a Male Actor in a Supporting Role 2016) 2015, Zootropolis (voice) 2016, Bastille Day 2016, The Jungle Book (voice) 2016, Star Trek Beyond 2016, A Hundred Streets 2016, Star Trek Beyond 2016, The Dark Tower 2017, Thor: Ragnarok 2017, Yardie (dir) (Nat. Film Award for Best Dir 2019) 2018. *Music video:* Lover of the Light, Mumford and Sons (producer and star) 2012. *Radio includes:* Journey Dot Africa (BBC Radio 2) 2014. *Television includes:* Space Precinct 1994, The Bill (series) 1994–95, Absolutely Fabulous 1995, Bramwell (mini-series) 1995, Crucial Tales (mini-series) 1996, Crocodile Shoes II 1996, Family Affairs (series) 1997–98, Silent Witness (series) 1997, Ultraviolet 1998, Dangerfield 1999, In Defence 2000, The Inspector 2002, The Wire (series) 2002–04, Girlfriends (series) 2005, Sometimes in April (film) 2005, Jonny Zero (series) 2005, World of Trouble (film) 2005, All in the Game (film) 2006, Queens Supreme (series) 2007, The No. 1 Ladies' Detective Agency (series) 2008, The Office 2009, Luther (series) (also producer) (NAACP Image Award for Outstanding Actor in a Television Movie, Mini-Series, or Dramatic Special 2011, Golden Globe Award for Best Actor–Miniseries or Television Film 2012, Black Reel Award for Best Actor: TV Movie/Cable 2012, Screen Actors Guild Award for Outstanding Performance by a Male Actor in a Television Movie or Miniseries 2016) 2010–, Call of Duty: Modern Warfare 3 (video game) 2011, Idris Elba's How Clubbing Changed the World (presenter) 2012, Idris Elba: King of Speed (presenter) 2013, Idris Elba: No Limits (presenter) 2015, Idris Elba: Fighter (presenter) 2017, Turn Up Charlie (also exec. producer) 2019; exec. producer: Walk Like a Panther (series) 2010, How Hip Hop Changed the World (documentary) 2011. *Recordings include:* EPs: Big Man 2006, Kings Among Kings 2009, High Class Problems Vol. 1 2010, Idris Elba Presents Mi Mandela 2014. *Leisure interest:* Arsenal Football Club. *Address:* c/o WME Entertainment, 100 New Oxford Street, London, WC1A 1HB, England (office). *Telephone:* (20) 8929-8400 (office). *Website:* wmeentertainment.com (office).

ELBAZ, Alber; Israeli designer; b. 12 June 1961, Casablanca, Morocco; partner Alex Koo; ed Shenkar Coll. of Textile Tech. and Fashion, Tel-Aviv; moved to New York, USA 1980s; worked for fashion firm for two years; worked for Geoffrey Beene, New York 1989–96, Guy Laroche, Paris, France 1997–98; designer of Rive Gauche ready-to-wear womenswear line, Yves Saint Laurent, Paris 1998–2001; designer for Krizia, Milan 2000–01; Creative Dir Lanvin, Paris 2001–15; Chevalier, Légion d'honneur 2007; Dr hc (Royal Coll. of Art) 2014; International Award, Council of Fashion Designers of America 2005, named amongst the 100 Most Influential People in the World by Time magazine 2007, Geoffrey Beene Fashion Impact Award 2013, Grande Médaille de Vermeil de la Ville de Paris 2009, Superstar Award, Fashion Group International 2015. *Publication:* a book of 3,000 photographs documenting the work of Lanvin 2012.

ELBEGDORJ, Tsakhiagiin, MA; Mongolian politician and fmr head of state; b. 30 March 1963, Zereg Som, Hovd Prov.; m.; two c.; ed Harvard Univ., USA; machinist, Erdenet copper mine 1981–82; army service 1982; mil. reporter, Mil. School, Lvov, Ukraine 1983–88; journalist, Ulaan-Od (Ministry of Defence newspaper) 1988–90; mem. Co-ordinating Council of Mongolian Democratic Union (MDU) 1989, Leader 1990; Deputy to People's Great Hural 1990–92, also mem. State Little Hural; mem. State Great Hural 1992–94, 1996, Vice-Chair. 1996–98; mem. Democratic Party–DP 1994, Leader 1996–2000, 2006–08, also Leader Democratic Union coalition in State Great Hural; Prime Minister of Mongolia April–Dec. 1998, 2004–06; Pres. of Mongolia 2009–17. *Address:* c/o State Palace, Ulan Bator 12 (office); Democratic Party, CPOB 578, Sükhbaatar District, Ulan Bator, Mongolia (office). *Telephone:* (11) 320355 (office). *Fax:* (11) 323755 (office). *E-mail:* info@demparty.mn (office). *Website:* www.demparty.mn (office).

ELDER, Sir Mark Philip, Kt, CH, CBE, BA, MA (Hons); British conductor; *Music Director, Hallé Orchestra;* b. 2 June 1947, Hexham; s. of John Elder and Helen Elder; m. Amanda Jane Stein 1980; one d.; ed Bryanston School and Corpus Christi Coll., Cambridge; mem. music staff, Wexford Festival 1969–70; Chorus Master and Asst Conductor Glyndebourne 1970–71; mem. music staff, Royal Opera House, Covent Garden 1970–72; Staff Conductor, Australian Opera 1972–74; Staff Conductor, ENO 1974–77, Assoc. Conductor 1977–79, Music Dir 1979–93; Prin. Guest Conductor London Mozart Players 1980–83, BBC Symphony Orchestra 1982–85, City of Birmingham Symphony Orchestra 1992–95; Music Dir Rochester Philharmonic Orchestra, NY 1989–94, Hallé Orchestra, Manchester, UK 2000–; Artistic Dir Opera Rara 2011–; Pres. London Philharmonic Choir 2014–; Hon. FRNCM; Hon. Fellow, Corpus Christi Coll., Cambridge 2010; Hon. mem. Royal Philharmonic Soc. 2011; Dr hc (Manchester) 2003, (Sheffield) 2006, (Open Univ.) 2009, (RAM) 2012; Olivier Award for Outstanding Contrib. to Opera 1990, Royal Philharmonic Soc. Award for Conductor 2006. *Recordings include:* with Hallé Orchestra, Choir and Youth Chorus: Elgar: The Apostles (BBC Music Magazine Choral Award and Recording of the Year 2013, Gramophone Choral Award 2013), Cilea: Adriana Lecouvreur (Int. Classical Music Award for DVD Performance 2013), Donizetti: Le Duc d'Albe 2016, Edward Elgar & Arnold Bax: For The Fallen 2017. *Address:* c/o Groves Artists Ltd, 7 St George's Court, 131 Putney Bridge Road, London, SW15 2PA, England (office); Hallé Concerts Society, The Bridgewater Hall, Manchester, M1 5HA, England (home). *Telephone:* (20) 8874-3222 (office). *E-mail:* info@grovesartists.com (office). *Website:* www.grovesartists.com (office); www.halle.co.uk (office).

ELDER, Murdoch George, DSc, MD, FRCS, FRCOG; British physician and academic; *Professor Emeritus of Obstetrics and Gynaecology, Imperial College London;* b. 4 Jan. 1938, Kolkata, India; s. of A. J. Elder and L. A. C. Elder; m. Margaret McVicker 1964; two s.; ed Edinburgh Acad. and Edinburgh Univ.; lecturer, Royal Univ. of Malta 1969–71; Sr Lecturer and Reader, Univ. of London, Charing Cross Hosp. Medical School 1971–78; Prof. of Obstetrics and Gynaecology, Univ. of London at Hammersmith Hosp. 1978–98; Dean, Royal Postgraduate Medical School Inst. of Obstetrics and Gynaecology 1985–95; Chair. Div. of Paediatrics, Obstetrics and Gynaecology, Imperial Coll. School of Medicine, Univ. of London 1996–98, Prof. Emer. 1998–; Visiting Prof. UCLA 1984, 1986, 1997, Univ. of Singapore 1987, Univ. of Natal 1988; consultant to WHO and other int. orgs; mem. WHO Scientific and Ethics Research Group; External Examiner to Univs of Edin., Cambridge, Oxford, London, Leeds, Bristol, Glasgow, Dundee, Malta, Malaya, Malaysia, Helsinki, Rotterdam, Cape Town, Singapore; Hon. Fellow, Imperial Coll. School of Medicine 2001; Silver Medal, Hellenic Obstetrical Soc. 1984, Bronze Medal, Helsinki Univ. 1996. *Publications include:* Human Fertility Control (co-author) 1979, Preterm Labor (co-ed.) 1981 and 1996, Obstetrics and Gynaecology 2002; more than 240 original publs in field of biochemistry of reproduction and clinical high-risk obstetrics. *Leisure interests:* travel, golf. *Address:* Burnholm, Broughton, Biggar, ML12 6HQ, Scotland. *Telephone:* (1899) 830359. *E-mail:* melder@eastercalzeat.fsnet.co.uk.

ELDERFIELD, John, PhD; American art historian and museum curator; *Allen R. Adler, Class of 1967, Distinguished Curator and Lecturer, Princeton University;*

b. 25 April 1943, Yorks., UK; ed Univ. of Leeds and Courtauld Inst. of Art, UK; joined Museum of Modern Art, New York 1975, has held several positions, including Chief Curator at Large –2003, Chief Curator of Painting and Sculpture 2003–08 (retd), Chief Curator Emer. 2008–; Ind. Curator and Art Historian, Gagosian Gallery 2012–; Allen R. Adler, Class of 1967, Distinguished Curator and Lecturer, Princeton Univ. 2015–; mem. Bd of Dirs Dedalus Foundation, Phillips Collection, American Advisory Cttee, Courtauld Inst. of Art, Asscn of Literary Scholars, Critics and Writers; Fellow, John Simon Guggenheim Memorial Foundation 1972; Visiting Fellow, Getty Research Inst. 2001; Assoc. Fellow, American Acad. in Rome 2006; Hon. mem. Proyecto Armando Reverón, Caracas; Officier des Arts et des Lettres 2006; Mitchell Prize in Twentieth-Century Art (for Kurt Schwitters) 1986. *Publications include:* Modern Painting and Sculpture: 1880 to Present at the Museum of Modern Art, Henri Matisse: A Retrospective, Helen Frankenthaler, Language of the Body; numerous scholarly articles. *Address:* Princeton University Art Museum, McCormick Hall, Princeton, NJ 08542, USA (office). *Telephone:* (609) 258-3788 (office). *Website:* artmuseum .princeton.edu (office).

ELDIN, Gérard, Licence ès Lettres, Licence en Droit; French civil servant and banker; b. 21 March 1927, Cannes; s. of Charles Eldin and Elise Eldin; m. Marie-Cécile Bergerot 1960; two s. two d.; ed Bethany Coll., USA, Univ. d'Aix-en-Provence and Ecole Nat. d'Admin, Paris; Insp. of Finances 1954–58; served in the Treasury 1958–63; Adviser to Minister of Finance and Econ. Affairs 1963–65; Deputy Dir Dept of Planning 1965–70; Deputy Sec.-Gen. OECD 1970–80; Deputy Gov. Crédit Foncier de France 1980–86; Chair. Foncier-Investissement 1982–86, Crédit-Logement 1986–87, 1995–96; Chair. Banque centrale de compensation 1987–90; Chair. Foncier-court terme Sicav 1988–96; Chair. and CEO Soc. d'études immobilières et d'expertises foncières (Foncier-Expertise) 1990–96; Dir Compagnie foncière de France 1980–93, Soc. immobilière Paix-Daunou 1987–93, Soc. des Immeubles de France 1993–2000; Hon. Inspecteur Général des Finances; Chevalier, Légion d'honneur, Commdr, Ordre nat. du Mérite. *Publications:* Avenue des Broussailes, Souvenirs d'enfance et de jeunesse (1927–1951) 2009. *Leisure interests:* singing, local history. *Address:* 32 rue des Archives, 75004 Paris, France (home). *Telephone:* 1-44-54-09-83 (home). *E-mail:* eldingmc@wanadoo.fr.

ELDON, David Gordon, CBE, JP, FCIB; British business executive; *Vice-Chairman, Noble Group;* with HSBC Group, based in Middle and Far East 1968–2005, mem. Bd of Dirs HSBC Holdings and Chair. Hongkong and Shanghai Banking Corpn Ltd –2005 (retd); currently Sr Adviser, PricewaterhouseCoopers, Hong Kong; mem. Bd of Dirs, Noble Group Ltd 2007, later Ind. Chair. (non-exec.), currently Vice-Chair.; Chair. (non-exec.), Dubai Int. Financial Centre Authority; Deputy Chair. Hong Kong Jockey Club; mem. Bd of Dirs, Mass Transit Railway Corpn, Hong Kong, Eagle Asset Man. Ltd, China Central Properties Ltd; fmr Chair. Hong Kong Gen. Chamber of Commerce; Founding mem. and Past Chair. Seoul Int. Business Advisory Council; Int. Council mem. Bretton Woods Cttee; Adviser to Unisys; Hon. Citizenship of Seoul 2005; Gold Bauhinia Star, Govt of Hong Kong Special Admin. Region 2004; Hon. DBA (City Univ. of Hong Kong); Dr hc (Hong Kong Acad. for Performing Arts) 2011; named DHL/SCMP Hong Kong Business Person of the Year 2003, Asian Banker Lifetime Achievement Award 2006. *Address:* Noble Group Ltd, 18th Floor, Mass Mutual Tower, 38 Gloucester Road, Hong Kong Special Administrative Region, People's Republic of China (office). *Telephone:* 2861-3511 (office). *Fax:* 2527-0282 (office). *E-mail:* noble@ thisisnoble.com (office). *Website:* www.thisisnoble.com (office).

ELDON, Sir Stewart Graham, KCMG, OBE, CMG, MSc, MIEE; British diplomatist; *Senior Adviser on Defence and Security, Transparency International;* b. 18 Sept. 1953, Accra, Ghana; m. Christine Mason 1978; one s. one d.; ed Pocklington School, Yorks. and Christ's Coll., Cambridge; entered FCO 1976, UK Mission New York 1976, Asst Desk Officer, UN Dept, FCO 1977–78, Third (later Second) Sec., British Embassy, Bonn 1978–82, Head of Section, Repub. of Ireland Dept, FCO 1982–83, Minister of State, FCO 1983–86, First Sec., Chancery, UK Mission, New York 1986–90, Deputy Head, Middle East Dept, FCO 1990–91, seconded to Cabinet Office 1991–93, Fellow, Center for Int. Affairs, Harvard Univ. 1993–94, Political Counsellor, UK Del. to NATO/WEU 1994–97, Dir of Confs, FCO 1997–98, Deputy Perm. Rep., UK Mission to UN, New York 1998–2002; Visiting Fellow, Yale Univ. 2002; Amb. to Ireland 2003–06; UK Perm. Rep. to NATO, Brussels 2006–10, NATO Subject Matter Expert on Building Integrity 2010–; Sr Adviser on Defence and Security, Transparency International 2010–; Ind. mem. Parole Bd for England and Wales 2010–; Partner, The Ambassador Partnership 2010–; Sr Civil Adviser, UK Higher Command and Staff Course 2012–; mem. Advisory Council, Joint Services Command and Staff Coll. 2013–; Visiting Fellow, Yale Univ. 2002. *Publication:* From Quill Pen to Satellite: Foreign Ministries in the Information Age 1994. *Leisure interests:* travel, good food, reading science fiction, breaking computers. *Address:* Transparency International, CAN Mezzanine, 32–36 Loman Street, London, SE1 0EH, England (office). *Telephone:* (20) 7922-7906 (office). *Fax:* (20) 7922-7907 (office). *E-mail:* enquiries@stewarteldon.com (office). *Website:* www.transparency.org (office); www.stewarteldon.com.

ELENOVSKI, Lazar, BA; Macedonian politician, diplomatist and international organization official; *Special Representative to NATO;* b. 19 March 1971, Skopje; s. of Akeksandar Elenovski and Mirusha Elenovski; m.; two c.; ed Faculty of Econs, Sts Cyril and Methodius Univ., Skopje; fmr Deputy CEO JSP (public transport co.); joined Social Democratic Alliance of Macedonia, f. Social Democratic Youth of Macedonia 1992, Sec.-Gen. 1996–99, Pres. 1999–2001; f. Young Europeans for Security (YES Macedonia) 1995; mem. Presidency, Social-Democratic Union of Macedonia 1997–2003; Sec.-Gen. Euro-Atlantic Club of Macedonia 2001–05; Pres. Euro-Atlantic Council of Macedonia 2005–12; Amb. to Belgium 2012–16; Co-founder Cen. and South Eastern European Security Forum (Balkan Mosaic); Minister of Defence 2006–08; Special Rep. of the Govt to NATO 2018–; mem. Atlantic Treaty Asscn, Vice-Pres. 2011–. *Publications:* numerous articles on the Euro-Atlantic integration process, the Balkan region, and security sector reforms. *Leisure interest:* philosophy. *Address:* Embassy of North Macedonia, 20 rue Vilain XIV, 1050 Brussels, Belgium (office). *Telephone:* (2) 734-56-87 (office). *Fax:* (2) 732-07-17 (office). *E-mail:* ambassade.mk@skynet.be (office); lazar.elenovski@ata-sec .org.

ELFMAN, Danny; American film music composer and musician (guitar); b. 29 May 1953, Amarillo, Tex.; m. Bridget Fonda 2003; lead singer, rhythm guitarist and songwriter eight-piece rock band, Oingo Bongo 1974–95; numerous songs and scores for films, TV programmes and computer games; Grammy Award for Best Instrumental Composition (for The Batman Theme) 1990, Frederick Loewe Award for Film Composing 2004, Hollywood Film Festival Composer of the Year 2008. *Music for film:* Forbidden Zone 1980, Fast Times at Ridgemont High 1982, Bachelor Party 1984, Surf II 1984, Beverly Hills Cop 1984, Weird Science 1985, Pee-Wee's Big Adventure 1985, Wisdom 1986, Something Wild 1986, Back to School 1986, Summer School 1987, Hot to Trot 1988, Big Top Pee-Wee 1988, Beetlejuice 1988, Midnight Run 1988, Scrooged 1988, 1989, Ghostbusters II 1989, Dick Tracy 1990, Nightbreed 1990, Darkman 1990, Edward Scissorhands 1990, Pure Luck 1991, Batman Returns 1992, Article 99 1992, Army of Darkness 1993, Sommersby 1993, The Nightmare Before Christmas (Saturn Award for Best Music 1993) 1993, Black Beauty 1994, Dolores Claiborne 1995, To Die For 1995, Dead Presidents 1995, Mission: Impossible 1996, The Frighteners 1996, Freeway 1996, Extreme Measures 1996, Mars Attacks! (Saturn Award for Best Music 1996) 1996, Men In Black (Saturn Award for Best Music 1997) 1997, Flubber 1997, Good Will Hunting 1997, Scream 2 1997, A Simple Plan 1998, A Civil Action 1998, My Favorite Martian 1999, Instinct 1999, Anywhere But Here 1999, Sleepy Hollow (Saturn Award for Best Music 1999) 1999, The Family Man 2000, Proof of Life 2000, Spy Kids 2001, Planet of the Apes 2001, Heartbreakers 2001, Mazer World 2001, Novocaine 2001, Spider-Man (Saturn Award for Best Music 2002) 2002, Men in Black II 2002, Red Dragon 2002, Chicago 2002, Hulk 2003, Big Fish 2003, Spider-Man 2 2004, Charlie and the Chocolate Factory 2005, Charlotte's Web 2006, Spider-Man 3 2007, Hellboy II: The Golden Army 2008, Wanted 2008, Standard Operating Procedure 2008, Milk 2008, Notorious 2009, Terminator Salvation 2009, Taking Woodstock 2009, The Wolf Man 2009, Men in Black III 2012, Dark Shadows 2012, Promised Land 2012, Hitchcock 2012, Oz the Great and Powerful 2013, Epic 2013, Mr Peabody & Sherman 2014, The Unknown Known 2014, Fifty Shades of Grey 2015, Avengers: Age of Ultron 2015, Goosebumps 2015, Before I Wake 2016, Alice Through the Looking Glass 2016. *Music for television:* Amazing Stories 1985, Alfred Hitchcock Presents 1985, Fast Times 1986, Sledge Hammer! 1986, Pee-Wee's Playhouse 1986, Tales from the Crypt 1989, The Simpsons 1989, Beetlejuice 1989, The Flash 1990, Batman 1992, Family Dog 1993, Weird Science 1994, Perversions of Science 1997, Dilbert 1999, Desperate Housewives (Emmy Award for Outstanding Main Title Theme Music 2005) 2004. *Recordings:* albums with Oingo Boingo: Only A Lad 1981, Nothing To Fear 1982, Good For Your Soul 1983, Dead Man's Party 1985, Boingo 1986, Skeletons In The Closet 1989, Dark At The End Of The Tunnel 1990, Article 99 1992. *Address:* c/o Kraft-Engel Management, 15233 Ventura Boulevard, Suite 200, Sherman Oaks, CA 91403, USA (office). *Telephone:* (818) 380-1918 (office). *E-mail:* info@ Kraft-Engel.com (office). *Website:* www.Kraft-Engel.com (office).

ELIA LOMURO, Martin; South Sudanese politician; *Minister of Cabinet Affairs;* b. Central Equatoria; ed Zagazig Univ., Egypt; went into exile after military takeover 1989; returned to South Sudan after independence 2005; Minister of Animal Resources and Fisheries (in first govt of Repub. of South Sudan) 2005; Minister of Cabinet Affairs 2015–, also Acting Minister of Foreign Affairs and Int. Co-operation April–July 2018; Chair. South Sudan Democratic Forum. *Address:* Ministry of Cabinet Affairs, Juba, South Sudan (office).

ELIADES, Demetris J.; Cypriot lawyer and politician; b. 1947, Lefkoniko, Famagusta Dist; m. Angeliki Hadjisavva; one s. one d.; ed Lefkoniko Greek Gymnasium, Univ. of Athens; founded Demetris J. Eliades & Co. LLC 1980, currently Advocate and Man. Dir; mem. House of Reps 1985–2001, Chair. Parl. Environment Cttee, mem. Law Cttee; Minister of Agric., Natural Resources and Environment 2010–11, of Defence 2011–13; mem. Bd of Dirs Hellenic Bank 2005–10; mem. Exec. Cttee Commonwealth Parl. Asscn; mem. European Exec. Cttee Commonwealth Parl. Asscn of Legislation 1990–; mem. European Asscn of Legislation 1990–. *Address:* Demetris J. Eliades & Co. LLC, 4 Agias Elenis Street, 5th Floor, Michaelides Building, 1060 Nicosia, Cyprus (office). *Telephone:* 22755100 (office). *Fax:* 22755106 (office). *E-mail:* d.eliades@delaw.com.cy (office). *Website:* www.delaw.com.cy (office).

ELIAS, Olufemi, BA, MA, LLM, PhD; Nigerian international lawyer and UN official; *Assistant Secretary-General and Registrar of the Mechanism, United Nations International Residual Mechanism for Criminal Tribunals (IRMCT);* b. Lagos; s. of Taslim Elias; ed Univ. of London, Univ. of Cambridge, Univ. of Oxford; Legal Adviser, UN Compensation Comm. 1998–05; Sr Legal Officer, Org. for the Prohibition of Chemical Weapons (OPCW) 2005–08, Legal Adviser and Dir 2013–16; Exec. Sec., World Bank Admin. Tribunal 2008–13, July–Nov. 2016; Asst Sec.-Gen. and Registrar of the Mechanism, UN Int. Residual Mechanism for Criminal Tribunals (IRMCT) 2017–; fmr Lecturer, King's Coll. London, Univ. of Buckingham; Visiting Prof. of Int. Law, Queen Mary Univ. of London; Sec.-Gen. African Asscn of Int. Law; mem. Exec. Council American Soc. of Int. Law; Assoc. mem. Institut de Droit Int.; mem. Nigerian Bar Asscn; Hon. Membership Award, American Soc. of Int. Law 2018. *Publications:* has written widely on various aspects of public int. law. *Address:* International Residual Mechanism for Criminal Tribunals, Haki Road, Plot No. 486, Block A, Lakilaki Area, Arumeru District, POB 6016, Arusha, Tanzania (office); Churchillplein 1, 2517 JW, The Hague, Netherlands (office). *Telephone:* (27) 2565791 (Arusha) (office); (70) 5125101 (Hague) (office). *E-mail:* mict-registryarusha@un.org (office). *Website:* www.irmct .org (office).

ELIAS, Rt Hon. Dame Sian, GNZM, PC, LLB, QC; New Zealand lawyer; m. Hugh Fletcher; ed Auckland Univ., Stanford Univ., USA; worked for Turner Hopkins & Partners 1972–75; barrister 1975–88; QC 1988; Law Commr and Chair. ICI Cttee of Inquiry 1989–90; apptd High Court Judge 1995; involved in litigation concerning Treaty of Waitangi 1987; sat on Court of Appeal 1998–99; Chief Justice 1999–2019 (retd); Acting Gov.-Gen. March–April 2001, Aug. 2006, Aug. 2011; mem. Motor Sports Licensing Appeal Authority 1984–88, Working Party on the Environment 1984; Commemorative Medal for Services to the Legal Profession 1990; Dame Grand Companion, NZ Order of Merit. *Address:* c/o Chief Justice's Chambers, DX SX 10084, Wellington, New Zealand (office).

ELÍAS AYUB, Alfredo, BS, MBA; Mexican civil servant and energy industry executive; *Chairman, Promociones Metropolis SA de CV;* b. 13 Jan. 1950, Mexico City; s. of Alfredo Elías Aiza and Sylvia Ayub; m. Begona Garcia; four s.; ed Anáhuac Univ., Harvard Univ., USA; has held numerous public sector posts including Exec. Co-ordinator of Urban Devt, Secr. of Public Works and Dir, Nat. Fund for Social Activities; worked for nine years at Secr. of Energy, Mines and Govt-controlled Industry holding positions on Coordinating Comm. of Advisors to Sec., Under-Secr. of Mines and Basic Industry, Under-Secr. of Energy; fmr CEO and Pres. Airports and Auxiliary Services; Gen. Dir Comisión Federal de Electricidad 1999–2011; Dir, Azteca Acquisition Corpn 2011–; Ind. Dir, Grupo Aeroportuario del Pacifico S.A.B. de CV 2012–14, Arcos Dorados Holdings, Inc. 2012–, Iberdrola USA, Inc. 2014–; currently Chair. Promociones Metropolis SA de CV (family real-estate business); mem. Deans' Bd of Advisors, Harvard Business School 2010–; fmr Dir School of Eng, Anáhuac Univ.; fmr Chair. Devt Bd, Anáhuac Univ., Mexico Foundation, Harvard Univ. *Address:* Iberdrola USA, Inc., 52 Farm View Drive, New Gloucester, ME 04260, USA (office). *Telephone:* (207) 688-6300 (office). *E-mail:* info@iberdrolausa.com (office). *Website:* www.iberdrolausa.com (office).

ELIASHBERG, Yakov, PhD; American (b. Russian) mathematician and academic; *Herald L. and Caroline L. Ritch Professor of Mathematics, Stanford University;* b. 11 Dec. 1946, Leningrad, Russian SFSR, USSR; ed Leningrad State Univ.; Assoc. Prof., Syktyvkar State Univ., Komi Repub., Russian SFSR 1972–79, Chair. Dept of Math. 1975–79; head of computer software group 1980–87; moved to USA 1988; with Math. Sciences Research Inst., Berkeley, Calif. 1988–89; Prof. of Math., Stanford Univ. 1989–2007, fmr Chair. Math. Dept, currently Herald L. and Caroline L. Ritch Prof. of Math.; Eilenberg Visiting Prof., Columbia Univ. 2007; mem. NAS 2002; Fellow, American Math. Soc. 2012; Dr hc (École normale supérieure, Lyon) 2009; Prize of Leningrad Math. Soc. 1972, Invited Speaker, Int. Congress of Mathematicians 1986, 1998, 2006 (Plenary Lecturer), Guggenheim Fellowship 1995, Oswald Veblen Prize in Geometry, American Math. Soc. 2001, Heinz Hopf Prize, ETH, Zurich (co-recipient) 2013, Crafoord Prize (Math.), Royal Swedish Acad. of Sciences 2016. *Publications:* numerous papers in professional journals. *Address:* Room 383-S, 450 Serra Mall, Building 380, Stanford University, Stanford, CA 94305-2125, USA (office). *Telephone:* (650) 723-4073 (office). *Fax:* (650) 725-4066 (office). *E-mail:* eliash@math.stanford.edu (office). *Website:* mathematics.stanford.edu (office).

ELIASSON, Jan Kenneth Glenn, MA; Swedish diplomatist, politician and UN official; *Chairman, Governing Board, Stockholm International Peace Research Institute;* b. 17 Sept. 1940, Göteborg; s. of John H. Eliasson and Karin Eliasson (née Nilsson); m. Kerstin Englesson 1967; one s. two d.; ed School of Econs, Göteborg; entered Foreign Service 1965; Swedish OECD Del., Paris 1967; at Swedish Embassy, Bonn 1967–70; First Sec. Swedish Embassy, Washington 1970–74; Head of Section, Political Dept, Ministry for Foreign Affairs, Stockholm 1974–75; Personal Asst to the Under-Sec. of State for Foreign Affairs 1975–77; Dir Press and Information Div., Ministry for Foreign Affairs 1977–80, Asst Under-Sec., Head of Div. for Asian and African Affairs, Political Dept 1980–82; Foreign Policy Adviser, Prime Minister's Office 1982–83; Under-Sec. for Political Affairs, Stockholm 1983–87; Perm. Rep. of Sweden to UN, New York 1988–92; Chair. UN Trust Fund for SA 1988–92; Personal Rep. to UN Sec.-Gen. on Iran-Iraq 1988–92; Vice-Pres. ECOSOC 1991–92; Under-Sec.-Gen. for Humanitarian Affairs, UN 1992–94; Chair. Minsk Conf. on Nagornyi Karabakh 1994; State Sec. for Foreign Affairs 1994–2000; Amb. to USA 2000–05; Pres. 60th UN General Ass. 2005–06; Minister of Foreign Affairs April–Oct. 2006; Special Envoy of the UN Sec.-Gen. for Darfur 2006–08; apptd Sr Visiting Scholar, US Inst. of Peace 2008; Deputy Sec.-Gen. UN 2012–16; Chair. Governing Bd, Stockholm Int. Peace Research Inst. (SIPRI) 2017–; Sec. to Swedish Foreign Policy Advisory Bd 1983–87; Expert, Royal Swedish Defence Comm. 1984–86; Dir Inst. for East–West Security Studies, New York 1989–93, Int. Peace Acad. 1989–2001; fmr Guest Prof., Uppsala Univ.; Chair. WaterAid, Sweden 2009–12; mem. of UN Sec.-Gen.'s Advocacy Group of the Millennium Development Goals; Dr hc (American Univ. Washington, DC) 1994, (Gothenburg) 2001, (Bethany Coll., Kansas) 2005, (Uppsala) 2006. *Leisure interests:* art, literature, sports. *Address:* Stockholm International Peace Research Institute, Signalistgatan 9, SE- 169 72 Solna, Sweden (office). *Telephone:* (8) 655-97-00 (office). *Website:* www.sipri.org (office).

ELIASSON, Olafur; Danish artist; b. 1967, Copenhagen; ed Royal Danish Acad. of Fine Arts, Copenhagen; est. Studio Olafur Eliasson as a lab. for spatial research in Berlin 1995; represented Denmark at 50th Venice Biennale 2003; installed The Weather Project in Turbine Hall of Tate Modern, London 2003; Prof., Berlin Univ. of the Arts, f. Institut für Raumexperimente (Inst. for Spatial Experiments) 2009–14; lives and works in Copenhagen and Berlin. *E-mail:* studio@olafureliasson.net. *Website:* www.olafureliasson.net.

ELIZABETH II, HM Queen (Elizabeth Alexandra Mary), (Queen of Great Britain and Northern Ireland and of Her other Realms and Territories), (see Reigning Royal Families section for full titles); b. 21 April 1926, London; d. of HRH Prince Albert, Duke of York (later HM King George VI) and Duchess of York (later HM Queen Elizabeth The Queen Mother); succeeded to The Throne following Her father's death 6 Feb. 1952; married 20 Nov. 1947, HRH The Prince Philip, The Duke of Edinburgh (q.v.), b. 10 June 1921; children: Prince Charles Philip Arthur George, Prince of Wales (q.v.) (heir apparent), b. 14 Nov. 1948; Princess Anne Elizabeth Alice Louise, The Princess Royal (q.v.), b. 15 Aug. 1950; Prince Andrew Albert Christian Edward, Duke of York (q.v.), b. 19 Feb. 1960; Prince Edward Antony Richard Louis, Earl of Wessex, b. 10 March 1964. *Address:* Buckingham Palace, London, SW1A 1AA; Windsor Castle, Berkshire, SL4 1NJ, England; Balmoral Castle, Aberdeenshire, AB35 5TB, Scotland; Sandringham House, Norfolk, PE35 6EN, England; Palace of Holyroodhouse, Edinburgh, Scotland. *Website:* www.royal.gov.uk.

ELIZONDO BARRAGÁN, Fernando, LicenDer, MJ, MBA; Mexican lawyer, business executive and politician; *Executive Director of State Government of the State of Nuevo León;* b. 6 Jan. 1949, Monterrey, Nuevo León; s. of Eduardo Elizondo; m. Verónica Ortiz Salinas; two d.; ed Centro Univ. Monterrey (CUM), Univ. of Nuevo León, New York Univ., USA; laywer, Monterrey 1972–79, 1986–94; various positions in legal div., Grupo Industrial Alfa 1979–89; Co-ordinator CANACO Monterrey, CAINTRA Nuevo León and COPARMEX Nuevo León 1988–92; mem. Civic Council of Nuevo León 1988–92; Exec. Pres. Grupo Salinas y Rocha 1995–97; Sec. of Finance and the Treasury, State of Nuevo León 1997–2003; Gov. (interim) of State of Nuevo León 2003; Sec. of Energy of Mexico and Chair. Petróleos Mexicanos (PEMEX) 2004–05; mem. Senate 2006–12; unsuccessful cand. for Gov. of Nuevo León 2009, 2015; Co-founder Panistas por México; Exec. Dir of State Govt of State of Nuevo León 2015–; del. to numerous int. confs and orgs. *Website:* www.nl.gob.mx (office).

ELKANN, John Jacob Philip; American/Italian automotive industry executive; *Chairman, Fiat Chrysler Automobiles NV;* b. 1 April 1976, New York, NY, USA; s. of Alain Elkann and Margherita 'Daisy' Agnelli de Pahlen; grandson of Gianni Agnelli (fmr Chair. of Fiat); m. Donna Lavinia Borromeo 2004; two s. one d.; ed Lycée Victor Duruy, Paris, Politecnico di Torino; spent his childhood travelling with his parents and siblings between UK, Brazil and France; mem. Bd of Dirs, Fiat 1997–; analyst, Gen. Electric Co. 2000, later mem. Corp. Audit Group 2001–02; returned to Turin to work with Fiat family business 2002, Vice-Chair. Fiat SpA 2004–10, Chair. 2010–, Chair. Fiat Chrysler Automobiles NV 2014–, Investment Man. IFIL SpA (investment co., one of Agnelli-family holding cos) 2003–06, Vice-Chair. 2006–; Chair. and CEO EXOR SpA; Chair. IFI SpA 2007–, Giovanni Agnelli e C. Sapaz 2010–; Chair. Cushman & Wakefield, Editrice La Stampa, PartnerRe, Italiana Editrice; mem. Bd, CNH Industrial, The Economist Group, News Corporation, Ferrari, Gruppo Banca Leonardo SpA; Vice-Chair. Fondazione Giovanni Agnelli, Italian Aspen Inst.; mem. Confindustria, Fondazione Italia-Cina; mem. Bd of Dirs Le Monde, News Corp 2013–; mem. Int. Advisory Council Brookings Inst., Museum of Modern Art, New York. *Leisure interest:* Juventus football club. *Address:* FCA Group, Via Nizza 250, 10126 Turin (office); EXOR SpA, Via Nizza 250, 10126 Turin, Italy (office). *Telephone:* (011) 006-2709 (Fiat) (office); (011) 5090248 (EXOR) (office). *Fax:* (011) 006-3796 (Fiat) (office); (011) 5090330 (EXOR) (office). *E-mail:* investor.relations@fcagroup.com (office); governance@exor.com (office). *Website:* www.fcagroup.com (office); www.exor.com (office).

ELLEDGE, Stephen Joseph, BSc, PhD; American geneticist, molecular biologist and academic; *Gregor Mendel Professor of Genetics, Harvard Medical School;* b. 7 Aug. 1956, Paris, Ill.; m. Prof. Mitzi Kuroda; ed Univ. of Illinois, Urbana-Champaign, Massachusetts Inst. of Tech.; apptd Post-doctoral Fellow, Stanford Univ. 1984; Asst Prof., Biochemistry Dept, Baylor Coll. of Medicine 1989–93, Assoc. Prof. 1993–95, Prof. 1995–2003, apptd Investigator, Howard Hughes Medical Inst. 1993; joined Genetics Dept, Harvard Medical School and Div. of Genetics, Brigham and Women's Hospital 2003, currently Gregor Mendel Prof. of Genetics; mem. NAS 2003–, American Acad. of Arts and Sciences 2003–, American Acad. of Microbiology 2005–, Inst. of Medicine 2006–; Michael E. Debakey Award for Research Excellence 2002, G.H.A. Clowes Memorial Award, American Asscn of Cancer Research 2001, inaugural Paul Mark's Prize in Cancer Research 2001, NAS Award in Molecular Biology 2001, John B. Carter, Jr Technology Innovation Award 2002, NIH Merit Award 2003, Genetics Soc. of America Medal 2005, Hans Sigrist Int. Prize, Bern Univ. 2005, Dickson Prize in Medicine 2012, American Italian Cancer Foundation Prize for Scientific Excellence in Medicine 2012, Lewis Rosenstiel Award for Distinguished Work in Basic Medical Sciences 2013, Gairdner Foundation Int. Award 2013, Albert Lasker Basic Medical Research Award, Lasker Foundation (co-recipient) 2015. *Publications:* numerous papers in professional journals on the genetic and molecular mechanisms of eukaryotic response to DNA damage. *Address:* Department of Genetics, Harvard Medical School, Division of Genetics, Brigham and Women's Hospital, Room 158D, NRB, 77 Avenue Louis Pasteur, Boston, MA 02115, USA (office). *Telephone:* (617) 525-4510 (office). *Fax:* (617) 525-4500 (office). *E-mail:* selledge@genetics.med.harvard.edu (office). *Website:* elledgelab.med.harvard.edu (office); genetics.med.harvard.edu (office); www.hhmi.org/scientists/stephen-j-elledge (office).

ELLEMANN-JENSEN, Uffe, MA; Danish politician and international organization official; *Honorary Chairman, Baltic Development Forum;* b. 1 Nov. 1941; s. of Jens Peter Jensen; m. Alice Vestergaard 1971; two s. two d.; ed Univ. of Copenhagen; Danish Defence staff 1962–64; Sec., Meat Producers' Asscn 1964–67; journalist on Berlingske Aftenavis 1967–70; econ. and political corresp. Danish TV 1970–75; Ed.-in-Chief and mem. Bd daily newspaper Borsen 1975–76; mem. Parl. 1977–2001 (Liberal), Party Spokesperson, Political Affairs 1978–82, Chair. Parl. Market Cttee 1978–79; mem. Exec. Cttee Liberal Party 1979, Chair. 1984–98; mem. Bd Cen. Bank 1978–81, 1996–99, Index Figures' Bd 1979–81, Inter-Parl. Union 1979–82; Minister of Foreign Affairs 1982–93; Vice-Pres. European Liberal Party 1985–95, Pres. 1995–2000; Co-founder and Chair. Baltic Devt Forum 1998–2011, Hon. Chair. 2011–; Chair. Foreign Policy Soc., Denmark 1993–, Danish Centre for Int. Studies and Human Rights 2002–06, BankInvest (investment and venture capital firm) 2003–; Adjunct Prof., Copenhagen Business School 2006–; Dir Reuters Founders Share Co. Ltd 2000–; Trustee, Int. Crisis Group 1999–; mem. Bd Royal Theatre 2004, The Vaccine Fund 2005; Grand Cross, Order of the Dannebrog 2002, 8th of September Order (Fmr Yugoslav Repub. of Macedonia) 2010; Dr hc (Univ. of Gdansk) 2002; Robert Schuman Prize 1987, Hansa Prize 1993. *Publications:* De nye millionaerer (The New Millionaires) 1971, Det afhaengige samfund (The Dependent Society) 1972, Hvad gør vi ved Gudenåen (We Ought to Do Something About Gudenåen) 1973, Den truede velstand (The Threatened Wealth) 1974, Økonomi (Economy) 1975, Da Danmark igen sagde ja til det falles (When Denmark Repeated its Yes to Europe) 1987, Olfert Fischer 1991, Et lille land – og dog (A Small Country – And Yet) 1991, Din egen dag er kort (Short is Your Own Day) 1996, Ude med snøren (Going Fishing) 2001, Østen for solen (East of the Sun) 2002, Fodfejl (Foot Fault) 2004, Fodfejl: Da Danmark svigtede under den kolde krig 2005, Og Vejen jeg valgte 2007; numerous articles in newspapers and periodicals. *Leisure interests:* fishing, hunting, opera. *Address:* Baltic Development Forum, Nygade 3, 5th Floor, PO Box 56, 1002 Copenhagen K, Denmark (office). *Telephone:* 7020-9394 (office). *Fax:* 7020-9395 (office). *E-mail:* uffe@ellemann.dk (home); bdf@bdforum.org (office). *Website:* www.bdforum.org (office).

ELLINGSRUD, Geir, CandReal, PhD; Norwegian mathematician, academic and fmr university rector; *Professor of Mathematics, University of Oslo;* b. 29 Nov. 1948; ed Univ. of Oslo, Stockholm Univ., Sweden; Asst Lecturer, Univ. of Oslo 1973–80, Assoc. Prof. 1985–89, Prof. of Math. 1992–, Rector Univ. of Oslo 2006–09; Guest Prof., Univ. of Strasbourg, France 1980–81, Univ. of Nice, France 1982–83; Lecturer, Stockholm Univ. 1983–84; Prof. of Math., Univ. of Bergen 1989–92; Chevalier, Légion d'Honneur 2014. *Address:* University of Oslo, Department of Mathematics, Room 629, PO Box 1053, Blindern, 0316 Oslo, Norway (office).

Telephone: 22-85-58-88 (office). *Fax:* 22-85-43-49 (office). *E-mail:* ellingsr@math.uio.no (office). *Website:* www.math.uio.no (office).

ELLIOTT, Sir John Huxtable, Kt, MA, PhD, FBA; British historian and academic; *Regius Professor Emeritus of Modern History, University of Oxford;* b. 23 June 1930, Reading, Berks., England; s. of Thomas Charles Elliott and Janet Mary Payne; m. Oonah Sophia Butler 1958; ed Eton Coll. and Trinity Coll., Cambridge; Asst Lecturer in History, Univ. of Cambridge 1957–62, Lecturer 1962–67; Prof. of History, King's Coll., Univ. of London 1968–73; Prof., School of Historical Studies, Inst. for Advanced Study, Princeton, NJ 1973–90; Regius Prof. of Modern History, Univ. of Oxford 1990–97, now Prof. Emer.; Fellow, Oriel Coll., Oxford 1990–97; Fellow, Trinity Coll., Cambridge 1954–67; mem. Scientific Cttee, Prado Museum 1996; Fellow, Royal Acad. of History, Madrid, American Acad. of Arts and Sciences, American Philosophical Soc., King's Coll., Univ. of London 1998, Accad. Naz. dei Lincei 2003, Accad. delle Scienze di Torino 2009, Académico de honor, Real Academia de Buenas Letras de Sevilla 2009; Foreign Corresp. Fellow, Real Academia Española 2016; Hon. Fellow, Trinity Coll. Cambridge 1991, Oriel Coll. Oxford 1997, Lady Margaret Hall, Oxford 2013; Hon. Trustee, Prado Museum 2015; Commdr, Order of Alfonso X El Sabio 1984, Commdr, Order of Isabel la Católica 1987, Grand Cross of Order of Alfonso X, El Sabio 1988, Grand Cross of Order of Isabel la Católica 1996, Cross of Sant Jordi (Catalonia) 1999; Dr hc (Universidad Autónoma de Madrid) 1983, (Genoa) 1992, (Portsmouth) 1993, (Barcelona) 1994, (Warwick) 1995, (Brown) 1996, (Valencia) 1998, (Lleida) 1999, (Madrid Complutense) 2003, (Coll. of William and Mary) 2005, (London) 2007, (Carlos III, Madrid) 2008, (Seville) 2011, (Alcalá) 2012, (Cambridge) 2013, (Cantabria) 2015; Visitante Ilustre of Madrid 1983, Leo Gershoy Award, American Historical Asscn 1985, Wolfson Literary Award for History and Biography 1986, Medal of Honour, Universidad Int. Menéndez y Pelayo 1987, Gold Medal for Fine Arts (Spain) 1991, Eloy Antonio de Nebrija Prize (Univ. of Salamanca) 1993, Prince of Asturias Prize in Social Sciences 1996, Gold Medal, Spanish Inst., New York 1997, Balzan Prize for History 1500–1800 1999, Francis Parkman Prize 2007, Premio Órdenes Españolas 2018. *Publications include:* Imperial Spain, 1469–1716 1963, The Revolt of the Catalans 1963, Europe Divided, 1559–1598 1968, The Old World and the New, 1492–1650 1970, The Diversity of History (co-ed. with H. G. Koenigsberger) 1970, Memoriales y Cartas del Conde Duque de Olivares 1978–80, A Palace for a King (with J. Brown) 1980 (revised edn 2003), Richelieu and Olivares 1984, The Count-Duke of Olivares 1986, Spain and Its World 1500–1700 1989, The Hispanic World (ed.) 1991, The World of the Favourite (co-ed.) 1999, The Sale of the Century (with J. Brown) 2002, Empires of the Atlantic World (Francis Parkman Prize 2007) 2006, Spain, Europe and the Wider World 1500–1800 2009, History in the Making 2012, Scots and Catalans:Union and Disunion 2018. *Leisure interest:* looking at paintings. *Address:* 122 Church Way, Iffley, Oxford, OX4 4EG, England (home). *Telephone:* (1865) 716703 (home). *E-mail:* john.elliott@history.ox.ac.uk (office).

ELLIOTT, Marianne, OBE, DPhil, FRHistS, FBA; Irish historian and academic; *Professor Emerita, Institute of Irish Studies, University of Liverpool;* b. 25 May 1948, Northern Ireland; d. of Terence J. Burns and Sheila O'Neill; m. Trevor Elliott 1975 (died 2013); one s.; ed Dominican Convent, Fort William, Belfast, Queen's Univ. Belfast and Lady Margaret Hall, Oxford; French Govt research scholar in Paris 1972–73; other research in Ireland, UK, France, Netherlands and USA; Lecturer in History, West London Inst. of Higher Educ. 1975–77; Research Fellow, Univ. Coll. Swansea 1977–82; Visiting Prof., Iowa State Univ. 1983, Univ. of South Carolina 1984; Research Fellow, Univ. of Liverpool 1984–87; Simon Fellow, Univ. of Manchester 1988–89; Lecturer, Birkbeck Coll., Univ. of London 1991–93; Andrew Geddes and John Rankin Prof. of Modern History, Univ. of Liverpool 1993–2008, Dir Inst. of Irish Studies 1997–2014, Blair Chair of Irish Studies 2008–14, now Prof. Emerita; mem. Int. Opsahl Comm. on the Conflict in NI 1993, Encounter 1998–; Fellow, British Acad. 2000, section mem. of Modern History; Hon. MRIA 2016; Leo Gershoy Award for History 1983, Sunday Independent/Irish Life Award for Biography 1989, James Donnelly Sr Award for History (American Conf. for Irish Studies) 1991, Ford's Lecturer, Univ. of Oxford 2005. *Publications:* Partners in Revolution: The United Irishmen and France 1982, Watchmen in Sion: The Protestant Idea of Liberty 1985, The People's Armies (translation) 1987, Wolfe Tone: Prophet of Irish Independence 1989, A Citizens' Inquiry: The Report of the Opsahl Commission on Northern Ireland 1993, The Catholics in Ireland: A History 2000, The Long Road to Peace in Northern Ireland (ed.) 2001, Robert Emmet: The Making of a Legend 2003, When God Took Sides. Religion and Identity in Ireland, Unfinished History 2009. *Leisure interests:* running, swimming, cycling, following the tangleweed of Northern Irish identities. *Address:* Institute of Irish Studies, University of Liverpool, 1 Abercromby Square, Liverpool, L69 7WY, England (office). *Telephone:* (151) 794-3830 (office). *E-mail:* melliott@liverpool.ac.uk (office); irro@liv.ac.uk (office). *Website:* www.liv.ac.uk/irish (office).

ELLIOTT, Marianne Phoebe, OBE; British theatre director; *Artistic Director, Elliott and Harper Productions;* b. 27 Dec. 1966, Westminster; d. of Michael Eliott and Rosalind Knight; m. Nick Sidi; one d.; ed Hull Univ.; Casting Director and Drama Sec., Granada Television; Artistic Dir Elliott and Harper Productions 2016–; fmr Assoc. Dir, Nat. Theatre. *Plays include:* Dir: Saint Joan (Laurence Olivier Award for Best Revival) 2008, War Horse (Tony Award for Best Direction of a Play) 2011, 2014, Alice 2010, 2011, All's Well That Ends Well 2009, The Curious Incident of the Dog in the Night-Time (multiple awards for direction, including Laurence Olivier Award for Best Dir 2013, Tony Award for Best Direction of a Play 2015) 2012, Angels in America Part Two-Perestroika, Angels in America Part One-Millennium Approaches 2017, Company 2018. *E-mail:* nada@elliottharper.com. *Website:* www.elliottandharper.com.

ELLIS, Alexander Wykeham, CMG; British diplomatist; *Director-General, Department For Exiting the European Union;* b. 5 June 1967; m. Maria Teresa Adegas; one s.; with Southern Africa Dept, FCO 1990–92, Third, later Second Sec., Lisbon 1992–96, First Sec. (Econ., later Insts), Perm. Rep., Brussels 1996–2001, Head of Enlargement Team, EU Directorate, FCO 2001–03, Counsellor and Head of EU and Global Issues Team, Madrid 2003–05, seconded as Adviser to Pres. of EC 2005–07, Amb. to Portugal 2007–10, Dir of Strategy, Policy Unit, Central Group, FCO 2010–13, Amb. to Brazil 2013–16, Dir-Gen. Dept for Exiting the EU 2017–. *Address:* Department of Exiting the European Union, 9 Downing Street, London, SW1A 2AS, England (office). *Website:* www.gov.uk/government/organisations/department-for-exiting-the-european-union (office).

ELLIS, Bret Easton, BA; American writer; b. 7 March 1964, Los Angeles; ed Bennington Coll.; mem. Authors Guild. *Films:* as screenwriter: The Informers 2008, The Canyons (Melbourne Underground Film Festival's Best Screenplay 2014) 2013, The Curse of Downers Grove 2016; as dir: All That Glitters 2010, Orphéus 2015. *Publications include:* Less Than Zero 1985, The Rules of Attraction 1987, American Psycho 1989, The Informers (short stories) 1994, Glamorama 1998, Lunar Park 2005, Imperial Bedrooms 2010, White 2019; contrib. to Rolling Stone, Vanity Fair, Elle, Wall Street Journal, Bennington Review. *Address:* c/o Amanda Urban, ICM Partners, 65 E 55th Street, New York, NY 10022, USA (office). *Telephone:* (212) 556-5600 (office). *E-mail:* mdyer@icmpartners.com (office). *Website:* breteastonellis.com.

ELLIS, George Francis Rayner, FRAS, PhD, FRS; British/South African professor of astrophysics and applied mathematics; *Professor Emeritus, Mathematics Department, University of Cape Town;* b. 11 Aug. 1939, Johannesburg; s. of George Rayner Ellis and Gwen Hilda Ellis (née MacRobert); m. 1st Sue Parkes 1963; one s. one d.; m. 2nd Mary Wheeldon 1978 (died 2007); m. 3rd Carole Bloch 2010; ed Michaelhouse, Univ. of Cape Town, Univ. of Cambridge, UK; Fellow, Peterhouse, Cambridge 1965–67; Asst Lecturer, then Lecturer, Univ. of Cambridge 1967–73; Prof. of Applied Math., Univ. of Cape Town 1974–88, 1990–2005, Prof. Emer. 2005–; Prof. of Cosmic Physics, SISSA, Trieste 1988–92; G.C. MacVittie Visiting Prof. of Astronomy, Queen Mary Coll., London 1987–; Chair. GR10 Scientific Cttee 1988; mem. Int. Cttee on Gen. Relativity and Gravitation; Pres., Int. Soc. of Gen. Relativity and Gravitation 1989–92; mem. Cttee (and Pres.) Royal Soc. of SA 1990–2000, Pres. 1992–96; Founding mem. and fmr mem. Council, Acad. of Science of SA; Fellow, Univ. of Cape Town, Inst. of Math. and its Applications, Third World Acad. of Science 2004; Jt Ed.-in-Chief International Journal of General Relativity and Gravitation 2006–11; Chair. Quaker Service, West Cape 1976–86, 1990–2004, 2011–15, Quaker Peacework Cttee 1978–86, 1990–95, SA Inst. of Race Relations, West Cape 1985–87; Clerk SA Yearly Meeting of Quakers 1986–88; Fellow, Univ. of Cape Town, Int. Soc. on Gen. Relativity and Gravitation at GR20 2013; mem. Bd of Dirs, Asscn for Educational Transformation, Early Learning Resource Unit, Philani Child Health and Nutrition Project; Hon. Fellow, Royal Soc. of SA 2008–; Order of Mapungubwe (Silver) 2006; Hon. DSc (Haverford Coll.) 1996, (Natal Univ.) 1998, (Queen Mary, Univ. of London) 2004, (Univ. of Cape Town) 2009, (Univ. Pierre and Marie Curie) 2017; Herschel Medal of Royal Soc. of SA, Gravity Research Foundation 1st Prize 1979, Templeton Prize 2004, Science-for-Society Gold Medal, Acad. of Science of South Africa 2005, Lemaitre Prize, Univ. Louvain 2019. *Publications:* The Large Scale Structure of Space-Time (with S. W. Hawking) 1973, The Squatter Problem in the Western Cape (with J. Maree, D. Hendrie) 1976, Low Income Housing Policy (with D. Dewar) 1980, Flat and Curved Space-Times (with R. Williams) 1988, Before the Beginning 1993, The Renaissance of General Relativity and Cosmology (co-ed.) 1993, The Dynamical Systems Approach to Cosmology (co-ed.) 1996, The Density of Matter in the Universe (with P. Coles) 1996, On the Moral Nature of the Universe: Cosmology, Theology and Ethics (with N. Murphy) 1996, Foundations of Space and Time: Reflections on Quantum Gravity (co-ed.) 2012, Relativistic cosmology (with R. Maartens and M. MacCallum) 2012, How Can Physics Underlie the Mind 2016, Beyond Evolutionary Psychology (with M. Solms) 2017. *Leisure interests:* climbing, gliding. *Address:* Department of Mathematics and Applied Mathematics, University of Cape Town, Rondebosch 7701, Cape Town, South Africa (office). *Telephone:* (21) 6502339 (office). *Fax:* (21) 6502334 (office). *E-mail:* george.ellis@uct.ac.za (office); gfrellis@gmail.com (home). *Website:* www.math.uct.ac.za/prof-george-ellis-0 (office).

ELLIS, Adm. (retd) James (Jim) Oren, Jr, MSc; American naval officer (retd) and aerospace engineer; b. 20 July 1947, Spartanburg, SC; m. Paula Matthews (died 2008); ed US Naval Acad., Georgia Inst. of Tech., Univ. of West Florida, Harvard Univ., US Naval Aviator Training, US Naval Test Pilot School, US Naval Nuclear Power Training; Naval Aviator 1971, carrier-based tours with Fighter Squadron 92, USS Constellation (CV 64) and Fighter Squadron 1, USS Ranger (CV 61); first CO of Strike/Fighter Squadron 131, USS Coral Sea (CV 43); served as experimental/operational test pilot, in Navy Office of Legis. Affairs, and F/A-18 Program Coordinator, Deputy Chief of Naval Operations (Air Warfare); served as Exec. Officer of USS Carl Vinson (CVN 70) and CO of USS LaSalle (AGF 3); assumed command of USS Abraham Lincoln (CVN 72) and participated in Operation Desert Storm while deployed during her maiden voyage 1991; Inspector-Gen. US Atlantic Fleet, served as Dir for Operations, Plans and Policy on staff of C-in-C US Atlantic Fleet 1993; Commdr Carrier Group Five/Battle Force Seventh Fleet 1995–96; Deputy Commdr and Chief of Staff, Jt Task Force Five (counter-narcotics force for US C-in-C in the Pacific); Deputy Chief of Naval Operations (Plans, Policy and Operations) 1996–98; C-in-C US Naval Forces, Europe, London, UK and C-in-C Allied Forces, Southern Europe, Naples, Italy 1998; C-in-C US Strategic Command, Offutt Air Force Base, Neb. 1998–2004; C-in-C, United States Strategic Command 2001–2002; Pres. and CEO Inst. of Nuclear Power Operations (INPO) 2005–12; mem. Bd of Dirs Lockheed Martin Corpn, Level 3 Communications, Inc. 2005–; Advisor to Bd, Inmarsat 2004, Bd of Dirs Inmarsat PLC 2005–; US Presidential appointee, Foreign Intelligence Advisory Bd 2006–09; currently Annenberg Distinguished Visiting Fellow, Hoover Inst., Stanford Univ.; Order of Merit (Hungary), Grand Order of Merit (Italy), Star of Merit and Honor (Greece); Defense Distinguished Service Medal (three awards), Navy Distinguished Service Medal, Legion of Merit (four awards), Defense Meritorious Service Medal, Meritorious Service Medal (two awards), Navy Commendation Medal; inducted into Georgia Inst. of Tech. Eng Hall of Fame. *Leisure interests:* running, cycling, hiking, fly-fishing, reading.

ELLIS, John Martin, BA, PhD; American professor of German literature; *Professor Emeritus of German Literature, University of California, Santa Cruz;* b. 31 May 1936, London, England; s. of John Albert Ellis and Emily Ellis; m. Barbara Rhoades 1978; two s. two d. one step-d.; ed City of London School and Univ. Coll., London; Royal Artillery 1954–56; Tutorial Asst in German, Univ. of Wales, Aberystwyth 1959–60; Asst Lecturer in German, Univ. of Leicester 1960–63; Asst Prof. of German, Univ. of Alberta, Canada 1963–66; Assoc. Prof. of German Literature, Univ. of Calif., Santa Cruz 1966–70, Prof. 1970–94, Prof. Emer. 1994–,

Dean, Graduate Div. 1977–86; Literary Ed. Heterodoxy 1992–2000; Sec.-Treas. Asscn of Literary Scholars and Critics 1994–2001; Pres. Calif. Asscn of Scholars 2007–14, Chair. 2014–; Guggenheim Fellowship, Nat. Endowment for the Humanities Sr Fellowship; Nat. Asscn of Scholars' Peter Shaw Memorial Award (for Literature Lost). *Publications include:* Narration in the German Novelle 1974, The Theory of Literary Criticism: A Logical Analysis 1974, Heinrich von Kleist 1979, One Fairy Story Too Many: The Brothers Grimm and Their Tales 1983, Against Deconstruction 1989, Language, Thought and Logic 1993, Literature Lost: Social Agendas and the Corruption of the Humanities 1997. *Leisure interests:* birdwatching, golf. *Address:* 144 Bay Heights, Soquel, CA 95073, USA (home). *Telephone:* (831) 476-1144 (home). *E-mail:* johnellis2608@att.net (office).

ELLIS, (Jonathan Richard) John, CBE, MA, PhD, FRS, FInstP; British physicist and academic; *Clerk Maxwell Professor of Theoretical Physics, King's College London;* b. 1 July 1946, Hampstead, London, England; s. of Richard Ellis and Beryl Lilian Ellis (née Ranger); m. Maria Mercedes Martinez Rengifo 1985; one s. one d.; ed Highgate School, King's Coll., Cambridge; Post-doctoral Research Fellow, Stanford Linear Accelerator Center, USA 1971–72; Richard Chase Tolman Fellow, California Inst. of Tech., USA 1972–73; Research Fellow, CERN, Geneva, Switzerland 1973–74, staff mem. 1974–, Leader, Theoretical Physics Div. 1988–94, Sr Staff Physicist 1994–, also Adviser to CERN Dir-Gen. on relations with non-mem. states; currently Clerk Maxwell Prof. of Theoretical Physics, King's Coll. London; Hon. Fellow, King's Coll., Cambridge 2006; Dr hc (Southampton) 1994, (Uppsala Univ.); Maxwell Medal, Royal Soc. 1982, Dirac Medal and Prize, Inst. of Physics 2005. *Publications:* more than 800 scientific publs in professional journals. *Leisure interests:* literature, music, travel, hiking, cinema. *Address:* Department of Physics, King's College London, The Strand, London, WC2R 2LS, England (office); Theory Division, CERN, 1211 Geneva 23 (office); 5 Chemin du Ruisseau, Tannay, 1295 Mies, Vaud, Switzerland (home). *Telephone:* (20) 7848-2470 (London) (office); (22) 7674142 (Geneva) (office); (22) 7764858 (home). *Fax:* (20) 7848-2420 (London) (office); (22) 7673850 (Geneva) (office); (22) 7764858 (Geneva) (home). *E-mail:* john.ellis@cern.ch (office). *Website:* www.cern.ch (office).

ELLIS, Reginald John, PhD, FRS; British biologist and academic; *Professor Emeritus of Biological Sciences, University of Warwick;* b. 12 Feb. 1935, Newcastle-under-Lyme, Staffs., England; s. of Francis Gilbert Ellis and Evangeline Gratton Ellis; m. Diana Margaret Warren 1963; one d.; ed Highbury Grove Grammar School, London and King's Coll., London; Agricultural Research Council Fellow, Dept of Biochemistry, Univ. of Oxford 1961–64; Lecturer, Depts of Botany and Biochemistry, Univ. of Aberdeen 1964–70; Sr Lecturer, Univ. of Warwick 1970–73, Reader 1973–76, Prof. of Biological Sciences 1976–96, Prof. Emer. 1996–, f. Molecular Chaperone Club; Sr Research Fellow, Science and Eng Research Council 1983–88; mem. European Molecular Biology Org. 1986–; Sr Visiting Research Fellow, St John's Coll. Oxford 1992–93; Academic Visitor, Oxford Centre for Molecular Sciences 1996–2000; Tate & Lyle Award 1980, Int. Gairdner Foundation Award 2004, Cell Stress and Chaperones Int. Medal 2007, Royal Soc. Croonian Lecture Prize 2011. *Publications:* Chloroplast Biogenesis (ed.) 1984, Molecular Chaperones (ed.) 1990, The Chaperonins (ed.) 1996, Molecular Chaperones Ten Years On (ed.) 2000, Protein Misfolding and Human Disease (ed.) 2004, How Science Works: Evolution 2010 (second edn 2016); 165 papers on plant and microbial biochemistry. *Leisure interests:* landscape photography, fell walking. *Address:* Life Sciences, University of Warwick, Coventry, Warwicks., CV4 7AL, England (office). *E-mail:* r.j.ellis@warwick.ac.uk (office). *Website:* www2.warwick.ac.uk/fac/sci/lifesci (office); www.cirs.info (office).

ELLIS, Richard Salisbury, CBE, DPhil, FRS, FRAS, FInstP; British astronomer and academic; *Professor of Astrophysics, University College London;* b. 25 May 1950, Colwyn Bay, Wales; s. of Capt. Arthur Ellis and Marion Ellis; m. Barbara Williams 1972; one s. one d.; ed Univ. Coll., London, Univ. of Oxford; researcher, Durham Univ. 1974–81, Lecturer 1981–83, Prof. of Astronomy 1985–93, Visiting Prof. 1994–; Plumian Prof., Univ. of Cambridge 1993–99, Visiting Prof. 2000–03, Dir Inst. of Astronomy 1994–99, Professorial Fellow, Magdalene Coll. Cambridge 1994–99; Prof. of Astronomy, California Inst. of Tech., USA 1999–2002, Steele Prof. of Astronomy 2002–15, Dir Palomar Observatory 2000–02, Caltech Optical Observatories 2002–05; Royal Soc. Prof., Univ. of Oxford 2008–09, Professorial Fellow, Merton Coll., Oxford 2008–09; Sr Research Fellow, Royal Greenwich Observatory 1983–85; Sr Scientist European Southern Observatory 2015–17; Prof. of Astrophysics, Univ. Coll. London 2015–; mem. American Astronomical Soc., Royal Astronomical Soc.; Fellow, Univ. Coll. London 1998; Hon. DSc (Durham) 2002; Bakerian Prize, Royal Soc. 1998, Gruber Cosmology Prize 2007, Gold Medal, Royal Astronomical Soc. 2011, Breakthrough Prize in Physics 2014, Carl Sagan Memorial Prize 2017. *Publications:* numerous articles in scientific journals; Observational Tests of Cosmological Inflation 1991, Large Scale Structure in the Universe 1999. *Leisure interests:* skiing, photography, travel. *Address:* Department of Physics & Astronomy, University College London, Gower Street, London, WC1E 6BT, England (office). *Telephone:* (20) 3108-7912 (office). *E-mail:* richard.ellis@ucl.ac.uk (office). *Website:* www.ucl.ac.uk/star/people/ellis (office).

ELLISON, Jane; British politician and international organization official; *Deputy Director-General for Corporate Operations, World Health Organization;* b. 15 Aug. 1964, Bradford; ed St Hilda's Coll., Oxford; joined John Lewis Partnership (JLP) as Graduate Trainee 1986, becoming Man., John Lewis customer magazine and Man., JLP Customer Direct Marketing –2010; mem. Council, London Borough of Barnet 2006–08; MP (Conservative) for Battersea 2010–17; Parl. Under-Sec. of State for Public Health 2013–16, Financial Sec. to the Treasury 2016–17; Deputy Dir-Gen. for Corp. Operations, WHO 2017–. *Address:* World Health Organization (WHO), 20 ave Appia, 1211 Geneva 27, Switzerland (office). *Telephone:* 227912111 (office). *Fax:* 227913111 (office). *E-mail:* info@who.int (office). *Website:* www.who.int (office).

ELLISON, Lawrence (Larry) J.; American software industry executive; *Chairman and Chief Technology Officer, Oracle Corporation;* b. 17 Aug. 1944, Bronx, New York; divorced; two c.; ed Univs of Illinois and Chicago; started as technician with Firemans' Fund, Wells Fargo Bank; with Ampex built databases; co-f. Software Devt Labs (later Oracle Corpn) 1977, CEO 1977–2014, Pres. 1978–96, mem. Bd of Dirs and Chair. 1990–92, 1995–2004, Chair. and Chief Tech. Officer 2014–; mem. Bd of Dirs Apple Computer Inc. 1997–2002, Tesla, Inc. 2018–. *Leisure interests:* racing sail boats, flying aeroplanes, playing tennis and guitar. *Address:* Oracle Corpn, 500 Oracle Parkway, Redwood Shores, CA 94065-1675, USA (office). *Telephone:* (650) 506-7000 (office). *E-mail:* info@oracle.com (office). *Website:* www.oracle.com (office).

ELLMAN, Michael, BA, MSc(Econ), PhD; British economist and academic; *Professor Emeritus, University of Amsterdam;* b. 27 July 1942, Ripley, Surrey; m. Patricia Harrison 1965; one s. one d.; ed Univ. of Cambridge, London School of Econs; Lecturer, Glasgow Univ. 1967–69; Research Officer then Sr Research Officer, Dept of Applied Econs, Univ. of Cambridge 1969–75; Prof. of Econs, Univ. of Amsterdam 1975–2007, Chair. Dept of Econs 2001–05, Chair. Business Studies 2007–12, Prof. Emer. 2012–; Visiting Prof., ISS, The Hague 1983, New Economic School, Moscow 1997; Fellow, Tinberg Inst.; Visiting Fellow, Fitzwilliam Coll., Cambridge 2005; Hon. Foreign mem. Russian Acad. of Econ. Sciences and Entrepreneurship; Kondratieff Prize 1998, Stapenning Hon. Award, Univ. of Amsterdam 2012. *Publications:* Planning Problems in the USSR 1973, Socialist Planning 1979, The Destruction of the Soviet Economic System (ed. with V. Kontovovich) 1998, Russia's Oil and Natural Gas: Bonanza or Curse? (ed.) 2006. *Leisure interests:* walking, cycling. *Address:* Department of Economics, Universiteit van Amsterdam, Roetersstraat 11, 1018 WB Amsterdam, Netherlands (office). *Telephone:* (20) 5254235 (office). *Fax:* (20) 5254254 (office). *E-mail:* m.j.ellman@uva.nl (office). *Website:* ellman.home.xs4all.nl/ellmanmj; www.feb.uva.nl (office).

ELLROY, James; American writer; b. (Lee Earle Ellroy), 4 March 1948, Los Angeles, Calif.; s. of Armand Ellroy and Geneva Odelia Hilliker Ellroy; m. 1st Mary Doherty 1988 (divorced 1991); m. 2nd Helen Knode 1991 (divorced 2006); ed John Burroughs Junior High School and Fairfax High School, Los Angeles. *Films include:* Dark Blue 2002, The Black Dahlia 2006, Street Kings (screenplay and story) 2008, Land of the Living 2008, Rampart 2011. *Publications include:* Brown's Requiem 1981, Clandestine 1982, Blood on the Moon (Lloyd Hopkins series) 1983, Because the Night (Lloyd Hopkins series) 1984, Killer on the Road 1986, Silent Terror 1986, Suicide Hill (Lloyd Hopkins series) 1986, The Black Dahlia (LA series) 1987, The Big Nowhere (LA series) 1988, LA Confidential (LA series) 1990, White Jazz (LA series) 1992, Hollywood Nocturnes (essays and stories) 1994, American Tabloid (Underworld USA series) (Time Magazine Novel of the Year) 1995, My Dark Places (memoir) (Salon.com Book of the Year) 1996, LA Noir 1998, Crime Wave (essays and stories) 1999, The Cold Six Thousand (Underworld USA series) 2001, Destination: Morgue (essays and stories) 2003, Blood's a Rover 2009, The Hilliker Curse: My Pursuit of Women 2010, The Best American Noir of the Century (co-ed) 2011, Shakedown 2012, Perfidia: A Novel 2014, LAPD '53 2015, This Storm 2019. *Address:* c/o Sobel Weber Associates Inc, 146 East 19th Street, New York, NY 10003-2404, USA (office). *Website:* www.randomhouse.com/knopf/authors/ellroy; jamesellroy.net.

ELLWOOD, David T., PhD; American economist and academic; *Scott M. Black Professor of Political Economy, John F. Kennedy School of Government, Harvard University;* b. 16 Sept. 1953, Minnesota; s. of Paul M. Ellwood, Jr; m. Marilyn Ellwood; two d.; ed Harvard Univ.; Research Asst, Cttee on Costs and Benefits of Auto Air Emission Controls, Nat. Bureau of Econ. Research 1974, Research Asst 1978–80, Research Assoc. 1988–; Research Asst to A. Mitchell Polinsky, Harvard Univ. 1974–75, to Prof. Martin S. Feldstein 1974–75, 1977, Teaching Fellow, Labor Econs 1977–79; Research Assoc., Health Policy Program, Univ. of California, San Francisco 1975–76; Asst Prof. of Public Policy, John F. Kennedy School of Govt, Harvard Univ. 1980–84, Assoc. Prof. of Public Policy 1984–88, Prof. of Public Policy 1988–92, Co-Dir Malcolm Wiener Center for Social Policy 1992–93, Academic Dean, 1992–93, 1995–97, Malcolm Wiener Prof. of Public Policy 1992–93, 1995–98, Dir Multidisciplinary Program in Inequality and Social Policy 1998–99, Lucius N. Littauer Prof. of Political Economy 1998–2003, Scott M. Black Prof. of Political Economy 2003–, Dean, John F. Kennedy School of Govt 2004–15; Asst Sec. for Planning and Evaluation, US Dept of Health and Human Services, Washington, DC 1993–95; Faculty Affiliate, Jt Center for Poverty Research, Northwestern Univ. and Univ. of Chicago 1997–; Sr Research Affiliate, Nat. Poverty Center, Gerald R. Ford School of Public Policy, Univ. of Mich. 2003–; mem. Nat. Acad. of Social Insurance 1990–, Nat. Acad. of Public Admin 2000–; mem. of Review Panel, Work and Welfare Demonstration, Manpower Demonstration Research Corpn 1985–; mem. Bd of Dirs Malcolm Hewitt Wiener Foundation 2000–, Abt Assocs 2001–; Fellow, American Acad. of Arts and Sciences; Morris and Edna Zale Award for Outstanding Distinction in Scholarship and Public Service, Stanford Univ., David Kershaw Award for Outstanding Contribution to Policy Analysis and Man., Asscn of Public Policy Analysis and Man. *Publications include:* A Working Nation?: Workers, Work and Government in the New Economy (co-ed.) 2000; contribs to The Economic Journal, Harvard Business Review, New England Economic Review, Bulletin of the New York Academy of Medicine, The American Prospect, Journal of Economic Perspectives, The New York Times, Washington Post, Los Angeles Times, Boston Globe; books: Poor Support: Poverty and the American Family 1988, Welfare Realities: From Rhetoric to Reform (co-author Mary Jo Bane) 1996. *Leisure interests:* hiking, sea kayaking, most outdoor activities. *Address:* John F. Kennedy School of Government, Harvard Kennedy School, 79 John F. Kennedy Street, Mail box 104 Cambridge, MA 02138, USA (office). *Telephone:* (617) 495-1121 (office). *Fax:* (617) 495-9118 (office). *E-mail:* david_ellwood@Harvard.edu (office). *Website:* www.hks.harvard.edu (office).

ELLWOOD, Sir Peter Brian, Kt, VLL, CBE, FCIB, FRSA; British business executive; b. 15 May 1943, Bristol; s. of Isaac Ellwood and Edith Ellwood (née Trotter); m. Judy Ann Windsor 1968; one s. two d.; ed King's School, Macclesfield; joined Barclays Bank 1961; worked in London and Bristol; Chief Exec. Barclaycard 1985; Dir Barclays Bank (UK) Ltd; Chief Exec. Retail Banking, TSB Bank PLC, Dir TSB Group PLC 1990–95, Chief Exec. 1992–95, Deputy Chief Exec. Lloyds TSB Group PLC 1995–97, Chief Exec. 1997–2003; Chair. ICI PLC 2004–08, mem. Supervisory Bd Akzo Nobel NV (after acquisition of ICI) 2008–14; Chair. (non-exec.) Rexam PLC 2008–12; Chair. Royal Parks Advisory Bd 2003, Royal Parks Foundation 2003; Deputy Chair. Royal Coll. of Music 2003; Chair. Visa Europe, Middle East and Africa 1992–96, Visa International 1994–99; Chair. Advisory Council, Royal Philharmonic Orchestra; Pres. Northampton Bach Choir; Dir (non-exec.) Sears PLC 1994–96; mem. Court, Univ. Coll., Northampton (fmrly Nene Coll.) 1989–; mem. Bd of Govs St Andrew's Healthcare 2008–, Trustee 2010–; Hon.

LLD (Leicester) 1994; Dr hc (Univ. of Central England) 1995. *Leisure interests:* music, theatre.

ELLWOOD, Susie, BSE; American publishing and media executive; *Executive Vice-President and General Manager, USA TODAY;* b. Ark.; m. Bill Ellwood; six c.; ed Arkansas State Univ., Jonesboro; fmr Dir Sales and Marketing, National Investors Life Insurance Co., Little Rock, Ark.; Vice-Pres. and Dir of Marketing, Arkansas Gazette (newspaper), Little Rock 1984–91; Vice-Pres. Market Devt, Detroit Media Partnership 1991–2004, Exec. Vice-Pres. and Gen. Man. Detroit Media Partnership 2006–09, CEO 2009–11; Vice-Pres. Market Devt, Gannett's Newspaper Div. 2004–06, Exec. Vice-Pres. and Gen. Man. USA TODAY 2011–; mem. Bd of Dirs Int. Newsmedia Marketing Asscn North America 2011–; mem. Bd Detroit Regional Chamber, Detroit Econ. Club, Inforum Center for Leadership, Make-A-Wish Foundation of Michigan, CATCH, Sparky Anderson's Charity for Children; mem. Int. Women's Forum; recipient of Newspaper Asscn of America's Distinguished Marketing Award and Lifetime Achievement Award, named Gannett's Manager of the Year 2009, nine-time winner of Gannett's President Ring. *Address:* USA TODAY, 7950 Jones Branch Drive, McLean, VA 22108-0605, USA (office). *Telephone:* (703) 854-3400 (office). *Fax:* (703) 854-2139 (office). *E-mail:* sellwood@usatoday.com (office). *Website:* www.usatoday.com (office).

ELMAN, Richard Samuel; British business executive; arrived in Asia from England mid-1960s; Regional Dir of Asia Operations, Phibro, New York, USA 1976–86, mem. Bd of Dirs for two years; Founder and CEO Noble Group Ltd (global commodity merchant) from 1986, apptd Exec. Dir 1994, Chair. –2010, Chair. Emer. Sept.–Nov. 2010, Chair. (non-exec.) Nov. 2010–17, Acting CEO 2011–12, Dir (non-exec.) –2018; Dir (non-exec.) Consolidated Minerals Ltd 2002–07; mem. Bd of Dirs, Territory Resources Ltd June–Dec. 2008; mem. Hong Kong Inst. of Dirs. *Address:* Noble Group Ltd, 18th Floor, MassMutual Tower, 38 Gloucester Road, Hong Kong Special Administrative Region, People's Republic of China (office). *Telephone:* 2861-3511 (office). *Fax:* 2527-0282 (office). *E-mail:* richard@thisisnoble .com (office). *Website:* www.thisisnoble.com (office).

ELMER, Michael B.; Danish lawyer and judge; *Vice-President, Danish Courts;* b. 26 Feb. 1949, Copenhagen; s. of Poul Chr. B. Elmer and Etly Elmer (née Andersson); m. Annette Elmer; one d.; ed Univ. of Copenhagen; civil servant, Ministry of Justice 1973–76, 1977–82, Head of Div. 1982–87, 1988–91, Deputy Perm. Sec., Head of Community Law and Human Rights Dept 1991–94; Assoc. Prof., Univ. of Copenhagen 1975–85; Deputy Judge, Hillerød 1976–77; Asst Public Prosecutor 1980–81; Judge, Court of Ballerup 1981–82; external examiner, Danish law schools 1985–; High Court Judge (a.i.), Eastern High Court, Copenhagen 1987–88; Vice-Pres. (a.i.), Danish Maritime and Commercial High Court, Copenhagen 1988, Vice-Pres., Pres. of Chamber 1997–2012, Frederiksberg 2015–; Pres. Iraq and Afghanistan Inquiry 2012–15; Rep. EC Court of Justice, Luxembourg 1991–94; Advocate-Gen. EC Court of Justice 1994–97; mem. Governing Council UNIDROIT, Rome 1999–2013; int. commercial arbitrator; Chair. and mem. numerous govt and int. orgs and cttees; Kt (First Degree), Order of the Dannebrog; Grand Cross, Order of Merit (Luxembourg). *Publications:* several books and articles on civil law, penal law, community law and the law on aliens (immigration). *Leisure interests:* travelling, collecting antiques, street and other Leica M photography. *Address:* Skovalléen 16, 2880 Bagsvaerd, Denmark (home). *Telephone:* 93-93-09-30. *E-mail:* michael@elmer.eu (office).

ELMI, Mohamed Hashi; Somali civil engineer and politician; b. 1938; f. Somali Nat. Movement (rebel group to overthrow the regime) in the 1980s; fmr Mayor of Hargeisa; Minister of Commerce and Industry, 'Somaliland' 2005, Minister of Finance 2010–12; Deputy Chair. Qaran (political grouping) (imprisoned for five months for involvement with banned group 2007).

ELOP, Stephen, BEngMgt; Canadian engineer and business executive; *Executive Vice-President, Devices Group, Microsoft Corporation;* b. 31 Dec. 1963, Ancaster, Ont.; m. Nancy Elop; five c. (including triplets and one adopted d.); ed McMaster Univ., Hamilton, Ont.; Chief Information Officer, Boston Chicken, Inc. 1992–98, Einstein Brothers Bagels, Inc. 1994–97; joined Macromedia 1998, held numerous sr positions, including COO, Exec. Vice-Pres. of Worldwide Field Operations, Gen. Man. eBusiness Div. and Pres. and CEO –2005, joined Adobe following acquisition of Macromedia Inc. 2005, Pres. Worldwide Field Operations 2005–06; COO Juniper Networks 2007–08; Pres. Microsoft Business Div., Microsoft Corpn 2008–10, mem. sr leadership team that set overall strategy and direction for Microsoft, oversaw the Information Worker, Microsoft Business Solutions and Unified Communications Groups, Exec. Vice-Pres. Microsoft Devices Group 2014–; Pres. and CEO Nokia Corpn (first non-Finn) 2010–13, Nokia Leadership Team mem. 2010–13, Chair. 2010–13, mem. Bd of Dirs 2011–13, Exec. Vice-Pres., Devices & Services (until his transfer to Microsoft following sale of business in Sept. 2013) 2013–14; Chair. NAVTEQ Corpn; Hon. LLD (McMaster Univ.). *Address:* Microsoft Corporation, 1 Microsoft Way, Redmond, WA 98052, USA (office). *Telephone:* (425) 882-8080 (office). *Fax:* (425) 706-7329 (office). *Website:* www.microsoft.com (office).

ELRINGTON, Hon. Wilfred Peter (Sedi), LLB, SC; Belizean lawyer and politician; *Minister of Foreign Affairs;* b. 20 Nov. 1948, Belize City; m. Barbara Wright; four c.; ed Univ. of the West Indies; Founding Sr Partner, Pitts and Elrington (law firm); served as a part-time Justice of Supreme Court of Belize; mem. United Democratic Party; contested Pickstock constituency as an ind. 2002, elected MP 2008–; served as a Senator and Leader of Govt Business; Minister of Foreign Affairs 2008–, Attorney-Gen. 2008–10, 2012–15; mem. Trinity Methodist Church. *Leisure interests:* teaching, farming, journalism. *Address:* Ministry of Foreign Affairs, NEMO Building, Second Floor, PO Box 174, Belmopan, Belize (office). *Telephone:* 822-2322 (office); 822-2167 (office). *Fax:* 822-2854 (office). *E-mail:* belizemfa@btl.net (office); agministrybze@yahoo.com (office). *Website:* www.mfa.gov.bz (office).

ELS, Theodore Ernest (Ernie); South African professional golfer; b. 17 Oct. 1969, Johannesburg; s. of Nils Els and Hettie Els; m. Leizl Els; one s. one d.; wins include South African Open 1992, 1996, US Open 1994, 1997, Toyota World Matchplay Championships 1994, 1995, 1996, South African PGA Championship 1995, Byron Nelson Classic 1995, Buick Classic 1996, 1997, Johnnie Walker Classic 1997, Bay Hill Invitational 1998, Nissan Open 1999, Int. presented by Quest 2000, Standard Life Loch Lomond 2000, Open Championship 2002, 2012, Genuity Championship 2002, sixth World Match Play title 2004, Mercedes Championship 2003, BMW International Open 2013; mem. Dunhill Cup Team 1992–2000, World Cup Team 1992, 1993, 1996, 1997, 2001; mem. President's Cup 1996, 1998, 2000; f. Ernie Els and Fancourt Foundation 1999, Els for Autism; South African Sportsman of the Year 1994, European Tour Player of the Year 1994, 2002, 2003, Lifetime Membership European Tour 1998, Payne Stewart Award 2015. *Leisure interests:* movies, reading, sport. *E-mail:* info@ernieels.com. *Website:* www.ernieels.com.

ELSTEIN, David Keith, MA; British broadcasting executive, author and producer; *Chairman, openDemocracy;* b. 14 Nov. 1944, Slough, Berks., England; ed Haberdashers' Aske's School, Gonville and Caius Coll. Cambridge; producer (BBC) The Money Programme, Panorama, Cause for Concern, People in Conflict 1964–68; (Thames TV) This Week, The Day Before Yesterday, The World At War 1968–72; (London Weekend) Weekend World 1972; Ed. This Week (Thames TV) 1974–78; f. Brook Productions 1982; Exec. Producer A Week in Politics 1982–86, Concealed Enemies 1983; Man. Dir Primetime TV 1983–86; Dir of Programmes, Thames TV 1986–92; Head of Programmes BSkyB 1993–96; Chief Exec. Channel 5 Broadcasting 1996–2000; Chair. Nat. Film and TV School 1996–2002, British Screen Advisory Council 1997–2008, Broadcasting Policy Group 2003–, Commercial Radio Cos Asscn 2004–06, Screen Digest 2004–10, XSN PLC 2004–08, Sparrowhawk Investments Ltd 2004–07, DCD Media PLC 2005–11, Luther Pendragon Holdings 2006–10, openDemocracy 2009–; Vice-Chair. Kingsbridge Capital Advisors Ltd 2004–16; Dir, Virgin Media Inc. 2003–08; Visiting Prof., Univ. of Stirling 1995–2000, Univ. of Oxford 1999, Univ. of Westminster 2000–05; Hon. Fellow, Gonville and Caius Coll.; Primetime Emmy Award for Best Limited Series, Concealed Enemies 1984. *Film:* IDA (producer) 2015. *Radio:* July 1914: Countdown to War 2014 (writer/producer). *Publications:* The Political Structure of UK Broadcasting 1949–1999 (Oxford Lectures) 1999, 2015, Beyond The Charter: The BBC After 2006 (Broadcasting Policy Group) 2004. *Leisure interests:* theatre, cinema, bridge, politics, reading. *E-mail:* elsteindavid@aol.com (home).

ELSTONE, Robert G., BA (Hons), MA (Econ), MCom; Australian investment banker, business executive and academic; ed Univs of London and Manchester, UK and Univ. of Western Australia, Sr Exec. Devt Programs at Harvard and Stanford Grad. Schools of Business, USA; career has spanned investment banking in 1980s, public co. CFO roles in 1990s, aviation and global resource materials sectors, and wholesale financial markets and risk man. in 2000s; managed Australian office of Paribas' int. capital markets activities in Paris, London and New York 1980s; Man. Dir and CEO SFE Corpn (holding co. for Sydney Futures Exchange prior to its merger with Australian Stock Exchange Ltd (ASX)) 2000–06, Man. Dir and CEO ASX 2006–11; Adjunct Prof., Business School, Univ. of Sydney; mem. Bd of Dirs Westpac Banking Corpn 2012–17; fmr mem. Bd of Dirs Nat. Australia Bank, SFE Clearing Corpn Ltd, Austraclear Ltd, Australian Clearing House Pty Ltd, ASX Settlement and Transfer Corpn Pty Ltd; mem. Future Fund Bd of Guardians 2006; Chair. Financial Sector Advisory Council 2007–08; served as consultant to Campbell Inquiry into Australian financial system in 1970s; Hon. Fellow, Finance and Treasury Asscn. *Address:* University of Sydney Business School, H70, Abercrombie Street and Codrington Street, Darlington, NSW 2006, Australia (office). *Telephone:* (2) 9351-3076 (office). *Website:* sydney.edu.au/business (office).

ELTON, Sir Arnold, Kt, KB, CBE, MS, FRCS, FRSM, FICS; British surgeon; *Health Adviser, Hospital Corporation of America Group of Hospitals;* b. 14 Feb. 1920; s. of Max Elton and Ada Elton; m. Billie Pamela Briggs 1952; one s.; ed Univ. Coll., London, Univ. Coll. Hosp. Medical School, London; House Surgeon, House Physician, Casualty Officer, Univ. Coll. Hosp. 1943–45; Sr Surgical Registrar, Charing Cross Hosp. 1947–51; Consultant Surgeon, Harrow Hosp. 1951–70, Mount Vernon Hosp. 1960–70, Wellington Hosp.; Consultant Surgeon, Northwick Park Hosp. and Clinical Research Centre 1970–85 (now Consulting Surgeon); Surgeon Emer. Clementine Churchill Hosp.; First Chair. Medical Staff Cttee Northwick Park Hosp., Chair. Surgical Div. and Theatre Cttee; Health Adviser, Wellington Hosp. 2000–; mem. Ethical Cttee Northwick Park Hosp., Govt Working Party on Breast Screening for Cancer 1985–; Surgical Tutor, Royal Coll. of Surgeons 1970–82; Nat. Chair. Conservative Medical Soc. 1975–92, Chair. European Group and Pres. 1992–97, Pres. Emer. 1997–, European Rep. 1994–, Ed. European Bulletin 1994–, also Chair. Educ. and Research Div.; Examiner, Gen. Nursing Council, Royal Coll. of Surgeons 1971–83; Medical Adviser Virgin Fitness Clubs, Adviser, Hospital Corpn of America Group of Hosps 2009–; Exec. Dir Healthy Living (UK) Ltd, Healthy Living (Durham) Ltd, Universal Lifestyle Ltd, Medical Consulting Services Ltd; Chair. Int. Medical and Scientific Fund-raising Cttee, British Red Cross, Medical and Science Div., World Fellowship Duke of Edinburgh Award 2013–; Fellow, Asscn of Surgeons of GB, Int. Coll. of Surgeons; Founding mem. British Asscn of Surgical Oncology; mem. Court of Patrons Royal Coll. of Surgeons 1986–, Int. Medical Parliamentarians Org. (Chair UK Div.), European Soc. of Surgical Oncology, World Fed. of Surgical Oncological Socs (adviser on int. affairs), European Fed. of Surgeons, Tricare Europe Preferred Provider Network (US Armed Forces and Families), Breast and Thyroid Surgery 1997–; Devt Consultant, Ridgeford Properties Ltd 2001; Health Exec. Bovis Lend Lease Ltd 2000–; Medical Consultant and Adviser, Keltbray Ltd 2003–; Health Consultant and Adviser, Clipfine, BDL; mem. Nat. Events Cttee of Imperial Cancer Research Fund; Gosse Research Scholarship; Health Consultant and Adviser to Sir Robert McAlpine Ltd; mem. Apothecaries and Carmen Liveries; Queen's Jubilee Medal for Community Services; Freeman, City of London. *Publications:* various medical publs. *Leisure interests:* tennis, music, cricket. *Address:* The Consulting Rooms, Wellington Hospital, Wellington Place, London, NW8 9LE (office); 58 Stockleigh Hall, Prince Albert Road, London, NW8 7LB, England (home). *Telephone:* (20) 7483-5275 (office). *Fax:* (20) 7722-6638 (office).

ELTON, Benjamin (Ben) Charles, BA; British writer and performer; b. 3 May 1959; s. of (Prof.) Lewis Richard Benjamin Elton and Mary Elton (née Foster); m. Sophie Gare 1994; ed Godalming Grammar School, S Warwicks. Coll. of Further Educ., Univ. of Manchester; first professional appearance at Comic Strip Club 1981; numerous tours as stand-up comic 1986–; British Acad. Best Comedy Show Awards 1984, 1987, Best New Comedy Laurence Olivier Award 1998. *Film:* Much Ado About Nothing (actor) 1993, Maybe Baby (writer and dir) 2000. *Television:* writer: Alfresco 1982–83, The Young Ones (jtly) 1982–84, Happy Families 1985, Filthy Rich and Catflap 1986, Blackadder II (jtly) 1986, Blackadder the Third (jtly)

1987, Blackadder Goes Forth (jtly) 1989, The Thin Blue Line (jtly) 1995–96, Blessed 2005, The Wright Way 2013, Upstart Crow 2016–; writer and performer: South of Watford (jtly, documentary series) 1984–85, Saturday Live 1985–87, Friday Night Live 1988, Ben Elton Live 1989, 1993, 1997, The Man from Auntie 1990, 1994, Stark 1993, The Ben Elton Show (jtly) 1998, Get a Grip 2007. *Theatre:* Gasping 1990, Silly Cow 1991, Popcorn 1996, Blast from the Past 1998, The Beautiful Game (musical, book and lyrics) 2000, We Will Rock You (story to musical) 2002, Tonight's the Night (story to musical) 2003, Love Never Dies 2010. *Recordings:* albums: Motormouth 1987, Motorvation 1989. *Publications:* novels: Bachelor Boys 1984, Stark 1989, Gridlock 1992, This Other Eden 1993, Popcorn 1996, Blast from the Past 1998, Inconceivable 1999, Dead Famous 2001, High Society 2002, Past Mortem 2004, The First Casualty 2005, Chart Throb 2006, Blind Faith 2007, Meltdown 2009, Two Brothers 2012, Time and Time Again 2014. *Leisure interests:* walking, reading, socializing.

ELTON, 2nd Baron, cr. 1934, of Headington; **Rodney Elton,** TD, MA; British politician and company director; *Backbench and Select Committee Member, House of Lords;* b. 2 March 1930, Oxford, England; s. of Godfrey Elton, 1st Baron and Dedi Hartmann; m. 1st Anne Frances Tilney 1958 (divorced 1979); one s. three d.; m. 2nd Susan Richenda Gurney, DCVO 1979; ed Eton Coll. and New Coll., Oxford; fmr Capt. Queen's Own Warwicks. and Worcs. Yeomanry; fmr Maj. Leics. and Derbyshire Yeomanry; farming 1957–73; Asst Mastership in History, Loughborough Grammar School 1962–67, Fairham Comprehensive School for Boys 1967–69; contested Loughborough div. of Leics. 1966, 1970; Lecturer, Bishop Lonsdale Coll. of Educ. 1969–72; joined House of Lords May 1973, Opposition Whip 1974–76, an Opposition Spokesman 1976–79, a Deputy Chair. of Cttees 1997–2008, Deputy Speaker 1999–2008, mem. House of Lords Select Cttee on the Scrutiny of Delegated Powers 1994–97, Select Cttee on the Constitution 2002–06, Ecclesiastical Cttee (of both houses) 2002–, Procedure Cttee 2005–09, Conventions (Jt Cttee) 2006, EU Sub-cttee B–Internal Market, Infrastructure and Employment 2012–13; Parl. Under-Sec. of State for NI 1979–81, Dept of Health and Social Security 1981–82, Home Office 1982–84, Minister of State 1984–85; Minister of State Dept of Environment 1985–86; Chair. Financial Intermediaries' Mans' and Brokers' Regulatory Asscn (FIMBRA) 1987–90; Dir Andry Montgomery Ltd 1977–79, Deputy Chair. 1978–79, 1986–99; Dir Overseas Exhbns Ltd 1977–79, Bldg Trades Exhbn Ltd 1977–79; mem. Panel on Takeovers and Mergers 1987–90; Chair. Ind. Inquiry into Discipline in Schools (Report 1989), Intermediate Treatment Fund 1990–93; Chair. DIVERT Trust 1993–2000, Pres. 2000–2002; Deputy Chair. Asscn of Conservative Peers 1986–93; Vice-Pres. Inst. of Trading Standards Admins 1990–; mem. Council Rainer Foundation 1990–96, City and Guilds of London Inst. 1991–97 (mem. Quality and Standards Cttee 1999–2004); Licensed Lay Minister, Oxford Diocese, Church of England 1999–; fmr Trustee, City Parochial Foundation and Trust for London; Conservative; Hereditary Peer 1999; Hon. Vice-Pres. Inst. of Trading Standards Officers; Hon. Fellow, City and Guilds Inst. of London. *Leisure interest:* painting. *Address:* House of Lords, Westminster, London, SW1A 0PW, England (office). *Telephone:* (20) 7219-3165 (office). *Fax:* (20) 7219-5979 (office). *E-mail:* eltonr@parliament.uk (office). *Website:* www.parliament.uk/biographies/lords/lord-elton/2812 (office).

ELWES, Cary; British actor and writer; b. (Ivan Simon Cary Elwes), 26 Oct. 1962, London; s. of Dominic Elwes and Tessa Kennedy; m. Marie Kurbikoff; one c.; ed Harrow School; stage debut in Equus 1981. *Films include:* Another Country 1984, Oxford Blues 1984, The Bride 1985, Lady Jane 1986, Maschenka 1987, The Princess Bride 1987, Glory 1989, Days of Thunder 1990, Hot Shots! 1990, Leather Jackets 1991, Bram Stoker's Dracula 1992, Robin Hood: Men in Tights 1992, The Crush 1993, Rudyard Kipling's Jungle Book 1994, The Chase 1994, Twister 1996, Liar Liar 1997, Kiss the Girls 1997, The Informant 1997, Quest for Camelot (voice) 1998, Cradle Will Rock 1999, Shadow of the Vampire 2000, Wish You Were Dead 2000, Saw 2004, Ella Enchanted 2004, The Bard's Tale (voice) 2004, Neo Ned 2005, Edison 2005, Pucked 2006, Walk the Talk 2007, Georgia Rule 2007, The Alphabet Killer 2008, A Christmas Carol (voice) 2009, Little Murder 2010, The Adventures of Tintin (voice) 2010, New Year's Eve 2011, The Story of Luke 2011, The Oogieloves in the Big Balloon Adventure (voice) 2012, Justice League: The Flashpoint Paradox (voice) 2013, Reach Me 2014, Teen Lust 2014. *Television includes:* Race Against Time 2000, The X Files (series) 2001–02, The Riverman 2004, Pope John Paul II 2005, Haskett's Chance 2006, Law & Order 2007, Psych 2009–14, Wonder Woman 2011, Leverage 2012, Perception 2012, The Anna Nicole Story 2013, Cosmos: A Spacetime Odyssey 2014, Granite Flats 2014. *Publication:* As You Wish: Inconceivable Tales from the Making of The Princess Bride 2014. *Address:* c/o Tavistock Wood, 45 Conduit Street, London, W1S 2YN, England. *Telephone:* (20) 7494-4767. *Fax:* (20) 7434-2017. *E-mail:* info@tavistockwood.com. *Website:* www.tavistockwood.com.

ELZUBAIR, Mohammad Khari, BSc, MA, PhD; Sudanese economist, government official and fmr central banker; *Economic Secretary, National Congress Party;* b. 1945; m.; five c.; ed Univ. of Khartoum, Univ. of Wales, UK; Financial Insp., Loans and Int. Aid Admin, Ministry of Finance and Nat. Economy 1968–73, First Insp., Ministry of Finance and Econ. Planning 1975–79, Dir of Commodity Aid 1983–86, Dir of External Loans, Econ. Planning Agency 1986–98, First Under-Sec. for Planning 1989–93, State Minister for Planning 1993–96; Chair. and Gen. Man. Sudanese Devt Corpn 1996–98; State Minister for Finance, Ministry of Finance and Nat. Economy 1998–2000, Minister of Finance and Nat. Economy 2000–01; Vice-Pres., Bank of Sahel and Sahara Community 2002–09; apptd Gov. Cen. Bank of Sudan 2011; currently Economic Sec., Nat. Congress Party (NCP).

EMADI, Ali Shareef al-, BFin; Qatari banking executive and politician; *Minister of Finance;* ed Univ. of Arizona, USA; began career at Qatar Nat. Bank 1990, held various positions, including in Banking Control Dept 1990–98, Sr Man. of Retail Banking 1998–2001, Asst Gen. Man. Credit 2001–05, Gen. Man. Risk Dept 2005, Acting CEO, then apptd Group CEO Qatar Nat. Bank SAQ 2005; Pres. Commr, PT Bank QNB Kesawan Tbk 2011; Vice-Chair. Nat. Mobile Telecommunications Co. (KSC); Minister of Finance 2013–; Deputy Chair. Qatar Telecom (Q-TEL) (QSC), Dir 1999; Vice Chair. Nat. Tourism Council 2018–; mem. Bd of Dirs Wataniya Telecom. *Address:* Ministry of Economy and Finance, al-Corniche Street, al-Souq, Doha, Qatar (office). *Telephone:* 44461444 (office). *Fax:* 44430239 (office). *E-mail:* info@baladiya.gov.qa (office). *Website:* www.mof.gov.qa (office).

EMAN, Jan Hendrik Albert (Henny); Aruban politician and lawyer; b. 20 March 1948; s. of Shon A Eman and Blanche Eman-Harthogh; brother of Michiel Godfried (Mike) Eman; ed Leiden Univ., Netherlands; founder and fmr Leader, Arubaanse Volkspartij (AVP); Prime Minister of Aruba and Minister of Gen. Affairs 1986–89, 1993–2001; Orden Francisco de Miranda, Orden del Libertador (Venezuela), Officier in de orde van de Nederlandse Leeuw (Netherlands).

EMAN, Michiel Godfried (Mike), LLB; Aruban lawyer and politician; b. 1 Sept. 1961, Oranjestad; s. of Albert (Shon A.) Eman and Blanche Eman-Harthogh; brother of Jan Hendrik Albert (Henny) Eman; m. Doina Neagoy; ed Univ. of the Netherlands Antilles; worked in pvt. law practice 1992–2001; mem. Arubaanse Volkspartij, Vice-Pres. 2001–03, Leader 2003–17; mem. Staten (Parl.), Leader of the Opposition 2005–09, Prime Minister and Minister of Gen. Affairs, Science, Innovation and Sustainable Devt 2009–17. *Website:* mikeeman.com.

EMANUEL, Elizabeth Florence, MA, DesRCA, FCSD; British fashion designer; b. 5 July 1953, London; d. of Samuel Charles Weiner and Brahna Betty Weiner; m. David Leslie Emanuel 1975 (divorced 2009); one s. one d.; ed City of London School for Girls, Harrow School of Art, Royal Coll. of Art; opened London salon 1978; co-designed wedding gown for HRH Princess of Wales 1981, costumes for Andrew Lloyd Webber's Song and Dance 1982, sets and costumes for ballet Frankenstein, The Modern Prometheus, Royal Opera House London, La Scala Milan 1985, costumes for Stoll Moss production of Cinderella 1985, costumes for film The Changeling 1995, Ros Beef 2004, uniforms for Virgin Atlantic Airways 1990, Britannia Airways 1995; launched int. fashion label Elizabeth Emanuel 1991; launched Bridal Collection for Berkertex Brides UK Ltd 1994; launched bridal collection in Japan 1994; opened new shop and design studio 1996; launched own brand label (with Richard Thompson) 1999; f. Art of Being (couture label) 2005; Founder and Creative Dir new luxury fashion co. Art of Being Ltd in Little Venice studio 2013; f. Emanuel Mayfair 2018. *Dance:* Frankenstein, The Modern Prometheus. *Films:* Middletons Changeling, Ros Beef. *Publications:* Style for All Seasons (with David Emanuel) 1982, A Dress for Diana (with David Emanuel) 2006. *Leisure interests:* ballet, cinema, writing, environmental and conservation issues. *Address:* c/o Limelight Management, 10, 75 Filmer Road, Fulham, London, SW6 7JF, England (office); Garden Studio, 51 Maida Vale, Little Venice, London, W9 1SD, England (office). *Telephone:* (20) 7384-9950 (office); (20) 7289-4545 (office). *E-mail:* roz@limelightmanagement.com (office); elizabeth@elizabethemanuel.co.uk (office). *Website:* www.limelightmanagement.com (office); www.elizabethemanuel.co.uk (office).

EMANUEL, Kerry Andrew, PhD; American meteorologist and academic; *Professor of Meteorology, Massachusetts Institute of Technology;* b. 21 April 1955, Cincinnati; ed Massachusetts Inst. of Tech.; Adjunct Asst Prof. then Asst Prof., UCLA 1978–81; Postdoctoral Fellow, Univ. of Oklahoma Cooperative Inst. for Mesoscale Meteorological Studies 1979; Asst Prof., Dept of Meterology and Physical Oceanography, MIT 1981–83, Asst Prof. then Assoc. Prof. Center for Meteorology and Physical Oceanography and Dept of Earth, Atmospheric and Planetary Sciences 1983–87, Prof. 1987–, Dir 1989–97; mem. NAS 2007–; Carl-Gustaf Rossby Research Medal. *Achievements include:* researcher in atmospheric dynamics, has specialized in atmospheric convection and mechanisms acting to intensify hurricanes. *Publications:* Atmospheric Convection 1994, Divine Wind: The History and Science of Hurricanes 2005, What We Know About Climate Change 2007; numerous scientific papers in professional journals. *Address:* Room 54-1620, Department of Earth, Atmospheric and Planetary Sciences, Massachusetts Institute of Technology, 77 Massachusetts Avenue, Cambridge, MA 02139-4307, USA (office). *Telephone:* (617) 253-2462 (office). *Fax:* (617) 253-6208 (office). *E-mail:* emanuel@mit.edu (office). *Website:* wind.mit.edu/~emanuel/home.html (office).

EMANUEL, Rahm Israel, BA, MA; American banking executive and politician; *Mayor of Chicago;* b. 29 Nov. 1959, Chicago; ed Sarah Lawrence Coll., Northwestern Univ.; mem. campaign team for Paul Simon's election to US Senate 1984; nat. campaign dir for Democratic Congressional Campaign Cttee 1988; Sr Adviser and chief fundraiser for Richard M. Daley's campaign for Mayor of Chicago 1988–89; Nat. Financial Dir Clinton/Gore Campaign 1991–92; Asst to Pres. Bill Clinton, also Dir of Political Affairs and Deputy Dir of Communications, The White House, Washington, DC 1993–95, Dir of Special Projects and Sr Adviser for Policy and Strategy 1995–98; Man. Dir Wasserstein Perella (now Dresdner Kleinwort), Chicago 1999–2002; mem. US House of Reps from Fifth Illinois Dist 2003–09, Chair. Democratic Congressional Campaign Cttee 2005–07, House Democratic Caucus 2007–08; Chief of Staff, The White House, Washington, DC 2009–10 (resgnd); Mayor of Chicago 2011–; mem. Bd of Dirs Fed. Home Loan Mortgage Corpn (Freddie Mac) 2000–01. *Publication:* The Plan: Big Ideas for Change in America (with Bruce Reed) 2009. *Address:* Office of the Mayor, City Hall, Room 507, 121 North LaSalle Street, Chicago, IL 60602-120, USA (office). *Telephone:* (313) 744-3300 (office). *Website:* www.ci.chi.il.us (office).

EMBALÓ, Umaro el-Mokhtar Sissoco; Guinea-Bissau politician and fmr military commander; b. 23 Sept. 1972, Bissau; ed Universidade Técnica de Lisboa, Universidad Complutense de Madrid; fmr mil. commdr (rank of Brig.-Gen. 2012); fmr Minister of African Affairs, Middle East and Cooperation; fmr Adviser to several heads of state including transitional Pres. Manuel Serifo Nhamadjo; Prime Minister 2016–18; mem. Partido Africano da Independência da Guiné e Cabo Verde (PAIGC). *Address:* c/o Office of the Prime Minister, Av. dos Combatentes da Liberdade da Pátria, CP 137, Bissau, Guinea-Bissau (office).

EMBAS, Datuk Douglas Uggah, BA, BEcons; Malaysian politician; *Deputy Chief Minister of Sarawak;* b. 28 July 1955, Spaoh, Sarawak; m. Datin Doreen Mayang; one s. two d.; ed Univ. of Malaya, Univ. of Tasmania, Australia; Pegawai Bank, Wah Tat Bank Bhd 1976–77; Setiausaha Politik kepada Ketua Menteri Sarawak 1977–86; Ahli Parlimen Kawasan Betong, Sarawak 1986; Setiausaha Parlimen di Jabatan Perdana Menteri 1990–95; Setiausaha Parlimen Kementerian Pembangunan Luar Bandar 1995–99; Timbalan Menteri di Jabatan Perdana Menteri 2000–03; mem. Parti Pesaka Bumiputera Bersatu Sarawak (PBB), Sr Vice-Pres.; mem. Parl. for Betong Constituency; fmr Deputy Transport Minister; Minister of Natural Resources and Environment 2008–13, of Plantation Industries and Commodities 2013–16; Deputy Chief Minister of Sarawak 2016–; Pegawai Bintang Sarawak 1984, Ahli Bintang Sarawak 1985, Ahli Mangku Negara 1989,

Pingat Gemilang Bumi Kenyalang 1998. *Address:* Office of the Chief Minister, 22nd Floor, Wisma Bapa Malaysia Petra Jaya, 93502 Kuching, Sarawak, Malaysia (office). *Telephone:* (82) 440801 (office). *Fax:* (82) 444566 (office). *E-mail:* cmo@sarawak.gov.my (office). *Website:* www.cm.sarawak.gov.my (office); www.kppk.gov.my (office).

EMBUREY, John Ernest; British professional cricket coach and fmr professional cricketer; b. 20 Aug. 1952, Peckham, London; s. of John Emburey and Rose Emburey (née Roff); m. 2nd Susan Elizabeth Ann Booth 1980; two d.; ed Peckham Manor Secondary School; right-hand late-order batsman, off-break bowler, slip or gully fielder; teams: Middx 1973–95, Western Prov. 1982–84, Northants. 1996–98 (player/chief coach and man.), England 1978–95 (Capt. 1988); played in 64 Tests (two as Capt.), scored 1,713 runs (average 22.53, highest score 75) and took 147 wickets (average 38.04), best bowling 7/78; scored 12,021 first-class runs (seven hundreds) and took 1,608 wickets, best bowling 8/40; toured Australia 1978–80, 1986–87, West Indies 1981, 1986, India 1981/82, 1992/93, Pakistan 1987, NZ 1988, Sri Lanka 1982, 1993; 61 One-Day Ints (ODIs, seven as Capt.); mem. seven County Championship winning teams with Middx 1976, 1977, 1980, 1982, 1985, 1990, 1993, Gillette Cup 1977, 1980, Benson and Hedges Cup 1983, 1986, Sunday League Winners' Trophy 1991, Natwest Trophy 1994, 1998; retd from playing 1997; coached Northamptonshire Co. Cricket Club; Head Coach Middx Co. Cricket Club 2001–06, Ahmedabad Rockets (Indian Cricket League) 2008; Sky TV commentator; Wisden Cricketer of the Year 1984. *Publications:* Emburey – A Biography 1987, Spinning in a Fast World 1989. *Leisure interests:* golf, fishing, reading.

EMEFIELE, Godwin, BSc, MBA; Nigerian banking executive and central banker; *Governor, Central Bank of Nigeria;* b. 4 Aug. 1961, Lagos; s. of Alice Emefiele; m. Margaret Emefiele; two c.; ed Univ. of Nigeria, Nsukka, Stanford Univ., Harvard Univ., Wharton School of Business, Univ. of Pennsylvania, USA; fmr Lecturer of Finance and Insurance, Univ. of Nigeria, Nsukka, Univ. of Port Harcourt; apptd Exec. Dir Zenith Bank 1990, Deputy Man. Dir 2001, Group Man. Dir and CEO Zenith Bank PLC 2010–14; Gov. Cen. Bank of Nigeria 2014–, also Chair. Bd of Dirs; Chair. West Africa Monetary Zone 2018–; Dir, ACCION Microfinance Bank Ltd; Hon. Fellowship, Chartered Inst. of Bankers of Nigeria 2014; Commdr of the Order of the Niger 2014; Democracy Heroes Award 2016. *Address:* Central Bank of Nigeria, Plot 33, Abubakar Tafawa Balewa Way, Central Business District, Cadastral Zone, PMB 0187, Garki, Abuja, Nigeria (office). *Telephone:* (9) 46239701 (office). *Fax:* (9) 46236012 (office). *E-mail:* info@cenbank.org (office). *Website:* www.cenbank.org (office).

EMERSON, Hon. David Lee, PC, OBC, PhD; Canadian public servant, politician and business executive (retd); b. 17 Sept. 1945, Montreal, PQ; s. of Bernard Emerson and Beulah Emerson; m. Theresa Emerson; one s. one d.; ed Univ. of Alberta, Queen's Univ.; Researcher, Econ. Council of Canada, Ottawa 1972; Deputy Minister of Finance, BC 1984, 1990, later Deputy Minister to Premier; fmr Pres. BC Trade Devt Corpn; Pres. and CEO Western and Pacific Bank of Canada, Vancouver 1986–90; Pres. and CEO Vancouver Int. Airport Authority 1992; Pres. and CEO Canfor Corpn 1998; fmr CEO Emerson Services Ltd; apptd BC trade envoy on softwood lumber 2017; mem. Conservative Party of Canada; MP (Vancouver Kingsway) 2004–08; Minister of Industry 2004, of Int. Trade and Minister for the Pacific Gateway and the Vancouver-Whistler Olympics 2006–08, Acting Minister for Foreign Affairs May–June 2008, Minister of Foreign Affairs 2008. *Telephone:* (604) 569-0237 (office). *E-mail:* emerson.services@shaw.ca (office).

EMERSON, E. Allen, BS, PhD; American computer scientist and academic; *Regents Chair and Professor Emeritus, Department of Computer Science, University of Texas;* b. 2 June 1954, Dallas, Tex.; ed Univ. of Texas, Harvard Univ.; apptd Prof., Dept of Computer Sciences, Univ. of Texas 1981, now Prof. Emer. and Regents Chair, also fmrly Endowed Prof.; mem. editorial bds of leading formal methods journals and conf. programme cttees; Kanellakis Prize, Asscn for Computing Machinery (ACM) 1998, CMU Newell Prize, IEEE LICS'06 Test-of-Time Award, ACM A.M. Turing Award 2007, an Information Sciences Inst. Highly Cited Researcher. *Achievements include:* co-inventor and co-developer of model checking, an algorithmic method of verifying nominally finite-state concurrent programmes. *Publications include:* Methods for Mu-calculus Model Checking: A Tutorial 1995; several book chapters and numerous scientific papers in professional journals on model checking, decision procedures and algorithmic methods of program synthesis. *Address:* Department of Computer Sciences, Gates-Dell Complex 3.720, University of Texas, Austin, TX 78712, USA (office). *Telephone:* (512) 471-9537 (office). *Fax:* (512) 471-8885 (office). *E-mail:* emerson@cs.utexas.edu (office). *Website:* www.cs.utexas.edu (office).

EMERSON, John B., BA, JD; American lawyer and diplomatist; b. New York, NY; ed Hamilton Coll., Univ. of Chicago; Partner, Manatt, Phelps & Phillips (law firm) –1987; Los Angeles Chief Deputy City Attorney 1987–93, selected by Friedrich Ebert Stiftung to visit Germany as part of American-German del.; served on Pres. Clinton's sr staff 1993–97, as Deputy Dir of Presidential Personnel, subsequently as Deputy Dir of Intergovernmental Affairs, also co-ordinated the Econ. Conf. of Clinton-Gore transition team and led efforts to obtain congressional approval of GATT Uruguay Round Agreement 1994 and extension of China's MFN trading status 1996; Pres. Capital Group Private Client Services 1997–2013; apptd to serve on Pres.'s Advisory Cttee for Trade Policy and Negotiations 2010; Amb. to Germany 2013–17; fmr Chair. Music Center of Los Angeles Co.; fmr Dir and Vice-Chair. Los Angeles Metropolitan YMCAs; fmr Trustee, The Buckley School; fmr Trustee and Pres. Bd of Marlborough School; fmr mem. Los Angeles Mayor's Trade Advisory Council, Pacific Council on Int. Policy, Council on Foreign Relations.

EMERY, Alan Eglin Heathcote, MD, PhD, DSc, FRCP, FRCPE, FACMG, FLS, FRSE; British physician and professor of human genetics; *Professor Emeritus, University of Edinburgh;* b. (Alan Eglin Heathcote-Emery), 21 Aug. 1928, Manchester, England; s. of Harold Heathcote Emery and Alice Eglin; m. 2nd Marcia Lynn Miller 1988; three s. three d. from previous m.; ed Manchester Central Grammar School, Chester Coll., Univ. of Manchester, Johns Hopkins Univ., USA; Postdoctoral Research Fellow, Johns Hopkins Univ., Baltimore 1961–64; Lecturer, then Reader in Medical Genetics, Univ. of Manchester 1964–68; Foundation Prof. and Chair., Dept of Human Genetics, Univ. of Edinburgh 1968–83, Prof. Emer. 1983–, Hon. Fellow 1990–; Research Dir European Neuromuscular Centre and Chair. Research Cttee 1990–99, Chief Scientific Adviser 1999–2012; Pres. British Clinical Genetics Soc. 1980–83; Visiting Prof., Univs of New York, Heidelberg, UCLA, Padua, Beijing, Duke, Cape Town, Warsaw, Royal Postgraduate Medical School, London, etc.; Harveian, Boerhaave, Jenner Lecturer etc.; mem. Scientific Cttee Int. Congress on Neuromuscular Diseases 1990, 1994, 1998, 2000; mem. Exec. Cttee Research Group on Neuromuscular Diseases of World Fed. of Neurology 1996–, Exec. Bd World Muscle Soc. 1999–; Adviser, Asian and Oceanian Myology Centre, Tokyo 2000–; Vice-Pres. Muscular Dystrophy Campaign of Great Britain 1999–; Pres. Section Medical Genetics, Royal Soc. of Medicine 2001–04 (Council mem. 2004–, Trustee 2007–08); Fellow, American Coll. of Medical Genetics; Hon. Clinical Prof., Univ. of Exeter; Hon. FRS (SA); Hon. Fellow, Green Templeton Coll., Oxford 1985, Gaetano Conte Acad. (Italy) 1991, Royal Soc. of Medicine; Hon. mem. Dutch Soc. of Genetics 1999, Asscn of British Neurologists 1999; Hon. MD (Naples, Würzburg, Athens), Hon. DSc (Univ. of Chester); Int. Award for Genetic Research (USA), Gaetano Conte Prize for Clinical Research 2000, Pro Finlandiae Gold Medal for contribs to Neuroscience 2000, Lifetime Achievement Award, WFN 2002, Double-day Award and Cockcroft Medal, School of Medicine, Univ. of Manchester 2007, Int. Honouree Award, Int. Congress on Neuromuscular Diseases 2010, Wall of Honour, Royal Soc. of Medicine 2010, Int. Award for Excellence in Educ., American Soc. of Human Genetics 2012, Lifetime Achievement Award, Muscular Dystrophy Campaign (UK) 2012, Lifetime Achievement Award, World Muscle Soc. 2015. *Publications:* Psychological Aspects of Genetic Counselling 1984, Methodology in Medical Genetics (second edn) 1986, Principles and Practice of Medical Genetics (second edn) 1991, Elements of Medical Genetics (eighth edn) 1992, The History of a Genetic Disease: Duchenne Muscular Dystrophy or Meryon's Disease 1995, Introduction to Recombinant DNA (second edn with S. Malcolm) 1995, Diagnostic Criteria for Neuromuscular Disorders (second edn) 1997, Neuromuscular Disorders: Clinical and Molecular Genetics 1998, The Muscular Dystrophies 2001, Medicine and Art (with M. L. H. Emery) 2003, Surgical & Medical Treatment in Art (with M. L. H. Emery) 2006, Mother & Child Care in Art 2007, Muscular Dystrophy: The Facts (third edn) 2008, The History of a Genetic Disease (with M. L. H. Emery) (second edn) 2011, Duchenne Muscular Dystrophy (fourth edn) 2015; several books of poetry, including haiku, 400 scientific papers. *Leisure interests:* ancient Greek history, oil painting, writing poems, particularly Haiku. *Address:* Green Templeton College, Woodstock Road, Oxford, OX2 6HG (office); 2 Ingleside Court, Budleigh Salterton, Devon, EX9 6NZ, England (home). *Telephone:* (1395) 445847 (home). *Fax:* (1395) 445847 (home). *E-mail:* alan.emery@gtc.ox.ac.uk (office).

EMERY, Lin; American sculptor; b. New York City; d. of Cornell Emery and Jean Weill; m. S. B. Braselman 1962 (deceased); one s.; ed Univs of Chicago and Sorbonne, Paris; worked in studio of Ossip Zadkine, Paris 1950; 54 solo exhbns in US museums and galleries 1957–2006; int. exhbns in Tokyo, Hong Kong, Manila, Sofia, Paris, London, Berlin, Brisbane, Kyoto and Frankfurt 1961–98; public sculpture erected in Civic Center, New Orleans 1966–70, Fidelity Center, Oklahoma City 1972, Humanities Center, Columbia, SC 1974, Federal Plaza, Houma, La. 1997, Marina Centre, Singapore 1986, City of Oxnard, Calif. 1988, Osaka Dome, Japan 1997, Mitre Corpn, Alexandra, Va 2001, Schiffer Publishing Co., Atglen, Pa 2002, Sterling Corpn, Las Colinas, Tex. 2002, etc.; Visiting Prof., Tulane School of Architecture, New Orleans 1969–70, Newcomb School of Art, New Orleans 1980; Visiting Artist and Lecturer, Art Acad. of Cincinnati, Louisiana State Univ., Univ. of New Orleans, Univ. of Texas at Austin, Univ. of Maine 1985–88; Chair. 9th Int. Sculpture Conf. 1976, Co-Chair. Mayor's Steering Cttees, New Orleans 1979–80; Studio Chair. Coll. Art Asscn 1979; Chair. Int. Sculpture Symposium, New Orleans 2004; mem. Bd Contemporary Arts Center, New Orleans 1997–; mem. Loyola Univ. Visiting Cttee 1996–99; adviser, Artists Guild, New Orleans 1997–99; mentor, Center for Creative Arts, New Orleans 1998; mem. Nat. Acad. of Design 2003–, Int. Women's Forum 2003–, Century Asscn, New York; Order of St Lazarus Companionate of Merit 2004; Hon. LHD (Loyola Univ) 2004; Mayor's Award for Achievement in the Arts, La 1980, Lazlo Aranyi Award for Public Art, Va 1990, Delgado Award for Artistic Excellence, La. 1997, Grand Prix for Public Sculpture (Japan) 1997, Gov.'s Arts Award, La. 2001, S. Simon Award, Nat. Acad. 2005. *Address:* 7520 Dominican Street, New Orleans, LA 70118, USA (home). *Telephone:* (504) 866-7775 (home). *Fax:* (504) 866-0144 (home). *E-mail:* lin@linemery.com (office).

EMIN, Tracey, CBE, RA; British artist; b. 3 July 1963, London; d. of Enver Emin and Pamela Cashin; ed John Cass School of Art, London, Maidstone Coll. of Art, Royal Coll. of Art; Eranda Prof. of Drawing, RA 2011–13; Dr hc (RCA) 2007, Hon. DLit (Univ. of Kent) 2007, Hon. PhD (London Metropolitan Univ.) 2007; Int. Award for Video Art, Baden-Baden 1997, Video Art Prize, Südwest Bank, Stuttgart 1997, Jury Prize, Cairo Biennale 2001. *Exhibitions include:* My Major Retrospective, White Cube, London 1993, Minky Manky, South London Gallery 1995, Exorcism of the Last Painting I Ever Made, Stockholm 1996, It's Not Me That's Crying, It's My Soul, Brussels 1996, I Need Art Like I Need God, South London Gallery 1997, Sobasex, Tokyo 1998, Tracey Emin Every Part of Me's Bleeding, NY 1999, What Do You Know About Love, Berlin 2000, Love is a Strange Thing, London 2000, You Forgot to Kiss My Soul, White Cube, London 2001, I Think It's In My Head, NY 2002, Ten Years, Amsterdam 2002, This Is Another Place, Oxford 2002, Tracey Emin, Sydney 2003, Memphis, Counter Gallery, London 2003, Fear, War and the Scream, Roslyn Oxley9, Sydney, and City Gallery, Wellington 2004, I'll Wait For You in Heaven, Galleria Lorcan O'Neill, Rome 2004, Tracey Emin, BP British Art Displays, Tate Britain, London 2004, Tracey Istanbul, Istanbul 2004, More Flow, Galleria Lorcan O'Neill, Rome 2006, Borrowed Light, Venice Biennale 2007, You Left Me Breathing, Gagosian Gallery, Beverly Hills 2007, Tracey Emin: 20 Years, Scottish Nat. Gallery of Art, Edinburgh, CAC, Malaga 2008, and Kunstmuseum Bern 2009, For You, Liverpool 2008, Strangeland, Berlin 2009, Those Who Suffer Love, White Cube, London 2009, Only God Knows I'm Good, Lehmann Maupin, NY 2009, Why Be Afraid?, Galleria Lorcan O'Neill, Rome 2010, Walking With Tears, RA, London 2010, Do Not Abandon Me, NY 2010, Praying to a Different God, Amanda Love Art, Sydney 2010, Do Not Abandon Me, London 2011, Love is What You Want, Hayward Gallery, London 2011, The Vanishing Lake, White Cube, London 2011, You Saved Me, Galleria Lorcan O'Neill, Rome 2012, You Don't Believe in Love But I Believe in

You, White Cube, Sao Paulo 2012, How it Feels, Buenos Aires 2012, She Lay Down Deep Beneath the Sea, Turner Contemporary, Margate 2012, Self Portrait, Aix-en-Provence 2013, Roman Standard, NY 2013, I Followed You To The Sun, NY 2013, The Last Great Adventure Is You, White Cube, London 2014, Tracey Emin/Egon Schiele: Where I Want To Go, Leopold Museum, Vienna 2015, Waiting To Love, Galleria Lorcan O'Neill, Rome 2015, BP Spotlight: Tracey Emin and Francis Bacon, Tate Britain, London 2015, Tracey Emin and William Blake in Focus, Tate Liverpool 2016, Stone Love, Lehmann Maupin, NY 2016, New Monotypes, Carolina Nitsch, NY 2016, I Cried Because I Love You, Lehmann Maupin, NY and White Cube, Hong Kong 2016, Surrounded By You, Chateau la Coste, Aix-en-Provence 2017, The Memory of Your Touch, Xavier Hufkens, Brussels 2017, Tracey Emin 'My Bed'/JMW Turner, Turner Contemporary, Margate 2017, The Distance of Your Heart, Amanda Love Art, Sydney 2018. *Work includes:* The Roman Standard (BBC public art comm. for Art05 Festival, Liverpool) 2005, The Distance of Your Heart (City of Sydney public art comm., Sydney) 2018, I Want My Time With You (Terrace Wires Art comm., St Pancras Int., London) 2018, A Moment Without You (Harbour Arts Sculpture Park, Hong Kong) 2018. *Films include:* Why I Never Became a Dancer, Top Spot (dir) 2004. *Publications include:* Exploration of the Soul 1995, Always Glad to See You 1997, Tracey Emin: Holiday Inn 1998, Tracey Emin on Pandaemonium 1998, Absolute Tracey 1998, Strangeland 2005, One Thousand Drawings 2009, Tracey Emin: My Life in a Column 2011, Angel Without You 2013, I Followed You To The Sun 2013, The Last Great Adventure is You 2014, Where I Want to Go 2015, I Cried Because I Love You 2016, The Memory of Your Touch 2017, Tracey Emin 2007–2017 2017. *Leisure interests:* writing poetry, watching sunsets. *Address:* c/o White Cube, 144–152 Bermondsey Street, London, SE1 3TQ, England (office). *Telephone:* (20) 7930-5373 (office). *E-mail:* enquiries@whitecube.com (office). *Website:* www.whitecube.com/artists/emin (office).

EMINEM, (Slim Shady); American rap artist and musician; b. (Marshall Bruce Mathers III), 17 Oct. 1972, St Joseph, Mo.; m. Kim Mathers (divorced); one d.; moved to Detroit aged 12; dropped out of high school to join local rap groups Basement Productions, D12; released debut album The Infinite on ind. label FBT; after releasing Slim Shady EP, made guest appearances with Kid Rock and Shabbam Shadeeq, leading to deal with Dr Dre's Aftermath Records; collaborations with artists, including Dr Dre, D12, Missy Elliott, Dido; Founder and Owner Slim Shady record label 1999–, Eight Mile Style publishing co.; f. Marshall Mathers Foundation (charity); MTV Annual American Music Awards Best Hip Hop Artist 2000, 2002, three Grammy Awards 2001, Best Pop/Rock Male Artist 2002, MTV Europe Music Awards for Best Male Act 2002, 2009, for Best Hip Hop Act 2002, 2013, for Global Icon 2013, BRIT Award for Best Int. Male Solo Artist 2003, 2005, American Music Awards for Best Male Pop/Rock Artist, Best Male Hip Hop/R&B Artist 2003, Acad. Award for Best Music (for Lose Yourself, from film 8 Mile) 2004, Grammy Award for Best Male Rap Solo Performance (for Lose Yourself) 2004, Grammy Award for Best Rap Song (for Lose Yourself) 2004, Grammy Award for Best Rap Performance by a Duo or Group (for Crack a Bottle with Dr Dre and 50 Cent) 2010, Grammy Award for Best Rap Solo Performance (for Not Afraid) 2011, Echo Award for Best Int. Hip Hop Artist, Germany 2005, Smash Hits Award for Best Hip-Hop Act 2005, American Music Award for Favorite Male Rap/Hip-Hop Artist 2005, 2006, Billboard Music Award for Top Rap Artist 2014, Grammy Award for Best Rap/Sung Collaboration (with Rihanna for The Monster) 2015, MTV Europe Music Awards for Best Hip Hop 2017. *Film:* 8 Mile 2002. *Recordings include:* albums: The Infinite 1997, The Slim Shady LP 1999, The Marshall Mathers LP (MTV Award for Best Album) 2000, The Eminem Show (MTV Award for Best Album 2002, Grammy Award for Best Rap Album, BRIT Award for Best Int. Album, American Music Awards for Best Pop/Rock Album, Best Hip Hop/R&B Album 2003) 2002, Eminem Is Back 2004, Encore 2004, Curtain Call 2005, Eminem Presents The Re Up 2006, Relapse (Grammy Award for Best Rap Album 2010) 2009, Relapse 2 2009, Recovery (Grammy Award for Best Rap Album 2011) 2010, The Marshall Mathers LP 2 (Billboard Music Award for Top Rap Album 2014, Grammy Award for Best Rap Album 2015) 2013, Revival 2017, Kamikaze 2018. *Publications:* Angry Blonde 2000, The Way I Am (auto-biog.) 2008. *Website:* www.shadyrecords.com; revival.eminem.com.

EMMERICH, Roland; German film director, screenwriter and film producer; b. 10 Nov. 1955, Stuttgart; film produced as student Das Arche Noah Prinzip (The Noah's Ark Principle) shown at 1984 Berlin Film Festival and sold to more than 20 countries; f. Centropolis Film Productions. *Films include:* Franzmann 1979, Das Arche Noah Prinzip 1984, Joey 1985, Hollywood-Monster 1987, Moon 44 1990, Eye of the Storm (producer) 1991, Universal Soldier 1992, Stargate 1994, The High Crusade (producer) 1994, Independence Day 1996, Godzilla 1998, The Thirteenth Floor (producer) 1999, The Patriot 2000, Eight Legged Freaks (producer) 2002, The Day After Tomorrow 2004, 10,000 BC 2008, 2012 2009, Dark Horse 2012, White House Down 2013, Stonewall 2015, Independence Day: Resurgence 2016. *Television includes:* (series) The Visitor (producer) 1997. *Address:* Centropolis Entertainment, Inc., 1445 North Stanley, 3rd Floor, Los Angeles, CA 90046, USA. *Telephone:* (323) 850-1212. *Fax:* (323) 850-1201. *Website:* www.centropolis.com.

EMMERT, Mark A., BA, PhD; American political scientist, academic and university administrator; *President, National Collegiate Athletic Association;* b. 16 Dec. 1952, Tacoma, Wash.; m. DeLaine S. Emmert; one s. one d.; ed Univ. of Washington, Maxwell School, Syracuse Univ.; various public service roles 1976–80; Univ. Fellow and Research Asst, Maxwell School, Syracuse Univ. 1980–83; Research Assoc., Center for Governmental Studies, then Asst Prof., Dept of Political Science, Northern Illinois Univ. 1983–85; held faculty and admin. positions at Univ. of Colorado, including Assoc. and Asst Prof., Grad. School of Public Affairs, Assoc. Dean Grad. School of Public Affairs, Assoc. Vice-Chancellor for Academic Affairs, Univ. of Colorado, Denver and Pres.'s Office, Boulder and Denver Campuses 1985–92; Prof. of Political Science, Provost and Vice-Pres. for Academic Affairs, Montana State Univ. 1992–95; Prof. of Political Science, Chancellor and Provost Univ. of Connecticut 1995–99; Prof., E. J. Ourso Coll. of Business Admin and Chancellor Louisiana State Univ. 1999–2004; Prof., Evans School of Public Affairs and Pres. Univ. of Washington 2004–10, mem. Univ. of Washington Medicine Bd; Pres. Nat. Collegiate Athletic Asscn 2010–; Guest of Ministry of Educ., People's Repub. of China; Visiting Scholar and Guest of Monash Univ., Melbourne, Australia; lectured and conducted training programs in Hong Kong, Okinawa, Panama City, Guam, US Micronesia, Germany, France and Mexico; consultant and trainer, Asscn of Governing Bds, San Antonio Art Inst., Colorado State Univ., Vision Hispanica, Colorado Gov.'s Business-Educ. Summit, Educ.-Policy Fellowship Program for the Inst. for Educational Leadership, Univ. of Oklahoma, Minnesota State Univ. System, Rochester Inst. of Tech.; Chair. Louisiana Univs Marine Consortium 2002; Chair. Pres.'s Council Southern Univs Research Asscn 2001–02; Co-Chair. Prosperity Partnership 2005–; mem. New England Council of Pres 1994–99, New England Asscn of Schools and Colls 1998–99, Educ. Comm. of the States, Commr for Louisiana 2000–04, Univ. Research Asscn (Pres Council 2000–04), Cttee Exec. Southeastern Conf. 2002–04, Exec. Council Southern Asscn of Schools and Colls 2000–04, Nat. Visiting Cttee Arizona State Univ. 2004–, American Asscn of Colls and Univs 2005–, Asscn of American Univs, Nat. Security Higher Educ. Advisory Bd 2005–, Asscn of Governing Bds of Univs and Colls Council of Pres 2005–, Nat. Asscn of State Univs and Land-Grant Colls (Co-Chair. Bd on Oceans and Atmosphere), American Council on Educ., Council of Fellows, Comm. on Leadership and Institutional Effectiveness, Nat. Collegiate Athletic Asscn Presidential Task Force on the Future of Intercollegiate Athletics Fiscal Responsibility Sub-cttee, Pac-10 Conf. of CEOs 2005–; Charter mem. Asscn of Pacific Rim Univs 2005–; fmr Dir Josephson Inst. of Ethics Bd, Louisiana Research Park Corpn, Shaw Center for the Arts, Baton Rouge Chamber of Commerce; Leadership mem. and Campaign Cabinet, Capital Area United Way; mem. Organizing Cttee Summer Nat. Sr Games 2001; mem. Advisory Bd Policy Consensus Center, Seattle Community Devt Roundtable 2005–, Gov.'s Global Competitiveness Council 2005– (mem. Research and Innovation Sub-cttee), Puget Sound Partnership; fmr mem. Bd of Dirs Baton Rouge Center for World Affairs; Trustee Greater Seattle Chamber of Commerce 2006–; mem. Conn. Acad. of Arts and Sciences; American Council on Educ. Fellow, J. W. Fulbright Admin. Fellow, Germany 1991, J. W. Fulbright Sr Admin. Seminar, Germany 1994, Gambit Magazine Baton Rouge Citizen of the Year 2000, Good Growth Award, Baton Rouge Business Report and Growth Council 2003, Marketer of the Year, Sales and Marketing Execs Asscn 2003. *Publications include:* numerous journal articles, monographs, book chapters and tech. reports. *Leisure interests:* boating, golf, scuba diving, fly-fishing, skiing, reading. *Address:* National Collegiate Athletic Association 700 West Washington Street, PO Box 6222, Indianapolis, IN 46206-6222, USA (office). *Telephone:* (317) 917-6222 (office). *Fax:* (317) 917-6888 (office). *Website:* www.ncaa.org (office).

EMMOTT, William (Bill) John, BA; British journalist; *Chairman, International Institute for Strategic Studies (IISS);* b. 6 Aug. 1956, Hammersmith, London, England; s. of Richard Emmott and Audrey Emmott; m. 1st Charlotte Crowther 1982 (divorced); m. 2nd Carol Barbara Mawer 1992; ed Latymer Upper School, Hammersmith and Magdalen and Nuffield Colls, Oxford; Brussels Corresp., The Economist 1980–82, Econs Corresp. 1982–83, Tokyo Corresp. 1983–86, Finance Ed. 1986–89, Business Affairs Ed. 1989–93, Ed.-in-Chief 1993–2006, Editorial Dir Economist Intelligence Unit May–Dec. 1992; Adviser, Swiss Re 2006–; Chair. London Library 2009–15, PeerIndex 2010–14; Visiting Prof., Shujitsu Univ., Okayama, Japan 2014–18; Visiting Fellow, All Souls Coll., Oxford 2017–18; Visiting Fellow, Blavatnik School of Govt, Oxford 2015–17; Dir, Development Consultants International 2006–09; Chair. The Wake Up Foundation 2013–; Chair. Japan Soc. of the UK 2019–; Chair. Trinity Long Room Hub Arts & Humanities Research Inst. 2019–; columnist, La Stampa 2010–, Nikkei Business 2015–; Trustee, IISS 2009–15, Chair. 2019–; Hon. Fellow, Magdalen Coll. Oxford 2002; Order of the Rising Sun, Gold Rays with Neck Ribbon (Japan) 2016; Hon. LLD (Warwick) 1999, (Northwestern) 2009, Hon. DLitt (City) 2001. *Films:* Girlfriend in a Coma (co-author and narrator) 2013, The Great European Disaster Movie (exec. producer) 2015. *Publications:* The Pocket Economist (with R. Pennant-Rea) 1983, The Sun Also Sets 1989, Japanophobia 1993, Kanryo no Taizai 1996, 20:21 Vision: The Lessons of the 20th Century for the 21st 2003, Hiwa Mata Noboru 2006, Japan's New Golden Age – of the next ten years 2006, Nihon no sentaku 2007, Sekai Choryu no Yomikata 2008, Rivals: How the Power Struggle between China, India and Japan will Shape our Next Decade 2008, Forza, Italia: Come Ripartire dopo Berlusconi 2010, Good Italy, Bad Italy 2012, The Fate of the West: The Battle to Save the World's Most Successful Political Idea 2017. *Leisure interests:* cricket, wine, dog-walking, journalism. *Address:* 5 Cranham Street, Oxford, OX2 6DD, England (office). *E-mail:* bill@billemmott.com (office); bill.emmott@japansociety.org.uk (office). *Website:* www.billemmott.com.

EMOMALI, Maj.-Gen. Rustam; Tajikistani politician and sports organization executive; *Mayor of Dushanbe;* b. (Rustam Emomalievich Rahmonov), 19 Dec. 1987, Danghara, Kulob Oblast (now Khatlon Viloyat), Tajik SSR, USSR; eldest s. of Pres. Emomali Rahmon (q.v.) and Azizmo Asadullayeva; m.; one s. one d.; ed Tajik State Nat. Univ., Diplomatic Acad. of Russian Ministry of Foreign Affairs, Moscow; co-f. FC Istiklol football club, Dushanbe 2007, played for it as a striker and served as its capt. –2012; Deputy Pres. Tajikistan Fotball Fed. 2011–12, Pres. 2012–; mem. Int. Relations Cttee, Olympic Council of Asia 2011–; mem. FIFA Devt Cttee 2012–14; apptd a leading specialist at Tajikistan's Org. for Co-operation with WTO 2006, a leading specialist in State Cttee on Investments and State Property 2009 (also adviser and later head of a dept); apptd a Deputy Head of the Youth Union (successor to Soviet-era Komsomol org.); has attended major int. summits and meetings with foreign dignitaries in Tajikistan 2009–; mem. Cen. Exec. Cttee, Hizbi Halki-demokratii Tojikiston (HDT) (People's Democratic Party of Tajikistan) 2010–; mem. Dushanbe Municipal Ass.; apptd Head of Anti-Smuggling Dept in Customs Service 2011–13, Head of Customs Service 2013–15; rank of Maj. 2011; rank of Maj.-Gen. 2013; Head of State Agency for Financial Control and Measures Against Corruption 2015–17; Mayor of Dushanbe 2017–. *Leisure interests:* car racing, collecting sports cars. *Address:* Office of the Mayor, 734000 Dushanbe, Xiyoboni Rudaki 80, Tajikistan (office). *Telephone:* (37) 2232214 (office). *Fax:* (37) 2232076 (office). *E-mail:* dushanbe80@yahoo.com (office). *Website:* www.dushanbe.tj/chairman/biography (office).

EMOVON, Emmanuel Uwumagbuhunmwun, PhD; Nigerian chemist, academic and fmr politician; b. 24 Feb. 1929, Benin City; s. of Gabriel A. Emovon and Oni Emovon; m. Princess Adesuwa C. Akenzua 1959; three s. three d.; ed Baptist School, Benin City, Edo Coll., Benin City, Univ. Coll., Ibadan, Univ. Coll., London Univ., UK; Lecturer in Chem., Univ. Coll. Ibadan 1959; Prof. of Chem., Univ. of Benin 1971; Vice-Chancellor Univ. of Jos 1978; Fed. Minister of Science and Tech. 1985–89; Co-ordinator, Sheda Science and Tech. Complex 1990–98 (retd); invested Chief Obayagbona of Benin 1991; fmr mem. numerous govt cttees and bds; fmr external examiner; Fellow Science Asscn of Nigeria, Nigerian Acad. of Science; nat. mem. ICSU 1986. *Publications:* numerous scientific papers. *Leisure interests:* photography, gardening, tennis, table tennis, cricket and football.

EMPEY, Baron (Life Peer), cr. 2011, of Shandon in the City and County of Belfast; **Reginald Norman Morgan Empey,** Kt, OBE, BSc; British politician; *Chairman, Ulster Unionist Party;* b. 26 Oct. 1947, Belfast, Co. Antrim, Northern Ireland; s. of Samuel Frederick Empey and Emily Winifred Empey (née Morgan); m. Stella Ethna Donnan 1977; one s. one d.; ed The Royal School, Armagh, Queen's Univ., Belfast; Publicity Officer, Ulster Young Unionist Council 1967–68, Vice-Chair. 1968–72; Chair. Vanguard Unionist Party 1974–75; mem. E Belfast NI Constitutional Convention 1975–76; mem. Belfast City Council 1985–2010; Deputy Lord Mayor 1988–89, Lord Mayor of Belfast 1989–90, 1993–94; mem. NI Ass. for Belfast East 1998–2002 (Ass. suspended Oct. 2002, restored May 2007), 2007–11; Minister of Enterprise, Trade and Investment 1999–2002; Acting First Minister of Northern Ireland July–Nov. 2001; Minister for Employment and Learning 2007–10; Deputy Leader United Ulster Unionist Party 1977–84; mem. Ulster Unionist Party (UUP), Deputy Leader UUP in NI Ass. 2003–05, Leader UUP 2005–10 (resgnd), Chair. 2012–; mem. Ulster Unionist Council 1987– (Hon. Sec. 1990–96, Vice-Pres. 1996–2002); Vice-Pres. Inst. of Export; Bd mem. Police Authority for NI 1992–2002, European Cttee of the Regions for NI 1994–2002; mem. House of Lords 2011–. *Leisure interests:* gardening, walking. *Address:* Ulster Unionist Party, 2 Belmont Road, Belfast, BT5 2AN, Northern Ireland (office); House of Commons, Westminster, London, SW1A 0PW, England. *Telephone:* (28) 9047-4630 (office); (28) 9065-2149 (office). *Fax:* (28) 9045-6899 (office). *E-mail:* empeyr@parliament.uk (office); uup@uup.org (office). *Website:* www.parliament.uk; www.uup.org (office).

EMSIS, Indulis, PhD; Latvian politician and biologist; *Consultant and Lecturer, Latvijas Universitate;* b. 2 Jan. 1952, Salacgrīva, Limbazi Dist; m.; one d.; ed Rīga First Secondary School, Univ. of Latvia, Moscow Scientific Research Inst.; Head, Lab. of Environmental Protection 1978–89; Deputy Chair. Nature Preservation Cttee 1989–90; mem. Supreme Council, Chair. Latvian Environmental Protection Cttee 1990–93; Minister of State, Ministry for Environmental Protection and Regional Devt 1993–98; Deputy Chair. SIA Eirokonsultants 1998–2000, Dir-Gen. SIA Eiroprojekts 2000–02; mem. Rīga City Council 2000–02, Deputy Chair. Devt Cttee; mem. 6th Saeima (Parl.) 1993–98, 8th Saeima 2002–04, 9th Saeima 2006–07, Speaker 2006–07; Prime Minister of Latvia March–Dec. 2004; mem. Latvian Green Party (part of Greens' and Farmers' Union) 1990–, also Co-Chair.; currently Consultant and Lecturer, Latvijas Universitate; Three Star Order (Third Degree) 1996; Award of the Baltic Sea Foundation for Outstanding Contribs to Protection of the Marine Environment, Certificate of Merit of the Cabinet of Ministers of the Repub. of Latvia. *Address:* Latvijas Universitate, Jelgava Street 1, Riga 1004, Latvia (office). *Telephone:* 6703-3920 (office). *E-mail:* indulis.emsis@lu.lv (office). *Website:* www.lu.lv (office).

ENARI, Atelina Ainuu, LLB, MSc; Samoan economist and central banker; *Governor, Central Bank of Samoa;* ed Univ. of Southern Queensland, Australia, Univ. of Wales, UK, Univ. of the South Pacific, Fiji and Vanuatu; joined Cen. Bank of Samoa 1991, apptd Man. Financial Markets Dept 2000, other positions included Economist, Research and Statistics Dept, Sr Economist and Asst Man. Int. Dept, Gov. and Chair. Cen. Bank of Samoa 2011–, also currently Chair. Samoa Int. Finance Authority. *Address:* Central Bank of Samoa, Private Bag, Apia, Samoa (office). *Telephone:* 34100 (office). *Fax:* 20293 (office). *E-mail:* centralbank@cbs.gov.ws (office). *Website:* www.cbs.gov.ws (office).

ENCINAS RODRÍGUEZ, Alejandro, BEcons; Mexican politician; *Senator of the State of Mexico;* b. 13 May 1954, Mexico City; ed Univ. Nacional Autónoma de México; mem. Cámara Federal de Diputados (Partido Revolucionario Institucional–PRI) 1985–88, mem. (Partido de la Revolución Democrática–PRD) 1991–94; adviser, ECLAC 1990, Inter-American Inst. for Co-operation on Agric. 1991; Head, Mexico City Govt 2005; Senator of the State of Mexico 2012–. *Address:* Senado (Senate), Av. Paseo de la Reforma 135, esq. Insurgentes Centro, Colonia Tabacalera, Cuauhtémoc, 06030 Mexico CP, Mexico (office). *Telephone:* (55) 5345-3000 (ext. 3112, 3961) (office). *E-mail:* aencinas@senado.gob.mx (office). *Website:* www.senado.gob.mx (office); www.alejandroencinas.com.mx.

ENDERBY, Sir John Edwin, Kt, KB, CBE, PhD, DSc, FRS; British scientist and academic; b. 16 Jan. 1931, Grimsby, Lincs.; s. of Thomas Edwin Enderby and Rheita Rebecca Enderby (née Hollinshead); m. Susan Bowles; one s. two d.; one s. (deceased) one d. from previous m.; ed Chester Grammar School, Westminster Coll., Birkbeck Coll., Univ. of London; Lecturer then Reader, Univ. of Sheffield 1960–69; Prof. and Head of Dept, Univ. of Leicester 1969–76; Prof. of Physics, Univ. of Bristol 1976–81, H.H. Wills Prof. 1981–96, Prof. Emer. 1996–, Head of Dept and Dir H.H. Wills Lab. 1981–94; Directeur-Adjoint, Inst. Laue-Langevin, Grenoble, France (on secondment) 1985–88; Ed. Proceedings of the Royal Society 'A' 1989–93; Ed.-in-Chief Journal of Physics: Condensed Matter 1997–2001; Physical Sec. and Vice-Pres. Royal Soc. 1999–2004; Pres. Inst. of Physics 2004–06, Hon. FInstP 2011; apptd Chair. Melys Diagnostics Ltd 2004; mem. Council Particle Physics and Astronomy Research Council 1994–98; Chief Scientific Adviser, Inst. of Physics Publishing 2002; Distinguished Argonne Fellow (USA); Foreign mem. Royal Holland Acad. of Science and Humanities 2001; Hon. Fellow, Birkbeck Coll., Univ. of London 2001; Hon. DSc (Loughborough) 1998, (Leicester) 2006, (Bristol) 2006, (Sheffield) 2007, (East Anglia) 2007, (Kent) 2008, (Huddersfield) 2011, (Chester) 2012; Guthrie Medal and Prize, Inst. of Physics 1995. *Publications:* numerous papers on liquids in academic journals. *Leisure interests:* travel, woodwork, music, reading. *Address:* H.H. Wills Physics Laboratory, University of Bristol, Tyndall Avenue, Bristol, BS8 1TL (office); 7 Cotham Lawn Road, Bristol, BS6 6DU, England (home). *Telephone:* (117) 928-8737 (Bristol) (office); (117) 973-3411 (home). *E-mail:* j.e.enderby@bristol.ac.uk (office). *Website:* www.bristol.ac.uk (office).

ENDERS, Thomas (Tom), PhD; German aeronautics industry executive; *CEO, Airbus Group NV;* b. 21 Dec. 1958; ed Univ. of Bonn, Univ. of California, Los Angeles, USA; served with 1st Airborne Div., Bundeswehr 1977–78, completed officer training, Maj. in Army Reserve Forces 1978–83; Asst, Fed. Parl., Bonn 1982–85; Research Assoc., Research Inst. of Konrad Adenauer Foundation, St Augustin 1985–87, Research Inst. of German Council on Foreign Affairs, Bonn 1988–89; Sr Research Assoc., IISS, London, UK 1989–90; mem. Planning Staff, Minister of Defence 1989–91; joined aeronautics mfr MBB (later Dasa and now part of EADS) 1991, served in various marketing posts 1991–95, Corp. Sec. and Head of Office of Chair. 1995–96, Dir of Corp. Devt and Tech. 1996–2000, apptd Head of Defence and Security Systems Div. 2000; mem. Exec. Cttee and CEO Defence and Security Systems Div., European Aeronautic Defence and Space Co. (EADS) NV 2000–05, Co-CEO EADS 2005–07, CEO Airbus SAS (subsidiary of EADS) 2007–12, CEO EADS (reorganized as Airbus Group NV Jan. 2014) 2012–; Pres. German Aerospace Industries Asscn (BDLI) 2005–12; Chair. Atlantik-Brücke e.V. 2005–09; mem. BDI Presidential Bd (German Industry Asscn) 2009–, Business Advisory Group of UK Prime Minister David Cameron 2011–15, Jt Advisory Council of Allianz SE 2013–. *Achievement:* performed a paradrop from the A400M Nov. 2010. *Address:* Airbus Group NV, PO Box 32008, 2303 DA Leiden, The Netherlands (office). *Telephone:* (71) 524-56-00 (office). *E-mail:* info@airbusgroup.com (office). *Website:* www.airbusgroup.com (office).

ENDICOTT, Timothy Andrew Orville, AB, MPhil, LLB, DPhil; Canadian lawyer and academic; *Professor of Legal Philosophy, University of Oxford;* ed Harvard Coll., USA, Univ. of Oxford, UK, Univ. of Toronto; barrister and solicitor, Osler, Hoskin & Harcourt LLP (law firm), Toronto 1988–91; Tutor in Law, Univ. of Oxford 1994–, Stipendiary Lecturer, Jesus Coll. 1994–95, Stipendiary Lecturer, St Anne's Coll. 1995–96, Lecturer, St Catherine's Coll. 1996–99, Fellow 1998–99, Fellow, Balliol Coll. 1999–, Dir of Grad. Studies, Faculty of Law 2004–07, Prof. of Legal Philosophy 2006–, Dean, Faculty of Law 2007–15; Rhodes Scholar, Univ. of Oxford 1983–85. *Publications:* Vagueness in Law 2000, Properties of Law (co-ed.) 2006, Administrative Law 2009. *Address:* Balliol College, University of Oxford, Oxford, OX1 3BJ, England (office). *Telephone:* (1865) 277754 (office). *E-mail:* timothy.endicott@law.ox.ac.uk (office). *Website:* www.law.ox.ac.uk (office).

ENDO, Akira, BA, PhD; Japanese biochemist and academic; *Director, Biopharm Research Laboratories Inc;* b. 14 Nov. 1933, Akita; ed Faculty of Agric., Tohoku Univ.; Research Investigator Sankyo Co. Ltd 1957–66, Sr Research Investigator 1969–78, later Head of Lab. of Fermentation Research Labs; Research Assoc., Albert Einstein Coll. of Medicine 1966–68; Assoc. Prof., Dept of Agricultural Chem., Faculty of Agric., Tokyo Univ. of Agric. and Tech. 1979–86, Prof. 1986–97, Distinguished Prof. Emer. 2008–; Dir Biopharm Research Laboratories, Inc. 1997–; Foreign Assoc., NAS 2011; Order of the Sacred Treasure, Gold and Silver Star 2012; Hon. DS (Univ. of Pennsylvania) 2012; Young Investigator Award in Agricultural Chem. (Japan) 1966, Heinrich Wieland Prize for the discovery of the HMG-CoA reductase inhibitors (FRG) 1987, Toray Science and Tech. Prize (Japan) 1988, Warren Alpert Foundation Prize, Harvard Medical School, USA) 2000, Massry Prize, Keck School of Medicine, Univ. of Southern California 2006, Japan Prize 2006, The Science and Tech. Foundation of Japan 2006, Lasker-DeBakey Clinical Medical Research Award 2008, inducted into Nat. Inventors Hall of Fame 2012, Prince Mahidol Award 2015, Hon. Lifetime Membership Award, Nat. Lipid Asscn, USA 2015, Canada Gairdner Int. Award 2017. *Achievements include:* discovered first cholesterol-lowering statin drug. *Publications:* numerous scientific papers in professional journals. *Address:* Biopharm Research Laboratories, Inc., 2-24-16, Nakacho Koganei, Tokyo, Japan (office). *E-mail:* aendo@biopharm.co.jp (office); aendo@cc.tuat.ac.jp (office). *Website:* biopharm.co.jp (office); endoakira.com.

ENDO, Nobuhiro; Japanese business executive; *Chairman and Representative Director, NEC Corporation;* b. 8 Nov. 1953; ed Grad. School of Science and Eng, Tokyo Inst. of Tech.; joined NEC Corpn 1981, Gen. Man. Mobile and Wireless Div. 2003–05, Sr Gen. Man. Mobile Network Operations Unit 2005–06, Sr Vice-Pres. and Exec. Gen. Man. 2006–09, Exec. Vice-Pres. 2009–10, mem. Bd of Dirs 2009–, Pres. 2010–16, Rep. Dir 2010–, Chair. 2016–; mem. Bd of Dirs MX Mobiling Co. 2006–, Japan Post Insurance Co. 2016–, Seiko Holdings Corpn 2017–. *Address:* NEC Corporation, 7-1, Shiba 5-chome, Minato-ku, Tokyo 108-8001, Japan (office). *Telephone:* (3) 3454-1111 (office). *Fax:* (3) 3798-1510 (office). *E-mail:* info@nec.com (office). *Website:* www.nec.com (office).

ENDZIŅŠ, Aivars, DrIur; Latvian lawyer, politician and academic; *Professor, Faculty of Law, Turiba University;* b. 8 Dec. 1940, Rīga; m. Inara Sturma 1963; two s.; ed Univ. of Latvia, Moscow State Univ.; Lecturer, then Assoc. Prof., Univ. of Latvia 1972–90, 1996–97; Assoc. Prof., Police Acad. 1998–2002, Prof. 2002–; mem. Supreme Council, Presidium Supreme Council 1990–93; mem. Saeima (Parl.), Vice-Chair. Legal Affairs Cttee 1993–96; Acting Chair., then Chair. Constitutional Court 1996–2007; unsuccessful cand. (Harmony Centre party) in presidential elections 2007; mem. Parl. Ass., Council of Europe 1995–96; Assoc. mem. Democracy Through Law Comm. (Venice Comm.) 1992–95, mem. 1995–, mem. Bureau 1991–2001; currently Prof., Faculty of Law, School of Business Administration, Turiba Univ., Riga; Order of Three Stars 2001, Grand Officer, Repub. of Italy 2004. *Publications include:* more than 60 academic publs. *Leisure interests:* fishing, hunting. *Address:* Faculty of Law, School of Business Administration, Turiba University, Graudu Street 68, Riga 1058 (office); No. 31 Drustu St, Rīga 1002, Latvia (home). *Telephone:* 6760-7662 (office); 793-4654 (home). *E-mail:* aivars.endzins@turiba.lv (office). *Website:* www.turiba.lv (office).

ENESTAM, Jan-Erik, MPolSci; Finnish politician; b. 12 March 1947, Västanfjärd; m. Solveig V. Dahlqvist 1970; three c.; ed Åbo Akademi Univ., Turku; tourism researcher, Åland Provincial Govt 1972–74; researcher, Finnish Tourist Bd 1974; Head of Office, Åland Provincial Govt 1974–78; Municipal Man. Västanfjärd 1978–83; Project Man. Nordic Council of Ministers 1983–91; mem. Regional Policy Advisory Bd 1987–91; mem. Parl. 1991–2007; Chair. Västanfjärd Municipal Council 1989–96; Special Adviser to Minister of Defence 1990–91; Minister of Defence and Minister at Ministry of Social Affairs (Equality) and Health Jan.–April 1995; Minister of the Interior 1995–99, of Defence, Nordic Co-operation and Foreign Affairs (Adjacent Areas) 1999–2003, of the Environment and Foreign Affairs (Nordic Co-operation) 2003–07; Deputy Chair. Cen. Fed. of Fishing Industry 1986–94; Vice-Pres. Svenska Folkpartiet (SFP—Swedish People's Party) Parl. Group 1991–94, Chair. SFP 1998–2006; Sec.-Gen. Nordic Council 2007–13; Commdr, Order of the White Rose of Finland 1996, Kt (Third Class), Order of Grand Duke Gediminas (Lithuania) 1997, Cross of Merit with Clasp, Armour Guild; Medal for Mil. Merit 1995, Medal of Merit, Cen. Chamber of Commerce of Finland. *Leisure interests:* literature, cross-country skiing, swimming, football, canoeing, cooking. *E-mail:* jee@kitnet.fi.

ENEX, Jean-Charles, MPA; Haitian academic, politician and fmr government official; b. 18 July 1960, Chansolme, Port-de-Paix; m.; three c.; ed Univ. Libre de Bruxelles, Belgium, Univ. of Missouri, USA; Prof. of Admin. Law, Faculty of Law and Econs, State Univ. of Haiti 1991–; Prof., Valparaiso Univ., Port-de-Paix 2006–; Sec.-Gen., Council of Ministers (with rank of minister) 2004–06; Special Adviser to Pres. René Préval 2007–11; Adviser to Pres. Michel Martelly 2011–16; Prime Minister 2016–17; fmr consultant to numerous nat. and int. insts regarding the organization, action and law related to political and admin. matters. *Publications include:* Haitian Administrative Law Manual; numerous articles and research reports on administrative policy development, local participation and decision-making in administrative matters. *Address:* c/o Office of the Prime Minister, 33 blvd Harry S Truman, BP 6114, Port-au-Prince, Haiti (office).

ENGEL, Klaus, Dr rer. nat; German business executive; *Chairman of the Executive Board and CEO, Evonik Industries AG;* b. 21 April 1956, Duisburg; ed Ruhr Univ., Bochum; with Chemische Werke Hüls AG, Marl 1984–89, VEBA AG, Düsseldorf 1989–94, Hüls AG, Marl 1994–98; Man. Dir Creanova Spezialchemie GmbH, Marl 1998; with Stinnes AG, Mülheim an der Ruhr 1998; mem. Exec. Bd Brenntag AG, Mülheim an der Ruhr 1999–2006, Chair. 2001–06, Chief Exec. Dir Brenntag Man. GmbH 2004–06; mem. Exec. Bd RAG AG, Essen 2006–07; Chair. Exec. Bd Degussa AG, Düsseldorf 2006–08, Chair. Bd of Man., Evonik Degussa GmbH, Essen 2007–08, mem. Exec. Bd Evonik Industries AG, Essen 2007–08, Chair. Exec. Bd and CEO 2009–. *Address:* Evonik Industries AG, Rellinghauser Straße 1–11, 45128 Essen, Germany (office). *Telephone:* (201) 177-01 (office). *Fax:* (201) 177-3475 (office). *E-mail:* info@evonik.com (office). *Website:* www.evonik.com (office); corporate.evonik.com (office).

ENGELBERT, Catherine (Cathy), BS, CPA; American accountant and business executive; *CEO, Deloitte, LLP;* b. 1964; m.; one s. one d.; ed Lehigh Univ.; joined Deloitte 1986, numerous leadership positions including Nat. Audit Man. Partner, Deloitte, LLP 1986, mem. Deloitte, LLP Bd of Dirs, mem. Strategic Investment, Finance & Audit, Risk, and Regulatory & Govt Relations Cttees, Chair. and CEO, Deloitte & Touche, LLP 2014–15, CEO Deloitte, LLP 2015–; mem. Financial Accounting Standards Advisory Council; mem. American Inst. of Certified Public Accountants; certified public accountant licensed in Pennsylvania, New York, and New Jersey. *Address:* Deloitte LLP, 100 Kimball Drive, Parsippany, NJ 07054-2176, USA (office). *Telephone:* (973) 602-6000 (office). *Fax:* (973) 602-5050 (office). *E-mail:* cathyengelbertdeloitteusceo@deloitte.com (office). *Website:* www.deloitte.com (office).

ENGELBRECHT, Jüri; Estonian physicist, mathematician and academic; *Head of Department, Institute of Cybernetics, Tallinn University of Technology;* b. 1 Aug. 1939, Tallinn; m.; two c.; ed Tallinn Tech. Univ.; part-time assoc., then Prof., Tallinn Univ. of Tech. 1974–92, 1994–, Head of Dept, Inst. of Cybernetics 1986–; mem. Estonian Acad. of Sciences 1990, Pres. 1994–2004, Vice-Pres. 2004–; Chair. Estonian Cttee for Mechanics 1991–; Adjunct Prof., Helsinki Univ. of Tech.; Visiting Prof., Czech Technical Univ. 1967–68, Newcastle-upon-Tyne Univ. 1979–80, 1986, Univ. of Messina 1981, 1987, Budapest Technical Univ. 1989, Univ. of Cambridge 1989, 1994, Univ. of Paris VI 1991, RWTH Aachen 1992, 1995, Univ. of Torino 1996, Univ. of Duisburg-Essen 2003; Pres. ALLEA (European Fed. of Nat. Acads of Sciences and Humanities) 2005–; For Ed.-in-Chief Proceedings of the Estonian Academy of Sciences 1991–95; Ed. Research Reports in Physics 1988–93; mem. Ed. Bd Prikladnaya Mekhanika and several other journals; mem. Estonian Soc. for Physics, Academia Scientiarum et Artium Europaea 1996–, Accad. Peloritana dei Pericolanti, Italy; Foreign mem. Latvian Acad. of Sciences 1996–, Gothenburg Royal Soc. of Sciences and Arts 1998–, Hungarian Acad. of Sciences 1998–, Bulgarian Acad. of Sciences 2007–; Fellow, World Innovation Foundation 2001–, Academia Europaea 2004–, Lisbon Acad. of Sciences 2010–, World Acad. of Arts and Sciences 2010–; Hon. mem. Estonian Naturalists Soc. 2003–; Kt White Rose 1st Class (Finland) 1999, Coat of Arms 4th Class (Estonia) 1999, Lion Grand Cross (Finland) 2001, Chevalier des Palmes Académiques 2003, Order of Merit (No 1) of Ministry of Educ. and Research 2004, Cavalier Cross of the Order of Merit (Poland) 2005, Order of the Nat. Coat of Arms 3rd Class 2007; Dr hc (Budapest) 1999; Estonian Science Prize 1992, Humboldt Research Award 1993, Medal of the Baltic Acads 2000, Marin Drinov Medal, Bulgarian Acad. of Sciences 2004, Nikolai Alumäe Medal, Estonian Acad. of Sciences 2005. *Publications:* Nonlinear Deformation Waves 1981, Nonlinear Wave Processes of Deformation in Solids 1983, Nonlinear Evolution Equations 1986, An Introduction to Asymmetric Solitary Waves 1991, Nonlinear Dynamics and Chaos 1993, Nonlinear Wave Dynamics: Complexity and Simplicity 1997, and more than 200 scientific articles. *Address:* Estonian Academy of Sciences, Kohtu 6, 10130 Tallinn (office); Institute of Cybernetics, Tallinn University of Technology, Akadeemia tee 21, 12618 Tallinn, Estonia (office). *Telephone:* (2) 644-20-13 (office). *Fax:* (2) 645-18-29 (office). *E-mail:* je@ioc.ee (office); J.Engelbrecht@akadeemia.ee (office). *Website:* www.akadeemia.ee (office); homes.ioc.ee/je (office).

ENGELL, Mikaela, MA; Danish government official; *High Commissioner of Greenland;* b. 4 Oct. 1956, Copenhagen; d. of Maj.-Gen. Hans Christian Blæsenborg Engell; four c.; ed Univ. of Copenhagen; teacher, Head of Dept, Greenland Teacher Training Coll. and Greenland Business School 1984–93; Head of Section, Greenland Home Rule Ministry of Health and the Environment 1993–95, Pvt. Sec. to the Minister 1995–99, Head of Office, Foreign Affairs, Greenland Home Rule 1999–2001, Acting Perm. Sec. 2001–03, Perm. Sec. for Foreign Affairs 2003–05, Counsellor, Danish Ministry of Foreign Affairs 2005–11, High Commr of Greenland (Danish External Territory) 2011–; mem. Danish-Greenland Cultural Foundation; Order of Dannebrog (Knight first class). *Address:* The High Commissioner of Greenland, PO Box 1030, 3900 Nuuk, Greenland (office). *Telephone:* 321001 (office). *Fax:* 324171 (office). *E-mail:* ro@gl.stm.dk (office). *Website:* www.rigsombudsmanden.gl (office).

ENGEN, Travis, BS; American business executive (retd); b. 1944, Calif.; m.; one d.; ed MIT; held various man. positions at Bell Aerospace including dir of electronics; Dir Marketing Republic Electronic Industries Group 1976–79; Dir Govt Avionics, Bendix Avionics Div. 1980–83; Vice-Pres. and Gen. Man., Bendix Gen. Aviation Avionics Div. 1983–85; Pres. and Gen. Man. ITT Avionics 1985–86, Pres. and CEO ITT Defence, Exec. Vice-Pres. ITT Corpn 1991–94, CEO ITT Industries, 1995; Dir Alcan Inc. 1996–2006, Pres. and CEO 2001–06 (retd); Dir Lyondell Chemical Co., Int. Aluminium Inst., Canadian Council of Chief Execs; mem. US Govt Defense Business Practice Implementation Bd; Chair. World Business Council for Sustainable Devt 2006–08; apptd Chair. Prince of Wales Int. Business Leaders Forum 2005, now mem. Int. Advisory Bd; SAM/SPG Sustainability Leadership Award 2006. *Leisure interest:* racing vintage cars. *Address:* c/o International Advisory Board, The Prince of Wales International Business Leaders Forum (IBLF), 15–16 Cornwall Terrace, Regent's Park, London, NW1 4QP, England (office).

ENGIBOUS, Thomas (Tom) J., MSc; American electronics industry executive (retd); b. 31 Jan. 1953, St Louis, Mo.; s. of James Engibous and Emma Engibous (née Buck); m. Wendy Engibous; three c.; ed Purdue Univ.; joined Texas Instruments Inc. (TI) 1976, Exec. Vice-Pres. 1993–96, Pres. Semiconductor group 1993–96, Pres. and CEO TI 1996–2004, mem. Bd of Dirs 1996–2008, Chair. 2004–08 (retd); Chair. Catalyst Inc. 2002–05, now Chair. Emer.; Chair. J. C. Penney Co. Inc. 2012–15; mem. Eng Visiting Cttee, Purdue Univ.; mem. Nat. Acad. of Eng, Inst. of Electrical and Electronics Engineers; Trustee Southern Methodist Univ.; Hon. Trustee, Southwestern Medical Foundation; Hon. DEng (Purdue Univ.) 1997; Woodrow Wilson Award 2004, inducted into Texas Business Hall of Fame. *Address:* 20 Shady Bend Drive, Melissa, TX 75434, USA.

ENGL, Walter L., Dr rer. nat, FIEEE; German professor of engineering; b. 8 April 1926, Regensburg; ed Technical Univ. of Munich; with Siemens Instrument and Control Div. 1950–63, latterly Head of Research Div.; Prof., Tech. Univ. of Aachen 1963–91, then Emer. Prof., Dean, Faculty of Eng 1968–69; Visiting Prof., Univ. of Arizona 1967, Stanford Univ. 1970, Univ. of Tokyo 1972, 1980; mem. Acad. of Science of North Rhine-Westphalia; mem. Int. Union of Radio Science; Foreign Assoc. mem. Eng Acad. of Japan; Hon. Prof., Univ. of Kiel 1992; VDE-Ehrenring (highest award of German Electrical Engineers Soc.). *Publications include:* 100 publs. *Address:* Zum Heider Busch 5, 52134 Herzogenrath, Germany (home). *E-mail:* w.l.engl@web.de.

ENGLAND, Philip Christopher, BSc, DPhil, FRS; British geophysicist and academic; *Professor of Geology, Department of Earth Sciences, University of Oxford;* b. 30 April 1951; ed Univ. of Bristol, Univ. of Oxford; NATO Postdoctoral Fellow, Norwegian Seismic Array, Kjeller, Norway 1976; NERC Research Fellow, Dept of Geodesy and Geophysics, Univ. of Cambridge 1977–79, Jr Research Fellow, Darwin Coll. 1978–80, IBM Research Fellow, Dept of Earth Sciences, Cambridge 1979–81; Asst and Assoc. Prof., Dept of Geological Sciences, Harvard Univ., USA 1981–86; Lecturer in Geophysics, Dept of Earth Sciences, Univ. of Oxford 1986–2000, Prof. of Geology 2000–; Gold Medal, Royal Astronomical Soc. 2016. *Address:* Department of Earth Sciences, University of Oxford, South Parks Road, Oxford, OX1 3AN, England (office). *Website:* www.earth.ox.ac.uk (office).

ENGLAND, Richard, BArch; Maltese architect, academic, artist and poet; *Director, England & England, Architects;* b. 3 Oct. 1937, Sliema; s. of Edwin England Sant Fournier and Ina Desain; m. Myriam Borg Manduca 1962; one s. one d.; ed St Edward's Coll., Univ. of Malta, Politecnico, Milan, Italy; student-architect in Gio Ponti's studio, Milan 1960–62; Dir England & England, Architects 1962–; Dean Faculty of Architecture, Head, Dept of Architecture, Univ. of Malta 1987–89; Prof., Int. Acad. of Architecture 1987–, Academician 1991–, Vice-Pres. 2009–; Visiting Prof., Univ. of Malta; Fellow, Inst. of Professional Designers, London, Foundation of Int. Studies, Malta, Royal Society of Arts, UK; Hon. Prof., Univ. of Georgia, Inst. of Advanced Studies, New York Univ., Univ. of Buenos Aires; Hon. Fellow, Univ. of Bath (UK); Hon. FAIA 1999; Hon. mem. World Forum of Young Architects, Colegio de Arquitectos, Jalisco, Mexico; Officer, Nat. Order of Merit (Malta) 1993; Dr hc (Univ. of Architecture, Civil Eng and Geodesy, Sofia, Bulgaria), (Spiru Haret Univ., Romania), (Univ. of Malta); Interarch 1985, 1989, 1991, 1993 and 1995 Laureate Prizes, Commonwealth Architects Regional Awards 1985, 1987, Gold Medal City of Toulouse 1985, Comité des Critiques d'Architecture Silver Medal 1987, USSR Biennale Laureate Prize 1988, IFRAA Prize (USA) 1991, Int. Prize, Costa Rica Biennale 1996, Gold Medal, Belgrade Architectural Biennale 2000, Grand Prix, Int. Acad. of Architecture 2006, Annual Prize, Int. Acad. of Architecture 2012. *Works include:* Manikata Church, Univ. of Malta Extension, Cen. Bank of Malta, Malta Parl., Millennium Chapel, St James Cavalier Centre for Creativity, Valletta; various commercial bldgs, hotels and banks in Malta and the Middle East. *Publications include:* Walls of Malta 1973, White is White 1973, Contemporary Art in Malta 1974, Carrier-Citadel Metamorphosis 1974, Island: A Poem for Seeing 1980, Uncaged Reflections: Selected Writings 1965–80, In Search of Silent Spaces 1983, Octaves of Reflection (with Charles Camilleri) 1987, Eye to I (selected poems) 1994, Sacri Luogi 1995, Mdina, Citadel of Memory (with Conrad Thake) 1996, Fraxions 1996, Gozo – Island of Oblivion 1997, Transfigurations: Places of Prayer (with Linda Schubert) 2000, Viaggio in Italia: Travel Sketches 2000, Gabriel Caruana Ceramics 2001, The Palette, Paintings of John Borg Manduca 2005, Norbert Attard 2007, Sanctuaries: Collected Poems 2007, Clavichords: Collected Poems 2009, Between Shadow & Stone: A Visual Exploration of Richard England's Architecture with Timmy Gambin 2011, Tapestries: Collected Poems 2012. *Leisure interests:* music and art in general. *Address:* England & England Architects, 26/1 Merchants Street, Valletta, VLT10 (office); 18 Oleander Street, The Gardens, St Julians, STJ 1912, Malta (home). *Telephone:* 27350171 (home); 21350171 (home). *E-mail:* richardengland@onvol.net (office). *Website:* www.architectrichardengland.com (office).

ENGLE, Robert F., BS, MS, PhD; American economist and academic; *Michael Armellino Professor in the Management of Financial Services, Leonard Stern School of Business, New York University;* b. 10 Nov. 1942, Syracuse, New York; s. of Robert Fry Engle, Jr and Mary Starr Engle; m. Marianne Eger Engle 1969; one s. one d.; ed Williams Coll., Cornell Univ.; Asst Prof., MIT 1969–74, Assoc. Prof. 1974–77; Assoc. Prof., Univ. of Calif., San Diego 1975–77, Prof. 1977–, Chair. Dept of Econs 1990–94, Chancellor's Assocs Chair. in Econs 1993–; Michael Armellino Prof. in the Man. of Financial Services, New York Univ. Stern School of Business 2000–, also Dir Volatility Inst.; Prin. Robert F. Engle Econometric Services; Co-Founding Pres. Soc. for Financial Econometrics; Nat. Bureau of Econ. Research Assoc. 1987–; Fellow, Econometric Soc. 1981– (mem. Council 1994–), AAAS 1995–, Inst. For Quantitative Research in Finance; mem. Int. Advisory Panel, Risk Man. Inst. 2012; Roger F. Murray Prize, Inst. for Quantitative Research in Finance 1991, Nobel Prize in Econs 2003 (jt recipient), Presidential Medal, Hofstra Univ. 2009, Distinguished Alumni Award, Dept of Statistical Science, Cornell Univ. 2011. *Publications include:* more than 100 academic papers and three books.

Address: Kaufman Management Center, 44 West 4th Street, KMC 9-62, New York, NY 10012-1126, USA (office). *Telephone:* (212) 998-0710 (office). *Fax:* (212) 995-4220 (office). *E-mail:* rengle@stern.nyu.edu (office). *Website:* www.stern.nyu.edu (office).

ENGLER, John Mathias, JD; American lawyer, association executive and fmr politician; *President Business Roundtable;* b. 12 Oct. 1948, Mount Pleasant, Mich.; s. of Mathias Engler and Agnes Engler (née Neyer); m. Michele Engler; three d.; ed Michigan State Univ. and Thomas M. Cooley Law School; mem. Mich. House of Reps 1971–78; mem. Mich. Senate 1979–90, Republican leader 1983, majority leader 1984–90; Gov. of Mich. 1990–2003; Pres. and CEO Nat. Asscn of Mfrs 2004–10; Pres. Business Roundtable 2011–; Chair. Advisory Bd Blackford Capital's Michigan Prosperity Fund 2013; mem. Annie E Casey Foundation; mem. Bd of Trustees and mem. Bd of Dirs, Universal Forest Products Inc.; Hon. LLD (Alma Coll.) 1984, (Western Mich.) 1991. *Address:* Business Roundtable, 300 New Jersey Avenue, NW, Suite 800, Washington, DC 20001, USA (office). *Telephone:* (202) 872-1260 (office). *Website:* www.businessroundtable.org (office).

ENGLERT, Baron; **François,** DèsSc; Belgian physicist and academic; *Professor Emeritus of Physics, Université Libre de Bruxelles;* b. 6 Nov. 1932, Etterbeek; m. Mira Nikomarow; one s. four d.; ed Université Libre de Bruxelles; Asst, Université Libre de Bruxelles 1959–60, Chargé de cours 1961–64, Prof. of Physics 1964–98, Co-Dir Theoretical Physics Group 1980–98, Prof. Emer. 1998–; Research Assoc., Cornell Univ., USA 1959–60, Asst Prof. 1960–61; Perm. Sackler Fellow and Sr Prof. by Special Appointment, Tel-Aviv Univ. 1992–, Visiting Prof., Inst. for Quantum Studies, Chapman Univ. 2011; Hon. mem., Solvay Insts 2006; Dr hc (Université de Mons-Hainaut) 2004, (Vrije Universiteit Brussels) 2005, (Université Blaise Pascal), (Univ. of Edinburgh), (Peking Univ.), (East China Normal Univ.), (Nat. Tech. Univ. of Athens), (Bar Ilan Univ.), (Hebrew Univ. Jerusalem); Prix de Sciences Mathematiques et Physiques, Acad. Royale de Belgique 1977, First Award of the Int. Gravity Contest (with R. Brout and E. Gunzig) 1978, Prix Franqui 1982, European Physical Soc. High Energy and Particle Physics Prize (with R. Brout and Peter W. Higgs) 1997, Wolf Prize in Physics (with R. Brout and Peter W. Higgs) 2004, J.J. Sakurai Prize (co-recipient), American Physical Soc. 2010, Prince of Asturias Award for Technical & Scientific Research 2013, Nobel Prize in Physics (co-recipient with Peter W. Higgs) 2013. *Publications include:* more than 115 articles in scientific journals. *Address:* Service de physique théorique, Université Libre de Bruxelles, Campus de la Plaine, CP 225, 2 Boulevard du Triomphe, 1050 Brussels, Belgium (office). *Telephone:* (714) 997-6815 (Chapman) (home); (2) 650-55-80 (office); (2) 375-46-49 (home). *Fax:* (2) 650-59-51 (office). *E-mail:* fenglert@ulb.ac.be (office).

ENGLISH, Hon. (Simon William) Bill, BA, BComm; New Zealand politician; b. 1961, Lumsden; m. Mary English; six c.; ed Univ. of Otago, Victoria Univ. of Wellington; fmr policy analyst and farmer; MP for Wallace 1990–93, for Clutha-Southland 1993–2014, Nat. Party list mem. 2014–18, Leader of the Opposition 2001–03, Oct. 2017–Feb. 2018; Parl. Under-Sec. for Health and Crown Health Enterprises 1993–96, Minister of Crown Health Enterprises, Assoc. Minister of Educ., Minister of Health 1996–99 and Assoc. Minister of Revenue 1997–99, Minister of Finance (including Responsibility for Govt Superannuation Fund) and of Revenue 1999, Assoc. Treas. 1998–99, Deputy Prime Minister and Minister of Finance 2008–16, Minister for Regulatory Reform, Minister for Infrastructure 2008–11, for HNZC (Housing New Zealand) 2014–16, Prime Minister 2016–17, also Minister of Ministerial Services and Minister of Nat. Security and Intelligence; Leader, New Zealand Nat. Party 2001–03, 2016–18, Deputy Leader 2006–16, Nat. Party Spokesman for Educ. 2003–08. *Leisure interests:* rugby, running, cycling. *Address:* c/o New Zealand National Party, 41 Pipitea St, Thorndon, Wellington 6011, New Zealand (office). *Telephone:* (4) 894-7016 (office). *Fax:* (4) 894-7031 (office). *E-mail:* hq@national.org.nz (office). *Website:* www.national.org.nz (office); www.billenglish.co.nz.

ENGLISH, Edmond J. (Ted), BA; American business executive; *CEO, Bob's Discount Furniture LLC;* b. 1954; ed Northeastern Univ. Coll. of Business Admin; joined TJC Companies Inc. 1983, held various merchandising positions 1983–95, Sr Vice-Pres. Merchandising 1995–97, Exec. Vice-Pres. Merchandising, Planning and Allocation, Marmaxx Group 1997–98, Sr Vice-Pres. and Group Exec. 1998–99, COO TJX 1999–2000, Chair. Marmaxx Group 2000–01, Pres. 1999–2005, CEO 2000–05 (resgnd); CEO Bob's Discount Furniture LLC, Manchester, Conn. 2006–; mem. Bd of Dirs Citizens Financial Group, BJ's Wholesale Club, Inc. 2006–; Hon. DIur (Framingham State Coll.) 2002; Sir Ernest Shackleton Award, Shackleton Schools 2002, named Business Leader of the Year, MetroWest Chamber of Commerce 2003. *Address:* Bob's Discount Furniture LLC, 428 Tolland Turnpike, Manchester, CT 06040-1715, USA (office). *Telephone:* (860) 645-3208 (office). *Fax:* (860) 645-4056 (office). *Website:* www.mybobs.com (office).

ENGLISH, Joseph Thomas, MD; American psychiatrist; *Professor and System Chairman, Department of Psychiatry and Behavioral Sciences, St. Vincent Catholic Medical Centers of New York;* b. 21 May 1933, Philadelphia, Pa; s. of Thomas J. English and Helen Gilmore English; m. Ann Carr Sanger 1969; two s. one d.; ed Jefferson Medical Coll.; intern, Jefferson Medical Coll. Hosp., Philadelphia 1958–59; Resident in Psychiatry, Inst. of Pa Hosp., Philadelphia 1959–61, Nat. Inst. of Mental Health, Bethesda, Md 1961–62; Chief Psychiatrist, US Peace Corps, Washington, DC 1962–66; Deputy Asst Dir of Health Affairs, Office of Econ. Opportunity 1966, Asst Dir 1966–68; Admin., Health Services and Mental Health Admin., US Dept of Health, Educ. and Welfare 1968–70; Pres. New York City Health and Hosps Corpn 1970–73; Chair.; Prof. and System Chair. Dept of Psychiatry and Behavioral Sciences, St Vincent Catholic Medical Centers of New York 1973–; Prof. of Psychiatry, New York Medical Coll. 1979–, Assoc. Dean 1979–; Adjunct Prof., Cornell Univ. School of Medicine 1975–; Lecturer in Psychiatry, Harvard Univ. 1978–89; Visiting Fellow, Woodrow Wilson Nat. Fellowship Foundation 1979–; Trustee, Sarah Lawrence Coll. 1986–90, Menninger Foundation 1993–; Pres. American Psychiatric Asscn 1992–93; mem. World Psychiatric Soc. (Chair. section on religion and psychiatry 1994–), American Medical Asscn, New York Psychiatric Soc., Hosp. Soc. of New York, Asscn for Acad. Psychiatry, New York State Medical Soc., American Asscn of Gen. Hosp. Psychiatrists, Group Advancement Psychiatry, American Coll. of Mental Health Admins, American Hosp. Asscn, Greater New York Hosp. Asscn (Chair. Mental Health and Substance Abuse Services Cttee 1975–), Catholic Health Asscn; mem. Joint Comm. Accreditation Hosps 1984–86, Vice-Chair. 1986–88, Chair. 1988–89, Commr 2002–; numerous awards. *Address:* Department of Psychiatry and Behavioral Sciences, St Vincent's Hospital and Medical Center, 203 West 12th Street, New York, NY 10011-7762, USA (office). *Telephone:* (212) 604-8252 (office). *Fax:* (212) 604-8794 (office). *Website:* www.svcmc.org (office).

ENGLISH, Sir Terence Alexander Hawthorne, Kt, KBE, MA, FRCS, FRCP; British cardiac surgeon (retd); *Patron, Primary Trauma Care Foundation;* b. 3 Oct. 1932, Pietermaritzburg, South Africa; s. of Arthur Alexander English and Mavis Eleanor Lund; m. 1st Ann Margaret Smart Dicey; two s. two d.; m. 2nd Judith Milne 2002; ed Witwatersrand Univ. and Guy's Hosp. Medical School, London; Intern, Demonstrator in Anatomy, Jr Surgical Registrar, Guy's Hosp. 1962–65; Resident Surgical Officer, Bolingbroke Hosp. 1966; Surgical Registrar, Brompton Hosp. 1967; Sr Surgical Registrar, Nat. Heart and London Chest Hosps 1968–72; Research Fellow, Cardiac Surgery, Univ. of Ala 1969; Consultant Cardiothoracic Surgeon to Papworth and Addenbrooke's Hosps 1973–95; Dir British Heart Foundation Heart Transplant Research Unit, Papworth Hosp. 1980–89; Consultant Cardiac Adviser, Humana Hosp. Wellington, London 1983–89; Master of St Catharine's Coll. Cambridge 1993–2000; Pres. Int. Soc. for Heart Transplantation 1984–85, Royal Coll. of Surgeons 1989–92; mem. Jt Consultants Cttee 1989–92, Standing Medical Advisory Cttee 1989–92, Audit Comm. 1993–99; Pres. BMA 1995–96; Gov. The Leys School 1993–2001; Trustee, Medical Aid for Palestinians, Steering Group, Healthcare Professionals for Assisted Dying, Dignity in Dying; Patron, Primary Trauma Care Foundation; Hon. Fellow, St Catharine's Coll., Cambridge, St Hugh's Coll., Cambridge, Worcester Coll., Oxford, King's Coll. London; Hon. DSc (Sussex), (York), (Oxford Brookes Univ.); Hon. MD (Nantes), (Mahidol, Bangkok), (Witwatersrand, S Africa); Man. of the Year, Royal Asscn for Disability and Rehabilitation 1980, Clement Price Thomas Award, Royal Coll. of Surgeons 1986, Lifetime Achievement Award, Soc. for Cardiothoracic Surgery of GB and Ireland 2009, Lifetime Achievement Award, International Soc. for Heart and Lung Transplantation 2014, Ray C Fish Award for Scientific Achievement, Texas Heart Inst. 2014. *Achievement:* performed Britain's first successful heart transplant in 1979. *Publications:* Follow Your Star from Mining to Heart Transplants: A Surgeon's Story 2011; more than 100 articles in scientific journals. *Leisure interests:* reading, hill walking, South African history. *Address:* 28 Tree Lane, Oxford, OX4 4EY, England (home). *Telephone:* (1865) 717708 (home). *E-mail:* tenglish@doctors.org.uk (office). *Website:* terenceenglish.com.

ENKHBAYAR, Jadambaagiin; Mongolian lawyer and politician; b. 16 Feb. 1973, Ulan Bator; s. of Shagalyn Jadambaa; ed Nat. Univ. of Mongolia, Maastricht School of Man., Netherlands; Dir-Gen. Gazar LLC 1992–2000; Head of Dept, Petroleum and Customs Authority 2000–02; Head of Dept and Vice-Chair., Ulan Bator Customs Authority 2002–03; Adviser, Customs Gen. Authority 2004–06; Vice-Chair. State Professional Inspection Authority 2006–08, Head of Secr. 2008; mem. Mongolian Great Khural (Parl.) for Govi-Altai 2008–, mem. Standing Cttee on Environment, Food and Agric.; Minister of Defence 2012–13; mem. Mongolian People's Party (fmrly Mongolian People's Revolutionary Party). *Address:* c/o Mongolian People's Party, Palace of Independence, Ulan Bator, Mongolia. *E-mail:* contact@mpp.mn.

ENKHBAYAR, Nambaryn; Mongolian politician and writer; b. 1 June 1958, Ulan Bator; s. of Baljinnyam Nambar and Radnaa Budkhand; m. Onon Tsolmon 1986; four c.; ed High School No. 23, Ulan Bator, Literature Inst., Moscow, Univ. of Leeds, UK; Ed. and Interpreter, Exec. Sec. and Head of Dept, Asscn of Mongolian Writers 1980–90; Vice-Pres. and Ed., Mongolian Interpreters' Union 1990–92; First Vice-Chair. Culture and Art Devt Cttee 1990–92; Minister of Culture 1992–96; Leader of the Opposition 1997–2000; mem. Great Hural (Parl.) 1992–, Speaker 2004–05; Prime Minister of Mongolia 2000–04; Pres. of Mongolia 2005–09, also C-in-C of Armed Forces; Chair. Mongolian People's Revolutionary Party (MPRP) 1997–2005; World Bank Adviser on Asian Culture and Buddhist Religion 1998–; Chair. Mongolia-India Friendship Asscn; Head of Nat. Council of Museums 1995–; Int. Pres. Alliance of Religions and Conservation 2003–; Govt of Mongolia Polar Star 1996, MPRP Politician of the Year 1997, Govt of Mongolia Star of the Flag for Work Achievements 2001. *Publications:* translated several classic Russian novels; About Mongolian Arts, Literature and Emptiness 1989, On the Indicators of Development from the Buddhist Point of View 1998, Some Thoughts on the Relationship between Buddhist Philosophy and Economics 1998, To Develop or Not to Develop 1998. *Leisure interests:* reading, tennis, basketball, volleyball. *Address:* c/o State Palace, Ulan Bator 12 (office); Ikh Tenger, Suite 50-3, Ulan Bator, Mongolia (home).

ENKHBOLD, Mieyeegombo, MEcon; Mongolian politician; b. 19 July 1964, Ulan Bator; m.; two c.; ed School of Economy, Nat. Univ. of Mongolia, studies in Japan and at Local Govt Training Inst., Germany; Economist, Public Service Office of Ulan Bator 1987–89; Expert, Ministry of Public Estate Service 1989–91; joined Mongolian People's Revolutionary Party (MPRP) 1990, Chair. MPRP Council, Ulan Bator 1997, Chair. MPRP (now Mongolian People's Party—MPP) 2005–07, 2013–17; Head of Estate Service Dept, Ulan Bator House of Reps 1991–92; Deputy Gov. Chingeltei Dist of Ulan Bator 1992–96; Chair. Presidium of Chingeltei Dists, Khural of Citizens Reps 1996–98; Gov. and Mayor of Ulan Bator 1998–2005; mem. Parl. 2005–; Prime Minister of Mongolia 2006–07 (resgnd); Deputy Prime Minister 2007–12; Deputy Chair. (Speaker) of the Parl. of Mongolia 2012–16, Chair. 2016–19; cand. in presidential election 2017; Full mem. Int. Acad. of Informatization of the UN 2003; Hon. Dr of State Admin (Guan Yun Univ., South Korea) 2005, (Guangdong Univ., South Korea) 2006; Dr hc (Orkhon Univ.). *Address:* Parliament, State Great Hural Mongolian, 14201, Ulaanbaatar, Mongolia (office). *Telephone:* (51) 267016 (office). *Fax:* (11) 327016 (office). *E-mail:* enkhboldm@parliament.mn (office). *Website:* www.parliament.mn (office); enkhboldm.parliament.mn (office).

ENKHBOLD, Nyamaa, MA; Mongolian politician; *Minister of Defence;* b. 6 Jan. 1957; m.; two c.; ed Press Inst. of Moscow, Russia, Political Inst., Moscow, Univ. of Sydney, Australia; mem. Mongolian People's Revolutionary Party; Economist, Ministry of Culture 1979–80, Expert, Planning Dept 1980–86; Deputy Dir State Printing House 1986–90; Gen. Dir Mongol Hevlel Corpn 1990–93; Adviser to Deputy Prime Minister 1993–95; Head of Press and Public Relations Dept, Office of the Pres. 1997–2000; mem. State Great Hural (Parl.) 2000–, Deputy Chair. 2008–12, fmr Chair. Mongolia-Indonesia Parl. Group, Vice-Chair. Mongolia-Japan

Parl. Group, Chair. Mongolian Parliamentarians Group for Population and Devt; Minister of Foreign Affairs 2006–07, of Defence 2017–; Head of Govt Affairs Directorate 2007–08; apptd Chair. Mongolian People's Party 2012–13; Pres. Mongolian Red Cross Soc.; Order Polar Star 2001. *Address:* Ministry of Defence, Government Building 7, Enkhtaivny Örgön Chölöö 51, Bayanzürkh District, Ulaanbaatar, Mongolia (office). *Telephone:* (51) 263531 (office). *Fax:* (11) 458112 (office). *E-mail:* info@mod.gov.mn (office); enkhbold@parliament.mn (office). *Website:* www.mod.gov.mn (office); enkhboldn.parliament.mn (office).

ENKHSAIKHAN, Jargalsaikhany, DJur; Mongolian diplomatist and researcher; *Chairman, Blue Banner;* b. (Enkhee), 2 Sept. 1950, Ulaanbaatar; s. of Jargalsaikhan Bayaryn and Martha Tserengiin; m. 1st Tuul Myagmarjavyn 1976 (divorced 1993); m. 2nd Batgerel Budjavyn 1994; two s. four d.; ed Moscow State Inst. for Int. Relations; has held numerous positions at Ministry of Foreign Affairs, including Third, then Second Sec., Treaty and Legal Affairs Dept 1974–79, Third, then Second Sec. Perm. Mission to UN, New York 1979–86, Acting Head, Policy Planning Dept and Treaty and Legal Affairs Dept 1986–88, Deputy Chief of Mission, Embassy in Moscow 1988–92; Foreign Policy and Legal Adviser to Pres. of Mongolia 1992–93; Exec. Sec. Nat. Security Council 1993–96; Mongolian Rep. at UN Conf. on Law of the Sea 1976–82; Perm. Rep. to UN, New York 1996–2003, Rapporteur Legal (Sixth) Cttee of UN Gen. Ass. 1983, Vice-Chair. 1984, Chair. 1998, Vice-Chair. Special Cttee on Non-Use of Force in Int. Relations 1983, Chair. Group of Land-Locked States 1997, Vice-Pres. 52nd session UN Gen. Ass. 1997, Vice-Chair. Disarmament Comm. 1997; Exec. Dir Mongolian Nat. Coalition for Int. Criminal Court 2004–06; Adviser and Lead Researcher, Inst. for Strategic Studies, Nat. Security Council 2007; Adviser to Minister of Foreign Affairs 2007–08; Focal Point and Co-ordinator of Mongolia's nuclear-weapon-free status 2008–; Amb. to Austria and Amb. and Perm. Rep. to UN, Vienna 2008–13 (also accred as Amb. to Italy 2009–12, to Croatia 2010–12), Perm. Rep. to FAO, Rome 2009–12, to OSCE 2012–13; Adviser, Ministry of Foreign Affairs 2013, Amb.-at-Large in charge of disarmament issues 2013–14; Chair. Blue Banner (non-governmental org. to promote Mongolia's nuclear-weapon-free status) 2015–; Gov. of Mongolia, Bd Govs, IAEA 2009–11, Pres. 54th Gen. Conf. of IAEA Sept. 2010; Chair. Working Group A, Comprehensive Test Ban Treaty Preparatory Comm. (CTBTO Prepcom) 2011–12; Adviser, Mongolia's Presidency of Community of Democracies 2013; Amb.-at-large of Mangolia 2013–14; State Merit Lawyer of Mongolia 2016; Hon. Prof. of Int. Relations 2006; Mongolian State Order of the Polar Star 1991, Mongolian Order of the Red Banner 2012, Order of Labour Merit 2012, Merited Lawyer of Mongolia 2015; Dr hc (SIRPA, Mangolian Nat. Univ.) 2018. *Publications:* articles on int. relations, int. law, foreign policy, nuclear disarmament-related issues, democratic reforms in Mongolia, role of civil society in Mongolia, etc. *Leisure interest:* reading. *Address:* BZD, 3 Horoo, 12 Horoolol, Building 55, Apt 9, Ulaanbaatar 13381, Mongolia (home). *Telephone:* 7717-3661 (office); 9931-3661 (mobile). *E-mail:* enkhee@bluebanner.org.mn (office).

ENKHSAIKHAN, Mendsaikhan, PhD; Mongolian economist, politician and diplomatist; *Ambassador to Sweden;* b. 4 June 1955, Ulan Bator; early work as an economist; mem. Mongolian Great Khural (Parl.) 1990–93, 2004–08; Chief of Staff to Pres. Ochirbat 1993–96; Prime Minister of Mongolia 1996–98, Deputy Prime Minister 2006–07; Dir Premier Int. Co. 1998–2003; Chair. Nat. Democratic Party 2003–05; Amb. to Sweden 2017–; fmr Minister of State. *Address:* Embassy of Mongolia, Svärdvägen 25b, 182 33 Danderyd, Sweden (office). *Telephone:* (8) 753-11-35 (office). *Fax:* (8) 753-11-38 (office). *E-mail:* stockholm@mfa.gov.mn (office). *Website:* stockholm.mfa.gov.mn (office).

ENNACEUR, Mohamed, PhD; Tunisian lawyer, diplomatist and politician; *President, Assembly of the Representatives of the People;* b. 21 March 1934, El Djem; m. Siren Möenstre; three s. two d.; ed Univ. of Tunis, Univ. of Paris (Sorbonne); early career as lawyer; Attaché, Ministry of Public Health and Social Affairs 1959–61, Chef du Cabinet 1961–64; Head of Transport Div., Ministry of Social Affairs 1964–67; Dir-Gen., Office for Professional Training and Employment 1967–72; Gov. of Sousse 1972–73; Minister of Labour and Social Affairs 1974–77, 1979–85; Pres. Econ. and Social Council of Tunisia 1985–91; Perm. Rep. to UN and other int. orgs, Geneva 1991–96; Minister of Social Affairs Jan.–Dec. 2011; Pres. Ass. of the Reps. of the People (Parl.) 2014–; Acting Pres. Nidaa Tounes (Call for Tunisia) 2014–; Co-ordinator, UN Pacte Mondial agreement in Tunisia 2005–; Chair. World Employment Conf. (ILO) 1976, 71st session of Int. Labour Conf. (ILO) 1985, 49th session of Human Rights Comm. (UN) 1993; Pres. Inst. Social-Consult; Ed. Tunisian Social Law Review; Hon. KBE; Grand Cordon of Order of Independence, Order of the Repub., Ordre de Léopold (Belgium), Ordre d'Orange-Nassau (Netherlands), Ordre du Grand-Duché (Luxembourg), Ordre National du Mérite (France), Ordre National du Mérite (Côte d'Ivoire), Commdr, Order of Merit (Germany). *Publications include:* Human Rights after the Vienna Conference 1993; articles on labour law, human rights and social policy in Int. Studies Review, Tunisian Social Law Review, Int. Review of the Red Cross and other publs. *Leisure interests:* sports, music. *Address:* Office of the President, Assembly of the Representatives of the People, Palais du Bardo, 2000 Tunis, Tunisia (office). *Telephone:* (71) 510-200 (office). *Fax:* (71) 514-608 (office). *E-mail:* anc@anc.tn (office). *Website:* www.arp.tn (office).

ENNIS-HILL, Dame Jessica, DBE, CBE, MBE, BSc; British track and field athlete; b. 28 Jan. 1986, Sheffield, Yorks., England; d. of Vinnie Ennis and Alison Powell; m. Andy Hill 2013; ed Univ. of Sheffield; competed at World Youth Championship, Sherbrooke 2003, World Junior Championship, Grosseto 2004; winner European Athletics Junior Championship, Kaunas 2005; bronze medal, Summer Universiade, Izmir 2005; bronze medal (heptathlon), Commonwealth Games, Melbourne 2006; bronze medal (100m hurdle), European Under-23 Championship, Debrecen 2007; finished sixth at European Indoor Championship (pentathlon), Birmingham 2007; finished fourth at World Championship, Osaka 2007; gold medal (heptathlon), World Championship, Berlin 2009; winner Int. Asscn of Athletics Feds (IAAF) World Combined Events Challenge, Desenzano del Garda 2009; gold medal (heptathlon), European Championship, Barcelona 2010; gold medal (pentathlon), World Indoor Championship, Doha 2010; winner (60m hurdle), five team int. meeting, Glasgow 2010; winner (heptathlon), Hypo-Meeting, Götzis 2010; seventh position (javelin throw), Diamond League, Gateshead 2010; silver medal (heptathlon), World Championship, Daegu 2011, awarded gold medal after Tatyana Chernova was stripped of title for doping offences 2016; winner (60m hurdle), Aviva Int. meeting, Glasgow 2011; winner (heptathlon), Hypo-Meeting, Götzis 2011; finished seventh (100m hurdle), eighth position (long jump), Diamond League, New York 2011; silver medal (pentathlon), World Indoor Championship, Istanbul 2012 (nat. record of 4,965 points); winner (heptathlon), IAAF World Combined Events Challenge, Götzis 2012; gold medal (heptathlon), Olympic Games, London 2012 (British and Commonwealth record of 6,995 points); double World Champion, first British woman to win world titles both indoors and outdoors; writes a column for The Times newspaper; Amb. for the Jaguar Acad. of Sport; Patron Sheffield Children's Hosp., Wells Sports Foundation; Hon. DLitt (Sheffield) 2010; Women's European Athletics Rising Star of the Year 2007, Sportswoman of the Year, British Sports Journalists Asscn 2009, 2010, Sportswoman of the Year, Ultimate Woman of the Year Awards, Cosmopolitan Magazine 2009, 2010, British Athlete of the Year, British Athletics Writers Asscn 2009, 2010, 2011, Outstanding Female Athlete, Commonwealth Sports Awards 2010, Dame Marea Hartman Award 2010, Most Inspirational Sportswoman of the Year, Jaguar Acad. of Sport Annual Awards 2010, Sportswoman of the Year, Glamour Magazine 2012, Sunday Times Sportswoman of the Year Award 2012, Women's European Athlete of the Year 2012, Laureus World Sportswoman of the Year 2012. *Publication:* Jessica Ennis: Unbelievable–From My Childhood Dreams to Winning Olympic Gold 2012. *Leisure interests:* cooking, shopping, listening to music, Sheffield United Football Club. *Address:* c/o United Kingdom Athletics, Athletics House, Alexander Stadium, Walsall Road, Perry Barr, Birmingham, B42 2BE, England. *Website:* www.jessicaennis.net.

ENO, Brian Peter George St John Baptiste de la Salle; British composer, artist, keyboard player and producer; b. 15 May 1948, Woodbridge, Suffolk; s. of William Arnold Eno and Maria Alphonsine Eno (née Buslot); m. 1st Sarah Grenville 1967; one d.; m. 2nd Anthea Norman-Taylor 1988; two c.; ed St Mary's Convent, St Joseph's Coll., Ipswich School of Art, Winchester Coll. of Art; Founder-mem. Roxy Music 1971–73; worked with guitarist Robert Fripp 1975–76; invented 'ambient music' 1975; Visiting Prof., RCA 1995–; Hon. Prof. of New Media, Berlin Univ. of Art 1998–; f. Long Now Foundation 1996; mem. PRS, BAC&S; Hon. DTech (Plymouth) 1995; Dr hc, Royal Coll. of Art 2007; Q Magazine Award for Best Producer (with others) 1993, BRIT Awards for Best Producer 1994, 1996, Frankfurter Musikpreis 1994, Inspiration Award (with David Bowie) 1995, Grammy Awards for Producer of Best Record of the Year 2000, 2009. *Recordings include:* albums: Here Come The Warm Jets 1974, Taking Tiger Mountain (By Strategy) 1974, Another Green World 1975, Discreet Music 1975, Before and After Science 1977, Music For Films 1978, Ambient 1: Music For Airports 1978, After the Heat 1978, My Life in the Bush of Ghosts (with David Byrne) 1981, Ambient 3: Day of Radiance 1981, Empty Landscapes 1981, Ambient 4: On Land 1982, Music For Films Vol. 2 1983, Apollo: Atmospheres and Soundtracks 1983, Begegnungen 1984, Thursday Afternoon 1985, Begegnungen II 1985, Music For Films Vol. 3 1988, Wrong Way Up 1990, Nerve Net 1992, The Shutov Assembly 1992, Neroli 1993, Headcandy 1994, Spinner 1995, The Drop 1997, Extracts from Music for White Cube 1997, Kite Stories 1999, I Dormienti 1999, Music for Onmyo-Ji 2000, Music for Civic Recovery Center 2000, Drawn From Life 2001, January 07003: Bell Studies for The Clock 2003, Another Day on Earth 2005, Everything that Happens will Happen Today (with David Byrne) 2008, Small Craft on a Milk Sea 2010, Lux 2012, Someday World (with Karl Hyde) 2014, The Ship 2016, Reflection 2017; with Robert Fripp: No Pussyfooting 1975, Evening Star 1976, The Equatorial Stars 2004, The Cotswold Gnomes 2006, Beyond Even 1992–2006 2007; numerous albums as producer, co-producer, collaborations, guest appearances on albums, and remixes including: U2, Coldplay, Paul Simon, David Bowie, David Byrne. *Publications include:* A Year with Swollen Appendices 1995, The Margin: A Canongate Diary for 2007 (ed.). *Address:* Opal Ltd, Regent House, 1 Pratt Mews, London, NW1 0AD, England. *Website:* www.enoshop.co.uk; www.brian-eno.net.

ENOKSEN, Hans; Greenlandic politician; *Minister of Fisheries, Hunting and Agriculture;* b. 7 Aug. 1956, Itilleq; mem. Siumut (Forward) Party, Chair. 2001–09; mem. Parl. 1995–; Minister for Fisheries, Hunting and Settlements 2001–02, 2016–; Prime Minister, Greenland Home Rule Govt 2002–09; re-elected to Inatsisartut (Progressive Party) in elections of Jan. 2014, broke with the party and founded Partii Naleraq March 2014; Greenland Home Rule Nersonaat in Gold 2003. *Address:* Partii Naleraq, Imaneq 2, 3900 Nuuk, Greenland (office). *Telephone:* 346233 (office). *E-mail:* hes@kni.gl (office); prp@inatsisartut.gl (office). *Website:* www.partiinaleraq.gl (office).

ENQUIST, Per Olov, (P.O. Enquist), MA; Swedish novelist, playwright, journalist and poet; b. 23 Sept. 1934, Hjoggböle; m. 2nd Lone Bastholm; ed Univ. of Uppsala; Visiting Prof., UCLA 1973; Svenska Dagbladet Prize 1966, Nordic Council Literary Prize 1969, Selma Lagerlöf Prize 1977, H.C. Andersen Prize 1992, Eyvind Johnson Prize 1994, August Award 1999, Deutsche Bücherpreis 2002, Premio Mondello 2002, Nelly Sachs Prize 2003, Independent Foreign Fiction Prize 2003, Premio Napoli 2007, Augustpriset 2008, Österreichischer Staatspreis für Europäische Literatur (Austrian State Prize for European Literature) 2009, Nordic Prize, Swedish Academy 2010, Budapest Grand Prize 2011. *Publications include:* Kristallögat 1961, Färdvägen 1963, Magnetisörens Femte Vinter 1964, Bröderna Casey 1964, Hess 1966, Sextiotalskritik 1966, Legionärerna 1968, Sekonden 1971, Katedralen i München 1972, Berättelser Från de Inställda Upprorens Tid (short stories) 1974, Tribadernas Natt 1975, Chez Nous (with Anders Ehnmark) 1976, Musikanternas Uttåg 1978, Mannen På Trottoaren 1979, Till Fedra 1980, Från Regnormarnas Liv 1981, En Triptyk 1981, Doktor Mabuses Nya Testamente (with Anders Ehnmark) 1982, Strindberg Ett Liv 1984, Nedstörtad Ängel 1985, Två Reportage om Idrott 1986, I Lodjurets Timma 1988, Kapten Nemos Bibliotek 1991, Hamsun (screenplay) 1996, Bildmakarna (play) 1998, Livläkarens Besök (The Visit of the Ryal Physician) 1999, Systrarna (play) 2000, Lewis Resa (Lewi's Journey) 2001, Boken om Blanche och Marie (The Story of Blanche and Marie) 2004, Et Annat Liv 2008, Liknelseboken: en kärlekshistoria 2013; contrib. to literary criticism in newspapers, including Uppsala Nya Tidning, Svenska Dagbladet, Expressen. *Address:* c/o Norstedts, Tryckerigatan 4, Box 2052, 103 12 Stockholm, Sweden (office).

ENRILE, Juan Ponce (see PONCE ENRILE, Juan).

ENSIGN, John E., BS, DMV; American politician and fmr veterinarian; b. 25 March 1958, Roseville, Calif.; s. of Mike Ensign and Sharon Ensign; m. Darlene Sciaretta; three c.; ed Ore. State Univ., Colo State Univ.; owner of animal hosp. in

Las Vegas; Gen. Man. Gold Strike Hotel and Casino 1991, Nevada Landing Hotel and Casino 1992; mem. US Congress from 1st Dist, Nev. 1994–98, mem. Ways and Means Cttee, Sub-Cttee on Health, Sub-Cttee on Human Resources, Comm. on Resources 1995–98; cand. for Senate 1998–99; Senator from Nev. 2001–11.

ENSOUR, Abdullah, PhD; Jordanian politician; b. 20 Jan. 1939, Salt, Transjordan (now Jordan); ed American Univ. of Beirut, Univ. of Paris (Sorbonne), France; Deputy in Parl. 1989–; Minister of Planning 1984, 1985, of Educ. 1989–91, of Foreign Affairs 1991–93, of Industry and Trade 1993–96, of Higher Educ. 1996–97; Deputy Prime Minister and Minister of Admin. Devt 1997–98; Deputy Prime Minister and Minister of Information 1998–2001; Senator in Jordanian Parl. –2001; Prime Minister and Minister of Defence 2012–16; Chair. Bd of Trustees, Al-Zaytoonah Univ. of Jordan –2001; fmr Gov. of Jordan to the World Bank, Deputy to IMF and Deputy Perm. Del. to UNESCO; mem. Bd Arab African Bank, Nuackchott (Pres.), Univ. of Jordan (Vice-Pres.), French Univs' Grads in Jordan (Hon. Pres.); Ind.; Istiqlal Medal of the First Order, Order of the Star of Jordan, Kawkab Medal of the First Order; Educ. Jordanian Medal – Excellent.

ENTHOVEN, Marius, MSc; Dutch civil servant and international organization official; b. 23 Nov. 1940, Baarn; s. of Emil S. Enthoven and Anna G. Schouten; m. Lidwine Kolfschoten 1965; four d.; ed Delft Tech. Univ., Princeton Univ., USA; Research Assoc., Princeton Univ. 1965–67; Research Fellow, Dutch Nat. Aerospace Labs (NLR) 1967–72; Head of Noise Abatement Dept, Ministry for Environment 1972–77, Dir Scientific Affairs 1977–80, Chief Insp. Environmental Protection 1980–88, Dir-Gen. Environmental Protection 1988–94; Dir-Gen. Environment, Nuclear Safety and Civil Protection, Directorate-Gen. XI, European Comm. 1994–98; Special Adviser to Sec.-Gen., European Comm. 1997–98; Exec. Dir NIB Capital Bank NV, The Hague 1998–2004, also Exec. Dir Research Inst.; Chair. Vereniging Oud-Leden Delftsch Studenten Corps 2008–; Chair. Alliance for UN Univ. for Peace (UPEACE) 2008–, mem. Bd of Dirs UN Univ. for Peace 2008–; Vice-Chair. Algemene Energieraad 2002–10; mem. Supervisory Bd Dura Vermeer Groep 2004–; mem. Energy Council (ind. advisory body that advises Dutch govt and parl. on energy policy) 2002–10; Kt Order of the Dutch Lion. *Publications include:* books and articles on environmental man. issues. *Leisure interests:* literature, theatre, music, tennis. *Telephone:* (70) 3268255 (office). *E-mail:* marius@enthoven.eu.

ENTHOVEN, Raphaël, PhD; French philosopher, academic and television producer; *Producer, Philosophie, ARTE France;* b. 9 Nov. 1975, Paris; s. of Jean-Paul Enthoven and Catherine David; m. Justine Lévy 1995; one s. with Carla Bruni; one c. with Chloé Lambert; one s. with Maud Fontenoy; ed École Normale Supérieure; taught for two years at Jean Moulin Univ. Lyon 3, then at Univ. of Paris VII-Jussieu, then at Université populaire de Caen 2002–03; Co-producer of radio show Les vendredis de la philosophie 2007–11, Gai savoir 2012–15; now teaches at École Polytechnique and Sciences Po; adviser to Ed. of Philosophie Magazine; producer of Philosophy programme, broadcast on Sundays on ARTE France 2008–; Columnist, L'Express 2008–11; Teacher, École Jeannine Manuel 2013–; joined Europe 1 2015; Chevalier, Ordre des Arts et des Lettres 2014. *Publications:* Un jeu d'enfant: la philosophie 2007, L'Endroit du décor 2009, La Dissertation de philo (essays) 2010, Le philosophe de service et autres textes 2011, La folie 2011, Lectures de Proust 2013, Matière Première 2013, Anagrammes pour lire dans les pensées (with Jacques Perry-Salkow and Chen Jiang Hong) 2016, Little Brother 2017, Morales provisoires 2018. *Address:* Philosophie, ARTE France, 8 rue Marceau, 92785 Issy-les-Moulineaux Cedex 9, France (office). *Telephone:* 1-55-00-77-77 (office). *Fax:* 1-55-00-77-00 (office). *Website:* www.arte.tv (office).

ENTRECANALES DOMECQ, José Manuel, Licenciado en Ciencias Económicas; Spanish business executive; *Chairman and CEO, Acciona SA;* b. 1 Jan. 1963, Madrid; ed Universidad Complutense de Madrid; Assoc., Merrill Lynch Europe Ltd Capital Markets, London and New York 1986–90; mem. Bd of Dirs Sefinco Ltd, New York 1990–92; Finance Dir Acciona SA 1992–2004, Chair. and CEO 2004–; Man. Dir Vodafone España 1994–2000, Chair. 2000–07, also Chair. Vodafone Foundation; Chair. Endesa SA 2007–09; Chair. Fundación Consejo España EEUU, José Manuel Entrecanales Foundation for Innovation in Sustainability, Acciona Microenergy Foundation; mem. of Bd Instituto de la Empresa Familiar (Chair. 2012–14); fmr mem. Bd Conferencia Española de Fundaciones, Guggenheim Foundation, Spanish Red Cross, Universal Library, Cotec Foundation for Technological Innovation, Reina Sofía Higher School of Music, Business and Society Foundation, Spain-US Chamber of Commerce, Spanish Institutional Foundation; mem. Advisory Bd UN Sustainable Energy for All initiative; Founding mem. Pro CNIC Foundation; Patron, Princess of Asturias Foundation, Prado Museum. *Address:* Acciona SA, Avda. de Europa, 18 Parque Empresarial La Moraleja, 28108 Madrid, Spain (office). *Telephone:* (91) 6632850 (office). *Fax:* (91) 6632851 (office). *Website:* www.acciona.com (office).

ENTREMONT, Philippe; French pianist and conductor; b. 7 June 1934, Reims; s. of Jean Entremont and Renée Entremont (née Monchamps); m. Andrée Ragot 1955; one s. one d.; ed Inst. Notre-Dame, Reims, Conservatoire Nat. Supérieur de Musique de Paris; has performed with numerous major orchestras world-wide 1953–; Pres. Acad. Int. de Musique Maurice Ravel, Saint-Jean-de-Luz 1973–80; apptd Chief Conductor and Music Dir Vienna Chamber Orchestra 1976, now Lifetime Musical Dir; Dir New Orleans Symphony Orchestra 1980–86; Prin. Conductor, Denver Symphony Orchestra 1986–88, Paris Orchestre Colonne 1987–90, Netherlands Chamber Orchestra 1993–2002; apptd Music Dir and Prin. Conductor, Israel Chamber Orchestra 1995, now Conductor Laureate; Dir American Conservatory Fontainebleau 1994; f. Santo Domingo Biennial Festival 1997; apptd Prin. Guest Conductor, Shanghai Broadcasting Symphony Orchestra 2001; Prin. Guest Conductor, Munich Symphony Orchestra 2005–06, Prin. Conductor 2006, apptd Lifetime Laureate Conductor 2010; Conductor, Super World Orchestra, Tokyo 2006; Prin. Conductor, Boca Raton Symphonia 2010–11; Dir Chamber Orchestra of École Normale Supérieure de Musique de Paris—Alfred Cortot 2014–; fmr Pres. Int. Certificate for Piano Artists, Fondation Bell'Arte, Brussels; fmr Pres. Ravel Acad., Paris; Dir American Conservatory of Fontainebleau 1994–2013; Officier, Ordre nat. du Mérite, Commdr, Légion d'honneur, Commdr des Arts et Lettres, Österreichisches Ehrenkreuz für Wissenschaft und Kunst (Arts and Sciences Cross of Honour, Austria); Harriet Cohen Piano Medal 1951, Grand Prix Int. Concours Marguerite Long-Jacques Thibaud 1953, four Grand Prix du Disque Awards, Edison Award 1960, Grammy Award 1972. *Publication:* Piano ma non troppo (autobiography) 2014. *Leisure interest:* golf. *Address:* c/o Emily Yoon, Columbia Artists Management Inc., 5 Columbus Circle, 1790 Broadway, New York, NY 10019-1412, USA (office); 10 rue de Castiglione, 75001 Paris, France (home). *Telephone:* (212) 841-9509 (office); 9-62-56-77-32 (office). *Fax:* (212) 841-9774 (office). *E-mail:* info@cami.com (office); p.entremont@free.fr (office); info@philippeentremont.com. *Website:* columbia-artists.com (office); www.philippeentremont.com.

ENTWISTLE, George Edward, BA; British media executive; b. 8 July 1962, Yorks., England; s. of Philip Entwistle and Wendy Entwistle; m. Jane Porter; one s. one d.; ed Durham Univ.; began career as writer and magazine ed., Haymarket Magazines 1984–89; joined BBC as Broadcast Journalism trainee 1989, Asst Producer, Panorama 1990–92, Producer, On The Record 1993–94, Asst Ed. and later Deputy Ed., Newsnight 1994–99, Deputy Ed., Tomorrow's World 1999–2001, Ed., Newsnight 2001–04, Exec. Ed. of Topical Arts on BBC Two and BBC Four 2004, Head and Commissioning Ed. of TV Current Affairs 2005, Acting Controller of BBC Four 2007, Controller of Knowledge Commissioning 2008–11, also Controller of Editorial Standards for BBC Vision, Dir, BBC Vision 2011–12, Dir-Gen. BBC Sept.–Nov. 2012 (resgnd); Trustee, Public Catalogue Foundation (now Art UK) 2013–; Advisory Chair. Edinburgh Int. TV Festival 2011.

ENTWISTLE, John Nicholas McAlpine, OBE; British solicitor and consultant; b. 16 June 1941, Southport, Lancs.; s. of Sir Maxwell Entwistle and Lady (Jean) Entwistle; m. Phillida Burgess; one s. one d.; ed Uppingham School, Rutland; qualified as solicitor 1963; Asst Attorney, Shearman & Sterling, New York, USA 1963–64; Partner, Maxwell Entwistle & Byrne 1966–91; mem. Liverpool City Council 1968–71; Nat. Vice-Chair. The Bow Group 1967–68; Parl. cand. (Conservative) for Huyton 1970; Consultant Solicitor, Davies Wallis Foyster 1992–2004; Lloyds underwriting mem. 1971–2000; Founder-Dir Merseyside TEC 1990–91; Dir (non-exec.) Rathbone Brothers PLC 1992–98; Deputy Dist Chair. Appeals Service 1992; Chair. Liverpool Chamber of Commerce & Industry 1992–94; Founder-Chair. NW Chambers of Commerce Asscn 1993–97; Pres. British Chambers of Commerce 1998–2000; mem. Chancellor of Exchequer's Standing Cttee on preparation for EMU 1998–2000, Council of Britain in Europe 1999–2004; Sec., Rainbow Property Co. Ltd 2009; Home Sec.'s rep. for appointments to Merseyside Police Authority 1994–2000; mem. Nat. Trust NW Regional Cttee 1992–98, Parole Bd 1994–2000, Disciplinary Cttee, Mortgage Compliance Bd 1999–2004, Criminal Injuries Compensation Appeals Panel 2000; fmr Tribunal Judge, Tribunal Service–Criminal Injuries Compensation; part-time asylum adjudicator 2000–05, part-time immigration judge 2005–10; Dir Friends of the Lake Dist 2014–; Trustee, Nat. Museums & Galleries on Merseyside 1990–97, Royal Acad. of Arts Trust 2006; DL for Merseyside 1992–2002; Hon. Fellow, Liverpool John Moores Univ. 2010. *Leisure interests:* collecting and painting pictures, gardening, shooting. *Address:* Low Crag, Crook, nr Kendal, Cumbria, LA8 8LE, England (home). *Telephone:* (15395) 68268 (home). *E-mail:* jentwistle@onetel.net (office).

ENYA; Irish singer, composer and musician (piano); b. (Eithne Ní Bhraonáin), 17 May 1961, Gweedore, Co. Donegal; d. of Leon Ó Braonáin and Máire Bean Uí Bhraonáin; keyboard and background vocals with family group, Clannad (traditional Irish music) 1980–82; formed Aigle Music (with producer and sound engineer Nicky Ryan and man. and lyricist Roma Ryan) 1982; performed at the Queen's 50th Wedding Anniversary, birthday celebrations of King Gustav of Sweden and privately for Pope John Paul II; numerous other live appearances, including the Acad. Awards 2002; Dr hc (Nat. Univ. of Ireland, Galway) 2007, (Univ. of Ulster) 2007; Ivor Novello Int. Achievement Award 1998, six World Music Awards including Best-Selling Artist in the World 2001, Japanese Grand Prix Award for New Artist of the Year, Hot Press Best Irish Solo Artist, Academy of Achievement of America Golden Plate Award, Billboard Artist Award, Echo Award (for Only Time), BMI Special Citation of Achievement (for Only Time, for Orinoco Flow, I Don't Wanna Know), Las Vegas Film Critics' Soc. Award for Best Original Song (for May It Be), Phoenix Film Critics' Award for Best Original Song (for May It Be), Broadcast Film Critics' Award for Best Song (for May It Be). *Recordings include:* albums: with Clannad: Crann Ull 1980, Fuaim 1982; as Enya: Enya 1987, Watermark (IFPI Platinum European Award) 1988, Shepherd Moons (IFPI Platinum European Award, Grammy Award, Billboard Music Award, NARM Best-Selling Album Award) 1991, The Celts 1992, The Memory of Trees (Grammy Award) 1995, Paint the Sky with Stars (Japanese Grand Prix Album of the Year) 1997, A Day Without Rain (Grammy Award, Japanese Grand Prix Album of the Year) 2000, Amarantine (Grammy Award for Best New Age Album 2007) 2005, And Winter Came 2008, Dark Sky Island 2015. *Address:* Treesdale, Church Road, Killiney, Co. Dublin, Ireland (office). *Website:* www.enya.com.

ENZENSBERGER, Hans Magnus, (Andreas Thalmayr), DPhil; German poet and writer; b. 11 Nov. 1929, Kaufbeuren; m. 1st Dagrun Averaa Christensen; one d.; m. 2nd Maria Alexandrowna Makarowa 1986; m. 3rd Katharina Bonitz; one d.; ed Univs of Erlangen, Freiburg im Breisgau, Hamburg and Paris; Third Programme Ed., Stuttgart Radio 1955–57; Lecturer, Hochschule für Gestaltung, Ulm 1956–57; Literary Consultant to Suhrkamp's (publrs), Frankfurt 1960; mem. 'Group 47', Ed. Kursbuch (review) 1965–75, Publr 1970–90; Ed. TransAtlantik (monthly magazine) 1980–82; Publr and Ed., Die Andere Bibliothek 1985–2005; apptd Artistic Dir Renaissance Theatre Berlin 1995; Ordre pour le Mérite 2000; Dr hc (Bard Coll., New York) 2012; Hugo Jacobi Prize 1956, Kritiker Prize 1962, Georg Büchner Prize 1963, Premio Pasolini 1982, Heinrich Böll Prize 1985, Kultureller Ehrenpreis der Stadt München 1994, Heinrich Heine Prize, Düsseldorf 1997, Príncipe de Asturias 2002, Griffin Trust for Excellence in Poetry's Lifetime Recognition Award 2009, and others. *Publications include:* poetry: Verteidigung der Wölfe 1957, Landessprache 1960, Blindenschrift 1964, Poems for People Who Don't Read Poems (English edn) 1968, Gedichte 1955–1970 1971, Mausoleum 1975, Gedichte 1950–2005 2006; essays: Clemens Brentanos Poetik 1961, Einzelheiten 1962, Politik und Verbrechen 1964; also: Deutschland, Deutschland unter Anderen 1967, Das Verhör von Habana (play) 1970, Freisprüche 1970, Der kurze Sommer der Anarchie (novel) 1972, Gespräche mit Marx und Engels 1973, Palaver 1974; Ed. Museum der Modernen Poesie 1960, Allerleirauh 1961, Andreas Gryphius Gedichte 1962, Edward Lears kompletter Nonsense (trans.) 1977, Raids and Reconstruction (essays, English edn), Der Untergang der Titanic (epic poem) 1978, Die Furie des Verschwindens 1980,

Politische Brosamen 1982, Critical Essays 1982, Der Menschenfreund 1984, Ach Europa! 1987, Mittelmass und Wahn 1988, Requiem für eine romantische Frau 1988, Der Fliegende Robert 1989, Zukunftsmusik (poems) 1991, Die grosse Wanderung 1992, Mediocrity and Delusion (English edn) 1992, Aussichten auf den Bürgerkrieg 1993, Diderots Schatten 1994, The Palace (libretto) 1994, Civil War (English edn) 1994, Selected Poems (English edn) 1994, Kiosk (poems) 1995 (English edn 1997), Voltaires Neffe (play) 1996, Der Zahlenteufel 1997, The Number Devil (English edn) 1998, Zickzack 1997, Wo warst du, Robert? (novel) 1998, Leichter als Luft (poems) 1999 (English edn 2001), Where were you, Robert? (English edn) 2000, Die Elixiere der Wissenschaft (essays and poems) 2002, Nomaden im regal (essays) 2003, Die Geschichte der Wolken (poems) 2003, Dialoge (prose) 2005, Hammerstein oder der Eigensinn 2008; as Andreas Thalmayr: Heraus mit der Sprache 2005. *Leisure interests:* early 17th century Flemish art, mathematics. *Address:* c/o Suhrkamp-Verlag, Lindenstr. 29, 60325 Frankfurt am Main, Germany (home).

ENZI, Michael (Mike) Bradley, BA, MBA; American politician; *Senator from Wyoming;* b. 1 Feb. 1944, Bremerton, Wash.; s. of Elmer Enzi and Dorothy Bradley Enzi; m. Diana Buckley 1969; one s. two d.; ed George Washington Univ. and Univ. of Denver; Staff Sergeant, Wyoming Air Nat. Guard 1967–73; Pres. NZ Shoes Inc., Gillette, Wyo. 1969–96, NZ Shoes of Sheridan Inc., Wyo. 1983–91; Acting Man. Dunbar Well Services, Gillette 1985–97; Chair. First Wyoming Bank, Gillette 1978–88; Dir, Black Hills Corpn 1992–96; Mayor of Gillette 1975–82; mem. Wyo. House of Reps 1987–91, Wyo. State Senate 1991–96; Senator from Wyo. 1997–, mem. Foreign Relations Cttee, Co-founder and Chair. USAF Caucus; Pres. Wyoming Asscn of Municipalities 1980–82; mem. Energy Council Exec. Cttee 1989–93, 1994–96, Educ. Comm. of the States 1989–93; Commr Western Interstate Comm. for Higher Educ. 1995–96; Republican; Distinguished Eagle Scout. *Publications include:* Harvard Journal on Legislation 1998. *Leisure interests:* fishing, fly tying, canoe making, reading. *Address:* 379A Russell Senate Office Building, Washington, DC 20510, USA (office). *Telephone:* (202) 224-3424 (office). *Fax:* (202) 228-0359 (office). *E-mail:* senator@enzi.senate.gov (office). *Website:* enzi.senate.gov (office).

EÖRSI, Mátyás, PhD; Hungarian lawyer and politician; b. 24 Nov. 1954, Budapest; s. of Gyula Eörsi and Marianna Eörsi; m. Katalin Eörsi; two s. one d.; ed Kossuth Zsuzsa High School and Eötvös Loránd Univ., Budapest; foreign trade lawyer 1981, worked as legal adviser and at int. trading co.; est. Eörsi & Partners 1987; mem. Nat. Ass. 1990–2010, Chair. Foreign Affairs Cttee 1994–97, Vice-Chair. Foreign Affairs Cttee 2002–06, Chair. European Affairs Cttee 2004–10, Chair. Foreign Affairs and Hungarian Minorities Abroad Cttee 2006–; Founding mem. Alliance of Free Democrats (SZDSZ) and mem. Nat. Cttee, also Legal Rep. 1988, mem. Nat. Governing Cttee 1991, 2003–12, Chair. SZDSZ Goodwill and Ethics Cttee 1993–98, Foreign Affairs Spokesman from 1994, Deputy Leader Parl. Group 2002–06, Leader Parl. Group 2007–10; mem. Demokratikus Koalíció (DK—Democratic Coalition, split from Hungarian Socialist Party—MSZP) 2012–; mem. Exec. Office Liberal International 1997–, Vice-Pres. 2002–; following regime change became regular mem. Council of Europe Parl. Ass.; Head of Hungarian del. with observer status, Ass. of WEU and Head of Del. to Parl. Ass. of Cen. European Initiative; State Sec. for Policy, Ministry of Foreign Affairs 1997–98; mem. Hungarian Parl. del. to Council of Europe 1998–; Leader, Liberal faction, Parl. Ass. of the Council of Europe (PACE) 2001–09, lead PACE observers mission during Ukrainian presidential elections 2009–10; Country Dir Nat. Democratic Inst., Lybia 2011; Sec.-Gen., Parl. Forum for Democracy 2013; Head of Admin, Finance and HR, Community of Democracies, Warsaw 2014–17; Head of Mission OSCE 2017, 2019. *Address:* 3881 Baskó, Gulyas koz 7/c, Hungary (home). *Telephone:* (20) 499-5005 (office). *E-mail:* matyas@eorsi.eu (office).

EÖTVÖS, Peter; German (b. Hungarian) composer, conductor and academic; b. 2 Jan. 1944, Székelyudvarhely, Hungary; s. of László Eötvös and Ilona Szücs; m. 1st Piroska Molnár 1968; one s.; m. 2nd Pi-Hsien Chen 1976; one d.; m. 3rd Maria Mezei 1995; ed Budapest Music Acad., Musik-hochschule, Cologne; played in Stockhausen's Ensemble, Cologne 1968–76; composer and producer at WDR Electronic Music Studio, Cologne 1971–79; Conductor and Musical Dir Ensemble Intercontemporain, Paris 1979–91; Prin. Guest Conductor BBC Symphony Orchestra, London 1985–88, Gothenburg Symphony Orchestra 2003–07; First Guest Conductor, Budapest Festival Orchestra 1992–95, ORF Radio Symphony Orchestra, Vienna 2009–12; Chief Conductor Netherlands Radio Chamber Orchestra 1994–2005; Prof., Musikhochschule Karlsruhe, Germany 1992–98, 2002–08, Cologne 1998–2001; f. Peter Eötvös Contemporary Music Foundation 1991; mem. Akad. der Künste, Berlin, Szechenyi Acad. of Art, Budapest, Sächsische Akad. der Künste, Dresden, Royal Swedish Acad. of Music, Stockholm; Commdr, Ordre des Arts et des Lettres 2003; Bartók Award, Budapest 1997, Stephan Kaske Prize, Munich 2000, Kossuth Prize, Hungary 2002, Royal Philharmonic Soc. Music Award 2002, Midem Classical Award 'Living Composer', Cannes 2004, European Composing Prize 2004, Frankfurter Musikpreis 2007, Prince Pierre of Monaco Prize in Musical Composition 2008, Golden Lion Award for Lifetime Achievement 2011, Echo Klassik Award for Choral Recording of the Year–20th/21st Century (for Ligeti Requiem) 2012, Goethe Medal 2018. *Compositions include:* for orchestra: Chinese Opera, Psychokosmos 1993, Atlantis, Ima, Jet Stream, CAP-KO, Zeropoints, Two Monologues, Replica, Konzert für zwei Klaviere, Levitation; for ensemble: Intervalles-Intérieurs, Windsequenzen, Steine, Triangel 1993, Shadows 1996, Octet, Sonata per sei; for string quartet: Korrespondenz, Encore, Da Capo 2014; for vocal ensemble: Three comedy madrigals, Schiller: energische Schönheit; for percussion: Psalm 151, Speaking Drums; for violin: Seven (Prix de Composition Musicale, Fondation Prince Pierre de Monaco 2008), Doremi; for violoncello: Cello Concerto Grosso; for musical theatre/opera: Radames, Harakiri, Three Sisters, As I Crossed a Bridge of Dreams 1998–99, Le Balcon 2001–02, Angels in America 2002–04, Lady Sarashina 2008, Love and Other Demons 2008, Die Tragödie des Teufels 2010, Paradise Reloaded, Der goldene Drache 2013–14. *Recordings include:* Bartók, Eötvös & Ligeti: Violin Concertos (Gramophone Recording of the Year 2013, Echo Klassik Prize 2013, Int. Classical Music Award for Concertos 2014). *Leisure interests:* pipe, jazz, walking. *Address:* c/o Harrison Parrott, The Ark, 201 Talgarth Road, London, W6 8BJ, England (office). *Telephone:* (20) 7229-9166 (office). *Fax:* (20) 7221-5042 (office). *E-mail:* info@harrisonparrott.co.uk (office); eotvos@eotvospeter.com (home). *Website:* www.harrisonparrott.com (office); www.eotvospeter.com (home).

EPHREM, Gen. Sebhat; Eritrean army officer and politician; *Minister of Energy and Mines;* b. 5 Sept. 1950, Asmara; m. Ruth Halle; three c.; ed Evangelical Lutheran High School, Asmara, Haile Selassie Univ., Ethiopia, Open Univ., UK; fmr Eritrean People's Liberation Front Commdr during Eritrean War of Independence; served in Eritrean Armed Forces –1992; Gov. of Asmara 1992–94; Minister of Health 1994–95; returned to the army May 1995; rank of Gen. 1995; apptd Minister of Defence; Minister of Energy and Mines 2014–; Grand Officiale (Italy) 1997. *Leisure interests:* reading, football. *Address:* Ministry of Energy and Mines, PO Box 5285, Asmara (office); Marsa Teklay Street, 17, Asmara, Eritrea (home). *Telephone:* (1) 168752 (office); (1) 122572 (home). *Fax:* (1) 127652 (office); (1) 1244548 (home). *E-mail:* asmeromht@yahoo.com. *Website:* www.moem.gov.er (office).

EPSTEIN, Sir (Michael) Anthony, Kt, CBE, MA, MD, DSc, PhD, FRCPath, FRS; British virologist and academic; b. 18 May 1921, London; ed St Paul's School, London, Trinity Coll., Cambridge, Middlesex Hosp. Medical School, London; House Surgeon, Middlesex Hosp. and Addenbrooke's Hosp., Cambridge 1944; commissioned RAMC 1945–47; Asst Pathologist, Bland Sutton Inst., Middlesex Hosp. Medical School 1948–65; Berkeley Travelling Fellow and French Govt Exchange Scholar, Inst. Pasteur, Paris 1952–53, Visiting Investigator, Rockefeller Inst., New York 1956; Reader in Experimental Pathology, Middlesex Hosp. Medical School and Hon. Consultant in Experimental Virology, Middlesex Hosp. 1965–68; Prof. of Pathology, Univ. of Bristol 1968–85, Head of Dept and Hon. Consultant Pathologist, Avon Area Health Authority (Teaching) 1968–82, Prof. Emer. 1985–; Prof., Nuffield Dept of Clinical Medicine, Univ. of Oxford 1985–2012, Prof. Emer. 2012–; Extraordinary Fellow, Wolfson Coll., Oxford 1986–2001, Hon. Fellow 2001–; mem. MRC Cell Bd 1979–84, Chair. 1982–84; Chair. CRC/MRC Jt Cttee for Inst. of Cancer Research 1982–87; mem. MRC 1982–86, Chair. MRC Tropical Medicine Research Bd 1985–88, Medical and Scientific Advisory Panel, Leukaemia Research Fund 1982–85, Council of Royal Soc. 1983–85, 1986–91; mem. UK Co-ordinating Cttee on Cancer Research 1983–87, Scientific Advisory Cttee, The Lister Inst. of Preventive Medicine 1984–86; Scientific Adviser, Charing Cross Medical Research Centre 1984–87; Foreign Sec. and Vice-Pres. Royal Soc. 1986–91, MRC Assessor 1987–91; mem. Expert Working Party on Bovine Spongiform Encephalopathy, Dept of Health 1988, mem. Exec. Bd Int. Council of Scientific Unions 1990–93, Chair. Cttee for Science in Cen. and Eastern Europe 1992–95; mem. Exec. Council European Science Foundation 1990–93; Special Rep. of Dir-Gen., UNESCO, for Science in Russia, Moscow 1992; mem. Programme Advisory Group, World Bank China Key Studies Project 1992–96; Hon. Prof., Zhongshan Medical Univ., People's Repub. of China 1981, Chinese Acad. of Preventive Medicine 1988, Hon. Fellow, Queensland Inst. of Medical Research 1983, Royal Coll. of Pathologists of Australasia 1995, Cancer Research UK 2004, Univ. of Bristol 2006, Hon. mem. Belgian Soc. for Study of Cancer 1979, Pathological Soc. 1987, Hon. FRSE 1991, Hon. FRCP 1986; Hon. MD (Edinburgh) 1986, (Charles Univ., Prague) 1998, Hon. DSc (Birmingham) 1996; Leeuwenhoek Prize Lecturer, Royal Soc. 1983; Markham Skerritt Prize (Univ. of Bristol) 1977, Paul Ehrlich and Ludwig Darmstaedster Prize and Medal (Frankfurt) 1973, Bristol-Myers Award (New York) 1982, Prix Griffuel (Paris) 1986, Gairdner Foundation Int. Award (Toronto) 1988, S. Weiner Distinguished Visitor Award (Univ. of Manitoba) 1988, Royal Medal, The Royal Soc. 1991. *Scientific achievements include:* discovered the Epstein-Barr virus (EBV) (first human cancer virus) 1964. *Publications includes:* more than 240 scientific papers in int. journals; numerous studies on EBV and other viruses; author and ed. of five scientific books; Jt Founder-Ed., Int. Review of Experimental Pathology 1962–86, Vols 1–28, Academic Press Inc., New York and London. *Address:* Wolfson College, University of Oxford, Linton Road, Oxford, OX2 6UD, England (office). *Telephone:* (1865) 250885 (office). *E-mail:* anthony.epstein@wolfson.ox.ac.uk (office).

EPSTEIN, Emanuel, BS, MS, PhD; American professor of plant nutrition and plant physiologist; *Edward A. Dickson Professor Emeritus, University of California, Davis;* b. 5 Nov. 1916, Duisburg, Germany; s. of Harry Epstein and Bertha Epstein (née Löwe); brother of Gabriel Epstein; m. Hazel M. Leask 1943; two c. (one deceased); ed Univ. of California, Davis, Univ. of California, Berkeley; served in US Army 1943–46; Plant Physiologist, US Dept of Agric., Beltsville, Md 1950–58; Lecturer and Assoc. Plant Physiologist, Univ. of California, Davis 1958–65, Prof. of Plant Nutrition and Plant Physiologist 1965–87, Research Prof. 1987–, Prof. of Botany 1974–87, Research Prof. 1987–, Edward A. Dickson Emer. Prof. 2009; Faculty Research Lecturer 1980; consultant to govt agencies, private orgs and publrs at various times; mem. NAS; Fellow, AAAS, Pres. Pacific Div. 1990–91; Guggenheim Fellow 1958, Fulbright Sr Research Scholar 1965–66, 1974–75; Gold Medal, Pisa Univ., Italy 1962, Charles Reid Barnes Life Membership Award, American Soc. of Plant Physiologists 1986, Univ. of California, Davis Coll. of Agricultural and Environmental Sciences Award of Distinction 1999, Cal Aggie Alumni Asscn Citation for Excellence 1999, Award of Honor, American Soc. of Agronomy, Calif. Chapter 2002. *Publications:* Mineral Nutrition of Plants: Principles and Perspectives 1972 (second edn, with A. J. Bloom 2005), The Biosaline Concept: An Approach to the Utilization of Underexploited Resources (co-ed.) 1979, Saline Agriculture: Salt-Tolerant Plants for Developing Countries (co-ed.) 1990; research papers, reviews and articles. *Leisure interests:* hiking, photography and history. *Address:* Department of Land, Air and Water Resources, Soils and Biogeochemistry, University of California, Davis, CA 95616-3630, USA (office). *E-mail:* eqepstein@ucdavis.edu (office). *Website:* lawr.ucdavis.edu (office).

ERAKAT, Saeb Muhammad Salih, BA, MA, PhD; Palestinian politician and journalist; *Secretary-General, Palestine Liberation Organization;* b. 28 April 1955, East Jerusalem; m. two s. two d.; ed San Francisco State Univ., USA and Bradford Univ., UK; fmr journalist, Al Quds daily; Lecturer in Political Science, An-Najah Univ. 1983, fmr Sec.-Gen. Arab Studies Soc.; mem. negotiating team Oslo Peace Process 1995; mem. Palestinian Parl. for Jericho 1996–; Head of Palestinian Negotiation Steering and Monitoring Cttee 1996–2011, Chief Palestinian Peace Negotiator 1995–2003 (resgnd), 2003–11 (resgnd), still holding the function July 2013; elected mem. Palestinian Legis. Council, Jericho 1996; Minister of Negotiation Affairs, Palestinian Nat. Authority (PNA) 2004–06; Sec.-Gen. Palestine Liberation Org. (PLO) 2015–; Hon. PhD (Peru) 2004. *Publications include:* eight books and numerous articles on foreign policy. *Address:* Palestine Liberation Organization (PLO), Negotiations Affairs Department, POB 4120, Ramallah,

Palestinian Autonomous Areas (office). *Telephone:* (2) 2963741 (office). *Fax:* (2) 2963740 (office). *Website:* www.nad-plo.org (office).

ERBSEN, Claude Ernest, BA; American journalist; *Senior Consultant, Innovation International Media Consultancy Group;* b. 10 March 1938, Trieste, Italy; s. of Henry M. Erbsen and Laura Erbsen; m. 1st Jill J. Prosky 1959; m. 2nd Hedy M. Cohn 1970; two s. one d.; ed Amherst Coll. Mass.; reporter and printer, Amherst Journal Record 1955–57; staff reporter, El Tiempo, Bogotá 1960; with Associated Press (AP) in New York and Miami 1960–65; reporter to Chief of Bureau, AP Brazil 1965–69; Exec. Rep. for Latin America, AP 1969–70; Business Man. and Admin. Dir AP-Dow Jones Econ. Report, London 1970–75; Deputy Dir AP World Services, New York 1975–80, Vice-Pres., Dir 1987–2003; Vice-Pres., Dir AP-Dow Jones News Services 1980–87; fmr Dir, Innovation Int. Media Consultancy Group, currently Sr Consultant; mem. Bd of Dirs World Press Inst. St Paul; mem. Int. Press Inst., Council on Foreign Relations; San Giusto d'Oro Award, City of Trieste 1995. *Publications:* Her Job: Planning Meals for 200! 1963. *Leisure interests:* reading, travel, folk art. *Address:* Innovation, 27 Stratton Road, Scarsdale, NY 10583-7556, USA (office). *Telephone:* (914) 725-1809 (office). *E-mail:* erbsen@innovation-mediaconsulting.com (office); headquarters@innovation-mediaconsulting.com (office). *Website:* www.innovation-mediaconsulting.com (office).

ERÇEL, Gazi; Turkish consultant and fmr central banker; *President, Erçel Global Advisory;* b. 20 Feb. 1945, Gelibolu; m. Zeynel Erçel; one d.; ed Ankara Univ., Vanderbilt Univ., USA; bank examiner, Ministry of Finance 1967–77; Deputy Dir-Gen. of Treasury 1977–82; Asst to Exec. Dir IMF, Washington, DC 1982–86; Dir-Gen. of Treasury and Foreign Trade 1987–89; Gov. Cen. Bank of Turkey 1996–2001; Founder and Pres. Erçel Global Advisory 2002–; fmr mem. Bd of Dirs Rhea Venture Capital Investment Trust (now Rhea Private Equity Investment Trust Inc.); mem. Policy and Econs Council, Gerson Lehrman Group; Lecturer, Faculty of Econs and Admin. Sciences, Istanbul Aydin Univ.; columnist, daily newspaper HaberTurk; Cen. Banker of the Year Award, Global Finance, Prague 2000. *Address:* Erçel Global Advisory, Abdi Ipekçi Caddesi No. 32/7, Nisantasi 80200, Istanbul, Turkey (office). *Telephone:* (212) 2919565 (office). *Fax:* (212) 2919566 (office). *E-mail:* gazi.ercel@erceladvisory.com (office). *Website:* www.erceladvisory.com (office).

ERDEI, Tamás; Hungarian banker; b. 1954; one c.; fmr Gen. Man. Br. Office, Nat. Savings Bank; Chief Officer in Banking Supervision, Ministry of Finance 1981–83; Chief Accountant, Hungarian Foreign Trade Bank (MKB) 1983–85, Exec. Dir 1985–90, Deputy Chief Exec. 1990–94, CEO 1994–97, Chair. and CEO 1997–2012; Pres. Hungarian Banking Assen 1997–2008; mem. Bd of Dirs OTP Bank 2012–. *E-mail:* otpbank@otpbank.hu. *Website:* www.otpbank.hu.

ERDENEBAT, Badarch, DEcon; Mongolian politician; *Chairman, Motherland Party;* b. 1959, Hövsgöl prov.; m. Sergelen; ed Novosibirsk Higher School of Geodesy and Cartography, Mongolian State Univ., Inst. of Econ. and Political Studies, Russian Acad. of Sciences; f. Erel Group (interests in banking, investment, mining and construction) 1989, Dir-Gen. –2000; Founder and Chair. Mongolian Democratic New Socialist Party (now Motherland Party) 1998–; elected mem. Mongolian Great Khural (Parl.) 2000; Minister of Defence 2004–06, of Fuel and Power 2006–07. *Address:* Motherland Party, Jukovyn Örgön Chölöö 7a, Ulaanbaatar, Mongolia (office). *Telephone:* 90150268 (office). *Fax:* (11) 453178 (office).

ERDENEBAT, Jargaltulga; Mongolian accountant and politician; b. 1973, Selenge Prov.; m.; one s. two d.; ed Inst. of Trade and Industry, Inst. of Professional Accountants and Man., Mongolian State Univ. of Agric.; worked as accountant 1996–97; mem. Audit Cttee, Selenge Prov. 1997–2000, Head of Finance, Econs and Policy Regulation Div., Selenge Prov. Admin 2000–04; Deputy Gov., Selenge Prov. 2004–05, Gov. 2008–12; apptd mem. Mongolian Great Khural (Parl.) 2012; Minister of Finance 2014–15, Prime Minister 2016–17; mem. Mongolian People's Party; 800 years of Mongolian Statehood Medal 2006, Honorary Labour Medal 2008, Order of the North Star 2010.

ERDENECHULUUN, Luvsangiin, MA; Mongolian diplomatist and politician; *Director, Human Security Policy Studies Centre;* b. 10 Oct. 1948, Ulaanbaatar; s. of Sonomyn Luvsan and Lhamsurengiin Baimanhand; m. Sukh-Ochiryn Solongo 1969; two s. one d.; ed State Inst. of Int. Relations, Moscow and Diplomatic Acad. Moscow; officer, Dept of Int. Relations, Ministry of Foreign Affairs 1972–80; First Sec., Perm. Mission to UN, New York 1980–84; Head of Press and Information Dept Ministry of Foreign Affairs 1985–86, Head of Dept of Int. Orgs 1988–90; Deputy Perm. Rep. to UN, New York 1990, Perm. Rep. 1992–96; Adviser to Pres. of Mongolia 1996–97; Minister of Foreign Affairs 2000–04; Dir Human Security Policy Studies Centre 2003–; mem. Exec. Bd of UNESCO 2007–; mem. Mongolian People's Party; Distinguished Service Medal, Order of Polar Star, Medal of Service Merit, Order of Friendship Among Nations (Russian Fed.), Order of Red Banner of Service Excellence. *Address:* Chingeltei District, 1st khoroo, M-100, 442, Ulaanbaatar, Mongolia (home). *Telephone:* 70110216 (office); 379151 (home). *Fax:* 70110215 (office). *E-mail:* hspsc@mongol.net (office); echuluun.unesco@yahoo.com (home).

ERDŐ, HE Cardinal Péter, DCL, DTheol; Hungarian ecclesiastic; *Archbishop of Esztergom-Budapest;* b. 25 June 1952, Budapest; ed Seminary of Esztergom, Theological Acad. of Budapest, Pontifical Lateran Univ., Rome; ordained priest by Bishop László Lékai 1975; Parish Priest, Parish of Dorog; Prof. of Theology and Canon Law, Seminary of Esztergom 1980–88; Prof., Faculty of Canon Law, Pontifical Gregorian Univ., Rome 1986–2002; Invited Prof., Faculty of Theology, Peter Pazmany Catholic Univ., Budapest 1988–2003, Rector 1998–2002; Auxiliary Bishop of Szekesfekhervar 1999; Titular Bishop of Puppi 1999; consecrated by Pope John Paul II, Vatican City 2000; Archbishop of Esztergom-Budapest 2002–; cr. Cardinal (Cardinal-Priest of Santa Balbina) 2003; participated in Papal Conclave 2005, 2013; Pres. Hungarian Catholic Bishops' Conf. 2005–, Consilium Conferentiarum Episcopalium Europae 2006–; mem. Hungarian Acad. of Sciences 2007; Galileo Galilei Prize, Italian Rotary Club 1999. *Publications:* 30 books, 400 articles.

ERDOES, Mary Callahan, BS, MBA; American business executive; *CEO, Asset Management, JPMorgan Chase & Company;* b. 13 Aug. 1967, Winnetka, Ill.; d. of Patrick Joseph Callahan Jr and Patricia Ann Callahan (née Henebry); m. Philip Erdoes; three d.; ed Georgetown Univ. and Harvard Business School; worked at Bankers Trust in corp. finance, merchant banking and high yield debt underwriting; Vice-Pres. with Meredith, Martin & Kaye –1996; Head of Fixed Income Group, J.P. Morgan Investment Management 1996–99, Head of Investment Man. and Alternative Solutions for the Pvt. Bank 1999, assumed responsibility for global suite of investment solutions and investment strategy for pvt. banking clients world-wide following J.P. Morgan/Chase merger 2000, CEO J.P. Morgan's Pvt. Bank 2005–08, Chair. and CEO Global Wealth Man., J.P. Morgan (comprises Pvt. Bank, Pvt. Wealth Man., Bear Stearns Pvt. Client Services) 2008–, CEO, Asset Man., JPMorgan Chase & Co. 2009–, also mem. JPMorgan Chase & Co.'s Exec. Cttee and Operating Cttee; mem. Bd of Dirs US Fund for UNICEF 2005–. *Leisure interests:* running, Dora the Explorer games, Ring Around the Rosie or whatever her daughters request. *Address:* JPMorgan Chase & Co., 270 Park Avenue, New York, NY 10017 (office); 41 River Terrace, New York, NY 10282-1113, USA. *Telephone:* (212) 270-6000 (office). *Fax:* (212) 270-1648 (office). *Website:* www.jpmorgan.com (office).

ERDOĞAN, Recep Tayyip, BA; Turkish politician and head of state; *President;* b. 26 Feb. 1954, Istanbul; m. Emine Gülbaran 1978; two s. two d.; ed Marmara Univ., Istanbul; professional footballer 1969–80; elected Chair. Nat. Salvation Party Youth Org. early 1970s, mem. Nat. Salvation Party –1981; mem. Welfare Party 1983–98, Chair. Istanbul Br. 1985; Mayor of Metropolitan Istanbul 1994–98, tenure of office ended by court decree 1998, convicted of having read a provocative poem in public, imprisoned for four months and banned for life from holding public office; mem. Virtue Party 1998–2001; Founder and Chair. AK Partisi – AKP (Justice and Devt Party) 2001–14, 2017–, ruling party in Turkey following 2002 elections, constitutional ban preventing him from holding public office overturned Jan. 2003; Prime Minister of Turkey 2003–14; Pres. of Turkey 28 Aug. 2014–, Chair. Turkey Wealth Fund 2018–; Founder Democratization and Action Movt; Hon. Citizen of Seoul, South Korea 2004, Tehran, Iran 2009, Prizren, Kosovo 2010; Freeman of the City of Tirana, Albania 2009; Order of the Golden Fleece (Georgia) 2010, Danaker Order (Kyrgyzstan) 2011; 31 hon. doctorates; European of the Year 2004, Agricola Medal, UN Food and Agric. Org. 2007. *Address:* Office of the President, Cumhurbaşkanlığı Genel Sekreterliği, 06689Çankaya, Ankara (office); AK Partisi, Genel Merkezi Ceyhun Atif Kansu Cad., No. 202 Balgat, Ankara, Turkey (office). *Telephone:* (312) 4701100 (office). *Fax:* (312) 4702433 (office). *E-mail:* cumhurbaskanligi@tccb.gov.tr (office). *Website:* www.cankaya.gov.tr (office); www.akparti.org.tr (office); www.rte.gen.tr.

ERDÖS, André; Hungarian diplomatist and academic; *Lecturer in International and Hungarian studies, University of Szeged;* b. 18 May 1941, Algiers, Algeria; s. of Gusztáv Erdős and Márta Czeichner; m. Katalin Pintér 1965; one d.; ed Moscow State Inst. for Int. Relations, Budapest School of Political Sciences; joined Ministry of Foreign Affairs 1965, attach, Morocco 1968–72, staff mem., CSCE Dept Ministry of Foreign Affairs 1972–78, assigned to Perm. Mission to UN, New York 1978–83, del. to UN Gen. Ass. 1984, 1985, 1989, Adviser to Minister of Foreign Affairs of Hungary 1984–86, Head of Hungary's del. to Vienna CSCE follow-up meeting 1986–89, Amb. and Perm. Rep. to UN, New York 1990–94, 1997–2002, Pres. UN Disarmament and Int. Security Comm. 2001–02, Hungarian Rep., UN Security Council 1992–93, Deputy State Sec. for Multilateral Affairs, Ministry of Foreign Affairs 1994–97, Amb. to France 2002–06, mem. Prime Minister's Council on Foreign and Security Policy 2007–09; currently Lecturer in Int. and Hungarian studies, Univ. of Szeged; Vice-Pres. Hungarian Atlantic Council; Vice-Pres. Hungarian UN Assen; appearances on several radio and TV programmes; Hon. Prof., Budapest Inst. for Grad. Int. and Diplomatic Studies 1999; Commdr's Cross, Order of Merit (Hungary), Order of Duke Branimir with Ribbons (Croatia), Commdr, Légion d'honneur (France), Grand Croix, Ordre nat. du Mérite (France). *Television:* Face to Face with History (Duna TV series) 2008–10. *Publications:* Co-operation in the United Nations between Socialist and Developing Countries 1981, Soviet-German Relations 1939–41 1984, The Circumstances of the Birth of the 1941 Soviet-German Non-Aggression Pact 1987, Geography vs. Political Reality at the United Nations 2001, Sorsfordító Esztendők (Crucial Years) 2004, Additions to the history of Hungarian foreign policy during the system change 2009; numerous articles on int. affairs. *Leisure interests:* philately, numismatics, collecting postcards, making video movies.

ERDRICH, (Karen) Louise, MA; American writer and poet; b. 7 June 1954, Little Falls, Minn.; d. of Ralph Louis Erdrich and Rita Joanne Erdrich (née Gourneau); m. Michael Anthony Dorris 1981 (died 1997); six c. (one s. deceased); ed Dartmouth Coll., Johns Hopkins Univ.; Visiting Poetry Teacher, ND State Arts Council 1977–78; Teacher of Writing, Johns Hopkins Univ. 1978–79; Communications Dir and Ed., Circle-Boston Indian Council 1979–80; textbook writer, Charles Merrill Co. 1980; mem. PEN (mem. Exec. Bd 1985–90); Guggenheim Fellow 1985–86; Owner, Birchbark Books bookstore, Minneapolis, Minn.; Dr hc (North Dakota) 2007, (Dartmouth) 2009; Nelson Algren Award 1982, Pushcart Prize 1983, Nat. Magazine Fiction Award 1983, 1987, First Prize, O. Henry Awards 1987, Lifetime Achievement Award, Native Writers Circle of the Americas 2000, Theodore Roosevelt Rough Rider Award 2013, PEN/Saul Bellow Award for Achievement in American Fiction 2014, Richard C. Holbrooke Distinguished Achievement Award, Dayton Literary Peace Prize 2014. *Publications include:* fiction: Love Medicine (Nat. Book Critics' Circle Award for best work of fiction) 1984, The Beet Queen 1986, Tracks 1988, The Crown of Columbus (with Michael Anthony Dorris) 1991, The Bingo Palace 1994, The Bluejay's Dance 1995, Tales of Burning Love 1996, The Antelope Wife 1998, The Birchbark House 1999, The Last Report on the Miracles at Little No Horse 2001, The Master Butcher's Singing Club 2003, Four Souls 2004, The Painted Drum 2005, The Plague of Doves (Anisfield-Wolf Book Award) 2008, The Red Convertible: Selected and New Stories 1978–2008 2009, Shadow Tag 2010, The Round House (Nat. Book Award for Fiction 2012) 2012, LaRose: A Novel 2016; poetry: Jacklight 1984, Baptism of Desire 1989, Original Fire: Selected and New Poems 2003; non-fiction: Imagination (textbook) 1980; contrib. short stories, children's stories, essays and poems to anthologies and journals, including American Indian Quarterly, Atlantic, Frontiers, Kenyon Review, Ms, New England Review, New York Times Book Review, New Yorker, North American Review, Redbook. *Address:* The Wylie Agency, 250 West 57th Street, Suite 2114, New York, NY 10107, USA (office); Birchbark Books,

2115 West 21st Street, Minneapolis, MN 55405, USA. *E-mail:* mail@wylieagency.com (office). *Website:* birchbarkbooks.com; www.harpercollins.com.

EREN, Halit, MA, PhD; Turkish institute director and academic; *Director-General, Research Centre for Islamic History, Art and Culture (IRCICA);* b. 1953, Gumulcine (Komotini, Greece); m.; two s. one d.; ed Inst. of Social Sciences and Inst. of Turkic Studies, Marmara Univ., Istanbul; apptd Sr Researcher and Head of Library and Documentation Dept, Research Centre for Islamic History, Art and Culture (IRCICA) 1981, Deputy Dir-Gen. 1984–2005, Co-ordinator/mem. Organizing Cttee of IRCICA's academic symposia relating to history of Caucasia, Cen. Asia and the Balkans, participated in Islamic Summit Confs, Islamic Confs of Ministers of Foreign Affairs, Culture, and Information, and other confs and cttees of OIC, Chair. Int. Calligraphy Competition, IRCICA jury 1986–2019, Dir-Gen. IRCICA 2005–, Ed.-in-Chief, IRCICA Journal 2015; Founder and Admin. Turkish-Islamic Asscn of England 1979–81; mem. Exec. Bd Cen. Office of the Solidarity Asscn of Western Thrace Turks, Istanbul 1984–94, Pres. 1992–94; Sec.-Gen. Foundation for Research on Islamic History, Art and Culture, Istanbul 1990–; Founding mem. Turkish Soc. for the History of Science 1989–, Rumeli (Eastern Europe) Foundation for Educ., Istanbul 1993–; mem. Preparatory Cttee Seventh Devt Plan of Turkey 1993; Second Pres. Cultural and Solidarity Asscn of East European Turks 1997–2001; Founding mem. Western Thrace Foundation for Educ., Culture and Health, Istanbul 1996, Vice-Pres. 1996–98, 2002–04; Founding mem. and Chair. (BALMED Asscn) Centre for Balkan Civilization 2007–; mem. Exec. Bd and Second Chair. Cultural and Solidarity Foundation of East European Turks 2001–; Adviser on Balkan Affairs to Minister of State of Repub. of Turkey 1997; Founder and Ed.-in-Chief Bati Trakya'nin sesi (The Voice of Western Thrace) journal 1987–94, Gen. Co-ordinator 1994–97; Ed. Rumeli Culture journal 2002–; Hon. Prof., UFA Bashkir State Univ., Bashkortostan 2010; Sultan Qaboos Order for Culture, Science and Art of the First Degree (Oman) 2012; Dr hc (Sh. Marjany History Inst. of Tatarstan Acad. of Sciences) 2006, (Tatarstan Repub. Kazan Federal Univ.) 2010; Russian Fed. State Medal 2006. *Publications include:* World Bibliography of Translations of the Meanings of the Holy Quran: 1515–1980 (compiler, jtly with Ismet Binark) 1986, Bati Trakya Türkleri (Western Thrace Turks) 1997; numerous articles in professional journals. *Address:* Research Centre for Islamic History, Art and Culture (IRCICA), Alemdar Cd. No. 15, Babıali Girişi, 34110, Cağaloğlu- Istanbul, Turkey (office). *Telephone:* (212) 402 0000 (office). *Fax:* (212) 2584365 (office). *E-mail:* ircica@ircica.org (office). *Website:* www.ircica.org (office).

ERESMAN, Randall K. (Randy), BSc; Canadian petroleum engineer and energy industry executive; b. Medicine Hat, Alberta; m. Shelly Eresman; two c.; ed Northern Alberta Inst. of Tech., Univ. of Wyoming, USA; joined Alberta Energy Co. (AEC) 1980, Vice-Pres. AEC Oil and Gas 1996–99, Pres. AEC Oil and Gas Partnership 1999–2002, Exec. Vice-Pres. EnCana Corpn (after merger of AEC and PanCanadian Energy Corpn), responsible for Onshore N America Div. Jan.–Dec. 2002, COO 2002–06, Pres. and CEO 2006–13 (retd); mem. Asscn of Professional Engineers, Geologists and Geophysicists of Alberta, Young Pres' Org., Canadian Council of Chief Execs; mem. Nat. Advisory Bd, Univ. of Wyoming's Coll. of Eng, Nat. Petroleum Council (an Oil and Natural Gas Advisory Cttee to US Sec. of Energy).

ERGEN, Charles (Charlie) W., BS, MBA; American communications industry executive; *Chairman and CEO, EchoStar Communications Corporation;* b. 1 March 1953, Oak Ridge, Tenn.; s. of William Krasny Ergen and Viola Siebenthal Ergen; m. Cantey McAdam; five c.; ed Univ. of Tennessee, Babcock Grad. School, Wake Forest Univ.; f. EchoStar Communications Corpn 1980, now Chair. and CEO, f. Dish Network (subsidiary of EchoStar Communications Corpn) 1996, Chair. and CEO 1998–; mem. Colorado Mountain Club; Home Satellite TV Asscn Star Award 1988, Rocky Mountain News Business Person of the Year 1996, 2001. *Achievements include:* has scaled Mount Kilimanjaro, Mount Aconcagua, Argentina, Mount Everest base camp, Nepal. *Leisure interests:* mountain climbing, poker, pick-up basketball. *Address:* EchoStar Communications Corporation, 100 Inverness Terrace, Englewood, CO 80112, USA (office). *Telephone:* (303) 723-1000 (office). *Fax:* (303) 723-1399 (office). *Website:* www.echostar.com (office); www.dishnetwork.com (office).

ERGIN, Mehmet, PhD; Turkish professor of physical chemistry; *Fellow, Islamic World Academy of Sciences;* b. 25 May 1936, Yozgat; m.; two c.; ed Ankara Gazi High School, Ankara Univ., Univ. of Glasgow, UK; researcher, Nuclear Chem. Lab., Atomic Energy Comm., Acting Dir 1963–66, fmr Pres.; research and training at IAEA Labs, Vienna; researcher, Inst. for Physics and Chem., Asscn for Meat Research, FRG, then Dept of Chem., Univ. of Glasgow; Lecturer, Asst Prof., then Prof. of Physical Chem., Dept of Chem., Hacettepe Univ.; Exec. Sec. Eng Dept, Turkish Scientific and Research Council (TUBITAK) 1974, Deputy Sec.-Gen. for Planning and Coordination 1985–87, Pres. 1987–90; currently Fellow, Islamic World Acad. of Sciences (Vice-Pres. 1986–99, 2009–13, Sec.-Gen. 1999–2009); mem. Bd of Trustees and Lecturer, Fatih Univ., Istanbul. *Address:* Islamic World Academy of Sciences, PO Box 830036, Amman, Jordan (office). *Telephone:* 5522104 (office). *Fax:* 5511803 (office). *E-mail:* secretariat@ias-worldwide.org (office). *Website:* www.ias-worldwide.org (office).

ERGMA, Ene, CandSci, DrSci; Estonian astrophysicist, academic and politician; b. 29 Feb. 1944, Rakvere; ed Viljandi Carl Robert Jakobson Secondary School No. 1, Secondary School, Lomonosov Moscow State Univ., Russia, Tartu Univ., Inst. of Space Research, Moscow; jr research assoc., Inst. of Physics and Astronomy, Estonian Acad. of Sciences 1972–74; jr research assoc., Exec. Sec., Sr and Leading Research Assoc., Astronomical Council, USSR Acad. of Science 1974–88; Prof. of Theoretical Physics and Astrophysics, Tartu Univ. 1988–92, Prof. of Astrophysics 1992–, Head of Theoretical Physics Inst. 1993–96, Head of Physics Dept 1993–98; fmr Vice-Chair. Educ. and Culture Cttee, Tartu City Council; Pres. (Speaker), Parl. of Estonia (Riigikogu) 2003–06, 2007–14, Vice-Pres. (Deputy Speaker) 2006–07; Gauss Prof., Göttingen Acad. of Sciences 1994; Guest Prof., Univ. of Amsterdam 1997; Guest Researcher, Univ. of Helsinki 2000; Descartes Grand Jury 2002–, Pres. 2003–05; mem. European Astronomical Union, Int. Astrophysical Union, Estonian Astronomical Cttee, Tartu Observatory Science Council, Estonian Physical Soc. Cttee, Estonian Acad. of Sciences 1997 (Vice-Pres. 1999–), Euroscience; Assoc. mem. Royal Astronomical Soc. 2001; Foreign mem. Royal Swedish Acad. of Eng Sciences; Order of the White Star, Fourth Class (Estonia) 2001, Grand Cross, Order of Infante Dom Henrique (Portugal) 2003, Grand Cross, Order of Merit (Italy) 2004, Commdr's Cross, Order of Repub. of Poland 2005, Royal Order of the North Star, First Class (Sweden) 2007, Order of Merit for Services Grand Gold Decoration of Austria 2007, Badge of Honour 'Jüriöö Star' 2007, Order of the Nat. Coat of Arms, Second Class 2008, Grand Cross, Order of Orange-Nassau (Netherlands) 2008, Grand Cross, Order of Crown (Belgium) 2008; Medal of the Baltic Ass., Estonian Repub. Science Award in Exact Sciences 2002, Grand Medal of Estonian Acad. of Sciences 2004. *Publications include:* more than 100 scientific articles in professional journals and articles in Estonian press and encyclopaedias. *Leisure interest:* tennis. *Address:* Riigikogu (State Assembly), Lossi plats 1A, 15165 Tallinn, Estonia (office). *Telephone:* 631-6301 (office). *E-mail:* ene.ergma@riigikogu.ee (office). *Website:* www.riigikogu.ee (office).

ERHÜRMAN, Tufan, BA, PhD; Turkish-Cypriot academic and politician; *Prime Minister, 'Turkish Republic of Northern Cyprus';* b. 1970, Nicosia; ed Ankara Univ.; Research Asst, Admin. Law Dept, Ankara Univ. 1995–2001; worked for Turkish Ministry of Justice 1999–2004; Instructor in Public Law, Eastern Mediterranean Univ. Faculty of Law 2001–06, Lecturer 2008–, Asst Dean, Faculty of Law 2001–06, Deputy Dean 2010–13; Instructor, Faculty of Law, Near East Univ. 2006–08; Assoc. Ed. Journal of Eastern Mediterranean Univ. Cyprus Research 2003–04; mem. Ass. of the Repub. (parl.) 2013–; Prime Minister, 'Turkish Repub. of Northern Cyprus' 2018–; mem. Republican Turkish Party (CTP), Pres. 2016–. *Publications:* numerous books on public law. *Address:* Prime Minister's Office, 3 Selçuklu Cad., Lefkoşa (Nicosia), Mersin 10, Turkey (office). *Telephone:* 2283141 (office). *Fax:* 2275281 (office). *E-mail:* info.basbakanlik@gov.ct.tr (office). *Website:* www.kktcbasbakanlik.org (office); www.tufanerhurman.com.

ERIAN, Mohamed El-, MA, DPhil; French/Egyptian/American business executive and investment analyst; *Chairman, US President's Global Development Council;* b. 19 Aug. 1958, New York, USA; ed schools in Cairo, New York, Paris and UK, Univs of Cambridge and Oxford, UK; lived in Egypt as a young child, family moved back to New York 1968, accompanied his diplomat father on postings abroad, settled in USA 1983; worked at IMF, Washington, DC 1983–98; Man. Dir, Citigroup, London, UK 1998–99; joined Pacific Investment Management Co. LLC (PIMCO) 1999, Sr mem. PIMCO's portfolio man. and investment strategy group, left co. 2005, re-joined PIMCO 2007, CEO and Co-Chief Information Officer –2014; apptd by Pres. Barack Obama as Chair. US Pres.'s Global Devt Council 2012–; Pres. and CEO Harvard Management Co. 2005–07; fmr mem. of Faculty, Harvard Business School; served on several bds and cttees, including US Treasury Borrowing Advisory Cttee, Int. Center for Research on Women, IMF's Cttee of Eminent Persons, Peterson Inst. for Int. Econs; mem. Bd Carnegie Endowment for Peace, Nat. Bureau of Econ. Research, Cambridge in America; writes a monthly column in Foreign Policy; regular op-ed contrib. to Project Syndicate; Dr hc (American Univ. in Cairo); Creative Leadership Award, Louise Blouin Foundation 2012. *Publications include:* When Markets Collide (Financial Times/Goldman Sachs Business Book of the Year 2008) 2008; columns have appeared in The Atlantic, Bloomberg, The Economist, Financial Times, Fortune, Newsweek, The Wall Street Journal, The Washington Post, The Financial Express, and other publs. *Leisure interests:* sports, supports NY Jets football team. *Address:* Global Development Council, 1600 Pennsylvania Ave, NW, Washington, DC 20500, USA (office). *Telephone:* (202) 456-1414 (office). *Website:* www.whitehouse.gov (office).

ERIKSEN SØREIDE, Ine Marie, Cand. jur; Norwegian politician; *Minister of Foreign Affairs;* b. 2 May 1976, Lørenskog, Akershus; d. of Egil Eriksen and Wenche Irene Hansen; m. Øystein Eriksen Søreide; ed Univ. of Tromsø; mem. Tromsø City Council 1995–99; Presenter, Metropol TV 2001; mem. Storting (Parl.) for Oslo 2005–, Chair. Standing Cttee on Educ., Research and Church Affairs 2005–09, Standing Cttee on Foreign Affairs and Defence 2009–13, Enlarged Foreign Affairs Cttee 2009–13; Minister of Defence 2013–17, of Foreign Affairs 2017–; mem. Conservative Party (Høyre), Chair., Young Conservatives in Norway 2000–04, mem. Conservative Party Central Exec. Cttee 2000–. *Address:* Ministry of Foreign Affairs, 7 juni pl./Victoria Terrasse, PO Box 8114 Dep., 0032 Oslo, Norway (office). *Telephone:* 23-95-00-00 (office). *Fax:* 23-95-00-99 (office). *E-mail:* post@mfa.no (office); udenriksminister@mfa.no (office). *Website:* www.regjeringen.no/no/dep/ud (office).

ERIKSSON, Per, MSc, PhD; Swedish telecommunications engineer and university administrator; b. 22 June 1949; ed Lund Univ.; Pres. and Chair. of several consultancies in signal processing and acoustics 1980–79; Asst Prof. of Telecommunications and Signal Processing, Faculty of Eng, Lund Univ. 1981, Prof. of Signal Processing 2007–, Dir of Undergraduate Studies in Electrical Eng 1981–87, Dean and Chair. of Undergraduate Studies 1983–88, Vice-Chancellor Lund Univ. 2009–14; Founding Pres. Blekinge Inst. 1989–2000; Dir-Gen. Swedish Govt Agency for Innovation Systems (Vinnova) 2001–08; mem. Royal Swedish Acad. of Eng Sciences; Royal Inst. of Tech. Janne Carlsson Prize for Academic Leadership 1999, Telecom City Prize of Honour 2001. *Address:* Lund University, PO Box 117, 221 00 Lund, Sweden (office). *Telephone:* (46) 222-00-00 (office). *Fax:* (46) 222-47-20 (office). *E-mail:* per.eriksson@eit.lth.se (office). *Website:* www.lunduniversity.lu.se (office).

ERIKSSON, Per-Olof, MSc (Eng); Swedish business executive; b. 1 March 1938, Seglora; s. of Gunhild Eriksson and Herbert Eriksson; m. Helena Eriksson Joachimsson 1962; two s. one d.; ed Royal Inst. of Tech., Stockholm; Dir and Head of Production and Materials Control, Sandvik Coromant 1975; Pres. Seco Tools AB 1976; Pres. and CEO Sandvik AB 1984–94; Chair., Ferronordic Machine AB, Odlander, Fredriksson & Co. AB; mem. Bd Kamstrup AB, Fed. Swedish Bridge; Hon. DTech. *Leisure interests:* orienteering, skiing, hunting, golf, bridge. *Address:* Hedåsvägen 57, 811 61 Sandviken, Sweden (home). *Telephone:* 26-27-02-02 (home). *Fax:* 26-27-02-02 (home). *E-mail:* per-olof.eriksson@healthcap.eu (office).

ERIKSSON, Sven-Göran; Swedish professional football manager; b. 5 Feb. 1948, Sunne; m. Ann-Christine Petterson 1977 (divorced); two c.; raised in Torsby, Värmland; player (right back) with Torsby IF 1966–71, SK Sifhälla 1971–73, KB Karlskoga 1973–75, Degerfors 1975, Asst Coach 1976, Coach 1977–78; Coach, IFK Gothenburg 1979–82 (won Swedish Cup 1979, Swedish League Champions 1981 1982, UEFA Cup 1982), Benfica 1982–84, 1989–92 (won Portuguese League Championship and Cup 1983, Portuguese League Championship 1984), AS Roma 1984–87 (won Italian Cup 1986), AC Fiorentina 1987–89, Sampdoria 1992–97 (won

Italian Cup 1994), Lazio 1997–2001 (won Italian Cup 1998, Italian Super Cup 1998, UEFA Cup 1999, UEFA Super Cup 1999, Italian League Champions 2000); Coach, England Nat. Team 2001–06; Man. Manchester City Football Club 2007–08; Head Coach, Mexican Nat. Team 2008–09; Dir of Football, Notts County FC 2009–10; Head Coach, Côte d'Ivoire Nat. Team 2010; Man. Leicester City 2010–11; Tech. Dir BEC Tero 2012, Al Nasr 2013; Man. Guangzhou R&F, People's Repub. of China 2013–14, SIPG Shanghai FC 2014–; Prince's Plaque (Swedish Govt Award) 2001, BBC Sports Coach of the Year 2001. *Publications:* Sven-Goran Eriksson on Football 2001, Sven: My Story 2013. *Address:* c/o Athole Still, Athole Still Ltd, Foresters Hall, 25–27 Westow Street, London, SE19 3RY, England (office). *Telephone:* (20) 8771-5271 (office). *Fax:* (20) 8771-8172 (office). *E-mail:* athole@atholestill.co.uk (office). *Website:* www.atholestill.co.uk (office).

ERJAVEC, Karl Viktor; Slovenian politician and government official; *Minister of Defence;* b. 21 June 1960, Aiseau, Belgium; m.; two d.; ed Univ. of Ljubljana; worked in pvt. business sector –1990; mem. Kranj Urban Municipality Ass. Exec. Council 1990–95, apptd Sec. for Gen. Admin and other Legal Affairs 1990; fmr Head, Office of Human Rights Ombudsman, Repub. of Slovenia 1995–2000, fmr Dir Expert Service; State Sec. for Judicial Admin, Ministry of Justice 2001–04, Minister of Defence 2004–08, 2018–, of the Environment and Physical Planning 2008–10, Deputy Prime Minister and Minister of Foreign Affairs 2012–18; Pres. Demokratična Stranka Upokojencev Slovenije (Democratic Party of Pensioners of Slovenia) 2005–. *Publications:* numerous articles on human rights and judicial system functions. *Leisure interests:* painting, sports. *Address:* Ministry of Defence, 1000 Ljubljana, Vojkova cesta 55 (office); Demokratikična Stranka Upokojencev Slovenije, 1000 Ljubljana, Kersnikova 6/VI, Slovenia. *Telephone:* (1) 4712211 (ministry) (office); (1) 4782231 (office). *Fax:* (1) 4712978 (ministry) (office). *E-mail:* glavna.pisarna@mors.si (ministry) (office); karl.erjavec@gov.si (office); info@desus.si (office). *Website:* www.mors.si (ministry) (office); www.desus.si (office).

ERKEBAYEV, Abdygany Erkibayevich, DPhilSci; Kyrgyzstani politician; *President, National Academy of Sciences, Kyrgyz Republic;* b. 9 Sept. 1953, Kara-Tent, Osh Oblast; m.; two s. one d.; ed Kyrgyz State Univ.; jr researcher, Inst. of World Literature, USSR Acad. of Sciences 1976–82; sr teacher, Kyrgyz Women's Pedagogical Inst. 1982–85; Deputy Ed. Kyrgyzstan Madanyaty (newspaper), Dir Inst. of Language and Literature, Kyrgyz Acad. of Sciences 1985–90; Deputy, Supreme Soviet, Kyrgyz SSR 1990–91; Minister of Press and Information, Kyrgyz Repub. 1991–92; Vice-Prime Minister 1992–93; Head, Osh Oblast Admin. 1993–95; mem. Zhogorku Kenesh (Parl.), apptd Chair. Cttee on Social Problems 1995, Chair. Zhogorku Kenesh 2000–05; Pres. Nat. Acad. of Sciences, Kyrgyz Repub. 2012–; Chair. Inter-Parl. Cttee of Russia, Belarus, Kazakhstan, Kyrgyzstan (Union of Four); Co-Chair. Union of Democratic Forces; Dank Medal. *Publications include:* eight books and more than 150 articles and reviews on problems of literature, arts and politics. *Leisure interest:* reading. *Website:* www.nas.aknet.kg (office).

ERLANDE-BRANDENBURG, Alain; French museum curator; b. 2 Aug. 1937, Luxeuil-les-Bains; s. of Gilbert Erlande and Renée Pierra; m. Anne-Bénédicte Mérel 1980; four c.; ed École des Chartes, École du Louvre section supérieure, École pratique des hautes études (IVe section); Curator Musée de Cluny and Musée d'Ecouen 1967, Chief Curator 1981; Dir of Studies École pratique des hautes études 1975; Prof., École du Louvre; Assoc. Prof., École Nationale des Chartes 1991–2000; Asst Dir, Musées de France 1987–92; Head of Musée Nat. du Moyen-Age 1991–94; Curator Musée Nat. de la Renaissance, Château d'Ecouen 1998–2005; Dir of Studies, L'Institut d'Etudes Supérieures des Arts 2005–07; Pres. Soc. française d'archéologie 1985–94; Dir French Archives, Ministry of Culture and the French Language 1994–98; Pres. French Soc. of Archaeology 1985–94, Nat. Soc. of French Antique Dealers 1995; Commdr, Ordre nat. du Mérite, Officier, Légion d'honneur, Commdr des Arts et des Lettres, Officier du Lion (Sénégal). *Publications include:* Paris monumental 1974, Le roi est mort 1975, Les rois retrouvés 1977, La dame à la licorne 1978, La cathédrale d'Amiens 1982, L'abbaye de Cluny 1982, L'art gothique 1984, Chartres 1986, La conquête de l'Europe 1260–1380 1987, La cathédrale 1989, Notre-Dame de Paris 1991, Quand les cathédrales étaient peintes 1993, Histoire de l'architecture française: Du Moyen Age à la Renaissance 1995, De pierre, d'or et de feu: la création artistique au Moyen Age 1999, Trois abbayes cisterciennes en Provence, Senanque, Silvacane, Le Thoronet 2000, Le Sacre de l'artiste. La création au Moyen Age 2000, Royaumont 2004, L'art gothique 2004, Qu'est-ce qu'une église? 2010, Cathédrales d'Europe 2012, Saint-Germain-des-Prés. An 1000 2012, La révolution gothique 2012, La cathédrale de Rouen 2012. *Address:* 143 rue de Rennes, 75006 Paris (home); Impasse de l'abbaye, 77120 Beautheil, France (home). *Telephone:* 1-44-45-95-38 (home). *E-mail:* alain.brandenburg@gmail.com.

ERLEN, Hubertus, Dr-Ing; German business executive; b. 7 June 1943, Troppau; m. Anna-Maria Erlen; two c.; ed Tech. Univ., Berlin; joined pharmaceutical manufacturing arm of Schering AG 1972, moved to Electroplating Div. 1981, Tech. Dir Feucht plant, Nuremberg 1981–84, mem. Div. Bd 1984–85, mem. Bd 1986–, CEO Schering AG 2001–06, Vice-Chair. Supervisory Bd Bayer Schering Pharma AG 2006–12; Chair. Foreign Econ. Cttee, European Econ. Asscn 2007–12; mem. Supervisory Bd Celesio AG, Invest in Germany GmbH; Chair. Robert-Koch-Stiftung; Vice-Chair. Schering-Stiftung; Order of Merit of Berlin 2005, Cross of Merit 1st Class 2012; Award for Understanding and Tolerance, Jewish Museum Berlin 2010. *Address:* Robert-Koch-Stiftung, Müllerstraße 178, Postfach RKS, 13342 Berlin, Germany (office).

ERMAKOVA, Nadezhda Andreevna; Belarusian local government official, banking executive and fmr central banker; *Chairman of the Supervisory Board, Bank BelVEB OJSC;* b. 19 April 1953, Mogilev Region; divorced; two d.; ed Pinsk Accounting Coll. of the State Bank of the USSR, V. V. Kuibyshev Belarusian State Inst. of Nat. Economy (now Belarus State Econ. Univ.), Minsk; Credit Inspector, later Chief Credit Inspector and Deputy Head, Khotimsk Br., Belarusian Republican Office of State Bank of USSR 1971–79, Deputy Head, Kirawsk Br. 1979–83, Head, Škłoŭ Br. 1983–84; Deputy Chair., Škłoŭ Town Municipal Exec. Cttee and Head of Planning Comm. 1984–90, Head, Financial Div. 1990–94; Head, Škłoŭ Br., Severo-Zapad Commercial Bank 1994; Head, Škłoŭ Br., JSCB Belagroprombank 1994–95; mem. Council of Repub. (upper house of parl.) 1996–2008; Deputy Chair., later Chair., JSC JSSB Belarusbank 1996–2011; Chief Financial Officer A&NN 2004–; mem. Bd Nat. Bank of Repub. of Belarus (central bank) 2006–10, Chair. 2011–14; Chair. Supervisory Bd Bank BelVEB OJSC 2014–; mem. Nat. Council for Gender Policy under Council of Ministers; apptd Chair. Belarusian Union of Women 1999; Honoured Economist of Repub. of Belarus, Honorary Worker of the Banking System of Repub. of Belarus, Order of Honour and two Certificates of Merit of Nat. Assembly, Certificate of Merit of Presidential Admin of Repub. of Belarus. *Address:* Bank BelVEB OJSC, 29, Pobediteley Avenue, 220004 Minsk, Belarus (office). *Telephone:* (17) 215-61-15 (office). *Fax:* (17) 309-62-12 (office). *Website:* eng.bveb.by (office).

ERMAN, Mateja Vraničar, MPA; Slovenian civil servant and politician; *State Secretary, Ministry of Finance;* b. 7 Nov. 1965, Ljubljana; ed Univ. of Ljubljana, John F. Kennedy School of Govt, Harvard Univ., USA; worked at Ministry of Foreign Affairs 1989–93; joined Ministry of Finance 1993, various roles in org. units of Ministry, responsible for customs and tax systems, becoming Head of Indirect Taxation Section and later Head, Dept for Tax and Customs Policy and Legislation in Directorate for Tax, Customs and Other Public Finance Revenues, State Sec., Ministry of Finance 2010–12, 2013–16, 2018–, apptd Head of Gen. Tax Matters and Analysis Dept 2012, Minister of Finance 2016–18. *Publications include:* Customs Legislation with Commentary 1993, New Customs Law with Commentary 1995, Implementing Legislation to the Customs Law with Commentary 1996, VAT Law with Commentary (co-author) 1999, 2007, Customs Code with Commentary 2001. *Address:* Ministry of Finance, 1000 Ljubljana, Župančičeva 3, Slovenia (office). *Telephone:* (1) 3696741 (office).

ERMEKBAEV, Nurlan Baiuzaqulı; Kazakhstani politician and diplomatist; *Minister of Defence;* b. 1 Jan. 1963, Shymkent, Kazakh SSR, Soviet Union; ed Mil. Inst. of the USSR Ministry of Defense, Kazakh Leading Acad. of Architecture and Civil Eng; served in the Mil. 1984–91; aide to Amb. to China 2001–03, Amb. to People's Repub. of China (also Accred to North Korea) April 2012–Oct. 2012; Deputy Minister of Foreign Affairs 2007–12; Asst to the Pres. 2007–12, 2018; Sec. of the Security Council 2014, 2018; Minister for Religious Affairs and Civil Society 2016–18, of Defence 2018–; Order of Kurmet 2005, Parasa lepida 2015. *Address:* Ministry of Defence, 010000 Nur-Sultan, 14, Dostyk Ave, Kazakhstan (office). *Telephone:* (7172) 72-13-84 (office); (7172) 72-13-85 (office). *E-mail:* mod@mod.gov.kz (office). *Website:* www.mod.gov.kz (office).

ERMITA, Eduardo; Philippine politician and fmr army officer; *Chairman LAKAS-CMD, Province of Batangas;* b. 13 July 1935, Balayan, Batangas; m. Elivra Ermita (née Ramos); one s. three d.; ed Naval Postgraduate School, Monterey, Calif., Kennedy Center, Fort Bragg, N Calif., Airborne School, Fort Benning, Ga, USA; Sr Mil. Asst, Office of the Under-Sec. of Nat. Defence 1976–85; Commdg Gen., Civil Relations Service, Armed Forces of the Philippines (AFP) 1985–86; Deputy Chief of Staff, AFP 1986–88, Vice-Chief of Staff 1988; Under-Sec., Dept of Nat. Defence 1988–92; Vice-Chair. Govt Peace Panel Negotiations with Moro Nat. Liberation Front 1992–96; Acting Sec. of Nat. Defence 2001; Presidential Adviser on Peace Process 2001–03; Chair. Govt Peace Negotiating Panel in Talks with Moro Islamic Liberation Front 2003; resgnd from AFP, rank of Gen. 2003; Sec. of Nat. Defence 2003–04; Exec. Sec. 2004–10; Prov. Chair. LAKAS-CMD, Prov. of Batangas 1992–, also Regional Chair. in Calabarzon; Chair. Inter-Agency Cttee for the Relief, Rehabilitation and Devt 2001; Chair., Vice-Chair. or mem. numerous Govt and Legis. Cttees 1992–2001; mem. Nat. Unification Comm. 1993–94; Pres. Repub. of Philippines Golf Asscn (RPGA) 1994–2000; Commdr, Legion of Honour (Philippines) 1988; Mil. Merit Medals, Outstanding Achievement Medal 1986, Distinguished Service Star 1986, Gold Cross Medal 1987, Distinguished Conduct Star 1988. *Address:* c/o Lakas-CMD, Unit AB, Lower Penthouse, One Burgundy Plaza Condominium, 307 Katipunan Avenue, Loyola Heights, Quezon City, Philippines.

ERMOTTI, Sergio P.; Swiss banking executive; *Group CEO, UBS AG and UBS Group AG;* b. 11 May 1960, Lugano; two c.; ed Advanced Man. Programme, Univ. of Oxford, UK; began career with Merrill Lynch 1987, held various positions in equity derivatives and capital markets, Co-Head of Global Equity Markets and mem. Exec. Man. Cttee for Global Markets and Investment Banking 2001–03; joined UniCredit as Head of Markets and Investment Banking Div. 2005–07, Deputy CEO UniCredit Group with responsibility for strategic business areas, Corp. and Investment Banking and Pvt. Banking 2007–10; mem. Group Exec. Bd April 2011–, Chair. and CEO UBS Group Europe, Middle East and Africa April–Nov. 2011, Acting Group CEO UBS AG Sept.–Nov. 2011, Group CEO Nov. 2011–, Group CEO UBS Group AG 2014–; Dir (non-exec.) London Stock Exchange Group plc; mem. Bd Global Apprenticeship Network; mem. Institut Int. d'Etudes Bancaires; mem. Saïd Business School Global Leadership Council, Univ. of Oxford. *Address:* UBS AG, Bahnhofstrasse 45, 8021 Zurich, Switzerland (office). *Telephone:* (44) 234-11-11 (office). *Fax:* (44) 239-91-11 (office). *E-mail:* info@ubs.com (office). *Website:* www.ubs.com (office).

ERNST, Joni Kay, BA, MPA; American politician and fmr army officer; *Senator from Iowa;* b. 1 July 1970, Red Oak, Ia; d. of Richard Culver and Marilyn Culver; m. Gail Ernst; three c.; ed Iowa State Univ., Columbus Coll.; volunteer crisis counsellor, ACCESS Women's Shelter 1991–92; saleswoman, Parisian Shoes 1993–95; human resources applicant tester, Blue Cross/Blue Shield 1996–97; Job Training Partnership Act Coordinator, Midlands Tech. Coll. 1997–99; Emergency Coordinator, Montgomery County, Ia 2001–03; served with US Army Reserve, attaining rank of Maj., Iowa Nat. Guard, Co. Commdr, Operation Iraqi Freedom, Kuwait 2003–04; Auditor, Montgomery County 2004–10; mem. Ia State Senate for Dist 48 2011–14; Senator from Iowa 2015–; Co-Chair. Montgomery County Republican Party 2006–12; Montgomery County Chair., Romney for President 2011–12. *Address:* 111 Russell Senate Office Building, Washington, DC 20510, USA (office). *Telephone:* (202) 224-3254 (office). *Website:* www.ernst.senate.gov (office).

ERNST, Richard R., DrScTech, PhD; Swiss chemist and academic; *Professor Emeritus, Laboratory of Physical Chemistry, Eidgenössischen Technischen Hochschule (ETH) Zürich;* b. 14 Aug. 1933, Winterthur; s. of Robert Ernst and Irma Brunner; m. Magdalena Kielholz 1963; one s. two d.; ed Edgenössische Technische Hochschule, Zürich; Scientific Collaborator, Physical-Chem. Lab., ETH, Zürich 1962–63; Scientist, Varian Associates, Palo Alto, Calif., USA 1963–68; tutor, then Asst Prof., Assoc. Prof., ETH, Zürich 1968–76, Prof. of Physical Chem. 1976–98, now Prof. Emer.; mem. editorial bd various journals on magnetic resonance; Pres. Research Council of ETH, Zürich 1990–94; Vice-Pres. Bd Spectrospin AG, Fällanden 1989–; Fellow American Physical Soc.; mem. Schweizer Chemikerverband, Int. Soc. of Magnetic Resonance, Schweizerische Chemische Gesellschaft, Deutsche Akad. der Naturforscher Leopoldina, Academia Europaea, Schweizerische Akad. der Technischen Wissenschaften, NAS, Royal Soc. London; Dr hc (ETH-Lausanne) 1985, (Zürich) 1994, (Antwerp) 1997, (Babes-Bolyai) 1998, (Montpellier) 1999, (Allahabad) 2000, (Prague) 2002, Hon. Dr rer. nat (Munich Tech. Univ.) 1989; several awards including Benoist Prize 1986, John Gamble Kirkwood Medal, Yale Univ. 1989, Ampere Prize 1990, Wolf Prize for Chem., Jerusalem 1991, Nobel Prize for Chem. 1991, Louisa Gross Horwitz Prize, Columbia Univ. 1991. *Publications include:* World of Invention (2nd Edn) 1999, Contemporary Authors Online 2006. *Leisure interests:* music, Tibetan art. *Address:* Laboratorium für Physikalische Chemie, ETH Zürich, HCI D 217, Vladimir-Prelog-Weg 1-5/10, 8093 Zürich (office); Kurlistr. 24, 8404 Winterthur, Switzerland (home). *Telephone:* 522427807 (home); 446324368 (office). *Fax:* 446321257 (office). *E-mail:* richard.ernst@nmr.phys.chem.ethz.ch (office). *Website:* www.chab.ethz.ch; www.richard-r-ernst.ch.

EROĞLU, Derviş, PhD; Turkish-Cypriot politician; b. 1938, Ergazi, Famagusta; m.; four d.; ed Univ. of Istanbul; internship, Ankara Gen. Hosp., later specialized in urology; worked at Famagusta State Hosp. 1972–76; Chair. Turkish Cooperative Bank for Famagusta Dist 1972–82; mem. Ass. of 'Turkish Federated State of Northern Cyprus' for Famagusta 1976–81, Minister of Educ., Culture, Youth and Sports 1976–77; mem. Legis. Ass. of 'Turkish Republic of Northern Cyprus' (TRNC) 1981–2009, mem. de facto TRNC Constituent Ass. Nov. 1983–; Leader of Ulusal Bırlık Partisi (UBP—Nat. Unity Party) for Famagusta Dist 1977–83, Chair. UBP 1983–2005, 2008–; Prime Minister 'Turkish Repub. of Northern Cyprus' 1985–93, 1996–2004, 2009–10, Pres. 2010–15; treated by UN as bona fide negotiator for the Turkish Cypriot community of the Repub. of Cyprus. *Address:* National Unity Party, 9 Atatürk Meydanı, Lefkoşa (Nicosia), Mersin 10, 'Turkish Republic of Northern Cyprus'. *Telephone:* (22) 73972. *E-mail:* info@kktcb.org (office). *Website:* www.kktcb.org (office).

EROĞLU, Veysel, PhD; Turkish civil engineer, academic and politician; b. 18 Aug. 1948, Şuhut dist, Afyonkarahisar Prov.; m.; four c.; ed Afyonkarahisar High School, Istanbul Tech. Univ.; Asst Lecturer, Hydraulics Dept, Eng Faculty, Yildiz Tech. Univ. 1976–77; Asst Lecturer, Dept of Environmental Eng, İstanbul Tech. Univ. 1980–81, Assoc. Prof. 1984–91, Full Prof. and Head of Dept 1991–; carried out postgraduate studies and research at Int. Inst. for Hydraulic and Environmental Eng, Delft, Netherlands 1981–82; Gen. Dir Istanbul Water and Sewerage Admin (İSKİ) 1994–2002; Dir-Gen. State Hydraulic Works (DSİ) 2003–06; cand. for Mayor of Istanbul 2004; mem. Parl. 2007–; Minister of Forestry and Water Works 2007–18; mem. Istanbul Council, Waters Foundation (SU VAKFI), History and Nature Foundation (TATAV), Turkish Hematological Asscn (THD), Turkish Nat. Cttee on Water Pollution Research (SKATMK), Civil Eng Asscn (IMO), Int. Water Asscn, ICOLD (Int. Comm. on Large Dams), Int. Comm. on Irrigation and Drainage, World Water Council, Int. Network on Participatory Irrigation Man., BENA (Balkan Environmental Asscn), Int. Hydropower Asscn; numerous prizes and certificates of appreciation. *Achievements include:* as Gen. Dir of Istanbul Water and Sewerage Admin credited with solving long-standing problem of Istanbul's drinking water supply. *Publications:* more than 250 academic works, including scientific and tech. reports, book chapters and conf. papers. *Leisure interests:* paper marbling, swimming, diving, reading, calligraphy. *Address:* c/o Grand National Assembly, TBMM 06543, Bakanlıklar, Ankara, Turkey.

EROKHIN, Vladimir Petrovich; Russian business executive; *Chairman, OJSC Surgutneftegas;* b. 1949; Deputy Gen. Dir on Drilling, Surgutneftegas (now OJSC Surgutneftegas) 2003–07, Chair. 2007–. *Address:* OJSC Surgutneftegas, Surgut 628415, ul. Kukuyevitskogo 1, Tyumen, Russia (office). *Telephone:* (3462) 42-61-33 (office). *Fax:* (3462) 33-32-35 (office). *E-mail:* secret_b@surgutneftegas.ru (office). *Website:* www.surgutneftegas.ru (office).

EROPKIN, Dmitriy P.; Russian economist and banker; *President, Rossiyskiy Kredit Bank;* b. 1970, Moscow; ed Moscow Aviation Univ., Financial Acad. to Govt of Russian Fed.; economist, JSC Rossiyskiy Kredit Bank 1994–95, Man. Int. Transfers Area, Int. Settlement Dept April–June 1995, Deputy Head of Int. Settlement Dept June–Sept. 1995, Deputy Dir Int. Settlement Div. and Head of Int. Settlement Dept Sept. 1995, also Head of Financial Trade and Documentary Business Dept March 1996, Dir Int. Settlement and Corresp. Relations Div. and Vice-Pres. JSC Rossiyskiy Kredit Bank responsible for devt programmes of rep. offices and subsidiary banks in UK, Switzerland, Hungary, China, Viet Nam and Bahrain 1996–97, Deputy Chair. and Dir Int. Div. 1997–2001, Chair. and Pres. Rossiyskiy Kredit Bank 2006–07, Pres. 2007–; Chair. JSC Impexbank 2001–04, Chair. and Pres. 2004–06; Chair. Supervisory Bd Unicor man. co. 2006; Chair. SV Group 2008–09; mem. Bd of Dirs B&N Bank 2015–; mem. Presidium of Council of Asscn of Russian Banks; mem. Cttee on Financial Markets and Credit Orgs, Chamber of Trade and Industry of Russian Fed.; Hon. Diploma, Asscn of Russian Banks 2004. *Address:* Rossiyskiy Kredit Bank, 26/9 Smolenskii Blvd, Moscow 119002, Russia (office). *Telephone:* (495) 967-34-43 (office). *Fax:* (495) 247-39-39 (office). *E-mail:* web-adm@roscredit.ru (office). *Website:* www.roscredit.ru (office).

ERRÁZURIZ OSSA, HE Cardinal Francisco Javier; Chilean ecclesiastic; *Archbishop Emeritus of Santiago de Chile;* b. 5 Sept. 1933, Santiago; ed German School of the Congregation of the Divine Word, Catholic Univ., Univ. of Fribourg, Switzerland; ordained priest 1961; first Superior of Secular Inst. of Schoenstatt (German-based Marian movt) in Chile, Spain and Ecuador 1965, Superior Gen. in Germany 1971–87; Sec. Vatican Congregation for Consecrated Life and Socs of Apostolic Life, Rome 1990; Titular Archbishop of Hólar 1990; Archbishop (Personal Title) of Valparaíso 1996–98, of Santiago de Chile 1998–2010, Archbishop Emer. 2010–; Pres. Chilean Bishops' Conf. 1998; cr. Cardinal (Cardinal-Priest of Santa Maria della Pace) 2001; participated in Papal Conclave 2005, 2013; mem. Council of Cardinals 2013–18; apptd Special Envoy to World Apostolic Congress Of Mercy III, Colombia 2014. *Address:* Archdiocese of Santiago de Chile, Casilla-30 D, Erasmo Escala 1884, Santiago, Chile (office). *Telephone:* (2) 6963275 (office); (2) 2744830 (home). *Fax:* (2) 6989137 (office); (2) 2092251 (home). *Website:* www.iglesiadesantiago.cl (office).

ERRERA, Gérard, CVO; French fmr diplomatist and business executive; *Chairman (France), Blackstone Group;* b. 30 Oct. 1943, Brive-la-Gaillarde (Corrèze); s. of Paul Errera and Bella Montekio; m. Virginie Bedoya; three c.; ed Inst. d'Etudes Politiques and Ecole Nat. d'Admin, Paris; First Sec. Washington, DC 1971–75; Special Adviser to Minister of Foreign Affairs 1975–77, 1980–81; Political Counsellor, Madrid 1977–80; Consul-Gen. San Francisco 1982–85; Dir of Int. Relations, French Atomic Energy Comm. and Gov. for France, IAEA 1985–90; Amb. to Conf. on Disarmament, Geneva 1991–95; Amb. and Perm. Rep. to NATO, Brussels 1995–98; Dir-Gen. of Political Affairs, Ministry of Foreign Affairs 1998–2002; Amb. to UK 2002–07; Sec.-Gen. Ministry of Foreign Affairs 2007–09; Dir, Areva, EDF 2007–09, Asscn des Arts Décoratifs 2012–; Sr Adviser to The Blackstone Group 2009–, Chair. (France) 2012–; mem. Orientation Council, Domaine Nat. de Chambord 2017–; mem. Advisory Cttee, Qwant; Officier, Légion d'honneur, Ordre nat. du Mérite. *Leisure interests:* skiing, tennis, guitar. *Address:* The Blackstone Group International Partners LLP, 278 Blvd Saint-Germain, 75007 Paris, France (office). *Telephone:* 1-70-98-23-30 (office). *E-mail:* ge@gerrera.com (office).

ERRÓ, Guðmundur; Icelandic artist; b. (Guðmundur Guðmundsson), 19 July 1932, Ólafsvík; s. of Guðmundur Einarsson and Soffía Kristinsdóttir; m. Myriam Bat-Yosef 1956 (divorced 1967); one c.; ed Reykjavík, Oslo, Ravenna and Florence Art Acads; painter since 1955, over 135 personal exhbns worldwide (six retrospective including Jeu de Paume, Paris 1999 and MAC-Lyon, Lyons 2014)) and has participated in over 250 group exhbns; works in numerous perm. public collections; Officier des Arts et Lettres; Gold Medal (Sweden), Falcon Medal (Iceland). *Publications include:* Sjalfsdadledsla (Mecapoème 1959) 1991, Easy is Interesting 1993, The Discontinued Story: Se Non E Vero E Ben Trovato (catalogue) 1996. *Leisure interests:* travelling (Far East), food, Cuban cigars, wine. *Address:* c/o Siwert Bergström, Galleri GKM, Stora Nygatan 30, 211 37 Malmö, Sweden. *E-mail:* office@gkm.se.

ERSEK, Hikmet; Turkish-American business executive; *President and CEO, The Western Union Company;* m. D Nayantara Ghosh Ersek; ed Wirtschaftsuniversität, Vienna, Austria; began career in financial services at Europay/MasterCard, Austria 1986, held a variety of progressively responsible roles in sales, marketing and banking relationships; with General Electric (GE) Capital 1996–99, responsible for retailer sales, finance and the card business, also represented GE Corpn as Nat. Exec. in Austria and Slovenia; joined Western Union 1999, has held several exec. roles, including as Regional Vice-Pres. for Southeastern Europe, Sr Vice-Pres., Europe, Middle East, Africa and South Asia 2004–06, Exec. Vice-Pres. 2006–08, assumed overall responsibility for EMEA-APAC region 2008, COO The Western Union Co. 2008–10, Pres. and CEO 2010–; mem. Bd of Dirs Teach for All (charity); Hon. Consul for Austria for Colo and Wyo.; Responsible CEO of the Year 2012, Opening Minds Corporate Leadership Award, Inst. of Int. Educ. and Corp. Responsibility 2012. *Address:* The Western Union Co., 12500 East Belford Avenue, Englewood, CO 80112, USA (office). *Telephone:* (720) 332-1000 (office). *Fax:* (720) 332-4753 (office). *Website:* corporate.westernunion.com (office).

ERSHAD, Lt-Gen. Hossain Mohammad; Bangladeshi politician and fmr army officer; *Chairman, Jatiya Party (National Party);* b. 1 Feb. 1930, Rangpur; s. of Maqbul Hussain and Begum Majida Khatun; m. Raushan Ershad 1956; one s. one adopted d.; ed Univ. of Dhaka, Officers Training School, Kohat, Pakistan; first appointment in 2nd E Bengal Regt 1952, several appointments in various units including Adjutant, E Bengal Regt Centre, Chittagong 1960–62, completed staff course, Quetta Staff Coll. 1966, promoted to Lt-Col 1969, Commdr 3rd E Bengal Regt 1969–70, 7th E Bengal Regt 1971–72, Adjutant-Gen. Bangladesh Army, promoted to Col 1973, attended Nat. Defence Coll., New Delhi, India 1975, promoted to Brig. 1975, Maj.-Gen. 1975, Deputy Chief of Army Staff 1975–78, Chief of Army Staff 1978–86, attained rank of Lt-Gen. 1979; led mil. takeover in Bangladesh March 1982, Chief of Martial Law Admin. and Pres. Council of Ministers 24 March 1982, adopted title of Prime Minister Oct. 1982, title of Pres. of Bangladesh Dec. 1983, elected Pres. of Bangladesh Oct. 1986, resigned Dec. 1990, also Minister of Defence 1986–90, of Information 1986–88; fmrly in charge of several ministries including Home Affairs; Chief Adviser, Bangladesh Freedom Fighters Asscn; fmr Chair. Bangladesh Olympic Asscn, Bangladesh Tennis Fed.; arrested, convicted and acquitted of several charges, sentenced to two years' imprisonment on corruption charges 2006, suspended due to time already served 2007; Chair. Jatiya Party (National Party) (fmrly Jana Dal, reorganized in 1986 following merger with four other parties of pro-Ershad National Front) 2009–; UN Population Award 1987, UN Environment Award 1988, Lifetime Achievement Award for Universal Courage and Heroism 2015. *Leisure interests:* golf, writing poems, art, literature, oriental music. *Address:* Jatiya Party (National Party), 75E, Rajni Gandha 17a, Banani, Dhaka 1213, Bangladesh (office). *Telephone:* (2) 9571658 (office). *Fax:* (2) 8813433 (office). *E-mail:* ershad@dhaka.agni.com (office). *Website:* www.jatiyo-party.org (office).

ERSKINE, Peter; British business executive; *Chairman, Ladbrokes Plc;* fmr European Vice-Pres. of Sales and Customer Service, Mars; fmr Sr Vice-Pres. of Sales and Marketing, UNITEL; sr positions with British Telecommunications (BT) 1993–, including Dir BT Mobile, Pres. and CEO Concert and Man. Dir BT Cellnet 1998–2001; CEO mmO2 2001–08, mem. Bd of Dirs Telefónica SA (parent co.) 2008–; mem. Bd of Dirs Ladbrokes Plc Jan. 2009–, Chair. May 2009–; mem. Advisory Bd Univ. of Reading Business School. *Address:* Ladbrokes Plc, Imperial House, Imperial Drive, Rayners Lane, Harrow, HA2 7JW, England (office). *Telephone:* (20) 8868-8899 (office). *Fax:* (20) 8868-8767 (office). *Website:* www.ladbrokesplc.com (office).

ERTL, Gerhard, Dr rer. nat, Dipl. Phys; German chemist and academic; *Professor Emeritus, Department of Physical Chemistry, Fritz-Haber-Institut der Max-Planck-Gesellschaft, Berlin;* b. 10 Oct. 1936, Stuttgart; m. Barbara Ertl; one s. one d.; ed Tech. Univ. of Stuttgart, Univ. of Paris, Ludwig-Maximilians Univ., Munich; Asst and Lecturer, Tech. Univ. of Munich 1965–68; Prof. and Dir, Inst. for Physical Chem., Tech. Univ., Hanover 1968–73; Prof. and Dir, Inst. for Physical Chem., Ludwig-Maximilians Univ., Munich 1973–86; Visiting Prof., Dept of Chemical Eng, Calif. Inst. of Tech., Pasadena, Calif., USA 1976–77; Visiting Prof., Dept of Physics, Univ. of Wis., Milwaukee 1979; Visiting Prof., Dept of Chem., Univ. of Calif., Berkeley 1981–82; Dir, Dept Physical Chem., Fritz-Haber-Institut der Max-Planck-Gesellschaft, Berlin 1986–2004, Prof. Emer. 2004–; mem. German

Acad. of Sciences Leopoldina 1986–, Academia Europaea 1992–, Berlin-Brandenburg Acad. of Sciences 1998–, Pontificia Academia Scientiarium 2010; Corresp. mem. Scientific Soc. of Braunschweig 1986, Nordrhein-Westfal Acad. of Sciences 1993, Bavarian Acad. of Sciences 1998, Austrian Acad. of Sciences 2001; Foreign mem. Polish Acad. of Sciences 2009, Bulgarian Acad. of Sciences 2010, Russian Acad. of Sciences 2011; Foreign Assoc. NAS 2002–; Foreign Hon. mem. American Acad. of Arts and Sciences 1993; Hon. FRSE 1985, FRSC 2007; Hon. mem. Deutsche Bunsengesellschaft für Physikalische Chemie 2006, Physikalischer Verein, Frankfurt 2008, European Acad. of Sciences and Art 2008, Berliner Wissenschaftliche Gesellschaft 2008, Gesellschaft Deutscher Chemiker 2008, Deutscher Hochschulverband 2009, Technische Universität Berlin 2009, German Physical Soc. 2012; Dr hc (Ruhr Univ. of Bochum) 1992, (Univ. of Münster) 2000, (Aarhus Univ.) 2003, (Univ. of Leuven) 2003, (Chalmers Univ. of Tech.) 2003 (Queen's Univ.) 2008, (Comenius Univ., Bratislava) 2009, (Univ. of Technology and Life Sciences, Bydgoszcz) 2011 and three others; Laurea hc Università di Pisa 2010; numerous awards, including E.W. Muller Award, Univ. of Wisconsin, Milwaukee 1979, C.F. Gauss Medal, Scientific Soc. of Braunschweig 1985, RSC Centenary Medal 1985, ACS Langmuir Lecturer 1986, Liebig Medal, German Chemical Soc. 1987, RSC Bourke Medal 1991, Prize of Science and Tech. Foundation of Japan 1992, Wolf Prize in Chem. 1998, Nobel Prize in Chem. 2007, Otto Hahn Prize 2007, Baker Lectureship 2007, Faraday Lectureship 2007, Nicolaus Copernicus Medal 2008, Barsanti & Matteucci Award 2010,. *Address:* Physical Chemistry Department, Fritz-Haber-Institut der Max-Planck-Gesellschaft, Faradayweg 4–6, 14195 Berlin, Germany (office). *Telephone:* (30) 8413-5100 (office). *Fax:* (30) 8413-5106 (office). *E-mail:* ertl@fhi-berlin.mpg.de (office). *Website:* www.rz-berlin.mpg.de (office).

ERTUĞRULOĞLU, Tahsin, BA; Turkish-Cypriot politician; b. 17 Aug. 1953, Lefkosa (Nicosia); m.; two c.; ed Univs of Arizona and Minnesota, USA; joined Ministry of Foreign Affairs and Defence 1983, Head of Political Affairs, 'Turkish Republic of Northern Cyprus' London Rep.'s Office 1986–91; Under-Sec. to Prime Minister 1991–94, re-apptd 1996–98; Counsellor, Office of the Prime Minister, Legis. Ass. 1994–96; Humphrey Fellowship, Univ. of Minnesota 1995–96; mem. Parl. for Lefkosa 1998–; Minister of Foreign Affairs and Defence 1998–2004, of Transport 2015–16, of Foreign Affairs 2016–18; Chair. Bayrak Radio and TV Exec. Cttee; Chair. Nat. Unity Party (UBP) 2006–08, rejoined UBP 2012–; ind. cand. in presidential election 2010; Founder and Chair. Democracy and Trust Party 2011–12; mem. Parl. for Lefkosa 2013–. *Leisure interests:* football, travelling, music. *Address:* c/o Ministry of Foreign Affairs, Selçuklu Rd, Lefkoşa (Nicosia), Mersin 10, Turkey (office).

ERWA, Lt-Gen. Elfatih Mohamed; Sudanese diplomatist and business executive; *CEO and Managing Director, Zain Sudan;* b. 11 May 1950, Khartoum; m. Kawther Amin Mohamed 1973; seven c.; ed Univ. of Khartoum, Sudan Military Coll.; fmr pilot; joined Nat. Security Services 1976; served as Consul General in Embassies in Moscow and Addis Ababa 1977–84; worked in pvt. sector in aviation field 1986–87; Nat. Security Adviser to Pres. 1989–95; State Minister for Nat. Defence 1995–96; Perm. Rep. to UN 1996–2005; Pres. TRANSAFRICA Inc 2005–08; CEO and Man. Dir Africa Operations, Zain Sudan 2008–, CEO Africa Operations, Mobile Telecommunications Co KSC (subsidiary) 2012–; Order of Bravery. *Leisure interests:* flying, reading, computers. *Address:* Zain Sudan, PO Box 13588, Khartoum, Sudan (office). *E-mail:* info@sd.zain.com (office). *Website:* www.sd.zain.com (office).

ERWIN, Alexander (Alec), BEcons; South African politician, academic, trade union official and investment executive; *Chairman, Ubu Investment Holdings;* b. 17 Jan. 1948; m.; ed Durban High School, Univ. of Natal; Lecturer, Dept of Econs, Univ. of Natal 1971–78; visiting lecturer, Centre of Southern African Studies, Univ. of York 1974–75; Gen. Sec. Trade Union Advisory and Co-ordinating Council 1977–79; Gen. Sec. Fed. of SA Trade Unions 1979–81; Br. Sec. Nat. Union of Textile Workers 1981–83; Educ. Sec. Fed. of SA Trade Unions 1983–85; Educ. Sec. Congress of SA Trade Unions 1986–88; Nat. Educ. Officer Nat. Union of Metalworkers 1988–93; Interim Exec. mem. ANC S Natal Region 1989; Exec. mem. ANC Western Areas Br. 1990–91; fmr mem. Devt and Reconstruction Cttee, Natal Peace Accord; fmr Congress of SA Trade Unions rep. at Nat. Econ. Forum; fmr Ed. ANC Reconstruction and Devt Programme; Deputy Minister of Finance 1994; Minister of Trade and Industry 1996–99, 1999–2004, of Public Enterprises 2004–08 (resgnd); currently Chair. Ubu Investment Holdings; mem. Int. Investment Council, Nigeria, Togo Presidential Investment Advisory Council. *Address:* Ubu Investment Holdings, Stonehouse, Ground Floor, Stand no 1021, 94 Sovereign Drive, Route 21 Corporate Park, Irene X31, South Africa (office). *E-mail:* info@ubuholdings.co.za (office). *Website:* ubuholdings.co.za (office).

ERWIN, Tami; American business executive; *Vice-President and Chief Marketing Officer, Verizon Wireless;* ed Pacific Union Coll.; began career as a customer service rep. for US WEST, Bellevue, Wash. 1987, later held a series of man. assignments in outbound calling, tech. operations, call centre admin, activations and service inquiries, also worked on an int. team responsible for implementing cellular service in Hungary; fmr Pres., Southwest Region, and Vice-Pres., Customer Service for the West Area, Verizon Wireless, later Pres., Wash./Baltimore/Va Region, later West Area Pres., currently Vice-Pres. and Chief Marketing Officer, Verizon Wireless; mem. Verizon Foundation Bd, Forbes Exec. Women's Bd, Paley Center for Media; cr. and leads a Women's Leadership Conf. to develop women for professional growth and advancement; three-time winner Verizon Pres.'s Cabinet Award for sales achievement, Women of Excellence Award in Community Service, Nat. Asscn of Female Execs 2011. *Address:* Verizon Wireless Corporate Office and Headquarters, 15 Federal Road, Brookfield, CT 06804, USA (office). *Telephone:* (203) 269-8858 (office). *E-mail:* info@verizonwireless.com (office). *Website:* www .verizonwireless.com (office).

ERZAN, Ayse, BA, PhD; Turkish physicist; b. 2 May 1949, Ankara; m. Orhan Silier; ed Bryn Mawr Coll. and State Univ. of NY at Stony Brook, USA; worked at univs and research inst. in Switzerland, Portugal, Germany, the Netherlands and Italy –1990; fmr Prof. of Physics, Istanbul Tech. Univ.; specialization in condensed matter physics, phase transitions and scaling behaviour in complex systems; recently involved in investigating math. models of evolution and biological networks; mem. Turkish Acad. of Sciences, Palestinian Acad. for Science and Tech., TWAS (fmrly Third World Acad. of Sciences); fmr mem. Editorial Bd, Journal of Statistical Physics; L'Oréal UNESCO Award for Women in Science 2003. *Address:* Department of Physics, Faculty of Sciences and Letters, Istanbul Technical University, Maslak, 34 469 Istanbul, Turkey (office). *Telephone:* (212) 2853277 (office). *Fax:* (212) 2856386 (office). *E-mail:* erzan@itu.edu.tr (office). *Website:* atlas.cc.itu.edu.tr/~erzan (office).

ERZEN, Jale Nejdet, MFA, PhD; Turkish art historian, painter and writer; *Professor of History of Art and Aesthetics, Middle East Technical University;* b. (Adile Jale Erzen), 12 Jan. 1943, Ankara; d. of Necdet Erzen and Selma Erzen; ed Art Center Coll. of Design, Los Angeles, USA, Istanbul Tech. Univ.; taught part-time at various univs in Turkey; lectured widely in USA, Italy and France; mem. staff, Faculty of Architecture, Middle East Tech. Univ. 1974–, Prof. (now part-time lecturer) of History of Art and Aesthetics 1992–; Visiting Prof., Univ. Bologna, Italy and Osaka Univ., Japan; Founder and Ed. Boyut Fine Arts Journal 1980–85; Founder and Pres. SANART Asscn of Aesthetics and Visual Culture; Gen. Sec. Int. Asscn of Aesthetics 1995–98, Vice-Pres. 2007–; adviser, Int. Asscn for Applied Aesthetics 1998–2001; work in collections in Europe, USA and in nat. and pvt. collections in Turkey; consultant, Istanbul Biennale 1992, Istanbul Contemporary Museum 1992–93, Ankara Contemporary Museum 2000–01; Fulbright Fellow, Lawrence Univ., Wis. 1985; Japan Soc. for the Promotion of Science Fellowship 2003; Organizer of Int. Congress of Aesthetics in Ankara 2007; consultant for various architectural journals; Chevalier, Ordre des Arts et des Lettres 1991; Best Author Award 2000, Best Critic Award, Istanbul Art Fair 2000, Contribution to Architecture Award, Turkish Chamber of Architects 2008. *Video:* Exhbn of Suleiman the Magnificent, Grand Palais, Paris (with Stephane Yerasimos) 1989. *Publications:* books on Ottoman architect Sinan, and Turkish artists Sabri Berkel, Erol Akyavas, Mehmet Aksoy; various articles on aesthetics, modern art, Ottoman architecture, environmental aesthetics, competitive aesthetics. *Leisure interests:* gardening, horse riding, poetry. *Address:* Faculty of Architecture, Middle East Technical University, Inönu blvd, 06531 Ankara (office); Sanart, Kenedi Cad. 42, Kavaklidere, 06660 Ankara, Turkey (home). *Telephone:* (312) 2102215 (office); (312) 4464761 (home). *Fax:* (312) 2101249 (office). *E-mail:* erzen@arch.metu.edu.tr (office). *Website:* www.metu.edu.tr (office).

ESAKI, (Reona) Leo, PhD; Japanese scientist, academic and university administrator; *President, Yokohama College of Pharmacy;* b. 12 March 1925, Osaka; s. of Soichiro Esaki and Niyoko Ito; m. 1st Masako Araki 1959; one s. two d.; m. 2nd Masako Kondo 1986; ed Univ. of Tokyo; with Sony Corpn 1956–60, conducted research on heavily-doped germanium and silicon which resulted in the discovery of tunnel diode; with IBM Corpn, USA 1960–92, IBM Fellow 1967–92, IBM T. J. Watson Research Center, New York, 1960–92, Man. Device Research 1962–92; Dir IBM-Japan 1976–92, Yamada Science Foundation 1976–; Pres. Univ. of Tsukuba, Ibaraki, Japan 1992–98, Chair. Science and Tech. Promotion Foundation of Ibaraki 1998; Dir-Gen. Tsukuba Int. Congress Center 1999; Pres. Shibaura Inst. of Tech. 2000–05; Pres. Yokohama Coll. of Pharmacy 2006–; Sir John Cass Sr Visiting Research Fellow, London Polytechnic 1981; mem. Japan Acad. 1975, American Philosophical Soc. 1991, Max-Planck Gesellschaft 1984; Foreign Assoc. NAS 1976, American Nat. Acad. of Engineering 1977; Order of Culture 1974, Grand Cordon Order of Rising Sun (First Class) 1998; Nishina Memorial Award 1959, Asahi Press Award 1960, Toyo Rayon Foundation Award 1961, Morris N. Liebmann Memorial Prize 1961, Stuart Ballantine Medal, Franklin Inst. 1961, Japan Acad. Award 1965, Nobel Prize for Physics 1973, US-Asia Inst. Science Achievement Award 1983, American Physical Soc. Int. Prize for New Materials (jtly) 1985, IEEE Medal of Honor 1991, Japan Prize 1998. *Achievements include:* at IBM pioneered (with co-workers) research on superlattices and quantum wells, triggering wide spectrum of experimental and theoretical investigations leading to emergence of new class of transport and optoelectronic devices. *Publications:* numerous articles in professional journals. *Address:* Office of the President, Yokohama College of Pharmacy, 601 Matanocho, Totsuka-ku, Yokohama, Kanagawa 245-0066; 12-6 Sanban-cho, Chiyoda-ku, Tokyo 102, Japan (home). *Telephone:* (1) 2076-8089 (office); (3) 3262-1788 (home). *Website:* hamayaku.jp (office).

ESCALANTE, Amat; Mexican film director, producer and screenwriter; b. (Amat Escalante Wool), 28 Feb. 1979, Barcelona, Spain; ed Centre d'Estudis Cinematogràfics de Catalunya, Spain, Int. School of Film and Television, Cuba. *Films include:* Amarrados (short, also producer and writer) (Award at Berlin Film Festival 2003) 2002, Sangre (also producer, screenwriter and ed.) 2005, Battle in Heaven (asst dir) 2005, Los bastardos (also producer, screenwriter and ed.) 2008, Revolución (segment 'El cura Nicolas colgado' 2010, Heli (also assoc. producer and screenwriter) (Palme d'Or for Best Dir, Cannes Film Festival, NHK Filmmaker Award) 2013, Esclava (short) 2014, De Hombres y Bestias (short, assoc. producer) 2014, La región salvaje (trans. as The Untamed) (Silver Lion for best dir, 2016 Venice Film Festival) 2016. *E-mail:* contacto@mantarraya.com. *Website:* mantarraya.com.

ESCANERO FIGUEROA, Mauricio; Mexican diplomatist; *Ambassador to Belgium;* b. 25 Nov. 1958, Mexico City; s. of Lunnasi Xi; m.; joined diplomatic service 1982, Analyst in Ministry of Foreign Affairs 1983–85, Second Sec., Embassy in Canberra 1985–87, Chargé d'affaires a.i., Embassy in Kingston, Jamaica 1988–89, Counsellor, Embassy in Washington, DC 1990–92, Counsellor, Embassy in Tokyo 1993–95, Minister, Embassy in Beijing 1995–97, Adviser to Undersecretary for Multilateral and Econ. Affairs 1991–98, Minister, Perm. Mission to UN, New York 1998–2003, Vice-Pres., Second Cttee, UN Gen. Ass., New York 1998, Facilitator of Monterrey Consensus and Conf. on Int. Financing for Devt 1999–2002, Consul Gen. in Shanghai 2003–07, Dir-Gen. of Int. Econ. Promotion 2007–08, Adviser to Undersecretary of Foreign Affairs 2008–09, Alt. Perm. Rep. to OAS, Washington, DC and to UNESCO, Paris 2009–11, Founding Pres. Subsidiary Cttee of the 1970 Convention of UNESCO Against Illicit Trafficking in Cultural Property 2013–15, Amb. to South Africa 2015–18; Amb. to Belgium (also accred to Luxembourg) 2018–, also Head Mexican Mission to EU 2018–. *Address:* Embassy of Mexico, 94 avenue F. D. Roosevelt, 1050 Brussels, Belgium (office). *Telephone:* (2) 629-07-77 (office). *Fax:* (2) 644-08-19 (office). *E-mail:* embamex@embamex.eu (office). *Website:* www.embamex.sre.gob.mx/ belgica (office).

ESCHENBACH, Christoph; German conductor and concert pianist; b. 20 Feb. 1940, Breslau (now Wrocław, Poland); ed Musikhochschulen, Cologne and

Hamburg; Musical Dir, Philharmonic Orchestra, Ludwigshafen 1979–83; Chief Conductor, Tonhalle Orchestra, Zürich 1982–86; Co-Artistic Dir Pacific Music Festival 1992–98; Artistic Dir Schleswig-Holstein Music Festival 1999–2002; Musical Dir Houston Symphony Orchestra 1988–99, Conductor Laureate 1999–; Musical Dir Ravinia Festival 1994–2003; Prin. Conductor, NDR Symphony Orchestra 1998–2004; Musical Dir Orchestre de Paris 2000–10, Philadelphia Orchestra 2003–08; Music Dir Nat. Symphony Orchestra, included role as Music Dir Kennedy Center 2010–17; Chief Conductor, Konzerthausorchester Berlin 2018–; has appeared as conductor with Boston Symphony, Chicago Symphony, Houston Symphony, LA Philharmonic, New York Philharmonic, Philadelphia Orchestra, San Francisco Symphony (US conducting debut 1975), Berlin Philharmonic, Danish Nat. Radio Orchestra, Hamburg NDR Symphony Orchestra, Kirov Orchestra, all five London orchestras, Orchestre de Paris, Vienna Philharmonic; as pianist with Atlanta Symphony, Radio Orchestras of Munich and Stuttgart, Israel Philharmonic and Israel Chamber Orchestras, NHK Orchestra Tokyo; operatic engagements include Bayreuth, Houston Grand Opera, NY Metropolitan Opera, Hessian State Theatre, Darmstadt (operatic conducting debut 1978); festivals include Bayreuth, Ravinia and Schleswig-Holstein; Officer's Cross with Ribbon, German Order of Merit 1990, Commdr's Cross 1993, Officer's Cross with Star, German Order of Merit 2002, Chevalier, Légion d'honneur 2002, Officier, Ordre national du Mérite 2006, Commdr, Ordre des Arts et des Lettres; 1st Prize, Steinway Piano Competition 1952, Munich Int. Competition 1962, Clara Haskil Competition 1965, Leonard Bernstein Award, Pacific Music Festival 1993, Ernst von Siemens Music Award 2015, Hindemith Prize, City of Hanau 2016, Brahms Prize, Brahms Soc. Schleswig-Holstein 2016. *Recordings include:* Mozart: The Piano Sonatas 1967, Schubert: Music for Piano Duet II 1997, Rachmaninov: Piano Concertos Nos. 1-4 2007, Tchaikovsky: Symphony No. 6, 'Pathétique' 2008, Hindemith: Violinkonzert; Symphonic Metamorphosis; Konzertmusik (Grammy Award for Best Classical Compendium 2014) 2013. *Address:* c/o David Foster, Opus 3 Artists, 470 Park Avenue South, 9th Floor North, New York, NY 10016, USA (office). *E-mail:* dfoster@opus3artists.com (office). *Website:* www.opus3artists .com (office); www.christoph-eschenbach.com.

ESCHENMOSER, Albert, DrScNat; Swiss chemist and academic; *Professor Emeritus, Swiss Federal Institute of Technology (ETH) Zurich;* b. 5 Aug. 1925, Erstfeld; s. of Alfons Eschenmoser and Johanna Eschenmoser (née Oesch); m. Elizabeth Baschnonga 1954; two s. one d.; ed Collegium Altdorf, Kantonsschule St Gallen, Swiss Federal Inst. of Tech. (ETH), Zürich; Privatdozent, Organic Chem., ETH Zurich 1956, Assoc. Prof. of Organic Chem. 1960, Prof. 1965–92, Prof. Emer. 1992–; Prof., Skaggs Inst. for Chemical Biology, La Jolla, Calif., USA 1996–2009; mem. Deutsche Akad. der Naturforscher Leopoldina (Halle) 1976, Pontifical Acad. (Vatican) 1986; Foreign Assoc. NAS 1973; Foreign mem. American Acad. of Arts and Sciences (Boston) 1966, Royal Soc. (London) 1986, Akad. der Wissenschaften (Göttingen) 1986, Academia Europaea (London) 1988, Croatian Acad. of Sciences and Arts 1994; Foreign Hon. mem. American Acad. of Arts and Sciences 1966, Pharmaceutical Soc. for Japan 1999; Hon. FRSC (London) 1981; Hon. mem. Gesellschaft Oesterreichischer Chemiker, Vienna 1997, Swiss Chemical Soc. 2009; Orden pour le mérite für Wissenschaften und Künste (Berlin) 1992, Österreich. Ehrenzeichen für Wissenschaft und Kunst (Vienna) 1993; Hon. Dr rer. nat (Fribourg) 1966; Hon. DSc (Chicago) 1970, (Edin.) 1979, (Bologna) 1989, (Frankfurt) 1990, (Strasbourg) 1991, (Harvard) 1993, (TSRI, La Jolla) 2000, (Innsbruck) 2010; ETH Kern Award 1949, Werner Award, Swiss Chemical Soc. 1956, ETH Ruzicka Award 1958, ACS Fritzsche Award 1966, Marcel Benoist Prize (Switzerland) 1973, R.A. Welch Award in Chem., Houston, Texas 1974, Kirkwood Medal, Yale 1976, A.W.v. Hofmann-Denkmünze, GDCh 1976, Dannie-Heinemann Prize, Akad. der Wissenschaften, Göttingen 1977, Davy Medal, Royal Soc., London 1978, Cliff S. Hamilton Award and Medal, Lincoln 1980, Tetrahedron Prize, Pergamon Press 1981, G. Kenner Award, Univ. of Liverpool 1982, ACS Arthur C. Cope Award 1984, Wolf Prize in Chem. (Israel) 1986, M.-M. Janot Medal (France) 1988, Cothenius Medal, Akad. Leopoldina 1991, Ciba-Drew Award, Madison 1994, H.H. Inhoffen Medal, Braunschweig 1995, Nakanishi Prize, Chemical Soc. of Japan 1998, Paracelsus Prize, New Swiss Chemical Soc. 1999, Grande Médaille d'Or, Acad. des Sciences, Paris 2001, A.I. Oparin Medal, Int. Soc. for the Origin of Life 2002, ACS Roger Adams Award 2003, Kitasato Microbial Chemistry Medal, Tokyo 2003, F.A. Cotton Medal, Texas A&M Univ. 2004, F. Westheimer Medal, Harvard Univ. 2004, RSC D.H.R. Barton Medal 2004, Benjamin Franklin Medal in Chem., Philadelphia 2008, Paul Karrer Medal, Univ. of Zurich 2009. *Publications:* numerous articles on organic synthesis and bio-organic chemistry in professional journals. *Address:* Laboratorium für Organische Chemie, ETH Hönggerberg HCI-H309, 8093 Zürich (office); Bergstrasse 9, 8700 Küsnacht (ZH), Switzerland (home). *Telephone:* (44) 6322893 (office); (44) 9107392 (home). *Fax:* (44) 6321043 (office). *E-mail:* eschenmoser@org.chem.ethz.ch (office).

ESCHWEY, Helmut Ludwig, DSc; German business executive; *Chairman of the Advisory Board, Atreus Interim Management;* b. 25 July 1949, Heidenheim/Brenz; m.; two s.; ed Freiburg Univ.; various man. roles with Henkel KGaA, Düsseldorf, Veith Pirelli AG, Höchst/Odenwald and Freudenberg Group, Weinheim 1975–92; mem. Man. Bd Battenfeld Holding 1992, Chair. 1993; mem. Man. Bd SMS Kunststofftechnik AG 1994, Pres. Plastics Tech. Group 1994–2003, mem. Advisory Bd; Chair. Bd of Man. Heraeus Holding GmbH 2003–08; Chair. Advisory Bd Atreus Interim Management 2008–, currently mem.; Dir Inst. of Plastics Processing (IKV), Rheinish-Westphalian Tech. Univ. (RWTH); mem. Supervisory Bd Altana AG 2007–12; fmr Chair. Plastics and Rubber Machinery Div., Verband Deutscher Maschinen- und Anlagenbau eV (VDMA, German Eng Fed.); Dir Novelis Inc. 2005–07, Exova Group, PLC 2014–17; mem. Bd of Trustees Business Ethics Inst. of the European Business School. *Address:* Atreus GmbH, Landshuter Allee 10, 80637 Munich, Germany (office). *Telephone:* (89) 452249540 (office). *E-mail:* eschwey@atreus.de (office). *Website:* www.atreus.de (office).

ESCOBAR CERDA, Luis, MPA; Chilean economist and academic; *Professor of Economics, University of Chile;* b. 10 Feb. 1927, Santiago; m. 2nd Helga Koch 1973; five c.; ed Univ. de Chile and Harvard Univ.; Dir School of Econs, Univ. de Chile 1951–55, Dean of Faculty of Econs 1955–64; Minister of Econ. Devt and Reconstruction 1961–63; mem. Inter-American Cttee for Alliance for Progress 1964–66; Exec. Dir IMF 1964–66, 1968–70, IBRD 1966–68; Special Rep. for Inter-American Orgs, IBRD 1970–75; Trustee of Population Reference Bureau 1968–73; mem. OAS Advisory Cttee on Population and Devt 1968–73; mem. Council Soc. for Int. Devt 1969–72; Deputy Exec. Sec. Jt Bank/Fund Devt Cttee 1975–79; Prof., Georgetown Univ. 1975–79, George Washington Univ. 1977, Dept of Econs, American Univ. 1978–79; CEO at pvt. banks 1979–84; Minister of Finance 1984–85; Amb. to UN and Int. Orgs, Geneva 1986–90; ind. consultant on econ. and financial matters 1990–; Prof., Univ. of Chile 1990–, Dean, Faculty of Business Admin., Iberoamerican Univ. for Sciences and Tech. 1997–2001, Acad. mem. for Life and Extraordinary Prof.; Prof., Univ. del Pacifico 2002–09, Univ. de Chile; Vice-Pres. Partido Radical Social Demócrata 1994–95; Gold Medal for Best Graduate in Econs and Honor Medal, Univ. of Chile; recognition for contribs to teaching and research in econs 1996. *Publications include:* The Stock Market 1959, Organization for Economic Development 1961, A Stage of the National Economic Development 1962, Considerations on the Tasks of the University 1963, Organizational Requirements for Growth and Stability 1964, The Role of the Social Sciences in Latin America 1965, The Organization of Latin American Government 1968, Multinational Corporations in Latin America 1973, International Control of Investments 1974, External Financing in Latin America 1976, 1978, Mi Testimonio 1991, Financial Problems of Latin American Economic Integration 1992, Globalization and Challenges of Globalization 2000–01; contrib. of articles to newspapers and reviews. *Leisure interests:* reading, tennis, skiing, reading. *Address:* 2979 Los Tulipanes, Providencia, Santiago, Chile (home). *Telephone:* (2) 7618635 (home); 56992314231 (mobile) (home). *E-mail:* escobarcerda@yahoo.com (home). *Website:* lecchile.wordpress.com (home).

ESKÉNAZI, Gérard André, MBA; French business executive; b. 10 Nov. 1931, Paris; s. of Roger Eskénazi and Léone Blanchard; m. Arlette Gravelin 1964; three s. one d.; ed studies in law and business admin; joined Banque de Paris et des Pays-Bas (now Banque Paribas) 1957, Pres. Cie Financière de Paribas 1978–82; Chair. of Bd and Chair. Exec. Cttee of Pargesa SA 1985–90; Deputy Chair. and Pres. Groupe Bruxelles Lambert SA 1982–90; Chair. Parfinance 1986–90; Deputy Chair. Banque Bruxelles Lambert 1982–90; Deputy Chair. Banque Internationale à Luxembourg 1984–90; Chair. Compagnie Industrielle Pallas (COMIPAR) 1991–95; Chair. Naviter 1999–; mem. Bd Schneider 1981–97, Petrofina 1986–90, Cie Financière Paribas 1988–90; Chevalier, Légion d'honneur and Ordre nat. du mérite. *Leisure interest:* horse riding. *Address:* 7 rue Maurice Ravel, 92210, Saint-Cloud, France (home).

ESKEW, Michael L., BEng; American business executive (retd); *Senior Advisor, RRE Ventures LLC;* b. 28 June 1949, Vincennes, Ind.; m. Molly Eskew; four c.; ed Purdue Univ., Univ. of Pennsylvania; joined UPS 1972, Industrial Eng Man., Ind. 1972, various man. positions including roles with UPS Germany and UPS Airlines, Corp. Vice-Pres., Industrial Eng 1994–96, Group Vice-Pres. for Eng 1996–99, Dir UPS 1998–2014, Exec. Vice-Pres. 1999–2002, also Vice-Chair. 2000–02, Chair. and CEO 2002–07 (retd); currently Sr Advisor, RRE Ventures LLC; mem. Bd of Dirs 3M Corpn 2003–, IBM Corpn 2005–, Eli Lilly Inc. 2008–, Allstate Corpn 2014–; Trustee, UPS Foundation, Annie E. Casey Foundation; mem. Pres.'s Export Council, Business Roundtable; Distinguished Engineering Alumnus Award, School of Engineering, Purdue Univ. 1998, Jet Corp. Leadership Award 2003. *Leisure interests:* golfing, writing. *Address:* RRE Ventures LLC, 130 East 59th Street, 17th Floor, New York, NY 10022, USA (office). *E-mail:* info@rre.com (office). *Website:* www.rre.com (office).

ESKIN, Alex, BS, PhD; American (b. Russian) mathematician and academic; *Arthur Holly Compton Distinguished Service Professor, University of Chicago;* b. 19 May 1965, Moscow, Russia; s. of Gregory I. Eskin; ed Univ. of California, Los Angeles, Massachusetts Inst. of Tech., Stanford Univ., Princeton Univ.; mem. Inst. of Advanced Study, Princeton 1993–94; Dickson Instructor, Univ. of Chicago 1994–96, Assoc. Prof. of Math. 1997–98, Prof. 1998–2012, Arthur Holly Compton Distinguished Service Prof. 2012–; DOE Scholarship 1991, Sloan Fellowship 1992, Packard Fellowship 1997–2002, Invited Speaker, Int. Congress of Mathematicians, Berlin 1998, Hyderabad 2010, Clay Research Prize 2007, Simons Investigator Award 2014. *Publications include:* numerous papers in academic journals. *Address:* Department of Mathematics, University of Chicago, 5734 University Avenue, Chicago, IL 60637-1514, USA (office). *Telephone:* (773) 702-7380 (office). *Fax:* (773) 702-9787 (office). *E-mail:* eskin@math.uchicago.edu (office). *Website:* www.math.uchicago.edu/~eskin (office).

ESKINDAROV, Mikhail A., DEcon; Russian economist, academic and university rector; *Rector, Financial University of the Government of the Russian Federation;* b. 15 Nov. 1951, Besleney Village, Karachayevo-Cherkess Autonomous Region, Stavropolsky Krai; m.; two s.; ed Moscow Finance Inst.; Deputy Dean, Dept of Finances and Econs, Moscow Finance Inst. (now Financial Univ.) 1981–82, Head of HR Dept 1982–84, Dean, Dept of Int. Econ. Relations 1984–87, Head of team of Soviet Profs, Univ. of Aden, Yemen 1987–91, Vice-Rector for Econs, Vice-Rector for Academic Affairs, First Vice-Rector for Academic Affairs and Assoc. Prof., Prof. Dept of World Economy and Int. Currency and Credit Relations 1991–2002, First Vice-Rector 2002–06, Rector 2006–; co-f. Earmarked Capital Endowment; mem. Bd of Dirs VTB group; mem. Russian Union of Rectors; mem. Presidium, Moscow Council of Rectors; Order of Friendship 1996, Honored Worker of Russian Higher Professional Educ. 1997, Honored Scholar of Russian Fed. 2009; Dr hc (Ryskulov Kazakh Econ. Univ.) 2009; Pres. of Russian Fed. Prize in Educ. 2000, Best Man. in Educ. 2001. *Publications include:* more than 180 research publications. *Address:* Office of the Rector, Finance University, Moscow 125993, 49–55 Leningradsky Prospect, Russia (office). *Telephone:* (495) 943-98-55 (office). *Fax:* (495) 157-70-70 (office). *E-mail:* academy@fa.ru (office). *Website:* www.fa.ru (office).

ESMAHAN D'AUBUISSON, Ricardo; Salvadorean politician; b. 3 Oct. 1964; Exec. Sec., Inter-party Comm. to Support the Peace Process 1989–92; Dir-Gen. Directorate Gen. for Consumer Protection 1994–95; Pres. El Salvador Chamber of Agric. and Agro-industry (CAMAGRO) 2003–08, Cen. American Fed. of Agric. and Agro-industry (FECAGRO) 2003–07; adviser to Exec. Cttee, Nat. Asscn of Pvt. Enterprise (ANEP) 2004–08; Minister of the Economy 2008–09; mem. COENA (Council Nat. Exec. ARENA) 2012–14.

ESMATI, Zabiullah; Afghan government official and business executive; fmrly lived in Calif., USA; Acting Dir-Gen. Ind. Admin Against Corruption (GIAAC) 2003–07; Pres. Ariana Afghan Airlines 2007–09; apptd Deputy Dir Project Coordination Unit, Emergency Irrigation Rehabilitation Project, Ministry of Energy and Water, Mazar Region 2009. *Address:* c/o Project Coordination Unit

Regional Office, Emergency Irrigation Rehabilitation Project, Ministry of Energy & Water, Deputy Director PCU Regional Office, Mew Tasadi Bridge, Mazar e Sharif City, Afghanistan (office). *Telephone:* 79-5399864 (mobile) (office).

ESONO ANGÜE, Simeón Oyono; Equatorial Guinean diplomatist and government official; *Minister of Foreign Affairs and Co-operation;* Amb. to Ethiopia and Perm. Rep. to African Union –2018; Pres. AU Sub-Cttee for Refugees and Displaced Persons, Addis Ababa 2017; Minister of Foreign Affairs and Co-operation 2018–. *Address:* Ministry of Foreign Affairs and Co-operation, Malabo, Equatorial Guinea (office). *Website:* www.mae-ge.org (office).

ESONO EDJO, Melchor; Equatorial Guinean economist, politician and business executive; *President, GVI Semaport;* nephew of Pres. Teodoro Obiang Nguema Mbasogo; ed studied econs in Morocco; State Paymaster-Gen. 1992–2001, Sec. of State for the Treasury 2001; apptd Pres. Ecuato Guineana de Aviación (airline co.) 2002; Minister of Finance and the Budget 2010–13; Pres. GVI Semaport 2013–; mem. Partido Democrático de Guinea Ecuatorial; Hon. Pres. Liste Mouvement Int. pour la Paix. *Address:* GVI Semaport, Edificio GVI, Apdo 540, Banapá, Malabo, Equatorial Guinea (office). *Telephone:* 222272105 (office). *Fax:* 333098300 (office). *E-mail:* gvigrupo@hotmail.com (office).

ESPADA, Rafael, MD; Guatemalan/American cardiac surgeon, academic and politician; *Vice-Chairman, Central American Parliament (PARLACEN);* b. 14 Jan. 1944, Guatemala City; ed Universidad San Carlos, Guatemala City, Baylor Coll. of Medicine, USA, specialist training from LeClub Mitrale, France; performed surgery internship residency training in gen. and thoracic surgery at Baylor Coll. of Medicine, Houston 1970–76, Instructor, Asst and Assoc. Prof. of Surgery 1977–97, Prof. of Cardiothoracic Surgery 1997, joined Methodist DeBakey Heart Center, Houston 1977, Deputy Chief of Cardiothoracic Surgery 2005–07; Vice-Pres. of Guatemala 2008–12; currently Vice-Pres. Central American Parliament (PARLACEN); currently Vice-Chair. Global Financial Integrity; Founder Unidad de Cirugía Cardiovascular de Guatemala (UNICAR) (cardiovascular hosp.), Guatemala City 1995; mem. Unidad Nacional de la Esperanza (UNE); Hon. Prof., Universidad LaSalle, Mexico; Dr hc (Univ. of Francisco Marroquin, Guatemala) 1992; Chest Foundation Gov.'s Award, Int. Rotary Soc. Paul Harris Award, Methodist Hosp. Humanitarian Award 2006, among others. *Achievements include:* believed to have been one of first surgeons ever to perform successfully a cardiac autotransplant. *Address:* Global Financial Integrity, 1100 17th Street, NW, Suite 505, Washington, DC 20036, USA (office). *Telephone:* (202) 293-0740 (office). *Fax:* (202) 293-1720 (office). *E-mail:* gfi@gfintegrity.org (office). *Website:* www.gfintegrity.org (office); www.parlacen.int (office).

ESPERSEN, Lene Feltmann, MSc(Econ); Danish politician; *CEO, Danish Association of Architectural Firms;* b. (Lene Espersen), 26 Sept. 1965, Hirtshals; d. of Ole Peter Espersen and Inger Tanggaard Espersen; m.; two s.; ed Hirtshals Municipal School, Hjørring Upper Secondary School, Lester B. Pearson United World Coll., Canada, Århus Univ.; Vice-Chair. Denmark Conservative Students 1986–88; market analyst, Aarhus Stiftsbogtrykkerie 1991–92; systems designer, Bankernes EDB Cen., Roskilde 1992–94; cand. for Conservative People's Party (DKF) in Ringkjøbing constituency 1993, Sæby constituency 1994; cand. for European Parl. 1994; mem. of Folketing (Parl.) for N Jutland Co. constituency 1994–2014; Political Spokesperson and mem. Parl. Party, DKF 1999–2001, Leader 2008–11; Minister of Justice 2001–08, of Econ. and Business Affairs 2008–10, of Foreign Affairs 2010–11; CEO Danish Asscn of Architectural Firms 2014–, mem. Bd of Dirs 2014–; Chair. Bd of Univ. of Aalborg, Baltic Devt Forum; mem. Bd, Formuepleje; Commander Cross; Outstanding Young Person, The Outstanding Young Persons of the World, JCI Denmark 1996, Tingprisen 2004, alle tiders kvinde 2009, Årets nordjyske erhvervskvindepris 2009. *Publications include:* Stygge Krumpen (children's book) 2005, Det er et yndigt land (with Villy Søvndal) 2008. *Leisure interests:* running, fitness, swimming, Olympic distance triathlon. *Address:* Danish Association of Architectural Firms, Vesterbrogade 1E, 2. sal, 1620 Copenhagen V, Denmark (office). *Telephone:* 23-27-69-26 (office). *E-mail:* le@danskeark.dk (office). *Website:* www.danskeark.dk (office).

ESPINA OTERO, Alberto Miguel; Chilean lawyer and politician; *Minister of National Defence;* b. 4 Nov. 1956, Santiago; s. of Alberto Espina Barros and María Eliana Otero Lathrop; m. María Elena Donoso Peña; three c.; ed Univ. of Chile; Asst Prof., Dept of Constitutional Law, Univ. of Chile 1980, Asst Prof., Dept of Procedural Law 1982–83; Prof. of Criminal Law and Police Procedure, Carabineros School (police training acad.) 1981; lawyer and partner, Otero law firm 1982–89; fmr lawyer with Espina, Hinzpeter, Zepeda and Pizarro (later Espina, Zepeda, Hermosilla, Acosta, Solís and Cía); Pnr, Espina, Zepeda, Acosta, Rodríguez and Tavolari Law Offices 1990–; mem. Chamber of Deputies (lower house of parl.) for Dist No. 21 (Ñuñoa and Providencia) 1990–2002; Senator for Circumscription 14, Araucanía Norte 2002–; Minister of Nat. Defence 2018–; Founder and Exec. Dir Oficina de Fiscalización contra el Delito (FICED, Office of Control Against Crime) 2000; mem. Renovación Nacional, mem. Political Comm. 1987–90, Pres. 1997–99. *Address:* Ministry of National Defence, Zenteno 45, 4°, Santiago, Chile (office). *Telephone:* (2) 2222-1202 (office). *Fax:* (2) 2633-0568 (office). *E-mail:* correo@defensa.cl (office). *Website:* www.defensa.cl (office).

ESPINAL, Flavio Dario, BL, MA, PhD; Dominican Republic lawyer and diplomatist; m. Minerva Del Risco de Espinal; two d.; ed Pontificia Universidad Católica Madre y Maestra, Univ. of Essex, UK, Univ. of Virginia, USA; fmr Co-ordinator Civil Society Agenda during the Summits of the Americas; fmr Prof. of Law, Dir Univ. Center of Political and Social Studies and Center for the Study, Prevention and Resolution of Conflicts, and Dean of the Law School, Pontificia Universidad Católica Madre y Maestra, Recinto Santo Tomás de Aquino, Santo Domingo; practised law in Santiago and Santo Domingo; consultant for both pvt. sector and various int. orgs; published weekly op-ed. column in El Caribe newspaper and co-produced En Contexto TV programme; Perm. Rep. to OAS 1996–2000, Chair. Perm. Council, Cttee on Legal and Political Issues, Cttee on Hemispheric Security, Amb. to USA 2005–09; Attorney, law firm Squire, Sanders & Dempsey LLP, Santo Domingo 2009–13; Founding Partner, Flavio Darío Espinal & Asociados, Santo Domingo 2013–. *Publications:* Constitutionalism and Political Processes in the Dominican Republic; numerous articles and essays on political and constitutional issues in various academic journals. *Address:* Flavio Darío Espinal & Asociados, Torre Forum, Ave. 27 de Febrero No. 495, 4to Piso, Suite 4-E, Santo Domingo, DN, Dominican Republic (office). *Telephone:* 530-6878 (office). *E-mail:* Info@fdelegal.com (office). *Website:* fdelegal.com (office).

ESPINASSE, Jacques Paul, MBA; Belgian business executive (retd); b. 12 May 1943, Alès; s. of Gustave Espinasse and Andrée Bernadel; m. Daniele Samat 1964; one s. one d.; ed Univ. of Michigan, USA; financial analyst, London and Brussels 1967–70; Consultant, Science Man. Int. 1970–73; Head, Control Dept Renault Véhicules Industriels 1973–78, Commercial Man. in charge of export in Europe 1979; Head, Int. Treasury Dept Régie Renault 1980; Financial Officer, Sommer Allibert 1981–82; Chief Financial Officer CEP Communication 1982–85; Chief Financial Officer Havas 1985–87, Exec. Vice-Pres. 1987–93; Consultant 1994–; Dir-Gen. Télévision par satellite (TPS) 1999–2002; Chief Financial Officer (CFO), Vivendi Universal (now Vivendi) 2002–07, mem. Man. Bd 2005–07; fmr CEO Fondation JED-Belgique; mem. Supervisory Bd Canal+ Group; mem. Bd of Dirs SFR, Vivendi Games, Inc., Veolia Environnement, Vivendi Universal Net, LBPAM –2017; currently Bd mem. Hammerson, AXA Belgium, AXA Bank Europe, SES, Fondation Epilepsie (FFRE); Chevalier, Légion d'honneur, Ordre nat. du Mérite, Kt, Order of Saint John (Malta); voted Institutional Investor's Best CFO (Media) 2005. *Leisure interests:* golf, skiing, reading, concerts, operas. *Address:* Avenue Louise 541, 1050 Brussels, Belgium (home). *Telephone:* (2) 649-47-10 (home). *Fax:* (2) 649-48-10 (home). *E-mail:* jacques@espinasse.eu (office).

ESPINOSA CANTELLANO, Patricia, MA; Mexican government official, politician, diplomatist and UN official; *Executive Secretary, United Nations Framework Convention on Climate Change;* b. 21 Oct. 1958, Mexico City; m. Juan Luis Rivera Ferrero; one s. one d.; ed Ibero-American Univ.; mem. Partido Acción Nacional (PAN) 1987–, Head Secr. of Political Promotion of Women, mem. Nat. Exec. Cttee, Head of Sub-coordination for Culture, Educ. and Information, PAN Parl. Group; mem. 57th Legislature, Chamber of Deputies 1997–2000, mem. Equity and Gender Cttee; Chair. Querétaro Municipal Directive Cttee, Head State Secr. of Political Promotion of Women, Head Secr. of Social Devt, Municipality of Querétaro 2000–01; Pres. Nat. Women's Inst. of Mexico (Inmujeres) 2001–06; Sec. of Foreign Affairs 2006–12; Amb. to Germany 2013–16; Exec. Sec., UN Framework Convention on Climate Change 2016–; participated in Non-Governmental Org. (NGO) Forums, Fourth World Conf. on Women, Beijing; Chair. of Bd, Regional Conf. on Women of Latin America and the Caribbean; mem. Mexican Asscn for the Integral Advancement of the Family. *Address:* United Nations Framework Convention on Climate Change (UNFCCC) Secretariat, UN Campus, Platz der Vereinten Nationen 1, 53113 Bonn, Germany (office). *E-mail:* secretariat@unfccc.int (office). *Website:* unfccc.int (office).

ESPINOSA GARCÉS, María Fernanda, PhD; Ecuadorean anthropologist, diplomatist, government official and poet; *President, UN General Assembly;* b. 7 Sept. 1964, Quito; m. Galo Mora; ed Catholic Univ. of Ecuador, Facultad Latinoamericana de Ciencias Sociales (FLACSO) and Rutgers Univ., USA; fmr Adjunct Prof. of Politics and Political Ecology, FLACSO; Sr Adviser on Biodiversity and Indigenous Peoples, Int. Union for the Conservation of Nature (IUCN) 1995–2005, Regional Dir for South America 2005–07; Minister of Foreign Affairs, Commerce and Integration Jan.–Dec. 2007 (resgnd); Amb. and Perm. Rep. to UN, New York 2008–09; Minister Co-ordinator of Natural and Cultural Heritage 2009–12; Minister of Nat. Defence 2012–14, Minister of Foreign Relations and Migration 2017–; Pres. Gen. Assembly, UN 2018–; research fellowships from Ford Foundation, Latin American Studies Asscn, Int. Soc. of Women Geographers, Rockefeller Foundation, Natura Foundation; mem. World Future Council; Premio Nacional de Poesía 1990. *Publications include:* poetry: Caymándote 1990, Tatuaje de Selva 1992, Loba Triste 2000; numerous newspaper and journal articles on environmental, cultural and political issues. *Address:* Office of the President of the United Nations General Assembly c/o United Nations, 405 East 42nd Street, New York, NY 10017, USA (office). *Telephone:* (212) 963-1234 (office). *Fax:* (212) 963-4879 (office). *Website:* www.un.org/en/ga (office); www.mariafernandaespinosa.com.

ESPIRITU, Edgardo B.; Philippine banking executive and diplomatist; m. Lydia Baskinas Espiritu; four c.; ed Univ. of Philippines; started career as Gen. Man. Marikina Rural Bank 1962; apptd Personnel Man. and Trust Officer, Metropolitan Bank and Trust Co. 1965; apptd Pres. Metrobank 1983; apptd Chair. National Power Corpn 1986; Pres. Philippine National Bank 1987–92 (resgnd); Finance Sec. 1998–2000 (resgnd), Gov. for the Philippines, World Bank 1999–2000; fmr Owner, Westmont Bank; fmr mem. Bd of Dirs First Philippine Fund; Co-Chair. ASEAN Special Jt Ministerial Meeting, Manila 1999; Amb. to UK and Perm. Rep. to IMO 2003–09; mem. Bd of Trustees, Philippine Inst. for Devt; Chair. CICI General Insurance Corpn; Banker's Asscn of the Philippines Banker of the Year, TOFIL Award for Banking 1988.

ESQUIVEL, Rt Hon. Sir Manuel, Kt, KCMG, PC; Belizean politician and fmr teacher; b. 2 May 1940, Belize City; s. of John Esquivel and Laura Esquivel; m. Kathleen Levy 1971; one s. two d.; ed Loyola Univ., New Orleans, USA, Univ. of Bristol, UK; teacher at St John's Jr Coll., Belize City –1984; f. United Democratic Party 1973, Chair. 1976–82; fmr Councillor, Belize City Council; mem. Senate 1979–84; Prime Minister of Belize 1984–89, 1993–98, also Minister of Finance, fmrly of Defence and of Econ. Devt; Leader of the Opposition 1989–93; Sr Financial Adviser, Office of the Prime Minister with the rank of Minister 2008–14 (resgnd); Chair. Cen. Bank of Belize 2011–13; mem. Bd of Dirs Belize Telecommunication Ltd, Belize Sugar Industries Ltd, Belize Petroleum & Energy Ltd; Order of Belize; Dr hc (Loyola Univ., New Orleans), USA) 1986. *Address:* c/o United Democratic Party, South End Bel-China Bridge, PO Box 1898, Belize City, Belize.

ESRAR, Air Marshal Abu; Bangladeshi air force officer; *Chief of Air Staff;* b. 1961, Gazipur dist; m. Tasneem Esrar; three d.; ed Bhawal BA Govt Coll., Air Command and Staff Coll., USA, Nat. Defence Coll., Asia Pacific Centre for Security Studies, USA; joined Bangladesh Air Force (BAF) 1978, commissioned in Gen. Duties (Pilot) branch 1981, has served in numerous command and instructional positions, including Officer Commdg, 8 Squadron, Officer Commdg, 25 Squadron, Officer Commdg, Training Wing, Officer Commdg, Flying Wing, Deputy Commdt, Bangladesh Air Force Acad., Dir Air Operations at Air Force Headquarters, Dhaka, Base Commdr, BAF Base Bangabandhu and BAF Base Zahurul Haque, Air Officer Commdg, BAF Base Bangabandhu, BAF Base Bashar, BAF Base Paharkanchanpur, has served as Defence Attache, Embassy in Moscow, Asst Chief of Air Staff (Operation and Training) 2009–15, Chief of Air Staff 2015–; mem. Bd of Dirs Biman Bangladesh Airlines; Biman Bahini Podok 2013. *Leisure interests:* painting, music. *Address:* Office of the Chief of Air Staff, Air Force Headquarters, Dhaka Cantonment, Dhaka, Bangladesh (office). *E-mail:* dce@baf.mil.bd (office). *Website:* www.baf.mil.bd/coas/coas.html (office).

ESSAYDI, Lalla, BFA, MFA; Moroccan photographer; b. 1956; ed Ecole des Beaux Arts, France and Tufts Univ. and School of the Museum of Fine Arts, Boston, USA; lives and works in New York; works held in numerous public collections including Brooklyn Museum of Art, Kodak Museum of Art, Rochester, NY, Williams Coll. Museum of Art, Longwood Center for the Visual Arts, Brooks Museum of Art, Chicago Art Inst., Santa Barbara Museum of Art, Museum of Fine Arts, Boston, Kresge Art Museum, East Lansing, Mich., Columbus Museum of Art, Museum of Fine Arts, Houston, Fries Museum, Leeuwarden, The Netherlands. *Address:* c/o Edwynn Houk Gallery, 745 Fifth Avenue, New York, NY 10151, USA (office). *Telephone:* (212) 750-7070 (office). *E-mail:* info@houkgallery.com (office). *Website:* www.houkgallery.com (office).

ESSEBSI, Béji Caïd; Tunisian lawyer, diplomatist, politician and head of state; *President;* b. 29 Nov. 1926, Sidi Bou Said; m.; two s. two d.; ed Univ. of Paris, France; called to bar, Tunisia 1952, worked as lawyer with Cour de cassation (Supreme Court of Judicature); active within Néo-destour Party (pro-independence political movt); joined govt following independence as adviser to Pres. Habib Bourguiba 1956; Dir-Gen. Sûreté nationale (police authority) 1963; Minister of the Interior 1965–69, of Defence 1969–70; Amb. to France 1970–71, to Germany 1987–90; Ed. Democracy (opposition magazine) –1980; Minister-Del. to Prime Minister 1980, Minister of Foreign Affairs 1981–86; Speaker, Majlis al-Nuab (Chamber of Deputies) 1989–91; Prime Minister Feb.–Dec. 2011; Pres. of Tunisia 2014–; fmr mem. Parti socialiste destourien (PSD); mem. Mouvement des démocrates socialistes (MDS) 1978–; f. Nidaa Tounes, Pres. 2012–. *Address:* Office of the President, Palais de Carthage, 2016 Carthage, Tunisia (office). *Website:* www.carthage.tn (office).

ESSENHIGH, Sir Nigel, Kt, KCB; British naval officer (retd) and business executive; b. 8 Oct. 1944; m. Susie Essenhigh; ed Royal Coll. of Defence Studies; joined Royal Navy 1963, qualified as Prin. Warfare Officer, specializing in navigation 1972, served in variety of ships, Commdr Type 42 Destroyers HMS Nottingham and HMS Exeter; Hydrographer of the Navy, Chief Exec. UK Hydrographic Office, with rank of Rear Adm.; several appointments at Ministry of Defence including Asst Chief of Defence Staff (Programmes); promoted to Adm., C-in-C Fleet; C-in-C E Atlantic (NATO) and Commdr Allied Naval Forces N (NATO); First Sea Lord and Chief of Naval Staff 2001–02; Chair. NGC UK Ltd (Northrop Grumman Corpn's UK holding co.) 2009–13, CEO Northrop Grumman Information Systems Europe; fmr Chair. Defence Strategy & Solutions (consultancy); mem. Bd of Dirs Babcock International Group plc 2003–12; Fellow, Nautical Inst., Royal Inst. of Navigation; mem. Advisory Bd Strategy and Security Inst., Univ. of Exeter; mem. Hon. Co. of Master Mariners; Younger Brothe, Trinity House; ADC; Freeman of Trinity House, Newcastle; Deputy Lieutenant, County of Devon.

ESSEX, David, OBE; British singer, actor and composer; b. (David Albert Cook), 23 July 1947, London; s. of Albert Cook and Doris Cook (née Kemp); m. Maureen Annette Neal 1971; one s. one d.; ed Shipman Secondary School, E London; started in music industry 1965; TV debut on Five O'Clock Club; has since made numerous TV appearances in UK, Europe and USA, including own BBC series 1977, The River BBC1 Series 1988; appeared on stage in repertory and later in Godspell 1971, Evita 1978, Childe Byron, Mutiny! (also wrote music) 1985, with Sir Peter Hall's Co. in She Stoops to Conquer tour and Queen's Theatre, London 1993–94; wrote score for Russian All Stars Co.'s Beauty and the Beast 1995–96; first concert tour of UK 1974, subsequent tours 1975 (including Europe, USA and Australia), 1976, 1977, 1978, 1979 (including Europe and USA), 1980, 1987, 1988, 1989/90 (World Tour); Amb. for Voluntary Service Overseas 1990–92; Pres. Stanstead Park Cricket Club; numerous gold and silver discs for LP and single records in Europe and USA; voted Best Male Singer and Outstanding Music Personality in Daily Mirror poll 1976; Variety Club of GB Award for Show Business Personality of the Year (joint) 1978 ASCAP Award 1989, BASCA Award for Composer 1994. *Films include:* Assault, All Coppers Are . . . 1971, That'll Be The Day (Variety Club Award) 1973, Stardust 1974, Silver Dream Racer 1979, Shogun Mayeda 1991. *Albums include:* Rock On 1974, All the Fun of the Fair 1975, Out on the Street 1976, Gold and Ivory 1977, Imperial Wizard 1979, Hot Love 1980, Be Bop the Future 1981, Stage Struck 1982, The Whisper 1983, This One's For You 1984 (all solo); Under Different Skies (album of musicians from developing countries); War of the Worlds (with Jeff Wayne, Richard Burton and others), From Alpha to Omega (with Cat Stevens) 1978, Silver Dream Racer (film soundtrack: composer/producer) 1979, Centre Stage 1986, Touching the Ghost 1989, David Essex Greatest Hits 1991, Cover Shot 1993, Back to Back 1994, Living in England 1995, A Night at the Movies 1997, The Very Best of David Essex 1998, I Still Believe 1999, Thank You 2000, Wonderful 2001, Forever 2002, Sunset 2003, It's Gonna Be Alright 2004, Greatest Hits 2006, Beautiful Day 2006, Happily Ever After 2007, All the Fun of the Fair 2008, Unplugged 2009, Reflections 2013. *Publications:* A Charmed Life 2003, Faded Glory 2016. *Leisure interests:* motorcycling, cricket, squash, flying helicopters. *Address:* David Essex Management, PO Box 390, Billingshurst, West Sussex, RH14 4BE, England. *Website:* www.davidessex.com.

ESSID, Habib, MEcon, MAgr; Tunisian politician; b. 1 June 1949, Sousse; m.; three c.; ed Tunis Univ., Univ. of Minnesota; various positions in Ministry of Agric. 1975–80, Chief of Staff to Minister of Agriculture 1993–97; CEO Office of Devt 1980–88; Chief of Agric. Devt, Bizerte 1989; Chief of Staff to Minister of Interior –2001, Sec. of State for Fisheries 2001–02, for Environment 2002–03; CEO Pipeline Transportation Co. (TRAPSA) 2003–04; Exec. Dir Int. Olive Oil Council 2004–10; Security Adviser, Tunisia Govt 2011; Minister of Interior March–Dec. 2011; Prime Minister 2015–16.

ESSIMI MENYE, Lazare; Cameroonian government official; b. Mfomakap; m.; four c.; ed Institut des Statistiques et d'Économie Appliquée, Morocco, Institut National des Sciences et Techniques Nucléaires, Saclay, France; UNDP adviser for Rwanda 1990–92; adviser to World Bank 1994; fmr govt adviser for IMF, Washington, DC; Minister-Del. in charge of the budget, Ministry of Finance and Economy 2006–07, Minister of Finance and Economy 2007–11, Minister of Agric. and Rural Devt 2011–15. *Address:* 6305 Shiplett Boulevard, Burke, VA 22015, USA.

ESSNER, Robert Alan, BA, MA; American pharmaceutical industry executive; *Senior Advisor, Carlyle Group;* b. 26 Oct. 1947, New York City; s. of Arthur Essner and Charlotte E. Levy; m. 1st Rosalind Essner (divorced); two c.; m. 2nd Anne Essner; three c.; ed Miami Univ., Univ. of Chicago; with Sandoz Pharmaceutical Corpn 1978–86, Vice-Pres. 1986–87, Pres. Sandoz Consumer HealthCare Group 1987; joined American Home Products (AHP) 1989, Pres. Wyeth-Ayerst Labs 1993–97, Pres. Wyeth-Ayerst Pharmaceuticals 1997–2000, Exec. Vice-Pres., mem. Bd of Dirs AHP (renamed Wyeth, then Pfizer) 1997–2007, Pres. and COO 2000–01, CEO 2001–07, Chair. 2003–08 (retd); Sr Advisor, Carlyle Group 2010–; Chair. Children's Health Fund 2012–; Exec.-in-Residence and Adjunct Prof., Columbia Business School; fmr Chair. Pharmaceutical Research and Mfrs of America; mem. Bd Dirs Mass Mutual Life Insurance Co., Amicus Therapeutics; mem. Business Roundtable, Business Council; Trustee, Mote Marine Laboratory; Prix Galien Suisse 2003, Science/Technology Medal, Research and Devt Council of New Jersey 2003. *Leisure interests:* antique photography. *Address:* Carlyle Group, 520 Madison Avenue, New York, NY 10022, USA (office). *Telephone:* (212) 813-4900 (office). *E-mail:* re2222@gsb.columbia.edu. *Website:* www.carlyle.com (office).

ESSO, Laurent; Cameroonian magistrate and politician; *Minister of State, Minister of Justice and Keeper of the Seals;* b. 10 Aug. 1942, Douala; Minister of Justice 1996–2000, of Public Health 2000–01; Minister Del. at the Presidency in charge of Defence 2001–04; Minister of State in charge of External Relations 2004–06; Minister of State and Sec.-Gen. at the Presidency 2006–11, Minister of State, Minister of Justice and Keeper of the Seals 2011–; mem. Rassemblement démocratique du peuple camerounais. *Address:* Ministry of Justice, Quartier Administratif, Yaoundé, Cameroon (office). *Telephone:* 2223-4292 (office). *Fax:* 2223-0005 (office). *E-mail:* jpouloumou@yahoo.fr (office). *Website:* minjustice.gov .cm (office).

ESSY, Amara, LLM; Côte d'Ivoirian diplomatist and international organization executive; *Chairman, International Institute for Water and Environmental Engineering (2iE) Foundation;* b. 20 Dec. 1944, Bouake; m. Lucie Essy 1971; three s. three d.; ed Univ. of the Carnegie Endowment for Int. Peace; Chief of Div. of Econ. Relations 1970; First Counsellor, Embassy in Brazil 1971–73, Perm. Misson to UN, New York 1973–75; Perm. Rep. to the UN Office, Geneva 1975–81, to UNIDO, Vienna 1975–81; Amb. to Switzerland 1978–81; Amb. and Perm. Rep. to UN (also accred as Amb. to Argentina and Cuba), New York 1981–91; Pres. UN Security Council 1990–91; Minister of Foreign Affairs 1990–98; Pres. 49th Session UN Gen. Ass. 1994–95; Minister of State, Minister of Foreign Affairs in charge of Int. Co-operation 1998–99; Sec.-Gen. OAU Sept. 2001–02, Chair. (interim) African Union 2002–03; currently Chair. Int. Inst. for Water and Environmental Eng (2iE) Foundation; fmr UN Special Envoy for Countries Affected by the War in the Democratic Repub. of the Congo; participated in the following UN confs: Law of the Sea (Caracas, Geneva, New York), Int. Women's Year (Mexico City), Econ. Co-operation among Developing Countries, UNCTAD (Nairobi, Manila) and of the codification of int. law; meetings of the Econ. and Social Council and Comm. on Human Rights; Grand Officier, Ordre Nat. (Côte d'Ivoire), Grand Croix, Ordre Nat. de Bolivar (Venezuela), Grand Officier, Ordre Nat. de San Carlos (Colombia), Grand Croix de Rio Branco (Brazil), Grand Croix, Ordre du Lion du Sénégal. *Address:* 2iE Foundation, rue de la Science, 01 BP 594, Ouagadougou 01, Burkina Faso (office). *Telephone:* 50-49-28-00 (office). *Fax:* 50-49-28-01 (office). *E-mail:* 2ie@2ie-edu.org (office). *Website:* www.2ie-edu.org (office).

ESTEFAN, Gloria Maria; American singer and songwriter; b. 1 Sept. 1957, Havana, Cuba; d. of Jose Fajardo and Gloria García; m. Emilio Estefan 1979; one s. one d.; ed Univ. of Miami; went to USA 1959; f. Gloria Estefan Foundation 1997; hon. law degree (Barry Univ., Miami) 2002, Hon. DMus (Berklee Coll. of Music, Boston) 2007; American Music Award 1987, Billboard Latin Music Award for Best Female Tropical Airplay Track (for Tu Fotografía) 2005, Latin Grammy Award for Best Tropical Song (for Pintame de Colores) 2008, Billboard Spirit of Hope Award 2011, Presidential Medal of Freedom 2015, Kennedy Center Honor 2018, Gershwin Prize for Popular Song, US Library of Congress 2019. *Recordings include:* albums: Primitive Love 1986, Let it Loose 1987, Anything For You 1988, Cuts Both Ways 1989, Coming Out of the Dark 1991, Greatest Hits 1992, Mi Terra 1993, Hold Me, Thrill Me, Kiss Me 1994, Destiny 1996, Gloria! 1998, Santo Santo 1999, Alma Caribeño: Caribbean Soul 2000, Greatest Hits: Vol. 2 2001, Unwrapped 2003, 90 Millas (Latin Grammy Award for Best Traditional Tropical Album 2008) 2007, Miss Little Havana 2011, The Standards 2013. *Address:* Estefan Enterprises Inc., 420 Jefferson Avenue, Miami Beach, FL 33139, USA. *Telephone:* (305) 695-7000. *Website:* www.estefan.com; www.gloriaestefan.com.

ESTEPA LLAURENS, HE Cardinal José Manuel; Spanish ecclesiastic; *Archbishop Emeritus of Spain, Military;* b. 1 Jan. 1926, Andújar, Prov. of Jaén; ordained priest, Diocese of Madrid 1954; Auxiliary Bishop of Madrid 1972–83; Titular Bishop of Tisili 1972–83; Archbishop of Spain, Mil. 1983–2003, Archbishop Emer. of Spain, Mil. 2003–; Titular Archbishop of Velebusdus 1983–89; Titular Archbishop of Italica 1989–98; cr. Cardinal (non-voting) 20 Nov. 2010 (installed as Cardinal-Priest of S. Gabriele Arcangelo all'Acqua Traversa 2011). *Address:* c/o Military Ordinariate of Spain, Calle Nuncio 13, 28005 Madrid, Spain.

ESTES, Richard; American painter; b. 14 May 1932, Kewanee, Ill.; s. of William Estes and Maria Estes; ed Chicago Art Inst.; began career as commercial artist working in publishing and advertising 1956; moved to Spain 1962; began to paint full-time 1966; currently living and working in New York and Maine; MECA Award for Achievement as a Visual Artist, Maine Coll. of Art 1996. *Address:* c/o Marlborough Gallery, 40 West 57th Street, New York, NY 10019, USA (office). *Telephone:* (212) 541-4900 (office). *Fax:* (212) 541-4948 (office). *E-mail:* mny@marlboroughgallery.com (office). *Website:* www.marlboroughgallery.com (office).

ESTEVE-COLL, Dame Elizabeth, DBE, BA, FRSA; British university chancellor and fmr museum director; *Chancellor Emerita, University of Lincoln;* b. 14 Oct. 1938; d. of P. W. Kingdon and Nora Kingdon; m. José Alexander Timothy Esteve-Coll 1960 (died 1980); ed Birkbeck Coll., London; librarian, London Borough of Merton, Kingston Coll. of Art, Kingston Polytechnic 1968–77; Head, Dept of Learning Resources, Kingston Polytechnic 1977–82; Univ. Librarian Univ. of Surrey, Chair. Arts Cttee 1982–85; Chief Librarian, Nat. Art Library, Victoria &

Albert Museum 1985–87; Dir Victoria & Albert Museum 1988–95; Vice-Chancellor Univ. of East Anglia 1995–97; Chancellor, Univ. of Lincoln 2001–10, Chancellor Emer. 2010–; Assoc. Library Asscn; Hon. LittD (E Anglia) 1997; Hon. DLitt (Hull) 1998. *Publication:* The Victoria and Albert Museum (with others) 1992. *Address:* c/o The Tabernacle, Millgate, Aylsham, Norfolk, NR11 6HR, England (home).

ESTEVES, (Maria da) Assunção; Portuguese judge and politician; b. 15 Oct. 1956, Valpaços; mem. Social Democratic Party (SDP), fmr Vice Pres., fmr mem. Nat. Political Cttee; mem. Assembleia da República (Assembly of the Republic) 1987–89, 2002–04, 2009–15, Chair. first Parl. Cttee 2002–04, Pres. Assembleia da República 2011–15; Judge, Constitutional Tribunal 1989–98; mem. European Parl., Brussels 2004–09; Asst Prof. of Public Law, Univ. of Lisbon 1989–99; Pres. Nat. Council of the European Movt; Vice-Pres. Sá Carneiro Inst.

ESTEVEZ, Emilio; American actor and film director; b. 12 May 1962, New York; s. of Martin Sheen (q.v.) and Janet Sheen (née Templeton); m. Paula Abdul (q.v.) 1992 (divorced 1994); one s. one d. *Films include:* Seventeen Going on Nowhere (actor) 1980, To Climb a Mountain (actor) 1981, In the Custody of Strangers (actor) 1982, Tex (actor) 1982, The Outsiders (actor) 1983, Nightmares (actor) 1983, Repo Man (actor) 1984, The Breakfast Club (actor) 1984, St Elmo's Fire (actor) 1984, That was Then, This is Now (actor, writer) 1985, Maximum Overdrive (actor) 1986, Wisdom (dir, actor, writer) 1986, Stakeout (actor) 1987, Young Guns (actor) 1988, Nightbreaker (actor) 1989, Young Guns II (actor) 1990, Men at Work (dir, actor, writer) 1989, Freejack (actor) 1992, The Mighty Ducks (actor) 1992, Loaded Weapon (actor) 1993, Another Stakeout (actor) 1993, Judgement Night (actor) 1993, D2: The Mighty Ducks (actor) 1994, Mission Impossible (actor) 1996, The War at Home (dir, actor, prod.) 1996, D3: Mighty Ducks (actor) 1996, Dollar for the Dead (actor) 1998, Late Last Night (actor) 1999, Rated X (dir, actor) 2000, Sand (actor) 2000, Los Reyes magos (voice) 2003, Culture Clash in AmeriCCa (dir) 2005, LA Riot Spectacular (actor) 2005, Bobby (dir, actor, writer) 2006, Arthur and the Invisibles (voice) 2006, The Way (dir, actor) 2010.

ESTLEMAN, Loren Daniel, BA; American writer; b. 15 Sept. 1952, Ann Arbor, Mich.; s. of Leauvett C. Estleman and Louise A. Estleman; m. Deborah Ann Green 1993; one step-s. one step-d.; ed Eastern Michigan, Univ.; police reporter, Ypsilanti Press 1972–73; Ed.-in-Chief, Community Foto News 1975–76; Special Writer, Ann Arbor News 1976; staff writer, Dexter Leader 1977–80; full-time novelist 1980–; Vice-Pres. Western Writers of America 1998–2000, Pres. 2000–02; Western Writers of America Spur Award, Best Historical Novel 1981, Spur Award, Best Short Fiction 1986, 1996, Private Eye Writers of America Shamus Award, Best Novel 1984, Shamus Award, Best Short Story 1985, 1988, Mich. Foundation of the Arts Award for Literature 1987, Mich. Library Asscn Authors Award 1997, Spur Award, Best Western Novel 1999, Western Heritage Award, Outstanding Western Novel 1998, 2001, Western Heritage Award, Outstanding Short Story 2000, Western Heritage Award for Outstanding Western Novel 2001, Shamus Award for Best Short Story 2003; Dr hc of Humane Letters (Eastern Mich. Univ.) 2002. *Publications include:* novels: The Oklahoma Punk 1976, The Hider, Sherlock Holmes vs. Dracula 1978, The High Rocks 1979, Dr. Jekyll and Mr. Holmes, Stamping Ground, Motor City Blue 1980, Aces and Eights, Angel Eyes, The Wolfer 1981, Murdock's Law, The Midnight Man 1982, Mister St John, The Glass Highway 1983, This Old Bill, Sugartown, Kill Zone, The Stranglers 1984, Every Brilliant Eye, Roses Are Dead, Gun Man 1985, Any Man's Death 1986, Lady Yesterday 1987, Bloody Season, Downriver 1988, Silent Thunder, Peeper 1989, Sweet Women Lie, Whiskey River 1990, Sudden Country, Motown 1991, King of the Corner 1992, City of Widows 1994, Edsel 1995, Stress 1996, Never Street, Billy Gashade 1997, The Witchfinder, Journey of the Dead, Jitterbug 1998, The Rocky Mountain Moving Picture Association 1999, The Hours of the Virgin 1999, White Desert 2000, The Master Executioner 2001, Sinister Heights 2002, Something Borrowed, Something Black 2002, Black Powder, White Smoke 2002, Poison Blonde 2003, Port Hazard 2004, Retro 2004, Little Black Dress 2005, The Undertaker's Wife 2005, Nicotine Kiss 2006, The Adventures of Johnny Vermillion, 2006, American Detective 2007, Amos Walker's Detroit 2007, Frames 2008, Gas City 2008, The Branch and the Scaffold 2009, Alone 2009, The Book of Murdock 2010, Amos Walker: The Complete Story Collection 2010, The Left-Handed Dollar 2010, Infernal Angels 2011, Burning Midnight 2012, The Confessions of Al Capone 2013, Alive! 2013, You Know Who Killed Me 2014, The Wister Trace 2014, Ragtime Cowboys 2014, Don't Look for Me 2014; non-fiction: The Wister Trace 1987, Writing the Popular Novel 2004; collections: General Murders 1988, The Best Western Stories of Loren D. Estleman 1989, People Who Kill 1993; anthologies: P.I. Files 1990, Deals with the Devil 1994, American West 2001. *Leisure interests:* collecting books, antiques, typewriters, records and old films on tape and DVD, movie posters. *Address:* c/o Tor/Forge Books, 175 Fifth Avenue, New York, NY 10010 (office); 5552 Walsh Road, Whitmore Lake, MI 48189, USA (home). *Website:* www.lorenestleman.com.

ESTRADA, Joseph Marcelo Ejercito (Erap); Philippine politician; *Mayor, City of Manila;* b. 19 April 1937, Tondo, Manila; m. Dr Luisa Pimentel; three c.; film actor 1960–89; Mayor of San Juan 1969–85; mem. Senate 1987, Vice-Pres. 1992; fmr Chair. Partido ng Masang Pilipino (PMP), now Founding Pres. Puwersa ng Masang Pilipino; Pres. of the Philippines 1998–2001; impeached for corruption by Congress Nov. 2000, on trial in Senate 2002, sentenced to life imprisonment Sept. 2007, granted exec. clemency and released Oct. 2007; f. ERAP (Educ., Research and Assistance Program) Foundation 1998; Mayor, City of Manila 2013–. *Website:* manila.gov.ph (office); erap.ph.

ESTRADA, Julio Héctor, BA, MBA; Guatemalan economist and politician; *Minister of Public Finance;* m.; two c.; ed Universidad Francisco Marroquín, INSEAD, France; Risk Control Officer Citibank, Zurich 1997; Co-Founder and Gen. Man. Palo Blanco Devt SA 1998–2003; Consultant A.T. Kearney Int. 2004; Asst Dir Latin America, World Econ. Forum, Geneva 2005–08; Exec. Dir Nat. Competitiveness Program (PRONACOM) 2008–10; Tech. Coordinator Mejoremos Guate 2010–12; Gen. Dir Desarrollo Palo Blanco 2010–12; Exec. Dir Nat. Agency for Devt of Econ. Infrastructure (ANADIE) 2012–15; Ed. monthly report for Guatemala, The Economist Intelligence Unit 2012; Minister of Public Finance 2016–; mem. Bd of Govs Inter-American Investment Corpn. *Address:* Ministry of Public Finance, Centro Cívico, 8a Avda y 21 Calle, Zona 1, Guatemala City, Guatemala (office). *Telephone:* 2322-8888 (office). *Fax:* 2248-5054 (office). *E-mail:* info@minfin.gob.gt (office). *Website:* www.minfin.gob.gt (office).

ETCHEGARAY, HE Cardinal Roger Marie Élie, DIurUtr; French ecclesiastic; *President Emeritus, Pontifical Council for Justice and Peace;* b. 25 Sept. 1922, Espelette; s. of Jean-Baptiste Etchegaray and Aurélie Dufau; ed Petit Séminaire, Ustaritz and Grand Séminaire, Bayonne; ordained priest 1947, served in Diocese of Bayonne 1947–60; Asst Sec., then Sec.-Gen. French Episcopal Conf. 1961–70, Pres. 1975–81; Auxiliary Bishop of Paris and Titular Bishop of Gemellae in Numidia 1969–70; Archbishop of Marseilles 1970–85, Archbishop Emer. 1985–; Pres. Council of European Episcopal Confs 1971–79; Prelate, Mission de France o Pontigny 1975–81; Titular Bishop of Porto-Santa Rufina; cr. Cardinal (Cardinal-Priest of San Leone I 1979, Cardinal-Bishop of Porto-Santa Rufina 1998); Pres. Pontifical Council for Justice and Peace 1984–98, Pres. Emer. 1998–; Vice-Dean (Sub-Dean), Coll. of Cardinals 2005–; Pres. Council Cor Unum 1984–95; Special Papal Emissary to Togo 1993, to Bethlehem to try to help end the standoff between Israeli forces and Palestinian gunmen in Church of the Nativity 2002; Pres. Cttee for Grand Jubilee of Year 2000; Officier, Légion d'honneur, Grand Croix 2014; Commdr, Ordre nat. du Mérite; Grand Cross, Nat. Order of Merit (FRG); Grand Cross, Nat. Order of Hungary; Dr hc from several univs in Europe and North America; Ladislaus-Laszt Ecumenical Prize, Ben-Gurion Univ. 1985. *Publications:* Dieu à Marseille 1976, J'avance comme un âne 1984, L'évangile aux couleurs de la vie 1987, Jésus, vrai homme, vrai Dieu 1997. *Address:* Pontifical Council for Justice and Peace, Piazza San Calisto 16, 00153 Rome, Italy. *Telephone:* (06) 69879911. *Fax:* (06) 69887205. *Website:* www.justpax.va; www.vatican.va/roman_curia/cardinals/index_it.htm.

ETCHEGARAY AUBRY, Alberto; Chilean civil engineer, politician and business executive; *Chairman, Empresas Red Salud SA;* b. 5 May 1945; s. of Alberto Etchegaray and Odette Etchegaray; m.; five s. two d.; ed Pontificia Universidad Catolica de Chile; Univ. Prof. of Business Admin.; Dir Dept of Studies, Unión Social de Empresarios Cristianos; co-ordinator of visit of Pope John Paul II to Chile; Dir Hogar de Cristo; mem. Council, Semanas Sociales de Chile (initiative of Episcopal Conf. of Chile); Minister of Housing and Urban Devt 1990–94; Pres. Nat. Council against Poverty 1994–98; Dir Cía. Seg. de Vida la Construcción SA; Pres. Fundación Nacional para la Superación de la Pobreza 1997–2000, Dir 2000–; Pres. Celulosa Arauco y Constitución 2005–07; Chair. SalfaCorp Ingienería Construcción Inmobiliaria SA 2007–15; Chair. Empresas Red Salud SA (operates clinics and medical centres) 2011–; Dir Banco del Desarollo. *Publication:* Poverty in Chile: The Challenge of Equity and Social Intergration. *Address:* Empresas Red Salud SA, Av. Nueva de Lyon 145, Piso 10, Providencia, Santiago, Chile (office). *Website:* www.redsalud.cl (office).

ETHERINGTON, William (Bill) A., BEE; Canadian banking executive; b. 1942; ed Univ. of Western Ontario; joined IBM Canada 1964, held several sales, services and staff positions 1964–80, served successively as Vice-Pres. Western Region, Vice-Pres. Sales, Vice-Pres. Finance and Chief Financial Officer 1980–88, Asst Gen. Man. IBM Latin America 1988–91, Pres. and CEO IBM Canada Ltd 1991–95, Global Gen. Man., Large Enterprise Sales, IBM Corpn 1995–97, Gen. Man. IBM Europe, Middle E and Africa 1997–98, Sr Vice-Pres. and Group Exec., Sales and Distribution, IBM Corpn and Chair., Pres. and CEO IBM World Trade Corpn 1998–2001; Chair. Canadian Imperial Bank of Commerce 2003–09, mem. Bd of Dirs Canadian Imperial Bank (USA) 1994–2009; mem. Bd of Dirs Celestica Inc. 2001–, MDS Inc. 2001–, SS Technologies Holdings Inc. 2006–, Onex Corpn 2007–, Allstream Inc., Dofasco Inc. 2002–06, MDS Inc.; Head of United Way Campaign of Greater Toronto 1993; Hon. LLD (Univ. of Western Ont.) 1998.

ETHERTON, Sir Terence Michael Elkan Barnet, Kt, QC; British barrister and judge; *Chancellor of the High Court;* b. 21 June 1951; ed St Paul's School, Corpus Christi Coll., Cambridge; called to the bar (Gray's Inn) 1974; Queen's Counsel 1990; worked as barrister, primarily at Chancery Bar; apptd a High Court Judge, Chancery Div. 2001; apptd a Lord Justice of Appeal 2008; Chancellor of the High Court (Pres. of the Chancery Div.) 2013–; Chair. The Law Comm. of England and Wales 2006–09; Pres. Council of the four Inns of Court 2009–12; Visiting Prof. of Law, Birkbeck, Univ. of London 2010; Chair. Trust Law Cttee 2012; Hon. Pres. Property Bar Asscn; Hon. Fellow, Royal Holloway Coll. 2005, Corpus Christi Coll., Cambridge 2007; Hon. Prof., Univ. of Kent 2011; Dr hc (City Univ., London) 2009. *Achievements include:* mem. British int. fencing team 1977–80, competed in World Championships 1977, 1978 and 1979. *Address:* High Court of Justice, The Royal Courts of Justice, Strand, London, WC2A 2LL, England (office). *Telephone:* (20) 7947-6000 (office). *Website:* www.justice.gov.uk (office).

ETIANG, Paul Orono, BA; Ugandan politician and diplomatist; b. 15 Aug. 1938, Tororo; s. of Kezironi Orono and Mirabu Adacat Adeke Achom; m. Zahra A. Foum 1967; two s. two d.; ed Busoga Coll. and Makerere Univ. Coll.; Dist Officer, Prov. Admin 1962–64; Asst Sec., Ministry of Foreign Affairs 1964–65, Third Sec., Uganda Embassy, Moscow 1965–66, Second Sec. 1966–67; First Sec., Uganda Perm. Mission to UN, New York 1967–68; High Commr to UK 1968–71; Chief of Protocol and Marshal of Diplomatic Corps, Uganda 1971; Perm. Sec., Ministry of Foreign Affairs 1971–73, Acting Minister of Foreign Affairs May–Oct. 1973; Minister of State for Foreign Affairs 1973–76, of Transport, Works and Communications 1976–78, for Regional Co-operation 1988–89, for Commerce 1989–91, for Information 1991–96, Third Deputy Prime Minister and Minister of Labour and Social Services 1996–97, Third Deputy Prime Minister and Minister for Disaster Preparedness and Refugees 1997–98; mem. Parl. 1998–2001; Asst Sec.-Gen. OAU, Addis Ababa 1978–87; Chair. Tororo Rock FM Radio 2001, Uganda Railways Corpn 2003–06; Dir Cairo Int. Bank 2004. *Leisure interests:* billiards, badminton, music, theatre.

ÉTIENNE, Philippe; French diplomatist; *Sherpa of President;* b. 24 Dec. 1955; ed École normale supérieure, École nationale d'admin, Institut nat. des langues et civilisations orientales; overseas postings include Embassy in Belgrade 1981–83, Embassy in Bonn 1985–87, Perm. Mission to EU, Brussels 1988–91, 1997–2002, Cultural Counsellor, Embassy in Moscow 1991–94, Amb. to Romania 2002–05, Dir-Gen. of Int. Co-operation and Devt 2004–07, Ministry of Foreign and European Affairs, Head of Cabinet of Minister of Foreign and European Affairs 2007–09, Amb. and Perm. Rep. to EU, Brussels 2009–14, Amb. to Germany 2014–17; Diplomatic Counsellor (Sherpa) of Pres. 2017–; Chevalier, Légion d'honneur 2003, Officier 2013, Officier, Ordre nat. du Mérite. *Address:* Office of the President, Palais de l'Élysée, 55 Rue du Faubourg Saint Honoré, 75008 Paris, France (office). *Telephone:* 1-42-92-81-00 (office). *Website:* www.elysee.fr (office).

ETO, Akinori, LLM; Japanese politician; b. 12 Oct. 1958, Towada, Aomori Dist; ed Nihon Univ.; joined Shiseikai (social welfare corpn) 1984, Vice-Pres. 1988–2002, Pres. 2002; mem. House of Reps (lower house of Parl.) for Aomori Second Dist 1996–2000, 2003–, Chair. Security Cttee 2013; Parl. Vice-Minister in Cabinet Office 2004–05, Deputy Minister of Defence 2007–08, 2012–13, Minister of Defence Sept.–Dec. 2014; mem. Liberal Democratic Party. *Address:* c/o Ministry of Defence, 5-1, Ichigaya, Honmura-cho, Shinjuku-ku, Tokyo 162-8801, Japan (office). *Website:* www.eto-akinori.jp.

ETO'O FILS, Samuel; Cameroonian professional footballer; b. 10 March 1981, Nkon; striker; teams played for include Real Madrid, Spain 1997–2000 (won Intercontinental Cup 1998), Leganes, Spain 1997–98 (on loan), Espanyol, Spain 1999 (on loan), Real Mallorca, Spain 1999–2004 (initially on loan and then part-owned by Real Madrid, won Copa del Rey 2003), FC Barcelona, Spain 2004–09 (won La Liga 2005, 2006, 2009, Supercopa de España 2006, 2007, UEFA Champions League 2006, 2009, Copa del Rey 2009), Internazionale, Italy 2009–11, Anzhi Makhachkala, Dagestan 2011–13, Chelsea 2013–14, Everton 2014–15, Sampdoria 2015, Antalyaspor 2015–; played for Cameroon Nat. Team 1996–2014, played in World Cups 1998, 2002, gold medal, Olympic Games, Sydney 2000, winner African Nations Cup 2000, 2002, fmr Capt. of nat. team; leading scorer for Real Mallorca in 2003–04 Primera Liga season, won Copa del Rey 2003; Confed. of African Football Footballer of the Year 2003, African Cup of Nations Top Scorer 2006, 2008, African Player of the Year 2003, 2004, 2005, 2010, FIFPro World XI 2004–05, 2005–06, UEFA Champions League Best Forward 2006, UEFA Team of the Year 2005, 2006, Spanish La Liga Top Scorer 2006, World XI Striker 2004–05, 2005–06, Most Goals Scored in Domestic League for RCD Mallorca 54 Goals, African Cup of Nations Top Scorer of All Time with 16 Goals, Most Goals Scored in History of Cameroon Nat. Team, FIFA World Player of the Year (Third Place) 2005, Golden Foot Award 2015.

ETTL, Harald; Austrian trade union official and politician; b. 7 Dec. 1947, Gleisdorf, Styria; m.; three c.; ed Higher Fed. Teaching and Experimental Coll. for Textile Industry, Vienna; military service 1968–69; Asst to Works Man., Eybl carpet factory, Ebergassing; Sec. Textile, Clothing and Leather Workers' Union 1971–73, Cen. Sec. 1973–84, Pres. 1984–2000; Vice-Pres. Metal-Textile Trade Union 2000; Vice-Pres. Int. Textile, Clothing and Leather Workers' Asscn 2004; Chair. Consumer Information Asscn 1993–2001; Minister for Health and the Civil Service 1989–92; MEP 1996–2009; Chair. Gen. Accident Insurance Scheme 1978–89; Pres. Accident Insurance Cttee, Fed. of Austrian Social Insurance Bodies 1978–89; Chair. Working Group for Integration in Austrian Trade Union Confed.; mem. Social Democratic Party; Grand Gold Decoration with Ribbon for Services to the Republic of Austria 1992.

EUBANK, Chris; British fmr professional boxer; b. 8 Aug. 1966, Dulwich, London; s. of Rachel Scollins; m.; four c.; WBC Int. Middleweight Boxing Champion March–Nov. 1990 two defences; WBO Middleweight Boxing Champion Nov. 1990–Aug. 1991 three defences; WBO World Super-Middleweight Boxing Champion Sept. 1991–March 1995 fourteen defences, lost title to Steve Collins, Cork Sept. 1995, failed to regain title against Joe Calzaghe, Sheffield Oct. 1997; unsuccessful fights for WBO Cruiserweight title against Carl Thompson, Manchester April 1998, Sheffield July 1998; Patron Breakthrough; numerous UK television appearances; Amb. for the Int. Fund for Animal Welfare; spokesperson for the Nat. Soc. for the Prevention of Cruelty to Children.

EUGENIDES, Jeffrey, BA, MA; American novelist; b. 8 March 1960, Detroit, Mich.; m.; one d.; ed Brown Univ., Stanford Univ.; Fellow, Berliner Künstlerprogramm 2002; Guggenheim Foundation Fellowship, Nat. Foundation for the Arts Fellowship, American Acad. in Berlin Prize Fellowship 2000–01; teacher in Creative Writing Program, Princeton Univ. 1999–2000, Prof. of Creative Writing, Peter B. Lewis Center for the Arts 2007– (on leave 2018–19); mem. American Acad. of Arts and Letters 2018; Fellow American Acad. of Arts and Sciences 2013; Hon. DLit (Brown Univ.) 2014; Whiting Writers' Award, American Acad. of Arts and Letters Harold D. Vursell Memorial Award. *Publications:* The Virgin Suicides 1993, Middlesex (Pulitzer Prize for Fiction 2003, WELT-Literaturpreis, Great Lakes Book Award) 2002, Air Mail 2005, My Mistress's Sparrow is Dead (Ed.) 2008, The Marriage Plot 2011, Fresh Complaint 2017; contrib. to The New Yorker, The Paris Review, The Yale Review, The Gettysburg Review, Best American Short Stories, Granta's Best of Young American Novelists. *Address:* New South Building, Floor 6, Princeton University, 185 Nassau Street, Princeton, NJ 08544, USA (office). *Telephone:* (609) 258-8561 (office). *Fax:* (609) 258-2230 (office). *E-mail:* jeugenid@princeton.edu (office). *Website:* www.princeton.edu/~visarts/cwr (office).

EUH, Yoon-dae, BA, MA, MBA, PhD; South Korean academic; *Professor Emeritus, Korea University;* b. 22 May 1945, Jinhae City; ed Korea Univ., Asian Inst. of Man., Univ. of Michigan, USA; Prof. of Int. Business and Finance, Korea Univ. 1979, now Prof. Emer., Chair. Dept of Int. Business and Trade 1982–86, Assoc. Dean Coll. of Business Admin 1986–89, Dean Academic Affairs 1991–93, Dir Inst. for Business Research and Educ. 1993–97, Dean Grad. School of Business Admin 1996–98, Pres. Korea Univ. 2003–06; Research Fellow, Inst. for Int. Commerce, Univ. of Michigan 1976–78; Visiting Prof., PAMI (Summer Program) Coll. of Business Admin, Univ. of Hawaii, USA 1982–87, Faculty of Commerce and Business Admin, Univ. of British Columbia, Canada 1989; Visiting Scholar, Inst. of Developing Economies, Japan 1985–86; Scholar, Faculty of Econs, Univ. of Tokyo, Japan 1990–91; adviser, Korea Inst. for Int. Econ. Policy 1997–, Korea Devt Inst. 1997–; Policy Adviser, Ministry of Foreign Affairs and Trade 1993–2004; Chair. Advisory Bd Ministry of Educ. and Human Resources 2003–05, Cttee for Future Korea, Ministry of Information and Communication 2006–; Co-Chair. Nat. Fed. for Cooperation between Univ. and Industry 2006–; Vice-Chair. Nat. Econ. Advisory Council 2005–; Founding Pres. Korea Center for Int. Finance 1999–2000; Dir (non-resident) Korea Inst. for Public Finance 1996–99; mem. Monetary Bd Bank of Korea 1992–95; mem. Bd of Dirs Korea Devt Bank 1996–97, Korea First Bank 1998–99, Hyundai Corpn 1998–2002, CJ Home Shopping 1999–2003; mem. (Minister) Public Fund Oversight Comm. 2001–03; Pres. Korean Acad. of Int. Business 1992–93, Korea Money and Finance Asscn 1995–96, Korean Academic Soc. of Business Admin 2002–03; Chair. Presidential Council on Nation Branding 2009–10, KB Financial Group 2010–13; Hon. Prof., Jilin Univ. 2005, Nanjing Univ. 2006; Hon. Fellow, Royal Holloway, Univ. of London 2005; Order of Service Merit (Blue Stripes); Hon. LLD (Weseda Univ.) 2005, Hon. PhD (Yonsei Univ.) 2006, Hon. DUniv (Griffith Univ.) 2006; Asian Inst. of Man. Triple A Award, A Merit, Les Insignes de Chevalier de l'Ordre nat. du Mérite, Global CEO Award 2006, Dasan Finance Prize 2012, Asian Banker Leadership Achievement Award 2013. *Address:* College of Business Administration, University of Korea, Anam-dong, Sungbuk-gu, Seoul 136-701, Republic of Korea (office). *Telephone:* (2) 3290-1916 (office). *Fax:* (2) 395-1976 (office). *E-mail:* ydeuh@korea.ac.kr (office). *Website:* www.korea.ac.kr (office).

EUSTACE, Arnhim Ulric; Saint Vincent and the Grenadines economist and politician; *Leader, New Democratic Party;* b. 1944; economist specializing in fiscal man.; mem. Parl. 1998–; fmr Minister of Finance; Prime Minister of Saint Vincent and the Grenadines 2000–01; Leader, New Democratic Party (NDP) 2000–. *Address:* Ratho Mill, PO Box 76, Kingstown; New Democratic Party, Murray Road, PO Box 1300, Kingstown, Saint Vincent and the Grenadines (office). *Telephone:* 456-2114 (office). *Fax:* 457-2647 (office). *E-mail:* ndp@caribsurf.com (office). *Website:* www.ndpsvg.com (office).

EUSTACE, Dudley Graham (D. G.), BA; British business executive; *Operating Partner, Tri-Artisan Capital Partners, LLC;* b. 3 July 1936; m. Carol Diane Zakrajsek; two c.; ed Univ. of Bristol; with John Barrit & Son, Hamilton, Bermuda 1962; with Int. Resort Facilities 1963; exec. positions with Alcan Aluminium Ltd in various locations including Montreal, Vancouver, Buenos Aires, Rio de Janeiro, Madrid and UK 1964–87; joined British Aerospace plc 1987, Financial Dir 1988–92; mem. Group Cttee, Royal Philips Electronics NV 1992–2001, Exec. Vice-Pres. and Chief Financial Officer 1993–97, Vice-Chair. Bd of Man. 1997–99; Deputy Chair. Smith & Nephew PLC 1999–2000, Chair. (non-exec.) 2000–06; mem. Supervisory Bd AEGON NV 1997–2010, Vice-Chair. –2005, Chair. 2005–10, fmr Chief Financial Officer AEGON Canadian NV; Operating Partner, Tri-Artisan Capital Partners, LLC; Exec. Vice-Pres. and mem. Corp. Exec. Bd Koninklijke Ahold NV (fmrly Royal Ahold) 2003–, Interim Chief Financial Officer March–June 2003; Chair. Supervisory Bd The Nielsen Co. (mem. 2006–); Vice-Chair. Supervisory Bd Royal KPN NV 2001– (mem. 2000–), Hagemeyer NV (mem. 1999–); fmr Chief Financial Officer Hagemeijer NV, Royal KPN NV (fmrly Koninklijke KPN NV), Smith and Nephew PLC, Sendo Holdings PLC, Sonae.com.SGPS, W&S Nederland BV; mem. Supervisory Bd KLM Royal Dutch Airlines 1999–, Hagemeyer NV 2001–, Stork NV 2007–, European Advisory Council of Rothschilds; mem. Export Guarantees Advisory Council, UK 1988, European Advisory Council for Rothschilds; mem. Bd Sonae.Com SGPS S.A. of Portugal, Council of Univ. of Surrey. *Address:* Tri-Artisan Capital Partners, LLC, 110 East 59th Street, 37th Floor, New York, NY 10022, USA (office). *Telephone:* (212) 610-1500 (office). *Fax:* (212) 610-1501 (office). *E-mail:* contact@tri-artisan.com (office). *Website:* www.tri-artisanpartners.com (office).

EVAN, Gerard, BA, MA, PhD, FRS, FMedSci; British/American biomedical scientist, cancer researcher and academic; *Sir William Dunn Professor of Biochemistry, University of Cambridge;* b. 17 Aug. 1955, London, England; s. of Robert Evan and Gwendoline Evan (née Groom); m.; one s. one d.; ed Univs of Oxford and Cambridge, UK, Univ. of California, San Francisco, USA; MRC Lab. of Molecular Biology, Univ. of Cambridge 1977–82, Research Fellowship, Downing Coll. Cambridge 1984–88, Asst Prof., Ludwig Inst. for Cancer Research, Cambridge 1984–88, Sir William Dunn Prof. of Biochemistry, Univ. of Cambridge 2009–, Fellow of Christ's Coll. 2010–; Dept of Microbiology and Immunology, Univ. of California, San Francisco 1982–84, Gerson and Barbara Bass Bakar Distinguished Prof. of Cancer Biology 1999–2009; Prin. Scientist, Imperial Cancer Research Fund 1988–99; Royal Soc. Napier Research Prof., Univ. Coll., London 1996–99, George Daniel Brooks Lectureship in Oncology 2010; mem. Scientific Advisory Bd EISAI London Research Labs 1994–97, Oxagen Inc. 1997–99, ESBA Tech 1998–2007, Genomic Health Inc.; Consultant Cantab Pharmaceuticals Ltd 1994–99, Ontogeny Inc., Boston 1998–2000, Cambridge Antibody Tech. Inc. 1998–99, Amersham/Nycomed 1998–99; mem. Scientific Review Bd DNAX 1998–2006, Oncology Advisory Bd Astra-Zeneca; mem. European Acad. of Sciences, European Molecular Biology Org.; Pfizer Prize in Biology 1995, Royal Soc. Napier Research Prof. of Cancer Biology 1996, Joseph Steiner Prize, Swiss Oncological Soc. 1997, Royal Soc. Wolfson Foundation Research Award 2009, Marguerite Vogt Lecturer, Salk Inst. 2010. *Radio includes:* participation in numerous science programmes for BBC. *Publications:* numerous academic publs. *Leisure interests:* sailing, music, white water rafting, hiking, skiing. *Address:* Sanger Building, Department of Biochemistry, 80 Tennis Court Road, Cambridge, CB2 1GA, England (office). *Telephone:* (1223) 765944 (office). *Fax:* (1223) 766082 (office). *E-mail:* gie20@cam.ac.uk (office). *Website:* www.bioc.cam.ac.uk/uto/evan.html (office).

EVANGELISTA, Linda; Canadian model; b. 10 May 1965, St Catharines, Ont.; m. Gerald Marie (divorced 1993); one s. with Francois-Henri Pinault; face of L'Oréal, Paris; numerous catwalk fashion shows. *Address:* c/o dna Model Management, 520 Broadway, 11th Floor, New York, NY 10012, USA (office). *Telephone:* (212) 226-0080 (ext. 4) (office). *E-mail:* info@dnamodels.com (office). *Website:* www.dnamodels.com (office).

EVANGELOU, Alecos C., Barrister-at-Law; Cypriot lawyer; *Senior Partner, Alecos Evangelou and Co.;* b. 23 July 1939, Kato Lakatamia; s. of Costas Evangelou and Theano A. Tsiappa; m. Nicoulla Protopapa 1965; one s. two d.; ed English School, Nicosia and Gray's Inn, London; called to the Bar, Gray's Inn, London 1967; worked in Nicosia Dist Admin. 1957–72, later at Ministry of Finance 1970–72; law officer, Attorney, Office of Attorney-Gen. 1972–93; Minister of Justice and Public Order 1993–97; fmr Chair. Appropriate Authority for Intellectual Property; fmr Pres. Supreme Sports Tribunal; Chair. two Commonwealth Ministerial Confs; fmr Chair. Cyprus Radio-TV Authority, Intensive Care Forum; Deputy Gov. American Biographical Inst., Inc.; currently Sr Partner, Alecos Evangelou and Co. (law firm). *Publications include:* legal studies and manuals on matters of public and private law. *Leisure interest:* gardening. *Address:* PO Box 29238, 1623 Nicosia, Cyprus (office). *Telephone:* (22) 879999 (office). *Fax:* (22) 879990 (office). *E-mail:* evangelou@evangelou.com.cy (office).

EVANS, Daniel Jackson, MS; American consultant and fmr politician; *Chairman, Daniel J. Evans Associates;* b. 16 Oct. 1925, Seattle, Wash.; s. of Daniel Lester and Irma Evans (née Ide); m. Nancy Ann Bell 1959; three s.; ed Roosevelt High School, Seattle and Univ. of Washington; USNR 1943–46; Lt on active duty

Korean War 1951–53; Asst Man. Mountain Pacific Chapter, Assoc. Gen. Contractors 1953–59; State Rep. King County 1956–64; Pnr, Gray and Evans (structural and civil engineers) 1959–64; Gov. of Washington State 1965–77; Chair. Western Govs Conf. 1968–69, Nat. Govs Conf. 1973–74; Senator from Washington 1983–89; mem. Advisory Comm. on Intergovernmental Relations 1972, Trilateral Comm. 1973; Keynote Speaker, Republican Nat. Convention 1968; mem. Pres.'s Vietnamese Refugee Comm. 1974; mem. Nat. Center for Productivity and Quality of Working Life 1975–76; mem. Carnegie Council on Policy Studies in Higher Educ. 1977; mem. Univ. of Washington Bd of Regents 1993–2005 (Pres. 1996–97); Trustee, Urban Inst. 1977, Carnegie Foundation for the Advancement of Teaching 1977; Pres. Evergreen State Coll. 1977–83; Chair. Daniel J. Evans Assocs (consulting firm), Seattle 1998–; mem. Bd of Dirs NIC Inc., Archimedes Technology Group, Costco Wholesale Corpn 2003–; mem. Univ. of Washington Bd of Regents 1993–2005, Vice-Pres. 1995–96, Pres. 1996–97; Republican; several hon. degrees; Nat. Municipal League Distinguished Citizen Award 1977. *Leisure interests:* skiing, sailing, mountain climbing. *Address:* Daniel J. Evans Associates, 4000 NE 41st Street, Seattle, WA 98105-5428, USA. *Telephone:* (206) 525-9090.

EVANS, David (see (The) Edge).

EVANS, David Albert, AB, PhD, FRSC; American chemist and academic; *Abbott and James Lawrence Professor Emeritus of Chemistry, Harvard University;* b. 11 Jan. 1941, Washington, DC; s. of Albert Edward Evans and Iris Hope Hill; m. Selena Anne Welliver 1962; one d.; ed Oberlin Coll., California Inst. of Tech.; Asst Prof. of Chem., UCLA 1967–72, Assoc. Prof. 1972–73, Prof. 1974; Prof. of Chem., Calif. Inst. of Tech. 1974–83; Prof. of Chem., Harvard Univ. 1983–90, Abbott and James Lawrence Prof. Emer. of Chem. 1990–, Chair. Dept of Chem. and Chemical Biology 1995–98, Arthur and Ruth W. Sloan Research Prof. 1999–; Consultant, Upjohn Co. 1972–74, Eli Lilly Co. 1974–89, Merck Research Lab. 1989–2008, Oxford Asymmetry Ltd 1994–2001, UK 1994–2001, Bristol-Myers Squibb Pharmaceuticals Co. 1994–2002, Amgen 2002–; visiting lecturer at numerous int. univs; mem. NAS 1984–, American Acad. of Arts and Sciences 1988–; mem. Editorial Bd, Journal of the American Chemical Soc. 1983–88, Topics in Stereochemistry 1989–, Chemical Reviews 1993–96, Organic Letters 1999–; Fellow, Alfred P. Sloan Foundation 1972–74, AAAS 1992–; Hon. MA (Harvard) 1983; Hon. DrSc (Oberlin); numerous awards, including Phila Organic Chemists Club Allen R. Day Award 1984, ACS Arthur C. Cope Scholar Award 1988, Ohio State Univ. Mack Award 1992, Univ. of Neb. C. S. Hamilton Award 1992, ACS Remsen Award 1996, Univ. of Tokyo Yamada Prize 1997, Royal Soc. of Chem. Robert Robinson Award 1998, Tetrahedron Prize 1998, Eidgenossische Technische Hochschule Prelog Medal 1999, ACS Arthur C. Cope Award 2000, Nagoya Medal, Nagoya Univ., Japan, 2003, Karl Ziegler Prize 2003, Willard Gibbs Award 2005, Ryoji Noyori Prize 2006, ACS Herbert C. Brown Award for Creative Research in Synthetic Methods 2007, Welch Prize in Chem. 2012, ACS Roger Adams Award 2013. *Address:* Department of Chemistry and Chemical Biology, Harvard University, 12 Oxford Street, Cambridge, MA 02138, USA (office). *Telephone:* (617) 823-7033 (mobile) (office). *E-mail:* evans@chemistry.harvard.edu (office). *Website:* chemistry.harvard.edu/people/david-evans (office); evans.rc.fas.harvard.edu (office).

EVANS, Donald Louis, BEng, MBA; American oil industry executive and fmr government official; *Chairman, Energy Future Holdings Corporation;* b. 27 July 1946, Houston, Tex.; s. of Samuel Rostron Evans and Betty Sue Timmerman Evans; m. Susie Marinis; three c.; ed Univ. of Texas; joined Tom Brown Inc. 1975, Pres. 1979, Chair. and CEO 1985–2001; advisor to George W. Bush's political campaigns, Nat. Finance Chair. 1999, Chair. Bush/Cheney campaign 2000; Sec. of Commerce 2001–05 (resgnd); CEO Financial Services Forum 2005–07; Chair. Energy Future Holdings Corpn (fmrly TXU Corpn) 2007–; Sr Partner, Quintana Energy Partners; mem. Univ. of Tex. System Bd of Regents 1995–2001, Chair. 1997–2001; Chair. United Way of Midland 1981, Pres. 1989; Chair. Beefeaters Ball, Midland Cerebral Palsy Center; mem. YMCA of Midland Metropolitan Bd 1988–94, Bd of Govs, Bynum School; mem. Bd of Dirs The Gladney Fund 1992–96, Scleroma Research Foundation 1992–2000, Young Presidents Org., Omicron Delta Kappa Soc., Texas Cowboys; mem. Midland Chamber of Commerce; mem. Exec. Cttee Young Life, Bd; Trustee, Memorial Hosp. and Medical Center; Hon. DHumLitt (Univ. of South Carolina) 2001; Midland Jaycees Distinguished Service Award and Boss of the Year 1980, Univ. of Texas at Austin Distinguished Alumni Awards (School of Eng) 1997, 2002, (McCombs School of Business) 2002, Nat. Foreign Trade Council World Trade Award 2002. *Leisure interest:* golf. *Address:* Energy Future Holdings Corporation, Energy Plaza, 1601 Bryan Street, Dallas, TX 75201, USA (office). *Telephone:* (214) 812-4600 (office). *Website:* www.energyfutureholdings.com (office).

EVANS, Hon. Gareth John, AC, QC, LLB, MA; Australian international organization official and fmr politician; *Chancellor, Australian National University;* b. 5 Sept. 1944, Melbourne, Vic.; s. of Allan O. Evans and Phyllis Evans (née Le Boeuf); m. Merran Anderson 1969; one s. one d.; ed Univ. of Melbourne, Magdalen Coll., Oxford; Lecturer and Sr Lecturer in Law, Univ. of Melbourne 1971–76; mem. Australian Reform Comm. 1975; Barrister-at-Law 1977–; Senator for Victoria 1978–96; Shadow Attorney-Gen. 1980–83; Attorney-Gen. 1983–84; Minister for Resources and Energy, Minister Assisting the Prime Minister and Minister Assisting the Minister for Foreign Affairs 1984–87; Minister for Transport and Communications 1987–88, for Foreign Affairs 1988–96; Deputy Leader of Govt in the Senate 1987–93, Leader 1993–96; MP for Holt, Vic. 1996–99; Deputy Leader of Opposition, Shadow Treas. 1996–98; Pres. and Chief Exec. Int. Crisis Group 2000–09, Pres. Emer. 2009–; Professorial Fellow, Univ. of Melbourne 2009–12; Chancellor, ANU 2010–, Hon. Professorial Fellow 2012–; Co-Chair. Int. Comm. on Intervention and State Sovereignty 2000–01, Int. Comm. on Nuclear Non-Proliferation and Disarmament 2008–10; mem. UN Sec.-Gen.'s High Level Panel on Threat, Challenges and Change 2003–04, Weapons of Mass Destruction Comm. 2004–06; Hon. Fellow, Magdalen Coll., Oxford 2004–, Hon. FASSA 2012; Chilean Order of Merit (Grand Cross) 1999; Companion, Order of O.R. Tambo (Silver) (South Africa) 2015; Hon. LLD (Melbourne) 2002, (Carleton Univ., Canada) 2005, (Sydney) 2008, (Queen's Univ., Canada) 2010; Australian Humanist of the Year 1990, ANZAC Peace Prize 1994, Grawemeyer Award for Ideas Improving World Order 1995, Roosevelt Inst. Freedom from Fear Award 2010. *Publications:* Labor and the Constitution 1972–75 (ed.) 1977, Law, Politics and the Labor Movement (ed.) 1980, Labor Essays 1980, 1981, 1982 (co-ed.), Australia's Constitution: Time for Change? (co-author) 1983, Australia's Foreign Relations (co-author) 1991, Co-operating for Peace 1993, The Responsibility to Protect 2008, Nuclear Weapons: The State of Play (co-ed.) 2013, Inside the Hawke-Keating Government: A Cabinet Diary 2014, Incorrigible Optimist: A Political Memoir 2017. *Leisure interests:* reading, writing, football, travel. *Address:* ANU House Level 11, 52 Collins Street, Melbourne, Vic. 3000, Australia (office). *Telephone:* (3) 9639-8197 (office). *Fax:* (3) 9639-8203 (office). *E-mail:* ge@gevans.org (office). *Website:* www.gevans.org (office).

EVANS, Sir Harold Matthew, Kt, KBE, MA; American (b. British) author, publisher, fmr newspaper editor and author; b. 28 June 1928, Manchester, England; s. of Frederick and Mary Evans; m. 1st Enid Parker 1953 (divorced 1978); one s. two d.; m. 2nd Christina Hambley (Tina) Brown (q.v.) 1982; one s. one d.; ed St Mary's Road Central School, Loreburn Coll., Manchester, Durham Univ.; Commonwealth Fund Fellow, Univ. of Chicago 1956–57; Lecturer, Workers' Education Assen 1959; Ed. Sunday Times, London 1967–81, The Times 1981–82; mem. Bd Times Newspapers Ltd, Dir 1978–82; Int. Press Inst. 1974–80; Dir Goldcrest Films and Television 1982–85; Visiting Prof., Duke Univ. 1983; Ed.-in-Chief Atlantic Monthly 1984–86, Contributing Ed. 1986–, Editorial Dir and Vice-Chair. 1998–; Ed. Dir U.S. News and World Report 1984–86, Contributing Ed. 1986–, Editorial Dir and Vice-Chair. 1998, currently Editor at Large, The Week; Vice-Pres. and Sr Ed. Weidenfeld and Nicolson 1986–87; Adviser to Chair. Condé Nast Publications 1986–; Founding Ed.-in-Chief, Condé Nast Traveler 1986–90; Pres. and Publr Random House Adult Trade Group 1990–97; Editorial Dir Mortimer Zuckerman's media properties 1997–; Editorial Dir and Vice-Chair. New York Daily News Inc. 1998–99, Fast Co. 1998–; Poynter Fellow, Yale Univ.; author, Little, Brown and Co., NY 2000–; writer and presenter A Point of View (BBC Radio 4) 2005–; Fellow, Soc. Industrial Artists, Inst. of Journalists; Hon. Visiting Prof., Journalism City Univ. 1978; Dr hc (Stirling) 1982, (Teesside, London Inst.), Hon. DCL (Durham) 1998; Journalist of the Year Prize 1973, Int. Ed. of the Year Award 1975, Inst. of Journalists Gold Medal Award 1979; Design and Art Dir, Pres.'s Award 1981, Ed. of Year Award, Granada 1982, Hood Medal, Royal Photographic Soc. 1981, Press Photographers of GB Award 1986; Gold Award for Achievement, British Press Awards 2000, World Press Freedom Hero, Int. Press Inst. 2000. *Radio:* Point of View BBC; Breakfast at Barneys literary conversations. *Television:* They Made America (four-part series, WGBH), Shots in the America (four-part series, WGBH), Mayor of America (BBC), What the Papers Say. *Publications:* Active Newsroom 1964, Editing and Design, Newsman's English 1970, Newspaper Design 1971, Newspaper Headlines 1973, Newspaper Text 1973, We Learned to Ski (co-author) 1974, Freedom of the Press 1974, Pictures on a Page 1978, Suffer the Children (co-author), How We Learned to Ski 1983, Good Times, Bad Times 1983, Front Page History 1984, The American Century 1998, They Made America 2004, We the People 2007, My Paper Chase 2009. *Leisure interests:* music, table tennis, swimming. *Address:* Little, Brown and Co., 1271 Avenue of the Americas, New York, NY 10020, USA (office). *Telephone:* (646) 717-9543 (office); (212) 371-1193 (home). *Fax:* (212) 302-9671 (office); (212) 754-4273 (home). *E-mail:* cindyquillinan@gmail.com (office); harold371@aol.com. *Website:* sirharoldevans.com (office).

EVANS, Jill, BA (Hons), MPhil; British politician; b. 8 May 1959, Ystrad Rhondda, Glamorgan, Wales; ed Tonypandy Grammar School, Univ. of Wales, Aberystwyth, Polytechnic of Wales, Trefforest (now Univ. of Glamorgan); worked as Research Asst at Polytechnic of Wales; Public Affairs Officer, Nat. Fed. of Women's Insts in Wales 1989–96; Wales Regional Organiser for CHILD – The Nat. Infertility Support Network 1997–99; elected to Rhondda Borough Council 1992–93, Mid-Glamorgan Co. Council 1993–96 and, following their abolition, to Rhondda Cynon Taf Council 1996–99; elected (Plaid Cymru) Alt. mem. Cttee of the Regions 1993–97; Chair. Plaid Cymru 1994–96, Vice-Pres. 2003–10, Pres. 2010–13, Party Spokesperson for European and Int. Issues, Chair. CND Cymru; MEP (Plaid Cymru) for Wales 1999–, mem. Group of the Greens/European Free Alliance (EFA), Pres. EFA and first Vice-Pres. Greens/EFA Group in European Parl., Vice-Chair. Cttee on Women's Rights and Equal Opportunities 1999–2004, mem. Cttee on the Environment, Public Health and Food Safety, Substitute mem. Cttee on Agric. and Rural Devt, Cttee on Women's Rights and Gender Equality, Del. for Relations with the Palestinian Legis. Council, Del. for Relations with Iraq; unsuccessful cand. in Rhondda constituency for Nat. Ass. for Wales election 2007; Assoc. mem. Glamorgan Women's Inst. *Leisure interests:* organic gardening, jigsaw puzzles. *Address:* European Parliament, Bâtiment Altiero Spinelli, 08H153, 60 rue Wiertz, 1047 Brussels, Belgium (office); 45 Heol Gelligaled, Ystrad, Rhondda Cynon Taf, CF41 7RQ, Wales. *Telephone:* (2) 284-51-03 (office). *Fax:* (2) 284-91-03 (office). *E-mail:* jill.evans@europarl.europa.eu (office). *Website:* www.europarl.europa.eu (home); www.plaidcymru.org (office); www.jillevans.net (office).

EVANS, John David Gemmill, MA, PhD, MRIA; British academic; *Professor of Logic and Metaphysics, Queen's University, Belfast;* b. 27 Aug. 1942, London; s. of John Desmond Evans and Babette Evans; m. Rosemary Ellis 1974; ed St Edward's School, Oxford, Queens' Coll., Cambridge; Research Fellow, Sidney Sussex Coll., Cambridge 1964–65, Fellow and Lecturer 1965–78; Visiting Prof., Duke Univ., NC 1972–73; Dean of Arts Faculty, Queen's Univ., Belfast 1986–89, Prof. of Logic and Metaphysics 1978–, Head of School of Philosophical Studies 2004–05; Dir of School of Philosophical and Anthropological Studies 1987–95; Bd mem. Arts Council of NI 1991–94; Council mem. Royal Inst. of Philosophy 1991–98; Chair. UK Nat. Cttee for Philosophy 1994–2003; mem. Exec. Cttee Int. Fed. of Philosophical Socs (FISP) 1988–, Aristotelian Soc. 1998–2001, Exec. Cttee British Philosophical Assen 2003–05, Bureau Centrale, Assen Int. des Professeurs de Philosophie 2000–. *Publications:* Aristotle's Concept of Dialectic 1977, 2010, Aristotle 1987, Moral Philosophy and Contemporary Problems 1987, Teaching Philosophy on the Eve of the Twenty-First Century 1997, Philosophy of Education (Proceedings of 21st World Congress of Philosophy vol. 4) 2006. *Leisure interests:* mountaineering, astronomy, travel, gardening. *Address:* School of Philosophical Studies, Queen's University, Room 101, 15 University Square, Belfast, BT7 1NN, Northern Ireland (office). *Telephone:* (28) 9097-3624 (office). *Fax:* (28) 9024-7895 (office). *E-mail:* jdg.evans@qub.ac.uk (office). *Website:* www.qub.ac.uk/phil (office).

EVANS OF WEARDALE, Baron (Life Peer), cr. 2014, of Toys Hill in the County of Kent, Sir; **Jonathan Douglas Evans,** Kt, KCB, DL; British government official; b. 1958; ed Univ. of Bristol; joined Security Service (MI5) 1980, worked on counter-espionage investigations 1980–85, moved to Protective Security Policy Dept serving in posts related to Irish-related counter terrorism, Head of Security Service's Secr. and attachment to Home Office 1985–99, moved to Int. Terrorism Dept 1999, Dir of Int. Counter Terrorism 2001–05, Deputy Dir-Gen. MI5 2005–07, Dir-Gen. 2007–13; Deputy Lt of Kent 2015–; mem. Bd of Dirs HSBC Holdings plc 2013–, Ark Data Centres Ltd. *Address:* House of Lords, London, SW1A 0PW, England (office). *E-mail:* contactholmember@parliament.uk (office).

EVANS, Sir Martin John, Kt, PhD, ScD, FRS, FMedSci; British scientist and academic; b. 1 Jan. 1941, Stroud, Glos.; s. of Leonard Wilfred Evans and Hilary Joyce Evans (née Redman); m. Judith Clare Williams 1966; two s. one d.; ed St Dunstan's Coll. Catford and Christ's Coll. Cambridge; Research Asst Dept of Anatomy and Embryology, Univ. Coll. London 1963–66, Asst Lecturer 1966–69, Lecturer 1969–78; Univ. Lecturer, Dept of Genetics, Univ. of Cambridge 1978–91, Reader in Mammalian Genetics 1991, Prof. of Mammalian Genetics 1994–99; Prof. of Mammalian Genetics and Dir, School of Biosciences, Cardiff Univ. 1999–2007, Pres. Cardiff Univ. 2009–12, Chancellor 2012–17, Prof. Emer. 2017–; mem. Advisory Bd Faraday Inst. for Science and Religion 2009–; Hon. Fellow, St Edmund's Coll., Cambridge 2002, Hon. Mem. Biochemical Soc.; Hon. DSc (Mount Sinai School of Medicine) 2002; March of Dimes Prize in Developmental Biology 1999, Albert Lasker Basic Medical Research Award 2001, Miami Nature Biotechnology Winter Symposium Special Achievement Award 2003, Nobel Prize in Physiology or Medicine (with Mario Capecchi and Oliver Smithies) 2007, Copley Medal, Royal Soc. 2009, Gold Medal, Royal Soc. of Medicine 2009, UCL Prize Lecture in Clinical Science 2011, named amongst 10 Britons Who Changed Our World by The Independent newspaper, School of Biosciences building re-named the Sir Martin Evans Building in his honour 2013. *Publications:* more than 150 scientific publs. *Leisure interests:* family, golf. *Address:* Cardiff University, Main Building, Park Place, Cardiff, CF10 3AT, Wales (office). *Telephone:* (29) 2087-4000 (office). *E-mail:* EvansMJ@cardiff.ac.uk (office). *Website:* www.cardiff.ac.uk (office).

EVANS, Nicholas, BA; British author; b. 26 July 1950, Bromsgrove, Worcs.; s. of Anthony and Eileen Evans; m. 2nd Charlotte Gordon Cumming; three s. one d.; ed Univ. of Oxford; previously journalist for Evening Chronicle, Newcastle upon Tyne and producer documentaries for London Weekend TV, writer and producer films for TV and cinema; now novelist. *Publications:* The Horse Whisperer 1995, The Loop 1998, The Smoke Jumper 2001, The Divide 2005, The Brave 2010. *Leisure interests:* tennis, skiing, books, cinema. *Address:* c/o Caradoc King at United Agents LLP, 12–26 Lexington Street, London, W1F 0LE, England (office). *Telephone:* (20) 3214-0800 (office). *Fax:* (20) 3214-0801 (office). *E-mail:* info@unitedagents.co.uk (office); nicholas@nicholasevans.com (office). *Website:* www.unitedagents.co.uk (office); www.nicholasevans.com.

EVANS, Paul, BSc; British insurance industry executive; *Group CEO, AXA UK;* b. 1965; m.; three c.; ed Imperial Coll., London; Dir PricewaterhouseCooper Insurance Div., London and Toronto, 1986–99; joined AXA 2000, Group Finance Dir and mem. Bd AXA UK 2001–03, CEO AXA Sun Life 2003–10, Group CEO AXA UK 2010–, Chair. AXA Corp. Solutions 2014–; Chair. Asscn of British Insurers 2014–; mem. Inst. of Chartered Accountants. *Address:* AXA UK, 5 Old Broad Street, London, EC2N 1AD, England. *Website:* www.axa.co.uk (office).

EVANS, Sir Richard John, Kt, MA, DPhil, LittD, FBA, FRSL, FLSW, FRHistS; British historian and academic; *Provost, Gresham College;* b. 29 Sept. 1947, Woodford, Essex; s. of Ieuan Trefor Evans and Evelyn Evans (née Jones); m. 1st Elín Hjaltadóttir 1976 (divorced 1993); m. 2nd Christine L. Corton 2004; two s.; ed Forest School, London, Jesus Coll., Oxford, St Antony's Coll., Oxford; Lecturer in History, Stirling Univ. 1972–76; Lecturer in European History, Univ. of East Anglia 1976–83, Prof. 1983–89; Prof. of History, Birkbeck Coll., London 1989–98, Vice-Master 1993–98, Acting Master 1997; Prof. of Modern History, Univ. of Cambridge 1998–, Regius Prof. of Modern History 2008–10, Regius Prof. of History 2010–14, currently Prof. Emer., Chair. Faculty of History 2008–10, Fellow, Gonville and Caius Coll., Cambridge 1998–2010; Visiting Assoc. Prof. of European History, Columbia Univ., New York 1980; Fellow, Alexander von Humboldt Foundation, Free Univ. of Berlin 1981, Humanities Research Centre, ANU, Canberra, Australia 1986; Gresham Prof. of Rhetoric, Gresham Coll. 2009–; Pres. Wolfson Coll., Cambridge 2010–17; Provost, Gresham Coll. 2014–; Fellow, Learned Soc. of Wales; Fellow, Birkbeck, Univ. of London 1999; Hon. Fellow, Jesus Coll., Oxford 1998, Birkbeck Coll. 1999, Hon. Fellow, Gonville and Caius Coll., Cambridge 2010; Hon. LitD (London) 2012; Stanhope Historical Essay Prize 1969, Wolfson Literary Award for History 1987, William H. Welch Medal, American Asscn for the History of Medicine 1988, Hamburg Civic Medal for Arts and Sciences 1993, Fraenkel Prize in Contemporary History 1994, History Honoree, Los Angeles Times Book Awards 2008, 2009, Norton Medlicott Medal of the Historical Asscn 2014. *Publications include:* The Feminist Movement in Germany 1894–1933 1976, The Feminists 1977, Society and Politics in Wilhelmine Germany (ed.) 1978, Sozialdemokratie und Frauenemanzipation im deutschen Kaiserreich 1979, The German Family (co-ed.) 1981, The German Working Class (co-ed.) 1982, The German Peasantry (co-ed.) 1986, The German Unemployed (co-ed.) 1987, Death in Hamburg 1987, Comrades and Sisters 1987, Rethinking German History 1987, In Hitler's Shadow 1989, Kneipengespräche im Kaiserreich 1989, Proletarians and Politics 1990, Rituals of Retribution 1996, Rereading German History 1997, In Defence of History 1997, Tales from the German Underworld 1998, Lying about Hitler 2001, The Coming of the Third Reich 2003, The Third Reich in Power 2005, The Third Reich at War 2008, Cosmopolitan Islanders 2009, Altered Pasts 2014; contrib. to scholarly journals, newspapers, magazines, radio and TV. *Leisure interests:* gardening, music, reading, travelling. *Address:* Gresham College, Barnard's Inn Hall, Holborn, London, EC1N 2HH, England (office). *Telephone:* (20) 7831-0575 (office). *E-mail:* rje36@cam.ac.uk (office). *Website:* www.richardjevans.com.

EVANS, Robert J.; American actor and film producer; b. (Robert J. Shapera), 29 June 1930, New York; s. of Archie Shapera and Florence Shapera; m. 1st Sharon Hugueny 1961 (divorced 1962); m. 2nd Camilla Sparv 1964 (divorced 1967); m. 3rd Ali McGraw 1969 (divorced 1973); one s.; m. 4th Phyllis George 1977 (divorced 1978); m. 5th Catherine Oxenberg 1998 (annulled); m. 6th Leslie Ann Woodward 2002 (divorced 2004); m. 7th Lady Victoria White 2005; child radio actor in more than 300 radio productions; partner in women's clothing firm Evan-Picone 1952–67; ind. producer at 20th Century-Fox 1966–76; Vice-Pres. (Production) Paramount Pictures Corpn 1966–69, Vice-Pres. (Worldwide Production) 1969–71, Exec. Vice-Pres. 1971–76 (resgnd); Prof. of Film, Brown Univ. 1976. *Films include:* as actor: The Man of 1000 Faces 1957, The Sun Also Rises 1957, The Fiend Who Walked the West 1958, The Best of Everything 1959, The Girl from Nagasaki 2013; as producer: Chinatown 1974, Marathon Man 1976, Black Sunday 1977, Players 1979, Popeye 1980, Urban Cowboy 1980, Cotton Club 1984, The Two Jakes 1989, Sliver 1993, Jade 1995, The Phantom 1996, The Saint 1997, The Out of Towners 1999, How to Lose a Guy in 10 Days 2003. *Television includes:* as actor: Kid Notorious 2003. *Publications include:* The Kid Stays in the Picture (autobiography) 1994, The Fat Lady Sang 2013.

EVANS, Robert John Weston, PhD, FBA; British historian and academic; *Regius Professor Emeritus of History, University of Oxford;* b. 7 Oct. 1943, Leicester; s. of T. F. Evans and M. Evans; m. Kati Robert 1969; one s. one d. (deceased); ed Dean Close School, Cheltenham and Jesus Coll., Cambridge; Research Fellow, Brasenose Coll., Oxford 1968–97, Univ. Lecturer in Modern History of East-Central Europe, Univ. of Oxford 1969–90, Reader 1990–92, Prof. of European History 1992–97, Regius Prof. of History 1997–2011, Emer. 2011–; Ed. English Historical Review 1985–95; Fellow, Hungarian Acad. of Sciences 1995, Austrian Acad. of Sciences 1997, Learned Soc. of Czech Repub. 2004, Learned Soc. of Wales 2010; Ehrenkreuz für Kunst und Wissenschaft (Austria) 2010; Dr hc (Charles Univ., Prague) 2005, (Eötvös Loránd Univ., Budapest) 2014, (Univ. of Cambridge) 2018; Wolfson Literary Award for History 1980, Anton Gindely-Preis (Austria) 1986, František Palacký Medal (Czechoslovakia) 1991. *Publications:* Rudolf II and His World 1973, The Wechel Presses 1975, The Making of the Habsburg Monarchy 1979, The Coming of the First World War (co-ed) 1988, Crown, Church and Estates (co-ed) 1991, The Revolutions in Europe 1848–9 (ed.) 2000, Austria, Hungary, and the Habsburgs, c. 1683–1867 2006, Curiosity and Wonder from the Renaissance to the Enlightenment (co-ed) 2007, Czechoslovakia in a Nationalist and Fascist Europe 1918-48 (co-ed) 2007, Wales and the Wider World (co-ed) 2010, The Uses of the Middle Ages in Modern European States (co-ed) 2011, The Holy Roman Empire, 1495–1806 (co-ed) 2011. *Leisure interests:* local history, wildlife, dogs, music. *Address:* Rowan Cottage, 45 Sunningwell, Abingdon, Oxon., OX13 6RD, England (home). *Telephone:* (1865) 736973 (office). *E-mail:* robert.evans@history.ox.ac.uk (office).

EVANS, Ronald M., BA, PhD; American biologist and academic; *March of Dimes Chair in Molecular and Developmental Biology, Professor and Director, Gene Expression Laboratory, Salk Institute for Biological Studies;* b. 17 April 1949, Los Angeles, Calif.; ed Univ. of California, Los Angeles; worked in Dept of Molecular Cell Biology, The Rockefeller Univ., New York 1975–78; Asst Research Prof., Tumor Virology Lab., Salk Inst. for Biological Studies, La Jolla, Calif. 1978–83, Assoc. Prof., Molecular Biology and Virology Lab. 1983–84, Sr Mem. 1984–86, Prof. and Dir Gene Expression Lab. 1986–, also March of Dimes Chair in Molecular and Developmental Biology, mem. Bd of Trustees 1990–94, 1996–99, Chair. Faculty 1993–94, 1997–98; apptd Adjunct Prof., Dept of Biology, Univ. of California, San Diego 1985, Adjunct Prof., Dept of Biomedical Sciences, School of Medicine 1989, Adjunct Prof., Dept of Neuro-sciences 1995; Investigator, Howard Hughes Medical Inst., Chevy Chase, MD 1985–; S. Richard Hill, Jr Visiting Prof., Univ. of Alabama 1995; Woodward Visiting Prof., Memorial Sloan-Kettering 1996; First Alvin Taurog Lectureship in Pharmacology, Southwestern Medical Center 1996; Burroughs Wellcome Visiting Prof., Univ. of Massachusetts 1998; f. Ligand Pharmaceuticals 1988 (Chair. Scientific Advisory Bd); Co-f. Syndax Pharmaceuticals, Inc. 2005, currently Advisor, Scientific Advisory Bd; Co-founder of several companies including X-Ceptor Pharmaceuticals, Xenopharm; Scientific Advisor, TaconicArtemis GmbH 2007–; mem. Scientific Advisory Bd SIBIA 1983, Nat. Advisory Cttee Pew Scholars Program in the Biomedical Sciences 1987–2000, External Scientific Advisory Bd Massachussets Gen. Hosp. 1996, Scientific Advisory Bd Dana Farber Cancer Inst. 1996–, Osaka Bioscience Inst. 1999, Aragon Pharmaceuticals, Inc. 2010, BrainCells, Inc., Mitobridge, Inc., Epizyme, Inc., Exelixis, Inc., Seragon Pharmaceuticals, Inc.; Assoc. Ed. Molecular Brain Research 1985–93, Journal of Neuroscience 1985–90, Neuron 1987–93; Co-Ed. Current Opinion in Cell Biology 1993; Ed. Molecular Endocrinology 1993–97; mem. Editorial Bd Genes and Development 1992, Hormones and Signalling (Academic Press series) 1996–; NIH Fellowship 1975–78; mem. NAS 1989, Inst. of Medicine 2004, American Asscn for Cancer Research, Harvey Soc., American Acad. of Microbiology, Soc. for Neuroscience, Soc. for Developmental Biology, Endocrine Soc., American Philosophical Soc.; Fellow, American Acad. of Microbiology 1993, American Acad. of Arts and Sciences 1997; Gregory Pincus Medal, Laurentian Soc. 1988, The Louis S. Goodman and Alfred Gilman Award, American Soc. for Pharmacology and Experimental Therapeutics 1988, Van Meter/Rorer Pharmaceuticals Prize, American Thyroid Asscn 1989, Eleventh C.P. Rhoads Memorial Award, American Asscn for Cancer Research 1990, Gregory Pincus Memorial Award, Worcester Foundation for Experimental Biology 1991, Rita Levi Montalcini Award, Fidia Research Foundation Neuroscience 1991, Osborne and Mendel Award, American Inst. of Nutrition 1992, Robert J. and Claire Pasarow Foundation Award for Cancer Research 1993, Edwin B. Astwood Lectureship Award, The Endocrine Soc. 1993, Transatlantic Medal, Soc. for Endocrinology 1994, California Scientist of the Year, California Museum of Science 1994, Dickson Prize in Medicine, Univ. of Pittsburgh 1994–95, Morton Lecture and Award, Biochemical Soc., Univ. of Liverpool, UK 1996, Gerald Aurbach Memorial Award, Asscn for Bone and Mineral Research 1997, Fred Conrad Koch Award, The Endocrine Soc. 1999, Bristol-Myers Squibb Award for Distinguished Achievement in Metabolic Research 2000, Lya and Harrison Latta Lecturer, UCLA 2000, Pezcoller International Award, American Asscn for Cancer Research 2001, Alfred P. Sloan Junior Prize, GM Cancer Research Foundation 2003, Albert Lasker Award for Basic Medical Research, Lasker Foundation 2004, Gairdner Foundation Int. Award 2006, Grande Médaille d'Or (France) 2005, Glenn T. Seaborg Medal 2005, Harvey Prize in Human Health 2006, Albany Medical Center Prize in Medicine and Biomedical Research (shared with Solomon H. Snyder and Robert J. Lefkowitz) 2007, Wolf Prize in Medicine 2012, Louisa Gross Horwitz Prize 2018. *Publications:* more than 260 publs in scientific journals. *Address:* Salk Institute for Biological Studies, Howard Hughes Medical Institute, 10010 N Torrey Pines Road, La Jolla, CA 92037, USA (office). *Telephone:* (858) 453-4100 ext. 1302 (office). *Fax:*

(858) 455-1349 (office). *E-mail:* evans@salk.edu (office). *Website:* www.salk.edu/faculty/evans.html (office).

EVANS, Stephen Nicholas, CMG, OBE, BA, MPhil; British diplomatist; b. 29 June 1950; s. of Vincent Morris Evans and Doris Mary Evans (née Braham); m. Sharon Ann Holdcroft 1975; one s. two d.; ed King's Coll., Taunton, Univ. of Bristol, Corpus Christi Coll., Univ. of Cambridge; Lt in Royal Tank Regt 1971–74; Third Sec., FCO 1974–75, language student (Vietnamese), SOAS, London 1975, Second Sec., FCO 1976–78, First Sec., Hanoi 1978–80, FCO 1980–82, language training (Thai), Bangkok 1982–83, First Sec., Bangkok 1983–86, FCO 1986–90, First Sec. (Political), Ankara 1990, Counsellor (Econ., Commercial, Aid), Islamabad 1993–96, seconded to UN Special Mission to Afghanistan 1996–97, Counsellor and Head of OSCE and Council of Europe Dept, FCO 1997–98, Counsellor and Head of South Asian Dept 1998–2001, Chargé d'affaires, Kabul 2001–02, High Commr to Sri Lanka 2002–06, Amb. to Afghanistan 2006–07, Dir Afghanistan Information Strategy, FCO 2007–08, High Commr to Bangladesh 2008–11; NATO Asst Sec.-Gen. for Operations 2011–18. *Leisure interests:* military, naval and South Asian history, cycling, golf.

EVANS, Ted, AC, BEcon (Hons); Australian banking executive; ed Queensland Univ.; began career in Postmaster-Gen.'s Dept, Ipswich, Queensland; joined Australian Treasury 1969, Deputy Sec. 1984–89, Sec. to Treasury 1993–2001, mem. Australian Perm. Del. to OECD, Paris 1976–79, Exec. Dir representing Australia, IMF 1989–93; Dir (Ind.) Westpac Banking Corpn 2001–11, Chair. 2007–11; Dir Commonwealth Bank of Australia 1993–96, Reserve Bank of Australia 1993–2001, IBT Education Ltd 2004–08, Navitas Ltd; apptd Chair. of Nomination Panel for appointments to Bds of Australian Broadcasting Corpn and Special Broadcasting Service 2016; Hon. DUniv (Griffith). *Address:* Nominations Panel, Australian Broadcasting Corporation and Special Broadcasting Service, c/o Department of Communications, GPOB 2154, Canberra, ACT 2601, Australia. *Website:* www.communications.gov.au.

EVANS OF BOWES PARK, Life Peer, cr. 2014; **Baroness Natalie Jessica Evans;** British politician; *Leader of the House of Lords and Lord Privy Seal;* b. 29 Nov. 1975; m. James Wild; ed New Hall, Cambridge; Deputy Dir, Conservative Research Dept 2000–02; Head of Policy, British Chambers of Commerce –2008; Deputy Dir, Policy Exchange 2008–11; Chief Operating Officer, New Schools Network (registered charity) 2011–13, Dir 2013–15; introduced to House of Lords 28 Oct. 2014; mem. House of Lords Selection Cttee 2016–, Procedure Cttee 2016–, Cttee for Privileges and Conduct 2016–, Liaison Cttee 2016–, House Cttee 2016–; Lord in Waiting (HM Household) (Whip) 2015–16; Leader of the House of Lords and Lord Privy Seal 2016–; mem. Conservative Party. *Address:* Office of the Leader of the House of Lords, House of Lords, Room 20, London, SW1A 0PW, England (office). *Telephone:* (20) 7219-3200 (office). *Fax:* (20) 7219-3051 (office). *E-mail:* psleaderofthelords@cabinetoffice.gov.uk (office). *Website:* www.gov.uk/government/organisations/office-of-the-leader-of-the-house-of-lords (office).

EVANS OF PARKSIDE, Baron (Life Peer), cr. 1997, of St Helens in the County of Merseyside; **John Evans;** British politician and engineer; b. 19 Oct. 1930; s. of James Evans and Margaret Evans (née Robson); m. Joan Slater 1959; two s. one d.; ed Jarrow Cen. School; apprentice marine fitter 1946–49, 1950–52; nat. service, Royal Engineers 1949–50; engineer, Merchant Navy 1952–55; joined Amalgamated Union of Eng Workers (later Amalgamated Eng Union) 1952; joined Labour Party 1955; worked as fitter in ship-building, steel and eng industries 1955–65, 1968–74; mem. Hebburn Union Dist Council 1962, Leader 1969, Chair. 1972; Sec./Agent Jarrow Co-operative Labour Party 1965–68; Labour MP for Newton 1974–83, for St Helens, North 1983–97; Asst Govt Whip 1978–79; Opposition Whip 1979–80; Parl. Pvt. Sec. to Leader of Labour Party 1980–83; Opposition Spokesman on Employment 1983–87; MEP 1975–78; Chair. Regional Policy, Planning and Transport Cttee 1976–78; mem. Labour Party Nat. Exec. Cttee 1982–96; retd from House of Lords 2015. *Leisure interests:* watching football, reading, gardening. *Address:* 6 Kirkby Road, Culcheth, Warrington, Cheshire, WA3 4BS, England (home).

EVATT, The Hon. Elizabeth Andreas, AC, LLB, LLM; Australian lawyer and human rights expert; b. 11 Nov. 1933, Sydney, NSW; d. of Clive R. Evatt and Marjorie H. Evatt (née Andreas); m. Robert Southan 1960; one d.; ed Univ. of Sydney and Harvard Univ.; called to Bar, Inner Temple; Chief Judge Family Court of Australia 1976–88; Deputy Pres. Conciliation and Arbitration Comm. 1973–89, Australian Industrial Relations Comm. 1989–94; Pres. Australian Law Reform Comm. 1988–93, mem. 1993–94; mem. UN Cttee on Elimination of Discrimination Against Women 1984–92, Chair. 1989–91; Chancellor, Univ. of Newcastle 1988–94; reviewed Aboriginal and Torres Strait Islander Heritage Protection Act 1984; Hearing Commr (part-time), Human Rights and Equal Opportunity Comm. 1995–98; mem. UN Human Rights Cttee 1993–2000, World Bank Admin. Tribunal 1998–2006; fmr Hon. Visiting Prof., Univ. of New South Wales Law School; fmr Chair. Public Interest Advocacy Centre, Sydney; Hon. mem., Int. Comm. of Jurists; Australian Human Rights Medal 1995. *Address:* Unit 2003, 184 Forbes Street, Darlinghurst, NSW 2010, Australia (home). *E-mail:* eevatt@bigpond.net.au (office).

EVE, Trevor John; British actor; b. 1 July 1951, Sutton Coldfield, Warwicks. (now West Midlands); s. of Stewart Frederick Eve and Elsie Eve (née Hamer); m. Sharon Patricia Maughan 1980; two s. one d.; ed Bromsgrove School, Kingston Art Coll., Royal Acad. of Dramatic Art; best known for playing the eponymous detective in BBC series Shoestring and for playing Detective Supt Peter Boyd in BBC series Waking the Dead; Patron, Childhope International; Hon. DLitt (Newman Univ.). *Theatre includes:* Children of a Lesser God (Olivier Award for Best Actor 1982) 1981, The Genius 1983, High Society 1986, Man Beast and Virtue 1989, The Winter's Tale 1991, Inadmissible Evidence 1993, Uncle Vanya (Olivier Award for Best Supporting Actor 1997) 1996. *Films include:* Children (short) 1976, Dracula 1979, The Terence Davies Trilogy 1983, Scandal 1989, In the Name of the Father (short) 1992, Aspen Extreme 1993, Don't Get Me Started 1994, Soup (short) 1996, Next Birthday (short) 1998, The Tribe 1998, Appetite 1998, Possession 2002, Troy 2004, She's Out of My League 2010. *Television includes:* 2nd House (series) 1974, Hindle Wakes (film) 1976, Sunday Night Drama (series) 1977, London Belongs to Me (series) 1977, Shoestring (series) 1979–80, Jamaica Inn (film) 1983, A Brother's Tale (film) 1983, Lace (film) 1984, The Corsican Brothers (film) 1985, Shadow Chasers (series) 1985, A Wreath of Roses (film) 1987, Life on the Flipside (film) 1988, Beryl Markham: A Shadow on the Sun (film) 1988, Dear John USA (series) 1989, The Stone Age (film) 1989, A Sense of Guilt (series) 1990, Coup de foudre (series) 1990, Parnell & the Englishwoman (mini-series) 1991, Murder, She Wrote (series) 1992, A Doll's House (film) 1992, Jack's Place (series) 1992, The President's Child (film) 1992, Murder in Mind (film) 1994, The Politician's Wife (series) 1995, No Man's Land (film) 1995, Ivana Trump's For Love Alone (film) 1996, Heat of the Sun (mini-series) 1998, An Evil Streak (series) 1999, Doomwatch: Winter Angel (film) 1999, David Copperfield (film) 1999, Waking the Dead (series) 2000–11, Lawless (film) 2004, The Family Man (film) 2006, Hughie Green, Most Sincerely (film) 2008, Framed (film) 2009, Bouquet of Barbed Wire (series) 2010, Kidnap and Ransom (series, actor and producer) 2011–12, The Farmer (film) 2013, Death Comes to Pemberley 2014, The Interceptor 2015, Unforgotten 2015. *Leisure interests:* golf, tennis, squash, painting. *Address:* c/o Independent Talent Group Ltd, Oxford House, 76 Oxford Street, London, W1D 1BS, England (office). *Telephone:* (20) 7434-1110 (office); (20) 7636-6565 (office). *Fax:* (20) 7323-0101 (office). *E-mail:* jojacob9@googlemail.com (office); info@independenttalent.com (office). *Website:* www.independenttalent.com (office).

EVERED, David Charles, MD, FRCP, FIBiol; British scientific administrator and physician; b. 21 Jan. 1940, Beaconsfield; s. of Thomas C. Evered and Enid C. Evered; m. 1st Anne Lings 1964 (died 1998); one s. two d.; m. 2nd Sheila Pusinelli 2000; ed Cranleigh School, Surrey and Middlesex Hosp. Medical School; jr hosp. appointments London and Leeds 1964–70; First Asst in Medicine, Wellcome Sr Research Fellow and Consultant Physician, Univ. of Newcastle-upon-Tyne and Royal Vic. Infirmary 1970–78; Dir The Ciba Foundation, London 1978–88; Second Sec., MRC, London 1988–96, Consultant 1996–; mem. Council Int. Agency for Research into Cancer 1988–96, Royal Post grad. Medical School 1994–96, Bd Hammersmith Hosps Nat. Health Service (NHS) Trust 1995–96, numerous cttees, socs and other professional bodies; Chair. NOC NHS Trust 1998–2001; Special Adviser Int. Agency for Research on Cancer, WHO, Lyon, France 2001–03. *Publications:* Diseases of the Thyroid 1976, Atlas of Endocrinology (with R. Hall and R. Greene) 1979, Collaboration in Medical Research in Europe (with M. O'Connor) 1981; numerous papers in professional journals. *Leisure interests:* reading, history, tennis, music. *Address:* Old Rectory Farm, Rectory Road, Padworth Common, Berks., RG7 4JD, England (home). *E-mail:* david_evered@hotmail.com (home).

EVERETT, Rupert; British actor; b. 29 May 1960, Norfolk; s. of Anthony Michael Everett and Sara Everett (née Maclean); ed Ampleforth School and Cen. School for Speech and Drama, London; apprenticed with Glasgow Citizen's Theatre 1979–82; has modelled for Versace, Milan; sometime image of Opium perfume for Yves Saint Laurent. *Stage appearances include:* Another Country 1982, The Vortex 1989, Private Lives, The Milk Train Doesn't Stop Here Anymore, The Picture of Dorian Gray 1993, The Importance of Being Earnest 1996, Some Sunny Day 1996. *Films include:* A Shocking Accident 1982, Another Country 1984, Dance with a Stranger 1985, The Right Hand Man 1985, Duet for One 1986, Chronicle of Death Foretold 1987, Hearts of Fire 1987, Haunted Summer 1988, The Comfort of Strangers 1990, Inside Monkey Zetterland 1992, Pret à Porter 1994, The Madness of King George 1995, Dunston Checks In 1996, My Best Friend's Wedding 1997, A Midsummer Night's Dream 1998, B Monkey 1998, An Ideal Husband 1999, Inspector Gadget 1999, The Next Best Thing 2000, Unconditional Love 2002, The Importance of Being Earnest 2002, To Kill a King 2003, Stage Beauty 2004, Separate Lies 2005, The Chronicles of Narnia: The Lion, the Witch and the Wardrobe (voice) 2005, Shrek the Third (voice) 2007, Stardust 2007, St Trinian's 2007, Wild Target 2010, Hysteria 2011, Justin and the Knights of Valour 2013, A Royal Night Out 2015, Miss Peregrine's Home for Peculiar Children 2016, The Happy Prince (Nat. Film Award for Best Actor 2019) 2018, Swords and Sceptres 2019. *Television includes:* Arthur the King, The Far Pavilions 1982, Princess Daisy 1983, Mr Ambassador 2003, Sherlock Holmes and the Case of the Silk Stocking 2004, Boston Legal 2005, Who Do You Think You Are? 2010, Parade's End 2012, Loose Women 2013, Quacks 2017, The Name of the Rose 2019. *Publications:* Hello Darling, Are You Working? 1992, The Hairdressers of St Tropez 1995, Red Carpets and Other Banana Skins (autobiog.) 2006, Vanished Years (autobiog.) 2012. *Address:* c/o Creative Artists Agency, 2000 Avenue of the Stars, Los Angeles, CA 90067, USA (office). *Telephone:* (424) 288-2000 (office). *Fax:* (424) 288-2000 (office). *Website:* www.caa.com (office).

EVERITT, Anthony Michael, BA; British writer, academic and fmr arts organization administrator; b. 31 Jan. 1940, Hunstanton, Norfolk, England; s. of Michael Everitt and Simone Vergriette; ed Cheltenham Coll. and Corpus Christi Coll. Cambridge; Lecturer, Nat. Univ. of Iran, SE London Coll. of Further Educ., Birmingham Coll. of Art, Trent Polytechnic 1963–72; Art Critic, The Birmingham Post 1970–75, Drama Critic 1974–79, Features Ed. 1976–79; Dir Midland Group Arts Centre, Nottingham 1979–80, E Midlands Arts Asscn 1980–85; Chair. Ikon Gallery, Birmingham 1976–79, Birmingham Arts Lab. 1977–79; Vice-Chair. Council of Regional Arts Asscns 1984–85; mem. Drama Panel, Arts Council of GB 1974–78, Regional Cttee 1979–80; mem. Cttee for Arts and Humanities, Council for Nat. Academic Awards 1986–87, Performing Arts Cttee 1987–92; mem. Gen. Advisory Council, IBA 1987–90; Deputy Sec.-Gen. Arts Council of GB 1985–90, Sec.-Gen. 1990–94; Visiting Prof. in Visual and Performing Arts, Nottingham Trent Univ. 1996–2006; Hon. Fellow, Dartington Coll. of Arts 1995; Companion, Liverpool Inst. of Performing Arts 2003. *Publications:* Abstract Expressionism 1974, In from the Margins 1997, Joining In 1997, The Governance of Culture 1997, The Creative Imperative 2001, Citizens: Towards a Citizenship Culture (contrib.) 2001, Cicero: A Turbulent Life 2000, Cicero: The Life and Times of Rome's Greatest Politician (USA), New Voices 2004, The First Emperor: Caesar Augustus and the Triumph of Rome 2006, Augustus: The Life of Rome's First Emperor (USA) 2006, Hadrian and the Triumph of Rome (USA) 2009, The Rise of Rome (UK and USA) 2012, SPQR: A Roman Miscellany 2014; contribs to newspapers and journals. *Address:* Westerlies, Anchor Hill, Wivenhoe, Essex, CO7 9BL, England.

EVERS, Tony, BA, MA, PhD; American educator and politician; *Governor of Wisconsin;* b. 5 Nov. 1951, Plymouth, Wis.; m. Kathy Evers; two s. one d.; ed Univ. of Wisconsin, Madison; Chief Admin., Cooperative Educational Service Agency 1992–2000; Deputy Supt, Dept of Public Instruction, Wis. 2001–09, Supt 2009–19; Gov. of Wis. 2019–; fmr Supt, Verona and Oakfield School Dist; Pres. Bd of Dirs,

Council of Chief State School Officers. *Telephone:* (608) 266-1212 (office). *E-mail:* EversInfo@wisconsin.gov (office). *Website:* www.evers.wi.gov (office).

EVERT, Christine (Chris) Marie; American fmr professional tennis player; b. 21 Dec. 1954, Fort Lauderdale, Fla; d. of James Evert and Colette Evert; m. 1st John Lloyd 1979 (divorced 1987); m. 2nd Andy Mill 1988 (divorced 2006); m. 3rd Greg Norman 2008 (divorced 2010); three s.; ed St Thomas Aquinas High School, Fort Lauderdale; amateur player 1970–72; professional 1972–89; Wimbledon Singles Champion 1974, 1976, 1981; French Champion 1974, 1975, 1979, 1980, 1983, 1985, 1986; US Open Champion 1975, 1976, 1977, 1978, 1980, 1982; Italian Champion 1974, 1975, 1980; South African Champion 1973; Colgate Series Champion 1977, 1978; World Champion 1979; played Wightman Cup for USA 1971–73, 1975–82, 1984–85; won 1,000th singles victory (first ever player) Australian Open Dec. 1984; played Federation Cup for USA 1977–82; ranked No. 1 in the world for seven years; won 1,309 matches in her career; won 157 singles titles and 18 Grand Slam titles (third best in history); Pres. Women's Tennis Asscn (WTA) 1975–76, 1983–91; Founder Chris Evert Charities for needy and drug-abusive mothers and their children 1989; Host and Organizer Annual Chris Evert Pro-Celebrity Tennis Classic 1989–; Pnr and coach, Evert Tennis Acad., Boca Raton, Fla; Owner, Evert Enterprises/IMG, Boca Raton, Fla 1989–; Dir and mem. Bd Pres.'s Council on Physical Fitness and Sports 1991; NBC TV sports commentator and host for numerous TV shows; mem. Bd Ounce of Prevention Fund of Florida, Make-A-Wish Foundation of S Florida, Florida Sports Foundation, United Sports Foundation of America, Save the Children, American AIDS Asscn, Women's Sports Foundation, The Don Shula Foundation, Nat. Cttee to Prevent Child Abuse, The Buoniconti Fund, Palm Beach Co. Sports Authority; Sports Illustrated Sportsman of the Year Award 1976, WTA Sportsmanship Award 1979 and Player Service Award 1981, 1986, 1987, named Greatest Woman Athlete of the Last 25 Years (Women's Sports Foundation) 1985, Flo Hyman Award 1990, Providencia Award 1991, Nat. High School Hall of Fame 1992, March of Dimes Lifetime Achievement Award 1993, Madison Square Garden Walk of Fame 1993, Int. Tennis Hall of Fame 1995, Int. Tennis Fed. Chartrier Award 1997, named by ESPN as One of Top 50 Athletes of the 20th Century 1999. *Publications:* Chrissie (autobiog.) 1982, Lloyd on Lloyd (with John Lloyd) 1985. *Leisure interests:* visiting Paris and the Great Barrier Reef in Hamilton Island. *Address:* Evert Enterprises/IMG, 7200 West Camino Real, Suite 310, Boca Raton, FL 33433; Evert Tennis Academy, 10334 Diego Drive South, Boca Raton, FL 33428, USA. *Telephone:* (561) 394-2400 (office); (561) 488-2055 (office). *Website:* www.chrisevert.org (office); www.evertacademy.com (office).

EVERY, Bob, AO, BSc, PhD; Australian business executive; *Non-Executive Chairman, Wesfarmers Ltd;* b. 18 June 1945; m. Sheryl Every; two s. two d.; ed Univ. of New South Wales; mem. Bd of Dirs Wesfarmers Ltd 2006–, Chair. (non-exec.) 2008–, Chair. Remuneration and Nomination Cttees, mem. Audit Cttee; Man. Dir and CEO OneSteel Ltd –2005; Chair. Iluka Resources Ltd 2004–10, Sims Group Ltd 2005–07; Deputy Chair. Boral Ltd 2007, Chair. 2007–10, Chair. (non-exec.) 2010–; fmr Chair. Steel & Tube Holdings Ltd, NZ; fmr Man. Dir Tubemakers of Australia Ltd; fmr Pres. BHP Steel; Adjunct Prof. Australian School of Business; fmr adviser to Proudfoot Consulting; mem. or fmr mem. Bd of Dirs O'Connell Street Assocs Pty Ltd, OCA Services Pty Ltd, OneSteel Ltd, CARE Australia; Chair. Malcolm Sargent Cancer Fund for Children in Australia Ltd (known as Redkite) –2012; Fellow, Australian Acad. of Technological Sciences and Eng, Australian Inst. of Co. Dirs; Centenary Medal of Australia. *Leisure interest:* golf. *Address:* Wesfarmers Ltd, 12th Floor, Wesfarmers House, 40 The Esplanade, Perth, WA 6000 (office); 6/28 Billyard Avenue, Elizabeth Bay, NSW 2011, Australia (home). *Telephone:* (8) 9327-4283 (office); (2) 9331-7551 (home). *Fax:* (8) 9327-4216 (office). *E-mail:* info@wesfarmers.com.au (office); bevery@wesfarmers.com.au (home). *Website:* www.wesfarmers.com.au (office).

EVES, Ernie, QC; Canadian investment banker and fmr politician; *Chairman, Timeless Herbal Care Ltd;* b. 1946, Windsor, Ont.; m.; one s. (deceased) one d.; ed Univ. of Toronto, Osgoode Hall Law School, York Univ.; first elected as MPP for Parry Sound, Ont. Legislature 1981, fmr Vice-Chair. Priorities, Policy and Communications Bd of Cabinet, fmr Vice-Chair. Man. Bd of Cabinet, fmr Govt House Leader, fmr Minister of Community and Social Services, fmr Minister of Skills Devt, Deputy Premier and Minister of Finance, Ont. 1995–2001, Leader Ont. Progressive Conservative Party March 2002–Sept. 2004, MPP for Dufferin-Peel-Wellington-Grey 2002–05 (resgnd), Premier of Ont. April 2002–Oct. 2003; Leader of the Official Opposition Oct. 2003–Sept. 2004; fmr Chair. Ont. Advisory Council on Int. Trade and Investment 2006; fmr Vice-Chair. and Sr Advisor, Credit Suisse First Boston (Canada); fmr Counsel, Borden Ladner Gervais, LLP; Exec. Chair. Jacob Securities Inc (investment bank), Toronto 2007–12; Chair. Timeless Herbal Care Ltd 2015–; Founder and Sec. Treas., Big Brothers Asscn of Parry Sound; mem. Advisory Bd Embassy of Hope; Co-founder and Chair. Justin Eves Foundation 1995–. *Address:* Timeless Herbal Care, 30 Dominica Drive, Suite 31A, Kingston 5, Saint Andrew, Jamaica (office). *Telephone:* (876) 754-2121 (office). *E-mail:* info@timelessherbalcare.com (office). *Website:* timelessherbalcare.com (office).

EVIN, Claude, DIur; French politician and organization official; *President, Institut des Hautes Etudes de Protection Sociale;* b. 29 June 1949, Le Cellier, Loire-Atlantique; s. of André Evin and Adrienne Lecommandeur; m. Françoise Guillet 1971; three d.; Sec. St-Nazaire Section, Parti Socialiste 1975–77, mem. Loire-Atlantique Fed. Cttee of Socialist Party 1975–, mem. Nat. Cttee 1991–; Mun. Counsellor and Deputy Mayor of St-Nazaire 1977; Deputy to Nat. Ass. 1978–88, 1997; MP Ass. of Council of Europe; Chair. Nat. Ass. Cultural, Family and Social Affairs Cttee 1981–86; mem. Social Security Audit Comm. 1985; Vice-Pres. Nat. Ass. 1986–88; Minister-Del. attached to Minister of Social Affairs and Employment with responsibility for Social Protection May–June 1988; Minister of Solidarity, Health and Social Protection 1988–91; Conseiller régional Pays de la Loire 1992–98; mem. Econ. and Social Council 1994–97, Parl. Ass., Council of Europe 1997–2007; Pres. Fédération hospitalière de France 2004–09; currently Pres. Institut des Hautes Etudes de Protection Sociale; Chevalier, Légion d'honneur. *Address:* Institut des Hautes Etudes de Protection Sociale, 77 Avenue de Segur, 75015 Paris, France (office). *Telephone:* 1-45-66-34-31 (office). *Fax:* 1-45-66-34-33 (office). *Website:* www.iheps.com (office).

ÉVORA, Nelson; Portuguese (b. Côte d'Ivoirian) athlete; b. 20 April 1984, Côte d'Ivoire; triple jumper and long jumper; triple jump Olympic and World Champion; relocated to Portugal aged five; represented Cape (now Cabo) Verde until June 2002, when became Portuguese citizen; still holds Cabo Verde records in both long jump (7.57m) and triple jump (16.15m); first coached by João Ganço; Gold Medal, triple and long jump, European Athletics Jr Championships, Tampere, Finland 2003; competed in triple jump at Athens Olympics 2004; Bronze Medal, triple jump, European Under-23 Championships 2005; finished first in long jump and second in triple jump, European Cup in Athletics, Thessaloniki 2006; finished sixth at Int. Asscn of Athletics Feds (IAAF) World Indoor Championships 2006; finished fourth in triple jump and sixth in long jump at European Athletics Championships, Gothenburg 2006 (set Portuguese triple jump record of 17.23m during qualification); finished fifth at European Athletics Indoor Championships, Birmingham 2007; finished first in triple jump, European Cup in Athletics, Milan 2007; Gold Medal, World Championships, Osaka 2007 (set personal best, Portuguese nat. record and second-best world mark of the year at 17.74m); Bronze Medal, triple jump (17.27m), IAAF World Indoor Championships, Valencia 2008; Gold Medal, triple jump (17.67m), Olympic Games, Beijing 2008; competes for S.L. Benfica (sports club), Lisbon. *Address:* c/o Federação Portuguesa de Atletismo, 15-B Largo da Lagoa, 2799-538 Linda a Velha, Portugal. *Telephone:* (21) 4146020. *Fax:* (21) 4146021. *E-mail:* comunicacao@fpatletismo.pt. *Website:* www.fpatletismo.pt.

EWALD, François, PhD; French insurance risk expert and academic; b. 29 April 1946, Boulogne-Billancourt; ed Univ. of Paris (Sorbonne), Institut d'Etudes Politiques; Asst to Michel Foucault, Coll. de France 1975–84; expert on issues of risk and responsibility, the formation of an insured soc. and the devt of the French Social Security System; fmr Professorial Chair of Insurance, Conservatoire nat. des arts et métiers (CNAM); fmr Dir École nationale d'assurances, Paris; Founder and Chair. Observatory of Precautionary Principle, Paris; currently Chair. Scientific Cttee, Universite de l'Assurance; Distinguished Visitor, Univ. of Connecticut Law School 2003; Founder and Pres. Michel Foucault Centre; mem. Acad. des Technologies; Fellow, French Technological Acad.; Legion d'Honneur 2006. *Publications include:* L'Etat providence 1986, Naissance du Code civil 1989, Le problème français des accidents thérapeutiques 1992, Le principe de précaution (jtly) 2001. *Address:* Université de l'Assurance, 20 Place de la Défense, 92071 Paris La défense cedex, France. *Website:* www.universite-assurance.org.

EWANGO, Corneille E. N., BSc, MSc, PhD; Democratic Republic of the Congo botanist and conservationist; *Director, Okapi Wildlife Reserve;* ed Univ. of Kisangani, Univ. of Missouri, St Louis, USA, Wageningen Univ., the Netherlands; staff mem., Congolese Inst. for the Conservation of Nature and Wildlife Conservation Soc. (WCS)'s Democratic Repub. of Congo (DRC) programme, responsible for Okapi Faunal Reserve's botany programme, Ituri Rainforest 1996–2003, currently Dir Okapi Wildlife Reserve; extensive research experience in DRC, Rwanda, Uganda and Cameroon; Dir WCS and Centre de Formation et de Recherche en Conservation Forestière (CEFRECOF), Ituri Landscape, DRC Programme 2006–07; Sr Botanist Researcher and Head of Botanical and Forest Ecology Programme, WCS-DRC Programme 2006; Goldman Environmental Prize 2005, Emerging Explorers Award—Africa, Nat. Geographic Soc. 2007, Invited Speaker, TEDGlobal 2007 Conf., Africa: The Next Chapter, Arusha, Tanzania 2007, Future for Nature Award 2011. *Achievements include:* helped lead effort to protect and preserve Okapi Reserve during civil war in DRC; uncovered 270 species of lianas and 600 tree species in the area. *Publications:* several scientific papers in professional journals on forest dynamics, tropical forest structure and functional ecology, lianas, biodiversity conservation, biology of epiphytes, and plant taxonomy and systematics. *E-mail:* ewango_corneille@yahoo.com.

EWING, Maria Louise; American singer (soprano); b. 27 March 1950, Detroit, Mich.; d. of Norman I. Ewing and Hermina M. Veraar; m. Sir Peter Hall 1982 (divorced 1989); one d.; ed Cleveland Inst. of Music; debut at Metropolitan Opera, New York singing Cherubino in The Marriage of Figaro 1976, closely followed by debuts with major US orchestras, including New York Philharmonic and at La Scala Milan; regular performances at Glyndebourne including the Barber of Seville, L'Incoronazione di Poppea and Carmen; repertoire also includes Pelléas et Mélisande, The Dialogues of the Carmelites, Così fan Tutte, La Perichole, La Cenerentola, The Marriage of Figaro (Susanna); performed Salome at Covent Garden 1988, 1992, Carmen at Earl's Court, London 1989, Tosca in Los Angeles 1989, Salome in Washington 1990, Madame Butterfly in Los Angeles, Tosca in Seville, Tosca in Los Angeles and Chicago, Salome in San Francisco, Madame Butterfly and Tosca in Vienna, The Trojans at the Metropolitan, New York 1993–94; also appears as concert and recital singer; debut Promenade Concerts, London 1987, Lady Macbeth of Mtsensk with Metropolitan Opera 1994. *Leisure interests:* home and family.

EWING, Rodney Charles, BS, MS, PhD; American geologist, materials scientist and academic; *Frank Stanton Professor in Nuclear Security, Stanford University;* b. 20 Sept. 1946, Abilene, Tex.; s. of Charles Ewing and Mary Cobos; ed Texas Christian Univ., Stanford Univ. (NSF Fellowship); mem. Faculty, Dept of Earth and Planetary Sciences, Univ. of New Mexico 1974–97, Chair. Dept 1979–84, Regents' Prof. Emer. 1997–; Prof., Dept of Nuclear Eng and Radiological Sciences, Univ. of Michigan 1997–2014, responsible for programme in radiation effects and nuclear waste man., also holds appointments in Geological Sciences and Materials Science and Eng, currently Donald R. Peacor Collegiate Prof., Dept of Geological Sciences; Adjungeret Prof., Univ. of Århus, Denmark; Councillor, Materials Research Soc. 1983–85, 1987–89, Sec. 1985–86; currently Frank Stanton Prof. in Nuclear Security, Stanford Univ.; Pres. Mineralogical Soc. of America 2002, Int. Union of Materials Research Socs 1997–98, New Mexico Geological Soc. 1981; mem. Bd of Dirs Caswell Silver Foundation 1980–84, Energy, Exploration, Education, Inc. 1979–84; Guest Scientist or Faculty mem. Battelle Pacific Northwest Labs, Oak Ridge Nat. Lab., Hahn-Meitner-Institut, Berlin, Dept of Nuclear Eng, Technion Univ., Haifa, Israel, Centre d'Études Nucléaires de Fontenay-Aux-Roses, Commissariat à l'Énergie Atomique (France), Charles Univ., Prague, Japan Atomic Energy Research Inst., Institut für Nukleare Entsorgungstechnik of Kernforschungszentrum Karlsruhe, Århus Univ., Mineralogical Inst., Tokyo Univ., Khlopin Radium Inst., St Petersburg, Russia; mem. Bd of Radioactive Waste Man., Nat. Research Council, Nat. Research Council cttees for NAS that reviewed Waste Isolation Pilot Plant in NM 1984–96, Remediation of Buried and

Tank Wastes at Hanford, Wash. and INEEL, Ida 1992–95, INEEL High-Level Waste Alternative Treatments 1998–99, sub-cttee on WIPP for the Environmental Protection Agency's Nat. Advisory Council on Environmental Policy and Tech. 1992–98; has served as invited expert to Advisory Cttee on Nuclear Waste of Nuclear Regulatory Comm.; fmr consultant to Nuclear Waste Tech. Review Bd; mem. Program Cttee, Materials Research Soc., Ed. or Assoc. Ed. proceedings vols for symposia on the 'Scientific Basis for Nuclear Waste Management', Berlin 1982, Boston 1984, Stockholm 1985, Berlin 1988, Strasbourg 1991, Kyoto 1994, Boston 1998, Sydney 2000; Fellow, Geological Soc. of America, Mineralogical Soc. of America; Dr hc (Université Pierre et Marie Curie) 2006; Guggenheim Fellowship 2002, Lomonosov Gold Medal, Russian Acad. of Sciences 2006, Roebling Medal, Mineralogical Soc. of America 2015, Ian Campbell Medal, American Geoscience Inst. 2015, Medal of Excellence, Int. Mineralogical Asscn 2015. *Publications include:* Radioactive Waste Forms for the Future (co-ed. and contributing author) 1988; ed. or co-ed. of seven monographs, proceedings vols or special issues of journals; author or co-author of more than 700 specialist research publs; holds patent for the development of a highly durable material for the immobilization of excess weapons plutonium. *Address:* Department of Geological Sciences, Stanford University, Stanford, CA 94305, USA (office). *E-mail:* rewing1@stanford.edu (office). *Website:* profiles.stanford.edu/rodney-ewing (office).

EWING, Rufus Washington, DM, MPH; Turks and Caicos physician and politician; b. 1972, Blue Hills, Providenciales Island; s. of Hilly Ewing and Jane Ewing; m. Dawn Perry 1993; one s.; ed Barbados Community Coll., Univ. of the West Indies, IWK Grace Health Center, Halifax, Canada, Johns Hopkins Univ. Bloomberg School of Public Health, Baltimore, USA; Deputy Chief Medical Officer, Turks and Caicos 2001–05, Chief Medical Officer and Dir of Health Services 2005–12; f. Omnicare (private medical practice), Providenciales 2001–; Pres. Civil Servants Asscn (trade union) 2011–12; Leader, Progressive Nat. Party; Premier of Turks and Caicos (first since suspension of office by UK in 2009) 2012–16; fmr Chair. Health Practitioners' Bd, Public and Environmental Health Bd, Nat. Insurance Medical Bd; fmr Dir Caribbean Health Research Council; Fellow, Royal Coll. of Surgeons of Edinburgh 1998. *Address:* c/o Office of the Premier, N. J. S. Francis Building, Government Square, Grand Turk, Turks and Caicos (office).

EYRE, Ivan, CM, OM, BFA; Canadian artist and academic; *Professor Emeritus of Drawing and Painting, University of Manitoba;* b. 15 April 1935, Tullymet, Sask.; s. of Thomas Eyre and Kay Eyre; m. Brenda Fenske 1957; two s.; mem. Faculty, Univ. of Manitoba, Winnipeg 1959–93, Head, Drawing Dept 1974–78, Prof. of Drawing and Painting 1975–93, Prof. Emer. 1994–; works represented in permanent collections at Winnipeg Art Gallery, Nat. Gallery, Ottawa, Edmonton Art Gallery, Montreal Museum of Fine Arts, Assiniboine Park Pavilion Gallery, Winnipeg, Man. etc.; Canada Council Sr Fellow 1966–77; Founder mem. Winnipeg Art Gallery 1996; mem. Royal Canadian Acad. of Arts; subject of books 'Ivan Eyre' by George Woodcock, 'Ivan Eyre Drawings' by Tom Lovatt and of various documentary films; Queen's Silver Jubilee Medal 1977, Academic of Italy with Gold Medal 1980, Jubilee Award, Univ. of Manitoba Alumni Asscn 1982, Queen's Golden Jubilee Medal 2002, Order of Manitoba 2007. *Publications include:* Ivan on Eyre (autobiog.). *Address:* 1098 Des Trappistes Street, Winnipeg, MB R3V 1B8, Canada (home). *Fax:* (204) 275-6650 (home).

EYRE, Sir Richard Hastings Charles, Kt, CH, KBE, CBE, BA, FRSL; British theatre, film and television director; b. 28 March 1943, Barnstaple, Devon, England; s. of Commdr R. G. H. G. Eyre, RN, Minna Mary Jessica Royds; m. Sue Birtwistle 1973; one d.; ed Sherborne School, Peterhouse, Cambridge; directed his first production, The Knack, at Phoenix Theatre, Leicester 1965; Asst Dir Phoenix Theatre 1967; Assoc. Dir Royal Lyceum, Edinburgh 1967–70, Dir of Productions 1970–72; Artistic Dir Nottingham Playhouse 1973–78; Producer-Dir Play for Today for BBC 1978–80; Assoc. Dir Nat. Theatre (now called Royal Nat. Theatre) 1980–86, Artistic Dir 1988–97; BBC Gov. 1995–2004; Cameron Mackintosh Visiting Professorship, St Catherine's Coll. Oxford 1997; Visiting Prof. of Drama, Univ. of Warwick 1999, Univ. of Sheffield 2000; Fellow Emer., St Catherine's Coll., Oxford 2003; Pres. Rose Bruford Coll. 2010; Chair. Channel 4 Playwrights' Award 2010–, Nat. Theatre Foundation 2014–; Hon. Fellow, Goldsmiths Coll. 1993, King's Coll. London 1994, Guildhall School of Music and Drama 1996, Peterhouse, Cambridge 2001; Officier des Arts et des Lettres 1998; Hon. DLitt (Nottingham Trent) 1992, (South Bank) 1994, Hon. BA (Surrey) 1998, Dr hc (Royal Scottish Acad. of Drama) 2000, (Liverpool) 2003, Hon. DUniv (Oxford Brookes Univ.) 2003, (Nottingham) 2008, (East Anglia) 2011; Patricia Rothermere Award 1995, STV Award for Best Dir 1969, 1970, 1971, Vittorio de Sica Award 1986, BAFTA Best Dir 1987, Special Award, Evening Standard Awards for Drama 1988, for Best Dir 1997, 2014, Special Award for running Nat. Theatre 1997, Critics Circle Award for Best Dir 1996, for Lifetime Achievement 1997, Laurence Olivier Award for Best Dir 1982, 1997, 2005, Best Revival 2005, 2014, for Outstanding Achievement 1997, South Bank Show Award for Outstanding Achievement 1997, Dir's Guild Award for Outstanding Achievement 1997. *Plays directed include:* Hamlet (Royal Court) 1980, Guys and Dolls (Olivier 1982, Soc. of West End Theatres and Evening Standard Awards for Best Dir 1982), The Beggar's Opera, Schweyk in the Second World War (Nat. Theatre) 1982, The Government Inspector (Nat. Theatre) 1985, Futurists (Nat. Theatre) (Time Out Award for Best Dir) 1986, Kafka's Dick (Royal Court) 1986, High Society (West End) 1987, The Changeling 1988, Bartholomew Fair 1988, Hamlet 1989, The Voysey Inheritance 1989, Racing Demon 1990, Richard III (Nat. Theatre, also nat. and int. tour) 1990, Napoli Milionaria 1991, Murmuring Judges 1991, White Chameleon 1991, The Night of the Iguana 1992, Macbeth 1993, The David Hare Trilogy – Racing Demon, Murmuring Judges, The Absence of War 1993 (Racing Demon, New York 1995), Johnny on a Spot 1994, Sweet Bird of Youth 1994, Skylight 1995, 1996 (New York 1996), La Grande Magia 1995, The Prince's Play 1996, John Gabriel Borkman 1996, Guys and Dolls 1996, 1997, King Lear 1997, Amy's View 1997 (New York 1999), The Invention of Love 1997, The Judas Kiss 1998 (New York 1998), The Novice 2000, The Crucible (New York) 2002, Vincent in Brixton 2002, Mary Poppins 2004, Hedda Gabler (London 2005), Mary Poppins (New York) 2006, The Reporter (Nat. Theatre) 2007, The Last Cigarette (Chichester and West End) 2009, The Observer (Nat. Theatre) 2009, Private Lives (Theatre Royal Bath, Vaudeville) 2010, (Toronto and Broadway) 2011, Welcome to Thebes (Nat. Theatre 2010), Flea in Her Ear (Old Vic) 2010, Betty Blue Eyes (Novello Theatre) 2011, The Last of the Duchess (Hampstead Theatre) 2011, Quartermaine's Terms (Wyndham's Theatre) 2013, The Pajama Game (Chichester) 2013, (Shaftesbury theatre) 2014, Liolá (Nat. Theatre), Ghosts (Almeida and Trafalgar Studios) 2013, Stephen Ward (Aldwych) 2013, Mr Foote's Other Leg (Haymarket Theatre) 2105, Little Eyolf (Almeida Theatre) 2015, The Stepmother (Chichester) 2017, Long Day's Journey Into Night (Wyndham's Theatre and USA tour) 2018, My Name Is Lucy Barton (Bridge Theatre) 2018. *Opera:* La Traviata, Covent Garden 1994, Le Nozze di Figaro, Aix-en-Provence, France 2001, Carmen, Metropolitan Opera 2009, Werther, Metropolitan Opera 2014, Manon Lescaut, Baden-Baden 2014, Le Nozze Di Figaro, Metropolitan Opera 2014, Manon Lescaut, Metropolitan Opera 2017. *Films:* The Ploughman's Lunch (Evening Standard Award for Best Film) 1983, Loose Connections 1984, Laughterhouse (Venice Film Festival Award for Best Film) 1984, Iris (co-dir and co-writer) (Special Mention for Excellence in Filmmaking Award, Nat. Bd of Review (NBR) 2001, Humanitas Screenwriting Award for screenplay 2002, Efebo D'Oro Award) 2001, Stage Beauty (NBR Award, Jury Prize, Abbeville Film Festival) 2004, Notes on a Scandal (NBR Award, Rotten Tomatoes Award, Best Gay Film, Berlin Festival) 2006, The Other Man (Official Selection at Toronto, San Sebastian and London Film Festivals) 2008, The children Act (Official Selection at Toronto) 2017. *Radio:* Macbeth (BBC Radio 3) 2000, Angel (BBC Radio 4) 2001, Ghosts (BBC Radio 3) 2013, Victory (BBC Radio 4) 2014. *Television includes:* producer: BBC Play For Today 1978, Just a Boy's Game, Long Distance Information, Chance of a Lifetime; dir: Waterloo Sunset 1979, Comedians 1979, The Cherry Orchard 1980, The Imitation Game 1980, Pasmore (own adaptation) 1981, Country 1982, Loose Connections 1984, Laughterhouse (Venice Film Festival Award for Best TV Film) 1984, Past Caring (Venice TV Prize Special Mention) 1985, The Insurance Man (Tokyo World TV Festival Special Prize) 1985, 'V' (RTS Award) 1987, Tumbledown (Italia RAI Prize 1988, BAFTA Award for Best TV Single Drama, Royal TV Soc. Award for Best Single Drama 1989, BPG Award) 1987, Suddenly Last Summer (BBC) 1993, The Absence of War (BBC) 1995, King Lear (BBC) (Peabody Award 1998) 1998, The Three Kings (Sky TV) 2009, Henry IV Parts 1 and 2 2012, The Dresser (BBC and Starz) 2015, King Lear (BBC and Amazon 2018). *Publications include:* Utopia and Other Places (memoirs) 1993 (revised edns 1994, 2003), The Eyre Review: The Future of Lyric Theatre in London 1998, Changing Stages (with Nicholas Wright) 2000, Iris (screenplay) 2002, National Service: Diary of a Decade (Theatre Book Award 2004) 2003, Hedda Gabler 2005, Talking Theatre: Interviews with Theatre People 2009, What Do I Know? 2014, Place to Place 2018. *Address:* c/o Judy Daish Associates Ltd, 2 St Charles Place, London, W10 6EG, England (office). *Telephone:* (20) 8964-8811 (office). *Fax:* (20) 8964-8966 (office). *E-mail:* judy@judydaish.com (office). *Website:* www.judydaish.com (office).

EYRE, Richard Anthony, CBE, MA; British media executive; *Chairman, Internet Advertising Bureau;* b. 3 May 1954; s. of Edgar Gabriel Eyre and Marjorie Eyre (née Corp); m. Sheelagh Colquhoun 1977; one s. one d.; ed King's Coll. School, Wimbledon, Lincoln Coll., Oxford; media buyer, Benton & Bowles 1975–79, media planner 1980–84; TV airtime salesman, Scottish TV 1979–80; Media Dir, Aspect 1984–86, Bartle Bogle Hegarty 1986–91; Chief Exec. Capital Radio PLC 1991–97, ITV 1997–2000, Pearson TV 2000–01; Dir of Strategy and Content, RTL Group 2000–01; Chair. (non-exec.), RDF Media 2001, GCap Media PLC 2007–08, Next 15; Adviser to 19 Group 2002–; currently Chair. Internet Advertising Bureau; Dir (non-exec.), MGt plc, Results International; mem. Bd Grant Thornton; Chair. Eden Project; fmr mem. Bd, Guardian Media Group; Mackintosh Medal 2013. *Address:* c/o Patricia Siakwang, Executive Assistant to the CEO, Internet Advertising Bureau, 14 Macklin Street, London, WC2B 5NF, England (office). *Telephone:* (20) 7050-6952 (office). *E-mail:* patricia@iabuk.net (office). *Website:* www.iabuk.net/about/iab-team (office).

EYSKENS, Mark, Bac. Philo., LLD, DEcon, MA; Belgian politician, academic and author; *Chairman, PA Europe International Foundation;* b. (Marc Maria Frans Eyskens), 29 April 1933, Louvain; s. of Gaston Eyskens and Gilberte Eyskens; m. Ann Rutsaert 1962; two s. three d.; ed Catholic Univ. of Louvain, Columbia Univ., New York; Prof., Catholic Univ. of Louvain; Econ. Adviser, Ministry of Finance 1962–65; mem. of Parl. (Christian People's Party (Belgium), now called Christian Democratic and Flemish) 1977–2003; Sec. of State for the Budget and Regional Economy and Minister of Co-operation 1976–80; Minister of Finance 1980–81; Prime Minister April–Dec. 1981; Minister for Econ. Affairs 1981–85, for Finance 1985–88, of Foreign Affairs 1989–92, Minister of State 1998–; Chair. Council of EC Ministers of Finance 1987; Gov. IMF, IBRD 1980–81, 1985–88; mem. Council of Europe 1995–2003; fmr Pres. Royal Acad. of Sciences (currently Hon. Pres.), Letters and Fine Arts, Centre for European Culture, Inst. for European Policy; Vice-Pres. Royal Inst. for Int. Relations, Ass. of WEU 1995–2003; Observer, European Convention 2002–; currently Chair. PA Europe Int. Foundation; Pres. Francqui Foundation, Music Festival of Flanders, Arenberg Foundation, Center European Culture; mem. Bd Int. Crisis Group, Itinera, several cos; numerous radio and TV interviews; numerous Belgian and foreign decorations; numerous Belgian and foreign awards, including Benelux-Europe Prize, J.M./Huyghe Prize, Scriptores Christiani Prize, Grande médaille d'or Acad. française des Arts, Sciences et Lettres. *Publications include:* author of 54 books including Algemene economie 1970, Economie van nu en straks 1975, Ambrunise 1976, Une planète livrée à deux mondes 1980, La source et l'horizon, Le redressement de la société européenne 1985, Economie voor iedereen 1987, Vie et mort du Professeur Mortal 1989, Buitenlandse zaken 1992, Affaires étrangères 1992, Le Fleuve et l'océan 1994, De Reis naar Dabar 1996, De lust van de verbeelding 1996, L'Affaire Titus 1998, Democratie tussen Spin en Web 1999, Het verdriet van het werelddorp 2000, Leven in tijden van Godsverduistering 2001, Het hijgen van de geschiedenis 2003, Omdat wij van de avond nooit genzen 2004, De oude prof en de zee 2005, Le vieux prof et la mer 2006, Mijn levens 2008, Absurdistan 2009; Mes vies. A la recherche du temps vécu 2010, Vonken in het duister (e-book) 2010, 1001 quotes 2011, Het land van ergens 2012, Macht en Gezag 2012, Zwarte melk in de politiek 2013, Le nationalisme, recul de l'histoire, Veelal: Een theorie van alles–Ideeënroman; has written more than 1,000 articles, prefaces, columns, poems and contribs. *Leisure interests:* painting, literature, music. *Address:* Royal Academy of Sciences and Arts, Hertogsstraat 1, 1000 Brussels (office); PA Europe, Franklin Street 106, 1000 Brussels, Belgium (office). *Telephone:* (2) 550-23-23 (Royal Acad.) (office); (2) 735-83-96 (PA Europe) (office). *Fax:* (1) 640-60-18 (home). *E-mail:* m.eyskens@skynet.be (office). *Website:* www.eyskens.com.

EYTON, Anthony John Plowden, RA, RWS, R.W.A.; British artist; b. 17 May 1923, Teddington, Middx; s. of Capt. John Seymour Eyton and Phyllis Annie Tyser; m. Frances Mary Capell 1960 (divorced); three d.; ed Twyford School, Canford School and Camberwell School of Art; part-time teacher, Camberwell Art School 1955–86, Royal Acad. Schools 1963–99; Resident Artist, Eden Project 1999–2009; mem. Royal Cambrian Acad., Royal Inst. Oil Painters (ROI); Hon. mem. Pastel Soc., Hon. Prof. and Fellow, Univ. of the Arts, London 2011; several awards and prizes. *Publications:* Indian Memories, Journal of P A Eyton (RA Publications) 1996, Eyton's Eye, a Life in Painting (by Jenny Perry, RA Publications) 2005. *Leisure interest:* gardening. *Address:* c/o Browse and Darby Ltd, 19 Cork Street, London, W1X 1HB, England (office).

EYYUBOV, Yaqub Abdulla oğlu; Azerbaijani oil engineer and politician; *First Deputy Prime Minister;* b. 28 Nov. 1945, Baku, Azerbaijan SSR, USSR; ed Azerbaijan Polytechnical Inst.; worked briefly at Lieutenant Schmidt Plant (now Sattarhan Plant) 1964; conscripted into Soviet Army 1964–67; returned to Baku 1968; Chair. Komsomol Cttee, Construction Studies Dept, Azerbaijan Tech. Univ. 1970–72, Deputy Chair. Party Cttee of the Univ. 1973–74; worked part-time as a Sr Prof., Asst Dean, Docent, Acting Dean and Pro-Rector on Scientific Issues and Dept Dir at Azerbaijan Architecture and Construction Univ. 1975–97; Chair. Regulation of Industrial Activities Safety Cttee and Highland Field Exploration Regulation Cttee 1997–99; Deputy Prime Minister 1999–2003, First Deputy Prime Minister 2003–; Head of Azeri-Saudi Inter-governmental Econ. Comm.; Co-chairs 13 comms under the Ministry of Econ. Devt; apptd to develop the oil and gas strategy of Azerbaijan by Pres. Ilham Aliyev 2009. *Address:* Office of the Prime Minister, 1066 Baku, Lermontov küç. 68, Azerbaijan (office). *Telephone:* (12) 492-84-19 (office). *Fax:* (12) 492-91-79 (office). *E-mail:* nk@cabmin.gov.az (office). *Website:* www.cabmin.gov.az (office).

EYZAGUIRRE GUZMAN, Nicolás, PhD; Chilean economist, international organization official and politician; b. 1954, Santiago; s. of Joaquín Eyzaguirre Edwards and Delfina Guzmán Correa; m. Bernardita Piedrabuena; three c.; ed Univ. of Chile, Harvard Univ., USA; worked at Cen. Bank of Chile 1990–97, positions included Adviser, Man. and Dir of Studies, also prin. adviser to the Pres. 1990–97; Exec. Dir IMF 1998; Minister of Finance 2000–06; Pres. Chilean Competitiveness Council 2006–; Minister of Educ. 2014–15, Minister, Sec.-Gen. of the Presidency 2015–17, Minister of Finance 2017–18; fmr mem. Bd of Dirs Banco Estado; mem. Latin American Advisory Bd Deutsche Bank AG 2008–; mem. Partido Por la Democracia—PPD. *Publication:* The Macroeconomy of Quasi-Fiscal Operations in Chile (with Osvaldo Larrañaga) 1990. *Address:* c/o Ministry of Finance, Teatinos 120, 12°, Santiago, Chile (office).

EZZATI ANDRELLO, HE Cardinal Ricardo, SDB; Chilean (b. Italian) ecclesiastic; *Archbishop of Santiago de Chile;* b. 7 Jan. 1942, Campiglia dei Berici, Vicenza, Italy; s. of Mario and Assunta; ed Novitiate of the Salesians, Quilpué, Valparaíso, Catholic Univ. of Valparaíso, Pontifical Salesian Univ., Rome, Institut de Pastoral Catéchetique, Strasbourg; arrived in Chile 1959; professed (Perpetual Vows) as mem. Salesians of St John Bosco 1966; ordained priest of Salesians of St John Bosco 1970; taught at Faculty of Theology, Pontifical Catholic Univ. of Chile; served as Vice-Pres. Conf. of Religious of Chile; participated in Gen. Chapters of the Salesian Congregation 1984, 1990; fmr Prof. of Religion and Philosophy, Catholic Univ. of Valparaíso; consecrated Bishop of Valdivia 1996–2001; apptd Titular Bishop of La Imperial 2001; Auxiliary Bishop of Santiago de Chile 2001–06; Archbishop of Concepción (Santissima Concezione) 2006–10; Archbishop of Santiago de Chile 2010–; cr. Cardinal (Cardinal-Priest of Santissimo Redentore a Valmelaina) 2014–; apptd an official of the Congregation for Insts of Consecrated Life and Socs of Apostolic Life 1991. *Address:* Erasmo Escala 1872, Santiago, Chile (office). *Telephone:* (2) 7875600 (office). *Fax:* (2) 7875633 (office). *E-mail:* info@iglesiadesantiago.cl (office). *Website:* www.iglesiadesantiago.cl (office).

F

FABIANO, Emmanuel, BEd, MSc, PhD; Malawi politician and fmr university administrator; *Minister of Foreign Affairs and International Co-operation;* ed Univ. of Malawi, Warwick Univ., Newcastle Univ.; started career as Staff Assoc., Univ. of Malawi, several sr positions including Prin., Chancellor Coll. 1994–98, 2005–09, Vice Chancellor, Univ. of Malawi 2009–13; mem. Nat. Ass. (Parl.) for Chiradzulu West 2014–; Minister of Educ., Science and Tech. 2014–17; Minister of Foreign Affairs and Int. Co-operation 2017–; mem. Democratic Progressive Party (DPP). *Address:* Ministry of Foreign Affairs and International Co-operation, POB 30315, Lilongwe 3, Malawi (office). *Telephone:* 1789088 (office); 1789115 (office). *Fax:* 1788482 (office); 1789112 (office). *E-mail:* foreign.affairs@foreignaffairs.gov.mw (office). *Website:* www.foreignaffairs.gov.mw (office).

FABIUS, Laurent; French politician; *President, Constitutional Council;* b. 20 Aug. 1946, Paris; s. of André Fabius and Louise Fabius (née Strasburger-Mortimer); m. Françoise Castro (divorced); two s.; one s. from previous relationship; ed Lycées Janson-de-Sailly and Louis-le-Grand, Paris, Ecole normale supérieure and Institut d'études politiques, Paris, Ecole nat. d'admin, Strasbourg; Auditor, Council of State 1973; First Deputy Mayor of Grand-Quevilly 1977–95, 2008–14, Mayor 1995–2000, mem. Grand-Quevilly municipal council 2014–16; Deputy (Seine-Maritime) to Nat. Ass. 1978–81, 1986–2000, 2002–12, Pres. Nat. Ass. 1997–2000; Nat. Sec. Parti Socialiste, in charge of press 1979–81, 1991–92, First Sec. 1992–93, Pres. Groupe Socialiste in Nat. Ass. 1995–97, mem. Nat. Bureau 1988–2002, 2006–07, 2009–12; Minister-Del. for the Budget, attached to Minister of Econ. and Finance 1981–83, Minister of Industry and Research 1983–84, of Econs, Finance and Industry 2000–02; Prime Minister 1984–86; Minister of Foreign Affairs 2012–16; Pres. Regional Council, Haute Normandie 1981–82; Pres. Syndicat intercommunal à vocations multiples (Sivom) 1989–2000; Pres. COP21 (UN climate talks) 2015–16; Pres. Constitutional Council 2016–; mem. Gen. Council, Seine-Maritime 2000–02; Commdr, Ordre nat. du Mérite 1984, Kt Grand Cross, Order of Merit of the Italian Repub. 1990, Grand Cross, Royal Norwegian Order of Merit 1995, Grand Cross, Order of the Star of Romania 1999, Grand Officier, Ordre de la Légion d'honneur 2008, Grand Cross, Order of Isabella the Catholic (Spain) 2015; Ewald von Kleist Award 2016. *Publications:* La France inégale 1975, Le coeur du futur 1985, C'est en allant vers la mer 1990, Les blessures de la vérité (Prize for Best Political Book 1996) 1995, Cela commence par une balade 2003, Une certaine idée de l'Europe 2005, Le Cabinet des douze (Prix Montaigne de Bordeaux 2011) 2010, 37, Quai d'Orsay – Diplomatie française 2012–2016 2016. *Address:* Conseil Constitutionnel, 2 rue de Montpensier, 75001 Paris, France (office). *Telephone:* 1-40-15-30-00 (office). *Fax:* 1-40-20-93-27 (office). *E-mail:* informatique@conseil-constitutionnel.fr (office). *Website:* www.conseil-constitutionnel.fr (office).

FABRE, Jan; Belgian artist, playwright and stage designer; b. 1958, Antwerp; ed Decorative Arts Inst., Royal Acad. of Fine Arts; began career as decorator and set designer; wrote a series of plays and produced black and white films 1970s; became active in the field of performance art 1976–81; produced a series of chamber plays 1980s; Founder and Artistic Dir Troublyn (creative work asscn) 1986–; fmr Artist-in-Residence, Museum of Natural History, London; decorated the Hall of Mirrors at the Royal Palace at the invitation of the Queen of Belgium 2003; productions have been staged in Europe, the USA, Japan and Australia; contrib. to numerous European museums and galleries including deSingel arts centre, Antwerp, Centre for Contemporary Art, Warsaw, Gallery of Modern and Contemporary Art, Bergamo. *Drawings include:* The Flying Cock, The Road from the Earth to the Stars is not Smooth, Hour of the Blue. *Sculptures include:* House of Flames III, Scissors' House. *Stage works include:* Body, Body on a Wall. *Plays include:* This is the Theatre One Should have Awaited and Expected 1982, The Power of Theatrical Frenzy (staged at Venice Biennial) 1984, Sweet Temptations, Universal Copyrights 1 & 9, Luminous Icons, The End Comes a Little Bit Earlier This Century. But Business as Usual 1998, The Values of Night 1999, Requiem für eine Metamorphose 2007, Another Sleepy Dusty Delta Day 2008, Orgy of Tolerance 2008. *Opera includes:* Glass in the Head will be Made of Glass (Flemish Opera House, Antwerp) 1990. *Ballet includes:* Sound of One Clapping Hand 1989, The Four Temperaments 1997. *Address:* Troubleyn/Jan Fabre VZW, Pastorijstraat 23, 2060 Antwerp, Belgium (office). *Telephone:* (3) 201-13-00 (office). *Fax:* (3) 233-15-01 (office). *E-mail:* info@troubleyn.be (office). *Website:* www.troubleyn.be (office); janfabre.be.

FABRIZI, Pier Luigi, BEcons; Italian professor of finance and banker; *Professor of Financial Markets, Bocconi University;* b. 23 April 1948, Siena; s. of Francesco Fabrizi and Bianca Corradeschi; m. Patrizia Vaselli; two c.; ed Università degli Studi di Siena; Asst Prof. of Banking, Università degli Studi di Parma 1974–82, Assoc. Prof. of Financial Markets 1982–87, Full Prof. of Banking 1987–89, Full Prof. of Financial Intermediaries 1990–93, Dean Faculty of Econs 1990–93; Full Prof. of Financial Markets, Bocconi Univ., Milan 1993–; mem. Bd of Dirs Banca Monte dei Paschi di Siena SpA 1997–2006, Chair. 1998–2006; mem. Bd of Dirs S. Paolo IMI SpA 1998–99, Olivetti SpA 1999–2001, Banca Monte Parma SpA 1999–2003, Banca Agricola Mantovana SpA 1999–2006, Banca Nazionale del Lavoro SpA 2001–06, Unipol Assicurazioni SpA 2001–07; Chair. Gruppo Monte Paschi Asset Man. SGR SpA 1999–2000, MPS Finance SpA 2000–01, CartaSi SpA 2006–09, SiHolding SpA 2006–09; Grande Ufficiale dell' Ordine al Merito. *Publications:* Il credito al consumo 1975, Il credito fondiario e il credito edilizio 1977, La politica degli investimenti in titoli nelle banche di deposito 1982, L'attività in titoli con clientela nelle banche di deposito (ed.) 1986, La gestione dei flussi finanziari nelle aziende di credito (ed.) 1990, La gestione integrata dell'attivo e del passivo nelle aziende di credito (ed.) 1991, Nuovi modelli di gestione dei flussi finanziari nelle banche (ed.) 1995, La formazione nelle banche e nelle assicurazioni 1998, Il futuro del sistema bancario italiano: atrategie e modelli organizzativi 2000, La gestione del risparmio privato (ed.) 2000, La crisi finanziaria globale: teoria e realtà a confronto 2009, Finanza 2013, Economia del mercato mobiliare (ed.) 2016. *Address:* Department of Finance, Università Bocconi, Via Roentgen 1, 2nd Floor, 20136 Milan (office); Via Adelaide Coari 11, 20141 Milan, Italy. *Telephone:* (02) 58365901 (office). *Fax:* (02) 58365920 (office). *E-mail:* pierluigi.fabrizi@unibocconi.it (office).

FADELL, Anthony (Tony) Michael, BS; American technology industry executive; *CEO, Nest Labs Inc.;* b. 22 March 1969; m. Danielle Fadell; ed Grosse Pointe South High School, Mich., Univ. of Michigan; CEO Constructive Instruments (while at univ.) –1992; Diagnostics Engineer and Systems Architect, General Magic 1992–95; Co-Founder, Chief Tech. Officer and Dir of Eng, Philips Electronics Mobile Computing Group 1995–98, Vice-Pres., Philips Strategy and Ventures 1998–99; f. Fuse Systems Inc. 1999; designed iPod for Apple Inc. 2001, Head of iPod and Special Projects Group 2001–04, Vice-Pres. iPod Engineering 2004–06, Sr Vice-Pres. iPod Div. 2006–08, Advisor to CEO 2008–10; Co-Founder and CEO Nest Labs Inc. 2010– (acquired by Google 2014–), apptd to served as Head of Google Glass Div., Google Inc., subsidiary of newly formed holding co. Alphabet Inc.) 2015; Alva Award 2012. *Address:* Nest Labs Inc., 3400 Hillview Avenue, Palo Alto, CA 94304, USA (office). *Website:* nest.com (office); www.google.com (office).

FADEYECHEV, Alexei Nikolayevich; Russian ballet dancer; *Choreographer, Teatr Wielki Opea Narodowa;* b. 16 Aug. 1960, Moscow; s. of Nikolay Fadeyechev (q.v.) and Nina Fetisova; m. Rastozguyeva Tatyana; ed Bolshoi Choreographic School; Prin. Dancer, Bolshoi Ballet 1978, Artistic Dir 1998–2000; co-f. (with Nina Ananiashvili q.v.) ballet co. Moscow Theatre of Dance 2000; Artistic Dir Rostov Musical Theatre ballet co. 2004–13; currently Choreographer, Teatr Wielki Opea Narodowa, Poland; has performed with Mariinsky (fmrly Kirov) Ballet, Royal Danish Ballet, Royal Swedish Ballet, Nat. Ballet of Netherlands, Nat. Ballet of Finland, Nat. Ballet of Portugal, Birmingham Royal Ballet, Boston Ballet, Tokyo Ballet and numerous others; People's Artist of Russia. *Performances as a dancer include:* Frantz in Coppelia, Prince Siegfried in Swan Lake, Prince Desire in The Sleeping Beauty, Prince in The Nutcracker, Jean de Brienne in Raimonda, Basil in Don Quixote, Albrecht in Giselle, title roles in Spartacus, Ivan the Terrible, Macbeth, Romeo and Juliet, Cyrano de Bergerac, Prince of the Pagodas, leading roles in Les Sylphides, Paquita. *Address:* Teatr Wielki, Polish National Opera, Plac Teatralny 1, 00-950, Warsaw, skrytka pocztowa 59, Poland. *Telephone:* (22) 6920200. *E-mail:* office@teatrwielki.pl. *Website:* teatrwielki.pl/en/ludzie/alexei-fadeyechev.

FADEYECHEV, Nikolay Borisovich; Russian ballet dancer; b. 27 Jan. 1933; m. 1st Nina Fetisova; m. 2nd Irina Kholina; two s.; ed Bolshoi Theatre Ballet School; Bolshoi Theatre Ballet Co. 1952–76, coach, Bolshoi Theatre 1977–; Order of Honour 2003; Vatslav Nijinsky Prize, Paris Acad. of Dance 1959, People's Artist of USSR 1976, Prize for selfless service to art of dance, Galina Ulanova Foundation 2004, Soul of Dance Prize, Ballet magazine 2004. *Roles include:* Siegfried (Swan Lake), Albert (Giselle), Jean de Brienne (Raimonde), Harmodius (Spartacus), Frondoso (Laurensia), Danila (Stone Flower), Romeo (Romeo and Juliet), Prince Desire (Sleeping Beauty), José (Carmen Suite), Karenin (Anna Karenina), Prince (Nutcracker), Illiys (Giselle), Vatslav.

FADHLI, Ahmad Obaid al-; Yemeni politician; Minister of Trade and Supply 1986; Deputy Minister of Finance 2012, Minister of Finance 2016–19; Gov., Arab Monetary Fund 2016–; Chair. Saudi–Yemeni Coordination Council Coordination and Follow-up Cttee 2017–; Dir Central Bank of Yemen. *Address:* c/o Ministry of Finance, POB 190, San'a, Yemen (office).

FADIAH, João Aladje Mamadu; Guinea-Bissau politician; Minister of the Economy and Finance 2004–05, 2016–18; fmr Nat. Dir for Guinea-Bissau, Banque Centrale des Etats de l'Afrique de l'Ouest (BCEAO). *Address:* c/o Ministry of the Economy and Finance, Av. dos Combatentes da Liberdade da Pátria, CP 67, Bissau, Guinea-Bissau (office).

FADNAVIS, Devendra Gangadharrao, LLB, MBM; Indian politician; *Chief Minister of Maharashtra;* b. 22 July 1970, Nagpur, Maharashtra; s. of Gangadharrao Fadnavis and Sarita Fadnavis; m. Amruta Ranade 2006; one d.; ed Dharampeth Junior Coll., Nagpur Univ., DSE (German Foundation for Int. Devt) Univ., Germany; mem. Akhil Bharatiya Vidyarthi Parishad (ABVP) 1986–89; joined Bharatiya Janata Yuva Morcha—BJYM (youth wing of Bharatiya Janata Party—BJP), apptd Ward Pres. 1989, Nagpur Pres. 1992, State Vice-Pres. 1994, Nat. Vice-Pres. 2001, Gen. Sec., BJP Maharashtra 2010–13, Pres. 2013; mem. Municipal Corpn of Nagpur 1992–2001; Mayor of Nagpur 1997–2001; mem. of Maharashtra Legis. Ass. 1999–; Chief Minister of Maharastra 2014–; Sec., Global Parliamentarians Forum on Habitat for Asia Region; Pres. Nagpur Dist Basketball Asscn; mem. Senate, Rashtra Sant Tukdoji Maharaj Nagpur Univ.; Best Parliamentarian Award, Commonwealth Parl. Asscn 2002–03, Rajyogi Neta Award by Prunavad Parivar, Nasik, Bose Prize in Hindu Law. *Publication:* How To Understand and Read State Budget. *Address:* Bharatiya Janata Party Nagpur, Tilak Statue, Mahal, Nagpur 440 002 (office); 276, Trikoni Park, Dharampeth, Nagpur 440 010, India (home). *Telephone:* (712) 2723994 (office); (712) 2533446 (home). *E-mail:* chiefminister@maharashtra.gov.in (office). *Website:* www.maharashtra.gov.in (office); www.devendrafadnavis.in.

FADOUL, Abdoulaye Sabre, LLD; Chadian politician; b. Biltine; m.; six c.; ed Univ. de N'Djamena, Univ. Paris-V-René-Descartes, Saint Cyr Mil. Acad., Saumur Cavalry School; Lecturer, Univ. Paris-V-René-Descartes and Univ. de Picardie 2003–09; returned to Chad 2009; Adviser on Legal Affairs to the Pres. 2009–11; Minister of Justice 2011–13, Minister of Justice and State Control 2012, Minister of Post and Telecommunications 2013, Sec.-Gen. of the Govt 2013–17, also responsible for Relations with Parl. and Reforms 2016–17, Minister of Finance and the Budget 2017–18.

FADUL, Francisco José, BA, BTh, MA, PhD; Guinea-Bissau lawyer, politician and academic; *President, Partido para a Democracia, Desenvolvimento e Cidadania (PADEC);* b. 15 Dec. 1953, Mansoa; s. of Ângelo Fadul and Adelina da Silva Gonçalves; m. Jóia Albino Ialá Fadul; five s. four d.; fmr adviser to Gen. Ansumane Mane; Prime Minister of Guinea-Bissau 1998–2000; Leader Partido Unido Social Democrático (PUSD) 2002–06 (resgnd); unsuccessful PUSD presidential cand. 2005; Personal Counsellor to Pres. of the Repub. 2005–06 (resgnd); Pres. Partido para a Democracia, Desenvolvimento e Cidadania (Party for Democracy, Devt and Citizenship—PADEC) 2007–; Pres. Tribunal of Accounts

2009–12; barred by Supreme Court as PADEC cand. in presidential election on the grounds that he was still Pres. of Tribunal of Accounts 2009; mem. UNESCO Int. Comm. for Peace Research; Amb. for Peace of Universal Peace Fed. *Publication:* O Desenvolvimento do Continente Africano na Era da Mundialização 2005. *Leisure interests:* literature, music, cinema, sport, gymnastics. *Address:* Partido para a Democracia, Desenvolvimento e Cidadania (PADEC), Apartado 415, 1032 Bissau Codex, Guinea-Bissau (office). *Telephone:* 92-5263801 (Portugal, mobile) (office). *E-mail:* fjfadul@hotmail.com (office).

FAGERNÄS, Peter, LLM; Finnish investment banker and business executive; *Managing Partner, Hermitage & Co Oy;* b. 1952; ed Univ. of Helsinki; Founder and Chair. Conventum Oyj (investment bank); Chair. Pohjola Group PLC 2001–03; Man. Pnr, Hermitage & Co. Oy and Chair. Oy Hermitage Ab 2003–; Chair., Fortum Corpn 2004–09 (resgnd), Taaleri PLC 2007–, Kesko 2018–; mem. Supervisory Bd Finnlines PLC, Trigon Capital; fmr mem. Bd of Dirs Merita Bank, Kansallis-Osake-Pankki; Vice-Chair. Helsinki Stock Exchange. *Address:* Hermitage & Co Oy, Erottajankatu 11 A 16, 00130 Helsinki, Finland (office). *Telephone:* (9) 6818180 (office). *Fax:* (9) 68181880 (office). *Website:* www.hermitage.fi (office).

FAGIN, Claire Muriel Mintzer, PhD, RN; American nurse; b. 25 Nov. 1926, New York; d. of Harry Mintzer and Mae Mintzer (née Slatin); m. Samuel Fagin 1952; two s.; ed Wagner Coll., Teachers' Coll., Columbia Univ. and New York Univ.; staff nurse, Sea View Hosp., Staten Island, New York 1947, Clinical Instructor 1947–48; Bellevue Hosp., New York 1948–50; Psychiatric Mental Health Nursing Consultant, Nat. League for Nursing 1951–52; Asst Chief, Psychiatric Nursing Service Clinical Center, NIH 1953–54, Supt 1955; Research Project Co-ordinator, Children's Hosp., Dept of Psychiatry, Washington, DC 1956; Instructor in Psychiatric-Mental Health Nursing, New York Univ. 1956–58, Asst Prof. 1964–67, Dir Grad. Programs in Psychiatric-Mental Health Nursing 1965–69, Assoc. Prof. 1967–69; Prof. and Chair. Nursing Dept, Herbert H. Lehman Coll. 1969–77; Dir Health Professions Inst., Montefiore Hosp. and Medical Center 1975–77; Dean, School of Nursing, Univ. of Pennsylvania, Philadelphia 1977–92, Prof. 1992–96, Interim Pres. 1993–94, Dean Emer., Prof. Emer. 1996–; mem. Task Force, Jt Cttee on Mental Health of Children 1966–69, Gov.'s Cttee on Children, New York 1971–75, Inst. of Medicine, NAS (Governing Council 1981–83), Comm. on Human Rights 1991–94, American Acad. of Nursing (Governing Council 1976–78), Expert Advisory Panel on Nursing, WHO 1974, Nat. Advisory Mental Health Council, Nat. Inst. of Mental Health 1983–87, Bd of Health Promotion and Disease Prevention 1990–94; Pres. American Orthopsychiatric Asscn 1985; Dir Salomon Inc. 1994–97; mem. Bd of Dirs Radian 1994–2002, Visiting Nurse Service of New York; Program Dir, Building Academic Geriatric Nursing Capacity Program, John A. Hartford Foundation 2000–05; Sr Advisor to Univ. of California, Davis School of Nursing; Pres. Nat. League for Nursing 1991–93; Sr Advisor to Jonas Center for Nursing; consultant to numerous foundations, public and pvt. univs, health-care agencies; speaker on radio and TV; Hon. Fellow, Royal Coll. of Nursing 2002; Hon. DSc (Lycoming Coll., Cedar Crest Coll., Univ. of Rochester, Medical Coll. of Pennsylvania, Univ. of Maryland, Loyola Univ., Wagner Coll., Case Western Reserve 2002), Hon. LLD (Pennsylvania), Hon. DHumLitt (Hunter Coll., Rush Univ., Johns Hopkins) 2003, Hon. DrIur (Toronto) 2004, (Syracuse) 2010, (New York Univ.) 2011; numerous awards and distinctions including American Acad. of Nursing Living Legend 1998, New York Univ. Pres.'s Medal 1998, American Nurses Foundation Nightingale Lamp Award 2002, named to American Nurses Asscn Hall of Fame 2010. *Publications:* numerous books including Nursing Leadership: Global Strategies (ed.) 1990, Essays in Nursing Leadership 2000, When Care Becomes a Burden 2001, and over 100 articles on nursing and health policy. *Leisure interests:* theatre, opera, art, sailing, snorkelling, gardening. *Address:* 200 Central Park South, Apartment 12E, New York, NY 10019-1415, USA (home). *Telephone:* (212) 581-4752 (office). *Fax:* (212) 581-4752 (office). *E-mail:* cfagin1@nyc.rr.com (office).

FAHEY, Hon. John Joseph, AC; Australian lawyer, politician and international organization official; b. 10 Jan. 1945, New Zealand; s. of Stephen Fahey and Annie Fahey; m. Colleen McGurran 1968; one s. two d.; ed St Anthony's Convent, Picton and Chevalier Coll. Bowral, Sydney Univ. Law Extension; mem. Parl. of NSW 1984–95; Minister for Industrial Relations and Employment and Minister Assisting Premier of NSW 1988–90; Minister for Industrial Relations, Further Educ., Training and Employment, NSW 1990–92; Premier and Treas. of NSW 1992; Premier and Minister for Econ. Devt of NSW 1993–95; Fed. mem. for Macarthur and Minister for Finance 1996–2001, for Admin. 1997–2001; Pres. World Anti-Doping Agency 2007–13; Chancellor, Australian Catholic Univ. 2014–; Chair. Australian Govt Reconstruction Inspectorate –2015; Chair. Sydney 2000 Olympic Bid Co. 1992–93; Dir Bradman Foundation 2001–. *Leisure interests:* rugby league, swimming and tennis. *Address:* Office of the Chancellor, Australian Catholic University, POB 968, North Sydney, NSW 2059, Australia (office).

FAHIM, Sulaiman Abdul Kareem Mohammad al-, MBA, PhD; United Arab Emirates business executive; *President and Chairman, Arab Union for Real Estate Development;* b. 1977, Dubai; m.; three c.; ed American Univ., Washington, DC, Kogod School of Business; Founder and CEO Hydra Properties (real estate co.) 2005–09; Pres. and Chair. Arab Union for Real Estate Devt 2009–; Rep., Abu Dhabi United Group for Devt and Investment (sovereign wealth fund), involved in takeover of Manchester City Football Club 2008; Chair. Portsmouth Football Club 2009–10; creator and host Hydra Executives (reality TV series) 2008–; Founder Intergovernmental Inst. for the use of Micro-algae Spirulina Against Malnutrition (IIMSAM) and IIMSAM's Amb. to the Kingdom of Spain; Dir Intergovernmental Renewable Energy Org. 2010, Royal Football Fund; Pres. UAE Chess Asscn; has been at the forefront of many green social housing initiatives in Saudi Arabia; Visionary Award, Middle East CEO magazine 2007, Gold Medal of Excellence, HM Tuanku Zainal Abidin (King of Malaysia) 2008. *Address:* Arab Union for Real Estate Development, 2 Alsiadla Buildings Smouha, Alexandria, Egypt (office). *Website:* sulaiman-al-fahim.blogspot.co.uk.

FAHRENSCON, Georg; German economist, politician and banking executive; *President, Deutscher Sparkassen- und Giroverband (German Savings Banks Association);* b. 8 Feb. 1968, Munich; m.; two c.; ed Univ. of Augsburg; involved in Youth Union (Jungen Union—JU) 1985–2003, including as mem. Fed. JU Germany, Dist Chair. Upper JU; mem. Christian Social Union (CSU) 1987–, Deputy Dist Chair. CSU, Munich-Land 1999–, Dist Treas. Upper Bavaria CSU 2003–, Deputy Chair. CSU Policy Comm. 2006–08, Chair. CSU (Econ.) 2008–; Councillor Neuried 1990–2002, Second Mayor of Neuried 2002; mem. Co. Council for Munich-Land 1996–; mem. Bundestag 2002–07; State Sec., Bavarian State Ministry of Finance 2007–08, Minister of Finance 2008–11; Pres. Deutscher Sparkassen- und Giroverband (German Savings Banks Asscn) 2012–; Chair. DekaBank Deutsche Girozentrale 2012–, Aufsichtsrates der Berliner Sparkasse 2012–, Deutschen Sparkassen Leasing Verwaltungs AG 2013–; Chair. Supervisory Bd Berlin Hyp AG 2013–; Vice-Pres. European Savings Banks Group 2012–; mem. Bd of Dirs KfW Bankengruppe 2012–, Landwirtschaftliche Rentenbank 2012–, Landesbank Hessen-Thüringen Girozentrale 2012–, Bundesverbandes Öffentlicher Banken 2012–; mem. Cen. Cttee of German Catholics 2004, Presidium of Ecumenical Church Congress, Munich 2010 2007, Sudeten Germans 2008; Founding mem. Soc. and mem. Bd of Trustees, air rescue 'Christoph 1' eV 2005. *Address:* Deutscher Sparkassen- und Giroverband (German Savings Banks Association), Charlottenstraße 47, 10117 Berlin, Germany (office). *Telephone:* (30) 202250 (office). *Website:* www.dsgv.de (office).

FAHRHOLZ, Bernd, LLB; German lawyer and banking executive; *Chairman of the Supervisory Board, Smartrac NV;* b. 4 Aug. 1947, Oldenburg, Lower Saxony; ed Univ. of Hamburg; joined Dresdner Bank as legal adviser 1977, with Domestic Corp. Customer Div. 1985–89, Man. Corp. Finance Div. 1989, later Co-Head, Int. Activities, Sr Gen. Man. 1996, Head of Global Finance, Investment Banking Div. 1997, mem. Bd of Man. Dirs 1998–2003, Chair. 2000–01, also Man. Dir Corp. Centre, Corp. Communications, Econs, Gen. Secr., Group Devt, Group Strategy, Human Resources and Legal Services, CEO 2000–03 (after acquisition of Dresdner Bank by Allianz AG forming Allianz-Dresdner AG); Partner, Dewey & LeBoeuf LLP (law firm), Frankfurt –2012; mem. Supervisory Bd Smartrac NV, Amsterdam 2009–, currently Chair.; mem. Supervisory Bd Fresenius Medical Care AG; mem. Advisory Council, Strategic Value Partners, LLC (SVP); Prof., Univ. of Frankfurt; mem. Frankfurt Bar Asscn; Hon. Prof., Johann Wolfgang Goethe Univ. 2002. *Address:* Supervisory Board, Smartrac NV, Strawinskylaan 851, 1077 XX, Amsterdam, The Netherlands (office). *Website:* www.smartrac-group.com (office).

FAHRNI, Fritz, PhD; Swiss academic and business executive; b. 7 Sept. 1942; m.; two d.; ed Swiss Fed. Inst. of Tech. (ETH), Zürich, Illinois Inst. of Tech., Chicago and Harvard Business School, USA; research worker, Ill. Inst. of Tech., NASA 1967–70; Team Leader, Research, Eng, Devt and Production Processes, CIBA-GEIGY 1971–76; Head, Research and Devt Gas Turbine Dept Sulzer Brothers 1976–80, Head, Gas Turbine Dept 1980–82, Head, Textile Machinery Group 1982–87, Pres. and CEO Sulzer Corpn 1988–99; Chair. Bd, Universität St Gallen, Institut für Technologiemanagement (ITEM-HSG) 1999–2007, Prof. of Practice in Tech. Man. and Entrepreneurship, ETH Zürich and Universität St Gallen 2000–07, now Prof. Emer.; Chair. LEM SA, Switzerland 1998–2004, u-blox Ltd 2008–14, INSYS Industriesysteme AG; mem. Bd of Dirs Univ. Hospital Balgrist; individual mem. Swiss Acad. of Technical Sciences; mem. Swiss Federal Counsel for Science and Technology 2000–12; Hon. mem. Swiss American Chamber of Commerce; Int. Entrepreneurial Leadership Award, Ill. Inst. of Tech. 2000; several times winner of 'Entrepreneur of the Month' and 'E of the Year' Awards, Switzerland. *Leisure interests:* sport, mountaineering, reading, music, garden. *Address:* Universität St Gallen, Institut für Technologiemanagement, Dufourstrasse 40A, 9000 St Gallen (office); ETH Zentrum, Kreuzplatz 5, 8032 Zürich, Switzerland (office). *Telephone:* (71) 224-73-00 (office); (44) 390-25-95 (home). *Fax:* (71) 224-73-01 (office). *E-mail:* fritz.fahrni@unisg.ch (office); ffahrni@ethz.ch (office). *Website:* www.item.unisg.ch (office).

FAINSILBER, Adrien, DPLG; French urban designer and fmr architect; b. 15 June 1932, Le Nouvion; s. of Sigismond Fainsilber and Fanny Moscovici; m. Julia Berg 1961; two s. one d.; ed Ecole Nationale Supérieure des Beaux Arts; architect, Univ. of Villetaneuse 1969–70, Univ. of Tech. of Compiègne 1973, Evry Hosp. 1980, La Géode, Parc de la Villette, Paris 1984, Cité of Science and Industry, Paris 1985, Water Treatment Plant, Valenton 1987, Museum of Beaux Arts, Clermont-Ferrand 1992, Town Hall, La Flèche 1994, HQ Unedic, Paris 1994, master plan and housing for Zac Richter, Port Marianne, Montpellier 1995, Montsouris Mutual Inst. Psychiatric Centre for Adolescents, Paris 1996, Museum of Modern and Contemporary Art, Strasbourg 1997, Children's Hosp., Purpan, Toulouse 1998, Courthouse Avignon 2000, Municipal Library, Marseille 2003, Extension, Water Treatment Plant, Valenton 2005, Obstetrical and Gynaecological Hospital, Lyon 2007; co. seat for Haut-Rhin 2004; mem. Int. Acad. of Architecture; Chevalier, Légion d'honneur 1987, Officier des Arts et des Lettres 1997; Bronze Medal, Soc. d'Encouragement à l'Art et à l'Industrie 1973, Silver Medal, Acad. of Architecture 1986, UIA Prix Auguste Perret 1990, Prix de Construction Metallique 2004. *Publications:* La Virtualité de l'Espace: Projets et Architecture 1962–1988, Adrien Fainsilber & Associés 1986–2002 by Christine Desmoulins. *Leisure interests:* swimming, travel. *Address:* 9 rue de Monttessuy, 75007 Paris, France. *Telephone:* 1-45-51-34-33. *E-mail:* adrienfainsilber@free.fr.

FAIRBANK, Richard (Rich) D., BEcons, MBA; American banking executive; *Chairman and CEO, Capital One Financial Corporation;* b. 18 Sept. 1950, Northampton, Mass; m.; eight c.; ed Stanford Univ., Stanford Grad. School of Business; consultant, Strategic Planning Assocs (later Mercer Management) 1981–87; Chair. and CEO Capital One Financial Corpn 1994–, Pres. 2003–; mem. US Region Bd of Dirs MasterCard 1995–2004 (Chair. 2002–04), mem. MasterCard International Global Bd of Dirs 2004–; Washingtonian Magazine Business Leader of the Year, Institutional Investor magazine Best CEO in specialty finance, American Banker magazine Banker of the Year Award 2006. *Address:* Capital One Financial Corporation, 1680 Capital One Drive, McLean, VA 22102-3407, USA (office). *Telephone:* (703) 720-1000 (office). *Fax:* (703) 720-2306 (office). *E-mail:* info@capitalone.com (office). *Website:* www.capitalone.com (office).

FAIREY, Michael (Mike) Edward, ACIB; British business executive; *Chairman, Hastings Group Holdings PLC;* b. 17 June 1948, Louth, Lincs.; s. of Douglas Fairey and Marjorie Fairey; m. Patricia Ann Dolby 1973; two s.; ed King Edward VI Grammar School; Asst Dir Watford Group, Barclays Bank 1967–86, Operations Dir Barclaycard 1986–88, Exec. Dir Barclays Card Services 1988–92; Dir Retail Credit and Group Credit Dir TSB Group 1992, Group Dir Credit Operations 1993–96, Information Tech. and Operations Dir 1996–97, Group Dir, Cen. Services, Lloyds TSB Group 1997–98, Deputy Group Chief Exec. 1998–2008 (retd); Chair. Vertex Data Science Ltd 2012–, OneSavings Bank PLC 2014–, Hastings Group Holdings PLC 2015–; Pres. British Quality Foundation; Chair. Race for Opportunity; mem. Bd of Dirs EST Holdings Ltd 2014–, Stonehaven UK Ltd 2014–; Trustee Consumer Credit Counselling Service. *Leisure interests:* tennis, opera, football. *Address:* Hastings Group, Conquest House, Collington Avenue, Bexhill-on-Sea, TN39 3LW, England (office); Churchfields House, Hitchin Road, Codicote, Herts., SG4 8TH, England (home). *Telephone:* (1438) 821710 (home). *Fax:* (1438) 821079 (home). *E-mail:* cosec@hastingsplc.com (office). *Website:* www.hastingsplc.com (office).

FAIRHEAD, Baroness (Life Peer), cr. 2017, of Yarm in the County of North Yorkshire; **Rona Alison Fairhead,** CBE, MA, MBA; British business executive and government official; *Minister of State, Department for International Trade;* b. (Rona Alison Haig), 28 Aug. 1961, Cumbria; m. Thomas Edwin Fairhead; three c.; ed Yarm Grammar School, Stockton-on-Tees, St Catharine's Coll., Cambridge, Harvard Business School, USA; worked for Bain & Co. 1983–87, Morgan Stanley 1988; sr exec. in aerospace industry, working for Bombardier/Shorts Aerospace and British Aerospace 1991–95; Exec. Vice-Pres. Strategy and Group Financial Control and mem. Exec. Bd, ICI PLC 1995–2001; Deputy Finance Dir, Pearson PLC 2001–02, Chief Financial Officer 2002–06, Chair. and Chief Exec. Financial Times Group 2006–13, also mem. Bd of Dirs, Pearson PLC and mem. Man. Cttee; Chair. Interactive Data Corpn 2007–10; non-exec. mem. Cabinet Office 2010–14 (resgnd); Chair. BBC Trust 2014–17; Minister of State, Dept of Int. Trade 2017–; Chair. (non-exec.) HSBC Northern America Holdings Inc., Dir (non-exec.), HSBC Holdings PLC 2004–16; Dir (non-exec.), PepsiCo, Inc. 2014–; UK Trade & Investment Business Amb. 2014–16. *Leisure interests:* flying (qualified pilot), scuba diving. *Address:* Department for International Trade, King Charles St, Whitehall, London, SW1A 2AH, England (office). *Telephone:* (20) 7215-5000 (office). *E-mail:* enquiries@trade.gsi.gov.uk (office). *Website:* www.gov.uk/government/organisations/department-for-international-trade (office).

FAIRUZ; Lebanese singer; b. (Nuhad Haddad), 21 Nov. 1935, Jabal Alarz; d. of Wadi Haddad and Liza Alboustani; m. Assi al-Rahbani 1954; two s. three d.; ed St Joseph School for Girls and Nat. Conservatory of Music, Beirut; also known as Fayrouz; started singing as mem. of chorus, then lead soloist, Lebanese Radio Station; early collaborations with brothers, Assi and Mansour al-Rahbani; first live appearance, the Baalbeck Int. Festival at Temple of Jupiter 1957; concerts and tours world-wide, including in USA, Canada, the Middle East, across Europe and in Mexico, Brazil, Argentina and Australia; has performed in numerous venues including the Royal Albert Hall, London 1962, Carnegie Hall, New York 1971, Shrine Auditorium, Los Angeles 1971, 1981, 2003, London Palladium 1978, L'Olympia de Paris 1979, Royal Festival Hall, London 1986, John F. Kennedy Center for the Performing Arts, Washington, DC 1981, 1987, amongst numerous others; Order of Merit 1962, Order of Cedars 1963, Order of Merit, First Class (Syria) 1967, Legion of Honour (Lebanon) 1970, Gold Medal of Honour (Jordan) 1975, Commdr, Ordre des Arts et des Lettres 1988, Chevalier, Légion d'honneur 1998; Dr hc (American Univ. of Beirut) 2005; Baalbeck Int. Festival Cavalier Medal 1957, Jerusalem Award 1997. *Films:* Biya al-Khawatim 1965, Safarbarlek 1966, Bint al-Harass 1967. *Recordings include:* over 80 album recordings include A Christmas Album, The Very Best of Fayrouz 1977, Fairuz sings Gibran, The Lady and the Legend 2005, Fayrouz: Live in Dubai 2008, Eh... fi amal 2010. *Website:* www.fairouz.com.

FAISAL, Ameen; Maldivian politician; *National Security Adviser;* b. 16 Jan. 1963; s. of Abdul Majeed Mahir and Ameena Ameen; grand-s. of Mohamed Ameen Didi, first Pres. of the Maldives; m. Aminath Mubarik; four c.; mem. Maldivian Democratic Party (MDP), mem. MDP Nat. Council and Pres. of MDP Malé Dhaairaa constituency 2007–08; arrested and detained for several weeks following Addu Boat Crisis Nov. 2006; arrested while attending funeral of Hussein Salah and detained in solitary confinement in Dhoonidhoo Prison April 2007; Shadow Defence Minister –2008; Minister of Defence and Nat. Security 2008–10; Nat. Security Adviser 2010–; Chair. Nat. Crime Prevention Cttee. *Address:* Ministry of Defence and National Security, Ameer Ahmed Magu, Malé 20-126, Maldives (office). *Telephone:* 3322601 (office). *Fax:* 3325525 (office). *E-mail:* admin@defence.gov.mv (office). *Website:* www.defence.gov.mv (office).

FAITHFULL, Marianne; British singer; b. 29 Dec. 1946, Ormskirk, Lancs.; d. of Glynn Faithfull and Eva Faithfull; m. 1st John Dunbar; one s.; m. 2nd Ben Brierley; m. 3rd Giorgio della Terza; made first recording (As Tears Go By) aged 17; Commdr, Ordre des Arts et des Lettres 2011. *Films:* I'll Never Forget Whatsisname 1967, Girl on a Motorcycle 1968, Hamlet 1969, Lucifer Rising 1972, Ghost Story 1974, Assault on Agathon 1975, When Pigs Fly 1993, The Turn of the Screw 1994, Shopping 1994, Moondance 1995, Crimetime 1996, Intimacy 2001, Far From China 2001, Alone in the Dark 2003, A Letter to True 2003, Nord-Plage 2004, Paris, je t'aime 2006, Marie Antoinette 2006, Irina Palm 2007. *Television:* Anna 1967, The Door of Opportunity 1970, The Stronger 1971, Who Do You Think You Are? 2012. *Stage appearances:* Three Sisters (London) 1967, Seven Deadly Sins (St Ann's Cathedral, New York) 1990, The Threepenny Opera (Gate Theatre, Dublin) 1992, The Seven Deadly Sins (Landestheatre, Linz) 2012. *Recordings include:* albums: Come My Way 1965, Marianne Faithfull 1965, Go Away From My World 1966, North Country Maid 1966, Faithfull Forever 1966, Love in a Mist 1967, Dreaming My Dreams 1977, Faithless (with the Grease Band) 1978, Broken English 1979, Dangerous Acquaintances 1981, A Child's Adventure 1983, Summer Nights 1984, Music for the Millions 1985, Strange Weather 1987, Rich Kid Blues 1988, Blazing Away 1990, A Secret Life 1995, 20th Century Blues 1997, The Seven Deadly Sins 1998, Vagabond Ways 1999, Stranger On Earth 2001, Kissin' Time 2002, Before the Poison 2004, Live In Hollywood 2005, Live At The BBC 2008, Easy Come Easy Go 2009, Horses And High Heels 2012, Give My Love To London 2014, No Exit 2016. *Publications:* Faithfull (autobiog.) 1994, Marianne Faithfull Diaries 2002. *E-mail:* assistante@mac.com (office). *Website:* www.mariannefaithfull.org.uk.

FAIVRE d'ARCIER, Bernard, LèsL; French civil servant and culture consultant; *CEO, BFA-Conseil;* b. 12 July 1944, Albertville; s. of Guy Faivre d'Arcier and Geneviève Teilhard de Chazelles; m. 1st Sylvie Dumont 1966; one s.; m. 2nd Madeleine Lévy 1991; m. 3rd Ophélie Orecchia 2012; ed Hautes études commerciales, Inst. d'études politiques and Ecole nat. d'admin; Civil Admin., Ministry of Culture 1972–79; Dir Festival d'Avignon 1979–84, Artistic Dir 1992–2003; Tech. Adviser to the Prime Minister's Cabinet 1984–86; Pres. la SEPT (TV Channel) 1986; Consultant, UNESCO 1987–88; Adviser to the Pres. of the Nat. Ass. 1988; Head of Dept of Theatre, Ministry of Educ. and Culture 1992–; Dir Nat. Centre for Theatre 1992; CEO BFA-Conseil (man. consultants); Commdr des Arts et des Lettres; Officier, Ordre nat. du Mérite, Légion d'honneur. *Leisure interests:* art, theatre. *Address:* 27 rue Michel Le Comte, 75003 Paris, France. *Telephone:* 1-72-76-42-11. *E-mail:* bernard.faivre-darcier@orange.fr.

FAIZASYAH, Teuku, PhD; Indonesian diplomatist; *Ambassador to Canada;* m.; three c.; ed Padjadjaran Univ., Univ. of Birmingham, UK, Univ. of Waikato, New Zealand; joined Ministry of Foreign Affairs 1990, served in various positions, including as Deputy Dir for Political, Social and Security Issues, Office of the Foreign Minister 2003–04, Section Chief of Econ. Data, Agency of Research and Devt 1998–2000, Section Chief, ASEAN's Tourism Devt, ASEAN Econ. Bureau 1994–95, staff mem., Directorate for American Affairs 1991–92, Head of Secr. of Presidential Advisors and Special Envoys 2003–04, staff mem., Econ. Section, Embassy in Washington, DC 1995–98, Political Counsellor and Head of Chancery, Embassy in Pretoria 2004–08, Chief of Staff, Office of the Foreign Minister and Spokesperson of Ministry of Foreign Affairs 2008–10, Special Staff for Int. Affairs (Foreign Policy Advisor) to Pres. Yudhoyono and Presidential Spokesperson for Int. Relations 2010–14, Amb. to Canada and Perm. Rep. to ICAO, Montreal 2014–. *Publications:* several opinion articles in Indonesian nat. media, including the Jakarta Post and Kompas. *Address:* Embassy of Indonesia, 55 Parkdale Avenue, Ottawa, ON K1Y 1E5, Canada (office). *Telephone:* (613) 724-1100 (office). *Fax:* (613) 724-1105 (office). *E-mail:* info@indonesia-ottawa.org (office). *Website:* www.indonesia-ottawa.org (office).

FAIZULLAEV, Alisher, (Alisher Faiz), PhD, DSc; Uzbekistani diplomatist and social and political scientist; *Director of Negotiation Laboratory and Professor, Department of Practical Diplomacy, University of World Economy and Diplomacy;* b. 10 Jan. 1957, Tashkent; s. of Omonulla Faizullaev and Nasiba Ashrapkhanova; m. Shakhnoz Faizullaeva; two s. two d.; ed Tashkent State Univ. and Inst. of Psychology, USSR Acad. of Sciences, Moscow; Lecturer, Uzbekistan Acad. of Sciences, Tashkent 1979–80, Sr Lecturer 1983–86; Visiting Fellow, Inst. of Psychology, USSR Acad. of Sciences 1986–87; Sr Lecturer, Tashkent State Univ. 1987–88; Head of Dept, Exec. Training Inst., Tashkent 1988–91; Intern, City Council of San Diego, CA 1989; Head of Dept, Inst. of Political Sciences and Man., Tashkent 1991–92; Distinguished Visiting Scholar, Western Washington Univ., Bellingham, USA 1992; Dir Inst. of Man., Univ. of World Economy and Diplomacy, Tashkent 1992–93, First Vice-Rector 2003–05, currently Dir of Negotiation Laboratory and Prof., Dept of Practical Diplomacy; Consultant on Political Affairs, then Chief Consultant on Int. Affairs and Foreign Econ. Relations, Office of the Pres. of Uzbekistan 1993–94; Deputy Minister of Foreign Affairs 1994–95; Amb. to Belgium and Head of Missions to EU and Euro-Atlantic Partnership Council/NATO 1995–98, concurrently Amb. to the Netherlands and Luxembourg with residence in Brussels 1997–98; State Adviser to Pres. of Uzbekistan on Int. Affairs and Foreign Econ. Relations 1998–99; First Deputy Minister of Foreign Affairs Feb.–Dec. 1999; Amb. to UK 1999–2003; Visiting Scholar, Centre of Int. Studies and Visiting Fellow, New Hall Coll., Cambridge 2005, Jesus Coll., Cambridge 2007; Fulbright Scholar, Fletcher School of Law and Diplomacy, Tufts Univ. and Inst. for the Study of Diplomacy, School of Foreign Service, Georgetown Univ. 2011–12; Visiting Scholar, McGill Univ., Canada 2014; USSR Young Social Scientists Prize 1987. *Publications:* Motivational Self-Regulation of Personality (in Russian) 1987, Human Being, Politics, Management (in Russian and Uzbek) 1995, Tabula rasa (short stories in Russian) 2004, Krugovorot (short stories in Russian) 2006, Diplomatic Negotiations (in Russian) 2007, As Power to Power: Politics of Interpersonal Relations (in Russian) 2010; numerous articles on behavioural, social and political sciences in academic journals. *Leisure interests:* tennis, fencing, Tai Chi. *Address:* University of World Economy and Diplomacy, 54 Buyuk Ipak Yuli, Tashkent 100113, Uzbekistan (office). *Telephone:* (71) 2676769 (office). *Fax:* (71) 2670900 (office). *E-mail:* alisher@faizullaev.com (home). *Website:* www.uwed.uz (office); www.faizullaev.com.

FAKHFAKH, Elyès; Tunisian engineer and politician; b. 1972, Tunis; ed Institut Nat. des Sciences Appliquées, Lyon, France; began career as engineer with Total France (petroleum co.), worked in Europe, USA and Asia, becoming Dir of new Total industrial plant in Poland 2004–06; fmr Deputy Dir Gen. Cortrel (Tunisian automotive parts mfr); Minister of Tourism 2011–12, of Finance 2012–14; mem. Forum démocratique pour le travail et les libertés (Ettakatol). *Address:* c/o Ministry of Finance, pl. du Gouvernement, La Kasbah, 1008 Tunis, Tunisia (office).

FAKI MAHAMAT, Moussa; Chadian politician; *Chairman, African Union Commission;* b. 21 June 1960, Biltine; early career as Prof. of Law, Chad Univ.; Dir-Gen. Nat. Sugar Soc. 1996–99; Minister of Transport and Public Works 2002; Prime Minister of Chad 2003–05; Minister of External Relations and African Integration 2008–17; Chair. African Union Comm. 2017–; mem. Patriotic Salvation Movement. *Address:* Commission of the African Union, Roosevelt Street, Old Airport Area, POB 3243, Addis Ababa, Ethiopia (office). *Telephone:* (11) 5517700 (office). *Fax:* (11) 5517844 (office). *E-mail:* webmaster@africa-union.org (office). *Website:* www.au.int (office).

FAKUDZE, Mtiti, BAgr; Swazi politician; ed Univ. of Swaziland; mem. House of Ass. (Parl.) for Dvokodvweni constituency; Minister of Agric. and Co-operatives 2003–08, of Public Service and Information 2008–11, of Foreign Affairs 2011–13; currently mem. Ludzidzini Council. *Address:* Ludzidzini Council, Mbabane, Eswatini (office).

FALCO, Edith (Edie); American actress; b. 5 July 1963, Brooklyn, New York; d. of Frank Falco and Judith Loney; one adopted s.; ed State Univ. of New York at Purchase. *Television includes:* The Sunshine Boys (film) 1995, Oz (series) 1997–99; The Sopranos (series – Emmy Award for Outstanding Lead Actress in A Drama Series 2000, 2003, Golden Globe Award for Best Performance by an Actress in a Drama Series 2000, SAG Award for Outstanding Performance by a Female Actor in a Drama Series 2000, 2008) 1999–2007, Jenifer (film) 2001, Fargo (film) 2003, 30 Rock 2007–08, Nurse Jackie 2009–15. *Films include:* The Unbelievable Truth 1989, Trust 1990, Laws of Gravity 1992, Time Expired 1992, Bullets Over Broadway 1994, Rift 1995, The Addition 1995, Breathing Room 1996, Hurricane

1997, Private Parts 1997, Cop Land 1997, Trouble on the Corner 1997, Cost of Living 1997, A Price above Rubies 1998, Judy Berlin 1999, Stringer 1999, Random Hearts 1999, Overnight Sensation 2000, Death of a Dog 2000, Sunshine State 2002, Family of the Year 2004, The Girl from Monday 2005, The Great New Wonderful 2005, The Quiet 2005, Freedomland 2006, Three Backyards 2009. *Plays:* 'night, Mother 2005. *Address:* c/o ICM, 10250 Constellation Boulevard, Los Angeles, CA 90067, USA (office).

FALCO, Randel (Randy) E., BBA, MBA; American media executive; *President and CEO, Univision Communications Inc.;* b. 26 Dec. 1953, Bronx, New York; m. Susan Falco; three c.; ed Iona Coll.; joined NBC 1975, several positions in Finance, Tech. Operations, Corp. Strategic Planning, Vice-Pres. Finance and Admin, NBC Sports 1986–91, Pres. Broadcast and Network Operations Div., NBC 1993–98, COO Olympics, Barcelona Olympics 1992, Atlanta Olympics 1996, Sydney Olympics 2000, Salt Lake City Olympics 2002, Pres. NBC TV Network 1998–2003, Group Pres. 2003–04, Pres. NBC Universal TV Networks Group 2004–06; Chair. and CEO AOL LLC (div. of Time Warner) 2006–09; Exec. Vice-Pres. and COO, Univision Communications Inc. Jan.–June 2011, Pres. and CEO 2011–; mem. Bd of Dirs Ronald McDonald House; mem. Advisory Bd Nat. Museum of American History; Dr hc (Iona Coll.) 2001; six Emmy Awards; MS Hope Award, Nat. Multiple Sclerosis Soc. 2013, Bd of Trustees' Award, Nat. Acad. of TV Arts and Sciences 2013, inducted into Broadcasting & Cable Hall of Fame 2013, Champion Award, KIND 2015, Civic Inspiration Award, Ballet Hispanico. *Address:* Univision Communications Inc., 5999 Center Drive, Los Angeles, CA 90045, USA (office). *Telephone:* (310) 348-3434 (office). *Website:* www.corporate.univision.com (office).

FALCONE, Jean-Marc, MA; French police officer and government official; *Director-General of the National Police;* b. 1 June 1953, Algiers, Algeria; ed École nationale supérieure de la police; began career as a police officer stationed at Lille 1979–83, then at Grenoble 1983–86, Head of Gen. Security, Dept of Urban Police Fort-de-France 1986–90, promoted within body of sub-prefects, Dir Office of the Prefect of the Territoire de Belfort 1990, Prefect of Cher 1991, Sec.-Gen., Pref. of Landes 1994, Chief of Staff of Prefect of Rhône-Alpes region 1996, Chief of Staff to Sec. of State for Overseas 1997–98, Sec.-Gen., Pref. of Réunion 1998–2000, Sub-prefect of Pointe-à-Pitre 2000–01, Deputy Chief of Staff, State Secr. for Overseas 2001–03, Sub-prefect of Saint-Nazaire 2003–06, Deputy to Alain Juillet responsible for econ. intelligence 2006–08, Prefect delegate for Security and Defence in Bordeaux 2008–10, Dir of Foresight and Planning of Nat. Security, Gen. Secr. of the Ministry of the Interior 2010–11, Special Asst to Sec.-Gen. of Ministry of the Interior, Overseas, Local Authorities and Immigration Sept.–Oct. 2011, Prefect of Tarn 2011–12, Adviser for Internal and Overseas Affairs to the Prime Minister 2012–14, Dir-Gen. Nat. Police 2014–; Chevalier, Légion d'honneur, Ordre nat. du Mérite, Ordre du Mérite agricole. *Address:* Directorate General of the National Police, Ministry of the Interior, place Beauvau, 75008 Paris (office). *Telephone:* 1-49-27-49-27 (office). *Fax:* 1-43-59-89-50 (office). *E-mail:* sirp@interieur.gouv.fr (office). *Website:* www.interieur.gouv.fr (office); www.police-nationale.interieur.gouv.fr (office).

FALCONER OF THOROTON, Baron (Life Peer), cr. 1997, in the County of Nottinghamshire; **Rt Hon. Charles Leslie Falconer,** PC, QC; British lawyer and politician; b. 19 Nov. 1951; s. of John Falconer and Anne Falconer; m. Marianna Hildyard 1985; three s. one d.; ed Trinity Coll., Glenalmond, Queen's Coll., Cambridge; called to the Bar 1974, took silk 1991; mem. (Labour), House of Lords 1997–; Solicitor-Gen. 1997–98; Minister of State Cabinet Office 1998–2001; Minister with responsibility for Millennium Dome 1998–2001; Minister of State for Housing and Planning 2001, for the Criminal Justice System 2002–03; Lord Chancellor 2003–07; also Sec. of State for Justice May–June 2007; Shadow Spokesperson (Justice) 2010–12; Shadow Spokesperson (Constitutional and Deputy Priministerial Issues) (Justice) 2011–15; Shadow Lord Chancellor and Shadow Sec. of State for Justice 2015–16; Chair. John Smith Memorial Trust 2007–, Amicus Horizon Housing Group 2008–, Chair. Ravensbourne Coll. 2011–, Comm. on Assisted Dying 2012–; Visitor Queens Coll., Cambridge 2008–; Trustee, Roy Castle Lung Cancer Foundation 2007–. *Address:* House of Lords, Westminster, London, SW1A 0PW, England (office). *Telephone:* (20) 7219-5353 (office). *Fax:* (20) 7219-5979 (office). *E-mail:* contactholmember@parliament.uk (office). *Website:* www.parliament.uk/biographies/lords/lord-falconer-of-thoroton/2758 (office).

FALCONES JAQUOTOT, Baldomero, MBA; Spanish business executive; b. 1946, Majorca; ed Universidad Politécnica de Madrid, Univ. of Navarra; fmr Gen. Man. and mem. Exec. Cttee and CEO, Banco Santander Central Hispano; mem. Bd of Dirs MasterCard International Worldwide 1997–2007, Vice-Chair. 2001–03, Chair. 2003–07; Founding Pnr, Magnum Industrial Partners 2007; Exec. Vice-Chair. and CEO Fomento de Construcciones y Contratas (FCC) SA 2007–08, Chair. and Man. Dir 2008; Co-founder Fomento y Expansión Empresarial (pvt. equity firm) 2013; mem. Bd of Dirs Unión Fenosa, Renta Corpn 2016–; mem. Advisory Bd Montana Capital Partners; Counsellor, APD; Chair. Plan Foundation; mem. Econ. Cttee, Fundación Albéniz. *Address:* Fomento y Expansion Empresarial Scr de Regimen Simplificado SA, Calle Apolonio Morales 21, Madrid 28036, Spain (office).

FALCONÍ BENÍTEZ, Fander, MSc, PhD; Ecuadorean economist, academic and politician; b. 19 Sept. 1962, Quito; ed Pontifical Catholic Univ. of Ecuador, Latin-American Faculty of Social Sciences, Autonomous Univ. of Barcelona; econs ed. for Punto de Vista newspaper 1987–91; econs analyst for Hoy newspaper 1987–89; adviser to Nat. Energy Inst. 1989–91; Tech. Asst Dept of Energy Planning and Dept for Subregional Andean Oil Integration Project, Latin American Energy Org. 1991–93; researcher, Ecuador Chamber of Commerce and Industry, Germany 1993–96; consultant to Petróleos del Ecuador SA 1995; Financial Man. Petróleos y Servicios 1995–96; Presidential adviser to Nat. Telecommunications Council 1996; UNDP adviser, Ministry of the Environment 2001; adviser to Fundación Natura 2001–02; Prof., Latin-American Faculty of Social Sciences (FLASCO) 2001–; Prof. of Agricultural Econs and Rural Devt, Central Univ. of Ecuador 2001–04; Prof., Nat. Polytechnic School 2002–04; Nat. Sec. for Planning and Devt 2007–08; Minister of External Relations, Trade and Integration 2008–10 (resgnd); Owner, Senplades 2011–13; Visiting Prof., San Simón Univ. 2003, Centro Bartolomé de las Casas 2004, Univ. of Guadalajara, Mexico 2004. *Website:* www.fanderfalconi.com.

FALDO, Sir Nicholas (Nick) Alexander, Kt, MBE; British professional golfer, golf course designer and television commentator; b. 18 July 1957, Welwyn Garden City, Herts.; m. 1st Melanie Rockall 1979 (divorced 1984); m. 2nd Gill Bennett 1986 (divorced 1998); one s. two d.; m. 3rd Valerie Bercher 2001 (divorced 2006); one d.; ed Sir Francis Osborne School, Welwyn Garden City; won England Boys' Int. 1974, England Youth Int. 1975, Herts. Co. Championship, Berkshire Trophy, Scrutton Jug, S African Golf Union Special Stroke Championship, was Co. Champion of Champions, mem. GB Commonwealth team, Sr England Int. 1975–; became professional 1976; won Skol Lager Int., Rookie of the Year (Best British Newcomer) 1977, Colgate PGA Championship 1978, 1980, 1981, five titles on PGA European Tour, Golf Writers' Asscn Trophy and Harry Vardon Trophy 1983, Open Championship, Muirfield 1987, French Open and Volvo Masters, Valderrama 1988, Masters, Augusta, Ga, USA 1989, French Open 1989, US Masters 1989, 1990, 1996, Open Championship, St Andrew's 1990, Irish Open 1991, 1992, 1993, Open Championship, Muirfield 1992, Toyota World Match Play Championship 1992, Scandinavian Masters 1992, European Open 1992, Johnnie Walker World Championship 1992, (seven tournament victories 1992), Alfred Dunhill Belgian Open 1994, Doral Ryder Open, USA 1995; World No. 1 1992–94, Johnnie Walker Asian Classic 1993, Los Angeles Open, USA 1997, World Cup 1998; named Capt. European Ryder Cup team beginning 2008; involved in Faldo Design, an int. golf course architectural co. 1991–; lead analyst for Golf Channel and CBS TV PGA tour coverage; joined BBC Sport for coverage of Open Championship 2012; BBC Sports Personality of the Year 1989, PGA Award for Outstanding Services to Golf 2003, Payne Stewart Award 2014. *Publications include:* In Search of Perfection (with Bruce Critchley) 1995, Faldo – A Swing for Life 1995, Life Swings: The Autobiography 2004. *Leisure interests:* fly fishing, helicopter flying, golf course design. *Address:* Faldo Enterprises, 19 Russell Street, Windsor, SL4 1HQ, England (office). *Telephone:* (1753) 829711 (office). *Fax:* (1753) 829712 (office). *E-mail:* info@nickfaldo.com (office). *Website:* www.nickfaldo.com (office).

FALIH, Khalid A. al-, BS, MBA; Saudi Arabian business executive and government official; *Minister of Petroleum and Mineral Resources;* b. 1960, Riyadh; m. Dr Najah Al-Garawi; two s. three d.; ed Texas A&M Univ., USA, King Fahd Univ. of Petroleum and Mineral Resources, Dhahran; joined Saudi Arabian Oil Co. (Saudi Aramco, fmrly Aramco) 1979, held various man. positions including Pres. Petron Corpn (jt venture with Philippine Nat. Oil Co.) 1999, Sr Vice-Pres. of Gas Operations and Industrial Relations, Head of New Business Devt 2003, Dir Aramco 2004–, Exec. Vice-Pres. for Operations 2007–08, Pres. and CEO Saudi Aramco 2009–15; Minister of Health 2015–16, of Petroleum and Mineral Resources 2016–; fmr Chair. South Rub' al-Khali (exploration co.), Dammam City Municipal Council; Dir Saudi Nat. Program for Devt of Industrial Clusters; mem. Saudi Arabian Supreme Council of Petroleum and Mineral Affairs, American Soc. of Mechanical Engineers, Int. Asscn for Energy Econs, Oxford Energy Policy Club; mem. Bd of Dirs US-Saudi Arabian Business Council; mem. Asia Business Council, JP Morgan International Council; Founding mem. Bd of Trustees, King Abdullah Univ. of Science and Tech. 2008–. *Address:* Ministry of Petroleum and Mineral Resources, PO Box 247, Al Ma'ather Street, Riyadh 11191, Saudi Arabia (office). *Telephone:* (1) 478-7777 (office). *Fax:* (1) 479-3596 (office). *E-mail:* info@mopm.gov.sa (office). *Website:* www.mopm.gov.sa (office).

FALK, Thomas J., BCom, MSc; American business executive; *Chairman and CEO, Kimberly-Clark Corporation;* b. 1958, Waterloo, Ia; m. Karen Falk; one s.; ed Univ. of Wisconsin, Stanford Univ. Grad. School of Business; accountant, Alexander Grant & Co. 1980–83; joined Audit Dept, Kimberly-Clark Corpn 1983, various man. positions, including Sr Auditor 1984, Sr Financial Analyst 1986, Dir of Corp. Strategy Analysis 1987, Operations Man. for Infant Care, Beech Island, SC 1989, Vice-Pres. Operations Analysis and Control 1990, Sr Vice-Pres. of Analysis and Admin 1991–93, Group Pres., Infant and Child Care 1993–95, Group Pres. N America Consumer Products 1995–98, Group Pres. Global Tissue and Paper 1998–99, COO 1999, Pres. 1999–2002, Dir 1999–2002, CEO 2002–, Chair. 2003–; mem. Bd of Dirs Lockheed Martin, Catalyst, Univ. of Wisconsin Foundation, Centex Corpn; mem., Dallas Regional Advisory Bd, JP Morgan Chase; Nat. Gov. Boys and Girls Clubs of America; Distinguished Accounting Alumnus, Dept of Accounting and Information Systems, Univ. of Wisconsin 2002, Patrick Henry Award, Nat. Guard Asscn of US 2003. *Address:* Kimberly-Clark Corpn, 351 Phelps Drive, Irving, TX 75038, USA (office). *Telephone:* (972) 281-1200 (office). *Fax:* (972) 281-1490 (office). *E-mail:* info@kimberly-clark.com (office). *Website:* www.kimberly-clark.com (office).

FALKENGREN, Annika; Swedish business executive; *President and Group CEO, SEB AB;* b. (Annika Bolin), m.; one c.; ed Univ. of Stockholm; joined SEB (Skandinaviska Enskilda Banken) AB as trainee in Stockholm br. 1987, Head, Corp. & Insts Div. 2001–05, Deputy CEO SEB AB 2005, Pres. and Group CEO 2005–; mem. Bd of Dirs Securitas AB 2003–; mem. Supervisory Bd Volkswagen Group 2011–. *Leisure interests:* golf, reading. *Address:* SEB AB, Kungsträdgårdsg 8, 106 40 Stockholm, Sweden (office). *Telephone:* (771) 62-10-00 (office). *E-mail:* seb@seb.se (office). *Website:* www.seb.se (office).

FALKINGHAM, Jane Cecelia, OBE, PhD; British social scientist and academic; *Professor of Demography and International Social Policy, University of Southampton;* Researcher/Lecturer/Reader, Dept of Social Policy, LSE 1986–2002, Dir ESRC SAGE Research Group 1999–2003; Prof. of Demography, Univ. of Southampton 2002–, later Deputy Head of Social Sciences and Assoc. Dean of the fmr Faculty of Law, Arts and Social Sciences, Dir ESRC Centre for Population Change 2009–, Dean, Faculty of Social and Human Sciences 2014–. *Publications:* several book chapters and more than 150 papers in professional journals. *Address:* Room 32/1027, Social Statistics & Demography, Social Sciences, University of Southampton, Southampton, SO17 1BJ, England (office). *Telephone:* (23) 8059-3192 (office); (23) 8059-3399 (office). *E-mail:* j.c.falkingham@soton.ac.uk (office). *Website:* www.southampton.ac.uk/demography (office); www.cpc.ac.uk (office).

FALL, Sir Brian James Proetel, GCVO, KCMG, MA, LLM; British diplomatist (retd); b. 13 Dec. 1937, London; s. of John William Fall and Edith Juliette Fall (née Proetel); m. Delmar Alexandra Roos 1962; three d.; ed St Paul's School, Magdalen Coll. Oxford, Univ. of Michigan Law School, USA; joined HM Foreign (now Diplomatic) Service 1962, UN Dept, Foreign Office 1963, Moscow 1965, Geneva 1968, Civil Service Coll. 1970, Eastern European and Soviet Dept and Western Orgs Dept, Foreign Office 1971, New York 1975, Harvard Univ. Center for Int.

Affairs 1976, Counsellor, Embassy in Moscow 1977–79, Head of Energy, Science and Space Dept, FCO 1979–80, Head of Eastern European and Soviet Dept, FCO 1980–81, Prin. Pvt. Sec. to Sec. of State for Foreign and Commonwealth Affairs 1981–84, Dir Cabinet Sec.-Gen. of NATO 1984–86, Asst Under-Sec. of State (Defence), FCO 1986–88, Minister, Embassy in Washington, DC 1988–89, High Commr to Canada 1989–92; Amb. to Russia (also accred to several mems of CIS) 1992–95; Prin. Lady Margaret Hall, Oxford 1995–2002; British Govt Special Rep. for S Caucasus 2002–12; Chair. MC Russian Market Fund 1996–2002; Adviser, Rio Tinto 1996–2012; Gov. St Mary's School, Calne 1996–2006; Hon. Fellow, Lady Margaret Hall 2002; Hon. LLD (York Univ., Toronto) 2002. *Leisure interest:* France. *Address:* 2 St Helena Terrace, Richmond, TW9 1NR, England (home).

FALL, Cheikh Ibrahima, MSc (Econ), MBA; Senegalese international civil servant and banker; b. 1 Oct. 1947, Louga; m. Marième Diouma Faye 1972; two s. one d.; financial analyst, Operations Dept Banque Ouest-Africaine de Développement (BOAD) 1978–79, Rural Devt and Infrastructural Operations Dept 1979–81, Officer-in-Charge of Dept 1981, Dir of Dept 1981–85, Dir Loans and Equity Dept 1985–86; Dir Office of Pres. of African Devt Bank (ADB) 1986–92, Dir Co. Programmes, S Region Dept 1992–95, Officer-in-Charge of Admin. and Gen. Services and ADB restructuring exercise 1995–96, Sec.-Gen. ADB 1996–99, 2004–06; Vice-Pres. and Corp. Sec., World Bank 1999–2004. *Leisure interests:* music, golf, reading.

FALL, François Louncény, LLM; Guinean politician and diplomatist; *Special Representative for Central Africa and Head of UN Regional Office of Central Africa;* b. 21 April 1949; m.; four c.; ed Univ. of Conakry; Asst Prof., Faculty of Law, Univ. of Conakry 1977–79; First Counsellor, Embassy in Cairo 1982–85, Abuja 1985–89, Paris 1989–90, Mission to UN, New York 1990–93; Head, Div. of Consular Affairs, Ministry of Foreign Affairs 1993, Deputy Dir of Legal and Consular Affairs 1995–96, Dir 1996–2000; Perm. Rep. to UN, New York 2000–02, Vice-Pres. 55th Session of UN Gen. Ass. 2000; Minister at the Presidency, in charge of Foreign Affairs 2002–04, Del. to UN Security Council during debate over US mil. action in Iraq, acted as Pres. of UN Security Council March 2003; Prime Minister Feb.–April 2004 (resgnd); mem. UN Cttee for the Elimination of Racial Discrimination 2000–02, Econ. Community of West African States (ECOWAS) Ministerial Cttee for Security and Mediation 2002–04; UN Sec.-Gen.'s Special Rep. for Somalia and Head of UN Political Office for Somalia (UNPOS), Nairobi, Kenya 2005–07, Special Rep. for Cen. African Repub. (CAR) and Head of UN Peacebuilding Office in CAR (BONUCA—Bureau de l'Organisation des Nations Unies en République Centrafricaine) 2007–09, Special Rep. for Cen. Africa and Head of UN Regional Office for Central Africa (UNOCA) 2017–; Minister of Foreign Affairs and Guineans Abroad 2012–16; Vice-Chair. Comm. for Monitoring and Evaluation of South Sudan Peace Agreement Jan.–Oct. 2016. *Address:* United Nations Regional Office for Central Africa, BP 23773, Cité de la Démocratie, Villas 55–57, Libreville, Gabon (office). *Telephone:* (241) 741-401 (office). *Fax:* (241) 741-402 (office). *Website:* unoca.unmissions.org (office).

FALL, Ibrahima D., LLM, PhD; Senegalese international organization official, politician and academic; b. 1942, Tivaouane, Thies; s. of Momar Khoudia Fall and Seynabou (Diakhate) Fall; m. Déguène Fall; five c.; ed Univ. of Dakar, Inst. of Political Science, Paris, Faculty of Law, Univ. of Paris, Acad. of Int. Law, The Hague, Netherlands; Prof. of Int. Law and Int. Relations, Cheikh Anta Diop Univ., Dakar 1972–81, Dean of Faculty of Law 1975–81; Minister of Higher Educ. 1983–84, of Foreign Affairs 1984–90; Adviser, Supreme Court of Senegal; Asst Sec.-Gen. for Human Rights and Dir UN Centre for Human Rights, Geneva 1992–97; Sec.-Gen. UN World Conf. on Human Rights, Vienna 1993; Asst Gen. Sec. UN Dept of Political Affairs 1997–2000, Special Envoy of UN Sec.-Gen. to Côte d'Ivoire 2000–02, Special Rep. for the Great Lakes Region 2002–08; Special Envoy of the Pres. of the Comm. of the African Union for Guinea 2008–10; fmr Resident Co-ordinator and Resident Rep., Deputy Special Rep. of UN Sec.-Gen. and UNDP Humanitarian Coordinator for Burundi, Bujumbura; consultant, UNESCO; Founding-mem. and Hon. Pres. Senegalese Asscn for African Unity; mem. African Council for Higher Educ.; unsuccessful candidate in 2012 Senegalese presidential election; Hon. Pres. Int. Acad. of Constitutional Law; Dr hc (Univ. of Picardie, France), (Univ. of Fort Hare, South Africa). *Publications:* articles on int. public law, constitutional law and political science in professional journals. *Address:* Sicap Fenêtre Mermoz, Dakar, Senegal (home). *E-mail:* fall5@un.org (office).

FALLAS VENEGAS, Helio; Costa Rican economist and politician; b. 1947, San Sebastián; s. of Helio Fallas Jiménez; m. Nuria Más; three c.; ed Univ. of Costa Rica, Univ. of the Andes; Minister of Planning 1990–94, of Housing 2002–05, Vice-Pres. 2014–18, Minister of Finance 2014–18; Prof. of Econs, Univ. of the Andes 1991–2011; independent econ. consultant 1991–2011; regular contribs to El País, La Nación, La Tribuna Democrática and other Central American newspapers; fmr mem. Social Christian Unity Party (PUSC); currently mem. Citizens' Action Party (PAC). *Address:* c/o Ministry of Finance, Edif. Antigüo Banco Anglo, Avda 2A, Calle 3A, San José, Costa Rica (office).

FALLIN, Mary, BS; American politician and fmr state governor; b. 9 Dec. 1954, Warrensburg, Mo.; d. of Joseph Newton Copeland and Mary Jo Copeland (née Duggan); m. 1st; one s. one d.; m. 2nd Wade Christensen; four c.; ed Tecumseh High School, Oklahoma Baptist Univ., Shawnee, Univ. of Cen. Oklahoma, Edmond, Oklahoma State Univ.; business man., Oklahoma Dept of Securities, Oklahoma City 1979–81; State Travel Coordinator, Oklahoma Dept of Tourism 1981–82; sales rep., Associated Petroleum 1982–83; Marketing Dir, Brian Head Hotel & Ski Resort, UT 1983–84; Dir of Sales, Residence Inn Hotel, Oklahoma City 1984–87; Dist Man., Lexington Hotel Suites 1988–90; Real Estate Assoc., Pippin Properties, Inc. 1990–94; mem. Oklahoma House of Reps 1990–94; Lt Gov. of Okla (first Republican and first woman) 1995–2007; mem. US House of Reps for 5th Congressional Dist of Okla 2007–11; Gov. of Okla (first woman) 2011–19; Chair. Nat. Governors Asscn 2013–14; fmr Chair. Nat. Conf. of Lt Govs; mem. and del., Oklahoma Fed. of Republican Women; mem. American Legis. Exchange Council, Nat. Conf. of State Legislatures; fmr mem. Bd United Way of Oklahoma City, YWCA; mem. Advisory Bd Trail of Tears; fmr Co-Chair. Festival of Hope; mem. Aerospace States Asscn (Chair. 2003–05); Republican; fmr Hon. Chair. Organ Donor Network; fmr Hon. Co-Chair. Indian Territory Arts and Humanities Council; Legislator of the Year 1993, Woman of the Year in Govt 1998, Women in Communication's Woman in the News Award, inducted into Okla Women's Hall of Fame and Okla Aviation Hall of Fame, Clarence E. Page Award, recognized by American Legis. Exchange Council as Legislator of the Year, named Guardian of Small Business by Nat. Fed. of Ind. Business. *Address:* c/o Office of the Governor, State Capitol Building, 2300 North Lincoln Blvd, Room 212, Oklahoma City, OK 73105, USA (office). *Website:* www.maryfallin.org.

FALLON, James (Jimmy) Thomas, BA; American actor, comedian, singer, musician and television host; b. 19 Sept. 1974, Brooklyn, New York; s. of James W. Fallon and Gloria Fallon; m. Nancy Juvonen 2007; one d.; ed Saugerties High School, New York, The Coll. of Saint Rose, Albany, New York; began career as stand-up comedian, after college did stand-up tours across USA; took improvisation classes with The Groundlings, Los Angeles; played at Caroline's Comedy Club, New York City; joined cast of Saturday Night Live as featured player 1998–2004, Weekend Update co-anchor with Tina Fey 2000–04; host, MTV Movie Awards 2001 (with Kirsten Dunst), 2005, MTV Video Music Awards 2002, Emmy Awards 2010; host, Late Night with Jimmy Fallon (NBC) 2009–14; host, The Tonight Show (NBC) (Primetime Emmy Award for Outstanding Creative Achievement in Interactive Media - Social TV Experience 2015) 2014–; Dr hc (The Coll. of Saint Rose) 2009. *Films include:* Almost Famous 2000, Anything Else 2003, The Entrepreneurs 2003, Taxi 2004, The Perfect Catch 2005, Doogal (voice) 2006, Arthur et les Minimoys (voice: English version) 2006, Factory Girl 2006, The Year of Getting to Know Us 2008, Whip It 2009, Arthur and the Great Adventure (voice) 2009, Arthur 3: The War of the Two Worlds (voice) 2010. *Television includes:* Saturday Night Live (series) 1998–2004, 2011, 2013 (Emmy Award for Outstanding Guest Actor in a Comedy Series 2014), Band of Brothers (mini-series) 2001, Saturday Night Live Christmas 2002 (film) (writer) 2002, Just for Laughs (series) (writer) 2009, Late Night with Jimmy Fallon (series) (writer) 2009–14, Guys with Kids (series) (writer and exec. producer) 2012–13. *Recordings include:* albums: The Bathroom Wall 2002, Blow Your Pants Off 2012; singles: Idiot Boyfriend 2002, Car Wash for Peace 2008, Drunk On Christmas (featuring John Rich) 2010. *Address:* The Tonight Show, NBC Studios, 30 Rockefeller Plaza, New York, NY 10112, USA (office). *Website:* www.nbc.com/the-tonight-show (office).

FALLON, John, BA; British publishing executive; *CEO, Pearson PLC;* b. Aug. 1962; m.; two c.; ed Univ. of Hull; held sr public policy and communications roles in British and UK local govts; fmr Dir of Corp. Affairs, Powergen PLC, mem. Exec. Cttee; Dir of Communications, Pearson PLC 1997–2003, Pres. Pearson Inc. 2000–03, CEO of Pearson's educational publishing businesses for Europe, Middle East and Africa 2003–08, Chief Exec. Int. Educ. Businesses 2008–12, mem. Pearson Man. Cttee, mem. Bd of Dirs and CEO Pearson PLC 2013–; mem. Bd of Dirs Interactive Data Corp. 2000–07. *Achievements include:* spearheaded partnership with Save the Children to offer education opportunities to Syrian children refugees 2015. *Address:* Pearson PLC, 80 Strand, London, WC2R 0RL, England (office). *Telephone:* (20) 7010-2000 (office). *Fax:* (20) 7010-6601 (office). *E-mail:* john.fallon@pearson.com (office). *Website:* www.pearson.com (office).

FALLON, Martin (see PATTERSON, Harry).

FALLON, Rt Hon. Sir Michael Cathel, KCB, PC, MA; British politician and business executive; b. 14 May 1952, Perth, Scotland; m. Wendy Elisabeth Payne 1986; two s.; ed Epsom Coll., Univ. of St Andrews; MP (Conservative) for Darlington 1983–92, for Sevenoaks 1997–; Asst Whip (HM Treasury) 1988–90, Lord Commr (Whip) 1990; Parl. Under-Sec., Dept for Educ. 1990–92; Shadow Spokesperson on Trade and Industry 1997, on the Treasury 1997–98; Deputy Chair. Conservative Party 2010–12; Minister of State for Business and Enterprise 2012–14; Minister of State for Energy 2013–14; Minister of State for Portsmouth Jan.–July 2014; Sec. of State for Defence 2014–17 (resgnd); Chair. Avanton Ltd 2018–; held positions on Treasury Select Cttee; mem. Bd of Dirs Bannatyne Fitness Ltd, Quality Care Homes PLC, Just Learning Ltd, Attendo AB, Tullett Prebon PLC 1992–97; mem. Int. Advisory Bd Investcorp Ltd 2018–. *Address:* House of Commons, Westminster, London, SW1A 0AA; Constituency Office, Becket House, 13 Vestry Road, Sevenoaks, TN14 5EL, England. *Telephone:* (20) 7219-6482 (Westminster); (1732) 452261 (Sevenoaks). *Fax:* (870) 051-8023 (Sevenoaks). *E-mail:* michael.fallon.mp@parliament.uk; office@sevenoakstory.org.uk. *Website:* www.michaelfallonmp.org.uk.

FALLON, Adm. William Joseph, BA, MA; American military officer (retd); *Chairman, CounterTack Inc.;* b. 30 Dec. 1940, East Orange, NJ; m. Mary Fallon; four c.; ed Naval War Coll., Newport, RI, Nat. War Coll., Washington, DC, Old Dominion Univ., Norfolk, Va, Villanova Univ., Pa; received comm. through USN ROTC Program, designated naval flight officer upon completion of training 1967; began Naval Aviation service flying RA-5C Vigilante with a combat deployment to Viet Nam; served in flying assignments with Attack Squadrons and Carrier Air Wings with deployment to the Mediterranean Sea, Atlantic, Pacific and Indian Oceans, in USS Saratoga, USS Ranger, USS Nimitz, USS Dwight D. Eisenhower, USS Theodore Roosevelt; Commdr Carrier Air Wing Eight, Operation Desert Storm 1991, Battle Force Sixth Fleet, Operation Deliberate Force, Bosnia 1995, other command posts included Attack Squadron Sixty Five on USS Dwight D. Eisenhower, Medium Attack Wing One at NAS Oceana, Va, Carrier Group Eight, Theodore Roosevelt Battle Group; Commdr, Second Fleet and Commdr, Striking Fleet Atlantic 1997–2000; shore duties have included Deputy Dir for Operations, Jt Task Force, Southwest Asia, Deputy Dir, Aviation Plans and Requirements, Staff of the Chief of Naval Operations, Washington, DC; flag officer assignments included Asst Chief of Staff, Plans and Policy, NATO Supreme Allied Commdr, Atlantic, Deputy and Chief of Staff, US Atlantic Fleet, Deputy C-in-C and Chief of Staff, US Atlantic Command; Vice-Chief of Naval Operations 2000–03; Commdr US Fleet Forces Command and US Atlantic Fleet 2003–05; Commdr US Pacific Command 2005–07; Commdr US Cen. Command (first naval officer to hold the position) 2007–08 (resgnd); f. William J. Fallon & Assoc., LLC (consultancy); Partner, Tilwell Petroleum LLC; CEO, CounterTack Inc. 2011–13, Chair. 2013–; Exec. Vice-Pres., Strategy, SM&A 2013; Sr Advisor to the Chair., Beau Dietl & Assoc. Inc.; mem. Bd of Dirs, American Security Project, Cylance Inc.; fmr Robert E. Wilhelm Fellow, MIT Centre for Int. Studies, now Chair. Advisory Bd; mem. Global Affairs Advisory Bd, Occidental Coll., Advisory Bd, Univ. of California, San Diego School of Int. Relations and Pacific Studies; Distinguished Fellow, Centre for Naval Analyses; mem., US Sec. of Defense Science Bd; fmr mem. Experts Group advising Congressional Comm. on the Strategic Posture of the US; fmr Co-Chair. Center for Strategic and Int. Studies Comm. on Smart Global Health Policy, Nat.

Asscn of Corp. Dirs 2009 Blue Ribbon Comm.; Defense Distinguished Service Medal, Distinguished Service Medal, Defense Superior Service Medal, Legion of Merit, Bronze Star, Meritorious Service Medal, Air Medal, Navy Commendation Medal; Dr hc (Villanova Univ.). *Address:* CounterTrack Inc., 100 Fifth Avenue, First Floor Waltham, MA 02451-1208, USA (office). *Telephone:* (855) 893-5428 (office). *Website:* www.countertack.com (office).

FALOMIR FAUS, Miguel, DFA; Spanish museum director; *Director, Museo Nacional del Prado;* b. 1966, Valencia; s. of Miguel Falomir and Adela Faus de Falomir; m. Luisa Elena Alcala Donegani; ed Univ. de Valencia, Inst. of Fine Arts, New York Univ.; Researcher in history of art, Council for Scientific Research, Madrid 1996; fmr Prof., Dept of History of Art, Univ. de Valencia; Head, Dept of Italian and French Paintings, Museo Nacional del Prado 1997, Deputy Dir for Conservation and Research 2015–17, Dir, Museo Nacional del Prado 2017–; Andrew Mellon Prof., Center for Advanced Study in the Visual Arts, Nat. Gallery of Art, Washington, DC 2008–10; Visiting Prof., Univ. of Udine, Italy, UCLA, USA; mem. Scientific Cttee Fondazione Tiziano, Italy. *Publications:* numerous exhbn catalogues. *Address:* Museo Nacional del Prado, Paseo del Prado, s/n, 28014 Madrid, Spain (office). *Telephone:* (91) 3302800 (office). *Website:* www.museodelprado.es (office).

FÄLTHAMMAR, Carl-Gunne, PhD; Swedish scientist and academic; *Professor Emeritus of Plasma Physics, Alfvén Laboratory, Royal Institute of Technology;* b. 4 Dec. 1931, Markaryd; s. of Oskar Fälthammar and Ingeborg Fälthammar; m. Ann-Marie Sjunnesson 1957; one s. one d.; ed Royal Inst. of Tech. (KTH), Stockholm; Asst Prof., KTH 1966–69, Chair. Dept of Plasma Physics 1967–97, Prof. of Plasma Physics 1975–97, Emer. 1997–; mem. Swedish Nat. Cttee for Radio Science 1970–96, Swedish Nat. Cttee for Geodesy and Geophysics 1973–96; Chair. Swedish Geophysical Soc. 1978–80; mem. Royal Swedish Acad. of Sciences, Int. Acad. of Astronautics, Academia Europaea; other professional affiliations; Hon. PhD (Oulu) 1989; Basic Sciences Award, Int. Acad. of Astronautics 1996, Golden Badge Award, European Geophysical Union 1996, Hannes Alfvén Medal, European Geophysical Soc. 1998. *Publications:* Cosmical Electrodynamics (with H. Alfvén) 1963, Magnetospheric Physics (with B. Hultqvist) 1990; papers in plasma physics and space physics. *Address:* Royal Institute of Technology (KTH), Teknikringen 31, Floor 4, Room 1515, 100 44 Stockholm (office); Bovägen 35, 18143 Lidingö, Sweden (home). *Telephone:* (8) 790-76-85 (office); (8) 7650862 (home). *E-mail:* carl-gunne.falthammar@ee.kth.se (office); carl-gunne.falthammar@telia.com (home). *Website:* www.kth.se/eecs (office).

FALTINGS, Gerd, PhD; German mathematician and academic; *Scientific Member and Managing Director, Max-Planck-Institut für Mathematik;* b. 28 July 1954, Gelsenkirchen-Buer; ed Westphalian Wilhelm Univ. of Münster; Postdoctoral Research Fellow, Harvard Univ., Cambridge, Mass, USA 1978–79; Prof. of Math., Univ. of Wuppertal 1979–85; mem. Faculty, Princeton Univ., NJ, USA 1985; Scientific Mem. Max-Planck-Institut für Mathematik, Bonn 1994–, Man. Dir 1995–; Bundesverdienstkreuz (First Class) 2009; Danny Heineman Prize, Akad. der Wissenschaften, Göttingen 1983, Fields Medal, Int. Congress of Mathematicians, Berkeley, Calif. 1986, Leibniz Prize, Germany 1996, Karl Georg Christian von Staudt Prize 2008, Heinz Gumin Prize 2010, King Faisal Int. Prize for Science 2014, Shaw Prize in Math. Sciences (co-recipient) 2015. *Publications:* numerous publs in math. journals. *Address:* Max-Planck-Institut für Mathematik, PO Box 7280, 53072 Bonn (office); Max-Planck-Institut für Mathematik, Vivatsgasse 7, 53111 Bonn, Germany (office). *Telephone:* (228) 402229 (office). *Fax:* (228) 402277 (office). *E-mail:* faltings@mpim-bonnmpgde (office); gerd@mpim-bonn.mpg.de (office). *Website:* www.hcm.uni-bonn.de/people/faculty/profile/gerd-faltings (office); www.mpim-bonn.mpg.de/node/102 (office).

FALTLHAUSER, Kurt, BEcons, Dr rer. pol; German politician; b. 13 Sept. 1940, Munich; m.; two c.; ed Ludwig-Maximilian-University; leader, Gen. Student Council, Univ. of Munich 1964–65; mem. Bavarian Landtag 1974–80, 1998–2008; State Minister and Head, Bavarian State Chancellery 1995–98, State Minister of Finance 1998–2007; mem. Bundestag 1980–95; Chair. Finance and Budget Committee, Christian Social Union (CSU); Financial Spokesman CDU/ CSU Parl. Group, also Deputy Chair.; Parl. State Sec. to the Fed. Minister of Finance; Chair. Bd of Admin Bayerische Landesbank; Hon. Prof., Faculty of Econs, Ludwig-Maximilian-University 1994. *Address:* Postfach 65 01 20, 81215 Munich; Maximilianeum, 81627 Munich, Germany (home). *Telephone:* (89) 41260 (home). *E-mail:* info@faltlhauser.de (home). *Website:* www.faltlhauser.de.

FÄLTSKOG, Agnetha Åse; Swedish singer and actress; b. 5 April 1950, Jönköping; m. 1st Björn Ulvæus 1971 (divorced 1979); m. 2nd Tomas Sonnenfeld 1990 (divorced 1993); solo recording artist aged 17; actress, Jesus Christ Superstar, Sweden; mem. pop group ABBA 1972–82; winner, Eurovision Song Contest 1974; worldwide tours; concerts include Royal Performance, Stockholm 1976, Royal Albert Hall, London 1977, UNICEF concert, New York 1979, Wembley Arena 1979; reunion with ABBA, Swedish TV This Is Your Life 1986; solo artist 1982–90, 2004–; World Music Award, Best Selling Swedish Artist 1993. *Films:* ABBA: The Movie 1977, Nöjesmaskinen 1982, Rakenstam 1983. *Recordings:* albums: with ABBA: Ring Ring 1973, Waterloo 1974, ABBA 1975, Greatest Hits 1976, Arrival 1976, The Album 1978, Voulez-Vous 1979, Greatest Hits Vol. 2 1979, Super Trouper 1980, The Visitors 1981, The Singles: The First Ten Years 1982, Thank You For The Music 1983, Absolute Abba 1988, Abba Gold 1992, More Abba Gold 1993, Forever Gold 1998, The Definitive Collection 2001; solo: Eleven Women In One Building 1975, Wrap Your Arms Around Me 1983, Eyes of a Woman 1985, I Stand Alone 1987, My Colouring Book 2004, A 2013; singles include: with Abba: Ring Ring 1973, Waterloo 1974, Mamma Mia 1975, Dancing Queen 1976, Fernando 1976, Money Money Money 1976, Knowing Me Knowing You 1977, The Name Of The Game 1977, Take A Chance On Me 1978, Summer Night City 1978, Chiquitita 1979, Does Your Mother Know? 1979, Angel Eyes/Voulez-Vous 1979, Gimme Gimme Gimme (A Man After Midnight) 1979, I Have A Dream 1979, The Winner Takes It All 1980, Super Trouper 1980, On and On and On 1981, Lay All Your Love On Me 1981, One Of Us 1981, When All Is Said and Done 1982, Head Over Heels 1982, The Day Before You Came 1982, Under Attack 1982, Thank You For The Music 1983; solo: I Was So In Love, The Heat Is On, Can't Shake You Loose, I Wasn't The One (Who Said Goodbye), If I Thought You'd Ever Change Your Mind 2004, My Colouring Book 2004, My Very Best 2008. *Publications:* As I Am (autobiography) 1997. *Website:* www.abbasite.com; www.agnetha.com.

FALUSI, Adeyinka Gladys, PhD; Nigerian geneticist and academic; *Professor of Haematology and Head of Genetic and Bioethics Research Unit, Institute for Medical Research and Training, College of Medicine, University of Ibadan;* m. A. O. Falusi; c.; has served as Visiting Scientist at numerous hosps including Hammersmith Hosp., London, UK 1983–84, John Radcliffe Hosp., Oxford, Memorial Sloan Kettering Cancer Center, New York, USA 1994–95, Humboldt Univ. Inst. for Tropical Medicine, Berlin 1998; currently Prof. and Head of Genetic and Bioethics Research Unit, Inst. for Advanced Medical Research and Training, Coll. of Medicine, Univ. of Ibadan, Acting Dir of Inst. 2001–02, Dir 2002–05, Chair. Univ. of Ibadan/Univ. Coll. Hosp. Institutional Review Cttee 2001–05; Country Coordinator for Nigeria, Networking for Ethics of Biomedical Research in Africa 2005–06; Founder and Vice-Pres. Sickle Cell Asscn of Nigeria; Founding Chair. Nigerian Bioethics Initiative; Fellow, Nigerian Acad. of Science 2009–; Trustee, Sickle Cell Hope Alive Foundation (currently Pres.); Nat. Productivity Order of Merit 2005, Kayode Fayemi 2013; L'Oréal-UNESCO Women in Science Award 2001, CEDPA/Nigerian News Rare Gems Award 2003, Vocational Excellence Award for Impact in Science 2004, Ekiti State Merit Award 2013. *Address:* College of Medicine, University of Ibadan, Ibadan, Nigeria (office). *Website:* com.ui.edu.ng (office).

FALZON, Michael, BArch; Maltese architect and politician; b. 17 Aug. 1945, Gzira; s. of Francis Falzon and Esther Cauchi; m. Mary Anne Aquilina; one s.; ed the Lyceum and Univ. of Malta; practised as architect; mem. Nat. Exec. Nationalist Party 1975, fmr Sec. of Information; Ed. The Democrat (weekly newspaper) 1975; mem. Parl. 1976–96; Shadow Minister for Information and Broadcasting 1976–81, for Industry 1981–87, Minister for Devt of Infrastructure 1987–92, for Environment 1992–94, for Educ. and Human Resources 1994–96; Ed. The People and People on Sunday (newspapers) 1997–98; Chair. Water Services Corpn 1998–2007; Pres. Malta Developers Asscn 2010–14, now Hon. Pres. and Consultant; columnist, MaltaToday. *Address:* c/o Malta Developers' Association, Triq l-Orsolini, Gwardamangia, Tal-Pietà PTA1227, Malta. *E-mail:* micfal@maltanet.net (home).

FAMA, Eugene F., BA; American economist and academic; *Robert R. McCormick Distinguished Service Professor of Finance, University of Chicago;* b. 14 Feb. 1939, Boston, Mass; m. Sally Fama; four c.; ed Tufts Univ.; Asst Prof. of Finance, Univ. of Chicago Grad. School of Business 1963–65, Assoc. Prof. 1966–68, Prof. 1968–73, Theodore O. Yntema Prof. of Finance 1973–84, Theodore O. Yntema Distinguished Prof. of Finance 1984–93, Robert R. McCormick Distinguished Service Prof. of Finance 1993–; Visiting Prof., Catholic Univ. of Leuven, Belgium 1975–76, Anderson Grad. School of Man., UCLA 1982–95; Assoc. Ed. Journal of Finance 1971–73, 1977–80, American Economic Review 1975–77, Journal of Monetary Economics 1984–96; Fellow, American Acad. of Arts and Sciences 1989, American Finance Asscn, Econometric Soc.; Hon. LLD (Leuven) 1985, (Rochester) 1987, (DePaul) 1989; Hon. DSc (Tufts) 2002; Dr hc (Univ. of Leuven, Belgium); Deutsche Bank Prize in Financial Econs 2005, Nicholas Molodovsky Award 2006, Morgan Stanley American Finance Asscn Award for Excellence in Finance 2007, Onassis Prize in Finance 2009, Nobel Prize in Econs (with Lars Peter Hansen and Robert Shiller) 2013. *Leisure interests:* windsurfing, golf, tennis, biking, old movies, opera. *Address:* 5807 South Woodlawn Avenue, Chicago, IL 60637-1610, USA (office). *Telephone:* (773) 702-7282 (office). *E-mail:* eugene.fama@chicagobooth.edu (office). *Website:* www.chicagobooth.edu/faculty/directory/f/eugene-f-fama (office).

FAN, Gen. Changlong; Chinese army officer and politician; *Vice-Chairman, Central Military Commission;* b. 1947, Donggang City, Liaoning Prov.; ed Beijing Mil. Acad.; sent to countryside to do manual work during Cultural Revolution 1968–69; joined PLA 1969, soldier, Ground Force 1969–71, Platoon Leader 1971–72, Political Dir, PLA Company Command 1973–76, Chief of Staff, Regt Command 1976–82, Chief of Staff, Div. Command 1985–90, Div. Commdr (Army) 1990–93, Chief of Staff, 16th Army Group 1993–95, Army Commdr, 16th Army Group 1995–2000, Chief of Staff, Shenyang Mil. Region 2000–03, Asst to Chief of PLA Gen. Staff 2003–04, Commdr, Jinan Mil. Region 2004–12; Vice-Chair., 18th CCP Cen. Cttee Cen. Mil. Comm. 2012–17; Vice-Chair., Cen. Mil. Comm. of the PRC 2013–; joined CCP 1969, alt. mem. 16th CCP Cen. Cttee 2002–07, mem. 17th CCP Cen. Cttee 2007–12, 18th CCP Cen. Cttee 2012–17, also mem. Politburo 2012–17; attained rank of Maj.-Gen. 1995, Lt-Gen. 2002, Gen. 2008. *Address:* Central Military Commission, 20 Jingshanqian Jie, Beijing 100009, People's Republic of China (office). *Telephone:* (10) 66730000 (office). *E-mail:* chinamod@chinamil.com.cn (office). *Website:* www.mod.gov.cn (office).

FAN, Jixiang; Chinese business executive; Group Pres. Sinohydro Corpn, Chair. Sinohydro Group Ltd; Chair. Power Construction Corpn of China (PowerChina, state-owned corpn) 2011–16. *Address:* c/o Power Construction Corporation of China, No. 7 & 8 Building, Beijing Xiyuan Hotel, 1 Sanlihe Road, Haidian District, Beijing 100040, People's Republic of China. *E-mail:* infocenter@powerchina.cn.

FAN, Zeng, BA MFA; Chinese painter, poet and writer; b. 5 July 1938, Nantong; ed Nankai Univ., Central Acad. of Fine Arts; worked at the Nat. Museum of Chinese History from 1962; Fan Zeng Art Gallery, Beijing was f. in his name 1984; Prof., Nankai Univ., Dir of the Dept of Chinese Painting 1993–, Dean 1993–, Prof. Emer. 1993–; Consultant UNESCO 2009; Hon. DLitt (Glasgow) 2011, (Alberta) 2012; received numerous awards in design and painting. *Address:* Century Avenue, Chongchuan Qu, Nantong Shi, Jiangsu Sheng 226000, People's Republic of China (office).

FAN HSU, Rita, CBE, JP, BA, MScS; Chinese politician; b. 20 Sept. 1945, Shanghai, People's Repub. of China; m. Stephen Fan Sheung-tak; two c.; ed St Stephen's Girls' Coll., Univ. of Hong Kong; mem. Legis. Council 1983–92, Exec. Council 1989–92; Chair. Bd of Educ. 1986–89, Educ. Comm. 1990–92; mem. Preliminary Working Cttee of the Preparatory Cttee for the Hong Kong Special Admin. Region (HKSAR) 1993–95, Preparatory Cttee for the HKSAR 1995–97; Deputy to the 9th Nat. People's Congress (NPC), People's Repub. of China 1998–2003, 10th NPC 2003–08, 11th NPC 2008–13, 12th NPC 2013–; Pres. Provisional Legis. Council 1997–98, First Legis. Council of HKSAR 1998–2000, Second Legis. Council 2000–04, Third Legis. Council 2004–08; Supervising Adviser, Hong Kong Fed. of Women; Hon. Advisor, Jr Chamber Int. Hong Kong; Gold Bauhinia Star 1998, Grand Bauhinia Medal 2007; Hon. LLD (China Univ. of

Political Science and Law) 2003; Hon. DScS (City Univ. of Hong Kong) 2005, (Hong Kong Univ.) 2009. *Website:* www.npcfan.hk.

FANG, Gen. Fenghui; Chinese army officer; *Chief of General Staff, People's Liberation Army;* b. 1951, Xianyang, Shaanxi Prov.; ed Univ. of Nat. Defence; joined PLA 1968, mem. Standing Cttee, Guangzhou Mil. Area Command and Chief of Staff, Guangzhou Mil. Area Command 2003–07, Commdr Beijing Mil. Area Command 2007–12, Chief of Gen. Staff, PLA 2012–; attained rank of Maj.-Gen. 1998, Lt-Gen. 2005, Gen. 2010; mem. 17th CCP Cen. Cttee 2007–12, 18th CCP Cen. Cttee 2012–; mem. 18th CCP Cen. Mil. Comm. 2012–; Deputy, 11th NPC 2008–13. *Address:* People's Liberation Army General Staff Headquarters, Beijing, People's Republic of China (office). *E-mail:* chinamod@chinamil.com.cn (office). *Website:* eng.mod.gov.cn (office).

FANG, Lijun; Chinese artist; b. 1963, Handan, Hebei; ed Hebei Univ. of Science and Tech., China Cen. Acad. of Fine Arts.

FANG, Shouxian; Chinese nuclear physicist; *Director, Beijing Electron Positron Collider National Laboratory;* b. 27 Oct. 1932, Shanghai; m. 1st Run Moyin (died 1965); m. 2nd Yao Mayli 1968, two d.; ed Fudan Univ., Shanghai; Prof. of Research, Nuclear Physics Inst., Academia Sinica 1982–; Project Dir, Beijing Electron Positron Collider (BEPC, first high energy accelerator in China) 1986, Dir Inst. of High Energy Physics 1988, Dir BEPC Nat. Lab. 1992–; mem. Chinese Acad. of Sciences 1991–; Hon. Nat. Natural Science Award 1990, Ho Leung Ho Lee Foundation Prize 1997, Asian Cttee for Future Accelerators Lifetime Prize 2013. *Address:* Institute of High Energy Physics, 19B YuquanLu, Shijingshan District, Beijing 100049, People's Republic of China (office). *Telephone:* (10) 88233093 (office). *Fax:* (10) 882333744 (office). *Website:* english.ihep.cas.cn (office).

FANG, Weizhong; Chinese economist; *Chairman, Chinese Macroeconomics Society;* b. 11 March 1928, Dongfeng Co., Jilin Prov.; three s.; ed Dongbei Univ., Northeast China Univ., Northeast China Teachers' Univ.; joined CCP 1950; Sec. Publicity Dept, CCP Northeast Bureau 1950–52; Deputy Dir Research and Editing Div., State Devt and Reform Comm. 1952–61; Researcher, General Office, CCP Cen. Cttee 1961–65; Vice-Minister, State Devt and Reform Comm. 1977–93; Prof., Beijing Univ., People's Univ. of China, Beijing; Deputy Ed. China Econ. Yearbook; Chief Ed. Chronicle of Major Econ. Events; Alt. mem. 12th CCP Cen. Cttee 1982–87; mem. 13th CCP Cen. Cttee 1987–92; Alt. mem. 14th CCP Cen. Cttee 1992–97; mem. CPPCC 8th Nat. Cttee 1993–98, 9th Nat. Cttee 1998–2003, Chair. Economy Sub-Cttee 1993–2003; Chair. Chinese Macroeconomics Soc. 1995–; Vice-Chair. China Planning Soc., China Enterprise Man. Asscn; mem. Council of People's Bank of China 1974–. *Leisure interest:* calligraphy. *Address:* Chinese Macroeconomics Society, 18th Floor B, Hua Zun Mansion, 29 Beisanhuan Zhonglu, Xicheng District, Beijing 100029, People's Republic of China (office). *E-mail:* Eng@macrochina.com.cn.

FANG, Gen. Zuqi; Chinese army officer; b. 1935, Jingjiang, Jiangsu Prov.; joined PLA 1951, took part in Korean War 1952; joined CCP 1956; worked as Asst, Cadre Dept, Army (or Ground Force), PLA Services and Arms, later Deputy Chief of Div. Org. Section; Deputy Regt Political Commissar, Army (or Ground Force), PLA Services and Arms 1969–70; fmr Dir Political Dept, PLA Shenyang and Beijing Mil. Area Command; Political Commissar, Nanjing Mil. Region 1993–2000; rank of Maj.-Gen. Group Army, PLA Services and Arms 1988–93, Lt-Gen. 1993–98, Gen. 1998–; mem. 15th CCP Cen. Cttee 1997–2002.

FANGIONO, Ciliandra, BA, MA; Indonesian business executive; *CEO, President and Director, First Resources Ltd;* b. 1976; s. of Martias Fangiono; m.; two c.; ed Univ. of Cambridge, UK; with Investment Banking Div., Merrill Lynch, Singapore 1999–2001; CEO First Resources Ltd (family palm oil plantation co.) 2002–, Pres. and Dir 2003–, Dir 2007–. *Address:* First Resources Ltd, Wisma 77, 7th Floor, Jalan Letjend, S. Parman Kav. 77, Slipi, Jakarta 11410, Indonesia (office). *Telephone:* (21) 53670888 (office). *Fax:* (21) 53671888 (office). *Website:* www.first-resources.com (office).

FANJUL, Oscar, PhD; Spanish business executive; *Vice-Chairman and CEO, Omega Capital;* b. 20 May 1949, Santiago, Chile; m. Curra Orozco; two c.; Founder, Chair. and CEO Repsol SA, now Hon. Chair.; fmr Chair. Hidroeléctrica del Cantábrico; currently Vice-Chair. and CEO Omega Capital; Vice-Chair. Lafarge-Holcom, mem. Bd of Dirs The Marsh and McLennan Companies, Ferrovial; fmr mem. Bd of Dirs Unilever, BBVA, London Stock Exchange, Areva, Acerinox, Partex; mem. Trilateral Comm.; mem. Bd, Museo Nacional Centro de Arte Reina Sofía; Trustee, International Financial Reporting Standards (IFRSs); Orden de Isabel la Católica, Ordre de la Couronne Belge. *Publications include:* several articles on industrial and financial matters. *Address:* Omega Capital, Paseo Eduardo Dato 18, Madrid 28010, Spain (office). *Telephone:* (91) 7027991 (office). *Fax:* (91) 3195733 (office). *E-mail:* ofanjul@omega-capital.com (office).

FANNING, Eric K., BA; American government official; b. 2 July 1968; ed Dartmouth Coll.; Research Asst, House of Reps Armed Services Cttee 1991–93; Special Asst to Sec., US Dept of Defense 1993–96; Assoc. Dir for Political Affairs, The White House 1996; Assoc. Producer, foreign and national desks, CBS News 1997–98; Sr Assoc., Robinson Lerer & Montgomery Communications 1998–99; Sr Vice-Pres., Operations & Strategy, 1800HomeCare.com 1999–2000; Regional Dir, Sr Vice-Pres. for Strategic Devt, Business Execs for Nat. Security 2001–07; Managing Dir, Communication Man. Group (strategic communications firm) 2007–08; Deputy Dir, Congress Comm. on the Prevention of Weapons of Mass Destruction Proliferation & Terrorism 2008–09; Special Asst to Sec. for White House Liaison, US Dept of Defense 2009, Deputy Under-Sec., Deputy Chief Man. Officer, Dept of the Navy 2009–13, Under-Sec. of the Air Force 2013–15, Acting Under-Sec. of the Army and Chief Man. Officer June–Nov. 2015, Acting Sec. of the Army 2015–16, Sec. of the Army 2016–17.

FANZHI, Zeng; Chinese artist; b. 1964, Wuhan, Hubei; ed Hubei Fine Arts Inst. *Publications:* Raw Beneath the Mask 2001, I, We 2003, Scapes – The Paintings of Zeng Fanzhi 1989–2004 2005, The Paintings of Zeng Fanzhi 2007, Idealism 2007, Tai Ping you xiang 2008. *Address:* c/o ShanghART Gallery, 50 Moganshan Road, Bldg 16, Shanghai, 200060, People's Republic of China (office). *Telephone:* (21) 6359-3923 (office). *Fax:* (21) 6359-4570 (office). *E-mail:* info@shanghartgallery.com (office). *Website:* www.shanghartgallery.com (office).

FAOURI, Refat al-, PhD; Jordanian university rector, international organization executive and academic; *Director-General, Arab Administrative Development Organization (ARADO);* ed Yarmouk Univ., Univ. of Southern California and Saint Louis Univ., USA; occupied several positions at Yarmouk Univ., including researcher and teaching asst, School of Econs, Asst Teacher, Public Relations Div., Co-teacher in Public Relations Div., Asst Dean of Faculty of Economy and Admin. Sciences, then Dean of School of Economics and Admin. Sciences and Prof. of Public Admin 1998–2003, Vice-Pres. for Admin., Academic and Quality Assurance 2003–07, Chair. Jordanian Studies Centre, Deputy Rector for Quality Affairs; has held numerous admin. posts, including mem. Bd of Dirs Public Admin Inst., Amman-Jordan, Dir Trust Council, Ministry of Higher Educ. and Scientific Research, Dir at Distinction Centre for Jordanian Office Services, mem. Informative Cttee for the Creativity and Distinction Fund Programme, Ministry of Admin. Devt, Jordan; Dir-Gen. Arab Admin. Devt Org. (ARADO) 2007–; mem. Advisory Bd OECD-MENA Region; mem. Higher Coordinating Cttee of Arab Cooperative Work; Oman Civil Order (Second Class) 2015. *Publications:* several books, including Management of Organizational Innovation; 36 research papers on business admin. *Address:* Arab Administrative Development Organization, 2 El Hegaz Street, PO Box 2692 al-Horreia, Heliopolis, Cairo, Egypt (office). *Telephone:* (2) 4175410 (office). *Fax:* (2) 4175407 (office). *E-mail:* arado@idsc.gov.eg (office); info@arado.org.eg (office). *Website:* www.arado.org.eg (office).

FARACI, John V.; American forest products industry executive; b. 1950; joined International Paper Co. in 1974 as financial analyst, various positions in Planning, Gen. Man. and Finance Depts, Vice-Pres. 1989, CEO and Man. Dir Carter Holt Harvey (subsidiary co.) 1995–99, Sr Vice-Pres. and Chief Financial Officer, International Paper Co. 1999–2000, Exec. Vice-Pres. and Chief Financial Officer 2000–03, Pres. Feb.–Nov. 2003, Chair. and CEO Nov. 2003–14; mem. Bd of Dirs United Technologies Corpn 2005–, ConocoPhillips 2015–, Grand Teton Nat. Park Foundation, Nat. Park Foundation; mem. Citigroup Int. Advisory Bd; mem. Business Round Table, Sustainable Forestry Bd; Trustee, Denison Univ.

FARAGE, Nigel Paul; British politician and business executive; *Leader, The Brexit Party;* b. 3 April 1964, Downe, Kent, England; s. of Guy Justus Oscar Farage and Barbara Farage (née Stevens); m. 1st Gráinne Hayes 1988 (divorced 1997); two s.; m. 2nd Kirsten Mehr 1999; two d.; ed Dulwich Coll., London; worked in City of London trading commodities at London Metal Exchange; joined US brokerage firm Drexel Burnham Lambert; transferred to Credit Lyonnais Rouse 1986; joined Refco 1994, Natexis Metals 2003; active in Conservative Party from school days, left party after signing of Maastricht Treaty 1992; Founding mem. UK Independence Party (UKIP) 1993, Chair. UKIP 1998–2000, Leader 2006–09 (resgnd to contest (unsuccessfully) parl. seat of Buckingham 2010), 2010–Sept. 2016 (resgnd), Interim Leader Oct.–Nov. 2016, left party 2018; Leader The Brexit Party 2019–; unsuccessful cand. for parl. seat of South Thanet, Kent 2015 (announced resignation but not accepted by party); MEP for South East England 1999–, Chair. Europe of Freedom and Direct Democracy group 2009–14, Co-Chair. Europe of Freedom and Direct Democracy 2014–; named Briton of the Year by The Times 2014. *Publications include:* Fighting Bull (Flying Free in paperback) 2010, The Purple Revolution: The Year That Changed Everything 2015. *Leisure interests:* cricket, fishing. *Address:* The Brexit Party, 83 Victoria Street, London, SW1H 0HW, England. *Website:* thebrexitparty.org (office); www.nigelfaragemep.co.uk.

FARAH, Ali Abdi; Djibouti politician; b. 16 Feb. 1947; mem. Rassemblement Populaire pour le Progrès (RPP), now part of Union pour la Majorité Présidentielle (UMP) coalition; fmr Minister for Industry, Energy and Minerals and Acting Minister for Public Works and Housing; Minister of Foreign Affairs, Int. Co-operation and Parl. Relations 1999–2005, of Communication and Culture 2005; fmr Govt Spokesperson. *Address:* Union pour la Majorité Présidentielle (UMP), Siège de l'UMP, Djibouti (office). *Telephone:* 21340056 (office). *E-mail:* lavictoire@ump.dj (office). *Website:* www.ump.dj (office).

FARAH, Col. Hassan Abshir; Somali government official, diplomatist and politician; b. 20 June 1945; m.; c.; ed Mil. Acad., Cairo, Egypt., Somali Nat. Univ.; Dist Commr of Mogadishu 1970–71, Vice-Mayor of Mogadishu 1971–73, Gov. and Mayor of Mogadishu 1973–76, 1982–87; Gov. of Middle Shabelle and Bakol 1976–82; Amb. to Germany (also accred to Austria) 1989–98; Minister of Internal Affairs and Security, Puntland Regional Govt 1998–2000; Minister of Water and Mineral Resources 2000–01; Chair. Somali Peace Conf. 2000; Prime Minister of Somalia 2001–03; Minister of Fishery and Marine Resources 2004–06; mem. Transitional Parl. 2006, mem. Fed. Parl. 2012–. *Address:* Federal Parliament, Mogadishu, Somalia.

FARAH, Sir Mohamed (Mo), Kt, CBE; British (b. Somali) track and field athlete; b. 23 March 1983, Mogadishu, Somalia; s. of Muktar Farah; m. Tania Nell 2010; one s. twin d. one step-d.; ed Feltham Community Coll., London; arrived in UK aged eight and grew up in West London; began cross country running in early teens; ran for Newham and Essex Beagles athletics club; finished ninth in English schools cross country 1996, then won first of five English school titles 1997; trained at St Mary's Univ. Coll., Twickenham 2001–11; began professional career 2005; relocated to Oregon, USA to further training with coach Alberto Salazar 2011; gold medal (individual), European Cross Country Championships, San Giorgio su Legnano 2006; silver medal, 5,000m, European Championships, Göteborg 2006; silver medal (individual), bronze medal (team), European Cross Country Championships, Brussels 2008; gold medal, 5,000m, European Team Championships, Leiria 2009; gold medal, 3000m, European Indoor Championships, Torino 2009; silver medal (individual, team), European Cross Country Championships, Dublin 2009; won 5,000m, Super Grand Prix, London 2009; gold medal, 5,000m, 10,000m, European Championships, Barcelona 2010 (became the fifth man in history of European Championships to win both 5,000m and 10,000m and the first in 20 years); ran 5,000m in 12:57.94, Diamond League, Zurich 2010 (became first British athlete to run under 13 minutes); winner, 5,000m, Diamond League, Birmingham 2011, Monaco 2011; also won 10,000m (in 26:46.57, new British and European record), Diamond League, Eugene 2011; gold medal, 3,000m, European Indoor Championships, Paris 2011; gold medal, 5,000m, European Championships, Helsinki 2012; gold medal, 5,000m, silver medal, 10,000m IAAF World Championships, Daegu 2011; gold medal, 5,000m, 10,000m, Olympic Games, London 2012, Rio 2016; winner, 5,000m, Diamond League, Eugene 2012; gold medal, 5,000m, 10,000m, IAAF World Championships, Moscow 2013; est. Mo

Farah Foundation 2011; Sponsor Muslim Writers' Awards; Male Athlete of the Year, British Athletics Writers' Asscn 2006, 2010, 2011, 2012, British Sr Athlete of the Year, UK Aviva Athletics Awards 2010, inducted into London Youth Games Hall of Fame 2010, Track-and Field Athlete of the Year, British Olympic Asscn 2010, European Athlete of the Year Award 2011, 2012, Premier Inn Celebrity Dad of the Year 2013; ranked by Arabian Business amongst the Power 500: The World's Most Influential Arabs (third) 2013. *Leisure interests:* spending time with his family, music. *E-mail:* info@mofarahfoundation.org.uk. *Website:* www.mofarah.com.

FARAH, Nuruddin; Somali writer; b. 24 Nov. 1945, Baidoa; s. of Farah Hassan and Fatuma Aleli; m. Amina Mama 1992 (divorced 2007); one s. one d.; ed Panjab Univ., Chandigarh, India, Univs of London and Essex, UK; Lecturer, Nat. Univ. of Somalia, Mogadishu 1971–74; Assoc. Prof., Univ. of Jos, Nigeria 1981–83; Writer-in-Residence, Univ. of Minn. 1989, Brown Univ., USA 1991; Prof., Makerere Univ., Kampala 1990; Rhodes Scholar St Antony's Coll., Oxford 1996; Visiting Prof., Univ. of Texas at Austin 1997; now full-time writer; mem. Union of Writers of the African People, PEN Int., Somali-Speaking PEN Centre; mem. Int. Advisory Bd, Bildhaan: An International Journal of Somali Studies, Macalester Coll., Minnesota; Hon. DLitt (Univ. of Kent at Canterbury) 2000; English-speaking Union Literary Prize 1980, Tucholsky Award 1991, Premio Cavour Award 1992, Zimbabwe Annual Award 1993, Neustadt Int. Literary Prize 1998, Festival Étonnant Voyageur St Malo, France 1998. *Plays include:* A Dagger in a Vacuum 1965, The Offering 1976, Yussuf and his Brothers 1982. *Publications include:* Why Die So Soon? (novella) 1965, From a Crooked Rib 1970, A Naked Needle 1976, Sweet and Sour Milk 1979, Sardines 1981, Close Sesame 1983, Maps 1986, Gifts 1992, Secrets (Prix de l'Astrolabe 2000) 1998, Yesterday, Tomorrow: Voices from the Somali Diaspora 1999, Territories 2000, Links 2004, Knots 2007, Crossbones 2011, Hiding in Plain Sight 2014, North of Dawn 2018; contrib. to Guardian, New African, Transition Magazine, New York Times, Observer, TLS, London Review of Books. *Address:* c/o Deborah Rogers, Rogers, Coleridge & White, 20 Powis Mews, London, W11 1JN, England (office). *Telephone:* (20) 7221-3717 (office). *Fax:* (20) 7229-9084 (office). *E-mail:* info@rcwlitagency.com (office). *Website:* www.rcwlitagency.com (office).

FAREMO, Grete, LLB; Norwegian lawyer, business executive, politician and UN official; *Executive Director, Office for Project Services, United Nations;* b. 16 June 1955, Byglandsfjord, Setesdal; d. of Osmund Faremo and Tora Aamlid; partner Magne Lindholm; one d.; ed Univ. of Oslo; with Ministry of Finance, Norwegian Agency for Devt Co-operation; Head of Div. Ministry 1984, Minister of Devt Co-operation 1990–92, of Justice 1992–96, of Oil and Energy 1996, of Defence 2009–11, of Justice and Public Security 2011–13; mem. Stortinget (Parl.) 1993–97; Dir Storebrand Insurance Co. 1997–98, Pres. 1997–2003; Dir of Legal and Corp. Affairs, Microsoft Northern Europe 2003–08; Chair. Norsk Folkehjelp 2003–08; Exec. Dir, United Nations Office for Project Services 2014–; mem. Bd Labour Party Forum for Art and Culture 1989–90, Int. Analysis 1997; mem. European Group, Trilateral Comm. 1998–2002; mem. Bd of Dirs Norsk Hydro 2006–09; Chief Negotiating Officer Aker Eiendom 1986; fmr Dir (of Cultural Affairs) Aker Brygge (business and leisure complex), Norsk Arbeiderpresse. *Address:* United Nations Office for Project Services Headquarters, Marmorvej 51, PO Box 2695, 2100 Copenhagen, Denmark (office). *Telephone:* 45-33-75-00 (office). *Fax:* 45-33-75-01 (office). *E-mail:* info@unops.org (office). *Website:* www.unops.org (office).

FARES, Farouk Saleh, BAgr, DEA, PhD; Syrian soil scientist, institute director and academic; b. 1945; m.; three c.; ed Damascus Univ., Paris Univ. VI in cooperation with the Nat. Agricultural Inst.-Nat. Higher School for Agric., Paris, INA-ENSA and ORSTOM, Nancy Univ. (France) in cooperation with Soil Research Centre (CNRS), Nancy, Nuclear Studies Centre (France), Nat. Inst. for Polytechnic, Lorraine and Biological Soil Research Centre (CNRS), Nancy, Pennsylvania State Univ., USA (Fulbright Scholarship), Environmental Resources Research Inst.; Dir-Gen. Arab Centre for the Study of Arid Zones and Dry Lands (ACSAD), Damascus, Syria 2004. *Address:* c/o Arab Centre for the Study of Arid Zones and Dry Lands (ACSAD), PO Box 2440, Damascus, Syria (office). *Website:* www.acsad.org (office).

FARES, Issam M.; Lebanese politician and business executive; b. 1937, Bayno, Akkar; m. Hala Fares; four c.; ed Tripoli Coll.; began as business exec. in Arabian Gulf, then moved to investment; f. numerous major business corpns in USA, Europe and Middle East including The Wedge Group, which includes Wedge Trust Corpn, Wedge Bank, Wedge Real Estate, Minefa Holdings, Farinvest; f. The Fares Foundation; mem. Parl., Deputy Prime Minister 2000–05; Chair. numerous governmental cttees; Order of the Prince Yaroslav the Wise, Second Rank (Ukraine), Grand Officer of the Nat. Order (Lebanon), Grand Cordon de Jean Baptiste (Antiochian Orthodox Church), Grand Cordon of Archon Depoutatos (Patriarchate of Constantinople), Grand Cordon of St Daniel (Patriarchate of Moscow and All Russia), Grand Officier de la Légion d'honneur (France), Grand Cross of the Phoenix (Greece), Grand Commdr Makarios the Third (Cyprus), Order of 'Stara Platina', First Rank (Bulgaria), Commandoria with Star of the Order of Merit (Poland) 2004; Dr hc (Diplomatic Acad., Moscow) 1997, (Tufts Univ., USA) 2000; Medal of Sts Peter and Paul (Antiochian Orthodox Patriarchate), World Maronite Foundation Gold Decoration, Antiochian Orthodox Christian Archdiocese of NY and N America Gold Medal of Merit, Maronite Cen. Council Gold Medal (Lebanon), Prize of the Int. Foundation for the Unity of Orthodox Nations (Patriarchate of Moscow and All Russia), UNESCO Gold Medal of Acropole, Alahd Nat. Merit (Algeria), Ministry of Youth and Sports Hon. Golden Medal (Bulgaria) 2003, Lifetime Achievement Award, American Task Force for Lebanon 2004, Shield of Honor, Casablanca Chamber of Trade, Industry and Services 2004, Award with jubilee decoration, Diplomatic Acad. of Russian Ministry of Foreign Affairs 2009. *Address:* Fares Foundation, Fares Foundation Bldg, Maameltein Highway, Jounieh, Lebanon (office). *Telephone:* (9) 639987 (office). *E-mail:* ffinfo@fares.org.lb (office). *Website:* www.issam-fares.org; www.fares.org.lb.

FARGETI, Mohamed Adan Ibrahim, MBA; Somali politician; b. 2 July 1964, Baidoa; ed Nat. Inst. of Statistics and Applied Econs, Univ. of Science Malaysia; moved to Australia early 2000s; CEO, Cumberland Housing Ltd, Australia 2004–08; Chair. Australian Somali Community Asscn 2009–12; returned to Somalia to work with Technical Selection Cttee as vetting expert (vetted 825 delegates who adopted new Fed. Constitution and mems of Somali Fed. Parl.) 2012; held numerous positions within Somali public sector, including with Ministry of Jubba Valley and Somalia Libya Agricultural Devt Co.; Minister of Posts and Telecommunications 2014–15, Minister of Finance 2015–17.

FARHADI, Asghar, BA, MA; Iranian film director and screenwriter; b. 1 Jan. 1972, Khomeyni Shahr County, Isfahan Prov.; m. Parisa Bakhtavar 1990; two c.; ed Tehran Univ., Tarbiat Modares Univ.; joined Iranian Young Cinema Soc. as student; began career working as screenwriter and dir for state broadcaster IRIB; f. Farhadi Film Production; mem. jury, 62nd Berlin Int. Film Festival 2012. *Television:* A Tale of a City (dir). *Films include:* Low Heights (screenwriter) 2001, Dancing in the Dust (Best Dir and Best Screenplay, Asia Pacific Film Festival 2003) 2003, The Beautiful City (Grand Prix, Warsaw Int. Film Festival 2004, Golden Peacock, Int. Film Festival of India 2004, FIPRESCI Prize, Split Film Festival 2005) 2004, Fireworks Wednesday 2006, About Elly (Silver Bear for Best Dir, Berlin Int. Film Festival 2009) 2009, Nader and Simin: A Separation (Acad. Award for Best Foreign Language Film 2012, Golden Globe for Best Foreign Film 2012, Golden Bear for Best Film, Berlin Int. Film Festival 2011) 2011, The Past 2013, The Salesman 2016, Everybody Knows 2018. *Address:* c/o United Talent Agency, 9336 Civic Center Drive, Beverly Hills, CA 90210, USA (office). *Website:* www.unitedtalent.com (office).

FARHANG, Mohammad Amin, BA, MA, PhD; Afghan economist, academic and fmr government official; b. 1940, Kabul; s. of Mir Mohammad Sediq Farhang; ed Esteqlal High School, Kabul Univ., Köln Univ., Germany; Prof. of Econs, Kabul Univ. and Dir Nat. Economy Inst. 1974–78; imprisoned due to opposition to Communist regime 1978–82; emigrated to Germany 1982; fmr Prof., Ruhr Univ., Co-ordinator Afghanistan Archive; returned to Afghanistan 2001; Minister of Reconstruction 2001, of Economy 2005–06, of Commerce and Industry 2006–08; currently Head, Kabul Attendants Inst. *Publications:* numerous articles.

FARINA, HE Cardinal Raffaele, PhD, SDB; Italian ecclesiastic; *Librarian and Archivist Emeritus of the Holy Roman Church;* b. 24 Sept. 1933, Buonalbergo; ed Pontifical Gregorian Univ., Rome; professed as mem. of Salesians of Saint John Bosco 1954; ordained priest of Salesians of Saint John Bosco 1958; Prof., Pontifical Salesian Univ., Rome for several years before becoming Dean of the Theology Faculty, Rector Pontifical Salesian Univ. 1977–83, 1992–97; Under-Sec. Pontifical Council for Culture 1983–92; Prefect of Vatican Library 1997–2007, Librarian of the Vatican Library and Archivist of the Vatican Secret Archives 2007–12, Librarian and Archivist Emer. 2012–; Titular Bishop of Opitergium 2007–08; cr. Cardinal (Cardinal-Deacon of San Giovanni della Pigna) 2007; participated in Papal Conclave 2013. *Address:* Vatican Library, 00120 Città del Vaticano (office). *Telephone:* (06) 6987-9530 (office). *Fax:* (06) 6987-9503 (office). *E-mail:* rfarina@vatlib.it (office). *Website:* www.vatlib.it (office).

FARISH, William; American business executive, racehorse owner and fmr diplomatist; b. 1938, Houston, Tex.; m. Sarah Sharp; one s. three d.; ed Univ. of Virginia; f. investment firm W. S. Farish & Co.; f. Lane's End Farm, Versailles, Ky (thoroughbred horse farm) 1978; Chair. Exec. Cttee Breeders Cup Ltd; Vice-Chair. US Jockey Club; Dir Thoroughbred Breeders and Owners Asscn; Chair. Bd Churchill Downs Inc., Ky; Amb. to UK 2001–04; Trustee, Keeneland Asscn 2006–. *Leisure interests:* horse breeding, hunting quail, polo. *Address:* c/o Lane's End, POB 626, Versailles, KY 40383; W. S. Farish & Co., Houston, Texas, USA (office). *E-mail:* bfarish@aol.com.

FARIZ, Ziad, BA, PhD; Jordanian economist, fmr government official and central banker; *Governor, Central Bank of Jordan;* b. 1943, Salt; ed Univ. of Baghdad, Arab Inst. for Planning, Kuwait, Keele Univ., UK; Minister of Planning 1989, 1991, of Industry and Trade 1989–91; Chair. Bd Bank of Export and Finance 1995; Gov. Cen. Bank of Jordan 1996–2001, 2012–; CEO Arab Banking Corpn 2001–05; Deputy Prime Minister and Minister of Finance 2005–07 (resgnd); Chair. Capital Bank 2007–09; Chair. First Investment Group, Amman 2009–12; fmr mem. Advisory Bd UNDP Regional Bureau for Arab States, Arab Human Devt Report. *Address:* Central Bank of Jordan, POB 37, King Hussein Street, Amman 11118, Jordan (office). *Telephone:* (6) 4630301 (office). *Fax:* (6) 4638889 (office). *E-mail:* info@cbj.gov.jo (office). *Website:* www.cbj.gov.jo (office).

FARLEY, Carole, MusB; American singer (soprano); b. 29 Nov. 1946, Le Mars, Ia; d. of Melvin Farley and Irene Farley (née Reid); m. José Serebrier 1969; one d.; ed Indiana Univ. and Hochschule für Musik, Munich (Fulbright Scholar); operatic debut in USA in title role of La Belle Hélène, New York City Opera 1969; debut at Metropolitan Opera as Lulu 1977; now appears regularly in leading opera houses world-wide and in concert performances with major orchestras in USA and Europe; Metropolitan Opera premiere of Shostakovich's Lady Macbeth of Mtsensk (Katerina Ismailova); Wozzeck (Marie), Toulouse Opera, Teatro Colón; f. Carole Farley International Vocal Coaching; mem. American Guild of Musical Artists; numerous awards and prizes including Grand Prix du Disque for Les Soldats Morts (by A. Lemeland) 1995 and Diapason d'Or (France) 1997, Abbiati Prize for Best Production of an Opera in Italy (for Berg's Lulu, Turin). *Recordings include:* Le Pré aux Clercs, Behold the Sun, French songs by Chausson, Duparc, Satie and Fauré, Prokofiev songs, Poulenc's La Voix Humaine, Menotti's The Telephone, Britten's Les Illuminations, Prokofiev's The Ugly Duckling, Kurt Weill songs, Milhaud songs (with John Constable), Strauss Songs and the Four Last Songs, Strauss Final Scenes from Daphne and Capriccio, Tchaikovsky opera arias, Delius songs with orchestra, Les Soldats Morts 1995 (Grand Prix du Disque), Grieg songs with orchestra, Serebrier Symphony No. 3, Ned Rorem Songs with Ned Rorem, Piano, Der Wampyr by Marschner, Songs of William Bolcom, Classic American Love Songs. *Roles include:* Monteverdi's Poppea, Massenet's Manon, Mozart's Idomeneo, roles in Don Giovanni, Entführung, Die Zauberflöte, Verdi's La Traviata, Puccini's La Bohème, Tosca, Lehar's The Merry Widow, Strauss' Zigeunerbaron, Berg's Lulu, Wozzeck, Weill's Mahagonny, Offenbach's Tales of Hoffmann, La Belle Hélène, Strauss's Salome, Capriccio, Die Frau ohne Schatten, Elektra, Shostakovich's Lady Macbeth of Mtsensk, Wagner's Parsifal, Die Walküre, Schönberg's Erwartung, Janáček's Macropoulos Case, Jenůfa, Katya Kabanova. *Leisure interests:* skiing, jogging, swimming, dancing, cooking, entertaining, reading. *Address:* Robert Lombardo Associates, Suite 6F, 61 West 62nd Street, New York, NY 10023, USA (office). *Telephone:* (212) 586-4453 (office). *Fax:* (212) 581-5771 (office). *E-mail:* Robert@robertlombardo.com (office); carole@

carolefarley.com (home). *Website:* www.lombardoassociates.org (office); www .carolefarley.com.

FARMER, (William John) Bill, AO, BA, MSc; Australian fmr diplomatist; b. 10 June 1947; m. Rev. Elaine Farmer; ed Univ. of Sydney, London School of Econs, UK; joined Foreign Service 1969; served in Embassy in Cairo 1969–71, in London 1972–75; Deputy High Commr to Fiji 1979–82; Minister, Perm. Mission to UN, New York 1984–87, Deputy Rep. of Australia on Security Council 1985–86; Amb. to Mexico (also accred to Cen. American countries and Cuba) 1987–89; High Commr to Papua New Guinea 1993–95, to Malaysia 1996–97; Deputy Sec., Dept of Foreign Affairs and Trade 1997–98, Sec., Dept of Immigration and Multicultural Affairs 1998–2001, Sec., Dept of Immigration and Multicultural and Indigenous Affairs 2001–05, also Sec., Dept of Reconciliation and Aboriginal and Torres Strait Islander Affairs; Amb. to Indonesia 2005–10; Counsellor, Dragoman Pty Ltd (consultancy) –2017; apptd to High-Level Panel of Review of Australian Aid Programme 2010, apptd to conduct Independent Review of Australian Livestock Export Industry 2011, apptd Chair. Ind. Review of Australian Centre for Int. Agricultural Research 2012; Sr Adviser to Australian Govt on the Kokoda Initiative between Australia and Papua New Guinea 2014–; mem. Bd of Dirs Asia Soc. Australia; mem. Bd of Trustees Queen Elizabeth Diamond Jubilee Trust Australia; mem. Northern Territory Chief Minister's Advisory Council; Centenary Medal 2003.

FARMER, Paul, MD, PhD; American physician, medical anthropologist and academic; *Kolokotrones University Professor, Harvard Medical School;* b. 26 Oct. 1959; m.; three c.; ed Harvard Medical School and Harvard Univ.; worked amongst dispossessed peasants in Haiti 1990s; fmr Maude and Lillian Presley Prof. of Medical Anthropology, Dept of Social Medicine, Harvard Medical School, Co-Dir Program in Infectious Diseases and Social Change, Kolokotrones Univ. Prof. 2010–, also Chair. Dept of Global Health and Social Medicine; divides his clinical time between Brigham and Women's Hosp. (Div. of Infectious Disease), where he is an attending physician, and Clinique Bon Sauveur charity hosp. in rural Haiti, where he serves as Medical Co-Dir; Founding Dir and Chief Strategist Partners in Health 1987; UN Deputy Special Envoy to Haiti 2009–12, Special Adviser to UN Sec.-Gen for Community Based Medicine and Lessons From Haiti 2012–; currently Chief of Div. Global Health Equity, Brigham and Women's Hosp.; Ed.-in-Chief Health and Human Rights Journal; visiting prof. at insts throughout USA as well as in France, Canada, Peru, Netherlands, Russia and Central Asia; has worked in communicable disease control in Americas for over a decade and is an authority on tuberculosis treatment and control; mem. Int. Scientific Cttee's Int. Conf. on AIDS, AIDS DOTS-Plus Working Group for the Global Tuberculosis Programme of WHO, Scientific Cttee of WHO Working Group on DOTS-Plus for MDR-TB, Commonwealth of Mass Bureau of Communicable Disease Control; Coordinator Int. Working Group on Multidrug-Resistant Tuberculosis; Chief Advisor, Tuberculosis Programs of the Open Soc. Inst.; Chief Medical Consultant, Tuberculosis Treatment Project in the Prisons of Tomsk (Siberia) for Public Health Research Inst.; has served on Scientific Review Bds of ten Int. Confs on AIDS; Fellow, American Acad. of Arts and Sciences 2009–; Hon. DH (North Adams State Coll.) 1995, Hon. DJur (Ohio Wesleyan Univ.) 2003, Hon. DMedSc (Brown Univ.) 2003 and many others; Duke Univ. Humanitarian Award, Margaret Mead Award, American Anthropological Asscn, Outstanding Int. Physician Award, American Medical Asscn, Heinz Humanitarian Award, John D. and Catherine T. MacArthur Foundation Genius Award 1993, Pedro Arrupe Medal for Outstanding Service 1996, Pro Bono Award, The Legal Aid Soc. of New York 2000, Award of Excellence, Haitian Studies Asscn 2001, Dr Jean Mayer Global Citizenship Award, Tufts Univ. 2002, Heinz Award in the Human Condition 2003 and numerous others. *Publications:* more than 75 publs including AIDS and Accusation 1992, The Uses of Haiti 1994, Infections and Inequalities 1998, Pathologies of Power 2003, Partner to the Poor: A Paul Farmer Reader 2010, Haiti After the Earthquake 2011, To Repair the World: Paul Farmer Speaks to the Next Generation 2013, Reimagining Global Health 2013; Co-Ed.: Women, Poverty, and AIDS (Eileen Basker 1997) 1996, The Global Impact of Drug-Resistant Tuberculosis 1999, Global Health in Times of Violence 2009. *Address:* Department of Social Medicine, Harvard Medical School, 641 Huntington Avenue, Boston MA 02115, USA (office). *Telephone:* (617) 432-1707 (office). *Website:* www.hms.harvard.edu/dsm (office).

FARMER, Richard Gilbert, MS, MD, MACP, MACG; American physician and professor of medicine; *Professor Emeritus of Medicine, Division of Gastroenterology and Hepatology, University of Rochester Medical Center;* b. 29 Sept. 1931, Kokomo, Ind.; s. of Oscar I. Farmer and Elizabeth J. Gilbert Farmer; m. Janice M. Schrank 1958; one s. one d.; ed Indiana Univ., Univ. of Maryland, Milwaukee Co. Hosp. (Marquette Univ.), Mayo Foundation, Rochester, Minn. and Univ. of Minnesota; mil. service 1960–62; staff, Cleveland Clinic Foundation and Cleveland Clinic Hosp. 1962–91, Chair. Dept of Gastroenterology 1972–82, Chair. Div. of Medicine 1975–91; Asst and Assoc. Clinical Prof., Case Western Reserve Univ. School of Medicine 1972–91; Sr Medical Adviser, Bureau for Europe, USAID 1992–94; consultant in health care, Eastern Europe and Soviet Union 1994–96; consultant, American Medico-Legal Foundation 1996–2003, Inst. for Health Policy Analysis 1996–2004; Clinical Prof. of Medicine, Georgetown Univ. Medical Center 1992–2004; Medical Dir Quality Health Int. 1997–98, Eurasian Medical Educ. Program (Russia) 1998–2004; medical consultant, Scandinavian Care Consultants, Stockholm 1998–2003; apptd Prof. of Medicine and Chief of Digestive and Liver Disease Unit, Univ. of Rochester Medical Center, New York 2004, Prof. Emer. of Medicine 2011–; mem. Inst. of Medicine, Nat. Advisory Bd, Nat. Foundation for Ileitis and Colitis, Nat. Comm. on Digestive Diseases 1977–79; Gov. for Ohio, American Coll. of Physicians 1980–84, Regent 1985–91; Chair. Health and Public Policy Comm. 1986–88; Pres. American Coll. of Gastroenterology 1978–79, Asscn of Program Dirs in Internal Medicine 1977–79; Interstate Postgraduate Medical Asscn 1983–84; mem. council to assess quality of care in the Medicare program, Gen. Accounting Office, US House of Reps, Washington, DC 1986–89; Special Citation, American Coll. of Physicians 1984, Mastership American Coll. of Gastroenterology 1991, American Coll. of Physicians 1993, mem. Int. Org. for Study of Inflammatory Bowel Disease (Deputy Chair. 1982–86); Founder's Award, Asscn of Program Dirs in Internal Medicine 1993, Jubilee Medal, Charles Univ. of Prague, Czech Repub. 1998, Mentor Award, American Gastroenterological Asscn 2007. *Publications:* author or co-author of 260 publs in the medical literature, primarily relating to digestive diseases with a specific interest in inflammatory bowel disease and health care in Eastern Europe and the fmr Soviet Union; author of six books and contrib. to others. *Leisure interests:* squash, tennis, running and reading (history and current events). *Address:* School of Medicine and Dentistry, Gastroenterology and Hepatology Division, University of Rochester Medical Center, 601 Elmwood Avenue, ACF 4-2071A, Rochester, NY 14642 (office); 9126 Town Gate Lane, Bethesda, MD 20817, USA (home). *Telephone:* (585) 275-7432 (office); (301) 365-5828 (home). *Fax:* (301) 365-6202 (home). *E-mail:* richard_farmer@urmc.rochester.edu (office). *Website:* www.urmc .rochester.edu (office).

FARNHAM, John Peter, AO; Australian (b. British) singer and entertainer; b. 1 July 1949, Essex, UK; m. Jillian Farnham 1973; two s.; ed Lyndale High School; settled in Australia 1959; apprenticed as plumber; lead singer for Strings Unlimited 1965; began recording 1967; television appearances including nature series Survival with Johnny Farnham for ABC; f. John Farnham Band 1978; lead singer for Little River Band 1982–85; 12 Gold Record Awards; ARIA Awards for Best Male Artist 1987, 1988, 1991, for Highest Selling Single (for You're the Voice) 1987, for Outstanding Achievement Award 1988, for Song of the Year 1991, Hall of Fame Award 2003, Australian of the Year, Bicentennial 1998. *Recordings include:* Sadie the Cleaning Lady 1967 (3 Gold Records), Friday Kind of Monday 1968, Rose Coloured Glasses 1968, One 1969, Raindrops Keep Falling on My Head 1969, Comic Conversation 1970, Rock Me Baby 1972, Don't You Know It's Magic 1973, Everything is Out of Season 1973, Uncovered 1980, The Net 1982, Playing to Win 1984, Whispering Jack (ARIA Awards for Highest Selling Album 1987, for Best Adult Contemporary Album 1987) 1986, Age of Reason (ARIA Award for Highest Selling Album 1989) 1989, Chain Reaction (ARIA Award for Highest Selling Album 1991) 1990, Full House 1991, Jesus Christ Superstar: The Album 1992, Then Again (ARIA Award for Highest Selling Album 1994) 1992, Romeo's Heart (ARIA Award for Best Adult Contemporary Album 1996) 1996, Anthology Series I, II and III 1997, 33⅓ 2001, The Last Time (ARIA Award for Best Adult Contemporary Album 2003) 2002, I Remember When I was Young 2005, Jack 2010, The Acoustic Chapel Sessions 2011, Two Strong Hearts 2015, The Complete Whispering Jack 2016, Friends for Christmas 2017. *Website:* www.johnfarnham .com.au.

FARNISH, Christine, CBE, BSc, MSc; British financial executive; *Chair, Zopa Ltd;* b. 21 April 1950, Ipswich, Suffolk; m. 1st; three s.; m. 2nd John Hayes; one d.; ed Ipswich High School, Univ. of Manchester; with Countryside Comm. 1972–76; London Borough of Lewisham 1983–86; London Research Centre 1986–88; joined Cambridge City Council 1988, Asst Chief Exec. –1994; Dir Consumer Affairs, Oftel 1994–98, Deputy Dir-Gen. 1998; Dir Consumer Div., Financial Services Authority (FSA) 1998–2002; Chief Exec. Nat. Asscn of Pension Funds 2002–06; Group Dir of Public Policy, Barclays PLC 2006–11; Chair. Family and Parenting Inst. 2010–, Consumer Focus 2010–, Peer to Peer Finance Asscn 2012–18; Chair. Zopa Ltd and NED Zopa Group Bd 2018–; Dir (non-exec.) Papworth NHS Trust 1998–2002, Office of Fair Trading 2003–06, Aggregate Industries Limited 2012–, Ofwat 2014–, Office for Gas and Electricity Markets (Ofgem) 2016–, Univ. Hospitals, Brighton, Sussex, AXA Group; Dir, ABTA 2010– (also Chair. Pension Trustee); mem. Council Advertising Standards Authority 2002–08; Trustee, FSA Pension Plan 1998–2002. *Address:* Zopa Ltd, 47-49, Cottons Centre, Tooley Street, London, SE1 2QG, England (office). *Website:* www.zopa.com (office).

FAROOQ, Qazi Muhammad, BL; Pakistani judge (retd) and government official; b. 6 Jan. 1938, Abbottabad; ed Dennys High School, Rawalpindi, Gordon Coll., Rawalpindi, Univ. Law Coll., Lahore, Nat. Inst. of Public Admin, Lahore, Inst. of Shariah and Legal Profession, Islamabad, Islamic Univ., Madina Munawwara; lawyer in Abbottabad –1967; joined PCS (Judicial Br.) 1967, worked as Civil Judge in Charsadda, Lakki Marwat, Bannu and as Sr Civil Judge, Mardan 1967–74, promoted as Additional Dist and Session Judge 1974, served at Haripur, Abbottabad and Mansehra 1974–77, promoted as Dist and Session Judge 1977, served at Mansehra, Bannu and Peshawar 1977–82; Prov. Election Commr NW Frontier Prov. 1982–88; Registrar, Peshawar High Court 1988–91, Judge of Peshawar High Court 1991–99, Chief Justice Peshawar High Court 1999–2000; Judge, Supreme Court of Pakistan 2000–03; Judge-in-Charge, Fed. Judicial Acad., Islamabad 2000–03; Chief Election Commr 2006–09; Chair. Cttee of Admin, Al-Mizan Foundation 2005–; mem. Law Reforms Comm. 2000–03, Law and Justice Comm. of Pakistan 2005–.

FAROOQI, Hamidullah, MA; Afghan economist, academic, business executive and government official; *Professor, National Economies Department, Kabul University;* b. 1953; ed Faculty of Econs, Kabul Univ., Int. Inst. of Foreign Trade, New Delhi, India, Queens Coll., City Univ. of New York, USA; fmr Prof. of Econs, Kabul Univ., now Prof., Nat. Economies Dept; Pres. and CEO United Molding Ltd., Global Export and Import Ltd,. and Hashmat Ltd, New York 1977–82; Pres. and CEO Hamed-Lais Construction Company, LLC, Kabul 2002–; Chair. Banke Millie Afghan (Afghan Nat. Bank) 2003–05; Pres. and CEO Afghanistan Int. Chamber of Commerce 2005–; Founder and Prin. Int. Model School (pvt. primary school teaching exclusively through English) 2005–08; Co-founder and Chair. Brishna (think tank) 2007–; Co-founder Mesbah Inst. 2008–; Founder and mem. Bd of Dirs Afghanistan Traders and Industrialists Centre 2000–; mem. Microfinance Investment Support Facility for Afghanistan 2006–, Afghanistan-Pakistan Peace Jerga 2007–; mem. Asscn for Democracy in Afghanistan 1995–, Afghanistan Artists Union 1998–, mem. Advisory Bd Kabul Centre for Strategic Studies 2007–; Minister of Transport and Civil Aviation 2009; apptd by Afghan Pres. Ashraf Ghani to lead an anti-corruption inquiry 2015–. *Address:* National Economies Department, Kabul University, Jamal Mina, Kabul, Afghanistan (office). *Website:* www.ku.edu.af (office).

FAROOQI, Khaled; Afghan politician; *Leader, Hizb-i Islami Afghanistan (Islamic Party of Afghanistan);* Leader of Hizb-i Islami (Islamic Party) in Paktika Prov., led breakaway faction that claimed to renounce violence and support US-trained Afghan Nat. Army, higher educ. for women, free elections and moves to disarm pvt. militias 2001, Leader, Hizb-i Islami Afghanistan (Islamic Party of Afghanistan) 2006–; mem. Parl. (Paktika Prov.) 2005–, Chair. Cttee on Communication, Urban Devt, Water, Power and Municipal Affairs 2005–. *Address:* Hizb-i Islami Afghanistan (Islamic Party of Afghanistan), Area A, Khushal Mena, Kabul, Afghanistan. *Telephone:* (79) 9421474.

FAROOQUI, Dewan M. Yousuf; Pakistani business executive; *Chairman, Dewan Mushtaq Group;* b. 13 March 1963, Karachi; Sindh Prov. Minister for Local Govt, Transport, Labour, Industries, Housing and Town Planning 2000–03; currently Chair. and Chief Exec. Dewan Mushtaq Group, and CEO Dewan Farooqui Motors Ltd, responsible for overseeing Dewan Motorcycles, Dewan Sugar Mills Ltd, Dewan Textile Mills Ltd, Dewan Salman Fiber Ltd; Chair. Pakistan Textile City 2004–09; Co-Chief Patron Pakistan-Korea Business Forum; mem. Bd of Dirs Pakistan Industrial Tech. Assistance Centre; mem. Pakistan Automotive Mfrs Asscn, Pakistan-France Business Alliance, Young Pres. Org., Int. Chamber of Commerce, Pakistan-India Business Forum; Pres. Sindh Squash Asscn; Sitara-i-Imtiaz Award for Public Service (Highest Industrial Investor), Pres. of Pakistan. *Address:* Dewan Mushtaq Group, Dewan Centre, 7th Floor Block A, Finance & Trade Centre, Shahrah-e-Faisal, Karachi, Pakistan (office). *Telephone:* (21) 35857862 (home); (21) 111364463 (office). *Fax:* (21) 35630814 (office). *E-mail:* dewanyousuf@dewangroup.com.pk (office). *Website:* www.dewangroup.com.pk (office).

FARQUHAR, Robin Hugh, BA (Hons), MA, PhD, FCCEA; Canadian academic and fmr university administrator; b. 1 Dec. 1938, Victoria, BC; s. of Hugh E. Farquhar and Jean MacIntosh; m. Frances Caswell 1963; three d.; ed Victoria High School, Victoria Coll., Univ. of British Columbia, Univ. of Chicago; teacher, counsellor and coach, Edward Milne Secondary School, Sooke, BC 1962–64; Assoc. Dir and Deputy Dir, Univ. Council for Educational Admin 1966–71; Chair., Dept of Educational Admin, Asst Dir, Ont. Inst. for Studies in Educ. and Assoc. Prof., then Prof., School of Grad. Studies, Univ. of Toronto 1971–76; Dean of Educ. and Prof., Univ. of Sask., Saskatoon 1976–81; Pres., Vice-Chancellor and Prof., Univ. of Winnipeg 1981–89, Pres. Emer. 1989–; Pres., Vice-Chancellor and Prof., Carleton Univ., Ottawa 1989–96, Prof. of Public Policy and Admin 1996–2004, then Prof. Emer.; int. consultant, higher educ. policy and man. 2004–, mem. Int. Advisory Cttee, Salzburg Seminar Univs Project, Institutional Evaluation Experts Pool, European Univ. Asscn, mem. General Council, Univ. of Madeira; Vice-Chair. Academics Without Borders-Universitaires sans Frontières; Fellow, Commonwealth Council for Educational Admin; Hon. mem. World Innovation Foundation; Hon. Citizen, City of Winnipeg, Hon. Scout, Scouts Canada; 125th Anniversary of the Confed. of Canada Commemorative Medal; Hon. Diploma in Adult Educ.; Award of Merit, Canadian Bureau for Int. Educ., Ottawa–Carleton Partnership Award of Excellence for Leadership. *Publications:* numerous books and monographs, over 100 published articles on educational admin. and higher educ. policy and management. *Address:* #700–636 Montreal Street, Victoria, BC V8V 4Y1, Canada (home). *Telephone:* (613) 878-1094 (home); (250) 361-3004 (home). *E-mail:* robin.farquhar@carleton.ca (home).

FARR, David N., BS, MBA; American business executive; *Chairman and CEO, Emerson Electric Company;* b. 1955; m.; two c.; ed Wake Forest Univ., Vanderbilt Univ.; joined Corp. Staff Dept, Emerson Electric Co. (later Emerson) 1981, becoming Man., Investor Relations, Vice-Pres., Corp. Planning and Devt, Pres. Ridge Tool Div., Group Vice-Pres. for Industrial Components and Equipment, Pres. Emerson Electric Asia-Pacific, Hong Kong 1994–97, Exec. Vice-Pres. Emerson 1997–99, Sr Exec. Vice-Pres. and COO 1999–2000, CEO 2000–, mem. Bd of Dirs and Chair. 2004–, Pres. 2005–10; mem. or fmr mem. Bd of Dirs Delphi Corpn, United Way of Greater St Louis (Chair. annual fund-raising campaign 2007, Chair. of its de Tocqueville Soc. 2010), US-China Business Council; mem. Bd of Dirs, IBM 2012; mem. Exec. Bd Municipal Theatre Asscn of St Louis (The Muny at Forest Park), Boy Scouts of America (Greater St Louis Area Council); mem. Civic Progress (current Pres.), The Business Council, Washington DC; Trustee, Webster Univ.; St Louis Citizen of the Year 2011, Semper Fidelis Award, Marine Scholarship Foundation 2012. *Address:* Emerson Electric Co., 8000 West Florissant Avenue, PO Box 4100, St Louis, MO 63136-8506, USA (office). *Telephone:* (314) 553-2000 (office). *Fax:* (314) 553-3527 (office). *E-mail:* info@emerson.com (office). *Website:* www.emerson.com (office).

FARRAKHAN, Louis; American religious leader; *Leader, Nation of Islam;* b. (Louis Eugene Wolcott), 11 May 1933, New York City; m. Betsy Wolcott; eight c.; ed Winston-Salem Teachers Coll.; joined Nation of Islam 1955, Leader and Nat. Spokesman, Nation of Islam Mosque, New York 1965–75, f. reorganized Nation of Islam 1977, Leader 1977–, f. The Final Call (official newspaper of Nation of Islam) 1979. *Achievements include:* organizer of Million Man March, Washington, DC 1995, Million Family March 2000. *Address:* Nation of Islam, 7351 South Stony Island Avenue, Chicago, IL 60649, USA. *Telephone:* (773) 324-6000 (office). *Website:* www.noi.org (office).

FARRANT, Jill, MSc, PhD; South African plant physiologist, molecular biologist and academic; *Research Chair in Molecular Physiology of Plant Desiccation Tolerance, University of Cape Town;* mem. Faculty, Univ. of Cape Town (UCT), initiated work on resurrection plants, Head of Molecular and Cell Biology Dept 2004–07, Research Chair in Molecular Physiology of Plant Desiccation Tolerance 2007–, mem. UCT Coll. of Fellows 2009–; Pres. South African Asscn of Botanists 2009–10; Harry Oppenheimer Memorial Trust Fellowship Award 2009, awarded an A-rating by the Nat. Research Foundation (first female researcher at UCT) 2009, Distinguished Woman in Science Award, Dept of Science and Tech. 2010, L'Oréal-UNESCO For Women in Science Award (Africa and the Arab States) (for the elucidation of mechanisms by which plants overcome drought conditions) 2012. *Publications:* numerous papers in professional journals. *Address:* Molecular and Cell Biology Department, University of Cape Town, Private Bag, Rondebosch 7701, South Africa (office). *Telephone:* (21) 6504496 (office). *Fax:* (21) 6501861 (office). *E-mail:* jill.farrant@uct.ac.za (office). *Website:* www.mcb.uct.ac.za (office).

FARRELL, Andrew (Andy), OBE; British rugby football coach and fmr rugby football player; b. 30 May 1975, Wigan, Lancs.; s. of Peter Farrell; m. to Colleen Farrell; loose forward, second row, prop forward or stand off; signed for Wigan Warriors 1992–2004 (sr debut versus Keighley Nov. 1991); became youngest player to win a Wembley final in 1993 aged 17 years and 11 months; won Harry Sunderland Trophy for Man of the Match in 1996 and 1997 Premiership finals (both against St Helens)—only Wigan player to have won the award twice; Super League record of 11 goals in a match versus St Helens 1997, repeated feat versus Paris St Germain 1997; highest Super League point scorer 1997; passed 3,000 points for Wigan in 2004 (second-highest total for the club); five caps for GB Acad., one cap for GB Under-21s, full GB debut versus Australia 1993 (youngest forward to win GB cap), 34 caps in total (fifth highest); GB Capt. 1998–2003 on 29 occasions (record); five caps for England; rep. Lancashire in 2003 Origin Match; awarded Wigan testimonial season 2001; retd from rugby league and joined Saracens in Rugby Football Union 2005–09 (retd), Skills and Backs Coach 2009; mem. runner-up team in Rugby World Cup, France 2007; Asst Coach, England Rugby Football Union Lions 2012–; Man of Steel 1995, 2004, selected for Super League Dream Team 2003, 2004, Rugby League World Golden Boot Award 2004 (only second British player to win prize). *Website:* www.rfu.com.

FARRELL, Colin; Irish actor; b. 31 May 1976, Castleknock, Dublin; s. of Eamon Farrell and Rita Farrell (née Monaghan); two c.; ed Gaiety School of Drama, Dublin. *Films include:* Drinking Crude 1997, Falling for a Dancer (TV) 1998, The War Zone 1999, Ordinary Decent Criminal 2000, Tigerland (Boston Soc. of Film Critics Best Actor Award) 2000, American Outlaws 2001, Hart's War (Shanghai Int. Film Festival Best Actor Award) 2002, Minority Report 2002, Phone Booth 2002, The Recruit 2003, Daredevil 2003, Veronica Guerin 2003, S.W.A.T. 2003, Intermission 2003, A Home at the End of the World 2004, Alexander 2004, The New World 2005, Ask the Dust 2006, Miami Vice 2006, Cassandra's Dream 2007, In Bruges (Golden Globe Award for Best Actor in a Musical or Comedy 2009) 2008, Pride and Glory 2007, The Imaginarium of Doctor Parnassus 2009, Ondine (Irish Film & TV Award for Best Actor) 2010, London Boulevard 2010, Total Recall 2012, Seven Psychopaths 2012, Dead Man Down 2013, Saving Mr. Banks 2013, Winter's Tale 2014, Miss Julie 2014, The Lobster 2015, Solace 2015, Fantastic Beasts and Where to Find Them 2016, The Killing of A Sacred Deer 2017, The Beguiled 2017, Widows 2018. *Television includes:* Ballykissangel 1996, Love in the 21st Century 1999, True Detective 2015. *Address:* c/o Creative Artists Agency, 2000 Avenue of the Stars, Los Angeles, CA 90067, USA (office). *Telephone:* (424) 288-2898 (office); (424) 288-2000 (office). *Fax:* (424) 288-2900 (office). *Website:* www.caa.com (office).

FARRELL, HE Cardinal Kevin Joseph, MBA, STL, MPhil; Irish/American ecclesiastic; *Camerlengo of the Apostolic Chamber;* b. 2 Sept. 1947, Dublin; ed Univ. of Salamanca, Pontifical Gregorian Univ., Rome, Univ. of Notre Dame; ordained priest by Congregation of the Legionaries of Christ 1978; served as Chaplain, Univ. of Monterrey, Mexico; incardinated in the archdiocese of Washington 1984, Priest of Washington DC 1984–2001, Auxiliary Bishop 2001–07, Asst Pastor, Parish of St Thomas the Apostle Church 1984–85, Dir Spanish Catholic Centre 1986, Acting Exec. Dir Catholic Charitable Orgs. 1987–88, Sec. of Financial Affairs 1989–2001, named Vicar-Gen. of archdiocese and Pastor of Annunciation Catholic Church 2001; apptd Titular Bishop of Rusuccuru 2001; ordained bishop 2002, Bishop of Dallas 2007–16; apptd Prefect of the Dicastery for Laity, Family and Life 2016; cr. Cardinal 2016, Cardinal-Deacon of San Giuliano Martire 2016–; Camerlengo (Chamberlain) of the Apostolic Chamber 2019–; mem. Admin of the Patrimony of the Apostolic See 2017, Pontifical Comm. for the Vatican City State 2017. *Address:* Apostolic Chamber, Palazzo Apostolico, 00120 Città del Vaticano, Rome, Italy (office). *Telephone:* (06) 69883554 (office). *Website:* www.vatican.va (office).

FARRELL, Norman, BA, LLB, LLM; Canadian lawyer and international organization official; *Chief Prosecutor, Special Tribunal for Lebanon;* ed Queen's Univ., Kingston, Ont., Columbia Univ., New York, USA; admitted to Law Soc. of Upper Canada, Ont. 1988; Crown Counsel (Criminal Div.) with Attorney-Gen. for Prov. of Ont. 1988–96; held several positions in ICRC, including as Del. and Co-ordinator in charge of dissemination of int. humanitarian law in Bosnia and Herzegovina, Legal Adviser on int. humanitarian law in Ethiopia and Kenya, Adviser on int. criminal law and int. humanitarian law in Switzerland 1996–99; Appeals Counsel, Int. Criminal Tribunal for the Fmr Yugoslavia 1999–2002, Head of Appeals Section and Sr Appeals Counsel 2002–05, Prin. Legal Officer, Office of the Prosecutor 2005–08, Deputy Prosecutor 2008–12, Head of Appeals Section and Sr Appeals Counsel, Int. Criminal Tribunal for Rwanda 2002–03, Chief Prosecutor, Special Tribunal for Lebanon 2012–; Lecturer on Int. Criminal Law, Faculty of Law, Queen's Univ. 2004–11, Int. Studies Centre, Herstmonceux, UK 2004–17. *Address:* Special Tribunal for Lebanon, Dokter van der Stamstraat 1, 2265 AC Leidschendam, Netherlands (office). *Telephone:* (70) 8003435 (office). *E-mail:* stl-pressoffice@un.org (office). *Website:* www.stl-tsl.org (office).

FARRELL, Patrick (Pat) M.; Irish business executive and fmr politician; *Head of Communications and Government Affairs, Bank of Ireland;* b. 30 Aug. 1957, Leitrim; s. of Bill Farrell and Mamie Casey; m. Margaret Logan 1988; one s. one d.; ed Columbia Business School; Gen. Man. Regional Hosp., Sligo 1981–86; CEO Galvia Hosp., Galway 1986–91; Gen. Sec. Fianna Fáil 1991–98; CEO Irish Banking Fed. 2004–13; Head of Communications and Government Affairs, Bank of Ireland 2013–; Chair. Bd of Dirs Sightsavers Ireland; Fellow, Inst. of Bankers. *Leisure interests:* current affairs, reading, writing, cycling. *Address:* Bank of Ireland, 40 Mespil Road, Dublin 4, Ireland (office). *E-mail:* Pat.Farrell@boi.com (office). *Website:* www.bankofireland.com (office).

FARRELL, Suzanne; American ballerina; *Artistic Director, Suzanne Farrell Ballet;* b. 16 Aug. 1945; ed School of American Ballet; fmr Prin. Dancer with New York City Ballet –1989; also danced with Béjart Ballet, Brussels; appeared in numerous Balanchine ballets choreographed for her including Mozartiana, Chaconne, Meditation, Vienna Waltzes; staged seven Balanchine ballets at John F. Kennedy Center for Performing Arts, Washington, DC 1995 and many other stagings of Balanchine's works; Founder-Artistic Dir Suzanne Farrell Ballet Co., Kennedy Center for the Performing Arts 2000–; répétiteur for Balanchine Trust, including Kirov Ballet, Royal Danish Ballet and Paris Opéra Ballet; mem. Advisory Panel Princess Grace Foundation, Sr Advisory Bd of Arthritis Foundation; EPPES Prof. of Dance, Florida State Univ.; trains ballet dancers in camp in The Adirondacks; several hon. degrees; Nat. Medal of the Arts 2003, Kennedy Center Honor 2005, Capezio Dance Award 2005. *Television:* Suzanne Farrell: Elusive Muse (documentary). *Publication:* Holding On To The Air (autobiography) 1990. *Address:* Suzanne Farrell Ballet, Kennedy Center for the Performing Arts, 2700 F Street, NW, Washington, DC 20566, USA (office). *Website:* www.kennedy-center.org/programs/ballet/farrell (office).

FARRELL, Sir Terence (Terry), Kt, CBE, MCP, MArch, MRTPI, RIBA, FCSD, FRSA; British architect; *Principal, Terry Farrell & Partners;* b. 12 May 1938; s. of Thomas Farrell and Molly Farrell (née Maguire); m. 1st Angela Rosemarie Mallam 1960; two d.; m. 2nd Susan Hilary Aplin 1973; two s. one d.; ed St Cuthbert's

Grammar School, Newcastle-upon-Tyne, Newcastle Univ., Univ. of Pennsylvania, USA; Harkness Fellow, Commonwealth Fund, USA 1962–64; Partner, Farrell Grimshaw Partnership 1965–80, Terry Farrell Partnership 1980–87; Prin. Terry Farrell & Partners 1987–; Visiting Prof., Univ. of Westminster 1998–2001; Hon. FAIA; Hon. DCL (Newcastle) 2000, Hon. DArts (Lincoln) 2003. *Major projects include:* Vauxhall Cross (MI6 Bldg), London, The Peak, Hong Kong, Charing Cross Station Redevelopment, London, Edinburgh Int. Conf. Centre, British Consulate and British Council Bldgs, Hong Kong, Dean Centre Art Gallery, Edin., Int. Centre for Life, Newcastle, Transportation Centre for Inchon Int. Airport, Seoul, The Deep 'Submarium' (aquarium), Hull, British Library masterplan, London 2009–, West Kowloon Cultural District. Hong Kong 2009–12, Kingkey 100, Shenzhen (Shenzhen's tallest building) 2011, Eagle House, London 2016, Embassy Gardens, Wandsworth, London (under construction). *Publications:* Architectural Monograph 1985, Urban Design Monograph 1993, Ten Years, Ten Cities: The work of Terry Farrell and Partners, 1991–2001 2002, Place 2005; articles in numerous journals. *Leisure interests:* walking, swimming. *Address:* Terry Farrell & Partners, 7 Hatton Street, London, NW8 8PL, England (office). *Telephone:* (20) 7258-3433 (office). *Fax:* (20) 7723-7059 (office). *E-mail:* tfarrell@terryfarrell.co.uk (office). *Website:* www.terryfarrell.co.uk (office).

FARRELL, Thomas Francis, II, BA, JD; American lawyer and business executive; *Chairman, President and CEO, Dominion;* b. 1954; m. Anne Garland Farrell (neé Tullidge); two s.; ed Univ. of Va; Pnr, McGuire Woods Beatle & Booth (law firm) 1981–95; joined Dominion Resources Inc. (now Dominion), Richmond 1995, Sr Vice-Pres. and Gen. Counsel 1995–97, Sr Vice-Pres. for Corp. Affairs 1997–99, Exec. Vice-Pres. 1999–2003, Pres. and COO 2002–05, Pres. and CEO 2006–07, Chair., Pres. and CEO 2007–, also CEO Va Power, Dominion Generation Inc., Pres. and COO Consolidated Natural Gas Co. (subsidiaries of Dominion); mem. Bd of Dirs Virginia Electric and Power Co., Inst. of Nuclear Power Operations (now Chair.), Edison Electric Inst. (Chair. 2011–12); fmr Chair. Colonial Williamsburg Foundation; mem. Va Bar Asscn, Va Law Foundation; fmr mem. Bd of Visitors, Univ. of Va; Trustee, Virginia Museum of Fine Arts, Virginia Foundation for Independent Colleges. *Address:* Dominion, 120 Tredegar Street, Richmond, VA 23219, USA (office). *Telephone:* (804) 819-2000 (office). *Fax:* (804) 819-2233 (office). *E-mail:* thomas_farrell@dom.com (office). *Website:* www.dom .com (office).

FARRINGTON, David Philip, OBE, MA, PhD, FBA, FMedSci; British psychologist, academic and criminologist; *Professor Emeritus of Psychological Criminology, Institute of Criminology, University of Cambridge;* b. 7 March 1944, Ormskirk, Lancs.; s. of William Farrington and Gladys Holden Farrington; m. Sally Chamberlain 1966; three d.; ed Univ. of Cambridge; mem. staff, Inst. of Criminology, Univ. of Cambridge 1969–, Prof. of Psychological Criminology 1992–2012, Prof. Emer. 2012–, Leverhulme Trust Emer. Fellow 2012–15; Visiting Fellow, US Nat. Inst. of Justice 1981; Chair. Div. of Criminological and Legal Psychology, British Psychological Soc. 1983–85; mem. Parole Bd for England and Wales 1984–87; Vice-Chair. US Nat. Acad. of Sciences Panel on Violence 1989–92; Visiting Fellow, US Bureau of Justice Statistics 1995–98; Co-Chair. US Office of Juvenile Justice and Delinquency Prevention Study Group on Serious and Violent Juvenile Offenders 1995–97, US Office of Juvenile Justice and Delinquency Prevention Study Group on Very Young Offenders 1998–2000, Campbell Collaboration Crime and Justice Group 2000–04; Chair. UK Dept of Health Advisory Cttee for Nat. Programme on Forensic Mental Health 2000–03; Fellow, Int. Soc. for Research on Aggression 2007–, Asscn for Psychological Science 2010–; mem. British Psychological Soc. 1974–, British Soc. of Criminology 1975– (Pres. 1990–93), American Soc. of Criminology 1983– (Pres. 1998–99, Fellow 1991, mem. Exec. Bd 1997–2000), European Asscn of Psychology and Law 1991– (Pres. (1997–99, mem. Exec. Cttee 1991–2002), Asscn of Univ. Teachers 1979–, Int. Asscn for Correctional and Forensic Psychology 2006–, European Soc. of Criminology 2008–; Hon. Fellow, British Psychological Soc. 2012; Sellin-Glueck Award, American Soc. of Criminology 1984, Sutherland Award, American Soc. of Criminology 2002, Joan McCord Award, Acad. of Experimental Criminology 2005, Beccaria Gold Medal, Criminology Soc. of German-Speaking Countries 2005, Hermann Mannheim Prize, Int. Centre for Comparative Criminology 2005, British Psychological Soc. (Div. of Forensic Psychology) Senior Prize 2007, European Asscn of Psychology and Law Award for Outstanding Career-Long Contributions to the Scientific Study of Law and Human Behaviour 2009, Jerry Lee Award, American Soc. of Criminology Div. of Experimental Criminology, for lifetime achievements in experimental criminology 2010, Robert Boruch Award, Campbell Collaboration for Contributions to Research that Informs Public Policy 2012, Stockholm Prize in Criminology 2013, Freda Adler Distinguished Scholar Award, American Soc. of Criminology, Div. of Int. Criminology 2013, Juvenile Justice Without Borders Int. Award, Int. Juvenile Justice Observatory, Belgium 2014, August Vollmer Award, American Soc. of Criminology, for outstanding contributions to justice or to the treatment or prevention of criminal or delinquent behaviour 2014. *Publications include:* numerous books and over 420 articles on criminology and psychology. *Address:* Institute of Criminology, University of Cambridge, Sidgwick Avenue, Cambridge, CB3 9DA (office); 7 The Meadows, Haslingfield, Cambridge, CB3 7JD, England (home). *Telephone:* (1223) 335360 (office); (1223) 872555 (home). *Fax:* (1223) 335356 (office). *E-mail:* enquiries@crim .cam.ac.uk (office). *Website:* www.crim.cam.ac.uk (office).

FARROW, Mia Villiers; American actress; b. 9 Feb. 1945, Los Angeles, Calif.; d. of John Villiers Farrow and Maureen O'Sullivan; m. 1st Frank Sinatra 1966 (divorced 1968); m. 2nd André Previn 1970 (divorced 1979); partner Woody Allen 1979–92; 15 c. (11 adopted); stage début in The Importance of Being Earnest, New York 1963; French Acad. Award for Best Actress 1969, David Donatello Award (Italy) 1969, Rio de Janeiro Film Festival Award 1969, San Sebastian Award. *Films include:* Guns at Batasi 1964, Rosemary's Baby 1968, Secret Ceremony 1969, John and Mary 1969, See No Evil 1970, The Great Gatsby 1973, Full Circle 1978, A Wedding 1978, Death on the Nile 1978, The Hurricane 1979, A Midsummer Night's Sex Comedy 1982, Zelig 1983, Broadway Danny Rose 1984, Purple Rose of Cairo 1985, Hannah and Her Sisters 1986, Radio Days 1987, September 1988, Another Woman 1988, Oedipus Wrecks 1989, Crimes and Misdemeanors 1989, Alice 1990, Shadows and Fog 1992, Husbands and Wives 1992, Widow's Peak 1994, Miami Rhapsody 1995, Private Parts 1997, Reckless 1995, Coming Soon 2000, Purpose 2002, The Omen 2006, Arthur and the Invisibles 2006, The Ex 2007, Be Kind Rewind 2007, Dark Horse 2011. *Television appearances:* Peyton Place 1964–66; Johnny Belinda 1965, Peter Pan 1975, Goodbye Raggedy Ann (film), Miracle at Midnight, The Secret Life of Zoey (film) 2002, Samantha: An American Girl Holiday (film) 2004. *Publication:* What Falls Away (autobiog.) 1996. *Leisure interests:* reading, mind wandering, listening to music and certain people. *Address:* c/o Sam Cohn, International Creative Management, 40 West 57th Street, New York, NY 10019, USA. *Website:* www .mia-farrow.com.

FARUQUE, Mohammad, BEng; Pakistani industrialist; *Chairman, Ghulam Faruque Group;* b. 14 Jan. 1930, Magpur, India; s. of Ghulam Faruque and Zulfara Faruque; two s. one d.; ed Univ. of Southern California, USA; Chair. Ghulam Faruque Group, conglomerate which includes Cherat Cement Co. Ltd, Mirpurkhas Sugar Mills Ltd, Greaves Pakistan (Pvt.) Ltd. *Leisure interests:* cricket, golf, reading. *Address:* Ghulam Faruque Group, Modern Motors House, Beaumont Road, Karachi 75530, Pakistan (office). *Telephone:* (21) 5682565 (office); (21) 5888889 (home). *Fax:* (21) 5682839 (office). *E-mail:* faruque@fascom.com (office). *Website:* www.gfg.com.pk (office).

FASCETTO, Jorge E.; Argentine journalist and international organization official; ed La Plata Nat. Univ.; apptd. Gen. Man. El Día newspaper, La Plata 1967, Chair. 1980; Founder and Chair. Diario Popular 1974–; Vice-Pres. Exec. Cttee Asociacíon de Diarios del Interior de la República Argentina 1985, Asociacíon de Entidades Periodísticas Argentinas 1986; mem. Exec. Cttee and Advisory Council, Inter-American Press Asscn (IAPA), Pres. IAPA Tech. Center 1989; Chair. Int. Press Inst. 2002–04. *Address:* El Día, Avda A, Diagonal 80 815, B1900CCI, La Plata, Argentina. *Website:* www.eldia.com.ar.

FASE, Martin M. G., PhD; Dutch banker, economist and academic; *Professor Emeritus of Monetary Economics, University of Amsterdam;* b. (Martinus Maria Gerard), 28 Dec. 1937, Boskoop; s. of A. P. Fase and G. J. M. de Groot; m. Lida E. M. Franse 1965; two s.; ed Univ. of Amsterdam; Research Assoc., Inst. of Actuarial Sciences and Econometrics, Amsterdam 1965–69; Ford Foundation Fellow, Dept of Econs, Univ. of Wisconsin, Madison, USA 1969–71; with De Nederlandsche Bank 1971–2001, Deputy Dir 1985–2001; Extraordinary Prof. of Business Statistics, Erasmus Univ., Rotterdam 1978–86; Extraordinary Prof. of Monetary Econs, Univ. of Amsterdam 1986–2003, Prof. Emer. 2003–; Man. Ed. De Economist 1998–2008, Chair. Editorial Bd 2003–08; Fellow, Royal Netherlands Acad. of Arts and Sciences 1987, Royal Hollandsche Maatschappij der Wetenschappen 1989; mem. Maatschappi der Nederlandse Letterkunde 2001; Officer, Order of Orange Nassau 1995; N.G. Pierson Medal 1996. *Publications include:* An Econometric Model of Age-Income Profiles: A Statistical Analysis of Dutch Income Data 1970, The Monetary Sector of the Netherlands in 50 Equations: A Quarterly Monetary Model for the Netherlands 1970–79, In Analysing the Structure of Econometric Models (ed. J. P. Ancot) 1984, Seasonal Adjustment as a Practical Problem 1991, Demand for Money and Credit in Europe 1999, Tussen behoud en vernieuwing 2000; articles in European Economic Review, Journal of International Economics and other journals; several monographs. *Leisure interests:* Dutch literature, hiking. *Address:* Ruysdaelweg 3B, 2051 EM Overveen, Netherlands (home). *Telephone:* (23) 5271700 (home). *E-mail:* mmg.fase@wxs.nl.

FASQUELLE, Jean-Claude; French publisher; *Chairman of the Board, Éditions Grasset et Fasquelle;* b. 29 Nov. 1930, Paris; s. of Charles Fasquelle and Odette Cyprien-Fabre; m. 1st Solange de la Rochefoucauld (divorced, died 2016); one d. (deceased); m. 2nd Nickla Jegher 1966; ed Ecole des Roches, Verneuil-sur-Avre, Sorbonne and Faculté de Droit, Paris; Pres.-Dir-Gen. Société des Editions Fasquelle 1953–60, Editions du Sagittaire 1958–; Admin.-Dir-Gen. Editions Grasset et Fasquelle 1960, Pres.-Dir-Gen. 1980–2000, Chair. of Bd 2000–; Dir Le Magazine littéraire (monthly) 1970–2004. *Address:* Éditions Grasset et Fasquelle, 61 rue des Saintes-Pères, 75006 Paris (office); 13 Square Vergennes, 75015 Paris, France (home). *Telephone:* 1-44-39-22-00 (office). *Fax:* 1-44-39-22-18 (office). *E-mail:* jcfasquelle@wanadoo.fr (home). *Website:* www.edition-grasset.fr (office).

FASSBENDER, Michael; Irish/German actor; b. 2 April 1977, Heidelberg, Baden-Württemberg, Germany; s. of Josef Fassbender and Adele Fassbender; ed St Brendan's Coll., Killarney, Drama Centre, London, UK; raised in Killarney, Co. Kerry, south-west Ireland, where his family moved in 1979; moved to London to study acting 1996; toured with Oxford Stage Co. performing Chekhov's Three Sisters; lives in London. *Films include:* 300 2006, Angel 2007, Hunger 2008, Eden Lake 2008, Fish Tank 2009, Blood Creek 2009, Centurion 2010, Jonah Hex 2010, Jane Eyre 2011, X-Men: First Class 2011, A Dangerous Method 2011, Shame 2011, Haywire 2011, Prometheus 2012, 12 Years a Slave 2013, The Counsellor 2013, Frank 2014, X-Men: Days of Future Past 2014, Slow West 2014, Macbeth 2015, Steve Jobs (Int. Star Award — Actor, Palm Springs Int. Film Festival 2016) 2015, X Men: Apocalypse 2016, The Light Between Oceans 2016, Trespass Against Us 2016, Assassin's Creed 2016, Song to Song 2017, Alien: Covenant 2017, The Snowman 2017. *Television includes:* Band of Brothers (mini-series) 2001, Carla (film) 2003, Gunpowder, Treason & Plot (film) 2004, Julian Fellowes Investigates: A Most Mysterious Murder – The Case of Charles Bravo (film) 2004, A Bear Named Winnie (film) 2004, Sherlock Holmes and the Case of the Silk Stocking (film) 2004, Hex (series) 2004–05, Our Hidden Lives (film) 2005, Trial & Retribution (series) 2006-07, Wedding Belles (film) 2007, The Devil's Whore (mini-series) 2008. *Leisure interest:* Formula 1 motor racing. *Address:* c/o Conor McCaughan, Troika Talent Agency, Cosmopolitan House, 10A Christina Street, London, EC2A 4PA, England (office); c/o Michael Cooper, Creative Artists Agency, 2000 Avenue of the Stars, Los Angeles, CA 90067, USA (office). *Telephone:* (20) 7336-7868 (London) (office); (424) 288-2000 (Los Angeles) (office). *Fax:* (424) 288-2900 (Los Angeles) (office). *E-mail:* info@troikatalent.com (office); info@caa.com (office). *Website:* www.troikatalent .com (office); www.caa.com (office); michael-fassbender-online.net.

FASSI, Abbas al-; Moroccan politician and diplomatist; b. 18 Sept. 1940, Berkane; m.; four c.; ed Univ. Mohammed V, Rabat; apptd Sec.-Gen. Moroccan Human Rights League 1972; mem. Exec. Cttee Istiqlal Party 1974–, Gen. Sec. 1998–2012; Minister of Housing 1977–81, of Handicrafts and Social Affairs 1981–85; Amb. to Tunisia and Perm. Rep. to League of Arab Nations 1985–90; Amb. to France 1990–94; Minister of Social Devt, Solidarity, Employment and Professional Training 2000–02, Minister of State 2002–07; Prime Minister of Morocco 2007–11; mem. Bd of Dirs Caisse Nat. de Sécurité Sociale, Entraide Nationale,

Social Devt Agency; Grand Officier, Order National de Mérite, Commdr, Ordre de la République (Tunisia).

FASSI-FIHRI, Ahmed, LenD; Moroccan civil servant and diplomatist; b. 6 Aug. 1936, Oujda; m. Touria El Ouazzani; two s. two d.; pvt. sec. of Minister of Interior 1956; Head of Office, Dept of Minerals and Geology 1958; Head, Office of Minister of Foreign Affairs 1959; Chargé d'affaires, Embassy in Berne 1960; Pres. Melnes Municipality 1963; Founder and Dir Nat. Documentation Centre 1967–98, Information Science School 1974, Multimedia Centre 1993; Order of Ridha, Officier, Wissam du trône 1993. *Publications:* articles in field of information science in Arabic and French. *Leisure interests:* listening to Arabic and classical music, reading of the Arabic intellectual literary productions.

FASSI-FIHRI, Taïb, PhD; Moroccan government official; *Advisor to H.M. King Mohammed VI;* b. 9 April 1958, Casablanca; m.; two c.; ed Lycée Descartes, Rabat, Institut Nat. de la Statistique et d'Economie Appliquée, Rabat, Université Panthéon-Sorbonne, Paris, Institut d'Etudes Politiques, Paris; Lecturer, Univ. of Paris VII, also Chargé d'Etudes at Institut Français des Relations Internationales 1983–84; attached to Dept of Planning, Ministry of Planning 1984, in charge of special duties in Cabinet of Minister in charge of relations with the EEC 1985–86; Chief of Div., Ministry of Foreign Affairs and Co-operation in charge of relations with EC 1986–89; Dir Office of the Minister of State in charge of Foreign Affairs and Co-operation 1989–93; Sec. of State for Foreign Affairs and Co-operation 1993–98; Head of Mission at Royal Cabinet 1998–99; Sec. of State for Foreign Affairs 1999–2000, for Foreign Affairs and Co-operation 2000–02, Coordinator, responsible for negotiation of free trade agreement between Morocco and USA 2002, Minister Del. for Foreign Affairs and Co-operation 2002–07, Minister of Foreign Affairs and Co-operation 2007–11; currently Advisor to H.M. King Mohammed VI; Officer, Wissam Al Arch Order 2001. *Address:* Cabinet Royal, el Michwar Essaid, Touarga, 10000, Rabat, Morocco (office).

FASSINO, Piero Franco Rodolfo, BSc; Italian politician; *Mayor of Turin;* b. 7 Oct. 1949, Avigliana; m.; local councillor Turin 1975–80, 1985–90, Prov. Councillor 1980–85; various posts within Turin Fed. of Partito Comunista Italiano (PCI) 1971–83, Prov. Sec. 1983–87, elected to PCI Exec. 1983, Co-ordinator Nat. Secr. 1987, then Head of party org. during transition to Partito Democratico della Sinistra (PDS), mem. Nat. Secr. and Int. Sec. PDS 1991–96, PDS Rep. to Socialist Int. 1992, PDS re-named Democratici di Sinistra (DS) 1998, Leader (Nat. Sec.) DS 2001–07, mem. Partito Democratico (formed after merger between Democratici di Sinistra, Democrazia è Libertà—La Margherita and other left-wing and centrist parties); Pres. Cen. and Western Europe Cttee Socialist Int. 1993, Chair. Cttee for Peace, Democracy and Human Rights 2004; fmr Vice-Pres. Socialist Group, Council of Europe; mem. Chamber of Deputies from Liguria (PDS) 1994–96, from Piedmont 1996–2011; Mayor of Turin 2011–; Under-Sec. Ministry for Foreign Affairs 1996–98; Minister for Foreign Trade 1998–2000, for Justice 2000–01; mem. Parl. Asscn for Cen. Europe Initiative; Vice-Pres. Italian-Israeli Parl. Friendship Asscn 1995; Chevalier, Légion d'honneur; Grand Medal of Merit, Gala Dinner Dance and Awards Ceremony. *Publication:* Per Passione 2003. *Address:* Piazza Palazzo di Città, 1, Turin, Italy (office). *Telephone:* (011) 4423000 (office). *Fax:* (011) 5625580 (office). *E-mail:* segreteria.sindaco@comune.torino.it (office). *Website:* www.comune.torino.it (office); www.pierofassinosindaco.it.

FAST, The Hon. Edward (Ed) Daniel, PC; Canadian lawyer and politician; b. 18 June 1955, Winnipeg; m. Annette Fast; four d.; ed Univ. of British Columbia; f. Linley Welwood (legal practice), Abbotsford, BC 1983; mem. Abbotsford School Bd 1985–90; mem. Abbotsford City Council 1996–2005; fmr Deputy Mayor of Abbotsford; mem. House of Commons for Abbotsford 2006–; Minister of Int. Trade and Minister for the Asia-Pacific Gateway 2011–15; mem. Conservative Party of Canada. *Address:* Conservative Party of Canada, 130 Albert Street, Suite 1720, Ottawa, ON K1P 5G4, Canada (office). *Telephone:* (613) 755-2000 (office). *Fax:* (613) 755-2001 (office). *E-mail:* info@conservative.ca (office); ed.fast@parl.gc.ca (office). *Website:* www.conservative.ca (office); www.edfast.ca.

FATEYEVA, Asya; Russian saxophonist; b. 9 March 1990, Kerch; ed Moscow Gnessin Middle Special School of Music, studied with Margarita Shaposhnikova, Musikhochschule, Cologne, studied with Daniel Gauthier, Conservatoire Nat. de Paris, Hamburg School of Music and Theatre, studied with Niklas Schmidt, also studied with Claude Delangle in Paris and Jean-Denis Michat in Lyons; began studying piano 1996; studied saxophone with Liliya Rusanova 2000–03; moved to Germany 2004; teacher of solo saxophone classes, Musikhochschule, Münster, Germany 2014–; numerous concert performances including concerts with Vienna Symphony Orchestra, Tchaikovsky Radio Symphony Orchestra, Ukrainian Nat. Philharmonic, Istanbul State Symphony Orchestra, Giuseppe Verdi Symphony Orchestra of Milan, orchestras from Bochum, Bonn, Frankfurt an der Oder, Kassel; ZEIT Foundation's Gerd Bucerius Scholarship, Orpheum Foundation Award, First Prize, Young Soloist Int. Competition, Gap, France 2002, 2005, Triumph Youth Prize 2004, First Prize, Jugend Musiziert, Germany 2006, First Prize, Yamaha Competition, Hamburg, Germany 2007, First Prize, Int. Gustav Bumcke Saxophone Competition, Nuremberg, Germany 2010, First Prize, Bonn Int. Music Competition 2012, Zonta Int. Foundation Prize 2012, Berenberg Bank Prize for Culture 2015, ECHO Klassik for Best Newcomer 2016. *Recordings include:* albums: Mishat, Ibert (for alto saxophone and orchestra) 2012, Albright and Decruck (for alto saxophone and piano) 2015, Fantasia (with Sabine Meyer and Alliage Quintet) 2016. *Address:* Reinicke Artists, Ludwigkirchplatz 11, 10719 Berlin, Germany (office). *Telephone:* (30) 8892-2566 (office). *E-mail:* mail@reinicke-artists.com (office); info@asyafateyeva.com. *Website:* www.reinicke-artists.com (office); www.asyafateyeva.com.

FATTOUH, Rawhi, (Abu Wisam), BA; Palestinian politician; b. 23 Aug. 1949, Barqa, Gaza; m.; one d. two s.; ed Damascus Univ.; moved from Gaza to Jordan in 1967, returned to Gaza 1994; elected to Palestinian National Council 1983; mem. Palestinian Legislative Council (Parl.) 1996–2006, Speaker 2004–06; Minister of Agric. 2003; elected mem. Fatah Revolutionary Council 1996; Acting Pres. Palestinian (Nat.) Authority 2004–05, then apptd aide to Pres. Mahmoud Abbas 2005. *Publications:* several articles in Arabic about the Middle East.

FAU, Yamandú; Uruguayan academic and politician; b. 21 March 1945, Montevideo; m. Yiya Daners; two c.; mem. Parl. 1984–2000; Minister of Educ. and Culture 2000; elected Senator 2000; Minister of Nat. Defence 2002–05; mem. Partido Colorado de Uruguay.

FAUCI, Anthony Stephen, MD; American medical researcher; *Director, National Institute of Allergy and Infectious Diseases;* b. 24 Dec. 1940, Brooklyn, New York; s. of Stephen Fauci and Eugenia Fauci; m. Christine Grady 1985; three d.; ed Coll. of the Holy Cross, Cornell Univ. Medical Coll.; Instructor in Medicine, Cornell Medical Coll. 1971–72; Medical Dir US Public Health Service 1968–70, 1972; Clinical Assoc., Lab. of Clinical Investigation, Nat. Inst. of Allergy and Infectious Diseases (NIAID) 1968–71, Sr Staff Fellow, Lab. of Clinical Investigation 1970–71, Sr Investigator 1972–74, Head of Physiology Section 1974–80, Deputy Clinical Dir NIAID 1977–84, Dir 1984–; Chief Resident in Medicine, New York Hosp., Cornell Univ. Medical Center 1971–72; Chief Lab. of Immunoregulation 1980–; Dir Office of AIDS Research and Assoc. Dir Nat. Inst. of Health for AIDS Research 1988–94; consultant, Naval Medical Center, Bethesda, Md 1972–; mem. NAS, American Philosophical Soc., Royal Acad. of Medicine (Spain), Royal Danish Acad., Inst. of Medicine, Asscn of American Physicians, American Soc. for Clinical Investigation, Infectious Diseases Soc. of America, Int. AIDS Soc., American Fed. for Clinical Research, American Soc. for Cell Biology, American Soc. for Virology, American Asscn of Immunologists; Dr hc (Harvard Univ.) 2009; numerous awards, including Squibb Award, Infectious Diseases Soc. of America 1983, Bristol Award, Infectious Diseases Soc. of America 1999, Int. Prize for Scientific Research, Fondazione PISO 1999, Frank Berry Prize in Fed. Medicine 1999, Timely Topics Award Lecture of the US and Canadian Acad. of Pathology 1999, Frank Annunzio Humanitarian Award, Christopher Columbus Fellowship Foundation 2001, Ellis Island Family Heritage Award, Statue of Liberty-Ellis Island Foundation 2003, Lifetime Achievement Award, American Asscn of Immunologists 2005, Nat. Science Medal, NSF 2007, Mary Woodard Lasker Award for Public Service 2007, Presidential Medal of Freedom 2008, Dr Paul Janssen Award for Biomedical Research 2010, Prince Mahidol Award (Medicine) 2013, Heroes in the Struggle Award, Black AIDS Inst. 2014, Lifetime Achievement Award for Scientific Contributions and Public Service, Inst. of Human Virology 2015, Canada Gairdner Int. Award 2016. *Publications include:* numerous articles. *Leisure interests:* jogging, tennis. *Address:* NIAID/NIH, 31 Center Drive MSC 2520, Bethesda, MD 20892-0001 (office); 3012 43rd Street NW, Washington, DC 20016, USA (home). *Telephone:* (301) 496-2263 (office). *Fax:* (301) 496-4409 (office). *E-mail:* afauci@niaid.nih.gov (office). *Website:* www.niaid.nih.gov (office).

FAUCON, Bernard; French photographer; b. 12 Sept. 1950, Apt; ed Lycée d'Apt, Univ. of Aix en Provence, Sorbonne, Paris; Grand Prix Nat. 1989. *Publications include:* Les Grandes Vacances 1980, Les Papiers qui Volent 1986, Les Chambres d'Amour 1987, Tables d'Amis 1991, Les Idoles et les Sacrifices 1991, Dernier Portrait 1991, Les Écritures 1993, Jours d'Image 1995, La Fin de l'Image 1997, Chambres d'Amour, Chambres d'Or 1998, La Peur du Voyage 1999, Le Plus Beau Jour de ma Jeunesse 2000, La Plus Belle Route du Monde 2000, Une Singulière Gourmandise 2003, Atelier Faucon à Pingyao 2004, Catalogue Raisonné 2005, Le Tour de Monde 2008, Été 2550 2009. *Leisure interests:* cookery, travelling. *Address:* 6 rue Barbanègre, 75019 Paris, France. *Telephone:* 1-40-05-99-70. *E-mail:* info.contact@bernardfaucon.net. *Website:* www.bernardfaucon.net.

FAUGÈRE, Jean-Paul; French civil servant, government official and business executive; *Chairman, CNP Assurances SA;* b. 12 Dec. 1956; ed École Polytechnique, Institut d'Études Politiques de Paris, École Nationale d'Admin; insurance commr and controller 1980–81; Auditor to Council of State 1983; Rapporteur for Special Pensions Appeal Cttee and Cen. Cttee for Social Assistance 1983–86; Maître des requêtes (Counsel) to Council of State 1986; Govt Commr for CCAS 1986–87; Deputy Sec.-Gen., Council of State 1986–87; tech. adviser to Minister of Infrastructure, Transport and Housing 1987–88; Govt Commr for Council of State's litigation ass. 1988–90, adviser to Gen. Admin. 1990, then Finance Dir Atomic Energy Comm. 1991–94; Dir of Civil Liberties and Legal Affairs, Ministry of Interior 1994–97; Prefect for Loir et Cher 1997–2001, for La Vendée 2001–02; State Councillor 1998; Head of François Fillon's Office (fmr Minister of Social Affairs, then Minister of Nat. Educ.) 2002–05; Prefect for Alsace-Bas Rhin region 2005–07; Head of Prime Minister's Office 2007–12; Chair. CNP Assurances SA 2012–. *Address:* CNP Assurances SA, 4 place Raoul Dautry, 75716 Paris Cedex 15, France (office). *Telephone:* 1-42-18-88-88 (office). *Fax:* 1-42-18-93-66 (office). *E-mail:* edmond.alphandery@cnp.fr (office). *Website:* www.cnp.fr (office).

FAUJOUR, Olivier; French business executive; *President, Yoplait International, and Vice-President, General Mills;* ed Lycée Hoche, Versailles, ESCP Europe Grad. School, Paris; worked for 12 years for Procter & Gamble, holding various marketing roles in Europe and Latin America, including as Marketing Dir in Brazil; worked for seven years for Danone, held various leadership positions at nat. and global levels, participated in the expansion of Danone in China, f. commercial and industrial operations in S Korea; joined General Mills as Vice-Pres. and Man. Dir for General Mills France, Benelux and Southern Europe Nov. 2010, led devt of Häagen-Dazs, Old El Paso and Green Giant, currently Vice-Pres., General Mills and Pres., Yoplait International, oversees the global Yoplait (yogurt) business outside USA, mem. Bd of Dirs, Yoplait Joint Venture with Sodiaal. *Address:* Number One General Mills Boulevard, Minneapolis, MN 55426-1347, USA (office). *Telephone:* (763) 764-76002 (office). *Fax:* (763) 764-8330 (office). *E-mail:* info@generalmills.com (office). *Website:* www.generalmills.com (office).

FAULKNER, John, BA, DipEd; Australian politician (retd); b. 12 April 1954, Leeton, NSW; m. Sandra Nori (divorced); two c.; ed Macquarie Univ.; mem. NSW Admin. Cttee, Australian Labor Party (ALP) 1978–89, Asst Gen. Sec. 1980–89, apptd mem. ALP Nat. Exec. 1989, Nat. Pres. ALP 2007–08; mem. Senate 1989–2015, Father of the Australian Senate 2014–15; Man. of Govt Business 1993–96, Leader of Opposition 1996–2004; Minister for Veterans' Affairs and Minister for Defence Science and Personnel 1993–94, for Sport and Territories March 1994, for Environment, Sport and Territories 1994–96; Shadow Minister for Social Security 1996–97, for Public Admin and Govt Services 1997–2001, for Territories 1997–98, for Olympic Coordination and Centenary of Fed. 1998–2001, for Public Admin and Home Affairs 2001–03, for Public Admin and Accountability 2003–04, for Defence 2009–10; Special Minister of State, Cabinet Sec. and Vice-Pres. of the Exec. Council 2007–09; mem. Macquarie Univ. Council 1984–92. *Publication:* True Believers (co-author).

FAULKS, Sebastian, CBE, MA, FRSL; British writer; b. 20 April 1953, Newbury, Berks.; s. of Peter Faulks and Pamela Lawless; m. Veronica Youlten 1989; two s. one d.; ed Wellington Coll. and Emmanuel Coll., Cambridge; reporter, Daily Telegraph newspaper 1979–83, feature writer, Sunday Telegraph 1983–86; Literary Ed. The Independent 1986–89, Deputy Ed. The Independent on Sunday 1989–90, Assoc. Ed. 1990–91; columnist, The Guardian 1992–97, Evening Standard 1997–99, Mail on Sunday 1999–2000; invited to write new James Bond 007 novel to celebrate centenary of Ian Fleming's birth 2008; Hon. Fellow, Emmanuel Coll., Cambridge 2007; Hon. DLitt (Tavistock Clinic, Univ. of East London). *Radio:* Panelist, The Write Stuff, BBC Radio 4 1998–2014. *Television:* Churchill's Secret Army 2000, Faulks on Fiction 2011. *Publications:* A Trick of the Light 1984, The Girl at the Lion d'Or 1989, A Fool's Alphabet 1992, Birdsong 1993, The Fatal Englishman 1996, Charlotte Gray 1998, On Green Dolphin Street 2001, Human Traces 2005, Pistache 2006, Engleby 2007, Devil May Care (writing as Ian Fleming) (British Book Award for Popular Fiction 2009) 2008, A Week in December 2009, Faulks on Fiction 2011, A Possible Life 2012, Jeeves and the Wedding Bells 2013, A Broken World (co-ed.) 2014, Where My Heart Used to Beat 2015, Pistache Returns 2016, Paris Echo 2018. *Leisure interests:* wine, sport. *Address:* c/o Clare Alexander, Aitken Alexander Associates Ltd, 18–21 Cavaye Place, London, SW10 9PT, England (office). *E-mail:* reception@aitkenalexander.co.uk (office). *Website:* www.sebastianfaulks.com.

FAURE, Danny, BA; Seychelles politician and head of state; *President, with additional responsibility for Defence, Legal Affairs, Information and Hydrocarbons;* b. 8 May 1962, Kilembe; m.; four c.; early career as teacher, Seychelles Polytechnic and Nat. Youth Service; fmr Chair. Seychelles People's Progressive Front; Leader of Govt Business, Nat. Ass. 1993–98; Minister for Educ. and Youth 1998–2006; Minister of Finance and Designated Minister 2006–10, Minister of Finance, Trade, Information Tech. and Public Admin 2010, also Gov., Int. Monetary Fund, World Bank, African Development Bank; Vice-Pres. of Seychelles, also Minister of Information Tech. and Public Admin and Youth and Civil Soc. 2010–16, Pres. of Seychelles, with additional responsibility for Defence, Legal Affairs, Information and Hydrocarbons 2016–. *Address:* Office of the President, State House, POB 55, Victoria, Seychelles (office). *Telephone:* 4224155 (office). *Fax:* 4224985 (office). *E-mail:* cps@statehouse.gov.sc (office). *Website:* www.statehouse.gov.sc (office).

FAURE, Philippe René Jean-Paul Yves; French fmr diplomatist and consultant; *Special Representative for Mexico;* b. 13 June 1950, Toulouse; s. of Maurice Faure; ed École Nationale d'Admin; Sec. of Foreign Affairs, Ministry of Foreign Affairs 1976–77, Asst Dir Cabinet of Sec.-Gen. 1977–79, tech. adviser to Minister of Foreign Affairs Jean François-Poncet 1979–81; served as Second Counsellor and Head of Press, Embassy in Washington, DC 1981–87, First Counsellor, Embassy in Madrid 1987–89; Dir-Gen., then Co-Pres. Cecar (insurance co.) 1990–97; Pres. Marsh McLennan France 1997–2000, Gault et Millau 1997–2000; Sec.-Gen. Ministry of Foreign Affairs 2006–08; Admin. AREVA and EDF (Électricité de France) public energy groups 2006–08; Amb. to Mexico 2000–04, to Morocco 2004–06, to Japan 2008–11 (retd), Special Rep. for Mexico 2012–; est. a consultancy to foreign cos 2011; Hon. Amb. of France 2012; Officier, Légion d'honneur, Ordre nat. du Mérite; Commdr, Ordre d'Isabelle la Catholique (Spain); Commdr, Order of Merit (FRG); Commdr du Wissam Al Alaoui (Morocco); Grand Officier de l'Aigle Aztèque (Mexico); Grand Cordon, Order of the Rising Sun (Japan). *Address:* Ministry of Foreign Affairs, 37 quai d'Orsay, 75351 Paris Cedex 07, France (office). *Telephone:* 1-43-17-53-53 (office). *Fax:* 1-43-17-52-03 (office). *Website:* www.diplomatie.gouv.fr (office).

FAURIE, Jorge Marcelo; Argentine lawyer, diplomatist and politician; *Minister of Foreign Affairs and Worship;* b. 24 Dec. 1951, Santa Fe; ed Univ. Nacional del Litoral, Instituto del Servicio Exterior de la Nación; with Treaties Dept, Ministry of Foreign Affairs, Int. Trade and Worship (MFA) 1975–76, Brazil Desk 1976–77, Third Sec., Embassy in Venezuela 1978–79, Chargé d'affaires, Embassy in Jamaica 1989, Chargé d'affaires, Embassy in Trinidad and Tobago 1979–80, Second, later First Sec., Embassy in Bucharest 1980–84, Coordinator, South America and Atlantic, MFA 1985, Counsellor, MFA 1985–87, Counsellor, Embassy in Brasilia 1987–89, Minister-Counsellor and Head of Chancellery, Embassy in Santiago 1989–92, with Gen. Secr., MFA 1992, Dir, MERCOSUR Dept, MFA 1992–94, Chief of Protocol 1994–97, 1998–99, Chef de Cabinet, MFA 1997–98, assigned to Office of Gov. of Province of Buenos Aires 2000–01, Sec. for Foreign Affairs, MFA 2002, Amb. to Portugal 2002–13, Amb. to France 2015–17; Minister of Foreign Affairs and Worship 2017–. *Address:* Ministry of Foreign Affairs, International Trade and Worship, Esmeralda 1212, C1007ABR Buenos Aires, Argentina (office). *Telephone:* (11) 4819-7000 (office). *E-mail:* info@cancilleria.gob.ar (office). *Website:* www.argentina.gob.ar/relacionesexterioresyculto (office).

FAUST, (Catharine) Drew Gilpin, BA, MA, PhD; American historian, academic and university president; b. 18 Sept. 1947, Clarke Co., Va; d. of McGhee Tyson Gilpin and Catharine Gilpin; m. 1st Stephen Faust (divorced); m. 2nd Charles E. Rosenberg; two d.; ed Concord Acad., Bryn Mawr Coll. and Univ. of Pennsylvania; Asst Prof. of History, Dept of American Civilization, Univ. of Pennsylvania 1976–80, Assoc. Prof. 1980–84, Prof. 1984–88, Stanley Sheerr Prof. of History 1988–89, Annenberg Prof. of History 1989–2000, Chair. Dept of American Civilization 1990–95, Dir Women's Studies Program 1996–2000; Dean, Radcliffe Inst. for Advanced Study, Harvard Univ. 2001–07, Lincoln Prof. of History 2003–07, Pres. Harvard Univ. (first woman) 2007–18; Chair. Presidential Cttee on Univ. Life, Univ. of Pennsylvania 1988–90; mem. American Acad. of Arts and Sciences 1994–, American Philosophical Soc. 2004–, Southern Historical Asscn (Pres. 1999–2000), American Historical Asscn (Vice-Pres. 1992–96), Exec. Bd Org. of American Historians 1999–2002, Exec. Bd Soc. of American Historians 1999–2002, Educational Advisory Bd Guggenheim Foundation, Pulitzer Prize for History jury 1986, 1990, 2004 (Chair.), Goldman Sachs 2018–; Trustee, Bryn Mawr Coll. 1997–, Nat. Humanities Center 2002–, Andrew W. Mellon Foundation 2003–, J Paul Getty 2018–; Hon. DHumLitt (Bowdoin Coll.) 2007, Dr hc (Univ. of Pennsylvania) 2008, Hon. DH (Yale Univ.) 2008, Hon. LLD (Princeton Univ.) 2010; Dread Void of Uncertainty named one of ten best history essays of 2005 by Org. of American Historians, selected by the Nat. Endowment for the Humanities for the Jefferson Lecture (US Fed. Govt's highest honour for achievement in the humanities) 2011, John W. Kluge Prize 2018. *Publications:* A Sacred Circle: The Dilemma of the Intellectual in the Old South 1977, The Ideology of Slavery: Proslavery Thought in the Antebellum South, 1830–1860 1981, James Henry Hammond and the Old South: A Design for Mastery 1985, The Creation of Confederate Nationalism: Ideology and Identity in the Civil War South 1989, Southern Stories: Slaveholders in Peace and War 1992, Mothers of Invention: Women of the Slaveholding South in the American Civil War (Soc. of American Historians' Francis Parkman Prize 1997) 1996, This Republic of Suffering – Death and the American Civil War (American History Book Prize 2008, Bancroft Prize, Columbia Univ. 2009) 2008. *Address:* c/o Office of the President, Harvard University, Massachusetts Hall, Cambridge, MA 02138, USA (office).

FAVILA, Peter B., BSc; Philippine banker and government official; *Vice-Chairman, Herma Group of Companies;* b. 27 Aug. 1948, Manila; m. Alice Arnaldo Favilo; two c.; ed Univ. of Santo Tomas, Wharton School of Business, Univ. of Pennsylvania, USA; fmr positions include Sr Vice-Pres. Metropolitan Bank and Trust Co., Pres. Philippine Nat. Bank 1995–98, Pres. Security Bank, Allied Bank 1998–2001; Chair. Philippine Stock Exchange 2001–05, Securities Clearing Corpn of the Philippines –2005; Presidential Adviser on Infrastructure Finance, Econ. Adviser to Speaker of House of Reps –2005; Sec. of Trade and Industry 2005–10; mem. Monetary Bd Bangko Sentral ng Pilipinas 2008–14, now Consultant; currently Vice-Chair. Herma Group of Companies; mem. Bd of Dirs GT Capital Holdings Inc. 2015–17; fmr mem. Bd of Dirs ASEAN Chamber of Commerce and Industry, Philippine Airlines, Bankers Asscn of the Philippines; Consultant for CDC Holdings, Inc.; mem. Advisory Council, Asian Bankers Asscn; mem. Bd of Advisors, Asian Inst. of Man. Policy Forum; mem. Bd of Trustees Ramos Peace and Development Foundation; mem. Man. Asscn of the Philippines, Philippine Chamber of Commerce and Industry, Rotary Club of Makati South; Order of Lakandula (with rank of Bayani), Gran Cruz Orden de Isabel la Catolica (Spain). *Address:* Herma Group of Companies, c/o Herma Corporation, 94 Scout Rallos, Bgy. Sacred Heart, Kamuning, Quezon City 1103, Philippines (office). *Website:* www.hermagroup.com.ph (office).

FAVRE, Brett Lorenzo; American professional football player; b. 10 Oct. 1969, Gulfport, Miss.; s. of Irvin Favre and Bonita Favre; m. Deanna Tynes 1996; two d.; ed Hancock North Cen. High School, Univ. of Southern Miss.; quarterback; drafted out of coll. by Nat. Football League (NFL) Atlanta Falcons 1991 (33rd pick overall); traded to Green Bay Packers 1992–2007 (retd) but returned to play with New York Jets 2008 (retd); led Packers to seven div. championships 1995, 1996, 1997, 2002, 2003, 2004, 2007, four NFC Championship Games 1995, 1996, 1997, 2007, winning two 1996, 1997, and two Super Bowl appearances, winning one, Super Bowl XXXI 1997; came out of retirement for second time and signed with Minnesota Vikings Aug. 2009, 30–23 victory over fmr team, Green Bay Packers, on 5 Oct. made him first quarterback in NFL history to defeat every one of league's 32 franchises since NFL first expanded to 32 franchises in 2002 and game was most-viewed TV programme, sports or otherwise, in history of cable TV, drawing a 15.3 rating and having 21.8m. viewers; selected Nat. Football Conf. (NFC) Pro Bowl squad 1992–2007, youngest quarterback in Nat. Football League (NFL) history to play in a Pro Bowl; set record of 38 touchdown passes 1995; holds record for consecutive starts with 282 (304 including playoffs), most consecutive starts by a position player (NFL) with 282, most career regular-season victories by a starting quarterback with 180 (regular-season record: 180-102), most career passing touchdowns with 491, most career passing yards with 68,468, most career pass completions with 6,015, most career pass attempts with 9,713, most career interceptions thrown with 316, most career games with at least three touchdown passes with 70, most career games with at least four touchdown passes with 22, most seasons with at least 30 touchdown passes with eight, most consecutive seasons with at least 30 touchdown passes with five, most seasons with at least 3,000 passing yards with 18, most consecutive seasons with at least 3,000 passing yards with 18, most AP NFL MVP awards with three (tied with Peyton Manning), most career playoff interceptions thrown with 28 (tied with Jim Kelly), most career playoff losses as starting quarterback with 10 (tied with Dan Marino); retired from NFL 2011; f. Brett Favre Forward Foundation 1996; Favre family owns and operates the Brett Favre's Steakhouse, Green Bay, Wis.; NFL Most Valuable Player (MVP) 1995, 1996, 1997 (jtly with Detroit Lions' Barry Sanders, only player to win AP MVP three consecutive times), Green Bay Chamber of Commerce's Community Service Award 1997, Sports Illustrated Sportsman of the Year 2007, selected to play in Pro Bowl ten times in his career, a six-time First- or Second-team All-Pro selection, named to NFL 1990s All-Decade Team, inducted into Green Bay Packers Hall of Fame 2015. *Film:* Reggie's Prayer 1996. *Publications:* For the Record (with Chris Havel) 1997, Most Valuable Player (with Marc Serota) 1999, Favre (with Bonita Favre and Chris Havel) 2004. *Leisure interest:* golf. *Address:* c/o The Brett Favre Forward Foundation, 1 Willow Bend, Hattiesburg, MS 39402, USA. *E-mail:* info@officialbrettfavre.com. *Website:* www.officialbrettfavre.com; www.vikings.com.

FAWCETT, Dame; **Amelia Chilcott,** DBE, CBE, BA, JD; British/American lawyer, investment banker and company director; *Chairman, Hedge Fund Standards Board;* b. 16 Sept. 1956, Boston, Mass; d. of Frederick John Fawcett II and Betsey Sargent Chilcott; ed Wellesley, Univ. of Virginia School of Law; worked for Sullivan and Cromwell law firm, New York 1983–85, Paris 1986–87; joined Morgan Stanley 1987, Vice-Pres. 1990, Exec. Dir 1992, Man. Dir and Chief Admin. Officer for European Operations 1996–2002, Vice-Chair. and COO, Morgan Stanley International Ltd 2002–06; Chair. Pensions First Group LLP 2007–10; Chair., London Int. Festival of Theatre 2002–, Hedge Fund Standards Bd 2011–, Prince of Wales' Charitable Foundation 2012–; Deputy Chair. Investment AB Kinnevik 2011–; Dir (non-exec.), State Street Corpn 2006–, Guardian Media Group 2006–13 (Chair. 2009–13), Court of Dirs, Bank of England (Chair. Audit Cttee) 2004–09, Business in the Community 2005–09, Millicom Cellular SA 2014–; mem. Financial Services Practitioner Forum 1999–2001, Council of Univ. of London (Chair. Audit Cttee) 2002–08, London Int. Festival of Theatre 2002–10; Trustee and Deputy Chair. Nat. Portrait Gallery 2002–11; Gov. London Business School 2009–; Dir Project Hope (UK) 2009–; Commr US–UK Fulbright Comm. 2010–; mem. Advisory Bd Cambridge Programme for Sustainability Leadership; mem. London Employers Coalition 1998–2002, Competitiveness Council (Dept of Trade and Industry) 1999–2000, New Deal Task Force, Nat. Employment Panel 1999–2005; Companion of the Chartered Management Inst.; Dr hc (American Univ. in London); Prince of Wales Amb. Award 2004. *Leisure interests:* fly fishing, sailing, hill walking, reading, farm in Wales. *Address:* Hedge Fund Standards Board, Somerset House – New Wing, Strand, London, WC2R 1LA, England (office). *Telephone:* (20) 3701-7560 (office). *E-mail:* info@hfsb.org (office). *Website:* www.hfsb.org (office).

FAXON, Roger, BA; American entertainment business executive; *Chairman, MirriAd;* ed Johns Hopkins Univ.; fmrly Sr Staff mem. US Congress; Exec. Vice-Pres. and COO Lucasfilm Ltd 1980–84; Founding Partner, The Mount Company 1984–86; worked at Tri-Star and Columbia Pictures 1986–90, rising to Sr Exec. Vice-Pres. Columbia Pictures Entertainment; fmrly COO Sotheby's North and South America, CEO Sotheby's Europe, Man. Dir Sotheby's 1990–94; Sr Vice-Pres. of Business Devt and Strategy EMI Music 1994–99, Exec. Vice-Pres. and Chief Financial Officer EMI Music Publishing 1999–2002, Chief Financial Officer EMI Group PLC 2002–05, Bd mem. 2002–05, 2006–, Pres. and COO EMI Music Publishing 2005–06, Jt CEO 2006–07, Chair. and CEO 2007–10, Univ. EMI Music Group 2010–12; Prin., A&R Investments 2012–; Chair., MirriAd 2013–; mem. Bd of Dirs Johns Hopkins Univ. 2011–, ITV PLC 2012–, Pandora Media 2015–, Songwriters Hall of Fame; fmr mem. Bd of Dirs Music Choice, American Soc. of Composers, Authors and Publishers, Lancit Media Entertainment Ltd; mem. Council Brookings Inst.; mem. Acad. of Motion Pictures Arts And Sciences, The Recording Acad. *Address:* MirriAd, 624 Hampton Drive, Venice, CA 90291, USA (office). *Telephone:* (310) 392-2828 (office). *E-mail:* press@mirriad.com (office). *Website:* www.mirriad.com (office).

FAYED, Mohamed al-; Egyptian business executive; *Honorary Chairman, Harrods Holdings;* b. 27 Jan. 1929, Alexandria; s. of Aly Aly Fayed; m. 1st Samira Khashoggi 1954 (divorced 1958); one s. (died 1997); m. 2nd Heini Wathen; four c.; f. co. in Alexandria 1956; involved in shipping, property, banking, oil and construction; Chair. and Owner, Ritz Hotel, Paris 1979–; Chair. Harrods Ltd, London 1985–2010, Harrods Holdings PLC 1994–2010, Hon. Chair. 2010–; Owner, Fulham Football Club, London 1997–2013; Founder, Balnagown Castle & Estates (devt firm), Scotland 1972; Hon. mem. Emmanuel Coll., Cambridge; Commdr, Order of Merit (Italy) 1990, Officier, Légion d'honneur 1993; La Grande Médaille de la Ville de Paris 1985, Plaque de Paris 1989.

FAYEZ, Eid al-, BA; Jordanian politician; b. 1945, Manja; m.; three c.; ed Beirut Arab Univ.; Dir-Gen. Jordanian-Iraqi Transport Co. 1983–86; Dir-Gen. Jordanian Ports Corpn, Aqaba 1986–90; Sec.-Gen. Ministry of Youth 1990–93; Adviser, Royal Hashemite Court 1993–99; Minister of Labour 1999–2002, also of Youth and Sports 2001–02, of the Interior 2005–07, 2007–09.

FAYEZ, Faisal al-, BSc, MA; Jordanian diplomatist and government official; *President of the Senate;* b. 1952; ed Univ. of Cardiff, UK, Boston Univ., USA; joined Ministry of Foreign Affairs upon graduation; fmr diplomat, Embassy in Brussels 1979–83; fmr Deputy Dir of Royal Protocol, Royal Court, Chief of Royal Protocol and Minister of the Royal Court 2003; Prime Minister and Minister of Defence 2003–05; Minister of the Royal Court of Jordan 2003–05; elected Speaker, House of Rep. (Parl.) 2010; mem. Senate 2007–, Pres. 2015–; Officer, Order of Independence (Order of Al-Istiqlal) 1987, Grand Officer, Order of Independence (Order of Al-Istiqlal) 1995, Grand Cordon, Order of the Star of Jordan (Order of Al-Kawkab Al-Urduni) 2000. *Address:* Senate of Jordan, POB 72, Amman 11101, Jordan (office). *Telephone:* (6) 5689313 (office). *Fax:* (6) 5664121 (office). *E-mail:* info@senate.jo (office). *Website:* www.senate.jo (office).

FAYEZ, Nora bint Abdullah Al-, BA, MA; Saudi Arabian educationalist, academic and politician; *Deputy Minister of Women's Education;* b. 1965, Shaqra; m.; three s. two d.; ed King Saud Univ., Utah State Univ., USA; served as Dir-Gen. of Girls' Schools at Kingdom Schools; Lecturer and Head of Training Techniques Centre, women's section of Inst. of Public Admin 1984–88, Dir-Gen. women's section 1993–2009; Assoc. Prof. in Educ. Techniques, Coll. of Educ., King Saud Univ. 1989–95; Controller of Educ. Techniques, Inst. of Pvt. Educ., Ministry of Educ. 1989–93, apptd to Council of Ministers (first woman) as Deputy Minister for Women's Educ. 2009–; Head of Women's Cttee of Human Resources Devt Forum under Human Resources Devt Fund, Riyadh 2004; mem. Women's Organizing Cttee of Janadriya Festival 1991, 1992, Bd of Dirs Coll. of Literature at Gen. Presidency of Girls Educ. 1994–2000, Cultural Advisory Cttee of Janadriya Festival 1995, Women's Cttee for King Abdul Aziz Museum (Darah) 1997–99, Consultative Council of Nat. Museum 1999–, Consultative Council of Supreme Comm. for Tourism 2001–03, Women's Cttee of King Abdul Aziz Foundation for Gifted Persons 2002–07, Women's Cttee of First Riyadh Econ. Forum 2003, Women's Science Cttee for the Cultural Season of the World Ass. of Muslim Youth 2005; adviser, Prince Salman Social Center 1998–2001, King Abdul Aziz Women's Charity Soc., Qassim 2000–03; has attended several nat. and int. seminars and courses, including The Effective Training Man. Workshop Course, Brussels, Belgium 1985, Man. Communication for Devt, Washington, DC, USA 1994, Distance Educ., Salzburg, Austria 1997, Man. Work Conf., Denver, USA 1997, Women in Man., Dubai 1998, The Art of Leadership, Advanced Management, Euromatech, Amsterdam, Netherlands 2003, Oxford Advanced Man. and Leadership Programme, Oxford Man. Centre, London, UK 2008; Dr hc (Utah State Univ.) 2012. *Address:* Ministry of Education, King Abdullah Road, Riyadh 12435, Saudi Arabia (office). *Telephone:* (1) 475-3000 (office). *E-mail:* contact@moe.gov.sa (office). *Website:* www.moe.gov.sa (office).

FAYMANN, Werner; Austrian politician; b. 4 May 1960, Vienna; m.; two c.; ed Univ. of Vienna; consultant, Zentralsparkasse 1985–88; Prov. Chair. Socialistic Youth Vienna 1985–94; mem. State Parl. and Municipal Council of Vienna 1994–2007, Exec. City Councillor for housing, housing construction and urban renewal; fmr Pres. Viennese Fund for Provision of Property and Urban Renewal; fmr Vice-Pres. Viennese Business Agency; Fed. Minister for Transport, Innovation and Tech. 2007–08; Fed. Chancellor 2008–16 (resgnd); Exec. Chair. Social Democratic Party of Austria (SPÖ) 2008–16 (resgnd). *Address:* Social Democratic Party of Austria, Löwelstr. 18, 1014 Vienna, Austria (office). *Telephone:* (1) 534-27-0 (office). *Fax:* (1) 535-96-83 (office). *E-mail:* werner.faymann@spoe.at (office). *Website:* www.spoe.at (office); www.das-ist-faymann.at.

FAYROUZ (see Fairuz).

FAYYAD, Salam Khaled Abdullah, BSc, MBA, PhD; Palestinian economist and politician; b. 1952, Tulkarm, West Bank; m.; three c.; ed American Univ. of Beirut, Lebanon, Univ. of Texas, USA; fmr Lecturer in Econs, Yarmuk Univ., Jordan; fmr official, US Fed. Reserve Bank, St Louis; joined IMF, Washington, DC 1987, various sr positions including Resident Rep. to Palestinian Authority (PA), Jerusalem 1995–2001; Regional Man. of West Bank–Gaza, Arab Bank 2001–02 (resgnd); Minister of Finance 2002–05 (resgnd), 2007–12, also of Foreign Affairs 2007–08; Prime Minister of Palestinian Autonomous Areas 2007–13 (resgnd); nomination as Special Rep. and Head UN Support Mission in Libya (UNSMIL) vetoed by USA Feb. 2017. *Publications include:* numerous research papers on Palestinian economy. *Address:* c/o Ministry of Foreign Affairs, POB 1336, Ramallah, Palestinian Autonomous Areas.

FAZIO, Antonio, BSc; Italian fmr central banker; b. 11 Oct. 1936, Alvito, Frosinone; s. of Eugenio Fazio and Maria Giuseppa Persichetti; m. Maria Cristina Rosati; one s. four d.; ed Univ. of Rome, Massachusetts Inst. of Tech., USA; Research Fellow, Research Dept, Banca d'Italia 1960, Consultant to Research Dept 1961–66, Deputy Head, then Head, Econometric Research Office 1966, Deputy Dir Research Dept's Monetary Section 1972, Head, Research Dept 1973–79, Cen. Man. for Econ. Research 1980, Deputy Dir-Gen. Banca d'Italia 1982–93, Gov. 1993–2005 (resgnd); Asst Prof. of Demography, Univ. of Rome 1961–66; Chair. Italian Foreign Exchange Office 1993–2005; mem. Bd of Dirs Bank for Int. Settlements 1993–2005; mem. Governing Council, European Cen. Bank (fmrly European Monetary Inst.), 1993–2005; Paul Harris Fellow, Rotary International; Hon. mem., Circolo St Thomas Aquinas, Aquino (Italy); Kt Grand Gross, Order of Merit of the Italian Repub.; Hon. DEcon (Bari) 1994, Hon. DLitt (Johns Hopkins) 1995, Hon. Dr rer. pol (Macerata) 1996, Hon. LLB (Cassino) 1999, Hon. Dr Statistics and Econs (Milan) 1999, Hon. Dr Computer Eng (Lecce) 2000, Hon. Dr Banking Econs (Verona) 2002, Hon. LLD (St John's) 2002, Hon. PhD (Catania) 2002, Hon. Dr Moral Theol. (Pontificia Salesiana) 2003; Ezio Tarantelli Prize for most original theory in Economic Policy, Club dell'economia 1995, Euromoney Cen. Banker of the Year 1996, St Vincent Prize for Econs 1997, 'Pico della Mirandola' Prize for Econs, Finance and Business 1997–98, Int. Award in the Humanities, Accad. di Studi Mediterranei 1999, Keynes Sraffa Prize (London) 2003, Fiaccola d'oro Award, Circolo San Tommaso d'Aquino 2012. *Publications include:* Econometric Model of the Italian Economy; Razionalità economica e solidarietà 1996, Globalizzazione: politica economica e dottrina sociale 2008, Enciclica Caritas in Veritate: prospettiva storica e attualità; Sviluppo e declino demografico in europa e nel mondo 2012; texts dealing mainly with monetary theory, econ. policy and monetary policy issues. *Address:* Bank of Italy, Via Nazionale 91, 00184 Rome, Italy (office). *Telephone:* (06) 47921 (office).

FEARON, Douglas Thomas, BA, MD, FRCP, FAAS, FRS, FMedSci; American immunologist, academic and physician; *Senior Group Leader, Cancer Research UK Cambridge Research Institute, University of Cambridge;* b. 16 Oct. 1942, Brooklyn, NY; s. of Henry Dana Fearon and Frances Fearon (née Eubanks); m. 2nd Clare M. Wheless 1977; one s. one d.; ed Williams Coll., Johns Hopkins Univ. School of Medicine; residency, Johns Hopkins Hosp. 1968–70; US Army Medical Corps 1970–72; Post-doctoral Fellowship, Harvard Medical School 1972–75, Instructor, Harvard Medical School 1975–76, Asst Prof. of Medicine 1976–79, Assoc. Prof. 1979–84, Prof. of Medicine 1984–87; Prof. of Medicine, Johns Hopkins Univ. School of Medicine 1987–93; Prof., Wellcome Trust Immunology Unit, Univ. of Cambridge, UK 1993–, Fellow, Trinity Coll., Cambridge 2001–, Sheila Joan Smith Prof. of Immunology 2004–11, Emer. 2011–, Sr Group Leader, Cancer Research UK Cambridge Research Inst. 2011–; mem. NAS 2001; Hon. Consultant, Addenbrooke's Hosp. Cambridge 1993–; Bronze Star (US Army); Lee C. Howley Prize, Arthritis Foundation. *Publications:* more than 100 articles in scientific journals. *Leisure interest:* golf. *Address:* Li Ka Shing Centre, Robinson Way, Cambridge, CB2 0RE, England (office). *Telephone:* (1223) 404473 (office). *Fax:* (1223) 404573 (office). *E-mail:* dtf1000@cam.ac.uk (office). *Website:* www.trin.cam.ac.uk (office).

FEDERER, Roger; Swiss professional tennis player; b. 8 Aug. 1981, Binningen, nr Basel; s. of Robert Federer and Lynette Federer (née Durand); m. Miroslava (Mirka) Vavrinec 2009; two s. (twins) two d. (twins); world rank No. 1 as jr 1998, won Wimbledon jr title that year; turned professional 1998; singles titles: Milan 2001, Hamburg TMS 2002, 2005, Sydney 2002, Vienna 2002, 2003, Marseille 2003, Tennis Masters Cup, Houston 2003, 2004, 2006, 2007, Wimbledon 2003, 2004, 2005, 2006, 2007, 2009, 2012, 2017, Halle 2003, 2004, 2005, 2006, 2008, 2013, 2014, 2015, 2017, Vienna 2002, 2003, Munich 2003, Dubai 2003, 2004, 2005, 2007, 2012, 2014, Australian Open 2004, 2006, 2007, 2010, 2017, 2018, Bangkok 2004, 2005, Canada AMS 2004, Gstaad 2004, Hamburg AMS 2004, 2007, Indian Wells AMS 2004, 2005, 2006, 2012, 2017, Toronto 2004, 2006, US Open 2004, 2005, 2006, 2007, 2008, Cincinnati 2005, 2007, 2009, 2010, 2012, 2014, 2015, Doha 2005, 2006, Miami 2005, 2006, 2017, Rotterdam 2005, Basel 2006, 2007, 2008, 2014, 2015, Madrid 2006, 2009, 2012, Tennis Masters Cup, Shanghai 2006, 2007, Tokyo 2006, Estoril 2008, French Open 2009, Barclays ATP World Tour Finals, London 2010, 2011, BNP Paribas Masters Open 2011, 2012, ABN AMRO World Tennis Tournament, Rotterdam 2012, Shanghai Rolex Master 2014, Brisbane Int. presented by Suncorp 2015, Istanbul Open 2015; doubles titles: Rotterdam 2001 (with Jonas Bjorkman), 2002 (with Max Mirnyi), Gstaad 2001 (with Marat Safin), Moscow 2002 (with Mirnyi), Vienna 2003 (with Yves Allegro), Miami TMS 2003 (with Mirnyi), Halle 2005 (with Yves Allegro), Beijing Olympics 2008 (with Stanislas Wawrinka); team competitions: won Hopman Cup (partnering Martina Hingis), Perth, Australia 2001, Davis Cup (with Stanislas Wawrinka, Marco Chiudinelli and Michael Lammer), Lille, France 2014; highest number (20) of Grand Slam singles titles won by a man; first player to be ranked World No. 1 for four consecutive (non-calendar) years 2004–08, highest number (303 as of Feb. 2018) of weeks as World No. 1; coached by Adolf Kacovsky 1991, Peter Carter 1991–2000, Peter Lundgren 2000–03, Tony Roche 2006–07, Severin Lüthi 2007–, José Higueras 2008, Paul Annacone 2010–13, Stefan Edberg 2014–15, Ivan Ljubicic 2016–; ITF Jr World Champion 1998, ATP European Player of the Year 2003, 2004, Swiss Sportsman of the Year 2003, 2004, 2006, 2007, Swiss Personality of the Year 2003, Michael-Westphal Award 2003, ITF World Champion 2004, 2005, 2006, 2007, ATP Player of the Year 2004, 2005, 2006, 2007, 2008, Laureus World Sportsman of the Year 2005, 2006, 2007, 2008, 2018, ESPY Best Male Tennis Player 2005, 2006, 2007, 2008, BBC Sports Personality of the Year (Overseas Personality) 2004, 2006, 2007, Stefan Edberg Sportsmanship Award 2004–09, 2011–14, Swiss Team of the Year (with Stanislas Wawrinka) 2008, Amb. of the Year, Int. Tennis Writers Asscn 2018, Laureus Comeback of the Year 2018. *Leisure* *interests:* golf, soccer, skiing, PlayStation, music, playing cards. *Address:* c/o Lynette Federer, PO Box 209, 4103 Bottmingen, Switzerland; IMG Tennis, IMG Center, 1360 East 9th Street, Suite 100, Cleveland, OH 44114, USA. *Telephone:* (61) 4215712. *Fax:* (61) 4215719. *E-mail:* management@rogerfederer.com. *Website:* www.rogerfederer.com.

FEDEROVSKI, Vladimir; Russian/French writer, academic and fmr diplomatist; *Professor of History, Hautes Etudes Commerciales;* b. 1950, Moscow; ed Inst. of Int. Relations, Moscow; attaché, Soviet Embassy in Nouakchott, Mauritius 1972; interpreter for Leonid Brezhnev, Sec.-Gen. of CP during 1970s; counsellor, Soviet Embassy in Paris 1985; Spokesperson, Movt for Democratic Reform 1985–91; attained French citizenship 1995; currently Prof. of History, Hautes Etudes Commerciales (HEC), Paris; adviser on Cold War history, Mémorial de Caen; Officier des Arts et des Lettres. *Publications include:* Histoire de la diplomatie française 1985, Histoire secrète d'un coup d'État 1991, Les Égéries russes 1993, Les Égéries romantiques 1995, Le Département du diable 1996, Les Deux Soeurs ou l'art d'aimer 1997, Le Triangle russe 1999, Les Tsarines: Les Femmes qui ont fait la Russie 1999, L'Histoire secrète des ballets russes 2002, Le roman de Saint-Petersbourg 2002, Le Roman du Kremlin 2004, Le Roman de la Russie insolite 2004, Paris-Saint-Petersbourg 2005, Le Roman de l'Orient-Express 2006, Regards sur la France 2006, Le Fantôme de Staline 2007. *Address:* 22C ave. des Courlis, 78110 Le Vésinet, France.

FEDIN, Vladimir, DChemSci; Russian chemist and academic; *Director, Nikolaev Institute of Inorganic Chemistry;* b. 5 Sept. 1954, Pensa; ed Russian Acad. of Sciences and Univ. of Moscow; currently Prof. and Dir Nikolaev Inst. of Inorganic Chem., Siberian Br. of Russian Acad. of Sciences; Prof. and Head of Chair of Inorganic Chem., Novosibirsk State Univ. *Publications:* numerous articles in professional journals. *Address:* Nikolaev Institute of Inorganic Chemistry, Siberian Branch of Russian Academy of Sciences, 3 Acad. Lavrentiev Avenue, Novosibirsk 630090, Russia (office). *Telephone:* (383) 330-94-90 (office); (383) 330-58-42 (home). *Fax:* (383) 330-94-89 (office). *E-mail:* cluster@niic.nsc.ru (office). *Website:* www.niic.nsc.ru (office).

FEDOR, Martin, MEconSc; Slovak politician; b. 4 March 1974, Považská Bystrica; m.; two c.; ed Comenius Univ., Dublin European Inst., Ireland; Dir Office of Prime Minister 1998–2000; Dir Int. Relations Section, SDKÚ 2000–02, Head of Dept of Foreign Policy and Integration 2000–, Deputy Chair. New Generation (SDKÚ Youth Org.) –2002; State Sec., Ministry of Defence 2003–06, Minister of Defence Feb.–July 2006; mem. Slovak Nat. Council (Národná Rada Slovenskej republiky) 2006–. *Address:* National Council of the Slovak Republic, nám. Alexandra Dubčeka 1, 812 80 Bratislava, Slovakia (office). *Telephone:* (2) 5972-1111 (office). *Fax:* (2) 5441-9529 (office). *E-mail:* martin_fedor@nrsr.sk (office). *Website:* www.nrsr.sk (office); martinfedor.blog.sme.sk.

FEDOROV, Alexey Innokentevich; Russian manufacturing executive; b. 14 April 1952, Irkutsk; ed Oklahoma City Univ. Business School, USA; design engineer, Irkutsk Aviation Industrial Asscn, Irkutsk, Siberia, USSR 1974, Pres. 1998–2005, Chair. 2005; Gen. Dir and Gen. Constructor Russian Aviation Construction Corpn MiG 2004; Pres. United Aviation Construction Corpn 2006–12; counsellor to CEO Russian Technologies State Corpn (Rostec) 2012–; Order Merit to Fatherland (Fourth Degree), Badge of Honour, Peter the Great Golden Symbol. *Address:* Russian Technologies State Corpn (Rostec), Moscow 119048, 24, Usacheva str., Russia. *Website:* rostec.ru/en.

FEDOROV, Igor Borisovich, DrTech; Russian engineer and university administrator; *President, Moscow Bauman Technical University;* b. 1940; m.; one d.; ed Moscow Bauman Tech. Univ.; engineer, asst, Docent, Head of Dept, Prorector for Scientific Work, Moscow Bauman Tech. Univ. –1991, Rector 1991–2010, Pres. 2010–; mem. Int. Acad. of Informatization, Int. Acad. of Eng, Asscn of Rectors of Europe, Eurasian Asscn of Univs, Russian Acad. of Natural Sciences, Int. Acad. of Higher Educ. Problems; Merited Worker of Science and Tech., Order for Merits before Fatherland; Dr hc (de Montfort) 1994; Prize of USSR Ministry of Educ. 1991, Prize of the Pres. of Russian Fed. 1998, Prize of the Govt of Russian Fed. 2002, 2004. *Publications include:* more than 140 scientific papers on higher education problems; five monographs and 15 patents. *Address:* Office of the President, Moscow Bauman Technical University, 105005 Moscow, ul. Baumanskaya 2-ya, 5/1, Russia (office). *Telephone:* (499) 263-63-91 (office). *Fax:* (499) 267-48-44 (office). *E-mail:* bauman@bmstu.ru (office). *Website:* www.bmstu.ru (office).

FEDOROV, Valentin Petrovich, DEcon; Russian politician and research institute director; *Deputy Director for Research, Institute of Europe, Russian Academy of Sciences;* b. 6 Sept. 1939, Zhatai, Yakutia; m.; two d.; ed G. Plekhanov Moscow Inst. of Nat. Econ., Inst. of World Econ. and Int. Relations, USSR Acad. of Sciences; worked in State Planning Cttee Yakutia 1964–78; jr researcher, Head of Div. and Corresp., Journal of Inst. of World Economy and International Relations in West Germany 1978–84; Pro-Rector on Int. Relations, Prof., G. V. Plekhanov Moscow Inst. of Nat. Econ. 1987–90; Gov. of Sakhalin Region; People's Deputy of Russia 1990–93; Deputy Minister of Econ. 1993–94; Prime Minister of Sakhá (Yakutia) Repub. 1997–98; mem. Political Council Movt for Democratic Reforms, Co-Chair. Duma of Russian Nat. Sobor; Vice-Pres. Russian Union of Industrialists and Entrepreneurs 1994–97, 1998–2000; Deputy Dir for Research, Inst. of Europe, Russian Acad. of Sciences, Moscow 2000–; mem. Russian Acad. of Natural Sciences, Russian Eng Acad.; Dr hc (Loyola Univ., Los Angeles). *Publications include:* FRG: Country and People 1991, The Tragedy of Russia: People Extinction and Territorial Vulnerability 2004, European Union – Russia: A Measure of Cooperation (with N.P.Shmelev) 2012; several plays, collections of poems, monographs on econs. *Address:* Institute of Europe, 125993 Moscow, 11-3 Mokhovaya str., Russia (office). *Telephone:* (495) 629-59-18 (office). *Fax:* (495) 629-92-96 (office). *E-mail:* vpfyodorov@mail.ru. *Website:* en.instituteofeurope.ru (office).

FEDOSEYEV, Vladimir Ivanovich; Russian conductor; *Principal Conductor and Artistic Director, Tchaikovsky Symphony Orchestra;* b. 5 Aug. 1932, Leningrad; s. of Ivan Fedoseyev and Elena Fedoseyeva; m. Olga Dobrokhotova; two c.; ed Gnesins Musical Academy, Tchaikovsky Conservatory with Leo Ginzburg; mem. CPSU 1963–91; Artistic Dir and Chief Conductor, Moscow Radio Symphony Orchestra of USSR Radio Network (now Tchaikovsky Symphony Orchestra) 1974–; Music Dir Vienna Symphony Orchestra 1997–2006; apptd Perm. Guest Conductor, Tokyo Philharmonic Orchestra 2000, Zürich Opera 1997, Radio France Orchestra 2001; Prin. Conductor, Orchestra Sinfonica di Milano Giuseppe Verdi 2009–; works with Bolshoi and Mariinsky Theatres, opera productions and concerts abroad, including Italy, France, Austria, Germany, Japan, Switzerland, Spain, UK, USA; People's Artist of USSR 1980, RSFSR State Prize 1989, Crystal Award of Asahi Broadcasting Corpn, Osaka 1989, Golden Orpheus, for recording of opera May Night, Gold Medal, Int. Gustav Mahler Soc. 2007, among others. *Recordings include:* Symphonies by Beethoven, Mahler, Shostakovich, Mussorgsky, Sviridov, Russian operas. *Address:* Tchaikovsky Symphony Orchestra, 121069 Moscow, Malaya Nikitskaya 24, Russia (office). *Telephone:* (495) 229-57-68 (Moscow) (home); (1) 503-84-77 (Vienna) (home). *E-mail:* tsom@fedoseyev.com (office). *Website:* www.bso.ru (office); www.fedoseyev.com (office).

FEDOSOV, Yevgeny Aleksandrovich, DTechSc; Russian automation and avionics specialist; *Research Adviser, State Research Institute of Aviation Systems (GosNIIAS);* b. 14 May 1929, Moscow; s. of Alexander Yefimovitch Fedosov and Nadezhda Anempodistovna Smirnova; m. Lydia Petrovna Vasilyeva; one d.; ed Bauman Tech. Inst.; post-grad. work at Inst. 1953–56; mem. CPSU 1959–91; Research Fellow, Head of Dept, Deputy Dir State Research Inst. of Aviation Systems (GosNIIAS) 1956–70, Dir Research and Tech. 1970–2001, Gen. Dir GosNIIAS 2001–06, Research Adviser 2006–; simultaneously Head of Dept of Physico-Tech. Inst. 1970–; Prof. 1969; Corresp. mem. USSR (now Russian) Acad. of Sciences 1979, mem. 1984–; Lenin Prize 1976, Hero of Socialist Labour 1983, B.N. Petrov Gold Medal, Acad. of Sciences 1989, Honoured Scientist of Russian Fed. 1996. *Publications:* works on analysis and synthesis of complex multi-level operational systems. *Leisure interests:* tennis, gardening. *Address:* State Research Institute of Aviation Systems (GosNIIAS), Viktorenko str. 7, 125319 Moscow, Russia (office). *Telephone:* (499) 157-70-47 (office). *Fax:* (499) 943-86-05 (office). *E-mail:* info@gosniias.ru (office). *Website:* www.gosniias.ru (office).

FEDOTOV, Maxim Viktorovich; Russian violinist, conductor and academic; b. 24 July 1961, Leningrad (now St. Petersburg); s. of Viktor Andreyevich Fedotov and Galina Nikolayevna Fedotova; m. Galina Yevgenyevna Petrova; one d.; ed Specialized Music School for Gifted Children in Leningrad, Moscow State Conservatory (with D. Tsyganov and I. Bezrodny); concert tours since 1975; Prof., Moscow State Conservatory 1987–2001; Prof. and Head, Violin and Viola Dept, Russian Gnesin Acad. of Music 2003–08; Artistic Dir and Chief Conductor, Russian Symphony Orchestra 2003–05, Russian Philharmonic Orchestra 2006–10; with Russian S.Prokofiev Symphony Orchestra, Symphony Orchestra of Tchaikovsky Foundation 2011–; as soloist plays with G. Petrova, regular recitals in Moscow and St Petersburg; performed in Madrid, Berlin, Leipzig, Frankfurt, Cologne, Milan, Chicago and other cities; took part in music festivals in Salzburg, Oakland, Bergen, Dresden, Klagenfurt; toured Australia, New Zealand, Korea, Turkey; Vice-Pres. Asscn of Laureates of P.I. Tchaikovsky Int. Competition 1995–, Pres. 1997–2003; mem. Peter the Great's Arts and Sciences Acad., St Petersburg; prizewinner, All-Union Music Competition Riga 1981, N. Paganini Competition, Genoa 1982, Vercelli 1984, P. Tchaikovsky, Moscow 1986, Tokyo 1986 (First Prize), People's Artist of Russia 2002. *Telephone:* (905) 518-74-55 (office). *E-mail:* maximfedotov@mail.ru (office). *Website:* fedotov-petrova.com/pages/en (office).

FEDOTOV, Mikhail Aleksandrovich, DJur; Russian politician and lawyer; *Chairman of the Presidential Council for Civil Society and Human Rights;* b. 18 Sept. 1949, Moscow; m. 3rd Maria Fedotova; one s. one d; ed Moscow State Univ., All-Union Inst. of Law; teacher of law, All-Union Inst. of Law 1973–90; Deputy Minister of Press and Mass Information of Russia 1991–92, Minister 1992–93; represented Pres. Yeltsin in Constitutional Court trial against CPSU 1992; Dir-Gen. Russian Agency of Intellectual Property (RAIS) Feb.–Dec. 1992; Russian rep. at UNESCO, Paris 1993–97; Sec., Russian Union of Journalists 2003–10; Adviser to the Pres. of Russian Federation and Chair. Presidential Council for Civil Soc. and Human Rights 2010–; Laureate Prize, Union of Journalists of the USSR 1990, UNESCO Medal in honour of the 50th anniversary of the Universal Declaration of Human Rights 1999. *Publications include:* more than 100 books and essays on human rights and constitutionalism, intellectual property and int. humanitarian co-operation. *Address:* c/o Office of the President, 103132 Moscow, Staraya pl. 4, Russia. *Telephone:* (495) 625-35-81. *Fax:* (495) 606-07-66. *Website:* www.kremlin.ru.

FEDOTOV, Yury Victorovich; Russian diplomatist and UN official; *Executive Director, United Nations Office on Drugs and Crime and Director-General, United Nations, Vienna;* b. 14 Dec. 1947, Moscow; ed Moscow State Inst. of Int. Relations; entered diplomatic service 1971, served in various posts in Ministry of Foreign Affairs and abroad (Algeria 1974–80, India 1983–88), Deputy Head, Dept of Int. Relations, Ministry of Foreign Affairs 1991–93, Deputy Perm. Rep. and Acting First Deputy Perm. Rep. to UN, New York 1993–99, Dir Dept of Int. Orgs, Ministry of Foreign Affairs 1999–2002, Deputy Minister of Foreign Affairs 2002–05, mem. Bd of Dirs 2000–05, Amb. to UK 2005–10; Exec. Dir UN Office on Drugs and Crime (UNODC) 2010–, also Dir-Gen. UN Office at Vienna (UNOV) 2010–. *Address:* United Nations Office on Drugs and Crime, Vienna International Centre, PO Box 500, 1400 Vienna, Austria (office). *Telephone:* (1) 26060-0 (office). *Website:* www.unodc.org (home).

FEFFER, Marc-André (Patrice), M.Droit pub; French television executive and lawyer; b. 22 Dec. 1949, Neuilly-sur-Seine; s. of Jacques Feffer and Marie-Jeanne Thirlin; m. Hélène Cataix 1976; three d.; ed Lycée Condorcet and Faculté de Droit, Inst. d'Etudes Politiques and Ecole Nat. d'Admin, Paris; official Conseil d'Etat 1976, Counsel 1980, now mem.; Sec.-Gen. Comm. des Sondages 1980; Adviser Office of Pres. of EEC 1981–84; Dir Centre Mondial Informatique et Ressource Humaine 1984; Head of Information (Legal and Tech.), Prime Minister's Staff 1985–88, Sr Defence Counsel, Information 1986–88; Sec.-Gen. Canal+ 1988–94, Gen. Man. 1994–95, Dir Exec. Cttee 1994, Exec. Vice-Pres. 1995–2003, Deputy Chair. Exec. Bd and Gen. Council 2000–03; apptd Dir-Gen. La Poste 2004; apptd Chair. Bd of Dirs Poste Immo 2007; Chevalier, Légion d'honneur, Commdr Ordre des Arts et des Lettres. *Leisure interests:* sailing, windsurfing.

FEFFERMAN, Charles, BS, PhD; American mathematician and academic; *Herbert Jones University Professor of Mathematics, Princeton University;* b. 18 April 1949, Washington, DC; ed Univ. of Maryland and Princeton Univ.; graduated univ. aged 17, doctorate aged 20, professor aged 22; Lecturer in Math., Princeton Univ. 1969–70, Prof. 1973–84, Herbert Jones Univ. Prof. of Math. 1984–, Chair. and Prof., Dept of Math. 1999–2002; Asst Prof. of Math., Univ. of Chicago 1970–71, Prof. 1971–73 (youngest full prof. ever appointed in USA); Wilson Elkins Visiting Professorship, Univ. of Maryland; Visiting Prof., Calif. Inst. of Tech., Courant Inst. of Math. Sciences, New York Univ., Univ. of Paris, France, Mittag-Leffler Inst., Djursholm, Sweden, Weitzmann Inst., Rehovot, Israel, Bar-Ilan Univ., Ramat-Gan, Israel Univ. of Madrid (Autónoma), Spain; mem. American Acad. of Arts and Sciences 1972, NAS 1979, American Philosophical Soc. 1989; mem. Editorial Bd Communications in Partial Differential Equations, Advances in Mathematics, Revista Mat. Iberoamericana, Journal of Fourier Analysis and Applications, Proceedings of the National Academy of Sciences, Journal d'Analyse; Hon. mem. London Mathematical Soc. 2009; Dr hc (Univ. of Maryland) 1979, (Knox Coll.) 1981, (Bar-Ilan Univ.) 1985, (Univ. of Madrid (Autónoma) 1990; NSF Fellowship 1966–69, Alfred P. Sloan Foundation Fellowship 1970, Nato Postdoctoral Fellowship 1971, Salem Prize 1971, First Recipient Alan T. Waterman Award 1976, Fields Medal, Int. Congress of Mathematicians, Helsinki 1978, American Math. Soc. Colloquium Lecturer 1983, Bergman Prize 1992; Bocher Memorial Prize 2008. *Publications:* Renewing U.S. Mathematics: A Plan for the Nineties (co-author); more than 80 publs in math. journals on multivariable complex analysis, partial differential equations and harmonic analysis. *Address:* 1102 Fine Hall, Department of Mathematics, Washington Road, Princeton University, Princeton, NJ 08544-1000, USA (office). *Telephone:* (609) 258-4200 (office). *Fax:* (609) 258-1367 (office). *E-mail:* cf@math.princeton.edu (office). *Website:* www.math.princeton.edu (office).

FEGAN-WYLES, Sally, BA, MS; Irish international civil servant and UN official; b. 1954, Dublin; m. John Wyles; ed Trinity Coll., London School of Econs and Political Science, UK, Harvard Univ., USA; Health Economist, then Programme Officer, UNICEF 1980–98, Rep. in Uganda 1986–91, Rep. in Zimbabwe 1991–95, Adviser on Change Man., New York 1995–98; UN Resident Coordinator and Resident Rep., UNDP, Tanzania 1998–2001; Dir UN Devt Group Office 2001–08; Sr Adviser on Peacebuilding, Office of UN Sec.-Gen. 2008–09, Sr Adviser on System-Wide Coherence, Office of Deputy Sec.-Gen., UN 2009–10, Sr Adviser on Transition, UN Women 2010–11; Asst Sec.-Gen. and Dir a.i., UNITAR 2012–15.

FEHRENBACH, Franz, BEng; German business executive; *Chairman of the Supervisory Board, Robert Bosch GmbH;* b. 1 July 1949, Kenzingen, Breisgau; m.; three s.; ed Univ. of Karlsruhe; trainee, Robert Bosch GmbH 1975–76, Man. Office of the Exec. Man., Electrical and Electronic Engine Equipment Div. 1976–78, Dir Material Planning and Logistics Dept 1978–80, Commercial Plant Man., Hildesheim 1980–82, Vice-Pres., Corp. Dept Planning and Control 1982–85, Commercial Plant Man., Robert Bosch Corpn, Automotive Group, USA 1985–88, Exec. Vice-Pres. 1988–89, Exec. Vice-Pres., Finance and Admin, Starters and Alternators Div. 1989–94, Pres., Starters and Alternators Div. 1994–96, Exec. Vice-Pres., Finance and Admin, Diesel Systems Div. 1996–97, Pres. Diesel Systems Div. 1997–99, Deputy mem. Bd of Man. 1999–2001, mem. 2001–03, Chair. 2003–12, Chair. Supervisory Bd 2012–, also Man. Partner, Robert Bosch Industrietreuhand KG 2003–; mem. Supervisory Bd BASF SE, Linde AG; mem. Advisory Bd of Stihl Holding AG and Co. K.G, Man. Bd VDA (German Asscn of the Automotive Industry), US Bd of Presiding Cttee of BDI (Fed. of German Industries), Asia Pacific Cttee of German Business, BBUG (Baden-Baden Entrepreneurs' Conf.); mem. Senate of Max Planck Soc.; Eco-Man. of the Year (cos category), WWF Deutschland and Capital magazine 2006, Hon. Golden Steering Wheel Prize, awarded to outstanding personalities by a German newspaper 2008, 'Yellow Angel' Personality of 2009 award, ADAC (German automobile asscn) 2009, environment award presented by BAUM (German Environmental Man. Asscn) 2009, Award for Understanding and Tolerance of the Jewish Museum, Berlin 2009, Greentech Man. of the Year 2011 Award, Capital magazine 2012. *Address:* Robert Bosch GmbH, Postfach 106050, 70049 Stuttgart, Germany (office). *Telephone:* 400-40990 (office). *Fax:* 400-40999 (office). *E-mail:* kontakt@bosch.de (office). *Website:* www.bosch.com (office).

FEI, Maj.-Gen. Junlong; Chinese astronaut; b. 5 May 1965, Suzhou, Jiangsu; m. 1991; one s.; joined PLA Air Force 1982, served as fighter pilot; selected to be astronaut, Shenzhou Program 1998; shortlisted to fly on board Shenzhou 5 (China's first manned space mission) 2003; debut space flight on board Shenzhou 6, with astronaut Nie Haisheng, launched from Jiuquan Satellite Launch Centre, Gobi Desert (China's second space mission) 12 Oct. 2005; asteroid 9512 Feijunlong named after him; rank of Maj.-Gen. 2011; Hon. Prof., Nanjing Audit Univ. 2011, Hon. mem. Chinese Soc. of Astronautics 2012; Merit Citation Class II 1996, Medal for Youth Having Outstanding Contributions 2005, Aerospace Achievement Medal 2005. *Address:* c/o China National Space Administration, Beijing, People's Republic of China.

FEIFFER, Jules Ralph; American cartoonist, writer and dramatist; b. 26 Jan. 1929, New York; s. of David Feiffer and Rhoda Davis; m. 1st Judith Sheftel 1961 (divorced 1983); one d.; m. 2nd Jennifer Allen 1983; two c.; m. 3rd JZ Holden 2016; ed Art Students' League, Pratt Inst.; asst to syndicated cartoonist Will Eisner 1946–51; cartoonist, author, syndicated Sunday page, Clifford, engaged in various art jobs 1953–56; contributing cartoonist Village Voice, New York 1956–97; cartoons published weekly in The Observer (London) 1958–66, 1972–82, regularly in Playboy (magazine); sponsor Sane; US Army 1951–53; mem. Dramatists' Guild (council 1970); currently Adjunct Prof., Program in Writing and Literature, Stony Brook Southampton Coll.; fmr teacher Yale School of Drama, Northwestern Univ.; fmr Sr Fellow, Columbia Univ. Nat. Arts Journalism Program; mem. American Acad. of Arts and Letters 1995–; Hon. Fellow, Inst. for Policy Studies 1987; Dr hc (Southampton Coll., Long Island Univ.) 1999; Acad. Award for Animated Cartoon (for Munro) 1961, Special George Polk Memorial Award 1962, Best Foreign Play, English Press (for Little Murders) 1967, Outer Critics Circle Award (Obie) 1969, (The White House Murder Case) 1970, Pulitzer Prize for Editorial Cartooning 1986, Writers Guild of America, East's Ian McLellan Hunter Award for Lifetime Achievement in Writing 2004, Nat. Cartoonist Soc. Milton Caniff Lifetime Achievement Award 2004, Benjamin Franklin Creativity Laureate Award 2006, Lifetime Achievement Award, Writers Guild of America 2010. *Plays:* Crawling Arnold 1961, Little Murders 1966, God Bless 1968, The White House Murder Case 1970, Feiffer on Nixon: The Cartoon Presidency 1974, Knock Knock 1975, Grown Ups 1981, A Think Piece 1982, Carnal Knowledge 1988, Anthony Rose 1989, Feiffer The Collected Works (vols 1, 2, 3) 1990, A Bad Friend 2003. *Screenplays:* Little Murders 1971, Carnal Knowledge 1971, Popeye 1980, I Want to Go Home (Best Screenplay, Venice Film Festival) 1989, I Lost My Bear 1998, Bark, George 1999. *Publications:* Sick, Sick, Sick 1959, Passionella and Other Stories 1960, The Explainers 1961, Boy, Girl, Boy, Girl, 1962, Hold Me! 1962, Harry, The Rat With Women (novel) 1963, Feiffer's Album 1963, The Unexpurgated Memoirs of Bernard Mergendeiler 1965, The Great Comic Book Heroes 1967, Feiffer's Marriage Manual 1967, Pictures at a Prosecution 1971, Ackroyd (novel) 1978, Tantrum 1980, Jules Feiffer's America: From Eisenhower to Reagan 1982, Marriage is an Invasion of Privacy 1984, Feiffer's Children 1986, Ronald Reagan in Movie America 1988, Elliott Loves (also play) 1990, The Man in the Ceiling (juvenile) 1993, A Barrel of Laughs, A Vale of Tears (juvenile) 1995, A Room with a Zoo (juvenile), The Daddy Mountain (juvenile), Explainers 2008, Backing into Forward: A Memoir 2010, Rupert Can Dance 2014, Kill My Mother 2014, Cousin Joseph 2016, The Ghost Script 2018. *Address:* Royce Carlton Inc., 866 United Nations Plaza, New York, NY 10017, USA (office); c/o Authors Guild, 31 East 32nd Street, 7th Floor, New York, NY 10016, USA. *Telephone:* (212) 355-7700 (office). *Fax:* (212) 888-8659 (office). *E-mail:* info@roycecarlton.com (office). *Website:* www.roycecarlton.com (office).

FEINENDEGEN, Ludwig E., DrMed; German professor of nuclear medicine; *Professor Emeritus, Department of Nuclear Medicine, University Hospital, Heinrich Heine University;* b. 1 Jan. 1927, Garzweiler; s. of Ludwig Feinendegen and Rosa Klauth; m. Jeannine Gemuseus 1960; two s.; ed Univ. of Cologne; Asst Physician and Scientist, Medical Dept, Brookhaven Nat. Lab., Upton, New York, USA 1958–63; Scientific Officer, Euratom, Brussels and Paris 1963–67; Dir Inst. of Medicine Research Center, Jülich GmbH and Prof. for Nuclear Medicine, Heinrich Heine Univ., Dept of Nuclear Medicine, Univ. Hosp., Düsseldorf 1967–93, Prof. Emer. 1993–; Prof. Emer. Catholic Univ., Seoul, Korea; Sr Scientist, Brookhaven Nat. Lab., USA 1993–98, Research Collaborator 1998–; Assignee, Dept of Energy, Washington, Wash., DC 1994–98; Fogarty Scholar, NIH, Bethesda 1998–99; mem. Advisory Council, Fed. Ministries of Interior Environment and Defence; mem. Cttee for meetings of Nobel Laureates 1978–2005; mem. Rhine Westfalian Acad. of Sciences (Vice-Pres. 1978–79); mem. Int. Comm. on Radiation Units and Measurements 1982–2006; Dist Gov. Rotary Int. 1992–93; Bundesverdienstorden, Ehrenkreuz Gold Deutsche Bundeswehr, Commdrs Cross, Order of Merit, Gy, Cross of Honor in Gold, German Armed Forces; numerous nat. and int. awards. *Publications include:* more than 700 publs in nat. and int. scientific journals and books on nuclear medicine and radiation biology. *Address:* Biosciences Department, Brookhaven National Laboratory, Upton, NY 11973, USA (office); Wannental 45, 88131 Lindau, Germany (home). *Telephone:* (8382) 75673 (home). *Fax:* (8382) 947626 (home). *E-mail:* feinendegen@gmx.net.

FEINGOLD, Russell (Russ) Dana, BA, BA (Oxon.), JD; American lawyer and politician; *Founder, Progressives United;* b. 2 March 1953, Janesville, Wis.; s. of Leon Feingold and Sylvia Feingold (née Binstock); m. 1st Susan Levine 1977 (divorced 1986); two d.; m. 2nd Mary Speerschneider 1991 (divorced 2005); two step-c.; ed Joseph A. Craig High School, Univ. of Wisconsin, Magdalen Coll., Oxford, UK (Rhodes Scholar), Harvard Univ. Law School; Assoc., Foley & Lardner (law firm), Madison 1979–82, LaFollette, Sinykin, Anderson & Munson, Madison 1983–85, Goldman & Feingold 1985–88; State Senator 1983–92; Senator from Wis. 1993–2011, mem. Foreign Relations Cttee; Founder Progressives United (political action cttee) 2011–; teaches at Marquette Univ. Law School, Milwaukee 2011–; Stephen Edward Scarff Distinguished Visiting Prof., Lawrence Univ. 2012–13; US Special Rep., African Great Lakes Region and Democratic Republic of the Congo 2013–15; announced candidacy for 2016 election for Senator from Wis. 2015; Democrat; John F. Kennedy Profile in Courage Award. *Publication:* While America Sleeps: A Wake-Up Call to the Post-9/11 2012. *Address:* Progressives United, 8025 Excelsior Drive, PO Box 620062, Madison, WI 53717 (office); 8383 Greenway Boulevard, Middleton, WI 53562, USA. *Telephone:* (608) 831-7877 (office). *Fax:* (608) 831-3192 (office). *E-mail:* info@progressivesunited.org (office). *Website:* www.progressivesunited.org (office).

FEINSTEIN, Dianne Goldman Berman; American politician; *Senator from California;* b. 22 June 1933, San Francisco, Calif.; d. of Leon Goldman and Betty Goldman (née Rosenburg); m. 1st Bertram Feinstein 1962 (deceased); one d.; m. 2nd Richard C. Blum 1980; ed Stanford Univ.; Intern in Public Affairs, Coro Foundation, San Francisco 1955–56; Asst to Calif. Industrial Welfare Comm., Los Angeles, also San Francisco 1956–57; Vice-Chair. Calif. Women's Bd Terms and Parole 1962–66; Chair. San Francisco City and Co. Advisory Comm. for Adult Detention 1967–69; Supervisor City and Co. of San Francisco 1970–78; Mayor of San Francisco 1978–88; served on Trilateral Comm. 1980s; Senator from California 1992–; mem. Council on Foreign Relations; Democrat; numerous hon. degrees; named by City and State Magazine the nation's Most Effective Mayor 1987, Woodrow Wilson Award for Public Service 2001, Nat. Distinguished Advocacy Award, American Cancer Soc. 2004, Women of Achievement Award, Century City Chamber of Commerce 2004, Funding Hero Award, Breast Cancer Research Foundation 2004, Outstanding Mem. of the US Senate Award, Nat. Narcotic Officers Asscns Coalition 2005, William Penn Mott Jr Park Leadership Award for singular outstanding achievement on behalf of Nat. Park protecting 2006, League of California Cities Congressional Leader of the Year Award 2006, Grammy on the Hill Award, Recording Acad. 2006, Charles Dick Medal of Merit, California Nat. Guard 2007, Legislator of the Year Award, California Co. Supts Educational Services Asscn 2007, Outstanding Int. Public Service Award, World Affairs Council 2012. *Address:* 331 Hart Senate Office Building, Washington, DC 20510-0001, USA (office). *Telephone:* (202) 224-3841 (office). *Fax:* (202) 228-3954 (office). *Website:* feinstein.senate.gov (office).

FEIREISS, Kristin; German art gallery director and writer; *Director, Aedes West;* b. 1942; Founder and Dir (with partner Hans-Jürgen Commercell) Aedes West Gallery (first pvt. forum for architecture in Germany), West Berlin 1980–, est. office in East Berlin 1995, over 250 exhbns shown including work of Peter and Alison Smithson, Peter Cook, Rem Koolhas, John Hejduk, over 200 catalogues published; Dir Netherlands Architecture Inst. 1996–2001; Bundesverdienstkreutz, Germany 1994; Literaturpreis für Baukultur, German Asscn of Architects and Engineers 1995. *Publications include:* Josef Paul Kleihues 1983, John Hejduk

1984, Fehling und Gogel 1986, Also Rossi 1989, Frank Gehry 1989, Nalbach und Nalbach 1990, Shin Takamatsu 1991, Syskowitz und Kowalski 1991, Zaha Hadid 1992, Hilde Léon Konrad Wohlhage 1992, Gustav Peichl: von der Skizze zum Bauwerk 1992, Sauerbruch und Hutton 1992, Daniel Libeskind: Erweiterung des Berlin Museums mit Abteilung Jüdisches Museum 1992, Ben van Berkel 1994, Christoph Mäckler 1995, Architekten Grüntuch/Ernst 1997, The Netherlands Architecture Institute 1999, Clorindo Testa 2001, Andre Poitiers 2002. *Address:* Aedes am Pfefferberg, Christinenstr. 18–19, 10119 Berlin, Germany. *Telephone:* (30) 282-7015 (office). *Fax:* (30) 2839-1466 (office). *E-mail:* aedes@baunetz.de (office). *Website:* www.aedes-arc.de (office).

FEITH, Pieter Cornelis, LicenPolSci, MA; Dutch diplomatist and international organization official; b. 9 Feb. 1945, Rotterdam; m.; three d.; ed Univ. of Lausanne, Switzerland, Fletcher School of Law and Diplomacy, Tufts Univ., USA; performed mil. service as reserve officer of Netherlands Marine Corps; with diplomatic service 1970–95, posted to Damascus, Bonn, New York (Mission to UN), Khartoum and Netherlands Mission to NATO and WEU, Brussels, also Chair. first UN Conf. of States Parties to the Chemical Weapons Convention, The Hague 1997; Personal Rep. of NATO Sec.-Gen. Lord Robertson for Yugoslavia, Dir of Crisis Man. and Operations Directorate, Head of NATO Balkans Task Force and Political Adviser to Commdr IFOR Bosnia-Herzegovina 1995–2001; Gen. Secr. of Council of EU, Deputy Dir-Gen. for Politico-Mil. Affairs 2001–10; Personal Rep. of EU High Rep., Javier Solana, for Sudan/Darfur 2004; Head of EU Expert Team for Iraq 2005; Head of EU-led Aceh Monitoring Mission (AMM) in Indonesia 2005–06; Civilian Operations Commdr for all civilian ESDP Crisis Man. Operations, Acting Dir of EU Civilian Planning and Conduct Capability 2007; led team of EU officials and approved the Constitution of the Repub. of Kosovo April 2008, EU Special Rep. in Kosovo 2008–11, Int. Civilian Rep. for Kosovo 2008–12; Distinguished Fellow, Center for Transatlantic Relations, Paul H. Nitze School of Advanced Int. Studies, Johns Hopkins Univ., Washington, DC 2013–; currently Sr Mediator, European Inst. of Peace, Brussels; Kt Commdr, Order of Orange-Nassau, Order Jasa Utama (Indonesia), Officer, Order of Merit (Germany), Order of Leopold II (Belgium). *Leisure interest:* playing tennis. *Address:* European Institute of Peace, rue des Deux Eglises 25, 1000 Brussels, Belgium (office); Kvesarum 4196, 24294 Horby, Sweden (home). *Telephone:* (4) 155-00-50 (office). *E-mail:* pcfeith@gmail.com (home); pieter.feith@eip.org (office). *Website:* www.pieterfeith.com.

FEKL, Matthias; French politician; *Partner, KGA Avocats, Paris;* b. 4 Oct. 1977, Frankfurt, Germany; ed Univ. Sciences-Po, Paris, Ecole nat. d'admin, Ecole Normale Supérieure-Lettres et Sciences Humaines; Admin Magistrate 2005–10; Deputy Mayor of Marmande, in charge of finances 2008–12; Vice-Pres. of Aquitaine region, responsible for econ. devt, employment and business 2010–12; Regional Councillor, Aquitaine 2010–15, Nouvelle Aquitaine 2016–; Chief of Staff to Chair. of Parl. Group in Senate 2010–11; Adviser to Pres. of Senate 2011–12; mem. Nat. Ass. (Socialist Party) for Lot-et-Garonne (2nd Dist) 2012–; Sec. of State for Foreign Trade, Tourism Promotion and French Abroad, Ministry of Foreign Affairs and Int. Devt 2014–17; Minister of the Interior March–May 2017; currently Partner, KGA Avocats, Paris; mem. Socialist Party (PS), First PS Fed. Sec. for Lot-et-Garonne 2012–15. *Address:* KGA Avocats Lawfirm, 44 Avenue des Champs-Elysées, 75008 Paris, France (office). *Telephone:* 1-44-95-20-87 (office). *Fax:* 1-49-53-03-97 (office). *E-mail:* m.fekl@kga.fr (office). *Website:* kga-avocats.fr (office).

FEKTER, Maria, DIur; Austrian politician; b. 1 Feb. 1956; ed Linz Univ.; Municipal Counsellor, Attnang-Puchheim 1986–90; State Sec., Fed. Ministry of Econ. Affairs 1990–94; mem. Nat. Council (Parl.) 1994–2007, 2008, 2013–17, Sec. 2004–07; Fed. Minister of the Interior 2008–11, of Finance 2011–13; mem. Econ. Comm. of European Union of Women 1994–2007, Chair. 2002–07, Country Chair. 2007–14; mem. Exec. Cttee Österreichischer Wirtschaftsbund 1990–2002, mem. Bd African Devt Bank 2011–13; Großes Silbernes Ehrenzeichen am Bande für Verdienste um die Republik Österreich 1994, Großes Goldenes Ehrenzeichen am Bande für Verdienste um die Republik Österreich 2011.

FELCHT, Utz-Hellmuth, PhD; German chemist and business executive; *Chairman of the Supervisory Board, Deutsche Bahn AG;* b. 8 Jan. 1947, Iserlohn; ed Univs of Mainz, Saarbrücken and Kaiserslautern; Scientific Asst, Univ. of Kaiserslautern 1977–; various man. positions at Hoechst AG Inc. 1977–91, mem. Bd, Hoechst AG 1991–98; Head of Div. Coordination, Corp. Staff Dept, Dir Cen. Research 2 and Deputy Head of Corp. Planning Dept, Ruhrkohle AG, Essen 1995–96; fmr Exec. Vice-Pres. and Pres. Advanced Tech. Group, Hoechst Celanese Corpn, Chatham, NJ, USA, responsible for Celanese Mexicana SA; Chair. Man. Bd, SKW Trostberg AG 1998–2000; Chair. Man. Bd, Degussa-Hls AG 2000–01, CEO Degussa AG, Chair. Man. Bd, 2001–06, Chair. Man. Bd, Degussa (China) Co. Ltd 2002–; Partner, One Equity Partners LLC 2007– (currently a Man. Dir), One Equity Partners Europe GmbH, Munich –2014; Chair. Supervisory Bd, Deutsche Bahn AG 2010–; Chair. Man. Bd, Essen, Wiesbaden, SKW Metallurgie AG, Ruetgers AG, Goldschmidt AG, SKW Stickstoffwerke Piesteritz GmbH; mem. Bd of Dirs, Süd-Chemie AG, CIBA Specialty Chemicals Holding, Inc.; mem. Man. Bd, Ruetgers AG 2003–, Goldschmidt AG, Ph. Holzmann AG; mem. and Chair. Supervisory Bd, Gerling-Group Globale Rückversicherungs AG, Gerling-Konzern Globale Rückversicherungs AG, Degussa Corpn (USA), Süd-Chemie AG, Munich 2008–11; mem. Supervisory Bd, SGL CARBON AG 1992–, Chair. 1992–2004; mem. Advisory Bd, Hapag-Lloyd AG; Dir (non-exec.), CRH PLC 2007–16; fmr mem. Supervisory Bd, RAG Coal International AG, fmr mem. Man. Bd, Rag AG; fmr Chair. Gesellschaft für Chemische Technik und Biotechnologie (DECHEMA); mem. Atlantic Bridge Asscn, Presidium of German Acad. of Science and Eng (Acatech); Hon. Prof., Tech. Univ. of Munich, Jilin Univ., Changchun, People's Repub. of China; Dr hc (Univ. of Rostock); DECHEMA Medal 2004. *Address:* Deutsche Bahn AG, Potsdamer Platz 2, 10785 Berlin (office); One Equity Partners Europe, Taunusanlage 21, 60325 Frankfurt am Main, Germany. *Telephone:* (30) 297-0 (Berlin) (office); (69) 5060-747-0 (Frankfurt) (office). *Fax:* (30) 297-61919 (Berlin) (office); (69) 5060-747-40 (Frankfurt) (office). *E-mail:* info@deutschebahn.com (office); oep.info@oneequity.com (office). *Website:* www.deutschebahn.com (office); www.bahn.de (office); www.oneequity.com (office).

FELD, Eliot; American dancer and choreographer; b. 5 July 1942, Brooklyn, New York; s. of Benjamin Feld and Alice Posner; ed High School of Performing Arts, New York; debut as Child Prince in Nutcracker, New York City Ballet 1954; mem. cast, West Side Story, Broadway 1958 (also appeared in film), I Can Get It For You Wholesale, Broadway 1962 and Fiddler on the Roof, Broadway; dancer and choreographer, American Ballet Theater 1963–68, first two ballets (choreographer) includes Harbinger and At Midnight 1967; Founder, Prin. Dancer and Choreographer, American Ballet Co. 1968–71; freelance choreographer, N America and Europe 1971–73; Founder, Artistic Dir and Choreographer, Field Ballets, New York; Founder, The New Ballet School 1977, The Joyce Theater 1982, Ballet Tech 1996; Co-founder, Lawrence A. Wien Center for Dance & Theater 1986; has choreographed over 140 ballets since 1967 including Yo Shakespeare 1997, Nodrog Doggo 2000, Coup de Couperin 2000, Organon 2001, Pacific Dances 2001, Skandia 2002, Pianola 2002, Lincoln Portrait 2002, Behold the Man 2002, KYDZNY, New York 2014; Guggenheim Fellow; Dance Magazine Award 1990; Dr hc (Juilliard) 1991. *Address:* c/o Ballet Tech, 890 Broadway, 8th Floor, New York, NY 10003-1211, USA (office). *Telephone:* (212) 777-7710 (office). *Fax:* (212) 353-0936. *Website:* www.ballettech.org.

FELDMAN, Jerome Myron, BS, MD; American physician, medical scientist and academic; *Professor Emeritus, Division of Endocrinology, Metabolism and Nutrition, Duke University Medical Center;* b. 27 July 1935, Chicago, Ill.; s. of Louis Feldman and Marian Feldman (née Swichkow); m. Carol B. Feldman; one s. two d.; ed Northwestern Univ., Michael Reese, Chicago and Duke Univ.; served as officer in Medical Corps, US Army Reserve 1965–67; Chief, Endocrinology and Metabolism, Durham Veteran's Admin. Hosp. 1971–2000, Staff Internist 1971–; Assoc. Prof. of Medicine, Duke Univ. 1972–98, Prof. of Medicine 1998–2000, Prof. Emer. 2000–, Dir Clinical Research Unit Core Lab. 1984; mem. Duke Comprehensive Cancer Center 1982–; Ed. Journal of Clinical Endocrinology and Metabolism 1983–89; Fellow, ACP; mem., Diabetes Asscn, Endocrine Soc. *Publications:* 218 research articles, book chapters and reviews dealing with hormone-secreting tumours, endocrinology and metabolism. *Leisure interests:* music, art. *Address:* Duke University Medical Center, Box 2963, Durham, NC 27710, (office); 2744 Sevier Street, Durham, NC 27705-5745, USA (home). *Telephone:* (919) 286-0411 (office). *E-mail:* feld002@duke.edu (office). *Website:* endocrine.duke.edu (office).

FELDMAN OF ELSTREE, Baron (Life Peer), cr. 2010, of Elstree in the County of Hertfordshire; **Andrew Feldman;** British politician, business executive and fmr barrister; b. 25 Feb. 1966; m. Gabrielle Gourgey; three c.; ed Haberdashers' Aske's School, Elstree, Herts., Brasenose Coll., Oxford; worked as man. consultant at Bain & Co. 1989–91; called to the Bar 1991; commercial barrister at chambers of Lord Grabiner QC 1991–95; left the Bar to take over running of family textile manufacturing and retail business 1995; acted as Treas. for and helped to run David Cameron's successful Conservative Party leadership campaign 2005; Deputy Treas. Conservative Party and Chair. Leaders Group 2005–08, Chief Exec. Conservative Party 2008–10, Chair. Party Bd and Co-Chair. Conservative Party 2010–15, Chair. Conservative Party 2015–16; Dir, Jayroma (London) Ltd, Conservative Party Foundation Ltd (endowment fund), C & UCO Properties Ltd, C & UCO Management Ltd, C & UCO Services Ltd. *Address:* House of Lords, Westminster, London, SW1A 0PW, England (office). *Telephone:* (20) 7219-5353 (office). *Fax:* (20) 7219-5979 (office). *E-mail:* chairman@conservatives.com (office). *Website:* www.conservatives.com (office).

FELDMANN, Sir Marc, Kt, MB BS, PhD, FRS, FRCP, FRCPath, FMedSci, FAA; Australian immunologist and rheumatologist; *Emeritus Professor, Kennedy Institute of Rheumatology, University of Oxford;* b. 2 Dec. 1944, Lvov, Poland; ed Univ. of Melbourne, Walter and Eliza Hall Inst. of Medical Research; family moved to France 1945, emigrated to Australia aged eight; Resident Medical Officer, Professorial Dept of Medicine and Surgery, St Vincent's Hosp., Melbourne 1968; Postdoctoral C.J. Martin Fellow, Dept of Zoology, Imperial Cancer Research Fund Tumour Immunology Unit, Univ. Coll. London, UK 1972–73, Sr Staff mem. 1974, Special Appointment Grade 1977; Deputy Dir and Head, Immunology Unit, Charing Cross Sunley Research Centre 1985–92; Prof. of Cellular Immunology, Univ. of London 1986; Wellesley Visiting Prof. and Distinguished Lecturer, Toronto, Canada 1988; mem. Scientific Advisory Bd and Consultant, Xenova PLC, Slough, UK 1989–99, Syntex Research (now Roche Bioscience), Palo Alto, Calif., USA 1991–, Centocor, Inc., Malvern, Pa, USA 1991–; Consultant, Sandoz, Basel, Switzerland 1991–98, Canji, Inc., La Jolla, Calif. 1994–, Alza Inc., Palo Alto 1994–, Ferring AS, Copenhagen, Denmark 1996–2000, Wyeth (fmrly Genetics Inst.), Boston, Mass, USA 1997–, Boehringer-Ingelheim 1999–, Novartis, Canfite, Inc., Receptor Biologix, Inc., Novo Nordisk 2003–; Head of Div., Imperial Coll. School of Medicine, Kennedy Inst. of Rheumatology 2000–11, Head of Kennedy Inst. of Rheumatology when it joined Univ. of Oxford 2011–, now Prof. Emer., Head of Dept of Cytokine Biology and Cellular Immunology 2000–11; Founder and Consultant, Synovis Ltd 2001–; Founder-mem. and Jr Councillor, Int. Cytokine Soc.; mem. British Soc. for Rheumatology (currently Pres), British Soc. of Immunologists, American Asscn of Immunologists, Autralian Immunology Soc.; mem. Research Sub-cttee, Arthritis Research Council, UK 1984–88 (mem. Scientific Consultative Cttee 2000–05), Oliver Bird Cttee, Nuffield Foundation 1991–96, Medical Research Advisory Cttee, Multiple Sclerosis Soc., UK 1991–2000 (Chair. 1999–2000), Scientific Advisory Bd, Jenner Inst. 2000–05, Scientific Advisory Cttee, Deutsches RheumaForschungsZentrum, Berlin, Germany 2002–06; Transmitting Ed. International Immunology 2001–; mem. Editorial Bd Journal of Experimental Pathology 1997–, Cytokines, Cytokine and Growth Factor Reviews, Journal of Autoimmunity, European Cytokine Network, Medical Immunology; mem. European Molecular Biology Org. 2005; Hon. mem. Scandinavian Soc. of Immunology, Polish Immunology Soc.; Hon. MD (Technical Univ., Munich) 2002; Univ. of Melbourne awards: Robert Gartley Healey Prize in Medicine, Hubert Sydney Jacobs Prize in Clinical Gynaecology, Sandoz Prize in Clinical Obstetrics, Fulton Scholarship, Clara Myers Prize in Surgical Pediatrics, Robert Garley Healey Prize in Surgery, Beaney Scholarship, Mead Johnson Prize in Pediatrics, Grieve Memorial Prize in Pediatrics; other awards: Margaret Ryan Prize in Surgery, Royal Australian Coll. of Surgeons, Marshall-Allen Prize in Obstetrics, Royal Coll. of Obstetricians and Gynaecologists, Michael Ryan Prize in Medicine Royal, Australian Coll. of Medicine, Watson-Smith Lecturer, Royal Coll. of Physicians (London) 1994, Canada Trust Distinguished Lecturer in Immunology (Toronto, Canada) 1998, Carol-Nachman Prize for Rheumatology Research (Germany) 1999, EULAR Prix Courtin-Clarins (jtly) 1999, Crafoord Prize (jtly), Royal Swedish Acad. 2000, Albert Lasker Clinical Medical Research Award (jtly) 2003, Cameron Prize, Univ. of Edinburgh (jtly) 2004, European Inventor of the Year, Lifetime Achievement Award, European Patent Office 2007, Curtin Medal,

ANU 2008, Dr Paul Janssen Award for Biomedical Research 2008, Ernst Schering Prize (jtly) 2010, Croonian Lecturer, Royal Coll. of Physicians 2012, Canada Gairdner Int. Award (jtly) 2014. *Publications include:* more than 600 publs in scientific journals and 90 patents. *Leisure interests:* tennis, hiking. *Address:* The Kennedy Institute of Rheumatology, University of Oxford, Roosevelt Drive, Headington, Oxford, OX3 7FY, England (office). *Telephone:* (1865) 612600 (office). *Fax:* (1865) 612601 (office). *E-mail:* marc.feldmann@kennedy.ox.ac.uk (office). *Website:* www.kennedy.ox.ac.uk/research/teams/feldmann/feldmann1.html (office).

FELDSTEIN, Martin Stuart (Marty), AB, BLitt, MA, DPhil; American economist and academic; *George F. Baker Professor of Economics, Harvard University;* b. 25 Nov. 1939, New York; s. of Meyer Feldstein and Esther Feldstein (née Gevarter); m. Kathleen Foley 1965; two d.; ed South Side High School, Rockville Centre, New York, Harvard Univ., Univ. of Oxford, UK; Research Fellow, Nuffield Coll. Oxford, UK 1964–65, Official Fellow 1965–67, Lecturer in Public Finance 1965–67, Hon. Fellow 1998–; Asst Prof. of Econs, Harvard Univ. 1967–68, Assoc. Prof. 1968–69, Prof. 1969–, George F. Baker Prof. of Econs 1984–; Research Assoc., Nat. Bureau of Econ. Research 1977–, Pres. and CEO 1977–82, 1984–2008, Pres. Emer. 2008–; Chair. Pres.'s Council of Econ. Advisers 1982–84; mem. Pres.'s Foreign Intelligence Advisory Bd 2006–09, Pres. Obama's Econ. Recovery Advisory Bd 2009–11; mem. Advisory Bd Congressional Budget Office, New York Fed. Reserve Bank, Boston Fed. Reserve Bank; mem. JP Morgan Int. Council 1984–93, 2001–; mem. Bd Dirs American International Group (AIG) 1988–2009, Eli Lilly 2001–; mem. Bd of Contribs, Wall Street Journal; mem. American Econ. Asscn Exec. Cttee 1980–82, Vice-Pres. 1988–89, Pres.-Elect 2003, Pres. 2004, Distinguished Fellow 2005; mem. Bd of Dirs Smith-Richardson Foundation 2007–; mem. Council on Foreign Relations 1986–, Dir 1998–, Trustee 1999–2007, 2009–, mem. Exec. Cttee 2002–; mem. Trilateral Comm. 1984– (mem. Exec. Cttee 1990–), Nat. Cttee on US-China Relations (Dir) 2001–, Group of Thirty Consultative Group on Int. Econ. and Monetary Affairs, Inc. (G-30), Washington, DC 2002– (mem. Exec. Cttee 2007–), Academic Advisory Council American Enterprise Inst. 2008–, Corpn of Massachusetts Gen. Hosp., New York Economic Club; mem. Bd of Contribs The Wall Street Journal; mem. Inst. of Medicine, NAS 1971–, American Philosophical Soc. 1989–; Foreign mem. Austrian Acad. of Sciences 1996; Fellow, Econometric Soc. 1970, American Acad. of Arts and Sciences 1977, Nat. Asscn of Business Economists 1980, European Econ. Asscn 2004; Corresp. Fellow, British Acad. 1998; Distinguished Fellow, Center for Naval Analysis 2009–; Hon. LLD (Univ. of Rochester) 1984, (Marquette) 1985, (Bentley Coll.) 1988, (Adelphi Univ.) 1991, (Dartmouth Coll.) 2009, Hon. Fellow (Brasenose Coll., Oxford) 2015–; Elizabeth Morgan Prize, Univ. of Chicago 1976, John Bates Clark Medal, American Econ. Asscn 1977, Fisher-Shultz Lecture, Econometric Soc. 1980, Joseph Schumpeter Prof., Univ. of Vienna March 1981, Distinguished Public Service Award, The Tax Foundation 1983, 1999, John R. Commons Prize, Omichron Delta Epsilon 1989, Jan Tinbergen Lecture, Netherlands Royal Econ. Soc. 1992, Adam Smith Lecturer, Nat. Asscn for Business Econs 1993, Bernhard Harms Prize, Weltwirtschafts Institut (Germany) 1994, Schumpeter Lecturer, European Econ. Asscn 1994, Richard Ely Lecturer, American Econ. Asscn 1996, Int. Prize of INA, Accad. Nazionale dei Lincei (Italy) 1997, Frank Geary Lecture, Econ. and Social Research Inst. (Ireland) 2000, Corp. America's Outstanding Directors Award, Year 2000 (Dir's Alert) 2000, Daniel M. Holland Award, Nat. Tax Asscn 2003, Money Marketeers Lifetime Achievement Award. *Publications:* more than 360 research articles in econs; regular contrib. to the Wall Street Journal. *Address:* National Bureau of Economic Research, 1050 Massachusetts Avenue, Cambridge, MA 02138 (office); 147 Clifton Street, Belmont, MA 02478, USA (home). *Telephone:* (617) 868-3905 (office). *Fax:* (617) 868-7194 (office). *E-mail:* mfeldstein@harvard.edu (office); msfeldst@nber.org (office). *Website:* www.nber .org (office).

FELDT, Kjell-Olof, PhD; Swedish politician; b. 18 Aug. 1931, Holmsund; m. Birgitta von Otter; three c.; ed Univs of Uppsala and Lund; Budget Sec., Ministry of Finance 1962–64, Budget Dir 1965, Under-Sec. 1967–70; Minister of Trade 1970–75, of Finance 1983–90; Minister without Portfolio 1975–76; mem. Parl. 1971–90; mem. Exec. Cttee Social Democratic Party 1978–90; Chair. Bank of Sweden 1967–70, 1994–99, Swedish Road Fed. 1992–, Vin & Sprit AB 1991–93; mem. Bd of Dirs Nordbanken 1991–94, Sandrew Theatre Co. 1990–. *Publication include:* Memoirs 1991, Save the Welfare State 1994, It Was No Big West - My Childhood and Upbringing 2002, My Road to Politics 2005, A Critical Study: If Social Democracy Victory and Crisis 2012, The Shy Entrepreneur 2012.

FELICI, Claudio; San Marino politician; b. 10 March 1960; m.; one c.; ed Università di Bologna; worked in eng design for 10 years; mem. Consiglio Grande e Generale (Parl.) 1998–; Sec. of State for Industry 2002–03, 2003–06, for Finance, the Budget, Postal Services and Relations with the Azienda Autonoma di Stato Filatelica e Numismatica 2012–14; mem. Del. to Council of Europe; mem. Partito Democratico Cristiano Sammarinese. *Address:* c/o Secretariat of State for Finance, the Budget, Postal Services and Relations with the Azienda Autonoma di Stato Filatelica e Numismatica, Palazzo Begni, Contrada Omerelli, 47890 San Marino (office).

FELIPE VI, HM The King of Spain Felipe Juan Pablo Alfonso de Todos los Santos de Borbón y de Grecia, LLB, MA; Spanish; b. 30 Jan. 1968, Madrid; s. of King Juan Carlos I and Queen Sofia of Spain; m. Letizia Ortiz Rocasolano 2004; d. Leonor, Princess of Asturias, b. 31 Oct. 2005; d., Princess (Infanta) Sofía, b. 29 April 2007; ed Santa Maria de los Rosales, Madrid, Lakefield Coll., Canada, Gen. Mil. Acad., Zaragoza, Naval Coll., Marin, Air Force Gen. Acad., San Javier, Madrid Autonomous Univ., Georgetown Univ., USA; fmrly Prince of Asturias, Prince of Viana, Prince of Girona, Duke of Montblanc, Count of Cervera and Lord of Balaguer, swore allegiance to the Constitution and to the King in the Spanish Parl. 30 Jan. 1986, succeeded to the throne on the abdication of his father 19 June 2014; Head of State and Capt.-Gen. (C-in-C) of the Armed Forces; received dispatches as Infantry Lt, Sub-Lt and Lt of the Air Arm 1989, held mil. ranks of Commdr of the Gen. Land Army Corps (Infantry), Lt Commdr in the Gen. Navy and Commdr of the Gen. Air Force; qualified helicopter pilot; numerous official visits to countries in Europe, Latin America, Middle East, Asia and Australasia 1995–; named Eminent Person for UN Int. Year of Volunteers 2001; mem. Spanish Olympic sailing team, Barcelona 1992; est. Prince of Asturias Foundation; plays role in promoting relations with Ibero-America; Hon. Pres. Codespa Foundation, Asscn of European Journalists, Spain. *Address:* The Royal Household of HM the King, Palacio de la Zarzuela, 28071 Madrid, Spain (office). *Website:* www.casareal.es (office).

FELIX, Allyson Michelle; American track and field athlete; b. 18 Nov. 1985, Los Angeles; d. of Paul Felix and Marlean Felix; ed Los Angeles Baptist High School, North Hills, Univ. of Southern California; competes internationally for USA, primarily in 200m but also at 100m and 400m; gold medal, 100m, World Athletics Youth Championships, Budapest 2001; gold medal, 4×100m relay, bronze medal, 200m, Pan American Games, Santo Domingo 2003; silver medal, 200m, Olympic Games, Athens 2004, gold medal, 4×400m relay, silver medal, 200m, Olympic Games, Beijing 2008, gold medal, 200m, 4×100m relay, 4×400m relay, Olympic Games, London 2012; World Athletics Championships: gold medal, 200m (youngest ever gold medallist sprinter), Helsinki 2005, gold medal, 200m, 4×100m relay, 4×400m relay, Osaka 2007, gold medal, 200m, 4×400m relay, Berlin 2009, gold medal, 4×100m relay, 4×400m relay, silver medal, 400m, bronze medal, 200m, Daegu 2011; World Athletics Final: gold medal, 200m, Monte Carlo 2005, gold medal, 200m, bronze medal, 100m, Stuttgart 2006; gold medal, 4×400m relay, World Indoor Athletics Championships, Doha 2010; personal bests: 60m 7.10s, Fayetteville, Ark. 2012, 100m 10.89s, London, UK 2012, 200m 21.69s, Eugene 2012, 300m 36.23s, Fayetteville, Ark. 2007, 400m 49.59s, Daegu, South Korea 2011; participant in US Anti-Doping Agency's 'Project Believe' programme; coached by Bobby Kersee 2005–; named by Track and Field News the nat. girls' High School Athlete of the Year 2003, Women's 200m Best Year Performance 2003, 2005, 2007, Women's Track & Field ESPY Award 2006, Jesse Owens Award 2007, 2010. *E-mail:* info@theevolveagency.com (office); allyson@allysonfelix.com. *Website:* www.theevolveagency.com (office); www.allysonfelix.com.

FELIX, HE Cardinal Kelvin Edward, OBE, MA; Dominican ecclesiastic; *Archbishop Emeritus of Castries, Saint Lucia;* b. 15 Feb. 1933, Roseau; ed St Francis Xavier Univ., Canada, Univ. of Notre Dame, USA, Univ. of Bradford, UK; ordained priest 1956; Prin., RC High School, Dominica 1972–75; Assoc. Gen. Sec. Caribbean Conf. of Churches 1975–81, Pres. 1981–86; consecrated Archbishop of Castries, Saint Lucia 1981–2008, Archbishop Emer. 2008–; cr. Cardinal (Cardinal-Priest of Santa Maria della Salute a Primavalle) 2014–; Pres. Antilles Episcopal Conf. 1991–97; Dominica Medal of Honour for Meritorious Service 1999, Medal of Honour (Gold) (SLMH), Order of Saint Lucia 2002; Hon. LLD (St Francis Xavier Univ.) 1986. *Address:* Archbishop's House, Nelson Mandela Drive, PO Box 267, Castries, Saint Lucia, West Indies (office). *Telephone:* (758) 4522416 (office). *Fax:* (758) 4523697 (office). *E-mail:* info@archdioceseofcastries.org (office). *Website:* www.archdioceseofcastries.org (office).

FELIX-BERKLEY, Linda; Grenadian banking executive; currently Country Dir Grenada Office, Eastern Caribbean Cen. Bank. *Address:* Eastern Caribbean Central Bank-Grenada Office, Monckton Street, Saint George's, Grenada (office). *Telephone:* 440-3016 (office). *Fax:* 440-6721 (office). *E-mail:* eccbgnd@spiceisle.com (office). *Website:* www.eccb-centralbank.org (office).

FELL, Sir David, Kt, KCB, BSc, DUniv, FIB, LLD; British business executive, banker and fmr government official; *Chairman, GMcG Belfast;* b. 20 Jan. 1943, Belfast, Northern Ireland; s. of Ernest Fell and Jessie McCreedy; m. Sandra J. Moore 1967; one s. one d.; ed Royal Belfast Academical Inst. and Queen's Univ. Belfast; Sales Man. Rank Hovis McDougall Ltd 1965–66; teacher 1966–67; Research Assoc. 1967–69; Dept of Agric. 1969–72, Asst Sec. 1971–81; Dept of Commerce 1972–82, Under-Sec. 1981–82; Deputy Chief Exec. Industrial Devt Bd 1982–84; Perm. Sec. Dept of Econ. Devt 1984–91; Second Perm. Under-Sec. NI Office and Head, NI Civil Service 1991–97; Chair. Northern Bank Ltd (subsidiary of Nat. Australia Bank) 1998–2005, Boxmore Int. PLC 1998–2000, Nat. Irish Bank Ltd 1999–2005; Dir Nat. Australia Group Europe Ltd 1998–, Dunloe Ewart PLC 1998–2002, Fred Olsen Energy ASA 1999–2003, Chesapeake Corpn 2000–08, Clydesdale Bank plc 2004–12; Chair. Prince's Trust, NI 1999, Harland & Wolff Group PLC 2001–02, Titanic Properties Ltd 2001–, Titanic Quarter Ltd 2001–, Goldblatt McGuigan (now GMcG Belfast) 2005–, Novenso Ltd 2010–; apptd Pro Chancellor Queen's Univ., Belfast 2005. *Leisure interests:* music, reading, golf, rugby. *Address:* GMcG Belfast, Alfred House, 19 Alfred Street, Belfast, BT2 8EQ, Northern Ireland (office). *Telephone:* (28) 9031-1113 (office). *Fax:* (28) 9031-0777 (office). *E-mail:* sirdavid@goldmac.com (office). *Website:* gmcgca.com (office).

FELLAG, Mohamed Said; Algerian actor and comedian; b. 31 March 1950, Kabylie; began career as classical actor; fmr Dir Théâtre Régional, Bougie; moved to Paris 1995; Prince Claus Award 1999, Raymond Devos Price 2003. *Films include:* Liberté, la nuit 1983, Le Gone du chaâba 1998, Inch'Allah dimanche 2001, Fleurs de sang 2002, Momo mambo 2003, Voisins, voisines 2005, Rue des figuiers (TV) 2005, Michou d'Auber 2007, L'ennemi intime 2007, Il faut sauver Saïd (TV) 2008, La veuve tatouée (TV) 2008, Les barons 2009, Monsieur Lazhar (Genie Award for Best Actor 2012) 2011, Zarafa 2012, Ce que le jour doit à la nuit 2012. *Shows include:* The Adventures of Tchop 1986, Khorotov Cocktail 1989, Djurdjurassic Bled 1998, Street of Small Bream 2001, Syndrome page 12 2002, Che bella vita! 2003, The Last Camel 2004, All the Algerians are Mechanics 2008, Small Shock of Civilizations 2011, Bled Runner 2016. *Television includes:* Rue des figuiers 2005, La Veuve tatouée 2008, Ni reprise, ni échangée 2010, Je vous ai compris 2013. *Website:* www.fellag.fr.

FELLEGI, Tamás László, PhD, JurD; Hungarian politician, jurist, political scientist and business executive; *Managing Director, EuroAtlantic Consulting and Investment Ltd.;* b. 7 Jan. 1956, Budapest; m. Ágnes Szokolszky; two s.; ed Ágoston Trefort high school, Budapest, Eötvös Loránd Univ. (ELTE), Budapest, Univ. of Connecticut, USA; Research Fellow, Inst. of Social Sciences (Társadalomtudományi Intézet), Hungarian Socialist Workers' Party 1981–87; Teaching Asst, then Adjunct, Dept of State and Law Theories, Faculty of Law and State, ELTE 1981–87, Dozent, Dept of Political Science 1993–97; Research Fellow, Harvard Univ., USA 1985–86; Int. Fellow and Teaching Asst, Univ. of Connecticut 1987–92; Sr Post-Doctoral Fellow, Univ. of Rochester 1992–93; Head of Advisory Body of Party Chair., Viktor Orbán, Fidesz 1993–94; Co-owner and Dir of Public Affairs, Press & Inform Public Relations Ltd; mem. Edelman Public Relations Worldwide 1994–95; Exec. Dir and Man. Partner, EuroAtlantic Business Development and Communication Consulting Ltd 1995–96, 2000–; Br. Dir, then Chief Officer for

Govt Relations, Regulatory and Public Affairs, Magyar Telekom (then Matáv Rt., subsidiary of Deutsche Telekom) 1996–2000, Perm. Invitee of Man. Bd; Man. Dir Kapsch Telematic Services Hungary 2007–09; Minister of Nat. Devt 2010–11; Minister without Portfolio, responsible for Liaison with certain Int. Financial Orgs 2011; Chair. American Chamber of Commerce, Budapest, Telecommunications Task Force Studies 1998–2000; Man. Dir EuroAtlantic Consulting and Investment Ltd 2012–; Pres. and CEO Hungary Initiatives Foundation, Washington 2012–; mem. Supervisory Bd, M-RTL Television Corpn (jt venture of Bertelsmann AG, RTL Television, Pearson Technologies and Magyar Telekom) 1997; Rep. of Magyar Telekom, Trans-Atlantic Business Dialogue (Brussels-Washington, DC) 1998–2000; mem. Presidium, Joint Venture Assen 2000–06; Fellow, New Westminster Coll. *Publications:* several book chapters and numerous articles in professional journals. *Address:* EuroAtlantic Consulting and Investment Limited, 1011 Budapest, Corvin tér 10, Hungary (office). *Telephone:* (1) 794-5818 (office). *Fax:* (1) 798-4403 (office). *E-mail:* info@euroatlanticconsulting.com (office).

FELLNER, Eric, CBE; British film producer; b. 10 Oct. 1959; four s. one d.; ed London Guildhall; Co-Chair. (with Tim Bevan) Working Title Films; Empire Film Award for outstanding contribution to British cinema (jtly) 2005, David O. Selznick Achievement Award in Theatrical Motion Pictures (with Tim Bevan) 2013, Zurich Film Festival Career Achievement Award (with Tim Bevan) 2013. *Films include:* Sid and Nancy 1986, Pascali's Island 1988, The Rachel Papers 1989, Hidden Agenda 1990, A Kiss Before Dying 1991, Liebstraum 1991, Wild West 1992, Posse 1993, Romeo is Bleeding 1993, Four Weddings and a Funeral 1994, The Hudsucker Proxy 1994, Loch Ness 1995, French Kiss 1995, Dead Man Walking 1995, Fargo (20/20 Award for Best Picture 2017) 1996, Bean 1997, The Borrowers 1997, Elizabeth (BAFTA Award for Best British Film 1999) 1998, The Big Lebowski 1998, Notting Hill 1999, Plunkett & Macleane 1999, O Brother, Where Art Thou? 2000, Billy Elliot 2000, Bridget Jones's Diary 2001, Captain Corelli's Mandolin 2001, The Man Who Wasn't There 2001, About a Boy 2002, The Guru 2002, 40 Days and 40 Nights 2002, Ali G Indahouse 2002, Long Time Dead 2002, My Little Eye 2002, Love Actually 2003, Calcium Kid 2003, Ned Kelly 2003, Shape of Things 2003, Johnny English 2003, Thirteen 2003, Shaun of the Dead 2004, Thunderbirds 2004, Wimbledon 2004, Bridget Jones: The Edge of Reason 2004, Gettin' Square 2004, Inside I'm Dancing 2004, Mickybo and Me 2005, The Interpreter 2005, Pride and Prejudice 2005, Nanny McPhee 2005, Middle of Nowhere 2006, Smokin' Aces 2006, United 93 (Best British Producer, London Film Critics' Circle Awards 2007) 2006, Hot Fuzz 2007, Atonement (BAFTA Award for Best Film 2008) 2007, Elizabeth: The Golden Age 2007, Definitely Maybe 2008, Wild Child 2008, Burn After Reading 2008, Frost/Nixon 2009, The Boat that Rocked 2009, The Soloist 2009, A Serious Man 2009, Green Zone 2010, Nanny McPhee and the Big Bang 2010, Senna 2011, Paul 2011, Johnny English Reborn 2011, Tinker Tailor Soldier Spy (BAFTA Award for Best British Film 2012) 2011, Les Miserables 2012, I Give It a Year 2013, Closed Circuit 2013, About Time 2013, Rush 2013, Anna Karenina 2013, The Theory of Everything (BAFTA Award for Best British Film 2015) 2014, Billy Elliot 2014, Trash 2014, Everest 2015, Legend 2015, The Danish Girl 2015, Hail, Caesar! 2016, Bridget Jones's Baby 2016, Baby Driver 2017, Darkest Hour 2017, Victoria & Abdul 2017, 7 days in Entebbe 2018, King of Thieves 2018, Johnny English Strikes Again 2018. *Address:* Working Title Films, 26 Aybrook Street, London, W1U 7AN, England (office); Working Title Films, 4th Floor, 9770 Wilshire Blvd, Beverly Hills, CA 90212, USA (office). *Telephone:* (20) 7307-3000 (London) (office); (310) 777-3100 (USA) (office). *Fax:* (20) 7307-3001 (London) (office); (310) 777-5243 (USA) (office). *Website:* www.workingtitlefilms.com (office).

FELLNER, Peter John, PhD; British pharmaceuticals and biotechnology executive; *Chairman, Vernalis PLC;* b. 31 Dec. 1943; s. of Hans Julius Fellner and Jessica Fellner (née Thompson); m. 1st Sandra Head (née Smith) 1969; one d. one step-s.; m. 2nd Jennifer Mary Zabel (née Butler) 1982; two step-s.; ed Univ. of Sheffield and Trinity Coll. Cambridge; Post-doctoral Research Fellow, Univ. of Strasbourg, France 1968–70, Assoc. Prof. 1970–73; Sr Research Investigator, Searle UK Research Labs 1973–77, Dir of Chem. 1977–80, Dir of Research 1980–84; Dir of Research Roche UK Research Centre 1984–86, Man. Dir Roche UK 1986–90; CEO Celltech PLC 1990–99, CEO Celltech Group (fmrly Celltech Chiroscience) PLC 1999–2003; Chair. Vernalis PLC (fmrly British Biotech PLC), Chair. (non-exec.) Celltech Group PLC 2003–, Ionix Pharmaceuticals Ltd, Astex Technology 2002–; Chair. Premier Research Group PLC 2007–; Dir (non-exec.) Colborn Dawes Ltd 1986–90, Synaptica Ltd 1999–2002, Qinetiq Group PLC 2004–, UCB SA 2005–, Evotec AG 2005–, Bespak PLC 2005–; mem. MRC 2000–07. *Leisure interest:* country walking. *Address:* Vernalis PLC, Oakdene Court, 613 Reading Road, Winnersh, RG41 5UA, England (office). *Telephone:* (118) 989-9312 (office). *Fax:* (118) 989-9369 (office). *Website:* www.vernalis.com (office).

FELLS, Ian, CBE, MA, PhD, FRSE, FREng, FIE, FIChemE; British professor of energy conversion; *Principal Consultant, Fells Associates;* b. 5 Sept. 1932, Sheffield, Yorks., England; s. of Dr H. Alexander Fells and Clarice Fells; m. Hazel Denton Scott 1957; four s.; ed King Edward VII School, Sheffield and Trinity Coll. Cambridge; Lecturer and Dir of Studies, Dept of Fuel Tech. and Chemical Eng, Univ. of Sheffield 1958–62; Reader in Fuel Science, King's Coll., Durham Univ. 1962; Prof. of Energy Conversion, Univ. of Newcastle-upon-Tyne 1975–; mem. Science Consultative Group, BBC 1976–81, Electricity Supply Research Council 1979–90; Exec., David Davies Inst. of Int. Affairs 1975–; Pres. Inst. of Energy 1978–79; Scientific Adviser, World Energy Council 1990–98; Life Vice-Pres. Int. Centre for Life 1995–; Chair. New and Renewable Energy Centre, Northumberland 2002–05; Prin. Consultant, Fells Associates; Adviser to House of Commons and House of Lords Select Cttee; numerous other professional appointments; Hatfield Memorial Prize 1974, Beilby Memorial Medal and Prize 1976, Royal Soc. Faraday Medal and Prize 1993, Melchett Medal 1999, John Collier Memorial Medal 1999, Kelvin Medal 2002. *Television series:* Young Scientist of the Year, The Great Egg Race, Men of Science, Earth Year 2050, Take Nobody's Word For It, What If the Lights Go Out?, Murphy's Law, Dr Priestley and the Breath of Life. *Radio:* extensive radio contribs. *Publications:* UK Energy Policy Post-Privatization 1991, Energy for the Future 1995, World Energy, 1923–1998 and Beyond 1998, Turning Point, An Independent Review of UK Energy Policy 2001, A Pragmatic Energy Policy for the UK 2008. *Leisure interests:* sailing, painting. *Address:* Fells Associates, 29 Rectory Terrace, Newcastle upon Tyne, NE3 1YB, England (office). *Telephone:* (191) 285-5343 (office); (191) 285-5343 (home). *Fax:* (191) 285-5343 (home). *E-mail:* ian@fellsassociates.com (office). *Website:* www.fellsassociates.com (office).

FELS, Gerhard, Dr rer. pol; German economist, academic and business executive; b. 17 June 1939, Baumholder; m. Baumholder Waltraut 1962; three c.; ed Univs of Bonn, Saarbrücken and the Saar; worked for Institut für Weltwirtschaft Kiel, Vice-Pres. 1976–83; Man. Dir and mem. Presidium, Institut der deutschen Wirtschaft, Cologne 1983; Prof., Univ. of Cologne 1985–2004; mem. German Expert Council on Overall Econ. Devt 1976–82, UN Cttee for Devt Planning 1978–82; has served on supervisory bds of several corpns, including Nestlé SA, Oppenheim KAG GmbH, Swiss Re Germany AG; apptd mem. Group of Thirty Consultative Group on Int. Econ. and Monetary Affairs, Inc. (G-30), Washington, DC 1988, now mem. Emer.; Hon. Prof., Univ. of Kiel 1974–85; Order of Merit (1st class) 1998; Bernhard Harms Medal, Kiel Inst. for World Economy 1986, Ludwig Erhard Prize for econ. journalism, Ludwig Erhard Foundation 2001. *Publications:* has written widely on applied econs and econ. policy. *Address:* c/o The Group of Thirty, 1726 M Street, NW, Suite 200, Washington, DC 20036, USA.

FELSENSTEIN, Joseph (Joe) Hua, BS, PhD; American geneticist and academic; *Emeritus Professor, Department of Genome Sciences, University of Washington;* b. 9 May 1942, Philadelphia, Pa; ed Central High School, Philadelphia, Univ. of Wisconsin, Nat. Insts of Health Trainee (Genetics Training Grant), Univ. of Chicago; NIH Postdoctoral Research Fellow, Inst. of Animal Genetics, Univ. of Edinburgh, UK 1967–68; Asst Prof., Dept of Genetics, Univ. of Washington, Seattle 1967–73 (on leave 1967–68), Assoc. Prof. 1973–78, Prof. 1978–2001, Prof., Dept of Genome Sciences 2001–17, Emer. Prof. 2018–, Adjunct Prof., Dept of Statistics 1981–2017, Adjunct Prof., Dept of Zoology 1990–2002, Prof. 2002–03 (on jt basis with Genome Sciences), Prof., Dept of Biology 2003–17 (on jt basis with Genome Sciences), Adjunct Prof., Dept of Computer Science and Eng 2003–17; Co-ordinator, Program in Computational Molecular Biology, Univ. of Washington 2001–06; Assoc. Ed. Theoretical Population Biology 1975–86, 1995–98, 2003–, Journal of Classification 1984–2015; mem. Editorial Bd, Molecular Phylogenetics and Evolution 1992–, Journal of Molecular Evolution 1993–, Journal of Computational Biology 1994–; Pres. Soc. for Study of Evolution 1993, Soc. of Molecular Biology and Evolution 2015–16; mem. American Acad. of Arts and Sciences 1992, NAS 1999, Washington State Acad. of Sciences 2008–, Soc. for Study of Evolution, Soc. of Systematic Biology Pres.; Hon. mem. Editorial Bd, Evolutionary Bioinformatics 2005–; Hon. DSc (Edinburgh) 2005; Sewall Wright Award, American Soc. of Naturalists 1993, Weldon Memorial Prize, Univ. of Oxford 2000, Pres.'s Award for Excellence in Systematics, Soc. of Systematic Biology 2002, Darwin-Wallace Medal, Linnean Soc. of London 2009, John J. Carty Award for the Advancement of Science, NAS 2009, Distinguished Scientist Award, American Inst. of Biological Sciences 2009, Int. Prize for Biology, Japan Soc. for the Promotion of Science 2013. *Publications:* more than 110 research papers in professional journals. *Address:* Department of Genome Sciences, University of Washington, Box 355065, Seattle, WA 98195-5065, USA (office). *Telephone:* (206) 543-0150 (office). *Fax:* (206) 685-7301 (office). *E-mail:* joe@gs.washington.edu (office). *Website:* www.gs.washington.edu (office).

FELTHEIMER, Jon, BA; American entertainment industry executive; *CEO, Lionsgate Entertainment Corporation;* b. 2 Sept. 1951, Brooklyn, New York; m.; three c.; ed Washington Univ., St Louis; moved to LA to become musician; joined New World Entertainment 1983, held various exec. positions including Pres. and CEO, Dir of Domestic and Int. Distribution Businesses, Man. New World TV Div., Marvel Productions and Learning Corpn of America Units; joined Sony Pictures Entertainment (SPE) 1991, launched interactive TV business 1996, cr. TriStar TV, Head of Columbia TriStar TV Group and Exec. Vice-Pres. SPE –2000; CEO Lionsgate Entertainment Corpn, Vancouver, Canada 2000–, Co-Chair. 2005–12; mem. Bd of Dirs Celestial Tiger Entertainment, Telltale Inc. 2015, Grupo Televisa, S.A.B. 2015; mem. Advisory Bd, EastWest Venture Group, JumpTV Inc.; Perosnality of the Year award, MIPCOM 2010, inducted in Hall of Fame, Broadcasting & Cable 2012, Brandon Tartikoff Legacy Award, Nat. Assen of TV Program Execs. (NATPE) 2014, Milestone Award, Producers Guild 2015. *Address:* Lionsgate Entertainment Corporation, 2700 Colorado Avenue, Suite 200, Santa Monica, CA 90404-5502, USA (office). *Telephone:* (310) 449-9200 (office). *Website:* www.lionsgate.com (office).

FELTMAN, Jeffrey D., BA, MA; American diplomatist and UN official; b. 1959; m. Mary Dale Draper; ed Ball State Univ., Fletcher School of Law and Diplomacy, Tufts Univ., Univ. of Jordan, Amman; career mem. Sr Foreign Service 1986–, Consular Officer, Embassy in Port-au-Prince, Haiti 1986–88, Econ. Officer, Embassy in Budapest 1988–91, Special Asst to Deputy Asst Sec. concentrating on coordination of US assistance to fmr Communist countries of Eastern and Cen. Europe 1991–93, joined Bureau of Near Eastern Affairs 1993, served in Embassy in Tel-Aviv 1995–98, responsible for econ. issues in the Gaza Strip 1998–2000, Chief of Political and Econ. Section, Embassy in Tunisia 2000, Special Asst on Peace Process issues, Embassy in Tel-Aviv 2000–01, Deputy Prin. Officer, US Consulate-Gen. in Jerusalem 2001–02, Acting Prin. Officer 2002–03, Head of Coalition Provisional Authority (CPA) office in Irbil Prov., Iraq and also served as Deputy Regional Coordinator for CPA northern area Jan.–April 2004, Amb. to Lebanon 2004–08, Deputy Asst Sec. of State for Near Eastern Affairs 2009–12, Under-Sec.-Gen. for Political Affairs, UN 2012–18.

FELTUS, Alan Evan, BFA, MFA; American artist and academic; b. 1 May 1943, Washington, DC; s. of Randolph Feltus and Anne Winter; m. Lani H. Irwin 1974; two s.; ed Tyler School of Fine Arts, Pa, Cooper Union for Advancement of Science and Art, Yale Univ.; instructor, School of Dayton Art Inst., Ohio 1968–70; Asst Prof., American Univ., Washington, DC 1972–84; full-time artist 1984–, represented by Forum Gallery, New York 1973–; occasional teaching workshops and lectures; resident in Italy since 1987; Artist-in-Residence, Maryland Inst. Coll. of Art, Baltimore 2006, Adjunct Prof. 2009–10; Rome Prize Fellowship, American Acad. in Rome 1970–72, Nat. Endowment for Arts Fellowship 1981, Louis Comfort Tiffany Foundation Grant in Painting 1980, Pollock-Krasner Foundation Grant in Painting 1992, 2005, Thomas B. Clarke Prize, Nat. Acad. of Design 1984, Benjamin Altman Prize 1990, Joseph S. Isidor Memorial Medal 1995, Raymond Neilson Prize 2001, Pollock-Krasner Foundation Grant in Painting 2005. *Address:* Porziano 68, 06081 Assisi, Perugia, Italy (home). *E-mail:* alan@feltus.com. *Website:* www.alanfeltus.com.

FENBY, Jonathan Theodore Starmer, CBE; British writer and journalist; *Managing Director, China Research, Trusted Sources;* b. 11 Nov. 1942, London, England; s. of Charles Fenby and June Fenby (née Head); m. Renée Wartski 1967; one s. one d.; ed King Edward's School, Birmingham, Westminster School and New Coll. Oxford; corresp. and ed., Reuters World Service, Reuters Ltd 1963–77; corresp. (France and Germany), The Economist 1982–86; Home Ed. and Asst Ed., The Independent 1986–88; Deputy Ed., The Guardian 1988–93; Dir Guardian Newspapers 1990–95; Ed., The Observer 1993–95; Ed., South China Morning Post 1995–99; Ed., Netmedia Group; Assoc. Ed., Sunday Business 2000–01; Ed., Business Europe 2000–01; Ed., www.earlywarning.com 2004–06; Founding Partner and Man. Dir China Research, Trusted Sources 2006–; mem. Bd European Journalism Centre, Belgian-British Colloquium; Chevalier, Ordre nat. du Mérite 1992. *Radio includes:* broadcasts on BBC, CBC and French and Swiss radio. *Television includes:* broadcasts on BBC, CNN, CNBC, Channel Four, FR2, Sky, Bloomberg. *Publications include:* The Fall of the House of Beaverbrook 1979, Piracy and the Public 1983, The International News Services 1986, On the Brink: The Trouble with France 1998 (new edn 2002), Comment peut-on être Français? 1999, Dealing With the Dragon: A Year in the New Hong Kong 2000, Generalissimo: Chiang Kai-shek and the China He Lost 2003, The Sinking of the Lancastria 2005, Alliance: The Inside Story of How Roosevelt, Stalin and Churchill Won One War and Began Another 2007, The Seventy Wonders of China 2007, The Penguin History of Modern China: The Fall and Rise of a Great Power (1850–2008) 2008, Dragon Throne: The Imperial Dynasties of China (co-author) 2008, The General: Charles De Gaulle and the France He Saved 2010, Tiger Head, Snake Tails: China Today, How It Got There and Where It Is Heading 2012; contrib. to newspapers and magazines in Europe, USA, Asia. *Leisure interests:* walking, jazz, belote. *Address:* Trusted Sources, 9 Orange Street, London, WC2H 7EA (office); 101 Ridgmount Gardens, Torrington Place, London, WC1E 7AZ, England (home). *Telephone:* (20) 3137-7261 (office). *Fax:* (20) 3137-3724 (office). *E-mail:* jtf@trustedsources.co.uk (office); jtfenby@hotmail.com (home). *Website:* www.trustedsources.co.uk (office).

FENCHEL, Tom Michael, DSci; Danish marine biologist and academic; *Professor Emeritus of Marine Biology, University of Copenhagen;* b. 19 March 1940, Copenhagen; s. of W. Fenchel and Käte Fenchel (née Sperling); m. 1st Anne Thane 1964; m. 2nd Hilary Adler 1978 (divorced 1989); one s. one d.; m. 3rd Ilse Duun 1995; ed Univ. of Copenhagen; Lecturer in Marine Biology, Univ. of Copenhagen 1964–70, Prof. of Marine Biology 1987–2010, Prof. Emer. 2010–; Prof. of Ecology and Zoology, Univ. of Aarhus 1970–87; mem. Danish Royal Soc. of Science and Letters, Royal Swedish Acad. of Science, Royal Soc., London, NAS, American Acad. of Microbiology; Hon. mem. Soc. for Gen. Microbiology; Gold Medal, Univ. of Copenhagen 1964, Ecology Inst. Prize 1987, Huntsmann Award for Oceanography 1987, A.G. Excellence in the Marine Sciences 1986, America Soc. of Limnology and Oceanography, Alfred C. Redfield Lifetime Achievement Award. *Publications include:* Theories of Populations in Biological Communities (with F. B. Christiansen) 1977, Bacteria and Mineral Cycling (with T. H. Blackburn) 1979, Ecology of Protozoa 1987, Ecology and Evolution in Anoxic Worlds (with B. J. Finlay), Bacterial Biochemistry (co-author), Bacterial Biogeochemistry (with G. M. King and T. H. Blackburn) 1998, 2012, Origin and Early Evolution of Life 2002. *Address:* Marine Biological Laboratory, University of Copenhagen, Strandpromenaden 5, 3000 Helsingor, Denmark (office). *Telephone:* 35-49-76-26-06 (home); 35-32-19-60 (office). *Fax:* 35-32-19-51 (office). *E-mail:* tfenchel@bio.ku.dk (office). *Website:* www.mbl.ku.dk (office).

FENDER, Sir Brian Edward Frederick, Kt, CMG, PhD; British chemist, academic and business consultant; *Chair, Mitchell Arts Centre, Stoke-on-Trent;* b. 15 Sept. 1934, Barrow, Cumbria; s. of George Clements Fender and Emily Goodwin; m. 1st 1956; one s. three d.; m. 2nd Ann Linscott 1986 (died 2011); ed Carlisle and Sale Grammar Schools, Imperial Coll., London; Research Instructor, Univ. of Washington, Seattle, USA 1959–61; Sr Research Fellow, Nat. Chemical Lab., Teddington 1961–63; Fellow, St Catherine's Coll., Oxford 1963–84, Lecturer in Inorganic Chem. 1965–80; Asst Dir Inst. Laue-Langevin, Grenoble 1980–82, Dir 1982–85; Vice-Chancellor, Keele Univ. 1985–95; Chief Exec. Higher Educ. Funding Council for England 1995–2001; Chair. BTG PLC 2003–08; Pres. and Chair. Inst. of Knowledge Transfer 2005–11; mem. Science and Eng Research Council 1985–90; Pres. Nat. Foundation for Educational Research 1999–2007; Chair. New Victoria Theatre, Staffs. 2003–15; Chair. London Waterway Partnership, Canal and River Trust 2012–18, Mitchell Arts Centre, Stoke-on-Trent 2018–; Dir Higher Aims Ltd; Hon. Fellow, St Catherine's Coll. Oxford, Imperial Coll. London, Cardiff Univ. *Publications:* scientific articles on neutron scattering and solid state chemistry. *Leisure interests:* theatre, gardens, cooking. *Address:* Bishops Offley Manor, Bishops Offley, Stafford, ST21 6ET, England (home). *E-mail:* fenderbrian1@gmail.com.

FENECH, Tonio, BCom, BA (Hons); Maltese accountant, auditor and politician; b. 5 May 1969; s. of Carmel V. Fenech and Helen Fenech (née Zarb); m. Claudine Ellul 1998; one s. one d.; ed St Aloysius' Coll., Birkirkara, Manoel Theatre Acad. of Dramatic Arts, Univ. of Malta; gained early work experience during school summer holidays at Multi Packaging Ltd; mem. Youth Fellowship 1987–96; with Price Waterhouse (later PricewaterhouseCoopers) 1993–2004, later became man. in audit practice, subsequently Sr Consultant in man. consultancy practice, several int. work experiences in Italy and Libya, including Instituto per le Opere Religiose (IOR), Vatican Bank; mem. Partit Nazzjonalista (Nationalist Party), mem. Exec. Cttee Nationalist Party Coll. of Councillors 1998–99, Sec.-Gen. Nationalist Party Coll. of Councillors 1999–2003, mem. Nationalist Party Exec. Cttee 1999–; elected as local councillor for Birkirkara 1996–98, Mayor of Birkirkara 1998–2003; MP from 8th Dist 2003–, apptd observer to European Parl. 2003–04; Parl. Sec., Ministry of Finance 2004–08 (participated in Malta's accession to EuroZone), Minister of Finance, Economy and Investment 2008–13; mem. Housing Authority Bd 1998–2003, e-Malta Comm. 2001–03. *Address:* Nationalist Party, Herbert Ganado Street, Pietà PTA 1541, Malta (office). *Telephone:* 21243641 (office); 79927302 (home); 27327302 (home). *Fax:* 21243640 (office). *E-mail:* admin@pn.org.mt (office); fenechtonio@gmail.com (home). *Website:* www.pn.org.mt (office); www.toniofenech.com (home).

FENECH-ADAMI, Edward, KUOM, BA, LLD; Maltese politician, lawyer and fmr head of state; b. 7 Feb. 1934, Birkirkara; s. of Luigi Fenech Adami and Josephine Pace; m. Mary Sciberras 1965 (deceased); four s. one d.; ed St Aloysius Coll., Univ. of Malta; entered legal practice 1959; Ed. Il-Poplu (weekly) 1962–69; mem. Nat. Exec. Nationalist Party 1961, Asst Gen. Sec. 1962–75, Pres. Gen. and Admin. Councils 1975–77, Leader 1977–2004; mem. Parl. 1969–2004; Leader of Opposition 1977–82, 1983–87, 1996–98; Prime Minister 1987–96, 1998–2004; Pres. of Malta 2004–09; Vice-Pres. European Union of Christian Democrat Parties 1979–99; Nat. Order of Merit 1990, Commander, Grand Cross of the Order of the Three Stars (Latvia) 2004, Order of Merit (Italy) 2005, Grand Order of King Tomislav (Croatia) 2006, Order of the White Eagle (Poland) 2009, Commandeur, Légion d'Honneur 2010.

FENEUILLE, Serge Jean Georges, PhD; French academic and company director; b. 16 Nov. 1940, Rheims; s. of Georges Feneuille and Marguerite Lemoine; m. Jeannine Large 1960; ed Coll. Moderne de Rheims, Ecoles Normales d'Instituteurs de Chalons-sur-Marne and Nancy, Ecole Normale Supérieure de St-Cloud; Maître-Asst, Univ. of Paris 1964–69; Maître de Recherche CNRS 1969–74, Dir of Research 1974–, Dir-Gen. CNRS 1986–88; Prof., Univ. Paris-Sud 1979–98; Dir of Research, Lafarge Coppée 1981–85, Scientific Dir and mem. Exec. Cttee 1985–86, Asst Dir-Gen. 1988–89, Dir-Gen. and Head of Research, Tech. and Strategy 1989–94, Special Adviser to Chair. and CEO 1995–2000; Man. Dir Centre Expérimental du Bâtiment et des Travaux Publiques 1998–2000; Pres. Admin. Council Ecole Normale Supérieure de Lyon 1986–94; Chair. Orsan (subsidiary of Lafarge Coppée) 1992–94, Innovation and Research Comm., Conseil Nat. du Patronat Français (CNPF) 1993–97; mem. Archaeological mission in Saggarah 2002–; mem. Sudanese Antiquities (French section) 2003–; Chair. High Council of Science and Tech. 2006–09; mem. French Acad. of Tech. 2000, European Acad. for Science, Arts and Letters 2010; Hon. Prof.; Officier, Ordre nat. du Mérite, des Palmes académiques, Chevalier Légion d'honneur; Prix Daniel Guinier de la Soc. Française de Physique, Bronze Medal, CNRS, Prix Servant de l'Acad. des Sciences, Prix Jaffé de l'Institut de France, Grand Prix, Soc. Française de Poésie. *Publications:* Paroles d'éternité 2007, Pensées égytiennes in Philosophies d'ailleurs (ed. R.-P. Droit) 2009, Paroles d'amour 2010, Paroles de sagesse 2012, Protocole d'étude des mortiers anciens (co-author) 2016; numerous articles in scientific journals. *Leisure interests:* egyptology, painting, literature. *Address:* 25 avenue du Maréchal Maunoury, 75016 Paris, France (home). *Telephone:* 1-45-27-14-50 (home); 6-12-97-49-28 (mobile) (home). *E-mail:* serge.feneuille@orange.fr (home).

FENG, Duan; Chinese physicist; *Professor of Physics, Nanjing University;* b. 27 April 1923, Suzhou City, Jiangsu Prov.; s. of Feng Zhou-bai and Yan Su-qing; m. Chen Lianfang 1955; three d.; ed Nat. Cen. Univ., Nanjing; Prof. of Physics, Nanjing Univ. 1978–; Dir of Grad. School of Nanjing Univ. 1984–88; Dir Nat. Lab. of Solid State Microstructures 1986–95; mem. Chinese Acad. of Sciences 1980–; Pres. Chinese Physical Soc. 1991–95; Fellow, the Third World Acad. of Sciences 1993–; State Prize for Natural Sciences 1982, 1995, 2003, 2004, State Prize for Progress of Science and Tech. 1997, 1998, Tan Kah Kee Prize in Math. and Physics 1999. *Publications:* Physics of Metals (Vols 1–4) 1987–99, New Perspective on Condensed Matter Physics 1992, Introduction to Condensed Matter Physics, Vol. I 2005. *Leisure interest:* literature. *Address:* Institute of Solid State Physics, Nanjing University, Nanjing 210008, Jiangsu Province, People's Republic of China. *Telephone:* (25) 83593705 (office); (25) 83592906 (home). *Fax:* (25) 83590535 (office); (25) 83300535. *E-mail:* duanf@netra.nju.edu.cn (home).

FENG, Gong; Chinese actor and film director; b. 6 Dec. 1957, Tianjin; m. Ai Hui; one s.; joined China Railway Art Work Troupe 1980; actor, China Broadcasting Art Troupe 1984–; performs comic dialogues with Niu Qun; Chair. China Literary and Art Volunteers' Asscn 2018; numerous prizes. *Films include:* Xiao po qing wang 1987, Li hun he tong 1990, Zhanzhi luo bie paxia 1993, Meishi touzhe le (Steal Happiness) 1998, Shui shuo wo bu zai hu (The Marriage Certificate) 2001, Eat Hot Tofu Slowly 2005, Getting Home 2007, A Simple Noodle Story 2009, Just Call Me Nobody 2010, The Founding of a Party 2011, The Grandmasters 2012, Happiness Is Coming 2018 (also dir and writer). *Address:* China Broadcasting Art Troupe, Beijing, People's Republic of China.

FENG, Jicai; Chinese writer and artist; *Director, Feng Jicai Research Institute of Arts and Literature;* b. 9 Feb. 1942, Tianjin, Zhejiang Prov.; s. of Feng Jifu and Ge Changfu; m. Gu Tongzhao; ed Tianjin Middle School; painter, Tianjin Calligraphic and Painting Studio 1962; writer, Tianjin Municipal Writers' Asscn 1978; joined China Asscn for Promoting Democracy 1983, currently Vice-Chair. 10th Cen. Cttee; Exec. Vice-Chair. China Fed. of Literary and Art Circles 1988, 2001–, Chinese Writers' Asscn 1986 (mem. Council 1986), Chinese Soc. for the Study of Folk Literature and Art 1986, UNESCO Int. Folk Arts Org.; apptd Chair. Fiction Soc. of China 2000; Dir Feng Jicai Research Inst. of Arts and Literature and Hon. Dean School of Social Sciences and Foreign Languages, Tianjin Univ. 2001–; Ed.-in-Chief Free Forum on Literature 1986; Ed. Artists; mem. 6th CPPCC Nat. Cttee 1983–88, 7th CPPCC Nat. Cttee 1988–93, 8th CPPCC Nat. Cttee 1993–98, Standing Cttee 9th CPPCC Nat. Cttee 1998–2003; Lifetime Achievement Award, China Fed. of Literary and Art Circles 2018. *Publications:* Magic Whip 1984, Three Inch Golden Lotus 1985, Gratitude to Life 1991, Legend of Magic Lamp, Tall Woman and Her Dwarf Husband, Sculpted Pipe, Crysanthemums and other stories. *Address:* Feng Jicai Research Institute of Arts and Literature, Weijin Road Campus, Tianjin University, No. 92 Weijin Road, Nankai District, Tianjin, People's Republic of China (office). *Website:* fengjicai.artron.net.

FENG, Mengbo; Chinese pop artist; b. 1966, Beijing; ed Print-Making Dept, Cen. Acad. of Fine Arts, Beijing; work consists of computer animations and paintings which resemble video-game screens; has exhibited at galleries in Germany, London, Sydney, Taipei and Hong Kong and at 45th Venice Biennale 1993; Interactive Art award, Prix Ars Electronica (Austria) 2004. *Works include:* Game Over: The Long March 1994, My Private Album (interactive installation) 1997, Q4U 2002, Taking Mount Doom by Strategy, Phantom Tales, Streetfighter (painting series), Long March Restart 2009. *Leisure interest:* collecting industrial antiques. *Address:* c/o Art So Close, No.7, Tianwei 4th Street, Tianzhu Airport Industrial Zone A Shunyi, Beijing 101312, People's Republic of China.

FENG, Xiaogang; Chinese screenwriter, director and actor; b. 1958, Beijing; m. 1st Zhang Di 1984 (divorced); m. 2nd Xu Fan 1999; ed Beijing Broadcasting Acad.; art designer, Beijing TV Art Centre 1985; began writing film and TV screenplays

1989. *Films include:* Zaoyu jiqing (Unexpected Passion) (writer) 1991, After Separation 1992, Yong shi wo ai (Lost My Love) (writer) 1994, The Funeral of a Famous Star, Living in Dire Strait, Jiafang yifang (The Dream Factory) (actor, dir) 1997, Bu jian bu san (Be There or Be Square) (writer, dir) 1998, Sorry, Baby 1999, Yi sheng tan xi (A Sigh) (writer, dir) 2000, Baba (Father) (actor) 2000, Da wan (Big Shot's Funeral) (writer, dir) 2001, Shui shuo wo bu zai hu (The Marriage Certificate) (actor) 2001, Shou ji (dir, producer) 2003, Ka la shi tiao gou (Cala, My Dog!) (exec. producer) 2003, Tian xia wu zei (A World Without Thieves) (writer, dir) 2004, Gong fu (actor) 2004, The Banquet 2006, The Assembly (Hundred Flowers Award for Best Dir 2008) 2007, Trivial Matters (actor) 2007, The Nobles (writer, dir) 2008, If You Are the One (Hundred Flowers Award for Best Dir 2010) 2008, Aftershock 2010, If You Are the One 2 (writer, dir) 2010, Let the Bullets Fly (actor) 2010, Back to 1942 (dir) 2012, The Monkey King: Uproar in Heaven (actor) 2012, Personal Tailor (dir) 2013, Mr. Six (actor) 2015. *Television:* Lend Me a Little Love, A Beijing Man in New York (TV Gold Eagle Award). *Publications:* After Separation 1992, A Born Coward 1994, Stories in the Editorial Office.

FENG, Ying; Chinese ballet dancer; *Director and Artistic Director, National Ballet of China;* b. 28 Feb. 1963, Harbin; m. James Y. Ho 1989; one d.; ed Beijing Dance Acad.; Paris Opera Ballet School 1982–83; apptd Prin. Dancer, Cen. Ballet of China 1980; leading role in many classical and Chinese ballets; Guest Artist, 2nd Paris Int. Ballet Competition 1986; toured USA, UK, Russia, Japan, Singapore, Hong Kong, Taiwan; left stage 1997 to concentrate on training new generation of dancers; Deputy Dir, Nat. Ballet of China 2004–09, Dir and Artistic Dir 2009–; mem. Chinese Dancers' Asscn 1982, China Ballet Art Soc. 1992; Leader Cen. Corps de Ballet 2008; First Prize Pas de Deux, Nat. Ballet Competition 1987, award at 5th Japan World Ballet Competition 1987, First Class Dancer of the State 1987. *Address:* Central Ballet of China, 3 Taiping Street, Beijing 100050, People's Republic of China. *Website:* www.ballet.org.cn/en (office).

FENG, Zhang, AB, PhD; American (b. Chinese) bioengineer and academic; *James and Patricia Poitras Professor of Neuroscience, Massachusetts Institute of Technology;* b. 22 Oct. 1981; s. of Guoqiang Zhang and Shujun Zhou; m. Yufen Shi; one d.; ed Harvard Coll., Stanford Univ.; moved from People's Repub. of China to USA with parents aged 11; joined Faculty, MIT 2011, fmr Asst Prof., Dept of Brain and Cognitive Science, later Assoc., and W. M. Keck Career Devt Prof. of Biomedical Eng, currently James and Patricia Poitras Prof. of Neuroscience, also core mem., MIT Broad Inst. and Investigator, McGovern Inst. for Brain Research 2011–; f. Editas Medicine (genome editing co.); Jr Fellow, Soc. of Fellows, Harvard 2009–10; Fellow, American Acad. of Arts and Sciences 2018–; mem. NAS; Robertson Investigator, New York Stem Cell Foundation; numerous awards including Perl/UNC Prize in Neuroscience (shared with Karl Deisseroth and Ed Boyden) 2012, NIH Dir's Pioneer Award 2012, Alan T. Waterman Award, Nat. Science Foundation (for CRISPR-Cas9 and Optogenetics) 2014, Jacob Heskel Gabbay Award in Biotechnology and Medicine (shared with Jennifer Doudna and Emmanuelle Charpentier) 2014, Soc. for Neuroscience Young Investigator Award (shared with Diana Bautista) 2014, Tsuneko & Reiji Okazaki Award, Nagoya Univ. 2015, Canada Gairdner Int. Award (for CRISPR-Cas9, shared with Jennifer Doudna and Emmanuelle Charpentier) 2016, Tang Prize 2017, Albany Medical Center Prize 2017, Keio Medical Science Prize Award 2018. *Achievements include:* pioneering work on CRISPR (gene editing technique) and development of optogenetics breakthrough technology. *Address:* Department of Brain and Cognitive Science, Room NE 30-10053, Massachusetts Institute of Technology, 77 Massachusetts Avenue, Cambridge, MA 02139-4307, USA (office). *Telephone:* (617) 714-7578 (office). *E-mail:* zhang_f@mit.edu (office). *Website:* be.mit.edu/directory/feng-zhang (office); zlab.mit.edu (office).

FENIC, František (Fero); Slovak producer, writer and media executive; *Director, FEBIO s.r.o.;* b. 20 March 1951, Nižná Šebastová; ed Comenius Univ., Bratislava, FAMU/Acad. of Musical Arts, Prague, Czech Repub.; mil. service 1978–79; Dir Studio of Short Films, Slovak Film Production, Bratislava 1979–83, 1985–86, Barrandov Film Studio Prague 1984; film-making interrupted for political reasons March 1984; freelance tourist guide, Youth Travel Agency 1986–92; f. FEBIO s.r.o. 1991, Dir 1992–; '1 June 1953' Journalism Award. *Films include:* over 20 documentary films and full-length films, including Vlak dospelosti, Praha slzám neverí, Noc, kdy se rospadl stát, Dzusový román (also screenwriter) 1984, Zvláštní bytosti (also screenwriter) 1990, Ceská soda 1998, Magický hlas rebelky (documentary) 2014. *Television includes:* GEN, GENUS, OKO, VIP – Influential People, Czech Soda, The Way We Live, Show Jana Krause 2015. *Publication:* Encyclopedia of Slovak Dramatic Arts 1989. *Leisure interest:* travel. *Address:* FEBIO s.r.o., Film and Television Company, Ruzová 13, 110 00 Prague 1 (office); Vejvodova 4, 11000 Prague 1, Czech Republic (home). *Telephone:* 221101111. *Fax:* 224214254. *Website:* www.ferofenic.cz.

FENTENER VAN VLISSINGEN, Annemiek M.; Dutch business executive; *Chairman of the Supervisory Board, SHV Holdings NV;* b. 14 April 1961; ed Univ. of Groningen; fmr Man. of Strategy and Business Devt, SHV Holdings NV, currently Chair. Supervisory Bd; mem. Supervisory Bd Draka Holding NV 2001– (Deputy Chair. 2006–), Flint Holding NV, Heineken NV 2006–; fmr mem. Bd of Dirs Ubbink/Buco; mem. Supervisory Bd Stadsherstel Amsterdam 2009–; mem. NPM Capital NV, Audit and Governance Cttee, Remuneration and Nomination Cttee. *Address:* SHV Holdings NV, Rijnkade 1, 3511 LC Utrecht, Netherlands (office). *Telephone:* (30) 233-88-33 (office). *Fax:* (30) 233-83-04 (office). *E-mail:* info@shv.nl (office). *Website:* www.shv.nl (office).

FENTIE, Dennis G.; Canadian politician and business executive; b. 8 Nov. 1950, Edmonton, Alberta; m. Lorraine Nixon; Owner and Man., Francis River Construction Ltd; elected MLA (New Democratic Party) for Watson Lake, Yukon Territory 1996–2011; joined Yukon Party May 2002, Leader June 2002–11; Premier of the Yukon 2002–11; fmr Dir Watson Lake Chamber of Commerce; fmr Commr Yukon Forest Comm.; mem. Bd of Dirs Golden Predator Mining Corpn 2014–15; fmr Dir Asscn of Yukon Forests. *Leisure interests:* baseball, hockey, history, current affairs.

FENTON, James Martin, MA, FRSL, FRSA, FSA; British poet, writer and journalist; b. 25 April 1949, Lincoln; s. of Rev. Canon J. C. Fenton and Mary Hamilton Ingoldby; partner Darryl Pinckney; ed Durham Choristers School, Repton School, Magdalen Coll., Oxford; Asst Literary Ed., New Statesman 1971, Editorial Asst 1972, Political Columnist 1976–78; freelance corresp. in Indo-China 1973–75; German Corresp., The Guardian 1978–79; Theatre Critic, Sunday Times 1979–84; Chief Book Reviewer, The Times 1984–86; Far East Corresp. The Independent 1986–88, columnist 1993–95; Prof. of Poetry, Univ. of Oxford 1994–99, Trustee, Nat. Gallery London 2002, Visitor, Ashmolean Museum 2003; Hon. Fellow, Magdalen Coll., Oxford 1999; Antiquary to the RA 2002; Newdigate Prize 1968, Southern Arts Literature Award for Poetry 1981, Queen's Gold Medal for Poetry 2007, PEN Pinter Prize (shared with Raif Badawi) 2015. *Publications include:* Our Western Furniture 1968, Terminal Moraine (Eric Gregory Award 1973) 1972, A Vacant Possession 1978, A German Requiem 1980, Dead Soldiers 1981, The Memory of War 1982, You Were Marvellous 1983, Children in Exile (Geoffrey Faber Memorial Prize 1984) 1984, Poems 1968–83 1985, The Fall of Saigon (in Granta 15) 1985, The Snap Revolution (in Granta 18) 1986, Cambodian Witness: The Autobiography of Someth May (ed.) 1986, Partingtime Hall (poems, with John Fuller) 1987, All the Wrong Places: Adrift in the Politics of Asia 1989, Manila Envelope 1989, Underground in Japan, by Rey Ventura (ed.) 1992, Out of Danger (poems) (Whitbread Prize for Poetry 1994) 1993, Collected Stories by Ernest Hemingway (ed.), Leonardo's Nephew: Essays on Art and Artists 1998, The Strength of Poetry: Oxford Lectures, An Introduction to English Poetry 2002, A Garden from a Hundred Packets of Seed, The Love Bomb & Other Musical Pieces 2003, Selected Poems 2006, Yellow Tulips: Poems 1968–2011 2012; trans.: Verdi's Rigoletto 1982, Simon Boccanegra 1985, Tamar's Revenge 2004; libretti: Haroun and the Sea of Stories (composer Charles Wuorinen) 2004, Tsunami Song Cycle (composer Dominic Muldowney) 2009; theatre: Pictures from an Exhibition 2009, The Orphan of Zhao (adaptation) 2012, Don Quixote (adaptation) 2016; contrib. to The Guardian, The Independent, The New York Review of Books. *Address:* c/o United Agents, 12–26 Lexington Street, London, W1F 0LE, England (office). *Telephone:* (20) 3214-0800 (office). *Fax:* (20) 3214-0801 (office). *E-mail:* info@unitedagents.co.uk (office). *Website:* www.unitedagents.co.uk (office); www.jamesfenton.com (home).

FENTY, Adrian Malik, BA, JD; American lawyer and fmr politician; *Business Development Manager, Perkins Coie LLP;* b. 6 Dec. 1970, Washington, DC; s. of Philip Fenty and Jan Fenty; m. Michelle Cross (divorced); twin s. one d.; ed Mackin Catholic High School, Oberlin Coll., Howard Univ. School of Law; called to DC Bar; worked as intern for US Senator from Ohio Howard Metzenbaum, Del. Eleanor Holmes Norton and Rep. Joseph P. Kennedy II before becoming involved in local Washington, DC politics, served as ANC 4C Commr and Treas. and Pres. 16th Street Neighborhood Civic Asscn; lead attorney and Counsel for Washington, DC City Council's Cttee on Educ., Libraries and Recreation –2000; mem. Washington, DC City Council representing Ward 4 2001–07, Chair. Cttee on Human Services, overseeing Dept of Youth Rehabilitation Services, Child and Family Services Agency, Dept of Human Services, and Office on Aging; Mayor of Dist of Columbia 2007–11; Adviser, Rosetta Stone Inc. 2011–12; Special Advisor, EverFi 2011–13; Special Counsel, Klores Perry Mitchell P.C. 2011–13; Special Advisor, Andreessen Horowitz (consultancy) 2013–; Business Development Man., Perkins Coie LLP, Palo Alto, Calif. 2013–; Distinguished Visiting Prof., Dept of African American Studies, Oberlin Coll. 2011; mem. Bd of Dirs College Track, Fight for Children; Democrat; named to Power 150, Ebony magazine 2008, Commitment to Social Justice Award, DC Acorn, Courageous Community Service Award, Fed. of Citizens. *Leisure interest:* takes part regularly in triathlons and other races in DC and throughout region. *Address:* Perkins Coie LLP, 3150 Porter Drive, Palo Alto, CA 94304-1212, USA (office). *Telephone:* (650) 838-4436 (office). *Fax:* (650) 838-4636 (office). *E-mail:* AFenty@perkinscoie.com (office). *Website:* www.perkinscoie.com (office).

FÉRAUD, Pierre; French retail executive; ed École des Hautes Etudes Commerciales, Institut d'Etudes Politiques, Paris; fmrly with UIC-SOFAL (commercial bank) and GMF (insurance co.); joined Groupe Euris 1991, apptd Pres. Foncière Euris SA 1991, Pres. and CEO –2010, Dir 2010–, Perm. Rep. of Euris on Bd of Dirs of Finatis; Chair. Carpinienne de Participations, Marigny Belfort, Matignon Marne La Vallée SAS, Mermoz Kléber SAS, Centre Commercial de l'Île Saint-Denis, Marigny Concorde, Marigny Elysées, Marigny Expansion, Marigny Foncière, Marigny Participations, Marigny Percier, Marigny Valbréon, Marigny Tours, Matignon Abbeville, Matignon Bail, Matignon Corbeil Centre, Les Moulins à Vent, Matignon Meylan, Matignon Moselle; Dir, Casino Guichard Perrachon & Cie SA –2009, Rallye Group SA 1995–2010, Mercialys 2006–; Vice-Chair. Supervisory Bd Les Nouveaux Constructeurs SA 2006–; Man. Centrum NS Sarl, Alexanderplatz Voltairestrasse GmbH, Alexa Holding GmbH, amongst others. *Address:* Foncière Euris SA, 83 rue du Faubourg Saint-Honoré, 75008 Paris, France (office). *Telephone:* 1-44-71-14-00 (office). *Fax:* 1-44-71-14-50 (office). *E-mail:* info@fonciere-euris.fr (office). *Website:* www.fonciere-euris.fr (office).

FERGESSA, Siraj, BSc, MA, MSc; Ethiopian politician; *Minister of Transportation;* b. 1971, Silt'e woreda (region); m.; ed Haremaya Univ., Azusa Pacific Univ. in Leadership, USA, Cranfield Univ., UK; fmr Chief Admin., Silt'e woreda (region); Minister of Fed. Affairs 2005–08, of Defence 2008–18, of Transportation 2018–; mem. South Ethiopian People's Democratic Movt, Deputy Chair. –2018; fmr mem. Exec. Cttee, Ethiopian People's Revolutionary Democratic Front (EPRDF). *Address:* Ministry of Transportation, Addis Ababa, Ethiopia (office). *Website:* www.motr.gov.et (office).

FERGUS-THOMPSON, Gordon, FRCM; British pianist and academic; *Professor of Piano, Royal College of Music;* b. 9 March 1952, Leeds, Yorks.; s. of George Thompson and Constance Webb; ed Temple Moor Grammar School, Leeds and Royal Northern Coll. of Music; debut at Wigmore Hall 1976; has appeared as soloist with orchestras including Orchestra of the Hague, Gothenburg Symphony Orchestra, Royal Liverpool Philharmonic, The Philharmonia, City of Birmingham Symphony, Hallé, BBC Symphony; extensive tours in Europe, N America, Australia, Far East and S Africa; Prof. of Piano, Royal Coll. of Music 1996–; Gulbenkian Foundation Fellowship 1978; MRA Prize for Best Instrumental Recording of the Year 1991, 1992. *Recordings include:* The Rachmaninov Sonatas 1987, Balakirev and Scriabin Sonatas 1987, Complete Works of Debussy (five vols), Complete Works of Scriabin (five vols) 1990–2001, Rachmaninov's Etudes-Tableaux 1990, Bach Transcriptions 1990, Complete Works of Ravel (two vols) 1992, Headington: Piano Concerto 1997, Bach Transcriptions 2016. *Leisure interests:* art, chess, cooking, tennis, humour. *Address:* 44 Courtfield Rise, West

Wickham, BR4 9BH, Kent, England (home). *Telephone:* 7590-515645 (mobile) (office). *E-mail:* gfergusthompson@rcm.ac.uk (office). *Website:* www.gordonfergusthompson.com.

FERGUSON, Sir Alexander (Alex) Chapman, Kt, CBE, OBE; British fmr professional football manager and fmr football player; b. 31 Dec. 1941, Govan, Glasgow, Scotland; s. of Alexander Beaton Ferguson and Elizabeth Hardy; m. Catherine Holding 1966; three s.; ed Govan High School; amateur player (striker) with Queen's Park 1958–60, professional player with St Johnstone 1960–64 (won Scottish First Div. 1962–63), Dunfermline Athletic 1964–67, Glasgow Rangers 1967–69, Falkirk 1969–73 (won Scottish First Div. 1969–70), Ayr United 1973–74 (two Scottish League caps); managed the following clubs: East Stirling 1974, St Mirren 1974–78 (First Div. Champions 1976–77), Aberdeen 1978–86 (winners UEFA European Cup Winners' Cup 1983, UEFA Super Cup 1983, Scottish Premier Div. Champions 1980, 1984, 1985, Scottish FA Cup 1982, 1983, 1984, 1986, Scottish League Cup 1986), Scottish Nat. Team (Asst Man.) 1985–86, Manchester United 1986–2013 (winners FA Cup 1990, 1994, 1996, 1999, 2004, League Cup 1992, 2006, 2009, 2010, UEFA European Cup Winners' Cup 1991, UEFA Super Cup 1991, FA Premier League Championship 1992/93, 1993/94, 1995/96, 1996/97, 1998/99, 1999/2000, 2000/01, 2002/03, 2006/07, 2007/08, 2008/09, 2010/11, 2012/13, League and FA Cup double 1994 and 1996 (new record), UEFA Champions League European Cup 1999, 2008, FA Charity/Community Shield 1990 (shared), 1993, 1994, 1996, 1997, 2003, 2007, 2008, 2010, 2011, European-S American Cup 1999, FIFA Club World Cup 2008), announced retirement May 2013, now a Dir and Amb. for the club; Vice-Pres. Nat. Football Museum, Preston, Lancs.; mem. Exec. Cttee League Mans Asscn (LMA); only man. to win top league honours and Double north and south of England-Scotland border (winning the Premiership with Manchester United and Scottish Premier League with Aberdeen); won 49 trophies as a manager, making him the most successful British football manager in history; Freeman, Cities of Aberdeen, Glasgow and Manchester; Hon. MA (Salford) 1996, (Manchester) 1997, Hon. LLD (Robert Gordon) 1997, (St. Andrews) 2002, Jt Hon. MSc (Manchester Metropolitan), (UMIST) 1998, Hon. DLitt (Glasgow Caledonian) 2001, Hon. DUniv (Glasgow) 2001, (Stirling) 2011, (Manchester) 2011, Hon. DBA (Manchester Metropolitan) 2009, Hon. DSc (Ulster) 2012; Man. of the Year Scotland 1983–85, Man. of the Year England 1993–94, 1996, World Soccer Magazine World Manager of the Year 1993, 1999, 2007, 2008, Football Writers' Asscn Tribute Award 1996, Onze d'Or Coach of the Year 1999, 2007, Mussabini Medal 1999, voted Best Coach in Europe, UEFA Football Gala 1999, UEFA Champions League Manager of the Year 1998–99, LMA Man. of the Year 1998–99, 2007–08, 2010–11, 2012–13, BBC Sports Personality of the Year Coach Award 1999, BBC Sports Personality of the Year Team Award 1999, IFFHS Club Coach of the Year 1999, LMA Manager of the Decade 1990s, Laureus World Sports Award for Team of the Year 2000, BBC Sports Personality of the Year Lifetime Achievement Award 2001, an inaugural inductee into English Football Hall of Fame 2002, inaugural recipient of FA Coaching Diploma 2003, Professional Footballers' Asscn Merit Award 2007, UEFA Team of the Year 2007, 2008, Premier League 10 Seasons Awards (1992/93–2001/02) (Manager of the Decade and Most Coaching Appearances — 392 games), Premier League Manager of the Year 1993–94, 1995–96, 1996–97, 1998–99, 1999–2000, 2002–03, 2006–07, 2007–08, 2008–09, 2010–11, LMA Special Merit Award 2011, Old Trafford North Stand officially renamed the Sir Alex Ferguson Stand in honour of his 25 years as manager 2011, bronze statue designed by Scottish sculptor Philip Jackson, and named after Ferguson, unveiled outside Old Trafford Nov. 2012. *Publications:* A Light in the North 1985, Alex Ferguson: Six Years at United 1992, Just Champion 1993, A Year in the Life: The Manager's Diary 1995, Alex Ferguson: 10 Glorious Years 1996, A Will to Win (co-author) 1997, Managing My Life: My Autobiography (co-author) 1999, The Unique Treble 2000, My Autobiography 2013, Leading (with Michael Moritz) 2015. *Leisure interests* golf, snooker, horse racing, fine wine. *Address:* ACF Sports Promotions Limited (office); Manchester United FC, Old Trafford, Manchester, M16 0RA, England (office). *Telephone:* (1625) 535294 (office). *E-mail:* lyn@acfpromotions.com (office). *Website:* www.manutd.com (office); www.mufcinfo.com/manupag/managers/mangers_pages/ferguson_alex.html.

FERGUSON, Iain, CBE; British business executive; *Chairman, Wilton Park Departmental Board and Advisory Council;* m. Catherine Ferguson; one d.; ed Univ. of St Andrews; Graduate Trainee, Unilever from 1977, various roles in operations, sales, industrial marketing, Chair. Plant Breeding International 1988–92, Chair. Unilever Plantation Group 1992–95, Exec. Chair. Birds Eye Walls 1995–2001, Sr Vice-Pres. Corp. Devt 2001–03; CEO Tate & Lyle PLC 2003–09; Chair. Wilton Park Departmental Board and Advisory Council 2009–; Commr Govt Comm. on the Future of Farming and Food 2001–02; fmr Pres. Food & Drink Fed., Inst. of Grocery Distribution; non-Exec. Dir Greggs PLC, Balfour Beatty PLC, Berendsen PLC, Rothamsted Research Ltd 1996–2005, Sygen International PLC 2002–06; mem. DEFRA Supervisory Bd; fmr mem. Dept of Trade and Industry Foresight Panel, Bd of Cos House; Hon. Vice-Pres. British Nutrition Foundation; Forbes magazine European Businessman of the Year 2004. *Address:* Wilton Park, Wiston House, Steyning, West Sussex, BN44 3DZ, England (office). *Telephone:* (1903) 817766 (office). *Fax:* (1903) 815931 (office). *E-mail:* iain.ferguson@wiltonpark.org.uk (office). *Website:* www.wiltonpark.org.uk (office).

FERGUSON, John, BCom, CA; Canadian chartered accountant and business executive; *Chairman, Princeton Ventures Ltd.;* b. 21 Dec. 1941, Edmonton, Alberta; ed Univ. of Alberta; Founder and Chair. Princeton Developments Ltd, Princeton Ventures Ltd, Edmonton, Alberta 1976–2006, Chair. 2006–; Chancellor Univ. of Alberta 2000–04, later Chancellor Emer. and Chair. Bd of Govs, mem. Business Advisory Council, School of Business; mem. Bd of Dirs Alberta Investment Man. Corp. (AIMCo) 2011–16; mem. Bd of Dirs Suncor Corpn 1995–14, Chair. 2007–14; mem. Bd of Dirs Fountain Tire Ltd, Royal Bank of Canada, Strategy Summit Ltd; Dir C.D. Howe Inst., Alberta Bone and Joint Inst.; Advisory mem. Canadian Inst. for Advanced Research; mem. World Presidents' Org.; Fellow, Alberta Inst. of Chartered Accountants, Inst. of Corp. Dirs; Hon. Lt Col, South Alberta Light Horse; Mem. of the Order of Canada 2011; Hon. LLD (Univ. of Alberta) 1996; Commemorative Medal for 125th Anniversary of Confed. of Canada 1992, inducted into Jr Achievement Alberta Business Hall of Fame 2001, Golden Jubilee Medal 2003, Alberta Centennial Medal 2005. *Address:* Princeton Ventures Ltd., 100 Avenue, NW, Edmonton, Alberta T5K 0J8, Canada (office). *Telephone:* (780) 423-7775 (office).

FERGUSON, Niall Campbell, MA, DPhil; British historian, writer, academic and television presenter; b. 18 April 1964, Glasgow, Scotland; s. of James Campbell Ferguson and Molly Hamilton; m. 1st Susan M. Douglas 1994 (divorced 2011); two s. one d.; m. 2nd Ayaan Hirsi Ali 2011; one s.; ed Univ. of Oxford; Fellow, Christ's Coll., Cambridge 1989–90, Peterhouse, Cambridge 1990–92, Jesus Coll. Oxford 1992–2013; Houblon Norman Fellowship, Bank of England 1998–89; Prof. of Political and Financial History, Univ. of Oxford 2000–02; Herzog Prof. of Financial History, Stern School of Business, New York Univ. 2002–04; Laurence A. Tisch Prof. of History, Harvard Univ. 2004–16, William Ziegler Prof. of Business Admin, Harvard Business School 2006–11; Sr Fellow, Hoover Inst., Stanford Univ. 2003–18; Founder Chimerica Media Ltd 2006–, Greenmantle LLC 2011–; Philippe Roman Visiting Prof., LSE 2010–11; Consultant, GLG Partners (hedge fund) 2007–11; Sr Adviser, Morgan Stanley 2007–09; Trustee, Museum of Financial History, New York 2008–15, New York Historical Soc. 2009–, American Acad. in Berlin 2011–14; Bd mem. Centre for Policy Studies, London 2009–; GetAbstract Int. Book Award 2009, Benjamin Franklin Award for Public Service 2010, Hayek Lifetime Achievement Award 2012, BBC Reith Lecturer 2012, Estoril Global Issues Distinguished Book Prize 2013, Ludwig Erhard Prize for Economic Journalism 2013, Philip Merrill Award for Outstanding Contributions to Liberal Arts Educ., American Council of Trustees and Alumni 2016, Arthur Ross Book Award, Council on Foreign Relations 2016. *Film:* Kissinger (Best Documentary, New York Film Festival 2011) 2011. *Television:* Empire: How Britain Made the Modern World 2003, American Colossus 2004, The War of the World 2006, The Ascent of Money (International Emmy for Best Documentary 2009) 2008, Civilization: Is the West History? 2011, China: Triumph and Turmoil 2012. *Publications include:* Paper and Iron: Hamburg Business and German Politics in the Era of Inflation 1897–1927 1995, (ed.) Virtual History: Alternatives and Counterfactuals 1997, The World's Banker: A History of the House of Rothschild (Wadsworth Prize for Business History 1998) 1998, The Pity of War 1998, The Cash Nexus: Money and Power in the Modern World 2001, Empire: How Britain Made the Modern World 2003, Colossus: the Price of America's Empire 2004, The War of The World: History's Age of Hatred 2006, The Ascent of Money: A Financial History of the World 2008, High Financier: The Lives and Times of Siegmund Warburg 2010, Civilization: The West and the Rest 2011, The Great Degeneration: How Institutions Decay and Economies Die 2012. *Leisure interests:* reading, hiking, playing the double bass, surfing, skiing. *Address:* Hoover Institution, 434 Galvez Mall, Stanford University, Stanford, CA 94305-6003, USA (office). *Telephone:* (650) 723-2063 (office). *E-mail:* niallf@stanford.edu (office). *Website:* www.niallferguson.com.

FERGUSON, Roger Walter, Jr, BA, JD, PhD; American business executive; *President and CEO, TIAA-CREF;* b. 28 Oct. 1951, Washington, DC; m. Annette Nazareth; two c.; ed Harvard Univ.; attorney with Davis Polk & Wardwell, New York 1981–84; Assoc. and Partner, McKinsey & Co. 1984–97, Dir of Research and Information Services; mem. Bd Govs US Fed. Reserve, Washington, DC 1997–2006, Vice-Chair. 1999–2006 (resgnd); Chair. America Holding Corpn and Head of Financial Services, Swiss Re 2006–08; Pres. and CEO TIAA-CREF (Teachers Insurance and Annuity Asscn-Coll. Retirement Equities Fund), New York 2008–, Overseer and TIAA Trustee 2008–; Co-Chair. Nat. Research Council panel on the Long-Run Macro-Econ. Effects of the Aging US Population 2010–; mem. Bd of Dirs Partnership for New York City; mem. Council on Foreign Relations, Econ. Club of New York, Group of Thirty Consultative Group on Int. Econ. and Monetary Affairs, Inc. (G-30), Pres. Obama's Econ. Recovery Advisory Bd 2009–, Business Higher Educ. Forum; mem. Bd of Overseers, Harvard Univ. (Pres. 2008–09), Bd of Dirs Harvard Alumni Asscn; mem. Bd of Trustees, Nat. Bureau of Econ. Research, Inst. for Advanced Study, Carnegie Endowment for Int. Peace, New America Foundation, Memorial Sloan-Kettering Cancer Center; Treas. Friends of Educ. (a Trustees' Cttee of The Museum of Modern Art), mem. Bd Int. Flavors & Fragrances, Inc. 2010, General Mills, Inc. 2015–, Alphabet, Inc. 2016–; mem. American Philosophical Soc.; mem. Bd of Regents, Smithsonian Inst.; mem. Advisory Bd New York State Insurance; Trustee, Cttee for Econ. Devt 2008, Co-Chair. 2011; Fellow American Acad. of Arts & Sciences, Co-Chair. Comm. on the Future of Undergraduate Educ. 2016–17; Hon. Fellow, Pembroke Coll. Cambridge; Dr hc (Lincoln Coll., Webster Univ.); numerous awards including The George Mitchell Payments Systems Excellence Award, NACHA—The Electronic Payments Asscn 2005, The William F. Butler Memorial Award, New York Asscn for Business Econs 2006, The Renaissance Award, Abyssinian Devt Corpn 2006, The Frederick Heldering Global Leadership Award, Global Interdependence Center 2006, first GAIM/CERF Global Financial Policy Award for significant contribs to effective governance of global capital markets, Global Alternative Investment Man. Forum (GAIM) and Cambridge Endowment for Research in Finance (CERF) 2007, Visionary Award, Council for Econ. Educ. 2009, Nat. Council of ISACs Critical Infrastructure Protection Award 2010, Business Achievement Award, African American Chamber of Commerce of NJ 2011, Leadership Award, St Aloysius School for outstanding public service and commitment to improving the lives of New York City's children and families 2011, Global Economic Achievement Award 2012, Adam Smith Award, Nat. Asscn for Business Econs 2013, Leadership Award, Nat. Urban League 2013, Jill Chaifetz Award from Advocates for Children of New York 2015, Honorary Leadership Award, American Fed. for Aging Research 2016, Harvard Medal 2016, Irving Kahn Lifetime Achievement Award, CFA Soc. of New York 2017, Foreign Policy Association Centennial Medal 2018. *Publications include:* International Financial Stability, Geneva Report No. 9 (co-author) 2007, The Structure of Financial Supervision: Approaches and Challenges in a Global Marketplace (co-author) 2008. *Address:* TIAA-CREF, 730 Third Avenue, New York, NY 10017, USA (office). *Telephone:* (212) 916-6240 (office). *Fax:* (212) 916-6230 (office). *E-mail:* trustees@tiaa-cref.org (office). *Website:* www.tiaa-cref.org (office).

FERGUSON-McHUGH, Mary Lynn, BS, MBA; American business executive; *Group President, Western Europe and Global Discounter & Pharmacy Channels, Proctor & Gamble;* b. 1 Oct. 1959, Oakland, Calif.; ed Univ. of the Pacific, Univ. of Pennsylvania Wharton School; with Doubleday & Co. 1981–84; joined Proctor & Gamble (P&G) 1986, Brand Asst to Asst Brand Man., Vicks NyQuil 1986–88, Asst Brand Man., Vicks 1988–90, Brand Man. 1990–91, Brand Man., Vicks NyQuil/

DayQuil 1991–93, Marketing Dir Global Speed Teams, Egham, UK 1993–94, Marketing Dir Managed Care Team 1994–95, Marketing Dir PHC US (Respiratory/GI) 1995–99, Gen. Man., North America, Personal Health Care 1999–2001, Vice-Pres. 2001–03, Vice-Pres. Global Personal Health Care 2003–05, Vice-Pres. North America, Family Care 2005–07, Pres. Family Care 2007–10, Group Pres. Global Family Care 2010–11, Group Pres. Western Europe and Global Discounter & Pharmacy Channels, P&G 2011–; mem. Advisory Bd, Center for Brand and Product Man., Univ. of Wisconsin; fmr Treas., New York City PanHellenic; fmr mem. Bd of Trustees, Art Acad. of Cincinnati; fmr mem. United Way of Greater Cincinnati; fmr Mentor with Cincinnati Youth Collaborative; fmr mem. Bd of Dirs YWCA. *Address:* The Procter & Gamble Co., Rutistrasse 26, 8952 Schlieren, Switzerland (office). *Telephone:* (58) 0046111 (office). *Website:* www.pg.com/fr_CH (office); www.pg.com/de_CH (office).

FERGUSON-SMITH, Malcolm Andrew, MB ChB, MA, FRS, FRSE, FRCPath, FRCP (Glas), FRCOG, FMedSci; British professor of pathology; *Professor Emeritus of Pathology, University of Cambridge;* b. 5 Sept. 1931, Glasgow, Scotland; s. of John Ferguson-Smith and Ethel May Ferguson-Smith (née Thorne); m. Marie Eva Gzowska 1960; one s. three d.; ed Stowe School, Univ. of Glasgow; Registrar in Lab. Medicine, Dept of Pathology, Western Infirmary, Glasgow 1958–59; Fellow in Medicine and Instructor, Johns Hopkins Univ. School of Medicine 1959–61; Lecturer, Sr Lecturer, then Reader in Medical Genetics, Univ. of Glasgow 1961–73, Burton Prof. of Medical Genetics 1973–87; Prof. of Pathology, Dept of Veterinary Medicine, Univ. of Cambridge 1987–98, Prof. Emer. 1998–; Fellow, Peterhouse Coll., Cambridge 1987–98; Dir West of Scotland Medical Genetics Service 1973–87, East Anglian Regional Clinical Genetics Service 1987–95; Pres. Clinical Genetics Soc. 1979–81, European Soc. of Human Genetics 1997–98, Int. Soc. for Prenatal Diagnosis 1998–2002, Asscn of Clinical Cytogeneticists 2003–05; Ed. Prenatal Diagnosis 1980–2006; mem. Johns Hopkins Univ. Soc. of Scholars; mem. BSE Inquiry Cttee 1997–2000; Foreign mem. Polish Acad. of Science 1988, Nat. Acad. of Medicine Buenos Aires 2002; Hon. Consultant in Medical Paediatrics, Royal Hosp. for Sick Children, Glasgow 1966–73, in Clinical Genetics, Yorkhill and Assoc. Hosps 1973–87, in Medical Genetics, Addenbrooke's Hosp., Cambridge 1987–98; Hon. Assoc., Royal Coll. of Veterinary Surgeons 2002; Hon. DSc (Strathclyde) 1992, (Glasgow) 2002; Bronze Medal, Univ. of Helsinki 1968, Makdougall-Brisbane Prize of Royal Soc. of Edinburgh 1984–86, San Remo Int. Prize for Research in Genetics 1990, Mauro Baschirotto Award for achievements in human genetics 1996, Sir James Y. Simpson Award 1998, J.B.S. Haldane Medal 2000, McLaughlin-Gallie Professorship, Royal Coll. of Physicians and Surgeons of Canada 2001, Pruzansky Lecture, American Coll. of Medical Genetics 2008. *Publications:* Early Prenatal Diagnosis (ed.) 1983, Essential Medical Genetics (co-author) 1984 (sixth edn 2011), Prenatal Diagnosis and Screening (co-ed.) 1992; papers on cytogenetics, gene mapping, human genetics, comparative genomics, evolutionary biology and prenatal diagnosis in medical and scientific journals. *Leisure interests:* swimming, sailing, fishing. *Address:* Department of Veterinary Medicine, University of Cambridge, Madingley Road, Cambridge, CB3 0ES, England (office). *Telephone:* (1223) 766496 (office). *Fax:* (1223) 766496 (office). *E-mail:* maf12@cam.ac.uk (office). *Website:* www.vet.cam.ac.uk/genomics (office).

FERIANTO, Djaduk; Indonesian composer and musician; b. 19 July 1964, Java; s. of Bagong Kussudiardja; brother of Butet Kertaredjasa; Founder and leader of group Kua Etnika 1996–; f. Padepokan Seni Bagong K Foundation; UNESCO Grand Prize 2000. *Films:* as composer: Clowns of the City 1993, Leaf on a Pillow 1998, Untuk Rena 2005, Drupadi 2008, Sarinah 2011, Soegija 2012, Gending Sriwijaya 2013; as actor: Sherina's Adventure 2000, Cewek saweran 2011. *Compositions include:* Kompi Susu (Milk Brigade), Brigade Mailing (Thieves' Brigade). *Recordings include:* albums: Orkes Sumpeg Nang Ning Nong 1997, Ritus Swara 2000, Parodi Iklan 2000, Komedi Putar 2002, Janji Palsu 2003, Maling Budiman 2006, Dia Sumber Gembiraku 2006, Pata Java.

FERINGA, Bernard Lucas (Ben), BSc, PhD, FRSC; Dutch chemist and academic; *Jacobus Van't Hoff Distinguished Professor of Molecular Sciences, Stratingh Institute for Chemistry, University of Groningen;* b. 18 May 1951, Barger-Compascuum; m. Betty Feringa; three d.; ed Univ. of Groningen; Research Scientist, Royal Dutch Shell, Shell Labs, Amsterdam 1978–82, Shell Biosciences Labs, Sittingbourne, UK 1982–83, Project Leader, Homogeneous Catalysis, Shell Research Labs, Amsterdam 1983–84; Lecturer, Hogere Analistenschool, Amsterdam 1979–82; Lecturer in Organic Chem., Univ. of Groningen 1984–88, Prof. of Organic Chem. 1988–, Chair. Dept of Organic and Molecular Inorganic Chem. 1991–95, Dir Stratingh Inst. for Chem. 2003–11, Jacobus Van't Hoff Distinguished Prof. of Molecular Sciences 2003–; mem. and Vice-Pres. Royal Netherlands Acad. of Science, Acad. Prof. and Chair. Science Div. 2008–; Founding Scientific Ed. Journal of Organic & Biomolecular Chemistry 2002–06; Chair. Editorial Bd, Chemistry World, RSC; mem. Editorial Advisory Bd, Chemical Communications, Chemistry, an Asian Journal, Journal of Organic Chemistry, Organic & Biomolecular Chemistry; mem. Editorial Bd, Faraday Transactions of the Royal Society, Advanced Synthesis and Catalysis, Advances in Physical Organic Chemistry, Topics in Stereochemistry; mem. Int. Advisory Bd, Macromolecular Rapid Communications –2010, Israel Journal of Chemistry; mem. Netherlands Acad. for Tech. and Innovation, Academia Europeae, ACS, Royal Netherlands Chemical Soc.; Foreign Hon. mem. American Acad. of Arts and Sciences; Hans Fischer Hon. Fellow, Inst. for Advanced Studies, Tech. Univ., Munich 2011; Kt, Order of the Netherlands Lion 2008; Koerber European Science Award 2003, Spinoza Award 2004, Prelog Gold Medal 2005, ACS Norrish Award 2007, Paracelsus Medal 2008, Chirality Medal 2009, RSC Organic Stereochemistry Award 2011, Humboldt Award 2012, Grand Prix Scientifique Cino del Duca, Acad. française 2012, Marie Curie Medal 2013, Nagoya Gold Medal 2013, Wilhelm August von Hofmann Medal 2015, Chemistry for the Future Solvay Prize 2015, Nobel Prize in Chem. (co-recipient with Jean-Pierre Sauvage and Sir James Fraser Stoddart) 2016. *Publications:* more than 650 papers in professional journals on homogeneous catalysis, stereochemistry, photochemistry and molecular switches/motors; more than 30 patents. *Address:* Stratingh Institute for Chemistry, Faculty of Mathematics and Natural Sciences, University of Groningen, Nijenborgh 4, 9747 AG Groningen, The Netherlands (office). *Telephone:* (50) 363-4278 (office). *Fax:* (50) 363-4296 (office). *E-mail:* b.l.feringa@rug.nl (office). *Website:* www.rug.nl/staff/b.l.feringa/research (office); www.benferinga.com.

FERLAND, E. James, BSc, MBA; American energy industry executive; *Chairman and CEO, Babcock & Wilcox Enterprises Inc.;* b. 19 March 1942, Boston, Mass; ed Univ. of Maine, Univ. of New Haven, Harvard Grad. School of Business Admin; began career as engineer, Hartford Electric Light Co., Conn. 1964–67; mem. operating staff, Millstone Nuclear Power Station 1967–76, Station Superintendent 1976–78; Dir of Rate Regulatory Project, Corp. HQ, Northeast Utilities 1978–80, Exec. Vice-Pres. and Chief Financial Officer 1980–83, Pres. and COO 1983–86; Chair., Pres. and CEO Public Service Enterprise Group Inc. (PSEG) 1986–2007, Chair. and CEO Public Service Electric and Gas Co. (PSE&G) 1986–91, Pres. 1986–91, Chair. and CEO PSEG Energy Holdings LLC 1989–2007; Sr Vice-Pres., Utility Operations, PNM Resources Inc. 2007; Pres., American Divisions, Westinghouse Electric Co. LLC 2010–12; CEO and Pres., Babcock & Wilcox Co. 2012–15, Chair. and CEO, Babcock & Wilcox Enterprises Inc. 2012–; fmr mem. Bd of Dirs Vermont Yankee Nuclear Power Corpn, Yankee Atomic Electric Co., Maine Yankee Atomic Power Co., The HSB Group Inc., Foster Wheeler Corpn; fmr mem. Bd Cttee for Econ. Devt; fmr Chair. NJ State Chamber of Commerce, Metro Newark Chamber of Commerce, Public Affairs Research Inst. of NJ, Inst. of Nuclear Power Operations, Electric Power Research Inst.; fmr mem. Bd NJ Performing Arts Center, Edison Electric Inst., Nuclear Energy Inst., American Gas Asscn, Asscn of Edison Illuminating Cos, NJ Utilities Asscn, United Way of Tri-State. *Address:* Babcock & Wilcox Enterprises Inc., 13024 Ballantyne Corporate Place, Suite 700, Charlotte, NC 28277, USA (office). *Telephone:* (704) 625-4900 (office). *Website:* www.babcock.com (office).

FERLINGHETTI, Lawrence, MA, PhD, DUniv; American writer and painter; b. 24 March 1919, Yonkers, New York; s. of Charles Ferlinghetti and Clemence Mendes-Monsanto; m. Selden Kirby-Smith 1951; one s. one d.; ed Columbia Univ., Univ. of Paris; served as Lt Commdr in USNR in World War II; co-f. (with Peter D. Martin) the first all-paperback bookshop in USA, City Lights Bookstore, San Francisco 1953; f. City Lights publishing co. 1955; arrested on obscenity charges following publ. of Allan Ginsberg's 'Howl' 1956 (later acquitted); participant One World Poetry Festival, Amsterdam 1980, World Congress of Poets, Florence 1986; First Poet Laureate of San Francisco 1998–99; Ed. City Lights Books; mem. Nat. Acad. of Arts and Letters 2003; Commdr, French Acad. of Arts and Letters 2007; Poetry Prize, City of Rome 1993, Premio Internazionale Flaiano, Italy 1999, Premio Internazionale di Camaiore, Italy 1999, Premio Cavour, Italy 2000, Los Angeles Times Book Festival Lifetime Achievement Award 2001, Poetry Soc. of America Robert Frost Medal 2003, Nat. Book Foundation Literarian Award 2005, Douglas MacAgy Distinguished Achievement Award, San Francisco Art Inst. 2012, Janus Pannonius Int. Poetry Prize 2012. *Publications include:* Pictures of the Gone World (poems) 1955, Selections from Paroles by Jacques Prévert, A Coney Island of the Mind (poems) 1958, Berlin 1961, Her (novel), Starting from San Francisco (poems) 1961, Where is Vietnam? 1965, An Eye on the World 1967, After the Cries of the Birds 1967, Unfair Arguments with Existence (seven plays), Routines (plays), The Secret Meaning of Things (poems) 1969, Tyrannus Nix? (poem) 1969, The Mexican Night (travel journal) 1970, Back Roads to Far Places (poems) 1971, Open Eye, Open Heart (poems) 1973, Who Are We Now? 1976, Northwest Ecolog 1978, Landscapes of Living and Dying (poems) 1979, Literary San Francisco: A Pictorial History from the Beginnings to the Present (with Nancy J. Peters) 1980, Leaves of Life: Drawings from the Model 1983, The Populist Manifestos 1983, Over All the Obscene Boundaries (poems) 1984, Endless Life: Selected Poems 1984, Seven Days in Nicaragua Libre 1984, Inside the Trojan Horse 1987, Love in the Days of Rage (novel) 1988, When I Look at Pictures (poems and paintings) 1990, These Are My Rivers: New and Selected Poems 1993, A Far Rockaway of the Heart 1997, How to Paint Sunlight: New Poems 2001, Americus (Book One) 2004, Poetry as Insurgent Art (prose and poetry) 2007, At Sea 2011, Time of Useful Consciousness 2012, I Greet You At The Beginning Of A Great Career: The Selected Correspondence of Lawrence Ferlinghetti and Allen Ginsberg 1955–1997 2015. *Address:* City Lights Bookstore, 261 Columbus Avenue, San Francisco, CA 94133, USA (office). *Telephone:* (415) 362-8193 (office). *Fax:* (415) 362-4921 (office). *Website:* www.citylights.com (office).

FERNALD, Ivan Christiaan; Suriname government official; b. 7 Dec. 1955; fmr Dir Inst. for Econ. Administrative Secondary Educ. (IMEAO); Minister of Defence 2005–10.

FERNANDES, Anthony (Tony) Francis, BSc; Malaysian airline executive and fmr music industry executive; *Group CEO, AirAsia;* b. 30 April 1964, Kuala Lumpur; ed Epsom Coll. and London School of Econs, UK; started as auditor London accountancy firm 1987; fmr Financial Analyst, Virgin, Financial Controller Virgin TV Div. 1987–89; joined Warner Music 1989, youngest ever Man. Dir Warner Music (Malaysia), Vice-Pres. ASEAN Region, 1999–2001; Co-founder Tune Air, bought AirAsia Sept. 2001, Group CEO AirAsia (Asia's first 'no frills' airline) and CEO Tune Air (parent co. of AirAsia) 2001–; Head, Team Lotus 2010–11; Head, Caterham F1 Team 2012–14; Co-Chair. and Owner, Queens Park Rangers Football Club 2015–18; awarded title Panglima Setia Mahkota by HRH King of Malaysia Yang Di Pertuan Agong Tuanku Mizan Zainal Abidin 2011; Hon. CBE 2011; Commdr, Légion d'honneur 2013; Airline Exec. of the Year, Centre for Aviation 2004, 2005, 2016, Airline CEO of the Year Award, Jane's Transport Finance 2009, Excellence in Leadership Award, Frost & Sullivan 2009, Legend Award (Aviation Hall of Fame), Centre for Aviation 2009, Businessman of the Year, Forbes Asia 2010, Nikkei Asia Prize 2010, Travel Business Leader Award, CNBC Asia Pacific 2011, Airline Industry Leader of the Year, Aviation 100 2014, TIME Magazine 100 List 2015, Fourth Pillar Award, US–ASEAN Business Council 2016, ASEAN Entrepreneurial Excellence Award by EY 2016. *Address:* AirAsia, RedQ, Jalan Pekeliling 5, Kuala Lumpur International Airport (KLIA2), 64000 Sepang, Selangor, Malaysia (office). *Telephone:* (3) 86604333 (office). *Fax:* (3) 87761100 (office). *E-mail:* tonyfernandes@airasia.com (office). *Website:* www.airasia.com (office).

FERNANDES DE ARAÚJO, HE Cardinal Serafim; Brazilian ecclesiastic; *Archbishop Emeritus of Belo Horizonte;* b. 13 Aug. 1924, Minas Novas; ordained priest 1949; Auxiliary Bishop of Belo Horizonte, Minas Gerais, 1959–82, Coadjutor Archbishop 1982–86, Archbishop of Belo Horizonte 1986–2004, Archbishop Emer. 2004–; Titular Bishop of Verinopolis 1959; Cardinal-Priest of S. Luigi Maria Grignion de Montfort 1998–. *Address:* c/o Archdiocese of Belo Horizonte, Cúria

Metropolitana, Av. Brasil 2079, CP 494, 30140-002 Belo Horizonte, MG, Brazil. *Telephone:* (31) 261-3400. *Fax:* (31) 261-5713.

FERNÁNDEZ, Alberto Angel; Argentine politician; b. 2 April 1959, Buenos Aires; m.; one s.; ed Universidad de Buenos Aires; Prof., Dept of Penal Rights, Universidad de Buenos Aires; Pres. Asociacíon de Superintendentes de Seguros de América Latina 1989–92; Exec. Vice-Pres. Grupo Banco Provincia 1997; mem. Parl. for Buenos Aires 2000; Cabinet Chief 2003–08 (resgnd); Industrialist of the Year in Insurance 1997, Millennium Prize for Industrialist of the Century 2000.

FERNÁNDEZ, Aníbal Domingo; Argentine accountant and politician; b. 9 Jan. 1957, Quilmes; m.; one s.; ed Universidad Nacional de Lomas de Zamora; adviser to Budget Cttee, Buenos Aires Prov. Senate 1983–85, Admin. Sec., Peronista bloc 1985–91, Senator 1995; Mayor of Quilmes 1991–95; Asst to Minister of Govt and Justice, Govt of Buenos Aires 1997–99; Sec. of Labour 1999–2001, Minister of Labour 2001–02; Sec.-Gen. to the Presidency Jan.–Oct. 2002; Minister of Production 2002–03, of the Interior 2003–07, of Justice and Human Rights 2007–09; Chief, Cabinet of Ministers 2009–11, Feb.–Nov. 2015; Senator, Upper House of Parl. 2011–14; mem. Alianza Frente para la Victoria; Senator of the Year 1996. *Address:* Partido Justicialista (PJ), Domingo Matheu 128/130, C1082ABD Buenos Aires, Argentina (office). *Telephone:* (11) 4954-2450 (office). *E-mail:* contacto@pj.org.ar (office). *Website:* www.pj.org.ar (office).

FERNÁNDEZ, Carlos Rafael, BEcons; Argentine economist and politician; b. 1954, Ciudad de la Plata; ed La Plata Nat. Univ.; Nat. Dir of tax co-ordination for provs 1989–97; Sub-Sec., tax co-ordination and policy for Buenos Aires prov. govt 1997, Under-Sec. for Fiscal Policy, Buenos Aires Prov. 2002–03, Interim Prov. Minister of Economy 2007; Treasury Sec. 2006; Under-Sec. for Relations with the Provs, Ministry of Economy 2007; Sub-Sec. of the Budget 2007–08; Dir Administración Fed. de Ingresos Públicos (tax agency) March–April 2008; Minister of the Economy and Production 2008–09. *Address:* c/o Ministry of the Economy and Public Finance, Hipólito Yrigoyen 250, C1086AAB Buenos Aires, Argentina. *E-mail:* ciudadano@mecon.gov.ar.

FERNANDEZ, Charles 'Max'; Antigua and Barbuda politician; m. Jill Fernandez; three s.; ed St Joseph's Acad., Univ. of the West Indies; appointed to Senate 1995–2004; mem. House of Reps (Parl.) for St John's Rural North 2009–; Minister of Foreign Affairs 2014–18; Chair. Free Trade and Processing Zone 1995–2002, Medical Benefits Scheme 2002–04; Man. and Dir Deluxe Theatre Ltd; mem. Antigua Labour Party 1984–. *Address:* c/o Ministry of Foreign Affairs, Queen Elizabeth Highway, St John's, Antigua and Barbuda (office).

FERNANDEZ, Dominique, DèsSc; French writer; b. 25 Aug. 1929, Neuilly-sur-Seine; s. of Ramon Fernandez and Liliane Chomette; m. Diane Jacquin de Margerie 1961 (divorced 1971); one s. one d.; ed Lycée Buffon, Paris and Ecole Normale Supérieure; Prof. Inst. Français, Naples 1957–58; Prof. of Italian, Univ. de Haute-Bretagne 1966–89; literary critic, L'Express 1959–84, Le Nouvel Observateur 1985–; music critic, Diapason 1977–85, Opera International 1978, Classical Repertoire 2000–; mem. Académie française 2007–; mem. Reading Cttee, Editions Bernard Grasset 1959–; Chevalier, Légion d'honneur, Commdr, Ordre nat. du Mérite, Cruzeiro do Sul (Brazil); Prix Médicis 1974, Prix Goncourt 1982, Grand Prix Charles Oulmont 1986, Prix Prince Pierre de Monaco 1986, Prix Méditerranée 1988, Prix Oscar Wilde 1988. *Publications:* Le roman italien et la crise de la conscience moderne 1958, L'écorce des pierres 1959, L'aube 1962, Mère Méditerranée 1965, Les Evènements de Palerme 1966, L'échec de Pavèse 1968, Lettre à Dora 1969, Les enfants de Gogol 1971, Il Mito dell'America 1969, L'arbre jusqu'aux racines 1972, Porporino 1974, Eisenstein 1975, La rose des Tudors 1976, Les Siciliens 1977, Amsterdam 1977, L'étoile rose 1978, Une fleur de jasmin à l'oreille 1980, Le promeneur amoureux 1980, Signor Giovanni 1981, Dans la main de l'ange 1982, Le volcan sous la ville 1983, Le banquet des anges 1984, L'amour 1986, La gloire du paria 1987, Le rapt de Perséphone (opera libretto) 1987, Le radeau de la Gorgone 1988, Le rapt de Ganymede 1989, L'Ecole du Sud 1991, Porfirio et Constance 1992, Séville 1992, L'Or des Tropiques 1993, Le Dernier des Médicis 1993, La Magie Blanche de Saint-Pétersbourg 1994, Prague et la Bohême (jtly) 1995, La Perle et le croissant 1995, Le Musée idéal de Stendhal 1995, Saint-Pétersbourg 1996, Tribunal d'honneur 1997, Le musée de Zola 1997, Le voyage d'Italie 1998, Rhapsodie roumaine 1998, Palerme et la Sicile 1998, Le loup et le chien 1999, Les douze muses d'Alexandre Dumas 1999, Bolivie 1999, Nicolas 2000, Errances solaires 2000, L'amour qui ose dire son nom 2001, Syrie 2002, La Course à l'abîme 2003, Dictionnaire amoureux de la Russie 2004, Rome 2004, Sentiment indien 2005, Sicile 2006, Jérémie! Jérémie! 2006, l'Art de raconter 2007, Place rouge 2008, Ramon 2009, Avec Tolstoï 2010, Pise 1951 2011, Transsibérien 2012, Dictionnaire amoureux de Stendhal 2013, On a sauvé le monde 2014, Amants d'Apollon. L'Homosexualité dans la culture 2015, Le Piéton de Rome, portrait souvenir 2015, Correspondance indiscrète 2016, La Société du mystère 2017, Où les eaux se partagent 2018, Stendhal 2018, Venise 2018, Le peintre abandonné 2019. *Leisure interest:* operatic music. *Address:* 14 rue de Douai, 75009 Paris (home); c/o Editions Bernard Grasset, 61 rue des Saints-Pères, 75006 Paris, France (office).

FERNANDEZ, Manuel (Manny) A., BEE; American business executive; *Managing Director, SI Ventures;* b. 22 April 1946; ed Univ. of Florida; began his career in engineering positions with Fairchild and Harris Corpn, fmr Group Exec. Vice-Pres., Fairchild Semiconductor; fmr Pres. and CEO Dataquest, Inc., Gavilan Computer Corpn, Zilog Inc.; Co-founder and Man. Dir SI Ventures 1996–; Chair., Pres. and CEO Gartner, Inc. (information tech. research and consulting co.) –2001, Chair. Emer. 2001–; mem. Bd of Dirs Sysco Corpn 2006–13, Chair. (non-exec.) 2009–12, Exec. Chair. 2012–13; mem. Bd of Dirs Brunswick Corpn, Flowers Foods, Inc., The Black & Decker Corpn, Florida Research Consortium and several pvt. cos and foundations; apptd by Pres. George W. Bush to serve on Pres.'s Information Tech. Advisory Cttee; Chair. Bd of Trustees, Univ. of Florida. *Address:* SI Ventures, 12600 Gateway Boulevard, Fort Myers, FL 33913, USA (office). *Telephone:* (239) 561-4760 (office). *Fax:* (239) 561-4916 (office). *E-mail:* info@siventures.com (office). *Website:* www.siventures.com (office).

FERNÁNDEZ, Margarita Cedeño de, LLD, LLM; Dominican Republic lawyer; *Vice-President;* b. 1 May 1965, Santo Domingo; d. of Luis Cedeño and Margarita Cedeño; m. Leonel Antonio Fernández Reyna (Pres. of Dominican Repub.) 2003; one d.; two c. from previous marriage; ed Universidad Autónoma de Santo Domingo, Pontifícia Universidad Católica Madre y Maestra; Assoc., Dr Abel Rodríguez del Orbe and Fernández y Asociados (law firms); legal adviser to Pres. 1996–2000; fmr consultant and Dir Legal Man. and Investment Bd, Office for the Promotion of Foreign Investment; First Lady of Dominican Repub. 2004–12, Vice-Pres. 2012–, acts as head of govt's social programmes centred on educ., tech., social solidarity and family devt; Founding mem. Digital Solidarity Fund, Geneva 2005; FAO Goodwill Amb. 2009–; primary cand. of Partido de la Liberación Dominicana for presidential election 2011; Hon. Pres. 40th Nat. Congress of Paediatrics 2009; Grande Ufficiale, Ordine della Stella della Solidarietà Italiana 2009; Dr hc (Univ. Centre of Brasília) 2005; ITU Union World Information Soc. Award 2007, Latin Pride Nat. Awards Woman of the Year 2009. *Address:* c/o Office of the President, Palacio Nacional, Avda México, esq. Dr Delgado, Gazcue, Santo Domingo, DN; Partido de la Liberación Dominicana (PLD), Avda Independencia 401, Santo Domingo DN, Dominican Republic (office). *Telephone:* 685-3540 (PLD) (office). *Fax:* 685-3540 (PLD) (office). *E-mail:* pldorg@pld.org.do (office). *Website:* www.pld.org.do (office); www.presidencia.gob.do (office).

FERNÁNDEZ AMUNATEGUI, Mariano, LLB; Chilean diplomatist, editor and UN official; b. 21 April 1945, Santiago; m. María Angélica Morales; two s. one d.; ed Universidad Católica de Santiago, Bonn Univ., Germany; joined Chilean Foreign Service 1967; Third Sec., Embassy in Germany 1971–74; in exile, Bonn, Germany 1974–82; Ed. Development and Cooperation (magazine) and Chief Ed. IPS-Dritte Welt Nachrichtenagentur (news agency) 1974–82; Chief Ed. Handbuch der Entwicklungshilfe 1974–76; returned to Chile 1982; Researcher and mem. Exec. Cttee Centre of Studies for Devt (CED) 1982–90; Amb. to EC 1990–92, to Italy (also accred to Malta) 1992–94, to Spain (also accred to Andorra) 2000–02, to UK 2002–06, to USA 2006–09; Under-Sec. of Foreign Affairs 1994–2000, Minister of Foreign Affairs 2009–10; Special Rep. of Sec.-Gen. for Haiti, UN 2011–13; Head UN Stabilization Mission in Haiti 2011–13; Pres. Int. Council of Latin-American Centre for Relations with Europe (CELARE), Santiago 1996–98; Vice-Pres. European-Latin American Relations Inst. (IRELA), Madrid, Spain 1992, Pres. 1992–94; Vice-Chair. Italian-Latin-American Inst. 1992–94; Commr Int. Whaling Comm. 2003–07; mem. Exec. Cttee Jacques Maritian Inst., Rome, Italy 1994–96; mem. Bd of Dirs Fintesa Financial Agency (Banco del Desarrollo) 1982–84, Radio Cooperativa 1982–90; mem. Editorial Bd Mensaje (magazine) 1984–86, Fortin Mapocho (newspaper) 1986–88, Apsi (magazine) 1986–89; mem. Political Science Asscn of Chile, Acad. Int. du Vin; Hon. Pres., Chilean Asscn of Sommeliers; Grand Cross (Argentina, Brazil, Colombia, Ecuador, Finland, Germany, Holy See, Italy, Mexico, Panama, Peru, Spain), Grand Officer (Croatia, Germany, Sweden). *Address:* c/o Ministry of Foreign Affairs, Teatinos 180, Santiago, Chile.

FERNÁNDEZ BERMEJO, Mariano, LicenDer; Spanish lawyer, professor of law and politician; b. 10 Feb. 1948, Ávila; ed Complutense Univ.; Public Prosecutor, Prov. Court of Santa Cruz de Tenerife 1974–76, Territorial Court of Cáceres 1976–81; Deputy Chief Prosecutor, Prov. Court of Segovia 1981–84, Chief Prosecutor 1984–86; exec. adviser to Ministry of Justice 1986–89; Prosecutor, Tribunal Supremo (Supreme Court) 1989–92, Chief Prosecutor, Chamber for Admin. Proceedings 2004–07; Chief Prosecutor, Madrid High Court of Justice 1992–2003; Minister of Justice 2007–09 (resgnd); Interim Adjunct Prof. of Criminal Law, Extremadura Univ. 1977–80; Prof., Nat. Univ. of Distance Learning (UNED) 1980–81; San Raimundo de Penafort Cross of Honour, Silver Cross Order of Merit of the Civil Guard; Jesús Vicente Chamorro Prize 2003, Political Merit Medal. *Publications include:* El concepto de desamparo 1987, Líneas generales de la Reforma del Derecho del Menor 1988, Adopción y acogimientos familiares 1988, El menor de edad en la legislación española 1994, La Mediación como solución alternativa al proceso y su significación respecto a la víctima 2000, La protección de los Derechos Humanos en los colectivos sociales marginales 2001, Contra la especulación del suelo 2003.

FERNÁNDEZ DE GURMENDI, Silvia Alejandra; Argentine lawyer, judge and fmr diplomatist; b. 24 Oct. 1954; ed Córdoba Univ., Univ. of Buenos Aires, Limoges Univ., France; joined Ministry of Foreign Affairs (MFA) 1987, with Legal Dept 1989–94, Legal Counsellor, Perm. Mission to UN, New York 1994–2000, Dir-Gen. for Human Rights, MFA 2006; represented Argentina before int. and regional human rights bodies and advised on justice issues related to the prevention of genocide and other int. crimes; Judge, Int. Criminal Court, The Hague 2010–, Pres. (first woman) 2015–18; fmr Prof. of Int. Criminal Law, Univ. of Buenos Aires; Visiting Prof., American Univ. Washington Coll. of Law.

FERNÁNDEZ DE KIRCHNER, Cristina Elisabet; Argentine politician, lawyer and fmr head of state; b. 19 Feb. 1953, La Plata, Buenos Aires; m. Néstor Carlos Kirchner (died 2010); one s. one d.; ed Universidad Nacional de La Plata; began political career in Tendencia Revolucionaria faction of Partido Justicialista 1970s; elected prov. rep. in Patagonian prov. of Santa Cruz 1989–95, Chair. Constitutional Affairs, Authorities and Regulations Cttee, Santa Cruz House of Reps 1989–95, First Vice-Chair. 1990; elected to represent Santa Cruz in Senate 1995–97, 2001–05, in Chamber of Deputies 1997, 2005–07, Senator representing Prov. of Buenos Aires (Front for Victory faction of party) 2005–07; Pres. of Argentina (first elected female Pres.) 2007–15; mem. Congress Partido Justicialista 1985, mem. Nat. Congress 1995, Pres. Congress Partido Justicialista 2004. *Address:* c/o General Secretariat to the Presidency, Balcarce 50, C1064AAB, Buenos Aires, Argentina. *Website:* www.cristina.com.ar.

FERNÁNDEZ DE LA VEGA, María Teresa, PhD; Spanish lawyer, judge and politician; b. 15 June 1949, Valencia; d. of Wenceslao Fernández de la Vega Lombán and Elena Sanz; ed Complutense Univ. of Madrid, Barcelona Central Univ.; started career as legal sec.; one of first women judges in Justicia Democrática movement during transition to democracy; served in Ministry of Justice 1980s; magistrate 1989; Sec. of State for Justice 1994; Deputy for Jaén, Congress of Deputies 1996–2000, for Madrid 2000–08, for Valencia 2008–10; First Deputy Prime Minister, Minister of the Presidency and Govt Spokesperson 2004–10; Assoc. Prof., Barcelona Central Univ., Complutense Univ. of Madrid; tutor, UNED Perm. mem. Consejo de Estado 2010–; fmr Pres. Fundación Mujeres por África; Permanent Counsellor, Spanish State Council 2010–; fmr Sec.-Gen., Socialist Group in Congress; Gran Cruz de la Orden de Carlos III 2010; Dr. hc (Univ. International Menéndez Pelayo) 2011; Gredos de Guisando Award 2004, Protagonistas Award 2004, Valores de la Ciudad de Valencia Award 2004, Tomás y Valiente Award 2006, Montblanc Mujer 2007, Naranja Especial Award 2008, Foro de Alta Dirección Award 2010, AMIT Award 2011, Colectivo 8 de Marzo Award 2011, Meridiana Award 2012, Premio Igualdad de la Agrupación Socialista de Pinto Award 2013. *Publications include:* Effects of Bankruptcy Procedures in the Labour Execution Process, Bankruptcy Procedures and Workers' Rights, Human Rights and Council of Europe. *Address:* Consejo de Estado C/ Mayor, 79, 28013 Madrid, Spain (office). *Telephone:* (91) 5166207 (office). *E-mail:* seccion7@consejo-estado.es (office). *Website:* www.consejo-estado.es (office).

FERNÁNDEZ DE SOTO VALDERRAMA, Guillermo; Colombian politician, international organization official and diplomatist; *Permanent Representative to United Nations;* b. 1956; m. 1st Consuelo Camacho, three c.; m. 2nd Alexandra Kling Mazuera, one s.; ed Pontificia Universidad Javeriana, Univ. of Bogotá, Georgetown Univ., USA, Harvard Univ.; Asst to Mayor of Santafé de Bogotá 1972–73; Exec. Sec. Circulo de Investigaciones para el Desarollo Económico y Social 1972–77; Gen. Man. Consultant, Corporación Financiera Popular 1973–76; Exec. mem. Esguerra Fernandez de Soto y Asociados 1976–77; Minister, Ministry of Foreign Affairs 1985–86; Consultant, UNDP 1987–91; Founder and Exec. Dir Int. Studies Center, Inter-American Forum 1988–91; Exec. Dir Presidential Campaign for Rodrigo Lloreda Caicedo 1990; Adviser to Minister of Foreign Affairs 1990–92; Pres. Chamber of Commerce of Bogotá and Pres. Colombian Cttee Int. Chamber of Commerce 1993–98; Minister of Foreign Affairs 1998–2002; f. Groupe de Contadora; Intermediate Sec. Groupe de Rio; Sec.-Gen. Andean Community of Nations 2002–03; Amb. to Netherlands 2004–09; mem. Inter-American Juridical Committee, OAS, Rio de Janeiro, Brazil 2008–11, Vice-Chair. 2009–11, Pres. 2011–12; Corp. Dir of Europe, Corporacion Andina de Fomento, Devt Bank of Latin America 2012–18; Perm. Rep. to UN 2018–, Pres. Peace Building Comm. 2019–; Founder, Center for Colombian Studies, Washington, DC; fmr Pres. Ibero-American Asscn of Chambers of Commerce; Pres. Colombian Cttee of Economic and Social Council for the Pacific Basin, Int. Relations Colombian Council; Dean of the Int. Relations Faculty, Jorge Tadeo Lozano Univ., Bogota; Dir Inter-American Comm. of Commercial Arbitration; Ordre nat. du Mérite 1985, numerous other decorations. *Address:* Permanent Mission of Colombia to United Nations in New York, 140 East 57th Street, New York, NY 10022, USA (office). *Telephone:* (212) 355-7776 (office). *Fax:* (212) 371-2813 (office). *Website:* nuevayork-onu.mision.gov.co (office).

FERNÁNDEZ DIAZ, Jorge; Spanish engineer and politician; b. 6 April 1950, Valladolid; m.; two c.; ed Escuela Técnica Superior de Barcelona, Escuela Superior de Marketing y Administración de Empresas, Barcelona; trained as industrial engineer; Deputy Del., later Del. of Ministry for Labour Affairs in Barcelona 1979–80; Civil Gov. of Asturias 1980–81, of Barcelona 1981–82; Councillor, Barcelona City Council 1983–84; mem. Regional Parl. of Catalonia 1984–89; Sec. of State for Regional Authorities 1996–99, for Educ., Univs, Research and Devt 1999–2000, for Parl. Relations 2000–04; mem. Congreso de los Diputados (Parl.) for Barcelona 1989–96, 2004–, Third Vice-Pres. (Deputy Speaker) 2008–11; Minister of the Interior 2011–16; mem. Partido Popular, mem. Nat. Exec. Cttee; Order of the Legion of Honour, Order of St Gregory the Great (Vatican City), Knight Grand Cross, Order of San Carlos (Colombia). *Address:* c/o Ministry of the Interior, Paseo de la Castellana 5, 2046 Madrid, Spain (office).

FERNÁNDEZ ESTIGARRIBIA, José Félix; Paraguayan lawyer, diplomatist, international organization official and academic; *Counsel for International Law, Ministry of Foreign Affairs;* b. 4 Feb. 1941; ed Nat. Univ. of Asunción, Universidad Católica, Int. Law Acad., The Hague, Netherlands; fmr Amb. to Mexico (also accred to Guatemala and the Dominican Repub.), fmr Amb. to the UN, New York; fmr Deputy to Nat. Ass., later Senator of the Nation; Minister of Foreign Affairs and mem. Advisory Council of the Chancellor 1999–2003, Minister of Foreign Affairs 2012–13, Counsel for Int. Law, Ministry of Foreign Affairs 2013–; Prof. of Public Int. Law, Latin American Faculty of Social Sciences (FLACSO), Asunción 2011, 2012, 2013; fmr Prof. of Int. Relations and Int. Law, Faculty of Juridical and Diplomatic Sciences, Universidad Católica; fmr Prof. of Int. Law, Faculty of Law and Social Sciences, Nat. Univ. of Asunción; fmr Prof. of Contemporary Int. System, Diplomatic and Consular Acad., Ministry of Foreign Affairs; taught at XVIII and XXIX Course on Int. Law, OAS, Rio de Janeiro, Brazil; served as Pres. Bar Asscn of Paraguay, Latin American Asscn of Lawyers for Human Rights (Paraguay Br.); fmr mem. Bd Diplomatic Acad. of Paraguay; Paraguayan Referee, Schedule for the Settlement of Disputes in MERCOSUR Protocol of Brasilia, mem. MERCOSUR Council of Inst. for European-Latin American Relations (IRELA); Sec.-Gen. Latin American Integration Asscn (Asociación Latinoamericana de Integración—ALADI) 2009–11; Corresp. mem. Inst. for Political and Constitutional Law, Nat. Univ. of La Plata, Inst. for Political and Econ. Integration of Latin America Studies, Nat. Univ. of Tucumán; Academic mem. Inst. for Legis. Studies, Argentina Fed. of Bar Asscns; Best Grad., Faculty of Law and Social Sciences, Nat. Univ. of Asunción 1963. *Publications include:* co-author: Las Transnacionales en el Paraguya; Política Internacional, Economía e Integración 1985, La Sociedad Internacional y el Estado Autoritario del Paraguay 1987. *Address:* Ministry of Foreign Affairs, Edif. Benigno López, Palma, esq. 14 de Mayo, Asunción, Paraguay (office). *Telephone:* (21) 49-3928 (office). *Fax:* (21) 49-3910 (office). *E-mail:* sistemas@mre.gov.py (office). *Website:* www.mre.gov.py (office).

FERNÁNDEZ-FAINGOLD, Hugo; Uruguayan diplomatist and fmr politician; b. 1 March 1947, Montevideo; m.; seven c.; ed Columbia Univ. and Georgetown Univ., USA; fmr Prof., Univ. of the Repub., Montevideo; Dean, School of Social Sciences, Nat. Univ. Costa Rica 1974–76; fmr consultant to several int. orgs including UNDP, ILO, Inter-American Inst. for Cooperation in Agriculture, Inter-American Devt Bank; mem. Nat. Convention and Montevideo Convention, Colorado Party 1985–, Sec.-Gen. Colorado Party Nat. Exec. Cttee 1995–2000; Minister of Labor and Social Security 1985–89; mem. Senate 1995–2000; Dir El Dia (daily newspaper) 1997–98; Vice-Pres. of Uruguay and Pres. of Gen. Ass. 1998–2000; Amb. to USA 2000–05. *Publications:* more than 70 articles and papers. *Leisure interests:* soccer, fencing.

FERNÁNDEZ FIGUEROA, Rosario del Pilar; Peruvian lawyer and politician; b. 9 Nov. 1955, Lima; d. of Joffre Fernandez Veldivieso; m. Ernest Coz; two d.; ed Pontifical Catholic Univ. of Peru; Pnr, Fernández, Heraud & Sánchez (law firm) 1988–2007; Vice-Chair. Lima Stock Exchange 1988–91; Treas. Lima Bar Asscn 1993–94; Minister of Justice 2008–09, 2010–11; Pres. Council of Ministers (Prime Minister) March–July 2011; teaches int. private law, Univ. of Lima. *Address:* c/o Fernández, Heraud & Sánchez, Independencia 663, Miraflores, Lima, Peru (office). *Telephone:* 1-242-6327 (office). *E-mail:* rfernandez@fhsabogados.com (office).

FERNÁNDEZ ORDÓÑEZ, Miguel Ángel, LicenDer, LicenCienEcon; Spanish economist, politician, fmr central banker and academic; b. 3 April 1945, Madrid; m. Inés Alberdi; two c.; ed Universidad Complutense de Madrid; mem. Socialist Workers' Party; Prof. of Political Economy Universidad Complutense de Madrid 1970–72; Chief of Section, Coyuntura de la Comisaría del Plan de Desarrollo 1970–72; economist, Dept of Econ. Studies, OECD 1973; Chief of Co-ordination Service, Ministry of Planning and Devt 1974–75; econ. consultant, Ministry of Finance 1976; Deputy Dir-Gen. of Conjunctural Analysis, Ministry of the Economy 1977; consultant to Exec. Dir World Bank 1978–80; Sec. Cttee of Public Investments, Ministry of the Economy 1980–82; Sec. of State for the Economy and Planning 1982–86; elected Deputy for Madrid 1986–88; Sec. of State for Commerce 1987–88; Exec. Dir IMF 1988–90; Pres. Icopostal, Sociedad de Valores y Bolsa 1990–91; mem. Council of Admin Banco Argentaria and Pres. Fundación Argentaria 1991–92; Pres. Court of Defence of Competition 1992–95; Pres. Comm. of Nat. Electric System 1995–99; econ. columnist, El País y Cinco Días, collaborator on TV programme Economía a Fondo, CNN+ and Dir radio programme Economía de los Negocios, SER 2000–03; Sec. of State for Internal Revenue 2004–06; Counsellor, Banco de España and mem. Exec. Comm. March–July 2006, Gov. Banco de España July 2006–12; mem. Cuerpo de Técnicos Comerciales and State Economists. *Publications include:* La Competencia; numerous articles on political economy, regulation, liberalization, privatization, defence of competition and the financial system.

FERNÁNDEZ RETAMAR, Roberto, Dr en Fil; Cuban writer; b. 9 June 1930, Havana; s. of José M. Fernández Roig and Obdulia Retamar; m. Adelaida de Juan 1952; two d.; ed Univ. de la Habana, Univ. of Paris (Sorbonne), France, Univ. of London, UK; Prof., Univ. de la Habana 1955–; Visiting Prof., Yale Univ. 1957–58; Dir Nueva Revista Cubana 1959–60; Cultural Counsellor of Cuba in France 1960; Sec., Union of Writers and Artists of Cuba 1961–65; Ed. Casa de las Américas 1965, now Pres.; Visiting Lecturer, Columbia Univ. 1957, Univ. of Prague 1965; Felix Varela Order of first grade 1981, Orden de Mayo, Argentina 1998; Nat. Prize for Poetry, Cuba 1952, Rúben Dario Latin American Prize 1980, Int. Prize for Poetry Nikola Vaptsarov, Bulgaria 1989, Nat. Literary Award, Cuban Book Inst. 1989, Int. Prize for Poetry, Pérez Bonalde, Argentina 1989, Official Medal of Arts and Letters (France) 1998, Int. José Martí Prize, UNESCO 2019. *Publications include:* poetry: Elegía como un Himno 1950, Patrias 1952, Alabanzas, Conversaciones 1955, Vuelta de la Antigua Esperanza 1959, Con las Mismas Manos 1962, Poesía Reunida 1948–1965 1966, Buena Suerte Viviendo 1967, Que veremos arder 1970, A quien pueda interesar 1970, Cuaderno paralelo 1973, Juana y otros temas personales 1981, Aquí 1995; studies: La Poesía contemporánea en Cuba 1954, Idea de la Estilística 1958, Papelería 1962, Ensayo de otro mundo 1967, Introducción a Cuba: la historia 1968, Caliban 1971, Lectura de Martí 1972, El son de Vuelo popular 1972, Introducción a Martí 1978. *Leisure interests:* reading, swimming. *Address:* Casa de las Américas, 3ra y G Street, El Vedado, Havana, Cuba (office). *E-mail:* webmaster@casa.cult.cu (office). *Website:* www.casadelasamericas.com (office).

FERNÁNDEZ REYNA, Leonel, DIur; Dominican Republic politician and fmr head of state; *President, Partido de la Liberación Dominicana;* b. 26 Dec. 1953, Santo Domingo; s. of José Antonio Fernández Collado and Yolanda Reyna Romero; m. Margarita Cedeño; one c. (two c. from previous m.); ed Universidad Autónoma de Santo Domingo; joined Partido de la Liberación Dominicana 1973, Pres. 2002–; cand. for Vice-Pres. 1994; Pres. 1996–2000, 2004–12. *Address:* Partido de la Liberación Dominicana, Avda Independencia 401, Santo Domingo, Dominican Republic (office). *Telephone:* 685-3540 (office). *Fax:* 687-5569 (office). *E-mail:* pldorg@pld.org.do (office). *Website:* www.pld.org.do (office).

FERNÁNDEZ SAAVEDRA, José Gustavo; Bolivian politician and diplomatist; b. 24 Sept. 1941, Cochabamba; m.; three c.; ed San Simón Univ.; Exec. Sec., Secr. of Integration, La Paz 1969–70; Head Legal Dept, Comm. on Cartagena, Lima, Peru 1970–76; Dir of Consultation and Latin American Co-ordination, Caracas, Venezuela 1976–77; Consulting Dir-Gen. Coprinco y Asociados Consultores 1977–78, Pres. 1979–80, 1982–83; Minister of Integration 1978, of Foreign Affairs 1979, 1984–85, 2001–02; Consultant to UNCTAD 1980–83, 1987–89, 1993–98; Rep. of Ministries of Industry and Foreign Affairs, Quito, Ecuador 1980–81, Geneva, Switzerland 1985–87; Amb. to Brazil 1983–84; Exec. Dir Muller y Asociados Consultores 1987–89, Network of Advising and Man. SA 1993; Vice-Presidential cand. 1989; Minister of the Presidency 1989–93; Co-ordinator, Nat. Dialogue 1997; Rep. Andean Corpn of Promotion in Peru 1998–99; Gen. Consul of Bolivia in Chile 2000–01; Special Rep. of the OAS Sec.-Gen. and Head, Misión Especial de Acompañamiento al Proceso Democrático y Electoral de la República de Nicaragua (Special Mission Accompanying the Democratic Process and Elections of Repub. of Nicaragua) 2006, Head of OAS Election Observation Mission (EOM) to El Salvador 2013–14. *Address:* Casilla 7ll, La Paz, Bolivia (home). *Telephone:* (2) 278-2614 (home). *Fax:* (2) 278-6793 (home). *E-mail:* gustavof@acelerate.com (home).

FERNÁNDEZ-TARANCO, Oscar; Argentine UN official; *Assistant Secretary-General for Peacebuilding Support, United Nations;* b. 1957; m. Aissata Traore; two c.; ed Cornell Univ., Massachusetts Inst. of Tech., USA; worked as UN Volunteer, Benin, Deputy Special Rep. of Admin. West Bank and Gaza Programme of Assistance 1994–98, Resident Rep., UN Resident Coordinator and Deputy Special Rep. of Sec.-Gen. in Haiti 1998–2001, Deputy Asst Admin. and Deputy Regional Dir Regional Bureau for Arab States, UNDP 2001–06, Asst Sec.-Gen. for Political Affairs 2009–14, for Peacebuilding Support 2014–; mem. Interpeace Governing Council. *Address:* Peacebuilding Support Office, United Nations Headquarters, 405 E 42nd Street, New York, NY 10017, USA (office). *Telephone:* (212) 963-1234 (office). *Fax:* (212) 963-4879 (office). *Website:* www.un.org (office).

FERNÁNDEZ VALDOVINOS, Carlos Gustavo, BEcons, MEconSc, PhD; Paraguayan economist, academic and central banker; b. 9 Feb. 1965, Asuncion; ed Federal Univ. of Parana, Univ. of Illinois and Univ. of Chicago, USA; served as Prof., Nat. Univ. of Asuncion, Catholic Univ., Our Lady of the Assumption, Paraguay, Univ. of San Andrés, Univ. of Chicago and Georgetown Univ., USA; Section Chief, Monetary Programming, Banco Central del Paraguay 1991–92,

Advisory Man., Econ. Studies 1999–2001, Man. of Econ. Studies 2001–04; Sr Economist for Argentina, World Bank 2004–06; Sr Economist, IMF for country missions to Africa, Europe, and Western Hemisphere 2006–11, Resident Rep. for Brazil and Bolivia 2011–13; Pres. Banco Central del Paraguay 2013–18; Best Central Banker, Global Finance 2015, 2016. *Publications include:* Policy Instruments to Lean Against the Wind in Latin America (co-ed.) 2011, Inflation Uncertainty and Relative Price Variability in WAEMU Countries (with Kerstin Gerling) 2011, Paraguay: Regulator Statement 2016. *Address:* c/o Banco Central del Paraguay, Avda Federación Rusa y Cabo 1° Marecos, Casilla 861, Barrio Santo Domingo, Asunción, Paraguay (office). *Telephone:* (21) 608-011 (office). *Fax:* (21) 611-118 (office).

FERNANDO, Kalupage Austin, BA, MBA; Sri Lankan diplomatist and government official; *High Commissioner to India;* b. 12 June 1942; m. Sylvia Fernando; ed Univ. of Ceylon, Univ. of Sri Jayewardenepura; Grad. Teacher 1963–67; Asst Commr, Matale and Batticaloa dist 1968–67; Commr and Registrar, Cooperative Societies, Ministry of Food and Cooperatives 1983–86; Sec., Ministry of Rehabilitation 1986–88; CEO Nat. Reconstruction Steering Cttee (UNDP Assignment) 1988–91; Chair. State Gem Corpn, Ministry of Finance 1991–92; Postmaster-Gen. of Sri Lanka 1992–93; Sec., Ministry of Cooperatives Prov. Councils, Home Affairs, Local Govt and Indigenous Medicine 1993–96; Sec., Ministry of Defence 2001–03; Exec. Dir, Resources Devt Consultants Ltd 2003–15; Adviser to the Prime Minister Nov. 2003–April 2004; Sr Adviser and freelance consultant, Japan Int. Corpn Agency 2004–15; Gov. of Eastern Prov. 2015–17; Sec. to the Pres. 2018; High Commr to India 2018–; mem. State Admin. Asscn (fmr Pres.) 1985; mem. Sri Lanka Evaluation Asscn 1999–. *Publication:* My Belly is White: Reminiscences of a Peacetime Secretary of Defence 2008. *Address:* High Commission of Sri Lanka, No. 27, Kautilya Marg, Chanakyapuri, New Delhi 110021, India (office). *Telephone:* (11) 23010201 (office); (11) 23010202 (office). *Fax:* (11) 23793604 (office). *E-mail:* slhc.newdelhi@mfa.gov.lk (office). *Website:* www.slhcindia.org (office).

FERNANDO, Merrill Joseph; Sri Lankan tea planter and business executive; *Founder and Chairman, MJF Group of Companies (Dilmah Tea);* b. 6 May 1930, Negombo; s. of P. Harry Fernando and Lucy Fernando; m.; two s.; ed Maris Stella Colles, Negombo; selected for training as tea taster, travelled to Mincing Lane, London, UK; worked in UK tea co. before returning to Sri Lanka; joined A. F. Jones and Co., becoming Man. Dir within two years, bought out British shareholders and ran business with another partner; supplied first ever consignment of Ceylon tea direct to then USSR 1950s; est. Merrill J. Fernando and Co. Ltd, supplied bulk tea to most of world's major tea brands 1960s–70s; lost tea plantation to nationalization 1970s, sold business with intention of emigrating from Sri Lanka, remained in Sri Lanka and est. M. J. F. Exports Ltd 1974; registered trademark DILMAH in face of opposition from bulk tea customers early 1980s; DILMAH Tea launched in Australia 1988, thereafter in New Zealand and to date in 94 countries worldwide; est. The Merrill J. Fernando Charitable Foundation. *Address:* MJF Group (Dilmah), 111 Negombo Road, Peliyagoda, Colombo 11830, Sri Lanka (office). *Telephone:* (11) 4822000 (office). *Fax:* (11) 4822001 (office). *E-mail:* info@dilmahtea.com (office); marketing@dilmahtea.com (office). *Website:* www.dilmahtea.com (office); www.mjffoundation.org; www.dilmahtea.com (office).

FERNANDO, Most Rev. Nicholas Marcus, BA, PhL, STD; Sri Lankan ecclesiastic; *Archbishop Emeritus of Colombo;* b. 6 Dec. 1932; s. of W. Severinus Fernando and M. M. Lily Fernando; ordained priest 1959; Rector, St Aloysius Minor Seminary 1965–73; Archbishop of Colombo 1977–2002 (resgnd), Archbishop Emer. 2002–; mem. Sacred Congregation for the Evangelization of Peoples 1989; Pres. Catholic Bishops' Conf. of Sri Lanka 1989–95. *Address:* c/o Archbishop's House, 976 Gnanartha Pradeepaya Mawatha, Colombo 8, Sri Lanka.

FERNANDO, Rear Adm. Sarath Palitha, PC, LLB, LLM; Sri Lankan lawyer, naval officer and government official; s. of Thomas Fernando and Sylvia Fernando; m. Lalinthi Fernando; two c.; ed Royal Coll., Sri Lanka Law Coll., Univ. of Colombo, Univ. of Bristol, UK; captained the Coll. English and Sinhala debating teams, served as Student Chair. Coll. English Literary Asscn and Gen. Sec. Sinhala Literary Asscn; Pres. Young Zoologists' Asscn of Sri Lanka 1976; joined Attorney Gen.'s Dept as acting State Counsel 1980–89, Sr State Counsel 1989–97, Deputy Solicitor Gen. 1997–2004; apptd Judge Advocate of Sri Lanka Navy, as a Cdre in Volunteer Naval Force to head legal br. 2004, served as prosecutor and Judge Advocate at several Courts Martial of all three Services, apptd President's Counsel by Pres. Mahinda Rajapaksa 2007, Solicitor Gen. 2011–12, Acting Attorney-Gen. June–July 2012, Attorney-Gen. July 2012–14 (retd); attained rank of Rear Adm. in Volunteer Naval Force; Visiting Lecturer, Open Univ. of Sri Lanka; mem. Faculty, Bandaranaike Centre for Int. Studies; mem. Pres.'s Council; Prize for Commercial Law and Hector Jayawardena Gold Medal, Sri Lanka Law Coll.

FERNEYHOUGH, Brian John Peter, DMus, ABSM, ARAM, FRAM, FBC; British composer and academic; *William H. Bonsall Professor in Music, Stanford University;* b. 16 Jan. 1943, Coventry, West Midlands; s. of Frederick George Ferneyhough and Emily May Ferneyhough (née Hopwood); m. 4th Stephanie Hurtik 1990; ed Birmingham School of Music, Royal Acad. of Music, Sweelinck Conservatory, Amsterdam, Music Acad., Basle; composition teacher, Musikhochschule, Freiburg, Germany 1973–78, Prof. of Composition 1978–86; Prin. Composition Teacher, Royal Conservatory of The Hague 1986; Prof. of Music, Univ. of California, San Diego 1987–99; Leader of Master Class in Composition, Civica Scuola di Musica, Milan 1982–86, Fondation Royaumont, France 1990–; Visiting Artist, DAAD, Berlin 1976–77; Guest Prof., Musikhögskolan, Stockholm 1980, 1981, 1982, 1985; Visiting Prof., Univ. of Chicago 1986; Lecturer in Composition, Darmstadt Int. Courses 1976–96, 2008–; Guest Prof. of Poetics, Mozarteum, Salzburg, Austria 1995; William H. Bonsall Prof. in Music, Stanford Univ. 2000–; Visiting Prof., Harvard Univ. 2007–08, S.L. Lee Visiting Professorial Fellow, Univ. of London 2012; Corresp. Mem. Bayrische Akademie der Schönen Künste 2005–; mem. Akademie der Künste, Berlin 1996–; mem. Bd Perspectives of New Music 1995–; Jury mem. Kranichsteiner Preis Jury, Darmstadt 1978–96; Hon. DMus (Goldsmiths Coll.) 2011, Dr hc (Royal Birmingham Conservatoire) 2018; Chevalier des Arts et des Lettres 1984; Koussevitsky Prize 1979, Grand Prix du Disque 1978, 1984, Ernst von Siemens Prize for Lifetime Achievement 2007, and other awards and prizes. *Compositions include:* Sonatas for String Quartet 1967, Firecycle Beta 1969–71, Transit 1972–74, Time and Motion Study III 1974, La Terre Est Un Homme 1976–79, Second String Quartet 1979–80, Lemma-Icon-Epigram 1981, Carceri d'Invenzione 1981–86, 3rd String Quartet 1987, Kurze Schatten II 1988, La Chute d'Icare 1988, Fourth String Quartet 1989–90, Allgebrah 1991, Bone Alphabet 1991, Terrain 1992, On Stellar Magnitudes 1994, String Trio 1995, Incipits 1995–96, Flurries 1997, Unsichtbare Farben 1999, Doctrine of Similarity 2000, Opus Contra Naturam 2000, Stele for Failed Time 2001, Shadowtime (opera) 2004, Plötzlichkeit 2005, Fifth String Quartet 2006, Dum transisset I–IV 2007, Exordium 2008, Chronos-Aion 2008, Renvois/Shards 2008, Sisyphus Redux 2008, Sixth String Quartet (Royal Philharmonic Soc. Chamber-scale Composition Prize 2011) 2009, Liber Scintillarum 2012, Finis Terrae 2012, Quirl 2013, Schatten aus Wasser und Stein 2013, Silentium 2013, Contraccolpi 2015. *Publications include:* Complete Writings on Music 1994, Collected Writings 1996; various articles published separately. *Leisure interests:* reading, cats, wife, wine (not in that order). *Address:* Office 231A, Department of Music, Braun Music Center, Stanford University, 541 Lasuen Mall, Stanford, CA 94305-3076, USA (office). *Telephone:* (650) 725-3102 (office). *Fax:* (650) 725-2686 (office). *E-mail:* brian.ferneyhough@stanford.edu (office). *Website:* music.stanford.edu (office).

FERRAGAMO, Ferruccio; Italian business executive; b. 9 Sept. 1945, Fiesole, Florence; s. of Salvatore Ferragamo and Wanda Ferragamo; m. Amanda Collingwood; five c.; began career working on production side of family business Salvatore Ferragamo Italia SpA, later involved in worldwide management of Ferragamo stores; finance and admin. from 1983, currently CEO Salvatore Ferragamo Italia SpA; Vice-Pres. Polimoda, Florence; mem. Bd Società Gaetano Marzotto & Fratelli, La Fondaria Assicurazioni, Banca Mercantile, Florence, Centro di Firenze per la Moda Italiana. *Leisure interests:* golf, shooting, sailing, tennis. *Address:* Salvatore Ferragamo Italia, SpA, Via Mercalli 201, Sesto Fiorentino, Florence 50019, Italy (office). *Telephone:* (055) 33601 (office). *Fax:* (055) 3360444 (office). *E-mail:* segreteria.societaria@ferragamo.com (office). *Website:* www.salvatoreferragamo.it (office).

FERRARA, Abel; American film director and actor; b. 19 July 1951, Bronx, New York; m. Nancy Ferrara; two d.; began making short films while at school; has used pseudonym Jimmy Laine; television work includes episodes of Miami Vice and pilot for NBC's Crime Story. *Films include:* Nicky's Film 1971, The Hold Up 1972, Could This Be Love? 1973, Nine Lives of a Wet Pussy 1976, Not Guilty: For Keith Richards 1977, Driller Killer (also acted) 1979, Ms.45 (also acted) 1981, Fear City 1984, China Girl 1987, Cat Chaser 1989, The King of New York 1990, Bad Lieutenant 1992, Body Snatchers 1993, Dangerous Game 1993, The Addiction 1995, The Funeral 1996, California 1996, The Blackout 1997, New Rose Hotel 1998, 'R Xmas 2001, Mary (Venice Film Festival Special Jury Prize) 2005, Go Go Tales 2007, Chelsea on the Rocks 2008, Napoli, Napoli, Napoli 2009, The Bad Lieutenant: Port of Call–New Orleans 2009 (writer), 4:44 - Last Day on Earth 2011, Welcome to New York 2014, Pasolini 2014. *Website:* abelferrara.com.

FERRARA, Napoleone, MD; Italian/American molecular biologist and academic; *Distinguished Professor of Pathology, University of California, San Diego;* b. 26 July 1956, Italy; ed Univ. of Catania Medical School, Univ. of California, San Francisco; Univ. Postdoctoral Research, Univ. of California, San Francisco; Internship, The Oregon Health Sciences; worked at Genentech, Inc., San Francisco 1988–2013; Distinguished Prof., Univ. of California, San Diego 2013–, Sr Deputy Dir for Basic Science, Moores Cancer Center; mem. NAS 2006, Nat. Acad. of Medicine (USA) 2015; Dr hc (Univ. of Eastern Piedmont, Italy) 2007; Discover Magazine Award 2004, Italian Asscn for Research and Therapy of Eye Disorders (AIRCMO) Prize 2004, American-Italian Cancer Foundation Prize 2004, Lefoulon-Delelande-Institut-de-France Prize 2005, AACR Bruce F. Cain Memorial Award 2005, Passano Award 2006, General Motors Cancer Research Award 2006, C. Chester Stock Award Lecturer, Memorial Sloan-Kettering Cancer Center 2007, Special Recognition for Scientific Achievement, Biotech Hall of Fame 2007, ASCO Science of Oncology Award 2007, Arnall Patz Award, Macula Soc. 2008, Pezcoller Foundation-AACR Int. Award 2009, Macula Soc.-Michaelson Award 2010, Lasker-DeBakey Clinical Medical Research Award 2010, Special Recognition, ARVO/AFER 2011, Dr Paul Janssen Award for Biomedical Research 2012, The Economist Innovation Award (Bioscience) 2012, Breakthrough Prize in Life Sciences 2013, Canada Gairdner Int. Award (co-recipient) 2014, A. Champalimaud Vision Award (co-recipient) 2014. *Publications:* numerous papers in professional journals. *Address:* Moore Cancer Center, University of California, San Diego, 3855 Health Sciences Drive, Mail Code #0819, La Jolla, CA 92093, USA (office). *Telephone:* (858) 822-6822 (office). *E-mail:* nferrara@ucsd.edu (office). *Website:* pathology.ucsd.edu/faculty/ferrara.htm (office).

FERRARI, Luca, BA; Italian diplomatist; *Ambassador to Saudi Arabia;* b. 28 Oct. 1961, Rome; m.; one s.; entered diplomatic service 1986, Head of Secr. of the Legal Service 1986–88, Sec.-Gen. 1988–90, with Cabinet of Minister of Foreign Affairs 1990–92, First Sec. (Commercial), Embassy in Moscow 1992, Head of Secr. of Amb. overseeing Office for Social, Consular and Judicial Affairs 1992–95, Counsellor and Head of Secr. of Amb., Embassy in Washington, DC 1995–99, Office of Minister of Foreign Affairs 1999–2000, rank of Counsellor 2000, Dir Middle East Office of Directorate Gen. for Countries of the Mediterranean and the Middle East 2001–05, First Counsellor for Political Affairs, Embassy in Washington, DC 2005–08, rank of Minister Plenipotentiary 2008, Minister-Counsellor, Spokesperson and Head of Press and Law 2008–09, Minister and Deputy Chief of Mission, Embassy in Madrid 2009–13, Deputy Dir-Gen. for Globalization and Global Issues, Ministry of Foreign Affairs 2013–16, Amb. to Saudi Arabia 2016–; Commdr, Order of Merit of the Italian Repub. 2005. *Address:* Embassy of Italy, PO Box 94389, Riyadh 11693, Saudi Arabia (office). *Telephone:* (11) 488-1212 (office). *Fax:* (11) 480-6964 (office). *E-mail:* segreteria1.riad@esteri.it (office). *Website:* www.ambriad.esteri.it (office).

FERRARI, Margaret Hughes, BL; Saint Vincent and the Grenadines lawyer and fmr diplomatist; b. 1 Jan. 1948; m.; three c.; ed Univ. of London, UK; Sec. and Legal Exec. Hughes and Cummings law firm 1967–90, Partner 1990–2008; called to Bar, Lincoln's Inn, London, UK 1990; fmr Pres. Bar Asscn of Saint Vincent and the Grenadines; Deputy Chair. Bd Saint Vincent Co-operative Bank Ltd; Dir Bottlers Ltd. (bottling co.); Perm. Rep. to UN, New York 2000–07.

FERREIRA, G(errit) T(homas), BCom, BBA, MBA; South African business executive; *Chairman, RMB Holdings;* b. 6 April 1948; m.; two c.; ed Stellenbosch Univ.; Co-founder Rand Consolidated Investments (RCI) 1977, Man. Dir Rand Merchant Bank (RMB) (acquired by RCI 1985) 1985–88, later Chair., Chair. (non-exec.) RMB Holdings (RMBH) 1987–, Chair. (non-exec.) FirstRand 1998–2008; mem. Bd of Dirs Glenrand M.I.B Ltd, VenFin Ltd, Remgro Ltd, Open Soc. of South Africa; mem. of Council, Univ. of Stellenbosch, Open Soc. Foundation of South Africa; Trustee, Univ. of Stellenbosch 2000 Trust; owns Tokara vineyard; Business Leader, Cape Town Chamber of Business 2010. *Address:* RMB Holdings, 3rd Floor, 2 Merchant Place, Corner Fredman Drive, Rivonia Road, Sandton, Johannesburg 2196, South Africa (office). *Telephone:* (11) 2821824 (office). *Fax:* (11) 2824210 (office). *Website:* www.rmbh.co.za (office).

FERREIRA, Murilo Pinto de Oliveira, BA, MBA; Brazilian business executive; *President and CEO, Vale;* ed Escola de Administração de Empresas, Fundação Getulio Vargas, EBAP-FGV; began career at Vale SA (Companhia Vale do Rio Doce—CVRD) as financial and econ. analyst 1977, Commercial and Financial Dir, Vale do Rio Doce Alumínio SA 1998, Aluvale (holding co. of CVRD that merged into CVRD 2003), held positions as Exec. Officer, Nickel Marketing & Sales of Copper & Aluminum and Exec. Dir, Nickel Business, Marketing and Sales of Copper and Aluminum, mem. Exec. Bd Vale SA (Companhia Vale do Rio Doce—CVRD), Exec. Dir, Holdings, Energy, Equities & Business Devt, Companhia Vale do Rio Doce (holding company of Vale Overseas Ltd) 2005–07, Pres. and CEO Vale Inc. (fmrly CVRD Inc. Ltd) (subsidiary of PT International Nickel Indonesia Tbk) 2007–08, Pres. and CEO Vale SA 2011–; worked at Aluminio Brasileiro SA (Albras) as Man. of Int. Financial Dept 1980–89; consultant 1990–97, worked on projects involving mergers and acquisitions and restructuring, especially related to Cia. Paulista de Ferro Ligas, Sibra Eletrosiderurgica and Alumina do Norte do Brasil SA (Alunorte); fmr CEO Albras and Alunorte; Chief Commr/Pres. Commr of Int. Nickel Indonesia tbk PT 2007–08, Commr–Dec. 2008; mem. Bd of Dirs, Mineracao Rio do Norte, Valesul Aluminio; Chair. Petróleo Brasileiro SA (Petrobras) 2015 (resgnd). *Address:* Vale, Av. Graça Aranha, 26, 20030-900 Rio de Janeiro RJ, Brazil (office). *Telephone:* (21) 3814-4477 (office). *Fax:* (21) 3814-4040 (office). *E-mail:* info@vale.com (office). *Website:* www.vale.com (office).

FERREIRA BRUSQUETTI, Manuel Adolfo; Paraguayan economist and politician; *President, MF Economía SA;* b. 20 Feb. 1964, Asunción; ed Universidad Católica Nuestra Señora de la Asunción, Univ. of Essex, UK, Univ. of Massachusetts, Amherst, USA; Partner, MCS Consulting Group 1998–2012; Pres. Investor Casa de Bolsa SA 2010–12; Minister of Finance 2012–13; Founding mem. Desarrollo en Democracia (Dende); Pres. MF Economía SA 2016–, Inversiones SA 2016–. *Address:* MF Economía SA, Paseo La Galeria, Torre 2, Piso 16, Asunción, Paraguay (office). *Telephone:* (21) 69-5585 (office). *E-mail:* mferreira@mf.com.py (office). *Website:* mf.com.py (office).

FERREIRA DE OLIVEIRA, Manuel, PhD; Portuguese engineer and business executive; *Vice-Chairman and CEO, Galp Energia SGPS SA;* b. 21 Dec. 1948, Fajões; s. of Henrique Soares De Oliveira and Maria José Gomes Ferreira; m. Maria Teresa Ferreira De Oliveira; two s.; ed Faculdade de Engenharia da Universidade do Porto (FEUP), Univ. of Manchester, UK; exec. responsibilities in LAGOVEN SA (subsidiary of Petroleos de Venezuela SA— PDVSA), including responsibilities as CEO and mem. Bd BP Bitor Energy, Nynas Petroleum and Ruhr Oel 1980–95; Chair. and CEO Petrogal – Petróleos de Portugal SA 1995–2000; Chair. and CEO UNICER – Bebidas de Portugal SGPS SA 2000–06; CEO Galp Exploração e Produção, Petrogal, GDP — Gás de Portugal, Galp Power and Galp Energia SA 2006–, Exec. Dir and COO Galp Energia SGPS SA 2006–07, Vice-Chair. and CEO Galp Energia SGPS SA 2007–, Chair. Fundação Galp Energia 2009–; Order of Francisco de Miranda (Venezuela) 1995, Grã-Cruz, Order of Merit (Portugal) 2006; Dr hc (Technical Univ. of Lisbon) 2001. *Address:* Galp Energia SGPS SA, Rua Tomás da Fonseca, Torre A, Edifício Galp Energia, 1600-209 Lisbon, Portugal (office). *Telephone:* (21) 724-25-00 (office); (21) 724-19-69 (office). *Fax:* (21) 003-90-80 (office). *E-mail:* presidencia@galpenergia.com (office). *Website:* www.galpenergia.com (office).

FERRELL, John William (Will); American comedian and actor; b. 16 July 1967, Irvine, Calif.; s. of Lee Ferrell and Kay Ferrell; m. Viveca Paulin 2000; two s.; ed Univ. of Southern California; started as mem. The Groundlings (improvisation group), Los Angeles; Mark Twain Prize for American Humor 2011. *Films include:* Men Seeking Women 1997, Austin Powers: International Man of Mystery 1997, The Thin Pink Line 1998, A Night at the Roxbury 1998, The Suburbans 1999, Austin Powers: The Spy Who Shagged Me 1999, Dick 1999, Superstar 1999, Drowning Mona 2000, The Ladies Man 2000, Jay and Silent Bob Strike Back 2001, Zoolander 2001, Old School 2003, Elf 2003, Anchorman: The Legend of Ron Burgundy 2004, Melinda and Melinda 2004, The Wendell Baker Story 2005, Kicking and Screaming 2005, Bewitched 2005, Winter Passing 2005, The Producers 2005, Wedding Crashers 2005, Curious George (voice) 2006, Talladega Nights: The Ballad of Ricky Bobby 2006, Stranger Than Fiction 2006, Blades of Glory 2007, Semi-Pro 2008, Step Brothers 2008, Land of the Lost 2009, The Other Guys 2010, Everything Must Go 2010, Tim and Eric's Billion Dollar Movie 2012, Casa de mi Padre 2012, The Campaign 2012, Anchorman 2: The Legend Continues 2013, Get Hard 2015. *Stage performance:* You're Welcome America: A Final Night with George W. Bush (Broadway) 2009. *Television includes:* cast mem. Saturday Night Live 1995–2002, Eastbound & Down (series) 2009–12, Funny or Die Presents 2010–11, The Office 2011, The Spoils of Babylon (mini-series) 2014. *Address:* c/o Creative Artists Agency, Inc., 2000 Avenue of the Stars, Los Angeles, CA 90067, USA (office). *Website:* www.facebook.com/WillFerrell.

FERRER, David; Spanish professional tennis player; b. 2 April 1982, Xàbia, Alicante; right-handed (two-handed backhand); moved to Gandia aged 13, to Barcelona to attend Catalan Tennis Fed. aged 15; spent nine months at Equelite, Juan Carlos Ferrero's Acad. in Villena; coached by Javier Piles; turned professional 2000, finishing as World No. 419, winning in Poland F1 and Spain F3, runner-up in Spain F1; won first career Challenger title in Sopot 2001; winner, Bucharest 2002, Stuttgart 2006, Tokyo 2007, Bastad 2007, Auckland 2007, 2011, 2012, 2013, 's-Hertogenbosch 2008, 2012, Valencia 2008, 2010, 2012, Acapulco 2010, 2011, 2012, Buenos Aires 2012, 2013, Abierto Mexicano Telcell, Acapulco 2012, SkiStar Swedish Open 2012, BNP Paribas Masters, Paris 2012, Qatar ExxonMobil Open 2015, Malaysian Open, Kuala Lumpur 2015, Erste Bank Open, Vienna 2015; runner-up, Tennis Masters Cup 2007; Grand Slam results: runner-up, French Open 2013, semi-finalist, US Open 2007, 2012, Australian Open 2011, quarter-finalist, French Open 2005, 2008, 2012, 2014, Australian Open 2008, Wimbledon 2012; finalist, ATP World Tour Finals 2007; mem. winning Spanish Davis Cup team 2008, 2009, 2011; doubles titles: Acapulco (with Santiago Ventura) 2005, Viña del Mar (with Ventura) 2005; first achieved a top-10 ranking 2006; lives in Valencia; Golden Bagel Award 2007. *Leisure interests:* soccer, basketball, supports Valencia Football Club, reading. *E-mail:* albert.molina@imgworld.com (office); aboutdavidferrer@gmail.com. *Website:* www.aboutdavidferrer.weebly.com.

FERRERO, Juan Carlos, (El Mosquito); Spanish professional tennis player (retd); b. 12 Feb. 1980, Onteniente; s. of Eduardo Ferrero and Rosario Ferrero; m. Eva Alonso; two c.; turned professional 1998; 12 singles titles: Mallorca 1999, Barcelona 2001, Dubai 2001, Estoril 2001, Rome Tennis Masters Series (TMS) 2001, Hong Kong 2002, Madrid TMS 2003, Monte Carlo TMS 2002, 2003, French Open 2003, Valencia 2003, Grand Prix Hassan II, Casablanca, Morocco 2009; runner–up French Open 2002, US Open 2003; ranked 4th Champions Race 2002, ranked 3rd in 2003; career winnings of more than US $12m.; nine Davis Cup ties 1999–2008; won Davis Cup with Spain in 2000; coached by Antonio Martinez and Samuel Lopez; f. Equalite J.C. Ferrero tennis school 2001; Asscn of Tennis Professionals Rookie of the Year 1999. *Leisure interests:* soccer, collecting cars and motorcycles. *Address:* Casas de Menor, 44, 03400 Villena, Alicante, Spain. *Telephone:* (96) 5340013. *E-mail:* info@juancarlosferrero.com. *Website:* www.juancarlosferrero.com.

FERRERO COSTA, Carlos; Peruvian politician; b. 7 Feb. 1941, Lima; m. Nina Ghislieri 1968; four c.; Congressional Speaker 2000–03; Prime Minister of Peru 2003–05 (resgnd); mem. Congreso (Perú Posible). *E-mail:* carfecos@gmail.com (office). *Website:* www.carlosferrero.org (office).

FERRERO-WALDNER, Benita Maria, DIur; Austrian diplomatist and politician; *President, Fundación Euroamerica;* b. 5 Sept. 1948, Salzburg; ed Univ. of Salzburg; export and sales managerial roles in German and US cos, Germany 1978–83; joined diplomatic service 1984, several posts in Ministry of Foreign Affairs, Vienna 1984–86, First Sec., Dakar, Devt Aid Dept, Vienna; Counsellor for Econ. Affairs, Deputy Head of Mission, Chargé d'affaires, Paris 1986–93; Deputy Chief of Protocol, Ministry of Foreign Affairs 1993; UN Chief of Protocol, Exec. Office of Sec.-Gen., New York 1994–95; State Sec., Ministry of Foreign Affairs 1995–2000, Minister of Foreign Affairs 2000–04; EU Commr for External Relations and European Neighbourhood Policy 2004–09, for Trade and European Neighbourhood Policy 2009–10; Pres. EU-Latin America and Caribbean Foundation (EU-LAC Foundation) 2011–15; Pres. Fundación Euroamerica 2011–; mem. Supervisory Bd Munich Re 2010–, Gas Natural Barcelona 2015–; Partner, Cremades and Calvo Sotelo Abogados, Madrid 2014–; mem. Bd of Trustees, Príncesa de Girona Foundation, Bertelsmann Foundation, Fundación para las Relaciones Internacionales y Diálogo (FRIDE) 2015; Grand Decoration of Honour in Gold with Sash for Services 2010; Dr hc (Lebanese American Univ., Beirut); Mérite Européen Gold Medal, European Diplomat of the Year, European Voice Magazine 2007, XVI Blanquerna Prize (Generalitat de Cataluña) 2009. *Publications:* The Future of Development Co-operation, Setting Course in a Changing World. *Leisure interests:* reading, yoga, cycling. *Address:* Fundación Euroamerica, Calle General Arrando 38, 28010 Madrid, Spain (office). *Telephone:* (91) 781-82-60 (office). *E-mail:* benita.ferrero.waldner@gmail.com (office). *Website:* euroamerica.org (office).

FERRES, Veronica Maria; German actress; b. 10 June 1965, Cologne; m. Martin Krug 2001; one d.; ed Ludwig-Maximilian-Univ., Munich; several awards including Golden Camera Award, Germany 1998, 2002, Bavarian TV Award 2002. 2004, Romy Award, Austria 2002, Video Award, Germany 2004. *Films include:* The Mask of Desire (Bambi Best Actress Award) 1992, Lateshow, The Ladies Room, Schtonk 1992, Superwoman 1996, Rossini 1997, Honeymoon 1997, The Parrot 1997, The Second Homeland 1997, The Bride (Best Actress Award 9th Int. Film Festival, Pescara 1999) 1999, Klimt 2006, Die Wilden Hühner 2006, Bye Bye Harry! 2006, Die Wilden Hühner und die Liebe 2007, Adam Resurrected 2008, Die Wilden Hühner und das Leben 2009, Unter Bauern – Retter in der Nacht 2009, Das Leben ist zu lang 2010. *Plays include:* Gold 1998, The Casket 2000, The Geierwally 2000, Talking With 2000, The Bernauerin 2000, Ghostride 2000, Everyman 2002–04. *Television includes:* Jack's Baby, The Chaos Queen, The Naughty Woman, Dr Knock, Catherine the Great, Tatort Fatal Motherlove, The Mountain Doctor, Bobby 2002, Sans Famille 2002, Les Misérables 2002, The Manns (Golden Grimme Award, Emmy Award) 2002, Forever Lost 2003, Anna's Return 2003, Stronger Than Death 2003, The Return of the Dancing Master 2004, Stars Even Shine At Day 2004, No Heaven Over Africa 2005, Neger, Neger, Schornsteinfeger 2006, Mein alter Freund Fritz 2007, Die Frau vom Checkpoint Charlie (mini-series) 2007, Das Wunder von Berlin 2008, Das Geheimnis der Wale 2010, Das blaue Licht 2010, Die lange Welle hinterm Kiel 2011, Tsunami – Das Leben danach 2012. *Leisure interests:* horseriding, skiing, fencing, golf, scuba diving, dancing. *Address:* Ferres Management, Kurfürstenstr. 18, 80801 Munich, Germany (office). *Telephone:* (89) 34020927 (office). *Fax:* (89) 38398689 (office); (89) 4702198 (office); (89) 399744 (home).

FERRETTI, Alberta; Italian fashion designer and retailer; b. 1951; m. 1968 (separated); two s.; made clothes and opened first boutique The Jolly Shop, Cattolica 1968, launched first collection under the name Alberta Ferretti 1974; began mfg clothes for other designers in 1970s; launched Alberta Ferretti line 1981, Philosophy line 1984, lingerie, accessories and beachwear lines 2001; opened flagship store in Los Angeles 2008; Owner and Vice-Pres. Aeffe fashion design and mfg co.; Cavaliere del Lavoro 1998; Dr hc (Bologna); Alta Roma Career Awards 2005. *Leisure interests:* swimming, reading, sailing. *Address:* AEFFE Spa, via Delle Querce, 15, 47842 San Giovani in Marignana; Via Donizetti 48, 20122 Milan, Italy (office). *Telephone:* (0) 760591 (office). *Fax:* (0) 782373 (office). *E-mail:* info@aeffe.com (office). *Website:* www.aeffe.com (office); www.albertaferretti.com (office).

FERRIER, Michael J.; St Maarten business executive and politician; fmr Chair. Windward Islands Airways Int. NV (Winair, govt-owned airline); fmr Chair. Carib Sky Alliance; Owner NAPA Auto Truck and Marine Parts; Minister of Finance

Jan.–June 2018; mem. Bd of Dirs St Maarten Marine Trades Asscn (SMMTA); mem. Democratic Party (DP, Democratische Partij) –2014, fmr Pres. *Address:* c/o Finance Department, POB 943, Clem Labega Square, Philipsburg, Sint Maarten (office). *E-mail:* Michael.Ferrier@sintmaartengov.org (office).

FERRO, Marc; French historian and academic; *Director of Studies in Social Sciences, École des hautes études en sciences sociales;* b. 24 Dec. 1924, Paris; noted for his studies of Russian and Soviet history as well as history of cinema; currently Dir of Studies in Social Sciences, École des hautes études en sciences sociales; Co-Dir French review Annales; Co-Ed. Journal of Contemporary History; Chevalier, Légion d'honneur. *Television:* directed and presented documentaries on the rise of the Nazis, Lenin and the Russian revolution and on the representation of history in cinema. *Publications include:* La Révolution de 1917 1967 (reprinted 1976, 1997) (English trans.: October 1917: A Social History of the Russian Revolution, translated by Norman Stone 1980), La Grande Guerre, 1914–1918 1968 (reprinted 1987) (English trans.: The Great War, 1914–1918, translated by Nicole Stone 1972), Cinéma et Histoire 1976 (reprinted 1993) (English trans.: Cinema and History, translated by Naomi Greene 1988), L'Occident devant la révolution soviétique 1980, Suez 1981, Comment on raconte l'histoire aux enfants à travers le monde 1983 (reprinted 1986), L'Histoire sous surveillance: science et conscience de l'histoire 1985 (reprinted 1987), Pétain 1987 (reprinted 1993, 1994), Les Origines de la Perestroïka 1990, Nicolas II 1991, Questions sur la Deuxième Guerre mondiale 1993, Histoire des colonisations, des conquêtes aux indépendances (XIIIe–XXe siècle) 1994, L'internationale 1996, Les sociétés malades du progrès 1999, Que transmettre à nos enfants (with Philippe Jammet) 2000, Les Tabous de l'histoire 2002, Le livre noir du colonialisme (ed.) 2003, Histoire de France 2003, Le choc de l'Islam 2003, Le Cinéma, une vision de l'histoire 2003, Les Tabous de L'Histoire, Pocket Vol. 11949 2004, Les individus face aux crises du XXe siècle-L'Histoire anonyme 2005, Mes histoires parallèles: Entretiens avec Isabelle Veyrat-Masson (Prix Saint-Simon 2011) 2011. *Address:* École des hautes études en sciences sociales, 54 blvd Raspail, 75244 Paris Cedex 13, France (office). *Telephone:* 1-49-54-25-25 (office). *E-mail:* ferro@ehess.fr (office). *Website:* ehess.fr (office).

FERRY, Bryan, CBE; British singer and songwriter; b. 26 Sept. 1945, Washington, Co. Durham, England; s. of Frederick Charles Ferry and Mary Ann Ferry (née Armstrong); m. 1st Lucy Margaret Mary Helmore 1982 (divorced 2003); four s.; m. 2nd Amanda Sheppard 2012 (divorced 2014); ed Newcastle Univ.; formed Roxy Music 1971; official debut, Lincoln Festival 1972; first US concerts 1972; first British and European tours 1973; Ivor Novello Award for Outstanding Contrib. to British Music 2003, BMI Icon Award 2008. *Recordings include:* albums: with Roxy Music: Roxy Music 1972, For Your Pleasure (Grand Prix du Disque, Golden Rose Festival, Montreux 1973) 1973, Stranded 1973, Country Life 1974, Siren 1975, Viva Roxy Music 1976, Manifesto 1979, Flesh & Blood 1980, Avalon 1982, The Atlantic Years 1983, Street Life – 20 Great Hits 1986; solo: These Foolish Things 1973, Another Time Another Place 1974, Let's Stick Together 1976, In Your Mind 1977, The Bride Stripped Bare 1978, Boys And Girls 1985, Bete Noire 1987, The Ultimate Collection 1988, Taxi 1993, Mamouna 1995, Bryan Ferry and Roxy Music Video Collection 1996, Frantic 2002, Dylanesque 2007, Olympia 2010, Avonmore 2014. *Address:* c/o Alistair Norbury, Studio One, Avonmore Place, London, W14 8RY, England (office). *E-mail:* info@denejesmond.co.uk (office); info@bryanferry.com (office). *Website:* www.bryanferry.com.

FERRY, Luc, Dr rer. pol; French philosopher, politician and academic; b. 3 Jan. 1951, Colombes; s. of Pierre Ferry and Monique Faucher; m. Marie-Caroline Becq de Fouquières 1999; three d. (one from previous m.); ed Lycée Saint-Exupéry, Centre nat. de télé-enseignement, Sorbonne, Univ. of Heidelberg; Lecturer, Teacher Training Coll., Arras, Asst Lecturer, Univ. of Reims 1977–79; Asst Lecturer, Ecole Normale Supérieure, Paris 1977–79, 1980–82; Research Attaché Nat., CNRS 1980–82; Asst Lecturer, Univ. of Paris I-Panthéon Sorbonne and Paris X-Nanterre 1980–88; Prof. of Political Sciences, Inst. of Political Studies, Univ. of Lyon II–Lumière 1982–88; Prof. of Philosophy, Univ. of Caen 1989–97; Asst Lecturer, Paris I 1989; Prof. of Philosophy, Univ. of Paris VI-Jussieu 1996–; Founder-mem. and Sec.-Gen. Coll. of Philosophy 1974–; responsible for Ideas section then Editorial Adviser, L'Express 1987–94; Pres. Nat. Curriculum Council (CNP) 1994–2002; Minister for Nat. Educ., Research and Tech. 1997–2002; Minister of Youth, Nat. Educ. and Research 2002–04; mem. Comm. for UNESCO 1997–2002; Pres. Conseil d'analyse de la société 2004; Dir Editions Grasset collection of Coll. of Philosophy; mem. Academic Bd fmr mem. Saint-Simon Foundation; columnist for Le Point 1995–; Telesio Galilei Acad. of Science Laureate for Philosophy 2013; Chevalier de la Dive Bouteille de Gaillac 2012, Chevalier, Légion d'honneur, Ordre des Arts et des Lettres Dr hc (Université de Sherbrooke, Canada). *Publications include:* Philosophie politique (three vols 1984–85), la Pensée 68, le Nouvel ordre écologique: l'arbre, l'animal et l'homme (Prix Jean-Jacques Rousseau) 1992, Homo aestheticus – L'Intervention du goût à l'âge démocratique 1990 (Prix Médicis 1992), l'Homme Dieu ou le sens de la vie (Prix Littéraire des Droits de l'Homme) 1996, La Sagesse des Modernes 1998, Le Sens du Beau 1998, Philosopher à dix-huit ans (co-author) 1999, Qu'est-ce que l'homme? (co-author) 2000, Lettres à tous ceux qui aiment l'école (co-author) 2003, Le Religieux après la religion 2004, Comment peut-on être ministre? 2005, Vaincre les peurs 2006, Apprendre à vivre 2006 (trans.: A Brief History of Thought: A Philosophical Guide to Living 2011), Kant. Une lecture des trois Critiques 2006, Familles, je vous aime 2007, Kant. L'oeuvre philosophique expliquée 2008, Nietzsche. L'oeuvre philosophique expliquée 2008, La tentation du christianisme (co-author) 2009, Quel devenir pour le christianisme (co-author) 2009, Face à la crise 2009, La révolution de l'amour: Pour une spiritualité laïque 2010, La Politique de la jeunesse (co-author) 2011, On Love: A Philosophy for the Twenty-first Century 2013, The Wisdom of the Myths: How Greek Mythology Can Change Your Life 2014, La révolution transhumaniste: Comment la technomédecine et l'uberisation du monde vont bouleverser nos vies 2017; numerous articles on philosophy. *Address:* c/o Berggruen Institute, Bradbury Building, 304 S Broadway, Suite 500, Los Angeles, CA 90013, USA.

FERSHT, Sir Alan Roy, Kt, MA, PhD, FRS, FMedSci; British chemist and academic; *Master and Life Fellow of Gonville and Caius College and Group Leader, MRC Laboratory of Molecular Biology, University of Cambridge;* b. 21 April 1943, London, England; s. of Philip Fersht and Betty Fersht; m. Marilyn Persell 1966; one s. one d.; ed Sir George Monoux Grammar School, Walthamstow, Gonville and Caius Coll., Cambridge; Research Fellow, Brandeis Univ., Waltham, Mass, USA 1968–69; Fellow, Jesus Coll., Cambridge 1969–72; mem. scientific staff, MRC Lab. of Molecular Biology, Cambridge 1969–77; Eleanor Roosevelt Fellow, Stanford Univ., Calif. 1978–79; Wolfson Research Prof. of Royal Soc. 1978–89; Prof. of Biological Chem., Imperial Coll., London 1978–88; Herchel Smith Prof. of Organic Chem., Univ. of Cambridge 1988–2010, Prof. Emer. 2010–, Dir Cambridge Interdisciplinary Research Centre for Protein Eng 1989–2010, Dir MRC Unit for Protein Function and Design 1989–2010, Group Leader, MRC Lab. of Molecular Biology 2010–; Professorial Fellow, Gonville and Caius Coll. Cambridge 1988–, Master 2012–; Co-founder and Sr Ed. Protein Engineering Design and Selection; Assoc. Ed. Proceedings of the National Academy Sciences; Co-founder Cambridge Antibody Technology 1989 (acquired by Astra-Zeneca 2006); Co-founder Cambridge Drug Discovery 1997 (acquired by Millennium Pharmaceuticals 2000); Co-founder Avidis (France) 2000; Pres. Cambridge Univ. Chess Club 1964–65; mem. European Molecular Biology Org. 1980, American Philosophical Soc. 2008 Foreign mem. Italian Nat. Acad.; Foreign Assoc. NAS 1993; Hon. Foreign mem. American Acad. of Arts and Sciences 1988; Hon. mem. Japanese Biochemical Soc. 2002; Hon. Fellow, Manchester Interdisciplinary Biocentre 2006; Hon. Prof., Sichuan Univ. 2006, Shanghai Inst. of Materia Medica 2008; Freeman of the Worshipful Co. of Clockmakers 2005; Hon. PhD (Uppsala) 1999, (Free Univ. of Brussels) 1999, (Weizmann Inst.) 2004, (Hebrew Univ.) 2006, (Aarhus) 2008; Fed. of European Biochemical Socs Anniversary Prize 1980, Novo Biotech. Award 1986, Charmian Medal for Enzyme Chem., RSC 1986, Gabor Medal, Royal Soc. 1991, Max Tishler Prize, Harvard Univ. 1992, Harden Medal, Biochemical Soc. 1993, Feldberg Foundation Prize 1996, Davy Medal, Royal Soc. 1998, Anfinsen Award, The Protein Soc. 1999, Laureate, 'Chaire Bruylants', Louvain 1999, RSC Natural Products Award 1999, Stein and Moore Award, The Protein Soc. 2001, ACS Bader Award 2005, Linderstrøm-Lang Prize and Medal 2005, Bijvoet Medal 2008, G.N. Lewis Medal, Berkeley 2008, Royal Medal, Royal Soc. 2008, Wilhelm Exner Medal, Austrian Asscn for SME (Oesterreichischer Gewerbeverein—OGV) (jtly) 2009. *Publications include:* Enzyme Structure and Mechanism 1977, Structure and Mechanism in Protein Science 1999: A Guide to Enzyme Catalysis and Protein Folding, Jaques Staunton Chess Sets 1849–1939: A Collectors Guide 2007; papers in scientific journals. *Leisure interests:* chess, horology. *Address:* Gonville and Caius College, Cambridge, CB2 1TA (office); MRC Laboratory of Molecular Biology, Francis Crick Avenue, Cambridge, CB2 0QH, England (office). *Fax:* (1223) 332431 (office). *E-mail:* master@cai.cam.ac.uk (office); arf25@cam.ac.uk (office); alan@mrc-lmb.cam.ac.uk (office). *Website:* www.cai.cam.ac.uk/people/alan-fersht (office); www2.mrc-lmb.cam.ac.uk/group-leaders/a-to-g/alan-fersht (office); www.ch.cam.ac.uk/person/arf25 (office).

FERT, Albert, PhD; French physicist and academic; *Scientific Director, Unité Mixte de Physique, Centre National de la Recherche Scientifique-Thales;* b. 7 March 1938, Carcassonne; m.; two c.; ed Ecole Normale Supérieure, Paris, Université de Paris, Université Paris-Sud; Asst, Univ. of Grenoble 1962–64; Asst Prof., Université Paris-Sud (Orsay) 1966–76; Prof. of Physics, Université Paris-Sud 1976, Prof. Emer. 2013–; Scientific Dir Unité Mixte de Physique, CNRS-Thales (Orsay) 1995–; mem. French Acad. of Sciences 2004; Grand Croix, Ordre nat. du Mérite, Commdr, Légion d'honneur; American Physical Soc. New Materials Prize (co-recipient) 1994, IUPAP Magnetism Award (co-recipient) 1994, Grand Prix de Physique Jean Ricard, Soc. Française de Physique 1994, Hewlett-Packard Europhysics Prize (co-recipient) 1997, CNRS Gold Medal 2003, Japan Prize (co-recipient) 2007, Wolf Foundation Prize for Physics (co-recipient) 2007, Nobel Prize in Physics (co-recipient) 2007, Prix Gay-Lussac Humboldt 2014, Humboldt Research Award 2015. *Achievements include:* discoverer (with Peter Grünberg) of giant magnetoresistance phenomenon, which has led to enormous increase in storage capacity of magnetic hard-disk drives and has triggered the devt of a new field of research and tech., spintronics, to which he has made seminal contribs; recent works on magnetic skyrmions and topological insulators. *Publications:* about 350 articles in scientific journals or chapters of books. *Leisure interests:* jazz, cinema, windsurfing, mountain-hiking. *Address:* UMR CNRS/Thales, TRT, 1 avenue A. Fresnel, 91767 Palaiseau, France (office). *Telephone:* 1-69-41-58-64 (office). *Fax:* 1-69-41-58-64 (office). *E-mail:* albert.fert@cnrs-thales.fr (office). *Website:* www.cnrs-thales.fr (office).

FERZAT, Ali; Syrian political cartoonist; b. 22 June 1951, Hama; ed Damascus Univ. Faculty of Fine Arts; early work appeared in state-run newspapers including al-Thawra and Tishreen 1970s; gained int. recognition after cartoons were published in Le Monde (French newspaper) 1980; exhbn at Institut du Monde Arabe, Paris 1989; published satirical review Domari (Lamplighter) 2001–03 (forced to close when licence revoked); fmr Pres. League of Arab Cartoonists; Prins Claus Prize (Netherlands) 2002, EU Sakharov Prize 2011, Index on Censorship Freedom of Expression Award (Arts) 2012. *Website:* www.ali-ferzat.com (office).

FETERIS, Maarten W. C.; Dutch lawyer; *President, Supreme Court;* b. 10 March 1960, The Hague; ed Haganum Gymnasium; Research Asst, Univ. of Leiden 1982–83; Judicial Employee, Social Insurance 1983–86; Deputy Justice, Court Den Bosch 1994–2008; Tax Consultant, PricewaterhouseCoopers 1986–2008; Counselor, Supreme Court of the Netherlands 2008–13, Vice-Pres. 2013–14, Pres. 2014–; Prof., Erasmus Univ., Rotterdam 1994–. *Address:* De Hoge Raad der Nederlanden, Korte Voorhout 8, 2511 EK The Hague, Netherlands (office). *Telephone:* (70) 3611311 (office). *Fax:* (70) 7530347 (office). *E-mail:* info@hogeraad.nl (office). *Website:* www.rechtspraak.nl/organisatie/hoge-raad.

FETISOV, Vyacheslav Aleksandrovich; Russian professional ice hockey coach and fmr professional ice hockey player; *Head, Federal Agency for Physical Culture and Sports;* b. 20 April 1958, Moscow; m. Lada Fetisova; one d.; played with Cen. Army Sports Club 1975–89; USSR champion 1975, 1979–89; seven times world champion with USSR teams 1977–91; Olympic champion 1984, 1988; played with Nat. Hockey League (NHL) New Jersey Devils 1989–95, Detroit Red Wings 1995–98 (team won Stanley Cup 1997); Asst Coach New Jersey Devils 1998–2001; Gen. Man. and Coach Russian Olympic hockey team Salt Lake City 2002 (won bronze medal); Chair. Fed. Agency on Physical Culture and Sports 2002–; mem. Council of Founders of World Anti-Doping Agency (WADA), Head, Cttee of Sportsmen of WADA; Soviet Honoured Masters of Sport Award 1984, 1986, 1990, inducted into Hockey Hall of Fame 2001, UNESCO Champion for Sport 2004. *Address:* Federal Agency of Physical Culture and Sport, Kazakova str. 18, 105064

Moscow, Russia (office). *Telephone:* (495) 105-72-50 (office). *Fax:* (495) 267-34-40 (office). *E-mail:* info@rossport.ru (office). *Website:* www.rossport.ru (office).

FETTER, Trevor, BEcons, MBA; American business executive; b. 16 Jan. 1960, San Diego, Calif.; m.; two c.; ed Stanford Univ., Harvard Business School; Investment Banker, Merrill Lynch Capital Markets –1988; Exec. Vice-Pres. and Chief Financial Officer, Metro-Goldwyn-Mayer Inc. 1988–95; joined Tenet Healthcare Corpn 1995, Exec. Vice-Pres. and later Chief Financial Officer 1996–2000, Pres. 2002–03, apptd Pres. and CEO 2003, Chair. and CEO 2015–17; Chair. and CEO Broadlane Inc. 1995–2000; mem. Bd of Dirs Hartford Financial Services Group Inc., Fed. of American Hosps; mem. Advisory Bd, Harvard Business School Healthcare; fmr Dir Catalina Island Conservancy, Santa Barbara Zoological Gardens, Neighborhood Youth Asscn; Hon. Bd mem., Greater Dallas Chamber of Commerce. *Address:* c/o Tenet Healthcare Corporation, 1445 Ross Avenue, Suite 1400, Dallas, TX 75202, USA (office).

FETTIG, Jeff M., BA, MBA; American business executive; *CEO, Whirlpool Corporation;* b. 1957, Tipton, Ind.; ed Indiana Univ.; joined Whirlpool Corpn as Operations Assoc. 1981, various man. positions in sales, planning, operations and product devt 1981–89, Vice-Pres. Marketing, KitchenAid Appliance Group 1989–90, Vice-Pres., Marketing, Philips Whirlpool Appliance Group, Whirlpool Europe BV 1990–92, Vice-Pres., Group Marketing and Sales, N American Appliance Group 1992–94, Exec. Vice-Pres. Whirlpool Corpn and Pres. Whirlpool Europe and Asia 1994–99, apptd Dir Whirlpool Corpn 1999, Pres. and COO 1999–2004, Chair., Pres. and CEO 2004–06, Chair. and CEO 2006–17, CEO 2017–; mem. Pres. Trump's American Manufacturing Council Jan.–Aug. 2017; mem. Bd of Dirs Dow Chemical Co., Kohler Co.; mem. Business Leaders for Mich., Business Roundtable Asscn; mem. Dean's Advisory Council, Ind. Univ. Kelley School of Business; Trustee, Midwest Region, Boys and Girls Club of America. *Address:* Whirlpool Corporation, 2000 North M-63, Benton Harbor, MI 49022-2692, USA (office). *Telephone:* (269) 923-5000 (office). *Fax:* (269) 923-5443 (office). *E-mail:* info@whirlpoolcorp.com (office). *Website:* www.whirlpoolcorp.com (office).

FETTING, Rainer; German painter and sculptor; b. 31 Dec. 1949, Wilhelmshaven; ed Hochschule der Künste, Berlin, with Prof. Jänisch; Co-founder Galerie am Moritzplatz with Helmut Middendorf, Salomé, Bernd Zimmer, Anne Jud and Berthold Schepers, Luciano Castelli 1977; lived in New York and Berlin 1983–94, lives and works in Berlin and Sylt 2006–; DAAD scholarship, Columbia Univ., New York 1978. *Works include:* Willy Brandt sculpture for Willy-Brandt-Haus, Berlin 1996, Seven scultpures of Helmut Schmidt 2006. *Website:* www.fetting.de.

FEUILLÉE, Marc; French editor and newspaper executive; *Director-General, Le Figaro;* b. 1 Sept. 1962, Paris; ed secondary school in Dijon, Univ. of Paris I-Panthéon-Sorbonne, École des hautes études commerciales, Institut d'études politiques de Paris; Business Analyst, Hachette, Lagardère Group 1987–90; Financial Dir, L'Express 1990–98, Gen. Man. 1998–2006, CEO 2006–10; Vice-Pres. of Magazine Distribution, Libre Service Actualités 1996–98; Head of Syndicat de la presse magazine, SPM 2010–11; Dir-Gen. (CEO) Le Figaro newspaper 2011–; mem. Bd and Treas., OJD; mem. Supervisory Bd Presstalis; Pres. Syndicat de la presse quotidienne nationale. *Address:* Le Figaro, 14 blvd Haussmann, 75009 Paris, France (office). *Telephone:* 1-42-21-62-00 (office). *Fax:* 1-42-21-64-05 (office). *E-mail:* info@lefigaro.fr (office). *Website:* www.lefigaro.fr (office).

FEULNER, Edwin (Ed) John, Jr, MBA, PhD; American research institute administrator; *President and Chief Executive Officer, Heritage Foundation;* b. 12 Aug. 1941, s. of Edwin John Feulner, Sr and Helen Joan Feulner (née Franzen); m. Linda Claire Leventhal; one s. one d.; ed Immaculate Conception High School, Elmhurst, Ill., Regis Univ., Georgetown Univ., Univ. of Edinburgh and London School of Econs, UK; Pres. Heritage Foundation, Washington, DC 1973–2013, Pres. and CEO 2017–, continues as Chung Ju-yung Fellow and Chair. Asian Studies Center, Chancellor, Heritage Foundation; Treas. and Trustee, Mont Pelerin Soc. (also fmr Pres.); Trustee and fmr Chair. Intercollegiate Studies Inst.; Dir Nat. Chamber Foundation; adviser to several US govt depts and agencies; fmr Consultant for Domestic Policy to US Pres. Ronald Reagan; US Rep. to UN Special Session on Disarmament 1982; mem. numerous govt comms, including Carlucci Comm. on Foreign Aid 1983, Pres.'s Comm. on White House Fellows 1981–83, Meltzer Comm. 1999–2000; mem. Bd of Visitors, George Mason Univ.; fmr Pres. Philadelphia Soc.; fmr Dir Sequoia Bank, Regis Univ., Council for Nat. Policy; Trustee, Acton Inst., Int. Republican Inst.; Dr hc (Nichols Coll.) 1981, (Univ. Francisco Marroquin, Guatemala) 1982, (Bellevue Coll.) 1987, (Gonzaga Univ.) 1992, (Grove City Coll.) 1994, (Pepperdine Univ.) 2000, (St Norbert Coll.) 2002, (Hillsdale Coll.) 2004, (Thomas More Univ.) 2005, (Edin.) 2006, (Hanyang Univ., Korea); Presidential Citizen's Medal 1989. *Publications include:* US–Japan Mutual Security: The Next Twenty Years (ed.), China: The Turning Point (ed.), Looking Back 1981, Conservatives Stalk the House 1983, The March of Freedom 1998, Intellectual Pilgrims 1999, Leadership for America 2000, Getting America Right 2006; regular contrib. to Chicago Sun Times, Chicago Tribune, New York Times, Washington Post. *Address:* Heritage Foundation, 214 Massachusetts Avenue NE, Washington, DC 20002-4999, USA (office). *Telephone:* (202) 546-4400 (office). *Fax:* (202) 544-0904 (office). *E-mail:* staff@heritage.org (office). *Website:* www.heritage.org/about/staff/f/edwin-feulner (office).

FFOWCS WILLIAMS, John Eirwyn, MA, PhD, ScD (Cantab.), CEng, FREng, FRAeS, FInstP, FIMA, FRSA; British engineer and academic; *Rank Professor Emeritus of Engineering, Emmanuel College, Cambridge;* b. 25 May 1935; m. Anne Beatrice Mason 1959; two s. one d.; ed Derby Tech. Coll., Univ. of Southampton; eng apprentice, Rolls-Royce Ltd 1951–55; Spitfire Mitchell Memorial Scholar to Southampton Univ. 1955–60 (Pres. Students' Union 1957–58); joined Aerodynamics Div., Nat. Physical Lab. 1960–62; with Bolt, Beranek & Newman, Inc. 1962–64; Reader in Applied Math., Imperial Coll. of Science and Tech. 1964–69, Rolls-Royce Prof. of Theoretical Acoustics 1969–72; Rank Prof. of Eng, Univ. of Cambridge 1972–2002, now Rank Prof. Emer., Master, Emmanuel Coll., Cambridge 1996–2002 (Professorial Fellow 1972–96, Life Fellow 2002); Chair. Concorde Noise Panel 1965–75, Noise Research Cttee, Airport Regions Conf. 1969–76, Topexpress Ltd 1979–89; Dir VSEL Consortium PLC 1987–95; Foreign Assoc. Nat. Acad. of Eng, USA 1995; Fellow, AIAA, Inst. of Acoustics, Acoustical Soc. of America; Hon. Prof., Beijing Inst. of Aeronautics and Astronautics 1992–, Foreign Hon. mem. American Acad. of Arts and Sciences 1989; Aero-Acoustics Medal, AIAA 1977, Rayleigh Medal, Inst. of Acoustics 1984, Silver Medal, Soc. Française d'Acoustique 1989, Gold Medal, Royal Aeronautical Soc. 1990, Per Bruel Gold Medal, ASME 1997, Sir Frank Whittle Medal, Royal Acad. of Eng. 2002. *Publications include:* Sound and Sources of Sound (with A.P. Dowling) 1983, numerous articles in professional journals; film on Aerodynamic Sound (jtly). *Leisure interests:* friends and cigars. *Address:* Emmanuel College, Cambridge, CB2 3AP, England (office). *Telephone:* (1223) 334200 (office). *E-mail:* jef1000@cam.ac.uk (office). *Website:* www.emma.cam.ac.uk (office).

FFRENCH-DAVIS MUÑOZ, Ricardo, PhD; Chilean economist, academic and UN official; *Professor of Economics, University of Chile;* b. 27 June 1936, Santiago; m. Marcela Yampaglia 1966; ed Catholic Univ. of Chile, Univ. of Chicago, USA; Researcher and Prof. of Econs, Econ. Research Cen., Catholic Univ. 1962–64; Prof. of Econs, Univ. of Chile 1962–73, 1984–; Deputy Man. Research Dept, Cen. Bank of Chile 1964–70; Research Dir Cen. on Planning Studies, Catholic Univ. 1970–75; Vice-Pres. and Dir Centre for Latin American Econ. Research (CIEPLAN), Santiago 1976–90; Research Dir, Cen. Bank of Chile 1990–92; mem. Acad. Council, Latin American Program, The Woodrow Wilson Center, Washington, DC 1977–80; mem. UN Cttee on Econ. Planning 1990–92; Prin. Regional Adviser, Econ. Comm. for Latin America and the Caribbean (ECLAC) 1992–2004; Chair. Cttee for Devt Policy, UN 2007–10; mem. Exec. Cttee Latin American Studies Asscn 1992–94, School of Econs, Univ. of Chile 2007–; Visiting Fellow, Univ. of Oxford 1974, 1979; Visiting Prof., Boston Univ. 1976; Pres. Acad. Circle, Acad. de Humanismo Cristiano, Chile 1978–81; Co-ordinator Working Group on Econ. Issues of Inter-American Dialogue 1985–86; mem. Editorial Bds Latin American Research Review, El Trimestre Económico and Colección Estudios Cieplan; Profesor Extraordinario, Universidad Católica de Valparaíso; Dr hc (Universidad de Talca); Ford Foundation Grants 1971, 1975, 2001, Social Science Research Council Grant 1976, Inter-American Dialogue Grant 1985–86, Nat. Prize for the Humanities and Social Sciences 2005. *Publications:* Políticas Económicas en Chile: 1952–70 1973, El cobre en el desarrollo nacional (co-ed.) 1974, Economía internacional: teorías y políticas para el desarrollo 1979, 1985, Latin America and a New International Economic Order (co-ed.) 1981, 1985, The Monetarist Experiment in Chile 1982, Relaciones financieras externas y la economía latinoamericana (ed.) 1983, Development and External Debt in Latin America (co-ed.) 1988, Debt-equity swaps in Chile 1990, Latin America and the Caribbean: Policies to Improve Linkages with the World Economy (ed.) 1998, Macroeconomics, Trade and Finance 2000, Financial Crisis in 'Successful' Emerging Economies (ed.) 2001, Economic Reforms in Chile: From Dictatorship to Democracy 2002 (second edn 2010 and six edns in Spanish), Stability with Growth 2006 (co-author); more than 150 articles on int. econs, Latin-American econ. devt and Chilean econ. policies in nine languages. *Address:* Department of Economics, Universidad de Chile, Diagonal Paraguay 257, Office 1502, Santiago (office); Casilla 179-D, Santiago, Chile (home). *Telephone:* (2) 2978-3407 (office). *E-mail:* rffrench@econ.uchile.cl (office). *Website:* www.econ.uchile.cl/es/academico/rffrench (office).

FIALA, Petr, MA, LLM, PhD; Czech political scientist, academic, politician and fmr university administrator; *Leader, Občanská demokratická strana (Civic Democratic Party);* b. 1 Sept. 1964, Brno, Czechoslovak Socialist Repub. (now Czech Repub.); ed J.E. Purkyně Univ. (now Masaryk Univ.), Nottingham Trent Univ., UK; historian, Museum of the Kroměříž region 1988–89; Ed. Lidová demokracie daily newspaper 1990; Ed. Atlantis publishing house 1990; Asst, Dept of Econs and Political Science, Faculty of Arts, Masaryk Univ. 1990–91, Asst Prof., Dept of Political Science 1991–96, Head, Dept of Political Science, Faculty of Social Studies (at Faculty of Arts –1997) 1993–2002, Assoc. Prof., Dept of Political Science, Faculty of Social Studies (at Faculty of Arts –1997) 1996–2002, Dir Int. Inst. of Political Science 1996–2004, Prof., Dept of Int. Relations and European Studies, Faculty of Social Studies 2002–, Head, Dept of Int. Relations and European Studies 2002–04, Vice-Dean for Int. Relations and Doctoral Study 2000–04, Dir Inst. for Comparative Political Research 2004–11, Dean, Faculty of Social Studies 2004, Rector, Masaryk Univ. 2004–11, Rector Emer. 2011–, Vice-Rector for Academic Affairs 2011–12, Dir Int. Inst. of Political Science 2012; Docent (Assoc. Prof.) in Political Science, Faculty of Social Sciences, Charles Univ., Prague 1996–2002; Pres. Czech Rectors Conf. 2009–11; Chief Scientific Adviser to Prime Minister 2011–12; Perm. Sr Fellow, Centre for European Integration Studies (ZEI), Bonn, Germany 2001–; Vice-Chair. of Research, Devt and Innovation Council, Govt of Czech Repub. 2011–; mem. Scientific Bd, Palacký Univ., Olomouc 2003–, Nat. Economy Faculty, Univ. of Econs, Prague 2006–, Comenius Univ., Bratislava, Slovakia 2007–, Univ. of Veterinary and Pharmaceutical Sciences, Brno 2007–; mem. Academic Bd, Academie Rerum Civilium – Political and Social Sciences Univ., Kolín 2005–; mem. Acad. Ass., Acad. of Sciences of the Czech Repub. 2006–; mem. Academic Council, CEVRO Inst., Prague 2007–; mem. Bd, Inst. for the Study of Totalitarian Regimes 2007–; mem. Research and Devt Council, Govt of Czech Repub. 2008–; mem. Council for Higher Educ. Reform, Ministry of Educ. 2009–; mem. Bd of Govs (Hochschulrat), Universität Regensburg, Germany 2012–; mem. Editorial Bd, Czech Journal of Political Science 1994–, German Policy Studies/Politikfeldanalyse (USA) 1999–; Minister of Educ., Youth and Sport 2012–13; Leader, Občanská demokratická strana (Civic Democratic Party) 2014–. *Publications:* 14 monographs, including Laboratoř sekularizace (The Laboratory of Secularization) 2007, Evropská unie (The European Union) (co-author) 2009, Evropský mezičas (European Meantime) 2007, 2010, Politika, jaká nemá být (What Politics Should Not Be) 2010; more than 200 papers in various languages. *Address:* Občanská demokratická strana, Polygon House, Doudlebská 1699/5, 140 00 Prague 4, Czech Republic (office). *Telephone:* (2) 34707111 (office). *Fax:* (2) 34707103 (office). *E-mail:* hk@ods.cz (office). *Website:* www.ods.cz (office).

FIASCHI, Lorenzo; Italian gallery director; *Co-Director and Partner, Galleria Continua;* co-f., with Mario Cristiani and Maurizio Rigillo, Galleria Continua in San Gimignano, Tuscany 1990, other locations include Beijing 2004 and Boissy-le-Châtel, France, 2007–; represents several major artists, including Daniel Buren, Kendell Geers, Anish Kapoor and Hans Op de Beeck. *Address:* Galleria Continua, Via del Castello 11, 53037 San Gimignano, Italy (office). *Telephone:* (0577) 943134 (office). *E-mail:* info@galleriacontinua.com (office). *Website:* www.galleriacontinua.com (office).

FICEAC, Bogdan; Romanian editor and newspaper executive; fmr Deputy Ed.-in-Chief, România Liberă (Free Romania), Bucharest, then Ed.-in-Chief; Reuters Foundation Fellow, John S. Knight Fellowship, Stanford Univ. *Publications include:* Cenzura comunista 1999, Tehnici de manipulare 2004.

FICO, Robert, JUDr, CSc; Slovak politician and lawyer; *Leader, Smer—Sociálna demokracia (Direction—Social Democracy);* b. 15 Sept. 1964, Topoľčany, Czechoslovak Socialist Repub. (now Slovakia); m. Svetlana Svobodová 1988; one s.; ed Comenius Univ., Bratislava; mem. staff Inst. of Laws, Ministry of Justice 1986–91; mem. CP 1987–90; mem. Strana Demokratickej Ľavice (SDĽ—Party of Democratic Left) 1990–99, Vice-Chair. 1998–99; mem. Nat. Council 1992–2006, 2010–12; Head of Slovak del. to Parl. Meeting of European Council, Rep. to European Cttee for Human Rights and European Court for Human Rights 1994–2000; Founder and Chair. Smer (Direction) party 1999– (absorbed Strana Občianskeho Porozumenia (Party of Civic Understanding) 2003, Sociálnodemokratická alternativa (Social Democratic Alternative), Sociálnodemokratická Strana Slovenksa (Social Democratic Party of Slovakia) and Strana demokratickej ľavice (Party of the Democratic Left) 2004, renamed Smer—Sociálna demokracia (Direction—Social Democracy) 2004, Pres. Parl. Mems' Club 2002–; Observer on behalf of European Socialists' faction at European Parl. 2002–04; Prime Minister 2006–10, 2012–18 (resgnd); unsuccessful cand. in presidential election 2014. *Publication:* Trest smrti (The Death Penalty). *Leisure interest:* sport. *Address:* Smer—Sociálna demokracia, Súmračná 25, 821 02 Bratislava, Slovakia (office). *E-mail:* generalny.manager@strana-smer.sk (office). *Website:* www.strana-smer.sk (office).

FIDAI, Muhammad Halim, MA, MBA; Afghan politician and journalist; b. 28 Dec. 1970, Paktika Prov.; m. Samina Fidai; four c.; ed High Teachers' Inst., Peshawar, Pakistan; worked with several NGOs in Afghanistan since 1990s, including Dir-Gen., American Center 1989–2002; Head of Media Dept, CARE International 1995–2003, also Ed.-in-Chief Pamlarana Magazine 1995–2003; Communication Man., Creative Assocs 2003–05; Media and Communication Dir Counterpart Int. 2005–08; Country Dir in Afghanistan, South Asia Free Media Asscn 2007–08; Gov. Wardak Prov. 2008–12. *Leisure interests:* reading and writing.

FIDALGO, José María; Spanish trade union official, orthopaedic surgeon and academic; b. 18 Feb. 1948, León; orthopaedic surgeon, Hosp. La Paz, Madrid; mem. trade union movt 1974–; mem. Confederación Sindical de Comisiones Obreras (CCOO) 1977–, Sec. of Institutional Policy 1987–2000, Gen. Sec. 2000–08; Gen. Sec. Fed. of Health Workers 1981–87; Dir Negocia, Negotiation and Mediation Centre, IE Law School, Madrid 2009–. *Address:* IE Law School, María de Molina, 11, 28006 Madrid, Spain (office). *Telephone:* (91) 5689600 (office). *Website:* www.ie.edu/IE/site/php/en/school_law.php (office).

FIELD, Sir Malcolm David, Kt; British business executive; b. 25 Aug. 1937, London; m. (divorced 1982); one d.; m. 2nd Rosemary Anne Charlton 2001; ed Highgate School and London Business School; joined W.H. Smith 1963, Wholesale Dir 1970–78, Man. Dir Retail Group 1978–82, Man. Dir 1982–93; Group Chief Exec. 1994–96; Chair. Civil Aviation Authority 1996–2001; apptd Policy Adviser to Dept of Transport, London and the Regions 2000; mem. Bd of Man. Navy, Army and Air Force Insts 1973–93, Chair. 1986–93; Dir (non-exec.) Marine Environment Protection Cttee 1989–99, Scottish & Newcastle PLC 1993–98, Phoenix Group 1994–97, The Stationery Office 1996–2001, Walker Greenbank PLC 1997–2001, Sofa Workshop Ltd 1998–2002, Beeson Gregory 2000–04, Odgers 2002–; Chair. (non-exec.) Tubelines Ltd 2003–06; Chair. Aricom PLC 2004–06; Sr Dir Hochschild Mining 2006–. *Leisure interests:* watching cricket, tennis, ballet, modern art, reading biographies, recreating garden in Devon. *Address:* 21 Embankment Gardens, London, SW3 4LW, England (office). *Telephone:* (20) 7351-7455 (office); (7740) 433744 (home). *Fax:* (20) 7351-7452 (office). *E-mail:* mdfield@netcomuk.co.uk (office).

FIELD, Sally; American actress and film producer; b. 6 Nov. 1946, Pasadena, Calif.; m. Alan Greisman 1984; three c.; ed Actor's Studio; co.-f. Fogwood Films Ltd (production co.) 1984. *Films include:* The Way West 1967, Stay Hungry 1976, Smokey and the Bandit 1977, Hooper 1978, Norma Rai (Cannes Film Festival Best Actress Award 1979, Acad. Award 1980) 1979, Beyond the Poseidon Adventure 1979, Smokey and the Bandit II 1980, Absence of Malice 1981, Places in the Heart (Acad. Award 1984) 1984, Murphy's Romance (also exec. producer) 1985, Punchline 1987, Steel Magnolias 1989, Not Without My Daughter 1991, Soapdish 1991, Dying Young (co-producer) 1991, Homeward Bound: The Incredible Journey (voice) 1993, Mrs Doubtfire 1993, Forrest Gump 1994, Eye for an Eye 1996, Homeward Bound II: Lost in San Francisco (voice) 1996, Where the Heart Is 2000, Time of Our Lives 2000, Say It Isn't So 2001, Legally Blonde 2: Red, White & Blonde 2003, Two Weeks 2006, The Amazing Spider-Man 2012, Lincoln 2012, The Amazing Spider-Man 2 2014, Hello, My Name Is Doris 2015, Little Evil 2017. *TV appearances include:* Gidget (series) 1965, The Flying Nun (series) 1967–69, Maybe I'll Come Home In the Spring 1971, Marriage: Year One 1971, Home for the Holidays 1972, The Girl With Something Extra (series) 1973, Bridges 1976, Sybil (Emmy Award 1977) 1976, A Woman of Independent Means (mini-series) 1995, Merry Christmas, George Bailey 1997, From the Earth to the Moon (mini-series) 1998, A Cooler Climate 1999, David Copperfield 2000, ER (series) 2000–06, The Court (series) 2002, Conviction 2005, Brothers & Sisters (Emmy Award for Best Actress in a Drama Series 2007) 2006–11. *Plays:* The Goat, or Who Is Sylvia? 2002, The Glass Menagerie 2017. *Address:* 9830 Wilshire Blvd, Suite 1000, Beverly Hills, CA 90212; c/o Creative Artists Agency, 2000 Avenue of the Stars, Los Angeles, CA 90067, USA.

FIELDING, Sir Leslie, Kt, KCMG, LLD, FRSA, FRGS; British fmr university vice-chancellor and diplomatist; b. 29 July 1932, London, England; s. of Percy Archer Fielding and Margaret Calder Horry; m. Sally Harvey 1978; one s. one d.; ed Emmanuel Coll., Cambridge, School of Oriental and African Studies, London, St Antony's Coll., Oxford; with HM Diplomatic Service (served Tehran, Singapore, Phnom Penh, Paris and London) 1956–73; Dir External Relations Directorate-Gen., European Comm., Brussels 1973–77; Visiting Fellow, St Antony's Coll., Oxford 1977–78; Head EC Del., Tokyo 1978–82; Dir-Gen. for External Relations, Brussels 1982–87; Vice-Chancellor Univ. of Sussex 1987–92; mem. Japan-EC Asscn 1988–98, UK-Japan 2000 Group 1993–2000; mem. House of Laity of Gen. Synod of Church of England 1990–92; Hon. Pres. Univ. Asscn for Contemporary European Studies 1990–2000; Hon. Fellow, Emmanuel Coll. Cambridge 1990–, Sussex European Inst. 1993; Grand Officer's Star, Order of St Agatha of San Marino 1987, White Rose of Finland 1988, Silver Order of Merit (Austria) 1989. *Publications:* Travellers' Tales (contrib.) 1999, More Tales from the Travellers' (contrib.) 2005, Before the Killing Fields: Witness to Cambodia and the Vietnam War 2008, Kindly Call Me God: The Misadventures of 'Fielding of the FO', Eurocrat Extraordinaire and Vice-Chancellor Semipotentiary 2009, Twilight over the Temples: The Close of Cambodia's Belle Epoque 2010, The Mistress of the Bees 2011, Mentioned in Despatches (Phnom Penh, Paris, Tokyo, Brussels): Is Diplomacy Dead? 2012. *Leisure interests:* country life, theology. *Address:* Wild Cherry Farm, Elton, nr Ludlow, Shropshire, SY8 2HQ, England. *E-mail:* fieldingleslie@aol.com.

FIELDS, Janice (Jan) L.; American business executive; m. Doug Fields; two c.; joined McDonald's as restaurant crew mem. 1978, worked in all facets of restaurant business, served as a Dir of Store Man. and Operations from 1978, apptd Regional Vice-Pres. Pittsburgh Region 1994, Vice-Pres. McDonald's Great Lakes Div. May 2000, Pres. Cen. Div., McDonald's USA –2006, Exec. Vice-Pres. and COO McDonald's USA, LLC 2006–10, Pres. 2010–12, Exec. Sponsor for Career Devt Program; mem. Bd of Dirs Monsanto Co. 2008–; Chair. and mem. Advisory Bd Catalyst, Inc. (women's org.); Dir of Ronald McDonald House Charities, Chicago Urban League; McDonald's Pres.'s Award 1988, McDonald's Golden Arch Partners Award 1988, McDonald's Women Operators Network Recognition Award 2001, McDonald's Women's Leadership Award 2002.

FIELDS, Mark, BA, MBA; American automotive industry executive; b. 24 Jan. 1961, Brooklyn, New York; s. of Gerald S. Fields and Elinor Fields; m. Jane Fields; two s.; ed Paramus High School, NJ, Rutgers Univ., Harvard Univ.; worked for IBM; joined Ford Motor Co. 1989, Man. Dir Ford of Argentina 1997–98, Sr Man. Dir of Marketing and Sales, Mazda Motor Corpn (subsidiary) 1998, CEO 1998–2002, Chair. Premier Automotive Group (luxury unit which included Lincoln, Aston Martin, Jaguar, Land Rover and Volvo Cars) 2002–04, Exec. Vice-Pres. Ford Europe 2004–05, Exec. Vice-Pres. and Pres. Americas Operations 2005–12, COO Ford Motor Co. 2012–14, mem. Bd of Dirs, Pres. and CEO 2014–17; mem. Bd of Dirs, IBM 2016–; Chair. US–China Business Council. *Address:* c/o Ford Motor Company, World Headquarters, One American Road, Dearborn, MI 48126-2798, USA (office).

FIENNES, Joseph Alberic; British actor; b. 27 May 1970, Salisbury; s. of Mark Fiennes and Jini Lash; brother of Ralph Fiennes (q.v.), Martha, Magnus, Sophie and Jacob Fiennes; m. María Dolores Diéguez 2009; one d.; ed Guildhall School of Music and Drama. *Theatre includes:* The Woman in Black, A Month in the Country, A View from the Bridge, Real Classy Affair, Edward II, Love's Labours Lost, Epitaph for George Dillon (Comedy Theatre, London) 2005–06, Cyrano de Bergerac (Chichester Festival Theatre) 2009. *RSC performances include:* Son of Man, Les Enfants Du Paradis, As You Like It, Troilus and Cressida, The Herbal Bed. *Television includes:* The Vacillations of Poppy Carew 1995, Animated Epics: Beowulf (voice) 1998, FlashForward 2009–10, Camelot (mini-series) 2011. *Radio:* Romeo and Juliet, Keith Douglas Poems. *Films include:* Stealing Beauty 1996, Shakespeare in Love 1998, Martha – Meet Frank, Daniel and Laurence 1998, Elizabeth 1998, Forever Mine 1999, Rancid Aluminium 2000, Enemy at the Gates 2001, Killing Me Softly 2001, Dust 2001, Leo 2002, Sinbad: Legend of the Seven Seas 2003, Luther 2003, Merchant of Venice 2004, Man to Man 2005, The Great Raid 2005, The Darwin Awards 2006, Running with Scissors 2006, Goodbye Bafana 2007, The Escapist 2007, Pretty/Handsome 2008, Spring 1941 2008, Against the Current 2009, The Games Maker 2014, Hercules 2014. *Address:* c/o Tracy Brennan, Creative Artists Agency, 2000 Avenue Of The Stars, Los Angeles, CA 90067, USA (office). *E-mail:* josephfiennesnet@gmail.com (office). *Website:* www.joseph-fiennes.net (office).

FIENNES, Ralph Nathaniel Twisleton Wykeham; British actor; b. 22 Dec. 1962, Ipswich, Suffolk; s. of Mark Fiennes and Jennifer (Jini) Lash; brother of Joseph Fiennes (q.v.); m. Alex Kingston 1993 (divorced 1997); partner Francesca Annis 1995–2006; ed St Kieran's Coll., Kilkenny and Newtown School, Co. Waterford, Ireland, Bishop Wordsworth's School, Salisbury, Chelsea School of Art, Royal Acad. of Dramatic Art, London; Jameson Empire Award 2015, European Achievement in World Cinema, European Film Awards 2018. *Theatre includes:* Open Air Theatre, Regent's Park: Twelfth Night, Ring Round the Moon 1985, A Midsummer's Night Dream 1985, 1986, Romeo and Juliet 1986; Royal Nat. Theatre: Six Characters in Search of an Author 1987, Fathers and Sons, Ting Tang Mine 1987, Man and Superman 2015; RSC: Much Ado About Nothing 1988, title role of Henry VI in The Plantagenets 1988, Playing with Trains 1989, King John 1989, The Man Who Came to Dinner 1989, Troilus and Cressida, King Lear 1990, Love's Labours Lost 1991; Almeida Theatre: Hamlet 1995, Ivanov 1997, Richard II 2000, Coriolanus 2000, Brand 2003, Oedipus 2008, The Tempest 2011; Man and Superman, Nat. Thatre, London 2015, The Master Builder, Old Vic 2016, Richard III, Almeida 2016. *Films include:* Wuthering Heights 1992, The Baby of Mâcon 1993, Schindler's List (BAFTA Award for Best Actor in a Supporting Role) 1993, Quiz Show 1994, Strange Days 1995, The English Patient 1996, Oscar and Lucinda 1997, The Avengers 1998, The Prince of Egypt (voice) 1998, Onegin (also exec. producer) 1999, Sunshine 1999, The End of the Affair 1999, Spider 2002, The Good Thief 2002, Red Dragon 2002, Maid in Manhattan 2002, The Chumscrubber 2005, Chromophobia 2005, Harry Potter and the Goblet of Fire 2005, The Constant Gardener 2005, The White Countess 2005, Wallace & Gromit in the Curse of the Were-Rabbit (voice) 2005, Land of the Blind 2006, Harry Potter and the Order of the Phoenix 2007, Bernard and Doris 2007, In Bruges 2008, The Duchess 2008, The Hurt Locker 2008, The Reader 2008, Cemetery Junction 2009, Clash of the Titans 2009, Harry Potter and the Half-Blood Prince 2009, Harry Potter and the Deathly Hallows: Part 1 2010, Coriolanus (actor and dir (debut)) 2010, Wrath of the Titans 2012, Great Expectations 2012, Skyfall 2012, The Invisible Woman 2013, The Grand Budapest Hotel 2014, Spectre 2015, A Bigger Splash 2015, Hail Caesar! 2016, The White Crow 2018, Holmes and Watson 2018. *Television includes:* Prime Suspect (film) 1991, Great Performances: A Dangerous Man: Lawrence after Arabia (series) 1992, Screen Two: The Cormorant (series) 1993, The Great War and the Shaping of the 20th Century (series) (voice of Wilfred Owen) 1996, How Proust Can Change Your Life (film) 2000, The Miracle Maker (voice) 2000, Freedom: A History of Us (series documentary) 2003, Page Eight (film) 2011, Rev. (series) 2011, Turks & Caicos 2014. *Address:* c/o Dalzell & Beresford Ltd, 26 Astwood Mews, London, SW7 4DE, England (office). *Telephone:* (20) 7341-9411 (office). *Fax:* (20) 7341-9412 (office). *E-mail:* mail@dbltd.co.uk (office). *Website:* www.dalzellandberesford.com (office).

FIENNES, Sir Ranulph Twisleton-Wykeham-, 3rd Bt, cr. 1916, OBE, DLitt; British travel writer, lecturer and explorer; b. 7 March 1944, Windsor; s. of Lt-Col Sir Ranulph Twisleton-Wykeham-Fiennes, DSO, 2nd Bt and Audrey Newson; m. 1st Virginia Pepper 1970 (died 2004); m. 2nd Louise Millington 2005; one d.; ed Eton; Lt Royal Scots Greys 1966, Capt. 1968, retd 1970; attached 22 SAS Regt 1966, Sultan of Muscat's Armed Forces 1968; Leader, British Expeditions to White Nile 1969, Jostedalsbre Glacier 1970, Headless Valley, BC 1971, (Towards) North Pole 1977; Leader, Transglobe Expedition (first polar circumnavigation of world on its polar axis) 1979–82; led first unsupported crossing of Antarctic continent and longest unsupported polar journey in history Nov. 1992–Feb. 1993; first man to reach both poles on land; discovered lost city of Ubar in Oman 1993; ran seven marathons on seven continents in seven days 2003; climbed north face of Mount Eiger 2007; climbed Mount Everest 2009; Exec. Consultant to Chair. of Occidental Petroleum Corpn 1984–90; Hon. mem. Royal Inst. of Navigation; Hon. DSc (Loughborough Coll.) 1986, Hon. DUniv (Univ. of Cen. England in Birmingham) 1995, (Univ. of Portsmouth) 2000, (Sheffield) 2005, (Univ. of Abertay, Dundee) 2007, Hon. DLitt (Glasgow Caledonian) 2002; Dhofar Campaign Medal 1969, Sultan's Bravery Medal 1970, Livingstone Medal, Royal Scottish Geographical Soc., Royal Inst. of Navigation 1977, Gold Medal of Explorers Club of New York 1983, Founders Medal Royal Geographical Soc. 1984, Polar Medal for Arctic and Antarctic, with Bars 1985, with clasp 1995, ITN Award for Int. Exploit of the Decade 1989, Explorers Club Millennium Award for Polar Exploration 2000, ITV1 Greatest Briton – Sportsman of the Year 2007. *Achievements include:* has raised £16 million for various charities (Just Giving Top Fundraiser 2011). *Film:* Killer Elite 2011 (based on The Feather Men). *Publications include:* A Talent for Trouble 1970, Ice Fall in Norway 1972, The Headless Valley 1973, Where Soldiers Fear to Tread 1975, Hell on Ice 1979, To the Ends of the Earth 1983, Bothie – The Polar Dog (with Virginia Twisleton-Wykeham-Fiennes) 1984, Living Dangerously 1987, The Feather Men 1991, Atlantis of the Sands 1992, Mind over Matter 1993, The Sett 1996, Fit for Life 1998, Beyond the Limits 2000, The Secret Hunters 2001, Captain Scott 2003, Mad Bad and Dangerous to Know (autobiography) 2007, Mad Dogs And Englishmen 2009, My Heroes 2011, Cold 2013. *Leisure interests:* langlauf, photography. *Address:* Greenlands, Exford, Minehead, West Somerset, TA24 7NU, England (office). *Telephone:* (1643) 831350 (office).

FIER, Florisvaldo, (Dr Rosinha); Brazilian physician, politician and international organization official; *High Representative General, Mercosur;* b. 12 Nov. 1950, Rolândia; ed Pontifícia Universidade Católica de Paraná; worked for several years in health clinics on outskirts of Curitiba during 1980s; Founder and Dir Union of Municipal Civil Servants (Sismuc); fmr Dir Brazilian Center for Health Studies; co-f. Partido dos Trabalhadores (PT) and Central Única dos Trabalhadores (central union confed.) early 1980s; Councillor, Curitiba 1989–91; State Rep., Paraná 1991–99; mem. Câmara dos Deputados (Parl.) for Paraná 1998–2015; Vice-Pres. Mercosur Parl. 2008–09, High Rep. Gen., Mercosur 2015–; Ordem de Rio Branco. *Address:* Edificio Mercosur, Luis Piera 1992, 1°, 11200 Montevideo, Uruguay (office). *Telephone:* 2412 9024 (office). *Fax:* 2418 0557 (office). *E-mail:* secretaria@mercosur.org.uy (office). *Website:* www.mercosur.int (office).

FIERSTEIN, Harvey Forbes; American actor and screenwriter; b. 6 June 1954, Brooklyn, New York; s. of Irving Fierstein and Jacqueline Harriet Gilbert; ed Pratt Univ.; began acting career as founding mem. The Gallery Players, Brooklyn; professional acting debut in Pork 1971; Fund for Human Dignity Award 1983, GLAAD Award for Visibility 1994, Humanitas Prize (in Children's Animation category) 2000; also three Drama Desk Awards, Drama League Award, New York Magazine Award, a special Obie, Theater World and LA Drama Critics Circle Award. *Films include:* Garbo Talks 1984, The Times of Harvey Milk (narrator) 1984, Torch Song Trilogy (also writer) 1988, The Harvest 1993, Mrs. Doubtfire 1993, Bullets Over Broadway 1994, Dr. Jekyll and Ms. Hyde 1995, White Lies 1996, Independence Day 1996, Everything Relative 1996, Kull the Conqueror 1997, Mulan (voice) 1998, Safe Men 1998, Jump 1999, Playing Mona Lisa 2000, Death to Smoochy 2002, Duplex 2003, Mulan II (voice) 2004, Farce of the Penguins (voice) 2007, The Samurai 2013, Foodfight! (voice) 2012, Animal Crackers (voice) 2017. *TV appearances include:* The Demon Murder Case (voice) 1983, Apology 1986, Tidy Endings 1988, In the Shadow of Love: A Teen AIDS Story 1992, Daddy's Girls (series) 1994, Happily Ever After: Fairy Tales for Every Child (voice) 1995, Stories from My Childhood (series, voice) 1998, X-Chromosome (series, voice) 1999, Double Platinum 1999, The Sissy Duckling (also writer, voice) 1999, Common Ground (also writer) 2000, Hairspray Live! (also writer, film) 2016. *Plays:* Torch Song Trilogy (writer and actor) (four Tony Awards including Best Actor (Play) and Author of Best Play 1983) 1982, La Cage aux Folles (librettist) (Tony Award for Best Book (Musical) 1984) 1983, Legs Diamond (author) 1988, Hairspray (Best Actor (Musical) 2003) 2003, Fiddler on the Roof 2005, A Catered Affair (also co-author) 2007, Newsies (author) 2012, Kinky Boots (author) (Tony Award for Best Musical 2013) 2012. *Leisure interests:* gay rights activist, painting, gardening, cooking. *Address:* c/o William Morris Agency, 1325 Avenue of the Americas, New York, NY 10019, USA.

FIFOR, Mihai-Viorel, BA, MA, MPA; Romanian politician; b. 10 May 1970, Turnu Severin; m. Adina Fifor; ed Univ. of Craiova, Univ. of Turku, Finland, Central European Univ., Budapest, Hungary, Leeds Univ., UK, Nat. School of Political and Admin. Studies, Bucharest, Nat. Defence Coll., Romanian Diplomatic Inst.; Sr Research Scientist, C.S. Nicolăescu-Plopşor Social and Human Research Inst., Romanian Acad., Craiova 1994–2002; Dir and Research Scientist, Dolj Traditional Culture Preservation and Promotion Centre 2001–04; Sr Lecturer, later Assoc. Prof., Faculty of Letters, Univ. of Craiova 2003; Gen. Man., Oltenia Museum, Craiova 2005–12; Sec. of State, Ministry of Admin and Interior Jan.–Oct. 2009, Sec. of State for Local Communities May–Dec. 2012; mem. Senate (upper house of parl.) (Partidul Social Democrat—PSD—Social Democratic Party) 2012–; Minister of Economy June–Sept. 2017; Minister of Nat. Defence 2017–18 (resgnd); Acting Prime Minister 16–29 Jan. 2018; mem. PSD. *Address:* 200390 jud. Doj, Craiova, Str. Mihail Kogălniceanu 19, Romania (office). *Telephone:* (78) 4072831 (office). *E-mail:* mihai@fifor.ro (office). *Website:* www.fifor.ro (office).

FIGALLI, Alessio; Italian mathematician; *Professor, ETH Zürich;* b. 2 April 1984, Rome; m.; ed Univ. of Pisa, Scuola Normale Superiore, Pisa, Ecole Normale Supérieure, Lyon; CNRS Researcher, Univ. of Nice 2007–08; Prof., Ecole Polytechnique, Palaiseau, France 2008–09; Assoc. Prof. and Harrington Faculty Fellow, Univ. of Texas at Austin 2009–10, Assoc. Prof. 2010–11, Full Prof. 2011–13, Full Prof. and R. L. Moore Chair 2013–16; Full Prof. and Chair, ETH Zürich 2016–; Fellow and Hon. mem. European Acad. of Sciences 2017; Foreign mem. Royal Spanish Acad. of Sciences 2018; Dr hc (Univ. Côte d'Azur) 2018; Kt, Order of Merit of the Italian Repub. 2018; Accademia Nazionale dei Lincei Giuseppe Borgia Prize 2008, Gioacchino Iapichino Prize 2010, Feltrinelli Prize 2017, European Math. Soc. Prize 2012, Stampacchia Gold Medal 2015, Int. Math. Union Fields Medal 2018. *Address:* Department of Mathematics, ETH Zürich, HG G 63.2, Rämistrasse 101, 8092 Zürich, Switzerland (office). *E-mail:* alessio.figalli@math.ethz.ch (office). *Website:* people.math.ethz.ch/~afigalli (office).

FIGEĽ, Ján, MSc, PhD; Slovak politician and research scientist; *Special Envoy for the promotion of freedom of religion outside the EU;* b. 20 Jan. 1960, Vranov nad Topľou; m.; four c.; ed Košice Tech. Univ., Georgetown Univ., USA, Universitaire Faculteiten Sint-Ignatius Antwerpen, Antwerp, Belgium, St Elisabeth Univ. of Health and Social Work, Bratislava; Research and Devt Scientist, ZPA Prešov 1983–92; mem. Parl. 1992–98, 2002–, mem. Foreign Affairs Cttee, Cttee for European Integration 1992–98, Chair. Foreign Affairs Cttee 2002–; mem. Krestansko-demokratické hnutie (KDH—Christian Democratic Movt) 1990–, mem. Party Presidium 1992–98, Deputy Chair. for Foreign Policy 1992–94, 1994–98, 2000–04, Chair. KDH 2010–16; State Sec., Ministry of Foreign Affairs 1998–2002; Chief Negotiator for Slovakia's accession to EU 1998–2003; mem. Presidium Slovak Democratic Coalition 1998–2000; Vice-Chair. European People's Party (EPP) in Parl. Ass. 1998; mem. Convention on the Future of Europe 2002–03; Head, Standing Del. of Observers of European Parl. 2003–04; Presidency mem. EPP-ED fraction in European Parl. 2003–04; mem. European Parl. Cttee on Econ. Affairs and Devt 2003–04, Vice-Chair. 2004; EU Commr without Portfolio Jan.–Nov. 2004, for Educ., Training, Culture and Multilingualism 2004–06, for Educ., Training, Culture and Youth 2007–09; First Deputy Prime Minister and Minister of Transport, Posts and Telecommunications 2010–11, First Deputy Prime Minister and Minister of Transport, Construction and Regional Devt 2011–12; Lecturer in Int. Relations, Univ. of Trnava 1995–2000; EC Special Envoy for the promotion of freedom of religion outside the EU 2016–; mem. Cen. European Forum, Int. Cttee for Support of Democracy in Cuba; Pres. Pan-European Union in Slovakia; mem. Bd of Dirs Slovak Soc. for Foreign Policy, Anton Tunega Foundation, Foundation for the Support of Social Change; mem. Council Cen. European Inst. for Econ. and Social Reforms; Hon. Pres., Centre for European Policy, Kolping Work Slovakia, Hon. Citizen of Ústí nad Topľou 2005, Hon. Prof., Tech. Univ. of Cluj-Napoca, Romania 2007, Hon. Chair., Centre for European Policy, Kolping Soc. in Slovakia; Chevalier, Légion d'honneur 2004; Dr hc (Tech. Univ. of Košice) 2006, (Dimitri Cantemir Christian Univ., Bucharest) 2008, (Univ. of Trnava) 2009; Andrew Elias Prize, Czechoslovak Soc. of Arts and Science, Washington, DC 2004, Gold Medal, Int. Relations Council of Christians and Jews, Cambridge, UK 2006, Prešov Region Prize 2006, Freedom Prize, Int. Peace Centre, Sarajevo 2007. *Publications:* Slovakia on the Road to EU Membership (co-author) 2002, Slovakia on the Road to the European Union (with Miroslav Adam) 2003, Ageing Europe 2005, Return Home 2009. *Address:* Directorate General for International Cooperation and Development, Rue de la Loi 41, 1049 Brussels, Belgium (office). *Telephone:* (2) 299-11-11 (office). *E-mail:* Virginia.manzitti@ec.europa.eu (office). *Website:* www.ec.europa.eu/europeaid/special-envoy-jan-figel_en (office); www.janfigel.eu.

FIGES, Orlando, PhD; British historian, writer and academic; *Professor of History, Birkbeck College, London;* b. 20 Nov. 1959; s. of John Figes and Eva Figes (née Unger); m. Stephanie Palmer 1990; two d.; ed Gonville and Caius Coll., Cambridge, Trinity Coll., Cambridge; Fellow, Trinity Coll., Cambridge 1984–89, Dir of Studies in History 1988–98, Lecturer in History, Univ. of Cambridge 1987–99; Prof. of History, Birkbeck Coll., Univ. of London 1999–; regular contrib. to New York Review of Books. *Publications include:* Peasant Russia, Civil War: the Volga Countryside in Revolution 1917–21 1989, A People's Tragedy: the Russian Revolution 1891–1924 (Wolfson History Prize, WHSmith Literary Award, NCR Book Award, Los Angeles Times Book Prize) 1996, Interpreting the Russian Revolution (co-author) 1999, Natasha's Dance: a Cultural History of Russia 2002, The Whisperers: Private Life in Stalin's Russia 2007, Crimea: The Last Crusade 2010, Just Send Me Word: A True Story of Love and Survival in the Gulag 2012. Revolutionary Russia, 1891–1991 2014; numerous review articles and contribs to other published books. *Leisure interests:* football, wine, gardening. *Address:* School of History, Classics and Archaeology, Birkbeck College, Malet Street, London, WC1E 7HX, England (office). *Telephone:* (20) 7631-6299 (office). *Fax:* (20) 7631-6552 (office). *E-mail:* o.figes@bbk.ac.uk (office). *Website:* www.bbk.ac.uk/hca/staff/orlandofiges (office); www.orlandofiges.com.

FIGGIS, Brian Norman, PhD, DSc, FAA; Australian chemist and academic; *Professor Emeritus of Inorganic Chemistry, University of Western Australia;* b. 27 March 1930, Sydney; s. of John N. E. Figgis and Dorice B. M. Figgis (née Hughes); m. Jane S. Frank 1968; one s. one d.; ed Univs of Sydney and New South Wales; Research Fellow, then Lecturer, Univ. Coll., London, UK 1957–62; Reader, Univ. of Western Australia 1963–69, Prof. 1969, now Prof. Emer.; Visiting Prof., Univ. of Texas, USA 1961, Univ. of Arizona 1968, Univ. of Florence, Italy 1975, Univ. of Sussex, UK 1975; Visiting Scientist, Institut Laue-Langevin, France, Brookhaven Nat. Lab., Upton, NY, USA, Argonne Nat. Lab., Ill. 1984, 1991; Inorganic Award, Royal Australian Chemical Inst. 1985, Walter Burfitt Prize, Royal Soc. of NSW 1986, H.G. Smith Medal, Royal Australian Chemical Inst. 1989, Centenary Medal 2003. *Publications:* Introduction to Ligand Fields 1966, Ligand Field Theory and Its Applications 2000; Ed. Transition Metal Chemistry (Vols 8 and 9) 1984–85; 220 articles in scientific journals. *Leisure interest:* DIY. *Address:* 9 Hamersley Street, Cottesloe, WA 6011, Australia. *Telephone:* (8) 9384-3032. *E-mail:* bnf@cyllene.uwa.edu.au.

FIGGIS, Mike; British film director, writer and musician; b. 28 Feb. 1949, Carlisle; two s.; studied music, performing in band Gas Board; musician in experimental theatre group The People Show in early 1970s; made ind. films including Redheugh, Slow Fade, Animals of the City; made film The House for

Channel 4 (UK); Inst. of Film Professionals Ind. Spirit Award 1996, Nat. Soc. of Film Critics Award. *Films include:* Stormy Monday (also screenplay and music) 1988, Internal Affairs (also music) 1990, Liebestraum (also screenplay and music) 1991, Mr. Jones 1993, The Browning Version 1994, Leaving Las Vegas (also screenplay and music) 1995, One Night Stand 1997, Flamenco Women 1997, Miss Julie 1999, The Loss of Sexual Innocence 1999, Time Code 2000, Hotel 2001, The Battle of Orgreave 2001, Cold Creek Manor 2003, Co/Ma 2004 (also writer), The 4 Dreams of Miss X 2007, Love Live Long 2008, The Co(te)lette Film 2010, Suspension of Disbelief 2012. *Website:* www.mikefiggis.co.uk.

FIGO, Luis Filipe Madeira Caeiro; Portuguese fmr professional footballer; b. 4 Nov. 1972, Lisbon; m. Helene Svedin; three d.; attacking midfielder/winger; youth player for União de Pastilhas and Sporting Clube de Portugal (CP); sr player for Sporting CP 1989–95 (won Cup of Portugal 1995, Portuguese SuperCup 1995), Barcelona 1995–2000 (won La Liga 1998, 1999, Copa del Rey 1997, 1998, Spanish SuperCup 1996, UEFA Cup Winners' Cup 1997, UEFA Super Cup 1997), Real Madrid (signed for then world record transfer fee) 1995–2000 (won La Liga 2001, 2003, Supercopa de España 2001, 2003, UEFA Champions League 2002, UEFA Super Cup 2002, Intercontinental Cup 2002), Inter Milan 2005–09 (won Serie A 2006, 2007, 2008, 2009, Italian Cup 2006, Italian SuperCup 2005, 2006, 2008) (retd); 127 caps and scored 32 goals with Portugal nat. team 1991–2006 (FIFA World Cup, (Fourth Place) 2006, European Football Championship (runner-up) 2004, (Third Place) 2000, FIFA U-20 World Cup 1991); jt seat holder with Carlos Queirós for A1 Team Portugal in A1 Grand Prix 2005–06; Officer, Order of Prince Henry, Order of the Immaculate Conception of Vila Viçosa (House of Braganza); Portuguese Golden Ball 1994, Portuguese Footballer of the Year 1995, 1996, 1997, 1998, 1999, 2000, Don Balón Award for Foreign Player of the Year in La Liga 1999, 2000, 2001, Ballon d'Or for Best Player of the Year 2000, FIFA European Footballer of the Year 2000, FIFA World Player of the Year 2001, FIFA 100, UEFA Team of the Year 2003, FIFA World Cup All-Star Team 2006, Golden Foot 2011. *Leisure interests:* the beach, rock music, spending time with friends.

FIGUEIREDO MACHADO, Luiz Alberto, LLB; Brazilian diplomatist and politician; *Ambassador to Portugal;* b. 17 July 1955; ed State Univ. of Rio de Janeiro; served in Perm. Mission to UN, New York 1986–89, Embassy in Santiago 1989–92, Head, Sea, Antarctic and Outer Space Affairs Div., Ministry of Foreign Affairs 1995–96, served in Embassy in Washington, DC 1996–99, Embassy in Ottawa 1999–2002, Head, Environmental Policy and Sustainable Devt Div. 2002–04, served in Mission to UNESCO 2003–05, Dir, Dept for Environment and Special Affairs 2005–11, Under-Sec. for Environment, Energy, Science and Tech. 2011–13, Amb. and Perm. Rep. to UN, New York 2013, Minister of Foreign Affairs 2013–14; Amb. to USA 2015–16, to Portugal 2016–; Exec. Sec. Rio+20 Nat. Comm.; served for many years as chief negotiator for Brazil at numerous int. confs on environmental issues. *Address:* Embassy of Brazil, Quinta de Mil Flores, Estrada das Laranjeiras 144, 1649-021 Lisbon, Portugal (office). *Telephone:* (21) 7248510 (office). *Fax:* (21) 7267623 (office). *E-mail:* geral@embaixadadobrasil.pt (office). *Website:* lisboa.itamaraty.gov.br (office).

FIGUERES, Christiana, MA; Costa Rican diplomatist, consultant and fmr UN official; b. (Karen Christiana Figueres Olsen), 1956, San José; d. of José Figueres Ferrer and Karen Olsen Beck; m. Konrad von Ritter; two d.; ed Swarthmore Coll., USA, London School of Econs, UK, Georgetown Univ., Gestalt Inst. of Cleveland, USA; Minister-Counsellor, Embassy in Bonn 1982–85; Dir of Int. Cooperation, Ministry of Planning 1987–88; Chief of Staff to Minister of Agriculture 1988–90; with corp. strategic communications, The Hawthorn Group 1993–94; Dir Technical Secr., Renewable Energy in the Americas, OAS 1994–96; Founder and Exec. Dir Centre for Sustainable Devt in the Americas (think tank) 1995–2003; ind. climate change adviser 2004–10, positions included Rep. of Latin America and the Caribbean on Exec. Bd Clean Development Mechanism, UN Framework Convention on Climate Change (UNFCCC) 2007, Vice-Chair Global Covenant of Mayors for Climate & Energy, Rating Cttee, Carbon Rating Agency 2008–10, Vice-Pres. Bureau of the Climate Convention 2008–09, Sr Advisor, C-Quest Capital 2009–10; Prin. Climate Change Adviser to ENDESA Latinoamérica 2008–10; Exec.-Sec. UNFCCC 2010–16; Founding Partner Global Optimism Ltd; Convernor Mission 2020; mem. Bd of Dirs Winrock International (NGO) 2005–10, International Inst. for Energy Conservation 2006–08, Voluntary Carbon Standard 2008–10; mem. Advisory Bd Eni SpA 2017–; mem. Scientific Advisory Panel, UNEP Risoe Centre, Project Catalyst Carbon Finance Working Group; Légion d'honneur 2015, Officer, Order of Orange-Nassau (The Netherlands) 2016, Order of Merit (Germany); Dr hc (Univ. of Massachusetts), (Univ. of Boston), (Concordia Univ.), (Georgetown Univ.); Hero for the Planet Award 2001, Medal of the City of Paris 2015, Ewald von Kleist Award 2016, President's Medal, Architectural League 2018, The Dan David Prize 2019. *Publications:* numerous contribs to journals and books. *Address:* c/o Marina Mansilla. *E-mail:* marina@globaloptimism.com. *Website:* www.christianafigueres.com; globaloptimism.com.

FIGUERES OLSEN, José María, MPA; Costa Rican/Spanish international organization official, business executive and fmr politician; *President, Carbon War Room;* b. 24 Dec. 1954, San José; s. of José Figueres Ferrer (fmr Pres. of Costa Rica); two c.; ed US Mil. Acad., West Point, New York, Kennedy School of Govt, Harvard Univ.; mem. Partido de Liberación Nacional; Minister of Agric. 1986–90; Pres. of Costa Rica 1994–98; Pres. Leadership for Environment and Devt (LEAD); Man. Dir World Econ. Forum 2000–03, Co-CEO 2003–04, CEO 2004; CEO Concordia 21, Madrid, Spain 2004–10; Chair. Water Supply and Sanitation Collaborative Council 2004–, Global Fairness Initiative 2008–14; Founder and Pres. Vía Costarricense - Proyecto País 2012–; Chair. Carbon War Room 2009–12, Pres. 2012–; Co-Chair. Global Ocean Comm. 2013–; mem. Bd Global Fairness Initiative, BT Global Services Strategy & Marketing Advisory Bd, Abraaj Capital Advisory Bd, Grupo San Cristobal, Dubai Recycling Park, Talal Abu-Ghazaleh Org., Earth Council Geneva, DARA (non-profit org.), Fundación para las Relaciones Internacionales y el Diálogo Exterior (FRIDE); mem. Dean's Alumni Council, Harvard Univ.; Bd Fellow, Thunderbird School of Man.; Int. Adviser, Global Environmental Action; Order of José Matías Delgado Grand Silver Cross (El Salvador) 1999; first recipient of Global Prize from World Bank's Global Environmental Fund 1988, Liberty Prize, Max Schmidheiny Foundation and St Gallen Univ. 1998, Award of the Climate Inst., Washington, DC 1998, Sustainability Award in Switzerland 2003. *Address:* Carbon War Room, 29 East 19th Street, 4th Floor, New York, NY 10003, USA. *Telephone:* (315) 266-9600 (office). *E-mail:* info@carbonwarroom.com (office); info@josemariafigueres.org. *Website:* www.carbonwarroom.com (office); www.josemariafigueres.org.

FIGUEROA, Adolfo, PhD; Peruvian economist, academic and international consultant; *Professor Emeritus and Senior Researcher, Centrum Graduate Business School, Catholic University of Peru;* b. 14 April 1941, Carhuaz; s. of José Manuel Figueroa and Modesta Figueroa; m. Yolanda Vásquez 1965; one s. one d.; ed Colegio Guadalupe (High School), Lima, San Marcos Univ., Lima, Vanderbilt Univ., Nashville, Tenn., USA; Prof. of Econs, Catholic Univ. of Peru, Lima 1970–2007, Head, Dept of Econs 1976–79, 1987–90, 1996–98, Dean Faculty of Social Sciences 2002–05, Prof. Emer. 2008–, also Sr Researcher, Centrum Grad. Business School 2008–; Dir Research Project on Productivity and Educ. in Agric. in Latin America, ECIEL Program 1983–85; Consultant to ILO, FAO, Inter-American Foundation, Ford Foundation, IFAD, IDB, World Bank; Visiting Prof., Univ. of Pernambuco, Brazil 1973, St Antony's Coll., Oxford 1976, Univ. of Ill., USA 1980, Econs Dept, Univ. of Nicaragua 1985, Univ. of Notre Dame, USA 1992, Univ. of Tex. 1997, Univ. of Wis. 2001; mem. Exec. Council Latin American Studies Asscn 1988–91, Editorial Advisory Bd, Journal of International Development 1988–92, World Devt 1997–2015, European Review of Latin American Studies 1997–2007, Journal of Human Devt and Capabilities 2008–; mem. Int. Network for Econ. Method; Award of Excellence in Grad. Teaching Univ. of Ill., USA 1980, Winner, Collaborative Research Grant Competition, MacArthur Foundation 1999, Winner, Tinker Professorship Competition, Univ. of Wis. 2001. *Publications:* Estructura del Consumo y Distribución de Ingresos en Lima 1968–1969 1974, Distribución del Ingreso en el Perú (co-author) 1975, La Economía Campesina de la Sierra del Perú 1981, Capitalist Development and the Peasant Economy in Peru 1984, Educación y Productividad en la Agricultura Campesina de América Latina 1986, Teorías Económicas del Capitalismo 1992, Crisis Distributiva en el Perú 1993, Social Exclusion and Inequality in Peru 1996, Reformas en sociedades desiguales 2001, La sociedad sigma: una teoría del desarrollo económico 2003, Nuestro mundo social, una introducción a la ciencia económica 2008, A Unified Theory of Capitalist Development 2009, Growth, Employment, Inequality, and the Environment: Unity of Knowledge in Economics (Vols I–II) 2015; articles in econ. journals on inequality and poverty, econ. growth, econ. devt, agric., labour markets, and econs of educ. *Leisure interests:* music, popular and classical guitar. *Address:* Centrum Graduate Business School, Universidad Católica del Perú, Jiron Alomia Robles 125, Surco, Lima 32 (office); Jirón Robert Kennedy 129, Lima 21, Peru (home). *Telephone:* (1) 626-7100 (office); (1) 261-6241 (home). *E-mail:* afiguer@pucp.edu.pe (office). *Website:* macareo.pucp.edu.pe/~afiguer/afiguer.htm (office).

FIGUEROA SERRANO, Carlos; Chilean lawyer, politician and diplomatist; b. 28 Nov. 1930, Angol; s. of Carlos Figueroa and Isabel Serrano; m. Sara Guzmán 1953; seven c.; ed Colegio de los Sagrados Corazones, School of Law, Universidad de Chile; practising lawyer 1957–, served at Appeals Court, Santiago 1971–72; Prof. of Procedural Law, Catholic Univ. of Chile 1960–76; joined Partido Demócrata Cristiano (PDC) 1957; Under-Sec. for Agric. 1967–69; Minister of Economy 1969–70; Acting Minister of Foreign Relations and of Finance on various occasions 1967–70; Pres. PDC Political Cttee 1980; Del. for Providencia to Prov. Bd of Eastern Santiago 1984–87; Head of Communications and Publicity, Patricio Aylwin's presidential campaign 1989; Amb. to Argentina 1990–93; Dir Communications and Publicity, Eduardo Frei's presidential campaign 1993; Minister for Foreign Affairs March–Sept. 1994, for Interior 1994–99; mem. Bd of Dirs CIC SA 1971, Financiera Condell 1986–90, Pesquera Guafo SA 1987–89; Gen. Man. VEEP SA (bldg contractors) 1980–86; Pres. Asociación Radiodifusoras de Chile 1972–78; Counsellor, Asociación Iberamericana de Radiodifusión 1973–79, Sec. Bd of Dirs 1975–77.

FILARDO, Leonor, MS; Venezuelan economist, banker and international finance official; b. 1944; d. of Jesus Filardo and Carmen Vargas de Filardo; m. (divorced); three d.; ed Caracas Catholic Univ., Univ. of Surrey, UK; worked for Cen. Bank of Venezuela 1970–75, Sr Vice-Pres., Int. Operations 1979–84; Sr Vice-Pres., Int. Finance, Venezuelan Investment Fund 1975–79; Exec. Dir, World Bank Exec. Bd 1984–86; Alt. Exec. Dir IMF 1986–88, Exec. Dir 1988–90; Rep. Office, Washington DC 1990; Vice-Pres. Cen. Bank of Venezuela 1993–94; Minister Counsellor, Embassy in Washington, DC 1994; fmr Adviser to Cen. American and Venezuelan govts on stabilization and structural adjustment programmes, participant in negotiations with IMF for External Fund Facility for Venezuela; mem. Centro de Divulgación del Conocimiento Económico—CEDICE (think tank); mem. Exec. Cttee Youth Orchestra of the Americas; Francisco de Miranda Medal, (1st Class) Venezuela 1990. *Leisure interests:* art, music, opera, travel, workout. *Address:* CEDICE, Avenida Andrés Eloy Blanco (Este 2), Edif. Cámara de Comercio de Caracas, Nivel Auditorio, Los Caobos, Caracas, Venezuela (office). *Telephone:* (212) 571-3357 (office). *E-mail:* cedice@cedice.org.ve (office). *Website:* www.cedice.org.ve (office).

FILARET, (Mykhailo Antonovych Denisenko); Ukrainian ecclesiastic; *Patriarch of Kyiv and All Rus-Ukraine;* b. 23 Jan. 1929, Blahodatne, Amvrosiivsky Raion, Donetsk Oblast, Ukrainian SSR, USSR; ed Odesa Seminary and Moscow Theological Acad.; monk and teacher from 1950; Rector Moscow Acad. 1954; moved to Saratov Seminary 1956, Kyiv Seminary 1957; fmr Chancellor Ukrainian Exarchate of Russian Orthodox Church – Moscow Patriarchate; apptd Bishop of Luga, Leningrad (now St Petersburg) Diocese 1962, Bishop of Vienna and Austria Nov. 1962, Bishop of Dmitrov, Moscow Diocese 1964; Rector Moscow's theological schools and Deputy Chair. Dept of External Church Relations 1964–66; Archbishop of Kyiv and Galicia 1966; Metropolitan of Kyiv 1968, dismissed May 1992; was instrumental in formation of Patriarchate of Kyiv and all Rus-Ukraine June 1992, Patriarch of Kyiv and All Rus-Ukraine 1995–; Order of Friendship of Peoples 1979, Order of the Red Banner of Labour 1988; Order of Liberty 2009, Order of Prince Yaroslav the Wise, Fifth Class 1999, Fourth Class 2001, Third Class 2004, Second Class 2006, First Class 2008, Cross of Ivan Mazepa 2010. *Address:* Ukrainian Orthodox Church (Kyiv Patriarchate), 01004 Kyiv, vul. Pushkinska 36, Ukraine (office). *Telephone:* (44) 234-10-96 (office). *Fax:* (44) 234-30-55 (home). *E-mail:* prescentr@gmail.com (office). *Website:* www.cerkva.info (office).

FILARET (see Philaret).

FILAT, Vladimir (Vlad); Moldovan business executive and politician; b. 6 May 1969, Lăpuşna, Hînceşti Dist, Moldovan SSR, USSR; m. 1st Nadejda Filat; one s. two d.; m. 2nd Sanda Filat (divorced 2012); m. 3rd Angela Gonţa 2014; one d.; ed Co-operation Coll., Chişinău, Alexandru Ioan Cuza Univ., Iaşi, Romania; served in Soviet army 1987–89; Man. Dir RoMold Trading SRL, Iaşi 1994–97; Pres. Admin. Council, Dosoftei Co., Iaşi 1997–98; Gen. Dir Dept of Privatization and State Property Admin, Ministry of Economy and Reform, Chişinău 1998–99; Minister of State, March Nov. 1999; mem. Partidul Democrat din Moldova (Democratic Party of Moldova) 1997–2007, Vice-Pres. 2000–07; mem. Parl. 1997–2007, Vice-Pres. Parl. Comm. for Security, Public Order and Defence 2005–09; unsuccessful cand. for Mayor of Chişinău 2007; Founder-mem. Partidul Liberal Democrat din Moldova (Liberal Democratic Party of Moldova) 2007–, Pres. 2007–15, party absorbed Alianţa Moldova Noastră (Our Moldova Alliance) April 2011; Prime Minister 2009–13; Acting Pres. of Moldova 28–30 Dec. 2010; stripped of immunity and handcuffed in Parl. Oct. 2015, under investigation for US $1,000m. bank fraud and accused of having taken bribes of approx. $250m., denied any wrongdoing and claimed allegations politically motivated, sentenced to nine years in prison June 2016. *Address:* c/o Partidul Liberal Democrat din Moldova (Liberal Democratic Party of Moldova), 2012 Chişinău, str. Bucureşti 88, Moldova (office). *Telephone:* (22) 81-51-54 (office). *Fax:* (22) 81-51-63 (office). *E-mail:* info@pldm.md (office). *Website:* www.pldm.md (office); filat.md.

FILI, Sunia Manu, BA; Tongan lawyer and politician; b. 1 Dec. 1965; m.; ed Univ. of the South Pacific; began career as lawyer and high school teacher before entering politics; mem. Legis. Ass. as People's Rep. for Eua 1999; Minister of Finance and Nat. Planning 2011–12, for Police, Prisons and Fire Services 2012; fmr mem. Human Rights and Democracy Movt. *Leisure interests:* tennis, reading, debating, swimming, gardening. *E-mail:* suniafili@gmail.com. *Website:* parliament.gov.to (office).

FILI-KRUSHEL, Patricia (Pat), BS, MBA; American media executive; *Chairman, NBCUniversal News Group, NBCUniversal;* ed St John's Univ., Fordham Univ.; worked for ABC Sports in various positions; held several positions with Home Box Office, later Vice-Pres. of Business Affairs and Production; with Lifetime Television as both Group Vice-Pres. of Hearst/ABC-Viacom Entertainment Services (HAVES) and Sr Vice-Pres. of Programming and Production of Lifetime Television 1988–93; joined ABC 1993, Pres. ABC Daytime 1993–98, responsible for introducing daytime talk show The View, Pres. ABC Television Network 1998–2000, conceived and orchestrated SoapNet (24-hour soap opera cable network); CEO WebMD Health 2000–01; Exec. Vice-Pres. of Admin, Time Warner Inc. 2001–12; Exec. Vice-Pres. NBCUniversal, Chair. NBCUniversal News Group 2012–; mem. Bd Dollar General Corpn; mem. Bd of Trustees, The Public Theater of New York (mem. Exec. Cttee and Chair. Nominating Cttee), The Paley Center for Media; mem. Mayor Bloomberg's Comm. on Women's Issues; Women in Film Muse Award 1993, recognized by New York Women in Communications, Inc. through their Matrix Awards for her contribution to the field of broadcasting, inducted into Museum of Television & Radio's "She Made It" Collection 2006, Vision Award, Crystal Apple Award, City of New York. *Address:* NBCUniversal Media LLC, 30 Rockefeller Plaza, New York, NY 10112, USA (office). *Telephone:* (212) 664-4444 (office). *Fax:* (212) 664-4085 (office). *E-mail:* info@nbcuni.com (office). *Website:* www.nbcuni.com (office).

FILIP, Pavel; Moldovan engineer, business executive and politician; *Prime Minister;* b. 10 April 1966, Pănăşeşti, Moldovan SSR, USSR; m. Tatiana Filip; two c.; ed Polytechnic Inst. of Moldova (now Tech. Univ. of Moldova), Chişinău, Int. Man. Inst., Chişinău; mil. service 1984–86; Chief Engineer, then Deputy Gen. Dir for Production and Issues, then Head of Div., Bucuria JSC 1991–2001, Dir-Gen. Bucuria JSC 2001–08; mem. Council, Nat. Confed. of Employers 2009–10; Dir-Gen. Tutun-CTC JSC, Chişinău 2008–11; Minister of Information Technologies and Communications 2011–16; Prime Minister of Moldova 2016–; mem. Partidul Democrat din Moldova (Democratic Party of Moldova) 2011–; affiliated with Aliănta pentru Integrare Europeană (Alliance for European Integration) 2009–13, 2013–15, 2015–; Order of Gloria Muncii 2014; Medal of ITU 2013. *Address:* Office of the Council of Ministers, 2033 Chişinău, Piaţa Marii Adunări Naţionale 1, Moldova (office). *Telephone:* (22) 25-01-01 (office). *Fax:* (22) 24-26-96 (office). *E-mail:* petitii@gov.md (office). *Website:* www.gov.md (office).

FILIP, Vojtěch; Czech politician; *Chairman, Komunistická strana Čech a Moravy (KSČM—Communist Party of Bohemia and Moravia);* b. 13 Jan. 1955, Jedovary, nr České Budějovice; m. Ludmila Filip 1979; one s. one d.; ed gymnasium in Trhové Sviny, Univ. of Jan Evangelista Purkyně, Brno (now Masaryk Univ.); worked as lawyer for Sfinx Budweis, returned following mil. service in Prague 1979–90; opened own law firm 1993, first as commercial lawyer, then as attorney specializing in commercial and constitutional law, political parties and human rights; worked for Socialistický Svaz Mládeže (SSM—Socialist Union of Youth) 1970–86; mem. Communist Party of Czechoslovakia (KSČ) from 1983, Komunistická Strana Čech a Moravy (KSČM—Communist Party of Bohemia and Moravia) 1990–, worked in Cen. Auditing Comm., later Chair. IP KSČM, České Budějovice and UV KSČM, mem. Exec. Cttee of Cen. KSČM from 1996, also worked as Chair. Comm. for legislation and human rights of UV KSČM, Vice-Chair. KSČM 2004–05, Chair. 2005–; mem. Municipal Cttee, České Budějovice 1984–90; mem. Fed. Ass. 1990–92; City Councillor, České Budějovice 1994–2002; mem. Parl. (KSČM) for South Bohemian Region 1996–2013, 2013–, Chair. Parl. Party 1996–2002, Vice-Pres. Chamber of Deputies 2002–06, 2006–10, 2013–; Prize for Human Rights, German Soc. for the Protection of Civil Rights and Human Dignity 2007. *Publications include:* numerous articles in professional journals and proceedings on the liability of relations in civil, commercial, labour and criminal law. *Leisure interests:* music (especially rock), nature, fishing, travelling. *Address:* Komunistická strana Čech a Moravy (Communist Party of Bohemia and Moravia), Politických vězňů 9, 111 21 Prague 1, Czech Republic (office). *Telephone:* (2) 22897111 (office). *Fax:* (2) 22897207 (office). *E-mail:* info@kscm.cz (office). *Website:* www.kscm.cz (office).

FILIPOVIĆ, Karlo; Bosnia and Herzegovina politician; b. 10 July 1954, Solakovicima; s. of Jozo Filipović and Mara Filipović; m.; one d.; ed Univ. of Sarajevo; Pres. Council of Municipalities, Sarajevo City Ass. 1987–89; mem. Cen. Cttee Communist League of Bosnia and Herzegovina 1988–91, elected mem. of presidency 1989; mem. of presidency Socialist Party of Bosnia and Herzegovina 1991–92; mem. of presidency of Social Democratic Party of Bosnia and Herzegovina (SDP BiH) 1992–95, Sec. 1995–97, Sec.-Gen. 1997–2001, Pres. Exec. Bd 2001; mem. House of Reps (Parl.) 1998–2001; Pres. Fed. of Bosnia and Herzegovina 2001–02, Vice-Pres. 2002–04.

FILIPPENKO, Aleksander Georgyevich; Russian actor; b. 2 Sept. 1944, Moscow; m. 2nd Marina Ishimbayeva; one d.; ed Moscow Inst. of Physics and Tech., Moscow, Shchukin Higher School of Theatre; Sr Engineer, Inst. of Geochemistry, USSR Acad. of Sciences 1967–69; actor in Amateur Theatre Nash Dom 1967–69, Taganka Theatre 1969–75, Vakhtangov Theatre 1975–94; Founder and actor, Experimental One-Man Theatre 1995–; staged Train to Chatanooga, Dead Souls, Fanbala; Merited Artist of Russia. *Films include:* Ostanovite Potapova! 1974, Kto zaplatit za udachu? 1980, Brosok 1981, Tam, na nevedomykh dorozhkakh 1982, Torpedonostsy 1983, Moy drug Ivan Lapshin 1984, Chyornaya strela 1985, Iz zhizni Potapova 1985, Oci ciornie 1987, Ubit drakona 1988, Es ist nicht leicht ein Gott zu sein 1989, Pod severnym siyaniyem 1990, The Inner Circle 1991, Ubiystvo v Sunshine Menor 1992, Anomaliya 1993, Master i Margarita 1994, Igra voobrazheniya 1995, Karera Arturo Ui 1996, Romanovy: Ventsenosnaya semya 2000, Ledi na den 2002, Aziris nuna 2006, Aziris nuna 2006, Leningrad 2007, My Fair Nanny 2008, Schastlivyy konets 2010, Peter the Great: The Testament 2011. *Television includes:* Oshibka Toni vendisa 1981, Vizit k Minotavru 1987, Prestuplenie lorda Artura 1991, Azbuka lyubvi 1992, Sledstvie vedut znatoki 23: Treteyskiy sudiya 2002, Bednaya Nastya 2003, Master i Margarita 2005, Zagovor 2007. *Address:* 103104 Moscow, Spiridonyevsky per. 8, Apt 17, Russia (home). *Telephone:* (495) 202-77-15 (home).

FILIPPETTI, Aurélie; French politician and novelist; b. 17 June 1973, Villerupt (Meurthe-et-Moselle); ed École normale supérieure de Fontenay-Saint-Cloud, agrégation in Classic Literature; fmr mem. Les Verts (Green Party), now mem. Parti socialiste (PS—Socialist Party); Tech. Adviser for Minister of Environment, Yves Cochet 2001–02; mem. (PS) Assemblée nationale for the Eight Dist of the Moselle département 2007–; Minister of Culture and Communication 2012–14 (resgnd); Commdr des Arts et des Lettres 2012. *Publications include:* Les derniers jours de la classe ouvrière (novel) 2003, wrote the script for theatre production Fragments d'humanité 2003, Un homme dans la poche 2006, L'école forme-t-elle encore des citoyens? (co-author) 2008, Si nous sommes vivants-le socialisme et l'écologie (co-author) 2010, J'ai 20 ans qu'est-ce qui m'attend? (co-author) 2012. *Address:* Assemblée nationale, 126 rue de l'Université, 75355 Paris Cedex 07, France (office). *Telephone:* 1-40-63-60-00 (office). *Fax:* 1-45-55-75-23 (office). *E-mail:* afilippetti@assemblee-nationale.fr (office). *Website:* www.assemblee-nationale.fr (office); aureliefilippetti.free.fr.

FILIPPOV, Vladimir Mikhailovich, Dr Physics-Math; Russian government official, mathematician, academic and university rector; *Rector, Peoples' Friendship University of Russia;* b. 15 April 1951, Uryupinsk; m.; one s. one d.; ed Patrice Lumumba Peoples' Friendship Univ., Steklov Math. Inst. USSR Acad. of Sciences; Asst, Chair of Higher Math., Chair. Council of Young Scientists and Head, Dept of Science, Patrice Lumumba Peoples' Friendship Univ. 1973–85, Prof., Head, Chair of Math. Analysis, Dean, Faculty of Natural Sciences 1985–93, Rector 1993–98; Minister of Gen. and Professional Educ. of Russian Fed. 1998–2000; Minister of Educ. 2000–04, Aide to Prime Minister 2004–05; Rector, Peoples' Friendship Univ. of Russia 2005–; Chair. Organizing Cttee, World Higher Educ. Conf. 2009; Chair. Higher Attestation Comm. 2013–; Vice-Pres. Euro-Asian Asscn of Univs; Presidium mem. Russian Acad. of Educ.; Order of the Friendship of People 1995, Order of King's Crown (Belgium) 2000, Order for Merits to Motherland, IV degree 2001, Chevalier, Légion d'honneur 2002, Belgian Inventor Medal, Mérite de l'Invention 2003, Order of Francisca de Paula Santander 2008, UNESCO Medal 2010, Order of Merit (Russia) 2015; Pres. Award in Educ. 2000, Govt Award in Educ. 2013. *Publications:* more than 240 scientific and methodological publications. *Address:* Peoples' Friendship University of Russia, 117198 Moscow, 6 Miklukho-Maklaya str., Russia (office). *Telephone:* (495) 434-70-27 (office). *Fax:* (495) 433-73-79 (office). *E-mail:* rector@rudn.ru (office). *Website:* www.rudn.ru (office).

FILIU, Jean-Pierre, PhD; French scholar and academic; *Associate Professor, Institute of Political Studies (Sciences Po);* b. 1961, Paris; ed Inst. of Political Studies (Sciences Po), Paris, Institut national de langues et civilisations orientales; fmr diplomatist and ministerial adviser; specializes in contemporary Islam, with an emphasis on jihadi movements and al-Qa'ida; Assoc. Prof., Inst. of Political Studies (Sciences Po), Paris 2006–, teaches in French, English and Arabic at Gilles Kepel's Middle East Chair; Visiting Prof., Columbia Univ., New York, Georgetown Univ., Washington, DC, USA 2008; mem. Scientific Bd, Maison méditerranéenne des Sciences de l'homme, Steering Cttee, Annuaire de la Méditerranée; mem. CERI (Centre d'études et de recherches internationales) 2009–. *Publications:* Mitterrand et la Palestine 2005, Les frontières du jihad 2006, L'Apocalypse dans l'Islam (Augustin-Thierry Prize, Rendez-vous de l'Histoire, Blois 2008) 2008, Mai 68 à l'ORTF 2008, Les neuf vies d'Al-Qaida 2009, La Révolution arabe, dix leçons sur le soulèvement démocratique 2011, Best of Enemies (with David B.) 2012; articles on the adaptation of Islam to globalized modernity. *Address:* Sciences Po, 27 rue Saint-Guillaume, 75337 Paris Cedex 07, France (office). *Telephone:* 1-45-49-51-47 (office). *Fax:* 1-42-22-31-26 (office). *E-mail:* jeanpierre.filiu@sciencespo.fr (office). *Website:* www.ceri-sciencespo.com/cerifr/cherlist/filiu.php (office); www.sciencespo.fr (office).

FILIZZOLA SERRA, Rafael, LLB; Paraguayan lawyer, academic and politician; b. 16 Feb. 1968, Asunción; m. Desirée Masi 1997; two c.; ed Univ. Católica Nuestra Señora de la Asunción; Sec.-Gen. Nat. Fed. of Univ. Students 1990–91; Deputy for Asuncion 1998–2003, 2003–08; Senator 2008 (resgnd); Minister of the Interior 2008–11; Founding mem. Asunción Para Todos (APT) and Constitución Para Todoa (CPT) (ind. political movt) 1991; Prof. of Political Law, Universidad Católica de Asunción; mem. Nat. Congress for Asunción 1998–2008; Founder and Pres. Partido Demorático Progresista (PDP) 2007–.

FILLON, François-Charles Amand, MA, DEA; French politician; b. 4 March 1954, Le Mans; s. of Michel Fillon and Anne Soulet; m. Penelope Clarke 1980; four s. one d.; ed Univ. of Le Mans, Univ. René-Descartes, Paris; Parl. Asst to Joël Le Theule 1976–77; served in Office of Minister of Transport 1978–80, Office of Minister of Defence 1980–81; Head of Legis. and Parl. Work, Ministry of Industry 1981; Town Councillor, Sablé-sur-Sarthe, Mayor 1983–2001; Pres. Conseil Général of Sarthe 1992–98, of Sablé-sur-Sarthe Dist 2001–12; Chair. Conseil Régional des Pays de la Loire 1998–2002; Municipal Councillor, Solesmes 2001–14; RPR/UMP Deputy to Nat. Ass. 1981–93, 1997–2002, 2007, 2012–; Senator for Sarthe 2004, 2005–07; Spokesman, Exec. Comm. RPR 1998, Political Adviser 1999–2001; Founder mem. Union en Mouvement 2002; Political Adviser to Nicolas Sarkozy (Union pour un Mouvement Populaire—UMP) 2004–07; Pres. Comm. for Nat. Defence and Armed Forces 1986–88; Minister for Higher Educ. and Research 1993–95; Minister of Information Tech. and Post May–Nov. 1995, Minister del. for Post, Telecommunications and Space 1995–97; Minister of Social Affairs, Labour and Solidarity 2002–04; Minister for Nat. Educ., Higher Educ. and Research 2004–05; Prime Minister 2007–12; Minister of Ecology, Sustainable Devt, Transport and Housing February–May 2012; unsuccessful cand. for Les Républicains in 2017 presidential election; Grand Croix, Ordre nat. du Mérite 2007, Grand Officier, Légion d'honneur 2012, Order of the Rising Sun (Japan) 2013. *Publications:* La France peut supporter la vérité 2006, Les Retraites 2007, Faire 2015, Vaincre le totalitarisme islamique 2016. *Leisure interests:* climbing, hiking, skiing, mountain biking, motor racing, running, cinema, reading. *Address:* Les Républicains, 238 rue de Vaugirard, 75015 Paris, France (office). *Telephone:* 1-40-76-60-00 (office). *E-mail:* equipe@fillon2017.fr. *Website:* www.blog-fillon.com; www.fillon2017.fr.

FILMON, Gary Albert, OC, PC, BSc, MSc; Canadian engineer, business executive and fmr politician; b. 24 Aug. 1942, Winnipeg, Man.; s. of Albert Filmon and Anastasia Filmon (née Dosckocz); m. Janice Wainwright 1963; two s. two d.; ed Sisler High School, Univ. of Manitoba; consulting engineer, Underwood McLellan Ltd 1964–69; Pres. Success/Angus Commercial Coll. 1969–80; Winnipeg City Councillor 1975–79; mem. Legis. Ass. for River Heights 1979–81, for Tuxedo 1981–2000; Minister of Consumer and Corp. Affairs and Environment and Minister Responsible for Man. Housing and Renewal Corpn 1981; Leader Man. Progressive Conservative Party 1983–88; Premier of Manitoba 1988–99, also Pres. Exec. Council, Minister of Fed. Prov. Relations; fmr Vice-Chair. Wellington West Capital Inc., Arctic Glacier Income Fund 2003–06; headed govt task force to evaluate emergency response to forest fires in BC 2004; fmr Chair. Bd of Trustees, Exchange Industrial Income Fund; fmr mem. Bd of Dirs F.W.S. Construction Ltd, Canadian Natural Resources Ltd, Manitoba Telecom Services Inc., Canada West Foundation, ParticipACTION Canada; mem. Security Intelligence Review Cttee 2001–06 (fmr Chair.); mem. Senate, Univ. of Manitoba; Community Service Award, Canadian Council of Professional Engineers, B'nai B'rith Canada Award of Merit, Distinguished Alumni Award, Univ. of Manitoba 2005.

FILO, David, BS, MS; American internet industry executive; *Chief Yahoo!, Yahoo! Inc.;* b. 20 April 1966, Moss Bluff, La.; m. Angela Buenning; ed Tulane Univ. and Stanford Univ.; co-created Yahoo! internet navigational guide 1994, Co-founder Yahoo! Inc. 1994, named Chief Yahoo!, mem. Bd of Dirs 1995–96, 2014–; f. Yellow Chair Foundation. *Address:* Yahoo! Incorporated, 701 1st Avenue, Sunnyvale, CA 94089, USA (home). *Telephone:* (408) 349-3300 (office). *Fax:* (408) 349-3301 (office). *Website:* www.yahoo.com (office).

FILONI, HE Cardinal Fernando, PhD, DCL; Italian ecclesiastic and diplomatist; *Prefect, Congregation for the Evangelization of Peoples;* b. 15 April 1946, Manduria, Taranto; ed Pontifical Lateran Univ., Rome; ordained priest, Diocese of Nardò-Gallipoli 1970; served in Nunciatures of Sri Lanka 1982–83, Iran 1983–85, Brazil 1989–92, the Philippines (based in Hong Kong) 1992–2001; apptd Titular Archbishop of Volturnum 2001; Apostolic Nuncio to Iraq and Jordan 2001–06, to Philippines 2006–07; Substitute (Sostituto) of Secr. of State 2007–11; Prefect of Congregation for Evangelization of Peoples 2011–13, 2013–; Pres. Interdicasterial Comm. for Consecrated Religious 2011–; Grand Chancellor, Pontifical Urbaniana Univ. 2011–; cr. Cardinal (Cardinal-Deacon of Nostra Signora di Coromoto in San Giovanni di Dio) 2012; participated in Papal Conclave 2013. *Address:* The Congregation for the Evangelization of Peoples, Palazzo di Propaganda Fide, Piazza di Spagna 48, 00187 Rome, Italy (office). *Telephone:* (06) 69879299 (office). *Fax:* (06) 69880118 (office); (06) 69880137 (office). *E-mail:* segreteria@propagandafide.va (office). *Website:* www.vatican.va/roman_curia/congregations/cevang (office).

FINALDI, Gabriele, BA, MA, PhD; British arts administrator and gallery director; *Director, National Gallery, London;* b. 1965, London; m. María Inés Guerrero; six c.; ed Dulwich Coll., Courtauld Inst. of Art; Curator of Italian and Spanish Paintings, Nat. Gallery, London 1992–2002, Dir, Nat. Gallery 2015–; Deputy Dir for Collections and Research, Museo Nacional del Prado, Madrid 2002–15. *Address:* The National Gallery, Trafalgar Square, London, WC2N 5DN, England (office). *Telephone:* (20) 7747-2885 (office). *Fax:* (20) 7747-2423 (office). *E-mail:* information@ng-london.org.uk (office). *Website:* www.nationalgallery.org.uk/about-us/organisation/director (office).

FINCHER, David; American film director; b. 28 Aug. 1962, Denver, Colo; s. of Jack Fincher; m. Donya Fiorentino 1990 (divorced); one d.; fmrly with Propaganda Films (video production co.) and Korty Films; worked at Industrial Light and Magic 1981–83; directed numerous music videos and commercials. *Films include:* Alien 3 1992, Se7en 1995, The Game 1997, Fight Club 1999, Panic Room 2002, Zodiac 2007, The Curious Case of Benjamin Button 2008, The Social Network (Golden Globe for Best Dir 2011, BAFTA Award for Best Dir 2011) 2010, The Girl with the Dragon Tattoo 2011, Gone Girl 2014. *Television includes:* House of Cards (Emmy Award for Best Dir in Drama Series) 2013–18, Manhunter 2017–. *Address:* c/o Creative Artists Agency, 2000 Avenue of the Stars, Los Angeles, CA 90067, USA (office).

FINCK, August von, Jr; German business executive; b. 11 March 1930, Munich; s. of August von Finck, Sr; m. Francine von Finck; four c.; grandfather f. Allianz insurance co. and Bankhaus Merck, Finck & Co., Munich, sold to Barclay's Bank 1990, Deutsche Spar- & Kreditbank AG, Munich, 1999; moved to Switzerland and acquired stakes in Mövenpick Holding AG, Von Roll, Alusuisse-Lonza, Oerlikon, SGS, Hochtief; mem. Bd of Dirs Generali Holding Vienna AG, SGS United Kingdom Ltd.

FINDLEY, Gbehzohngar Milton, BSc, MSc; Liberian business executive and politician; *Minister of Foreign Affairs;* b. 2 July 1960, Buchanan City, Grand Bassa County; s. of Joseph Findley and Gertrude Findley; m. Kaddiey Findley; two c.; ed Franklin Univ., USA, Lund Univ., Sweden; Owner, produce packaging co. exporting coffee and cocoa; mem. Senate (upper house of parl.) for Grand Bassa 2005–14, Pres. pro tempore of Senate 2012–14; Minister of Foreign Affairs 2018–; mem. Bd of Dirs Univ. of Liberia, Grand Bassa County Community Coll. *Address:* Ministry of Foreign Affairs, Mamba Point, POB 10-9002, 1000 Monrovia, 10, Liberia (office). *Website:* www.mofa.gov.lr (office).

FINE, Anne, OBE, BA, FRSL; British writer; b. (Anne Laker), 7 Dec. 1947, Leicester; d. of Brian Laker and Mary Baker; m. Kit Fine 1968 (divorced 1991); two d.; ed Northampton High School for Girls and Univ. of Warwick; Children's Laureate 2001–03; mem. Soc. of Authors; Scottish Arts Council Writer's Bursary 1986, Scottish Arts Council Book Award 1986, Publishing News' British Book Awards Children's Author of the Year 1990, 1993, Nasen Special Educational Needs Book Award 1996, Prix Sorcière 1998, Prix Versele 1999, 2000, Boston Globe Horn Book Award 2003, Silver Medal, Nestlé Children's Book Prize 2007, Winner, Good Writing Award 2010. *Publications include:* for older children: The Summer House Loon 1978, The Other Darker Ned 1978, The Stone Menagerie 1980, Round Behind the Icehouse 1981, The Granny Project 1983, Madame Doubtfire 1987, Goggle-Eyes (Guardian Children's Fiction Prize, Carnegie Medal 1990) 1989, The Book of the Banshee 1991, Flour Babies (Whitbread Children's Book of the Year, Carnegie Medal 1993) 1992, Step by Wicked Step 1995, The Tulip Touch (Whitbread Children's Book of the Year 1997) 1996, Very Different (short stories) 2001, Up on Cloud Nine 2002, Frozen Billy 2004, The Road of Bones 2006, The Devil Walks 2011; for younger children: Scaredy-Cat 1985, Anneli the Art Hater 1986, Crummy Mummy and Me 1988, A Pack of Liars 1988, Stranger Danger 1989, Bill's New Frock (Smarties Prize 1990) 1989, The Country Pancake 1989, A Sudden Puff of Glittering Smoke 1989, A Sudden Swirl of Icy Wind 1990, Only a Show 1990, Design-a-Pram 1991, A Sudden Glow of Gold 1991, The Worst Child I Ever Had 1991, The Angel of Nitshill Road 1991, Poor Monty (picture book) 1991, The Same Old Story Every Year 1992, The Chicken Gave It to Me 1992, The Haunting of Pip Parker 1992, Press Play 1994, How to Write Really Badly 1996, Countdown 1996, Jennifer's Diary 1996, Care of Henry 1996, Loudmouth Louis 1998, Charm School 1999, Roll Over Roly 1999, Bad Dreams 2000, Ruggles (picture book) 2001, Notso Hotso 2001, How to Cross the Road and Not Turn into a Pizza 2002, The More the Merrier 2003, Ivan the Terrible 2007, Eating Things on Sticks 2009, Trouble in Toadpool 2012; Killer Cat series: The Diary of a Killer Cat 1994, The Return of the Killer Cat 2003, The Killer Cat Strikes Back 2006, The Killer Cat's Birthday Bash 2008, The Killer Cat's Christmas 2009; Jamie and Angus series: The Jamie and Angus Stories 2002, Jamie and Angus Together 2008, Jamie and Angus Forever 2009; adult fiction: The Killjoy 1986, Taking the Devil's Advice 1990, In Cold Domain 1994, Telling Liddy 1998, All Bones and Lies 2001, Raking the Ashes 2005, Fly in the Ointment 2008, Our Precious Lulu 2009; non-fiction: Telling Tales: an Interview with Anne Fine 1999. *Leisure interests:* reading, walking. *Address:* c/o David Higham Associates, 7th Floor, Waverley House, 7–12 Noel Street, London, W1F 8GQ, England (office). *Telephone:* (20) 7434-5900 (office). *Fax:* (1833) 908127 (home). *Website:* www.annefine.co.uk.

FINE, Kit, BA, PhD, FBA, AAAS; British philosopher, mathematician and academic; *University Professor and Silver Professor of Philosophy and Mathematics, New York University;* b. 26 March 1946, Farnborough, Hants., England; s. of Maurice Fine and Joyce Cicely Woolf; two d.; ed Cheltenham Grammar School for Boys, Balliol Coll. Oxford, Univ. of Warwick; Prof., Univ. of Michigan, Ann Arbor, USA 1978–88; Prof., UCLA 1988–97; Univ. Prof. and Silver Prof. of Philosophy and Math., New York Univ. 1997–; Ed. Journal of Symbolic Logic 1978–87, Notre Dame Journal of Formal Logic 1984–87, Studies in Logic 1989–93; Guggenheim Fellow 1978–79; Fellow, American Council of Learned Socs 1981–82, American Acad. of Arts and Sciences; Corresponding Fellow, British Acad.; Dr hc (Bucharest). *Publications include:* Worlds, Times and Selves (with A. N. Prior) 1977, Reasoning with Arbitrary Objects 1985, Limits of Abstraction 2002, Modality and Tense 2005, Semantic Relationism 2007. *Leisure interests:* music, gardening, cooking. *Address:* Department of Philosophy, New York University, 5 Washington Place, New York, NY 10003, USA (office). *Telephone:* (212) 998-3558 (office). *Fax:* (212) 995-4179 (office). *E-mail:* kit.fine@nyu.edu (office). *Website:* philosophy.fas.nyu.edu (office).

FINE, Leon Gerald, MB, ChB, FRCP, FACP, FRCP (Glas), FMedSci; American physician and professor of medicine; *Chairman, Department of Biomedical Sciences and Director, Graduate Research Education, Cedars-Sinai Medical Center;* b. 16 July 1943, Cape Town, South Africa; s. of Matthew Fine and Jeanette Lipshitz; m. Brenda Sakinovsky 1966; two d.; ed Univ. of Cape Town, South Africa; residency, Tel-Aviv Univ. 1968–70; postgraduate clinical and research training, Albert Einstein Coll. of Medicine, New York 1972–76, Univ. of Miami 1976–78; Chief, Div. of Nephrology, UCLA 1978–91; Head, Dept of Medicine, Univ. Coll. London Medical School 1991–2002, Prof. of Medicine 1991–2007, Emer. Prof. 2007–, Dean, Faculty of Clinical Sciences, Royal Free and Univ. Coll. Medical School 2002–06; joined staff of Cedars-Sinai Medical Center, Los Angeles 2007, Chair. Dept of Biomedical Sciences and Dir Grad. Research Educ. 2007–, Prof. of Medicine and Prof. of Biomedical Sciences 2008–, Vice-Dean, Research and Grad. Research Educ. 2011–17, Dir History of Medicine Program 2018–; Ed.-in-Chief Experimental Nephrology 1993–2002; numerous invited lectureships; Founding Fellow, Acad. of Medical Sciences, UK 1998; mem. Bd of Dirs Nat. Inst. for Clinical Excellence 2002. *Publications:* over 100 articles in the area of kidney disease and renal biology. *Leisure interest:* collecting private press books and fine printing, photo books, post-war and contemporary art. *Address:* Cedars-Sinai Medical Center, 8700 Beverly Blvd, Los Angeles, CA 90048, USA (office). *E-mail:* leon.fine@cshs.org (office). *Website:* www.cedars-sinai.edu (office).

FINEBERG, Harvey Vernon, BA, MPP, MD, PhD; American physician and professional society administrator; *President, Gordon and Betty Moore Foundation;* b. 15 Sept. 1945; s. of Saul Fineberg and Miriam Fineberg (née Pearl); m. Mary Elizabeth Wilson 1975; ed Harvard Univ.; Intern, Beth Israel Hosp., Boston 1972–73; Asst Prof., School of Public Health, Harvard Univ. 1973–78, Assoc. Prof. 1978–81, Prof. 1981–2002, Dean 1984–97, Provost, Harvard Univ. 1997–2001; physician at E Boston Health Center 1974–76, Harvard St Health Center 1976–84; Jr Fellow, Harvard Univ. 1974–75, Mellon Fellow 1976; Pres. Gordon and Betty Moore Foundation 2014–; Trustee, Newton Wellesley Hosp., Mass. 1981–86; mem. Public Health Council, Mass. 1976–79; mem. Bd of Dirs American Foundation for

AIDS Research 1986–97; mem. NAS Inst. of Medicine 1983– (Pres. 2002–14); Hon. Assoc., Mexican Foundation for Health 1998; Hon. DrSc (New York Medical Coll.) 2004, (Univ. of Arkansas for Medical Sciences) 2005, (George Washington Univ.) 2007; Hon. DrMed (Univ. of South Florida) 2006; Joseph W. Mountin Lecture Prize, Centers for Disease Control 1988, Wade Hampton Frost Lecture Prize, Epidemiology Section, American Public Health Asscn 1988, James A. Shannon Lecturer, NIH 2003, The Harvard Medal, Harvard Alumni Asscn 2009, Frank A. Calderon Prize in Public Health, Columbia Univ. 2011. *Publications include:* Clinical Decision Analysis (co-author) 1980, The Epidemic that Never Was 1983, Innovators in Physician Education 1996; numerous articles in professional journals. *Address:* Gordon and Betty Moore Foundation, 1661 Page Mill Road, Palo Alto, CA 94304, USA (office). *Telephone:* (650) 213-3000 (office). *Fax:* (650) 213-3003 (office). *E-mail:* info@moore.org (office). *Website:* www.moore.org (office).

FINEMAN, S. David, BA, LLB, JD; American lawyer and business executive; *Co-founder and Manager, Fineman Krekstein & Harris P.C.;* ed American Univ., George Washington Univ.; fmr Lecturer on Business Law, Temple Univ.; Co-founder and Man. Pnr, Fineman & Bach, PC (law firm), now Fineman, Krekstein & Harris, P.C. Phila; served as Special Counsel to Phila Parking Authority, Sec. of Banking of Commonwealth of Pa, Insurance Commr of Commonwealth of Pa; fmr mem. Phila Planning Comm., Phila Mayor Edward Rendell's Intergovernmental Task Force, Mayor W. Wilson's Transition Team 1987; apptd Gov., US Postal Service by Pres. Bill Clinton 1995, Vice-Chair. Bd of Govs 2001–03, Chair. 2003–05; Chair. DHL Global Mail—Americas 2010–; mem. Bd Dirs MDI Entertainment LLC 1998–2003, SkyShop Logistics Inc. 2008–09, CCA Industries, Inc. 2015–; apptd to Center City Advisory Bd, Jefferson Bank 1999; fmr mem. Industry Policy Advisory Cttee, US Secr. of Commerce; mem. ABA, Phila Bar Asscn; mem. Urban Land Inst. (fmr Chair. Public Policy Cttee). *Address:* Fineman, Krekstein & Harris, Ten Penn Center, 1801 Market Street, Suite 1100, Philadelphia, PA 19103, USA (office). *Telephone:* (215) 893-8701 (office). *Fax:* (215) 893-8719 (office). *E-mail:* SDFineman@finemanlawfirm.com (office). *Website:* www.finemanlawfirm.com (office).

FINI, Gianfranco; Italian politician; b. 3 Jan. 1952, Bologna; fmr journalist; mem. Movimento Sociale Italiano-Destra Nazionale (MSI) 1987–94, Alleanza Nazionale 1994–2008, Chair. 1994–2008; Vice-Pres. Council of Ministers (Deputy Prime Minister) 2001–04; Minister of Foreign Affairs 2004–06; Pres. Camera dei Deputati (Chamber of Deputies) 2008–13; Co-founder Popolo della Libertà (People of Freedom) 2009, then Founder and Leader, Generazione Italia (Generation Italy) 2010; Pres. Future and Freedom for Italy 2011–13; Rep. to EU Special Convention on Pan-European Constitution 2002–06. *Publications include:* Un'Italia civile 1999, L'Europa che verrà 2003, Progetto per l'Italia 2009, Il Futuro della Libertà 2009, L'Italia che vorrei 2011, Il ventennio Io Berlusconi e la destra tradita 2013.

FINIKASO, Taukelina T., LLB; Tuvaluan diplomatist and politician; *Minister of Foreign Affairs, Environment, Trade, Labour and Tourism;* ed Univ. of Sydney, Australia; High Commr to Fiji (non-resident to Papua New Guinea and Samoa) 2001–06; MP for Vaitupu 2006–; Minister of Works, Communications and Transport 2006–10, for Communications, Transport and Fisheries Sept.–Dec. 2010, Minister of Foreign Affairs, Environment, Trade, Labour and Tourism 2013–. *Address:* Ministry of Foreign Affairs, Vaiaku, Funafuti, Tuvalu (office). *Telephone:* 20102 (office). *Fax:* 20820 (office).

FINK, Gerald R., BA, MS, PhD; American geneticist and professor of genetics; *American Cancer Society Professor of Genetics, Massachusetts Institute of Technology;* b. 1 July 1940, Brooklyn, New York; s. of Rebecca Fink and Benjamin Fink; m. Rosalie Lewis 1961; two d.; ed Amherst Coll., Yale Univ.; Postdoctoral Fellow, NIH 1965–66, 1966–67; Instructor, NIH Grad. Program 1966; Instructor, Cold Spring Harbor Summer Program 1970; Asst Prof. of Genetics, Cornell Univ. 1967–71, Assoc. Prof. 1971–76, Prof. 1976–79, Prof. of Biochemistry 1979–82; Prof. of Molecular Genetics, MIT 1982–; American Cancer Soc. Prof. of Genetics 1979–; Founding mem. Whitehead Inst. for Biomedical Research 1982–, Dir 1990–2001; Sec. Genetics Soc. of America 1977–80, Vice-Pres. 1986–87, Pres. 1988–89; Fellow, American Acad. of Arts and Sciences; mem. NAS, American Philosophical Soc., Inst. of Medicine 1996, American Acad. of Microbiology 1996; Hon. DSc (Amherst Coll.) 1982, (Cold Spring Harbor) 1999; NAS-US Steel Prize in Molecular Biology 1981, Genetics Soc. of America Medal 1982, Yale Science and Eng Award 1984, Emil Christian Hansen Foundation Award for Microbiological Research 1986, Wilbur Lucius Cross Medal, Yale Univ. 1992, Bristol-Myers Squibb Infectious Disease Research Award 1993, Ellison Medical Foundation Sr Scholar Award 2001, George W. Beadle Award, Genetics Soc. of America 2001, Yeast Genetics and Molecular Biology Lifetime Achievement Award 2002, Genetics Prize, Peter and Patricia Gruber Foundation 2010. *Publications:* numerous scientific publs. *Address:* Department of Biology, Massachusetts Institute of Technology, 77 Massachusetts Avenue 68-132, Cambridge, MA 02139, USA (office). *Telephone:* (617) 258-5215 (office). *E-mail:* gfink@wi.mit.edu (office). *Website:* www.biology.mit.edu (office).

FINK, Jonathan, BA, PhD, FAAS; American volcanologist, academic and administrator; *Professor of Geology, Portland State University;* b. (Jonathan Harry Fink), 2 May 1951, New York City; s. of Max Fink and Martha Fink; m. Nina DeLange; two c.; ed Colby Coll., Stanford Univ.; has held post-doctoral appointments in Dept of Applied Math., Weizmann Inst., Israel, and in Planetary Geology group, Arizona State Univ.; joined Arizona State Univ. 1979, Prof. 2006–09, Emer. Prof. 2011–, School of Earth and Space Exploration, Coll. of Liberal Arts and Sciences and School of Sustainability 1982–2006, Chair. Geology Dept (now part of School for Earth and Space Exploration) 1995–97, Vice-Provost for Research 1997–2002, Vice-Pres. for Research and Econ. Affairs 2002–07, Julie A. Wrigley Dir Global Inst. of Sustainability 2007–09, Dir, Center for Sustainability Science Applications 2009–11, also Univ. Sustainability Officer, Office of the Pres. 2007–09; held adjunct faculty position in Dept of Chemical Eng, Univ. of Colorado; Dir Geochemistry and Petrology Program, NSF 1992–93; Vice-Pres. for Research and Strategic Partnerships, Portland State Univ. 2010–16, Prof., Dept of Geology 2011–, apptd Sr Advisor to the Pres. 2016, Dir Earth, Environment, Soc. PhD Program; Visiting Prof. of Urban Analytics, Dept of Earth, Ocean and Atmospheric Sciences, Univ. British Columbia 2017–; fmr Visiting Fellow, Research School of Earth Sciences, ANU, Australia; fmr Visiting Scientist, Smithsonian Inst. Nat. Museum of Natural History; mem. Bd of Dirs, The Nature Conservancy, Arizona 2008–13, Oregon 2014–; mem. Bd of Advisors, Smithsonian Inst. Nat. Museum of Natural History, Bd of Trustees, Oregon Museum of Science and Industry, Bd of Advisors, KB Home; Fellow, Geological Soc. of America 1997. *Publications include:* books edited: The emplacement of silicic domes and lava flows 1987, Lava flows and domes: Emplacement mechanisms and hazard implications 1990, Remote sensing of active volcanoes 2000; numerous scientific papers in professional journals on fluid mechanics, remote sensing, isotope geochemistry to study volcanic eruptions on Earth and other planets, and problems of urban sustainability. *Leisure interests:* bicycling, skiing, swimming, hiking, bird watching. *Address:* Toulan School of Urban Studies and Planning, Portland State University, Portland, OR 97207, USA (office). *Telephone:* (503) 725-9995 (office). *E-mail:* jon.fink@pdx.edu (office); jon.fink@ubc.ca. *Website:* www.pdx.edu (office).

FINK, Laurence (Larry) Douglas, BA, MBA; American investment banker; *Chairman and CEO, BlackRock, Inc.;* ed Univ. of California, Los Angeles and UCLA Anderson School of Man.; began career in bond trading div. of The First Boston Corpn 1976, became one of first mortgage-backed securities traders on Wall Street, later Co-head, Taxable Fixed Income Div., started Financial Futures and Options Dept and headed Mortgage and Real Estate Products Group, mem. Man. Cttee and a Man. Dir The First Boston Corpn aged 28; f. BlackRock 1988, mem. Bd of Dirs 1999–, Chair. and CEO BlackRock, Inc. 1998–, Chair. Exec. Cttee, Man. Cttee, mem. Nominating and Governance Cttee, Chair. and CEO Blackrock Financial Management Inc., CEO and Dir BlackRock International Ltd, Chair. and CEO BlackRock Advisors, Chair. Nomura BlackRock Asset Man. (jt venture in Japan), Trustee and Pres. BlackRock Funds, Dir several of BlackRock's offshore funds and alternative investment vehicles; mem. Pres.'s Strategic and Policy Forum Jan.–Aug. 2017; mem. Bd of Trustees New York Univ., Chair. Financial Affairs Cttee and mem. Exec. Cttee, Ad Hoc Exec. on Bd Governance, Cttee on Trustees; Co-Chair. and mem. Exec. Cttee Mount Sinai New York Univ. Health Bd of Trustees, New York Univ. Hosps Center Bd of Trustees (Chair. Devt/Trustee Stewardship Cttee and mem. Finance Cttee); mem. Bd Execs New York Stock Exchange (now NYSE Next), mem. an advisory panel 2003–. *Address:* Corporate Communications Department, BlackRock, Inc., 55 East 52nd Street, New York, NY 10055, USA (office). *Telephone:* (212) 810-5300 (office). *Fax:* (212) 810-8760 (home). *E-mail:* blackrockbod@blackrock.com (office). *Website:* www2.blackrock.com (office).

FINK, Baron (Life Peer), cr. 2011, of Northwood in the County of Middlesex; **Stanley Fink;** British banking and finance executive and philanthropist; *CEO, International Standard Asset Management;* b. 12 Sept. 1957; m. Barbara Fink; three c.; ed Manchester Grammar School, Trinity Hall, Cambridge; qualified as chartered accountant 1982; with Mars 1982–83; Vice-Pres. Citibank NA 1983–86; joined Man Group PLC 1987, mem. Bd of Dirs with responsibility for planning, strategy and mergers and acquisitions 1988–91, Group Finance Dir 1991–96, led Man's initial public offering on London Stock Exchange 1994, Man. Dir small fund man. business 1996–2000, Group Chief Exec. 2000–07, Deputy Chair. –2008; CEO International Standard Asset Management in partnership with Lord Levy 2008–; Chair. Earth Capital LLP; Chair. Absolute Return for Kids 2009–; Co-Treas. Conservative Party 2009–10, Treas. 2010–. *Address:* International Standard Asset Management, 52 Queen Anne Street, London, W1G 8HL (office); House of Lords, Westminster, London, SW1A 0PW, England (office). *Telephone:* (20) 7258-9940 (office); (20) 7219-3000 (House of Lords) (office). *Fax:* (20) 7258-9941 (office); (20) 7219-5979 (House of Lords) (office). *Website:* www.isamfunds.com (office).

FINKE, Nikki; American journalist; b. 1953; m. Jeffrey W. Greenberg 1980 (divorced 1982); ed Wellesley Coll.; worked in Washington, DC for New York congressman Ed Koch; later joined the Associated Press (AP) and worked in Baltimore, Boston, the foreign desk at New York City headquarters, Moscow and London; later worked for The Dallas Morning News; joined staff of Newsweek as corresp. in Washington, DC and Los Angeles; later worked at Los Angeles Times as staff writer covering entertainment and features; West Coast Ed. for The New York Observer and then New York Magazine and wrote Hollywood business columns 1995–2000; has also written for The New York Times, Vanity Fair, Esquire, Harper's Bazaar, Elle, The Washington Post, Salon.com, Premiere and Los Angeles magazine; began writing LA Weekly column, Deadline Hollywood 2002, began Deadline (Deadline Hollywood Daily –2009) blog as daily online version of weekly column 2006, Founder, Ed.-in-Chief and Gen. Man. Deadline.com –2013; sold Deadline to Jay Penske's Mail.com Media Corpn under an agreement by which she continued as the writer and ed. of the website 2009–13; LA Weekly columns won First Place in the Alternative Weekly Awards for the category Media Reporting/Criticism, Circulation >50,000 2006, Los Angeles Press Club's Southern California Journalism Award for Entertainment Journalist of the Year 2007, Deadline won Second Place in AltWeekly Awards 2007. *Website:* nikkifinke.com (office).

FINKEL, Alan Simon, AO, FAA, PhD; Australian neuroscientist, engineer and entrepreneur; *Chief Scientist of Australia;* b. 17 Jan. 1953; m. Elizabeth Finkel; ed Monash Univ.; neuroscience research fellow, John Curtin School of Medical Research, Australian Nat. Univ. 1981–83; f. Axon Instruments (medical devices business), California 1983; Chief Tech. Officer, Molecular Devices (after it acquired Axon Instruments) 2004; Founder and Exec. Publr Cosmos (science magazine) 2004–; led amalgamation of fmr Howard Florey Inst., Brain Research Inst. and Nat. Stroke Research Inst. to form Florey Neuroscience Insts 2007; Chancellor, Monash Univ. 2008–16; Chief Scientist of Australia 2016–; Chief Tech. Officer, Better Place Australia 2009–11; co-f. Stile Education (educ. tech. co.) 2012; fmr Chair. Australian Centre of Excellence for All-Sky Astrophysics (CAASTRO), Manhattan Investment Group, Speedpanel Australia; Dir Cogstate Ltd (diagnostics co.) 2015–; Fellow, Australian Acad. of Tech. Sciences and Eng (ATSE) 2006–, Pres. 2013–15; Patron, Australian Science Media Centre 2014–; hon. mem. Monash Golden Key Soc. 2008; Inst. of Eng and Tech. Mountbatten Medal (UK) 2015. *Address:* Office of the Chief Scientist, Industry House, 10 Binara Street, Canberra, ACT 2601, Australia (office). *Fax:* (2) 6213-6558 (office). *Website:* www.chiefscientist.gov.au (office).

FINLAY, B. Brett, OC, BSc, PhD, FRSC; Canadian microbiologist and academic; *Peter Wall Distinguished Professor, University of British Columbia;* ed Univ. of Alberta, Stanford Univ. School of Medicine, USA; Assoc. Prof., Biotechnology Lab., Univ. of British Columbia 1989–96, Prof., Michael Smith Labs and Dept of

Biochemistry and Molecular Biology and Dept of Microbiology and Immunology 1996–, Peter Wall Distinguished Prof. 2002–; Dir SARS Accelerated Vaccine Initiative; Co-founder Inimex Pharmaceuticals, Inc.; mem. several editorial and advisory bds; mem. Canadian Centres of Excellence for Bacterial Diseases 1989; Fellow, American Acad. of Microbiology 2003, Canadian Acad. of Health Sciences 2005; Hon. mem. Univ. of British Columbia Golden Key Int. Honour Soc. 2001; Distinguished Scientist Seminar Award, Univ. of Southern Alabama 1991, Howard Hughes Medical Inst. Int. Research Scholar 1991, 1997, 2000, 2001, Fisher Scientific Award, Canadian Soc. of Microbiologists 1991, Killam Research Prize, Univ. of British Columbia 1993, Soc. Scientist Award 1996, 21st Annual Joseph E. Smadel Lecturer, Infectious Diseases Soc. of America 1997, E.W.R. Steacie Prize 1998, Howard Hughes Medical Inst. Holiday Lectures Presenter (first non-American) 1999, Dr Cam Coady Foundation Lectureship 2001, CIHR Distinguished Investigator Award 2001, 3M Distinguished Lectureship, Univ. of Western Ontario 2001, Distinguished Lecture in Biochemistry Award and Plaque, Univ. of Alberta 2001, Celebrate Research citation, Univ. of British Columbia 2001–04, James W. McLaughlin Distinguished Speaker, Univ. of Texas Medical Br. at Galveston 2002, Nat. Merit Award, Ottawa Life Sciences Council 2003, chosen by Time Canada as one of five Best in Medicine 2003, British Columbia Biotechnology Award for Innovation and Achievement 2003, featured in Maclean's The 2003 Watch List 2003, Solutions Through Research Award, British Columbia Innovation Council 2004, Squibb Award, Infectious Diseases Soc. of America 2004, Michael Smith Prize in Health Research 2004, CIHR Partnership Award for Sars Accelerated Vaccine Initiative 2005, awarded US $5.7m. from Genome Canada for the PREPARE (Proteomics for Emerging Pathogen Response) project 2005, Gates Foundation Award in Global Disease Fight 2005, Jacob Biely Faculty Research Prize, Univ. of British Columbia 2006, Killam Prize, Canada Council for the Arts 2006, RSC Flavelle Medal 2006. *Publications:* numerous scientific papers in professional journals on host–pathogen interactions at the molecular level. *Address:* Michael Smith Laboratories, Room #333, 2185 East Mall, University of British Columbia, Vancouver, BC V6T 1Z4, Canada (office). *Telephone:* (604) 822-2210 (office). *Fax:* (604) 822-9830 (office). *E-mail:* bfinlay@msl.ubc.ca (office). *Website:* www.finlaylab.msl.ubc.ca (office).

FINLAYSON, Chris, BA, LLM, LTCL; New Zealand lawyer and politician; b. 4 Dec. 1956, Wellington; ed Victoria Univ.; admitted to Bar 1981; Partner, Brandon Brookfield (law firm) 1986–90; Lecturer in Law, Victoria Univ. 1987–2002; Law Soc. Rep., New Zealand Council of Law Reporting 1990–98, New Zealand Council of Legal Educ. 1992–98, High Court Rules Cttee 1999–2005; Partner, Bell Gully 1991–2003; Barrister 2003–; mem. New Zealand Nat. Party 1974–, mem. Rules Cttee 1997–2001, Regional Chair. Lower North Island 2001–03, Electorate Chair. Mana Electorate 2003–05, Policy Chair. 2005; Assoc. Spokesman Treaty of Waitangi Issues and Maori Affairs 2005–06, Arts, Culture and Heritage 2005–06; Deputy Chair. Justice and Electoral Cttee 2005–08; Attorney-Gen. 2008–17, also Minister in Charge of Treaty of Waitangi Negotiations 2008–17, Minister for Arts, Culture and Heritage 2008–14, Minister in Charge of the New Zealand Security Intelligence Service, Minister Responsible for the Govt Communications Security Bureau (GCSB) and Assoc. Minister for Maori Devt 2014; Chair. Arts Board 1998–2001; Trustee Theatre Arts Charitable Trust, New Zealand Symphony Orchestra Foundation. *Address:* New Zealand National Party, 41 Pipitea St, Thorndon, Wellington 6011, New Zealand (office). *Telephone:* (4) 894-7016 (office). *Fax:* (4) 894-7031 (office). *E-mail:* hq@national.org.nz (office). *Website:* www.national.org.nz (office).

FINLAYSON, Max, BSc, PhD; Australian ecologist, academic and international organization official; *Professor of Ecology and Biodiversity and Director, Institute for Land, Water and Society, Charles Sturt University;* b. Mt Barker, WA; ed Univ. of Western Australia, James Cook Univ., Townsville; worked with CSIRO Irrigation Research at Griffith on aquatic weed control and using water plants to treat waste water 1980–83; worked at Office of the Supervising Scientist, Alligator Rivers Region, Kakadu, Northern Territory researching effects of uranium mining on floodplain environment 1983–89, research/managerial job 1993–2000; worked with Int. Waterbird and Wetland Research Bureau, Slimbridge, Glos., UK 1989–93, worked on wetlands conservation projects and capacity building in USSR, Eastern Europe, Eastern Africa and the Mediterranean; worked in S Africa arguing against expansion of mineral sands mining into St Lucia Nature Reserve; Dir Environmental Research Inst. for Office of Supervising Scientists, Darwin 2000–05; Prin. Researcher (Ecology), Int. Water Man. Inst., Colombo, Sri Lanka 2005–07; Prof. of Ecology and Biodiversity and Dir Inst. for Land, Water and Society, Charles Sturt Univ. 2007–; Adjunct Prof., Inst. for Water Educ., UNESCO; Pres. Supervisory Council, Wetlands International 2001–07; mem. Scientific Advisory Council to Biological Station Tour Du Valat, Camargue, France 2007–; Recognition of Excellence, Ramsar Wetland Conservation Awards 2002. *Publications:* more than 200 book chapters, journal articles, reports, guidelines and proceedings on wetland ecology and management. *Address:* Institute for Land, Water and Society, Charles Sturt University, Albury-Wodonga (Thurgoona) Campus, Elizabeth Mitchell Drive, PO Box 789, Albury, NSW 2640, Australia (office). *Telephone:* (2) 6051-9779 (office). *Fax:* (2) 6051-9797 (office). *E-mail:* mfinlayson@csu.edu.au (office); m.finlayson@unesco-ihe.org (office). *Website:* www.csu.edu.au/research/ilws (office); www.maxfinlaysonresearch.com.

FINLEY, The Hon. Diane, PC, BA, MBA; Canadian politician; b. 1957, Hamilton, Ont.; m. Doug Finley; ed Port Dover Composite School, Univ. of Western Ont.; fmr Admin. Univ. of Western Ont. French immersion school; positions in health care, transportation, agricultural equipment manufacturing, publishing, aviation; fmrly with Laidlaw Group of Cos; mem. House of Commons (Parl.) for Haldimand–Norfolk 2004–; Official Opposition Critic for Agric. and Agri-food 2004; Minister of Human Resources and Skills Devt 2006–07, 2008–13, of Citizenship and Immigration 2007–08, of Public Works and Government Services 2013–15. *Address:* Conservative Party of Canada, 130 Albert Street, Suite 1720, Ottawa, ON K1P 5G4, Canada (office). *Telephone:* (613) 755-2000 (office). *Fax:* (613) 755-2001 (office). *E-mail:* info@conservative.ca (office). *Website:* www.conservative.ca (office).

FINLEY, Gerald Hunter, OC, MA (Cantab.), ARCM, FRCM, CBE; Canadian opera singer (bass-baritone) and conductor; b. 1960, Montreal; s. of Eric Gault Finley and Catherine Rae Finley; m. 1st Louise Winter 1990 (divorced 2009); two s.; m. 2nd Heulwen Keyte 2010; one d.; ed Glebe Collegiate Inst., Univ. of Ottawa, Royal Coll. of Music, UK, Nat. Opera Studio, London, King's Coll., Cambridge; chorister, St Matthew's Church, Ottawa 1969–78; mem. Ottawa Choral Soc., Cantata Singers, Ont. Youth Choir 1977–78, Glyndebourne Festival Chorus, UK 1986–89; professional debut as opera soloist, Antonio (Le nozze di Figaro), Ottawa 1987 and Papageno (Die Zauberflöte), London 1989; debut at Glyndebourne with Glyndebourne Touring Opera as Kuligin (Katya Kabanova) 1988, Sid (Albert Herring) 1989, English Clerk (Death in Venice) 1989, Fiorello, Figaro (Il barbiere di Siviglia) 1989, Papageno 1990, with Glyndebourne Festival Opera as Count Dominik (Arabella) 1989, Kuligin 1990, Guglielmo 1992, Figaro at opening of new Glyndebourne opera house 1994, Owen Wingrave 1997, Olivier (Capriccio) 1998, Nick Shadow (The Rake's Progress) 2000, Agamemnon (Iphigénie en Aulide) 2002, Don Giovanni 2010, Hans Sachs (Meistersinger) 2011, 2016; debut at Canadian Opera Co. as Sid 1991, Figaro 1993, Falstaff 2014; debut at Festival d'Aix-en-Provence as Demetrius (A Midsummer Night's Dream) 1991; Amsterdam as Demetrius 1993, Count Almaviva (Le nozze di Figaro) 2001; debut at Covent Garden as Flemish Deputy (Don Carlo) 1989, Figaro 1995, Achilla (Giulio Cesare) 1997, Pilgrim (Pilgrim's Progress) 1997, Creonte (L'anima del filosofo) 2001, Forester (Cunning Little Vixen) 2003, Don Giovanni 2005, 2012, Count Almaviva (Le nozze di Figaro) 2006, Yeletsky (Pique Dame) 2006, Golaud (Pelléas et Mélisande) 2007, Onegin (Eugene Onegin) 2008, Frank/Fritz (Die tote Stadt) 2009, Zurga (Les pêcheurs de perles) 2010, Howard K. Stern (Anna Nicole) 2011; debut at Opéra de Paris as Valentin (Faust) 1997, Sharpless (Madama Butterfly) 1998, Papageno 2001, Figaro 2003, Don Giovanni 2003, Count Almaviva (Le nozze di Figaro) 2003, Olivier 2004, Hans Sachs 2016; debut at Metropolitan Opera, New York as Papageno 1998, 2000, Marcello 2001, 2010, Don Giovanni 2005, Golaud 2010, Count Amaviva (Le nozze di Figaro) 2013, Nick Shadow 2015; debut at Lyric Opera Chicago as Olivier 1994, Papageno 2002, Wolfram (Tannhäuser) 2015; debut at Los Angeles Opera as Figaro 1995, Belcore (L'elisir d'amore) 1996, Mr Fox (Fantastic Mr Fox) 1998; debut at ENO as Harry Heegan (The Silver Tassie) 2000, Chou-en-lai (Nixon in China) 2004, Onegin 2005, Balstrode (Peter Grimes) 2009; debut at San Francisco Opera as J. Robert Oppenheimer (Dr Atomic) 2005, Amsterdam 2007, Chicago 2008, Metropolitan Opera 2008, Atlanta 2008, ENO 2009; debut at Salzburg Festival as Count Almaviva (Le nozze di Figaro) 2007, 2009, Don Giovanni 2011, Don Alfonso 2013; debut at Bayerische Staatsoper as Don Giovanni 2010, 2013, Escamillo (Carmen) 2011, Count Almaviva (Le nozze di Figaro) 2014; Don Giovanni at Tel Aviv 2000, Vienna TAW 2006, Prague 2006, Budapest 2006, Rome 2006, Iago (Otello), London Symphony Orchestra, London 2009; Guillaume Tell, Accad. di Santa Cecilia 2010; debut at Vienna State Opera as Count Almaviva (Le nozze di Figaro) 2012, Forester 2014; Chou-en-lai (Nixon) BBC Symph. Orch. London, Berlin 2012; Il prigioniero New York Phil. 2013, Bayer. Rundf. Ork, 2013; Golaud Berlin Phil. 2015, LSO 2016; title role in Falstaff, Canadian Opera Co. 2014; performed world premiere of True Fire by Kaija Saariaho 2015; concert soloist and lieder singer; Visiting Prof., Royal Coll. of Music 2000–; Hon. DLitt (Saskatchewan) 2015; John Christie Award, Glyndebourne 1989, Juno Award for Best Vocal Performance (Canada) 1998, 2011, 2015, Singer Award, Royal Philharmonic Soc. 2001, Opera News Award 2009, Opera Canada Ruby Award 2013, DORA Award, Outstanding Opera Performance – Male (for Falstaff Canadian Opera, Toronto) 2015. *Films include:* Owen Wingrave 2001, L'amour de loin 2006, Doctor Atomic 2008, Die Meistersinger von Nürmberg 2012. *Recordings include:* albums include: Papageno, Guglielmo, Sid, Masetto, Haydn's Creation, Brahms' Requiem, Handel Messiah, Bach Weihnachtsoratorium, The Silver Tassie, Pilgrim's Progress, Dido and Aeneas, Songs of Travel 1998, Schubert Complete Songs 1817–1821, Complete Songs of Henri Duparc 2002, Songs of Charles Ives 2005, 2008, Stanford – Orchestral Songs (Editor's Choice Award, Gramophone Awards) 2006, Barber – Songs (Gramophone Award for Best Solo Vocal 2008), Schumann – Dichterliebe, etc. (Gramophone Award for Best Solo Vocal Performance 2009), Ravel – Songs 2009, Opera Arias in English (Juno Award 2011) 2010, Otello 2010, LSO, Britten Songs & Proverbs of William Blake (Gramophone Award for Best Solo Vocal Recording) 2011, The Ballad Singer 2011, Doctor Atomic (with Alan Gilbert, Meredith Arwady, Richard Paul Fink, Sasha Cooke, Thomas Glenn, Eric Owens and Jay David Saks) (Grammy Award for Best Opera Recording 2012) 2012, Schubert's Winterreise (with Julius Drake) (Juno Award-Vocal or Choral Performance) 2015) 2014, Liszt Songs 2015, Sibelius Songs 2016. *Radio:* numerous recordings with BBC, CBC, ORF and BR. *Achievements include:* climbed Mount Kilimanjaro in 2014 to raise funds for UK-based Musicians' Charity. *Leisure interests:* wine, reading, ice skating. *Address:* c/o IMG Artists, Capital Tower, 91 Waterloo Road, London, SE1 8RT, England (office); Alison Pybus, 10395 Wetherburn Road, Ellicott City, MD 21163, USA (office). *Telephone:* (20) 7957-5800 (London) (office); (410) 480-2095 (office). *Fax:* (20) 7957-5801 (London) (office). *E-mail:* salmansi@imgartists.com (office); alisonpybus73@gmail.com (office). *Website:* www.imgartists.com (office); www.geraldfinley.com.

FINN, Maj.-Gen. Michael, BComm; Irish army officer (retd) and UN official; b. 3 March 1953, Aughervilla, Claremorris; m. Helen Cummins; three c.; ed Nat. Univ. of Ireland, Galway, Irish Defence Forces Command and Staff Coll.; served in Irish Defence Forces –2015; served in various positions with UN peacekeeping forces overseas, served three tours of duty with UN Interim Force in Lebanon (UNIFIL) 1980–98, Mil. Observer with UN Truce Supervision Organisation (UNTSO), including Observer Group Golan, UN Disengagement Observer Force (UNDOF) and Observer Group Lebanon, UN Interim Force in Lebanon (UNIFIL) 1993–95, Commdr, first Irish infantry force with KFOR (Kosovo Force) mission, Kosovo 2003–04; Dir of Logistics, EU Mil. Staff, Brussels 2007–10; Asst Chief of Staff (Support) 2010–12, Gen. Officer commanding Second Infantry 2012–13; Head of Mission and Chief of Staff, UN Truce Supervision Org. (UNTSO) 2013–15. *Leisure Interests:* reading, foreign travel, Gaelic football, rugby.

FINN, Victor Konstantinovich, DrSc; Russian philosopher, logician and computer scientist; b. 15 July 1933, Moscow; m. Irina Yevgenyevna Yavchunovskaya-Belova; one d.; ed Moscow State Univ.; researcher, Head of Sector, Lab. of Electromodelling, USSR Acad. of Sciences 1957–59; Head of Lab. All-Union Inst. for Scientific and Tech. Information (VINITI) 1959–, currently Head, Dept of Intelligent Information Systems and Dept of Intelligent Systems for the Humanities; Lecturer, Moscow State Univ. 1967–68; Prof., Head Dept of Artificial Intelligence, Moscow State Inst. of History and Archives (now Russian Humanitarian Univ.) 1979–; mem. Bd int. journals Studia Logica, Foundation of Science; mem. Council Russian Assn of Artificial Intelligence; Honoured Science Worker 2007. *Publications:* over 100 scientific papers and books including Logical Problems of Information Search 1976, Epistemological and Logical Problems of History (with K. Khvostova) 1995, Intellectual Systems and Society 2001. *Address:* 1st Miusskaya str. 20, Apt. 19, 125047 Moscow, Russia (home); Usievitcha str., 20, 125190 Moscow, Russia (office). *Telephone:* (499) 251-08-99 (home); (499) 152-61-13 (office). *Fax:* (499) 152-54-47 (office); (499) 943-00-60 (office). *E-mail:* finn@viniti.ru (office); ira.finn@gmail.com (home). *Website:* www2.viniti.ru (office).

FINNBOGADÓTTIR, Vigdís; Icelandic politician and fmr head of state; b. 15 April 1930, Reykjavik; d. of Finnbogi Rutur Thorvaldsson and Sigridur Eiriksdóttir; m. (divorced); one adopted d.; ed Junior Coll., Menntaskólinn i Reykjavik, Univs of Grenoble and Paris (Sorbonne), France, Univ. of Iceland; Press Officer, Nat. Theatre of Iceland 1954–57, 1961–64; teacher, Reykjavík Grammar School 1962–67, Hamrahlíð Grammar School 1967–72; taught French at Jr Colls, Menntaskólinn i Reykjavik, Menntaskólinn vid Hamrahlid; fmr Head of Guide Training, Iceland Tourist Bureau; Dir Reykjavik Theatre Co. 1972–80; taught French drama, Univ. of Iceland; worked for Icelandic State TV; fmr Chair. Alliance Française; mem. Advisory Cttee on Cultural Affairs in Nordic Countries 1976–80, Chair. 1978–80; Pres. of Iceland 1980–96; UNESCO Goodwill Amb. for Languages 1998–; mem. Club of Madrid; Hon. GCMG 1982; Dr hc (Grenoble) 1985, (Bordeaux) 1987, (Smith Coll., USA) 1988, (Luther Coll., USA) 1989, (Manitoba) 1989, (Nottingham) 1990, (Tampere) 1990, (Gothenburg) 1990, (Gashuin, Tokyo) 1991, (Miami) 1993, (St Mary's, Halifax) 1996, (Leeds) 1996, (Memorial, St John) 1997, (Guelph) 1998, (Iceland) 2000. *Leisure interest:* theatre.

FINNEGAN, John D., BA, JD, MBA; American business executive; *Chairman, President and CEO, The Chubb Corporation;* b. 31 Jan. 1949, Jersey City, NJ; m. Kathleen Finnegan; two c.; ed Princeton, Rutgers and Fordham Univs; began career with General Motors (GM) 1976, various positions including Vice-Pres. GM and Pres. GM Acceptance Corpn 1997–99, Exec. Vice-Pres. GM and Pres. and Chair. GM Acceptance Corpn 1999–2002; apptd Dir The Chubb Corpn 2002, Pres. and CEO 2002–03, Chair., Pres. and CEO 2003–; mem. Bd United Negro Coll. Fund. *Address:* The Chubb Corporation, 15 Mountain View Road, Warren, NJ 07061-1615, USA (office). *Telephone:* (908) 903-2000 (office). *Fax:* (908) 903-3402 (office). *Website:* www.chubb.com (office).

FINNIS, John Mitchell, LLB, DPhil, FBA; Australian/British academic and barrister; *Professor Emeritus of Law and Legal Philosophy, University of Oxford;* b. 28 July 1940, Adelaide, South Australia; s. of Maurice M. S. Finnis and Margaret McKellar Stewart; m. Marie Carmel McNally 1964; three s. three d.; ed St Peter's Coll., Adelaide, St Mark's Coll., Univ. of Adelaide, Univ. Coll., Oxford, UK; Fellow and Praelector in Jurisprudence, Univ. Coll., Oxford 1966–2010, Stowell Civil Law Fellow 1973–2007, Vice-Master 2001–10; Lecturer in Law, Univ. of Oxford 1966–72, Rhodes Reader in the Laws of the Commonwealth and the United States 1972–89, Prof. of Law and Legal Philosophy 1989–2010, then Prof. Emer., mem. Philosophy Sub-Faculty 1984–2010, Chair. Bd of Faculty of Law 1987–89; Prof. and Head of Dept of Law, Univ. of Malawi 1976–78; Biolchini Family Prof. of Law, Univ. of Notre Dame, Ind., USA 1995–, Adjunct Prof. of Philosophy 1999–; barrister, Gray's Inn 1970–; Gov., Plater Coll., Oxford 1972–92; Consultor, Pontifical Commission Iustitia et Pax 1977–89, mem. 1990–95; Special Adviser, Foreign Affairs Cttee, House of Commons, on role of UK Parl. in Canadian Constitution 1980–82; mem. Catholic Bishops' Jt Cttee on Bio-ethical Issues 1981–89, Int. Theological Comm. (Vatican) 1986–92; Gov. Linacre Centre for Medical Ethics 1981–96, 1998– (Vice-Chair. 1987–96, 1998–2008); Huber Distinguished Visiting Prof., Boston Coll. Law School 1993–94; mem. Pontifical Acad. Pro Vita 2001–; Hon. Queen's Counsel 2017. *Publications include:* Halsbury's Laws of England (fourth edn) Vol. 6 (Commonwealth and Dependencies) 1974, 1990, 2003, (fifth edn) Vol. 13 (Commonwealth and Dependencies) 2009, Natural Law and Natural Rights 1980, Fundamentals of Ethics 1983, Nuclear Deterrence, Morality and Realism (with Joseph Boyle and Germain Grisez) 1987, Moral Absolutes 1991, Aquinas: Moral, Political and Legal Theory 1998, The Collected Essays of John Finnis 2011; articles on constitutional law, legal philosophy, ethics, moral theology and late 16th century history. *Address:* University College, Oxford, OX1 4BH, England (office); Notre Dame Law School, South Bend, IN 46556, USA (office). *Telephone:* (574) 631-5989 (South Bend) (office).

FINO, Bashkim Muhamet; Albanian economist and politician; b. 12 Oct. 1962, Gjirokaster; m.; two c.; ed Tirana Univ. and studies in USA; economist, Economic Data Inst., Gjirokaster Dist 1986–89, Dir 1989–92; Mayor of Gjirokaster (Socialist Party of Albania) 1992–96; Prime Minister of Albania March–July 1997; Deputy Prime Minister 1997–98; mem. Kuvendi Popullor (People's Ass.) for Berat 2005–. *Address:* Kuvendi Popullor (People's Assembly), Bulevardi Dëshmorët e Kombit 4, Tirana, Albania. *Telephone:* (4) 2264887. *Fax:* (4) 2221764. *E-mail:* marlind@parlament.al. *Website:* www.parlament.al.

FINSCHER, Ludwig, PhD; German musicologist, lexicographer and academic (retd); b. 14 March 1930, Kassel; ed Univ. of Göttingen; Asst Lecturer, Univ. of Kiel 1960–65, Univ. of Saarbrücken 1965–68; Ed. Die Musikforschung 1961–68, Co-Ed. 1968–74; Prof. of Musicology, Univ. of Frankfurt am Main 1968–81, Univ. of Heidelberg 1981–95; mem. Akad. der Wissenschaften, Heidelberg, Akad. der Wissenschaften und der Literatur, Mainz, Academia Europaea; Corresp. mem. American Musicological Soc.; Hon. mem. Int. Musicological Soc., Gesellschaft für Musikforschung; Hon. Foreign mem. Royal Musical Assn, London 1978; Ordre pour le Mérite 1994, Grand Order of Merit (Germany) 1997; Dr hc (Athens) 2002, (Zürich) 2003, (Saarbrücken) 2009; Akad. der Wissenschaften Prize, Göttingen 1968, Balzan Prize 2006. *Publications include:* Collected Works of Gaffurius (ed., two vols) 1955, 1960, Collected Works of Compère (ed., five vols) 1958–72, Loyset Compère (c. 1450–1518): Life and Works 1964, Geschichte der Evangelischen Kirchenmusik (co-ed., second edn) 1965, Studien zur Geschichte des Streichquartetts: I, Die Entstehung des klassischen Streichquartetts: Von den Vorformen zur Grundlegung durch Joseph Haydn 1974, Collected Works of Hindemith (co-ed. with K. von Fischer) 1976–, Renaissance-Studien: Helmuth Osthoff zum 80. Geburtstag (ed.) 1979, Quellenstudien zu Musik der Renaissance (ed., two vols) 1981, 1983, Ludwig van Beethoven (ed.) 1983, Claudio Monteverdi: Festschrift Reinhold Hammerstein zum 70. Geburtstag (ed.) 1986, Die Musik des 15. und 16. Jahrhunderts: Neues Handbuch der Musikwissenschaft (ed., Vol. 3/1–2) 1989–90, Die Mannheimer Hofkapelle im Zeitalter Carl Theodors (ed.) 1992, Die Musik in Geschichte und Gegenwart (ed., second edn, 26 vols) 1994–2007, Joseph Haydn 2000, Geschichte und Geschichten: Ausgewählte Aufsätze zur Musikhistorie 2003; contrib. editorially to the complete works of Mozart and Gluck, contrib. to scholarly books and journals. *Address:* Am Walde 1, 38302 Wolfenbüttel, Germany (home). *Telephone:* (5331) 32713 (home). *Fax:* (5331) 33276 (home).

FIONDA, Andrew, MA, M.Design; British fashion designer; b. 8 Feb. 1967, Middlesbrough, Cleveland; s. of Frederick Fionda and Sarah Park; ed Nottingham Trent Univ., Royal Coll. of Art, London; designer for fashion houses in UK and for John McIntyre, Hong Kong; Co-founder, with Reynold Pearce (q.v.), Owner and Designer, Pearce Fionda 1994–2013, Dir 2013–, first capsule collection for Spring/Summer 1995 shown in New Generation show during London Fashion Week; also designs PIIF collection for Designers at Debenhams range 1997–, duo now concentrate on evening wear range and children's bridesmaid creations; teacher, Univ. of Brighton 1996–98; Fashion Ed. at Brighton Visitor 2009–13; Fashion Lecturer, Northbrook Coll. Sussex 2015–; exhbns include Design of the Times, RCA 1996, The Cutting Edge of British Fashion 1997; with Reynold Pearce received Newcomers Award for Export, British Knitwear Clothing Export Council and Fashion Weekly 1994, New Generation Award, Lloyds Bank British Fashion Awards 1995, World Young Designers Award, Int. Apparel Fed. 1996, Glamour Award, Lloyds Bank British Fashion Awards 1997. *Leisure interests:* cinema, gym, music, reading. *Telephone:* 7889-602317 (mobile). *E-mail:* info@pearcefionda.com. *Website:* pearcefionda.com.

FIORASO, Geneviève, BA, MA, MA (Econ); French politician and fmr teacher; b. 10 Oct. 1954, Amiens (Somme); ed Univ. of Amiens; worked as an English teacher in Amiens; left teaching and moved to Grenoble 1978, served as Information Officer, then managing Documentation and Press for the City of Grenoble; became parl. attaché to Mayor Hubert Dubedout 1983; participated in cantonal electoral campaign 1985; mem. management team of Corys (startup of the CEA) 1989–95; Chief of Staff to Mayor of Grenoble, Michel Destot 1995; Dir Agence Régionale du Numérique (set up by the digital network of cities of Rhône-Alpes region) 1999–2001; Sr Marketing Man., France Telecom 2001–04; Deputy Asst for the Economy, Innovation, Trade and Craft, and First Vice-Pres. Metro-Agglomeration community of the Grenoble Alpes Métropole, in charge of econ. devt 2003–08, Deputy for the Economy, Universities and Research for the City Council of Grenoble 2008–; CEO S.E.M. Minatec Entreprises (public-pvt. venture, entrusted with the marketing of high-tech building of Minatec) 2003–; Chair. Institut d'Admin des Entreprises Grenoble; Deputy (Parti socialiste—PS) to Nat. Ass. for First Dist of Isère 2007–, Bd mem. Socialist, Radical, Citizen and other groups, mem. Cttee on Econ. Affairs, the Environment and Territory, mem. Parl. Office for Scientific and Technological Choices (OPECST); Minister of Higher Educ. and Research 2012–14.

FIORELLO, Rosario Tindario; Italian singer and radio and television presenter; b. 16 May 1960, Catania; began career working in tourist villages, first as barman and then as singer, mimic and entertainer; spotted by talent scout Claudio Cecchetto late 1980s; began hosting show Viva Radio Deejay; host TV show Karaoke, went on to host various other shows, first on Mediaset networks, then with RAI with Stasera Pago Io 2001, 2002, 2004; Co-host, with Marco Baldini, Francesco Bozzi and Enrico Cremonesi, radio show Viva Radio 2 2002–08. *Recordings include:* Veramente falso 1992, Nuovamente falso 1992, Spiagge e lune 1993, Karaoke 1993, Finalmente tu 1995, Sarò Fiorello 1996, Dai miei amici cantautori 1997, Batticuore (CD Bianco) 1998, Batticuore (CD Rosso) 1998, I miei amici cantautori 2000, Fiorello The Greatest 2002, Uno è famoso, l'altro no: Il meglio di Viva Radio 2 (CD and book) 2002, Viva Radio 2 (il meglio del 2003) 2003, A modo mio 2004, Viva Radio 2 (il meglio del 2005) 2005. *E-mail:* info@rosariofiorello.it. *Website:* www.rosariofiorello.it.

FIORENTINO, Linda; American actress and photographer; b. 9 March 1960, Philadelphia, Pa; ed Rosemont Coll., Circle in the Square Theatre School; mem. Circle in the Square Performing Workshops. *Films include:* Vision Quest 1985, Gotcha! 1985, After Hours 1985, The Moderns 1988, Queens Logic 1991, Shout 1991, Wildfire 1992, Chain of Desire 1993, The Desperate Trail 1994, The Last Seduction (New York Film Critic's Circle Award for Best Actress 1994 and multiple other best actress awards) 1994, Bodily Harm 1995, Larger Than Life 1996, Jade 1995, Unforgettable 1997, The Split 1997, Men in Black 1997, Kicked in the Head 1997, Body Count 1998, Dogma 1999, Ordinary Decent Criminal 2000, Where the Money Is 2000, What Planet Are You From? 2000, Liberty Stands Still 2002, Once More with Feeling 2009. *Television films include:* The Neon Empire 1989, The Last Game 1992, Acting on Impulse 1993, Beyond the Law 1994, The Desperate Trail 1995. *Website:* www.lindafiorentino.com.

FIORI, Publio; Italian politician and lawyer; b. 25 March 1938; elected mem. Rome City Council (Christian Democrat) 1971, Lazio Regional Council 1975; Deputy (Christian Democrat) 1979–94, Deputy (Alleanza Nazionale) 1994, Vice-Pres., Chamber of Deputies 2001; resgnd Alleanza Nazionale 2005, joined Democrazia Cristiana per le Autonomie then resgnd 2006; Founder and Leader Rifondazione Democristiana 2006; fmr mem. Parl. Comm. on Finance, Under-Sec. for Posts and Telecommunications, for Health; Minister of Transport 1994–95.

FIORINA, Carleton (Carly) S., BA, MS, MBA; American computer industry executive and politician; *Chairman and CEO, Carly Fiorina Enterprises;* b. (Cara Carleton Sneed), 6 Sept. 1954, Austin, Tex.; d. of Joseph Tyree Sneed III and Madelon Montross (née Juergens); m. 1st Todd Bartlem 1977 (divorced 1984); m. 2nd Frank Fiorina 1985; two step-d.; ed attended secondary schools in Ghana, UK, N Carolina, and Calif., Charles E. Jordan High School, Durham, NC, Stanford Univ., Robert H. Smith School of Business at Univ. of Maryland, Sloan School of Man. at Massachusetts Inst. of Tech.; began career with entry-level job, Hewlett-Packard Shipping Dept; fmr English teacher in Italy and seller of telephone services to fed. agencies; spent nearly 20 years at AT&T Corpn and Lucent Technologies Inc., Exec. Vice-Pres. Computer Operations, oversaw formation and spin-off of Lucent Technologies from AT&T, served as Lucent's Pres. Global Service Provider Business and Pres. Consumer Products; Pres., CEO and Dir Hewlett-Packard Co. 1999–2000, Chair. and CEO 2000–05; Chair. and CEO Carly Fiorina Enterprises; mem. Bd of Dirs US-China Bd of Trade, PowerUp, Revolution Health Group 2005–, Cybertrust 2005–, Taiwan Semiconductor Manufacturing

Co. Ltd 2006–; Gen. Business News Contrib., Fox Business Network 2007–; econ. adviser to Senator John McCain's campaign for US Pres. 2008; Republican nominee for US Senate representing Calif. June 2010; mem. Exec. Bd NY Stock Exchange; Adviser, US Space Comm.; mem. Bd of Dirs Revolution Healthcare Group LLC, Taiwan Semiconductor Manufacturing; fmr mem. Bd of Dirs Cisco Systems, Kellogg Co., Merck & Co., Telecommunications Industry Asscn, USA-Repub. of China Econ. Council, Goldstar Information & Communications Inc., Seoul, S Korea, AT&T Taiwan Telecommunications, Taipei; Chair. Good360; Founder One Woman Initiative; Global Amb. for Opportunity International; announced candidacy for Republican nomination for Pres. of US May 2015; Hon. Fellow, London Business School 2001; Appeal of Conscience Award 2002, Concern Worldwide 'Seeds of Hope' Award 2003, Private Sector Council Leadership Award 2004. *Publication:* Tough Choices: A Memoir 2006. *Leisure interests:* piano, gardening. *Address:* 3150 South Street NW, No. 3B, Washington, DC 20007, USA (home). *E-mail:* contact@carlyfiorina.com (office). *Website:* www.carlyfiorina.com; www.carlyforca.com.

FIORINI, Matteo; San Marino civil engineer and politician; b. 10 Feb. 1978, San Marino city; m. Marina Spadini 2011; ed Univ. of Bologna; Project Man. Gruppo SIT (packaging co.); mem. Consiglio Grande e Generale (Parl.) 2008–, mem. Foreign Affairs Standing Cttee; Captain-Regent (head of govt) 2011–12, 2017–18; Sec. of State for Land and Environment, Agric., Telecommunications, Youth, Sport, Civil Defence and Relations with the Azienda Autonoma di Stato di Produzione (AASP) 2012–14; mem. Alleanza Popolare. *Leisure interest:* theatre. *Website:* www.sanmarino.sm (office).

FIQI, Abdihakim Mohamed Haji; Somali diplomatist and politician; b. Bay Region, S Somalia; held diplomatic posting in Canada; Minister of Defence 2010–11, 2012–14, also Deputy Prime Minister 2010–11.

FIRE, Andrew Z., BA, PhD; American microbiologist and academic; *Professor of Pathology and Genetics, School of Medicine, Stanford University;* b. 27 April 1959, Santa Clara Co., Calif.; ed Univ. of California, Berkeley and Massachusetts Inst. of Tech.; Researcher, Univ. of Cambridge, UK 1983–86; mem. of staff, Dept of Embryology, Carnegie Inst. of Washington, Baltimore, Md 1986–2003, Carnegie Investigator 2003–; Prof. of Pathology and Genetics, Stanford Univ. School of Medicine 2003–; Adjunct Prof., Dept of Biology, Johns Hopkins Univ., Baltimore 2003–; Fellow, American Acad. of Arts and Sciences; mem. Inst. of Medicine, NAS; Genetics Soc. of America Medal, Maryland Distinguished Young Scientist Award 1997, NAS Award in Molecular Biology (jtly) 2003, Wiley Prize in the Biomedical Sciences, Mellon Lecturer, Univ. of Pittsburgh 2003, Bernard Cohen Memorial Lecturer, Univ. of Pennsylvania School of Medicine 2004, Dr H.P. Heineken Prize for Biochemistry and Piophysics 2004, Gairdner Foundation Int. Award 2005, Nobel Prize in Medicine (with Craig C. Mello) 2006. *Publications:* numerous publs in scientific journals. *Address:* Departments of Pathology and Genetics, Stanford University School of Medicine, 300 Pasteur Drive, L235, Stanford, CA 94305-5324, USA (office). *Telephone:* (650) 723-2885 (office). *Fax:* (650) 725-9070 (office). *E-mail:* afire@stanford.edu (office). *Website:* genome-www.stanford.edu/group/fire (office).

FIRTASH, Dmytro (Dmitrii); Ukrainian business executive; *Executive Chairman, Group DF;* b. 2 May 1965; m. Maria Firtash (divorced); expert in gas trading and distribution business in Eastern and Cen. Europe; secured gas deal with Turkmenistan Govt in exchange for supplies of fresh produce 1993; est. Highrock Holdings, partnership with gas trader Itera to oversee trade between Turkmenistan and Ukrainian state energy-provider Naftogaz 2001; f. Eural Trans Gas 2002 (replaced Highrock Holdings 2003); through his co. Centragas Holdings AG est. partnership with Russian energy corpn Gazprom to set up RosUkrEnergo (headquartered in Switzerland) 2004, which distributes gas from Cen. Asian states to Ukraine and EU; f. OSTCHEM Holding AG 2004, to consolidate his investments in titanium, soda ash, mineral fertilizers and other chemical products; f. Group DF in 2007 to bring together business interests in energy, chemicals and property with other cos including Hungarian gas trader Emfesz and Estonian fertilizer manufacturer Nitrofert, currently Exec. Chair.; took over Nadra Bank 2011; Chair. Fed. of Employers of Ukraine 2010–. *Address:* Group DF, 01601 Kyiv, 23rd Floor, Business Center Parus Street, Mechnikov 2A, Ukraine. *E-mail:* info@groupdf.com (office). *Website:* www.groupdf.com (office); www.dmitryfirtash.com.

FIRTH, Colin Andrew, CBE; British actor; b. 10 Sept. 1960, Grayshott, Hants.; s. of David Firth and Shirley Firth; m. Livia Giuggioli 1997, two s.; one s. by Meg Tilly; ed Montgomery of Alamein School, Winchester and Drama Centre, London; Commdr, Order of the Star of Italian Solidarity 2005. *Theatre includes:* Another Country 1983, Doctor's Dilemma 1984, The Lonely Road 1985, Desire Under the Elms 1987, The Caretaker 1991, Chatsky 1993, Three Days of Rain 1999. *Films include:* Another Country 1983, Camille 1984, A Month in the Country 1986, Apartment Zero 1988, Valmont (title role) 1988, Wings of Fame 1989, Femme Fatale 1990, The Hour of the Pig 1992, Good Girls 1994, Circle of Friends 1995, The English Patient 1996, Fever Pitch 1996, Shakespeare in Love 1998, The Secret Laughter of Women 1999, My Life So Far 1999, Relative Values 1999, Londinium 2000, Bridget Jones's Diary 2000, The Importance of Being Earnest 2002, Hope Springs 2003, Love Actually 2003, Trauma 2004, Bridget Jones: The Edge of Reason 2004, Where the Truth Lies 2005, Nanny McPhee 2005, The Last Legion 2007, And When Did You Last See Your Father? 2007, St Trinian's 2007, In Prison My Whole Life 2007, Then She Found Me 2007, The Accidental Husband 2008, Mamma Mia! 2008, Genova 2008, Easy Virtue 2008, Dorian Gray 2009, A Single Man (Volpi Cup for Best Actor, 66th Venice Int Film Festival 2009, BAFTA Award for Leading Actor 2010) 2009, A Christmas Carol 2009, St Trinian's 2: The Legend of Fritton's Gold 2009, The King's Speech (Golden Globe Award for Best Actor 2011, BAFTA Award for Leading Actor 2011, Acad. Award for Actor in a Leading Role 2011) 2010, Main Street 2010, Tinker, Tailor, Soldier, Spy 2011, Stars in Shorts 2012, Gambit 2013, The Railway Man 2014, Magic in the Moonlight 2014, Kingsman: The Secret Service 2015, Genius 2016, Bridget Jones's Baby 2016, Kingsman: The Golden Circle 2017, The Happy Prince 2018, The Mercy 2018, Mama Mia! Here We Go Again 2018, Mary Poppins Returns 2018. *Radio includes:* Richard II in Two Planks and a Passion 1986, Rupert Brooke in The One Before The Last 1987. *Television appearances:* Dutch Girls 1984, Lost Empires (series) 1985–86, Robert Lawrence in Tumbledown (Radio Times Best Actor Award) 1987, Out of the Blue 1990, Hostages 1992, Master of the Moor 1993, The Deep Blue Sea 1994, Mr Darcy in Pride and Prejudice (Best Actor Award, Broadcasting Press Guild 1996) 1994, Nostromo 1997, The Turn of the Screw 1999, Donovan Quick 1999, Celebration 2006, Born Equal 2006. *Publication:* The Department of Nothing (appeared in 'Speaking with the Angel' short story collection) 2000.

FIRTH, Peter; British actor; b. 27 Oct. 1953, Bradford; s. of Eric Firth and Mavis Firth; m. Lindsey Readman 1990; two s. one d.; has appeared with Nat. Theatre in Equus, Romeo and Juliet, Spring Awakening; Broadway appearances include role of Mozart in Amadeus; Hon. DLitt (Univ. of Bradford) 2009; Acad. Award for Best Supporting Actor, Tony Award, Golden Globe for Best Supporting Actor (all for Equus) and numerous other awards. *Films include:* Fratello sole, sorella luna 1972, Daniele e Maria 1973, King Arthur, the Young Warlord 1975, Aces High 1976, Joseph Andrews 1977, Equus 1977, When You Comin' Back, Red Ryder? 1979, Tess 1979, Feuer und Schwert: Die Legende von Tristan und Isolde 1982, White Elephant 1983, Born of Fire 1983, Letter to Brezhnev 1985, Lifeforce 1985, A State of Emergency 1986, Prisoner of Rio 1988, Tree of Hands 1989, Trouble in Paradise 1989, The Laughter of God 1990, The Hunt for Red October 1990, Burndown 1990, The Rescuers Down Under (voice) 1990, The Pleasure Principle 1991, White Angel 1993, El Marido perfecto 1993, Shadowlands 1993, An Awfully Big Adventure 1995, Marco Polo: Haperek Ha'aharon 1996, Merisairas 1996, Gaston's War 1997, Amistad 1997, Woundings 1998, Mighty Joe Young 1998, Chill Factor 1999, Pearl Harbor 2001, The Greatest Game Ever Played 2005, Ancient Rome: The Rise and Fall of an Empire 2006, World Without End 2010, Mayday 2013, Spooks: The Greater Good 2014. *TV includes:* The Flaxton Boys (series) 1969, Here Come the Double Deckers (series) 1970, Her Majesty's Pleasure 1973, Diamonds on Wheels 1974, The Picture of Dorian Gray 1976, The Lady of the Camellias 1976, The Flipside of Dominick Hide 1980, Another Flip for Dominick 1982, The Aerodrome 1983, Northanger Abbey 1986, Blood Royal: William the Conqueror 1990, The Incident 1990, Children Crossing 1990, Murder in Eden (mini-series) 1991, Prisoner of Honor 1991, Heartbeat (series) 1994, Resort to Murder (mini-series) 1995, The Witch's Daughter 1996, And the Beat Goes On (series) 1996, The Garden of Redemption 1997, The Broker's Man (series) 1997, Holding On (mini-series) 1997, That's Life (series) 2000, Spooks (series) 2002–09, Me & Mrs Jones 2002, Hawking 2004, The Battle for Rome (mini-series) 2006. *Leisure interests:* cookery, sailing.

FISCHER, Ádám; Hungarian conductor; *Principal Conductor, Düsseldorf Symphoniker;* b. 9 Sept. 1949, Budapest, Hungary; m. Doris Fischer 1979; one s. one d.; ed Budapest School of Music; conducting and composition studies in Budapest and Vienna with Swarowsky; held posts at Graz Opera, Karlsruhe; Gen. Music Dir Freiburg 1981–83; work with Bavarian State Opera; regular conductor with Vienna State Opera 1973–, and with Zurich Opera; major debuts Paris Opera 1984, La Scala 1986, Royal Opera House 1989, ENO 1991, San Francisco Opera 1991, Chicago Lyric Opera 1991, Metropolitan Opera, New York 1994; has conducted numerous world-class orchestras, particularly Helsinki Philharmonic, Boston and Chicago Symphonies and LA Philharmonic and Vienna Chamber Orchestra; concert tours to Japan and USA; Music Dir Kassel Opera 1987–92, founder and Artistic Dir, first Gustav Mahler Festival, Kassel 1989; f. Austro-Hungarian Haydn Orchestra (AHHO) and Festival, Eisenstadt, Austria 1987, currently Music Dir AHHO; Chief Conductor, Danish Nat. Chamber Orchestra 1999–; Conductor, Bayreuth Festival (Ring Cycle) 2001; Music Dir, Orchestra of the Hungarian Radio 2004–; f. Wagner Days festival 2006; Music Dir, Hungarian State Opera 2007–10, Prin. Guest Conductor 2010–; Prin. Conductor, Düsseldorf Symphoniker 2015–; Order of Merit of the Repub. of Hungary with Star 2009, Order of Dannebrog; first prize (jtly) Milan Cantelli Competition 1973, Kossuth Prize 2008, Wolf Prize for Music 2018. *Film:* BBC TV film of Bartók's Bluebeard's Castle with London Philharmonic Orchestra (Italia Prize 1989 and Charles Heidsieck Prize). *Recordings include:* complete Haydn symphonies, Mozart: Complete Symphonies (Int. Classical Music Award for Best Collection 2015), Lucio Silla and Des Knaben Wunderhorn with Danish Radio Sinfonietta, Mahler: Symphony No. 7 2016. *Address:* c/o Angelika Csillag, Raab und Böhm Agentur, Plankengasse 7, 1010 Vienna, Austria (office). *Telephone:* (1) 5120501 (office). *Fax:* (1) 5127743 (office). *E-mail:* csillag@rbartists.at (office). *Website:* www.rbartists.at (office).

FISCHER, Alain, MD, PhD; French paediatrician, immunologist and academic; *Professor, Collège de France;* b. 11 Sept. 1949, Paris; ed Université Paris Descartes and Université Paris Jussieu; Postdoctoral Fellowship in Immunology, Univ. Coll., London, UK 1980–81; Group Leader, Institut nat. de la santé et de la recherche médicale (INSERM) Unit 132, Hôpital Necker-Enfants malades, Paris 1981–91, tenured clinical position in Dept of Paediatric Immunology 1984–88; Prof. of Paediatric Immunology, Université Paris Descartes 1988–2013, Dir INSERM Unit 768 for Normal and Pathological Development of the Immune Ssystem, Hôpital Necker-Enfants malades 1991–2013, Dir Dept of Paediatric Immunology, Hôpital Necker-Enfants malades 1996–2012, Dir Institut Imagine (Institut des maladies génétiques), Hôpital Necker-Enfants malades, Université Paris Descartes, Inserm U1163 2007–; Prof., Institut Universitaire de France 2006–; Prof., Collège de France (Chaire de médecine expérimentale) 2014–; Ed. European Journal of Immunology, International Immunology, EMBO Journal, Clinical and Experimental Immunology, Annual Review of Immunology, Science; mem. European Molecular Biology Org. 2002, Acad. des sciences 2002, Academia Europea 2009; Officier, Légion d'honneur 2010; Dr hc (Univ. of Zurich) 2005; Halpern Prize 1984, Prix Behring-Metchnikoff 1992, Prix du Comité du Rayonnement français 1994, Jung Prize for Medicine 1998, Prix Pierre Royer 2000, NRJ Foundation–Institut de France Award 2000, Louis Jeantet Prize for Medicine (co-recipient) 2001, Novartis Prize for Clinical Immunology 2001, A. Philipson Prize 2003, Descartes Prize, European Community 2005, INSERM Grand Prix 2008, Sr Advanced Grant, European Research Council 2011, Avery Landsteiner Prize 2012, Grand Prix Claude Bernard de la Ville de Paris 2013, Sanofi-Pasteur Prize 2013, Robert Koch Prize 2014, Japan Prize (co-recipient) 2014. *Publications:* more than 490 papers in professional journals. *Address:* Collège de France, 11 place Marcelin Berthelot, 75231 Paris Cedex 05, France (office). *Website:* www.college-de-france.fr/site/alain-fischer (office).

FISCHER, Andreas, PhD; Swiss professor of philology and university administrator; *President Emeritus, University of Zurich;* b. 1947; ed Univ. of Basel,

Durham Univ., UK; Prof. of English Philology, Univ. of Basel 1981; Visiting Prof., Univ. of Michigan, USA 1984–85; Prof. of English Philology, Univ. of Zurich 1985–2008, Deputy Dean, Faculty of Arts 2002–04, Dean 2004–06, Pres. (Rector) Univ. 2008–13, Pres. Emer. 2014–; Gen. Ed. Swiss Papers in English Language and Literature 1995–2007; mem. Advisory Bd Journal of Historical Pragmatics, Inst. for Historical Study of Language, Dept of English Language, Univ. of Glasgow; mem. Zurich James Joyce Foundation. *Publications:* Engagement, Wedding and Marriage in Old English 1986, Dialects in the South-West of England 1991, Es begann mit Scott und Shakespeare: Eine Geschichte der Anglistik an der Universität Zürich 2016; co-ed.: Schweizer Anglistische Arbeiten/Swiss Studies in English, Englisch-deutsche Studienausgabe der Dramen Shakespeares. *Address:* Office of the President, University of Zurich, Künstlergasse 15, 8001 Zurich, Switzerland (office). *Telephone:* (44) 6342211 (office). *E-mail:* rektor@uzh.ch (office). *Website:* www.uzh.ch/about/management/unileitung_en.html (office).

FISCHER, Debra (Deb) Strobel, BS; American politician and rancher; *Senator from Nebraska;* b. 1 March 1951, Lincoln, Neb.; d. of Jerry Strobel; m. Bruce Fischer 1972; three s.; ed Univ. of Nebraska, Lincoln; mem. Nebraska Legislature from 43rd Dist 2005–13, Chair. Transportation and Telecommunications Cttee, mem. Exec. Bd and Revenue Cttee; Senator from Nebraska 2013–; with husband, runs the family ranch, Sunny Slope Ranch, nr Valentine, Neb.; Republican. *Address:* United States Senate, Washington, DC 20510, USA (office). *Telephone:* (202) 224-3121 (office). *Website:* www.senate.gov (office).

FISCHER, Edmond H., DèsSc; American biochemist and academic; *Professor Emeritus of Biochemistry, University of Washington;* b. April 1920, Shanghai, China; s. of Oscar Fischer and Renee C. Fischer (née Tapernoux); m. Beverley B. Bullock; two s.; ed Univ. of Geneva; Asst, Labs of Organic Chem., Univ. of Geneva 1946–47; Fellow, Swiss Nat. Foundation 1948–50; Research Fellow, Rockefeller Foundation 1950–53; Privat-dozent, Univ. of Geneva 1950; Research Assoc., Div. of Biology, Calif. Inst. of Tech., USA 1953; Asst Prof., Univ. of Washington, USA 1953–56, Assoc. Prof. 1956–61, Prof. of Biochemistry 1961–90, Prof. Emer. 1990–; mem. numerous cttees, professional orgs etc.; Gov. Basel Inst. for Immunology 1996–, Weizmann Inst. of Science, Rehovot, Israel 1997–; Hon. Pres. World Cultural Council 2007–14; mem. NAS, AAAS, American Acad. of Arts and Sciences, Swiss Chem. Soc., British Biochemical Soc.; Dr hc (Montpellier) 1985, (Basel) 1988; co-recipient Nobel Prize in Physiology or Medicine (with Edwin G. Krebs) 1992, several other awards and honours. *Leisure interests:* classical piano, flying (pvt. pilot). *Address:* Department of Biochemistry, University of Washington, 1959 NE Pacific Street, HSB J-405, Seattle, WA 98195-7350 (office); 5540 NE Windermere Road, Seattle, WA 98105, USA (home). *Telephone:* (206) 523-7372 (home). *E-mail:* efischer@u.washington.edu (office). *Website:* depts.washington.edu/biowww (home).

FISCHER, Heinz, DIur; Austrian politician and fmr head of state; b. 9 Oct. 1938, Graz; m. Margit Fischer; two c.; ed Univ. of Vienna; Assoc. Prof. of Political Science, Univ. of Innsbruck 1978–94, Prof. 1994–; Sec. Socialist Parl. Party 1963–75, Exec., Floor Leader 1975–83, 1987–90, Deputy Chair. Socialist Party 1979–2004; mem. Nationalrat (Parl.) for Vienna 1971–2004, Pres. Nationalrat 1990–2002, Second Pres. 2002–04; Fed. Minister for Science and Research 1983–87; Deputy Chair. European Socialist Party 1992–2004; Pres. of Austria 2004–16; Co-Ed. Europäische Rundschau; fmr mem. Nat. Security Council and Foreign Affairs Council; Pres. Nat. Fund of the Repub. of Austria for Victims of Nat. Socialism 1995–2002, Austrian Friends of Nature –2005, Austrian Univ. Extension Asscn; Vice-Pres. Inst. for Advanced Studies –2004. *Publications:* Positions and Outlook 1977, The Kreisky Era 1993, Reflexionen 1999, Times of Change: An Austrian Interim Report 2003; numerous books and articles on law and political science.

FISCHER, Iván; Hungarian/Dutch conductor; *Music Director, Budapest Festival Orchestra;* b. 20 Jan. 1951, Budapest; s. of Sándor Fischer and Evelin Boschán; two s. two d.; ed B. Bartók Music Conservatory, Budapest and Wiener Hochschule für Musik under Hans Swarowsky, Mozarteum, Salzburg under Nikolaus Harnoncourt; Jt Music Dir Northern Sinfonia of England, Newcastle 1979–82; Music Dir and Artistic Dir, Kent Opera 1982–2000; Prin. Guest Conductor, Cincinnati Symphony Orchestra 1989–96; Music Dir Lyon Opera House 2000–03; Prin. Conductor, Nat. Symphony Orchestra, Washington, DC 2008–10; Co-founder and Music Dir Budapest Festival Orchestra 1983–; Music Dir Konzerthaus and Konzerthausorchester, Berlin 2012–17; concerts with London Symphony Orchestra, Berlin Philharmonic Orchestra, Concertgebouw Orchestra, others; main performances in USA: Los Angeles Philharmonic, Cleveland, Philadelphia, San Francisco Symphony and Chicago Symphony Orchestras; operas: Idomeneo, Don Giovanni, Julius Caesar, La Bohème, La Clemenza di Tito, Marriage of Figaro, Magic Flute in London, Paris, Vienna; Co-founder Hungarian Mahler Soc.; Patron British Kodály Acad.; Hon. Citizen of Budapest; Hon. RAM 2013; Chevalier des Arts et des Lettres; Premio Firenze 1974, Rupert Foundation Award, BBC, London 1976, Gramophone Award for Best Orchestral Recording of the Year (for The Miraculous Mandarin) 1998, Golden Medal, Republic of Hungary 1998, Crystal Award, World Econ. Forum 1998, Kossuth Prize 2006, Gramophone Editor's Choice Award (for Mahler's Second Symphony) 2007, Royal Philharmonic Soc.'s Conductor Award 2011, Dutch Ovatie Prize 2011, Abu Dhabi Festival Award 2015. *Compositions include:* The Red Heifer 2014. *Address:* Budapest Festival Orchestra, Alkotás utca 39/c., 1123 Budapest, Hungary (office). *Telephone:* (1) 489-4330 (office). *Fax:* (1) 355-4049 (office). *E-mail:* bfofound@mail.datanet.hu (office). *Website:* www.bfz.hu (office).

FISCHER, Jan; Czech economist, statistician and politician; b. 2 Jan. 1951, Prague; m.; two s. one d.; ed Univ. of Econs, Prague; researcher, Research Inst. of Socio-econ. Information (part of Fed. Statistical Office) 1974–82; with Fed. Statistical Office 1982–90, Vice-Pres. 1990–92; Vice-Pres. Czech Statistical Office 1993–2000, Pres. 2003–09; Production Dir, Taylor Nelson Sofres Factum Co. 2000–02; Prime Minister 2009–10 (resgnd); Deputy Prime Minister and Minister of Finance 2013–14; Pres. European Council 2009; mem. Czech Statistical Soc., Academic Council and Bd of Dirs Univ. of Econs, Prague, Academic Council J.E. Purkyne Univ., Usti nad Labem; mem. Int. Statistical Inst., Statistical Programme Cttee, UN Statistical Comm., UN Economic Comm. for Europe, Cttee on Statistics, and others.

FISCHER, Joschka; German academic, consultant and fmr politician; *Managing Partner, Joschka Fischer & Company;* b. (Joseph Martin Fischer), 12 April 1948, Gerabronn; m. 1st Edeltraud Fischer 1967 (divorced 1984); m. 2nd Inge Peusquens 1984 (divorced 1987); m. 3rd Claudia Bohm 1987 (divorced 1998); m. 4th Nicola Leske 1999 (divorced 2003); m. 5th Minu Barati 2005; one s. one d.; joined Green Party 1982, fmr Leader; mem. German Bundestag 1983–85; Minister of the Environment and Energy, Hesse 1985–87, of the Environment, Energy and Fed. Affairs 1991–94; Deputy Bundesrat 1985–87, Chair. Green Parl. Group, Hesse Parl. 1987–91; Deputy Minister-Pres. of Hesse 1991–98; Speaker Parl. Group Alliance 90/Greens, Bundestag 1994–98; Vice-Chancellor of Germany and Minister of Foreign Affairs 1998–2005; Sr Fellow, Liechtenstein Inst. on Self-Determination, Princeton Univ. 2006–07, also Frederick H. Schultz Class of 1951 Prof. of Int. Econ. Policy, Woodrow Wilson School of Public and Int. Affairs and Fellow, European Union Program; Sr Strategic Counsel, Albright Group LLC and Strategic Consultant to Albright Capital Management LLC, Washington, DC 2008–; Co-founder and Man. Partner, Joschka Fischer and Co. 2009–; mem. Int. Advisory Bd Tilray Inc. 2018–; mem. Bd of Dirs International Crisis Group, European Council on Foreign Relations. *Publication:* The Red-Green Years: German Foreign Policy from Kosovo to Sept. 11 2007. *Address:* Joschka Fischer & Company, Markgrafenstrasse 34, 10117 Berlin, Germany (office). *Telephone:* (30) 206253320 (office). *E-mail:* tybussek@joschkafischer.de (office). *Website:* www.jfandc.de (office).

FISCHER, Stanley, BSc (Econ), MSc (Econ), PhD; American/Israeli economist and central banker; b. 15 Oct. 1943, Lusaka, Northern Rhodesia (now Zambia); s. of Philip Fischer and Ann Kopelowitz; m. Rhoda Keet 1965; three s.; ed London School of Econs, UK, Massachusetts Inst. of Tech.; Postdoctoral Fellow, Univ. of Chicago 1969–70, Asst Prof. of Econs 1970–73; Assoc. Prof., MIT 1973–77, Prof. 1977–88, 1990, Killian Prof. 1992–94, Head of Dept 1993–94; Vice-Pres. and Chief Economist, IBRD (World Bank), Washington, DC 1988–90; Visiting Sr Lecturer, Hebrew Univ., Jerusalem 1972; Fellow, Inst. for Advanced Studies, Princeton, NJ 1976–77, Visiting Prof. 1984; Visiting Scholar, Hoover Inst., Stanford Univ. 1981–82; consultant on Israeli economy, US Dept of State 1984–87, 1991–94; First Deputy Man. Dir IMF 1994–2001; Vice-Chair. Citigroup 2002–05, Head of Public Sector Group 2004–05, Chair. Country Risk Cttee, Pres. Citigroup International 2002–05; Gov. Bank of Israel 2005–13; Vice-Chair. Bd of Govs, Fed. Reserve System, Washington, DC 2014–17; Research Assoc., Nat. Bureau of Econ. Research (NBER); Ed. NBER Macroeconomics Annual 1986–94 (Co-Ed. with O. Blanchard 1989–93, with J. Rotemberg 1994); Assoc. Ed. Journal of Monetary Economics 1975–94 (mem. Advisory Bd 1995–, Assoc. Ed. Journal of Economic Theory 1973–75, Journal of Money, Credit and Banking 1973–75, Econometrica 1975–87, Journal of Economic Literature 1982–84, Journal of Economic Perspectives 1986–88, Journal of Comparative Economics 1994–; mem. Editorial Advisory Bd The World Economy 1990–; mem. Editorial Bd Journal of Policy Reform 1994–; newspaper columnist, Il Messaggero (monthly), Rome, Italy 1990–93; mem. Council on Foreign Relations, Group of Thirty Consultative Group on Int. Econ. and Monetary Affairs, Inc. (G-30), Washington, DC, Trilateral Comm., Bilderberg Group; fmr mem. Bd Inst. for Int. Econs, Women's World Banking, Int. Crisis Group; fmr mem. Int. Advisory Bd New Econ. School, Moscow; Guggenheim Fellow; Fellow, Econometric Soc., American Acad. of Arts and Sciences; Hon. Adviser, Inst. for Monetary and Econ. Studies, Bank of Japan 1987–94; Hon. Prof., Faculty of Econs, St Petersbug State Univ., Russian Fed. 2003, Acad. of Nat. Economy under Govt of Russian Fed. 2004; Hon. Fellow, LSE; Distinguished Fellow, Council on Foreign Relations; Dr hc (Tbilisi State Univ.) 1996, (Ben Gurion Univ.) 1998, (Tel-Aviv Univ.) 2001, (LSE) 2002, (Univ. of Sofia, Bulgaria) 2004, (Hebrew Univ.) 2006; Cen. Bank Gov. of the Year, Euromoney magazine 2010. *Publications include:* Rational Expectations and Economic Policy (ed.) 1980, Indexing, Inflation and Economic Policy 1986, Macroeconomics and Finance: Essays in Honor of Franco Modigliani (co-ed.) 1987, Economics (with Rudiger Dornbusch and Richard Schmalensee; 2nd edn) 1987, Inflation Stabilization (co-ed.) 1988, Lectures in Macroeconomics (with O. Blanchard) 1989, Lessons of Economic Stabilization and Its Aftermath (co-ed.) 1990, Economic Reform in Sub-Saharan Africa (co-ed.) 1991, Adjustment Lending Revisited (co-ed.) 1992, Monetary Theory and Thought: Essays in Honor of Don Patinkin (co-ed.) 1993, The Economics of Middle East Peace (co-ed.) 1993, Macroeconomics (with Rudiger Dornbusch) 1994 (ninth edn with R. Dornbusch and R. Startz 2004), Securing Peace in the Middle East: Project on Economic Transition (co-ed.) 1994, IMF Essays From a Time of Crisis: The International Financial System, Stabilization, and Development 2004, Living Standards and the Wealth of Nations (co-ed. with Leszek Balcerowicz) 2006; reports: World Bank: Responsibility for World Development Report 1988, 1989, 1990, Report on Adjustment Lending, I 1988, II 1990, Report on Trade Policy Reform 1989, participated in jt (IMF, IBRD, OECD, EBRD) study of the Soviet economy 1990; numerous publs on int. econ. and macroeconomic issues.

FISCHER, Thomas R., BEcons, PhD; German banker and business executive; b. 6 Oct. 1947, Berlin; ed Univ. of Freiburg, Breisgau; fmr amateur boxer, employed in family-owned business 1965–68, 1973–76; Research Asst, Univ. of Freiburg, Breisgau 1980–81; Head of Controlling, VARTA Batterie AG 1981–85; Deputy Dir Group Devt Dept, Deutsche Bank AG, Hanover 1985–91, Man. Dir Deutsche Immobilien Anlagegesellschaft mbH (subsidiary of Deutsche Bank) 1991–92, Global Head of Derivatives Deutsche Bank AG, Frankfurt 1992–95, Chair. Risk Man. Cttee, mem. Bd Man. 1999–2002; Vice-Chair. Landesgirokasse, Stuttgart 1995–96, Chair. 1996–98; Chair. WestLB AG 2004–07, CEO –2007; Pres. Asscn of German Public Sector Banks 2004–07; Chair. Supervisory Bd RWE AG 2006–09; mem. Bd (non-exec.) RWE 2010.

FISCHER, Timothy Andrew, AC; Australian politician and diplomatist; b. 3 May 1946, Lockhart, NSW; s. of J. R. Fischer and Barbara Mary Fischer; m. Judy Brewer 1992; two s.; ed Boree Creek School, Xavier Coll., Melbourne; joined Army 1966, officer with First Bn, Royal Australian Regt, Australia and Viet Nam 1966–69; farmer, Boree Creek, NSW; mem. NSW Legis. Ass. 1970–84; MP for Farrer, NSW 1984–2002 (retd); Shadow Minister for Veterans' Affairs 1985–89 and Deputy Man. of Opposition Business 1989–90; Leader Nat. Party of Australia 1990–99; Shadow Minister for Energy and Resources 1990–93, for Trade 1993–96; Deputy Prime Minister and Minister for Trade 1996–99; Chair. Tourism Australia 2004–07; Nat. Chair. Flying Doctor Service 2007; Amb. to the Holy See 2009–12,

Special Envoy to South Sudan, Special Envoy to the Kingdom of Bhutan; mem. Advisory Bd Cognita Singapore, Global Crop Diversity Trust; Grand Cross of the 'Orden de Mayo al Merito' (Argentina), Grand Cross of the 'Orden de Bernardo O'Higgins' (Chile), Grand Officer of the National Order of the Southern Cross (Brazil), Blue Ribbon, Most Exalted Order of the White Elephant (Thailand) and numerous other decorations; Hon. DLit (ANU) 2005. *Publications:* several books, including Bold Bhutan Beckons (with Tshering Tashi), Outback Heroes (with Peter Rees). *Leisure interests:* chess, tennis, skiing, water skiing, bush-walking, mountaineering.

FISCHER, Urs; Swiss artist; b. 2 May 1973, Zürich; m. Tara Subkoff 2014 (divorced); ed Schule für Gestaltung Zürich; Artist in Residence, Delfina Studio Trust 1999; Providentia Prize, YoungArt 1999. *E-mail:* info@ursfischer.com (office). *Website:* www.ursfischer.com (office).

FISCHER-APPELT, Peter, DrTheol; German university administrator and educator; b. 28 Oct. 1932, Berlin; s. of Hans Fischer-Appelt and Margret Fischer-Appelt; m. Hildegard Zeller 1959; two s. one d.; ed Schubart-Oberschule, Aalen and Univs of Tübingen, Heidelberg and Bonn; Scientific Asst, Protestant Theology Faculty, Univ. of Bonn 1961–70; Pastor, Cologne-Mülheim 1964–65; Co-founder and Chair. Bundesassistentenkonferenz, Bonn 1968–69; Pres. Univ. of Hamburg 1970–91, Pres. Emer. 1991–, teaching assignment in Systematic Theology 1972–; Pres. 'Cyril and Methodius' Int. Foundation, Sofia 1992–98, Hon. Pres. 2002; mem. Exec. Cttee Inter-Univ. Centre for Postgrad. Studies, Dubrovnik 1974–81, Chair. of Council 1981–98, Hon. mem. 1998; mem. Standing Conf. on Univ. Problems, Council of Europe 1987–94, Deputy Chair. 1987–88, Chair. 1989–90; Chair. Steering Group, Higher Educ. Legislation Reform Programme for Cen. and Eastern Europe 1992–98; mem. and Chair. Bd of Trustees UNESCO Inst. for Educ., Hamburg 1992–96; mem. German Comm. UNESCO 1991–2002, Hon. mem. 2002; mem. Bd of Trustees, Deutscher Akad. Austauschdienst 1972–2007 and various other comms, etc.; mem. European Acad. of Sciences and Arts, Salzburg; Horseman of Madara (First Class), Order of Cyril and Methodius (First Class), Bulgaria, Order of the Croatian Star with the Effigy of Rudjer Bošković; numerous hon. degrees including Hon. LHD (Temple Univ.), Hon. LittD (Purdue Univ.), Hon. LLD (Indiana Univ.), Dr hc (Technical Univ., Varna), (Technological Univ., Sofia), (Kliment Ohridski Univ., Sofia); Gold Medal, Bulgarian Acad. of Sciences, Pro Cultura Hungarica Medal, Medal of the Comm. of Nat. Educ., Poland 2000, Medal Pro Merito of the Council of Europe 2000. *Achievements:* annual Peter Fischer-Appelt Award for eminent achievements in acad. teaching, Univ. of Hamburg 1991, annual Prof. Dr Peter Fischer-Appelt Awards for best Bulgarian school teachers in Bulgarian, German, Spanish, Classic languages Cyril and Methodius Int. Foundation, Sofia 2004. *Publications:* Metaphysik im Horizont der Theologie Wilhelm Herrmanns 1965, Albrecht Ritschl und Wilhelm Herrmann 1968, Rechtfertigung 1968, Wissenschaft und Politik 1971, Zum Verständnis des Glaubens in der liberalen und dialektischen Theologie 1973, Zum Gedenken an Ernst Cassirer 1975, Integration of Young Scientists into the University 1975, Wilhelm Herrmann 1978, Hiob: oder die Unveräusserlichkeit der Erde 1981, The Future of the University as a Research Institution 1982, Was darf ich hoffen? Erwartungen an das Musiktheater 1982, Die Oper als Denk- und Spielmodell 1983, Die Kunst der Fuge: Ein deutsches Forschungsnetz im Aufbau 1984, Dialogue and Co-operation for World Peace Today 1985, Die Universität zwischen Staatseinfluss und Autonomie 1986, The University in the 21st Century 1988, Die Ostpolitik der Universitäten 1992, Die Universität im Prozess der Humanisierung der Gesellschaft 1994, Wer hat Angst vor den Wandlungen der Universität 1994, Die Erhellung des Mythos durch die Sprache der Musik 1995, The University: Past, Present and Future 1996, Concepts of the University 1997, Die Buchstaben und Europa 1997, One Europe to Tend 2000, Gottes Sein im Werden des Wissens 2000, Hochschulpolitik als Sozialpolitik 2001, Wissenschaft in der Kaufmannsrepublik 2002, Das Modell Byzanz und seine Einflüsse auf die Lebenswelt Osteuropas 2003, Felix Mendelssohn Bartholdy und Arnold Schönberg 2003, Hermann Cohen und Arnold Schönberg 2003, Die Göttlichen Stimmen in Schönberg's oper Moses und Aron 2003, Wie weit reicht Europa? 2004, The University of Reason 2004, Curt Kosswig, ein Wegbereiter der Türkei nach Europa 2004, Der Präsident in der Rolle des Mitmenschen und Übermenschen 2007, Die stille Erhebung Bulgariens 2010, Die neue Universität 2011, Die Aufhebung der Epoche aus des verlorenen Gedanken der Einzigkeit Gottes 2011, Wilhelm Herrmann und Hermann Cohen 2012, Die Universität als Kunstwerk 2012, Albrecht Ritschl/Wilhelm Herrmann: Briefwechsel 1875–1889 (co-ed.) 2013. *Leisure interests:* chess, skiing, music, opera, theatre. *Address:* Waldweg 22, 25451 Quickborn-Heide, Germany. *Telephone:* (4106) 71212 (home). *Fax:* (4106) 78637 (home). *E-mail:* peter.fischerappelt@fischerappelt.de (home).

FISCHER BOEL, (Else) Mariann; Danish politician; b. 15 April 1943, Aasum, Funen; d. of Hans Boel and Valborg Boel; ed Tietgen Business School, Odense; Man. Sec. at export co., Copenhagen 1965–67, Finance Man. 1967–71; mem. Munkebo Municipal Council 1982–91, 1994–97, Second Deputy Mayor 1986–90; Chair. Liberal Party Kerteminde constituency 1987–89; mem. Folketing for Funen Co. 1990–, Chair. Food, Agric. and Fisheries Cttee 1994–98, Trade and Industry Cttee 1998–99, Fiscal Affairs Cttee 1998–99; Minister of Food, Agric. and Fisheries 2001–04; EU Commr for Agric. and Rural Devt 2004–10; mem. Cen. Bd, Liberal Party 1990–, mem. Man. Cttee Parl. Liberal Party 1990; Chair. High Schools' Secr. 1993; mem. Nat. Assessment Council 1994–98, Nat. Tax Tribunal 1998–2001; mem. Cttee of Reps Østifterne 1991; mem. Bd of Govs Boel Fund 1992–; mem. Aarhus Univ. Bd; European of the Year, Danish Europe Movement (Europabevægelsen) 2008. *Address:* Dr. Tværgade 59, 3. sal, 1302 Copenhagen K, Denmark.

FISCHL, Eric, BFA; American artist; b. 9 March 1948, New York; ed Phoenix Junior Coll., Ariz., Ariz. State Univ., Tempe, Calif. Inst. of the Arts; moved to Chicago and worked as guard at Museum of Contemporary Art; taught painting at Nova Scotia Coll. of Art and Design, Halifax 1974–78; moved to New York 1978. *Address:* c/o Mary Boone Gallery, 745 Fifth Avenue, New York, NY 10151, USA. *Telephone:* (212) 941-1304. *Fax:* (212) 941-8674. *E-mail:* fischlstudio@gmail.com. *Website:* www.ericfischl.com.

FISCHLER, Franz, Dipl.Ing, PhD; Austrian fmr politician and consultant; *President, European Forum Alpbach;* b. 23 Sept. 1946, Absam, Tyrol; m. Heidi Fischler; two s. two d.; ed Franciscan secondary school, Tyrol, Agricultural Univ., Vienna; Asst, Dept of Agricultural Man., Univ. of Vienna 1973–79; Dept Head, Tyrolean Prov. Chamber of Agric. 1979, Sec. 1982, Dir 1985–89; Minister of Agric. and Forestry 1989–94; EU Commr for Agric. and Rural Devt 1995–99, for Agric., Rural Devt and Fisheries 1999–2004; consultancy work, Franz Fischler Consult GmbH 2005–; Pres. EcoSocial Forum Europe 2012, European Forum Alpbach 2012; ten hon. degrees; Mansholt Award. *Publications:* as co-author: Europa Der Staat, den keiner will 2006, Erinnerungen 2006. *Leisure interests:* skiing, mountaineering. *Address:* Franz Fischler Consult GmbH, Dörferstrasse 30B, 6067 Absam, Austria (office). *Telephone:* (5223) 57075 (office). *Fax:* (5223) 57076 (office). *E-mail:* ffc@franz-fischler-consult.co.at (office). *Website:* www.franz-fischler-consult.co.at (office).

FISCHLI, Peter; Swiss artist; b. 8 June 1952, Zurich; ed Accad. di Belle Arti, Urbino, Acad. di Belle Arti, Bologna, Italy; collaboration with David Weiss 1979–; works held in many int. galleries including Tate Gallery, London, Solomon R. Guggenheim Museum, New York; Leopold-Hoesch-Museum Günther Peill Prize 2000, Roswitha Haftmann Prize 2006, Wolfgang-Hahn Prize 2010 (with David Weiss). *Films:* Der rechte Weg (The Right Way) 1983, Der Lauf der Dinge (The Way Things Go) 1987, Kanalvideo (Sewage Video) 1992, Arbeiten im Dunkeln (Works in the Dark) 1995, Büsi (Kitty) 2001, Hunde (Dogs) 2003. *Address:* c/o Matthew Marks Gallery, 523 West 24 Street, New York, NY 10011, USA (office). *Telephone:* (212) 243-0200 (office). *E-mail:* info@mathewmarks.com (office). *Website:* www.matthewmarks.com (office).

FISHBURNE, Laurence; American actor; b. 30 July 1961, Augusta, Georgia; s. of Laurence John Fishburne, Jr and Hattie Bell Crawford Fishburne; m. Hanja Moss 1985 (divorced); one s. one d.; Global Philanthropist Award, UNICEF 2017. *Stage appearances include:* Short Eyes, Two Trains Running, Riff Raff (also writer and dir). *Television includes:* One Life to Live (series, debut aged 11), Pee-wee's Playhouse, Tribeca (Emmy Award 1993), A Rumour of War, I Take These Men, Father Clements Story, Decoration Day, The Tuskegee Airmen, Miss Ever's Boys, Always Outnumbered, CSI: Crime Scene Investigation (series) 2008–, Thurgood (film) 2011. *Films include:* Cornbread Earl and Me 1975, Fast Break, Apocalypse Now, Willie and Phil, Death Wish II, Rumble Fish, The Cotton Club, The Color Purple, Quicksilver, Band of the Hand, A Nightmare on Elm Street 3: Dream Warriors, Gardens of Stone, School Daze, Red Heat, King of New York, Cadence, Class Action, Boyz 'N the Hood, Deep Cover, What's Love Got to Do With It? Searching for Bobby Fischer, Higher Learning, Bad Company, Just Cause, Othello, Fled, Hoodlums (also exec. producer), Event Horizon, Welcome to Hollywood, The Matrix 1999, Michael Jordan to the Max 2000, Once in the Life (also writer) 2000, Osmosis Jones 2001, The Matrix Reloaded 2003, The Matrix Revolutions 2003, Mystic River 2003, Assault on Precinct 13 2005, Akeelah and the Bee 2005, Mission: Impossible III 2006, Five Fingers 2006, Bobby 2006, TMNT (voice) 2007, The Death and Life of Bobby Z 2007, Fantastic Four: Rise of the Silver Surfer (voice) 2007, 21 2008, Tortured 2008, Days of Wrath 2008, Black Water Transit 2009, Armored 2009, Predators 2010. *Address:* c/o Sam Gores, Paradigm, 10100 Santa Monica Boulevard, 25th Floor, Los Angeles, CA 90067, USA.

FISHER, Joel, BA; American sculptor and academic; *Head of Sculpture, Northumbria University;* b. 6 June 1947, Salem, Ohio; s. of James R. Fisher and Marye Fisher (née Giffin); m. 1st Pamela Robertson-Pearce 1977 (divorced); one s.; m. 2nd Gabrielle Wambaugh 2003; one d.; ed Kenyon Coll., Ohio; Artist in Residence, Univ. of Auckland 2000; currently Head of Sculpture, Northumbria Univ.; Kress Foundation Art History Award 1967, 1968, Gast der Berliner Kunstler Program des DAAD (German Academic Exchange Service) 1973–74, 1994, George A. and Eliza Gardner Howard Foundation Fellow 1987, Guggenheim Fellow 1993, Pollock-Krassner Foundation Award 1993, Henry Moore Fellowship (Newcastle upon Tyne) 2001–03. *Publications:* A Shadow of the Earth 1968, Double Camouflage 1970, Berliner Book 1974, Instances of Change 1975, False History 1978, Between Two and Three Dimensions – Drawings and Objects Since 1979 1984, Little Buttercup: Happiest Bear in the World (photos) 2004. *Address:* 29 Goldspink Lane, Newcastle upon Tyne, NE2 1NQ, England; P.O. Box 349, River Road, North, Troy, VT 05859, USA (home). *Telephone:* (191) 227-3140 (office); (191) 230-0370 (home); (802) 988-2870 (home). *E-mail:* joel.fisher@unn.ac.uk (office); jfisher@together.net (office).

FISHER, Kenneth (Ken) L., BA; American business executive and writer; *Founder and Chairman, Fisher Investments Inc.;* b. 29 Nov. 1950, San Francisco; s. of Philip A. Fisher and Dorothy Whyte; m. Sherrilyn Fisher; three s.; ed Humboldt State Univ.; began career in father's investment firm; founder, CEO and Chief Investment Officer Fisher Investments Inc. 1978–2016, currently Chair. and Co-Chief Investment Officer, f. Fisher Investments Europe 2000, Gruner Fisher 2008; columnist, Forbes Magazine 1984–; est. Kenneth L. Fisher Chair in Redwood Forest Ecology, Humboldt State Univ. 2006; mem. Bd of Advisors, Forbes School of Business, Ashford Univ. 2015–; Bernstein Fabozzi/Jacobs Levy Award for outstanding published research article of the year 2000, Tiburon CEO Summit Award for Challenging Conventional Wisdom 2009. *Publications include:* Super Stocks 1984, The Wall Street Waltz 1987, 100 Minds that Made the Market 1996, The Only Three Questions that Count 2006, The Ten Roads To Riches 2008, How to Smell a Rat: The Five Signs of Financial Fraud (with Lara Hoffmans) 2009, Debunkery 2010, Markets Never Forget 2011, Plan Your Prosperity 2012, The Little Book of Market Myths 2013, Beat the Crowd 2015; various research papers on investment and stocks. *Address:* Fisher Investments Inc., 13100 Skyline Boulevard, Woodside, CA 94062-4547, USA (office). *Fax:* (650) 529-1436 (office). *E-mail:* info@fi.com (office). *Website:* www.fisherinvestments.com (office).

FISHER, Mark Andrew, BA, MBA; British banker; b. 29 April 1960; ed Warwick Business School; joined NatWest in 1981, joined Royal Bank of Scotland (RBS) (following its acquisition of NatWest in 2000), Chief Exec. RBS Manufacturing Div. 2000–07, mem. Bd of Dirs RBS Group 2006–, Chair. Man. Bd and CEO ABN AMRO (bank partially owned by RBS) 2007–09; Fellow, Chartered Inst. of Bankers in Scotland. *Address:* c/o ABN AMRO Holding NV, Gustav Mahlerlaan 10, 1082 PP Amsterdam, Netherlands (office). *Telephone:* (20) 628-9393 (office). *Fax:* (20) 629-9111 (office). *E-mail:* info@abnamro.com (office). *Website:* www.abnamro.com (office).

FISHER, Michael Ellis, BSc, PhD, FRS; British theoretical scientist, university teacher and researcher and consultant; b. 3 Sept. 1931, Trinidad, West Indies; s. of Harold Wolf Fisher and Jeanne Marie Fisher (née Halter); m. Sorrel Castillejo

1954 (died 2016); three s. one d.; ed King's Coll., London; Lecturer in Math., RAF Tech. Coll. 1952–53; London Univ. Postgraduate Studentship 1953–56; Dept of Scientific and Industrial Research Sr Research Fellow 1956–58; Lecturer in Theoretical Physics, King's Coll., London 1958–62, Reader in Physics 1962–64, Prof. of Physics 1965–66, Fellow 1981; Prof. of Chem. and Math., Cornell Univ., USA 1966–73, Horace White Prof. of Chem., Physics and Math. 1973–89, Chair. Dept of Chem. 1975–78; Wilson H. Elkins Prof., Inst. for Science and Tech., Univ. of Md 1987–93, Distinguished Univ. Prof. and Univ. System of Md Regents Prof. 1993–2012, Prof. Emer. 2012–; Guest Investigator, Rockefeller Inst., New York 1963–64; Visiting Prof. of Applied Physics, Stanford Univ., USA 1970–71; Walter Ames Prof., Univ. of Wash. 1977; Visiting Prof. of Physics, MIT 1979; Sherman Fairchild Distinguished Scholar, Caltech 1984; Visiting Prof. of Theoretical Physics, Oxford 1985; Lorentz Prof., Univ. of Leiden 1993; Visiting Prof., Nat. Inst. of Standards and Tech., Gaithersburg, Md 1993; Foreign Assoc., NAS, American Philosophical Soc.; Foreign mem. Brazilian Acad. of Sciences, Royal Norwegian Soc. of Sciences and Letters; Fellow, American Acad. of Arts and Sciences, American Philosophical Soc.; performer and teacher of the flamenco guitar and writer about flamenco; Hon. FRSE; Hon. Fellow, Indian Acad. of Sciences (Bangalore) 2000; Distinguished Lecturer in Theoretical Physics, The Technion 2004; Hon. DSc (Yale) 1987; Hon. DPhil (Tel-Aviv) 1992, (Weizmann Inst. of Science) 2009, (École Normale Supérieur de Lyon) 2012; Jr Collectors Silver Cup, British Philatelic Exhbn 1946, Irving Langmuir Prize in Chemical Physics, American Physical Soc. 1970, John Simon Guggenheim Memorial Fellow 1970–71, 1978–79, Award in Physical and Math. Sciences, New York Acad. of Sciences 1978, Guthrie Medal, Inst. of Physics 1980, Wolf Prize in Physics, Israel 1980, Michelson-Morely Award, Case-Western Reserve Univ. 1982, James Murray Luck Award, NAS 1983, Boltzmann Medal, IUPAP 1983, Festschrift and Conf. in honour of 60th Birthday: Current Problems in Statistical Mechanics 1991, Lars Onsager Medal, Norwegian Inst. of Tech. 1993, Joel H. Hildebrand Award for Chem. of Liquids 1995, Hirschfelder Prize in Theoretical Chem., Univ. of Wisconsin 1995, First Lars Onsager Memorial Prize, American Physical Soc. 1995, G.N. Lewis Memorial Lecture Award, Univ. of California 1995, George Fisher Baker Lecturer, Cornell Univ. 1997, Centennial Speaker, American Physical Soc. 1998, Royal Medal, Royal Soc. of London 2005, Oppenheimer Lecturer, Univ. of California, Berkeley 2006; Raman Lecturer, Indian Inst. of Science, Bangalore 2007, Bhabha Lecturer, Tata Inst., Mumbai 2007, Hudspeth Centenial Lecturer, Univ. of Texas, Austin 2007, Kac Memorial Lecturer, Los Alamos 2008, Sherman Memorial Lecturer, Indiana Univ. 2009, BBVA Foundation, Madrid 2009, Frontiers of Knowledge Award in Basic Sciences 2010, inaugural James S. Kouvel Memorial Lecturer, Univ. of Illinois, Chicago 2013, Joe L. Franklin Memorial Lecturer, Rice Univ. 2014, Rudranath Capildeo Award for Applied Science and Tech., Trinidad and Tobago, West Indies 2015. *Publications include:* Analogue Computing at Ultra-High Speed (with D. M. MacKay) 1962, The Nature of Critical Points 1964 (also in Russian 1968), Excursions in the Land of Statistical Physics 2016; more than 420 contribs to scientific journals, proceedings and reviews. *Leisure interests:* flamenco guitar, travel, art work. *Address:* Institute for Physical Science and Technology, University of Maryland, College Park, MD 20742, USA (office). *Telephone:* (301) 405-4819 (office). *Fax:* (301) 314-9404 (office). *E-mail:* xpectnil@umd.edu (home).

FISHER, Robert (Bob) J.; American retail executive; b. 1955; s. of Donald G. Fisher and Doris F. Fisher; m. Elizabeth S. Fisher; three c.; ed Phillips Exeter Acad., Princeton Univ., Stanford Univ. School of Business; Man. The Gap, Inc. 1980–85, Exec. Vice-Pres. of Merchandise, Banana Republic 1985–89, Pres. 1989–90, mem. Bd of Dirs The Gap Inc. 1990–99, Exec. Vice-Pres. 1992–99, COO 1992–93, 1995–97, CFO 1993–95, Pres. Gap Div. 1997–99 (resgnd), Chair. The Gap Inc. 2004–07, currently mem. Bd of Dirs, Interim CEO 2007; mem. Bd of Dirs Sun Microsystems Inc.; mem. Bd of Trustees, Golden Gate Nat. Park Asscn, Natural Resources Defense Council, Conservation Int., San Francisco Museum of Modern Art.

FISHLOW, Albert, PhD; American economist, academic and fmr government official; *Professor Emeritus of International and Public Affairs, Columbia University;* b. 21 Nov. 1935, Philadelphia; m. Harriet Fishlow 1957; one s. two d.; ed Univ. of Pennsylvania, Harvard Univ.; Acting Asst Prof., Assoc. Prof., then Prof., Univ. of California, Berkeley 1961–77, Prof. of Econs 1983, Chair. Dept of Econs 1973–75, 1985–89, Dean Int. and Area Studies 1990, Dir Int. House 1990, now Prof. Emer.; Visiting Fellow, All Souls Coll. Oxford, UK (Guggenheim Fellow) 1972–73; Prof. of Econs, Yale Univ. 1978–83; Prof. Emer. of Int. and Public Affairs, fmr Dir Columbia Inst. of Latin American Studies and Center for Study of Brazil, Columbia Univ., New York; mem. Berkeley Foundation Trustees Int. Cttee 1990–; Co-Ed. Journal of Devt Econs 1986–; Dir-at-Large, Bd of Social Science Research Council 1990–; Deputy Asst Sec. of State for Inter-American Affairs 1975–76; mem. Council on Foreign Relations 1975–, Paul A. Volcker Sr Fellow for Int. Econs –1999; Consultant to Rockefeller, Ford and other foundations, fmr Consultant to World Bank, IDB, UNDP; Nat. Order of the Southern Cross (Brazil) 1999; David Wells Prize, Harvard 1963, Arthur H. Cole Prize, Econ. History Asscn 1966, Joseph Schumpeter Prize, Harvard 1971, Outstanding Service Award, Dept of State 1976. *Publications include:* American Railroads and the Transformation of the Ante Bellum Economy 1965, International Trade, Investment, Macro Policies and History: Essays in Memory of Carlos F. Diaz-Alejandro (co-ed.) 1987; numerous articles. *Address:* 834 International Affairs Building, Columbia University, Mail Code 3323, New York, NY 10027, USA (office). *Telephone:* (212) 854-1555 (office). *Fax:* (212) 864-4847 (office). *E-mail:* af594@columbia.edu (office). *Website:* sipa.columbia.edu (office).

FISHMAN, Gerald (Jerry) Jay, BS, MS, PhD; American astrophysicist; *Chief Scientist, Marshall Space Flight Center;* b. 10 Feb. 1943, St Louis, Mo.; s. of Irwin Fishman and Minnie Fishman; m. Nancy Neyman 1967; two d.; ed Univ. of Missouri, Rice Univ.; fmr Research Asst/Research Assoc., Space Science Dept, Rice Univ.; began career as a Sr Scientist working on aerospace projects at Research Labs, Teledyne Brown Engineering, Huntsville, Ala; Research Scientist, NASA Marshall Space Flight Center, Huntsville 1974–78, Chief Scientist 1979–, Staff Scientist, Astrophysics Div., Office of Space Science, NASA HQ 1978–79, Prin. Investigator of Burst and Transient Source Experiment (BATSE), Compton Gamma Ray Observatory, currently a Co-Investigator of Gamma-ray Burst Monitor, Fermi Gamma-ray Space Telescope 2008–; Fellow, American Physical Soc. 1995; NASA Medal for Outstanding Scientific Achievement 1982, 1991, 1992, Alan Berman Research Publs Award, Naval Research Lab. 1992, Sigma Xi Research Scientist of the Year, Huntsville 1993, Distinguished Alumnus Award, Univ. of Missouri 1994, Bruno Rossi Prize, High Energy Astrophysics Div., AAS 1994, NASA Exceptional Service Medal 2011, Shaw Prize in Astronomy (co-recipient) 2012. *Publications:* more than 900 publs, including encyclopedia articles, published proceedings, published abstracts, reports and patents. *Address:* NASA Marshall Space Flight Center, Redstone Arsenal, Huntsville, AL 35812, USA (office). *Website:* www.nasa.gov/centers/marshall/home (office).

FISIAK, Jacek, OBE, PhD, DLitt; Polish philologist, linguist and academic; *Head, School of English, Warsaw Division, Academy of Management in Łódź;* b. 10 May 1936, Konstantynów Łódzki; s. of Czesław Fisiak and Jadwiga Fisiak; m. Liliana Sikorska; ed Warsaw Univ.; staff mem. Łódź Univ. 1959–67, Asst Prof. 1962–67; staff mem. Adam Mickiewicz Univ., Poznań 1965–, Head of English Dept 1965–69, Head of Dept of History of English, School of English 1969–, Extraordinary Prof. 1971–77, apptd Prof. 1977–, Rector 1985–88; Head, School of English, Warsaw Div., Acad. of Man., Łódź 2007–; Chair. Comm. on Modern Languages and Literature, Ministry of Higher Educ. 1974–88; Minister of Nat. Educ. 1988–89; participant in Round Table debates 1989; Visiting Prof., UCLA 1963–64, Univ. of Kan. 1970, Univ. of Fla 1974, State Univ. of New York 1975, American Univ., Washington, DC 1979–80, 1991–92, Univ. of Kiel 1979–80, Vienna Univ. 1983, 1988–89, 1990–91, Univ of Zürich 1984, 1994, Univ. of Tromsø 1986, Univ. of Jyväskylä 1987, Univ. of Saarbrücken 1990, 1993, Univ. of Bamberg 1994; Ed. Studia Anglica Posnaniensia 1967–, Papers and Studies in Contrastive Linguistics 1972–, Ed.-in-Chief Folia Linguistic Historica 1978–; Pres. Int. Asscn of Univ. Profs of English 1974–77, Societas Linguistica Europaea 1982–83, Int. Soc. for Historical Linguistics 1981–83; Chair. Neophilological Cttee, Polish Acad. of Sciences 1981–93; mem. Finnish Acad. of Sciences and Humanities 1990, Academia Europaea 1990, Finnish Acad. of Arts and Sciences, Norwegian Acad. of Sciences 1996, New York Acad. of Sciences 1996, Medieval Acad. of America 2001, Polish Acad. of Sciences 2004; Pres. Polish-British Friendship Soc. 1989–; mem. editorial bds of numerous foreign and int. philological journals, numerous scientific socs; consultant, Ford Foundation, IREX, Swedish Govt, Austrian Ministry of Higher Educ., Encyclopaedia Britannica (Chicago); Dr. hc (Jyväskylä) 1982, (Opole) 2005; Commdr.'s Cross of the Order Polonia Restituta with Star, Grand Cross of the Order Polonia Restituta, Officer's Cross of the Order of the British Empire (OBE), Nat. Educ. Comm. Medal, Commdr's Cross of Lion of Finland Order, Officier, Ordre des Palmes Académiques and numerous other decorations. *Publications:* 177 publs, 50 books including Morphemic Structure of Chaucer's English 1965, A Short Grammar of Middle English 1968, 1996, Recent Developments in Historical Phonology (ed.) 1978, Historical Syntax (ed.) 1983, A Bibliography of Writings for the History of English 1987, Historical Dialectology (ed.) 1990, An Outline History of English 1993, 2000, Medieval Dialectology 1995, Linguistic Change Under Contact Conditions 1995, Studies in Middle English Linguistics 1997, Typology and Linguistics Reconstruction 1997, East Anglia (co-author with P. Trudgill) 2001, The New Kościuszko Foundation Dictionary (English–Polish, Polish–English) 2003, Foreign Influences on Medieval English (co-ed. with M. Bator) 2011. *Leisure interests:* history, sport. *Address:* School of English, Warsaw Division, Academy of Management, Sienkiewicza 9, 90-050 Łódź (office); School of English, A Mickiewicz Univ., Al. Niepodleglosci 4, 61-874 Poznan, Poland (office). *Telephone:* (42) 6325023 (office); (61) 8293536 (office); (61) 8243153 (home); (61) 8293510 (office). *Fax:* (61) 8523103 (office); (61) 8243159 (home). *E-mail:* fisiak@amu.edu.pl (office); office@swspiz.pl (office). *Website:* www.swspiz.pl (office); www.amu.edu.pl (office).

FISICHELLA, Domenico; Italian politician and academic; b. 15 Sept. 1935, Messina, Sicily; m. Loredana Fisichella; two d.; Prof. of Political Science, Univ. of Florence, Università La Sapienza and Libera Università Internazionale degli Studi Sociali (LUISS), Rome; co-f. Alleanza Nazionale Party 1992, elected Senator 1994, Vice-Pres. of Senate 1996–2006; Minister of Culture 1994–95; Gold Medal for achievement in field of culture, education and art, Carlo Casalegno Journalism Prize 1985, Culture Prize for essays 1988, Guido and Roberto Cortese Prize for essays 1996. *Publications include:* Denaro e democrazia: Dall'antica Grecia all'economia globale (Money and Democracy: From Ancient Greece to Global Economy) 2000, Totalitarismo: Un regime del nostro tempo (Totalitarianism: A Regime of Our Times) 2002, Politica e mutamento sociale (Politics and Social Changes) 2002, La destra e l'Italia (The Right and Italy) 2003, Lineamenti di scienza politica: Concetti, problemi, teorie (Fundamentals of Political Science: Concepts, Problems, Theories) 2003, Contro il federalismo (Against Federalism) 2004, and numerous articles in nat. dailies.

FISK, David John, CB, ScD, CEng, FREng, FInstP; British engineer and academic; *BP/Royal Academy of Engineering Professor of Engineering for Sustainable Development, Department of Civil and Environmental Engineering, Imperial College London;* b. 9 Jan. 1947; s. of John Howard Fisk and Rebecca Elizabeth Fisk (née Haynes); m. Anne Thoday 1972; one s. one d.; ed Stationers' Co. School, Hornsey, St John's Coll. Cambridge and Univ. of Manchester; joined Bldg Research Establishment, Sr Prin. Scientific Officer, Head, Mechanical and Electrical Eng Div. 1978–84; with Dept of Environment, then Dept of the Environment, Transport and the Regions, then Dept for Transport, Local Govt and the Regions, now Office of the Deputy Prime Minister 1984–2005, Asst Sec. Cen. Directorate of Environmental Protection 1984–87, Under-Sec. 1987, Deputy Chief Scientist 1987–88, Chief Scientific Adviser 1988– (Dir Air Climate and Toxic Substances Directorate 1990–95, Environment and Int. Directorate 1995–98, Cen. Strategy Directorate 1999–2002); Visiting Prof., Univ. of Liverpool 1988–2002; Dir Watford Palace Theatre 2000–; apptd Royal Acad. of Eng Prof. of Eng for Sustainable Devt, Imperial Coll. London 2002, now BP/RA Eng Chair in Eng for Sustainable Devt, also Co-Dir BP Urban Energy Systems Project; mem. Gas and Electricity Markets Authority 2009–; Hon. Fellow, Chartered Inst. of Bldg Service Engineers, RIBA. *Publications include:* Thermal Control of Buildings 1981; numerous papers on bldg science, systems theory and econs. *Leisure interests:* theatre, music. *Address:* Department of Civil and Environmental Engineering, Imperial College, 436 Skempton Building, South Kensington Campus, London, SW7 2BU, England (office). *Telephone:* (20) 7594-6109. *Fax:* (20) 7594-6049. *E-mail:* d.fisk@imperial.ac.uk (office). *Website:* www.cv.ic.ac.uk (office).

FISMER, Christiaan (Chris) Loedolff; South African politician and government official; b. 30 Sept. 1956, Pretoria; s. of William Fismer and Elizabeth Fismer; m. Linda Mills; twin d.; ed Univ. of Pretoria; served in mil. service; admitted to Pretoria Bar 1986; practised as advocate 1986–87; fmr Chair. Student Rep. Council, Univ. of Pretoria, Pres. Afrikaanse Studentebond (umbrella org. for univ. governing bodies); mem. Nat. Party; co-f. Nat. Party Youth Action; MP for Rissik 1987, Sr Transvaal Whip of Nat. Party 1989; apptd party rep. to Conf. for a Democratic S Africa working group on implementation of decisions 1991; Prov. Leader Nat. Party in Eastern Transvaal 1994; fmr Deputy Minister in Office of State Pres. F. W. de Klerk; Deputy Minister of Justice 1994–95; Minister of Gen. Services 1995–96, of Provincial and Constitutional Affairs March–May 1996; Chair. Nat. Gaming Board of SA 1998–2009 (retd); Univ. of Pretoria Gold Medal.

FISZEL, Roland Henri Léon; French engineer; b. 16 July 1948, Paris; s. of Jean Fiszel and Marie Eber; m. Nadine Kohn 1974; one s. two d.; ed Lycée Pasteur, Neuilly-sur-Seine, Ecole polytechnique, Massachusetts Inst. of Tech., USA; Head of Housing Dept, Ministry of Construction 1974–77; Head of Studies and Planning Group, Infrastructure Div., Hauts-de-Seine 1977–81; Deputy Sec.-Gen. Codis-Cidise, in charge of Treasury 1981–82; Tech. Adviser, Office of Minister of Social Affairs and Nat. Solidarity 1983–84, then of Minister of the Economy and Finance 1984–86; Dir Nat. Printing Office 1986–92; Adviser to Chair. of Euris 1996, mem. Bd of Dirs 2002–06; Pres. and Dir-Gen. Société francaise de production 1997–2001; Ingénieur en chef des ponts et chaussées; Dir representing State, Agence Havas 1986–87; Dir Antenne 2 1988–92; fmr Sec.-Gen. Caisse nationale du Crédit agricole. *Leisure interests:* skiing, tennis. *Address:* 4 rue Jobbé Duval, 75015 Paris, France (home). *E-mail:* roland@fiszel.fr.

FITERMAN, Charles; French politician; b. 28 Dec. 1933, St-Etienne; s. of Moszek Fiterman and Laja Rozenblum; m. Jeannine Poinas 1953; Departmental Sec. Jeunesse Communiste 1952; Sec. CGT, St-Etienne SFAC 1958–62; Dir Cen. School, Parti Communiste Français (PCF) 1963–65; elected to PCF Cen. Cttee 1972, to Political Bureau and Cen. Cttee Sec. 1976; Gen. Councillor, Head, Econ. Section and PCF Rep. to Liaison Cttee of Signatory Parties to Common Programme of the Left 1977; Deputy (Val-de-Marne) to Nat. Ass. 1978–81; Minister of State, Minister of Transport 1981–84; Deputy for Rhône 1986–88; Mayor of Tavernes 1989–; f. Refondations Movt 1990, Convention pour une alternative progressiste 1994; Pres. Forum Alternatives Européennes 1994–99; mem. Socialist Party 1998–, Conseil Economique et Socialde France; Chevalier, Légion d'honneur. *Publications include:* Profession de foi: pour l'honneur de la politique 2005.

FITIAL, Benígno Repeki, BBA; American politician, fmr state governor and business executive; b. 27 Nov. 1945, Saipan, Northern Mariana Islands (NMI); m. Josepina (Josie) Padiermos; six c.; ed Mt Carmel High School, Univ. of Guam; govt positions include News Dir, KJQR Radio Station; Budget Analyst, Trust Territory Govt; Budget Officer, 1st NMI Legislature; Chief Admin. Officer, 1st NMI Legislature, Minority Leader, 2nd and 4th NMI Legislature, Vice-Speaker, 5th NMI Legislature, Speaker of the House of Reps, 3rd, 12th and 14th NMI Legislature; business positions include Pres. Bank of Saipan, Century Insurance Corpn, Century Travel Corpn, Consolidated Transportation Services Inc., Pacific Oriental Inc., Home Improvement (MPI); Vice-Pres. Tan Holdings Corpn; Special Consultant, L&T Corpn; Founder CNMI Covenant Party; Chair. Northern Marianas Republican Party, Bush for President Cttee for the CNMI, CNMI Zoning Bd, NMI Trusteeship Termination Task Force, 1st CNMI Civil Service Comm., Saipan Municipal Scholarship Bd; mem. CNMI Tax Task Force, Republican Presidential Task Force (US); Del., 1st Northern Marianas Constitutional Convention; Chair. Constitutional Convention Cttee (s) on Tax, Public Debt, Educ. and Local Govt; Gov. of the Commonwealth of the Northern Mariana Islands (CNMI) 2006–13 (impeached 11 Feb. 2013, resgnd 20 Feb. 2013); Republican –2001, 2011–, Covenant Party 2001–11; Distinguished Alumni, Univ. of Guam. *Address:* c/o Office of the Governor, Juan A. Sablan Memorial Building, Capital Hill, Caller Box 10007, Saipan, MP 96950, Commonwealth of the Northern Mariana Islands (office).

FITOUSSI, Jean-Paul Samuel, DèsScEcon; French economist and academic; *Research Director, Observatoire Français des Conjonctures Economiques (OFCE);* b. 19 Aug. 1942, La Goulette; s. of Joseph Fitoussi and Mathilde Cohen; m. Anne Krief 1964; one s. one d.; ed Acad. Commerciale, Univs of Paris and Strasbourg; Asst Lecturer, Univ. of Strasbourg 1968–71, Dir of Studies 1971–73, Maître de Conférence Agrégé 1974–75, Prof. 1975–78, Titular Prof. 1978–82, Dean, Faculty of Econ. Science and Dir Dept of Econ. Science 1980–81; Prof. in charge of research programme on foundation of macroeconomic policy, Inst. Universitaire Européen, Florence 1979–83, External Prof., Univ. Européenne, Florence 1984–93, mem. Research Council 2003–; Prof., Inst. d'Etudes Politiques, Paris 1982, now Prof. Emer.; also currently Prof., LUISS Guido Carli Univ., Rome; Dir Dept of Studies Observatoire Français des Conjonctures Economiques (OFCE) 1982–89, Chair. 1990–2010, now Research Dir; mem. French Comm. Economique de la Nation 1995–; mem. Conseil d'Analyse Economique of the French Prime Minister 1997–2012; Expert, Comm. of the European Parl. 2000–09; mem. UN Research Inst. for Social Devt 2001–, Exec. Cttee, Aspen Inst. Italia 2001–, Comité nationale d'évaluation de la politique de la ville 2002–, Comité national d'initiative et de proposition pour la recherche 2004–, Scientific Bd Austrian Inst. of Economic Research 2004–; Sec.-Gen. Int. Econ. Asscn 1984; mem. Bd of Dirs Telecom Italia SpA 2004–, École Normale Supérieure 2004–, Pirelli & C. SpA 2013–; mem. Supervisory Bd Intesa SanPaolo SpA 2010–; mem. Advisory Bd Centre on Capitalism and Soc., Columbia Univ. 2004–, Cttee for Evaluation of Research 2005–; columnist, Le Monde and La Repubblica; Hon. Prof., Univ. of Trento, Italy; Officier, Ordre nat. du Mérite, Chevalier, Légion d'honneur, Grand Officier, Ordre de l'Infant Henri (Portugal); Dr hc (Buenos Aires), (Tres de Febrero); Prix Asscn Française de Sciences Economiques, Prix Acad. des Sciences Morales et Politiques. *Publications:* Inflation, équilibre et chômage 1973, Le fondement macroéconomique de la théorie Keynesienne 1974, Modern Macroeconomic Theory 1983, Monetary Theory and Economic Institutions (with N. de Cecco) 1985, The Slump in Europe (with E. Phelps) 1988, Competitive Disinflation (with others) 1993, Pour l'emploi et la cohésion sociale 1994, Le débat interdit: monnaie, Europe, pauvreté 1995, Economic Growth, Capital and Labour Markets 1995, Le nouvel âge des inégalités (with Pierre Rosanvallon) 1996, Rapport sur l'état de l'Union européenne 1999, 2000, 2002, Réformes structurelles et politiques macroéconomique: les enseignements des modèles de pays (with O. Posset) 2000, contrib. to collected publs, L'enseignement supérieur de l'économie en question, Rapport au ministre de l'éducation nationale 2001, Rapport sur l'état de l'union européenne 2002; La Règle et le choix 2002, How to Reform the European Central Bank (with J. Creel) 2002, Il dittatore benevolo 2003, Rapport sur l'état de l'union europénne 2004, Les inégalités 2003, La démocratie et le marché 2004, L'ideologie du monde 2004, Ségrégation urbaine et intégration sociale (jtly) 2004, Macroeconomic Theory and Economic Policy 2004, La politique de l'impuissance 2005, Report on the State of the European Union 2005. *Leisure interests:* travel, cinema, guitar, scuba-diving. *Address:* Observatoire Français des Conjonctures Economiques, 69 quai d'Orsay, 75340 Paris Cedex 07 (office); 47 rue de boulainvilliers, 75016 Paris, France (home). *Telephone:* 1-44-18-54-01. *Fax:* 1-44-18-54-71. *E-mail:* presidence@ofce.sciences-po.fr (office). *Website:* www.ofce.sciences-po.fr (office).

FITRAT, Abdul Qadeer, BA, MA; Afghan banker; b. 1 May 1963, Badakhshan; ed secondary school, Kabul, Int. Islamic Univ., Islamabad, Pakistan, Wright State Univ., Dayton, Ohio, USA; fmr Asst Research Co-ordinator for USAID-supported project, ESSP, Peshawar, Pakistan; fmr Chair. Bank-e-Millie Afghan, Kabul early 1990s; Consultant Economist, IMF, Washington, DC, USA in late 1990s; First Deputy Gov. Da Afghanistan Bank (Cen. Bank of Afghanistan) 1995, Gov. 1996, Gov. and Chair. Supreme Council (Supervisory Bd) 2007–11; fled to USA 2011, warrant for his arrest issued by Afghan Govt June 2011, ordered by Pres. Karzai to return to Afghanistan Oct. 2012; consumer banker to First Union Nat. Bank, northern Va 2000–01; Adviser to Exec. Dir, World Bank 2004–07.

FITSCHEN, Jürgen, MBA; German business executive; b. 1948, Harsefeld; ed Univ. of Hamburg; worked at Citibank in various positions in Hamburg and Frankfurt am Main 1975–87, mem. Exec. Cttee Germany 1983–87; joined Deutsche Bank 1987, held executive positions in Thailand, Japan and Singapore before becoming mem. of the Global Corps and Insts Div. Bd, Frankfurt 1997–98, London 1998–2001, mem. Bd of Man. Dirs 2001–09, responsible for Corp. and Investment divs, mem. Group Exec. Cttee 2002–, Head of Regional Man. team world-wide, CEO Germany and Chair. Man. Cttee Germany, Frankfurt 2005–12, mem. Man. Bd, Deutsche Bank AG 2009–16, Co-Chair. Man. Bd and Co-CEO 2012–16; mem. Bd of Dirs, Kuehne + Nagel International AG; mem. Supervisory Bd, METRO AG, Schott AG. *Address:* c/o Deutsche Bank AG, Taunusanlage 12, 60262 Frankfurt am Main, Germany. *E-mail:* info@db.com.

FITTIPALDI, Emerson; Brazilian fmr racing driver; b. 12 Dec. 1946, São Paulo; s. of Wilson Fittipaldi and Juze Fittipaldi; m. 1st Maria Helena Dowding 1970; one s. two d.; m. 2nd Teresa Hotte 1995; one s. one d.; m. 3rd Rossana Fanucchi 2001; one s. one d.; ed scientific studies; Brazilian champion Formula V and Go-Kart 1967; Formula 3 Lombard Championship 1969; Formula 1 World Champion 1972 (youngest ever), 1974; second in World Championship 1973, 1975; won Indianapolis 500 1989, 1993; retd (following injury) 1996 with 17 Indy Car victories; owns Fittipaldi Motoring Accessories, 500,000-acre orange plantation and exports orange concentrate; has Mercedes-Benz partnership in Brazil; Pnr, Hugo Boss fashion retailer; set up the Fittipaldi Foundation to help impoverished children in Brazil; runs Fittipaldi-Dingman Racing; mem. Bd Laureus World Sports Acad. *Leisure interests:* sport, music, water-skiing, flying. *Address:* Av. Rebouças, 3551, Jardim Paulistano, São Paulo, SP 05401-400, Brazil. *Telephone:* (11) 3215-6050; (11) 3215-6072 (office). *Fax:* (11) 3215-6051. *Website:* www.emersonfittipaldi.com.

FITZGERALD, Frances Mary, B.Soc.Sci, MSc; Irish politician; b. (Frances Ryan), 1 Aug. 1950, Croom, Co. Limerick; m. Michael Fitzgerald; three s.; ed Univ. Coll. Dublin, London School of Econs; fmr social worker (worked in Mater Hosp., St James' Hosp. and Ballymun Child and Family Centre for 10 years); fmr mem. Dublin City Council; mem. Dáil Éireann (parl.) for Dublin South-East 1992–2002, for Dublin Mid West 2011–; mem. Seanad (Senate) 2007–11, Leader of Fine Gael in the Seanad 2007–11; Minister for Children and Youth Affairs 2011–14, for Justice and Equality 2014–17, for Enterprise and Innovation June–Nov. 2017; Tánaiste (Deputy Prime Minister) 2016–17; Chair. Nat. Women's Council of Ireland 1988–92; mem. Fine Gael.

FITZGERALD, Mgr Michael Louis, BA, DTheol; British ecclesiastic and diplomatist (retd); b. 17 Aug. 1937, Walsall, West Midlands; s. of Dr Thomas Walter Fitzgerald and Dr Nora Josephine Fitzgerald (née Twomey); ed Pontifical Gregorian Univ., School of Oriental and African Studies, Univ. of London; ordained priest, Soc. of Missionaries of Africa (White Fathers) 1961; teacher, Makerere Univ., Kampala, Uganda 1969–71, Pontifical Inst. of Arabic and Islamic Studies, Rome 1971–78; pastoral work, Sudan 1978–80; mem. Gen. Council of Missionaries of Africa 1980–86; Sec. Secr. for Non-Christians (now renamed Pontifical Council for Inter-Religious Dialogue) 1987–2002, Pres. 2002–06; Apostolic Nuncio in Egypt and Del. to the Arab League 2006–12; Titular Bishop of Nepte 1992–2002, Titular Archbishop of Nepte 2002–; presented von Hügel Lecture on Christian-Muslim Relations, Cambridge 2002; Conventual Chaplain ad honorem of the Sovereign Mil. Order of Malta; Officier, Légion d'honneur 2005; Dr hc (Catholic Univ. of Australia) 2014, (Heythrop Coll., Univ. of London) 2017; Mohammed Nafi Tschelebi Medienpreis 2004, Pax Christi Award, St John's Abbey and Univ., Cellegeville, Minn. 2007. *Publications include:* Signs of Dialogue: Christian Encounter with Muslims (co-author) 1992, Catalysts (co-author) (second edn) 1998, Dieu reve d'unité. Les catholiques et les religions: les leçons du dialogue. Entretiens avec Annie Laurent 2005, Interfaith Dialogue – A Catholic View (co-author) 2006, Praise the Name of the Lord – Meditations on the Most Beautiful Names of God 2015, Christian-Muslim Dialogue (co-ed.) 2017; numerous specialist articles and lectures. *Address:* St Vincent's Presbytery, 13 Hardy Street, Liverpool, L1 5JN, England (office). *Telephone:* (07780) 014218 (office).

FITZGERALD, Niall, FRSA, BComm; Irish business executive; *Chairman, Hakluyt & Company Ltd;* b. 13 Sept. 1945; m.; two s. two d.; ed Univ. Coll., Dublin; joined Unilever 1967, various man. roles including CEO, Unilever Food Div., S Africa, early 1980s, later Treasurer, Unilever, London, Dir Unilever PLC and Unilever NV 1987–2004, Financial Dir 1987–89, Co-ordinator, Edible Fats and Dairy 1989–90, mem. Foods Exec. 1989–91, Co-ordinator, Detergents 1991–95, Vice-Pres. Unilever PLC 1994–96, Chair. 1996–2004, also becoming Vice-Chair. Unilever NV 1996–2004; Dir Reuters Group 2003–08, Chair. 2004–08, Deputy Chair. Thomson Reuters (following acquisition of Reuters) 2008–11; Pres. Advertising Asscn 2000–05; Chair. Hakluyt & Co. Ltd 2008–, The Conf. Bd

2003–05; mem. World Econ. Forum, Int. Advisory Bd 1999–2011, Council on Foreign Relations, Trilateral Comm., EU–China Cttee, US Business Council; Gov. Nat. Inst. of Econ. and Social Research; Chair. Bd of Trustees, British Museum 2006–14; Trustee, Leverhulme Trust; Sr Advisor to Allen & Co.; Hon. KBE. *Leisure interests:* jazz, opera, football, rugby, golf. *Address:* Hakluyt & Company Ltd, 34 Upper Brook Street, London, W1K 7QS, England (office). *Website:* hakluyt.co.uk (office).

FITZGERALD, Peter Gosselin, AB, JD; American banker, lawyer and fmr politician; *Chairman, Chain Bridge Bancorp Inc.;* b. 20 Oct. 1960, Elgin, Ill.; s. of Gerald Francis Fitzgerald and Marjorie Fitzgerald (née Gosselin); m. C. Nina Kerstiens 1987; one s.; ed Dartmouth Coll., Univ. of Michigan; called to Bar Ill. 1986; with US Dist Court Ill. 1986; Assoc. Isham, Lincoln & Beale 1986–88; Pnr, Riordan, Larson, Bruckert & Moore 1988–92; Counsel, Harris Bankmont Inc. 1992–96; mem. Ill. Senate 1993–98, Chair. State Govt Operations Cttee 1997–99, US Senator from Illinois 1999–2005 (retd), Chair. Senate Sub-Cttee on Consumer Affairs and Product Safety 2003–05, Sub-Cttee on Financial Man., the Budget and Int. Security 2003–05; Chair. Chain Bridge Bancorp Inc. 2006–; mem. N American Advisory Bd, Transurban Group; Advisory Bd, Financial Services Partners Fund I, LLC. *Address:* Chain Bridge Bancorp Inc., 1445-A Laughlin Avenue, McLean, VA 22101-5737, USA (office). *Telephone:* (703) 748-2005 (office). *Fax:* (703) 748-2007 (office). *E-mail:* info@chainbridgebank.com (office). *Website:* www.chainbridgebank.com (office).

FITZGERALD, Stephen Arthur, AO, BA, PhD; Australian scholar and diplomatist; b. 18 Sept. 1938, Hobart, Tasmania; s. of F.G. FitzGerald; m. Helen Overton; one s. two d.; ed Tasmania Univ., Australian Nat. Univ.; Dept of Foreign Affairs 1961–66; Research Scholar, ANU 1966–69, Research Fellow 1969–71, Fellow 1972–73, Professorial Fellow 1977–, Head Dept of Far Eastern History 1977–79, Head Contemporary China Centre, Research School of Pacific Studies 1977–79; Amb. to People's Repub. of China (also accred to Democratic People's Repub. of Korea) 1973–76; Ed. Australian Journal of Chinese Affairs; Deputy Chair. Australia–China Council 1979–86; mem. Australian Acad. of Science Sub-Cttee on Relations with China; Trustee, Australian Cancer Foundation 1985–99; Chair. Asian Studies Council 1986–91; Chair. and Man. Dir Stephen Fitzgerald and Co. Ltd; Chair. Asia-Australia Inst., also Prof. Univ. of NSW 1990–; Co-Chair. Jt Policy Cttee on Relations between Northern Territory and Indonesia; currently adviser to Australian govt-funded China-Australia Governance Program; Fellow, Australian Inst. of Int. Affairs 2009; mem. council Musica Viva Australia; Dunlop Asia Medal 1999, Australia-China Council Award 1999. *Publications:* China and the Overseas Chinese 1972, Talking with China 1972, China and the World 1977, Immigration: A Commitment to Australia (jtly) 1988, A National Strategy for the Study of Asia in Australia (jtly) 1988, Asia in Australian Education (jtly) 1989, Australia's China (jtly) 1989, Ethical Dimension to Australia's Engagement with Asia 1993, Is Australia an Asian Country? 1997, East View-West View: Divining the Chinese Business Environment 1999, Comrade Ambassador: Whitlams' Beijing Envoy 2015.

FITZGERALD, Tara; British actress; b. 18 Sept. 1969, Sussex; d. of Michael Callaby and Sarah Geraldine Fitzgerald; stage debut in Our Song, London; appeared in London as Ophelia in Hamlet 1995, Antigone 1999. *Theatre:* Our Song, London, Hamlet (Drama Desk Award Best Supporting Actress 1995), New York, A Streetcar Named Desire 1999, The Doll's House 2003, And Then There Were None, Gielgud Theatre, London 2005, A Doll's House, Donmar Theatre, London 2009, The Misanthrope, The Comedy Theatre, London 2009–10. *Films:* Hear My Song 1991, Galleria 1993, Sirens 1994, A Man of No Importance 1994, The Englishman Who Went up a Hill but Came Down a Mountain 1995, Brassed Off 1996, Conquest 1998, The Snatching of Bookie Bob 1998, Childhood 1999, New World Disorder 1999, Rancid Aluminium 2000, Dark Blue World 2001, I Capture the Castle 2003, Five Children and It 2004, Secret Passage 2004, In a Dark Place 2006, Legend 2015, Una 2016. *Television includes:* Six Characters in Search of an Author 1992, The Camomile Lawn (mini-series) 1992, Anglo Saxon Attitudes 1992, Fall from Grace 1994, The Vacillations of Poppy Carew 1995, The Tenant of Wildfell Hall 1996, The Woman in White 1997, The Student Prince 1997, Little White Lies 1998, Frenchman's Creek (Best Actress Award, Reims Int. TV Festival 1999) 1998, In the Name of Love 1999, Love Again 2003, Marple: The Body in the Library 2004, Like Father Like Son 2005, The Virgin Queen (mini-series) 2005, Jane Eyre (mini-series) 2006, Waking the Dead (series) 2007–11, U Be Dead 2008, The Body Farm 2011, Game of Thrones 2013–15, In the Club 2014, Requiem 2018, The ABC Murders 2018. *Address:* c/o Lindy King, United Agents, 12–26 Lexington Street, London, W1F 0LE, England (office). *Telephone:* (20) 3214-0800 (office). *Fax:* (20) 3214-0801 (office). *E-mail:* info@unitedagents.co.uk (office). *Website:* www.unitedagents.co.uk (office).

FITZGIBBON, Joel; Australian politician; b. 16 Jan. 1962, Bellingen, NSW; m. Dianne Fitzgibbon; one s. two d.; ed Univ. of New England, NSW, Univ. of Newcastle; automotive electrician 1978–90; Dir Hunter-Manning Tourist Authority 1987–89; Deputy Mayor of Cessnock 1989–90; part-time Lecturer, Tech. and Further Educ. (TAFE); Del. Hunter Region Assen of Councils 1994–95; MP (Australian Labor Party) for Hunter 1996–, various portfolios including Small Business, Tourism, Banking and Financial Services, Forestry, Mining and Energy, Asst Treas., Shadow Minister for Defence; Minister for Defence 2007–09 (resgnd), Minister for Agric., Fisheries and Forestry July–Sept. 2013, Shadow Minister for Agric. Oct. 2013–, Shadow Minister for Rural Affairs Oct. 2013–, Spokesperson for Country Caucus Oct. 2013–. *Address:* Parliament House, R1 48, Canberra, ACT 2600, Australia (office). *Telephone:* (2) 6277-4550 (office). *Fax:* (2) 6277-8422. *E-mail:* Joel.Fitzgibbon.MP@aph.gov.au (office). *Website:* www.joelfitzgibbon.com.

FITZPATRICK, Sean; New Zealand fmr rugby union player; *Chairman, Laureus World Sports Academy;* b. 4 June 1963, Auckland; s. of Brian Fitzpatrick; ed Sacred Heart Coll., Auckland; hooker for New Zealand All Blacks 1986–97, capt. 1992–97; int. debut 28 June 1986; final appearance before retirement 29 Nov. 1997; rugby consultant to NZ Rugby Football Union 1999–; Man. Auckland Blues Super 12 Team 2001–03; second-most capped NZ player of all time, most consecutive int. rugby union appearances (63 in 1986–95), missed only two test matches during his career; totals: 128 All Blacks games, including 92 tests (55 test points, including 12 tries); f. www.whatwecanbe.com (motivational speaking co.); Deputy Chair. Laureus Sport for Good Foundation, Chair. Laureus World Sports Acad. 2016–; Dir Front Row Group; Officer, New Zealand Order of Merit 1997. *Publication:* Turning Point – The Making of a Captain. *Address:* Laureus World Sports Academy, 460, Fulham Road, London, SW6 1BZ, England. *Telephone:* (20) 7514 2762 (office). *Fax:* (20) 7514-2837 (office). *Website:* www.laureus.com (office).

FITZWATER, Marlin, BA; American journalist, writer and fmr government official; b. 24 Nov. 1942, Salina, Kan.; s. of Max Fitzwater and Phyllis Seaton; m. Melinda Andrews; two c.; ed Kansas State Univ.; served with USAF 1968–70; speechwriter, US Dept of Transportation, Washington, DC 1970–72; with press relations dept, US Environmental Protection Agency 1972–74, Dir Press Office 1974–81; Deputy Asst Sec. for Public Affairs, Dept of Treasury 1981–83; Deputy Press Sec. to Pres. of US 1983–85, Press Sec. to Vice-Pres. of US 1985–87, Prin. Deputy Press Sec. to Pres. 1987–89, Press Sec. to Pres. 1989–93; Advertising Pres. Fitzwater & Tutweiler, Inc. 1993; mem. Bd of Trustees Franklin Pierce Coll. 1999–, mem. Advisory Bd, Marlin Fitzwater Center for Communication; fmr mem. Bd, Woodrow Wilson School for Int. Scholars; Dr hc (Kansas State Univ.) 2015; Presidential Merit Award 1992. *Publications include:* Call the Briefing (memoir) 1995, Esther's Pillow (novel) 2001, Death In The Polka Dot Shoes (novel) 2011.

FJÆRVOLL, Dag Jostein; Norwegian politician; b. 20 Jan. 1947, Hadsel; s. of Edmund Fjærvoll; m.; two c.; fmr teacher; Head Teacher, Melbu School 1984; mem. Hadsel Municipal Council 1975, mem. Exec. Bd 1980, Mayor 1980–85; mem. Storting Nordland Co. 1985–97, mem. Standing Cttee on Local Govt and the Environment 1985–89, on Shipping and Fisheries 1989–93, on Scrutiny and the Constitution 1993–97; Vice-Pres. Lagting 1989–93, Odelsting 1993–97; Minister of Defence 1997–99, of Transport and Communications 1999–2000; mem. Kristelig Folkeparti (Christian Democratic Party).

FLACH, Christian; German business executive; *Chairman of the Executive Board and CEO, Marquard & Bahls AG;* joined Marquard & Bahls AG 1993, held several man. positions at Marquard & Bahls, Oiltanking and Mabanaft in Germany as well as abroad, Man. Dir Mabanaft GmbH & Co. KG 2006–11, mem. Bd of Dirs Marquard & Bahls AG 2008–, Chair. Exec. Bd and CEO 2011–; Chair. AFM+E (Aussenhandelsverband für Mineralöl und Energie e.V.); Dir Enterprise Products Holdings LLC 2016–. *Address:* Marquard & Bahls AG, Admiralitaetstr. 55, 20459 Hamburg, Germany (office). *Telephone:* (40) 370040 (office). *Fax:* (40) 37004141 (office). *E-mail:* office@marquard-bahls.com (office). *Website:* www.marquard-bahls.com (office).

FLAHAUT, André, MA; Belgian politician; *Minister of Budget, Government of French Community;* b. 18 Aug. 1955, Walhain; ed Université Libre de Bruxelles; Asst to Emile Vandervelde Inst. 1979, Man. 1989; Councillor of Walhain 1982–94; Chair. Parti Socialiste Fed. of Wallon Brabant 1983–95; Prov. Councillor of Brabant 1987–91; Chair. Office de la Naissance et de l'Enfance 1989–95; Vice-Chair. of Intercommunale des Oeuvres Sociales du Brabant Wallon 1993–95; Chair. Mutualité Socialiste du Brabant Wallon 1993; Parl. Rep. 1994; Minister for Civil Service 1995–99, for Defence 1999–2007; Pres. Chambre des Représentants (Chamber of Reps) 2010–14; currently Minister of Budget, Govt of French Community. *Website:* www.pcf.be.

FLAKE, Jeffry (Jeff) Lane, BA, MA; American foundation director and politician; b. 31 Dec. 1962, Snowflake, Ariz.; s. of Dean Maeser Flake and Nerita Flake (née Hock); m. Cheryl Flake 1985; five c.; ed Brigham Young Univ.; served as Mormon missionary for The Church of Jesus Christ of Latter-day Saints in South Africa early 1980s, worked in public affairs sector after college and served as Exec. Dir Foundation for Democracy in Namibia and of Goldwater Inst. –2001; mem. US House of Reps for 1st Congressional Dist of Ariz. 2001–03, 6th Congressional Dist 2003–13, mem. Cttee on Appropriations; Senator from Arizona 2013–19; Republican. *Address:* c/o United States Senate, Washington, DC 20510, USA (office). *Website:* jeffflake.com.

FLAMMARION, Charles-Henri, LèsL, LèsLet, MBA; French publishing executive; b. 27 July 1946, Boulogne-Billancourt; s. of Henri Flammarion and Pierrette Chenelot; m. Marie-Françoise Mariani 1968; one s. two d.; ed Lycée de Sèvres, Univ. of Paris (Sorbonne), Institut d'Etudes Politiques and Columbia Univ., USA; Asst Man., Editions Flammarion 1972–81, Gen. Man. 1981–85, Pres. Flammarion SA 1985–2003; Pres. Editions J'ai Lu 1982–2003, Audie-Fluide Glacial 1990–2003; mem. Bureau du Syndicat Nat. de l'Edition 1979–88, 1996–2003; Vice-Pres. Cercle de la Librairie 1988–94, Pres. 1994–2003; Pres. Casterman 1999–2003. *Leisure interests:* cooking, travel, skiing, walking. *Address:* 15 rue des Barres, 75004 Paris, France (home). *E-mail:* flammarionch@gmail.com (home).

FLANAGAN, Andrew Henry, CA; British chartered accountant, media industry executive and charity executive; *Chairman, Scottish Police Authority;* b. 15 March 1956, Glasgow, Scotland; s. of Francis Desmond Flanagan and Martha Donaldson Flanagan; m. Virginia Walker 1972; one s. one d.; ed Univ. of Glasgow; chartered accountant with Touche Ross 1976–79, Price Waterhouse 1979–81; Financial Control Man. ITT 1981–86; Finance Dir PA Consulting Group 1986–91; Group Finance Dir and Chief Financial Officer BIS Ltd 1991–94; Finance Dir Scottish TV PLC 1994–96, Man. Dir 1996–97; Chief Exec. Scottish Media Group (later SMG PLC) 1997–2006; Dir ITV Network Ltd, Heart of Midlothian PLC, Scottish Rugby Union 2000; CEO Nat. Soc. for the Prevention of Cruelty to Children (NSPCC), London 2009–13; Chair. Scottish Police Authority 2015–. *Leisure interests:* golf, cinema, reading, skiing. *Address:* Scottish Police Authority, 1 Pacific Quay, Glasgow, G51 1DZ, Scotland (office). *E-mail:* enquiries@spa.pnn.police.uk (office). *Website:* www.spa.police.uk (office).

FLANAGAN, Charles (Charlie), BA; Irish politician and fmr solicitor; *Minister for Justice and Equality;* b. 1 Nov. 1956, Mountmellick; s. of Oliver J. Flanagan; m. Mary Flanagan; two d.; ed Knockbeg Coll., Univ. Coll. Dublin, Inc. Law Soc. of Ireland; several years' practise as solicitor; mem. Dáil Éireann (Parl.) for Laois-Offaly (now Laois) constituency 1987–2002, 2007–, Fine Gael (FG) Chief Whip 2000–02, Chair. FG Parl. Party 2011–14, FG Leader on Constitutional Convention, FG Front Bench Spokesperson on Justice, Equality and Defence 2007–10, on Children and Youth Affairs 2010–11; mem. Laois County Council 1987–2004; Vice-Chair. British-Irish Parl. Group 1997–2000; Minister of Foreign Affairs and Trade 2014–17, Minister for Justice and Equality 2017–; mem. Fine Gael, Party Spokesperson on N Ireland 1997–2000. *Address:* Department of Justice and Equality, 51 St Stephen's Green, Dublin D02 HK52, Ireland (office). *Telephone:* (1)

6028202 (office). *Fax:* (1) 6615461 (office). *E-mail:* info@justice.ie (office). *Website:* www.justice.ie (office).

FLANAGAN, Richard Miller, BA (Hons), MLitt; Australian writer and film director; b. July 1961, Longford, Tasmania; m. Majda Smolej; three d.; ed Univ. of Tasmania, Worcester Coll., Oxford, UK (Rhodes Scholar); grew up in remote mining town of Rosebery on Tasmania's west coast; left school aged 16; Pres. Tasmania Univ. Union 1983; fmr river guide; scriptwriter, journalist, novelist. *Films include:* The Sound of One Hand Clapping (dir, co-writer), Australia (co-writer) 2008. *Publications include:* non-fiction: A Terrible Beauty: A History of the Gordon River County 1985, The Rest of the World Is Watching–Tasmania and the Greens (co-ed.) 1990, Codename Iago: The Story of John Friedrich (co-author) 1991, Parish-Fed Bastards: A History of the Politics of the Unemployed in Britain, 1884–1939 1994, And What Do You Do, Mr Gable? 2011, Notes on an Exodus 2016; novels: Death of a River Guide (Victorian Premier's Award for Fiction) 1995, The Sound of One Hand Clapping 1998, Gould's Book of Fish (Commonwealth Writer's Prize) 2002, The Unknown Terrorist 2007, Wanting (Queensland Premier's Prize, Western Australian Premier's Prize, Tasmania Book Prize) 2008, The Narrow Road to the Deep North (Man Booker Prize 2014, Australian Prime Minister's Literary Prize 2014, Queensland Premier's Literary Award for Fiction 2014) 2013, First Person 2017; contribs to numerous publs, including the New Yorker, Le Monde, Süddeutsche Zeitung, la Repubblica. *Address:* c/o The Wylie Agency, 250 West 57th Street, Suite 2114, New York, NY 10107, USA (office). *Telephone:* (212) 246-0069 (office). *Fax:* (212) 586-8953 (office). *E-mail:* mail@wylieagency.com (office). *Website:* www.wylieagency.com (office); www.randomhouse.com.au/authors/richard-flanagan.aspx.

FLANAGAN, William F., JD, DEA, LLM; Canadian professor of law; *Dean, Faculty of Law, Queen's University;* ed Univ. of Toronto, Columbia Univ., USA, Univ. Paris I, France; began career as law clerk to Hon. Justice W. Z. Estey, Supreme Court of Canada, Ottawa 1986–87; joined Law Faculty, Queen's Univ., Kingston, Ont. 1991, Queen's Nat. Scholar 1996, becoming Prof. of Law, also Dir and Founder, Int. Law Spring Program, Queen's Univ. Int. Study Centre, Herstmonceux, UK 2001–05, Dean Faculty of Law 2005–, Co-Chair. Queen's Annual Business Law Symposium 1998; Vice-Chair. Workplace Safety and Insurance Appeals Tribunal 1991–2003; Co-founder and Exec. Dir Canada AIDS Russia Project 2001–04; Pres. Canadian Council of Law Deans 2010–; mem. National Action Cttee on Access to Justice 2011–. *Publications include:* several casebooks on property law, int. human rights, int. trade law and business law. *Address:* Office of the Dean, Faculty of Law, Queen's University, Kingston, ON K7L 3N6, Canada (office). *Telephone:* (613) 533-6000 (ext. 74285) (office). *Fax:* (613) 533-6509 (office). *E-mail:* w.flanagan@queensu.ca (office). *Website:* law.queensu.ca (office).

FLANDERS, Stephanie Hope, BA (Hons), MPA; British investment analyst, economist and fmr broadcast journalist; *Chief Market Strategist for the UK and Europe, J.P. Morgan Asset Management;* b. 5 Aug. 1968; d. of Michael Flanders and Claudia Flanders (née Cockburn); granddaughter of Claud Cockburn; partner John Arlidge; one s. one d.; ed St Paul's Girls' School, Balliol Coll., Oxford, Harvard Univ., USA (Kennedy Scholar); began career as an economist at London Business School and Inst. for Fiscal Studies; leader writer and columnist, Financial Times 1994–97; speechwriter and adviser to US Treasury Sec. Lawrence H. Summers 1997–2001; with New York Times 2001–02; Econs Ed., BBC Newsnight 2002–08, Econs Ed., BBC 2008–13; Chief Market Strategist for the UK and Europe, J.P. Morgan Asset Man. 2013–; Visiting Fellow, Nuffield Coll., Oxford 2008–; Dr hc (Leeds) 2013; Harold Wincott Foundation Award for Broadcast Journalist and Online Journalist of the Year 2011, Bob Friend Memorial Lecturer, Pilkington Lecture Theatre, Univ. of Kent's Medway Campus, Chatham 2013. *Television:* Masters of Money (documentary series) (BBC Two) 2012. *Radio:* Stephanomics (discussion series) (BBC Radio 4) 2011–13. *Leisure interest:* cycling. *Address:* J.P. Morgan Asset Management, 60 Victoria Embankment, London, EC4Y 0JP, England (office). *Telephone:* (20) 7742-6000 (office). *E-mail:* Stephanie.Flanders@jpmorgan.com. *Website:* www.jpmorgan.com/pages/jpmorgan/am (office).

FLANNERY, John L., BS, MBA; American business executive; b. 1962, Alexandria, Va; m.; three c.; ed Fairfield Univ., Univ. of Pennsylvania Wharton School of Business; joined General Electric Co. 1987, worked for GE Capital, Latin America 1997, Pres. and CEO, GE Equity 2002–04, Man. Dir and Business Leader, Bank Loan Group, GE Capital 2004–05, Pres. and CEO, Asia GE Capital 2006–09, Pres. and CEO, GE India 2009–13, Sr Vice Pres., Corp. Business Devt, GE 2013–14, Pres. and CEO, GE Healthcare 2014–17, Chair. and CEO General Electric Co. 2017–18. *Address:* c/o General Electric Company, 41 Farnsworth St, Boston, MA 02210, USA (office).

FLANNERY, Timothy (Tim), BSc, MSc, PhD; Australian mammalogist, palaeontologist and academic; *Professorial Fellow, Melbourne Sustainable Society Institute, University of Melbourne;* b. 28 Jan. 1956; m. Alexandra Szalay; ed La Trobe Univ., Monash Univ., Univ. of New South Wales; fmr Prof., Univ. of Adelaide; fmr Dir South Australian Museum, Adelaide; fmr Prin. Research Scientist, Australian Museum; fmr Chair in Australian Studies, Harvard Univ., USA; fmr adviser on environmental issues to Australian Fed. Parl.; Chief Commr, Climate Comm. 2011–13; mem. Climate Risk Concentration of Research Excellence and Prof., Macquarie Univ. 2007–13; currently Professorial Fellow, Melbourne Sustainable Society Inst., Univ. of Melbourne; Chair. Copenhagen Climate Council; mem. Wentworth Group of Concerned Scientists; Order of Saint-Charles, Monaco; Greater Monkey-faced Bat (*Pteralopex flanneryi*) named after him 2005, named Australian of the Year 2007, Leidy Award 2010. *Television series:* with John Doyle: Two Men in a Tinnie 2006, Two in the Top End 2008, Two on the Great Divide 2012, Two Men in China 2014. *Achievements include:* surveyed mammals of Melanesia, discovered 16 new species 1990s. *Publications include:* Mammals of New Guinea 1990, The Future Eaters: An Ecological History of the Australasian Lands and People 1994, Mammals of the South-West Pacific & Moluccan Islands 1995, Throwim Way Leg: An Adventure 1998, The Eternal Frontier: An Ecological History of North America and Its Peoples 2001, A Gap in Nature (co-author) 2001, Astonishing Animals (co-author) 2004, Country: A Continent, a Scientist & a Kangaroo 2005, The Weather Makers: The History & Future Impact of Climate Change (Book of the Year, New South Wales Premier's Literary Awards 2006) 2006, Chasing Kangaroos: A Continent, a Scientist, and a Search for the World's Most Extraordinary Creature 2007, Now or Never: Why We Must Act Now to End Climate Change and Create a Sustainable Future 2009, Here on Earth 2010, Among the Islands: Adventures in the Pacific 2011, Atmosphere of Hope: Searching for Solutions to the Climate Crisis 2015; as Ed.: The Birth of Melbourne, The Birth of Sydney, The Explorers, Watkin Tench, 1788, Terra Australis – Matthew Flinders' Great Adventures in the Circumnavigation of Australia, John Morgan – The Life and Adventures of William Buckley, John Nicol – Life and Adventures: 1776–1801, Joshua Slocum – Sailing Alone Around the World; more than 90 scientific papers in professional journals. *Address:* Melbourne Sustainable Society Institute, Level 3, Room 303, Melbourne School of Design, University of Melbourne, Masson Road, Parkville, Vic 3010, Australia (office). *Telephone:* (3) 9035-8235 (office). *E-mail:* timothy.flannery@unimelb.edu.au (office). *Website:* www.sustainable.unimelb.edu.au (office).

FLAVELL, Richard Anthony, PhD, DSc, FRS; British immunobiologist and academic; *Sterling Professor of Immunobiology, Yale University;* b. 23 Aug. 1945, Chelmsford, Essex, England; s. of John Trevor Flavell and Iris Flavell (née Hancock); m. Madlyn Nathanson 1987; one d.; two s. from previous m.; ed Univ. of Hull, Univ. of Amsterdam and Univ. of Zurich, Wetenschappelijk Medewerker, Univ. of Amsterdam, The Netherlands; Head, Lab. of Gene Structure and Expression, Nat. Inst. for Medical Research, Mill Hill, London 1979–82; Pres. and Chief Scientific Officer, Biogen NV 1982–88; Sterling Prof. of Immunobiology, Yale Univ. School of Medicine 1988–, Chair. Dept of Immunobiology 1988–2016; Investigator, Howard Hughes Medical Inst., USA 1988–; Adjunct Prof., Scripps Research Inst., Fla 2009; mem. NAS 2002–, Inst. of Medicine 2006–, Henry Kunkel Soc. 2007, European Research Inst. for Integrated Cellular Pathology (ERI-ICP) 2009, Yale Comprehensive Cancer Center, Yale Univ. 2010; Hon. Dir Int. Immunology Center, Biomedical Translational Research Inst., Jinan Univ., Guangzhou, China 2013; Fed. of European Biochemical Socs Anniversary Prize 1980, Colworth Medal 1980, Darwin Trust Prize 1995, Distinguished Service Award, Miami Nature Biotechnology Winter Symposia 2001, Rabbi Shai Shacknai Memorial Prize and Lectureship in Immunology and Cancer Research 2008, AAI-Invitrogen Meritorious Career Award 2008, Andrew Lazarovitz Award, Canadian Soc. of Transplantation, Québec 2011, Cell Signaling Networks in Merida, Yucatan, Mexico 2011, Gold Medal and Certificate of Honour for "outstanding contribs to understanding of the immune system using reverse genetics in the mouse" 2011, Vilcek Prize in Biomedical Science 2013, Star of Hope Award, JDRF Connecticut Chapter 2014, AAI Excellence in Mentoring Award, American Association of Immunologists 2016. *Publications include:* more than 1,200 scientific articles. *Leisure interests:* music, tennis, horticulture. *Address:* Department of Immunobiology, Yale University School of Medicine, TAC S-569, PO Box 208011, 300 Cedar Street, New Haven, CT 06520, USA (office). *Telephone:* (203) 785-7024 (office). *Fax:* (203) 737-2958 (office). *E-mail:* richard.flavell@yale.edu (office). *Website:* medicine.yale.edu/lab/flavell (office).

FLAY, Jennifer; New Zealand/French gallery owner and director; *Director, Foire Internationale d'Art Contemporain (FIAC);* b. New Zealand; studied art history; worked in several contemporary art galleries, including with Catherine Issert at St-Paul-de-Vence 1982–91, then with Daniel Templon and Ghislaine Hussenot in Paris; operated own Paris gallery, Galerie Jennifer Flay 1991–2003; among the first to exhibit the work of Felix Gonzalez-Torres, Andrea Zittel, John Currin, Karen Kilimnik, Dominque Gonzalez-Foerster and Claude Closky; one of pioneer dealers to move to rue Louise-Weiss art dist, 13th arrondissement, now home to several leading art galleries; scholar of contemporary art and author of several publs and numerous articles on art history; Artistic Dir Foire Internationale d'Art Contemporain (FIAC—Int. Contemporary Art Fair), Paris 2004–, Dir 2010–; mem. Conseil d'admin, Ecole nationale supérieure des Beaux-Arts de Paris, Palais de Tokyo, Printemps de Septembre; mem. Jury, Prix Meurice, Prix Liliane Bettancourt pour l'Intelligence de la Main; Officier des Arts et des Lettres 2012, Officier, Légion d'honneur 2015; Frontier Art Prize. *Telephone:* 1-47-56-64-26 (office). *E-mail:* jennifer.flay@reedexpo.fr (office). *Website:* www.fiac.com (office).

FLECK, James (Jim) Douglas, CC, BA, DBA; Canadian business executive, academic and fmr government official; *M. Wallace McCutcheon Professor Emeritus of Business Government Relations, Faculty of Management, University of Toronto;* b. 10 Feb. 1931, Toronto; m. Margaret Evelyn Humphrys; three s. one d.; ed Univ. of Toronto Schools, Univ. of Western Ontario, Harvard Univ., USA; Founder, Chair. and CEO Fleck Manufacturing Inc. 1954–94; Prof. and Assoc. Dean, Faculty of Admin Studies and Dir, MBA Program, York Univ. 1966–70; CEO, Office of the Premier, Govt of Ont. 1972–74, Sec. of Cabinet 1974–75, Deputy Minister of Industry and Tourism, Govt of Ont. 1976–78; William Lyon Mackenzie King Visiting Prof. of Canadian Studies, Business and Public Man., John F. Kennedy School of Govt, Harvard Univ. 1978–79; M. Wallace McCutcheon Prof. of Business Govt Relations, Faculty of Man., Univ. of Toronto and Sr Fellow, Massey Coll., now Prof. Emer.; Chair. NGRAIN Corpn; Chair. Alias Research Inc. –1995, ATI Technologies Inc. –2006; mem. Bd of Dirs Promis Systems Corpn Ltd –2000; Chair., Minister's Advisory Council for Arts and Culture (Ont.); Pres. Art Gallery of Ontario Foundation; Founding Dir Public Policy Forum; Hon. LLD (Toronto) 2002, Hon. DSL (Trinity Coll.) 2010; Edmund C. Bovey Award for Leadership Support of the Arts 2003, Queen's Silver Jubilee Medal 1977, Queen's 50th Anniversary Medal 2002. *Leisure interests:* tennis, fine arts. *Address:* Joseph L. Rotman School of Management, 105 St George Street, Toronto, ON M5S 3E6, Canada (office). *Telephone:* (416) 978-5703 (office). *Website:* www.rotman.utoronto.ca (office).

FLEISCHER, Ari; American public relations consultant and fmr government official; b. 13 Oct. 1960; m. Becki Davis 2002; two c.; ed Middlebury Coll.; Press Sec. for Senator Pete Domenici 1989–94; Deputy Communications Dir for Pres. George H. W. Bush's 1992 re-election campaign; fmr Communications Dir for Elizabeth Dole; White House Press Sec. for Pres. George W. Bush 2001–03; f. Ari Fleischer Sports Communications LLC 2008; sports marketing consultant with IMG 2004–; Spokesman Don't Take My Bat Away coalition; consultant for US Olympic Cttee 2009–. *Publications:* Taking Heat: The President, the Press and My Years in the White House 2005. *Address:* Ari Fleischer Sports Communications LLC, 50 Main Street, Suite 1625, White Plains, NY 10606, USA (office). *Telephone:* (212) 255-3000 (office). *Fax:* (646) 688-1607 (office). *E-mail:* info@fleischersports.com (office). *Website:* www.fleischersports.com (office).

FLEISCHMANN, Peter; German film director and producer; b. 26 July 1937, Zweibrücken; s. of Alexander Fleischmann and Pascal Fleischmann; two c.; ed Inst. de Hautes Etudes Cinématographiques, Paris; fmrly asst to dir of short feature films, documentaries and animations; Co-founder Hallelujah Film with Volker Schlondorff; now produces and directs feature and documentary films; consultant to Studio Babelsberg; Pres. Fédération Européene des Réalisateurs Audiovisuels; Chair. European Audiovisual Centre, Babelsberg; mem. EC Expert Council for reform of audiovisual politics. *Films include:* Alexander und das Auto ohne linken Scheinwerfer 1965 (animation), Herbst der Gammler 1967 (documentary), Jagdszenen aus Niederbayern (feature) 1968, Der Dritte Grad 1971 (feature), Hamburger Krankheit 1979 (feature), Frevel 1983 (feature), Al Capone von der Pfalz 1984 (documentary), Es ist nicht leicht ein Gott zu sein 1988 (feature), Deutschland, Deutschland 1991 (documentary), Mein Onkel, der Winzer 1993 (documentary), Mein Freund, der Mörder 2006. *Address:* Europäisches Filmzentrum Babelsberg, August-Bebel-Strasse 26-53, 14482 Potsdam, Germany (office). *Telephone:* (331) 7062700 (office). *Fax:* (331) 7062710 (office). *Website:* www.studiobabelsberg.com (office).

FLEMING, Graham Richard, PhD, FRS; American (b. British) chemist and academic; *Professor of Chemistry and The Melvin Calvin Distinguished Professor of Chemical Biodynamics, University of California, Berkeley;* b. 3 Dec. 1949, Barrow-in-Furness, Cumbria, England, UK; s. of Maurice N. H. Fleming and Lovima E. Winter; m. Jean McKenzie 1977; one s.; ed Univs of London and Bristol, UK; Research Fellow, California Inst. of Tech. 1974–75; Univ. Research Fellow, Univ. of Melbourne, Australia 1975, Australian Research Grants Cttee Research Asst 1976; Leverhulme Fellow, Royal Inst., London 1977–79; Asst Prof., Univ. of Chicago 1979–83, Assoc. Prof. 1983–85, Prof. 1985–87, Arthur Holly Compton Distinguished Service Prof. 1987–97; Prof. of Chem., Univ. of California, Berkeley 1997–, The Melvin Calvin Distinguished Prof. of Chemical Dynamics 2002–, Dir Physical Biosciences Div., Lawrence Berkeley Nat. Lab. 1997–2004, Assoc. Lab. Dir for Physical Sciences, Deputy Lab. Dir 2004–07, Vice-Chancellor for Research 2009–15; Dir California Inst. for Quantitative Biosciences Research 2001; mem. NAS, American Philosophical Soc.; Foreign mem. Indian Nat. Science Acad.; Visiting Fellow, Magdalen Coll., Oxford 2019; Fellow, American Acad. of Arts and Sciences; A.P. Sloan Foundation Fellow; Hon. foreign mem. Chemical Soc. of Japan, Hon. mem. Inst. Solvay; Hon. DSc (Bristol); Dr hc (Vilnius Univ.); Guggenheim Fellowship, RSC Marlow Medal, Coblentz Award, Tilden Medal, ACS Nobel Laureate Signature Award for Grad. Educ. in Chem., ACS Peter Debye Award in Physical Chem., ACS Harrison Howe Award, Earle K. Pyler Prize, American Physical Soc., George Porter Medal, ACS A.H. Zewail Prize, ACS Hildebrand Award, ACS Remsen Award, RSC Faraday Award. *Leisure interest:* climbing mountains, music. *Address:* Department of Chemistry, 221 Hildebrand, University of California, Berkeley, CA 94720, USA (office). *Telephone:* (510) 643-2735 (office). *Fax:* (510) 642-6340 (office). *E-mail:* fleming@berkeley.edu (office); grfleming@lbl.gov (office). *Website:* chemistry.berkeley.edu/faculty/chem/fleming (office).

FLEMING, Gregory (Greg) James, BA, JD; American business executive; *President and CEO, Rockefeller Capital Management;* b. 1964, New York; s. of Neil S. Fleming and Patricia Fleming; m. Melissa Danne Shaw 1990; ed Colgate Univ., Yale Law School; Prin., Booz Allen Hamilton Inc. 1988–92; Pres. and COO, Merrill Lynch 1992–2009, Exec. Vice-Pres. 2003–07; Head, US Financial Insts Group 1999–2001; Co-Head, Global Financial Insts Group 2001–03; Pres. Morgan Stanley Investment Man. 2010–15, Wealth Man. 2011–15; Vice-Chair. Harlem RBI; Pres. and CEO, Rockefeller Capital Man. 2018–, also mem. Bd of Dirs; mem. Bd of Govs., Financial Industry Regulatory Authority; Sr Research Scholar and Distinguished Visiting Fellow, Yale Law School 2009, 2016–, also mem. Bd of Advisors; mem. Bd of Dirs Great-West Life & Annuity Insurance Co. 2016–, Colgate Univ., Turn2 Foundation, Asia Soc., Ronald McDonald House, Putnam Investments, LLC BlackRock; Trustee, Deerfield Acad. 2014–, Rippowam Cisqua School. *Address:* Rockefeller Capital Management, 10 Rockefeller Plaza, New York, NY 10020, USA (office). *Telephone:* (212) 549-5100 (office). *E-mail:* info@rockco.com (office). *Website:* www.rockco.com (office).

FLEMING, Osbourne Berrington; Anguillan/British politician and business executive; b. 18 Feb. 1940, East End; m. Ruby Fleming; ed Valley Secondary School; Customs Officer, Saint Kitts 1959–64; lived in St Thomas, US Virgin Islands 1964–68, Saint Kitts 1968–81; f. Fleming's Transport (transport and shipping co.), St Croix 1974; MP (People's Progressive Party) 1981–85, MP (Anguilla Nat. Alliance—ANA) 1985–89, ind. MP 1989–94, rejoined ANA, Leader Opposition in House of Ass. 1994–2000; Minister of Tourism, Agric. and Fisheries 1981–85, of Finance 1985–89, of Finance and Econ. Devt 1989–94; Chief Minister 2000–10, also Minister of Minister of Home Affairs, Tourism, Agric., Fisheries and Environment 2000–08, of Home Affairs, Natural Resources, Lands and Physical Planning 2008–10 (retd); fmr Chair. Caribbean Commercial Bank (CCB). *Leisure interests:* playing draughts, dominoes and cards. *Address:* Sea Feathers, East End, Anguilla (home). *Telephone:* 497-4783 (home).

FLEMING, Renée, MMus; American singer (soprano); b. 14 Feb. 1959, Indiana, Pa; d. of Edwin Davis Fleming and Patricia (Seymour) Alexander; m. Richard Lee Ross 1989 (divorced 2000); two d.; ed Potsdam State Univ., Eastman School of Music of Univ. of Rochester, Juilliard School American Opera Center; debuts Houston Grand Opera in Marriage of Figaro 1988, Spoleto Festival, Charleston and Italy 1987–90, New York City Opera in La Bohème 1989, San Francisco Opera, Metropolitan Opera, Paris Opera at Bastille, Teatro Colón, Buenos Aires all in Marriage of Figaro 1991, Glyndebourne in Cosi fan tutte 1992, La Scala Milan in Don Giovanni 1993, Vienna State Opera in Marriage of Figaro 1993, Lyric Opera of Chicago in Susannah 1993, San Diego Opera in Eugene Onegin 1994, Paris Opera 1996, Massenet's Thaïs at Nice and Gounod's Marguerite at the Met 1997, Floyd's Susannah at the Met 1999, Louise at Barbican Hall, London and the Marschallin at Covent Garden 2000; premiered Previn's A Streetcar Named Desire 1998; recital tour with Jean-Yves Thibaudet 2001–02; London Proms 2002, Dvořák's Rusalka in concert at Covent Garden 2003, Bellini's Il Pirata at the Met 2003; Fulbright Scholar to Germany 1984–85; sang The Star-Spangled Banner (first opera singer), Super Bowl opening ceremony 2014; Hon. mem. RAM 2003; Chevalier, Légion d'honneur 2005; Dr hc Juilliard School, New York 2003, Hon. DMus (Harvard) 2015; Fulbright Scholar 1984–85, George London Prize 1988, Richard Tucker Award 1990, Solti Prize, Acad. du Disque Lyrique 1996, Prix Maria Callas Acad. du Disque Lyrique 1997, 2004, Musical America Vocalist of the Year 1997, Prize Acad. du Disque Lyrique 1998, Grammy Awards 1999, 2002, 2010, creation of the dessert 'La Diva Renée' by Master Chef Daniel Boulud 1999, Classical BRIT Awards for Top-selling Female Artist 2003, for Outstanding Contribution to Music 2004, LOTOS Medal of Merit 2005, Polar Music Prize 2008, Opera News Award 2008, Nat. Medal of Arts 2012, Female Artist of the Year, BRIT Awards 2018. *Plays:* Living on Love (Williamstown Theatre Festival 2014, Broadway debut in Longacre Theatre 2015). *Recordings include:* Sacred Songs 2005, R. Strauss's Daphne (with Cologne Radio Chorus and Symphony Orchestra) 2005, Love Sublime (with Brad Mehldau) 2006, Homage: The Age of the Diva 2006, Four Last Songs 2008, Verismo Arias (Grammy Award for Best Classical Vocal Performance) 2009, Dark Hope 2010, Ravel/Messiaen, Dutilleux: Poèmes (ECHO Klassik Award for Female Singer of the Year) (Grammy Award for Best Classical Vocal Solo 2013) 2012, Christmas in New York 2014, Distant Light 2017. *Publication:* The Inner Voice: The Making of a Singer (autobiog.) 2005. *Address:* c/o Alec C. Treuhaft, IMG Artists, Pleiades House, 7 West 54th Street, New York, NY 10019, USA (office). *Telephone:* (212) 994-3500 (office). *Fax:* (212) 994-3550 (office). *E-mail:* atreuhaft@imgartists.com (office). *Website:* www.imgartists.com (office); www.renee-fleming.com.

FLEMING, Stephen Paul; New Zealand professional cricketer (retd); b. 1 April 1973, Christchurch, Canterbury; s. of Pauline Fleming; m. Kelly Payne 2007; one s. one d.; ed Waltham Primary School, Cashmere High School, Christchurch Teachers' Coll.; left-handed batsman; teams: Canterbury 1991–2000, New Zealand 1994–2008 (Capt. 1997–2007), Wellington 2000–08, Middx 2001, Yorks. 2003, Notts. 2005–07 (Capt.), Chennai Super Kings 2008; First-class debut: 1991/92; Test debut: NZ v India, Hamilton 19–23 March 1994; ODI debut: NZ v India, Napier 25 March 1994; T20I debut: NZ v Australia, Auckland 17 Feb. 2005; youngest Capt. in NZ history; NZ's highest run-scorer in ODIs; holds NZ record for number of Test caps, Test runs and Test catches; retired from int. cricket 26 March 2008; Coach, Melbourne Stars of the Big Bash League 2015. *Publication:* Cricketing Safari (with Nathan Astle) 2000. *Leisure interests:* golf, computer games, reading. *Address:* Melbourne Stars, PO Box 327, East Melbourne 3002, Australia. *Website:* www.melbournestars.com.au.

FLETCHER, Ernest (Ernie) Lee, BS, MD; American physician and fmr politician; *Founder and CEO, Alton Healthcare LLC;* b. 12 Nov. 1952, Mount Sterling, Ky; m. Glenna Foster; one s. one d.; ed Univ. of Kentucky Coll. of Eng and Coll. of Medicine; served in USAF as F-4E Aircraft Commdr and N American Aerospace Defense Command (NORAD) Alert Force Commdr 1980s; physician in family practice 1983–95; CEO St Joseph Medical Foundation 1997–99; mem. Ky State Legislature for 78th Congressional Dist 1995–99, mem. Ky Comm. on Poverty, Task Force on Higher Educ.; mem. US House of Reps from 6th Congressional Dist 1999–2003, mem. House Cttee on Energy and Commerce, Chair. Policy Sub-Cttee on Health; Gov. of Kentucky 2003–07; Founder and CEO Alton Healthcare LLC, Cincinnati 2008–; fmr Chair. Southern States Energy Bd; mem. Bd of Dirs Achieve, Inc.; Republican. *Address:* Alton Healthcare LLC, 290 Country Club Drive, Suite 220, Stockbridge, GA 30281, USA (office). *Telephone:* (678) 284-6300 (office). *Fax:* (678) 284-6336 (office). *Website:* www.altonhealthcare.com (office).

FLETCHER, Graham, BA; Australian diplomatist; *Ambassador to People's Republic of China;* ed Univ. of Sydney; Counsellor, Embassy in Beijing 1986–88, 1997–2000, Deputy Head of Mission (DHOM) 2004–08; DHOM, Embassy in Washington, DC 2011–13; First Asst Sec., Free Trade Agreement Div., Dept of Foreign Affairs and Trade (DFAT) 2014, also lead negotiator for China–Australia Free Trade Agreement; First Asst Sec., North Asia Div., DFAT, with responsibility for relations with China, Japan, Korean Peninsula and Mongolia 2015–19; Amb. to People's Repub. of China 2019–. *Address:* Embassy of Australia, 21 Dong Zhi Men Wai Dajie, San Li Tun, Beijing 100600, People's Republic of China (office). *Telephone:* (10) 51404111 (office). *Fax:* (10) 51404204 (office). *E-mail:* pubaff.beijing@dfat.gov.au (office). *Website:* www.china.embassy.gov.au (office).

FLETCHER, Hugh Alasdair, BSc, MCom (Hons), MBA; New Zealand company director and fmr university administrator; *Chairman, Fletcher Brothers Limited;* b. 28 Nov. 1947, Auckland; s. of Sir James Muir Cameron Fletcher and Margery V. Fletcher (née Gunthorp); m. Rt Hon. Dame Sian Seerpoohi Elias (Chief Justice of New Zealand) 1970; two s.; ed Auckland Univ., Stanford Univ.; CEO Fletcher Holdings Ltd 1980, Man. Dir Fletcher Challenge Ltd 1981, CEO 1987–97, Dir Fletcher Building 2002–12, currently Chair. Fletcher Brothers Ltd; Chair. Air New Zealand 1985–89; mem. Prime Minister's Enterprise Council 1992–98, Asia-Pacific Advisory Cttee, New York Stock Exchange 1995–2004; Chancellor, Univ. of Auckland 2004–08; Chair. Ministerial Inquiry into Telecommunications 2000–01; mem. Council, Univ. of Auckland 1999–2011; mem. Bd of Dirs Rubicon 2002–, IAG New Zealand 2003–, Reserve Bank of New Zealand 2003–12, Vector 2007–, IAG 2008–, Dilworth Trust 2008–, L.E.K. Australasian Advisory Bd 2010–13; Harkness Fellowship 1970–72; Hon. LLD (Auckland) 2011; Distinguished Alumni Award, Univ. of Auckland 1996. *Leisure interests:* horse riding, hunting, breeding, racing. *Address:* PO Box 11468, Ellerslie, Auckland 1542, New Zealand (office). *Telephone:* (2) 1369016 (office); (9) 579-4226 (office); 21-369016 (mobile) (office). *E-mail:* hugh.fletcher@xtra.co.nz (office).

FLETCHER, John E.; Australian business executive; *Chairman, DP World Australia Ltd;* b. 1952, Melbourne, Vic.; m. Nola Fletcher; three c.; held accounting, operating and sr man. positions, Brambles Industries 1974–82, Gen. Man. Transport Div. 1982–84, Commercial Dir, Europe 1984–86, Man. Dir CHEP Australia 1986–88, Man. Dir Brambles Australia 1988–93, CEO Brambles Industries 1993–2001; CEO and Man. Dir Coles Myer Ltd (renamed Coles Group Ltd 2006) 2001–07; Chair. DP World Australia 2016–; mem. Bd of Dirs Telstra Corpn 2001–06. *Leisure interests:* golf, tennis, skiing. *Address:* DP World Australia Ltd, Level 21, 400 George Street, Sydney, NSW 2000, Australia (office). *Telephone:* (2) 9270-8800 (office). *Website:* www.dpworldaustralia.com.au (office).

FLETCHER, Philip John, CBE, MA; British public servant; b. 2 May 1946, London; s. of Alan Philip Fletcher and Annette Grace Fletcher (née Wright); m. Margaret Anne Boys; two d. (one deceased); ed Marlborough Coll., Trinity Coll., Oxford; joined Civil Service 1968, Under-Sec. of Housing, Water and Cen. Finance,

Dept of the Environment 1986–90; Planning and Devt Control 1990–93; Chief Exec. PSA Services 1993–94; Deputy Sec. Cities and Countryside Group 1994–95; Receiver for the Metropolitan Police Dist 1996–2000; Dir-Gen. of Water Services 2000–06, Chair. Water Services Regulation Authority (Ofwat) 2006–12; Reader, Church of England; mem. Archbishops' Council for the Church of England; Dir (non-exec.) Ofqual Bd. *Leisure interest:* walking.

FLEURY, Gen. (retd) Jean André; French fmr air force officer and aeronautics industry executive; b. 1 Dec. 1934, Brest; s. of René Fleury and Blanche-Marie Marsille; m. 1st Madeleine Fleury (deceased); m. 2nd Margaret Hadlington; Commdt, Saint Dizier Air Base 1977–78; Head, Office of Supply, Air Force Gen. Staff 1978–81; Deputy Chief of Planning, Armed Forces Gen. Staff 1983–85; Commdt, Strategic Air Forces 1985–87; Chief of Staff to Pres. of Repub. 1987–89; Chief of Staff of Air Force 1989–91; mem. Supreme Council of Army and Air Forces 1989; Pres. Aéroports de Paris 1992–99; Chair. Airports Council Int. 1998–99; aeronautics consultant 2000–09; mem. Econ. and Social Regional Council of Britanny 2001–07; Grand Croix, Légion d'honneur; Commdr, Ordre nat. du Mérite; Croix de la Valeur militaire; Commdr, Legion of Merit (USA). *Publications include:* Faire face: Memoires d'un chef d'état major 1996, Le Général qui pensait comme un civil 2004, Le mystère de la Chesnaie 2007, Les guerres du Golfe 2009, Le bourbier afghan 2011, Crise libyenne: la nouvelle donne géopolitique 2012, La France en guerre au Mali 2013. *Address:* Les Mirages, 2 La Combe de Haut, 56140 Pleucadeuc, France (office). *Telephone:* (2) 97-26-96-85 (office). *E-mail:* fleurygeneral@wanadoo.fr (office).

FLIER, Jeffrey S., BS, MD; American endocrinologist and academic; *George C. Reisman Professor of Medicine, Harvard Medical School;* b. 27 Feb. 1948, New York; m. Dr Eleftheria Maratos-Flier; two c.; ed City Coll. of New York, Mount Sinai School of Medicine; intern, Mount Sinai Hosp., New York 1972–73, residency training in internal medicine 1973–74; Clinical Assoc., NIH, Bethesda, Md 1974–78; Asst Prof. of Medicine, Harvard Medical School 1978–82, Assoc. Prof. 1982–93, Prof. 1993–, George C. Reisman Prof. of Medicine 1999–, Chief of Endocrine Div. 1990, Chief Academic Officer, Beth Israel Deaconess Medical Center (BIDMC) 2002–07, also Carolyn Shields Walker Prof. of Medicine, Harvard Medical School, Dean, Faculty of Medicine 2007–16; Chief of Diabetes Unit, Beth Israel Deaconess Medical Center 1998–2002; Visiting Scientist, Whitehead Inst., MIT 1985–86; Fellow, American Acad. of Arts and Sciences; mem. AAAS, NAS Inst. of Medicine (Pres. 2001), Co-Chair., Scientific Advisory Bd, Alinea Pharmaceuticals Inc.; mem. Bd of Dirs Broad Inst. of MIT and Harvard; Hon. MD (Univ. of Athens) 1997, Hon. DS (Univ. of Edinburgh); American Diabetes Asscn Eli Lilly Award, American Physiological Soc. Berson Lecture, American Diabetes Asscn Banting Medal 2005. *Publications:* over 200 scholarly papers and reviews. *Address:* Israel Deaconess Medical Center, 330 Brookline Avenue, Mailstop EFN202, Boston, MA 02215, USA (office). *Telephone:* (617) 667-9050 (office). *Fax:* (617) 667-9054 (office). *E-mail:* jflier@bidmc.harvard.edu (office).

FLIGHT, Baron (Life Peer), cr. 2011, of Worcester in the County of Worcestershire; **Howard Emerson Flight,** MA (Cantab.), MBA, FRSA; British politician and investment manager; *Director, Metrobank;* b. 16 June 1948, London; m. Christabel Flight 1973; one s. three d.; ed Brentwood School, Magdalene Coll., Cambridge, Univ. of Michigan Ross School of Business, USA; worked as investment adviser and dir 1970–98; Jt Man. Dir Guinness Flight 1986–98 (acquired by Investec); MP (Conservative) for Arundel and South Downs 1997–2005; Shadow Econ. Sec. to the Treasury 1999–2001, Shadow Paymaster Gen. 2001–02, Shadow Chief Sec. to the Treasury 2002–04; Deputy Chair. Conservative Party 2004–05 (resgnd); mem. (Conservative), House of Lords 2011–; Chair. CIM Investment Management Ltd 2006–16, Downing Four VCT PLC 2009, Aurora Investment Trust PLC 2011, EIS Asscn; Chair. Flight and Partners 2007; mem. Bd of Dirs, Investec Asset Management Ltd 1998, Marechale Capital 2006, Edge Performance VCT PLC 2011, R5FX Ltd 2015, Mercantile Ports and Logistics Ltd; Dir (non-exec.), Metrobank PLC 2010; Commr Guernsey Financial Services Comm.; consultant, TISA (previously PIMA), Duff and Phelps, Arden Partners; mem. Advisory Bd Guinness Renewable Energy EIS Funds, Praesidian Europe, Financial Services Forum; Gov., Brentwood School, Essex; Chair. Croome Court Nat. Trust Appeal Cttee; Vice-Pres. and Trustee, Elgar Foundation; Liveryman of the Carpenters' Co. *Publications:* All You Need to Know about Exchange Rates 1988, The City in Europe and the World 2005 (contrib.). *Leisure interests:* classical music/opera, skiing, gardening, India. *Address:* House of Lords, Westminster, London, SW1A 0PW, England (office). *Telephone:* (20) 7222-7559 (office). *Fax:* (20) 7976-7059 (office). *E-mail:* hflight@btinternet.com (office); flighth@parliament.uk (office). *Website:* www.parliament.uk/biographies/lords/lord-flight/4211; www .howardflight.com.

FLIMM, Jürgen; German theatre director; *Director, Staatsoper Unter den Linden;* b. 17 July 1941, Giessen; s. of Werner Flimm and Ellen Flimm; m. Susanne Ottersbach 1990; early work at Munich Kammerspiele; Dir Nationaltheater, Mannheim 1972–73; Prin. Dir Thalia Theater, Hamburg 1973–74, 1985–2000; Dir Cologne Theatre 1979–85; Acting Dir Salzburg Festspiele 2001–06, Artistic Dir 2007–10; Artistic Dir Festival Ruhrtriennale 2005–08; Artistic Dir Salzburg Festival 2007–12; Dir Staatsoper Unter den Linden (Berlin State Opera) 2010–; Pres. German Bühnenverein 1999–2003; mem. Acad. of Arts in Hamburg, Munich, Berlin, Frankfurt; Bundesverdienstkreuz 1992; Dr hc (Hildesheim) 2002; Konrad-Wolf-Preis 1995, Grimme Prize, Medal for the Arts and Sciences of Free Hanseatic City of Hamburg, Max-Brauer-Prize, Alfred Toepfer Foundation F.V.S. *Films:* Wer zu spät kommt – die letzten Tage des Politbüros 1990, Käthchens Traum 2004. *Publications:* Götterdämmerung 2000, Theatergänger 2004, Theaterbilder 2008, Das Salzburger Kapitel 2010, Die gestürzte Pyramide 2010. *Address:* Staatsoper Unter den Linden, Unter den Linden 7, 10117 Berlin, Germany (office). *Website:* staatsoper-berlin.de (office).

FLINT, Sir Douglas J., Kt, CBE, BAcc (Hons); British business executive; b. July 1955, Scotland; m.; three c.; ed Univ. of Glasgow, Harvard Business School, USA; fmr Partner, KPMG; joined HSBC as Exec. Dir 1995, Chief Financial Officer and Exec. Dir, Risk and Regulation Feb.–Dec. 2010, Group Chair. HSBC Holdings 2010–17; Chair. Financial Reporting Council's review of the Turnbull Guidance on Internal Control 2004; Co-Chair. Counterparty Risk Man. Policy Group III 2008; mem. Standards Advisory Council of Int. Accounting Standards Bd 2001–04; fmr mem. Accounting Standards Bd, Large Business Forum on Tax and Competitiveness, Consultative Cttee of the Large Business Advisory Bd of HM Revenue and Customs; Dir (non-exec.), BP PLC 2005–11; Dir, The Hong Kong Asscn 2011–; Chair. (fmrly Vice-Chair.) Inst. of Int. Finance 2012–; Ind. External mem. Financial Services Trade and Investment Bd –2015; British Business Amb. 2014–; mem. Inst. of Chartered Accountants of Scotland, Asscn of Corp. Treasurers; Fellow, Chartered Inst. of Man. Accountants. *Leisure interest:* golf.

FLINTOFF, Andrew (Freddie), MBE; British fmr professional cricketer; b. 6 Dec. 1977, Preston, Lancs., England; s. of Colin Flintoff; m. Rachel Wools 2005; two s. one d.; ed Ribbleton Hall High School; all-rounder; right-hand batsman; right-arm fast bowler; played for Lancs. 1995–2010, 2014, England 1998–2009 (Capt. 2006, 2006–07), Int. Cricket Council (ICC) World XI 2006, Chennai Super Kings 2009, Brisbane Heat 2014–; First-class debut: 1995; Test debut: England v S Africa, Nottingham 23–27 July 1998; One-Day Int. (ODI) debut: England v Pakistan, Sharjah 7 April 1999; T20I debut: England v Australia, Southampton 13 June 2005; has played in 79 Tests, taken 226 wickets and scored 3,845 runs (five centuries, 26 half-centuries), highest score 167, average 31.77, best bowling (innings) 5/58, (match) 8/156; ODIs: 141 matches, scored 3,394 runs, average 32.01, highest score 123, took 169 wickets, average 24.38, best bowling 5/19; First-class: 183 matches, 9,027 runs, average 33.80, highest score 167, took 350 wickets, average 31.59, best bowling 5/24; retd from Test cricket at conclusion of Ashes series 2009; announced retirement from all cricket 16 Sept. 2010; had one professional boxing engagement in Manchester, beating American Richard Dawson on a points decision Nov. 2012; came out of retirement to play Twenty20 cricket for Lancs. again May 2014; holds the record for the most sixes (68) scored for England 2006; only the seventh player to have batted on all five days of a Test match 2006; one of only seven players to be on both the batting and bowling honours boards at Lord's; Brand Amb. for fashion brand Jacamo 2011; Freedom of the City of Preston 2006; NBC Denis Compton Award 1997, Cricket Writers' Club Young Cricketer of the Year 1998, Walter Lawrence Trophy 1999, Wisden Cricketer of the Year 2004, Wisden Leading Cricketer in the World 2005, ICC One-Day Player of the Year 2004, PCA Player of the Year 2004, 2005, ICC World One-Day XI 2004, 2005, 2006, BBC Sports Personality of the Year (Third Place) 2004, Beard of the Year Award, Beard Liberation Front 2004 (jt winner) 2005, ICC Player of the Year 2005, Compton-Miller Medal 2005, Sir Garfield Sobers Trophy 2005, BBC Sports Personality of the Year 2005, MCC Spirit of Cricket Award 2005, ICC World Test XI 2006. *Achievements:* currently holds 14 Guinness World Records in aid of Sport Relief, including the fastest time zorbing 100m, farthest distance to score a bull's-eye and popping the most party poppers in a minute. *Radio:* host show on BBC Radio Five Live on Monday nights. *Television:* team capt., A League of Their Own (Sky1) 2010, guest commentator, PDC World Darts Championship 2010, Freddie Flintoff versus The World (ITV 4) 2011, guest commentator, World Matchlay 2012, Freddie Flintoff: Hidden Side of Sport (BBC 1) 2012, judge on ITV talent show Let's Get Gold 2012. *Publications include:* Being Freddie, Freddie, Andrew Flintoff – My Life in Pictures, Ashes to Ashes 2009. *Leisure interests:* rugby (both codes), Manchester City Football Club. *Address:* c/o Katie Lydon, Merlin Elite Ltd, Hammersmith Studios, 55 Yeldham Road, Hammersmith, London, W6 8JF, England (office). *Telephone:* (20) 7259-1460 (office). *Website:* www.mcsaatchimerlin.com (office).

FLOCKHART, Calista; American actress; b. 11 Nov. 1964, Freeport, Ill.; d. of Ronald Flockhart and Kay Flockhart; m. Harrison Ford; one adopted s. *Films include:* Naked in New York 1993, Quiz Show 1994, Getting In 1994, Pictures of Baby Jane Doe 1995, Drunks 1995, The Birdcage 1996, Telling Lies in America 1997, Milk and Money 1997, A Midsummer Night's Dream 1999, Like a Hole in the Head 1999, Bash 2000, Things You Can Tell Just By Looking At Her 2000, The Last Shot 2004, Fragile 2005. *Plays on Broadway include:* The Glass Menagerie, The Three Sisters. *Television work includes:* The Guiding Light 1978, Darrow 1991, An American Story 1991, Life Stories: Families in Crisis 1992, Ally McBeal (Best Actress Award, Golden Globes 1998) 1997–2002, Bash: Latter-Day Plays 2000, Brothers and Sisters (series) 2006–11, Full Circle 2015, Supergirl (series) 2015–. *Address:* c/o Bill Butler, The Gersh Agency, 9465 Wilshere Blvd, 6th Floor, Beverly Hills, CA 90212, USA (office).

FLOOD, Philip James, AO, BEc (Hons); Australian diplomatist (retd); *President, The Order of Australia Association;* b. 2 July 1935, Sydney, NSW; s. of Thomas C. Flood and Maxine S. Flood; m. 2nd Carole Henderson 1990; two s. one d. from previous m.; ed North Sydney Boys High School, Univ. of Sydney; mem. Mission to EEC and Embassy, Brussels 1959–62, Rep. to OECD Devt Assistance Cttee, Paris 1966–69, Asst Sec., Dept of Foreign Affairs 1971–73, High Commr to Bangladesh 1974–76, Minister, Embassy, Washington, DC 1976–77, CEO Dept Special Trade Representations 1977–80; First Asst Sec., Dept of Trade 1980–84, Deputy Sec., Dept of Foreign Affairs and Trade 1985–89, Amb. to Indonesia 1989–93, Dir-Gen. Australian Int. Devt Assistance Bureau (AusAID) 1993–95, Dir-Gen. Office of Nat. Assessments 1995–96, Sec., Dept of Foreign Affairs and Trade 1996–98; High Commr to UK 1998–2000; Head of Inquiry into Immigration Detention 2000–01; Chair. Australia-Indonesia Inst. 2001–04; Head of Inquiry into Australian Intelligence Agencies 2004; Chair. Inquiry into Plasma Fractionation 2006; Advisor, Nat. Human Rights Consultation 2009; Pres. The Order of Australia Asscn; mem. Bd Asialink 2004–09, CARE Australia 2003–11; Fellow, Royal Australian Inst. Public Admin., Australian Inst. of Int. Affairs; Bintang Jasa Utama (Indonesian Order of Merit) 1993, Centenary Medal 2003. *Publications:* Odyssey by the Sea 2005, Dancing with Warriors – A Diplomatic Memoir 2011. *Leisure interests:* reading, music, walking, tennis, swimming.

FLORES ALEMÁN, (José) Armando; Salvadorean politician; *Minister of the Economy;* ed Universidad de El Salvador; Coordinator, Dept of Educ., Consumer Fed. of Cooperatives of El Salvador 1989–90; Co-founder Centro para la Defensa del Consumidor (Centre for Consumer Protection), Deputy Dir 1991–95, Exec. Dir 1997; Coordinator, Consumers Int. in Central America 1996; fmr Deputy Minister of Trade and Industry, Minister of the Economy 2012–. *Address:* Ministry of the Economy, Edif. C1–C2, Centro de Gobierno, Alameda Juan Pablo II y Calle Guadalupe, San Salvador, El Salvador (office). *Telephone:* 2231-5600 (office). *Fax:* 2221-5446 (office). *E-mail:* info@minec.gob.sv (office). *Website:* www.minec.gob.sv (office).

FLORES FACUSSÉ, Carlos Roberto, BEng, MIntEcon, PhD; Honduran politician and fmr head of state; b. 1 March 1950, Tegucigalpa; s. of Oscar A.

Flores and Margarita Facussé de Flores; m. Mary Carol Flake; one s. one d.; ed American School, Tegucigalpa and Louisiana State Univ.; Rep. for Francisco Morazan to Liberal Convention, Pres. Departmental Liberal Council, Francisco Morazan; Finance Sec. Nat. Directorate Movimiento Liberal Rodista; Congressman, Nat. Ass. for Francisco Morazan 1980–97; Presidential Sec. 1982–83; Gen. Co-ordinator, Movimiento Liberal Florista; fmr Pres. Cen. Exec. Council Partido Liberal de Honduras; Pres. of Honduras 1998–2002; Co-owner, Man. and mem. Editorial Bd La Tribuna, Co-owner and Man. Lithopress Industrial; fmr Man. CONPACASA; fmr Prof., School of Business Admin, Nat. Univ. of Honduras, Cen. American Higher School of Banking; fmr mem. Bd of Dirs Honduran Inst. of Social Security, Cen. Bank of Honduras, Inst. Nacional de Formación Profesional; mem. Industrial Eng Asscn of Honduras, Nat. Asscn of Industries, Consejo Hondureño de la Empresa Privada (COHEP), Honduran Inst. of Inter-American Culture. *Publication:* Forjemos Unidos el Destino de Honduras.

FLORES FLAKE, Mary Elizabeth, BA; Honduran lawyer, journalist, politician and diplomatist; *Permanent Representative, United Nations;* b. 6 Dec. 1973; d. of Carlos Roberto Flores (Pres. of Honduras 1998–2002) and Mary Flores; one s. one d.; ed Univ. of Loyola, New Orleans, USA, Nat. Autonomous Univ. of Honduras; First Vice-Pres. of Nat. Congress 2006–10, Pres. Ethics and Transparency Cttee; Amb. and Perm. Rep. to UN, New York 2010–, Vice-Pres. UN Gen. Ass. 2012–13; Pres. Exec. Bd, Int. Asscn of Perm. Reps., New York 2016; Vice-Pres. of Admin of Asscn of Newspapers and Magazines (PYRSA); participated in Fifth Language Congress sponsored by Royal Language Acad. (Spain), published paper on Intercultural Bilingual Educ. as a tool in devt of the indigenous groups in Latin America; presided over Support Cttee of Nat. Inst. of Thorax Hosp. for more than ten years; mem. Friedrich Naumann Foundation; chosen by World Econ. Forum to be part of the Young Global Leaders initiative 2007; mem. Rotary Club International of Nueva Tegucigalpa; Kappa Tae Alpha Award, Press Soc. of US for High Academic Standing 1997. *Address:* Permanent Mission of Honduras to the United Nations, 866 United Nations Plaza, Suite 417, New York, NY 10017, USA (office). *Telephone:* (212) 752-3370 (office). *Fax:* (212) 223-0498 (office). *E-mail:* honduras_un@hotmail.com (office). *Website:* www.un.int/wcm/content/site/honduras (office).

FLOSSE, Gaston; French Polynesian politician and fmr head of state; b. 24 June 1931, Rikitea (Gambier archipelago); m. 1st Barbara Cunningham, six c.; m. 2nd Marie-Jeanne Mao 1994, three c.; Pres. City Council Pirae 1963–65, Mayor 1965–2000; Govt Councillor in charge of Agric. 1965–67; mem. French Polynesian Territorial Ass. for Windward Islands 1967, Pres. 1972–77; Pres. Tahoeraa Huiraatira Party 1971; Deputy for French Polynesia, Nat. Ass., France 1978–97; Sec. of State in charge of S Pacific Affairs, France 1986–88; Vice-Pres. Govt Council 1982–84, Pres. Governing Council 1984–87, 1991–2004; apptd Senator of French Repub. 1998; Pres. of French Polynesia Feb.–June 2004, Oct. 2004–05, 2008, 2013–14 (removed from office after a corruption conviction became final); mem. Cen. Cttee Union des Democrates pour la République (UDR), France, then Founder-mem. RPR; Chevalier, Légion d'honneur, Ordre nat. du Mérite, First 'Grand Maître', Order of Tahiti Nui; Dr hc (Kyung Hee Univ., Korea) 1985. *Address:* c/o Office of the President of the Government, avenue Pouvana'a A Opa, BP 2551, 98713 Papeete, French Polynesia.

FLUG, Karnit, MA (Econs), PhD; Israeli economist and central banker; b. 9 Jan. 1955, Poland; m. Saul Lach; two c.; ed Hebrew Univ. of Jerusalem, Columbia Univ., USA; Economist, IMF 1984–88; joined Research Dept, Bank of Israel 1988, Deputy Dir, Research Dept 1997–2001, Dir and mem. Sr Man. 2001–11, Deputy Gov. 2011–13, Acting Gov. July–Jan. 2013, Gov. 2013–18; Sr Research Economist, Inter-American Devt Bank 1994–96; fmr mem. Cttee on Increasing Competitiveness in the Economy, Cttee for Social and Econ. Change, Cttee for the Defense Budget, Cttee to Study Raising the Retirement Age for Women.

FLUTUR, Cristina; Romanian film and theatre actress; b. Iaşi; ed Alexandru Ioan Cuza Univ., Babes-Bolyai Univ.; mem. Ludic Theatre (amateur theatre co. for students); performed for several years in theatre productions, both in Romania at Radu Stanca Nat. Theatre, Sibiu from 2004, and abroad on tour to Kiev, Sarajevo, Helsinki, Turku, St Petersburg, Skopje, Trabzon, Ljiubljana, Naples, Bogota and Rome; also performed at Sibiu Int. Theatre Festival; Diploma for Excellency, Ministry of Culture 2010, Woman of the Year (category Amb. of Romanian Arts Abroad), Avantaje magazine 2012. *Theatre includes:* Platonov, Time for Love, Time for Death, Turandot, The Guide of a Regained Childhood, Metamorphosis, Love Factory, Life with an Idiot, Othello, Today is No Smoking Day, The Seagull, Plasticine, Rhinoceros, Pantagruel's Sister-in-Law, The Human Voice (solo show), Sweet Thursday, The Clouds. *Films include:* Beyond the Hills (Best Actress Award (jtly with Cosmina Stratan), Cannes Film Festival) 2012. *Television includes:* Cinema 3 (series) 2012, Résistance (mini-series) 2014. *Address:* Agence Elizabeth Simpson, 62 boulevard du Montparnasse, 75015 Paris, France (office). *Telephone:* 1-42-22-85-50 (office). *Fax:* 1-42-22-85-56 (office). *E-mail:* contact@agencesimpson.com (office). *Website:* www.agencesimpson.fr (office).

FLYNN, Lt Gen. (retd) Michael (Mike) Thomas, BSc, MA, MBA; American army officer (retd) and fmr government official; *Chairman and CEO, Flynn Intel Group Inc.;* b. Dec. 1958, Middletown, RI; s. of Charles Flynn and Helen Flynn (née Andrews); m. Lori Andrade; two s.; ed Univ. of Rhode Island, US Army Command and Gen. Staff Coll., Naval War Coll.; commissioned into US Army as Second Lt in mil. intelligence 1981, multiple tours at Fort Bragg, NC, with 82nd Airborne Div., XVIII Airborne Corps and Jt Special Operations Command, roles included Asst Chief of Staff, G2 2001, Dir of Intelligence, Jt Task Force 180, Afghanistan 2001–02, Commdr, 111th Mil. Intelligence Brigade 2002–04, Dir of Intelligence, Jt Special Operations Command 2004–07, Dir of Intelligence, US Cen. Command 2007–08, Dir of Intelligence, Jt Staff 2008–09, Dir of Intelligence, Int. Security Assistance Force, Afghanistan 2009–10, Asst Chief of Staff, G2 2010–11, Asst Dir of Nat. Intelligence 2011–12, Dir, Defense Intelligence Agency 2012–14 (retd); CEO Flynn Intel Group LLC 2014–, Chair. Flynn Intel Group Inc. 2015–; Nat. Security Advisor, The White House Jan.–Feb. 2017 (resgnd); appeared in court Dec. 2017, admitted making false statements to FBI; numerous mil. decorations, including Defense Meritorious Service Medal, Defense Superior Service Medal, Legion of Merit, Bronze Star Medal, Meritorious Service Medal, Jt Service Commendation Medal, Army Commendation Medal; Dr hc (Inst. of World Politics, Washington, DC); Ellis Island Medal of Honor, Asscn of Special Operations Professionals Man of the Year Award 2012. *Publication:* The Field of Fight: How We Can Win the Global War against Radical Islam and Its allies (co-author) 2016. *Address:* Flynn Intel Group Inc., 44 Canal Center Plaza, #400, Alexandria, VA 22314, USA (office). *Telephone:* (703) 313-7040 (office). *E-mail:* info@flynnintelgroup.com (office). *Website:* www.flynnintelgroup.com (office).

FOALE, Marion Ann, RCA; British designer; b. 13 March 1939, London; d. of S. D. Foale; one s. one d.; ed South West Essex Tech and School of Art, RCA; designed Queen's mantle for OBE dedication ceremony 1960; Founding pnr (with Sally Tuffin) Foale and Tuffin Ltd 1961–72; signed with Puritan Fashion Corps, NY 1965–70; designed clothes for films, including for Susannah York in Kaleidoscope 1966 and Audrey Hepburn in Two for the Road 1966; f. own label Marion Foale-Knitwear Designer 1982; exhibition at Fashion and Textile Museum, London 2009–10. *Leisure interests:* studying fine art, painting. *Address:* Foale Ltd, The Cottage, 133A Long Street, Atherstone, Warwicks., CV9 1AD, England (office). *Telephone:* (1827) 720333 (office). *Fax:* (1827) 720444 (office). *E-mail:* foale@talk21.com (office). *Website:* marionfoale.com.

FODOR, Gen. (retd) Lajos; Hungarian army officer (retd) and diplomatist; b. 29 July 1947, Debrecen; m. Éva Kovács; one s. one d.; ed Lajos Kossuth Land Forces Mil. Acad., Szentendre, Frunze Mil. Acad., Moscow, Defence Language Inst., San Antonio, American Nat. Defence Univ.; infantry officer, 1970, platoon leader, 14th Mechanized Infantry Regt Nagykaniza 1971, Bn Commdr 63rd Mechanized Infantry Regt Nagyatád 1971–79, Deputy Commdr 1981–83, Regt Commdr 1983–85, Brig. 26th Mechanized Infantry Regt Lenti 1985–87, Deputy Chief and Chief of Mechanized Infantry and Armoured Service, Gen. Dir of Training 1989, Deputy Commdr 5th Army, Székesfehérvár, Deputy Commdr and Maj.-Gen. of Hungarian Army 1992, Dir of Mil. Intelligence Office 1993, Deputy Chief of Defence Staff 1996–99, Chief 1999–2003, also Under-Sec. for Policy, Ministry of Defence, Amb. to Australia and New Zealand 2003–07, Sec. of State for Administration 2007–13; Order of John Hunyadi 2001, Commdr's Cross of the Order of Merit of the Republic of Hungary 2003.

FOFANA, Ibrahima Kassory, PhD; Guinean politician; *Prime Minister;* b. 1954; ed Université IPGAN, Conakry, American Univ., Washington, DC; started as Economist Trainee, Econ. Div., Presidency of Repub. of Guinea, Conakry 1978, Gen. Admin. of Major Projects 1994–96; Asst Prof. Université de Conakry 1978–79; Deputy Dir Research Office, Ministry of Planning and Int. Cooperation 1978–79, Head, Div. of Bilateral Relations with the American Continent 1982–84, Div. of Multilateral Relations 1984–86, Dir-Gen. Int. Cooperation 1986–91, Nat. Dir of Public Investment 1991–94; Minister of Budget and Restructuring of Parapublic Sector 1996–98, of Economy and Finance 1998–2000, Minister of State in charge of Investment Issues and Public-Private Partnerships 2014–18; Prime Minister 2018–; Gov. Banque Africaine de Développement 1996–2000; Dir for Guinea, IMF 1998–2000; Chair. Bd of Dirs, Société d'Exploitation des Eaux de Guinée 1993–95, Société Guinéenne d'Electricité 1993–96, Société de Télécommunications de Guinée 1993–96; Chair. Steering Cttee TOKTEN Program, UNDP 1984–86; mem. Bd of Dirs Banque Internationale pour l'Afrique en Guinee 1991–93, Compagnie de Bauxite de Guinée 1991–94, Société Guinéenne de Palme et Hévéa 1993–96. *Address:* BP 5141, Conakry, Guinea (office). *Telephone:* 300-41-51-19 (office). *Fax:* 300-41-52-82 (office). *Website:* www.gouvernement.gov.gn (office).

FOFANA, Mohamed Said; Guinean economist and politician; b. 1952, Forécariah, Lower Guinea; ed Inst. Polytechnique Gamal Abdel Nasser, Centre Demographique de l'ONU-Roumanie, Romania, WTO Graduate Inst., Switzerland; Lecturer in Econs, Tabossi Coll., Fria 1976–77; served in various posts with Ministry of Planning and Statistics 1977–84; Sec.-Gen. Chamber of Trade and Industry 1985, Nat. Dir for Trade and Competition 2003–08, Nat. Dir for Foreign Trade 2008–09, Dir for Co-ordination of Projects, Ministry of Trade and Industry 2009; Prime Minister 2010–15; participated in negotiations with several int. orgs including WTO, ICC, UNCTAD, EU. *Address:* c/o Office of the Prime Minister, BP 5141, Conakry, Guinea.

FOGARTY, Thomas James, BS, MD; American thoracic surgeon and academic; *Clinical Professor of Surgery, Stanford University Medical Center;* b. 25 Feb. 1934, Cincinnati, Ohio; ed Xavier Univ., Univ. of Cincinnati; worked as scrub technician, Good Samaritan Hosp., Cincinnati; Peripheral Vascular Fellowship, Univ. of Cincinnati Coll. of Medicine 1962; Intern, Univ. of Oregon Medical School 1960–61, Residency in Gen. Surgery, 1965; Clinical Assoc. for NIH Surgery Br. 1967; Advanced Research Fellow in Cardiovascular Surgery, Stanford Univ. Medical Center 1969, Instructor of Surgery, Div. of Cardiovascular Surgery 1969–70, Asst Prof. of Surgery, Volunteer Clinical Faculty 1970–71, Asst Clinical Prof. of Surgery, Medical Center 1971–73, pvt. practice in Stanford Medical Center 1973–78, Pres. of Medical Staff 1977–79, Clinical Prof. of Surgery 1993–; Dir of Cardiovascular Surgery, Sequoia Hosp., Redwood City, Calif. 1980–93; Pres. Fogarty Eng Lab.; Co-founder Three Arch Pnrs (venture capital firm) 1993; f. Fogarty Medical Foundation 2000; est. Thomas Fogarty Winery and Vineyards, Santa Cruz, Calif. 1978; Co-Ed.-in-Chief Journal of Endovascular Therapy; mem. numerous professional socs including American Bd of Surgery, American Bd of Thoracic Surgery, American Coll. of Surgeons, American Medical Asscn, Calif. Medical Soc., San Francisco Surgical Soc., Soc. of Vascular Surgery; Dr hc (Xavier Univ.) 1987; San Francisco Patent and Trademark Asscn Inventor of the Year 1980, Lemelson-MIT Prize 2000, inducted into Nat. Inventors Hall of Fame 2001, Medical Design Excellence Awards Lifetime Achievement Award 2012, Nat. Medal of Tech. and Innovation 2014. *Medical inventions include:* Fogarty® Embolectomy Balloon Catheter 1961, Medtronic/AneuRx Endovascular Aortic Stent-Graft, Fogarty® Surgical Clips and Clamps, Hancock Tissue Heart Valve (with Warren Hancock); holds 63 US patents for medical devices; founder or co-founder of over 30 start-up cos mfg medical devices. *Publications:* chapters in numerous surgical textbooks, over 150 articles in professional journals in fields of cardiac, vascular and gen. surgery. *Leisure interests:* fishing, model-building, wine-making, inventing, design. *Address:* Stanford University School of Medicine, 291 Campus Drive, Li Ka Shing Building, Stanford, CA 94305 (office); Thomas Fogarty Winery & Vineyards, 19501 Skyline Blvd, Woodside, CA 94062, USA (office). *Telephone:* (650) 723-4000 (office); (650) 851-6777 (office). *E-mail:* tjf@fogartybusiness.com (office); info@fogartywinery.com (office). *Website:* med.stanford.edu (office); www.ctsnet.org (office).

FOGELBERG, Graeme, MCom, MBA, PhD; New Zealand university administrator; b. 10 Dec. 1939, Wellington; s. of Frederick Edward Fogelberg and Evelyn Fogelberg (née Greenwell); m. (divorced); three s. two d.; ed Wellington Coll., Victoria Univ. of Wellington and Univ. of Western Ontario, Canada; Prof. of Business Admin., Victoria Univ. of Wellington 1970, Dean, Faculty of Commerce Admin. 1977–82, Deputy Vice-Chancellor 1986–92; professorial appointments at Univ. of Western Ont. 1975–76, 1986–87 and Pennsylvania State Univ., USA 1992–93; Vice-Chancellor Univ. of Otago, Dunedin 1994–2004; Chair. NZ Vice-Chancellors Cttee 1999–2000; Chair. and Trustee, New Zealand Univs' Superannuation Scheme –2008; fmr Chair. Asscn of Commonwealth Univs; Fellow, New Zealand Inst. of Dirs; Pres. Rotary Club of Wellington 1988–89; Companion, New Zealand Order of Merit 2004; Hon. LLD (Otago) 2004. *Publications include:* several business study books and articles in accounting, business, man. and econs journals. *Leisure interests:* tennis, skiing, fine New Zealand wines, travel. *Address:* PO Box 2937, Wellington 6140, New Zealand (home). *Telephone:* (21) 320752 (home). *E-mail:* graemefogelberg@gmail.com (home).

FOGELHOLM, Markus, MA; Finnish banker and business executive; b. 11 March 1946, Helsinki; s. of Eila Fogelholm and Georg Fogelholm; m. Saara RI Suokas 1969; one s. one d.; ed Univ. of Helsinki; joined Bank of Finland 1972, Head of Foreign Financing Dept 1984–87, Market Operations Dept 1992–2001; Special Asst to Exec. Dir of UN Centre on Transnational Corpns 1978–81; Alt. Exec. Dir IMF 1987–89, Exec. Dir 1989–91; Man. Dir Finnish Bankers' Asscn 2001–06; mem. Bd of Dirs Julius Tallberg Real Estate Corpn 2008; Hon. mem. Forex Finland. *Leisure interests:* wine, music, tennis, hiking, skating.

FOGERTY, John Cameron; American singer, composer, songwriter and musician (guitar); b. 28 May 1945, Berkeley, Calif.; mem. Blue Velvets, renamed the Golliwogs 1959–67, then renamed Creedence Clearwater Revival 1967–71; solo artist 1972–. *Recordings include:* albums: with Creedence Clearwater Revival: Creedence Clearwater Revival 1968, Bayou Country 1969, Green River 1969, Willie and The Poor Boys 1969, Cosmo's Factory 1970, Pendulum 1970, Mardi Gras 1972, Live In Europe 1973, Live At The Royal Albert Hall 1980; solo: The Blue Ridge Rangers 1973, John Fogerty 1975, Centerfield 1985, Eye of a Zombie 1986, Premonition 1998, Blue Moon Swamp 2004, Deja Vu All Over Again 2004, The Long Road Home 2005, Revival 2007, The Blue Ridge Rangers Rides Again 2009, Wrote a Song For Everyone 2013. *Website:* www.johnfogerty.com.

FOING, Bernard H., MS, PhD (Habil.); French space scientist, technologist, academic and explorer; *Chairman, ESTEC Staff Committee and Chief Scientist, SMART-1 Project, European Space Agency;* ed Lycee Louis-Le-Grand, Paris, Ecole Normale Superieure Cachan, ENSET, Observatoire de Paris-Meudon, Univ. of Paris, Laboratoire de Physique Stellaire et Planétaire, CNRS France, Sac Peak, New Mexico, Boulder and Harvard Univ., USA; Chair. ESTEC Staff Cttee, Chief Scientist and Sr Research Coordinator, ESA, Exec. Dir Int. Lunar Exploration Working Group (ILEWG), Co-Investigator, Mars Express, Exomars, COROT, Int. Space Station, Head of Research Div., ESA Research and Scientific Support Dept, SMART-1 Lead Project Scientist; Convener int. conferences for EGS/EGU 1997–, Cttee on Space Research (COSPAR) 1992–, ILEWG 2000–; numerous radio and TV interviews on space and lunar exploration; fmr Researcher at CNRS and European Southern Observatory ESO Chile; mem. Int. Acad. of Astronautics, Cttee on Space Research (COSPAR); Extraordinary Prof., Vrije Universiteit Amsterdam, Distinguished Research Prof., Florida Inst. of Tech.; Space Visionaries, ILEWG Tech. Award, SMART-1 Team Award, ESA service, Ames Honor for Team. *Films:* Black Sun Highlights, documentaries on space and lunar exploration, Naked Science (TV Series documentary) - Earth Without the Moon 2010. *Music:* plays viola (superior studies), guitar and piano accompaniment (classical/jazz), performer in int. amateur orchestras, quartet and chamber music groups. *Play:* JJ Rousseau's opera Devin du Village (co-production). *Publications include:* more than 600 publs, including more than 200 refereed papers on space science and tech., lunar and planetary exploration; more than 5,400 citations; main ed. 20 books on space science and exploration, including: Multi-Site Continuous Spectroscopy Workshops Proceedings (co-ed.) 1988, 1990, 1994, Helioseismology from Space (Advances in Space Research (ASR), Vol. 11, No. 4) 1991, Astronomy and Space Research, from the Moon (ASR Vol. 14, No. 6) 1994, Special Issue, Open Session on Solar & Heliospheric Physics, Journal of Physical Chemistry of Earth 1996, Missions to the Moon, Advances in Moon and Exploring the Cold Universe (ASR Vol. 18, No. 11) 1998, Solar Seismology and Variability (ASR Vol. 24, No. 2) 1999, The Moon and Mars (ASR Vol. 23, No. 11), Lunar Exploration 2000 (ASR Vol. 30, No. 8) in Special Issue on Lunar Exploration (Planetary and Space Science, Vol. 50, Issue 14–15) 2002, Earth-Like Planets and Moons 2002, ESA report to COSPAR 2002, The Next Steps in Exploring Deep Space 2003, The Moon and Near-Earth Objects (ASR Vol. 37, No. 1, co-ed.) 2006, 9th ILEWG ed. on Exploration and Utilisation of the Moon (abstracts) 2007, The Moon: Science, Exploration and Utilisation 2008; Organiser/Ed. Forum ed. Française des Spécialistes en Astronomie (1987): ESA Horizon 2000. *Address:* ESTEC/SRE-S, Postbus 299, 2200 AG Noordwijk, Netherlands (office). *Telephone:* (71) 565-5647 (office). *Fax:* (71) 565-4697 (office). *E-mail:* bfoing@rssd.esa.int (office); bernard.foing@esa.int (office). *Website:* www.esa.int (office); sci.esa.int/smart-1 (office); sci.esa.int/ilewg (office).

FOK, Canning Kin-ning, BA, CA; Hong Kong telecommunications executive; *Group Managing Director and Executive Director, Hutchison Whampoa Ltd;* b. 1951; four c.; ed St John's Univ., Minn., USA, Univ. of New England, Australia; began career with Cheung Kong (real estate co.) 1979; joined Hutchison Whampoa Group 1984, Exec. Dir Hutchison Whampoa Ltd 1984–, Group Man. Dir 1993–, also Chair. Hutchison Telecom Int., Hutchison Harbour Ring Ltd, Hutchison Telecommunications International Ltd, Hutchison Telecommunications (Australia) Ltd, Hutchison Global Communications Holdings Ltd, Partner Communications Co. Ltd, Hongkong Electric Holdings Ltd; Partner and Co-Chair. Husky Energy Inc. 2000–; Deputy Chair. Cheung Kong Infrastructure Holdings Ltd; Dir, Cheung Kong (Holdings) Ltd, Hutchison Whampoa Finance (CI) Ltd; mem. Australian Inst. of Chartered Accountants. *Address:* Hutchison Whampoa Ltd, 22nd Floor, Hutchison House, 10 Harcourt Road, Hong Kong Special Administrative Region, People's Republic of China (office). *Telephone:* 2128-1188 (office). *Fax:* 2128-1705 (office). *E-mail:* info@hutchison-whampoa.com (office). *Website:* www.hutchison-whampoa.com (office).

FOK, Chun-wan Ian, BS, MBA; Hong Kong business executive; *CEO, Fok Ying Tung Group;* b. (Fok Chun-wan), s. of Henry Fok; ed Univ. of British Columbia, Canada; CEO Fok Ying Tung Group; Deputy 12th Nat. People's Congress, People's Repub. of China; Vice-Chair. 11th All-China Gen. Chamber of Industry & Commerce, China Overseas Friendship Asscn, Guangdong Overseas Friendship Asscn; mem. Standing Council, China Overseas Exchange Asscn; Councillor, China Council for the Promotion of Peaceful Nat. Reunification; Pres. Hong Kong GuangFoZhao Fraternity Asscn Ltd; Gov. and Chair. of Standing Cttee, Hong Kong Pei Hua Educ. Foundation; Man. Dir Fok Ying Tung Foundation Ltd; Pres. Hong Kong Wushu Union, Wushu Fed. of Asia; mem. Exec. Cttee Int. Wushu Fed.; fmr mem. Hong Kong Trade and Devt Council; mem. Advisory Council Boao Forum for Asia; mem. Court, Hong Kong Univ. of Science & Tech.; mem. Univ. Assembly, Univ. of Macau; Deputy Chair., 7th Bd of Dirs, Guangzhou Jinan Univ.; mem. Advisory Bd, Sun Yat-Sen Univ.; Trustee, Chinese Univ. of Hong Kong United Coll. 1996–2005; Hon. Citizen of Panyu, Guangzhou and Ganzhou, Hon. Univ. Fellow, Open Univ. of Hong Kong, Chinese Univ. of Hong Kong; Life Hon. Chair. Chinese Gen. Chamber of Commerce in Hong Kong; Silver Bauhinia Star 2005. *Address:* Fok Ying Tung Group, Units 1105–1112, West Tower Shun Tak Centre, 168–200 Connaught Road Central, Hong Kong Special Administrative Region, People's Republic of China (office). *Telephone:* 2522-7131 (office). *Fax:* 2526-9858 (office).

FOK, Timothy, JP; Hong Kong business executive; *President, Hong Kong Football Association;* b. (Fok Tsun-ting), 14 Feb. 1946, Hong Kong; s. of Henry Fok and Lui Yin-nei; m. Loletta Chu (divorced 2006); three s.; ed Millfield Coll., UK, Univ. of Southern California, USA; Man. Dir Yau Wing Co. Ltd, Chair. Fok Ying Tung Group; Pres. Sports Fed. and Olympic Cttee of Hong Kong, Hong Kong Football Asscn 2015–; Vice-Pres. Olympic Council of Asia; Gov. Fok Ying Tung Foundation; Justice of the Peace 1998, Hon. mem. IOC 2001–; Silver Bauhinia Star Medal 1999, Grand Bauhinia Star Medal 2004. *Address:* Hong Kong Football Association, 55 Fat Kwong Street, Homantin, Kowloon, Hong Kong Special Administrative Region, People's Republic of China (office). *Telephone:* 27129122 (office). *Fax:* 27688825 (office). *E-mail:* hkfa@hkfa.com (office). *Website:* www.hkfa.com (office).

FOKAIDES, Christoforos, MA; Cypriot economist, political scientist and politician; b. June 1973, Famagusta; ed Univ. of Cyprus, Univ. of Kent, UK; Pres. NEDISY (youth br. of Democratic Rally) 2005–09; mem. Dimokratikos Synagermos (Democratic Rally), mem. Exec. Bd and Policy Planning Sec., Dir of Communications and Deputy Press Spokesman 2009–; Minister of Defence 2014–18; Lecturer in Politics, European Univ., Nicosia 2005–; fmr Visiting Scholar, Yale Univ., USA. *Address:* c/o Ministry of Defence, 4 Emmanuel Roides Avenue, 1432 Nicosia, Cyprus (office).

FOKIN, Valery Vladimirovich; Russian theatre and film director; *Artistic Director, Alexandrinsky Theater;* b. 28 Feb. 1946, Moscow; m. Tatiana Krivenko; two s.; ed Moscow Shchukin Theatre School; Stage Dir Moscow Sovremennik Theatre 1971–85; Chief Stage Dir Yermolova Theatre 1985–90; Artistic Dir M. Yermolova Theatre Centre 1990–2000; Founder, Artistic Dir and Dir-Gen. Meyerhold Artistic Centre 1991–, Artistic Dir Russian State Pushkin Acad. Drama Theatre (Alexandrinsky Theatre) 2006–; Order of Service to the Fatherland, IV degree 2006; Theatre Prize, BITEF Prize, State's Prize, Honoured Art Worker of Poland, three Crystal Turandot awards including for Last Night of the Tsar, Hon. Badge of Service to St Petersburg for outstanding contribution to the devt of Russian theatre, The Golden Mask (Russian Nat. Theatre Award) 2008, Special Jury's Prize for the renaissance of the Alexandrinsky Theatre 2009. *Film:* The Metamorphosis. *Theatre includes:* (Stage Dir) Valentin and Valentina, I'll Go and Go, Inspector, Provincial Anecdotes, Lorenzacchio, Who's Afraid of Virginia Woolf, In Spring I Shall Come Back to You, Transformation, (Chief Stage Dir) Speak Up, Second Year of Freedom, Sports Scenes of 1980, Invitation to Punishment (Artistic Dir), Hotel Room in Town N (Best Dir), (Dir) Artand and His Double, The Queen of Spades (opera). *Television:* over 25 films and performances. *Publications:* Hotel Room in Town N, The Metamorphosis; numerous articles and speeches. *Address:* Vsevolod Meyerhold Centre, Novoslobodskaya str. 23, Moscow (office); Triohprudniy pereulok 13/11, 5, Moscow, Russia (home). *Telephone:* (495) 363-10-46 (office); (495) 299-16-76 (home). *Fax:* (495) 363-1041 (office). *Website:* en.alexandrinsky.ru/articles/about/artistic_director (office).

FOKIN, Vitold Pavlovych; Ukrainian politician; b. 25 Oct. 1932, Novomikolaivka, Zaporozhye region; m.; one s. one d.; ed m. Dnepropetrovsk Mining Inst.; fmr mem. CP; mining engineer 1954–71; Deputy Chair. Council of Ministers of Ukraine 1987–90; Chair. State Cttee for Econs Aug.–Nov. 1990; Chair. Council of Ministers (Prime Minister) of Ukraine 1990–92; Sr Researcher, Inst. of World Econ. and Int. Relations 1993–, Pres. Int. Fund for Humanitarian and Econ. Relations with Russian Fed. 1993–; mem. Higher Econ. Council of Pres. of Ukraine 1997–; People's Deputy 1998–; Prof. Nat. Acad. of Mines; Chair. Supervisory Bd DEWON Inc. 2000–; Miner's Glory Order 1st, 2nd, 3rd class 1961–63, Decoration of Honour 1967, two Orders of Working Red Banner 1970, 1975, Order of St Prince Volodymyr 2002, Order of Yaroslav the Wise 2002, Order of Honour 2004; Laureate of State Prize of Ukraine 1983, Medal for Services 2004, seven medals. *Publications:* about 30 published works and articles in social, political and technical journals and books. *Leisure interests:* hunting, fishing, tennis, tourism. *Address:* Flat 266, 13 Suvorova Street, 01010 Kyiv, Ukraine (home). *Telephone:* (44) 290-52-55 (home). *E-mail:* vitold.fokin@dewon.com.ua.

FOKIN, Yuri Yevgenyevich; Russian diplomatist; b. 2 Sept. 1936, Gorky (now Nizhny Novgorod); m.; one s. one d.; ed Moscow Inst. of Int. Relations; on staff, USSR Ministry of Foreign Affairs 1960–; with USSR Mission in UN 1960–65, Secr. of Minister of Foreign Affairs 1966–73, Sr Adviser, Dept of Planning of Int. Events 1973–76; Deputy Perm. Rep. of USSR to UN 1976–79; Deputy Dir-Gen. Ministry of Foreign Affairs 1979–80, Dir-Gen. 1980–86; Amb. to Cyprus 1986–90, to Norway 1995–97, to UK 1997–2000; Head, Second European Dept, Russian Ministry of Foreign Affairs 1990–92, Dir Second European Dept 1991–95; on staff, Ministry of Foreign Affairs 1995–, Rector, Diplomatic Acad. of Ministry of Foreign Affairs –2006; decorations from Russia, Austria, Norway. *Publications:* Diplomatic Yearbook 2000–12, State & Diaspora: A Record of Interaction, A Word of the President (A. A. Akaev). *Leisure interests:* reading, ballet, theatre. *Address:* c/o Diplomatic Academy of the Ministry of Foreign Affairs, 53/2 Ostozhenka, 119992

Moscow, Russia. *Telephone:* (499) 940-13-56; (499) 246-47-56; (499) 255-80-34. *E-mail:* yuri.fokine@dipacademy.ru.

FOLBRE, Nancy, MA, PhD; American economist and academic; *Professor of Economics, University of Massachusetts;* ed Univ. of Texas, Univ. of Massachusetts; consultant, Maine Comm. for Women 1981, Kenya Fuelwood Project 1981, Beijer Inst. 1981, 1983, Royal Swedish Acad. of Science 1981, 1983, Zimbabwe Energy Planning Project, 1983, Int. Center for Research on Women 1989–90, The Population Council 1989–94, ILO 1992, World Bank 1994–95; Asst Prof. of Econs, Bowdoin Coll. 1980–83; Assoc. Prof. of Econs, Univ. of Mass 1984–91, Prof. of Econs 1991–, Chair. Dept of Econs 2003–04; Visiting Assoc. Prof., American Univ. 1991; Visiting Lecturer, Eugene Havens Center, Univ. of Wisconsin 1991; Visiting Scholar, Women's Research and Resource Center, Univ. of California, Davis 1992, Gender Inst., LSE, UK 1995; Visiting Chair. in American Studies, Ecole des Hautes Etudes en Sciences Sociales, Paris, France 1995–96; Visiting Research Fellow, ANU 2000, 2002, Adjunct Prof., Social and Political Theory Program 2003–; Phi Beta Kappa Visiting Scholar 2000–01; Visiting Fellow, Russell Sage Foundation 2005–06; Co-founder and CEO The Dancing Monkey Project 1998–; Pres. Int. Asscn for Feminist Econs 2002–; Staff Economist, Center for Popular Econs 1979–; Consultant to UN Human Devt Office 2005; Assoc. Ed. Feminist Economics 1995–; mem. Bd Foundation of Child Devt; mem. NAS; French-American Foundation Fellow 1995–96, MacArthur Foundation Fellow 1998–2003; Olivia Schieffelin Nordberg Award 1999, Distinguished Visiting Scholar Award, Univ. of Massachusetts 2002. *Publications include:* A Field Guide to the US Economy 1988, Issues in Contemporary Economics, Vol. 4 (co-ed.) 1991, Who Pays for the Kids? Gender and the Structures of Constraint 1994, The New Field Guide to the US Economy 1995, War on the Poor: A Defense Manual 1996, The Economics of the Family (ed.) 1996, De la différence des sexes en économie politique 1997, The Ultimate Field Guide to the US Economy 2000, The Invisible Heart: Economics and Family Values 2001, Family Time (co-ed.) 2003, Greed, Lust and Gender 2009, Valuing Children: Rethinking the Economics of the Family 2010, Saving State U 2010; numerous articles in professional journals, chapters in books and newspaper articles. *Address:* Department of Economics, Thompson Hall, University of Massachusetts, Amherst, MA 01003, USA (office). *Telephone:* (413) 545-3283 (office). *Fax:* (413) 545-2921 (office). *E-mail:* folbre@econs.umass.edu (office). *Website:* people.umass.edu/~folbre/folbre (office).

FOLEY, Lt-Gen. John Paul, Kt, KCB, KStJ, CB, OBE, MC, DL; British business executive, fmr civil servant and fmr army officer; *Vice Lord-Lieutenant of Herefordshire;* b. 22 April 1939, London; s. of Henry Thomas Hamilton Foley and Helen Constance Margaret Foley (née Pearson); m. Ann Rosamond Humphries 1972; two d.; ed Bradfield Coll., Berks., Army Staff Coll., Camberley, Royal Coll. of Defence Studies, London; nat. service with Royal Green Jackets (RGJ) 1959–61, then Regimental Service 1962–70, attached to Staff Coll. 1971; Brig.-Maj. 1974–75; instructor, Staff Coll. 1976–78; CO 3 RGJ 1978–80, Commdt, Jr Div. Staff Coll. 1981–82, Dir SAS 1983–85, Royal Coll. of Defence Studies 1986; Chief, British Mission to Soviet Forces, E Germany 1987–89; Deputy Chief, Defence Intelligence 1989–91, Chief, Defence Intelligence 1994–97; Commdr British Forces Hong Kong 1992–94, retd 1997; Lt-Gov. of Guernsey 2000–05; High Sheriff of Herefords. and Worcs. 2006–07; Vice Lord-Lt of Herefords. 2010–; mem. Security Comm.; mem. Int. Advisory Bd, Group 4 1998–2000; Chair. British Greyhound Racing Bd 1999–2000; Dir AD Systems (UK) Ltd 2009–; US Legion of Merit (Officer). *Leisure interests:* gardening, reading, walking, tennis, bird watching, golf.

FOLEY, Thomas C., BA, MBA; American business executive and fmr diplomatist; b. 9 Jan. 1952; one s.; ed Harvard Univ., Harvard Business School; worked for McKinsey & Co., New York, later for Citicorp Venture Capital, New York; f. NTC Group (pvt. equity investment business) 1985, Chair. 2009; Dir of Pvt. Sector Devt for Coalition Provisional Authority, Iraq 2003–04, Amb. to Ireland 2006–09; recently served as Trustee, Kennedy Center for the Performing Arts, Washington, DC and two Conn. State Comms involving educ. and children's rights; Cand. for Gov. of Conn. 2014; Dept of Defense Distinguished Public Service Award for service in Iraq 2004. *Leisure interest:* charity work. *Address:* c/o Tom Foley for Governor, PO Box 2014, Stamford, CT 06906, USA. *Telephone:* (860) 637-8039. *E-mail:* press@tomfoleyct.com. *Website:* www.tomfoleyct.com.

FØLLESDAL, Dagfinn, PhD; Norwegian academic; *Clarence Irving Lewis Professor of Philosophy, Emeritus, Stanford University;* b. 22 June 1932, Askim; s. of Trygve Føllesdal and Margit Teigen; m. Vera Heyerdahl 1957; five s. one d.; ed Univs of Oslo and Göttingen and Harvard Univ.; Research Asst in Ionospheric Physics, Norwegian Research Council 1955–57; Instructor and Asst Prof. of Philosophy, Harvard Univ. 1961–64; Prof. of Philosophy, Univ. of Oslo 1967–99; Prof. of Philosophy, Stanford Univ. 1968–76, Clarence Irving Lewis Prof. of Philosophy 1976, now Prof. Emer.; Prof. Coll. de France 1977; Guggenheim Fellow 1978–79; Fellow, Center for Advanced Study in Behavioral Sciences 1981–82, American Council of Learned Socs 1983–84, Inst. for Advanced Study, Princeton 1985–86, Wissenschaftskolleg, Berlin 1989–90, Centre for Advanced Study, Oslo 1995–96, 2003–04; mem. American Acad. of Arts and Sciences, Academia Europaea and scientific acads in Norway, Denmark, Sweden and Finland; Pres. Norwegian Acad. of Science 1993, 1995, 1997; Univ. of Oslo Research Prize 1995, Alexander von Humboldt Research Award 1997, Lauener Prize 2006. *Publications:* Husserl und Frege 1958, Referential Opacity and Modal Logic 1966, Argumentasjonsteori språk og vitenskapsfilosofi (with L. Walløe and J. Elster) 1977; Ed. Journal of Symbolic Logic 1970–82, Philosophy of Quire, 5 vols 2000; numerous articles on philosophy of language, phenomenology, existentialism, action theory, educational and ethical issues. *Leisure interests:* skiing, running. *Address:* Department of Philosophy, Building 90, Stanford University, Stanford, CA 94305-2155, USA (office); Filosofisk institutt, Universitetet i Oslo, PB 1024, Blindern 0317, Oslo (office); Staverhagan 7, 1314 Slependen, Norway (home). *Telephone:* (650) 723-2587 (office); (47) 67-55-00-01 (home). *Fax:* (47) 67-55-00-02 (home). *E-mail:* dagfinn@csli.stanford.edu (office). *Website:* www-philosophy .stanford.edu (office); www.hf.uio.no/filosofi/organisasjon/ansatte/follesdal.html (office).

FOLLETT, Kenneth (Ken) Martin, CBE, BA; British writer; b. 5 June 1949, Cardiff, Wales; s. of Martin Dunsford Follett and Lavinia Cynthia (Veenie) Follett (née Evans); m. 1st Mary Elson 1968 (marriage dissolved 1985); one s. one d.; m. 2nd Barbara Broer 1985; one step-s. two step-d.; ed Harrow Weald Grammar School, Univ. Coll. London; trainee journalist, South Wales Echo, Cardiff 1970–73; reporter, London Evening News 1973–74; Editorial Dir Everest Books, London 1974–76, Deputy Man. Dir 1976–77; full-time writer 1977–; Fellow, Univ. Coll. London 1994; Chair. Nat. Year of Reading 1998–99, Advisory Cttee, Reading is Fundamental UK 2003–07; Pres. Dyslexia Inst. 1998–2008; Vice-Pres. Stevenage Borough Football Club 2000–02; Trustee, Stevenage Community Trust 2002– (Chair. 2005–13, Pres. 2013–); Chair. Govs, Roebuck Primary School and Nursery 2001–05; mem. Council, Nat. Literary Trust 1996–2010 (Trustee 2005–10); Bd mem. Nat. Acad. of Writing 2003–10; Dir, Stevenage Leisure Ltd 1997–2005; Patron, Stevenage Home-Start 2000–; mem. Yr Academi Gymreig 2000 (Fellow 2011); Hon. DLitt (Glamorgan) 2007, (Saginaw Valley State) 2007, (Exeter) 2008; Olaguibel Prize, Colegio Oficial de Arquitectos Vasco-Navarro 2008, Thriller Master Award, Int. Thriller Writers 2010, Grand Master, Mystery Writers of America 2013. *Publications include:* Eye of the Needle (Edgar Award, Mystery Writers of America) 1978, Triple 1979, The Key to Rebecca 1980, The Man from St Petersburg 1982, On Wings of Eagles 1983, Lie down with Lions 1986, The Pillars of the Earth 1989, Night over Water 1991, Mrs Shiblak's Nightmare (pamphlet) 1992, A Dangerous Fortune 1993, A Place Called Freedom 1995, The Third Twin 1997, The Hammer of Eden 1998, Code to Zero 2000, Jackdaws (Corine Buchpreis 2003) 2001, Hornet Flight 2002, Whiteout 2004, World Without End 2007, Fall of Giants (Libri Golden Book Award, Hungary 2010, Que Leer Prize 2011) 2010, Winter of the World 2012, Edge of Eternity 2014, A Column of Fire 2017; various articles, screenplays and short stories. *Leisure interests:* bass guitarist in a blues band; Labour Party supporter and campaigner. *Address:* The Follett Office, Follett House, Primett Road, Stevenage, Herts., SG1 3EE, England. *Telephone:* (1438) 810400 (office). *E-mail:* ken@ken-follett.com (office). *Website:* www.ken-follett .com.

FØLSGAARD, Mikkel Boe; Danish actor; b. 1 May 1984, Rønne; one s.; ed Statens Teaterskole, Copenhagen; Shooting Star Award, Berlin Int. Film Festival 2013. *Theatre includes:* Hov? Tjek! Tjekhov 2010, Melampe 2010, Twelfth Night or What You Will 2010, Three Sisters 2010, Metamorphoser 2010, Mænd der hader kvinder 2010, Creatures of the Wind 2011, Sådan Går 5 År 2011, Sans 2011, Inga & Lutz 2012, Nero 2013. *Films include:* En Kongelig Affære (A Royal Affair) (Silver Bear for Best Actor, Berlin Int. Film Festival 2012, Årets Svend Award for New Upcoming Talent 2012, Lauritzen – Believe in You Award for Outstanding Performance 2012, Danish Film Acad. Award 'Robert' for Best Supporting Actor 2013, Danish Critics' Asscn Award 'Bodil' for Best Actor 2013) 2012, The Keeper of Lost Causes 2013, Rosita 2014, Land of Mine 2015, Sommeren '92 2015, De Standhaftige 2015, A Serious Game 2016, Fuglene over sundet 2016, Du Forsvinder 2017, Den Bedste Mand 2017, Kein Problem 2017, En helt almindelig familie 2019. *Television includes:* Bryggeren (mini-series) 1997, Den som dræber (Those Who Kill) (series) 2011, Dicte (series) 2013, Arvingerne (The Legacy) (series) 2014–17, The Rain 2018. *Address:* Lindberg Management ApS, Lavendelstræde 5–7, Baghuset 4.sal, 1462 Copenhagen K, Denmark (office). *Telephone:* 33-11-15-57 (office). *E-mail:* info@lindbergmanagement.com (office). *Website:* www .lindbergmanagement.com (office).

FOLT, Carol L., BS, PhD; American environmental scientist, academic and university administrator; b. 1951, Akron, Ohio; m. Prof. David Peart; one s. one d.; ed Univ. of California, Santa Barbara, Univ. of California, Davis; postdoctoral work at W.K. Kellogg Biological Station, Michigan State Univ.; mem. Faculty, Dartmouth Coll. 1983, later Dartmouth Prof. of Biological Sciences, Ivy League Inst., Assoc. Dir Toxic Metals Research Program 1998–2000, Assoc. Dir Center for Environmental Health Sciences 2000–01, Dean of Grad. Studies and Assoc. Dean of Faculty for Interdisciplinary Programs 2001–04, Dean 2004–09, Acting Provost Dartmouth Coll. 2009–10, Provost 2010–12, Interim Pres. 2012–13; Chancellor Univ. of North Carolina, Chapel Hill 2013–19; Fellow, AAAS. *Address:* c/o Office of the Chancellor, University of North Carolina, 103 South Building, Campus Box 9100, Chapel Hill, NC 27599-9100, USA.

FOMENKO, Anatoly Timofeevich, PhD; Russian mathematician and academic; *Professor and Head of Department of Mathematics and Mechanics, Moscow State University;* b. 13 March 1945; m.; ed Moscow State Univ.; Asst, Sr Researcher, now Prof. and Head, Dept of Math. and Mechanics, Moscow State Univ.; Corresp. mem. USSR (now Russian) Acad. of Sciences 1990, mem. 1994; research in theory of minimal surfaces, topology of multidimensional manifolds, simplectic geometry and theory of topological classifications of integrable differential equations; Chair. Moscow Math. Soc.; Award of Moscow Math. Soc. 1974, Award of Presidium of Russian Acad. of Sciences 1987, State Award of Russian Fed. 1996. *Publications include:* Simplectic Geometry: Methods and Applications 1988, The Plateau Problem 1990. *Leisure interests:* statistical analysis of historical texts, painting. *Address:* Department of Mathematics and Mechanics, Moscow State University, 119991 Moscow, GSP-1, Leninskiye Gory, 1, Main Building, Russia (office). *Telephone:* (495) 939-39-40 (office). *E-mail:* mmmf@mech.math .msu.su (office). *Website:* www.math.msu.su (office); www.anatoly-fomenko.com.

FONDA, Bridget; American actress; b. 27 Jan. 1964, Los Angeles; d. of Peter Fonda (q.v.) and Susan Fonda; m. Danny Elfman 2003; one s.; ed New York Univ. theater programme; studied acting at Lee Strasberg Inst. and with Harold Guskin; workshop stage performances include Confession and Pastels. *Films:* Aria (Tristan and Isolde sequence) (début) 1987, You Can't Hurry Love 1988, Shag 1988, Scandal 1989, Strapless 1989, Frankenstein Unbound 1990, The Godfather: Part III 1990, Doc Hollywood 1991, Out of the Rain 1991, Single White Female 1992, Singles 1992, Bodies Rest and Motion 1993, Point of No Return 1993, Little Buddha 1994, It Could Happen To You 1994, Camilla 1994, The Road to Welville 1994, Rough Magic 1995, Balto (voice) 1995, Grace of My Heart 1996, City Hall 1996, Drop Dead Fred, Light Years (voice), Iron Maze, Army of Darkness, Touch, Jackie Brown, Finding Graceland, The Break Up, South of Heaven West of Hell, Lake Placid 1999, Delivering Milo, Monkey Bone 2001, Kiss of the Dragon 2001, The Whole Shebang 2001. *Television includes:* Leather Jackets 1991, In the Gloaming 1997, After Amy 2001, No Ordinary Baby 2001, The Chris Isaak Show 2002, Snow Queen 2002. *Address:* 114 Fremont Place, Los Angeles, CA 90005, USA.

FONDA, Jane; American actress and activist; b. 21 Dec. 1937, New York City; d. of Henry Fonda and Frances Seymour; sister of Peter Fonda (q.v.); m. 1st Roger

Vadim 1967 (divorced 1973, died 2000); one d.; m. 2nd Tom Hayden 1973 (divorced 1989, died 2016); one s.; m. 3rd Ted Turner 1991 (divorced 2001); ed Emma Willard School, Troy, NY, Vassar Coll.; studied with Lee Strasberg and became mem. Actors Studio, New York; Founder and Chair. Georgia Campaign for Adolescent Pregnancy Prevention 1995–; est. Jane Fonda Center for Adolescent Reproductive Health, Emory Univ. School of Medicine 2002; produced 23 home exercise videos including Jane Fonda's Workout 1982 (top-grossing home video of all time); Acad. Award for Best Actress 1972, 1979, Golden Globe Award 1978, Great Medal of Paris 2010, Lumière Award 2018. *Films include:* Tall Story 1960, A Walk on the Wild Side 1962, Period of Adjustment 1962, Sunday in New York 1963, The Love Cage 1963, La Ronde 1964, Cat Ballou 1965, Histoires extraordinaires 1967, Barefoot in the Park 1967, Hurry Sundown 1967, Barbarella 1968, They Shoot Horses Don't They? 1969, Klute 1970, Steelyard Blues 1972, Tout va bien 1972, A Doll's House 1973, The Blue Bird 1975, Fun with Dick and Jane 1976, Julia 1977, Coming Home 1978, California Suite 1978, The Electric Horseman 1979, The China Syndrome 1979, Nine to Five 1980, On Golden Pond 1981, Roll-Over 1981, Agnes of God 1985, The Morning After 1986, The Old Gringo 1988, Stanley and Iris 1990, Monster-in-Law 2005, Georgia Rule 2007, All Together 2011, Peace, Love & Misunderstanding 2011, The Butler 2013, Better Living Through Chemistry 2014, This Is Where I Leave You 2014, Youth 2015, Fathers and Daughters 2015, Our Souls at Night 2017, Book Club 2018; producer Lakota Woman 1994. *Plays include:* There Was a Little Girl, Invitation to a March, The Fun Couple, Strange Interlude, 33 Variations (Broadway) 2009. *Television:* The Dollmaker (ABC-TV) (Emmy Award) 1984, The Newsroom (series) 2012–14, The Simpsons (voice) 2014, Grace and Frankie (series) 2015–. *Publications:* Jane Fonda's Workout Book 1982, Women Coming of Age 1984, Jane Fonda's New Workout and Weight Loss Program 1986, Jane Fonda's New Pregnancy Workout and Total Birth Program 1989, Jane Fonda Workout Video, Jane Fonda Cooking for Healthy Living 1996, My Life So Far (autobiography) 2005. *Address:* c/o Kim Hodgert, Creative Artists Agency, 9830 Wilshire Boulevard, Beverly Hills, CA 90212-1825 (office); Georgia Campaign for Adolescent Pregnancy Prevention, 100 Auburn Avenue, Suite 200, Atlanta, GA 30303, USA (office). *Telephone:* (310) 288-4545 (office). *Fax:* (310) 288-4800 (office).

FONDA, Peter; American film actor, director and producer; b. 23 Feb. 1939, New York; s. of Henry Fonda and Frances Seymour; brother of Jane Fonda; m. 1st Susan Brewer (divorced 1974); two c.; m. 2nd Portia Rebecca Crockett (divorced 2011); m. 3rd Margaret DeVogelaere; ed Univ. of Nebraska, Omaha. *Films include:* Tammy and the Doctor 1963, The Victors 1963, Lilith 1964, The Young Lovers 1964, The Wild Angels 1966, The Trip 1967, Easy Rider (also co-screenplay writer, co-producer) 1969, The Last Movie 1971, The Hired Hand (also dir) 1971, Two People (also dir) 1973, Idaho Transfer (dir) 1973, Dirty Mary, Crazy Larry 1974, Race with the Devil 1975, 92 in the Shade 1975, Killer Force 1975, Fighting Mad 1976, Futureworld 1976, Outlaw Blues 1977, High Ballin' 1978, Wanda Nevada (also dir) 1979, Open Season, Smokey and the Bandit II 1980, The Cannonball Run (cameo) 1981, Split Image 1982, Spasms 1983, Dance of the Dwarfs (also known as Jungle Heat) 1983, Peppermint-Frieden 1983, Certain Fury 1985, Mercenary Fighters 1987, The Rose Garden 1989, Fatal Mission 1990, South Beach 1992, Deadfall 1993, Nadja 1994, Love and a 45 1994, Painted Hero 1996, Escape from LA 1996, Ulee's Gold 1997, Reckless, Diajobu My Friend, Family Spirit, Bodies Rest and Motion, Molly and Gina, The Limey 1999, South of Heaven, West of Hell 2000, Thomas and the Magic Railroad 2000, Second Skin 2000, Wooly Boys 2001, The Laramie Project 2002, The Heart Is Deceitful Above All Things 2004, Ghost Rider 2007, Wild Hogs 2007, 3:10 to Yuma 2007, Japan 2008, The Perfect Age of Rock 'n' Roll 2009, The Boondock Saints II: All Saints Day 2009, The Trouble with Bliss 2011, Smitty 2012, Harodim 2012, The Ultimate Life 2013, The Harvest 2013, Cooperhead 2013, As Cool as I Am 2013, House of Bodies 2013, The Runner 2015, The Ballad of Lefty Brown 2017, Boundaries 2018. *Television films:* The Hostage Tower 1980, Don't Look Back 1996, A Reason to Live, A Time of Indifference, Sound, Certain Honorable Men, Montana, The Maldonado Miracle 2003, Capital City 2004, A Thief of Time 2004, Back When We Were Grownups 2004, Supernova (mini-series) 2005, The Gathering (mini-series) 2007, Journey to the Center of the Earth 2008, HR 2014. *Other work includes:* Grand Theft Auto: San Andreas (video game, voice) 2004. *Publication:* Don't Tell Dad (autobiography) 1998. *Address:* IFA Talent Agency, 8730 West Sunset Boulevard, Suite 490, Los Angeles, CA 90069, USA (office).

FONSECA, Jorge Carlos de Almeida, MA; Cabo Verde lawyer, politician and head of state; *President;* b. 20 Oct. 1950, Mindelo; m.; three c.; ed Univ. of Lisbon; Dir Gen. of Emigration 1975–77; Sec. Gen., Ministry of Foreign Affairs 1977–79, Minister of Foreign Affairs 1991–93; Teaching Asst, Faculty of Law, Univ. of Lisbon 1982–90; Guest Prof. of Criminal Law, Inst. of Forensic Medicine, Lisbon 1987; Resident Dir and Guest Assoc. Prof., Law Course and Public Admin, Univ. da Ásia Oriental, Macau 1989, 1990; unsuccessful cand. in presidential election 2001; Founder and Dir Direito e Cidadania (journal), Inst. of Legal and Social Science 2004–; Pres. of Cabo Verde 2011–; mem. Editorial Bd Revista de Economia e Direito; Combatente da Liberdade da Pátria. *Publications:* several books and over 50 scientific and technical works in the field of law; two books of poetry. *Address:* Palácio da Presidência da República de Cabo Verde, CP 100, Plateau, Praia, Ilha de Santiago, Cabo Verde (office). *Telephone:* (261) 2445 (office); (261) 2829 (office). *Fax:* (261) 4356 (office). *E-mail:* presidencia.cv@gmail.com (office). *Website:* presidenciadarepublica.blogs.sapo.cv (office).

FONSECA, Ralph H.; Belizean politician; b. 9 Aug. 1949; m.; three c.; ed St John's Coll.; fmr Asst Gen. Man. Texaco, Belize; fmr Area Gen. Man. Cardinal Distributors, Canada; fmr Research Engineer, Control Data; fmr Systems Analyst, Prescribe Data System; fmr gen. man. brewing co.; fmr Man. Dir Hillbank Agroindustry; fmr Chair. Belize Electricity Co.; fmr Chair. Belize Telecommunications Authority Ltd; fmr Pres. Consolidated Electricity Services; mem. Parl. 1993–2008; Minister of Budget Man., Investment and Home Affairs 1999–2003, Minister of Finance and Home Affairs 2003–05; Minister of Home Affairs and Public Utilities 2005–08, of Housing 2007–08.

FONSECA, Rubem; Brazilian writer and screenwriter; b. 11 May 1925, Juiz de Fora, Minas Gerais; m. Théa Maud (deceased 1996); three c.; ed Escola de Policia, Rio de Janeiro, Fundação Getúlio Vargas, New York Univ.; started career as police officer, apptd Police Commr São Cristóvão (RJ) 1952; Premio Camões 2003, Premio Juan Rulfo 2003. *Television:* Mandrake 1983, 2005, Agosto 1993. *Films:* Lúcia McCartney, Uma Garota de Programa 1971, Relatório de Um Homem Casado 1974, A Extorsão 1975, Stelinha 1990, A Grande Arte 1991, Bufo & Spallanzani 2001, The Man of the Year 2003, O Caso Morel 2006, El cobrador: In God We Trust 2006. *Publications:* Os prisioneiros 1963, A coleira do cão 1965, Lucía McCartney 1967, O caso Morel 1973, O homen de fevereiro ou março 1973, Feliz ano novo 1975, O cobrador (Prêmio Estácio de Sá) 1979, A grande arte (Prêmio Goethe, Prêmio Jabuti) 1983, Buffo & Spallanzani 1986, Vastas emoções e pensamentos imperfeitos (Prêmio Pedro Nava) 1988, Agosto 1990, Romance negro e outras histórias 1992, Contos reunidos 1994, O selvagem da ópera 1994, O buraco na parede (Prêmio Jabuti) 1995, Romance negro, Felis ano novo e outras histórias 1996, Histórias de amor 1997, E do meio do mundo prostitute só amores guardei ao meu charuto (Prêmio Machado de Assis) 1997, Confraria dos espadas (Prêmio Eça de Queiroz) 1998, O doente Molière (Prêmio de melhor romance do ano, Associação Paulista de Críticos de Arte) 2000, Secreções, excreções, desatinos 2001, Pequenas criaturas 2002, Diário de um fescenino 2003, 64 contos de Rubem Fonseca 2004, Ela e outras mulheres 2006, Los mejores relatos 2007, O Seminarista 2009, José 2011, Axilas e Outras Histórias Indecorosas 2011, Ianka, meu amor 2013, Histórias Curtas 2015, Carne Crua 2018; contrib. to numerous anthologies.

FONSEKA, Field Marshal Sarath; Sri Lankan politician and fmr army officer; *Minister of Sustainable Development, Wildlife and Regional Development;* b. 18 Dec. 1950, s. of Peter Fonseka and Piyawathie Fonseka; m. Anoma Indumathi Munasinghe; two c.; ed Dharmasoka Coll., Ambalangoda, Ananda Coll., Colombo; joined army 1970; has held numerous staff appointments, involved in operations Balawegaya and Jayasikuru which led to capture of Elephant Pass and Mankulam, wounded in Yaldewee operation 1993, as a Col, commanded 23 Brigade of Sri Lankan Army at Polonnaruwa 1993, led troops in Operation 'Midnight Express' to rescue besieged troops in Jaffna Fort 1993, as Deputy GOC, captured Jaffna from Tamil Tigers (LTTE) 1995, among other appointments held were Col, Gen. Staff Army HQ, Sri Lankan Army, Centre Commdt, Sri Lanka Sinha Regt, Brigade Commdr in Operation Ballavegaya, Deputy Commdt-5 Brigade Group, Mannar and Co-ordinating Officer for Gampaha Gum Gumaga, Sri Lanka Army, Chief of Staff of Sri Lankan Army, relinquished post to become Commdr of the Army, Chief of Defence Staff July–Nov. 2009 (resgnd); mem. New Democratic Front 2009–10, Democratic Nat. Alliance 2010–13, Democratic Party 2013–16, United Nat. Party 2016–; MP, Sri Lanka (Colombo Dist) April–Oct. 2010, (Nationalist) 2016–; United Nat. Party cand. for Pres. 2010; Minister of Defence 2015–16, of Regional Devt 2016–, of Sustainable Devt and Wildlife 2018–; numerous decorations including Rana Wickrama Padakkama, Rana Sura Padakkama, Vishista Seva Vibhushanaya, Uttama Seva Padakkama, Desha Putra Sammanaya, Riviresa Campaign Services Medal, Poorna Bhoomi Padakkama, North and East Operations Medal, Desha Putra Sammanaya, and several others. *Address:* Ministry of Regional Development, Sino Lanka Tower, No.1090 Sri Jayawardenapura Road, Rajagiriya, Sri Lanka (office). *Telephone:* (11) 2879273 (office). *Fax:* (11) 2879274 (office). *Website:* www.cabinetoffice.gov.lk (office).

FONTANA, Bernard, BEng; French business executive; *CEO, Areva NP;* b. 1961; ed Ecole Polytechnique and the Ecole Nationale Supérieure des Techniques Avancées in Paris; began career with Groupe SNPE in France, Head of US operations 1998–2001, mem. Exec. Cttee 2001–04; joined ArcelorMittal 2004, given responsibility for HR, IT and Business Devt at Flat Carbon 2004–06, mem. Exec. Cttee ArcelorMittal with responsibility for Automotive Worldwide Business Unit 2006–07, mem. Group Man. Cttee responsible for HR and global alliance with Nippon Steel 2007–10; CEO Aperam (spun off from ArcelorMittal 2010) 2010–11; CEO Holcim Ltd 2012–15; CEO Areva NP 2015–. *Address:* Areva NP, 1 place Jean Millier, 92400 Paris Courbevoie, France (office). *Telephone:* 1-34-96-00-00 (office). *Fax:* 1-34-96-66-06 (office). *Website:* www.areva.com (office).

FONTANELLI, Paolo, MBA, PhD; Italian business executive; *CEO, MCM Holdings AG;* ed Univ. of Florence, Cornell Univ., USA), Bocconi Univ., Milan, Advanced Man. Program, Harvard Business School, USA; conducted research in astrophysics and achieved fellowships from Cornell Univ., Observatoire de Paris, Arecibo Observatory, Puerto-Rico and Nat. Radio Astronomy Observatory, Va, USA 1982–85; Payload Expert, Sax satellite project at Aeritalia SpA (Italian aerospace co.) 1986–88; Controller Eli Lilly Italia SpA 1988–89, Treasury Man. 1989–90; Chief Financial Officer, Industrie Puccioni SpA 1991–95; Asst to the CEO, Salvatore Ferragamo Italia SpA 1995–98, Group Chief Financial Officer 1998–99; Chief Financial Officer, Giorgio Armani Group 1999–2007, Pres. and CEO Giorgio Armani Hong Kong and Greater China 2000–07; CEO Furla 2007–10; currently CEO MCM Holdings AG. *Address:* MCM Holdings AG, Bahnhofstr. 11, 6300 Zug, Switzerland (office). *Telephone:* 417102066 (office). *Website:* www.mcmworldwide.com (office).

FOON, Momodou S.; Gambian economist, academic and government official; ed Haverford Coll., USA, Univ. of Glasgow, Scotland; fmr Asst Lecturer, Dept of Econs, Univ. of The Gambia; fmr consultant to UNDP on macroeconomic issues; joined Central Bank of The Gambia 1979, becoming Prin. Economist and Head of Money and Credit Div., Economic Research Dept, later Special Asst to Gov., Cen. Bank of The Gambia; Sr Policy Adviser to Minister of Finance and Econ. Affairs 1993–95; joined West African Inst. for Financial and Econ. Man. (WAIFEM), Lagos, Nigeria 1999, becoming Dir, Macroeconomic Man. Dept, Acting Dir-Gen., WAIFEM Feb.–May 2009; Perm. Sec., Ministry of Econ. Planning and Industry – March 2010, Minister of Finance and Econ. Affairs March–July 2010.

FOOT, Michael David Kenneth Willoughby, CBE, MA, FCIB; British financial services industry executive and fmr financial regulator; *Global Vice-Chairman, Promontory Financial Group (UK) Ltd;* b. 16 Dec. 1946; s. of Kenneth Willoughby Foot and Ruth Joan Foot (née Cornah); m. Michele Annette Cynthia Macdonald 1972; one s. two d.; ed Pembroke Coll., Cambridge and Yale Univ.; joined Bank of England 1969, Man. 1978, Sr Man. 1985; seconded to IMF, Washington, DC as UK Alt. Exec. Dir 1985–87; Head of Foreign Exchange Div., Bank of England 1988–90, European Div. 1990–93, Banking Supervision Div. 1993–94, Deputy Dir Supervision and Surveillance 1994–96, Exec. Dir 1996–98; Man. Dir Financial Services Authority 1998–2004; Inspector of Bank and Trust Cos, Cen. Bank of the Bahamas 2004–07; Global Vice-Chair. Promontory Financial Group (UK) Ltd, London 2007–; Dir Prescot Management Co. Ltd 2008–11; Hon. Pres. ACI (UK) 2002–04.

Publications include: essays on monetary econs in various books and professional journals. *Leisure interests:* choral singing, tennis. *Address:* Promontory Financial Group (UK) Ltd, 2nd Floor, 30 Old Broad Street, London, EC2N 1HT (office); Cordons Windsor Lane, Little Kingshill, Great Missenden, HP16 0DZ, England. *Website:* www.promontory.com (office).

FOOTE, Huger, BA; American photographer and artist; b. 13 Nov. 1961, Memphis, Tenn.; s. of Shelby Foote and Gwyn Foote; ed Sarah Lawrence Coll., New York; began photography aged 12; photo assistant, Paris 1983–87; freelance photographer, New York 1987–93; began working as professional artist, Memphis 1993–98; moved to London 1998; has held exhbns across Europe and the USA. *Solo exhibitions include:* Ledbetter Lusk Gallery, Memphis 1996, Gallery of Contemporary Photography, Santa Monica 1997, Dorothy de Pauw Gallery, Brussels 2000, Patrick de Brock Gallery, Knokke 2001, Sight Unseen, David Lusk Gallery, Memphis 2004, Hamilton's Gallery, London 2005, These 18 2011, Sixteen 2013, David Lusk Gallery 2015. *Group exhibitions include:* Ledbetter Lusk Gallery 1995, Memphis Coll. of Art 1996, Artfair Seattle 1997, Memphis Arts Council 1997, The Armory, New York 1998, River Gallery, Chatanooga 1999, Belgian Art Fair 1999, Hamiltons Gallery, Brussels 2000, Sotheby's, London 2000, Contemporary Art Center of Virginia 2000, Houldsworth Fine Art, London 2000, Hamiltons Gallery, London 2005, David Lusk Gallery, Miami 2011, Dixon Gallery and Gardens, Memphis 2013. *Publications:* Seasons 1997, Sleep (photo essay) 2000, My Friend From Memphis (monograph) 2000, It's Always the Day After, Hamiltons 2002; contribs to Wall Street Journal, Vanity Fair, Vogue etc. *Leisure interests:* cycling, travelling in Africa and Pakistan. *Address:* c/o David Lusk Gallery, 4540 Poplar Avenue, Memphis, TN 38117, USA (office).

FOOTE, Judy M., PC, MP, BA, BEd; Canadian journalist and politician (retd); *Lieutenant Governor of Newfoundland and Labrador;* b. 23 June 1952, Grand Bank, Newfoundland; m. Howard Foote; one s. two d.; ed Memorial Univ., Lambton Coll.; began career as TV journalist with CBC, working on public affairs programme Here & Now; mem. Newfoundland and Labrador House of Ass. for Grand Bank 1996–2007, Prov. Minister of Devt and Rural Renewal 1996–97, of Industry, Trade and Tech. 1997–98, of Educ. 1998–2000, 2001–03, of Industry, Trade and Rural Devt Feb.–Nov. 2003; mem. House of Commons (Parl.) for Random–Burin–St George's 2008–15, for Bonavista–Burin–Trinity 2015–, Liberal Deputy House Leader 2010–11, Liberal Whip 2011–15; Minister of Public Services and Procurement 2015–17; Lt-Gov. of Newfoundland and Labrador 2018–; mem. Liberal Party of Canada. *Address:* Government House, 50 Military Rd, POB 5517, St. John's, NL, A1C 5W4, Canada (office). *E-mail:* governmenthouse@gov.nl.ca. *Website:* www.govhouse.nl.ca (office).

FORAU SOALAOI, Clay; Solomon Islands politician; b. 10 Oct. 1976; ed Solomon Islands Coll. of Higher Educ.; worked in educ. before entering politics; mem. Nat. Parl. for Temotu Vatud 2006–, Chair. Constitution Review Cttee 2008–, Leader of the Independent Mems 2010–11; Minister for Justice and Legal Affairs April–May 2006, for Health and Medical Services 2006–07, for Police, Nat. Security and Correctional Services April–Nov. 2011, Nov. 2011–Feb. 2012, for Foreign Affairs and Trade Relations 2012–14; fmr mem. Social Credit Party; mem. People's Federation Party. *Address:* Committee Secretariat, Constitution Review Committee, National Parliament, PO Box G19, Honiara, Solomon Islands (office). *Telephone:* 28520 (office). *Fax:* 24272 (office).

FORBES, Adm. (retd) Sir Ian, Kt, KCB, CBE; British naval officer (retd) and business executive; *Senior Adviser, Booz & Company;* ed RAF Staff Coll., Bracknell, Royal Coll. of Defense Studies (RCDS); joined RN 1965, tours in HM Yacht Britannia and on American Exchange with USS WH Standley; qualified as Prin. Warfare Officer 1979; specialized as Anti Air Warfare Officer 1978; fmr Commdr HMS Kingfisher, HMS Diomede, HMS Chatham, HMS Invincible (involved in NATO bombing campaign over Bosnia 1995, Operation Desert Fox in Gulf 1999), HMS Illustrious; engaged in active operations off Iceland, the Falklands, the Gulf and Adriatic; Staff Officer Operations to Comas Wsrikfor 1986–88; participant in Standing Naval Force Atlantic; promoted Rear Adm. 1995; served as Mil. Adviser to High Rep. in Sarajevo and Chief of Staff, Office of the High Rep., Bosnia; Commdr UK maritime contribs to NATO operations in Kosovo 1999; Flag Officer Surface Flotilla, NATO 2000, Deputy Saclant 2001, Adm. Supreme Allied Command Atlantic 2002–04; retd from service 2004; Pres. Forces Pension Soc. 2013–; Sr Adviser, Booz & Co. 2006–; Assoc. Fellow, Royal United Services Inst.; Mentor to Sr Mil. Command Courses; mem. Windsor Leadership Trust; Gov. Portsmouth High School for Girls; Chair. Council, Eastbourne Coll. 2005–; NATO Meritorious Service Medal, HRH Queen's Commendation for Valuable Service 1995. *Address:* Booz & Company, 7 Savoy Court, Strand, London, WC2R 0JP, England (office). *Telephone:* (20) 7393-3333 (office). *Fax:* (20) 7393-0025 (office). *Website:* www.booz.com (office).

FORBES, Kristin J., BA, PhD; American economist and academic; *Member, Monetary Policy Committee, Bank of England;* b. 21 Aug. 1970, New York, NY; m.; three c.; ed Williams Coll., Massachusetts Inst. of Tech.; early career as financial analyst Morgan Stanley Mergers and Acquisitions, NY 1992–93; Project Asst in Dept of Dir, Policy Research Dept, World Bank 1993–94; Research Fellow, Macroeconomics Group, Nat. Council of Applied Econ. Research, New Delhi 1996; Asst Prof. in Applied Econs Group, Sloan School of Man., MIT 1998–2002, Mitsubishi Career Devt Chair of Int. Man. 2001–04, Assoc. Prof. of Econs 2002–04, Assoc. Prof. of Econs with tenure 2004–09, Jerome and Dorothy Lemelson Prof. of Man. and Global Econs 2009–14; Deputy Asst Sec. of Quantitative Policy Analysis, Int. Affairs, US Treasury Dept 2001–02, Deputy Asst Sec. of Quantitative Policy Analysis, Latin American and Caribbean Nations 2002; mem. Monetary Policy Cttee, Bank of England 2014–; mem. Pres.'s Council of Econ. Advisors, Washington, DC 2003–05, Advisory Council Peterson Inst. of Int. Econs, Advisory Council Center for Global Devt; Research Assoc., Nat. Bureau of Econ. Research; mem. Council on Foreign Relations; mem. Trilateral Comm.; fmr Visiting Scholar US Fed. Reserve Bd, IMF; named a Young Global Leader by the World Econ. Forum, Davos, Switzerland, MIT Solow Prize for Excellence in Research and Teaching, Milken Award for Distinguished Econ. Research, numerous teaching awards. *Publications:* International Financial Contagion (co-ed.) 2001; numerous articles in magazines and journals. *Leisure interests:* hiking, tennis, skiing. *Address:* Bank of England, Threadneedle Street, London, EC2R 8AH, England (office). *Telephone:* (20) 7601-4444 (office). *Fax:* (20) 7601-4771 (office). *E-mail:* enquiries@bankofengland.co.uk (office). *Website:* www.bankofengland.co.uk.

FORBES, Malcolm Stevenson (Steve), Jr, LHD; American publishing executive; *Chairman and Editor-in-Chief, Forbes Media;* b. 18 July 1947, Morristown, NJ; s. of Malcolm Forbes and Roberta Laidlaw; m. Sabina Beekman 1971; ed Princeton Univ. and Lycoming Coll. Jacksonville Univ.; with Forbes Inc., New York 1970–, Pres. and COO 1980–90, Pres. and CEO 1990, Deputy Ed.-in-Chief, Forbes magazine 1982–90, apptd Ed.-in-Chief 1990, Chair. 2008, Chair. Forbes Newspapers 1989, now Chair. and Ed.-in-Chief of Forbes Media; mem. Bd for International Broadcasting 1983–93, Chair. 1985–93; mem. Advisory Council, Dept of Econs Princeton Univ. 1985–; mem. Bd of Dirs FreedomWorks 2006–; mem. Bd of Trustees, Heritage Foundation; several hon. degrees. *Film:* Some Call It Greed (scriptwriter) 1977. *Publications include:* Fact and Comment (ed.) 1974, A New Birth of Freedom 1999, Flat Tax Revolution: Using a Postcard to Abolish the IRS 2005, How Capitalism Will Save Us: Why Free People and Free Markets Are the Best Answer in Today's Economy (with Elizabeth Ames) 2009, Power Ambition Glory: The Stunning Parallels between Great Leaders of the Ancient World and Today... and the Lessons You Can Learn (with John Prevas) 2009. *Address:* Forbes Inc., 60 Fifth Avenue, New York, NY 10011, USA (office). *E-mail:* sforbes@forbes.com (office). *Website:* www.forbes.com (office).

FORD, Anna, BA, FRGS; British company director and fmr broadcaster; b. 2 Oct. 1943; d. of John Ford and Jean Beattie Winstanley; m. 1st Alan Holland Bittles (divorced 1976); m. 2nd Charles Mark Edward Boxer (died 1988); two d.; ed Minehead Grammar School, White House Grammar School, Brampton and Univ. of Manchester; work for students' interests, Univ. of Manchester 1966–69; Lecturer, Rupert Stanley Coll. of Further Educ., Belfast 1970–72; staff tutor, Social Sciences, NI Region, Open Univ. 1972–74, 1974–78; presenter and reporter, Man Alive (Granada TV), Tomorrow's World (BBC); newscaster, ITN 1978–80; with TV-AM 1980–83; freelance broadcasting and writing 1983–86; BBC News and Current Affairs 1989–2006; mem. Bd of Dirs J Sainsbury PLC 2006–12; Trustee, Royal Botanic Gardens, Kew 1995–; Chancellor, Univ. of Manchester 2001–04, Co-Chancellor 2004–08; Fellow, Royal Geographical Soc.; Hon. Fellow, Open Univ. 1998; Hon. Bencher Middle Temple 2002; Hon. BA (Cen. Lancs.) 1998, Hon. LLD (Manchester) 1998, Dr hc (Univ. of St Andrews) 2006. *Publication:* Men: A Documentary 1985. *Leisure interests:* talking, walking, drawing. *Address:* 1 Upper Butts, Brentford, TW8 8BU, England (home).

FORD, Hon. Anthony David, LLB; New Zealand judge; b. 8 May 1942, Hokitika; s. of Tom Ford and Cath Ford; m. Valda Ford; five d. two s.; ed Auckland Univ.; Judge, Supreme Court of Tonga 2000–06, Chief Justice of Tonga 2006–10; Judge, Fijian Court of Appeal 2005–07; Pres. Tonga Court of Appeal 2006–10; Judge, Employment Court of New Zealand 2010–15; Grand Cross of the Order of Queen Salote, Queen's Service Medal for services to Tonga and the Judiciary 2015.

FORD, Bruce; American singer (tenor); b. Lubbock, Tex.; m. H. Ypma 1982; one s.; ed West Texas State Univ., Texas Tech. Univ., Houston Opera Studio; sings in major opera houses in N America and Europe, specializing in Mozart and bel canto composers; Rossini's Otello (Covent Garden), Ermione (Glyndebourne), Zelmira, Ricciardo e Zoraide (Pesaro) revived for him; concert appearances include La Scala, Edinburgh Festival, Covent Garden, San Francisco Opera, Düsseldorf Symphonic, Chicago Lyric Opera and Amsterdam Concertgebouw; extensive recording career including many rare 19th-century operas; Seal of Texas Tech. Univ. 1997. *Leisure interests:* scuba diving, sailing. *Address:* c/o Athole Still Opera Ltd, 25–27 Westow Street, London, SE19 3RY, England (office). *Website:* www.atholestill.co.uk (office); tenorbruceford.com. *E-mail:* tenorbruceford@gmail.com; hetty.ford@gmail.com.

FORD, David Frank, MA, PhD, STM, OBE; Irish professor of divinity; *Regius Professor Emeritus of Divinity, University of Cambridge;* b. 23 Jan. 1948, Dublin; s. of George Ford and Phyllis Woodman; m. Deborah Hardy 1982; one s. two d. (one d. deceased); ed High School, Dublin, Trinity Coll., Dublin, St John's Coll., Cambridge, Yale Univ., USA, Univ. of Tübingen, Germany; Lecturer in Theology, Univ. of Birmingham 1976–90, Sr Lecturer 1990–91; apptd Regius Prof. of Divinity, Univ. of Cambridge 1991, now Regius Prof. of Divinity Emer., Chair. Faculty Bd of Divinity 1993–95, apptd Fellow, Selwyn Coll. Cambridge 1991, apptd Foundation mem. Trinity Coll. Cambridge 1991, mem. Syndicate Cambridge University Press 1993, Chair. Man. Cttee Centre for Advanced Religious and Theological Studies, Univ. of Cambridge 1995; Chair. Council, Westcott House Theological Coll. 1991–2006; mem. Archbishop of Canterbury's Urban Theology Working Group 1991–96; Fellow, Center of Theological Inquiry, Princeton Univ. 1993; Founding mem. and mem. Man. Cttee Soc. for Scriptural Reasoning 1996; Pres. Soc. for the Study of Theology 1997–98; mem. Postgraduate Panel in Philosophy and Theology, Humanities Research Bd of The British Acad. 1997–99, Church of England Doctrine Comm. 1998–2003; Founding Dir Cambridge Inter-Faith Programme 2002–; Academic mem. World Econ. Forum Council of 100 Leaders for West-Islamic World Dialogue 2003–; mem. Arts and Humanities Research Council Peer Review Coll. 2005–; mem. Advisory Bd Centre for Christian Studies, Hong Kong 2006–, Advisory Bd of ResponsAbility 2007–; mem. Bd of Advisors, John Templeton Foundation 2008–; Trustee, Golden Web Foundation 2006–, Center of Theological Inquiry, Princeton 2007–, Murray Cox Foundation 2007–; Lay Canon Theologian of Birmingham Cathedral 2006–; Hon. DD (Birmingham) 2000. *Publications include:* Barth and God's Story 1981, Jubilate: Theology in Praise (with D. W. Hardy) 1984, Meaning and Truth in 2 Corinthians (with F. M. Young) 1987, The Modern Theologians 1997, The Shape of Living 1997, Self and Salvation: Being Transformed 1999, Theology: A Very Short Introduction 1999, Jesus (ed. with M. Higton) 2002, Reading Texts, Seeking Wisdom (co-ed. with Graham Stanton) 2003, Fields of Faith: Theology and Religious Studies for the Twenty-First Century (co-ed. with Ben Quash and Janet Martin Soskice 2005, The Promise of Scriptural Reasoning (co-ed. with C. C. Pecknold) 2006, Musics of Belonging: The Poetry of Micheal O'Siadhail (co-ed. with Marc Caball) 2006, Christian Wisdom: Desiring God and Learning in Love 2007, Shaping Theology: Engagements in a Religious and Secular World 2007. *Leisure interests:* literature, walking, ball games, kayaking, family and friends. *Address:* Faculty of Divinity, West Road, Cambridge, CB3 9BS, England (office). *Telephone:* (1223) 763031 (office). *Fax:* (1223) 763003 (office). *E-mail:* dff1000@cam.ac.uk (office). *Website:* www.divinity.cam.ac.uk/directory/david-ford (office).

FORD, Douglas Robert; Canadian politician; *Premier of Ontario;* b. 20 Nov. 1964, Etobicoke, Ont.; s. of Doug Ford, Sr and Ruth Diane Campbell; m. Karla Middlebrook; four d.; ed Scarlett Heights Collegiate Inst.; Toronto City Councillor 2010–14; joined Progressive Conservative Party of Ontario 2014, Party Leader 2018–; Minister of Intergovernmental Affairs 2018–; mem. Ontario Prov. Parl. for Etobicoke North 2018–; mem. Bd of Dirs Toronto Transit Infrastructure Ltd. *Address:* Government of Ontario, Legislative Building, Queen's Park, Toronto, ON M7A 1A1, Country (office). *E-mail:* premier@ontario.ca (office). *Website:* www.ontario.ca (office).

FORD, Harrison; American actor; b. 13 July 1942, Chicago, Ill.; m. 1st Mary Ford; two s.; m. 2nd Melissa Ford (divorced 2004); one s. one d.; m. 3rd Calista Flockhart 2010; one s.; ed Ripon Coll.; Cecil B. DeMille Award, Golden Globes 2002, American Film Inst. Lifetime Achievement Award 2000, Jane Alexander Global Wildlife Amb. Award 2018. *Films include:* Dead Heat on a Merry-Go-Round 1966, Luv 1967, A Time for Killing 1967, Journey to Shiloh 1968, The Long Ride Home 1967, Getting Straight 1970, Zabriskie Point 1970, The Conversation 1974, American Graffiti 1974, Star Wars 1977, Heroes 1977, Force 10 from Navarone 1978, Apocalypse Now 1979, Hanover Street 1979, Frisco Kid 1979, The Empire Strikes Back 1980, Raiders of the Lost Ark 1981, Blade Runner 1982, Return of the Jedi 1983, Indiana Jones and the Temple of Doom 1984, Witness 1985, The Mosquito Coast 1986, Working Girl 1988, Frantic 1988, Indiana Jones and the Last Crusade 1989, Presumed Innocent 1990, Regarding Henry 1991, The Fugitive 1992, Patriot Games 1992, Clear and Present Danger 1994, Sabrina 1995, The Devil's Own 1996, Air Force One 1996, Six Days and Seven Nights 1998, Random Hearts 1999, What Lies Beneath 2000, K-19: The Widowmaker (also exec. producer) 2002, Hollywood Homicide 2003, No True Glory: The Battle for Fallujah 2006, Firewall 2006, Indiana Jones and the Kingdom of the Crystal Skull 2008, Crossing Over 2009, Extraordinary Measures 2010, Morning Glory 2010, 42 2013, Paranoia 2013, Ender's Game 2013, Anchorman 2: The Legend Continues 2013, The Expendables 3 2014, The Age of Adaline 2015, Star Wars: The Force Awakens 2015, Blade Runner 2049 2017. *Address:* c/o United Talent Agency, 9560 Wilshire Blvd, Beverly Hills, CA 90212, USA (office).

FORD, Richard, BA, MFA; American writer and academic; *Emmanuel Roman and Barrie Sardoff Roman Professor of the Humanities, Columbia University School of the Arts;* b. 16 Feb. 1944, Jackson, Miss.; s. of Parker Carrol Ford and Edna Ford; m. Kristina Hensley Ford 1968; ed Michigan State Univ., Univ. of California, Irvine; Lecturer, Univ. of Michigan, Ann Arbor 1974–76; Asst Prof. of English, Williams Coll. 1978–79; Lecturer, Princeton Univ. 1980–81; Prof., Trinity Coll., Dublin 2008; Prof., Univ. of Mississippi 2011; Prof. of Writing, Columbia Univ. School of the Arts 2012–, currently Emmanuel Roman and Barrie Sardoff Roman Professor of the Humanities; Guggenheim Fellowship 1977–78; Nat. Endowment for the Arts Fellowships 1979–80, 1985–86; mem. American Acad. of Arts and Letters, PEN, Writers' Guild, American Acad. of Arts and Sciences; Commdr, Ordre des Arts et des Lettres; Dr hc (Rennes, Michigan, Maine); Miss. Acad. of Arts and Letters Literature Award 1987, American Acad. and Inst. of Arts and Letters Award for Literature 1989, American Acad. of Arts and Letters Award in Merit for the Novel 1997, PEN-Malamud Award for Short Fiction 2001, Fitzgerald Award for Achievement in American Literature 2015, Princess of Asturias Award for Literature 2016, Siegfried Lenz Prize 2018, Premio la Lettura 2018. *Screenplays include:* American Tropical 1983, Bright Angel 1991. *Publications:* A Piece of My Heart (novel) 1976, The Ultimate Good Luck (novel) 1981, The Sportswriter (novel) 1986, Rock Springs (short stories) 1987, My Mother in Memory (ed.) 1988, The Best American Short Stories (ed.) 1990, Wildlife (novel) 1990, The Granta Book of the American Short Story (ed.) 1992, Independence Day (novel, Pulitzer Prize for Fiction 1996, PEN/Faulkner Award for Fiction 1996) 1995, Women with Men (short stories) 1997, The Granta Book of the American Long Story (ed.) 1999, A Multitude of Sins (short stories) 2002, The Lay of the Land (novel) 2006, The New Granta Book of the American Short Story (ed.) 2007, Canada (novel, Prix Femina Etranger 2013, Andrew Carnegie Medal for Excellence in Fiction 2013) 2012, Let Me Be Frank With You (four linked novellas) 2014, Between Them: Remembering My Parents (memoir) 2017. *Address:* c/o International Creative Management, 825 Eighth Avenue, New York, NY 10019, USA (office); Columbia University School of the Arts, 415 Dodge Hall, Mail Code 1808, 2960 Broadway, New York, NY 10027, USA (office). *Telephone:* (212) 854-4391 (office). *Website:* arts.columbia.edu (office).

FORD, Tom; American fashion designer and film-maker; *President and CEO, Tom Ford International;* b. 27 Aug. 1962, Texas; ed New York Univ., Parsons School of Design; fmrly acted in TV commercials, asst to designer Cathy Hardwick, with Perry Ellis Co.; joined Gucci Group 1990, Design Dir 1992–94, Creative Dir 1994–2004, Vice-Chair. Man. Bd 2002–04; Creative Dir, Yves St Laurent Rive Gauche and YSL Beauté 2000–04; est. Tom Ford Int. 2005, currently Pres. and CEO, launched menswear collection Spring 2007; involved in fund-raising in US and Europe; four Council of Fashion Designers of America awards, five VH-1/Vogue Fashion awards, two Fashion Editor's Club of Japan awards, two US Accessory Council awards, Best Fashion Designer, Time Magazine 2001, GQ Designer of the Year 2001, Fashion Design Achievement Award, Cooper Hewitt Museum 2002, Andre Leon Talley Lifetime Achievement Award, Savannah Coll. of Art and Design 2005, Geoffrey Beene Lifetime Achievement Award 2014, Fashion Award for Menswear Designer of the Year 2015, Council of Fashion Designers of America (CFDA). *Films:* A Single Man (dir) 2009, Noctural Animals (dir, producer and writer) 2016. *Address:* Tom Ford HQ, 845 Madison Avenue, New York, NY 10021-4908, USA (office). *Telephone:* (212) 359-0300 (office). *Fax:* (212) 359-0301 (office). *Website:* www.tomford.com (office).

FORD, William Clay, Jr, BA, MS; American automobile industry executive; *Executive Chairman, Ford Motor Company;* b. 3 May 1957, Detroit, Mich.; s. of William Clay Ford and Martha Firestone Ford; m. Lisa Ford; four c.; ed Princeton Univ., Massachusetts Inst. of Tech.; joined Ford Motor Co. as product-planning analyst 1979, then various positions in mfg, sales, marketing, product devt and finance; served on Ford's Nat. Bargaining Team in Ford–United Auto Workers talks 1982; Planning Man., Car Product Devt 1985–86; Dir, Comm. Vehicle Marketing, Ford of Europe 1986–87; Chair. and Man. Dir, Ford of Switzerland 1987–89; elected to Bd of Dirs Ford Motor Co. 1988, Chair. Bd Finance Cttee, mem. Bd's Sustainability and Innovation Cttee, Chair. of Bd 1999–, Vice-Pres. Ford Motor Co. 1994, CEO 2001–06, Exec. Chair. 2006–; Exec. Dir Business Strategy, Ford Automotive Group 1991–92, Gen. Man., Climate Control Div. 1992–94, Head of Commercial Truck Vehicle Centre 1994–95; mem. World Econ. Forum's Global Leaders for Tomorrow 1995; Chair. Detroit Econ. Club; mem. Bd of Dirs, Business Leaders for Michigan; Trustee, Henry Ford Health System, The Henry Ford (fmrly Henry Ford Museum); Vice-Chair. Detroit Lions Inc. (professional football team); Co-Chair. Country Music Hall of Fame Capital Campaign 2011; mem. Bd of Dirs, eBay Inc. 2005–15, Princeton Varsity Club 2013–; Founding Partner, Fontinalis Partners, LLC, Mich.; Hon. Chair. Southeast Mich. Consortium for Water Quality 2001, Hon. mem. Golden Key Int. Honour Soc. 2006; Hon. D.Env (Koc Univ., Istanbul) 2006; Hon. LLD (Univ. of Michigan) 2011; Hon. LHD (Bradley Univ.) 2012; Automotive Exec. of the Year 2006, Boneh Kehillah Award, Jewish Community Center of Detroit 2007, inducted into Irish America Hall of Fame 2011, Amb. for Humanity Award, USC Shoah Foundation 2015. *Leisure interests:* fly-fishing, Tae Kwon Do black belt, playing ice hockey and tennis, cars. *Address:* Ford Motor Company, World Headquarters, One American Road, Dearborn, MI 48126-2798, USA (office). *Telephone:* (313) 322-3000 (office). *Fax:* (313) 594-1593 (office). *E-mail:* mculler@ford.com (office). *Website:* www.ford.com (office).

FORDE, Sir Henry de Boulay, Kt, PC, QC, LLM, KA; Barbadian politician and lawyer; b. 20 March 1933, Christ Church; adopted s. of Courtley Ifill and Elise Ifill; m. Cheryl Wendy Roach; four s.; ed Harrison Coll., Barbados, Christ's Coll., Cambridge, Middle Temple, London; Research Asst, Dept of Criminology, Univ. of Cambridge 1958, Research Student, Int. Law, worked on British Digest of Int. Law, Univ. of Cambridge 1958–59, Supervisor and Tutor in Int. Law, Emmanuel Coll., Cambridge 1958–59; called to English Bar 1959, to Barbadian Bar 1959; Lecturer, Extra-Mural Programme, Univ. of West Indies 1961–68, part-time Lecturer, Caribbean Studies 1964–69; mem. House of Ass. for Christ Church West 1971–2003; Minister of External Affairs and Attorney-Gen. 1976–81; Minister of State 1993; Leader of the Opposition 1986–89, 1991–93; mem. Privy Council 1976–92, 1996–; Chair. and Political Leader, Barbados Labour Party 1986–93; Chair. Commonwealth Observer Group to the Seychelles 1991, to Fiji Islands 2001; mem. Commonwealth Cttee on Vulnerability of Small States 1985, Commonwealth Parl. Asscn, Editorial Bds of The Round Table, Int. Comm. of Jurists 1987–92, Barbados Bar Asscn, Hon. Soc. of Middle Temple, Int. Tax Planning Asscn, Interparliamentary Human Rights Network, Barbados Nat. Trust, Int. Acad. of Estate and Trust Law, Int. Inst. for Democracy and Electoral Assistance, Inter-American Comm. on Human Rights; Kt of St Andrew, Order of Barbados; Hon. LLD (Univ. of the West Indies) 2013. *Leisure interests:* reading, walking, gardening. *Address:* Juris Chambers, Parker House, Wildey Business Park, Wildey Road, St Michael, Barbados (office); Codrington Court, Society, St John, Barbados, West Indies (home). *Telephone:* 429-5320 (office); 429-2203 (office); 423-3881 (home). *Fax:* 429-2206 (office); 423-3949 (home). *E-mail:* shf@jurischambers.com (office).

FORE, Henrietta H., BA, MSc; American politician, business executive and UN official; *Executive Director, United Nations Children's Fund (UNICEF);* b. 9 Dec. 1948; m.; four c.; ed Univ. of Northern Colorado, Univ. of Oxford, UK, Stanford Univ. Graduate School of Business; Chair., Stockton Products 1977–2017, Middle East Investment Initiative 2015–17; Chair. and CEO Holsman Int. 1993–2017; Co-Chair. Global Bd of Dirs, Asia Soc. 1993–2017; Dir US Mint, Dept of Treasury 2001–05, Under-Sec. of State for Man. 2005–07, Admin. US Agency for Int. Devt (USAID) 2007–09; Co-Chair. Women Corp. Dirs Foundation 2009–15; Exec. Dir UNICEF 2018–; mem. Bd of Trustees, Aspen Inst. 1993–2017, Center for Strategic and Int. Studies (CSIS) 1995–2017, Cttee for Econ. Devt 2010–17; mem. Bd, CECP 1993–2017, Center for Global Devt 2011–17; mem. Bd of Dirs, Theravance Biopharma US, Inc. 2010–17, ExxonMobil 2012–17, Gen. Mills 2014–17, Essilor Int. SA 2016–17; Women Redefining Leadership Award 1997, CRDF Global's George Brown Award for Int. Scientific Cooperation 2013, Circle of Achievement Award 2014. *Leisure and interests:* sailing, collecting antiques. *Address:* United Nations Children's Fund (UNICEF), 3 United Nations Plaza, New York, NY 10017, USA (office). *Telephone:* (212) 326-7000 (office). *Fax:* (212) 888-7465 (office). *E-mail:* info@unicef.org (office). *Website:* www.unicef.org (office).

FOREHAND, Joe W., BS, MSc; American business executive; m.; two s.; ed Auburn Univ., Purdue Univ.; joined Accenture, Atlanta 1972, made Pnr 1982, held various man. positions including Leader, Global Communications and High Tech. Group, CEO 1999–2004, Chair. 2001–06 (retd); Sr Advisor, Kohlberg Kravis & Roberts 2006–10; Interim CEO First Data Corp. March–Oct. 2010, Chair. 2010–14; mem. Bd of Dirs Aricent Inc. 2006–, Chair. 2008–12; mem. Hands On Network Advisory Council; fmr mem. Business Roundtable; Dr hc (Purdue Univ.); Carl S. Sloane Award for Excellence in Man. Consulting 2003, Morgan Stanley Leadership Award 2003.

FOREMAN, Amanda, BA, PhD, FRSL; British historian, writer and journalist; b. 30 June 1968, London, England; d. of Carl Foreman; m.; one s. four d.; ed Sarah Lawrence Coll., USA, Lady Margaret Hall, Oxford; Henrietta Jex-Blake Sr Fellowship, Lady Margaret Hall, Oxford 1993; TV and radio presenter 1998–; Visiting Sr Research Fellow in History, Faculty of Arts, Queen Mary, Univ. of London 2004–; mem. Bd of Dirs, American Friends of the Nat. Theatre 2011–, American Friends of Policy Exchange 2012–; Judge, Orange Prize For Women's Fiction 2000, Nat. Book Award – Non Fiction 2009, PEN/Hessell-Tiltman History Prize 2011–12, Dan David Prize 2012, Man Booker Prize 2012 (Chair. 2015); mem. Advisory Council, Lady Margaret Hall, Oxford 2005–, New York Public Library 2009–, American Friends of Policy Exchange 2012–, Americans for Oxford 2015, The Whiting Foundation 2015–; writes column Historically Speaking in Wall Street Journal. *Television:* The Ascent of Woman (documentary series) 2014. *Publications include:* Georgiana: Duchess of Devonshire (Whitbread Award for Biography of the Year) 1998, Georgiana's World 2001, A World on Fire: An Epic History of Two Nations Divided (Fletcher Pratt Award for Excellence in Civil War History Writing 2012) 2010. *Address:* c/o The Wylie Agency, 17 Bedford Square, London, WC1B 3JA, England (office). *E-mail:* mail@wylieagency.co.uk (office). *Website:* www.wylieagency.co.uk (office); www.amanda-foreman.com.

FOREMAN, George; American fmr professional boxer; b. 10 Jan. 1949, Marshall, Tex.; s. of J.D. Foreman and Nancy Foreman; m. five times; five s. seven d.; Olympic heavyweight champion Mexico 1968; world heavyweight champion 1973–74, 1994–95; lost title to Muhammad Ali (knockout in 8th round) in 1974;

recaptured it on 5 Nov. 1994 at age 45 with a 10-round knockout of WBC/IBF champion Michael Moorer, becoming oldest man to win heavyweight crown; successfully defended title at age 46 against Axel Schulz; gave up IBF title after refusing rematch with Schulz; now an evangelical minister; f. a youth and community centre; has diverse business interests, has endorsed or sold numerous products such as hamburgers, hot dogs and grilling machines and rotisseries; AP Male Athlete of the Year 1994, inducted into Int. Boxing Hall of Fame 2003. *Publications include:* By George (autobiograpahy),Knock-Out-the-Fat Barbecue and Grilling Cookbook 1996, Book of Grilling, Barbecue, and Rotisserie (with Barbara Witt) 2000, Indoor Grilling Made Easy (with Kathryn Kellinger) 2004, Let George Do It! 2005, God's in My Corner (with Ken Abraham) 2007, Going the Extra Smile 2007, Fatherhood By George 2008, Knockout Entrepreneur (with Ken Abraham) 2009. *Leisure interests:* raising livestock, breeding horses. *Address:* c/o The Church of Lord Jesus Christ, 2501 Lone Oak, Houston, TX 77093, USA. *E-mail:* george@biggeorge.com. *Website:* www.biggeorge.com.

FORGEARD, Noël, LèsScEcon; French mining engineer and business executive; b. 8 Dec. 1946, Ferté-Gaucher; s. of Henri Forgeard and Laurence Duprat; m. Marie-Cécile de Place 1972; one s. three d.; ed Lycée Louis-le-Grand, Ecole Polytechnique, Paris; qualified as mining engineer; entered mining industry in Clermont-Ferrand, industry rep. to Auvergne prefecture 1972–73; Asst Sec.-Gen. Dept of Mining, Ministry for Industry 1973–76, Sec.-Gen. 1976–78; Tech. Adviser to Minister of Transport 1978–80, of Defence 1980; Head of Industrial Affairs and Armaments, Ministry of Defence 1980–81; Deputy Pres., Asst Gen. Man. Compagnie française des aciers spéciaux (CFAS) 1982–84, Prés., Dir-Gen. 1984–86; Man. Dir then Pres., Dir-Gen. Ascometal 1985–86; Chair. Asfor Steel Products 1986–87; Tech Adviser and Head of Industrial Affairs, Office of the Prime Minister 1986–87; Man. Defence and Space Divs Matra 1987, Pres., Dir-Gen. Matra-défense espace finance co. (Sofimades), Matra Hautes technologies, Matra Bac Dynamics, mem. Exec. and Strategy Cttee and Gen. Man. Lagardère SCA 1993–98; Man. Dir Airbus Industrie 1998–2005, CEO 2000–05, Jt CEO European Aeronautic Defence and Space Co. EADS NV (main shareholder of Airbus) 2005–06; Dir Matra systèmes et information, Snecma, Matra-Marconi Space NV; Vice-Pres. Groupement des industries de l'aéronautique et de l'espace (Gifas); Officier, Légion d'honneur, Ordre nat. du Mérite; Public Enterprise Foundation Award 1971. *Leisure interests:* modern art, swimming. *Address:* 85 avenue de Wagram, 75017 Paris (home); Le Roc, 35800 St-Briac-sur-Mer, France (home).

FORIEL-DESTEZET, Philippe, MBA; French business executive; *Honorary President, Adecco SA;* b. 12 Sept. 1935; m.; four c.; ed Hautes Etudes Commerciales; Founder Ecco SA, Lyon 1964, Dir, Adecco Group 1996–2006, Co-Chair. 2004–05, Jt Chair. Adecco SA 1996–2002, Hon. Pres. 2006–; Chair. Akila Finance, Luxembourg; Chevalier, Légion d'honneur. *Address:* PFD Office, 16 rue Jean Pierre Brasseur, 1258 Luxembourg, Luxembourg (office). *Telephone:* 27-44-92-80 (office). *Fax:* 27-44-92-81 (office). *E-mail:* secretariat@pfd-office.lu (office). *Website:* www.adecco.com (office).

FORMIGONI, Roberto, MA; Italian politician; b. 30 March 1947, Lecco; s. of Emilio Formigoni and Doralice Baroni; ed Catholic Univ. of Milan, Univ. of Sorbonne, Paris; co-f. Movimento Popolare (political arm of Catholic Movt Comunione e Liberazione), Nat. Pres. 1976–87; MEP (Christian Democratic Party) 1984–94, Vice-Chair. Presidential Office 1989–94; elected Deputy 1987, 1992, 1994 (Christian Democratic Party); Under-Sec., Ministry of Environment 1993–94; Pres. Lombardy Region 1995–2013; Laurea hc (Libera Univ. di Lingue e Comunicazione, Milan) 2004; award for devt cooperation of Lombardy Region. *Leisure interests:* yachting, jogging. *Address:* c/o Palazzo della Regione Lombardia, Via Fabio Filzi 22, 20124 Milan, Italy. *Website:* www.formigoni.it.

FORMUZAL, Mihail; Moldovan politician and government official; b. 7 Nov. 1959, Beşghioz, Ceadîr-Lunga dist; m.; three c.; ed M.V. Frunze Mil. High School of Artillery, Odesa, Ukrainian SSR, Public Admin Acad., Chişinău; specialist, public admin; mil. service 1977–94, achieved rank of Maj.; Deputy Mayor of Ceadîr-Lunga 1995–99, Mayor 1999–2007; Chair. People's Republican Party (Respublika Halk Partiyası) 2005; Başkan (Gov.) Autonomous Territory of Găgăuz-Yeri 2006–15; numerous awards.

FORNÉ MOLNÉ, Marc; Andorran lawyer and politician; b. 30 Dec. 1946, La Massana; m. Maria Lluïsa Gispert Boronat; one s.; ed Univ. of Barcelona, Spain; fmr Ed. Andorra 7 magazine; mem. Partit Liberal d'Andorra (fmr Leader); Head of Govt of Andorra 1994–2005; Commdr, Légion d'honneur 2003. *Address:* Partit Liberal d'Andorra (PLA), Carrer Babot Camp 13, 2°, Andorra la Vella, AD500, Andorra (office). *Telephone:* 807715 (office). *Fax:* 869728 (office). *E-mail:* advocatsforne@andorra.ad (office). *Website:* www.partitliberal.ad (office).

FORREST, Andrew; Australian business executive; *Chairman, Fortescue Metals Group Ltd;* b. 1961; s. of Donald Forrest and Judith Forrest; m. Nicola Forrest; three c.; early career as investment banker; Founding CEO and Deputy Chair. Anaconda Nickel Ltd (now Minara Resources Ltd) 1994, also Chair. Murrin Murrin Jt Venture; fmr Chair. Moly Mines Ltd, Siberia Mining Corpn Ltd; Founder and CEO Fortescue Metals Group Ltd 2003–11, Chair. 2003–05, 2011–; Chair. Poseidon Nickel Ltd, Australian Children's Trust; Founder GenerationOne; fmr Chair. Athletics Australia; fmr Dir West Australian Chamber of Minerals and Energy; Fellow, Australian Inst. of Mining and Metallurgy. *Address:* Fortescue Metals Group Ltd, Level 2, 87 Adelaide Terrace, East Perth, WA 6004, Australia (office). *Telephone:* (8) 6218-8888 (office). *Fax:* (8) 6218-8880 (office). *E-mail:* fmgl@fmgl.com.au (office). *Website:* www.fmgl.com.au (office).

FORREST, Sir (Andrew) Patrick McEwen, Kt, MD, ChM, FRCS, FRCPE, FRSE; British surgeon; b. 25 March 1923, Mount Vernon, Scotland; s. of Andrew J. Forrest and Isabella Pearson; m. 1st Margaret B. Hall 1955 (died 1961); m. 2nd Margaret A. Steward 1964; one s. two d.; ed Dundee High School and St Andrew's Univ.; Mayo Foundation Fellow, Rochester, Minn. 1952–53; Lecturer, then Sr Lecturer, Univ. of Glasgow 1954–62; Prof. of Surgery, Welsh Nat. School of Medicine 1962–71; Regius Prof. of Clinical Surgery, Univ. of Edinburgh 1970–88, Prof. Emer. 1989–, Hon. Fellow, Faculty of Medicine 1989–95; Visiting Scientist, NIH 1989–90; Assoc. Dean (Clinical Studies) Int. Medical Coll., Kuala Lumpur 1993–96; mem. MRC 1975–79; Chief Scientist, Scottish Home and Health Dept (part-time) 1981–87; mem. Advisory Bd for Research Councils 1982–85; Hon. FACS; Hon. FRACS; Hon. FRCS (Canada); Hon. FRCR; Hon. FFPH; Hon. DSc (Wales, Chinese Univ. of Hong Kong); Hon. LLD (Dundee); Gimbernat Prize, Catalonian Surgical Asscn 1996; European Inst. of Oncology Breast Cancer Award 2000; Lister Medal 1987, Gold Medal, Netherlands Surgical Asscn 1988. *Publications:* Prognostic Factors in Breast Cancer (jtly) 1968, Principles and Practice of Surgery (jtly) 1985, Breast Cancer: The Decision to Screen 1990; over 250 publs in scientific and medical journals. *Leisure interests:* golf, sailing. *Address:* 19 St Thomas Road, Edinburgh, EH9 2LR, Scotland (home). *Telephone:* (131) 667-3203 (home). *Fax:* (131) 662-1193 (home). *E-mail:* patforresthome@aol.com (home).

FORSEE, Gary D., BS; American university administrator and fmr telecommunications industry executive; *CEO, AirGate PCS Inc.;* b. 10 April 1950, Kansas City; m. Sherry Forsee; two d.; ed Missouri Univ. of Science and Tech.; with Southwestern Bell Telephone 1972–80; with AT&T 1980–89; Vice-Pres. and Gen. Man. Govt System Div., Sprint Corpn 1989–91, Pres. Govt System Div., Business Services Group 1991–93, Sr Vice-Pres. of Staff Operations, Long Distance Div. 1993–95, Interim CEO Sprint PCS 1995, Pres. and COO Sprint Long Distance Div. 1995–98, Pres. and CEO Sprint Corpn (now Sprint Nextel Corpn) 2003–07 (resgnd), Pres. and CEO Global One (subsidiary co.), Brussels, Belgium 1998–2000; Chief Staff Officer and Exec. Vice-Pres. BellSouth Int. 1999–2000, Pres. 2000–01, Vice-Chair. Domestic Operations, BellSouth Corpn 2002–03; Chair. Cingular Wireless 2001–02; Pres. Univ. of Missouri 2007–11; currently CEO, AirGate PCS Inc.; mem. Bd of Dirs Goodyear Tire & Rubber Co., Great Plains Energy Inc. 2008–; Nat. Exec. Bd, Boys Scouts of America. *Address:* AirGate PCS Inc., 233 Peachtree Street, NE, Harris Tower, Suite 1700, Atlanta, GA 30303, USA (office). *Telephone:* (404) 525-7272 (office). *Fax:* (404) 525-7922 (office).

FORSÉN, K. Sture, MSc, DTech; Swedish chemist and academic; *Senior Scientific Adviser, Pufendorf Institute for Advanced Studies, Lund University;* b. 12 July 1932, Piteå; s. of Helmer Forsén and Signe Forsén; m. Dr Gunilla Isaksson 1973 (divorced 1986); ed Royal Inst. of Tech., Stockholm; Assoc. Prof. of Chemical Physics, Royal Inst. of Tech. 1963–67, Prof. of Physical Chem., Lund Univ. 1966, now Prof. Emer.; mem. Bd of Dirs Swedish Natural Science Research Council 1983–86, Perstorp AB 1986–, Swedish Nat. Chemicals Inspectorate 1989–; Fairchild Scholar, Calif. Inst. of Tech. 1986–87, Fogarty Scholar, NIH, USA 1987–94, Visiting Investigator, Scripps Research Inst., La Jolla 1990–; Man. Dir SWEGENE (postgenomic consortium) 2000–05; mem. Bd of Dirs Wallenberg Global Learning Network 2005–; Scientific Adviser to Rectrix Magnifica Boel Flodgrenthe, Lund Univ. 1998–2000, to Rector Magnificus Goran Bexell 2004–09, Sr Scientific Adviser, Pufendorf Inst. for Advanced Studies, Lund Univ. 2009–; mem. Scientific Advisory Council of Volvo Research Foundation 1987–92; mem. Royal Swedish Acad. of Sciences 1973–, Nobel Cttee for Chem. 1976–95; mem. Royal Swedish Acad. of Eng Sciences 1986–; Celsius Gold Medal, Royal Soc. of Uppsala 1979. *Publications include:* co-author of two books on NMR spectroscopy 1972, 1976; over 300 scientific articles, at present mainly concerning biophysical studies of calcium-binding proteins, in int. journals. *Leisure interests:* music from Frescobaldi to Keith Jarrett, renovating old farmhouses. *Address:* Pufendorf Institute, Lund University, PO Box 117, 221 00 Lund, Sweden (office). *Telephone:* (46) 222-62-01 (office). *E-mail:* sture.forsen@pi.lu.se (office). *Website:* www.pi.lu.se (office).

FORSTER, Carl-Peter, BSc; German automobile industry executive; b. 9 May 1954, London, England; m.; three c.; ed Bonn Univ., Munich Tech. Univ.; raised in London, Bonn and Athens; consultant, McKinsey and Co., Munich 1982–86; Head of Planning and Logistics, Tech. Devt Dept, BMW AG 1986–88, Systems and Project Man. 5-series 1988–90, Head of Dept for Test and Pilot Car Mfg, Tech. Devt Centre 1990–93, Head of 5-series 1993–96, Man. Dir BMW (SA) Pty Ltd 1996–99, mem. Man. Bd BMW AG 1999–2000; Chair. and Man. Dir Opel AG 2001–04, Chair. 2004–09, Chair. Supervisory Bd 2004–09; mem. Bd of Dirs Fiat-GM Motors Powertrain 2001–09, GM Vice-Pres. and Pres. General Motors Europe 2004–09, Chair. Saab 2005–09, GM Group Vice-Pres. 2006–09; Group CEO and Man. Dir Tata Motors Ltd 2010–11, Dir (non-exec.) 2011–; Dir Geely Automotive Holdings and Volvo Cars 2013–, Rexam PLC 2014–; Adviser, Geely Holding Group 2011–. *Leisure interests:* skiing, regatta-sailing.

FORSTMOSER, Peter, LLM, DrIur; Swiss lawyer and business executive; *Partner, Niederer Kraft and Frey AG;* b. 22 Jan. 1943, Zurich; s. of Alois Forstmoser-Locher and Ida Forstmoser-Locher; two s.; ed Zurich Univ. Law School, Harvard Law School, USA; admitted to the Bar 1971; attorney 1971–, Partner, Niederer Kraft and Frey AG 1975–; Lecturer, Faculty of Law and Political Science, Univ. of Zürich 1971–74, Assoc. Prof., Univ. of Zürich Law School 1974–78, Full Prof. of Civil, Corp. and Capital Market Law 1978–2008, Prof. Emer. 2008–; mem. Bd of Dirs Swiss Reinsurance Co. (Swiss Re) 1990–2009, Chair. 2000–09; Chair. Leonteq AG 2012–; Chair. and mem. various corp. bds. *Publications include:* Schweizer Aktienrecht 1996, Organisation und Organisationsreglement der Aktiengesellschaft 2011, Schweizer Gesellschaftsrecht 2012, Einführung in das Recht 2012 and numerous other publs on Swiss company and capital market law. *Leisure interests:* sports, modern art. *Address:* Niederer Kraft and Frey AG, Bahnhofstrasse 13, 8001 Zurich, Switzerland (office). *Telephone:* (58) 800-80-00 (office). *Fax:* (58) 800-80-80 (office). *E-mail:* peter.forstmoser@nkf.ch (office). *Website:* www.nkf.ch (office).

FORSYTH, Frederick, CBE; British writer; b. 25 Aug. 1938, Ashford, Kent; m. 1st Carole Cunningham 1973; two s.; m. 2nd Sandy Molloy; ed Tonbridge School, Univ. of Granada, Spain; served with RAF 1956–58; reporter, Eastern Daily Press, Norfolk 1958–61; joined Reuters 1961, reporter, Paris 1962–63, Chief of Bureau, E Berlin 1963–64; radio and TV reporter, BBC 1965–66; Asst Diplomatic Corresp., BBC TV 1967–68; freelance journalist, Nigeria and Biafra 1968–69; Diamond Dagger Award (for lifetime achievement), Crime Writers Asscn 2012. *Television appearances include:* Soldiers (narrator) 1985, Frederick Forsyth Presents 1989. *Film appearance:* I Have Never Forgotten You: The Life and Legacy of Simon Wiesenthal 2006. *Publications include:* fiction: The Day of the Jackal (Edgar Allan Poe Award for Best Novel, Mystery Writers of America 1971) 1971, The Odessa File 1972, The Dogs of War 1974, The Shepherd 1975, The Devil's Alternative 1979, No Comebacks (short stories) 1982, The Fourth Protocol 1984, The Negotiator 1988, The Deceiver 1991, Great Flying Stories (ed.) 1991, The Fist of God 1993, Icon 1996, The Phantom of Manhattan 1999, Quintet 2000, The Veteran and Other Stories 2001, Avenger 2003, The Afghan 2006, The Cobra 2010, The Kill List 2013; non-fiction: The Biafra Story 1969 (revised edn as The Making of an

African Legend: The Biafra Story 1977), Emeka 1982, I Remember: Reflections on Fishing in Childhood 1995. *Leisure interests:* sea angling, reading. *Website:* www .frederickforsyth.co.uk.

FORSYTH, William (Bill) David; British film director; b. 29 July 1946, Glasgow, Scotland; one s. one d.; ed Nat. Film School, Beaconsfield; Hon. DLitt (Glasgow) 1984; Hon. DUniv (Stirling) 1989; BAFTA Award for Best Screenplay 1982, for Best Dir 1983. *Films include:* That Sinking Feeling 1979, Gregory's Girl 1980, Andrina (TV film) 1981, Local Hero 1982, Comfort and Joy 1984, Housekeeping 1987, Breaking In 1988, Being Human 1994, Gregory's Two Girls 1999.

FORSYTH MEJÍA, Harold Winston; Peruvian journalist, politician and diplomatist; *Ambassador to Japan;* b. 27 May 1951, Lima; s. of Willy Forsyth Cauvi and Lucciola Mejía de Forsyth; m. María Verónica Sommer Mayer; two s. one d.; ed Pontifical Catholic Univ. of Peru, Diplomatic Acad. of Peru; Third Sec., Embassy in Santiago 1977–78, Second Sec. and Chargé d'affaires a.i., Embassy in Sofia 1978–79, Second Sec., Embassy in Caracas 1980–82, Chief of Cabinet of Perm. Sec., Sistema Económico Latinoamericano y del Caribe (SELA) 1982–84, First Sec., Chief of Evaluation and Control, Diplomatic Acad. of Peru 1984–85, Under-Dir of Latin-American Cooperation, Ministry of Foreign Affairs (MFA) 1986, Counsellor, Embassy in Ottawa 1987–89, Minister-Counsellor, Embassy Berlin 1990–92, Amb. to Colombia 2001–04, to Italy 2004–06, Deputy Minister and Sec.-Gen. of Foreign Affairs 2006, MFA Adviser 2006–09, Amb. to People's Repub. of China 2009–11, to USA 2011–15, to Japan 2017–; mem. Congreso (Parl.) for Lima 1995–2000; numerous int. honours, including Grand Cross, Order of Bernardo O'Higgins (Chile) 2001, Peruvian Cross for Naval Merit 2003, Order Francisco de Miranda, First Class (Venezuela) 2003, Grand Cross, Simón Bolívar Order of Democracy 2004, Grand Cross, José Gregorio Paz Soldán Order 2006, Grand Cross, Peruvian Order of Merit for Distinguished Service 2006. *Publication:* Conversation with Javier Pérez de Cuéllar 2001; contrib. to El Comercio and Caretas. *Address:* Embassy of Peru, 2-3-1, Hiroo, Shibuya-ku, Tokyo 150-0012, Japan (office). *Telephone:* (3) 3406-4243 (office). *Fax:* (3) 3409-7589 (office). *E-mail:* embperutokyo@embperujapan.org (office). *Website:* embajadadelperuenjapon.org (office).

FORSYTH OF DRUMLEAN, Baron (Life Peer), cr. 1999, of Drumlean in Stirling; **Rt Hon. Michael Bruce Forsyth,** Kt, PC, MA; British fmr politician and investment banker; b. 16 Sept. 1954, Montrose, Scotland; s. of John Forsyth and Mary Watson; m. Susan Jane Clough 1977; one s. two d.; ed Arbroath High School, St Andrews Univ.; MP for Stirling 1983–97; Minister of State for Health/Educ. (Scotland) 1981–92, Minister of State, Dept of Employment 1992–94, Home Office 1994–95, Sec. of State for Scotland and Lord Keeper of the Great Seal of Scotland 1995–97; apptd mem. House of Lords 1999, mem. House of Lords' Economic Affairs Cttee 2007–11, 2015–; Dir Flemings 1997–2000; Vice-Chair. Investment Banking (Europe), JP Morgan 2000–02, Deputy Chair. JP Morgan (UK) 2002–05, Evercore Partners International LLP 2005–12; Chair. Hyperion Insurance Group (merged with RKH Group) –2015, Safor Ltd; mem. Bd of Dirs J & J Denholm Ltd, Secure Trust Bank; Parliamentarian of the Year 1996. *Publications include:* Reservicing Britain 1980, The Myths of Privatisation 1983. *Leisure interests:* mountaineering, astronomy, gardening, art, fly fishing, photography. *Address:* House of Lords, London, SW1A 0PW, England (office). *Telephone:* (20) 7219-5353 (office). *Fax:* (20) 7219-5979 (office).

FORSYTHE, William; American choreographer; *Artistic Advisor, Choreographic Institute, Glorya Kaufman School of Dance, University of Southern California;* b. 30 Dec. 1949, New York; ed Jacksonville Univ., Joffrey Ballet School; joined Stuttgart Ballet 1973, dancer, then choreographer; choreographed works commissioned by cos including New York City Ballet, San Francisco Ballet, Nat. Ballet of Canada, Royal Ballet, Covent Garden and Nederlands Dans Theater; Founder and Dir Ballett Frankfurt 1984–2004, Ballett Frankfurt and TAT 1999–2004; f. The Forsythe Co. 2005; Prof. of Dance and Artistic Advisor, Choreographic Inst., Glorya Kaufman School of Dance, Univ. of Southern California 2014–; Assoc. Choreographer, Paris Opera Ballet 2015–; Hon. Fellow, Laban Centre for Movt and Dance, London; Chevalier des Arts et Métiers 1991, Commdr des Arts et Lettres 1999; Dr hc (The Julliard School in New York); Harlekin Preis, Frankfurt 1986, Bessie Award 1988, 1998, 2004, 2007, Deutscher Kritikerpreis 1988, Olivier Award 1992, Evening Standard Award 1999, Golden Lion for Lifetime Achievement, Venice Biennale 2010, American Dance Festival Award for Lifetime Achievement 2012, Swedish Carina Ari Medal 2014 and numerous other awards. *Ballets include:* Urlicht 1976, Gänge 1983, Artifact 1984, Impressing the Czar 1988, Limb's Theorem 1991, The Loss of Small Detail 1991, Eidos: Telos 1995, Endless House 1999, Kammer/Kammer 2000 (Paris 2002), Decreation 2003, Three Atmospheric Studies 2005, You made me a monster 2005, Human Writes 2005, Heterotopia 2006, The Defenders 2007, Yes we can't 2008, 2010 (second version), I don't believe in outer space 2008, The Returns 2009, Sider 2011. *Films include:* Berg Ab 1984, Solo 1995, From a Classic Position 1997. *Address:* Glorya Kaufman School of Dance, University of Southern California, 837 Downey Way, STO 322, Los Angeles, CA 90089-0851, USA (office). *Telephone:* (213) 740-9327 (office). *Website:* kaufman.usc.edu (office).

FORT-BRESCIA, Bernardo, BA, MArch, FAIA; American (b. Peruvian) architect; *Founding Principal, Arquitectonica International Corporation;* b. 19 Nov. 1951, Lima, Peru; s. of Paul Fort and Rosa Brescia; m. Laurinda Spear 1976; five s. one d.; ed Princeton Univ., Harvard Univ.; moved to Fla 1975; Visiting Prof. of Architecture and Planning, Univ. of Miami 1975–77; co-f. (with Laurinda Spear) Arquitectonica Int. Corpn, Miami, Fla 1977–, also Founding Prin.; projects in USA, Europe, S America, Cen. America, Asia and Caribbean; Prof. Univ. of Miami 1975–77; mem. Advisory Bd Univ. of Miami School of Architecture; mem. Bd of Dirs New World Symphony, Wolfsonian-FIU Museum; numerous AIA Awards and Honors for Design Excellence; Founder's Award, Salvadori Center 2000. *Publications:* Arquitectonica 1991, numerous articles in specialist and non-specialist journals. *Address:* Arquitectonica International Corporation, 2900 Oak Avenue, Miami, FL 33131-2517, USA (office). *Telephone:* (305) 372-1812 (office). *Fax:* (305) 372-1175 (office). *E-mail:* bfort@arquitectonica.com (office). *Website:* www .arquitectonica.com (office).

FORTE, Sir Rocco, Kt, MA, FCA; British hotel industry executive; *Chairman and CEO, The Rocco Forte Collection;* b. 18 Jan. 1945; s. of Lord Forte; m. Aliai Ricci 1986; one s. two d.; ed Downside and Pembroke Coll., Oxford; Dir of Personnel, Trusthouse Forte 1973–78, Deputy Chief Exec. 1978–82, Jt Chief Exec. 1982–83; Chief Exec. Trusthouse Forte PLC 1983–92; Chair. Forte PLC 1992–96; Chair. and CEO Rocco Forte Collection 1996–; mem. Chairs' Cttee Savoy Group 1994–96; Trustee, London Symphony Orchestra; Prin. Patron Hospitality Action; fmr Vice-Pres. Commonwealth Games Council for England; Cavaliere di Gran Croce al Merito della Republica 2005. *Achievements include:* represented Britain within his age group at World Triathlon Championships 2005, 2006, 2007, 2009. *Leisure interests:* shooting, golf. *Address:* The Rocco Forte Collection, 70 Jermyn Street, London, SW1Y 6NY, England (office). *Telephone:* (20) 7321-2626 (office). *Fax:* (20) 7321-2424 (office). *E-mail:* cwilliams@roccofortehotels.com (office). *Website:* www.roccofortehotels.com (office).

FORTEY, Richard Alan, BA, PhD, DSc, FRS, FRSL; British palaeontologist and writer; *Research Associate, Natural History Museum;* b. 15 Feb. 1946, London; s. of Frank Allen Fortey and Margaret Fortey (née Wilshin); m. 1st Bridget Elizabeth Thomas (divorced); one s.; m. 2nd Jacqueline Francis 1977; one. s. two d.; ed Ealing Grammar School for Boys, King's Coll., Cambridge; Sr Scientific Officer, Dept of Paleontology, Natural History Museum, London 1973–80, Prin. Scientific Officer 1980–86, Individual Merit Researcher 1986–2002, 2003–06, Research Assoc. 2006–; Howley Visiting Prof., Memorial Univ. of Newfoundland, Canada 1977–78; Visiting Prof. of Palaeobiology, Univ. of Oxford 2000–; Collier Chair in Public Understanding of Science and Tech., Univ. of Bristol 2002–03; Prof., Nanjing Inst. of Geology and Paleontology 2010; mem. Geological Soc. of London 1972– (Pres. 2007), British Mycological Soc. 1980–; Hon. Fellow, BAAS 2008, Royal Soc. Biology 2016; Dr hc (St Andrews) 2007, (Open Univ.) 2007, (Birmingham) 2010, (Leicester) 2012; Natural World Book of the Year Award 1994, Lyell Medal, Geological Soc. of London 1996, Frink Medal, Zoological Soc. of London 2001, Lewis Thomas Prize, Rockefeller Univ. 2003, Linnean Medal for Zoology 2006, Michael Faraday Prize, Royal Soc. 2006, T.N. George Medal, Glasgow Geological Soc. 2007, Linnean Legacy Lecturer, Univ. of Arizona 2009, Lapworth Medal, Palaeontological Association 2014, Lapworth Medal, Paleontological Soc. of America 2016, Silver Medal, Zoological Soc. of London 2017. *Television:* Survivors 2012, Fossil Wonderlands 2014, Islands of Evolution 2016. *Publications include:* The Roderick Masters Book of Money Making Schemes (as Roderick Masters) 1981, Fossils: The Key to the Past 1982, The Hidden Landscape 1993, Life: An Unauthorised Biography 1997, Trilobite! 2000, The Earth: An Intimate History 2004, Dry Store Room No. 1: The Secret Life of the Natural History Museum 2008, Horseshoe Crabs and Velvet Worms: The Story of the Animals and Plants That Time Has Left Behind 2012, The Wood for the Trees 2016. *Leisure interests:* mycology, humorous writing, walking. *Address:* Department of Palaeontology, Natural History Museum, Cromwell Road, London, SW7 5BD, England (office). *Telephone:* (20) 7942-5493 (office). *Fax:* (20) 7942-5546 (office). *E-mail:* r.fortey@nhm.ac.uk (office). *Website:* www.nhm.ac.uk/palaeontology (office).

FORTIER, L. Yves, CC, PC, OQ, QC, BCL, LLD; Canadian lawyer, diplomatist and business executive; b. 11 Sept. 1935, Québec City; s. of François Fortier and Louise Fortier (née Turgeon); m. Cynthia Carol Eaton 1959; one s. two d.; ed Univ. of Montréal, McGill Univ., Univ. of Oxford, UK; called to Bar, Québec 1960; Chair. and Sr Partner, Ogilvy, Renault (law firm), Montréal; Pres. Jr Bar Asscn Montréal 1965–66, Jr Bar Section, Canadian Bar Asscn 1966–67; mem. Gen. Council, Bar of Québec 1966–67; Councillor, Bar of Montréal 1966–67; Amb. and Perm. Rep. to UN, New York 1988–91, Pres. UN Security Council 1989, Vice-Pres. UN Gen. Ass. 1990; Pres. London Court of Int. Arbitration 1998–2001; Chair. and Sr Partner, Ogilvy Renault LLP (then Norton Rose), Montréal 1992–2008, Chair. Emer. 2008–11; Chair. Hudson's Bay Co. 1997–2006; Chair. Alcan Inc., Montréal 2002–07; f. Cabinet Yves Fortier 2012; mem. Council, Canadian Section, 1st Comm. of Jurists 1967–87; mem. Canadian Bar Asscn (Pres. Québec br. 1975–76, Nat. Pres. 1982–83); Founding Dir Canadian Bar Asscn Law for the Future Fund; fmr mem. Bd of Dirs Royal Bank of Canada, Manulife, Northern Telecom Ltd, Rio Tinto Ltd, Alcan Inc., Westinghouse Inc., Trans-Canada Pipelines Ltd, Nova Chemicals Inc.; mem. Permanent Court of Arbitration, The Hague 1984–89; Pres. London Court of Int. Arbitration 1998–2001; Chair. World Bank Sanctions Bd 2012–15; Chair. EBRD Enforcement Cttee 2016–; mem. Security and Intelligence Review Cttee of Canada 2013; mem. Privy Council of Canada 2013; Fellow, American Coll. of Trial Lawyers (Regent 1992–96); Dir Canadian Inst. of Advanced Legal Studies, Canadian Law Inst. of the Pacific Rim 1986–88; mem. Int. Trade Advisory Council Canada; Adviser to UN Sec.-Gen. on territorial dispute between Gabon and Equatorial Guinea 2003; Gov. McGill Univ. 1970–85; Dir Canadian Asscn of Rhodes Scholars (Pres. 1975–77); Hon. mem. ABA; Dr hc (Université Laval) 2008; Walter S. Tarnopolsky Award 2008. *Leisure interests:* skiing, tennis, golf, reading. *Address:* Cabinet Yves Fortier, 1 place Ville Marie, Suite 2822 Montréal, PQ H3B 4R4 (office); 19 Rosemount Avenue, Westmount, PQ H3Y 3G6, Canada (home). *Telephone:* (514) 286-2011 (office). *Fax:* (514) 286-2019 (office). *E-mail:* yves.fortier@yfortier.ca (office). *Website:* www.yfortier.ca (office).

FORTIER, Hon. Michael M., PC; Canadian financier, lawyer and politician; *Vice-Chairman, RBC Capital Markets;* b. 10 Jan. 1962; m. Michelle Setlakwe; six c.; joined Ogilvy Renault law firm, Montréal 1985–99, managed office in London, UK 1992–96; joined Credit Suisse First Boston 1999, Man. Dir and Sr Adviser and headed Montréal office –2004; Man. Dir (Québec) TD Securities (subsidiary of TD Bank Financial Group) 2004–06; Pres. Progressive Conservative Party of Canada 1990s, cand. in leadership election 1998, cand. for party in gen. election 2000, mem. Conservative Party of Canada 2003–, Co-Chair. Stephen Harper's nat. leadership campaign 2004, Co-Chair. Conservative nat. elections campaign 2004, 2006; Minister of Public Works and Govt Services 2006–08, of Int. Trade 2008; mem. Senate from Rougemont, Québec 2006–08; Vice-Chair. RBC Capital Markets 2010–. *Address:* RBC Capital Markets, Bureau 300, 1 place Ville Marie, Montréal, PQ H3B 4R8, Canada (office). *Telephone:* (514) 878-7000 (office). *Website:* www .rbccm.com (office).

FORTIER, Suzanne, BSc, PhD; Canadian chemist, academic and university administrator; *Principal and Vice-Chancellor, McGill University;* b. St-Timothée, Québec; ed McGill Univ.; Postdoctoral Assoc., Medical Foundation of Buffalo, Inc. 1976–78, Research Scientist 1980–82; Research Assoc., Nat. Research Council of Canada 1978–79; Prof. of Chem. and of Computing and Information Science, Queen's Univ., Kingston, Ont. 1982–2013, Assoc. Dean of Grad. Studies and

Research, Vice-Prin. (Research) 1995–2000, Vice-Prin. (Academic) 2000–05; Pres. Natural Sciences and Eng Research Council of Canada, Ottawa 2006–13; Prin. and Vice-Chancellor, McGill Univ. 2013–; mem. Minister of Finance's Advisory Council on Econ. Growth 2016–, World Econ. Forum's Global Univ. Leaders Forum 2016–; fmr mem. Protein Eng Network of Centres of Excellence, Inst. for Robotics and Intelligent Systems, Communications and Information Tech. Ontario, Bd of Dirs Ontario Centres of Excellence Inc., Bd Govs Royal Mil. Coll. of Canada, Fed. Govt's Council of Science and Tech. Advisors; mem. Bd of Dirs Canada Foundation for Innovation, Strategic Cttee of Investissements d'Excellence Bordeaux, Steering Cttee of the Networks of Centres of Excellence, Ontario Task Force on Competitiveness, Productivity and Economic Econ.; Fellow, AAAS; Specially Elected Fellow, Royal Soc. of Canada 2015; Officier, Ordre nat. du Mérite; Hon. DLitt Thompson Rivers Univ., BC 2006; Entrance Scholarship and R.P.D. Graham Scholarship, McGill Univ., Clara Benson Award for distinguished contributions to chemistry by a woman 1997, Entrepreneurship Award, Communications and Information Tech. Ontario 1997, Queen's Univ. Distinguished Service Award 2005, Queen Elizabeth II Diamond Jubilee Medal 2012. *Publications:* more than 80 scientific publs on protein crystallography. *Address:* Office of the Principal and Vice-Chancellor, Room 506, James Administration Building, McGill University, 845 Sherbrooke Street West, Montréal, PQ H3A 0G4, Canada (office). *Telephone:* (514) 398-4180 (office). *Fax:* (514) 398-4768 (office). *E-mail:* suzanne.fortier@mcgill.ca (office). *Website:* www.mcgill.ca/principal (office).

FORTOV, Vladimir Yevgenyevich; Russian physicist; b. 23 Jan. 1946, Noginsk, Moscow Region; m.; one d.; ed Moscow Inst. of Physics and Tech.; researcher, Head of Lab., Inst. of Chemical Physics USSR (now Russian) Acad. of Sciences 1971–86; Head of Div., Inst. of High Temperature Physics, USSR Acad. of Sciences 1986–92; apptd Dir Inst. for High Energy Densities, Russian Acad. of Sciences 1992; Chair. Russian Foundation for Basic Research 1993–97; Deputy Chair., then Chair. State Cttee on (now Ministry of) Science and Tech. of Russian Fed. 1996–98; Corresp. mem. USSR (now Russian) Acad. of Sciences 1987, mem. 1992, Vice-Pres. 1996–2001, apptd Head, Div. for Energetics, Machinery, Mechanics and Control Systems, Russian Acad. of Sciences 2002, Pres. 2013–17; Chair. Tech. Cttee of Judges for the prize 'Novaya generatsiya' (New Generation) 2004–; mem. Advisory Academic Panel Skolkovo Foundation 2010–; mem. Presidium Russian Nat. Prize Russkie sozidateli (Russian Creators) 2005–; Corresp. mem. Int. Asscn on Physics and Tech. of High-Pressures; Fellow, US Nat. Acad. of Eng; mem. American Physics Soc., European Acad. of Arts and Sciences, Int. Acad. of Astronautics, Max Plank Soc., Royal Acad. of Eng of GB, Royal Acad. of Eng, Sweden; Order of Merit of the Fed. Repub. of Germany 2006, Order of Légion d'Honneur 2006, Order of Honour of Russian Fed. 2007, Order of Friendship of Russian Fed. 2010; State Award of Russian Fed., P. Bridgeman Prize for High Pressure Technology, Max Plank Award, A. Einstein Gold Medal UNESCO, Hannes Alfven Prize, EPS, Shock Compression Science Award, APS, Medal of the Pres. of Chechen Repub. for Personal Contrib. to Peace and Co-operation in the Caucasus 2004. *Publications:* numerous works on thermophysics of extremely high temperatures and pressures, physics of gas dynamics and physics of strong shock waves. *Leisure interests:* skiing, sailing. *Address:* c/o Presidium of the Russian Academy of Sciences, Leninski prospekt 32A, 119991 Moscow (office). *Telephone:* (495) 938-18-14 (Acad.) (office).

FORTUÑO BURSET, Luis Guillermo, BSFS, JD; American lawyer, politician and fmr state official; *Partner, Steptoe & Johnson LLP;* b. 31 Oct. 1960, San Juan, Puerto Rico; s. of Luis Fortuño Moscoso and Shirley Joyce Burset de Mari; m. Lucé Vela-Gutierrez 1984; two s. one d. (triplets); ed Colegio Marista, Guaynabo, Georgetown Univ., Univ. of Virginia Law School; Pres. Puerto Rico Statehood Students Asscn 1980–81; Exec. Dir Puerto Rico Tourist Co. and Pres. Hotel Devt Corpn 1993–94; Sec., Puerto Rico Dept of Econ. Devt and Commerce 1994–96; Pnr, Correa, Collazo, Herrero, Jiménez and Fortuño (law firm) 1996–2005; Resident Commr of Puerto Rico 2005–09; mem. US House of Reps for Puerto Rico 2005–09, Vice-Chair. Congressional Hispanic Conf. 2005–07, Chair. 2007–09; Gov. of the Commonwealth of Puerto Rico 2008–13; Partner, Steptoe & Johnson LLP 2013–; mem. Partido Nuevo Progresista (PNP—New Progressive Party, affiliated to the Republican Party), currently Pres.; Pres. Southern Governors Asscn 2011–12, Council of State Govts 2012; mem. Republican Nat. Cttee; Orden de Isabel la Católica, Grand Cross with Collar (Spain) 2009. *Address:* Steptoe & Johnson LLP, 1330 Connecticut Avenue, NW, Washington, DC 20036, USA. *Telephone:* (202) 429-8015. *Fax:* (202) 429-3902 (office). *E-mail:* lfortuno@steptoe.com (office). *Website:* www.steptoe.com (office).

FOSHEE, Douglas L., BBA MBA; American oil industry executive; *Chairman, President and CEO, Sallyport Investments, LLC;* b. 1960; ed Southwest Texas State Univ., Jesse E. Jones Grad. School, Rice Univ., Southwestern Methodist Univ.; began career in commercial banking; various finance and business venture positions at ARCO Int. Oil and Gas Co. –1993; joined Torch Energy Advisers Inc. 1993, held positions successively as Vice-Pres. Special Projects, Exec. Vice-Pres. Acquisitions and Financial Analysis, Pres., COO, CEO 1993–97; Pres., CEO and Chair. Nuevo Energy Co. 1997–2001; Exec. Vice-Pres. and Chief Financial Officer, Halliburton Co. 2001–03, Exec. Vice-Pres. and COO 2003; Pres., CEO and Dir El Paso Corpn 2003–12; currently Chair., Pres. and CEO, Sallyport Investments, LLC; mem. Bd of Dirs Cameron International Corpn, El Paso Pipeline Pnrs, LP, Goodwill Industries, Small Steps Nurturing Center; mem. Ind. Petroleum Asscn of America, Nat. Petroleum Council; mem. Council of Overseers, Jesse E. Jones Grad. School, Rice Univ.; Distinguished Alumni, Texas State Univ. 2008; Ellis Island Medal of Honor 2007. *Address:* Sallyport Investments LLC, 3743 Ingold Street, Houston, TX 77005, USA (office). *Telephone:* (713) 396-0687 (office).

FOSS, Per-Kristian; Norwegian politician; b. 19 July 1950, Oslo; m. Jan Erik Knarbakk 1952; ed Univ. of Oslo; journalist 1971–73; mem. Høyre (Conservative Party), Chair. Høyre Municipal Council 1973–77, Chair. Unge Høyre (Young Conservatives) 1973–77, Chair. Høyre Cttee on Party Programme 1981–85, Chair. Høyre Cttee on Cultural Objectives and Strategies 1983–85, Deputy Chair. Høyre Party Parl. Mems' Group 1993–2001, Leader of Høyre 2002; mem. Storting (Parl.) for Oslo 1977–2013, mem. Cttee on Energy and Industry 1981–89 (Second Vice-Chair. 1985–89), mem. Standing Cttee on Finance 1989–2001 (Chair. 1989–93, Vice-Chair. 1993–97), mem. Enlarged Foreign Affairs Cttee 1997–2001, Second Vice-Pres. 2009–; Minister of Finance 2001–2005; Auditor Gen. 2014–16; Ed. of Kontur (periodical) 1979–80; Consultant, Norges Rederforbund (Norwegian Shipowners' Asscn) 1980–81; mem. Lillehammer Olympic Organizing Cttee 1994; Commdr of the St Olav 2005.

FOSSE, Jon Olav, Cand. Philol; Norwegian writer, dramatist and poet; b. 29 Sept. 1959, Haugesund; ed Univ. of Bergen; teacher of creative writing, Acad. of Writing, Bergen 1987–93; professional writer 1993–; Hon. mem. Norwegian Actors' Soc., Det Norske Samlaget, Norwegian Dramatists' Soc.; Chevalier, Ordre nat. du Mérite 2003, Commdr, St Olavs Orden 2005; Dr. hc (Univ. of Bergen) 2015; Nynorsk Literature Prize 1988, Noregs Mållags Prize for Children's Books 1990, Andersson-Rysst Fondet 1992, Prize for Literature in New Norwegian 1993, 2003, Samlags Prize 1994, Ibsen Prize 1996, Sunnmoers Prize 1996, Melsom Prize 1997, Asshehoug Prize 1997, Dobloug Prize 1999, Gyldendal Prize 2000, Nordic Prize for Dramatists 2000, Nestroy Prize 2001, Scandinavian Nat. Theatre Prize 2002, Norwegian Council of Culture Prize of Honour 2003, Norwegian Theatre Prize of Honour (Hedda) 2003, UBU Prize for best foreign play, Italy 2004, Norwegian Prize for Literature of Honour (Brage) 2005, Anders Jahre Prize for Culture 2006, Nordic Prize, Swedish Acad. 2007, Deutscher Jugendliteraturpreis 2007, Bergen Prize for Artists 2009, Medal from Benedict XVI for participation in Meeting with the Artist in The Sistine Chapel 2009, Int. Ibsen Award 2010, given Grotten as hon. residence from Norwegian Govt 2011, European Prize for Literature 2014, Literature Prize, Nordic Council 2015, Willy Brandt Prize 2016, The City of Münster Int. Prize for Poetry 2017. *Plays include:* Og aldri skal vi skiljast 1994, Namnet 1995, Nokon kjem til å komme 1996, Barnet 1996, Mor og barn 1997, Sonen 1997, Natta syng sine songar 1997, Ein sommars dag 1999, Gitarmannen 1999, Draum om hausten 1999, Besoek 2000, Vinter 2000, Ettermiddag 2000, Vakkert 2001, Doedsvariasjonar 2002, Jenta i sofaen 2003, Suzannah 2004, Sa ka la, 2004, Varmt 2005, Svevn 2005, Rambuku 2006, Skuggar 2006, Eg er vinden 2007, Desse auga 2008, Jente i gul regnjakke 2009, Hav 2014, Tre librettoar 2015. *Publications include:* fiction: Raudt, svart 1983, Stengd gitar 1985, Naustet 1989, Flaskesamlaren 1991, Bly og vatn 1992, Melancholia I 1995, Melancholia II 1996; shorter prose: Blod. Steinen er Forteljing 1987, To forteljingar 1993, Prosa frå ein oppvekst. Kortprosa 1994, Eldre kortare prosa 1997, Morgon og kveld 2000, Det er Ales 2004, Andvake 2007, Kortare prosa 2011, Olvas draumar 2012, Kveldsvævd 2014, Trilogien 2014, Levande stein. Kortare prosa og ei hymne 2015; poetry: Engel med vatn i augene 1986, Hundens bevegelsar 1990, Hund og engel 1992, Nye dikt 1997, Ange i vind 2003, Songar 2009, Stein til stein 2013; essays: Frå telling via showing til writing 1989, Gnostiske essays 1999, Når ein engel går gjennom scenen og andre 2014, Poesiar. Etter Henrik Wergeland 2016; also books for children. *Address:* c/o Winje Agency, Skiensgate 12, 3912 Porsgrunn, Norway (office); Colombine Teaterförlag, Gaffelgränd 1A, 111 30 Stockholm, Sweden (office).

FOSTER, Brendan, CBE, MBE, BSc; British sports commentator, business executive and fmr athlete; *Chairman, Nova International;* b. 12 Jan. 1948, Hebburn, Co. Durham, England; s. of Francis Foster and Margaret Foster; m. Susan Margaret Foster 1972; one s. one d.; ed Univ. of Sussex, Carnegie Coll., Leeds; competed at Olympic Games, Munich 1972, 5th in 1,500m; Montreal 1976, won bronze medal in 10,000m, 5th in 5,000m, Moscow 1980, 11th in 10,000m; competed in Commonwealth Games, Edinburgh 1970, won bronze medal at 1,500m; Christchurch 1974, won silver medal at 5,000m; Edmonton 1978, won gold medal at 10,000m and bronze medal 5,000m; European Champion at 5,000m 1974 and bronze medallist at 1,500m 1971; has held world record at 3,000m and 2 miles, European record at 10,000m, Olympic record at 5,000m; Dir Recreation, Gateshead 1982; Man. Dir Nike International 1982–86, Vice-Pres. Marketing (Worldwide) and Vice-Pres. (Europe) 1986–87; Chair. Nova International; BBC TV commentator 1980–; Hon. Fellow, Sunderland Polytechnic; Hon. MEd (Newcastle), Hon. DLitt (Sussex) 1982, Hon. DArts (Leeds Metropolitan), Hon. DCL (Northumbria); BBC Sports Personality of the Year 1974. *Publications include:* Brendan Foster (with Cliff Temple) 1978, Olympic Heroes 1896–1984 1984. *Leisure interests:* sport and running every day. *Address:* Nova International, Newcastle House, Albany Court, Monarch Road, Newcastle upon Tyne, NE4 7YB, England (home). *Telephone:* (191) 272-7033 (home). *Website:* www.greatrun.org.

FOSTER, Brian, OBE, BSc, MA, DPhil, CPhys, FInstP, FRS; British physicist and academic; *Alexander von Humboldt Professor, University of Hamburg;* b. 4 Jan. 1954, Crook, Co. Durham; s. of John Foster and Annie Foster; m. Sabine Margot Foster 1983; two s.; ed Wolsingham Secondary School, Co. Durham, Queen Elizabeth Coll., Univ. of London, Univ. of Oxford; Research Assoc., Rutherford Appleton Lab., Chilton, Oxon. 1978–82; Research Assoc., Dept of Physics, Imperial Coll., London 1982–84; Lecturer, Dept of Physics, Univ. of Bristol 1984–92, Reader 1992–96, Particle Physics and Astronomy Research Council (PPARC) Advanced Fellow 1991–97, Head of Particle Physics Group 1992–2003, Lecturer Fellow 1999–2000, Prof. of Experimental Physics 1996–2003, Prof. Emer. 2003–; Prof. of Experimental Physics, Univ. of Oxford 2003–16, Donald. H. Perkins Prof. of Experimental Physics 2016–, Head of Particle Physics Dept 2004–11, Professorial Fellow, Balliol Coll. 2003–; Alexander von Humboldt Prof., Univ. of Hamburg and Leading Sr Scientist, Deutsches Elektronen Synchrotron (DESY), Hamburg, Germany 2011–; European Dir Global Design Effort for Int. Linear Collider 2005–13; European Dir Linear Collider Collaboration 2013–16; guest lecturer at numerous int. univs; mem. Scientific Council, DESY 1999–2010 (Group Leader, Bristol group on TASSO 1984–90, Group Leader, Bristol group on ZEUS experiment 1985–2003); Chair. Inst. of Physics Nuclear and Particle Physics Div. 1989–93; mem. CERN Large Hadron Collider Cttee, Geneva, Switzerland 1996–99; Acting Dir John Adams Inst. for Accelerator Science 2004–05; mem. numerous expert cttees including European Cttee for Future Accelerators 1992–96 (Chair. 2002–05, ex officio CERN Council, CERN Scientific Policy Cttee), PPARC Council 2001–06 and numerous PPARC cttees including Science Cttee, Inst. of Physics Council 2009–13; mem. Council, Royal Soc. 2016–, Public Engagement Cttee 2016–18, Vice-Pres. 2018–; Admin. Dir and Chair. of Trustees, Oxford May Music; Consultant Ed. for particle physics, Inst. of Physics Publishing 1991–2005, Taylor & Francis Ltd 2005–15; Editor-in-Chief Oxford Research Encyclopedia of Physics, Oxford Univ. Press 2017–; mem. BAAS (now the British Science Asscn) 1993; Special European Physical Soc. Prize in Particle Physics 1995, Alexander von Humboldt Foundation Research Prize 1999, Max Born Medal and Prize 2003, Alexander von Humboldt Professorship 2010. *Radio:* Einstein's Fiddle (BBC Radio 4) 2008, Private Passions (BBC Radio 3) 2008, Essential Classics (BBC Radio 3)

2012. *Publications include:* Topics in High Energy Physics 1988, 40 Years of Particle Physics 1988, Electron-Positron Annihilation Physics 1990. *Leisure interests:* sport, history and politics, music (violin), collecting first edns of books. *Address:* Gruppe FLA, Room 01E/O2.518, DESY, Notkestrasse 85, 22607 Hamburg, Germany (office); 2 Hillview Cottage, Blackford, nr Wedmore, Somerset, BS28 4NL, England (home). *Telephone:* (40) 8998-3201 (office); (1934) 712699 (home). *Fax:* (40) 8998-3282 (Hamburg) (office); (1865) 273417 (Oxford) (office). *E-mail:* brian.foster@physics.ox.ac.uk (office). *Website:* www.physics.ox.ac.uk/users/foster (office).

FOSTER, Sir Christopher David, Kt, MA; British economist; b. 30 Oct. 1930, London; s. of George Cecil Foster and Phyllis Joan Foster (née Mappin); m. Kay Sheridan Bullock 1958; two s. three d.; ed Merchant Taylors School and King's Coll., Cambridge; Fellow and Tutor, Jesus Coll., Cambridge 1964–66; Dir-Gen. of Econ. Planning, Ministry of Transport 1966–70; Head, Unit for Research in Urban Econs, LSE 1970–76, Prof. of Urban Studies and Econs 1976–78, Visiting Prof. 1978–86; Gov. Centre for Environmental Studies 1967–70, Dir 1976–78; Visiting Prof. of Econs MIT 1970; Head of Econ. and Public Policy Div. Coopers & Lybrand (fmrly Coopers & Lybrand Assocs, then Coopers & Lybrand Deloitte) 1978–84, Public Sector Practice Leader and Econ. Adviser 1984–86, Dir and Head Econs Practice Div. 1988–, Partner 1988–94, mem. Man. Cttee 1988–90, Adviser to Chair. 1990–92, 1994–99; Special Adviser to Sec. of Transport on Privatization of British Rail 1992–94; mem. Bd Railtrack 1994–2000; Commercial Adviser to Bd of British Telecommunications PLC 1986–88; Chair. RAC (Royal Automobile Club) Foundation 1999–2003; Hon. Fellow, Jesus Coll., Cambridge 1992. *Publications include:* The Transport Problem 1963, Politics, Finance and the Role of Economics: The Control of Public Enterprise (jtly) 1972, Local Government Finance 1980, Privatization, Public Ownership and the Regulation of Natural Monopoly 1992, The State Under Stress 1996, British Government in Crisis 2005; papers in various econ. and other journals. *Leisure interests:* theatre, reading. *Address:* 6 Holland Park Avenue, London, W11 3QU, England. *E-mail:* cd@foster46.fsnet.co.uk.

FOSTER, David Manning, BSc, PhD; Australian writer; b. 15 May 1944, Katoomba, NSW; m. 1st Robin Bowers 1964; one s. two d.; m. 2nd Gerda Busch 1975; one s. two d.; ed Univ. of Sydney, Australian Nat. Univ., Univ. of Pennsylvania, USA; professional fiction writer 1973–; NSW Premier's Fellowship 1986, Keating Fellowship 1991–94, James Joyce Foundation Award 1996, Patrick White Award 2010. *Publications include:* The Pure Land (The Age Award 1974) 1974, The Empathy Experiment 1977, Moonlite (Australian Nat. Book Council Award 1981) 1981, Plumbum 1983, Dog Rock: A Postal Pastoral 1985, The Adventures of Christian Rosy Cross 1986, Testostero 1987, The Pale Blue Crochet Coathanger Cover 1988, Mates of Mars 1991, The Glade Within the Grove (Miles Franklin Award 1997) 1996, In the New Country (Courier Mail Award 1999) 1999, The Land Where Stories End 2001, Sons of the Rumour 2009, Man of Letters 2012; poetry: The Fleeing Atalanta 1975, The Ballad of Erinungarah 1997, Sunset on Santorini 2012. *Leisure interests:* gardening, bush walking. *Address:* PO Box 57, Bundanoon, NSW 2578, Australia (office).

FOSTER, Ian T., BSc PhD; American computer scientist and academic; *Arthur Holly Compton Distinguished Service Professor of Computer Science, University of Chicago;* Distinguished Fellow and Assoc. Div. Dir, Math. and Computer Science Div., Argonne Nat. Lab., Head of Distributed Systems Lab.; Arthur Holly Compton Distinguished Service Prof. of Computer Science, Univ. of Chicago 2004–; Dir Computation Inst. (jt project between Univ. of Chicago and Argonne Nat. Lab.) 2006–16, Argonne Distinguished Fellow 2006–, Dir Data Science and Learning Div., Argonne Nat. Lab. 2017–; co-f. Globus Project 1995; open source strategist, Open Grid Forum and Globus Alliance; co-f. Univa Corpn, Elmhurst, Ill. 2004 (merged with United Devices to form Univa UD 2007); mem. Advisory Bd for IOCOM Communications; Fellow, AAAS 2003, British Computer Soc., Asscn for Computing Machinery; Lovelace Medal, British Computer Soc., Gordon Bell Prize for high-performance computing 2001, Tsutomu Kanai Award, IEEE 2011, High Performance Parallel and Distributed Computing Achievement Award 2012. *Achievements include:* called "the father of the Grid"; research resulted in devt of techniques, tools and algorithms for high-performance distributed computing and parallel computing; led research and devt of software for I-WAY wide-area distributed computing experiment across N America 1995. *Publications:* numerous influential documents on Grid architecture and principles. *Address:* Department of Computer Science, University of Chicago, 1100 E 58th Street, Ryerson Physical Laboratory, Chicago, IL 60637 (office); Argonne National Laboratory, 9700 South Cass Avenue, Building 221-D156, Argonne, IL 60439, USA (office). *Telephone:* (773) 702-6614 (Chicago) (office); (630) 252-4619 (Argonne) (office). *Fax:* (773) 702-8487 (Chicago) (office). *E-mail:* foster@cs.uchicago.edu (office); foster@mcs.anl.gov (office). *Website:* www-fp.mcs.anl.gov/~foster (office); ianfoster.typepad.com; www.cs.uchicago.edu/directory/ian-foster (office).

FOSTER, Jodie (Alicia Christian), BA; American actress, film director and producer; b. 19 Nov. 1962, Los Angeles; d. of Lucius Foster and Evelyn Foster (née Almond); Pnr Cydney Bernard 1993–2008; two s.; m. Alexandra Hedison 2014; ed Yale Univ.; acting début in TV programme Mayberry R.F.D. 1968; owner and Chair. EGG Pictures Production Co. 1990–; Hon. DFA (Yale) 1997; Cecil B DeMille Award, Golden Globe Awards, Hollywood Foreign Press Association 2012. *Films include:* Napoleon and Samantha 1972, Kansas City Bomber 1972, One Little Indian 1973, Tom Sawyer 1973, Alice Doesn't Live Here Any More 1975, Taxi Driver 1976, Echoes of a Summer 1976, Bugsy Malone 1976, Freaky Friday 1976, The Little Girl Who Lives Down the Lane 1977, Candleshoe 1977, Foxes 1980, Carny 1980, Hotel New Hampshire 1984, The Blood of Others 1984, Siesta 1986, Five Corners 1986, The Accused (Acad. Award for Best Actress 1989) 1988, Stealing Home 1988, Catchfire 1990, The Silence of the Lambs (Acad. Award for Best Actress 1992) 1990, Little Man Tate (also dir) 1991, Shadows and Fog 1992, Sommersby 1993, Maverick 1994, Nell 1994, Home for the Holidays (dir, co-producer only) 1996, Contact 1997, The Baby Dance (exec. producer only) 1997, Waking the Dead (exec. producer only) 1998, Anna and the King 1999, Panic Room 2001, The Dangerous Lives of Altar Boys (also producer) 2002, Un long dimanche de fiançailles 2004, Flightplan 2005, Inside Man 2006, The Brave One (also producer) 2007, Nim's Island 2008, The Beaver (also dir) 2010, Carnage 2011, Elysium 2013, Money Monster (dir) 2016. *Address:* EGG Pictures Production Co., Jerry Lewis Annex, 5555 Melrose Avenue, Los Angeles, CA 90038-3112, USA.

FOSTER, Kent B., BS, MS MBA; American computer distribution industry executive (retd); b. 1944; ed North Carolina State Univ., Univ. of South Carolina; worked 29 years with GTE Corpn, becoming Dir 1992–99, Vice-Chair. 1993–99, Pres. 1995–99; CEO and Pres. Ingram Micro Inc. 2000–05, Chair. 2000–05, Chair. 2005–07 (retd); mem. Bd of Dirs Campbell Soup Co. Inc., J. C. Penney Co. Inc., New York Life Insurance Co.; mem. Dallas Opera Exec. Bd; mem. Bd of Govs, Dallas Symphony Asscn; Personal Trustee, GTE Foundation; Distinguished Eng Alumnus Award, North Carolina State Univ. 1993.

FOSTER, Lawrence Thomas; American conductor; b. 23 Oct. 1941, Los Angeles, Calif.; m. Angela Foster 1972; one d.; ed studied with Fritz Zweig and Karl Böhm and at Bayreuth Festival and Tanglewood Master Classes; Music Dir, Young Musicians Foundation, Los Angeles 1960–64; Conductor, San Francisco Ballet 1960–64; Asst Conductor, LA Philharmonic Orchestra 1965–68; Chief Guest Conductor, Royal Philharmonic Orchestra, London 1969–74; Music Dir, Houston Symphony Orchestra 1971–78; Music Dir, Orchestre Philharmonique, Monte Carlo 1978–96; Music Dir, Duisburg Orchestra, FRG 1982–86; Music Dir, Chamber Orchestra of Lausanne 1985; conductor, Jerusalem Symphony Orchestra 1990; Music Dir, Aspen Music Festival and School 1990–96; Music Dir, Orquestra Ciutat de Barcelona 1995–2002, Prin. Guest Conductor 2002–; Artistic Dir, Georg Enescu Festival 1998–2001; Music Dir, Gulbenkian Orchestra, Lisbon 2002–13, Orchestre et Opéra Nat. de Montpellier 2009–12, Opéra de Marseille and Orchestre Philharmonique de Marseille 2013–; Artistic Dir and Chief Conductor, Polish Nat. Radio Symphony Orchestra (2019–); Pres.'s decoration for services to Romanian music 2003; Koussevitsky Memorial Conducting Prize, Tanglewood 1966, Orfée d'Or, Académie National du Disque Lyrique (for his recording of Vincent D'Indy's L'Etranger with Opera et Orchestre National de Montpellier Languedoc Roussillon) 2013. *Film appearance:* Belle toujours 2006. *Leisure interests:* reading history and biographies, films. *Address:* c/o HarrisonParrott, The Ark, 201 Talgarth Road, London, W6 8BJ, England (office). *Telephone:* (20) 3725-9131 (office). *E-mail:* linda.marks@harrisonparrott.co.uk (office). *Website:* www.harrisonparrott.com/artists/lawrence-foster (office).

FOSTER, Maria das Graças Silva, MSc, MBA; Brazilian chemist and oil company executive; b. (Maria das Graças), 26 Aug. 1953, Morro do Adeus, Rio de Janeiro; m. Colin Foster; two c.; ed Universidade Federal Fluminense, Universidade Federal do Rio de Janeiro, Fundação Getulio Vargas; joined Petróleo Brasileiro SA (Petrobras) as trainee 1978, Exec. Dir of Natural Gas and Energy 2007–12, Pres. and CEO 2012–15 (resgnd); Sec. of Oil, Natural Gas and Renewable Fuels, Ministry of Mines and Energy 2003–05; CEO Petroquisa-Petrobras Quimica SA 2005–06; CEO and Chief Financial Officer, Petrobras Distribuidora SA 2006–07; Chair. of Bd Transportadora Associada de Gas SA; mem. Bd of Dirs, Transpetro-Petrobras Transporte SA, Petrobras Biocombustivel SA, Braskem SA; Commdr, Rio Branco Order, Ministry of External Affairs 2007, Kt Commdr, Admiralty Order of Merit 2011, Inconfidência Medal, State of Minas Gerais 2012; named Executive of the Year by Inst. of Brazilian Finance Execs 2008, Tiradentes Medal, Legis. Ass. of State of Rio de Janeiro 2009, voted the best CEO in Latin America in Institutional Investor magazine's oil, gas and petrochemical industry ranking 2013, State of Minas Gerais Inconfidência Medal 2012. *Address:* c/o Petrobras Brasil, Av. Republica do Chile #65, Centro, Rio de Janeiro, Brazil.

FOSTER, Robert Fitzroy (Roy), FBA; Irish historian, writer and academic; b. 16 Jan. 1949, Waterford; s. of Frederick Ernest Foster and Elizabeth Fitzroy; m. Aisling O'Conor Donelan; one s. one d.; ed Trinity Coll. Dublin; Prof. of Modern British History, Birkbeck Coll., London 1989–91; Carroll Prof. of Irish History and Fellow, Hertford Coll., Oxford 1991–2016; visiting fellowships include St. Anthony's Coll., Oxford, Inst. for Advanced Study, Princeton, New Jersey, Princeton Univ.; Parnell Fellow, Magdalene Coll., Cambridge 2015–16; Hon. Fellow, Birkbeck Coll., Univ. of London 2005; Hon. DLitt (Aberdeen) 1997, (Queen's, Belfast) 1998, (Trinity Coll. Dublin) 2003, (Nat. Univ. of Ireland) 2004; Dr hc (Queen's Univ., Kingston, Ont.); James Joyce Award, Nat. Univ. of Ireland 2011, British Acad. Medal 2015. *Publications include:* biographies of Charles Stewart Parnell 1976 and Lord Randolph Churchill 1981, Modern Ireland 1600–1972 1988, The Oxford Illustrated History of Ireland 1989, Paddy and Mr Punch 1997, W. B. Yeats: A Life, Vol. I: The Apprentice Mage 1865–1914 2001, The Irish Story: Telling Tales and Making it Up in Ireland (Christian Gauss Award from Phi Beta Kappa 2003) 2001, W. B. Yeats: A Life, Vol. II: The Arch-Poet 1915–1939 2003, Conquering England: the Irish in Victorian London (with Fintan Cullen) 2005, Luck and the Irish 2007, Words Alone: Yeats and His Inheritances 2011, Vivid Faces: The Revolutionary Generation in Ireland, 1890–1923 2014. *Address:* Hertford College, Catte Street, Oxford, OX1 3BW, England (office). *Telephone:* (1865) 279400 (office). *E-mail:* roy.foster@hertford.ox.ac.uk (office). *Website:* www.hertford.ox.ac.uk (office).

FOSTER OF THAMES BANK, Baron (Life Peer), cr. 1999 of Reddish in the County of Greater Manchester; **Norman Robert Foster,** Kt, OM, MArch, RA, RIBA; British architect; *Chairman and Founder, Foster + Partners;* b. 1 June 1935, Manchester; s. of Robert Foster and Lilian Foster; m. 3rd Elena Ochoa 1996; ed Manchester Univ. School of Architecture and City Planning, Yale Univ. School of Architecture; Urban Renewal and City Planning Consultants work 1962–63; pvt. practice, as Team 4 Architects (with Wendy Cheesman, Georgie Wolton, Lord Rogers of Riverside) London 1963–67, Foster Associates (now Foster + Partners), offices Berlin, Singapore 1967–, Chair. Foster + Partners 1967–; collaboration with Buckminster Fuller 1968–83; Consultant Architect to Univ. of E Anglia 1978–87; fmr External Examiner RIBA Visiting Bd of Educ.; fmr mem. Architectural Asscn Council (Vice-Pres. 1974); fmr teacher Univ. of Pa, Architectural Asscn, London, London Polytechnic, Bath Acad. of Arts; FCSD 1975; IBM Fellow, Aspen Design Conf. 1980; Council mem. RCA 1981–; mem. Int. Acad. of Architecture (IAA), European Acad. of Sciences and Arts, American Acad. of Arts and Sciences; mem. Order of French Architects, Akad. der Kunst, Royal Acad. of Fine Arts, Sweden; Hon. FAIA 1980, Royal West of England Academician; Hon. Fellow Royal Acad., Inst. of Structural Engineers, Royal Coll. of Eng, Kent Inst. of Art and Design, Hon. mem. Bund Deutscher Architekten (BDA), Royal Designer for Industry (RDI), Assoc. Acad. Royale de Belgique; Hon. LittD (Univ. of E Anglia) 1980, Hon. DSc (Bath) 1986, (Humberside) 1992, (Valencia) 1992, (Manchester) 1993, Dr hc (Royal Coll. of Art) 1991, (Tech. Univ. Eindhoven) 1996, Hon. DLitt. (Oxford) 1996, (London) 1997; numerous awards including Architectural Design Projects Awards

1964, 1965, 1966, 1969, Financial Times Industrial Architecture Awards 1967, 1974, 1984, RIBA Awards 1969, 1972, 1977, 1978, 1992, 1993, 1997, 1998, 1999; RSA Business and Industry Award 1976, 1991, Int. Design Awards (Brussels) 1976, 1980, R. S. Reynolds Int. Memorial Awards (USA) 1976, 1979, 1986, Structural Steel Awards 1972, 1978, 1984, 1986, 1992, 1999, 2000, Ambrose Congreve Award 1980, Royal Gold Medal for Architecture 1983, Civic Trust Award 1984, 1992, 1995, 1999, 2000, Constructa-European Award Program for Industrial Architecture 1986, Premio Compasso d'Oro Award 1987, Japan Design Foundation Award 1987, PA Innovations Award 1988, Annual Interiors Award (USA) 1988, 1992, 1993, 1994, Kunstpreis Award, Berlin 1989, British Construction Industry (BCI) Award 1989, 1991, 1992, 1993, 1997, 1998, Mies van der Rohe Award, Barcelona 1991, Gold Medal, Acad. Française 1991, Concrete Soc. Award 1992, 1993, 1999, American Inst. of Architects (AIA) Gold Medal 1994, Queen's Award for Export Achievement 1995, AIA Award 1995, 1997, 'Mipim' Man of the Year 1996, 'Building' Construction Personality of the Year 1996, Silver Medal of Chartered Soc. of Designers 1997, Pritzker Prize for Architecture 1999, Visual Arts Award 2000, Praemium Imperiale 2002, British-German Asscn Medal of Honour for Services to Anglo-German Relations 2006, China Friendship Award from Chinese State Admin of Foreign Experts Affairs 2008, Premio Príncipe de Asturias, Spain 2009, American Prize for Design 2018; German Federal Order of Merit 1999, Officier, Ordre des Arts et des Lettres (France), Order of N Rhine-Westphalia. *Major works include:* Pilot Head Office for IBM, Hampshire 1970, Tech. Park for IBM, Greenford 1975, Willis, Faber and Dumas, Ipswich 1975, Sainsbury Centre for Visual Arts, Norwich 1977, Renault Centre UK 1983, Hong Kong Bank HQ 1986, Third London Airport Terminal Stansted 1991, Century Tower Tokyo 1991, Barcelona Telecommunications Tower 1992, Sackler Galleries, Royal Acad. 1991, Cranfield Univ. Library 1992, Arts Centre, Nîmes 1993, Lycée, Fréjus 1993, Microelectronics Park, Duisburg 1993, Bilbao Metro System 1995, Univ. of Cambridge Faculty of Law 1996, American Air Museum, Duxford 1997, Commerzbank HQ Frankfurt 1997, Chek Lap Kok Airport, Hong Kong 1998, new German Parl. (Reichstag), Berlin 1999, Great Court, British Museum 2000, Al Faisaliah Complex, Riyadh 2000, Research Facility, Stanford Univ. Calif. 2000, Greater London Authority Bldg, London, Millennium Bridge, London, Swiss Re Tower (RIBA Stirling Prize 2004) 2002–03, Wembley Stadium, London 2003–07, Torre Caja Madrid 2004–08, Millau Viaduct, France 2005, Supreme Court, Singapore 2005, Petronas Univ. Campus, Malaysia, Hearst Headquarters tower, New York 2006, Khan Shatyr Entertainment Center, Astana, Kazakhstan 2006–10, Museum of Fine Arts, Boston, Opera House, Dallas, Smithsonian Inst. Courtyard, Washington, DC 2007, The Bow, Calgary, Canada 2007–10, SSE Hydro, Glasgow 2005–13, Dolder Grand Hotel, Zürich 2008, Beijing Int. Airport Terminal 3, China 2008, Ombrelle, Old Port, Marseille 2013, Tower 2 of planned reconstruction of World Trade Center, New York City (under construction); work exhibited in Moscow, Antwerp, Barcelona, Berlin, Bilbao, Bordeaux, London, Lyon, Madrid, Milan, Munich, New York, Paris, Tokyo, Valencia, Venice, and Zürich; work in perm. collection of Museum of Modern Art, New York and Centre Georges Pompidou, Paris. *Publications include:* Norman Foster: Buildings and Projects Vols 1, 2, 3, 4, On Foster ... Foster On 2000 and numerous contribs to the architectural and tech. press. *Leisure interests:* flying, skiing, running. *Address:* Foster + Partners, Riverside Three, 22 Hester Road, London, SW11 4AN, England (home). *Telephone:* (20) 7738-0455 (home). *Fax:* (20) 7738-1107 (home). *E-mail:* info@fosterandpartners.com (office). *Website:* www.fosterandpartners.com (office).

FOTIOU, Fotis, BBA; Cypriot accountant and politician; b. 1960, Larnaca; m. Maro Arestis; three s.; ed American Acad., Larnaca, Eastern Michigan Univ., USA; began career as chartered accountant, auditor and business consultant, worked for several int. auditing firms including PriceWaterhouseCoopers and Deloitte Haskins & Sells, and for Inland Revenue Dept of Ministry of Finance; Founder and Man. Partner, PKP Consultants; Minister of Agric., Natural Resources and Environment 2006–08, Minister of Defence 2013–14; mem. Dimokratiko Komma (DIKO—Democratic Party), Spokesman 2008–13; mem. Cyprus Inst. of Certified Accountants, Inst. of Financial Accountants; Dir Electricity Authority of Cyprus 1993–99, Cyprus Tourism Org. 2000–03 (Chair. 2003); mem. Chamber of Commerce and Industry of Larnaca; fmr Vice-Pres. and Sec. to Bd AEK Larnaca (football club).

FOTTRELL, Patrick, BSc, MSc, PhD, DSc, MRIA; Irish biochemist, academic, business executive and fmr university administrator; *Chairman, Westgate Biological Ltd;* b. 26 Sept. 1933, Youghal, Co. Cork; s. of Matthew Fottrell and Mary Fottrell (née O'Sullivan); m. Esther Kennedy 1963; two s. two d.; ed Christian Brothers School, Youghal and North Mon Schools, Univ. Coll., Cork, Univ. of Glasgow, UK, Univ. Coll., Galway; Sr Research Officer, Agric. Inst., Johnstown Castle, Wexford 1963–65; Lecturer, later Assoc. Prof., Prof. of Biochemistry, Univ. Coll., Galway 1965, Pres. Univ. Coll., Galway 1996–2000; currently Chair. Westgate Biological Ltd, Science Foundation Ireland 2003–12; Visiting Prof., Harvard Univ., USA 1972, 1982; fmr Chair. Dublin Inst. of Tech.; fmr Chair. Irish Council of Bioethics; fmr Vice-Pres. Royal Irish Acad.; Beit Memorial Fellow; EEC Science Writers Award, Conway Medal, Royal Acad. of Medicine (Ireland). *Publications include:* Perspectives on Coeliac Disease (co-author); more than 100 scientific publs in int. journals on biochemistry. *Leisure interests:* walking, music, soccer. *Address:* Westgate Biological Ltd, 56, Sir Rogerson's Quay, Dublin 2 (office); Bunowen, Taylorshill, Galway, Ireland (home). *Telephone:* (23) 54944 (office); (91) 21022 (home). *Website:* www.westgate.ie (office).

FOTYGA, Anna; Polish politician; b. 12 Jan. 1957, Lębrok; m.; two c.; ed Univ. of Gdańsk; worked in Int. Dept, Nat. Election Comm., NSZZ Trade Union (Solidarity) 1981, Dir 1989–91; mem. Man. Bd, Modem Co. 1987–89; worked at Przekaz publishing house 1992–94; involved in World Bank projects, GPEC Gdańsk 1994–96, Consultant 1996; Vice-Chair. Supreme Supervisory Bd, Social Insurance Inst. (ZUS) 1998–2002; European Integration Adviser to Pres. of Office of Health Insurance Oversight 1999–2001; Int. Affairs Adviser to Prime Minister 2000; Dir Dept of Int. Affairs, Chancellery of the Prime Minister 2001; mem. City Council of Gdańsk 2002, Council Vice-Pres. (Deputy Mayor) responsible for Econ. Affairs 2002–04; mem. European Parl. 2004–05, coordinated Union for Europe of the Nations Group in Cttee on Foreign Affairs; Sec. of State, Ministry of Foreign Affairs 2005–06, Minister of Foreign Affairs 2006–07, Chair. Cttee on European Integration 2006–07, mem. Nat. Security Council 2006–10, Chief Office of the Pres. 2007–08; mem. Nat. Parl. 2011–14; Vice-Pres. Alliance of European Conservatives and Reformists 2012–; mem. European Parl. 2014–, Chair. Sub-Cttee on Security and Defence 2014–. *Address:* Prawo i Sprawiedliwość, ul. Nowogrodzka 84/86, 02-018 Warszawa, Poland (office). *Telephone:* (22) 6215035 (office). *Fax:* (22) 6216767 (office). *E-mail:* biuro@pis.org.pl (office). *Website:* www.pis.org.pl (office).

FOU, Ts'ong; British (b. Chinese) pianist; b. 10 March 1934, Shanghai; s. of Fu Lei; m. 1st Zamira Menuhin 1960 (divorced 1970); one s.; m. 2nd Hijong Hyun 1973 (divorced 1978); m. 3rd Patsy Toh 1987; one s.; ed studied in China with Mario Paci, Warsaw Conservatory with Zbigniew Drzewiecki; debut with Shanghai Municipal Orchestra, playing Beethoven's Emperor Concerto 1951; gave 500 concerts in E. Europe while studying in Poland 1953–58; moved to UK 1958, London debut 1959; solo appearances in Europe, Scandinavia, the Far East, Australia and New Zealand, North and South America; currently Visiting Prof., Int. Foundation for Pianists, Como, Italy and Shanghai Conservatory, China; mem. jury, Chopin Competition 1985, 2010; Dr hc (Hong Kong Univ.); Third Prize, Bucharest Piano Competition 1953, Int. Chopin Competition, Warsaw 1955. *Solo piano CDs:* Bach, Chopin, Debussy, Handel, Mozart, Scarlatti, Schubert and Schumann. *Piano concerto CDs:* Chopin and Mozart. *Leisure interests:* bridge, sport, oriental art. *Address:* 62 Aberdeen Park, London, N5 2BL, England (home). *Telephone:* (20) 7226-9589 (home). *Fax:* (20) 7704-8896 (home).

FOUDA, Yosri; Egyptian journalist; b. 1964; ed American Univ. in Cairo; taught mass communication and various media courses, Cairo Univ. 1986–92; producer for Arabic-language TV Service, BBC, London, UK –1996; reporter, Al Jazeera London Bureau, UK 1996–2009, Bureau Chief –2009 (resgnd), also presenter, Top Secret TV programme; Ed. and Presenter, Last Word TV programme, ONTV 2009–14; worked with Deutsche Welle 2016–18; Pan-Arab Cairo Radio and TV Production Festival Award 1998, AUC's Outstanding Professional Performance Award 2000. *Publication:* Masterminds of Terror: The Truth Behind the Most Devastating Attack The World Has Ever Seen (with Nick Fielding) 2003, Capture or Kill: The Pursuit of the 9/11 Masterminds and the Killing of Osama bin Laden (with Nick Fielding) 2011, In Harm's Way: From the Stronghold of al-Qaida to the Heart of ISIL 2015, A Testimony of Hope on Egypt's Revolution 2016. *E-mail:* yosri21@talk21.com.

FOURCADE, Jean-Pierre; French politician; b. 18 Oct. 1929, Marmande; s. of Raymond Fourcade and Germaine Fourcade (née Raynal); m. Odile Mion 1958; one s. two d.; ed Coll. de Sorèze, Bordeaux Univ. Faculté de Droit, Inst. des Etudes politiques; student, Ecole Nat. d'Admin. 1952–54; Insp. des Finances 1954–73; Chargé de Mission to Sec. of State for Finance (later Minister of Finance) 1959–61, Conseiller technique 1962, Dir Adjoint du Cabinet 1964–66; Asst Head of Service, Inspection gén. des Finances 1962; Head of Trade Div., Directorate-Gen. of Internal Trade and Prices 1965, Dir-Gen. 1968–70; Asst Dir-Gen. Crédit industriel et commercial 1970, Dir-Gen. 1972–74, Admin. 1973–74; Admin., later Pres. and Dir-Gen. Soc. d'Epargne mobilière 1972–74; Admin. Banque transatlantique 1971–74, Soc. commerciale d'Affrètement et de Combustibles 1972–74; Minister of Econ. and Finance 1974–76, of Supply 1976–77, of Supply and Regional Devt 1977; Mayor of St-Cloud 1971–92, of Boulogne-Billancourt 1995–2007; Conseiller-Gén., canton of St-Cloud 1973–89; Conseiller Régional, Ile de France 1976, Vice-Pres. 1982–86, First Vice-Pres. 1986–95; Senator, Hauts de Seine 1977–2011; Pres. Comité des Finances Locales 1980–2004, Comm. des Affaires Sociales du Sénat 1983–99; Pres. Clubs Perspectives et Réalités 1975–82; mem. Union pour la Démocratie française (UDF) 1978–, Vice-Pres. 1978–86; mem. UMP Parl. group 2002–; mem. Admin. Council of RATP 1984–93, Epad 1985–95, SNCF 1993–98; Pres. Conseil de Surveillance de la Caisse Nat. des Allocations Familiales 2002–04; Vice-Pres. Asscn des Maires des Grandes Villes de France 2002–; Pres. Comm. Consultative d'Evaluation des Charges 2005–; Commdr, Ordre nat. du Mérite. *Publications:* Et si nous parlions de demain 1979, la Tentation social-démocrate 1985, Remèdes pour l'assurance maladie 1989, Mon expérience peut-elle éclairer l'avenir 2015. *Address:* 8 Parc de Béarn, 92210 St-Cloud, France (home). *E-mail:* jeanpierre.fourcade92@gmail.fr (home).

FOURNEYRON, Valérie; French physician and politician; b. (Valérie Absire), 4 Oct. 1959, Le Petit-Quevilly (Seine-Maritime); m.; four c.; sports doctor, CHU de Rouen 1981–89, Rouen ice-hockey team 1984–90; Regional Insp. for Youth and Sports 1989–90; Chief of Mission, Sport Medicine, Ministry for Youth and Sport 1989–91; Dir Regional Centre of Sports Medicine, Sotteville-le-Rouen and doctor to French volleyball team 1991–95; mem. interdepartmental group for sports medicine and doping and participant of working group on development of new legislation on doping 1998; doctor to Rouen professional basketball team 2002–05; Regional Councillor for Haute-Normandie 1998–2007; Gen. Councillor for Rouen 5 2004–08; Deputy (Parti socialiste) to Nat. Ass. for First Dist of Seine-Maritime 2007–12; Mayor of Rouen 2008–12; Minister for Sport, Youth, Popular Educ. and Community Life 2012–14; holds several other elected political offices.

FOURNIER, Guy, OC; Canadian author, screenwriter, producer and broadcasting executive; *Administrator, Canada Media Fund;* b. 23 July 1931, Waterloo, Québec; m. Maryse Beauregard; has written TV drama as well as films, has also produced dramatic films and documentaries; mem. Bd of Dirs and Chair. CBC 2005–06 (resgnd); currently TV commentator and columnist, Le Journal de Montréal; mem. Bd of Dirs and Admin., Canada Media Fund 2009–; Gold Medal Cuisine (Canada), five Gemini Awards, Gérard Philippe Medal (France). *Plays:* C'est maintenant qu'il faut boire, L'amour ou la vie, Soleil, maudit soleil, Je t'aime clés en main (adaptation). *Film screenplays include:* Y'a toujours moyen de moyenner! (There's Always a Way to Find a Way) 1973, La mer mi-sel 1974, Maria Chapdelaine 1983, Mon amie Max 1994, Histoire de famille 2006. *Television screenplays include:* Les enquêtes Jobidon (series) 1962, Ti-Jean caribou (series) 1963, Bidule de Tarmacadam (series) 1969, Jo Gaillard (series) 1975, Jamais deux sans toi (series) 1977, Rue de l'anse (series) 1983, Manon (series) 1985, L'or et le papier (series) 1990, Coeur à prendre 1994, Jamais deux sans toi (series) 1996, Les parfaits (series) 2001, Trudeau II: Maverick in the Making (mini-series) 2005. *Publications:* has published poems, humorous essays, novels, cookbooks and children's books. *Address:* 150 Berlioz, Verdun, PQ H3E 1K3, Canada (office); c/o Canadian Television Fund, 50 Wellington Street East, 4th Floor, Toronto, ON M5E 1C8, Canada. *Telephone:* (514) 762-1785 (office); (416) 214-4400. *E-mail:* gfmb@

videotron.ca (office); ctf@ctf-fct.ca. *Fax:* (416) 214-4420. *Website:* www.canadiantelevisionfund.ca.

FOURNIER, Jacques, LenD; French lawyer; b. 5 May 1929, Épinal; s. of Léon Fournier and Ida Rudmann; m. 1st Jacqueline Tazerout (deceased); three s.; m. 2nd Michèle Dubez 1980 (divorced); m. 3rd Noëlle Fréaud-Lenoir 1989 (divorced); ed Inst. for Political Studies, Paris and Nat. School of Admin; Civil Servant, French State Council 1953, Master of Petitions 1960, State Councillor 1978; Legal Adviser, Embassy in Morocco 1961–64; Head of Dept of Social Affairs, Gen. Planning Office 1969–72; Asst Sec.-Gen. to Pres. of France 1981–82; Sec.-Gen. of the Govt 1982–86; Pres. of Admin. Council of Gaz de France 1986–88; Pres. SNCF 1988–94, Centre européen des entreprises publiques 1988–94, Sceta 1989–94, Ciriec-France 1994; Chair. Carrefour 1992–98; fmr mem. Council of State, renewed mem. 1994–98; mem. Conseil supérieur de la magistrature 1998–2002; Chevalier, Ordre Nat. du Mérite; Commdr, Légion d'honneur. *Publications:* Politique de l'Education 1971, Traité du social, situations, luttes politiques, institutions 1976, Le Pouvoir du social 1979, Le travail gouvernemental 1987, le Train, l'Europe et le service public 1993. *Address:* 19 rue Presbourg, 75116 Paris, France (home). *E-mail:* jfrnier@easynet.fr (home).

FOWLER, Sir (Edward) Michael Coulson, Kt, MArch, FNZIA, ARIBA; New Zealand architect; b. 19 Dec. 1929, Marton; s. of William Coulson Fowler and Faith Agnes Fowler (née Netherclift); m. Barbara Hamilton Hall 1953 (died 2009); two s. one d.; ed Christ's Coll., Christchurch, Auckland Univ.; with Ove Arup & Pnrs, London 1954–55; Pnr, Gray Young, Morton Calder & Fowler, Wellington 1959; Sr Pnr, Calder, Fowler & Styles 1960–89; travelled abroad to study cen. banking systems' security methods; work includes Overseas Terminal, Wellington, Reserve Bank, Wellington, Dalmuir House, Wellington Club, office bldgs, factories, houses, churches; mem. Wellington City Council 1968–74; Chair. NZIA Educ. Cttee 1967–73; Mayor of Wellington 1974–83; Chair. Queen Elizabeth II Arts Council of New Zealand 1983–86; architectural consultant 1983–; regular dealer at gallery exhbns and sales of paintings; Hon. Pres. New Zealand Youth Hostel Asscn 1983–86; Award of Honour, New Zealand Inst. of Architects 1983, Alfred O. Glasse Award, New Zealand Planning Inst. 1984. *Publications:* Country Houses of New Zealand 1972, Wellington Sketches: Folios I, II 1973, The Architecture and Planning of Moscow 1980, Eating Houses in Wellington 1980, Wellington-Wellington 1981, Eating Houses of Canterbury 1982, Wellington Celebration 1983, The New Zealand House 1983, Buildings of New Zealanders 1984, Michael Fowler's University of Auckland 1993. *Leisure interests:* sketching, writing, history, politics. *Address:* 1 May Street, Wellington (office); 30 Goring Street, Thorndon, Wellington, New Zealand (home). *Telephone:* (4) 499-9991 (office); (4) 473-0888 (home). *Fax:* (4) 471-0017 (office). *E-mail:* michael.fowler@xtra.co.nz (home).

FOWLER, Baron (Life Peer), cr. 2001, of Sutton Coldfield in the Co. of West Midlands; **Rt Hon. (Peter) Norman,** Kt, PC, MA; British politician; *Speaker ofHouse of Lords;* b. 2 Feb. 1938; s. of N. F. Fowler and Katherine Fowler; m. 1st Linda Christmas 1968; m. 2nd Fiona Poole 1979; two d.; ed King Edward VI School, Chelmsford, Trinity Hall, Cambridge; Nat. Service Comm., Essex Regt 1956–58; joined The Times 1961, Special Corresp. 1962–66, Home Affairs Corresp. 1966–70; mem. Council, Bow Group 1967–69, Editorial Bd, Crossbow 1962–69; Vice-Chair. N Kensington Conservative Asscn 1967–68; Chair. E Midlands Area, Conservative Political Centre 1970–73; MP for Nottingham S 1970–74, for Sutton Coldfield 1974–2001, mem. Parl. Select Cttee on Race Relations and Immigration 1970–74; Jt Sec. Conservative Parl. Home Affairs Cttee 1971–72, Vice-Chair. 1974; Parl. Pvt. Sec. NI Office 1972–74; Opposition Spokesman on Home Affairs 1974–75; Chief Opposition Spokesman on Social Services 1975–76, on Transport 1976–79; Minister of Transport 1979–81, Sec. of State for Transport 1981, for Social Services 1981–87, for Employment 1987–90; Chair. Conservative Party 1992–94; Opposition Front Bench Spokesman on Environment, Transport and the Regions 1997–98, on Home Affairs 1998–99; mem. House of Lords 2001–, Chair. Select Cttee on Future of BBC 2005–06, Chair. Select Cttee on Communications 2005–10, Chair. Select Cttee on HIV/AIDS 2011–, Speaker 2016–; mem. Lloyds 1989–98; Chair. Nat. House Bldg Council 1992–98, Midland Ind. Newspapers 1992–98, Regional Ind. Media (the Yorkshire Post Group) 1998–2002, Numark Ltd 1998–2005, Aggregate Industries 2000–06; mem. Bd Group 4 Security 1990–93; Dir NFC 1990–97; Dir (non-exec.) Holcim Ltd (Switzerland) 2006–09, ABTA the Travel Business 2000–, Aggregate Industries 2010–14; Dr hc (City of Birmingham) 2011. *Publications:* The Cost of Crime 1973, The Right Track 1977, After the Riots: The Police in Europe 1979, Ministers Decide: A Memoir of the Thatcher Years 1991, A Political Suicide: The Conservatives' Voyage into the Wilderness 2008, AIDS: Don't Die of Prejudice 2014. *Address:* House of Lords, Westminster, London, SW1A 0PN, England (office). *Telephone:* (20) 7219-3525 (office). *E-mail:* fowlern@parliament.uk (office). *Website:* www.parliament.uk/biographies/lords/lord-fowler/315 (office).

FOX, Edward, OBE; British actor; b. 13 April 1937; s. of Robin Fox and Angela Fox; brother of James Fox (q.v.); m. 1st Tracy Pelissier 1958 (divorced 1961); one d.; m. 2nd Joanna David; one s. one d.; ed Ashfold School, Harrow School and Royal Acad. of Dramatic Art; actor since 1957; started in provincial repertory theatre 1958 and has since worked widely in films, stage plays and TV; recipient of several awards for TV performance as Edward VIII in Edward and Mrs Simpson 1978. *Stage appearances include:* Knuckle 1973, The Family Reunion 1979, Anyone for Denis 1981, Quartermaine's Terms 1981, Hamlet 1982, The Dance of Death 1983, Interpreters 1986, The Admirable Crichton 1988, Another Love Story 1990, The Philanthropist 1991, My Fair Lady, Father 1995, A Letter of Resignation 1997, The Chiltern Hundreds 1999, The Browning Version 2000, The Twelve Pound Look 2000, An Evening with Anthony Trollope 2010. *Films include:* The Go-Between 1971, The Day of the Jackal 1973, A Doll's House 1973, Galileo 1976, A Bridge Too Far (BAFTA Award for Best Supporting Actor) 1977, The Duellists 1977, The Cat and the Canary 1977, Force Ten from Navarone 1978, The Mirror Crack'd 1980, Gandhi 1982, Never Say Never Again 1983, Wild Geese 1984, The Bounty 1984, The Shooting Party 1989, Return from the River Kwai 1989, Prince of Thieves 1990, They Never Slept 1991, A Month by the Lake 1996, Prince Valiant 1997, Nicholas Nickleby 2002, The Republic of Love 2003, Stage Beauty 2004, Lassie 2005, Katherine of Alexandria 2014. *Television includes:* Circles of Deceit 1989, Daniel Deronda 2002, Oliver Twist 2007, Marple 2010, Midsomer Murders: Dark Secrets 2011, Lewis: Intelligent Design 2013, The Dresser 2015. *Leisure interest:* playing the piano.

FOX, James; Canadian diplomatist and government official; b. 1952; m. Nurys Estrella-Fox; joined Dept of Foreign Affairs 1976, assignments have included positions as Deputy Dir of Int. Relations and G8 Co-ordinator and postings to Zimbabwe, Cuba and Spain, Exec. Asst to Asst Under-Asst of External Affairs with special responsibilities for man. issues 1991–93, Amb. to Guatemala and El Salvador 1993–96, Dir APEC Div., Dept of Foreign Affairs 1996–98, Dir Japan Div. 1998–2002, Dir-Gen. for S and SE Asia and Sr Official for Canada's relations with ASEAN 2002–06, Asst Deputy Minister for Bilateral Relations, responsible for overseeing relations with all countries except USA, Mexico and Afghanistan 2006–08, Asst Deputy Minister for Europe, the Middle East and Maghreb 2008–09, Amb. to Italy (also accred to Albania and San Marino and as High Commr to Malta) 2008–13. *Address:* Foreign Affairs, Trade and Development Canada, Lester B. Pearson Building, 125 Sussex Drive, Ottawa, ON K1A 0G2, Canada (office). *Telephone:* (613) 944-4000 (office). *Fax:* (613) 996-9709 (office). *E-mail:* enqserv@international.gc.ca (office). *Website:* www.international.gc.ca (office).

FOX, James; British actor; b. 19 May 1939, London; s. of Robin Fox and Angela Fox (née Worthington); brother of Edward Fox (q.v.) and Robert Fox; m. Mary Elizabeth Fox 1973; four s. one d.; ed Ashfold Prep. School and Harrow School. *Films include:* Mrs Miniver 1952, The Servant 1963, King Rat 1965, Those Magnificent Men in Their Flying Machines 1965, Thoroughly Modern Millie 1966, Isadora 1967, Performance 1969, A Passage to India 1984, Runners 1984, Farewell to the King 1987, Finding Mawbee (video film as the Mighty Quinn) 1988, She's Been Away 1989, The Russia House 1990, Afraid of the Dark 1991, Patriot Games 1991, As You Like It 1992, The Remains of the Day 1993, Elgar's Tenth Muse 1995, Anna Karenina 1997, Mickey Blue Eyes 1998, Jinnah 1998, Up at the Villa 1998, The Golden Bowl 1999, Sexy Beast 2000, The Mystic Masseur 2001, The Prince and Me 2004, The Freediver 2004, Charlie and the Chocolate Factory 2005, Goodbye Mr Snuggles 2006, Mister Lonely 2006, Sherlock Holmes 2009, W.E. 2011, Cleanskin 2012, Effie Gray 2013, The Double 2013, A Long Way From Home 2013. *Plays include:* Uncle Vanya 1995. *Television includes:* A Question of Attribution 1991, Gulliver's Travels 1995, The Lost World 2001, The Falklands Play 2002, Cambridge Spies 2003, Colditz 2005, Celebration 2006, Waking the Dead 2007, New Tricks 2008, Margaret 2009, Midsomer Murders 2010, Law & Order: UK 2011, Merlin 2012, Utopia 2013, Death in Paradise 2015, 1864 2015. *Publications include:* Comeback: An Actor's Direction 1983. *Leisure interests:* Russian language and culture.

FOX, Kerry; New Zealand actress; b. 30 July 1966; m. Jaime Robertson; ed New Zealand Drama School; fmr lighting designer. *Television appearances include:* Mr Wroe's Virgins, A Village Affair, Saigon Baby, The Affair, 40, Footprints in the Snow 2005, Nostradamus 2006, The Shooting of Thomas Hurndall 2008, Cloudstreet (mini-series) 2011, Sex & Violence 2013–15, The Crimson Field 2014, National Treasure 2016. *Films include:* The Affair 1973, The Decline of Western Civilization 2: The Metal Years 1988, An Angel at My Table (Elvira Notari Best Performance Award) 1991, The Last Days of Chez Nous 1992, Rainbow Warrior 1993, The Last Tattoo 1994, Friends 1994, Shallow Grave 1995, Country Life 1995, The Affair 1995, Saigon Baby 1995, Welcome to Sarajevo 1997, Hanging Garden 1997, Immortality 1998, The Sound of One Hand Clapping 1998, The Wisdom of Crocodiles 1998, The Darkest Light 1998, Fanny and Elvis 1999, To Walk With Lions 1999, The Point Men 2001, Intimacy 2001, Black and White 2002, The Gathering 2002, So Close to Home 2003, Niceland 2004, Rag Tale 2005, The Ferryman 2007, Intervention 2007, He Said 2007, Inconceivable 2008, Storm 2009, Bright Star 2009, Burning Man 2011, Intruders 2011, Mental 2012, Trap for Cinderella 2013, Patrick's Day 2014, War Book 2014, Holding the Man 2015, Downriver 2015, The Dressmaker 2015, The Rehearsal 2016, Mayhem 2017. *Address:* c/o Hamilton Hodell, Fifth Floor, 66–68 Margaret Street, London, W1W 8SR, England.

FOX, Rt Hon. Liam, MB, ChB; British physician and politician; *Secretary of State for International Trade;* b. 22 Sept. 1961, East Kilbride, Scotland; s. of William Fox and Catherine Young; m. Jesme Fox; ed St Bride's High School, E Kilbride, Univ. of Glasgow; civilian army medical officer, Royal Army Educ. Corps 1981–91; gen. practitioner, Beaconsfield 1987–91; Div. Surgeon, St John's Ambulance 1987–91; contested Roxburgh and Berwickshire 1987; MP for North Somerset (fmrly Woodspring) 1992–, mem. Scottish Affairs Select Cttee 1992–93, Sec., Conservative Backbench Health Cttee 1992–93, Parl. Pvt. Sec. to Home Sec. Michael Howard 1993–94, Asst Govt Whip 1994–95, Lord Commr, HM Treasury (Sr Govt Whip) 1995–96, Parl. Under-Sec. of State, FCO 1996–97, Opposition Front Bench Spokesman on Constitutional Affairs 1997–98, Shadow Sec. for Constitutional Affairs 1998–99, Shadow Sec. of State for Health 1999–2003, Shadow Foreign Sec. 2005, Shadow Defence Sec. 2005–10, Sec. of State for Defence 2010–11 (resgnd), Sec. of State for Int. Trade and Pres. Bd of Trade 2016–; Co-Chair. Conservative Party 2003–05; Pres. Glasgow Univ. Conservative Club 1982–83; Nat. Vice-Chair. Scottish Young Conservatives 1983–84; mem. Conservative Political Centre; Sec., Conservative West Country Mems Group 1992–93. *Publications include:* Making Unionism Positive 1988, Bearing the Standard (contrib.) 1991, contrib. to House of Commons Magazine, Rising Tides 2013. *Leisure interests:* tennis, swimming, cinema, theatre. *Address:* House of Commons, Westminster, London, SW1A 0AA (office); Constituency Office, 71 High Street, Nailsea, North Somerset, BS48 1AW, England (office). *Telephone:* (20) 7219-4198 (Westminster) (office); (1275) 790090 (Nailsea) (office). *Fax:* (1275) 790091 (Nailsea) (office). *E-mail:* douglasi@parliament.uk (office). *Website:* admin@northsomersetconservatives.com (office); www.liamfox.co.uk.

FOX, Marye Anne, BS, MS, PhD; American chemist and university chancellor; *Chancellor Emeritus and Distinguished Professor of Chemistry, University of California, San Diego;* b. 9 Dec. 1947, Canton, Ohio; m. James K. Whitesell; three s. two step-s.; ed Notre Dame Coll., Cleveland State Univ., Dartmouth Coll.; Postdoctoral Fellow, Univ. of Maryland 1974–76; Asst Prof. of Organic Chem., Univ. of Texas 1976–81, Assoc. Prof. 1981–85, Prof. 1985–86, Rowland Pettit Centennial Prof. 1986–91, Dir Center for Fast Kinetics Research 1986–91, M. June and J. Virgil Waggoner Regents Chair in Chem. 1991–98, Vice-Pres. for Research, Univ. of Texas 1994–98; Chancellor and Distinguished Univ. Prof. of Chem., North Carolina State Univ. 1998–2004; Chancellor Univ. of California, San Diego

2004–12, currently Chancellor Emer. and Distinguished Prof. of Chem.; Visiting Scholar, Harvard Univ. 1989, Univ. of Iowa 1993; Professeur Invitée, Université Pierre et Marie Curie, Paris VI 1992; Visiting Prof., Chem. Research Promotion Center, Nat. Science Council, Taipei, Taiwan 1993; Morris S. Kharasch Visiting Prof., Univ. of Chicago 1997; consultant/contrib., McGraw-Hill Encyclopedia of Science and Technology 1992–94; mem. Bd of Dirs Asscn for Advancement of Tech. in Biomedical Sciences 1989–90, Boston Scientific, Inc. (Audit and Strategic Planning Cttee) 2001–, PPD, Inc. 2002–, Red Hat, Inc. 2002–, W. R. Grace, Inc.; mem. Camille and Henry Dreyfus Foundation Bd 1990–2002, Nat. Science Bd (Chair. Cttee on Programs and Plans 1993–96, mem. Exec. Cttee 1993–94) 1991–96, Associated Western Univs 1996–98, Council NAS (Exec. Cttee) 1996–99, Environmental Defense Fund (Texas Bd) 1996–98, Oak Ridge Associated Univs 1996–98, Oak Ridge Foundation Bd 1996–98, Nat. Research Council Governing Bd 1997–99, Kenan Inst. for Eng, Tech., and Science (Chair.) 1998–, Microelectronic Center of N Carolina (Chair. 2001) 1998–, Raleigh Cooperating Colls 1998–, Research Triangle Inst. Bd Govs 1998–2003, Robert A. Welch Foundation Scientific Advisory Bd 1998–, Univ. of Texas-Battelle Man. Bd of Oak Ridge Nat. Lab. (Chair. Science and Tech. Cttee) 1999–, Nat. Inst. for the Environment 2001–, Pres.'s Council of Advisors on Science and Tech. 2001–, Burroughs-Wellcome Fund 2002–, North Carolina Bd of Science and Tech. 2002–, Nat. Asscn of State Univs and Land Grant Colls 2003–; Assoc. Ed. Journal of the American Chemical Soc. 1986–95; Invited Expert Analyst, Chemtracts 1989–96; mem. Editorial Advisory Bd Journal of Organic Chemistry 1984–89, Molecular Structure and Energetics 1985–88, American Chemical Soc. Symposium Series and Advances in Chemistry 1986–89, CRC Critical Reviews in Surface Chemistry 1988, New Journal of Chemistry 1995–99, The Chemical Intelligencer 1997–2001, Organic Letters 1999; mem. Advisory Bd Heterogeneous Chemistry Reviews 1993–96, Chemical and Engineering News 1994–99, Chemical Reviews 1994–2002, Issues in Science and Technology 1996–2002; mem. Int. Advisory Bd Contemporary Concepts in Chemistry 1994–96; mem. numerous advisory and scientific bds and review cttees; mem. ACS, Inter-American Photochemical Soc., NAS 1994, American Philosophical Soc. 1996; Foreign Corresp. mem. Royal Acad. of Science and Arts, Barcelona 1996; Fellow, AAAS 1993, American Acad. of Arts and Sciences 1994, American Women in Science 2001, ACS 2010–; Trustee, Univ. of Notre Dame 2002–; Hon. DSc (Notre Dame Coll.) 1994, (Cleveland State Univ.) 1998, Hon. JD (Sandhills Community Coll.) 2000, Hon. DUniv (Univ. of Ulster) 2002, Hon. DHumLitt (Texas A&M Univ.) 2002, Dr hc (Université Pierre et Marie Curie—Paris VI) 2001, (Universidad Nacional de Educacion a Distancia, Madrid) 2003; numerous awards including Honour Scholarship, Notre Dame Coll. 1965–69, Outstanding Freshman Chemist Award, Chemical Rubber Co. 1965, NSF Undergraduate Research Fellow, Illinois Inst. of Tech. 1968, Medal of Excellence, American Inst. of Chemists 1969, Dartmouth Fellow 1972–73, Goodyear Tire Fellow 1973–74, Postdoctoral Fellow (NSF and RANN), Univ. of Maryland 1974–76, Alfred P. Sloan Research Fellow 1980, Distinguished Alumna Award, Notre Dame Coll. 1981, Agnes Fay Morgan Research Award, Selection, Teaching Excellence Award, Univ. of Texas Coll. of Natural Sciences 1986, ACS Garvan Medal 1988, Döbereiner Medal, Friedrich Schiller Univ., Jena, GDR 1988, ACS Arthur C. Cope Scholar Award 1989, Medallion for Contribs to Photographic Sciences, Inst. of Chemical Physics, USSR Acad. of Sciences, Moscow 1990, Havinga Medal, Gorleaus Laboratoria der Rijksuniversiteit, Leiden 1991, ACS Research Award (Southwest Region) 1993, Paul Harris Fellowship, Raleigh Rotary Club 1999, Citation as Outstanding Woman in Science by the Women's History Cttee of New York Acad. of Science 1999, Distinguished Mem. Nat. Soc. of Collegiate Scholars 2001, Hall of Honor, Coll. of Natural Sciences Foundation Advisory Council, Univ. of Texas at Austin 2001, Nat. Order of Omega 2001, Gov.'s Old North State Award (North Carolina) 2004, ACS Parsons Award for Public Service 2005, Nat. Medal of Science 2010. *Publications include:* Orbital Symmetry Concepts in Organic Chemistry 1987, Photoinduced Electron Transfer (four vols, co-ed.) 1988, Organic Chemistry (co-author) 1994, Supplemental Problems for Organic Chemistry (co-author) 1995, Instructor's Resource Manual of Tests and Additional Problems to Accompany Organic Chemistry (co-author) 1995, Organic Chemistry (co-author) 1997, Cultivating Academic Careers (co-author) 1998, Containing the Threat from Illegal Bombings (co-author) 1998, Transforming Undergraduate Education in Science, Mathematics, Engineering, and Technology 1999, Evaluating, Rewarding, and Improving Quality Teaching in Science, Mathematics, Engineering, and Technology (co-author) 2007; nearly 30 book chapters, 49 policy papers, three patents and more than 400 scientific papers, mostly on organic photochemistry and electrochemistry. *Address:* c/o Chancellor's Office, University of California San Diego, Department of Chemistry and Biochemistry, 2050 Urey Hall Addition, 9500 Gilman Drive, MC 0358, La Jolla, CA 92093-0332, USA. *Telephone:* (858) 534-5871 (office). *Fax:* (858) 534-0202 (office). *E-mail:* mafox@ucsd.edu (office). *Website:* www-chem.ucsd.edu (office).

FOX, Michael J., OC; Canadian/American actor; b. (Michael Andrew Fox), 9 June 1961, Edmonton, Alberta, Canada; s. of Bill Fox and Phyllis Fox; m. Tracy Pollan 1988; one s. two d.; ed Burnaby Cen. High School, Vancouver, BC, Canada; f. Michael J. Fox Foundation for Parkinson's Research 2000; inducted into Canadian Hall of Fame 2000, Goldene Kamera für Lebenswerk, German film and TV Award 2011, CSHL Double Helix Medal Honoree 2012; Hon. DFA (New York Univ.) 2008; Hon. DJur (Univ. of British Columbia) 2008, (Justice Inst. of British Columbia) 2012; Dr hc (Karolinska Inst.) 2010. *TV appearances include:* Leo and Me 1976, Palmerstown USA 1980, Family Ties (series) (Emmy Awards 1987, 1988) 1982–89, Spin City (series) 1996–2000, Otherwise Engaged (exec. producer) 2002, Hench at Home (writer) 2003, Scrubs 2004, The Magic 7 (voice) 2009, The Good Wife 2010, The Michael J. Fox Show 2013–14. *TV films include:* Letters from Frank 1979, Poison Ivy 1985, High School USA 1985. *Film appearances include:* Midnight Madness 1980, Class of '84 1981, Back to the Future 1985, Teen Wolf 1985, Light of Day 1986, The Secret of My Success 1987, Bright Lights, Big City 1988, Back to the Future II 1989, Back to the Future III 1989, The Hard Way 1991, Doc Hollywood 1991, The Concierge 1993, Give Me a Break 1994, Greedy 1994, The American President 1995, Mars Attacks! 1996, The Frighteners 1996, Stuart Little (voice) 1999, Atlantis: The Lost Empire (voice) 2001, Interstate 60 2002, Stuart Little 2 (voice) 2002, Stuart Little 3: Call of the Wild (voice) 2005, The Magic 7 (voice) 2009, Drew: The Man Behind the Poster (documentary) 2013, Annie 2014, Back in Time 2015. *Publications:* Lucky Man: A Memoir 2002, Always Looking Up: The Adventures of an Incurable Optimist 2009, A Funny Thing Happened on the Way to the Future: Twists and Turns and Lessons Learned 2010. *Address:* Michael J. Fox Foundation for Parkinson's Research, Grand Central Station, POB 4777, New York, NY 10163, USA (office). *Website:* www.michaeljfox.org (office).

FOX, Sir Paul Leonard, Kt, CBE; British media executive; b. 27 Oct. 1925; m. Betty R. Nathan 1948; two s.; ed Bournemouth Grammar School; with Parachute Regt 1943; reporter, Kentish Times 1946, The People 1947; scriptwriter, Pathe News 1947; BBC TV scriptwriter 1950; Ed. Sportsview 1953, Panorama 1961; Head, BBC TV Public Affairs Dept 1963, Current Affairs Group 1965; Controller, BBC 1 1967–73; Dir of Programmes, Yorkshire TV 1973–84, Man. Dir Yorkshire TV 1977–89; Dir Independent Television News 1977–86, Chair. 1986–89; Man. Dir BBC TV 1988–91; Chair. BBC Enterprises 1988–91, Stepgrades Consultants 1991–2002; Chair. ITV Network Programme Cttee 1978–80, Council, Independent Television Cos Asscn Ltd 1982–84; mem. Royal Comm. on Criminal Procedure 1978–80; Pres. Royal TV Soc. 1985–92; Dir Channel Four 1985–88, World TV News 1986–88, Thames TV Ltd 1991–95; Chair. Racecourse Asscn Ltd 1993–97, Racecourse Tech. Services 1994–, Disasters Emergency Cttee 1996–99; Dir British Horse Racing Bd 1993–97, Horserace Betting Levy Bd 1993–97, Barnes TV Trust Ltd 1997–; consultant, Oflot 1994–; mem. Cttee Nat. Museum of Photography, Film and TV 1985–95, Cinema and TV Benevolent Fund 1986–92, Pres. 1992–95; Hon. LLD (Leeds) 1984; Hon. DLitt (Bradford) 1991. *Leisure interests:* television, attending race meetings.

FOX, Peter Kendrew, MA; British fmr librarian; *University Librarian Emeritus, University of Cambridge;* b. 23 March 1949, Beverley, Yorks., England; s. of Thomas Kendrew Fox and Dorothy Wildbore; m. Isobel McConnell 1983; two d.; ed Baines Grammar School, Poulton-le-Fylde, Lancs., King's Coll. London, Univ. of Sheffield; Asst Library Officer, Univ. of Cambridge Library 1973–77, Asst Under-Librarian 1977–78, Under-Librarian 1978–79, Univ. Librarian 1994–2009, currently Univ. Librarian Emer.; Deputy Librarian, Trinity Coll., Dublin 1979–84, Librarian 1984–94; Fellow, Selwyn Coll., Cambridge 1994–; mem. British Library Project on Teaching and Learning Skills for Librarians 1978–79, Soc. of Coll., Nat. and Univ. Libraries (SCONUL) Advisory Cttee on Information Services 1979–91 (Chair. 1987–91), An Chomhairle Leabharlanna (Ireland) 1982–94, Cttee on Library Co-operation in Ireland 1983–94 (Chair. 1990–91), Nat. Preservation Advisory Cttee, British Library 1984–95 (mem. Man. Cttee 1996–2002, mem. Bd 2002–09, Chair. 2002–05), Brotherton Collection Advisory Cttee, Univ. of Leeds 1995–2002, 2009–12 (Chair. 1999–2002), Wellcome Trust Library Advisory Cttee 1996–2005, Chair. 2000–05, Consortium of Univ. Research Libraries (Chair. 1997–2000), Lord Chancellor's Advisory Council on Public Records 2001–06, Legal Deposit Advisory Panel (DCMS) 2005–08, External Advisory Bd Trinity Coll. Dublin Long Room Hub 2008–11; Assoc., King's Coll., London; Visiting Fellow, Trinity Coll. Dublin 2011. *Publications include:* Reader Instruction Methods in Academic Libraries 1974, User Education in the Humanities in US Academic Libraries 1979, Trinity College Library Dublin 1982, Trinity College Library Dublin: A History 2014; Ed.: Library User Education – Are New Approaches Needed? 1980, Second (and Third) Int. Conf. on Library User Educ. Proc. 1982 (and 1984), Treasures of the Library – Trinity College Dublin 1986, Commentary Volume: Book of Kells Facsimile 1990, Cambridge University Library: The Great Collections 1998; co-ed. An Leabharlann: The Irish Library 1982–87; contribs to books and journals.

FOX, Simon; British retail executive; *Chief Executive, Trinity Mirror PLC;* m.; three c.; graduate trainee, Security Pacific Bank; worked at Boston Consulting Group and Sandhurst Marketing PLC; founder office supplies retailer, Office World; joined Kingfisher 1998, held various posts, including CEO for Electricals, Man. Dir Comet (during de-merger with Kingfisher); fmr COO, Kesa Electricals PLC, with responsibility for Comet UK; Group Chief Exec., HMV Group PLC 2006–12; Chief Exec., Trinity Mirror PLC 2012–. *Address:* Trinity Mirror PLC, One Canada Square, Canary Wharf, London, E14 5AP, England (office). *Telephone:* (20) 7293-3000 (office). *Website:* www.trinitymirror.com (office).

FOX QUESADA, Vicente; Mexican politician, business executive and fmr head of state; b. 2 July 1942, Mexico City; s. of José Luis Fox and Mercedes Quesada; m. 1st (divorced); two s. two d.; m. 2nd Marta Sahagún 2001; ed Universidad Iberoamericana, Mexico City, Harvard Univ.; worked for Coca Cola Group, first as route supervisor, becoming Regional Pres. for Mexico and Latin America; also worked as farmer and shoemaker; joined Partido Acción Nacional (Nat. Action Party—PAN); Fed. Deputy 1988; Gov. of Guanajuato 1995–2000; Pres. of Mexico 2000–Dec. 2006; Co-Pres. Centrist Democratic International, Rome 2007; f. Vicente Fox Center of Studies, Library and Museum. *Publication:* Revolution of Hope: The Life, Faith and Dreams of a Mexican President 2007. *Address:* Vicente Fox Center of Studies, Library and Museum, Carretera León-Cuerámaro Km. 13, CP. 36440 San Fco. del Rincón, Guanajuato, México. *Website:* centrofox.org.mx.

FOXX, Jamie; American actor, comedian and singer; b. (Eric Marlon Bishop), 13 Dec. 1967, Terrell, Tex.; s. of Darrell Bishop and Louise Annette Talley Dixon; adopted and raised by his mother's adoptive parents, Mark Talley and Esther Marie Talley (née Nelson); two d.; began playing the piano aged five; made TV debut in comedy series In Living Color 1991; writer, performer, dir and producer on The Jamie Foxx Show 1996–2001; writer, performer and producer, two songs on Any Given Sunday film soundtrack 1999; tours: The Unpredictable Tour 2006, The Blame It Tour 2009; Image Award for Best Musical Artist 2006, BET Award for Best Duet/Collaboration (for Gold Digger, with Kanye West) 2006, American Music Award for Favorite Male Soul/R&B Artist 2006, Grammy Award for Best R&B Performance by a Duo or Group with Vocals (for Blame It with T-Pain) 2010. *Films include:* Toys 1992, The Truth About Cats and Dogs 1996, The Great White Hype 1996, Booty Call 1997, The Players Club 1998, Held Up 1999, Any Given Sunday 1999, Bait 2000, Date from Hell 2001, Ali 2001, Shade 2003, Redemption: The Stan Tookie Williams Story 2004, Breakin' All the Rules 2004, Collateral (BET Award for Best Supporting Actor) 2004, Ray (Best Actor in a Musical or Comedy, Golden Globe Awards 2005, Best Actor, Screen Actors Guild Awards 2005, Best Actor in a Leading Role, BAFTA Awards 2005, Best Actor, Acad. Awards 2005) 2004, Stealth 2005, Jarhead 2005, Miami Vice 2006, Dreamgirls 2006, The Kingdom 2007, The Soloist 2009, Law Abiding Citizen 2009, Valentine's Day 2010, Malice N Wonderland (video short) 2010, Due Date 2010, I'm Still Here 2010, Rio (voice) 2011, Horrible Bosses 2011, Django Unchained 2012, White House Down 2013, Rio 2 (voice) 2014, The Amazing Spider-Man 2 2014, Horrible Bosses 2 2014, Annie

2014, Sleepless 2017. *Television includes:* In Living Colour 1991–94, C-Bear and Jamal (voice) 1996, The Jamie Foxx Show 1996–2001, Jamie Foxx: I Might Need Security (HBO Comedy Special) 2002. *Recordings include:* Peep This 1994, Unpredictable (Soul Train Award for Best R&B/Soul Album by a Male Artist 2007) 2005, Intuition 2008, Best Night of My Life 2010. *Address:* Foxxhole Productions, Inc., 15821 Ventura Boulevard 525, Encino, CA 91436, USA (office). *Telephone:* (310) 205-2800 (office). *Website:* www.jamiefoxxmusic.com.

FRACKOWIAK, Richard S. J., MA, MB, BChir, MD, DSc, FRCP, FMedSci; British neurologist, clinical neuroscientist and academic; *Professeur ordinaire ad hominem, University of Lausanne;* b. 26 March 1950, London, England; s. of Jozef Frackowiak and Wanda Frackowiak (née Majewska); m. 1st Christine Frackowiak (divorced 2003); one s. two d.; m. 2nd Laura Spinney; ed Latymer Upper School, Peterhouse, Cambridge, Middx Hosp. Medical School; MRC Clinical Scientist 1989–94; Asst Dir MRC Cyclotron Unit; Prof. of Cognitive Neurology, Univ. Coll., London 1994–2009, Dean, Inst. of Neurology 1998–2002; Dir Leopold Muller Functional Imaging Lab. 1994–2002; Chair. Wellcome Dept of Cognitive Neurology 1994–2002; Prin. Clinical Research Fellow and programme grant holder, Wellcome Trust 1994–2004; Vice-Provost Univ. Coll., London 2002–09; Prof. of Neurology and Chair., Dept of Clinical Neuroscience, Centre Hospitalier Universitaire Vaudois, Univ. of Lausanne, Switzerland 2009–15, currently Professeur ordinaire ad hominem; also Professeur titulaire, Ecole Polytechnique de Lausanne; Dir Departement d'Etudes Cognitives, Ecole Normale Superieure, Paris 2005–09; Adjunct Prof., Cornell Univ. Medical School 1992–; Visiting Prof., Univ. Catholique de Louvain, Yale Medical School, Beth Israel & MGH Boston, La Sapienza, Rome; Hon. Dir Neuroimaging Unit, Fondazione Santa Lucia, Rome 2002–10; Scientific Adviser and Pres.-Dir-Gen. Institut Nat. de la Santé et Recherche Médicale, France 2005–14; fmr MRC Training Fellow; Hon. mem. NAS, American Neurological Asscn, Royal Belgian Acad. de Medicine, French Nat. Acad. de Médecine, Inst. of Medicine (USA), Academia Europaea, Acad. of Medicine (UK), Polish Acad. of Sciences; Hon. MD (Liège); Ipsen Prize, Feldberg Prize, Zulch Prize, Rossi Prize. *Publications include:* Human Brain Function 1997, Brain Mapping: The Disorders 2000, Le Grand Atlas du Cerveau 2018; numerous papers in scientific journals. *Leisure interests:* reading, travel, politics. *Address:* 9, Chemin des Mines Biotech Campus EPFL ENT BBP/HBP B1-05, CH- 1202 Geneva, Switzerland (office). *E-mail:* richard.frackowiak@gmail.com (office). *Website:* www.unil.ch/lren/en/home/menuinst/lab-members/honorary-pis/richard-frackowiak.html (office).

FRADKOV, Mikhail Yefimovich; Russian politician; b. 1 Sept. 1950, Kurumoch, Kuibyshev (now Samara) Oblast, Russian SFSR, USSR; m. Yelena Ludenko-Fradkova; two c.; ed Moscow Inst. of Machines and Tools, USSR Acad. of Foreign Trade; on staff, office of Counsellor on econ. affairs, USSR Embassy to India 1973–75; on staff, Foreign Trade Agency Tyazhpromeksport, USSR State Cttee on Econ. Relations 1975–84; Deputy, later First Deputy Dir of Dept, USSR State Cttee on Econ. Relations 1985–91; Deputy Perm. Rep. of Russian Fed. to GATT 1991–92; Sr Adviser, Perm. Mission of Russian Fed. to UN; Deputy, First Deputy Minister of External Econ. Relations 1993; Interim Acting Minister of External Econ. Relations 1997, Minister of External Econ. Relations and Trade 1997–98; Chair. Bd of Dirs Ingosstrakh 1998–99, Dir-Gen. 1999; Minister of Trade 1999–2000; First Deputy Sec., Security Council of Russia 2000–01; Head, Fed. Service of Tax Police 2001–03; Plenipotentiary Rep. to EU 2003–04; apptd Special Rep. of the Pres. of the Russian Fed. on the Devt of Relations with the EU June 2003; Chair. of the Govt (Prime Minister) of Russian Fed. 2004–07; Dir Fed. Foreign Intelligence Service (SVR) of Russian Fed. 2007–16; Medal 'For Valiant Labour. To commemorate the 100th anniversary of Lenin's birth', Medal 'In Commemoration of the 850th Anniversary of Moscow', Order of Honour, Order of Merit for the Fatherland (Second Class) 2005, (First Class) 2007.

FRAGA NETO, Armínio, PhD; Brazilian economist and banker; *Founding Partner, Gavea Investimentos Ltda.;* b. 20 July 1957, Rio de Janeiro; m.; two c.; ed Pontificia Univ. Católica do Rio de Janeiro, Princeton Univ., USA; trainee, Atlantica-Companhia de Seguros Boavista 1976–77, Banco do Estado do Rio de Janeiro 1979–80, Int. Finance Div., Fed. Reserve Bd, Washington, DC 1984; Chief Economist and Operations Man. Banco de Investimentos Garantia 1985–88; Vice-Pres. Salomon Brothers, New York 1988–91; consultant IBRD 1988–89; Dir responsible for Int. Affairs, Banco Cen. do Brasil 1991–92, Gov. 1999–2002; Man. Dir Soros Fund Man., New York 1993–99; Founding Partner, Gavea Investimentos Ltda, Rio de Janeiro 2003–, also Chief Investment Officer, Chair. and Pres.; mem. Int. Council, JP Morgan Chase & Co. 2004–; Prof., Grad. School in Econs, Fundação Getúlio Vargas 1985–88, 1999–; Visiting Asst Prof., Finance Dept, Wharton School, Pennsylvania Univ. 1988–89; Adjunct Prof. of Int. Affairs, Columbia Univ., New York 1993–99; mem. Bd Pro-Natura USA 1993–99; mem. Council on Foreign Relations, Princeton Univ. Center for Econ. Policy Studies 1993–, Group of Thirty Consultative Group on Int. Econ. and Monetary Affairs, Inc. (G-30), Washington, DC 2001–, Int. Advisory Council of Chinese sovereign wealth fund China Investment Corpn 2009–; Banco Boavista Award. *Publications:* numerous articles on banking and econs. *Address:* Gavea Investimentos Ltda., Rua Ataulfo de Paiva, 1.100, 7th floor, Leblon CEP, 22440-035 Rio de Janeiro, Brazil (office). *Telephone:* (21) 3206-9000 (office). *Fax:* (21) 3206-9001 (office). *E-mail:* arminio@fgv.br (office); faleconosco@fgv.br (office). *Website:* www.gaveajus.com (office); www.gaveainvestimentos.com.br (office).

FRALEY, Robert T., PhD; American plant biotechnologist and business executive; b. 25 Jan. 1953, Wellington, Ill.; ed Univ. of Illinois, Univ. of California, San Francisco; successive positions at Monsanto include Sr Research Specialist, Monsanto Biological Sciences Program, Dir Plant Science Research Group, Vice-Pres. of Tech. for Crop Chemical and Plant Biotechnology R&D, Group Vice-Pres. and Gen. Man., New Products Div. 1993–95, Pres. Ceregen Business Unit (before merger with Pharmacia and Upjohn) 1995–97, Co-Pres. Agricultural Sector 1998–2000, Exec. Vice-Pres. and Chief Tech. Officer 2000–18; fmr mem. Agric. Biotechnology Research Advisory Cttee, NIH Molecular Cytology Study Section; tech. adviser to numerous govt and public agencies, including US Dept of Agric., NSF, Office of Tech. Assessment, CAST, Agency for Int. Devt, NAS of Science, Int. Service for Acquisition of Agri-Biotech Applications; Fellow, AAAS; Monsanto Thomas and Hochwalt Award, Monsanto Edgar M. Queeny Award, Man of the Year, Progressive Farming magazine 1995, Kenneth A. Spencer Award for Outstanding Achievement in Agricultural and Food Chem. 1995, Nat. Award for Agricultural Excellence in Science, Nat. Agri-Marketing Asscn 1995, Nat. Medal of Tech. 1999, World Food Prize (co-recipient) 2013. *Publications:* more than 100 publs and patent applications. *Address:* c/o Monsanto Co., 800 North Lindbergh Blvd, St Louis, MO 63167, USA (office).

FRAME, Ronald William Sutherland, MA, MLitt; British author; b. 23 May 1953, Glasgow, Scotland; s. of Alexander D. Frame and Isobel D. Frame (née Sutherland); ed The High School of Glasgow, Univ. of Glasgow, Jesus Coll., Oxford; full-time author 1981–; many recent Scottish-set short stories published in UK, N America and Australia; regular weekly 'Carnbeg' short story in The Herald (Scotland) 2008, 'Carnbeg Days' in The Scotsman (Scotland) 2008–09, regular contrib. Scottish Review of Books (Sunday Herald); Betty Trask Prize (jt first recipient) 1984, Samuel Beckett Prize 1986, TV Industries' Panel's Most Promising Writer New to TV Award 1986, Saltire Scottish Book of the Year 2000, Barbara Gittings Honor Citation for Fiction, American Library Asscn 2003, Muriel Spark Soc. Lecturer 2015. *Radio scripts include:* Winter Journey 1985, Twister 1986, Rendezvous 1987, Cara 1989, A Woman of Judah 1991, The Lantern Bearers 1997, The Hydro (serial) 1997–99, Havisham 1998, Maestro 1999, Pharos 2000, Don't Look Now (adaptation) 2001, Sunday at Sant' Agata 2001, Greyfriars 2002, The Servant (adaptation) 2005, The Razor's Edge (adaptation) 2005, A Tiger for Malgudi (adaptation) 2006, The Blue Room (adaptation) 2007, The Shell House 2008, Blue Wonder 2008, Monsieur Monde Vanishes (adaptation) 2009, Pinkerton 2010, Sunday (adaptation) 2010, Striptease (adaptation) 2010, The Other Simenon 1 (three adaptations) 2011, The Dreamer 2012, The Other Simenon 2 (three adaptations) 2012, Before the Fact (adaptation) 2013, The Other Simenon 3 (three adaptations) 2014. *Television screenplays include:* Paris 1985, Out of Time 1987, Ghost City 1994, A Modern Man 1996, M R James: Four Ghost Stories for Christmas (adaptation) 2000, Darien: Disaster in Paradise 2003, Cromwell 2003, The Two Loves of Anthony Trollope (script contrib.) 2004. *Publications include:* Winter Journey 1984, Watching Mrs. Gordon 1985, A Long Weekend with Marcel Proust 1986, Sandmouth People 1987, Paris (TV play) 1987, A Woman of Judah 1987, Penelope's Hat 1989, Bluette 1990, Underwood and After 1991, Walking My Mistress in Deauville 1992, The Sun on the Wall 1994, The Lantern Bearers 1999, Permanent Violet 2002, Time in Carnbeg 2004, Unwritten Secrets 2010, A Carnbeg Affair, Carnbeg Piccalilli, Mysteries of Carnbeg (Kindle) 2011, Havisham 2012, Room 17 2018. *Leisure interests:* swimming, film, walking in the wind. *Address:* c/o Laura Macdougall, Tibor Jones & Associates, 2–6 Atlantic Road, London, SW9 8HY, England (office); c/o Faber & Faber Ltd, Bloomsbury House, 74–77 Great Russell Street, London, WC1B 3DA, England. *Telephone:* (20) 7733-0555 (office); (20) 7927-3800. *E-mail:* laura@tiborjones.com (office). *Fax:* (20) 7927-3801. *Website:* www.carnbeg.com.

FRAMLINGHAM, Baron (Life Peer), cr. 2011, of Eye in the County of Suffolk; **Michael Nicholson Framlingham,** Kt, MA; British politician and company director; b. 17 Oct. 1938, South Manchester; m. Jennifer Margaret Childs 1965; one s. one d.; ed William Hulme's Grammar School, Whalley Range, Manchester, Christ's Coll., Cambridge; Dir Power Line Maintenance Ltd 1966–68; f. Lords Tree Services Ltd 1968; Councillor, Bedford Borough Council (fmrly N Beds. Borough Council) 1974–77, Beds. Co. Council 1981–83; Parl. cand. for Manchester Gorton 1979; arboricultural consultant 1983–; MP (Conservative) for Suffolk Cen. 1983–97, for Cen. Suffolk and N Ipswich 1997–2010, Parl. Pvt. Sec. to John MacGregor 1984–87, Deputy Speaker of House of Commons 1997–2005, Second Deputy Chair. of Ways and Means 1997–2010; Fellow and Past Pres. Arboricultural Asscn; Cambridge Rugby Blue. *Address:* House of Lords, Westminster, London, SW1A 0PW, England (office). *Telephone:* (20) 7219-5353 (office). *Fax:* (20) 7219-5979 (office).

FRAMPTON, Kenneth, A.A.Dip., ARIBA; British architect and academic; *Ware Professor of Architecture, Graduate School of Architecture, Planning and Preservation, Columbia University;* ed Architectural Asscn, London; Tech. Ed. Architectural Design (magazine) 1962–65; emigrated to USA 1964; Faculty mem., School of Architecture, Princeton Univ. 1964–72; Faculty mem., Dept of Architecture, Columbia Univ. 1972–, Chair. Div. of Architecture 1986–89, Dir Postgraduate Program in History and Theory of Architecture 1993–, also Ware Prof. of Architecture; Faculty mem., RCA, London 1974–77; Visiting Prof. at numerous schools of architecture including Berlage Inst., Amsterdam, ETH, Switzerland, Chinese Univ. of Hong Kong, Univ. della Svizzera Italiana, Mendrisio, Switzerland; mem. jury Alvar Aalto Medal Cttee 1988; Pres. EEC Jury, Mies van der Rohe Foundation, Barcelona; presented Raoul Wallenberg Lecture 1999; Fellow, Graham Foundation 1969–72; Loeb Fellow, Harvard Univ. Grad. School of Design 1972; Guggenheim Fellow 1975; Fellow, Inst. for Architecture and Urban Studies, New York; Fellow, Wissenschaftskolleg, Berlin 1986, American Acad. of Arts and Sciences 1993; Dr hc (Royal Inst. of Tech., Stockholm) 1991, (Univ. of Waterloo) 1995, (Calif. Coll. of Arts and Crafts) 1999; AIA Nat. Honors Award 1985, Acad. d'Architecture Gold Medal 1987, AIA New York Chapter Award of Merit 1988, ASCA Topaz Award 1990, President's Medal, Architectural League of New York 2007, Architectural Award, American Acad. of Arts and Letters 2008, Schelling Architecture Theory Prize 2012. *Design work includes:* Duplex apartment building, London 1962–65, Low-Rise High Density, Brownsville, Brooklyn USA 1972–75. *Publications include:* Modern Architecture: A Critical History 1980, 2008, Modern Architecture and the Critical Present 1993, American Masterworks 1995, Studies in Tectonic Culture 1995, Latin American Architecture: Six Voices (co-author) 2002, Le Corbusier 2002, Labor, Work and Architecture 2002, Evolution of 20th Century Architecture: A Synoptic Account 2007, A Genealogy of Modern Architecture: Comparative Critical Analysis of Built Form (with Ashley Simone) 2015. *Address:* Graduate School of Architecture, Planning and Preservation, Columbia University, 1172 Amsterdam Avenue, New York, NY 10027, USA (office). *Telephone:* (212) 854-4699 (office). *E-mail:* Kf7@columbia.edu (office). *Website:* www.arch.columbia.edu (office).

FRANÇA, José-Augusto, DèsLitt et Sc Hum, DHist; Portuguese writer, art historian and academic; *Professor Jubilado, Department of Art History, University of Lisbon;* b. 16 Nov. 1922, Tomar; s. of José M. França and Carmen R. França; m. 2nd Marie-Thérèse Mandroux; one d. (by previous m.); ed Lisbon Univ., Ecole des Hautes Etudes and Univ. of Paris; travels in Africa, Europe, Americas and Asia 1945–; Ed., Lisbon literary review Unicornio 1951–56, Co-Ed., Cadernos de Poesia

1951–53; Founder-Dir Galeria de Marco, Lisbon 1952–54; art critic 1946–; film critic 1948–; lexicographical publr 1948–58; Ed., Pintura & Não 1969–70, Colóquio Artes 1970–96; Prof., Cultural History and History of Art, Dir Dept of Art History, New Univ. of Lisbon 1974–92, Prof. Jubilado 1992–, Dir elect Faculty of Social Sciences 1982; Dir Fondation C. Gulbenkian, Centre Culturel Portugais, Paris 1983–89; Visiting Prof., Univ. of Paris III 1985–89; Vice-Pres. Int. Asscn of Art Critics 1970–73, Pres. 1985–87, Hon. Pres. 1987–; Vice-Pres. Acad. Européenne de Sciences, Arts et Lettres Paris 1985–2000, Hon. Pres. 2000–; City Councillor, Lisbon 1974–75; mem. of City Ass. Lisbon 1990–93; Pres. Inst. Cultura Portuguesa 1976–80, World Heritage Cttee, UNESCO 1999–2005, J-A F's art collection Museu of Tomar 2004; mem. Int. Asscn of Art Critics, Int. Cttee of Art History, PEN Club, Soc. Européenne de Culture, Soc. de l'Histoire de l'Art français, Acad. Nacional de Belas Artes (Pres. 1977–80, Emer. 2012–), Acad. das Ciencias de Lisboa (Emer. 2012–), Acad. Européenne de Sciences, Arts et Lettres, World Acad. of Arts and Science, Acad. Nat. Sciences, Arts et Lettres de Bordeaux, Ateneo Veneto, Real Acad. Bellas Artes San Fernando (Spain); Hon. mem. Union Journalistes Cinéma 2008, Ordem dos Arquitectos 2009; Officier, Ordre nat. du Mérite, Chevalier, Ordre des Arts et des Lettres, Commdr, Ordem Rio Branco (Brazil), Grand Cross Order of Public Instruction, Grand Cross Ordem Infante Dom Henrique, Officer, Ordem Santiago; Medals of Honour (Lisbon, Tomar), Medal of Cultural Merit 2012. *Publications include:* Natureza Morta (novel) 1949, Charles Chaplin–the Self-Made Myth 1952, Amadeo de Souza-Cardoso 1957, Azazel (play) 1957, Despedida Breve (short stories) 1958, Situação da Pintura Ocidental 1959, Da Pintura Portuguesa 1960, Dez Anos de Cinema 1960, Une ville des lumières: La Lisbonne de Pombal 1963, A Arte em Portugal no Século XIX 1967, Oito Ensaios sobre Arte Contemporânea 1967, Le romantisme au Portugal 1972, Almada, o Português sem Mestre 1972, A Arte na Sociedade Portuguesa no Século XX 1972, Antonio Carneiro 1973, A Arte em Portugal no século XX 1974, Zé Povinho 1975, Manolo Millares 1977, Lisboa: Urbanismo e Arquitectura, O Retrato na Arte Portuguesa, Rafael Bordalo Pinheiro, O Português tal e qual 1980, Malhoa & Columbano, Historia da Arte Occidental 1780–1980 1987, Os Anos 20 em Portugal 1992, Bosch ou le visionnaire intégral, Thomar revisited 1994, (In) definições de Cultura 1997, Lisboa 1998, Memorias para o Ano 2000 2000, Monte Olivete, minha aldeia 2001, Buridan (novel) 2002, Regra de Três (novel), Cem Cenas, quadros e contos (short stories) 2003, A Bela Angevina (novel), Historia da Arte em Portugal 1750–2000 2004, José e os outros (novel), Exercícios de Passamento (short stories) 2005, Ricardo Coraçao de Leão (novel) 2007, João sem Terra (novel) 2008, Lisboa: história física e moral 2008, Guerra e Paz (novel) 2009, Ano X–Lisboa 1936 (essay) 2010, Mina e as coincidencias (novel) 2011, Ano XX–Lisboa 1946 (essay) 2012, Memórias após o Ano 2000 2012, Memórias do Conselheiro Adalberto (essay) 2014, Dialogo entre o Autor e o Critico (essay) 2015. *Leisure interests:* travel and detective stories. *Address:* Av. Infante Santo, 17/8D, 1350-175 Lisbon, Portugal (home); 12 route de Beauvau, 49140 Jarzé, France (home). *Telephone:* (21) 3953512 (Lisbon) (home); 2-41-95-40-04 (Jarzé) (home). *Fax:* 2-41-95-40-04 (Jarzé) (home).

FRANCESCHI, Patrice, PhD; French writer, sailor and aviator; *Honorary President, Société des explorateurs français;* b. 18 Dec. 1954, Toulon; ed Univ. of Paris (Sorbonne), Aix-Marseille Univ.; explorer and humanitarian activist; sponsored by UNESCO to promote dialogue between different cultures; journeys in Guyana 1974, Congo 1975, the Amazon 1976, Burundi, Tanzania, Uganda and Egypt 1978, Viet Nam 1979, New Guinea 1989, SE Asia 1999–2000; descended the Nile on foot 1978; first world tour in ultra-light motorized vessel 1984–97; world exploration tour with tall ship La Boudeuse 2004–07; Founding mem. and Pres. Solidarités aid agency, has engaged in numerous humanitarian missions in Thailand 1980, Romania 1989–90, Kurdistan 1991–92, Sarajevo 1992, Rwanda 1996, Afghanistan 1979–99, Bosnia and Herzegovina 1997; Coordinator French Governmental Aid in Somalia 1992–93; currently Hon. Pres. Soc. des explorateurs français; Chevalier, Légion d'honneur; Medal, Acad. de la Marine 1980, Lauréat de l'Acad. Française 1981, Gold Medal Acad. des sports 1987, Écrivain de Marine 2014. *Television:* 18 documentary films about exploration of New Guinea, Amazon, Nagaland, Pacific, SE Asia etc. *Publications include:* Au Congo jusqu'au cou 1977, Terre farrouche 1977, L'exode vietnamien 1979, Ils ont choisi la liberté 1981, Guerre en Afghanistan 1984, Un capitane sans importance 1987, La folle équipée 1987, Qui a bu l'eau du Nil 1989, Raid papou 1990, Chasseurs d'horizons 1991, Quelque chose qui prend les hommes 1992, Tout l'or du fleuve 1995, De l'esprit d'aventure (with J-C Guilbert, G. Chaliand) 2003, La Boudeuse en Amazonie (illustrator N. Clérice) 2005, La Grande Aventure de La Boudeuse 2008, Le chemin de la mer 2009, Le regard du singe 2013, Première personne du singulier (Prix Goncourt de la Nouvelle 2015) 2014, Il est minuit, monsieur K 2016. *Leisure interests:* literature, philosophy, science, exploration. *Address:* Société des explorateurs français, 184 blvd Saint-Germain, 75006 Paris, France (office). *Telephone:* 1-45-49-03-51 (office). *E-mail:* navire@la-boudeuse.org (office). *Website:* www.la-boudeuse.org (office).

FRANCHET, Yves Georges; French statistician and international public servant; *Chairman, PEKEA (Political and Ethical Knowledge in Economic Activities);* b. 4 March 1939, Paris; m. Marie Bernard Robillard; two s.; ed Ecole polytechnique, Paris, Université Paris I, Ecole nationale de la statistique et de l'admin économique de Paris; Dir Statistics Office, UDEAC, Brazzaville, Congo 1964–68; mem. govt econ. planning staff 1968–69; economist, World Bank, Washington, DC 1969–74; Head of Planning, Co-operation Div., Inst. Nat. de la Statistique et des Etudes Economiques (INSEE) 1974–77; Dir Ecole Nat. de la statistique et de l'admin économique (ENSAE) 1977–80; Deputy Dir European Office of World Bank, Paris 1980–83; Vice-Pres. IDB, Washington, DC 1983–87; Dir-Gen. Statistical Office of the European Communities (EUROSTAT) 1987–2003; Chair. Exec. Cttee and Bd of Dirs, PEKEA (Political and Ethical Knowledge in Econ. Activities); Chevalier, Légion d'honneur; Commdr, Order of Merit (Niger); Dr hc (Bucharest). *Address:* PEKEA, 110 rue de la Poterie, 35 200 Rennes, France (office); 7 rue J. P. Brasseur, 1258 Luxembourg Ville, Luxembourg (home). *Telephone:* (2) 99-86-17-35 (office). *Fax:* (2) 99-86-17-35 (office). *E-mail:* yves.franchet@wanadoo.fr (home); pekea@pekea-fr.org (office). *Website:* www .pekea-fr.org (office).

FRANCIONI, Reto, PhD; Swiss business executive; *Chairman, Swiss International Air Lines Limited;* b. 18 Aug. 1955, Zürich; m.; two s.; ed Univ. of Zurich; with UBS 1981–85, Credit Suisse 1985–88, mem. Bd of Dirs UBS AG 2013–; Deputy CEO of Man., Asscn Tripartite Bourses 1988–92; Dir, Corp. Finance Div., Hofmann-La Roche 1992–93; mem. Exec. Bd, Deutsche Börse AG 1993–2000, Deputy CEO 1999–2005, CEO 2005–15; Co-CEO and Spokesman, Consors 2000–02; Pres. and Chair. SWX Swiss Exchange 2002–05; Adjunct Prof. of Economics and Finance, Zicklin School of Business, New York, USA 2003–05; Prof. of Applied Capital Markets Theory, Univ. of Basel 2006–; Sr Ind. Dir Coca-Cola HBC AG 2016–, also mem. Bd of Dirs; Chair. and Dir SIX Swiss Exchange Ltd 2005; Chair. Swiss Int. Air Lines 2016–; Deputy Chair. Eurex Clearing AG, also mem. Supervisory Bd; mem. Bd Francioni AG; mem. Supervisory Bd Conrad Holding GmbH, Hirschau Consors España SV, SA, Consors ONline Broker SIM SpA, Italy Consors AG, ONBanca SpA, Berliner Effektengesellschaft AG; mem. Advisory Bd Moscow Int. Financial Center, Instituto de Empresa. *Publications:* Equity Markets in Action (co-author) 2004, The Equity Trader Course (co-author) 2006. *Address:* Swiss International Air Lines Ltd., Corporate Communications, PO Box CH-8058, Zurich, Switzerland (office). *Telephone:* 445644414 (office). *Website:* www.swiss.com/corporate/en/company/about-us/cv/cv-reto-francioni (office).

FRANCIS, Hermangild, LLB; Saint Lucia politician and fmr police officer; *Minister of Home Affairs, Justice and National Security;* b. Vieux-Fort; ed Univ. of the West Indies, Cave Hill Campus; Trainee Man., Hotel La Toc 1970–72; joined Royal St Lucia Police Force 1975, becoming Deputy Commr of Police 1975–2008; Security Dir, Windjammer Landing Villa Beach Resort 2009–16; apptd Senator 2016; Minister of Home Affairs, Justice and Nat. Security 2016–; Pres. Referees Asscn 1998–2001. *Address:* Ministry of Home Affairs, Justice and National Security, Sir Stanislaus James Bldg, Ground Floor, Waterfront, Castries LC04 301, Saint Lucia (office). *Telephone:* 468-3600 (office). *Fax:* 468-3617 (office). *E-mail:* homeaffairs@gosl.gov.lc (office). *Website:* homeaffairs.govt.lc (office).

FRANCIS, Julian W., OBE, BSc, MBA; Bahamian financial services industry executive and fmr central banker; *Chairman, Providence Advisors Ltd;* m.; two s.; ed New York Univ., USA; Accounting Officer and Credit Officer, SFE Banking Corpn, Nassau 1969–72, Asst Vice-Pres. Credit Dept 1976–79; worked for Barclays Bank, Nassau and Eleuthera; with Banque de la Soc. Financière Européenne, Paris, France 1980–92, positions include Asst Man. for Business Devt in Latin America, Deputy Man. for Assets Man., Man. of Assets Trading Dept, Cen. Man. for Corp. Finance, Jt Gen. Man. and mem. Man. Cttee; Deputy Gov. and mem. Bd of Dirs Cen. Bank of the Bahamas 1993–97, Gov. 1997–2005; Co-Chair. and CEO Grand Bahama Port Authority 2005; currently Chair. Providence Advisors Ltd; mem. Bd of Dirs Butterfield Bank Group 2007–, Bahamas Cancer Centre; Vice-Chair. Securities Bd; Chair. The Bridge Authority; Bahamian jt negotiator on Competition Policy, Free Trade of the Americas negotiations 1997; fmr Vice-Chair. Securities Market Task Force. *Leisure interests:* reading, fishing, tennis. *Address:* Providence Advisors Ltd, Goodman's Bay Corporate Centre, 1st Floor, PO Box AP 59223, Slot 409, West Bay Street, Nassau, The Bahamas (office). *Telephone:* 328-7115 (office). *Fax:* 328-7129 (office). *E-mail:* info@providenceadvisors.net (office). *Website:* www.providenceadvisors.net (office).

FRANCIS I, His Holiness Pope (Jorge Mario Bergoglio), SJ; Argentine ecclesiastic; b. 17 Dec. 1936, Buenos Aires; ed San José Major Coll.; ordained priest of Soc. of Jesus 1969; at Prov. San José Major Coll. 1973–79, Rector 1980–86; Auxiliary Bishop of Buenos Aires 1992–97, Coadjutor Bishop of Buenos Aires 1997–98, Archbishop of Buenos Aires 1998–2013; Titular Bishop of Auca May–June 1992; Vicar Gen. Archdiocese of Buenos Aires 1993; apptd Bishop of Argentina 1998; Ordinary of the Ordinariate for the Faithful of the Eastern Rites in Argentina 1998–2013; cr. Cardinal (Cardinal-Priest of S. Roberto Bellarmino) 2001; Pres. Argentine Episcopal Conf. 2005–08; participated in Papal Conclave March 2013, elected Pope and Bishop of Rome 2013– (first non-European in more than 1,200 years and first Jesuit priest ever to become Pope); Grand Chancellor, Universidad Católica Argentina; mem. Congregation for Divine Worship and Discipline of Sacraments, Congregation for the Congregation for the Clergy, Congregation for Insts of Consecrated Life and Socs of Apostolic Life, Pontifical Council for the Family, Episcopal Comm. for Latin America; met with Patriarch Kirill I (Head of Russian Orthodox Church) at José Martí Int. Airport, Havana, Cuba and signed a 30-point joint declaration on global issues, including their hope for re-establishment of full unity, the persecution of Christians in the Middle East, the Syrian Civil War and church organization in Ukraine, this was the first meeting between a Pope and a Russian Orthodox Patriarch since the Western and Eastern branches of Christianity split in the Great Schism of 1054 AD 12 Feb. 2016. *Publications include:* Meditaciones para religiosos 1982, Reflexiones sobre la vida apostólica 1986, Reflexiones de esperanza 1992, Diálogos entre Juan Pablo II y Fidel Castro 1998, Educar: exigencia y pasión 2003, Ponerse la patria al hombro 2004, La nación por construir 2005, Corrupción y pecado 2006, Sobre la acusación de sí mismo 2006, El verdadero poder es el servicio 2007, Mente abierta, corazón creyente 2012, The Name of God Is Mercy 2016. *Address:* Palazzo Apostolico Vaticano, 00120 Città del Vaticano, Rome, Italy (office). *Website:* www.vatican.va (office).

FRANCO, James Edward, MFA; American actor, director and screenwriter; b. 19 April 1978, Palo Alto, California; s. of Douglas Franco and Betsy-Lou Franco; ed Columbia Univ.; early acting experience in school plays; career breakthrough with leading role in TV series Freaks and Geeks 1999; f. own production co. Rabbit Bandini Productions. *Television includes:* Freaks and Geeks (series) 1999, James Dean (TV film) (Broadcast Film Critics Asscn Award for Best Actor in TV Film, Golden Globe Award for Best Actor - Miniseries or TV Film) 2001. *Films include:* At Any Cost 2000, Whatever It Takes 2000, Spider-Man 2002, City by the Sea 2002, Sonny 2002, The Company 2003, Spider-Man 2 2004, The Ape 2005, Annapolis 2006, Flyboys 2006, Good Time Max (writer and dir) 2007, Spider-Man 3 2007, Pineapple Express 2008, Milk 2008, Eat Pray Love 2010, 127 Hours 2010, The Broken Tower (actor and dir) 2011, Oz the Great and Powerful 2013, This Is the End 2013, As I Lay Dying 2013, Spring Breakers (Best Supporting Actor, Nat. Soc. of Film Critics) 2013, The Disaster Artist (Golden Globe Award for Best Performance by an Actor in a Motion Picture, Musical or Comedy 2018) 2017. *Address:* c/o James/Levy/Jacobson Management, Inc., 3500 West Olive Avenue, Suite 1470 Burbank, CA 91505, USA (office). *Telephone:* (818) 955-7070 (office). *Fax:* (818) 955-7073 (office).

FRANCO GOMEZ, Julio César, PhD; Paraguayan physician and politician; *President, Partido Liberal Radical Auténtico (PLRA);* b. 17 April 1951; ed Nat. Univ. of Cordoba, Argentina, Asunción Univ.; Senator 1998; Pres. of the Comm. for

Public Health, Social Security and Drug Control 1999; Vice-Pres. of Paraguay 2000–03; fmr Chair. Partido Liberal Radical Auténtico (PLRA), PLRA presidential cand. 2003, Pres. PLRA 2016–. *Address:* Partido Liberal Radical Auténtico, Iturbe N° 936, casi Manuel Dominguez, Asunción, Paraguay (office). *Telephone:* (21) 49-8441 (office). *Fax:* (21) 49-8443 (office). *Website:* www.plra.org.py (office).

FRANCO GÓMEZ, Luis Federico, DrMed; Paraguayan surgeon, politician and fmr head of state; b. 23 July 1962, Asunción; m. Emilia Alfaro Patricia de Franco; four c.; ed Nat. Univ. of Asunción; Head of Interns and Residents, 1CCM Univ. Hosp. de Clínicas, Asunción 1990–91, also Chief of Emergency, Instructor in Medicial Semiology 1991–92; Chief of Nat. Guard Hosp. MSP and BS, 1994–96, also Chief Resident of Internal Medicine and Chief of Cardiology; Town Councillor Fernando de la Mora 1991–96, also becoming Pres. of Legislation and Pres. of Health, Hygiene and Social Services, Mayor, Fernando de la Mora 1996–2001; mem. Partido Liberal Radical Auténtico, apptd Dir 2002; Gov. Cen. Prov. 2003–08; Vice-Pres. of Paraguay 2008–12, Pres. 2012–13; mem. Paraguayan Soc. of Internal Medicine. *Address:* c/o Office of the President, Palacio de los López, Asunción, Paraguay (office).

FRANCON, Nathalie; French business executive; *CEO and Owner, NFP Fashion and Luxury Advisor;* fmr exec. with Chanel; COO Christian Lacroix –2007; CEO Azzaro 2007–12; currently CEO and Owner NFP Fashion and Luxury Advisor. *Telephone:* 9-67-37-06-43 (office). *Website:* www.nfp-paris.com (office).

FRANGIALLI, Francesco; French international organization official; b. 23 Jan. 1947, Paris; m. Leila Niiranen; two s. one d.; ed Université de Paris, Institut d'Études Politiques de Paris, École Nationale d'Admin; Lecturer, Institut d'Études Politiques de Paris 1972–89; extensive background in public admin; Dir Tourism Industry, govt ministry responsible for tourism 1986–90; Perm. Rep. to World Tourism Org. 1986–89, Deputy Sec.-Gen. 1990–96, Sec.-Gen. a.i. 1996–97, Sec.-Gen. 1998–2009, led the org.'s conversion to a specialized agency of the UN 2003. *Publications:* La France dans le tourisme mondial 1991, Tourisme et loisirs – Une question sociale (co-author), published in Observations on International Tourism 1997–2000, and in International Tourism: The Great Turning Point 2001–2003; numerous articles, speeches and papers.

FRANGOU, Angeliki, BEng, MEng; Greek business executive; *Chairman and CEO, Navios Maritime Holdings;* ed Fairleigh Dickinson Univ. and Columbia Univ., USA; analyst on trading floor of Republic National Bank of New York 1987–89; CEO Franser Shipping SA, Piraeus 1990–2001, CEO Maritime Enterprises Management SA, Piraeus 2001–05; Chair., Pres. and CEO International Shipping Enterprises Inc. (ISE) 2004–05, Chair. and CEO Navios Maritime Holdings (following acquisition of Navios Holdings by ISE) 2005–, Chair. and CEO Navios Maritime Partners LP (affiliate of Navios Holdings) 2007–, Navios Maritime Acquisition Corpn 2008–, Chair. Navios South American Logistics 2007–; Chair. Proton Bank, Athens 2006–08, IRF European Finance Investments Ltd; mem. Bd of Dirs Emporiki Bank of Greece 2004–05; mem. Bd The United Kingdom Mutual Steam Ship Assurance Asscn (Bermuda) Ltd; Vice-Chair. China Classification Soc. Mediterranean Cttee; mem. Hellenic and Black Sea Cttee of Bureau Veritas, Greek Cttee of Nippon Kaiji Kyokai. *Address:* Navios Maritime Holdings, 85 Akti Miaouli Street, Piraeus 185 38, Greece (office); Navios Corporation, 825 Third Avenue, 34th Floor, New York, NY 10022, USA (office). *Telephone:* (210) 417-2050 (Piraeus) (office); (212) 223-7000 (New York) (office). *Fax:* (210) 417-2070 (Piraeus) (office); (212) 223-7650 (New York) (office). *E-mail:* info@navios.com (office). *Website:* www.navios.com (office).

FRANGULYAN, Georgy; Russian sculptor; b. 29 May 1945, Tbilisi, Georgia; m. Yelena Maximova; four c.; ed Moscow Stroganov Higher School of the Arts; Diploma of Russian Acad. of Fine Arts 1999; Grekov Medal 1979, Grand Prix Int. Competition of Plastic Arts, Hungary 1982, Grand Prix Int. Competition of Sculpture, Poznań, Poland 1987, Jury Prize at the Int. Competition of Sculpture, Ravenna, Italy 1988, Silver Medal of Russian Acad. of Fine Arts 1996, Gold Medal of Russian Acad. of Fine Arts 1996, Pushkin Gold Medal of Union of Russian Artists 1999, Honoured Artist of Russia 2004, People's Artist of Russia 2011. *Address:* 119121 Moscow, Zemledelchesky per. 9, Building 1, Russia (home). *Telephone:* (495) 248-24-67 (home). *Website:* www.georgy-frangulyan.ru.

FRANK, Charles Raphael, Jr, PhD; American banker, economist, government official and business executive; b. 15 May 1937, Pittsburgh, Pa; s. of Charles Raphael Frank and Lucille Frank (née Briscoe); m. 1st Susan Patricia Buckman (divorced 1976); one s. one d.; m. 2nd Eleanor Sebastian 1976; two s.; one step-s. one step-d.; ed Rensselaer Polytechnic Inst. and Princeton Univ.; Sr Research Fellow, East African Inst. for Social Research, Makerere Univ. Coll., Kampala 1963–65; Asst Prof. of Econs, Yale Univ. 1965–67; Assoc. Prof. of Econs and Int. Affairs, Princeton Univ. 1967–70, Prof. 1970–74; Assoc. Dir Research Programme on Econ. Devt, Woodrow Wilson School 1967–70, Dir 1970–74; Sr Fellow, Brookings Inst. 1972–74; mem. Policy Planning staff and Chief Economist, US Dept of State 1974–77, Deputy Asst Sec. of State for Econ. and Social Affairs 1977–78; Vice-Pres. Salomon Bros, Inc. 1978–87; Pres. Frank & Co., Inc. 1987–88; Vice-Pres. and Man. Dir for Structured Finance GE Capital Corpn, Stamford, Conn. 1988–97; First Vice-Pres. EBRD 1997–2001; currently Adviser, Sabre Capital, RAO UES; Chair. Baneasa Investments, SA; mem. Bd of Dirs Central European Media Enterprises Ltd 2001–09, 2010–, Chief Financial Officer 2009–10; mem. Bd of Dirs Mittal Steel Galati, Romanian-American Enterprise Fund; mem. Investment Cttee Darby Converging Europe Mezzanine Fund; mem. Council on Foreign Relations. *Publications include:* The Sugar Industry in East Africa 1965, Production Theory and Indivisible Commodities 1969, Economic Accounting and Development Planning (with Brian Van Arkadie) 1969, Debt and the Terms of Aid 1970, Statistics and Econometrics 1971, American Jobs and Trade with the Developing Countries 1973, Foreign Exchange Regimes and Economic Development: The Case of South Korea 1975, Foreign Trade and Domestic Adjustment 1976, Income Distribution and Economic Growth in the Less Developed Countries (jtly) 1977. *Address:* Flat 5, 70–72 Cadogan Square, London, SW1X 0EA, England (home).

FRANK, Joachim, PhD; American (b. German) biophysicist and academic; *Professor, Department of Biochemistry and Molecular Biophysics, College of Physicians and Surgeons, Columbia University;* b. 9 Dec. 1940, Weidenau/Sieg, Germany; m.; two c.; ed Univ. of Freiburg, Germany, Ludwig Maximilians Univ. Munich, Technische Hochschule München; Research Asst, Dept of Physics, Ludwig Maximilians Univ. Munich 1964–67; Research Asst, Max-Planck Institut für Eiweiss-und Lederforschung (now Max-Planck Inst. for Biochemistry) 1967–70, Visiting Scientist 1972–73; Sr Research Asst, Cavendish Lab., Dept of Physics, Univ. of Cambridge 1973–75; Sr Research Scientist, Wadsworth Center, New York State Dept of Health 1975–98; Visiting Assoc. Prof., Computer Science Dept, State Univ. of New York (SUNY) 1976–80, Biology Dept 1982–, Prof., Dept of Biomedical Sciences, School of Public Health, SUNY 1986–2007, apptd Distinguished Prof. 2007; Lab. Chief, Lab. for Computational Biology and Molecular Imaging 1994–2007; Investigator, Howard Hughes Medical Inst. 1998–; Sr Lecturer, Dept of Biochemistry and Molecular Biophysics, Columbia Univ. Coll. of Physicians and Surgeons 2003–08, Prof. 2008–, also Prof., Dept of Biological Sciences, Columbia Univ. Coll. of Arts and Sciences 2008–; mem. Protein Soc., RNA Soc., American Soc. for the Advancement of Science, Nat. Acad. of Sciences; Fellow, American Acad. for Arts and Sciences, American Acad. of Microbiology, American Asscn for the Advancement of Science 1997, Biophysical Soc. 2001, Microscopy Soc. of America 2009; The Harkness Fellowship 1970; Fogarty Sr Int. Fellowship 1987; Humboldt Fellowship 1994; Award for Excellence in Research, Univ. Albany 2001, Scientific Merit Award, New York State Dept of Health 2001, Franklin Medal for Life Science 2014, Wiley Prize in Biomedical Sciences 2017, Nobel Prize in Chemistry (co-recipient) 2017. *Publications include:* Three-Dimensional Electron Microscopy of Macromolecular Assemblies 2006, Electron Tomography 2006, Molecular Machines in Biology: Workshop of the Cell 2011, Found in Translation – Collection of Original Articles on Single-Particle Reconstruction and the Structural Basis of Protein Synthesis 2014. *Address:* Department of Biological Sciences, Columbia University, 650 West 168th Street, Black Building 2-221, New York, NY 10032, USA (office). *Telephone:* (212) 305-9510 (office). *Fax:* (212) 305-9500 (office). *E-mail:* jf2192@cumc.columbia.edu (office). *Website:* biology.columbia.edu.

FRANK, Mary E., MD; American physician and academic; b. New Jersey; ed Fairleigh Dickinson Univ., Teaneck, NJ, Penn State Univ., Hershey, Pa; residency and teaching fellowship, Medical Univ. of S Carolina; joined a family practice, Charleston, Calif. 1977; in full-time practice 1977–; fmr Residency Program Dir, Sutter Hosp., Santa Rosa, Calif.; fmr Clinical Instructor of Family, Community and Preventive Medicine, Stanford Univ., Calif.; fmr Facility Medical Dir, Primary Care Assocs, Rohnert Park; currently Assoc. Clinical Prof. of Ambulatory and Community Medicine, Univ. of Calif., San Francisco; mem. American Acad. of Family Physicians (AAFP) 1973–, served as Chair. Comm. on Legislation and Govt Affairs, Cttee on Women, liaison to Carnegie Foundation Conf. on Healthy Youth for the 21st Century, American Coll. of Obstetricians and Gynaecologists Cttee on Adolescent Health, Rep. to Nat. Quality Forum, Nat. Conf. of State Legislatures, Pres. Calif. Acad. of Family Physicians, mem. Bd of Dirs AAFP 2000–03, Pres. (first woman) 2003–05, Chair. 2005–06; Fellow, American Acad. of Family Physicians; mem. Bd of Dirs Comm. on Office Lab. Accreditation (COLA); Vice-Chair. Council on Scientific Affairs, Calif. Medical Asscn; mem. Sonoma Co. Medical Asscn; volunteer, Special Olympics 1994–; regular speaker, Nat. Youth Leadership Forum; nominated Local Legend, American Medical Women's Asscn. *Leisure interests:* photography, reading mystery novels, hiking. *Address:* American Academy of Family Physicians, 11400 Tomahawk Creek Parkway, Leawood, KS 66211-2680 (office); American Academy of Family Physicians, PO Box 11210, Shawnee Mission, KS 66207-1210, USA (office). *Telephone:* (800) 274-2237 (office); (913) 906-6000 (office). *Fax:* (913) 906-6075 (office). *Website:* www.aafp.org (office).

FRANK, Sergey Ottovich; Russian business executive and politician; *General Director, Sovkomflot;* b. 13 Aug. 1960, Novosibirsk; m.; one s.; ed Far East Higher Marine School of Eng, Far East State Univ., Higher School of Commerce, Ministry of Foreign Econ. Relations of Russian Fed.; Sec., Comsomol Cttee, later Deputy Head, Far East Higher Marine School; mem. staff, Far East Marine Navigation Agency 1989–93, Deputy Dir-Gen. 1993–95; Deputy Head, Dept of Marine Transport, Ministry of Transport 1995–96; First Deputy Minister of Transport 1997–98, Minister 1998–2004, First Deputy Minister of Transport and Communications 2004; Gen. Dir Sovkomflot 2004–. *Address:* Sovcomflot, 6 Gasheka str., 125047 Moscow, Russia (office). *Telephone:* (495) 626-1434 (office). *Fax:* (495) 626-1850 (office). *E-mail:* moscow@sovcomflot.ru (office). *Website:* www.sovcomflot.ru (office).

FRANKEL, Bethenny; American television personality, author, entrepreneur and natural foods chef; b. 4 Nov. 1970; d. of Robert J. Frankel and Bernadette Burke; m. 1st Peter Sussman 1996 (divorced); m. 2nd Jason Hoppy 2010 (divorced); one d.; ed Pine Crest School, Fort Lauderdale, Fla, Nat. Gourmet Inst. for Healthy and Culinary Arts, New York, New York Univ., Boston Univ.; began career appearing in short film Soiree Sans Hors D'oeuvres 1993; an original cast mem. on series The Real Housewives of New York City 2008–18; appeared on The Apprentice: Martha Stewart show 2005, one of two finalists; launched own co. Skinnygirl Cocktails 2009; starred in Bravo reality show Bethenny Getting Married? 2010; host of series Bethenny 2012–14; Founder, B Real Productions 2015; named one of the Top 100 Most Powerful Celebrities, Forbes magazine. *Films include:* actor: Hollywood Hills 90028 1994, Wish Me Luck 1995. *Publications:* Naturally Thin: Unleash Your SkinnyGirl and Free Yourself from a Lifetime of Dieting 2009, The Skinnygirl Dish: Easy Recipes for Your Naturally Thin Life 2009, Body by Bethenny: Body-sculpting Workouts to Unleash Your SkinnyGirl 2010, A Place of Yes: 10 Rules for Getting Everything You Want Out of Life 2011. Skinnygirl Cocktails: 100 Fun & Flirty Guilt-Free Recipes 2014, Cookie Meets Peanut 2014, I Suck at Relationships So You Don't Have To: 10 Rules for Not Screwing Up Your Happily Ever After 2015. *Website:* www.bethenny.com.

FRANKEL, Max, MA; American journalist; b. 3 April 1930, Gera, Germany; s. of Jacob A. Frankel and Mary Frankel (née Katz); m. 1st Tobia Brown 1956 (died 1987); two s. one d.; m. 2nd Joyce Purnick 1988; ed Columbia Univ.; mem. staff, The New York Times 1952, Chief Washington Corresp. 1968–72, Sunday Ed. 1973–76, Editorial Pages Ed. 1977–86, Exec. Ed. 1986–94, 1994–95, also columnist, New York Times magazine 1995–2000; Pulitzer Prize for Int. Reporting 1973. *Publications include:* The Time of My Life and My Life with the Times 1999, High Noon in the Cold War: Kennedy, Khrushchev and the Cuban Missile Crisis 2004.

FRANKEN, Alan (Al) Stuart, BA; American comedian, author and politician; b. 21 May 1951, New York; s. of Joseph Franken and Phoebe Kunst Franken; m.

Franni Franken; one s. one d.; ed Harvard Univ.; grew up in St Louis Park, Minn.; performed stand-up comedy and stage shows with pnr Tom Davis at Harvard Univ. in early 1970s; Franken and Davis signed by Lorne Michaels for TV show Saturday Night Live, New York 1975–80, 1985–95; wrote several unproduced screenplays; political satirist at Democratic Nat. Convention, Atlanta, Ga 1988; co-anchored Comedy Central's election coverage 1992, 1996; wrote and starred in Lateline (NBC) 1998–99; has given speeches to hundreds of corpns, univs and other orgs and has twice been keynote speaker at White House Correspondents' Dinner for Pres. Clinton, Nat. Press Club, USO tours, DNC dinners and commencement speaker at Harvard Univ. 2002; Host, The Al Franken Show (Air America Radio) 2004–07; Fellow, Harvard Univ. Kennedy School of Govt, Shorenstein Center on the Press, Politics and Public Policy; Senator from Minn. 2009–18 (resgnd); mem. Democratic-Farmer-Labor Party; five Emmy Awards (four writing and one producing), Stewart B. McKinney Award 2013. *Films include:* Tunnel Vision 1976, Trading Places 1983, One More Saturday Night (also writer) 1986, When a Man Loves a Woman (also writer and exec. producer) 1994, Stuart Saves His Family (also writer) 1995, The Definite Maybe 1997, Harvard Man (as himself) 2000, Outfoxed 2004, Al Franken: God Spoke (documentary) 2006, Hot Coffee (documentary) 2011. *Television includes:* as writer: The Paul Simon Special 1977, Saturday Night Live (series) 1975–80, 1985–95, The Coneheads 1983, Franken and Davis at Stockton State 1984, Best of John Belushi 1985, Best of Dan Aykroyd 1986, Saturday Night Live Goes Commercial 1991, Politically Incorrect (series) 1996, Lateline (series) 1998, Saturday Night Live: Presidential Bash 2000; as producer: Saturday Night Live 1985–95, Saturday Night Live Goes Commercial 1991, Lateline (exec. producer) 1998, Saturday Night Live: Presidential Bash (consulting producer) 2000. *Publications include:* I'm Good Enough, I'm Smart Enough and Doggone It, People Like Me 1992, Rush Limbaugh is a Big Fat Idiot (Grammy Award for audio version) 1996, A Father and Son Learn From Newt's Mistakes 1997, Why Not Me? – The Making and Unmaking of the Al Franken Presidency 1999, Franken Sense 1999, Home-Fried Franken 2000, Block That Rush 2000, Is George W. Bush Dumb? 2000, Oh, The Things I Know: A Guide to Success, Or, Failing That, Happiness 2002, Norm and the Other 1 Percent 2003, Lies and the Lying Liars Who Tell Them: A Fair and Balanced Look at the Right (Grammy Award for audio version) 2003, The Truth (With Jokes) 2005. *Website:* www.alfranken.com (office).

FRANKEN, Hendrik (Hans), PhD; Dutch lawyer and academic; *Professor Emeritus of Information Law, University of Leiden;* b. 17 Sept. 1936, Haarlem; s. of Albert J. Franken and Catherine G. Weijland; m. 1st Boudewine D.M. Bonebakker 1966 (divorced 1993); two s. one d.; m. 2nd Ingrid L. E. Sanders 1995 (died 2008); ed Univ. of Leiden, Univ. of Paris (Sorbonne), France, Univ. of Amsterdam; Sec., Mil. Tribunal 1960; Asst Prosecutor, Dist Court, Rotterdam 1964; mem. Rotterdam Bar 1967; judge 1969; Prof. of Jurisprudence, Erasmus Univ., Rotterdam 1974, of Jurisprudence, Univ. of Leiden 1977–98, of Information Law 1987–98, Dean Leiden Law Faculty 1995–98, now Prof. Emer.; Prof. of Information Law, Univ. of Groningen 1989–95; mem. State Council 1982–87, Court of Appeal, The Hague 1977–2006; Chair. Nat. Cttee of Information Tech. and Law; mem. Social Econ. Council 1988–2004, Sec.-Gen. Royal Acad. of Arts and Sciences 1998–2001; mem. Senate (Eerste Kamer) 2004–15; Kt of Netherlands Lion 1995; Modderman Prijs 1973, Wolffert van Borselenpenning 1982. *Publications include:* Vervolgingsbeleid: The Policy of Public Prosecutors 1973, Maat en Regel 1975, Jurimetrics and the Rule of Law 1975, The New Law and Economics 1982, Models of Contracts in Information Law 1992, Introduction to the Law (10th edn) 2003, Trusted Third Parties 1996, Law and Computer (5th edn) 2004, Independence and Responsibility of the Judge 1997, Nemo Plus 2001. *Address:* Faculty of Law, University of Leiden, Kamerlingh Onnes Gebouw, Steenschuur 25, 2311 ES Leiden (office); Weipoortseweg 95A, 2381 NJ Zoeterwoude, Netherlands (home). *Telephone:* (71) 5277841 (office); (71) 5804764 (home). *Fax:* (71) 5809794 (home). *E-mail:* h.franken@law.leidenuniv.nl (office); h.franken@xs4all.nl. *Website:* www.universiteitleiden.nl/en/law (office).

FRANKL, Peter; British pianist and academic; b. 2 Oct. 1935, Budapest, Hungary; s. of Tibor Frankl and Laura Frankl; m. Annie Feiner 1958; one s. one d.; ed Franz Liszt Acad. of Music, Budapest with Profs Hernadi, Kodály and Weiner; began career on int. circuit 1960s, London debut 1962, New York debut with Cleveland Orchestra 1967; has performed with numerous orchestras in USA (Chicago, Philadelphia, Boston, Washington, Los Angeles, San Francisco, Pittsburgh etc.), Berlin Philharmonic, Leipzig Gewandhaus, Amsterdam Concertgebouw, Orchestre de Paris, Israel Philharmonic, all London orchestras and many others in Europe and all parts of the world; has appeared with conductors including Abbado, Ashkenazy, Barbirolli, Blomstedt, Boulez, Chailly, Davis, Dorati, Fischer, Haitink, Kempe, Kertesz, Leinsdorf, Maazel, Masur, Muti, Sanderling, Solti, Szell, among others; numerous tours to Japan, Australia, NZ and South Africa, playing with orchestras, in recitals and in chamber music concerts; more than 20 appearances at BBC Promenade Concerts, London; regular participant at Edinburgh, Cheltenham, Aldeburgh, Verbier, Kuhmo, Naantali and Casals Festivals; soloist at Enescu Festival, Bucharest with Budapest Festival Orchestra at one of the last concerts Yehudi Menuhin ever conducted; regular guest artist at summer festivals in Aspen, Chautauqua, Hollywood Bowl, Marlboro, Norfolk, Ravinia, Santa Fe and Yellow Barn, USA; toured with Frankl-Pauk-Kirshbaum Trio world-wide; frequent performances with string quartets including Amadeus, Bartók, Borodin, Fine Arts, Guarneri, Lindsay, Panocha, Takacs, Tokyo and Vermeer; master-classes world-wide, including RAM and Royal Coll. of Music, London, Liszt Acad., Budapest, Van Cliburn Inst., Texas, in Berlin, Madrid, Beijing, Hong Kong and Seoul; mem. numerous jury panels at int. piano competitions, including Van Cliburn, Rubinstein, Leeds, Santander, Hilton Head, William Kappell, Hong Kong, Clara Haskil, Paderewski, Marguerite Long, Cleveland, Shanghai, Manchester and Brussels (Queen Elisabeth); apptd mem. Faculty, Yale Univ. School of Music 1987, Prof. of Piano –2017 (retd); Hon. Prof., Franz Liszt Acad. of Music; Officer's Cross 1972, Middle Cross (Hungary) 2005; won first prize in several int. competitions, Distinguished Visitors Medal, Univ. of Toronto. *Recordings include:* complete Schumann and Debussy piano works (with Andras Schiff, the Schumann two-piano and four-hand repertoire); both Brahms Concerti and the Violin Sonatas (with Kyung Wha Chung) and Piano Trios; Piano Concerti, Violin Sonatas and four-hand works by Mozart; Bartók solo and violin pieces; Piano Quintets by Brahms, Schumann, Dvořák, Martinů and Dohnányi. *Leisure interests:* football, opera, theatre, tennis. *Address:* c/o Donald E. Osborne, California Artists Management, 449 Springs Road, Vallejo, CA 94590-5359, USA (office); 5 Gresham Gardens, London, NW11 8NX, England (home). *Telephone:* (415) 362-2787 (office); (20) 8455-5228 (home). *E-mail:* camdon@aol.com (office); info@peterfrankl.co.uk. *Website:* www.calartists.com (office); www.peterfrankl.co.uk; music.yale.edu/faculty/frankl-peter. *Fax:* (20) 8455-2176 (home).

FRANKLIN, Barbara Hackman, BA, MBA; American business executive and fmr government official; *President and CEO, Barbara Franklin Enterprises;* b. (Barbara Ann Hackman), 19 March 1940, Lancaster, Pa; d. of Arthur A. Hackman and Mayme M. Hackman (née Haller); m. Wallace Barnes 1986; ed Pennsylvania State Univ., Harvard Business School; with Singer Co., New York 1964–68; Asst Vice-Pres. Citibank, New York 1969–71; White House Staff Asst to the Pres. for Recruiting Women to Govt, Washington, DC 1971–73; Commr and Vice-Chair. US Consumer Product Safety Comm., Washington, DC 1973–79; Sr Fellow and Dir Govt and Business Program, Wharton School, Univ. of Pa 1980–88; Pres. and CEO Franklin Assocs, Washington, DC 1984–92, Pres. and CEO Barbara Franklin Enterprises 1995–; US Sec. of Commerce, Dept of Commerce, Washington, DC 1992–93; mem. Pres.'s Advisory Cttee for Trade Policy and Negotiations 1982–86, 1989–92; mem. US Comptroller Gen.'s Consultant Panel 1984–92; mem. Bd of Dirs Aetna Inc. 1979–92, 1993–, Dow Chemical Co. 1980–92, 1993–2012, Pathway Genomics 2015–; Chair. Emer. Bd of Trustees, Econ. Club of New York; mem. Bd of Dirs Nat. Asscn of Corp. Dirs (NACD), Chair. 2009–12; fmr Vice-Chair. US-China Business Council, now Dir; fmr Chair. Asian Studies Advisory Council, Heritage Foundation; Dir or Trustee of three funds in American Funds Family of Mutual Funds; Dir Nat. Cttee for US–China Relations, Nat. Symphony Orchestra, The Richard Nixon Foundation; mem. Council on Foreign Relations, Int. Women's Forum (founding mem.), Foreign Policy Asscn, US-China Policy Foundation, Cttee for Econ. Devt; mem. Int. Advisory Bd LafargeHolcim Inc.; mem. Advisory Council Public Co. Accounting Oversight Bd, Management Executives Soc.; several hon. degrees, including from Briarwood Coll., Univ. of Hartford, Drexel Univ., Bryant Coll.; numerous awards for professional achievement, including John J. McCloy Award, NACD Dir of the Year Award 2000, Bd Alert Outstanding Dir 2003, Woodrow Wilson Award for Public Service 2006, recognized by Directorship as one of the 100 most influential people in corp. governance 2007, 2009, CT Women's Hall of Fame Inductee 2013, NACD Directorship 100 Hall of Fame 2014, Financial Executives Int. Hall of Fame 2015, PSU Distinguished Alumni Award, HBS Alumni Achievement Award. *Television:* regular commentator, Nightly Business Report, Public Broadcasting Service 1997–2012. *Leisure interests:* exercise, hiking, reading, painting. *Address:* Barbara Franklin Enterprises, 2600 Virginia Avenue NW, Suite 506, Washington, DC 20037, USA (office). *Telephone:* (202) 337-9100 (office). *Fax:* (202) 337-9104 (office). *E-mail:* bhfranklin@bhfranklin.com (office). *Website:* www.bhfranklin.com (office).

FRANKLIN, Kirk; American singer, songwriter and record company executive; b. (Kirk Smith), 26 Jan. 1970, Fort Worth, Tex.; m. Tammy Collins 1996; four c.; Choir Dir Greater Strangers Rest Baptist Church, Fort Worth 1988; worked with Dallas-Fort Worth Mass Choir on albums I Will Not Let Nothing Separate Me 1991, Another Chance 1993; f. choir group The Family; Founder, Chair. and CEO Fo Yo Soul Entertainment, Inc., Dallas, Tex. 2004–; BET Award for Best Gospel Artist 2006, 2007, American Music Award for Favorite Contemporary Inspirational Artist 2006, Grammy Awards for Best Gospel Song (for Imagine Me) 2007, (for Help Me Believe) 2009, (for Hello Fear) 2012, (for God Provides) 2017, (for Never Alone) (co-winner) 2019, Billboard Music Award for Top Gospel Artist 2016. *Film soundtrack contributions include:* My Life is in Your Hands (for Get on the Bus 1996), Joy (for The Preacher's Wife 1996). *Recordings include:* albums: with The Family: Kirk Franklin and The Family 1992, Christmas 1995, Watcha Lookin' 4 (Grammy Award for Best Contemporary Soul Gospel Album 1997) 1996; solo: God's Property from Kirk Franklin's Nu Nation (Grammy Award for Best Gospel Album by a choir or chorus 1998) 1997, The Nu Nation Project (Grammy Award for Best Contemporary Soul Gospel Album 1999) 1998, Kirk Franklin and the Family 2001, The Rebirth of Kirk Franklin 2002, Hero (Grammy Award for Best Contemporary R&B Gospel Album 2007) 2006, Songs from the Storm, Vol. 1 2006, The Fight of My Life (Grammy Award for Best Contemporary R&B Gospel Album 2009) 2007, Hello Fear (Grammy Award for Best Gospel Album 2012) 2011, Losing My Religion (Grammy Award for Best Gospel Album 2017) 2016, Dying to Live 2019. *Publications include:* Church Boy: My Music and My Life (autobiography) 1998, The Blueprint: A Plan for Living Above Life's Storms 2010. *E-mail:* info@foyosoulentertainment.com. *Website:* www.foyosoulentertainment.com; www.kirkfranklin.com.

FRANKLIN, Melissa Jeanette (Missy); American fmr swimmer; b. 10 May 1995, Pasadena, Calif.; d. of Dick Franklin and D. A. Franklin; began swimming aged five; competed at Olympic Team Trials 2008 aged 13; competed in six individual events Nat. Championships 2010; won first int. medal at Fédération Internationale de Natation (FINA) World Championships, Dubai 2010; silver medal, 100m, 200m backstroke, 4×100m medley relay, Pan Pacific Swimming Championships 2010; gold medal, 200m freestyle, 200m backstroke, 4×100m medley relay, silver medal, 4×100m freestyle relay, bronze medal, 50m backstroke, World Aquatics Championships, Shanghai 2011; winner, 100m backstroke, 100m backstroke freestyle, US Nat. Championships 2011; winner 200m backstroke, FINA Swimming World Cup 2011; gold medal, 4×100m medley relay, Duel in the Pool, Atlanta 2011; gold medal, 100m backstroke, 200m backstroke, 4×200m freestyle relay, 4×100m medley relay, bronze medal, 4×100m freestyle relay, Olympic Games, London 2012; gold medal, 100m backstroke, 200m backstroke, 200m freestyle, 4×100m medley relay, 4×100m freestyle relay, 4×200m freestyle relay, FINA World Championships, Barcelona 2013; bronze medal, 200m freestyle, 4×200m freestyle relay, 200m backstroke, bronze medal, 4×100m freestyle relay, FINA World Cup 2015; gold medal 4×200m freestyle relay, Olympic Games Rio 2016; holds a record of winning 11 gold medals at World Aquatics Championships (broken by Katie Ledecky in 2017); swam for Colorado Stars; retd from competitive swimming 2018; Breakout Performer of the Year Award at Golden Goggle Awards 2010, Female Athlete of the Year and Race of the Year Award (200m backstroke) and Relay Performance of the Year (4×100m medley relay), Swimming's Annual Awards Night 2011, Best Female Swimmer, FINA Aquatics World Magazine 2011, FINA Swimmer of the Year 2011–12, World Swimmer of the Year 2012, American

Swimmer of the Year 2012, Women's Sports Foundation Female for Athlete of the Year 2013, ESPY Award for Best Female Olympic Athlete 2013. *Leisure interests:* reading, dancing. *Website:* www.coloradostars.org; www.missyfranklin.com.

FRANKLIN, Raoul Norman, CBE, DSc, FREng; British scientist, academic and university administrator; b. 3 June 1935, Hamilton, NZ; s. of N. G. Franklin and T. B. Franklin (née Davis); m. 1st Faith Ivens 1961 (died 2004); two s.; m. 2nd Christine Penfold 2005; ed Auckland Grammar School, Univ. of Auckland, Univ. of Oxford; Sr Research Fellow, Royal Mil. Coll. of Science 1961–63; Tutorial Fellow, Keble Coll., Oxford 1963–78, Univ. Lecturer, Eng Science, Oxford Univ. 1967–78; Consultant, UKAEA Culham Lab. 1968–; Vice-Chancellor, City Univ., London 1978–98, Prof. Plasma Physics and Tech. 1986–98; Visiting Prof., Open Univ. Oxford Research Unit 1998; Chair. City Tech. Ltd 1978–93; Chair. Assoc. Examining Bd 1994–98, Assessment and Qualifications Alliance (AQA) 1998–2003; Vice-Chair. Gen. Bd of the Faculties, Oxford Univ. 1971–74; mem. of Hebdomadal Council, Oxford Univ. 1971–74, 1976–78, of Science Bd, Science and Eng Research Council 1982–85, of London Pensions Fund Authority 1989–95, of Bd Arab-British Chamber of Commerce 1995–2002; mem. Council Gresham Coll. 1980–98; mem. Int. Cttee of ESCAMPIG (Europhysics Conf. on Atomic & Molecular Physics of Ionized Gases) 1993–96; Gov. Ashridge Man. Coll. 1986–99, Council City & Guilds 1996–2000, Council Univ. of Buckingham 2001–; Foundation Master, Guild of Educators 2001–02; Trustee, Trust Fund 2009; Master, Worshipful Co. of Curriers 2002–03; Hon. Fellow, Keble Coll., Coll. of Preceptors, Guildhall School of Music and Drama, Royal Inst. of Chartered Surveyors; Freeman, City of London; Distinguished Alumni Award, Univ. of Auckland 2004. *Publications:* Plasma Phenomena in Gas Discharges 1976, Physical Kinetics, Vol. XII 1981, Interaction of Intense Electromagnetic Fields with Plasmas (ed.) 1981. *Leisure interests:* walking, gardening. *Address:* 12 Moreton Road, Oxford, OX2 7AX, England (home). *Telephone:* (1865) 558311 (home). *E-mail:* raoulnf_1935@gmail.com (home).

FRANKLYN, Gregor; Saint Lucia banking executive; currently Country Dir St Lucia Office, Eastern Caribbean Cen. Bank. *Address:* Eastern Caribbean Central Bank-Saint Lucia Office, Colony House, Unit 5, John Compton Highway, POB 295, Castries LC04 101, Saint Lucia (office). *Telephone:* 452-7449 (office). *Fax:* 453-6022 (office). *E-mail:* eccbslu@candw.lc (office). *Website:* www.eccb-centralbank.org (office).

FRANKS, Gen. (retd) Tommy Ray, KBE, MS; American army officer (retd); b. 17 June 1945, Wynnewood, Okla; m. Cathryn Carley 1969; one d.; ed Univ. of Texas, Shippensburg Univ., Pa, Armed Forces Staff Coll., US Army War Coll.; commissioned 2nd Lt 1967; served with 9th Infantry Div., Viet Nam, 2nd Armored Cavalry Regt, FRG; Commdr 2nd Bn 78th Field Artillery, FRG 1981–84; Deputy Asst G3, III Corps, Fort Hood, Tex. 1985–87; Commdr Div. Artillery, 1st Cavalry Div. 1987–88; Chief of Staff 1st Cavalry Div. 1988–89; Asst Div. Commdr (Maneuver), 1st Cavalry Div., Operation Desert Shield/Desert Storm, Saudi Arabia, Iraq 1990–91; Asst Commdt Field Artillery School, Fort Sill, Okla 1991–92; Dir La. Maneuvers Task Force, Office Chief of Staff US Army, Fort Monroe, Va 1992–94; Asst Chief of Staff Combined Forces Command and US Forces Korea 1994; Commdr 2nd Infantry Div., Korea 1995–97, Commdr 3rd US Army, Fort McPherson, Ga 1997–2000; promoted Gen., C-in-C US Cen. Command, MacDill Air Force Base, Fla 2000–03; lead American and Coalition troops in Operation Enduring Freedom in Afghanistan 2001 and Operation Iraqi Freedom in Iraq 2004; f. Franks & Assocs LLC 2003; mem. William Penn Univ.; Advisor to the Gen Franks Leadership Inst. and Museum, Hobart Okla; Defense Distinguished Service Medal, Distinguished Service Medal (with oak leaf cluster), Legion of Merit (with three oak leaf clusters), Bronze Star Medal (with 'V' device and three oak leaf clusters), Purple Heart (with two oak leaf clusters), Air Medal (with 'V' device), Presidential Medal of Freedom 2004; Hon. Co-Chair. Flight 93 Nat. Memorial 2005. *Publications:* American Soldier 2004. *Leisure interests:* country music, Mexican food, Harley road trips. *Address:* 4 Star Ranch, Roosevelt, OK 73564, USA (office). *E-mail:* admin@tommyfranks.com. *Website:* www.tommyfranks.com; www.tommyfranksmuseum.org (office). *Telephone:* (580) 639-2526 (office).

FRANZ, Christoph, Dr rer. pol; German business executive; *Chairman, Roche Group;* b. 2 May 1960, Frankfurt am Main; ed Ecole Centrale de Lyon and Ecole Supérieure de Commerce de Lyon, France, Darmstadt Tech. Univ., Univ. of California, Berkeley, USA; joined Deutsche Lufthansa AG 1990, initially involved in strategy, sales and controlling projects in Germany, France and Turkey, later mem. staff team of then-CEO Jürgen Weber 1992–94, mem. Exec. Bd, Deutsche Lufthansa AG and CEO Lufthansa German Airlines 2009–10, served as Deputy to Exec. Bd Chair. and CEO, Chair. Exec. Bd and CEO Deutsche Lufthansa AG 2011–14, mem. Supervisory Bd, Lufthansa Technik and Swiss International Air Lines; with Deutsche Bahn AG 1994, held various exec. functions 1994–2003, mem. Exec. Bd and CEO Passenger Transport Div. 2004; CEO Swiss International Air Lines (SWISS) 2004–09; mem. Admin. Bd, Roche, Chair. Roche Holding Ltd (Roche Group) 2014–; mem. Bd, Stadler Rail AG, Lufthansa Technik AG, Zurich Insurance Group Ltd; mem. Bd of Trustees, Avenir Suisse, Ernst Göhner Foundation; mem. Advisory Bd, Univ. of St Gallen (HSG). *Address:* Roche Holding Ltd, Grenzacherstrasse 124, 4070 Basel, Switzerland (office). *Telephone:* (61) 688-11-11 (office). *Fax:* (61) 691-93-91 (office). *E-mail:* info@roche.com (office). *Website:* www.roche.com (office).

FRANZ, Judy R., BA, MS, PhD; American physicist and academic; *Executive Officer Emeritus, American Physical Society;* b. (Judy Rosenbaum), 3 May 1938, Chicago, Ill.; m. Frank A. Franz; one s.; ed Cornell Univ., Univ. of Ill.; Research Scientist, IBM Research Labs, Switzerland 1965–67; Asst Prof. of Physics, Indiana Univ., Bloomington 1968–74, Assoc. Prof. 1974–79, Prof. 1979–87, Assoc. Dean, Coll. of Arts and Sciences 1980–82; Prof. of Physics, Univ. of West Virginia 1987–94; Prof. of Physics, Univ. of Alabama 1994–2007; Visiting Prof., Cornell Univ. 1985–86, 1988, 1990; Councillor-at-Large, American Physical Soc. 1984–88, Exec. Officer 1994–2007, Exec. Officer Emer. 2007–; Councillor-at-Large, Asscn for Women in Science (AWIS) 1981–83; mem. Editorial Bd, American Journal of Physics 1985–88; mem. Exec. Bd Council of Scientific Soc. Presidents 1990; Pres. American Asscn of Physics Teachers 1990; mem. Council, AAAS 1995–98; Assoc. Sec.-Gen., IUPAP 1999–2002, Sec.-Gen. 2002–08; mem. Governing Bd, Exec. Cttee of American Inst. of Physics; Rep. to US Nat. Cttee to UNESCO 2004–08; mem. Bd, ASTRA; Fellow, American Physical Soc., AAAS, Asscn of Anatomical Pathology Technologists, AWIS; Distinguished Teaching Award, Ind. Univ. 1978, Humboldt Research Fellowship, Munich, Germany 1978–79, Alumni Honor Award for Distinguished Service, Coll. of Eng, Univ. of Illinois, Urbana-Champaign 1997, Melba Newell Phillips Medal, American Asscn of Physics Teachers 2008. *Publications:* Physics in the 20th Century (co-ed.) 1999; numerous contribs to Physics Review, Journal of Physics and other professional journals. *Leisure interests:* hiking, reading, gardening, concerts. *Address:* 1177 22nd Street NW, #5K, Washington, DC 20037, USA (office). *Telephone:* (202) 296-3736 (office). *E-mail:* franz@aps.org (office).

FRANZEN, Jonathan, BA; American writer; b. 17 Aug. 1959, Western Springs, Ill.; partner Kathryn Chetkovich; ed Swarthmore Coll., Free Univ. of Berlin, Germany; fmrly worked part-time in seismology lab., Harvard Univ. Dept of Earth and Planetary Sciences; currently full-time novelist, essayist, and journalist affiliated with The New Yorker; mem. American Acad. of Arts and Letters 2012–; Hon. DHumLitt (Swarthmore Coll.) 2005; Whiting Award 1988, Guggenheim Fellowship, American Acad. Berlin Prize 2000, Granta Best Young American Novelist, Carlos Fuentes Medal, Guadalajara International Book Fair 2012, Budapest Grand Prize, Int. Book Festival Budapest 2015. *Publications include:* The Twenty-Seventh City (Whiting Award) 1988, Strong Motion 1991, The Corrections (Nat. Book Award for Fiction, New York Times Ed.'s Choice, James Tait Black Memorial Prize for Fiction 2003) 2001, How to be Alone (essays) 2002, The Discomfort Zone: A Personal History 2006, Spring Awakening (new trans. of Frank Wedekind play) 2007, Freedom (Heartland Prize, John Gardner Fiction Award 2011, Int. Author of the Year 2010, Specsavers Nat. Book Awards 2010) 2010, Farther Away (essays) 2012, The Kraus Project (non-fiction) 2013, Purity 2015, The End of the End of the Earth: Essays (essays) 2018. *Address:* c/o Steven Barclay Agency, 12 Western Avenue, Petaluma, CA 94952, USA (office). *Telephone:* (707) 773-0654 (office). *Fax:* (707) 778-1868 (office). *E-mail:* info@barclayagency.com (office). *Website:* www.barclayagency.com (office); us.macmillan.com/author/jonathanfranzen.

FRASE, Jeffrey Scott, BS; American business executive; ed Lehigh Univ.; Man. Dir and Global Head of Crude Oil and Derivatives Trading, Goldman Sachs 1990–2007; Head of Global Oil, Lehman Brothers 2007–08; Man. Dir and Global Head of Oil Trading, JP Morgan, New York 2008–13; Co-Head of Global Energy, Noble Americas 2013–15, Exec. Dir and Co-CEO Noble Group 2015–17; Commodity Exec., Advisor and Bd Mem., Frase and Co. 2017–.

FRASER, Lady Antonia, CH, DBE, CBE, MA, FRSL; British writer; b. (Antonia Margaret Caroline Pakenham), 27 Aug. 1932, London, England; d. of the 7th Earl and Countess of Longford; m. 1st Hugh Fraser 1956 (divorced 1977, died 1984); three s. three d.; m. 2nd Harold Pinter 1980 (died 2008); one step-s.; ed Dragon School, Oxford, St Mary's Convent, Ascot and Lady Margaret Hall, Oxford; mem. Cttee English PEN 1979–88 (Pres. 1988–89, Vice-Pres. 1990–), Crimewriters Asscn 1980–86, Writers in Prison Cttee, Chair. 1985–88, 1990; Hon. DLitt (Hull) 1986, (Sussex) 1990, (Nottingham) 1993, (St Andrew's) 1994; Prix Caumont-La Force 1985, Norton Medlicott Medal, Historical Asscn 2000. *TV plays include:* Charades 1977, Mister Clay 1985. *Publications:* King Arthur 1954, Robin Hood 1955, Dolls 1963, History of Toys 1966, Mary, Queen of Scots (James Tait Black Memorial Prize 1969) 1969, Cromwell: Our Chief of Men 1973, King James VI of Scotland and I of England 1974, Scottish Love Poems, A Personal Anthology 1974, Kings and Queens of England (ed.) 1975, Love Letters (anthology) 1976, King Charles II 1979, Heroes and Heroines (ed.) 1980, Oxford In Verse (ed.) 1982, The Weaker Vessel (Wolfson History Prize 1984) 1984, Boadicea's Chariot: The Warrior Queens 1988, The Six Wives of Henry VIII 1992, Charles II: His Life and Times 1993, The Gunpowder Plot (St Louis Literary Award 1996, CWA Non-Fiction Gold Dagger 1996) 1996, The Lives of the Kings and Queens of England 1998, Marie Antoinette: The Journey (Enid McLeod Literary Prize, Franco-British Soc. 2001) 2001, Love and Louis XIV 2006, Must You Go? My Life with Harold Pinter 2010, Perilous Question: The Drama of the Great Reform Bill 1832 2013, My History: A Memoir of Growing Up 2015, The King and the Catholics: The Fight for Rights 1829 2018; Jemima Shore novels: Quiet as a Nun (TV adaptation 1978) 1977, The Wild Island 1978, A Splash of Red 1981, Cool Repentance 1982, Oxford Blood 1985, Jemima Shore's First Case 1986, Your Royal Hostage 1987, The Cavalier Case 1990, Jemima Shore at the Sunny Grave 1991, Political Death: A Jemima Shore Mystery 1994; anthologies (ed.): Scottish Love Poems 1975, Love Letters 1976; ed. The Pleasure of Reading 1992, 2015. *Leisure interests:* cats, grandchildren. *Address:* c/o Jonathan Lloyd, Curtis Brown Group Ltd, Haymarket House, 28–29 Haymarket, London, SW1Y 4SP, England (office). *Telephone:* (20) 7393-4418 (office). *E-mail:* sabhbh.curran@curtisbrown.co.uk (office). *Website:* www.curtisbrown.co.uk/client/antonia-fraser (office).

FRASER, Bernard (Bernie) William, BA; Australian economist, central bank governor and business executive; b. 26 Feb. 1941, Junee, NSW; s. of K. Fraser; m. Edna Gallogly 1965 (divorced); one s. two d.; ed Junee High School, NSW, Univ. of New England, Armidale, NSW, Australian Nat. Univ., ACT; joined Dept of Nat. Devt 1961; joined Dept of Treasury 1963, Treasury Rep., London, UK 1969–72, First Asst Sec. 1979, Sec. Dept 1984–89; with Dept of Finance 1976; mem. Bd of Dirs Nat. Energy Office 1981–83, Queensland Treasury Corpn; Chair. and Gov. Reserve Bank of Australia 1989–96; Chair. Govt Superannuation Office of Victoria, Members Equity; Trustee and Dir Construction and Bldg Unions Superannuation Trust (C+BUS) 1996, Superannuation Trust of Australia 1996, Australian Retirement Fund 1996; Chair. Members Equity Bank (ME Bank) 2000–15 (retd); Hon. Prof. of Econs, Univ. of Canberra; Dr hc (Univ. of New England), (Charles Sturt Univ.). *Leisure interest:* farming.

FRASER, Brendan; American actor; b. 3 Dec. 1968, Indianapolis, Ind.; m. Afton Smith; two s.; ed Cornish Inst. *Films include:* My Old School (TV) 1991, Dogfight 1991, Child of Darkness, Child of Light (TV) 1991, Guilty Until Proven Innocent (TV) 1991, Encino Man 1992, School Ties 1992, Twenty Bucks 1993, Younger and Younger 1993, With Honors 1994, Airheads 1994, The Scout 1994, The Passion of Darkly Noon 1995, Mrs Winterbourne 1996, Glory Daze 1996, George of the Jungle 1997, The Twilight of the Golds (TV) 1997, Still Breathing 1997, Gods and Monsters 1998, Blast from the Past 1999, The Mummy 1999, Dudley Do-Right 1999, Sinbad: Beyond the Veil of Mists (voice) 2000, Bedazzled 2000, Monkeybone 2001, The Mummy Returns 2001, The Quiet American 2002, Revenge of the

Mummy: The Ride 2004, Crash 2004, Beach Bunny (voice) 2005, Journey to the End of the Night 2006, The Last Time 2006, The Air I Breathe 2007, Journey to the Center of the Earth 2007, The Mummy: Tomb of the Dragon Emperor 2008, Inkheart 2008, Extraordinary Measures 2010, Stand Off 2012, Escape from Planet Earth (voice) 2013, A Case of You 2013, Gimme Shelter 2013, The Nut Job (voice) 2014. *Television includes:* My Old School 1991, Fallen Angels 1995, Duckman (voice) 1997, The Simpsons (voice) 1998, King of the Hill 2000, Scrubs 2002, Wishology (voice) 2009. *Website:* www.brendanfraser.com.

FRASER, Dawn, AO, MBE, JP; Australian fmr swimmer; b. 4 Sept. 1937, Balmain, near Sydney; d. of Kenneth Fraser and Rose Miranda Fraser; m. Gary Ware (divorced); one d.; first female swimmer to win gold medals in three consecutive Olympic Games 1956, 1960, 1964; broke women's 100m freestyle world record nine times 1956–64; first female to break 60 seconds in 100m freestyle; shares record for most Olympic medals won by a woman swimmer (four gold, four silver); set 39 world records; banned for 10 years (later rescinded) after Tokyo Games for allegedly stealing an Olympic Flag from Japanese Imperial Hotel, forcing retirement; became involved in coaching, business ventures, politics; mem. NSW Parl. for Balmain 1988–91; attaché to Australian Olympic Team 2000; mem. Int. Swimming Hall of Fame Selection Cttee; dedicates most of her time to her sponsors; also guest speaking for a wide range of causes; Dir DF Prom., NRMA M&S, Wests Tigers NRL Football Club; Australian of the Year 1965, Int. Swimming Hall of Fame 1965, Olympic Order Award 1981, honoured as one of the greatest Olympians of all time at Atlanta Olympics 1996, named Nat. Living Treasure by Australian Govt, voted Athlete of the Century 1999. *Publication:* Below the Surface: Australian Title Gold Medal Girl (autobiog., with Harry Gordon) 1965, Dawn: One Hell of a Life (autobiog.) 2001. *Leisure interests:* spending time with grandson, jet skiing, cycling, walking the dogs. *Address:* PO Box 118, Balmain, NSW 2041, Australia (office). *Telephone:* (417) 900040 (office). *E-mail:* info@dawnfraser.com.au (office). *Website:* www.dawnfraser.com (office).

FRASER, Hon. John Allen, PC, OC, OBC, CD, QC; Canadian organization official and fmr politician; b. 15 Dec. 1931, Yokohoma, Japan; m. Catherine Findlay; three d.; ed Univ. of BC; law practice, Vic., Powell River, Vancouver 1955–72; mem. House of Commons 1972–94, Speaker of the House of Commons 1986–94; Minister of the Environment and Postmaster Gen. 1979–80; Minister of Fisheries and Oceans 1984–85 (resgnd); Amb. for the Environment 1994–98; Chair. Pacific Fisheries Resource Conservation Council 1998–2005, now mem. Council; Chair. Nat. Defence Minister's Monitoring Cttee on Change 1996–2003, Pacific Fisheries Resource Conservation Council 1998–2005, BC Pacific Salmon Forum 2004–09; Co-Chair. Advisory Council, Equitas Soc.; Hon. Lt-Col, Seaforth Highlanders of Canada 1994, now Hon. Col; Hon. LLD (St Lawrence Univ.) 1999, (Simon Fraser Univ.) 1999, (Univ. of BC) 2004; Vimy Award, Conf. of Defence Asscns Inst. 2002. *Publication:* The House of Commons at Work 1993.

FRASER-PRYCE, Shelly-Ann, OD, BSc; Jamaican athlete; b. (Shelly-Ann Fraser), 27 Dec. 1986, Kingston; d. of Maxine Simpson; m. Jason Pryce 2011; ed Wolmer's High School For Girls, Univ. of Technology; first Jamaican woman in history to win an Olympic gold medal in the 100m, Beijing Olympics 2008 (personal best time of 10.78 seconds); gold medal, 100m, World Athletics Final, Stuttgart 2008, silver medal, Thessaloniki 2009; gold medal, 100m, 4×100m. relay, World Championships, Berlin 2009, silver medal, 4×100m. relay, World Championships, Daegu 2011, gold medal, 100m, 200m., 4×100m. relay, World Championships, Moscow 2013, gold medal, 100m, 4×100m. relay, World Championships, Beijing 2015; gold medal, 60m, World Indoor Championships, Sopot 2014; gold medal, 4×100m. relay, Commonwealth Games, Glasgow 2014; gold medal, 100m, silver medal, 200m., 4×100m. relay, London Olympics 2012; bronze medal, 100m, silver medal, 4×100m. relay, Rio Olympics 2016; coached by Stephen Francis, MVP Track & Field Club; Order of Distinction; first UNICEF Nat. Goodwill Amb. for Jamaica 2010, Grace Goodwill Amb. for Peace 2010, Golden Cleats Award for Female Athlete of the Year 2010, 2013, IAAF Female Athlete of the Year 2013. *Address:* Jamaica Athletics Administrative Association Ltd, PO Box 272, Kingston 5, Jamaica. *Telephone:* 978-7102. *Fax:* 946-0003. *E-mail:* athleticsja@cwjamaica.com.

FRASYNIUK, Władysław; Polish politician and trade union official; b. 25 Nov. 1954, Wrocław; s. of Stanisław Frasyniuk and Zofia Frasyniuk; m. 1978; one s. three d.; driver, mechanic Municipal Transport, Wrocław, organizer of strike in bus depot, Wrocław Aug. 1980; press spokesman Founding Cttee of Ind. Self-Governing Trade Union; Chair. Solidarity Trade Union, Lower Silesia 1981–90 (resgnd); mem. Nat. Consultative Comm. of Solidarity; active underground under martial law, Jt Founder Provisional Exec. Cttee of Solidarity; arrested 1982, amnestied 1984; arrested again Feb. 1985, sentenced to over 4 years, amnestied 1986; mem. Provisional Council of Solidarity 1986–87, Nat. Exec. Comm. of Solidarity 1987–90; mem. Citizens' Cttee of Solidarity, Chair. 1988–90; took part in Round Table talks, Comm. for Trade Union Pluralism Feb.–April 1989; among founders and leaders of Citizens' Movt for Democratic Action (ROAD) 1990–91; mem. Social-Liberal faction of Democratic Union 1991–94; Vice-Chair. Democratic Union 1991–94; mem. Freedom Union (now Democratic Party (Partia Demokratyczna), Chair. 2005–06; Deputy to Sejm (Parl.) 1991–2001; Hon. Citizen of Wroclaw 2011, Hon. Citizen of Lower Silesia 2014; Kt's Cross, Order of Polonia Restituta 1990, Grand Cross, Order of Polonia Restituta 2006, Chevalier, Légion d'honneur 2016; United Wroclaw 1995, Polish-Indian Award, Delhi 1996. *Leisure interests:* dogs, individual sports, history of Russia.

FRATTINI, Franco, LLB; Italian lawyer and politician; *President, Società Italiana Organizzazione Internazionale (Italian Society for International Organization);* b. 14 March 1957, Rome; s. of Alberto Frattini and Lea Frattini; ed Sapienza - Università di Roma; State Attorney 1981, Attorney, State Attorney-Gen.'s Office 1984; Magistrate, Regional Admin. Tribunal, Piedmont 1984–86, Council of State Judge 1986–; Legal Adviser to Minister of the Treasury 1986, to Deputy Prime Minister 1990–91, to Prime Minister 1992; Deputy Sec.-Gen., Office of Prime Minister 1993, Sec.-Gen. 1994; Minister for Civil Service and Regional Affairs 1995–96; mem. Camera dei Deputati (Parl.) (Forza Italia) 1995–96, 2001–04, Pres. Parl. Cttee for Intelligence and Security Services and State Secrets 1996–2004; City Councillor, Rome 1997–2000; Minister for Civil Service and for Co-ordination of Intelligence and Security Services 2001–02, for Foreign Affairs 2002–04, 2008–11; Vice-Pres. European Comm., Commr for Justice, Freedom and Security 2004–08; Pres. Foundation Alcide De Gasperi 2011–13, Società Italiana Organizzazione Internazionale (SIOI—Italian Soc. for Int. Org.) 2012–, High Court of Sport Justice (CONI); Special Adviser to the Serbian Govt for the EU Integration Process; Justice and Chamber Pres., Italian Supreme Admin. Court; Special Rep. of OSCE Chair. for transdniestrian settlement process; Kt Grand Cross, Order of Merit of the Italian Repub.; Commdr, Légion d'honneur; Golden Neck-chain of the Olympic Order (IOC), Order of Friendship of the Russian Fed. *Publications include:* numerous specialist articles on law and public works. *Address:* Società Italiana Organizzazione Internazionale, Piazza di San Marco, 51, 00186 Rome, Italy (office). *Telephone:* (06) 6920781 (office). *E-mail:* f.frattini@sioi.org (office). *Website:* www.sioi.org (office); francofrattinidiarioitaliano.blogspot.it (home).

FRAYLING, Sir Christopher John, Kt, MA, PhD; British historian, arts administrator, broadcaster and academic; *Professor Emeritus, Royal College of Art;* b. 25 Dec. 1946; m. Helen Anne Snowdon; ed Repton School, Churchill Coll., Cambridge; Lecturer, Univ. of Bath, Univ. of Exeter during 1970s; Prof. of Cultural History, RCA 1979–2009, Prof. Emer. 2009–, f. Dept of Cultural History, Rector 1996–2009; mem. Arts Council England 1987–2000, Chair. 2004–09; Chair. Design Council, Crafts Study Centre, Royal Mint Advisory Cttee; fmr Gov. BFI; mem. Arts & Humanities Research Bd; Trustee, Victoria & Albert Museum; Hon. FRSA 2004, Hon. FRIBA 2005; several hon. doctorates, including Dr hc (Sheffield Hallam) 2010. *Television includes:* The Art of Persuasion (New York Film and Television Festival Gold Medal), The Face of Tutankhamun, Strange Landscape, Nightmare: The Birth of Horror 1996. *Radio includes:* The Rime of the Bounty (Sony Radio Award, Soc. of Authors Award). *Publications include:* Napoleon Wrote Fiction 1973, The Vampyre 1976, Spaghetti Westerns 1980, The Face of Tutankhamun 1992, Clint Eastwood: A Critical Biography 1993, Strange Landscape: A Journey through the Middle Ages 1995, Nightmare: The Birth of Horror 1996, Sergio Leone: Something to Do with Death 2000, Ken Adam: The Art of Production Design 2005, Mad, Bad and Dangerous? The Scientist and Cinema 2006, On Craftsmanship: Towards a New Bauhaus 2011, The Yellow Peril: Dr Fu Manchu and the Rise of Chinophobia 2014, Inside the Bloody Chamber: On Angela Carter, the Gothic and Other Weird Tales 2015. *Telephone:* (78) 0107-4181 (office). *E-mail:* hedda@hlaagency.co.uk (office). *Website:* www.hlaagency.co.uk (office); www.rca.ac.uk (office). *Address:* Royal College of Art, 15--25 Howie Street, London, SW11 4AS, England (office).

FRAYN, Michael, BA, FRSL; British playwright and author; b. 8 Sept. 1933, London; s. of Thomas A. Frayn and Violet A. Lawson; m. 1st Gillian Palmer 1960 (divorced 1989); three d.; m. 2nd Claire Tomalin (q.v.) 1993; ed Kingston Grammar School and Emmanuel Coll., Cambridge; reporter, The Guardian 1957–59, columnist 1959–62; columnist, The Observer 1962–68; Cameron Mackintosh Prof. of Contemporary Theatre, Univ. of Oxford 2009–10; Hon. Fellow, Emmanuel Coll., Cambridge, Emer. Fellow, St Catherine's Coll., Oxford; Order of Merit (Germany) 2004; Hon. DLitt (Cambridge) 2001; Heywood Hill Literary Prize 2002, Golden PEN Award 2003, Saint Louis Literary Award 2006, McGovern Award 2006, Companion of Literature 2007, Writers' Guild Lifetime Achievement Award 2010. *Stage plays include:* The Two of Us 1970, The Sandboy 1971, Alphabetical Order (Evening Standard Best Comedy of the Year 1975) 1975, Donkeys' Years (Laurence Olivier Award for Best Comedy 1976, Soc. of West End Theatre Comedy of the Year 1976) 1976, Clouds 1976, Balmoral 1978, Liberty Hall (new version of Balmoral) 1980, Make and Break 1980 (Evening Standard Best Comedy of the Year 1980), Noises Off (Evening Standard Best Comedy of the Year 1982, Laurence Olivier Award for Best Comedy 1982, Soc. of West End Theatre Comedy of the Year 1982) 1982, Benefactors (Laurence Olivier/BBC Award for Best New Play 1984) 1984, Look Look 1990, Here 1993, Now You Know 1995, Copenhagen (Evening Standard Award for Best Play of the Year 1998, West End Critics' Circle Best New Play Award 1998, Prix Molière Best New Play 1999, Tony Award for Best Play 2000) 1998, Alarms and Excursions 1998, Democracy (Evening Standard Theatre Award for Best Play, Critics' Circle Award for Best Play 2003) 2003, Afterlife 2007, Matchbox Theatre 2015. *TV includes:* plays: Jamie, on a Flying Visit (BBC) 1968, Birthday (BBC) 1969; documentary series: Second City Reports (with John Bird, Granada) 1964, Beyond a Joke (with John Bird and Eleanor Bron) 1972, Making Faces 1975; documentaries: One Pair of Eyes 1968, Laurence Sterne Lived Here 1973, Imagine a City Called Berlin 1975, Vienna: The Mask of Gold 1977, Three Streets in the Country 1979, The Long Straight (Great Railway Journeys of the World) 1980, Jerusalem 1984, Magic Lantern, Prague 1993, Budapest: Written in Water 1996 (all BBC documentaries); films: First and Last 1989, A Landing on the Sun 1994. *Cinema:* Clockwise 1986, Remember Me? 1997. *Plays translated include:* The Cherry Orchard, Three Sisters, The Seagull, Uncle Vanya, Wild Honey, The Sneeze (Chekhov), The Fruits of Enlightenment (Tolstoy), Exchange (Trifonov), Number One (Anouilh). *Publications include:* novels: The Tin Men (Somerset Maugham Award 1966) 1965, The Russian Interpreter (Hawthornden Prize 1967) 1966, Towards the End of the Morning 1967, A Very Private Life 1968, Sweet Dreams 1973, The Trick of It 1989, A Landing on the Sun (Sunday Express Book of the Year) 1991, Now You Know 1992, Headlong 1999, Spies (Whitbread Award for Best Novel) 2002, Skios 2012; non-fiction: Constructions (philosophy) 1974, Speak after the Beep 1995, Celia's Secret (with David Burke) 2000, The Human Touch: Our Part in the Creation of the Universe 2006, Stage Directions: Writing on Theatre 1970–2008 2008; Travels with a Typewriter 2009, My Father's Fortune: A Life (J. R. Ackerley Prize for Autobiography 2011) 2010, Matchbox Theatre 2015; several vols of collections of columns, plays and trans. *Address:* c/o Greene & Heaton Ltd, 37A Goldhawk Road, London, W12 8QQ, England (office).

FRAZIER, Kenneth C., BA, JD; American lawyer and business executive; *Chairman and CEO, Merck & Company, Inc.;* ed Pennsylvania State Univ., Harvard Law School; Pnr, Drinker Biddle & Reath (law firm), Philadelphia –1992; Vice-Pres., Gen. Counsel and Sec., Astra Merck Group 1992–94, Vice-Pres. of Public Affairs 1994–99, Asst Gen. Counsel, Corp. Staff 1997–99, Vice-Pres. and Deputy Gen. Counsel, Merck & Co., Inc. Jan.–Dec. 1999, Sr Vice-Pres. and Gen. Counsel 1999–2006, Exec. Vice-Pres. and Gen. Counsel 2006–07, Exec. Vice-Pres. and Pres. Global Human Health 2007–10, Pres. Merck & Co., Inc. 2010–11, CEO Jan. 2011–, Chair. Dec. 2011–; mem. Bd of Dirs, Exxon Mobil Corpn, Pennsylvania State Univ., Cornerstone Christian Acad., Philadelphia, Pa; mem. Council on Foreign Relations, Council of the American Law Inst., ABA; mem. Pres.'s

American Manufacturing Council –Aug. 2017 (resgnd). *Address:* Merck & Co. Inc., 1 Merck Drive, PO Box 100, Whitehouse Station, NJ 08889-0100, USA (office). *Telephone:* (908) 423-1000 (office). *Fax:* (908) 735-1253 (office). *E-mail:* info@merck.com (office). *Website:* www.merck.com (office).

FRCKOVSKI, Ljubomir; Macedonian lawyer, academic and fmr politician; *Professor of International Law and Theory of International Relations, SS Cyril and Methodius University;* b. 2 Dec. 1957; ed Skopje Univ., Univ. of Ljubljana; Prof. of Int. Law and Theory of Int. Relations, SS Cyril and Methodius Skopje Univ. 1984–; co-author of new Constitution of Repub. of Macedonia 1991; Minister without Portfolio 1990–92, Minister of Interior 1992–96, of Foreign Affairs 1996–97; Exec. Dir Foundation for strategic analyses Kiro Gligorov 2000–01; adviser to Pres. Boris Trajkovski 2000–04; unsuccessful cand. (Social Democratic Alliance of Macedonia) in 2009 presidential election; Fellow, Schloss Leopoldskron, Salzburg, 21st Century Trust, London; mem. Inst. Francais des Relations Int., Paris, Int. Law Asscn Skopje, Forum for Human Rights Macedonia. *Publications:* International Public Law 2012, Negotiation Identity Conflicts 2013, Restless Nationalism 2015, Human Rights and Psychoanalysis 2018. *Address:* Faculty of Law, SS Cyril and Methodius University of Skopje, Bul. Krste Misirkov bb, 1000 Skopje (office); Perisa Savelic 5, 1000 Skopje, North Macedonia (home). *Telephone:* (23) 117244 (office). *E-mail:* frckoski@pf.ukim.edu.mk (office); frckoski@unet.com.mk. *Website:* www.pf.ukim.edu.mk (office).

FREARS, Stephen Arthur; British film director; b. 20 June 1941, Leicester; s. of Russell E. Frears and Ruth M. Frears; m. Mary K. Wilmers 1968 (divorced 1974); two s.; partner Anne Rothenstein; one s. one d.; ed Gresham's School, Holt, Trinity Coll., Cambridge; Asst Dir Morgan, a Suitable Case for Treatment 1966, Charlie Bubbles 1967, If... 1968; worked in TV for 13 years, including several TV films and plays in collaboration with Alan Bennett; Chair. jury Cannes Film Festival 2007; Commdr, Ordre des Arts et des Lettres 2009; Hon. LittD (East Anglia, Norwich); Santa Fe Film Festival Lifetime Achievement Award 2003, Golden Duke for Lifetime Achievement, Odessa International Film Festival 2014, Jaeger-LeCoultre Prize 2017. *Films include:* Gumshoe 1971, Bloody Kids 1980, Going Gently 1981, Walter 1982, Saigon 1983, The Hit 1984, My Beautiful Laundrette 1985, Prick Up Your Ears 1986, Sammy and Rosie Get Laid 1987, Dangerous Liaisons 1989, The Grifters 1990, Hero 1992, The Snapper 1992, Mary Reilly 1996, The Van 1996, The Hi-Lo Country 1999, High Fidelity 2000, Liam 2000, Dirty Pretty Things (British Ind. Film Awards Best British Film, Best Dir, Best Screenplay) 2002, Mrs Henderson Presents 2005, The Queen (Best Film and co-winner Best Dir, Toronto Film Critics Asscn 2006, Goya Award for Best European Film 2007, Evening Standard Alexander Walker Special Award 2007, Attenborough Award for British Film of the Year 2007, Best British Dir, London Film Critics' Circle Awards 2007, BAFTA Award for Best Film 2007) 2006, Cheri 2009, Tamara Drewe 2010, Lay the Favourite 2011, Philomena 2013, The Program 2015, Florence Foster Jenkins 2016, Victoria & Abdul 2017. *Television includes:* Fail Safe 2000, The Deal 2003, Mohammed Ali's Greatest Fight 2012. *Address:* c/o Jenne Casarotto, Casarotto Ramsay and Associates Ltd., Waverley House, 7–12 Noel Street, London, W1F 8GQ, England (office). *Telephone:* (20) 7287-4450 (office). *Fax:* (20) 7287-9128 (office). *E-mail:* jenne@casarotto.co.uk (office). *Website:* www.casarotto.co.uk (office).

FRÉCHET, Jean M. J., BS, MS, PhD, PhD; French chemist and academic; *Professor Emeritus of Chemistry and of Chemical Engineering and Henry Rapoport Chair Emeritus of Organic Chemistry, University of California, Berkeley;* b. 19 Aug. 1944, Burgundy; m. Janet Fréchet; ed Institut de Chimie et Physique Industrielles, Lyon, Coll. of Environmental Sciences and Forestry, State Univ. of NY and Syracuse Univ., USA; Asst/Assoc. Prof. of Chem., Univ. of Ottawa, Canada 1973–82, Prof. of Chem. 1982–87, Vice-Dean, School of Grad. Studies and Research 1983–87; Visiting Scientist, IBM Research Lab., San Jose, Calif. 1979, 1983; IBM Prof. of Chem., Cornell Univ., Ithaca, NY 1987–95, Peter J. Debye Chair of Chem. 1995–98; Faculty Sr Scientist, E.O. Lawrence Berkeley Nat. Lab., Berkeley, Calif. 2000–11, Scientific Dir The Molecular Foundry 2004–11; Prof. of Chem., Univ. of California, Berkeley 1996–2011, Prof. Emer. 2011–, Prof. of Chemical Eng 2003–11, Prof. Emer. 2011–, Henry Rapoport Chair of Organic Chem. 2003–11, Emer. 2011–; Vice-Pres. Research, King Abdullah Univ. of Science and Tech. (KAUST), Saudi Arabia 2010–; mem. NAS 2000–, Nat. Acad. of Eng 2000–, Academia Europaea 2009–; Fellow, ACS 2010, American Acad. of Art and Sciences 2000, AAAS 2000, PMSE Div. of ACS 2000; Hon. DSc (Université de Lyon I) 2002, (Univ. of Liverpool, UK) 2008; Hon. DUniv (Univ. of Ottawa) 2004; IUPAC Canadian Nat. Cttee Award 1983, Lecture Award, Polymer Soc. of Japan 1986, ACS Doolittle Award in Polymer Materials Science and Eng 1986, ACS Cooperative Research Award in Polymer Science 1994, ACS Award in Applied Polymer Science 1996, Kosar Memorial Award, Soc. of Imaging Science and Tech. 1999, ACS Award in Polymer Chem. 2000, ACS Cope Scholar Award 2001, ACS Salute to Excellence Award 2001, Chemical Communications 40th Anniversary Award 2005, Esselen Award for Chem. in the Service of the Public 2005, Macro Group UK Medal (jt RSC and Soc. of Chemical Industry award for outstanding achievement in the field of Macromolecular Chem.) 2006, ACS Arthur C. Cope Award for Outstanding Achievement in the Field of Organic Chem. 2007, Dickson Prize in Science, Carnegie Mellon Univ. 2007, Inst. of Industrial Science Medal (Japan) 2007, Arun Guthikonda Memorial Award, Columbia Univ. 2009, Carothers Award for "Outstanding contributions and advances in industrial applications of chemistry" 2009, ACS Herman Mark Award 2009, Remsen Award, Maryland Section of the ACS 2009, Nagoya Gold Medal 2009, Int. Award for the "Development of functional polymers from fundamentals to applications", Soc. of Polymer Science of Japan 2010, Erasmus Medal, Academia Europaea 2010, Grand Prix de la Maison de la Chimie, Paris 2010, Japan Prize 2013, King Faisal Prize for Chemistry 2019. *Achievements include:* with Donald A. Tomalia and Fritz Vögtle, invented and developed dendritic polymers. *Publications:* more than 900 publs and patents. *Address:* 718 Latimer Hall, Department of Chemistry, University of California, Berkeley, CA 94720-1460, USA (office). *Telephone:* (510) 643-3077 (office). *Fax:* (510) 643-3079 (office). *E-mail:* frechet@cchem.berkeley.edu (office); frechet@berkeley.edu (office). *Website:* chemistry.berkeley.edu/faculty/chem/emeriti/fréchet (office); www.kaust.edu.sa/en/study/faculty/jean-frechet (office); www.frechet.com.

FREDA, Fabrizio, BA, MBA; Italian/American business executive; *President and CEO, Estée Lauder Companies Inc.;* m.; two c.; ed Univ. of Naples; directed marketing and strategic planning for Gucci SpA 1986–88; worked for Procter & Gamble 1988–2008, responsible for various operating, marketing and strategic efforts, including as Pres. Global Snacks; mem. Bd of Dirs, Pres. and COO, Estée Lauder Companies Inc. 2008–09, Pres. and CEO 2009–; mem. Bd of Dirs BlackRock, Inc. 2012–; mem. Advisory Bd McDonough School of Business Global Business Initiative, Georgetown Univ. 2013; Cavaliere del Lavoro 2015. *Address:* Estée Lauder Companies Inc., 767 Fifth Avenue, New York, NY 10153, USA (office). *Telephone:* (212) 572-4200 (office). *Fax:* (212) 893-7782 (office). *Website:* www.elcompanies.com (office).

FREDERIK ANDRÉ HENRIK CHRISTIAN, HRH The Crown Prince of Denmark, Count of Monpezat, MSc; b. 26 May 1968, Copenhagen; s. of HM Queen Margrethe II and HRH Prince Consort Henrik of Denmark; m. HRH Crown Princess Mary Elizabeth (née Donaldson) 2004; two s. two d.; ed Krebs' Skole, École des Roches, France, Øregaard Gymnasium, Univ. of Århus and Harvard Univ., USA; heir to the throne of Denmark; began mil. service with Royal Life Guard 1986, apptd Lt Reserve Army 1988, Reconnaissance Platoon Commdr Royal Guard Hussars' Regt 1988, First Lt Reserve Army 1989, completed training with the Royal Danish Navy Frogman Corps 1995, First Lt Reserve Navy 1995, Capt., Reserve Army 1997, Lt Commdr, Reserve Navy 1997, Royal Danish Air Force Flying School 2000, Capt., Reserve Air Force 2000, Command and General Staff Course Royal Danish Defence Coll. 2001–02, Maj., Reserve Army and Air Force 2002, Commdr, Reserve Navy 2002, Staff Officer, Defence Command Denmark 2002–03, Sr Lecturer, Inst. of Strategy, Royal Danish Defence Coll. 2003, Commdr Sr Grade in the Navy, Lt-Col in the Army and Air Force 2004, Capt. (Navy), Col (Air Force, Army) 2010, Rear Adm. (Navy), Maj.-Gen. (Air Force, Army) 2015; served at Danish UN Mission, New York 1994, First Sec. Embassy in Paris 1998–99; participated in expedition to Mongolia 1986, Expedition Sirius 2000 to Greenland 2000; Pres. Royal Danish Geographical Soc.; patronages include Danish Red Cross, Deaf Asscn, Royal Acad. of Music, Århus, Save the Children Fund, Asscn of Fine Arts, Comm. for Scientific Research in Greenland, Dyslexia Org., Foreign Policy Soc., Georg Jensen Prize, Greenlandic Soc., Cold Hawaii PWA World Cup; mem. IOC 2009–, Int. Sailing Fed. Events Cttee, Young Global Leaders; f. Crown Prince Frederik's Foundation; finished first in his class boat in Fyn Cup in Denmark 2010; Hon. Vice-Pres. Siam Soc. in Thailand; hon. memberships include Asscn of Cavalry Officers, Mongolian Soc., Naval Asscn, Ancient Guild of Christian IV, Aalborg, Guards' Asscn, Copenhagen, Royal Danish Yacht Club, Sailors' Soc. of 1856; Kt Grand Cross with Collar, Order of the Elephant, Kt Grand Commdr, Order of the Dannebrog, Recipient of the Cross of Honour, Order of the Dannebrog, Recipient of the Nersornaat Medal for Meritorious Service, First Class (Greenland), Commemorative Medal of the 50th Anniversary of HM Queen Ingrid's arrival in Denmark, Badge of Honour, Officers of the Reserve, Commemorative Medal of HM Queen Margrethe II and HRH Prince Consort Henrik's Silver Wedding, Silver Jubilee Medal of HM Queen Margrethe II, Danish Mil. Athletic Asscn Medal, King Frederik IX Centenary Medal, Royal Medal of Recompense with Crown, Commemorative Medal of Queen Ingrid, Greenland Home Rule Medal, Medal of Merit of Greenland Nersornaat, Grand Cross, Order of Honourable Service (Italy), Adolph of Nassau Civilian and Mil. Service Order, Grand Cross (Luxembourg), Orders of Ojaswi Rajanya, Grand Cross (Nepal), Seraphim (Sweden), Saint Olav Grand Cross (Norway), White Roses Grand Cross (Finland), Terra Mariana Grand Cross (Estonia), Three Stars Grand Cross (Latvia), Leopold Grand Cross (Belgium), Grand Cross, Order of the Falcon (Iceland), Renaissance Grand Cross (Jordan), Chrysanthemum (Japan), Southern Cross (Brazil), Rio Branco Grand Cross (Brazil), Chula Chom Klao Grand Cross (Thailand), Stara Planina First Class (Bulgaria), Order of Service for the FRG, Grand Cross, Order of the Star of Romania, Grand Cross, Commemorative 75th Birthday Medal of HRH The Prince Consort 2009, Commemorative 70th Birthday Medal of HM The Queen 2010, Commemorative Ruby Jubilee Medal of HM The Queen 2012. *Achievement:* completed the KMD Ironman Copenhagen in the time of 10:45:32 (first royal to complete an Ironman) 2013. *Leisure interest:* sailing. *Address:* Court of TRH The Crown Prince and Crown Princess of Denmark, Christian VIII Palace, Amalienborg Slotsplads 7, 1257 Copenhagen K (home); Court of TRH The Crown Prince and Crown Princess of Denmark, PO Box 2143, 1015 Copenhagen K, Denmark (home). *Telephone:* 33-40-10-10 (home). *Fax:* 33-40-11-15 (home). *Website:* kongehuset.dk/en/the-royal-house/crown-prince-couple.

FREDERIKSEN, Claus Hjort, LLM; Danish politician; *Minister of Defence;* b. 4 Sept. 1947, Copenhagen; s. of Niels Frederiksen and Elna Frederiksen (née Hjort); m. Christina Hall Frederiksen; two s.; ed Univ. of Copenhagen; Sec., Venstre (Liberal Party) Parl. Group 1973–77; Head of Div., Ministry of Food, Agric. and Fisheries 1977–79; Sec.-Gen. Asscn of Industrial Employers 1979–83; Admin Man., Venstre 1983–85, Sec.-Gen. 1985–2001; Minister for Employment 2001–09, of Finance 2009–11, 2015–16, of Defence 2016–; mem. (Venstre), Folketing (Parl.) for Copenhagen Co. 2005–07, for North Zealand 2007–. *Address:* Ministry of Defence, Holmens Kanal 9, 1060 Copenhagen K, Denmark (office). *Telephone:* 72-81-00-00 (office). *Fax:* 72-81-03-00 (office). *E-mail:* fmn@fmn.dk (office). *Website:* www.fmn.dk (office).

FREDERIKSEN, Suka K., BCom; Greenlandic politician; *Minister for Independence, Foreign Affairs and Agriculture;* b. 18 July 1965, Narsaq; m. Sofus Frederiksen; four c.; began career with Savaatillit Allaffiat (Sheep Farming Office) 1987–92; with Neqi A/S (meat producer) and Royal Greenland (fishery co.) 1992–94; Dir, Eskimo Pels (sealskin clothing mfr) 2000–01; Prin., Culture and Educ., Narsap Municipality 1994–2004, mem. municipal council, Narsap Municipality 2005–09; Admin Man., Kujalleq Municipality 2007–13, Labour Market Man. 2013–15; mem. Inatsisartut (Greenland Parl.) 2014–; Minister of Independence, Environment, Nature and Agric. 2016–17, Minister for Independence, Foreign Affairs and Agric. 2017–; mem. Siumut. *Address:* Grønlands Selvstyre (Naalakkersuisut), Imaneq 4, POB 1015, 3900 Nuuk, Greenland (office). *Telephone:* 345000 (office). *Fax:* 325002 (office). *E-mail:* govsec@nanoq.gl (office). *Website:* www.nanoq.gl (office).

FREDRIKSEN, John; Cypriot (b. Norwegian) shipping industry executive; *Chairman and President, Frontline Ltd;* b. 10 May 1944, Oslo, Norway; m.; two c.; began as trainee in shipbrokering co.; owner of tanker fleet with more than 70 oil tankers, and major interests in oil rigs and fish farming; f. investment cos Hemen Holdings Ltd and Meisha; Chair. and CEO Old Frontline –1997, Chair., apptd Pres. and CEO Frontline Ltd 1997, now Chair. and Pres.; Chair. Seadrill Ltd 2005–; mem. Bd of Dirs Seatankers Man. Co. Ltd, Golar LNG Ltd. *Leisure interest:* collecting classic Norwegian art. *Address:* Frontline Management AS, Bryggegata 3, PO Box 1327-VIKA, 0112 Oslo, Norway (office). *Telephone:* 23-11-40-00 (office). *Fax:* 23-11-40-40 (office). *E-mail:* Frontline@front.bm (office). *Website:* www.frontline.bm (office).

FREED, Karl Frederick, BS, AM, PhD; American chemist and academic; *Henry G. Gale Distinguished Service Professor Emeritus, James Franck Institute and Department of Chemistry, University of Chicago;* b. 25 Sept. 1942, Brooklyn, NY; m. Gina Freed; two d.; ed Columbia Univ., Harvard Univ.; Asst Prof., James Franck Inst., Univ. of Chicago 1968–73, Assoc. Prof. 1973–76, Prof. 1976–, Henry G. Gale Distinguished Service Prof. 2006–12, Prof. Emer. 2012–, Dir 1983–86; Visiting Scientist, Centre Nucléaires, Strasbourg, France 1977, Inst. of Physical and Chemical Research, Saitama, Japan 1979; Visiting Prof., Univ. of Minn. 1984, Univ. of Strasbourg 1991; Visiting Scientist, IBM Research Labs 1993; Chair. Gordon Conf. on Polymer Physics 1996; mem. Editorial Bd Journal of Statistical Physics 1976–78, Chemical Physics 1979–82, Journal of Chemical Physics 1982–85, Advances in Chemical Physics 1984–, International Journal of Quantum Chemistry 1995; Fellow, Alfred P. Sloan Foundation 1969–71, John S. Guggenheim Foundation 1972–73, American Physical Soc. 1983–, American Acad. of Arts and Sciences 2007–; Chemical Soc. Marlow Medal 1973, Award in Pure Chem. 1976, Case Centennial Scholar Medal 1980, Polymer Physics Prize, American Physics Soc. 2014. *Publications include:* Renormalization Group Theory of Macromolecules; more than 600 articles in scholarly journals. *Address:* James Franck Institute, University of Chicago, 929 East 57th Street, Chicago, IL 60637, USA (office). *Telephone:* (773) 702-7202 (office). *Fax:* (773) 702-5863 (office). *E-mail:* freed@uchicago.edu (office). *Website:* freedgroup.uchicago.edu (office).

FREEDBERG, Hugh; British business executive; b. 18 June 1945, Cape Town, South Africa; ed Univ. of Witwatersrand, Univ. of South Africa, Harvard Univ., Amos Tuck School of Business Admin, Dartmouth Coll., USA; Book Club Assocs, UK 1973–75; Marketing and Sales Dir for UK Card Div. American Express 1975–78, Gen. Man. 1978–86, Head of Divs in Benelux countries, Southern Europe, Middle East and Africa, UK, Ireland, SE Asia; joined Salomon Inc. 1986, CEO Mortgage Corpn –1990; joined TSB Group 1990, Exec. Dir, CEO Insurance and Investment Services Div., Deputy CEO 1992–96; CEO Hill Samuel Group (bought by TSB Group) 1991–96, then CEO Hill Samuel Bank Ltd (div. of Lloyds TSB Group PLC), Dir Macquarie Bank, Australia 1994–96; Man. Partner, Financial Services Practice, Korn Ferry Int. 1996–98; CEO London Int. Financial Futures and Options Exchange (now NYSE Liffe) 1998–2009, Chair. 2009–12, Group Exec. Vice-Pres. and Head of Global Derivatives 2007–09, mem. Supervisory Bd AtosEuronext SBF SA 2004–05, Atos Euronext Market Solutions Holding S.A.S. 2005–07. *E-mail:* hugh@hughfreedberg.com. *Website:* www.hughfreedberg.com.

FREEDMAN, Sir Lawrence David, Kt, KCMG, CBE, DPhil, FRSA, FRHistS, FBA, FKC; British academic; *Professor Emeritus, King's College London;* b. 7 Dec. 1948, Tynemouth, England; s. of Lt-Commdr Julius Freedman and Myra Robinson; m. Judith Hill 1974; one s. one d.; ed Whitley Bay Grammar School and Univs of Manchester, Oxford and York; Research Assoc., IISS 1975–76; Research Fellow, Royal Inst. of Int. Affairs 1976–78, Head of Policy Studies 1978–82; Fellow, Head Dept of War Studies, King's Coll. London 1978–2006, Prof. 1982–2014, now Prof. Emer., Head School of Social Science and Public Policy 2001–, Vice-Prin. (Strategy and Devt) 2003–; Visiting Prof. Univ. of Oxford 2013–; mem. Council, IISS 1984–92, 1993–2002, School of Slavonic and E European Studies 1993–97; Chair. Cttee on Int. Peace and Security, Social Science Research Council (USA) 1993–98; occasional newspaper columnist; Trustee Imperial War Museum 2001–09; cttee mem. The Iraq Inquiry 2009–; Hon. Dir Centre for Defence Studies 1990–2003; Silver Medallist, Arthur Ross Prize, Council on Foreign Relations (USA) 2002, RUSI Chesney Gold Medal 2006, Lionel Gelber Prize 2009, Duke of Westminster Prize for Military History 2009, W. J. McKenzie Prize 2014. *Publications include:* US Intelligence and Soviet Strategic Threat 1978, Britain and Nuclear Weapons 1980, The Evolution of Nuclear Strategy 1981, 1989, Nuclear War and Nuclear Peace (co-author) 1983, The Troubled Alliance (ed.) 1983, The Atlas of Global Strategy 1985, The Price of Peace 1986, Britain and the Falklands War 1988, US Nuclear Strategy (co-ed.) 1989, Signals of War (with V. Gamba) 1989, Europe Transformed (ed.) 1990, Military Power in Europe (essays, ed.) 1990, Britain in the World (co-ed.) 1991, Population Change and European Security (co-ed.) 1991, War, Strategy and International Politics (essays, co-ed.) 1992, The Gulf Conflict 1990–91, Diplomacy and War in the New World Order (with E. Karsh) 1993, War: A Reader 1994, Military Intervention in Europe (ed.) 1994, Strategic Coercion (ed.) 1998, The Revolution in Strategic Affairs 1998, The Politics of British Defence Policy 1979–1998 1999, Kennedy's Wars 2000, The Cold War 2001, Superterrorism (ed.) 2002, Deterrence 2004, The Official History of the Falklands Campaign 2005, A Choice of Enemies 2009, Strategy: A History 2013; articles etc. *Leisure interests:* grandchildren, political cartoons. *Address:* King's College London, Strand, London, WC2R 2LS, England (office). *Telephone:* (20) 7836-5454 (office). *E-mail:* lawrence.freedman@kcl.ac.uk.

FREEDMAN, Michael H., PhD; American mathematician and academic; *Director, Microsoft Station Q, University of California, Santa Barbara;* b. 21 April 1951, Los Angeles, Calif.; ed Univ. of California, Berkeley, Princeton Univ.; Lecturer in Math., Univ. of California, Berkeley 1973–75; mem. of staff, Inst. for Advanced Study, Princeton, NJ 1975–76, 1980–81; Asst Prof. of Math., Univ. of California, San Diego 1976–79, Assoc. Prof. 1979, Prof. 1982–2004, Charles Lee Powell Prof. of Math. 1985–2004; Sr Researcher and Dir Microsoft Station Q, Univ. of California, Santa Barbara 2004–; mem. NAS, American Acad. of Arts and Sciences, New York Acad. of Sciences 1984; Fellow, MacArthur Foundation 1984; Sloan Fellowship, California Scientist of the Year 1984, Fields Medal, Int. Congress of Mathematicians, Berkeley 1986, Veblen Prize, American Math. Soc. 1986, Nat. Medal of Science 1987, Humboldt Award 1988, Guggenheim Fellowship 1994. *Publications:* numerous publs in math. journals and physics journals. *Address:* Microsoft Station Q, CNSI Bldg, Office 2243, University of California, Santa Barbara, CA 93106-6105, USA (office). *Telephone:* (805) 893-8818 (office). *Fax:* (425) 708-1426 (office). *Website:* research.microsoft.com/en-us/labs/stationq/ (office).

FREEDMAN, Wendy L., BSc, MSc, PhD; American (b. Canadian) astronomer; *University Professor, Department of Astronomy and Astrophysics, University of Chicago;* b. 17 July 1957, Toronto, Ont.; m.; one s. one d.; ed Univ. of Toronto; Postdoctoral Fellow, Carnegie Observatories, Pasadena, Calif. 1984, mem. Scientific Staff 1987, Crawford H. Greenewalt Chair, Dir 2003–14, Chair. Bd of Dirs, Giant Magellan Telescope 2003–15; Univ. Prof., Dept of Astronomy and Astrophysics, Univ. of Chicago 2014–; mem. NAS 2003, American Astronomical Soc., American Physical Soc.; Fellow, American Acad. of Arts and Sciences 2000, American Philosophical Soc. 2007, American Physical Soc. 2011; Hon. DSc (Toronto) 2013; hon. degree from Univ. of Chicago 2014; Marc Aaronson Prize 1994, Cosmos Club Award 2000, John P. McGovern Award 2000, American Philosophical Soc. Magellanic Prize 2002, Gruber Cosmology Prize 2009, Dannie Heinemann Prize in Astrophysics 2015. *Address:* Department of Astronomy and Astrophysics, University of Chicago, 5640 South Ellis Avenue, Chicago, IL 60637, USA (office). *Telephone:* (773) 834-5651 (office). *E-mail:* wfreedman@uchicago.edu (office). *Website:* astro.uchicago.edu/people/wendy-freedman.php (office).

FREEH, Louis J., JD, LLM; American lawyer, judge, consultant and fmr government official; *Chairman and Treasurer, Freeh Group International Solutions LLC;* b. 6 Jan. 1950, Jersey City, New Jersey; m. Marilyn Freeh; six s.; ed Rutgers Coll., Rutgers Law School and New York Univ. Law School; special agent, FBI 1975–81, Dir 1993–2001; apptd Asst US Attorney, Attorney-Gen.'s Office for Southern District of New York 1980, later Chief of the Organized Crime Unit, Assoc. US Attorney and Deputy US Attorney 1981–90; Judge, US Dist Court for Southern NY 1991–93; Gen. Counsel for MBNA America Bank 2001–06; Founder and Sr Man. Partner, Freeh Group International Solutions LLC (consulting firm) 2006–, also Chair. and Treasurer; Founding Pnr, Freeh, Sporkin & Sullivan (law firm), Washington, DC, firm acquired by Pepper Hamilton LLP 2012, Chair. Pepper Hamilton 2013–14, now Partner; Advisor, Millennium Partners LP; mem. Bd of Dirs, Bristol-Myers Squibb Co. 2006–13, Max Planck Florida Inst., US Naval Acad. Foundation, Nat. Italian American Foundation, Int. Asscn of Chief of Police Foundation; John Marshall Award for Preparation of Litigation 1984, Attorney-Gen.'s Award for Distinguished Service 1987, 1991, Fed. Law Enforcement Officers Asscn Award 1989. *Achievements include:* lead prosecutor in the Pizza Connection case, one of the largest and most complex narcotics investigations ever undertaken by the US Fed. Govt; investigations and prosecutions relating to racketeering, drugs, organized crime, fraud, white collar crime and terrorism. *Publication:* My FBI 2005. *Address:* Freeh Group International, 3711 Kennett Pike, Suite 130, Wilmington, DE 19807 (office); Pepper Hamilton LLP, Hercules Plaza, Suite 5100, 1313 Market Street, POB 1709, Wilmington, DE 19899-1709, USA (office). *Telephone:* (302) 824-7139 (Freeh Group) (office); (302) 777-6500 (Pepper Hamilton) (office). *Fax:* (302) 824-7148 (Freeh Group) (office); (302) 421-8390 (Pepper Hamilton) (office). *E-mail:* Bescript@FreehGroup.com (office). *Website:* www.pepperlaw.com (office); www.freehgroup.com (office).

FREELAND, Chrystia, MA; Canadian newspaper editor and politician; *Minister of Foreign Affairs;* b. 8 Feb. 1969, Peace River, Alberta; m. Graham Bowley; three c.; ed Harvard Univ., USA, St Anthony's Coll. Oxford, UK; corresp. for Financial Times, The Economist and Washington Post in Kiev, Ukraine 1991–93; Eastern Europe Corresp. Financial Times (FT), London 1994–95, Moscow Bureau Chief 1995–96, UK News Ed. 1998–99, Ed. FT.com 2001–02, oversaw launch of subscription services 2002, Ed. FT Weekend (Saturday edn) 2002–03, Deputy Ed. FT 2003–08, US Man. Ed. 2008–10; Deputy Ed. The Globe & Mail, Toronto, Canada 1999–2001; Global Ed.-at-Large, Reuters 2010–11, then Ed. Thomson Reuters Digital, then Man. Dir and Ed. of Consumer News –2013; MP for Toronto Centre 2013–15, for University–Rosedale 2015–; Minister of Int. Trade 2015–17, of Foreign Affairs 2017–; fmr Sr Fellow, Int. Security Program, Belfer Center for Science and Int. Affairs, John F Kennedy School of Govt, Harvard Univ.; Rhodes Scholarship 1993, Business Journalist of the Year Award for Best Energy Submission 2004. *Publications include:* Sale of the Century: Russia's Wild Side from Communism to Capitalism 2000, Plutocrats: The Rise of the New Global Super-Rich and the Fall of Everyone Else (Lionel Gelber Prize 2013, National Business Book Award 2013) 2012. *Address:* Foreign Affairs, Trade and Development Canada, Lester B. Pearson Bldg, 125 Sussex Dr., Ottawa, ON K1A 0G2 (office); House of Commons, Ottawa, ON K1A 0A6, Canada (office). *Telephone:* (613) 944-4000 (office); (613) 992-5234 (office). *Fax:* (613) 996-9709 (office); (613) 996-9607 (office). *E-mail:* chrystia.freeland@parl.gc.ca (office); enqserv@international.gc.ca (office). *Website:* www.dfait-maeci.gc.ca (office); www.chrystiafreeland.ca (office).

FREEMAN, Catherine (Cathy) Astrid; Australian fmr athlete; b. 16 Feb. 1973, Mackay; d. of Norman Freeman and Cecilia Barber; m. 1st (Sandy) Alexander Bodecker 1999 (divorced 2003); m. 2nd James Murch; one d.; works as public relations adviser; winner Australian 200m 1990–91, 1994, 1996, Australian 100m 1996, Amateur Athletics Fed. 400m 1992, 200m 1993; gold medallist 4×100m Commonwealth Games 1990; gold medallist 200m, 400m, silver medallist 4×100m Commonwealth Games 1994; silver medallist 400m, Olympic Games, Atlanta 1996; winner World Championships 400m, Athens 1997 (first Aboriginal winner at World Championships); gold medallist 400m, Olympic Games, Sydney 2000; set 2 Australian 200m records, 5 Australian 400m records 1994–96; took break from athletics in 2001; returned to int. competition Commonwealth Games Manchester 2002, winning a gold medal in the 4×400m relay; retd from athletics 2003; f. Catherine Freeman Foundation; Media and Communications Officer, Australia Post; Hans Christian Andersen Amb. 2003–; numerous nat. awards including Young Australian of the Year 1990, Australian of the Year 1998 (only person to have been awarded both honours). *Leisure interests:* family, pets, children, movies. *Address:* c/o Jane Cowmeadow, Communications & Management, Bron Madigan, PO Box 5138, Ringwood, Vic. 3134, Australia. *Website:* www.cathyfreeman.com.au; www.cathyfreemanfoundation.org.au.

FREEMAN, Hon. Charles (Chas) Wellman, Jr, BA, JD; American fmr diplomatist and fmr government official; *Chairman, Projects International, Inc.;* b. 2 March 1943, Washington, DC; s. of Charles W. Freeman and Carla Park; m. 1st Patricia Trenery 1962 (divorced 1993); three s. (one deceased) one d.; m. 2nd Margaret Van Wagenen Carpenter 1993; ed Milton Acad., Milton, Mass., Nat.

Autonomous Univ. of Mexico, México, Yale Univ., Harvard Law School, Harvard Univ., Foreign Service Inst. School of Chinese Language and Area Studies; entered US Foreign Service 1965, Vice-Consul, Madras, India 1966–68, Taiwan 1969–71, State Dept, China Desk 1971–74, Visiting Fellow, E Asian Legal Research, Harvard Univ. 1974–75, Deputy Dir, Taiwan Affairs, US Dept of State 1975–76, Dir Public Programs, Dept of State 1976–77, Plans and Man. 1977–78, Dir US Information Agency programs 1978–79, Acting US Co-ordinator for Refugee Programs 1979, Dir, Chinese Affairs, Dept of State 1979–81, Minister, Embassy in Beijing 1981–84, Embassy in Bangkok 1984–86, Prin. Deputy Asst Sec. of State for African Affairs 1986–89, Amb. to Saudi Arabia 1989–92; Asst Sec. of Defense (Int. Security Affairs) 1993–94; Chair. Projects International, Inc. 1995–, Cttee for the Repub. 2003–; Vice-Chair. Atlantic Council of USA 1996–2008; Co-Chair. US-China Policy Foundation 1996–2009; Pres. Middle East Policy Council 1997–2009; Distinguished Fellow, Inst. for Nat. Strategic Studies, Nat. Defense Univ. 1992–93; US Inst. of Peace, Washington, DC 1994–95; mem. American Acad. of Diplomacy 1995, mem. Bd 2001–10; mem. Bd, Washington World Affairs Council 1998–2009, Pacific Pension Inst. 2001–06, Asscn for Diplomatic Studies and Training 2001–09, Inst. for Defense Analyses, Carnegie Endowment for Int. Peace 2009–17; Overseer, Roger Williams Univ. 2006–09; Advisor, MIT Centre for Security Studies 2009–14, Centre for Naval Analysis 2009–12; Sr Fellow, Watson Inst. for Int. and Public Affairs, Brown Univ. 2015–; Order of King Abd Al-Aziz (First Class) 1992; Forrest Prize, Yale Univ., Superior Honor Awards 1978, 1982, Presidential Meritorious Service Awards 1984, 1987, 1989, Group Distinguished Honor Award 1988, Sec. of Defense Award for Meritorious Civilian Service 1991, Distinguished Honor Award 1991, Sec. of Defense Awards for Distinguished Public Service 1994. *Publications include:* Cooking Western in China 1987, The Diplomat's Dictionary 1994 (revised edn 2010), Arts of Power: Statecraft and Diplomacy 1997, America's Misadventures in the Middle East 2010, Interesting Times: China, America, and the Shifting Balance of Prestige 2013, America's Continuing Misadventures in the Middle East 2016. *Leisure interests:* swimming, sailing, reading, computers, cookery. *Address:* Projects International, Inc., Farragut Square, 888 17th Street NW, Suite 1250, Washington, DC 20006 (office); Watson Institute for International and Public Affairs, Brown University, 219 Stephen Roberts, 62 Hall, Providence, RI 02912, USA (office); 2853 Ontario Road NW, Suite 605, Washington, DC 20009, USA (home). *Telephone:* (202) 333-1277 (office); (202) 248-3919 (home). *E-mail:* cfreeman@projectsinternational.com (office); chas_freeman@brown.edu (office); CWFResidence@gmail.com. *Website:* watson.brown.edu/people/fellows/freeman (office); www.chasfreeman.net.

FREEMAN, John Patrick George, CMG; British diplomatist; *Governor of Turks and Caicos Islands;* m. Corinna Freeman; two c.; Head of South Africa Section, FCO 1986–89, Senate Liaison, British Mil. Govt in Berlin, and subsequently Head of Political Section, Berlin Office of the British Embassy 1989–91, Deputy Head of Eastern (later Cen.) European Dept and, secondly, Head of the Security Co-ordination Dept, FCO 1991–94, attached to Trade Promotion Div., Dept of Trade and Industry, Singapore 1994, Deputy High Commr and Commercial and Econ. Counsellor 1994–97, Amb. and Perm. Rep. to UN agencies, Vienna 1997–2001, Deputy Perm. Rep. at NATO and Alt. Rep. on North Atlantic Council, Brussels 2001–04, Amb. and Perm. Rep. to UN Conf. on Disarmament, Geneva 2004–06, Amb. for Multilateral Arms Control, Geneva 2005–06, Secondment, Deputy Dir-Gen. OPCW, The Hague 2006–11, Amb. to Argentina (also accred to Paraguay 2012–13) 2012–16, Gov., Turks and Caicos Islands 2016–. *Address:* Office of the Governor, Government House, Waterloo, Grand Turk, Turks and Caicos Islands (office). *Telephone:* 946-2308 (office). *Fax:* 946-2308 (office). *E-mail:* governorgt@fco.gov.uk (office).

FREEMAN, Kenneth, BSc, PhD, FAA, FRS, AC; Australian astronomer, astrophysicist and academic; *Duffield Professor of Astronomy, Research School of Astronomy and Astrophysics, Mount Stromlo Observatory, Australian National University;* b. (Kenneth Charles Freeman), 27 Aug. 1940, Perth, WA; s. of Herbert Anthony Freeman and Herta Elizabeth Freeman; m. Margaret Leigh Elizabeth; one s. three d.; ed Univ. of Western Australia, Univ. of Cambridge, UK; postdoctoral appointment at Univ. of Texas, USA; Research Fellowship at Trinity Coll., Cambridge; returned to Australia as a Queen Elizabeth Fellow at Mount Stromlo Observatory, ANU 1967, currently Duffield Prof. of Astronomy, Research School of Astronomy and Astrophysics, ANU Coll. of Physical and Math. Sciences; Distinguished Visiting Scientist, Space Telescope Science Inst.; Oort Prof., Leiden Univ., The Netherlands 1994; Visiting Fellow, Merton Coll., Oxford, UK 1997; Tinsley Prof., Univ. of Texas 2001; Blaauw Prof., Univ. of Groningen 2003; Assoc., Royal Astronomical Soc. in Australia 2002; Hon. DSc (Univ. of Western Australia); Pawsey Medal, Australian Acad. of Science 1972, Aaronson Lecturer, Univ. of Arizona 1990, Dannie Heineman Prize, American Inst. of Physics and American Astronomical Soc. 1999, Bishop Lecturer, Columbia Univ. 2001, Robert Ellery Lecturer, Astronomical Soc. of Australia 2001, Centenary Medal, Australian Govt 2003, Antoinette de Vaucouleurs Lecture and Medal, Univ. of Texas 2004, Prime Minister's Prize for Science 2012, Henry Norris Russell Lectureship, American Astronomical Soc. 2013, Cosmology Prize, Peter Gruber Foundation (co-recipient) 2014, Dirac Medal 2016, Foreign Assoc. US Nat. Acad. of Sciences 2017. *Achievements include:* a pioneer of a branch of astronomy now called Near Field Cosmology. *Publications include:* In Search of Dark Matter (with Geoff McNamara) 2006; numerous papers in professional journals. *Address:* Room D109, Research School of Astronomy and Astrophysics, ANU College of Physical and Mathematical Sciences, Mount Stromlo Observatory, Cotter Road, Weston Creek, ACT 2611, Australia (office). *Telephone:* (2) 6125-0264 (office). *E-mail:* kenneth.freeman@anu.edu.au (office). *Website:* rsaa.anu.edu.au/people/ken-freeman (office); researchers.anu.edu.au/researchers/freeman-kc (office).

FREEMAN, Martin John Christopher; British actor; b. 8 Sept. 1971, Aldershot, Hants., England; s. of Geoffrey Freeman and Philomena Freeman; fmr pnr Amanda Abbington; one s. one d.; ed Central School of Speech and Drama, London; joined a youth theatre group aged 15, professional actor from the age of 17; has appeared in numerous TV series, theatre productions and several radio productions. *Films include:* I Just Want to Kiss You (short) 1998, The Low Down 2000, Fancy Dress (short) 2001, Ali G Indahouse 2002, Love Actually 2003, Call Register (short) 2004, Shaun of the Dead 2004, Blake's Junction 7 (short) 2005, The Hitchhiker's Guide to the Galaxy 2005, Round About Five (short) 2005, Long Hot Summer 2006, Confetti 2006, Breaking and Entering 2006, Dedication 2007, The Good Night 2007, Hot Fuzz 2007, Lonely Hearts (short) (voice) 2007, The All Together 2007, Rubbish (short) 2007, Nightwatching 2007, HIV: The Musical (short) 2009, Wild Target 2009, Nativity! 2009, The Girl Is Mime (short) 2010, The Voorman Problem (short) 2011, Swinging with the Finkels 2011, What's Your Number? 2011, The Pirates! In an Adventure with Scientists! (voice) 2012, Animals 2012, The Hobbit: An Unexpected Journey 2012, Svengali 2013, The Hobbit: The Desolation of Smaug 2013, The Hobbit: There and Back Again 2014, The Hobbit: The Battle of the Five Armies 2014, Whiskey Tango Foxtrot 2016, Captain America: Civil War 2016, Ghost Stories 2017, Cargo 2017, Black Panther 2018. *Television includes:* The Bill (series) – Man Trap 1997, This Life (series) – Last Tango in Southwark 1997, Casualty (series) – She Loved the Rain 1998, Picking up the Pieces (series) 1998, Bruiser (series) 2000, Lock, Stock... (series) 2000, Black Books (series) – Cooking the Books 2000, Men Only (film) 2001, World of Pub (series) 2001, The Office (series) 2001–03, Helen West (series) 2002, Linda Green (series) – Easy Come, Easy Go 2002, Comic Relief 2003: The Big Hair Do (film) (Blankety Blank sketch) 2003, The Debt (film) 2003, Margery and Gladys (film) 2003, Charles II: The Power & the Passion (mini-series) 2003, Hardware (series) 2003–04, Pride (film) (voice) 2004, Not Tonight with John Sergeant 2005, The Robinsons (series) 2005, Comedy Showcase (series) – Other People 2007, The Old Curiosity Shop (film) 2007, Svengali (film) 2009, Boy Meets Girl (mini-series) 2009, Micro Men (film) 2009, Sherlock (series) (as Dr John Watson) (BAFTA Award for Best Supporting Actor 2011, Primetime Emmy Award for Outstanding Supporting Actor in a Miniseries or a Movie 2014) 2010–17, The Life of Rock with Brian Pern (mini-series) 2014, Fargo (series) 2014–15, The Eichmann Show (film) 2015, Robot Chicken (series) (voice) 2015, Stick Man (voice) 2015, StartUp 2016–. *Leisure interest:* Motown music. *Address:* c/o Creative Artists Management, 4th Floor, 111 Shoreditch High Street, London, E1 6JN, England (office). *Telephone:* (20) 7292-0600 (office). *E-mail:* reception@cam.co.uk (office). *Website:* www.cam.co.uk (office).

FREEMAN, Morgan; American actor and director; b. 1 June 1937, Memphis, Tenn.; s. of Grafton Freeman and Mayme Revere; m. 1st Jeanette Bradshaw 1967 (divorced 1979); two s. from previous relationships; m. 2nd Myrna Colley-Lee 1984 (divorced 2010); one adopted d. one c.; ed Los Angeles City Coll.; stage debut in Niggerlover 1967; other stage appearances include: Hello Dolly, Broadway 1967, Jungle of Cities 1969, The Recruiting Officer 1969, Purlie, ANTA Theatre, New York 1970, Black Visions 1972, Mighty Gents 1978 (Clarence Derwent Award, Drama Desk Award) 1978, White Pelicans 1978, Coriolanus, New York Shakespeare Festival 1979, Mother Courage and Her Children 1980, Othello Dallas Shakespeare Festival, 1982, Medea and the Doll 1984, The Gospel at Colonus (Obie Award), Driving Miss Daisy 1987, The Taming of the Shrew; Co-founder Revelations Entertainment (production co.) 1996, ClickStar (broadband entertainment co.) 2006; hon. degrees from Rhodes Coll. (Hon. Alumnus) 1997, (Brown Univ.) 2010; Crystal Globe Award for Outstanding Artistic Contrib. to World Cinema, Karlovy Vary Int. Film Festival 2003, Spencer Tracy Award, UCLA 2006, Guest of Honour, Cairo Int. Film Festival 2006, Lifetime Achievement Award (co-recipient with his wife), Mississippi Inst. of Arts and Letters 2007, Outstanding Contrib. To Film and TV Gong, Screen Nation Film and TV Awards 2007, Kennedy Center Honor 2008, Lifetime Achievement Award, American Film Inst. 2011, chosen as Favorite Movie Icon, People's Choice Awards 2012, Cecil B. DeMille Award, Golden Globe Awards 2012. *Films include:* Who Says I Can't Ride a Rainbow? 1971, Brubaker 1980, Eyewitness 1980, Harry and Son 1983, Teachers 1984, Street Smart 1987, Clean and Sober 1988, Lean On Me 1989, Johnny Handsome 1989, Driving Miss Daisy (Golden Globe Award) 1989, Glory 1989, Robin Hood 1991, Unforgiven 1992, The Power of Ore 1992, Chain Reaction 1993, The Shawshank Redemption 1994, Outbreak 1995, Se7en 1996, Moll Flanders, Amistad (NAACP Image Award) 1997, Kiss the Girls 1997, Hard Rain 1998, Deep Impact 1998, Water Damage 1999, Mutiny 1999, Under Suspicion 2000, Nurse Betty 2000, Along Came a Spider 2000, High Crimes 2002, The Sum of All Fears 2002, Levity 2003, Dreamcatcher 2003, Bruce Almighty 2003, Guilty by Association (video) 2003, The Big Bounce 2004, Million Dollar Baby (Best Supporting Actor, Screen Actors Guild Awards 2005, Acad. Awards 2005) 2004, A Remarkable Promise (short) (narrator) 2004, Unleashed 2005, Batman Begins 2005, War of the Worlds (voice) 2005, Danny the Dog 2005, An Unfinished Life 2005, Edison 2005, Magnificent Desolation: Walking on the Moon 3D (documentary short) 2005, Lucky Number Slevin 2006, 10 Items or Less 2006, The Contract 2006, Evan Almighty 2007, Gone Baby Gone 2007, Feast of Love 2007, The Bucket List 2007, Wanted 2008, The Dark Knight 2008, The Code 2009, The Maiden Heist 2009, Invictus (Nat. Bd of Review Award for Best Actor) 2009, Red 2010, Wish Wizard (short) 2011, Conan the Barbarian 2011, Dolphin Tale 2011, We the People 2011, The Dark Knight Rises 2012, The Summer of Monte Wildhorn 2012, Olympus Has Fallen 2013, Oblivion 2013, Transcendence 2014, Momentum 2015, Now You See Me 2 2016, Going in Style 2017; dir: Bopha! 1993. *Television includes:* American Masters (series documentary) 2000, Freedom: A History of Us (series documentary) 2003, Slavery and the Making of America (series) (narrator) 2005, A Raisin in the Sun (film) 2008, 30 for 30 (series) 2010. *Address:* Revelations Entertainment, 301 Arizona Avenue, Suite 303, Santa Monica, CA 90401; Clickstar Inc., 520 Broadway, #100, Santa Monica, CA 90401; c/o WME Entertainment, 9601 Wilshire Boulevard, Beverly Hills, CA 90210, USA (office). *Telephone:* (310) 394-3131 (Revelations); (310) 285-9000 (office). *Fax:* (310) 394-3133 (Revelations); (310) 883-6402 (Clickstar); (310) 285-9010 (office). *Website:* www.wma.com (office).

FREEMAN, Raymond (Ray), MA, DPhil, DSc, FRS; British chemist and academic; *Professor Emeritus, University of Cambridge;* b. 6 Jan. 1932, Long Eaton, Derbyshire, England; s. of Albert Freeman and Hilda F. Freeman; m. Anne-Marie Périnet-Marquet 1958; two s. three d.; ed Nottingham High School and Lincoln Coll., Oxford; Ingénieur, French Atomic Energy Comm., Centre d'Etudes Nucléaires de Saclay 1957–59; Sr Scientific Officer, Nat. Physical Lab. 1959–63; Research Scientist, Instrument Div., Varian Assocs, Palo Alto, Calif. 1963–73; Univ. Lecturer in Physical Chem. and Fellow, Magdalen Coll., Oxford 1973–87, Aldrichian Praelector in Chem. 1982–87; John Humphrey Plummer Prof. of Magnetic Resonance, Univ. of Cambridge 1987–99, Prof. Emer. 1999–, Fellow, Jesus Coll., Cambridge 1987–99, Fellow Emer. 1999–; Hon. DSc (Durham) 1998; Leverhulme Medal, Royal Soc. 1990, RSC Longstaff Medal 1999, Queen's Medal, Royal Soc. 2002, Laukien Prize Experimental NMR Conf. 2005, Varian Prize 2015. *Publications:* A Handbook of Nuclear Magnetic Resonance 1987, Spin Choreography: Basic Steps in High Resolution NMR 1997, Magnetic Resonance in Chemistry and Medicine 2003; several scientific papers on nuclear magnetic resonance spectroscopy in various journals. *Leisure interests:* swimming, traditional jazz. *Address:* Jesus College, Cambridge, CB5 8BL (office); 29 Bentley Road, Cambridge, CB2 8AW, England (home). *Telephone:* (1223) 323958 (home). *E-mail:* rf110@hermes.cam.ac.uk (office). *Website:* www.ray-freeman.org (office).

FREEMAN, Richard B., PhD; American economist and academic; *Ascherman Professor of Economics, Harvard University;* b. 29 June 1953, Newburgh, NY; m. Alida Castillo; one s. one d.; ed Dartmouth and Harvard Univs; fmr Program Dir, Science and Eng Workforce Project, Nat. Bureau of Econ. Research (NBER); fmr Faculty Co-Dir Labor and Worklife Program, Harvard Law School; fmr Sr Research Fellow, Centre for Econ. Performance, LSE, London, UK; fmr Fairchild Distinguished Research Prof., California Inst. of Tech.; fmr Asst Prof. of Econs, Yale Univ.; fmr Asst Prof. of Econs, Univ. of Chicago; fmr Asst Prof., then Assoc. Prof. of Econs, Harvard Univ., Ascherman Prof. of Econs 2009–; Frances Perkins Fellow, American Acad. of Political and Social Science 2011–; has served on eight panels of the NAS, including Cttee on Assuring a Future US-based Nuclear Chem. Expertise, Cttee on Nat. Statistics Panel on Developing Science, Tech. and Innovation Indicators for the Future, Cttee on Capitalizing on the Diversity of the Science and Eng Workforce in Industry, Cttee on Nat. Needs for Biomedical and Behavioral Scientists, and jt NAS, Nat. Acad. of Eng and Inst. of Medicine Study on Policy Implications of Int. Grad. Students and Postdoctoral Scholars in the US, has also served on the Sub-cttee on Biomedical Research Workforce Modeling, an NIH Advisory Cttee to the Dir; mem. AAAS 2004 (Fellow 2007), American Acad. of Arts and Sciences; Hon. Professorial Fellow, Univ. of Melbourne 2013–14; Mincer Lifetime Achievement Prize, Soc. of Labor Econs 2006, IZA Prize in Labor Econs 2007. *Lectures:* Clarendon Lecturer, Univ. of Oxford 1994, Lionel Robins Lecturer, LSE 1999, Luigi Einauidi Lecturer, Cornell Univ. 2002, Okun Lecturer, Yale Univ. 2003, World Econ. Annual Lecturer, Univ. of Nottingham 2003, Dr Heinz Kienzl Lecturer, OeNB, Vienna 2003, Roco C. Siciliano Lecturer, Univ. of Utah 2004, W.J. Usery Lecturer, Georgia State Univ. 2005, Ernst Fraenkel Distinguished Lecturer, Freie Universität, Berlin 2006, Public Lecturer, LSE 2006, Public Lecturer, Inst. for Legal Research, Univ. of California, Berkeley 2007, Sawyer Lecturer, Stanford Univ. 2007, Jefferson Memorial Lecturer, Univ. of California, Berkeley 2007–08, Donald Wood Hon. Lecturer, Queen's Univ., Kingston, Canada 2008, Angelo Costa Lecturer, Universita LUISS Guido Carli, Rome 2008, Annual Kenneth M. Piper Lecturer, Chicago-Kent Law School 2009, Rupert Johnson Lecturer, Washington and Lee Univ., Va 2009, Ralph Milliband Public Lecturer, LSE 2012, V.V. Giri Memorial Lecturer, 53rd Annual Conf. of Indian Soc. of Labour Economists, Mohanlal Sukhadia Univ., Udaipur, Rajasthan, India 2012. *Publications:* The Over-Educated American 1976, What Do Unions Do? 1984, Labor Markets in Action 1989, Working Under Different Rules 1994, What Workers Want 1999 (revised second edn with Joel Rogers 2007), Can Labor Standards Improve Under Globalization? (co-author) 2003, America Works: The Exceptional Labor Market 2007, What Workers Say: Employee Voice in the Anglo American World (co-author) 2007, International Differences in the Business Practices & Productivity of Firms (co-author) 2009, Science and Engineering Careers in the United States (co-author) 2009, Reforming the Welfare State: Recovery and Beyond in Sweden (co-author) 2010, Shared Capitalism at Work: Employee Ownership, Profit and Gain Sharing, and Broad-based Stock Options (co-author) 2010, The Citizen's Share: Putting Ownership Back into Democracy 2013. *Leisure interest:* professional wrestling. *Address:* National Bureau of Economic Research, 1050 Massachusetts Avenue, Cambridge, MA 02138, USA (office). *E-mail:* rbfreeman@gmail.com (office). *Website:* users.nber.org/~freeman (office).

FREETH, Peter, RA, RE; British artist and printmaker; b. 15 April 1938, Birmingham; s. of Alfred William Freeth and Olive Freeth (née Walker); m. Mariolina Meliadó 1967; two s.; ed King Edward's Grammar School, Aston, Birmingham, Slade School, London, British School, Rome; tutor, Etching Royal Acad. Schools 1966–; works on display in British Museum, Victoria & Albert Museum, Arts Council of England, Fitzwilliam Museum, Cambridge, Ashmolean Museum, Oxford, Nat. Gallery, Washington, DC, USA, Metropolitan Museum, New York, Hunterian Gallery, Glasgow; mem. Royal Soc. of Painter-Printmakers and Royal Academician 1991; Prix de Rome (engraving) 1960, Best Print, Royal Acad. 1986, Drawing/Print Prize 2002, Hunting Art Prizes, Royal Coll. of Art 2004, 2005. *Publication:* Printmakers' Secrets (contrib.) 2009. *Leisure interests:* books, music, grandchildren. *Address:* 83 Muswell Hill Road, London, N10 3HT, England (home).

FREI RUIZ-TAGLE, Eduardo; Chilean civil engineer and fmr head of state; b. 24 June 1942, Santiago; s. of Eduardo Frei Montalva (fmr Pres. of Chile) and María Ruiz-Tagle; m. María Larraechea; ed Univ. of Chile; joined Christian Democrat (CD) Party 1958, fmr Pres.; CD presidential cand., Dec. 1993, Pres. of Chile 1994–2000; C-in-C of Armed Forces 1998–2000; Senator for Los Rios region 1989–2014, Pres. of Senate 2006–08; Pres. Fundación Eduardo Frei Montalva 1982–93; unsuccessful CD presidential cand. 2010; Partner, Sigdo Koppers SA (engineering co.).

FREIER, Philip, BD, MEdSt, PhD; Australian ecclesiastic; *Archbishop of Melbourne;* b. 9 Feb. 1954, Brisbane; m. Joy Freier; two c.; ed Melbourne College of Divinity, University of Newcastle, James Cook University, University of Queensland, Queensland Institute of Technology; employed as a teacher at Thursday Island, Kowanyama, and Yarrabah, later as an advisory teacher in Aboriginal education with Queensland Educ. Dept; Deacon 1983–84, Priest 1984–99, Examining Chaplain to Archbishop of Brisbane 1993–99, Area Dean of the Burnett, Diocese of Brisbane; Rector, Christ Church Bundaberg, Diocese of Brisbane; Rector, St Oswald's Banyo, Diocese of Brisbane, Bishop of Northern Territory 1999–, Chaplain, Royal Australian Air Force Reserve 2001–, Archbishop of Melbourne 2006–, Anglican Primate of Australia 2014–; Chair. Board of Delegates, Australian College of Theology 2002–07; currently Chair. Doctrine Commission, General Synod; Fellow, Australian Inst. of Co. Directors 1995–; Hon. Fellow, Faculty of Law, Business and Arts, Northern Territory Univ. 2000–03; Chaplain Most Venerable Order of St John, Order of St John Service Medal; Australian Centenary Medal. *Leisure Interests:* bush-walking, reading, visual arts. *Address:* 209 Flinders Lane, Melbourne Vic 3000, Australia (office). *E-mail:* archbishopsoffice@melbourneanglican.org.au (office). *Website:* www.melbourneanglican.org.au (office); www.anglicanprimate.org.au (office).

FREIJ, Col Gen. Fahd Jassem al-; Syrian army officer and politician; b. 17 Jan. 1950, Hama; m.; three c.; ed Homs Mil. Acad.; joined Syrian Arab Army 1968, graduated as an Armoured Corps Lt 1971, rank of Lt Gen. 2001, Gen. 2009, Col Gen. 2012, Deputy Chief of Staff, Syrian Arab Army 2005, Chief of Staff 2011–12, commanded Syrian Army Special Forces in regions of Daraa, Idlib and Hama; Minister of Defence 2012–18, also Deputy C-in-C of Army and Armed Forces 2012–18; several mil. decorations.

FREITAS DO AMARAL, Diogo de, PhD; Portuguese politician and academic (retd); b. 21 July 1941, Póvoa de Varzim; s. of Duarte P.C. Freitas do Amaral and Maria Filomena Campos Trocado; m. Maria José Salgado Sarmento de Matos 1965; two s. two d.; Prof. of Admin. Law, Lisbon Univ. 1968, Head, Dept of Public Law and Prof., Portuguese Catholic Univ. 1978; mem. Council of State 1974–75; mem. Parl. 1975–82, 1992–93; Pres. Centre Democrat Party 1974–82, 1988–91; Pres. European Union of Christian Democrats 1981–82; Prime Minister of Portugal (interim) 1980–81, Minister of Foreign Affairs 1980–81, Deputy Prime Minister and Minister of Defence 1981–83, Minister of Foreign Affairs 2005–06; unsuccessful presidential cand. 1986; Pres. 50th Gen. Ass. of UN 1995–96; Minister of Foreign Affairs and Portuguese Communities Abroad 2005–06 (resgnd); Founder and Chair. School of Law, Universidade Nova de Lisboa 1996–2001; Pres. Fundação Portugal Século XXI 1986–90, PETROCONTROL 1992–2000; Order of Christ, Order of Santiago, Order of Henry the Navigator, Order of Saint James of the Sword 2003, Order of the White Star of Estonia 2006; Calouste Gulbenkian Prize (twice), Henry the Navigator Prize. *Plays:* O Magnífico Reitor 2001, Viriato 2002. *Publications include:* A Utilização do Domínio Público Pelos Particulares 1965, A Execução das Sentenças dos Tribunais Administrativos 1967, Conceito e natureza do recurso hierárquico 1981, Uma Solução para Portugal 1985, Curso de Direito Administrativo I, 1986, II 2001, O Antigo Regime e a Revolução (Memórias Políticas: 1941–76) 1995, História das Ideias Políticas, Vol. I 1998, D. Afonso Henriques. Biografia 2000, Estudios de Direito Público (two vols) 2004, Manual de Introdução ao direito (Vol. I) 2004, Quinze meses no Ministério dos Negócios Estrangeiros 2006, A crise no Conselho de Justiça da Federação Portuguesa de Futebol 2008. *Leisure interests:* music, horses, reading, theatre, writing, political philosophy. *E-mail:* gab.dfamaral@gmail.com.

FRENCH, Dawn; British actress and comedienne; b. 11 Oct. 1957, Holyhead, Wales; m. 1st Lenny Henry (q.v.) 1984 (divorced 2010); one d. (adopted); m. 2nd Mark Bignell 2013; ed Manchester Univ., London Cen. School of Speech and Drama; stage shows and TV series with Jennifer Saunders (q.v.); co–founder and Man. Sixteen 47 Ltd (fashion business); Hon. Rose, Montreux 2002, Acad. Fellowship, BAFTA 2009. *Stage appearances include:* Silly Cow, When We are Married 1996, My Brilliant Divorce 2003, Smaller (Lyric Theatre, London and UK tour) 2006. *Radio:* guest appearances on numerous talk shows. *TV appearances include:* The Comic Strip (Strike, Consuela, Five Go Mad in Dorset, Supergrass, Ken, The Yob, Susie) 1982–90, French and Saunders 1987–2006, Murder Most Horrid 1991–99, The Vicar of Dibley 1994–2007, Tender Loving Care 1993, Sex and Chocolate 1997, Jam & Jerusalem 2006–08, A Bucket o' French and Saunders 2007, Lark Rise to Candleford 2008, Psychoville 2009, Roger and Val Have Just Got In 2010–12; presenter: Swank 1987, Scoff 1988 (UK Channel 4), Little Big Shots 2017. *Films include:* The Supergrass 1985, Eat the Rich 1987, The Adventures of Pinocchio 1996, Maybe Baby 2000, Harry Potter and the Prisoner of Azkaban 2004, The Chronicles of Narnia: The Lion, the Witch and the Wardrobe (voice) 2005, Love and Other Disasters 2006, Coraline (voice) 2009. *Publications include:* Dear Fatty (auto-biog.) 2008, A Tiny Bit Marvellous (novel) (Galaxy Nat. Book Award for Popular Fiction Book of the Year 2011) 2010, Oh Dear Silvia 2012, According to Yes 2015. *Address:* c/o Maureen Vincent, United Agents, 12–26 Lexington Street, London, W1F 0LE, England (office). *Telephone:* (20) 3214-0800 (office). *Fax:* (20) 3214-0801 (office). *E-mail:* info@unitedagents.co.uk (office). *Website:* unitedagents.co.uk (office).

FRENCH, James (Jim), CBE, FRAeS; British airline industry executive; b. 4 July 1953; m.; three c.; began aviation career with Caledonian Airways 1970, then sr positions with Air UK; joined Jersey European Airways (now Flybe) 1990, CEO 2002–13, Chair. 2005–13; Chair. CBI South West Region 2010–12; Founder Jim French and Associates Ltd 2005–; Gov. Exeter Mathematics School 2014–; Trustee, Calvert Trust - Exmoor 2014–; Dr hc (Exeter) 2011; inducted into British Travel Industry Hall of Fame 2011.

FRENDO, Michael, Diploma Notary Public, LLM, LLD; Maltese lawyer, business executive and fmr politician; *Managing Director, Frendo Advisory;* b. 29 July 1955; s. of Joseph Frendo and Josephine Frendo (née Felice); m. Irene Brincat 1984; one s. two d.; ed Univ. of Malta and Univ. of Exeter, UK; admitted to the Bar 1977; Sr Lecturer, Faculty of Law, Univ. of Malta 1977–; Dir Press and Media Relations and Editorial Dir (newspapers) of Partit Nazzjonalista (Christian Democrat) 1982–85; MP 1987–2013, Chair. Foreign and European Affairs Cttee, House of Reps 2008–10, Speaker (Pres.), House of Reps (Parl.) 2010–13; mem. of Parl. Ass. of Council of Europe 1987–92; mem. Malta Parl. Del. to European Parl. 1987–90, 1996–98 (Chair. 1990–92); Parl. Sec. for Youth, Culture and Consumer Protection 1990–92; Minister for Youth and the Arts 1992–94, for Transport, Communications and Tech. 1994–96; Minister of Foreign Affairs 2004–08; First Vice-Chair. Jt Parl. Cttee, European Parl. and Malta Parl. 1999–2004; Nationalist Party (Christian Democrat, European People's Party); mem. European Convention (EU) 2000–02; signatory to European Convention Draft Treaty establishing a Constitution for Europe 2002, to Treaty establishing a Constitution for Europe 2004, to Treaty of Lisbon 2007; Chair. Commonwealth Ministerial Action Group 2005–07, Commonwealth Connects Programme 2005–07, cand. for post of Sec.-Gen. of Commonwealth 2007; consultant, Salamander (Consultancy) Ltd 2008–12; Prin., Frendo Advocates 2010–12; Dir Scordis Papapetrou and Co. Consultants Ltd 2012–; Man. Partner, Frendo Legal 2015–, currently Man. Dir Frendo Advisory Ltd; Chair. (non-exec.) Banif Bank (Malta) Plc 2013–; mem. Council of Europe European Comm. on Democracy through Law (Venice Comm.) 2014–, Pres. 2017–; several decorations from Spain, Portugal, Italy, Tunisia, Austria, Cyprus, Latvia and other countries, including Grand Cross of the Order of Isabella la Católica (Spain) 2009; Parl. Ass. of the Mediterranean Award 2011. *Publications include:* several books; articles in local and int. magazines and journals. *Leisure interests:*

reading, listening to 'talking books'. *Address:* 41 St Christopher Street, Valletta VLT 1464, Malta (office). *Telephone:* 79-790790 (mobile) (office). *Fax:* (2123) 4444 (office). *E-mail:* m.frendo@scordispapapetrou.com (office); michaelfrendo@gmail.com (home); michael.frendo@parlament.mt (home). *Website:* www.scordispapapetrou.com (office).

FRENI, Mirella; Italian singer (soprano); b. (Mirella Fregni), 27 Feb. 1935, Modena; d. of Ennio Fregni and Gianna Fregni (née Arcelli); m. 1st Leone Magiera 1955; one d.; m. 2nd Nicolai Ghiaurov (died 2004); debut 1955 as Micaëla in Carmen, debut at Glyndebourne Festival 1961, Royal Opera House, Covent Garden 1961, La Scala, Milan 1962, Metropolitan Opera, NY 1965; has sung at Vienna State Opera, Rome Opera, Barcelona Gran Teatro del Liceo, Boston Opera, La Scala and at Salzburg Festival and leading opera houses throughout the world; retd from the stage 2005; frequent master-classes, including extended classes in voice at Acad. of Vocal Studies, Vignola, Italy; Midem Classical Award for Lifetime Achievement 2010, Opera News Award for invaluable contribution to opera 2012. *Recordings include:* Carmen, Falstaff, La Bohème, Madame Butterfly, Tosca, Verdi Requiem, Aïda, Don Giovanni. *Major roles include:* Nanetta in Falstaff, Mimi in La Bohème, Zerlina in Don Giovanni, Susanna, Adina in L'Elisir d'amore, Violetta in La Traviata, Desdemona in Otello. *Address:* c/o Jack Mastroianni, IMG Artists, Pleiades House, 7 West 54th Street, New York, NY 10019, USA (office). *Telephone:* (212) 994-3553 (office). *E-mail:* jmastroianni@imgartists.com (office). *Website:* imgartists.com/roster/mirella-freni (office).

FRENK MORA, Julio José, MA, PhD, MD; Mexican physician, academic, public health administrator, university administrator and fmr government official; *President, University of Miami;* b. 20 Dec. 1953, Mexico City; m. Dr Felicia Knaul; three c.; ed National Autonomojus Univ. of Mexico, Univ. of Michigan, USA; Founding Dir Centre of Public Health Research, Ministry of Health 1984–87; Founding Dir Gen. Nat. Inst. of Public Health of Mexico 1987–92; Visiting Prof., Harvard Center for Population and Devt Studies 1992–93; Exec. Vice Pres. and Dir Centre for Health and Economy, Mexican Health Foundation 1995–98; Exec. Dir Evidence and Information for Policy, WHO, Geneva 1998–2000; Sec. of Health 2000–06; Pres. Carso Health Inst., Mexico City 2006–09; Sr Fellow in Global Health Program, Bill & Melinda Gates Foundation 2006–09; Dean of Faculty and T & G Angelopoulos Prof. of Public Health and Int. Devt, Harvard School of Public Health 2009–15; Pres. Univ. of Miami 2015–; Chair. Inst. for Health Metrics and Evaluation, Univ. of Washington; Vice-Pres. for Latin America, American Public Health Asscn; fmr Pres. Mexican Soc. for Quality in Health Care; Nat. Researcher, Mexican Research System 1984–98; mem. Nat. Acad. of Medicine of Mexico, US Inst. of Medicine and numerous other professional orgs; mem. editorial bds of 10 journals; Int. Fellow in Health, W.K. Kellogg Foundation 1986–89; Fellow, Mich. Soc. of Fellows, Univ. of Mich. 1982–84; Cecilio A. Robelo Award for Scientific Research (State of Morelos) 1993, Clinton Global Citizen Award 2008. *Publications include:* author of 28 books and monographs and 103 articles in cultural magazines and newspapers. *Address:* Office of the President, University of Miami, PO Box 248006, Coral Gables, FL 33124, USA (office). *Telephone:* (305) 284-5155 (office). *Website:* www president.miami.edu (office).

FRENKEL, Jacob Aharon, BA, MA, PhD; Israeli economist, academic and business executive; *Chairman, JPMorgan Chase International;* b. 8 Feb. 1943, Tel-Aviv, British Mandate of Palestine; m. Niza Frenkel 1968; two d.; ed Univ. of Chicago, USA, Hebrew Univ. of Jerusalem; on staff, Univ. of Chicago 1973–87, held various positions including David Rockefeller Prof. of Int. Econs and Ed. Journal of Political Economy; Econ. Counsellor and Dir of Research, IMF 1987–91; joined Tel-Aviv Univ. 1991, Weisfeld Prof. of Econs of Peace and Int. Relations 1994–; Gov. Bank of Israel 1991–2000, 2013–; Sr Vice-Pres. and Vice-Chair. Merrill Lynch International Inc. 2000–04, Chair. Sovereign Advisory Group and Global Financial Insts Group 2000–04; Vice-Chair. Global Econ. Strategies, American International Group (AIG) 2004–09; Chair. JPMorgan Chase International 2009–; Chair. and CEO Group of Thirty Consultative Group on Int. Econ. and Monetary Affairs, Inc., Washington, DC 2001–11; Co-Chair. Israeli del. to multilateral peace talks on Regional Econ. Devts 1991; Chair. Bd of Govs Inter-American Devt Bank 1995–96; Vice-Chair. Bd of Govs EBRD, London 1999–2000; mem. Bd of Dirs Nat. Bureau of Econ. Research, Inst. for Int. Econs, Boston Properties Inc. 2010–; mem. Int. Advisory Bd Council on Foreign Relations, Trilateral Comm., Bd of The Council for the United States and Italy, Investment Advisory Council of the Prime Minister of Turkey, Int. Advisory Council of the China Devt Bank; mem. Int. Bd of Govs Peres Center for Peace, Israel; Distinguished mem. Advisory Cttee Inst. for Global Econs, Korea; Fellow, Econometric Soc.; Hon. Pres. Israel Asscn of Grads in the Social Sciences and Humanities; Foreign Hon. mem. American Acad. of Arts and Science, Japan Soc. of Monetary Econs; Gran Cruz, Orden de Mayo al Mérito (Argentina), Order of Merit (in the rank of Cavaliere di Gran Croce) (Italy); several hon. doctoral degrees; Karel Englis Prize in Econs (Czech Repub.), Hugo Ramniceanu Prize for Econs, Tel-Aviv Univ., Economic Policy Award, Emerging Markets 1993, Euromoney Cen. Banker of the Year Award 1997, Israel Prize 2002. *Publications:* numerous books and articles on int. econs and macro-econs. *Address:* JPMorgan Chase & Co., 270 Park Avenue, New York, NY 10017, USA (office); Bank of Israel, PO Box 780, Kiryat Ben-Gurion, Jerusalem 91007, Israel (office). *Telephone:* (212) 270-6000 (New York) (office); (2) 6552211 (Jeruslaem) (office). *Fax:* (212) 270-1648 (New York) (office); (2) 6528805 (Jeruslaem) (office). *E-mail:* info@bankisrael.gov.il (office). *Website:* www.jpmorgan.com (office); www.bankisrael.gov.il (office).

FRENZEL, Michael, Dr iur.; German business executive; *President, Federal Association of the German Tourism Industry (BTW);* b. 2 March 1947, Leipzig; ed Ruhr Univ., Bochum; joined Westdeutsche Landesbank (WestLB), Düsseldorf 1981, Man. Industrial Holdings Dept 1983–85, Man. Equity Holdings Div. 1985–88; mem. Bd of Dirs Preussag AG (renamed TUI AG 2002) 1988–, Vice-Chair. 1992–93, Chair. Exec. Bd 1994–2013, Chair. Hapag-Lloyd AG 1998–, also Chair. TUI Travel PLC 2007–13; Chair. Creditanstalt AG, Vienna; Pres. Fed. Asscn of German Tourism Industry (BTW) 2012–; mem. Supervisory Bd AWD Holding AG, AXA Konzern AG, Hapag-Lloyd AG (Chair.), TUIfly GmbH (Chair.), TUI Cruises GmbH, TUI Deutschland (Chair.), Volkswagen AG, Hochtief AG, Deutsche Bahn AG, AXA Konzern AG; mem. Bd TUI China Travel Co. Ltd, TUI Travel PLC (Chair.); Chair. Exec. Cttee, World Travel & Tourism Council (WTTC) 2012–16, WTTC Amb. 2018–. *Address:* Federal Association of the German Tourism Industry, Am Weidendamm 1A, 10117 Berlin, Germany (office). *Telephone:* (307) 26254 (office). *Fax:* (307) 2625444 (office). *E-mail:* info@btw.de (office). *Website:* www.btw.de (office).

FRÈRE, Gérald; Belgian business executive; *Chairman (non-executive), Compagnie Nationale à Portefeuille SA (CNP);* b. 17 May 1951, Charleroi; s. of Baron Albert Frère; joined Frère-Bourgeois Group (family co.) 1972, later Man. Dir; Chair. (non-exec.) Compagnie Nationale à Portefeuille SA (CNP) 1988–; also Chair. Diane SA, Filux SA, Gesecalux SA, Loverfin SA, Stichting Administratie Kantoor Bierlaire, TVI SA; Vice-Chair. Pargesa Holding SA (Dir 1992–); Chair. and Man. Dir Haras de la Bierlaire SA, Groupe Bruxelles Lambert SA 1993– (Exec. Dir 1982–); Man. Dir Financière de la Sambre SA; Dir Power Financial Corpn 1990–, Compagnie Benelux Paribas SA, COBEPA SA (Belgium), Erbe SA, Fingen SA, Fonds Charles-Albert Frère asbl (fmrly Fondation Charles Albert Frère asbl), GBL Finance SA, Stichting Administratie Kantoor Frère-Bourgeois (NL), Suez-Tractebel SA, Fomento de Construcciones y Contratas, GIB SA, Clt-Ufa SA, AXA Holding SA, AXA Royale Belge SA, Corporation Financière Power (CDN), Frabepar, Hexane, PetroFina SA, Taittinger SA, Suez-Tractebel SA (Belgium), Lafarge SA 2008–; Dir (non-exec.) RTL Group SA 2000–06; Man. Agriger SPRL; mem. Bd of Regency, Nationale Bank van België (Banque Nationale de Belgique SA); mem. Supervisory Bd, Financial Services Authority, Brussels; fmr Exec. Officer, Chrome Corpn Ltd (fmrly Preston Resources Ltd); fmr Dir Electrafina SA, Soc. Générale de Belgique SA; mem. Bd of Trustees Belgian Governance Inst.; Hon. Consul of France. *Address:* Compagnie Nationale à Portefeuille, rue de la Blanche Borne 12, 6280 Gerpinnes (Loverval) (office); Groupe Bruxelles Lambert SA, avenue Marnix 24, 1000 Brussels, Belgium (office). *Telephone:* (71) 60-60-60 (Gerpinnes) (office); (2) 547-23-52 (Brussels) (office). *Fax:* (71) 60-60-70 (Gerpinnes) (office); (2) 547-22-85 (Brussels) (office). *E-mail:* info@cnp.be (office); info@gbl.be (office). *Website:* www.cnp.be (office); www.gbl.be (office).

FRÉROT, Antoine, PhD; French business executive; *Chairman and CEO, Veolia Environnement;* b. 3 June 1958, Fontainebleau; ed Ecole Polytechnique, Ecole Nationale des Ponts et Chaussées (ENPC); began career as a research engineer at Bureau Cen. d'études pour l'Outre-Mer; Project Man., Centre d'Études et de Recherche de l'ENPC (Cergrene) 1983, Deputy Dir 1984–88; worked for the Crédit National 1988–90; Head of Mission, Compagnie Générale des Eaux 1990–95; CEO Compagnie Générale d'Entreprises Automobiles (CGEA) and CGEA Transport 1995–2000; mem. Bd of Dirs Vivendi Environnement (VE) and CEO CONNEX Transport Div., VE 2000–03, CEO Veolia Eau-Compagnie Générale des Eaux, mem. Exec. Cttee VE and Deputy Man. Dir Veolia Environment 2003–, CEO Veolia Transport 2005–09, CEO Veolia Environnement 2009–, Chair. 2010–, also Dir of Veolia Transport, Veolia Propreté, Veolia Environnement 2010–, SARP and Sade CGTH, and Chair. Compagnie des Eaux et de l'Ozone and Veolia Water Solutions & Technologies, also acts as a Veolia Rep. on Bd of Soc. des Eaux de Marseille. *Address:* Veolia Environnement, 36–38 avenue Kléber, 75116 Paris, Cedex 8, France (office). *Telephone:* 1-71-75-00-00 (office). *Fax:* 1-71-71-15-45 (office). *E-mail:* info@veoliaenvironnement.com (office). *Website:* www.veoliaenvironnement.com (office).

FRESTON, Thomas (Tom) E., BA, MBA; American media executive; b. 22 Nov. 1945, New York; s. of Thomas E. Freston and Winifred Geng; m. 1st Margaret Badali 1980; two s.; m. 2nd Kathy Freston (divorced); Dir of Marketing, MTV, MTV Networks, New York 1980–81; Dir of Marketing, The Movie Channel 1982–83; Vice-Pres. Marketing MTV, MTV Networks 1983–84, Vice-Pres. of Marketing 1984–85, Sr Vice-Pres. and Gen. Man. of Affiliate Sales, Marketing 1985, Sr Vice-Pres. and Gen. Man. MTV, VH-1 1985–86, Pres. Entertainment 1986–87, Pres. and CEO 1987–89, Chair. and CEO MTV Networks 1989–2004; Co-Pres. and Co-COO Viacom Inc. 2004–05, CEO Viacom (after split of Viacom Inc.) 2005–06; currently Prin. Firefly3 LLC (media consultancy); mem. Bd of Dirs Cable Advertising Bureau 1987–, Museum of Natural History, Rock and Roll Hall of Fame 1986–, Viacom Inc. 2005–06; DreamWorks Animation SKG Inc. 2007–, American Museum of Nat. History; mem. Stategic Advisory Bd, Shelter Capital Partners; mem. Advisory Bd, Raine Group LLC; mem. Smithsonian Comm. Music in America 1987–, Cable TV Admin. and Marketing Asscn, Nat. Acad. of Cable Programming; Trustee, Asia Soc.; Gov.'s Award, Nat. Acad. of Cable Programming, Personality of the Year, MIPCOM, Pres. Award, Cable TV Public Affairs Asscn, Humanitarian of the Year Award, T.J. Martell Foundation; inducted into Cable TV Hall of Fame 2005. *Leisure interests:* photography, travel, antique rugs.

FRETTON, Anthony (Tony); British architect; *Principal Emeritus, Tony Fretton Architects;* b. 17 Jan. 1945, London; s. of Thomas C. Fretton and May Frances Diamond; m. Susan Pearce 1963 (divorced 1988); one s. one d.; ed Architectural Asscn School of Architecture; Prin. Tony Fretton Architects 1982; Visiting Prof., Berlage Inst., Amsterdam, Netherlands 1996, Ecole Polytechnique de Lausanne, Switzerland 1994–96; apptd Prof. of Architectural and Interior Design, Tech. Univ. of Delft, Netherlands 1999, now Prof. Emer.; Prof., Univ. of East London 2013–; Visiting Lecturer, Harvard Design School, USA 2004–05, ETH Zurich 2010–12, TU Vienna 2013; Corp. mem. RIBA; Trustee, Docomomo UK 2016–; Dr hc (Oxford Brookes) 2006. *Major projects include:* Lisson Gallery, London 1992, Artsway Centre for Visual Arts, Sway, Hampshire 1996, Quay Arts Centre, Newport, Isle of Wight 1998, Two Apartments, Groningen, Netherlands 2001, The Red House, Chelsea, London (Stone Fed. of GB Natural Stone Award 2002, RIBA Award 2003, Chicago Athenaeum Int. Architecture Award 2006), Faith House, Holton Lee Centre for Disability in the Arts, Poole, Dorset (ACE/RIBA Awards for Religious Architecture 2003, Guardian Best British Building of the Year Award) 2002, Arts Council Sculpture Gallery, Yorkshire Sculpture Park 2003, Camden Arts Centre, London 2004, Constantijn Huygenstraat, Amsterdam 2004–11, House for Two Artists, Clerkenwell, London 2005, Stroud Valley Arts Space 2007, House for Anish Kapoor 2008, Vassall Road Housing, London 2008, Fuglsang Kunstmuseum, Lolland, Denmark (RIBA Award 2009) 2008, British Embassy, Warsaw, Poland (RIBA Award 2010) 2009, de Prinsendam, Amsterdam 2010, Tietgens Grund, Copenhagen 2010, Andreas Ensemble, Amsterdam 2010. *Publications include:* Building and Project: Four British Architects, 9H Gallery 1990, Tony Fretton 1995, Tony Fretton Architects: Abstraction and Familiarity 2001,Designing the Warsaw Embassy: Tony Fretton Architects 2006, 2G Monographs 2009, Tony Fretton 2009, Architects 2010, Buildings and their Territories 2014; numerous exhbn catalogues. *Leisure interests:* travel, film, visual arts, poetry. *Address:* Tony Fretton Architects, Highgate Studios, 53–79 Highgate Road, London, NW5 1TL, England (office). *Telephone:* (20) 7284-2000 (office). *Fax:* (20) 3227-1055 (office). *E-mail:* studio@tonyfretton.com (office). *Website:* www.tonyfretton.com (office).

FREUD, Anthony Peter, OBE, LLB; British/American opera administrator and barrister; *General Director, President and CEO, Lyric Opera of Chicago;* b. 30 Oct. 1957, London, England; s. of Joseph Freud and Katalin Freud (née Löwi); m. Colin Ure; ed King's Coll. School, Wimbledon, King's Coll., London; trained as barrister before becoming theatre man. at Sadler's Wells Theatre Co. 1980–84; Co. Sec., Welsh Nat. Opera 1984, Head of Planning 1989–92, Gen. Dir 1994–2005; Chair. Opera Europe 2001–05; Gen. Dir and CEO Houston Grand Opera, Tex., USA 2006–11; Gen. Dir, Pres. and CEO Lyric Opera of Chicago 2011–; Exec. Producer, Opera, Philips Classics 1992–94; Chair. OPERA America 2008–12; Jury Chair., BBC Cardiff Singer of the World Competition 1995–2005; Trustee, Nat. Endowment for Science, Tech. and the Arts 2004–05; Hon. Fellow, Univ. of Cardiff 2002, Royal Welsh Coll. of Music and Drama 2005. *Leisure interests:* music, theatre, cinema, visual arts, travel, cookery. *Address:* Lyric Opera of Chicago, 20 North Wacker Drive, Chicago, IL 60606, USA (office). *Telephone:* (312) 827-3550 (office). *Fax:* (312) 332-0503 (office). *E-mail:* afreud@lyricopera.org (office). *Website:* www.lyricopera.org (office).

FREUDENTHAL, David (Dave) Duane, BA, JD; American lawyer, politician and fmr state governor; *Senior Counsel, Crowell & Moring LLP;* b. 12 Oct. 1950, Thermpolis, Wyo.; m. Nancy D. Freudenthal; two s. two d.; ed Amherst Coll., Mass, Univ. of Wyoming Coll. of Law; economist, Wyo. Dept of Econ. Planning and Devt 1973–75, apptd State Planning Co-ordinator 1975–80; f. law office, Cheyenne 1980; Chair. Wyoming State Democratic Cen. Cttee 1981–85; US Attorney, Wyo. 1994–2001; Gov. of Wyo. 2003–11; Sr Counsel, Crowell & Moring LLP 2011–; fmr Chair. Greater Cheyenne Chamber of Commerce; Founder-Dir Wyo. Student Loans Corpn; mem. Bd of Dirs Arch Coal, Inc. 2011–; mem. Wyoming Futures Project 1984–87, Wyo. State Econ. and Devt and Stabilization Bd 1985–89, Educ. Policy Implementation Council 1989–90, Bd Wyo. Community Foundation, Laramie Co. Community Action; Gov. Substance Abuse and Violent Crime Advisory Bd 1994–2001; Democrat. *Address:* Crowell & Moring LLP, 1604 Pioneer Avenue, Cheyenne, WY 82001-4414, USA (office). *Telephone:* (307) 996-1401 (office). *E-mail:* dfreudenthal@crowell.com (office). *Website:* www.crowell.com (office).

FREY, Bruno S., PhD; Swiss economist and academic; *Permanent Visiting Professor, University of Basel;* b. 4 May 1941, Basel; s. of Leo Frey and Julie Frey (née Bach); ed Univ. of Basel and Univ. of Cambridge, UK; Assoc. Prof. of Econs, Univ. of Basel 1969–2006; Prof. of Econs, Univ. of Konstanz 1970–77, Univ. of Zurich 1977–2012; Distinguished Prof. of Behavioural Science, Warwick Business School, Univ. of Warwick, UK 2010–13; Sr Prof. of Econs, Zeppelin Univ., Friedrichshafen, Germany 2013–15; Perm. Visiting Prof., Univ. of Basel 2015–; Visiting Fellow, All Souls Coll., Oxford, UK 1983; Fellow, Coll. of Science, Berlin, FRG 1984–85; Visiting Research Prof., Univ. of Chicago, USA 1990; Guest Prof., Univ. of St Gallen 1993–2006, 2010; Visiting Prof., Univ. of Rome, Italy 1996–97, Antwerp Univ., Belgium 1999, Univs of Gothenburg, Stockholm, Linz, Klagenfurt, Siena, Kiel, Valencia, Groningen, Research School of Social Sciences, ANU, Queensland Univ. of Tech., ETH-Zürich 2007–09; Research Dir CREMA – Centre for Research in Econs, Man. and the Arts, Zurich 2000–; First Jelle Zijlstra Professorial Fellow, Inst. of Advanced Study, Wassenaar 2003; Distinguished Fellow, CESifo Research Network 2005; Academic Affiliate, Judge School of Business, Univ. of Cambridge, UK 2005; Man. Ed. Kyklos 1969–; mem. numerous editorial bds; Fellow, Public Choice Soc. 1998, Collegium Budapest 2002, European Econ. Asscn 2004; mem. European Acad. of Sciences and Arts (Academia Scientiarum et Artium Europaea); Corresp. FRSE 2005; Distinguished Fellow, Asscn for Cultural Econs, International 2010; Hon. DEcon (St Gallen) 1998, (Gothenburg) 1998, (Vrije Universiteit Brussel, Belgium) 2009, (Université Paul Cézanne Aix-Marseille III, France) 2010, (Univ. of Innsbruck, Austria) 2011; Genossenschaftspreis, Philosophical-Historical Faculty, Univ. of Basel 1965, Vernon Prize, Asscn for Public Policy and Man. (USA) 1996, Stolper Prize of Verein für Socialpolitik 2007, Friedrich von Wieser-Prize, Prague Conf. on Political Economy 2008, Röpke Prize for Civil Soc. Liberal Inst. 2012. *Publications include:* Economics as a Science of Human Behaviour 1992, Not Just for the Money: An Economic Theory of Personal Motivation 1997, The New Democratic Federalism for Europe 1999, Arts and Economics: Analysis and Cultural Policy 2000, Managing Motivation: Wie Sie die neue Motivationsforschung für Ihr Unternehmen nutzen können (co-author) 2000, Inspiring Economics: Human Motivation in Political Economy 2001, Successful Management by Motivation – Balancing Intrinsic and Extrinsic Incentives 2002, Happiness and Economics: How the Economy and Institutions Affect Human Well-Being 2002, Dealing with Terrorism: Stick or Carrot? 2004, Economics and Psychology 2007, Happiness: A Revolution in Economics 2008, Glück – Die Sicht der Ökonomie (with Claudia Frey Marti) 2010, Recent Developments in the Economics of Happiness (co-ed.) 2013. *Leisure interest:* travel. *Address:* Centre for Research in Economics, Management and the Arts, Suedstrasse 11, 8008 Zurich, Switzerland (office). *Telephone:* (44) 3800078 (office). *E-mail:* bruno.frey@bsfrey.ch (office). *Website:* www.unibas.ch/crew (office); www.crema-research.ch (office); www.bsfrey.ch.

FREY JENSEN, Hugo, MEconSc; Danish economist and central banker; *Governor, Danmarks Nationalbank;* b. 11 Jan. 1958; m. Helle Frey Jensen 1984; ed Univ. of Århus; Asst Lecturer, Univ. of Århus 1980–84, Univ. of Copenhagen 1984–88, Copenhagen Business School 1989–92; Asst Admin. and Man. in various depts, Danmarks Nationalbank (central bank) 1984–93, Head of Monetary Policy Office and Econs Dept 1994–2000, later Head of Capital Markets Dept, Deputy Dir 2010, Gov. 2011–; Dir European Central Bank 1993–2001, 2008–10; mem. EU Econ. Policy Cttee 1997–2000, European Central Bank Supervision Cttee 2001–07, Banking Advisory Cttee 2001–03; Dir Fondsrådet (Danish Securities Council) 2003–07, 2010–11; mem. Bd of Dirs Bankernes Kontantservice (BKS) 2013–16, Nets Holding 2013–14; Danish Ship Finance 2014–15, VP Securities 2014–; mem. Advisory Tech. Cttee, ESRB 2011; Chair. Danmarks Nationalbank's Pension Fund 2011–, Betalingsrådet 2012–15; Observer, Bankernes EDB Central (BEC) 2011–. *Address:* Board of Governors, Danmarks Nationalbank, Havnegade 5, 1093 Copenhagen K, Denmark (office). *Telephone:* 33-63-63-63 (office). *Fax:* 33-63-71-03 (office). *E-mail:* nationalbanken@nationalbanken.dk (office). *Website:* www.nationalbanken.dk (office).

FREYRE, Angela Mariana, BA, DEJG, LLM, JD; American (b. Cuban) lawyer and business executive; *Senior Vice-President and General Counsel, Export-Import Bank of the United States (Ex-Im Bank);* b. 18 Sept. 1954, Havana, Cuba; ed Wellesley Coll., Mass, Université de Droit d'Economie et des Sciences Sociales de Paris, Georgetown Univ., Washington, DC; admitted to NY Bar 1984; Assoc., Mudge, Rose, Guthrie, Alexander & Ferdon LLP, New York and Paris 1984–95; Pnr, Coudert Brothers LLP, New York (int. corp. finance firm) 1995–2005; Sr Vice-Pres. and Deputy Gen. Counsel for Legal and Strategic Affairs, The Nielsen Co. (global information services co.) 2005–11; Sr Vice-Pres. and Gen. Counsel, Export-Import Bank of the US (Ex-Im Bank), Washington, DC 2011–; mem. City of New York Conflicts of Interest Bd; Trustee, LongHouse Reserve Ltd 2000–; mem. Bar Asscn, City of New York; Fulbright Scholar. *Address:* Export-Import Bank of the United States, 811 Vermont Avenue, NW, Washington, DC 20571, USA (office). *Telephone:* (202) 565-3946 (office). *Fax:* (202) 565-3380 (office). *E-mail:* info@exim.gov (office). *Website:* www.exim.gov (office).

FRICK, Aurelia, Lic.iur., DrIur; Liechtenstein lawyer and politician; *Minister of Foreign Affairs, Justice and Culture;* b. 19 Sept. 1975; m.; two c.; ed Univ. of Fribourg, Univ. of Basel; admitted to Zürich Bar 2004; attorney, Haymann & Baldi, Zürich 2004–05; Assoc., Bjørn Johansson Assocs AG, Zürich 2006–07; man. consultant 2008–09; Minister of Foreign Affairs, Justice and Culture 2009–13, 2017–, Educ. and Cultural Affairs 2013–17; mem. Progressive Citizens' Party 2009–. *Leisure interests:* music, sport, culture, arts. *Address:* Regierungsgebäude, Postfach 684, 9490 Vaduz, Liechtenstein (office). *Telephone:* 2366111 (office). *Fax:* 2366022 (office). *E-mail:* office@liechtenstein.li (office). *Website:* www.liechtenstein.li (office).

FRICK, Mario, DrIur; Liechtenstein lawyer, politician and civil servant; *Partner, Seeger, Frick & Partner AG;* b. 8 May 1965, Balzers; s. of Kuno Frick-Kaufmann and Melita Frick-Kaufmann; m. Andrea Haberlander 1992; one s. one d.; ed Univ. of St Gallen, Switzerland; State Admin. Legal Service 1991–93; mem. Municipal Council of Balzers 1991–93; Deputy Head of Govt May–Dec. 1993, Head of Govt 1993–2001, also Minister of Finance and Construction; currently Partner, Seeger, Frick & Partner AG (law firm); Trustee, Univ. of St Gallen 2002–; Chair. Bank Frick & Co. *Leisure interests:* football, tennis, biking. *Address:* Seeger, Frick & Partner AG, Landstrasse 81, 9494 Schaan, Liechtenstein (office). *Telephone:* 2652225 (office). *Fax:* 2652232 (office). *E-mail:* mario.frick@sfplex.li (office). *Website:* www.sfplex.li (office); www.bankfrick.li (office).

FRIDERICHS, Hans, Dr rer. pol; German politician and business executive; b. 16 Oct. 1931, Wittlich; s. of Paul Friderichs and Klara Neuwinger; m. Erika Wilhelm; two d.; Man. Rhineland-Hesse Chamber of Industry and Trade 1959–63; Deputy Business Man. FDP 1963–64, Business Man. 1964–69; mem. Bundestag 1965–69, 1976–77; Sec. of State, Ministry of Agric., Viniculture and Protection of the Environment for Rhineland Palatinate 1969–72; Fed. Minister of Econs 1972–77; Deputy Chair. FDP 1974–77; Dir Dresdner Bank 1977–85, Chair. Bd Man. Dirs 1978–85 (resgnd); mem. Supervisory Bd AEG Telefunken 1979, Chair. 1980–84; Chair. Supervisory Bd allit AG Kunststofftechnik, Goldman Sachs Investment Management GmbH, Frankfurt, Germany, Leica Camera AG, Solms, Germany, Racke-Dujardin GmbH & Co. KG, Bingen, Germany, C.A. Kupferberg & Cie. KGaA, Mainz, Germany; Deputy Chair. Supervisory Bd adidas AG –2007, Chair. 2007–09; Deputy Chair. Supervisory Bd IIC The New German Länder Industrial Investment Council GmbH, Berlin, Germany; Chair. Univ. Council, Univ. of Mainz –2013; mem. Supervisory Bd Schneider Electric S.A., Paris, France –2005. *Leisure interests:* art, sport.

FRIDMAN, Mikhail Maratovich; Russian business executive; *Chairman, L1 Holdings;* b. 21 April 1964, Lviv, Ukrainian SSR, USSR; m.; two c.; ed Moscow Inst. of Steel and Alloys; with Elektrostal Eng Construction Factory, Elektrostal City, Moscow Oblast 1986–88; Founder Alfa-Foto, Alfa-Eco, Alfa-Capital 1988, Chair. Alfa-Bank (later Alfa-Group) from 1991, Alfa-Consortium from 1996, Alfa Commercial Bank from 1998, now Chair. Supervisory Bd Alfa Group Consortium, Interim CEO TNK-BP (joint venture between BP and Alfa-Access-Renova) 2009–11, Exec. Chair. 2011–13 (co. acquired by Rosneft); Co-founder LetterOne Group (L1) Group, Luxembourg 2013, Chair. L1 Holdings and L1 Investment Holdings 2013–; mem. Bd of Dirs, Russian Public TV (ORTV) 1995–98, Oil Co. SIDANKO 1996–2000, Perekrestok Trade House 1998–, VimpelCom; mem. Supervisory Bd, X5 Retail Group NV, DEA Deutsche Erdoel AG, Hamburg (acquired by L1 Energy 2015); Founder and Vice-Pres. Russian Jewish Congress 1996–, Head of Cttee on Culture 1996–; mem. Council on Banking Activity, Fed. Govt 1996–, Council on Business, Council of Ministers 2001–; mem. Bureau of Man. Bd, Russian Council of Industrialists and Entrepreneurs; elected to Russia's Public Chamber 2005; Founder and Chair. Genesis Philanthropy Group; mem. Int. Advisory Bd, Council of Foreign Relations; Golden Plate Award, Int. Acad. of Achievement, Washington, DC 2003. *Address:* Alfa-Bank, 107078 Moscow, ul. Kalanchevskaya 27, Russia (office); LetterOne Holdings SA, 3 Blvd de la Foire, 1528 Luxembourg Ville, Luxembourg (office). *Telephone:* (495) 929-91-91 (Moscow) (office); (26) 38771 (Luxembourg). *Fax:* (495) 788-69-81 (Moscow) (office); (26) 387799 (Luxembourg) (office). *E-mail:* mail@alfabank.ru (office); contact@letterone.lu (office). *Website:* www.alfagroup.org (office); www.letterone.lu (office).

FRIDRIKSSON, Fridrik Thor; Icelandic film director; b. 12 May 1954; s. of Fridrik Gudmundson and Gudridur Hjaltested; m. (divorced); one s. one d.; Founder Reykjavik Film Festival; est. Icelandic Film Corp. (production co.) 1984. *Films:* Eldsmiðurinn (The Blacksmith) 1981, Rokk í Reykjavik (Rock in Reykjavik) 1982, Kúreakr norðursins (Icelandic Cowboys) 1984, Hringurinn (The Circle) 1985, Skytturnar (White Whales) 1987, Flugþrá (Sky Without Limit) 1989, Englakroppar (Pretty Angels) 1990, Börn náttúrunnar (Children of Nature) 1991, Bíódagar (Movie Days) 1994, Á köldum klaka (Cold Fever) 1995, Djöflaeyjan (Devil's Island) 1996, Englar alheimsins (Angels of the Universe) 2000, Fálkar 2002, Næsland 2004, The Boss of It All 2006, Mamma Gógó 2010. *Address:* Icelandic Film Corporation, Hverfisgata 46, 101 Reykjavik (office); Bjarkargata 8, 101 Reykjavik, Iceland (home). *Telephone:* 5512260 (office); 5528566 (home). *Fax:* 5525154 (office). *E-mail:* amk@icecorp.is (office); f.thor@vortex.is (home).

FRIED, Charles, LLB, MA; American lawyer and academic; *Beneficial Professor of Law, Harvard Law School;* b. (Karel Fried), 15 April 1935, Prague, Czechoslovakia; s. of Anthony Fried and Marta Fried (née Wintersteinova); m. Anne Sumerscale 1959; one s. one d.; ed Princeton and Columbia Univs, Univ. of Oxford, UK; law clerk to Assoc. Justice John M. Harlan, US Supreme Court 1960; mem. Faculty, Harvard Law School 1961–, Prof. of Law 1965–85, Carter Prof. of Gen. Jurisprudence 1981–85, 1989–95, Prof. Emer., Distinguished Lecturer 1995–, Beneficial Prof. of Law 1999–; Deputy Solicitor-Gen. and Counselor to Solicitor-Gen. 1985, Solicitor-Gen. of USA 1985–89; Assoc. Justice Supreme Judiciary Court of Mass, Boston 1995–99; Fellow, American Acad. of Arts and Sciences; started HarvardX MOOC (open online course): From trust to promise to contract 2015. *Publications include:* An Anatomy of Values 1970, Medical Experimentation: Personal Integrity and Social Policy 1974 (second edn 2016), Right and Wrong 1978, Contract as Promise: A Theory of Contractual Obligation 1981 (second edn 2015), Order and Law: Arguing the Reagan Revolution 1991, Making Tort Law (with David Rosenberg) 2003, Saying What the Law Is: The Constitution in the Supreme Court 2004, Modern Liberty 2006, Because it is Wrong: Torture, Privacy and Presidential Power in the Age of Terror (with Gregory Fried) 2010; contribs to legal and philosophical journals. *Address:* Harvard Law School, 1563 Massachusetts Avenue, Cambridge, MA 02138, USA (office). *Telephone:* (617) 495-4636 (home). *Fax:* (617) 496-4865 (office). *E-mail:* fried@law.harvard.edu (office). *Website:* www.law.harvard.edu (office).

FRIED, Jonathan T., BA, LLB, LLM; Canadian diplomatist and international organization official; b. 19 Aug. 1953, Edmonton, Alberta; m. Paula Vaillancourt; ed Univ. of Toronto, Columbia Univ., New York, Parker School of Foreign and Comparative Law (Program in Int. Business Law); articles of clerkship and pvt. practice with Field, Owen, Barristers and Solicitors, Edmonton, Alberta 1977–78; UN Sixth Cttee (Legal) 1980; Asst Sec. to Canadian Del. to Ottawa Summit 1981; Second Sec. and Vice-Consul, Embassy in Brasilia 1981–83; Counsel, Econ. Law and Treaty Div., Legal Affairs Bureau, Foreign Affairs and Int. Trade Canada 1983–86, Asst Gen. Counsel, Trade Negotiations Office 1986–87; Counselor for Congressional and Legal Affairs, Embassy in Washington, DC 1987–91; Prin. Legal Counsel, N American Free Trade Agreement (NAFTA) Bureau, Foreign Affairs and Int. Trade Canada 1991–93, Dir-Gen., Trade Policy Bureau and Coordinator for NAFTA 1995–97, Asst Deputy Minister, Trade, Econ. and Environmental Policy 1997–2000, Sr Asst Deputy Minister and G7 Deputy for Canada, Finance Canada 2000–03, Assoc. Deputy Minister, Foreign Affairs and Int. Trade Canada 2003; Sr Foreign Policy Advisor and Head, Canada-US Secr. to the Prime Minister of Canada, Privy Council Office 2003–06; Exec. for Canada, Ireland and the Caribbean, IMF 2006–08; Amb. to Japan 2008–12, Amb. and Perm. Rep. to WTO, Geneva 2012–17; mem. Law Soc. of Alberta.

FRIED, Linda Phyllis, BA, MD, MPh; American physician, academic and university administrator; *DeLamar Professor of Public Health and Dean, Mailman School of Public Health, Columbia University;* b. 1949, New York City; ed Hunter Coll. High School, New York, Rush Medical Coll., Chicago, Johns Hopkins Univ., Colgate Univ.; intern, Rush Presbyterian St Luke's Medical Center, Chicago 1979–80, resident in internal medicine 1980–82; Fellow in Gen. Internal Medicine, Johns Hopkins Medical Inst., Baltimore 1982–85, Fellow in Epidemiology 1983–85, Fellow in Geriatrics 1985–86, Prof. of Medicine, Epidemiology and Health Policy 2003–08, Mason F. Lord Prof. of Geriatric Medicine 2003-08, Dir Div. of Geriatric Medicine and Gerontology 2003–08, Medical Insts' Center of Excellence for Aging Research –2008, Center on Aging and Health –2008, Dir Program Epidemiology of Aging, Bloomberg School of Public Health –2008; Dean, Mailman School of Public Health, Columbia Univ. 2008–, DeLamar Prof. of Public Health 2008–, Prof. of Epidemiology 2008–, Sr Vice-Pres. Columbia Univ. Medical Center 2008–; Co-founder Experience Corps, Baltimore 2002; mem. Nat. Advisory Council on Aging 2003–; mem. Inst. of Medicine, NAS; mem. World Econ. Forum Council on Challenges of Gerontology; Herbert DeVries Distinguished Research Award, Council on Aging and Adult Devt 2000, Mary Betty Stevens Award, ACP 2007, Archstone Award, American Public Health Asscn, Maxwell Pollack Award, Gerontological Soc. of America, American Geriatrics Soc.'s Henderson Award, Merit Award from Nat. Inst. on Aging. *Address:* Office of the Dean, Mailman School of Public Health, Columbia Univ., 722 West 168th Street, R1408, New York, NY 10032, USA (office). *Telephone:* (212) 305-9300 (office). *Fax:* (212) 305-9342 (office). *E-mail:* lpfried@columbia.edu (office). *Website:* www.mailman.columbia.edu (office).

FRIEDBERG, Aaron L., AB, AM, PhD; American academic; *Professor of Politics and International Affairs, Woodrow Wilson School, Princeton University;* b. 1956, Pittsburgh; ed Harvard Univ.; joined Woodrow Wilson School, Princeton Univ. 1987, currently Prof. of Politics and Int. Affairs; Henry A. Kissinger Chair in Foreign Policy and Int. Relations, John W. Kluge Center, Library of Congress 2001–02; fmr Fellow, Woodrow Wilson Int. Center for Scholars, Smithsonian Inst., Norwegian Nobel Inst. 1998, Harvard Univ. Center for Int. Affairs; Deputy Asst for Nat. Security Affairs, Office of the Vice-Pres., Washington, DC 2003–05; Chair. Bd of Counselors, Kenneth B. and Anne H.H. Pyle Center for Northeast Asian Studies, Nat. Bureau of Asian Research. *Publications include:* The Weary Titan: Britain and the Experience of Relative Decline 1895–1905 (Edgar Furniss Nat. Security Book Award 1988), In the Shadow of the Garrison State: America's Anti-Statism and Its Cold War Grand Strategy 2000, Strategic Asia 2001–02: Power and Purpose (co-ed.) 2001, A Contest for Supremacy: China, America, and the Struggle for Mastery in Asia 2011, Beyond Air-Sea Battle: The Debate Over US Military Strategy in Asia 2014. *Address:* Woodrow Wilson School, Bendheim 013, Princeton University, Princeton, NJ 08544-1013, USA (office). *Telephone:* (609) 258-9891 (office). *E-mail:* alf@princeton.edu (office). *Website:* www.princeton.edu (office).

FRIEDEN, Luc, LLM; Luxembourg politician; *Chairman, Banque Internationale à Luxembourg (BIL);* b. 16 Sept. 1963, Esch-sur-Alzette; m.; two c.; ed Lycée de garçons, Esch-sur-Alzette, Athénée de Luxembourg, Centre universitaire de Luxembourg, Université de Paris I (Panthéon Sorbonne), France, Univ. of Cambridge, UK, Harvard Law School, USA; commentator RTL, Luxembourg Radio 1981–94; attorney-at-law Luxembourg Bar (Barreau de Luxembourg) 1989–98, 2016–; fmr teacher Centre Universitaire de Luxembourg; mem. Parl. 1994–, Chair. Finance and Budget Cttee, Cttee on Constitutional Affairs 1994–98; Minister of Justice, of the Budget and for Relations with Parl. 1998–99; Minister of Justice 1998–2009, of Treasury (in charge of financial services and budget) 1999–2009, also Minister of Defence 2004–05, Minister of Finance 2009–13; Gov. World Bank 1998, Asian Devt Bank 2003–04; Vice-Chair. Deutsche Bank AG and Chair. Supervisory Bd Deutsche Bank Luxembourg SA 2014–16; Chair. (acting) Bd of Govs. IMF 2013; Chair. Banque Internationale à Luxembourg (BIL) 2016–; Pnr (attorney-at-law) Elvinger Hoss Prussen 2016–; mem. moral sciences and politics section, Institut Grand-Ducal; Hon. LLD (Sacred Heart Univ., USA) 2006. *Address:* Banque Internationale à Luxembourg SA, 69 Route d'Esch, 2953, Luxembourg (office). *Telephone:* 45-90-50-00 (office). *E-mail:* contact@bil.com (office). *Website:* www.bil.com (office).

FRIEDEN, Thomas R., BA, MD, MPH; American physician and public health official; *Director, Centers for Disease Control and Prevention;* ed Oberlin Coll., Columbia Univ., Yale Univ.; began career as Epidemic Intelligence Service Officer, New York City Health Dept 1990–92; Head of New York City tuberculosis control programme 1992–96; worked on tuberculosis control programme for WHO, India 1996–2002; Commr, New York City Health Dept 2002–09; Dir Centers for Disease Control and Prevention and Admin., Agency for Toxic Substances and Disease Registry 2009–; fmr advisor on health to New York City Mayor Michael Bloomberg; numerous awards and honours; Dr hc (Tufts Univ.) 2011; Hon. DrSc (Oglethorpe Univ.) 2015. *Publications:* more than 200 scientific articles. *Address:* Office of the Director, Centers for Disease Control and Prevention, 1600 Clifton Road, Atlanta, GA 30333, USA (office). *Telephone:* (404) 639-7000 (office). *E-mail:* Tomfrieden@cdc.gov (office). *Website:* www.cdc.gov (office).

FRIEDKIN, William; American film director, producer and screenwriter; b. 29 Aug. 1939, Chicago, Ill.; s. of Louis Friedkin and Rae Green; m. 1st Jeanne Moreau (divorced); m. 2nd Lesley-Anne Down (divorced); one s.; m. 3rd Kelly Lange (divorced); m. 4th Sherry Lansing; Lifetime Achievement Award, Saturn Awards 2013, Special Lion, Venice Film Festival 2013. *Films directed include:* Good Times 1967, The Night They Raided Minsky's 1968, The Birthday Party 1968, The Boys in the Band 1970, The French Connection 1971 (Acad. Award for Best Picture, 1971), The Exorcist 1973, Sorcerer 1977, The Brinks Job 1979, Cruising 1980, Deal of the Century 1983, To Live and Die in LA 1985, C.A.T. Squad 1986, The Guardian 1990, Rampage 1992, Blue Chip 1993, Jade 1995, Twelve Angry Men 1997, Rules of Engagement 2000, Night Train 2000, The Hunted 2003, Bug 2006, Killer Joe (Golden Mouse, Venice Film Festival 2011, Grand Prix, Belgian Film Critics Asscn 2013, Saturn Award for Best Dir 2013) 2011; several TV films. *Publication:* The Friedkin Connection (memoir) 2013.

FRIEDMAN, David Melech, JD; American lawyer; *Ambassador to Israel;* s. of Morris S. Friedman and Addi Friedman; m. Tammy Deborah Sand 1981; ed Columbia Univ., New York Univ. School of Law; mem. New York bar 1982–; Founding Pnr, Kasowitz, Benson, Torres & Friedman (law firm) 1994–, Head, Creditors' Rights and Bankruptcy Practice Group; Pres. American Friends of Bet El Inst.; columnist for Israeli newspapers Arutz Sheva and The Jerusalem Post; Amb. to Israel 2017–. *Address:* US Embassy, 71 Hayarkon St, Tel-Aviv 6343229, Israel (office). *Telephone:* 3-5197475 (office). *E-mail:* nivtelaviv@state.gov (office). *Website:* il.usembassy.gov (office).

FRIEDMAN, Jack; American business executive; ed Muscatine Community Coll.; Dir, FCStone from 1996, fmr Vice-Chair., Dir of International Assets following merger with International Assets Holding Corpn 2009, Chair. INTL FCStone Inc. 2009–12; Partner, Innovative Ag Services, Monticello, Ia (or with its predecessor) for 21 years, then CEO, retd 2012; Man. Swiss Valley Ag Center, Monticello 1995–; mem. Bd of Dirs Western Dubuque Biodiesel LLC, Iowa Inst. of Cooperatives, Dyerville Plannig and Zoning Bd.

FRIEDMAN, Jeffrey M., MD, PhD; American molecular geneticist and academic; *Head, Laboratory of Molecular Genetics, The Rockefeller University;* b. 20 July 1954, Orlando, Fla; m.; two d.; ed Hewlett High School, Rensselaer Polytechnic Inst., Albany Medical Coll. of Union Univ., Cornell Univ., The Rockefeller Univ.; completed two residencies at Albany Medical Center Hosp.; Assoc. Physician and Postgraduate Fellow, The Rockefeller Univ. 1980, Asst Prof. 1986–91, Assoc. Prof. 1991–95, Head of Lab. of Molecular Genetics 1991–, Prof. 1995–, Marilyn M. Simpson Prof. 1999–, also Dir Starr Center for Human Genetics, co-Dir Kavli Neural Systems Institute 2015–16; Asst Investigator, Howard Hughes Medical Inst. 1986–92, Assoc. Investigator 1992–96, Investigator 1996–; mem. Inst. of Medicine, NAS 2001, American Acad. of Arts and Sciences 2013, Nat. Acad. of Medicine; Foreign mem. Royal Swedish Acad. of Sciences 2005; Assoc. mem. European Molecular Biology Org.; Fellow American Asscn for the Advancement of Science; Bristol-Myers Squibb Award 2001, Gairdner Foundation Int. Award 2004, Passano Foundation Award 2004, Danone Int. Prize for Nutrition 2007, Jessie Stevenson Kovalenko Medal 2007, Keio Medical Science Prize, Shaw Prize (co-recipient) 2009, Albert Lasker Basic Medical Research Award 2010, named Thomson Reuters Citation Laureate in Medicine 2010, Robert J. and Claire Passano Foundation Award 2010, Fondation IPSEN 11th Endocrine Regulation Prize 2012, UCL Prize Lecture in Clinical Science 2012, Sanofi-Institut Pasteur Award 2012, Frontiers of Knowledge Award in Biomedicine, BBVA Foundation (Spain) (co-recipient) 2013, King Faisal Int. Prize in Medicine (co-recipient) 2013, Harrington Prize for Innovation in Medicine 2016. *Achievements include:* with Douglas Coleman, discovered leptin, a hormone that regulates appetite and metabolism. *Address:* The Rockefeller University, Laboratory of Molecular Genetics, 1230 York Avenue, New York, NY 10065, USA (office). *Telephone:* (212) 327-8000 (office). *Fax:* (212) 327-7974 (office). *E-mail:* jeffrey.friedman@rockefeller.edu (office). *Website:* www.rockefeller.edu/research/faculty/labheads/JeffreyFriedman (office).

FRIEDMAN, Jerome Isaac, BA, PhD; American physicist and academic; *Institute Professor Emeritus, Massachusetts Institute of Technology;* b. 28 March 1930, Chicago, Ill.; s. of Selig Friedman and Lillian Warsaw; m. 1st 1956; two s. two d.; m. 2nd Tania Baranovsky 1972; ed Univ. of Chicago; Research Assoc., Univ. of Chicago 1956–57, Stanford Univ. 1957–60; Asst Prof. then Assoc. Prof., MIT 1960–67, Prof. of Physics 1967, Dir Lab. of Nuclear Science 1980–83, Head, Dept of Physics 1983–88, William A. Coolidge Prof. 1988–90, Inst. Prof. 1990, now Inst. Prof. Emer.; mem. NAS; Fellow, American Acad. of Arts and Sciences, American Physical Soc.; Hon. Prof., Faculty of Physics, Univ. of Belgrade; Hon. DSc (Trinity Coll.); Dr hc (Univ. of Belgrade) 2008; W. K. H. Panofsky Prize (American Physical

Soc.) (jt recipient) 1989, Nobel Prize in Physics (jt recipient) 1990. *Publications include:* numerous articles in professional journals. *Leisure interests:* painting, Asian ceramics, African art. *Address:* Department of Physics, Room 4-304, Massachusetts Institute of Technology, 77 Massachusetts Avenue, Cambridge, MA 02139-4307 (office); 75 Greenough Street, Brookline, MA 02146, USA (home). *Telephone:* (617) 253-4800 (office). *Fax:* (617) 253-8554 (office). *E-mail:* jif@mit.edu (office). *Website:* web.mit.edu/physics (office).

FRIEDMAN, Stephen, BA, LLB; American lawyer, financial services industry executive and fmr government official; *Chairman, Stone Point Capital LLC;* b. 21 Dec. 1937; m. Barbara Benioff Friedman; one s. two d.; ed Cornell Univ., Columbia Univ. Law School; fmr law clerk to Fed. Dist Court judge; attorney, New York City 1963–66; joined Goldman Sachs & Co. 1966, Pnr 1973–92, Vice-Chair. and Co-COO 1987–90, Co-Chair. 1990–92, Chair. and Sr Pnr 1992–94, Dir 2002, 2005–13; Sr Prin., Marsh & McLennan Capital Inc. 1998–2002; Sr Advisor, Stone Point Capital LLC 1998–2002, Chair. 2004–; Asst to Pres. for Econ. Policy and Dir Nat. Econ. Council, The White House, Washington, DC 2002–04; mem. Pres.'s Foreign Intelligence Advisory Bd 1993–95, Chair. 2006–09; Chair. Fed. Reserve Bank of New York 2008–09; mem. Bd of Dirs Trident Fund, Cross Ocean Partners Man. LLC, Duff & Phelps Corpn, NXT Capital Inc.; fmr mem. Bd of Dirs Fannie Mae, Wal-Mart Stores; Trustee, Council on Foreign Relations, Aspen Inst. 2006–, Memorial Sloan-Kettering Cancer Center; Chair. Emer. Bd of Trustees, Columbia Univ., Exec. Cttee, The Brookings Inst.; Eastern Collegiate Wrestling Champion 1959, AAU Nat. Wrestling Champion 1961, Maccabiah Games Gold Medal 1961, NCAA Silver Anniversary Medal for outstanding athletic and career achievements 1984. *Address:* Stone Point Capital LLC, 919 Third Avenue, 30th Floor, New York, NY 10022, USA (office). *Telephone:* (203) 862-2900 (office). *Fax:* (203) 625-8357 (office). *Website:* www.stonepoint.com (office).

FRIEDMAN, Thomas Lauren, BA, MPhil; American journalist and writer; *Foreign Affairs Columnist, New York Times;* b. 20 July 1953, St Louis Park, Minneapolis, Minn.; m. Ann Bucksbaum; two d.; ed St Louis Park High School, Brandeis Univ., St Antony's Coll. Oxford, UK; joined London bureau of United Press Int., dispatched a year later to Beirut –1981; joined The New York Times 1981, Beirut Bureau Chief 1982–84, Israel Bureau Chief 1984–88, Washington Chief Diplomatic Corresp., Chief White House Corresp., Chief Econs Corresp., Foreign Affairs Columnist 1995–; Visiting Lecturer, Harvard Univ. 2000–05; mem. Bd of Trustees, Brandeis Univ.; mem. Pulitzer Prize Board 2004–; Hon. OBE 2004; hon. degrees from several US univs; Pulitzer Prize for Int. Reporting 1983, 1988, for Distinguished Commentary 2002, Lifetime Achievement Award, Overseas Press Club 2004, Lifetime Achievement Award, Nat. Press Club 2009. *Television includes:* documentaries include: Searching for the Roots of 9/11, 2003, Straddling the Fence 2003, The Other Side of Outsourcing 2004, Does Europe Hate Us? 2005, Addicted to Oil 2006, Green: The New, Red, White and Blue 2007. *Publications include:* From Beirut to Jerusalem (Nat. Book Award for Non-Fiction, Overseas Press Club Award) 1989 (revised edn 1990), The Lexus and the Olive Tree: Understanding Globalization (Overseas Press Club Award for Best Non-Fiction Book on Foreign Policy 2000) 1999 (revised edn 2000), Longitudes and Latitudes: Exploring the World After September 11 2002 (reprinted as Longitudes and Attitudes: The World in the Age of Terrorism 2003), The World is Flat: A Brief History of the Twenty-first Century (Financial Times/Goldman Sachs Business Book Award) 2005 (expanded edn 2006, revised edn 2007), Hot, Flat and Crowded: Why We Need a Green Revolution – And How It Can Renew America 2008, That Used To Be Us (with Michael Mandelbaum) 2011. *Address:* The New York Times, 1627 Eye Street, NW, Suite 700, Washington, DC 20006, USA (office). *Telephone:* (202) 862-0300 (office). *Fax:* (202) 862-0340 (office). *Website:* www.nytimes.com (office); www.thomaslfriedman.com.

FRIEDMANN, Theodore, AB, MD, MA; American paediatrician and academic; *Professor of Pediatrics, University of California, San Diego;* b. 16 June 1935, Austria; m. Ingrid Friedmann; two c.; ed Univ. of Pennsylvania, Univ. of Oxford, UK; Children's Hosp. Medical Center, Boston, Mass 1960–62; Capt., USAF, 10th Tac., Hosp., Alconbury, UK 1962–63; Research Fellow in Colloid Science, Univ. of Cambridge, UK 1963–64; Children's Hosp. Medical Center, Boston and Teaching and Research Fellow, Harvard Univ. 1964–65; Staff Scientist, NIH, Bethesda, Md 1965–68; Asst Prof. of Pediatrics, Univ. of California, San Diego 1969–73, Assoc. Prof. of Pediatrics 1973–81, Prof. of Pediatrics 1981–; Pres. American Soc. of Gene Therapy 2006; Chair. Gene Doping Expert Group, World Anti-Doping Agency; mem. AAAS; Cross of Honour for Science and the Arts (Austria) 1996; Faculty Research Lecturer Award, Univ. of California, San Diego 1984–85, Chancellor's Assocs Award for Excellence in Research, Univ. of California 1992, H.C. Jacobæus Prize, Nordic Research Cttee and Nordic Insulin Foundation, Lund, Sweden 1995, Salvador Zubiran Medal (Mexico) 1996, Newton-Abraham Visiting Professorship, Univ. of Oxford 1996, NIH Award of Merit 2003, Distinguished Grad. Award, Univ. of Pennsylvania 2006, Japan Prize (co-recipient) 2015. *Publications:* numerous papers in professional journals. *Address:* Department of Pediatrics, University of California, San Diego, 9500 Gilman Drive, La Jolla, CA 92093-0634, USA (office). *Telephone:* (858) 534-4268 (office); (858) 822-1013 (office). *E-mail:* tfriedmann@ucsd.edu (office). *Website:* biomedsci.ucsd.ed (office); www.pediatrics.ucsd.edu/research/Friedmann_Lab (office).

FRIEDRICH, Hans-Peter, PhD; German lawyer and politician; *Federal Minister of Food and Agriculture;* b. 10 March 1957, Naila, Bavaria; m.; three c.; ed Univ. of Augsburg; Higher Exec. Officer, Industrial Policy Directorate-Gen., Fed. Ministry of Econs 1988–90; seconded to Econs and Science Dept, Embassy in Washington, DC 1990–91; worked for CDU/CSU Parl. Group 1991–93, Pvt. Sec. to Chair. of CSU Parl. Group 1993–98; mem. Bundestag (Parl.) 1998–, Chair. Bundestag electoral district ass., Hof/Wunsiedel 1998–, Deputy Chair., CDU/CSU Parl. Group in Bundestag 2005–09; Deputy Chair., CSU in Upper Franconia 1999–; Fed. Minister of the Interior 2011–13, Acting Fed. Minister of Food, Agric. and Consumer Protection Sept.–Dec. 2013, Fed. Minister of Food and Agric. 2013–; mem. Christlich-Soziale Union. *Address:* Federal Ministry of Food and Agriculture, Wilhelmstrasse 54, 11055 Berlin, Germany (office). *Telephone:* (30) 185290 (office). *Fax:* (30) 185294262 (office). *E-mail:* poststelle@bmelv.bund.de (office). *Website:* www.bmelv.de (office).

FRIEND, Cynthia M., BS, PhD; American chemist and academic; *Theodore William Richards Professor of Chemistry and Professor of Materials Science, Harvard University;* ed Univ. of California, Davis, Univ. of California, Berkeley, Stanford Univ.; Post-Doctoral Research Fellow, Stanford Univ. 1981–82; Asst Prof., Harvard Univ. 1982–86, Assoc. Prof. 1986–88, Morris Kahn Assoc. Prof. 1988–89, Prof. of Chem. 1989–98, Theodore William Richards Prof. of Chem. 1998–, Prof. of Materials Science 2002–, Assoc. Dir, Harvard Materials Research Science and Eng Center 2001–, Assoc. Dean, Faculty of Arts and Sciences 2002–05, Chair., Dept of Chem. and Chemical Biology 2004–; Visiting Prof. in Chemical Eng, Stanford Univ. 2001; Trustee, Radcliffe Coll. 1990–93; mem. numerous professional cttees, panels and bds including NATO Advisory Panel on Organic Chemistry 1987, NSF Chem. Advisory Panel 1989–92, Advanced Light Source Users' Exec. Cttee 1990–93, Bd on Chemical Science and Tech., Nat. Research Council 1992, 56th Annual Conf. on Physical Electronics Cttee 1995–96, Chemical and Eng (C&EN) Advisory Bd 2001–02, Claire Booth Luce Fellowship Selection Bd 2000–, Council of Gordon Research Confs 2002–05, US Dept of Energy Cttee of Visitors, Office of Basic Energy Sciences 2005; Gen. and Program Chair., Biennial Inorganic Chem. Symposium, Molecular Design of Materials 1987, Program Chair., New England Catalysis Soc. 1987–89, Chair., Richards Medal Award Cttee 1994–96; Chair., Canvassing Cttee, ACS Award for Creative Research in Catalysis 1999–2000; US rep., Int. Union of Pure and Applied Chem. 2000–03; Co-Chair., Opportunities in Nanocatalysis Workshop 2005; chair. of numerous academic bds including Harvard Faculty of Arts and Sciences Standing Cttee on Women 1991–94, Elected Docket Cttee, Harvard Univ. 1998–2000; consultant to Lord Corpn, Cary, NC 1987–90, Advanced Tech. Materials, Danbury, Conn. 1988–92, Texaco Lubricants Div. 1995–98, Ryoka Systems, Tokyo, Japan 1995–2003, Kaelow and Assocs LLP 1998–99, Pennie and Edmonds LLP 2002–03, Paul Hastings LLP 2004, Mitsubishi Chemical Co. 2005–07; mem. ACS, American Vacuum Soc., AAAS, American Physical Soc., Iota Sigma Pi; mem. of several editorial bds including Journal of Cluster Science 1990–94, Langmuir 1991–2001, The Chemical Intelligencer 1997–, Surface Science 2000–, Chemical Eng News 1999–2001, e-Journal of Surface Science and Nano tech. (EJSSNT) 2005–; IBM Faculty Devt Award 1983–85, Presidential Young Investigator Award 1985–90, Union Carbide Innovation Recognition Program 1988-89, Distinguished Young Alumni Award, Univ. of Calif.-Davis 1990, Garvan Medal of ACS 1991, Iota Sigma Pi Agnes Fay Morgan Research Award 1991, Smithsonian Inst. Chosen Scientist for Perm. Exhibit "Science and American Life" 1992–. *Publications:* numerous articles in professional journals. *Address:* Harvard University, Department of Chemistry and Chemical Biology, 12 Oxford Street, Office M018, Cambridge, MA 02138, USA (office). *Telephone:* (617) 495-4198 (office). *Fax:* (617) 496-8410 (office). *E-mail:* cfriend@seas.harvard.edu (office). *Website:* (office); www.seas.harvard.edu/friend.

FRIEND, Lionel; British conductor; *Music Director, British Youth Opera;* b. 13 March 1945, London; s. of Norman A. C. Friend and Moya L. Dicks; m. Jane Hyland 1969; one s. two d.; ed Royal Grammar School, High Wycombe, Royal Coll. of Music, London Opera Centre; with Welsh Nat. Opera 1969–72, Glyndebourne Festival/Touring Opera 1969–72; Second Kapell-meister, Staatstheater Kassel, West Germany 1972–75; Conductor, ENO 1976–89; Musical Dir New Sussex Opera 1989–96; Conductor-in-Residence, Birmingham Conservatoire 2003–10; Music Dir British Youth Opera 2015–; Guest Conductor, BBC Symphony, Philharmonia, Royal Philharmonic, Nash Ensemble, Scottish Chamber, Royal Ballet etc. and in Australia, Belgium, Brazil, Denmark, France, Germany, Hungary, The Netherlands, New Zealand, Norway, Spain, Sweden, USA; Hon. Fellow, Birmingham Conservatoire. *Leisure interests:* reading, theatre. *Address:* c/o Robert Gilder & Co., N102 Westminster Business Square, 1-45 Durham Street, London, SE11 5JH, England (office); 136 Rosendale Road, London, SE21 8LG, England (home). *Telephone:* (20) 7580-7758 (office); (20) 8761-7845 (home). *Fax:* (20) 7580-7739 (office). *E-mail:* rgilder@robert-gilder.com (office); lionelfriend@hotmail.com. *Website:* www.robert-gilder.com (office); lionelfriend.com; www.byo.org.uk (office).

FRIEND, Sir Richard Henry, Kt, PhD, FRS, FREng; British physicist and academic; *Cavendish Professor of Physics, University of Cambridge;* b. 18 Jan. 1953; ed Trinity Coll., St John's Coll., Cavendish Lab., Univ. of Cambridge; Research Assoc., Laboratoire de Physique des Solides, Université Paris-Sud 1977–78; Research Fellow, St John's Coll., Cambridge 1977–80, Demonstrator in Physics 1980–85, Dir of Studies in Physics 1984–86, Lecturer in Physics 1985–93, Tutor in Physics 1987–91, Reader in Experimental Physics 1993–95, Cavendish Prof. of Physics 1995–; Tan Chin Tuan Centennial Prof., Nat. Univ. of Singapore; Visiting Prof., Univ. of California, Santa Barbara 1986–87; Assoc. Chair, Centre de Recherche sur les Très Basses Temperatures, CNRS 1987; Chief Scientist, Cambridge Display Technology Ltd 1996–; Consultant, Epson Cambridge Lab. 1998–; Chief Scientist and Dir Plastic Logic Ltd 2000–; Mary Shepard B. Upson Visiting Prof., Cornell Univ. 2003; mem. Tech. Advisory Council, British Petroleum PLC 1998–2003; Nuffield Foundation Science Research Fellowship 1992–93; Hon. FRSC 2004; Dr hc (Linkoping, Sweden) 2000, (Mons-Hainault, Belgium) 2002; Charles Vernon Boys Prize, Inst. of Physics 1988, RSC Interdisciplinary Award 1991, Hewlett-Packard Prize, European Physical Soc. 1996, Rumford Medal, Royal Soc. of London 1998, Italgas Prize 2001, Silver Medal, Royal Acad. of Eng 2002, McRobert Prize, Royal Acad. of Eng 2002, IEE Faraday Medal 2003, Gold Medal, European Materials Research Soc. 2003, EC Descartes Prize 2003, King Faisal Int. Prize for Science (co-recipient) 2009, Millennium Tech. Prize for the devt of plastic electronics 2010, Harvey Prize, Technion, Israel 2011. *Publications:* more than 600 papers in scientific journals. *Address:* Room K32, Kapitza Building, Cavendish Laboratory, University of Cambridge, Madingley Road, Cambridge, CB3 0HE, England (office). *Telephone:* (1223) 337218 (office). *Fax:* (1223) 764515 (office). *E-mail:* rhf10@cam.ac.uk (office). *Website:* www.phy.cam.ac.uk/people/friendr.php (office); www.oe.phy.cam.ac.uk/people/oestaff/rhf10.htm (office).

FRIES, Charles; French diplomatist; *Ambassador to Turkey;* b. 30 Dec. 1962; ed École nat. d'admin, Institut d'études politiques, Univ. of Paris I (Panthéon-Sorbonne), Ecole normale de musique (piano); Directorate for Econ. and Financial Affairs, Ministry of Foreign Affairs (MFA) 1989–93, Adviser for European Affairs to Minister of Foreign Affairs, Alain Juppé 1993–95, First Sec., Embassy in London (Embassy Spokesperson) 1995–98, Deputy Dir of Internal Community Affairs, MFA 1998–2000, Deputy Dir for External Relations of the Community 2000–02, Adviser for European Affairs to Pres. Jacques Chirac 2002–06, Amb. to Czech

Repub. 2006–09, Sec.-Gen. for European Affairs, MFA 2011–12, Diplomatic Adviser to Prime Minister François Fillon 2009–12, Amb. to Morocco 2012–15, to Turkey 2015–. *Address:* Embassy of France, Paris Caddesi 70, 06540 Kavaklıdere, Ankara, Turkey (office). *Telephone:* (312) 4554545 (office). *Fax:* (312) 4554527 (office). *E-mail:* ambaank@yahoo.fr (office). *Website:* www.ambafrance-tr.org (office).

FRIESEN, Dawna; Canadian broadcast journalist; *Anchor and Executive Editor, Global National with Dawna Friesen;* b. 8 Oct. 1964, Winnipeg; m. Tom Kennedy; one s.; ed Red River Coll.; fmr newspaper journalist, Portage Daily Graphic and news reporter at several radio and TV stations in western Canada, including Brandon, Saskatoon and Winnipeg; fmr Nat. News Corresp. and Anchor, CTV, Ottawa 1997–99 and CBC, Vancouver; London-based Foreign Corresp., NBC News, Today Show and MSNBC 1999–2010; Anchor and Exec. Ed. Global National with Dawna Friesen, Global Television 2010–; Univ. of Toronto Southam Fellowship for Journalists 1993, Emmy Award (for team coverage of US presidential campaign of Barack Obama) 2009, Gemini Award (now Canadian Screen Award) for best news anchor 2011, Best National Newscast, Canadian Screen Awards 2015. *Address:* Global National, 7850 Enterprise Street, Burnaby, BC V5A 1V7, Canada (office). *E-mail:* viewers@globalnational.com (office). *Website:* www.globalnational.com (office).

FRIGGIERI, Oliver, BA, MA, PhD; Maltese academic, writer, poet and literary critic; *Professor of Maltese Literature, University of Malta;* b. 27 March 1947, Furjana; s. of Charles Friggieri and Mary Galea; m. Eileen Cassar; one d.; ed Univ. of Malta, Catholic Univ. of Milan; Prof. of Maltese Literature, Univ. of Malta 1987–, Head of Dept of Maltese 1987–2004; Founder-mem. Academia Internationale Mihai Eminescu, Craiova 1995; mem. Asscn Int. des Critiques Littéraires, Paris; participant and guest speaker at 70 int. congresses throughout Europe; guest poet at numerous poetry recitals in major European cities; Co-founder Saghtar (nat. student magazine) 1971; Literary Ed. In-Nazzjon 1971–82; Nat. Order of Merit 1999; First Prize for Literary Criticism XIV Concorso Silarus 1982, Premio Internazionale Mediterraneo, Palermo 1988, Malta Govt Literary Award 1988, 1996, 1997, 1999, Premio Sampieri per la Poesia 1995, Premio Internazionale Trieste Poesia 2002, Gold Medal Award Malta Soc. of Arts, Manufactures and Commerce 2003, Premio Faber (Italy) 2004. *Radio includes:* weekly cultural programme presenter (Radio Malta). *Television includes:* regular appearances on Maltese and other networks. *Publications include:* novels: Il-Gidba 1977, L-Istramb 1980, Fil-Parlament ma Jikbrux Fjuri 1986, Gizimin li Qatt ma Jiftah 1998, It-Tfal Jigu bil-Vapuri 2000, The Lie 2007; short stories: Stejjer ghal Qabel Jidlam Vol. I 1979, Vol. II 1983 (combined, enhanced edn) 1986, Fil-Gżira Taparsi jikbru l-Fjuri 1991, Koranta and Other Short Stories from Malta 1994, À Malte, histoires du crépuscule 2004; poetry: Mal-Fanal Hemm Harstek Tixghel 1988, Rewwixta (play-poem) 1990, Poeziji 1998, Il-Kliem li Tghidlek Qalbek 2001, Il-Poeziji Migbura 2002, A Poet's Creed 2006; literary criticism: Kittieba ta' Zmienna 1970, Ir-Ruh fil-Kelma 1973, Il-Kultura Taljana f'Dun Karm 1976, Fl-Gharbiel 1976, Storja tal-Letteratura Maltija 1979, Saggi Kritici 1979, Ellul Mercer f'Leli ta' Haz-Zghir Mir-Realta' ghall-Kuxjenza 1983, Gwann Mamo Il'Kittieb tar-Riforma Socjali 1984, Dizzjunarju ta' Termini Letterarji 1986, L'Idea tal'Letteratura 1986, Mekkanizmi Metaforici f'Dun Karm 1988, Dun Karm 'Il-Jien u Lil hinn Minnu' 1988, Il-Kuxjenza Nazzjonali Maltija 1995, L-Istudji Kritici Migbura 1995, L'Istorja tal-Poezija Maltija 2001; numerous works translated into various languages, poems in anthologies and articles in academic journals and newspapers. *Leisure interest:* gardening. *Address:* Faculty of Arts, University of Malta, Room 249, Old Humanities Building, Msida, MSD 2080, Malta (office). *Telephone:* 23402944 (office). *Website:* www.um.edu.mt/arts/malti (office).

FRIIS, Lotte; Danish fmr swimmer; b. 9 Feb. 1988, Blovstrød; ed Marie Kruses gymnasium, Farum; European Championships (short course), Vienna 2004: silver medal, 800m freestyle, Debrecen 2007: gold medal, 800m freestyle, Rijeka 2008: bronze medal, 800m freestyle, Istanbul 2009: gold medal, 800m freestyle, silver medal, 400m freestyle, Szczecin 2011: gold medal, 800m freestyle, silver medal, 400m freestyle; European Championships (long course), Eindhoven 2008: bronze medal, 1,500m freestyle, Budapest 2010: gold medal, 800m freestyle, 1,500m freestyle, bronze medal, 400m freestyle; Olympic Games, Beijing 2008: bronze medal, 800m freestyle; World Championships (long course), Rome 2009: gold medal, 800m freestyle, silver medal, 1,500m freestyle, Shanghai 2011: gold medal, 1,500m freestyle, silver medal, 800m freestyle, Barcelona 2013: silver medal, 800m freestyle, 1,500m freestyle; swims for Herlev club; coach: Paulus Wildeboer. *Address:* c/o f. reklame AS, Klosterstræde 23, 1157 Copenhagen K, Denmark. *Telephone:* 33-12-72-44. *E-mail:* info@f-reklame.dk. *Website:* www.lottefriis.net.

FRISELL, Bill; American jazz musician (guitar) and composer; b. 18 March 1951, Baltimore, Md; one d.; ed Univ. of Northern Colorado, Berklee Coll. of Music; played with numerous artists, including Eberhard Weber, Mike Gibbs, Jan Garbarek, Charlie Haden, Carla Bley, John Scofield; David Sylvian, Bono, Marianne Faithfull, Robin Holcomb, Gavin Bryars, Brian Eno, Daniel Lanois, Paul Simon, Van Dyke Parks, Vic Chesnutt, Elvis Costello, Suzanne Vega, Loudon Wainwright III, Ron Carter, Dave Douglas, Rinde Eckart, Wayne Horvitz, Ginger Baker, Rickie Lee Jones, Laurie Anderson, Vernon Reid, Ron Sexsmith, Caetano Veloso, Vinicius Cantuaria, Mark Ribot, Ron Carter, T-Bone Burnett, The Campbell Brothers, Chip Taylor & Carrie Rodriquez, Buddy Miller and Renée Fleming; fmr mem., Power Tools, John Zorn's Naked City, The Paul Bley Quintet, Paul Motian Trio; Music Dir, Century of Song Ruhr Triennale Arts Festival 2003–05; Harris Stanton Guitar Award, Downbeat Critics' Poll Guitarist of the Year 1998, Deutsche Schallplatten Preis 1998, 2005, Critics' Award for Best Guitarist, Industry Award for Best Guitarist 1998, Jazz Journalists' Asscn Award for Guitarist of the Year 2013, 2014. *Compositions include:* Tales from the Far Side (music to TV series). *Recordings include:* albums: In Line 1983, Theoretically (with Tim Berne) 1984, Rambler 1985, News For Lulu (with John Zorn, George Lewis) 1987, Strange Meeting (with Power Tools) 1987, Lookout For Hope 1988, Before We Were Born 1989, Is This You? 1990, Where In The World? 1991, More News For Lulu (with John Zorn, George Lewis) 1992, Grace Under Pressure (with John Scofield) 1992, Have A Little Faith 1993, Music From The Films of Buster Keaton 1995, Going Home Again (with Ginger Baker Trio) 1995, Deep Dead Blue: Live At Meltdown (with Elvis Costello) 1995, Quartet 1996, Nashville 1997, Gone, Just Like a Train 1998, Songs We Know 1998, The Sweetest Punch (with Elvis Costello) 1999, Good Dog, Happy Man 1999, Ghost Town 2000, Blues Dream 2001, Bill Frisell With Dave Holland and Elvin Jones 2001, Selected Recordings 2002, The Willies 2002, The Intercontinentals 2003, Unspeakable 2004, Petra Haden's Bill 2004, Richter 858 2005, East/West 2005, Bill Frisell, Ron Carter, Paul Motian 2005, Floratone 2007, History, Mystery 2007, All Hat 2008, Hemispheres (with Jim Hall) 2008, Disfarmer 2009, Beautiful Dreamers 2010, Lágrimas Mexicanas (with Vinicius Cantuária) 2011, Sign of Life: Music for 858 Quartet 2011, All We Are Saying... 2011, The Kentucky Derby Is Decadent and Depraved 2012, Window & Door 2012, Enfants Terribles: Live at the Blue Note 2012, Quiver 2012, Silent Comedy 2013, John Zorn: The Mysteries 2013, Big Sur 2013, Guitar in the Space Age! 2014, When You Wish Upon a Star 2016. *Publication:* Bill Frisell: An Anthology. *Address:* c/o Phyllis Oyama, Songline/Tone Field Productions, 1649 Hopkins Street, Berkeley, CA 94707, USA (office). *Telephone:* (510) 528-1191 (office). *Fax:* (510) 528-1193 (office). *E-mail:* phyllis.oyama@songtone.com (office). *Website:* www.songtone.com (office); www.billfrisell.com.

FRIST, William (Bill) Harrison, MD; American transplant surgeon, business executive and fmr politician; b. 22 Feb. 1952, Nashville, Tenn.; m. Karyn McLaughlin; three s.; ed Montgomery Bell Acad., Nashville, Princeton Univ., Harvard Medical School; worked in Powell lab., Mass Gen. Hosp. 1977–78, Resident in Surgery 1978–83, Chief Resident and Fellow in Cardiothoracic Surgery 1984–85; worked at Southampton Gen. Hosp., Southampton, England 1983; Sr Fellow and Chief Resident in Cardiac Transplant Service and Cardiothoracic Surgery, Stanford Univ. School of Medicine 1985–86; mem. Faculty, Vanderbilt Univ. Medical Center 1986–89, est. centre for new therapies of heart and lung transplantation, also served as Staff Surgeon, Nashville Veterans Admin Hospital; f. Vanderbilt Transplant Center 1989; Senator from Tennessee 1995–2007 (retd), Senate Majority Leader 2002–07, fmr Chair. Nat. Representative Senatorial Cttee; Frederick H. Schultz Class of 1951 Prof. of Int. Econ. Policy, Princeton Univ. 2007–08 Chair. Volunteer Political Action Cttee (VOLPAC) 2007–; Republican. *Publications:* Tennessee Senators, 1911–2001: Portraits of Leadership in a Century of Change 1999, When Every Moment Counts: What You Need To Know About Bioterrorism From the Senate's Only Doctor 2002, Good People Beget Good People: A Genealogy of the Frist Family (co-author) 2003. *Address:* c/o Woodrow Wilson School of Public and International Affairs, Princeton University, Robertson Hall, Princeton, NJ 08544-1013, USA (office).

FRITCH, Édouard; French Polynesian engineer and politician; *President;* b. 4 Jan. 1952, Papeete, Tahiti; s. of Edgar Fritch and Tetuahirau Richmond, Winfred Édouard Tereori Fritch; ed Collège La Mennais, École des ingénieurs de la ville de Paris, France; carried out municipal works in city of Pirae before directing territorial office of social housing 1982 and territorial agency of reconstruction in Polynesia –1984; mem. Ass. of French Polynesia 1986–, Speaker 2007–08, Feb.–April 2009; served as Minister in French Polynesian Govt several times 1984–2011, Vice-Pres. of the Govt 1995–2005, 2009–11; Mayor of Pirae 2000–08, 2014–, Municipal Councillor 2000–12; Co-Pres. Tahoera'a Huiraatira (pro-French political party); unsuccessful cand. in French Polynesian presidential election 2009; mem. Nat. Ass. of France in 1st Constituency of French Polynesia 2012–14 (sat in Union for Democrats and Independents group); Pres. of French Polynesia 2014–. *Address:* Office of the President, Avenue Bruat, BP 2551-98713, Papeete, French Polynesia (office). *Telephone:* 40-47-20-00 (office). *Fax:* 40-41-02-71 (office). *E-mail:* courrier@presidence.pf (office). *Website:* www.presidence.pf (office).

FRITZ, Johann P.; Austrian journalist and broadcasting executive; *Director Emeritus, International Press Institute;* b. 15 April 1940, Ober-Eggendorf; s. of Johann Fritz and Amalia Piringer; m. Brigitte Weick 1964; one d.; ed Univ. of Vienna, Case Western Reserve Univ., Cleveland, Ohio and Hochschule für Welthandel, Vienna; Sec.-Gen. Österreichische Jungarbeiterbewegung 1964–67, Exec. Vice-Pres. 1967–70; Ed. Der Jungarbeiter 1964–70, MC Report 1970–75; Deputy Sec.-Gen. Österreichischer Wirtschaftsbund 1970–75; Man. Dir Die Presse 1975–91; Man. Dir Kabel TV Wien 1975–83; Founder and Co-Man. Radio Adria 1977–84, Consultant 1984–90; Co-founder, Sec.-Gen. and Report Ed. Man.-Club 1970–75; Founder and Chair. Cable TV Asscn, Austrian Chamber of Commerce 1980–90; mem. Supervisory Bd Telekabel Wien GmbH 1983–98; mem. Bd Austrian Press Agency 1982–91; Dir Int. Press Inst. (IPI) 1992–2007, currently Dir Emer. Austrian Chapter of IPI, Vienna; Publr Jazz Information (monthly) 1967–70, Cable TV: Project Study for Austria 1975, iPi Report 1992–97; Chair. of the Jury, Int. Book Award on Human Rights 2009–15; life-time title 'Senator' conferred by Int. Asscn for Newspaper and Media Tech. 1980; life-time title Prof. conferred by Austrian Fed. Ministry of Science and Research 2000; Kommerzialrat Award 1991, Gold Medal for Meritorious Service to Province of Vienna 2003, Special Award, Austrian Press Club Concordia 2003. *Television:* scripts for jazz productions 1968–73. *Publication:* Little Jazzbook of Vienna. *Leisure interests:* skiing, ice-skating, jazz, art deco, jugendstil. *Address:* International Press Institute (IPI), Austrian Chapter, Hasenauerstrasse 37/E, 1180 Vienna, Austria.

FROGIER, Pierre Edouard Nahéa; New Caledonian politician; b. 16 Nov. 1950, Nouméa; m. Annick Morault; three c.; ed Lycée Lapérouse, Nouméa and Faculty of Law, Dijon, France; elected mem. Ass. Territoriale 1977–78, Congress 1977–88; Mayor of Mont-Dore 1987–2001; Sec.-Gen. Rassemblement pour la Calédonie dans la République (RPCR) 1989; Territorial Sec., Rassemblement pour la République (RPR) 1995–97; Deputy for New Caledonia in French Nat. Ass. 1993–97, 2002–11; Pres. of New Caledonia 2001–04; Pres. Rassemblement-UMP 2005–18; mem. French Senate for New Caledonia 2011–; Pres. Ass., South Prov. 2009–12; Chevalier, Ordre nat. du Mérite. *Address:* Senate (Sénat), 15 rue de Vaugirard, 75291 Paris Cedex 06, France (office). *E-mail:* p.frogier@senat.fr (office). *Website:* www.senat.fr (office).

FRÖHLICH, Fritz W.; German business executive; b. 1942; fmr Chief Financial Officer and Vice-Chair. of Exec. Bd AkzoNobel NV; mem. Supervisory Bd Randstad Holding NV 2003–15, Chair., also mem. Audit Cttee and Chair. Remuneration and Nomination Cttee; Chair. Supervisory Bd Altana AG, Draka Holding NV; mem. Supervisory Bd ASML Holding NV 2004–15, Rexel SA 2007–, Allianz Nederland Groep NV, Aon Jauch & Hübener GmbH, Prysmian 2011–; mem. Investment Cttee ABP Vermogensbeheer.

FROHNMAYER, John Edward, MA, JD; American fmr lawyer, civil servant and writer; b. 1 June 1942, Medford, Ore.; s. of Otto Frohnmayer and Marabel Frohnmayer; m. Leah Thorpe 1967; two s.; ed Stanford Univ., Univs of Chicago and Oregon; Assoc., Johnson, Harrang & Mercer, Eugene, Ore. 1972–75; Pnr, Tonkon, Torp, Galen, Marmaduke & Booth, Portland 1975–89; Chair. Ore. Arts Comm. 1980–84; Chair. Nat. Endowment for the Arts, Washington, DC 1989–92; Visiting Professional Scholar, The Freedom Forum, 1st Amendment Center, Vanderbilt Univ. 1993; fmr Chair. Oregon Humanities; fmr mem. Art Selection Cttee, Ore. State Capitol Bldg; currently Affiliate Prof. of Liberal Arts, Oregon State Univ.; trial lawyer in pvt. practice, Bozeman, Mont. 1995–; Republican; People for the American Way, 1st Amendment Award 1992, Oregon Gov.'s Award for the Arts 1993; Intellectual Freedom Award, Montana Library Asscn 1998. *Publications:* Leaving Town Alive 1993, Out of Tune: Listening to the First Amendment 1994. *Leisure interests:* skiing, rowing, reading, music. *Address:* College of Liberal Arts, Oregon State University, Advising Office, 213 Gilkey Hall, Corvallis, OR 97331, USA (office). *Website:* liberalarts.oregonstate.edu (office).

FROLOV, Alexander V., PhD; Russian physicist and business executive; *CEO, Evraz Group;* b. 1964; m.; one c.; ed Moscow Inst. of Physics and Tech.; worked as Research Fellow at I.V. Kurchatov Inst. of Atomic Energy, Moscow; Chair. Evraz Group 2006–08, CEO 2007–. *Address:* Evraz Group SA, 1 allée Scheffer, 2520 Luxembourg, R.C.S. LuxembourgB 105615 (office); EvrazHolding OOO, 127006 Moscow, ul. Dolgorukovskaya 15, Bldgs 4 and 5, Russia (office). *Telephone:* (495) 234-46-31 (Moscow) (office). *Fax:* (495) 232-13-59 (Moscow) (office). *E-mail:* info@evraz.com (office). *Website:* www.evraz.com (office).

FROMAN, Michael, BA, MA, PhD, JD; American lawyer and fmr government official; *Distinguished Fellow, Council on Foreign Relations;* b. 20 Aug. 1962, San Rafael, California; m. Nancy Goodman; two s. (one deceased) one d.; ed Princeton Univ., Oxford Univ., Harvard Law School; Dir for Int. Econ. Affairs, Nat. Econ. Council and Nat. Security Council 1993–95; Deputy Asst Sec. for Eurasia and the Middle East, US Dept of Treasury Jan.–Dec. 1996, Treasury Chief of Staff 1997–99; Chief of Staff, Office of the Chair. and COO of Internet Operating Group, Citigroup 1999–2001, later becoming Pres. and CEO, CitiInsurance, Head of Emerging Markets Strategy, and COO and Man. Dir, Citigroup Infrastructure Investors at Citigroup Alternative Investments; Asst to the Pres. and Deputy Nat. Security Advisor for Int. Econ. Affairs, The White House 2009–13, US Trade Rep. 2013–17; served as US sherpa for several Group of Twenty and Group of Eight summits; Distinguished Fellow, Council on Foreign Relations 2017–; James R. Schlesinger Distinguished Prof., Univ. of Virginia Miller Center of Public Affairs 2017–18; Resident Fellow, German Marshall Fund. *Address:* Council on Foreign Relations, 58 East 68th Street, New York, NY 10065, USA (office). *Telephone:* (202) 509-8570 (office). *E-mail:* kevanoff@cfr.org (office). *Website:* www.cfr.org/experts/michael-froman (office).

FROMANTIN, Jean-Christophe; French politician and business executive; *Mayor of Neuilly-sur-Seine;* b. 30 Aug. 1962, Nantes (Loire-Atlantique); m.; four c.; ed secondary schools in Saintes, Dunkerque and Strasbourg, École supérieure libre des sciences commerciales appliquées, Paris; nat. service in Lisbon 1987–88; f. Eurochallenge (service and advice for import/export) 1989–94, Head of newly created company, Export Entreprises, following merged with Interex 1994–, participated in launch of Globaltrade.net 2009 (public-pvt. partnership between US Dept of Commerce and Fed. of Int. Trade Asscns); Mayor of Neuilly-sur-Seine 2008–; elected mem. Paris Métropole jt asscn 2009–, co-host Comm. 'Economic Development and Solidarity', Vice-Pres. Paris Métropole 2010–; Gen. Councillor, Hauts-de-Seine, canton of Neuilly-sur-Seine-Nord 2011–; launched political party Territoires en mouvement 2011–; Deputy to Assemblée Nationale (Parl.) 2012–. *Publications:* Mon village dans un monde global: la place de la France dans la mondialisation 2011, Le temps des Territoires 2012. *Leisure interests:* won the sailing Tour de France with the crew of the Dunkirk belonging to Damien Savatier 1980, marathon runner, regularly participates in Paris Marathon, 100 km Millau or the Transbaie (crossing Bay of Somme on bitumen, water, sand and mud). *Address:* Hôtel de Ville, 96 avenue Achille Peretti, 92522 Neuilly-sur-Seine Cedex, France (office). *Telephone:* 1-40-88-88-88 (office). *E-mail:* mr.lemaire@ville-neuillysurseine.fr (office). *Website:* www.ville-neuillysurseine.fr (office); www.territoiresenmouvement.com; www.fromantin.com.

FROMHERZ, Peter, Dr rer. nat; German biophysicist; *Director Emeritus, Max Planck Institute for Biochemistry;* b. 8 Oct. 1942, Ludwigshafen; ed Technische Hochschule, Karlsruhe, Univ. Marburg; Postdoctoral Fellow, Max Planck Inst. for Biophysical Chem., Göttingen 1970–81; Chair. of Experimental Physics, Univ. of Ulm 1978–94, Full Prof. of Experimental Physics 1981–; Scientific Mem., Max Planck Soc. 1994, apptd Dir Max Planck Inst. for Biochemistry, Martinsried 1994, now Dir Emer.; Hon. Prof. of Physics, Technische Universität Munich 1994–; Pres. German Biophysical Soc.; mem. Heidelberg Acad. of Sciences 1992–; Julius Springer Prize for Applied Physics 1998, Philip Morris Research Award 2004. *Publications:* 150 research papers. *Address:* Max-Planck-Institut für Biochemie, Abteilung Membran- und Neurophysik, Am Klopferspitz 18, D- 82152 Martinsried, Germany (office). *Telephone:* (89) 8578-2820 (office). *Fax:* (89) 8578-2822 (office). *E-mail:* fromherz@biochem.mpg.de (office). *Website:* www.biochem.mpg.de/en/eg/fromherz (office).

FROST, David George Hamilton, CMG; British diplomatist (retd) and business executive; *Chief Executive, Scotch Whisky Association;* b. 21 Feb. 1965, Derby, England; m. 1st Jacqueline Elizabeth Dias (divorced 2018); one s. one d.; m. 2nd Harriet Lucy Mathews 2018; ed Nottingham High School, St John's Coll., Oxford; joined FCO 1987, Desk Officer for Afghanistan, S Asia Dept 1987–88, Third Sec. (Political), Nicosia 1988–90, Desk Officer for NATO and WEU, Security Policy Dept 1992–93, First Sec. (Econ.), UK Representation to EU 1993–96, First Sec. (Human Rights), UK Mission to UN, New York 1996–98, Pvt. Sec. to Perm. Under-Sec., FCO 1998–99, Deputy Head of EU (External) Dept 1999–2001, Econ. and EU Counsellor, Paris 2001–03, Head of EU (Internal) Dept, FCO 2003–04, Dir EU (Internal) 2004–06, Amb. to Denmark 2006–08, Dir Directorate of Strategy, Policy Planning and Analysis, FCO 2008–10, on loan to Dept for Business, Innovation and Skills as Dir for Europe, Trade and Int. Affairs 2010–13; tax consultant, KPMG, London 1990–92; Chief Exec. Scotch Whisky Asscn 2014–; mem. Advisory Council, Open Europe, Exec. Cttee, Scottish Council for Devt and Industry, Exec. Group, Scotland Food & Drink. *Leisure interests:* languages and linguistics, medieval history, modern politics and economics, detective fiction and ghost stories, Richard Wagner, football. *Address:* The Scotch Whisky Association, Quartermile Two, 2 Lister Square, Edinburgh, EH3 9GL, Scotland (office). *Telephone:* (131) 222-9200 (office). *E-mail:* dfrost@swa.org.uk (office). *Website:* www.scotch-whisky.org.uk (office).

FROTSCHER, Michael, MD; German neuroscientist and academic; *Professor and Head, Institute for Structural Neurobiology, Centre for Molecular Neurobiology Hamburg (ZMNH), University Medical Centre Hamburg-Eppendorf;* b. 3 July 1947, Dresden; ed East-Berlin Humboldt Univ.; started scientific career at Inst. of Anatomy, East-Berlin Humboldt Univ., GDR; fled to FRG 1979, started new career at Max Planck Inst. of Brain Research, Frankfurt; fmr Prof. and Head of Dept, Inst. of Anatomy and Cell Biology, Albert-Ludwigs-Universität, Freiburg; currently Prof. and Head, Inst. for Structural Neurobiology, Centre for Molecular Neurobiology Hamburg (ZMNH), Univ. Medical Centre Hamburg-Eppendorf; hon. doctorate; German Research Foundation Leibniz Prize 1993, Max Planck Research Award for International Cooperation 2000, Ernst Jung Prize for Medicine 2002, Jacob Henle Medal 2013. *Publications:* numerous publs in medical and scientific journals. *Address:* Institute for Structural Neurobiology, Centre for Molecular Neurobiology Hamburg (ZMNH), University Medical Centre Hamburg-Eppendorf, Martinistr. 52, 20246 Hamburg, Germany (office). *Telephone:* (40) 741055028 (office). *Fax:* (40) 741040213 (office). *E-mail:* michael.frotscher@zmnh.uni-hamburg.de (office). *Website:* www.zmnh.uni-hamburg.de (office).

FROWEIN, Jochen Abraham, DJur, MCL; German professor of law; *Director Emeritus, Max-Planck-Institut für ausländisches öffentliches Recht und Völkerrecht;* b. 8 June 1934, Berlin; s. of Abraham Frowein and Hilde Frowein (née Matthis); m. Lore Flume 1962; one s. two d.; ed Univs of Kiel, Berlin, Bonn and Univ. of Michigan Law School, Ann Arbor, USA; Research Fellow, Max-Planck-Inst. for Comparative Public and Int. Law 1962–66; Prof., Ruhr-Univ., Bochum 1967–69, Univ. of Bielefeld 1969–81; Dir Max-Planck-Inst. and Prof., Univ. of Heidelberg 1981–2002, now Dir Emer.; Visiting Prof., Univ. of Michigan Law School 1978, Georgetown Univ. Law Faculty, Washington, DC 2003; Expert of European Parl. for Beneš-Decrees 2002; mem. European Comm. on Human Rights 1973–93 (Vice-Pres. 1981–93), Arbitration Tribunal for BIS 2001; Vice-Pres. German Research Foundation 1977–80; Pres. Vereinigung Deutscher Staatsrechtslehrer (German Public Law Teachers Asscn) 1999–2001; Vice-Pres. Max Planck Soc. 1999–2002; Commr, Int. Comm. of Jurists, Geneva 1998, mem. Exec. Cttee 2002–06, Vice-Pres. 2006–; Grosses Bundesverdienstkreuz 1994; Dr hc (Seville) 1984, (Louvain) 1997, (Szeged) 1998, (Bielefeld) 1999, (Univ. Panthéon-Assas Paris II) 2000. *Publications:* Das de facto-Regime im Völkerrecht 1968, EMRK-Kommentar (with W. Peukert) 1985; numerous articles and contribs. *Address:* Max-Planck-Institut für ausländisches öffentliches Recht und Völkerrecht, Im Neuenheimer Feld 535, 69120 Heidelberg, Germany (office). *Telephone:* (6221) 4821 (office). *Fax:* (6221) 48288 (office). *E-mail:* jfrowein@mpil.de (office). *Website:* www.mpil.de (office).

FRUNZĂVERDE, Sorin, PhD; Romanian engineer and politician; b. 26 April 1960, Bocsa, Caras-Severin Co.; m.; one c.; ed Faculty of Metallurgy, Polytechnic Inst., Bucharest, Western Univ., Timişoara, Nat. Defence Univ., Bucharest; Chief of Workshop, Resita Siderurgical Works 1985–88, Head Dept for Quality Control-Labs 1988–90; Pres. and Gen. Man. Chamber for Trade and Industry of Caraş-Severin 1991–96; County Counsellor, Sec., Comm. for Budget and Finances Cttee 1992–96; Chair. Caras-Severin Co. Council 1996–97, 2004–06; Minister of Environment, Waters Man. and Forests 1997–98, of Tourism 1998; Chair. Nat. Authority for Tourism 1999–2000; Minister of Nat. Defence 2000, 2006–07; mem. Chamber of Deputies for Caras-Severin Electoral Ward 2000–04; mem. Partidul Democrat (PD) (later Democratic Liberal Party), Vice-Pres. 1993–2012; mem. National Liberal Party (PNL) 2012–.

FRY, Sir Graham Holbrook, Kt, KCMG; British diplomatist (retd); b. 20 Dec. 1949, Shrewsbury, Shropshire, England; m. Toyoko Fry; two s.; ed Brasenose Coll., Oxford; joined FCO 1972, with Rhodesia Dept 1972–73, full-time language training, UK 1973–74, Kamakura 1974–75, Second Sec., Information, Embassy in Tokyo 1975–76, Second Sec., Commercial, Embassy in Tokyo 1976–79; with Invest in Britain Bureau, Dept of Trade and Industry 1979–81, EC Dept (Internal), FCO 1981–83; First Sec., (Political), Embassy in Paris 1983–87; with Western European Dept, FCO 1987–89; Political Counsellor, Embassy in Tokyo 1989–93; Head of Far Eastern and Pacific Dept, FCO 1993–95, Dir Northern Asia and Pacific 1995–98; High Commr to Malaysia 1998–2001; Dir-Gen. (Econ.), FCO 2001–04; Amb. to Japan 2004–08 (retd); fmr Pres. Cambridge and Oxford Soc.; mem. Governing Body, SOAS, Univ. of London; Council mem. Wildfowl and Wetlands Trust 2010–12. *Address:* c/o Governing Body, School of Oriental and African Studies, University of London, Thornhaugh Street, Russell Square, London, WC1H 0XG, England (office).

FRY, Hedy, PC; Canadian physician and politician; b. 6 Aug. 1941, Trinidad; three s.; ed Coll. of Physicians and Surgeons, Dublin, Ireland; fmr family physician, Vancouver Centre, BC; MP for Vancouver Centre 1993–; Parl. Sec. to Minister of Health 1993–96; Sec. of State (Multiculturalism, Status of Women) 1996–2002; Parl. Sec. to Minister of Citizenship and Immigration with special emphasis on Foreign Credentials 2003–04; Parl. Sec. to Minister of Citizenship and Immigration and Minister of Human Resources and Skills Devt with special emphasis on the Internationally Trained Workers Initiative 2004–06; Critic for Sport Canada in Liberal shadow cabinet 2006–; Vice-Chair. Task Force on Canada–US Relations 2002; Chair. BC Caucus 2002–2004, 2006–, Standing Cttee on Health 2002–03, Special Cttee on non-medical use of drugs 2002, Standing Cttee on the Status of Women 2009–11, Standing Cttee on Canadian Heritage 2016–; fmr Pres. BC Medical Asscn. *Leisure interests:* drama, racquetball, reading, swimming. *Address:* Confederation Building, Room 583, House of Commons, Ottawa, ON K1A 0A6 (office); Constituency Office, 1030 Denman Street, Suite 106, Vancouver, BC V6G 2M6, Canada (office). *Telephone:* (613) 992-3213 (office); (604) 666-0135 (Constituency). *Fax:* (613) 995-0056 (office); (604) 666-0114 (Constituency). *E-mail:* contact@hedyfry.com; fryh0@parl.gc.ca (office). *Website:* www.hedyfry.com (office).

FRY, Jonathan Michael, MA; British business executive (retd); b. 9 Aug. 1937, Jerusalem; s. of Stephen Fry and Gladys Yvonne Blunt; m. Caroline Mary

Dunkerly 1970 (divorced 1997); four d.; m. 2nd Marilyn Russell 1999; ed Repton School, Trinity Coll., Univ. of Oxford; Account Exec., Pritchard Wood Ltd 1961–65; Account Supervisor, Norman Craig & Kummel Inc. 1965–66; Consultant, McKinsey & Co. 1966–73; Devt/Marketing Dir Unigate Foods Div. 1973, Man. Dir 1973, Chair. 1976–78; Group Planning Dir Burmah Oil Trading Ltd 1978–81, Chief Exec. Burmah Speciality Chemicals Ltd 1981–87, Chair. Burmah Castrol PLC 1998–2000 (Man. Dir 1990–93, Chief Exec. 1993–98), Chief Exec. Burmah Castrol Trading Ltd 1993–98, Chair. 1998–2000 (Man. Dir 1990–93), Chair. Castrol Int. (fmrly Castrol Ltd) 1993–96 (Chief Exec. 1987–93); Deputy Chair. Northern Foods PLC 1996–2002, Dir (non-exec.) 1991–2002; Chair. Christian Salvesen PLC 1997–2003, Dir (non-exec.) 1995–2003; Chair. Elementis PLC (fmrly Harrisons & Crosfield PLC) 1997–2004; Chair. Control Risks Group Holdings Ltd 2000–07. *Leisure interests:* cricket, skiing, archaeology. *Address:* Beechingstoke Manor, Pewsey, Wilts., SN9 6HQ, England (home). *Telephone:* (167285) 1669 (home).

FRY, Stephen John, MA; British actor, comedian, writer, journalist and television and radio presenter and director; b. 24 Aug. 1957, Hampstead, London; s. of Alan John Fry and Marianne Eve Fry (née Newman); m. Elliott Spencer 2015; ed Uppingham School, Queens' Coll., Cambridge; columnist, The Listener 1988–89, Daily Telegraph 1990–; wrote first play Latin, performed at Edinburgh Festival 1980 and at Lyric Theatre, Hammersmith 1983; appeared with Cambridge Footlights in revue The Cellar Tapes, Edinburgh Festival 1981; re-wrote script Me and My Girl, London, Broadway, Sydney 1984; Chair. Criterion Theatre Trust 2010–; Pres. Friends for Life Terrence Higgins Trust; mem. Amnesty International, Comic Relief; co-f. SamFry Ltd 2008; Co-owner, with Gina Carter and Sandi Toksvig, Sprout Pictures (ind. film and TV co.); mem. Bd Norwich City Football Club 2010–; Distinguished Supporter, British Humanist Asscn 2010–; Freedom of the City of London 2013; Hon. LLD (Dundee) 1995, (East Anglia) 1999, Hon. DLit, Dr hc (Anglia Ruskin) 2005; Lifetime Achievement Award in Cultural Humanism, Humanist Chaplaincy at Harvard Univ. 2011, ranked fourth on the World Pride Power list 2014. *Plays include:* Forty Years On, Chichester Festival and London 1984, The Common Pursuit, London 1988 (TV 1992), three one-man shows in Australia 2010, stand-up performance, Royal Albert Hall, London 2010, Twelfth Night, Shakepeare's Globe 2012 (transferred to the West End). *Films include:* The Good Father 1985, A Fish Called Wanda 1988, A Handful of Dust 1988, Peter's Friends 1992, IQ 1995, Wind in the Willows 1996, Wilde 1997, Cold Comfort Farm 1997, A Civil Action 1997, Whatever Happened to Harold Smith? 2000, Relative Values 2000, Discovery of Heaven 2001, Gosford Park 2002, Bright Young Things (writer, dir, exec. producer) 2003, Mirrormask 2004, A Cock and Bull Story 2005, V for Vendetta 2005, Stormbreaker 2006, Little Claus and Big Claus 2006, Eichmann 2007, St Trinian's 2007, House of Boys 2009, Alice in Wonderland (voice) 2010, Animals United (voice) 2010, Sherlock Holmes: A Game of Shadows 2011, Wagner & Me 2012, Cicada Princess (short) 2012, The Look of Love 2013, The Hobbit: The Desolation of Smaug 2013, Stephen Fry Live: More Fool Me 2014, The Hobbit: The Battle of the Five Armies 2014, The Man Who Knew Infinity 2015, Rocky Horror Show Live (narrator) 2015, The Brits Are Coming 2016, Tomorrow 2016, Love and Friendship 2016, Alice Through the Looking Glass (voice) 2016. *Radio:* Loose Ends 1986–87, Whose Line Is It Anyway? 1987, Saturday Night Fry 1987, 1998, Absolute Power 2000–06, Fry's English Delight (BBC Radio 4, presenter) 2015–, Desert Island Discs (BBC Radio 4) 2015. *Television includes:* series: There's Nothing to Worry About 1982, Alfresco 1983–84, The Young Ones 1984, Happy Families 1985, Blackadder II 1985, Saturday Live 1986–87, A Bit of Fry and Laurie 1987–95, Blackadder's Christmas Carol 1988, Blackadder Goes Forth 1989, Jeeves and Wooster 1990–93, Stalag Luft 1993, Laughter and Loathing 1995, Gormenghast 2000, Absolute Power 2003–05, QI (presenter) 2003–16, Kingdom 2007–09, Bones 2007–09, Stephen Fry in America 2008, Last Chance to See 2009, Fry's Planet Word 2011, Playhouse Presents – The Man 2012; other: Doors Open (film) 2012, Stephen Fry: Out There (Best Presenter Award, Royal Television Soc. Programme Awards) 2014, This Is Jinsy (series) 2014, Lily's Driftwood Bay (series) 2014, 24: Live Another Day (mini-series) 2014, American Dad! (series) 2014, Marked (film) 2014, Danger Mouse (series) 2015. *Publications include:* Paperweight (collected essays) 1992, Stephen Fry Mixed Shrinkwrap 1993, X10 Hippopotamus Shrinkwrap 1993, The Liar (novel) 1993, The Hippopotamus 1994, A Bit of Fry and Laurie (with Hugh Laurie) 1994, 3 Bits of Fry and Laurie (with Hugh Laurie) 1994, Fry and Laurie 4 (with Hugh Laurie) 1994, Paperweight Vol. II (collected essays) 1995, Making History 1996, Moab is My Washpot (autobiography) 1997, The Stars' Tennis Balls (novel) 2000, The Salmon of Doubt by Douglas Adams (ed.) 2002, Revenge (novel) 2002, Rescuing the Spectacled Bear (novel) 2002, Incomplete & Utter History of Classical Music (with Tim Lihoreau) 2005, The Ode Less Travelled: Unlocking the Poet Within 2005, Stephen Fry in America 2008, The Fry Chronicles: An Autobiography (Galaxy Nat. Book Awards Biography of the Year) 2010, More Fool Me: A Memoir 2014. *Leisure interests:* smoking, drinking, swearing, pressing wild flowers. *Address:* c/o Hamilton Hodell Ltd, Fifth Floor, 66–68 Margaret Street, London, W1W 8SR, England (office); c/o Toni Howard, ICM, 8942 Wilshire Blvd, Beverly Hills, CA 90211-1908, USA (office). *Telephone:* (20) 7636-1221 (London) (office); (212) 556-5673 (Beverly Hills) (office). *Fax:* (20) 7636-1226 (London) (office). *Website:* www.stephenfry.com.

FRYDENBERG, Josh, LLB, MPhil, MPA; Australian lawyer and politician; *Treasurer of Australia;* b. 17 July 1971, Melbourne; m. Amie Frydenberg; two c.; ed Monash Univ., Oxford Univ., Harvard Univ.; Articled Clerk, Mallesons Stephen Jaques (law firm) 1996–99; ministerial adviser in Canberra 1999–2005, including as Policy Adviser to Prime Minister John Howard 2003–05; Dir of Global Banking, Deutsche Bank 2005–10; MP (Liberal) for Kooyong 2010–; Parl. Sec. to Prime Minister 2013, Asst Treasurer 2014–15, Minister for Resources, Energy and Northern Australia 2015–16, Minister for the Environment and Energy 2016–18, Treasurer of Australia 2018–; mem. Liberal Party of Australia 1999–. *Leisure interests:* tennis (represented Australia at two World Univ. Games), photography. *Address:* Department of the Treasury, Langton Cres., Parkes, ACT 2600, Australia (office). *Telephone:* (2) 6263-2111 (office). *Fax:* (2) 6263-2869 (office). *E-mail:* department@treasury.gov.au (office). *Website:* www.treasury.gov.au (office); joshfrydenberg.com.au.

FU, Chengyu, BSc, MSc; Chinese oil industry executive; b. 1951; ed Northeast Petroleum Inst., Univ. of Southern California, USA; fmr oil engineer, worked in Daqing, Liaohe and Huabei oilfields; joined China Nat. Offshore Oil Corpn (CNOOC) 1982, chair. several jt ventures, Vice-Pres. CNOOC Nanhai East Corpn 1994–95; Vice-Pres. Phillips China Inc. 1995; Gen. Man. Xijiang Devt Project 1995; Pres. CNOOC Nanhai East Corpn 1999, Exec. Dir, Exec. Vice-Pres. and COO CNOOC Ltd 1999, Vice-Pres. CNOOC 2000–02, Pres. CNOOC Ltd 2002–03, Chair. and CEO China Oilfield Services Ltd (subsidiary) 2002–11, Chair. and CEO CNOOC Ltd 2003–10, Chair. 2003–11, Pres. and Party Leadership Group Sec. CNOOC Ltd 2003–11; Chair. China Petrochemical Corpn (Sinopec Group) 2011–15, Sec. Party Cttee; mem. 17th CCP Cen. Cttee Cen. Comm. for Discipline Inspection 2007–12.

FU, Jianhua, MA; Chinese banking executive; ed Dongbei Univ. of Finance and Econs; Chair. Bank of Shanghai –2006; Vice-Chair., Pres. and Deputy Party Sec., Shanghai Pudong Development Bank Co. Ltd 2006–15; Dir (non-exec.), Shanghai Commercial Bank Ltd 2004–09.

FU, Mingxia; Chinese diver; b. Aug. 1978, Wuhan, Hubei Prov.; m. Antony Leung 2002; two s. one d.; ed Qinghua Univ., Beijing; youngest ever 10m platform diving world champion at the age of 12; first woman to win five Olympic diving medals; 10m platform diving gold medallist World Championships, Perth 1991, Rome 1994; 10m platform diving gold medallist at Olympics, Barcelona 1992, Olympics, Atlanta 1996 (also won 3m platform gold medal), 3m springboard gold medallist at Sydney Olympics 2000; 3m springboard silver medallist Asian Games, Hiroshima 1994, 10m platform diving bronze medallist, Asian Games, Beijing 1990; mem. bid cttee Beijing Olympics 2008; Nation's Best 10 Athletes Award.

FU, Qifeng; Chinese writer and former acrobat; b. 15 March 1941, Chengdu, Sichuan; d. of Fu Tianzheng and Ceng Qingpu; m. Xu Zhuang 1961; one s. one d.; performer, acrobatics troupe, Beijing 1960–70; Founder and Deputy Chief Ed. Acrobatics and Magic (journal); mem. Research Dept, Asscn of Chinese Acrobats 1987–, Council mem. 1991–; mem. Editorial Cttee Acrobatics, in series Contemporary China 1991–; mem. China Magic Cttee 1993–. *Publications include:* Chinese Acrobatics Through the Ages 1986, The Art of Chinese Acrobatics 1988; (with brother) Acrobatics in China 1983, History of Chinese Acrobatics 1989, History of Chinese Artistic Skills (in Japanese) 1993; (co-author) Literature and Art Volume of China Concise Encyclopedia 1994, Secret of Spiritualist Activities 1995, Illusions and Superstitions 1997, A Primer of Chinese Acrobatics 2003. *Address:* Chinese Acrobats Association, No.10, Nanli, Nongzhanguan (AgriCultural Exhibition Hall), Beijing 100026 (office); 5-2-501 Hongmiao Beili, Jintai Road, Beijing 100025, People's Republic of China. *Telephone:* 65005662 (office); 65002547.

FU, Gen. Quanyou; Chinese army officer (retd); b. Nov. 1930, Yuanping Co., Shanxi Prov.; ed Mil. Acad. of the Chinese PLA; joined PLA 1946, took part in Yanqing Campaign; joined CCP 1947; Deputy Co. Commdr Northwest Field Army, PLA Services and Arms 1948–50, Co. Commdr and Bn Chief-of-Staff 1950–52; soldier, Korean War 1953, Bn Commdr Chinese People's Volunteers 1953–58; Regt Chief-of-Staff, Chengdu Mil. Region, PLA 1961–64, Div. Chief-of-Staff 1968–69, Div. Commdr 1978–80, Army Chief-of-Staff 1981–83, Army Commdr 1983–85, Commdr 1985–88, Lt-Gen. 1988–93, Commdr Lanzhou Mil. Region 1990–92, Dir Gen. Logistics Dept 1992–95, Gen. 1995–2002, Chief of Gen. Staff 1995–99; Vice-Chair. Nat. Afforestation Cttee; Deputy Dir Nat. Cttee for the Patriotic Public Health Campaign 1994–98; mem. 12th CCP Cen. Cttee 1983–87, 13th CCP Cen. Cttee 1987–92, 14th CCP Cen. Cttee (mem. Cen. Mil. Comm.) 1992–97, 15th CCP Cen. Cttee 1997–2002; mem. Cen. Mil. Comm. of People's Repub. of China 1993–2003.

FU, Tianlin; Chinese poet; b. 24 Jan. 1946, Zizhong Co., Sichuan Prov.; ed Chongqing Electronic Tech. High School; worked in orchard Chongqing 1962–79; clerk, Beibei Cultural Centre 1980–82; Ed. Chongqing Publishing House 1982–; Vice-Pres. Poetry Inst. of China (PIC), Pres. PIC Chongqing; First Prize of Chinese Poetry 1983, voted as one of China's Ten Outstanding Poets by Poetry 1983 periodical 2008. *Publications include:* The Sweat (Nat. Outstanding Young Poet Award 1981), Green Musical Notes (First Chinese Nat. Poetry Works Award 1983) 1981, Between Children and the World 1983, Island of Music 1985, Red Strawberry 1986, Selected Poems of Seven Chinese Poets 1993, Futianlin Selected Works (Second Chinese Female Literature Award 2003) 2002, Lemon Leaves (Lu Xun Literature Award 2010) 2009. *E-mail:* futianlin023@163.com.

FU, Ying; Chinese diplomatist; b. Jan. 1953, Hohhot, Inner Mongolian Autonomous Region; m.; one d.; ed Foreign Languages Inst., Beijing, Univ. of Kent, UK; Attaché, Embassy in Romania 1978–82; Attaché, Dept of Translation and Interpretation, Ministry of Foreign Affairs 1982–85, Deputy Dir 1986–90, Deputy Dir, Dept of Asian Affairs 1990–92, Dir and Counsellor 1993–97, Dir-Gen. 2000–04; staff mem. UN Transitional Authority, Cambodia 1992–93; Minister Counsellor, Embassy in Jakarta 1997–98, Amb. to the Philippines 1998–2000, to Australia 2004–07, to UK 2007–09; Vice-Minister of Foreign Affairs 2009–13; Chair. Foreign Affairs Cttee, Nat. People's Congress 2013–18. *Publication:* A Dialogue with the World 2018.

FU, Yuning, PhD; Chinese business executive; *Chairman, China Resources (Holdings) Company Limited;* b. March 1957; ed Dalian Inst. of Tech., Brunel Univ., UK; worked as a postdoctoral research fellow at Brunel Univ.; fmr Asst Man. Dir Shenzhen Chiwan Petroleum Supply Base Co. Ltd, fmr Chair. Shenzhen Chiwan Wharf Holdings Ltd; fmr Chair. Union Bank of Hong Kong Ltd; fmr Gen. Man. China Nanshan Devt Group Inc., currently Chair.; fmr Vice-Pres. and Pres. China Merchants Group Ltd, Chair. –2014, Dir (non-exec.), China Merchants Bank Co. Ltd 1999–2014, Chair. 2010–14, also Chair. China Merchants Holdings (International) Co. Ltd; Chair. China Resources (Holdings) Ltd 2014–; Ind. Dir (non-exec.), Li & Fung Ltd; Exec. mem. Hong Kong Gen. Chamber of Commerce; mem. 12th Nat. Cttee of the CPPCC. *Address:* China Resources (Holdings) Co. Ltd, Floor 49, CRC Building, 26 Harbour Road, Wanchai, Hong Kong Special Administrative Region, People's Republic of China (office). *Telephone:* 28797888 (office). *Fax:* 28275774 (office). *E-mail:* crc@crc.com.hk (office). *Website:* www.crc.com.hk (office).

FU, Zhihuan; Chinese engineer and politician; b. March 1938, Haicheng Co., Liaoning Prov.; ed Moscow Railways Inst., USSR; technician, later Deputy Chief, later Chief, later Deputy Dir Zhuzhou Electric Eng Research Inst., Ministry of

Railways 1961; joined CCP 1966; Chief Engineer, Science and Tech. Bureau, Ministry of Railways 1983, Dir 1985; Dir Harbin Railway Bureau 1989; Vice-Minister of Railways 1990–97, Minister 2002–03; Chair. Financial and Econ. Cttee, NPC 2003–08; mem. CCP Cen. Comm. for Discipline Inspection 1997–2002; mem. 15th CCP Cen. Cttee 1997–2002; Academician, Chinese Acad. of Engineering. *Address:* Chinese Academy of Engineering, 2 Bingjiaokou Hutong, Xicheng District, Beijing 100088, People's Republic of China (office). *Telephone:* (10) 59300264 (office). *Fax:* (10) 59300140 (office). *E-mail:* info@cae.cn (office). *Website:* www.cae.cn (office).

FUCHS, Alain, PhD, FRSC; French chemical engineer, academic and national organization official; *President, Centre National de la Recherche Scientifique;* b. 10 April 1953, Lausanne; ed École polytechnique fédérale de Lausanne, Univ. of Paris-Sud, Orsay, France; Sr Prof. of Chem., Univ. of Paris-Sud 1995, Dir Chimie physique des matériaux amorphes (Physical Chem. of Amorphous Materials) lab. 1997–2000, Founder-Dir Orsay Laboratoire de chimie physique (Lab. of Physical Chem.) 2000–06; Dir Ecole Nationale Supérieure de Chimie de Paris (Chimie ParisTech) 2006–10; Visiting Prof., Univ. of California, USA 1999; several industrial collaborations; Pres. Section 13 (Physical Chem.—Molecules, Environments), Nat. Cttee of Scientific Research, based at CNRS 2004–07, mem. Scientific Cttee of CNRS's Science and Citizens programme 1997–99, Sr Adviser on calculation to CNRS Chem. Dept 1997–2003, Pres. CNRS 2010–; Pres. Physical Chem. Div., Soc. française de chimie 2002–05, Soc. française de physique 2002–05; mem. Bd of Dirs Int. Adsorption Soc.; mem. CDEFI permanent (Conférence des directeurs des écoles françaises d'ingénieurs) 2007–, Educational Bd Institut nat. des sciences et techniques nucléaires (affiliated with French Atomic Energy Comm.), Comité de coordination des formations en sciences et technologies du nucléaire 2009–, Scientific Bd CECAM Lyon (Centre européen de calcul atomique et moléculaire) 1999–2008; Chevalier des Palmes académiques 1996, Chevalier légion d'honneur; Dr hc, Univ. of Québec in Montréal. *Publications include:* numerous papers in professional journals on the modelization and molecular simulation of the behaviour of confined fluids. *Address:* CNRS, Campus Gérard-Mégie, 3 rue Michel-Ange, 75794 Paris Cedex 16, France (office). *Telephone:* 1-44-96-48-23 (office). *Fax:* 1-44-96-49-13 (office). *E-mail:* presidence.secretariat@cnrs-dir.fr (office). *Website:* www.cnrs.fr (office).

FUCHS, Elaine, BS, PhD; American cell biologist and academic; *Rebecca C. Lancefield Professor, Laboratory of Mammalian Cell Biology and Development, The Rockefeller University;* b. 5 May 1950, Chicago, Ill.; m. Dr David Hansen; ed Univ. of Illinois, Princeton Univ.; Postdoctoral Researcher, MIT 1977–80; Amgen Prof. of Basic Sciences, Univ. of Chicago 1980–2002; Rebecca C. Lancefield Prof., Lab. of Mammalian Cell Biology and Devt, The Rockefeller Univ. 2002–; Assoc. Investigator, Howard Hughes Medical Inst. 1988–93, Investigator 1993–; mem. Bd Damon Runyon Cancer Research Foundation; Pres. American Soc. for Cell Biology 2001; mem. NAS Inst. of Medicine 1994, NAS 1996, American Acad. of Arts and Sciences 1994, American Acad. of Microbiology 1997, German Soc. of Dermatology 2001, New York Acad. of Sciences 2004, American Philosophical Soc. 2005; Foreign mem. European Molecular Biology Org. 2010; Fellow, Harvey Soc. 2004, AAAS 2008, Acad. of American Asscn for Cancer Research 2013; Dr hc (Mount Sinai School of Medicine, New York Univ.) 2003, (Univ. of Illinois) 2006; Sr Women's Career Achievement Award, Women in Cell Biology 1997, Cartwright Award, Columbia Univ. 2002, Novartis/Drew Award in Biomedical Research 2002, Dickson Prize in Medicine 2004, Award for Scientific Excellence, Fed. of American Socs for Experimental Biology 2006, Nat. Medal of Science 2009, Bering Award 2006, Laureate for North America, L'Oréal-UNESCO Awards for Women in Science 2010, Charlotte Friend Award 2010, Madison Medal 2011, Passano Prize 2011, Prize in Medicine and Biomedical Research, Albany Medical Center 2011, Biomedical Research Award, New York Acad. of Medicine 2012, March of Dimes Prize in Developmental Biology 2012, Lifetime Achievement Award, American Skin Asscn 2013, Pasarow Award in Cancer Research 2013, Pezcoller Foundation-AACR Int. Award for Extraordinary Achievement in Cancer Research 2014, E. B. Wilson Medal, American Soc. for Cell Biology 2015, Vanderbilt Prize in Biomedical Science 2016, Howard Taylor Ricketts Award 2017, McEwen Award for Innovation 2017. *Publications:* numerous papers in professional journals. *Address:* Laboratory of Mammalian Cell Biology and Development, The Rockefeller University, 1230 York Avenue, New York, NY 10065, USA (office). *Telephone:* (212) 327-8000 (office). *E-mail:* elaine.fuchs@rockefeller.edu (office). *Website:* www.rockefeller.edu/our-scientists/heads-of-laboratories/1166-elaine-fuchs (office).

FUCHS, Victor Robert, MA, PhD; American economist and academic; *Henry J. Kaiser, Jr Professor Emeritus of Economics, Stanford University;* b. 31 Jan. 1924, New York; s. of Alfred Fuchs and Frances S. Fuchs (née Scheiber); m. Beverly Beck 1948; two s. two d.; ed New York and Columbia Univs; Assoc. Prof. of Econs, New York Univ. 1959–60; Program Assoc. Econs Ford Foundation 1960–62; Research Assoc., Nat. Bureau of Econ. Research 1962–; Prof. of Community Medicine, Mount Sinai School of Medicine 1968–74; Prof. of Econs, CUNY Grad. Center 1968–74; Prof. of Econs (in Depts of Econs and Health Research and Policy), Stanford Univ. 1974–95, Henry J. Kaiser, Jr Prof. 1988–95, Prof. Emer. 1995–; Pres. American Econ. Asscn 1995; mem. Inst. of Medicine, American Philosophical Soc.; Fellow, American Acad. of Arts and Sciences; Distinguished Fellow, American Econ. Asscn 1990; Madden Memorial Award 1982, John R. Commons Award 2002 and other awards. *Publications:* The Economics of the Fur Industry 1957, Changes in the Location of Manufacturing in the US since 1929 1962, The Service Economy 1968, Production and Productivity in the Service Industries 1969, Who Shall Live? Health, Economics and Social Choice 1974 (expanded edn 1998), Economic Aspects of Health (ed.) 1982, How We Live 1983, The Health Economy 1986, Women's Quest for Economic Equality 1988, The Future of Health Policy 1993, Individual and Social Responsibility: Child Care, Education, Medical Care and Long Term Care in America (ed.) 1996. *Address:* National Bureau of Economic Research, 30 Alta Road, Stanford, CA 94305 (office); 796 Cedro Way, Stanford, CA 94305, USA (home). *Telephone:* (650) 326-7639 (office); (650) 858-1527 (home). *Fax:* (650) 328-4163 (office); (650) 858-0411 (home). *E-mail:* vfuchs@stanford.edu (office). *Website:* www-econ.stanford.edu (office).

FUDGE, Ann Marie, BA, MBA; American advertising executive (retd); b. 23 April 1951, Washington, DC; m. Richard E. Fudge 1971; two s.; ed Simmons Coll. and Harvard Univ. Grad. School of Business; began career as marketing asst with General Mills, Inc., later Marketing Dir; Pres. Beverage, Desserts and Post Div., Kraft Foods –2003; Chair. and CEO Young & Rubicam Brands and Y&R Advertising 2003–05, Chair. and CEO Y&R Brands 2003–06; Chair. US Programs Advisory Panel, Bill and Melinda Gates Foundation; mem. Bd of Dirs General Electric 1999–, Novartis 2008–, Buzzient, Inc. 2009–, Unilever 2009–, Infosys 2011–; Hon. Dir Catalyst; mem. Bd of Govs Boys and Girls Club of America; fmr mem. Bd of Dirs Marriott International, The Advertising Council, Advertising Educational Foundation; mem. Harvard Bd of Overseers, Committee of 200, Council on Foreign Relations; mem. Nat. Comm. on Fiscal Responsibility and Reform 2010; Trustee, Brookings Inst., Rockefeller Foundation, Morehouse Coll.; Matrix Award for Advertising, New York Women in Communication, Leadership Awards, Minneapolis and New York City YWCA, Alumni Achievement Award, Harvard Business School 1998, Achievement Award, Executive Leadership Council 2000, Candace Award from Nat Coalition of 100 Black Women. *Address:* 2400 Beacon Street, PH1, Chestnut Hill, MA 02467, USA.

FUENTES KNIGHT, Juan Alberto, MA, PhD; Guatemalan economist, politician and international organization official; *Chairman, Oxfam International;* ed McGill Univ. and Univ. of Toronto, Canada, Univ. of Geneva, Switzerland, Univ. of Sussex, UK; served for 20 years as economist with UN, becoming Co-ordinator, Guatemalan Human Devt Report, UNDP; Founder and Exec. Dir and Research Co-ordinator, Instituto Centroamericano de Estudios Fiscales (Cen. American Inst. for Fiscal Studies) 2005–07; Minister of Public Finance 2008–10 (resgnd); apptd Regional Advisor, ECLAC, Dir Div. of Econ. Devt, Santiago, Chile 2012; Prof., Universidad Rafael Landivar 2014; Chair. Oxfam International 2015–. *Publications:* numerous articles in econ. journals. *Address:* Oxfam International, Oxfam House, John Smith Drive, Oxford, OX4 2JY, England (office). *Telephone:* (1865) 780100 (office). *Website:* www.oxfam.org (office).

FUENTES MENJÍVAR, Nelson Eduardo; Salvadorean economist, researcher and politician; *Minister of Finance;* b. 29 Sept. 1978; ed University of José Simeón Cañas, Univ. of Madrid, Spain; Project Coordinator Dept of Macroeconomy and Devt, Nat. Foundation for Devt (FUNDE) 2001–04, Programme Coordinator for Employment and Growth 2006–10, for Financing for Devt 2006–10; Adviser to Dir of Econ. and Fiscal Policy, Ministry of Finance 2010–14, Dir of Econ. and Fiscal Policy 2014–18; Minister of Finance 2018–. *Address:* Ministry of Finance, Blvd Los Héroes 1231, San Salvador, El Salvador (office). *Telephone:* 2244-3000 (office). *Fax:* 2244-6408 (office). *E-mail:* info@mh.gob.sv (office). *Website:* www.mh.gob.sv (office).

FUGARD, Athol, OIS; South African actor, playwright and academic; b. (Harold Athol Lanigan Fugard), 11 June 1932, Middelburg; s. of Harold David Fugard and Elizabeth Magdelene Potgiefer; m. Sheila Fugard 1956 (divorced); one d.; Co-f. The Circle Players 1956; worked as stage man., Nat. Theatre Org.; f. Serpent Players theatre co. 1960s; leading role in Meetings with Remarkable Men (film) 1977, The Guest (BBC production) 1977; acted in and wrote script for Marigolds in August (film); fmr Adjunct Prof. of Playwriting, Acting and Directing, Univ. of California, San Diego; Hon. DFA (Yale Univ.) 1973, Dr hc (Wittenberg Univ.) 1992, (Univ. of the Witwatersrand) 1993, (Brown Univ.) 1995, (Princeton Univ.) 1998, (Univ. of Stellenbosch) 2006, (Univ. of Cape Town, Georgetown Univ., New York Univ., Univ. of Pennsylvania, CUNY); Hon. DLit (Natal and Rhodes); winner Silver Bear Award, Berlin Film Festival 1980, Commonwealth Award for Contrib. to American Theatre 1984, Tony Award for Lifetime Achievement 2018. *Plays:* The Blood Knot, Hello and Goodbye, People are Living Here, Boesman and Lena 1970, Sizwe Banzi is Dead 1973, The Island 1973, Statements After an Arrest Under the Immorality Act 1974, No Good Friday 1974, Nongogo 1974, Dimetos 1976, The Road to Mecca 1984, My Children, My Africa, The Guest (film script) 1977, A Lesson from Aloes (author and dir Broadway production 1980) (New York Critics Award 1981) 1979, Master Harold and the Boys 1981 (London Evening Standard Award 1983), A Place with the Pigs (actor and dir) 1988, Playland 1992, Sign of Hope 1992, Valley Song (actor and dir) 1996, The Captain's Tiger 1999, Sorrows and Rejoicings 2001, Exits and Entrances 2004, Victory 2007, Coming Home 2009, The Train Driver 2010, The Shadow of the Hummingbird 2014, The Painted Rocks at Revolver Creek 2016. *Films include:* acted in films: Boesman and Lena 1973, Meetings with Remarkable Men 1979, Marigolds in August 1981, Gandhi 1982, The Guest 1984, The Killing Fields 1984, Road to Mecca 1991 (also co-dir). *Publications:* Notebooks 1960–77, Playland 1992; novel: Tsotsi 1980; plays: Road to Mecca 1985, A Place with the Pigs 1988, Cousins: A Memoir 1994. *Address:* c/o ICM Partners, 65 E 55th Street, New York, NY 10022, USA (office). *Website:* www.icmpartners.com (office).

FUJIMORI, Alberto Kenyo; Peruvian/Japanese fmr head of state and academic; b. 28 July 1938, Lima; s. of Nagochi Minami and Matsue Inomoto; m. 1st Susana Higushi (divorced 1996); two s. two d.; m. 2nd Satomi Kataoka 2006; ed Nat. School of Agric., Univ. of Wisconsin; fmr Rector, Nat. Agrarian Univ.; Pres. Nat. Ass. of Rectors 1984–89; Founder-mem. Cambio '90 (political party); Pres. of Peru 1990–2000; in exile in Japan Nov. 2000–05; arrested and charged in connection with state-sponsored murders, torture of a journalist, and embezzlement of public funds and dereliction of duty Sept. 2001, Peruvian Govt submitted 700-page document to back its charges 2003, Japanese Govt seeking further evidence in connection with Peruvian Govt's extradition request 2004; returned to Chile and arrested Nov. 2005; sentenced to six years in prison for abuse of power Dec. 2007; sentenced to 25 years in prison for ordering crimes against humanity during his presidency April 2009; Dr hc (Glebloux, Belgium, San Martín de Porres, Lima).

FUJIMORI, Fumio; Japanese business executive; joined Aisin Seiki Co. Ltd 1971, Exec. Vice-Pres. and Dir of First Devt 2005–09, Pres. and Rep. Dir 2009–15, Vice-Chair. 2015–16; Dir Exedy Corpn, ADVICS Co. Ltd, Aisin AW Co. Ltd, Aisin Chemical Co. Ltd.

FUJIMORI, Keiko Sofia Higuchi, MBA; Peruvian lawyer and politician; b. 25 May 1975; d. of Alberto Fujimori (fmr Pres. of Peru) and Susana Higuchi; m. Mark Villanella 2004; two c.; ed Stony Brook Univ., Boston Univ. School of Man., Columbia Univ. Business School, USA; served as First Lady of Peru during presidency of her father 1994–2000; Pres. Fundación por los Niños del Perú 1994–2000; mem. Congress for Lima constituency 2006–11; Pres. Fuerza Popular 2010–; unsuccessful cand. in 2011 presidential election and in 2016 presidential election. *Address:* Fuerza Popular, Paseo Colón 422, Cercado de Lima, Lima, Peru (office). *Telephone:* 999383300 (mobile) (office). *E-mail:* contacto@fuerza2011.com (office). *Website:* www.fuerzapopular.pe (office).

FUJIMOTO, James G., SB, SM, PhD; American electrical engineer and academic; *Elihu Thomson Professor of Electrical Engineering and Computer Science, Massachusetts Institute of Technology;* b. 1957, Chicago, Ill.; ed Massachusetts Inst. of Tech.; mem. Faculty, MIT 1985–, Prin. Investigator, Research Lab. of Electronics and Dept of Electrical Eng and Computer Science, currently Elihu Thomson Prof. of Electrical Eng and Computer Science; Adjunct Prof. of Ophthalmology, Tufts Univ. School of Medicine; Co-Chair. SPIE Biomedical Optics Symposium 2003–; Co-founder, Advanced Ophthalmic Devices, LightLabs Imaging; mem. Bd of Dirs Optical Soc. of America 2000–03; Fellow, NAS, Nat. Acad. of Eng, AAAS, Optical Soc. of America; Dr hc (Nicolaus Copernicus Univ., Poland) 2015; Presidential Young Investigator Award 1985, NAS Baker Award for Initiative in Research 1990, Discover Magazine Award for Technological Innovation 1999, Rank Prize in Optoelectronics (co-recipient) 2001, Hounsfield Lecturer, Imperial Coll. London 2009, Zeiss Research Award 2011, Champalimaud Vision Award (co-recipient) 2012, SPIE Britton Chance Biomedical Optics Award 2013, Frederic Ives Medal/Quinn Prize, Optical Soc. of America 2015. *Publications:* author or editor of nine books; more than 400 papers in professional journals on biomedical imaging, optical coherence tomography, advanced laser technologies and applications in ophthalmology, endoscopy, cancer detection, surgical guidance and developmental biology; numerous US patents. *Address:* Room 36-361, Massachusetts Institute of Technology, 77 Massachusetts Avenue, Cambridge, MA 02139, USA (office). *Telephone:* (617) 253-8528 (office). *E-mail:* jgfuji@mit.edu (office). *Website:* www.rle.mit.edu/people/directory/james-fujimoto (office); www.rle.mit.edu/boib (office).

FUJISHIMA, Akira, PhD; Japanese chemist, academic and university administrator; *President, Tokyo University of Science;* b. 10 March 1942; ed Yokohama Nat. Univ., Univ. of Tokyo; Lecturer, Kanagawa Univ. 1971, Asst Prof. 1973; Lecturer, Univ. of Tokyo 1975; Postdoctoral Fellow, Univ. of Texas 1976–77; Assoc. Prof., Univ. of Tokyo 1978, Prof. 1986, Prof. Grad. School 1994–2003, Prof. Emer. 2003–, Special Univ. Prof. Emer. 2005–; Chair. Kanagawa Acad. of Science and Tech. 2003; Pres. Chemical Soc. of Japan 2006; Pres. Tokyo Univ. of Science 2010–; Pres. Electrochemical Soc. of Japan 2003; advisory mem. Japanese Photochemistry Asscn; mem. Academia Europaea 2009–; Dr hc (Univ. of Turin) 2012; Asahi Prize 1983, Inoue Harunari Prize 1998, Chemical Soc. of Japan Prize 2000, Japan Prize (jtly) 2004, The Japan Academy Prize 2004, Nat. Commendation for Invention Award 2006, Kanagawa Culture Award 2006. *Address:* Office of the President, Tokyo University of Science, 1-3, Kagurazaka, Shinjuku-ku, Tokyo 162-8601, Japan (office). *Telephone:* (3) 5228-7413 (office). *E-mail:* koho@admin.tus.ac.jp (office). *Website:* www.sut.ac.jp/en/info/president (office).

FUJITA, Hiroyuki, PhD; Japanese scientist (retd) and academic; b. 13 Dec. 1952, Tokyo; s. of Shigeru Fujita and Tokiko Fujita; m. Yumiko Kato 1982; ed Univ. of Tokyo; Lecturer, Inst. of Industrial Science, Univ. of Tokyo 1980–81, Assoc. Prof. 1981–93, Prof., Fujita Lab. 1993; Visiting Scientist, Francis Bitter Nat. Magnet Lab., MIT, USA 1983–85; M. Hetényi Award for Experimental Mechanics 1987. *Publications:* contribs to books and numerous scientific papers in professional journals. *Leisure interests:* reading, skiing, tennis. *Address:* c/o Fujita Laboratory, Room No. Ew304, 4-6-1 Komaba, Meguro-ku, Tokyo 153-8505 (office); 1-9-14 Senkawa, Toshima-ku, Tokyo 171, Japan (home).

FUJITA, Makoto, BS, MS, PhD; Japanese chemist; *Professor, Department of Applied Chemistry, University of Tokyo;* b. 28 Sept. 1957; ed Chiba Univ., Tokyo Inst. of Tech.; Research Fellow, Sagami Chemical Research Centre 1982–87; Asst Prof., Faculty of Eng, Chiba Univ. 1988–91, Lecturer 1991–94, Assoc. Prof. 1994–97, Assoc. Prof., Inst. of Molecular Science 1997–99; Prof., Grad. School of Eng, Nagoya Univ. 1999–2002; Prof., Dept of Applied Chemistry, Univ. of Tokyo 2002–; Visiting Prof., Div. of Advanced Materials Science, Pohang Univ. of Science and Tech. 2012–13; Medal with Purple Ribbon (Govt of Japan) 2014; Tokyo Techno Forum 21 Gold Medal 2001, Japan IBM Award 2001, Nagoya Silver Medal 2003, Izatt-Christensen Award 2004, Japan Soc. of Coordination Chemistry (JSCC) Award 2010, Chemical Soc. of Japan Award 2013, Int. Soc. for Nanoscale Science, Computation, and Eng (ISNSCE) Nanoprize 2014, Fred Basolo Medal (Northwestern Univ.) 2014, Wolf Prize in Chemistry (with Omar Yaghi) 2018. *Address:* The Fujita Laboratory, University of Tokyo Department of Applied Chemistry, School of Engineering, 7-3-1, Hongo, Bunkyo-ku, Tokyo 113-8656, Japan (office). *Website:* fujitalab.t.u-tokyo.ac.jp (office).

FUJITA, Yuzuru; Japanese insurance industry executive; b. 24 Nov. 1941; joined Asahi Mutual Life Insurance Co. 1964, named Dir 1992, Man. Dir 1994–96, Pres. and Rep. Dir 1996–2008, Chair. 2008, now Sr Adviser; mem. Bd of Dirs and Auditor, Furukawa Electric Co., Ltd; Auditor, Zeon Corpn; outside statutory auditor, Yokohama Rubber Co., Ltd 2000–; Chair. Japan Nat. Cttee for UWCs.

FUKAYA, Koichi; Japanese automotive parts executive; joined DENSO Corpn 1966, becoming Gen. Man., Production Eng and Research and Devt Depts, later Pres. DENSO Manufacturing Michigan Inc., Man. Dir Thermal Systems Product Group, mem. Bd of Dirs DENSO Corpn 1995–2013, Sr Man. Dir, Production Promotion Centre 2002–03, Pres. and CEO DENSO Corpn 2003–08, Vice-Chair. 2008–09, Chair. 2009–13 (retd); fmr Corp. Auditor, Toyota Boshoku Corpn; mem. Bd of Dirs Brother Industries Ltd 2012–; mem. Bd ADVICS Co.; mem. Bd of Govs. Nippon Hoso Kyokai; mem. Audit and Supervisory Bd JTEKT Corpn, also Corp. Auditor.

FUKSAS, Massimiliano; Italian architect; b. 9 Jan. 1944, Rome; ed Univ. 'La Sapienza', Rome; teaching and research activities, Inst. of History of Architecture, Faculty of Architecture, Univ. 'La Sapienza', Rome; est. architecture practice, Rome 1967, Paris, France 1989, Vienna, Austria 1993; Consultant Architect, Town Planning Advisory Council, Berlin, Germany 1994–97, Planning Council, Salzburg, Austria 1994–97; Adviser, Admin Bd, Institut Français d'Architecture 1997–; writes architecture column of weekly publ. L'Espresso 2000–; Visiting Prof., Staatliche Akad. der Bildenden Kunste, Stuttgart, Germany 1988, Ecole Spéciale d'Architecture, Paris 1990, Columbia Univ., New York, USA 1990–91, Institut für Entwerten und Architektur, Hanover, Germany 1993, Akad. der Bildenden Kunste, Vienna 1995–97; mem. Accademico Nazionale di San Luca 2000; Hon. Fellow, American Inst. of Architects 2002; Hon. mem. RIBA 2006; Commandeur, Ordre des Arts et Lettres (France) 2000; numerous awards including Vitruvio a la Trayectoria, Buenos Aires 1998, Grand Prix d'Architecture Française 1999, Golden Cube Architecture Prize, Naples 2007, Ignazio Silone Int. Prize for Culture 2011. *Projects include:* Chamber of Commerce and Industry of Nîmes-Uzès-Le Vigan, Nîmes, France 1991, redevt of areas along bank of Seine, Clichy-la-Garenne, France 1991, renovation of Luth area, Gennevilliers, France 1991, Ecole Nat. Superieure de Mecanique et Aeronautique Futuroscope, Poitiers, France 1991, renovation of Allones town centre, France 1991, urban renovation, Port-de-Bouc, Marseille, France 1991, A tower on 11 towers, Frankfurt, Germany 1991, Ecole Nat. d'Ingenieurs and Institut Scientifique, Brest, France 1991–92, Saint-Exupéry Coll., Noisy-le-Grand, France 1991–93, renovation of old harbour area, Nagasaki, Japan 1993, European Inst. of Interior Design and Architecture, students' housing, Rouen, France 1991–93, Lu Jiazui, Int. Trade Centre, Pudong, China 1991, RIVP devt, Paris 1991–96, Faculty of Law and Econs, Limoges, France 1991–96, restoration and extension of Hotel Dieu, Chartres, France 1991–96, redevt of Domaine Bâti du Petit Arbois, Europole Méditerranéenne Programme, Aix-Les-Milles, France 1992, ZAC Berges-de-Seine, new quarter 'Cables de Lyon', Clichy, France 1992, renovation of Town Hall area, Limoges 1992, Centre Ville Univ., Brest 1992–94, renovation of Cité des Aigues Douces, Marseille 1992–95, residential complex, Clichy-la-Garenne 1992–96, Maison des Arts, exhbn centre, Bordeaux Univ., France 1992–95, masterplan of Tremblay in airport section of Roissy-Charles de Gaulle, Paris 1993–2001, Europark shopping centre, Salzburg 1994–97, Place des Nations, Geneva, Switzerland 1995, Maximilien Perret Coll., Alfortville, Paris 1995–98, Twin Tower, HQ for Wienerberger, Vienna 1995–2001, students and professors' housing, Alfortville, Paris (jtly with D. Mandrelli) 1997–98, Ilot Cantagrel, Paris XIII 1997–2000, harbour and urban rearrangement, Castellammare di Stabia, Italy 1998, Tuscolo Museum, Frascati, Rome 1998–2000, office bldg Hanse-Forum, Axel Springer Platz, Hamburg, Germany 1998–2002, residential and office complex, Alsterfleet, Hamburg 1998–2002, new commercial pavilion, Porta Palazzo, Turin 1998–2004, Peres Peace Centre, Jaffa, Israel 1998–2004, Piazza Mall complex, Eindhoven, Netherlands 1999–2004, Italia Congress and exhbn centre, Roma-Eur, Rome 1999–2003, residential centre, Brachmule, Vienna 2000, houses and commercial area, Rimini 2000–02, HQ Italian Space Agency (ASI), Rome 2000–07, devt of integrated cultural dist at West Kowloon Reclamation, Hong Kong 2001, Queensland Gallery of Modern Art, Brisbane, Australia 2001, devt of Water Front, Hong Kong West 2001, new HQ for Piedmont Region, Turin 2001–05, Emporio Armani Showroom, Hong Kong 2001–02, Europark Insein, Salzburg 2001–05, new HQ for Ferrari SpA, Maranello, Italy 2001–04, new Trade Fair Centre, Pero-Rho Milan 2002–05, inner city devt, Prague, Czech Repub. 2002, Canal+, Louveciennes, Paris 2002, new HQ for Bortolo Nardini Co., Bassano del Grappa, Vicenza, Italy 2002–04, MAB Zeil, Frankfurt, Germany 2002–06, exhbn centre, Rho-Pero, Milan 2002–05, new HQ for Miroglio-Vestebene, Alba, Italy 2003, Concert Hall Zenith, Amiens, France 2003–05, concept store for Palmers, Austria 2003, opera house, Astana, Kazakhstan 2003, Emporio Armani Showroom, Shanghai, China 2004, Sankei Bldg, Osaka, Japan 2004, exhbn complex for new capital of Kazakhstan, Astana 2004–06, tourist port, Marina di Stabia 2004, new HQ for FATER SpA, Pescara, Italy 2004, regeneration of Salford, UK 2005, tourist port at Margonara, Albissola, Savona, Italy 2005, African Inst. of Science and Tech., Abuja, Nigeria 2006, Montecatini Thermal Spa Devt, Italy 2007, Fujeirah Islands Masterplan, UAE 2007, New Silk Road Park, Xi'an, China 2007, Shenzhen Int. Airport, China 2008, Residential Complex Duca d'Aosta, Brescia, Italy 2009, Lyon Islands - Housing, France 2010, Palatino Centre Shopping Mall 2011, Tbilisi Public Service Hall, Georgia 2012, New Nat. Archives of France, Paris 2013, Bory Mall Shopping Center, Slovakia 2014. *Address:* Massimiliano Fuksas architetto, Piazza del Monte di Pietà 30, 00186 Rome, Italy (office). *Telephone:* (06) 68807871 (office). *Fax:* (06) 68807872 (office). *E-mail:* office@fuksas.it (office). *Website:* www.fuksas.it (office).

FUKUDA, Yasuo; Japanese politician; b. 16 July 1936, Tokyo; s. of Takeo Fukuda (fmr Prime Minister of Japan); m. Kiyoko Fukuda; two s. one d.; ed Waseda Univ.; with Maruzen Oil (now Cosmo Oil) petroleum refining and marketing co. 1959–76; Chief Sec. to Prime Minister Takeo Fukuda (father) 1977–78, Pvt. Sec. 1979–89; Dir Kinzai Inst. for Financial Affairs 1978–89; mem. LDP, Pres. 2007–08; mem. House of Reps for Gunma 4th Dist 1996–2012; Parl. Vice-Minister of Foreign Affairs 1995–96; Minister of State, Chief Cabinet Sec., Dir-Gen. Okinawa Devt Agency 2000–01; Chief Cabinet Sec. (Gender Equality) and Minister of State 2001–04 (resgnd); Deputy Sec.-Gen. LDP 1997–98, Chair. Finance Cttee 1998, Dir-Gen. Treasury Bureau 1999–2000, Deputy Chair. Policy Research Council 2000–, Prime Minister 2007–08 (resgnd); Grand Order of Queen Jelena with the Sash and the Croatian Morning Star (Croatia) 2008.

FUKUDA, Yoshitaka; Japanese business executive; *President, CEO and Representative Director, Aiful Corporation;* b. 1948; m.; three c.; est. sole proprietorship as consumer finance co. 1967; est. Marutaka Inc. 1978, absorbed three related cos and changed name to Aiful Corpn 1982, currently Pres., CEO and Rep. Dir. *Address:* Aiful Corporation, 381-1 Takasago-cho, Gojo-agaru, Karasuma-Dori, Shimogyo-kyu, Kyoto 600-8420, Japan (office). *Telephone:* (75) 201-2000 (office). *Website:* www.ir-aiful.com (office).

FUKUI, Takeo, BS; Japanese automotive industry executive; *Adviser, Honda Motor Company;* b. 28 Nov. 1944, Tokyo; ed Waseda Univ.; joined Honda Motor Co. 1969, engineer 1969–79, Chief Engineer, Honda R&D Co. 1979–82, Chief Engineer, Honda Racing Corpn 1982–83, Dir 1983–85, Exec. Vice-Pres. 1985–87, Pres. 1987–88, Dir 1988–90, Gen. Man. Motorcycle Devt 1991–92, Gen. Man. Motorcycle Operations, Hamamatsu Factory 1992–94, Exec. Vice-Pres. and Dir Honda of America Manufacturing Inc., Ohio, USA 1994–96, Man. Dir 1996–98, Sr Man. and Rep. Dir 1999–2003, Pres. and CEO 2003–09, Adviser 2009–. *Address:* Honda Motor Company, 2-1-1 Minami-Aoyama, Minato-ku, Tokyo 107-8556, Japan (office). *Telephone:* (3) 3423-1111 (office). *Fax:* (3) 5412-1515 (office). *E-mail:* info@honda.com (office). *Website:* www.honda.co.jp (office); world.honda.com (office).

FUKUI, Toshihiko; Japanese central banker (retd); b. 7 Sept. 1935, Osaka; ed Univ. of Tokyo; joined Bank of Japan 1958, Rep. in Paris 1970–77, Dir, Head of Planning Div., Coordination and Planning Dept 1977–80, Gen. Man. Takamatsu Br. 1980–81, Deputy Gen. Man. Osaka Br. 1981–83, First Deputy Dir-Gen. Personnel Dept 1984–85, Dir-Gen. Research and Statistics Dept 1985–86, Dir-

Gen. Banking Dept 1986–89, Dir-Gen. Policy Planning Dept 1989, Exec. Dir 1989–94, Deputy Gov. 1994–98, Gov. 2003–08 (retd); Chair. Fujitso Research Inst. 1998–2002; Vice-Chair. Japan Asscn of Corp. Execs (Keizai Doyukai) 2001–03.

FUKUJIN, Kunio; Japanese business executive; b. March 1944; Rep. Dir, Chair. and Pres. Alfresa Corpn –2009, apptd Rep. Dir and Chair. 2009, fmr Rep. Dir, Pres. and CEO Alfresa Holdings Corpn, later Chair., Hon. Chair. –2016, mem. Bd of Dirs –2016.

FUKUKAWA, Shinji; Japanese business executive; b. 8 March 1932, Tokyo; s. of Tokushiro Fukukawa and Maki Fukukawa; m. Yoriko Kawada 1961; two d.; ed Univ. of Tokyo; served at Ministry of Int. Trade and Industry (MITI) 1955–88, Deputy Vice-Minister 1983–84, Dir-Gen. Industrial Policy Bureau 1984–86, Vice-Minister 1986–88; Pvt. Sec. to fmr Prime Minister Ohira 1978–80; Sr Adviser to MITI 1988–90, to Japan Industrial Policy Research Inst. 1988–90, to Global Industrial and Social Progress Research Inst. 1988–, to Nomura Research Inst. 1989–90; Exec. Vice-Pres. Kobe Steel Ltd 1990–94; CEO Dentsu Inst. for Human Studies 1994–2002, Exec. Adviser, Dentsu Inc. 2002–04; Adviser, Global Industrial and Social Progress Research Inst., NHK International, Inc.; Chair. TEPIA (Machine Industry Memorial Foundation). *Publications:* Japan's Role in the 21st Century: Three Newisms 1990, Industrial Policy 1998, The Thinking of Successful Businessmen in the IT Age 2000, A Warning to Japan 2003. *Leisure interests:* tennis, golf, classical music, reading. *Address:* 7-11, Okusawa 8-chome, Setagaya-ku, Tokyo 158-0083, Japan (home). *Telephone:* (3) 3701-4956 (home). *Fax:* (3) 3701-4956 (home).

FUKUSHIMA, Mizuho, LLB; Japanese lawyer and politician; *Deputy Head, Social Democratic Party of Japan;* b. 24 Dec. 1955, Nobeoka, Miyazaki Pref.; one d.; ed Univ. of Tokyo; called to the Bar 1987; fmr commentator on weekly TV show; entered politics 1998, mem. House of Councillors 1998–, mem. Cttee on Health, Welfare and Labour, Cttee on the Budget, Comm. on the Constitution, Research Cttee on Society of Cooperative Way of Life and Regional Vitalization; mem. Social Democratic Party, Sec.-Gen. 2001–03, Chair. 2003–13, Deputy Leader 2013–; Minister of State for Consumer Affairs and Food Safety, Social Affairs and Gender Equality 2009–10; Vice-Chair. Socialist Int.; Visiting Prof., Gakushuin Women's Coll. *Address:* Social Democratic Party of Japan, 2-4-3-7F, Nagata-cho, Chiyoda-ku, Tokyo 100-0014 (office); Member's Office Building, House of Councillors, 2-1-1, Nagata-cho, Chiyoda-ku, Tokyo 100-8962, Japan (office). *Telephone:* (3) 5253-2111 (office). *E-mail:* kokusai@sdp.or.jp (office). *Website:* www.cao.go.jp (office); www.mizuhoto.org (office); www.sdp.or.jp (office).

FUKUYAMA, Francis, (Frank), PhD; American political scientist, writer and academic; *Director, Center on Democracy, Development, and the Rule of Law, Stanford University;* b. 27 Oct. 1952, Chicago, Ill.; s. of Yoshio Fukuyama and Toshiko Fukuyama (née Kawata); m. Laura Holmgren; three c.; ed Cornell and Harvard Univs; fmrly Sr Social Scientist, RAND Corpn, Washington, DC 1979–80, 1983–89, 1995–96; Deputy Dir US State Dept's Policy Planning Staff 1981–82, 1989; Hirst Prof. of Public Policy, George Mason Univ., Fairfax 1996–2001; Bernard L. Schwartz Prof. of Int. Political Economy, Paul H. Nitze School of Advanced Int. Studies, Johns Hopkins Univ. 2001–10; Olivier Nomellini Sr Fellow, Freeman Spogli Inst. for Int. Studies, Stanford Univ. 2010–, Dir Center on Democracy, Devt, and the Rule of Law; Chair. Editorial Bd The American Interest (magazine); mem. Bd of Govs, Pardee Rand Grad. School; mem. Pres.'s Council on Bioethics 2001–04; mem. Advisory Bd, Journal of Democracy; mem. American Political Science Asscn, Council on Foreign Relations; mem. US del. to Egyptian-Israeli talks on Palestinian autonomy 1981–82; Dr hc (Connecticut Coll.), (Doane Coll.), (Doshisha Univ., Japan), (Kansai Univ., Japan), (Århus Univ., Denmark), (Rand Grad. School); Los Angeles Times Book Award, Democracy Service Medal, Founders Award, Skytte Prize in Political Science. *Publications include:* The End of History and the Last Man 1992, Trust: The Social Virtues and the Creation of Prosperity 1996, The Great Disruption: Human Nature and the Reconstitution of the Social Order 1999, Our Posthuman Future 2002, State-Building: Governance and World Order in the 21st Century 2004, Nation-Building: Beyond Afghanistan and Iraq (ed.) 2005, America at the Crossroads: Democracy, Power, and the Neoconservative Legacy 2006, Falling Behind: Explaining the Development Gap between Latin American and the US 2008, The Origins of Political Order 2011, Political Order and Political Decay: From the Industrial Revolution to the Globalization of Democracy 2014. *Address:* Freeman Spogli Institute for International Studies, Encina Hall, 616 Serra Street, Stanford, CA 94305-6055, USA (office). *Telephone:* (650) 723-3214 (office). *Fax:* (650) 725-2592 (office). *E-mail:* f.fukuyama@stanford.edu (office). *Website:* cddrl.fsi.stanford.edu (office); www.francisfukuyama.com.

FULD, Richard (Dick) S., Jr, BA, BS, MBA; American investment banking executive; b. 26 April 1946; ed Univ. of Colorado, New York Univ. Stern School of Business; joined Lehman Brothers 1969, various man. positions, including Dir Lehman Brothers Inc. 1984–2008, Vice-Chair. Shearson Lehman Brothers Inc. 1984–90, Pres. and Co-CEO 1990–93, Dir Lehman Brothers Holdings Inc. 1990–2008 (after Chapter 11 filing by Lehman Brothers and acquisition by Barclays Capital); Pres. and COO 1993–94, CEO 1993–2008, Chair. 1994–2008, also Chair. Lehman Brothers Inc. 1994–2008; f. Matrix Advisors (consultancy) 2009; with Legend Securities, New York 2010–12; fmr mem. The Business Council, Exec. Cttee NY City Partnership, Univ. of Colorado Business Advisory Council; Trustee, Middlebury Coll., New York-Presbyterian Hosp.

FÜLE, Štefan; Czech diplomatist, politician and fmr EU official; b. 24 May 1962, Sokolov; m. Hana Füleová; one s. two d.; ed Charles Univ., Prague, Moscow State Inst. of Int. Relations, USSR, UN disarmament study programme; Desk Officer, UN Dept, Fed. Ministry of Foreign Affairs, Czechoslovakia 1987–90; First Sec., Mission of Czech Repub. to UN, New York 1990–95, mem. Del./Alt. Rep. to Security Council 1994–95; Dir UN Dept, Ministry of Foreign Affairs 1995–96, Security Policy Dept 1996–98; Amb. to Lithuania 1998–2001, NATO Point of Contact Amb. to Lithuania 2000–01; First Deputy Minister, Ministry of Defence 2001–02; Amb. to UK 2003–05; Amb. and Perm. Rep. to NATO and WEU, Brussels 2005–09; Minister for European Affairs May–Nov. 2009; Commr for Enlargement and European Neighbourhood Policy, EC, Brussels 2010–14; UN Disarmament Fellow 1988; Cross of Merit of Minister of Defence, Grade I 2001, Order of Grand Duke Gediminas, Third Class (Lithuania) 2002, Medal of Golden Lime Tree, Minister of Defence 2008.

FULFORD, Sir Adrian Bruce, QC; British barrister and judge; *Lord Justice of Appeal and Senior Presiding Judge for England and Wales;* b. 8 Jan. 1948; ed Elizabeth Coll., Guernsey, Univ. of Southampton; called to the Bar, Middle Temple, London 1978; apptd QC 1994; Recorder (Judge in Crown Court) 2001–; Judge, Queen's Bench Div. of High Court of England and Wales 2002–; Judge, Trial Div., Int. Criminal Court 2003–12; Lord Justice of Appeal 2013–, Sr Presiding Judge for England and Wales 2016–; Lecturer in Advocacy, Middle Temple 1994–; Lecturer to the Bar and Judiciary 1999–2001; mem. Cttee of Criminal Bar Asscn 1997–99, 2001–; Chair. Disciplinary Procedures for Bar Council 1997–; Housing Adviser, Shelter Housing Aid Centre 1975–77; Legal Adviser, N Lambeth Law Centre 1979–80; fmr Contrib. Ed., Archbold Criminal Pleading, Practice and Evidence, Atkins Court Forms; Hon. LLD (Univ. of Southampton) 2011. *Publications include:* A Criminal Practitioner's Guide to Judicial Review and Case Stated (co-author) 1999, United Kingdom Human Rights Reports (co-ed.) 2000–, Judicial Review: A Practical Guide (co-author) 2004; articles in professional journals and papers for Criminal Bar Asscn. *Address:* Judicial Office, 11th Floor, Thomas More Building, Royal Courts of Justice, Strand, London, WC2A 2LL, England. *Website:* www.judiciary.gov.uk (office).

FULLANI, Ardian; Albanian fmr central banker; b. 15 Jan. 1955, Tirana; ed Univ. of Tirana; began career at State Bank of Albania 1985, Deputy Dir Foreign Dept 1987–90; Head of Foreign Relations Dept, Albanian Commercial Bank 1990–92; Deputy Gov. Bank of Albania (Banka e Shqipërisë) 1992–93, Head of Foreign Relations Dept 1993–96, Gov. and Chair. Supervisory Council 2004–14; focused on consultancy in nat. and int. devt projects 1996–97; Deputy Gen. Man. and Head of Financial Dept, Italian-Albanian Bank 1997–2000, Gen. Man. 2000–04; also held positions including Pres. Albanian Asscn of Banks, Chair. Inst. of Banking Studies and Assistance, Commr Albanian Securities Comm.; acquitted in 2016 of theft of Bank of Albania funds; Commendatore dell'Ordine della Stella della solidarietà italiana 2007. *Publications include:* Growth in Albania and South East Europe: The Way Ahead 2013; numerous articles and scientific papers on economic and financial issues.

FULLER, H. Laurance (Larry), BS, JD; American lawyer and business executive (retd); b. 8 Nov. 1938, Moline, Ill.; m. Nancy Fuller 1961; one s. two d.; ed Cornell Univ., DePaul Univ.; Dir Amoco Corpn 1981–2000, Chair. and CEO 1991–2000, Co-Chair. BP Amoco 2000 (retd); mem. Bd of Dirs Security Capital Group Inc. 1991–, Cabot Microelectronics Corpn 2002–, Abbott Labs; fmr mem. Bd of Dirs JPMorgan Chase & Co., Motorola Inc., Catalyst, American Petroleum Inst., Rehabilitation Inst. of Chicago; Trustee, Orchestral Asscn, Cornell Univ.

FULLER, Kathryn S., BA, MS, JD; American attorney, international organization executive and environmentalist; *Chairman, Board of Directors, Ford Foundation;* b. 8 July 1946, New York; m. Stephen Paul Doyle 1977; two s. one d.; ed Brown Univ., Univs of Maryland and Texas; law clerk, New York, Houston and Austin, Tex. 1974–76, to Chief Justice John V. Singleton, Jr, US Dist Court, Southern Dist of Tex. 1976–77; called to Bar, DC and Tex.; attorney and adviser, Office of Legal Counsel, Dept of Justice, Washington, DC 1977–79, attorney, Wildlife and Marine Resources Section 1979–80, Chief Wildlife and Marine Resources Section 1981–82; Exec. Vice-Pres. and Dir TRAFFIC USA 1982–89; Pres. and CEO World Wildlife Fund US 1989–2005, now mem. Advisory Council; Chair. Ford Foundation 2004–10; currently Man. Partner, Doyle Property Partners LLC, Washington, DC; Chair. Advisory Bd National Museum of Natural History, Smithsonian Inst., Washington, DC; Public Policy Scholar, Woodrow Wilson Int. Center for Scholars 2005–06; mem. Bd of Dirs Alcoa Inc. (Compensation and Benefits Cttee, Governance and Nominating Cttee, Public Issues Cttee) 2002–, Robert Wood Johnson Foundation 2011–; mem. Council on Foreign Relations, Int. Council of Environmental Law, Overseas Devt Council; Trustee, Summit Foundation, Greater Himalayas Foundation; fmr Trustee, Brown Univ. Corpn; Hon. DSc (Wheaton Coll.) 1990; Hon. LLD (Knox Coll.) 1992; Hon. DHumLitt (Brown Univ.) 1992; William Rogers Outstanding Grad. Award, Brown Univ. 1990, UNEP Global 500 Award 1990. *Publications include:* numerous articles in journals. *Address:* Doyle Property Partners LLC, 3718 Morrison Street, NW, Washington, DC 20015-1734, USA (office). *Website:* www.mnh.si.edu.

FULLER, Simon; British music promoter, business executive and artist manager; b. 17 May 1960, Hastings, East Sussex; m. Natalie Swanston 2008; Founder and Dir 19 Group 1985–2005 (comprising 19 Brands, 19 Entertainment, 19 International Sports Management, 19 Management, 19 Merchandising, 19 Productions, 19 Recordings, 19 Songs, 19 Touring, 19 TV, Brilliant 19), sold to CFX 2005 (mem. Bd of Dirs 2005–); Founder, XIX Entertainment 2010–; current or fmr man. of numerous artists, including Annie Lennox, Emma Bunton, Will Young, Gareth Gates, Kelly Clarkson, Paul Hardcastle (1985), Madonna, Cathy Dennis, Spice Girls (–1997), 21st Century Girls and S Club 7 (later S Club, including TV series and S Club Juniors); dr hc (Univ. of Sussex) 2014; GQ Magazine Entrepreneur of the Year 2006, Music Managers Forum Peter Grant Award 2008, Producers Guild of America Visionary Award 2008, Anglo-American Cultural Award 2012. *Television includes:* creator of Popstars (ITV 1), Pop Idol (ITV 1), American Idol (series) 2002–16, So You Think You Can Dance (series) 2005–12, Popstars – The Rivals (ITV 1). *Address:* XIX Management, 9000 West Sunset Blvd., Penthouse, West Hollywood, CA 90069, USA (office); XIX Management, Unit 33, Ransomes Dock, 35–37 Parkgate Road, London, SW11 4NP, England (office). *Telephone:* (20) 7801-1919 (London) (office). *E-mail:* info@xixentertainment.com (office). *Website:* xixentertainment.com (office).

FULLERTON, William Hugh, CMG, MA; British diplomatist and consultant; b. 11 Feb. 1939, Wolverhampton; s. of Maj. A. H. T. F. Fullerton and M. Fullerton (née Parker); m. Arlene Jacobowitz 1968; one d.; ed Cheltenham Coll. and Queens' Coll., Cambridge; with Shell Int. Petroleum Co., Uganda 1963–65; joined Foreign Office 1965; with MECAS, Shemlan, Lebanon 1965–66; Information Officer, Jeddah 1966–67; at Perm. Mission to UN, New York 1967; with FCO 1968–70; Head of Chancery, High Comm., Jamaica (also accred to Haiti) 1970–73, Head of Chancery, Embassy in Ankara 1973–77; at FCO 1977–80; Counsellor, Embassy in Islamabad 1980–83, Consul-Gen. 1981–83; Amb. to Somalia 1983–87; on loan to Ministry of Defence 1987–88; Gov. Falkland Islands, Commr for South Georgia and South

Sandwich Islands 1988–92, concurrently High Commr, British Antarctic Territory 1988–89; Amb. to Kuwait 1992–96, to Morocco and Mauritania 1996–99; mem. advisory bd Intrinsic Value Investors (IVI) LLP; Trustee, Arab-British Centre, London 2002–12, Soc. for the Protection of Animals Abroad 2000–15, Lord Caradon Lecture Trust; mem. Nat. Trust, Campaign for the Protection of Rural England, World Wildlife Fund, RSPB; Kuwait Medallion (First Class) 1995, Alaouite Decoration (Morocco) 1999. *Leisure interests:* travelling in remote places, reading, sailing, music, the environment. *Address:* c/o Travellers' Club, 106 Pall Mall, London, SW1Y 5EP, England. *Telephone:* (20) 7832-1310 (office).

FULTON, Daniel (Dan) S., BA, MBA; American business executive; b. 1948; ed Miami Univ., Univ. of Washington, Stanford Univ.; fmr Officer, USN Supply Corps; mem. Investment Evaluation Dept, Weyerhaeuser Co. 1976–78, Planning Man. Weyerhaeuser Real Estate Co. 1978–79, Investment Man. Weyerhaeuser Venture Co. 1978–87, Chief Investment Officer Weyerhaeuser Realty Investors Inc. 1994–95, COO 1996–97, Pres. and CEO 1998–2000, Weyerhaeuser Real Estate Co. 2001–08, Pres. and CEO Weyerhaeuser Co. 2008–13, mem. Bd of Dirs 2008–13, Exec. Vice-Chair. Aug.-Oct. 2013; mem. Bd of Dirs TRI Pointe Group Inc. (also TRI Pointe Homes Inc.) 2014–, Saltchuk Resources Inc. 2014–, Sustainable Forestry Initiative Inc.; mem. Advisory Bd Univ. of Washington Business School, Policy Advisory Bd Jt Center of Housing with Harvard Univ.; mem. Bd of Govs. Lambda Alpha Int. Land Econs Soc., Nat. Asscn of Homebuilders.

FULTON, Lt Gen. Sir Robert, Kt, KBE; British Royal Marines officer and diplomatist; *CEO, Global Leadership Foundation;* b. 21 Dec. 1948, London, England; s. of James Fulton and Cynthia Fulton; m.; two s.; ed Eton Coll. and Univ. of East Anglia; joined Royal Marines 1972, has occupied several sr positions within the force, including Commdt-Gen. 1998–2001; moved to Ministry of Defence 2001, promoted to Lt-Gen. on appointment as Deputy Chief of Defence Staff (for Equipment Capability) 2003–06; Gov. and C-in-C of Gibraltar 2006–09; CEO Global Leadership Foundation 2010–. *Leisure interests:* sailing, cricket, rugby, golf, military history, theatre, music. *Address:* Global Leadership Foundation, 10 Brick Street, London, W1J 7HQ, England (office). *Telephone:* (20) 3457-1320 (office). *Fax:* (20) 7681-2263 (office). *E-mail:* secretariat@g-l-f.org (office). *Website:* www.g-l-f.org (office).

FUMAROLI, Marc, DèsL; French historian; *Honorary Chairman, Rhetoric and European Society of the 16th and 17th Centuries, Collège de France;* b. 10 June 1932, Marseille; ed Lycée Thiers Marseille, Univ. Aix-en-Provence, Univ. Sorbonne; Prof. Sorbonne, Paris 1976; Titular Prof., Chair of Rhetoric and European Soc. of 16th and 17th Centuries, Collège de France 1986–2002, now Hon. Chair.; Prof., Univ. of Chicago 1996–2006; Chair. Instituit européen d'histoire de la Republique de Lettres, Société d'Histoire litterature de la France 2001–; Dir XVIIe siècle (journal) 1981–88; mem. Advisory Council, Bibliothèque Nationale 1988–92; fmr Pres. Soc. Int. d'Histoire de la Rhétorique; Pres. Soc. of Friends of the Louvre 1996–; mem. Acad. Française 1995–, High Cttee of Nat. Celebrations 1998–; Corresp. mem. British Acad., mem. US Acad. of Sciences, Letters and Arts, Accad. dei Lincei; Officier, Légion d'honneur, Commdr, Ordre des Palmes académiques, Ordre nat. du Mérite, Cmmdr des Arts et des Lettres; Dr hc (Naples 1996, Bologna 1999, Madrid 2004); numerous other academic prizes; Balzan Prize 1995. *Publications include:* L'Age de l'éloquence 1980, Héros et Orateurs 1990, L'Etat Culturel: Une Religion Moderne 1991, La Diplomatie de l'esprit 1994, L'école du silence 1994, Trois institutions littéraires 1994, la Période 1600–1630 1994, Fables de Jean de la Fontaine (ed., Vol. I 1985, Vol. II 1995), Le Poète et le roi, Jean de La Fontaine et son siècle 1997, Poussin: Sainte Françoise Romaine 2001, Quand l'Europe parlait français 2001, Chateaubriand: Poésie et Terreur 2003, Exercises de lecture: De Rabelais à Valery 2006, De Rome à Paris: peinture et pouvoir aux XVIIe et XVIIIe siècles 2007, Paris-New York et retour. Voyage dans les arts et les images 2009, Le livre des métaphores 2012; numerous articles in professional journals; numerous pamphlets, essays and articles. *Leisure interest:* travel. *Address:* Collège de France, 11 place Marcelin Berthelot, 75231 Paris cedex 05 (office); 11 rue de l'Université, 75007 Paris, France (home). *Telephone:* 1-44-27-10-17 (office). *Fax:* 1-44-27-13-29 (office). *E-mail:* catherine.fabre@college-de-france.fr (office). *Website:* www.college-de-france.fr (office).

FUNADA, Hajime; Japanese politician; b. 22 Nov. 1953, Utsunomiya City, Tochigi Pref.; s. of Yuzuru Funada and Masako Funada; m. Rumi Funada 1978; one s. two d.; ed Keio Univ.; mem. House of Reps from Tochigi 1979–; Head, Youth Section of Nat. Organizing Cttee, LDP 1985–86; State Sec. for Man. and Co-ordination Agency 1986–87, for Ministry of Educ. 1987–88; Dir Educ. Div. of Policy Research Council, LDP 1988–89; Dir Foreign Affairs Div. 1990–92; Chair. Sub-Cttee of Counselling Japan Overseas Co-operation Volunteers 1989–90; Minister of State for Econ. Planning 1992–93; Co-Founder of Japan Renewal Party (Shinseito) 1993, Deputy Sec.-Gen. for Organizational Affairs 1993–94, Deputy Sec.-Gen. for Political Affairs 1994; Vice-Chair. Diet Man. Cttee, 'Reform' In-House Grouping (Kaikaku) 1994; Co-Founder New Frontier Party (Shinshinto) 1994, Vice-Chair. Org. Cttee 1994–95, Deputy Sec.-Gen. 1995, Assoc. Chair. Gen. Council 1995–96, resgnd from party 1996; Head of '21st Century' In-House Grouping (21seiki) 1996; rejoined Liberal Democratic Party 1997, Chair. Sub-Cttee on Asia and the Pacific, mem. Policy Deliberation Comm., mem. Gen. Council 1997–; mem. Ruling Parties Consultative Cttee on Guidelines for Japan–US Defence Co-operation 1997–; Dir Cttee on Health and Welfare, House of Reps 1998–. *Leisure interests:* astronomy, driving. *Address:* Shugiin Daini Giinkaikan, Room 412, 2-1-2 Nagata-cho, Chiyoda-ku, Tokyo 100, Japan. *Telephone:* (3) 3508-7412. *Fax:* (3) 3500-5612.

FUNAR, Gheorghe, PhD; Romanian politician; b. 29 Sept. 1949; m. Sabina Funar; one s.; ed Faculty of Econ. Science, Univ. of Cluj-Napoca; began career as agronomist, specializing in collective arm system; joined Party of Romanian Nat. Unity (PRNU) 1990, Leader 1992–97; Mayor of Cluj-Napoca 1992–2004; cand. in presidential elections 1992; Sec.-Gen. Greater Romanian Party (PRM–Partidul România Mare) 2000–13, Chair. 2013–15.

FUNDANGA, Caleb M., BA, MA, PhD; Zambian economist, international organization official and central banker; *Executive Director, Macro Economic and Financial Management Institute (MEFMI);* b. 28 Feb. 1953, Mufulira; s. of James Mailoni Fundanga and Alita Mutaya Fundanga; m. Rosario Chailunga Fundanga; one s. two d.; ed Univ. of Zambia, Univ. of Manchester, UK, Konstanz Univ., Germany; Lecturer in Econs, Univ. of Zambia 1985–87; served as Perm. Sec. wth Zambian Ministry of Econs and Finance; Exec. Dir ADB, Abidjan, Côte d'Ivoire, representing Lesotho, Malawi, Mauritius, South Africa, Swaziland and Zambia 1995–98, Sr Adviser to Pres. of ADB 1998–2002; Gov. and Chair. Bank of Zambia 2002–11, Alt. Gov., IMF 2002–11 (retd); Pres. Inst. for Finance and Econs 2011–; Exec. Dir Macro Economic and Financial Management Institute (MEFMI) for Eastern and Southern Africa 2014–; mem. Bd of Dirs Zambia Revenue Authority, Afreximbank; fmr Chair. COMESA Cttee of Cen. Bank Govs; fmr mem. Advisory Comm., African Econ. Research Consortium 2002, Chair. Programme Cttee 2005–; fmr Pres. World Univ. Service International; Cen. Banker of the Year (Global and Africa), The Banker magazine 2007, Cen. Banker of the Year (Africa), Emerging Markets Magazine 2007, Cen. Banker of the Year (Africa), Annual Meetings Daily 2008. *Publications:* as contrib.: The IMF, the World Bank and the African Debt: The Economic Impact 1979, Planners and History: Negotiating Development in Rural Zambia 1994, Economic Development and Democracy: Critical Issues in the Third Republic 1994, Domination or Dialogue?: Experiences and Prospects for African Development Cooperation 1996; articles for Southern Africa, Southern Review, Issues on the Zambian Economy. *Address:* Macro Economic and Financial Management Institute (MEFMI), Alexander Park, Harare, Zimbabwe (office). *Telephone:* (4) 745988 (office). *E-mail:* capacity@mefmi.org (office); cfundanga@gmail.zm (office). *Website:* www.mefmi.org (office).

FUNES CARTAGENA, Carlos Mauricio; Salvadorean broadcast journalist, politician and fmr head of state; b. 18 Oct. 1959, San Salvador; s. of Roberto and María Mirna Funes; m. Vanda Pignato; one s.; ed Colegio Externado San José, Universidad Centroamericana José Simeón Cañas; began career as TV reporter, Canal 10 1986; Dir of News, Canal 12 1987; 15 years as Corresp., CNN Español; selected as Frente Farabundo Martí para la Liberación Nacional (FMLN) presidential cand. 2007, Pres. of El Salvador 2009–14.

FUNG, Victor K(wok-king), CBE, BS, MS, PhD; American (b. Chinese) business executive and fmr international organization official; *Group Chairman, Fung Group;* b. 1945, Hong Kong; brother of William Fung; m. Julia Fung; three c.; ed Massachusetts Inst. of Tech., Harvard Business School, Harvard Univ., USA; Prof. of Finance, Harvard Business School 1972–76; joined Li & Fung 1973, Man. Dir 1981–89, Chair. 1989, currently Group Chair. Fung Group; Chair. Asia Advisory Bd Prudential Financial, Inc., Hong Kong Trade Devt Council 1991–2000, Hong Kong Airport Authority 1999–2008, Greater Pearl River Delta Business Council 2004–13, Hong Kong Univ. Council 2001–09, Airport Authority Hong Kong 1999–2008, Hong Kong-Japan Business Co-operation Cttee; Co-Chair. China Centre for Int. Econ. Exchanges; Vice-Chair. ICC 2007–08, Chair. 2008–10; mem. Bd of Dirs China Petrochemical Corpn, Bank of China Ltd, Chow Tai Fook Jewellery Group Ltd, Koc Holding AS; mem. Bd of Dirs Baosteel Group Corpn 2005–13; mem. Int. Business Leaders Advisory Council for Mayor of Beijing, Hong Kong Judicial Officers Recommendation Cttee –2006, Asian Business Advisory Council, CPPCC, Exec. Cttee of Hong Kong Govt Comm. on Strategic Devt of Hong Kong Special Admin. Region Govt, Advisory Bd of School of Econs and Man., Tsinghua Univ., WTO Panel on Defining the Future of Trade 2012–13; Hong Kong Rep. on APEC Business Advisory Council 1996–2003, Task Force on Econ. Challenges 2008–; Econ. Advisor to People's Govt of Nanjing; Hon. Trustee Peking Univ., Hon. Prof., Renmin Univ.; Hong Kong Businessman of the Year 1995, Top 25 Managers in BusinessWeek magazine 1995, Harvard Medal 2001, Gold Bauhinia Star 2003, Businessman of the Year, Forbes Asia magazine 2005, Grand Bauhinia Medal 2010, MIT Sloan Dean's Award for Excellence in Leadership 2011. *Address:* Li & Fung Group, Li Fung Tower, 888 Cheung Sha Wan Road, Kowloon, Hong Kong Special Administrative Region, People's Republic of China (office). *Website:* www.lifunggroup.com (office).

FUNKE, Cornelia Caroline; German children's writer; b. 1958, Dorsten, Westphalia; m. Rolf Funke (died 2006); one s. one d.; ed Hamburg Univ., Hamburg State Coll. of Design; worked as designer of board games, illustrator of children's books; began writing/illustrating full-time aged 28; also works for ZDF state TV channel; numerous awards including Wildweibchenpreis for collected works 2000, Roswitha Prize 2008. *Publications include:* Monstergeschichten 1993, Die Wilden Hühner 1993, Rittergeschichten 1994, Zwei wilde kleine Hexen 1994, Kein Keks für Kobolde 1994, Greta und Eule, Hundesitter 1995, Der Mondscheindrache 1996, Die Gespensterjäger auf eisiger Spur 1996, Die Wilden Hühner auf Klassenfahrt 1996, Hände weg von Mississippi 1997, Drachenreiter (trans. as Dragon Rider) (Kalbacher Klapperschlange 1998, Sakura Medal 2006) 1997, Prinzessin Isabella (trans. as The Princess Knight) 1997, Tiergeschichten 1997, Das verzauberte Klassenzimmer 1997, Die Wilden Hühner Fuchsalarm 1998, Dachbodengeschichten 1998, Potilla und der Mützendieb 1998, Dicke Freundinnen 1998, Igraine Ohnefurcht (trans. as Igraine the Brave) 1998, Strandgeschichten 1999, Das Piratenschwein (trans. as Pirate Girl) 1999, Herr der Diebe (trans. as The Thief Lord) (Swiss Youth Literature Award, Zurich Children's Book Award, Venice House of Literature Book Award, Kalbacher Klapperschlange 2001, Preis der Jury der jungen Leser 2001, Evangelischer Buchpreis 2002, Mildred L. Batchelder Award 2003) 2000, Lilli und Flosse 2000, Mick und Mo im Wilden Westen (trans. as Mick and Mo in the Wild West) 2000, Die Wilden Hühner und das Glück der Erde 2000, Kleiner Werwolf (Nordstemmer Zuckerrübe 2003) 2001, Als der Weihnachtsmann vom Himmel fiel 2001, Dicke Freundinnen und der Pferdedieb 2001, Die Gespensterjäger im Feuerspuk 2001, Die Gespensterjäger in der Gruselburg 2001, Die Gespensterjäger in grosser Gefahr 2001, Der geheimnisvolle Ritter Namenlos 2001, Die Wilden Hühner Bandenbuch 2001, Emma und der blaue Dschinn 2002, Die schönsten Erstlesegeschichten 2002, Die Glücksfee 2003, Hinter verzauberten Fenstern 2003, Käpten Knitterbart 2003, Tintenherz (trans. as Inkheart) (Phantastik-Preis der Stadt Wetzlar 2004, Kalbacher Klapperschlange 2004, Book Sense Children's Literature Award 2004) 2003, Kribbel Krabbel Käferwetter 2003, Der wildeste Bruder der Welt 2003, Der verlorene Wackelzahn 2003, Die Wilden Hühner und die Liebe 2003, Die Wilden Hühner Tagebuch 2004, Tintenblut (trans. as Inkspell) 2005, When Santa Fell to Earth 2006, Tintentod (trans. as Inkdeath) 2008, Reckless 2010, Saving Mississippi 2010, Reckless 2 2012, Ghost Night 2012, The New Girl 2012, Summer Gang 2012, Fearless 2013, Young Werewolf 2013, Sea Urchins and Sand Pigs 2014, The Moonhouse Dragon 2014, Heartless 2015, The Golden Yarn 2016. *Leisure interests:* reading, drawing, painting, knitting, travelling. *Address:* c/o Chicken House, 2 Palmer Street, Frome, Somerset, BA11 1DS, England (office); 9663 Santa

Monica Blvd, Beverly Hills, CA 90210, USA. *E-mail:* info@corneliafunke.com. *Website:* www.corneliafunke.com.

FURCHTGOTT-ROTH, Harold W., SB, PhD; American economist and fmr government official; *President, Furchtgott-Roth Economic Enterprises;* b. 13 Dec. 1956, Knoxville, Tenn.; s. of Ernest Furchtgott and Mary A. Wilkes Furchtgott; m. Diana E. Roth; five s. one d.; ed Massachusetts Inst. of Tech., Stanford Univ.; Research Analyst, Center for Naval Analyses, Alexandria, Va 1984–88; Sr Economist, Economists Inc., Washington, DC 1988–95; Chief Economist, US House Cttee on Commerce 1995–97; Commr, Fed. Communications Comm. 1997–2001; Visiting Fellow, American Enterprise Inst. 2001–03; Founder and Pres. Furchtgott-Roth Economic Enterprises 2003–; Co-founder and Chair. Oneida Broadband LLC 2005–; Founder and Dir Center for the Economics of the Internet; Sr Fellow, Hudson Inst.; Expert, Analysis Group (consultancy); mem. Bd of Dirs, MRV Communications Inc. 2005–09; mem. Washington Legal Foundation's Legal Policy Advisory Bd; mem. Advisory Bd Catalyst Investors. *Publications:* International Trade in Computer Software (co-author) 1993, Economics of a Disaster: The Exxon Valdez Oil Spill (co-author) 1995, Cable TV: Regulations or Competition (co-author) 1996, A Tough Act to Follow 2003, Telecommunications Act of 1996 2006. *Address:* Furchtgott-Roth Economic Enterprises, 1200 New Hampshire Avenue, NW, Suite 800, Washington, DC 20036 (office); 2705 Daniel Road, Chevy Chase, MD 20815, USA (home). *Telephone:* (202) 776-2032 (office); (301) 229-3593 (home). *E-mail:* hfr@furchtgott-roth.com (office). *Website:* www.furchtgott-roth.com (office).

FURLAN, Luiz Fernando, BEng; Brazilian business executive and government official; b. 1945; m. Ana Maria Gonçalves Furlan 1973; one s. one d.; ed São Paulo Univ., Univ. of Santana, INSEAD, France, Georgetown Univ., USA; joined Sadia SA (now Brasil Foods after merger with Perdigao 2009) 1976, mem. Bd 1978–2002, Exec. Vice-Pres. and Dir Investor Relations 1978–83, Chair. 1993–2002, 2008–09; Minister of Devt, Industry and Trade 2003–07; Chair. BRF Brasil Foods SA 2009–11; Co-Chair. BNDES 2003–07; Chair. Fundacao Amazonas Sustentavel FAS 2008–; Pres. Entrepreneurial Leaders Forum 2000–02; Pres. Brazilian Asscn of Open Cos 1991–94, Brazilian Asscn of Producers and Exporters of Chicken 1997–2001; fmr Pres. Mercosul European Business Forum; fmr Vice-Pres. Brazilian Foreign Trade Asscn; mem. Bd of Dirs Telefonica Brasil SA, Telefonica SA, AGCO Corpn; mem. Advisory Bd Panasonic, Walmart, McLarty & Assocs, ABERTIS Infraestructuras SA, Brasmotor SA, ABN-Amro Bank Brazil, Global Ocean Comm.; mem. Global Corp. Governance Forum, Nat. Council of Human Rights, Int. Council INSEAD, France; fmr mem. Brazil-USA Business Devt Council. *Address:* Fundacao Amazonas Sustentavel, Rua Álvaro Braga, 351, Park Ten November, Manaus AM 69055-660, Brazil. *Website:* fas-amazonas.org.

FURSE, Dame Clara Hedwig Frances, DBE, BSc, CIMgt; British/Canadian banking executive; *Chairman, HSBC UK;* b. 16 Sept. 1957, Jonquière, Québec, Canada; m. Richard Furse 1981; two s. one d.; ed schools in Colombia, Denmark and St James's School, West Malvern, London School of Econs; began career as broker, Heinold Commodities Ltd 1979; commodity broker, Philips & Drew 1983, Dir 1988, Exec. Dir 1992, Man. Dir UBS Philips & Drew (formed from merger with Union Bank of Switzerland; named changed to UBS following merger with Swiss Bank 1998) 1995–98, Global Head of Futures 1996–98; Deputy Chair. London Int. Financial Futures and Options Exchange (LIFFE) 1992–99 (mem. Bd 1992–99, Chair. Strategy Working Group 1994–95, Membership and Rules Cttee 1995–97, Finance Cttee 1998–99); Group Chief Exec. Crédit Lyonnais Rouse 1998–2000; Chief Exec. London Stock Exchange PLC 2001–09; mem. Financial Policy Cttee, HM Treasury 2013–; Chair. HSBC UK, Birmingham 2016–; mem. Bd of Dirs LCH.Clearnet SA, 2005–09; Euroclear PLC 2006–09, Fortis 2006–09, Legal & General Group PLC 2009–13, Nomura Holdings Inc. 2009–, Amadeus IT Holdings SA 2010–, Dept for Work and Pensions, UK 2011–; mem. Panel of Sr Advisers, Chatham House 2012–; mem. Shanghai Int. Financial Advisory Council 2006–09; mem. Advisory Council Prince's Trust; Trustee, RICS Foundation 2002–05. *Address:* c/o Financial Policy Committee, HM Treasury, 1 Horse Guards Road, London, SW1A 2HQ (office); HSBC UK, 2 Arena Central, Birmingham, England.

FURSENKO, Andrei Aleksandrovich, DrPhys; Russian scientist and politician; b. 17 July 1949, Leningrad (now St Petersburg); ed Leningrad State Univ.; Head of Lab., Deputy Dir for Scientific Research, Chief Scientific Researcher Moscow Ioffe Physico-Tech. Inst. 1971–91; Vice-Pres. Centre of Prospective Techs and Elaborations, St Petersburg 1991–93; Gen. Dir Regional Fund for Scientific Tech. Devt 1994–2001; Deputy Minister of Science, Industry and Technology 2001–03, First Deputy Minister 2002, Acting Minister 2003, Minister of Industry, Science and Technologies 2003–04, Minister of Educ. and Science 2004–12; Aide to the Pres. 2012; mem. Advisory Bd Graduate School of Man., St Petersburg State Univ.; mem. Bd of Trustees Russian Int. Affairs Council (RIAC).

FURSTENBERG, Hillel (Harry), BA, MSc, PhD; Israeli mathematician and academic; *Professor of Mathematics, Hebrew University of Jerusalem;* b. 29 Sept. 1935, Berlin, Germany; s. of Sally Furstenberg and Berta Grzyb; m. Rochelle Furstenberg; three s. two d.; ed Yeshiva and Princeton univs, USA; emigrated to USA as a child; began academic career at Univ. of Minnesota; moved to Israel 1965; Prof. of Math., Hebrew Univ. of Jerusalem 1965–; mem. Israel Acad. of Sciences and Humanities, NAS; Rothschild Prize 1978, Technion Harvey Prize 1993, Israel Prize 1993, Wolf Foundation Prize in Math. 2007. *Publications include:* Stationary Processes and Prediction Theory, Recurrence in Ergodic Theory and Combinatorial Number Theory, Ergodic Theory and Fractal Geometry. *Address:* Einstein Institute of Mathematics, Edmond J. Safra Campus, Givat Ram, The Hebrew University of Jerusalem, Jerusalem 91904 (office); 7 Alfasi Street, Jerusalem 92302, Israel (home). *Telephone:* 2-6584142 (office); 2-5617641 (home). *Fax:* 2-5630702 (office). *E-mail:* harry@math.huji.ac.il (office). *Website:* www.ma.huji.ac.il (office).

FURTH, Warren Wolfgang, AB, JD; American lawyer, consultant and international official (retd); b. 1 Aug. 1928, Vienna, Austria; s. of John W. Furth and Hedwig von Ferstel; m. Margaretha F. de la Court 1959; one s. one d.; ed Harvard Coll., Harvard Law School and Sloan School of Management, Massachusetts Inst. of Tech.; law clerk, Palmer, Dodge, Gardner, Bickford & Bradford, Boston, Mass 1951; admitted to New York Bar 1952; law clerk to Hon. H. M. Stephens, Chief Judge, US Court of Appeals, DC Circuit 1952–53; served in US Army 1953–57; Assoc. Cravath, Swaine & Moore (law firm) 1957–58; with ILO, Geneva 1959–70, Exec. Asst to Dir-Gen. 1964–66, Chief of Tech. Co-operation Branch and Deputy Chief, Field Dept 1966–68, Deputy Chief, later Chief, Personnel and Admin. Services Dept 1968–70; Asst Dir-Gen. WHO (Admin. Services; Co-ordinator, Special Programme for Research and Training in Tropical Diseases and responsibility for Special Programme for Research, Devt and Research Training in Human Reproduction) 1971–89; int. health consultant to US Govt, World Bank and pharmaceutical industry 1989–94; Assoc. Exec. Dir American Citizens Abroad 1994–2000; Chair. American Democrats Abroad, Switzerland 2001–03. *Address:* 13 route de Presinge, 1241 Puplinge (Geneva), Switzerland. *Telephone:* (22) 3497267. *Fax:* (22) 3493826. *E-mail:* wfurth@bluewin.ch.

FURUKAWA, Masaaki; Japanese business executive; b. 3 March 1940; joined Toyota Tsusho Corpn 1962, apptd Dir 1987, Man. Dir 1993–97, Sr Man. Dir 1997–99, Exec. Vice-Pres. 1999–2001, Pres. 2001–05, Chair. and Rep. Dir 2005–; Rep. Dir and Pres. Furukawa MFG Co. Ltd; Exec. Officer, Aderans Company Ltd –2015, Dir in charge of Overseas Business Group 2016–. *Address:* Aderans Company Ltd, Sumitomo Fudosan Yotsuya Building 6F, 7F, 13-4 Araki-cho, Shinjuku-ku, Tokyo 160-0007, Japan (office). *Website:* www.aderans.co.jp (office).

FUTAMIYA, Masaya, LLB; Japanese business executive; *Representative Director and Chairman, NKSJ Holdings Inc.;* b. 25 Feb. 1952; ed Chuo Univ.; joined Nippon Fire and Marine Insurance Co. Ltd (Nipponkoa Insurance Co. Ltd (Nipponkoa)) 1974, Gen. Man. Secr. Office 1998–2001, Gen. Man. Secr. Office of Nipponkoa 2001–02, Gen. Man. Chief Exec. Office and IR Office 2002–03, Exec. Officer and Gen. Man. Chief Exec. Office and IR Office 2003–04, Exec. Officer and Gen. Man. Chief Exec. Office and Customer Relationship Planning Dept April–June 2004, Man. Exec. Officer 2004–05, Dir and Man. Exec. 2005–09, Rep. Dir and Sr Man. Exec. Officer 2009–11, Rep. Dir, Pres. and CEO NKSJ Holdings, Inc. (following establishment of jt holding co. by Sompo Japan Insurance Inc. and Nipponkoa Insurance Co. Ltd 2010) 2011–12, Rep. Dir and Chair. 2012–, Exec. Officer 2012, Pres. 2014–16. *Address:* NKSJ Holdings Inc., 26-1, Nishi-Shinjuku 1-chome, Shinjuku-ku, Tokyo 160-8338, Japan (office). *Telephone:* (3) 3349-3111 (office). *Fax:* (3) 3349-4697 (office). *E-mail:* info@nksj-hd.com (office). *Website:* www.nksj-hd.com (office).

FUWA, Tetsuzo; Japanese politician; *President, Social Sciences Institute, Japanese Communist Party;* b. 26 Jan. 1930, Tokyo; ed Tokyo Univ.; mem. Secr. Fed. of Iron and Steel Workers' Union 1953; mem. Cen. Cttee, Japanese Community Party 1966–, Secr. Head 1970, Chair. Exec. Cttee 1982, Chair. Cen. Cttee 2000–06, Pres. Social Sciences Inst. *Publications include:* Stalin and the Great Power Chauvinism 1994, Interference and Betrayal 1994, Remaking Japan 1998, Nuclear Deception: Japan–USA Secret Agreements 2000, On Marx's Scientific View 2001, Re-reading Critique of the Gotha Programme: Marx and Engel's View of a Future Society 2003, Lenin's State and Revolution: A Critical Approach 2003, Asia, Africa and Latin America in the Present-Day World 2005, Seven Days in Tunisia 2005, Breaking Japan's Diplomatic Stalemate 2005, The 21st Century World and Socialism 2006, Japan's War: History of Expansionism 2006, Engels and The Capital 1997, Lenin and The Capital 1998, Five Days in Beijing—JCP-CPC Theoretical Discussion 2002, Marx and The Capital 2003, Invitation to Marx and Engels's Works 2008, Study on Theory of Revolution by Marx and Engels 2010. *Address:* Central Committee of the Japanese Communist Party, 4-36-7 Sendagaya, Shibuya-ku, Tokyo 151-8586, Japan (office). *Telephone:* (3) 3403-6111 (office). *E-mail:* info@jcp.or.jp (office). *Website:* www.jcp.or.jp (office).

FYODOROV, Nikolai Vasilievich, DrSci; Russian/Chuvash lawyer and politician; *Deputy Chairman, Federation Council;* b. 9 May 1958, Chuvash Repub.; m. Svetlana Fyodorova; one s. one d.; ed Kazan State Univ., Inst. of State and Law, USSR Acad. of Sciences; worked in legal bodies since 1983; teacher, Chuvash State Univ. 1980–82, 1985–89; USSR People's Deputy 1989–91; Deputy Chair. Legis. Comm. Supreme Soviet 1989–90; Minister of Justice of RSFSR (later Russia) 1990–93; Pres. Chuvash Repub. 1994–2010; Minister of Agriculture 2012–15; Presidential Counsellor April–Sept. 2015; Deputy Chair. Federation Council 2015–; mem. Council of Fed. 1996–2002; Order for Merits to Fatherland 1998, 2003; State Prize of Russia 1999. *Publications include:* more than 100 articles and several books on problems of democratic and federative structure of the state, freedom of mass media, independent judicial power and economic policy. *Leisure interests:* karate, swimming, skiing, water-skiing, chess. *Address:* Federation Council (Sovet Federatsii), 103426 Moscow, ul. B. Dmitrovka 26, Russia (office). *Telephone:* (495) 629-70-09 (office). *Fax:* (495) 629-67-43 (office). *E-mail:* post_sf@gov.ru (office). *Website:* www.council.gov.ru (office).

G

GABAGLIO, Emilio, BA (Econs); Italian trade union official; *Chairman, National Labour Forum, Partito Democratico;* b. 1 July 1937, Como; m.; two d.; ed Catholic Univ., Milan; fmr high school teacher; mem. Italian Workers Christian Asscn, Nat. Pres. 1969–72; Officer, Italian Workers Unions Confed. (CISL) 1974–, elected to Nat. Secr. 1983–, represented CISL in ILO and in Exec. Cttees of European Trade Union Confed. (ETUC) and ICFTU; Gen. Sec. ETUC 1991–2003; mem. European Convention 2002–03; Int. Dir Culture of Work' Section, World Forum of Cultures, Barcelona 2004; Chair. EU Employment Cttee 2007–09; mem. Notre Europe Steering Cttee 2006–; Chair. Nat. Labour Forum, Partito Democratico 2010–; Order of Merit (Poland) 1997, Légion d'honneur 2000. *Address:* Partito Democratico, via del Tritone 87, 00187 Rome, Italy (office). *Telephone:* (06) 91712424 (office); 331-1713379 (mobile). *E-mail:* emilio.gabaglio@partitodemocratico.it (office). *Website:* www.partitodemocratico.it (office).

GABAIX, Xavier, MA, PhD; French economist and academic; *Pershing Square Professor of Economics and Finance, Harvard University;* b. 1 Aug. 1971; s. of Julien Gabaix and Pierrette Gabaix; ed École Normale Supérieure, Paris, Harvard Univ., USA; Asst Prof. of Econs, MIT 1999–2003, Rudi Dornbusch Career Devt Asst, then Assoc. Prof. of Econs 2004–07; Assoc. Prof. of Finance, Stern School of Business, New York Univ., USA 2007–09, Prof. of Finance 2009–10, Martin J. Gruber Prof. of Finance 2010–16; Pershing Square Prof. of Econs and Finance, Harvard Univ. 2016–; mem. Conseil d'Analyse Economique 2010–12; Fellow, Econometric Soc. 2011; David A. Wells Prize for outstanding doctoral dissertation, Harvard Univ. 1999, Young Scientist Award for Socio- and Econophysics 2006, listed by The Economist amongst the top eight young economists in the world 2008, Bernacer Prize for the best European economist under 40 working in macro-finance 2010, TIAA-CREF Paul A. Samuelson Award: Certificate of Excellence 2011, Prix du meilleur jeune économiste de France, Le Cercle des Economistes/Le Monde 2011, Prize for Best Financial Economist under 40 2011, Fischer Black Prize, American Finance Asscn 2011 Lagrange Prize for research on complex systems 2012, Maurice Allais Prize 2015. *Publications:* numerous papers in professional journals on asset pricing, behavioural economics, executive compensation, macroeconomics and the origins and consequences of scaling behaviour. *Address:* Economics Department, Littauer Center, Harvard University, 1805 Cambridge Street, Cambridge, MA 02138, USA (office). *E-mail:* xgabaix@fas.harvard.edu (office). *Website:* economics.harvard.edu/people/xavier-gabaix (office).

GABBANA, Stefano; Italian fashion designer; *President, Dolce & Gabbana;* b. 14 Nov. 1962, Milan; early career as asst in Milan atelier; with Domenico Dolce opened fashion consulting studio 1982, selected to take part in Milano Collezioni new talents show 1985; Co-f. Dolce & Gabbana 1985, launched first maj. women's collection 1985, knitwear 1987, beachwear, underwear 1989, men's wear 1990, women's fragrance 1992, men's fragrance 1994, eyewear 1995; est. Dolce & Gabbana Industria production units 1999–2000; acquired and renovated Cinema Metropol in Milan for fashion shows and exhibitions 2005; opened boutiques in major cities in Europe, America and Asia; with Domenico Dolce, Woolmark Award 1991, Perfume Acad. Int. Prize for Best Feminine Fragrance of Year 1993, Best Masculine Fragrance of Year 1995, French "Oscar des Parfums", FHM magazine Designers of the Year 1996, Footwear News Designers of the Year 1997, Harper's Bizarre Russia Style Award 1999, T de Telva Award for Best Designers of the Year, GQ magazine (US) Best Designers of the Year 2003, Elle Magazine (UK) Best Int. Designers 2004, Premio Risultati 2004, GQ magazine (Russia) Best Int. Designers 2005. *Publications:* with Domenico Dolce, 10 Years Dolce and Gabbana 1996, Wildness 1997, Dolce and Gabbana Mémoires de la Mode 1998, Hollywood 2003, Calcio 2004, Music 2004, 20 Years Dolce & Gabbana 2005. *Leisure interests:* boxing, gym, taking vacations. *Address:* Dolce & Gabbana, Via San Damiano 7, 20122 Milan, Italy (office). *Telephone:* (02) 774271 (office). *Fax:* (02) 76020600 (office). *Website:* www.dolcegabbana.it (office).

GABBAY, Avraham (Avi), BA, MBA; Israeli politician; *Chairman, Israel Labour Party;* b. 22 Feb. 1967, Jerusalem; s. of Moïse Gabbay and Sara Gabbay; m. Ayelet Gabbay; three s.; ed Hebrew Univ. of Jerusalem; Liaison and Communications Officer, Budget Dept, Ministry of Finance 1995–99; Sr Asst to CEO, Bezeq (telecommunications co.) 1999, becoming Vice-Pres. of Econs and Strategy –2003, CEO, Bezeq International 2003–07, CEO, Bezeq Group 2007–13; Minister of Environmental Protection 2015–16; mem. Israel Labour Party 2016–, Chair. 2017–. *Address:* Israel Labour Party, POB 62033, Tel-Aviv 61620, Israel (office). *Telephone:* 3-6899444 (office). *Fax:* 3-6899420 (office). *E-mail:* mifkad@havoda.org.il (office). *Website:* www.havoda.org.il (office); avigabbay.co.il.

GABR, Shafik, BA, MA; Egyptian business executive; *Chairman and Managing Director, Artoc Group for Investment and Development;* b. 5 Nov. 1952, Cairo; m.; one d.; ed American Univ. in Cairo, Univ. of London, UK; Grad. Asst, Econs Dept, American Univ. in Cairo 1972–73; with Manufacturers Hanover Trust Bank, UK 1973–74; Chair. and Man. Dir Artoc Group for Investment and Devt 1976–; Chair. Int. Econ. Forum, Cairo, Arab Business Council, COMESA (Common Market for East and South Africa) Business Council; mem. Bd Egypt–US Business Council, World Econ. Forum Council, Geneva, Holding Co. for Metallurgical Industries, Egyptian Center for Econ. Studies, World Bank Council of Advisers for the MENA Region; mem. Advisory Bd Int. Org. for Migration 2005–; mem. Exec. Bd Int. Chamber of Commerce, Paris; mem. Zurich Financial Services Advisory Bd 2007–; mem. Egyptian Businessmen's Asscn (Dir 1996–98); Founding mem. American Chamber of Commerce in Egypt (Pres. 1995–97); mem. Initiative for Peace and Co-operation in the Middle East, Council Faith Community; Chair. Mohamed Shafik Gabr Foundation for Social Devt. *Address:* Artoc Group, 7 Hassan Al-Akbar Street, Mokattam, Cairo 11571, Egypt (office). *Telephone:* (2) 5055777 (office). *Fax:* (2) 5053222 (office). *E-mail:* chairman@artoc.com (office). *Website:* www.artoc.com (office).

GABRIADZE, Revaz (Rezo) Levanovich; Georgian scriptwriter, film director, sculptor and artist; b. 29 June 1936, Kutaisi; m. 2nd Yelena Zakharyevna Dzhaparidze; one s. one d.; ed Tbilisi State Univ., Higher Courses of Scriptwriters and Film Directors in Moscow; worked as corresp. for Molodezh Gruzii; with Gruzia Film Studio 1970–; wrote scripts for over 35 films including Do Not Grieve 1969, Serenade (after M. Zoshchenko) 1969, Jug (after L. Pirandello) 1970, Unusual Show 1970, White Stone 1973, Cranks 1974, Road, Mimino 1978, Kin-dza-dza; Founder and Artistic Dir Tbilisi Puppet Theatre (now Rezo Gabriadze Theatre) 1981, wrote and produced plays Traviata, Diamond of Marshal Fantier, Fall of Our Spring (USSR State Prize), Daughter of the Emperor of Trapezund; puppet productions in Switzerland and France 1991–94 including Ree Triste la Fin de l'Allee (Lausanne), Kutaisi (Rennes); Artistic Dir Cen. Puppet Theatre, Moscow 1994–95; Dir St Petersburg Satire Theatre 1996; productions include Song of the Volga 1996, Battle of Stalingrad, Forbidden Christmas or The Doctor and the Patient; numerous monumental and miniature sculptures including Chizhik-Pyzhik, Nose (after N. Gogol) ceramics exhibited in St Petersburg, Rabinovich (Odessa); graphic and painting shows in Moscow, St Petersburg, Paris, Rennes, Berlin, Lausanne; in Dijon and St Petersburg; illustrated works of A. Pushkin; Commdr, Ordre des Arts et des Lettres 1997; State Prize of Georgia 1987, USSR State Prize 1989, Shota Rustaveli State Prize of Georgia 1989, Golden Soffit Theatre Award 1997, Golden Mask 1997, Triumph Award 1997. *Screenplays include:* Don't Grieve 1969, Mimino 1977, Kin-dza-dza! 1986, Passport (Nika Award for the Best Screenplay 1991) 1990. *Publications include:* The White Bridge 1987, Kutaisi is a City 2002, The Eccentrics 1983 2002, Chito TK-49-54 or a Doctor and a Patient 2003. *Address:* Rezo Gabriadze Theatre, 0105 Tbilisi, 13 Shavteli St., Georgia (office). *Telephone:* (32) 98-65-93. *Fax:* (32) 98-65-89. *E-mail:* gabriadzetheater@yahoo.com (office). *Website:* www.gabriadze.com.

GABRIEL, Edward M., BS; American business executive and fmr diplomatist; *President and CEO, Gabriel Company LLC;* b. 1 March 1950, Olean, New York; m. Kathleen Linehan; ed Gannon Univ.; fmr Owner and Pres. Gabriel Group; fmr Sr Vice-Pres. in charge of Corp. Public Affairs, CONCORD Corpn; fmr Pres. and CEO Madison Public Affairs Group; Amb. to Morocco 1997–2001; Pres. and CEO Gabriel Company, LLC, Washington, DC 2002–; Pres. and CEO American Task Force for Lebanon; Advisor on Middle East policy for General Wesley Clark's presidential campaign 2004; currently Visiting Fellow, Middle East Program, Center for Strategic and Int. Studies; Sr Counsellor, Middle Eastern and Russian Issues, Center for Democracy; Founding mem. Exec. Cttee and Bd of Dirs, American Task Force on Lebanon; Dir Keystone Center; mem. Advisory Bd Guggenheim Partners; mem. Bd of Dirs Tri-Valley Corpn, American School of Tangier, Casablanca American School; mem. Global Advisory Bd, George Washington Univ. *Address:* Gabriel Company, LLC, 1220 L Street, NW, Suite 411, Washington, DC 20005, USA. *Telephone:* (202) 887-1113. *Fax:* (202) 887-1115. *Website:* www.thegabrielco.com.

GABRIEL, Mariya; Bulgarian politician and EU official; *European Commissioner for Digital Economy and Society;* b. (Mariya Ivanova Nedelcheva), 20 May 1979, Gotse Delchev; m. François Gabriel 2012; one s.; ed Plovdiv Univ., Inst. of Political Studies, Bordeaux; Teaching and Research Asst, Inst. of Political Studies, Bordeaux, France 2004–08; mem. European Parl. for Bulgaria 2009–17, Vice-Pres., European People's Party Group (EPP Group) and Head of Bulgarian del. in EPP Group 2014–17; European Commr for Digital Economy and Soc. 2017–. *Address:* European Commission, 200 Rue de la Loi/Wetstraat 200, 1049 Brussels, Belgium (office). *Telephone:* (2) 299-11-11 (switchboard) (office). *E-mail:* cab-gabriel-contact@ec.europa.eu (office). *Website:* ec.europa.eu/commission (office); mariya-gabriel.eu.

GABRIEL, Michal; Czech sculptor; b. 25 Feb. 1960, Prague; s. of František Gabriel and Jarmila Gabrielová; m. Milada Dočekalová 1987; two s. one d.; ed Secondary School of Applied Arts, Acad. of Fine Arts, Prague; apprenticed in timber industry; worked as skilled joiner 1975–78; graduated as woodcarver 1982, as sculptor 1987; Founding mem. creative group Tvrdohlaví ('The Stubborn' group) 1987; First Prize for statue Pegasus, Prague 1988, for gates for Nat. Gallery Bldg 1989 (completed 1992); Angel Sculpture (bronze), Bank in Opava 1995, 'The Winged Leopard', gilded bronze sculpture, entrance Pres.'s Office, Prague Castle 1996; City Hall windows, České Budějovice 2000; Fountain (metal), Hradec Králové 2001; 'Trunk' sculpture, Philosophy Faculty Brno 2002; Indonesian sculpture, Prague Zoo 2003; lecturer, Faculty of Performing Arts, Czech Univ. of Tech., Brno 1999–; Co-f. new exhbn hall, Palace Lucerne, Prague 2000; Jindřich Chalupecký Prize 1994. *Publication:* Tvrdohlaví 2000. *Address:* Dlouhá 32, 110 00 Prague 1, Czech Republic (home). *Telephone:* (2) 22314644 (home). *Fax:* (2) 22314644 (home). *E-mail:* michalgabriel@hotmail.com. *Website:* www.michal-gabriel.cz; www.ffa.vutbr.cz/gabriel.

GABRIEL, Peter; British rock singer and songwriter; b. 13 Feb. 1950, Woking, Surrey; m. 1st Jill Gabriel; two d.; m. 2nd Meabh Flynn 2002; two s.; ed Charterhouse School; Founder-mem., rock band Genesis 1966–75; solo artist 1975–; f. World of Music, Arts and Dance (WOMAD) featuring music from around the world 1982; f. Real World Group to develop interactive projects in arts and tech. 1985, Real World Studios 1986, Real World Records (world music record label) 1989, Real World Multimedia 1994; launched 'Witness' Human Rights Programme 1992; co-f. Europe digital music wholesaler OD2; co-f., with Brian Eno, the Magnificent Union of Digitally Downloading Artists (MUDDA) 2004; co-f., with Richard Branson, the Elders. org. 2000, launched by Nelson Mandela 2007; Dr hc (City Univ.) 1991; Hon. MA (Univ. Coll., Salford) 1994; Hon. DMus (Bath) 1996; Ivor Novello Award for Outstanding Contribution to British Music 1983, Ivor Novello Award for Best Song (for Sledgehammer) 1987, BRIT Award for Best British Music Video (for Sledgehammer) 1987, for Best British Male Artist 1987, for Best Producer 1993, Grammy Awards for Best New Age Performance 1990, for Best Short Form Music Video 1993,1994, for Best Long Form Music Video 1996, for Best Song Written for Motion Picture (for Down to Earth from Wall-E) 2009, for Best Instrumental Arrangement (for Define Dancing from Wall-E) 2009, Q Award for Lifetime Achievement 2006, Frankfurter Musikpreis 2006, Ivor Novello Lifetime Achievement Award 2007, BMI Icon 2007, Amb. of Conscience, Amnesty International 2008, Quadriga Award 2008, Time 100 Most Influential People Award 2008, Polar Music Prize 2009, inducted into Rock and Roll Hall of Fame (with Genesis) 2010, (as solo artist) 2014. *Film scores:* Birdy 1985, Last Temptation of Christ 1989, Long Walk Home (from Rabbit-Proof Fence) 2002, Wall-E (two Grammy Awards 2009) 2008, A Year Ago in Winter 2008, Inside Job 2010, The Reluctant Fundamentalist 2012. *Recordings include:* albums: with Genesis: From Genesis To Revelation 1969, Foxtrot 1972, Genesis Live 1973, Selling England By The Pound 1973, Nursery Crime 1974, The Lamb Lies Down On Broadway 1974; solo: Peter Gabriel I 1977, II 1979, III 1980, IV 1982, Peter Gabriel Plays Live 1983, So 1986, Passion 1989, Shaking The Tree 1990, Us 1992, Revisited 1992, Secret World 1995, Come Home to Me Snow 1998, Ovo 2000, Up 2002, Hit 2003, Big Blue Ball 2008, Scratch My Back 2010, New Blood 2011, Live Blood 2012, Scratch My Back/And I'll Scratch Yours 2013, Courage 2013, Rated PG 2019. *Publication:* Genesis: Chapter and Verse (with other band mems) 2007. *Address:* Real World Holdings Ltd, Box Mill, Mill Lane, Box, Wiltshire, SN13 8PL, England (office). *Telephone:* (1225) 740600 (office). *Website:* www.petergabriel.com; www.realworld.co.uk; www.realworldrecords.com; www.realworldmultimedia.com.

GABRIEL, Sigmar; German politician; b. 12 Sept. 1959, Goslar; m. 1st (divorced), one d.; m. 2nd Anke Stadler 2012, two d.; ed Göttingen Univ.; children and youth work in Sozialistische Jugend Deutschlands – die Falken 1976–89; joined SPD 1977; adult educ. lecturer 1983–88; teacher, Saxony Adult Educ. Inst. 1989–90; Dist Councillor for Goslar 1987–98, City Councillor 1991–99, Chair. Environmental Cttee 1991–96, Econ. Affairs and Tourism Cttee 1996; mem. Lower Saxony Parl. 1990–2005, mem. Environment Cttee 1990–94, Deputy Chair. SPD Parl. Group 1997–98, Chair. 1998–99, 2003–05; SPD Speaker for Home Affairs 1994–97; mem. Exec. Cttee SPD 1999–2005, Chair. SPD 2009–17; Minister-Pres. of Lower Saxony 1999–2003; mem. Bundestag for constituency 49 (Salzgitter-Wolfenbüttel) 2005–; Fed. Minister of the Environment, Nature Conservation and Nuclear Safety 2005–09, Fed. Vice-Chancellor 2013–18, also Fed. Minister of Econs and Energy 2013–17, of Foreign Affairs 2017–18. *Leisure interests:* cycling, sailing. *Address:* Sozialdemokratische Partei Deutschlands, Willy-Brandt-Haus, Wilhelmstr. 141, 10963 Berlin, Germany (office). *Telephone:* (30) 25991500 (office). *Fax:* (30) 25991507 (office). *Website:* www.spd.de (office); www.sigmargabriel.de (office).

GABRIELLI DE AZEVEDO, José Sergio, PhD; Brazilian economist, academic and business executive; b. 3 Oct. 1949, Salvador, Bahia; ed Fed. Univ. of Bahia, Boston Univ., USA; fmr Deputy Dir of Research and Postgraduate Studies, Fed. Univ. of Bahia, fmr Dir Faculty of Econ. Sciences, currently Prof. on leave; fmr Supt Foundation for Research and Extension Support; Visiting Research Scholar, LSE, UK 2000–01; Chief Financial Officer and Investor Relations, Dir Petróleo Brasileiro SA (Petrobras) 2003–05, Pres. and CEO 2005–12, mem. Bd of Dirs Petrobras Participaciones SA (PEPSA), Petrobras Energia SA (PESA); Sec. of Planning, Bahia 2012–14; Non-Resident Fellow, Center on Global Energy Policy, Columbia Univ. 2013; Brazilian Inst. of Finance Execs Equilibrist Award 2004, Nat. Assen of Execs in Finance, Admin and Accounting Professional of the Year 2004, Int. Stevie Business Awards Best Finance Exec. in Latin America 2005, named by Revista Época as one of the 100 most influential Brazilians of 2009, Global Energy Award, World Energy Council 2010, Petroleum Executive of the Year, Energy Intelligence 2011, Executive Entrepreneur of the Year, Ernst & Young 2011, most outstanding executive in trade relations between Brazil-Japan, Chamber of Commerce Brazil-Japan 2012. *Publications include:* numerous books and articles on productive restructuring, the labour market, macroeconomics and regional development.

GABRIELSE, Gerald, BS, MS, PhD; American physicist and academic; *George Vasmer Leverett Professor of Physics, Harvard University;* b. 1951; ed Calvin Coll., Univ. of Chicago; teaching asst, Calvin Coll., Grand Rapids, Mich. 1971–72, research asst 1972–73; grad. student, Univ. of Chicago 1973–78; Research Assoc., Univ. of Washington, Seattle 1978–82, Research Asst Prof. 1985–86, Assoc. Prof. 1986–87; George Vasmer Leverett Prof. of Physics, Harvard Univ. 1987– (Chair. Physics Dept 2000–03); Physicist, CERN, leader of ATRAP antimatter physics research project, Geneva, Switzerland; Consultant, Intermagnetics General Corpn 1995, PolyChip Inc. 1999; Scientist in Residence, Lexington Christian Acad. 1995–96; mem. NAS 2007–; Distinguished Fellow, Cockcroft Inst., Liverpool, UK 2007–; Levenson Prize, Harvard Univ. 2000, Davisson-Germer Prize, American Physical Soc. 2002. *Lectures include:* around 200 lectures at scientific confs and univs. *Publications include:* more than 100 scientific publs. *Address:* Department of Physics, Harvard University, 17 Oxford Street, Cambridge, MA 02138, USA (office). *Telephone:* (617) 495-4381 (office). *E-mail:* gabrielse@physics.harvard.edu (office). *Website:* physics.harvard.edu (office).

GABRIELYAN, Vache, MPA, PhD; Armenian political scientist, academic, politician and fmr business executive; *Adjunct Assistant Professor, American University of Armenia;* b. 24 Nov. 1968, Yerevan, Armenian SSR, USSR; m.; two c.; ed Yerevan State Univ., Rutgers Univ., USA; expert, Supreme Soviet Standing Comm. on Financial Credit and Fiscal Policy 1990–92; Reader, Depts of Public Admin and Political Sciences, Rutgers Univ., USA and Deputy Dir Nat. Center for Public Efficiency 1994–98; Reader, Econs Dept, Yerevan State Univ. and Faculty of Political Sciences, American Univ. of Armenia 1998–, also Adjunct Asst Prof.; Adviser to Pres. of CBA 1998–99, mem. Bd CBA 1999–2008, Vice-Pres. CBA 2008–10; Minister of Finance 2010–13; Minister-Chief of Govt Staff 2013–14; Chief Adviser to Prime Minister April–Nov. 2014; Deputy Prime Minister and Minister of Int. Econ. Integration and Reform 2014–18; mem. Hayastani Hanrapetakan Kusaktsutyun (HHK—Republican Party of Armenia). *Publications:* scientific papers in Armenia and abroad. *Address:* American University of Armenia, 0019 Yerevan, 136W, Paramaz Avedisian Building, 40 Marshal Baghramyan Avenue, Armenia (office). *Telephone:* (60) 61-26-71 (office). *E-mail:* vache.gabrielyan@aua.am (office). *Website:* www.psia.aua.am (office).

GABURICI, Chiril; Moldovan telecommunications industry executive and politician; *Minister of Economy and Infrastructure;* b. 23 Nov. 1976, Logănești, Hincești Dist, Moldovan SSR, USSR; m. Irina Gaburici; two c.; ed Slavonic Univ. of Moldova, Chișinău; worked for Moldcell mobile network co. from 2001, Moldovan Man. 2009–12; CEO Azercell (part of TeliaSonera group), Azerbaijan 2012–14; mem. Partidul Liberal Democrat din Moldova (PLDM—Liberal Democratic Party of Moldova); Prime Minister of Moldova Feb.–June 2015 (resgnd); Minister of Economy and Infrastructure 2017. *Address:* Office of the Council of Ministers, 2033 Chișinău, Piața Marii Adunări Naționale 1 (office); Partidul Liberal Democrat din Moldova (Liberal Democratic Party of Moldova), 2012 Chișinău, str. București 88, Moldova (office). *Telephone:* (22) 25-01-01 (office); (22) 81-51-54 (office). *Fax:* (22) 24-26-96 (office); (22) 81-51-63 (office). *E-mail:* petitii@gov.md (office); info@pldm.md (office). *Website:* www.pldm.md (office); www.gov.md (office).

GACHHADAR, Bijaya Kumar; Nepalese politician; b. Sunsari; m. Nirmala Gachhadar; elected mem. Nepalese Constituent Ass. 2008; mem. Madhesi Jana Adhikar Forum 2008–09 (expelled); Founder and Chair. Madhesi Jana Adhikar Forum Nepal—Loktantrik (MPRFN—Democratic) 2009–17; Chair. Nepal Democratic Forum April–Oct. 2017 (dissolved and merged into Nepali Congress); fmr Minister of Water Resources, Deputy Prime Minister and Minister for Physical Planning and Works 2009–11, Minister of Home Affairs 2011–13, of Physical Infrastructure and Transportation 2015–16, of Federal Affairs and Local Development 2017–18.

GACIYUBWENGE, Maj.-Gen. Pontien; Burundian army officer and politician; b. Mwaro Prov.; long career with Forces de défense nationales (FDN), positions included Commdr, Army Bn, Bujumbura, Commdr, Southern Mil. Region 2003, Commdr, Fifth Mil. Region 2005, later Chief of Staff in charge of training; Minister of Nat. Defence and War Veterans 2010–15. *Address:* c/o Ministry of National Defence and War Veterans, Bujumbura, Burundi.

GADDAFI, Seif al-Islam, BSc; Libyan foundation executive; b. 25 June 1972, Tripoli; s. of Col Mu'ammar Muhammad al-Gaddafi and Safia Farkash; ed Al-Fateh Univ., Tripoli, IMADEC Univ., Vienna, Austria, London School of Econs, UK; Co-owner Nat. Eng Service and Supplies Co.; Chair. Gaddafi Int. Charity and Devt Foundation (paid US $2,700m. compensation to families of the 270 victims of Lockerbie bombing); fmr Pres. Libyan Nat. Assen for Drugs and Narcotics Control; warrant issued for his arrest by Int. Criminal Court, The Hague on charges of crimes against humanity following popular uprising in Libya June 2011; arrested in southern Libya Nov. 2011, held in detention in Zintan, sentenced to death in absentia by Tripoli court July 2015, released from detention 2016.

GADDIS, John Lewis, PhD; American historian and academic; *Robert A. Lovett Professor of Military and Naval History, Yale University;* b. 2 April 1942; m. (divorced); two s.; m. 2nd Toni Dorfman 1997; ed Univ. of Texas, Austin; Lecturer and later Prof., Dept of History, Ohio Univ. 1969–94, Distinguished Prof. 1983, f. Contemporary History Inst., Ohio 1987; Sr Fellow, Hoover Inst. 2000–02; Robert A. Lovett Prof. of Mil. and Naval History, Yale Univ. 1997–; fmr Lecturer, US Naval War Coll., Univ. of Helsinki, Finland, Princeton Univ., Univ. of Oxford (Harmsworth Prof. of American History 1992); George Eastman Visiting Prof., Balliol Coll., Oxford, UK 2000–01; mem. Editorial Bd Foreign Affairs; mem. Advisory Bd Cold War Int. History Project; Pres. Soc. for Historians of American Foreign Relations 1992; Fellow, American Acad. of Arts and Sciences 1995; Stuart L. Bernath Prize 1973, Nat. Historical Soc. Prize 1973, Bancroft Prize 1973, Fulbright Scholar to Finland 1980, Guggenheim Fellowship 1986, Wilson Center Fellowship 1995, Fulbright Scholar to Poland 1996, Nat. Humanities Medal 2005, Harry S. Truman Book Award 2006. *Publications include:* The United States and the Origins of the Cold War 1941–47 1972, Russia, The Soviet Union and the United States: An Interpretive History 1978, Strategies of Containment: A Critical Appraisal of Postwar American National Security Policy 1982, The Long Peace: Inquiries into the History of the Cold War 1987, The United States and the End of the Cold War: Reconsiderations, Implications, Provocations 1992, We Now Know: Rethinking Cold War History 1997, The Landscape of History: How Historians Map the Past 2002, Surprise, Security, and the American Experience 2004, The Cold War: A New History 2006, George F. Kennan: An American Life (Nat. Book Critics' Circle Award for Biography 2011, Pulitzer Prize for Biography 2012, American History Book Prize 2012) 2011, On Grand Strategy 2018; several book chapters and numerous articles in professional journals. *Address:* Department of History, Yale University, PO Box 208324, New Haven, CT 06520-8353, USA (office). *Telephone:* (203) 432-1374 (office). *Fax:* (203) 432-7587 (office). *E-mail:* john.gaddis@yale.edu (office). *Website:* history.yale.edu/people/john-gaddis (office).

GADE JENSEN, Søren, MSc, CandEcon; Danish politician and organization official; b. 27 Jan. 1963, Holstebro; s. of Poul Jørgensen and Anna Gade Jørgensen; ed Århus Univ.; served as Officer, Jutland Regiment of Dragoons 1983–85, Reserve Officer, rank of Maj. 1985–; UN Observer in Middle East, UNTSO 1990–91; Int. Market Analyst, Cheminova Agro A/S 1991–93; Man., Bilka 1993–95; teacher, Holstebro Business Coll. 1997–98; Chief Operating Finance Officer, Færch Plast A/S 1995–2001; Head of Centre, RAR Regnskabscenter 2001–03; cand. for Holstebro Constituency (Liberal Party) 1995; mem. (temp.) Folketing for Ringkøbing County Constituency Oct.–Nov. 1999, mem. 2001–, Deputy Chair. Defence Cttee 2001; Minister of Defence 2004–10 (resgnd); CEO Landbrug & Fødevarer 2012–14; Commdr, Order of Danneborg.

GADGIL, Madhav, MSc, PhD; Indian ecologist, conservationist and academic; b. 24 May 1942; ed Univ. of Poona, Bombay Univ., Harvard Univ., USA; main contrib. to establishment of India's first biosphere reserve in the Western Ghats; worked at Indian Nat. Science Acad. from 1973; fmr IBM Fellow and Lecturer in Biology, Harvard Univ.; Visiting Prof., Stanford Univ., USA; fmr Distinguished Lecturer, Univ. of California, Berkeley, USA; Founder and Prof., Centre for Ecological Sciences, Bangalore, Indian Inst. of Science 1973–2004; mem. Science Advisory Council to Prime Minister 1986–90, Karnataka State Planning Bd; Vice-Pres. Scientific Advisory Bd to Convention on Biological Diversity 1995; Chair. Scientific and Tech. Advisory Panel of Global Environment Facility; represents Govt of India on Subsidiary Body on Scientific, Tech. and Technological Advice to Int. Convention on Biological Diversity; currently Chair. Cttee Environmental School Educ. Curriculum; fmr Chair. Fuel and Fodder Study Group of Planning Comm., Biodiversity Task Force of Dept of Biotechnology, Expert Group on Eastern and Western Ghats, Ministry of Environment and Forests; fmr mem. Steering Cttee Project Tiger, Steering Cttee Indian Bd for Wild Life, Silent Valley Cttee, Bastar Pine Plantation Cttee; Fellow, Indian Acad. of Sciences, Indian Nat. Science Acad., Third World Acad. of Sciences; Foreign Assoc., NAS; Hon. mem. British Ecological Soc., Ecological Soc. of America; Padma Shri 1981, Shanti Swarup Bhatnagar Award, Vikram Sarabhai Award, Iswarchandra Vidyasagar Award, Rajyotsava Award 1983, Centennial Medal, Harvard Univ. 2002, Govt of Karnataka, Volvo Environment Prize 2003, Padma Bhushan 2006, Firodia Award 2007, Tyler Prize for Environmental Achievement, Univ. of Southern California (co-recipient) 2015.

Publications: This Fissured Land, Ecology and Equity, Diversity: The Cornerstone of Life, Nurturing Biodiversity: An Indian Agenda, Ecological Journeys, People's Biodiversity Registers: A Methodology Manual; more than 215 research papers (two of them recognized as Citation Classics) on population biology, conservation biology, human ecology and ecological history; writes regularly for popular media in English and Indian languages. *Address:* c/o Centre for Ecological Sciences, Indian Institute of Science, Bangalore 560 012, India (office). *Telephone:* (80) 23600985 (office). *Fax:* (80) 23601428 (office). *E-mail:* madhav@ces.iisc.ernet.in (office); madhav.gadgil@gmail.com. *Website:* ces.iisc.ernet.in/hpg/cesmg (office).

GADIESH, Orit, MBA; Israeli business executive; *Chairperson, Bain & Company;* ed Hebrew Univ., Jerusalem, Harvard Business School, USA; joined Israeli army age 17, worked as Aide to Deputy Chief of Staff Ezer Weizman; taught at Hebrew Univ., Jerusalem Inst. of Man.; joined Bain & Co. (consultancy firm), Boston 1977, worked in steel industry and automotive industry sectors, Chair. 1993–; mem. Bd Harvard Business School, Haute Ecole Commerciale, Paris, Peres Inst. for Peace, Fed. Reserve Bank of New England, WPP Group; mem. Harvard Medical School Advisory Council for Cell Biology and Pathology, Harvard Business School Visiting Cttee, Metropolitan Museum of Art Cttee, New York; mem. Bd of Trustees Eisenhower Fellowships; mem. Foundation Bd World Economic Forum (WEF), also mem. WEF International Business Council; Baker Scholar, Harvard Business School; Brown Award for Outstanding Marketing Student, Harvard Business School 1977, Harvard Business School Alumni Achievement Award 2000, IDC Univ. Distinguished Leadership Award 2000, 25th Annual Golden Door Award, Int. Inst. of Boston 2002, Lifetime Achievement Award from Consulting magazine 2007. *Publications:* series of articles for Harvard Business Review. *Leisure interests:* reading. *Address:* Bain & Company Inc., 131 Dartmouth Street, Boston, MA 02116, USA (office). *Telephone:* (617) 572-2000 (office). *Fax:* (617) 572-2427 (office). *Website:* www.bain.com (office).

GADIO, Cheikh Tidiane, BA, PhD; Senegalese international organization official and government official; *President, Institut Panafricain de Stratégies;* b. 16 Sept. 1956, Saint-Louis; ed Ohio State Univ., USA, Univ. of Montréal, Canada, Univ. of Paris, France; Ed.-in-Chief, Tribune Africaine, Paris 1980–84; Head of Audiovisual section, Festival Panafricain des Arts et de la Culture (FESPAC) 1987–88; various econ. and telecommunications devt advisory posts, World Bank Inst.; Adviser, UN Office for Project Services 1998; Regional Dir for Africa, School for International Training, Vt, USA 1998–99; Co-ordinator for Africa, World Bank Inst. Jan.–April 2000; Minister of State, of Foreign Affairs, African Unity and Senegalese Abroad 2000–09; Chair. and CEO Sarata Holding (consultancy), Dakar 2009–; Founder and Pres. Mouvement politique citoyen (political party), unsuccessful cand. for Pres. of Senegal 2012; Founder and Pres. Pan-African Strategies Inst. (Institut Panafricain de Stratégies—IPS), Dakar 2012–; mem. Bd of Dirs African Democratic Inst.; mem. Council, Sustainable Devt Solutions Network. *Address:* Sarata Holding, Almadies Zone 15, Rond-Point Ngor, Dakar, Senegal. *Website:* www.sarata-holding.net.

GADJIYEV, Gadis Abdullayevich, DJur; Russian/Dagestan lawyer, judge and academic; *Justice, Constitutional Court of Russian Federation;* b. 27 Aug. 1957, Shovkra; m.; four s.; ed Moscow State Univ.; teacher Dagestan State Univ. 1975–79; legal consultant Supreme Soviet Dagestan ASSR 1979–80, Head Legal Dept Admin. 1980–90, Chair. Comm. on Law and Local Self-Man. 1990–91; Justice, Constitutional Court of Russian Fed. 1991–; apptd Prof., Faculty of Law, Nat. Research Univ. Higher School of Econs—HSE 2008, Ordinary Prof. 2013–; Chair. Bd of Trustees of the Law and Public Policy Inst.; Lawyer Emer. of the Russian Fed. *Publications include:* over 80 scientific publs including 4 monographs on constitutional law. *Leisure interest:* pigeon raising. *Address:* Constitutional Court of Russian Federation, 190000 St. Petersburg, 1, Pl. Senatskaya, Russia (office). *Telephone:* (812) 404-33-11 (office). *Fax:* (812) 404-31-99 (office). *E-mail:* ggadzhiev@hse.ru; ksrf@ksrf.ru (office). *Website:* www.ksrf.ru (office).

GADKARI, Nitin Jairam, MCom, LLB; Indian politician, lawyer, business executive and agriculturalist; *Minister of Road Transport and Highways, of Shipping and of Water Resources, River Development and Ganga Rejuvenation;* b. 27 May 1957, Nagpur; m. Kanchan Gadkari; two s. one d.; ed studies in Maharashtra; as a teenager, worked for Bharatiya Janata Yuva Morcha and student union Akhil Bharatiya Vidyarthi Parishad (ABVP) 1976–77; Co-ordinator for Purogami Lokashahi Aghdadi's Vidarbha region after state of emergency was lifted 1977; elected as Vidarbha Region Sec. of ABVP 1979 (re-elected 1980); Pres. Bharatiya Janata Yuva Morcha, Nagpur City Unit 1981, Sec. Bharatiya Janata Party, Nagpur City Unit 1985–86, Gen. Sec. 1988–89; elected to Maharashtra Govt Legis. Council from graduates constituency, Nagpur Region 1989 (re-elected 1990, 1996, elected unopposed 2002); Minister of Public Works Dept, Govt of Maharashtra 1995–99, est. Maharashtra State Road Devt Corpn (govt-owned co.) to undertake construction work; Guardian Minister for Nagpur Dist, Govt of Maharashtra 1995–99; mem. High Power Cttee for Privatization, Govt of Maharashtra 1995–99; Leader of Opposition, Maharashtra Legis. Council 1999–2004; Gen. Sec. Bharatiya Janata Party (BJP), Maharashtra 1992–94, State Pres. BJP, Maharashtra 2004–09, Pres. BJP (elected unanimously) 2009–13; Minister of Road Transport and Highways 2014–, of Shipping 2014–, of Water Resources, River Development and Ganga Rejuvenation 2017–; Founder-Chair. Maharashtra State Road Devt Corpn 1995–99; Chair. Mining Policy Implementation Cttee, Govt of Maharashtra 1995–99, Metropolis Beautification Cttee, Govt of Maharashtra 1995–99, Nat. Rural Road Devt Cttee; Chair. Nat. Rural Road Devt Cttee, Govt of India 1995–99, Review Cttee of Central Public Works Dept, Govt of India 1995–99; Chair. Purti Group of Cos; Founder-Chair. Poly Sack Industrial Soc. Ltd; Promoter and Dir Nikhil Furniture and Appliances Pvt. Ltd; Founder-Chair. Empress Employees Co-operative Paper Mills Ltd; Founder-mem. Atyodaya Trust; exports fruits to various countries under the banner Ketaki Overseas Trading Co., constructed series of roads, highways and flyovers across the state, including Mumbai–Pune Expressway and Bandra–Worli Sea Link; Mumbai Bhushan Award. *Address:* Ministry of Road Transport and Highways, Parivahan Bhavan, 1 Parliament Street, New Delhi 110 001, India (office). *Telephone:* (11) 23714104 (office). *Fax:* (11) 23356669 (office). *E-mail:* ifcmost@nic.in (office). *Website:* morth.nic.in (office); www.nitingadkari.org.

GADONNEIX, Pierre, DEcon; French business executive; *President of the Supervisory Board, Groupe Latécoère;* b. 1943, New York, USA; m.; three c.; ed École Polytechnique, Paris, Ecole Nationale Supérieure du Pétrole et des Moteurs, Harvard Business School, USA; began career as engineer, Groupe Elf Aquitaine 1966–69; f. SEFI 1969, Dir 1970–72; Dir Inst. de Développement Industriel (IDI) 1972–76; Tech. Adviser, Ministry of Industry 1976–78, Dir Mechanical and Metallurgical Industries Div. 1978–87; Pres. and Man. Dir Groupe Gaz de France 1987–96, Chair. and CEO 1996–2004; Chair. and CEO Électricité de France (EDF) 2004–09, Hon. Chair. 2009–; Pres. Supervisory Bd Groupe Latécoèref 2010–; Chair. World Energy Council 2007–10; mem. Bd Dirs Elf-Erap 1988–95, Renault 1978–86, SNCF 1983–87, France Télécom 1998–2003; Pres. Conseil Français de l'Energie 1993–99, Harvard Business School club de France 2010–; fmr Pres. Eurogas (trade asscn), Fondation Gaz de France 1996–2004; Lecturer, École Polytechnique 1983–92; mem. Conseil Economique et Social, Bd of Fondation Nationale des Sciences Politiques; Commdr, Légion d'honneur, Ordre nat. du Mérite, Ordre des Arts et des Lettres. *Address:* Groupe Latécoère, 135 rue de Periole, BP 5211, 31079 Toulouse Cedex 5, France (office). *Website:* www.latecoere-group.com/en (office).

GAEHTGENS, Thomas Wolfgang, DPhil; German art historian and academic; *Director, The Getty Research Institute;* b. 24 June 1940, Leipzig; m. Barbara Feiler 1969; two s.; ed Univs of Bonn and Freiburg and Univ. of Paris, France; Lecturer, Univ. of Göttingen 1970–72, Prof. of Art History 1972–78; Prof. and Chair. of Art History, Freie Univ., Berlin 1980–2006; Founder and Dir German Centre for the History of Art, Paris 1997–2007; Research Fellow, Inst. for Advanced Study, Princeton 1979–80; Visiting Scholar, The Getty Research Inst., Los Angeles, 1985–86, Dir 2007–18; Pres. Comité Int. d'histoire de l'art 1992–96; mem. Akad. der Wissenschaften, Göttingen, American Acad. of Arts and Sciences 2011; Chevalier, Légion d'honneur; Dr hc (Courtauld Inst. of Art) 2004, (Univ. Paris-Sorbonne) 2011; Grand Prix de la Francophonie 2009. *Publications include:* Napoleon's Arc de Triomphe 1974, Versailles als Nationaldenkmal 1984, Joseph-Marie Vien 1988, Anton von Werner 1990, Die Berliner Museuminsel im Deutschen Kaiserreich 1992. *Leisure interests:* art, history. *Address:* The Getty Research Institute, 1200 Getty Center Drive, Suite 1100, Los Angeles, CA 90049-1688, USA (office). *Telephone:* (310) 440-7335 (office). *E-mail:* reference@getty.edu (office). *Website:* www.getty.edu/research (office).

GAFT, Valentin Iosifovich; Russian actor; b. 2 Sept. 1935, Moscow; m. Olga Mikhailovna Ostroumova; ed Studio-School of Moscow Art Theatre; worked in Mossoviet Theatre, Na Maloy Bronnoy, Lenkom, Satire Theatre 1959–69; leading actor Sovremennik Theatre 1969–; Order of Friendship 1995, Order of Merit for the Fatherland 2005, 2010; People's Artist of Russia 1984, Laureate, Theatrical Prize I. Smoktunovskii 1995. *Theatre roles include:* Glumov (Balalaikin and Co.), Lopatin (From the Notes of Lopatin), George (Who's Afraid of Virginia Woolf?), Governor (Inspector), Vershinin (Three Sisters), Bridegroom (Something Like a Comedy), Husband, Wife and Lover (Trusotsii), The Government Inspector (Gorodnichii). *Film roles include:* Murder on Dante Street 1956, First Courier 1968, Crazy Gold 1977, Centaurs 1979, Parade 1980, Fuette 1986, Thieves by Law 1988, Blessed Heavens 1991, Khochu v Ameriku 1993, Tayna Marchello 1997, Nebo v almazakh 1999, Staryye klyachi 2000, Nezhnyy vozrast 2001, 12 2007, Kniga masterov 2009, Leningrad 2009, Käshbasshy zholy 2013, Yolki 3 2013. *Television includes:* Buddenbrooks, The Mystery of Edwin Drood, Archipelago Lenoire, Kings and Cabbage, Po tu storonu volkov (mini-series) 2002, Master i Margarita (mini-series) 2005. *Publications include:* Poetry and Epigrams 1989, Life is Theatre (with Leonid Alekseevich Filatov) 1998, Garden of Forgotten Memories 1999, Poems. Epigrams 2003. *Leisure interests:* writing verses and epigrams. *Address:* T. Shchevchenko nab. 1/2, Apt 62, 121059 Moscow, Russia (home). *Telephone:* (495) 243-76-67 (home).

GAGE, Fred H., (Rusty), BS, MS, PhD; American geneticist and academic; *Professor and Vi and John Adler Chair for Research on Age-Related Neurodegenerative Diseases, Salk Institute for Biological Studies;* b. 8 Oct. 1950, Virginia, USA; ed Univ. of Florida, Johns Hopkins Univ.; Nat. Inst. of Mental Health Predoctoral Fellow, Johns Hopkins Univ., Baltimore 1974–76; Asst, later Assoc. Prof., Texas Christian Univ. 1976–80; Assoc. Prof., Dept of Histology, Univ. of Lund, Sweden 1981–85; Assoc. Prof., Dept of Neurosciences, Univ. of California, San Diego 1985–88, Prof. 1988–; Prof. and Vi and John Adler Chair for Research on Age-Related Neurodegenerative Diseases, Lab. of Genetics, Salk Inst. for Biological Studies 1995–; co-f. StemCells Inc. 1988; Pres. Int. Soc. for Stem Cell Research 2011–12; Fellow, NAS, Inst. of Medicine, American Acad. of Arts and Sciences; mem. Soc. for Neuroscience (Pres. 2001); mem. American Philosophical Soc. 2010–; mem. Science Advisory Bd, Genetics Policy Inst.; numerous awards including Bristol-Myers Squibb Neuroscience Research Award 1987, IPSEN Prize in Neuronal Plasticity 1990, Christopher Reeve Research Medal 1997, Max Planck Research Prize 1999, MetLife Award for Medical Research 2002, Max Planck Soc. Klaus Joachim Zulch-Preis 2003, Keio Medical Science Prize 2008. *Address:* Salk Institute for Biological Studies, 10010 North Torrey Pines Road, La Jolla, CA 92037, USA (office). *Telephone:* (858) 453-4100 (office). *E-mail:* gage@salk.edu (office). *Website:* www.salk.edu (office).

GAGEY, Frédéric N. P. P., MA (Econ); French airline executive; *Chief Financial Officer, Air France-KLM;* b. 1956, Neuilly-sur-Seine; ed Ecole Polytechnique, École nationale de la statistique et de l'admin économique, Univ. of Paris 1 Panthéon-Sorbonne; began career at Bureau of Statistics (INSEE) and Ministry of Finance; Vice-Pres., Budget and Control, Air Inter 1994–97, Vice-Pres. for Privatization and Financial Communication, Air France (following merger 1997) 1997–99, Vice-Pres., Finance from 1999, Exec. Vice-Pres. of Fleet Man. and Purchasing, Air France-KLM SA 1999–2016, Man. Dir and Chief Financial Officer, KLM 2005–13, Chair. and CEO Air France 2013–16, Chief Financial Officer, KLM 2016–, interim CEO 2018–, mem. Man. Bd KLM Royal Dutch Airlines; Dir, Nat. Inst. of Statistics and Econ. Studies (INSEE); Chevalier, Légion d'honneur 2013. *Address:* Groupe Air France, 45 rue de Paris, 95747 Roissy CDG Cedex, France (office). *Telephone:* 1-41-56-61-65 (office). *Fax:* 1-41-56-61-59 (office). *E-mail:* info@airfrance.com (office). *Website:* corporate.airfrance.com (office); www.airfrance.com (office).

GAGNÈRE, Olivier; French designer; b. 1952, Boulogne; began career working with Ettore Sottsass and Memphis design group, Milan 1980; worked in Murano, Italy 1989, Arita, Japan 1989–92; collaborated with Bernardaud Porcelain 1992, Cristalleries St Louis 1995; decorated Cafe Marly at Louvre Museum, Paris 1994; designed reception areas of Hotel Marignan Champs-Elysées; designs include lighting, furniture, china, glassware, accessories; works are included in collections of major museums including MOMA, New York, Museum of Decorative Arts, Paris, Nat. Center of Art and Culture Georges Pompidou, FNAC (Fonds Nat. d'Art Contemporain), Museum of Modern Art, San Francisco; Maison & Objet Designer of the Year 1998. *Exhibitions include:* retrospective exhibition, Nat. Museum of Fine Arts, Beijing and Museum of Modern Art, Shanghai 2006. *Address:* 47 Blvd St Jacques, 75014 Paris, France (office). *Telephone:* 1-45-80-79-67 (office). *Fax:* 1-45-80-79-67 (office). *E-mail:* olivier@gagnere.net (office). *Website:* www.gagnere.net (office).

GAGNON, Jean-Marie, MBA, PhD, FRSC; Canadian academic; *Professor Emeritus of Finance, Laval University;* b. 16 July 1933, Fabre; s. of Pierre Gagnon and Yvette Langlois; m. Rachel Bonin 1959; three s.; ed Univ. of Chicago and Laval Univ.; chartered accountant, Clarkson, Gordon, Cie 1957–59; Prof. of Finance, Laval Univ. 1959–2000, Prof. Emer. 2004–; mem. Royal Soc. of Canada; Visiting Prof., Faculté Universitaire Catholique, Mons, Belgium 1972–74, Univ. of Nankai, People's Repub. of China 1985; Médaille Alfred Houle, Prix Hermès de la recherche. *Publications include:* Income Smoothing Hypothesis 1970, Traité de gestion financière (co-author) 1981, 1982, 1987, Belgian Experience with Mergers 1982, Taxes and Financial Decisions (co-author) 1988, Taxes and Dividends (co-author) 1988, 1989, Corporate Governance Mechanisms and Board Composition 1995, Distribution of Voting Rights and Takeover Resistance (co-author) 1995, Tax Benefits of Hedging for Small and Medium Size Businesses (co-author) 2010. *Address:* Département de finance et assurance, Faculté des sciences de l'administration, Pavillon Palasis-Prince, Bureau 3690, Université Laval, Québec, QC G1V 0A6, Canada (office). *Telephone:* (418) 656-5535 (office). *Fax:* (418) 656-2164 (office). *E-mail:* jean-marie.gagnon@fas.ulaval.ca (office). *Website:* www4.fsa.ulaval.ca/enseignants/jean-marie-gagnon (office).

GAGOSIAN, Lawrence (Larry) Gilbert; American gallery owner and art dealer; b. 19 April 1945, Los Angeles, Calif.; s. of Ara Gagosian and Ann Louise Tonkin; ed Univ. of California, Los Angeles; fmr literary agent with William Morris Agency; began career in art by selling posters in Santa Monica 1970s; Founder and Owner Gagosian Galleries in New York, Beverly Hills, Calif., London, Paris, Rome, Athens, Geneva and Hong Kong; represents the estate of Andy Warhol. *Address:* Gagosian Gallery, 980 Madison Avenue, New York, NY 10075, USA (office); Gagosian Gallery, 6–24 Britannia Street, London, WC1X 9JD, England (office). *Telephone:* (212) 744-2313 (New York) (office); (20) 7841-9960 (London) (office). *E-mail:* newyork@gagosian.com (office); london@gagosian.com (office). *Website:* gagosian.com (office).

GAHMBERG, Carl G., MD, DMedSc; Finnish biochemist and academic; *Professor Emeritus of Biochemistry, University of Helsinki;* b. 1 Dec. 1942, Helsinki; s. of Gustaf-Adolf Gahmberg and Marie-Louise Gahmberg; m. Marianne Gripenberg-Gahmberg; one s. one d.; ed Univ. of Helsinki; Post-doctoral Fellow, Univ. of Washington 1972–74; Docent of Cell Biology, Univ. of Helsinki 1974; Prof. of Biochemistry, Åbo Akad. 1979–81, Univ. of Helsinki 1981–2012, Prof. Emer. 2012–; Research Prof., Acad. of Finland 1986–91; Visiting Prof., La Jolla Cancer Research Foundation 1988–89; Vice-Chair. Finnish Medical Asscn 1998–99, Chair. 2000–01; Exec. Ed. Biochimica et Biophysica Acta 2000–08; mem. Finnish Acad. of Science, Finnish Soc. of Sciences and Letters (Perm. Sec.), European Molecular Biology Org., Academia Europaea, World Cultural Council; foreign mem. Royal Swedish Acad. of Science, Royal Soc. of Arts and Sciences, Göteborg; Kt of the Finnish White Rose (First Class), Commdr; Order of the Finnish Lion; Chevalier, Ordre des Palmes académiques, Order of the White Rose of Finland; Komppa Prize 1971, Scandinavian Jahre Prize 1981, 150th Anniversary Prize, Finnish Medical Asscn 1985, Prof. of the Year in Finland 1995, Finnish Ayräpää Prize for Medicine 1997, J.W. Runeberg Prize for Medicine 2010. *Publications include:* 270 int. publs on cell membrane, glycoproteins, cell adhesion, cancer research. *Leisure interests:* nature, classical music, gardening. *Address:* University of Helsinki, Department of Biosciences, Division of Biochemistry, PO Box 56, Viikinkaari 5, 00014 Helsinki, Finland (office). *Telephone:* (9) 1915-9028 (office). *Fax:* (9) 1915-9068 (office). *E-mail:* carl.gahmberg@helsinki.fi (office).

GAI, Dame Pratibha L., DBE, MSc, PhD, CEng, CPhys, FInstP, FRSC, FRS; British physicist and academic; *JEOL Professor, Yorkshire Forward Chair of Electron Microscopy and Co-Director, York JEOL Nanocentre, University of York;* b. India; ed Univ. of Cambridge; began career as Postdoctoral Researcher, Univ. of Oxford; worked at DuPont and Univ. of Delaware, USA for 18 years; currently JEOL Prof., Yorkshire Forward Chair of Electron Microscopy and Co-Dir York JEOL Nanocentre, Univ. of York; Gabor Medal and Prize, Inst. of Physics 2010, Laureate for Europe, L'Oréal-UNESCO Awards For Women in Science 2013. *Publications:* nine co-authored books and more than 250 papers in professional journals. *Address:* Department of Chemistry, University of York, Heslington, York, YO10 5DD (office); York JEOL Nanocentre, Helix House, University of York, Heslington, York, YO10 5DD, England (office). *Telephone:* (1904) 328403 (office). *Fax:* (1904) 322516 (office); (1904) 328485 (office). *E-mail:* pratibha.gai@york.ac.uk (office). *Website:* www.york.ac.uk/physics/people/gai (office); www.york.ac.uk/chemistry/staff/academic/d-g/pgai (office).

GAI, Taban Deng; South Sudanese politician; *First Vice-President;* b. 1959; worked for Chevron Oil Co. before joining Sudan People's Liberation Army (SPLA) 1980s; amongst commdrs who joined breakaway faction after 1991 'Nasir' Split in SPLA, rejoined SPLA before 2005 Comprehensive Peace Agreement (CPA); Gov. Unity State 2005–13; Minister of Mining 2016–, also First Vice-Pres. of S Sudan 2016–. *Address:* Office of the Vice-President, Juba, South Sudan (office). *Website:* www.goss.org (office).

GAICIUC, Brig.-Gen. Victor, DrHistSc; Moldovan army officer, government official and diplomatist; b. 12 March 1957, Melons, Singerei dist; m.; two c.; ed Kharkov Aviation School, Moscow Acad. of Mil.-Political Dept (Air Force), NATO Coll., Rome, Italy; pilot, main pilot, patrol commdr, deputy commdr regimental aviation squadron in mil. dists Zabaikalie and Belarus 1978–86; Head of Deputy Commdr Aviation Regt, responsible for staff training in mil. dist of Belarusian Soviet Army 1989–93, returned to Moldova and apptd Chief Specialist, Head of Dept for Humanitarian Training, Training Directorate, Ministry of Defence 1993–97; Deputy Minister of Defence 1997–99 (removed from position), Commr in Dept of Mil. Admin, Ministry of Defence 1999–2000, Deputy Minister of Defence 2000–01, Minister of Defence 2001–04 (dismissed); promoted to rank of Brig.-Gen. 2002; Amb. to Belgium and Perm. Rep. NATO (also accred as Amb. to the Netherlands) 2005–10; mil. decorations from Moldova, Russia, Kazakhstan and Ukraine, Order of Fatherland, Service Class III 2007. *Publications:* Constituirea Armatei Naţionale (cronica evenimentelor 1989–1992) (ed.) 1999; several articles. *Address:* c/o Ministry of Foreign Affairs and European Integration, 2012 Chişinău, str. 31 August 80, Moldova (office). *Telephone:* (22) 57-82-07 (office). *Fax:* (22) 23-23-02 (office). *E-mail:* secdep@mfa.md (office). *Website:* www.mfa.gov.md (office).

GAILANI, Fatima, BA, MA; Afghan politician and international organization official; *President, Afghan Red Crescent Society;* b. 1954, Kabul; d. of Pir Sayed Ahmed Gailani (leader of Nat. Islamic Front of Afghanistan during 1980s); m. 1st Hamid Nasser-Zia (divorced); m. 2nd Awar ul Haq Ahadi; one d.; ed Malalai High School, Kabul, Nat. Univ. of Iran, Muslim Coll., London, England; lived in exile during Soviet invasion of Afghanistan and acted as spokesperson in London for Afghan Mujahideen; attended Bonn Conf. on Afghanistan 2001; returned to Afghanistan, chosen as del. to Emergency Loya Jirga (Grand Council) 2002, apptd as constitution drafting and ratifying commr; Pres. Afghan Red Crescent Soc. 2004–. *Publications:* Mosques of London, A Biography of Mohammed Mosa Shafi. *Address:* Afghan Red Crescent Society, Afshar-e Silo, PO Box 3066, Shar Naw, Kabul, Afghanistan (office). *Telephone:* (75) 2014446 (office); 79-9385533 (mobile) (office). *Fax:* (75) 2023476 (office). *E-mail:* int.relation.arcs@gmail.com (office). *Website:* arcs.org.af/en/page/706 (office).

GAIMAN, Neil Richard; British writer, journalist, screenwriter, producer and director; b. 10 Nov. 1960, Portchester, Hants.; s. of David Gaiman and Sheila Gaiman; m. 1st Mary McGrath 1985 (divorced 2007); three c.; m. 2nd Amanda Palmer 2011; one s.; creator and writer of Sandman comics (75 issues, collected in ten vols); collaborations with Dave McKean, Terry Pratchett; adult novelist and children's author; Fellow, Univ. of Liverpool; Patron Open Rights Group, The Science Fiction Foundation, The Bookend Trust (Tasmania); Int. Horror Critics' Guild Award for Best Collection, Eagle Award for Best Graphic Novel 1988, Best Writer of American Comics 1990, Will Eisner Comic Industry Award 1991–94, Diamond Distributors' Gem Award 1993, GLAAD Award for Best Comic 1996, Julia Verlanger Award (France) 1999, Bram Stoker Award 1999, 2002–03, 4-11 Award for Best Children's Illustrated Book 2003, Eagle Award 2004, World Fantasy Award for Best Short Story 1992, Mythopoeic Award for Best Adult Novel 1999, 2005, Audie Award 2002, Jim Henson Honours 2007, Galaxy Award (China) 2008, 2009, Newbery Medal (USA) 2008, Carnegie Medal (UK) 2009. *Films include:* Princess Mononoke (writer of English version) 1997, A Short Film About John Bolton (writer, dir) 2003, MirrorMask (writer) 2004, Beowulf (writer of adaptation, exec. producer) 2007, Stardust (producer) 2007, Coraline (based on novel) 2009, Jay & Silent Bob's Super Groovy Cartoon Movie (voice) 2013, The Making of a Superhero Musical (short film) 2015, How to Talk to Girls at Parties (exec. producer) 2018. *Play:* Wolves in the Walls 2006. *Radio:* Signal to Noise 1996, Mr Punch 2005. *Television:* Neverwhere (BBC) 1996, Babylon 5 (episode) 1997, Statuesque (writer, dir) 2009, Doctor Who (The Doctor's Wife) (BBC) 2010, Neil Gaiman's Likely Stories (exec. producer) 2016, American Gods (exec. producer) 2017, The Big Bang Theory 2018. *Publications include:* non fiction: Duran Duran 1984, Ghastly Beyond Belief 1985, Don't Panic 1987, Make Good Art 2013, The View from the Cheap Seats 2016, Norse Mythology 2017; fiction: Violent Cases 1987, Black Orchid 1988, Good Omens 1990, Miracleman – The Golden Age 1992, Signal to Noise 1992, Death – The High Cost of Living 1993, Neverwhere 1997, Stardust 1998, Sandman – The Dream Hunters 1999, American Gods (Hugo, Nebula, SFX Stoker and Locus Awards 2001) 2001, Sandman – Endless Nights 2003, Anansi Boys (Mythopoeic Award 2007) 2005, The Ocean at the End of the Lane (Book of the Year, Nat. Book Awards 2013) 2013; juvenile fiction: The Day I Swapped My Dad for Two Goldfish 1997, Coraline (also film) (Hugo, Nebula and Locus Awards 2003) 2002, Elizabeth Burr/Worzalla Award 2003) 2002, The Wolves in the Walls (with Dave McKean) (BSFA Best Short Fiction, Liber Award 2003, Andersen Award 2004) 2003, The Graveyard Book (John Newbery Medal 2009, Hugo Award for Best Novel 2009, Elizabeth Burr/Worzalla Award 2009, Booktrust Teenage Prize 2009, Carnegie Medal 2010) 2008, Odd and the Frost Giants 2009, Crazy Hair 2009, Instructions 2010, Chu's Day 2013, Fortunately, the Milk 2013, The Silver Dream 2013, Eternity's Wheel 2015; short stories: A Study in Emerald (Hugo Award for Best Short Story 2005) 2003, Fragile Things 2006, Who Killed Amanda Palmer: A Collection of Photographic Evidence (with Kyle Cassidy and Beth Hommel) 2009, Click-Clack the Rattlebag 2013; other: The Absolute Sandman 2006; ed.: Now We Are Sick 1991, Stories: All-New Tales (co-ed.) 2010; contrib. to Time Out, The Sunday Times, Comic Relief, Punch, The Observer, The Face, BBC Radio 3, BBC Radio 4, NPR, New York Times, Washington Post, Wired. *Leisure interests:* blogging, beekeeping. *Address:* c/o Merrilee Heifetz, Writers House, 21 West 26th Street, New York, NY 10010, USA (office). *Telephone:* (212) 685-2400 (office). *Fax:* (212) 685-1781 (office). *E-mail:* heifetz@writershouse.com (office). *Website:* www.writershouse.com (office); www.neilgaiman.com.

GAINES, Ernest James, BA; American writer and academic; b. 15 Jan. 1933, River Lake Plantation, Pointe Coupee Parish, La; m. Dianne Saulney; ed San Francisco State Univ., Stanford Univ.; Writer-in-Residence, Denison Univ. 1971, Stanford Univ. 1981; Visiting Prof., Whittier Coll. 1983, Writer-in-Residence 1986; Prof. of English and Writer-in-Residence, Univ. of Louisiana, Lafayette (fmrly Univ. of Southwestern Louisiana) 1983, now Writer-in-Residence Emer.; Fellow, American Acad. of Arts and Letters, Stanford Univ. (Creative Writing Program) 1958; Chevalier, Ordre des Arts et des Lettres 1996; Dr hc (Bard Coll.), (Brown Univ.), (Denison Univ.), (Louisiana State Univ.), (Loyola Univ.), (Savannah Coll. of Art and Design), (Tulane Univ.), (Univ. of Miami), (Univ. of the South, Sewanee), (Whittier Coll.); Black Acad. of Arts and Letters Award 1972, Commonwealth Club of Calif. Fiction gold medals 1972, 1984, American Acad. and Inst. of Arts and Letters Award 1987, La Humanist of the Year 1989, John Dos Passos Prize for Literature 1993, Louisiana Center for the Book Award 2000, Nat. Govs' Asscn Award for Distinguished Service in the Arts 2000, La Govs' Award for Lifetime Achievement 2000, Louisiana Writers' Award 2000, Nat. Humanities Medal 2000, Anisfield-Wolf Book Award for Lifetime Achievement 2000, Academy of Achievement Golden Plate Award 2001, Sidney Lanier Prize for Southern Literature 2012, Nat. Medal of Arts 2012. *Publications include:* Catherine Carmier 1964, Of Love and Dust 1967, Bloodline (short stories) 1968, The Autobiography of Miss Jane Pittman 1971, A Long Day in November 1971, In My Father's House 1978, A

Gathering of Old Men 1983, A Lesson Before Dying (Nat. Book Critics Circle Award 1994, Southern Writers Conference Award 1994, La Library Asscn Award 1994) 1993, Mozart and Leadbelly 2005. *Address:* c/o Tanya Bickley Enterprises Inc., PO Box 1656, New Canaan, CT 06840, USA (office). *Telephone:* (203) 966-5216 (office). *Fax:* (203) 966-6340 (office). *E-mail:* tbickley@optonline.net (office).

GAINUTDIN, Ravil Ibn Ismail, PhD; Russian (Tartar) religious leader; *Chairman, Council of Muftis of Russia;* b. 25 Aug. 1959, Tatarstan; m.; two d.; ed Islam Medrese Mir-Arab Bukhara, Russian Acad. of State Service, Moscow; First Imam-Khatyb Kazan Mosque Nur Islam; Exec. Sec. Ecclesiastical Dept of Moslems, European Section of USSR and Siberia, Ufa 1985–87; Imam-Khatyb Moscow Mosque 1987–88; Chief Imam-Khatyb 1988–; Pres. Islam Cen. of Moscow and Moscow Region 1991–; currently Chair. Council of Muftis of Russia; Chair. Religious Bd of Muslims of European Part of Russia; Prof., Moscow Higher Islam Coll.; mem. Public Chamber, Russian Fed.; mem. Int. Acad. of Sciences of Eurasia, Int. Slavic Acad., Int. Acad. of Information; mem. Council on Co-operation with Religious Unions, Russian Presidency, Public Chamber of the Russian Fed.; Order of Friendship 1987, 1997, Order of Honour 2004, Public Recognition 2006. *Publications include:* Islam in Russia, Elections in Russia: The Muslims' Choice; books on Moslem dogma and rituals. *Address:* Religious Board of European Region of Russia, Council of Mufties of Russia, Vypolzov per. 7, 129090 Moscow, Russia (office). *Telephone:* (495) 681-49-04 (office); (495) 207-53-07 (home). *Fax:* (495) 681-49-04 (office). *E-mail:* info@muslim.ru (office). *Website:* www.muslim.ru (office).

GAKHARIA, Giorgi, MPolSci, MBA; Georgian business executive and politician; *Vice-Prime Minister and Minister of Internal Affairs;* b. 19 March 1975, Tbilisi, Georgia SSR, USSR; m.; one d.; ed Javakhishvili Tbilisi State Univ., Lomonosov Moscow State Univ.; Dir Gen., SFK Group 2004–08; Visiting Lecturer in Applied Biotechnology, Moscow State Univ. 2006–09; Business Devt Dir for Eastern Europe, CIS countries and Russian Fed., Lufthansa Service Holding AG 2008–13; Business Ombudsman of Georgia March–July 2013; Econ. Advisor to Prime Minister and Sec., Econ. Council 2014–16; mem. Sakartvelos Parlamenti (parl.) 2016–; Minister of Economy and Sustainable Devt 2016–17; Vice-Prime Minister and Minister of Internal Affairs 2017–. *Address:* Ministry of Internal Affairs, 0114 Tbilisi, Gulua 10, Georgia (office). *Telephone:* (32) 241-19-93 (office). *Fax:* (32) 241-19-93 (office). *E-mail:* miapr@mia.gov.ge (office). *Website:* police.ge (office).

GAKOSSO, Jean-Claude; Republic of the Congo politician; *Minister of Foreign Affairs and Co-operation;* b. 25 July 1957, Inkouélé, Gamboma Dist; ed Univ. of Paris (Sorbonne), France; fmr lecturer on journalism, Marien Ngouabi Univ., Brazzaville; Communications Adviser to Pres. Denis Sassou Nguesso 1997–2002; mem. Ass. Nat. (Congolese Labour Party) for Ongogni constituency 2007–; Minister of Culture, Arts and Tourism 2002–15, Minister of Foreign Affairs and Co-operation 2015–; Pres. Steering Cttee, Panafrican Music Festival, Brazzaville 2005. *Publication:* The New Congolese Press: From the Gulag to the Agora 1997. *Address:* Ministry of Foreign Affairs and Co-operation, BP 2070, Brazzaville, Republic of the Congo (office). *Telephone:* 22-281-10-89 (office). *Fax:* 22-281-41-61 (office).

GALA, Antonio, LicenDer; Spanish writer; b. 2 Oct. 1930, Brazatortas, Ciudad Real; s. of Luis Gala and Adoración Velasco; ed Univs of Seville and Madrid; Founder-Pres., Fundación Antonio Gala para jóvenes artistas 2002–; Hijo Predilecto de Andalucía (Favorite Son of Andalusia) 1985; Dr hc (Univ. of Córdoba); Nat. Prize for Literature, Hidalgo PrizeAthenaeum Medal, numerous other literary and theatre awards. *Publications include:* plays: Los Verdes Campos del Edén, El caracol en el espejo (Premio Ciudad de Barcelona 1965) 1964, El sol en el hormiguero 1966, Noviembre y un poco de hierba 1967, Canatr del Santiago para todos 1971, Los buenos días perdidos (Premio Mayte 1973) 1972, Suerte, campeón 1973, Anillos para una Dama 1973, Las cítaras colgadas de los árboles 1974, Por qué corres Ulises? 1975, Petra regalada 1980, Le vieja señorita del paraíso 1980, El Cementerio de los Pájaros 1982, Trilogía de la libertad 1983, Samarkanda 1985, El hotelito 1985, Séneca o el beneficio de la duda 1987, Carmen Carmen 1988, La Truhana 1992, Los Bellos Durmientes 1994, Café Cantante 1997, Las manzanas del viernes 2000, Inés desabrochada 2003; novels: El Manuscrito Carmesí (Planeta Prize 1990) 1990, La Pasión Turca 1993, Más Allá del Jardín 1995, La Regla de Tres 1996, El Corazón Tardío 1998, Las Afuneras de Dios 1999, El imposible olvido 2001, Los invitados al jardin 2002, El dueño de la herida 2003, El pedestal de las estatuas 2007, Los papeles de agua 2008, Cosas nuestras 2008; poetry: Enemigo Intimo 1959, 11 Sonetos de la Zubia 1981, Poemas Cordobeses 1994, Testamento andaluz 1994, Poemas de amor 1997, El poema de Tobías desangelado 2005; essays: Charlas con Troylo 1981, En Propia Mano 1985, Cuaderno de la Dama de Otoño 1985, Dedicado a Tobias 1988, El águila bicéfala 1993, Troneras 1996, Quintaesencia de Antonio Gala 2012. *Address:* Fundación Antonio Gala, Calle Ambrosio de Morales 20, 14003 Córdoba, Spain (office). *Telephone:* (957) 487395 (office). *Fax:* (957) 487423 (office). *E-mail:* info@fundacionantoniogala.org (office). *Website:* www.fundacionantoniogala.org (office); www.antoniogala.es.

GALADARI, Rashid Abdul Wahab; United Arab Emirates business executive; *Chairman, R.A.W. Galadari Group;* b. 1976; s. of Abdul Wahab Galadari; f. Galvest (holding group for large family-owned business) 2005, Chair. R.A.W. Galadari Group, subsidiaries include Galadari Investment Office (GIO) (luxury real estate and property devt co.) 2005–. *Address:* GIO Investments, PO Box 214472, Building # 4 Sheikh Zayed Road, Dubai, United Arab Emirates (office). *Telephone:* (4) 3689991 (office). *E-mail:* info@gio.ae (office). *Website:* www.gio.ae (office); www.rawgaladari.com (office).

GALAL, Ahmed, BCom, MEconSc, PhD; Egyptian economist and politician; ed Cairo Univ., Ain Shams Univ., Boston Univ., USA; served for 18 years with World Bank, becoming Sr Economist, Vice-Pres. and Adviser on Middle East and N Africa 2006–07; Exec. Dir and Dir of Research, Egyptian Centre for Econ. Studies 1996–97, 2000–06; Man. Dir Econ. Research Forum, Cairo 2007–; Minister of Finance and the Budget 2013–14; mem. Int. Bd of Govs Int. Devt Research Centre, Canada 2007–; Founding Co-Chair. MENA Health Policy Forum, Jordan; Founding Bd mem. Zewail City for Science and Tech. 2011; mem. Forum Euroméditerranéen des Instituts de Sciences Économiques, France; Econ. and Social Sciences Prize, Kuwait Foundation for Advancement of Sciences 2004. *Publications include:* The Road Not Traveled: Education Reform in the Middle East and North Africa (co-author) 2007, Rethinking the Role of the State: Industrial Policy in the Middle East and North Africa (ed.) 2008, Do Governments Pick Winners or Losers? An Assessment of Industrial Policy in Egypt (co-author) 2008. *Address:* c/o Ministry of Finance, Ministry of Finance Towers, Cairo, (Nasr City), Egypt (office).

GALAL, Mohamed Noman, BA, MA, PhD; Egyptian diplomatist and academic; *Political Adviser, Bahrain Ministry of Foreign Affairs;* b. April 1943, Assiut; m. Kawther Elsherif 1969; two s.; ed Univ. of Cairo; joined Egyptian Ministry of Foreign Affairs 1965; Third Sec., Embassy in Amman 1969–72; Vice-Consul, Kuwait 1972; Consul, Abu Dhabi 1972–73; Second Sec. Oslo 1975–79; Lecturer, Diplomatic Inst. 1979–80; First Sec., New Delhi 1980, Counsellor 1981–85; Counsellor, Cabinet of Deputy Prime Minister and Minister of Foreign Affairs 1985–87; Counsellor, Egyptian Mission at UN 1987–90, Minister and Deputy Perm. Rep. 1990–92; Perm. Rep. to League of Arab States, Cairo 1992–95; Amb. to Pakistan 1995–98, to People's Repub. of China 1998–2001; Visiting Lecturer, Farleigh Dickinson Univ., New Jersey, USA 1989–91, Univ. of Cairo 1994–95; fmr Deputy Dir Centre for Int. Studies, Univ. of Bahrain; Adviser for Strategic Int. Studies and Dialogue of Civilizations, Bahrain Centre for Studies and Research 2003–10; fmr Advisor, Sec.-Gen., Gulf Cooperation Council; Political Adviser, Ministry of Foreign Affairs, Bahrain 2010–; mem. Egyptian Council for Foreign Affairs 1996–, Arab Thought Forum 2003–, Nat. Council on Human Rights, Egypt 2004–10, World Cultural Forum, Beijing 2008–, Egyptian Asscn for Historical Studies 2010–, Chinese Forum of Int. Scholars of Chinese Studies, Shanghai Social Sciences Acad. 2008; mem. Bd Confucius Int. Asscn 2014–; St Olav Medal (Norway) 1972, Nat. Medal for Merit (Egypt) 1982. *Publications include:* more than 50 publs in Arabic and English on Arab and int. affairs, foreign policy, human rights, Egypt, Middle East, Pakistan, China, non-alignment, Islam in a changing world, human rights and Islam, Egyptian revolution of 25 Jan. 2011 etc.; contrib. to several Egyptian, Bahraini and Chinese newspapers. *Leisure interests:* travelling, swimming, Asian, Europe, US and Arab regions. *Address:* PO Box 547, Manama, Bahrain (office). *Telephone:* (17) 200858 (office); (17) 625072 (home). *Fax:* (17) 226862 (office); (17) 208531 (office); (17) 623492 (home). *E-mail:* mjalal@mofa.gov.bh (office); galal_m@hotmail.com (home). *Website:* www.mofa.gov.bh (office); mohamed-n-galal.com.

GALANTE, Edward G., BSc; American oil industy executive; b. 1951, Inwood, New York; m. Cathie Galante; four c.; ed Northeastern Univ.; joined Exxon Co. 1972, Man. Baton Rouge Refinery, LA 1988, CEO and Gen. Man. Esso Caribbean and Central America 1992, Exec. Asst to Chair. Exxon Corpn 1995, Chair. and Man. Dir Esso (Thailand) Public Co. Ltd, Bangkok 1997, Exec. Vice-Pres. Exxon Mobil Chemical Co., Houston, Tex. 1999, Sr Vice-Pres. Exxon Mobil Corpn 2001–06 (retd); Vice-Chair. US Council for Int. Business 2004; mem. Bd of Dirs Foster Wheeler AG 2008–; fmr Dir Nat. Council, Northeastern Univ., Council for the US and Italy, Council of the Americas, Jr Achievement Int., US–China Business Council. *Address:* 6414 Waggoner Drive, Dallas, TX 75230, USA.

GALASSI, Jonathan White, MA; American publishing executive; *President, Farrar, Straus & Giroux Inc.;* b. 4 Nov. 1949, Seattle, Wash.; s. of Gerard Goodwin Galassi and Dorothea Johnston Galassi (née White); m. Susan Grace Galassi 1975 (divorced 2011); two d.; ed Harvard Univ., Univ. of Cambridge, UK; Ed. Houghton Mifflin Co., Boston, New York 1973–81; Sr Ed. Random House, Inc., New York 1981–86; Exec. Ed. and Vice-Pres. Farrar, Straus & Giroux Inc., New York 1986–87, Ed.-in-Chief and Sr Vice-Pres. 1988–93, Exec. Vice-Pres. 1993–99, Publr 1999–, Pres. 2002–; Poetry Ed. Paris Review 1978–88; Guggenheim Fellow 1989; mem. Acad. of American Poets (Dir 1990–2002, Pres. 1994–99, Chair. 1999–2002, Hon. Chair. 2002–); Fellow, American Acad. of Arts and Sciences 2002; Roger Klein Award for Editing, PEN 1984, Award in Literature, American Acad. of Arts and Letters 2000; Chevalier des Arts et des Lettres. *Publications include:* The Second Life of Art: Selected Essays of Eugenio Montale (ed., trans.) 1982, Otherwise: Last and First Poems of Eugenio Montale (ed., trans.) 1986, Morning Run (poetry) 1988, Eugenio Montale, Collected Poems 1916–56 (ed., trans.) 1998 (revised edn 2012), North Street (poetry) 2000, Eugenio Montale, Posthumous Diary 2001, Giacomo Leopardi, Canti (ed, trans.) 2010, Left-handed (poetry) 2012, Muse (novel) 2015, Primo Levi, Collected Poems (trans.) 2015. *Address:* Farrar, Straus & Giroux Inc., 175 Varick Street, New York, NY 10014, USA (office). *Telephone:* (212) 741-6900 (office). *Website:* www.fsgbooks.com (office).

GALATERI DI GENOLA, Count Gabriele, DIur, MBA; Italian business executive; *Non-Executive Chairman, Assicurazioni Generali SpA;* b. 11 Jan. 1947, Rome; s. of Gen. Angelo Galateri di Genola and Carla Fontana; m. Evelina Christillin; one d.; ed Liceo Ennio Quirino Visconti, Rome, Univ. of Rome, Columbia Univ., New York; Asst Lecturer in Econ. Science, Univ. of Rome 1969–70; Head Financial Analysis Dept, later Int. Financing Dept, Banco di Roma 1971–74; Financial Dir Saint Gobain, Italy, then Asst to Financial Group Dir, Paris 1974–77; Head of Foreign Finance Div., Fiat SpA 1977–83, Financial Dir 1983–86, CEO 2002–03; CEO Ifil SpA 1986–93; CEO and Gen. Man. IFI 1993–2002; Chair. Mediobanca SpA 2003–07; Chair. Telecom Italia SpA 2007–11, mem. Bd of Dirs –2014; Vice-Chair. Assicurazioni Generali SpA 2003–10, Chair. (non-exec.) 2011–; Chair. TIM Brasil Serviços e Paricipações SA; Vice-Chair. RCS MediaGroup SpA; Dir (non-exec.) Lavazza SpA, Edenred SA, Giorgio Cini Foundation; Chair. Exec. Cttee Italian Inst. of Tech., Studium Marcianum Foundation; mem. Int. Advisory Bd of Columbia Business School; Cavaliere del Lavoro. *Leisure interests:* arts, music, tennis, skiing, gym. *Address:* Assicurazioni Generali SpA, Piazza Duca degli Abruzzi 2, 34132 Trieste, Italy (office). *Telephone:* (040) 6711 (office). *Fax:* (040) 671600 (office). *E-mail:* info@generali.com (office). *Website:* www.generali.com (office).

GALAYR, Ali Khalif, BA, MA, PhD; Somali politician and academic; *President of Khatumo State;* b. 15 Oct. 1941, Las Anod; ed Boston Univ. and Syracuse Univ., USA; Political Officer, Ministry of Interior 1965–67; Training and Research Officer, Somali Inst. of Public Admin 1970–73, Dir-Gen. 1973–74; Dir-Gen. Jowhar Sugar Enterprise 1974–76; Exec. Chair. Juba Sugar Project 1976–80; Minister of Industry 1980–82; Fellow, Center for Int. Affairs, Harvard Univ., USA 1982–84, Fellow, Center for Middle Eastern Studies 1984–86; consultant on devt issues 1986–89; Asst Prof., Dept of Public Admin, Maxwell School, Syracuse Univ. 1989–91, Assoc. Prof. 1991–94, Prof. of Public Admin and Int. Relations 1994–96; Chair. and CEO SOMTEL., Sharjah, UAE 1996–2000; Prime Minister of Somalia 2000–01; Visiting Prof., Humphrey Inst., Univ. of Minnesota 2002–06; unsuccessful presidential cand. 2009; mem. Fed. Parl. 2012–; Pres. Khatumo State 2014–.

GALBUR, Andrei; Moldovan diplomatist and government official; b. 5 July 1975, Chişinău, Moldovan SSR, USSR; ed Int. Free Univ. of Moldova, Dept of Int. Law and Int. Econ. Relations, Faculty of Law, Vienna Diplomatic Acad., Austria; Attaché, Directorate-Gen. for Europe and North America (DGEAN), Ministry of Foreign Affairs and European Integration 1995–97, Second Sec., DGEAN 1997–99, Counsellor, DGEAN 1999–2000, First Sec., Embassy in Vienna and Deputy Resident Rep. to Int. Orgs in Vienna 2000–04, Head, Gen. Directorate for Int. Security 2004–05, Head, Dept for Multilateral Co-operation 2005–07, Minister-Counsellor and Deputy Chief of Mission, Embassy in Washington, DC 2007–09, Chargé d'affaires a.i. 2009–10, Head, Gen. Directorate for Multilateral Co-operation 2010–13, Amb. to Russia 2013–15, Deputy Minister of Foreign Affairs and European Integration 2015–16, Deputy Prime Minister and Minister of Foreign Affairs and European Integration 2016–17. *Address:* c/o Ministry of Foreign Affairs and European Integration, 2012 Chişinău, str. 31 August 1989 80, Moldova (office).

GALEA, Ċensu; Maltese architect and politician; b. 28 Aug. 1956; s. of Joseph Galea; m. Grace Sammut; two s. two d.; ed Lyceum and Univ. of Malta; practising architect 1982; Sec.-Gen. then Pres. of Nationalist Party Youth Section 1978–81; mem. House of Reps (Parl.) (Nationalist Party) 1987–2017, Deputy Speaker 2010–17; Exec. Chair. Building Industry Consultative Council (BICC) 2010–13; Parl. Sec., Ministry for Social Security 1992–94; Minister for Food, Agric. and Fisheries 1994–96, for Transport and Communications 1998–2004, for Competitiveness and Communications 2004–08; Shadow Minister and Opposition Spokesman for Transport and Ports 1996–98; Sec. and Whip Nationalist Party Parl. Group 1997–98. *Address:* 526 Triq San Pawl, San Pawl Il-Bahar SPB 3418, Malta (home). *Telephone:* 99423149 (office).

GALEA, Louis, BA, LLD; Maltese lawyer and politician; b. 2 Jan. 1948, Mqabba; s. of Joseph Galea and Joan Galea (née Farrugia); m. Vincienne Zammit 1977; one s. three d.; mem. Gen. Council and Exec. Cttee Nationalist Party 1972–, Gen. Sec. 1977–87; mem. Parl. 1976–2008; Minister for Social Policy including Health 1987–92, for Home Affairs and Social Devt including Health 1992–95, Minister for Social Devt 1995–96; Shadow Minister for Educ. 1996–98; Minister of Educ. 1998–2008; Speaker, House of Reps 2008–10; apptd Auditor, European Court of Auditors 2010. *Leisure interests:* reading, music, tennis.

GALEYEV, Albert Abubakirovich, Dr PhysMathSC; Russian/Bashkir physicist; *Honorary Director, Institute of Space Research, Russian Academy of Sciences;* b. 19 Oct. 1940, Ufa; m.; two c.; ed Univ. of Novosibirsk; worked at USSR Acad. of Sciences Inst. of Nuclear Physics 1961–70; Sr researcher at Acad. of Sciences Inst. of High Temperatures 1970–73; mem. CPSU 1976–91; Corresp. mem. USSR (now Russian) Acad. of Sciences 1987–92, mem. 1992; Head of Section at Acad. of Sciences Inst. of Space Research 1973–88, Dir 1988–2002, now Hon. Dir; Ed.-in-Chief Earth Research from Space; Lenin Prize 1984, Order the Badge of Honour 2002. *Publications include:* works on physics of plasma and cosmic physics. *Address:* Institute of Space Research, 117997 Moscow, Profsoyuznaya 84/32, Russia (office). *Telephone:* (495) 333-25-88 (office); (495) 135-10-94 (home). *Fax:* (495) 333-33-11 (office). *E-mail:* agaleyev@iki.rssi.ru (office).

GALGUT, Damon; South African playwright and novelist; b. 12 Nov. 1963, Pretoria; CNA Award 1992, Univ. of Johannesburg Prize 2008. *Plays:* Echoes of Anger, Party for Mother, Alive and Kicking, The Green's Keeper. *Publications include:* A Sinless Season 1984, Small Circle of Beings 1988, The Beautiful Screaming of Pigs 1991, The Quarry 1995, The Good Doctor (Commonwealth Writers Prize for Best Book, Africa Region 2004) 2003, The Impostor 2008, In a Strange Room 2010, Arctic Summer (Barry Ronge Fiction Prize 2015) 2014. *Address:* Felicity Bryan Associates, 2a North Parade Avenue, Oxford, OX2 6LX, England (office). *Telephone:* (1865) 513816 (office). *Fax:* (1865) 310055 (office). *E-mail:* agency@felicitybryan.com (office). *Website:* www.felicitybryan.com (office).

GALIBIN, Aleksander Vladimirovich; Russian actor and theatre director; b. 28 Sept. 1955, Leningrad; m.; three d.; ed Leningrad State Inst. of Theatre, Music and Cinematography, A. Vasilyev Drama School, Moscow; actor, Komissarzhevskaya Drama Theatre 1977–79; Stage Dir Aleksandrinsky Theatre 1995–; Meritorious Artist of the RSFSR 1991, People's Artist of Russian Fed. 2006. *Films include:* acted in more than 35 films 1976–, including Pyatnitskaya Street, Courage, Silver Strings, Letters from the Front, Red Crown, Ragin 2004, Master and Margarita 2005, The First Rule of the Queen 2005, Him, Her and Me 2007, Revenge 2007, 40 2007, Adel 2008, 22 minuty 2014. *Theatre includes:* (stage dir) Three Sisters, Harp of Greeting, City Romance, Pupil, Tsar Piotr and His Dead Son Aleksey. *Television includes:* The Master and Margarita (mini-series) 2005, Vyzhit posle (series) 2016.

GALIL, Zvi, BSc, MSc, PhD; Israeli computer scientist, academic and university administrator; *John P. Imlay Jr. Professor and Dean of Computing, College of Computing, Georgia Institute of Technology;* b. 26 June 1947, Tel-Aviv; m. Bella Gorenstein Galil; one s.; ed Tel-Aviv Univ., Cornell Univ., USA; conducted postdoctoral research at IBM Thomas J. Watson Research Center, Yorktown Heights, New York 1975; Faculty mem. Computer Science Dept, Tel-Aviv Univ. 1976–81, Full Prof. 1981–95, Dept Chair. 1979–82; Prof., Dept of Computer Science, Columbia Univ., New York City 1982–2006, Chair. Dept of Computer Science 1989–94, Julian Clarence Levi Prof. of Math. Methods and Computer Science, School of Eng and Applied Sciences 1987–2006, Dean, Fu Foundation School of Eng and Applied Sciences, Columbia Univ. 1995–2006; Pres. Tel-Aviv Univ. 2007–09 (resgnd); John P. Imlay Jr Dean of Computing and Prof., Coll. of Computing, Georgia Inst. of Tech. 2010–; Area Ed. Journal of the ACM (Asscn for Computing Machinery) 1984–2004; Ed. in Chief Journal of Algorithms 1988–2004; Man. Ed. SIAM (Soc. for Industrial and Applied Math.) Journal on Computing 1991–97; Chief Computer Science Adviser in the US to Oxford University Press 1992–2003; mem. Nat. Acad. of Eng 2004; Fellow, American Acad. of Arts and Sciences 2005, Asscn for Computing Machinery 1995; Dir Guglielmo Marconi Int. Fellowship Foundation 1997–; Guarantor, Italian Acad. for Advance Studies in America 1997–; Dr hc (Univ. of Waterloo) 2012; Pupin Medal 2005, Great Teacher Award, Columbia Soc. of Graduates 2009. *Publications include:* Combinatorial Algorithms on Words (co-ed.) 1985, SIAM Journal of Computing Special Issue on Cryptography (ed.) 1988, Theory of Computing and Systems, Lecture Notes in Computer Science 601 (co-ed.) 1992, Combinatorial Pattern Matching III, Lecture Notes in Computer Science 644 (co-ed.) 1992, Pattern Matching Algorithms (co-ed.) 1997; has written more than 200 scientific papers. *Address:* Georgia Institute of Technology, College of Computing, 801 Atlantic Avenue, NW, Atlanta, GA 30332, USA (office). *E-mail:* galil@cc.gatech.edu (office). *Website:* www.cc.gatech.edu (office).

GALIMOV, Erik Mikhailovich, PhD, DSc; Russian geochemist; *Director, V.I. Vernadsky Institute of Geochemistry and Analytical Chemistry, Russian Academy of Sciences;* b. 29 July 1936, Vladivostok; s. of Mikhail Piskunov and Zeya Galimova; m. 1st; one d.; m. 2nd Galina Andriukhina; two d.; ed Moscow Inst. of Oil and Gas; operational engineer 1959–60; head of geophysics expeditions 1960–63; sr researcher 1965–73; Dir V. I. Vernadsky Inst. of Geochemistry and Analytical Chem. 1992– (Head of Lab. 1973–92); Prof., Moscow State Univ.; Chair. Geochemistry Council of Russian Acad. of Sciences, Int. Lunar Exploration Working Group; Vice-Pres. Int. Asscn of Geochemical Cosmochemistry 1996–2000, Pres. 2000–04; Ed.-in-Chief International Geochemistry; mem. Editorial Bd Chemical Geology, Astrobiology; Corresp. mem. USSR (now Russian) Acad. of Sciences 1991, mem. 1994–, mem. Presidium 2002–, Chair. Meteorite Cttee; Foreign mem. German Acad. of Sciences and Literature 1998; Geochemical Fellow 1998; research in geochemistry of stable isotopes, organic geochemistry and oil and gas geology, lunar and planetary research, origin of life; Order of Honour 1988, 1996; Vernadsky Prize 1984, Alfred Treibs Medal 2004. *Achievement:* developed theory of ordered isotope distribution in biological systems, devt of isotope thermodynamics, cavitational synthesis of diamond, isotope identification of oil and gas sources, new concept of sustaining ordering as a mechanism of life emerging and evolution, new model of Earth and the Moon formation as a twin system. *Publications:* more than 400 scientific works including Geochemistry of Stable Carbon Isotopes 1968, Carbon Isotopes in Oil and Gas Geology 1973, Biological Isotope Fractionation 1985, Sources and Mechanism of Formation of Natural Gases 1988, Kimberlite Magmatism and Diamond Formation 1991, Evolution of the Biosphere 1995, Origin of the Moon 1996, Origin of the Moon: New Concept—Geochemistry and Dynamics (co-author) 2012. *Address:* V.I. Vernadsky Institute of Geochemistry and Analytical Chemistry, Kosygin Street 19, 119991 Moscow (office); Nikitski Blvd 5–5, 119019 Moscow, Russia (home). *Telephone:* (495) 137-41-27 (office); (495) 291-48-60 (home). *Fax:* (495) 938-20-54 (home). *E-mail:* galimov@geokhi.ru (office). *Website:* www.geokhi.ru/eng (office).

GALIN, Alexander; Russian playwright, actor, film and theatre director and writer; b. (Alexander Mikhaylovich Pourer), 10 Sept. 1947, Rostovskaja Oblast, USSR; s. of Mikhail Pourer and Lubov Pourer; m. Galina Alekseyevna Pourer 1950; one s.; ed Inst. of Culture, Leningrad; factory worker, later actor in puppet theatre; freelance writer 1978–; Amb. of the Arts, Fla 1989. *Plays include:* The Wall 1971, Here Fly the Birds 1974, The Hole 1975, The Roof 1976, The Delusion 1977, Retro 1979, The Eastern Tribune 1980, Stars in the Morning Sky 1982, The Toastmaster 1983, The Librarian 1984, Jeanne 1986, Group 1989, Sorry 1990, The Title 1991, The Czech Photo 1993, The Clown and the Bandit 1996, The Anomaly 1996, Sirena and Victoria 1997, The Accompanist 1998, The Competition 1998, Sea of Rain Rendevous 2000, Cash & UFO 2005, The Heroine's Dream 2005, Dzinrikisya 2009, Golden Age, or Reading 'Kandid' 2010, The Face 2013, The Parade 2015, This Night 2018; plays translated into several languages. *Films include:* The Last Escape (scriptwriter) 1979, The Ring (scriptwriter) 1982, Casanova's Coat (The Delegation) (scriptwriter and dir) 1993, The Barbarian (screenplay) 1995, The Anomaly (screenplay) 1996, The Toastmaster (screenplay) 1998, The Wedding (scriptwriter, with Pavel Lungin) 1999, Photo (scriptwriter, actor and dir) 2003, My Last Will (screenplay) 2004, The Casualty (scriptwriter and dir) 2009. *Publications include:* Selected Plays 1989, Do-re-mi-do-re-do Novel 2013. *Address:* Gorohovsky per. 15, Apt 11, 103064 Moscow, Russia (home). *E-mail:* galinalexander@gmail.com (home). *Website:* www.a-galin.ru.

GALJAARD, Hans, MD, PhD; Dutch professor of cell biology (retd); b. 8 April 1935, Leiden; m. Henriette H. van Boven 1960; two s. one d.; ed State Univ. Leiden; radiobiology training at Medical Biology Lab. Nat. Defence Org. Rijswijk 1962–65 and Atomic Energy Research Establishment, Harwell, England 1965; apptd Prof. of Cell Biology, Erasmus Univ. Rotterdam 1966, now Prof. Emer. of Human Genetics, Chair. Dept of Clinical Genetics, Univ. Hosp. 1980; apptd Dir Rotterdam Foundation of Clinical Genetics 1980; mem. Nat. Health Council, Nat. Council for Science Policy, Advisory Council on Tech.; consultant for WHO and UNFPA; mem. Royal Dutch Acad. of Sciences 1984–, Acad. Europaea; Hon. mem. Dutch Soc. for Human Genetics, Indian Soc. for Prenatal Diagnosis and Therapy; Carter Memorial Medal, British Clincial Genetics Soc., Van Walree Prijs 1997, Van Barneveld Medal 2000. *Publications include:* The Life of the Dutch 1981, Alle mensen zijn ongelijk 1994, Erfelijke aanleg 1995, Prenatal Testing: New Developments and Ethical Dilemmas 2004, Gezondheid kent geen grenzen 2008; approximately 400 articles in scientific journals, book chapters and monographs. *Leisure interests:* writing, filming, sailing. *Address:* c/o Department of Cell Biology, Erasmus University, Faculty Building, PO Box 2040, 3000 CA Rotterdam, Netherlands.

GALKO, L'ubomír; Slovak software engineer and politician; b. 14 Feb. 1968, Klieština; m.; two c.; ed Technical High School of Mechanical Eng, Comenius Univ., Bratislava; Computer Programmer, Computer Tech. Enterprise, Bratislava 1991–92; Programmer-Analyst, CK Arrangement and Consulting Ltd, Bratislava 1992–93; man. with chain of retail and wholesale stores, responsible for software applications devt, Bratislava 1993–2001; Dir Kaufland Hypermarket, Bratislava 2001–03; Deputy Dir Interfruct Slovakia Co., Bratislava 2003–04; Dir DONA DN Co. (jt stock co.), Bratislava 2004–10; Minister of Defence 2010–11 (dismissed); Deputy, Nat. Council of the Slovak Repub. (Parl.) 2012–, mem. Defence and Security Cttee, Mil. Intelligence Special Cttee; mem. Freedom and Solidarity party 2009–. *E-mail:* lubomir_galko@nrsr.sk (office). *Website:* www.lubomirgalko.sk.

GALL, Hugues R.; French arts executive; *Director, Claude Monet Foundation;* b. 18 March 1940, Honfleur; s. of Max Gall and Geneviève Carel; ed Inst. des Sciences Politiques, Univ. of Paris (Sorbonne); fmr official, Ministries of Agric., Educ. and Culture; Sec.-Gen. Réunion des Théâtres Lyriques 1969–73; Deputy Dir-Gen. Paris Opéra 1973–80; Dir-Gen. Grand Theatre, Geneva 1980–94; Dir-Gen. Paris Opéra 1995–2004; Chair. Bd of Dirs Institut pour le Financement du Cinéma et des Industries Culturelles 2004–10; Conseiller d'État 2005–09; Dir École du Louvre 2004, Fondation Noureev 2004–09, Fondation d'entreprise Veolia Environnement

2004–11, Théâtre de l'Opéra-Comique 2004; Pres. Orchestre Français des Jeunes 2007; Dir Claude Monet Foundation 2008–; elected mem. Acad. des Beaux-Arts, Inst. de France 2002–; mem. conseil de l'ordre de la Légion d'honneur 2008–, Conseil économique, social et environnemental 2011–; Officier des Palmes académiques, Chevalier du Mérite agricole, Commdr des Arts et des Lettres, Légion d'honneur, Ordre nat. du Mérite, Bourgeois d'honneur de Genève, Switzerland; Prix Montaigne 1996, Prix Grand Siècle-Laurent Perrier 1999, Médaille Beaumarchais de la SACD 2004. *Address:* Claude Monet Foundation, 84 rue Claude Monet, 27260 Giverny, France (office). *E-mail:* contact@fondation-monet.com (office). *Website:* fondation-monet-giverny.fr (office).

GALL, Joseph Grafton, BS, PhD; American biologist and academic; *American Cancer Society Professor of Developmental Genetics, Department of Embryology, Carnegie Institution;* b. 14 April 1928, Washington, DC; s. of John C. Gall and Elsie Gall (née Rosenberger); m. 1st Dolores M. Hogge 1955; one s. one d.; m. 2nd Diane M. Dwyer 1982; ed Yale Univ.; Instructor, Asst Prof., Assoc. Prof., Prof., Dept of Zoology, Univ. of Minnesota 1952–64; Prof. of Biology and Molecular Biophysics and Biochemistry, Yale Univ. 1964–83; mem. staff Dept of Embryology, Carnegie Inst. 1983–, American Cancer Soc. Prof. of Developmental Genetics 1984 (lifetime appointment); mem. Cell Biology Study Section, NIH 1963–67, Chair. 1972–74; Pres. American Soc. for Cell Biology 1968, Soc. for Developmental Biology 1984–85; mem. Bd of Scientific Counsellors, Nat. Inst. of Child Health and Human Devt, NIH 1986–90; mem. Bd of Scientific Advisers, Jane Coffin Childs Memorial Fund for Medical Research 1986–94; Visiting Prof., St Andrews Univ., UK 1960, 1968, Univ. of Leicester 1971; Visiting Scientist, Max Planck Inst., Tübingen, Germany 1960; mem. NAS, AAAS, American Acad. of Arts and Sciences, American Philosophical Soc., Accad. Naz. dei Lincei (Rome) 1988; Fellow, Yale Corpn 1989–95; Hon. DrMed (Charles Univ., Prague) 2002; E.B. Wilson Medal, American Soc. for Cell Biology 1983, Wilbur Cross Medal of Yale Univ. 1988, AAAS Mentor Award for Lifetime Achievement 1996, Jan E. Purkyne Medal, Czech Acad. of Science 1999, Lifetime Achievement Award, Soc. for Developmental Biology 2004, Albert Lasker Special Achievement in Medical Science Award 2006, Louisa Gross Horwitz Prize (co-recipient) 2007. *Publications:* scientific articles on chromosome structure, nucleic acid biochemistry, cell fine structure, organelles of the cell. *Leisure interest:* collecting books on the history of biology. *Address:* Department of Embryology, Carnegie Institution for Science, 3520 San Martin Drive, Baltimore, MD 21218 (office); 5702 Ainsley Garth, Baltimore, MD 21212, USA (home). *Telephone:* (410) 246-3017 (office). *Fax:* (410) 243-6311 (office). *E-mail:* gall@carnegiescience.edu (office). *Website:* www.carnegiescience.edu (office).

GALLACH, Cristina; Spanish journalist and UN official; *High Commissioner for the 2030 Agenda of Spain;* b. 1960, Barcelona; m.; two c.; ed Universidad Autonoma, Barcelona, Columbia Univ., USA; began career as reporter with TVE Barcelona 1983–84; USA Corresp., Avui (Catalan daily newspaper) 1984–86; Corresp., El Periodico, Barcelona 1986–90; Sr Corresp. with EFA (Spanish news agency), Moscow 1990–92, Brussels 1993–96; Chief Media Adviser to Sec.-Gen., NATO, Brussels 1996–99; Spokesperson and Chief Media Adviser to EU High Rep. for Common Foreign and Security Policy, Brussels 1999–2009; Spokesperson of Spanish Govt for EU rotating Presidency 2010; Head of Public Relations Unit, Council of EU, Directorate-Gen. for Information and Communication, Brussels 2010–14; Under-Sec.-Gen. for Communications and Public Information, UN 2014–17; High Commr for the 2030 Agenda of Spain 2018–. *Website:* www.agenda2030.gob.es (office).

GALLAGHER, Katy, BA; Australian social worker, trade union organizer and politician; b. 17 March 1970, Weston Creek, Canberra, ACT; partner Dave Skinner; one s. one d. and one d. with fiancé Brett Seaman (died 1997); ed Melrose High School, Stirling Coll., Australian Nat. Univ.; started career as social worker; worked as an advocate for People First ACT 1994–97; joined Community and Public Sector Union 1997, initially working as a case manager and then as a nat. organizer; mem. ACT Legis. Ass. (Australian Labor Party) for Molonglo constituency 2001–; Deputy Chief Minister of ACT with responsibilities including Disability and Community Services, and Women 2006–11, for Children and Young People 2007–11; ACT Minister for Health 2006–14; Treas. of ACT 2008–11; Minister for Industrial Relations 2009–11; Chief Minister of ACT 2011–14; Senator for ACT 2015–18. *Address:* ACT Legislative Assembly, GPO Box 1020, Canberra, ACT 2601, Australia (office). *Telephone:* (2) 6205-0840 (office). *Fax:* (2) 6205-3030 (office). *E-mail:* gallagher@act.gov.au (office). *Website:* www.act.gov.au (office); www.katygallagher.net.

GALLAGHER, Liam (William John Paul); British singer, musician (guitar, keyboards) and producer; b. 21 Sept. 1972, Burnage, Manchester; s. of Peggy Gallagher; brother of Noel Gallagher (q.v.); m. 1st Patsy Kensit 1997 (divorced 2000); one s.; one d. (with Lisa Moorish); m. 2nd Nicole Appleton 2008 (divorced 2014); one s.; ed St Mark's High School, Didsbury, Manchester; Founder-mem., Oasis 1991–2009; f. and recorded for Big Brother Records 2000–; Founder-mem., Beady Eye 2009–14; numerous concert and festival appearances; regular tours UK, Europe and USA; Q Awards for Best New Act 1994, Best Live Act 1995, BRIT Awards for Best Newcomers 1995, Best Single, Best Video, Best British Group 1996, NME Awards for Best UK Band, Artist of the Year 2003, Q Award for Best Act in the World Today 2006, BRIT Award for Outstanding Contribution to Music 2007. *Recordings include:* albums: with Oasis: Definitely Maybe 1994, (What's The Story) Morning Glory? (BRIT Award for Best Album 1996) 1995, Be Here Now 1997, The Masterplan 1998, Standing On The Shoulder of Giants 2000, Familiar To Millions (live) 2001, Heathen Chemistry 2002, Don't Believe The Truth (Q Award for Best Album) 2005, Stop the Clocks 2006, Dig Out Your Soul 2008; with Beady Eye: Different Gear, Still Speeding 2011, BE 2013; solo: As You Were 2017. *Website:* www.oasisinet.com; www.liamgallagher.com.

GALLAGHER, Noel Thomas David; British singer, songwriter and musician (guitar); b. 29 May 1967, Burnage, Manchester; s. of Peggy Gallagher; brother of Liam Gallagher (q.v.); m. 1st Meg Matthews 1997 (divorced 2001); one d.; m. 2nd Sara MacDonald 2011; two s.; fmrly worked as guitar technician for Inspiral Carpets 1990–93; mem., Oasis 1991–2009; f. and recorded for Big Brother Records 2000–; mem., Noel Gallagher's High Flying Birds 2011–; numerous concert and festival appearances; regular tours UK, Europe and USA; numerous collaborations with other artists including Ian Brown, the Chemical Brothers, Goldie, Miles Kane, Paul Weller; Founder Sour Mash Records 2001–; mem. Tailgunner; Q Awards for Best New Act 1994, for Best Live Act 1995, for Best Act in the World Today 2006, for Best Solo Artist 2018, Brit Awards for Best Newcomers 1995, for Best Single, for Best Video, for Best British Group 1996, for Outstanding Contribution to Music 2007, Ivor Novello Award 1995, Music Week Award for Top Songwriter 1996, Grammy Award for Best Song (Wonderwall) 1997, NME Awards for Best UK Band, Artist of the Year 2003. *Recordings include:* albums: Definitely Maybe 1994, (What's The Story) Morning Glory? (BRIT Award for Best Album 1996) 1995, Be Here Now 1997, The Masterplan 1998, Standing On The Shoulder of Giants 2000, Familiar To Millions (live) 2001, Heathen Chemistry 2002, Don't Believe The Truth (Q Award for Best Album) 2005, Stop the Clocks 2006, Dig Out Your Soul 2008; with Noel Gallagher's High Flying Birds: Noel Gallagher's High Flying Birds 2011, Chasing Yesterday (Q Best Album Award 2015) 2015, Who Built the Moon? 2017. *Leisure interest:* supporting Manchester City football club. *Address:* Ignition Management, 54 Linhope Street, London, NW1 6HL, England (office). *Telephone:* (20) 7298-6000 (office). *Fax:* (20) 7258-0962 (office). *E-mail:* info@ignition.co.uk (office). *Website:* www.ignition.co.uk/management.php (office); www.oasisinet.com; www.noelgallagher.com.

GALLAGHER, Most Rev. Paul Richard, DCL; British ecclesiastic, diplomatist and Vatican official; *Secretary for Relations with States;* b. 23 Jan. 1954, Liverpool; ed St Francis Xavier's Coll., Pontifical Ecclesiastical Acad.; ordained RC priest 31 July 1977; apptd Asst Priest, Holy Name parish, Fazakerley, Liverpool, also chaplain, Fazakerley Hosp.; joined Papal Diplomatic Service 1984, Diplomatic Attaché, Tanzania 1984–87, Sec., Apostolic Nunciature, Uruguay 1987–91, Auditor, Apostolic Nunciature, Philippines 1991–94, Counsellor, Dept for Relations with States, Vatican Secr. of State 1994–2000, Perm. Observer, Council of Europe, Strasbourg 2000–04, Apostolic Nuncio to Burundi 2004–09, to Guatemala 2009–12, to Australia 2012–14; Sec. for Relations with States 2014–; Titular Archbishop of Hodelm 2004–. *Address:* Secretariat of State, Roman Curia, Palazzo Apostolico Vaticano, Citta del Vaticano 00120 Rome, Italy (office). *Telephone:* (06) 69883014 (office). *Fax:* (06) 69885364 (office). *E-mail:* vati032@relstat-segstat.va (office). *Website:* www.vatican.va/roman_curia/secretariat_state (office).

GALLAND, Yves; French politician and business executive; *President, Boeing France;* b. 8 March 1941; s. of Jean Galland and Suzanne Vershave; m. Anne Marie Chauvin 1967; one s. two d.; pres. of publishing and publicity cos 1969; mem. European Parl. 1979–, Vice-Pres. 1989–91; Deputy Mayor of Paris in charge of housing 1983–95, of architecture 1995–98; Minister of Local Affairs and Decentralization 1986–88, of Industry 1995, of Finance and Foreign Trade 1995–97; Pres. Valoise Radical Party 1988–94; mem. Nat. Council Union pour la démocratie française (UDF), del. to Paris 1979, mem. Nat. Political Bureau 1984–, Pres. Liberal Group, European Parl. 1991–94; Pres. UDF Group 1998–; Chair. European Assistance Group 2000–03; Vice-Pres. Int. Relations, Boeing Corpn 2003–, Pres. Boeing France 2003–. *Address:* Boeing, 75 rue du Faubourg Saint-Honoré, 75008 Paris (office); 6 rue des Haudriettes, 75003 Paris, France. *Telephone:* 1-70-37-07-47 (office). *E-mail:* BoeingFranceCommunication@boeing.com (office). *Website:* www.boeing.fr (office).

GALLANT, Hon. Brian Alexander, BA, LLB, LLM; Canadian lawyer and politician; b. 27 April 1982, Shediac Bridge, NB; s. of Pierre Gallant and Marilyn Gallant (née Scholten); ed Polyvalente Louis-J.-Robichaud, Université de Moncton, McGill Univ.; Pres. Student Fed., Université de Moncton; practised corp. and commercial law with firm Stewart McKelvey; later became Partner at Veritas Law, Dieppe; unsuccessful cand. in Moncton East by-election 2006; Leader of the Liberal Party 2012–; MLA of New Brunswick for Kent 2013–14, for Shediac Bay-Dieppe 2013–, Leader of the Opposition 2013–14; Premier of New Brunswick 2014–18 (resgnd). *Address:* c/o Office of the Premier, Centennial Building, PO Box 6000, 675 King Street, Fredericton, NB E3B 5H1, Canada (office). *Website:* nbliberal.ca/meet-brian.

GALLIANO, John, CBE; British fashion designer; *Creative Director, Maison Margiela;* b. (Juan Carlos Antonio Galliano Guillén), 28 Nov. 1960, Gibraltar; s. of John J. Galliano and Anita Guillén; ed Wilson's Grammar School, Wallington, Central St Martin's Coll. of Art and Design, London; moved to Streatham, southwest London 1966, and later to Brockley; designer collections 1985–; worked on Courtelle project 1985; first British designer ever to show collection in Paris at the Louvre during Paris Fashion Week 1990; moved to Paris and introduced Galliano's Girl 1991; designer of costumes for Ballet Rambert 1990, Kylie Minogue's Let's Get to It UK tour 1991; Chief Designer Givenchy 1995–96, Christian Dior 1996–2011, launched 'galliano' womenswear collection 2007; recreated some of Dior's period clothing for Madonna in film Evita; other clients have included Charlize Theron, Riley Keough (granddaughter of Elvis Presley), Kate Moss, Cate Blanchett, Nicole Kidman, Daphne Guinness and the late Princess Diana; found guilty by a French court of racial insults and fined Sept. 2011; currently Creative Dir Maison Margiela; British Designer of Year Award, British Council 1987, 1994, 1995, 1997 (co-recipient), Dress of the Year, Fashion Museum, Bath 1988, Int. Womenswear Designer of the Year, CFDA 1997, VH1 Womenswear Designer of the Year 1997, Int. Designer Award, Council of Fashion Designers of America 1998, Royal Designer for Industry 2002, appeared on The Independent on Sunday's 'pink list' for being one of "the most influential gay people in Britain" 2007 and other awards. *Address:* Maison Margiela, 163 rue Saint Maur, 75011 Paris (office); John Galliano, 384–386 rue St Honoré, 75001 Paris; 60 rue d'Avron, 75020 Paris, France. *Telephone:* 1-44-53-63-00 (office); 1-55-35-40-40. *E-mail:* reception@margiela.com (office). *Website:* www.maisonmargiela.com (office); www.johngalliano.com.

GALLIENNE, Guillaume; French actor and film director; b. 8 Feb. 1972, Neuilly-sur-Seine (Hauts-de-Seine); ed Conservatoire national; mem. Comédie-Française co. 1998–, Sociétaire 2005–; collaborated on writing of ballet Le Riche for Paris Opera 2005; staged Huis Clos by Jean-Paul Sartre at Tessenkaï Noh Theatre, Tokyo 2006, Sur la Grand-rout by Anton Chekhov at Studio-Théâtre, Comédie-Française 2007; cr. Les Garçons et Guillaume, à table! (Molière de la Révélation Théâtrale Masculine 2010, Prix Nouveau Talent Humour/One Man Show, SACD 2010, Prix du Jeune Théâtre Béatrix, Dussane-André Roussin 2010) 2008; Chevalier, Ordre nat. du Mérite; Officier des Arts et des Lettres. *Theatre includes:* numerous plays including Fantasio (Alfred de Musset) 2008, Les trois soeurs (Chekhov) 2010–11, Un fil a la patte (Georges Feydeau) 2013. *Films include:* List of Merite 1992, Sabrina 1995, Un samedi sur la terre 1996, Jeunesse 1997, The Tango

Lesson 1997, Monsieur Naphtali 1999, Une pour toutes 1999, Mon plus beau mariage (short) 1999, The Dancer 2000, Jet Set 2000, Fils de personne 2000, Le coeur sur la main (short) 2001, En scène! (short) 2001, Fanfan la tulipe 2003, Monsieur Ibrahim 2003, The Secret Adventures of Gustave Klopp 2004, Tu vas rire, mais je te quitte 2005, Orchestra Seats 2006, Marie Antoinette 2006, U (voice) 2006, The Jungle 2006, The Colonel 2006, Le dernier épisode de Dallas (short) 2006, The Candidate 2007, Sagan 2008, Musée haut, musée bas 2008, The Concert 2009, Ensemble, nous allons vivre une très, très grande histoire d'amour... 2010, L'Italien 2010, De la table à la scène (documentary) (producer) 2011, Confession of a Child of the Century 2012, Astérix and Obélix: God Save Britannia 2012, Me, Myself and Mum (also writer, dir and producer) (Art Cinema Award and Prix SACD, Cannes Film Festival) 2013, Yves Saint Laurent 2014, Down by Love 2016, Cézanne and I 2016. *Television includes:* Elles et moi (mini-series) 2008, Les Bonus de Guillaume (series) (also writer) 2008, Farewell De Gaulle, Farewell (film) 2009, The Little Prince (series) 2010–13, Hard (series) 2011, Le débarquement (series) 2013, Oblomov (film) (also dir) 2017. *Address:* c/o Cécile Felsenberg, UBBA, 6 rue de Braque, 75003 Paris, France (office). *Telephone:* 1-44-54-26-40 (office). *Fax:* 1-44-54-08-44 (office). *E-mail:* info@ubba.eu (office). *Website:* www.ubba.eu (office).

GALLINGER, Yuri Yiosifovich, DrMed; German surgeon; b. 3 Sept. 1939, Krasnaarmejsk, Saratov Region, Russian Federation; s. of Joseph Gallinger and Yekaterina Roor; m.; one s.; ed Kishinev Inst. of Medicine; gen. practitioner in polyclinics, then in 59th Clinic Hosp., Moscow 1962–67; researcher, Moscow Medical Univ., apptd Head Dept of Endoscopic Surgery, B. V. Petrovsky Nat. Research Center for Surgery 1986; Pres. Russian Scientific Soc. of Endoscopic Surgery; mem. European Asscn of Endoscopic Surgery, Pirogov Asscn of Surgeons, New York Acad. of Sciences; State Prize of Russian Fed. 1990. *Publications include:* over 200 scientific publs. *Leisure interests:* detective films and literature.

GALLO, Robert C., MD; American biomedical scientist and academic; *Professor and Director, Institute of Human Virology, University of Maryland;* b. 23 March 1937, Waterbury, Conn.; m. Mary Jane Hayes 1961; two s. one d.; ed Providence Coll., Jefferson Medical Univ., Philadelphia, Yale Univ., Univ. of Chicago; Intern and Resident in Medicine, Univ. of Chicago 1963–65; Clinical Assoc. Nat. Cancer Inst. Bethesda, Md 1965–68, Sr Investigator 1968–69, Head, Section on Cellular Control Mechanisms 1969–72, Chief, Lab. of Tumor Cell Biology, Div. of Cancer Etiology 1972–93; apptd Prof. and Dir Inst. of Human Virology, Univ. of Md, Baltimore 1993, currently Co-founder and Dir Inst. of Human Virology, Homer and Martha Gudelsky Distinguished Prof. in Medicine, Co-founder and Scientific Dir Global Virus Network; Rep. World Conf. Int. Comparative Leukemia and Lymphoma Asscn 1981–; mem. Bd of Govs Franco-American AIDS Foundation, World AIDS Foundation 1987; Co-founder Global Virus Network 2011; mem. NAS 1988, US Inst. of Medicine 1989; Hon. Prof., Johns Hopkins Univ. 1985–, Karolinska Inst., Stockholm 1998–; 30 hon. doctorates from 13 countries; numerous honours and awards including First Dameshek Award, American Soc. of Hematology 1974, Lasker Award for Basic Medical Research 1982, Otto Herz Cancer Prize, Tel Aviv Univ. 1982, Rabbi Shacknai Immunology Award, Hebrew Univ., Israel 1985, Gen. Motors Cancer Research Award 1984, Armand Hammer Cancer Research Award 1985, Lasker Award for Clinical Medical Research 1986, Gairdner Foundation Int. Award 1987 and other awards for cancer research, Japan Prize for Science and Technology 1988, 1st Dale McFarlin Award for Research, Int. Retrovirology Asscn 1994, Promesa Award 1997, Nomura Prize for AIDS and Cancer Research (Japan) 1998, Warren Alpert Prize, Harvard Univ. 1998, Paul Erlich Award (Germany) 1999, Príncipe de Asturias Award (Spain) 2000, Frank Annunzio Award in Science 2000, World Health Award 2001, Dan David Prize, Tel Aviv Univ. 2009, Award for Distinguished Research in the Biomedical Sciences, Asscn of American Medical Colls 2009, Most Cited Scientist in the World, Inst. of Scientific Information 1980–90. *Achievements include:* co-discoverer of HIV virus and first human retroviruses; discoverer of one of the first known cytokimes IL-2 (with co-workers); discoverer of Human Herpes Virus-6 (HHV-6) (with co-workers). *Publications:* over 1,200 scientific publs. *Leisure interests:* swimming, reading historical novels, tennis, theatre, biking. *Address:* Office of the Director, Institute of Human Virology, 725 West Lombard Street, Suite S307, Baltimore, MD 21201, USA (office). *Telephone:* (410) 706-8614 (office). *Fax:* (410) 706-1952 (office). *E-mail:* rgallo@ihv.umd.edu (office). *Website:* www.ihv.org (office).

GALLOGLY, James (Jim) L., BA, LLB; Canadian business executive; b. St John's, Newfoundland; ed Univ. of Colorado, Univ. of Oklahoma, Advanced Exec. Program, J.L. Kellogg Grad. School of Man., Northwestern Univ.; began career with Phillips Petroleum Co. 1980, served in a variety of legal, finance and operational roles, including Man. of Business Services of N America Exploration and Production and Finance Man. 1990–93, Man. Ekofisk II, Norway 1993–95, Vice-Pres. of N America 1995–97, Vice-Pres. of Plastics 1997–98, of Olefins and Polyolefins 1998–99, Sr Vice-Pres. of Chemicals, ConocoPhillips 1999–2000, Exec. Vice-Pres. of Refining, Marketing and Transportation 2006–08, of Exploration and Production 2008–09, mem. Bd of Dirs, Pres. and CEO Chevron Phillips Chemical Co. 2000–06; CEO LyondellBasell Industries 2009–15, Chair. Man. Bd 2010–15; Dir, DuPont 2015–; mem. Bd of Dirs, American Petroleum Inst.; fmr mem. Bd of Dirs, American Chemical Council, American Plastics Council, Nat. Petrochemical and Refiners' Asscn; mem. Univ. of Oklahoma Coll. of Eng Bd of Visitors, Univ. of Colorado Eng Advisory Council, Univ. Cancer Foundation Bd of Visitors at the Univ. of Texas M.D. Anderson Cancer Center; mem. Colorado, Oklahoma and Texas Bar Asscns; Chair. Junior Achievement of Southeast Texas. *Address:* E.I. DuPont de Nemours & Co., 1007 Market Street, Wilmington, DE 19898, USA (office). *Telephone:* (302) 774-1000 (office). *E-mail:* info@dupont.com (office). *Website:* www.dupont.com (office).

GALLOIS, Louis; French business executive and fmr government official; *Chairman of the Supervisory Board, PSA Peugeot Citröen SA;* b. 26 Jan. 1944, Montauban, Tarn-et-Garonne; s. of Jean Gallois and Marie Prax; m. Marie-Edmée Amaudric du Chaffaut 1974; one s. two d.; ed École des Hautes Études Commerciales, Paris, École Nat. d'Admin, Strasbourg; Head of Bureau, Treasury 1972; Dir of Cabinet of Jean-Pierre Chevènement (Minister of Research and Tech. 1981–82, Minister of Research and Industry 1982); Dir-Gen. for Industry, Ministry of Research and Industry 1983; Civil Admin., Ministry of Econ. and Finance 1986; Dir of Civil and Mil. Cabinet, Minister of Defence 1988–89; Pres., Dir-Gen. Soc. Nationale d'Etude et de Construction de Moteurs d'Aviation (SNECMA) 1989–92; Pres. (Econ. Interest Group) Avion de Combat européen-Rafale 1989; Pres., Dir-Gen. Aérospatiale 1992–96; Chair. Soc. Nationale des Chemins de Fer Français (SNCF) 1996–2006; Co-CEO European Aeronautic Defence and Space Co. (EADS) NV 2006–07, CEO 2007–12, CEO Airbus SAS 2006–07; Commr Gen. of Investment –2014; Chair. Supervisory Bd, PSA Peugeot Citröen SA 2014–; Pres. Soc. Gestion de Participations Aéronautiques (SOGEPA) 1993–96; Vice-Pres. Supervisory Council Airbus-Industrie 1992–96; Pres. Communauté des chemins de fer européens 1999–, Fondation Villette-Entreprises; mem. Dassault aviation 1992–; Chevalier, Ordre nat. du Mérite; Commdr, Légion d'honneur. *Address:* PSA Peugeot Citroën SA, 75 avenue de la Grande-Armée, 75116 Paris, France (office). *Telephone:* 1-40-66-42-96 (office). *E-mail:* louis.gallois@mpsa.com (office). *Website:* www.psa-peugeot-citroen.com (office).

GALLOWAY, David A., BA, MBA; Canadian financial services industry executive; m.; two c.; ed Univ. of Toronto, Harvard Business School, USA; Founding Partner, Canada Consulting Group; joined Torstar Corpn 1981, Pres. and CEO 1988–2002, also CEO Harlequin Books 1982–88; joined Bd of Dirs Bank of Montréal (BMO) Financial Group 1998, Chair. BMO Financial Group 2004–12; mem. Bd of Dirs, E.W. Scripps Co. 2002–, Toromont Industries Ltd 2002–, Cognos Inc. 2007–, Shred-it Canada Corpn 2014–; fmr mem. Bd of Dirs Clearnet Communications Inc., Visible Genetics, Westburne Inc., Harris Bankmont, Corel Corpn 2001–03 Hudson's Bay Co. 2003–06, Abitibi Consolidated Inc. 2006–07, Shell Canada Ltd 2006–07; Founding Dir Canadian Film Centre (fmr Chair.); Chair. Bd of Trustees, Hosp. for Sick Children, Toronto 2002–05. fmr mem. Bd of Govs Trent Univ.

GALLOWAY, James N., BS, PhD; American chemist, environmental scientist and academic; *Sidman P. Poole Professor in Environmental Science and Professor, Department of Environmental Sciences, University of Virginia;* b. 26 Oct. 1944, Annapolis, MD; ed Whittier Coll., Calif., Univ. of California, San Diego; Postdoctoral appointment, Cornell Univ.; apptd Asst Prof., Univ. of Virginia, Charlottesville 1976, currently Sidman P. Poole Prof. in Environmental Science and Prof., Dept of Environmental Sciences, Pres. Bermuda Biological Station for Research 1988–95, Chair. Dept of Environmental Sciences 1996–2001; currently Chair. Int. Nitrogen Initiative (sponsored by Scientific Cttee on Problems of the Environment and the Int. Geosphere-Biosphere Programme); mem. US Environmental Protection Agency's Science Advisory Bd; currently researching acidification of streams in Shenandoah Nat. Park, Va, composition of precipitation in remote regions, air-sea interactions and Asia's impact on global biogeochemistry; Fellow, AAAS 2002, American Geophysical Union 2008; Tyler Prize for Environmental Achievement (co-recipient) 2008, Alumnus Achievement Award, Whittier Coll. 2011. *Publications:* Asian Change in the Context of Global Climate Change: Impact of Natural and Anthropogenic Changes in Asia on Global Biogeochemical Cycles (co-ed.) 1998, Biogeochemical Cycling of Sulfur and Nitrogen in the Remote Atmosphere (co-ed.) 2002; numerous scientific papers in professional journals on biogeochemistry and chem. of natural waters at the watershed, regional and global scales, effects of nitrogen in the environment. *Address:* PO Box 400123, Clark Hall 210, Department of Environmental Sciences, University of Virginia, Charlottesville, VA 22903, USA (office). *Telephone:* (434) 924-1303 (office). *Fax:* (434) 982-2137 (office). *E-mail:* jng@virginia.edu (office). *Website:* www.evsc.virginia.edu (office).

GALSWORTHY, Sir Anthony Charles, Kt, KCMG, MA; British organization official and fmr diplomatist; b. 20 Dec. 1944, London, England; s. of Sir Arthur Galsworthy and Lady Galsworthy; m. Jan Dawson-Grove 1970; one s. one d.; ed St Paul's School, London, Corpus Christi Coll., Cambridge; Foreign Office, London 1966, Third Sec., Hong Kong 1967, Third, later Second Sec., Beijing 1970, Second, later First Sec., FCO, London 1972, First Sec., Rome 1977, First Sec., later Counsellor, Beijing 1981, Counsellor and Head Hong Kong Dept, FCO 1984, Prin. Pvt. Sec. to Sec. of State for Foreign and Commonwealth Affairs 1986, with Royal Inst. of International Affairs, London 1988, British Sr Rep., Jt Liaison Group, Hong Kong 1989, Cabinet Office 1993, Deputy Under-Sec. of State, FCO 1995, Amb. to People's Repub. of China 1997–2002; Adviser on China, Standard Chartered Bank 2002–14; Dir Earthwatch, Europe 2002–06; Dir Bekaert SA 2004–14, WWT (Consulting) Ltd 2009–; Scientific Assoc. Nat. History Museum, London 2001–; Trustee, Wildfowl and Wetland Trust 2002–09, British Trust for Ornithology 2002–06; Hon. Fellow, Royal Botanic Gardens, Edin. 2002, Kunming Inst. of Botany 2001; Linnean Soc. Medal for Taxonomy 2000. *Leisure interests:* wildlife, entomology.

GALTUNG, Johan Vincent, PhD (Math.), PhD (Sociology); Norwegian professor of peace studies and mediator; *Peace Mediator and Professor of Peace Studies, Transcend;* b. 24 Oct. 1930, Oslo; s. of August Galtung and Helga Holmboe; m. 1st Ingrid Eide 1956 (divorced 1968); two s.; m. 2nd Fumiko Nishimura 1969; one s. one d.; ed Univ. of Oslo; Prof. of Sociology, Columbia Univ., New York, USA 1957–60; Founder and Dir Int. Peace Research Inst., Oslo 1959–69; Prof. of Peace Research, Univ. of Oslo 1969–77; Prof., Princeton Univ., USA 1985–89; Prof. of Peace Studies, Univ. of Hawaii 1985–2004; Prof. of Peace and Co-operation Studies, Univ. of Witten-Herdecke, Germany; Olof Palme Prof. of Peace, Stockholm, Sweden 1990–91; Prof. of Peace Studies, Univ. of Alicante, Spain 2005–; Founder and Dir Transcend (peace devt network) 1993–, Rector Transcend Peace Univ., also Prof. of Peace Studies; mediator in more than 100 conflicts world-wide; Hon. Prof., Berlin, Alicante, Sichuan, Witten/Herdecke; Dr hc (Finland, Romania, Uppsala, Tokyo, Hagen, Alicante, Osnabrück, Turin, Puebla, Complutense Madrid); Alternative Nobel Peace Prize (Right Livelihood Award 1987), Bajaj Int. Gandhi Prize 1993, Korean DMZ Peace Prize, Abdul Ghaffar Khan Int. Peace-Builder Prize, Premio Hidalgo 2005, Erik Byes Minnepris 2011, The People's Nobel Peace Prize 2017. *Play:* Globalizing God 2011. *Publications include:* Theory and Methods of Social Research (four vols) 1967, 1977, 1980, 1988, There are Alternatives 1983, Hitlerism, Stalinism, Reaganism 1984; Essays in Peace Research Vols I–VI 1974–88, Human Rights in Another Key, Peace by Peaceful Means: Peace, Conflict, Development, Civilization, Conflict Transformation by Peaceful Means 2000, Johan uten land: På fredsveien gjennom verden (Norwegian Brage Literary Prize) 2000, 50 Years: 100 Peace & Conflict Perspectives 2008, 50 Years: 2 Intellectual Landscapes Explored 2008, The Fall of the US Empire – And Then What? 2009, Globalizing God (with Graeme MacQueen) 2009, A Theory of

Conflict 2010, A Theory of Development 2010, Reconciliation (with Joanna Santa Barbara and Diane Perlman) 2012, Peace Mathematics (with Dietrich Fischer) 2012, Peace Economics 2012, The Art of Peace 2018. *Leisure interests:* travel, writing. *Address:* 6 Carrer Marfil Urb. Escandinavia, ALFAZ Del Pi, 03580 Alicante, Spain (home); Garden Court, Apt 912, Kawaramachi/Shomen, Kyoto 600, Japan (home). *Telephone:* (96) 5889919 (Alicante) (home). *Fax:* (96) 5889919 (Alicante) (home). *E-mail:* galtung@transcend.org (office). *Website:* www.transcend.org (office).

GALUŠKA, Vladimír, JUDr; Czech diplomatist and lawyer; b. 2 Oct. 1952, Prague; s. of Miroslav Galuška and Milena Galušková (née Králová); m. Marcela Wintrová 1975; two s.; ed Charles Univ., Prague; Legal Counsel, Škoda Praha Enterprise 1975–85, Head of Legal Dept, Škoda Praha 1985–90; Consul, Embassy in Washington, DC 1990–91, Political Counsellor 1991–92, Acting Perm. Rep. to UN, New York 1993, Deputy Chief of Mission, Embassy in Washington, DC 1993–94, Dir Personnel Dept, Ministry of Foreign Affairs 1994–97, Amb. and Perm. Rep. to UN, New York 1997–2001, Dir Dept of American States, Ministry of Foreign Affairs 2001–02, Dir-Gen., Section of Bilateral Relations 2002–04, Amb. to Slovakia 2004–09, Dir Gen., Consular Section, Ministry of Foreign Affairs 2009–10, Deputy Minister of Foreign Affairs 2010–13, Amb. and Perm. Rep. to UN, OSCE and other Int. Orgs, Vienna 2013–18; Pres. ECOSOC 1997, Exec. Bd UNDP/UNFPA 2000; Chair. Third Cttee, 54th UN Gen. Ass. 1999.

GALVÁN GALVÁN, Gen. Guillermo, BA, MA; Mexican army officer and government official; b. 19 Jan. 1943, Mexico City; ed Colegio Militar, Colegio de Defensa Nacional, Monterrey Inst. of Tech. and Higher Educ.; has been Commdr in numerous mil. zones, including Fifth Zone in state of Chihuahua, 30th in Tabasco, 21st in Tabasco and 17th in Querétaro; fmr Mil. and Air Defence Attaché, Embassy in Madrid; fmr Rector Universidad del Ejército y Fuerza Aérea Mexicanos; has served as Asst Operating Staff Dir, as Head of Centre for the Co-ordination of Air Operations of Nat. Defence Staff, as Head of Fifth Section of Nat. Defence Staff; Under-Sec. of Nat. Defence 2004–06, Sec. of Nat. Defence 2006–12. *Address:* c/o Secretariat of State for National Defence, Blvd Manuel Avila Camacho, esq. Avenida Industria Militar, 3°, Col. Lomas de Sotelo, Del. Miguel Hidalgo, 11640 México, DF, Mexico. *E-mail:* ggalvang@mail.sedena.gob.mx.

GALWAY, Sir James, Kt, KBE, FRCM, FRCO, FGSM; British flautist and conductor; b. 8 Dec. 1939, Belfast; s. of James Galway and Ethel Stewart Galway (née Clarke); m. 1st 1965; one s.; m. 2nd 1972; one s. two d. (twins); m. 3rd Jeanne Cinnante 1984; ed Mountcollyer Secondary School, Royal Coll. of Music, Guildhall School of Music, Conservatoire National Supérieur de Musique, France; first post in Wind Band of Royal Shakespeare Theatre, Stratford-on-Avon; later worked with Sadler's Wells Orchestra, Royal Opera House Orchestra, BBC Symphony Orchestra; Prin. Flute, London Symphony Orchestra and Royal Philharmonic Orchestra; Prin. Solo Flute, Berlin Philharmonic Orchestra 1969–75; int. soloist 1975–; soloist/conductor 1984–; Prin. Guest Conductor, London Mozart Players 1997–; performances worldwide include appearances in The Wall, Berlin, and at Nobel Peace Prize Ceremony, 1998; as conductor, toured Germany with Wurttembergisches Kammerorchester and Asia with Polish Chamber Orchestra, 2000–01; has premiered many contemporary flute works commissioned by and for him; f. First Flute online educational network 2013; Amb. to European Brain Council; Prince Consort Professor, Royal College of Music; Officier, Ordre des Arts et des Lettres 1987, Commdr, Ordre des Arts et des Lettres 2018; Hon. MA (Open Univ.) 1979, Hon. DMus (Queen's Univ., Belfast) 1979, (New England Conservatory of Music) 1980, (St Andrew's Univ.), (Birmingham Conservatoire) 2016; Grand Prix du Disque 1976, 1989, Nat. Acad. Recording, Arts & Sciences Pres. Merit Award 2004, Classical BRIT Award for Outstanding Contribution to Music 2005, Artist Laureate, Ulster Orchestra 2009, Lifetime Achievement Award, National Concert Hall Dublin 2013, Gramophone Award for Lifetime Achievement 2014, Gold Medal in the Arts, Kennedy Center International Committee on the Arts 2016. *Recordings include:* Vivaldi The Four Seasons, Sometimes When We Touch, Mozart Concerto No. 1, Andante and Concerto for Flute and Harp, Song Of The Seashore 1979, Annie's Song 1981, Man With The Golden Flute 1982, The Wayward Wind 1982, Nocturne 1983, James Galway Plays Mozart 1984, In The Pink 1984, In Ireland 1986, Christmas Carol 1986, J.S. Bach Suite No. 2 Concerto - Trio Sonatas 1987, Mercadante Concertos 1987, James Galway Plays Beethoven 1988, The Enchanted Forest 1988, James Galway Plays Giuliani 1988, Quantz 4 Concertos 1989, C.P.E. Bach 3 Concertos 1989, The Concerto Collection 1990, Over The Sea To Skye 1990, J.S. Bach Suite No. 2 Concerto for Flute, Violin and Harpsichord 1991, Italian Flute Concertos 1991, In Dulci Jubilo 1991, The Wind Beneath My Wings 1991, Mozart Flute Quartets 1991, Mozart Concerto for Flute and Harp and Sonatas for Flute and Piano 1992, At The Movies 1992, The Magic Flute 1992, Danzi 1993, Dances For Flute 1993, Seasons 1993, The Classical James Galway 1993, Bach Sonatas 1993, Pachelbel Canon 1994, Wind Of Change 1994, The Lark In The Clear Air 1994, The French Recital 1994, Mozart Concerto for Flute and Harp, Concerto No. 1 and Concerto No. 2 1995, Bach Vol. 2 Trio Sonatas 1995, The Celtic Minstrel 1996, James Galway plays the music of Sir Malcolm Arnold 1996, Music for my Friends 1997, James Galway plays Lowell Liebermann 1997, Legends 1997, Flute Sonatas 1997, Meditations 1998, Serenade 1998, Tango del Fuego 1998, Winter's Crossing 1998, Unbreak My Heart 1999, Sixty Years-Sixty Flute Masterpieces Collection 1999, Love Song 2001, Hommage à Rampal 2001, A Song of Home: An American Musical Journey 2002, The Very Best of James Galway 2002, Music for my Little Friends 2002, Wings of Song 2004, My Magic Flute 2006, Ich war ein Berliner 2006, The Essential James Galway 2006, Celebrating 70: A Collection of Personal Favourites 2009, James Galway Plays Flute Concertos (12-cd set) 2011, The Man with the Golden Flute 2014. *Film music:* flute soloist, soundtrack of Lord of the Rings – Return of the King. *Publications:* James Galway: An Autobiography 1978, Flute (Menuhin Music Guide) 1982, James Galway's Music in Time 1983, Flute Studies – Boehm 12 Grand Studies 2003. *Leisure interests:* music, walking, swimming, films, theatre, TV, computing, chess, backgammon, talking to people. *Address:* c/o Stephen Wright, International Classical Artists Ltd, 26–28 Hammersmith Grove, 6th Floor, London, W6 7BA, England (office). *E-mail:* swright@icartists.co.uk (office). *Website:* www.jamesgalway.com; www.firstflute.com.

GAMA, Jaime José Matos da; Portuguese politician and business executive; *Chairman, Novo Banco dos Açores;* b. 8 June 1947, Azores; Founding mem. Partido Socialista 1977, unsuccessful cand. for leadership 1986, 1988; Pres. Parl. Comm. for Int. Business 1976–78, of Parl. Comm. for Nat. Defence 1985–91, of Parl. Comm. for European Affairs and Foreign Politics 2002–05; Minister of Home Affairs 1978, Minister of Foreign Affairs 1983–85, 1995–2002; Minister of Nat. Defence 1999; Minister of State 1999–2002; Pres. Assembleia da República (Parl.) 2005–11; Sr Strategic Counsel, Albright Stonebridge Group; currently Chair. Novo Banco dos Açores; mem. General Council, Univ. of Lisbon; mem. Int. Advisory Bd Tilray, Inc. 2018–; numerous decorations including Grand Cross, Order of Christ, Order of Prince Henry (Ordem do Infante Dom Henrique), Order of Liberty, Order of St Michael and St George. *Address:* Novo Banco dos Açores., R. Hintze Ribeiro 2–8, 9500-049 Ponta Delgada, Portugal (office). *Telephone:* (707) 296-365 (office). *Fax:* (296) 307-000 (office). *E-mail:* info@novobancodosacores.pt (office). *Website:* www.novobancodosacores.pt (office).

GAMARNIK, Andrea V., PhD; Argentine molecular virologist; *Head of Molecular Virology Laboratory, Fundación Instituto Leloir, Argentinean Council of Investigation (CONICET);* b. 5 Oct. 1964; ed Univ. of Buenos Aires, Univ. of California, San Francisco, USA; Postdoctoral Researcher, Univ. of California, San Francisco 1994–99; Scientist, Research and Devt Dept, ViroLogic Inc. 2000–01; returned to Argentina to work at Leloir Inst., est. first Lab. of Molecular Virology; Int. Research Scholar, Program of Infectious Diseases, Howard Hughes Medical Inst., USA 2005–11; currently Int. Investigator, Argentinean Council of Investigation (CONICET); Assoc. Ed., PLoS Pathogens; mem. Editorial Bd, Virology for the Leloir Institute; mem. American Acad. of Microbiology; Golda Meir Award for Distinguished Women in Arts, Humanities, and Sciences (Argentina) 2009, Nat. L'Oreal-UNESCO-CONICET Award For Women in Science (Argentina) 2009, Hon. Declaration for Achievements in Science, City of Buenos Aires, Law 3407-2010 2010, L'Oréal-UNESCO Award for Women in Science (South America) 2016. *Publications:* numerous papers in professional journals. *Address:* Fundación Instituto Leloir, Avenida Patricias Argentinas 435, Buenos Aires, CP C1405BWE, Argentina (office). *Telephone:* (11) 5238-7500 (office). *Fax:* (11) 5238-7501 (office). *E-mail:* info@leloir.org.ar (office). *Website:* www.leloir.org.ar/gamarnik-en/head-of-laboratory (office).

GAMATIÉ, Ali Badjo; Niger economist and politician; Head of Nat. Accounts Div. 1982–84, Dir-Gen. Institut nat. de la Statistique 1986–89; with Tech. Dept, World Bank, Washington, DC, USA 1989; with Centre Européen de Coopération Statistique, Luxembourg 1990–94, Bureau Régional de Coopération Statistique pour l'Afrique de l'Ouest et du Centre, Abidjan, Côte d'Ivoire and Ouagadougou, Burkina Faso 1995–99; Minister of the Economy and Finance 2000–03; Vice-Gov. Banque centrale des Etats de l'Afrique de l'Ouest (BCEAO) 2003–09; Special Adviser on Mineral Affairs to Pres. 2008; Prime Minister 2009–10 (ousted following coup d'état Feb. 2010); mem. Mouvement nat. pour la société de développement; Grand Officier, Légion d'honneur, Grand Officier, Ordre du mérite du Niger, Commdr, Ordre du mérite de l'enseignement supérieur de Côte d'Ivoire 2005; Robert Schuman Medal.

GAMBA, Virginia, BA, MSc; Argentine security consultant and UN official; *Special Representative of the Secretary-General for Children and Armed Conflict, United Nations;* b. 1954; ed Univ. of Newcastle upon Tyne, Univ. Coll. of Wales; fmr Sr Lecturer in Latin American Security Studies, Dept of War Studies, King's Coll., London; Dir, Disarmament and Conflict Resolution Programme, UN Inst. for Disarmament Research, Geneva 1992–96; Deputy Dir, Inst. for Security Studies (ISS), South Africa 1996–2001; Dir for South-South Interactions, SaferAfrica (int. ind. not-for-profit org.), South Africa 2001–07; Expert Consultant to EU and African Union on devt of implementation strategy for the African Common Approach to Combat Illicit Small Arms Trafficking 2007–09; Deputy Dir, Safety and Security, Inst. for Public Safety, Buenos Aires City Govt Ministry of Justice 2009–12; Dir and Deputy to High Rep. for Disarmament Affairs, UN Office for Disarmament Affairs 2012–15, Asst Sec.-Gen. and Head, Org. for the Prohibition of Chemical Weapons OPCW-UN Jt Investigative Mechanism 2015–17; Special Rep. of the Sec.-Gen. for Children and Armed Conflict 2017–. *Address:* Office of the Secretary-General, United Nations, New York, NY 10017, USA (office). *Telephone:* (212) 963-1234 (office). *Fax:* (212) 963-4879 (office). *Website:* www.un.org/sg (office).

GAMBARI, Ibrahim Agboola, CFR, BSc, MA, PhD; Nigerian diplomatist, academic and UN official; b. 24 Nov. 1944, Ilorin, Kwara State; m. Fatima Oniyangi 1969; two s. one d.; ed Kings Coll., Lagos, London School of Econs, UK, Columbia Univ., New York, USA; Lecturer, Queen's Coll., CUNY 1969–74; Asst Prof., State Univ. of New York (Albany) 1974–77; Sr Lecturer, Ahmadu Bello Univ., Zaria 1977–80, Assoc. Prof. 1980–83, Prof. 1983–89, fmr Chair. Dept of Political Science and Founder, Undergraduate Programme in Int. Studies (first in Nigeria); Dir-Gen. Nigerian Inst. of Int. Affairs 1983–84; Minister for Foreign Affairs 1984–85; Visiting Prof., Johns Hopkins Univ. School of Advanced Int. Studies, Howard Univ., Georgetown Univ. and Brookings Inst. 1986–89; Resident Scholar, Rockefeller Foundation Bellagio Study and Conf. Centre, Italy Nov.–Dec. 1989; Perm. Rep. to UN, New York 1990–99, Chair. Special Cttee against Apartheid; UN Under-Sec.-Gen. and Special Adviser on Africa 1999–2005, Special Rep. of the Sec.-Gen. and Head of UN Mission to Angola 2002–03, Under-Sec.-Gen. for Political Affairs 2005–07, Special Adviser to the Sec.-Gen. on the Int. Compact with Iraq and Other Political Issues 2007–09, Special Envoy to Myanmar 2007–09, Jt Special Rep. to African Union/UN Hybrid Operation in Darfur (UNAMID) 2010–13; Chancellor, Kwara State Univ. 2013–; Founder Savannah Centre for Diplomacy, Democracy and Devt (think tank), Abuja, Nigeria; fmr Guest Scholar, Wilson Centre for Int. Scholars, Smithsonian Inst., USA; Chair. Nat. Seminar to Commemorate 25th Anniversary of OAU, Lagos 1988; mem. Soc. of Scholars, Johns Hopkins Univ. 2002–; Hon. Prof., Chugsan Univ., Guangzhou, People's Repub. of China 1985; Commdr, Fed. Repub. of Nigeria 2002; Hon. DHumLitt (Univ. of Bridgeport) 2002, (Fairleigh Dickinson Univ.) 2006, Dr hc (Chatham Univ.) 2008; Special Recognition for Int. Devt and Diplomacy Award, Africa-America Inst. 2007, Distinguished Service Award 2008, Harry Edmonds Award for Lifetime Achievement 2009. *Publications include:* Party Politics and Foreign Policy in Nigeria During the First Republic 1981, Theory and Reality in Foreign Policy Making: Nigeria After the Second Republic 1989, Political and Comparative Dimensions of Regional Integration: The Case of ECOWAS 1991, Report of the Security Council Mission to Rwanda 1995, United Nations 21: Better Service,

Better Value, Better Management, Progress Report of the Efficiency Board to the Secretary-General (co-author) 1996. *Address:* Kwara State University, PMB 1530, Malete 00234, Kwara State, Nigeria (office).

GAMBHIR, Gautam; Indian professional cricketer; b. 14 Oct. 1981, Delhi; s. of Deepak Gambhir; m. Natasha Jain 2011; ed Modern School, New Delhi, Hindu Coll., Univ. of Delhi, Nat. Cricket Acad., Bangalore; opening batsman; left-handed batsman; right-arm leg-break bowler; plays for Delhi 1999–, India 2003–, Delhi Daredevils 2008–10, 2018– (Capt. Jan.–April 2018), Kolkata Knight Riders 2011–17, India Red, Indian Bd Pres.'s XI, Rajasthan Cricket Asscn Pres.'s XI; First-class debut: 1999/2000; Test debut: India v Australia, Mumbai 3–5 Nov. 2004; One-Day Int. (ODI) debut: Bangladesh v India, Dhaka 11 April 2003; T20I debut: India v Scotland, Durban 13 Sept. 2007; has played in 54 Tests and scored 4,021 runs (9 centuries, 21 fifties), highest score 206, average 44.18; ODIs: 147 matches, scored 5,238 runs, highest score 150 not out, average 39.68; First-class: 155 matches, 12,225 runs, highest score 233 not out, took seven wickets, best bowling 3/12; mem. Indian team, ICC (Int. Cricket Council) World Twenty20 2007, winning Indian team, ICC Cricket World Cup 2011; scored centuries in five consecutive test matches 2009–10; No. 1 ranked batsman in ICC Test rankings for ten days July 2009; fmr Captain, Delhi Ranji Team; Arjuna Award 2008, Best Asian Batsman T20 Castrol Asian Cricket Award 2008, ICC Test Player of the Year 2009. *Address:* c/o Delhi & District Cricket Association, Ferozeshah Kotla Grounds, New Delhi 110 002, India. *Telephone:* (11) 23319323; (11) 23312721; (11) 23313143. *Fax:* (11) 23722097. *E-mail:* generalenquiry@ddca.co. *Website:* www.ddca.in.

GAMBHIR, Sanjiv Sam, BS, MD, PhD; American (b. Indian) physician, scientist and academic; *Virginia and D.K. Ludwig Professor in Cancer Research, Chairman, Department of Radiology, School of Medicine and Professor by Courtesy, Departments of Bioengineering and Materials Science and Engineering, Stanford University;* b. 23 Nov. 1962, Ambala, India; m. Aruna Bodapati Gambhir; ed Arizona State Univ., Univ. of California, Los Angeles; family moved to USA 1969, raised in Phoenix, Ariz.; Internship, UCLA Medical Center 1994, Residency 1995, Fellowship 1996; Bd Certification in Nuclear Medicine, American Bd of Nuclear Medicine 1996; Prof., Dept of Radiology and Bio-X Program, Stanford Univ. 2003–, Dir Molecular Imaging Program at Stanford (MIPS) 2003–, Virginia and D.K. Ludwig Prof. for Clinical Investigation in Cancer Research 2009–, Prof. by Courtesy, Dept of Bioengineering 2005–, Dept of Materials Science and Eng 2009–, Dir Canary Center at Stanford for Cancer Early Detection 2009–, mem. Stanford Leadership Acad. 2011–12, Chair. Dept of Radiology, School of Medicine 2011–; serves on numerous editorial and advisory bds and cttees; mem. American Inst. for Medical and Biological Eng 2006, American Soc. of Clinical Investigation 2008, Inst. of Medicine of the Nat. Acads 2008; Taplin Award, Soc. of Nuclear Medicine (SNM) 2002, Holst Medal, Philips Corpn and TU/e, The Netherlands 2003, Distinguished Basic Scientist of the Year Award, Acad. of Molecular Imaging 2004, Achievement Award, Soc. for Molecular Imaging (SMI) 2004, Distinguished Clinical Scientist Award, Doris Duke Charitable Foundation 2004, SNM Image of the Year 2005, AMI Top Clinical Abstract Award, Acad. of Molecular Imaging (AMI) 2005, Hounsfield Medal, Imperial Coll., London 2006, SNM Paul C. Aebersold Award 2006, SNM Best Clinical Article 2007, Co-host, Nobel Symposium on Molecular Imaging, Nobel Cttee, Stockholm 2007, Best Essay Award, American Coll. of Neuropsychopharmacology/SNM 2007, Most Influential Radiology Researcher, Aunt Minnie 2006, Tesla Medal, Royal Coll. of Radiologists (UK) 2008, Parmley Prize, American Coll. of Cardiology Foundations 2009, Outstanding Researcher Award, Radiological Soc. of North America 2009, SNM Georg Charles de Hevesy Nuclear Pioneer Award 2011, Distinguished Scientist Award for Distinguished Contribs to Nuclear Medicine, 37th Annual Western Regional Meeting, SNM 2012, Award of Soc. of Asian American Scientists in Cancer Research 2013, Lifetime Achievement Award, American Asscn of Indian Scientists in Cancer Research 2014, J. Allyn Taylor Int. Prize in Medicine, Robarts Research Inst. 2015, Benedict Cassen Prize 2018. *Publications:* author or co-author of several textbooks; more than 550 papers in professional journals; 52 patents. *Address:* Nuclear Medicine, 300 Pasteur Drive, H2200 MC 5281, Stanford, CA 94305 (office); MIPS, The James H. Clark Center, 318 Campus Drive, East Wing, 1st Floor, Stanford, CA 94305-5427, USA (office). *Telephone:* (650) 725-2309 (Nuclear Medicine) (office); (650) 725-6175 (MIPS) (office). *Fax:* (650) 725-6175 (Nuclear Medicine) (office); (650) 724-4948 (MIPS) (office). *E-mail:* sgambhir@stanford.edu (office). *Website:* med.stanford.edu (office); mips.stanford.edu/research/mmil.html (office); www.canaryfoundation.org (office).

GAMBI, Gen. Antoine; Central African Republic army officer and government official; Chief of Gen. Staff, Armed Forces 2002–06; Coordinator, Nat. Comm. Against the Proliferation of Small Arms and Light Weapons to the Disarmament and Reintegration (CNPDR) 2006–09; Pres. Nat. SSR Cttee (security reform preparatory group) 2007–08; Minister of Foreign and Francophone Affairs and Regional Integration 2009–13, Minister-Del. to Minister of Nat. Defence, in charge of Restructuring of the Armed Forces and the Programme of Disarmament, Demobilization and Reintegration 2013–14. *Address:* c/o Ministry of National Defence, War Veterans, War Victims and the Restructuring of the Armed Forces, Bangui, Central African Republic (office).

GAMBIER, Dominique, DèsSc Econ; French academic and politician; *Mayor of Déville-les-Rouen;* b. 14 Aug. 1947, Rouen; s. of Michel Morel and Yvette Morel; two d.; ed Lycée Corneille, Rouen and Ecole Centrale de Paris; Asst Univ. of Rouen 1972–81; Prof., Ecole Centrale de Paris 1981–83; special assignment, Commissariat Général au Plan 1983–84; Maître de conférences and Dir Inst. of Research and Documentation in Social Sciences (IRED), Univ. of Rouen 1984–87; expert adviser, EEC, Brussels 1980–81; scientific adviser, Observatoire français des conjonctures économiques (OFCE) 1981–83; Regional Councillor, Haute-Normandie 1986–, Vice-Pres. of Regional Council 1998–; Pres. Univ. of Rouen 1987–88; Deputy for Seine Maritime 1988–93; Mayor of Déville-les-Rouen 1995–; Officier des Palmes académiques. *Publications include:* Analyse conjoncturelle du chômage, Théorie de la politique économique en situation d'incertitude 1980, Le marché du travail 1991, L'emploi en France 1997; numerous articles on economy of work and labour etc. *Leisure interests:* football, tennis, skiing. *Address:* 5 allée du Houssel, 76130 Mont-St-Aignan, France (home). *Telephone:* 2-35-76-88-18 (office). *E-mail:* elus@mairie-deville-les-rouen.fr (office); dominiquegambin@free.fr. *Website:* www.deville-les-rouen.fr (office); dominiquegambier.fr.

GAMBLE, Christine Elizabeth, PhD; British consultant on culture and sport and fmr diplomatist; b. 1 March 1950, Rotherham, South Yorks., England; d. of Albert Edward Gamble and Kathleen Laura Wallis; m. Edward Barry Antony Craxton; ed Royal Holloway Coll., Univ. of London; worked in Anglo-French cultural org. 1974–75; Office of the Cultural Attaché, Embassy in Moscow 1975–76; joined British Council, New Delhi 1977, UK 1979, Harare 1980–82, Regional Officer for Soviet Union and Mongolia 1982–85, Deputy Dir Athens 1985–87, Corp. Planning Dept 1988–90, Head, Project Pursuit Dept and Dir Chancellor's Financial Sector Scheme 1990–92, Dir Visitor's Dept 1992–93, Gen. Man. Country Services Group and Head European Services 1993–96, Cultural Councillor, Embassy in Paris and Dir British Council, France 1996–98; Dir Royal Inst. of Int. Affairs, London 1998–2002; Co. Sec., Ind. Football Comm. 2002–05; Consultant to Comm. for Racial Equality 2005–10; Order of Rio Branco, Brazil 2000. *Leisure interests:* literature, art, music, theatre, sport. *Address:* Syke Fold House, Dent, Sedbergh, Cumbria, LA10 5RE, England (home). *Telephone:* (1539) 625518 (home). *Fax:* (1539) 625518 (home). *E-mail:* cgamble@gmdsolutions.co.uk.

GAMBLIN, Jacques; French actor; b. 16 Nov. 1957, Granville, Manche; ed Centre dramatique de Caen; wrote the theatre play Quincaillerie. *Films include:* Train d'enfer (Hell Train, USA) 1985, Périgord noir 1988, Il y a des jours… et des lunes (There Were Days… and Moons) 1990, Pont et soupirs 1992, La belle histoire (The Beautiful Story) 1992, Adeus Princesa (Goodbye Princess) 1992, Tout ça… pour ça! (All That… for This?!) 1993, La femme à abattre 1993, Fausto (aka À la mode (USA), aka In Fashion) 1993, Naissances 1994, Les braqueuses (Girls with Guns) 1994, Sans souci 1995, Les misérables (aka Les misérables du vingtième siècle) 1995, À la vie, à la mort! (Til Death Do Us Part) 1995, Au petit Marguery 1995, Mon homme (My Man) 1996, Pédale douce 1996, Une histoire d'amour à la con 1996, Tenue correcte exigée 1997, Mauvais genre 1997, Kanzo sensei (Dr. Akagi, USA) 1998, Au coeur du mensonge (The Color of Lies, USA) 1999, Les enfants du marais (The Children of the Marshland) (Best Actor Award, Cabourg Romantic Film Festival 1999) 1999, Mademoiselle 2001, Bella ciao 2001, Laissez-passer (Safe Conduct) (Silver Berlin Bear for Best Actor, Berlin Int. Film Festival 2002) 2002, Carnages (Carnage) 2002, À la petite semaine (Nickel and Dime) 2003, Dissonances 2003, 25 degrés en hiver (25 Degrees in Winter) 2004, Holy Lola 2004, L'enfer (Hell) 2005, Les brigades du Tigre (The Tiger Brigades) 2006, Serko 2006, Les irréductibles 2006, Fragile(s) 2007, Nos retrouvailles (aka In Your Wake) 2007, Enfin veuve (A Widow at Last) 2008, Bellamy 2009, The Names of Love (César Award for Best Actor 2011) 2010, Holidays by the Sea 2011, Le premier homme 2012, The Finishers 2013. *Television includes:* La double inconstance 1984, L'Été 36 1986, Le vagabond des mers (mini-series) 1990, Années de plumes, années de plomb 1991, C'est mon histoire: Présumé coupable 1992, Un cercueil pour deux 1993, Les brouches 1994, Couchettes express 1994, La bougeotte 1996, Les clients d'Avrenos 1996, Le voyageur sans bagage 2004, Les oubliées (mini-series) 2007, L'Infiltré 2011, Ils ont libéré 2014, Pétain 2015.

GAMBLING, William Alexander, BSc, PhD, DSc, FRS, FREng; British electrical engineer and industrial consultant; b. 11 Oct. 1926, Port Talbot, Glamorgan, Wales; s. of George Alexander Gambling and Muriel Clara Gambling; m. 1st Margaret Pooley 1952 (separated 1987); one s. two d.; m. 2nd Barbara Colleen O'Neil 1994; ed Univs of Bristol and Liverpool; Lecturer in Electric Power Eng, Univ. of Liverpool 1950–55; Fellow, Nat. Research Council, Univ. of BC 1955–57; Lecturer, Sr Lecturer and Reader, Univ. of Southampton 1957–64, Prof. of Electronics 1964–80, Dean of Eng and Applied Science 1972–75, Head of Dept 1974–79, British Telecom Prof. of Optical Communication 1980–95, Dir UK Nat. Optoelectronics Research Centre 1989–95; Royal Soc. Visiting Prof. and Dir, Optoelectronics Research Centre, City Univ. of Hong Kong 1996–2001; Dir of Optoelectronics Research and Devt, LTK Industries Ltd 2002–05, Consultant 2005–07; Consultant in Optoelectronics, COTCO Holdings Ltd; Visiting Prof., Univ. of Colo 1966–67, Bhabha Atomic Research Centre, India 1970, Osaka Univ., Japan 1977; Pres. I.E.R.E. 1977–78; Chair. Comm.D, Int. Union of Radio Science 1981–84, Eng Council 1983–88; mem. Bd, Council of Eng Insts 1974–79, Electronics Research Council 1977–80, Nat. Electronics Council 1977–78 and 1984–89; Dir York Ltd 1980–97; mem. British Nat. Cttee for Radio Science 1978–87, Educational Advisory Council, IBA 1980–82, Eng Industries Training Bd 1985–88; mem. Council, Royal Acad. of Eng 1989–92; Selby Fellow, Australian Acad. of Science 1982; Foreign mem. Polish Acad. of Sciences 1985; Liveryman, Worshipful Co. of Engineers 1988; Fellow Hong Kong Acad. of Eng Sciences (Vice-Pres. 2004–); Hon. FIEE; Hon. Prof., Huazhong Univ. of Science and Tech., Wuhan, 1986–, Beijing Univ. of Posts and Telecommunications, Shanghai Univ. 1991–, Shandong Univ. 1999–; Hon. Dir Beijing Optical Fibres Lab., People's Repub. of China 1987–; Freeman, City of London 1988; Dr hc (Madrid) 1994, (Aston) 1995, (Bristol) 1999, (Southampton) 2005; Academic Enterprise Award 1982, IEE J. J. Thomson Medal 1982, IEE Faraday Medal 1983, Churchill Medal, Soc. of Engineers 1985, Simms Medal, Soc. of Engineers 1988, Micro-optics Award (Japan) 1989, Dennis Gabor Award (USA) 1990, Rank Prize for Optoelectronics 1991, C & C Medal (Japan) 1993, Mountbatten Medal 1993, Royal Soc./Inst. of Civil Engineers James Alfred Ewing Medal 2002; six awards for outstanding research publs, 11 int. prizes and medals for research in optical fibre communications tech. *Publications:* some 400 research papers on electrical discharges, microwave devices, quantum electronics, optical fibre communication and education. *Leisure interests:* reading, music, the Bible, Christian literature. *Address:* LTK Industries, 6/F Photonics Centre, Hong Kong Science Park, Sha Tin, Hong Kong Special Administrative Region, People's Republic of China (office). *Telephone:* 2410-3009 (office). *Fax:* 2943-1709 (office). *E-mail:* wag@ltkcable.com (office); wagconl@yahoo.com (office). *Website:* www.ltkcable.com (office).

GAMBON, Sir Michael John, Kt, CBE; British actor; b. 19 Oct. 1940, Dublin, Ireland; s. of Edward Gambon and Mary Gambon; m. Anne Miller 1962; one s.; ed St Aloysius School for Boys, London; fmr mechanical engineer; Trustee Royal Armouries 1995–98; Hon. DLitt 2003. *Theatre includes:* first stage appearance with Edwards/Mácliammoir Co., Dublin 1962; Nat. Theatre, Old Vic 1963–67; Birmingham Repertory and other provincial theatres 1967–69, title roles including Othello, Macbeth, Coriolanus; RSC Aldwych 1970–71; The Norman Conquests 1974, Otherwise Engaged 1976, Just Between Ourselves 1977, Alice's Boys 1978,

The Caretaker 2000; with Nat. Theatre 1980, appearing in Galileo (London Theatre Critics' Award for Best Actor), Betrayal, Tales from Hollywood; with RSC, Stratford and London 1982–83, title roles in King Lear, Antony and Cleopatra, Old Times 1985, A Chorus of Disapproval, Nat. Theatre 1985 (Olivier Award for Best Comedy Performance), A Small Family Business 1987, Uncle Vanya 1988, Mountain Language 1988, Othello 1990, Taking Steps 1990, Skylight (play) 1995, Volpone (Evening Standard Drama Award) 1995, Tom and Clem 1997, The Unexpected Man 1998, Cressida 2000 (Variety Club Award for Best Actor), A Number, Jerwood Theatre, Royal Court, London 2002, End Game 2004, Henry IV parts I and II, Nat. Theatre 2005, Eh Joe 2006, No Man's Land 2008–09, Krapp's Last Tape 2010. *Films include:* The Beast Must Die 1975, Turtle Diary 1985, Paris by Night 1988, The Cook, The Thief, His Wife and Her Lover 1989, A Dry White Season 1989, The Rachel Papers 1989, State of Grace 1989, Mobsters 1992, Toys 1992, Clean Slate 1993, Indian Warrior 1993, The Browning Version 1993, Mary Reilly 1994, Midnight in Moscow 1994, A Man of No Importance 1995, The Innocent Sleep 1995, All Our Fault 1995, Two Deaths 1996, Nothing Personal 1996, The Gambler 1996, Dancing at Lughnasa 1997, Plunket and McClean 1997, The Last September 1998, Sleepy Hollow 1999, Dead On Time 1999, The Insider, End Game 1999, High Heels and Low Lifes 2001, Gosford Park 2001, Charlotte Gray 2001, Ali G Indahouse 2001, Path to War 2001, Christmas Carol: The Movie (voice) 2001, The Actors 2003, Open Range 2003, Sylvia 2003, Standing Room Only 2004, Harry Potter and the Prisoner of Azkaban 2004, Being Julia 2004, Sky Captain and the World of Tomorrow 2004, Layer Cake 2004, The Life Aquatic with Steve Zissou 2004, Harry Potter and the Goblet of Fire 2005, My Boy 2005, Elizabeth Rex 2005, The Good Sheperd 2006, Amazing Grace 2006, John Duffy's Brother 2006, The Good Night 2007, The Baker 2007, The Alps (voice) 2007, Harry Potter and the Order of the Phoenix 2007, Brideshead Revisited 2008, Harry Potter and the Half-Blood Prince 2009, Fantastic Mr Fox (voice) 2009, Harry Potter and the Deathly Hallows: Part 1 2010, The King's Speech 2010, Harry Potter and the Deathly Hallows: Part 2 2011, Quartet 2012, Dad's Army 2016, Victoria and Abdul 2017, King of Thieves 2018, Judy 2019. *Television includes:* Ghosts, Oscar Wilde, The Holy Experiment, Absurd Person Singular, The Borderers, The Singing Detective (BAFTA for Best Actor 1987), The Heat of the Day, Maigret 1992, The Entertainer, Truth, Wives and Daughters (BAFTA for Best Actor 2000), Longitude 2000 (BAFTA for Best Actor 2001), Perfect Strangers (BAFTA Best Actor 2002), Cranford 2007, Emma 2009, Doctor Who (series) 2010, Page Eight (film) 2011, Luck (series) 2012, Restless (film) 2012, National Theatre Live (series) – 50 Years on Stage 2013, Lucan (film) 2013, Fortitude (series) 2014, Quirke (mini-series) 2014, Common (film) 2014, The Casual Vacancy (mini-series) 2015, The Hollow Crown (film) 2016, Little Women (mini-series) 2017. *Leisure interests:* flying, gun collecting, clock making. *Address:* c/o Independent Talent Group Ltd, 40 Whitfield Street, London, W1T 2RH, England (office). *Telephone:* (20) 7636-6565 (office). *Website:* www.independenttalent.com (office).

GAMEDZE, Chief Mgwagwa; Swazi government official; Minister of Home Affairs 2008–11, of Justice and Constitutional Affairs 2011–13, of Foreign Affairs 2013–18; mem. Senate. *Address:* c/o Ministry of Foreign Affairs, POB 518, Mbabane, Eswatini (office).

GAMES, David Edgar, PhD, DSc, CChem, FRSC; British scientist and academic; *Professor Emeritus, Mass Spectrometry Research Unit, University of Wales, Swansea;* b. 7 April 1938, Ynysddu; s. of Alfred William Games and Frances Elizabeth Bell Games (née Evans); m. Marguerite Patricia Lee 1961; two s.; ed Lewis School, Pengam, King's Coll., Univ. of London; Lecturer, Sr Lecturer, Reader and Personal Chair., Univ. Coll., Cardiff 1965–89; Prof. of Mass Spectrometry and Dir of Mass Spectrometry Research Unit, Univ. of Wales at Swansea 1989–2003, now Prof. Emer., Head Dept of Chem. 1996–2001; fmr Chair. British Mass Spectrometry Soc.; Royal Soc. of Chem. Award in Analytical Separation Methods 1987, The Chromatographic Soc. Martin Medal 1991, Royal Soc. of Chem. SAC Gold Medal 1993, J. J. Thomson Gold Medal, Int. Mass Spectrometry Cttee 1997, Aston Medal, British Mass Spectrometry Soc. 1999. *Leisure interests:* swimming, walking. *Address:* 9 Heneage Drive, West Cross, Swansea, SA3 5BR, Wales (home). *Telephone:* (1792) 405192 (home).

GAMKRELIDZE, Thomas V.; Georgian linguist and cultural historian; *President, Georgian National Academy of Sciences;* b. 23 Oct. 1929, Kutaisi, Georgia; s. of Valerian Gamkrelidze and Olimpiada Gamkrelidze; m. Nino Javakhishvili 1968; one s. one d.; ed Ivane Javakhishvili Tbilisi State Univ.; post-grad. work 1952–55; Lecturer, Georgian Acad. of Sciences, Inst. of Linguistics 1956–60, Head of Dept 1960–73, Dir The Oriental Inst. 1973–; Head of Dept, Tbilisi State Univ. 1966–72; main work in area of theoretical linguistics, Kartvelian, Semitic and Indo-European linguistics and semiology; People's Deputy of the USSR 1989–91; mem. Parl., Repub. of Georgia 1992–; Ed.-in-Chief Voprosy Jazykoznanija (Russian Acad. of Sciences) 1988–94; mem. Georgian Nat. Acad. of Sciences 1974, Pres. 2005–; mem. USSR (now Russian) Acad. of Sciences 1984, Austrian Acad. of Sciences, Academia Europaea 2006, World Acad. of Art and Science 2007, Academia Scientiarum et Artium Europaea 2009; Corresp. FBA; Foreign Assoc., NAS 2006; Foreign mem. Sächsische Akad. der Wissenschaften, Latvian Acad. of Sciences 2007; Foreign Hon. mem. American Acad. of Arts and Sciences; Hon. mem. Indogermanische Gesellschaft, Linguistic Soc. of America, Societas Linguistica Europaea (Pres. 1986), Hungarian Acad. of Sciences 2007, Académie Internationale de Philosophie des Sciences 2009; Dr hc (Bonn, Chicago); Lenin Prize 1988, Humboldt Prize (FRG) 1989, Javakhishvili Prize, Tbilisi Univ. 1992. *Publications:* Indo-European and the Indo-Europeans (two vols) (with V. V. Ivanov) 1984, Alphabetic Writing and the Old Georgian Script – Typology and Provenance of Alphabetic Writing Systems 1989. *Leisure interests:* music, tennis. *Address:* Georgian National Academy of Sciences, Rustaveli Avenue 52, Tbilisi 0108 (office); Jac. Nikoladze Street 6, 380009 Tbilisi, Georgia (home). *Telephone:* (32) 99-88-91 (office); (32) 22-64-92 (home). *Fax:* (32) 99-88-23 (office). *E-mail:* t.gamkrelidze@science.org.ge (office). *Website:* www.science.org.ge (office).

GANBAATAR, Adiya; Mongolian politician, academic and diplomatist; b. 8 Feb. 1959, Ulan Bator; s. of Adiya Ganbaatar and Ichinkhorlo Ganbaatar; m.; three d.; ed Univ. of Łódź, Poland; Lecturer, Mongolian State Univ. 1983–90; Chair. Democratic Socialist Movt 1990; mem. State Great Hural (Parl.) 1992–2000, Chair. Standing Cttee on the Budget 1997; fmr Ed.-in-Chief UG (journal); Vice-Chair. Cen. Asia Devt Foundation 1992; Pres. Mongolian Tennis Asscn 1997; Amb. to Poland 2012–15 (also accred to Latvia, Lithuania 2013–15); Distinguished Officer, Banking and Finance 1999, Distinguished Officer, Educ. 2000; Commander's Cross of the Order of Merit (Poland) 2015. *Publications include:* three books on mathematics. *Leisure interests:* chess, tennis.

GANBOLD, Davaadorjiin, MSc (Econs), PhD; Mongolian politician; b. 26 June 1957, Ulan Bator; s. of Tsedevsuren Davaadorj and Lodongiin Oyun; m. M. Tserengav Oyun; two d.; ed Moscow State Univ., USSR; Asst to Prof. of Political Econ., Mongolian State Univ. 1979–84; Prof. of Political Econ., State and Social Studies Acad. 1988–90; Founder-mem. Nat. Progress Party, Chair. Party Council; First Deputy Prime Minister 1990; mem. Great Hural (legislature) 1992–2000; Chair. Standing Cttee on Budget, Finance and Econs; Chair. Mongolian Nat. Democratic Party (merger of four opposition parties) 1992–96, Deputy Leader 1998; fmr Economic Policy Adviser to Prime Minister; fmr Nat. Security Adviser to the Pres. and mem. Nat. Security Council; Chair. Railway Authority of Mongolia. *Leisure interests:* fishing, cycling, collecting stamps and model cars.

GANDEL, John, AO; Australian business executive; *Chairman, Gandel Group of Companies;* b. 1935; m. Pauline Gandel; four c.; ed Univ. of Melbourne; inherited retailer Sussan from parents, sold co. to brother-in-law 1985, used proceeds to build business in shopping malls, currently Chair. Gandel Group Pty Ltd, fmr Chair. Gandel Retail Trust, Gandel Retail Management; f. Gandel Charitable Trust 1978; Chair. Jewish Museum of Australia 1983–93, currently Chair. Bd of Govs; fmr mem. Bd of Dirs Australian CSIRO; Fellow, Australian Inst. of Man., Australian Inst. of Co. Dirs; Patron Gandel Inst. for Adult Jewish Learning, Hebrew Univ. of Jerusalem; Dr hc (Tel-Aviv Univ.) 2006; Nat. Defense Medal 1994, Nat. Service Commemorative Medal 2002, Centenary Medal 2003. *Address:* Gandel Group Pty Limited, Level 3, 1341 Dandenong Road, Chadstone Shopping Centre, Melbourne, Vic. 3148, Australia (office).

GANDHI, Maneka Sanjay; Indian politician; *Minister of Women and Child Development;* b. 26 Aug. 1956, New Delhi; d. of Col T. S. Anand and Amteshwar Anand; m. Sanjay Gandhi 1974 (died 1980); one s.; ed Lady Shri Ram Coll. for Women; Ed. Surya (Sun) magazine 1977–80; Founder and Leader of political party Rashtriya Sanjay Manch (merged with Janata Party 1988) 1983; Minister of State for the Environment and Forests 1989–91; mem. Lok Sabha (lower house of Parl.) for Pilibhit 1989–2008, for Aonla 2008–; Minister for Social Justice and Empowerment 1999–2001; Minister of State for Statistics and Programme Implementation 2002–04; Minister of Women and Child Devt 2014–; Chair. People for Animals Trust, Cttee on Control and Supervision of Experiments on Animals, Soc. for Prevention of Cruelty to Animals; Founder Greenline Trees; Special Adviser to Voice (consumer action forum); cr. environmental film series New Horizons; writer and anchorwoman nat. TV programmes on animals, Heads and Tails, Maneka's Ark, Jeene ki Raah; Pres. Ruth Cowell Trust, Sanjay Gandhi Animal Care Centre; Patron Worldwide Fund for Nature; Chair. RUGMARK; Lord Erskine Award, Royal Soc. for the Prevention of Cruelty to Animals 1991, Vegetarian of the Year Award, Vegetarian Soc. 1995, Prani Mitra Award, Nat. Animal Welfare Bd 1997, Marchig Prize, Marchig Animal Welfare Trust (GB) 1997, Venu Menon Lifetime Achievement Award 1999, Bhagwan Mahavir Award 1999, Diwaliben Charitable Trust Award 1999, Dinanath Mangeshkar Aadishakti Puruskar 2001, Woman of the Year, Int. Women's Asscn 2001. *Publications include:* Sanjay Gandhi 1980, Mythology of Indian Plants, Animal Quiz, Penguin Book of Hindu Names, The Complete Book of Muslim and Parsi Names, First Aid for Animals, Animal Laws of India, Rainbow and Other Stories, Natural Health for Your Dog, Heads and Tails, Wise and Wonderful Animal Alphabet Quiz Book, Definitive Etymological Works, Animal Activism and Laws. *Leisure interests:* reading, writing, animal welfare, environmental protection, gardening, charity. *Address:* Ministry of Women and Child Development, Shastri Bhavan, Dr Rajendra Prasad Rd, New Delhi (office); A-4, Maharani Bagh, New Delhi 110 005, India (home). *Telephone:* (11) 23383586 (office). *Fax:* (11) 23381495 (office). *E-mail:* secy.wcd@nic.in (office). *Website:* wcd.nic.in (office).

GANDHI, Rahul, BA, MPhil; Indian politician; *President, Indian National Congress;* b. 19 June 1970, New Delhi; s. of Rajiv Gandhi and Sonia Gandhi; brother of Priyanka Gandhi-Vadra; ed St Stephen's Coll., New Delhi, Harvard Univ., Rollins Coll., USA, Trinity Coll., Cambridge, UK; worked in London with strategy consultancy firm Monitor Group; returned to India in 2002; Dir Backops Services Pvt. Ltd 2002; canvassed for Congress Party on behalf of his mother in Amethi constituency, UP 1999; election campaign in parl. elections supervised by his sister Priyanka Gandhi 2004; MP (Lok Sabha) for Amethi constituency 2004–, fmr mem. Parl. Standing Cttee on Home Affairs and Human Resource Devt, Consultative Cttee for the Ministry of Civil Aviation, currently mem. Parl. Standing Cttee on External Affairs, Consultative Cttee, Ministry of Finance and Corporate Affairs; mem. Indian Nat. Congress, Gen. Sec. 2007–13, mem. Congress Working Cttee 2007–, Vice-Pres. 2013–17, Pres. 2017–, Chair. Indian Youth Congress 2007–17, Nat. Students Union of India; Trustee, Rajiv Gandhi Foundation, Rajiv Gandhi Charitable Trust; Videocon India Youth Icon Award 2009, CNN-IBN Indian of the Year Award 2009. *Address:* Indian National Congress, 24 Akbar Road, New Delhi 110 011 (office); 10, Janpath, New Delhi 110 011, India. *Telephone:* (11) 23019080 (office); (11) 23012686 (home). *Fax:* (11) 23017047 (office); (11) 23018550 (home). *Website:* www.congress.org.in (office).

GANDHI, Sonia; Indian (b. Italian) politician; b. (Edvige Antonia Albina Maino), 9 Dec. 1946, Lusiana, nr Vicenza, Veneto, Italy; d. of Stefano Maino and Paola Maino; m. Rajiv Gandhi 1968 (fmr Prime Minister of India) (died 1991); one s. one d.; ed Univ. of Cambridge, UK, Nat. Gallery of Modern Art, Delhi; mem. Indian Nat. Congress Cttee, Pres. 1998–2006 (resgnd), reappointed 2007–17; Chair. Nat. Advisory Council 2004–06 (resgnd), reappointed 2010; elected MP (Lok Sabha) for Bellary constituency 1999, for Rae Bareli constituency 2004, 2009, Leader of Opposition –2004; Chair. United Progressive Alliance, Rajiv Gandhi Foundation, Indira Gandhi Memorial Trust, Jawaharlal Nehru Memorial Fund, Rajiv Gandhi Inst. for Contemporary Studies; Pres. Swaraj Bhavan Trust, Kamla Nehru Memorial Hosp. Soc.; Trustee, Jalianwala Bagh Nat. Memorial Trust; mem. Nehru Memorial Museum and Library. *Publications:* Rajiv 1992, Rajiv's World 1994. *Leisure interests:* reading, gardening, art, music. *Address:* Indian National Congress, 24 Akbar Road, New Delhi 110 011 (office); Rajiv Gandhi Foundation, Jawahar Bhawan, Dr Rajendra Prasad Road, New Delhi 110 001; 10 Janpath, New Delhi 110 011, India (home). *Telephone:* (11) 23019080 (office); (11) 23014161 (home); (11) 23755117. *Fax:* (11) 23017047 (office). *E-mail:* aicc@congress.org.in (office); soniagandhi@sansad.nic.in (office). *Website:* www.congress.org.in (office); www.soniagandhi.org (home).

GANDOIS, Jean Guy Alphonse; French business executive; b. 7 May 1930, Nieul; s. of Eugène and Marguerite Gandois (née Teillet); m. Monique Testard 1953; two s.; ed École Polytechnique, Paris; Civil Engineer, Ministry of Public Works, French Guinea 1954–58; mem. of tech. co-operation missions to Brazil and Peru 1959–60; Asst to Commercial Dir Wendel & Cie 1961, Econ. Dir 1966; Econ. and Commercial Dir Wendel-Sidelor 1968; Gen. Man. Sacilor 1973; Pres., Dir-Gen. Sollac 1975; Dir-Gen. Rhône-Poulenc SA 1976, Vice-Pres. 1977–79, Chair. and CEO 1979–82 (resgnd); Chair. and CEO Pechiney 1986–94; Chair. Cockerill-Sambre (Belgium) 1987–99; Pres. CNPF (Nat. Council of French Employers) 1994, Hon. Pres. 2000–01; Chair. Supervisory Bd Suez-Lyonnaise des Eaux 2000–01, Vice-Chair. 2001–05; mem. Bd of Dirs, Eurazéo (fmrly Eurafrance); Hon. mem. Order of Australia, Commdr, Légion d'honneur, Grand Cordon, Ordre de Léopold, Grand Croix, Ordre de la Couronne (Belgium), Grand Officier, Couronne du Chêne (Luxembourg); Dr hc (Liège, Louvain). *Address:* 55 quai des Grands Augustins, 75006 Paris, France (home). *Telephone:* 1-42-96-29-85 (home). *E-mail:* jeangandois@aol.com.

GANELLIN, Charon Robin, PhD, DSc, FRS, FRSC; British scientist and academic; *Smith Kline and French Professor Emeritus of Medicinal Chemistry, University College London;* b. 25 Jan. 1934, London; s. of Leon Ganellin and Beila Cluer; m. 1st Tamara Greene 1956 (died 1997); one s. one d.; m. 2nd Dr Monique Garbarg 2003; ed Harrow County Grammar School for Boys and Queen Mary Coll., Univ. of London; Research Assoc., MIT, USA 1960; Research Chemist in Medicinal Chem., Smith Kline and French Labs Ltd (UK) 1958–59, Head of Dept 1961–75, Dir of Histamine Research, Smith Kline and French Research Ltd 1975–80, Vice-Pres. Research 1980–84, Vice-Pres. Chemical Research 1984–86; Advisory Tutor in Chem., Polytechnic of North London 1979–83; Hon. Lecturer, Dept of Pharmacology, Univ. Coll., London 1975–86, Hon. Research Fellow, Chem. 1985–86, Hon. Research Fellow, Pharmacology 1986–87, Smith Kline and French Prof. of Medicinal Chem. 1986–2003, Prof. Emer. 2003–; Fellow, Queen Mary and Westfield Coll., Univ. of London 1992; Pres. IUPAC Medicinal Chem. Section 2000–01, Chair. IUPAC Subcommittee Medicinal Chem. Drug Devt 2002–12, IUPAC Div. VII Fellow Emer. 2014–; Chair. UK Govt Home Office Advisory Council on Misuse of Drugs 2002–07; Corresp. Academician, Académia Nacional Farmacia España 2006; Hon. Prof. of Medicinal Chem., Univ. of Kent 1979–89, Hon. mem. Sociedad Española de Química Terapéutica 1982, European Histamine Research Soc. 2007; Hon. DSc (Aston) 1995; UK Chemical Soc. Medallion in Medicinal Chem. 1977, Prix Charles Mentzer, Soc. de Chimie Thérapeutique (France) 1978, ACS (Div. of Medicinal Chem.) Award 1980, Royal Soc. of Chem. Tilden Medal 1982, Soc. for Chemical Industry Messel Medal 1988, Soc. for Drug Research Award 1989, Nat. Inventors Hall of Fame (USA) 1990, Royal Soc. of Chem. Adrien Albert Medal 1999, European Fed. for Medicinal Chem. Nauta Award in Pharmacochemistry 2004, Società Chimica Italiana Pratesi Gold Medal 2006, ACS (Div. of Medicinal Chem.) Hall of Fame 2007. *Achievements include:* co-discoverer of histamine H2 receptors, co-inventor of Cimetidine (Tagamet®) 1970s, co-inventor of Pitolisant (Wakix®) 2000s. *Publications include:* Pharmacology of Histamine Receptors 1982, Frontiers in Histamine Research 1985, Dictionary of Drugs 1990, Medicinal Chemistry 1993, Dictionary of Pharmacological Agents 1997, Analogue-based Drug Discovery Vol. I 2006, Vol. II 2010, Vol. III 2013, Practical Studies for Medicinal Chemistry (Web edn) 2007, Introduction to Biological and Small Molecule Drug Research and Development 2013; research papers and reviews in various journals. *Leisure interests:* sailing, swimming, walking, ballroom dancing, music. *Address:* Department of Chemistry, University College London, 20 Gordon Street, London, WC1H 0AJ, England (office). *Telephone:* (20) 7679-4624 (office). *Fax:* (20) 7679-7463 (office). *E-mail:* c.r.ganellin@ucl.ac.uk (office). *Website:* www.ucl.ac.uk/silva/chemistry/staff/emeritus/robin_ganellin (office).

GANGA, Gobind, BA, MA, PhD; Guyanese economist and central banker; *Governor, Bank of Guyana;* m. Devika Ganga; one d.; ed Univ. of Winnipeg and Univ. of Manitoba, Canada; Dir Research Dept Bank of Guyana 1995–2003, apptd Deputy Gov. 2005, Acting Gov. May–Nov. 2014, Gov. 2014–; Alt. Exec. Dir World Bank, Washington, DC 2003–05; fmr Lecturer in Econs, Univ. of West Indies, Mona, Jamaica, Adjunct Prof., Consortium Graduate School at Mona, Jamaica; fmr Sr Researcher/Lecturer, Univ. of Guyana, Turkeyen Campus. *Publications include:* numerous articles on economic issues, including monetary policy and macroeconomics. *Address:* Bank of Guyana, 1 Church Street and Avenue of the Republic, POB 1003, Georgetown, Guyana (office). *Telephone:* 226-3250 (office). *Fax:* 227-2965 (office). *E-mail:* communications@bankofguyana.org.gy (office). *Website:* www.bankofguyana.org.gy (office).

GANGULY, Ashok S., MS, PhD, FRSC; Indian business executive and scientist; *Chairman, ABP Private Limited;* b. 28 July 1935, Patna, Bihar; s. of Sekhar Nath Ganguly and Binapani Ganguly; m. Rooma Ganguly; two d.; ed Jaihind Coll., Mumbai Univ., Univ. of Illinois, USA; Chair. Hindustan Lever Ltd 1980–90, Chief Tech. Officer and Dir Unilever 1990–97; Chair. ICI India Ltd 1996–2003; Chair. ICICI OneSource Ltd (I-OneSource, later Firstsource Solutions Ltd) –2010; currently Chair. ABP Pvt. Ltd (Ananda Bazar Patrika Group); Dir Cen. Bd Reserve Bank of India 2000–09; mem. (nominated) Rajya Sabha (Parl.) 2009–15; Dir (non-exec.) British Airways PLC 1996–2005, ICICI Knowledge Park Ltd, Mahindra & Mahindra Ltd, Tata AIG Life Insurance Co. Ltd; Ind. Dir Wipro Corpn 1999–; mem. Governing Council Centre for Advanced Financial Research and Learning; mem. Science Advisory Council to Prime Minister of India 1985–89, UK Advisory Bd of Research Councils 1991–94, Advisory Bd Microsoft Corpn (I) Pvt. Ltd, Hemogenomics Pvt. Ltd, Prime Minister's Council on Trade and Industry, Investment Comm., Nat. Knowledge Comm., India-USA CEO Council, Rajiv Gandhi Foundation; Trustee, Lever Hulme Trust UK 2000–16; Hon. Prof., Chinese Acad. of Science, Shanghai 1996; Padma Bhushan 1988, Hon. CBE, UK 2006, Padma Vibhushan 2009; Business Man of the Year, India 1996, Madhuri and Jagdish N. Sheth Int. Alumni Award for Exceptional Achievement 2003, Economic Times Lifetime Achievement Award 2008, Outstanding Alumnus, Coll. of Food and Nutrition, Univ. of Illinois 1997, Int. Alumni Award, Univ. of Illinois 2003–04. *Publications include:* Industry and Liberalisation 1994, Strategic Manufacturing for Competitive Advantage 1998, Business Driven R&D: Managing Knowledge to Create Wealth 1999. *Leisure interests:* classical music, reading, golf. *Address:* ABP Private Ltd, Gandhi Mansion, 4th Floor, 20 Altamount Road, Mumbai 400 026 (office); N-6, Pemino Altamount Road, Mumbai 400 026, India (home). *Telephone:* (22) 23532331 (office); (22) 23538471 (home). *E-mail:* ashok.ganguly01@gmail.com (home).

GANGULY, Sourav Chandidas, MBA; Indian professional cricketer; *President;* b. 8 July 1972, Calcutta (now Kolkata), Bengal; s. of Chandidas Ganguly and Nirupa Ganguly; m. Dona Roy; one d.; ed St. Xavier's, Calcutta; left-handed middle-order batsman, right-arm medium-pace bowler; played for Bengal 1989–2007, India 1992– (Capt. 2000–06), Lancs. 2000, Glamorgan 2005, Northants. 2006, Kolkata Knight Riders 2008–; First-class debut 1989/90; Test debut: England v India, Lord's 20–24 June 1996; ODI debut: India v West Indies, Brisbane 11 Jan. 1992; has played in 113 tests (49 as Capt.), scored 7,212 runs (average 42.17, highest score 239) with 16 hundreds and took 32 wickets; scored 15,025 First-class runs (average 43.93, highest score 239) with 31 hundreds and took 164 wickets (best bowling 6/46); 311 ODIs, scored 11,363 runs (average 41.02, highest score 183 v Sri Lanka at Taunton, England) with 22 hundreds and took 100 wickets; led India to second place at World Cup 2003; currently Pres. Cricket Asscn of Bengal, Editorial Bd, Wisden India; mem. Governing Council and Technical Cttee, Indian Premier League; Arjuna Award 1997, Padma Shri 2004, Banga Bibhushan Award 2013. *Address:* 2/6 Biren Roy Road, Behala, Kolkata 700 008, India (home). *Website:* www.cricketassociationofbengal.com (office).

GANIĆ, Ejup, DSc; Bosnia and Herzegovina engineer, academic and politician; *Chancellor and Rector, Sarajevo School of Science and Technology;* b. 3 March 1946, Novi Pazar; m. Fahrija Ganić; one s. one d.; ed Univ. of Belgrade, Massachusetts Inst. of Tech., USA; Asst Prof., Univ. of Illinois, Chicago 1977–80, Assoc. Prof. 1980–82; returned to Bosnia and Herzegovina 1982; Prof. of Mechanical Engineering, Univ. of Sarajevo 1982–85; Exec. Dir UNIS Co. 1984–90; mem. Presidency of Bosnia and Herzegovina 1990–96, Vice-Pres. 1992–96, Vice-Pres. Fed. of Bosnia and Herzegovina 1994–96, Co-Pres. 1996–2002; Founder, Chancellor and Rector, Sarajevo School of Science and Tech. 2004–, also Prof. of Engineering Science; Founder and Pres. MET Foundation. *Publications:* Handbook of Heat Transfer Applications 1985, Handbook of Heat Transfer Fundamentals 1985, Handbook of Essential Engineering Information and Data 1991, Engineering Companion 2003; more than 100 scientific papers. *Address:* Office of the President, Sarajevo School of Science and Technology, Hrasnicka 3A, 71000 Sarajevo, Bosnia and Herzegovina (office). *Telephone:* (33) 617205 (office). *Fax:* (33) 617205 (office). *E-mail:* ejup.ganic@ssst.edu.ba; ejup_ganic@hotmail.com. *Website:* ssst.edu.ba (office).

GANIEV, Rivner Fazilovich; Russian mechanical engineer; *Scientific Director, Non-linear Wave Mechanics and Technology Centre, Russian Academy of Sciences;* b. 1 April 1937, Bashkiriya; m. Galina Mikhailovna Antonovskaya; two s.; ed Ufa Aviation Inst.; engineer constructor, jr, sr researcher, Head of Dept, Inst. of Mechanics Ukrainian Acad. of Sciences 1959–78; Head of Lab., Research Inst. of Machine Devt 1978–89, Deputy Dir 1989–95; Scientific Dir of Non-linear Wave Mechanics and Tech. Centre, Russian Acad. of Sciences 1995–; Head, Applied Physics Faculty, Moscow Aviation Inst.; Chair. Council of Dirs, United Inst. of Automobile Mechanics and Tech. in Oil Extraction of the Russian Acad. of Sciences and the Acad. of Sciences of the Repub. of Bashkortostan; mem. Scientific Council on Problem Reliability of Machines; Corresp. mem. USSR (now Russian) Acad. of Sciences 1987, mem. 1994; specialist in applied math., theoretical and applied mechanics, mechanical eng; more than 100 inventions and patents; research in theory of resonance phenomena at nonlinear spatial oscillations of solid and deformable matter, theory of nonlinear oscillations of multiphase systems, vibration and wave processes and tech. *Publications include:* Dynamics of Particles under Influence of Vibrations 1975, Solid Matter Oscillations 1976, Oscillatory Phenomena in Multiphase Media and their Applications to Technology 1980; more than 300 other published works, including 15 monographs and numerous articles in scientific journals. *Leisure interests:* sport, skiing. *Address:* Non-linear Wave Mechanics and Technology Centre, Russian Academy of Sciences, 4, Maly Kharitonievskiy Pereulok, 101990 Moscow, Russia (office). *Telephone:* (495) 135-55-93 (office). *Fax:* (495) 135-61-05 (office). *E-mail:* info@imash.ru (office). *Website:* www.eng.imash.ru (office).

G'ANIYEV, Elyor Majidovich; Uzbekistani politician; b. 7 Jan. 1960, Syrdarya Prov.; m.; five c.; ed Tashkent Polytechnic Inst.; Asst, Tashkent Polytechnic Inst. 1981–85; service in the Armed Forces 1985–90; Sr Adviser, State Cttee for Foreign Econ. and Trade Relations 1990–92; Head of Dept, Ministry of Foreign Econ. Relations 1992–93; Head of Div., Inst. for Strategic and Regional Studies under Pres. of Uzbekistan 1993–94; Deputy Minister of Foreign Econ. Relations 1994–95, First Deputy Minister 1995–97, Minister of Foreign Econ. Relations 1997–2002; Deputy Prime Minister and Chair. Agency for Foreign Econ. Relations 2002–05; Deputy Prime Minister and Minister of Foreign Affairs 2005–06, 2010–12, Minister of Foreign Econ. Relations, Investment and Trade 2006–09, 2013, Deputy Prime Minister and Minister of Foreign Econ. Relations 2009–10, Deputy Prime Minister, Minister of Foreign Affairs, responsible for Foreign Econ. Activities, the Attraction of Foreign Investment and the Localization of Production 2010–12; Pres. Volleyball Fed. of Uzbekistan. *Address:* c/o Ministry of Foreign Trade, 100047 Tashkent, 51, str. Istiqlal, Uzbekistan.

GANNUSHKINA, Svetlana; Russian mathematician; b. 6 March 1942, Moscow; d. of Alexei Petrovich Gannushkin and Elena Grigorievna Gannushkina; m.; one s. one d.; ed Moscow State Univ.; Lecturer, later Assoc. Prof. of Math., Historical and Archive Inst., Moscow (now Russian State Humanities Univ.) 1970–2000; involved in human rights work since late 1980s, including partnership with UNHCR and Secours Catholique (French charity), MSF, Norwegian Helsinki Cttee, etc.; Co-founder Grazhdanskoe Sodeistvie (Civic Assistance, regional charity helping refugees) 1990; Founding mem. Memorial Human Rights Centre 1993, Migration Rights Network 1996; went to Chechnya, Dagestan, North Ossetia and Ingushetia to provide humanitarian aid and help establish legal advice centres; mem. Expert Council under the Office of the High Commr for Human Rights in Russia; mem. Presidential Council for Civil Society and Human Rights 2002–12; mem. Civil Soc. Insts and Human Rights Council 2002–, Govt Comm. on Migration Policy; For Faith and Service of Russia Order 2010, Chevalier, Légion d'honneur 2011; Open

Society Institute (Soros Fund) Award 1997, Award of German section of International Amnesty 2003, UNHCR Nansen Award for Refugees 2004, Homo Homini Award 2006, Norwegian Helsinki Human Rights Cttee Sakharov Award 2007, Shyur Lindebrekkes Award for Democracy and Human Rights (Norway) 2012, Stig Larsson Award (Sweden) 2014, Heinz Schwarzkopf Young Europe Fund Award (Hamburg) 2014, Medal for Protection of Human Rights in the Republic of Ingushetia 2014. *Address:* Civil Society Institutions and Human Rights Council, 103132 Moscow, 4, Staraya Square, Russia (office). *Telephone:* (495) 606-49-14 (office).

GANONGO, Calixte; Republic of the Congo business executive and politician; *Minister of Finance and Budget;* b. Oyo; ed Jean Moulin Univ. of Lyon III; Head Collection Services, Social Security Insp., Accountant of Deposit and Guarantee Fund, Nat. Social Security Fund (CNSS) 1990–97; Head Dept of Finance and Accounting, Nat. Petroleum Co. of Congo (SNPC) 1998–2010, Deputy Dir-Gen. Finance and Accounting 2010; Minister of Finance and Budget 2016–. *Address:* Ministry of Finance and the Budget, ave de l'Indépendance, croisement ave Foch, BP 2083, Brazzaville, Republic of the Congo (office). *Telephone:* 22-281-45-24 (office). *Fax:* 22-281-43-69 (office). *E-mail:* mefb-cg@mefb-cg.net (office).

GANSER, Gérard Roger Gaston; French civil servant; b. 6 Jan. 1949, Montreuil-Sous-Bois; s. of Pierre Ganser and Simone Braillon; m. Aimée Fontaine (divorced); one s.; ed Lycées Paul Valéry and Louis le Grand, Ecole polytechnique, Ecole nat. d'admin; Auditor, Cour des comptes 1976–80, Public Auditor 1980, Chief Adviser 1993–98, Sec.-Gen. 1998–99; with Interministerial Mission of the Sea 1979–80; commercial adviser in Mexico 1981–82; with Ministry of Agric. 1983, Jt Dir Ministry of Trade and Tourism 1983–84, with Ministry of Industrial Redeployment and Trade 1984, Ministry for Communications 1988, Dir 1989–91; Jt Dir-Gen. Commercial Affairs Télédiffusion de France 1984–86; reporter to Constitutional Council 1987–88; Pres. and Chair. Soc. financière de radiodiffusion (Sofirad) 1991–94; Vice-Pres. Radio Monte Carlo 1991–94; Auditor, European Examinations Office 1995; Auditor, Inst. des hautes études de la défense nat. 1996; Chevalier Ordre nat. du Mérite.

GANTAR, Pavel, MA, PhD; Slovenian sociologist and politician; *President, For Real—New Politics (Zares);* b. 26 Oct. 1949, Gorenja vas, Škofja Loka, Upper Carniola, Yugoslavia (now Slovenia); ed professional school for carpentry, Faculty of Political Sciences, Univ. of Ljubljana, Univ. of Essex, UK, Univ. of Zagreb, Croatia; as student, Co-founder student group 'November 13th' 1971; Asst Prof., Faculty of Social Sciences, Univ. of Ljubljana 1974–94; mem. Urban Planning Council of Ljubljana 1970s; mem. Editorial Bd Journal for the Critique of Science (Časopis za kritiko znanosti, ČKZ) 1976; columnist, Mladina magazine 1980s; Pres. SKUC-Forum (org. for alternative culture) 1980s; studied in UK 1984; apptd Chair. CP cell, Faculty of Social Sciences, Univ. of Ljubljana 1984, expelled from CP of Slovenia for using his position to defend essayist Spomenka Hribar accused of denigration of Yugoslav People's Liberation War 1985; among first scholars of contemporary underground social movts in Slovenia and Yugoslavia late 1980s, actively involved in 'Slovenian Spring'; Founding mem. Cttee for the Protection of Human Rights 1988–90; joined Liberal Democratic Party 1990; elected to Državni zbor (Nat. Ass.) 1990 (re-elected 2004, 2008), Chair. 2008–11; Minister of the Environment and Spatial Planning 1994–2000, of Information Society 2001–04; Founding mem. For Real—New Politics (Zares) 2007–, Pres. 2012–. *Publications include:* several articles on civil society under the socialist regime, theories of social planning, spatial planning, information society. *Address:* For Real—New Politics (Zares), 1000 Ljubljana, Župančičeva 8, Slovenia (office). *Telephone:* (1) 2428750 (office). *Fax:* (1) 2428753 (office). *E-mail:* info@zares.si (office). *Website:* www.zares.si (office).

GANTNER, Carrillo Baillieu, AO, MFA; Australian theatre manager, director, actor and business executive; *Chairman, Sidney Meyer Fund;* b. 17 June 1944, San Francisco, Calif., USA; s. of Vallejo Gantner and Neilma Gantner; m. 1st Nancy Black 1971 (divorced 1982); two s. one d. (deceased); m. 2nd Dr Jennifer Webb; two s.; ed Melbourne Grammar School and Melbourne, Stanford and Harvard Univs; Fellow, Stanford Univ. 1968–69; Asst, Admin. Adelaide Festival of Arts 1969–70; Drama Officer, Australian Council for the Arts 1970–73; Gen. Man. Melbourne Theatre Co. 1973–75; Exec. Dir Playbox Theatre Co. Ltd 1976–84, The CUB Malthouse; Cultural Counsellor, Australian Embassy, Beijing 1985–87; Artistic Dir Playbox Theatre Centre 1988–93, Chair. Playbox Malthouse Ltd 1994–96; Councillor, City of Melbourne 1996–99 (Chair. Planning and Devt Cttee 1996–98, Docklands Cttee 1998–99, Deputy Chair. Finance and Service Cttee and Audit Cttee 1998–99); Chair. Performing Arts Bd Australia Council 1990–93, Nat. Circus Summit 1990, Nat. Dance Summit 1991, Nat. Advisory Council, Musica Viva 1993, Melbourne Int. Comedy Festival 1995–, Victorian Art Centre 2000–09; Pres. Melbourne Chapter of URASENKE 1995–; Dir Myer Foundation 1984–92 (Vice-Pres. 1992), Asialink 1990–92 (Chair. 1992), Mayfair Hanoi Ltd (Hong Kong) 1996–98, Deputy Chair. 1999; Trustee, Sidney Myer Fund 1991–, currently Chair.; mem. Australia–China Council 1989–94, Australia Abroad Council 1991–95, Exec. Cttee Asia Pacific Philanthropy Consortium 1994, Nat. Advisory Council, Adelaide Festival 1996; Corresp. mem. The Hague Club 1994–; Gov. Fed. for Asian Cultural Promotion 1994; Japan Foundation Visitors Program 1991; mem. Working Group to establish an Asian Business Council for the Arts 1997–98; Chair. Arts Man. Course Advisory Cttee, Victorian Coll. of the Arts 1996–98; Chair. Barclay Investment Pty Ltd, Myer Investment Pty Ltd 1998–; Hon. Fellow, Australian Acad. of the Humanities 2008; Dorothy Crawford Award 2007, Victorian of the Year 2007. *Publications:* articles in professional journals. *Leisure interests:* viticulture, tennis. *Address:* Sidney Myer Fund, PO Box 21676, Little Lonsdale Street, Melbourne, Victoria 8011, Australia (office). *Telephone:* (3) 8672-5555 (office). *Fax:* (3) 8672-5556 (office). *E-mail:* admin@myerfoundation.org.au (office). *Website:* www.myerfoundation.org.au (office).

GANTZ, Gen. Benjamin (Benny), BA, MA; Israeli army officer and politician; b. 9 June 1959, Kafar Ahim; m. Revital Gantz; four c.; ed Tel Aviv Univ., Univ. of Haifa, Nat. Defense Univ., USA; drafted into Israel Defense Forces (IDF) 1977, becoming Commdr, 890 Echis Airborne Bn 1987–89, Shaldag Unit 1989–92, Reserve Paratroopers Brigade 1992–94, Judea Regional Brigade 1994–95, Paratroopers Brigade 1995–97, Ground Forces Command 2005–07; Mil. Attaché in USA 2007–09; Deputy Chief of Gen. Staff of IDF 2009–10, Chief of Gen. Staff 2011–15; Chair. Bd of Dirs Fifth Dimension (computer security and law enforcement tech. co.) 2015–18; f. Israel Resilience (Hosen L'Yisrael) 2018 (merged with Telem party to form Blue and White Alliance 2019); Commdr, Legion of Merit (USA). *Website:* www.telem-il.org.

GAO, Bo; Chinese architect and photographer; b. 1964, Chongqing, Sichuan Prov.; m. Delphine Gao; ed Sichuan Fine Arts Inst., Central Acad. of Art and Design, Beijing, Catholic Inst. of Paris, France; architect, Beijing 1996–; Dir Beijing Boart Culture Devt Co. Ltd; f. China Heritage Soc.; worked as photographer for Agence VU (photographic agency), Paris 1989–95; mem. Chinese Photographers' Inst.; Winner, People's Daily Photography Competition 1986. *Works include:* Portraits and Masks Duality Series 1964, Faint Memory 2006, Unlimited Scenery 2007, Searching 2007. *Exhibitions include:* Int. Festival of Photography, Pingyao, Sichuan 2002, Arles Festival, France 2003, Museum of New Art, Pontiac, Michigan 2004, Three Shadows Photography Art Center, Beijing 2007, 2008, From New Photography to Rookie Award: Three Shadows Collection, Guangzhou 2013–14, Chinese Photography: Twentieth Century and Beyond, Berlin 2015, Family Tree, Guangzhou 2016, 40 Years of Chinese Contemporary Photography 1976–2017, Shanghai 2017, Resident Alien, Paris 2017–18. *Publications include:* GB Vol. 1-4 2017, volumes of photographs on rural China, Tibet and Tiananmen Square. *Address:* c/o Agence Vu, 17 boulevard Henri IV, 75004 Paris, France (office).

GAO, Changli; Chinese fmr politician; b. July 1937, Yutai, Shandong Prov.; ed Chinese People's Univ.; joined CCP 1956; cadre Yutai Co. People's Govt, cadre Office of CCP Jining Pref. Cttee; Vice-Sec. CCP Yishui Co. Cttee, Sec. CCP Rizhao Co. Cttee, Vice-Chief Sec. then Chief Sec. CCP Shandong Prov. Cttee 1976–87; Vice-Gov. Shandong Prov. and Sec. Political and Legal Cttee of CCP Shandong Prov. Cttee; mem. Trial Cttee of Supreme People's Court; Vice-Chair. Supreme People's Court 1993–98; Minister of Justice 1998–2000; Alt. mem. 14th CCP Cen. Cttee 1992–97, 15th CCP Cen. Cttee 1997–2002.

GAO, Dezhan; Chinese state official and engineer; b. 6 Aug. 1932, Qixia, Shandong Prov.; ed Dalian Eng Inst., Liaoning Prov.; joined CCP 1950; engineer and Dir China Sugar Refinery, Jilin Prov. 1954–58; Deputy Chief Engineer and Deputy Dir Petrochemical Bureau, Jilin Prov. 1961–76; Dir Jilin Prov. Econ. Comm. 1980–81; Vice-Gov. Jilin Prov. 1983–85, Gov. 1985–87; Deputy Sec. CCP Jilin Prov. Cttee 1985–87; Minister of Forestry 1987–93; Vice-Chair. All-China Greening Cttee 1988–93, Deputy Head Cen. Forest Fire Prevention 1988–93; Deputy Head State Leading Group for Comprehensive Agricultural Devt 1990–; Deputy Head Cen. Forest Fire Prevention 1988–93; Alt. mem. 12th CCP Cen. Cttee 1982–87, 13th CCP Cen. Cttee 1987–92, mem. 14th CCP Cen. Cttee 1992–97; Sec. Tianjin City CCP Cttee 1993–97; Deputy, 8th NPC 1993–98, mem. 9th Standing Cttee of NPC 1998–2003, Chair. Agric. and Rural Affairs Cttee of NPC 1998–2003; Special Gold Prize for Chinese Greening Science and Tech. 1993. *Address:* c/o Standing Committee of the National People's Congress, Beijing, People's Republic of China.

GAO, Guofu, PhD; Chinese business executive; *Chairman, Shanghai Pudong Development Bank Co. Ltd;* b. June 1956; ed Shanghai Jiao Tong Univ.; fmr Gen. Man. Shanghai Urban Construction Investment and Devt Corpn; fmr Gen. Man. Shanghai Waigaoqiao Free Trade Zone Devt Co.; fmr Acting Pres. Shanghai Wanguo Securities Co.; fmr Sec. China Pacific Insurance (Group) Co. Ltd, Exec. Dir and Chair. 2006–17, mem. Bd of Dirs –2017, Sec. CCP China Pacific Insurance Group Cttee 2017–; Chair. Shanghai Pudong Devt Bank Co. Ltd 2017–. *Address:* Shanghai Pudong Development Bank, 12, Zhongshan Dong Yi Road, Shanghai, Shanghai Province, People's Republic of China (office). *Telephone:* (21) 61618888 (office). *Fax:* (21) 63232036 (office). *Website:* www.spdb.com.cn (office).

GAO, Hucheng, DSc; Chinese fmr government official; b. 1951, Shuozhou, Shanxi Prov.; ed Beijing Second Foreign Languages Inst., Nat. Univ. of Zaire (now Univ. of Kinshasa), Democratic Repub. of the Congo, Univ. Paris VII, France; Commercial Officer, Embassy in Kinshasa, Zaire (now Democratic Repub. of the Congo) 1977–80; Sec., China Nat. Machinery and Equipment Import and Export Corpn (CMEC) 1980–82, Operations Man. and Deputy Gen. Man., CMEC French Office, Paris 1982–87, Deputy Chief, Financial Dept, CMEC 1987–89, Chief 1989–90; Deputy Gen. Man. China Nat. Resources Corpn 1992–94, also Sec., CCP Party Cttee; Head, Planning and Finance Dept, Ministry of Foreign Trade and Econ. Cooperation 1994–97, Asst to Minister 1997–2002, also mem. CCP Leading Party Group 1997–2002; Vice-Chair., People's Govt, Guangxi Zhuang Autonomous Region 2002–03; Vice-Minister of Commerce 2003–13, Minister 2013–17, mem. Ministry of Commerce CCP Leading Party Group 2003–09; Alt. mem. 18th CCP Cen. Cttee 2012–17.

GAO, Jianping, BA; Chinese economist and business executive; *Chairman, Industrial Bank Company Limited;* served as Deputy Gen. Man. Gen. Office of Industrial Bank, Dir of Industrial Bank's Office in Fuzhou Econ. and Technological Devt Zone, Gen. Man. Office of Industrial Bank, Head of Industrial Bank's Shanghai Br. Preparatory Team, Vice-Pres. of Industrial Bank and Pres. of Industrial Bank's Shanghai Br., Vice-Pres. of Industrial Bank (in charge of overall management), Sec. of CP Cttee, mem. Bd of Dirs, Industrial Bank Co. Ltd 2007–, currently also Chair. *Address:* Industrial Bank Co. Ltd, 154 Hudong Road, Fuzhou 350003, People's Republic of China (office). *Telephone:* (591) 87839338 (office). *Fax:* (591) 87841932 (office). *E-mail:* webmaster@cib.com.cn (office). *Website:* www.cib.com.cn (office).

GAO, Shangquan; Chinese government official and professor of economics; b. Sept. 1929, Jia Ding Co., Shanghai; s. of Gao Ruyu and Xiang Shi; m. Cha Peijun 1958; one s.; ed St John's Univ., Shanghai; worked as researcher, Deputy Div. Chief, Div. Chief, Bureau for Machine-Bldg Industry of Ministry of Industry of local North-Eastern People's Govt; Policy Research Dept, First Ministry of Machine-Bldg Industry; Research Dept, Ministry of Agricultural Machine-Bldg Industry; Office of Agricultural Mechanization, State Council; Policy Research Dept, State Comm. of Machine-Bldg Industry; Research Fellow, Research Centre for Agricultural Devt and Sr Economist, State Comm. of Machine-Bldg Industry; State Comm. for Restructuring Econ. System 1982, then Deputy Dir and Head, Research Inst. of Restructuring the Econ. System 1985–93; Vice-Minister in charge of State Comm. for Restructuring the Econ. System 1985–93; mem. preliminary working Cttee of preparatory Cttee of the Hong Kong Special Admin. Region and Head of Econ. Panel 1993–97, 9th Nat. Cttee of CPPCC 1998–2003;

mem. Sino-Japanese Econ. Exchange Comm.; Vice-Group-Leader, Leading Group for Restructuring Housing System, under State Council; Pres. China Research Soc. for Restructuring the Econ. Systems, China Soc. of Enterprise Reform and Devt, China Inst. for Reform & Devt, China Reform Foundation, China Soc. of Urban Housing System Reform, Asscn of Future Market of China; Vice-Pres. Asscn of China's Urban Economy, Asscn of China's Industrial Economy, Asscn for Study of China's Specific Condition, Asscn of Social and Economics Publs; Chair. Research Group for Rural and Urban Housing Reform 1995–; mem. UN Cttee for Devt Policy; Doctorate Supervisor, Prof., Beijing Univ. and Shanghai Jiaotong Univ.; Dean Man. School, Zhejiang Univ.; Prof. Nankai Univ., Chinese People's Univ., Shanghai Univ. of Finance and Econs; MBA programme adviser of Nat. Univ. of Australia; Outstanding Scholar Award Hong Kong Polytechnic. *Publications:* Enterprises Should Enjoy Certain Autonomy 1956, Follow A Road of Our Own in Agricultural Modernization 1982, Nine Years of Reform in China's Economic System 1987, A Road To Success 1987, Selected Works of Gao Shangquan 1989, China: A Decade of Economic Reform 1989, The Reform of China's Economic System 1991, Lead to a Powerful Country 1991, On Planning and Market in China 1992, From Planned Economy to the Socialist Market Economy 1993, An Introduction to Socialist Market Economy 1994, China: The Second Revolution 1995, China's Economic Reform 1996, Extensive Talk About China's Market Economy 1998, The Second Revolution 1998, Market Economy and China's Reform 1999, Two Decades of Reform in China 1999; also ed. of numerous publications. *Address:* c/o State Commission for Restructuring the Economic System, 22 Xianmen Street, Beijing 100017, People's Republic of China.

GAO, Xingjian, BA; French (b. Chinese) writer and dramatist; b. 4 Jan. 1940, Ganzhou, Jiangxi Prov., People's Republic of China; ed Dept of Foreign Languages, Beijing; translator, China Reconstructs (magazine), later for Chinese Writers Asscn; spent five years in re-education during Cultural Revolution; Artistic Dir People's Art Theatre, Beijing 1981; left China 1987 after work banned in 1985, living in Paris 1988–, became French citizen 1998; Chevalier des Arts et des Lettres 1992, Légion d'honneur 2000; Prix Communauté française de Belgium 1994, Prix du Nouvel An Chinois 1997, Nobel Prize for Literature 2000. *Publications include:* plays: Absolute Signal 1982, Bus Stop 1983, Wild Man 1990, The Other Shore 1999, Fugitives 1993, Tales of Mountains and Seas 1993, The Man Who Questions Death 2003; novels: Soul Mountain 1999, Return to Painting 2001, One Man's Bible 2002; other: Snow in August (opera) 2002, Buying a Fishing Rod for my Grandfather (short stories) 2004. *Address:* c/o HarperCollins, 77–85 Fulham Palace Road, London, W6 8JB, England (office).

GAO, Xiqing, BA, LLM, JD; Chinese lawyer and banking executive; b. Sept. 1953; ed Univ. of Int. Business and Econs, Beijing, Duke Univ. School of Law, USA; worked as Assoc. at Mudge Rose Guthrie Alexander & Ferdon (law firm), Wall Street, New York; returned to China 1988; Deputy Chair. and CEO Bank of China International (Holdings) Ltd 1990s; Gen. Counsel and Dir-Gen. Public Offering Supervision Dept, China Securities Regulatory Comm. (CSRC) 1992–95, later Vice-Chair. 1999–2003; Deputy Chief Exec. Hong Kong-Macao Regional Office, Bank of China 1997–99; later Vice-Chair. Nat. Council for the Social Security Fund; Vice-Chair. and Pres. China Investment Corpn 2007–14; mem. Bd of Trustees, Duke Univ. 2008–. *Achievements include:* first Chinese citizen to pass New York State Bar exam. *Address:* c/o Board of Trustees, Duke University, 217 Allen Building, Durham, NC 27708, USA.

GAO, Yan; Chinese government official and engineer; b. 1942, Yushu Co., Jilin Prov.; joined CCP 1965; Deputy Dir Jilin Thermal Power Plant 1965–74 (also Sec. CCP and Communist Youth League); Sr Engineer and Deputy Dir, later Dir Electricity Bureau 1975; Head Org. Dept, CCP Jilin Prov. Cttee 1988–95, Deputy Sec. Jilin CCP Jilin Prov. Cttee 1988–95; Vice-Gov. of Jilin Prov. 1988–92, Gov. 1992–95; Sec. CCP Cttee, Yunan Prov. 1995–97; Dir Political Dept, Chinese People's Armed Police Force; Sec. CCP 6th Yunnan Prov. Cttee; mem. 14th CCP Cen. Cttee 1992–97, 15th CCP Cen. Cttee 1997–2002; Deputy Gen. Man. State Electrical Power Corpn 1997–98, Gen. Man. 1998–2002; Vice Minister of Power Industry 1997–98.

GAO, Yaojie, MD; Chinese physician and activist; b. 19 Dec. 1927, cen. Henan Prov.; m.; several c.; ed Henan Univ.; retd gynaecologist from Henan Coll. of Traditional Chinese Medicine who discovered wide-scale HIV infection among citizens of Henan Prov. in early 1990s, alerted govt authorities 1996 but no action taken; spent much of her pension printing pamphlets to educate rural residents and to buy medicine for the sick; placed under house arrest 2007; living in exile in USA as a result of her campaigns in relation to China's AIDS epidemic 2009–; Jonathan Mann Award for Global Health and Human Rights, Global Health Council 2001, Ramon Magsaysay Award for Public Service 2003, named one of 10 People Who Moved China in 2003, Touching China Award from China Central TV 2004, Vital Voices Global Partnership Global Leadership Award, Women Changing Our World 2007, New York Acad. of Sciences Heinz R. Pagels Human Rights of Scientists Award 2007, Liu Binyan Conscience Award 2014. *Publications:* Ten Thousand Letters (First Chinese Publications and Media Award 2005) 2004, The Soul of Gao Yaojie 2008, My Experience of AIDS Prevention (in Chinese) 2011. *Address:* China AIDS Orphan Fund, The Minneapolis Foundation, 800 IDS Center, 80 South Eighth Street, Minneapolis, MN 55402, USA (office). *Website:* www.chinaaidsorphanfund.org (office).

GAO, Ying; Chinese author and poet; b. 25 Dec. 1929, Jiaozuo, Henan; s. of Gao Weiya and Sha Peifen; m. Duan Chuanchen 1954; one s. two d.; Vice-Chair. Sichuan Br. and mem. Council, Chinese Writers Asscn; Deputy Dir Ed. Bd, Sichuan Prov. Broadcasting Station 1983; mem. Sichuan Political Consultative Conf. *Publications include:* The Song of Ding Youjun, Lamplights around the Three Gorges, High Mountains and Distant Rivers, Cloudy Cliff (novel), Da Ji and her Fathers (novel and film script), The Orchid (novel), Loving-Kindness of the Bamboo Storey (collection of prose), Mother in my Heart (autobiographical novel), Songs of Da Liang Mountains (poems), Frozen Snowflakes (poems), Reminiscences, Xue Ma (novel), Gao Ying (short stories). *Leisure interests:* painting, music.

GAO, Youxi; Chinese physicist; b. 1920; ed Nat. Central Univ.; Dir Plateau Atmospheric Physics Inst., Lanzhou 1981; mem. Dept of Earth Sciences, Academia Sinica 1985; Nat. Science Award 1989.

GAO, Zhanxiang; Chinese party official; b. 1935, Tongxian Co., Hebei Prov.; joined CCP 1953; mem. Communist Youth League Cen. Cttee 1964, Sec. 1978–83; Vice-Chair. All-China Youth Fed. 1978–83; Deputy Sec. CCP Cttee, Hebei Prov. 1983–86; Dir State Ethnic Affairs Comm. 1986–89; Vice-Minister of Culture 1986–96; Sec. Secr. China Fed. of Literary and Art Circles 1990, Vice-Chair. 1990; Pres. Soc. of Mass Culture 1990–93; Vice-Chair. Chinese Asscn for Promotion of Popular Culture 1993, Hon. Chair. 1996; Adviser, China Int. Tea Cultures Soc. 1993; Chair. Soc. of Photographic Arts 1994; Vice-Chair. China Soc. of Tourism Culture 1994; Dir, Ed.-in-Chief Chinese Arts 1994; Alt. mem. 12th CCP Cen. Cttee 1982–87; Del., 13th CCP Nat. Congress 1987–92, 14th CCP Nat. Congress 1992–97, 15th CCP Nat. Congress 1997–2002; mem. 7th CPPCC Nat. Cttee 1988–93, Standing Cttee of 8th CPPCC Nat. Cttee 1993–98 (mem. Educ. and Culture Sub-cttee), Standing Cttee of 9th CPPCC Nat. Cttee 1998–2003; Hon. Chair. Soc. for the Promotion of Chinese Culture 1996–. *Publications:* author of several literary anthologies.

GAPONOV-GREKHOV, Andrey Viktorovich; Russian physicist and academic; *Scientific Chief Supervisor, Institute of Applied Physics, Russian Academy of Sciences;* b. 7 June 1926, Moscow; m.; one d.; ed Gorky State Univ.; Instructor, Gorky Polytech. Inst. 1952–55; Sr Scientific Assoc., Gorky (now Nizhny Novgorod) State Univ. 1955–, Head of Dept of Radio Physics, Inst. of Applied Physics 1977–2003, Scientific Chief Supervisor 2003–; Corresp. mem. USSR (now Russian) Acad. of Sciences 1964–68, mem. 1968–; USSR People's Deputy 1989–91; Hero of Socialist Labour 1986; State Prize 1967, 1983, 2003. *Publications:* numerous theoretical and experimental works in the field of electrodynamics and electronics of inducted cyclotronic radiation, which led to development of a new class of electronic instruments – masers with cyclotronic resonance. *Address:* Institute of Applied Physics, Ulyanova str. 46, Nizhny Novgorod 603950, Russia (office). *Telephone:* (831) 436-66-69 (office); (831) 436-36-67 (home). *Fax:* (831) 436-20-61 (office). *E-mail:* gapgr@appl.sci-nnov.ru (office). *Website:* www.ipfran.ru (office).

GARAIKOETXEA URRIZA, Carlos, LicenDer; Spanish (Basque) lawyer, economist and fmr politician; b. 2 June 1939, Pamplona; s. of Juan Garaikoetxea and Dolores Urriza; m. Sagrario Mina Apat 1966; three s.; mem. Inst. Príncipe de Viana, org. to protect and promote Basque culture, Navarra Dist Council 1971; Chair. Navarra Chamber of Commerce and Industry 1971; Chair. Nat. Council PNV 1977, re-elected 1978; mem. Navarra Dist Parl. 1979; Pres. Gen. Council of the Basque Country 1979; elected to Basque Parl. as PNV cand. for Guipúzcoa March 1980; Pres. of Basque Govt 1980–86; European Deputy 1987; Pres. Eusko Alkartaruna Party 1987–99. *Publications:* Euskadi: la transición inacabada, Memorias Políticas. *Leisure interests:* music (especially classical), skiing, Basque pelota, reading (especially political essays and history).

GARANG MABIORDIT WOL, Salvatore; Sudanese government official; *Minister of Finance and Economic Planning* ed Univ. of Liberia, Univ. of Birmingham; Dir of Int. Audit and Inspection, Council of Ministers, Wau, Bahr al Ghazal 1983–91, fmr Dir of accounts, Regional Ministry Of Finance; Dir-Gen. of Finance, Ministry of Finance, Warrap, Tonj State 1994–95; Asst Admin. of Médecins Sans Frontières Switzerland, Marial Lou Hospital, Tonj 2001–02; Interpreter in Australia 2004–08; Undersecretary, Ministry of Finance and Econ. Planning 2008–18, Minister of Finance and Econ. Planning 2018–. *Address:* Ministry of Finance and Economic Planning, POB 80, Juba, South Sudan (office). *Telephone:* 122249178 (office). *E-mail:* kitoundo@hotmail.com (office). *Website:* grss-mof.org.

GARAVANI, Valentino; Italian fashion designer; b. 11 May 1932, Voghera, nr Milan; pnr Giancarlo Giammetti; ed Ecole des Beaux-Arts, Paris, Ecole de la Chambre Syndicale de la Couture, Paris; asst designer at Paris fashion houses of Jean Dessès 1950–55, Guy Laroche 1956–58; est. Valentino fashion house with Giancarlo Giammetti in Rome 1960, debut collection 1962, opened boutiques in Rome, Milan, Paris, New York, Tokyo and other cities; launched first Valentino perfume 1978; designed kit for Italian Olympic team 1984; designed costumes for opera The Dream of Valentino, J. F. Kennedy Center, USA 1994; sold Valentino fashion house to HdP 1998; announced decision to retire 2008; f. Valentino Acad. 1990; f. L.I.F.E for AIDS research and assistance to victims of the disease 1990; retrospective exhbn of creations in Rome 1991, at Columbus Festivities, New York 1992; Grande Ufficiale dell'Ordine al Merito della Repubblica Italiana 1985, Cavaliere del Lavoro 1996, Légion d'honneur, France 2005; Neiman Marcus Prize 1967, Premio speciale dell'arte nella moda, Florence 1995, CFDA Lifetime Achievement Award 2000, Medaille de Vermeil 2008. *Address:* c/o Li.ter Ltd, 26 Upper Brook Street, London W1K 7QE, England (office). *Telephone:* (20) 7409-1606 (office). *Fax:* (20) 7409-3110 (office). *E-mail:* ronaldfeijen@btconnect.com. *Website:* www.valentino.com.

GARAYEV, Tamerlan; Azerbaijani politician and diplomatist; *Ambassador to Indonesia;* b. 30 Jan. 1952, Gasimly, Agdam Region; s. of Yelmar Garayev and Khalida Garayeva; m. Farida Garayeva 1976; two s.; ed Azerbaijan Univ.; public prosecutor 1973–78; Lecturer, Azerbaijan Univ. 1978–91; became involved in opposition politics late 1980s; leader, moderate wing Popular Front, elected Deputy to Supreme Soviet 1990, Deputy Chair., First Deputy Chair. 1991–93; Amb. to China 1993–2000, to India 2004–11, to Indonesia 2011–; mem. Org. for the Liberation of Karabakh. *Leisure interest:* golf. *Address:* Embassy of Azerbaijan, Jalan Karang Asem Tengah, Blok C-5, Kav. 20, Kuningan Timur, Jakarta 12950, Indonesia (office). *Telephone:* (21) 25554408 (office). *Fax:* (21) 25554409 (office). *E-mail:* jakarta@mission.mfa.gov.az (office). *Website:* www.jakarta.mfa.gov.az (office).

GARBER, Judith G., BS; American diplomatist; *Ambassador to Cyprus;* m.; two c.; ed Georgetown Univ.; worked at Bd of Govs, Fed. Reserve and Dept of Treasury, Washington, DC; joined Foreign Service 1984, Dept of State Secr. and Bureau of Econ. Affairs, overseas postings include Econ. Counsellor, Embassy in Madrid, Deputy Econ. Counsellor, Embassy in Tel-Aviv, Econ. Officer, Embassies in Prague, Mexico City, Vice Consul, Embassy in Seville, Dir for Overseas Devt Finance, Bureau of Econ. and Business Affairs, Dept of State, Dir Office of North Cen. Europe –2007, Deputy Asst Sec. of State, Bureau of European and Eurasian Affairs 2007–09, Amb. to Latvia 2009–12; Acting Asst Sec., Bureau of Oceans and Int. Environmental and Scientific Affairs 2014–18; Amb. to Cyprus 2019–; Order of the Three Stars (Latvia) 2012. *Address:* US Embassy, Metochiou & Ploutarchou Street, Engomi, 2407 Nicosia, Cyprus (office). *Telephone:* 22393939 (office). *Fax:*

22780944 (office). *E-mail:* infonicosia@state.gov (office). *Website:* cy.usembassy.gov (office).

GARCÉS CÓRDOBA, Mariana, LLB; Colombian lawyer and politician; b. Cali, Valle del Cauca; ed Universidad de los Andes, Universidad Icesi, Cali; Co-founder and fmr Gen. Man. Telepacífico (regional TV channel); Sec. of Culture and Tourism, City of Cali 2005–07; Minister of Culture 2010–18; fmr Dir Cali Int. Art Festival; Exec. Dir Asscn for the Advancement of the Arts (Proartes), Cali, Orchestre Philharmonique de Cali 2002–10; fmr mem. Nat. TV Comm.

GARCETTI, Eric Michael, BA; American politician; *Mayor of Los Angeles;* b. 4 Feb. 1971, Los Angeles; s. of Gil Garcetti and Sukey Roth; m. Amy Wakeland; one d.; ed Columbia Univ., London School of Econs, Queen's Coll., Oxford, UK; fmr Visiting Instructor, Dept of Int. Affairs, Univ. of Southern California; fmr Asst Prof., Occidental Coll., LA; mem. Council for Dist 13, Los Angeles City Council 2001–13, Pres. 2006–12; Mayor, City of Los Angeles 2013–. *Address:* Office of the Mayor, 200 North Spring Street, Los Angeles, CA 90012, USA (office). *Telephone:* (213) 978-0600 (office). *E-mail:* mayor.garcetti@lacity.org (office). *Website:* www.lamayor.org (office).

GARCIA, Andy; Cuban/American actor, producer and director; b. (Andres Arturo Garcia Menendez), 12 April 1956, Havana; s. of Rene Garcia and Amelie Garcia; m. Marivi Lorido Garcia; one s. three d.; ed Florida Int. Univ.; moved to USA 1961; several years acting with regional theatres Fla; Hon. DFA (St John's Univ. NY) 2000; numerous awards including Harvard Univ. Foundation Award 1994, Lifetime Achievement Award, American Cancer Soc. 1996, Spirit of Hope Award 2001, Desert Palm Award, Palm Springs Film Festival 2002, Imagen Foundation Creative Achievement Award 2002. *Films include:* The Mean Season 1985, 8 Million Ways to Die 1986, The Untouchables 1987, Stand and Deliver 1987, American Roulette 1988, Black Rain 1989, Internal Affairs 1990, The Godfather III 1990, Dead Again 1991, Jennifer Eight 1992, When A Man Loves A Woman 1994, Steal Big Steal Little (also producer) 1995, Things to Do in Denver When You're Dead 1995, Night Falls on Manhattan 1997, The Disappearance of García Lorca 1997, Hoodlum 1997, Desperate Measures 1998, Just the Ticket (also producer) 1999, The Unsaid (also producer) 2000, The Man from Elysian Fields (also producer) 2000, Oceans Eleven 2001, Confidence 2003, Blackout 2003, Twisted 2004, The Lazarus Child 2004, Ocean's Twelve 2004, The Lost City 2005, Smokin' Aces 2006, The Air I Breathe 2007, Ocean's Thirteen 2007, Beverly Hills Chihuahua (voice) 2008, New York, I Love You 2009, La linea 2009, City Island 2009, The Pink Panther 2 2009; dir: Cachao, Like His Rhythm There Is No Other 1993. *Albums produced include:* Cachao Master Sessions, Vol. I 1993 (Grammy Award 1994), Vol. II 1994 (Down Beat Critics Poll Winner 1996), Just the Ticket (soundtrack) 1999, Cachao-Cuba Linda 2000, For Love Or Country: The Arturo Sandoval Story (soundtrack) 2000, Score (Emmy Award) 2001. *Television appearances include:* Hill Street Blues, Brothers, Foley Square, Clinton and Nadine, Swing Vote (also producer) 1999, For Love Or Country: The Arturo Sandoval Story (also producer) 2000. *Leisure interests:* golf, fishing. *Address:* Paradigm, c/o Clifford Stevens, 200 West 57th Street, New York, NY 10019, USA. *Telephone:* (212) 246-1030 (office). *Fax:* (212) 246-1521 (office). *E-mail:* cineson@cineson.com (office). *Website:* www.cineson.com (office).

GARCIA, Jeannette M., BS, PhD; American polymer chemist; *Researcher in Materials, Polymer Synthesis and Characterization, IBM Almaden Research Center;* ed Univ. of Seattle, Boston Coll.; joined IBM Almaden Research Center, San Jose, Calif. 2012, postdoctoral researcher on high performance and recyclable materials –2013, currently Researcher in Materials, Polymer Synthesis and Characterization 2013–; IBM Master Inventor, MIT Tech Review's 35 Innovators Under 35 2015, one of Business Insider's 17 IBM Research Rock Stars, World Tech. Award (Materials) 2015. *Publications:* 28 papers in professional journals; more than 70 patents. *Address:* IBM Almaden Research Center, 650 Harry Road, San Jose, CA 95120, USA (office). *Telephone:* (408) 927-1602 (office). *E-mail:* jmgarcia@us.ibm.com (office). *Website:* www.almaden.ibm.com (office).

GARCÍA, Paulina, (Pali García); Chilean actress, theatre director and playwright; b. (Paulina García Alfonso), 27 Nov. 1960, Santiago; m. Juan Carlos Zagal; three c.; ed Pontifical Catholic Univ. of Chile; debut at Catholic Univ. Theatre 1983; TV debut 1984. *Stage roles include:* El último fuego 2009, Gertrudis, el grito 2009, Las analfabetas 2010, Fábula del niño y los animales que se mueren 2012. *Plays written:* Peso negro; Frágil 2002. *Plays directed include:* Recordando con ira (Look Back in Anger), Anhelo del corazón (A Heart's Desire) 2004, El neoproceso 2006, La gran noche 2008, Apoteosis final: BBB up 2009, Orates 2010, La mantis religiosa, Cerca de Moscú 2013. *Films include:* Three Nights on a Saturday 2002, Cachimba 2004, Casa de Remolienda 2007, The Wall 2012, Gloria (Silver Bear for Best Actress, Berlin Int. Film Festival, Platino Award for Best Actress) 2013, Génesis Nirvana 2013, Las analfabetas (Kikito for Best Actress, Festival de Cinema de Gramado – Brazil 2014) 2013, I Am from Chile 2013, Un concierto inolvidable: Nueva Ola, la película 2014, I'm Not Lorena 2014, La voz en off 2014, The 33 2015. *Television includes:* Huaiquimán y Tolosa (mini-series) 2006, Héroes (mini-series) 2007, Cárcel de mujeres (mini-series) (APES Award for Best Actress, Altazor Award for Best Actress 2008) 2007–08, Los simuladores (mini-series) 2010, Los archivos del cardenal (mini-series) 2011–14.

GARCÍA-BERDOY Y CEREZO, Juan Pablo, LLB; Spanish diplomatist; *Permanent Representative to European Union;* b. 9 March 1961, Madrid; m.; two c.; Consul in Manila, Phillippines 1988–90, Tech. Adviser, Ministry of Foreign Affairs 1987–88, 1990, Cen. and Eastern Europe, Secr. of State for the European Communities Dec. 1990–Nov. 1991, Counsellor Spanish Embassy, Bonn, Germany 1991–96, Dir, Cabinet of Sec. of State for Foreign Policy 1996–2000, Cabinet of Presidency of Congress of Deputies 2000–02, Dir-Gen. of Foreign Policy for Europe 2003–04; Amb. to Romania 2005–09, to Germany 2012–16, Perm. Rep. to EU 2016–; Founder and Sec.-Gen., Aspen Inst. Spain 2010–12; Patron ICO Foundation. *Address:* Permanent Representation of Spain, Blvd du Régent 52, 1000 Brussels, Belgium (office). *Telephone:* (2) 509-86-11 (office). *Fax:* (2) 511-19-40 (office). *E-mail:* reper.bruselasue@reper.maec.es (office). *Website:* es-ue.org (office).

GARCÍA BERNAL, Gael; Mexican actor; b. 30 Nov. 1978, Guadalajara, Jalisco; s. of José Angel García; partner Dolores Fonzi 2008–14; one s. one d.; ed Cen. School of Speech and Drama, UK; Founding mem. Canana production Co.; Dinosour Award, Ganovia (with Brad Pitt for the Movie Babel) 2007, Excellence in Acting Award, Provincetown International Film Festival 2008, Human Rights Award, Washington Office on Latin America 2011, Best Actor Award, Abu Dhabi Film Festival 2012. *Films include:* De tripas, corazón 1996, Cerebro 2000, Amores perros (Best Actor, Ariel Awards, Best Actor, Chicago Int. Film Festival) 2000, Y tu mamá también (Marcello Mastroianni Award, Venice Int. Film Festival) 2001, El Ojo en la nuca 2001, Vidas privadas 2001, Sin noticas de Dios 2001, The Last Post 2001, El Crimen del padre Amaro (The Crime of Father Amaro) 2002, I'm With Lucy 2002, Dot the I 2003, Dreaming of Julia 2003, Diarios de motocicleta (The Motorcycle Diaries) 2004, La Mala educación (Bad Education) 2004, Babel 2006, La Science des Rêves (The Science of Sleep) 2006, Déficit (also Dir) 2007, El pasado 2007, Blindness 2008, Rudo y Cursi 2008, Mammoth 2009, The Limits of Control 2009, Letters to Juliet 2010, Even the Rain 2010, Miss Bala 2011, A Little Bit of Heaven 2011, The Loneliest Planet 2011, No 2012, Deserted Cities 2013, The Ardor 2014, Desierto 2015. *Television includes:* Teresa 1989, El Abuelo y yo 1992, Fidel 2002, Soy tu fan 2006, Mozart in the Jungle (Golden Globe Award for Best Actor in a TV Series 2016) 2014–. *Plays include:* Blood Wedding (Almeida Theatre, London) 2005. *Address:* c/o William Morris Endeavor Entertainment, 9601 Wilshire Blvd, 3rd Floor, Beverly Hills, CA 90212-5213, USA (office). *Telephone:* (310) 285-9000 (office). *Fax:* (310) 248-2020 (office). *Website:* www.wmeentertainment.com (office).

GARCÍA CARNEIRO, Gen. Jorge Luis; Venezuelan politician and army officer (retd); *Governor of Estado Vargas;* b. 8 Feb. 1952; m. María del Valle de García; three s.; two d.; ed Mil. Acad. Venezuela; fmr Commdt Pelotón, Batallion; Commdt and teacher, Mil. Acad. Venezuela; Commdt and teacher, Army Tech. Coll.; Commdt First Co. Ricaurte Infantry Battalion; Second in Command, Carabobo Battalion Edo. Táchira; First Commdt GB José Ignacio Pulido, San Juan de Colon, Edo. Táchira; Commdt Barinas, Mérida, Caracas and Táchira garrisons; Chief of Staff, Acquisition of War Materials USA; First Commdt, Ministry of Defence HQ; Dir, Mil. Acad. Venezuela; Minister of Nat. Defence –2005; Gov. of Estado Vargas 2008–; mem. United Socialist Party of Venezuela (Partido Socialista Unido de Venezuela—PSUV); numerous decorations including Order Francisco de Miranda, Order Rafael Urdaneta, Order Nat. Defence, Order Estrella de Carabobo, Order of Merit Army, Civil Defence, Order José de Cruz Carrillo, Order Tulio Febres Cordero, Order García d'Hevia, Order Bicentenaria de la Ilustre Universidad de Los Andes, Order Rómulo Gallegos. *Address:* Office of the Governor, La Guaira, Estado Vargas, Venezuela (office). *Website:* estadovargas.gob.ve; www.garciacarneiro.com.

GARCÍA COCHAGNE, Manuela Esperanza; Peruvian lawyer and politician; b. 12 Dec. 1961; ed Universidad de San Martín de Porres, Lima; has worked for 28 years in Ministry of Labour, Minister of Labour and Employment 2009–11, Dir of Employment Promotion and Labour Training 2011–14, Dir of Prevention and Solution of Conflicts and of Corporate Social Responsibility 2014–. *Address:* Ministry of Labour and Employment, Avda Salaverry 655, cuadra 8, Jesús María, Lima 11, Peru (office).

GARCÍA DE ALBA ZEPEDA, Sergio Alejandro, BA, MA; Mexican business executive, government official and academic; ed Instituto Tecnológico y de Estudios Superiores de Occidente, Guadalajara, IPADE, Mexico City; Prof. of Finance, Instituto Tecnológico y de Estudios Superiores de Occidente 1980–84; Pres. Regional Chamber of Manufacturing Industry of Jalisco 1993–94; Vice-Pres. Confed. of Industrial Chambers of Mexico 1993–95; Founding mem. and Dir-Gen. Fibrart –1995; Sec. of Econ. Promotion, Jalisco state 1995–2001; Regional Vice-Pres. Axtel 2001; Under-Sec. for Small and Medium-Sized Businesses, Secr. of the Economy 2003–05, Sec. of the Economy 2005–06; Pres. Instituto para la Innovación, Competitividad y Desarrollo Empresarial, Tecnológico de Monterrey 2007–09; CEO American Industries Guadalajara 2011–; Econ. Policy Advisor, Govt of Jalisco 2012–; CAREINTRA Outstanding Businessman Award 1989, Asscn of Sales and Marketing Execs of Guadalajara Exec. of 1993, Ocho Columnas newspaper Columna de Oro 1999, COPARMEX Jalisco Efraín González Luna Prize for Political Merit 2005. *Website:* www.americanindustriesgroup.com/guadalajara.html.

GARCÍA DE ARNOLD, María Liz; Paraguayan academic, human rights lawyer and politician; b. 22 Nov. 1955, Asunción; d. of Antonio García Gómez and Teresa Ramona Frasquerí de García; m. Don Aníbal Arnold del Puerto; one s. two d.; ed Univ. Paranaense, Umuarama, Brazil, Univ. Tecnológica Intercontinental, Asunción, Instituto de Altos Estudios Estratégicos, William J. Perry Center for Hemispheric Defense Studies, Washington, DC; worked for 20 years at Colegio Americano de Asunción; Rector, Universidad Metropolitana de Asunción –2012, Founder and Dir, Post-Graduate School of Devt, Security, Defense and Human Rights; Minister of Nat. Defence 2012–13; Vice-Pres. Paraguayan Asscn of Private Univs; Founder and Dir Metropolitan Inst. of Languages, Asscn of Metropolitan Studies and Research; mem. Paraguayan Nat. Human Rights Comm., Never Again to State Terrorism, Nat. Comm. for UNESCO, Org. of Women Politicians for Democracy and Power; Peace Amb., El Mensajero de la Paz, William J Perry Award for Excellence in Security and Defense Education 2013. *Publication:* Con rostro de mujer. Memorias de una gestión gubernamenta. *Address:* c/o Post-Graduate School of Development, Security, Defense, and Human Rights, Metropolitan University, Asunción, Paraguay.

GARCÍA-HERRERA, Trinidad Jiménez, LLB; Spanish politician; b. 4 June 1962, Málaga; m. (divorced 1995); ed Universidad Autonoma de Madrid; Co-founder Socialist Students Asscn 1983, joined Partido Socialista Obrero Español (PSOE) 1984, Sec. Int. Policy of Exec. Cttee PSOE Federal 2000, re-elected 2004, 2008, 2011; Rep. to North American NATO Youth Exchange Program 1989, also headed New Programs and Devt Dept, Spanish Del. of American Field Service; Officer in Charge of Political Relations with America, PSOE Int. Relations Secr. 1996–2000; chosen as PSOE cand. for Mayor of Madrid 2003; Sec. of State for Latin America 2006; Minister of Health and Social Policy 2009–10, of Foreign Affairs and Cooperation 2010–11; fmr Prof. of Political Law, Universidad Nacional de Educación a Distancia, Spanish school in Bata. *Address:* c/o Ministry of Foreign Affairs and Co-operation, Plaza de la Provincia 1, 28012 Madrid, Spain. *E-mail:* trinidad.jimenez@congreso.es.

GARCÍA LINERA, Álvaro Marcelo; Bolivian mathematician, sociologist, academic and politician; *Vice-President;* b. 19 Oct. 1962, Cochabamba; m. Claudia

Fernández Valdivia 2012; ed Colegio San Agustin, Nat. Autonomous Univ. of Mexico; fmr Prof. of Sociology, Universidad Mayor de San Andrés, La Paz; mem. Tupaj Katari guerilla group, served five years in prison 1992–97; fmr political commentator; mem. Movt Toward Socialism party; Vice-Pres. of Bolivia 2006–. *Publications:* several books and articles. *Address:* Office of the Vice-President, Edif. de la Vicepresidencia del Estado, Calle Ayacucho, esq. Mercado 308, Casilla 7056, La Paz, Bolivia (office). *Telephone:* (2) 214-2000 (office). *Fax:* (2) 220-1211 (office). *E-mail:* despacho@vicepresidencia.gov.bo (office). *Website:* www.vicepresidencia.gob.bo (office).

GARCÍA-LÓPEZ LOAEZA, Agustín, BA, MA; Mexican diplomatist; *Executive Director, Agencia Mexicana de Cooperación Internacional para el Desarrollo (AMEXCID);* b. 5 March 1962, Valle de Bravo, Mexico State; m. Katya Anaya de la Fuente; two s.; ed Baccalaureate in Philosophy and Literature from Vienna, Austria, Columbia Univ., USA; joined Ministry of Foreign Affairs 1986, mem. Foreign Service 1991–, Adviser to Minister of Foreign Affairs on Econ. Affairs 1986–89, Econ. Affairs and Foreign Policy Officer, Embassy in London 1989–93, Dir of Financial Affairs for North America, the Caribbean and the Pacific, Ministry of Finance 1993–95, Dir-Gen. for the OECD and Econ. Analysis, Ministry of Foreign Affairs 1995–98, Dir-Gen. for Econ. Co-operation 1998–2000, Dir-Gen. for Int. Financial Affairs, Ministry of Finance 2000, Exec. Dir for Mexico and Dominican Repub. to IDB and Inter-American Investment Corpn, Washington, DC 2000–07, Perm. Rep. to OECD, Paris 2007–13, Amb. to France 2013–15, to Canada 2015–17, Exec. Dir Agencia Mexicana de Cooperación Internacional para el Desarrollo (AMEXCID) 2017–; Univ. Prof. of Econs, Nat. Univ. of Mexico, has served as a prof. in master's degree programme on Mexico–US Relations, Nat. Univ. of Mexico, Acatlán campus; taught at Ibero-American Univ., Mexico; ed. for Cross-currents magazine, Rockefeller Foundation, New York. *Publications include:* The New Mexican Policy on Co-operation (co-author) 1999. *Address:* AMEXCID, Plaza Juárez 20, Col. Centro, 06010 Ciudad de México, CP, Mexico (office). *Telephone:* (55) 3686-5100 (office). *E-mail:* gobmx@funcionpublica.gob.mx (office). *Website:* www.gob.mx (office).

GARCÍA LUNA, Genaro, BSc, MBA; Mexican police officer and politician; b. 10 July 1968, Mexico City; ed Autonomous Metropolitan Univ., Univ. of Miami; researcher, Sub-Dept of Foreign Affairs, Center for Research and Nat. Security (CISEN) 1988–98; Gen. Intelligence Coordinator for Prevention, Fed. Preventive Police Force 1998–2000; Dir-Gen. of Planning and Operations, Fed. Judicial Police (now Fed. Investigations Agency) 2000–03, Co-ordinator Tech. Cttee 2003–04; Chair. Strategic Information Sub-cttee, Interpol 2004–05; Sec. of Public Security 2006–12. *Publications:* The New Public Security Model for Mexico 2011.

GARCÍA-MARGALLO Y MARFIL, José Manuel, LLB, LLM, LLD; Spanish lawyer and politician; b. 13 Aug. 1944, Madrid; ed Univ. of Deusto, Bilbao, Univ. Miguel Hernández, Alicante, Harvard Univ.; joined Inspectorate of Finance 1968, becoming Head of Research and Programming, Technical Secr., Ministry of Finance 1974; Dir-Gen. of Community Devt, Ministry of Culture 1977–79; mem. Congreso de los Diputados (Parl.) 1977–82, 1986–94, Chair. Cttee on Petitions 1979–82, Spokesperson for Economy and Finance 1986–89, 1989–93, 1993–94; practising attorney 1990–; mem. European Parl., Brussels 1994–2011, Vice-Chair. Sub-Cttee on Monetary Affairs 1994–99, Cttee on Econ. and Monetary Affairs 1999–2004, Chief Observer for EU Election Observation Mission in Togo 2010, mem. parl. dels to China, India, Japan, New Zealand, Egypt, Namibia, Argentina, Brazil and Uruguay; Minister of Foreign Affairs and Co-operation 2011–16; fmr Lecturer, Faculty of Law, Univ. of Deusto, San Sebastian; mem. Partido Popular; Gran Cruz del Mérito Civil 1982, Orden del Mérito Constitucional 1983. *Address:* c/o Ministry of Foreign Affairs and Co-operation, Plaza de la Provincia 1, 28012 Madrid, Spain (office).

GARCÍA PADILLA, Alejandro Javier, BA, JD; Puerto Rican lawyer, politician and fmr state governor; b. 3 Aug. 1971, Coamo, Puerto Rico; s. of Luis Gerardo García Sánchez and María de los Angeles Padilla Passalacqua; m. Wilma Pastrana 2001; one s. two d.; ed Univ. of Puerto Rico, Río Piedras, Interamerican Univ., San Germán; began career as law clerk at Court of Appeals, then worked as attorney, specializing in property, estates, contracts and admin. law; also Prof. of Law, Interamerican Univ., Prof. of Law, American Univ. 2000–02; later served as legis. aide for Cttees on Internal Affairs, Women's Affairs and on Agric., amongst others; Sec. Puerto Rico Dept of Consumer Affairs 2005–07 (resgnd): Senator-at-Large 2008–13; Gov. of the Commonwealth of Puerto Rico 2013–17; fmr mem. Bd Puerto Rico Bar Asscn. *Address:* Popular Democratic Party, PO Box 9020436, San Juan 00902-0436, Puerto Rico (office). *Telephone:* (787) 721-2000 (office). *Fax:* (787) 725-9734 (office). *Website:* www.ppdpr.net (office); www.alejandrogarciapadilla.com.

GARCÍA RAMÍREZ, Sergio, PhD; Mexican politician, lawyer and judge; b. 1 Feb. 1938, Guadalajara; ed Nat. Univ. of Mexico; Research Fellow and teacher of penal law, Inst. of Juridical Research, Nat. Univ. of Mexico 1966–76; Dir Correction Centre, State of Mexico and Judge, Juvenile Courts; Asst Dir of Govt Ministry of Interior; Attorney-Gen. of Fed. Dist; Under-Sec. Ministries of Nat. Resources, Interior, Educ., Industrial Devt; Dir Prevention Centre of Mexico City; fmr Minister of Labour; Attorney-Gen. 1982–88; Pres. Inter-American Court of Human Rights (IACHR) (Corte Interamericana de Derechos Humanos), OAS, San José, Costa Rica 2004–07; Advisor, Federal Electoral Inst. 2011–13; mem. Mexican Acad. of Penal Sciences, Mexican Inst. of Penal Law, Nat. Inst. of Public Admin., Ibero-American Inst. of Penal Law; mem. Governing Bd, UNAM 1993; Orden del Mérito Civil, España, Gran Cruz de la Orden de San Raimundo de Peñafort, España, Medalla Ambrosio Paré, Medalla Alfonso Quiroz Cuarón. *Publications include:* Teseo Alucinado 1966, Asistencia a Reos Liberados 1966, El Artículo 18 Constitucional 1967, La Imputabilidad en el Derecho Penal Mexicano, El Código Tutelar para Menores del Estado Michoacán 1969, La Ciudadanía de la Juventud 1970, La Prisión 1975, Los Derechos Humanos y el Derecho Penal 1976, Legislación Penitenciaria y Correccional Comentada 1978, Otros Minotauros 1979, Cuestiones Criminológicas y Penales Contemporáneas 1981, Justicia Penal 1982, El museo del hombre 1986, La autonomía universitaria en la Constitución y en la ley 2005. *Address:* Circuito Maestro Mario de la Cueva s/n, Cd. Universitaria, CP 04510, Mexico City, Mexico (office). *Telephone:* (55) 5622-7474 (office). *E-mail:* sgr@servidor.unam.mx (office); sgriijunam@gmail.com. *Website:* www.juridicas.unam.mx (office).

GARCÍA RODRÍGUEZ, Enrique, BEcons, MEcons; Bolivian economist and banking executive; *Executive President and CEO, Development Bank of Latin America;* ed St Louis Univ., American Univ.; fmr Operations Man., Banco Industrial SA; mem. Bd several industrial and financial cos; served as an officer of IDB for 17 years, including as Treas.; fmr Gov. for Bolivia in World Bank Group, IDB and Financial Fund for the River Plate Basin; Deputy Minister of Planning and Coordination and mem. Bd Bolivian Cen. Bank 1970s; Minister of Planning and Coordination and Head of Econ. and Social Cabinet 1989–91; Exec. Pres. and CEO CAF (Corporación Andina de Fomento—Devt Bank of Latin America) 1991–; fmr mem. Devt Cttee of IBRD and IMF representing Bolivia, Chile, Argentina, Peru, Uruguay and Paraguay; Vice-Pres. Canning House; mem. Bd Inter-American Dialogue, Advisory Council of the Center for Latin American Studies at Georgetown Univ., Policy Council of George Washington Univ.; mem. Center for Latin America and the Caribbean, Florida Int. Univ., Advisory Council of the Latin American Program at the Woodrow Wilson Center, Dean's Council at the Kennedy School, Harvard Univ.; Trustee, Doña Maria de las Mercedes Foundation (Spain); fmr Prof., Universidad Mayor de San Andrés, La Paz, Catholic Univ., La Paz; mem. Bolivian Acad. of Econs, Council of Science and Tech. of the Bolivian Acad. of Sciences; Sovereign Order of Malta; decorations from Govts of Argentina, Bolivia, Brazil, Colombia, Ecuador, Peru, Venezuela; hon. doctorates and degrees from several univs; numerous awards, including being selected as Person of the Year by Última Hora newspaper 1990, Award for Latin American Integration, Business Council of Latin America—CEAL 2001, Award for Excellence in Regional Integration, América Economía magazine 2004, Americas Award for Excellence in Public Service, CIFAL Atlanta 2010. *Address:* CAF, Avenida Luis Roche, Torre CAF, Altamira, Caracas, Venezuela (office). *Telephone:* (212) 209-2111 (office). *Fax:* (212) 209-2444 (office). *E-mail:* Infocaf@caf.com (office). *Website:* www.caf.com (office).

GARCÍA-SAYÁN LARRABURE, Diego, LLB, LLM; Peruvian lawyer, judge, academic and government official; *United Nations Special Rapporteur on the Independence of Judges and Lawyers;* b. (Diego García-Sayán), 2 Aug. 1950, New York, NY, USA; three s.; ed Pontificia Universidad Catolica del Peru, Lima, Univ. of Texas, USA; Exec. Dir Andean Comm. of Jurists 1982–92, 1994–2000, Dir-Gen. 2003–; Prof. of Law, Pontificia Universidad Catolica del Peru, Lima 1987–2004; with UN in Guatemala 1991–92; Dir of Human Rights Div., UN Observer Mission in El Salvador 1992–94; Prof., Peruvian Univ. of Applied Sciences 1998–2000; Minister of Justice 2000–01, of Foreign Affairs 2001–02; Judge, Inter-American Court of Human Rights, San José, Costa Rica 2004–09, Vice-Pres. 2008–09, Pres. 2010–13; UN Special Rapporteur on the Independence of Judges and Lawyers 2016–; Chair. UN Working Group on Enforced or Involuntary Disappearances 1988–; mem. Bd of Dirs American Inst. of Human Rights, San José, Costa Rica 1994–; fmr Visiting Prof., Univ. of Richmond, American Univ., Instituto de Altos Estudios de América Latina, Univ. of Paris (Sorbonne); Founding mem. Peruvian Centre for Int. Studies (CEPEI); mem. Exec. Cttee Int. Comm. of Jurists, Geneva 1996–2000; mem. Lima Bar Asscn (mem. Bd of Dirs 1985–86), Peruvian Soc. of Int. Law. *Address:* Los Sauces 285, Lima 27, Peru (office); Office of the United Nations High Commissioner for Human Rights, 8–14 avenue de la Paix, 1211 Geneva 10, Switzerland (office). *Telephone:* (1) 4215675 (Peru) (office); 997356077 (mobile) (office). *Fax:* (1) 2027199 (Peru) (office); (22) 917-9006 (Switzerland) (office). *E-mail:* dgs@rocketmail.com (home). *Website:* www.ohchr.org (office).

GARCÍA-VALDECASAS Y FERNÁNDEZ, Rafael, BL, DJur; Spanish lawyer and judge; b. 9 Jan. 1946, Granada; m. Rosario Castaño Parraga 1975; ed Univ. of Granada; lawyer, Office of Attorney-Gen. 1976; mem. Office of Attorney-Gen. Tax and Judicial Affairs Office, Jaén 1976–85; mem. Office of Attorney-Gen. Econ. and Admin. Court of Jaén 1979–85; mem. Jaén Bar 1979–89, Granada Bar 1981–89; mem. Office of Attorney-Gen. Econ. and Admin. Court of Córdoba 1983–85, Tax and Judicial Affairs Office of Granada 1986–87; Head, Spanish State Legal Service for cases before EC Court of Justice (Ministry of Foreign Affairs) 1987–89; Judge, Court of First Instance of the European Communities (now Gen. Court) 1989–2007; currently govt lawyer; Encomienda de la Orden Civil del Mérito Agrícola 1982, Encomienda de la Orden de Isabel la Católica 1990, Gran Cruz de la Orden del Mérito Civil 1999. *Publications include:* Comentarios al Tratado de Adhesión de España a la C.E.: La Agricultura 1985, El 'acquis' comunitario 1986, El medio ambiente: conservación de espacios protegidos en la legislación de la CE 1992, La Jurisprudencia del Tribunal de Justicia CE sobre la libertad de establecimiento y libre prestación de servicios por los abogados 1993, El Tribunal de Primera Instancia de las Comunidades Europeas 1993, El respeto del derecho de defensa en materia de competencia 1997, El desarollo normativo de los reglamentos comunitarios 1999; also papers in books and learned journals. *Leisure interests:* swimming, cycling, fishing.

GARDE DUE, Ulrik, BA; Danish business executive; *President, Living Division, Fiskars Corporation;* b. 14 Jan. 1963, Copenhagen; ed Koebmandskolen, Copenhagen, Schiller Int. Univ., Paris/London, CESDIP (CPA), Paris, Corp. Finance Programme, London Business School; Commercial Asst and Ship Broker, Holm & Wonsild ApS (EAC), Copenhagen 1981–83; Oil Broker, Fretoil (Hunting Group), Paris and London 1984–86; Commercial Counsellor and Export Consultant for the Danish Ministry of Foreign Affairs, Danish Embassy, Paris 1986–89; Commercial Officer in charge of launch/real-estate promotion of the WTC, CNIT (SARI), La Défense, Paris 1989–90; Commercial Officer, Europe Distribution, Wholesale, Licensees and DFS, Celine SA (LVMH), Paris 1990; Commercial Dir of SE Asia, Celine SA (LVMH), Tokyo, Vice-Pres. Celine Inc. (LVMH) N America, New York 1993–97; Int. Dir of Marketing and Sales, Cerruti 1881 GmbH (Escada Group), Paris, global responsibility for Marketing and Sales in SE Asia, the Middle East and USA 1997–98; Sr Vice-Pres., Int. Sales, Burberry Ltd, London 1998–2007, Gen. Man. role in brand turn-around; Dir (non-exec.) Royal Copenhagen (Axcel), Copenhagen 2004–10; Pres. and CEO Georg Jensen 2007–13; CEO Temperley London 2013–16; Pres., Living Div., Fiskars Corpn 2016–; mem. Bd of Dirs Danish Jewellery Asscn 2010–12, Day Birger et Mikkelsen, Fashion 2011–12. *Address:* Fiskars Corporation, Hämeentie 135 A, PO Box 130, 00561 Helsinki, Finland (office). *Telephone:* (2) 043910 (office). *Fax:* (9) 604053 (office). *E-mail:* info@fiskars.fi (office). *Website:* www.fiskarsgroup.com (office).

GARDEL, Louis; French publishing editor, novelist and screenwriter; b. 8 Sept. 1939, Algiers, Algeria; s. of Jacques Gardel and Janine Blasselle; m. 1st Béatrice Herr (deceased) 1963; m. 2nd Hélène Millerand 1990; two s. two d.; ed Lycée Bugeaud, Algeria, Lycée Louis-le-Grand and Institut d'Etudes Politiques; Head of Dept, Inst. des Hautes Etudes d'Outre-Mer 1962–64; Man. Soc. Rhône-Progil 1964–74; Head of Dept Conseil Nat. du Patronat 1974–80; Literary Consultant, Editions du Seuil 1980, Literary Ed. 1980–; mem. juries Prix Renaudot, Conseil Supérieur de la Langue Française; Chevalier, Légion d'honneur. *Film screenplays:* Fort Saganne, Nocturne Indien, Indochine, La Marche de Radetzky 1996, Est.Ouest, Himalaya 1999, Princesse Marie 2005, Gaspard le bandit 2006, Le temps des secrets 2007, Le temps des amours 2007, La baie d'Alger 2012, La chartreuse de Parme 2012. *Publications include:* L'Eté Fracassé 1973, Couteau de chaleur 1976, Fort Saganne 1980 (Grand Prix du Roman de l'Acad. française), Notre Homme 1986, Le Beau Rôle 1989, Darbaroud 1993. L'Aurore des Bien-Aimés 1997, Grand-Seigneur 1999, La Baie d'Alger 2007, Le scénariste 2012. *Leisure interest:* horses. *Address:* Editions du Seuil, 27 rue Jacob, 75006 Paris (office); 25 rue de la Cerisaie, 75004, Paris, France (home). *Telephone:* 1-40-46-50-50 (office). *E-mail:* froumens@seuil.com (office).

GÄRDENFORS, Peter, PhD; Swedish philosopher, cognitive scientist, academic and author; *Professor of Cognitive Science, Lund University;* b. 21 Sept. 1949, Degeberga; s. of Torsten Gärdenfors and Ingemor Gärdenfors (née Jonsson); m. Annette Wald 1975 (divorced 2002); three s. one d.; ed Lund Univ., Princeton Univ., USA; Lecturer in Philosophy, Lund Univ. 1974–80, Reader in Philosophy of Science 1975–77, Reader in Philosophy 1980–88, Prof. of Cognitive Science 1988–; Visiting Fellow, Princeton Univ., USA 1973–74, ANU, Australia 1986–87; Visiting Scholar, Stanford Univ., USA 1983–84; Visiting Prof., Univ. of Buenos Aires 1990, École Normale Superieur, Cachan 1992, Rome University La Sapienza 1995, Univ. of California, San Diego 2005, Cà Foscari Univ. of Venice 2005, Univ. of Technology, Sydney 2006, Humboldt Universität, Berlin 2011–; Visiting Scholar, CREA, Paris 1999, British Acad. 2005; Fellow, SCASSS, Uppsala 2003–04; Ed. Theoria 1978–86, Journal of Logic, Language and Information 1991–96; Vice-Chair. Natur och Kultur Foundation 2007–; mem. Prize Cttee, Nobel Prize in Econ. Sciences 2011–; mem. Royal Swedish Acad. of Letters, Academia Europaea, Leopoldina Deutsche Akad. für Naturforscher 2004, Royal Swedish Acad. of Science 2009; Hon. Adjunct Prof., Univ. of Tech., Sydney 2012–; Rausing Prize 1986, Hermann Lotze Prize 2012, Universitatis Lodziensis Amico Medal 2012. *Publications include:* Generalized Quantifiers (ed.) 1986, Knowledge in Flux 1988, Decision, Probability and Utility (with N.-E. Sahlin) 1988, Belief Revision (ed.) 1992, Blotta Tanken 1992, Fangslande Information 1996, Cognitive Semantics (with J. Allwood) 1998, Conceptual Spaces 2000, How Homo Became Sapiens 2003, The Dynamics of Thought 2005, The Geometry of Meaning 2014. *Leisure interests:* botany, walking, climbing. *Address:* Department of Philosophy, Lund University, Box 192, 221 00 Lund, Sweden (office). *Telephone:* (46) 222-48-17 (office). *Fax:* (46) 222-44-24 (office). *E-mail:* peter.gardenfors@lucs.lu.se (office). *Website:* www.fil.lu.se/en/person/PeterGardenfors (office).

GARDINER, Sir John Eliot, Kt, CBE, MA, FRSA; British conductor and music director; *President, Bach-Archiv Foundation;* b. 20 April 1943, Fontmell Magna, Dorset; s. of Rolf Gardiner and Marabel Gardiner (née Hodgkin); m. 1st Cherryl Anne ffoulkes 1971 (divorced 1981); m. 2nd Elizabeth Suzanne Wilcock 1981 (divorced 1997); three d.; m. 3rd Isabella de Sabata 2001; ed Bryanston School, King's Coll., Cambridge, King's Coll., London, and in Paris and Fontainebleau with Nadia Boulanger; Founder and Artistic Dir Monteverdi Choir 1964, Monteverdi Orchestra 1968, the English Baroque Soloists 1978, Orchestre Révolutionnaire et Romantique 1990; concert debut Wigmore Hall, London 1966; youngest conductor at Henry Wood Promenade Concerts, Royal Albert Hall 1968; operatic debut Sadler's Wells Opera, London Coliseum 1969; Prin. Conductor CBC Vancouver Orchestra 1980–83; Musical Dir Lyon Opera 1982–88, Chef fondateur 1988–; Artistic Dir Göttingen Handel Festival 1981–90, Veneto Music Festival 1986; Prin. Conductor, NDR Symphony Orchestra, Hamburg 1991–94; residency at Théâtre du Châtelet, Paris 1999–2003; Bach Cantata Pilgrimage, with performances throughout Europe 2000; Guest Conductor, Royal Opera House, Covent Garden, La Scala, Milan; regular guest conductor with London Symphony Orchestra, and other major orchestras in Amsterdam, Paris, Dresden, Leipzig, Prague, Vienna, Berlin, Chicago, Cleveland, Pittsburgh; Domaine privé, Cité de la musique, Paris 2007; appearances at European music festivals, including Aix-en-Provence, Aldeburgh, Bath, Berlin, Edinburgh, Flanders, Netherlands, London, Salzburg, BBC Proms; Pres., Bach-Archiv Foundation, Leipzig 2014–; Visiting Fellow, Peterhouse Coll., Cambridge 2007–08; Christoph Wolff Distinguished Visiting Scholar, Harvard Univ. 2015; Hon. Fellow, King's Coll., London 1992, Royal Acad. of Music 1992, King's Coll., Cambridge 2015; Commdr, Ordre des Arts et des Lettres 1997, Officer's Cross of the Order of Merit (Germany) 2005, Chevalier, Légion d'honneur 2011; Dr hc (Univ. Lumière de Lyon) 1987, (Complutense Univ. of Madrid) 2001, (New England Conservatoire) 2005, (Pavia) 2006; Hon. DMus (St Andrews) 2014, (Cambridge) 2015; 17 Gramophone awards, including Record of the Year 1991, 2005, Artist of the Year 1994, eight Edison Awards, four Grands Prix du Disque, three Prix Caecilia, two Arturo Toscanini Music Critics' awards, two Grammy Awards, three Deutscher Schallplattenpreis, Buxtehude Prize Lübeck 1994, Robert Schumann Preis Zwickau 2001, Halle Handel Prize 2001, La Medalia Internacional Complutense Univ. of Madrid 2001, Classic FM Gramophone Award 2005, Léonie Sonning Music Prize 2005, City of Leipzig and Bach Archiv Bach Medal for lifetime achievement in the performance of music by J. S. Bach 2005, Royal Acad. of Music/Kohn Foundation Bach Prize 2008, Diapason d'Or de l'année 2011, Harvard Glee Club Medal 2015. *Recordings include:* over 250 albums including Bach Cantatas (Gramophone Award for Specialist Achievement 2011, J. C. Bach: Welt, gute Nacht (ECHO Klassik Award for Choral Recording of the Year – 16th/17th Century 2012) 2011, Bach Motets (Gramophone Award for Baroque Vocal 2013), Mendelssohn: Symphony 1 & 4, Beethoven: Missa Solemnis (Int. Classical Music Award for Choral Works 2015), Mendelssohn: A Midsummer Night's Dream 2017. *Publications:* Music in the Castle of Heaven: A Portrait of Johann Sebastian Bach 2013. *Leisure interests:* forestry, organic farming. *Address:* Intermusica Artists' Management Ltd, 36 Graham Street, Crystal Wharf, London, N1 8GJ, England (office). *Website:* www.intermusica.co.uk/gardiner (office).

GARDNER, Anthony Luzzatto, BA, MPhil, MA, JD; American business executive and diplomatist; b. 16 May 1963; ed Harvard Univ., Balliol Coll., Oxford, UK, Columbia Law School, London Business School, UK; worked with Treuhandanstalt (German Privatization Ministry), Berlin, with Comm. des Operations de Bourse, Paris, and as intern at Directorate-Gen. for Competition Policy at European Comm., Brussels; Dir for European Affairs, Nat. Security Council 1994–95; worked as a Sr Assoc. at int. law firms in London, Paris, New York and Brussels; Exec. Dir in leveraged finance depts of Bank of America and GE Capital, London and as a Dir in int. acquisitions group of GE International, London –2008; Man. Dir Palamon Capital Partners, London 2008–14; Amb. to EU, Brussels 2014–17; Visiting Fellow, Coll. of Europe, Bruges 2017; mem. Council on Foreign Relations; fmr mem. Bd, Peggy Guggenheim Collection in Venice; fmr Trustee, Guggenheim UK Charitable Trust. *Publications:* A New Era in U.S.–EU Relations?: The Clinton Administration and the New Transatlantic Agenda; numerous articles on EU affairs.

GARDNER, Cory Scott, BA, JD; American lawyer and politician; *Senator from Colorado;* b. 22 Aug. 1974, Yuma, Colo; m. Jamie Gardner; one d.; ed Colorado State Univ., Univ. of Colorado; farm equipment dealer 1997–98, 2005–11; Communications Dir to US Senator Wayne Allard, Washington, DC 2001–02, Legislative Dir 2002–05; mem. Colo House of Reps for Dist 63 2007–11, Minority Whip 2007–11; mem. US House of Reps for 4th Colo Dist 2011–15, mem. House Energy and Commerce Cttee; Senator from Colorado 2015–; Republican. *Address:* Senate Dirksen Office Building SD-B40B, Washington, DC 20510, USA (office). *Telephone:* (202) 224-5941 (office). *Fax:* (202) 224-6524 (office). *Website:* www.gardner.senate.gov (office).

GARDNER, David Pierpont, BSc, MA, PhD; American professor of education, foundation executive and fmr university president; *President Emeritus, University of California;* b. 24 March 1933, Berkeley, Calif.; s. of Reed S. Gardner and Margaret Pierpont Gardner; m. 1st Elizabeth Fuhriman 1958 (died 1991); four d.; m. 2nd Sheila Sprague Gardner 1995; ed Brigham Young Univ., Univ. of Calif., Berkeley; Admin. Asst, Personnel Man. and Prin. Asst to Chief Admin. Officer, Calif. Farm Bureau Fed., Berkeley 1958–60; Field and Scholarship Dir Calif. Alumni Asscn, Univ. of Calif., Berkeley 1960–62, Dir Calif. Alumni Foundation 1962–64; Asst to Chancellor Univ. of Calif., Santa Barbara 1964–67, Asst Chancellor and Asst Prof. of Higher Educ. 1967–69, Vice-Chancellor, Exec. Asst and Assoc. Prof. of Higher Educ. 1969–70; Vice-Pres. Univ. of Calif. and Prof. of Higher Educ. (on leave from Univ. of Calif., Santa Barbara) 1971–73; Pres. Univ. of Utah and Prof. of Higher Educ. 1973–83, Pres. Emer. 1983–; Pres. Univ. of Calif. 1983–92 (Pres. Emer. 1993–), Prof. of Higher Educ., Univ. of Calif., Berkeley 1983–92, Chair. Nat. Comm. on Excellence in Educ. 1981–83; Pres. William and Flora Hewlett Foundation, Menlo Park Calif. 1993–99; Chair. Bd of Trustees, J. Paul Getty Trust, LA 2000–04; Visiting Fellow, Clare Hall, Cambridge Univ. 1979, Life Mem. 1979–, Hon. Fellow 2002; numerous professional appointments, directorships, trusteeships etc.; Fellow, American Acad. of Arts and Sciences, Nat. Acad. of Public Admin.; mem. Nat. Acad. of Educ., American Philosophical Soc.; Fulbright Fellow, Japan 1987, Fulbright 40th Anniversary Distinguished Fellow, Japan 2000–04; Chevalier Légion d'honneur 1985, Kt Commdr's Cross Order of Merit (Germany) 1992; 12 hon. degrees; numerous awards and distinctions including James Bryant Conant Award, Educ. Comm. of USA 1985. *Publications:* The California Oath Controversy 1967, Earning My Degree: Memoirs of an American University President 2005; numerous articles in professional journals. *Leisure interests:* fly fishing, travel. *Address:* c/o Center for Studies in Higher Education, Evans Hall, University of California, Berkeley, CA 94720, USA (office). *Telephone:* (510) 642-5040 (office).

GARDNER, Edward, OBE; British conductor; *Chief Conductor, Bergen Philharmonic Orchestra;* b. 22 Nov. 1974, Gloucester; ed King's Coll., Cambridge and Royal Acad. of Music; fmr Asst Conductor Hallé Orchestra; Music Dir Glyndebourne Touring Opera 2004–06, with productions including La Bohème 2004, La Cenerentola 2005, The Turn of the Screw 2006, Fidelio 2006; has conducted Camerata Salzburg, London Philharmonic, Melbourne Symphony, Belgrade Philharmonic, Royal Scottish Nat. Orchestra, BBC Symphony Orchestra, Philharmonia, Alabama Symphony, Orchestre de Bretagne; season 2005–06 appearances included BBC Scottish Symphony Orchestra, BBC Nat. Orchestra of Wales, Vancouver Symphony, Orquestra Nacional do Porto, MDR Leipzig, Orchestre Philharmonique de Liège; opera highlights include Tchaikovsky's Eugene Onegin with Glyndebourne Touring Opera 2002, Meyerbeer's L'Africaine with Strasbourg Opera 2004, Mozart's Così fan tutte with ENO 2005, Adams' The Death of Klinghoffer with Scottish Opera 2005, Weill's Seven Deadly Sins with Paris Opéra 2005, Royal Opera debut Il re pastore 2006, Donizetti's L'Elisir d'amore, Paris Opéra 2006, Stravinsky's The Rake's Progress, Paris 2007–08; Music Dir, ENO 2006–15; Prin. Guest Conductor, City of Birmingham Symphony Orchestra 2011–; Guest Conductor, Bergen Philharmonic Orchestra, Chief Conductor 2015–; co-f. (with tenor Toby Spence) song recital series Wardsbrook Concerts 2013; Royal Philharmonic Soc. Award for Best Young Artist 2005, for Best Conductor 2008, Olivier Award for Outstanding Achievement in Opera 2009. *Recordings include:* works by Mendelssohn, Walton, Lutoslawski, Britten, Grieg, Berio vocal and orchestral works and Verdi's Macbeth with ENO, Janáček: Glagolitic Mass 2016. *Address:* c/o Celia Willis, Askonas Holt Ltd, 15 Fetter Lane, London, EC4A 1BW, England (office). *Website:* www.askonasholt.co.uk (office).

GARDNER, Sir Richard Lavenham, Kt, MA, PhD, FRS; British scientist and academic; *Honorary Professor, University of York;* b. 10 June 1943, Dorking; s. of Allan Constant and Eileen May Gardner; m. Wendy Joy Cresswell 1968; one s.; ed St John's School, Leatherhead, NE Surrey Coll. of Tech., St Catharine's Coll. Cambridge; Research Asst, Physiological Lab., Cambridge 1970–73; Lecturer in Devt and Reproductive Biology, Dept of Zoology, Oxford 1973–77, Research Student, Christ Church 1974–77, Ordinary Student 1978–2008, Royal Soc. Henry Dale Research Prof. 1978–2008, Royal Soc. Edward Penley Abraham Research Prof. 2003–08; Hon. Prof., Dept of Biology, Univ. of York 2007–; Hon. Dir Imperial Cancer Research Fund Developmental Biology Unit 1986–96; mem. Advisory Bd for the Research Councils 1990–93; Pres. Inst. of Biology (now Soc. for Biology) 2006–08; Chair. AS-ET; Leverhulme Emer. Fellowship; Hon. DSc (Univ. of Cambridge) 2012; Scientific Medal, Zoological Soc. 1977, March of Dimes Prize in Developmental Biology 1999, Royal Medal, Royal Soc. 2001, Albert Brachet Prize,

Belgian Royal Acad. of Sciences, Letters and Fine Arts. *Publications include:* various scientific papers. *Leisure interests:* ornithology, music, sailing, gardening, painting. *Address:* Department of Biology, University of York, Heslington, York, YO10 5DD, England (office). *Telephone:* (1904) 328500 (office). *Fax:* (1904) 328505 (office). *E-mail:* rg534@york.ac.uk (office). *Website:* www.york.ac.uk/biology (office).

GARDNER, Sir Roy Alan, Kt, FCCA, FRAeS, FRSA; British business executive; *Chairman, Compass Group PLC;* b. 20 Aug. 1945, Chiswick, London, England; s. of Thomas Gardner and Iris Gardner; m. Carol Gardner 1969; one s. two d.; ed Strodes School, Egham; Finance Dir, Marconi Space and Defence Systems 1975–84, Marconi 1984–85; Finance Dir STC PLC, Man. Dir STC Communications Ltd 1986–91, mem. Bd Dirs STC PLC 1986–91; COO Northern Telecom Europe Ltd 1991–92; Man. Dir GEC-Marconi Ltd 1992–94; Dir GEC PLC 1994; Finance Dir British Gas PLC 1994–95, Exec. Dir 1995–96; CEO Centrica 1997–2005; Sr Ind. Dir (non-exec.) Compass Group 2005–06, Chair. 2006–, Chair. Nomination Cttee, mem. Corp. Responsibility Cttee; Chair. (non-exec.) Connaught PLC –2010; Chair. Plymouth Argyle Football Club –2010; Chair. Spice Ltd 2010–; Dir (non-exec.) Manchester United PLC (Chair. (non-exec.) 2002–05), Willis Group Holdings Ltd, Mainstream Renewable Power Ltd (Chair. 2011–); fmr Dir (non-exec.) Laporte PLC; Sr Advisor, Credit Suisse; Pres. Energy Inst., Carers UK; Chair. Advisory Bd of Energy Futures Lab., Imperial Coll. London; Chair. Apprenticeship Ambassadors Network, EnServe Group Ltd; mem. Int. Advisory Bd IESE Business School at Univ. of Navarra –2011. *Leisure interests:* golf, running family. *Address:* Compass Group PLC, Compass House, Guildford Street, Chertsey, Surrey KT16 9BQ, England (office). *Telephone:* (1932) 573000 (office). *Fax:* (1932) 573184 (office). *E-mail:* info@compass-group.com (office). *Website:* www.compass-group.com (office).

GARDNER, Susan (Sue) P., BA; Canadian journalist and media executive; b. 11 May 1967, Bridgetown, Barbados; m.; ed Ryerson Polytechnic Inst.; began career as producer with CBC's As It Happens news and current events radio programme 1990, worked for more than a decade as a producer, reporter and documentary-maker for CBC Radio current affairs and for Newsworld International, focusing on pop culture and social issues, Sr Dir of CBC.ca website 2006–07; began consulting for WikiMedia Foundation (non-profit org.) as special adviser on operations and governance May 2007, Exec. Dir WikiMedia Foundation Dec. 2007–14; mem. Bd The Ada Initiative 2011–. *Address:* c/o WikiMedia Foundation, 149 New Montgomery Street, Third Floor, San Francisco, CA 94105, USA (office). *Website:* suegardner.org.

GARDOCKI, Lech; Polish judge (retd) and professor of law; b. 13 April 1944, Rydzewo; s. of Józef Gardocki and Filomena Gardocki; one s. two d.; ed Univ. of Warsaw; Deputy Head, Inst. of Criminal Law, Warsaw Univ. 1977–81, 1981–84, Asst Prof. of Law 1980–91, held Chair, Dept of Comparative Studies in Criminal Law 1985–95, Prof. Extraordinary 1991–, Prof. in Legal Art 1992–, holds Chair, Dept of Material Criminal Law 1996–; Justice of the Supreme Court 1996–2011, First Pres. 1998–2010; mem. Int. Advisory Cttee on Zeitschrift für die gesamte Strafrechtswissenschaft magazine; Order of Polonia Restituta 2010; First Degree Award in competition organized by State and Law magazine 1979. *Publications:* more than 80 publs including An Outline of International Criminal Law (Second Degree Award of Ministry of Educ.) 1985, Problems of Theory of Criminalization 1990, Criminal Law (Award of Minister of Educ.) 1994. *Leisure interest:* film.

GAREYEV, Gen. Makhmud Akhmedovich; Russian army officer and historian; b. 23 July 1923; m.; two c.; ed Tashkent Infantry School, M. Frunze Mil. Acad., Gen. Staff Acad.; involved in mil. operations on Western Front, officer Operative Div., Gen. Staff of Far E Army at end of Second World War; Commdr of Regt, Tank Div. Belarus Mil. Command, Head of Gen. Staff Urals Mil. Command, then officer Gen. Staff; Head Mil. Scientific Dept, then Deputy Head of Chief Operative Dept, apptd Deputy Head of Gen. Staff 1974; Chief Mil. Counsellor, Afghanistan, then Commdr 1989–; mem. Russian Acad. of Mil. Sciences (Pres. –2015), Council on Interaction with Orgs of War Veterans; Order of Lenin and numerous other decorations and medals. *Publications:* Frunze – Military Theoretician, General Army Exercises, Marshal G. Zhukov and more than 60 scientific works. *Leisure interest:* athletics. *Address:* Academy of Military Sciences, Myasnitskaya str. 37, 103175 Moscow, Russia (office). *Telephone:* (495) 293-33-55 (office).

GARFIELD, Andrew; American-British actor; b. 20 Aug. 1983, Los Angeles, Calif.; s. of Richard Garfield and Lynn Garfield (née Hillman); ed Cen. School of Speech and Drama, Univ. of London; began acting in youth theatre productions; first professional roles were on stage 2005; made British TV debut 2005. *Films include:* Boy A (BAFTA Award for Best Actor 2007) 2007, Lions for Lambs 2007, The Imaginarium of Doctor Parnassus 2009, Never Let Me Go (Saturn Award for Best Supporting Actor 2010, Best Supporting Actor, British Independent Film Awards 2010) 2010, The Social Network 2010, The Amazing Spider-Man 2012, The Amazing Spider-Man 2 2014, 99 Homes 2014, Hacksaw Ridge (AACTA Award for Best Actor 2016, Satellite Award for Best Actor–Motion Picture 2016) 2016, Silence 2016, Breathe 2017, Under the Silver Lake 2018. *Television includes:* Sugar Rush (series) 2005, Doctor Who (series) 2007, Red Riding: The Year of Our Lord 1974 (film) 2009, Red Riding: The Year of Our Lord 1980 (film) 2009. *Address:* Gordon and French (Talent Agency), 12–13 Poland Street, London, W1F 8QB, England (office). *Telephone:* (20) 7734-4818 (office). *Fax:* (20) 7734-4832 (office). *Website:* www.gordonandfrench.co.uk (office).

GARFUNKEL, Arthur (Art), MA; American singer and actor; b. 5 Nov. 1941, Forest Hills, NY; m. 1st Linda Marie Grossman 1972 (divorced 1975); m. 2nd Kim Cermak 1988; one s.; ed Columbia Univ.; mem. singing duo Simon & Garfunkel (with Paul Simon) 1964–71; solo artist 1972–; Britannia Award for Best International Pop LP and Single 1977, six Grammy Awards, inducted into Rock and Roll Hall of Fame (with Paul Simon) 1990, Nat. German Sustainability Award 2015. *Films include:* Catch 22 1970, Carnal Knowledge 1971, Bad Timing 1980, Good To Go 1986, Boxing Helena 1993, 54 1998, The Rebound 2010. *Recordings include:* albums: as Simon & Garfunkel: Wednesday Morning 3am 1964, Sounds of Silence 1966, Parsley, Sage, Rosemary and Thyme 1966, The Graduate (film soundtrack) (two Grammy Awards) 1968, Bookends 1968, Bridge Over Troubled Water (six Grammy Awards 1971) 1970, Concert in Central Park (live) 1982, Early Simon & Garfunkel 1993, Old Friends 1997; solo: Angel Clare 1973, Breakaway 1975, Watermark 1977, Fate for Breakfast (Doubt for Dessert) 1979, Art Garfunkel 1979, Scissors Cut 1981, The Animals' Christmas 1986, Lefty 1988, Garfunkel 1989, Up Till Now 1993, Across America 1997, Songs from a Parent to a Child 1997, Everything Waits to be Noticed 2002, Some Enchanted Evening 2007. *Publication:* Still Water 1989. *E-mail:* contact@artgarfunkel.com. *Website:* www.artgarfunkel.com.

GARGANAS, Nikolaos C., MSc (Econ), PhD; Greek economist and fmr central banker; *Honorary Governor, Bank of Greece;* b. 20 Jan. 1937, Soufli; m. Maria L. Kokka; one d.; ed Athens School of Econs and Business Studies, London School of Econs and Univ. Coll., London, UK; Head, Research Unit, Agricultural Bank of Greece 1964–66; Research Officer, Nat. Inst. of Econ. and Social Research, London 1968–75; Lecturer, Brunel Univ., Uxbridge, UK 1970–71; Sr Economist, Bank of Greece 1975–84, Dir/Adviser, Econ. Research Dept 1984–93, Econ. Counsellor (Chief Economist) 1993–96, Deputy Gov. Bank of Greece 1996–2002, mem. Monetary Policy Council 1998–2008, Gov. 2002–08, currently Hon. Gov.; Chief Econ. Adviser, Ministry of Nat. Economy and mem. Council of Econ. Experts 1985–87; mem. Governing Bd Centre of Econ. Planning and Research (KEPE) 1985–87; mem. Prime Minister's Cttee for Examination of Long-Term Econ. Policy 1996–97; Chair. Deposit Guarantee Fund in Greece 1996–2002; Greek Rep. to OECD Econ. Policy Cttee of EC 1975–88, Econ. Policy Cttee of EC 1982–85, EC Monetary Cttee 1985–87, 1994–98, EU Econ. and Financial Cttee 1998–2002; mem. European Cen. Banks' Governing Council and Gen. Council 2002–08; Hon. Fellow, LSE. *Publications include:* Greece's Economic Performance and Prospects (co-ed. and contrib.) 2001; books and articles on macro-economics, economic modelling, European economic and monetary union, monetary policy. *Address:* Bank of Greece, Leoforos E. Venizelos 21, 102 50 Athens, Greece (office). *Telephone:* (210) 3203680 (office). *Fax:* (210) 3222784 (office). *E-mail:* ngarganas@bankofgreece.gr (office).

GARHY, Amr Abdel Aziz el-; Egyptian banker and politician; ed Cairo Univ.; fmr Deputy CEO, Ahli Bank, Qatar; fmr Man. Dir, EFG Hermes (regional investment bank); fmr Man. Dir for Investment Banking, Fleming-CIIC (fund man. firm); fmr Exec. Dir, Commercial International Investment Co.; fmr Sr Credit Man., Commercial International Bank; fmr Vice-Chair. and Man. Dir, Nat. Investment Bank; Man. Dir, Agrifoods Div. and Head of Corp. Finance and Investment Review Function, Qalaa Holdings (investment co.) –2016; Minister of Finance 2016–18. *Address:* c/o Ministry of Finance, Ministry of Finance Towers, Cairo (Nasr City), Egypt (office).

GARIBASHVILI, Irakli; Georgian business executive and politician; b. 28 June 1982, Tbilisi, Georgian SSR, USSR; m. Nunu Tamazashvili; three s. one d.; ed Ivane Javakhishvili Tbilisi State Univ., Univ. Paris 1 Panthéon-Sorbonne, France; Probationer, Foreign Affairs Cttee, Parl. 2001–02; Man., External Purchase Office of Logistics Dept, Burji Ltd (Cartu Group) 2004–05, Asst to Pres., JSC Cartu Group 2005–08, Head, Bd of Admin. and Gen. Dir, Cartu Int. Charity Fund 2005–12; mem. Supervisory Bd, JSC Cartu Bank 2007–12; Dir Georgian Dream Ltd (record label) 2009–12; Co-founder-mem. Qartuli Ocneba—Demokratiuli Sakartvelo (Georgian Dream-Democratic Georgia) party, also Head of Review Cttee 2012, Chair. 2013–15; Minister of Internal Affairs 2012–13; Prime Minister of Georgia 2013–15 (resgnd). *Address:* Qartuli Ocneba-Demokratiuli Sakartvelo (Georgian Dream-Democratic Georgia), 0105 Tbilisi, Erekle II Moedani 3, Georgia (office). *Telephone:* (32) 219-77-11 (office). *Website:* 41.ge (office).

GARLAND, Greg C., BS (ChemEng); American chemical engineer and business executive; *Chairman and CEO, Phillips 66;* ed Texas A&M Univ.; began career with Phillips as project engineer for Plastics Technical Center 1980, later worked as sales engineer for Phillips' plastics resins, Business Service Man. for Advanced Materials, Business Devt Dir, and Olefins Man. for Chemicals, Man. of K-Resin® Business Unit 1992–94, Man. of Planning and Devt in Planning and Tech. 1994–95, Gen. Man. of Natural Gas Liquids 1995–97, apptd Gen. Man. Qatar/Middle East 1997; Sr Vice-Pres., Planning and Specialty Chemicals, Chevron Phillips Chemical Co. (now a jt venture between Phillips 66 and Chevron), Pres. and CEO –2010; Sr Vice-Pres., Exploration and Production, Americas for ConocoPhillips 2010–13, Chair. and CEO Phillips 66 (refining arm of ConocoPhillips) 2013–; mem. Bd of Dirs DCP Midstream; mem. Bd and Exec. Cttee American Petroleum Inst., Junior Achievement for Southeast Texas; mem. Bd Greater Houston Partnership; mem. Eng Advisory Bd Texas A&M Univ. *Address:* Phillips 66, PO Box 4428, Houston, TX 77210, USA (office). *Telephone:* (281) 293-6600 (office). *E-mail:* info@phillips66.com (office). *Website:* www.phillips66.com (office).

GARLAND, Merrick Brian, AB, JD; American lawyer and judge; *Chief Judge, US Court of Appeals;* b. 13 Nov. 1952, Chicago, Ill.; s. of Cyril Garland and Shirley Garland; m. Lynn Rosenman 1987; two d.; ed Harvard Univ., Harvard Law School; law clerk for Judge Henry J. Friendly, US Court of Appeals for the Second Circuit 1977–78, for Justice William J. Brennan, Jr, US Supreme Court 1978–79; Special Asst to Attorney-Gen., US Dept of Justice, Washington, DC 1979–81, Assoc. Ind. Counsel 1987–88, Asst US Attorney 1989–92, Deputy Asst Attorney-Gen. (criminal div.) 1993–94, Prin. Assoc. Deputy Attorney-Gen. 1994–97, Judge, US Court of Appeals, DC Circuit 1997–, Chief Judge 2013–; nominated by Pres. Barack Obama as Assoc. Justice of US Supreme Court March 2016; Assoc., Arnold & Porter LLP, Washington, DC 1981–85, Partner 1985–89, 1992–93; Lecturer, Harvard Univ. Law School 1985–86; mem. American Law Inst. *Address:* US Court of Appeals, 333 Constitution Avenue, NW, Washington, DC 20001-2866, USA (office). *Telephone:* (202) 216-7000 (office). *Website:* www.cadc.uscourts.gov (office).

GARN, Edwin Jacob (Jake), BS; American business executive and fmr politician; b. 12 Oct. 1932, Richfield, Utah; s. of Jacob E. Garn and Fern Christensen; m. 1st Hazel R. Thompson 1957 (died 1976); two s. two d.; m. 2nd Kathleen Brewerton 1977; two s. one d.; ed Univ. of Utah; private pilot then USN pilot on active duty for four years; USAF pilot for 20 years; Special Agent, John Hancock Mutual Life Insurance Co., Salt Lake City 1960–61; Asst Man. Home Life Insurance Co. New York, Salt Lake City 1961–66; Gen. Agent, Mutual Trust Life Insurance Co., Salt Lake City 1966–68; City Commr Salt Lake City 1968–72, Mayor 1972–74; Dir Metropolitan Water Dist 1968–72; Senator from Utah 1974–93; Congressional observer and payload specialist space shuttle Discovery Mission STS-51-D 1985; Vice-Chair. Huntsman Chemical Corpn, Salt Lake City 1993–99; Man. Dir Summit Ventures LLC, Salt Lake City 2000–04; currently self-employed consultant; Chair. Primary Children's Medical Center Foundation; mem. Bd of Dirs United Space Alliance, Franklin Covey Co., Headwaters, Inc., Nu Skin Enterprises, Inc.; Republican; six hon. doctorate degrees; Wright Brothers Memorial Trophy. *Publication:* Night Launch 1989. *Address:* 1267 Chandler Circle, Salt Lake City, UT 64103, USA.

GARNAUT, Ross Gregory, AO, BA, PhD; Australian economist and fmr diplomatist; *Professorial Research Fellow in Economics, University of Melbourne;* b. 28 July 1946, Perth, WA; s. of L. Garnaut and P. W. Garnaut; m. Jayne Potter 1974; two s.; ed Perth Modern School, WA and Australian Nat. Univ. (ANU), Canberra; Research Fellow, Sr Research Fellow and Sr Fellow, Econs Dept, Research School of Pacific Studies, ANU 1972–75, 1977–83, Prof. of Econs, Head of Dept, Research School of Pacific Studies 1989–, Dir Asia Pacific School of Econs and Man. 1998–, Chair. China Economy and Business Program 1989–2009; Vice-Chancellor's Fellow, Univ. of Melbourne 2008–13; First Asst Sec.-Gen., Financial and Econ. Policy, Papua New Guinea Dept of Finance 1975, 1976; Research Dir ASEAN-Australia Econ. Relations Research Project 1980–83; Sr Econ. Adviser to Prime Minister Bob Hawke 1983–85; Amb. to People's Repub. of China 1985–88; econs adviser to Prime Minister Kevin Rudd 2007–10; has led numerous high-level govt reviews and comms; apptd ind. expert adviser to the Multi-Party Climate Change Cttee 2010; has led Australian diplomatic missions interacting at heads of govt level to Asian countries on trade policy 1984, to Korea 1989, ANC in South Africa; Chair. Aluminium Smelters of Victoria 1988–89, Primary Industry Bank of Australia 1988–94, Rural and Industries Bank of Western Australia 1988–95, Australian Centre for Int. Agric. Research 1994–, Lihir Gold 1995–2010, Papua New Guinea Sustainable Devt Program Ltd 2002–12 (its nominee Dir to Ok Tedi Mining Ltd 2002–13, Chair. 2011–13); Hon. DLit (ANU) 2009; Hon. DS (Univ. of Sydney) 2013. *Publications:* Irian Jaya: The Transformation of a Melanesian Economy 1974, ASEAN in a Changing Pacific and World Economy 1980, Indonesia: Australian Perspectives 1980, Taxation and Mineral Rents 1983, Exchange Range and Macro-Economic Policy in Independent Papua New Guinea 1984, The Political Economy of Manufacturing Protection: Experiences of ASEAN and Australia 1986, Australian Protectionism: Extent, Causes and Effects 1987, Australia and the Northeast Asian Ascendancy (report to Prime Minister) 1989, Economic Reform and Internationalization 1992, Grain in China 1992, Structuring for Global Realities (report on Wool Industry to Commonwealth Governments) 1993, The Third Revolution in the Chinese Countryside 1996, Open Regionalism: An Asian Pacific Contribution to the World Trading System 1996, East Asia in Crisis 1998, Private Enterprise in China (co-author) 2001, Social Democracy in Australia's Asian Future (co-author) 2001, Resource Management in Asia Pacific Developing Countries (ed.) 2002, China 2002: WTO Entry and World Recession (co-ed.) 2002, China: New Engine of World Growth (co-ed.) 2003, China: Is Rapid Growth Sustainable? (co-ed.) 2004, China's Third Economic Transformation (co-ed.) 2004, China's Ownership Transformation (co-author) 2005, The China Boom and its Discontents (co-ed.) 2005, The Turning Point in China's Economic Development (co-ed.) 2006, China: Linking Markets for Growth (co-ed.) 2007, The Garnaut Climate Change Review 2008 (updated 2010), The Great Crash of 2008 (co-author) 2009, China: The Next 20 Years of Reform and Development (co-ed.) 2010, The Garnaut Review 2011: Australia in the Global Response to Climate Change 2011, China: A New Model for Growth and Development (co-ed.) 2013, Dog Days: Australia After the Boom 2013, Deepening Reform for China's Long-Term Growth and Development (co-ed.) 2014, China's Domestic Transformation in a Global Context (co-ed.) 2015. *Leisure interests:* cricket, tennis, Australian football, the history of humanity. *Address:* Melbourne Institute of Applied Economic and Social Research, Faculty of Business and Economics Building, University of Melbourne, 111 Barry Street, Melbourne, Vic. 3010, Australia (office). *Telephone:* (2) 6125-3100 (office). *E-mail:* ross.garnaut@unimelb.edu.au (office). *Website:* www.rossgarnaut.com.au.

GARNEAU, Marc, OC, BSc, DEng; Canadian astronaut, politician and fmr naval engineer; *Minister of Transport;* b. 23 Feb. 1949, Quebec City; ed Royal Mil. Coll., Kingston, Imperial Coll. of Science and Tech., London, UK, Canadian Forces Command and Staff Coll., Toronto; Combat Systems Engineer, HMCS Algonquin 1974–76; Instructor in Naval Weapon Systems, Canadian Forces Fleet School, Halifax 1976–77, with Naval Eng Unit 1980–82; Project Engineer in Naval Weapon Systems, Ottawa 1977–80; promoted Commdr 1982; Design Authority for Naval Communications and Electronic Warfare Equipment and Systems, Ottawa 1983–86; promoted Capt. 1986; retd from Navy 1989; selected to be astronaut 1983; seconded to Canadian Astronaut Program from Dept of Nat. Defence 1984; first Canadian to fly in space as Payload Specialist on Shuttle Mission 41-G, Oct. 1984; Deputy Dir Canadian Astronaut Program 1989; selected to be Mission Specialist 1992; trained at NASA's Johnson Space Center 1992–93, worked on tech. issues, Astronaut Office Robotics Integration Team, Capsule Communicator (CAPCOM) in Mission Control during Shuttle flights; served as Mission Specialist on flight STS-41G 1984, STS-77 1996 and STS-97 2000; has logged 677 hours in space; Exec. Vice-Pres., then Pres. Canadian Space Agency 2001–06; MP for Westmount–Ville-Marie, Ottawa 2008–15, for Notre-Dame-de-Grâce–Westmount 2015–; Minister of Transport 2015–; Co-Chair. Liberal International Affairs Council of Advisors 2013–; Chancellor Carleton Univ. 2003–; Pres. Bd McGill Univ. Chamber Orchestra; mem. Asscn of Professional Engineers of Nova Scotia, Navy League of Canada, Int. Acad. of Astronauts 2002; Hon. Fellow, Canadian Aeronautics and Space Inst., Nat. Hon. Patron of Hope Air and Project N Star, Hon. mem. Canadian Soc. of Aviation Medicine 1998; Canadian Mil. Decoration 1980; Hon. PhD (Univ. of Laval, Tech. Univ. of Nova Scotia, Royal Mil. Coll. of Kingston) 1985, (Royal Mil. Coll. of St-Jean) 1990, (Univ. of Ottawa) 1997, Hon. DSci (Univ. of Lethbridge) 2001, (York Univ.) 2002; Athlone Fellowship 1970, NASA Space Flight Medals 1984, 1996, 2000, F.W. Baldwin Award, Canadian Aeronautics and Space Journal 1985, NASA Exceptional Service Medal 1997, Queen's Golden Jubilee Medal 2002, Prix Montfort en sciences 2003. *Achievements include:* first Canadian to fly on a NASA mission to space 1984. *Address:* Transport Canada, 330 Sparks Street, Ottawa, ON K1A 0N5, Canada (office). *Telephone:* (613) 990-2309 (office). *Fax:* (613) 954-4731 (office). *E-mail:* GarneM@parl.gc.ca (office). *Website:* www.tc.gc.ca (office); www.marcgarneau.ca.

GARNER, Alan, OBE, FSA, FRSL; British writer; b. 17 Oct. 1934, Cheshire, England; s. of Colin Garner and Marjorie Garner (née Greenwood Stuart); m. 1st Ann Cook 1956 (divorced); one s. two d.; m. 2nd Griselda Greaves 1972; one s. one d.; ed Manchester Grammar School, Magdalen Coll., Oxford; mil. service with rank of Lt, RA; mem. Editorial Bd Detskaya Literatura Publrs, Moscow; Visiting Prof., School of Applied Sciences, Univ. of Huddersfield; Co-founder The Blackden Trust; Hon. DLitt (Warwick), (Salford), (Manchester Metropolitan), Hon. DUniv (Huddersfield); Carnegie Medal 1968, Guardian Award 1968, Lewis Carroll Shelf Award, USA 1970, Chicago Int. Film Festival Gold Plaque 1981, Phoenix Award, Children's Literature Asscn of America 1996, Karl Edward Wagner Award 2003, World Fantasy Lifetime Achievement Award 2012. *Plays:* Holly from the Bongs 1965, Lamaload 1978, Lurga Lom 1980, To Kill a King 1980, Sally Water 1982, The Keeper 1983, Pentecost 1997, The Echoing Waters 2000. *Dance drama:* The Green Mist 1970. *Libretti:* The Bellybag 1971, Potter Thompson 1972, Lord Flame 1996. *Screenplays:* The Owl Service 1969, Red Shift 1978, Places and Things 1978, Images 1981 (First Prize, Chicago Int. Film Festival), Strandloper 1992. *Publications include:* The Weirdstone of Brisingamen 1960, The Moon of Gomrath 1963, Elidor 1965, Holly from the Bongs 1966, The Old Man of Mow 1967, The Owl Service (Library Asscn Carnegie Medal 1967, Guardian Award 1968) 1967, The Book of Goblins (ed.) 1969, Red Shift 1973, The Breadhorse 1975, The Guizer 1975, The Stone Book Quartet (Phoenix Award, Children's Book Asscn of USA 1996) 1976–78, Tom Fobble's Day 1977, Granny Reardun 1977, The Aimer Gate 1978, Fairy Tales of Gold 1979, The Lad of the Gad 1980, A Book of British Fairy Tales (ed.) 1984, A Bag of Moonshine 1986, Jack and the Beanstalk 1992, Once Upon a Time 1993, Strandloper 1996, The Little Red Hen 1997, The Voice That Thunders 1997, The Well of the Wind 1998, Thursbitch 2003, Collected Folk Tales 2011, Boneland 2012, The Beauty Things (co-author) 2016, Where Shall We Run To? 2018. *Leisure interest:* work. *Address:* c/o Curtis Brown Ltd, 28–29 Haymarket, London, SW1Y 4SP, England (office). *Telephone:* (20) 7393-4400 (office). *Fax:* (20) 7393-4401 (office). *E-mail:* info@curtisbrown.co.uk (office). *Website:* www.curtisbrown.co.uk (office); alangarner.atspace.org.

GARNETT, Tony; British television producer; b. 3 April 1936, Birmingham; ed Central Grammar School, Univ. Coll., London; began career as TV actor; producer of numerous TV programmes and films; worked in USA 1980–90; Co-founder and Chair. World Productions 1990–2012; Visiting Prof. of Media Arts, Royal Holloway Coll., Univ. of London 2000–. *TV appearances include:* Dixon of Dock Green 1960s. *TV productions include:* Up the Junction 1965, Cathy Come Home 1966, The Resistable Rise of Arturo Ui 1972, Hard Labour 1973, The Enemy Within 1974, Days of Hope 1975, Law and Order 1978, Between the Lines 1992, Cardiac Arrest 1994, Ballykissangel 1996, This Life 1996–97, The Cops 1998, Attachments 2000. *Films produced include:* Kes 1969, Handgun 1983, Earth Girls are Easy 1989, Shadow Makers 1989. *Address:* Flat 60, Arlington House, Arlington Street, London, SW1A 1RL, England. *Website:* tonygarnett.info.

GARNIER, Rt Hon. Sir Edward Henry, Kt, QC, PC, BA, MA; British barrister and politician; b. 26 Oct. 1952, Germany; s. of Col William D'Arcy Garnier and hon. Lavender Hyacinth Garnier; m. Anna Caroline Mellows 1982; two s. one d.; ed Wellington Coll., Jesus Coll., Oxford, Coll. of Law, London; called to the Bar, Middle Temple 1976, QC 1995, Bencher 2001; practising barrister specializing in defamation, media law and corp. crime; Crown Court Asst Recorder 1998, Recorder (part-time Circuit Judge) 2000; fmr lawyer for The Guardian newspaper; contested Hemsworth constituency 1987; MP for Harborough 1992–2010, for Harborough (revised boundary) 2010–, Sec., Conservative House of Commons Foreign Affairs Cttee 1992–94, mem. Home Affairs Select Cttee 1992–95; Parl. Pvt. Sec. to Alastair Goodlad and David Davis as Ministers of State, FCO 1994–95, to Sir Nicholas Lyell as Attorney-Gen. and to Sir Derek Spencer as Solicitor Gen. 1995–97, to Roger Freeman as Chancellor of the Duchy of Lancaster 1996–97; Shadow Minister, Lord Chancellor's Dept 1997–99; Shadow Attorney-Gen. 1999–2001, 2009–10; Shadow Minister for Home Affairs 2005–07, for Justice 2007–09; HM Solicitor Gen. for England and Wales 2010–12; Hon. Sec. Foreign Affairs Forum 1988–92, Vice-Chair. 1992–; Treas. Macleod Group of Conservative MPs 1995–97; mem. Exec. 1922 Committee 2002–05; Chair. Exec. Cttee Soc. of Conservative Lawyers 2003–09; Dir, GB-China Centre 1998–2010; mem. Privy Council 2015; Visiting Parl. Fellow, St Antony's Coll., Oxford 1996–97; mem. Advisory Bd, Samaritans 2013–; Trustee, China-Oxford Scholarship Fund 2013–, Prison Reform Trust 2015–, Freeman of City of London 2015; Conservative. *Publications include:* Facing the Future 1993; contribs to Halsbury's Laws of England 1985, Bearing the Standard: Themes for a Fourth Term 1991, Lissack and Horlick on Bribery 2014. *Leisure interests:* cricket, history, music, shooting. *Address:* House of Commons, Westminster, London, SW1A 0AA (office); Constituency Office, 24 Nelson Street, Market Harborough, Leics., LE16 9AY, England. *Telephone:* (20) 7219-4034 (office); (20) 7353-8845 (office). *Fax:* (1858) 410013. *E-mail:* edward.garnier.mp@parliament.uk (office); garniere@parliament.uk (office); eg@onebrickcourt.com (office). *Website:* www.edwardgarnier.co.uk.

GARNIER, Jean-Pierre (JP), PhD, MBA; French business executive; b. 31 Oct. 1947, Le Mans; m.; three d.; ed Univ. of Louis Pasteur, Stanford Univ., USA; joined Schering-Plough 1975, numerous man. positions including Gen. Man. of numerous overseas subsidiaries, then Vice-Pres. of Marketing, US Pharmaceutical Products Div. 1983, then Sr Vice-Pres. and Gen. Man. with responsibility for sales and marketing for US prescription business, then Pres. US business; Pres. pharmaceutical business in N America, SmithKline Beecham 1990, mem. Bd Dirs 1992, Chair. Pharmaceuticals 1994–95, COO 1995–2000, CEO GlaxoSmithKline PLC 2000–08; CEO Pierre Fabre SA 2008–10; Chair. NormOxys Inc. 2010–11; mem. Bd of Dirs United Technologies Corpn, Eisenhower Exchange Fellowships Inc., INSEAD, Global Business Coalition on HIV/AIDS, John Hopkins Univ., Hole in the Wall Foundation, Cttee to Encourage Corp. Philanthropy; mem. Quaker BioVentures Int. Business Advisory Council for UK; mem. Advisory Bd Newman's Own Foundation; Hon. KBE 2008; Officier, Légion d'honneur 2007; Oliver R. Grace Award for distinguished service in advancing cancer research 1997, named a Star of Europe, Business Week 2001, Marco Polo Award 2001, Corporate Citizenship Award, Henry H. Kessler Foundation, Sabin Vaccine Inst. Humanitarian Award 2002, CNBC Leadership Award 2007. *Leisure interests:* competitive tennis and paddle playing, squash, golf, windsurfing.

GAROFANO, Giuseppe, MBA; Italian engineer and business executive; *President, Industria e Innovazione SpA;* b. 25 Jan. 1944, Nereto, Teramo; m.; three c.; ed Milan Polytechnic Inst., Bocconi Univ. Business School; Man. Dir Cotonificio Cantoni 1981–84; Vice-Chair. and Man. Dir Iniziativa META SpA

1984–88, Chair. and CEO 1988; Man. Dir Ferruzzi Finanziaria SpA 1988–92, Vice-Chair. 1989; Vice-Chair. Milano Assicurazioni SpA 1987, Fondiaria SpA 1989, La Previdente Assicurazioni SpA 1991; Vice-Chair. Montedison SpA 1989–90, Chair. 1990–92; Chair. Reno de Medici SpA 2003–09; Founder and Vice-Chair. Alerion Cleanpower SpA 2002–; Pres., Industria e Innovazione SpA 2010–, RCR Cristalleria Italiana SpA, Manucor SpA; mem. Bd of Dirs Realty Vailog SpA, RCR Cristalleria Italiana SpA, Efibanca SpA Autostrada Torino—Milano SpA, Miroglio SpA. *Address:* Industria e Innovazione SpA, Via San Vittore n. 40, 20123 Milan, Italy (office). *Telephone:* (06) 62460 (office). *Fax:* (6) 62409 (office). *Website:* www.industriaeinnovazione.it (office).

GAROUSTE, Gérard; French painter and sculptor; b. 10 March 1946, Paris; s. of Henri Garouste and Edmée Sauvagnac; m. Elizabeth Rochline 1970; two s.; ed Acad. Charpentier, Beaux-Arts de Paris; cr. nine sculpted bronze doors, 23 rue de l'université, Paris; Chevalier, Ordre des Arts et Lettres, Légion d'honneur, Officier, Ordre Nat. du Mérite, Commdr, Ordre des Arts et Lettres, Officier, Légion d'honneur 2015; Prix Francine et Antoine Bernheim pour les arts, les lettres et les sciences 2015. *Theatre includes:* Le classique et l'indien (Théâtre du rondpoint, Paris) 2010. *Publications include:* L'Intranquille (co-author) 2009. *Address:* La Mésangère, 27810 Marcilly-sur-Eure, France (home). *Telephone:* (2) 37-48-47-18 (home).

GARRÉ, Nilda, BA; Argentine lawyer and politician; b. 3 Nov. 1945, Buenos Aires; m. Juan Manuel (divorced); three c.; ed Universidad del Salvador; active in Juventud Peronista in 1970s; elected to prov. ass. Buenos Aires as rep. of Frente Justicialista de Liberación 1973–76; lawyer and human rights activist 1976–82; participated in Renovación Peronista of Partido Justicialista 1983; joined Frente del País Solidario; mem. Cámara de Diputados (Parl.) 1995–2000, 2015–; Deputy Interior Minister 2000–01; elected to Senado 2001–05; Amb. to Venezuela June 2005; Minister of Defence 2005–10, of Security 2010–13; Rep. of Nat. Chamber of Deputies to UN on Penal Legislation 1997; Vice-Pres. Fundación Carlos Auyero 1997–2002, Pres. 2004–05; mem. Advisory Cttee on Penal Reform 2003–04; Perm. Rep. to OAS 2013–15; Gen. Coordinator Centre for Research and Public Policy Advice (CEAPP). *Address:* Cámara de Diputados, Av. Rivadavia 1864, Buenos Aires, Argentina (office). *Telephone:* (11) 4127-7100 (office). *Website:* www.diputados.gov.ar (office).

GARRETT, Lesley, CBE, FRAM; British singer (soprano); b. 10 April 1955; d. of Derek Arthur Garrett and Margaret Wall; m. 1991; one s. one d.; ed Thorne Grammar School, Royal Acad. of Music, Nat. Opera Studio; performed with Welsh Nat. Opera, Opera North, at Wexford and Buxton Festivals and at Glyndebourne; joined ENO (Prin. Soprano) 1984; Gov. RAM; Hon. DArts (Plymouth) 1995; winner Kathleen Ferrier Memorial Competition 1979, Gramophone Award for Best Selling Classical Artist 1996. *Television:* appeared in BBC TV series Lesley Garrett... Tonight, The Lesley Garrett Show. *Major roles include:* Susanna in The Marriage of Figaro, Despina in Così Fan Tutte, Musetta in La Bohème, Jenny in The Rise and Fall of The City of Mahagonny, Atalanta in Xerxes, Zerlinda in Don Giovanni, Yum-Yum in The Mikado, Adèle in Die Fledermaus, Oscar in A Masked Ball, Dalinda in Ariodante, Rose in Street Scene, Bella in A Midsummer Marriage, Eurydice in Orpheus and Eurydice, and title roles in The Cunning Little Vixen and La Belle Vivette; numerous concert hall performances in UK and abroad (including Last Night of the Proms). *Recordings include:* albums: Diva! A Soprano at the Movies 1991, Prima Donna 1992, Simple Gifts 1994, Soprano in Red 1995, Soprano in Hollywood 1996, A Soprano Inspired 1997, Lesley Garrett 1998, I Will Wait for You 2000, Travelling Light 2001, The Singer 2002, So Deep is the Night 2003, When I Fall in Love 2007, Amazing Grace 2008, You'll Never Walk Alone: The Collection 2010, A North Country Lass 2012, Centre Stage: The Musicals Album 2015, The Very Best of Lesley Garrett 2015. *Publication:* Notes From a Small Soprano (autobiog.) 2001. *Leisure interest:* watching cricket. *Address:* The Music Partnership Ltd, 58 Howe Drive, Beaconsfield, Buckinghamshire, HP9 2BD, England (office). *Telephone:* (20) 7840-9590 (office). *E-mail:* office@musicpartnership.co.uk (office). *Website:* www.musicpartnership.co.uk (office); www.lesleygarrett.co.uk.

GARRETT, Malcolm, BA (Hons), FISTD, FRSA; British graphic designer; *Creative Director, Images&Co Ltd;* b. 2 June 1956, Northwich, Cheshire; ed Univ. of Reading, Manchester Polytechnic; f. Assorted Images Design Co. 1978, renamed Assorted Images Ltd 1983, Design Dir 1978–94, designed for artists such as the Buzzcocks, Duran Duran, Culture Club and Simple Minds, and pioneered digital and interactive work with Peter Gabriel; Founder and Creative Dir AMX Digital Ltd 1994–2001; joined Havas Advertising (re-named AMX Studios, then AMX) 1998, Chair. 1999–2001; Consultant Creative Dir i-mmersion, Toronto 2003–05; Creative Dir Applied Information Group 2005–11; Creative Dir 53K LLP 2011–12; Creative Dir Images&Co, London 2013–; Visiting Prof., Univ. of the Arts, London (fmrly London Inst.); Visiting Prof. in Interactive Communication, RCA 2000–03; Co-founder annual Design Manchester festival; mem. Sir Misha Black Awards Cttee, APDIG Advisory Bd, Science Museum Advisory Bd, Eye Magazine Editorial Bd 2007–; Founder-mem. 5D World Builders, Univ. of Southern California; Amb. for Manchester School of Art 2012–; Hon. Fellow, Int. Soc. of Typographic Designers 2009–; Hon. MA (Salford Univ.) 1999, Hon. Dr of Design (Robert Gordon Univ.) 2005, (Univ. of the Arts London) 2013, (London South Bank Univ.) 2015; Master of the Faculty, RSA Faculty of Royal Designers for Industry 2013–15, inducted into Design Week Hall of Fame 2015. *Publications include:* Duran Duran: Their Story (with Kasper de Graaf) 1982, When Cameras go Crazy: Culture Club (with Kasper de Graaf) 1983, Duran Duran Unseen: Photographs by Paul Edmond (with Kasper de Graaf) 2005. *Address:* Images&Co Ltd, The Clarence Centre, 6 St George's Circus, London, SE1 6FE, England (office). *Website:* www.images.co.uk (office); www.malcolmgarrett.com.

GARRETT, Peter Robert, AM, BA, LLB; Australian environmentalist, musician and politician; b. 16 April 1953, Wahroonga, NSW; s. of Peter Maxwell Garrett and Betty Garrett; m.; three d.; ed Barker Coll., Hornsby, Australian Nat. Univ., Univ. of New South Wales; mem. Rock Island Line; lead singer, Midnight Oil 1973–2002; benefit concerts for Aboriginal Rights Assen, Tibet Council, Rainforest Action Network, other orgs; Exxon Valdez oil spill protest concert 1990; ran for Australian Senate, Nuclear Disarmament Party 1984; Pres. Australian Conservation Foundation 1989–91, 1998–2004; mem. Bd Greenpeace International 1991–93; mem. Australian Labor Party 2004–; MP for Kingsford Smith 2004–13; Minister for the Environment, Heritage and the Arts 2007–10, for School Educ., Early Childhood and Youth 2010–13; Officier des Arts et des Lettres 2009; Hon. DLitt (Univ. of NSW) 2001; four Australian Record Industry Assen Awards 1991, Sony Music Crystal Globe Award 1991, Australia's Living Treasures Award, Nat. Trust of Australia 1999, Australian Humanitarian Foundation Award (Environment category) 2000, Leaders for a Living Planet Award, WWF Australia and International 2010. *Recordings:* albums with Midnight Oil: Midnight Oil 1978, Head Injuries 1979, Bird Noises 1980, Place Without A Postcard 1981, Red Sails In The Sunset 1982, 10 9 8 7 6 5 4 3 2 1 1983, Diesel and Dust 1987, Blue Sky Mining 1990, Scream In Blue - Live 1992, Earth, Sun and Moon 1993, Breathe 1996, 20,000 Watt RSL - The Midnight Oil Collection 1997, Redneck Wonderland 1998, The Real Thing (live) 2000, Capricornia 2002, Best of Both Worlds 2004, Essential Oils 2012; solo: A Version of Now 2016. *Publications:* Political Blues 1987, Big Blue Sky (memoir) 2015. *Leisure interests:* surfing, Australian literature. *Website:* www.petergarrett.com.au.

GARRICK, Sir Ronald (Ron), Kt, CBE, FREng, FRSE, FIMechE; British business executive; b. 21 Aug. 1940, Springburn, Glasgow, Scotland; ed Albert Secondary School; chartered engineer; joined Weir Group as grad. trainee 1962, CEO 1982–99, Chair. 1999–2002; Deputy Chair. Scottish Enterprise 1992–96; Dir (non-exec.) Bank of Scotland PLC 2000–09, Chair. 2005–06, Dir (non-exec.) HBOS PLC 2001–09, Deputy Chair. 2003–09, Chair. Irish Unit of HBOS PLC 2005–09, Sr Ind. Dir (non-exec.) 2004–09, Chair. Nomination Cttee 2001–02, Dir, Halifax Group Ltd 2001–07, Dir (non-exec.) Bank of Scotland (Ireland) Ltd 2007–09, Red Eye Devts (Park Terrace) Ltd 2010–13; fmr mem. Bd of Dirs Shell UK, Scottish Power PLC 1992–99; Hon. Sec. for Mechanical Eng, Royal Acad. of Eng 1991–94; Hon. DUniv (Paisley) 1993, (Strathclyde) 1994; Hon. DEng (Univ. of Glasgow) 1998.

GARTON ASH, Timothy John, CMG, MA, FRSA, FRHistS, FRSL; British writer and academic; *Professor of European Studies, University of Oxford;* b. 12 July 1955, London; m. Danuta Maria 1982; two s.; ed Exeter Coll., Oxford, St Antony's Coll., Oxford; editorial writer, The Times 1984–86; Foreign Ed. The Spectator 1984–90; Fellow, Woodrow Wilson Int. Center for Scholars, Washington, DC 1986–87; Sr Assoc. mem., St Antony's Coll., Oxford 1987–89, Fellow and Sr Research Fellow in Contemporary European History 1990–, currently Prof. of European Studies, Isaiah Berlin Professorial Fellow, and Hon. Chair. St Antony's Coll. European Studies Centre; columnist, The Independent 1988–90, The Guardian 2002–; Sr Fellow, Hoover Inst., Stanford Univ. 2000–; Fellow, Acad. of Sciences, Berlin-Brandenburg, European Acad. of Arts and Sciences; Corresp. Fellow, Inst. for Human Sciences, Vienna; mem. PEN, Soc. of Authors; Golden Insignia of Order of Merit (Poland) 1992, Kt's Cross of Order of Merit (Germany) 1995, Order of Merit (Czech Repub.) 2000; Hon. DLitt (St Andrew's) 2004; Soc. of Authors Somerset Maugham Award 1984, Veillon Foundation Prix Européen de l'Essai 1989, David Watt Memorial Prize 1989, Granada Award for Commentator of the Year 1989, Friedrich Ebert Stiftung Prize 1991, Imre Nagy Memorial Plaque, Hungary 1995, Premio Napoli 1995, Orwell Prize for Journalism 2006, Ischia Prize for Int. Journalism 2008. *Publications include:* 'Und willst du nicht mein Bruder sein...': Die DDR heute 1981, The Polish Revolution: Solidarity 1983, The Uses of Adversity: Essays on the Fate of Central Europe 1989, We the People: The Revolution of '89 Witnessed in Warsaw, Budapest, Berlin and Prague 1990, In Europe's Name: Germany and the Divided Continent 1993, Freedom for Publishing for Freedom: The Central and East European Publishing Project (ed.) 1995, The File: A Personal History 1997, History of the Present 1999, Free World 2004, Facts are Subversive: Political Writing from a Decade Without a Name 2009, Free Speech: Ten Principles for a Connected World 2016; contribs to books, newspapers and magazines. *Address:* St Antony's College, Oxford, OX2 6JF, England (office). *Telephone:* (1865) 274474 (office). *Fax:* (1865) 274478 (office). *E-mail:* tga.pa@sant.ox.ac.uk (office). *Website:* www.sant.ox.ac.uk (office); www.timothygartonash.com.

GARWIN, Richard L., MS, PhD; American physicist; b. 19 April 1928, Cleveland, Ohio; s. of Robert Garwin and Leona S. Garwin; m. Lois E. Levy 1947; two s. one d.; ed Case Western Reserve Univ., Univ. of Chicago; Instructor and Asst Prof. of Physics, Univ. of Chicago 1949–52; mem. staff, IBM Watson Lab., Columbia Univ. 1952–65, Dir of Applied Research 1965–66, Lab. Dir 1966–67, Fellow 1967–93, Fellow Emer. 1993–; apptd Adjunct Prof. of Physics, Columbia Univ. 1957; Phillip D. Reed Sr Fellow for Science and Tech., Council on Foreign Relations 1994–2004; mem. Defense Science Bd 1966–69; mem. President's Science Advisory Cttee 1962–66, 1969–72; mem. IBM Corporate Tech. Cttee 1970–71; Prof. of Public Policy, Kennedy School of Govt, Harvard Univ. 1979–81, apptd Adjunct Research Fellow 1982; Andrew D. White Prof.-at-Large, Cornell Univ. 1982–87; mem. NAS 1966–, Inst. of Medicine 1975–81, Nat. Acad. of Eng 1978–, American Philosophical Soc. 1979–, Council on Foreign Relations; Consultant to Los Alamos 1950–93, to Sandia Nat. Lab. 1994; Fellow, American Physical Soc. American Acad. of Arts and Sciences; Ford Foundation Fellow, CERN, Geneva 1959–60; Dr hc (Case Western Reserve Univ.) 1966, (Rensselaer Polytechnic Inst.), (State Univ. of New York); R. V. Jones Intelligence Award (Nat. Foreign Intelligence Community) 1996, Enrico Fermi Award 1997, Nat. Medal of Science 2002, Presidential Medal of Freedom 2016. *Publications include:* Nuclear Power Issues and Choices (co-author) 1977, Nuclear Weapons and World Politics 1977, Energy, the Next Twenty Years (co-author) 1979, The Dangers of Nuclear Wars 1979, Unresolved Issues in Arms Control 1988, A Nuclear-Weapon-Free World: Desirable? Feasible? 1993, Managing the Plutonium Surplus: Applications and Technical Options 1994, U.S. Intervention Policy for the Post-Cold War World: New Challenges and New Responses 1994, Feux Follets et Champignons Nucléaires (with G. Charpak) 1997; about 200 published papers and 42 US patents. *Leisure interests:* skiing, military technology, arms control, social use of technology.

GARZA, Antonio O., Jr, BBA, JD; American lawyer, diplomatist, politician and business executive; *Partner, ViaNovo LP;* b. 7 July 1959; m. 1st María Aramburuzabala Larregui 2005 (divorced 2010); m. 2nd Liz Beightler 2012; ed Univ. of Texas, Southern Methodist Univ. School of Law; elected to US House of Reps for S Texas 1988; Tex. Sec. of State and Sr Adviser to Tex. Gov. George W. Bush 1994–1997, later Chief Elections Officer; served on presidential dels to observe elections in Nicaragua and El Salvador; Cameron Co. Judge –1995; Partner, Bracewell & Patterson LLP (law firm), Austin –1998; Tex. Railroad

Commr 1998–2002; Amb. to Mexico 2002–09; Partner, ViaNovo LP (man. and communications consultancy) 2009–, also Chair. ViaNovo Ventures (cross-border business devt unit); serves as Counsel, White & Case (law firm), Mexico City 2010–; mem. Bd of Dirs Basic Energy Services 2009–16; Trustee, Southern Methodist Univ.; mem. Advisory Bd Bush School of Govt and Public Service, Texas A&M Univ., FameCast, Maguire Energy Inst.; Dr hc Austin College 2008; Distinguished Public Servant Award, Texas Tech. Univ. 1999, SMU Distinguished Alumnus Award 2001, Distinguished Alumni Award, Texas, SMU 2007, Distinguished Diplomat Award, Univ. of Denver 2005, Joe Kilgore Award, Greater Austin Crime Commission 2005, Azteca Aguila Award (Mexico) 2009. *Address:* ViaNovo LP, 327 Congress, Suite 450, Austin, TX 78701 (office); PO Box 685284, Austin, TX 78768, USA; White & Case, S.C., Torre del Bosque - PH, Blvd. Manuel Avila Camacho #24, Col. Lomas de Chapultepec, 11000 México, DF, Mexico (office). *Telephone:* (512) 744-0044 (ViaNovo LP) (office). *E-mail:* agarza@vianovo.com (office); antonio.garza@whitecase.com (office); aog@tonygarza.com. *Website:* www .tonygarza.com.

GARZÓN, Angelino; Colombian politician and fmr trade unionist; b. 29 Oct. 1946, Buga, Valle del Cauca; m. Monserrat Muñoz 1979; two c.; ed Univ. Jorge Tadeo Lozano, Bogotá, Univ. de Salamanca, Spain, Int. Labour Org. Training Centre, Turin, Italy; fmr mem. Exec. Cttee, Partido Comunista Colombiano; fmr Vice-Pres. Unión Patriótica; fmr Sec.-Gen. of various trade unions including Federación Nacional de Trabajadores al Servicio del Estado (Fenaltrase), Confederación Sindical de Trabajadores de Colombia (CSTC), Central Unitaria de Trabajadores (CUT), Geneva; mem. Asamblea Nacional Constituyente (responsible for writing new Constitution of Colombia) 1991; Minister of Work and Social Security 2000–02; Gov. Valle del Cauca Dept 2004–07; Rep. of Colombia to UN 2009–10; Vice-Pres. of Colombia 2010–14.

GARZÓN, Baltasar; Spanish judge; b. 26 Oct. 1955, Villa de Torres (Jaen); m. Rosario Serrano 1980; one s. two d.; ed Univ. of Seville; prov. judge 1978-87, Audiencia Nacional (Nat. Court) 1987–2012; mem. Parl. 1993–94; has investigated numerous high-profile cases involving drug trafficking, Basque terrorism, govt corruption, Spain's security forces and human rights abuses, and Islamic fundamentalism; issued arrest warrant for Gen. Augusto Pinochet Ugarte to face charges of genocide, terrorism and torture 1998; banned Basque politicial party Batasuna Aug. 2002; recruited as head of Wikileaks legal team 2012; Hon. DJur (New York Univ.) 2007. *Publications include:* Christmas Carol: A different World is Possible 2002, A World without Fear 2005, The Fight against Terrorism and its Limits 2006, The Soul of the Executioners 2007, React 2011.

GARZÓN, Luis Eduardo (Lucho); Colombian politician and fmr trade union official; b. 11 Feb. 1951, Bogota; s. of Eloísa Garzón; ed Universidad Libre; early work experience as caddie, carpenter and street trader; fmr messenger, Public Relations Div., Ecopetrol; fmr leader Unión Sindical Obrera (USO), later Vice-Pres.; fmr leader Central Unitaria de Trabajadores (CUT); fmr presidential cand., coalición Polo Democrático; fmr mem. Comité Central del Partido Comunista Colombiano; mem. Polo Democrático Independiente (PDI); Mayor of Bogota 2004–07; mem. several official cttees including Consejo Nacional de Paz, Comisión de Conciliación Nacional, Comité de Búsqueda de la Paz, Comisión Facilitadora par los diálogos con el Eln; AFL-CIO George Meany-Lane Kirkland Prize 2001.

GASCOIGNE, Paul John, (Gazza); British fmr professional footballer; b. 27 May 1967, Dunston, Gateshead, Tyne and Wear; s. of John Gascoigne and Carol Gascoigne (née Harold); m. Sheryl Failes 1996 (divorced 1998); one s. and two step-c.; ed Heathfield Sr School; midfielder; youth player with Newcastle United 1980–85 (won FA Youth Cup 1985), sr player 1985–88 (won FA Cup 1991); played for Tottenham Hotspur 1988–92 (FA Cup Winners' Medal 1991), Lazio, Italy 1992–95, Rangers 1995–98 (won Scottish League Championship 1995/96, 1996/97, Scottish Cup 1996, Scottish League Cup 1996), Middlesbrough 1998–2000, Everton 2000–02, Burnley 2002; signed as player-coach for Gansu Tianma (Gansu Sky Horses), Chinese B-League 2003; Wolverhampton Wanderers reserves 2003; player-coach, Boston United 2004; played for England, 13 Under-21 caps and five goals 1987–88, four England B caps and one goal 1989, 57 full caps and ten goals 1988–98 (won Rous Cup 1989, Tournoi de France 1997, FIFA World Cup (Fourth Place)/FIFA Fair Play Award 1990); Man. Kettering Town 2005, Garforth Town Asscn Football Club 2010; played for team England at Soccer Aid 2006; began playing amateur football for team Sunday League Div. Four, Bournemouth 2014; Professional Footballers' Asscn Young Player of the Year 1988, BBC Sports Personality of the Year 1990, World Cup All-Star Team Player 1990, Scottish Players' Player of the Year 1996, Scottish Football Writers' Player of the Year 1996, inducted into English Football Hall of Fame 2002. *Publications:* Paul Gascoigne (autobiography with Paul Simpson) 2001, Gazza: My Story (with Hunter Davies) (British Book Award for Sports Book of the Year 2005) 2004. *Leisure interests:* football, fishing, tennis, swimming. *Address:* c/o Sharron Elkabas, MN2S, 79-81 Borough Road, London, SE1 1DN, England (office). *Telephone:* (20) 7234-9455 (office). *Website:* mn2s.com (office).

GASHI, Bejtush, PhD; Kosovo politician; b. 27 July 1957, Prishtina, Autonomous Region of Kosovo, People's Repub. of Serbia, Fed. People's Repub. of Yugoslavia; m. Ajna Gashi; four c.; ed Univ. of Belgrade, Univ. of Zagreb, Spiro Moisiu Defence Acad., Tirana; Lecturer, Faculty of Civil Eng and Architecture, Univ. of Prishtina 1984–2001; Sr Emergency Planning Dir, Dept of Civil Security and Emergency Preparedness, Ministry of Internal Affairs 2001–06, Dir Dept of Internal Policies 2006–07; Lecturer, School of European Integration, Prishtina 2006–08; Dir, Inst. for Security and Integration Studies, Katana Complex, Obilić 2007–11; Deputy Minister of Kosovo Security Force 2011–14; Dean, Public Safety Faculty, Kosovo Acad. for Public Safety 2014–18; Minister of Internal Affairs April–Oct. 2018; mem. Aleanca Kosova e Re (New Kosovo Alliance). *Publications:* several scientific works in the field of security, defence, counterterrorism and civil emergencies; co-author of four u univ. textbooks: The Yugoslav Army and Its Presence in Kosovo in the Period 1945–1990 2006, International and Interethnic Conflicts 2008, Crisis Management System 2012, The Role and Responsibilities of the Police in the Internal Security System in Kosovo 2012.

GASHI, Dardan; Kosovo politician; *Deputy Prime Minister and Minister of Diaspora and Strategic Investment;* b. 3 July 1969; ed Univ. of Vienna, Austria; early career during 1990s as journalist for various orgs including Zëri (weekly periodical), BBC, Deutsche Welle, Der Standard (Austrian daily newspaper), Tribuna (Prishtina daily newspaper); fmr Election Supervisor with Org. for Security and Co-operation in Europe (OSCE) Mission in Bosnia and Herzegovina, becoming Election Officer and Head of Field Office in Brcko Fed. 1997, OSCE Spokesman in Sarajevo, Human Rights Monitor, Kosovo 1997, Public Information Liaison Officer, Kosovo Verification Mission, OSCE Secr. Liaison Office, Vienna 1999; worked at Int. Crisis Group and UN Criminal Tribunal for Fmr Yugoslavia (ICTY) 2000; fmr adviser, The European Stability Initiative (ind. think tank); various roles in office of the Deputy Prime Minister/Ministry of Local Govt Admin 2005–08, including Chair. decentralization working group and Sr Adviser, Vienna Negotiations on Status of Kosovo; Deputy Minister of European Integration 2010–11; Minister of Environment and Spatial Planning 2011–14; Deputy Prime Minister and Minister of Diaspora and Strategic Investment 2017–; mem. Aleanca Kosova e Re (New Kosovo Alliance). *Address:* Ministry of the Diaspora and Strategic Investment, 10000 Prishtina, Sheshi Nënë Terezë, Kosovo (office). *Telephone:* (38) 20017031 (office). *E-mail:* sabrie.grainca@rks-gov.net (office). *Website:* med.rks-gov.net (office).

GAŠIĆ, Bratislav; Serbian business executive and politician; b. 30 June 1967, Kruševac; m.; three s.; ed Univ. of Niš; engaged in private enterprise as owner and dir of private cos Grand kafa, Saco and Santos 1989–2012; Mayor of Kruševac 2012–14; fmr Vice-Pres. of Man. Bd Nat. Alliance for Local Econ. Devt; mem. People's Assembly (Narodna skupština) 2014–; Minister of Defence 2014–16; Co-founder Serbian Progressive Party (Srpska napredna stranka), currently Vice-Pres.

GASKÓ, István; Hungarian trade union official; b. 21 July 1954, Sajòszentpèter; m.; one s.; ed Econ. Univ., Budapest; mem. Democratic Trade Union of Scientific Workers 1988; f. Social Democratic Party 1989; f. Free Trade Union of Railway Workers (VDSZSZ) 1989, Pres. 1991–2015; Pres. Democratic League of Ind. Trade Unions (LIGA) 1996–2016. *Leisure interests:* reading, music, film, theatre, travelling.

GASPAR, Vítor Louçã Rabaça, DEcon; Portuguese economist and politician; b. 9 Nov. 1960; s. of Vítor Manuel Rabaça Gaspar and Maria Laura Seixas Louçã; m. Sílvia Luz; three d.; ed Univ. Católica Portuguesa, Univ. Nova de Lisboa; Dir of Econ. Studies, Ministry of Finance 1989–92; Adviser to the Bd and Dir Research and Statistics Dept, Banco de Portugal 1993–98, Adviser, Banco de Portugal 2005–06, Special Adviser 2010–11; Dir-Gen. of Research, European Central Bank 1998–2004; Head, Bureau of European Policy Advisers 2007–10; Minister of State and Finance 2011–13; Ind. *Publications:* several books and articles in econ. journals. *Address:* c/o Ministry of State and Finance, Av. Infante D. Henrique 1, 1149-009 Lisbon, Portugal.

GASPARD, Patrick H.; American government official and diplomatist; *President, Open Society Foundations;* held several positions with the City of New York, including Special Asst, Office of the Manhattan Borough Pres. and Special Asst, Office of Mayor Dinkins; Chief of Staff, New York City Council 1998–99; Nat. Deputy Field Dir for Dean for America 2003–04; Nat. Field Dir for America Coming Together 2004; Exec. Vice-Pres. and Political Dir, Service Employees Int. Union from 2004; Nat. Political Dir, Obama for America –2009; Asst to Pres. and Dir Office of Political Affairs 2009–11; Exec. Dir Democratic Nat. Cttee 2011–13; Amb. to South Africa 2013–16; Pres. Open Soc. Foundations 2017–. *Address:* Open Society Foundations, 224 W 57th Street, New York, NY 10019, USA (office). *Telephone:* (212) 548-0600 (office). *Fax:* (212) 548-4600 (office). *E-mail:* media@opensocietyfoundations.org (office). *Website:* www.opensocietyfoundations .org (office).

GASPARI, Mitja, MSc; Slovenian economist, fmr central banker and politician; b. 25 Nov. 1951, Ljubljana; ed Univ. of Ljubljana, Univ. of Belgrade, Serbia; Research Economist, Nat. Bank of Slovenia 1975–81, Head of Research 1981–87, Deputy Gov. 1987–88; Deputy Gov., Nat. Bank of Yugoslavia 1988–91; Sr Financial Economist, Trade and Finance Div., Tech. Dept Europe and USSR, The World Bank 1991–92; Minister of Finance 1992–2000; mem. Parl. 2000–01; Gov. Bank of Slovenia 2001–07; Minister without Portfolio, responsible for Devt and European Affairs 2008–12. *Publications:* numerous articles on fiscal studies.

GASPARINI, Massimo; Italian business executive; has over 20 years of experience working for Italian and multinational cos; has worked in fashion since 2001, overseeing Gucci's watch and jewellery div. –2006; CEO Missoni SpA, Milan 2007–09.

GAŠPAROVIČ, Ivan, JUDr, CSc; Slovak politician, lawyer and fmr head of state; b. 27 March 1941, Poltár, Lučenec Dist; s. of Vladimír Gašparovič and Elena Gašparovič; m. Silvia Beníková 1964; one s. one d.; ed Comenius Univ., Bratislava; clerk, Prosecutor's Office, Martin Trenčín 1965–66; Municipal Public Prosecutor, Bratislava 1966–68; teacher, Faculty of Law, Comenius Univ., Bratislava 1968–90, Vice-Rector 1990–; Gen. Prosecutor of CSFR 1990–92; mem. Movt for Democratic Slovakia 1992–2002 (movt became a political party 2000); Deputy to Slovak Nat. Council 1992–2002, mem. of Presidium; Chair. of Slovak Nat. Council 1992–98; Chair. Special Body of Nat. Council of Slovakia for Control of Slovak Intelligence Services 1993–98; Acting Pres. of Slovakia (served alongside Vladimír Mečiar) March–Oct. 1998; Founder and Leader Movt for Democracy 2002–; Pres. of Slovakia 2004–14; a leader of the ice hockey club Slovan ChZJD (later called HC Slovan Bratislava); fmr Vice-Pres. Int. Comm. of the Czechoslovak Ice Hockey Union, hockey team of the sports unit ŠK Slovan Bratislava; Order of the White Double Cross, Order of Ľudovít Štúr, Pribina Cross, Cross of Milan Rastislav Štefánik, Order of Andrej Hlinka; Grand Cross of the Order of Vytautas the Great (Lithuania) 2005, Kt Grand Cross with Grand Cordon, Order of Merit of the Italian Repub. 2007, Order of the Netherlands Lion 2007, Order of Isabella the Catholic (Spain) 2007, Kt Grand Cross, Grand Order of King Tomislav (Croatia) 2008, Order Orła Białego (Poland) 2009, Order of St Olav (Norway) 2010, Collar of the Order of the Cross of Terra Mariana (Estonia) 2011, Kt of the Order of the Elephant (Denmark) 2012, Order of the Repub. of Serbia 2013, Order of the White Lion (Czech Repub.) 2013. *Publications:* author and co-author of many univ. textbooks, numerous articles and reviews on criminal law. *Leisure interests:* American basketball, Korean cars, tennis, ice hockey, motoring. *Address:* c/o Office of the President, Hodžovo nám. 1, PO Box 128, 810 00 Bratislava, Slovakia. *E-mail:* informacie@prezident.sk.

GASPIN, Jeff, BA, MBA; American media executive; *Chairman, TAPP TV;* b. 29 Dec. 1960, Bayside, Long Island, New York; m. Karen Gaspin; two s. one d.; ed State Univ. of New York, New York Univ. Grad. School of Business Admin; Dir of Financial Planning, NBC News 1988–89, Vice-Pres. of Programming and Devt 1989–94; Sr Vice-Pres. Programming, QVC 1994–96; Sr Vice-Pres. Programming and Production, VH1 1996–98, Exec. Vice-Pres. 1998–2001; Exec. Vice-Pres. Alternative Series, Longform, Specials and Program Strategy, NBC Entertainment 2001–02; Pres. Bravo 2002–04; Pres. Cable Entertainment, NBC Universal 2004–07, Pres. Cable and Digital Content 2007, Pres. and COO NBC Universal TV Group 2007–09, Chair. NBC Universal TV Entertainment 2009–10; Co-founder and Chair. TAPP TV 2013–; numerous awards including Brandon Tartifoff Legacy Award, Humanitarian Award, Anti-Defamation League 2010, GLAAD Fairness Award. *E-mail:* info@tapptv.com (office). *Website:* tapptv.com (office).

GASS, Michelle, BS, MBA; American business executive; *Chief Customer Officer, Kohl's Corporation;* m.; two c.; ed Worcester Polytechnic Inst., Univ. of Washington; worked with Procter & Gamble in marketing and new product devt –1996; joined Starbucks as Marketing Man. for Frappuccino blended beverages 1996, various man. positions 1996–2004, Sr Vice-Pres. and US Category Man. 2004–07, Sr Vice-Pres. Global Product and Brand 2007–08, served a special assignment in Office of the CEO leading the Global Strategy function Jan.–July 2008, Sr Vice-Pres., Marketing and Category July–Nov. 2008, Exec. Vice-Pres. 2008–09, Pres. Seattle's Best Coffee 2009–11, Pres. Europe, Middle East and Africa, Starbucks 2011–13; Chief Customer Officer, Kohl's Corpn 2013–; mem. Bd of Dirs Ann, Inc. *Address:* Kohl's Corporation, N56 W17000 Ridgewood Drive (Greenway Circle), Menomonee Falls, WI 53051, USA (office). *Telephone:* (262) 703-7000 (office). *Website:* kohlscorporation.com (office).

GAST, Alice Petry, BSc, MSc, PhD; American engineer, academic and university administrator; *President, Imperial College London;* b. 25 May 1958, Houston, Tex.; m. Bradley J. Askins; one s. one d.; ed Univ. of Southern California, Princeton Univ.; Prof. of Chemical Eng, Stanford Univ. (affiliated with Stanford Synchrotron Radiation Lab.) 1985–2001; Vice-Pres. for Research and Assoc. Provost and Robert T. Haslam Chair. in Chemical Eng, MIT 2001–06; Pres., Lehigh Univ., Philadelphia 2006–14; Pres. Imperial Coll., London 2014–; US Science Envoy to Caucasus and Central Asia 2010–; mem. Nat. Acad. of Eng 2001–, American Acad. of Arts and Sciences 2002– (Fellow 2007); mem. Bd of Trustees, King Abdullah Univ. of Science and Tech. (KAUST), Thuwal, Saudi Arabia 2011–12; mem. Bd of Dirs Chevron Corpn 2012–; mem. Academic Research Council for Singapore Ministry of Educ.; mem. Global Science and Innovation Advisory Council to Prime Minister of Malaysia; Dr hc (Univ. of Western Ont.) 2010; Camille and Henry Dreyfus Teacher Scholar Award, Guggenheim Fellowship 1991, NAS Award for Initiatives in Research 1992, AIChE Colburn Award 1992. *Address:* Office of the President, Imperial College, South Kensington Campus, London, SW7 2AZ, England (office). *Telephone:* (20) 7589-5111 (office). *Website:* www.imperial.ac.uk (office).

GATES, (William Henry) Bill, III; American software industry executive and foundation executive; *Founder and Technology Advisor, Microsoft Corporation;* b. (William Henry Gates, III), 28 Oct. 1955, Seattle, Wash.; s. of William H. Gates II and Mary M. Gates (née Maxwell); m. Melinda Gates 1994; one s. two d.; ed Lakeside School, Seattle, Harvard Univ.; while at Harvard developed version of BASIC programming language for MITS 1975; programmer for Honeywell 1975; Co-founder, with Paul Allen, Microsoft Corpn 1975, Gen. Partner 1975–77, Pres. 1977–82, Chair. 1981–2014 (part-time, non-exec. Chair. 27 June 2008–14), Chief Software Architect 1999–2006, CEO –2000, Technology Advisor 2014–; f. Corbis (digital archive of art and photography) 1989; co-f. Bill and Melinda Gates Foundation 1994, currently Co-Chair. and Trustee; f. Gates Library Foundation 1997, name changed to Gates Learning Foundation 1999, merged with Bill and Melinda Gates Foundation 2000; mem. Bd of Dirs ICOS (biotechnology co.) 1990–, Berkshire Hathaway Inc. 2004–; Hon. KBE (UK) 2005; Hon. DJur (Harvard) 2007; Howard Vollum Award, Reed Coll. Portland, Ore. 1984, Nat. Medal for Tech. from US Commerce Dept 1992, CEO of the Year, Chief Executive Magazine 1994, named by Time magazine amongst Persons of the Year 2005, Prince of Asturias Award for Int. Cooperation (co-recipient with wife) 2006, voted by New Statesman magazine eighth in list of Heroes of Our Time 2006, Bower Award for Business Leadership, The Franklin Inst. 2010, Buffalo Award, Boy Scouts of America 2010, Presidential Medal of Freedom 2016, numerous other awards. *Publications include:* The Future 1994, The Road Ahead 1995, Business @ the Speed of Thought 1999. *Leisure interests:* reading, golf, tennis, bridge. *Address:* Microsoft Corporation, 1 Microsoft Way, Redmond, WA 98052-6399 (office); Bill and Melinda Gates Foundation, 500 Fifth Avenue North, Seattle, WA 98109, USA. *Telephone:* (425) 882-8080 (office). *Fax:* (425) 936-7329 (office). *E-mail:* info@gatesfoundation.org. *Website:* www.microsoft.com/en-us/news/exec/billg (office); www.gatesfoundation.org; www.gatesnotes.com.

GATES, Henry Louis, Jr, BA, MA, PhD; American academic, author and editor; *Alphonse Fletcher University Professor and Director, W. E. B. DuBois Institute for African and African-American Research, Harvard University;* b. 16 Sept. 1950, Piedmont, W Va; s. of Henry-Louis Gates and Pauline Augusta Gates (née Coleman); m. Sharon Lynn Adams 1979; two d.; ed Yale Univ. and Clare Coll., Cambridge; fmr European corresp. for Time magazine; Lecturer in English, Yale Univ. 1976–79, Asst Prof. English and Afro-American Studies 1979–84, Assoc. Prof. 1984–85; Prof. of English, Comparative Literature and Africana Studies, Cornell Univ. 1985–90; John Spencer Bassett Prof. of English, Duke Univ. 1990–91; W. E. B. DuBois Prof. of the Humanities and Chair. Dept of African and African-American Studies, Harvard Univ. 1991–2006, Alphonse Fletcher Univ. Prof. 2006–, also Dir W. E. B. DuBois Inst. for African and African-American Research, Walter Channing Cabot Fellow 2011; Pres. Afro-American Acad. 1984–; Ed.-in-Chief, Oxford African American Studies Center 2006–, TheRoot.com 2008–; Co-founder and Co-owner, AfricanDNA.com 2008–; contrib. New Yorker, New York Times; MacArthur Fellowship 1981–86; mem. American Acad. of Arts and Letters 1999–, Pulitzer Prize Bd; Hon. Citizenship of Benin 2001; numerous hon. degrees; numerous awards, including Zora Neale Hurston Soc. Award for Cultural Scholarship 1986, Candle Award, Morehouse Coll. 1989, Norman Rabb Award, American Jewish Cttee 1994, Tikkun Nat. Ethics Award 1996, Roger Joseph Prize, Hebrew Union Coll. 1997, Nat. Humanities Medal 1998, Henry James Award, Edith Wharton Soc. 2004, Carl Sandburg Literary Award 2004, Jay B. Hubbell Award for Lifetime Achievement in American Literary Studies, Modern Language Asscn 2006, National Arts Club, Lifetime Achievement Award 2007, Gondobay Manga Foundation Sankofa Award 2009, Ralph Lowell Award 2009, Leon H. Sullivan Honors Award 2009, Madison Freedom Award 2009, Lifetime Achievement Award in Genealogy and Genetics, New England Historical and Genealogical Soc. 2010, Media Bridge-Builder Award, Tanenbaum Center, 2011, Public Interest Law Asscn Award, CUNY 2012, Benjamin Franklin Creativity Laureate Award 2018. *Television includes:* African American Lives 2006, African American Lives 2 2008, Faces of America 2010, Finding Your Roots 2012. *Publications include:* Figures in Black (literary criticism) 1987, The Signifying Monkey (American Book Award 1989) 1988, Loose Canons (literary criticism) 1992, Colored People (short stories) 1994, The Future of the Race (with Cornel West) 1996, Thirteen Ways of Looking at a Black Man 1998, Africana (jtly) (TV documentary) 1999, Wonders of the African World 1999, The Civitas Anthology of African-American Slave Narratives, The African-American Century 2000; Encarta Africana Encyclopaedia (co-ed.) 1999; as ed. The Bondswoman's Narrative 2002, America Behind the Color Line 2004, In Search of Our Roots: How Nineteen Extraordinary African Americans Reclaimed Their Past 2009, Tradition and the Black Atlantic: Critical Theory in the African Diaspora 2010, Black in Latin America 2011, Life Upon These Shores 2011, Dictionary of African Biography (co-ed.) 2011. *Address:* W.E.B. Du Bois Institute, 104 Mount Auburn Street, Room 3R, Cambridge, MA 02138, USA (office). *Telephone:* (617) 496-5468 (office). *Fax:* (617) 495-9490 (office). *E-mail:* gates@harvard.edu (office). *Website:* www.aaas.fas.harvard.edu (office).

GATES, Holly G.; American computer engineer; *Senior Hardware Engineer, E Ink Corporation;* ed Weihai Br. of Shandong Univ., China, Massachusetts Inst. of Tech., Massachusetts Coll. of Art, Harvard Univ.; worked for Brown Innovations Inc., Boston Mass 1995–96; Lecturer, MIT Edgerton Center, Cambridge, Mass 1996–97; worked for Zond Systems Inc., Searsburg, Vt June–Aug. 1997; worked for MIT Media Lab., Cambridge, Mass 1996–98; Hardware Engineer, E Ink Corpn, Cambridge, Mass 1998–2002, Sr Hardware Engineer 2002–; First Prize for robot called 'dog' (built with Leila Hasan), 6.270 LEGO Robotics Competition 1998, Rudenberg Memorial Fund 1998, World Tech. Award in Information Tech. (Hardware), World Tech. Network 2005. *Publications include:* papers in professional journals and several patents. *Leisure interests:* welding, renovating, dancing, mountaineering, electronics, sculpture, clothing design, fashion devices. *Address:* E Ink Corporation, 733 Concord Avenue, Cambridge, MA 02138 (office); 189 Summer Street, Apartment 2, Somerville, MA 02145, USA (home). *Telephone:* (617) 499-6000 (office). *Fax:* (617) 499-6200 (office). *E-mail:* info@eink.com (office). *Website:* www.eink.com (office); www.positron.org/people/hgates (office).

GATES, Melinda, BSc, BEcons, MBA; American foundation executive; *Co-Director, Bill and Melinda Gates Foundation;* b. (Melinda Ann French), 15 Aug. 1964, Dallas, Tex.; m. William (Bill) Henry Gates III 1994; one s. two d.; ed Ursuline Acad., Dallas, Duke Univ. and Duke Univ. Fuqua School of Business; several positions at Microsoft Corpn 1987–96, including Product Unit Man. Microsoft Publisher, Microsoft Bob, Microsoft Encarta and Microsoft Expedia; co-f. Bill and Melinda Gates Foundation 1994; mem. Bd of Dirs Drugstore.com –2006, The Washington Post –2010; attends the Bilderberg Group; Trustee, Duke Univ. 1996–2003; Hon. DBE 2013; named by TIME magazine amongst Persons of the Year 2005, Prince of Asturias Award for Int. Co-operation (co-recipient with husband) 2006, Padma Bhushan (co-recipient with husband) 2015, Presidential Medal of Freedom 2016. *Address:* Bill and Melinda Gates Foundation, PO Box 23350, Seattle, WA 98102, USA (office). *Telephone:* (206) 709-3100 (office). *E-mail:* info@gatesfoundation.org (office). *Website:* www.gatesfoundation.org (office).

GATES, Hon. Robert M., PhD; American government official and fmr academic administrator; *Chancellor, College of William & Mary;* b. 25 Sept. 1943, Wichita, Kan.; m. Becky Gates; two c.; ed Coll. of William & Mary, Indiana Univ., Georgetown Univ.; service with USAF 1966–68; career training programme, CIA 1968, intelligence analyst 1969–72, mem. staff of Special Asst to the Dir of Central Intelligence for Strategic Arms Limitations 1972–73, Asst Nat. Intelligence Officer for Strategic Programs 1973–74, mem. staff, Nat. Security Council The White House 1974–76, mem. staff, Center for Policy Support 1976–77, Special Asst to Pres. for Nat. Security Affairs 1977–79, Dir Strategic Evaluation Center 1979–80, Exec. Asst to Dir of Cen. Intelligence and Dir of the Exec. Staff, Dir of Office of Policy and Planning and Nat. Intelligence Officer for the Soviet Union and Eastern Europe 1980–81, Deputy Dir for Intelligence 1982–86, Chair. Nat. Intelligence Council 1982–86, Acting Dir of Central Intelligence 1986–87, Deputy Dir of Central Intelligence 1986–89, Asst to the Pres. and Deputy for Nat. Security Affairs The White House 1989–91, Dir CIA 1991–93; Interim Dean, George Bush School of Govt and Public Service, 1999–2001, Pres. Texas A&M Univ. 2002–06; US Sec. of Defense 2006–11; Chancellor Coll. of William & Mary 2012–; Nat. Pres. Boy Scouts of America 2014–; mem. Bd of Dirs Starbucks Corpn 2012–; fmr mem. Bd of Dirs NACCO Industries Inc., Brinker International Inc., Parker Drilling Co. Inc.; fmr mem. Bd of Trustees The Fidelity Funds; mem. Iraq Study Group, US Inst. for Peace 2006; Fellow, American Acad. of Arts and Sciences 2009; Hon. PhD (Kansas State Univ.); Hon. DHumLitt (Coll. of William & Mary, Georgetown Univ., Indiana Univ., Univ. of Oklahoma, Yale Univ.); Hon. LLD (Univ. of Notre Dame); Hon. Dr of Public Admin (Univ. of South Carolina); Nat. Intelligence Distinguished Service Medal (twice), Distinguished Intelligence Medal (three times), Intelligence Medal of Merit, Arthur S. Fleming Award, Nat. Security Medal, Presidential Citizen's Medal, Presidential Medal of Freedom, Eagle Scout, Distinguished Eagle Scout Award, Silver Buffalo Award, Vigil Honor, Order of the Arrow, Robert C. Vance Distinguished Lecturer, Central Connecticut State Univ. 2011. *Publication:* From the Shadows: The Ultimate Insider's Story of Five Presidents and How They Won the Cold War 1996. *Address:* Chancellor, College of William & Mary, c/o Office of the President, PO Box 8795, Williamsburg, VA 23187-8795, USA (office). *Website:* www.wm.edu/about/administration/chancellor (office).

GATES, Theaster, BS, MA, MS; American installation artist and curator; b. 28 Aug. 1973, Chicago, Ill.; ed Iowa State Univ., Univ. of Cape Town, S Africa; Transit Arts Planner and Special Projects Man., Chicago Transit Authority 2000; Dir of Educ. and Outreach, Little Black Pearl 2005; Co-ordinator of Arts Programming, Humanities Div., Univ. of Chicago 2007, Lecturer, Dept of Visual Arts 2008, Dir of

Arts Program Devt, Office of the Provost, and Artist-in-Residence, Dept of Visual Arts 2009, apptd Dir and Project Leader, Arts and Public Life Initiative 2011, currently Prof., Dept of Visual Arts; Loeb Fellowship, Harvard Grad. School of Design, Int. Studio and Curatorial Program, New York Arts/Industry Residency Program, John Michael Kohler Arts Center, Sheboygan, Wis., Gestures of Resistance, Museum of Contemporary Craft, Portland 2010; Global Residency, Creative Time, New York 2013; mem. Bd Hyde Park Alliance for the Arts, Chicago, Univ. of Chicago Arts Council, Experimental Station, Chicago, South Side Community Art Center, Chicago; mem. Artspeaks, Chicago; artistic practice includes space devt, object making and performance; Fellow, United States Artists 2012; Joyce Award, The Joyce Foundation, Chicago 2009, Artadi a Award, Artadia: The Fund for Art and Dialogue, New York 2009, Artist Grant, Graham Foundation, Chicago 2009, 2011, Harpo Foundation Grant, Bemis Center for Contemporary Arts, Omaha, Nebraska 2010, USA Kippy Fellow – Visual Arts, USA Projects, Los Angeles 2012, Innovator of the Year – Art Award, Wall Street Journal 2012, Vera List Center Prize, The New School, New York 2012, Creative Capital Visual Arts Grant 2012, Armory Show Artist Commission 2012, Prize for Arts and Politics, Vera List Center, Parsons The New School for Design, New York 2013, Artes Mundi Prize 2015. *Address:* University of Chicago, 5801 South Ellis Avenue, ADM 510, Chicago, IL 60637 (office); 6918 South Dorchester Avenue, Chicago, IL 60637, USA (home). *Website:* theastergates.com; www.kavigupta.com/artist/theastergates; www.theastergates.com; whitecube.com/artists/theaster_gates.

GATETE, Claver; Rwandan economist, diplomatist, government official and fmr central banker; *Minister of Infrastructure;* m. Jeanne Gatete; worked in Canada as an economist 1991–97, Agric. and Agri-food Canada (Statistics), Univ. of British Columbia and Algonquin Coll.; Nat. Economist, UNDP– Kigali-Rwanda 1997–2000; fmr Sr Adviser and Personal Rep. of Pres. Paul Kagame to NEPAD (New Partnership for Africa's Devt) Steering Cttee; Dir-Gen. for Social and Econ. Affairs and mem. Presidential Advisory Council, Office of the Pres. 2000–03; Sec.-Gen. Ministry of Finance and Econ. Planning and Sec. to the Treasury 2003–05; Amb. to UK (also accred to Ireland, Denmark, Norway and Sweden) 2005–09; mem. Bd of Dirs Nat. Bank of Rwanda 2003–05, Deputy Gov. 2009–11, Gov. 2011–13; Minister of Finance and Econ. Planning 2013–18, of Infrastructure 2018–; Chair. Rwanda Revenue Authority 2001–03, School of Finance and Banking 2003–05, Nat. Privatization Tech. Cttee 2003–05, Nat. Treasury Man. Cttee 2003–05; Vice-Chair. Community Devt Fund 2003–05; Co-Chair. Development Partners Coordination Group 2004–05. *Publications include:* Canadian Agri-food Medium Term Policy Baseline (with Merritt Cluff, Hsin Huang, Rebecca Ewing and Mitch Wensley 1997, Pacific Food Outlook (with Brad Gilmour and Lars Brink) 1997; several papers in professional journals. *Address:* Ministry of Infrastructure, KG7 Ave, POB 24, Kigali, Rwanda (office). *Telephone:* 252585503 (office). *E-mail:* info@mininfra.gov.rw (office). *Website:* www.mininfra.gov.rw (office).

GATISS, Mark, BA; British actor, screenwriter and novelist; b. 17 Oct. 1966, Sedgefield, County Durham; s. of Maurice Gatiss and Winifred Gatiss (née O'Kane); m. Ian Hallard 2008; ed Bretton Hall Coll.; co-creator and performer BBC TV comedy series The League of Gentlemen; writer and actor BBC TV series Doctor Who and Sherlock; frequent appearances in BBC Radio productions; numerous stage appearances in London; Hon. DLitt (Huddersfield) 2003. *Television appearances include:* The League of Gentlemen 1995–2002, 2017, Randall & Hopkirk 2001, The League of Gentlemen's Apocalypse (feature film) 2005, The Wind in the Willows 2007, Doctor Who 2007, 2011, 2017, Jekyll 2007, Sense and Sensibility 2008, A History of Horror 2010, Being Human 2012, Game of Thrones 2014–, Wolf Hall 2015, Denial 2016, Taboo 2017. *Theatre appearances include:* The League of Gentlemen (Edinburgh Festival Perrier Award 1997) 1995–2002, All About My Mother (Old Vic Theatre) 2007, Season's Greetings (Royal Nat. Theatre) 2010–11, Coriolanus (Donmar Warehouse) 2013, Three Days In The Country (Nat. Theatre) (What'sOnStage Best Supporting Actor in a Play 2016, Olivier Award for Best Supporting Actor 2016) 2015. *Radio includes:* On the Town with The League of Gentlemen 1997. *TV Screenplays include:* as writer or co-writer: The League of Gentlemen (19 episodes) 1999–2002, Randall & Hopkirk 2001, Doctor Who (nine episodes) 2005–17, Crooked House 2004, Sherlock (seven episodes) 2010–17. *Publications:* Doctor Who novels: Nightshade 1992, St Anthony's Fire 1994, The Roundheads 1997, Last of the Gaderene 2013; Lucifer Box novels: The Vesuvius Club 2005, The Devil in Amber 2007, Black Butterfly 2009; non-fiction: James Whale: A Biography 1995, They Came From Outer Space!: Alien Encounters In The Movies 1996. *Address:* PBJ Management, 22 Rathbone Street, London W1T 1LG, England (office). *Telephone:* (20) 7287-1112 (office). *Website:* www.pbjmanagement.co.uk/artists/mark-gatiss (office).

GATLAND, Warren David, OBE; New Zealand rugby union coach and fmr rugby union player; *Head Coach, Wales National Rugby Union Team;* b. 17 Sept. 1963, Hamilton; ed Hamilton Boys' High School, Waikato Univ.; hooker; played for Waikato 1986–94, record-holder for most games for Waikato near end of 1994 season, finished with 140 games in total and announced retirement before start of 1995 season; played 17 non-int. matches for NZ; Coach, Galwegians RFC 1989–94, Thames Valley 1994–96, Connacht Rugby 1996–98, Ireland 1998–2001, London Wasps 2002–05, Waikato 2005–07; Head Coach, Wales Nat. Rugby Union Team 2007– (won RBS Six Nations Grand Slam 2008, 2012), British and Irish Lions 2013 (won series against Australia 2–1); UK Coach of the Year, UK Coaching Awards 2013. *Address:* Welsh Rugby Union, Millennium Stadium, Westgate Street, Cardiff, CF10 1NS, Wales (office). *E-mail:* info@wru.co.uk (office). *Website:* www.wru.co.uk (office).

GATLIN, Justin; American sprinter; b. 10 Feb. 1982, Brooklyn, New York; s. of Willie Gatlin and Jeanette Gatlin; ed Woodham High School, Fla, Univ. of Tennessee; first athlete since 1957 to win consecutive Nat. Collegiate Athletic Assn (NCAA) titles in both 100m and 200m; five NCAA titles in total; US Jr Champion on three occasions; finished second in 60m (beating Maurice Greene) on professional debut at Verizon Millrose Games 2003; secured US $500,000 by winning Moscow Challenge 100m 2003; World Indoor Champion and US Champion 60m 2003; gold medal, 100m (in a personal-best time of 9.85 seconds), bronze medal 200m Olympic Games, Athens 2004; received four-year ban from athletics for positive doping test 2006; silver medal, 4×100m relay, bronze medal, 100m, Olympic Games, London 2012; USA Track and Field Jesse Owens Award 2004. *Website:* justingatlinusa.com.

GATSINZI, Gen. Marcel, BSc; Rwandan army officer and politician; b. 9 Jan. 1948, Kigali; s. of Phocas Mpagazehe and Anastasie Nyirabagahe; m. Irene Mukanaho; six c.; ed Ecole de Guerre, Brussels, Belgium, Inst. of World Politics, Washington, DC, USA; served in Rwandan Armed Forces, rank of Gen.; fmr Deputy Chief of Staff, then Chief of Staff, Nat. Gendarmerie; mem. Neutral Mil. Observer Group of fmr OAU (now the African Union) 1992–93; Sec.-Gen., Nat. Security Council 2002; Minister of Defence 2002–10, of Disaster Man. and Refugee Affairs 2010–13; rep. to numerous int. negotiations and meetings including African Union, Easbrig, Golden Spear, East African Community, UN Consultative Cttee on Security Matters in Cen. Africa.

GATT, Austin, LLD; Maltese politician and lawyer; b. 29 July 1953; m. Marisa Zammit Maempel; two s.; ed Lyceum and Univ. of Malta; practised law 1975–82; Nationalist Party org. 1980; Chair. Man. Bd Independence Print Co. Ltd 1982–87; Head, Legal Office of Nationalist Party 1982–87, Sec.-Gen. 1988–98; Chair. Euro Tours Co. Ltd; MP 1996, Opposition Spokesman for Justice, Local Councils and Housing 1996–98; Parl. Sec. Office of Prime Minister 1998–99; Minister for Justice and Local Govt 1999–2003, for Information Technology and Investment 2004–08, for Infrastructure, Transport and Communications 2008–13. *Address:* c/o Nationalist Party, Herbert Ganado Street, Pietà PTA 1541, Malta (office).

GATTI, Daniele; Italian conductor; *Director, Teatro dell'Opera di Roma;* b. 6 Nov. 1961, Milan; ed Giuseppe Verdi Conservatory; debut at La Scala, Milan with Rossini's L'occasione fa il Ladro 1987–88 season; US debut with American Symphony Orchestra, Carnegie Hall, New York 1990; Covent Garden debut with I Puritani 1992; Music Dir Accad. di Santa Cecilia, Rome 1992–97; Prin. Guest Conductor, Royal Opera House, Covent Garden 1994–97; debut at Metropolitan Opera, New York with Madama Butterfly 1994–95 season; debut with Royal Philharmonic Orchestra 1994, Music Dir 1995–2009, Conductor Laureate 2009–; debut with New York Philharmonic 1995; Music Dir Teatro Communale, Bologna 1997–2007; Music Dir, Orchestre Nat. de France 2008–16; Music Dir, Opernhaus Zürich 2009–12; Chief Conductor, Royal Concertgebouw Orchestra 2016–18; Artistic Adviser, Mahler Chamber Orchestra 2016–; Dir Teatro dell'Opera di Roma 2018–; has led many orchestras in Europe and USA, including Vienna Philharmonic, Staatskapelle Dresden, Bavarian Radio Symphony, Munich Philharmonic, London Philharmonic, New York Philharmonic, Boston and Chicago Symphonies, Filarmonica della Scala, Milan and Accademia Santa Cecilia, Rome; Grande Ufficiale, Merito della Repubblica Italiana, Chevalier, Légion d'honneur 2016; Franco Abbiati Prize 2005, 2016. *Recordings include:* Tchaikovsky's Fourth and Fifth Symphonies, Pathétique Symphony No. 6 2005. *Address:* Teatro dell'Opera di Roma, Piazza Beniamino Gigli, 1, 00184 Rome, Italy (office). *Website:* www.operaroma.it (office); danielegatti.eu.

GATTI, Gabriele, MA; San Marino politician; b. 27 March 1943, Domagnano; m. Gina Fiorini; two d.; ed Univ. of Urbino; mem. Parl. 1978; Deputy Sec. Christian Democratic Party 1979–85, Sec.-Gen. 1985–87; Sec. of State for Foreign Relations and Political Affairs 1986–2002; Pres. Ministerial Chief, Council of Europe; mem. Gen. Comm. of the Inst. for Social Security, Urban Comm.; Sec. of State for Finance, the Budget, Post and Relations with the Azienda Autonoma di Stato Filatelica e Numismatica 2008–11; Captain Regent (Jt head of state) 2011–12.

GATTING, Michael (Mike) William, OBE; British professional cricket coach and fmr professional cricketer; b. 6 June 1957, Kingsbury, Middx; m. Elaine Mabbott 1980; two s.; ed John Kelly High School; right-hand batsman and right-arm medium bowler; played for Middx 1975–99 (Capt. 1983–97), MCC 1978–87; 79 Tests for England 1977–95 (23 as Capt. 1986–88), scoring 4,409 runs (average 35.55, highest score 207) including 10 hundreds, took four wickets; 92 One-Day Ints (37 as Capt.), scoring 2,095 runs (average 29.50, highest score 115 not out) including one hundred; scored 36,549 first-class runs (94 hundreds), average 49.52, highest score 258; toured Australia 1986–87 (Capt.), 1987–95; Capt. rebel cricket tour to SA 1989–90; mem. England Selection Cttee 1997–99; Dir of Coaching, Middx Cricket Club 1999–2000, mem. Exec. Bd 2015–; Dir Ashwell Leisure 2001–; Pres. Lord's Taverners 2005–06; mem. MCC Cttee; Grand Cru Travel Consultant; Wisden Cricketer of The Year 1984. *Radio includes:* analyst on Test Match Special. *Publications include:* Limited Overs 1986, Triumph in Australia 1987, Leading from the Front (autobiog.) 1988. *Leisure interests:* golf, soccer and sport in general. *Address:* 8A Village Road, Enfield, Middx, EN1 2DH, England (home).

GATTUNG, Theresa Elizabeth, CNZM, BA, LLB; New Zealand business executive; b. 11 April 1962; ed Univ. of Waikato, Victoria Univ. of Wellington; fmr Chief Man. of Marketing, Nat. Mutual; Chief Man. of Marketing, Bank of New Zealand –1994; Gen. Man. Marketing, Telecom Corpn Ltd (largest co. in New Zealand) 1994–96, Group Gen. Man. Services 1996–99, Chief Exec. and Man. Dir Telecom Corpn of New Zealand Ltd 1999–2007; mem. Bd of Dirs, AIA Australia (insurance co.) 2009–, Chair. 2010–; Chair. Wool Partners Int. 2008–11, Co-founder My Food Bag Ltd 2013; Co-founder and Trustee, Eva Doucas Charitable Trust; Chair. Wellington Bd of Soc. for the Prevention of Cruelty to Animals; Patron Cambodia Charitable Trust, Cambodia Charitable Trust; Companion of the NZ Order of Merit 2015. *Publication:* Bird On a Wire 2010. *Address:* Office of the Chairman, AIA Australia Ltd, 553 St Kilda Road, Melbourne, Vic. 3000, Australia (office). *Telephone:* (3) 9009-4000 (office). *E-mail:* chris@theresagattung.com (home). *Website:* www.aia.com.au (office); www.theresagattung.com.

GATZOULIS, Michael Athanasios, MD, PhD, FESC, FACC; Greek/British cardiologist; *Academic Head, Adult Congenital Heart Centre and Centre for Pulmonary Hypertension, Royal Brompton Hospital; Professor of Cardiology and Congenital Heart Disease, National Heart and Lung Institute;* b. 10 April 1958, Drama, Greece; s. of Dr Athanasios K. Gatzoulis; m. Julie Kohls-Gatzoulis; two s.; ed Aristotelian Univ., Thessaloniki, Greece, MRCPCH, London, Univ. of London, UK; fmr Staff Cardiologist and Asst Prof., Univ. of Toronto Congenital Cardiac Centre for Adults; currently Prof. of Cardiology, Congenital Heart Disease and Consultant Cardiologist and Academic Head, Adult Congenital Heart Centre and Centre for Pulmonary Hypertension, Royal Brompton Hosp.; Prin. Investigator, Adult Congenital Heart Programme, Nat. Heart and Lung Inst., Imperial Coll. School of Medicine, also Prof. of Cardiology and Congenital Heart Disease 2005–;

Visiting Prof., Vanderbilt Univ. 2006, Stanford Univ. 2006, Harvard Univ. 2007, Erasmus Univ. and Thorax Centre, Rotterdam, Netherlands, Japan Heart Inst. and Univ. of Tokyo, King Faisal Specialist Hosp. and Research Center, Jeddah, Leiden Univ., Netherlands, Univ. of Athens, Aristotelian Univ. of Thessaloniki; Idriss Distinguished Prof., Northwestern Univ.; Assoc. Ed., Int. Journal of Cardiology 2003–; mem. Int. Editorial Bd and Guest Ed., European Heart Journal; Section Ed., Congenital Heart Disease, Hellenic Journal of Cardiology 2002–; Journal Reviewer, Heart 1994–, Circulation 1997–, Clinical Science 1998–, European Heart Journal 1999–, Arch Dis Child 2001–, Europace 2002–, Lancet, 2003–, American Heart Journal 2003–, Cardiology Young 1994–, Journal of the American College of Cardiology 1997–, International Journal of Cardiology 1999–, Drugs 2000–; Sec.-Gen. Int. Soc. of Adult Congenital Cardiac Disease 2000–01, Pres. 2004–05; ESC Nucleus and UK Rep. EuroHeart Survey for Adult Congenital Heart Disease 2001–03. *Publications include:* The Adult with Tetralogy of Fallot 2001, Diagnosis and Management of Adult Congenital Heart Disease 2003, Adult Congenital Heart Disease: A Practical Guide 2004, Heart Disease and Pregnancy 2006; co-ed. 40th Edn of Gray's Anatomy; author of more than 150 peer-reviewed scientific papers, including articles in Nature, New England Journal of Medicine, The Lancet, and Circulation. *Leisure interests:* tennis, skiing, model rail (Marklin), windsurfing, sailing. *Address:* Royal Brompton Hospital, Sydney Street, London, SW3 6NP, England (office). *Telephone:* (20) 7352-8602 (PA Mrs Rachel Collumbell) (office); (20) 7351-8227 (direct line) (office). *Fax:* (20) 7351-8629 (office). *E-mail:* m.gatzoulis@imperial.ac.uk (office); m.gatzoulis@rbh.nthames.nhs.uk (office). *Website:* www.rbh.nthames.nhs.uk (office).

GAUCK, Joachim; German politician, Lutheran pastor and fmr head of state; b. 24 Jan. 1940, Rostock; four c.; family suffered discrimination under communist regime of East Germany; became Lutheran pastor and anti-communist human rights activist under the communist state; Co-founder New Forum opposition movement in East Germany 1989, contributed to the downfall of the Soviet-backed dictatorship of the Socialist Unity Party of Germany (SED); mem. only freely elected People's Chamber (Volkskammer) for the Alliance 90 March–Oct. 1990; mem. Bundestag following reunification 3–4 Oct. 1990 (stepped down following appointment as Special Rep. of Fed. Govt); first Fed. Commr for Stasi Archives 1991–2000, earned recognition for exposing crimes of the fmr communist political police; founding signatory of Prague Declaration on European Conscience and Communism, together with Václav Havel and other statesmen, and Declaration on Crimes of Communism; unsuccessful cand. of SPD and the Greens for Pres. of Germany in 2010 election; selected as non-partisan consensus cand. for Pres. of Germany in 2012 election by the govt parties CDU, Christian Social Union in Bavaria (CSU) and Free Democratic Party, and opposition SPD and the Alliance '90/The Greens Feb.–March 2012, Pres. of Germany 2012–17; Chair. Gegen Vergessen—Für Demokratie 2003–12; Guest Prof., Heinrich Heine Univ. Düsseldorf 2018; mem. Man. Bd, European Monitoring Centre on Racism and Xenophobia 2001–04; Hon. Chair. Gegen Vergessen – Für Demokratie 2017–, Hon. Citizen, Berlin, Rostock; Fed. Cross of Merit 1995, Collar Grand Cross, Order of Merit of the Italian Repub. 2013, Grand Cross, Royal Norwegian Order of St Olav 2014, Hon. Knight Grand Cross, Order of the Bath (UK) 2015, Grand Cordon, Order of Leopold (Belgium) 2016, Knight, Order of the Seraphim (Sweden) 2016; Dr hc (Rostock) 1999, (Augsburg) 2005, (Maastricht) 2017; Theodor Heuss Medal 1991, Hermann Ehlers Prize 1996, Hannah Arendt Prize 1997, Imre Nagy Prize (Hungary) 1999, Dolf Sternberger Prize 2000, Erich Kästner Prize 2001, 'Goldenes Lot' des Verbandes Deutscher Vermessungsingenieure 2002, Courage Prize (Osnabrück) 2003, Thomas Dehler Prize 2008, Das Glas der Vernunft 2009, Geschwister-Scholl Prize 2010, Ludwig Börne Prize 2011, Leo Baeck Medal 2014, Ewald von Kleist Award 2017, Reinhard Mohn Prize 2018, Charles IV Prize 2018. *Publications include:* Die Stasi-Akten. Das unheimliche Erbe der DDR 1991, Von der Würde der Unterdrückten (contrib.) 1992, Verlust und Übermut. Ein Kapitel über den Untertan als Bewohner der Moderne (contrib.) 1993, Das Schwarzbuch des Kommunismus – Unterdrückung, Verbrechen und Terror (contrib. of the chapter 'Vom schwierigen Umgang mit der Wahrnehmung', on political oppression in East Germany) 1998, Reite Schritt, Schnitter Tod! Leben und Sterben im Speziallager Nr. 1 des NKWD Mühlberg/Elbe (contrib.) 2007, Winter im Sommer – Frühling im Herbst: Erinnerungen 2009, Freiheit: Ein Plädoyer 2012, Nicht den Ängsten folgen, den Mut wählen: Denkstationen eines Bürgers 2013. *Address:* Gegen Vergessen – Für Demokratie, Stauffenbergstraße 13–14, 10785 Berlin, Germany (office). *Telephone:* (30) 2639783 (office). *Fax:* (30) 26397840 (office). *E-mail:* info@gegen-vergessen.de (office). *Website:* www.gegen-vergessen.de (office); www.joachim-gauck.de.

GAUDET, Tracy W., BA, MD; American obstetrician, gynaecologist, academic and author; *Director of Office of Patient Centered Care and Cultural Transformation, Department of Veterans Affairs;* one s.; ed Univ. of Texas Medical School, San Antonio; practised and taught at Univ. of Texas, San Antonio –1996; Founding Exec. Dir Univ. of Arizona Program in Integrative Medicine 1996–2000; joined faculty of Duke Univ. 2000, Exec. Dir Duke Integrative Medicine, Duke Univ. Medical Center 2001–11, Asst Prof. of Obstetrics and Gynaecology, Duke Univ. Medical Center; Dir Office of Patient Centered Care and Cultural Transformation, US Dept of Veterans Affairs, Washington, DC 2011–; Co-founder Consortium of Academic Health Centers for Integrative Medicine, Chair. Membership Cttee 2002–04, mem. Steering, Exec., Educ. and Policy Cttees; mem. of Editorial Bds, Clinical Acupuncture and Oriental Medicine, Integrative Medicine Journal, Seminars in Integrative Medicine; columnist, Body + Soul magazine. *Publications include:* Consciously Female 2004, Body, Soul and Baby 2007. *Address:* US Department of Veterans Affairs, 810 Vermont Avenue, NW, Washington, DC 20420 (office); Duke Integrative Medicine, Duke Center for Living Campus, 3475 Erwin Road, Durham, NC 27705, USA (office). *Telephone:* (866) 313-0959 (Durham) (office); (919) 660-6826 (Durham) (office). *Website:* www.va.gov (office); www.dukeintegrativemedicine.org (office).

GAUKE, Rt Hon. David Michael; British solicitor and politician; *Lord Chancellor and Secretary of State for Justice;* b. 8 Oct. 1971, Ipswich; m. Rachel Gauke; three s.; ed St Edmund Hall, Oxford, Chester Coll. of Law; qualified as solicitor 1997; with Macfarlanes (law firm) 1999–2005; MP (Conservative) for SW Hertfordshire 2005–, mem. Procedure Cttee 2005–07, Treasury Cttee 2006–07, Tax Law Rewrite Bills (Jt Cttee) 2009; Shadow Minister (Treasury) 2007–10, Exchequer Sec. (HM Treasury) 2010–14, Financial Sec. (HM Treasury) 2014–16, Chief Sec. to the Treasury 2016–17, Sec. of State for Work and Pensions 2017–18, Lord Chancellor and Sec. of State for Justice 2018–. *Address:* Ministry of Justice, 102 Petty France, London, SW1H 9AJ; House of Commons, London, SW1A 0AA, England (office). *Telephone:* (20) 3334-3555 (ministry); (20) 3267-5144 (office). *E-mail:* general.queries@justice.gsi.gov.uk; david@davidgauke.com. *Website:* www.gov.uk/government/organisations/ministry-of-justice (office); www.davidgauke.com.

GAULAND, Alexander Eberhardt; German lawyer, journalist and politician; *Leader of AfD in the Bundestag;* b. 20 Feb. 1941, Chemnitz; s. of Alexander Gauland; pnr Carola Hein; one d. from previous m.; ed Marburg Univ.; worked for Federal Press Office 1970–72; Press Attaché, Consulate Gen. in Edinburgh 1974–75; Dir, Office of the Mayor of Frankfurt am Main 1977–86; Sec. of State, Hesse State Chancellery 1987–91; Ed. Märkische Allgemeine (local newspaper), Potsdam 1991–2006; mem. CDU 1973–2013; mem. Brandenburg Landtag (AfD) 2014–; mem. Bundestag for Frankfurt (Oder)–Oder-Spree 2017–; Founder mem. Alternative for Germany (AfD) 2013, Chair. AfD Brandenburg 2014–, Deputy Leader of AfD 2015–, co-Lead Cand. at 2017 election, AfD Leader in the Bundestag 2017–; regular contributor to Berlin Tagesspiegel, Criticon, New Society, Frankfurter Allgemeine Zeitung, Frankfurter Rundschau. *Publications include:* Was ist Konservativismus? 1991, Helmut Kohl: Ein Prinzip 1994, Anleitung zum Konservativsein 2002, Die Deutschen und ihre Geschichte 2009. *Address:* Alternative für Deutschland, Schillstr. 9, 10785 Berlin, Germany (office). *Telephone:* (30) 22056960 (office). *Fax:* (30) 220569629 (office). *E-mail:* bgs@alternativefuer.de (office). *Website:* www.afd.de (office); www.afd.de/dr-alexander-gauland/.

GAULTIER, Jean-Paul; French fashion designer; b. 24 April 1952, Arcueil, Paris; s. of Paul Gaultier; first show in 1976; launched first commercial collection with his Japanese pnr 1978; since then known on int. scale for his women's and men's collections as well as haute couture from 1997; first jr collection 1988; costume designs for film The Cook, The Thief, His Wife and Her Lover 1989, for ballet Le Défilé de Régine Chopinot 1985, Madonna's World Tour 1990; released record How to Do That (in collaboration with Tony Mansfield) 1989; designed costumes for Victoria Abril (q.v.) in Pedro Almodóvar (q.v.) 's film Kika 1994, film La Cité des Enfants Perdus 1995, The Fifth Element 1996; two more collaborations with Almodóvar with Bad Education 2005 and The Skin I Live In 2011; launched perfume brands Jean-Paul Gaultier 1993, Le Mâle 1995, Fragile 1999, Madame 2008, Kokorico 2011; women's wear Design Dir, Hermès 2004–11; exhbn spanning 35 years of his career opened in Montréal 2011, Dallas and San Francisco 2012; Chevalier, Légion d'honneur; Fashion Oscar 1987, Progetto Leonardo Award for How to Do That 1989. *Leisure interests:* film, theatre, ballet. *Address:* 325 rue Saint-Martin, 75003 Paris, France. *Telephone:* 1-72-75-83-00 (office). *Website:* www.jeanpaulgaultier.com.

GAUR, Varsh Shri Babulal, BA, LLB; Indian politician; b. 2 June 1930, UP; s. of Shri Ramprasad; fmr trade union activist; elected mem. MP Legis. Ass. 1974–, Leader of Opposition 2002–03; fmr MP State Minister of Local Admin, Legal Affairs, Legis. Affairs, Bhopal Gas Tragedy Relief, Public Relations, Urban Admin and Devt 2003; Chief Minister MP 2004–05; currently MP Minister of Urban Admin and Devt; Founder mem. Bhartiya Majdoor Sangh; Sec. Bharatiya Jansangh; mem. Bharatiya Janata Party; Swatantrata Sangram Senani Samman 1974. *Address:* Urban Administration and Development Department, Palika Bhawan, Shivaji Nagar, Bhopal, India (office). *Telephone:* (755) 2552396 (office). *Website:* www.mpurban.gov.in (office).

GAUTAM, Bam Dev; Nepalese politician; b. 11 July 1944, Dakhakwadi-1, Pyuthan; s. of Kabi Raj Gautam and Padma Devi Gautam; m.; joined Communist Party of Nepal (CPN) 1964, Dist Sec. Rupandehi CPN 1972–79, became W Cttee Sec. 1979–80, mem. CPN Central Cttee 1980–97, fmr Deputy Sec.-Gen. Communist Party of Nepal–Unified Marxist Leninist (CPN–UML), split from CPN–UML and co-f. CPN–ML 1998, apptd Gen. Sec. CPN–ML, party failed to win a seat in next election and then rejoined CPN–UML, elected Vice-Chair. CPN–UML 2009; mem. Parl. for Bardiya Constituency 1991–; Deputy Prime Minister and Minister of Home Affairs 1997–99, 2008–11, 2014–15.

GAUTRAND, Manuelle; French architect; *Partner and Principal Architect, Manuelle Gautrand Architecture;* b. 14 July 1961, Marseille; d. of Alain Gautrand and Janine Gautrand; m. Marc Blaising; two s.; ed Ecole Nationale Supérieure d'Architecture, Montpellier; qualified as an architect 1985, est. practice in Paris 1991; numerous projects, ranging from housing and offices to cultural bldgs, business premises and leisure facilities; clients include public contracting authorities as well as private firms, in France and abroad; earned int. recognition for C42 Citroën Flagship Showroom bldg, Champs-Elysée, Paris; Pres. Acad. of Architecture, Paris 2017; mem. Int. Council of the Van Alen Inst., New York 2016; Chevalier des Arts et des Lettres 2007, Légion d'honneur 2010; Albums de la Jeune Architecture Award, Ministry of Culture 1992, Silver Medal, Acad. d'Architecture 2002, Trophée de la Construction, Asscn des Journalistes de la Construction 2003, Prix Montgolfier 2013, ARVHA Prix Femme Architecte 2014, German Design Award 2017, European Prize for Architecture 2017. *Major works include:* footbridge, Lyon 1993, Le Fellini four-screen cinema, Villefontaine 1994, Univ. Inst. of Professional Educ., Annecy-le-Vieux 1996, restructuring of admin. unit of Georges Pompidou Centre, Paris 1996, restructuring of two-screen cinema, Saint-Priest 1996, Laurent-Mourguet School, Ecully 1997, toll plazas on A16 motorway 1998, airport catering bldg, Nantes (Award for Architecture and Work Places, Architecture et Maîtrise d'Ouvrage Asscn and Ministry of Culture 2000) 1998, Nat. Drama Theatre, Béthune 1998, Univ. Inst. of Professional Educ., Lieusaint 1999, La Coupole cultural centre, Saint-Louis 2000, two metro stations for the Val line, Rennes 2002, complex of 104 ecological apartments, Rennes 2006, Citroën showroom, Champs-Élysées, Paris (MIPIM Architectural Review Future Project Award 2005, Third Prize for int. Interior Design Competition, Int. Interior Design Asscn (USA) 2008, Int. Interior Design Asscn Interior Design Award 2008, AIT Magazine (Germany) Int. Contract World Award 2009, World Architecture News Architecture Award (commercial category) 2009, European Contractworld Award, AIT Magazine 2009) 2007, block of 35 apartments, Boulogne-Billancourt 2007, shopping mall, Bangkok (first building abroad) 2009, Lille Museum of Modern, Contemporary and Outsider Art 2010, Origami office bldg, Paris 2010, Business Centre in Saint-Etienne (The Chicago Athenaem Award 2011, "des plus beaux ouvrages de construction métallique" Award 2011) 2010, Le Monolith office bldg in Lyon 2010, housing block in Acigné, restructuring and reconversion of the old theatre Gaîté Lyrique into an interactive platform for 21st-century music and arts 2011, facade, Galeries Lafayette, Metz (Lightening Conception Award, ACE) 2014, restructuring Comédie de Béthune 2014, cultural, sports and community centre, Saint-Louis Alsace 2015. *Films include:* L'Art et la Manière 2008, Chic 2008. *Publications include:* La coupole a Saint-Louis 2003, Unaccustomed – Manuelle Gautrand 2004, Manuelle Gautrand Architectures 2005, Manuelle Gautrand Architect 2006, Manuelle Gautrand 2007, Monograph Manuelle Gautrand Architect 2008, Ré-enchanter la Ville 2008, LaM, le Musée d'Art Moderne de Lille Métropole 2010, Ceux que j'ai (déjà) construits – Those I Have (Already) Built 2011, La Gaîté du Lyrique au Numérique 2011. *Address:* Manuelle Gautrand Architecture, 36 boulevard de la Bastille, 75012 Paris, France (office). *Telephone:* 1-56-95-06-46 (office). *Fax:* 1-56-95-06-47 (office). *E-mail:* contact-com@manuelle-gautrand.com (office). *Website:* www.manuelle-gautrand.com (office).

GAVASKAR, Sunil ('Sunny') Manohar, BA; Indian business executive, sports administrator and fmr professional cricketer; b. 10 July 1949, Bombay (now Mumbai), Maharashtra; s. of Manohar Keshav Gavaskar and Meenal Manohar Gavaskar; m. Marshniel Mehrotra 1974; one s.; ed St Xavier's High School, Bombay, St Xavier's Coll., Bombay Univ.; right-hand opening batsman; played for Mumbai 1967–87, Somerset 1980; 125 Tests for India 1970–97 (47 as Capt.), scoring 10,122 runs (average 51.12, highest score 236 not out) with 34 hundreds and holding 108 catches; toured England 1971, 1974, 1975 (World Cup), 1979, 1982, 1983 (World Cup); One-Day Ints: first player to score more than 10,000 Test runs 1987; first player to score over 2,000 runs against three countries 1987; only man to play in a 100 successive Tests; nominated to Rajya Sabha 1992; Match Referee Int. Cricket Council (ICC) 1993–94; f. Sunil Gavaskar Foundation for Cricket in Bengal 1996; Chair. ICC Cricket Cttee –2008, Indian Nat. Cricket Acad. 2001–05; Interim Pres. BCCI 2014; Sheriff of Mumbai 1994; Dr hc (D.Y. Patil Univ.) 2009; India's Best Schoolboy Cricketer of the Year 1966, Arjuna Award 1975, Padma Bhushan 1980, Wisden Cricketer of The Year 1980, Col C K Nayudu Lifetime Achievement Award for Cricket 2012, Padma Shri. *Films include:* Premachi Saavli, Maalamal. *Publications include:* Sunny Days – An Autobiography 1976, Idols (autobiog.) 1982, Runs 'n' Ruins 1984, One-day Wonders, The Sunil Gavaskar Omnibus 1999.

GAVIDIA, Yolanda Mayora de; Salvadorean economist, civil servant and international organization official; m.; ed Cen. American Inst. of Business Admin, INCAE; worked with various nat. devt orgs; mem. Panel of Econ. Advisers, Ministry of Social Planning 1990–92; Tech. Sec.-Gen. for Econ. and Social Policy, Ministry of Planning 1993–95; Program Coordinator for Improvement of Competitiveness, Presidential Comm. for Modernization of the Public Sector 1995–97; joined Ministry of the Economy 1996, Minister of the Economy 2004–08; Sec.-Gen. Secretaría de Integración Económica Centroamericana (SIECA), Guatemala City, Guatemala 2009–11 (resgnd); Exec. Dir Carlos F. Novella Foundation. *Address:* c/o Secretaría de Integración Económica Centroamericana (SIECA), 4A Avda 10–25, Zona 14, Apdo 1237, 01901 Guatemala City, Guatemala.

GAVIN, Michelle D., BA, MPhil; American diplomatist and institute director; *Managing Director, The Africa Center;* b. June 1973, Ariz.; d. of Michael Gavin and Jeanette Gavin; m. David Bonfili; one d.; ed Georgetown Univ. School of Foreign Service (Truman Scholar), Univ. of Oxford, UK (Rhodes Scholar); served as Staff Dir of Senate Foreign Relations Cttee's Sub-cttee on African Affairs; Primary Foreign Policy Adviser to Senator Russ Feingold (Democrat-Wis.) 1999–2005; Legis. Dir to US Senator from Colo Ken Salazar 2005–06; Adjunct Fellow for Africa and an Int. Affairs Fellow, Council on Foreign Relations 2007–09; Special Asst to the Pres. and Sr Dir for Africa, Nat. Security Staff, The White House 2009–11; Amb. to Botswana 2011–14; Man. Dir, The Africa Center, New York 2015–. *Address:* The Africa Center, 1280 5th Avenue, New York, NY 10029, USA (office). *Website:* www.theafricacenter.org (office).

GAVIRIA TRUJILLO, César; Colombian economist, politician and fmr international organization official; b. 31 March 1947, Pereira; s. of Byron Gaviria Londoño and Mélida Trujillo Trujillo; m. Ana Milena Muñoz de Gaviria 1978; two c.; ed Univ. of the Andes; mem. town council of Pereira, later Mayor; mem. Chamber of Deputies (Partido Liberal Colombiano) and Dir Comm. for Econ. Affairs 1974; Vice-Minister for Econ. Devt 1978; Speaker of Parl. 1983; journalist in early 1980s; Minister of Finance and Public Credit 1986–87, of the Interior 1987–89; Pres. of Colombia 1990–94; Sec.-Gen. OAS 1994–2004; Pres. Partido Liberal Colombiano 2005–09; mem. Inter-American Dialogue, Club de Madrid, La Conférence de Montréal; est. Nueveochenta (art gallery), Bogotá; Hon. Prof., Universidad ICESI, Colombia, Univ. of Miami, USA, Universidad Libre Colombia 1990, Universidade Estácio de Sá, Rio de Janeiro 1991, Northeastern Univ., USA 2002; Hon. LLB (Univ. Libre de Colombia); Hon. DCL (Northeastern Univ.) 2002; W. Averell Harriman Democracy Award 2002, Nat. Democratic Inst. Democracy Award 2002, Washington Times Int. Courage in Leadership Award 2002. *Publications include:* La Deuda Latinoamericana 1982, Reflexiones para una nueva Constitución 1990, La Revolución Pacífica 1990, Las Bases de la Nueva Colombia: El Revolcón Institucional 1990–1994 1994, Reformas Económicas 1990–1994 1994, Plan de Desarrollo Económico y Social 1990–1994 1994, A New Vision of the OAS 1995, Toward the New Millennium: The Road Travelled 1994–1999 1999; book chapters and articles in journals. *Address:* c/o Partido Liberal Colombiano, Avda Caracas, No 36-01, Bogotá, DC, Colombia (office).

GAVRIISKI, Svetoslav; Bulgarian government official and banker; *CEO, Allianz Bank Bulgaria;* b. 18 Dec. 1948, Svishtov; ed Karl Marx Higher Inst. of Econs, Sofia; economist, Ministry of Finance 1972; Sr Expert, Nat. Balance Sheets Directorate, Ministry of the Economy and Planning 1988; Sr Expert in Int. Financial Relations, Ministry of Finance 1990, Head of Int. Finance Dept 1991–92; Deputy Minister of Finance 1992–97, Minister Feb.–May 1997; Gov. of Bulgaria to IMF 1992–96, 1997, to IBRD, EBRD and European Investment Bank 1997, to Black Sea Trade and Devt Bank 1998; Leader Group Negotiations on Bulgaria's External Debt 1991–94; mem. Man. Bd Bulbank 1991–97; Gov. Bulgarian Nat. Bank 1997–2003; CEO Allianz Bank Bulgaria 2006–, also now Chair., also Exec. Vice-Pres. Allianz Bulgaria Holding; Man. mem. Int. Bank for Econ. Co-operation, Moscow 1992, Int. Investment Bank, Moscow 1992; mem. Bd of Dirs Bank Consolidation Co. 2001–; mem. Supervisory Bd Municipal Bank 2005–; unsuccessful Cand. in mayoral elections in Sofia 2005. *Address:* Allianz Bank Bulgaria, 1202 Sofia, 79, Maria Louisa Blvd, Bulgaria (office). *Telephone:* (2) 921-54-04 (office). *Fax:* (2) 981-93-07 (office). *E-mail:* admin@bank.allianz.bg (office). *Website:* bank.allianz.bg (office).

GAVRIN, Alexander Sergeyevich, PhD; Russian engineer and politician; b. 22 July 1953, Orlovo, Zaporozhye Region, Ukraine; ed Tumen Industrial Inst., Tumen State Inst. of Oil and Gas; army service 1972–74; controller, master Zaporozhye plant Radiopribor 1974–79; controlling master, Manuylsky Research Inst., Kiev 1979–80; engineer constructor, Kiev plant generator 1980–81; technician, Kiev production co. 1981–83; electrician, Povkhneft Kogalym, Tumen Region 1983–88; engineer and head of group, Kogalymneftegas Co., Tumen Region 1988–89; Chair. Trade Union LUKOil-Kogalymneftegas 1989–93; Head of Admin. Kogalym., Tumen Region 1993–96; Mayor of Kogalym 1996–2000; Minister of Energy of Russian Fed. 2000–01; fmr Senator of the Russian Fed.; mem. Bd of Dirs PetroAlliance Services Co. Ltd, Bankhaus Erbe; fmr Rep. of Tumen Region to Council of Fed., Russian Fed. Ass.

GAWANAS, Bience, LLB, MBA (Exec.); Namibian lawyer, government official and UN official; *Special Adviser on Africa, United Nations;* b. 1956; d. of Philemon Gawanab and Hilde Rheiss; m.; three c.; ed Univ. of Western Cape, SA, Univ. of Warwick, UK, Univ. of Cape Town, SA; worked as Barrister at Lincoln's Inn, London 1988; Lawyer, Legal Assistance Centre 1990–91; Commr Public Service Comm., Namibia 1991–96; Sec.-Gen. Namibia Nat. Women's Org. 1993–99; Lecturer on Gender Law, Univ. of Namibia 1995–97; Ombudswoman of Namibia 1996–2003; Chair. Women's Action for Devt 2001–02; Commr for Social Affairs of Head of Govt, African Union Ass. 2003–12; Co-Chair. Global Leadership Group of Maternal Mortality 2009; mem., Global Comm. of HIV and Law, UNDP 2010, Comm. on Accountability and Information, WHO, Special Adviser on Africa to UN 2018–; Special Adviser to Minister of Health and Social Services 2013, also to Minister of Poverty Eradication and Social Welfare –2018; fmr Dir of Bd, Cen. Bank of Namibia; mem., Int. Advisory Reference Group 2009, SWAPO Youth League; Patron Nat. Fed. of Persons with Disabilities 2001–10; went into exile in Zambia, Angola and Cuba; Hon. LLD (Univ. of Western Cape) 2012. *Address:* United Nations Headquarters, 405 E 42nd Street, New York, NY 10017, USA (office). *Telephone:* (212) 963-1234 (office). *Fax:* (212) 963-4879 (office). *Website:* www.un.org (office).

GAWANDE, Atul, MD, MPH; American surgeon, public health researcher and writer; *Samuel O. Thier Professor of Surgery, Harvard Medical School;* b. 5 Nov. 1965, Brooklyn, New York; m. Kathleen Hobson; three c.; ed Stanford Univ., Balliol Coll., Oxford, UK, Harvard Medical School; surgeon, gen. and endocrine surgery depts, Brigham and Women's Hosp. 2003–; Prof., Dept of Health Policy and Management, Harvard T.H. Chan School of Public Health, also Samuel O. Thier Prof. of Surgery, Harvard Medical School; Sr Health Policy Adviser to Bill Clinton's presidential campaign and subsequently The White House 1992–93; Dir, WHO Safe Surgery Saves Lives programme 2007–; Exec. Dir Ariadne Labs; Chair. Lifebox (non-profit org.); staff writer, The New Yorker 1998–; BBC Reith Lecturer 2014; writes Notes of a Surgeon column, New England Journal of Medicine; MacArthur Fellow 2006, Hastings Center Fellow 2009; two Nat. Magazine Awards, AcademyHealth's Impact Award for highest research impact on healthcare, Lewis Thomas Award for Writing about Science 2014. *Publications include:* Complications: A Surgeon's Notes on an Imperfect Science 2002, Better 2007, The Checklist Manifesto 2009, Being Mortal: Medicine and What Matters in the End 2014. *Address:* Department of Health Policy and Management, Harvard T.H. Chan School of Public Health, 677 Huntington Avenue, Boston, MA 02115, USA (office). *E-mail:* atul@atulgawande.com (office). *Website:* atulgawande.com (office); www.hsph.harvard.edu/atul-gawande.

GAWN, Maj.-Gen. Arthur David (Dave), MBE; New Zealand military commander and UN official; *Chief Executive, Pike River Recovery Agency;* b. 17 May 1958, Marton; s. of Donald Gawn; m. Anne Mary Wheeler; two s. one d.; ed Deakin Univ., Centre for Defence and Strategic Studies, US Army Command and Gen. Staff Coll., Fort Leavenworth, Kansas, School of Advanced Warfighting, Quantico, Virginia; joined New Zealand Army Aug. 1978, becoming Second Lt, Royal NZ Infantry Regt (RNZIR) 1980, Platoon Commdr, 1st Bn RNZIR, Singapore 1981–84, Staff Officer, Air and Special Duties, HQ Army Training Group, Waiouru 1984–85, Staff Officer, Grade Three Co-ordination, HQ Land Force Command, Takapuna 1985–87, Officer Commanding, 1st Ranger Co. 1987–89, Staff Officer, Grade Three Peacekeeping, Land Force Command HQ 1989–90, NZ Instructor, Australian Defence Force Acad., Canberra 1990–92, Co. Commdr, 1st Battalion RNZIR 1992–94, Officer Commanding, Kiwi Co., NZFOR UNPROFOR, Santici Camp, Bosnia 1994–95, Instructor, Tactical School, Waiouru 1997, Staff Officer, Grade Doctrine and Capability Devt Br., Army Gen. Staff 1998, Commanding Officer, 3rd NZ Bn Group, NZ UN Transitional Authority 2000–01, Asst Chief of Staff, Devt Br., Army Gen. Staff 2002–05, Commdr, 3rd Land Force Group, Burnham Mil. Camp 2005–07, Land Component Commdr, Jt Forces NZ HQ 2007–10, Deputy Chief of Army 2010–11, Commdr, Jt Forces NZ 2011–13, Chief of Army of NZ 2013–15; Head of Mission and Chief of Staff, UN Truce Supervision Org. (UNTSO) 2015–17; attained rank of Capt. 1987, Lt-Col 1998, Col 2001, Maj.-Gen. 2011; Chief Exec. Pike River Recovery Agency 2017–; Force Commdr's Commendation (for his role in Timor-Leste) 2001. *Address:* Pike River Recovery Agency, PO Box 414, Greymouth 7840, New Zealand (office). *E-mail:* info@pikeriverrecovery.govt.nz (office). *Website:* www.pikeriverrecovery.govt.nz (office).

GAYAN, Anil Kumarsingh, LLB, LLM; Mauritian lawyer and politician; b. 22 Oct. 1948; m. Sooryakanti Nirsimloo; three c.; ed Royal Coll., Port Louis, London School of Econs and Univ. of London, UK; called to the Bar, Inner Temple, London 1972; mem. Mauritius Bar and Seychelles Bar 1972–73, pvt. practice 1973–74, 1982, 1986–90, 1995–2000; Chair. Bar Council 1989–90; joined Chambers of Mauritius Attorney-Gen. as Crown Counsel 1974, Sr Counsel 1995; Del. to UN Conf. on the Law of the Sea 1974–82; mem. Parl. 1982–86, Minister of External Affairs, Tourism and Emigration 1983–86, Foreign Affairs and Regional Co-operation 2000–03; Lecturer, Univ. de la Réunion 2008–14; Founder and Leader Front Nat. Mauricien (FNM) party 2009; Special Adviser to Comoros 2011; Chair. African Union panel on qualifications of African Union Commrs 2011; Adviser to Govt of Seychelles on UN Security Council Matters 2013; apptd jtly by African Union and UN to chair investigation cttee into circumstances surrounding the assassination of Paramount Chief Deng in Abyei area 2013; Minister of Health and Quality of Life 2014; mem. Nat. Ass. (Parl.) for Constituency No. 20 Beau Bassin and Petit Riviere 2014–; Chair. Council of Univ. of Mauritius 1983; Consultant for Geneva-based Centre for Human Rights, consultancy work in Bhutan, Mongolia, Armenia and Togo 1991; Hon. Minister, Hon. Teaching Fellow, Dept of Primary Care and Public Health, School of Public Health, Imperial Coll., London 2016. *Address:* National Assembly, Parliament House, Place d'Armes, Port Louis (office); 223, Royal Road, Forest Side, Curepipe, Mauritius (home). *Telephone:* 201-1414 (office). *Fax:* 212-8364 (office). *E-mail:* agayan@govmu.org (office). *Website:* mauritiusassembly.govmu.org (office).

GAYDAMAK, Arcadi Alexandrovich; Russian/Israeli business executive; b. 8 April 1952, Moscow; moved from USSR to Israel aged 20, moved to France 1973, to Israel 2000; f. Gaydamak Translations, Paris; Owner, Moskovskie Novosti newspaper 2005–08, Beitar Jerusalem FC football team 2005–09, Tiv Taam supermarkets 2007–; Pres. Hapoel Jerusalem professional basketball team; organized and paid for emergency accommodation for civilians in northern Israel affected by conflict with Lebanon 2006; Founder and Leader Social Justice (Tzedek Hevrati—Za'am) political party 2007–; unsuccessful cand. for Mayor of Jerusalem 2008; Pres. Congress of Jewish Religious Communities and Orgs of Russia; warrant issued for his arrest by French authorities in connection with alleged arms dealing with Angola 2000, acquitted by Court of Appeal 2011; Hon. Pres. World Betar.

GAYE, Lt-Gen. Babacar; Senegalese army officer, diplomatist and UN official; b. 31 Jan. 1951, Saint Louis; s. of Amadou Karim Gaye; m.; two c.; ed École Spéciale Militaire de Saint-Cyr, École Supérieure de Guerre, France; served with UN Emergency Force 1974–75, Commdr, Senegalese contingent, UN Interim Force in Lebanon 1979–80; several posts working for Govt of Senegal, including Dir of Information and Public Relations 1993–94, Dir of Documentation and External Security 1994–97, Commdr, Mil. Zone 6 1997–2000, Chief of Defence Staff 2000–03; Amb. to Germany 2004–05; Commdr UNO Mission in the Democratic Repub. of the Congo 2005–10, UN Mil. Adviser for Peacekeeping Operations 2010–13, Special Rep. to UN Sec.-Gen. for Central African Repub. (BINUCA) 2013–14, Special Rep. to UN Sec.-Gen. and Head, Multidimensional Integrated Stabilization Mission in the Central African Repub. (MINUSCA) 2014–15; attained rank of Lt 1979, Capt. 1981, Commdr 1984, Lt-Col 1988, Col 1991, Brig-Gen. 2000, Div.-Gen. 2002, currently Lt-Gen.; numerous awards including Grand Officier, Ordre nat. du Lion, Croix de la Valeur Militaire, Officier, Légion d'honneur, Officier, Ordre du Mérite (Gabon), several UN medals. *Address:* c/o Department of Peacekeeping Operations, Room S-3727B, United Nations, New York, NY 10017, USA (office).

GAYLE, Christopher Henry (Chris); Jamaican professional cricketer; b. 21 Sept. 1979, Kingston; pnr Natasha Berridge; one d.; all-rounder; left-handed opening batsman; right-arm off-break bowler; plays for Jamaica (domestic) 1998–2008, 2010–, West Indies 1999– (Capt. 2007–08, 2009–10), Worcestershire 2005, Kolkata Knight Riders 2008–10, Western Warriors 2009–11, Royal Challengers Bangalore 2011–17, Sydney Thunder 2011–13, Barisal Burners 2012, Melbourne Renegades 2015–16, St Kitts and Nevis Patriots 2017, Kings XI Punjab 2018–, Multan Sultans 2018–, ICC (Int. Cricket Council) World XI, Stanford Superstars; First-class debut: 1998/99; Test debut: West Indies v Zimbabwe, Port of Spain 16–20 March 2000; One-Day Int. (ODI) debut: India v West Indies, Toronto 11 Sept. 1999; T20I debut: NZ v West Indies, Auckland 16 Feb. 2006; played 103 Tests (to Sept. 2014), scored 7,214 runs (average 42.18) and took 73 wickets (average 42.73) with two triple centuries, one double century, 15 centuries and 37 fifties, highest score 333 against Sri Lanka, Galle 2010, with two five-wicket performances, best bowling 5/34 against England, Birmingham 2004; played 284 ODIs (to July 2018), scored 9,727 runs (average 37.12) and took 165 wickets (average 35.33) with one double century, 23 centuries and 49 fifties, highest score 215 against Zimbabwe, Canberra 2015, with one five-wicket performance, best bowling 5/46 against Australia, St George's 2003; played 56 T20Is (to May 2018), scored 1,607 runs (average 33.47) and took 17 wickets (average 22.17) with two centuries and 13 fifties, highest score 117 against South Africa, Johannesburg 2007, best bowling 2/15 against Australia, Hobart 2010; played 180 First-class matches (to Sept. 2014), scored 13,226 runs (average 44.83) and took 132 wickets (average 39.34) with 32 centuries and 64 fifties, with two five-wicket performances; mem. of the victorious West Indies team that won ICC World Twenty20 Championship in Sri Lanka Oct. 2012; f. The Chris Gayle Acad. 2015; named Player of the Champions Trophy 2006. *Achievements include:* first batsman to score a century in a Twenty20 Int., scoring 117 against S Africa in first match of ICC World Twenty20, South Africa 2007; became first int. player to 'carry his bat' (not out) through entire innings in this format of the game in semi-final match against Sri Lanka in World Twenty20 Tournament 2009; made jt 12th highest Test score of 333 v Sri Lanka, Galle 16 Nov. 2010, one of only four players to have scored two triple centuries at Test level (including 317 against South Africa 2005); first batsman to score a century in three formats of int. cricket; first ever batsman to hit a six off the opening ball of a Test match, against Bangladesh off-spinner Sohag Gazi in Dhaka 14 Nov. 2012; set a new record for the fastest century in professional cricket by reaching 100 off 30 balls for Royal Challengers Bangalore in Indian Premier League T20 against Pune Warriors 2013, went on to record the highest T20 score of 175 not out (17 sixes and 13 fours off 66 balls); first batsman in Cricket World Cup history and fourth cricketer ever to score a double century in ODI history when he reached 200 off 138 balls during the Cricket World Cup v Zimbabwe 2015, finished on 215 runs, partnership with Marlon Samuels was the most productive wicket in Cricket World Cup history, producing 372 runs. *Address:* c/o West Indies Cricket Board Inc., PO Box 616 W, St John's, Antigua. *Telephone:* 481-2450. *Fax:* 481-2498. *E-mail:* wicb@windiescricket.com. *Website:* www.windiescricket.com; www.thechrisgaylefoundation.com.

GAYMARD, Clara; French business executive and author; *President and CEO, General Electric France;* b. 27 Jan. 1960, Paris; d. of Jérôme Lejeune; m. Hervé Gaymard; nine c.; ed Institut d'Études Politiques, Ecole Nationale d'Admin, Paris; Admin. attaché, Office of Mayor of Paris 1982–84; served as auditor and counsellor, State Audit Office 1986–90; Commercial Counsel, Econ. and Commercial Section, embassy in Cairo 1991–93; Head of Europe Bureau 1993–95; Dir Office of Minister for Solidarity between Generations Colette Codaccioni 1995–96; Sub-Dir for Regional Action, PME 1996–99, Head of PME 1999–2003; Chair. Invest in France Agency 2003–06; Pres. and CEO General Electric (GE) France 2006–, Pres. Northwest Europe Region 2008–, Vice-Pres. GE International 2009–, Vice-Pres. in charge of Govt and Cities 2010–; lecturer in public law and general culture; Auditor of 53rd session of IHEDN; Chair. American Chamber of Commerce in France; Pres. Women's Forum for the Economy and Society; Founding mem. Fondation Jérôme Lejeune; mem. bd French-American Foundation; mem. Trilateral Commission; Officier Ordre nat. du mérite, Chevalier Légion d'honneur, Commendatore della Repubblica Italiana. *Publications:* (as Clara Lejeune): La vie est un bonheur, Jérôme Lejeune, mon père 1997, Histoires de femme autres simples bonheurs 1999, S'il suffisait d'aimer 2003. *Leisure interests:* sport, travel, reading. *Address:* General Electric France, 2 rue Pillet Will, 75009 France (office). *Telephone:* 1-43-12-16-16 (office); 1-43-12-78-27 (office). *Fax:* 1-43-12-78-40 (office); 1-47-65-76-90 (office). *E-mail:* alexandra.panseri@ge.com (office). *Website:* www.ge.com/fr (office).

GAYMARD, Hervé, LenD; French politician; *Chairman, Savoie General Council;* b. 31 May 1960, Bourg-Saint-Maurice (Savoie); m.; eight c.; ed Ecole Nationale d'Admin and Institut d'Etudes Politiques, Paris; worked at Budget Ministry 1986–90; Financial Attaché, Cairo Embassy 1990–92; Deputy for Savoie to Nat. Ass. 1993– (RPR then UMP 2002–), mem. Finance Cttee, Vice-Chair. RPR Group; Minister of State for Finance May–Nov. 1995; Minister of State with responsibility for Health and Social Security 1995–97; Minister for Agric., Food, Fisheries and Rural Affairs 2002–04; Minister of the Economy, Finance and Industry 2004–05 (resgnd); Chair. Savoie Gen. Council 1999–2002, 2008–, Vice-Chair. 2002–08; mem. Cttee RPR 1995–98, Political Bureau 1995–2002 (then UMP 2002–05); regional counsellor Rhône Alpes 2004–07; Pres. Assemblée du Pays de Tarentaise Vanoise 2005–; mem. Bd Centre Georges Pompidou. *Publications:* Pour Malraux 1996, La route des Chapieux 2004, Un nouvel usage du monde – Mille et une nuits 2007, Nation et engagements 2010. *Address:* Secrétariat Parlementaire, BP 78 - 5, place Ferdinand Million, 73203 Albertville Cedex (office); Assemblee Nationale, 126 rue de l'Université, 75355 Paris Cedex 07, France (office). *Telephone:* 4-79-32-03-68 (office); 1-40-63-60-00 (office). *Fax:* 4-79-37-82-74 (office); 1-45-55-75-23 (office). *E-mail:* infos@assemblee-nat.fr (office); hervegaymard.savoie@cg73.fr (office). *Website:* www.gaymard-rolland-savoie.com; www.assemblee-nationale.fr (office).

GAYOOM, Maumoon Abdul, MA; Maldivian politician, diplomatist and fmr head of state; *Founder and Chairman, Progressive Party of Maldives (PPM);* b. 29 Dec. 1937, Malé; m. Nasreena Ibrahim 1969; two s. two d.; ed Al-Azhar Univ., Cairo, Egypt; Research Asst in Islamic History, American Univ. of Cairo 1967–69; Lecturer in Islamic Studies and Philosophy, Abdullahi Bayero Coll., Ahmadu Bello Univ., Nigeria 1969–71; teacher, Aminiya School 1971–72; Man. Govt Shipping Dept 1972–73; writer and trans., Press Office 1972–73, 1974; Under-Sec. Telecommunications Dept 1974; Dir Telephone Dept 1974; Special Under-Sec. Office of the Prime Minister 1974–75; Deputy Amb. to Sri Lanka 1975–76; Under-Sec. Dept of External Affairs 1976; Perm. Rep. to UN 1976–77; Deputy Minister of Transport 1976, Minister 1977–78; Pres. of Repub. of Maldives and C-in-C of the Armed Forces and of the Police 1978–2008; Gov. Maldives Monetary Authority 1981–2004; Minister of Defence and Nat. Security 1982–2004, of Finance 1989–93, of Finance and Treasury 1993–2004; Founder and Interim Chair. Progressive Party of Maldives (PPM) 2011–13, Chair. 2013–; mem. Constituent Council of Rabitat Al-Alam Al-Islami; Hon. Leader, Dhivehi Rayyithunge Party (DRP—Maldivian People's Party); Grand Order of Mugunghawa 1984, Hon. GCMG 1997; Hon. DLitt (Aligarh Muslim Univ. of India) 1983, Hon. DrLit (Jamia Millia Islamia Univ., India) 1990, Hon. DLit (Pondicherry Univ.) 1994; UNEP Global 500 Honour Roll 1988, Man of the Sea Award, Lega Navale Italiana 1991, WHO Health-for-All Gold Medal 1998, DRV Int. Environment Award 1998, Al-Azhar Univ. Shield 2002. *Publication:* The Maldives: A Nation in Peril. *Leisure interests:* astronomy, calligraphy, photography, badminton, cricket. *Address:* Progressive Party of Maldives (PPM), Office B, 8th Floor, Sakeenaa Manzil, Medhuziyaaraiyy Magu, Malé 20127, Maldives (office). *Telephone:* 3303838 (office). *E-mail:* ppm.head .office@gmail.com (office). *Website:* www.ppm.mv (office).

GAYSSOT, Jean-Claude; French politician and trade union official; b. 6 Sept. 1944, Béziers (Hérault); s. of Clotilde Founau; m. Jacqueline Guiter 1963; three c.; ed Lycée Technique, Béziers; worked as technician, SNCF (French state railways); official in Railworkers' Union, then in Conféd. générale du travail (CGT) 1976–79; mem. Parti Communiste Français 1963–, mem. Nat. Secr. 1985–, head dept for relations with other political parties and trade union and community movt 1994–; elected municipal councillor, Bobigny (Seine-Saint-Denis) 1977; Nat. Ass. Deputy for 5th Seine-Saint-Denis Constituency 1986–97; Minister for Public Works, Transport and Housing 1997–2002; Mayor of Drancy 1997–2002; Chevalier, Légion d'honneur 2006, Officier, Légion d'honneur 2015; Trombinoscope Prize for Minister of the Year 2000. *Publications:* Le Parti communiste français 1989, Sur ma route 2000. *Address:* Parti Communiste Français, 2 place du Colonel Fabien, 75940 Paris, France.

GAZALI, Lihadh al-, MB, ChB, DCH, MSc, MRCP, FRCP (I), FRCPCH; British geneticist and academic; *Professor in Clinical Genetics and Paediatrics, UAE University;* b. Baghdad, Iraq; ed Baghdad Medical Coll. and Baghdad Univ., Iraq, Royal Coll. of Physicians and Univ. of Edinburgh, UK, Royal Coll. of Physicians, Ireland; Clinical Research Fellow in Clinical Genetics, Univ. of Leeds, UK 1986–90; Asst Prof. in Clinical Genetics, FMHS, UAE Univ. 1990–97, Assoc. Prof. in Clinical Genetics 1997–2003, Prof. in Clinical Genetics and Paediatrics 2003–; Fellow, Royal Coll. of Physicians (Ireland) 1993, Royal Coll. of Paediatrics and Child Health (UK) 1997; Distinguished Performance Award in Research and Clinical Services, UAE Univ. 2003, Laureate for Africa and the Arab States, L'Oréal-UNESCO Awards for Women in Science 2008, Sheikh Hamdan Award for Medical Sciences 2008, Takreem Award in Science & Technology 2014. *Publications:* more than 200 papers in professional journals. *Address:* College of Medicine and Health Sciences, UAE University, PO Box 17666, Al-Ain, United Arab Emirates (office). *Telephone:* (3) 7137415 (office). *Fax:* (3) 7672022 (office). *E-mail:* l.algazali@uaeu.ac.ae (office). *Website:* www.cmhs.uaeu.ac.ae (office).

GAZIT, Maj.-Gen. (retd) Shlomo, MA; Israeli army officer (retd) and university administrator; *Chairman, Galili Centre for Defence-Haganah Studies;* b. 22 Oct. 1926, Turkey; s. of Efrayim Gazit and Zippora Gazit; m. Avigayil-Gala Gazit; one s.

two d.; ed Tel-Aviv Univ.; joined Palmach 1944, Co. Commdr Harel Brigade 1948; Dir Office of Chief of Staff 1953; Liaison Officer with French Army Del., Sinai Campaign 1956; Instructor, Israel Defence Forces (IDF) Staff and Command Coll. 1958–59; Gen. Staff 1960–61; Deputy Commdr Golani Brigade 1961–62; Instructor, Nat. Defence Coll. 1962–64; Head of IDF Intelligence assessment div. 1964–67; Co-ordinator of Govt Activities in Administered Territories, Ministry of Defence 1967–74; attained rank of Maj.-Gen. 1973; Head of Mil. Intelligence 1974–79; Fellow, Center for Int. Affairs, Harvard Univ. 1979–80; Pres. Ben Gurion Univ. of the Negev 1981–85; Dir-Gen. Jewish Agency, Jerusalem 1985–88; Sr Research Fellow, Jaffee Centre for Strategic Studies, Tel-Aviv Univ. 1988–94; Fellow, Woodrow Wilson Center, Washington, DC 1989–90; Distinguished Fellow, US Inst. of Peace, Washington, DC 1994–95; Adviser to Israeli Prime Minister on Palestinian Peace Process 1995–96; Chair. Galili Centre for Defence-Haganah Studies 1996–; Ben-Gurion Award 2012. *Publications include:* Estimates and Fortune-Telling in Intelligence Work 1980, Early Attempts at Establishing West Bank Autonomy 1980, Insurgency, Terrorism and Intelligence 1980, On Hostages' Rescue Operations 1981, The Carrot and the Stick – Israel's Military Govt in Judea and Samaria 1985, The Third Way – The Way of No Solution 1987, Policies in the Administered Territories 1988, Intelligence Estimates and the Decision Maker 1988, (ed.) The Middle East Military Balance 1988–89, 1990–91, 1993–94, Trapped Fools: 30 Years of Israeli Policy in Judea, Samaria and Gaza Strip 2003, The Arab-Israeli Wars: War and Peace in the Middle East 1948–2005 2005, Decisive Junctions - From Palmach to Head IDF Intelligence 2016, Savta Tarngolet (with Osnat-Anita Yoshpe) 2016. *Address:* 58 Enzo Sireni Street, Kfar-Saba 44285 (home); 40 Levanon Street, Tel-Aviv, Israel (office). *Telephone:* (3) 6400400 (ext. 478) (office); (9) 7466554 (home). *Fax:* (3) 7447589 (office); (9) 7416815 (home). *E-mail:* shagaz@inss.org.il (office). *Website:* www.galili.org.il (office).

GAZIZULLIN, Farit Rafikovich, CPhilSc, DSc; Russian/Tatar engineer and politician; b. 20 Sept. 1946, Zelenodolsk, Tatar ASSR; m.; one s.; ed Gorky (now Nizhny Novgorod) Inst. of Water Transport Eng; engineer, Zelenodolsk 1965–67; Comsomol and CP work 1967–87, including First Chair. City Cttee of the Komsomol, Sec., Tatar Oblast Cttee VLKSM, Second Sec., Komsomol Rayon Cttee in Naberezhnye Chelny, Chair. Exec. Cttee of Komsomol Rayon Council; Head of Dept, First Deputy Chair., State Planning Cttee Tatar Autonomous Repub. 1987–95; Vice-Prime Minister of Tatarstan, Chair. State Cttee on Property 1995–96; First Deputy Chair. Cttee on State Property of Russian Fed. 1996–97; Deputy Chair. Govt of Russian Fed. 1997–98; Minister of State Property (temporarily Ministry of Property Relations) 1997–2004; Prof. 2004; mem. Bd of Dirs OAO Gazprom 1998–. *Address:* c/o Board of Directors, OAO Gazprom, 117997 Moscow, 16 Nametkina str., Russia.

GAZMIN, Lt-Gen. (retd) Voltaire Tuvera; Philippine diplomatist, government official and fmr army officer; b. Moncada, Tarlac; s. of Segundo L. Gazmin and Petra T. Gazmin; m. Rhodora Hernandez 1969; ed Univ. of the Philippines, Philippine Mil. Acad., US Army Command and General Staff Coll., Manuel L. Quezon Univ.; served 32 years in various positions in Philippine Army, including Commdr of three Battalions in Mindanao (45th Infantry Bn, 4th Infantry Div. 1979, 26th Infantry Bn, 4th Infantry Div. 1980, 2nd Scout Ranger Bn, First Scout Ranger Regt), Commdr, Presidential Security Group (PSG) 1986–92, Commanding Gen., Philippine Army 1999–2000, retd with rank of Lt-Gen. 2000; fmr Defense and Armed Forces Attaché, Embassy in Washington, DC; Amb. to Cambodia 2002–04; Sec. of Nat. Defense 2010–16; numerous mil. hons including Philippine Legion of Honor. *Publications include:* Defense and Security: Challenges and Prospects 2013, Under the Shadow of the Flag 2014. *Address:* c/o Department of National Defense, DND Building, 3rd Floor, Camp Aguinaldo, Quezon City, 1110 Metro Manila, Philippines (office).

GBAGBO, Laurent, MA, PhD; Côte d'Ivoirian fmr head of state; b. 31 May 1945, Central-Western Prov.; m.; four c.; ed Univ. of Abidjan, Univ. of Lyon, Sorbonne, Paris VII Univ.; taught history and geography at Lycée Classique d'Abidjan 1970–71; imprisoned for unauthorized political activities 1971–73; worked in Dept of Educ. 1973–79; exile in France 1982–88; f. Front populaire Ivoirien (FPI) in secret 1982, FPI Sec.-Gen. 1988–96; mem. Parl. for Ouragahio 1990–2000; arrested Feb. 1992, sentenced to three years' imprisonment under anti-riot law, granted presidential pardon Aug. 1992; Pres. of Côte d'Ivoire Oct. 2000–11 (re-elected Dec. 2010 but election disputed by int. observers including UN Security Council); arrested April 2011 and charged with crimes against humanity; acquitted by Int. Criminal Court (ICC) in The Hague Jan. 2019.

GBEHO, James Victor; Ghanaian lawyer, international organization official and fmr diplomatist; b. 12 Jan. 1935, Keta; s. of Philip Gbeho; worked in Ghana Foreign and Commonwealth Service and later in Ministry of Foreign Affairs and served in various capacities at diplomatic missions abroad as well as in Accra, postings to Missions in China, India, Nigeria, New York (UN), Germany, UK and Geneva (UN), Deputy High Commr to UK 1972–76, Amb. and Perm. Rep. to UN, Geneva, also accred to UNIDO, Vienna 1978–80, IAEA, Vienna, held several posts, including Chair. UNCTAD IV's Cttee on Econ. Cooperation Among Developing Countries (ECDC) held in Manila, Philippines 1979, Chair. Geneva-based UNCTAD Preparatory Cttee for the establishment of the Common Fund for Commodities 1980–82; Perm. Rep. to UN, New York 1980–90, also accred to Cuba, Jamaica and Trinidad and Tobago, held several positions at UN, including Chair. First Cttee (Political and Security), Chair. Fourth Cttee (Decolonisation), Chair. Disarmament Cttee, mem. Anti-Apartheid Cttee and Chair. Sub-cttee on the Implementation of Sanctions against Apartheid South Africa, Chair. Exec. Council of the Int. Convention against Apartheid in Sports, elected to UN Security Council 1986–87, served twice as Pres. of the Council; also served on or led dels of Ghana to Sessions of UN Gen. Ass., Summit Meetings of the Commonwealth Heads of Govt, Commonwealth Ministerial Action Group, Non-Aligned Summit and Ministerial Meetings; has attended several Ministerial and Summit Meetings of OAU, African Union, Econ. Community of West African States (ECOWAS); Dir Non-Aligned Movement Secr., Ministry of Foreign Affairs from 1990, also Dir of State Protocol and also Acting Chief Dir of the Ministry; Special Rep. of UN Sec.-Gen. in Somalia 1994–95; Special Rep. of Chair. of ECOWAS in Liberia 1995–96, led ECOWAS Team that negotiated the Status of Forces Agreement with Govt of Charles Taylor 1996; Deputy Minister of Foreign Affairs 1996–97, Minister of Foreign Affairs 1997–2001; mem. Parl. for Anlo Constituency 2001–04; worked in offices of Flight-Lt Jerry John Rawlings as the fmr Pres.'s Special Asst 2005–08; Adviser on Foreign Affairs to Pres. of Ghana 2008–10; Pres. ECOWAS Comm. 2010–12. *Address:* c/o Ministry of Foreign Affairs and Regional Integration, Treasury Road, PO Box M53, Accra, Ghana. *E-mail:* ghmaf00@ghana.com.

GBEZERA-BRIA, Michel, BL; Central African Republic politician, diplomatist and banker; *Ambassador to France;* b. 1 Jan. 1946, Bossongoa; m.; five c.; ed Brazzaville School of Law, Caen School of Econs and Int. Inst. of Public Admin.; with civil service 1973–, Vice-Minister Sec.-in-charge of diplomatic missions 1975; Deputy Minister of Foreign Affairs 1976; Minister of Public Works, Labour and Social Security 1976–77, of Foreign Affairs 1977–78, of Public Works and Social Security 1978–79; State Comptroller 1979–80, Perm. Rep. to UN, Geneva 1980–83, New York 1983–89; Minister of Justice 1987–88, of Foreign Affairs 1988–90; Prime Minister of Cen. African Repub. 1997–99; Cabinet Dir of the Presidential Palace and Minister of State 2008; Chair. Ecobank Centrafrique 2006–08; Dir Econ. Man. Project 1991; Amb. to France 2015–; received several Hons. *Publications include:* several Publs in Cen. Press. *Leisure interests:* sports, walking. *Address:* Embassy of Central African Republic, 30 rue des Perchamps, 75016 Paris, France (office). *Telephone:* 1-45-25-39-74 (office). *Fax:* 1-55-74-40-25 (office). *E-mail:* accueil@amb-rcaparis.org (office); contact@ambarca-paris.org (office). *Website:* www.ambarca-paris.org/en/node/2 (office).

GBIAN, Jonas Aliou; Benin economist and politician; b. 25 March 1965, Ina, Borgou; m.; three c.; ed Centre Ouest africain de Formation et d'Etudes Bancaires, Dakar, Université Nationale du Bénin; 15 years with Banque Centrale des Etats de l'Afrique de l'Ouest; fmr adviser on econ. affairs to Pres.; Minister of Energy, Mining and Petroleum Research, Water and the Devt of Renewable Energy Sources 2011–12, of Economy and Finance 2012–14. *Address:* c/o Ministry of the Economy and Finance, BP 302, Cotonou, Benin (office).

GBOWEE, Leymah Roberta, AA, MA; Liberian social worker, peace activist and women's rights advocate; *President, Gbowee Peace Foundation Africa;* b. 1 Feb. 1972, Monrovia; d. of Joseph Gbowee and Rachel Gbowee; six c.; ed Mother Patern Coll. of Health Sciences, Monrovia, Eastern Mennonite Univ., Harrisonburg, Va, USA, certifications: Conflict Prevention and Peacebuilding Training at UNITAR, the Healing Victims of War Trauma Centre in Cameroon, Non-Violent Peace Educ. in Liberia; Co-founder and Exec. Dir Women Peace and Security Network Africa (WIPSEN-A); Founding mem. and fmr Liberia Coordinator of Women in Peace-building Network/West Africa Network for Peacebuilding (WIPNET/WANEP); Founder and Pres. Gbowee Peace Foundation Africa; her leadership of Women of Liberia Mass Action for Peace brought together Christian and Muslim women in a non-violent movement that played a pivotal role in ending Liberia's civil war 2003; Commr-designate for the Liberia Truth and Reconciliation Comm. 2004–05; selected by Pres. Johnson Sirleaf to serve as Head of the Liberia Reconciliation Initiative; Africa columnist, Newsweek Daily Beast; Advocate, Sustainable Devt Goals, UN, mem. Sec.-Gen.'s High-Level Advisory Bd on Mediation 2017–; mem. Bd of Dirs Nobel Women's Initiative, PeaceJam Foundation; mem. African Women Leaders Network for Reproductive Health and Family Planning; Hon. LLD (Rhodes Univ., SA), (Univ. of Alberta, Canada); Blue Ribbon for Peace, John F. Kennedy School of Govt, Harvard Univ. 2007, Women's eNews Leaders for the 21st Century Award 2008, Gruber Prize for Women's Rights 2009, John F. Kennedy Profile in Courage Award 2009, John Jay Medal for Justice, John Jay Coll. of Criminal Justice 2010, Living Legends Award for Service to Humanity 2010, Joli Humanitarian Award, Riverdale Country School 2010, Villanova Peace Award, Villanova Univ. 2010, Nobel Peace Prize (jtly) for "non-violent struggle for the safety of women and for women's rights to full participation in peace-building work" 2011, flag-bearer for the Olympic Games Opening Ceremony, London 2012, Oxfam America Right the Wrong Award 2014. *Film:* central character in documentary film Pray the Devil Back to Hell (shown at Tribeca Film Festival, New York) 2008. *Publication:* Mighty Be Our Powers: How Sisterhood, Prayer and Sex Changed a Nation at War (autobiog.). *Address:* Gbowee Peace Foundation Africa, Doe Apartment Bldg, 2nd Floor Suites, Congo Town, Monrovia, Liberia (office). *Telephone:* 776-976584 (mobile) (office). *E-mail:* info@gboweepeaceafrica.org (office).

GE, Honglin; Chinese business executive; *Chairman and CEO, Aluminum Corporation of China (CHALCO); President, China Aluminum Corporation (CHINALCO);* b. 1956, Nantong; ed Beijing Univ. of Science and Tech.; joined CCP 1986; mem. Bd of Dirs and Vice Pres., Shanghai Metallurgical Holdings 1995–98; Mayor of Chengdu City 2001–14; Exec. Chair. and Exec. Dir, Aluminum Corpn of China Ltd (CHALCO) 2015–, Pres. China Aluminum Corpn (CHINALCO) 2015–; fmr Dir and Vice-Gen. Man., Baosteel Group; mem. 13th Nat. Cttee, CPPCC 2018–. *Address:* Aluminum Corporation of China (CHALCO), 62 North Xizhimen Street, Haidian District, Beijing 100082, People's Republic of China (office). *Telephone:* (10) 8229-8103 (office). *Fax:* (10) 8229-8081 (office). *E-mail:* webmaster@chalco.com.cn (office). *Website:* www.chalco.com.cn (office).

GE, You; Chinese actor; b. 19 April 1957, Beijing; s. Ge Cunzhuang and Wenxin Shi; m. Cong He 1987; joined All-China Fed. of Trade Unions Art Troupe 1979. *Films include:* Farewell My Concubine 1993, After Separation (Golden Rooster Award for Best Actor 1993) 1993, To Live 1994 (Cannes Film Festival for Best Actor 1994), The Emperor's Shadow 1996, A World without Thieves 2004, Suffocation 2005, Shanghai Red 2006, The Banquet 2006, Crossed Lines 2007, Let the Bullets Fly 2010, Sacrifice 2010, Personal Tailor 2013, Gone with the Bullets 2014, The Wasted Times 2016.

GEBBIA, Joe, BFA; American designer and business executive; *Co-founder and Chief Product Officer, Airbnb, Inc.;* b. 21 Aug. 1981, Atlanta, Ga; s. of Joe Gebbia and Eileen Gebbia; ed Rhode Island School of Design, Brown Univ.; first job as Designer, Chronicle Books, San Francisco; Co-founder and Chief Product Officer, Airbnb, Inc. 2008–; fmr part-time design partner, Y Combinator (seed fund co.); mem. Bd of Trustees Rhode Island School of Design. *Address:* Airbnb Inc., 888 Brannan Street, Suite 400, San Francisco, CA 94103-4932, USA (office). *Website:* www.airbnb.co.uk (office); joegebbia.com.

GEBEYEHU, Workneh, BA, MA, PhD; Ethiopian politician; *Director-General, United Nations Office at Nairobi (UNON);* b. 16 July 1968, Shashemene, Oromia; ed Addis Ababa Univ., Univ. of South Africa; Dist Chief, Security, Immigration and Refugees Affairs Authority 1993–94, Head of Security, Oromiya Region 1994–96, regional states of Ethiopia 1996–98; Head of Admin and Cabinet mem., Oromiya Regional Council Admin 1999–2000; Commr-Gen., Ethiopian Fed. Police Comm. 2001–12; mem. House of Peoples' Reps (lower house of parl.) 2005–12; mem. Addis Ababa City Council 2012–16; Minister of Transport 2012–16, of Foreign Affairs 2016–19; Dir-Gen. UN Office at Nairobi (UNON) 2019–; mem. Ethiopian People's Revolutionary Democratic Front (EPRDF) and Oromo Peoples' Democratic Org. (OPDO) 1991–, mem. Exec. Cttees 2012–. *Address:* United Nations Office at Nairobi, POB 67578, Nairobi, Kenya (office). *Telephone:* (20) 7621234 (office). *Website:* www.unon.org (office).

GEBREAB, Newaye-Kirstos; Ethiopian central banker; *Chairman, National Bank of Ethiopia;* b. Adwa, Tigray; ed Addis Ababa Univ. Coll., Sidist Kilo; fmr econ. adviser to Prime Minister Meles Zenawi; currently Chair. Nat. Bank of Ethiopia; Order of the Rising Sun, Gold and Silver Star (Japan) 2016. *Address:* Office of the Chairman, National Bank of Ethiopia, Sudan Avenue, POB 5558, Addis Ababa, Ethiopia (office). *Telephone:* (11) 5517438 (office). *Fax:* (11) 5514588 (office). *E-mail:* nbe.gov@ethionet.et (office). *Website:* www.nbe.gov.et (office).

GEBREMARIAM, Haile Tilahun; Ethiopian UN official and fmr military officer; *Head of Mission, United Nations Interim Security Force for Abyei (UNISFA);* b. 1954; m.; three c.; ed Open Univ., UK; long career with Ethiopian Ministry of Defence, including as Chief of Logistics 1996–97, Chief of Admin 1997–98, Deputy Commdr, Ethiopian Air Force 1998–2001, State Minister of Defence 2003–06; several roles in private sector including adviser to Gen. Man. of an engineering co. 2006–11, adviser to an internal audit man. co. 2011–13; Head of Logistics, Ambasel Trading House (agri-business trader), Ethiopia 2013–14; Head of Mission, UN Interim Security Force for Abyei (UNISFA) 2015–. *Address:* United Nations Interim Security Force for Abyei (UNISFA), Abyei Town, Sudan (office). *Website:* www.un.org/en/peacekeeping/missions/unisfa (office).

GEBRSELASSIE, Haile; Ethiopian fmr professional athlete; *President, Ethiopian Athletics Federation;* b. 18 April 1973, Arssi; m. 1996; two c.; set 21 world records or best times indoors and outdoors 1994–98, including world 5,000m and 10,000m records 1997, 1998; silver medal World Jr Cross Country Championships 1992; gold medals World Jr Championships 5,000m and 10,000m 1992; silver medal World Championships 5,000m 1993; gold medal World Championships 10,000m 1995, 1997; gold medal World Indoor Championships 3,000m 1995, 1999, 2003; gold medal Olympic Games 10,000m 1996, 2000, silver medal 2004; winner IAAF World Half-Marathon Championship, England 2001; bronze medal World Championships 10,000m 2001; silver medal World Championships 10,000m 2003; winner Berlin Marathon 2006, 2007, 2008, 2009; 5,000m (indoor and outdoor), 10,000m, 10km road race world record holder, one-hour running event world record holder 2007; indoor record holder for two miles; previous world record holder marathon: 2.03.59; Pres. Ethiopian Athletics Fed. 2016–; IAAF Athlete of the Year 1998. *Leisure interests:* boxing, soccer. *Address:* c/o Jos Hermens, Global Sports Communication, Snelliusstraat 10, 6533 TD Nijmegen, Netherlands (office); Ethiopian Athletics Federation, Gurd Sholla, PO Box 13336, Addis Ababa, Ethiopia (office). *E-mail:* gsc@global-sports-comm.nl (office). *Website:* www.globalsportscommunication.nl (office); www.eaf.org.et (office). *Telephone:* (11) 6479765 (office). *Fax:* (11) 6450879 (office).

GEDVILAS, Vydas, PhD; Lithuanian basketball coach, medical scientist and politician; b. 17 May 1959, Užgiriuose, Kelme dist; m. Elena Gevilienė; one s. one d.; ed Lithuanian State Inst. of Physical Educ.; teacher, Lithuanian Acad. of Physical Educ. (LVKKI) from 1981, Asst Coach, LVKKI men's basketball team 'Atletas' (three times Lithuanian champions) 1988–93, Chief Coach, LKKA women's basketball team 'Viktorija' (Lithuanian and Baltic women's basketball champions) 1993–2004, Vice-Rector LVKKI 2001–04; Head Coach, Lithuanian women's basketball team (European champions) 1996–2002; mem. Labour Party (Darbo Partija) 2004–; mem. Seimas (Parl.) 2004–, Chair. (Speaker) 2012–13, First Deputy Speaker 2013–, mem. Conf. of Chairs 2012–13, Chair. Seimas Del. to the Ass. of Mems of the Seimas of the Repub. of Lithuania, the Sejm and Senate of the Repub. of Poland and the Verkhovna Rada of Ukraine 2012–13; mem. Kaunas City Council 2011–12; mem. Lithuanian Basketball Coaches Asscn; Hon. Pres. Exec. Cttee, Lithuanian Basketball Fed.; Hon. Coach of Lithuania; Order of Grand Duke Gediminas, Third Class. *Publications:* research papers on methodological tools for students and at numerous int. scientific confs. *Address:* Seimas (Parliament), Gedimino pr. 53, Vilnius 01109 (office). *Telephone:* (5) 239-6341 (office). *Fax:* (5) 239-6289 (office). *E-mail:* vydas.gedvilas@lrs.lt (office). *Website:* www.lrs.lt (office).

GEE, E. Gordon; American lawyer and university administrator; b. 2 Feb. 1944; m. 1st Elizabeth D. Gee; one d.; m. 2nd Constance Gee (divorced); ed Columbia Univ.; completed a fed. judicial clerkship; served as Asst Dean for Univ. of Utah Coll. of Law; fmr Judicial Fellow and Sr Staff Asst for US Supreme Court Chief Justice Warren Burger; fmr Assoc. Dean and Prof., J. Reuben Clark Law School, Brigham Young Univ.; Dean Law School, West Virginia Univ. 1979, Pres. West Virginia Univ. 1981–85; Pres. Univ. Colorado at Boulder 1985–90; Pres. Ohio State Univ. 1990–97, 2007–13; Pres. Brown Univ. 1997–2000; Chancellor Vanderbilt Univ. 2000–07; mem. Bd of Dirs Freedom Forum Diversity Inst., Inc., Montgomery Bell Acad., Tennessee Coll. Asscn; mem. Advisory Cttee Nashville Alliance for Public Educ., Pres.'s Council for Imagining America: Artists and Scholars in Public Life, Bd Christopher Isherwood Foundation, Business-Higher Educ. Forum, Nat. Cttee to Unite a Divided America; has carried out research on behalf of Ford Foundation, Guy Anderson Foundation, American Bar Foundation, and others; mem. Circle of Hope; currently Dir or Trustee The Jason Foundation, Nat. Hospice Foundation, Historic Black Coll. and Univ. Advisory Cttee Kresge Foundation, Hasbro, The Limited, Dollar General Corpn, Massey Energy Corpn, Gaylord Entertainment Co.; Trustee Harry S. Truman Scholarship Foundation 1995–; Mellon Fellow, Aspen Inst. for Humanistic Studies, W.K. Kellogg Fellow, Distinguished Alumnus Award, Univ. of Utah 1994, Distinguished Alumnus Award, Teachers' Coll., Columbia Univ. 1994, Outstanding Promotion of Diversity Award, Nashville Br., Nat. Asscn for the Advancement of Colored People, Nashville Women's Political Caucus' Good Guy Award 2004, Apollo Award for Communications Leadership, Public Relations Soc. of America (Nashville chapter) 2004. *Publications:* co-author of six books; numerous papers and articles in fields relating to both law and education. *Address:* c/o Office of the President, Ohio State University, 205 Bricker Hall, 190 North Oval Mall, Columbus, OH 43210-1357, USA.

GEE, Maurice Gough, MA; New Zealand novelist; b. 22 Aug. 1931, Whakatane; m. Margaretha Garden 1970; one s. two d.; ed Avondale Coll., Auckland, Auckland Univ.; school teacher, librarian, other casual employment 1954–75; Robert Burns Fellow, Univ. of Otago 1964; Writing Fellow, Vic. Univ. of Wellington 1989; Katherine Mansfield Memorial Fellow, Menton, France 1992; Hon. DLitt (Victoria) 1987, (Auckland) 2004; NZ Fiction Award 1976, 1979, 1982, 1991, 1993, NZ Book of the Year Award (Wattle Award) 1979, 1993, James Tait Black Memorial Prize 1979, NZ Children's Book of the Year Award 1986, 1995, Prime Minister's Award for Literary Achievement 2004. *Publications include:* Plumb 1978, Meg 1981, Sole Survivor 1983, Collected Stories 1986, Prowlers 1987, The Burning Boy 1990, Going West 1992, Crime Story 1994, Loving Ways 1996, Live Bodies 1998, Ellie and the Shadow Man 2001, The Scornful Moon 2004, Blindsight (Deutz Medal for Fiction 2006, Montana New Zealand Book Award for Fiction 2006) 2005; juvenile fiction includes: Under the Mountain 1979, The O Trilogy 1982–85, The Fat Man 1994, Salt (New Zealand Book Awards for Young Adult Fiction 2008) 2007, Gool 2008, Access Road 2009, The Limping Man 2010; also scripts for film and TV. *Address:* 56 Nile Street, 7010 Nelson, New Zealand (home).

GEENS, Koenraad (Koen) Frans Julia, DrIur; Belgian lawyer, academic and politician; *Minister of Justice;* b. 22 Jan. 1958, Brasschaat; m. Griet Dupré; three c.; ed Univ. of Antwerp, Katholieke Universiteit (KU) Leuven, Harvard Univ., USA; Lecturer, Faculty of Law, KU Leuven 1986–93, Assoc. Prof. 1993–, Dir Jan Ronse Inst. for Company Law 1986–, Chair. Dept of Econ. Law 2009–, mem. Organizing Govt, KU Leuven and KU Leuven Asscn 2010–; Chair. Bd of Govs. Thomas More Colls (Antwerp, Mechelen and Kempen) 2010–; Founding Partner Eubelius (law firm) 1994–2013; Chief of Staff for Flemish Minister-Pres. Kris Peeters 2007–09; Minister of Finance and of Sustainable Devt, in charge of the Civil Service 2013–14, Minister of Justice 2014–; mem. Chamber of Reps; Co-ordinator, Flanders in Action 2020 2007–09, Chair. Council of the Wise 2010–13; Pres. Fed. of Liberal and Intellectual Professions 1999–2005; mem. Flemish Council for Science and Innovation 2010–12, Belgian Corp. Governance Cttee 2007–13; Founding Co-Ed. Tijdschrift voor Rechtspersoon en Vennootschap; Co-Ed. Beginselen van Belgisch privaat recht 2013–; mem. Bd of Dirs Thomas More Colls Antwerp, Mechelen and Kempen 2010–, VZW Le Concert Olympique 2010– (Chair. 2010–13), BNP Paribas Fortis NV 2011–13; mem. Christen-Democratisch en Vlaams (CD&V); mem. Royal Flemish Acad. of Belgium for Science and Arts, Humanities Class 2012, Academia Europaea 2013. *Publications include:* Vennootschapsrecht (in Beginselen van Belgisch Privaat Recht) (with M. Wyckaert), Encyclopaedia of Laws, Corporations and Partnerships (co-ed.), Commentaar Vennootschapsrecht (co-ed.), Wetboeken Story Scienta (ed.), Overzichten van rechtspraak vennootschapsrecht, Tijdschrift voor Privaatrecht (co-author), Beginselen van Belgisch privaat recht (co-ed.) 2013. *Address:* Federal Public Service of Justice, 115 Blvd de Waterloo, 1000 Brussels, Belgium (office). *Telephone:* (2) 542-80-11 (office). *Fax:* (2) 542-80-03 (office). *E-mail:* info@just.fgov.be (office). *Website:* www.just.fgov.be (office); www.koengeens.be.

GEERLINGS, Perry F. M.; St Maarten politician; *Minister of Finance;* b. 22 Nov. 1960; ed Amsterdam Univ., Netherlands Inst. of Int. Relations, Clingendael, European Acad. for Taxes, Econs and Law; Chair. Supervisory Bd, Stichting Kadaster en Hypotheekwezen, St Maarten 2004–11; Policy Advisor and Deputy Dir, Cabinet of Minister Plenipotentiary 2011–12, Cabinet Dir 2013–17; Chair. Stichting Soualiga (non-profit org.) 2011–; Country Expert, Royal Tropical Inst., Amsterdam 2012–; mem. States (Parl.) 2017–; Minister of Finance 2018–; mem. United Democrats. *Address:* Ministry of Finance, Government Administration Building, 1 Soualuiga Road, Great Bay, Sint Maarten (office). *E-mail:* perrysxm@yahoo.com (office). *Website:* www.sintmaartengov.org; perrygeerlings.com (office).

GEFFEN, David Lawrence; American film, recording and theatre executive; b. 21 Feb. 1943, Brooklyn, New York; s. of Abraham Geffen and Batya Geffen (née Volovskaya); ed New Utrecht High School, Brooklyn, Univ. of Texas, Brooklyn Coll.; joined William Morris talent agency as mail clerk 1964, promoted to jr agent; launched new film studio with Steven Spielberg (q.v.) and Jeffrey Katzenberg (q.v.); f. music publishing co. Tunafish Music, with Laura Nyro; joined Ashley Famous Agency, then apptd Exec. Vice-Pres. Creative Man. (now Int. Creative Man.) 1968; f. Asylum Records and Geffen-Roberts Man. Co. with Elliot Roberts 1970, sold Asylum to Warner Communications, but remained Pres. 1971, merged it with Elektra, signed Bob Dylan and Joni Mitchell, Vice-Chair. Warner Brothers Pictures 1975–76; taught business studies at Yale Univ.; f. Geffen Records, Pres. 1980, signed Elton John, John Lennon and Yoko Ono and many others, sold label to Music Corpn of America Inc. 1990; f. Geffen Film Co.; Co-producer musical Dreamgirls 1981–85, Cats 1982, M. Butterfly 1986, Social Security, Chess 1990, Miss Saigon; f. DGC record label 1995; Co-founder and Prin. Dreamworks SKG 1994–2008; f. David Geffen Foundation 1986; Ahmet Ertegun Award, inducted into Rock and Roll Hall of Fame 2010, President's Merit Award for Indelible Contrib. to the Music Industry, Nat. Acad. of Recording Arts and Sciences 2011. *Address:* c/o David Geffen Foundation, 12011 San Vincente Blvd., Suite 606, Los Angeles, CA 90049-4926, USA.

GEHLOT, Ashok, BSc, LLB, MA; Indian politician; *Chief Minister of Rajasthan;* b. 3 May 1951, Mahamandir, Jodhpur, Rajasthan; s. of Lachman Singh Gehlot; m. Sunita Gehlot 1977; one s. one d.; worked in refugee camps at Bangaon and 24 Parganas dists (West Bengal) during liberation war of Bangladesh 1971; Pres. Rajasthan Nat. Students' Union of India 1974–79; City District Congress Cttee 1979–82; mem. Indian Nat. Congress party; mem. Lok Sabha (Parl.) 1980–89, 1991–99, Public Accounts Cttee 1980–82, Consultative Cttee on Communication 1991–96, Standing Cttee on Railways 1991–98, Consultative Cttee on External Affairs 1996–98; mem. Rajasthan Legis. Ass. 1999–; Union Deputy Minister, Dept of Tourism 1982–83, of Tourism and Civil Aviation 1983–84, 1984–85, of Sports 1984; Minister Dept of Home and Public Health Eng, Govt of Rajasthan 1989; Union Minister of State, Dept of Textiles 1989; Chief Minister of Rajasthan 1998–2003, 2008–13, 2018–; Gen. Sec. Rajasthan Pradesh Congress Cttee (Pres. 1997–99); Gen. Sec. in-Charge for Gujarat Congress 2017–; mem. various Indian dels abroad, including to China as mem. All India Congress Cttee del. 1994, Leader Indian del. to Commonwealth Youth Affairs to Cyprus, Indian del. to Bulgaria, visited various countries, including Bangkok, Ireland, Frankfurt, USA (as mem. Indian del. to UN and for RIC convention), Canada, Hong Kong, UK, Italy, Dubai, France; Founder-Pres. Bharat Seva Sansthan; Chair. Rajiv Gandhi Study Circle,

New Delhi. *Address:* Chief Minister Office, Secretariat, Jaipur 302005 (office); 13, Civil Lines, Jaipur 302006 (home); Gujarat Pradesh Congress Committee, Rajiv Gandhi Bhavan, Sanskar Kendra Marg, Ellisbridge, Ahmedabad 380 006, India (office). *Telephone:* (141) 2227656/47 (Jaipur) (office); (141) 2229900/4400 (Jaipur) (home); (79) 26578212/13 (office). *Fax:* (141) 2227687 (Jaipur) (office); (141) 2222521 (Jaipur) (home). *E-mail:* cmrajasthan@nic.in (office); gpcc1234@gmail.com (office); cmoffice.rajasthan.gov.in. *Website:* www.gujaratcongress.in (office).

GEHRIG, Bruno, Dr rer. pol; Swiss economist, academic and insurance industry executive; b. 26 Dec. 1946; m.; three c.; ed Univ. of Berne, Univ. of Rochester, NY, USA; Asst, then Lecturer on Econs, Univ. of Berne 1970–78, Asst Prof. 1978–80; Head of Econs Section, Union Bank of Switzerland (UBS) 1981–84, with Stock Markets and Securities Sales Div., UBS Group 1986–88, Head of Div. 1988–89, mem. Bd of Dirs UBS AG 2008–12; Chair. Exec. Bd, Bank Cantrade, Zürich 1989–91; Prof. of Business Admin and Head of Swiss Inst., Univ. of St Gallen 1992–96; apptd mem. Governing Bd, Swiss Nat. Bank 1996, Head of Dept III 1996–2001, Vice-Chair. Governing Bd 2001–03; Chair. Swiss Life Holding 2003–09; Deputy Chair. F. Hoffmann-La Roche AG 2003–13; Chair. Swiss International Airlines Ltd 2010–16; Chair. Econ. Policy Study Group, Swiss Christian Democratic Party (CVP) 1984–91; Chair. Bd of Trustees Swiss Air Transport Foundation; mem. Swiss Fed. Banking Comm. 1992–96; mem. Bd of Dirs Maerki Baumann & Co. AG 2014–, Kartause Ittingen, Canton of Thurgau, Switzerland, Investec Bank AG; mem. Bd of Trustees Antidoping Switzerland; Hon. LLD (Univ. of Rochester, NY) 2006.

GEHRING, Gillian Anne, OBE, MA, DPhil, FInstP; British physicist and academic; *Professor Emeritus of Physics, University of Sheffield;* b. 19 May 1941, Nottingham, England; d. of H. L. (Max) Murray and F. Joan Murray; m. Karl A. Gehring 1968; two d.; ed Univs of Manchester and Oxford; Leverhulme Postdoctoral Research Fellowship, St Hugh's Coll., Oxford 1965–67; NATO Fellowship, Univ. of California, Berkeley, USA 1967–68; Fellow and Tutor in Physics, St Hugh's Coll., Oxford 1968–70; CUF Lecturer in Theoretical Physics, Univ. of Oxford 1970–89; Prof. of Physics, Univ. of Sheffield 1989–2007, Prof. Emer. 2007–; Leverhulme Emer. Fellow 2007–09, 2012–14; Hon. mem. European Physical Soc. 2010, Hon. Fellow, St Hugh's Coll., Oxford, Hon. Fellow, Inst. of Physics; Hon. DSc (Salford) 1994, (Sheffield) 2012, (Hull) 2013. *Publications:* research papers on theoretical condensed matter physics. *Leisure interest:* family activities. *Address:* Department of Physics and Astronomy, University of Sheffield, Hicks Building, Hounsfield Road, Sheffield, S3 7RH (office); Flat 3, West Royd, 119 Manchester Road, Sheffield, S10 5DN, England (home). *Telephone:* (114) 222-4299 (office). *E-mail:* g.gehring@sheffield.ac.uk (office). *Website:* www.shef.ac.uk/physics/people/ggehring (office).

GEHRY, Frank Owen, CC, BArch, FAIA; Canadian/American architect; b. (Ephraim Owen Goldberg), 28 Feb. 1929, Toronto, Canada; s. of Irving Gehry and Thelma Caplan; m. 1st Anita Snyder (divorced); two d.; m. 2nd Berta Aguilera 1975; two s.; ed Univ. of Southern California and Harvard Univ. Grad. School of Design; designer, Victor Gruen Assocs, LA 1953–54, Planning, Design and Project Dir 1958–61; Project Designer and Planner, Pereira & Luckman, LA 1957–58; Design Prin. Frank O. Gehry & Assocs, Santa Monica, Calif. 1962–; f. Gehry Partnership LLP 2002; f. Gehry Technologies Inc. (building industry tech. co.); architect for Temporary Contemporary Museum 1983, Calif. Aerospace Museum 1984, Loyola Law School 1981–84, Frances Howard Goldwyn Regional Br. Library 1986, Information and Computer Science Eng Research Facility, Univ. of Calif. Irvine 1986, Vitra Furniture Mfg Facility and Design Museum, Germany 1989, Chiat/Day HQ, Venice, Calif. 1991, American Center, Paris 1992–94, Weisman Art Museum, Minneapolis 1993, Disney Ice, Anaheim 1995, EMR Communication & Tech. Centre, Bad Oeynhausen, Germany 1995, Team Disneyland Admin., Anaheim 1996, ING Office Bldg, Prague 1996, Guggenheim Museum, Bilbao 1997, Experience Music Project, Seattle 2000, Walt Disney Concert Hall, LA 2003, Maggie's Cancer Care Centre, Dundee 2003, bandshell, Millennium Park, Chicago 2004, IAC HQ 2006; Fellow, American Inst. of Architects, American Acad. of Arts and Letters, American Acad. of Arts and Sciences; Charlotte Davenport Chair. Yale Univ. 1982, 1989; Eliot Noyes Design Chair. Harvard 1984; currently Distinguished Prof., Grad. School of Architecture, Planning and Preservation, Columbia Univ.; Dr hc (Calif. Coll. of Arts and Crafts) 1987, (Rhode Island School of Design) 1987, (Tech. Univ. of Nova Scotia) 1989, (Calif. Inst. of Arts), (Otis Art Inst., Parsons School of Design) 1989, (Occidental Coll.) 1993, (Whittier Coll.) 1995, (Southern Calif. Inst. of Architecture) 1997, (Univ. of Toronto) 1998, (Univ. of Edinburgh) 2000, (Univ. of Southern Calif.) 2000, (Yale Univ.) 2000, (Harvard Univ.) 2000, (School of The Art Inst. of Chicago) 2004; Arnold W. Brunner Memorial Architecture Prize 1983, Pritzker Architecture Prize 1989, shared Wolf Prize 1992, Imperial Prize (Japan) 1992, Lillian Gish Award 1994, National Medal of Arts 1998, Kiesler Prize for Architecture and the Arts 1998, Gold Medal of Inst. of Architects 1999, Gold Medal for Architecture, American Acad. of Arts and Letters 2002, Royal Fine Art Comm. Trust Building of the Year Award 2004, Woodrow Wilson Award for Public Service 2004, Prince of Asturias Award for Arts 2014, Presidential Medal of Freedom 2016. *Film appearance:* The Cool School 2007. *Publications:* Individual Imagination and Cultural Conservatism 1995, Gehry Draws 2005. *Address:* Gehry Partners LLP, 12541 Beatrice Street, Los Angeles, CA 90066 (office); Frank O. Gehry & Associates, 1520-B Cloverfield Boulevard, Santa Monica, CA 90404 (office). *Telephone:* (310) 482-3000 (office). *Fax:* (310) 482-3006 (office). *Website:* www.gehrypartners.com (office).

GEIDUSCHEK, E(rnest) Peter, PhD; American biologist and academic; *Consulting Professor, Department of Structural Biology, Stanford University;* b. 11 April 1928, Vienna, Austria; s. of Sigmund Geiduschek and Frieda Tauber; m. Joyce B. Brous 1955; two s.; ed Columbia and Harvard Univs; Instructor in Chem., Yale Univ. 1952–53, 1955–57; Asst Prof. of Chem., Univ. of Mich. 1957–59; Asst Prof. of Biophysics and Research Assoc. in Biochemistry, Univ. of Chicago 1959–62, Assoc. Prof. of Biophysics and Research Assoc. in Biochemistry 1962–64, Prof. of Biophysics and Research Assoc. in Biochemistry 1964–70; Prof. of Biology, Univ. of Calif., San Diego 1970–94, Chair. 1981–83, Acting Chair 1994, Research Prof., Dept of Biological Sciences 1994–2014, Prof. Emer. 2014–; Consulting Prof., Dept of Structural Biology, Stanford Univ. 2014–; mem. Bd of Scientific Counselors, Nat. Cancer Inst., NIH 1998–2003; European Molecular Biology Org. (EMBO) Lecturer 1977, Hilleman Lecturer, Univ. of Chicago 1978, Paul Doty Lecturer, Harvard Univ. 1993, Adriano Buzzati-Traverso Lecture, Rome 1996; Jean Weigle Lecture, Geneva 2001; Lalor Foundation Faculty Fellow, Yale 1957, Guggenheim Fellow, Inst. de Biologie Moléculaire, Geneva 1964–65; mem. NAS, American Acad. of Arts and Sciences; Fellow, AAAS, Acad. of Microbiology (USA); Grande Ufficiale, Ordine al Merito della Repubblica Italiana 1997; Gregor Mendel Medal, Acad. of Sciences of the Czech Repub. 2004. *Publications include:* primarily numerous articles on molecular biology, biochemistry and virology. *Address:* Stanford University, Department of Structural Biology, Fairchild Center, 229 West Campus Drive, Stanford, CA 94305, USA (office). *Telephone:* (650) 728-9246 (office). *E-mail:* epg@stanford.edu (office); epg@ucsd.edu (office). *Website:* www.biology.ucsd.edu (office).

GEIGER, Helmut; German banker and lawyer; b. 12 June 1928, Nuremberg; m.; one s. one d.; ed Univs of Erlangen and Berlin; legal asst, Deutsche Bundestag and asst lawyer, Bonn 1957–59; lawyer in Bonn and man. of office of Öffentliche Bausparkassen 1959–66; Man. Dir Deutsche Sparkassen-und Giroverband 1966–72, Pres. 1972–93; Pres. Int. Inst. der Sparkassen (Int. Savings Bank Inst.), Geneva 1978–84; Pres. EEC Savings Banks Group, Brussels 1985–88; Chair. Sparkassenstiftung für Int. Kooperation 1992–98; mem. Bundestag 1965; Chair. and mem. of various charitable and professional bodies; Grand Fed. Cross of Merit; Dr hc (Cologne). *Publications include:* Herausforderungen für Stabilität und Fortschritt 1974, Bankpolitik 1975, Gespräche über Geld 1986, Die deutsche Sparkassenorganisation 1992 and numerous publs on banking matters. *Address:* Simrockstr. 4, 53113 Bonn, Germany. *Telephone:* (228) 9703610.

GEIM, Sir Andre Konstantinovich, Kt, MSc, PhD, FRS; British/Dutch (b. Russian) physicist and academic; *Royal Society 2010 Anniversary Research Professor and Regius Professor of Physics, University of Manchester;* b. 21 Oct. 1958, Sochi, Russian SFSR, USSR; s. of Konstantin Alekseyevich Geim (Heim) and Nina Nikolayevna Bayer; m. Irina V. Grigorieva; ed Moscow Inst. of Physics and Tech., Inst. of Solid State Physics, USSR (now Russian) Acad. of Sciences, Chernogolovka; worked as research scientist at Inst. for Microelectronics Tech., Russian Acad. of Sciences, Chernogolovka 1987–90, then as post-doctoral fellow at Univs of Nottingham and Bath, UK and at Univ. of Copenhagen, Denmark 1990–94; Assoc. Prof., Radboud Univ., Nijmegen 1994–2001, Prof. of Innovative Materials and Nanoscience 2010–; Prof. of Physics, Univ. of Manchester, UK 2001–07, Langworthy Research Prof. of Physics 2007–13, Royal Society 2010 Anniversary Research Prof. 2010–, Regius Prof. of Physics 2013–, Dir Manchester Centre for Mesoscience and Nanotechnology 2002–; EPSRC Sr Research Fellow 2007–; Prof. of Innovative Materials and Nanoscience, Radboud Univ. Nijmegen 2010–; Foreign Assoc. NAS 2012; Corresponding mem. Royal Netherlands Acad. of Arts and Sciences; Hon. Prof., Nat. Univ. of Singapore, Moscow Phys-Tech, Univ. of Nijmegen; Einstein Prof., Chinese Acad. of Sciences; Hon. FInstP; Hon. FRSC; Hon. Fellow, Singapore Inst. of Physics; Kt Commdr, Order of the Netherlands Lion 2010; Dr hc (Delft Univ. of Tech., ETH Zurich, Univ. of Antwerp, Univ. of Manchester); Ig Nobel Prize (jtly) 2000, Mott Prize, Inst. of Physics 2007, Europhysics Prize (jtly) 2008, Körber European Science Award 2009, named by Thomson-Reuters amongst the top 10 most active, "hottest" researchers 2009–11, NAS John J. Carty Award for the Advancement of Science 2010, Hughes Medal 2010, Royal Soc. 2010 Anniversary Research Professorship 2010, Nobel Prize in Physics (with Konstantin Novoselov) 2010, Niels Bohr Medal 2011, Copley Medal, Royal Soc. 2013. *Achievements include:* best known for his discovery, with Konstantin Novoselov, of two-dimensional crystals made of carbon atoms (and most notably graphene) in 2004 at Univ. of Manchester; original jt paper on graphene in Science in 2004 acknowledged by ISI citation index as "one of the most cited recent papers in the field of physics"; earlier experiments on diamagnetic levitation publicized by worldwide media and featured in textbooks, famously levitated a frog; also well known for demonstrating a new microfabricated adhesive based on the same physics mechanism underlying the climbing ability of geckos. *Publications:* more than 150 peer-refereed research papers, including many in Nature and Science, on condensed matter physics. *Address:* Room 2.14, Schuster Building, The School of Physics and Astronomy, University of Manchester, Manchester, M13 9PL, England (office). *Telephone:* (161) 275-4120 (office). *E-mail:* andre.k.geim@manchester.ac.uk (office). *Website:* www.manchester.ac.uk/research/Andre.k.geim (office); www.condmat.physics.manchester.ac.uk/people/academic/geim (office).

GEINGOB, Hage Gottfried, MA; Namibian politician; *President;* b. 3 Aug. 1941, Grootfontein Dist; m. Loine Kandume 1993 (divorced); one s. three d. from previous m.; ed Augustineum Coll. Okahandja, Temple Univ., Fordham Univ. and The New School, New York, USA, Univ. of Leeds, UK; joined SWAPO 1962; teacher, Tsumeb 1962; exiled for political activities Dec. 1962; became SWAPO Asst Rep. Botswana 1963–64; subsequently moved to USA, studied at Fordham Univ. and New School for Social Research, New York and became SWAPO Rep. at UN –1971; mem. SWAPO Politburo 1975, Vice-Pres. SWAPO 2007–; Dir UN Inst. for Namibia, Lusaka, Zambia 1975–89; returned to Namibia as Election Dir 1989; Chair. Constituent Ass. and Namibia Independence Celebrations Cttee 1989; Prime Minister 1990–2002, 2012–15; Pres. 2015–; Exec. Sec., Global Coalition for Africa, Washington, DC 2003–04; mem. Parl. 2004–; Minister of Trade and Industry 2008–12; Chair. 14th Meeting of Experts on the UN Programme in Public Admin and Finance 1998; mem. Int. Bd of Govs, Centre for Int. Governance Innovation of Canada 2004–; mem. Bd of Dirs, Trustco Group Holdings 2006–; Officier des Palmes académiques 1980; Ongulumbashe Medal for bravery and long service 1987; Order of Carlos Manuel de Cespedes (Cuba) 1994; Order of the Sun, 1st Class (Namibia) 1994; Hon. LLD (Colby Coll., Chicago) 1994, (Univ. of Delhi) 1995, (Univ. of Namibia) 1997; Hon. DHumLitt (American Univ. of Rome) 1998; African Gender Award 2018. *Leisure interests:* playing tennis, reading, watching soccer and rugby. *Address:* Office of the Prime Minister, Robert Mugabe Avenue, PMB 13338, Windhoek, Namibia (office). *Telephone:* (61) 2879111 (office). *Fax:* (61) 226189 (office). *Website:* www.opm.gov.na (office).

GEISS, Johannes, Dr rer. nat; Swiss physicist and academic; *Honorary Director, International Space Science Institute;* b. 4 Sept. 1926, Stolp, Pomerania, Poland; s. of Hans Geiss and Irene Wilke; m. Carmen Bach 1955; one d.; ed Univ. of Göttingen, Germany; Research Assoc., Enrico Fermi Inst., Univ. of Chicago, USA 1955–56; Assoc. Prof., Marine Lab., Univ. of Miami, USA 1958–59; Assoc. Prof., Univ. of Berne 1960, Prof. of Physics 1964–91, Dir Inst. of Physics 1966–90;

Visiting Scientist, NASA Goddard Inst. for Space Studies, New York 1965, NASA Manned Spacecraft Center, Houston 1968–69; Chair. Launching Programme Advisory Cttee, ESA, Paris 1970–72; Visiting Prof., Univ. of Toulouse 1975; Chair. Space Science Cttee, European Science Foundation 1979–86; Exec. Dir Int. Space Science Inst. 1995–2002, Hon. Dir 2003–; Adjunct Prof., Univ. of Michigan; Rector, Univ. of Berne 1982–83; Fellow, American Geophysical Union; Foreign mem. American Acad. of Arts and Sciences, NAS, Max-Planck-Inst. für Aeronomie, Int. Acad. of Astronautics, Max-Planck-Inst. für Kernphysik, Austrian Acad. of Sciences, Academia Europaea; Dr hc (Univ. of Chicago); NASA Medal for Exceptional Scientific Achievement, Leonard Medal 1983, Allan D. Emil Memorial Award 1989, Sir Harry Massey Medal 1992, Albert Einstein Medal 2001, William Bowie Medal 2004. *Publications:* over 300 publs on nucleosynthesis, cosmology, the origin of the solar system, geochronology, climatic history of the earth, the age of meteorites and lunar rocks, comets, solar wind, solar terrestrial relations. *Address:* International Space Science Institute, Hallestr. 6, 3012 Berne, Switzerland (office). *Telephone:* (31) 6313253 (office). *Fax:* (31) 6314897 (office). *E-mail:* Geiss@issibern.ch (office). *Website:* www.issibern.ch (office).

GEITHNER, Timothy Franz, AB, MA; American banking executive, economist and fmr government official; *President and Managing Director, Warburg Pincus LLC;* b. 18 Aug. 1961, Brooklyn, New York; m. Carole M. Sonnenfeld; one s. one d.; ed Dartmouth Coll., Johns Hopkins School of Advanced Int. Studies; worked for Kissinger Assocs, Inc., Washington, DC 1985–88; joined US Treasury Dept 1988, served in several positions in Int. Affairs Div. including Under-Sec. of Treasury for Int. Affairs 1999–2001; Sr Fellow in Int. Econs, Council on Foreign Relations, Washington, DC Feb.–Aug. 2001; Dir Policy Devt and Review Dept, IMF, Washington, DC 2001–03; Pres. and CEO Fed. Reserve Bank of New York 2003–09, Vice-Chair. and Perm. mem. Fed. Open Market Cttee 2003–09; US Sec. of the Treasury, Washington, DC 2009–13; Pres. and Man. Dir Warburg Pincus LLC (pvt. equity firm) 2014–, also mem. Exec. Man. Group; mem. Council on Foreign Relations, Distinguished Fellow 2013–; mem. Bd of Dirs Center for Global Devt, Washington, DC, Nat. Acad. Foundation 2007–; mem. Bd of Trustees RAND Corpn 2006–08; Trustee, Econ. Club of New York. *Publication:* Stress Test: Reflections on Financial Crises 2014. *Address:* Warburg Pincus LLC, 450 Lexington Avenue, New York, NY 10017, USA (office). *Telephone:* (212) 878-0600 (office). *Fax:* (212) 878-9351 (office). *Website:* www.warburgpincus.com (office).

GELB, Bruce S., MBA, Hon. PhD; American business executive and administrator; *Chairman, Council of American Ambassadors;* b. 24 Feb. 1927, New York; s. of Lawrence M. Gelb and Joan Gelb; m. Lueza Gelb; four c.; ed Yale Univ., Harvard Business School; served in the US Navy; Vice-Chair. Bristol-Myers Co. 1977–85, now Sr Consultant; Dir US Information Agency 1989–91, Amb. to Belgium 1991–93; Commr for the UN, Consular Service and Int. Business, New York 1994–97; Pres. Wilson Council (pvt. sector advisory group for Woodrow Wilson Int. Center for Scholars) —2006, also mem. Wilson Center Bd of Trustees 2003–; fmr mem. Pres. Bush's Arts and Humanities Cttee; fmr mem. Bd of Trustees John F. Kennedy Center for the Performing Arts, Howard Univ.; Vice-Chair. Exec. Cttee Madison Square Boys' and Girls' Club; Life Trustee Choate Rosemary Hall School, CT; mem. Bd of Dirs UN Devt Corpn for New York City; currently Chair. Council of American Ambassadors. *Address:* Council of American Ambassadors, 888 17th Street, NW, Suite 306, Washington, DC 20006, USA (office). *Telephone:* (202) 296-3757 (office). *Fax:* (202) 296-0926 (office). *E-mail:* council@americanambassadors.org (office). *Website:* www.americanambassadors .org (office).

GELB, Peter; American business executive, film and television producer and arts administrator; *General Manager, Metropolitan Opera;* b. 1953; s. of Arthur Gelb and Barbara Gelb; m. Keri-Lynn Wilson; two s. (from a previous m.); fmr Man., Vladimir Horowitz; Pres. Sony Classical USA 1993–95, Pres. Sony Classical Int. Operations 1995–2005; Gen. Man. Metropolitan Opera, New York 2006–; Officier, Ordre des Arts et des Lettres 2010, Chevalier, Légion d'honneur 2013; Dr hc (Macaulay Honors Coll., CUNY) 2008; Emmy Award for Outstanding Classical Program in the Performing Arts 1987, 1990, 1991, Emmy Award for Outstanding Individual Achievement in Int. Programming 1991, Int. Documentary Asscn Award 1991, Grammy Award 2002, Diplomacy Award, Foreign Policy Asscn 2012, Sanford Prize, Yale School of Music 2013. *Address:* The Metropolitan Opera, Lincoln Center, New York, NY 10023, USA (office). *Telephone:* (212) 799-3100 (office). *Website:* www.metopera.org (office).

GELBER, (J.) David, BA; American media executive; *Co-founder and Managing Director, Roaring Fork Films;* b. 1941, New York; s. of Isaac Gelber and Florence Gelber; m. Kyoko Inouye 2001; two d.; ed Swarthmore Coll.; worked several years with Pacifica Radio in 1970s; fmr TV reporter and producer, Boston, Chicago and New York; fmr Exec. Producer, Peter Jennings Reporting, ABC News; consultant, Soros Foundation 1996; with CBS News 1976–2011, Exec. Producer, Ed Bradley on Assignment and 60 Minutes; mem. Bd of Mans Swarthmore Coll.; Co-founder and Man. Dir Roaring Fork Films 2011–; Peabody Award 2000. *TV productions include:* While America Watched: The Bosnia Tragedy (Emmy, DuPont Award), The Peacekeepers: How the UN Failed in Bosnia (Emmy, DuPont Award), Ed Bradley on Assignment: Town Under Siege 1997 (named by Time Magazine Award as one of 10 Best TV shows of the year), CBS News 60 Minutes II: The Church on Trial 2003 (Emmy Award for Outstanding Coverage of a Feature News Story in a News Magazine), Years of Living Dangerously (Emmy Award for Outstanding Documentary or Nonfiction Series, Environmental Media Awards for Outstanding Achievement for Environmental Content) 2014. *Address:* Roaring Fork Films, 630 9th Avenue, New York, NY 10036-3708, USA (office). *Telephone:* (646) 410-0440 (office). *Website:* www.roaringforkfilms.com (office).

GELDOF, Bob; Irish rock singer and songwriter; b. 5 Oct. 1954, Dublin; m. Paula Yates 1986 (divorced 1996, died 2000); three d. (one deceased); ed Blackrock Coll.; worked in several casual jobs, including lorry driving, busking, teaching English, working in factory, etc., then journalist on pop music paper, Georgia Strait, Vancouver, Canada; later journalist for New Musical Express, Melody Maker; returned to Dublin and f. rock group, Boomtown Rats 1975–84; solo artist 1986–; organized recording of Do They Know It's Christmas? by Band Aid, raising money for African famine relief Nov. 1984, f. Band-Aid Trust (incorporating Live Aid, Band Aid, Sport Aid) to distribute proceeds 1984, Chair.; organized Live Aid concerts in Wembley Stadium, London and JFK Stadium, Philadelphia, USA with int. TV link-up by satellite 13 July 1985, raised £40 million for famine relief in Africa; f. Live Aid Foundation, USA; organized publ. of Live Aid book The Greatest Show on Earth 1985; Owner, Planet 24 (TV production co.) 1990–99; Co-founder and Dir (non-exec.) Ten Alps PLC (now Zinc Media) 2001–; mem. Africa Comm. 2004–; organized re-recordings of Do They Know It's Christmas?, raising money for African famine relief 2004, 2014; organized Live 8 concerts in London, Philadelphia, Paris, Rome and Berlin, with int. TV link-up by satellite, to highlight ongoing problem of global poverty and debt 2 July 2005, The Long Walk to Justice, Edinburgh, Scotland, to present leaders of G8 Summit at Gleneagles with plan to double aid, drop debt and make trade laws fair 6 July 2005; Patron, Exeter Entrepreneurs Society, Univ. of Exeter; Freeman of Ypres 1986; Hon. KBE 1986, Elder of the Repub. of Tanzania; Dr hc (Ghent) 1986, (Univ. Coll. Dublin) 2005; Hon. DLit (London) 1987; Hon. DCL (Newcastle) 2007; Hon. MA (Univ. for the Creative Arts) 2010; Hon. DPhil (Ben-Gurion Univ. of the Negev) 2011; Order of Two Niles (Sudan), Order of Leopold II (Belgium), Irish Peace Prize, UN World Hunger Award, EEC Gold Medal, four Ivor Novello Awards, MTV Video Awards Special Recognition Trophy 1985, American Music Awards Special Award of Appreciation 1986, Third World Prize 1986, BRIT Award for Outstanding Contrib. to Music 2005, Golden Rose Charity Award (Switzerland) 2005, MTV Europe Free Your Mind Award 2005, Man of Peace Award 2005, Nichols-Chancellor's Medal, Vanderbilt Univ. 2008. *Film appearances include:* Pink Floyd – The Wall 1982, Number One 1985, Sketches of Frank Gehry 2006, Oh My God 2009. *Recordings include:* albums: with Boomtown Rats: The Boomtown Rats 1977, A Tonic For The Troops 1978, The Fine Art Of Surfacing 1979, Mondo Bongo 1981, V Deep 1982, In the Long Grass 1984; solo: Deep In The Heart Of Nowhere 1986, The Vegetarians Of Love 1990, The Happy Club 1993, Sex Age And Death 2001, How to Compose Popular Songs That Will Sell 2011. *Publications include:* Is That It? (autobiog.) 1986, Geldof in Africa 2005. *Address:* c/o Amanda Hon, PO Box 13995, London, W9 2FL, England (office); Zinc Media, 13th Floor, Portland House, Bressenden Place, London, SW1E 5BH, England. *Telephone:* (20) 7289-7331 (office). *E-mail:* amanda .hon@dsl.pipex.com (office); enquiries@bobgeldof.com. *Website:* www.bobgeldof .com.

GELDYMYRADOV, Khojamyrat; Turkmenistani politician; Deputy Minister of the Economy and Finance 2005–07, Co-ordinator of Int. Tech. Aid to Turkmenistan 2005–07, Deputy Prime Minister responsible for Econ. Affairs 2007–09.

GELETA, Bekele, BA, MEconSc; Ethiopian/Canadian fmr diplomatist and international organization official; b. 1 July 1944, Nedjo, Oromia; s. of Geleta and Alemi Dinsa; m. Tsehay Mulugeta; four s.; ed Addis Abba Univ., Univ. of Leeds, UK; began career with Ethiopian Roads Authority; fmr Gen.-Man. Franco-Ethiopian Railway Co.; political prisoner, Addis Ababa 1978–81; Urban Devt Officer, Irish Concern Int. 1982; Sec.-Gen., Ethiopian Red Cross 1984–88; Vice-Minister of Transport and Communications 1988–91; Amb. to Japan 1991; moved to Canada as refugee 1992; programme man. for Kenya and Somalia, Care Canada 1995–96; various positions within Int. Fed. of Red Cross and Red Crescent Socs (IFRC) 1996–2007 including Head of Africa Dept 1996, Secr., Geneva, Deputy Head, IFRC del. to UN, New York, Head of regional del. in Bangkok 2004, Gen.-Man. Int. Operations, Canadian Red Cross, Sec.-Gen. IFRC 2008–14.

GELL-MANN, Murray, PhD; American physicist and academic; *Professor and Distinguished Fellow, Sante Fe Institute;* b. 15 Sept. 1929, New York City; s. of Arthur Gell-Mann and Pauline (Reichstein) Gell-Mann; m. 1st J. Margaret Dow 1955 (died 1981); one s. one d.; m. 2nd Marcia Southwick 1992 (divorced 2005); one step-s.; ed Yale Univ., Massachusetts Inst. of Tech.; mem. Inst. for Advanced Study, Princeton 1951, 1955, 1967–68; Instructor, Asst Prof. and Assoc. Prof., Univ. of Chicago 1952–55; Assoc. Prof., Calif. Inst. of Tech. 1955–56, Prof. 1956–66, R. A. Millikan Prof. of Theoretical Physics 1967–93, R. A. Millikan Prof. Emer. 1993–; Research Assoc. Univ. of Illinois 1951, 1953; Visiting Assoc. Prof. Columbia Univ. 1954; Visiting Prof. Collège de France and Univ. of Paris 1959–60, Mass. Inst. of Tech. 1963, European Council for Nuclear Research 1971–72, 1979–80, Univ. of NM 1995–; Consultant, Inst. for Defense Analyses, Arlington, Va 1961–70, RAND Corpn, Santa Monica, Calif. 1956; Overseas Fellow, Churchill Col, Cambridge, England 1966; mem. NASA Physics Panel 1964, President's Science Advisory Cttee 1969–72, Council on Foreign Relations 1975–, President's Council of Advisors on Science and Tech. 1994–2001; Consultant to Los Alamos Scientific Laboratory, Los Alamos, NM 1956–, Laboratory Fellow 1982–; Citizen Regent, Smithsonian Inst. 1974–88; Chair. Western Center, American Acad. of Arts and Sciences 1970–76; Chair. of Bd Aspen Center for Physics 1973–79; Founding Trustee Santa Fe Inst. 1982, Chair. Bd of Trustees 1982–85, Co-Chair. Science Bd 1985–2000, Prof. and Distinguished Fellow 1993–; mem. Bd Calif. Nature Conservancy 1984–93, J. D. and C. T. MacArthur Foundation 1979– (Chair. World Environment and Resource Cttee 1982–97), Lovelace Insts 1993–95; mem. Science and Grants Cttee, Leakey Foundation 1977–88, NAS, American Physical Soc. 1960–, American Acad. of Arts and Sciences 1964–, American Philosophical Soc. 1993–, Science Advisory Cttee, Conservation Inst. 1993, AAAS 1994–, Advisory Bd Network Physics 1999–; Hon. mem. French Physical Soc. 1970; Foreign mem. Royal Soc. 1978–, Pakistan Acad. of Sciences 1985–, Indian Acad. of Sciences 1985–, Russian Acad. of Sciences 1993–; Hon. ScD (Yale) 1959, (Chicago) 1967, (Illinois) 1968, (Wesleyan) 1968, (Utah) 1970, (Columbia) 1977, (Cambridge Univ.) 1980, (Oxford Univ.) 1992, (Southern Illinois Univ.) 1993, (Univ. of Florida) 1994, (Southern Methodist Univ.) 1999; Dr hc (Turin, Italy) 1969; Dannie Heineman Prize, American Physical Soc. 1959, Ernest O. Lawrence Award 1966, Franklin Medal 1967, John J. Carty Medal, NAS 1968, Nobel Prize in Physics 1969, Research Corpn Award 1969, UNEP Roll of Honor for Environmental Achievement 1988, Erice Prize 1990, Sigma Xi Procter Prize for Scientific Achievement 2004, Ellis Island Family Heritage Award 2005, Albert Einstein Medal 2005. *Achievements include;* developed strangeness theory, theory of neutral K mesons, eightfold way theory of approximate symmetry; current algebra, quark scheme; contributed to theory of dispersion relations, theory of weak interaction and formulation of quantum chromodynamics. *Publications:* (with Yuval Ne'eman) The Eightfold Way 1964, The Quark and the Jaguar 1994. *Leisure interests:* historical linguistics, wilderness trips, ornithology, numismatics. *Address:* c/o Santa Fe Institute, 1399 Hyde Park Road, Santa Fe, NM 87501, USA (office). *Telephone:* (505) 984-8800. *Fax:* (505) 982-0565. *E-mail:* mgm@santafe.edu (office). *Website:* www.santafe.edu/sfi/people/mgm (office).

GELLERT, Jay M., BA; American healthcare industry executive; *President and CEO, Health Net Inc.;* b. 13 March 1954, New York; ed Stanford Univ.; Sr Vice-Pres. and COO California Healthcare System 1985–88; Pres. and CEO Bay Pacific Health Corpn (HMO) 1988–91; Advisor, Shattuck Hammond Pnrs –1996; Pres. and COO Health Systems Int. Inc. (HIS, later Health Net Inc.) 1996–97, Dir 1996–97, Exec. Vice-Pres. and COO Health Net Inc. April–May 1997, Pres. and CEO 1998–, also COO May–Aug. 1998; mem. Bd of Dirs Ventas 2001–, America's Health Insurance Plans (Chair. 2008–), Council for Affordable Quality Healthcare. *Address:* Health Net Incorporated, 21650 Oxnard Street, Woodland Hills, CA 91367, USA (office). *Telephone:* (818) 676-6000 (office). *Fax:* (818) 676-8591 (office). *E-mail:* jay.m.gellert@health.net (office). *Website:* www.healthnet.com (office).

GEMAYEL, Amin Pierre; Lebanese politician; b. 10 Nov. 1942, Bikfayya; s. of Pierre Gemayel; brother of Bashir Gemayel; m. Joyce Tyan; two s. (one deceased) one d.; ed St Joseph Univ., Beirut; mem. Parl. 1970–82; Pres. of Lebanon 1982–88; moved to USA 1988, to France 1989, back to Lebanon 2000; The House of the Future, The Amin Gemayel Educational Foundation, Le Reveil newspaper; Pres. Al-Kataeb (Lebanese Social Democratic Party) 2008–15. *Address:* Al-Kataeb, POB 992, place Charles Hélou, Beirut, Lebanon (office). *Telephone:* (1) 584107 (office). *Website:* www.kataeb.org (office).

GEMEDA, Gen. Abedula, MA; Ethiopian army officer and politician; b. (Minasse Woldegiorgis), 5 July 1958, Arsi; ed Defense Univ. of China, Century Univ., Greenwich Univ.; career in Ethiopian Armed Forces, fmr Head of Operation and Information Dept, fmr Head of Defence Intelligence Unit –2001 (resgnd); fmr Minister of Defence; Chair. Oromo People's Democratic Org.; Pres. Oromia Regional Govt 2005–10; Speaker, House of People's Reps (Parl.) 2010–17.

GEMKOW, Stephan, MBA; German business executive; *Chairman of the Managing Board, Franz Haniel & Cie. GmbH;* b. 23 Jan. 1960; ed Universität Paderborn, St Olaf Coll., Northfield, MN; began career as man. consultant for BDO Deutsche Warentreuhand AG; held various management positions at Lufthansa Group from 1990, mem. Man. Bd responsible for Finances 2006–12, for Aviation Services 2009–12; Chair. Man. Bd and Group Human Resources Officer, Franz Haniel & Cie. GmbH 2012–; Chair. Supervisory Bd Lufthansa Systems AG 1990, Celesio AG 2012–14; mem. Supervisory Bd Evonik Industries AG 2007–17, GfK SE 2009–11; mem. Bd of Dirs Amadeus IT Group 2006–13, 2018–, JetBlue Airways Corpn 2008–, Flughafen Zürich AG 2017–; mem. Advisory Bd Takkt AG 2013–, HSBC Trinkaus & Burkhardt AG 2014–; mem. Comm. of Exchange Experts. *Address:* Franz Haniel & Cie. GmbH, Franz-Haniel-Platz 1, 47119 Duisburg, Germany (office). *Telephone:* (203) 806-0 (office). *Fax:* (203) 806-496 (office). *E-mail:* info@haniel.de (office). *Website:* www.haniel.de (office).

GENACHOWSKI, Julius, BA, JD; American lawyer, business executive and fmr government official; *Managing Director, The Carlyle Group;* b. 19 Aug. 1962; m. Rachel Goslins; ed Columbia Coll., Columbia Univ., Harvard Law School; Law Clerk to Chief Judge Abner Mikva, US Court of Appeals for DC Circuit 1991–92, to US Supreme Court Justice William J. Brennan Jr 1992, to US Supreme Court Justice David Souter 1993–94; Chief Counsel to Chair. Fed. Communications Comm. (FCC) 1994–97, fmr Sr Official, Chair. FCC 2009–13 (resgnd); worked with mems of US Congress 1995–98, including as mem. Congressional Cttee investigating Iran-Contra Affair; Gen. Counsel and Sr Vice-Pres. of Business Devt, USA Broadcasting 1997–2000; Vice-Pres. of Corp. Devt Ticketmaster Online-Citysearch, Inc. 2000; Sr Vice-Pres. and Gen. Counsel USA Networks Inc, InterActiveCorp 2000–02, Exec. Vice-Pres. and Gen. Counsel 2002, Chief of Business Operations and mem. Office of the Chair. IAC/InterActive Corpn 2003–06; Special Adviser, General Atlantic LLC, Greenwich, Conn. 2006–09; Man. Dir The Carlyle Group 2014–; mem. Bd of Dirs The Motley Fool, Web.com, Mark Ecko Enterprises, Beliefnet, Common Sense Media; fmr mem. Bd of Dirs Expedia, Hotels.com, Ticketmaster, Truveo, Rapt; mem. of Advisory Bd Environmental Entrepreneurs (E2); fmr Sr Fellow, Aspen Inst. *Address:* The Carlyle Group, 1001 Pennsylvania Avenue, NW, Washington, DC 20004, USA (office). *Telephone:* (202) 729-5800 (office). *Website:* www.carlyle.com (office).

GENBA, Koichiro; Japanese politician; b. 20 May 1964, Tamura, Fukushima Pref.; ed Sophia Univ., Matsushita Inst. of Govt and Man.; mem. Fukushima Prefectural Ass. 1991–93; mem. House of Reps for Fukushima No. 2 Dist (New Party Sakigake) 1993–96, for Tōhoku (Democratic Party of Japan—DPJ) 1996–2000, for Fukushima No. 3 Dist 2000–; mem. New Party Sakigake 1993–96; Founder mem. DPJ 1996–, fmr Deputy Sec.-Gen., Chair. Election Campaign Cttee, Policy Research Council 2010–11; Minister of State for Civil Service Reform 2010, for Social Affairs and Gender Equality 2010, for Nat. Policy 2010–11, for Space Policy and Science and Tech. Policy 2011, Minister of Foreign Affairs 2011–12. *Leisure interests:* watching films, reading, sports. *Address:* Democratic Party of Japan, 1-11-1, Nagata-cho, Chiyoda-ku, Tokyo 100-0014, Japan (office). *Telephone:* (3) 3595-9988 (office). *Fax:* (3) 3595-9961 (office). *E-mail:* dpjenews@dpj.or.jp (office). *Website:* www.dpj.or.jp (office).

GENDREAU-MASSALOUX, Michèle; French public servant and organization official; *Rector Emeritus, Agence Universitaire de la francophonie (AUF);* b. 28 July 1944, Limoges; d. of François Massaloux and Marie-Adrienne Delalais; m. Pascal Gendreau 1970; ed Ecole Normale Supérieure de Jeunes Filles, Sèvres, Inst. d'Etudes Politiques, Paris; univ. teacher, Sorbonne, Villetaneuse (Paris XIII), then Univ. of Limoges (fmr Vice-Pres.); Rector Acad. d'Orléans-Tours 1981–84; Tech. Adviser to Secr.-Gen. for Nat. Educ. and Univs., Presidency of the Repub., then to Secr.-Gen. for Admin. Reform and Improvement of Relations between Public Services and their Users, Deputy Sec.-Gen. 1985–88, Spokesperson 1986–88, Head of Mission May 1988; Rector, Acad. de Paris 1989–98; Conseiller d'Etat 1998; mem. Comm. Nat. de la Communication et des Libertés 1988–89, French Comm. for UNESCO 1991, Conseil orientation Ecole du Louvre 1991, Council, Coll. Univ. Français de Moscou 1991, Council, Coll. Univ. Français de Saint-Petersbourg 1992, Conseil Scientifique de la Cinquième 1996; mem. Comm. de contrôle des sondages 1999; Rector, Agence Universitaire de la francophonie (AUF), Paris 1999–2007, now Emer.; mem. interministerial mission, Union for the Mediterranean, in charge of higher education, research, training and health issues; Prof. Univ. Paris VIII–Vincennes St-Denis 1999–; Dr hc (Univ. of Aberdeen, Univ. of Chile, Laval Univ., Univ. of Moldova, New York Univ., Univ. of Toronto, Univ. of Sofia, Univ. of Bucharest, Univ. of Moncton, Univ. of Ouagadougou); Chevalier, Légion d'honneur, Officier, Ordre Nat. du Mérite, Chevalier, Ordre des Palmes Académiques. *Publication:* Recherche sur l'Humanisme de Francisco de Quevedo 1977, works and translations concerning the Spanish Golden Age. *Leisure interest:* music. *Address:* Agence Universitaire de la francophonie (AUF), 4 place de la Sorbonne, 75005, Paris (office); Conseil d'Etat, 75100 Paris 01 SP (office); 34 rue de Penthièvre, 75008 Paris, France (home). *Telephone:* 1-44-41-18-18 (office). *Fax:* 1-44-41-18-19 (office). *E-mail:* recteur@auf.org (office). *Website:* www.auf.org (office).

GENERALOV, Sergey Vladimirovich; Russian politician and business executive; *President, Industrial Investors;* b. 7 Sept. 1963, Simferopol; ed Moscow Inst. of Energy, Higher School of Man. at State Acad. of Man.; Commercial Dir TET 1991–92; Deputy Chair. NIPEBANK 1992–93; Head of Div., Head of Dept, Promradtechbank 1993; Vice-Pres. YUKOS Oil Co., 1993–97, ROSPROM-YUKOS 1997; Deputy Chair. MENATEP 1997–98; Minister of Fuel and Power Eng of Russian Fed. 1998–99; mem. State Duma 1999–2003, faction Right-Wing Forces; Head State Duma Comm. for Protection of Investors' Rights –2002; Dir Fuel and Energy Complex Investments Agency 1999–2000; Co-Chair., Russian Public Asscn 2001–; Chair. Int. Advisory Bd, Russia Partnership for Responsible Business Practices 2006–; Pres. Industrial Investors 2003–; Pres. and CEO, FESCO Transportation Group Ltd 2009–12; Pres. and CEO Far-Eastern Shipping Co. PLC 2011–12, Chair. 2012–13; mem. Transport and Telecommunications Devt Comm. 2008–, Maritime Bd 2011–. *Address:* Industrial Investors, Berkeley Square House, 8th Floor, London, W1J 6DB, England (office). *Telephone:* (20) 76474000 (office). *Fax:* (20) 76474001 (office). *E-mail:* contact@industrial-investors.com (office). *Website:* www.industrial-investors.com (office).

GENG, Huichang; Chinese politician; b. 1951, Hebei Prov.; Deputy Dir Univ. of Int. Relations, American Research Dept, Beijing Municipality 1985–90, Dir 1990–92; Head, China Inst. of Contemporary Int. Relations 1992–98; Vice-Minister of State Security 1998–2007, Minister of State Security 2007–16; mem. Nat. Energy Comm. 2010–; Deputy Dir Subcommittee for Hong Kong, Macao, Taiwan and Overseas Chinese, CPPCC 2016–; mem. 17th CCP Cen. Cttee 2007–12, 18th CCP Cen. Cttee 2012–, Cen. Politics and Law Comm., CCP 2017–, Leading Small Group (LSG) for Foreign Affairs Work, CCP 2017–, LSG for Taiwan Affairs, CCP 2017–.

GENISARETSKY, Oleg Igorevich; Russian sociologist and organization executive; b. 28 Feb. 1942, Kovrov, Vladimir region; ed Moscow Inst. of Physics and Eng, Moscow State Univ.; researcher, All-Union Inst. of Tech. Aesthetics 1965–93; apptd Deputy Dir Inst. of Man., Russian Acad. of Sciences 1993; Pres. Open Museum Asscn, Russian Asscn of Visual Anthropology; CEO Inst. of Synergetic Anthropology; Prof., Inst. of Corp. Entrepreneurship, Higher School of Econs; Triumph Prize. *Publications include:* numerous publs on theory and methods of system and artistic design, ecology of culture, aesthetic educ., theoretical sociology of culture and psychology of creativity.

GENNETTE, Jeffrey, BA; American retail executive; *Chairman and Chief Executive Officer, Macy's, Inc.;* b. 1961, San Diego; m.; one d.; ed Stanford Univ.; joined Macy's West, San Francisco as Exec. Trainee 1983, becoming Vice Pres. and Div. Merchandise Man. for men's collections, later Sr Vice Pres. and Gen. Merchandise Man. for men's and children's collections, Exec. Vice Pres. and Dir of Stores, Macy's Central, Atlanta 2004, Chair. and CEO Macy's Northwest, Seattle 2006–08, Chair. and CEO, Macy's West 2008–09, Chief Merchandising Officer, Macy's, Inc. 2009–14, Pres., Macy's, Inc. 2014–17, CEO 2017–, also Chair. 2018–; mem. Bd of Trustees, Brooklyn Public Library 2011–16; mem. Bd and Exec. Cttee, Partnership For New York City 2016–. *Address:* Macy's, Inc., 7 West Seventh Street, Cincinnati, Ohio 45202, USA (office). *Telephone:* (513) 579-7000 (office). *Fax:* (513) 579-7095 (office). *Website:* www.macysinc.com (office).

GENNIMATA, Fofi; Greek politician; *Chairman, Panellínio Socialistiko Kinima (PASOK—Panhellenic Socialist Movement);* b. 17 Nov. 1964, Athens; d. of Georgios Gennimatas; m. Andreas Tsounis; three c.; ed Univ. of Athens; mem. socialist student union at univ.; mem. Panellínio Socialistiko Kinima (PASOK—Panhellenic Socialist Movement), mem. Cen. Cttee 2001–04, mem. Exec. Bureau and the Political Council 2003–09, Pres. Super-Pref. of Athens and Piraeus 2002, 2006, Spokesperson for PASOK 2012, Chair. PASOK 2015–; mem. Vouli (Parl.) for Athens A 2000–02, for Athens B State list 6–19 May 2012, 2015–; blocked by Supreme Court from standing as a PASOK cand. in legis. elections because she had not finished her term as a local govt official 2007; Deputy Minister of Health and Welfare 2009–10; Alt. Minister of Educ., Lifelong Learning and Religious Affairs 2010–11. *Address:* Panellínio Socialistiko Kinima (PASOK), Odos Hippocrates 22, 106 80 Athens, Greece (office). *Telephone:* (210) 3665000 (office). *Fax:* (210) 3665209 (office). *E-mail:* pasok@pasok.gr (office); f.gennimata@parliament.gr (office); gennimata@gmail.com. *Website:* www.pasok.gr (office); www.fofigennimata.gr.

GENOVÉS, Juan; Spanish artist; b. 31 May 1930, Valencia; ed Escuela Superior de Bellas Artes, Valencia; has taken part in numerous group exhbns; solo exhbns in Spain, Portugal, USA, Italy, Germany, Netherlands, Japan, UK, Cuba, Puerto Rico, Canada, Switzerland, France and S America 1957–; took part in Paris Biennale 1961, Venice Biennale 1962, 1966, São Paulo Biennale 1965; works in collections and museums in Germany, SA, Guinea, Australia, Austria, Belgium, Brazil, Canada, Colombia, Cuba, Spain, Finland, France, Netherlands, England, Israel, Italy, Japan, Mexico, Nicaragua, Poland, Switzerland, USA and Venezuela; Gold Medal, San Marino Biennale 1967, Premio Marzotto Internazionale 1968, Premio Nacional de Artes Plásticas 1984, Valencian Art Prize 2002, Gold Medal, Spanish Culture Dept 2005, Personalities Award, Centre for Contemporary Culture 2010, Julian Besteiro Award 2012, Valencia Arts Award, Awards of Culture 2013. *Address:* Arandilla 17, 28023 Aravaca, Madrid, Spain (home). *Website:* www.juangenoves.com/en.

GENSLER, Gary, BS, MBA; American fmr government official; b. 18 Oct. 1957, Baltimore, Md; s. of Sam Gensler and Jane Gensler (née Tilles); m. Francesca Danieli 1986 (died 2006); three d.; ed Wharton School, Univ. of Pennsylvania; joined The Goldman Sachs Group, LP (int. investment banking firm) in 1979, worked in Mergers and Acquisition Dept 1979–84, assumed responsibility for firm's efforts advising media cos 1984–88, Pnr 1988–97, joined Fixed Income Div. and directed Goldman's Fixed Income and Currency trading efforts in Tokyo –1995, Co-head of Finance for Goldman Sachs world-wide 1995–97; Asst US Sec. of the Treasury for Financial Markets, Washington, DC 1997–99, also served as a sr mem. Treasury Financing Group and Working Group on Financial Markets, Under-Sec. of the Treasury for Domestic Finance 1999–2001; fmr Sr Advisor to US Senator Paul Sarbanes; Sr Advisor to Senator Hillary Clinton's presidential campaign and, after Democratic Primary, to Barack Obama's presidential campaign 2008; Chair. US Commodity Futures Trading Comm., Washington, DC 2009–14; Chief Financial Officer, Hillary Clinton's presidential campaign 2015–; Tamar Frankel Fiduciary Prize 2014. *Publication:* The Great Mutual Fund Trap: An Investment Recovery Plan (with Gregory Arthur Baer) 2002. *Leisure interests:* running, mountain climbing. *Website:* www.hillaryclinton.com (office).

GENTIL DA SILVA MARTINS, António (Tony), MD; Portuguese pediatric and plastic surgeon and pediatric oncologist; b. 10 July 1930, Lisbon; s. of António Augusto da Silva Martins and Maria Madalena Gentil da Silva Martins; m. Maria Guilhermina Ivens Ferraz Jardim 1963; three s. five d.; ed Univ. of Lisbon; Medical Faculty 1953, Univ. of Lisbon, Course of Pedagogical Sciences 1954; intern, Hospitais Civis, Lisbon; fmr House Surgeon, Hosp. for Sick Children, London and Registrar, Alder Hey Children's Hosp., Liverpool, UK; Founder and Head, Pediatric Oncology multidisciplinary Dept, Instituto Português de Oncologia de Lisboa Francisco Gentil 1960–87, apptd Consultant in Surgical Pediatric Oncology 1987; Pediatric surgeon, Hosp. D. Estefânia (Children's Hosp.), Lisbon 1965, Dir of Pediatric Surgery 1987–2000; Assoc. Prof. of Pediatric Surgery, Faculty of Medical Sciences, Lisbon 1986–2000; Temporary Consultant, Pediatric Cancer, WHO 1977, EEC 1991; Pres. Portuguese Soc. of Plastic and Reconstructive Surgery 1968–74, Ordem dos Médicos (Portuguese Medical Asscn) 1978–86, Portuguese Asscn of Pediatric Surgeons 1975–84, 1991–94, World Medical Asscn 1981–83, Southern Br. Portuguese League Against Cancer 1988–94, Portuguese League Against Cancer 1995–97; Founder-Acreditar Int. Confed. of Children's Cancer Parents Orgs, Council Deputy mem. 1994–95; Founder and Hon. mem. Int. Soc. of Pediatric Oncology (SIOP), Int. Soc. of Pediatric Surgical Oncology (IPSO); Hon. mem. and Vice-Pres. Gen. Ass., Nat. Confed. of Portuguese Family Asscns 2004–08; Founder and Hon. mem. Portuguese Fed. of Badminton 1956, Int. Coll. of Surgeons 1965, Vice-Pres. 2004–06 (Founder and Pres. Portuguese Section 2005–07); mem. Exec. Council World Fed. of Asscns of Pediatric Surgeons 1983–89, Council Int. Conf. of Childhood Cancer Parent Orgs 1994–95; Founder and Pres. Portuguese Olympic Athletes Asscn 2003–12, 2017–; Founder CAVITOP (Center for Support of Victims of Torture Portugal) 2002–; Pres. Gen. Ass. PASC-Casa da Cidadania (Platform of Socs. Civil Society-House of Citizenship); mem. Emer. Portugal Acad. of Medicine; mem. numerous other professional socs; Hon. mem. Portuguese League against Cancer, AMI (Int. Medical Assistance), Portuguese Cancer League; mem. of Merit Int. Football Club (CIF); Grande Oficial da Ordem do Infante D. Henrique 1980, Great Cross 2009, Order of Henry the Navigator; Silva Pereira Award 1972, awarded Silver Plate for film on separation of conjoined twins 1980, Keys of Miami and Dale County 1983, Diploma of Honour, Cuban Medical Asscn in Exile 1983, Gold Medal Ministry of Health 2001, Medal of Honour, Portuguese Medical Asscn 2002, Ordem dos Médicos 2002, Medal of Our Lady of Vila Viçosa 2007; Merit Prize for prevention in oncology 2014, Miller Guerra Prize for Hospital Humanism 2015, Prize for Ethics in Sports and numerous other awards. *Achievements include:* separation of six pairs of conjoined twins with nine survivors, developed multiple surgical techniques. *Films:* Separation of Siamese Twins, Vaginoplasty with Labia Minora, Partial Nephrectomy for Unilateral Wilms Tumours, A So-called Inoperable Neuroblastoma, and others. *Publications include:* Le Médecin et les droits de l'homme (co-author) 1982, textbook on Plastic Surgery of the Ibero-Latin-American Foundation of Plastic Surgery (co-author) 1986 (revised edn 2008), Head and Neck Cancer in Children, Elementos de Psiquiatria da Criança e do Adolescente, O Médico e a Eutanásia, Atlas of Pediatric Surgery (co-author), Psychosocial Issues in Pediatric Cancer (co-author), Educação pelo Desporto; Pediatric chapter in Textbook of Surgery 2006, Atlas of Pediatric Surgery (co-author), Medical Associations and Human Rights, Pediatric Urology (co-author). *Leisure interests:* target-shooting (rapid fire pistol, Olympics, Rome 1960, Portuguese rifle champion and record holder), volleyball (Portuguese champion), lawn tennis (Portuguese Jr Champion, men's doubles), table tennis, badminton (Lisbon Champion Mix-Doubles), table tennis, collecting stamps and coins, music (classical), photography. *Address:* Rua de Campolide 166G, 1070-037 Lisbon (office); Av. Almirante Reis 242, 000-057 Lisbon, Portugal (home). *Telephone:* (21) 384-1860 (office); (21) 848-9540 (home); 93-9555162 (mobile). *E-mail:* agentilmartins@gmail.com.

GENTILI, Stève; French business executive; *Vice-Chairman of the Supervisory Board, Groupe BPCE;* ed Collège des sciences sociales et économiques; began career at French Ministry of Finance; dir of a major agribusiness co. –2004; Chair. Bred Banque Populaire 2004–; Vice-Chair. Supervisory Bd Groupe BPCE –2014, 2015–, Chair. 2014–15; adviser, Bd of Dirs Natixis; Chair. Econ. Org. of the Summit of the Heads of State of French-speaking countries. *Address:* Groupe BPCE, 50 avenue Pierre Mendès France, 75201 Paris Cedex 13, France (office). *Telephone:* 1-58-40-41-42 (office). *E-mail:* info@bpce.fr (office). *Website:* www.bpce.fr (office).

GENTILONI SILVERI, Paolo; Italian journalist and politician; b. 22 Nov. 1954, Rome; m. Emanuela Mauro; ed Liceo Tasso, Rome; Ed. La Nuova ecologia (monthly journal) 1984–93; fmr Spokesman for Mayor of Rome and Councillor for Tourism and the Jubilee; mem. Chamber of Deputies (Parl.) for Lazio 1 2001–, mem. Foreign Affairs Cttee 2013–, Chair. Italy-USA Inter-Parl. Union; Minister of Communications 2006–08, of Foreign Affairs 2014–16, Prime Minister 2016–18, acting Minister for Regional Affairs and Autonomy 2017–18; Chair. Supervisory Cttee RAI (public broadcasting co.) 2005–06; fmr mem. Ulivo political group, Campaign Dir 2001; mem. La Margherita (political party) 2002–07; mem. Partito Democratico (PD) 2007–, mem. Founding Cttee. *Leisure interests:* tennis, opera. *Address:* Partito Democratico, Via Sant'Andrea delle Fratte 16, 00187 Rome, Italy (office). *Website:* www.partitodemocratico.it (office).

GENTLE, Angus, BSc, BSc (Hons), BE, PhD; Australian physicist and academic; *Research Officer and Lecturer, School of Mathematical and Physical Sciences, University of Technology Sydney;* worked at Univ. of Tech. Sydney 2000, undertook part-time research during undergraduate degrees; postdoctoral work at School of Photovoltaics and Renewable Energy Eng, Univ. of New South Wales 2008; Postdoctoral Fellow, Univ. of Tech. Sydney 2009, currently Research Officer and Lecturer, School of Math. and Physical Sciences; World Tech. Award (Environment) (co-recipient) 2015. *Publications:* numerous papers in professional journals. *Address:* University of Technology Sydney, City Campus, 15 Broadway, Ultimo, NSW 2007, Australia (office). *Telephone:* (2) 9514-7373 (office). *E-mail:* angus.gentle@uts.edu.au (office). *Website:* www.uts.edu.au/staff/angus.gentle (office).

GENTZ, Manfred, LLB, LLD; German business executive; b. 22 Jan. 1942, Riga, Latvia; ed Univ. of Berlin, Univ. of Lausanne, Switzerland, Berlin Free Univ.; joined Daimler-Benz AG 1970, mem. Man. Bd 1983–90, CEO Daimler-Benz Interservices 1990–95, Chief Financial Officer Daimler-Benz AG 1995–98, mem. Man. Bd Daimler Chrysler AG (after merger of Daimler-Benz and Chrysler Corpn) 1998–2004; Chair. Zurich Financial Services Ltd and Zurich Insurance Co. Ltd 2005–12; Chair. Supervisory Bd Eurohypo AG 2005–06, Deutsche Börse AG 2008–; mem. Bd of Supervisors Hannoversche Lebensversicherung AG 1985–2005 (Proxy Chair. 1990–2005), Agrippina Versicherung AG 1987–95, DWS Investment GmbH 1995–2009, Zurich Beteiligungs-AG (Deutschland) 1996–2005, Deutsche Börse AG 2003–12 (Chair. 2008–12), Adidas AG 2004–09; mem. Exec. Bd ICC, Chair. German Nat. Cttee 2014; Chair. Curatorship of Technische Universität Berlin 2007–10; mem. Comm. for German Corporate Governance Kodex 2006– (Chair. 2013–17) mem. several scientific and cultural insts. *Address:* Alte Potsdamer Straße 5, 10785 Berlin, Germany (office). *Telephone:* (30) 25941500 (office); (30) 25941505 (office). *E-mail:* manfred.gentz@mg-office-berlin.com (office).

GENZEL, Reinhard, PhD; German astrophysicist and academic; *Director and Scientific Member, Max Planck Institute for Extraterrestrial Physics;* b. 24 March 1952, Bad Homburg vor der Höhe; ed Univs of Freiburg and Bonn, Max Planck Inst. for Radio Astronomy; Postdoctoral Fellow, Harvard-Smithsonian Center for Astrophysics, Cambridge, Mass, USA 1978–80, Miller Fellow 1980–82; Assoc. Prof. of Physics and Assoc. Research Astronomer, Space Sciences Lab., Univ. of California, Berkeley 1981–85, Prof. of Physics 1985–86, 1999–; Dir and Scientific mem., Max Planck Inst. for Extraterrestrial Physics, Garching 1986–; lectured at Ludwig Maximilians Univ., Munich; mem. US and German Astronomical and Physical Socs; Foreign mem. NAS 2000, Acad. des sciences (Institut de France) 1998, Royal Spanish Acad. of Sciences 2011, Royal Soc.; mem. Deutsche Akad. der Naturforscher Leopoldina 2002, European Acad. of Sciences 2002; Sr mem. Bayerische Akad. der Wissenschaften 2003; Fellow, American Physical Soc. 1985; Hon. Prof., Univ. of Munich 1988; Dr hc (Leiden); Otto Hahn Medal, Max Planck Gesellschaft 1980, NSF Presidential Young Investigator Award 1984, Newton Lacy Pierce Prize, American Astronomical Soc. 1986, Gottfried Wilhelm Leibniz Prize, Deutsche Forschungsgemeinschaft 1990, De Vaucouleurs Medal, Univ. of Texas 2000, Prix Jules Janssen, French Astronomical Soc. 2000, Stern Gerlach Medal for experimental physics, Deutsche Physikalische Gesellschaft 2003, Balzan Prize for Infrared Astronomy 2003, Petrie Prize, Canadian Astronomical Soc. 2005, Albert Einstein Medal 2007, Shaw Prize (co-recipient) 2008, 'Galileo 2000' Prize 2009, Karl Schwarzschild Medal, Deutsche Astronomische Gesellschaft 2011, Crafoord Prize, Royal Swedish Acad. of Sciences (co-recipient) 2012, Harvey Prize, Technion, Israel (co-recipient) 2014. *Publications:* numerous papers in professional journals. *Address:* Max-Planck-Institut für extraterrestrische Physik, PO Box 1312, 85741 Garching, Germany (office). *Telephone:* (89) 30000-3280 (office). *Fax:* (89) 30000-3601 (office). *E-mail:* genzel@mpe.mpg.de (office); genzel@socrates.berkeley.edu (office). *Website:* www.mpg.de/463069/extraterrestrische_physik_wissM1 (office); physics.berkeley.edu/people/faculty/reinhard-genzel (office).

GEOANĂ, Mircea Dan, LLB, PhD; Romanian diplomatist, politician and international organization official; *President, Aspen Institute Romania;* b. 14 July 1958, Bucharest; m. Mihaela Geoană; one s. one d.; ed Bucharest Polytechnic Inst., Univ. of Bucharest, Ecole Nat. d'Admin, Paris, France, Harvard Univ., USA, Acad. for Econ. Studies, Bucharest; joined Ministry of Foreign Affairs 1990, Dir European Affairs Dept, Head of Romanian Del. to CSCE Cttee of Sr Officials 1991, Ministry Spokesperson 1993–95, Dir-Gen. for Asia, Latin America, Middle East and Africa 1994, Dir-Gen. for Europe, N America, Asia, Latin America, Middle East and Africa 1995; Amb. to USA 1996–2000; Minister of Foreign Affairs 2000–05; Chair.-in-Office OSCE 2001–; cand. for Mayor of Bucharest 2004; mem. Senate (Partidul Social Democrat (PSD—Social Democratic Party) 2004–11, (Ind.) 2011–, Pres. of Senate 2008–11; Pres. PSD 2005–10, dismissed from party for refusing to stand down as Pres. of the Senate Nov. 2011, rejoined party 2012–14; unsuccessful presidential cand. 2009; Prof., Nat. School for Political and Admin Sciences, Nicolae Titulescu Univ., Bucharest; Founding mem. and Pres. Aspen Inst. Romania 2006–; Founder and fmr Acting Pres., Partidul Social Românesc 2015–; NATO Fellow on Democratic Insts 1994; Hon. Chair. George C.Marshall Asscn; Commdr, Nat. Order Star of Romania 2000, Commdr, Legion d'honneur 2002, Stella della Soliedarita (Italy) 2013. *Publications include:* several books including Romanian Foreign Policy in the Beginning of the XXIst Century, The Road to Europe and Transatlantic World, America, Europe and Romania's Modernization: Bases for a Romanian Societal Model, The Romanian Social Model: The Way towards a New Romania, Trust; numerous articles on Euro-Atlantic integration. *Address:* Aspen Institute Romania, Bucharest 020974, 25, Italiana Street, 1st Floor, Romania (office). *Telephone:* (21) 3164279 (office). *Fax:* (21) 3173443 (office). *Website:* www.aspeninstitute.ro (office).

GEOGHEGAN, Michael F., CBE; British banking executive; b. 4 Oct. 1953, Windsor; m.; two s.; joined HSBC (Hong Kong and Shanghai Banking Corpn) Group 1973, spent 12 years in N and S America, eight years in Asia, seven years in Middle East, Pres. HSBC Bank Brasil SA/Banco Múltiplo 1997–2003, responsible for all of HSBC's business throughout S America 2000–03, Chief Exec. HSBC PLC 2004–06, Exec. Dir HSBC Holdings 2004–10, Group Chief Exec. 2006–10 (resgnd), Chair. Group Man. Bd, Chair. The Hongkong and Shanghai Banking Corpn Ltd 2010, Chair. HSBC Bank USA, N.A. –2009, HSBC USA Inc. –2009, HSBC Bank Canada, Deputy Chair. HSBC Bank PLC, a Dir of HSBC France, HSBC North America Holdings Inc., HSBC Nat. Bank USA, HSBC Latin America Holdings (UK) Ltd (Chair. –2009); Dir (non-exec.) and Chair. Young Enterprise UK.

GEOGHEGAN-QUINN, Máire; Irish politician, fmr EU official and fmr business consultant; b. 5 Sept. 1950, Carna, Co. Galway; d. of John Geoghegan and Barbara Folan; m. John V. Quinn 1973; two s.; ed Carysfort Teacher Training Coll. Blackrock, Co. Dublin; fmr primary school teacher; mem. Galway City Council 1985–92; mem. Dáil Éireann (Parl.) 1975–97; Parl. Sec. to Minister of Industry,

Commerce and Energy 1977–78; Minister of State with responsibility for Consumer Affairs, Ministry of Industry, Commerce and Energy 1977–78; Minister for the Gaeltacht 1979–81; Minister of State with responsibility for Youth and Sport, Dept of Educ. March–Dec. 1982; Minister of State for European Affairs 1987, 1991; Minister for Tourism, Transport and Communications 1992, of Justice 1993; columnist, Irish Times 1997–2000; mem. Audit Devt and Reports Group, Court of Auditors of the EC 2000–10; Commr for Research, Innovation and Science, EC, Brussels 2010–14; consultant to several cos; fmr Chair. The Saffron Initiative; fmr Vice-Pres. Fianna Fáil; fmr Dir (non-exec.) The Ryan Hotel Group, Aer Lingus; fmr TV broadcaster. *Publication:* The Green Diamond (novel) 1996. *Leisure interests:* reading, writing and travel. *Address:* c/o European Commission, 200 rue de la Loi/Wetstraat 200, 1049 Brussels, Belgium (office).

GEORGE; British artist; b. (George Passmore), 8 Jan. 1942, Devon; ed Dartington Hall Adult Educ. Centre, Dartington Hall Coll. of Art, Oxford Art School, St Martin's School of Art, London; began working with Gilbert (Proesch) in 1967 as Gilbert & George; est. reputation as performance artists, presenting themselves, identically dressed, as living sculptures; later work includes large composite drawings and vividly coloured photo-pieces often featuring likenesses of the artists; work underpinned by 'Art for all' philosophy; works address social issues, taboos and artistic conventions; work held in public collections in UK and abroad; Dr hc (London Metropolitan Univ.) 2008, (Univ. of East London) 2010, (Open Univ.) 2012, (Plymouth Univ.) 2013; Magister Artium Gandensis (University Coll. Ghent) 2010; Turner Prize 1986. *Publications include:* Manifesto: What Our Art Means, Gilbert and George: The Complete Pictures 2007. *Address:* White Cube, 144–152 Bermondsey Street, London, SE1 3TQ, England (office). *Telephone:* (20) 7930-5373 (office). *E-mail:* g-and-g@dircon.co.uk (office). *Website:* www.whitecube .com (office).

GEORGE, Andrew Neil; British diplomatist; b. 9 Oct. 1952, Scotland; m. Watanalak George; one s. one d.; Desk Officer, S American Dept, FCO 1980–81, Second Sec., Chancery, Bangkok 1976–80, Desk Officer, West African Dept 1981–82, 1974–75, Under-Sec./Dir-Gen. 1982–84, First Sec., Chancery, Canberra 1984–88, First Sec. and Head of Chancery, Bangkok 1988–92, Asst Head, Repub. of Ireland Dept 1993–94, Asst Head, Eastern Dept 1994–95, Head of Section, Counter Proliferation Dept 1995–98, Amb., Asencion 1998–2001, Commercial Counsellor, Jakarta 2002, Asst Dir with Human Resources Directorate 2003–05, Gov. and C-in-C of Anguilla 2006–09.

GEORGE, Jennie, BA; Australian trade union official and politician; b. 20 Aug. 1947, Italy; ed Burwood Girls High School, Univ. of Sydney; Gen. Sec. NSW Teachers Fed. 1980–82, Pres. 1986–89, Life mem.; mem. Exec. Australian Council of Trade Unions 1983, Vice-Pres. 1987, Asst Sec. 1991–95, Pres. 1996–2000; Asst Nat. Dir Trade Union Training Authority 1989–91; Fed. MP for Throsby 2001–10.

GEORGE, Marcus, MEng, PhD; Iraqi/Canadian civil engineer and business executive; *CEO, EC Consulting Engineers;* ed Baghdad Univ., Univ. of Glamorgan, UK; early career working in Kuwait and Canada; worked several years in Iraqi public sector, worked with numerous int. construction cos including Skidmore Owings Merrill Architects; moved to Dubai 1992; f. Engineering Consortium (EC) Consulting Engineers 1997, currently CEO. *Address:* EC Consulting Engineers, Dubai, United Arab Emirates (office). *Fax:* (4) 2830771 (office). *Website:* www.ec -uae.com (office).

GEORGE, Peter J., CM, BA, MA, PhD; Canadian economist, academic and university administrator; *Professor Emeritus, McMaster University;* b. 12 Sept. 1941, Toronto, Ont.; m. 1st Gwendolyn Schar –1997; m. 2nd Allison Barrett 1998; one s. two d.; ed Univ. of Toronto; Lecturer, McMaster Univ. 1965–67, Asst Prof. 1967–71, Assoc. Prof. 1971–80, apptd Prof. of Econs 1980, Assoc. Dean of Grad. Studies 1974–79, Dean Faculty of Social Sciences 1980–89, Pres. and Vice-Chancellor, McMaster Univ. 1995–2010, now Prof. Emer.; Pres. Council of Ont. Univs 1991–95; fmr Chair. Council of Deans of Arts and Science of Ont.; fmr mem. Ont. Council on Univ. Affairs; mem. Bd of Dirs C. D. Howe Inst., Golden Key Int. Honour Soc., Foundation for Educ. Exchange between Canada and USA, Ont. Inst. for Cancer Research; Trustee, Univ. Sharjah, UAE; Hon. mem., Alumni Asscn, McMaster Univ. 1996; mem. Order of Ontario 2007; Hon. DUniv, Hon. DLitt, Hon. LLD. *Publications:* Government Subsidies and the Construction of the Canadian Pacific Railway 1981, The Emergence of Industrial America: Strategic Factors in American Economic Growth Since 1870 1982. *Leisure interests:* fishing, golf.

GEORGE, Susan; British actress, producer, photographer, author and horse breeder; b. (Susan Melody George), 26 July 1950, London, England; d. of Norman Alfred George and Eileen Percival; m. Simon MacCorkindale 1984 (died 2010); began acting career 1954; Owner, Georgian Arabians, Somerset, Amy Int. Productions, London; Dir SG Naturally Ltd, Susan George Photography Ltd. *Theatre:* The Sound of Music 1962, The Country Girl 1984, Rough Crossing 1987. *Films include:* Cup Fever, Davey Jones' Locker, Billion Dollar Brain, Twinky 1969, Spring and Port Wine 1970, Eyewitness 1970, Straw Dogs 1971, Dirty Mary and Crazy Larry 1974, Mandingo 1975, Out of Season 1975, A Small Town in Texas 1977, Tomorrow Never Comes 1978, Venom 1980, A Texas Legend 1981, The House Where Evil Dwells 1982, The Jigsaw Man 1984, Czechmate 1985, Lightning, The White Stallion 1986, Stealing Heaven (producer) 1987, That Summer of White Roses (also producer) 1988, The House That Mary Bought (also producer) 1994, Diana and Me 1997, In Your Dreams 2008, City of Life 2009. *Television appearances include:* Swallows and Amazons, Human Jungle, The Right Attitude 1968, Dr Jekyll and Mr Hyde 1973, Lamb to the Slaughter 1979, Royal Jelly 1979, The Bob Hope Special 1979, Pajama Tops 1982, Masquerade 1983, Hotel 1985, Blacke's Magic 1986, Jack the Ripper 1988, The Castle of Adventure 1990, Counterstrike 1990, Cluedo 1992, Stay Lucky 1992, Tales of Mystery and Imagination – The Black Cat 1995, EastEnders 2001. *Publication:* illustrated book of poetry 1987. *Leisure interests:* singing, riding, homeopathy, travel. *Address:* c/o Chatto & Linnit Ltd, 123 King's Road, Chelsea, London, SW3 4PL, England (office); Georgian Arabians, PO Box 55, Minehead, Somerset, TA24 7WA, England (office). *Telephone:* (20) 7352-7722 (office); (1398) 371187 (office). *Fax:* (20) 7636-2888 (office). *E-mail:* info@georgianarabians.com. *Website:* www .georgianarabians.com (office); www.susangeorgeofficialwebiste.co.uk; www .sgnaturally.com.

GEORGE-WOUT, Lucille Andrea; Curaçao politician; *Governor of Curaçao;* b. 26 Feb. 1950; m. Herman George; began career as youth social worker 1971–80; Sec., Partido MAN (Movementu Antia Nobo) 1979; mem. Island Council of Curaçao (Parl.) 1980–84, 1986–90; Co-founder Partido Alternativo Real (PAR) (Real Alternative Party) 1993; Speaker, States (Parl.) of Netherlands Antilles 1994–98; fmr Commr of Finance, Island Territory of Curaçao; Minister for Work and Social Affairs, Netherlands Antilles 1999–2001; Gov. of Curaçao (first female) 2013–. *Address:* Office of the Governor, Fort Amsterdam 2, Willemstad, Curaçao (office). *Telephone:* (9) 461-2148 (office). *Fax:* (9) 461-2045 (office). *E-mail:* adjudant@kgcur.org (office). *Website:* www.gouverneurvancuracao.org (office).

GEORGEL, Pierre, DEnLett; French museum director; b. 14 Jan. 1943, Safi, Morocco; s. of Lucien Georgel and Santia Maria Georgel (née Santini); m. Chantal Martinet 1985; ed Univs of Montpellier, Paris and Lille, Ecole du Louvre, Paris; Asst, Musée du Louvre 1966–70; seconded to CNRS, Paris 1970–74; Curator of Graphic Art, Musée Nat. d'Art Moderne 1974–79; Dir Musée des Beaux-Arts, Dijon 1980–86; Dir Musée Picasso, Paris 1986–89; Chief Curator of French Museums (based at Musée Picasso) 1989–93; Dir Musée nat. de l'Orangerie des Tuileries 1993–2007; Prof., Ecole du Louvre 1980–85, 1995–96; Conservateur-général du Patrimoine 2000. *Publications include:* Dessins de Victor Hugo 1971, La Gloire de Victor Hugo 1985, La Peinture dans la peinture 1987, Courbet: le Poème de la nature 1995, Monet: le Cycle Nymphéas 1999.

GEORGELIN, Gen. Jean-Louis; French military officer; *Grand Chancellor, Ordre National de la Légion d'honneur;* b. 30 Aug. 1948, Aspet (Haute-Garonne); ed Prytanée Nat. Militaire, Mil. Acad. of St Cyr, Command and Gen. Staff Coll., Fort Leavenworth, Kan., USA, Centre for Advanced Mil. Studies, Paris; First Lt, Platoon Leader, 9th Airborne Infantry Bn 1970–73; Instructor, Infantry School, Montpellier 1973–76; Capt. Co. Cadre, 153rd Infantry Bn 1976–79; Dept of Mil. Intelligence 1979–80; ADC to Army Chief of Staff 1980–82; promoted to Maj. 1982, to Lt Col 1985, to Col 1988; Chief of Financial Planning Office, Army Staff 1988–91; Commdr 153rd Infantry Bn 1991–93; Army Asst to Chief of Mil. Cabinet of the Prime Minister 1994–97; promoted to Brig. Gen. 1997; Second-in-Command 11th Airborne Div., then Chief J5, Stabilization Force (SFOR) in fmr Yugoslavia 1997–98; Chief of Plans and Programmes Div., Jt Defence HQ 1998–2001; promoted to Maj.-Gen. 2000, to Lt-Gen. 2002; Chief of Mil. Staff 2002–06; promoted to Army Gen. (France) 2003; Chief of Defence Staff 2006–10; Grand Chancellor, Ordre nat. de la Légion d'honneur and Chancellor, Ordre nat. du Mérite 2010–; Grand' Croix, Légion d'honneur, Ordre nat. du Mérite; numerous other foreign decorations. *Address:* Grande chancellerie de la Légion d'honneur, 1 rue de Solférino, 75700 Paris 07 SP, France (office). *Telephone:* 1-40-62-83-13 (office). *Fax:* 1-45-56-02-98 (office). *Website:* www.legiondhonneur.fr (office).

GEORGES, Michel A. J., MSc; Belgian geneticist and academic; *Professor of Genetics, Faculty of Veterinary Medicine, University of Liège;* b. 1959, Schoten; ed Univ. of Liège, Univ. of Brussels; Asst Prof., Univ. of Liège 1983–88, Prof. of Genetics, Faculty of Veterinary Medicine 1994–; specializes in animal genetics and genomics; Assoc. Prof., Dept of Human Genetics, Univ. of Utah, USA 1991–93; mem. Belgian Royal Acad. of Medicine; Wolf Foundation Prize in Agric. 2007, Francqui Prize 2008. *Address:* Université de Liège, Faculty of Veterinary Medicine, 9 place du 20 Août, Liège 4000, Belgium (office). *Telephone:* (4) 366-21-11 (office). *E-mail:* michel.georges@ulg.ac.be (office). *Website:* www.ulg.ac.be/ fmv (home).

GEORGESCU, Florin, PhD; Romanian economist, politician and central banker; b. 25 Nov. 1953, Bucharest; ed Acad. of Econ. Studies, Bucharest; Fulbright Scholar, Kansas City Univ., USA 1991–92; Assoc. Prof., Acad. of Econ. Studies; Sec. of State, Ministry of Finance 1992, Minister of State 1992–96; mem. Chamber of Deputies (Social Democratic Party) for Olt Electoral Constituency 1996–2004, Pres. Chamber of Deputies Comm. for Budget, Finance and Banks 2000–04, mem. Del. to Parl. Ass. of Black Sea Econ. Cooperation, Parl. Group of Friendship with Repub. of Slovenia 2000–, Pres. Parl. Group of Friendship with Repub. of Bulgaria 2000; First Deputy Gov. and Vice-Chair. Nat. Bank of Romania (Banca Naţională a României) 2004–12; Deputy Prime Minister and Minister of Public Finance May–Dec. 2012; Prof., Bucharest Univ. of Econ. Studies; Kt, Order of the Star of Romania 2002, Order of Industrial and Commercial Merit 2007, Grand Officer, Order of the Star of Romania 2010. *Publications include:* more than 200 studies and papers. *Address:* Faculty of Economics, Bucharest University of Economic Studies, 71131 Bucharest, 15–17 Dorobanti Avenue, District 1, Romania (office). *Telephone:* (21) 3191900 (office). *Fax:* (21) 3129549 (office). *E-mail:* international@ ase.ro (office). *Website:* www.ase.ro (office).

GEORGESCU, Peter Andrew, BA, MBA; American (b. Romanian) advertising executive (retd); *Chairman Emeritus, Young & Rubicam Inc.;* b. 9 March 1939, Bucharest, Romania; s. of V.C. Georgescu and Lygia Bocu; m. Barbara A. Armstrong 1965; one s.; ed Princeton and Stanford Univs; joined Young & Rubicam Inc., New York 1963, Dir of Marketing 1977–79, Exec. Vice-Pres. and Dir Cen. Region, Young & Rubicam Inc., Chicago 1979–82, Pres. Young & Rubicam Int., New York 1982–86, Young & Rubicam Advertising, New York 1986–99, Pres. Young & Rubicam Inc. 1994–2000, Chair. and CEO 1994–99, Chair. Emer. 2000–; f. Constant Choice website; Vice-Chair. New York Presbyterian Hosp.; mem. Bd of Dirs Briggs & Stratton Inc.; mem. Council on Foreign Relations; Dr hc (Univ. of Alabama), (Cornell Coll.); Ellis Island Medal of Honor 1997. *Publications include:* The Source of Success 2006, The Constant Choice: An Everyday Journey from Evil Toward Good 2013. *Website:* theconstantchoice.com.

GEORGHADJI, Chrystalla, MA; Cypriot economist and central banker; b. 13 July 1956, Famagusta; two c.; ed Univ. of Athens, Greece, Univ. of Southampton, UK, Univ. of Chicago, USA; apptd Econ. Officer, Ministry of Finance 1981, later Econ. Officer A, then Sr Econ. Officer 1991; Deputy Pres. SEC of Cyprus 1993–98; Asst Supt of Insurance, Cyprus 1995–96, Head of Service 1996–98; Auditor-Gen. of Cyprus 1998–2014; Gov. Cen. Bank of 'Turkish Repub. of Northern Cyprus' 2014–19, also mem. Governing Council, European Cen. Bank; Hon. mem. ACCA 2000. *Address:* c/o Central Bank of Cyprus, 80 Kennedy Avenue, 1076 Nicosia, Cyprus.

GEORGIADES, Haris, BA, MA; Cypriot politician; *Minister of Finance;* b. 9 April 1972, Nicosia; m. Eva Yiangou Georgiades; one d.; ed English School, Nicosia, Univ. of Reading, UK; postgraduate researcher, Inst. of European and Int. Studies,

Univ. of Reading, UK 1996–98; Gen. Sec. NEDISY (DISY—Democratic Rally Youth Org.) 2001–03, Dir, DISY Pres.'s Office 2006–11, DISY Press Spokesman 2009–13, also Deputy Head, DISY Econ. Policy Div.; mem. House of Reps (Parl.) (DISY—Democratic Rally) for Nicosia constituency 2011–13, mem. Financial and Budgetary Affairs Cttee, Watchdog Cttee, Communications and Public Works Cttee; Minister of Labour and Social Insurance March–April 2013, of Finance April 2013–; Chair. Bd of Govs European Bank for Reconstruction and Development 2014–15; mem. (Ex-Officio) Bd of Govs, EIB, European Stability Mechanism, IMF, Multilateral Investment Guarantee Agency, World Bank; mem. DISY Exec. Council and Political Bureau; mem. Young Leaders Group for Europe, World Econ. Forum. *Address:* Ministry of Finance, cnr Michalakis Karaolis Street and Gregoriou Afxentiou Street, 1439 Nicosia, Cyprus (office). *Telephone:* 22601104 (office); 22601105. *Fax:* 22602741 (office). *E-mail:* registry@mof.gov.cy (office); info@harrisgeorgiades.com.cy. *Website:* ww.mof.gov.cy (office); harrisgeorgiades .com.cy.

GEORGIEV, Georgii Pavlovich; Russian molecular biologist; *Adviser and Scientific Director, Institute of Gene Biology, Russian Academy of Sciences;* b. 4 Feb. 1933, Leningrad (now St Petersburg); s. of Pavel K. Georgiev and Anastasia Georgieva; m. Nekrasova Anastasia A.; one s. one d.; ed First Moscow Medical Inst.; qualified as medical doctor; researcher, A. Severtsev Inst. of Morphology of Animals, USSR (now Russian) Acad. of Sciences 1956–63, Head of Lab., V. Engelhart Inst. of Molecular Biology 1963–90, Founder and Dir Inst. of Gene Biology 1990–2006, currently Adviser and Scientific Dir; Corresp. mem. USSR (now Russian) Acad. of Sciences 1970, mem. 1987; mem. Academia Europaea, Royal Acad. of Spain, German Acad. Leopoldina, Scientific Acad. of Norway, European Molecular Biology Org.; research in molecular biology and genetics; author of discoveries of hnRNA and study of nuclear RNP particles containing hnRNA and investigation of a new type of nucleoprotein complex structure; first description of nuclear skeleton components; discovery of mobile elements in animals; studies of chromosome structure and transcription-active chromatin, tumour metastasis genes and cancer gene therapy; Lenin Prize 1976, USSR State Prize 1983, Russian State Prize 1996, Engellhardt Gold Medal 2009. *Publications include:* Genes of Higher Organisms and their Expression 1989; more than 500 scientific articles. *Leisure interest:* mountain climbing. *Address:* Institute of Gene Biology, Russian Academy of Sciences, Vavilov str. 34/5, 119334 Moscow (office); App. 75, home 7, Gubkin str., 117312 Moscow, Russia (home). *Telephone:* (499) 135-60-89 (office); (499) 125-74-54 (home). *Fax:* (495) 135-41-05 (office). *E-mail:* georgiev@igb.ac.ru (office). *Website:* www.igb.ac.ru (office).

GEORGIEVA, Kristalina Ivanova, MA, PhD; Bulgarian economist, international organization official and politician; *CEO, International Bank for Reconstruction and Development, World Bank Group;* b. 13 Aug. 1953, Sofia; m.; one c.; ed Karl Marx Higher Inst. of Econs (now Univ. of Nat. and World Economy), Sofia, Harvard Business School and Massachusetts Inst. of Tech., USA; Assoc. Prof. of Econs, Univ. of Nat. and World Economy, Sofia 1977–93; Research Fellow, Dept of Econs, LSE, UK 1987–88; Consultant, Environmental Policy Services for Central and Eastern Europe, Environomics and Merser Management Consulting, Inc. 1992; Environmental Economist/Sr Environmental Economist, Environment Div., Europe and Cen. Asia, The World Bank Group 1993–97, Sector Man., Environment, East Asia and Pacific Region, responsible for regional environmental programmes, environmental projects (investments and tech. assistance) 1997–98, Sector Dir, Environment and Social Devt, East Asia and Pacific Region, responsible for social devt operations, including extensive work on social safety nets, community devt and women's empowerment, global environment projects, and regional initiatives in areas of social devt and environment 1998–99, Dir Environment Dept, in charge of World Bank environmental strategy, policies and lending 2000–04, Dir and Resident Rep., Russian Fed., based in Moscow, responsible for World Bank projects in more than 40 regions of the Fed. 2004–07, Dir, Strategy and Operations, Sustainable Devt, in charge of overall directions and delivery of World Bank policy and lending operations in infrastructure, urban devt, agriculture, environment and social devt, including co-ordination of World Bank support to fragile and conflict-affected countries 2007–08, Vice-Pres. and Corp. Sec., World Bank Group 2008–10; Commr for Int. Co-operation, Humanitarian Aid and Crisis Response, EC 2010–14, for Budget and Human Resources 2014–16, Vice-Pres., EC 2014–16; CEO IBRD and IDA, World Bank Group 2017–, Interim Pres., World Bank Group Feb.–April 2019; apptd by UN Sec.-Gen. as Co-Chair. of High-Level Panel on Humanitarian Financing 2015; Visiting Prof. at numerous insts, including ANU 1991, Yale Univ., Harvard Univ., MIT, Tsinghua Univ., Univ. of the South Pacific, Fiji 1991; mem. Bd of Trustees, Inst. for Sustainable Communities 2003–05, LEAD International 2003–09, Univ. of Nat. and World Economy 2009–; European Voice Commr of the Year 2010, European of the Year 2010. *Publications include:* textbook on microeconomics; more than 100 publs on environmental policy and sustainable devt. *Leisure interests:* travelling, guitar playing, dancing, cooking exotic dishes. *Address:* International Bank for Reconstruction and Development, World Bank Group, 1818 H Street NW, Washington, DC 20433, USA (office). *Website:* www.worldbank.org/en/about/what-we-do/brief/ibrd (office); ida.worldbank.org (office).

GEORGIOU, Andreas, BA, PhD; Greek economist; b. 1960, Patras; one d.; ed Amherst Coll., Univ. of Michigan; economist with IMF 1989–2010, including as Deputy Div. Chief, Statistics Dept 2004–10; Pres. Hellenic Statistical Authority (ELSTAT) 2010–15; fmr lecturer in econs, Univ. of Michigan; Visiting Prof., Econs Univ. of Bratislava; Chair. EU Council Working Party on Statistics 2014; mem. Partnership Group, European Statistical System 2012–14; mem. Int. Statistical Inst. 2013; faced criminal charges of undermining the nat. interest by inflating budget deficit and debt figures 2013, charges dropped by Court of Appeal 2015 but this decision overturned by Supreme Court 2016.

GEPHARDT, Richard (Dick) Andrew, BS, JD; American lawyer and fmr politician; *President and CEO Gephardt Group;* b. 31 Jan. 1941, St Louis, Mo.; s. of Louis Andrew Gephardt and Loreen Estelle Gephardt (née Cassell); m. Jane Ann Byrnes 1966; one s. two d.; ed Northwestern Univ. and Univ. of Michigan Law School; called to the Mo. Bar 1965; Pnr, Thompson and Mitchell (law firm), St Louis 1965–76; Alderman 14th Ward, St Louis 1971–76, Democratic Committeeman 1968–71; mem. US House of Reps from Third Mo. Dist 1979–2005, Democratic Leader 1989–2002; cand. for Democratic nomination to US presidency 1988, 2004; Pres. and CEO Gephardt Group 2005–; apptd Sr Counsel, DLA Piper Rudnick Gray Cary US LLP, Washington, DC 2005; Chair. National Endowment for Democracy; Pres. Children's Hematology Research Asscn, St Louis Children's Hosp. 1973–76; mem. Labor Advisory Bd, American Income Life Insurance Co. 2005–; mem. Advisory Bd Int. Conservation Caucus Foundation; Advisory Bd Chair. Richard A. Gephardt Inst. for Public Service, Washington Univ. in St. Louis; mem. Council on Foreign Relations, Young Lawyers Soc. (Chair. 1972–73). *Address:* Gephardt Group, 2496 Jett Ferry Road, Suite 102, Atlanta, GA 30338, USA. *Telephone:* (678) 205-1310. *Website:* www.gephardtgroup.com.

GERASHCHENKO, Victor Vladimirovich; Russian banker (retd) and fmr politician; b. 21 Dec. 1937, Leningrad (now St Petersburg); s. of Vladimir Gerashchenko and Anastasia Klinova; m. Nina Drozdkova 1960; one s. one d.; ed Moscow Financial Inst.; Man. Div. of Foreign Exchange Dept, USSR Bank for Foreign Trade (BFT) 1960–65, Man. Dir of Dept 1972–74, Man. Dir Foreign Exchange Dept 1982–83, Deputy Chair. 1983–89; Dir Moscow Narodny Bank Ltd, London 1965–67, Deputy Gen. Man., then Gen. Man. Beirut 1967–71, Gen. Man. Singapore 1977–82; Chair. Bd Ost-West Handelsbank, Frankfurt am Main 1974–77; Chair. Bd State Bank of USSR 1989–91, Head of Dept Fund Reforma 1991–92; Chair. Cen. Bank of Russian Fed. 1992–94, 1998–2002 (resgnd), Adviser 1994–96; Chair. Bd Moscow Int. Bank (MIB) 1996–98; Chair. Supervisory Bd Vneshtorgbank 1998–2003; mem. State Duma (Parl.) 2003–04; Co-Chair. Party of the Russian Regions (Partiya Rossiiskikh Regionov–PRR), now Motherland (Rodina) 2004; mem. Bd of Dirs Yukos 2004; now retd; Order of Banner of Labour (twice), Order of Merit for the Fatherland 2000, Order of the Red Banner of Labour, Order of Friendship of People. *Leisure interest:* literature.

GERASIMOV, Gen. Valerii Vasilevich; Russian army officer and government official; *Chief of the General Staff;* b. 8 Sept. 1955, Kazan, Tatar ASSR, Russian SFSR, USSR; m. (divorced); one s.; ed Kazan Suvorov Mil. School, Kazan Higher Tank Command School, Malinovskii Mil. Acad. of Armoured Forces, Mil. Acad. of the Gen. Staff of the Armed Forces of Russia; following graduation, became commdr of a platoon, co. and bn of the Eastern Mil. Dist; later a chief of staff of a tank regt, then of a motorized rifle div. in Baltic Mil. Dist; commdr of a motorized infantry div. in North Western Force 1993–95; First Deputy Army Commdr in Moscow Mil. Dist and Commdr of 58th Army in North Caucasus Mil. Dist during Chechen War 1999–; Commdr Leningrad Mil. Dist 2006–09, Moscow Mil. Dist 2009–12, Cen. Mil. Dist 2012; ran Victory Day parades in Moscow 2009–12; Deputy Chief of Gen. Staff 2010–12, First Deputy Defence Minister and Chief of Gen. Staff 2012–; rank of Gen. of the Army 2014; Order of the Friendship of Peoples, Medals For 'Impeccable Service' (1st, 2nd and 3rd degrees), Medal '200 Years of the Ministry of Defence', Medal 'For Strengthening of Brotherhood in Arms', Medal For Valour (First Class), Medal '60 Years of the Armed Forces of the USSR', Medal '70 Years of the Armed Forces of the USSR, Medal for Battle Merit', Merit for Motherland in the USSR Armed Forces (Third Grade), Merit for Motherland (Fourth Grade), Order of Mil. Merit. *Address:* Ministry of Defence, 119169 Moscow, ul. Znamenka 19, Russia (office). *Telephone:* (495) 696-71-71 (office); (495) 696-84-36 (office). *Website:* eng.mil.ru/en/management/deputy/more .htm?id=11113936@SD_Employee (office).

GERBERDING, Julie Louise, BA, MD, MPH; American professor of medicine; *Associate Adjunct Professor of Medicine (Infectious Diseases), University of California, San Francisco;* b. 22 Aug. 1955, Estelline, SDak; m. David Rose; one step-d.; ed Case Western Reserve Univ., Cleveland, Ohio; internship and residency in internal medicine, Univ. of California, San Francisco (UCSF); Fellowship in Clinical Pharmacology and Infectious Diseases, UCSF; Faculty mem. and Dir of Prevention Epicentre, UCSF –1998; Dir Healthcare Quality Promotion Div., Nat. Center for Infectious Diseases (NCID) 1998–2001, Acting Deputy Dir NCID 2001–02; Dir Centers for Disease Control and Prevention (CDC) and Admin. Agency for Toxic Substances and Disease Registry 2002–09; currently Assoc. Adjunct Prof. of Medicine (Infectious Diseases), UCSF and Assoc. Clinical Prof. of Medicine (Infectious Diseases), Emory Univ.; Scientific Advisor, Edelman 2009–10; Pres., Merck Vaccines, Merck & Co., Inc. 2010–; Dir, MSD Wellcome Trust Hilleman Laboratories Pvt. Sec. Ltd (jt initiative between Merck and The Wellcome Trust); Assoc. Ed. American Journal of Medicine; mem. Editorial Bd Annals of Internal Medicine; fmr mem. Bd of Scientific Counselors, Nat. Center for Infectious Diseases, CDC HIV Advisory Cttee, Scientific Program Cttee, Nat. Conf. on Human Retroviruses; mem. American Soc. for Clinical Investigation, American Coll. of Physicians, Soc. for Healthcare Epidemiology of America, American Epidemiology Soc.; Fellow, Infectious Diseases Soc. of America, also Chair. Cttee on Professional Devt and Diversity and mem. Nominations Cttee; consultant to Nat. Insts of Health, American Medical Asscn, Occupational Safety and Health Admin, Nat. AIDS Comm., Congressional Office of Tech. Assessment, WHO; Alice Paige Cleveland Award 1981, Surgeon Gen.'s Medallion 2007, Global Health Leadership Award 2008. *Publications:* more than 140 peer-reviewed publs and textbook chapters. *Leisure interests:* scuba diving, reading on the beach, gardening. *Address:* Box 0811, University of California, San Francisco, CA 94143-0811 (office); Merck Corporate Headquarters, One Merck Drive, PO Box 100, Whitehouse Station, NJ 08889-0100, USA (office). *Telephone:* (908) 423-1000 (Whitehouse Station) (office). *Website:* www.ucsf.edu (office); www.merck.com/product/vaccines (office).

GERDAU JOHANNPETER, André; Brazilian business executive; *CEO, Metalúrgica Gerdau;* b. 17 March 1963; s. of Jorge Gerdau Johannpeter and Erica Johannpeter (neé Bier); s. of Jorge Gerdau Johannpeter; m.; three c.; ed Catholic Univ. of Rio Grande do Sul, Univ. of Toronto, Canada, Univ. of Pennsylvania, USA; joined Metalúrgica Gerdau 1981, Asst to Exec. Pres., Gerdau Ameristeel (US operation), Cambridge, Mass 1992–94, Business Devt Dir 2001–02, COO Canada operations 2002–03, COO 2002–03, Vice-Pres. Gerdau Ameristeel 2003–04, Exec. Vice-Pres. Metalúrgica Gerdau 2002–07, Dir of Marketing and Sales, Raw Materials, Procurement, Logistics, Human Resources, and Organizational Devt 2004–07, CEO 2007–, also Pres. Gerdau Exec. Cttee; mem. Brazilian Olympic Equestrian Team 1996–2000. *Sporting achievements:* won Olympic bronze medal for equestrianism 1996, 2000. *Leisure interest:* riding horses. *Address:* Gerdau Grupo, Avenida Farrapos 1811, Floresta, 90220-005 Porto Alegre, Rio Grande do Sul, Brazil (office). *Website:* www.gerdau.com.br (office).

GERDAU JOHANNPETER, Jorge; Brazilian business executive; *Chairman Gerdau Group;* b. 8 Dec. 1936, Rio de Janeiro; s. of Curt Johannpeter and Helda Gerdau; m. 1st Erica Bier; five s. including Andre Gerdau Johannpeter; m. 2nd Cristina Harbich; m. 3rd Maria Helena; ed Fed. Univ. of Rio Grande do Sul; began career at Metalúrgica Gerdau (now Gerdau Group) as steelworker 1950, Dir 1973–, CEO 1983–2006, Chair. 1983–; Pres. Quality and Productivity Programme, Rio Grande do Sul; Pres. Council for Competitive Brazilian Devt 2001–; Coordinator, Brazilian Business Action; mem. Bd of Dirs and Human Resources Cttee, Petrobras; mem. Exec. Cttee Int. Iron and Steel Inst.; mem. Council on Econ. and Social Devt; Grand Cross, Nat. Scientific Order of Merit 2002; Willy Korf Steel Vision Award 2001. *Leisure interests:* race horse training, surfing. *Address:* Presidência Grupo Gerdau, Avenida Farrapos 1811, Floresta, 90220-005 Porto Alegre, Rio Grande do Sul, Brazil (office). *E-mail:* jorge.gerdau@gerdau.com.br (office). *Website:* www.gerdau.com.br (office).

GERDZHIKOV, Ognian; Bulgarian jurist, professor of commercial law and politician; b. 19 March 1946, Sofia; s. of Tinka Gerdzhikova; m.; one c.; ed Sofia Univ. St Kliment Ohridski, Univ. of Vienna, Austria, Max Planck Inst. for Comparative Public Law and Int. Law, Hamburg, Germany; began career as Lecturer at Faculty of Law, Sofia Univ. 1979, Prof. of Civil and Commercial Law 1994–; twice mem. Nat. Ass. (Narodno Sobraniye—Parl.) (Natsionalno dvizhenie za stabilnost i vazhod (NDSV—Nat. Movt for Stability and Progress)), Chair. Nat. Ass. 2001–05, Chair. Standing Parl. Cttee for Human Rights and Religious Denominations; Prime Minister of Caretaker Govt Jan.–May 2017; Pres. Court of Arbitration of the Bulgarian Industrial Asscn; Order of Stara Planina. *Publications:* numerous textbooks, monographs and articles in the field of civil, commercial and company law. *Leisure interests:* table tennis, football, travelling. *Address:* c/o Council of Ministers, 1594 Sofia, bul. Dondukov 1, Bulgaria (office). *Telephone:* (2) 940-29-99 (office). *Fax:* (2) 980-21-01 (office). *E-mail:* gis@government.bg (office). *Website:* www.government.bg (office).

GERE, Richard; American actor and activist; b. 31 Aug. 1949, Philadelphia, Pa; s. of Homer George Gere and Doris Ann Gere (née Tiffany); m. 1st Cindy Crawford (q.v.) 1991 (divorced 1995); m. 2nd Carey Lowell 2002 (divorced 2016); one s. one step-d.; ed Univ. of Massachusetts; fmrly played trumpet, piano, guitar and bass and composed music with various groups; stage performances with Provincetown Playhouse and off-Broadway; appeared in London and Broadway productions of The Taming of the Shrew, A Midsummer Night's Dream and Broadway productions of Habeas Corpus and Bent; film debut 1975; Founding Chair. and Pres. Tibet House, New York 1987–91; f. Gere Foundation 1991; mem. Bd of Dirs Int. Campaign for Tibet 1992–, Chair. 1995–; Founder and Dir Healing the Divide Foundation 2001–; Hon. DLit (Leicester) 1992; Eleanor Roosevelt Humanitarian Award 2000, Marian Anderson Award 2007, George Eastman Award 2012, Medal of Gratitude, Albania 2012. *Films include:* Report to the Commissioner 1975, Baby Blue Marine 1976, Looking for Mr Goodbar 1977, Days of Heaven 1978, Blood Brothers 1978, Yanks 1979, American Gigolo 1980, An Officer and a Gentleman 1982, Breathless 1983, Beyond the Limit 1983, The Cotton Club 1984, King David 1985, Power 1986, No Mercy 1986, Miles From Home 1989, 3000 1989, Internal Affairs 1990, Pretty Woman 1990, Rhapsody in August 1991, Final Analysis 1991, Sommersby (co-exec. producer) 1993, Mr Jones (co-exec. producer) 1994, Intersection 1994, First Knight 1995, Primal Fear 1996, Red Corner 1997, Burn Hollywood Burn 1998, Runaway Bride 1999, Dr T. and the Women 2000, Autumn in New York 2000, The Mothman Prophecies 2002, Unfaithful 2002, Chicago (Golden Globe for Best Actor in a Musical 2003) 2002, Shall We Dance? 2004, Bee Season 2005, The Hoax 2006, The Flock 2007, The Hunting Party 2007, I'm Not There 2007, Nights in Rodanthe 2008, Amelia 2009, Hachiko: A Dog's Story 2009, Brooklyn's Finest 2010, The Double 2011, Arbitrage 2012, Time Out of Mind 2014, The Second Best Exotic Marigold Hotel 2015. *Publication:* Pilgrim Photo Collection 1998. *Address:* c/o Andrea Jaffe Inc., 9229 Sunset Boulevard, Suite 414, Los Angeles, CA 90069, USA; Healing the Divide Foundation, 341 Lafayette Street, #4416, New York, NY 10012, USA (office). *Website:* www.healingthedivide.org.

GERGAWI, HH Mohammed bin Abdullah al-, BBA; United Arab Emirates business executive and politician; *Minister of Cabinet Affairs and the Future;* b. 1963, Dubai; m.; three c.; ed Eastern Michigan Univ., USA; Sec.-Gen., Exec. Council, Govt of Dubai 2002–06; CEO Dubai Holding (manages cos, including Dubai Properties, Dubai International Properties, Jumeirah International, Dubai International Capital, Dubai Internet City, Dubai Media City, Dubai Knowledge Village, Dubai Industrial City, Dubai Humanitarian City) 2004–; Minister of State for Cabinet Affairs, UAE Council of Ministers (now Minister of Cabinet Affairs and the Future) 2006–; fmr Sec.-Gen. Govt of Dubai Exec. Council; fmr Chair. Dubai Devt & Investment Authority (DDIA); CEO Exec. Office of HH Sheikh Muhammad bin Rashid al-Maktoum, ruler of Dubai; Chair. Arab Strategy Forum; Chair. Young Arab Leaders; mem. Bd of Dirs Dubai Media Inc., UAE Univ., London Business School, UK; Founder Dubai Autism Centre, UAE Disabled Sports Fed.; Vice-Chair. Handicapped Club; Royal Order of Merit (Morocco); American Business Council Award 2000, Key to Dubai, RE Con Award 2014. *Address:* Ministry of Cabinet Affairs and the Future, POB 899, Abu Dhabi (office); Dubai Holding, PO Box 66000, Dubai, United Arab Emirates (office). *Telephone:* (2) 4039999 (Ministry) (office); (4) 3300300 (office). *Fax:* (2) 6777399 (Ministry) (office); (4) 3300303 (office). *E-mail:* contactus@moca.gov.ae (office). *Website:* www.moca.gov.ae (office); www.dubaiholding.com (office).

GERGEN, David Richmond, BA, LLB, JD; American academic and fmr govt official; *Professor of Public Service and Director, Center for Public Leadership, John F. Kennedy School of Government, Harvard University;* b. 9 May 1942, Durham, North Carolina; s. of Dr John Jay Gergen and Aubigne Munger Gergen; m. Anne Elizabeth Gergen 1967; one s. one d.; ed Yale and Harvard Univs; staff asst, Nixon Admin, Washington, DC 1971–72, Special Asst to Pres. and Chief, White House writing/research team 1973–74, Special Counsel to Pres. Ford and Dir White House Office Communications 1975–77; Research Fellow, American Enterprise Inst., Man. Ed. American Enterprise Inst. Public Opinion magazine 1977–81; Asst to Pres. Ronald Reagan, Staff Dir, White House 1981, Asst to Pres. Reagan for Communications 1981–83; Research Fellow, Inst. of Politics, John F. Kennedy School of Govt, Harvard Univ. 1983–85, Prof. of Public Service 1999–, Dir Center for Public Leadership 2000–; Man. Ed. US News & World Report, Washington, DC 1985–86, Ed.-at-Large 1986–; Commentator, ABC News Nightline 2000–, Marketplace 2002–; Moderator, World @ Large PBS discussion series 2000–02; Advisor to Pres. Bill Clinton 1993–2001, for Foreign Policy 1994–95, to Sec. of State 1994; Visiting Prof., Duke Univ. 1995–98; currently Sr Political Analyst CNN; Sr Fellow, Aspen Inst.; mem. Bd of Dirs American Assembly, Nat. Council Against Teenage Pregnancy, Center for Study of Presidency, Duke Univ., City Year, Kenan Inst. for Ethics; mem. Advisory Bd Intel Corpn, Leadership Center at Morehouse Coll., Harvard Grad. School of Educ.; mem. DC Bar, Council on Foreign Relations, Trilateral Comm.; several hon. degrees. *Publications include:* Eyewitness to Power: The Essence of Leadership – Nixon to Clinton 2000. *Address:* J.F. Kennedy School of Government, Harvard University, 79 J.F. Kennedy Street, Cambridge, MA 02138 (office); 31 Ash Street, Cambridge, MA 02138, USA (home). *E-mail:* David_Gergen@harvard.edu (office). *Website:* www.ksg.harvard.edu/leadership (office); www.davidgergen.com.

GERGIEV, Valery Abesalovich; Russian conductor; *General Director and Artistic Director, Mariinsky Theatre;* b. 2 May 1953, Moscow; m. Natalia Gergieva; two s. one d.; ed Leningrad Conservatory; Chief Conductor Armenian State Orchestra 1981–84; Asst Conductor (to Yuriy Temirkanov) Kirov Opera, Leningrad; Music Dir Kirov (now Mariinsky) Opera Theatre Orchestra 1988–, also Artistic and Gen. Dir 1996–; Prin. Guest Conductor Rotterdam Philharmonic 1989–92, Prin. Conductor 1992–2008, Music Dir 1995–2008; Prin. Guest Conductor New York Metropolitan Opera 1998–2008; Prin. Conductor London Symphony Orchestra 2007–15; Chief Conductor, Munich Philharmonic 2015–; Artistic Dir St Petersburg Stars of the White Nights Festival, Moscow Easter Festival, Gergiev Festival Rotterdam, Mikkeli Int. Festival, Finland; tours extensively in Europe and the USA; has guest-conducted Berlin Philharmonic, Dresden Philharmonic, Bayerischer Rundfunk, Royal Concertgebouw, London Philharmonic, City of Birmingham Symphony, Royal Philharmonic, London Symphony, Orchestra of Santa Cecilia, Japan Philharmonic, orchestras of Boston, Chicago, Cleveland, New York, San Francisco and Toronto, operas at Covent Garden, Metropolitan and San Francisco; Dean of the Faculty of Arts, St Petersburg State Univ. 2010–; Hon. Pres. Edinburgh International Festival 2011; Dr hc (Moscow State Univ.) 2012; prize winner at All-Union Conductors' Competition, Moscow (while still a student) and at Karajan Competition, Berlin, State Prize of Russia 1994, 1999, 1998, 2001, 2016, Musical Life Magazine Musician of the Year 1992, 1993, Classical Music Award 1994, Musical America Yearbook Conductor of the Year 1996, People's Artist of Russia 1996, Triumph Prize 1999, Order of Friendship, Russia 2000, Order of St Mesrop Mashtots, Armenia 2000, Russian Presidential Prize 2002, UNESCO Artist of the World 2003, Nat. Pride of Russia Award 2003, For Work and the Fatherland Award 2003, World Econ. Forum Crystal Prize 2004, People's Artist of Ukraine 2004, Royal Swedish Acad. of Music Polar Music Prize 2005, Royal Philharmonic Soc. Award for Best Conductor 2009, Hero of Labour of the Russian Federation 2013, Int. Classical Music Award for Choral Works 2011. *Recordings include:* numerous recordings of operas and ballets including Shostakovich War Symphonies (Nos 4–9) 2005, Prokofiev Complete Symphonies (Gramophone Award for Best Orchestral Recording 2007) 2006, Tchaikovsky Swan Lake 2007, Shostakovich The Nose 2009, Wagner Parsifal 2010, Prokofiev: The Gambler (Int. Classical Music Award for DVD Performance 2014), Stravinsky Firebird 2016, Rachmaninov: Symphony No. 1 2016, Russian Heart 2016. *Address:* Columbia Artists Management, 1790 Broadway, New York, NY 10019-1412, USA (office); Mariinsky Theatre, Teatralnaya pl. 1, St Petersburg, 190000, Russia. *Telephone:* (212) 841-9500 (office); (812) 326-41-41. *Fax:* (212) 841-9744 (office); (812) 314-17-44. *E-mail:* info@cami.com (office); post@mariinsky.ru. *Website:* www.cami.com (office); lso.co.uk; mariinsky.us/valery-gergiev.

GËRGURI, Gani, MBA; Kosovo economist and central banker; *Governor, Central Bank of the Republic of Kosovo;* b. 1960, Istog; m. Muzafere Gërguri; two s.; ed Univ. of Prishtina, Univ. of Zagreb, Croatia, Univ. of Sheffield, UK; started career in Statistics and Analysis Dept, Nat. Bank of Kosovo 1983; Head of Research and Statistics Dept, Central Bank of the Repub. of Kosovo 2000–04, Chief Operations Officer 2004–06, Deputy Man. Dir 2006–08, Deputy Gov. 2008–10, Acting Gov. 2010–11, Gov. 2011–; Co-Chair. Nat. Payments Council; mem. Bd Financial Intelligence Unit of Kosovo (ind. nat. inst. within Ministry of Finance and Economy). *Address:* Office of the Governor, Central Bank of the Republic of Kosovo, 10000 Prishtina, Rruga Garibaldi 33, Kosovo (office). *Telephone:* (38) 222055 (office). *Fax:* (38) 243763 (office). *E-mail:* publicrelations@cbak-kos.org (office). *Website:* www.bqk-kos.org (office).

GERHARDT, Wolfgang, PhD; German politician; *President, Friedrich-Naumann-Foundation;* b. 31 Dec. 1943, Ulrichstein-Helpershain; m.; two c.; ed Univ. of Marburg; mem. State Parl., Hesse 1983–94, Hessian Minister for Science and Art and Deputy Prime Minister 1987–91, Party Whip FDP; mem. Bundestag (Parl.) 1994–2013, Chair. FDP Parl. Group in Bundestag 1998–2006; Nat. Chair. FDP 1995–2001; Vice-Pres. Liberal Int. 2002–12; Pres. Friedrich Naumann Foundation for Liberty 2006–; Chair. Bd of Trustees Theodor-Heuss-Haus-Stiftung Foundation 2006–; Reinhold-Maier Medal 2008, Wilhelm-Leuschner Medal 2011. *Publication:* Es geht: wir haben alle Chancen 1997. *Address:* Friedrich Naumann Foundation, Karl-Marx-Strasse 2, 14482 Potsdam, Germany (office). *Telephone:* (30) 22012634 (office). *Fax:* (30) 69088102 (office). *E-mail:* service@freiheit.org (office). *Website:* www.freiheit.org (office).

GERINGER, James E. (Jim), BS; American business executive and fmr politician; *Director of Policy, Environmental Systems Research Institute (ESRI);* b. 24 April 1944, Wheatland, Wyo.; m. Sherri Geringer; five c.; ed Kansas State Univ.; fmr farmer and substitute teacher; officer USAF, Space Devt Programs; fmr Wyo. State Rep. Platte Co.; mem. Wyo. State Senate for Platte Co., Dist 3 until 1995; Gov. of Wyoming 1994–2003; Dir Policy, Environmental Systems Research Institute (ESRI) (software firm) 2003–; fmr Chair. Western Govs Asscn, Educ. Comm. of States; Co-Chair. Nat. Policy Consensus Center 2009; mem. Bd of Dirs Dakota Gasification Co. 2012–; mem. Bd of Trustees, Western Govs Univ., Chair. 2005–. *Address:* ESRI, 380 New York Street, Redlands, CA 92373-8100, USA. *Telephone:* (909) 793-2853. *Website:* www.esri.com (office).

GERMAIN, Philippe; New Caledonian business executive and politician; *Prime Minister;* b. 1 Jan. 1967, Nouméa; ed studied management and accountancy in Paris and Nice, France; joined Biscochoc (chocolate producer) as accountant 1990, becoming Chief Accountant, Dir of Finance and Dir-Gen. –2008; Pres. Fédération des industries de Nouvelle-Calédonie 2004–09; Minister for Labour, Monitoring of Monetary and Credit Affairs and Social Dialogue 2009–11, Minister for Relations with Econ., Social and Environmental Council and for Energy and Audiovisual Communications June–Dec. 2014, Minister for Economy, External Trade, Commercial Law, Fiscal Affairs and Customs 2014, also Pres., Council of Ministers (Prime Minister) 2015–, also Minister for Judicial Protection of Children and Youth, and Civil Security 2015–17; mem. Calédonie ensemble. *Address:* Présidence du Gouvernement, 8 route des Artifices, Artillerie, BP M2, 98849 Nouméa Cedex, New Caledonia (office). *Telephone:* 246565 (office). *Fax:* 246580 (office). *E-mail:* presidence@gouv.nc (office). *Website:* www.gouv.nc (office).

GERMAIN, Sylvie, PhD; French writer; b. 8 Jan. 1948, Châteauroux; ed Univ. of Paris (Sorbonne), Univ. of Paris X Nanterre; civil servant, attached to Ministry of Culture 1981–86, taught at L'École française, Prague 1986–93, full-time novelist 1994–; Prix mondial Cino Del Duca 2016. *Publications:* novels: Le Livre des nuits 1985, Nuit d'Ambre 1987, Jours de colère (Prix Femina) 1989, Opéra muet 1989, L'Enfant Méduse 1991, La Pleurante des rues de Prague 1992, Immensités (Louis-Guilloux Award 1994) 1993, Eclats de sel 1996, L'Encre du poulpe 1998, Tobie des marais 1998, La Chanson des mal-aimants 2002, Ateliers de lumière 2004, Magnus (Prix Goncourt des Lycéens) 2005, Frères 2006, L'inaperçu 2008, Hors Champ 2009, Petites scènes capitales 2013, À la table des hommes 2015; non-fiction: Les Echos du silence (prix de littérature religieuse 1997) 1996, Céphalophores 1996, Patience et songe de lumière: Vermeer 1996, Bohuslav Reyneck à Petrov: un nomade en sa demeure 1998, Etty Hillesum 1999, Mourir un peu 2000, La Grande nuit de Toussaint, Le Temps qu'il fait 2000, Cracovie à vol d'oiseau 2000, Célébration de la Paternité 2001, J'ai envie de rompre le silence (with René Vouland and Gérard Vouland) 2001, Songes du temps 2003, Les Personnages 2004, Patinir, Paysage avec Saint Christoph 2010, Quatre actes de présence 2011, Chemin de croix (with Tadeusz Kluba) 2011, Le monde sans vous 2011, Rendez-vous nomades 2012. *Address:* c/o Albin Michel, 22 rue Huyghens, 75014 Paris, France (office). *Website:* www.albin-michel.fr (office).

GERMÁN, Alejandrina; Dominican Republic academic and politician; *Secretary of State for Women;* b. Duarte Prov.; d. of Tomás Germán García and Teodora Mejía de Germán; m. José María Sosa Vásquez; two s.; ed Universidad Autónoma de Santo Domingo; Prof., Dept of Pedagogy, Universidad Autónoma de Santo Domingo (UASD) 1976–, fmr Pres. Asscn of UASD Humanities Profs; Pres. Nat. Council of Higher Educ., with rank of Sec. of State 1996–99; Sec. of State for the Presidency 1999–2000, for Educ. 2004–08, for Women 2008–; Adviser, UNDP Education Programme 1990–96; Consultant, Universidad Iberoamericana; mem. Partido de la Liberación Dominicana 1974–, mem. Cen. Cttee 1990, mem. Political Cttee 1994–. *Address:* Secretariat of State for Women, Edif. de Ofs. Gubernamentales, Bloque D, 2°, Avda México, esq. 30 de Marzo, Santo Domingo DN, Dominican Republic (office). *Telephone:* 685-3755 (office). *Fax:* 686-0911 (office). *E-mail:* info@mujer.gob.do (office). *Website:* www.mujer.gob.do (office).

GERNANDT LUNDIUS, Marianne; Swedish lawyer and judge; *President, Supreme Court;* b. (Marianne Lundius), 28 April 1949, Malmö; court clerk 1976–78; Pnr, Lagerlof & Leman Attorneys 1978–98; mem. Supreme Court of Sweden 1998–, Pres. (first woman) 2010–; Vice-Chair. Fideikommiss; replacement of Chair. of Oil Crisis Bd, Vice-Chair. Bd for support to financial Insts; Vice-Chair. Bd of Nomination of Judges; Vice-Pres. Disciplinary Cttee, Stockholm Stock Exchange, OMX Nasdaq, Disciplinary Cttee, Swedsec AB; Vice-Chair. Securities Council; Vice-Chair. Heijne Foundation; Prin. Stockholm Nursing Home Foundation; Head of Heart-Lung Foundation, Swedish Nat. Asscn against Heart and Lung Diseases, King Oscar II Jubilee Foundation; Chair. Sven and Lilly Lawskis Fund for Scientific Research; mem. Royal Physiographic Soc. in Lund; Hon. LLD (Univ. of Lund). *Address:* Högsta domstolen (Supreme Court), PO Box 2066, 103 12 Stockholm (office); Högsta domstolen, Riddarhustorget 8, 111 28 Stockholm, Sweden (office). *Telephone:* (8) 561-666-00 (office). *Fax:* (8) 561-666-86 (office). *E-mail:* hogsta.domstolen@dom.se (office). *Website:* www.hogstadomstolen.se (office).

GERONZI, Cesare; Italian banking executive; *Chairman, Fondazione Assicurazioni Generali SpA;* b. 15 Feb. 1935, Marino, Rome; m. Giuliana Iozzi; two d.; hired by Bank of Italy 1960, continued to work there until 1980; moved to Banco di Napoli 1980, arranged first bank merger in Italy, between Cassa di Risparmio di Roma, Banco di Santo Spirito and Banco di Roma, whose subsequent merger with Mediocredito Centrale, Banco di Sicilia and Bipop-Carire gave rise to the Capitalia banking group, directed takeover of Capitalia by the Unicredit Group 2007; Vice-Chair. UniCredit SpA (fmrly Unicredito Italiano SpA) 2007; Deputy Chair. Mediobanca SpA 2001–06, Deputy Chair. Supervisory Bd Jan.–June 2007, Chair. Mediobanca SpA 2007–10; Chair. Assicurazioni Generali SpA 2010–11 (resgnd); Chair. Fondazione Assicurazioni Generali SpA 2011–; mem. Bd of Dirs Telecom Italia SpA (fmrly Olivetti SpA and Stet-Società Finanziaria Telefonica p.A.) 2001–, RCS Mediagroup SpA 2004–, Capitalia SpA 2007–, RCS Quotidiani, Italian Bankers Asscn, CASPIE; mem. governing bodies of various pvt. law orgs and insts, including Istituto della Enciclopedia Italiana Treccani, Assonime, Associazione 'Guido Carli', Aspen Inst. Italia, Fondazione di Diritto Vaticano dell'Ospedale Bambino Gesù; Hon. Fellow, Tel-Aviv Museum of Art; numerous honours, including High Official of Order of Merit of the Repub. of Italy, Commdr, Holy Order of St Gregory the Great, Commdr's Cross of Maltese Order of Merit of Sovereign Mil. Hospitaller Order of St John of Jerusalem of Rhodes and of Malta; hc (Bari Univ.). *Address:* Fondazione Assicurazioni Generali SpA, Piazza Duca degli Abruzzi 2, 34132 Trieste, Italy (office). *Telephone:* (06) 42009046 (office). *Fax:* (06) 42009045 (office). *E-mail:* segreteria@fondazionegenerali.it (office); info@cesaregeronzi.it. *Website:* www.fondazionegenerali.eu (office); www.cesaregeronzi.it.

GERSHON, Sir Peter, Kt, KBE, CBE, FREng, FRAeS; British business executive and fmr civil servant; *Chairman, National Grid;* b. 10 Jan. 1947; m.; three c.; ed Univ. of Cambridge; joined Int. Computers Ltd and worked in the computer industry 1969–86; held sr line managerial positions in the telecommunications industry 1987–94; apptd Main Bd Dir of GEC PLC 1994–2000; Chief Exec. of the Office of Govt Commerce 2000–04; Chair. Premier Farnell PLC 2004–11, Symbian Ltd; fmr Man. Dir Marconi Electronic Systems; fmr Chair. Tate & Lyle PLC; mem. Bd of Dirs and Deputy Chair. National Grid Aug.–Dec. 2011, Chair. 2012–; fmr mem. UK Defence Acad. Advisory Bd, HM Govt Efficiency Bd; Chair. Aircraft Carrier Alliance Man. Bd; fmr Dir (non-exec.) HM Treasury; mem. Council Royal Acad. of Eng, Imperial Coll. London; served as adviser to the Conservative Party at the time of the 2010 gen. election; Fellow, British Computer Soc., Chartered Inst. of Purchasing and Supply; Companion, Chartered Man. Inst.; Hon. FIEE; Hon. Fellow, Asscn for Project Man.; Liveryman, Worshipful Co. of Information Technologists; Hon. DTech (Kingston Univ.). *Achievements include:* known for conducting the Gershon Review which recommended savings across the UK's public services 2004–05. *Leisure interests:* skiing, swimming, reading, travel, the theatre. *Address:* National Grid PLC, 1–3 The Strand, London, WC2N 5EH, England (office). *Telephone:* (20) 7004-3000 (office). *Fax:* (20) 7004-3004 (office). *E-mail:* info@nationalgrid.com (office). *Website:* www.nationalgrid.com (office).

GERSIE, Glenn; Suriname banking executive and central banker; *Governor, Centrale Bank van Suriname;* held several positions at Centrale Bank van Suriname for over three decades, including as Dir Monetary and Econ. Affairs, Gov. Centrale Bank van Suriname 2016–, also; currently mem. Bd of Govs IMF; mem. Strategic Man. Cttee, Caribbean Centre for Money and Finance. *Address:* Centrale Bank van Suriname, Waterkant 20, POB 1801, Paramaribo, Suriname (office). *Telephone:* 473741 (office). *Fax:* 476444 (office). *E-mail:* info@cbvs.sr (office). *Website:* www.cbvs.sr (office).

GERSON, Allan, MA, JD, LLM, JSD; American lawyer and academic; *Chairman, Gerson International Law Group;* b. Uzbekistan; m. Joan Nathan; three c.; ed New York Univ. Law School, Hebrew Univ. of Jerusalem, Israel, Yale Univ.; joined US Dept of Justice 1977, joined Office of Special Investigations (OSI) to prosecute Nazi collaborators 1979; apptd Counsel to US Ambs to UN Jeane Kirkpatrick and Gen. Vernon Walters 1981; fmr Deputy Asst Attorney-Gen. for Legal Counsel and Counsellor for Int. Affairs, US Dept of Justice; brought first lawsuit against Libya on behalf of families of victims of 1988 Pan Am Lockerbie bombing, led lawsuit against Saudi Royal family and Govt of Sudan on behalf of families of victims of World Trade Center bombing 2001; Sr Fellow, American Enterprise Inst. 1986–89; Distinguished Prof. of Int. Law and Transactions, George Mason Univ. 1989–95; currently Chair. Gerson Int. Law Group PLLC, Washington, DC; fmr Research Prof. of Int. Relations, George Washington Univ. and Co-Dir Inst. for Peace-building and Devt, Elliott School of Int. Affairs; fmr Exec. Dir Morocco-US Council on Trade and Investment; Sr Fellow for Int. Law and Orgs, Council on Foreign Relations 1998–2000; fmr Resident Scholar, American Enterprise Inst. *Publications include:* Israel, the West Bank and International Law 1978, Lawyers' Ethics: Contemporary Dilemmas 1980, The Kirkpatrick Mission: Diplomacy without Apology 1991, The Price of Terror: One Bomb. One Plane. 270 Lives. The History-Making Struggle for Justice After Pan Am 103 (co-author) 2001, Privatizing Peace: From Conflict to Security 2002; articles in professional and popular publs. *Address:* Gerson International Law Group, 2131 S Street, NW, Washington, DC 20008, USA (office). *Telephone:* (202) 234-9717 (office).

GERSON, Mark; British photographer; b. 3 Oct. 1921, London; s. of Bernard Gerson and Esther Gerson; m. Renée Cohen 1949; two d.; ed Cen. Foundation School for Boys, London and Regent Polytechnic, London; served in RAF 1941–46; taught photography under EVT scheme while serving in RAF in Paris 1946; specialist portrait photographer concentrating on literary personalities and industrialists; ran photographic studio 1947–87; now freelance photographer; major exhbns Fox Talbot Museum, Lacock, Wilts. 1981, Shaw Theatre, London 1983, Writers Observed, Nat. Theatre, London 1984, The Poetry Library, Royal Festival Hall 1991, Literati, Nat. Portrait Gallery, London 1996; Fellow, British Inst. of Professional Photography. *Leisure interests:* cinema, theatre. *Address:* 3 Regal Lane, Regent's Park, London, NW1 7TH, England. *Telephone:* (20) 7485-6437 (home). *E-mail:* mark@reneegerson.plus.com. *Website:* www.markgersonphotography.com.

GERSTNER, Louis Vincent, Jr, BE, MBA; American business executive; *Senior Advisor, Carlyle Group;* b. 1 March 1942, Mineola, New York; s. of Louis Vincent Gerstner and Marjorie Rutan Gerstner; m. Elizabeth Robins Link 1968; one s. one d.; ed Dartmouth Coll. and Harvard Univ.; Dir McKinsey & Co., New York 1965–78; Exec. Vice-Pres. American Express Co., New York 1978–81, Vice-Chair. 1981–83, Chair. Exec. Cttee 1983–85, Pres. 1985–89, Chair., CEO RJR Nabisco 1989–93; Chair., CEO IBM 1993–2002; Vice-Chair. New American Schools Devt Corpn Bd 1991–98; Dir The New York Times Co. 1986–97, Bristol-Myers Squibb Co.; mem. Exec. Cttee, Bd of Trustees Jt Council on Econ. Educ. 1975–87, Chair. 1983–85; mem. Bd of Dirs Memorial Sloan Kettering Hosp. 1978–89, 1998–, Vice-Chair. 2000–; Chair. Computer Systems Policy Project 1999–2001; Advisory Bd DaimlerChrysler 2001–, Sony Corpn 2002–; Chair. Carlyle Group 2002–08, currently Sr Advisor; mem. Policy Cttee, Business Roundtable 1991–98; mem. Bd of Overseers Annenberg Inst. for School Reform, Brown Univ.; mem. Business Council, American China Soc., Council on Foreign Relations, Nat. Security Telecommunications Advisory Cttee 1994–97, Advisory Cttee for Trade Policy and Negotiations 1995–, Nat. Acad. of Eng; Trustee NY Public Library 1991–96, American Museum of Natural History 2004–; Co-Chair. of Achieve 1996–2002; Founder and Chair. The Teaching Commission 2003–; Fellow, American Acad. of Arts and Sciences; Hon. KBE 2001; Hon. DBA (Boston Coll.) 1994; Hon. LLD (Wake Forest, Brown) 1997; Hon. DEng (Rensselaer Polytechnic Inst.) 1999; Washington Univ. Acad. for Excellence in Business, Eng and Technology 1999; numerous awards for work in educ. *Publications iclude:* Reinventing Education (with Roger D. Semerad) 1994; Who Says Elephants Can't Dance: Inside IBM's Historic Turnaround 2002. *Address:* Carlyle Group, 1001 Pennsylvania Avenue, NW, Suite 220 South, Washington, DC 20004-2505 (office); Teaching Commission, 365 Fifth Avenue, Suite 6200, New York, NY 10016, USA. *Telephone:* (202) 347-2626 (office). *Fax:* (202) 347-1818 (office). *Website:* www.thecarlylegroup.com (office); www.theteachingcommission.org.

GERTH, Donald R., BA, MA, PhD; American academic and university administrator; *President Emeritus, California State University, Sacramento;* b. 4 Dec. 1928, Chicago, IL; s. of George C. Gerth and Madeleine A. Canavan; m. Beverly J. Hollman 1955; two d.; ed Georgetown Univ., Univ. of Chicago; Field Rep. for Southeast Asia, World Univ. Service 1950; served in USAF 1952–56; Lecturer in History, Univ. of the Philippines 1953–54; Admissions Counselor, Univ. of Chicago 1956–58; Assoc. Dean of Students, Admissions and Records and mem. Dept of Govt, San Francisco State Univ. 1958–63; Assoc. Dean of Institutional Relations and Student Affairs, California State Univ. system 1963–64; Dean of Students,

California State Univ., Chico 1964–68, Prof. of Political Science 1964–76, Co-Dir Danforth Foundation Research Project 1968–69, Coordinator, Inst. for Local Govt and Public Service and of Public Admin. 1968–70, Assoc. Vice-Pres. for Acad. Affairs and Dir Int. Programs (Dir of Center at Univ. of Skopje, Yugoslavia) 1969–70, Vice-Pres. for Acad. Affairs 1970–76, Pres. and Prof. of Political Science and Public Admin., California State Univ., Dominguez Hills 1976–84, Pres. and Prof. of Public Policy and Admin., California State Univ., Sacramento 1984–2003, Prof. Emer. 2003–; Pres. Int. Asscn of Univ. Presidents 1996–99; numerous other appointments; Hon. Prof.; numerous hon. doctorates. *Publications:* The Invisible Giant 1971, The People's University: A History of the California State University 2010; numerous articles. *Leisure interest:* international affairs. *Address:* 7132 Secret Garden Loop, Roseville, CA 95747-8041, USA (home). *Telephone:* (916) 771-3412 (home). *Fax:* (916) 771-3413 (home). *E-mail:* dongerth@csus.edu. *Website:* www.calstate.edu (office).

GERTLER, Meric, PhD, FRSC, AcSS, MCIP; Canadian professor of geography, academic and university administrator; *President, University of Toronto;* ed Harvard Univ., USA; Vice-Dean, Grad. Educ. and Research, Faculty of Arts & Science, Univ. of Toronto –2008, Dean 2008–13, Pres. Univ. of Toronto 2013–, Founding Co-Dir Program on Globalization and Regional Innovation Systems (PROGRIS), Munk School of Global Affairs, served as Dir Dept of Geography's Program in Planning, holds the Goldring Chair in Canadian Studies; visiting appointments at Univ. of Oxford, UK, Univ. Coll., London, UCLA and Univ. of Oslo; has served as adviser to local, regional and nat. govt in Canada, USA and Europe, and to OECD and EU; mem. Expert Panel on Business Innovation established by Council of Canadian Acads 2009; Academician, Acad. of Social Sciences (UK) 2012; mem. Canadian Inst. of Planners; Hon. PhD (Lund Univ., Sweden) 2012; Award for Scholarly Distinction, Canadian Asscn of Geographers 2007. *Publications:* six books, including Manufacturing Culture: The Institutional Geography of Industrial Practice, Innovation and Social Learning (co-ed.), Oxford Handbook of Economic Geography (co-ed.) (Outstanding Academic Book Award, Choice Magazine); more than 80 journal articles and book chapters on the geography of innovative activity and the economies of city regions. *Address:* Office of the President, University of Toronto, 27 King's College Circle, Room 206, Toronto, ON M5S 1A1, Canada (office). *Telephone:* (416) 978-4163 (office). *E-mail:* president@utoronto.ca (office). *Website:* www.president.utoronto.ca (office).

GERTZE, Neville Melvin, MBA; Namibian diplomatist and government official; *Permanent Representative to United Nations;* b. 5 Aug. 1966, Windhoek; m.; two c.; ed Univ. of Cape Town; Desk officer Asia and Pacific, Ministry of Foreign Affairs 1990; First Sec. Embassy of Namibia, Washington DC 1991–95; Personal Asst to Minister of Foreign Affairs 1995–97; Counsellor, South Africa 1997–2003; High Commr to Malaysia 2003–08, Amb. (non-resident) to Philippines and Thailand 2008, Amb. to Germany 2009–15; Chief of Protocol, Ministry of Int. Relations and Cooperation 2015–17; Perm. Rep. to UN 2017–. *Address:* Permanent Mission of Namibia, 135 E 36th Street, New York, NY 10016, USA (office). *Telephone:* (212) 685-2003 (office). *Fax:* (212) 685-1561 (office). *E-mail:* namibia@un.int (office). *Website:* www.un.int/namibia (office).

GERVASI, (Alexander) Sacha Simon; British film director, journalist and screenwriter; b. 1966, London; s. of Sean Gervasi and Milli Kasoy; m. Jessica de Rothschild 2010; one d. with Geri Halliwell; ed Westminster School, King's Coll., London, Univ. of California, Los Angles Film School; befriended Canadian metal band Anvil 1981, toured London and became a roadie for the band on three tours, left band 1986; original mem. of alternative rock group Future Primitives (now Bush); worked for the Poet Laureate of England, Ted Hughes at Arvon Writing Foundation; subsequently worked for John Calder of the Samuel Beckett archive; moved to Los Angeles to attend grad. screen-writing programme at UCLA Film School 1995; worked as journalist, writing for newspapers and magazines, including The Sunday Times, The Observer and Punch; the voice of Jaguar cars on US radio and TV 1999–2000; began writing for film as co-writer with Craig Ferguson for The Big Tease 1999; twice won the BAFTA/LA scholarship. *Films directed:* Anvil: The Story of Anvil (documentary) (also exec. producer) (Evening Standard British Film Award for Best Documentary 2009, Int. Documentary Asscn Award for Best Documentary Feature 2010, Ind. Spirit Award for Best Documentary 2010, Emmy Award for Outstanding Arts and Cultural Programming 2010) 2008, Hitchcock 2012. *Screenplays:* The Big Tease (also exec. producer) 1999, The Terminal 2004, Henry's Crime (also exec. producer) 2010, My Dinner with Hervé 2013, November Criminals 2017.

GESCHKE, Charles M. (Chuck), AB, MS, PhD; American computer industry executive; b. 11 Sept. 1939, Cleveland, Ohio; m. Nancy Geschke 1964; several c.; ed Saint Ignatius High School, Xavier Univ., Carnegie-Mellon Univ.; fmr Prin. Scientist and Researcher, Xerox Palo Alto Research Center (PARC), f. PARC Imaging Sciences Lab. 1980; Co-founder, with John Warnock, Adobe Systems Inc. 1982, COO 1986–94, Pres. 1989–2000, Co-Chair. 1997–2017; Dir Rambus, Inc.; mem. Nat. Acad. of Eng, Govt-Univ. Industry Research Roundtable, Nat. Acad. of Sciences; mem. Bd of Govs San Francisco Symphony, Commonwealth Club of Calif., Egan Maritime Foundation, Nat. Leadership Roundtable on Church Man., Nantucket Boys and Girls Club, Tableau Software; mem. Advisory Bd Carnegie-Mellon Univ., Princeton Univ.; mem. Bd of Trustees Univ. of San Francisco (Chair. –2010); mem. Nat. Acad. of Eng 1995, American Acad. of Arts and Sciences 2008; Fellow, Asscn for Computing Machinery (ACM) 1999, Computer History Museum 2002; Hon. DHumLitt (John Carroll Univ.) 2012; honoured by several orgs, including ACM, Nat. Computer Graphics Asscn, Rochester Inst. of Tech., John W. Gardner Leadership Award, Entrepreneur of the Year Award, Medal of Achievement, American Electronics Asscn (with John Warnock) 2006, Computer Entrepreneur Award, IEEE Computer Soc. (with John Warnock) 2008, Nat. Medal of Tech. and Innovation (with John Warnock) 2008, Marconi Prize (with John Warnock) 2010. *Address:* c/o Adobe Systems Inc., 345 Park Avenue, San Jose, CA 95110-2704, USA.

GESSEN, Maria Alexandrovna (Masha); Russian/American journalist, author and translator; b. 13 Jan. 1967, Moscow, USSR; d. of Alexander Gessen and Yelena Gessen; m. 1st Svetlana Generalova 2004 (divorced); m. 2nd Darya Oreshkina; two s. one d.; ed Rhode Island School of Design, Cooper Union, New York; Ed.-in-Chief, The Snob Magazine 2008–11, Vokrug Sveta 2011–12; Russian Service Dir, Radio Svoboda 2012–13, Radio Free Europe/Radio Liberty, USA 2012–13; Visiting Prof. Amherst Coll., MA 2017–, John J. McCloy '16 Prof. of American Inst. and Int. Diplomacy 2017–18, 2018–19; staff writer The New Yorker 2017–; Wallenberg Medal, Univ. of Michigan 2015, Hitchens Prize 2018. *Publications:* The rights of lesbians and gay men in the Russian Federation: an International Gay and Lesbian Human Rights Commission report 1994, Dead Again: The Russian Intelligentsia After Communism 1997, Ester and Ruzya: How My Grandmothers Survived Hitler's War and Stalin's Peace 2004, Blood Matters: From Inherited Illness to Designer Babies, How the World and I Found Ourselves in the Future of the Gene 2008, Perfect Rigor: A Genius and the Mathematical Breakthrough of the Century 2009, The Man Without a Face: The Unlikely Rise of Vladimir Putin 2012, Words Will Break Cement: The Passion of Pussy Riot 2014, Gay Propaganda: Russian Love Stories 2014, Brothers: The Road to An American Tragedy 2015, Where the Jews Aren't: The Sad and Absurd Story of Birobidzhan, Russia's Autonomous Region 2016, The Future is History: How Totalitarianism Reclaimed Russia (Nat. Book Award for Nonfiction 2017) 2017, Never Remember: Searching for Stalin's Gulags in Putin's Russia 2018. *Address:* Amherst Coll., 210 Webster Hall, 220 South Pleasant Street, Amherst, MA 01002 USA (office). *Telephone:* (413) 542-5963 (office). *E-mail:* mgessen@amherst.edu (office). *Website:* www.amherst.edu/people/facstaff/mgessen (office).

GETTU, Tegegnework; Ethiopian economist and UN official; *Under-Secretary-General and Associate Administrator, United Nations Development Programme (UNDP);* b. 1952; m.; two c.; fmr Fellow and Asst Prof., Columbia Univ.; fmr Lecturer, Univ. of Rochester, New York; fmr Country Dir for Southern Africa and Indian Ocean countries, Acting Resident Rep. in Liberia and Sierra Leone –2003, UN Resident Coordinator and UNDP Resident Rep. in Nigeria 2003–06, Chief of Staff and Dir, Exec. Office, UNDP 2006–09, Asst Sec.-Gen. and Regional Bureau Dir for Africa, UNDP 2009–13, Under-Sec.-Gen. for Gen. Ass. and Conf. Man., UN 2013–15, Under-Sec.-Gen. and Assoc. Admin., UNDP 2015–; fmr Asst Prof. and Lecturer, Univ. of Rochester, Hunter Coll., Addis Ababa Univ.; also served as Sr Econ. and Political Adviser, UNDP Africa Bureau, New York, Sr Adviser, Ministry of Planning and Econ. Devt. *Address:* United Nations Development Programme, One United Nations Plaza, New York, NY 10017, USA (office). *Website:* www.undp.org (office).

GETTY, Mark; American business executive; *Co-Founder, Getty Images, Inc.;* b. 9 July 1960, Oxfordshire, UK; s. of Sir Paul Getty, Jr and Abigail Harris Getty; m. Domitilla Harding; two s. one d.; fmr investment banker, Kidder Peabody, New York, then Hambros Bank Ltd, London 1991; Co-Founder Getty Investments LLC 1993; Co-founder Getty Images Inc. 1995, Chair. 1995–2015; Trustee, Nat. Gallery, London. *Address:* c/o Getty Images Inc., 605 5th Avenue S, Suite 400, Seattle, WA 98104, USA (office). *Telephone:* (206) 925-5000 (office). *Fax:* (206) 925-5001 (office). *Website:* www.gettyimages.com (office).

GEVORGYAN, Armen, MA; Armenian politician and foundation director; *CEO, Initiatives for Development of Armenia (IDeA) Charitable Foundation;* b. 8 July 1973, Yerevan; m.; two s. one d.; ed School No. 28, Yerevan, Orenburg State Pedagogical Inst., Russia, St Petersburg Inst. of Public Service, Russia, Twente Univ., Netherlands, St Petersburg Gertsen Russian Pedagogical Inst., Russia; Asst to the Prime Minister 1997–98; Asst to the Pres. of Armenia and First Deputy Head of Admin 1998–2000, First Asst to the Pres. 2000–06; Chief of Staff to the Pres. 2006–08; Sec. Nat. Security Council, Pres.'s Office 2007–08; Deputy Prime Minister and Minister of Territorial Admin 2008–14; CEO Initiatives for Devt of Armenia (IDeA) Charitable Foundation 2014–; mem. CIS Econ. Council 2008–. *Address:* Initiatives for Development of Armenia (IDeA) Charitable Foundation, 0019 Yerevan, 6 Baghramyan avenue, Armenia (office). *Telephone:* (60) 70-08-00 (office). *E-mail:* a.gevorgyan@idea.am (office). *Website:* www.idea.am/en/our-team (office).

GHABBAN, Mohammed Salem al-; Iraqi politician; ed Univs in Tehran and London, Univ. of Baghdad; longtime opponent of Saddam Hussain, detained in 1979, later lived in exile in Iran; mem. Badr Org., State of Law Coalition; Minister of the Interior 2014–16.

GHADHBAN, Thamir Abbas al-, BSc, MSc; Iraqi petroleum engineer; *Deputy Prime Minister for Energy Affairs and Minister of Oil;* b. 1945, Babil; ed Univ. Coll. London and Imperial Coll., London Univ., UK; worked for Ministry of Oil 1973–2003, first as reservoir engineer, then Head of Petroleum and Reservoir Eng –1989, Dir-Gen. of Reservoir and Field Devt 1989–90, Dir-Gen. of Studies and Planning 1991–92, Tech. Advisor to Oil Ministry 1993–2001, Dir-Gen. of Planning 2002–03, Chief Geologist and CEO 2003–04; Interim Minister of Oil 2004–05; Acting Chair. Nat. Investment Comm. 2009; Chair. Advisory Cttee to Prime Minister 2008–16; Advisor to Prime Minister 2016–18; Deputy Prime Minister for Energy Affairs and Minister of Oil 2018–; Order of the Rising Sun, Gold and Silver Star (Japan) 2016; OAPEC Distinguished Science Award 2000. *Publications include:* author and co-author of more than 50 studies and technical papers. *Address:* Ministry of Oil, Oil Complex Building, Port Said Street, Baghdad, Iraq (office). *Telephone:* (1) 817-7000 (office). *Fax:* (1) 747-0341 (office). *E-mail:* ministryofoil@oil.gov.iq (office). *Website:* www.oil.gov.iq (office).

GHADIRIAN, Shadi, BA; Iranian photographer; b. 1974, Tehran; m. Peyman Hooshmand-zadeh; ed Islamic Azad Univ., Tehran; Man. www.fanoosphoto.com (first Iranian specialized photography website); Photo Ed. Women in Iran website (www.womeniniran.com); collaborates with Akskhaneh Shahr (Museum of Photography), Tehran; works held in several int. public collections including Museum of Contemporary Art, Tehran, British Museum, Victoria and Albert Museum and Satchi Gallery, London, Musée des Arts Contemporains, Centre Georges Pompidou, Paris, Museum Moderner Kunst Stiftung Ludwig, Vienna, Los Angeles County Museum of Art, Sackler Gallery, Smithsonian Inst., Washington DC, Devi Art Foundation, Delhi. *Address:* c/o Silk Road Art Gallery, 103 Lavasani Avenue, 19368-39631 Tehran, Iran (office). *E-mail:* info@shadighadirian.com (office). *Website:* shadighadirian.com (office).

GHAFERI, Amal Al, BSc, PhD; United Arab Emirates physicist and academic; *Assistant Professor, Materials Science and Engineering, Masdar Institute of Science and Technology;* ed UAE Univ., Univ. of Pittsburgh, USA; Asst Prof., Physics Dept, UAE Univ., Al Ain 2007–10; Asst Prof., Materials Science and Eng, Masdar Inst. of Science and Tech. 2010–; Visiting Scholar, MIT, USA 2010–; Sheikh Rashid Scientific Distinction Award 2000, 2007, UK Prime Minister's

Initiative Award – PMI2 2009, Women in Science and Tech. Fellowship (USA) 2009. *Publications:* numerous papers in professional journals on implementing nanotechnology in renewable energy. *Address:* Masdar Institute of Science and Technology, Masdar City, Adu Dhabi, United Arab Emirates (office). *Telephone:* (2) 810-9103 (office). *Fax:* (2) 810-9901 (office). *E-mail:* aalghaferi@masdar.ac.ae (office). *Website:* www.masdar.ac.ae (office).

GHAFOOR MOHAMED, Abdul, BA, MA; Maldivian diplomatist and international organization official; b. 20 Nov. 1959, Malé; m.; one s. one d.; ed Univ. of Tasmania, Australia, The Fletcher School of Law and Diplomacy, Tufts Univ., USA; career diplomat; Programme Officer, Ministry of Foreign Affairs 1983, Asst Under-Secretary 1985, Asst Dir (Political Affairs) 1989, Deputy Dir (Foreign Relations) 1992, Dir (Foreign Relations) 1994; Dir (Maldives), South Asian Asscn for Regional Cooperation Secr., Kathmandu, Nepal 1997–2000; Dir-Gen. (Foreign Relations), Ministry of Foreign Affairs 2000; Counsellor, Embassy in Colombo 2003; Asst Exec. Dir, Ministry of Foreign Affairs 2005; Deputy High Commr to Sri Lanka 2005, to Malaysia 2006; Exec. Dir, Ministry of Foreign Affairs 2007; Perm. Rep. to UN, Geneva 2007–09; Perm. Rep. to WTO 2008–09; Amb.-at-Large, Ministry of Foreign Affairs, seconded to Office of the Pres. 2009–10; Amb. and Perm. Rep. to UN, New York (also accred as Amb. to USA) 2010–12 (resgnd). *Address:* Ministry of Foreign Affairs, Boduthakurufaanu Magu, Malé 20-077, Maldives (office). *Telephone:* 3323400 (office). *Fax:* 3323841 (office). *E-mail:* admin@foreign.gov.mv (office). *Website:* www.foreign.gov.mv (office).

GHAI, Dharam Pal, PhD; Kenyan international civil servant and economist; b. 29 June 1936, Nairobi; s. of Basti Ghai and Widya Wati; m. Neela Korde 1963; one s. two d.; ed Queen's Coll., UK, Yale Univ., USA; Lecturer in Econs, Makerere Univ., Uganda 1961–65; Visiting Fellow, Econ. Growth Center, Yale Univ. 1966–67; Research Prof. and Dir of Econs Research, Inst. of Devt Studies, Univ. of Nairobi 1967–71, Dir Inst. of Devt Studies 1971–74; Sr Economist, Comm. on Int. Devt (Pearson Comm.), Washington, DC 1968–69; Chief, World Employment Programme Research Br., Employment and Devt Dept, ILO, Geneva 1973–74, Chief, Tech. Secr., World Employment Conf. 1975–76, Chief, Rural Employment Policies Br., Employment and Devt Dept 1977–87; Dir UN Research Inst. for Social Devt 1987–97; Coordinator ILO Transition Team 1998–99; Adviser, Int. Inst. of Labour Studies; Fellow, African Acad. of Sciences. *Publications include:* Collective Agriculture and Rural Development in Soviet Central Asia (with A. R. Khan) 1979, Planning for Basic Needs in Kenya (co-author) 1979, Agricultural Prices, Policy and Equity in Sub-Saharan Africa (with Lawrence Smith) 1987, Labour and Development in Rural Cuba (co-author) 1987, Social Development and Public Policy (ed.), Renewing Social and Economic Progress in Africa (ed.); contrib. to UN Intellectual History Project; co-ed. and contrib. to several other books. *Leisure interests:* photography, gardening, swimming. *Address:* 32 chemin des Voirons, 1296 Coppet, Vaud, Switzerland (home). *Telephone:* (22) 7765281 (home). *Fax:* (22) 7765282 (home). *E-mail:* ghai@bluewin.ch.

GHAI, Yash P., BA, LLM, DCL; Kenyan constitutional lawyer, academic and UN official; b. 20 Oct. 1938; m. Jill Cottrell; ed Univ. of Oxford, UK, Harvard Univ., USA; barrister, Middle Temple, London, UK 1962; Lecturer, Univ. of Dar-es-Salaam 1963–66, Sr Lecturer 1966–69, Prof. and Dean 1969–70; Sr Fellow and Lecturer, Yale Univ., USA 1971–73; Prof., Univ. of Warwick, UK 1974–89; Sir Y. K. Pau Prof. of Public Law, Univ. of Hong Kong 1989–95, Prof. Emer. 1995–; involved in drafting constitutions for Papua New Guinea, Fiji, Solomon Islands and others; Chair. Constitution of Kenya Review Comm. 2000–03; UN Sec.-Gen.'s Special Rep. for Human Rights in Cambodia 2005–08 (resgnd); fmr Head of UNDP Constitution Advisory Support Unit in Nepal; Researcher, Ethnicity and Democratic Governance Project, Queen's Univ., Canada; Hon. Fellow, Soc. for Advanced Legal Studies 1997, Hon. Life mem. Law Soc. of Kenya 1998; Dr hc Univ. of the South Pacific 1995; Distinguished Researcher Award, Univ. of Hong Kong 2001. *Publications include:* Public Law and Political Change in Kenya 1970, Asians in East Africa 1971, Hong Kong's New Constitutional Order: The Resumption of Chinese Sovereignty and Basic Law 1997, Hong Kong's Constitutional Debate: Conflict over Interpretation (co-author) 1999, Autonomy and Ethnicity: Negotiating Competing Claims in Multi-Ethnic States (ed. and contrib.) 2000, Public Participation and Minorities 2001.

GHALIB, Omar Arteh; Somali politician; b. 1930, Hargeisa; s. of Arteh Ghalib and Sahra Sheikh Hassan; m. Shakri Jirdeh Hussein 1954; six s. six d.; ed St Paul's Coll., Cheltenham, UK and Univ. of Bristol; teacher 1946–49; Headmaster of various elementary schools 1949–54; Vice-Prin. Intermediate School, Sheikh, Somalia 1954–56; Prin. Intermediate School, Gabileh 1958; Officer in charge of Adult Educ. 1959; District Commr in Public Admin 1960–61; First Sec. Somali Embassy, Moscow 1961–62; Rapporteur, Special Cttee on SW Africa, UN 1962–63; Counsellor, Perm. Mission of Somalia at UN, New York 1964; Amb. to Ethiopia 1965–68; mem. Somali Nat. Ass. 1969; Sec. of State for Foreign Affairs 1969–76; Minister of Culture and Higher Educ. 1976–78, in the Pres.'s Office 1978–80; mem. Cttee for Social and Political Thought 1976; Speaker, People's Ass. 1982–91; Prime Minister of Somalia 1991–93; numerous awards and decorations. *Publications include:* Back from the Lion of Judah. *Leisure interests* reciting the Koran, writing, poetry, horse riding, social welfare activities.

GHALIBAF, Mohammad Baqer, PhD; Iranian politician; b. 23 Sept. 1961, Mashhad; m.; two s. one d.; ed Tarbiat Modares Univ., Tehran; Chief of IRI (Islamic Repub. of Iran) Police Forces 2000–05 (resgnd); unsuccessful cand. in presidential election 2005; Mayor of Tehran 2005–17. *Publication:* Local Government in Iran. *Leisure interests:* reading (novels, history, politics), horse-riding, tennis, swimming. *Website:* www.ghalibaf.ir.

GHANDOUR, Fadi, BA; Jordanian business executive; *Co-founder and Vice-Chairman, Aramex International Ltd;* b. 1 Jan. 1959; s. of Ali Ghandour; m. Rula Atalla; two s.; ed George Washington Univ., Washington, DC, USA; Co-founder Aramex International Ltd 1982, CEO 1982–2012, Vice-Chair. 2012–; Founding Pnr, Maktoob.com; Middle East and North Africa Area Chair. Young Presidents' Org. 2003–05; fmr Vice-Chair. Bd of Trustees, Jordan River Foundation; fmr Chair. Nat. Microfinance Bank, Jordan; Founder Ruwwad Devt; mem. Bd of Dirs Abraaj Capital; Founding Bd mem. Endeavor Jordan; mem. Advisory Bd Suliman S. Olayan School of Business, American Univ. of Beirut. *Address:* Aramex International Ltd, PO Box 960913, Amman 11196, Jordan (office). *Telephone:* (6) 5522192 (office). *Fax:* (6) 5527461 (office). *Website:* www.aramex.com (office); www.fadighandour.com.

GHANDOUR, Ibrahim; Sudanese politician; b. 6 Dec. 1952; ed Univ. of Khartoum; fmr Vice-Chancellor, Univ. of Khartoum, also Dean, Faculty of Dentistry; Pres. All Sudan Workers Trade Unions Fed. 2001; fmr consultant to WHO; Asst to Pres. of Sudan 2013–15; Minister of Foreign Affairs 2015–18; mem. Nat. Congress Party (NCP), fmr Sec. for Political Affairs and Head of External Relations, currently NCP Vice-Pres. *Address:* c/o Ministry of Foreign Affairs, POB 873, Khartoum, Sudan (office).

GHANI, Ashraf, MPh, PhD; Afghan anthropologist, academic, university administrator, government official and head of state; *President;* b. (Ashraf Ghani Ahmadzai), 12 Feb. 1949, Logar; m. Rula Ghani; two c.; ed American Univ. of Beirut, Lebanon, Columbia Univ., USA; has taught at Århus Univ., Denmark and Univ. of California, Berkeley, USA; fmr Adjunct Prof. of Anthropology, Johns Hopkins Univ., USA; broadcasts on BBC and Voice of America Persian and Pashto services 1982–; anthropologist at World Bank 1991–2001; Special Adviser to UN Sec.-Gen.'s Special Rep. for Afghanistan 2001 (adviser during Bonn process and establishment of first post-Taliban admin in Afghanistan); Minister of Finance, Transitional Authority 2002–04; Chancellor, Kabul Univ. 2004–08; unsuccessful cand. in presidential elections 2009; apptd Chair. of govt comm. on transition 2010; Pres. of Afghanistan 2014–; Co-founder and Chair. Inst. for State Effectiveness 2005–11; fmr mem. Comm. on Legal Empowerment of the Poor (UNDP initiative); Chair. Global Agenda Council on Fragile States, World Econ. Forum; mem. Bd of Dirs World Justice Project. *Publication:* Fixing Failed States: A Framework for Rebuilding a Fractured World (co-author) 2008. *Address:* Office of the President, Gul Khana Palace, Presidential Palace, Kabul, Afghanistan (office). *Telephone:* (20) 2141135 (office). *E-mail:* aimal.faizi@arg.gov.af (office). *Website:* www.president.gov.af (office); ps.ashrafghani.com.

GHANI, Nasimul; Bangladeshi television industry executive; fmr Dir-Gen. Prime Minister's Office; Dir-Gen. Bangladesh TV (govt controlled) 2006–08; mem. Advisory Council Citigroup Microentrepreneurship Awards 2006.

GHANI, Owais Ahmed; Pakistani engineer and government official; *Senior Fellow, Global Think Tank Network, National University of Sciences and Technology;* b. 5 Feb. 1951; s. of Sardar Abdul Ghani; m. Ghazala Owais Ghani; Kakar Pushtun by tribe; fmr Fed. Minister for Labour in Musharraf-led mil. govt and later Minister for Industries in North West Frontier Prov. –2003; Gov. of Balochistan 2003–08, of North West Frontier Prov. (renamed Khyber Pakhtunkhwa April 2010) 2008–11; Pres. Pakistan Red Crescent Soc. Balochistan Br.; Chancellor Balochistan Univ. of Information Tech. and Man. Sciences; Sr Fellow and mem. Bd of Dirs, Global Think Tank Network (GTTN), Nat. Univ. of Sciences and Technology 2013–. *Publications:* Pakistan, 2013: Views on Statecraft Politics & Governance 2013. *Address:* Global Think Tank Network, National University of Sciences and Technology, Islamabad, Pakistan (office). *E-mail:* info.gttn@nust.edu.pk (office). *Website:* www.nust.edu.pk (office).

GHANNOUCHI, Muhammad; Tunisian politician; b. 18 Aug. 1941, Sousse, French Protectorate of Tunisia; m.; two c.; ed Tunis Univ.; Minister of Finance and the Economy 1989–92, of Int. Co-operation and Foreign Investment 1992–99; Prime Minister of Tunisia 1999–2011 (resgnd); Acting Pres. of Tunisia following the fall of Pres. Zine El Abidine Ben Ali in the wake of popular protests 14–15 Jan. 2011; mem. Constitutional Democratic Rally party –2011; Ind. 2011–; Kt, Order of Independence; Grand Cordon, Order of the Repub.; Grand Cordon, Order of 7 November. *Address:* c/o Bureau du Premier Ministre, place du Gouvernement, La Kasbah, 1030 Tunis, Tunisia. *E-mail:* boc@pm.gov.tn.

GHARBI, El Mostafa, LLB; Moroccan international postal official; b. 9 Feb. 1935, El Jadida; m. Lalla Hafida Regragui 1962; three d.; ed Ecole Nat. Supérieure des Postes, Télégraphes et Téléphones, Paris; various positions, Ministry of Posts, Telegraphs and Telephones, Rabat 1956–65, Dir of Postal and Financial Services 1965–71; Counsellor, Universal Postal Union (UPU), Berne 1971–78, Sr Counsellor 1978–81, Asst Dir-Gen. in charge of postal services and studies 1981–90, in charge of legal and admin. questions 1990, later Asst Dir-Gen., Int. Bureau; Médaille de Chevalier. *Publications include:* The UPU: Present Situation—Main Policies 1990; other books on postal services and strategies. *Leisure interests:* reading, sport.

GHARIANI, Muhammad; Tunisian diplomatist; b. 13 Aug. 1962, Kairouan; m. Olfa Ghariani; two d.; ed Univ. of Tunis; activist in youth wing of Democratic Constitutional Rally (RCD) 1980s, Sec.-Gen. RCD Students' party 1987, Deputy Sec.-Gen. for Youth, Educ. and Culture 1995–96; mem. Econ. and Social Council 1992–96; Gov. southern Tunisian prov. of Sidi Bouzid 1996–2001; Deputy Sec.-Gen. for Relations with Orgs and Asscns 2001–05; Amb. to UK (also accred to Ireland) 2005–07; Sec.-Gen. Rassemblement constitutionnel démocratique (political party) 2008–11; arrested on charges of embezzlement 2011; Political Adviser 2013; joined Nat. Initiative destourienne 2016; Officer, Order of the Republic, Officer, Order of November 7, Grand Officer, Order of Merit. *Leisure interest:* literature.

GHASEMI, Brig.-Gen. (retd) Rostam; Iranian military officer and government official; b. 22 May 1964, Shiraz, Fars Prov.; ed Aryamehr Univ. of Tech.; joined Army of the Guardians of the Islamic Revolution 1981, participated in Iran–Iraq War 1980s; later joined Khatam Anbia Troops (Guards' eng and construction co.), Deputy Commdr 2001–07, Chief Commdr Iranian Revolutionary Guard 2007–11 (retd); elected mem. Parl. 1988, re-elected 1992, 1996; Minister of Petroleum 2011–13; Adviser to Minister of Defence 2013–; Chair. Iranian Marine Industrial Co. (SADRA), Khalij Fars Shipbuilding Complex (ISOICO); Man. Iran Sepah Marine Eng Div.; Man. Dir Khatam-Ul-Anbia Construction HQR (upstream and downstream oil, gas and petrochemical projects) 2006–11; Pres. of the Conf., OPEC; mem. Iran Chamber of Commerce, Industries and Mines, Bd of Dirs Industrial Devt and Renovation Org. of Iran. *Address:* Ministry of Defence and Armed Forces Logistics, Shahid Yousuf Kaboli St, Sayed Khandan Area, Tehran, Iran (office). *Telephone:* (21) 26126988 (office). *E-mail:* info@mod.ir (office). *Website:* www.mod.ir (office).

GHAZAL, Mohammed Iyad, BEng; Syrian government official; b. Aleppo; ed Univ. of Aleppo; Pres. and Gen. Dir Syrian Railways 1999–2005; Gov. Homs Governorate 2005–11.

GHAZANFAR, Hosna Banu, BA, MA, PhD; Afghan politician, academic and poet; b. 1 Feb. 1957, Balkh; d. of Abdul Ghafar; ed Sultan Razia High School, Mazar-e-Sharif, Stawarpool Qafqaaz Univ., St Petersburg Univ., Russia; fmr Lecturer in Literature, Kabul Univ. for two years, fmr Dean of Faculty of Literature and Language; Minister of Women's Affairs (first female minister in cabinet) 2006–15; mem. High Council of Ministry of Higher Educ., Speranto Int. Asscn of Women, Int. Asscn of Turk Zabanan, Bd of Dirs Hakim Naser Khesro Balkhi Asscn. *Publications include:* The Human Fate, Predations in the 21st Century, The Secrets of Beauty and Attraction, Self Realization (trans.); scientific articles and essays published in nat. and int. newspapers.

GHAZOUANI, Mohamed Ould Cheikh Mohamed Ahmed Ould El; Mauritanian politician; b. 1957; ed Meknes Royal Military Acad., Morocco; Chief of Staff of the Armed Forces 2008–18; Minister of Defence 2018–19; presidential candidate, Union pour la République, 2019. *Address:* c/o Ministry of Defence, Nouakchott, Mauritania.

GHAZZALI, Dato' Sheikh Abdul Khalid, BEcons; Malaysian diplomatist and consultant; *Senior Advisor, Malaysia, Bower Group Asia;* b. 20 March 1946; m. Datin Faridah Ghazzali; ed Univ. of La Trobe, Australia; fmr Deputy Perm. Rep. to UN and Security Council, New York, fmr Deputy High Commr to UK, fmr High Commr to Zimbabwe, fmr Dir-Gen. Inst. of Diplomacy and Foreign Relations, Malaysia, fmr Deputy Sec.-Gen., Ministry of Foreign Affairs, Amb. to USA 1999–2006, Amb.-at-Large, Ministry of Foreign Affairs 2006–10; currently Sr Advisor, Malaysia, Bower Group Asia; ASEAN-US Eminent Person for Malaysia; mem. Bd of Trustees Axiata Foundation. *Leisure interests:* reading, walking. *Address:* Bower Group Asia, 11350 Random Hills Road, Suite 400, Fairfax, VA 22030, USA (office). *Telephone:* 19-3817564 (mobile). *E-mail:* tansrighazzali@bowergroupasia.com (office). *Website:* bowergroupasia.com (office).

GHEIT, Ahmed Aboul, BSc; Egyptian diplomatist, politician and international organization official; *Secretary-General, League of Arab States;* b. 12 June 1942, Heliopolis; m.; two c.; ed Ainshams Univ., Cairo; joined Ministry of Foreign Affairs 1965; Attaché-Third Sec., Embassy in Cyprus 1968–72; staff mem. of Adviser to Pres. on Nat. Security Affairs 1972–74; Second-First Sec., Perm. Mission to UN, New York 1974–77; Counsellor, Special Aide, Cabinet of Minister of Foreign Affairs 1977–79; Political Counsellor, Embassy in Moscow 1979–82; Political Adviser to Minister of Foreign Affairs 1982–84, 1989–90, to Prime Minister 1984–85; Counsellor, Perm. Mission to UN 1985–87, Deputy Perm. Rep. 1987–89; Chef de Cabinet, Minister of Foreign Affairs 1990–92, Asst Foreign Minister for Cabinet Affairs 1996–99; Amb. to Italy, Macedonia, San Marino and Rep. to FAO, Rome 1992–96; Perm. Rep. to UN 1999–2004; Minister of Foreign Affairs 2004–11; Sec.-Gen., League of Arab States 2016–. *Publications:* My Testimony 2013. *Address:* League of Arab States, PO Box 11642, Arab League Building, Tahrir Square, Cairo 11211, Egypt (office). *Telephone:* (2) 575-0511 (office). *Fax:* (2) 574-0331 (office). *E-mail:* communication.dept@las.int (office). *Website:* www.lasportal.org (office).

GHEORGHE, Mariana; Romanian business executive; *President of the Executive Board and CEO, OMV Petrom SA;* ed Acad. of Econ. Studies, Univ. of Bucharest Law School, London Business School, UK; worked for Ministry of Finance 1991–93, held position of Deputy Gen. Dir, Int. Finance Dept; apptd Assoc. Banker, EBRD, London 1993, later Sr Banker, South-Eastern Europe and the Caucasus Group, Banking; currently Pres. Exec. Bd and CEO OMV Petrom SA, Dir, Snp Petrom SA. *Address:* OMV Petrom SA, 239 Calea Dorobantilor Sector 1, 010567 Bucharest, Romania (office). *Telephone:* (21) 2125001 (office). *Fax:* (21) 3155166 (office). *E-mail:* info@petrom.com (office). *Website:* www.petrom.com (office); www.omv.com/portal/01/com/omv/OMV_Group/Business_Segments/OMV_Gas_and_Power/Subsidiaries/OMV_Petrom_SA (office).

GHEORGHIU, Angela; Romanian singer (soprano); b. 7 Sept. 1965, Adjud; m. 1st Andrei Gheorghiu 1988; m. 2nd Roberto Alagna (q.v.) 1996 (divorced 2013); ed Bucharest Acad., studied with Mia Barbu; debut at Bucharest as Solveig in Grieg's Peer Gynt 1983; appearances at Covent Garden from 1992, Met debut 1993, and in Washington, Vienna, Monte Carlo, Berlin, Nat. Opera Cluj; Tosca, Royal Opera House, Wiener Staatsoper, Staasoper Berlin 2016; repertoire includes Zerlina, Mimi, Nina (all in Cherubin), Suzel (L'Amico Fritz), Juliette (Roméo et Juliette), Magda (La Rondine), Nedda (Pagliacci), Tosca, Manon, and roles in Don Giovanni, La Bohème (Mimi), Turandot, Carmen, La Traviata (Violetta), L'Elisir d'Amore, Falstaff; Officier, Ordre des Arts et Lettres, Chevalier, Ordre des Arts et Lettres, Nihil Sine Deo 2012; Dr hc (Univ. of Arts, Iasi); Belvedere Prize, Vienna, Schatzgraber-Preis, Hamburg State Opera, Gulbenkian Prize, La Medaille Vermeille de la Ville de Paris, Star of Romania 2010, European Culture Award 2015. *Recordings include:* La Traviata (as Violetta) 1994, Casta Diva 2001, Tosca (solo) 2001, Diva 2004, Manon 2007, Live From La Scala 2007, My Puccini 2008, Madama Butterfly 2009, Puccini Opera Arias 2010, Fedora 2011, Homage to Maria Callas 2011, Solti: The Legacy 1937–97 2012, Tosca (Puccini) (BBC Music Magazine DVD Performance Award 2014) 2012, O, ce veste minunata! Colinde romanesti 2013, The Complete Recitals 2017. *Address:* c/o IMG Artists, Pleiades House, 7 West 54th Street, New York, NY 10019, USA (office). *Telephone:* (212) 994-3500 (office). *Fax:* (212) 994-3550 (office). *Website:* www.imgartists.com (office); www.angelagheorghiu.com. *E-mail:* agerdanovits@gmx.net.

GHERMAN, Natalia, MA; Moldovan diplomatist and government official; *Special Representative and Head, United Nations Regional Centre for Preventive Diplomacy for Central Asia;* b. 20 March 1969, Chişinău, Moldovan SSR, USSR; d. of Mircea Snegur (fmr Pres. of Moldova) and Georgette Snegur; m. Artur Gherman; one c.; ed Moldova State Univ., Nat. School of Political and Admin. Studies, Romania, King's Coll., London, UK; Second Sec., Dept of Int. Orgs, Ministry of Foreign Affairs (MFA) 1991–92, First Sec., Dept of European Orgs 1992–94, Counsellor and Deputy Head of Perm. Del. of Moldova to OSCE and other Int. Orgs in Vienna 1994–97, Deputy Head, Dept of European Security and Political-Military Affairs, MFA 1997–2001, Minister-Counsellor, Embassy in Brussels and Deputy Head, Mission of Moldova to NATO 2001–02, Amb. to Austria, also Perm. Rep. to OSCE and other Int. Orgs in Vienna 2002–06, Amb. to Sweden (also accred to Norway and Finland) 2006–09, Deputy Minister of Foreign Affairs and European Integration 2009–13, Deputy Prime Minister and Minister of Foreign Affairs and European Integration 2013–16, Acting Prime Minister June–July 2015; Special Rep. and Head, UN Regional Center for Preventive Diplomacy for Central Asia (UNRCCA) 2017–; mem. Partidul Liberal Democrat din Moldova (Liberal Democratic Party of Moldova). *Address:* Partidul Liberal Democrat din Moldova (Liberal Democratic Party of Moldova), 2012 Chişinău, str. Bucureşti 88, Moldova (office); United Nations Regional Centre for Preventive Diplomacy for Central Asia, 744036 Ashgabat, 43 Archabil Avenue, Turkmenistan (office). *Telephone:* (22) 81-51-54 (office). *Fax:* (22) 81-51-63 (office). *E-mail:* info@pldm.md (office). *Website:* www.pldm.md (office); unrcca.unmissions.org (office).

GHESQUIÈRE, Nicolas; French fashion designer; *Creative Director, Louis Vuitton;* b. 9 May 1971, Comines, Nord Département; internship with agnès b. (Paris-based fashion designer) 1986; Asst to designer Jean-Paul Gaultier 1990–92; fmr stylist with designers Thierry Mugler and Trussardi; fmr designer, Pôles (Parisian knitwear manufacturer); joined fashion house Balenciaga as licensed product designer 1995, becoming Artistic Dir 'Le Dix' womenswear collection 1997, Creative Dir, Balenciaga 1997–2012; joined Louis Vuitton 2013, becoming Creative Dir (women's collections) 2013–; Chevalier, Ordre des Arts et des Lettres 2007; Avant-Garde Designer of the Year, VHI/Vogue Fashion Awards 2000, Womenswear Designer of the Year, Council of Fashion Designers of America 2001. *Address:* Louis Vuitton, 22 avenue Montaigne, 75008 Paris, France (office). *Telephone:* (1) 44-13-22-22 (office). *Fax:* (1) 44-13-21-19 (office). *Website:* www.louisvuitton.com (office).

GHEZ, Andrea Mia, BS, PhD; American physicist, astronomer and academic; *Professor of Physics and Astronomy and Lauren B. Leichtman & Arthur E. Levine Chair in Astrophysics, University of California, Los Angeles;* b. 16 June 1965, New York, NY; ed Massachusetts Inst. of Tech., California Inst. of Tech.; Hubble Postdoctoral Research Fellow, Steward Observatory, Univ. of Arizona 1992–93; Asst Prof. of Physics and Astronomy, UCLA 1994–97, Assoc. Prof. 1997–2000, Prof. 2000–; mem. American Acad. of Arts and Sciences 2004, NAS 2004; Packard Fellowship 1996, UCLA Physics Dept Teaching Award 1997, 1998, 2005, Newton Lacy Pierce Prize, American Astronomical Soc. 1998, Maria Goeppert-Mayer Award, American Physical Soc. 1999, Sackler Prize 2004, Aaronson Award 2006, MacArthur Fellowship 2008, Crafoord Prize in Astronomy, Royal Swedish Acad. of Sciences (co-recipient) 2012. *Publications:* more than 160 papers in professional journals. *Address:* Department of Physics and Astronomy, 430 Portola Plaza, University of California, Los Angeles, CA 90095-1547, USA (office). *Telephone:* (310) 206-0420 (office). *E-mail:* ghez@astro.ucla.edu (office). *Website:* www.astro.ucla.edu/~ghez (office).

GHEZALI, Salima; Algerian newspaper editor; *Editor-in-Chief, La Nation;* b. 1958, Bouïra; m. (divorced); two c.; worked as schoolteacher and trade unionist 1983–90; Ed.-in-Chief La Nation weekly newspaper 1994–96, 2001–, newspaper suspended by Algerian authorities 1996–2001; f. Women of Europe and North Africa Asscn, Asscn for Women's Emancipation 1989, Women's Solidarity of Europe and the Maghreb Asscn 1992; f. Nyssa magazine 1990; mem. of Parl. 2017–; mem. Front des forces socialistes (FFS) 2017–18; Dr hc (Univ. L'Aquila, Italy) 1999; Int. Press Club Award 1996, Sakharov Human Rights Prize 1997, Olof Palme Prize 1997, Theodor Haecker Prize 1999. *Publications include:* Le Reve Algérien 1999, Los amantes de Sherezade 2000, Disquiet Days/Jours intranquilles (co-author) 2009. *Address:* La Nation, 33 rue Larbi Ben M'hidi, Algiers, Algeria (office). *Telephone:* (21) 43-21-76 (office).

GHEZZI SOLIS, Piero Eduardo, BEcon, PhD; Peruvian economist and government official; *Minister of Production;* b. 8 April 1968, Lima; m. Mariane Barton Martinelli; three c.; ed Univ. del Pacífico, Univ. of California, Berkeley, USA; fmr Head of Emerging Markets Research, JPMorgan Chase & Co.; adviser to Ministry of Economy 1995–96; fmr Macroeconomic Consultant, IDB; Asst Prof. of Int. Macroeconomics, Johns Hopkins Univ.; joined Deutsche Bank AG as Head of Research Dept for Emerging Markets 1999, becoming Head of Latin America Strategy, Deutsche Bank AG, New York 2004–07; Head of Global Economics, Emerging Markets and Foreign Exchange Research and Man. Dir, Research Div., Barclays PLC 2007–13; Partner, Macrocapitales SAFI SA; Minister of Production 2014–. *Address:* Ministry of Production, Calle Uno Oeste 60, Urb. Córpac, San Isidro, Lima 27, Peru (home). *Telephone:* (1) 6162222 (office). *E-mail:* portal@produce.gob.pe (office). *Website:* www.produce.gob.pe (office).

GHIGO, Enzo; Italian politician; b. 24 Feb. 1953, Turin; m. Anna Casale; one s.; fmr Scientific Ed., UTET (publishing co.), Turin; self-employed in tech. components industry –1982; joined Pubblitalia '80 (advertising co.) 1982, Man. 1986–90, Area Man. for Veneto and Marche 1990; Regional Co-ordinator, Forza Italia 1993; mem. Parl. for Piedmont 2 1994, Pres. Piedmont 1995–2005, Vice-Pres. Regional Presidential Congress 1997; Pres. Conf. of Presidents of Italian Regions 2000–05; Vice-Pres. Foundation Italia in Japan 2001; Senator 12th Standing Cttee 2008; Co-ordinator, Piedmont Blue 2008; Grand'Ufficiale al merito della Repubblica Italiana 1999, Cavaliere di Gran Croce 2002. *Leisure interests:* cinema, reading, cycling.

GHIMIRE, Madhav Prasad, MSc, MBA; Nepalese civil servant, diplomatist and politician; b. 7 Feb. 1961, Tansen Municipality-12, Palpa; ed Tribhuvan Univ., Asian Inst. of Tech., Thailand; joined civil service as Planning Officer at Nat. Planning Comm. 1985–92, Under-Sec. 1992–98, Jt Sec. 1998–2004, responsible for overall human resource management at Ministry of Water Resources, also served as Chief Admin. Officer at Dept of Irrigation, introducing and institutionalizing VAT system in Nepal, headed Foreign Aid Co-ordination Div. of Ministry of Finance 1998–2003, architect of Nepal Devt Forum, Paris 2000, Kathmandu 2002, Consul Gen. to Hong Kong and Macao Special Admin. Regions of People's Repub. of China 2003, Sec. to Ministry of Gen. Admin 2004–06, to Ministry of Culture, Tourism and Civil Aviation 2006–09, to Ministry of Peace and Reconstruction 2008–09, Chief Sec. of the Govt 2009–12; Minister for Home Affairs and Minister for Foreign Affairs 2013–14; Suprabal Gorkha Daxinbahu, Fourth Medal, and Suprabal Gorkha Daxinbahu, Third Medal from the then King of Nepal, Rastra Deep (Light of the Nation) from Pres. Dr Ram Baran Yadav; Best Youth of the Year, Nepal Jaycees 1999, Best Civil Service Employee of the Year, Govt of Nepal 2001, Best Alumnus, Asian Inst. of Tech. Alumni Asscn Annual Meeting, Indonesia 2005. *Publications include:* Bibliography on Environmental Studies (co-ed.) 1993; several articles in journals, mostly on economic reforms, governance, foreign aid management and peace-building. *Address:* c/o Ministry of Foreign Affairs, Narayanhiti, Kathmandu, Nepal.

GHIMPU, Mihai; Romanian lawyer and politician; *Chairman, Partidul Liberal (PL—Liberal Party);* b. 19 Nov. 1951, Coloniţa, Moldovan SSR, USSR; s. of Toader Ghimpu and Irina Ursu; m. Dina Ghimpu; ed Moldova State Univ.; served in Soviet army –1972; began career as legal counsel, becoming head of legal dept of several state enterprises; Judge, Sectorul Rîşcani, Chişinău 1978–90; Founder mem. Popular Front of Moldova 1988–93; mem. Parl. (Popular Front) 1990–94, (Bloc of the Intellectuals) 1994–98, Vice-Chair. Parl. Legal Cttee, Chair. (Speaker) 2009–10; mem. Party of Reform 1993–, Chair. 1998– (renamed Partidul Liberal—Liberal Party 2005); Alderman, Chişinău Municipal Council 2007–09, Chair. 2007–08; Acting Pres. of Moldova 2009–10. *Address:* Partidul Liberal (Liberal Party), 2012 Chişinău, str. Nicolae Iorga 15, Moldova (office). *Telephone:* (22) 24-35-69 (office). *Fax:* (22) 22-80-97 (office). *E-mail:* liberal@pl.md (office). *Website:* pl .md (office).

GHINEA, Cristian, MA; Romanian journalist, political scientist and politician; ed Nat. School of Political Science and Public Admin, Bucharest, London School of Econs, UK; wrote a political column for Dilema Veche weekly magazine –2015, also co-ordinated int. policy page; also wrote a column for Cotidianul daily and a syndicated editorial for Employers Publrs' Asscn and local media; also wrote a weekly column for Romania Libera newspaper 2011; Dir and later mem. Bd of Dirs, Romanian Centre for European Policies; Councillor of State for European Affairs, Romanian Govt Office 2015–16; Minister of European Funds April–Oct. 2016; worked on various projects for Academic Soc. of Romania, APADOR-CH, Freedom House – Romania, Centre for Ind. Journalism. *Publications:* I Vote DNA! Why It Is Worth Defending Anti-Corruption Institutions (in Romanian) 2012; book chapters. *Address:* c/o Ministry of European Funds, 011171 Bucharest 1, Bd Ion Mihalache 15–17, Romania. *E-mail:* contact.minister@fonduri-ue.ro.

GHIZ, Robert, BA; Canadian politician; b. 21 Jan. 1974, Charlottetown; s. of Joseph Ghiz (fmr Premier of PEI); m. Dr Kate Ellis; one d.; ed Bishop's Univ.; Special Asst to Minister of Canadian Heritage 1997–98; lobbyist for Bank of Nova Scotia, Ottawa 1998–2001; Atlantic Canada Advisor, Office of the Prime Minister, Ottawa 2001–03; Leader PEI Liberal Party 2003–; MLA for Charlottetown-Rochford Square 2003–07, for Charlottetown-Brighton 2007–, Leader of the Opposition 2003–07; Premier of PEI 2007–15. *Address:* c/o Office of the Premier, Shaw Building, 5th Floor South, 95 Rochford Street, PO Box 2000, Charlottetown, PE C1A 7N8, Canada (office).

GHIZZONI, Federico; Italian business executive; *CEO, UniCredit Group;* b. 14 Oct. 1955, Piacenza; ed Univ. of Law, Parma; began career as Customer Relations Man. at Credito Italiano's Piacenza Br. 1980, worked as Head of Credit and Marketing Dept, later Br. Dir, Trieste 1988–89, Dir Seriate Br. 1990–92, Deputy Gen. Man. Credito Italiano's London Office 1992–95, Gen. Man. Singapore Office 1995–2000, Exec. Dir responsible for Corp. and Int. Banking, Bank Pekao SA (affiliate of UniCredit Group) 2000–02, worked at Koç Financial Services (joint venture with UniCredit Group) 2003, COO and Exec. Bd mem. Koç Financial Services and COO & Vice-Chair. Yapi ve Kredi Bankasi (following acquisition by Koç Financial Services), Head of Poland's Markets Div. at UniCredit, Head of CEE Banking Operations and Bd mem. responsible for CEE Banking Div., Bank Austria AG 2007–10, Deputy CEO and Deputy Gen. Man. UniCredit Aug.–Sept. 2010, CEO UniCredit 2010–, mem. Perm. Strategic Cttee, Corp. Governance, HR and Nomination Cttee, Chair. Supervisory Bd UniCredit Bank AG, Munich 2011–; Chair. Orchestra Filarmonica della Scala Asscn, Milan; mem. Int. Monetary Conf., Washington, DC, Institut Int. d'Etudes Bancaires, Brussels. *Address:* UniCredit Group, Piazza Cordusia, 20123 Milan, Italy (office). *Telephone:* (02) 88621 (office). *Fax:* (02) 88628503 (office). *E-mail:* info@unicreditgroup.eu (office). *Website:* www .unicreditgroup.eu (office).

GHONDA MANGALIBI, Antoine; Democratic Republic of the Congo politician; b. 19 Feb. 1965, Leuven, Belgium; Minister of Foreign Affairs and Int. Co-operation 2003–04; Amb. for Pres. Kabila 2005; mem. Nat. Ass. 2006–. *Address:* c/o National Assembly, Brazzaville, Democratic Republic of the Congo (office). *Website:* www.assemblee-nationale.cg/ (office).

GHOSE, Gautam; Indian film director and actor; b. 24 July 1950, Calcutta (now Kolkata); s. of Prof. Himangshu Ghosh and Santana Ghosh; m. Neelanjana Ghosh 1978; one s. one d.; ed Cathedral Mission School, Calcutta, City Coll., Calcutta and Calcutta Univ.; mem. Int. Jury (Oberhausen) 1979; official del., Cannes and London Film Festivals 1982, Venice and Tokyo Film Festivals 1984; mem. Nat. Jury 1985; Exec. Dir Nat. Film Inst. 1987; Dir Nat. Film Devt Corpn, West Bengal Film Devt Corpn; Knighthood of the Star of the Italian Solidarity 2006; Pres. Award (five times), Human Rights Award (France), Silver Medal and UNESCO Award, Grand Prix Award (USSR), Vittori Di Sica Award, several Nat. and Int. awards. *Films include:* Hungry Autumn 1974, Maabhoomi 1980, Dakhal 1981, Paar 1984, Antarjali Yatra 1987, Padma Nadir Majhi 1992, Patang 1993, Gudiya 1997, Dekha 2001, Abar Aranye 2003, Yatra 2006, Kaalbela 2009, Moner Manush 2010, Baishe Srabon 2011, Shunyo Awnko: Act Zero 2013, Chotushkone 2014, Sankhachil 2016. *Publications include:* numerous articles on the cinema. *Leisure interests:* music, reading, travel. *Address:* Block 5, Flat 50, 28/1A Gariahat Road, Kolkata 700 029, India. *Telephone:* (33) 4405630 (home). *Fax:* (33) 4640315 (home).

GHOSH, Amitav, BA, MA, DPhil; Indian writer and academic; b. 11 July 1956, Calcutta (now Kolkata); m. Deborah Baker; two c.; ed St Stephen's Coll., Univ. of Delhi, Institut Bourguiba des Langues Vivantes, Tunisia and Univ. of Oxford, UK; Visiting Fellow, Centre for Social Sciences, Trivandrum, Kerala 1982–83; Research Assoc., Dept of Sociology, Univ. of Delhi 1983–87, Lecturer, Dept of Sociology 1987; Visiting Prof., Depts of Literature and Anthropology, Univ. of Virginia, Charlottesville 1988, South Asia Centre, Columbia Univ. 1989, Dept of Anthropology, Univ. of Pennsylvania 1989; Fellow, Centre for Studies in Social Science, Kolkata 1990–92; Adjunct Prof., Dept of Anthropology, Columbia Univ. 1993, Visiting Prof. 1994–97; Distinguished Visiting Prof., American Univ. in Cairo 1994; taught fiction workshop, Sarah Lawrence Coll., New York 1996; Distinguished Prof., Dept of Comparative Literature, Queens Coll., CUNY 1999–2003; Visiting Prof., Dept of English and American Literature and Language, Harvard Univ. 2004; Best American Essays Award 1995, Padma Shri 2007, Pushcart Prize 1999, Grinzane Cavour Prize 2007, Dan David Prize 2010, Jnanpith Award 2018. *Publications include:* The Circle of Reason (New York Times Notable Book 1987, Prix Médicis Étranger 1990) 1986, The Shadow Lines (Sahitya Akademi Award, Ananda Puraskar 1990) 1988, In an Antique Land (non-fiction) (New York Times Notable Book of 1993) 1992, The Calcutta Chromosome (Arthur C. Clark Award 1997) 1996, Dancing in Cambodia and At Large in Burma (essays) 1998, Countdown 1999, The Glass Palace (Frankfurt International e-Book Awards Grand Prize for Fiction, New York Times Notable Book, Los Angeles Times Notable Book, Chicago Tribune Favourite Book 2001) 2000, The Imam and the Indian (essays) 2002, The Hungry Tide (Hutch Crossword Book Prize 2006) 2004, Sea of Poppies (Indiaplaza Golden Quill Awards for Best Book, Readers' Choice Award for Fiction, Vodafone Crossword Book Award 2009) 2008, River of Smoke 2011, Flood of Fire 2015, Gun Island 2019; contrib. to articles in Ethnology, Granta, The New Republic, New York Times, Public Culture, Subaltern Studies, Letra Internacional, Cultural Anthropology, Observer Magazine, Wilson Quarterly, The New Yorker, Civil Lines, American Journal of Archaeology, Kenyon Review, Desh. *E-mail:* amitav@amitavghosh.com (office). *Website:* www .penguinbooksindia.com/amitavghosh; www.amitavghosh.com.

GHOSH, Asim, B.Tech, MBA; Canadian business executive; *President and CEO, Husky Energy;* b. 7 Dec. 1947, New Delhi, India; s. of Amalananda Ghosh and Sudha Ghosh; m. Sanjukta Ghosh; two c.; ed Indian Inst. of Tech., Delhi, Wharton School, Univ. of Pennsylvania, USA; began career with Procter & Gamble in Canada; then Sr Vice-Pres., Carling O'Keefe; later became Founding CEO Pepsi Foods' start-up operations in India; subsequently served in sr exec. positions and as CEO of AS Watson consumer packaged goods subsidiary of Hutchison Whampoa, managed a group of 13 business units 1991–98, expanded group's operations from Hong Kong to China and Europe; fmr Man. Dir and CEO Vodafone Essar Ltd; mem. Bd of Dirs Husky Energy 2009–, Pres. and CEO 2010–; mem. Bd of Dirs Kotak Mahindra Bank Ltd 2008–16; Dir, Li Ka Shing (Canada) Foundation. *Address:* Husky Energy, 707 Eighth Avenue SW, Box 6525, Station D, Calgary, AB T2P 1H5, Canada (office). *Telephone:* (403) 298-6111 (office). *Fax:* (403) 298-7464 (office). *E-mail:* info@huskyenergy.com (office). *Website:* www .huskyenergy.com (office).

GHOSN, Carlos, BEng; Brazilian/French/Lebanese automotive industry executive; b. 9 March 1954, Porto-Velho, Brazil; m. Rita Ghosn; one s. three d.; ed Collège Notre-Dame de Jamhour, Beirut, Ecole Polytechnique, Ecole des Mines, Paris; moved to Beirut, Lebanon with his mother 1960; trained as mining eng; Man. Dir Michelin Le Puy factory 1981, CEO Michelin Brazil 1985, Michelin North America 1989; Asst Dir-Gen. Renault Group 1996, Dir (non-exec.) 2001–, Pres. and CEO Renault SA 2005–19, Chair. 2008–18; COO Nissan Motor Co. Ltd 1999–2001, Dir 1999–2018, Pres. 2000–17, CEO 2001–17, Co-Chair. 2003–08, Chair. 2008–18, Pres. and CEO Nissan N America –2007; Chair. Alliance Bd Renault-Nissan b.v.; Chair. Mitsubishi Motors Corpn 2016–18; mem. Bd of Dirs, Alcoa Inc. 2002–11, Alcoa of Australia Ltd 2002–, Alcoa Automotive Inc. 2002–, Closure Systems International Inc. 2002–, Sony Corpn 2003–, IBM Corpn 2004–05, Mirant Corpn, Public Jt Stock Co. AVTOVAZ, Public Jt Stock Co. AvtoVAZ (Chair. 2013–16); mem. Int. Advisory Bd, Itaú Unibanco Holding SA; Pres. European Automobile Mfrs Asscn (ACEA) 2009, 2014–; arrested in Japan and charged with financial misconduct Dec. 2018; Hon. KBE 2006; voted Man of the Year by Fortune magazine's Asian edn 2003, Japan Automotive Hall of Fame 2004, named by CEO Quarterly Magazine as one of the Most Respected CEOs 2010, named by Forbes as one of the Seven Most Powerful South Americans 2010. *Publications include:* Renaissance 2001, Shift: Inside Nissan's Historic Revival 2005.

GHOSN, Fayiz, BA, MA; Lebanese politician; b. 28 June 1950, Kousba; m.; two d.; ed Lebanese Univ., St Joseph Univ., Beirut; mem. Majlis al-Nuab (Nat. Ass.) for Koura 1992–2005, mem. Lebanese-French Parl. Cttee; Minister of Nat. Defence 2011–14; mem. El-Marada Movt, currently Vice-Pres. *Address:* El-Marada Movement, Zgharta, Lebanon (office). *E-mail:* info@elmarada.org (office). *Website:* elmarada.org (office).

GHOSSOUB, Joseph; Lebanese marketing executive; *Chairman and CEO, MENA Communications Group (MENACOM);* b. Beirut; m. Daad Rahme 1977; three c.; f. Low One (night club), Reyfoun 1974; opened restaurant, Kaslik 1976; worked in Saudi Arabia 1980–83; worked in advertising in Lebanon 1983–85; moved to Dubai 1985; f. Team Advertising 1994, CEO 1993, affiliated with Young and Rubicam 1997, consolidated all businesses under The Holding Group (THG) 2000, renamed MENA Communications Group (MENACOM) 2009, currently Chair. and CEO; Chair. and World Pres. Int. Advertising Asscn 2004–08; fmr Pres. Lebanese Business Council in the UAE; mem. Bd Arab Forum for Environment and Devt; Dir Dubai Media Inc. 2003, 2007–; fmr Dir American Univ. in Dubai; Kt, Nat. Order of the Cedar 2004, Presidency Shield of the Repub. of Lebanon 2006, Pontifical Equestrian Order of St Gregory the Great (Vatican) 2009; Campaign Middle East's Man of the Year Award 2006, Dubai Lynx Advertising Personality of the Year 2008, Arabian Business Achievement Award for Business Leadership 2008, Arab Ad Man of the Year 2012. *Leisure interest:* golf. *Address:* MENA Communications Group, 2nd Floor, Arjaan Office Tower, Office No. 201, Dubai, United Arab Emirates (office). *Telephone:* (4) 4354211 (office). *Fax:* (4) 4341739 (office). *Website:* www.wpp.com (office); josephghossoub.com.

GHOZALI, Sid Ahmed; Algerian politician and diplomatist; b. 31 March 1937, Marnia; ed Ecole des Ponts et Chaussées, Paris; fmr Dir of Energy, Ministry of Industry and Energy; Adviser, Ministry of the Economy 1964; Under-Sec., Ministry of Public Works 1964–65; Pres., Dir-Gen. Soc. nationale pour la recherche, la production, le transport, la transformation et la commercialisation des hydrocarbures (SONATRACH) 1966–84, Chair., Man. Dir; Minister of Hydraulics March–Oct. 1979, of Foreign Affairs 1989–91; Prime Minister of Algeria 1991–92; Amb. to Belgium 1987–89, to France 1992–93; mem. Cen. Cttee Front de Libération Nat.; Chair. Front Démocratique 2000; mem. Org. technique de mise en valeur des richesses du sous-sol saharien 1962; unsuccessful cand. in presidential election 1999, 2004.

GHUKASYAN, Arkadi Arshavirovich, MA; Armenian politician, diplomatist and fmr journalist; *Special Envoy of the President of Armenia;* b. 21 June 1957, Stepanakert, Azerbaijan; m.; two c.; ed Yerevan State Univ., Armenia; reporter, Sovetskii Karabakh newspaper (Russian edn) 1979–81, First Deputy Ed. 1981–88;

sr mem. Karabakh Movt 1988; elected Deputy to Supreme Soviet (Supreme Council) of Nagornyi Karabakh 1992; Minister of Foreign Affairs of 'Repub. of Nagornyi Karabakh' 1993–98; Pres. of 'Repub. of Nagornyi Karabakh' 1997–2007 (sustained serious injuries as result of assassination attempt 2000); Special Envoy of the Pres. of Armenia; Vice-Chair. Bd of Trustees All-Armenian Hayastan Fund 2009–; Hon. mem. Acad. of Sciences on Security, Defence and Law and Order, Acad. of Sciences on Int. Relations, Acad. of Sciences on Nature and Society, Acad. of Sciences on Nat. Security Problems, Acad. of Spiritual Unity of Nations; Golden Eagle Order of the Hero of Artsakh; Dr hc (Artsakh State Univ.) 2003. *Address:* All-Armenian Hayastan Fund, Government Building #3, 0010 Yerevan, Armenia (office). *E-mail:* info@himnadram.org (office); a.ghukasyan@president.am. *Website:* www.himnadram.org (office).

GHUNAIM, Maha K. al-, BSc; Kuwaiti business executive; *Chairperson and Managing Director, Global Investment House;* m.; four c.; ed San Francisco State Univ., USA; began career with Kuwait Foreign Trading Contracting & Investment Co. 1982–98; Founder, Vice-Chair. and Man. Dir Global Investment House, Kuwait 1998–2006, Chair. and Man. Dir 2006–; Pres. Kuwait Chapter, Young Arab Leaders Org.; mem. Bd of Dirs Nat. Industries Group, BankMuscat International (Bahrain); Chair. Global Bahrain; Vice-Chair. Al-Soor Finance Co., Shurooq Investment Services Co. (Oman); mem. DEPA United Group, UAE; mem. Practitioner Cttee Dubai Int. Financial Exchange; Gulf Excellence Award 2005, Arabian Business magazine Business Women of the Year Award 2005. *Address:* Global Investment House, Souk Al-Safat Bldg, 2nd Floor, PO Box 28807, Safat 13149, Kuwait (office). *Telephone:* 804242 (office). *Fax:* 2400661 (office). *E-mail:* maha@global.com.kw (office). *Website:* www.globalinv.net (office).

GHURAIR, Abd al-Aziz Abdullah al-, BEng; United Arab Emirates banking executive; *CEO, Mashreq Bank;* b. 12 Nov. 1954; s. of Abdullah al-Ghurair; m.; three s.; ed California Polytechnic State Univ., USA; joined Mashreq Bank 1977, apptd Exec. Dir 1989, CEO 1990–; Chair. UAE Banking Federation, Oman Insurance Co.; Vice-Chair. DIFC; mem. Bd of Dirs Al Ghurair Group, Masafi Mineral Water, Dubai Int. Financial Centre, Emirates Foundation, Dubai Econ. Council; Chair. Arab Business Angels Network 2006; Speaker of the House, UAE Fed. Nat. Council (Parl.) 2007–11; fmr mem. Bd of Dirs Emaar, Dubai Investments, Visa Int., MasterCard, Dubai Chamber of Commerce and Industry; Lifetime Achievement Award, CEO Middle East Awards, Achievement Award, Arab Bankers Asscn of N America 2008, Innovator of the Year Award, Gulf Business Industry Awards 2014. *Address:* Mashreq Bank Building, Omar Bin Al Khatab Street, Dubai, United Arab Emirates (office). *Telephone:* (4) 2223333 (office). *Fax:* (4) 2226061 (office). *E-mail:* info@mashreqbank.com (office). *Website:* www.mashreqbank.com (office).

GIAEVER, Ivar, PhD; American physicist and academic; *CEO, Applied BioPhysics, Inc.;* b. 5 April 1929, Bergen, Norway; s. of John A. Giaever and Gudrun M. Skaarud; m. Inger Skramstad 1952; one s. three d.; ed Norwegian Inst. of Tech., Rensselaer Polytechnical Inst., NY; Norwegian Army 1952–53; Patent Examiner, Norwegian Patent Office 1953–54; Mechanical Engineer, Canadian Gen. Electric Co. 1954–56; Applied Mathematician, Gen. Electric Co. 1956–58; Physicist, Gen. Electric Research and Devt Center 1958–88; Inst. Prof., Physics Dept, Rensselaer Polytechnic, NY 1988–; Prof., Univ. of Oslo 1988–; co-f. Applied Biophysics Inc. 1991, currently CEO; mem. NAS 1974–; eight Hon. PhD degrees; Oliver E. Buckley Prize 1965, Nobel Prize for Physics 1973, Zworkin Award 1974. *Publications in Physics Review Letters:* Energy Gap in Superconductors Measured by Electron Tunneling 1960, Study of Superconductors by Electron Tunneling 1961, Detection of the AC Josephson Effect 1965, Magnetic Coupling Between Two Adjacent Superconductors 1965, The Antibody-Antigen Reaction: A Visual Observation 1973, A Morphological Biosensor for Mammalian Cells 1993, Cell Adhesion Force Microscopy 1999. *Leisure interests:* skiing, sailing, tennis, hiking, camping, playing Go. *Address:* Applied BioPhysics, Inc., 175 Jordan Road, Troy, NY 12180 (office); 2080 Van Antwerp Road, Schenectady, NY 12309, USA (home). *Telephone:* (518) 880-6860 (office). *Fax:* (518) 880-6865 (office). *E-mail:* giaever@biophysics .com (office). *Website:* www.biophysics.com (office).

GIAMATTI, Paul, MFA; American actor; b. (Paul Edward Valentine Giamatti), 6 June 1967, New Haven, Conn.; s. of A. Bartlett Giamatti and Toni Smith; m. Elizabeth Giamatti 1997; one s.; ed Choate Rosemary Hall prep school, Yale Univ.; began career in regional theatre before developing a successful film career. *Films include:* Singles 1992, Past Midnight 1992, Mighty Aphrodite 1995, Sabrina 1995, Breathing Room 1996, Ripper 1996, Donnie Brasco 1997, Private Parts 1997, My Best Friend's Wedding 1997, Deconstructing Harry 1997, A Further Gesture 1997, Arresting Gena 1997, The Truman Show 1998, Doctor Dolittle 1998, Saving Private Ryan 1998, The Negotiator 1998, Safe Men 1998, Cradle Will Rock 1999, Man on the Moon 1999, Big Momma's House 2000, Duets 2000, Storytelling 2001, Planet of the Apes 2001, Big Fat Liar 2002, Thunderpants 2002, Confidence 2003, American Splendor 2003, Paycheck 2003, Sideways (Best Male Lead, Ind. Spirit Awards 2005) 2004, The Cinderella Man (Critics' Choice Award for Best Supporting Actor 2006, Screen Actors Guild Award for Best Supporting Actor 2006) 2005, Robots (voice) 2005, The Fan and the Flower (voice) 2005, The Hawk Is Dying 2006, Asterix and the Vikings (voice) 2006, The Illusionist 2006, Lady in the Water 2006, The Ant Bully (voice) 2006, The Nanny Diaries 2007, Shoot 'Em Up 2007, Fred Claus 2007, Pretty Bird 2008, Cold Souls 2009, The Haunted World of El Superbeasto (voice) 2009, Duplicity 2009, The Last Station 2009, Barney's Version (Golden Globe Award for Best Actor in a Comedy or Musical 2011) 2010, Ironclad 2011, Win Win 2011, The Ides of March 2011, Turbo (voice) 2013, 12 Years a Slave 2013, Straight Outta Compton 2015, Private Life 2018. *Television includes:* Tourist Trap 1998, Winchell 1998, If These Walls Could Talk 2 2000, The Pentagon Papers 2003, The Amazing Screw-On Head (voice) 2006, John Adams (series, HBO) (Golden Globe Award for Best Actor in a Mini-Series 2009) 2008, 30 Rock (series) 2010, Billions 2016–. *Address:* c/o WME Entertainment, 9601 Wilshire Boulevard, Beverly Hills, CA 90210, USA (office). *Telephone:* (310) 285-9000 (office). *Fax:* (310) 285-9010 (office). *Website:* www.wma.com (office).

GIAMBASTIANI, Adm. (retd) Edmund P., Jr; American naval officer (retd) and business executive; *President and CEO, Giambastiani Group LLC;* b. 4 May 1948, Canastota, NY; s. of Edmund P. Giambastiani, Sr and Adele Grilli Giambastiani; m. Cindy Giambastiani; one s. one d.; ed US Naval Acad.; assignments included Program Man. Navy Recruiting Command HQ, Washington, DC, Special Asst to Deputy Dir of Intelligence, CIA, Deputy Chief of Staff for Resources, Warfare Requirements and Assessments, US Pacific Fleet, Dir Submarine Warfare Div., Naval Operations, Deputy Chief of Naval Operations for Resources, Requirements and Assessments; fmr Commdr Submarine NR-1 (nuclear-powered deep diving submarine), USS Richard B. Russell (nuclear-powered attack submarine); fmr Leader Submarine Devt Squadron Twelve; fmr First Dir Strategy and Concepts, Naval Doctrine Command; fmr Commdr Atlantic Fleet Submarine Force, Anti-Submarine and Reconnaissance Forces Atlantic; Sr Mil. Asst to Sec. of Defense Donald Rumsfeld –2003; Commdr US Jt Forces Command and Supreme Allied Commdr Transformation (SACT), NATO 2003–05; Vice-Chair. Jt Chiefs of Staff, Washington, DC 2005–07, also served as Chair. Jt Requirements Oversight Council, Vice-Chair. Defense Acquisition Bd, mem. Nat. Security Council Deputies Cttee, Nuclear Weapons Council; f. Giambastiani Group LLC 2007; Sr Advisor, ValueOptions, Inc. 2007–; Sr Advisor, SG Blocks, Inc –2015; Chair. Alenia North America Inc. 2008–09; mem. Bd of Dirs Boeing Co. 2009–, Monster Worldwide, Inc. (Chair. 2015–); mem. Bd of Trustees and Advisory Bd, Oppenheimer Funds; mem. Advisory Bd Maxwell School of Citizenship and Public Affairs, Syracuse Univ. 2012–; mem. Advisory Council, Business Executives for National Security; Trustee, Mitre Corpn 2008–; numerous awards including Defense Distinguished Service Medal, Jt Meritorious Unit Award, eight Battle Efficiency E's, five Navy Unit Commendations, five Navy Meritorious Unit Commendations. *Address:* Giambastiani Group LLC., 690 Budds Landing Road, Warwick, MD 21912, USA (office). *Telephone:* (410) 275-8048 (office).

GIAMPIETRI ROJAS, Adm. (retd) Luis; Peruvian naval officer (retd) and politician; b. 31 Dec. 1940, Bellavista; s. of Luis Giampietri Berenice and Rosa Rojas Lapoint; m. Lida Marcela Ramos Seminario; four c.; ed Peruvian Naval School; joined Peruvian Navy as ensign in 1960, positions included Commdr Gen. Naval Zones, Commdr Gen. Defence Coast, Dir Peruvian Naval School; fmr Deputy Rep. of Perm. Del. to OAS; fmr del. to Inter-American Defence Council, Washington, DC; Chair. Peruvian Sea Inst. 1996–2000, Chair. Multi-Sector Cttee in charge of Nat. Study of El Niño (ENFEN), mem. Nat. Environment Comm., Perm. Comm. for the Pacific SE, Nat. Comm. for Antarctic Affairs; Councillor for Lima 1998–2002; First Vice-Pres. of Peru 2007–11; mem. Mexican Acad. of Sciences, Inst. of Maritime History, Peruvian Centre of Mil. Maritime History.

GIANNITSIS, Anastasios; Greek economist, academic, business executive and government minister; *Chairman, LAMDA Development;* b. 1944; Prof. of Devt and Int. Econs, Univ. of Athens –2011, now Prof. Emer.; Chief Econ. Advisor to the Prime Minister, Minister of Labor 2000–01; Alt. Foreign Minister 2001–04; Minister of the Interior 2011–12; Chair. Hellenic Petroleum SA 2009, LAMDA Devt SA 2015–; mem. Panhellenic Socialist Movt (PASOK); mem. Bd of Dirs Lambrakis Press SA. *Publications:* numerous publs on industrial issues, int. integration, specialization and competitiveness, foreign investment, social policy, technology-innovation and technology policy and on Greek econ. policy issues. *Address:* LAMDA Development SA, 37A Kifissias Avenue (Golden Hall), 151 23 Maroussi, Greece (office). *Telephone:* (210) 7450600 (office). *Fax:* (210) 7450645 (office). *E-mail:* lamda@lamdadev.com (office).

GIANOTTI, Fabiola, PhD; Italian physicist; *Director-General, European Organization for Nuclear Research (CERN);* b. 29 Oct. 1962; ed Univ. of Milan, CERN, Switzerland; originally trained as humanist and pianist at Milan Conservatory; joined CERN 1987, worked on various experiments including UA2 experiment and ALEPH on the Large Electron Positron Collider (precursor to Large Hadron Collider), ATLAS experiment physics coordinator 1999–2003, Head of ATLAS 2009–13, Dir-Gen., CERN (first female) 2016–; mem. Physics Advisory Cttee Fermilab (particle physics lab.), Batavia, Ill., USA; corresponding mem. Accad. dei Lincei, USA National Acad. of Sciences, French Acad. of Sciences; Hon. Prof., Univ. of Edinburgh 2013–; Commendatore, Ordine al Merito della Repubblica Italiana 2009, Grande Ufficiale, Ordine al Merito della Repubblica Italiana 2012; Dr hc (École polytechnique fédérale de Lausanne) 2013, (Univ. of Uppsala), (Univ. of Oslo), (Univ. of Edinburgh), (Univ. of Roma Tor Vergata); City of Milan Ambrogino d'oro 2012, Special Fundamental Physics Prize 2012, Premio Nonino 2013, Niels Bohr Inst. Medal of Honour 2013, Società Italiana di Fisica Premio Enrico Fermi 2013, Wilhelm Exner Medal 2017. *Leisure interests:* jogging, playing the piano. *Address:* European Organization for Nuclear Research (CERN), Geneva 23, Switzerland (office). *Telephone:* 22-76-761-11 (office). *Fax:* 22-76-765-55 (office). *E-mail:* fabiola.gianotti@cern.ch (office). *Website:* consult.cern.ch (office); atlas.ch (office).

GIANVITI, François Paul Frédéric, DenD; French lawyer, academic and international organization official; *Judge, Qatar Financial Centre Regulatory Tribunal;* b. 2 Aug. 1938, Paris; s. of Dominique Gianviti and Suzanne Fournier; m. Barbara Zawadsky 1965; one s. two d.; ed Lycées Henri IV and Louis-le-Grand, Paris, Facultés des Lettres et de Droit, Paris and New York Univ. School of Law; Asst, Faculté de Droit, Paris 1963–67; Lecturer, Faculté de Droit, Nancy 1967–68, Caen 1968–69; Maître de conférences, Faculté de Droit, Besançon, on secondment to IMF 1970–74; Maître de conférences, Univ. of Paris XII 1974–75, Prof. of Law 1975, Dean 1979–85; Dir of Legal Dept, IMF 1986–2004, Gen. Counsel 1987–2004 (retd); mem. Monetary Cttee, Int. Law Asscn; Judge, Qatar Financial Centre Regulatory Tribunal, Doha 2011–; Chevalier, Ordre Nat. du Mérite, Chevalier des Palmes académiques. *Publication:* Les Biens 1984; numerous book chapters and journal articles. *Address:* Qatar International Court and Dispute Resolution Centre, QFC Tower 2, Omar Al Mukhtar Street, West Bay, PO Box 13667, Doha, Qatar (office). *E-mail:* info@qicdrc.com.qa (office). *Website:* qicdrc.com.qa (office).

GIBARA, Samir G., BBA, MBA; French business executive (retd); b. 23 April 1939, Cairo, Egypt; s. of Selim Gibara and Renée Bokhazi; m. Salma Tagher 1968; ed Cairo Univ., Harvard Business School, USA; Adviser, Inst. for Int. Trade, Paris 1967–70; Pres. and Man. Dir Goodyear France 1983; Pres. and CEO Goodyear Canada 1989; Vice-Pres. and Gen. Man. Goodyear Europe 1990; Vice-Pres. Strategic Planning and Acting Chief Financial Officer, Goodyear Tire & Rubber Co. 1992, Exec. Vice-Pres. N American Operations 1994, Pres. and COO 1995–96, Chair., Pres. and CEO Jan. 1996, Chair. and CEO July 1996–2003 (retd); mem. Bd of Dirs Int. Paper Co. 1999–2011, Sumitomo Rubber Industries 1999–2002, Dana Corpn 2004–08, W & T Offshore, Inc. 2008–13, Edgen Group Inc. 2012–; mem. Bd of Dean's Advisors, Harvard Business School 2007–11; mem. Advisory Bd Proudfoot Consultants; Trustee, Univ. of Akron Foundation; Chevalier, Ordre nat. du Mérite, Chevalier du Tastevin. *Publications:* articles in Le Monde and business journals. *Leisure interests:* theatre, music, reading, tennis, swimming.

GIBB, Sir Barry Alan Crompton, Kt, CBE; British/American singer, songwriter and record producer; b. 1 Sept. 1946, Isle of Man; s. of Hughie Gibb and Barbara Gibb; m. Linda Gray 1970; five c.; emigrated to Australia 1958, returned to UK 1967; formed The Bee Gees (with brothers Robin, Maurice and Andy) 1958; started singing in nightclubs, Australia; numerous performances at major venues around the world; Hon. degree (Univ. of Manchester) 2004; seven Grammy awards, American Music Award for Int. Achievement 1997, BRIT Award for Outstanding Contribution to Music 1997, World Music Award for Lifetime Achievement 1997, Q Lifetime Achievement Award 2005, Ivor Novello Acad. Fellowship 2006, BMI Icon Award 2007, Freeman of the Borough of Douglas (Isle of Man) 2009. *Compositions include:* writer or co-writer, producer or co-producer of numerous songs for other artists including: Elvis Presley (Words), Cliff Richard (I Cannot Give You My Love), Sarah Vaughan (Run To Me), Al Green, Janis Joplin, Barbra Streisand (Guilty album), Diana Ross (Chain Reaction), Dionne Warwick (Heartbreaker), Dolly Parton and Kenny Rogers (Islands In The Stream), Ntrance (Staying Alive), Take That (How Deep Is Your Love), Boyzone (Words), Yvonne Elliman (If I Can't Have You). *Recordings include:* albums: with The Bee Gees: Bee Gees Sing and Play 14 Barry Gibb Songs 1965, Monday's Rain 1966, Bee Gees 1st 1967, Horizontal 1968, Idea 1968, Odessa 1969, Cucumber Castle 1970, Marley Purt Drive 1970, Sound of Love 1970, Two Years On 1971, Melody (OST) 1971, Trafalgar 1971, To Whom It May Concern 1972, Life in a Tin Can 1973, Mr Natural 1974, Main Course 1975, Children of the World 1976, Here at Last... Bee Gees Live 1977, Saturday Night Fever (OST) 1977, Spirits Having Flown 1979, SWALK 1979, Living Eyes 1981, Staying Alive (OST) 1983, E.S.P. 1987, One 1989, High Civilization 1991, Size Isn't Everything 1993, Still Waters 1997, One Night Only 1998, This Is Where I Came In 2001, Harmonies Down Under 2002, Alone 2002, In the Beginning 2003, Merchants of Dream 2003, Bee Gees Number Ones 2004; solo: Now Voyager 1984, Hawks 1988, In the Now 2016. *Address:* c/o Crompton Songs, 5820 North Bay Road, Miami Beach, FL 33140, USA. *Telephone:* (305) 672-2390. *Fax:* (305) 531-8041. *E-mail:* middleear@earthlink.het. *Website:* www.barrygibb.com.

GIBBARD, Allan Fletcher, BA, PhD; American academic; *Richard B. Brandt Distinguished University Professor of Philosophy, University of Michigan;* b. 7 April 1942, Providence, RI; s. of Harold A. Gibbard and Eleanor Reid Gibbard; m. 1st Mary Elizabeth Craig 1972 (died 1990); m. 2nd Beth Genné 1991; two s.; ed Swarthmore Coll., Harvard Univ.; teacher of math. and physics with US Peace Corps, Achimota School, Ghana 1963–65; Asst Prof. then Assoc. Prof. of Philosophy, Univ. of Chicago 1969–74; Assoc. Prof. of Philosophy, Univ. of Pittsburgh 1974–77; apptd Prof. of Philosophy, Univ. of Michigan 1977, Richard B. Brandt Prof. 1992–94, Richard B. Brandt Distinguished Univ. Prof. 1994–, Sr Fellow, Michigan Soc. of Fellows 1990–94, Nelson Fellow, Dept of Philosophy 1991–; Vice-Pres. Cen. Div., American Philosophical Asscn 2000–01, Pres. 2001–02, Past Pres. 2002–03; Fellow, Econometric Soc. 1984; mem. American Acad. of Arts and Sciences 1990–, NAS 2009–; Membre Titulaire, Institut International de Philosophie 1999–; Goldsmith Prize, Harvard Univ. 1968–69, Emily and Charles Carrier Prize, Harvard Univ. 1971. *Publications include:* Manipulation of Voting Schemes: A General Result 1973, Wise Choices, Apt Feelings: A Theory of Normative Judgement 1990, Thinking How to Live 2003, Reconciling our Aims: In Search of Bases for Ethics 2008, Meaning and Normativity 2012; articles in journals. *Address:* Department of Philosophy, University of Michigan, Angell Hall, 435 South State Street, Ann Arbor, MI 48109-1003, USA (office). *Telephone:* (313) 764-6285 (office); (313) 769-2628 (home). *Fax:* (313) 763-8071 (office). *E-mail:* gibbard@umich.edu (office). *Website:* www-personal.umich.edu/~gibbard (office).

GIBBON, Gary, BA; British journalist; *Political Editor, Channel 4 News;* b. 15 March 1965; s. of Robert Gibbon and Elizabeth Gibbon; m. Laura Pulay 1993; two s.; ed Balliol Coll., Oxford; fmr journalist, BBC; joined Channel 4 News 1990, Political Producer 1992–94, Political Corresp. 1994–2005, Political Ed. 2005–; RTS Home News Award 2006, Political Studies Asscn Political Broadcaster of the Year Award 2008, Specialist Broadcaster of the Year Award, Royal TV Soc. 2010. *Address:* Channel 4 News, 200 Gray's Inn Road, London, WC1X 8XZ, England (office). *Telephone:* (20) 7430-4996 (office). *E-mail:* gary.gibbon@itn.co.uk (office). *Website:* www.channel4.com/news (office).

GIBBONS, Gary William, PhD, FRS; British theoretical physicist and academic; *Professor of Theoretical Physics, University of Cambridge;* b. 1 July 1946, Coulsdon, Surrey; m. Christine Gibbons (néé Howden); two c.; ed Purley Co. Grammar School, Old Coulsdon, Surrey, St Catharine's Coll., Cambridge, Univ. of Cambridge; elected Denman-Baynes Student, Clare Coll., Cambridge 1971–75; SRC Research Asst, Dept of Applied Math. and Theoretical Physics, Univ. of Cambridge 1975–76, 1977–78, SRC Advanced Fellow 1978–80, Univ. Lecturer 1980–90, Reader in Theoretical Physics 1990–97, Prof. of Theoretical Physics 1997–, Fellow, Trinity Coll. Cambridge 2002–; Max Planck Institut für Physik und Astrophysik, Munich, FRG 1976–77; mem. Inst. of Theoretical Physics, Univ. of California, Santa Barbara, USA Jan.–April 1980; sabbatical leave at Observatoire de Meudon and Ecole Normale Superieure, Paris, France 1986–87, at IHES, Bures-sur-Yvette, France Jan.–April 1990, as Kramers Prof. at Inst. for Theoretical Physics, Univ. of Utrecht, Netherlands April–June 1992, at Laboratoire de Physique Théorique, Ecole Normale Superieure, Paris Oct.–Dec. 1999, as Yukawa Prof. at Yukawa Inst. for Theoretical Physics, Kyoto Univ., Japan Jan.–April 2000; Le Studium Prof., LMTP, Univ. of Tours, France 2013–17; Visiting Prof., Center for Theoretical Physics, MIT, USA Sept.–Dec. 2003, Dept of Physics, Univ. of Pennsylvania, USA 2013–16. *Publications include:* Euclidean Quantum Gravity 1993; numerous articles in professional journals on supergravity, p-branes and M-theory. *Leisure interest* art and music, history of science. *Address:* Pavilion B, Room B1.24, Department of Applied Mathematics and Theoretical Physics, Centre for Mathematical Sciences, Wilberforce Road, Cambridge, CB3 0WA, England (office). *Telephone:* (1223) 337899 (office). *Fax:* (1223) 764984 (office). *E-mail:* G.W.Gibbons@damtp.cam.ac.uk (office). *Website:* www.damtp.cam.ac.uk (office).

GIBBONS, Michael Gordon, MBE, BSc, BEng, MSc, PhD; Canadian academic; *Honorary Professor, Science and Technology Policy Research, University of Sussex;* b. 15 April 1939, Montreal; s. of Albert Gordon Gibbons and Dorothy Mildred Gibbons; m. Gillian Monks 1968; one s. one d.; ed Concordia Univ., McGill Univ., Queens Univ., Univ. of Manchester, UK; Lecturer, Univ. of Manchester 1967–72, Sr Lecturer 1972–75, Prof. 1975–92, Head of Dept 1975–92; Dir Univ. of Manchester Inst. of Science and Tech. (UMIST) Pollution Research Unit, UK 1979–86, Chair. and Founding Dir Policy Research in Eng, Science and Tech. 1979–92, Dir Research Exploitation and Devt, Vice-Chancellor's Office 1984–92; Dean Grad. School and Dir Science Policy Research Unit (now Science and Tech. Policy Research), Univ. of Sussex 1992–96, Dir 2004, now Hon. Prof.; Sec.-Gen. Asscn of Commonwealth Univs 1996–2004; Visiting Prof., Univ. of Montréal 1976–81, Univ. of Calif., Berkeley 1992; Special Adviser to House of Commons Science and Tech. Cttee 1993; mem. Council, ESRC 1997; mem. Research Priorities Bd 1994, Chair. 1997; Consultant, Cttee of Science and Tech. Policy, OECD, Paris; Fellow, Royal Swedish Acad. of Eng Sciences 2000; Hon. LLD (Univ. of Ghana, Legon) 1999, (Concordia Univ., Montréal) 2004; Hon. DUniv (Univ. of Surrey) 2005; Lt-Gov.'s Silver Medal 1959, Govt of Canada Commemorative Medal 2002. *Publications include:* Wealth from Knowledge (jtly) 1972, Science as a Commodity 1984, Post-Innovation Performance: Technical Development and Competition 1986, The Evaluation of Research: A Synthesis of Current Practice 1987, The New Production of Knowledge 1994, Re-thinking Science 2000. *Leisure interests:* classical music, American football. *Address:* 24 Fletsand Road, Wilmslow, Cheshire, SK9 2AB, England (home). *Telephone:* (1625) 527924 (home). *E-mail:* michael_gibbons@onetel.net.

GIBBS, Anthony Matthews, BA, BLitt, MA, FAHA; Australian academic; *Professor Emeritus of English, Macquarie University;* b. 21 Jan. 1933, Vic.; s. of J. F. L. Gibbs and S. T. Gibbs; m. 1st Jillian Irving Holden 1960; m. 2nd Donna Patricia Lucy 1983; two s. one step d.; ed Ballarat Church of England Grammar School, Trinity Coll., Univ. of Melbourne, and Magdalen Coll., Oxford; Lecturer in English, Univ. of Adelaide 1960–66, Univ. of Leeds 1966–69; Prof. of English, Univ. of Newcastle, NSW 1969–75; Prof. of English, Macquarie Univ. 1975–98, Prof. Emer. 1999–; mem. Exec. Cttee Int. Asscn for the Study of Anglo-Irish Literature 1973–78, Exec. Cttee English Asscn (Sydney br.) 1975–91, Founding Council, Int. Shaw Soc. 2004; Vice-Pres. Australian Acad. of Humanities 1988–89; Ed. 1989–93; Rhodes Scholarship 1956, Centenary Medal 2003. *Publications includes:* Shaw 1969, Sir William Davenant 1972, The Art and Mind of Shaw 1983, Shaw: Interviews and Recollections 1990, Bernard Shaw: Man and Superman and Saint Joan 1992, Heartbreak House: Preludes of Apocalypse 1994, A Bernard Shaw Chronology 2001, Bernard Shaw: A Life 2005. *Leisure interests:* theatre, cooking. *Address:* 4 Acacia Close, Turramurra, NSW 2074, Australia (home). *Telephone:* (2) 9449-2668 (office). *E-mail:* gibbston@gmail.com (home). *Website:* www.engl.mq.edu.au (office).

GIBBS, Herschelle Herman; South African fmr professional cricketer; b. 23 Feb. 1974, Green Point, Cape Town, Cape Prov.; m. Tennielle Povey 2007 (divorced 2007); ed St Joseph's Marist Coll., Diocesan Coll., Rondebosch; right-handed top order batsman; right-arm bowler; Jr Rep. Cricket: WP Nuff 1989–92, SA Schools 1991–92; played for Western Prov. 1990–2004, S Africa 1996–2010, Cape Cobras 2004–06, Deccan Chargers 2008–10, Glamorgan 2008, Yorkshire 2010, Northern Districts 2010, Perth Scorchers 2011–12, Mumbai Indians 2012, Durham Dynamos 2012; First-class debut: 1990/91; Test debut: India v S Africa, Kolkata 27 Nov.–1 Dec. 1996; One-Day Int. (ODI) debut: Kenya v S Africa, Nairobi (Gym) 3 Oct. 1996; T20I debut: S Africa v NZ, Johannesburg 21 Oct. 2005; played 90 Tests, scored 6,167 runs (average 41.95) with 14 centuries and 26 fifties, highest score 228 against Pakistan, Cape Town 2003; played 248 ODIs, scored 8,094 runs (average 36.13) with 21 centuries and 37 fifties, highest score 175 against Australia, Johannesburg 2006; played 23 T20Is, scored 400 runs (average 18.18) with three fifties, highest score 90 not out against West Indies, Johannesburg 2007; played 193 First-class matches, scored 13,425 runs (average 42.21) with 31 centuries and 60 fifties; awarded citizenship of Saint Kitts and Nevis 2007. *Achievements include:* first player to hit six sixes in one over in ODI cricket, doing so against the Netherlands off bowling of Daan van Bunge in Cricket World Cup 2007; with Graeme Smith, only pair in Test history to break 300 on three occasions; also holds S African second wicket record, a partnership of 315 not out with Jacques Kallis; one of only three batsmen in ODI history to score hundreds in three consecutive innings.

GIBBS, Lancelot (Lance) Richard; Guyanese sports organizer and fmr professional cricketer; b. 29 Sept. 1934, Georgetown, British Guiana (now Guyana); s. of Ebenezer Gibbs and Marjorie Gretna Gibbs (née Archer); cousin of cricketer Clive Lloyd; m. Joy Roslyn Margarete Rogers 1963; one s. one d.; ed St Ambrose Anglican Primary School and Day Commercial Standard High School; right-arm off-spin bowler; played for British Guiana/Guyana 1953/54–74/75, Warwickshire 1967–73, S Australia 1969–70; played in 79 Tests for West Indies 1957/58–75/76, taking then world record 309 wickets (average 29.09), best bowling (innings) 8/38, (match) 11/157; only bowler to take 100 or more wickets against both England and Australia; toured England 1963, 1966, 1969, 1973, 1975 (World Cup); took 1,024 First-class wickets, average 27.22, best bowling (innings) 8/37; Man. 1991 West Indies tour of England; now a sports organizer based in USA, which he represented against Canada 1983; Chair. of Lauderhill, Fla bid to host Cricket World Cup in 2007; man. posts in transportation business including Booker Shipping, Guyana and Kent Line, Canada; Cricketer of the Year, Indian Cricket 1967, Player of the Year, Professional Cricketers Asscn 1971, Wisden Cricketer of The Year 1972. *Leisure interests:* reading, all sports.

GIBBS, Nancy, MA; American author, journalist and publishing executive; *Managing Editor, Time magazine;* b. 1960; m.; two c.; ed Yale Univ., New Coll., Oxford, UK; began career as fact checker in int. section, Time Inc. 1985–88, becoming Feature writer 1988–91, Sr Ed. 1991–96, Chief political writer 1996–2002, Ed.-at-Large 2002, Exec. Ed., Deputy Man. Ed. 2011–13, Man. Ed. 2013–; Ferris Prof., Princeton Univ. 1993, 2006. *Publications include:* The Preacher and the Presidents: Billy Graham in the White House (with Michael Duffy) 2007, The Presidents Club: Inside the World's Most Exclusive Fraternity (with Michael Duffy) 2012. *Address:* Time Inc, 1271 Avenue of the Americas, New York, NY 10020, USA (office). *Website:* www.time.com/time (office).

GIBBS, Robert L., BA; American political consultant, fmr government official and business executive; *Executive Vice-President and Global Chief Communications Officer, McDonald's Corporation;* b. 29 March 1971, Auburn, Ala; s. of Robert Gibbs and Nancy Jean Gibbs (née Lane); m. Mary Catherine Gibbs; one s.; ed

North Carolina State Univ.; Press Sec. for US Congressman Bob Etheridge 1997; spokesman for Fritz Hollings' senatorial campaign 1998; Press Sec. for John Kerry's presidential campaign 2004; Communications Dir Democratic Senatorial Campaign Cttee and Barack Obama's senatorial campaign 2004; Communications Dir for Senator Barack Obama, Washington, DC 2004–08; Communications Dir Senator Barack Obama's presidential campaign 2007–08; White House Press Sec. 2009–11; Founding Partner, Incite Agency 2013–; Exec. Vice-Pres. and Global Chief Communications Officer, McDonald's Corpn 2015–. *Address:* McDonald's Corporation, 2111 McDonald's Drive, Oak Brook, IL 60523, USA (office). *Website:* www.mcdonalds.com (office).

GIBSON, Charles DeWolf, AB; American newscaster; b. 9 March 1943, Evanston, IL; s. of Burdett Gibson and Georgiana Gibson (née Law); m. Arlene Joy Gibson 1967; two d.; ed Princeton Univ.; Washington Producer, RKO Network, Washington, DC 1966; News Dir Station-WLVA-TV, Lynchburg, Va 1967–69; anchorman, reporter Station-WMAL-TV (now WJLA-TV), Washington, DC 1970–73; corresp., TVN, Inc. (TV News, Inc.) 1974–75; joined ABC News 1975, White House Corresp., Washington, DC 1976–77, Corresp., gen. assignment 1977–81, Capitol Hill Corresp. 1981–87; Co-host Good Morning America, ABC TV, New York City 1987–98, 1999–2006, Anchor, World News Tonight with Charles Gibson 2006–09 (retd); mem. Bd of Dirs Knight-Wallace Fellows at Mich. 1988; Trustee Princeton Univ. 2006–15; Nat. Journalism Fellow, Nat. Endowment of the Humanities, Univ. of Mich. 1973–74, John Maclean Fellowship, Princeton Univ. 1992.

GIBSON, Sir Ian, Kt, BSc, CBE; British business executive; *Chairman, William Morrison Supermarkets PLC;* m. 1st Joy Musker (divorced); two d.; m. 2nd Sue Wilson (divorced); one s.; ed Univ. of Manchester; joined Ford Motor Co., 1968, served several exec. positions in UK and Germany –1984; joined Nissan Motor Manufacturing (UK) Ltd as purchasing and production control dir 1984, Man. Dir and CEO 1989–98, Chair. 1998, Pres. Nissan Europe and Sr Vice-Pres. Nissan Motor Co. Ltd 1999–2001; Deputy Chair. (non-exec.) William Morrison Supermarkets PLC 2007–08, Chair. 2008–; Chair. (non-exec.) Trinity Mirror PLC 2006–; fmr Chair. BPB PLC; fmr Deputy Chair. Asda Group PLC; fmr mem. Bd of Dirs Chelys Ltd; fmr Sr Dir (non-exec.) Northern Rock PLC; fmr Dir (non-exec.) GKN PLC, Greggs PLC; fmr mem. Court of the Bank of England. *Address:* William Morrison Supermarkets PLC, Hilmore House, Gain Lane, Bradford, BD3 7DL (office); Trinity Mirror PLC, One Canada Square, Canary Wharf, London, E14 5AP, England (office). *Telephone:* (845) 611-5000 (Morrisons) (office); (20) 7293-3000 (Trinity Mirror) (office). *Fax:* (20) 7510-3000 (Trinity Mirror) (office). *E-mail:* info@morrisons.co.uk (office); info@trinitymirror.com (office). *Website:* www.morrisons.co.uk (office); www.trinitymirror.com (office).

GIBSON, Mel, AO; Australian actor, director and producer; b. 3 Jan. 1956, Peekskill, New York, USA; s. of Hutton Gibson and Anne Gibson; m. Robyn Moore (divorced 2011); six s. one d.; (with subsequent partners) one s. one d.; ed Nat. Inst. for Dramatic Art, Sydney; f. ICONS Productions; Commdr, Ordre des Arts et des Lettres. *Films include:* Summer City, Mad Max 1979, Tim 1979, Attack Force Z, Gallipoli 1981, The Road Warrior (Mad Max II) 1982, The Year of Living Dangerously 1983, The Bounty 1984, The River 1984, Mrs. Soffel 1984, Mad Max Beyond Thunderdome 1985, Lethal Weapon, Tequila Sunrise, Lethal Weapon II, Bird on a Wire 1989, Hamlet 1990, Air America 1990, Lethal Weapon III 1991, Man Without a Face (also dir) 1992, Maverick 1994, Braveheart (also Dir, co-producer, Acad. Award for Best Picture 1996) 1995, Ransom 1996, Conspiracy Theory 1997, Lethal Weapon IV 1998, Payback 1997, The Million Dollar Hotel 1999, The Patriot 2000, What Women Want 2000, We Were Soldiers 2002, Signs 2002, The Singing Detective 2003, The Passion of the Christ (dir, producer; US People's Choice Award for Best Drama 2005) 2004, Apocalypto (dir) 2006, Edge of Darkness 2010, The Beaver 2011, How I Spent My Summer Vacation 2012, Machete Kills 2013, The Expendables 3 2014, Blood Father 2016, Hacksaw Ridge (dir) 2016. *Plays include:* Romeo and Juliet, Waiting for Godot, No Names No Pack Drill, Death of a Salesman. *Address:* ICONS Productions, 808 Wilshire Blvd, 4th Floor, Santa Monica, CA 90401, USA (office).

GIBSON, Rt Hon. Sir Peter (Leslie), Kt; British judge; *Chairman, Detainee Inquiry;* b. 10 June 1934; s. of Harold Leslie Gibson and Martha Lucy Gibson (née Diercking); m. Dr Katharine Mary Beatrice Hadow 1968 (died 2002); two s. one d.; ed Malvern Coll., Worcester Coll., Oxford; Nat. Service 2nd Lt RA 1953–55; called to Bar, Inner Temple 1960; Bencher, Lincoln's Inn 1975; Second Jr Counsel to Inland Revenue (Chancery) 1970–72; Jr Counsel to the Treasury (Chancery) 1972–81; Judge of the High Court of Justice, Chancery Div. 1981–93; Chair. Law Comm. for England and Wales 1990–92; Judge, Employment Appeal Tribunal 1984–86; Lord Justice of Appeal 1993–2005; Intelligence Services Commr 2006–10; Chair. Detainee Inquiry 2010–; conducted Omagh bombing intelligence review 2008; Judge, Qatar Financial Centre Civil and Commercial Court 2007–; Chair. Trust Law Cttee 2005–; Treas., Lincoln's Inn 1996; Hon. Fellow, Worcester Coll., Oxford 1993, Hon. Mem. Soc. of Legal Scholars. *Address:* Office of the Chairman, The Detainee Inquiry, 35 Great Smith Street, London, SW1A 3BQ, England (office). *Telephone:* (20) 7276-5544 (office). *E-mail:* secretariat@detaineeinquiry.org.uk (office). *Website:* www.detaineeinquiry.org.uk (office).

GIBSON, Richard F., Sr; St Maarten lawyer and politician; b. 1944, Oranjestad, Aruba; ed Univ. of Netherlands Antilles; admitted to legal practice within jurisdiction of Jt Court of Justice of Aruba, Curaçao, St Maarten, Bonaire, St Eustatius and Saba 1969; Partner, Gibson & Assocs (law firm); Supervisory Dir, Central Bank of Netherlands Antilles 1982–89; Pres., Netherlands Antilles Red Cross 1984–87; fmr Minister of Constitutional and Interior Affairs, Netherlands Antilles; Minister of Finance (of St Maarten) 2015–18, also Acting Minister of Justice 2015–16; mem. Netherlands Antilles Criminal Code Revision Cttee; fmr mem. Netherlands Antilles Bar Asscn; mem. St Maarten Bar Asscn (Pres. 1982–94); mem. Int. Acad. of Trial Lawyers; Kt, Order of Orange-Nassau 2006. *Address:* c/o Department of Finance, POB 943, Clem Labega Square, Philipsburg, St Maarten (office).

GIBSON, Robert Dennis, AO, MSc, PhD, DSc, FTS, FAIM; Australian academic and university chancellor; *Professor of Functional Food Science, University of Adelaide;* b. 13 April 1942, Newcastle, UK; s. of Edward Gibson and Euphemia Gibson; m. 1st. Eileen Hancox 1964; one s. two d.; m. 2nd Catherine Bull 1994; ed Univs of Hull and Newcastle, UK; Prof. and Head, School of Math. and Computing, Newcastle Polytechnic 1977–82; Deputy Dir Queensland Inst. of Tech. 1982–83, Dir 1983–88; Vice-Chancellor Queensland Univ. of Tech. (QUT) 1989–2003; Chancellor RMIT (fmrly Royal Melbourne Inst. of Tech.) 2003–10; currently Prof. of Functional Food Science, Univ of Adelaide; Chair. Grad. Careers Council of Australia 1999–2005, M&MD Ltd 2003; Premier of Queensland SMART Awards Panel 2003; mem. Bd of Dirs Int. Soc. of Study of Fatty Acids and Lipids (ISSFAL) 2006; Fellow, Australian Inst. of Co. Dirs mem. Australian Research Council 1988–93; Hon. DSc (CNAA) 1984, Hon. DUniv (USC) 2000, (QUT) 2003; Alexander Leaf Distinguished Scientist Award 2012. *Publications:* over 80 publs in mathematical modelling. *Leisure interests:* cricket, running. *Address:* University of Adelaide, GN 20, Waite Building, Adelaide, SA 5005 (office); 173/350 St Kilda Road, Melbourne, VIC 3004, Australia (office). *Telephone:* (8) 8313-4333 (office). *Fax:* (8) 8313-7135 (office). *E-mail:* robert.gibson@adelaide.edu.au (office). *Website:* www.adelaide.edu.au (office).

GIBSON, Toby J., PhD; British biologist and biochemist; *Team Leader, European Molecular Biology Laboratory;* ed Univ. of Cambridge; on staff, Lab. of Molecular Biology, Cambridge 1981–86; Team Leader, Gibson Team, Structural and Computational Biology Unit, European Molecular Biology Lab., Heidelberg, Germany 1986–. *Publications include:* numerous publs in scientific journals. *Address:* European Molecular Biology Laboratory, Meyerhofstrasse 1, 69117 Heidelberg, Germany (office). *Telephone:* (6221) 3870 (office). *Fax:* (6221) 387-8306 (office). *E-mail:* toby.gibson@embl.de (office). *Website:* www.embl.org/aboutus (office).

GIBSON-SMITH, Christopher (Chris) Shaw, CBE, BSc, MS, PhD; British business executive; *Chairman, Partnership;* m. Marjorie Gibson-Smith; two c.; ed Univs of Durham and Newcastle and Stanford Business School, USA; with British Petroleum (BP) 1970–2001, positions include COO BP Chemicals, CEO BP Exploration Europe, Group Man. Dir 1997–2001; Chair. Nat. Air Traffic Services 2001–05; Chair. London Stock Exchange 2003–15; Chair. Partnership 2013–; mem. Bd of Dirs (non-exec.) Lloyds TSB Group PLC 1999–2005, Powergen UK PLC 2001–02, Qatar Financial Centre Authority 2006–12, British Land Co. PLC 2003–07 (Chair. 2007–12); Business Amb., UK Trade and Investment Org. 2008–10; fmr Chair. Calif. Marine Mammal Centre; Chair. Advisory Bd Reform 2012–; served on UK Government Advisory Comms on Aviation and on Oil and Gas; Sloan Fellow, Stanford Business School 1984–85, fmr mem. Advisory Bd Stanford Business School; fmr mem. Council CBI Scotland, Sustainability Comm.; Gov. London Business School 2005–12; fmr Trustee, Arts and Business, Inst. of Public Policy Research; Hon. Fellow, Univ. Coll. Durham . *Leisure interests:* skiing, golf, music, the arts. *Address:* Office of the Chairman, Partnership, Regent House, 1–3 Queensway, Redhill, RH1 1QT, England (office). *Telephone:* (20) 7398-5933 (office). *E-mail:* info@partnership.co.uk (office). *Website:* www.partnership-group.com (office).

GIDDENS, Baron (Life Peer), cr. 2004, of Southgate in the London Borough of Enfield; **Anthony Giddens,** PhD; British sociologist; b. 18 Jan. 1938, Edmonton, London; m. Jane Ellwood 1963; two d.; ed Minchenden School, Southgate, Univ. of Hull, London School of Economics, Univ. of Cambridge; Lecturer in Sociology, Univ. of Leicester 1961–70; Visiting Asst Prof., Simon Fraser Univ., Vancouver 1967–68, UCLA 1968–69; Lecturer in Sociology and Fellow, King's Coll., Cambridge 1970–84, Reader in Sociology 1984–86, Prof. of Sociology 1986–96, now Political Science Fellow; Dir LSE 1997–2003, Prof. Emer. 2004–; Founder Polity Press Ltd 1985, apptd Dir Blackwell-Polity Ltd 1985; Dir Centre for Social Research 1989– (fmr Chair.); BBC Reith Lecturer 1999; numerous visiting professorships; Founder of 'The Third Way'; mem. Russian Acad. of Sciences, American Acad. of Science; Hon. Fellow, LSE 2004, Chilean Acad., Chinese Acad. of Social Sciences; Nat. Order of the Southern Cross (Brazil), Grand Cross, Order of the Infante Dom Henrique (Portugal); Hon. DLitt (Univ. of Anglia), (Open Univ.), (Univ. of Salford), (South Bank Univ.), (Univ. of Hull), (Univ. of Leicester), Hon. DScS (Univ. of Helsinki), Dr hc (Vesalius Coll., Vrije Univ. Brussels), (Univ. of Buenos Aires, Argentina), (Univ. of Twente, Netherlands); German British Forum Award 1999, Prince of Asturias Award (Spain) 2002, Gold Medal, Norwegian Acad. *Publications include:* Capitalism and Modern Social Theory 1971, Politics and Sociology in the Thought of Max Weber 1972, Emile Durkheim: Selected Writings (ed. and trans.) 1972, The Class Structure of the Advanced Societies 1973, Positivism and Sociology (ed.) 1973, Elites and Power in British Society (with P. H. Stanworth) 1974, New Rules of Sociological Method 1976, Studies in Social and Political Theory 1977, Emile Durkheim 1978, Central Problems in Social Theory 1979, A Contemporary Critique of Historical Materialism 1981, Sociology: A Brief but Critical Introduction 1982, Classes, Conflict and Power (with D. Held) 1982, Classes and the Division of Labour (with G. G. N. Mackenzie) 1982, Profiles and Critiques in Social Theory 1983, The Constitution of Society: Outline of the Theory of Structuration 1984, The Nation-State and Violence 1985, Durkheim on Politics and the State 1986, Social Theory and Modern Sociology 1987, Social Theory Today (with Jon Turner) 1988, Sociology 1988, The Consequences of Modernity 1990, Modernity and Self-Identity 1991, Human Societies 1992, The Transformation of Intimacy 1992, Beyond Left and Right 1994, Reflexive Modernisation (with Ulrich Beck and Scott Lash) 1994, Politics, Sociology and Social Theory 1995, In Defence of Sociology 1996, Conversations with Anthony Giddens: Making Sense of Modernity (with Christopher Pierson) 1998, The Third Way: The Renewal of Social Democracy 1998, Runaway World: How Globalisation is Reshaping Our Lives 1999, The Third Way and its Critics 2000, On the Edge: Living with Global Capitalism (ed with Will Hutton) 2000, The Global Third Way Debate 2001, The Progressive Manifesto 2003, Essentials of Sociology 2006, Europe In The Global Age 2007, Over to You, Mr Brown - How Labour Can Win Again 2007, The Politics of Climate Change 2009, Turbulent and Mighty Continent: What Future for Europe? (European Book Prize 2014) 2013; contrib. of articles, review articles and book reviews to professional journals and newspapers. *Leisure interests:* theatre, tennis, cinema. *Address:* House of Lords, London, SW1A 0PW; Polity Press, 65 Bridge Street, Cambridge, CB2 1UR, England (office). *Telephone:* (1223) 324315 (Cambridge) (office). *E-mail:* editorial@politybooks.com (office). *Website:* www.polity.co.uk (office).

GIDDINGS, Hon. Larissa (Lara) Tahireh, BA, LLB; Australian politician; b. 14 Nov. 1972, Goroka, Papua New Guinea; ed Univ. of Tasmania; worked in

Australian Senate as Whip's Clerk, then as an electorate officer with Senator Sue Mackay; travelled to UK to carry out temporary admin. work in London, later worked as a parl. research officer for Helen Eadie MSP, Edinburgh; mem. Tasmanian House of Ass. (Australian Labor Party) for Lyons 1996–98, for Franklin 2002–, worked for Tasmanian Premier as speech writer and media asst; Minister for Econ. Devt and the Arts 2004–06, for Health and Human Services 2006–10, for Infrastructure and Econ. Devt April–Nov. 2010; Deputy Premier of Tasmania, Attorney-Gen. and Minister for Justice 2008–11, Treas. of Tasmania and Minister for the Arts 2010–14, Premier (first woman) 2011–14. *Address:* 1/17 Bligh Street, Rosny, Clarence, Tasmania 7018, Australia (office). *Telephone:* (3) 6212-2361 (office). *E-mail:* lara.giddings@parliament.tas.gov.au (office).

GIELGUD, Maina Julia Gordon, AO, BEPC; British ballet director, teacher and dance coach; b. 14 Jan. 1945, London, England; d. of Lewis Gielgud and Elisabeth Grussner; with Cuevas Co. and Roland Petit Co. –1963; Grand Ballet Classique de France 1963–67; Béjart Co. 1967–71; Berlin 1971; London Festival Ballet 1972–76; ballerina, Sadler's Wells Royal Ballet 1976–78; freelance ballerina and guest artist 1978–82; Rehearsal Dir London City Ballet 1982; Artistic Dir The Australian Ballet 1983–96; Ballet Dir Royal Danish Ballet 1997–99; Artistic Assoc., Houston Ballet 2003–05; freelance dir, regular guest répétiteur and teacher, English Nat. Ballet 2006–12; Artistic Adviser, Hungarian Nat. Ballet 2014–; guest teacher/stager, Boston Ballet, Nat. Ballet of Canada, La Scala, Milan, The Australian Ballet, Rome Opera and other ballet cos and schools world-wide; freelance stager, guest teacher, coach and jury mem.; Hon. AO 1991. *Plays:* L'Heure Exquise (Maurice Bejart, after Happy Days by Samuel Beckett). *Film:* L'Age en Fleurs. *Ballets produced:* Steps Notes and Squeaks 1968; for The Australian Ballet: The Sleeping Beauty 1985, Giselle 1987; for Boston Ballet: Giselle 2002, 2007; for Ballet du Rhin: Giselle 2003; for Houston Ballet: Giselle 2005; for Conservatoire of Ballet Christine Walsh: Coppelia 2015. *Ballets performed:* L'Heure Exquise. *Publications:* various articles for Dance Europe as well as blogs. *Address:* 1/9 Stirling Court, 3 Marshall Street, London, W1F 9BD, England. *Telephone:* (20) 7734-6612. *E-mail:* mainagielgud@gmail.com. *Website:* www.mainagielgud.com.

GIENOW, Herbert Hans Walter, DIur; German business executive; b. 13 March 1926, Hamburg; s. of Günther and Margarethe Gienow; m. Imina Brons 1954 (divorced 2013); one s. one d.; ed Hamburg Univ.; Head Clerk, Deutsche Warentreuhand AG, mem. Man. Bd 1959; mem. Hamburg Bar; chartered accountant 1961; mem. Man. Bd, Klöckner-Werke AG 1962, Chair. Exec. Bd 1974–91; Pres. ALSTOM Germany 1991–98; Sr Adviser, Gen. Capital Group, Munich; Chair. Supervisory Bd ALSTOM GmbH 1994–99, SteelDex AG 2001–16; fmr Chair. Consultative Cttee Deutsche Bank AG, Essen; Hon. mem. World Steel Inst., Brussels 1992, Hon. Pres. Academia Baltica 2008; Commdr, Confrèrie des Chevaliers du Tastevin, Dijon 1982, Chevalier, Légion d'honneur 1998. *Leisure interests:* books, shooting, model soldiers. *Address:* An der Pönt 51, 40885 Ratingen (office); Am Adels 7, 40883 Ratingen, Germany (home). *Telephone:* (2102) 126903 (office); (2102) 60692 (home). *Fax:* (2102) 126909 (office). *E-mail:* woneigoffice@t-online.de (office).

GIEROWSKI, Stefan; Polish painter; b. 21 May 1925, Częstochowa; s. of Józef Gierowski and Stefania Gierowska (née Wasilewska); m. Anna Golka 1951; one s. one d.; ed Acad. of Fine Arts, Kraków, Jagiellonian Univ.; worked with Gallery Krzywe 1956–61; Docent, Acad. of Fine Arts, Warsaw, Dean of Painting Dept 1975–80, Extraordinary Prof. 1976–96; mem. Union of Polish Artists and Designers, Sec.-Gen. 1957–59, Pres. of Painting Section 1959–61, 1963–66; mem. Organizing Cttee, Congress of Polish Culture 1981; Kt's and Officer's Cross of Order of Polonia Restituta; Silver Medal, Third Festival of Fine Arts, Warsaw 1978, Prize of Chair. Council of Ministers (1st class) 1979, Jan Cybis Prize 1980. *Address:* ul. Gagarina 15 m. 97, 00-753 Warsaw, Poland. *Telephone:* (22) 8411633.

GIERTYCH, Roman, MA, LLM; Polish politician and lawyer; *Principal, Kancelaria Adwokacka Roman Giertych;* b. 27 Feb. 1971, Srem; s. of Maciej Giertych and Antonina Giertych; m. Barbara Giertych; four c.; ed Adam Mickiewicz Univ., Poznań; owner of a legal practice, Warsaw; reactivated All-Polish Youth (Młodziej Wszechpolska), Chair. 1989–93 (resgnd), then Hon. Chair.; mem. Nat. Democratic Party (Stronnictwo Narodowo-Demokratyczne) and Nat. Party (Stronnictwo Narodowe), Vice-Pres. Bd Nat. Party 1994, both parties merged with several others orgs to form League of Polish Families 2001, Pres. Congress of League of Polish Families (Liga Polskich Rodzin) 2002; Deputy to Sejm (Parl.) 2001–07; Deputy Prime Minister and Minister for Nat. Educ. 2006–07; apptd Vice-Chair. PKN Orlen Investigation Comm. (to investigate biggest corruption scandal in modern Polish political history) 2004; currently Prin., Kancelaria Adwokacka Roman Giertych (law firm); mem. Polish Academic Union 1988. *Publications include:* Kontrrewolucja mlodych (Counter-Revolution of the Young) 1994, Pod walcem historii. Polityka zagraniczna ruchu narodowego 1938–1945 (Under History's Roller. Foreign Policy of the National Movement 1938–1945) 1995, Lot orla (Flight of the Eagle) 2000, Możemy wygrać Polskę (We Can Win Poland) 2001; numerous articles, including several publs in Nasz Dziennik, Mysl Polska. *Leisure interests:* historical books, chess (Champion of Poznań Voivodship), tennis. *Address:* Kancelaria Adwokacka Roman Giertychm ul. Nowy Świat 35 lokal 4, Warsaw, Poland (office). *Telephone:* (22) 4240736 (office). *E-mail:* biuro@giertych-kancelaria.pl (office). *Website:* giertych-kancelaria.pl (office).

GIESBERT, Franz-Olivier; French/American journalist and author; *Editor, Le Point;* b. 18 Jan. 1949, Wilmington, Del., USA; s. of Frederick Giesbert and Marie Allain; m. 1st Christine Fontaine (divorced); two s. one d.; m. 2nd Natalie Freund 2000; one s. one d.; ed Centre de Formation des Journalistes; journalist, Le Nouvel Observateur 1971, Sr Corresp. in Washington, DC 1980, Political Ed. 1981, Ed.-in-Chief 1985–88; Ed.-in-Chief, Le Figaro 1988–2000, Figaro Magazine 1997–2000, mem. Editorial Bd 1993–2000, Figaro Magazine 1997–2000; Ed. Le Point (weekly news magazine) 2000–; Dir/presenter 'le Gai savoir' TV programme, Paris Première cable channel 1997–2001, Dir Culture et Dépendances France 3 TV channel 2001–06; Editorial Dir La Provence 2017–; mem. jury Prix Théophraste Renaudot 1998–, Prix Louis Hachette, Prix Aujourd'hui; mem. Conseil Admin Musée du Louvre Paris 2000; Aujourd'hui Best Essay Prize 1975, Prix Gutenberg 1987, Prix Pierre de Monaco 1997, Prix Richelieu 1999, Prix Itheme for Best Talk Show 1999. *Television includes:* host: Chez FOG (France 5) 2006–09, Vous aurez le dernier mot (France 2) 2009–10, Semaine critique! (France 2) 2010–11, Les grandes questions (France 5) 2011–13, Le monde d'après (France 3) 2012–. *Publications:* François Mitterrand ou la tentation de l'Histoire (essay) 1977, Monsieur Adrien (novel) 1982, Jacques Chirac (biog.) 1987, Le Président 1990, L'Affreux (novel) (Grand Prix du Roman de l'Acad. française) 1992, La Fin d'une Époque 1993, La Souille (novel) (William the Conqueror and Interallié Prize), Le Vieil homme et la Mort 1996, François Mitterrand, une vie 1996, Le Sieur Dieu (novel) (Prix Jean d'Heurs de Nice Baie des Anges) 1998, Mort d'un berger (novel) 2002, L'Abatteur (novel) 2003, L'Américain (novel) 2004, L'Immortel (novel) 2007, La Tragédie du président: scènes de la vie politique 2006, Le Huitième Prophète (novel) 2008, Le lessiveur (novel) 2009, Un très grand amour (novel) 2010, Dieu, ma mère et moi (novel) 2012, La cuisinière d'Himmler (novel) 2013, L'amour est éternel tant qu'il dure (novel) 2014, L'Arracheuse de dents (novel) 2016, Belle d'amour (novel) 2017, Le théâtre des incapables (essay) 2017, Une journée particulière (essay) 2017, La dernière fois que j'ai rencontré Dieu (essay) 2018. *Address:* Le Point, 74 avenue du Maine, 75014 Paris Cedex, France (office). *Telephone:* 1-44-10-10-10 (office). *Fax:* 1-44-10-12-49 (office). *E-mail:* fogiesbert@lepoint.tm.fr (office). *Website:* www.lepoint.fr (office).

GIEVE, Sir John, Kt, BA, CB, MPhil; British civil servant and financial executive; *Chairman, VocaLink;* b. 20 Feb. 1950; m.; two c.; ed New Coll., Oxford; several positions at HM Treasury 1978–2001, including working in Dept of Employment, Pvt. Sec. to the Chief Sec., Treasury Press Sec., Prin. Pvt. Sec. to the Chancellor; Perm. Sec. Home Office 2001–05; Deputy Gov. and mem. Monetary Policy Cttee, Bank of England 2006–09, with responsibility for Bank's Financial Stability work; Chair. VocaLink 2009–; Sr Adviser, GLG Partners LP 2010–12; Visiting Prof., Dept of Political Science, University Coll. London 2012–; fmr mem. Bd Financial Services Authority; mem. Bd of Dirs CLS, Morgan Stanley International, Homerton Hospital Trust; Gov. Islington Primary School; Chair. Bd of Trustees Clore Social Leadership 2009–; Trustee Nesta 2011–; Hon. Fellow, Regent's Univ. London. *Address:* VocaLink, 1 Angel Lane, London, EC4R 3AB, England (office). *Website:* www.vocalink.com (office).

GIFFORD, Charles (Chad) K., BA; American banking executive; b. 8 Nov. 1942, Providence, RI; s. of Clarence H. Gifford and Priscilla Kilvert Gifford; m. Anne Dewing; four c.; ed Princeton Univ.; Chair., Pres. and CEO BankBoston 1995–96, CEO 1996–97, Chair. and CEO 1997–99; Pres. and COO FleetBoston Financial Corpn 1999–2001, Pres. and CEO 2001–02, Chair. and CEO 2002–04; Chair. Bank of America Corpn (following acquisition of FleetBoston) 2004–05 (retd), now Chair. Emer. and mem. Bd of Dirs; mem. Bd of Dirs Mass Mutual Life Insurance Co., CBS Corpn; Chair. Bd of Trustees, BPE (fmrly Boston Plan for Excellence); Trustee, NSTAR, Dana-Farber Cancer Inst., Eversource Energy (fmrly Northeast Utilities/Northeast Utilities System) 2012–; Hon. Dir Greater Boston Chamber of Commerce.

GIGABA, Malusi Knowledge Nkanyezi, MA; South African party official and politician; b. 30 Aug. 1971, Eshowe, KwaZulu-Natal; s. of Jabulani Gigaba and Nomthandazo Gigaba; ed Univ. of Durban-Westville; joined African Nat. Congress (ANC), South African Communist Party (SACP) and ANC Youth League (ANCYL) 1990, Provincial Sec., ANCYL 1994–96, Pres. ANCYL 1994–2004; Office Asst, Public Affairs Dept, Univ. of Durban-Westville 1993; Consultant, Macsteel Co. 1997; mem. Nat. Ass. (ANC) 1999–2001, 2004–18; Deputy Minister of Home Affairs 2009–10, Minister of Public Enterprises 2010–14, Minister of Home Affairs 2014–17, Feb.–Nov. 2018, Minister of Finance 2017–18; Patron OASIS for Hope Hospice; mem. ANC, mem. Nat. Working Cttee.

GIJSBERTHA, Kenneth; Curaçao politician; *Minister of Finance;* b. 8 March 1953, Kòrsou; ed Maria Immaculata Lyceum, Willemstad; mem. Movementu Antia Nobo (MAN, Movt for a New Antilles), Parl. Leader, Island Council of Curaçao (territorial governing body as part of Netherlands Antilles) 1996–2002, Pres. MAN 1999–2000, Political Leader 2000–02; Materials Superintendent, Refineria Isla Curacao BV 1997–2014, Public Relations Man. 2008–16; Deputy Lt Gov., Island Territory of Curaçao 2004–06, 2010; Minister of Traffic and Telecommunication 2006, of Finance 2016–; Chair. Supervisory Bd, Nieuwe Post Nederlandse Antillen NV 2011–16, United Telecommunication Services UTS 2012–16. *Address:* Ministry of Finance, Pietermaai 17, Willemstad, Curaçao (office). *Telephone:* (9) 432-8000 (office). *Fax:* (9) 461-3339 (office). *E-mail:* directie.financien@gobiernu.cw (office).

GIL, Gilberto; Brazilian politician, musician (guitar, accordion) and singer; b. (Gilberto Passos Gil Moreira), 26 June 1942, Salvador, Bahia State; s. of José Gil Moreira and Claudina Passos Gil Moreira; ed Fed. Univ., Bahia; began playing accordion aged eight; composed songs for TV advertisements in early 1960s; appeared in Nós Por Exemplo (show directed by Caetano Veloso) 1964; moved to São Paulo 1965; had first hit when Elis Regina recorded Louvação; participated in Tropicalia movt, sang protest songs that proved controversial with mil. dictatorship; imprisoned 1968; forced to leave Brazil on release and moved to UK; worked with groups such as Pink Floyd, Yes, Incredible String Band and Rod Stewart's band in London clubs; returned to Brazil in 1972; toured with Caetano Veloso, Gal Costa and Maria Bethânia; recorded album Nightingale in USA 1978; appearances at Montreux Jazz Festival; Pres. Fundação Gregorio de Matos, Salvador 1987; mem. Council of City Hall of Salvador 1988–92, Pres. Environmental Defence Cttee 1989; mem. Advisory Council Fundação Mata Virgem and Fundação Alerta Brasil Pantanal; Pres. Negro-Mestizo Reference Centre (CERNE); mem. Green Party 1989, later mem. Nat. Exec. Cttee; mem. Parl. for Salvador; Minister of Culture 2003–08 (resgnd); fmr Pres. Fundação Onda Azul (Blue Wave Foundation); Cruz da Ordem de Rio Branco, Chevalier, Ordre des Arts et des Lettres, Grand Officier, Légion d'honneur 2005; Shell and Sharp Prize 1990, UNESCO Artist for Peace 1999, Polar Music Prize 2004, 2005. *Recordings include:* albums: Louvação 1967, Gilberto Gil 1968, Tropicália ou Panis et Circensis 1968, Gilberto Gil 1969, Expresso 2222 1972, Barra 69 1972, Temporada de Verão 1974, Gilberto Gil ao Vivo 1974, Gil Jorge Ogum Zangô 1975, Refazenda 1975, Doces Bárbaros 1976, Refavela 1977, Refestança 1978, Antologia do Samba-Choro: Gilberto Gil e Germano Mathias 1978, Gilberto Gil ao Vivo em Montreux 1978, Nightingale 1978, Realce 1979, A Gente Precisa Ver o Luar 1981, Brasil: João Gilberto Gil, Caetano e Bethânia 1981, Um Banda Um 1982, Extra 1983, Quilombo 1984, Vamos Fugir (with The Wailers) 1984, Raça Humana 1984, Dia Dorim Noite Neon 1985, Gilberto Gil em Concerto 1987, Ao Vivo Em Tóquio 1987, Soy Loco por Ti, América 1987, O Eterno Deus Mu Dança 1989, Parabolicamará 1992, Tropicália 2 1993,

Gilberto Gil Unplugged 1994, Quanta 1997, O sol de Oslo 1998, Ensaio Geral 1999, Cidade do Salvador 1999, O Viramundo 1999, Gilberto Gil – Satisfação 1999, Gil & Milton 2000, São João Vivo 2001, Kaya N'Gan Daya 2002, Eletracústico (Grammy Award for Best Contemporary World Music Album 2006) 2005, Gil Luminoso 2006, Banda Larga de Cordel 2008, BandaDois (Latin Grammy Award for Best Música Popular Brasileira Album 2010) 2009, Fé na Festa (Latin Grammy Award for Best Native Brazilian Roots Album) 2010, Concerto de cordas & máquinas de ritmo 2012, Gilbertos Samba Ao Vivo 2014, Gilbertos Samba 2014, Caetano Veloso e Gilberto Gil - Dois Amigos, Um Século de Música 2015. *Address:* Gege Produções, Estrada de Gávea 135, 22451-260 Rio de Janeiro, RJ, Brazil (office). *Telephone:* (21) 3323-1600 (office). *Fax:* (21) 2239-9727 (office). *E-mail:* atendimento@gege.com.br (office). *Website:* www.gege.com.br (office); www.gilbertogil.com.br.

GIL-DÍAZ, Francisco, BSc, PhD; Mexican economist, government official and telecommunications industry executive; *CEO, Telefonica Moviles Mexico, SA De C V;* b. 2 Sept. 1943, Mexico City; m.; four c.; ed Instituto Tecnológico Autónomo de México (ITAM), Univ. of Chicago, USA; Prof., ITAM 1970–76, now Prof. Emer., Co-ordinator, ITAM Econs Program 1973–78; Prof., Colegio de México 1970–84; economist, Bank of Mexico 1973, Dir-Gen. of Econ.-Treasury Studies, Secr. of Treasury 1976, Head of Org. and Analysis of Econ. Information 1977–78, Dir-Gen. of Income Policy, Secr. of Treasury 1978–82; Asst Dir Bank of Mexico 1982–85, Dir of Econ. Research 1985–88; Under-Sec. of Revenue 1988–94 and later Gen. Man. for Econ. and Financial Studies, Finance and Public Credit Secr., then Gen. Dir of Revenue Policy; Gen. Man. Avantel SA (telecommunications co.) 1997–2000; Sec. of State for Finance and Public Credit 2000–06; CEO Telefónica México and Central América (Telefonica Moviles Mexico) 2007–; mem. Bd of Dirs Corporacion Geo SAB de CV 2008–, Bolsa Mexicana de Valores SAB de CV 2008–; mem. Advisory Bd BandwidthX Inc. *Address:* Telefonica Moviles Mexico, SA De C V, Prolg Paseo De La Reforma No 1200, Pisos 8–14, Santa Fe Cruz Manca, Cuajimalpa 05349 México DF, Mexico (office). *Website:* www.telefonica.com.mx (office).

GILAD, Nir, BA, MA; Israeli business executive and fmr government official; ed Hebrew Univ., Jerusalem, Bar Ilan Univ.; fmr Chief Financial Officer Israel Aircraft Industries; fmr Accountant Gen. and Deputy Head of Budget Div., Ministry of Finance; Sr Vice-Pres., Migdal Insurance Co., CEO Migdal Investment Man. Ltd and Chair. Migdal Capital Markets Ltd; Sr Vice-Pres. for Business Devt and Strategy, Israel Corpn –2006, Pres. and CEO 2006–15, Chair. Israel Chemicals—ICL (subsidiary) 2008–16; Chair. Friends of Soroka Medical Center Asscn 2014–; mem. Bd of Dirs Zim Integrated Shipping Services Ltd, Tower Semiconductors Ltd, Chery Quantum Ltd; mem. Yedidei Atidim Asscn; holds rank of Lt-Col in Israel Defense Force reserves.

GILANI, Makhdoom Syed Yousaf Raza, BA, MA; Pakistani politician; b. 9 June 1952, Karachi; s. of Alamdar Hussain Gilani; m. Elahi Gilani; four s. one d.; ed Univ. of the Punjab, Lahore; mem. Cen. Leadership Muslim League, Pakistan 1978; mem. Pakistan People's Party 1988–, Vice-Chair. Cen. Exec. Cttee 1998–2015 (resgnd); cabinet mem. in three-year Govt of Prime Minister Muhammad Khan Junejo, Minister of Housing and Works 1985–86, of Railways Jan.–Dec. 1986; Chair. Dist Council, Multan; mem. Nat. Ass. from Multan 1985–, Speaker 1993–97; served in cabinet of fmr Prime Minister, the late Benazir Bhutto, as Minister of Tourism 1989–90, of Housing and Works Jan.–Aug. 1990; tried on charges of abusing his authority by govt anti-corruption agency 1997, accused of putting more than 500 unqualified people from his constituency on govt payroll when he was House Speaker, imprisoned 2001–06; Prime Minister of Pakistan 2008–12 (indicted by Pakistan Supreme Court for contempt for failing to pursue corruption charges against Pres. Asif Ali Zardari April 2012, disqualified from holding office and from parl. June 2012). *Publication:* Reflections of Yusuf's Well. *Address:* Gilani House, Ghaus-al-Azam Road, Multan, 155-B, Phase-I, Defence, Lahore, Pakistan. *E-mail:* makhdoomyrgillani@hotmail.com (home).

GILAURI, Nikoloz (Nika) Zurabis, BA, MA; Georgian economist and politician; b. 14 Feb. 1975, Tbilisi; m. Marine Shamugia 2010; one d.; ed Ivane Javakhishvili Tbilisi State Univ., Bournemouth Coll., UK, Limerick Univ., Ireland, Temple Univ., Philadelphia, USA, Univs of Paris and Tokyo; worked at Dublin Int. Finance Centre as an Admin./Man. Invesco assets man. corpn 1999; financial consultant for energy conservation projects at Philadelphia Small Business Devt Center 2000; financial consultant, Georgia Telecom 2001; financial consultant, Spanish corpn Iberdrola (Georgian energy market man. contractor) 2002; worked for SBE (Ireland) as man. contractor and financial controller of Georgian state electricity 2003–04; Minister of Energy 2004–07, of Finance 2007–09; First Deputy Prime Minister 2008–09, Prime Minister 2009–12; Head of JSC Partnership Fund (state-owned stock fund) 2012–. *Address:* JSC Partnership Fund, 0108 Tbilisi, 8 Rustaveli Avenue (Old Parliament Building), Georgia (office). *Telephone:* (322) 99-04-48 (office). *E-mail:* info@fund.ge (office). *Website:* www.fund.ge (office).

GILBERT; British artist; b. (Gilbert Proesch), 17 Sept. 1943, Dolomites, Italy; ed Wolkenstein School of Art, Hallein School of Art, Munich Acad. of Art, St Martin's School of Art, London; began working with George (Passmore) in 1967 as Gilbert & George; est. reputation as performance artists, presenting themselves, identically dressed, as living sculptures; later work includes large composite drawings and vividly coloured photo-pieces often featuring likenesses of the artists; work underpinned by 'Art for all' philosophy; works address social issues, taboos and artistic conventions; work held in public collections in UK and abroad; Dr hc (London Metropolitan Univ.) 2008, (Univ. of East London) 2010, (Open Univ.) 2012, Hon. (Plymouth Univ.) 2013, Magister Artium Gandensis (University Coll. Ghent) 2010; Turner Prize 1986. *Publications include:* What Our Art Means, Gilbert and George: The Complete Pictures 2007. *Address:* White Cube, 144–152 Bermondsey Street, London, SE1 3TQ, England (office). *Telephone:* (20) 7930-5373 (office). *E-mail:* g-and-g@dircon.co.uk (office). *Website:* www.whitecube.com (office).

GILBERT, Kenneth Albert, OC, DMus, FRCM, FRSC; Canadian/Austrian harpsichordist, organist and academic; b. 16 Dec. 1931, Montreal; s. of Albert George Gilbert and Reta Mabel (née Welch); ed Conservatoire de Musique, Montréal and Conservatoire Nat. Supérieur de Musique, France; Prof., Conservatoire de Musique, Montreal 1957–74, McGill Univ. 1964–72; Assoc. Prof., Laval Univ., Québec 1970–76; Artist-in-Residence, Univ. of Ottawa 1969–70; Guest Prof., Royal Antwerp Conservatory, Belgium 1971–73; Dir Early Music Dept Conservatoire de Strasbourg, France 1981–85; Prof., Staatliche Hochschule für Musik, Stuttgart, Germany 1981–89, Paris Conservatoire 1988–96; Prof., Hochschule Mozarteum, Salzburg, Austria 1984–2000, Prof. Emer. 2000–; apptd Adjunct Prof. of Harpsichord and Organ, McGill Univ., Montreal 1998; Visiting Prof., RAM and Royal Coll. of Music, London; instructor at other music acads, summer schools etc.; Pres. Editions de l'Oiseau-Lyre, Monaco 2001–12; mem. RSC; Hon. RAM; Hon. FRCO; Officier des Arts et des Lettres, Cross of Honour 1st Class (Austria); Hon. DMus (McGill), (Melbourne), (Laval); Fellowships from Canada Council 1968, 1974, and Calouste Gulbenkian Foundation 1971, Prix Opus Québec 2006. *Recordings include:* complete harpsichord works of F. Couperin, Scarlatti and Rameau, Suites and Partitas of J.S. Bach, Well-Tempered Clavier and Concertos for 2, 3 and 4 Harpsichords by Bach. *Publications:* editions of complete harpsichord works of Couperin, Scarlatti and Rameau, Bach's Goldberg Variations, Frescobaldi Toccatas, Kapsberger's lute works transcribed for harpsichord. *Address:* Strathcona Music Building, Schulich School of Music, McGill University, 555 West Sherbrooke Street, Montréal, PQ H3A 1E3, Canada (office). *E-mail:* kenneth.gilbert@mcgill.ca (office). *Website:* www.mcgill.ca/music (office).

GILBERT, Walter, AB, MA, PhD; American molecular biologist, investment company executive and artist; *General Partner, BioVentures Investors;* b. 21 March 1932, Boston, Mass; s. of Richard V. Gilbert and Emma Gilbert (née Cohen); m. Celia Stone 1953; one s. one d.; ed Harvard Univ., Univ. of Cambridge, UK; NSF Postdoctoral Fellow, Harvard Univ. 1957–58, Lecturer in Physics 1958–59, Asst Prof. of Physics 1959–64, Assoc. Prof. of Biophysics 1964–68, Prof. of Biochemistry 1968–72; American Cancer Soc. Prof. of Molecular Biology 1972–81, Prof. of Biology 1985–86; H. H. Timken Prof. of Science 1986–87; Carl M. Loeb Univ. Prof. 1987–2002, Prof. Emer. 2002–, Chair. Dept of Cellular and Developmental Biology 1987–93; Chair. Scientific Bd, Biogen NV 1978–83, Co-Chair. Supervisory Bd 1979–81, Chair. Supervisory Bd and CEO 1981–84; Vice-Chair. Myriad Genetics, Inc. 1992–; Chair. Paratek Pharmaceuticals, Inc. 1996–2014; mem. Bd of Dirs Amylyx Pharmaceticals, Inc. 2012–; Gen. Partner BioVentures Investors, Cambridge, Mass 2002–; mem. NAS, American Physical Soc., American Soc. of Biological Chemists, American Acad. of Arts and Sciences; Foreign mem. Royal Soc.; V.D. Mattia Lectureship, Roche Inst. of Molecular Biology 1976; Smith, Kline and French Lecturer, Univ. of California, Berkeley 1977; Hon. Fellow, Trinity Coll. Cambridge, UK 1991; Hon. DSc (Univ. of Chicago, Columbia Univ.) 1978, (Univ. of Rochester) 1979, (Yeshiva Univ.) 1981, (Tulane Univ.) 2011; Guggenheim Fellowship, Paris 1968–69, US Steel Foundation Award in Molecular Biology, NAS 1968, Ledlie Prize, Harvard Univ. (with M. Ptashne) 1969, Warren Triennial Prize, Massachusetts Gen. Hosp. (with S. Benzer) 1977, Louis and Bert Freedman Award, New York Acad. of Sciences 1977, Prix Charles-Léopold Mayer, Acad. des Sciences, Inst. de France (with M. Ptashne and E. Witkin) 1977, Harrison Howe Award of the Rochester br. of ACS 1978, Louisa Gross Horwitz Prize, Columbia Univ. (with F. Sanger) 1979, Gairdner Foundation Annual Award 1979, Albert Lasker Basic Medical Research Award (with F. Sanger 1979), Prize for Biochemical Analysis, German Soc. for Clinical Chem. (with A. M. Maxam, F. Sanger and A. R. Coulsen) 1980, Sober Award, American Soc. of Biological Chemists 1980, Nobel Prize for Chem. (with F. Sanger and P. Berg) for work on deoxyribonucleic acid (DNA) 1980, New England Entrepreneur of the Year Award 1991, Ninth Nat. Biotechnology Ventures Award 1997. *Address:* BioVentures Investors, 70 Walnut Street, Suite 302, Wellesley, MA 02481 (office); 1 Fitchburg Street, C319, Somerville, MA 02143, USA (home). *Telephone:* (617) 252-3443 (office). *Fax:* (617) 497-1503 (office); (617) 621-7993 (office). *E-mail:* wgilbert@bioventureinvestors.com (office). *Website:* www.bioventuresinvestors.com (office); wallygilbert.com (home).

GILCHRIST, Adam Craig, AM; Australian fmr professional cricketer; b. 14 Nov. 1971, Bellingen, NSW; m. Melanie Gilchrist; one s. one d.; left-handed batsman and wicketkeeper; teams played for include NSW 1992–94, Western Australia 1994–2008 (Capt. since 2001), Australia 1996–2008 (retd), Deccan Chargers 2008–10, Kings XI Punjab 2011–13; test debut versus Pakistan at Brisbane 5–9 Nov. 1999; One-Day Int. (ODI) debut: Australia v S Africa, Faridabad, Pakistan 25 Oct. 1996; T20I debut: NZ v Australia, Auckland 17 Feb. 2005; scored 5,570 runs in 96 tests (average 47.60) with 17 hundreds and 26 fifties, highest score 204 not out; 9,619 runs in 287 ODIs (average 35.89) with 16 hundreds and 55 fifties; 10,334 runs in 190 First-class matches; holds record for most wicketkeeping dismissals in ODIs; fastest strike-rate in test-cricket history for a batsman scoring over 2,000 runs; captained Australia to first test-series victory in India for 34 years; mem. Australia's World Cup winning side 2003; retd from int. cricket March 2008; Wisden Cricketer of the Year 2002, Allan Border Medal 2003, One-Day Int. Player of the Year 2003, 2004, Wisden Australia Cricketer of the Year 2003, awarded a record total of six Carlton & United Beverages Gold Cups as Western Australia's best player; selected in Richie Benaud's Greatest XI, inducted into Sport Australia Hall of Fame 2012, ICC Hall of Fame 2013. *Publications:* One-Day Cricket: Playing the One-Day Game 2000, Walking to Victory 2003; newspaper columns for Sydney Morning Herald, Melbourne Age and West Australian. *Address:* c/o Western Australian Cricket Association, WACA Ground, PO Box 6045, East Perth, WA 6892, Australia. *Telephone:* (8) 9265-7222. *Fax:* (8) 9221-1823. *E-mail:* info@waca.com.au. *Website:* www.waca.com.au; www.adamgilchrist.info.

GILES, Alan James, MA, MS, OBE; British business executive; b. 4 June 1954, Dorchester, Dorset, England; m. Gillian Rosser 1978; two d.; ed Blandford School, Dorset, Merton Coll. Oxford, Stanford Univ., USA; buyer, Boots the Chemists 1975–78, Promotions Man. 1978–80, Asst Merchandise Controller 1980–82; Retail Devt Man., WHSmith 1982–85, Merchandise Controller (Books) 1985–88, Operations & Devt Dir, Do It All 1988–92; Man. Dir Waterstone's Booksellers 1992–99; CEO HMV Group PLC 1998–2006; Chair. (non-exec.) Fat Face 2006–13, Dir (non-exec.) 2013–; mem. Bd of Dirs, Somerfield PLC 1993–2004, Wilson Bowden PLC 2004–07, Rentokil Initial PLC 2006–17, Book Tokens Ltd 2007–13, The Office of Fair Trading 2007–14, The Competition & Markets Authority 2013–, Perpetual Income & Growth Investment Trust 2015–; Assoc. Fellow, Said Business School, Univ. of Oxford 2007–; Hon. Visiting Prof., Cass Business School. *Leisure interests:* watching football, cycling, walking.

GILIOMEE, Hermann Buhr, MA, DPhil; South African historian, academic and political columnist; *Extraordinary Professor of History, University of Stellenbosch;*

b. 4 April 1938, Sterkstroom; s. of Gerhardus Adriaan Giliomee and Catherine Geza Giliomee; m. Annette van Coller 1965; two d.; ed Porterville High School and Univ. of Stellenbosch; diplomatic service 1963–64; Lecturer in History, Univ. of Stellenbosch 1967–83, Extraordinary Prof. of History 2002–; Prof. of Political Studies, Univ. of Cape Town 1983–2002; recipient of Fellowships to Yale Univ., USA 1977–78, Univ. of Cambridge, UK 1982–83, Woodrow Wilson Center for Int. Scholars, Washington, DC 1992–93; Pres. South African Inst. of Race Relations 1995–97; f. Die Suid-Afrikaan journal 1984; political columnist for Cape Times, Rand Daily Mail, and other periodicals 1980–97; currently writes political column for Die Burger, Beeld and Volksblad morning newspapers; Stals Prize for Political Sciences 2001, Stals Prize for History 2004. *Publications:* The Shaping of South African Society 1652–1820 1979, Ethnic Power Mobilized: Can South Africa Change? 1979, Afrikaner Political Thought 1750–1850 1983, Up Against the Fences: Poverty, Passes and Privilege 1985, From Apartheid to Nation-building 1990, The Bold Experiment: South Africa's New Democracy 1994, Liberal and Populist Democracy in South Africa 1996, Surrender Without Defeat 1997, The Awkward Embrace: Dominant-Party Rule and Democracy in Semi-Industrialized Countries 1999, Kruispad 2001, The Afrikaners – Biography of a People 2003, Die Afrikaners: in Biografie 2004. *Leisure interest:* tennis. *Address:* 5 Dennerandweg, Stellenbosch 7600, South Africa (home). *Telephone:* (21) 8832964 (home). *Fax:* (21) 8878026 (home). *E-mail:* hgiliome@mweb.co.za (home).

GILL, Michael; Australian editor and media executive; *Chairman, SkillsDMC;* ed Univ. of Newcastle; presenter, Business Sunday (TV) 1988–90; sr writer, The Australian Financial Review 1990–93, Deputy Ed. 1993–96, Gen. Man. Business Devt, John Fairfax Holdings Ltd 1996–98, Publr and Ed.-in-Chief; Publr and Ed.-in-Chief Fairfax Business Media 1998–2007, CEO 2007–09, CEO Financial Review Group 2009–11; Pres. UNICEF Australia 2008–14, also mem. Bd of Dirs; Counsellor, Dragoman 2011–; Adviser, Liverwire Markets 2013–14; Prin. Adviser, Changepond Technologies 2014–15; Chair. SkillsDMC 2016–; mem. Bd of Dirs Tall Poppies Foundation Ltd 2008–, Royal Fast West 2015–; mem. Advisory Bd Subscribility 2015–; fmr Chair. Australian Associated Press, Nat. Inst. of Econ. and Industry Research; fmr Dir The Ian Potter Museum of Art, Victorian Community Foundation, Blue Mountains Festival, Circus Oz. *Address:* SkillsDMC, Tower 1, Level 1, Suite 2, 475–495 Victoria Avenue, Chatswood, NSW 2067, Australia (office). *E-mail:* skillsdmc@skillsdmc.com.au (office). *Website:* www.skillsdmc.com.au (office).

GILL, (Robert) Bates, PhD; American political scientist and research institute director; *CEO, United States Studies Centre, University of Sydney;* m. Dr Sarah Palmer; ed Woodrow Wilson Dept of Government and Foreign Affairs, Univ. of Virginia; assignments have included directing the East Asia programmes at the Center for Nonproliferation Studies, Monterey Inst. of Int. Studies, Monterey, Calif.; also held Fei Yiming Chair in Comparative Politics, Johns Hopkins Univ. Center for Chinese and American Studies, Nanjing Univ., People's Repub. of China; fmr Sr Fellow in Foreign Policy Studies and inaugural Dir Center for Northeast Asian Policy Studies, Brookings Inst., Washington, DC; Freeman Chair in China Studies, Center for Strategic and Int. Studies, Washington, DC 2002–07; Dir Stockholm Int. Peace Research Inst. (first American) 2007–12, initiated and led the East Asia Arms Control and Security Project 1993–97; CEO US Studies Centre, Univ. of Sydney 2012–; mem. Council on Foreign Relations, IISS; has consulted for several multinational corpns and govt agencies; Commdr, Royal Order of the Polar Star (Sweden). *Publications include:* author: Chinese Arms Transfers 1992, Contrasting Visions: U.S., China, and World Order 2006, Rising Star: China's New Security Diplomacy 2007 (revised edn 2010); co-author: China's Arms Acquisitions from Abroad: A Quest for "Superb and Secret Weapons" 1995, Chinese Arms Exports: Policy, Players, and Process 2004, China: The Balance Sheet – What the World Needs to Know Now About the Emerging Superpower 2006, Asia's New Multilateralism: Cooperation, Competition, and the Search for Community 2009; co-ed.: Weathering the Storm: Taiwan, Its Neighbours, and the Asian Financial 2000; more than 120 other publs, including monographs, book chapters, journal articles, essays, magazine columns and opinion pieces. *Address:* United States Studies Centre, University of Sydney, Institute Building H03, City Road, NSW 2006, Australia (office). *Website:* www.ussc.edu.au (office).

GILLAM, Sir Patrick, Kt, BA; British business executive; b. 15 April 1933, London; s. of Cyril B. Gillam and Mary J. Gillam; m. Diana Echlin 1963; one s. one d.; ed London School of Econs; Foreign Office 1956–57; joined British Petroleum (BP) 1957, Vice-Pres. BP North America Inc. 1971–74, Gen. Man. Supply Dept 1974–78, Dir BP Int. Ltd 1978–82, Chair. BP Shipping Ltd 1981–88, BP Minerals Int. Ltd 1981–88, Man. Dir BP Co. 1981–91, Chair. BP Africa Ltd 1982–88, BP Coal Inc. 1988–90, BP Nutrition 1989–91, BP America 1989–91, BP Oil 1990–91; Chair. Booker Tate Ltd 1991–93, Asda Group PLC 1991–96, Royal and Sun Alliance 1997–2003; Deputy Chair. Standard Chartered Bank Africa PLC 1988–89, Standard Chartered Overseas Holdings Ltd 1988–89, Standard Chartered Bank Aug.–Nov. 1988, Chair. 1993–2003, Standard Chartered PLC 1991–92, Chair. 1993–2003 (Dir 1988–2002); Chair. Asia House 2003–05; Consultant, CMi; Dir Commercial Union PLC 1991–96; Chair. ICC (UK) 1989–98; apptd mem. of Court of Govs, LSE 1989, Hon. Fellow 2000. *Leisure interest:* gardening. *Address:* 3 St Leonards Terrace, London, SW3 4QA, England.

GILLAN, Rt Hon. Dame Cheryl Elise Kendall, PC, DBE, FCIM; British politician and marketing consultant; b. 21 April 1952, Llandaff, Cardiff, Wales; m. John Coates (Jack) Leeming 1985; ed Cheltenham Ladies Coll., The Coll. of Law; marketing exec. for International Management Group 1977–84; Dir, British Film Year 1984–86; Sr Marketing Consultant, Ernst & Young 1986–91; Marketing Dir, Kidsons Impey 1991–93; Chair. Bow Group 1987–88; contested Greater Manchester Cen. in European Parl. Elections 1989; MP for Chesham and Amersham, Bucks. 1992–2010, for Chesham and Amersham (revised boundary) 2010–, mem. (Select Cttees), Science and Tech. 1992–95, Procedure 1994–95, Public Accounts 2003–04, Public Administration and Constitutional Affairs 2015–, Speaker's Cttee on the Independent Parliamentary Authority 2015–, Panel of Chairs 2015–; Parl. Pvt. Sec. to Viscount Cranborne as Leader of House of Lords and Lord Privy Seal 1994–95; Parl. Under-Sec. of State, Dept of Educ. and Employment 1995–97; Shadow Minister for Trade and Industry 1997–98, for Foreign and Commonwealth Affairs 1998–2001, for Int. Devt 1998–2001; Opposition Whip 2001–03; Shadow Minister for Home Affairs 2003–05; Shadow Sec. of State for Wales 2005–10; Sec. of State for Wales 2010–12; mem. Conservative Party (also, mem. Bd 2018–), Vice-Chair. Conservative backbench (1922 Cttee) 2015–; Asst Chair. Int. Democratic Union 2018–; mem. Exec. Cttee UK Br., Commonwealth Parl. Asscn 1998–, UK Rep. British Islands and Mediterranean region 1999–2004, Int. Treas. 2004–06; mem. NATO Parl. Ass. 2003–05; Fellow, Chartered Inst. of Marketing; Freeman of the City of London 1991; mem. Worshipful Co. of Marketors. *Leisure interests:* singing, gardening, golf, keeping chickens. *Address:* House of Commons, Westminster, London, SW1A 0AA (office); Constituency Office, 7A Hill Avenue, Amersham, Bucks., HP6 5BD, England (office). *Telephone:* (20) 7219-4061 (London); (1494) 721577 (Amersham). *E-mail:* cheryl.gillan.mp@parliament.uk (office); shawmj@parliament.uk (office). *Website:* www.parliament.uk/biographies/commons/mrs-cheryl-gillan/18 (office); www.cherylgillan.co.uk.

GILLAN, Michael J., DPhil; British physicist and academic; *Emeritus Professor of Physics, University College London;* ed Univ. of Oxford, Univ. of Minnesota, USA; early position as post-doctoral researcher, Univ. of Minn.; mem. staff, Atomic Energy Research Establishment, Harwell 1970–88; Prof. of Theoretical Physics, Univ. of Keele 1988–98; Prof. of Condensed Matter and Materials Physics, Physics and Astronomy Dept, Univ. Coll. London 1998, now Prof. Emer., London Centre for Nanotechnology, UCL; mem. Peer Review Coll. of UK Eng and Physical Sciences Research Council; Dirac Prize and Medal, Inst. of Physics 2006. *Publications:* numerous scientific papers in professional journals on theory of condensed matter, with a strong emphasis on computer simulation. *Address:* London Centre for Nanotechnology, Room 3.C1, University College London, 17–19 Gordon Street, London, WC1H 0AH, England (office). *Telephone:* (20) 7679-7049 (office). *Fax:* (20) 7679-7145 (office). *E-mail:* m.gillan@ucl.ac.uk (office). *Website:* www.london-nano.com (office).

GILLARD, Julia Eileen, BA, LLB; Australian lawyer and politician; b. 29 Sept. 1961, Barry, Wales, UK; d. of John Gillard and Moira Gillard; ed Univ. of Adelaide, Univ. of Melbourne; solicitor, Slater & Gordon, Werribee 1987–95, Partner 1990–95; Del. Australian Labor Party (ALP) State Conf. (Victoria) 1982–, Pres. ALP Carlton Br. 1985–89, Co-Convenor, Affirmative Action Working Party 1993–94, mem. Admin. Cttee 1993–97, Deputy Leader Fed. ALP 2006–07; Chief of Staff to Vic. Leader of Opposition J. Brumby 1995–98; MP (Australian Labor Party) for Lalor, Vic. 1998–; Shadow Minister for Population and Immigration 2001–03, for Reconciliation and Indigenous Affairs 2003, for Health 2003–06, for Employment, Industrial Relations and Social Inclusion 2006–07, Deputy Leader of Opposition 2006–07; Deputy Leader of the Labor Party 2006–10, Leader 2010–13; Deputy Prime Minister and Minister for Educ., Employment and Workplace Relations, and Social Inclusion 2007–10; Prime Minister 2010–13; Hon. Visiting Prof., Univ. of Adelaide 2013–; Chair. beyondblue 2017–, Global Inst. for Women's Leadership, Kings Coll., London 2018–. *Publications:* My Story 2014. *Address:* c/o Australian Labor Party, PO Box 6222, Kingston, ACT 2604, Australia. *Website:* juliagillard.com.au.

GILLESPIE, Norman, BA (hons), PhD; British arts administrator and business executive; *CEO, UNICEF Australia;* b. 1957, Lurgan, NI; m. Nicole Gillespie; one d.; ed Queen's Univ. Belfast, Univ. of London, Harvard Business School, USA, Chinghua Univ., Beijing, China; grad. trainee UK civil service; joined BP (British Petroleum) 1987, various positions including Tax Controller for North Sea Operations, Glasgow, mem. Group Strategy Team, London, Head of Pvt. Office of CEO and Chair. 1990–91, US Man. of Planning and Reporting, Houston, Tex. 1992–94; Dir of Group Planning and Financial Control, Cable & Wireless, London 1994–97, Head of Group Strategy 1995–97; Chief Financial Officer Cable & Wireless Optus (following merger of Cable & Wireless and Optus 1997), Sydney, Australia 1997–2002, Deputy CEO 1997–2002; Deputy Chair. Australian Brandenburg Orchestra 1999–2012; Deputy Chair. NSW Div., Australian Business Arts Foundation 2001–07, mem. Bd of Dirs 2003–07; CEO UNICEF Australia 2010–, Sydney Opera House 2002–07, Australian Jockey Club 2007–09; mem. Bd of Dirs Sydney Convention and Visitors Bureau 2002–05; Bd mem. Pinchgut Opera 2013; mem. Editorial Advisory Cttee The Global Mail 2012–14. *Leisure interests:* early music, opera, contemporary dance, mountain trekking. *Address:* UNICEF Australia, Level 4, 280 Pitt Street, Sydney, NSW 2000, Australia (office). *Telephone:* (2) 9261-2811 (office). *Fax:* (2) 9261-2844 (office). *E-mail:* unicef@unicef.org.au (office). *Website:* www.unicef.org.au (office).

GILLESPIE, Ronald James, PhD, DSc, FRS, FRSC, FRSC (UK), FCIC, CM; Canadian/British chemist and academic; *Professor Emeritus of Chemistry, McMaster University;* b. 21 Aug. 1924, London, England; s. of James A. Gillespie and Miriam Gillespie (née Kirk); m. 1st Madge Ena Garner 1950 (died 2008); two d.; m. 2nd Marcelle Roy 2011; ed Univ. Coll., London; Asst Lecturer, Dept of Chem., Univ. Coll., London 1948–50, Lecturer 1950–58; Commonwealth Fund Fellow, Brown Univ., RI, USA 1953–54; Assoc. Prof., Dept of Chem., McMaster Univ., Hamilton, Ont., Canada 1958–60, Prof. 1960–88, Prof. Emer. 1988–, Chair. Dept of Chem. 1962–65; Assoc. Prof., Univ. des Sciences et Techniques de Languedoc, Montpellier, France 1972–73; Visiting Prof., Univ. of Geneva, Switzerland 1976, of Göttingen, FRG 1978; mem. The Chemical Soc., ACS; Hon. LLD (Concordia) 1988, (Dalhousie) 1988; Dr hc (Montpellier) 1991; Hon. DSc (McMaster Univ.) 1993, (Lethbridge) 2007; numerous medals and awards. *Publications:* Molecular Geometry 1972, Chemistry (co-author) 1986, 1989, The VSEPR Model of Molecular Geometry (with I. Hargittai) 1991, Atoms, Molecules and Reactions: An Introduction to Chemistry (co-author) 1994, Chemical Bonding and Molecular Geometry: From Lewis to Electron Densities (co-author) 2001; papers in scientific journals. *Leisure interests:* chess, travel. *Address:* Department of Chemistry, McMaster University, Hamilton, ON L8S 4M1 (office); 50 Hatt Street, Dundas, ON L9H 0A1, Canada (home). *Telephone:* (905) 628-1502 (office); (905) 628-1502 (home). *Fax:* (905) 522-2509 (office). *E-mail:* ronald.gillespie@sympatico.ca (home).

GILLIAM, Terry Vance, BA; British (b. American) film director, animator, actor, illustrator and writer; b. 22 Nov. 1940, Minn.; s. of James Hall Gilliam and Beatrice Gilliam (née Vance); m. Margaret Weston 1973; one s. two d.; ed Occidental Coll., Calif.; Assoc. Ed. HELP! magazine 1962–64; freelance illustrator 1964–65, advertising copywriter/art dir 1966–67; Chevalier, Ordre des Arts et des Lettres 2013; Hon. Dr of Arts (Occidental Coll.), (Wimbledon Coll. of Art, London) 2000; Hon. DFA (Royal Coll. of Art, London) 1989; BAFTA Fellowship 2009, Dir with Unique Visual Sensitivity Award 2009. *Television:* Do Not Adjust Your Set (series writer) 1967, Marty (series writer) 1968, Broaden Your Mind (series writer) 1968, Monty Python's Flying Circus (series writer, actor) 1969–74, presenter The Last Machine (series) 1995. *Films include:* Storytime (dir) 1968, Monty Python's And Now for Something Completely Different (writer, actor, animator) 1971, The Miracle of Flight (dir) 1974, Monty Python and the Holy Grail (writer, actor, dir) 1975, Jabberwocky (screenplay, actor, dir) 1977, Monty Python's Life of Brian (writer, actor, animator) 1979, Time Bandits (writer, dir) 1981, Monty Python Live at the Hollywood Bowl (writer, actor) 1982, Monty Python's The Meaning of Life (writer, actor, dir) 1983, The Crimson Permanent Assurance (writer, actor, dir) 1983, Brazil (screenplay, actor, dir) 1985, Spies Like Us (actor) 1985, The Adventures of Baron Munchausen (screenplay, actor, dir) 1988, The Fisher King (dir) 1991, Twelve Monkeys (dir) 1995, Fear and Loathing in Las Vegas (screenplay, dir) 1998, Lost in La Mancha (appeared in documentary about film project The Man Who Killed Don Quixote) 2002, Tideland (writer, dir) 2005, The Brothers Grimm (dir) 2005, Enfermés dehors (actor) 2006, The Imaginarium of Doctor Parnassus (co-writer, dir, producer) 2009, The Zero Theorem 2013, Monty Python Live 2014. *Publications include:* Monty Python's Big Red Book, Monty Python's Papperbok 1977, Monty Python's Scrapbook 1979, Animations of Mortality 1979, Monty Python's The Meaning of Life, Monty Python's Flying Circus – Just the Words (co-ed.) 1989, The Adventures of Baron Munchhausen 1989, Not the Screenplay of Fear and Loathing in Las Vegas 1998, Gilliam on Gilliam 1999, Dark Nights and Holly Fools 1999, The Pythons Autobiography (co-author) 2003. *Address:* c/o Jenne Casarotto, National House, 60–66 Wardour Street, London, W1V 4ND, England (office). *Telephone:* (20) 7287-4450 (office). *Fax:* (20) 7287-9128 (office). *E-mail:* jenne@casarotto.co.uk (office). *Website:* www.casarotto.co.uk (office).

GILLIBRAND, Kirsten Elizabeth Rutnik, AB, JD; American attorney and politician; *Senator from New York;* b. 9 Dec. 1966, Albany, NY; d. of Douglas P. Rutnik and Polly Noonan Rutnik; m. Jonathan Gillibrand; two s.; ed Acad. of Holy Names, Emma Willard School, Troy, Dartmouth Coll., Univ. of California, Los Angeles School of Law; fmr intern for Senator Alfonse D'Amato; fmr law clerk for Judge Roger Miner, US Court of Appeals for the Second Circuit 1992–93; Sr Assoc. Davis, Polk & Wardell; fmr Special Counsel, US Sec. of Housing and Urban Devt, Washington, DC 2000–01; Pnr, Boies, Schiller & Flexner LLP, Albany 2001–07; mem. US House of Reps 2007–09, mem. Cttees on House Armed Services, on Agric., Nutrition and Forestry, on Environment and Public Works, Special Cttee on Aging; Senator from NY (apptd to replace Senator Hillary Clinton) 2009– (elected at special election 2010, re-elected for full term 2012). *Address:* 478 Russell Senate Office Building, Washington, DC 20510, USA (office). *Telephone:* (202) 224-4451 (office). *Fax:* (202) 228-0282 (office). *Website:* gillibrand.senate.gov (office); www.kirstengillibrand.com.

GILLICK, Liam, BA; British artist; b. 1964, Aylesbury, Bucks.; ed Univ. of London, Goldsmiths Coll., London; staged first solo exhbn, 84 Diagrams, Karsten Schubert, London 1989; has exhibited in galleries and insts in Europe and USA, including collaborative projects with other artists, architects, designers and writers; selected to produce artworks for the canopy, glass facade, kiosks, entrance ikon and vitrines of Home Office bldg, Marsham Street, London 2002; represented Germany at Venice Biennale 2009; mem. Grad. Cttee Center for Curatorial Studies and Art in Contemporary Culture, Bard Coll., Annandale-on-Hudson, New York, USA; mem. Faculty, School of the Arts, Columbia Univ., New York 1997–; lives and works in New York; Paul Cassirer Kunstpreis, Berlin, Germany 1998. *Films include:* Margin Time 2012, The Heavenly Lagoon 2013, Hamilton: A Film by Liam Gillick 2014, Exhibition (dir Joanna Hogg) 2014. *Publications include:* Proxemics (Selected Writing 1988–2006), 2007, Factories in the Snow by Lilian Haberer (monograph) 2007, Meaning Liam Gillick (critical reader) 2009, Allbooks (anthology of his artistic writing) 2009, Why Work? 2010, Memoirs of the Twentieth Century/Prevision: Should the Future Help the Past 2010, Weapons Grade Pig Work 2015, Industry and Intelligence: Contemporary Art Since 1820 2016; contrib. to numerous art magazines and journals, including Parkett, Frieze, Art Monthly, October and Art Forum. *Address:* c/o Maureen Paley, 21 Herald Street, London, E2 6JT, England (office); c/o Casey Kaplan, 525 West 21st Street, New York, NY 10011, USA (office). *Telephone:* (20) 7729-4112 (office); (212) 645-7335 (office). *Fax:* (20) 7729-4113 (office); (212) 645-7835 (office). *E-mail:* info@maureenpaley.com (office); info@caseykaplangallery.com (office). *Website:* www.maureenpaley.com (office); www.caseykaplangallery.com (office); www.liamgillick.info.

GILLIES, Pamela Ann, CBE, BSc, PGCE, MEd, MMedSci PhD, FRSE, FRSA, FFPH, FAcSS; British public health scientist, academic and university administrator; *Principal and Vice-Chancellor, Glasgow Caledonian University;* b. 13 Feb. 1953, Scotland; ed Univs of Aberdeen and Nottingham; Lecturer in Public Health Medicine, Univ. of Nottingham 1980s, later Pro-Vice-Chancellor 2001–06; Abbott Fellowship for AIDS Research, San Francisco 1988; mem. WHO Global Programme on AIDS, Geneva 1989–90; Harkness Fellow, Commonwealth Fund of New York and Visiting Prof. in Health and Human Rights, Harvard Univ., USA 1992–93; seconded as first Exec. Dir of Research, Health Educ. Authority for England, London 1996–99; Prin. and Vice-Chancellor Glasgow Caledonian Univ. (GCU) 2006–, mem. Bd INTO GCU, the Foundation Coll. for the Univ., Pres. New York Campus; mem. Bd of Trustees, British Council 2008–; Founding Trustee, Grameen Scotland Foundation; Founding Bd mem. Grameen Caledonian of Nursing, Dhaka, Bangladesh (partnership with Grameen Healthcare Trust) 2010–; mem. London Higher Group of Univs; Founding Patron of a school for children of sex workers in Domjur, Kolkata; Academician, Acad. for the Social Sciences 2005; Fellow, Faculty of Public Health of the Royal Coll. of Physicians of London 2002; Hon. Fellow, Royal Coll. of Physicians and Surgeons (Glasgow) 2007. *Publications include:* numerous articles on HIV/AIDS, health development, and inequalities in health focusing on the potential of social action for health. *Leisure interests:* tennis, gardening. *Address:* Office of the Principal, Glasgow Caledonian University, Britannia Building, City Campus, Cowcaddens Road, Glasgow, G4 0BA, Scotland (office). *Telephone:* (141) 331-3113 (office); (141) 331-3112 (Julie Burns, PA) (office). *Fax:* (141) 331-3174 (office). *E-mail:* pamela.gillies@gcu.ac.uk (office); julie.burns@gcu.ac.uk (office). *Website:* www.gcu.ac.uk (office).

GILLINGWATER, Richard, CBE; British business executive; *Chairman, SSE PLC;* b. July 1956; worked in corporate finance and investment banking for more than a decade; fmr Chair. European Investment Banking at CSFB; served as Chief Exec. of the Shareholder Executive; later Dean of Cass Business School, London; served as Chair. CDC Group; fmr Dir (non-exec.), P&O, Debenhams, Tomkins, Qinetiq Group, Kidde; Sr Ind. Dir, Hiscox Ltd –2015 (resgnd); Dir (non-exec.), Wm Morrison Supermarkets PLC –2015 (resgnd); mem. Bd of Dirs, SSE PLC 2007–, Chair. 2015–, Chair. Nomination Cttee, mem. Remuneration Cttee; Chair. Henderson Group PLC; Sr Ind. Dir, Helical Bar PLC. *Address:* SSE PLC, Inveralmond House, 200 Dunkeld Road, Perth, PH1 3AQ, Scotland (office). *Telephone:* (1738) 456000 (office). *E-mail:* info@sse.com (office). *Website:* www.sse.com (office); www.hydro.co.uk (office).

GILLINSON, Sir Clive Daniel, Kt, CBE, ARAM, FRAM, FRNCM; British cellist and arts administrator; *Executive and Artistic Director, Carnegie Hall;* b. 7 March 1946, Bangalore, India; m. 1st Penny Gillinson (divorced); one s. two d.; m. 2nd Anya Deutsch 2018; ed Frensham Heights School, Queen Mary Coll., Univ. of London, Royal Acad. of Music, London; played in Nat. Youth Orchestra of GB 1963–65, Philharmonia Orchestra –1970, London Symphony Orchestra 1970–84; elected to Bd of Dirs London Symphony Orchestra 1976–79, 1983–, Finance Dir 1979, Man. Dir 1984–2005; Exec. and Artistic Dir Carnegie Hall, New York 2005–; owned an antique shop, Hampstead, London 1978–86; Chair. Asscn of British Orchestras 1992–95; Gov. and mem. of Exec. Cttee Nat. Youth Orchestra 1995–2004; Founding Partner, Masterprize 1997–; Founding Trustee, Nat. Endowment for Science, Tech. and the Arts 1998–2004; mem. Int. Music Council of the Children's Hearing Inst., New York 1998–, Brubeck Inst. Hon. Bd 2007–, Curtis Inst. Bd of Overseers 2007–08; Visiting Fellow, St. Catherine's Coll., Oxford 2012; Hon. GSMD 1992; Freeman of the City of London 1993; Hon. Fellow, Guildhall School; Honorary Bd mem. Brubeck Inst. of the Univ. of the Pacific; Grand Decoration of Honor in Silver (Austria); Dr hc (City Univ.) 1995, (Curtis Inst.) 2007; Hon. DHumLitt (Skidmore Coll.) 2010; RAM May Mukle Cello Prize, ABSA Garrett Award 1992, Luminary Award, Eastman School of Music 2010, Int. Citation of Merit, Int. Soc. for the Performing Arts 2012, Theodore S. Kesselman Award, New York Youth Symphony 2014, Gift of Music Award, The Orchestra of St. Luke's 2015. *Publication:* Better to Speak of It (co-author) 2016. *Leisure interests:* reading, theatre, cinema, sport. *Address:* Carnegie Hall, 881 Seventh Avenue, New York, NY 10019-3210, USA (office). *Telephone:* (212) 903-9820 (office). *Fax:* (212) 903-0820 (office). *E-mail:* cgillinson@carnegiehall.org (office). *Website:* www.carnegiehall.org (office).

GILMARTIN, Raymond V., MBA; American business executive and academic; b. 6 March 1941, Washington, DC; m. Gladys Higham 1965; one s. two d.; ed Union Coll. and Harvard Univ.; Devt Engineer, Eastman Kodak 1963–67; various exec. positions at Becton Dickinson & Co. 1976–92, Chair., Pres. and CEO 1992–94; Chair., Pres. and CEO Merck & Co. Inc. 1994–2005 (resgnd); Adjunct Prof., Harvard Business School 2006–, also fmr mem. Bd of Dean's Advisors; fmr Chair. Healthcare Leadership Council, Pharmaceutical Research and Mfrs of America, Council on Competitiveness, United Negro College Fund; fmr Pres. Int. Fed. of Pharmaceutical Mfrs; mem. Bd of Dirs General Mills Inc. 1997– (currently presiding Dir), Microsoft 2001–12, National Association of Corporate Directors 2013–; mem. Transatlantic Business Dialogue, Trade and Poverty Forum, German Marshall Fund.

GILMORE, Eamon, BA; Irish politician and fmr trade unionist; *Special Envoy for Peace in Colombia, European Union;* b. 24 April 1955, Caltra, Co. Galway; m. Carol Hanney; two s. one d.; ed St Joseph's Coll., Garbally, Co. Galway, Univ. Coll. Galway; Pres. Union of Students in Ireland 1976–78; joined staff of Irish Transport & General Workers' Union (now SIPTU) 1978, Sec., Professional and Managerial Staffs Br. 1981–89; TD, Dáil Éireann (Irish Parl.) for Dun Laoghaire 1989–2016; Minister of State at Dept of the Marine 1994–97; Tánaiste (Deputy Prime Minister) and Minister for Foreign Affairs and Trade 2011–14; Chair. OSCE 2012; Pres. Gen. Affairs Council of EU 2013; EU Special Envoy for Peace in Colombia 2015–; fmr mem. Workers' Party; co-f. Democratic Left 1992 (merged with Labour Party 1999); mem. Labour Party, Labour Party Spokesperson on Environment, Housing and Local Govt 2002–07, Labour Party Leader 2007–14; mem. Parl. Ass. of Council of Europe 2005–07; Adjunct Prof., DCU 2016–; Visiting Prof., CEU Budapest 2017; Officer, Legion d'honneur; Hon. DIur (Nat. Univ. of Ireland, Galway); named as one of the Leading Global Thinkers by Foreign Policy Magazine Dec. 2015. *Publications include:* Leading Lights: People Who've Inspired Me 2010, Inside the Room: The Untold Story of Ireland's Crisis Government 2015. *Address:* 1 Corbawn Close, Shankill, Dublin 18, Ireland (home). *Telephone:* 86-7947624 (mobile) (home). *E-mail:* eamon.gilmore@eeas.europa.eu (office); egil@eircom.net (home). *Website:* www.gilmore.ie.

GILMORE, James (Jim) Stuart, III, BA, LLB, JD; American lawyer and fmr politician; *President, Gilmore Global Group, LLC;* b. 6 Oct. 1949, Richmond, Va; s. of James Stuart Gilmore, Jr and Margaret Kandle Gilmore; m. Roxane Gatling Gilmore; two s.; ed Univ. of Virginia; served in US Army as counterintelligence agent in West Germany 1971–74; Partner, Benedetti, Gilmore, Warthen and Dalton (law firm) 1977–80, 1984–87; fmr Commonwealth's Attorney, Henrico Co., Va; fmr Attorney-Gen. State of Va; Gov. of Virginia 1997–2001; Chair. Repub. Nat. Cttee 2001–02; Chair. Congressional Advisory Panel to Assess Domestic Response Capabilities for Terrorism Involving Weapons of Mass Destruction 1999–2003; Partner, Kelley Drye and Warren (law firm) 2002–08, Chair. Homeland Security Practice Group; Founder and Pres. Gilmore Global Group LLC (consultancy) 2009–; Pres. and CEO Free Congress Foundation 2009–; Founder and Pres. USA Secure; fmr Chair. Nat. Council on Readiness and Preparedness, Bd of Visitors, Air Force Acad.; mem. Bd of Dirs CACI Int. Inc. 2009–; mem. Bd of Advisors Lucent Technologies Inc., Unisys, Abraxas Corpn; announced candidacy for Republican nomination for Pres. of US 2015. *Address:* Gilmore Global Group, LLC, PO Box 865, Alexandria, VA 22313, USA (office). *Website:* www.gilmoreglobalgroup.com (office); www.usasecure.org.

GILMORE, Rosalind E. J., CB, MA, FRSA; British fmr business executive and civil servant; b. 23 March 1937, London; d. of Sir Robert Fraser and Lady (Betty) Fraser; m. Brian Terence Gilmore 1962; ed King Alfred School, N London, Univ. Coll., London and Newnham Coll., Cambridge; entered HM Treasury 1960; Exec. Asst to Econs Dir IBRD 1966–67, HM Treasury 1968–74, Cabinet Office 1974; Asst Sec. HM Treasury 1975, Head Financial Insts. Div. 1977–80; Press Sec. to Chancellor of Exchequer 1980–82; Gen. Man. Corp. Planning, Dunlop Ltd

1982–83; Dir of Marketing, Nat. Girobank 1983–86; Directing Fellow, St George's House, Windsor Castle 1986–89; Dir Mercantile Group PLC 1986–89, Mercantile Credit Co. Ltd 1986–89, London and Manchester Group PLC 1986–89; Marketing Consultant, FI Group PLC (Software) 1986–89; mem. Financial Services Act Tribunal 1986–89; Deputy Chair. and Commr Bldg Socs Comm. 1989–91, Chair. and First Commr; Chief Registrar of Friendly Socs and Industrial Insurance Commr 1991–94; Chair. Homeowners Friendly Society Ltd 1996–98, CLT Broadcasting subsidiaries 1989–98; Dir Moorfields Eye Hosp. Trust 1994–2000, BAT Industries PLC 1996–98, Zurich Financial Services AG (Zurich) 1998–2007; mem. Securities and Investment Bd 1993–96; mem. Prudential Regulatory Authority 2013–14; Dir Leadership Foundation 1997–2009 (Pres. 2005–07), Trades Union Fund Mans 2000–06, Int. Women's Forum 2005–07; fmr mem. Court, Cranfield Univ. and Advisory Bd, Cranfield School of Man.; mem. Bd Opera North 1993–96; mem. Lloyd's Regulatory Bd 1994–98 (Dir Regulatory Services, Lloyds 1994–95); mem. Council Royal Coll. of Music 1997–2007; mem. Winton Centre for Financial History, Univ. of Cambridge; Hon. Fellow, Univ. Coll., London 1988, Newnham Coll. Cambridge 1993; Hon. mem. Royal Coll. of Music 2008. *Achievements include:* mem. Cambridge Univ. Swimming Team (blue 1960), Cambridge Univ. Squash Team. *Publication:* Mutuality for the Twenty-first Century 1998. *Leisure interests:* music, reading, house in Greece, languages (Greek, French and Spanish). *Address:* 3 Clarendon Mews, London, W2 2NR, England. *Telephone:* (20) 7402-8554. *Fax:* (20) 7402-8554. *E-mail:* rosalindgilmore@btinternet.com.

GILMOUR, Andrew James, BA, MA, MSc; British UN official; *Assistant Secretary-General for Human Rights and Head, Office of the United Nations High Commissioner for Human Rights;* b. 22 March 1964; s. of Ian Gilmour (Lord Gilmour of Craigmillar) and Lady Caroline Gilmour; m. Emma Williams; four c.; ed Balliol Coll., Oxford, London School of Econs; journalist, Jordan Times, Amman 1983; Foreign Policy and Defence Adviser to leader of Social Democratic Party, London 1987–88; Adjunct Fellow, Center for Strategic and Int. Studies, Washington, DC 1988–89; joined UN 1989, Asst to Personal Rep. of Sec.-Gen. for Humanitarian Affairs in Afghanistan, then Iraq–Kuwait, Geneva 1989–91, Special Asst to Personal Rep. of Sec.-Gen., Afghanistan and Pakistan, Islamabad and Kabul 1991–92, various positions in Dept of Political Affairs, Security Council, Offices of Asst Sec.-Gen. and Under-Sec.-Gen., New York 1992–2000, Sr Political Advisor to UNHCR Special Envoy to Balkans, Skopje, Pristina May–Aug. 1999, Head of Regional/Political Unit, UN Special Coordinator for the Middle East Peace Process, Lebanon, later Beirut, Gaza and Jerusalem 2000–02, Sr Political Advisor, UN Office for W Africa, Dakar 2002–06, Deputy Dir (Political, Peacekeeping, Humanitarian), Exec. Office of the Sec.-Gen., New York 2006–07 (Acting Dir March–Aug. 2007), Deputy Special Rep. of Sec.-Gen. (Political), UN Assistance Mission for Iraq (UNAMI), Baghdad 2007–09, Rep. of Sec.-Gen. in Serbia, Belgrade 2009–12, Acting Deputy Head, UN Political Office for Somalia (UNPOS), Nairobi April–May 2010, Deputy Special Rep. of Sec.-Gen. (Political), UN Mission in S Sudan (UNMISS), Juba Oct.–Dec. 2011, Dir for Political, Peacekeeping, Humanitarian and Human Rights Affairs in Exec. Office of the Sec.-Gen. 2012–16, Asst Sec.-Gen. for Human Rights and Head, OHCHR 2016–; mem. Governing Council Interpeace. *Publications:* has written for numerous publs including The Times (London), Middle East International, The Spectator, The Nation, Newsweek. *Leisure interests:* environmental issues, classical piano, trees, history, literature. *Address:* Office of the UN High Commissioner for Human Rights, United Nations, New York, NY 10017, USA (office). *E-mail:* InfoDesk@ohchr.org (office). *Website:* www.ohchr.org (office).

GILMOUR, David, CBE; British singer, musician (guitar) and composer; b. 6 March 1946, Cambridge; m. Polly Samson 1994; eight c.; mem. Pink Floyd 1968–; numerous live performances, festival appearances; Exec. Producer for Kate Bush's album, The Kick Inside; solo artist; Nordoff-Robbins Music Therapy Silver Clef Award 1980, MTV Music Video Award 1988, Ivor Novello Award for Outstanding Contribution to British Music 1992, Q Award for Best Live Act 1994, Grammy Award for Producer in Best Instrumental Performance (for Marooned), Polar Music Prize 2008. *Recordings include:* albums: with Pink Floyd: A Saucerful Of Secrets 1968, More (film soundtrack) 1969, Ummagumma 1969, Atom Heart Mother 1970, Relics 1971, Meddle 1971, Obscured By Clouds 1972, The Dark Side Of The Moon 1973, Wish You Were Here 1975, Animals 1977, The Wall 1979, The Final Cut 1983, A Momentary Lapse Of Reason 1987, The Delicate Sound Of Thunder 1988, Shine On (box set) 1992, The Division Bell 1994, Pulse 1995, Echoes: The Very Best Of Pink Floyd 2001, The Endless River 2014; solo: David Gilmour 1978, About Face 1984, Live In Concert 2002, On An Island 2006, Metallic Spheres (with The Orb) 2010, Rattle That Lock 2015. *Address:* Steve O'Rourke, EMKA Productions Ltd, 43 Portland Road, Holland Park, London, W11 4LJ, England (office). *Website:* www.pinkfloyd.com/index2.php; www.davidgilmour.com; www.davidgilmourblog.com.

GILMOUR, Matthew, BSc, PhD; Canadian microbiologist, academic and public health official; *Scientific Director-General, National Public Health Laboratories;* ed Univ. of Alberta, Canadian Coll. of Medical Microbiologists; Asst Prof., Univ. of Manitoba 2004–; Chief, Enteric Diseases Program, Public Health Agency of Canada 2004–12, Dir, Bacteriology and Enteric Diseases 2010–13; Clinical Microbiologist, Diagnostic Services of Manitoba 2013–15; Scientific Dir-Gen., Nat. Public Health Labs (Nat. Microbiology Public Health Lab., Winnipeg and Lab. for Foodborne Zoonoses, Guelph) 2015–; Sec.-Treas., Canadian Asscn for Clinical Microbiology and Infectious Diseases 2010–; Assoc. Ed., Journal of Medical Microbiology 2008–, BMC Microbiology 2008–; Health Canada Deputy Minister's Award for Excellence in Science 2009, Queen Elizabeth II Diamond Jubilee Medal 2012, Killam Prize 2014. *Address:* Public Health Agency of Canada, 1015 Arlington Street, Winnipeg MB, R3E 3R2, Canada (office). *Telephone:* (204) 789-2070 (office). *E-mail:* Matthew.Gilmour@phac-aspc.gc.ca (office). *Website:* www.phac-aspc.gc.ca (office).

GIMBRONE, Michael Anthony, Jr, AB, MD; American pathologist, vascular biologist and academic; *Elsie T. Friedman Professor of Pathology, Harvard Medical School;* b. 16 Nov. 1943, Buffalo, NY; ed Cornell Univ., Ithaca, NY, Harvard Medical School, Boston, Mass; NSF Summer Fellow, Roswell Park Memorial Inst., Buffalo 1960–63; Summer Research Fellow, Dept of Physiology, New York Univ. Medical School 1964; Summer Research Fellow, Depts of Anatomy, Biochemistry and Surgery, Harvard Medical School 1965–67 (ind. study and research 1968–69); Intern in Surgery, Massachusetts Gen. Hosp., Boston 1970–71; Research Fellow, Dept of Surgery, Children's Hosp. Medical Center, Boston 1971–72; Commissioned Officer, NIH US Public Health Service, Bethesda, Md 1972–74, Staff Assoc., Lab. of Pathophysiology, Nat. Cancer Inst., NIH 1972–74; Resident in Pathology, Peter Bent Brigham Hosp., Boston 1974–76; Instructor, Dept of Pathology, Harvard Medical School 1975–76, Asst Prof. 1976–79, Assoc. Prof. 1979–85, Prof. 1985, Elsie T. Friedman Prof. of Pathology 1987–2007, 2012–, Ramzi S. Cotran Prof. of Pathology 2007–12; Adjunct Faculty, W. Alton Jones Cell Science Center, Lake Placid, New York 1976–78; Assoc. in Pathology, Brigham and Women's Hosp., Boston 1976–79, Head, Vascular Pathophysiology Research Lab. 1976–85, Assoc. Pathologist 1979–80, Pathologist 1980, Dir Vascular Research Div. 1985, Dir Center for Excellence in Vascular Biology 1998, mem. Bd of Dirs Brigham and Women's Hosp. Pathology Foundation, Inc. 1998, Vice-Chair. for Research and Academic Affairs, Dept of Pathology 2000–01, Chair. Dept of Pathology 2002–12; Special Consultant, Hypertension Task Force, Nat. Heart, Lung and Blood Inst., Bethesda 1977, Consultant, Arteriosclerosis Task Force 1979; Visiting Prof., Cardiovascular Research Div., Cleveland Clinic Foundation 1980, Johns Hopkins Univ. School of Medicine, Baltimore, Md 1988–90, Washington Univ. School of Medicine, St Louis, Mo. 1988–90, 1994, Univ. of Pennsylvania School of Medicine, Philadelphia 1988–90, Univ. of South Carolina School of Medicine, Columbia 1988–90, Medical Coll. of Wisconsin, Milwaukee 1996, Bowman Gray School of Medicine, Wake Forest Univ., Winston-Salem, NC 1998; Johanaoff Visiting Prof., Mario Negri Inst. of Pharmacological Research, Milan, Italy 1982; Visiting Scholar in Pulmonary Medicine, Duke Univ. Medical Center and Univ. of North Carolina School of Medicine Research, Triangle Park, Nat. Inst. of Environmental Health Sciences, NC 1988; Pfizer Visiting Professorship in Cardiovascular Medicine, Univ. of Minnesota-Duluth School of Medicine 1991; First Annual Vascular Visiting Prof., Cornell Univ. Medical Coll., New York Hosp. 1992; Distinguished Visiting Prof., Johns Hopkins Univ. School of Medicine 1993, Nat. Cardiovascular Research Inst., Osaka, Japan 1996, Kyoto Univ., Japan 1996, Yamanashi Medical Univ., Japan 1996, Tokyo Medical and Dental Univ., Japan 1996; Woznicki Lecturer and Visiting Prof. in Pathology, Baylor Coll. of Medicine Houston, Tex. 1994; Hans Selye Visiting Prof., Univ. of California, Irvine Medical School 1996; Co-Founder North American Vascular Biology Org. 1994, Pres. 1994–95, Past Pres. 1995–96; mem. Editorial Bd numerous journals; mem. Cttee of Profs, Harvard Medical School 1985–; mem. American Heart Asscn 1975 (Fellow 2001), American Soc. for Investigative Pathology 1975 (Vice-Pres. 1991–92, Pres. 1992–93), Tissue Culture Asscn 1976, American Soc. for Cell Biology 1976, Massachusetts Medical Soc. 1978, New York Acad. of Sciences 1979, Int. Soc. on Thrombosis and Haemostasis 1979, American Soc. of Haematology 1980, American Fed. for Clinical Research 1981, American Soc. for Clinical Investigation 1986, Int. Acad. of Pathology 1987, European Vascular Biology Asscn 1991, Asscn of American Physicians 1992, Microcirculatory Soc. 1996, NAS 1997, Inst. of Medicine of NAS 1999, American Acad. of Arts and Sciences 1999, New England Soc. of Pathologists, Inc. 2002, European Acad. of Science and Arts 2015; Trustee, Karin Grunebaum Cancer Research Foundation 1990–; Council of Academic Deans, Harvard Medical School & Faculty Dean for Academic Affairs, Partners HealthCare System 2003–05, 2008–11; Distinguished Scientist, American Heart Asscn 2007; Professeur Invité, Collège de France 2013; Harvard Medical School awards: Karin Grunebaum Research Award 1968–69, Soma Weiss Research Prize 1969, Leon Reznick Research Prize 1970, Mellon Faculty Award 1975–77; other awards include: Herbert I. Horowitz Memorial Lecturer, New York Univ. Medical Center 1977, Established Investigator Award, American Heart Asscn 1977–82, Warner-Lambert/Parke-Davis Award in Experimental Pathology, American Asscn of Pathologists 1982, Erst Roche Distinguished Lecturer, Hoffman-La Roche Co. 1986, Rufus Cole Lecturer in Medicine, Rockefeller Univ. 1990, Dutkevich Memorial Lecturer, Toronto Acad. of Medicine and Univ. of Toronto 1992, Basic Research Prize, American Heart Asscn 1993, MERIT Award, Nat. Heart, Lung and Blood Inst. 1994, Cardiovascular Research Award, Bristol-Myers Squibb Research Inst. 1994, Remold Memorial Lecturer, European Soc. for Clinical Investigation 1995, Simon Dack Plenary Lecturer, American Coll. of Cardiology 1995, Pasarow Foundation Award in Cardiovascular Disease 1996, J. Allyn Taylor Int. Prize in Medicine (co-recipient) 1999, Bristol-Myers Squibb Award for Distinguished Achievement in Cardiovascular Research 2001, Earl Benditt Lifetime Achievement Award in Vascular Biology (NAVBO) 2002, King Faisel International Prize in Medicine 2006, Distinguished Scientist, American Heart Asscn 2006, Rous-Whipple Award, American Soc. for Investigative Pathology 2008, Distinguished Achievement Award, Soc. for Cardiovascular Pathology 2013. *Publications:* more than 450 publs in medical journals. *Address:* Center for Excellence in Vascular Biology, Brigham and Women's Hospital, 77 Avenue Louis Pasteur, NRB-752, Boston, MA 02115-6110, USA (office). *Telephone:* (617) 525-4325 (office). *E-mail:* mgimbrone@partners.org (office).

GIMÉNEZ DUARTE, Lea Raquel, MA, BEcons, PhD; Paraguayan economist and politician; b. 1981; ed Univ. of Iowa, Columbia Univ., New York, Lehigh Univ., Pa; fmr Asst Prof. of Econs, Lehigh Univ.; fmr Lecturer, Univ. of Iowa; Int. Consultant and Economist for World Bank, including Economist, Econ. Policy and Poverty Team, S Asia Region 2011–13, Economist, Poverty Global Practice 2013–15, Consultant, Macro Global Fiscal Practice 2015–16; Vice Minister of Economy and Integration 2016–17, Minister of Finance 2017–18. *Address:* c/o Ministry of Finance, Chile 252, entre Palma y Presidente Franco, Asunción, Paraguay (office).

GIMFERRER, Pere; Spanish writer and literary manager; b. 22 June 1945, Barcelona; s. of Pere Gimferrer and Carmen Torrens; m. 1st María Rosa Caminals 1971 (died 2003); m. 2nd Cuca de Cominges 2006; ed Univ. of Barcelona; Head of Literary Dept, Editorial Seix Barral 1970, Literary Consultant 1973, Literary Man. 1981–; Academician, Real Acad. Española 1985–, Acad. Européenne de Poésie, Luxembourg, World Acad. of Poetry, Verona; Nat. Prize for Poetry 1966, 1989, Critic's Prize 1983, 1989, Premio Nacional de las Letras Españolas 1998, Queen Sofía Prize for Iberoamerican Poetry 2000, Int. Octavio Paz Prize for Poetry and Essay 2006, Prize for Bullfighting 2010. *Publications:* Arde el Mar 1966, L'Espai Desert 1977, Dietari 1981, Fortuny 1983, El Vendaval 1988, La Llum 1991, The Roots of Miró 1993, Complete Catalan Work, Vol. I 1995, Vol. II 1995, Vol. III 1996, Vol. IV 1996, Vol. V 1997, Masquerade (poem) 1996, L'Agent

Provocador 1998, Marea Solar, Marea Lunar 2000, El Diamant dins l'Aigua 2001, Interludio azul 2006, Amor en vilo 2006, Tornado 2008, Rapsodia (poem) 2011, Alma Venus (poem) 2013, El Castell de la Puresa 2014. *Leisure interests:* cinema, travel. *Address:* Editorial Seix Barral, Diagonal 662, Barcelona 08034 (office); Rambla de Catalunya 113, Barcelona 08008, Spain (home). *Telephone:* (93) 4967003 (office); (93) 2150242 (home). *Fax:* (93) 4967004 (office).

GINER DE SAN JULIAN, Salvador, MA, PhD; Spanish sociologist and academic; *Professor Emeritus of Sociology, University of Barcelona;* b. 10 Feb. 1934, Barcelona; m. Montserrat Sariola 1966; one s. one d.; ed Int. School Barcelona, Univs of Barcelona, Cologne, Germany and Chicago, USA; Visiting Prof., Univ. of Puerto Rico 1962–63; Lecturer, Univ. of Reading, UK 1965–70; Sr Lecturer, Univ. of Lancaster, UK 1970–76; Reader, then Prof. and Head Dept of Sociology and Social Anthropology, Brunel Univ., West London, UK 1976–87; Prof. and Head, Dept of Sociology, Univ. of Barcelona 1987–90, Prof. Emer. 2005–; Dir Inst. of Advanced Social Studies, Higher Council for Scientific Research 1988–97, Barcelona Metropolitan Region Sociological Survey 2001–02; Pres. Spanish Sociological Asscn 1986–91; Vice-Pres. Inst. of Catalan Studies, Barcelona 2000–05, Pres. 2005; Ed. Revista Internacional de Sociología 1992; Asst Ed. European Journal of Social Theory 1988; mem. Scientific Cttee European Prize for Social Science (Amalfi Prize) 1989; Pres. Acad. of Sciences and Humanities of Catalonia, Barcelona; Order of Civil Merit (Spain) 1987, Creu de Sant Jordi 1995, St George's Cross, Catalonia 1998; Dr hc (Universitat Nacional d'Educació a Distància) 2016. *Publications include:* Contemporary Europe (Vol. I) 1971, (Vol. II) 1978, Mass Society 1976, Ensayos Civiles 1985, El Destino de la Libertad 1988, España: Sociedad y Política 1990, La Gobernabilidad 1992, Religión y Sociedad en España 1994, Carta sobre la Democracia 1996, Buen Gobierno y Política Social 1997, La Societat Catalana (Coll. of Economists Prize 1999) 1998, Diccionario de Sociología (ed.) 1998, Sociology (revised edn) 2001, Historia del Pensamiento Social (revised edn) 2002, Teoría Sociológica Clásica 2001, 2006, Carisma y Razón 2003, Teoría Sociológica Moderna 2004. *Address:* Department of Sociology, University of Barcelona, Diagonal 690, 08034 Barcelona, Spain (office). *Telephone:* (93) 4035553 (office). *Fax:* (93) 4021894 (office). *E-mail:* sginer@ub.edu (office); sginer@iec.cat (office). *Website:* www.ub.edu/sociologia (office).

GINGRICH, Newton (Newt) Leroy, BA, MA, PhD; American politician, business executive and writer; b. 17 June 1943, Harrisburg, Pa; s. of Newton Searles McPherson and Kathleen (Kit) Daugherty (later Gingrich), adopted s. of Robert Bruce Gingrich; m. 1st Jackie Battley 1962 (divorced 1980); two d.; m. 2nd Marianne Ginther 1981 (divorced 2000); m. 3rd Callista Bisek 2000; ed Baker High School, Columbus, Ga, Emory Univ., Tulane Univ.; mem. Faculty, West Georgia Coll., Carrollton 1970–78, Prof. of History –1978; mem. US House of Reps from 6th Dist of Ga, Washington, DC 1979–92, House Republican Whip 1989, Speaker of House 1994–98, co-f. Congressional Mil. Reform Caucus, Congressional Space Caucus; Adjunct Prof., Reinhardt Coll., Waleska, Ga 1994–95; Chair. GOPAC, now Chair. Emer.; Gen. Chair. American Solutions for Winning the Future 2007–12; cand. for Republican US presidential nomination 2012; mem. US Comm. on Nat. Security in 21st Century 1999; Founder and CEO Gringrich Group LLC (communications and consulting firm) 1999–2011; Co-Chair. Nat. Comm. for Quality Long Term Care; mem. AAAS; mem. Advisory Bd Agency for Healthcare Quality and Research; mem. Bd of Regents, Nat. Library of Medicine; fmr Sr Fellow, American Enterprise Inst., Distinguished Visiting Fellow, Hoover Inst.; mem. Int. Advisory Bd, Barrick Gold Corpn 2015–; March of Dimes Georgian of the Year 1995, Georgia Breast Cancer Coalition Honoree 1996, Mental Health Asscn Advocacy Award 1996, Juvenile Diabetes Foundation Advocate of the Year 1997, American Asscn of Endocrinologists Patients Advocate of the Year 1998, American Diabetes Asscn Charles Best Medal 1998, Nat. Asscn of Community Health Centers Diabetes Healthcare Advocate of the Year 1998, Health Quality Award, Nat. Cttee for Quality Assurance 2005, Louis Sullivan Award, Workgroup for Electronic Data Interchange 2005, HIMSS Advocacy Award 2005, Nat. Hispanic Youth Initiative Award for Leadership 2006, Indispensible Person of the Year Award, Alliance on Aging 2008. *Film:* Nine Days that Changed the World 2010. *Publications include:* Window of Opportunity, 1945 1995, To Renew America 1995, Winning the Future: A 21st Century Contract with America 2005, Pearl Harbor: A Novel of December 8th (with William R. Forstchen) 2007, A Contract with the Earth (co-author) 2007, Rediscovering God in America 2007, Real Change: From the World That Fails to the World That Works 2008, To Try Men's Souls (co-author) 2009, To Save America (co-author) 2010, Valley Forge (co-author) 2010, A Nation Like No Other: Why American Exceptionalism Matters 2011, Victory at Yorktown: A Novel (co-author William R. Forstchen) 2012, Duplicity: A Novel (co-author Pete Earley) 2015. *Address:* Gingrich Productions, 4501 North Fairfax Drive, Suite 900, Arlington, VA 22203, USA (office). *Telephone:* (703) 678-2231 (office). *Website:* www.gingrichproductions.com (office).

GINKAS, Kama Mironovich; Russian theatre director; *Professor, Swedish Theatre Academy, Helsinki;* b. 7 May 1941, Kaunas, Lithuania; m. Yanovskaya Henrietta Yanovna; one s.; ed Leningrad Inst. of Theatre, Music and Cinema; worked in Krasnoyarsk Theatre of Young Spectators 1971–73; accused of aestheticism and barred from working in theatres; currently Prof., Swedish Theatre Acad., Helsinki; teaches directing at Moscow Art Theatre School. *Theatre includes:* Little Car, Moscow Art Theatre 1981, Hedda Gabler, Moscow Mossoviet Theatre 1984, Performing Crime, Moscow Theatre of Young Spectators 1991, Love is Wonderful, Finland, K.I. from Crime, Moscow Theatre of Young Spectators, Idiot (opera), Germany, Lady with a Lapdog 1995, Macbeth, Finland. *Publications:* Provoking Theater (with John Freedman) 2003. *Address:* Moscow Art Theatre School, Tverskaya str., 6, Bldg 7, 125009 Moscow (office); Tishinsky per. 24, Apt 7, Moscow, Russia (home). *Telephone:* (495) 299-53-60 (office); (495) 253-43-15 (home). *Website:* mhatschool.theatre.ru (office).

GINÓBILI, Emanuel (Manu) David; Argentine professional basketball player; b. 28 July 1977, Bahía Blanca; s. of Jorge Ginóbili; m. Marianela Oroño; three s.; professional debut with Andino 1995–96; with Estudiantes Bahía Blanca 1996–98, Basket Viola Reggio Calabria 1998–2000, Virtus Bologna 2000–02; titles: Italian League Championship 2001, Italian Cup 2001, 2002, Euroleague 2001, Americas Championship 2001; joined Nat. Basketball Asscn (NBA) San Antonio Spurs 2002–; mem. gold medal-winning Nat. Team, FIBA Americas Championships, Neuquén 2001, silver medal-winning team, San Juan 2003; mem. silver medal-winning All-Tournament Team, World Championships 2002; NBA Championship 2003, 2005, 2007; mem. Argentine Nat. Team 1998–, gold medal, Olympic Games, Athens 2004, bronze medal, Olympic Games, Beijing 2008; UNICEF Goodwill Amb. 2007–; Italian League All-Star 1999, 2000, 2001, Italian League Most Improved Player 2000, 2001, 2002, Euroleague Finals Most Valuable Player 2001, Italian Cup Most Valuable Player 2002, NBA All-Star 2005, All-Tournament Team, FIBA World Championship 2002, 2006, Ideal Olympics Team 2004, Summer Olympic Games Most Valuable Player 2004, Olimpia de Oro 2003, 2004 (shared with Carlos Tévez), 50 Greatest Euroleague Contributors 2008, NBA Sixth Man of the Year Award 2008, All-NBA Third Team 2008, 2011. *Address:* San Antonio Spurs, One SBC Center, San Antonio, TX 78219, USA (office). *Telephone:* (210) 444-5000 (office). *Website:* aol.nba.com/spurs (office); www.manuginobili .com.

GINOLA, David; French professional footballer (retd), actor and model; b. 25 Jan. 1967, Gassin, Var; s. of René Ginola and Mireille Collet; m. Coraline Delphin 1991; one s. two d.; ed Lycée du Parc Impérial, Nice; winger; played for first div. Toulon clubs 1985–88, Racing Club Paris 1988–90, Brest 1990–92, Paris Saint-Germain 1992–95 (French nat. champions 1993/94, winners Coupe de France 1993, 1995, Coupe de la ligue 1995), Newcastle United, England 1995–97, Tottenham Hotspur 1997–2000 (winners Football League Cup 1999), Aston Villa 2000–02, Everton 2002; 17 caps for France, scored three goals 1990–95; anti-landmine campaigner for Red Cross 1998–; f. The Centre (retreat) 2004; Club Player of Year 1998, Professional Football Asscn Player of the Year 1999, Football Writers' Asscn Player of the Year 1999. *Films include:* Rosbeef 2004, Mr Firecul 2004, The Last Drop 2005, Soccer Aid (TV) 2006. *Television includes:* cameo appearance in first episode of ITV drama series At Home with the Braithwaites, playing himself and announcing results of first ever Euro Lottery 2000; also appeared in episode 22 of Channel 4's Coach Trip (acted as tour guide of Ste Maxime); cameo appearance as Daveed Ginjola in Beezly'n'Cool comic Sept. 2009. *Publication:* David Ginola: The Autobiography (with Neil Silver) 2000. *Leisure interests:* golf, tennis, skiing, car racing.

GINSBURG, Ruth Joan Bader, BA, LLB; American lawyer, academic and judge; *Associate Justice, United States Supreme Court;* b. 15 March 1933, Brooklyn, New York; d. of Nathan Bader and Celia Bader (née Amster); m. Martin D. Ginsburg 1954 (died 2010); one s. one d.; ed Cornell Univ. and Harvard and Columbia Law Schools; admitted New York Bar 1959, DC Bar 1975, US Supreme Court Bar 1967; Law Sec. to Judge, US Dist Court (southern Dist), New York 1959–61; Research Assoc., Columbia Law School, New York 1961–62, Assoc. Dir project on int. procedure 1962–63; Asst Prof., Rutgers Univ. Law School, Newark 1963–66, Assoc. Prof. 1966–69, Prof. 1969–72; Prof. Columbia Univ., School of Law, New York 1972–80; Fellow, Center for Advanced Study in Behavioral Sciences, Stanford, Calif. 1977–78; Gen. Counsel, American Civil Liberties Union 1973–80; US Circuit Judge, US Court of Appeals, DC Circuit, Washington, DC 1980–93; Assoc. Justice, US Supreme Court 1993–; mem. ABA, AAAS, American Law Inst., Council on Foreign Relations; numerous hon. degrees; Genesis Lifetime Achievement Award, Israel 2018. *Publications:* Civil Procedure in Sweden (with A. Bruzelius) 1965, Swedish Code of Judicial Procedure 1968, Sex-Based Discrimination (with others); articles in legal journals. *Address:* United States Supreme Court, One First Street, NE, Washington, DC 20543, USA (office). *Telephone:* (202) 479-3000 (office). *E-mail:* info@supremecourt.gov (office). *Website:* www.supremecourt.gov (office).

GINWALA, Frene Noshir, LLB, DPhil; South African journalist and politician; b. 25 April 1932, Johannesburg; ed Univs of Oxford and London, UK; left SA in 1960 to establish external mission of the African National Congress (ANC), fmr ANC Spokeswoman, UK; contrib. to The Guardian, The Economist and the BBC, UK; Ed. Tanzania Standard and Sunday News, Tanzania; returned to SA 1991; mem. Secr., Office of Pres. of ANC, Head of ANC Research Dept 1991–94; Speaker, Nat. Ass. 1994–2004; Chancellor, Univ. of KwaZulu-Natal 2005–09; Chair. (SA), Commonwealth Parliamentary Asscn, Southern African Devt Community Parliamentary Forum, International Parliamentary Union (SA), ANC Archives Cttee; Co-Chair. Global Coalition for Africa (GCA); apptd to head enquiry into Nat. Dir of Public Prosecutions Vusi Pikoli's fitness to hold office 2007–08; Pres. South African Speakers Forum; Chair. Presidential Award for Youth Empowerment; Hon. Fellow, Linacre Coll. Oxford, UK; Grand Officier, Ordre nat. (Côte d'Ivoire) 1998, Grand Cordon of the Order of the Rising Sun (Japan) 2008; Dr hc (Rhodes) 1996, (Natal) 1996, (Cape Town) 1997, (Connecticut, USA) 2002, (Nelson Mandela Metropolitan Univ.) 2003; Global Award for Outstanding Contrib. to the Promotion of Human Rights and Democracy, Priyadarshni Acad., India 2000, Black Man. Forum Leadership Award 2000, Woman of the Year Award (Univ. of Pretoria Law Faculty) 2000, North-South Prize 2003. *Publications include:* Sanctions in South Africa in Question, Gender and Economic Policy in a Democratic South Africa, Women and the Elephant: Putting Women on the Agenda. *Leisure interest:* reading. *Address:* c/o African National Congress of South Africa, POB 61884, Marshalltown 2107, South Africa. *Telephone:* (11) 3761000. *Fax:* (11) 3761242. *E-mail:* communications@anc.org.za. *Website:* www.anc.org.za.

GIOIA, (Michael) Dana, BA, MA, MBA; American poet and academic; *Judge Widney Professor of Poetry and Public Culture, University of Southern California;* b. 24 Dec. 1950, Los Angeles, Calif.; s. of Michael Gioia and Dorothy Gioia (née Ortiz); m. Mary Hiecke 1980; three s. (one deceased); ed Stanford and Harvard Univs; fmr Visiting Writer, Colorado Coll., Johns Hopkins Univ., Wesleyan Univ.; Chair. Nat. Endowment for the Arts 2003–09; Dir Harman-Eisner Program in the Arts, Aspen Inst. 2009–11, Harman-Eisner Sr Fellow in the Arts 2011–; Judge Widney Prof. of Poetry and Public Culture, Univ. of Southern California 2011–; Calif. State Poet Laureate 2015–; mem. Bd and Vice-Pres. Poetry Soc. of America; mem. Wesleyan Univ. Writers' Conf., Citizens' Stamp Advisory Cttee (USA) 2009–12; mem. US Del. to UNESCO 2003–09; California Poet Laureate 2015; 11 hon. doctorates; Esquire Best of New Generation Award 1984, Frederick Bock Prize for Poetry 1985, American Book Award 2001, Smithsonian Latino Legacy Award 2007, Nat. Civilian's Medal 2009, Laetare Medal 2010, John Carroll Medal 2011, Aiken-Taylor Poetry Award 2014, Levertov Award 2016. *Dance:* Counting the Children 1994. *Operas:* Nosferatu 2001, Tony Caruso's Final Broadcast 2008, The Three Feathers (operas) 2014. *Song cycles:* Becoming a Redwood 2004, Prayer 2012, For Love or Money 2015, Sung with Words 2015, Speaking of Love 2017.

Radio: Nat. Endowment for the Arts Big Read radio shows (32 episodes), contrib./writer, BBC 1992–2012. *Publications include:* The Ceremony and Other Stories 1984, Daily Horoscope 1986, Mottetti: Poems of Love (trans.) 1990, The Gods of Winter 1991, Can Poetry Matter? 1992, An Introduction to Poetry 1994, The Madness of Hercules (trans.) 1995, Interrogations at Noon (American Book Award 2002) 2001, Nosferatu (opera libretto with Alva Henderson) 2001, The Barrier of a Common Language (essays) 2003, Twentieth-century American Poetry 2004, Twentieth-century American Poetics 2004, 100 Great Poets of the English Language 2005, Literature for Life 2012, Pity the Beautiful 2012, 99 Poems: New and Selected (Poets' Prize 2018) 2016; also ed. of several works of literary criticism; regular contrib. to various journals, reviews and periodicals, including San Francisco magazine (classical music critic). *Leisure interests:* opera, jazz, book collecting. *Address:* Taper Hall 314, University of Southern California, 3501 Trousdale Parkway, Los Angeles, CA 90089-0354 (office); 7190 Faught Road, Santa Rosa, CA 95403, USA (home). *Telephone:* (213) 740-2797 (office). *E-mail:* gioia@usc.edu (office). *Website:* priceschool.usc.edu/dana-gioia (office); capoetlaureate.net (office); www.danagioia.com.

GIOJA, José Luis; Argentine politician and lawyer; *President, Partido Justicialista;* b. 4 Dec. 1949, San Juan Prov.; m. Rosa Palacio; four c.; ed Escuela Normal de Jáchal, San Juan and Nat. Univ. of Cuyo; Pres. Agrupación Nacional de Estudiantes Universitarios 1972–73; Pvt. Sec. to Gov. Eloy Camus 1973; Sec.-Gen. Juventud Peronista, Partido Justicialista de San Juan 1975, Congresal Prov. 1975–76; Interventor Instituto Prov. de la Vivienda 1974–75; Pres. Unidad Básica del Barrio Edilco 1983; Cand., Departamento de Rawson 1983; Pres. Junta Departamental de Rawson 1984–85; mem. Consejo Nacional Justicialista 1987–93, Consejo Prov. Justicialista 1987–93; Prov. Deputy and Vice-Pres. Justicialista Bloc, Chamber of Deputies, San Juan Prov. 1987–91, Pres. Comisión de Minería, Obras Públicas y Recursos Hídricos; Deputy in Nat. Ass. 1991–99, Pres. Jt Party Comm. Argentina–Chile 1993; Senator 1995–2002, Pres. Comisión Bicameral de Minería y de Coparticipación Fed. de Impuestos, Pres. Senate Justicialistas Bloc 2000–02, Pres. (provisional) of Senate 2002; Gov. of Province of San Juan 2003–15; Pres. Partido Justicialista 2016–. *Address:* Partido Justicialista, Domingo Matheu 128/130, C1082ABD, Buenos Aires, Argentina (office). *Telephone:* (11) 4954-2450 (office). *Fax:* (11) 4954-2421 (office). *E-mail:* contacto@pj.org.ar (office). *Website:* www.pj.org.ar (office).

GIONI, Massimiliano; Italian curator and art critic; *Artistic Director, Fondazione Nicola Trussardi;* b. 1973, Milan; m. Cecilia Alemani; US Ed. Flash Art (magazine) 2000–02; Co-Dir The Wrong Gallery, New York 2002–05; Artistic Dir Fondazione Nicola Trussardi, Milan 2003–; Assoc. Dir of Exhbns, New Museum of Contemporary Art, New York 2007–; Founder Family Business, New York 2012–; Artistic Dir 55th Venice Biennale 2013; Ed. Charley and Wrong Times (visual magazines); columnist, Domus magazine, Wired Italy, Rolling Stone Italy; contrib., Flash Art magazine, Artforum, Frieze, Parkett, ArtPress. *Exhibitions curated include:* Uniform. Order and Disorder, PS1, New York 2001, The Fourth Sex. Adolescent Extremes, Pitti Discovery, Florence 2002, Yesterday Begins Tomorrow, Deste Foundation, Athens 2003, Short Cut (Elmgreen and Dragset), Milan 2003, The Zone, 50th Venice Biennale 2003, If I Had You (Darren Almond), Milan 2003, Untitled (Maurizio Cattelan), Milan 2004, Manifesta 5, San Sebastian, Spain (co-curator) 2004, Monument to Now, Athens 2004, Meechfieber (John Bock), Milan 2004, Jet Set Lady (Urs Fisher), Milan 2005, Long Sorrow (Anri Sala), Milan 2005, Of Mice and Men, Berlin Biennial (co-curator) 2006, I Like Things (Martin Creed), Milan 2006, My Religion Is Kindness (Paola Pivi), Milan 2006, One of Many (Pawel Althamer), Milan 2007, The Fractured Figure, Athens 2007, Altri fiori e altre domande (Fishli and Weiss), Milan 2008, After Nature, New York 2008, Tino Sehgal, Milan 2008, The Generational: Younger Than Jesus, New York 2009, Urs Fischer: Marguerite de Ponty, New York 2009, Still Life (Tacita Dean), Milan 2009, Pig Island (Paul McCarthy), Milan 2010, 10,000 Lives, 8th Gwangju Biennale 2010, Alighiero e Boetti Day, Turin 2011, Lynda Benglis, New York 2011, Gustav Metzger, New York 2011, Apichatpong Weerasethakul, New York 2011, Ostalgia, New York 2011, Parasimpatico (Pipilotti Rist), Milan 2011, Carsten Höller, New York 2012, Ego (Takashi Murakami), Doha, Qatar 2012, Tacita Dean, New York 2012, Klara Liden, New York 2012, Rosemarie Trockel, New York 2012, Ghosts in the Machine, New York 2012, Rubble and Revelation (Cyprien Gaillard), Milan 2012, NYC 1993. Experimental Jet Set, Trash and No Star, New York 2013, The Encyclopedic Palace, 55th Venice Biennale 2013, Fault Lines (Allora & Calzadilla), Milan 2013. *Publications:* numerous articles and books on contemporary art, several monographs. *Address:* Fondazione Nicola Trussardi, Piazza della Scala 5, 20121 Milan, Italy (office). *Telephone:* (02) 8068821 (office). *Fax:* (02) 80688281 (office). *E-mail:* info@fondazionenicolatrussardi.com (office). *Website:* www.fondazionenicolatrussardi.com (office).

GIORDANA, Marco Tullio; Italian film director and screenwriter; b. 1 Oct. 1950, Milan. *Films include:* Forza Italia! (screenwriter) 1978, Maledetti vi amerò (To Love the Damned) (also screenwriter) 1980, Car Crash (screenwriter) 1980, La caduta degli angeli ribelli (also screenwriter) 1981, Notti e nebbie (TV) (also screenwriter) 1984, Appuntamento a Liverpool (also screenwriter) 1988, La domenica specialmente (Especially on Sunday, USA) 1991, L'unico paese al mondo 1994, Pasolini, un delitto italiano (Pasolini, an Italian Crime) (also screenwriter) 1995, I cento passi (The Hundred Steps) (also screenwriter) 2000, Un altro mondo è possibile (Another World Is Possible, USA) 2001, Il cineasta e il labirinto (as himself) 2002, La meglio gioventù (The Best of Youth) (Un certain Regard, Cannes Film Festival 2003) 2003, Quando sei nato non puoi più nasconderti (Once You're Born You Can No Longer Hide, UK) 2004, Wild Blood 2008, Piazza Fontana: The Italian Conspiracy 2012. *Television:* as dir: Notti e nebbie (TV movie) 1984, Alfabeto italiano (Series) 1998, Lea (TV movie) 2015.

GIORDANI, Jorge A.; Venezuelan economist, academic and politician; b. 1940, San Pedro de Macoris, Dominican Republic; ed Univ. of Bologna, Italy, Univ. of Sussex, UK; fmr Prof., Universidad Central de Venezuela, also Dir of Grad. Studies, Ciencias Económicas y Sociales; fmr Dir Cordiplan (Cen. Office of Co-ordination and Planning); Minister of Planning and Devt –2010, of Planning and Finance 2010–13, of Planning 2013–14. *Publications:* Human Development in Venezuela 2004.

GIORDANO, Richard Vincent, BA, LLB, PhD; American business executive; b. 24 March 1934, New York; s. of Vincent Giordano and Cynthia Giordano (née Cardetta); m. Barbara Claire Beckett 1956 (divorced); one s. two d.; ed Stuyvesant School, New York, Harvard Univ. and Columbia Univ. Law School; admitted to New York Bar 1961; Assoc., Shearman and Sterling (law firm), New York 1959–63; Asst Sec., Air Reduction Co. Inc., New York 1963–64, Vice-Pres. Distribution of Products Div. 1964–65, Exec. Vice-Pres. 1965–67, Group Vice-Pres. 1967–71, Pres. and COO 1971–74, CEO 1977–79; Dir BOCI 1974; Man. Dir and CEO BOC Group 1979–84, Chair. 1985–92, CEO 1985–91, Chair. (non-exec.) 1991–96; apptd Chair. British Gas PLC 1994, implemented de-merger into three cos, continued as Chair. BG PLC –2003; Chair. Carnegie Endowment for International Peace 2009–13; mem. Bd of Dirs Cen. Electricity Generating Bd 1982–89, Georgia Pacific Corpn 1984–2006, Grand Metropolitan 1985–97 (Deputy Chair. 1991–97), Reuters 1991–94, RTZ (renamed Rio Tinto PLC, Deputy Chair. 1992–2005), Lucas Industries 1993–94, Oxara Energy Group Ltd 2006–13; mem. Bd of Trustees, Cicely Saunders International; Hon. Fellow, Royal Coll. of Anaesthetists, London Business School; Hon. KBE 1989; Hon. DCS (St John's Univ., USA); Hon. LLB (Bath) 1998. *Leisure interests:* sailing, opera.

GIOVANNI, Nikki, BA; American poet and academic; *University Distinguished Professor, Virginia Polytechnic Institute and State University;* b. (Yolande Cornelia Giovanni), 7 June 1943, Knoxville, Tenn.; d. of Jones Giovanni and Yolande Watson; one s.; ed Fisk Univ., Univ. of Cincinnati and Univ. of Pennsylvania; Asst Prof. of Black Studies, City Coll. of New York 1968; Assoc. Prof. of English, Rutgers Univ. 1968–72; Prof. of Creative Writing, Coll. Mt St Joseph on the Ohio 1985; Prof. of English, Va Polytechnic Inst. and State Univ. 1987–, Gloria D. Smith Prof. of Black Studies 1997–99, Univ. Distinguished Prof. 1999–; Founder, Nixtom Ltd 1970; Visiting Prof., Ohio State Univ. 1984; recipient of numerous awards and hon. degrees. *Publications include:* Black Feeling, Black Talk 1968, Black Judgement 1968, Re: Creation 1970, Poem of Angela Yvonne Davis 1970, Spin A Soft Black Song 1971, Gemini 1971, My House 1972, A Dialogue: James Baldwin and Nikki Giovanni 1973, Ego Tripping and Other Poems for Young Readers 1973, A Poetic Equation: Conversations Between Nikki Giovanni and Margaret Walker 1974, The Women and the Men 1975, Cotton Candy on a Rainy Day 1978, Vacationtime 1980, Those Who Ride the Night Winds 1983, Sacred Cows... and other Edibles 1988, Conversations with Nikki Giovanni 1992, Racism 101 1994, Grand Mothers 1994, Selected Poems of Nikki Giovanni 1996, Shimmy Shimmy Shimmy Like My Sister Kate 1996, Nikki in Philadelphia 1997, Love Poems 1997, Blues: For All the Changes 1999, Grand Fathers 1999, Quilting the Black-Eyed Pea: Poems and Not-Quite Poems 2002, The Collected Poetry of Nikki Giovanni 2003, The Prosaic Soul of Nikki Giovanni 2003, The Girls in the Circle 2004, Rosa 2005, Acolytes 2007, On My Journey Now 2007, The Grasshopper's Song 2008, Lincoln and Douglass: An American Friendship 2008, Hip Hop Speaks to Children 2008, Bicycles: Love Poems 2009, Best African American Fiction 2010 (co-ed.) 2009, Chasing Utopia: A Hybrid 2013; Children's Book: Spin a Soft Black Song 1971, Ego-Tripping and Other Poems For Young People 1973, The Girls in the Circle (Just for You!) 2004, Poetry Speaks to Children: A Celebration of Poetry with a Beat 2005, Lincoln and Douglass: An American Friendship 2008, Hip Hop Speaks to Children: A Celebration of Poetry with a Beat 2008, I Am Loved 2018. *Address:* Department of English, Virginia Polytechnic Institute and State University, 323 Shanks Hall, Blacksburg, VA 24061, USA (office). *Telephone:* (540) 231-9453 (office). *E-mail:* info@nikki-giovanni.com. *Website:* www.english.vt.edu (office); www.nikki-giovanni.com.

GIRALDO, Luis Guillermo, LLB; Colombian lawyer, economist, politician and fmr diplomatist; b. 1 May 1944, Manizales; ed Pontificia Universidad Javeriana, Bogota; Sec.-Gen. of Treasury, Manizales 1967; mem. House of Reps 1970–78; Mayor of Manizales 1978–79; Senator 1978–98, Pres. of Senate 1989–90; Amb. to Germany 1990–91, to Venezuela 1998–99; Chief of Presidential Campaign of Alvaro Uribe 2002, then mem. team preparing Govt Plan of Action –2003; Perm. Rep. to UN, New York 2003, Amb. to Mexico 2003–05; Sec.-Gen. Partido Social de la Unidad Nacional (Partido de la U) 2005–08; mem. Peace Negotiations 1999. *Publications:* Contrapuntos del Poder y la Fama, Algunas Palabras, De Relojes y de Nostalgias, El Antiheroe.

GIRARD, Jean-François, MD, MSc; French fmr civil servant and professor emeritus of medicine; *Adviser to the President, SATT IdFInnov;* b. 20 Nov. 1944, Luçon (Vendée); one s. two d.; ed Univ. of Paris; Prof. of Medicine 1979–97, Prof. Emer. 1997–; Dir-Gen. Ministry of Health 1986–97; Chair. Exec. Council WHO 1992, 1993; Conseiller d'Etat 1997–2013; Pres. Inst. de recherche pour le développement 2001–09; Pres. Pôle de recherche et d'enseignement supérieur, Sorbonne Paris Cité 2010–13; Adviser to the Pres. of SATT Île-de-France Innov (IdFInnov—pvt. tech. transfer org.) 2013–; Officier, Légion d'honneur; Commdr, Ordre nat. du Mérite. *Publications:* Quand la santé devient publique 1998, La maladie d'Alzheimer 2000. *Leisure interest:* sailing. *Address:* PRES Sorbonne Paris Cité, 190 avenue de France, 75013 Paris, France (office). *Telephone:* 1-49-54-83-41 (office). *E-mail:* jean-francois.girard@sorbonne-paris-cite.fr (office).

GIRARD-diCARLO, David F., BA, JD; American lawyer and fmr diplomatist; *Partner, Cozen O'Connor;* b. 1942, Philadelphia, Pa; m. Constance B. Girard-diCarlo; ed St Joseph's Univ., Villanova Univ. School of Law; began career as an Assoc. with Wolf Block LLP before moving on to Dilworth Paxon LLP, later Partner; Chair. South Eastern Pennsylvania Transportation Authority –1981; returned to law firm 1981; began work for Blank Rome LLP, served for 16 years as Man. Partner and CEO, later Chair. for six years; appointed Man. Dir Blank Rome Govt Relations LLC (subsidiary and lobbying br. of law firm), Washington, DC; Chair. Bush-Cheney election campaign 2000; Co-Chair. Republican Convention in Philadelphia 2000; Pennsylvania Chair. Bush-Cheney campaign 2004; Amb. to Austria 2008–09; currently Partner, Cozen O'Connor (law firm), Philadelphia; Pres. The Pennsylvania Soc.; Trustee, Saint Joseph's Univ.; mem. Bd of Consultors, Villanova Univ. School of Law; mem. Philadelphia School Reform Comm. 2009–11; mem. Council of American Ambs, Diplomatic Council on Energy Security; fmr Chair. Bd and Chair. Exec. Cttee Greater Philadelphia Chamber of Commerce; Hon. DrIur (Drexel Univ.) 2010; Kt of St Gregory the Great from Pope John Paul 2003; named to PoliticsPA list of 'Sy Snyder's Power 50' list of politically influential individuals 2003, 2004. *Address:* Cozen O'Connor, 1650 Market Street Suite 2800, Philadelphia, PA 19103, USA (office). *Telephone:* (215) 665-2000 (office). *Fax:* (215) 665-2013 (office). *E-mail:* dgirarddicarlo@cozen.com (office). *Website:* www.cozen.com (office).

GIRARDET, Herbert, BSc (Econ); German ecologist, consultant, writer and television producer; *Co-founder, Honorary Member and Senior Consultant, World Future Council;* b. 28 May 1943, Essen; s. of Dr Herbert Girardet and Ingrid Girardet; m. Barbara Hallifax 1967; two s.; ed Tübingen and Berlin Univs, London School of Econs, UK; consultant to Town and Country Planning Asscn, London 1976–86, environment consultant Channel 4 TV, London 1987–89, consultant to UN Habitat II Conf., Istanbul 1995–96; Visiting Prof. of Environmental Planning, Middlesex Univ. 1995–2003; Visiting Prof. of Sustainable Urban Devt, Univ. of Northumbria 2003–06; Visiting Prof. of Cities and the Environment, Univ. of the West of England 2004–; Thinker-in-Residence, Adelaide 2003; Dir Under the Sky Urban Regeneration Co., Bristol 2004–; Co-founder and Dir of Programmes, World Future Council 2004–11, Hon. mem. and Sr Consultant 2011–; Chief Consultant to Shanghai City Govt on design of Dongtan Eco-City on Chongming Island; mem. Balaton Group of int. environment experts 1993–; Sr Consultant, Saudi Sustainability Initiative 2009; Chair. The Schumacher Soc., UK 1994–2006; Trustee, The Sustainable London Trust 1996–2004; Patron The Soil Asscn, UK 1990–; Hon. FRIBA 2000; UN Global 500 Award for Outstanding Environmental Achievements, prizes for TV documentaries. *Television:* initiator and researcher: Far from Paradise (series) 1983–86; writer and producer: Jungle Pharmacy 1988, Halting the Fires 1989, Metropolis 1994, Urban Best Practices 1996, UN Habitat 1996, Deadline 2000 (28 three-minute films) 1997–99; series consultant: The People's Planet 1999–2000. *Publications include:* Far From Paradise: The Story of Human Impact on the Environment (co-author) 1986, Blueprint for a Green Planet (co-author) 1987, Earthrise 1992, The Gaia Atlas of Cities 1992, Making Cities Work (co-author) 1996, Getting London in Shape for 2000 1997, Creating a Sustainable London (co-author) 1998, Creating Sustainable Cities 1999, Tall Buildings and Sustainable Development (co-author) 2001, Creating a Sustainable Adelaide 2003, Cities, People, Planet 2004, Shanghai Dongtan: An Ecocity (co-author) 2006, Surviving the Century (ed.) 2007, A Renewable World, Energy, Ecology, Equality 2009 (co-author), Regenerative Cities 2010, Creating Regenerative Cities 2014. *Leisure interests:* gardening, country walking. *Address:* World Future Council, Trafalgar House, 100 Pall Mall, London, SW1Y 4AU, England (office); Forest Cottage, Trelleck Road, Tintern, Chepstow, Monmouthshire, NP16 6SN, Wales (home). *Telephone:* (20) 7321-3810 (office); (1291) 689392 (home). *Fax:* (20) 7321-3738 (office); (1291) 689392 (home). *E-mail:* herbie@worldfuturecouncil.org (office). *Website:* www.worldfuturecouncil.org (office).

GIRKIN, Igor Vsevolodovich, (Igor Ivanovich Strelkov); Russian fmr security agent and rebel leader; b. 17 Dec. 1970, Moscow; fought on fed. side in Russian counter-separatist campaigns in Chechnya and on pro-Russian separatist side in conflict in Moldova's breakaway region of Transnistria; took part in Bosnian War as a volunteer on Serb side, and in Chechnya under contract; claimed to have served in Russian Fed. Security Service (FSB) 1996–2013, including in Chechnya 1999–2005; prominent mem. of Russian Mil. Historical Soc.; participated in events in Crimea 2014; key figure behind War in Donbass (aka War in Eastern Ukraine) as the mil. commdr of 'Donetsk People's Repub.' rebellion April 2014; charged by Ukraine authorities with terrorism; sanctioned by EU for his leading role in insurgency in eastern Ukraine; confirmed in an interview that he is col of FSB Dec. 2014. *Publication:* published memoirs of the fighting in Bosnia and Herzegovina 1999. *E-mail:* info@icorpus.ru. *Website:* icorpus.ru.

GIROLAMI, Sir Paul, Kt, BCom, FCA; British/Italian chartered accountant and company chairman (retd); b. (Paolo Girolami), 25 Jan. 1926, Fanna, Italy; s. of Pietro Girolami and Assunta Bertossi; m. Christabel Mary Gwynne Lewis 1952; two s. one d.; ed London School of Econs; with Chantrey and Button (Chartered Accountants) 1950–54, Cooper Brothers 1954–65; mem. Bd Glaxo 1965–94, Finance Dir 1965–80, Chief Exec. 1980–86, Exec. Chair. 1985–94; Pres. Glaxo Finanziaria SpA Italy; mem. Bd of Dirs Nippon Glaxo Ltd, Japan 1975–94, Glaxo-Sankyo Ltd 1984–94, Credito Italiano Int. 1990–93, Forte PLC 1992–96, UIS France 1994–2000; mem. CBI Council 1986–93; Chair. Senate for Chartered Accountants in Business 1990–; Chair. Council Goldsmith's Coll., Univ. of London 1995–2002; Dir American Chamber of Commerce (UK) 1983; mem. Appeal Cttee of Inst. of Chartered Accountants 1987, Stock Exchange Listed Cos Advisory Cttee 1987–92, Open Univ. Visiting Cttee 1987–89; mem. Worshipful Co. of Apothecaries, Worshipful Co. of Chartered Accountants, Court of Assts of The Worshipful Co. of Goldsmiths (Prime Warden) 1986; Pres. British-Italian Soc.; Freeman, City of London Liveryman 1980, Hon. Fellow, LSE 1989, Goldsmiths Coll., Emmanuel Coll., Cambridge 1994; Grande Ufficiale, Ordine al Merito della Repubblica Italiana 1987, Insignia of the Order of the Rising Sun (Japan), Cavaliere del Lavoro (Italy) 1991, Grand Cross, Order of the Holy Sepulchre; Dr hc (Trieste) 1991, Hon. DSc (Aston) 1991, (Sunderland) 1991, (Bradford) 1993, Hon. LLD (Singapore) 1993, (Warwick) 1996; City and Guilds Insignia Award in Tech. (hc) 1988, Public Service Star, Singapore 2000. *Leisure interests:* reading, music. *Address:* Piazza Conte Nicolo' di Maniago 16, Maniago (PN), Italy (office). *Telephone:* (0427) 709005 (office). *E-mail:* paolo.girolami@alice.it.

GISCARD D'ESTAING, Valéry Marie René George; French politician, civil servant and fmr head of state; b. 2 Feb. 1926, Koblenz, Germany; s. of Edmond Giscard d'Estaing and May Bardoux; m. Anne-Aymone de Brantes 1952; two s. two d.; ed Ecole Polytechnique, Ecole Nat. d'Admin; Official, Inspection des Finances 1952, Insp. 1954; Deputy Dir du Cabinet of Prés. du Conseil June–Dec. 1954; Deputy for Puy de Dôme 1956–58, re-elected for Clermont 1958, for Puy de Dôme 1962, 1967, 1984, 1986, 1988, resgnd 1989; Sec. of State for Finance 1959, Minister for Finance and Econ. Affairs 1962–66, 1969–74; Pres. Comm. des Finances, de l'Economie général et du plan 1967–68; Pres. Cttee des Affaires Etrangères 1987–89; Pres. of the French Repub. 1974–81; Founder-Pres. Fed. Nat. des Républicains Indépendants (from May 1977 Parti Républicain) 1965; Del. to UN Gen. Ass. 1956, 1957, 1958; Chair. OECD Ministerial Council 1960; mem. (ex officio) Conseil Constitutionnel 1981–; Conseiller gen., Puy-de-Dôme 1982–88; Pres. Regional Council of Auvergne 1986–2004; Pres. Union pour la democratie française (UDF) 1988–96; Deputy to European Parl. 1989–93; Pres. European Movt Int. 1989–97; Pres. Council of European Municipalities and Regions 1997–2004; Deputy for Puy-de-Dôme 1993–2002; Pres. Comm. of Foreign Affairs, Nat. Ass. 1993–97; Chair. EU Convention on the Future of Europe 2002–03; mem. Royal Acad. of Econ. Science and Finance (Spain) 1995–, Acad. française 2003–; Grand Croix, Ordre de la Légion d'honneur, Grand Croix, Ordre nat. du Mérite, Croix de guerre, Kt Grand Cross, Order of St Olav (Norway) 1962, Kt Grand Cross, Order of Merit of the Italian Repub. 1973, Grand Collar, Order of St James of the Sword (Portugal) 1975, Gran Cruce, Ordén de Isabel la Católica 1976, Kt, Order of the Elephant (Denmark) 1978, Grand Collar, Order of Prince Henry (Portugal) 1978, Kt, Order of the Seraphim (Sweden) 1980, Baillif Grand Cross of Honour and Devotion of the Sovereign Mil. Order of Malta, Hon. Kt, Grand Cross of the Order of the Bath (England); Nansen Medal 1979, Onassis Foundation Prize 2000, Trombinoscope Prize for Political Personality of the Year 2000, Jean Monnet Foundation Medal 2001, Trombinoscope European of the Year 2002, Charlemagne Prize 2002, Ewald von Kleist Award 2014. *Publications include:* Démocratie française 1976, Deux français sur trois 1984, Le Pouvoir et la vie, Vol. I 1988, Vol. II: L'Affrontement 1991, Vol. III: Choisir 2006, Le Passage 1994, Dans cinq ans, l'an 2000 (essay) 1995, Les Français 2000, La Princesse et le Président 2009, La victoire de la Grande Armée 2010, Matilda 2011. *Leisure interests:* shooting, skiing. *Address:* 199 blvd Saint-Germain, 75007 Paris, France (office). *Telephone:* 1-45-44-30-30 (office). *Fax:* 1-45-49-11-16 (office). *E-mail:* secretariat@cab-vge.fr (office); international @cab-vge.fr (office).

GISKE, Trond; Norwegian politician; b. 7 Nov. 1966, Trondheim; s. of Bjørn Giske and Norunn Illevold Giske; m. Haddy N'jie 2014; one d; one d with Anne Grethe Moe; ed Univ. of Oslo, Norwegian Univ. of Science and Tech.; joined Labour Party 1989, Leader, Labour Youth League, Sør-Trøndelag Co. 1989–90, mem. Cen. Exec. Cttee 1990–96, Leader, Labour Youth League 1992–96, mem. Labour Party Cen. Exec. Cttee 1992–96, mem. Parl. Election Cttee 1997–2001, Deputy Chair. of Labour Party 2015–18; mem. Storting (Parl.) for Sør-Trøndelag Co. 1997–, mem. Standing Cttee on Finance and Econ. Affairs 1997–2001, Standing Cttee on Family, Cultural Affairs and Govt Admin 2001–05, Labour Party Parl. Group 2001–05; Minister of Educ., Research and Church Affairs 2000–01, of Culture and Church Affairs 2005–09, of Trade and Industry 2009–13; del. to UN Gen. Ass. 1999. *Address:* Arbeiderpartiet (Labour Party), Youngstorget, PO Box 0028, 0030 Oslo, Norway (office). *Telephone:* 24-14-40-00 (office). *Fax:* 24-14-40-01 (office). *E-mail:* post@arbeiderpartiet.no (office). *Website:* www.arbeiderpartiet.no (office).

GÍSLADÓTTIR, Ingibjörg Sólrún, BA; Icelandic politician; *Regional Director for Europe and Central Asia and Representative in Afghanistan, UN Women;* b. 31 Dec. 1954, Reykjavík; m. Hjörleifur Sveinbjörnsson; two s.; ed Univ. of Iceland, Univ. of Copenhagen, Denmark; began political career in Samtök um kvennalista (Women's Alliance), which she represented in Reykjavík's City Council 1982–88; mem. Althing (Parl.) for Reykjavík 1991–94, for Reykjavík North 2005–07, for Reykjavík South 2007–09, mem. Cttee on Foreign Affairs 1991–93, Cttee on Health and Social Security 1991–94, Cttee on Social Affairs 1991–94 (Vice-Chair. 1993–94), Cttee on Economy and Trade 2005–06, Icelandic Del. to EFTA and European Econ. Area Parl. Cttees 2005–; Founding mem. Samfylkingin (Social Democratic Alliance) 2000, Deputy Leader 1994–2003, Leader 2003–05, Chair. 2005–09; Mayor of Reykjavík 1994–2003 (resgnd); Minister for Foreign Affairs and External Trade 2007–09 (resgnd); currently Regional Dir for Europe and Cen. Asia and Rep. in Afghanistan, UN Women; Ed. Vera (feminist journal) 1988–90; mem. Exec. Bd Cen. Bank of Iceland 2003–05; mem. Hon. Bd, UN Women for Peace Asscn, Inc., Spirit of Humanity Forum. *Publication:* Þegar sálin fer á kreik. *Address:* Europe and Central Asia Regional Office, UN Women, Hakkı Yeten Cad. Selenium Plaza No: 10/C, 18th Floor, Beşiktaş, İstanbul, Turkey (office); c/o Samfylkingin, Hallveigarstíg 1, 101 Reykjavík, Iceland. *E-mail:* eca.operations@unwomen.org (office). *Website:* www.unwomen.org/en (office).

GITHAE, Robinson Njeru, LLB; Kenyan lawyer, politician and diplomatist; *Ambassador to USA;* b. 1957, Central Prov.; m. Alice Githae; three s. (one deceased); ed Univ. of Nairobi, Kenya School of Law; began work in financial industry as Co. Sec., Diamond Trust Bank –1986; Co. Sec., CFC Bank 1986–91; Gen. Man. Pan African Insurance 1991–2001; mem. Nat. Ass. (Parl.) for Ndia constituency 2002–13; Asst Minister for Transport 2006–08, for Local Govt 2008–10, Minister of Metropolitan Devt 2010–12, Minister of Finance 2012–13; Amb. to USA 2014–; mem. Party of National Unity (PNU). *Address:* Kenyan Embassy, 2249 R Street, NW, Washington, DC 20008, USA (office). *Telephone:* (202) 387-6101 (office). *Fax:* (202) 462-3829 (office). *E-mail:* washington@mfa.kz (home). *Website:* www.kenyaembassy.com (office).

GITONAS, Constantinos I.; Greek politician; b. Lagadia, Arcadia; m.; two d.; ed Nat. Tech. Univ. of Athens; Gen. Sec. Ministry of Public Works 1981–85; Deputy Minister of Environment, Land Use and Public Works 1985–86, Alt. Gen. Dir Pvt. Political Office of Prime Minister 1986–89; elected Parl. for Athens B 1989, First Vice-Pres. of Parl. 2000–04; Deputy Minister of Public Order 1993–94, Alt. Minister of Environment, Land Use and Public Works 1994–96, Minister of Public Order 1996, Minister of Health and Welfare 1996–98, Minister of State (attached to Prime Minister) 1998–2000; mem. Cen. Cttee PASOK (Panhellenic Socialist Movt).

GIULIANI, Rudolph (Rudy) William Louis, BA, JD; American lawyer, fmr government official and fmr politician; *Cyber Security Advisor to President;* b. 28 May 1944, Brooklyn, New York; s. of Harold Angelo Giuliani and Helen Giuliani (née D'Avanzo); m. 1st Regina Peruggi (divorced); m. 2nd Donna Hanover (divorced 2002); one s. one d.; m. 3rd Judith Nathan 2003; ed Manhattan Coll., New York Univ. School of Law; law clerk to Hon. Lloyd Francis McMahon, US Dist Court, New York City 1968–70; Asst US attorney, Southern Dist, New York, US Dept of Justice 1970–73, Chief of Narcotics Unit, US Attorney's Office 1973–75 Assoc. Deputy Attorney-General and Chief of Staff to Deputy Attorney-General, US Dept of Justice 1975–77; Attorney, Patterson, Belknap, Webb & Tyler, New York 1977–81; Assoc. Attorney-General, Dept of Justice 1981–83, Asst US Attorney, Southern Dist, New York, US Attorney 1983–89; Attorney, White & Case, New York 1989–90; Attorney, Patterson, Belknap, with Anderson Kill Olick & Oshinsky, New York 1990–93; Mayor of New York 1994–2001; Chair. and CEO Giuliani Partners LLC, New York 2002–, Giuliani Advisors LLC (investment advisory firm) 2004–07 (acquired by Macquarie Group 2007); Sr Partner, Bracewell & Giuliani LLP (law firm), Houston 2005–16; Chair. Cybersecurity, Privacy and Crisis Man. Practice and Sr Advisor to Exec. Chair., Greenberg Traurig LLP, New York 2016–18; Chair. Bd of Advisors, Leeds Weld and Co. 2002–; unsuccessful cand. for Republican nomination for US Pres. 2007–08; Cyber Security Advisor to the Pres. 2017–; Hon. KBE 2002; Dr hc (Loyola Coll., Md), (Middlebury Coll.) 2005, (The Citadel) 2007, (Drexel School of Law) 2009; Richard A. Cook Gold Medal Award, 100 Year Asscn of New York 1998, Time Magazine

Person of the Year 2001, Ronald Reagan Freedom Award 2002, Christopher Leadership Award 2002, Fiorello LaGuardia Public Service Award for Valor and Leadership in the Time of Global Crisis 2002, US Senator John Heinz Award for Outstanding Public Service by an Elected or Appointed Official 2002, Pete du Pont Individual Freedom Award 2007, Special Achievement Award for Public Service, National Italian American Foundation 2007, Margaret Thatcher Medal of Freedom 2007. *Publication:* Leadership 2002. *Address:* Department of Homeland Security, NIAC Secretariat, 245 Murray Lane, SW, Washington, DC 20528-0075, USA (office). *Telephone:* (703) 235-2888 (office). *E-mail:* niac@dhs.gov (office). *Website:* www.dhs.gov/national-infrastructure-advisory-council (office).

GIULIANO, Louis J., BA, MBA; American business executive; *Senior Advisor, The Carlyle Group;* m. Barbara Giuliano; two d.; ed Syracuse Univ.; served in numerous positions with Allied-Signal, including as Pres. Avionics Systems Group; joined ITT Corpn as Vice-Pres. of Corpn and Vice-Pres. of Defense Operations at ITT Defense 1988, later Pres. and CEO ITT Corpn; Sr Advisor, Carlyle Group 2005–; mem. Bd of Govs US Postal Service 2005–, Vice-Chair. 2009–10, Chair. 2010–11; Chair. Vectrus Inc. 2014–, Meadowkirk Retreat Center; mem. Bd of Dirs Accudyne Industries; mem. CEO Forum, Advisory Bd Princeton Univ. Faith and Work Initiative; Hon. Chair. Westchester County Red Cross Armed Forces Emergency Services. *Address:* The Carlyle Group, 520 Madison Avenue, New York, NY 10022, USA (office). *Website:* www.carlyle.com (office); vectrus.com (office).

GIURANNA, Bruno; Italian violist and conductor; *Viola Professor, Fondazione Stauffer, Cremona;* b. 6 April 1933, Milan; ed Coll. S. Giuseppe and Conservatorio di Musica Santa Cecilia, Rome and Conservatorio di Musica S. Pietro a Maiella, Naples; Founder-mem. I Musici 1951–61; Prof., Conservatorio G. Verdi, Milan 1961–65, Conservatorio S. Cecilia, Rome 1965–78, Accad. Chigiana, Siena 1966–83, 2004–, Nordwest-deutsche Musik-akademie, Detmold, Germany 1969–83, Hochschule der Künste, Berlin 1981–98, Fondazione Stauffer, Cremona 1985–, RAM, London 1994–96, Accad. S. Cecilia, Rome 1995–97; mem. Int. Music Competition jury, Munich 1961–62, 1967, 1969, Geneva 1968, Budapest 1975; soloist at concerts in festivals including Edinburgh and Holland Festivals, and with orchestras including Berlin Philharmonic, Amsterdam Concertgebouw and Teatro alla Scala, Milan; Artistic Dir Orchestra da Camera di Padova 1983–92; Academician of Santa Cecilia 1974; Pres. European String Teachers Asscn 2011; Cavaliere, Gran Croce della Repubblica Italiana 1987; Hon. DLit (Univ. of Limerick) 2003. *Address:* Via Bembo 96, 31011 Asolo, Treviso, Italy (home). *Telephone:* (0423) 529913 (home). *E-mail:* brgiuranna@gmail.com (home). *Website:* www.giuranna.com.

GIURGIU, Tudor, (Todor Giurgiu); Romanian film director and broadcasting executive; b. 1972, Cluj-Napoca; m. Oana Giurgiu; one c.; fmr Dir Transylvania Film Festival; Pres. and Dir-Gen. Televiziunea Română (TVR) 2005–07; Matei Brancoveanu Award, Alexandrion Foundation 2015. *Films:* Vecini (Neighbours) (dir) 1993, È pericoloso sporgersi (aka Don't Lean Out the Window) (asst set designer) 1994, Prea târziu (aka Too Late (USA)) (first asst dir) 1996, The Midas Touch (first asst dir) 1997, The Shrunken City (video) (first asst dir) 1998, Train de vie (Train of Life) (casting: Romania) 1998, Phantom Town (video) (casting: Romania) 1999, Tuvalu (casting: Bucharest; as Todor Giurgiu) 1999, Popcorn Story (dir and producer) 2001, Marele jaf comunist (aka Great Communist Bank Robbery) (producer) 2004, Legaturi bolnavicioase (aka Love Sick) (dir and producer) 2006, Agentul VIP (as himself, Episode 1.46) 2007, Cendres et sang (aka Ashes and Blood) 2009, Why Me? 2015, Nelly's Adventure (exec. producer) 2016.

GJEDREM, Svein, MA; Norwegian business executive, academic and fmr central banker; *Chairman, Helse Bergen HF;* b. 25 Jan. 1950; ed Univ. of Oslo; Exec. Officer, Norges Bank (Cen. Bank of Norway) 1975–79, Head, Div. for Banking and Monetary Affairs, Ministry of Finance and Customs 1979–82, Deputy Dir 1982–86, Dir-Gen. and Head of Econ. Policy Dept 1986–95, Sec.-Gen. 1996–98, Gov. Norges Bank (Cen. Bank of Norway) 1999–2010, Admin. Leader, Ministry of Finance 2011–15; Chair. Helse Bergen HF 2016–; visiting engagement, EU Comm., Brussels 1994–95; Lecturer, Norwegian School of Econs and Business Admin, Bergen. *Address:* Helse Bergen HF, Haukelandsveien 22, 5021 Bergen, Norway (office). *E-mail:* Svein.Gjedrem@nhh.no (office); postmottak@helse-bergen.no (office). *Website:* helse-bergen.no (office); www.nhh.no/en/departments/economics (office).

GJINUSHI, Skënder, PhD; Albanian politician; *Chairman, Social Democratic Party of Albania;* b. 24 Dec. 1949, Vlorë; ed Univ. of Tirana; univ. lecturer in science 1973–87; mem. Kuvendi Popullor (People's Ass.) 1992–, Speaker 1997–2001; Minister of Educ. 1987–90, Deputy Prime Minister and Minister of Labour and Social Affairs 2002–05; currently Chair. Social Democratic Party of Albania. *Address:* Social Democratic Party of Albania, Rruga Asim Vokshi 26, Tirana, Albania (office). *Telephone:* (4) 226540 (office). *Fax:* (4) 227485 (office). *E-mail:* info@psd-al.org (home). *Website:* www.psd-al.org (office).

GJOSHA, Klajda, BA, MA; Albanian politician; b. 28 July 1983, Tirana; m. Ardian Gjoni; ed Strode Coll. and Univ. of Reading, UK; held various offices in insts including Tirana Municipality, Tirana Regional Employment Directorate and Nat. Tourism Agency; Deputy Chair. Lëvizja Socialiste për Integrim (LSI—Socialist Movt for Integration) and mem. Chairmanship 2012, also Chair. LSI Women Forum; has attended training courses and internships in various orgs, including Japanese Int. Co-operation Agency, European Parl. at office of Doris Pack MEP, Brussels; Deputy Minister of Labour, Social Affairs and Equal Opportunities 2012–13; Minister of European Integration 2013–17. *Address:* Lëvizja Socialiste për Integrim, Rr. Sami Frasheri, Godina 20/10, Tirana, Albania (office). *Telephone:* (4) 2270412. *E-mail:* info@lsi.al.

GLADDEN, Lynn Faith, CBE, OBE, BSc, PhD, FRS, FREng; British chemical engineer and academic; *Shell Professor of Chemical Engineering Science, University of Cambridge;* b. 30 July 1961; d. of John Montague Gladden and Sheila Faith Deverell; ed Univs of Bristol and Cambridge; currently Shell Prof. of Chemical Eng Dept of Chemical Eng and Biotechnology, Univ. of Cambridge, fmr Head of Dept, Lead Researcher at Magnetic Resonance Research Centre, Fellow, Trinity Coll. 1999; Miller Visiting Prof., Univ. of California, Berkeley, USA 1996; apptd Foreign mem. USA Nat. Acad. of Eng 2015; Dir (non-Exec.) British Land Co. plc 2015–; Beilby Medal, Univ. of Cambridge 1995, Tilden Lectureship and Silver Medal, Royal Soc. of Chem. 2000. *Publications:* numerous papers in professional journals on multi-component adsorption, diffusion and flow processes. *Address:* Department of Chemical Engineering and Biotechnology, University of Cambridge, West Cambridge Site, Philippa Fawcett Drive, Cambridge, CB3 0AS, England (office). *Telephone:* (1223) 334762 (office). *E-mail:* lfg1@cam.ac.uk (office). *Website:* www.ceb.cam.ac.uk (office).

GLADSTONE, Barbara; American gallery owner, art dealer and film producer; *Owner and Director, Gladstone Gallery;* b. (Barbara Levitt), m. Elliot B. Regen (deceased); three s. (one deceased); first opened in SoHo, New York in 1979, Owner and Dir Gladstone Gallery, represents many contemporary artists, including film-maker Shirin Neshat, photographer and installation artist Sarah Lucas and sculptor and film-maker Matthew Barney. *Films include:* producer: Cremaster 1 1996, Cremaster 5 1997, Cremaster 2 1999, Cremaster 3 2002, Drawing Restraint 9 (exec. producer) 2005, De Lama Lamina 2007, Women Without Men (exec. producer) 2009; appears in Drawing Restraint 13, a later film by Barney. *Address:* Gladstone Gallery, 515 West 24th Street, New York, NY 10011, USA (office). *Telephone:* (212) 206-9300 (office). *Fax:* (212) 206-9301 (office). *E-mail:* info@gladstonegallery.com (office). *Website:* www.gladstonegallery.com (office).

GLADYSZ, John A., BS, PhD, FRSC; American chemist and academic; *Distinguished Professor of Chemistry and Dow Chair in Chemical Invention, Texas A&M University;* b. 13 Aug. 1952, Kalamazoo, Mich.; s. of Edward Matthew Gladysz and Margean Alice Gladysz (née Worst); m. Janet Bluemel 1997; ed Western Michigan Univ., Univ. of Michigan, Stanford Univ.; Asst Prof., UCLA 1974–82; Assoc. Prof., Univ. of Utah 1982–85, Prof. 1985–88; Prof. Ordinarius and Chair., Organic Chem., Friedrich-Alexander-Universität Erlangen-Nürnberg, Germany 1998–2007; Distinguished Prof. of Chem. and Dow Chair. in Chemical Invention, Texas A&M Univ. 2008–; Visiting Assoc. in Chem., California Inst. of Tech. 1989; consultant or fmr consultant to several cos and corpns, including Gas Research Inst., Chicago, G.D. Searle & Co., Chicago, Procter & Gamble Co., Monsanto Corpn, Union Camp Corpn, Exxon Research and Eng, Kimberly Clark Corpn, 3M Corpn, Rhodia (Rhône-Poulenc) Corpn, Lyon, France, Total/Fina/Elf, Paris, France; mem. Editorial Bd, Organometallics 1990–92 (Ed.-in-Chief 2010–14), New Journal of Chemistry 2000–12; Assoc. Ed., Chemical Reviews 1984–2010; mem. ACS 1970 (Fellow 2009), The Chemical Soc. 1974 (Fellow 2014), AAAS 1975 (Fellow 2004), German Chemical Soc. 1997; Alfred P. Sloan Foundation Fellow 1980–84, Camille and Henry Dreyfus Scholar and Grantee 1980–85, Arthur C. Cope Scholar 1988, Univ. of Utah Distinguished Research Award 1992, Humboldt Award 1994, ACS Award in Organometallic Chemistry 1994, Int. Fluorous Technologies Award 2007, Texas A&M Distinguished Achievement Award in Research 2013, RSC Award in Organometallic Chemistry 2013. *Address:* Department of Chemistry, Texas A&M University, 318 Reed McDonald Building, 580 Ross Street, College Station, TX 77843, USA (office). *Telephone:* (979) 845-1399 (office). *Fax:* (979) 845-5629 (office). *E-mail:* gladysz@mail.chem.tamu.edu (office). *Website:* www.chem.tamu.edu/rgroup/gladysz (office).

GLANVILLE, Brian Lester; British writer and journalist; b. 24 Sept. 1931, London; s. of James A. Glanville and Florence Manches; m. Elizabeth De Boer 1959; two s. two d.; ed Charterhouse School; first sports columnist and football corresp., Sunday Times 1958–92; sports columnist, The People 1992–96; football writer, The Times 1996–98, Sunday Times 1998–; literary adviser, Bodley Head 1958–62. *Plays for radio:* The Rise of Gerry Logan 1963, 1965, Visit to the Villa 1981, The Diary 1987, I Could Have Been King 1988. *Television includes:* original writer of That Was The Week That Was 1962; wrote BBC documentary European Centre Forward (winner Silver Bear Award, Berlin Film Festival) 1963. *Publications include:* novels: Along the Arno 1956, The Bankrupts 1958, Diamond 1962, The Rise of Gerry Logan 1963, A Second Home 1965, A Roman Marriage 1966, The Artist Type 1967, The Olympian 1969, A Cry of Crickets 1970, The Comic 1974, The Dying of the Light 1976, The Catacomb 1988, Dictators 2001; sport: Soccer Nemesis 1955, Champions of Europe 1991, Story of the World Cup 1993, The Arsenal Stadium History 2006, England Managers: The Toughest Job in Football 2007, For Club and Country (Obits) 2008, The Real Arsenal 2009; short stories: A Bad Streak 1961, The Director's Wife 1963, The King of Hackney Marshes 1965, The Thing He Loves 1985, Love Is Not Love; plays: A Visit to the Villa 1981, Underneath the Arches (musical, co-author) 1982, The Diary (radio play) 1986; other: Football Memories (autobiog.) 1999. *Address:* 160 Holland Park Avenue, London, W11 4UH, England (home). *Telephone:* (20) 7603-6908 (home). *E-mail:* grandpam21@aol.com (home).

GLAPIŃSKI, Adam, DEcon; Polish economist, politician and central banker; *President, National Bank of Poland;* b. 9 April 1950, Warsaw; m.; ed Warsaw School of Econs; joined Faculty, Warsaw School of Econs 1974, positions included Prof. of Econs and Dir Dept of Political Economy and History of Econ. Thought; Lecturer, Polish Acad. of Sciences 1978–83, Inter-Univ. Centre of Postgraduate Studies, Dubrovnik 1986–89; Deputy Sejm 1991–93; Minister of Construction and Spatial Planning Jan.–Dec. 1991; Minister of Foreign Econ. Cooperation Dec. 1991–June 1992; Dir Inst. of Econs and Political Freedom 1993–2001; mem. Senate, Tarnów Voivodeship 1997–2001, fmr Deputy Chair. Nat. Econ. Cttee, mem. Jt Parl. Cttee, EU–Poland; Visiting Lecturer, Univ. of Colorado 1993–98, Institut Superieur de Gestion 1994–2005, US Business and Industrial Council, Univ. of Missouri 1996, Univ. of Kansas 1996; Prof., Edward Lipinski Higher School of Econs and Law, Kielce 2004–07; Founder Warsaw Branch, Democratic Centre Asscn 1989; Co-founder Centre Agreement 1990, Co-Chair. 1991–93; Co-founder Warsaw Branch, Liberal Democratic Congress 1990; apptd Chair. Export Devt Bank 2007, KGHM Polish Copper 2007; Pres. and Gen. Dir Polkomtel SA 2007–08; Econ. Advisor to Pres. of Poland 2009–10; mem. Monetary Policy Council 2010–16; mem. Bd of Dirs Nat. Bank of Poland Feb.–June 2016, Pres. 2016–; mem. Int. Joseph A. Schumpeter Soc. 2002–, European Soc. of Econ. Thought 2007–; scholarship, Société historique et littéraire polonaise, Paris 1988. *Publications include:* Transforming Economic Systems: The Case of Poland 1991, Economics of Independence 2000, Capitalism, Democracy and the Crisis of State Taxes 2004, Meanders of the History of Economics 2012, Methodological Issues: Evolutionary Approach in Economics 2013. *Address:* National Bank of Poland, 00-919 Warsaw, ul. Świętokrzyska 11/21, POB 1011, Poland (office). *Telephone:* (22) 6531000 (office). *Fax:* (22) 6208518 (office). *E-mail:* listy@nbp.pl (office). *Website:* www.nbp.pl (office).

GLASENBERG, Ivan, BAcc, MBA; South African chartered accountant and business executive; *CEO, Glencore PLC;* ed Univ. of the Witwatersrand, Univ. of Southern California, USA; worked at Levitt Kirson Chartered Accountants 1979–84; joined Glencore International PLC 1984, worked in coal/coke commodity dept in SA as a marketer 1984–87, head of Asian coal/coke commodity div., Australia 1987–88, Man. and Head of Glencore's Hong Kong and Beijing offices and Head of Coal Marketing in Asia 1988–89, Head of worldwide coal business for both marketing and industrial assets 1990–2002, CEO Glencore International PLC (merged with Xstrata PLC to form Glencore Xstrata PLC May 2013, now called Glencore PLC) 2002–; mem. Bd of Dirs United Co. Rusal PLC 2007–18, JSC Zarubezhneft. *Address:* Glencore PLC, Baarermattstrasse 3, 6340 Baar, Switzerland (office). *Telephone:* (41) 7092000 (office). *Fax:* (41) 7093000 (office). *E-mail:* info@glencore.com (office). *Website:* www.glencore.com (office).

GLASER, Robert (Rob) Denis, BA, BS, MA; American software industry executive; *Founding Chairman and CEO, RealNetworks Inc.;* b. 16 Jan. 1962, New York City; m. 2nd Sarah Block 2000; ed Yale Univ.; joined Microsoft Corpn 1983, head of multimedia tech. and consumer digital appliances, Vice-Pres. Multimedia and Consumer Systems, –1994; Founding Chair. and CEO RealNetworks Inc. (internet software co.) 1994–2010, hiatus 2010–12, Interim CEO 2012–14, CEO 2014–, cr. RealAudio 1995, RealVideo and RealPlayer; co-owner Seattle Mariners professional baseball team; Founding Chair. Atrium Group, US Library of Congress; apptd to Advisory Cttee on Public Interest Obligations of Digital TV Broadcaster by Pres. Bill Clinton; Venture Partner, Accel Partners 2010–; Trustee, Glaser Progress Foundation; mem. Bd of Dirs Electronic Frontier Foundation, Wash. Public Affairs Network, Foundation for Nat. Congress, Target Margin Theater Co. of NY, Dwight Hall (Yale Univ. Student Community Service), TVW 1994–; Music Visionary Award (co-recipient David Munns), Music for Youth Foundation and United Jewish Appeal 2004. *Address:* RealNetworks Inc., 1501 1st Avenue South, Suite 600, PO Box 91123, Seattle, WA 98111-9223, USA. *Telephone:* (206) 674-2700. *Fax:* (206) 674-2696. *Website:* www.realnetworks.com.

GLASHOW, Sheldon Lee, AB, PhD, FAAS; American physicist and academic; *Arthur G. B. Metcalf Professor, Physics Department, Boston University;* b. 5 Dec. 1932, New York; s. of Lewis Glashow and Bella Rubin; m. Joan Shirley Alexander 1972; three s. one d.; ed Bronx High School of Science, Cornell and Harvard Univs; NSF Post-Doctoral Fellow, Univ. of Copenhagen 1958–60; Research Fellow, Calif. Inst. of Tech. 1960–61; Asst Prof., Stanford Univ. 1961–62; Assoc. Prof., Univ. of Calif., Berkeley 1962–66; Prof. of Physics, Harvard Univ. 1967–84, Higgins Prof. 1979–2000, Mellon Prof. of Sciences 1988–93, Prof. Emer. 2000–; Visiting Prof., Boston Univ. 1983–84, Distinguished Visiting Scientist 1984–2000, Arthur G. B. Metcalf Prof. 2000–; Alfred P. Sloan Foundation Fellowship 1962–66; Visiting Scientist, CERN 1968; Visiting Prof., Univ. of Marseille 1970, MIT 1974, 1980–81; Consultant, Brookhaven Lab. 1966–73, 1975–; Affiliated Sr Scientist, Univ. of Houston 1983–96; Univ. Scholar, Texas A&M Univ. 1983–86, Einstein Prof., Chinese Acad. of Science 2003–; Fellow, American Physical Soc.; Pres. Int. Sakharov Cttee 1980–85; mem. American Acad. of Arts and Sciences, NAS, American Philosophical Soc.; Sponsor, Fed. of American Scientists (FAS) and Bulletin of the Atomic Scientists; mem. Advisory Council, American Acad. of Achievement 1979–, Science Policy Cttee, CERN 1979–84; Founding Ed. Quantum (magazine) 1989–2000; Hon. Prof., Univ. of Nanjing 1998–; Dr hc (Univ. of Aix-Marseille) 1982; Hon. DSc (Yeshiva Univ.) 1978, (Bar Ilan Univ., Gustavus Adolphus Coll., Adelphi Univ.) 1989, (Case Western Reserve Univ.) 1995, (Bologna) 2005; Oppenheimer Memorial Medal 1977, George Ledlie Award 1978; shared Nobel Prize for Physics with Abdus Salam and Steven Weinberg (q.v.) for work on elementary particles 1979, European Physical Soc. Prize 2011. *Publications include:* Interactions (with Ben Bova) 1989, Charm of Physics 1990, From Alchemy to Quarks 1994; over 200 articles on elementary particle physics. *Address:* Department of Physics, Boston University, Physics Research Building, 3 Cummington Mall Room 567, Boston, MA 02215 (office); 30 Prescott Street, Brookline, MA 02446, USA (home). *Telephone:* (617) 353-9099 (office). *E-mail:* slg@bu.edu (office). *Website:* buphy.bu.edu (office).

GLASMAN, Baron (Life Peer), cr. 2011, of Stoke Newington and of Stamford Hill in the London Borough of Hackney; **Maurice Glasman,** MA, PhD; British political scientist and academic; *Senior Lecturer in Political Theory, London Metropolitan University;* b. 8 March 1960, Walthamstow, London; ed JFS Comprehensive School, Univs of Cambridge and York, European Univ. Inst., Florence, Italy; fmr Prof., Johns Hopkins Univ.; Sr Lecturer in Political Theory, London Metropolitan Univ., also Dir Faith and Citizenship Programme; Visiting Lecturer, Univ. of Oxford, Queen Mary's Coll., London; Gov., Simon Marks Primary School, Hackney, London; three-year Arts and Humanities Research Council Grant to study religion and politics in London (in partnership with Dr Luke Bretherton, King's Coll. London). *Publications include:* Unnecessary Suffering 1996. *Address:* House of Lords, Westminster, London, SW1A 0PW (office); London Metropolitan University, Faculty of Social Sciences and Humanities, Room TM1-33, 166–220 Holloway Road, London, N7 8DB, England (office). *Telephone:* (20) 7219-5353 (House of Lords) (office); (20) 7133-5107 (office). *E-mail:* socialscience@londonmet.ac.uk (office). *Website:* www.londonmet.ac.uk/faculties/faculty-of-social-sciences-and-humanities (office).

GLASS, David D., BA; American retail executive; b. 1935, Liberty, Mo.; s. of Marvin Glass and Myrtle Van Winkle; m. Ruth Glass; three c.; ed Southwest Missouri State Univ.; Gen. Man. Crank Drug Co. 1957–67; Vice-Pres. Consumers Markets Inc. 1967–76; Exec. Vice-Pres. Wal-Mart Stores Inc. –1976, Chief Financial Officer 1976–84, Pres. 1984–2000, COO 1984–88, CEO 1988–2000, Chair. Exec. Comm. 2000–06, also Dir; Chair. and CEO Kansas City Royals professional baseball team 1993, became sole owner 2000; Chair. MLB Advanced Media, LP 2010–; mem. Bd of Dirs Nat. Baseball Hall of Fame and Museum 2000–; Retailer of the Year 1986, 1991. *Address:* Kansas City Royals, Kauffman Stadium, One Royal Way, Kansas City, MO 64129-1695, USA (office). *Website:* kansascity.royals.mlb.com (office).

GLASS, Philip; American composer; b. 31 Jan. 1937, Baltimore, Md; s. of Benjamin Glass and Ida Glass (née Gouline); m. 1st JoAnne Akalaitis (divorced); m. 2nd Luba Burtyk (divorced); one s. one d.; m. 3rd Candy Jernigan (died 1991); m. 4th Holly Critchlow 2001; two s. one d.; ed Peabody Conservatory, Univ. of Chicago and Juilliard School of Music; Composer-in-Residence, Pittsburgh Public Schools 1962–64; studied with Nadia Boulanger, Paris 1964–66; f. Philip Glass Ensemble 1968; f. record co. Chatham Square Productions, New York 1972, Dunvagen Music Publishers, Orange Mountain Music record co. 2002; Richard and Barbara Debs Composer's Chair, Carnegie Hall 2017; mem. ASCAP; BMI Award 1960, Lado Prize 1961, Benjamin Award 1961, 1962, Ford Foundation Young Composer's Award 1964–66, Fulbright Award 1966–67, Musical America Magazine Musician of the Year 1985, New York Dance and Performance Award 1995, Nat. Endowment for the Arts Opera Honor 2010, Glenn Gould Prize 2015, Nat. Medal of Arts 2015, Kennedy Center Honor for Lifetime Contribution to American culture through the performing arts 2018. *Film scores include:* North Star 1977, Koyaannisqatsi 1983, Mishima 1985, Powaqqatsi 1987, The Thin Blue Line 1988, Hamburger Hill 1989, Mindwalk 1990, A Brief History of Time 1991, Anima Mundi 1991, Candyman 1992, The Voyage 1992, Orphée 1993, Candyman II: Farewell to the Flesh 1994, Monsters of Grace 1998, Bent 1998, Kundun 1998, The Hours (BAFTA Anthony Asquith Award 2003, Classical BRIT Award for Contemporary Music 2004) 2002, Cassandra's Dream 2007, Mr Nice 2010, They Were There 2011, Fantastic Four 2015, Jane 2017. *Compositions include:* String Quartets (1–4), Violin Concerto, Low Symphony, The Palace of the Arabian Nights, Einstein on the Beach 1976, Madrigal Opera: The Panther 1980, Satyagraha 1980, The Photographer 1982, The Civil Wars: A Tree Is Best Measured When It Is Down 1983, Akhnaten 1983, The Juniper Tree 1985, A Descent Into The Maelstrom 1986, In The Upper Room 1986, Violin Concerto 1987, The Light for Orchestra 1987, The Making of the Representative for Planet 8 1988, The Fall of The House Of Usher 1988, 1,000 Airplanes on the Roof (with David Henry Hwang) 1988, Mattogrosso 1989, Hydrogen Jukebox (with Allen Ginsberg) 1989, The White Raven 1991, Orphée, chamber opera after Cocteau 1993, La belle et la bête, after Cocteau 1994, Witches of Venice (ballet) 1995, Les enfants terrible (dance opera) 1996, The Marriages Between Zones Three, Four and Five 1997, Symphony No. 5 1999, Symphony No. 6 (Plutonian Ode) 2000, In the Penal Colony (theatre) 2000, Tirol Concerto, piano and orchestra 2000, Concerto Fantasy for two timpanists and orchestra 2000, Voices for Organ, Didgeridoo and Narrator 2001, Concerto for Cello and Orchestra 2001, Danassimo 2001, The Man in the Bath 2001, Passage 2001, Diaspora 2001, Notes 2001, Galileo Galilei (opera) 2002, Waiting for the Barbarians (opera) 2005, Appomattox (opera) 2007, The American Four Seasons 2010, The Perfect American 2013, The Trial 2014. *Publications:* Music by Philip Glass 1987, Opera on the Beach 1988, Words Without Music: A Memoir (Chicago Tribune Literary Award 2016, Grand Prix France Music Muses Award 2018) 2015. *Address:* Dunvagen Music Publishers, 40 Exchange Place, Suite 1906, New York, NY 10005, USA (office). *Telephone:* (212) 979-2080 (office). *Fax:* (212) 473-2842 (office). *E-mail:* info@dunvagen.com (office). *Website:* www.philipglass.com (office).

GLASSCOCK, Larry Claborn, BA; American insurance executive; *Chairman, Zimmer Biomet Holdings, Inc.;* b. 4 April 1948, Cullman, Ala; m. Lee Ann Roden 1969; one s. one d.; ed Cleveland State Univ., Commercial Bank Man. Program, Columbia Univ., New York, School of Int. Banking, participated in American Bankers Asscn Conf. of Exec. Officers; served in US Marine Corps 1970–76; Vice-Pres. of Personnel, AmeriTrust Corpn, Cleveland, OH 1974–75, Vice-Pres. Nat. Div. 1976–78, Vice-Pres. and Man. Credit Card Center 1978–79, Sr Vice-Pres. Consumer Finance 1980–81, Sr Vice-Pres. Nat. Div. 1981–83, Exec. Vice-Pres. Corp. Banking Admin 1983–87, Group Exec. Vice-Pres. AmeriTrust Corpn and AmeriTrust Co. 1987–92; fmr Pres. and CEO Essex Holdings, Inc.; fmr Pres. and COO First American Bank; Pres. and CEO Blue Cross and Blue Shield, Nat. Capital Area 1993–98; COO CareFirst, Inc. Jan.–April 1998; Sr Exec. Vice-Pres. and COO Anthem Insurance (renamed Wellpoint, Inc. following merger with WellPoint Health Networks 2004) 1998–99, Pres. and CEO 1999–2007, Chair. 2005–10; Dir Zimmer Biomet Holdings, Inc. 2001–, Chair. 2013–; mem. Bd Dirs Sprint Corpn (fmrly Sprint Nextel Corpn) 2007–13, BCS Financial Services Corpn, Blue Cross and Blue Shield Asscn, Council for Affordable Quality Healthcare (Chair. 2002–03), Nat. Inst. for Health Care Man., Cen. Indiana Corp. Partnership, United Way of Cen. Indiana, Greater Indianapolis Progress Cttee; fmr Pres. Cleveland State Univ. Alumni Asscn; Indiana Ernst & Young Entrepreneur of the Year Award (jtly) 2003. *E-mail:* investor.zimmerbiomet.com.

GLASSER, Robert, PhD; Australian UN official; b. 1959; m.; three c.; ed Australian Nat. Univ.; fmr Asst Dir-Gen., Australian Agency for Int. Devt; Chief Exec., CARE Australia 2003–07, Sec.-Gen., CARE International 2008–15; inaugural Chair. CHS International Alliance 2015; Special Rep. of UN Sec.-Gen. for Disaster Risk Reduction 2016–18; worked on int. energy and environmental policy for US Dept of Energy; worked on peace and conflict issues at several insts including Cornell Univ. Peace Studies Program and Univ. of California Centre for Int. and Strategic Affairs; mem. Bd of Dirs Global Call for Climate Action; Fellow, Geneva Centre for Security Policy. *Publications:* several publications on environment, peace and conflict and development.

GLATZ, Ferenc, PhD; Hungarian historian; *Professor Emeritus, Hungarian Academy of Sciences;* b. 2 April 1941, Csepel; m. Katalin; one s. one d.; ed Eötvös Loránd Univ.; Research Fellow, Inst. of History of Hungarian Acad. of Sciences 1968–, Scientific Deputy Dir 1986–88, apptd Dir of Inst. 1988, now Prof. Emer., Corresp. mem. Hungarian Acad. of Sciences 1993, full mem. 2000, Pres. 1996–2002; Pres. Scientific Council, Teleki László Foundation 1990–98; apptd Prof., Eötvös Loránd Univ., Budapest 1974; Minister for Culture and Educ. 1989–90; Organizer and Dir Europa Inst., Budapest 1990; Ed.-in-Chief, História 1979; Founding Ed. Természettörténet 2007; mem. Bd of Dirs Holy Crown 1999–2002; Grand Cross of Honour 2003 (Germany), Grand Cross of Honour (Hungary) 2004; Szèchenyì Prize 1995, Herder Prize 1997, Presidential Silver Medal (Italy) 2003. *Publications:* numerous studies and books on 19th- and 20th-century history of Hungarian and European culture and historiography, including Hungarians and Their Neighbors in Modern Times 1867–1950 (ed.) 1995. *Leisure interests:* tennis, gardening. *Address:* c/o Institute of History, Hungarian Academy of Sciences, Ùri Utca 53, 1014 Budapest, Hungary.

GLAUBER, Robert R., BA, PhD; American economist, academic, business executive and fmr government official; *Senior Advisor, Peter J. Solomon Company;* b. 22 March 1939, New York City; m.; two c.; ed Harvard Univ.; Lecturer, Harvard

Business School 1964–65, Asst Prof. of Finance 1965–68, Assoc. Prof. of Finance 1968–72, Prof. of Finance 1972–2000, Lecturer, John F. Kennedy School of Govt 1992–2000, currently Adjunct Lecturer, Visiting Prof., Harvard Law School; Under-Sec. for Finance, US Treasury Dept, Washington, DC 1989–92; Exec. Dir Pres. Reagan's Task Force on Market Mechanisms ('Brady Commission') 1987–88, consultant to Bush Admin. 1989; Dir XL Group PLC 1998–2005, Ind. Dir 2006–18, Chair. (non-exec.) 2009–15, currently Dir XL Capital Ltd; Prof., Nat. Asscn of Securities Dealers 2000–01, CEO 2000–06, Chair. 2001–06; Sr Advisor, Peter J. Solomon (investment bank), New York 2006–; Chair. Bd Northeast Bancorp 2010–; mem. Bd of Dirs Moody's Corpn 1998–14, Freddie Mac 2006–11 (interim Chair. 2009–11), Fed. Reserve Bank of Boston, Investment Co. Inst., Dreyfus Municipal Income Inc. 1988–2000, 2006–, Fed. Home Loan Mortgage Corpn 2006–12, Ocean Reinsurance Ltd, Circuit City Stores, Inc., Quadra Realty Trust Inc. 2007–, Pioneer Global Asset Man. SpA; mem. Council on Foreign Relations, Boston Cttee on Foreign Relations, Cttee on Capital Markets Regulation, Int. Advisory Bd Korean Financial Supervisory Service; fmr Pres. Boston Econ. Club; Trustee, Int. Accounting Standards Cttee Foundation. *Address:* Peter J. Solomon Company, 520 Madison Avenue, New York, NY 10022, USA; XL Group PLC, 1 Hatch Street Upper, Dublin 2, Ireland (office). *Telephone:* (212) 508-1600 (New York). *Fax:* (212) 508-1633 (New York). *E-mail:* rglauber@pjsolomon.com. *Website:* www.pjsolomon.com; www.xlgroup.com (office).

GLAVCHEV, Dimitar Borisov, MA; Bulgarian registered auditor, certified accountant and politician; b. 15 Aug. 1963, Sofia; s. of Boris Dimitrov Glavchev and Mariya Dimitrova Glavchev; m. Pavlina Andreeva Glavchev; ed Univ. of Nat. and World Economy; financier 1991–; mem. Grazhdani za Evropeysko Razvitie na Balgariya (GERB—Citizens for European Devt of Bulgaria); mem. (GERB), Narodno Sobraniye (Parl.) for 23-SOFIA 1 2009–, Deputy Chair. GERB Parl. Group and Chair. of several parl. cttees, Chair. Narodno Sobraniye April–Nov. 2017, mem. Del. to Inter-Parl. Union 2017–, Del. to Parl. Ass. of the South-East European Co-operation Process 2017–. *E-mail:* dimitar.glavchev@parliament.bg (office). *Website:* www.parliament.bg (office).

GLAVIN, William F., BA, MBA; American business executive and academic administrator; *President Emeritus, Babson College;* b. 29 March 1932, Albany, NY; s. of John Glavin; m. Cecily McClatchy 1955; three s. four d.; ed Coll. of the Holy Cross, Worcester and Wharton Graduate School Univ. of Pennsylvania; fmr Exec. Int. Business Machines and Vice-Pres. Operations, Service Bureau Corpn (an IBM subsidiary); Exec. Vice-Pres. Xerox Data Systems 1970, Group Vice-Pres. 1972, Man. Dir and COO 1974, Exec. Vice-Pres. Xerox 1980, Exec. Vice-Pres. for Reprographics and Operations 1982, Pres. Business Equipment Group 1983–89, Vice-Chair. Xerox Corpn 1985–89; Pres. Babson Coll., Wellesley, Mass. 1989–97, now Pres. Emer.; mem. Bd of Dirs Gould Inc., State Street Boston Corpn, Norton Co.; mem. Bd of Trustees and Pres.'s Council Coll. of the Holy Cross; Trustee Emer., Franklin W. Olin Coll. of Engineering; Dr hc (College of the Holy Cross), (Babson College); Distinguished Alumni Award, Univ. of Pennsylvania. *Leisure interests:* golf, reading, art, music.

GLAZ'IEV, Sergey Yurievich, BA, MA, DrEcSc; Russian economist and politician; b. 1 Jan. 1961, Zaporozhye, Ukrainian SSR, USSR; m.; three c.; ed Moscow State Univ.; Head of Lab., Cen. Econ. Math. Inst. 1986–91; First Deputy Chair. Cttee on External Econ. Relations Ministry of Foreign Affairs 1991–92; First Deputy Minister of External Econ. Relations of Russia 1992, Minister 1992–93; mem. State Duma (Parl.) 1993–95, (CP of Russian Fed. faction) 1999–2007, Chair. Cttee for Econ. Policy 1994–95, 2000–07; Chair. Nat. Cttee of Democratic Party of Russia 1994–97; Head of Econ. Dept, Security Council 1996; Head, Information-Analytical Bd, Council of Fed. (Parl.) 1996–; Co-Chair. Partiya Rossiiskikh Regionov (PRR—Party of the Russian Regions) –2004; unsuccessful cand. in presidential election 2004; Head of Motherland election bloc, then For a Worthy Life Org.; Co-founder Rodina party; apptd by Pres. Vladimir Putin as presidential aide for the co-ordination of the work of federal agencies in developing the Customs Union of Belarus, Kazakhstan and Russia 2012; author of econ. programme for CP of Russian Fed. for Parl. Elections 1999; vigorous opponent of moves to integrate Ukraine with EU; one of first seven persons placed under executive sanctions by Pres. Barack Obama, following the Crimean status referendum, freezing his assets in USA and banning him from entering the country March 2014; criminal action brought against him July 2014; Corresp. mem. Russian Acad. of Sciences 2000, Full mem. 2008; Gold Kondratieff Medal, Int. N.D. Kondratieff Foundation and Russian Acad. of Natural Sciences 1995. *Publications include:* more than 40 books, including Economic Theory of Technical Development 1993, Economy and Politics 1994, One and a Half Years in the Duma 1995, Under the Critical Level 1996, Genocide: Russia and the New World Order 1998, I'm Just Paying My Debt 2007; hundreds of pamphlets and research papers. *E-mail:* glaziev-press@yandex.ru. *Website:* www.glazev.ru.

GLEAN, Sir Carlyle Arnold, GCMG, BEd, MA; Grenadian educator and government official; b. 11 Feb. 1932; s. of George Glean and Olive McBurnie; m. Norma Glean (née DeCoteau) 1955; one s. five d. (one deceased); ed Univ. of Calgary, Canada; began career as teacher, St John's RC School 1950; Principal, Happy Hill RC School 1964–65, 1967; tutor, Grenada Teachers Coll. 1970–72; fmr Prin. Grenada Teachers Coll.; fmr Lecturer, Univ. of the West Indies, Barbados; fmr Asst Chief Examiner, Caribbean Examinations Council; Minister of Educ. 1990–95 (retd); Gov.-Gen. 2008–13. *Publications include:* Heinemann Social Studies for Lower Secondary (three vols, jtly): The Caribbean: Our Land and People, The Caribbean: Our Changing Environment, The Caribbean and the Wider World; for infants: Our Family, Home and School, Our Neighbourhood.

GLEESON, Hon. (Anthony) Murray, AO, BA, LLB; Australian lawyer and judge; *Non-Permanent Judge, Court of Final Appeal, Hong Kong Special Administrative Region;* b. 30 Aug. 1938, Wingham, NSW; s. of L. J. Gleeson; m. Robyn Gleeson 1965; one s. three d.; ed Univ. of Sydney; called to the Bar 1963; tutor in law, St Paul's Coll., Univ. of Sydney 1963–65, Lecturer in Co. Law 1965–74; apptd QC 1974; mem. Council NSW Bar Asscn 1979–86, Pres. 1984–86; Chief Justice, Supreme Court NSW 1988–98; Pres. Judicial Comm. NSW 1988–98; Lt-Gov. NSW 1989–98; Chief Justice, High Court of Australia 1998–2008 (retd); Non-Perm. Judge, Court of Final Appeal, Hong Kong Special Admin. Region 2009–; mem. Perm. Court of Arbitration 1999; Hon. Bencher Middle Temple 1989; Dr hc (Univ. of Sydney) 1999; Centenary Medal 2001. *Publications include:* The Rule of Law and the Constitution. *Leisure interests:* tennis, skiing. *Address:* Court of Final Appeal, Court of Final Appeal Building, 8 Jackson Road, Central, Hong Kong Special Administrative Region, People's Republic of China (office). *Telephone:* 21230123 (office). *Fax:* 21210300 (office). *E-mail:* cfaenquiries@hkcfa.hk (office). *Website:* www.hkcfa.hk/en/home/index.html (office).

GLENDENING, Parris Nelson, MA, PhD; American fmr state governor; *President, Leadership Institute, Smart Growth America;* b. 11 June 1942, Bronx, NY; m. 1st Frances A. Hughes 1976; one s.; m. 2nd Jennifer E. Crawford; one d.; ed Florida State Univ. Fort Lauderdale and Tallahassee; Asst Prof., Univ. of Maryland, College Park 1967–72, Assoc. Prof. 1972–95; Co. Exec. Prince George's Co. Council, Upper Marlboro, Md 1982–94; various public appointments at co. level; Dir World Trade Center 1990–97; Gov. of Maryland 1995–2003; Pres. Smart Growth Leadership Inst., Washington DC 2003–; Chair. Bd Dirs Smart Growth Investments 2003–; Chair. Nat. Govs' Asscn 2001–03; mem. Adjunct Faculty, Johns Hopkins Carey Business School 2018–; mem. AAAS, American Political Science Asscn; Democrat; Hon. Mem., AIA 2010; Hon. LLD (Bowie State) 1995, (Baltimore) 1996, (Maryland at Baltimore) 1998; Hon. Dr of Public Service (Washington Coll.) 1995, (Carroll Community Coll.) 1997, (Maryland Univ. Coll.) 2000, (Bridgewater State Coll.) 2003; Hon. DHumLitt (Towson) 2000; numerous awards including Public Official of the Year Award Governing magazine 1990, 2000, Donald C. Stone Award American Soc. for Public Admin 1995, American Soc. of Landscape Architects' Olmstead Award, Harward Innovations in American Govt Award 2000, Hubert H. Humphrey Award 2002, Morris H. Blum Humanitarian Award 2006, Bridge Builders Award, Partners for Livable Communities 2008. *Publications:* Controversies of State and Local Political Systems (with M. M. Reeves) 1972, Pragmatic Federalism 1977; articles in professional publs. *Address:* Leadership Institute, Smart Growth America, 1152 15th Street NW, Suite 450, Washington, DC 20005, USA (office). *Telephone:* (202) 207-3355 (office). *E-mail:* info@smartgrowthamerica.org (office). *Website:* www.smartgrowthamerica.org (office).

GLENDON, Mary Ann, BA, MCompL, JD; American academic, lawyer, writer and fmr diplomatist; *Learned Hand Professor of Law, Harvard University;* b. 7 Oct. 1938, Pittsfield, Mass; m. Edward R. Lev 1970 (died 2013); three d.; ed Univ. of Chicago, Université Libre, Belgium; early career included period as volunteer civil rights attorney; practised law with Mayer, Brown and Platt, Chicago 1963–68; Prof. of Law, Boston Coll. Law School 1968–86; Prof. of Law, Harvard Law School 1986–93, Learned Hand Prof. of Law 1993–; Amb. to the Holy See (Vatican) 2008–09; fmr Visiting Prof., Univ. of Chicago Law School 1974, Gregorian Univ., Rome; fmr Pres. UNESCO-sponsored Int. Asscn of Legal Science 1991; mem. Pontifical Acad. of Social Sciences 1994–, Pres. 2004–13, US Comm. on Int. Religious Freedom 2012–16; mem. Bd of Supervisors, Inst. of Religious Works 2013–18, Int. Acad. of Comparative Law; mem. American Acad. of Arts and Sciences 1991; Head of Del. of Holy See to UN Women's Conf., Beijing 1995; hon. doctorates from Univ. of Chicago, Univ. of Louvain and others; Nat. Humanities Medal 2006, Premio Capalbio, Premio Capri-San Michele. *Publications:* as author: The New Family and the New Property 1981, Abortion and Divorce in Western Law (Scribes Book Award) 1987, The Transformation of Family Law (Order of the Coif Triennial Book Award) 1989, Rights Talk: The Impoverishment of Political Discourse 1991, Law of Decedent's Estates (co-author) 1991, A Nation Under Lawyers 1994, Seedbeds of Virtue (co-author) 1995, Comparative Legal Traditions (co-author) 1999, A World Made New: Eleanor Roosevelt and the Universal Declaration of Human Rights 2001, Traditions in Turmoil 2006, The Forum and the Tower: How Scholars and Politicians Have Imagined the World, from Plato to Eleanor Roosevelt 2011. *Address:* Hauser Hall 504, Harvard Law School, 1575 Massachusetts Avenue, Cambridge, MA 02138, USA (office). *Telephone:* (617) 495-4769 (office). *E-mail:* glendon@law.harvard.edu (office). *Website:* www.hls.harvard.edu (office).

GLENDONBROOK, Baron (Life Peer), cr. 2011, of Bowdon in the County of Cheshire; **Michael David Bishop,** Kt, CBE; British business executive and foundation administrator; *Chairman, The Michael Bishop Foundation;* b. 10 Feb. 1942, Bowdon, Cheshire, England; s. of Clive Leonard Bishop; ed Mill Hill School, North London; first job as a baggage handler at Manchester Airport; joined Mercury Airlines, Manchester 1963, British Midland Airways Ltd 1964–; Chair. British Midland PLC 1978–2009 (sold stake and renamed bmi, British Midland International to Lufthansa); Chair. Manx Airlines 1982–2001, British Regional Airlines Group PLC 1982–2001; Deputy Chair. Channel 4 TV Corpn 1991–93, Chair. 1993–97; Chair. D'Oyly Carte Opera Trust Ltd 1989–; Deputy Chair. Airtours PLC 1996– (Dir 1987–2001); Dir Williams PLC 1993–2000, Kidde PLC 2000–02; Founder and Chair. The Michael Bishop Foundation 1989–; mem. (Conservative), House of Lords 2011–; Hon. DTech (Loughborough Univ. of Tech.) 1989, Hon. DLitt (Salford) 1991, Hon. LLD (Nottingham) 1993, Hon. DUniv (Cent. England) 1993, Hon. DLitt (Coventry) 1994, Hon. LLD (Univ. of Leicester) 2007. *Leisure interests:* music, reading. *Address:* House of Lords, Westminster, London, SW1A 0PW, England (office). *Telephone:* (20) 7219-5353 (office). *Fax:* (20) 7219-5979 (office). *E-mail:* contactholmember@parliament.uk (office). *Website:* www.parliament.uk/biographies/lords/lord-glendonbrook/4236 (office).

GLENNIE, Dame Evelyn Elizabeth Ann, CH, DBE, GRSM, FRAM, FRCM, FRNCM; British percussionist, composer, consultant and motivational speaker; b. 19 July 1965, Aberdeen, Scotland; d. of Isobel Glennie and Herbert Arthur Glennie; ed Ellon Acad., Aberdeenshire, Royal Acad. of Music, London; solo debut at Wigmore Hall, London, 1986; concerto, chamber and solo percussion performances worldwide; gave Promenade concerts' first-ever percussion recital 1989; numerous TV appearances, three documentaries on her life including Touch the Sound 2004 (BAFTA Award); composer of music for TV and radio; many works written for her by composers, including Bennett, Rouse, Heath, Macmillan, McLeod, Muldowney, Daugherty, Turnage and Musgrave; performed at opening ceremony of London Olympics 2012; Hon. mem. Royal Philharmonic Soc. 2015; Hon. Patron, Univ. Philosophical Soc., Dublin 2015; Hon. Fellow, Homerton Coll. 2016; Hon. DMus (Aberdeen) 1991, (Bristol, Portsmouth) 1995, (Leicester, Surrey) 1997, (Queen's, Belfast) 1998, (Southampton) 2000, (Williams Coll., USA) 2005, (Binghampton) 2007, (Edinburgh Napier Univ.) 2009, (Cambridge) 2010, (Robert Gordon Univ., Scotland) 2016; Hon. DLitt (Warwick) 1993, (Loughborough) 1995, (Salford) 1999; Hon. LLD (Dundee) 1996; Hon. DUniv (Essex, Durham) 1998,

(Open) 2007, (Queen Margaret, Edinburgh) 2008; Dr hc (Moravian Coll., Pa, USA) 2015; Munster Trust Scholarship 1986; numerous int. prizes and awards, including Shell/LSO Music Gold Medal 1984, Queen's Commendation Prize at RAM 1985, Grammy Award 1988, Scotswoman of the Decade 1990, Charles Heidsieck Soloist of the Year, Royal Philharmonic Soc. 1991, Personality of the Year, Int. Classical Music Awards 1993, Young Deaf Achievers Special Award 1993, Best Studio Percussionist, Rhythm Magazine 1998, 2000, 2002, 2003, 2004, Best Live Percussionist, Rhythm Magazine 2000, Classic FM Outstanding Contribution to Classical Music 2002, Walpole Medal of Excellence 2002, Musical America 2003, Tartan Clef Award 2005, Scotland with Style Classical Award 2005, Best Orchestral Percussionist, Drummies Readers' Poll Awards 2005, 2009, Incorporated Soc. of Musicians Distinguished Musician Award 2006, Sabian Lifetime Achievement Award 2006, inducted into PASIC Hall of Fame 2008, Percuaction Lifetime Achievement Award 2014, Grammy Award 2013, Polar Music Prize 2015. *Films:* wrote and played music for The Trench, Touch the Sound (Critics' Prize, Locarno Int. Film Festival), Golf in the Kingdom. *Play:* Playing from the Heart. *Recordings include:* Rhythm Song, Dancin', Light in Darkness, Rebounds, Veni Veni Emmanuel, Wind in the Bamboo Grove, Drumming, Her Greatest Hits, The Music of Joseph Schwantner, Sonata for Two Pianos and Percussion (Bartók), Last Night of the Proms—100th Season, Street Songs, Reflected in Brass, Shadow Behind the Iron Sun, African Sunrise, Manhattan Rave, UFO: The Music of Michael Daugherty, Bela Fleck-Perpetual Motion, Oriental Landscapes, Fractured Lines, Michael Daugherty: Philadelphia Stories/ UFO, Philip Glass: The Concerto Project 2004, Christopher Rouse 2004, Touch the Sound soundtrack 2004, Margaret Brouwer: Aurolucent Circles 2006. *Television includes:* music for Trial and Retribution 1–5 (Yorkshire TV), music for Mazda commercial Blind Ambition, Survival Special (Anglia) and others. *Publications:* Good Vibrations (autobiography) 1990, Great Journeys of the World, Beat It!, African Dances, Marimba Encores, 3 Chorales for Marimba. *Leisure interests:* reading, walking, cycling, antiques, collecting musical instruments, psychology, designing jewellery, pets. *Address:* Evelyn Glennie Office, Unit 6, Ramsay Court, Hinchingbrooke Business Park, Huntingdon, Cambs., PE29 6FY, England (office). *Telephone:* (1480) 459279 (office). *Fax:* (1480) 451610 (office). *E-mail:* admin@ evelyn.co.uk (office); brenda@evelyn.co.uk (office). *Website:* www.evelyn.co.uk (office).

GLICKMAN, Daniel (Dan) Robert, BA, JD; American lawyer, association executive and fmr politician; *Vice-President and Executive Director, Congressional Program, Aspen Institute;* b. 24 Nov. 1944, Wichita, Kan.; s. of Milton Glickman and Gladys A. Glickman (née Kopelman); m. Rhoda J. Yura 1966; one s. one d.; ed Univ. of Michigan, George Washington Univ.; called to Kan. Bar 1969, Mich. Bar 1970; trial attorney, SEC, Washington, DC 1969–70; Assoc. then Partner, Sargent, Klenda & Glickman, Wichita 1971–76; mem. US House of Reps from 4th Kansas Dist 1977–95; US Sec. of Agric. 1995–2001; Partner, Akin, Gump, Strauss, Hauer & Feld LLP 2001–04, Advisor 2008; Dir Inst. of Politics, John F. Kennedy School of Govt, Harvard Univ. 2002–04; Pres. and CEO Motion Picture Asscn of America 2004–11 (retd); Exec. Dir Congressional Program, Aspen Inst., Washington, DC 2011–, Vice-Pres. 2012–; Sr Fellow, Bipartisan Policy Center; Sr Counselor, APCO Worldwide; mem. Bd of Dirs Chicago Mercantile Exchange 2001–, Hain-Celestial Corpn, Ready Pac Produce Corpn, Communities in Schools, America's Second Harvest, Food Research and Action Center, RFK Memorial Foundation; mem. Int. Advisory Bd of The Coca-Cola Co.; co-Chair. US Consensus Council, The Pew Initiative on Food and Biotechnology; Co-Chair. Chicago Council's Global Agricultural Development Initiative. *Address:* Aspen Institute, One Dupont Circle, NW, Suite 700, Washington, DC 20036-1133, USA (office). *Telephone:* (202) 736-5800 (office). *Fax:* (202) 467-0790 (office). *Website:* www.aspeninstitute .org (office).

GLIMCHER, Laurie Hollis, BA, MD; American immunologist, academic and university administrator; *President and CEO, Dana-Farber Cancer Institute;* b. 17 April 1951, Rochester, NY; d. of Melvin Jacob Glimcher and Geraldine Lee Glimcher (née Bogolub); m. Gregory Petsko; three c.; ed Radcliffe Coll., Harvard Univ., Harvard Univ. Medical School; Intern, Massachusetts Gen. Hosp., Boston 1976–77, Resident 1977–78, Fellow 1982–83; fmr Sr Rheumatologist, Brigham and Women's Hosp., Boston; Prof. of Medicine, Harvard Medical School 1990–2011, also Irene Heinz Given Prof. of Immunology, Harvard School of Public Health 1990–2011; Stephen & Suzanne Weiss Dean, Weill Cornell Medical Coll., New York 2012–16; Pres. and CEO Dana-Farber Cancer Inst. 2016–; Fellow, American Acad. of Arts and Sciences; mem. NAS, AAAS, American Asthma Foundation, American Asscn of Immunologists (fmr Pres.), American Soc. of Clinical Investigation, American Asscn of Physicians; numerous awards including Leukemia Soc. Stohlman Memorial Scholar Award, Arthritis Foundation Lee S. Howley Award, New York Acad. of Sciences Klemper Award 2003, American Asscn of Univ. Women Sr Scholar Award 2006, American Coll. of Rheumatology Distinguished Investigator Award 2006, Laureate for North America, L'Oréal-UNESCO Women in Science Awards 2014. *Address:* Office of the President, Dana-Farber Cancer Institute, 450 Brookine Avenue, Dana 1628, Boston, MA 02215, USA (office). *Telephone:* (617) 632-4266 (office). *Fax:* (617) 632-2161 (office). *E-mail:* laurie_glimcher@dfci.harvard.edu (office). *Website:* www.dana-farber.org (office).

GLIMCHER, Marc; American art gallery executive; *President and CEO, Pace Gallery;* b. 16 Sept. 1963; s. of Arnold Glimcher and Millie Glimcher; m. 1st Andrea Bundonis 2003 (divorced 2013); m. 2nd Fairfax Dorn 2015; ed Harvard Univ., Johns Hopkins Univ.; Exec. Producer The Paint Job 1992; Assoc. Dir Pace Gallery (fmrly PaceWildenstein Gallery) 1985, Pres. and CEO 2011–; past exhbns include Keith Tyson, Chuck Close, Donald Judd, Bridget Riley, Mark Rothko, Julian Schnabel; f. Artifex Press LLC 2008; Creative Time Art Gala Award 2010. *Address:* Pace Gallery, 32 East 57th Street, 2nd Floor, New York, NY 10022, USA (office). *Telephone:* (212) 421-3292 (office). *Fax:* (212) 421-0835 (office). *E-mail:* info@ pacegallery.com (office). *Website:* www.pacegallery.com (office).

GLIŃSKI, Piotr Tadeusz, MA, PhD; Polish sociologist, academic and politician; *Deputy Prime Minister and Minister of Culture and National Heritage;* b. 20 April 1954, Warsaw; m.; one d.; ed Bolesław Prus High School, Warsaw, Inst. of Econ. Sciences and Inst. of Sociology of Univ. of Warsaw, Inst. of Philosophy and Sociology of Polish Acad. of Sciences; active at Inst. of Philosophy and Sociology of Polish Acad. of Sciences from late 1970s, fmr Head of Dept of Civil Society; Prof. and Head of Dept of Sociology of Social Structure, Inst. of Sociology, Univ. of Bialystok 1998–; actively involved with non-governmental orgs since 1980s; Co-founder and Pres. Social Ecological Inst., co-organized All-Polish Congresses of the Environmental Movt; Co-founder and mem. Bd, KLON/JAWOR Asscn; mem. Acad. for the Devt of Philanthropy in Poland; activist of democratic opposition and NSZZ Solidarność (mem. Intervention and Mediation Cttee of Mazowieckie Voivodship) 1970s and 1980s; cand. for election to the Sejm from list of Freedom Union as part of Environmental Leaders Electoral Cttee; mem. Freedom Union 1998–2000; mem. Prawo i Sprawiedliwość (Law and Justice) party 2010–, Chair. Program Council 2014–; currently Deputy to the Sejm (Ass.–Parl.); Deputy Prime Minister and Minister of Culture and Nat. Heritage 2015–; lecturer at numerous European univs; Pres. Polish Sociological Asscn 2005–11; Officer's Cross, Order of Polonia Restituta 2011; Stanford Univ. Ford Foundation scholarship. *Publications include:* Człowiek-środowisko-zdrowie. Problemy polskie z prognostycznego punktu widzenia 1985, Społeczne aspekty ochrony i kształtowania środowiska w Polsce 1990, Polscy Zieloni. Ruch społeczny w okresie przemian 1996, Samoorganizacja społeczeństwa polskiego. III sektor i wspólnoty lokalne w jednoczącej się Europie 2002, Teorie wspólnotowe a praktyka społeczna. Obywatelskość, polityka, lokalność 2005, Civil Society in the Making 2006, Style działań organizacji pozarządowych w Polsce. Grupy interesu czy pożytku publicznego? 2006, Socjologia i Siciński. Style życia, społeczeństwo obywatelskie, studia nad przyszłością 2009, Kulturowe aspekty struktury społecznej. Fundamenty, konstrukcje, fasady 2010, Katastrofa smoleńska, Reakcje społeczne, polityczne i medialne 2011. *Address:* Ministry of Culture and National Heritage, 00-071 Warsaw, ul. Krakowskie Przedmieście 15/17, Poland (office). *Telephone:* (22) 4210100 (office). *Fax:* (22) 4210131 (office). *E-mail:* minister@mkidn.gov.pl (office). *Website:* www.mkidn.gov.pl (office); www.sejm.gov.pl/sejm8.nsf/posel.xsp?id=101 (office).

GLOAG, Ann Heron, OBE; British business executive; b. 10 Dec. 1942; d. of Iain Souter and Catherine Souter; m. 1st Robin N. Gloag 1965 (deceased); one s. (deceased) one d.; m. 2nd David McCleary 1990; ed Perth High School; trainee nurse, Bridge of Earn Hosp., Perth 1960–65, Theatre Sister 1969–80; ward sister, Devonshire Royal Hosp., Buxton 1965–69; Founding Partner, Gloagtrotter (renamed Stagecoach Express Services) 1980–83, Co-Dir Stagecoach Ltd 1983–86, Dir Stagecoach Holdings PLC 1986–, Exec. Dir 1986–2000, Man. Dir 1986–94; Trustee Princess Royal Trust for Carers; mem. Int. Bd Mercy Ships; Dir (non-exec.) OPTOS, The Balcraig Foundation, The Gloag Foundation, The Freedom From Fistula Foundation; Scottish Marketing Woman of the Year, Scottish Univs 1989, UK Businesswoman of the Year, Veuve Clicquot and Inst. of Dirs 1989–90, Susan B. Anthony Award, Nat. Council of Women of the United States 2009. *Leisure interests:* family, travel, charity support. *Address:* Stagecoach Group PLC, 10 Dunkeld Road, Perth, PH1 5TW, Scotland (office). *Website:* www .stagecoachgroup.com.

GLOBUS, Yoram; Israeli film producer; b. 7 Sept. 1943; m. Lea Globus 1993; one c.; f. Noah Films with Menahem Golan 1963; bought Cannon Films (USA) with Menahem Golan 1979 and produced over 100 motion pictures, Chair., CEO Cannon Entertainments –1989, Officer Cannon Group Inc. –1989; Co-Pres. Pathé Communications Corpn, Chair., CEO Pathé Int. 1989–1991; fmr mem. Bd of Dirs MGM Studios; f. GG Studios, Israel 1993; currently Pres. Globus Max. *Films produced include:* Over the Top, Barfly, Dancers, Missing in Action I, II & III, Death Wish IV, The Assault (winner of 1986 Acad. Award for Best Foreign Language Film), Surrender, Runaway Train, Hanna's War 1988, Masters of the Universe, King Lear, Tough Guys Don't Dance 1987, Shy People 1987, A Cry In The Dark 1988, Lelakek Tatut, Tipat Mazal, Mashehu Matok, Rak Klavim Ratzim Hofshi. *Website:* globusmax.co.il.

GLOCER, Thomas (Tom) Henry, BA, JD; American lawyer and business executive; b. 8 Oct. 1959, NY; s. of Walter Glocer and Ursula Glocer (née Goodman); m. Maarit Leso 1988; one s. one d.; ed Columbia Univ., Yale Univ. Law School; mergers and acquisitions lawyer, Davis Polk and Wardwell, New York, Paris and Tokyo 1985–93; joined Reuters 1993, mem. Legal Dept Gen. Counsel, Reuters America Inc., New York 1993–96, Exec. Vice-Pres., Reuters America Inc. and CEO Reuters Latin America 1996–98, CEO Reuters business in the Americas 1998–2001, Reuters Inc. 2000–01, CEO Reuters Group PLC (Thomson-Reuters following merger with Thomson 2007) 2001–12; mem. Bd of Dirs Merck & Co. Inc. 2007–, Morgan Stanley, K2 Intelligence, Council on Foreign Relations; fmr mem. Bd of Dirs Instinet Corpn, Partnership for New York; fmr mem. Business Council, Int. Business Council of World Econ. Forum, Advisory Bd of Judge Inst. of Man. at Univ. of Cambridge, European Business Leaders Council, Atlantic Council, Corporate Advisory Bd of Tate Britain, Madison Council of US Library of Congress; New York Hall of Science Award 2000, John Jay Alumni Award 2001. *Publications include:* author of computer software, including Coney Island: A Game of Discovery (co-author) 1983. *Website:* www.tomglocer.com (home).

GLOS, Michael; German politician and banking executive; b. 14 Dec. 1944, Brünnau; m.; three c. (one died 1997); served apprenticeship as miller and passed professional examination 1967; managed family flour mill, Prichsenstadt 1968–70; mem. CSU (Christlich-Soziale Union in Bayern) 1970–, first Chair. CSU-chapter, Prichsenstadt 1972–75, Chair. CSU-Dist of Kitzingen 1975–93, mem. Exec. Bd CSU Lower Franconia 1976, mem. Presidency of CSU Bavaria 1976, Chair. CSU Bavaria and Asst Chair. CDU/CSU Parl. Group 1993–2005; mem. Dist Council of Prichsenstadt 1972–78; mem. Council of Dist (Kreistag) of Kitzingen 1975–93; mem. Bundestag (Parl.) 1976–2013; Fed. Minister for Econs and Tech. 2005–09 (resgnd); Chair. Bd of Supervisory Dirs and Chair. Exec. Cttee KfW Bankengruppe 2008–09; Adviser, WEC GmbH, Prichsenstadt; Hon. Chair., Dist Asscn 1993; Bundesverdienstkreuz am Bande 1985, Bundesverdienstkreuz 1989, Bayerischer Verdienstorden 1992, Großes Bundesverdienstkreuz 1996, Ehrenzeichen für Verdienste um die Republik Österreich (Austria) 2001, Großkreuz, Orden Bernardo O'Higgins (Chile) 2011, Mittelkreuz, Ungarischer Verdienstorden (Hungary) 2014; Medal for Outstanding Service to Bavaria 2005, Georg-Schulhoff-Prize 2008, Bavarian Constitution Medal 2010. *Address:* Schulinstrasse 17, 97357 Prichsenstadt (office); Friedrich Straße 50-55, 10117 Berlin, Germany (office). *E-mail:* buero@glos.de. *Website:* www.glos.de.

GLOUCESTER, HRH The Duke of Richard Alexander Walter George, Earl of Ulster and the Baron Culloden, KG, GCVO; b. 26 Aug. 1944, Northampton,

England; s. of Duke of Gloucester (third s. of HM King George V) and Lady Alice Montagu-Douglas-Scott (d. of the 7th Duke of Buccleuch); m. Birgitte van Deurs 1972; one s. (Alexander, Earl of Ulster) two d. (the Lady Davina Windsor and the Lady Rose Windsor); ed Wellesley House, Broadstairs, Eton Coll. and Magdalene Coll., Cambridge; Corp. mem. RIBA 1972; Commdr-in-Chief St John Ambulance Brigade 1972–74; Col-in-Chief Glos. Regt 1974–94, Deputy Col-in-Chief Royal Glos., Berks. and Wilts. Regt 1994; Royal Col The Rifles 1993; Deputy Col-in-Chief The Royal Logistic Corps 1993; Col in Chief Royal Army Medical Corps 2003, NZ Army Medical Corps 2008, The Royal Anglian Regt 2006; Hon. Col Royal Monmouthshire Royal Engineers (Militia) 1977; Hon. Air Cdre RAF Odiham 1993; Grand Prior Order of St John 1975; Pres. The London Soc., Cancer Research Campaign 1973, Nat. Asscn of Clubs for Young People (now Ambition) 1974, Christ's Hosp. 1975, St Bartholomew's Hosp. 1975, Royal Smithfield 1975, British Consultants and Construction Bureau (now British Expertise) 1978, Cambridge House 1983, Britain Nepal Soc. 1989, Public Monuments and Sculpture Asscn 1998, Royal Agricultural Benevolent Inst. 2010, Crown Agents 2011; Jt Pres. Cancer Research UK 2002; Vice-Pres. LEPRA 1971; Commr Historic Buildings and Monuments Comm. for England 1983–2001; Royal Bencher, Gray's Inn 2000; Chancellor Univ. of Worcester 2008; Royal Trustee, British Museum 1973–2003; Royal Patron Peace and Prosperity Trust 2010, Global Heritage Fund 2012; Patron in Chief Scottish Veterans Residences 2005; Patron Action on Smoking and Health (ASH) 1971, Pestalozzi Int. Village Trust 1973, London Playing Fields Foundation 1975, Nuffield Farming Scholarships Trust 1975, Richard III Soc. 1980, Kensington Soc. 1981, Heritage of London Trust 1982, Int. Council on Monuments and Sites (ICOMOS) 1983, Fortress Study Group 1985, Normandy Veterans Asscn 1986, Construction Youth Trust 1987, London Chorus 1991, Building Centre Trust 1992, Japan Soc. 1994, Habitat for Humanity 1997, Severn Valley Railway 1997, St George's Soc. of New York 2000, British Limbless Ex-Service Men's Asscn (BLESMA) 2005, Architects Benevolent Soc. 2011; Co-Patron Abbotsford Trust 2009; Vice-Patron Nat. Churches Trust 2007; Sr Fellow, RCA 1984; Hon. Pres. Somme Asscn 2005, 20-Ghost Club 2012. *Publication:* On Public View, The Face of London, Oxford and Cambridge. *Address:* Kensington Palace, London, W8 4PU, England. *Telephone:* (20) 7368-1000 (office). *Fax:* (20) 7368-1019 (office). *Website:* www.royal.gov.uk.

GLOVER, Danny; American actor; b. 22 July 1946, San Francisco, Calif.; s. of James Glover and Carrie Glover; m. Asake Bomani; one d.; ed San Francisco State Univ.; researcher, Office of Mayor, San Francisco 1971–75; Head, TransAfrica (African-American Lobby) 2002–; mem. American Conservatory Theater's Black Actor Workshop; f. Carrie Productions (film production co.); with his wife f. Bomani Gallery, San Francisco; mem. Bd of Dirs Jazz Foundation of America; Dr hc (San Francisco State Univ.); Hon. DHumLitt (Utah State Univ.), (Starr King School for the Ministry) 2010; Chair.'s Award, Nat. Asscn for the Advancement of Colored People (NAACP) 2003. *Plays include:* Master Harold . . . and the Boys 1982, other stage appearances include: The Blood Knot 1982, The Island, Sizwe Banzi is Dead, Macbeth, Suicide in B Flat, Nevis Mountain Dew, Jukebox. *Films include:* Escape from Alcatraz 1979, Chu Chu and the Philly Flash 1981, Out 1982, Iceman 1984, Places in the Heart 1984, Birdy 1984, The Color Purple 1984, Silverado 1985, Witness 1985, Lethal Weapon 1987, Bat 21 1988, Lethal Weapon II 1989, To Sleep with Anger 1990, Predator 2 1990, Flight of the Intruder 1991, A Rage in Harlem 1991, Pure Luck 1991, Grand Canyon 1992, Lethal Weapon III 1992, The Saint of Fort Washington 1993, Bopha 1993, Angels in the Outfield 1994, Operation Dumbo Drop 1995, America's Dream 1996, The Rainmaker 1997, Wings Against the Wind 1998, Beloved 1998, Lethal Weapon IV 1998, Prince of Egypt (voice) 1998, Antz (voice) 1998, The Monster 1999, Bàttu 2000, Boseman and Lena 2000, Wings Against the Wind 2000, Freedom Song 2000, 3 A.M. 2001, The Royal Tenenbaums 2001, Saw 2004, The Cookout 2004, Missing in America 2005, Manderlay 2005, The Shaggy Dog 2006, The Adventures of Brer Rabbit (voice) 2006, Bamako 2006, Dreamgirls 2006, Barnyard (voice) 2006, Shooter 2007, Honeydripper 2007, Be Kind Rewind 2007, Blindness 2008, Gospel Hill 2008, This Life 2008, Night Train 2009, The Harimaya Bridge 2009, 2012 2009, Down for Life 2009, Death at a Funeral 2010, Dear Alice 2010, I'm Still Here 2010, Legendary 2010, Mooz-Lum 2010, I Want to Be a Soldier 2010, Five Minarets in New York 2010, Son of Morning 2011, Age of the Dragons 2011, Donovan's Echo 2011, Mysteria 2011, Heart of Blackness 2011, LUV 2012, The Children's Republic 2012, The Bouquet 2013, From Above 2013, Highland Park 2013, The Shift 2013, Space Warriors 2013, Tula: The Revolt 2013, Extraction 2013, Ninja Immovable Heart 2014, Beyond the Lights 2014, Supremacy 2014, Day of the Mummy 2014, This Changes Everything 2015, Toxin 2015, Bad Ass 3: Bad Asses on the Bayou 2015, About Scout 2015, Consumed 2015, Checkmate 2015, Gridlocked 2015, Waffle Street 2015, Diablo 2015. *Television includes:* The Henry Lee Project 2003, Legend of Earthsea 2004, The Exonerated 2005, Hannah's Law (film) 2012, Touch (series) 2012, A Way Back Home (film) 2013. *Address:* Carrie Productions Inc., 2625 Alcatraz Avenue, # 243, Berkeley, CA 94705, USA. *Telephone:* (510) 450-2500.

GLOVER, Donald McKinley, (Childish Gambino); American rapper, DJ, singer and songwriter, screenwriter, actor and director; b. 25 Sept. 1983, Calif.; s. of Donald Glover, Sr and Beverly Glover (née Smith); ed DeKalb School of the Arts, New York Univ.; recording career (as Childish Gambino) 2008–; numerous live appearances as performer in comedy and music; actor and writer for television and film; created television series Atlanta 2016; Grammy Award for Best Traditional R&B Performance (for Redbone) 2018, Grammy Award for Record of the Year, Song of the Year and Best Rap/Sung Performance (for This is America) 2019. *Films:* as actor: Mystery Team (also writer) 2009, The Lazarus Effect 2015, Magic Mike XXL 2015, The Martian 2015, Spider-Man: Homecoming 2017, Solo: A Star Wars Story 2018. *Television:* as writer: 30 Rock 2006–09; as actor: Community 2009–13, Atlanta (also series creator) (Golden Globe Awards for Best Television Series—Musical or Comedy 2017, for Best Actor—Television Series Musical or Comedy 2017, Primetime Emmy Awards for Outstanding Directing in a Comedy Series 2017, for Outstanding Lead Actor in a Comedy Series 2017) 2016–. *Recordings:* albums: Sick Boi 2008, Poindexter 2009, I Am Just a Rapper 2010, I Am Just a Rapper 2 2010, Culdesac 2010, Camp 2011, Because the Internet 2013, "Awaken, My Love!" 2016. *Address:* c/o Chad Taylor, Wolf and Rothstein Artist Management (office). *E-mail:* info@wolfandrothstein.com (office). *Website:* wolfandrothstein.com (office).

GLOVER, Jane Alison, CBE, MA, DPhil, FRCM; British conductor and academic; *Felix Mendelssohn Emeritus Professor of Music, Royal Academy of Music;* b. 13 May 1949; d. of Robert Finlay Glover and Jean Muir; ed Monmouth School for Girls and St Hugh's Coll., Oxford; Jr Research Fellow, St Hugh's Coll. 1973–75, Lecturer in Music 1976–84, Sr Research Fellow 1982–84; Lecturer, St Anne's Coll., Oxford 1976–80, Pembroke Coll. 1979–84; mem. Univ. of Oxford Faculty of Music 1979–; professional conducting debut at Wexford Festival 1975; operas and concerts for BBC, Glyndebourne 1982–, Royal Opera House 1988–, Covent Garden, ENO 1989–, London Symphony Orchestra, London Philharmonic Orchestra, Royal Philharmonic Orchestra, Philharmonia, Royal Scottish Orchestra, English Chamber Orchestra, Royal Danish Opera, Glimmerglass Opera, New York 1994–, Australian Opera 1996– and many orchestras in Europe and USA; Prin. Conductor London Choral Soc. 1983–2000; Artistic Dir London Mozart Players 1984–91; Prin. Conductor Huddersfield Choral Soc. 1989–96; Music Dir, Music of the Baroque, Chicago, USA 2002–; Dir of Opera, RAM 2009–16, Felix Mendelssohn Emer. Prof. of Music 2016–; mem. BBC Cen. Music Advisory Cttee 1981–85, Music Advisory Cttee, Arts Council 1986–88; Gov. RAM 1985–90, BBC 1990–95; Hon. DMus (Exeter) 1986, (CNAA) 1991, (London) 1992, (City Univ.) 1995, (Glasgow) 1996; Hon. DLitt (Loughborough) 1988, (Bradford) 1992; Dr hc (Open Univ.) 1988, (Brunel) 1997. *Television:* documentaries and series and presentation, especially Orchestra 1983, Mozart 1985. *Radio:* talks and series including Opera House 1995, Musical Dynasties 2000. *Publications:* Cavalli 1978, Mozart's Women: His Family, His Friends, His Music 2005; contribs to The New Monteverdi Companion 1986, Monteverdi 'Orfeo' Handbook 1986; articles in numerous journals. *Leisure interests:* The Times crossword puzzle, theatre, skiing, walking. *Address:* Music International, 13 Ardilaun Road, Highbury, London, N5 2QR, England (office); Royal Academy of Music, Marylebone Road, London, NW1 5HT, England (office). *E-mail:* neil@musicint.co.uk (office); j.glover@ram.ac.uk (office). *Telephone:* (20) 7873-7373 (office). *Website:* www.ram.ac.uk (office); www.janeglover.co.uk; www.baroque.org.

GLÜCK, Louise Elisabeth; American poet, writer and academic; *Rosenkranz Writer-in-Residence, Yale University;* b. 22 April 1943, New York City; d. of Daniel Glück and Beatrice Glück (née Grosby); m. 1st Charles Hertz (divorced); one s.; m. 2nd John Dranow 1977 (divorced 1996); ed Sarah Lawrence Coll., Columbia Univ.; Artist-in-Residence, Goddard Coll., Plainfield, Vt 1971–72, Faculty mem. 1973–74; Poet-in-Residence, Univ. of North Carolina at Greensboro 1973; Visiting Prof., Univ. of Iowa 1976–77; Elliston Prof. of Poetry, Univ. of Cincinnati 1978; Visiting Prof., Columbia Univ. 1979; Holloway Lecturer, Univ. of California, Berkeley 1982; Faculty mem. and Bd mem. MFA Writing Program at Warren Wilson Coll., Swannoa, North Carolina 1980–84; Visiting Prof., Univ. of California, Davis 1983; Scott Prof. of Poetry, Williams Coll., Mass 1983, part-time Sr Lecturer in English 1984–97, Parish Sr Lecturer in English 1997–; Regents Prof. of Poetry, UCLA 1985–88; Baccalaureate Speaker, Williams Coll. 1993; Poet Laureate of Vt 1994; Visiting Mem. of Faculty, Harvard Univ. 1995; Hurst Prof., Brandeis Univ. 1996; Special Consultant in Poetry at Library of Congress, Washington, DC 1999–2000; Poet Laureate of USA 2003–04; currently Rosenkranz Writer-in-Residence, Yale Univ.; mem. American Philosophical Soc. 2015; Fellow, American Acad. of Arts and Sciences; mem. PEN, American Acad. and Inst. of Arts and Letters, Acad. of American Poets (mem. Bd of Chancellors 1999–2006); Hon. LLD (Williams Coll.) 1993, (Skidmore Coll.) 1995, (Middlebury Coll.) 1996; Acad. of American Poets Prize 1967, Rockefeller Foundation Grant 1968–69, Nat. Educ. Asscn grants 1969–70, 1979–80, 1988–89, Nat. Endowment for the Arts Fellowships 1969–70, 1979–80, 1988–89, Vt Council for the Arts Grant 1978–79, Lannan Foundation Grant, Eunice Tietjens Memorial Prize 1971, Guggenheim Foundation Grant 1975–76, 1987–88, American Acad. and Inst. of Arts and Letters Literary Award 1981, Nat. Book Critics' Circle Award for poetry 1985, Poetry Soc. of America Melville Cane Award 1986, Wellesley Coll. Sara Teasdale Memorial Prize 1986, Bobbitt Natil Prize, Library of Congress 1992, William Carlos Williams Award 1993, PEN/Martha Albrand Award 1995, New Yorker Magazine Award in Poetry 1999, English Speaking Union Amb. Award 1999, 2001, Bollingen Prize 2001, Wallace Stevens Award 2008, Gold Medal in Poetry, American Acad. of Arts and Letters 2015, Nat. Humanities Medal 2015. *Publications:* poetry: Firstborn 1968, The House on the Marshland 1975, The Garden 1976, Descending Figure 1980, The Triumph of Achilles 1985, Ararat 1990, The Wild Iris (Pulitzer Prize for Poetry 1993) 1992, Proofs and Theories: Essays on Poetry 1994, The First Four Books of Poems 1995, Meadowlands 1996, Vita Nova 1999, The Seven Ages 2001, October 2004, Averno 2007, A Village Life 2009, Poems 1962–2012 (Los Angeles Times Book Prize) 2012, Faithful and Virtuous Night (Nat. Book Award 2014) 2014, American Originality: Essays on Poetry 2017; contrib. to many anthologies and periodicals. *Address:* c/o Steven Barclay Agency, 12 Western Avenue, Petaluma, CA 94952, USA (office); 14 Ellsworth Park, Cambridge, MA 02139, USA (home). *Telephone:* (707) 773-0654 (office). *Fax:* (707) 778-1868 (office). *Website:* www.barclayagency.com (office).

GLUSHENKO, Yevgeniya Konstantinovna; Russian actress; b. 4 Sept. 1952, Rostov-on-Don; d. of Konstantin Ivanovich and Olga Anatolyevna; m. Aleksandr Kalyagin; one s. one d.; ed Shchepkin Theatre School; worked with Maly Theatre 1974–97, 2000–, Russian Army Theatre 1997–2000; mem. All-Russian Theatrical Soc. 1979, Union of Theatre Workers 1989; Hon. mem. Russian Fed.; Order of Friendship 2004; People's Artist of Russia 1995, State Prize of Russia 2004. *Films include:* Unfinished Play for Mechanical Piano 1977, Profile and Front-View 1979, Oblomov 1980, First-Time Married 1980, In Love of One's Own Accord (Moscow and West Berlin Film Festival Prizes 1983) 1982, Unikum 1983, Zina-Zinulya 1986, Politseiskiye i vory 1997, Proshchaniye v iyune 2003, Live and Remember 2008. *Stage roles:* Liza in Misfortune from Sense 1975, Cordelia in King Lear 1979, Masha in The Savage 1990, Yefrosinya in Infanticide 1991, Matrena in The Hot Heart 1992, Susanna in A Criminal Mother or the Second Tartuffe 1993, Glafira in The Feast of Victors 1995, Vera in The Heart is not a Stone 1997, Vasilisa in The Lower Depths 1998, Emilia in Othello 1999, Kupavina in Sheep and Wolves 2000, Josephine in The Corsican Fury 2001, Zinaida Savishna in Ivanov 2002, Mavra Tarasovna in Truth is Dear, but Happiness is Yet Dearer 2003, Belina in The Imaginary Invalid 2005, Melanya in Children of the Sun 2008. *Television includes:* Zhizn Klima Samgina (series) 1986, Zhenshchiny, kotorym povezlo (miniseries) 1989, Koroleva Margo (series) 1996, Zal ozhidaniya (series) 1998, S novym schastiem! (series) 1999. *Leisure interests:* reading, listening to music, painting, visiting museums and exhibitions. *Address:* Apt 95, Building 17-2, Lavrushinsky Alley, Moscow, Russia (home). *Telephone:* (495) 959-07-52 (home). *E-mail:* dkaliaguin@hotmail.com (home).

GLVÁČ, Martin, JUDr; Slovak lawyer, business executive and politician; b. 20 Nov. 1967, Bratislava; m.; three c.; ed Comenius Univ., Bratislava; Asst Head of Inventory Dept, Otex sp. 1986–87; lawyer, Davao sro 1992–94; Exhbn Man., UAE 1994–97; Business Man., DONAR as 1997–98; Man., VOSS Slovakia sro 1998–2001; pvt. practice as lawyer 2001–06; Sec. of State, Ministry of Construction and Regional Devt 2006–10; mem. Slovak Nat. Council (Parl.) 2010–12; Minister of Defence 2012–16. *Leisure interests:* basketball, tennis, skiing, cinema. *Address:* c/o Ministry of Defence, Kutuzovova 8, 832 47 Bratislava, Slovakia (office).

GLYNN, Ian Michael, MD, PhD, FRS, FRCP; British scientist and academic; *Professor Emeritus of Physiology, University of Cambridge;* b. (Ian Galinsky), 3 June 1928, London; s. of Hyman Glynn and Charlotte Glynn; m. Jenifer Muriel Franklin 1958; one s. two d.; ed City of London School, Trinity Coll. Cambridge, Univ. Coll. Hosp., London; House Physician, Cen. Middlesex Hosp. 1952–53; Nat. Service, RAF Medical Br. 1956–57; MRC Scholar, Physiological Lab., Cambridge 1956, Fellow, Trinity Coll. 1955–, Demonstrator in Physiology 1958–63, Lecturer 1963–70, Reader 1970–75, Prof. of Membrane Physiology 1975–86, Prof. of Physiology 1986–95, Prof. Emer. 1995–, Vice-Master Trinity Coll. 1980–86; Visiting Prof., Yale Univ. 1969; mem. British MRC 1976–80, Council of Royal Soc. 1979–81, 1991–92, Agric. Research Council 1981–86; Chair. Editorial Bd Journal of Physiology 1968–70; Hon. Foreign mem. American Acad. of Arts and Sciences 1984, American Physiological Soc.; Hon. MD (Århus) 1988. *Publications:* The Sodium Pump (with J. C. Ellory) 1985; An Anatomy of Thought: the Origin and Machinery of the Mind 1999; The Life and Death of Smallpox (with Jenifer Glynn) 2004, Elegance in Science 2010; papers in scientific journals. *Address:* Trinity College, Cambridge, CB2 1TQ, England (office). *Telephone:* (1223) 353079 (office). *E-mail:* img10@cam.ac.uk (office). *Website:* www.trin.cam.ac.uk (office).

GLYNN, Robert (Bob) D., Jr, BS, MS; American energy industry executive; b. 1942, Orange, New Jersey; s. of Robert D. Glynn and Helen Josephine Glynn; m.; ed Manhattan Coll., Long Island Univ.; early career with Long Island Lighting Co. and Woodward-Clyde Consultants; joined Pacific Gas & Electric Co. 1984, Pres. and COO 1995–97, Pres. and CEO Pacific Gas & Electric Corpn 1997–2004, Chair. 1998–2005; mem. Bd of Govs San Francisco Symphony; mem. Business Council, Calif. Comm. for Jobs and Econ. Growth, Calif. Business Roundtable.

GNANAM, Arumugham, BSc, MA, MSc, PhD; Indian scientist; b. 5 Oct. 1932, Veeracholagan, Tamil Nadu; s. of Arumugham Pillai; m. Saratham Gnanam 1953; one s. three d.; ed Loyola Coll., Annamalai Univ., North Carolina State Univ. and Cornell Univ., USA; Fullbright Research Trainee 1963–68; Asst Prof. of Plant Sciences, Cornell Univ. 1967–68; Lecturer, Annamalai Univ. 1968–69; Reader, Madurai Kamaraj Univ. 1969–73, Prof. 1973–85, Dir Centre for Plant Molecular Biology 1990–91; Vice-Chancellor, Pondicherry Univ. 1991–99; Vice-Chancellor, Bharathidasan Univ., Trichy 1985–88, Univ. of Madras 1988–90; Sr Scientist, Indian Nat. Science Acad. 1997–2001; fmr Pres. Asscn of Indian Univs; elected Founder Fellow, Tamil Nadu Acad. of Sciences 1976; Nat. Fellow, Univ. Grants Comm. 1978, Nat. Lecturer in Botany 1980; Fellow, Indian Nat. Science Acad., New Delhi 1984, Nat. Acad. of Sciences, Allahabad 1985, fmr Chair. Nat. Assessment and Accreditation Council; several hon. degrees; Rafi Ahmed Kidwai Award, Best Teacher Award, Govt of Tamil Nadu. *Publications include:* numerous scientific papers. *Leisure interests:* photography, music, pets. *Address:* No. 12 Mother Farm House, Banyan Beach Resort Enclave, Old Madra Road, Kottakuppam 605 104, Tamil Nadu, India (home). *E-mail:* gnanama32@yahoo.com.

GNASSINGBÉ, Faure Essozimna, MBA; Togolese politician and head of state; *President;* b. 1966; s. of Gnassingbe Eyadéma (fmr Pres.); ed Paris-Dauphine, France, Georgetown Univ., USA; fmr Deputy, Nat. Ass.; Minister of Public Works, Mines and Telecommunications 2003–05; Pres. of Togo 2005–. *Address:* Office of the President, Palais Présidentiel, ave de la Marina, Lomé, Togo (office). *Telephone:* 221-27-01 (office). *Fax:* 221-18-97 (office). *E-mail:* presidence@republicoftogo.com (office). *Website:* www.republicoftogo.com (office).

GNEDOVSKY, Yuri Petrovich, PhD; Russian architect; *President, Theatre Architects Partnership;* b. 3 July 1930, Sverdlovsk (Ekaterinburg); m. Elena Andreyevna Borisova; one s. one d.; ed Moscow Inst. of Architecture, Acad. of Architecture; Sr Researcher Research Inst. of Public Bldgs Acad. of Architecture 1957–63; Head of div., Deputy Dir Cen. Research Inst. of Public Bldg Design 1964–82; Sec. Bd USSR Union of Architects 1982–91; Pres. Russian Union of Architects 1992–2008; Pres. Theatre Architects Partnership 1992–; mem. Council of Int. Union of Architects 1996–2002, fmr Vice-Pres.; mem. Presidium; Fellow, Russian Acad. of Architecture and Construction Sciences, Int. Acad. of Architecture Sofia; author of projects of numerous bldgs including Taganka Theatre, Meyerhold Cen., Russian Cultural Cen. Red Hills in Moscow, Moscow Int. Music House; Hon. Pres., Union of Architects of Russia 2008–; Pres.'s Prize for Arts and Literature 1999, People's Architect of Russia 2002. *Publications include:* Architecture of Soviet Theatre, Architecture of Public Buildings, World Architecture: A Critical Mosaic 1900–2000 (Vol. 7) 2000, over 60 articles. *Address:* c/o Union of Architects of Russia, 123001 Moscow, Granatny per. 12, Russia (office). *Telephone:* (495) 6911834 (office); (495) 6997057 (home). *Fax:* (495) 6911834 (office). *E-mail:* archunion-russia@mail.ru (office). *Website:* www.uar.ru (office).

GNEHM, Edward William, Jr, (Skip), MA; American diplomatist (retd) and academic; *Kuwait Professor of Gulf and Arabian Peninsula Affairs, Elliott School of International Affairs, George Washington University;* b. 10 Nov. 1944, Ga; s. of Edward W. Gnehm, Sr and Beverly Thomasson; m. Margaret Scott 1970; one s. one d.; ed George Washington Univ. (GWU) and American Univ. Cairo; Head, Liaison Office, Riyadh 1976–78, Deputy Chief of Mission, Embassy in San'a 1978–81, Dir Jr Officer Div. Personnel, Washington, DC 1982–83, Dir Secr. Staff 1983–84, Deputy Chief of Mission, Amman 1984–87, Deputy Asst Sec. of Defense for Near East and S Asia 1987–89, Deputy Asst Sec. of State, Bureau of Near East and S Asian Affairs, Washington, DC 1989–90, Amb. to Kuwait 1990–94, to Australia 2000–01, to Jordan 2001–04, Deputy Perm. Rep. to UN, New York 1994–97, Dir-Gen. of Foreign Service, Dir of Personnel, US Dept of State, Washington, DC 1997–2000; J.B. and Maurice C. Shapiro Visiting Prof. of Int. Affairs, Elliott School of Int. Affairs, GWU, Washington, DC 2004–06, Kuwait Prof. of Gulf and Arabian Peninsula Affairs and Dir Middle East Policy Forum 2006–, Vice Dean, Elliott School of Int. Affairs 2017–; mem. Middle East Inst., American Philatelic Soc., American Foreign Service Asscn, American Acad. of Diplomacy, Diplomatic and Consular Officers Retired, American Center for Oriental Research – Jordan, American Near East Refugee Agency, Bd of Sultan Qaboos Cultural Center, Washington, Senior Living Foundation, Arab Gulf States Inst., Washington, DC; Order of Independence, First Class (Jordan); Decoration of Medallion, Special Class (Kuwait); Presidential Distinguished Service Award 2000, Dept of Defense Meritorious Service Award 1989 and 1994, Dept of State Superior Honor Award 1991, Sec. of State Distinguished Service Award 2004, Harry Harding Teaching Prize, Elliott School of Int. Affairs, GWU, GW President's Medal. *Leisure interests:* history, foreign policy, cycling, stamps, hiking. *Address:* Elliott School of International Affairs, George Washington University, 1957 East Street NW, Suite 512, Washington, DC 20052, USA (office). *Telephone:* (202) 994-0155 (office). *Fax:* (202) 994-4055 (office). *E-mail:* ambgnehm@gwu.edu (office).

GNEUSS, Helmut Walter Georg, DPhil; German academic; *Professor Emeritus of English, University of Munich;* b. 29 Oct. 1927, Berlin; s. of Kurt Gneuss and Margarete Gneuss (née Grimm); m. Mechthild Gretsch 1974; ed Freie Universität Berlin, St John's Coll., Cambridge; Lecturer, German Dept, Univ. of Durham 1955–56, Dept of English, Freie Univ., Berlin 1956–62, Heidelberg Univ. 1962–65; Prof. of English, Univ. of Munich 1965–, now Prof. Emer.; Visiting Professorial Fellow, Emmanuel Coll., Cambridge 1970; Visiting Prof., Univ. of N Carolina, Chapel Hill 1974; mem. Bayerische Akad. der Wissenschaften, British Acad., Österreichische Akad. der Wissenschaften, Medieval Acad. of America; Vice-Pres. Henry Bradshaw Soc. *Publications:* Lehnbildungen und Lehnbedeutungen im Altenglischen 1955, Hymnar und Hymnen im englischen Mittelalter 1968, English Language Scholarship 1996, Language and History in Early England 1996, Books and Libraries in Early England 1996; Handlist of Anglo-Saxon Manuscripts 2001, Ælfric of Eynsham 2009. *Address:* Institut für Englische Philologie, Universität Munich, Schellingstrasse 3, 80799 Munich, Germany (office). *Telephone:* (89) 21803388 (office). *Fax:* (89) 2180 3399 (office). *E-mail:* department3@anglistik.uni-muenchen.de (office). *Website:* www.anglistik.uni-muenchen.de (office).

GNININVI, Léopold Messan Kokou, PhD; Togolese physicist and politician; *Secretary-General, Convention Démocratique des Peuples Africains;* b. 19 Dec. 1942, Aného, Lacs Pref.; ed Univ. of Dijon, France; Head of Solar Energy Lab., Univ. of Lomé 1978–93, Prof. 1981–97; Dir Nat. Inst. of Educational Science 1979–88, Nat. Dir of Scientific Research 1987–93; Sec.-Gen. Convention Démocratique des Peuples Africains (CDPA) 1991–; three years in exile 1995–98; unsuccessful CDPA cand. in presidential election 1998; Minister of State for Mines and Energy 2006–07, for Foreign Affairs and Regional Integration 2007–08, for Industry, Crafts, and Technological Innovations 2008–09. *Address:* Convention démocratique des peuples africains, 5 rue Djidjollé, BP 13963, Lomé, Togo (office). *Telephone:* 22-25-38-46. *E-mail:* cdpa-bt.cdpa-bt@orange.fr (office).

GNUDI, Piero, BEcons; Italian business executive; b. 17 May 1938, Bologna; m. Francesca Pagnini; ed Univ. of Bologna; mem. Bd Credito Italiano 1980–83, STET 1984–94, EniChem 1992–93; mem. Bd Istituto per la Ricostruzione Industriale (IRI) (state holding co.) 1994–99, Resp. for Privatization 1997–99, Chair. and CEO 1999–2000, Chair. Bd of Liquidators 2000–, Chair. IRI Foundation 2000–; Chair. Enel SpA (electricity co.) 2002–11; Minister of Regional Affairs, Tourism and Sport 2011–13; mem. Bd ENI (state energy co.) 1995–96; Econ. Counsellor to Ministry of Industry 1995–96; Deputy Chair. Rolo Banca 1473 SpA, Bologna 1994–; Chair. Locat SpA 1995–99, Profingest School of Man. 1995–99, Credito Fondiario SpA, Nomisma Società di Studi Economics SpA; Chair. Bd of Auditors, Marino Golinelli & C. Sapa; Vice-Chair. Consorzio Alma; mem. Econ. Policy Comm., Consiglio Nazionale dell'Economia e del Lavoro (CNEL) 2000–; Extraordinary Commr Ilva SpA; mem. Bd Dirs Unicredito Italiano, Il Sole 24 Ore SpA, Alfa Wassermann SpA, D & C Compagnia di Importazione prodotti Alimentari, Dolciari, Vini e Liquori SpA, Galotti SpA, ACB Group SpA, Ferrero, Gnudi, Guatri, Uckmar; mem. Exec. Cttee Confindustria, Steering Cttee Assonime (asscn of Italian corpns), Cttee in charge of strategic devt of the Italian Financial Markets, Exec. Cttee of Aspen Inst., Cttee on corp. governance of listed cos reconstituted on initiative of Borsa Italiana; Pres. Mediterranean Energy Observatory, 'e8' (org. of chairmen of major electricity production cos in the world); Chair. Emittenti Titoli; mem. Gen. Council, Bologna Business School; Cavaliere, gran croce dell'Ordine al merito della Repubblica italiana 2002. *Address:* UniCredit SpA, Piazza Cordusio, 20123 Milan, Italy (office). *Telephone:* (02) 88621 (office). *Fax:* (02) 8862-8652 (office). *E-mail:* info@unicredit.eu (office); azionisti@unicredit.eu (office). *Website:* www.unicreditgroup.eu (office).

GOBA, John; Sierra Leonean artist; b. 1944, Mattru Jong; sculptor, based in Freetown. *Address:* Magnin-A, 107 Blvd Richard-Lenoir, 75011 Paris, France (office). *Telephone:* 1-43-38-13-00 (office). *E-mail:* info@magnin-a.com (office). *Website:* www.magnin-a.com/en/artistes/presentation/68/john-goba (office).

GOBER, Robert; American sculptor; b. 12 Sept. 1954, Wallingford, Conn.; ed Middlebury Coll., Vt, Rome campus of Tyler School of Art (div. of Temple Univ.); arrived in New York 1976, worked as carpenter and handyman; also worked as asst to painter Elizabeth Murray; first solo exhbn at Paula Cooper Gallery, New York, consisting of single work titled Slides of a Changing Painting (1982–83) 1984; began creating three-dimensional works 1980s–90s; in recent years sculptures have become more conceptual, with photography in installations; represented USA at Venice Biennale 2001; Curator, Whitney Biennial 2012; Larry Aldrich Foundation Award 1996, Skowhegan Medal for Sculpture 1999, Artist's Space Honoree, Spring Benefit 2002, AICA Award 2005, honoured by Hammer Museum Gala in the Garden 2013. *Address:* c/o Marianne Boesky Fine Art, 535 West 22nd Street, New York, NY 10011, USA.

GOCHIYEV, Annamuhammet; Turkmenistani politician; b. 1973, Bendesen, Balkan Velayat; ed Turkmen State Inst. of Nat. Economy; Deputy Chair. Aşgabat Bakery Products 'Kuvvat' Co.; accountant and economist at 'Arvana' Co. specializing in agricultural statistical analysis; Chief Financial Insp. and Deputy Chair. 'Türkmenillinasabat' Nat. Inst. of Statistics and Forecasting 1997–2001; Head of Dept of Finance and Econs, Land Resources Service, Ministry of Agric., Chief Controller/Insp. in Control and Revision section, Ministry of Economy and Finance, then Head of Law Enforcement, Mil. and State Structures, Ministry of

Economy and Finance 2001–07; Deputy Minister of Finance 2007–08, Minister of Finance 2008–11; Deputy Chair. of the Govt, responsible for Econ. Affairs 2011–15. *Address:* c/o Office of the President and the Council of Ministers, 744000 Aşgabat, Galkynyş köç. 20, Turkmenistan. *E-mail:* nt@online.tm.

GOCKLEY, (Richard) David, BA, MBA; American opera director; *General Director Emeritus, San Francisco Opera;* b. 13 July 1943, Philadelphia, Pa; s. of Warren Gockley and Elizabeth Gockley; m. Adair Lewis; one s. two d.; ed Brown Univ., Columbia Univ., New England Conservatory; Dir of Music, Newark Acad. 1965–67; Dir of Drama, Buckley School, New York 1967–69; Box Office Man., Santa Fe Opera 1969–70; Asst Man. Dir Lincoln Center, New York 1970; Business Man., Houston Grand Opera 1970–71, Assoc. Dir 1971–72, Gen. Dir 1972–2006; Co-founder Houston Opera Studio 1977; Gen. Dir San Francisco Opera 2006–16, Gen. Dir Emer. 2016–; mem. Bd of Dirs Texas Inst. of Arts in Educ.; mem. Opera America (Pres. 1985–); fmr Chair. Houston Theater Dist; Hon. DHL (Univ. of Houston) 1992, Hon. DFA (Brown Univ.) 1993; League of New York Theaters and Producers Tony Award 1977, Columbia Business School Dean's Award 1982, Nat. Inst. of Music Theater Award 1985, Brown Univ. William Rogers Award 1995. *Operas produced include:* Pasatieri's The Seagull 1974, Porgy and Bess (Grammy Award 1977) 1976, Floyd's Bilby's Doll 1976, Willie Stark 1981, Harvey Milk (by Stewart Wallace and Michael Korie), Philip Glass's Akhnaten 1984, John Adams' Nixon in China (Emmy Award 1988) 1987, Tippett's New Year 1989, The Passion of Jonathan Wade 1991, Meredith Monk's Atlas 1991, Robert Moran's Desert of Roses 1992, Florencia en el Amazonas, Treemonisha, A Quiet Place, Resurrection, Carmen. *Leisure interest:* tennis. *Address:* San Francisco Opera, 301 Van Ness Avenue, San Francisco, CA 94102-4509, USA (office). *Telephone:* (415) 861-4008 (office). *Website:* www.sfopera.com (office).

GODAHEWA, Nalaka, BSc, MBA, PhD; Sri Lankan academic and business executive; *Chairman, Helicon Corporate Consultancy;* b. 7 June 1965; ed Univs of Moratuwa, Sri Jayawardenapura, South Australia; started career at Unilever, held various positions including Head of Business Devt; fmr Marketing Dir Suntel, Gen. Man. MAS Shadowline, CEO MAS Holdings; Man. Dir Sri Lanka Insurance Corpn 2009–10; Chair. Sri Lanka Tourism Devt Authority 2010–12, Sri Lanka Tourism Promotions Bureau 2010–12, Sri Lanka Inst. of Tourism and Hotel Man. 2010–12, Sri Lanka Convention Bureau 2010–12, Securities Exchange Comm. 2012–15, Asia Commerce Pvt. Ltd, Asscn of Licensed Banker Operations of Sri Lanka; Pres. Sri Lanka Br., Inst. of Certified Man. Accountants of Australia, currently Helicon Corp. Consultancy; mem. Certified Man. Accountants, Australia; Visiting Lecturer, Univ. of Colombo, Univ. of Keleniya, Univ. of Sri Jayewardenepura; mem. Bd of Dirs Seylan Bank PLC 2009–10, Urban Devt Authority, Colombo Land Pvt. Ltd, Sri Lanka Handicrafts Bd, Lanka Hospitals Pvt. Ltd, Sri Lankan Catering Pvt. Ltd; Fellow, Chartered Inst. of Marketing, UK, Inst. of Chartered Man. Accountants, UK; mem. Industry Consultative Cttee, Faculty of Eng, Univ. of Moratuwa; fmr Chair. Imperial Coll. of Business Studies; Hon. Pres. Global Marketing Network in Sri Lanka. *Address:* Helicon Corporate Consultancy, 6/2, Liberty Plaza, 250, R.A. De Mel Mawatha, Colombo 03 (office); 12-1, Park Tower, Havelock City, 324 Havelock Road, Colombo 05, Sri Lanka (home). *Telephone:* (77) 7418943 (office). *Fax:* (11) 2573667 (office). *E-mail:* info@helicon.lk (office). *Website:* www.helicon.lk (office).

GODAL, Bjørn Tore; Norwegian diplomatist and politician; b. 20 Jan. 1945, Skien; s. of Kari Godal and Aksel Godal; m. Gro Balas 1988; one c.; ed Oslo Univ.; office clerk, Skien 1964–65; Pres. Labour League of Youth 1971–73 (Sec. for org. 1970–71), Fritt Forum (Labour Party's Student Org.) 1967–68; research officer, Labour Party 1973–80, Sec.-Gen. Oslo Labour Party 1980–82, Leader 1982–90 (mem. Cen. Cttee Labour Party 1983–90); Pres. Council of European Nat. Youth Cttees 1973–75; Head of Secr. Labour Party Group of the Oslo Municipal Council 1986; Deputy Rep. Storting (Parl.), then elected Rep.; Minister of Trade and Shipping 1991–94, of Foreign Affairs 1994–97, of Defence 2000–01; Amb. to Germany 2003–07; Special Adviser on int. energy and climate issues, Ministry of Foreign Affairs 2007–10; currently Chair. Council of the Norwegian Defense Univ. Coll.; mem. Bd of Dirs Statoil ASA 2010–; Sr Adviser, Inst. of Political Science, Univ. of Oslo 2002–03; mem. Council for the Study of Power Distribution in Norway 1972–80, Standing Cttee on Finance 1986–89, on Foreign and Constitutional Affairs 1989–91, on Defence 1997–2000, Storting; Chair. Middle East Cttee 1997–2000, Socialist Int.; mem. North Atlantic Ass. 1997–2000. *Address:* Council of the Norwegian Defense University College, PO Box 800, Postmottak 2617, Lillehammer, Norway (office).

GODARD, Jean-Luc; French/Swiss film director; b. 3 Dec. 1930, Paris; s. of Paul Godard and Odile Monad; m. 1st Anna Karina 1961 (divorced); m. 2nd Anne Wiazemsky 1967; ed Lycée Buffon and Faculté des Lettres, Paris; journalist and film critic; film dir 1958–; mem. Conseil supérieur de la langue française 1989–; often identified with the 1960s French film movement La Nouvelle Vague, or New Wave; Chevalier, Ordre nat. du Mérite; Jury's Special Prize and Prix Pasinetti, Venice Festival 1962, Diploma of Merit, Edin. Film Festival 1968 for Weekend, Grand Prix Nat. 1982, Hon. César 1987, 1998, Grand Prix Nat. de la culture 1999, Hon. Academy Award, Acad. of Motion Picture Arts and Sciences 2010, Special Palme d'Or, Cannes Film Festival 2018. *Films include:* Opération Béton 1954, Une femme coquette 1955, Tous les garçons s'appellent Patrick 1957, Charlotte et son Jules 1958, Une histoire d'eau 1958, À bout de souffle (Prix Jean Vigo 1960) 1959, Le petit soldat 1960, Une femme est une femme 1961, Les sept péchés capitaux 1961, Vivre sa vie 1962, RoGoPaG 1962, Les carabiniers 1963, Le mépris 1963, Les plus belles escroqueries du monde 1963, Paris vu par . . . 1963, Bande à part 1964, Une femme mariée 1964, Alphaville 1965, Pierrot le fou 1965, Masculin-féminin 1966, Made in USA 1966, Deux ou trois choses que je sais d'elle 1966, La chinoise 1967, Loin du Vietnam 1967, Weekend 1967, Le plus vieux métier du monde 1967, Vangelo '70 1967, Le gai savoir (TV) 1968, Un film comme les autres 1968, One Plus One 1968, One American Movie – 1 a.m. 1969, British Sounds 1969, Le vent d'est 1969, Lotte in Italia 1970, Vladimir et Rosa 1971, Tout va bien 1972, Numéro deux 1975, Ici et ailleurs 1976, Bugsy 1979, Sauve qui peut 1980, Passion 1982, Prénom Carmen 1983, Detective 1984, Je vous salue, Marie 1985, Soigne ta droite 1987, Aria (segment) 1987, Nouvelle Vague 1989, Allemagne neuf zero 1991, Hélas pour moi 1993, JLG/JLG 1995, Forever Mozart 1996, De l'origine du XXIème siècle 2000, Eloge de l'amour 2001, Liberté et patrie 2002, Ten Minutes Older: The Cello 2002, Notre musique 2004, Vrai faux passeport 2006, Prière pour refusniks (1) 2006, Prière pour refusniks (2) 2006, Une Catastrophe 2008, Film Socialisme 2010, Les trois désastres (segment from 3X3D, omnibus film with Peter Greenaway and Edgar Pera) 2013, The Bridge of Sighs (short in omnibus film Les Ponts de Sarajevo) 2014, Khan Khanne (short) 2014, Adieu au Langage (Jury Prize, Cannes Film Festival 2014, Best Film, US Nat. Soc. of Film Critics 2014) 2014. *Publication:* Introduction à une véritable histoire du cinéma 1980. *Address:* 26 avenue Pierre 1er de Serbie, 75116 Paris, France; 15 rue du Nord, 1180 Roulle, Switzerland (home).

GODBER, John Harry, OBE, BEd, MA, PhD, FRSA; British playwright, film and theatre director and actor; b. 18 May 1956, Upton, Yorks.; s. of Harry Godber and Dorothy Godber; m. Jane Thornton; two d.; ed Minsthorpe High, Bretton Hall Coll., Wakefield, Univ. of Leeds; fmr Head of Drama, Minsthorpe High; Artistic Dir Hull Truck Theatre Co. 1984–; apptd Prof. of Contemporary Theatre, Liverpool Hope Univ. 2004, currently Sr Lecturer, Dance, Drama and Performance Studies Dept; fmr Prof. of Drama, Univ. of Hull; est. John Godber Co.; Hon. Lecturer, Bretton Hall Coll.; Hon. DLitt (Hull) 1988, (Lincoln) 1997, Hon. DUniv; Sunday Times Playwright Award 1981, Olivier Award 1984, Joseph Jefferson Award, Chicago 1988, Fringe First Winner (five times), BAFTA Awards for Best Schools Drama and for Best Original Drama 2005. *Plays include:* Happy Jack 1982, September in the Rain 1983, Up 'n' Under (Laurence Olivier Comedy of the Year Award 1984) 1984, Bouncers (seven Los Angeles Critics' Awards 1986) 1985, Blood, Sweat and Tears 1986, Shakers, Teechers 1987, Salt of the Earth 1988, On the Piste 1990, Happy Families 1991, April in Paris 1992, The Office Party, Passion Killers 1994, Lucky Sods 1995, Dracula 1995, Gym and Tonic 1996, Weekend Breaks 1997, It Started with a Kiss 1997, Unleashed 1998, Perfect Pitch, Thick as a Brick (music by John Pattison) 1999, Big Trouble in Little Bedroom 1999, Seasons in the Sun 2000, On a Night Like This 2000, This House 2001, Departures 2001, Moby Dick 2002, Men of the World 2002, Reunion 2002, Next Best Thing 2007, Sold 2007, Our House 2008, Funny Turns 2009, 20,000 Leagues Under the Sea 2010, The Debt Collectors 2011, The Sculptor's Surprise 2011, Lost and Found 2012, Losing The Plot 2013, A Kind of Loving 2013, Shafted 2015, This Might Hurt 2016; also radio plays and TV programmes. *Film:* Up 'n' Under (writer and dir) 1998. *Television:* The Ritz (BBC 2 series) 1987, The Continental (BBC Christmas Special), My Kingdom for a Horse (BBC film) 1991, Chalkface (BBC series) 1991, Bloomin' Marvellous (BBC comedy series) 1997, Thunder Road (BBC 4 film) 2001, Portas, Os 2005; has also written numerous episodes of Brookside, Crown Court and Grange Hill. *Leisure interests:* skiing, sport, literature, reading. *Address:* c/o Alan Brodie Representation Ltd, Paddock Suite, The Courtyard, 55 Charterhouse Street, London, EC1M 6HA, England (office); St Nicholas Swanland, North Ferriby, HU14 3QY, England (home). *Telephone:* (1482) 633854 (home). *E-mail:* johnhgodber@hotmail.com.

GODDARD, Joseph Evan, DLS, MSc, JP; Barbadian industrial relations consultant and diplomatist; b. 5 Aug. 1942, Bequest, St Philip; s. of Tilveal Ishmael and Violet Leotta Goddard; m. Nadine Pamela Goddard; one s. one d.; ed Ruskin Coll. and London School of Econs, UK; Asst Gen. Sec. Nat. Union of Public Workers 1973–77, Gen. Sec. 1977–2007; Gen. Sec. Caribbean Public Services Asscn 1982–97, Exec. Mem. 1997–2006; mem. Exec. Bd Public Services Int. (PSI) 1994–97, Regional Rep., PSI Public Sector Working Group 2003–06; Amb. and Perm. Rep. to UN, New York 2010–15; mem. Bd Barbados Nat. Productivity Council 1996–2006, Barbados Airport Inc. 2000–06, Congress of Trade Unions and Staff Asscns of Barbados (CTUSAB) 1998–2006 (Vice-Pres. 2000–04); mem. Bd of Dirs Barbados Consumer Research Org. 2005–; Keys to City of Shanghai, Govt of China 2001; numerous awards, including Award of Excellence, Caribbean Congress of Labour 2007, Pride of Barbados Award 2007, CTUSAB Lifetime Award 2008, Gold Crown of Merit 2017.

GODDARD, William (Bill) Andrew, III, BS, PhD, FRSC; American chemist, materials scientist, applied physicist and academic; *Charles and Mary Ferkel Professor of Chemistry, Materials Science and Applied Physics and Director, Materials and Process Simulation Center, Beckman Institute, California Institute of Technology;* b. 29 March 1937, El Centro, Calif.; s. of William A. Goddard II and Barbara Worth Bright; m. Yvonne Amelia Goddard; one s. three d.; ed Univ. of California, Los Angeles, California Inst. of Tech.; Asst Prof. of Theoretical Chem., California Inst. of Tech. 1965, Assoc. Prof. and Prof. –1978, Prof. of Chem. and Applied Physics 1978–84, Dir NSF Materials Research Group 1984–90, Charles and Mary Ferkel Prof. of Chem. and Applied Physics 1984–2001, Charles and Mary Ferkel Prof. of Chem., Materials Science and Applied Physics 2001–, Dir Materials and Process Simulation Center, Beckman Inst. 1990–, Dir NSF Grand Challenges Applications Group 1992–97; World Class Univ. Prof., Energy Environment Water Susceptibility Grad. School, KAIST, Daejeon, S Korea 2009–13; Centenary Prof., Indian Inst. of Science, Bengaluru 2015; Co-founder Molecular Simulations Inc. (now Accelrys) 1984 (Dir 1984–95, Chair. 1984–91), Schrödinger Inc. 1990 (Dir 1990–2000), AquaNano LLC 2010, VelvEtch LLC 2018; Chair. Material Science Advisory Bd; mem. Materials Research Soc., ACS, NAS 1984, Int. Acad. of Quantum Molecular Science 1988; Fellow, American Physical Soc. 1988, AAAS 1990, American Acad. of Arts and Sciences 2010; Hon. Philosophia Doctorem, Chem. (Uppsala) 2004; ACS Buck-Whitney Medal 1978, ACS Award for Computers in Chem. 1988, Calif. Inst. of Tech. Richard M. Badger Teaching Prize in Chem. 1995, Foresight Inst. Feynman Prize 1999, NASA Space Sciences Award 2000, 2009, 2012, ACS Richard Chase Tolman Prize 2000, ISI most Highly-Cited Chemist 1981–99, Inst. of Molecular Manufacturing Prize in Computational Nanotechnology Design 2002, ACS Award in Theoretical Chem. 2007, Award for Distinguished Scientific Achievement in Catalysis, 7th World Congress on Oxidation Catalysis 2013, appeared on list of ISI most highly-cited chemists 2014, 2015, 2016. *Publications:* 1,040 publs in scientific books and journals. *Address:* Beckman Institute (139–74), California Institute of Technology, 1200 East California Boulevard, Pasadena, CA 91125, USA (office). *Telephone:* (626) 395-3093 (office). *Fax:* (626) 395-8100 (office). *E-mail:* wag@wag.caltech.edu (office). *Website:* www.wag.caltech.edu (office).

GODDIO, Franck, BSc; French archaeologist; *President, Institut Européen d'Archéologie Sous-Marine (IEASM);* b. 1947, Casablanca, Morocco; ed Ecole Nat. de la Statistique Admin. Economique, Paris; adviser to various int. orgs; gained experience in marine archaeology in late 1970s; Pres. Institut Européen d'Archéologie Sous Marine, Paris (IEASM) 1987–; excavated historically important sunken ships and discovered submerged ruins of Alexandria, sunken cities of Thonis-Heracleion and Canopus in Aboukir Bay off the coast of Egypt; Sr Visiting Lecturer, School of Archaeology, Univ. of Oxford 2009, Visiting Prof. of Maritime Archaeology 2018; Légion d'honneur 2009. *Publications:* several books and scientific articles. *Address:* Institut Européen d'Archéologie Sous-Marine, 75, rue de Grenelle, 75007 Paris, France (office). *E-mail:* info@franckgoddio.org (office). *Website:* www.franckgoddio.org (office).

GODFREY, Malcolm Paul Weston, CBE, MB, BS, FRCP; British medical practitioner (retd); b. 11 Aug. 1926, London; s. of Harry Godfrey and Rose Godfrey; m. Barbara Goldstein 1955; one s. two d. (one deceased); ed Hertford Grammar School, King's Coll., London, King's Coll. Hosp. Medical School; various appointments in Nat. Health Service 1950–60; Fellow in Medicine and Asst Physician, Johns Hopkins Hosp. Baltimore, Md 1957–58; HQ staff, MRC 1960–74; Dean, Royal Postgraduation Medical School, Hammersmith Hosp. 1974–83; Second Sec., MRC 1983–88; Queen's Hon. Physician 1987–90; Chair. Public Health Lab. Service Bd 1989–96, United Medical and Dental Schools of Guys and St Thomas' Hosps 1996–98; mem. Soc. of Scholars, Johns Hopkins Univ. (USA) 2000; Fellow, Royal Postgraduate Medical School 1985, Imperial Coll. School of Medicine 1999, King's Coll., London 2000; Pres. King's Coll. London Asscn 2002–04; Univ. of London Gold Medal 1950. *Publications include:* articles on cardio-respiratory disorders in medical and scientific journals. *Leisure interests:* theatre, reading, current affairs, walking. *Address:* 17 Clifton Hill, St John's Wood, London, NW8 0QE, England (home). *Telephone:* (20) 7624-6335 (home). *Fax:* (20) 7328-9474 (home). *E-mail:* malcolmpgodfrey@talktalk.net.

GODLEE, Fiona N., MB, BChir, FRCP; British physician, editor, writer and publisher; *Editor-in-Chief, British Medical Journal;* b. 4 Aug. 1961; m.; two c.; ed Univ. of Cambridge; apptd Asst Ed., British Medical Journal (BMJ) 1990, Editorial Dir, establishing open-access online publr BioMed Central, Current Science Group 2000–03, Head of Knowledge Div. BMJ Publishing Group 2003–04, Ed.-in-Chief British Medical Journal 2005–; Harkness Fellow, Harvard Univ. 1994–95; Co-Ed. Peer Review in Health Sciences; fmr Pres. World Asscn of Medical Eds 1998–2000; Chair., Cttee on Publication Ethics 2003–05; Vice-Chair. Climate and Health Council; mem. Advisory Bd Nordic Cochrane Centre, Health Improvement Studies Inst., Peer Review Congress, Evidence Live, UK Health Alliance on Climate Change; Sr Visiting Fellow, Inst. of Public Health, Univ. of Cambridge; Hon. Prof. Netherlands School for Primary Care Research, Hon. Fellow, Royal Coll. of General Practitioners. *Address:* BMJ Publishing Group Ltd, BMA House, Tavistock Square, London, WC1H 9JR, England (office). *Telephone:* (20) 3655-5352 (office). *E-mail:* fgodlee@bmj.com (office). *Website:* www.bmj.com (office).

GODMANIS, Ivars, DrPhys; Latvian scientist and politician; b. 27 Nov. 1951, Rīga; s. of Teodors Godmanis and Ingrida Godmanis; m. Ramora Godmanē 1978; two s. one d.; ed Univ. of Latvia; mem. staff, Inst. of Solid-State Physics, Univ. of Latvia 1973–86, Lecturer, Univ. of Latvia 1986–90; involved in Movt for Independence of Latvia, Deputy Chair., People's Front; Chair. Council of Ministers of Repub. of Latvia (Prime Minister) 1990–93; with commercial co. Software House 1994–95; Vice-Chair. Asscn of Commercial Banks of Latvia 1995–96; Pres. Latvia Savings Bank (jt stock co.) 1996–97; mem. Saeima (Parl.) 1998–2009; Minister of Finance 1998–99, of the Interior 2006–07, Prime Minister of Latvia 2007–09 (resgnd); MEP 2009–; Programme Man. JSC Radio SWH 2003–; Chair. Latvia's Way (Latvijas ceļš) 2004–07, Co-Chair. Latvian First Party/Latvian Way (Latvijas Pirmā Partija/Latvijas ceļš) 2007–; mem. Bd JSC Latvian Shipping Co. 1997–98, JSC Saliena Real 2002–04; Order of the Three Stars (Second Class); Commemorative medal for participation in the barricades of 1991. *Leisure interest:* tennis. *Address:* European Parliament, ASP 10G153, 60, rue Wiertz, 1047 Brussels, Belgium (office). *E-mail:* ivars.godmanis@europarl.europa.eu (office). *Website:* www.europarl.europa.eu (office).

GODOVSKY, Yan; Russian ballet dancer; *Assistant Ballet Artistic Director, Bolshoi Ballet;* b. 29 April 1974, Tbilisi, Georgia; ed Moscow Coll. of Choreography (now Moscow Acad. of Choreography); joined Bolshoi Theatre Co. 1993, becoming leading soloist, Asst Ballet Artistic Dir 2011–; Golden Mask Nat. Theatre Prize 2006, Ballet magazine Soul of Dance Prize 2008. *Roles danced include:* He-Devil (Nutcracker) 1993, Conrad (Tikhon Khrennikov's Love for Love) 1994, Peasant Pas de Deux (Giselle) 1994, Boy (La Sylphide) 1994, Jig (Don Quixote) 1994, Fool (Swan Lake) 1995, Pas d'Action (Giselle) 1997, Mime (Spartacus) 1997, Friend to Prince (Swan Lake) 1998, French Doll (Nutcracker) 1999, Nutcracker-Prince (Nutcracker) 2000, Alain (La Fille mal gardée) 2002, Magedaveya, Dance with drum (La Bayadère) 2002, Romeo (Romeo and Juliet) 2003, Tarantella 2004, Yan (Dmitry Shostakovich's Bolt) 2005, Soloist (Igor Stravinsky's Jeu de cards) 2005, Pas d'Esclaves (Le Corsaire) 2007, James (La Sylphide) 2008. *Address:* Bolshoi Theatre, 125009 Moscow, Teatralnaya sq., 1, Russia (office). *Telephone:* (495) 692-08-18 (office). *Fax:* (495) 692-33-67 (office). *E-mail:* pr@bolshoi.ru (office). *Website:* www.bolshoi.ru (office).

GODREJ, Adi Burjor, MS; Indian industrialist; *Chairman, Godrej Group;* b. 3 April 1942, Bombay (now Mumbai); s. of Dr Burjor Pirojsha Godrej and Jai Burjor Godrej; m. Parmeshwar Mader 1966; one s. two d.; ed St Xavier's High School and Coll., Bombay, Massachusetts Inst. of Tech., USA; Chair. Godrej Group, Godrej Industries Ltd, Godrej Consumer Products Ltd, Godrej Properties Ltd, Godrej Hershey Ltd; mem. Bd of Dirs Godrej & Boyce Manufacturing Co. Ltd, Godrej Agrovet Ltd, Godrej International Ltd; fmr Chair. and Pres. Indian Soap & Toiletries Makers' Asscn, Central Org. for Oil Industry and Trade, Solvent Extractors' Asscn of India, Compound Livestock Feeds Mfrs' Asscn, Indo-American Soc., Governing Council of Narsee Monjee Inst. of Man. Studies; fmr mem. Dean's Advisory Council, MIT Sloan School of Man., Wharton Asian Exec. Bd; Chair. Bd, Indian School of Business; fmr Pres. Confed. of Indian Industry; Patron Himalayan Club; Rajiv Gandhi Award 2002, Entrepreneur of the Year, Asia Pacific Entrepreneurship Awards 2010, Best Businessman of the Year, GQ Men of the Year Awards 2010, Chemexcil's Life Time Achievement Award 2010, AIMA-JRD Tata Corp. Leadership Award 2010, American India Foundation Leadership in Philanthropy Award 2010, BMA Management Man of the Year Award 2010–11, Qimpro Platinum Standard Award for Business 2011, Ernst & Young Entrepreneur of the Year 2012, Padma Bhushan 2013, Asian Awards Entrepreneur of the Year 2013, All India Man. Asscn Business Leader of the Year 2014, 2015, The Clinton Global Citizen Award 2016, The Lifetime Achievement Award, CNBC Awaaz Real Estate Awards 2016, Global Leadership Award, US India Business Council Leadership Summit 2017, Lifetime Achievement Award, Forbes India Leadership Awards 2017. *Leisure interests:* boating, waterskiing, windsurfing, horse riding, bridge. *Address:* Godrej Industries Ltd, Pirojshanagar, Eastern Express Highway, Vikhroli, Mumbai 400 079 (office); Aashraye Godrej House, 67-H Walkeshwar Road, Mumbai 400 006, India (home). *Telephone:* (22) 25188060 (office); (22) 25188010 (office); (22) 23642956 (home). *Fax:* (22) 25188062 (office); (22) 23645159 (home). *E-mail:* abg@godrej.com (office); ab.godrej@godrejcp.com (office). *Website:* www.godrejindustries.com (office).

GODSELL, Robert (Bobby) Michael, BA, MA; South African business executive; *Chairman, Business Leadership South Africa;* b. 14 Sept. 1952, Boksburg; s. of Cyril H. Godsell and Winnefred Godsell (née Stephens); m. Gillian Hall 1975; three d.; ed Grosvenor Boys' High School, Univ. of Natal, Univ. of Cape Town; Deputy Prov. Leader Progressive Party, Natal 1969–70, Nat. Youth Chair. 1975–76; Dir Industrial Relations and Public Affairs, Anglo-American Corpn 1974–95, CEO Gold Div. 1995–2007, Deputy Chair. 1995–96, Chair. 1996–99, Dir (non-exec.) 1999–2008, Chair. and CEO AngloGold Ltd 2000–04, CEO AngloGold Ashanti (after Anglo merger with Ashanti Goldfields Co. Ltd) 2004–07; Chair. (non-exec.) Eskom Holdings Ltd 2008–09, World Gold Council 2001–02, Business Unity SA, Business Leadership SA, Freeworld Coatings; Co-Chair. Millennium Labour Council; Vice-Pres. Chamber of Mines 1991–97, Pres. 1992, 1997–98; currently Chair. Business Leadership South Africa; Co-Chair. Millennium Labour Council; mem. Bd of Dirs Optimum Coal Holdings Ltd 2010–12, Industrial Devt Corpn of South Africa Ltd 2011–, JSC Polymetal 2011–; fmr mem. Bd of Dirs (non-exec.) Standard Bank Group Ltd, Housing for Africa; apptd mem. Nat. Econ. Forum 1994, Nat. Planning Comm. 2010–; fmr mem. Buthelezi Comm.; Hon. Prof., Wits Business School. *Publications include:* A Future South Africa: Visions, Strategies and Realities 1988 (co-ed.). *Leisure interest:* squash. *Address:* Business Leadership South Africa, PO Box 7006, Johannesburg 2000, South Africa (office). *Telephone:* (11) 3564650 (office). *Fax:* (11) 7264705 (office). *E-mail:* businessleadership@businessleadership.org.za (home). *Website:* www.businessleadership.org.za (office).

GODSOE, Peter C., OC, BSc, MBA, FCA; Canadian business executive; b. 2 May 1938, Toronto; s. of Joseph Gerald Godsoe and Margaret Graham Cowperthwaite; m. Shelagh Cathleen Reburn 1963; one s. two d.; ed Univ. of Toronto, Harvard Univ., USA; fmr Deputy Chair., Pres. and CEO Bank of Nova Scotia, Chair. and CEO 1995–2004, also Chair. Bank of Nova Scotia Int. 1995–2004, now Hon. Dir fmr Chair. and Dir Scotia Centre Ltd, Scotia Futures Ltd, Scotia Mortgage Corpn; fmr Vice-Chair. and Dir Bank of Nova Scotia Properties Inc., Scotia Properties Québec Inc., Scotia Realty Ltd; Chair. Sobeys Inc., Fairmont Hotels and Resorts Inc. 2004–06; Vice-Chair. Atlantic Inst. for Market Research; mem. Bd of Dirs Barrick Gold Corpn 2004–10, Ingersoll-Rand Co. Ltd 1998–13, Onex Corpn 2004–, Rogers Communications Inc. 2004–14, Templeton Emerging Markets Investment Trust PLC 2003–08, Canadian Council of Christians and Jews, Mount Sinai Hosp., Lonmin PLC 2001–10, Warranty Group, Miller Thomson Foundation; fmr Chair. Canadian Bankers Asscn; Chancellor, Univ. of Western Ontario 1996–2000; Fellow, Inst. of Chartered Accountants; Hon. Commdr, OJ 2004; Order of Ontario 2009; Dr hc (Univ. of King's Coll.) 1993, (Concordia Univ.) 1995, (Univ. of Western Ontario) 2001, (Dalhousie Univ.) 2004; elected to Canadian Business Hall of Fame 2002, Ivey Business Leader Award, Univ. of Western Ontario 2005.

GODSON, Anthony; British fmr diplomatist and charity administrator; b. 1 Feb. 1948, London; s. of Percival Lawrence Godson and Kathleen Elizabeth Godson (née Jennings); m. Maryan Jane Margaret Godson (née Hurst); joined FCO 1968, Attaché, Bucharest 1970–71, Third Sec., Kuala Lumpur 1972–73, Jakarta 1973–76, Pvt. Sec. to British High Commr, Canberra 1976–79, Cen. African Dept, FCO 1980–82, Second, later First Sec., UK Perm. Mission, New York 1983–86, First Sec. and Consul, Kinshasa 1987–88, Head of Indo-China Section, later Deputy Head of SE Asian Dept, FCO 1988–89, Deputy Head of Mission, Bucharest 1989–91, First Sec., UK Mission, Geneva 1992–95, Deputy Head of Eastern European and Cen. Asia Dept, FCO 1996–98, Counsellor, Later Deputy Head of Mission and Consul General, Jakarta 1998–2002, FCO 2003–04, High Commr to Mauritius (also accred as Amb. to the Comoros and to Madagascar) 2004–07, Sensitivity Reviewer, FCO 2012–; Exec. Dir Prospect Burma (charity) 2007–10. *Leisure interests:* tennis, skiing, walking, classical music, reading, photography.

GODWIN, Gail Kathleen, PhD; American writer; b. 18 June 1937, Birmingham, Ala; d. of Mose Godwin and Kathleen Krahenbuhl; m. 1st Douglas Kennedy 1960 (divorced 1961); m. 2nd Ian Marshall 1965 (divorced 1966); ed Peace Jr Coll., Univs of North Carolina and Iowa; news reporter, Miami Herald 1959–60; reporter and consultant, US Travel Service, London 1961–65; Editorial Asst, Saturday Evening Post 1966; Fellow, Center for Advanced Study, Univ. of Illinois 1971–72; Lecturer, Iowa Writers Workshop 1972–73, Vassar Coll. 1977, Columbia Univ. Writing Program 1978, 1981; American specialist, USIS 1976; Guggenheim Fellow 1975–76; mem. PEN, Authors Guild, Authors League, Nat. Book Critics' Circle; American Acad. and Inst. of Arts and Letters Literature Award 1981. *Publications include:* novels including: The Perfectionists 1970, Glass People 1972, The Odd Woman 1974, Violet Clay 1978, A Mother and Two Daughters 1982, The Finishing School 1985, A Southern Family 1987, Father Melancholy's Daughter 1991, The Good Husband 1994, Evensong 1998, Evenings At Five 2003, Queen of the Underworld 2005, Unfinished Desires 2009, Flora 2013; non-fiction: Heart 2001; The Making of A Writer: Journals (ed.) 1961–63 Vol. 1 2006, Vol. 2 2011, Publishing: A Writer's Memoir 2015; also short stories, uncollected stories, novellas and librettos. *Address:* PO Box 946, Woodstock, NY 12498-0946, USA (office). *E-mail:* gail@gailgodwin.com (office). *Website:* www.gailgodwin.com.

GOEDGEDRAG, Frits Martinus de los Santos, LLM; Dutch government official; b. 1 Nov. 1951, Aruba; m. Dulcie Yvonne Terborg; three s.; ed High School, Colegio Arubano, Catholic Univ. of Nijmegen; legal adviser, Dept of Legal and General Affairs 1977–81; Sec. to the Island Territory of Bonaire 1981–92; Sec. to Council of Govs 1981–92; Gov. of Island Territory of Bonaire 1992–98; Attorney-Gen. 1998–2002; Gov. of Netherlands Antilles 2002–10 (last gov. before dissolution of Netherlands Antilles); Gov. of Curaçao 2010–12; Pres. Requisition Cttee Public Prosecutor, Application Comm. for the position of Dir of Dept of Justice; Pres. Judicial Governmental Del. to Netherlands 1998, to Belgium 2000, to Italy 2001;

mem. State Council 2013–; mem. Supervisory Bd Drug Rehabilitation Centre (Brasami), Curaçao, Selection Cttee for Public Servants Judicial Trainees (RAIO), and numerous other govt cttees; mem. Supervisory Bd Antillean Airlines Co., ALM, Cttee of Appeal of Football League of Bonaire, Bd Nat. Parks Foundation (Stinapa), Bonaire, Recompression Tanks Foundation, Zuster Maria Höppner Foundation, Jumpers basketball team, Bonaire; Hon. mem. Rotary Club of Curaçao 2004–; Kt, Order of Orange Nassau 1998; Naval Medal 'Almirante Luis Brion' for Distinguished Services Rendered to Venezuelan Navy 1994; Person of the Year, Bonaire Lions Club 1992.

GOEHR, Alexander, MA; British composer and academic; *Professor Emeritus of Music, University of Cambridge;* b. 10 Aug. 1932, Berlin, Germany; s. of Walter Goehr and Laelia Goehr; m. 1st Audrey Baker 1954; m. 2nd Anthea Felicity Staunton 1972; m. 3rd Amira Katz; one s. three d.; ed Berkhamsted School, Royal Manchester Coll. of Music, Paris Conservatoire (with Olivier Messiaen) and privately with Yvonne Loriod; composer, teacher, conductor 1956–; held classes at Morley Coll., London; part-time post with BBC, responsible for production of orchestral concerts 1960–; works performed and broadcast world-wide; awarded Churchill Fellowship 1968; Composer-in-Residence, New England Conservatory, Boston, Mass. 1968–69; Assoc. Prof. of Music, Yale Univ. 1969–70; Prof., West Riding Chair of Music, Univ. of Leeds 1971–76; Prof. of Music, Univ. of Cambridge 1976–99, Prof. Emer. 1999–, Fellow of Trinity Hall, Cambridge 1976–; Reith Lecturer 1987; Hon. Prof., Beijing Univ. 2001; Hon. mem. American Acad. and Inst. of Arts and Letters; Hon. ARCM 1976; Hon. FRNCM 1980; Hon. FRCM 1981; Hon. DMus (Southampton) 1973, (Manchester), (Nottingham) 1994, (Siena) 1999; Dr hc (Cambridge) 2000. *Compositions include:* Songs of Babel 1951, Sonata 1952, Fantasias 1954, Capriccio 1957, The Deluge 1957–58, La belle dame sans merci 1958, Four Songs from the Japanese 1959, Sutter's Gold 1959–60, Hecuba's Lament 1959–61, Suite 1961, A Little Cantata of Proverbs 1962, Two Choruses 1962, Virtutes 1963, Little Symphony 1963, Little Music for Strings 1963, Five Poems and an Epigram of William Blake 1964, Pastorals 1965, Piano Trio 1966, Arden muss sterben (Arden Must Die, opera) 1966, Warngedichte 1967, Romanza 1968, Naboth's Vineyard 1968, Nonomiya 1969, Paraphrase 1969, Symphony in One Movement 1970, Shadowplay 1970, Sonata about Jerusalem 1970, Concerto for Eleven Instruments 1970, Chaconne for Wind 1974, Lyric Pieces 1974, Metamorphosis/Dance 1974, Fugue on the Notes of the Fourth Psalm 1976, Romanza on the Notes of the Fourth Psalm 1977, Prelude and Fugue for three clarinets 1978, Chaconne for organ 1979, Das Gesetz der Quadrille 1979, Babylon the Great is Fallen 1979, Behold the Sun 1984, Two Imitations of Baudelaire 1985, Symphony with Chaconne 1986, Eve Dreams in Paradise 1987, Carol for St Steven 1989, ...in real time 1989, Sing, Ariel 1989, Still Lands 1990, Bach Variations 1990, The Death of Moses 1991, The Mouse Metamorphosed into a Maid 1991, Colossus or Panic 1992, I Said, I Will Take Heed 1993, Cambridge Hocket 1993, Arianna (opera) 1995, Schlussgesang 1997, Kantan (opera) 2000, Piano Quintet 2001, Second Musical Offering (GFH) 2002, Marching to Carcassonne 2003, Adagio (Autoporträt) 2003, Dark Days 2004, Fantasie 2005, Broken Lute 2006, Since Brass, Nor Stone (British Composer Award for Best Chamber Music Composition 2009) 2008, Manere 2008, Broken Psalm 2009, TurmMusik/Tower Music 2009–10, from Shadow of Night 2009–10, Hymn to Night 2010, When Adam Fell 2010–11, Cities and Thrones and Powers 2011, Pomfret. The Dungeon of the Castle 2012, Largo Siciliano 2012, To These Dark Steps/The Fathers Are Watching 2012, ...between the Lines/...zwischen den Zeilen 2013, Seven Impromptus 2014, Vanishing Word 2014–15. *Address:* c/o Schott Music, 48 Great Marlborough Street, London, W1F 7BB, England (home). *E-mail:* promotions@schott-music.com (home). *Website:* www.schott-music.com.

GOEI, Glen, BA, MA; Singaporean film and theatre director; *Associate Artistic Director, W!ld Rice Theatre Co.;* b. 22 Dec. 1962; ed Univ. of Cambridge, UK, New York Univ., USA; f. Mu-Lan Arts, London, Artistic Dir 1990–98; Creative Dir, Singapore Nat. Day Parade 2003, 2004, Singapore Pavilion for World Expo, Nagoya, Japan 2005; Assoc. Artistic Dir W!ld Rice Theatre Co.; Dir Dream Academy; Nat. Youth Council Award (Excellence) 1994. *Plays include:* with Mu-Lan Arts: Madame Mao's Memories 1991, 1993, Porcelain (London Fringe Awards Best Play, Best Production) 1992, The Magic Fundoshi (Best Comedy) 1993, 1994, Three Japanese Women 1993; in Singapore: Into the Woods 1994, Kampong Amber (Singapore Arts Festival headline event) 1994, Land of a Thousand Dreams 1995; with W!ld Rice: Blithe Spirit 2001, Boeing Boeing 2002, 2005, The Magic Fundoshi 2006, The Importance of Being Earnest 2009; with Dream Academy: Revenge of the Dim Sum Dollies 2004, The History of Singapore, The Little Shop of Horrors 2006. *Films:* Forever Fever (writer, dir and producer) 1998, The Blue Mansion 2009, I Have Loved (actor) 2011, Pontianak 2015. *Publications include:* Little Red in the Hood 2014. *Address:* W!ld Rice Theatre Co, 3A Kerbau Road, 219142, Singapore. *Telephone:* 6292-2695 (office). *Fax:* 6292-2249 (office). *E-mail:* info@wildrice.com.sg (office). *Website:* www.wildrice.com.sg (office).

GOEMAERE, Eric, MSc, MD; Belgian physician and international organization executive; *HIV/TB Unit Coordinator, South African Medical Unit;* ed Leuven Univ., Inst. of Tropical Medicine, Antwerp; fmr Head Mission in South Africa, Médecins Sans Frontières (MSF – Doctors Without Borders); currently HIV/TB Unit Coodinator, South African Medical Unit (SAMU); est. training programme for primary health care, Univ. of Cape Town; Co-founder Jt Civil Soc. Monitoring Forum; fmr adviser to WHO; Lecturer, Univ. of Witwatersrand; mem. South African AIDS Council; Hon. Sr Lecturer, School of Public Health and Family Medicine; Hon. DrSci (Univ. of Cape Town) 2008. *Address:* South African Medical Unit, Office 303 A&B, Building 20, Waverley Business Park, Wyecroft Road, Mowbray 7925, Cape Town, South Africa (office). *Telephone:* (21) 448-1058 (office). *E-mail:* tandi.gadla@joburg.msf.org (office). *Website:* www.samumsf.org (office).

GOENKA, Harsh Vardhan, MBA; Indian business executive; *Chairman, RPG Group;* b. 10 Dec. 1957, Calcutta; s. of Rama Prasad Goenka and Sushila Goenka; m. Mala Sanghi 1977; one s. one d.; ed St Xavier's Coll., Calcutta, IMD (Int. Inst. of Managerial Devt), Lausanne, Switzerland; joined family business RPG Enterprises, Vice-Chair. CEAT Ltd (part of RPG group) 1983, Chair. RPG Enterprises (now RPG Group) 1988–, also Chair. RPG Life Science, KEC Int. Ltd, RPG Cables, Bayer (India) Ltd, Zensar Technologies Ltd, CEAT Ltd; Dir (non-exec.) Bajaj Electricals; mem. Exec. Cttee Fed. of Indian Chambers of Commerce and Industry; Bd mem. IMD, Lausanne, Switzerland; fmr Pres. Indian Merchants' Chamber; mem. Bd of Govs Nat. Inst. of Industrial Eng; Lakshya Business Visionary Award. *Leisure interests:* sports, art. *Address:* RPG Group, RPG House, 463 Dr Annie Besant Road, Worli Mumbai 400 030, India. *Telephone:* (22) 24930621 (office); (22) 23630873 (home). *Fax:* (22) 24938933 (office). *E-mail:* hgoenka@rpg.in (office). *Website:* www.rpg.in (office).

GOENKA, Viveck; Indian engineer and newspaper executive; *Chairman, Press Trust of India;* b. (Vivek Khaitan), s. of A. M. Khaitan and Krishna Khaitan; m. 1st Ananya Goenka; m. 2nd Zita Goenka; Chair. and Man. Dir The Indian Express Ltd; mem. Exec. Cttee and fmr Pres. Indian Newspaper Soc. (INS); mem. Bd of Dirs United News of India; mem. Bd of Dirs The Press Trust of India Ltd, Chair. 2017–; mem. Council, Audit Bureau of Circulation. *Address:* The Press Trust of India Limited, PTI Building, 4, Parliament Street, New Delhi 110 001, India (office). *Telephone:* (11) 23716621 (office). *Fax:* (11) 23718714 (office). *E-mail:* trans@pti.in (office). *Website:* www.ptinews.com (office).

GOERENS, Charles; Luxembourg politician; b. 6 Feb. 1952, Ettelbruck; m.; three c.; ed Lycée Technique Agricole; mem. Parl. (Northern Dist constituency) for Parti Démocratique 1979; mem. European Parl. (Liberal and Democratic Group) 1982–84, (Group of the European Liberal, Democrat and Reform Party) 1994–99, (Group of the Alliance of Liberals and Democrats for Europe) 2009–; Pres. Ass. of WEU (Interparliamentary European Security and Defence Ass.) 1987–90, 2004; Chair. Parti Démocratique 1989–94, Chair. Political Group 2006–09; Minister for Co-operation, Humanitarian Action and Defence, and for the Environment 1999–2004, of Foreign Affairs 20–31 July 2004; Pres. Sahel and West Africa Club, OECD 2006–09; mem. Consultative Ass. of Council of Europe. *Address:* European Parliament, Bât. Altiero Spinelli, 09G157, 60 rue Wiertz, 1047 Brussels, Belgium (office). *Telephone:* (2) 284-56-12 (office). *Fax:* (2) 284-96-12 (office). *E-mail:* anne.daems@europarl.europa.eu (office). *Website:* www.europarl.europa.eu/meps/en/840/CHARLES_GOERENS_home.html (office); www.charlesgoerens.eu.

GOERNE, Matthias; German singer (baritone); b. 31 March 1967, Weimar; s. of Dieter Görne (former intendant of Dresdner Schauspielhaus) and Jutta Görne; ed Leipzig Univ. of Music and Theatre 'Felix Mendelssohn Bartholdy' with Prof. Hans-Joachim Beyer, then with Dietrich Fischer-Dieskau and Elisabeth Schwarzkopf; performed with the children's choir at Chemnitz Opera; sang in Bach's St Matthew Passion under Kurt Masur, Leipzig 1990; appearances with NDR Symphony Orchestra Hamburg; further engagements under Horst Stein, with Bamberg Symphony Orchestra and in Hindemith's Requiem under Wolfgang Sawallisch; concerts at Leipzig Gewandhaus under Helmuth Rilling and in Amsterdam and Paris; Lieder recitals and records with pianists Eric Schneider, Vladimir Ashkenazy, Alfred Brendel, Christoph Eschenbach and Leif Ove Andsnes at Wigmore Hall, London, Carnegie Hall, New York, festivals in Edinburgh, Lucerne, and Salzburg; sang title role in Henze's Prinz von Homburg, Cologne 1992, Marcello in La Bohème at Komische Oper, Berlin 1993, Wolfram in Tannhäuser, Cologne 1996, Die Schöne Müllerin, Bath 1997; Papageno in Die Zauberflöte, Salzburg Festival 1997; Wozzeck at The Royal Opera House, Covent Garden 2002; role of Kasim in Henze's L'Upupa 2003, Salzburg Festival 2003, repeated in Teatro Real, Madrid 2004; Wozzeck at Saito Kinen Festival with Ozawa in 2004; Papageno at Metropolitan Opera 2005; debut at Vienna State Opera as Wolfram 2010; Bluebeard in Bartók's Duke Bluebeard's Castle at Saito Kinen Festival 2011 and Maggio Musicale in Florence 2012; debut as Kurwenal at Bavarian State Opera, Munich 2012; roles of Kurwenal, Amfortas, and Wozzeck at Vienna State Opera, 2013–14; "Wozzeck", Metropolitan Opera New York 2014; debut as Wotan in Wagner's Rheingold in Hong Kong; concert performances with all major orchestras in Europe and US including Amsterdam Concertgebouworkester, Berliner Philharmoniker, Boston Symphony, Chicago Symphony, London Symphony, London Philharmonic, Los Angeles Philharmonic, New York Philharmonic, Orchestre de Paris; tour with Wiener Philharmoniker 2011; Prof. of Lieder Interpretation, Schumann Hochschule, Dusseldorf 2001–05. *Recordings include:* Matthäuspassion 1994, Winterreise 1997, Entarte Musik, Arias, J.S. Bach Cantatas, Eisler's Deutsche Sinfonie, The Hollywood Songbook, Mahler's Des Knaben Wunderhorn, Mendelssohn's Paulus Oratorio op. 36, Schubert's Schwanengesang, Die Schöne Müllerin, Winterreise, Goethe-Lieder, Messe D950, Liederkreis, Schumann's Dichterliebe; Performances and recordings: of Bartók's Bluebeard and Britten's War Requiem, first performances of works by Hans Werner Henze L'upupa, Thomas Larcher Böhmen liegt am Meer, and Marc-André Dalbavie; championing 20th-century composers Karl Amadeus Hartmann (Gesangsszene) and Bernd Alois Zimmermann (Ekklesiastische Aktion), Schubert: The Complete Matthias Goerne Lieder Edition 2016, Mahler, Berio: Sinfonia: 10 Frühe Lieder (ECHO Klassik Male Singer of the Year Award 2017) 2016. *Address:* Michael Kocyan Artists Management, Alt-Moabit 104A, 10559 Berlin, Germany (office). *Telephone:* (30) 31004940 (office). *Fax:* (30) 31004984 (office). *E-mail:* artists@kocyan.de (office). *Website:* www.kocyan.de (office); www.matthiasgoerne.de.

GOFF, Gregory J., BS, MBA; American business executive; *Executive Vice Chairman, Marathon Petroleum Corporation;* ed Univ. of Utah; joined Conoco 1981, held several positions in transportation as well as in supply, logistics and trading, served internationally in Europe, Asia and Latin America, Sr Vice-Pres., Commercial, ConocoPhillips 2008–10; Pres. and CEO Andeavor (previously Tesoro Corpn) 2010–18, Exec. Vice-Chair. Marathon Petroleum Corpn (merged with Andeavor in 2018) 2018–; Chair. American Fuel & Petrochemical Manufacturers 2015–; mem. Bd of Dirs DCP Midstream, LLC 2008–10, PolyOne Corpn 2011, MPLX GP LLC 2018–; currently mem. Advisory Bd David Eccles School of Business and Univ. of Utah, Nat. Soc. of High School Scholars. *Address:* Marathon Petroleum Corporation, 539 South Main Street, Findlay, OH 45840, USA (office). *Telephone:* (419) 421-2121 (office). *E-mail:* mediarelations@marathonpetroleum.com (office). *Website:* www.marathonpetroleum.com (office).

GOFF, Philip (Phil) Bruce, MA, MP; New Zealand politician; b. 22 June 1953, Auckland; s. of Bruce Charles Goff and Elaine Loyola Goff; m. Mary Ellen Moriarty 1979; two s. one d.; ed Papatoetoe High School, Univ. of Auckland, Nuffield Coll., Univ. of Oxford; Lecturer in Political Science, Auckland Univ.; field officer in Insurance Workers' Union; fmr Chair. Labour Youth Council; MP for Roskill 1981–90, 1993–96, for New Lynn 1996–99, for Mt Roskill 1999–; Minister of Housing, for the Environment, responsible for Government Life Insurance Corpn, in charge of the Public Trust Office 1986–87, of Employment, of Youth Affairs and Assoc. Minister of Educ. 1987–89, Minister of Tourism 1987–88, of Educ. 1989–90, of Foreign Affairs and Trade and of Justice 1999–2005, Minister of Defence 2005–08; Minister of Trade, of Pacific Island Affairs and for Disarmament and Arms Control Oct. 2005–08, of Corrections 2007–08; British Council Scholarship to Nuffield Coll. 1992; mem. Labour Party 1969–, Leader 2008–11, Leader of the Opposition 2008–11. *Leisure interests:* sports, gardening. *Address:* Executive Wing, Parliament Buildings, Wellington (office); Creightons Road RD 2, Papakura, Auckland, New Zealand (home). *Telephone:* (9) 624-2278 (office); (9) 292-8377 (home). *Fax:* (4) 624-1058 (office). *E-mail:* phil.goff@parliament.govt.nz (office). *Website:* www.labour.org.nz (office).

GOGGIN, Brian J., MSc; Irish banking executive; ed Trinity Coll. Dublin; joined Bank of Ireland 1969, various sr man. roles within Bank of Ireland Group in USA, UK and Ireland, CEO Corp. and Treasury 1996, apptd to Court of Bank of Ireland 2000, CEO Wholesale Financial Services 2002–03, CEO Asset Man. Services 2003–04, Group Chief Exec. 2004–09 (resgnd), also apptd Chair. Bristol & West PLC (subsidiary co.) 2005; Pres. Irish Chapter, Ireland-US Council; Dir Post Office Ltd.

GOGGINS, Colleen A.; American business executive; *Worldwide Chairman, Consumer and Personal Care Group, Johnson & Johnson;* ed Kellogg School of Man., Northwestern Univ.; began working at Johnson & Johnson 1981, has held several sr posts, including Dir of Marketing, Johnson & Johnson GmbH, Germany 1990–92, Pres. Johnson & Johnson Canada 1992–94, Pres. Consumer Products Co. 1995–98, Co. Group Chair. 1998–2001, Worldwide Chair. Consumer and Personal Care Group and mem. Exec. Cttee, Johnson & Johnson 2001–; mem. Exec. Advisory Bd Center for Brand and Product Man., School of Business, Univ. of Wis.-Madison. *Address:* Johnson & Johnson, 1 Johnson & Johnson Plaza, New Brunswick, NJ 08933, USA (office). *Telephone:* (732) 524-0400 (office). *Fax:* (732) 524-3300 (office). *Website:* www.jnj.com (office).

GOGOI, Tarun, BA, LLB; Indian lawyer and politician; b. 1 April 1936, Rangajan Tea Estate, Jorhat Dist; s. of Kamaleswar Gogoi; m. Dolly Gogoi 1972; one s. one d.; ed Gauhati Univ.; mem. Jorhat Municipal Council 1968–71, Leader Assam Youth Community 1971; elected to Lok Sabha 1971–; Jt Sec. All India Congress Cttee 1976, Gen. Sec. 1985; Pres. Assam Pradesh Congress (I) Cttee 1986–90, 1996–2001, Vice-Pres. 1991; Minister of Food 1991–93; Minister of State for Food Processing Industry 1993–95; mem. Assam Legis. Ass. 1997–98; Chief Minister of Assam (Asom) 2001–16 (resgnd); fmr Chair. Assam Small Industrial Devt Corpn, Bharat Yuvak Samaj; fmr Dir Vayudoot; fmr Jt Sec. Jorhat Law Coll.; fmr Commdr Student Volunteer Corps; mem. Consultative Cttee, Ministry of Petroleum and Natural Gas 1998–99, Cttee on Railways 1999–2000, Bar Council Assam, Cttee on Govt Assurances, Cttee on External Affairs; Universal Smile Award 2009. *Leisure interests:* travelling, reading, gardening. *Address:* Nazir Ali, Jorhat 785 001, India (home).

GOH, Chok Tong, MA; Singaporean politician; *Emeritus Senior Minister and Senior Adviser, Monetary Authority of Singapore;* b. 20 May 1941, Pasir Panjang; s. of Goh Kah Khoon and Quah Kwee Hwa; m. Tan Choo Leng 1965; one s. one d. (twins); ed Raffles Inst., Univ. of Singapore and Williams Coll., USA; with Singapore Admin. Service 1964–69, Neptune Orient Lines Ltd 1969–77; MP 1976–; Minister, Ministries of Finance, Trade and Industry, Health and Defence 1977–90, Deputy Prime Minister 1985–90; Prime Minister of Singapore 1990–2004; Sr Minister in Prime Minister's Office 2004–11, Emer. Sr Minister 2011–; Chair. Monetary Authority of Singapore 2004–11, Sr Adviser 2011–; mem. Central Exec. Cttee People's Action Party 1979–2011, Sec.-Gen. 1992–2004; Chair. Governing Bd, Lee Kuan Yew School of Public Policy, Nat. Univ. of Singapore 2017–; Perm. mem. Pres.'s Council for Minority Rights; Patron for Advancement, Singapore Univ. of Tech. and Design 2012; Grand Knight Cordon (Special Class) of the Most Exalted Order of the White Elephant (Thailand) 1997, Hon. Companion of the Order of Australia 2005, Order of the Rising Sun (Japan) 2011; Hon. DIur (Nat. Univ. of Singapore) 2015; Medal of Honour, Nat. Trade Union Congress (NTUC) 1987, Distinguished Comrade of Labour Award 2001, Jawaharlal Nehru Award for Int. Understanding (India) 2004, Distinguished Fellow, Econ. Devt Bd (EDB) Soc. 2015. *Leisure interests:* tennis, golf. *Address:* Monetary Authority of Singapore (MAS), 10 Shenton Way, MAS Bldg, Singapore 079117; Emeritus Senior Minister's Office, Orchard Road, Istana, Singapore 238823 (office). *Telephone:* 62255577 (MAS); 62358577 (office). *Fax:* 62299491 (MAS); 67324627 (office). *E-mail:* Goh_Chok_Tong@pmo.gov.sg (office); webmaster@mas.gov.sg. *Website:* www.pmo.gov.sg (office); www.mas.gov.sg.

GOH, Kun, MS; South Korean politician; b. 2 Jan. 1938, Seoul; m.; three s.; ed Kyung Ki High School, Seoul Nat. Univ.; Pres. Gen. Students' Council, Seoul Nat. Univ. 1959; Asst Jr Official Ministry of Home Affairs 1962–65, Asst Dir Planning Office 1965–68; Dir Interior Dept Jeonbuk Prov. 1968–71; Commr New Village Movt 1971–73; Vice-Gov. Gangwon Prov. 1973; Gov. of S Jeolla Prov. 1975–79; Chief Sec. of Political Affairs to the Pres., Chong Wa Dae (The Blue House) 1979–80; Chief Adviser, Korea Research Inst. for Human Settlement 1980; Minister of Transportation 1980–81, of Agric. and Marine Affairs 1981–82; Visiting Fellow, Harvard Univ. 1983; Visiting Prof., MIT 1984; mem. Nat. Ass. 1985–88; Minister of Home Affairs 1987; Dir Local Admin. Bureau 1973–75; Mayor, Seoul Metropolitan Govt 1988–90; Pres. Myong Ji Univ. 1994–97; Co-Pres. Korea Fed. for Environment Movt 1996–97; Prime Minister of Repub. of Korea 1997–98, 2003–04 (resgnd); Mayor of Seoul 1998–2002; Acting Pres. of South Korea March–May 2004; Pres. Transparency Int. Korea 2002–04 (resgnd); Head, Social Unity Council 2009; Hon. LLD (Won Kwang Univ.) 1992, (Syracuse Univ.) 2001; Order of Service Merit (Blue Stripes) 1972, (Red Stripes) 1982; Outstanding Policy-Maker Award, Korea Univ. 2000, Transparency Int. Global Integrity Medal 2001, Polestar Order from the Mongolian Pres. 2002.

GOICOECHEA LUNA, Emilio Rafael José; Mexican business executive, politician and diplomatist; b. 22 Oct. 1948, Mazatlan, Sinaloa; ed Instituto Tecnológico y de Estudios Superiores de Monterrey; served as Pres. Confederación Nacional de Cámaras de Comercio (Confed. of Nat. Chambers of Commerce), Instituto Mexicano de Mercadotecnia A.C. (Mexican Marketing Inst.) and mem. Consejo Coordinador Empresarial (Entrepreneurial Coordinating Council), Confederación Patronal de la República Mexicana (Employers' Confed. of Mexico); fmr adviser/consultant to nat. orgs including Centro de Estudios Económicos del Sector Privado, Instituto Mexicano de Comercio Exterior, Instituto Mexicano del Seguro Social, Instituto del Fondo Nacional de la Vivienda para los Trabajadores, Fondo Nacional de Fomento al Turismo, Ferrocarriles Nacionales de México, Asociación Nacional de Importadores y Exportadores, Confederación Nacional de Cámaras Industriales; began political career as Senator 1994–2000, mem. Fed. Chamber of Deputies 2000–03, Under-Sec. of Tourism 2003, Chief of Staff to Pres. Vicente Fox 2004–06; Amb. to Canada 2007–09; mem. Partido Acción Nacional (mem. Nat. Exec. 1996–); Pres. Asscn of Scouts of Mexico; Acapulco Chamber of Commerce's Exec. of the Year, Key to the City of Miami, Inst. for Promotion of Free Enterprise Golden Eagle Award.

GOIRIGOLZARRI TELLAECHE, José Ignacio, DEcon; Spanish banking executive; *President, Bankia SA;* b. 4 Feb. 1954, Bilbao; m.; two c.; ed Universidad de Deusto, Univ. of Leeds, England; joined the Banco de Bilbao 1978, worked in Strategic Planning, worked with Banco Bilbao Vizcaya Holdings, apptd Gen. Man. 1992, Man. Dir Retail Banking 1995–2000, Man. Dir Banco Bilbao Vizcaya Argentaria (BBVA) SA, US Div. 2000–01, Pres. and COO BBVA SA 2001–09, mem. Bd of Dirs 2001–09 (retd); Vice-Pres. Repsol YPF 2002–03; Dir and Pres. Bankia SA 2012–; Chair. Banco Financiero y de Ahorros 2012–; mem. Bd of Dirs Telefonica SA 2000–03, Asociación para el Progreso de la Dirección. *Address:* Bankia SA, Pintor Sorolla nº 8, 46002 Valencia, Spain (office). *Website:* www.bankia.es (office).

GOJKOVIĆ, Maja; Serbian lawyer and politician; *President, Narodna Skupština Republike Srbije (Parliament);* b. 22 May 1963, Novi Sad, Socialist Autonomous Province of Vojvodina, Socialist Repub. of Serbia, Socialist Fed. Repub. of Yugoslavia; ed Jovan Jovanović Zmaj Gymnasium, Novi Sad Law School; began working in family's law firm 1990; mem. Parl. of Fed. Repub. of Yugoslavia from 1992; mem. Vojvodina Parl. 1996–2000; Minister without portfolio in Serbian Govt 1998, 1999; Vice-Chair. Fed. Govt of Yugoslavia 1999; held a seat in Fed. Parl. of State Union of Serbia and Montenegro; Mayor of Novi Sad, Vojvodina 2004–08; Co-founder Srpska Radikalna Stranka (Serbian Radical Party), held position of Sec.-Gen., then Vice-Pres. Exec. Council, then Vice-Pres. of party, acted as Vojislav Šešelj's legal adviser before Int. Criminal Tribunal for Fmr Yugoslavia, left party following disagreement with leadership 2006; f. Grupa Građana – Maja Gojković (Maja Gojković Citizens' Group) 2008, later Co-leader Ujedinjeni Regioni Srbije (United Regions of Serbia) (expelled from party); mem. Srpska Napredna Stranka (Serbian Progressive Party); Pres. Narodna Skupština Republike Srbije (Parl.) 2014–. *Address:* Office of the President, People's Assembly (Narodna Skupština), 11000 Belgrade, Trg Nikole Pasića 13, Serbia (office). *Telephone:* (11) 3026100 (office). *E-mail:* nsrs@parlament.rs (office). *Website:* www.parlament.gov.rs (office).

GOKHALE, Vijay, MA; Indian diplomatist; *Foreign Secretary;* b. 24 Jan. 1959; m. Vandana Gokhale; one s.; ed Delhi Univ.; joined Foreign Service 1981, postings include Hong Kong, Hanoi, Beijing and New York, served as Deputy Sec. (Finance), Dir (China and East Asia) and Jt Sec. (East Asia) during stint at Ministry of External Affairs, High Commr to Malaysia 2010–13, Amb. to Germany 2013–16, to China 2016–17; Foreign Sec. 2017–. *Address:* Ministry of External Affairs, South Block, 110 011 New Delhi, India (office). *Telephone:* (11) 23011127 (office). *Fax:* (11) 23013254 (office). *E-mail:* eam@mea.gov.in (office). *Website:* www.mea.gov.in (office).

GOKONGWEI, John L., Jr, MBA; Philippine business executive; *Founder and Chairman Emeritus, JG Summit Holdings Inc.;* b. 4 July 1926, Xiamen, China; m. Elizabeth Yu Gokongwei; one s. five d.; ed San Carlos Univ., Cebu, De La Salle Univ., Manila, Harvard Business School, USA; f. Amasia Trading (import co.) 1946; f. Universal Corn Products (corn milling plant) 1957, renamed Universal Robina Corpn 1966, currently Dir and Chair. Emer.; Dir and Chair. Emer. Robinsons Land Corpn, JG Summit Petrochemical Corpn; Chair. Emer. Robinsons Bank; Founder, JG Summit Holdings Inc., Chair. and CEO –2001, now Dir and Chair. Emer.; Chair. and CEO Robinsons Retail Holdings, Inc.; Chair. Gokongwei Brothers Foundation, Inc.; Deputy Chair. United Industrial Corpn Ltd, Singapore Land Ltd (Singland); mem. Bd of Dirs Oriental Petroleum and Minerals Corpn, A. Soriano Corpn, JG Summit Olefins Corpn, Cebu Air, Inc. *Address:* JG Summit Holdings, Inc., 44/F Robinsons Equitable Tower, ADB Avenue, corner Poveda Road, Ortigas Center, Pasig City, Philippines (office); JG Summit Holdings, Inc., 44/F Robinsons Equitable Tower, ADB Avenue, corner Poveda Road, Ortigas Center, Pasig City, Philippines. *Telephone:* (2) 6337631 (office). *Fax:* (2) 3952607 (office). *Website:* www.jgsummit.com.ph (office).

GOLANI, Rivka; Canadian/Israeli violist and painter; b. 22 March 1946, Israel; d. of Jacob Gulnik and Lisa Gulnik; m. Jeremy Fox 1993; one s.; ed Univ. of Tel-Aviv, Rubin Music Acad., studied with Oedon Partos; concerts as soloist world-wide; has inspired many new works including viola concerti by Holloway, Hummel, Fontajn, Colgrass, Holmboe, Yuasa and Turner, solo works by Holliger, Holmboe and others; has collaborated with composers as a visual artist in presenting multimedia performances; art exhbns in Israel, UK, Germany and N America; Artistic Dir Fort Macleod International Chamber Music Festival; currently mem. Faculty, Strings Dept, Trinity Laban Conservatoire of Music and Dance, London; named Amb. of Canadian Music by Canadian Music Centre; Dr hc (Lethbridge Univ., Alberta, Canada) 2013; Grand Prix du Disque 1985, Medal Pro Artibus, Artijus Foundation, Musician of the Year, Artijus Music Foundation of Hungary 2011, named 'A woman who sings from a high place' by Blackfoot First Nations People of Canada 2016. *Recordings include:* three-album set of solo works by J. S. Bach; Hidden Treasure (Hungarian Classical Disc of the Year, Gramofon Award) 2013, Russian Concert 2015. *Publication:* Birds of Another Feather (book of drawings). *Address:* Marilyn Gilbert Artists Management, 705 King Street West, Suite 1713, Toronto, ON M5V 2W8, Canada (office); Trinity Laban Conservatoire of Music and Dance, Faculty of Music, King Charles Court, Old Royal Naval College, Greenwich, London, SE10 9JF, England (office). *E-mail:* r.golani@trinitylaban.ac.uk (office). *Website:* www.trinitylaban.ac.uk (office).

GOLD, Christina A.; Canadian business executive; ed Carleton Univ.; Founder, The Beaconsfield Group 1970–98; joined Avon Products, Inc. 1970, Pres. Avon Canada 1989–93, Pres. Avon North America 1993–97, Exec. Vice-Pres. of Global Devt 1997–98; Pres. and CEO Excel Communications 1999–2002; Pres. First Data Corpn (fmr parent co. of Western Union) 2002–06, Pres. and CEO Western Union

Financial Services, Inc. 2006–10 (retd); mem. Bd of Dirs ITT Industries 1998–, New York Life Insurance Co. 2001–, Safe Water Network 2010–, IFF 2013–, Torstar Corpn 1998–2007; Batisseur hon. degree (Professional Business School of Montreal); Award of Distinction, Faculty of Commerce and Admin, Concordia Univ., Montréal.

GOLD, David; British business executive; *Owner and Chairman, Gold Group International;* b. 15 Jan. 1937, Stepney, East London; m.; two d.; jt owner (with brother Ralph) Gold Group International 1965–2008, sole owner and Chair. 2008–, parent co. of retailer Ann Summers and lingerie chain Knickerbox, Gold Aviation, Greenwich House Properties, York Place and West Ham United Football Club; Chair. Birmingham City Football Club 1997–2009; acquired (with David Sullivan) 62% share of West Ham United Football Club, London 2010, Jt Chair. 2010–; Winner, Gozo Beacon 1979, Winner, Int. Malta Air Rally 1981, 1982 (runner up on three occasions). *Publication:* Pure Gold (with Bob Harris) 2005. *Leisure interests:* fixed wing pilot for 37 years, helicopter pilot for seven years. *Address:* Gold Group International, Gold Group House, Godstone Road, Whyteleafe, Surrey, CR3 0GG, England (office). *Telephone:* (1883) 629629 (office). *Fax:* (1883) 629220 (office). *Website:* www.davidgold.co.uk; www.whufc.com.

GOLD, Phil, CC, OQ, BSc, MSc, MDCM, PhD, FRCP(C), MACP, FRSC; Canadian physician and academic; *Douglas G. Cameron Professor of Medicine and Professor of Physiology and of Oncology, McGill University;* b. 17 Sept. 1936, Montréal, Québec; s. of Jack Gold and Rose Gold; m. Evelyn Katz; three c.; ed McGill Univ.; postgraduate training and research, The McGill Univ. Medical Clinic of The Montréal Gen. Hosp.; Medical Research Council of Canada Centennial Fellow 1967–68, Assoc. and Career Scientist 1969–80; Lecturer, Teaching Fellow, Asst and Assoc. Prof., Dept of Physiology and Dept of Medicine, McGill Univ. 1965–73, Prof. of Medicine and Clinical Medicine 1973–, of Physiology 1974–, of Oncology 1989–, Chair. Dept of Medicine 1985–90, Douglas G. Cameron Prof. of Medicine 1987–, Dir McGill Cancer Centre 1978–80, Sr Physician and Dir Clinical Research Centre, McGill Univ. Health Centre 1980–, Exec. Dir Clinical Research Centre, RIMUHC 1995–; Sr Physician, The Montréal Gen. Hosp. 1973–, Physician-in-Chief 1980–95, Sr Investigator Hosp. Research Inst.; Hon. Consultant, Royal Victoria Hosp., Montréal 1981–; mem. numerous professional socs, scientific research bds and orgs etc. including RSC, American Soc. for Clinical Investigation, Asscn of American Physicians; Hon. mem. Golden Key Int. Soc. 2012; Order of Montréal; Hon. DSc (McMaster); numerous honours and awards, including Sir Arthur Sims Commonwealth Travelling Professorship 1998, Carl Govesky Memorial Award 1999, 20th Anniversary of L'Actualité Medicale Award for Outstanding Contrib. to Medicine 2000, Montréal Gen. Hosp. Corpn Merit Award 2002, Queen's Golden Jubilee Medal 2002, honoured as Founding Dir of McGill Cancer Centre's 25th Anniversary 2003, Edwin F. Ullman Award, American Asscn of Clinical Chem. 2004, Award of Exception Merit, Canadian Soc. for Immunology 2004, Alpha Omega Achievement Medal, Alpha Omega Int. Dental Fraternity 2006, Isaak Walton Killam Award in Medicine of the Canada Council, Nat. Cancer Inst. of Canada R.M. Taylor Medal, Heath Medal of the MD Anderson Hosp., Inaugural Ernest C. Manning Foundation Award, Johann-Georg-Zimmerman Prize for Cancer Research, Medizinische Hochschule, Germany, Abbott Award (ISOBM), Japan, inauguration of Phil Gold Chair in Medicine, McGill Univ. Health Centre 2006, inducted into Canadian Medical Hall of Fame 2010, McGill Faculty of Medicine Global Award for Lifetime Achievement 2011, Queen's Diamond Jubilee Medal 2012, Lifetime Achievement Award, Dept of Oncology, McGill Univ. 2012, Prix du Québec, Wilder-Penfield 2013, Einstein Legacy Award 2017. *Publications:* 150 articles in professional journals since 1965. *Leisure interests:* photography, sailing, cinema, music, literature. *Address:* Montréal General Hospital, Suite D13 173, 1650 Cedar Avenue, Montréal, QC H3G 1A4, Canada (office). *Telephone:* (514) 934-1934 (ext. 43061) (office). *Fax:* (514) 934-8338 (office). *E-mail:* phil.gold@mcgill.ca (office). *Website:* www.medicine.mcgill.ca/oncology (office).

GOLDBERG, RoseLee, BA, MA; South African art historian, author and curator; *Founding Director and Curator, Performa;* b. 1947, Durban; ed Univ. of the Witwatersrand, Courtauld Inst. of Art, London, UK; fmr Dir RCA Gallery, London; fmr Curator, The Kitchen, New York; Clinical Assoc. Prof. of Visual Arts Admin New York Univ. 1987–; Founding Dir and Curator, Performa (arts org.), New York 2004–; frequent guest lecturer at Architectural Asscn and Tate Modern, London, California Inst. of the Arts, Guggenheim Museum, New York, Whitney Museum of American Art, Mori Museum, Tokyo, Yale Univ., Princeton Univ., Columbia Univ., Kyoto Univ. of Art and Design; regular contrib. to several magazines including Artforum; Chevalier des Arts et des Lettres 2006; Agnes Gund Curatorial Award 2010. *Publications:* Performance Art: From Futurism to the Present 1979, Performance Since 1960 1998, Laurie Anderson 2000, Shirin Neshat 2002, Performa 2007, Performance Now: New Art, New Dance, New Media 2007; contrib. to numerous journals and anthologies. *Address:* Performa, 100 West 23rd Street, 5th Floor, New York, NY 10011, USA (office); Department of Art and Art Professions, New York University Steinhardt, 34 Stuyvesant Street, New York, NY 10003, USA (office). *Telephone:* (212) 366-5700 (office); (212) 998-5700 (office). *Fax:* (646) 607-0811 (office). *E-mail:* info@performa-arts.org (office); roselee.goldberg@nyu.edu (office). *Website:* performa-arts.org (office); steinhardt.nyu.edu (office).

GOLDBERG, Whoopi; American comedienne, actress and author; b. (Caryn Johnson), 13 Nov. 1955, New York, NY; d. of Robert Johnson and Emma Harris; m. 2nd Dave Claessen 1986 (divorced 1988); one d.; m. 3rd Lyle Trachtenberg 1994 (divorced 1995); first stage appearance, aged 8, Hudson Guild Theater, New York; worked with Helena Rubinstein Children's Theater; moved to San Diego 1974; co-f. San Diego Repertory Theater, appeared in Mother Courage (Brecht) and Getting Out (Marsha Norman); moved to San Francisco, became mem. Blake St Hawkeyes Theater; toured USA in The Spook Show; co-wrote and appeared in Moms (one-woman show); Broadway debut, Lyceum Theater 1984; f. One Ho Productions (production co.) 1992; Grammy Award for Best Comedy Album 1985, Hans Christian Andersen Award for Outstanding Achievement by a Dyslexic, Mark Twain Prize for American Humor, Kennedy Center for Performing Arts 2001. *Plays include:* A Funny Thing Happened on the Way to the Forum, Ma Rainey's Black Bottom 2003. *Films include:* The Color Purple (Image Award from NAACP, Golden Globe Award, Hollywood Foreign Press Asscn 1985), Jumpin' Jack Flash 1986, Burglar 1987, Fatal Beauty 1987, Ghost 1990, Soapdish 1991, Sarafina 1992, Sister Act 1992, The Player 1992, Made in America 1992, Alice 1993, Sister Act II 1993, Corrina Corrina 1993, The Lion King (voice) 1994, Boys on the Side 1994, Moonlight and Valentino, Bogus, Eddie, The Associate 1996, The Ghost of Mississippi 1996, How Stella Got Her Groove Back 1998, Deep End of the Ocean 1999, Girl Interrupted 1999, Rat Race 2001, Kingdom Come 2001, Monkeybone 2001, Golden Dreams 2001, Star Trek: Nemesis 2002, More Dogs Than Bones 2002, Good Fences 2003, Blizzard (voice) 2003, Pinocchio 3000 (voice) 2004, Jiminy Glick in La La Wood 2004, Racing Stripes (voice) 2005, Doogal (voice) 2006, Homie Spumoni 2006, Everyone's Hero (voice) 2006, Farce of the Penguins (voice) 2006, If I Had Known I Was a Genius 2007, Snow Buddies (video) (voice) 2008, Madea Goes to Jail 2009, Toy Story 3 (voice) 2010, For Colored Girls 2010, A Little Bit of Heaven 2011, The Little Engine That Could (voice) 2011, The Contradictions of Fair Hope 2012, Teenage Mutant Ninja Turtles 2014, Black Dog, Red Dog 2014, Big Stone Gap 2014, Savva: Heart of the Warrior 2015. *Television includes:* In the Gloaming 1997, Cinderella 1997, A Knight in Camelot 1998, Alice in Wonderland 1999, Jackie's Back! 1999, The Magical Legend of the Leprechauns 1999, What Makes a Family 2001, Call Me Claus 2001, It's a Very Merry Muppet Christmas Movie 2002, Good Fences 2003, Whoopi (series) 2003–04, Littleburg (series) 2004, Whoopi: Back to Broadway – The 20th Anniversary (film) 2005, Bear in the Big Blue House (series) 2005, So Notorious (series) 2006, 30 Rock (series) 2007–09, Entourage (series) 2008, A Muppets Christmas: Letters to Santa (film) 2008, The Cleaner (series) 2009, Glee 2010–12, Robot Chicken (series) (voice) 2012, Sensitive Men (film) 2014, Delores & Jermaine (film) 2015; co-hostess The View (series) 2005–; producer, Hollywood Squares 1998–2002. *Publications include:* children's books: Sugar Plum Ballerinas series: Plum Fantastic 2008, Toeshoe Trouble 2009, Perfectly Prima 2010, Terrible Terrel 2010, CATastrophe 2011, Dancing Divas 2012; non-fiction: Alice 1992, Is It Just Me? Or Is It Nuts Out There? 2010, Whoopi's Big Book of Relationships: I Sucked at a Lot of Them So Now You Don't Have To 2015. *Address:* One Ho Productions, 375 Greenwich Street, Tribeca Film Center, New York, NY 10013; c/o Brad Cafarelli, Bragman/Nyman/Cafarelli, 9171 Wilshire Blvd, #300, Beverly Hills, CA 90210, USA.

GOLDBLUM, Jeff; American actor; b. 22 Oct. 1952, Pittsburgh, Pa; s. of Harold L. Goldblum and Shirley Goldblum (née Temeles); m. 1st Patricia Gaul (divorced); m. 2nd Geena Davis (q.v.) (divorced); two s.; m. 3rd Emilie Livingston 2014; ed Neighborhood Playhouse School of Theatre, New York; taught acting at Playhouse West, North Hollywood; Founding mem. The Fire Dept, theatre co., New York 2006. *Plays include:* The Pillowman (Broadway) 2005, The Prisoner of Second Avenue (Old Vic, London) 2010. *Films include:* California Split 1974, Death Wish 1974, Nashville 1975, Next Stop Greenwich Village 1976, Annie Hall 1977, Between the Lines 1977, The Sentinel 1977, Invasion of the Bodysnatchers 1978, Remember My Name 1978, Thank God it's Friday 1978, Escape from Athena 1979, The Big Chill 1983, The Right Stuff 1983, Threshold 1983, The Adventures of Buckaroo Banzai 1984, Silverado 1985, Into the Night 1985, Transylvania 6-5000 1985, The Fly 1986, Beyond Therapy 1987, The Tall Guy 1989, Earth Girls are Easy 1989, The Mad Monkey 1990, Mister Frost 1991, Deep Cover 1992, The Favour, the Watch and the Very Big Fish 1992, Father and Sons 1993, Jurassic Park 1993, Hideaway 1995, Nine Months 1995, Independence Day 1996, The Lost World 1997, Holy Man 1998, Popcorn 1999, Chain of Fools 2000, Angie Rose 2000, Cats and Dogs 2001, Igby Goes Down 2002, Dallas 362 2003, Spinning Boris 2003, Incident at Loch Ness 2004, The Life Aquatic with Steve Zissou 2004, Mini's First Time 2006, Fay Grim 2006, Man of the Year 2006, The Switch 2010, Zambezia 2012, Le Week-End 2013, The Grand Budapest Hotel 2014, Mortdecai 2015. *Television includes:* Tenspeed and Brown Shoe (series) 1980, Captain Planet and the Planeteers (series) 1990–91, Raines (series) 2007, Law & Order: Criminal Intent (series) 2009–10, Portlandia (series) 2012–15, Susan 313 (film) 2013. *Address:* c/o The Gersh Agency, 9465 Wilshire Blvd, 6th Floor, Beverly Hills, CA 90212 (office); c/o Keith Addis, Industry Entertainment, 955 Carrillo Drive Suite 300, Los Angeles, CA 90048, USA (office).

GOLDEMBERG, José, BSc, PhD; Brazilian physicist, academic and government official; b. 27 May 1928, Santo Ângelo; ed Universidade de São Paulo, Univ. of Saskatchewan, Canada, Univ. of Illinois, USA; Asst Prof., Universidade de São Paulo 1955, Assoc. Prof. 1955–67, Full Prof. of Physics 1967–, Dir Inst. of Physics 1970–78, Rector Universidade de São Paulo 1986–89; Research Assoc., High Energy Physics Lab., Stanford Univ., USA 1962–63; Assoc. Prof., Univ. of Paris (Orsay) 1964; Prof. of Physics, Univ. of Toronto, Canada 1972–73; Sr Research Assoc., Princeton Univ., USA several periods 1977–82; Visiting Prof., Woodrow Wilson School, Princeton Univ. 1993–94, Int. Acad. of the Environment, Geneva, Switzerland 1995, Center for Latin American Studies, Stanford Univ. 1996–97; Pres. Energy Co. of State of São Paulo 1983–86; Sec. of State for Science and Tech., Fed. Govt 1990–91; Minister of State for Educ., Fed. Govt 1991–92; Acting Sec. of State for Environment, Fed. Govt 1992; Sec. of State for the Environment, State of São Paulo 2002–06; Chair. Bd International Energy Initiative 1995–, World Energy Assessment 1998; mem. Advisory Bd Alliance for Global Sustainability 1997–, Environmental Advisory Bd Asea Brown Boveri (ABB) 1998, World Comm. on Dams 1998, Nat. Council for Energy Policy of Brazil 1999–2001, Sustainable Energy Inst.; Pres. Brazilian Asscn for the Advancement of Science 1979–81; mem. Brazilian Acad. of Sciences, Third World Acad. of Science; Ordem Nacional Do Mérito Científico 1995; Hon. DSc (Technion – Israel Inst. of Tech.) 1991; Mitchell Prize for Sustainable Devt (co-recipient) 1991, José Goldemberg Chair in Atmospheric Physics est. at Tel-Aviv Univ. 1994, Volvo Environment Prize (co-recipient) 2000, Blue Planet Prize, Asahi Glass Foundation 2008. *Publications:* several books and numerous scientific papers on nuclear physics, environment and energy in professional journals. *Address:* Centro Nacional de Referência Em Biomassa, Iee, Av. Professor Luciano Gualberto 1289, Cidade Universitária, 05508-010 Sao Paulo, SP, Brazil (office). *Telephone:* (11) 34836983 (office). *Fax:* (11) 30912649 (office). *E-mail:* goldemb@iee.usp.br (office). *Website:* www.iee.usp.br (office).

GOLDENBERG SCHREIBER, Efrain; Peruvian business executive, lawyer and fmr politician; b. 28 Dec. 1929, Lima; s. of Aron Goldenberg and Charna Schreiber; m. Irene Pravatiner 1952; one s. four d.; ed San Andrés (fmrly Anglo-Peruvian) School, Universidad Nacional Mayor de San Marcos; Minister of Foreign Affairs 1993–94, Pres. Council of Ministers (Prime Minister) and Minister of Foreign Affairs 1994–95; work in pvt. sector 1995–99; Minister of Econ. and

Finance 1999–2000; fmr Pres. Sociedad Nacional de Pesquería; fmr Dir Fondo para la Promoción de Exportaciones; fmr mem. Lima Jewish Community Asscn. *Address:* Miguel Dasso 144, Of. 2b, Lima 27, Peru (home). *Telephone:* (1) 4224291 (office). *E-mail:* efrain.goldenberg@gmail.com (office).

GOLDFAJN, Ilan, BEcons, MA, PhD; Brazilian/Israeli academic, economist and central banker; *President, Banco Central do Brasil;* b. 12 March 1966, Haifa, Israel; ed Federal Univ. of Rio de Janeiro, Catholic Univ. of Rio de Janeiro, Massachussetts Inst. of Tech., USA; Asst Prof., Brandeis Univ. 1995–96; Economist, IMF 1996–99; Asst Prof., Dept of Econs, Pontifical Catholic Univ. of Rio de Janeiro 1999–2009; Dir, Econ. Policy, Banco Central do Brasil (Cen. Bank of Brazil) 2000–03; Partner and Economist, Gávea Investimentos 2003–06; Partner, Ciano Investimentos 2007–08; Dir Inst. of Econ. Policy Studies, Inst., Casa das Garças 2006–09; Economist, Ciano Assessoria Econômica 2008–09; Chief Economist and Partner, Itaú Unibanco 2009–16; Pres. Banco Central do Brasil (Cen. Bank of Brazil) 2016–; Central Banker Of The Year, The Banker Awards 2018. *Publications include:* Inflation Targeting, Debt, and the Brazilian Experience, 1999 to 2003 2005. *Address:* Banco Central do Brasil, SBS, Quadra 03, Mezanino 01, Bloco B, 70074-900 Brasília, DF, Brazil (office). *Telephone:* (61) 3414-1414 (office). *Fax:* (61) 3414-2553 (office). *E-mail:* cap.secresecre.surel@bcb.gov.br (office). *Website:* www.bcb.gov.br (office).

GOLDIE, Sue J., BS, MD, MPH; American medical researcher and professor of public health; *Roger Irving Lee Professor of Public Health, Director of the Center for Health Decision Science, Harvard School of Public Health and Director of the Harvard Institute for Global Health, Harvard University;* b. 14 Dec. 1961, Wash.; m. Dr Aaron Bradley Waxman 1986; two s.; ed Union Coll., Albany Medical Coll., Harvard Univ., Certificate, Nat. Bd of Examiners, Diploma, American Bd of Internal Medicine; Intern in Internal Medicine, Yale New Haven Hosp., Yale Univ. School of Medicine 1988–89, Resident in Internal Medicine 1989–91; Fellow, Agency for Health Care Research and Quality Policy, Harvard School of Public Health, Boston 1995–97; Attending Physician, Yale New Haven Hosp. 1990, Brigham and Women's Hosp. 1998; Clinical Asst Prof. of Medicine, Yale Univ. School of Medicine 1994–98; Instructor in Medicine, Harvard Medical School, Boston 1998, Asst Prof. of Health Policy and Health Decision Science, Harvard School of Public Health 1998, Roger Irving Lee Prof. of Public Health and Dir Center for Health Decision Science, Co-Dir Exec. Cttee, Harvard Inst. of Global Health, Cambridge, Mass 2007–10, Dir 2010–; Prin. Investigator, NIH, Centers for Disease Control and Prevention, Bill & Melinda Gates Foundation, Doris Duke Foundation; mem. Inst. of Medicine, NAS (mem. Bd of Global Health) 2009, Soc. of Medical Decision Making (Editorial Bd), American Program Directors of Internal Medicine, Soc. of Gen. Internal Medicine, American Coll. of Physicians; Everett Mendelsohn Excellence in Mentoring Award, Harvard Univ., Dana Scholar, Charles A. Dana Foundation 1981, Dana Fellow 1982–84, Charles P. Drumm and Harold C. Wiggers Merit Scholar 1984–88, Original Investigation Competition Award for innovative programmes in medical educ., American Program Directors of Internal Medicine 1995, Larry Lynn Award, Soc. of Gen. Internal Medicine 1998, MacArthur Fellow, John T. and Catherine MacArthur Foundation 2005, John Eisenberg Award 2009. *Publications:* more than 150 papers in professional journals. *Leisure interests:* Tae Kwon Do, skiing, climbing, training her two golden retrievers. *Address:* Center for Health Decision Science, Harvard School of Public Health, 2nd Floor, 718 Huntington Avenue, Boston, MA 02115-5924, (office); Harvard Institute for Global Health, 3rd Floor, 104 Mount Auburn Street, Cambridge, MA 02138, USA (office). *Telephone:* (617) 432-2010 (Boston) (office); (617) 495-8222 (Cambridge) (office). *Fax:* (617) 432-0190 (Boston) (office); (617) 495-8231 (Cambridge) (office). *E-mail:* sue_goldie@harvard.edu (office); chds@hsph.harvard.edu (office); globalhealth@harvard.edu (office). *Website:* www.hsph.harvard.edu/faculty/sue-goldie (office); www.chds.hsph.harvard.edu (office); www.globalhealth.harvard.edu (office).

GOLDIN, Daniel S., BSc; American scientist and business executive; *Chairman, President and CEO, Intellisis Corporation;* b. 23 July 1940, New York City; m. Judith Kramer; two d.; ed City Coll. of New York; research scientist, NASA Lewis Research Center, Cleveland 1962–67; joined TRW Space & Tech. Group, Redondo, Calif. 1967, Vice-Pres. and Gen. Man. –1992; Admin., NASA 1992–2001; Founder and Chair., Pres. and CEO Intellisis Corpn 2005–; Sr Fellow, Neurosciences Inst., La Jolla, Calif.; Distinguished Fellow, Council on Competitiveness 2001–; Fellow, American Inst. of Aeronautics and Astronautics; mem. Bd of Dirs Lucent Technologies Inc. 2002–06, AOptix Technologies Inc.; mem. Bd of Trustees Nat. Geographic Soc.; mem. Advisory Council, Scripps Inst. of Oceanography; mem. Nat. Acad. of Engineers; numerous awards. *Address:* Intellisis Corporation, 10350 Science Center Drive, Suite 140, San Diego, CA 92121, USA (office). *Telephone:* (858) 500-8140 (office). *Fax:* (858) 500-8179 (office). *E-mail:* info@intellisis.com. *Website:* www.intellisis.com (office).

GOLDING, (Orrett) Bruce, BSc; Jamaican fmr politician; b. 5 Dec. 1947; s. of Tacius Golding and of Enid Golding (née Bent); m. Lorna Golding 1972; one s. two d.; ed St George's Coll., Jamaica Coll., Univ. of the West Indies; as a student served as Vice-Chair. Jamaica Labour Party (JLP) Constituency Exec. for West St Catherine and mem. Bd of Dirs, Nat. Lotteries Comm., selected as JLP parl. cand. for West St Catherine 1969, elected to JLP Cen. Exec. 1969, Co-founder Young Jamaica group 1970, elected as youngest-ever MP 1972, defeated in elections 1976, JLP Gen. Sec. 1974–84, Chair. 1984–95; apptd to Senate 1977, re-apptd 1980, Minister of Construction 1980–83; elected MP for South Central St Catherine 1983, re-elected 1989, 1993; left JLP and f. Nat. Democratic Movt (NDM) 1995, Pres. 1995–2002, left NDM and rejoined JLP 2002, Chair. JLP 2003–05, Leader 2005–11; Prime Minister 2007–11 (resgnd), also Minister of Planning and Devt and of Defence. *Radio:* host, Disclosure 2002. *Address:* Jamaica Labour Party, 20 Belmont Road, Kingston 5, Jamaica (office). *Telephone:* 929-1183 (office). *Website:* www.jamaicalabourparty.com (office).

GOLDMARK, Peter Carl, Jr, BA; American newspaper executive and consultant; b. 2 Dec. 1940, New York; s. of Peter Carl Goldmark and Frances Charlotte Trainer; m. Aliette Marie Misson 1964; three d.; ed Harvard Univ.; worked for US Office of Econ. Opportunity, Washington, DC; fmr teacher of history, Putney School, Vt; worked at Budget Office, City of New York for four years, later Asst Budget Dir Program Planning and Analysis then Exec. Asst to Mayor 1971; Sec., Human Services, Commonwealth of Mass. 1972–75; Dir of Budget, NY State 1975–77; Exec. Dir Port Authority of NY and NJ 1977–85; joined Times Mirror Co., Los Angeles 1985, fmr Sr Vice-Pres. Eastern Newspapers Div.; Pres. Rockefeller Foundation 1988–97; Chair. and CEO Int. Herald Tribune 1998–2003; Program Dir, Climate and Air Program, Environmental Defense Fund 2003–10; currently ind. consultant; columnist, Newsday; mem. Bd of Dirs Financial Accounting Foundation, Lend Lease Corpn 1999–2003; mem. Strategic Advisory Council, NewWorld Capital Group LLC; Trustee Whitehead Inst. for Biomedical Research 2000–07; Resolution Amb., The Resolution Project; Légion d'Honneur; Wilson Wyatt National Award for Urban Revitalization. *Address:* Newsday, 235 Pinelawn Road, Melville, NY 11747, USA (office). *Website:* www.newsday.com/opinion/columnists/peter-goldmark (office); www.petercgoldmark.com.

GOLDREICH, Peter, BSc, PhD; American scientist and academic; *Professor Emeritus, School of Natural Sciences, Institute for Advanced Study;* b. 14 July 1939, New York; s. of Paul Goldreich and Edith Rosenfield Goldreich; m. Susan Kroll 1960; two s.; ed Cornell Univ.; Post-Doctoral Fellow, Univ. of Cambridge 1963–64; Asst Prof. Astronomy and Physics, UCLA 1964–66, Assoc. Prof. 1966; Assoc. Prof. of Planetary Science and Astronomy, Calif. Inst. Tech. 1966–69, Prof. 1969–81, Lee Du Bridge Prof. of Astrophysics and Planetary Physics 1981–2002, Prof. Emer. 2002–, Acting Chair. Div. of Geological and Planetary Sciences 1989; Prof., School of Natural Sciences, Inst. for Advanced Study, Princeton, New Jersey 2003–09, Prof. Emer. 2009–; Sackler Lecturer, Univ. of Toronto 1998, Harvard Univ. 2004; Harris Lecturer, MIT 2005; Andrew Dixon White Fellowship 1960–61; Fellow, NSF 1961–63, Nat. Acad. of Sciences, Nat. Research Council 1963–64, Sloan Foundation 1968; Regents Fellow, Smithsonian Inst. 1988–90; mem. NAS 1972–; Foreign mem. Royal Soc. 2004–; Dr hc (Weizmann Inst. of Science) 2008; Hon. Woodrow Wilson Fellowship 1960–61; California Scientist of the Year Award 1981, Chapman Medal, Royal Astronomical Soc. 1985, Dirk Brouwer Award, American Astronomical Soc. 1986, Kuiper Prize, American Astronomical Soc. 1992, Gold Medal, Royal Astronomical Soc. 1993, Nat. Medal of Science 1995, Antoinette de Vaucouleurs Medal, Univ. of Texas 1999, Grande médaille, French Acad. of Sciences 2006, Shaw Prize, 2007, Albert Einstein Memorial Lecturer, Israel Acad. of Sciences and Humanities 2014. *Publications include:* on planetary dynamics, pulsar theory, radio emission from Jupiter, galactic stability and interstellar masers. *Leisure interest:* competitive athletics. *Address:* School of Natural Sciences, Institute for Advanced Study (IAS), Princeton, NJ 08540 (office); California Institute of Technology, 1200 East California Boulevard, Pasadena, CA 91125 (office); 471 S Catalina Avenue, Pasadena, CA 91106, USA (home). *Telephone:* (609) 734-8016 (IAS) (office). *Fax:* (609) 951-4402 (IAS) (office). *E-mail:* pmg@ias.edu (office). *Website:* www.sns.ias.edu (office); www.gps.caltech.edu (office).

GOLDSCHMIDT, Pinchas, MA, MSc; Russian (b. Swiss) rabbi and spiritual leader; *Chief Rabbi of Moscow;* b. 21 July 1963, Zurich, Switzerland; s. of Solomon Goldschmidt and Elizabeth Goldschmidt; m. Dara Lynn Brodie; seven c.; ed Ponevezh Yeshiva, Telshe Yeshiva, Chicago, Shevet Umechokek Inst. for Rabbinical Judges, Harry Fischel Inst. for Rabbinical Judges, Ner Israel Rabbinical Coll., Johns Hopkins Univ.; ordained 1987; worked in the rabbinate of Nazeret-Ilit 1987–89; Lecturer, Inst. for the Study of Judaism, USSR Acad. of Sciences 1989; Founder and Head, Moscow Rabbinical Court 1989–; Chief Rabbi of Moscow, Moscow Choral Synagogue 1993–; Pres. Conf. of European Rabbis (CER) 2011–, Chair. Standing Cttee; established European Council for Muslim and Jewish Leaders (MJLC) 2016; Officer, Russian Jewish Congress; Visiting Scholar, Davis Centre, Harvard Univ. 2009; Chevalier, Ordre Nat. de la Légion d'honneur 2016; Jerusalem Prize 2002. *Address:* Moscow Choral Synagogue, Moscow, Bolshaya Spasoglinischevsky per., 10 pp. 1, Russia (office). *Telephone:* (495) 623-47-88 (office). *Website:* centralsynagogue.ru.

GOLDSMITH, Harvey, CBE; British music promoter; b. 4 March 1946, London; s. of Sydney Goldsmith and Minnie Goldsmith; m. Diana Goldsmith 1971; one s.; ed Christ's Coll. and Brighton Coll. of Tech.; joined Big O Posters, Kensington Market 1966; organized open-air free concerts, Parliament Hill Fields 1968; in partnership with Michael Alfandary opened Round House, London 1968; organized 13 Garden Party concerts at Crystal Palace, London 1969; merged with John Smith Entertainment 1970–75; formed Harvey Goldsmith Entertainment promoting rock tours by Elton John, Rolling Stones etc.; in partnership with Ed Simons, rescued Hotel Television Network 1983; formed Allied Entertainment Group as public co. 1984–86, returned to pvt. ownership 1986; subsidiary Harvey Goldsmith Entertainment promotes some 250 concerts per year; formed Classical Productions with Mark McCormack, promoting shows at Earls Court including Pavarotti concert and productions of Aida 1988, Carmen 1989, Tosca 1991; produced Bob Dylan Celebration, New York 1992, Mastercard Masters of Music (Hyde Park), The Eagles (Wembley), Three Tenors (Wembley), Lord of the Dance (world tour) 1996, Music for Montserrat (Royal Albert Hall), Boyzone (tour), Paul Weller (tour), Pavarotti (Manchester), Cirque du Soleil (Royal Albert Hall) 1997, Alegria (Royal Albert Hall), The Bee Gees (Wembley), Ozzfest (Milton Keynes Bowl), Paul Weller (Victoria Park) 1998; Chair. Nat. Music Day; Vice-Chair. Prince's Trust Bd; Vice-Pres. React 1989–; Trustee, Gret, Band Aid 1985–, Live Aid Foundation 1985–; Dir Pres.'s Club, London First, London Tourist Bd; Amb. for London Judges Award 1997; Chair. Ignition International 2006–; mem. Advisory Group Red Cross; Music Industry Trust Award 2006, Queen's Diamond Jubilee Award 2012. *Leisure interest:* golf. *Address:* Harvey Goldsmith Entertainments Ltd, 3rd Floor, 113 Great Portland Street, London, W1W 6QQ, England (office). *Telephone:* (20) 7224-1992 (office). *Fax:* (20) 7580-1853 (office). *Website:* www.harveygoldsmith.com.

GOLDSTEIN, Jeffrey Alan, BA, MPh, PhD; American international civil servant, economist, government official and private equity investor; *Managing Director, Hellman & Friedman LLC;* b. 2 Dec. 1955, Pennsylvania; m. Nancy Coles; two s. one d.; ed Yale Univ., Vassar Coll., London School of Econs, UK; Research Asst, Brookings Inst., Washington, DC 1977–78; Int. Economist, Office of Int. Monetary Affairs, US Dept of Treasury, Washington, DC 1979; Consultant, Securities Group, New York 1980–81; Vice-Chair. Wolfensohn & Co. Inc., New York, then Co-Chair. BT Wolfensohn, New York 1984–99; Man. Dir and Chief Financial Officer, World Bank, Washington, DC 1999–2004; Man. Dir Hellman & Friedman LLC (pvt. equity firm) 2004–09, 2012–; Under-Sec. for Domestic Finance and Counselor to the Sec., US Dept of Treasury, Washington, DC 2009–11; mem. Bd LPL Financial, Advisory Bd Grosvenor Capital Management LLP 2012–,

Council on Foreign Relations; mem. Bd of Trustees, Vassar Coll.; Virginia Swinburn Brownell Prize in Political Econ. Studies, Alexander Hamilton Award 2011. *Address:* 390 Park Avenue, 21st Floor, New York, NY 10022, USA (office). *Telephone:* (212) 871-6681 (office). *Fax:* (212) 871-6688 (office). *E-mail:* jgoldstein@hf.com (office).

GOLDSTEIN, Joseph Leonard, BS, MD; American geneticist, physician and academic; *Regental Professor and Chairman, Department of Molecular Genetics, University of Texas Southwestern Medical Center;* b. 18 April 1940, Sumter, South Carolina; s. of Isadore E. Goldstein and Fannie A. Goldstein; ed Washington and Lee Univ., Univ. of Texas Southwestern Medical Center; Intern, then Resident in Medicine, Mass. Gen. Hosp., Boston 1966–68; Clinical Assoc., NIH 1968–70; Postdoctoral Fellow, Univ. of Washington, Seattle 1970–72; joined Faculty, Univ. of Texas Southwestern Medical Center, Dallas 1972, apptd Paul J. Thomas Chair in Medicine and Chair. Dept of Molecular Genetics 1977, Harvey Soc. Lecturer 1977, Regental Prof. 1985–, also Julie and Louis A. Beecherl, Jr. Distinguished Chair in Biomedical Research; Chair. Albert Lasker Medical Research Awards Jury 1996–; mem. Advisory Bd Howard Hughes Medical Inst. 1985–90, Chair. 1995–2002, Trustee 2002–; Fellow (non-resident), The Salk Inst. 1983–93; Welch Foundation 1986–; mem. Bd of Dirs Passano Foundation 1985–; mem. Editorial Bd Cell, Arteriosclerosis and Science; mem. Scientific Advisory Bd Welch Foundation, Memorial Sloan-Kettering Cancer Center, Scripps Research Institute, Van Andel Inst., Massachusetts General Hospital; mem. NAS (mem. Council 1991–94), American Acad. of Arts and Sciences, American Philosophical Soc., Inst. of Medicine, Asscn of American Physicians, American Soc. of Clinical Investigation (Pres. 1985–86), American Soc. of Human Genetics, American Soc. of Biological Chemists, American Fed. of Clinical Research; Foreign mem. Royal Soc., London; Trustee, Howard Hughes Medical Institute, The Rockefeller University; Hon. DSc (Univ. of Chicago, Rensselaer Polytechnic Inst., Washington and Lee Univ., Univ. of Paris-Sud, Univ. of Buenos Aires, Southern Methodist Univ., Univ. of Miami, Rockefeller Univ.); Heinrich-Wieland Prize 1974, ACS Pfizer Award in Enzyme Chem. 1976, Passano Award, Johns Hopkins Univ. 1978, Gairdner Foundation Award 1981, Award in Biological and Medical Sciences, New York Acad. of Sciences 1981, Lita Annenberg Hazen Award 1982, Research Achievement Award, American Heart Asscn 1984, Louisa Gross Horwitz Award 1984, 3M Life Sciences Award 1984, Albert Lasker Award in Basic Medical Research 1985, Nobel Prize in Physiology or Medicine 1985, Trustees' Medal, Mass Gen. Hosp. 1986, US Nat. Medal of Science 1988, Albany Medical Center Prize in Medicine and Biomedical Research 2003, Woodrow Wilson Award for Public Service 2005, Builders Science Award, Research America 2007, Stadtman Distinguished Scientist Award, American Soc. for Biochemistry and Molecular Biology 2011. *Publications include:* The Metabolic Basis of Inherited Disease (co-author) 1983. *Address:* Department of Molecular Genetics, University of Texas Southwestern Medical Center at Dallas, 5323 Harry Hines Blvd, Dallas, TX 75390-9046 (office); 3831 Turtle Creek Boulevard, Apt 22-B, Dallas, TX 75219, USA (home). *Telephone:* (214) 648-2141 (office). *Fax:* (214) 648-8804 (office). *E-mail:* joe.goldstein@utsouthwestern.edu (office). *Website:* www.utsouthwestern.edu/education/medical-school/departments/molecular-genetics/index.html (office).

GOLDSTONE, David Joseph, CBE, LLB; British property executive; b. 21 Feb. 1929, Swansea, South Wales; s. of Solomon Goldstone and Rebecca Goldstone (née Degotts); one s. two d.; ed Dynevor Secondary School, Swansea and London School of Econs; admitted as solicitor 1955; legal practice 1955–66; Chief Exec. Regalian Properties PLC 1970–2001, Chair. 1990–2001; Dir Swansea Sound Commercial Radio 1974–95, London Welsh Rugby Football Club 1997–2001, Wales Millennium Centre; Chair. Coram Family 2001–05, now Hon. Vice-Pres.; fmr Chair. Swanbourne Development Services Ltd; currently Adviser to Minister for Health and Social Services and to Minister for Business, Enterprise, Technology and Science, Welsh Ass.; Special Adviser, Welsh Rugby Union; mem. Court of Govs LSE 1985–2009 (Fellow 1996), Gov. Emer. 2009–; mem. Bd Football Asscn of Wales 1970–72, Welsh Nat. Opera 1984–89, Univ. of London 1994– (Deputy Chair. 2002–); mem. Council Royal Albert Hall 1998–2006 (Hon. Vice-Pres. 2007–), Capital Advisory Group, Welsh Ass. Govt 2009–14; Trustee, Civil Liberties Trust 2009–. *Leisure interests:* reading, sport. *Address:* Flat 4, Grosvenor Hill Court, 15 Bourdon Street, London, W1K 3PX, England (home). *Telephone:* (20) 7499-4525 (home). *E-mail:* djg@davstone.co.uk (office).

GOLDSTONE, Jeffrey, MA, PhD, FRS; British physicist and academic; *Cecil and Ida Green Professor Emeritus of Physics, Massachusetts Institute of Technology;* b. 3 Sept. 1933, Manchester, England; s. of Hyman Goldstone and Sophia Goldstone; m. Roberta Gordon 1980; one s.; ed Manchester Grammar School and Trinity Coll., Cambridge; Research Fellow, Trinity Coll., Cambridge 1956–60, Staff Fellow 1962–82; Univ. Lecturer, Applied Math. and Theoretical Physics, Univ. of Cambridge 1961–76, Reader in Math. Physics 1976; Prof. of Physics, MIT, USA 1977–83, Dir Center for Theoretical Physics 1983–89, Cecil and Ida Green Prof. of Physics 1983–2004, Cecil and Ida Green Prof. Emer. 2004–; Fellow, American Acad. of Arts and Sciences, American Physical Soc.; Hon. Fellow, Trinity Coll., Cambridge 2000; Heineman Prize, American Physical Soc. 1981, Guthrie Medal, Inst. of Physics 1983, Dirac Medal, Int. Centre for Theoretical Physics 1991. *Publications include:* articles in scientific journals. *Address:* Department of Physics, 6-407, Massachusetts Institute of Technology, Cambridge, MA 02139, USA (office). *Telephone:* (617) 253-6263 (office). *Fax:* (617) 253-8674 (office). *E-mail:* goldston@mit.edu (office). *Website:* web.mit.edu/physics/people/faculty/goldstone_jeffrey.html (office).

GOLDSTONE, Richard J., LLB; South African judge; b. 26 Oct. 1938, Boksburg, Gauteng Prov.; m. Noleen Behrman 1962; two d.; ed King Edward VII School, Johannesburg and Univ. of the Witwatersrand; admitted to Johannesburg Bar 1963, Sr Counsel 1976; Judge, Transvaal Supreme Court 1980–89; Judge, Appellate Div. Supreme Court of SA 1989–94; Justice, S African Constitutional Court 1994–2003; Chief Prosecutor, Int. Criminal Tribunal for Fmr Yugoslavia and Int. Criminal Tribunal for Rwanda 1994–96; mem. Ind. Int. Comm. on Kosovo 1999–2001, Int. Group of Advisers of the ICRC 1999–2003; apptd Co-Chair. Int. Bar Asscn Task Force on Int. Terrorism 2001; mem. UN Cttee of Inquiry into Iraq Oil for Food Programme (Volcker Cttee); Head UN Fact Finding Mission on the Gaza Conflict 2009; Eminent Leader in Residence, Joan B. Kroc Inst. for Peace and Justice (IPJ) 2005, Univ. of San Diego, now mem. IPJ Int. Council; fmr Visiting Prof., New York Univ. Law School, Fordham Univ. Law School, Harvard Univ. Law School; Distinguished Visitor from the Judiciary, Georgetown Univ. Law Center 2014; Nat. Pres. Nat. Inst. for Crime Prevention and Rehabilitation of Offenders 1982–99; Founding Chair. Inst. for Historical Justice and Reconciliation; fmr Chair. Standing Advisory Cttee on Co. Law Chair. Exec. Cttee World ORT (Pres. 1997–2004), Advisory Bd of Int. Center for Transitional Justice, Human Rights Inst. of SA 1994–2003 (now Trustee); Gov. Hebrew Univ. of Jerusalem 1982–2009; Chair. Bradlow Foundation 1989–2005; mem. Faculty, Salzburg Seminar 1996–2006; mem. Council, Univ. of Witwatersrand 1988–94, Chancellor 1995–2007; Int. mem. American Acad. of Arts and Sciences; Fellow, Centre for Int. Affairs, Harvard Univ. 1989; Hon. mem. Bar Asscn of New York; Hon. Bencher, Inner Temple, London; Hon. Fellow, St John's Coll. Cambridge; Hon. Pres. Human Rights Inst. of Int. Bar Asscn; 25 hon. degrees including Hon. LLD (Cape Town) 1993, (Natal, Hebrew Univ. of Jerusalem, Witwatersrand) 1994, (Wilfred Laurier Univ.) 1995, (Tilburg Univ.) 1996, (Univ. of Glasgow, Notre Dame Univ.) 1997, (Univ. of Calgary) 1998, (Emory Univ.) 2001; several awards including Toastmasters Int. Communication and Leadership Award 1994, Int. Human Rights Award (American Bar Asscn) 1994, MacArthur Award for Int. Justice 2009. *Publication:* For Humanity: Reflections of a War Crimes Investigator. *Leisure interests:* reading, walking, wine. *Address:* PO Box 396, Morningside 2057 (home); 22 West Road South, Morningside, South Africa (home). *Fax:* (11) 8035472 (home). *E-mail:* rjgoldstone@iafrica.com (home).

GOLDSTRAW, Peter, MB, ChB, FETCS; British thoracic surgeon (retd); *Professor Emeritus of Thoracic Surgery, Imperial College London;* b. 1945; m. Denise Mary Bowyer 1968; one s. one d.; ed Univ. of Birmingham; Consultant Thoracic Surgeon, Royal Brompton Hospital 1979–, fmr Dir of Surgery, Head of Thoracic Surgery Section; civilian adviser to Royal Navy, RAF; fmr Hon. Consultant, Benenden Chest Hospital; Prof. of Thoracic Surgery, Imperial Coll., London, now Prof. Emer.; Chair. Int. Staging Cttee of Int. Asscn for the Study of Lung Cancer, UK Cardiothoracic Training Cttee; Nat. Rep. European Union of Medical Specialists; mem. Man. Bd European Bd of Thoracic and Cardiovascular Surgery; UK Rep. UEMS Section of Cardiothoracic Surgery; Chair. Cardiothoracic SHC; mem. Belgian Asscn for Cardio-Thoracic Surgery, Cardiothoracic Surgery Network, European Asscn for Cardio-Thoracic Surgery, European Soc. of Thoracic Surgeons, Soc. of Cardiothoracic Surgeons of Great Britain and Ireland, American Asscn for Thoracic Surgery, Soc. of Thoracic Surgeons; mem. Editorial Bd Thorax, Annals of Thoracic Surgery; Assoc. Ed. Lung Cancer; Fellow, Royal Colls of Edinburgh and England; Hon. mem. European Soc. of Thoracic Surgeons 2007; Clement Price-Thomas Award Royal Coll. of Surgeons of England 2004, Merit Award, Int. Asscn for the Study of Lung Cancer 2007, Lifetime Achievement Award, Soc. for Cardiothoracic Surgery in GB and Ireland 2010. *Publications include:* contrib. to 44 textbooks on thoracic surgery; more than 200 articles in scientific journals; fmr Exec. Ed. Handbook of Staging in Thoracic Oncology. *Leisure interests:* sailing, fishing. *Address:* Royal Brompton Hospital, 3062 Sydney Street, London, SW3 6NP (office); Imperial College London, South Kensington Campus, London, SW7 2AZ, England (office). *Telephone:* (1803) 834171 (office). *E-mail:* p.goldstraw@imperial.ac.uk (office). *Website:* www.imperial.ac.uk/people/p.goldstraw (office).

GOLDSWORTHY, Andrew (Andy) Charles, OBE, BA; British sculptor; b. 25 July 1956, Cheshire; s. of Fredrick Alan Goldsworthy and Muriel Goldsworthy (née Stanger); m. Judith Elizabeth Gregson (divorced) 1982; partner Tina Fiske; two s. two d.; ed Bradford and Lancaster Art Colls; has exhibited in USA, France, Australia, Germany and Japan; numerous public and pvt. comms since 1984 including pieces for Grizedale Forest, Cumbria 1984, 1985, 1991, Enclosure, Royal Botanic Gardens, Edinburgh 1990, Seven Holes, Greenpeace, London 1991, Steel Cone, Gateshead 1991, Black Spring, Botanical Gardens, Adelaide 1992, Fieldgate, Poundridge, New York 1993, Laumeier Sculpture Park 1994, two pieces for Nat. Museum of Scotland, Edin. 1998; works represented in collections at Michael Hue-Williams Fine Arts Ltd, London, Galerie Lelong, New York and Paris, Haines Gallery, San Francisco, Galerij S65, Belgium, Springer and Winckler Galerie, Berlin; residency Yorks. Sculpture Park 1988; featured on Royal Mail Spring issue stamps 1995; Sr Lecturer in Fine Art and Craft, Univ. of Herts. 1996; Andrew D. White Prof.-at-Large, Cornell Univ., USA 2000–08; Visiting Prof., Crichton Coll., Univ. of Glasgow 2000–; collaborated with Cirque du Soleil, Montréal 1998; mem. Cass Sculpture Foundation; Hon. Fellow, Univ. of Cen. Lancs. 1995; Hon. BA (Bradford) 1993; North West Arts Award 1979, Yorks. Arts Award 1980, Northern Arts Award 1981, 1995, Scottish Arts Council Award 1988. *Dance includes:* Vegetal, with Regine Chopinot 1995, La danse du Temps, with Regine Chopinot and Ballet Atlantique 2000. *Film includes:* Two Autumns (for Channel 4) 1991, Rivers and Tides 2000. *Publications include:* A Collaboration with Nature 1989, Hand to Earth 1991, Touching North 1994, Stone 1994, Wood 1996, Time 2000, Passage 2005, Enclosure 2007, Ephemeral Works: 2004–2014 2015. *Leisure interests:* fishing, reading, listening to music.

GOLDTHORPE, John Harry, CBE, BA, Fil. Dr, FBA; British sociologist and academic; *Fellow Emeritus, Nuffield College, Oxford;* b. 27 May 1935, Barnsley, South Yorks.; s. of Harry and Lilian Eliza Goldthorpe; m. Rhiannon Esyllt Harry 1963; one s. one d.; ed Wath-upon-Dearne Grammar School, Univ. Coll. London, London School of Econs; Asst Lecturer, Dept of Sociology, Univ. of Leicester 1957–60; Fellow, King's Coll., Cambridge 1960–69; Asst Lecturer, then Lecturer in Faculty of Econs and Politics, Univ. of Cambridge 1962–69; Official Fellow, Nuffield Coll., Oxford 1969–2002, Fellow Emer. 2002–; mem. British Econ. and Social Research Council 1988–91; mem. Academia Europaea 1989; Foreign mem. Royal Swedish Acad. of Sciences 2001; Visiting Professorial Fellow, Centre for Longitudinal Studies, Inst. of Education, London 2006–10; Hon. Fellow, Royal Statistical Soc. 2016; Hon. Fil. Dr (Stockholm Univ.) 1990; Helsinki Univ. Medal 1990. *Publications include:* The Affluent Worker series (three vols) (with David Lockwood et al.) 1968–69, The Social Grading of Occupations (with Keith Hope) 1974, The Political Economy of Inflation (with Fred Hirsch, eds) 1978, Social Mobility and Class Structure 1980, Order and Conflict in Contemporary Capitalism (ed. and contrib.) 1984, Die Analyse sozialer Ungleichheit: Kontinuität, Erneuerung, Innovation (with Hermann Strasser; ed. and contrib.) 1985, The Constant Flux: a Study of Class Mobility in Industrial Societies (with Robert Erikson) 1992, The Development of Industrial Society in Ireland (with Christopher T. Whelan; ed. and contrib.) 1992, On Sociology: Numbers, Narratives and the

Integration of Research and Class Theory 2000 (second, two-vol. edn 2007), Sociology as a Population Science 2015. *Leisure interests:* lawn tennis, bird watching, computer chess, cryptic crosswords. *Address:* Nuffield College, Oxford, OX1 1NF (office); 32 Leckford Road, Oxford, OX2 6HX, England (home). *Telephone:* (1865) 278559 (office); (1865) 556602 (home). *E-mail:* john.goldthorpe@nuffield.ox.ac.uk (office).

GOLDWASSER, Shaffi, BS, MS, PhD; American/Israeli computer scientist and academic; *RSA Professor of Electrical Engineering and Computer Science, Massachusetts Institute of Technology;* b. 1958, New York, NY; m. Nir Shavit; two s.; ed Carnegie Mellon Univ., Univ. of California, Berkeley; Bantrel Postdoctoral Fellowship, MIT 1983, Asst Prof. 1983–87, Assoc. Prof. 1987–92, Prof. of Electrical Eng and Computer Science 1992–, RSA Prof. of Electrical Eng and Computer Science 1997–, Co-leader Cryptography and Information Security Group and mem. Complexity Theory Group within Theory of Computation Group and Computer Science and Artificial Intelligence Lab.; Prof. of Computer Science and Applied Math., Weizmann Inst. of Science 1993–; Dir Simons Inst. for the Theory of Computing, Univ. of California 2018–; Fellow, American Acad. of Arts and Sciences 2001, NAS 2004, Nat. Acad. of Eng 2005, Int. Asscn for Cryptologic Research 2012; IBM Young Faculty Devt Award 1983–85, NSF Presidential Young Investigator Award 1987–92, NSF Award for Women in Science 1991–96, SIGACT Gödel Prize (co-recipient) 1993, 2001, Grace Murray Hopper Award, Asscn for Computing Machinery (ACM) 1996, RSA Award in Math. for Outstanding Math. Contribs to Cryptography 1998, Levenson Prize in Math., Weizmann Inst. 1999, Distinguished Alumnus Award in Computer Science and Eng, Univ. of California, Berkeley 2006, Athena Lecturer, ACM Cttee on Women in Computing 2008, Benjamin Franklin Medal in Computer and Cognitive Science 2010, IEEE Emanuel R. Piore Award 2011, ACM A.M. Turing Award (with Silvio Micali) 2012. *Publications:* numerous papers in professional journals. *Address:* Room 32-G682, Computer Science and Artificial Intelligence Laboratory, Massachusetts Institute of Technology, 77 Massachusetts Avenue, Cambridge, MA 02139, USA (office). *Telephone:* (617) 253-5914 (office). *E-mail:* shafi@csail.mit.edu (office). *Website:* www.csail.mit.edu/user/733 (office).

GOLIKOVA, Tatyana Alekseyevna; Russian economist and government official; *Deputy Chairman of the Government;* b. 9 Feb. 1966, Mytischi, Moscow Oblast, Russian SFSR, USSR; m. Viktor Khristenko; ed Moscow Inst. of Nat. Economy (Plekhanov Inst.); served as economist in Ministry of Finance 1990–98, Head of Budget Dept 1998–99, 2007, Deputy then First Deputy Minister of Finance 1999–2007; Minister of Health and Social Devt 2007–12; Head of Accounts Chamber of Russian Fed. 2013–18; Deputy Chair., Govt of the Russian Fed. 2018–; Medal of the Order of Merit to the Fatherland (First Degree) 2004; Medal of Honour 2006, Medal of Friendship 2006. *Address:* Office of the Government, 103274 Moscow, Krasnopresnenskaya nab. 2, Russian (office). *Telephone:* (495) 985-42-80 (office). *Fax:* (495) 605-53-62 (office). *E-mail:* duty_press@aprf.gov.ru (office). *Website:* www.government.ru (office).

GOLITSYN, Georgy Sergeyevich; Russian physicist; b. 23 Jan. 1935, Moscow; s. of Sergei Golitsyn and Claudia Golitsyna; m. Ludmila Lisitskaya; two d.; ed Moscow State Univ.; Head of Lab., then Head of Div., Inst. of Atmospheric Physics, USSR (now Russian) Acad. of Sciences, apptd Dir Inst. of Atmospheric Physics 1958; Corresp. mem. USSR (now Russian) Acad. of Sciences 1979, mem. 1987, mem. Presidium 1988–2001; Chair. Council, Int. Inst. of Applied Systems Analysis 1992–97; main research on geophysical fluid dynamics, climate theory; Hon. Scholar, Int. Inst. for Applied Systems Analysis 1997, Hon. mem. Alfred Wegener 2005, Hon. Fellow, Royal Meteorological Soc. 2011; A. Friedmann Prize 1990, Demidov Prize 1996, Alfred Wegener Prize 2005. *Publications include:* Introduction to Dynamics of Planet Atmospheres 1973, Study of Convection with Geophysical Applications and Analogies 1980, Global Climate Catastrophes 1986, Convection of Rotating Fluids 1995, Dynamics of Natural Processes 2004, Micro and macrocosm, and Harmony 2008. *Leisure interests:* history, art, literature. *Address:* c/o A.M. Obukhov Institute of Atmospheric Physics, Russian Academy of Sciences, Pyzhyevsky per. 3, 119017 Moscow, Russia (office).

GOLL, Gerhard, JD; German lawyer, politician, business executive and academic; b. 18 June 1942, Stuttgart; m.; two c.; ed Univs of Tübingen and Freiburg; Judge, Regional Court of Stuttgart; with Ministry of Culture of Baden-Württemberg 1972–75; joined Ministry of Finance of Baden-Württemberg 1975, Head of Centre 1976–77, Head of Gen. Office of Budget Dept 1977–78; Sec., CDU Group, Parl. of Baden-Wuerttemberg 1980; joined Landeskreditbank Baden-Württemberg 1982, apptd mem. Bd of Dirs and Deputy CEO 1984; CEO Badenwerk AG, Karlsruhe 1993–97; joined Schwaben AG 1997, subsequently merged with Energie Baden-Württemberg (EnBW) AG, Chair. Energie Baden-Württemberg (EnBW) AG 1998–2003; Lecturer, Karlshochschule Int. Univ. 2008, then Chair. Foundation Bd; apptd Chair. Advisory Bd, Schwarzwald Nationalpark 2014; mem. Advisory Bd Landesverband Baden-Württemberg, German Alpine Asscn; Trustee Karlshochschule International Univ.

GOLLAKOTA, Shyamnath, BTech, MS, PhD; American (b. Indian) computer scientist and academic; *Assistant Professor, Department of Computer Science and Engineering, University of Washington;* ed Indian Inst. of Tech. (IIT), Madras, India, Massachusetts Inst. of Tech.; currently Asst Prof., Dept of Computer Science and Eng, Univ. of Washington, Adjunct Asst Prof. of Electrical Eng, Head of Networks and Mobile Systems Lab.; Inst. Award in Computer Science, IIT Madras 2006, William A. Martin SM Thesis Award 2008, Best Paper Award, Asscn for Computing Machinery (ACM) Special Interest Group on Data Communications (SIGCOMM) 2008, ACM SIGCOMM Doctoral Dissertation Award 2012, ACM Doctoral Dissertation Award 2012, George M. Sprowls Award for Best Dissertation in Computer Science, MIT 2013, ACM SIGCOMM Best Paper Award 2013 ACM MOBICOM Best Paper Award 2013, Technology Review TR35, Innovators Under the Age of 35 2014, Forbes 30 under 30 Energy 2015, Alfred Sloan Fellowship 2015, NSF Career Award 2015, CoMotion Presidential Innovation Fellow 2015, World Tech. Award (Communication Tech.) 2015, 10 Tech Breakthroughs, MIT Tech Review 2016, NSDI Best Paper Award 2016, Visionaries 2020, CNN 2016, SIGCOMM Best Paper Award 2016, Popular Science Brilliant Ten 2016. *Publications:* numerous papers in professional journals. *Address:* Room 550, Networks & Mobile Systems, Paul G. Allen Center, University of Washington, Box 352350, Seattle, WA 98195, USA (office). *E-mail:* gshyam@cs.washington.edu (office). *Website:* homes.cs.washington.edu/~gshyam (office).

GÖLLNER, Theodor, PhD, DrPhil, Habil.; German musicologist and academic; *Director, Commission of Music History, Bavarian Academy of Sciences;* b. 25 Nov. 1929, Bielefeld; s. of Friedrich Göllner and Paula Brinkmann; m. Marie Louise Martinez 1959; one s. one d.; ed Univs of Heidelberg and Munich; Lecturer, Univ. of Munich 1958–62, Asst Prof. 1962–67, Assoc. Prof. 1967, Prof. and Chair. Inst. of Musicology 1973–97, now Prof. Emer.; Prof., Univ. of Calif., Santa Barbara 1967–73; Dir Comm. of Music History, Bavarian Acad. of Sciences 1982–; mem. European Acad. of Sciences and Arts 1991–. *Publications:* Formen früher Mehrstimmigkeit 1961, Die mehrstimmigen liturgischen Lesungen 1969, Die Sieben Worte am Kreuz 1986, Et incarnatus est in Bachs h-moll-Messe und Beethovens Missa solemnis 1996, Die Tactuslehre in den deutschen Orgelquellen des 15. Jahrhunderts 2003, Münchner Veröffentlichungen zur Musikgeschichte (ed.) 1977–2006, Münchner Editionen zur Musikgeschichte 1979–97, Die psalmodische Tradition bei Monteverdi und Schütz 2006. *Address:* Institute of Musicology, University of Munich, Geschwister-Scholl-Platz 1, 80539 Munich (office); Bahnweg 9, 82229 Seefeld, Germany (home). *Telephone:* (1089) 21802364 (office). *E-mail:* TheodorGoellner@aol.com (home).

GOLODETS, Olga Yuryevna, PhD (Econ); Russian politician; *Deputy Chairman of the Government;* b. 1 June 1962, Moscow, Russian SFSR, USSR; m.; two c.; ed Lomonosov Moscow State Univ.; Researcher at Cen. Research Lab. of Labour Resources, R&D Inst. of Labour and Russian Acad. of Sciences' Employment Problems Inst. 1984–97; Social Programmes Dir, Reformugol Foundation 1997–99; Dir Social Policy and Human Resources Dept, Mining and Metallurgical Co. Norilsk Nickel 1999–2001, Deputy Dir-Gen. for Human Resources and Social Policy 2002–08; Deputy Gov. for Social Affairs, Taimyr (Dolgano-Nenets) Autonomous Okrug (in Krasnoyarsk Krai) 2001; Pres. All-Russian Inter-industry Asscn of Employers –Nat. Alliance of Nickel and Precious Metals Mfrs; Chair. Soglasiye Insurance Co. 2008–10; Deputy Moscow Mayor for Educ. and Healthcare and mem. Moscow City Govt 2010–12; Deputy Chair. of the Govt 2012–. *Address:* Office of the Chairman of the Government, 103274 Moscow, Krasnopresnenskaya nab. 2, Russia (office). *Telephone:* (495) 605-53-29 (office). *Fax:* (495) 605-52-43 (office). *E-mail:* duty_press@aprf.gov.ru (office). *Website:* government.ru/en/gov/persons/186/events (office).

GOLOMBEK, Diego Andrés, PhD; Argentine biologist and academic; *Regular Full Professor, Department of Science and Technology, Universidad Nacional de Quilmes;* b. 22 Nov. 1964, Buenos Aires; ed Univ. of Buenos Aires; Independent Researcher and Prin. Investigator, Consejo Nacional de Investigaciones Científicas y Técnicas (CONICET) 2001–; Coordinator, Cellular and Molecular Biology Area, Universidad Nacional de Quilmes (UNQ) 2001, Post-Grad. Sec. 2003–04, Regular Full Prof., Dept of Science and Tech. 2004–, Departmental Counsellor, Center for Studies and Research 2005–, also Dir New Approaches in Science and Tech., Editorial of UNQ; Dir PICT Subsidy, Agencia Nacional de Promoción de Ciencia y Tecnología 2000, 2004, Co-Dir 2003; Visiting Prof. at various univs including Toronto, São Paulo, Campinas, Virginia, Santander; Ed.-in-Chief, Ciencia que ladra…; mem. Editorial Cttee, Circadian Rhythm Research 2003; mem. Bd of Dirs Sociedad Argentina de Neuroquímica 2000–02, Int. Soc. for Chronobiology 2000–06; Premio Bernardo Houssay, Sociedad Argentina de Biología 2002, Premio Nacional de Ciencias B. Houssay, Secretaría de Ciencia y Técnica, Universidad Adventista del Plata busca 2003, Prize to the Best Book of Education, Book Foundation 2005, Ig Nobel Prize 2007, Kalinga Prize, UNESCO 2015, Konex Platinum Award 2017. *Publications:* Cronobiología humana (ed) 2002, El cocinero científico: Apuntes de alquimia culinaria 2002, ADN: 50 años no es nada 2004, Hoy las ciencias adelantan que es una barbaridad 2005, Sexo, drogas y biología 2006, Cavernas y palacios 2011, Así en la tierra (fiction) 2012, Demoliendo papers. La trastienda de las publicaciones científicas 2012, El nuevo cocinero científico. Cuando la ciencia se mete en la cocina 2012, Las neuronas de Dios. Una neurociencia de la religión, la espiritualidad y la luz al final del túnel 2014. *Address:* Department of Science and Technology, Universidad Nacional de Quilmes, Roque Sáenz Peña 180, Barnel, B1876BXD Buenos Aires, Argentina (office). *Telephone:* (11) 4365-7100 (ext. 154) (office). *Fax:* (11) 4365-7132 (office). *E-mail:* dgolombek@unq.edu.ar (office). *Website:* www.unq.edu.ar/comunidad (office).

GOLU, Mihail, MA, PhD; Romanian politician and scientist; *Professor and Head, Department of Psychology, Spiru Haret University;* b. 4 March 1934, Bumbe-Pitic, Gorj Co.; s. of Ion Golu and Gheorghita Golu; m. Elena Filip 1957; two s.; ed Psychology Coll., Bucharest and Lomonosov Univs; worked as psychologist, Prof., Bucharest Univ.; Researcher, Carnegie-Mellon Univ., USA 1973–74; Deputy (ind. cand.) 1990–92, Party of Social Democracy 1992–96; Minister of Educ. and Science 1991–92, of Culture 1992–93; Deputy, Parl. Ass. of Council of Europe 1993–96; currently Prof. and Head, Dept of Psychology, Spiru Haret Univ.; Pres. Romanian Asscn of Psychologists 1990–2004, Nat. Soc. for Educ. 1993; Vice-Pres. Nat. Foundation for Gifted Children and Young People 2004; Nat. Comm. for UNESCO 1990–95; mem. Acad. of Scientists 1998–, New York Acad. of Science; Order of Merit 2004; Romanian Acad. Prize 1981, Pablo Picasso Medal, UNESCO 1991, Jan Amos Komenius Medal, Czech Acad. 1992, Nat. Merit Award 2004. *Publications:* Sensibility 1970, Principles of Cybernetic Psychology 1975, Dynamics of Personality 1993, Neuropsychology 2000, Fundamentals of Psychology 2000, General Psychology 2003; scientific papers and articles. *Leisure interests:* reading biographies of famous people, classical music. *Address:* Bulevardul Libertatii 22, Bloc 102, Scara 5, Apt. 89, Bucharest, Romania (home). *Telephone:* 318-77-91 (home). *E-mail:* mgolu@spiruharet.ro.

GOLUB, Harvey, BS; American business executive; b. 16 April 1939, New York; s. of Irving Golub and Pearl Fader; m. Roberta Glunts 1980; one s. and two s. one d. by previous m.; Jr Partner, McKinsey & Co., New York 1967–74, Sr Partner 1977–83; Pres. Shulman Air Freight, New York 1974–77; Sr Officer, American Express Co., New York 1983–84, Vice-Chair. 1990–93, CEO and Chair. 1993–2001; Chair. and Pres. IDS Financial Services (now American Express Financial Advisors), Minn. 1984–90, Chair. and CEO 1990–2001; Chair., Campbell Soup Co. 2004–09 (now Dir); Chair. American International Group (AIG) 2009–10 (resgnd); Chair. Ripplewood Holdings (pvt. equity firm), Marblegate Asset Management LLC; fmr Chair. Reader's Digest Association Inc.; mem. Bd of Dirs

Hess Corpn 2013–; fmr mem. Bd of Dirs Dow Jones & Company; mem. Advisory Bd Miller Buckfire & Co. LLC 2004–11. *Address:* Ripplewood Holdings, 1 Rockefeller Plaza, 32nd Floor, New York, NY 10020, USA (office). *Telephone:* (212) 582-6700 (office). *Fax:* (212) 582-4110 (office).

GOLUTVA, Alexander Alekseyevich; Russian film producer; b. 18 March 1948, Liepaya, Latvia; m.; one d.; ed Moscow State Univ.; fmr teacher; taught philosophy at Leningrad Ulyanov-Lenin Electro-technical Inst. (LETI) 1973–74; fmr Lecturer, Div. of Propaganda and Agitation, Petrograd Exec. CP Cttee 1974–80, then Instructor, then Head; consultant, House of Political Educ. 1980–83; Head of Sector, Div. of Culture, Leningrad Regional CP Cttee 1983–85; Ed.-in-Chief Lenfilm Film Studio 1985–87, Dir 1987–96; First Deputy Chair. State Cttee on Cinematography 1996–97, State Sec. then First Deputy Chair. 1997–99, Chair. 1999–2000; First Deputy Minister of Culture, Head of Cinema Dept 2000–04; mem. Presidential Council for Culture and Art; ORKF 'Kinotvar' Best Producer of Russia 1995, Badge of Honour of Russian Fed. 1998, Nika Prize of Russian Fed. 1995, 1999, 2000. *Films produced include:* Taxi Blues 1990, Mif o Leonide 1991, Gadzho 1992, Barabaniada 1993, Lyubov, predvestie pechali 1994, Peculiarities of the National Hunt 1995, Istoriya pro Richarda, milorda i prekrasnuyu Zhar-ptitsu 1997, Khrustalyov, My Car! 1998, Marigolds in Flower 1999, His Wife's Diary 2000, Shizofreniya 2001, Anton's Right Here (documentary) 2012, Slide 2013, White Chief (documentary) 2014.

GOLYSHEV, Vyacheslav Arkadevich, PhD; Uzbekistani government official; *State Adviser of the President for Socioeconomic Policy Issues;* First Deputy Presidential Adviser for Econ. Affairs –2005; Deputy Prime Minister, Head of the Econ. Sector and Foreign Econ. Relations Sector, Minister of the Economy 2005–06; State Adviser of the Pres. for Socioeconomic Policy Issues 2006–. *Address:* Office of the President, 100163 Tashkent, O'zbekiston shoh ko'ch. 43, Uzbekistan (office). *Telephone:* (71) 239-54-04 (office). *Fax:* (71) 239-53-25 (office). *E-mail:* presidents_office@press-service.uz (office). *Website:* www.press-service.uz/en (office).

GOMA, Col Louis Sylvain; Republic of the Congo politician and army officer; b. 24 June 1941; ed Versailles and Saint-Cyr; Asst Dir of Mil. Engineers –1968; Chief of Staff of Congolese People's Nat. Army 1968, promoted Capt. 1968; mem. Parti Congolais du Travail (PCT) 1969, Cen. Cttee 1970, Special Gen. Staff of Revolution 1974, Political Bureau; Sec. of State for Defence 1969–70; Minister of Public Works and Transport 1970–74; promoted Maj. 1973; Chief of Gen. Staff of Armed Forces 1974; Prime Minister 1975–84, 1991, responsible for Plan 1975–79; mem. Council of State 1975–77; mem. PCT Mil. Cttee (Second Vice-Pres.) 1977–79; Sec.-Gen. Econ. Community of Cen. African States 1999–2012; mem. Nat. Transitional Council 1997; Crans Montana Award 2010.

GOMARD, Bernhard, DJur; Danish lawyer and academic; *Professor of Law, Copenhagen Business School;* b. 9 Jan. 1926, Karise; s. of C. J. Gomard and Karen Gomard (née Magle); m. 1st 1974; one s.; m. 2nd Marianne Rosen 1994 (died 2000); ed Univ. of Copenhagen; Legal Adviser, Danish Dept of Justice 1950–58, Danish Atomic Comm. 1956–76, Danish Insurance Cos 1958–2002; Prof. of Law, Univ. of Copenhagen 1958–96; Prof. of Law, Copenhagen Business School 1996–; mem. Bd of Dirs Danske Bank 1974–96; mem. and Chair. numerous Govt cttees; mem. Danish Acad. of Sciences 1975, Academia Europaea 1989, Inst. of International Business Law and Practice; Hon. Prof., Univ. of Freiburg 1970; Commdr, Order of Dannebrog; Hon. DrIur (Univ. of Lund) 1982; Nordic Jurists Prize 1987, Oersted Medal 1995. *Publications:* articles and treatises on contract and company law, civil procedure, with particular emphasis on Danish law. *Leisure interests:* opera, French art and literature. *Address:* Centre for Financial Law, Copenhagen Business School, Solbjergvej 3, 1, 2000 Frederiksberg C (office); 3 Hammerensgade, 1267 Copenhagen K, Denmark (home). *Telephone:* 38-15-26-42 (office); 33-32-80-20 (home). *Fax:* 38-15-26-60 (office). *E-mail:* bg.ckk@cbs.dk (office).

GOMELAURI, Vakhtang; Georgian police officer and government official; *Head, State Security Service;* b. 24 Dec. 1975, Tbilisi, Georgian SSR, USSR; m.; two c.; ed Nat. Sports Acad.; Special State Protection Service of Georgia 1994–2003; Security Police of Ministry of Internal Affairs 2003–13; Deputy Minister of Internal Affairs 2013–Dec. 2014, First Deputy Minister of Internal Affairs Dec. 2014–Jan. 2015, Minister of Internal Affairs Jan.–July 2015; Head of State Security Service July 2015–. *Address:* Ministry of Internal Affairs, 0114 Tbilisi, Kakheti 38, Georgia (office). *Telephone:* (32) 241-84-44 (office). *Fax:* (32) 241-10-17 (office). *E-mail:* monitoringi@mia.gov.ge (office). *Website:* www.police.ge (office).

GOMERSALL, Sir Stephen John, Kt, KCMG, MA; British business executive and fmr diplomatist; *Deputy Chairman, Hitachi Europe Limited;* b. 17 Jan. 1948, Doncaster, S Yorks., England; s. of Harry Raymond Gomersall and Helen Gomersall; m. Lydia Veronica Parry 1975; two s. one d.; ed Forest School, Snaresbrook, Queens' Coll., Cambridge, Stanford Univ., USA; entered diplomatic service 1970; in Tokyo 1972–77; Rhodesia Dept, FCO 1977–79; Pvt. Sec. to Lord Privy Seal 1979–82; Washington, DC 1982–85; Econ. Counsellor, Tokyo 1986–90; Head of Security Policy Dept, FCO 1990–94, Dir Int. Security 1998–99; Deputy Perm. Rep., Perm. Mission to the UN 1994–98; Amb. to Japan 1999–2004; Chief Exec. for Europe, Hitachi Ltd 2004–13, Exec. Officer 2006–, Group Chair. 2011–13, Deputy Chair. Hitachi Europe Ltd 2013–, Dir, Hitachi Ltd; mem. Advisory Council, London Symphony Orchestra. *Leisure interests:* music, golf. *Address:* 24 Windsor Court, Moscow Road, London, W2 4SN, England (home). *Telephone:* (1628) 585705 (home). *Fax:* (1628) 585710 (home). *E-mail:* sjgomersall@hotmail.com (home); stephen.gomersall@hitachi-eu.com (office). *Website:* www.hitachi.eu (office).

GOMES, Aristides; Guinea-Bissau politician; *Prime Minister and Minister of Economy and Finance;* b. 8 Nov. 1954; s. of Lawrence Gomes and Hope Baticã Gomes Ferreira; ed Univ. of Paris VIII, France; Dir-Gen. Televisão Experimental da Guiné-Bissau 1990–92; fmr Minister of Planning and Int. Cooperation; Prime Minister 2005–07 (resgnd), 2018–, also Minister of Economy and Finance 2018–; Founder and Pres. Partido Republicano para a Independência e o Desenvolvimento 2008–; fmr mem. Partido Africano da Independência da Guiné e Cabo Verde (PAIGC—African Party for the Independence of Guinea and Cape Verde). *Address:* Office of Prime Minister, Av. dos Combatentes da Liberdade da Pátria, CP 137, Bissau (office); Partido Republicano para a Independência e o Desenvolvimento, Bissau, Guinea-Bissau (office). *Telephone:* 443211308 (office). *Fax:* 443201671 (office). *Website:* www.gov.gw.

GOMES, Patrick Ignatius, MA, PhD; Guyanese diplomatist and international organization official; *Secretary-General, African, Caribbean and Pacific Group of States (ACP);* b. 3 Nov. 1941, Georgetown; ed Fordham Univ. and Univ. of Chicago, USA; Sr Adviser in Human Resources Devt, UN Economic Comm. for Latin America and the Caribbean/Caribbean Devt Cooperation Cttee (ECLAC/CDCC) 1990–92; Exec. Dir Caribbean Centre for Devt Admin (CARICAD) 1992–2003; Consultant Project Man. for FAO/CARICOM/CARIFORUM/Govt of Italy-funded Project on Promotion of Food Security and Food Safety 2003–05; Amb. to Belgium and the EC and Rep. to WTO and FAO 2005–15; Sec.-Gen., African, Caribbean and Pacific Group of States (ACP) 2015–, fmr Chair. ACP Working Group on Future Perspectives; fmr Chair. European Centre for Devt Policy Management (think tank), Maastricht. *Publications:* numerous publications in the areas of devt and social policy analysis. *Address:* ACP Secretariat, Avenue Georges Henri 451, 1200 Brussels, Belgium (office). *Telephone:* (2) 743-06-00 (office). *Fax:* (2) 735-55-73 (office). *E-mail:* info@acp.int (office). *Website:* www.acp.int (office).

GOMÈS, Philippe; New Caledonian politician; *Leader, Calédonie Ensemble;* b. 27 Oct. 1958, Algiers, Algeria; mem. Congress 1988–99, 1999–2004; mem. Perm. Comm. 1988–89, 1990–95; Mayor of La Foa 1989–2008; mem. Govt responsible for Employment and Vocational Training 1999–2001; Pres. Agricultural Pricing Comm. 1995; Pres. South Prov. Ass. 2004–09; mem. L'Avenir Ensemble –2008, co-f. Calédonie Ensemble 2008; Pres. of the Govt, also responsible for Mining, Air Transport and Int. Affairs 2009–11; Leader, Calédonie Ensemble (CE) party 2008–; mem. Ass. Nat. (French Parl.) for 2nd New Caledonia constituency 2012–. *Address:* Calédonie Ensemble, 13 route de Vélodrome, 98800 Nouméa, New Caledonia (office). *Telephone:* 288905 (office). *Fax:* 288906 (office). *Website:* www.caledonieensemble.nc (office).

GOMES, Rui Augusto; Timor-Leste economist and politician; *Minister of Planning and Finance;* b. 21 Sept. 1958, Dili; ed London South Bank Univ.; fmr staff mem., Bappeda (Indonesian regional planning bd), Dili; fmr Policy Advisor, Poverty Reduction & Community Devt Unit, UN Devt Program (UNDP), becoming Asst Country Dir for Timor-Leste; fmr IMF-funded consultant to Ministry of Finance; fmr advisor to Pres. on econ. affairs; Chef de Cabinet to fmr Pres. Taur Matan Ruak 2015; Minister of Planning and Finance 2017–. *Address:* Ministry of Planning and Finance, Palácio do Governo, Edif. 5, Av. Presidente Nicolau Lobato, Dili, Timor-Leste (office). *Telephone:* 3339646 (office). *E-mail:* info@mof.gov.tl (office). *Website:* www.mof.gov.tl (office).

GOMES CRAVINHO, João, BSc (Econ), MSc (Econ), DPhil; Portuguese academic, government official and diplomatist; *Minister of Defence;* b. 16 June 1964; ed United World Coll. of the Atlantic, South Wales, London School of Econs and St Antony's Coll., Oxford, UK; Research Assoc., Inst. of Int. and Strategic Studies, Lisbon 1995–96; Guest Lecturer, African Studies, Instituto Superior de Ciências do Trabalho e da Empresa, Lisbon 1996–99; Guest Lecturer, Faculty of Law, Nova Univ., Lisbon 1997–99; Research Assoc., Nat. Defence Inst., Lisbon 1997–99; Advisor to Sec. of State for Int. Affairs and Co-operation, Ministry of Foreign Affairs 1999–2000; Visiting Fellow, Dept of Govt, Georgetown Univ., Washington, DC 2000; Pres. Portuguese Inst. for Devt Assistance, Ministry of Foreign Affairs 2001–02; Lecturer in Int. Relations, Faculty of Econs, Univ. of Coimbra 1995–2005; Sec. of State for Foreign Affairs and Co-operation 2005–11; Amb. of the EU to India 2011–15, to Brazil 2015–18; Minister of Defence 2018–; numerous consultancies. *Publications:* Visões do Mundo: a disciplina de relações internacionais e o mundo contemporâneo (Visions of the World: The Discipline of International Relations and the Contemporary World) (third edn) 2002; numerous articles for Portuguese newspapers and magazines on int. politics. *Address:* Ministry of Defence, Esplanada dos Ministérios, Bloco Q, 70049-900 Brasília, DF, Brazil (office). *Telephone:* (61) 3312-4000 (office). *Fax:* (61) 3225-4151 (office). *E-mail:* faleconosco@defesa.gov.br (office). *Website:* www.defesa.gov.br (office).

GOMES CRAVINHO, João, MSc, DPhil; Portuguese diplomatist and politician; *Minister of National Defence;* b. 16 June 1964, Coimbra; s. of João Cardona Gomes Cravinho; ed London School of Econs, St Antony's Coll., Oxford; Research Assoc., Inst. for Strategic and Int. Studies, Lisbon 1995–96; Prof. of Int. Relations, Univ. of Coimbra 1995–2000, 2002–05; Visiting Prof., Higher Inst. of Labour and Enterprise Sciences (ISCTE), Lisbon 1996–99, New Univ., Lisbon 1997–99; Deputy Researcher, Nat. Defence Inst., Lisbon 1997–99; Adviser to Sec. of State for Foreign Affairs and Cooperation, Ministry of Foreign Affairs (MFA) 1999–2000; Visiting Prof., Georgetown Univ. July–Dec. 2000; Pres., Inst. for Portuguese Cooperation, MFA 2001–02; Sec. of State for Foreign Affairs and Cooperation 2005–11; Amb. of EU to India 2012–15, to Brazil 2015–18; Minister of Nat. Defence 2018–; mem. Partido Socialista. *Publication:* Visões do Mundo 2002. *Address:* Ministry of National Defence, Av. Ilha da Madeira 1, 1400-204 Lisbon, Portugal (office). *Telephone:* (21) 3034500 (office). *E-mail:* gabinete.ministro@mdn.gov.pt (office).

GOMES FURTADO, HE Cardinal Arlindo; Cabo Verde ecclesiastic; *Bishop of Santiago de Cabo Verde;* b. 15 Nov. 1949, Santa Catarina; ed theological studies in Portugal; ordained priest, Diocese of Santiago de Cabo Verde 1976; Bishop of Mindelo 2003–09, consecrated 2004; Bishop of Santiago de Cabo Verde 2009–; cr. Cardinal (Cardinal-Priest of San Timoteo) 2015. *Address:* C.P. 46, Avenida Amilcar Cabral, Largo 5 de Outubro, Praia 7600, Cabo Verde (office). *Telephone:* 2611119 (office). *Fax:* 2612126 (office).

GOMES JÚNIOR, Carlos, (Cadogo); Guinea-Bissau politician; b. 19 Dec. 1949, Bolama; s. of Carlos Domingos Gomes and Maria Augusta Ramalho; m. Salomea Neves; four c.; fmr banker and business exec.; elected to Parl. 1994, First Vice-Pres. 1996; mem. African Party for the Independence of Guinea-Bissau 1991–, Sec. for Foreign Affairs and Int. Co-operation 1999–2002, apptd Leader 2002; Prime Minister of Guinea-Bissau May 2004–05, 2009–12 (resgnd); cand. in presidential election 2012 then military coup, sent to live in Portugal and Cape Verde (now Cabo Verde), then returned.

GÓMEZ MONT URUETA, Fernando Francisco, LicenDer; Mexican lawyer and politician; *Partner, Zínser Esponda y Gómez Mont SC;* b. 11 Jan. 1963; s. of Felipe Gómez Mont; ed Escuela Libre de Derecho; mem. Cámara Federal de

Diputados 1991–94, Chair. Justice Comm. 1991–94; adviser to Pres. Ernesto Zedillo 1994–2000; mem. Partido Acción Nacional, fmr mem. Nat. Exec. Council and Policy Comm., Rep. in Fed. Electoral Inst. –1995 (resgnd); Partner, Zínser Esponda y Gómez Mont SC, (law firm), Mexico City 1995–2008, 2010–; Sec. of Interior 2008–10. *Address:* Zínser Esponda y Gómez Mont SC, Sierra Nevada 156, Col. Lomas de Chapultepec, México DF, C.P. 11000, Mexico (office). *E-mail:* contacto@zegm.mx (office). *Website:* www.zegm.mx (office).

GÓMEZ PICKERING, Diego, KCVO, BA, MA; Mexican writer, journalist and diplomatist; *Consul General to New York;* b. 1977, Mexico City; ed Instituto Tecnológico Autónomo de México, Univ. of Columbia, Indian Inst. of Mass Communications, Jawaharlal Nehru Univ., India; fmr journalist for CNN in Mexico City and for Americas edn of the Wall Street Journal; fmr int. corresp. for Panamanian newspaper La Prensa, wrote for various other Mexican and Hispano-American publs, including Reforma, Excelsior and El Universal in USA, Mexico, East Africa and the Middle East; has been engaged with UN activities as a consultant and adviser to several agencies, including UNESCO, UN Public-Pvt. Alliance for Rural Devt, ILO, Office for Humanitarian Affairs Co-ordination (OCHA), Cttee for the Elimination of Discrimination against Women; Cultural Attaché, Embassy in Nairobi 2007–08; worked as a communications consultant for UNRWA, Damascus, Syria 2008–11; Dir for Foreign Media, Office of the Pres. –2013, acted as Head of Foreign Press Co-ordination for both the presidential campaign and throughout the transition period; Amb. to UK 2013–16, Consul General to New York 2016–; Assoc., Mexican Council for Int. Affairs (COMEXI); mem. Bd Child's Fund Mexico, American Soc. of Mexico; Honorary Knight Commander of the Royal Victorian Order 2015. *Publications include:* Los jueves en Nairobi (Thursdays in Nairobi) 2010, La primavera de Damasco (Spring in Damascus) 2013; more than a dozen books of prose and fiction; numerous editorials and academic and journalistic articles for journals from Mexico, Latin America, Spain and USA, including Foreign Affairs, Journal of International Affairs, Letras Libres; work has been translated into English, French, Swahili, Arabic and Russian. *Address:* Consulate General of Mexico, 27 E 39th Street, New York, NY 10016, USA (office). *Telephone:* (212) 217-6400 (office). *Fax:* (212) 217-6493 (office). *E-mail:* titularny@sre.gob.mx (office). *Website:* consulmex.sre.gob.mx/nuevayork (office).

GOMEZ-PIMIENTA, Bernardo, MArch, DArch; Mexican architect and academic; *Principal, bgp arquitectura;* b. 18 Aug. 1961, Brussels, Belgium; s. of Jose Luis Gomez-Pimienta and Danielle Magar; m. Loredana Dall'Amico; one d. one s.; ed Universidad Anáhuac, Mexico City, Columbia Univ., USA, European Univ. of Madrid; draftsman, George Wimpey Contractors Ltd, London, UK 1980–81; Founding Partner and Co-Dir TEN Arquitectos 1987–2003; f. bgp arquitectura 2003; apptd Dir Furniture Design, Visual Int. 1995; Prof. of Architecture, Universidad Iberoamericana 1987–89, Universidad Anáhuac 1989, Universidad Nacional Autónoma de México 1992–96, 1998–2002 (Federico E. Marcial Chair of Architecture 2002); Visiting Prof., Southern Calif. Inst. of Architecture 1994, Univ. of Illinois 1996–97; currently Dir School of Architecture, Universidad Anáhuac; mem. Mexican Coll. of Architects 1990; mem. Editorial Bd and Founding mem. Arquine Review 1997; mem. Bd Architecture Cttee, Colegio de Arquitectos de la Ciudad de Mexico AC 1998–; mem. Editorial Bd Periódico Reforma 2002; mem. Jury AIA Design Honour Awards (New Mexico) 1997, (Iowa) 1999, (San Juan) 1999, Premios Alfher 2000, Fere Ambiente, Frankfurt 2002, Il Bienal Nacional de Diseño 2003; mem. Academia Nacional de Arquitectura 2003, Nat. Creator System, Council for Culture and Arts; Hon. Fellow, Royal Architectural Inst. of Canada, Hon. mem. AIA; Chevalier, Légion d'honneur 2007; over 40 architectural awards from Mexico, USA, Ecuador, UK and Argentina. *Architectural works include:* House 'O' 1992, Televisa Services Bldg 1994, Museum of Natural History, Mexico City 1996, Nat. Centre of the Arts, Mexico City 1996, Casa IA 2001, Hotel Habita 2002, Educare 2002, Arquine 2002, Mesa Lupa 2002, Perchero Ti 2002, Mesa Lobe 2002, Silla IA 2002. *Publications include:* numerous books, monographs, periodicals, catalogues and reviews. *Address:* bgp arquitectura, 23 Ave Maria Street Sta. Catarina, Coyoacán, Mexico City 04010 (office); School of Architecture, Universidad Anáhuac, 46, Col. Lomas Anáhuac, 52786 Huixquilucan, Mexico (office). *Telephone:* (52) 5523-3468 (bgp arquitectura) (office); (55) 5627-0210 (office). *E-mail:* im@bgp.com.mx (office). *Website:* bgp.com.mx (office); www.anahuac.mx/arquitectura (office).

GÓMEZ-POMPA, Arturo, BSc, DrSc; Mexican biologist, botanist and academic; *University Professor Emeritus and Distinguished Professor Emeritus of Botany, University of California, Riverside;* b. 21 Oct. 1934, Mexico City; m. Norma Edith Barrero; ed Universidad Nacional Autónoma de México (UNAM—Nat. Autonomous Univ. of Mexico); fmr Prof. of Botany, Univ. of California, Riverside, USA, fmr Univ. Prof. and Distinguished Prof. of Botany, now Univ. Prof. Emer. and Distinguished Prof. Emer. of Botany, fmr Dir Inst. of Univ. of California to Mexico and US (UC MEXUS); Founder and CEO Inst. for Research on Biotic Resources (INIREB), Xalapa, Veracruz; Head of Dept of Botany, UNAM-Inst. of Biology, Prof. of Ecology and Botany, Faculty of Nat. Univ.; Founder and first Pres. Asociación Mexicana de Jardines Botánicos, AC (Mexican Asscn of Botanic Gardens, AC) 1983; Pres. Bd El Edén Ecological Reserve, AC; mem. Bd, American Inst. of Biological Sciences, Exec. Council Tyler Prize, Botanical Research Inst. of Texas (BRIT); mem. Awards Cttee Acad. of Sciences for the Developing World, Int. Scientific Advisory Bd INBio, Costa Rica; fmr Vice-Chair. Species Survival Comm. of Int. Union for Conservation of Nature (IUCN); fmr Pres. Int. Coordinating Council of UNESCO's MAB Programme; currently Scientific Advisor, Centro de Investigaciones Tropicales de la Universidad Veracruzana; fmr mem. Bd of Govs The Nature Conservancy; Founder and Exec. Dir US-Mexico Foundation for Science; fmr mem. Advisory Cttee on Science, Space and Tech. of US House of Reps, Bd Smithsonian Inst., Washington, DC; Founder and mem. Bd Pronatura, AC; mem. acads of Mexico, Latin American, Third World and American Acad. of Arts and Sciences; Dr hc (Autonomous Univ. of Morelos); Medal of Merit, Univ. of Veracruz, Tyler Prize for Environmental Achievement, Chevron Conservation Medal, Luis Elizondo Prize in Science and Tech., Instituto Tecnológico de Estudios Superiores de Monterrey, Arca de Oro Medal (Netherlands) 1984, Alfonso L. Herrera Medal, Mexican Inst. of Renewable Natural Resources, Botanical Merit Medal, Botanical Soc. of Mexico. *Publications include:* more than 200 scientific papers in professional journals on tropical ecology, ethnobotany, conservation and man. of tropical forests. *Address:* 3133 Batchelor Hall, Department of Botany and Plant Sciences, University of California, 900 University Avenue, Riverside, CA 92521, USA (office). *Telephone:* (951) 827-4686 (office). *Fax:* (951) 827-4748 (office). *E-mail:* floramex@ucr.edu (office). *Website:* www.plantbiology.ucr.edu (office); www.agomezpompa.org (office).

GÓMEZ URRUTIA, José Antonio; Chilean lawyer and politician; b. 18 Dec. 1953, Santiago; s. of José Gómez López and Cecilia Urrutia Concha; m. Ximena Passi; four c.; ed Universidad de Chile; Councillor, Las Condes 1991–94; Adviser to Minister of Justice 1995, Deputy Attorney-Gen. 1996–99, Minister of Justice 1999–2003; mem. Senado for Antofagasta 2006–15, Vice-Pres. 2010–11, 2013–14; Sec. of State for Justice 2014–15; Minister of Nat. Defence 2015–18; mem. Chilean Del. to UN Conf. for Establishment of Int. Criminal Court, Rome and UN Comm. on Crime Prevention and Criminal Justice, Austria; mem. Comm. on Political Imprisonment and Torture 2004; mem. Partido Radical Socialdemócrata de Chile (PRSD). *Address:* c/o Ministry of National Defence, Edif. Diego Portales, 22°, Villavicencio 364, Santiago, Chile (office).

GOMORY, Ralph Edward, BA, MA, PhD; American mathematician, academic, business executive and foundation executive; *Research Professor, Stern School of Business, New York University;* b. 7 May 1929, Brooklyn Heights, NY; s. of Andrew L. Gomory and Marian Schellenberg; m. 1st Laura Secretan Dumper 1954 (divorced 1968); two s. one d.; m. 2nd Lilian Wu; ed Williams Coll., King's Coll., Cambridge and Princeton Univ.; Lt, USN 1954–57; Higgins Lecturer and Asst Prof., Princeton Univ. 1957–59; joined IBM 1959, Fellow 1964, filled various managerial positions including Dir Math. Science Dept, Dir of Research 1970–86, Vice-Pres. 1973–84, Sr Vice-Pres. 1985–89, mem. Corp. Man. Bd 1983–89, Sr Vice-Pres. for Science and Tech. 1986–89 (retd); Andrew D. White Prof.-at-Large, Cornell Univ. 1970–76; Pres. Alfred P. Sloan Foundation, New York 1989–2007, Pres. Emer. 2007–; Research Prof., Stern School of Business, New York Univ. 2008–; Dir Bank of New York 1986–88, Industrial Research Inst. 1986–91; mem. Bd of Dirs Washington Post Co. 1989–, Lexmark Int. Inc. 1991–; mem. NAS, Nat. Acad. of Eng, American Acad. of Arts and Sciences, Council on Foreign Relations, White House Science Council 1986–89, Visiting Cttee, Harvard Univ. Grad. School of Business 1995–; Fellow, Econometric Soc., American Acad. of Arts and Sciences 1973; Trustee, Hampshire Coll. 1977–86, Princeton Univ. 1985–89; Hon. DSc (Williams Coll.) 1973, (Polytechnic Univ.) 1987, (Syracuse Univ.) 1989, (Carnegie Mellon Univ.) 1989; Hon. LHD (Pace Univ.) 1986; Lanchester Prize, Operations Research Soc. of America 1964, John von Neumann Theory Prize 1984, Harry Goode Memorial Award 1984, IRI Medal 1985, IEEE Eng Leadership Recognition Award 1988, Nat. Medal of Science 1988, Presidential Award (New York Acad. of Sciences) 1992, Arthur M. Bueche Award, Nat. Acad. of Eng 1993, Heinz Award 1998, Madison Medal 1999, Harold Larnder Prize, Canadian Operational Research Soc. 2006. *Publications:* Global Trade and Conflicting National Interests 2001 (co-author); published more than 80 articles. *Address:* Leonard N. Stern School of Business, Kaufman Management Center, 44 West 4th Street, Room 8-179, New York, NY 10012 (office); 260 Douglas Road, Chappaqua, NY 10514, USA (home). *Telephone:* (212) 998-0100 (office). *E-mail:* rgomory@stern.nyu.edu (office). *Website:* www.stern.nyu.edu (office).

GOMRINGER, Eugen; Swiss poet and academic; b. 20 Jan. 1925, Cachuela Esperanza, Bolivia; s. of Eugen Gomringer and Delicia Rodriguez; m. 1st Klara Stöckli 1950; m. 2nd Nortrud Ottenhausen; five s. one d.; ed Kantonsschule, Zürich and Univ. of Berne; Sec. and Docent, Hochschule für Gestaltung, Ulm 1954–58; Art Dir Swiss Industrial Abrasives 1959–67; Man. Dir Schweizer Werkbund, Zürich 1961–67; Man. of Cultural Relations, Rosenthal AG, Germany 1967–85; Prof. of Aesthetics, Düsseldorf Art School 1976–90; Man. Int. Forum for Design, Ulm 1988–; co-f. first museum for concrete art in Ingolstadt 1992; f. Inst. für Konstruktive Kunst und Poesie IKKP Rehau 1999; Hon. Prof., Univ. of Zwickau; mem. Akad. der Künste, Berlin, PEN; Bayerischer Verdienstorden 2008. *Publications include:* several books of poetry and monographs in the art field; many publs for Concrete Poetry, beginning with Constellations, Bern 1953. *Leisure interests:* mountaineering, art collecting, farming, dogs. *Address:* Institute for Constructive Art and Concrete Poetry, Kirchgasse 4, 95111 Rehau, Germany (office). *Telephone:* 9283-899485 (office); 9283-1234 (home). *Fax:* 9283-899487 (office); 9283-1234 (home). *E-mail:* info@kunsthaus-rehau.de (office). *Website:* www.kunsthaus-rehau.de (office).

GOMUŁKA, Stanisław, DEcon; Polish/British economist and academic; *Chief Economist, Business Centre Club;* b. 10 Sept. 1940, Krężoły; s. of Władysław Gomułka and Zofia Gomułka; m. Joanna Gomułka; one s.; ed Warsaw Univ.; Dept of Econs, Warsaw Univ. 1962–65; Researcher, Dept of Econs, Århus Univ., Denmark 1970, 1973; Reader in Econs, LSE, London 1970–2005; Fellow, Netherlands Inst. for Advanced Studies 1980–81; Prof., Dept of Econs, Univ. of Pennsylvania, USA 1985–86; Fellow, Stanford Univ. 1986, Columbia Univ. 1987, Harvard Univ., USA 1989–90; Prof., Central European Univ., Dept of Econs 1995–2000; Prof., Natolin Coll. of Europe 1995–2000; Chief Economist, PZU Group (insurance co.) 2002–07; Under-Sec. of State, Ministry of Finance Jan.–April 2008; currently Chief Economist, Business Centre Club, Warsaw; econ. adviser to Polish Govts 1989–2002, to Chair. Nat. Bank of Poland 1996–97, to Russian Govt 1991; fmr econ. adviser to IMF, OECD, EU; Corresp. mem. Polish Acad. of Sciences 2013; Polonia Restituta; Dr hc (Poznań Econs Univ.). *Publications include:* Inventive Activity, Diffusion and the Stages of Economic Growth 1971, Growth, Innovation and Reform in Eastern Europe 1986, Economic Reforms in the Socialist World (co-ed.) 1989, The Theory of Technological Change and Economic Growth 1990, Polish Paradoxes (co-ed.) 1990, Emerging from Communism – Lessons from Russia, China, and Eastern Europe (co-ed.) 1998, The Theory of Technological Change and Economic Growth (e-book) 2002, Transformacja polska, dokumenty i analizy, Vol. I 2010, Vol. II 2011, Vol. III 2013; chapters in some 50 books and numerous articles in professional journals. *Leisure interests:* chess, bridge, walks. *Address:* Business Centre Club, 00-136 Warsaw, Plac Żelaznej Bramy 10, Poland (office). *Telephone:* (22) 6253037 (office). *Fax:* (22) 6218420 (office). *E-mail:* stanislaw.gomulka@bcc.org.pl (office). *Website:* www.bcc.org.pl (office).

GONÇALVES LOURENÇO, Maj.-Gen. João Manuel; Angolan party official, politician and head of state; *President;* b. 6 March 1954, Lobito Municipality, Central Benguela Prov.; m. Aga Afonso Dias; five c.; mem. Movimento Popular de Libertação de Angola (MPLA), First Sec., Prov. Party Cttee and Gov., Moxico Prov. 1984–87, First Sec., Prov. Party Cttee and Gov., Benguela Prov. 1987–90, mem.

MPLA Cen. Cttee 1985–, mem. Political Bureau 1990–, Sec., MPLA Information Div. 1992–97, Sec.-Gen., MPLA 1998–2003, Vice-Pres. MPLA 2016–; mem. Assembleia Popular (People's Ass., fmr Parl.) 1984–92, Chair. MPLA Parl. Group 1993–98, Pres. Constitutional Comm. 1998–2003; Head FAPLA (Forças Armadas Populares de Libertação de Angola, armed wing of MPLA) Nat. Policy Directorate 1990–92; First Vice-Pres., Assembleia Nacional (Parl.) 2012–14; Minister of Nat. Defence 2014–17; Pres. of Angola 2017–; attained rank of Maj.-Gen. 1989. *Address:* Office of the President, Rua 17 de Setembro, Palácio do Povo, Luanda, Angola (office). *Telephone:* 222332939 (office). *Fax:* 222339855 (office). *Website:* www.governo.gov.ao (office).

GONCHAR, Nikolai Nikolayevich, CEconSc; Russian politician; b. 16 Oct. 1946, Murmansk; m.; one d.; ed Moscow Energy Inst.; engineer, then head of div. Moscow City Council on research activities of students 1972–75; Head of Div. Research Inst. of Complex Devt of Nat. Econs of Moscow 1976–82; Deputy, then First Deputy Chair. Exec. Cttee of Deputies, Soviet of Bauman Region of Moscow 1987–89, Chair. 1990–91; Sec. Regional CPSU Cttee 1989–90; Deputy Chair. Moscow City Soviet of People's Deputies 1990–91, Chair. 1991–93; mem. Council of Fed. 1993–95, Deputy Chair. Cttee on Budget and Financial Regulations 1994–95; mem. State Duma 1995–, mem. Cttee on Budget Issues and Taxes; Chair. Cttee on Financial Markets, US-Russia Business Council. *Address:* State Duma, Okhotny Ryad 1, 103265 Moscow Russia (office). *Telephone:* (495) 292-75-08 (office). *E-mail:* gonchar@duma.gov.ru (office). *Website:* www.duma.gov.ru (office).

GONCHIGDORJ, Radnaasumberel R., PhD, DSc; Mongolian mathematician and politician; b. 29 Dec. 1953, Tsakhir Dist, Arkhangai Prov.; s. of Radnaasumberel Gonchigdorj; m. Damdinsurengiin Hishigt 1977; two s. two d.; ed Mongolian State Univ., Inst. of Math., Belorussian Acad. of Sciences; Lecturer in Math., Mongolian State Univ. 1975–88; Dir Inst. of Math., Mongolian Acad. of Sciences 1988–90; Chair. Exec. Cttee Mongolian Social Democratic Movt 1990, Chair. Mongolian Social Democratic Party 1994, now mem. Democratic Party (DP); Deputy to Great People's Hural 1990–92; Vice-Pres. of Mongolia and Chair. State Little Hural 1990–92; mem. State Great Hural 1992–96, Chair. 1996–2000, Deputy Speaker 2013–16; presidential cand. 2001.

GONDWE, Goodall; Malawi politician and economist; *Minister of Finance, Economic Planning and Development;* fmr Gen. Man. Reserve Bank of Malawi; fmr Sr Vice-Pres. and Acting Pres. African Devt Bank; Dir of African Div., IMF 1998; fmr Econ. Adviser to Pres. of Malawi; Minister of Finance 2004–09, of Local Govt and Rural Devt 2009–11, of Natural Resources, Energy and the Environment 2011–12, of Econ. Planning and Devt 2012–13, of Finance, Econ. Planning and Devt 2014–; Vice-Pres. Democratic Progressive Party 2011–. *Address:* Ministry of Finance, Economic Planning and Development, Capital Hill, POB 30049, Lilongwe 3, Malawi (office). *Telephone:* 1789355 (office). *Fax:* 1789173 (office). *E-mail:* finance@finance.gov.mw (office). *Website:* www.finance.gov.mw (office).

GONDWE, Michael M., MBA; Zambian business executive and fmr central banker; ed Univ. of Zambia, Univ. of Virginia, USA, Moi Univ., Kenya Coll. of Accountancy, Advanced Man. Programme, Univ. of Oxford, UK; worked for Zambia Industrial Mining Corpn (ZIMCO) and Bank of Zambia –1986; served in sr positions in Eastern and Southern African Trade and Devt Bank (PTA Bank), a COMESA inst. 1986–2001, Pres. Eastern and Southern African Trade and Development Bank (PTA) Bank 2001–12; Chair. Zep Re Pta Reinsurance Co. 2009–13; Chair. and Gov. Bank of Zambia 2011–15; fmr Dir Athi River Mining Ltd, Gulf African Bank; Hon. Fellow, Zambia Inst. of Banking and Financial Services 2015; Central Bank Governor of the Year, Africa Investor (Ai) Investment and Business Leader Awards 2014.

GONG, Ke; Chinese engineer, academic and university administrator; b. 1955, Beijing; ed Beijing Inst. of Tech., Tech. Univ. Graz, Austria; Prof., Tsinghua Univ. 1994, also Chair. Dept of Electronic Eng 1997, Dir Chinese Nat. Lab. on Microwave and Digital Communications 1998, Vice-Pres. Tsinghua Univ. 1999, also Dean, School of Information 2004, Dir Tsinghua Nat. Lab. for Information Science and Tech. 2005; Pres. Tianjin Univ. 2006–11, Nankai Univ. 2011–18, currently mem. Bd of Dirs Academic Cttee; Pres.-Desig. World Fed. of Eng Orgs 2018; Vice-Pres. Chinese Inst. of Electronics, Chinese Inst. of Communication, China Inst. of Measurement and Instrumentations; Exec. mem. China Asscn of Science and Tech., Tech. Advisory Cttee, Ministry of Industry and Informatization; Fellow, Russian Acad. of Aerospace Sciences 2002–; Pan Wen Yuan Foundation Award for Outstanding Research in 2006. *Publications:* author or co-author of more than 100 papers in wireless communication, radiowave propagation, digital TV transmission, microsatellites and their applications, etc. *Address:* c/oNankai University, 94 Weijin Road, Nankai District, Tianjin 300071, People's Republic of China (office); World Federation of Engineering Organizations, Maison de l'Unesco 1, rue Miollis, 75015 Paris, France (office). *Website:* www.wfeo.org (office).

GONG, Yuzhi; Chinese politician; b. 26 Dec. 1929, Xiangtan, Hunan Prov.; ed Tsinghua Univ.; joined CCP 1948; researcher, CCP Cen. Cttee Propaganda Dept 1952–66; Deputy Office Dir Cttee for Editing and Publishing Works of Mao Zedong 1977–80; Deputy Dir CCP Cen. Cttee Party Documents Research Office 1982; Deputy Dir CCP Cen. Cttee Propaganda Dept 1988; mem. 5th to 8th CPPCC Nat. Cttee 1978–98 (Vice-Chair. Sub-cttee of Study 1993–98), Standing Cttee 9th CPPCC Nat. Cttee 1998–2003 (Vice-Chair. Sub-cttee of Cultural and Historical Data 1998–2003); Vice-Pres. CCP Cen. Cttee Cen. Party School 1994–96, Soc. of Research on History of CCP (Pres. 1999), China Soc. of Dialectics of Nature, China Anti-Cult Asscn 2000; Dir Research Centre for Theory of Building Socialism with Chinese Characteristics; Exec. Deputy Dir Cen. Party History Research Centre; fmr mem. Academic Council, Inst. of Philosophy, Chinese Acad. of Social Sciences; fmr Guest Prof., Beijing and Tsinghua Univs. *Publications:* Some Questions on the Law of Development for Natural Sciences, On Science, Philosophy and Society, From New Democracy to Primary Stage of Socialism.

GONO, Gideon, MBA, PhD; Zimbabwean business executive and central banker (retd); b. 29 Nov. 1959, Buhera Dist; m. Hellin Gono 1982; two s. two d.; ed Univ. of Zimbabwe; began career with ZimBank; held several positions at Jewel Bank (fmrly Commercial Bank of Zimbabwe) including CEO; Gov. Reserve Bank of Zimbabwe 2003–13; acquired Modus Publications 2000; f. Lunar Chickens (poultry firm) 2007; Head, Univ. of Zimbabwe Council; fmr Chair. Zimbabwe Broadcasting Holdings; Chair. Bd Special Economic Zone (SEZ) 2017–; Dr hc (Univ. of Zimbabwe).

GONSALVES, Ralph E., PhD; Saint Vincent and the Grenadines politician and lawyer; *Prime Minister and Minister of National Security, Grenadines Affairs and Legal Affairs;* b. 1946; ed Univ. of West Indies, Victoria Univ. of Manchester, UK; called to Bar, Gray's Inn, London; practised law at Eastern Caribbean Supreme Court; fmr Lecturer, Depts of Govt, Political Science and Sociology, Univ. of W Indies; Leader United People's Movt (UPM) 1979–82, Movt for Nat. Unity (MNU) 1994–98; Leader United Labour Party (ULP); Prime Minister of Saint Vincent and the Grenadines and Minister of Finance, Planning, Econ. Devt, Labour and Information 2001–10, Minister of Nat. Security 2005–10, Prime Minister and Minister Nat. Security 2010–, also Minister of Grenadines Affairs and Legal Affairs, and of Finance 2010–17. *Address:* Office of the Prime Minister, Administrative Building, 4th Floor, Bay Street, Kingstown, Saint Vincent and the Grenadines (office). *Telephone:* 451-2939 (office). *Fax:* 457-2152 (office). *Website:* pmosvg@caribsurf.com (office).

GÖNÜL, Mehmet Vecdi; Turkish politician; b. 1939, Erzincan; m.; three c.; ed Faculty of Political Science, Ankara Univ.; participated in state training programme for recruiting dist govs 1967; Dist Gov. in several areas of Turkey 1967–76; Gov. of Kocaeli 1976–77, later of Izmir; Dir-Gen. of Nat. Security (Police) Directorate 1977–79; Gov. of Ankara 1979–88; Under-Sec., Ministry of the Interior 1988–91; apptd Head of State Court of Accounts 1991; mem. Parl. for Kocaeli 1999–2002, for İzmir 2007–11, for Antalya 2011–, Deputy Speaker of Parl. 1999–2001; joined AK Party 2001; Minister of Nat. Defence 2002–11, July–Nov. 2015; Del. to EU Parl. Ass. *Address:* c/o Ministry of National Defence, Milli Savunma Bakanlığı, 06100, Ankara, Turkey (office).

GONZALES, Alberto (Al) R., BA, JD; American lawyer and fmr government official; *Dean and Doyle Rogers Distinguished Professor, College of Law Belmont University;* b. 4 Aug. 1955, San Antonio, Tex.; s. of Pablo M. Gonzales and Maria Rodriguez Gonzales; m. Rebecca Gonzales; three s.; ed Rice Univ., Harvard Law School; served in USAF 1973–75, attended USAF Acad. 1975–77; joined Vinson & Elkins LLP, Houston, Tex. 1982, Partner –1994; Adjunct Prof. of Law, Univ. of Houston –1994; Gen. Counsel to Tex. Gov. George W. Bush 1994–97; Sec. of State for Tex. 1977–99; Justice of Supreme Court of Tex. 1999–2001; Legal Counsel to the White House, Washington, DC 2001–04, Attorney-Gen. US Dept of Justice 2004–07; Visiting Prof., Dept of Political Science, Texas Tech Univ. 2009–11; Founder and Prin. Alberto R. Gonzales P.C. (consultancy) 2009–12; Of Counsel, Waller Lansden (law firm), Nashville, Tenn. 2011–14; Dean and Doyle Rogers Distinguished Prof., Coll. of Law, Belmont Univ. 2012–; Pres. Houston Hispanic Bar Asscn 1990–91, Leadership Houston 1993–94; Chair. Comm. for Dist Decentralization, Houston Ind. School Dist 1994; mem. Bd of Dirs United Way of Tex. Gulf Coast 1993–94; mem. Cttee on Undergraduate Admissions, Rice Univ. 1994; mem. Bd State Bar of Tex. 1991–94, Bd of Trustees, Tex. Bar Foundation 1996–99; mem. American Law Inst. 1999–; Hispanic Salute Award, Houston Metro Ford Dealers 1989, Outstanding Young Lawyer of Tex., Tex. Young Lawyers Asscn 1992, Presidential Citation, State Bar of Tex. 1997, Latino Lawyer of the Year, Hispanic Nat. Bar Asscn 1999, Distinguished Alumnus of Rice Univ. 2002, Harvard Law School Asscn Award 2002, Hispanic Scholarship Fund Alumni Hall of Fame 2003, Good Neighbour Award, US–Mexico Chamber of Commerce 2003, Pres.'s Award, US Hispanic Chamber of Commerce 2003, Pres.'s Award, League of United Latin American Citizens 2003. *Publications include:* A Conservative and Compassionate Approach to Immigration Reform (with David N. Strange) 2014; numerous articles in professional journals. *Address:* Belmont University College of Law, 1901 15th Avenue South, Nashville, TN 37212, USA. *Telephone:* (615) 460-8259. *E-mail:* alberto.gonzales@belmont.edu. *Website:* www.belmont.edu/law.

GONZALES POSADA, Luis; Peruvian lawyer and politician; b. 30 July 1945, Pisco; s. of Carlos Gonzales Posada and Zurmira Zully Eyzaguirre; m. Maria Luisa de Cossio de Vivanco; three c.; ed Claretian Coll., Leoncio Prado Military Acad., Nat. Univ. of San Marcos; fmr Legal Adviser, Banco Industrial, Corporación Financiera de Desarrollo, Electricidad del Perú and of Social Security Dept; mem. Bd of Dirs Seguro Social Obrero, Seguro Social del Empleado, Empresa Nacional de Turismo del Perú, La Crónica, Futura and Visión Peruana publishing cos; Founder and Dir daily Hoy and the weekly Visión; has been on staff of La Tribuna, La Prensa, Correo and La Crónica; mem. Colegio de Abogados de Lima (Pres. Foreign Affairs Comm. 1999) and of Colegio de Periodistas de Lima; Minister of Justice 1985–86, of Foreign Affairs 1988–89; Perm. Rep. to OAS 1987; mem. Congreso 2001–11, Pres. 2007–08.

GONZÁLEZ ANAYA, José Antonio, PhD; Mexican economist and politician; b. 7 June 1967, Coatzacoalcos, Veracruz; m. Gabriela Gerard; ed Massachusetts Inst. of Tech. and Harvard Univ., USA; fmr economist for the World Bank; fmr Researcher and Prof., Center for the Analysis of Devt, Stanford Univ., USA; various roles in Secr. of Finance and Public Credit, including Chief of Staff for Sec. of Finance and Public Credit and the Unit responsible for Insurance, Securities and Pensions, Fed. Entities Co-ordinator, Undersecretary of Revenue, Dir Gen., Mexican Social Security Inst. 2012–16, apptd Sec. of Finance and Public Credit 2017–18; CEO Petróleos Mexicanos (PEMEX) 2016–17. *Address:* c/o Secretariat of State for Finance and Public Credit, Palacio Nacional, Plaza de la Constitución, Col Centro, Del. Cuauhtémoc, 06000 México, DF, Mexico (office).

GONZÁLEZ CASANOVA, Pablo, MA, PhD; Mexican researcher and academic; b. 11 Feb. 1922, Toluca; s. of Pablo González Casanova and Concepción del Valle; m. Natalia Henríquez Ureña 1947; three s.; ed El Colegio de México, Escuela Nacional de Antropología, Univ. Nacional Autónoma de México and Univ. de Paris, France; Asst Researcher, Inst. de Investigaciones Sociales, Univ. Nacional Autónoma de México (UNAM) 1944–50, Researcher 1950–52, Full-time Researcher 1973–78; Researcher, El Colegio de México 1950–54; Sec.-Gen. Asscn of Univs 1953–54; Titular Prof. of Mexican Sociology, Escuela Nacional de Ciencias Políticas y Sociales, UNAM 1952–66, of Gen. Sociology 1954–58; Dir Escuela Nacional de Ciencias Políticas y Sociales 1957–65, Full-time Titular Prof. 1964–65, Titular Prof. of Research Planning 1967–; Dir Inst. Investigaciones Sociales, UNAM 1966–70; Rector UNAM 1970–72, Prof. Emer. 1984–; Visiting Prof., Univ. of Cambridge, UK 1981–82; Pres. Admin. Cttee Facultad Latinoamericana de Ciencias Sociales, Santiago and Centro Latinoamericano de Investigaciones

Sociales, Rio de Janeiro, UNESCO 1959–65; Consultant UN Univ. 1983–87; Dir Centro de Investigaciones Interdisciplinarias en Humanidades Univ. Nacional Autónoma de Mexico 1986; mem. Asscn Int. de Sociologues de Langue Française, Comité Int. pour la Documentation des Sciences Sociales, Acad. de la Investigación Científica; Pres. Asociación Latinoamericana de Sociología 1969–72; Dr hc (Universidad Autonoma de Queretaro) 2007; Nat. Award for Social Sciences 1984, José Martí Int. Prize, UNESCO 2003. *Publications:* El misoneísmo y la modernidad cristiana 1948, Satira del Siglo XVIII (with José Miranda) 1953, Una utopia de América 1953, La literatura perseguida en la crisis de la Colonia 1958, La ideología norteamericana sobre inversiones extranjeras 1955, Estudio de la técnica social 1958, La Democracia en México 1965, Las categorías del desarrollo económico y la investigación en ciencias sociales 1967, Sociología de la explotación 1969, América Latina: Historia de Medio Siglo 1925–1975 (two vols, ed.) 1977, Historia del Movimiento Obrero en América Latina, Siglo XX 1981, El Estado y los Partidos Políticos en México 1981, El Poder al Pueblo 1985, América Latina, Hoy 1990, El Estado y la Política en el Sur del Mundo 1994. *Address:* Peña Pobre 28, Tlalpan, México, DF 14050, Mexico. *Telephone:* 5506702.

GONZÁLEZ FERNÁNDEZ, Cosme Mariano, LLB; Peruvian lawyer and government official; b. 26 April 1968, Lima; ed Univ. Nacional San Agustín, Arequipa, George Washington Univ., USA; several years' private legal practice including as Attorney and Partner, Gazette Consultores SA, Partner at Gonzalez & Assocs, Lawyers and Assoc. Attorney, Study Cornejo Chavez; fmr Chief of Staff to Advisers in Ministry of Defence 2011–12 and Ministry of the Interior 2012; fmr Exec. Dir Nat. Superintendence of Migration (migration agency under Ministry of Interior); fmr Adviser to Congress Parl. Intelligence Cttee; fmr consultant for several int. orgs including UNDP and Global Fund to Fight AIDS, Tuberculosis and Malaria (The Global Fund); fmr Gen. Coordinator, Office of Social Communication of the Presidency of Council of Ministers; Chair. Cttee on Infractions and Sanctions of Peruvian Agency for Int. Cooperation; fmr Adviser to Bd of Dirs Sisol (health agency), Metropolitan Municipality of Lima; Minister of Defence July–Nov. 2016; mem. Peruanos por el Kambio. *Address:* c/o Ministry of Defence, Edif. Quiñones, Avda de la Peruanidad s/n, Jesús María, Lima 1, Peru (office).

GONZÁLEZ FERNÁNDEZ, Margarita Marlene; Cuban engineer and politician; *Minister of Labour and Social Security;* b. 20 July 1964; spent several years working in construction industry; Vice-Minister, Ministry of Labour and Social Security 2001–03, First Vice-Minister 2001–09, Minister of Labour and Social Security 2009–; mem. Communist Party of Cuba. *Address:* Ministry of Labour and Social Security, Calle 23, esq. Calles O y P, Vedado, Municipio Plaza de la Revolución, Havana, Cuba (office). *Telephone:* (7) 838-0022 (office). *E-mail:* webmaster@mtss.cu (office). *Website:* www.mtss.cu (office).

GONZÁLEZ GONZÁLEZ, (Jaime) Ignacio; Spanish politician; b. 19 Oct. 1960, Madrid; s. of Pablo Gonzalez Liberal; m. Lourdes Cavero Mestre; three d.; ed Autonomous Univ. of Madrid; Under-Sec., Ministry of Culture, Educ. and Sports 1996–99; Sec. of State for Public Admin, Ministry of Public Admin 1999–2002; Sec. of State for Immigration, Ministry of Interior 2002–03, also Govt Commr for Foreigners and Immigration 2002–03; mem. Partido Popular (PP), Sec.-Gen., PP in Madrid 2011–16; First Deputy Prime Minister, Community of Madrid 2003–12, Minister of Culture and Sports, Community of Madrid 2009–12, Pres. Community of Madrid 2012–15. *Address:* c/o Partido Popular, C/Genova 13, 28004 Madrid, Spain.

GONZÁLEZ MACCHI, Luis Angel, (Lucho); Paraguayan lawyer and fmr head of state; b. 13 Dec. 1947, Asunción; s. of Dr Saúl González and Julia Macchi; m. Susana Galli; two d.; ed Univ. Nacional de Asunción; fmr Pres. Nat. Congress; fmr Chair. Nat. Vocational Service, Ministry of Justice and Labour; Dir-Gen. and Pres. of Exec. Council, Servicio Nacional de Promoción Profesional (SNPP) 1993–98; Pres. Chamber of Senators –1999; Pres. of Paraguay 1999–2003; sentenced to eight years in prison for fraud and embezzlement 2006, successfully appealed sentence; mem. Asociación Nacional Republicana—Partido Colorado.

GONZÁLEZ MÁRQUEZ, Felipe; Spanish lawyer and politician; b. 5 March 1942, Seville; m. Mar García Vaquero; two s. one d.; ed lower and high school, school of law, continued studies at Catholic Univ. of Louvain, Belgium; opened first labour law office to deal with workers' problems in Seville 1966; mem. Spanish Socialist Youth 1962; mem. Spanish Socialist Party (Partido Socialista Obrero Español, PSOE) 1964–, mem. Seville Prov. Cttee 1965–69, Nat. Cttee 1969–70, mem. Exec. Bd 1970, First Sec. 1974–79 (resgnd), re-elected Sept. 1979, then Sec.-Gen. –1997; mem. Congress of Deputies for Madrid 1977–2004, fmr Chair. Socialist Parl. Group; Prime Minister of Spain and Pres. Council of Ministers 1982–96; fmr EU Special Rep. for Fed. Repub. of Yugoslavia; mem. Club of Madrid, Circle of Montevideo, InterAcción Council, Shimon Peres Int. Council for Peace, Japanese Bonsai Asscn; Grand Cross of the Order of Mil. Merit 1984, Order of Isabel the Catholic 1996, Golden Cross of Merit (Austria) 1997; Dr hc (Louvain) 1995, Charlemagne Prize 1993, Carlos V Prize, Academia Europaea 2000. *Publications include:* What is Socialism? 1976, P.S.O.E. 1977, El futuro no es lo que era (with J. Cebrián) 20011, Memorías del Futuro 2003, Mi idea de Europa 2010, ¿Aún podemos entenernos? (with Miquel Roca) 2011. *Leisure interests:* reading, bonsai plants, jewellery. *Address:* c/o Partido Socialista Obrero Español (PSOE), Ferraz 68 y 70, 28008 Madrid (office); Fundación Progreso Global, Gobelas 31, 28023 Madrid, Spain. *Telephone:* (91) 5820444 (office). *Fax:* (91) 5820422 (office). *E-mail:* infopsoe@psoe.es (office). *Website:* www.psoe.es (office).

GONZÁLEZ RODRÍGUEZ, Francisco; Spanish banking executive; *Group Executive Chairman, Banco Bilbao Vizcaya Argentaria SA;* b. 19 Oct. 1944, Chantada (Lugo); m.; two d.; ed Universidad Complutense de Madrid; began career as computer programmer, Nixdorf, Germany 1970s; fmrly with FG Inversiones Bursátiles; led restructuring and privatization of Argentaria (collection of state banks) 1996, Argentaria merger with Banco Bilbao Vizcaya (BBA) 2000; Co-Chair. Banco Bilbao Vizcaya Argentaria (BBVA) SA 2000–02, Group Exec. Chair. 2002–, Chair. Fundación BBVA; Dir, Inst. for Int. Finance; Global Counsellor The Conf. Bd; Gov. Red Cross, Guggenheim Museum Bilbao, Museo de Bellas Artes, Fundación Principe de Asturias, Real Instituto Elcano, Foundation for Terrorism Victims, Foundation for Help Against Drug Addiction; mem. European Financial Services Roundtable, Institut Européen d'Etudes Bancaires, IMF Capital Markets Consultative Group, Int. Monetary Conf. *Leisure interest:* golf. *Address:* Banco Bilbao Vizcaya Argentaria SA, Plaza San Nicolás 4, Bilbao 48005, Vizcaya (office); Banco Bilbao Vizcaya Argentaria SA, Paseo de la Castellana 81, 28046 Madrid, Spain (office). *Telephone:* (944) 875555 (Vizcaya) (office); (915) 5377690 (Madrid) (office). *Fax:* (944) 876161 (Vizcaya) (office); (91) 3747610 (Madrid) (office). *Website:* www.bbva.com (office); www.bbva.es (office).

GONZÁLEZ SANZ, Manuel, LLD, LLM; Costa Rican lawyer and politician; b. 2 April 1968, San José; ed Univ. of Costa Rica, Columbia Univ., USA; Adviser to Vice-Pres. on Relations with Int. Financial Agencies 1992–94; mem. several dels to high-level meetings of UN 2002–03; Amb. and Perm. Rep. to UN Agencies in Geneva 2002–04; Head of Del. to Ass. of Human Rights Comm., Geneva 2003–04; Chair. Bd of Dirs PROCOMER (foreign trade promotion bd) 2004–06; Minister of Foreign Trade 2004–06, of Foreign Relations 2014–18; Vice-Pres. Chamber of Exporters of Costa Rica; mem. Advisory Panel on Latin American Affairs, World Econ. Forum; mem. Bar Asscn of Costa Rica for more than 20 years; Prof., School of Business Admin and Law, Univ. of Costa Rica. *Address:* c/o Ministry of Foreign Relations, Avda 7 y 9, Calle 11 y 13, Apdo 10027, 1000 San José, Costa Rica (office).

GONZÁLEZ SEGOVIA, Roberto Eudez; Paraguayan politician; b. 1959, Piribebuy; m. Miriam Benítez de González; four c.; ed Universidad Nacional de Asunción; practised as lawyer from 1986; Legal Adviser, various nat. pvt. enterprises; mem. Students' Rights Centre UNA; Students' Rep. of Hon. Council Bd Law and Social Sciences UNA; apptd Minister of Home Affairs 2002; Minister of Nat. Defence 2004-08; Minister for Public Works and Communications 2008; mem. Asociación Nacional Republicana.

GONZI, Lawrence, LLD, KBE; Maltese politician and lawyer; *Senior Legal Partner, Gonzi & Associates, Advocates;* b. 1 July 1953, Valletta, Malta; s. of Louis Gonzi and Inez Gonzi (née Galea); m. Catherine Gonzi (née Callus); two s. one d.; ed Malta Univ.; practised law 1975–88; Speaker House of Reps 1988–92, 1992–96; MP (Nationalist Party) 1996–2013; Leader Nationalist Party 2004–13, Whip, Parl. Group 1997–99, Sec.-Gen. 1997–98; Shadow Minister and Opposition Spokesman for Social Policy 1996–98; Leader of the House and Minister for Social Policy 1998–99, Deputy Prime Minister and Minister for Social Policy 1999–2004, Prime Minister and Minister of Finance 2004–08, 2008–13; Gen. Pres. Malta Catholic Action 1976–86; Chair. Pharmacy Bd 1987–88, Nat. Comm. for Persons with Disabilities 1987–94 (Pres. 1994–96), Nat. Comm. for Mental Health Reform 1987–96, Electoral System (Revision) Comm. 1994–95, Chair., Mizzi Org. Bd of Dirs 1989–97; mem. Prisons Bd 1987–88; mem. Bd of Dirs Fondazione Centesimus Annus Pro Pontifice; mem. Hon. Bd Wilfried Martens Centre for European Studies; mem. Global Leaders Foundation; Patron, World Sustainable Devt Forum; Hon. Companions of Honour (KUOM). *Publications:* Gonzi and Malta's Break with Gaddafi: Recollections of a Premier 2013. *Address:* Gonzi & Associates, Advocates, 115B, Old Mint Street, Valletta VLT1515, Malta (office). *Telephone:* 20157000 (office). *Fax:* 20157010 (office). *E-mail:* lawrence.gonzi@gonzi.com.mt (office). *Website:* www.gonzi.com.mt (office).

GOOCH, Graham Alan, OBE; British professional cricket coach and fmr professional cricketer; b. 23 July 1953, Leytonstone, Essex; s. of Alfred Gooch and Rose Gooch; m. Brenda Daniels 1976; three d.; ed Norlington Junior High School, Leytonstone, Redbridge Tech. Coll.; right-hand opening batsman, right-arm medium bowler; played for Essex 1973–97 (Capt. 1986–87, 1989–94), MCC 1975–2000, Western Prov. 1982–83, 1983–84; played in 118 Tests for England 1975–1994/95, 34 as Capt., scoring 8,900 runs (England record) (average 42.58) including 20 hundreds (highest score 333 and record Test match aggregate of 456 against India, Lord's 1990, becoming only batsman to score a triple century and a century in a first-class match) and holding 103 catches; scored 44,846 First-class runs (128 hundreds), average 49.01 and held 555 catches; toured Australia 1978–79, 1979–80, 1990–91 (Capt.) and 1994–95; 125 One-Day Ints, including 50 as Capt. (both England records), scoring 4,290 runs (average 36.98, highest score 142) including eight hundreds; mem. England Selection Cttee 1996–99; Man. England Tour to Australia 1998–99; Head Coach, Essex County Cricket Club 2001–05, now Essex County Cricket Club Amb.; inducted into Fed. of Int. Cricketers Asscn Hall of Fame 2000, into ICC Cricket Hall of Fame 2009; Dr hc (Univ. of East London) 2011; Wisden Cricketer of the Year 1980, Indian Cricket Cricketer of the Year 1988, Professional Cricketers' Association Player of the Year 1990. *Publications include:* Testing Times 1991, Gooch: My Autobiography 1995. *Leisure interests:* squash, golf, football. *Address:* Essex County Cricket Club, The Essex County Ground, New Writtle Street, Chelmsford, Essex, CM2 0PG, England. *Website:* www.essexcricket.org.uk.

GOOD, Anthony Bruton Meyrick, OBE, FID; British public relations consultant and marketing consultant; *Chairman, Cox and Kings (UK and India) Limited;* b. 18 April 1933, Sutton, Surrey, England; s. of Meyrick G. B. Good and Amy M. Trussell; m. (divorced); two d.; ed Felsted School, Essex; man. trainee, Distillers Group 1950–52; Editorial Asst Temple Press 1952–55; Public Relations Officer, Silver City Airways; Public Relations and Marketing Man., Air Holdings Group 1955–60; Founder and Chair. Good Relations Ltd (previously Good Relations Group PLC) 1961–89; Dir Cox and Kings Travel Ltd 1971–, Chair. 1975–; Chair. Good Relations (India) Ltd 1988–, Cox and Kings (UK and India) Ltd 1988–, Good Consultancy Ltd 1989–, Flagship Group 1999–2011, The Tranquil Moment Ltd 2000–07, Sage Organics 2000–09, Miller Insurance Group 2000–04, Outright Marketing and Distribution Ltd (fmrly Q-Link International Ltd) 2000–, Tulip Star Hotels Ltd 2000–, Relish Events Ltd 2001–06, Neutrahealth PLC 2004–, Marlin Group Holdings PLC 2012–; Dir (non-exec.), Arcadian International PLC 1995–98, Care First Group PLC 1996–98, Gowrings PLC 2003–05, Obento Ltd 2004–, Indo-British Partnership Network 2005–, Benney Watches PLC 2007–, I-Connections UK Ltd 2008–, DQ Entertainment PLC 2008–13, Outright Communication Ltd 2009–, All About Brands PLC 2010–12; Founder Dir International Motors; Dir UK India Business Council (India) Ltd 2005– (Chair. 2009–13); currently Adviser, Marks & Spencer PLC, Adam & Co. PLC, Early Learning Centre, Scottish & Newcastle PLC; Fellow, Inst. of Public Relations. *Leisure interests:* travel, reading, theatre. *Address:* Clench House, Wootton Rivers, Marlborough, Wilts., SN8 4NT, England (home). *Telephone:* (1672) 810126 (office); (1672) 810670 (home). *Fax:* (1672) 810869 (office); (1672) 810149 (home). *E-mail:* anthony.good@btinternet.com.

GOODALE, Rt Hon Ralph Edward, PC, BA, LLB; Canadian politician; *Minister of Public Safety and Emergency Preparedness;* b. Wilcox, Sask.; m. Pamela Goodale; ed Univ. of Regina, Sask. and Univ. of Saskatchewan; MP for Assiniboia constituency 1974–79, for Wascana 1997–2015, for Regina-Wascana 2015–; Leader, Sask. Liberal Party 1980s; mem. Sask. Legis. Ass. 1986–88; Minister of Agric. and Agri-Food 1993–97, of Natural Resources 1997–2002, Minister of State and Leader of the Govt in House of Commons Jan.–May 2002, Minister of Public Works and Govt Services, Minister responsible for the Canadian Wheat Bd, Fed. Interlocutor for Métis and Non-Status Indians, Minister responsible for Indian Residential Schools Resolution, Minister responsible for Communication and with regional responsibilities for Sask. and the North 2002–03, Minister of Finance 2003–06, Minister of Public Safety and Emergency Preparedness 2015–; Opposition House Leader, Liberal Party 2006–10, Deputy Leader 2010–. *Address:* Public Safety Canada, 269 Laurier Ave West, Ottawa, ON K1A 0P8, Canada (office). *Telephone:* (613) 944-4875 (office). *Fax:* (613) 954-5186 (office). *E-mail:* www.publicsafety.gc.ca (office); goodale@sasktel.net (office). *Website:* www.ralphgoodale.ca.

GOODALL, Dame Jane, DBE, PhD; British primatologist, ethologist and anthropologist; *Founder, Jane Goodall Institute;* b. (Valerie Jane Morris-Goodall), 3 April 1934, London; d. of Mortimer Herbert Morris-Goodall and Vanne Morris-Goodall (née Joseph); m. 1st Hugo Van Lawick 1964 (divorced 1974); one s.; m. 2nd M. Derek Bryceson 1975 (died 1980); ed Uplands School, Univ. of Cambridge; Sec., Univ. of Oxford; Asst Sec. to Louis Leakey, worked in Olduvai Gorge, then moved to Gombe Stream Game Reserve (now Gombe Nat. Park), Tanzania 1960, camp became Gombe Stream Research Centre 1964, Dir of Research, Gombe Nat. Park 1972–2003; Scientific Dir Gombe Stream Research Centre 1967–2003; studied social behaviour of the spotted hyena, Ngorongoro Conservation Area 1968–69; Founder, mem. Bd of Dirs and Trustee, Jane Goodall Inst. for Wildlife Research, Educ. and Conservation, USA 1976–; Scientific Gov. Chicago Acad. of Sciences 1981–; Int. Dir ChimpanZoo (research programme involving zoos and sanctuaries world-wide), USA 1984–; Vice-Pres. Animal Welfare Inst., British Veterinary Asscn, UK 1987–; Dir Humane Soc. of US 1989–; mem. Int. Advisory Bd of Teachers Without Borders, USA 2001–; mem. Bd Orangutan Foundation, USA 1994–, Save the Chimps/Center for Captive Chimpanzee Care 2000–, North American Bear Center 2001–; mem. Hon. Cttee Farm Sanctuary, USA 2001–; mem. Bd of Dirs Cougar Fund 2002–, The Many One Foundation, USA 2002–; mem. Advisory Panel World Summit on Sustainable Devt 2002, and numerous other advisory bds and cttees; Visiting Prof., Dept of Psychiatry and Program of Human Biology, Stanford Univ. 1971–75; Adjunct Prof., Dept of Environmental Studies, School of Veterinary Medicine, Tufts Univ. 1987–88; Assoc., Cleveland Natural History Museum 1990; Distinguished Adjunct Prof., Depts of Anthropology and Occupational Therapy, Univ. of Southern California 1990; A.D. White Prof.-at-Large, Cornell Univ. 1996–2002; Scientific Fellow, Wildlife Conservation Soc., USA 2002–; Trustee, L. S. B. Leakey Foundation 1974–, Jane Goodall Inst., UK 1988–, Jane Goodall Inst., Canada 1993–; mem. Explorer's Club, New York 1981, American Philosophical Soc. 1988, Soc. of Women Geographers, USA 1988, Deutsche Akad. der Naturforscher Leopoldina 1990, Academia Scientiarium et Artium Europaea, Austria 1991; Foreign mem. Research Centre for Human Ethology, Max Planck Inst. for Behavioural Physiology 1984; Hon. Foreign mem. American Acad. of Arts and Sciences 1972; Hon. Fellow, Royal Anthropological Inst. of GB and Ireland 1991; Hon. mem. Ewha Acad. of Arts and Sciences 2006; Ordre nat. de la Légion d'honneur 2006; 22 hon. degrees; numerous awards including Franklin Burr Award, Nat. Geographic Soc. 1963–64, Conservation Award, New York Zoological Soc. 1974, Order of the Golden Ark, World Wildlife Award for Conservation 1980, J. Paul Getty Wildlife Conservation Prize 1984, Albert Schweitzer Award, Int. Women's Inst. 1987, Nat. Geographic Soc. Centennial Award 1988, Anthropologist of the Year Award 1989, AMES Award, American Anthropologist Asscn 1990, Gold Medal, Soc. of Women Geographers 1990, Inamori Foundation Award 1990, Washoe Award 1990, Kyoto Prize in Basic Science 1990, Rainforest Alliance Champion Award 1993, Hubbard Medal for Distinction in Exploration, Discovery, and Research, Nat. Geographic Soc. 1995, Lifetime Achievement Award, In Defense of Animals 1995, Silver Medal, Zoological Soc. of London 1996, Tanzanian Kilimanjaro Medal 1996, Conservation Award, Primate Soc. of GB 1996, William Proctor Prize for Scientific Achievement Kilimanjaro 1996, Commonwealth Award for Public Service 1997, Royal Geographical Soc./Discovery Channel Europe Award for A Lifetime of Discovery 1997, Roger Tory Peterson Memorial Medal, Harvard Museum of Natural History 2001, 2007, Benjamin Franklin Medal in Life Science 2003, Award of Harvard Medical School Center for Health and the Global Environment 2003, Prince of Asturias Award for Tech. and Scientific Achievement 2003, Life Time Achievement Award, Int. Fund for Animal Welfare 2004, UNESCO 60th Anniversary Gold Medal 2006, Lifetime Achievement Award, Jules Verne Adventures 2006, Hon. Medal of the City of Paris 2007, Lifetime Achievement Award, Heart of Green Awards 2011. *Films:* Miss Goodall and the Wild Chimpanzees 1963, Among the Wild Chimpanzees 1984, People of the Forest (with Hugo van Lawick) 1988, Chimpanzee Alert 1990, Chimps, So Like Us 1990, The Life and Legend of Jane Goodall 1990, The Gombe Chimpanzees 1990, Fifi's Boys 1995, My Life with the Wild Chimpanzees 1995, Chimpanzee Diary 1995, Animal Minds 1995, Jane Goodall: Reason For Hope 1999, Chimps R Us 2001, Jane Goodall's Wild Chimpanzees 2002, Jane Goodall's Return to Gombe 2004, Jane Goodall's State of the Great Ape 2004, Jane Goodall – When Animals Talk 2005, Jane Goodall's Heroes 2006. *Publications include:* My Friends the Wild Chimpanzees 1967, Innocent Killers (with H. van Lawick) 1971, In the Shadow of Man 1971, The Chimpanzees of Gombe: Patterns of Behavior (R. R. Hawkins Award for the Outstanding Tech., Scientific or Medical Book of 1986, The Wildlife Soc. (USA) Award for Outstanding Publ. in Wildlife Ecology and Man. 1986) 1986, Through a Window: 30 Years Observing the Gombe Chimpanzees 1990, Visions of Caliban (with Dale Peterson) (New York Times Notable Book for 1993, Library Journal Best Sci-Tech Book for 1993) 1993, Brutal Kinship (with Michael Nichols) 1999, 40 Years at Gombe 2000, Africa in My Blood: An Autobiography in Letters (ed. by Dale Peterson) 2000, Beyond Innocence: An Autobiography in Letters, the Later Years (ed. by Dale Peterson) 2001, Performance and Evolution in the Age of Darwin: Out of the Natural Order 2002, Ten Trusts: What We Must Do to Care for the Animals We Love (with Marc Bekoff) 2002, Hope for Animals and Their World: How Endangered Species Are Being Rescued from the Brink (with Thane Maynard and Gail Hudson) 2009; for children: Grub: The Bush Baby 1972, My Life with the Chimpanzees (Reading-Magic Award for Outstanding Book for Children 1989) 1988, The Chimpanzee Family Book (UNICEF Award for the Best Children's Book of 1989, Austrian State Prize for Best Children's Book of 1990) 1989, Jane Goodall's Animal World: Chimps 1989, Animal Family Series, Jane Goodall: With Love 1994, Dr. White (illustrated by Julie Litty) 1999, The Eagle & the Wren (illustrated by Alexander Reichstein) 2000, Chimpanzees I Love: Saving Their World and Ours 2001, Rickie and Henri: A True Story (with Alan Marks) 2004; numerous book chapters and articles in scientific journals. *Address:* The Jane Goodall Institute for Wildlife Research, Education and Conservation, 4245 North Fairfax Drive, #600, Arlington, VA 22203, USA (office). *Telephone:* (703) 682-9220 (office). *Fax:* (703) 682-9312 (office). *E-mail:* info@janegoodall.org (office). *Website:* www.janegoodall.org.

GOODBY, John William, BSc, PhD, DSc, FRS, CChem, FRSC, FRMS; British materials chemist and academic; *Professor Emeritus, University of York;* b. 4 Oct. 1952, Warwicks.; s. of John Goodby and Constance Ruth Goodby (née Merkin); m. Ann Houghton 1976; one s. two d.; ed Univ. of Hull; Postdoctoral Fellow, Univ. of Hull 1977–79, Reader in Chem. 1988–90, apptd Prof. of Organic Chem. 1990; mem. Tech. Staff, AT&T Bell Labs, Murray Hill, NJ, USA 1979–84, Supervisor 1984–88; fmr Chair. of Materials Chem., Dept of Chem., Univ. of York, now Prof. Emer.; Research Advisor to ERATO Programme on Liquid Crystals, Japan 2000–04; Co-ordinator of EU-RTN Programme SAMPA 2002–06, ESF SONS II Project LC-NANOP 2007–11; Pres. Int. Liquid Crystal Soc. 2000–04; Vice-Chair. British Liquid Crystal Soc. 2000–03, 2005–06, Chair. 2003–05; Vice-Chair. Anglo-Japanese Liquid Crystal Soc. Conf., York 2001; Exec. Chair. 19th Int. Liquid Crystal Soc. Conf., Edinburgh 2002, Organizing Cttee for Seventh Materials Conf. (MC7) of RSC, Edinburgh 2005, Organizing Cttee for Royal Soc. Meeting on New Directions in Liquid Crystals UK; mem. EPSRC Coll. since its inception; Co-Ed., Taylor and Francis Series in Liquid Crystals, Philosophical Transactions for a Royal Society Discussion Meeting; mem. Editorial Bd, Journal of Liquid Crystals; Fellow, World Tech. Network 2004, World Innovation Foundation 2005; Hon. mem. Int. Liquid Crystal Soc. 2010; Hon. ScD (Trinity Coll. Dublin) 2002, Hon. DSc (INSA, Lyon) 2015; G.W. Gray Medal, British Liquid Crystal Soc. 1996, RSC Tilden Lectureship 2002–03, RSC Interdisciplinary Award 2007, RSC Materials for Industry–Derek Birchall Award 2013, AkzoNobel UK Science Award 2014, Frederiksz Medal, Russian Liquid Crystal Soc. 2015, Royal Medal, Royal Soc. 2016, Pierre Gilles de Gennes Prize, Int. Liquid Crystal Soc. 2018. *Publications:* Smectic Liquid Crystals: Textures and Structures 1984, Ferroelectric Liquid Crystals: Principles and Applications 1991, Handbook of Liquid Crystals (ed.) 1994 (second ed. 2014); more than 530 papers in professional journals. *Leisure interests:* cricket, football, woodwork. *Address:* Department of Chemistry, University of York, Heslington, York, YO10 5DD, England (office). *Telephone:* (1904) 322589 (office). *E-mail:* john.goodby@york.ac.uk (office). *Website:* www.york.ac.uk/chemistry (office).

GOODE, Anthony William, MD, FRCS FACS; British surgeon; b. 3 Aug. 1945, Newcastle-upon-Tyne; s. of William Henry Goode and Eileen Veronica Goode; m. Patricia Josephine Flynn 1987; ed Corby School and Univ. of Newcastle-upon-Tyne; held clinical surgical posts in Newcastle Hosps Group 1968–76; Univ. of London Teaching Hosps 1976–; Prof. of Endocrine and Metabolic Surgery, Univ. of London; Hon. Consultant Surgeon, Royal London Hosp.; Consultant Surgeon, Whitechapel and St Bartholomew's Hosp.; Hon. Prof., Centre for Biological and Medical Systems, Imperial Coll. London 1982–; Clinical Dir Helicopter Emergency Medical Service, London 1998–2000; Ed.-in-Chief Medicine, Science and the Law 1996–; Asst Sec., Gen. British Acad. of Forensic Science 1982–87, Pres. 1999–; Hon. Sec., British Asscn of Endocrine Surgeons 1983–96; Fellow, Royal Soc. of Medicine 1971–, American Coll. of Surgeons 2000; mem. Int. Soc. of Surgery 1984–, Int. Soc. of Endocrine Surgeons 1984–, New York Acad. of Sciences 1986–, MCC 1982–, Hunterian Soc. 1998 (Orator 1998), British Acad. of Forensic Sciences; Trustee, Smith and Nephew Foundation 1990–; Liveryman, Worshipful Soc. of Apothecaries of London; Freeman City of London 1992. *Publications include:* numerous papers and articles on nutrition in surgical patients, endocrine diseases, metabolic changes in manned spaceflight and related topics. *Leisure interests:* cricket, music (especially opera), literature.

GOODE, Charles Barrington, AC, BCom (Hons), MBA; Australian business executive; b. 26 Aug. 1938; ed Scotch Coll., Melbourne, Univ. of Melbourne, Columbia Univ., USA, Monash Univ.; mem. Bd of Dirs Australia and New Zealand Banking Group Ltd (ANZ) 1991–2010, Chair. 1995–2010; mem. Bd of Dirs Woodside Petroleum Ltd 1988–2007 (Chair. 1999–2007), Australian United Investment Co. Ltd, Diversified United Investment Ltd, Ian Potter Foundation Ltd, Howard Florey Inst. of Experimental Physiology and Medicine, Singapore Airlines 1999–2006; Chair. Grosvenor Australia Properties Pty Ltd 2008–12; fmr Pres. Inst. of Public Affairs; fmr mem. Council of Monash Univ., Finance Cttee of Australian Acad. of Science, Investment Cttee of Melbourne Univ. Grad. School of Man. Foundation; fmr Dir Melbourne Business School Foundation; Hon. LLD (Melbourne and Monash Univs); Melbourne Business School Award 2006.

GOODE, Richard Stephen, DipMus, BSc; American pianist; b. 1 June 1943, New York; m. Marcia Weinfeld 1987; ed Mannes Coll. of Music, Curtis Inst., studied with Nadia Reisenberg and Rudolf Serkin; debut, New York Young Concert Artists 1962; Carnegie Hall recital début 1990; mem. Boston Symphony Chamber Players 1967–69; Founding mem. Chamber Music Soc. of the Lincoln Center 1969–79, 1983–89; mem. Piano Faculty, Mannes Coll. of Music 1969–; concerts and recitals in USA, Europe, Japan, South America, Australia, Far East; has played with Baltimore, Boston, Chicago, Cleveland, New York, Philadelphia, Berlin Radio, Finnish Radio and Bamberg Symphony Orchestras, New York, Los Angeles, Baltimore, Orpheus, Philadelphia, ECO and Royal Philharmonic Orchestras; Co-Artistic Dir with Mitsuko Uchida, Marlboro Music (series of chamber music festivals) 1999–2013; Young Concert Artists Award, First Prize Clara Haskil Competition 1973, Avery Fischer Prize 1980, Grammy Award (with clarinettist Richard Stoltzman), Jean Gimbel Lane Prize Northwestern Univ. School of Music 2006. *Leisure interests:* book collecting, museums. *Address:* Frank Salomon Associates, 121 West 27th Street, Suite 703, New York, NY 10001, USA (office). *E-mail:* info@franksalomon.com (office). *Website:* www.franksalomon.com (office); www.richardgoodepiano.com.

GOODE, Sir Royston (Roy) Miles, Kt, OBE, CBE, QC, LLD, FBA, FRSA; British fmr professor of law and author; *Emeritus Professor of Law and Fellow, St John's College, University of Oxford;* b. 6 April 1933, London; s. of Samuel Goode and Bloom Goode; m. Catherine A. Rueff 1964; one d.; ed Highgate School and Univ. of London; admitted as solicitor 1955; Partner, Victor Mishcon & Co. (solicitors) 1966–67; called to Bar, Inner Temple 1988, Hon. Bencher 1992–; Prof. of Law, Queen Mary Coll., London 1971–73, Crowther Prof. of Credit and Commercial Law 1973–89, Head of Dept and Dean of Faculty of Laws 1976–80, Dir and Founder, Centre for Commercial Law Studies 1980–89; Norton Rose Prof. of English Law, Univ. of Oxford 1990–98, Prof. Emer. 1998–, Fellow, St John's Coll., Oxford 1990–98, Fellow Emer. 1998–; G.J. Wiarda Visiting Prof., Univ. of Utrecht 2003; Pres. Council of Int. Postgraduate Law School, Belgrade 2003–; mem. Monopolies and Mergers Comm. 1981–86, Council of Banking Ombudsman 1989–92; Chair. Pension Law Review Cttee 1992–93; mem. Council and Chair. Exec. Cttee JUSTICE 1994–96; mem. Governing Council, Int. Inst. for Unification of Private Law (UNIDROIT) 1989–2003; mem. Crowther Cttee on Consumer Credit; Hon. Fellow, Queen Mary and Westfield Coll., London 1991–, Hon. mem. Int. Inst. for Unification of Private Law 2003–, Hon. Pres. Centre for Commercial Law Studies 1990–, Oxford Inst. of Legal Practice 1994–, Uniform Law Foundation 2003–14; Hon. DSc (London) 1997; Hon. LLD (Univ. of E Anglia) 2003; Hon. DrIur (The College of Law) 2011. *Publications include:* Consumer Credit 1978, Commercial Law 1982 (2nd edn 1995, 3rd edn 2004, 4th edn 2009), Legal Problems of Credit and Security 1982 (2nd edn 1988, 3rd edn 2003, 4th edn 2008, 5th edn 2013), Payment Obligations in Commercial and Financial Transactions 1983, Proprietary Rights and Insolvency in Sales Transactions 1985, Principles of Corporate Insolvency Law 1990 (2nd edn 1997, 4th edn 2011), Proprietary Rights and Insolvency in Sales Transactions (3rd edn 2010), Consumer Credit Law and Practice (looseleaf), Commercial Law in the Next Millennium; books on hire purchase; contribs. to Halsbury's Laws of England (4th edn). *Leisure interests:* chess, reading, walking, browsing in bookshops. *Address:* Faculty of Law, University of Oxford, St Cross Building, St Cross Road, Oxford, OX1 3UL, England (office). *Telephone:* (1865) 271491 (home). *Fax:* (1865) 271493 (home). *E-mail:* roy.goode@law.ox.ac.uk (office). *Website:* www.law.ox.ac.uk.

GOODEN, Linda, BS; American business executive; *Executive Vice-President, Information Systems and Global Solutions, Lockheed Martin Corporation;* ed Youngstown State Univ., San Diego State Univ., Univ. of Maryland Univ. Coll., Exec. Program Manager course at Defense Systems Management Coll.; has held positions of increasing responsibility since joining Lockheed Martin Corpn, Vice-Pres. Software Support Services unit from 1994, later Pres. Information Tech., Exec. Vice-Pres. Information Tech. & Global Services –2007, Exec. Vice-Pres. Information Systems & Global Services, Gaithersburg, Md and Officer of Lockheed Martin Corpn 2007–; mem. Bd of Dirs ADP, Inc.; mem. Eisenhower Fellowships Bd of Trustees, Armed Forces Communications and Electronics Asscn International, Information Tech. Asscn of America, Univ. of Maryland's A. James Clark School of Eng, Prince George's Community Coll. Foundation; Hon. Doctor of Public Service (Univ. of Maryland Univ. Coll.) 2005; Federal 100 'Eagle' Award, Federal Computer Week 2002, Corp. Leadership Award, Women in Technology 2002, Black Engineer of the Year, U.S. Black Engineer and IT magazine 2006, Exec. of the Year, Greater Washington Govt Contractor Awards 2007, inducted into Maryland Business Hall of Fame 2008, named to Corporate Board Member magazine's Top 50 Women in Technology 2008, inducted into Career Communications Hall of Fame 2011. *Address:* Lockheed Martin Corporation, 6801 Rockledge Drive, Bethesda, MD 20817-1877, USA (office). *Telephone:* (301) 897-6000 (office). *Fax:* (301) 897-6704 (office). *E-mail:* info@lockheedmartin.com (office). *Website:* www.lockheedmartin.com (office).

GOODENOUGH, John Bannister, BA, PhD; American physicist, materials engineer and academic; *Professor of Mechanical and Electrical Engineering, University of Texas, Austin;* b. 25 July 1922, Jena, Germany; s. of Erwin R. Goodenough and Helen M. Lewis Goodenough; m. Irene J. Wiseman 1951; ed Yale Univ., Univ. of Chicago; Research Engineer, Westinghouse Electric Corpn 1951–52; Group Leader and Residential Physicist, Lincoln Lab., MIT 1952–76; helped develop computer memories for USAF; conducted groundbreaking research on behaviour of metal oxides; Prof. and Head of Inorganic Chem. Lab., Univ. of Oxford, UK 1976–86; Prof. of Mechanical and Electrical Eng, Univ. of Tex. 1986–, apptd Virginia H. Cockrell Centennial Chair in Eng; conducted research on energy and high-temperature superconductivity; mem. NAS, Nat. Acad. of Eng, ACS, AAAS, Acad. des Sciences de l'Inst. de France, RSC, Physical Soc. of Japan; Fellow, American Physical Soc.; Foreign Assoc., Indian Acad. of Sciences, Acad. de Ciencias Exactas, Físicas y Naturales, Spain; Foreign mem. Royal Soc., London; Centenary Lecturer, Royal Soc. of Chem. 1976; Hon. PhD (Univ. of Bordeaux) 1967, (Univ. of Santiago de Compostela) 2002; Solid State Chem. Prize, Royal Soc. of Chem. 1980, Von Hippel Award, Materials Research Soc. 1989, Sr Research Award, American Soc. for Eng Educ. 1990, Medal for Distinguished Achievement, Univ. of Pennsylvania 1996, John Bordeen Award, Mining, Metallurgy & Materials Soc. 1997, Olin Palladium Award, Electrochemical Soc. 1999, Japan Prize 2001, Hocott Award, Univ. of Tex. 2002, Enrico Fermi Award 2009, IEEE Medal for Environmental and Safety Technologies 2012, Nat. Medal of Science 2012, Nat. Alliance for Advanced Technology Batteries Lifetime Achievement Award 2012, Charles Stark Draper Prize, Nat. Acad. of Eng 2014, Thomson Reuters Citation Laureate 2015, The Eric and Sheila Samsun Prime Minister's Prize for Innovation in Alternative Fuels for Transportation 2015. *Publications include:* Magnetism and the Chemical Bond 1963, Les Oxydes des métaux de transition 1973, Witness to Grace 2008, Solid Oxide Fuel Cell Technology: Principle, Performance, and Operation (with K. Huang) 2009; numerous articles in scientific journals. *Leisure interests:* travel, Episcopal Church. *Address:* University of Texas, Department of Mechanical Engineering and Materials Science, 204 East Dean Keeton Street, Stop C2200, Austin, TX 78712-1592, USA (office). *Telephone:* (512) 471-1646 (office). *Fax:* (512) 475-8482 (office). *E-mail:* jgoodenough@mail.utexas.edu (office). *Website:* www.engr.utexas.edu (office).

GOODFELLOW, Peter Neville, DPhil, FRS, FMedSci; British geneticist; *Senior Adviser, Abingworth Management Ltd;* b. 4 Aug. 1951; s. of Bernard Clifford Roy Goodfellow and Doreen Olga Goodfellow (née Berry); m. Julia Mary Lansdall 1972; one s. one d.; ed Univs of Bristol and Oxford; MRC Postdoctoral Fellow, Univ. of Oxford 1975–76; Jane Coffin Childs Postdoctoral Fellow, Stanford Univ. 1976–78; Sr Fellow, American Cancer Soc. 1978–79; Staff Scientist, Imperial Cancer Research Foundation 1979–83, Sr Scientist 1983–86, Prin. Scientist 1986–92; Arthur Balfour Prof. of Genetics, Univ. of Cambridge 1992–96; Sr Vice-Pres. of Biopharmaceuticals and Neuroscience, Smithkline Beecham Pharmaceuticals 1996–2001, Sr Vice-Pres. Discovery Research, GlaxoSmithKline PLC 2001–06; Visiting Scholar, Rockfeller Univ. 2007; currently Sr Adviser Abingworth Man. Ltd; Visiting Prof., Univ. of Kent, Univ. College London, Bristol Univ., Univ. of Hong Kong; fmr mem. Bd of Dirs Decode Genetics; mem. Bd of Advisers Beaton Inst., Max Plank Inst. Berlin; mem. Scientific and Clinical Advisory Bd Prosensa Therapeutics BV; mem. Bd Inst. of Cancer Research, Muscular Dystrophy Campaign; Hon. DSc (Univ of Bristol) 2002; Amory Prize 1997, Louis Jeantet Prize. *Publications include:* The Mammalian Y Chromosone: Molecular Search for the Sex Determining Gene (co-ed.) 1987, Cystic Fibrosis (ed.) 1989, Molecular Genetics of Muscular Disease (co-ed.) 1989, Sex Determination and the Y Chromosone (co-ed.) 1991, Mammalian Genetics (co-ed.) 1992; numerous reviews and specialist articles in learned journals. *Leisure interests:* science, football. *Address:* Abingworth Management Ltd, 38 Jermyn Street, London SW1Y 6DN, England (office). *Telephone:* (20) 7534-1500 (office). *Fax:* (20) 7287-0480 (office). *Website:* www.abingworth.com (office).

GOODHART, Charles Albert Eric, CBE, PhD, FBA; British economist and academic; *Norman Sosnow Professor Emeritus of Banking and Finance, London School of Economics;* b. 23 Oct. 1936, London, England; s. of Sir A. L. Goodhart; m. Margaret (Miffy) Smith 1960; one s. three d.; ed Eton Coll., Trinity Coll., Cambridge, Harvard Univ., USA; Asst Lecturer, Dept of Econs, Univ. of Cambridge and Prize Fellow, Trinity Coll.; Economist, Dept of Econ. Affairs, London 1965–66; Lecturer, LSE 1966–68, Norman Sosnow Prof. of Banking and Finance 1985–2002, Prof. Emer. 2002–, mem. Financial Markets Group 1987– (Deputy Dir 2002–04), Hon. Fellow 2006; Adviser on Monetary Affairs, Bank of England 1968–85, External mem. Monetary Policy Cttee 1997–2000; Adviser to Gov. of Bank of England on Financial Regulation 2002–04; mem. Exchange Fund Advisory Council, Hong Kong 1988–97. *Publications include:* Money, Information and Uncertainty 1989, The Evolution of Central Banks 1985, The Central Bank and the Financial System 1995, The Emerging Framework of Financial Regulation (ed.) 1998, The Foreign Exchange Market (with R. Payne) 2000, Financial Crises, Contagion and the Lender of Last Resort (co-ed with G. Illing) 2002, Intervention to Save Hong Kong (with Lu Dai) 2003, Financial Development and Economic Growth (ed) 2004, House Prices and the Macroeconomy (with B. Hofmann) 2006, The Regulatory Response to the Financial Crisis 2009, The Basel Committee on Banking Supervision: A History of the Early Years, 1974–1997 2011, Financial Stability in Practice: Towards an Uncertain Future (with D. Tsomocos) 2012, The Challenges of Financial Stability: A New Model and its Applications (with D. Tsomocos) 2012. *Leisure interest:* sheep farming. *Address:* Financial Markets Group, Room 107b, Connaught House, London School of Economics, Houghton Street, London, WC2A 2AE (office); 27 Abbotsbury Road, London, W14 8EL, England (home). *Telephone:* (20) 7955-7555 (office); (20) 7603-5817 (home). *E-mail:* c.a.goodhart@lse.ac.uk (office). *Website:* fmg.lse.ac.uk (office).

GOODING, Cuba, Jr.; American actor; b. 2 Jan. 1968, Bronx, New York; s. of Cuba Gooding, Sr and Shirley Gooding (née Sullivan); m. Sara Kapfer; three c.; started as backup break dancer 1984; two Nat. Asscn for the Advancement of Colored People (NAACP) Awards. *Television appearances include:* Kill or Be Killed 1990, Murder with Motive: The Edmund Perry Story 1992, Daybreak 1993, The Tuskegee Airmen 1995, Gifted Hands: The Ben Carson Story (film) 2009, Firelight (film) 2012, Summoned (film) 2013, Guilty (film) 2013, The Book of Negroes (mini-series) 2015, Big Time in Hollywood, FL (series) 2015, Forever (series) 2015, American Crime Story: The People v. O. J. Simpson 2016. *Films include:* Coming to America 1988, Sing 1989, Boyz N the Hood 1991, Gladiator 1992, A Few Good Men 1992, Hitz 1992, Judgement Night 1993, Lightning Jack 1994, Losing Isaiah 1995, Outbreak 1995, Jerry Maguire (Acad. Award, Best Supporting Actor 1997, Chicago Film Critics Award, Screen Actor Guild Award) 1996, The Audition 1996, Old Friends 1997, As Good As It Gets 1997, What Dreams May Come 1998, A Murder of Crows 1999, Instinct 1999, Men of Honor 2000, Pearl Harbor 2001, Rat Race 2001, In the Shadows 2001, Snow Dogs 2002, Boat Trip 2002, The Fighting Temptations 2003, Radio 2003, Home on the Range (voice) 2004, Shadowboxer 2005, Dirty 2005, Lightfield's Home Videos 2006, End Game 2006, Norbit 2007, Daddy Day Camp 2007, American Gangster 2007, Hero Wanted 2008, Lies and Illusions 2009, Wrong Turn at Tahoe 2009, Red Tails 2012, One in the Chamber 2012, Don Jon 2013, Life of a King 2013, Absolute Deception 2013, The Butler 2013, Machete Kills 2013, Freedom 2014, Selma 2014. *Plays:* The Trip to Bountiful, Broadway 2013, Chicago, London 2018.

GOODING, Valerie (Val) Francis, CBE, BA, CIMgt; British business executive; *Chairman, Premier Farnell PLC;* b. 14 May 1950; d. of Frank Gooding and Gladys Gooding; m. Crawford Macdonald 1986; two s.; ed Leiston Grammar School, Suffolk, Univ. of Warwick, Kingston Univ.; Reservations Agent, British Airways PLC 1973–76, Man. Trainer 1977–80, Personnel Trainer 1980–83, Reservations Man. 1983–86, Head of Cabin Services 1987–92, Head of Marketing 1992–93, Dir of Business Units 1993–96, Dir Asia Pacific 1996; Man. Dir UK Operations, BUPA 1996–98, CEO 1998–2008; Chair. Premier Farnell PLC 2011–; mem. BBC Exec. Bd; mem. Bd of Dirs J Sainsbury PLC 2007–, Standard Chartered Bank PLC 2005–, Lawn Tennis Asscn, Home Office (UK); Pres. Int. Fed. of Health Plans 2002–04; fmr mem. Bd Asscn of British Insurers; mem. Advisory Bd Univ. of Warwick Business School; Trustee, British Museum, Rose Theatre; Hon. DBA (Bournemouth) 1999. *Leisure interests:* theatre, travel, tennis, keeping fit, family life. *Address:* Office of the Chairman, Premier Farnell PLC, Farnell House, Forge Lane, Leeds, LS12 2NE, England (office). *Website:* www.premierfarnell.com (office).

GOODISON, Sir Nicholas Proctor, Kt, PhD, FBA, FSA, FRSA; British stockbroker and banker; b. 16 May 1934, Radlett; s. of Edmund Harold Goodison and Eileen Mary Carrington Proctor; m. Judith Abel Smith 1960; one s. two d.; ed Marlborough Coll. and King's Coll., Cambridge; joined H. E. Goodison & Co. (now Quilter & Co. Ltd) 1958–88, partner 1962, Chair. 1975–88; mem. Council The Stock Exchange 1968–88, Chair. 1976–88; Pres. British Bankers Asscn 1991–96; Pres. Int. Fed. of Stock Exchanges 1985–86; Chair. TSB Group PLC 1989–95, TSB Bank PLC 1989–2000, Deputy Chair. Lloyds TSB Group PLC 1995–2000; Dir (non-exec.) Corus Group PLC (fmrly British Steel PLC) 1989–2001 (Deputy Chair. 1993–99); Dir Ottoman Bank 1986–92; Dir-Gen. Accident 1987–95; Trustee, Nat. Heritage Memorial Fund 1988–97; Vice-Chair. Bd of English Nat. Opera 1980–98 (Dir 1977–98); Chair. Nat. Art-Collections Fund 1986–2002, Courtauld Inst. 1982–2002, Crafts Council 1997–2005, Burlington Magazine Publs 2001–09, Nat. Life Story Collection 2003–15; Hon. Keeper of Furniture, Fitzwilliam Museum, Cambridge; Pres. Furniture History Soc.; Pres. Walpole Soc.; Gov. Marlborough Coll. 1981–97; mem. Royal Comm. on Long-term Care of the Elderly 1997–99; Leader and Author Goodison Review: Securing the Best for our Museums; Private Giving and Govt Support (HM Treasury) 2003; Sr Fellow, RCA 1991; Hon. FRIBA 1992; Hon. Fellow, King's Coll. Cambridge 2001, Courtauld Inst. of Art 2003, Royal Acad. of Arts; Chevalier, Légion d'honneur 1990; Hon. DLitt (City Univ.) 1985; Hon. LLD (Exeter) 1989; Hon. DSc (Aston Univ.) 1994; Hon. DArt (De Montfort Univ.) 1998; Hon. DCL (Univ. of Northumbria) 1999; Hon. DLit (Univ. of London) 2003. *Publications:* English Barometers 1680–1860 1968 (revised 1977), Ormolu: the Work of Matthew Boulton 1974 (revised as Matthew Boulton: Ormolu 2003), Hotspur: Eighty Years of Antiques Dealing (ed with Robin Kern) 2004, These Fragments 2005; many papers and articles on the history of furniture, clocks and barometers. *Leisure interests:* visual arts, history of furniture and decorative arts, music and opera, walking. *Address:* PO Box 2512, London, W1A 5ZP, England.

GOODLAD, Baron (Life Peer), cr. 2005, of Lincoln in the County of Lincolnshire; **Alastair Goodlad,** Kt, KCMG, PC, LLB, MA; British politician and fmr diplomatist; *Honorary President, Overseas Services Pensioners' Association;* b. 4 July 1943; s. of Dr John F. R. Goodlad and Isabel Goodlad (née Sinclair); m. Cecilia Hurst 1968; two s.; ed Marlborough Coll., King's Coll., Cambridge; MP for Norwich 1974–83, for Eddisbury 1983–99; Lord Commr of the Treasury 1981–84; Parl. Under-Sec. of State for Energy 1984–87; Comptroller HM Household 1989–90; Treas., HM Household and Deputy Chief Whip 1990–92; Minister of State for FCO 1992–95; Govt Chief Whip 1995–97; Shadow Sec. of State for Int. Devt 1997–98; High Commr to Australia 2000–05; mem. (Conservative), House of Lords 2005–, Chair. Constitution Cttee 2006–10, Merits of Statutory Instruments Cttee 2010–12, Secondary Legislation Scrutiny Cttee (fmrly Merits Cttee) 2012–; Chair. Asia House 2006–07, Britain-Australia Soc. 2006–07, Australian Opera Capital Fund, UK; Trustee, Sir Robert Menzies Memorial Trust; Hon. Pres., Overseas Services Pensioners' Asscn 2012–. *Address:* House of Lords, Westminster, London, SW1A 0PW, England (office). *Telephone:* (20) 7219-3427 (office). *Website:* www.parliament.uk/biographies/lords/lord-goodlad/670 (office).

GOODMAN, John, BFA; American film actor; b. 20 June 1952, St Louis; s. of Leslie Francis Goodman and Virginia Roos Goodman (née Loosmore); m. Annabeth Hartzog 1989; one d.; ed Meramac Community Coll. and SW Missouri State Univ.; Broadway appearances in Loose Ends 1979, Big River 1985. *Films include:* The Survivors 1983, Eddie Macon's Run 1983, Revenge of the Nerds 1984, C.H.U.D. 1984, Maria's Lovers 1985, Sweet Dreams 1985, True Stories 1986, The Big Easy 1987, Burglar 1987, Raising Arizona 1987, The Wrong Guys 1988, Everybody's All-American 1988, Punchline 1988, Sea of Love 1989, Always 1989, Stella 1990, Arachnophobia 1990, King Ralph 1990, Barton Fink 1991, The Babe 1992, Born Yesterday 1993, The Flintstones 1994, Kingfish: A Story of Huey P. Long 1995, Pie in the Sky, Mother Night 1996, Fallen 1997, Combat! 1997, The Borrowers 1997, The Big Lebowski 1998, Blues Brothers 2000 1998, Dirty Work 1998, The Runner 1999, Bringing Out the Dead 1999, Coyote Ugly 2000, O Brother Where Art Thou 2000, The Adventures of Rocky and Bullwinkle 2000, One Night at McCool's 2000, Emperor's New Groove (voice) 2000, Happy Birthday 2001, My First Mister 2001, Storytelling 2001, Monsters Inc. (voice) 2001, Mike's New Car (voice) 2002, Dirty Deeds 2002, Masked and Anonymous 2003, The Jungle Book 2 (voice) 2003, Home of Phobia 2004, Clifford's Really Big Movie (voice) 2004, Beyond the Sea 2004, Marilyn Hotchkiss' Ballroom Dancing and Charm School 2005, Cars (voice) 2006, Evan Almighty 2007, Death Sentence 2007, Bee Movie (voice) 2007, Speed Racer 2008, Gigantic 2008, Confessions of a Shopaholic 2009, The Artist 2011, Trouble with the Curve 2012, Argo (Screen Actors Guild Award for Outstanding Performance in a Motion Picture 2013) 2012, Flight 2012, The Hangover Part III 2013, Inside Llewyn Davis 2013, Monsters University (voice) 2013, The Monuments Men 2014, Transformers: Age of Extinction 2014, The Gambler 2014, Curious George 3: Back to the Jungle 2015, Trumbo 2015, Christmas with the Coopers 2015, 10 Cloverfield Lane 2016, Once Upon a Time in Venice 2017. *Television includes:* The Mystery of Moro Castle, The Face of Rage, Heart of Steel, Moonlighting, Chiefs (mini-series), The Paper Chase, Murder Ordained, The Equalizer, A Streetcar Named Desire 1995, Kingfish: A Story of Huey P. Long 1995, Roseanne (series) (American Comedy Award for Funniest Male Performer in a TV Series — Leading Role 1989, 1990) 1988–97, 2018–, Normal, Ohio (People's Choice Award for Favorite Male Performer in a New Television Series 2001) 2000, Pigs Next Door 2000, Father of the Pride (voice) 2004–05, Center of the Universe (series) 2004–05, Studio 60 on the Sunset Strip (Emmy Award for Outstanding Guest Actor in a Drama Series 2007) 2006, The Year Without a Santa Claus 2006, You Don't Know Jack 2010, Damages 2011, Alpha House (Satellite Award for Best Actor in a Television Series Musical or Comedy 2014) 2013–14. *Address:* c/o Fred Specktor, CAA, 2000 Avenue of the Stars, Los Angeles, CA 90067, USA.

GOODMAN, Marian; American art gallery owner; *President, Marian Goodman Gallery;* b. New York, NY; ed Columbia Univ.; f. Multiples 1965, publr of prints, multiples and publs by artists including Richard Artschwager, John Baldessari, Dan Graham, Sol Lewitt, Roy Lichtenstein, Claes Oldenburg, Robert Smithson and Andy Warhol, worked with European artists, introducing early edns by Joseph Beuys, Marcel Broodthaers, Blinky Palermo and Gerhard Richte 1968–75; est. Marian Goodman Gallery, New York 1977, relocated 1981, currently Pres.; est. Galerie Marian Goodman, Paris 1999; hon. degree from CUNY Grad. Center 2012. *Address:* Marian Goodman Gallery, 24 West 57th Street, New York, NY 10019, USA (office); Galerie Marian Goodman, 79 rue du Temple, 75003 Paris, France (office). *Telephone:* (212) 977-7160 (New York) (office); 1-48-04-70-52 (Paris) (office). *Fax:* (212) 581-5187 (New York) (office); 1-40-27-81-37 (Paris) (office). *E-mail:* goodman@mariangoodman.com (office). *Website:* www.mariangoodman.com (office).

GOODNIGHT, James (Jim) H., PhD; American software industry executive; *Chairman and CEO, SAS Institute Inc.;* b. 6 Jan. 1943, Salisbury, North Carolina; s. of Albert Goodnight and Dorothy Patterson Goodnight; m. Ann Goodnight; three c.; ed North Carolina State Univ.; mem. Faculty, North Carolina State Univ. 1972–76, Adjunct Prof. 1976–; Co-Founder and Co-owner (with John Sall), SAS Inst. Inc. (software co.) 1976–, currently Chair. and CEO; Co-Founder (with wife) Cary Acad. 1996; Fellow, American Statistics Asscn; Owner, Prestonwood Country Club, Umstead Hotel and Spa; CEO of the Year, Triangle Business Journal 2015. *Address:* SAS Institute Inc., 100 SAS Campus Drive, Cary, NC 27513-2414, USA (office). *Telephone:* (919) 677-8000 (office). *Fax:* (919) 677-4444 (office). *E-mail:* software@sas.com (office). *Website:* www.sas.com (office).

GOODWIN, Doris Helen Kearns, BA, PhD; American historian and writer; b. 4 Jan. 1943, Brooklyn, New York; m. Richard Goodwin 1973, three s.; ed Colby Coll., Harvard Univ.; Research Assoc., US Dept of Health, Educ. and Welfare, 1966; Special Asst, US Dept of Labor 1967; White House Fellow, 1967, Special Asst to Pres. Lyndon B. Johnson, 1968, Special Consultant to fmr Pres. Lyndon B. Johnson 1969–73; Asst Prof., Harvard Univ. 1969–71, Asst Dir, Inst. of Politics, 1971, Assoc. Prof. of Government 1972; mem. American Political Science Asscn, Council on Foreign Relations, Group for Applied Psychoanalysis, Signet Soc., Women Involved; Fulbright Fellow, 1966; numerous TV appearances; Presidential Award, New England Ind. Booksellers Asscn 2003, Lincoln Leadership Prize 2016, Charles Frankel Prize, Nat. Endowment for the Humanities, Sara Josepha Hale Medal, Carl Sandburg Literary Award. *Publications include:* Lyndon Johnson and the American Dream 1976, The Fitzgeralds and the Kennedys: An American Saga 1987, No Ordinary Time: Franklin and Eleanor Roosevelt: The Home Front in World War II (Pulitzer Prize for History 1995, Harold Washington Literary Award, New England Bookseller Asscn Award, Ambassador Book Award, The Washington Monthly Book Award) 1994, Wait Till Next Year: A Memoir, 1997, Every Four Years: Presidential Campaigns and the Media Since 1896 2003, Team of Rivals (Lincoln Prize, Book Prize for American History) 2005, The Political Genius of Abraham Lincoln 2009, The Bully Pulpit: Theodore Roosevelt, William Howard Taft, and the Golden Age of Journalism (Andrew Carnegie Medal for Excellence in Nonfiction 2014) 2013, Leadership: In Turbulent Times 2018. *Address:* c/o Beth Laski and Associates, 12930 Ventura Boulevard, Suite 513, Studio City, CA 91604, USA (office). *Telephone:* (818) 986-1105 (office). *Fax:* (818) 986-1106 (office). *E-mail:* beth@bethlaski.com (office). *Website:* www.doriskearnsgoodwin.com.

GOODWIN, Frederick (Fred) Anderson, LLB, CA, FCIB, FIB; British chartered accountant and banker; b. 17 Aug. 1958, Paisley, Scotland; m. Joyce Elizabeth McLean 1990; two c.; ed Paisley Grammar School, Univ. of Glasgow; with Touche Ross & Co. 1979–95, Partner 1988–95; CEO Clydesdale Bank 1995–98, Yorkshire Bank 1997–98; Deputy CEO The Royal Bank of Scotland Group PLC 1998–2000, Group CEO and Exec. Dir 2000–08 (resgnd); Adviser, RMJM (architectural firm) 2010; Chair. The Prince's Trust; Dir (non-exec.) Bank of China Ltd; Fellow, Chartered Inst. of Bankers in Scotland 1996– (fmr Pres.); Hon. Fellow, London Business School 2008; knighted for services to banking 2004, knighthood cancelled and annulled 2012; Hon. LLD (St Andrews) 2004; Forbes Businessman of the Year 2002, No. 1 in Scotland on Sunday's Power 100 2003–06, European Banker of the Year 2003. *Leisure interests:* restoring classic cars, golf, Formula One racing fan, shooting.

GOODYEAR, Charles W. (Chip), BSc, MBA, FCPA; American business executive; *President, Goodyear Capital Corporation;* b. 18 Jan. 1958, Hartford, Conn.; s. of Charles W. Goodyear III; m. Elizabeth Goodyear; one s. one d.; ed Yale Univ., Wharton School of Finance, Univ. of Pennsylvania; Assoc., Kidder Peabody Co. 1983–85, Asst Vice-Pres. 1986–89; Vice-Pres. of Corp. Finance, Freeport-McMoRan Copper & Gold Inc. 1989–93, Sr Vice-Pres. and Chief Investment Officer 1993–95, Exec. Vice-Pres. and Chief Financial Officer 1995–97; Pres. Goodyear Capital Corpn 1997–99, 2015–; Chief Financial Officer, BHP Group (BHP Billiton from 2001), London 1999–2001, Chief Devt Officer 2001–03, CEO, Melbourne, Australia 2003–07, Dir BHP Billiton Ltd and BHP Billiton PLC 2001–07; mem. Bd of Dirs Temasek Holdings Ltd, Singapore March–Oct. 2009, Anadarko Petroleum Corpn 2012–15; mem. Int. Council on Mining and Metals, Nat. Petroleum Council; mem. Yale Tomorrow Campaign Cttee, President's Council on Int. Activities; Trustee, Jackson Inst. Council, 2011–; Fellow, Yale Univ. *Leisure interests:* cycling, tennis, fishing, skiing. *Address:* Goodyear Capital Corporation, 210 Baronne Street, New Orleans, LA 70112, USA.

GOOLAGONG, Evonne Fay (see CAWLEY, Evonne).

GOOLSBEE, Austan Dean, BA, MA, PhD; American economist, academic and fmr government official; *Robert P. Gwinn Professor of Economics, Booth School of Business, University of Chicago;* b. 18 Aug. 1969, Waco, Tex.; s. of Arthur Goolsbee and Linda Catherine Goolsbee (née Dean); m. Robin Winters 1997; two s. one d.; ed Milton Acad., Yale Univ., Massachusetts Inst. of Tech.; mem. Macro econ. Task Force for Polish Econ. Restructuring, Warsaw, Poland 1990; mem. Econ. Staff of Senator David Boren, Washington, DC 1991; Asst Prof. of Econs, Grad. School of Business, Univ. of Chicago 1995–99, Assoc. Prof. of Econs 1999–2001, Prof. of Econs 2001–09, 2011–, Robert P. Gwinn Prof. of Econs, Booth School of Business 2005–; Staff Dir and Chief Economist, President's Econ. Recovery Advisory Bd, The White House, Washington, DC 2009–10, also mem. Council of Econ. Advisors, Chair. Council of Econ. Advisors 2010–11; Research Assoc., Nat. Bureau of Econ. Research 2001–; mem. Panel of Econ. Advisors to Congressional Budget Office 2007–11; Research Fellow, American Bar Foundation 1996–2009; Alfred P. Sloan Fellow 2000–02; Fulbright Scholar 2006–07; mem. Panel of Econ. Advisors, Federal Reserve Bank of New York 2012–; Chair. Advisory Bd, Yale Program on Financial Stability 2013–, mem. Advisory Council, Jackson Inst. for Int. Affairs, Yale Univ. 2012–; fmr columnist, Slate.com; columnist, New York Times 2006–08; Peter Lisagor Award for Exemplary Journalism 2006. *Television:* History's Business (History Channel). *Publications include:* numerous papers in professional journals and chapters in books. *Leisure interests:* improv comedy, triathlons. *Address:* Booth School of Business, University of Chicago, 5807 South Woodlawn Avenue, Chicago, IL 60637, USA (office). *Telephone:* (773) 702-5869 (office). *Fax:* (773) 702-0458 (office). *E-mail:* goolsbee@chicagobooth.edu (office). *Website:* www.chicagobooth.edu (office).

GOONETILEKE, Air Chief Marshal W. D. R. M. J.; Sri Lankan air force officer; b. 28 Feb. 1956; s. of Harry Goonetileke; m. Nelun Goonetileke; one s. one d.; ed St Peter's Coll., Bambalapitiya, Air Command and Staff Coll., USAF Air Univ., Alabama, USA, Pakistan Nat. Defence Coll.; joined Sri Lanka Air Force as Officer

Cadet, Gen. Duties Pilot Br. 1978, rank of Pilot Officer 1979, served as Operational Pilot and CO, No. 03 Maritime Squadron and later No. 04 Helicopter Wing, several sr operational command appointments including Zonal Commdr, North Zone, later East Zone, Commdr Air Force Bases, Katunayake, Anuradapura and China Bay, Dir of Operations/Deputy Chief of Staff Operations, becoming 12th Commdr Sri Lanka Air Force 2006–11, rank of Air Chief Marshal 2009, Chief of Sri Lanka Defence Staff 2009–13; Chair. Civil Aviation Authority 2009–11; Pres. Sri Lanka Rugby Football Union 2010–12; Chair. Bd Waters Edge Ltd; Fellow, Inst. of Man. of Sri Lanka; Uttama Seva Padakkama, Rana Wickrama Padakkama, Vishista Seva Vibhushanaya (Distinguished Service Decoration); Hon. PhD (Univ. of Kelaniya) 2009. *Address:* c/o Ministry of Defence, 15/5 Baladaksha Mawatha, PO Box 572, Colombo 03, Sri Lanka.

GOOSBY, Eric Paul, MD; American professor of medicine, UN official and fmr state official; *Special Envoy on Tuberculosis, United Nations;* b. 28 Aug. 1952; ed Univ. of California, San Francisco; Attending Physician, AIDS Activity Div., San Francisco Gen. Hosp. 1986, Assoc. Medical Dir, AIDS Clinic 1987; Dir of HIV Services, Health Resources and Services Admin, US Dept of Health and Human Services 1991–94, Dir, Office of HIV/AIDS Policy 1994–2000; Interim Dir, Nat. AIDS Policy Office, The White House 1997, Acting Deputy Dir 2000; CEO and Chief Medical Officer, Pangaea Global AIDS Foundation 2001–09; Amb.-at-large and Coordinator, US Govt Activities to Combat HIV/AIDS Globally, US Dept of State 2009–13; Prof. in Global Health Sciences, Dept of Medicine, Univ. of California, San Francisco, also Dir for Global Health Delivery and Diplomacy 2013–; UN Special Envoy on Tuberculosis 2015–. *Address:* UCSF Global Health Sciences Mission Hall, Global Health and Clinical Sciences Building 550, 16th Street, San Francisco, CA 94158, USA (office). *Telephone:* (415) 476-5494 (office). *E-mail:* communications@globalhealth.ucsf.edu (office). *Website:* globalhealthsciences.ucsf.edu (office).

GOOSEN, Retief; South African golfer; b. 3 Feb. 1969, Polokwane (fmrly Pietersburg); s. of Theo Goosen; m. Tracy Goosen; one s. one d.; turned professional 1990; sr victories, Iscor Newcastle Classic 1991, Spoornet Classic 1992, Bushveld Classic 1992, Witbank Classic 1992, Mount Edgecombe Trophy 1993, Phillips South African Open 1995, Slaley Hall Northumberland Challenge 1996, Peugeot Open 1997, Dunhill Cup 1997, 1998 (both times with Ernie Els and David Frost), Novotel Perrier Open 1999, Lancome Trophy 2000, 2003, Scottish Open 2001, Telefonica Open 2001, EMC World Cup (with Ernie Els) 2001, WGC World Cup (with Ernie Els) 2001, US Open 2001, 2004, Johnnie Walker Classic 2002, Dimension Data Pro-Am 2002, BellSouth Classic 2002, Chrysler Championship 2003, European Open 2004, The Tour Championship 2004, Nedbank Challenge 2004, Linde German Masters 2005, VW Masters 2005, Int. Tournament, South African Airways Open 2005; mem. Dunhill Cup team 1996–2000, World Cup team 1993, 1995, 2000, 2001, Presidents Cup team 2000, 2003, 2011, Iskandar Johor Open 2008, Africa Open 2009; Hon. mem. European Tour 2002–; f. Retief Goosen Acad. 2000; Hon. Patron, Make a Difference Charity, South African Disabled Golf Asscn; Springbok Colours Award 1990, Volvo Order of Merit 2001, 2002 (first non-European to retain title), Harry Vardon Trophy 2001, Goose Sauvignon Blanc 2008, Decanter World Wine Award 2009. *Leisure interests:* water skiing, wines. *Address:* IMG, McCormack House, Hogarth Business Park, Burlington Lane, Chiswick, London, W4 2TH, England (office). *E-mail:* angela.jones@imgworld.com (office). *Website:* www.retiefgoosen.com.

GOPAKUMAR, Rajesh, PhD; Indian physicist and academic; *Director, International Centre for Theoretical Sciences;* b. 1967, Trivandrum; m. Rukmini Dey; ed Indian Inst. of Tech., Kanpur, Princeton Univ., USA; Post-doctoral Fellow, Univ. of Calif., Santa Barbara 1997–98, Harvard Univ. 1998–2001; Visiting mem. Inst. of Advanced Study, Princeton, NJ 2001–05; Invited Lecturer, Strings, TIFR, Mumbai 2001, Collège de France, Paris 2004, Beijing 2006, Uppsala 2011; mem. Organizing Cttee Asia-Pacific School on String Theory, Seoul, S Korea 2001, 2004, 2005; fmr Prof., Harish-Chandra Research Inst., Allahabad; mem. Adjunct Faculty, Indian Inst. of Tech., Kanpur, Tata Inst. of Fundamental Research, Mumbai, Int. Centre for Theoretical Sciences, Bangalore (also Dir); Founding mem. Global Young Acad. 2010; Fellow, Indian Acad. of Sciences 2009, Indian Nat. Science Acad. 2010, World Acad. of Sciences; Best Graduating Student Award in Physics, Indian Inst. of Tech., Kanpur 1992, B. M. Birla Science Prize 2004, ICTP Prize 2006, Swarnajayanthi Fellowship 2006, Shanti Swarup Bhatnagar Award 2009, G. D. Birla Prize 2013, World Acad. of Sciences Award for Physical Sciences 2013. *Achievement:* discovered Gopakumar-Vafa invariants and Gopakumar-Vafa duality. *Publications:* numerous scientific papers in professional journals on string theory, particularly AdS/CFT correspondence, topological string theories, large N field theories and noncommutative field theories. *Address:* International Centre for Theoretical Sciences, G-303, Survey No. 151, Shivakote, Hesaraghatta Hobli, Bengaluru 560 089, India (office). *Telephone:* (80) 67306021 (office); (80) 46536021 (office). *E-mail:* rajeshgopakumar@icts.res.in (office). *Website:* www.icts.res.in (office).

GOPAL, Satya; Indian civil servant and government official; mem. Indian Admin. Service; Admin. Union Territories of Dadra and Nagar Haveli and of Daman and Diu –2011; Chair. Chandigarh Housing Bd 2011–14; Prin. Sec., Dept of Information, Govt of Arunachal Pradesh 2014–. *Address:* Department of Information, Government of Arunachal Pradesh, Itanagar, 791111, India (office). *Website:* arunachalipr.gov.in/GovtSeBureaucrats.htm (office).

GOPALAKRISHNAN, Adoor; Indian film-maker and writer; *Chairman, Public Service Broadcasting Trust of India;* b. (Gopalakrishnan), 3 July 1941, Adoor, Kerala; s. of Madhavan Unnithan and Gouri Kunjamma; m. R. Sunanda 1972; one d.; ed Gandhigram Rural Univ., Film Inst. of India; mem. Working Group on Nat. Film Policy 1979–80; Dir Nat. Film Devt Corpn 1980–83; Faculties of Fine Arts, Univ. of Kerala, Calicut and Mahatma Gandhi Univs 1985–89; Chair. Film & Television Inst. of India 1987–89, 1993–96; Chair. 7th Int. Children's Film Festival of India 1991; currently Chair. Public Service Broadcasting Trust of India; mem. Advisory Cttee Nat. Film Archive of India 1988–90; Chair. Jury, Singapore Int. Film Festival; Chair. Cairo Int. Film Festival, Fribourg Int. Film Festival; mem. Jury, Int. Film Festival of India 1983, Venice Int. Film Festival 1988, Bombay Int. Festival 1990, Hawaii Int. Film Festival, Sochi Int. Film Festival, Alexandria Int. Film Festival; Commdr des Arts et des Lettres 2003; Hon. DLitt (Mahatma Gandhi Univ.) 2006, (Univ. of Kerala) 2013, (Viswabharati Univ.) 2015; UNICEF Film Prize, OCIC Film Prize, Interfilm Prize, Padma Shri 1984, Dadasaheb Phalke Award 2004, Padma Vibhushan 2006, Lifetime Achievement Award, Cairo, Denver and New Jersey, Colombo, Mumbai int. film festivals, numerous other int. film awards. *Plays:* Vaiki Vanna Velicham, Ninte Rajyam Varunnu. *Films include:* Swayamvaram (Nat. Film Award) 1972, Kodiyettam (Nat. Film Award, Kerala State Film Award) 1977, Elippathayam (British Film Inst. Award, London Film Festival 1982, Nat. Film Award, Kerala State Film Award) 1981, Mukhamukham (Int. Film Critics' Prize, New Delhi, Nat. Film Award, Kerala State Film Award) 1984, Anantaram (Int. Film Critics' Prize, Karlovy Vary, Nat. Film Award, Kerala State Film Award) 1987, Mathilukal (Int. Film Critics' Prize, Venice, Nat. Film Award) 1989, Vidheyan (Int. Film Critics' Prize, Singapore, Nat. Film Award, Kerala State Film Award) 1993, Kathapurushan 1995 (Int. Film Critics' Prize, Mumbai, Nat. Film Award), Nizhalkkuthu 2002 (Int. Film Critics' Prize, Mumbai, Nat. Film Award), Naalu Pennungal (Nat. Film Award), Oru Pennum Randaanum (Kerala State Film Award), Pinneyum 2016, more than 24 short and documentary films. *Publications include:* plays: Vaiki vanna velicham 1961, Ninte rajyam varunnu 1963; books: The World of Cinema (Nat. Award for Best Book on Cinema 1984) 1983, The Experience of Cinema (Kerala State Award 2004), Film, Literature and Life (Sahitya Akademi Award) 2005, Adoor Gopalakrishnan-A Compendium of Essays on Cinema in Malayalam; screenplays of Rat-trap, Face to Face, Monologue and all 11 film collections of essays. *Leisure interest:* reading. *Address:* Darsanam, Thiruvananthapuram, 695 017 India. *Telephone:* (471) 551144; (471) 2446567. *E-mail:* adoorg@gmail.com. *Website:* www.adoorgopalakrishnan.com.

GOPALAKRISHNAN, Senapathy (Kris), MSc, MTech; Indian business executive; *Chairman, Axilor Ventures;* ed Indian Inst. of Tech., Madras; software engineer for Patni computer systems, Mumbai 1979, Asst Project Man. 1981; Co-founder and Dir Infosys Technologies, Bangalore 1981–, Tech. Dir –1987, Tech. Vice-Pres. KSA/Infosys, USA 1987–94, Head of Tech. Support Services 1994, Head of Client Delivery and Tech. 1996–98, fmr COO, Deputy Man. Dir –2006, Pres. and Jt Man. Dir 2006–07, CEO and Man. Dir 2007–11, Exec. Co-Chair. 2011–13, Exec. Vice-Chair. 2013–14; Co-founded Axilor Ventures 2014, Chair. 2015–; Chair. IIT Madras Growth Fund, Confed. of Indian Industry (CII) Nat. Cttee on E-commerce, Indian Inst. of Information Tech. and Man., Kerala; Vice-Chair. Bd for Information Tech. Educ. Standards; Vice-Chair. CII Southern Regional Council; mem. Asscn for Computing Machinery, IEEE, IEEE Computer Soc.; IIT Madras Distinguished Alumnus Award 1998, Padma Bhushan 2011. *Address:* Axilor Ventures Pvt Ltd, 15th Cross Road, KR Layout, JP Nagar Phase 6, JP Nagar, Bengaluru 560 078, Karnataka, India (office). *E-mail:* accelerator@axilor.com (office). *Website:* www.axilor.com (office).

GOPALASWAMI, N., MSc; Indian government official (retd); *President, Vivekananda Educational Society;* b. 21 April 1944, Needamangalam (then in Thanjavur dist), Tamil Nadu; ed St Joseph's Coll., Tiruchirappalli, Univ. of Delhi, Univ. of London, UK; mem. Indian Admin. Service 1966–, served in state of Gujarat in various capacities 1967–92, including Dist Magistrate in dists of Kutch and Kheda, Municipal Commr, Surat, Dir of Relief, Dir Higher Educ. and Jt Sec. (Home Dept) Govt of Gujarat, Man. Dir Gujarat Communication and Electronics Ltd, Vadodara, mem. (Admin and Purchase) Gujarat Electricity Bd, Sec. to Govt (Science and Tech. in Tech. Educ.) and Sec. Dept of Revenue; served Govt of India 1992–2004, worked as Adviser (Educ.) in Planning Comm., Jt Sec., Dept of Electronics, in charge of Software Devt and Industry Promotion Div. and also Head of Software Tech. Park of India Soc. and SATCOMM India Soc., Sec. Dept of Culture, Sec.-Gen. Nat. Human Rights Comm., Union Home Sec. –2004; Election Commr 2004–06, Chief Election Commr (with rank of Judge of the Supreme Court) 2006–09 (retd); Chair. Kalakshetra 2014–; Chancellor, Rashtriya Sanskrit Vidyapeetha 2015–; currently Pres. Vivekananda Educational Soc.; Vice-Pres. Samskrit Promotion Foundation, New Delhi; mem. Delimitation Comm. 2005–; int. observer in USA during presidential election Nov. 2004, gen. election in Mauritius July 2005; Prof. Mitra Gold Medal, Univ. of Delhi (first recipient) 1965, Padma Bhushan 2015. *Leisure interests:* listening to Carnatic music (classical music from South India), photography. *Address:* 77 Lodhi Estate, New Delhi 110 003 (home); Vivekananda Educational Society, 'Sri Paduka', H Block Krishna Apartments, 1053, Poonamalle High Road, Chennai 600 084, India (office). *Telephone:* (44) 23452120 (office). *E-mail:* info@vesonline.org (office). *Website:* www.vesonline.org (office).

GOPALSAMY, V., (Vaiko), BA, MA, BL; Indian lawyer and politician; *Leader, Marumalarchi Dravida Munnetra Kazhagam;* b. 22 May 1944, Kallingappatti, Tamil Nadu; s. of Vaiyapuri Gopalsamy and Mariammal Gopalsamy; m. Renugadevi Gopalsamy; one s. two d.; ed St Xavier's Coll., Presidency Coll., B.L Law Coll.; Propaganda Sec., Dravida Munnetra Kazhagam (DMK) Party for Tirunelveli and Kanyakumari dists 1972–73, DMK Election Campaign Sec. 1984–93; mem. Rajya Sabha (Parl.) 1978–96, Lok Sabha (Parl.) 1998–2004; Founder and Leader Marumalarchi Dravida Munnetra Kazhagam; arrested on charges of terrorism July 2002, Oct. 2008, released both times; Pres. Citizen's Forum for Rehabilitation of Physically Handicapped; f. Marumalarchi Blood Donors Asscn; Convener, Voluntary Blood Donors Asscn, Tirunelveli 1983; mem. Railway Convention Cttee 1982–84, Cttee on the Welfare of Scheduled Castes and Scheduled Tribes 1983–84, Cttee on Petitions 1986–87, Cttee on Papers Laid on the Table 1986–87, Cttee on External Affairs 1998–99, Consultative Cttee, Ministry of Industry, Cttee of Privileges 1999–2000, Cttee on Defence 1999–2000, Cttee Science and Technology, Environment and Forests 1999–2000, Cttee on Ethics 2000–01; Gold Medal in Econs. *Address:* AL-Block, New No. 20, 4th Cross Street, 11th Main Road, Anna Nagar, Chennai 600 040; Marumalarchi Dravida Munnetra Kazhagam, 'Thayagam', 141 Rukmani Lakshmi Pathi Salai, Egmore, Chennai 600 008; Kalingappatti Village, Thiruvengadam, Tirunelveli District 627 724, India. *Telephone:* (44) 26214252; (46) 36282127. *Website:* www.mdmk.org.in.

GOPEE-SCOON, Paula, BSc, LLB (Hons); Trinidad and Tobago politician and business executive; b. 18 April 1958, Point Fortin; m. (divorced); three c.; ed St Joseph's Convent, San Fernando, Univ. of the West Indies, Cave Hill, Barbados, Univ. of London, UK; professional experience includes teaching (Point Fortin Intermediate Roman Catholic School), banking and finance (Republic Bank and Royal Bank of Trinidad and Tobago), along with sales, marketing and customer service (BioChem Trinidad and Tobago Ltd and Sunspots Plastics Ltd); MP (People's Nat. Movt—PNM) for Point Fortin 2007–; Minister of Foreign Affairs

2007–10; mem. Dyslexia Asscn Bursary Fund Cttee, St Joseph's Convent (Port of Spain) Support Group. *Leisure interests:* art collecting, Caribbean culture, Scrabble, charitable work. *Address:* House of Representatives, Port of Spain (office); 66 Cherry Crescent, Westmoorings, Trinidad and Tobago (home). *Telephone:* (868) 648-1086 (office); (868) 637-1244 (home). *Fax:* (868) 648-1086 (office); (868) 637-1249 (home). *E-mail:* scoongp@gmail.com (home). *Website:* www.ttparliament.org/members.php?mid=54&id=PGO01 (office).

GOPINATH, Capt. G. R.; Indian airline executive and fmr army officer; *Chairman, Deccan Charters Ltd;* b. 13 Nov. 1951, Gorur, Karnataka; m. Bhargavi Gopinath; two d.; ed Nat. Defence Acad., Indian Mil. Acad.; first army assignment during Bangladesh War 1971; f. Malnad Mobikes; launched India's first low-cost airline Air Deccan 2003; unsuccessful cand. in nat. parl. elections 2009; Founder-Chair. Deccan Charters Ltd 2009–; Chevalier, Legion d'honneur 2007; Rolex Int. Award 1996, Rajyotsava Award 2005, Personality of the Decade Award, K.G. Foundation, WIPRO PRSI Award, Sir M Visvesvaraya Memorial Award, Fed. of Karnataka Chambers of Commerce and Industry. *Publications:* Simply Fly: A Deccan Odyssey 2010. *Address:* Deccan Charters Ltd, G11, G Block Market, Hauz Khas, New Delhi 110 016 India (office). *Telephone:* (11) 26520035 (office); (11) 26520036 (office). *Fax:* (11) 26520034 (office). *E-mail:* delops@deccanair.com (office). *Website:* www.deccanair.com (office).

GOPINATH, Shyamala, MCom; Indian banker; *Chairperson, Advisory Board on Bank, Commercial and Financial Frauds, Central Vigilance Commission;* b. 20 June 1949; joined Reserve Bank of India 1972, held several positions including Exec. Dir 2003–04, Deputy Gov. 2004–11, on secondment to IMF 2001–03; Chair. Advisory Bd on Bank, Commercial and Financial Frauds, Central Vigilance Comm. 2012–; Chair. (non-exec.) HDFC Bank 2015–; fmr mem. Bd of Dirs Union Bank of India 1998–2001, Bank of Maharashtra 1994–96, State Bank of India Ltd 2004–11, Nat. Housing Bank, Export-Import Bank of India; Ind. Dir (non-exec.) Ernst & Young 2011–; Ind. Dir, Indian Oil Corpn Ltd 2012–; Exec. Dir Nat. Stock Exchange of India Ltd 2012–14; mem. Indian Advisory Bd Catalyst Inc.; Additional Ind. Dir (non-exec.) Tata Elxsi Ltd 2011–, GAIL (India) Ltd 2012–15; fmr Del. Asian Clearing Union, BIS; Convenor and mem. Working Group on Financial Conglomerates; Assoc., Indian Inst. of Bankers. *Address:* Central Vigilance Commission, Satarkata Bhavan, A-Block, GPO Complex, INA, New Delhi 110 023, India (office). *Telephone:* (11) 24651001 (office). *Fax:* (11) 24651010 (office). *E-mail:* vigilance@nic.in (office). *Website:* cvc.nic.in (office).

GORA, Jo Ann M., MA, PhD; American sociologist, academic and university president; *President, Ball State University;* b. New York; m. Roy Budd; one s. one step-d.; ed Vassar Coll., Rutgers Univ.; prof. of sociology with specialization in criminology, medical sociology and organizational behaviour; Provost and Vice-Pres. for Academic Affairs, Old Dominion Univ. 1992–2001; Chancellor Univ. of Massachusetts, Boston 2001–04; Pres. Ball State Univ. 2004–; mem. Cttee on Leadership and Institutional Effectiveness, American Council on Educ.; mem. Bd Nat. Asscn of State Univs and Land Grant Colls; mem. Cen. Indiana Corp. Partnership 2004–; mem. Bd of Dirs Ball State Univ. Foundation, First Merchants Corpn, Ball Memorial Hosp., Muncie Innovator Connector, Muncie Symphony Orchestra; Dr hc (Yeungnam Univ., South Korea) 2008; Sagamore of the Wabash, Gov. of Ind. 2005, Torchbearer Award, Indiana Comm. for Women 2005, one of Women of Wonder, Indiana Minority Business Magazine 2008, 2009, Mira Trailblazer Award (TechPoint) 2009. *Publications:* The New Female Criminal: Empirical Reality or Social Myth?, Emergency Squad Volunteers: Professionalism in Unpaid Work; numerous articles in professional journals. *Leisure interests:* photography, tennis, golf, reading. *Address:* Office of the President, Ball State University, AD Building 101, Muncie, IN 47306, USA (office). *Telephone:* (765) 285-5555 (office). *Fax:* (765) 285-1461 (office). *E-mail:* president@bsu.edu (office). *Website:* cms.bsu.edu/about/administrativeoffices/president (office).

GORANOV, Vladislav Ivanov, MA; Bulgarian politician; *Minister of Finance;* b. 30 April 1977, Pleven; ed Geo Milev Mathematics High School, Pleven, Dimitar Apostolov Tsenov Acad. of Econs, Svishtov; Specialist, Extra-Budgetary Accounts and Funds Div., also Expert and Dir of Financial Policy Directorate, Ministry of Agric., Forestry and Agrarian Reform 1998–2001; Chief Expert, Financing of State Bodies, Programs and Insurance Funds Directorate, Ministry of Finance 2001, Head of Social Expenditures and Public Finance Man. Div. 2001–09, Deputy Minister of Finance 2009–13, Minister of Finance 2014–17, 2017–; mem. Nat. Ass. (parl.) for 24-Sofia 2 2013–14, mem. Econ. Policy and Tourism Cttee, Budget and Finance Cttee; Exec. Dir and mem. Man. Bd Municipal Bank PLC Feb.–Nov. 2014; mem. Bd of Govs., EIB 2017–; mem. Grazhdani za Evropeysko Razvitie na Bălgarija (GERB—Citizens for European Devt of Bulgaria). *Address:* Ministry of Finance, 1040 Sofia, ul. G.S. Rakovski 102, Bulgaria (office). *Telephone:* (2) 985-92-684 (office). *Fax:* (2) 980-68-63 (office). *E-mail:* feedback@minfin.bg (office). *Website:* www.minfin.bg (office).

GÖRANSSON, Bengt; Swedish politician; b. 25 July 1932, Stockholm; s. Gustaf Göransson and Gertrude Göransson; ed Univ. of Stockholm; Reso Ltd (travel org.) 1960–71; Chair. Manilla School for the Deaf 1970–78; Head, Community Centre Asscn 1971; Chair. of Bd Nat. Theatre Centre 1974–82; mem. various official cttees; Chair. of Bd Fed. of Workers' Educational Asscn 1980–82; Minister for Cultural Affairs 1982–89, Minister of Educ. and Cultural Affairs 1989–91; Chair. Ansvar Insurance Co. 1991–97, Int. Inst. of Alcohol Policy 1996–99, Center for Biotechnology 1996–98, Parl. Cttee on Democracy 1997–2000; Chair. Dalhalla Festival Stage 1994–2002, Norden Asscn 2000–07; Visiting Prof., Univ. of Gothenburg 2010; Dr hc (Gothenburg); 10GT Veteran Medal 1997, Illis quorum Govt Medal 2000, Royal Gold Medal 2008. *Publications include:* Thoughts on Politics 2010. *Leisure interests:* culture, politics, education, sports. *Telephone:* (8) 6616607 (home); (70) 5616608 (home). *E-mail:* a.b.goransson@telia.com (home).

GORBACH, Hubert; Austrian business executive and fmr politician; b. 27 July 1956, Frastanz; m.; one s. one d.; ed secondary school in Feldkirch and commercial Coll.; mil. service 1978, cadre and sergeant's training; Export Man., Elektra Bregenz 1978–79; Head of Dept, Authorized Agent, Co. Sec., mem. Bd Textilwerke Ganahl 1979–87; CEO Kolb GmbH 1987–93; mem. Bd prov. Hosp.-GmbH 1999–2003; mem. OW Cttee 2000–01; mem. Freiheitspartei Österreichs (FPÖ—Freedom Party Austria) 1975–2005; Prov. Sec. Ring freiheitlicher Jugend 1976–82, Gen. Sec. 1980–85, mem. Prov. Party Exec. 1975, Prov. Party Cttee 1984, Prov. Deputy Gen. Sec. 1984–92, Local Party Rep., Frastanz 1986–92, Dist Rep., Feldkirch 1988–92, Prov. Party Rep., Vorarlberg 1992–2004, mem. Party Leaders' Group 1980–92, Party Exec. 1980–85, Party Cttee 1992–2005, Deputy Gen. Sec. 2000–02; mem. Frastanz Dist Council 1985–92, Frastanz Local Council 1990–92; mem. State Parl. of Vorarlberg 1989–93, Vorarlberg Prov. Govt 1993–2003; Deputy Head of Prov. 1999–2003; Fed. Minister of Transport, Innovation and Tech. 2003–07; Vice-Chancellor of Austria 2003–07; Chair. Walter Klaus Holding 2007; Founder and Prin. Gorbach Consulting GmbH 2007–; Foundation mem. Bündnis Zukunft Österreich (BZÖ—Alliance Future Austria) 2005–, mem. Fed. Party Man.; Carinthian Order in Gold 2006. *Leisure interests:* skiing, horse riding (pres. prov. horse riding club), tennis, jogging, reading, wine culture, shooting, flying (pvt. pilot's licence). *Address:* Gorbach Consulting GmbH, Obere Lände 1, 6820 Frastanz, Austria (office). *Telephone:* (5522) 522-22-12 (office). *Fax:* (5522) 522-22-16 (office). *E-mail:* h.gorbach@gorbach-consulting.com (office). *Website:* www.gorbach-consulting.com (office).

GORBACHEV, Mikhail Sergeyevich; Russian organization official, politician and fmr head of state; b. 2 March 1931, Privolnoye, Krasnogvardeiskii Dist, Stavropol Krai; s. of Sergei Andreevich Gorbachev and Maria Panteleimonovna Gorbachev (née Gopcalo); m. Raisa Titarenko 1953 (died 1999); one d.; ed Faculty of Law, Moscow State Univ. and Stavropol Agricultural Inst.; began work as machine operator 1946; joined CPSU 1952; Deputy Head, Dept of Propaganda, Stavropol Komsomol (V. I. Lenin Young Communist League) Territorial Cttee 1955–56, Second, then First Sec. 1958–62; First Sec., Stavropol Komsomol City Cttee 1956–58; del. to CPSU Congress 1961, 1971, 1976, 1981, 1986, 1990; Party Organizer, Stavropol Territorial Production Bd of Collective and State Farms 1962; Head, Dept of Party Bodies of CPSU Territorial Cttee 1963–66; First Sec., Stavropol City Party Cttee 1966–68; Second Sec., Stavropol Territorial CPSU Cttee 1968–70, First Sec. 1970–78; mem. CPSU Cen. Cttee 1971–91, Sec. for Agric. 1978–85, Alt. mem. Political Bureau CPSU, Cen. Cttee 1979–80, mem. 1980–91, Gen. Sec., CPSU Cen. Cttee 1985–91; Deputy Supreme Soviet of USSR 1970–89 (Chair. Foreign Affairs Comm. of Soviet Union 1984–85), mem. Presidium 1985–88, Chair. 1988–89, Supreme Soviet of RSFSR 1980–90, elected to Congress of People's Deputies of USSR 1989, Chair. 1989–90; Pres. of USSR 1990–91; Head, Int. Foundation for Socio-Economic and Political Studies (Gorbachev Foundation) 1992–; Head Int. Green Cross/Green Crescent 1993–; presidential cand. 1996; Co-founder and Co-Chair. Social Democratic Party of Russia 2000–04 (resgnd); Founder and Leader, Union of Social Democrats 2007–; syndicated columnist for numerous newspapers world-wide 1992–; Hon. Citizen of Berlin 1992, Freeman of Aberdeen 1993; Order of Lenin 1971, 1973, 1981, Orders of Red Banner of Labour 1947, Order of the Badge of Honour 1966, Order of St Andrew 2011, numerous other decorations; Nobel Peace Prize 1990, Albert Schweitzer Leadership Award (jt recipient) 1992, Ronald Reagan Freedom Award 1992, Urania-Medaille (Berlin) 1996, Augsburg Peace Prize 2005, numerous other awards. *Recording:* Peter and the Wolf: Wolf Tracks (Grammy Award, Best Spoken Word Album for Children (jtly) 2004) 2003. *Publications:* A Time for Peace 1985, The Coming Century of Peace 1986, Speeches and Writings 1986–90, Peace Has No Alternative 1986, Moratorium 1986, Perestroika: New Thinking for Our Country and the World 1987, The August Coup (Its Cause and Results) 1991, December 1991: My Stand 1992, The Years of Hard Decisions 1993, Life and Reforms 1995. *Leisure interests:* literature, theatre, music, walking. *Address:* The Gorbachev Foundation, 125167 Moscow, Leningradskii pr. 39/14, Russia (office). *Telephone:* (495) 945-74-01 (office). *Fax:* (495) 945-74-01 (office). *E-mail:* gf@gorby.ru (office). *Website:* www.gorby.ru (office); sdorg.ru (office).

GORBUNOVS, Anatolijs; Latvian politician and fmr head of state; b. 10 Feb. 1942, Pilda, Riga Co.; s. of Valerians Gorbunovs and Aleksandra Gorbunova (née Mekša); m. Lidija Klavina; one s.; ed Riga Polytech. Inst., Moscow Acad. of Social Sciences; early job as builder on a state farm; Sr Mechanic, Riga Polytech. Inst. 1959–62; served in Red Army 1962–65; various posts in the structure of the Latvian CP 1974–88; Pres. of Latvia (Chair. Supreme Council of Latvia) 1988–93; Chair. Saeima (Parl.) 1993–95; mem. Parl. for Latvijas ceļš (Latvian Way, now Latvian First Party/Latvian Way) –2002, Chair. Saeima Cttee on European Affairs Feb.–Aug. 1996; Minister of Environmental Protection and Regional Devt and Deputy Prime Minister 1996–98; Minister of Communications 1998, of Transport 1999–2004; Chair. Latvian–Russian Intergovernmental Comm. 1996; Order of the Three Stars 1995. *Leisure interests:* hunting, gardening.

GORDER, Joseph (Joe) W., BBA, MBA; American business executive; *Chairman, President and CEO, Valero Energy Corporation;* ed Univ. of Missouri-St Louis, Our Lady of the Lake Univ.; fmr Vice-Pres. of Business Devt, Ultramar Diamond Shamrock, also Dir of Commercial/Industrial Sales, Asst Treas. and Dir of Information Systems; Sr Vice-Pres. for Corp. Devt and Strategic Planning 2003–06, Exec. Vice-Pres., Marketing and Supply 2006–12, Chief Commercial Officer and Pres. Valero-Europe 2011–12, Pres. and COO Valero Energy Corpn 2012–14, Pres. and CEO May 2014–, Chair. Dec. 2014–, Dir, Valero Energy Partners Group Llc 2013–. *Address:* Valero Corporate Headquarters, PO Box 696000, One Valero Way, San Antonio, TX 78269-6000, USA (office). *Telephone:* (210) 345-2000 (office). *Fax:* (210) 345-2646 (office). *E-mail:* info@valero.com (office). *Website:* www.valero.com (office).

GORDEYEV, Aleksei Vassilyevich, CandEconSci; Russian economist and politician; *Deputy Chairman of the Government;* b. 28 Feb. 1955, Frankfurt an der Oder, German Democratic Republic; m.; one s. one d.; ed Acad. of Nat. Econs, USSR Council of Ministers; Sr Supervisor SU-4 Govt Glavmosstroi 1980–81, Chief Expert, Head of Div., then Deputy Head Dept of Glavagrostroi 1981–86; Deputy Dir-Gen. Moskva (agro-industrial co.), Moscow Oblast 1986–92; Deputy Head of Admin., Lyubertsy Dist, Moscow Oblast 1992–97; Head, Dept of Econs, mem. Exec. Bd Ministry of Agric. and Food 1997–98, First Deputy Minister of Agric. and Food 1998–99, Minister of Agric. 1999–2009, Deputy Chair., Govt of Russian Fed. 2000–04, 2018–; Gov. of Voronezh Oblast 2009–17; Presidential Rep., Cen. Federal Okrug 2017–18; Merited Econ. of Russian Fed. *Address:* Office of the Government, 103274 Moscow, Krasnopresnenskaya nab. 2, Russia (office). *Telephone:* (495) 985-42-80 (office). *Fax:* (495) 605-53-62 (office). *E-mail:* duty_press@aprf.gov.ru (office). *Website:* www.government.ru (office).

GORDEYEV, Viacheslav Mikhailovich; Russian ballet dancer and choreographer; *Artistic Director, Russian State Ballet Theatre of Moscow;* b. 3 Aug. 1948,

Moscow; s. of Mikhail Gordeyev and Lyubov Gordeyeva; m. 2nd Maya Saidova 1987; one s. one d.; ed Moscow State Univ., State Inst. of Theatrical Arts; Leading Dancer, Bolshoi Theatre 1968–87; mem. CPSU 1977–90; Artistic Dir Russian State Ballet; Founder and Artistic Dir Russian State Ballet Theatre of Moscow 1984–; Head, Ballet Co. of Bolshoi Theatre 1995–97; Deputy of Duma, Moscow Area 2007–11; First Prize, Moscow Int. Ballet Competition 1973, USSR People's Artist 1984, Best Choreographer of the Year 1992–93 (Germany), Maurice Béjart Special Prize for Best Choreography 1992. *Roles include:* Prince, Désiré (Tchaikovsky's Nutcracker, Sleeping Beauty), Romeo (Prokofiev's Romeo and Juliet), Spartacus, Ferhat (Melnikov's Legend of Love), Albreht (Giselle), Basil (Minkus's Don Quixote), Prince (Tchaikovsky's Swan Lake). *Choreographic works:* Revived Pictures, Memory, Surprise Manoeuvres, or Wedding with the General and more than 30 choreographic compositions; own versions of classical ballets Paquita, Don Quixote and Walpurgisnacht, Nutcracker 1993, Last Tango (Bolshoi Theatre) 1996, Sleeping Beauty (Russian State Ballet) 1999, Cinderella (Russian State Ballet) 2001. *Leisure interests:* classical music, athletics, tennis. *Address:* Volgogradsky Prospekt 121, Moscow 109443 (office); Tverskaya str. 9, Apt 78, Moscow 103009, Russia (home). *Telephone:* (495) 379-94-82 (office); (495) 379-43-24 (office); (495) 629-13-36 (home). *Fax:* (495) 379-43-24 (office). *E-mail:* dilyarsb@gmail.com (office); dilyarsb@yandex.ru. *Website:* www.russballet.ru (office).

GORDHAN, Pravin Jamnadas, BPharm; South African pharmacist and politician; *Minister of Public Enterprises;* b. 12 April 1949, Durban; m. Vanitha Raju; two c.; ed Univ. of Durban Westville; mem. African Nat. Congress (ANC), fmr Sec., Operation Vula (ANC underground network); pharmacist, King Edward VII Hosp., Durban 1974–81 (expelled after detention by police); Exec. mem. Natal Indian Congress 1974–90; took part in Convention for Democratic South Africa (Codesa) 1991–94; mem. Nat. Ass. (Parl.) (ANC) 1994–98; Deputy Commr, South African Revenue Service 1998–99, Commr 1999–2009; Human Resources Dir, Telkom 1999; Minister of Finance 2009–14, 2015–17, of Cooperative Governance and Traditional Affairs 2014–15, of Public Enterprises 2018–; Chair. Council of World Customs 2000–06; Hon. DComm (Univ. of SA) 2007, Hon. LLD (Cape Town) 2007. *Address:* Ministry of Public Enterprises, Infotech Bldg, Suite 401, 1090 Arcadia St, Hatfield, Pretoria 0083 South Africa (office). *Telephone:* (12) 4311000 (office). *Fax:* (86) 5012624 (office). *E-mail:* info@dpe.gov.za (office). *Website:* www.dpe.gov.za (office).

GORDILLO, Elba Esther; Mexican union leader and politician; b. 6 Feb. 1945, Comitán, Chiapas; joined Sindicato Nacional de Trabajadores de la Educación—SNTE (Nat. Union of Educ. Workers) 1960, held succession of full-time positions 1971–89, Pres. SNTE 1989–95, Head of Finance 1995, Pres. Nat. Exec. Cttee 2004–13; elected to Chamber of Deputies 1979, re-elected 1985, 2003, Leader Partido Revolucionario Institucional (PRI) in Lower Chamber 2003; party elected to Senate 1994, Chair. Educ. Cttee; Pres. CNOP (org. that marshals pro-PRI orgs in movt) 1996–2003, Sec. Org. of the Nat. Exec. Council 1986–87, Gen. Sec. Council of Nat. Popular Orgs 1997–2002, Sec.-Gen. PRI 2003–05 (resgnd); Co-founder Nueva Alianza party 2005. *Publications:* La construcción de un proyecto sindical 1995, El paseo de las Reformas, la batalla por México 2005. *Address:* Sindicato Nacional de Trabajadores de la Educación, República de Venezuela No. 44, Col. Centro, 5to. Piso., México, DF (office); c/o Nueva Alianza, Durango 199, Col. Roma, Del. Cuauhtémoc, 06700 México, DF, Mexico. *Telephone:* (55) 5704-7000 (office). *E-mail:* info@snte.org.mx (office). *Website:* www.snte.org.mx (office).

GORDIN, Yakov Arkadyevich; Russian writer and historian; b. 23 Dec. 1935, Leningrad; m.; one s.; ed Moscow Ore Inst.; freelancer specializing in ind. historical research of crisis situations in Russian political history of 18th–20th centuries; Dir and Co-Ed. Zvezda (literary journal), St Petersburg. *Publications:* numerous articles and books, including Space, The Death of Pushkin, The Events and People of 14 December, Between Slavery and Freedom, Duels and Duelists, Coup of the Reformers, etc. *Address:* Mokhovaya str. 36, Apt 24, 191028 St Petersburg, Russia (home). *Telephone:* (812) 273-05-27 (home). *E-mail:* ariev@cityline.spb.ru.

GORDON, Alexander G.; Russian actor and journalist; b. 20 Feb. 1964, Obninsk, Moscow region; m.; ed Shchukin Theatre School; actor, Ruben Simonov Studio Theatre 1987–89; emigrated to USA, worked as waiter, asst cameraman of RTN TV co.; Sr Corresp., WMNB Corpn 1989–93; staff mem. Vostok Entertainment Co. 1993–94; writer and narrator of TV shows New York, New York (TV-6, Moscow); writer of some 100 TV programmes; returned to Russia 1997; staff mem., radio programme Silver Rain 1997; Founder-mem. and Sec.-Gen. Party of Public Cynicism 1998–; writer and narrator of publicity programmes on ORT TV channel, including Treasury of Mistakes, Gordon (NTV); actor, Theatre of the Contemporary Play; Head, Moscow Inst. Workshop of Journalism TV and Radio; TEFI, Russian TV Industry 2007, 2008, 2010, 2011. *Film directed:* Shepherd of his Sheep. *Leisure interest:* football.

GORDON, Sir Donald, Kt; South African/British business executive; *Honorary Life President, Liberty International PLC;* b. 24 June 1930, Johannesburg; s. of Nathan Gordon and Sheila Gordon; m. Peggy Cowan 1958; two s. one d.; ed King Edward VII School, Johannesburg; Chartered Accountant, Partner Kessel Feinstein 1955–57; Founder Liberty Life Asscn of Africa Ltd, Chair. 1957–99, Chair. Liberty Holdings Ltd 1968–99, Liberty Investors Ltd 1971–99, Guardian Nat. Insurance Co. Ltd 1980–99; Deputy Chair. Standard Bank Investment Corpn Ltd 1979–99, Premier Group Holdings Ltd 1983–96; Dir Guardbank Man. Corpn Ltd 1969–99, Guardian Royal Exchange Assurance PLC (UK) 1971–94, Charter Life Insurance Co. Ltd 1985–99, The South African Breweries Ltd 1982–99, Beverage & Consumer Industry Holdings Ltd 1989–99, GFSA Holdings Ltd 1990–94, Sun Life Corpn PLC (UK) 1992–95, Chair. Liberty Int. PLC (fmrly Transatlantic Holdings PLC) 1981–2005, Capital & Counties PLC (UK) 1982–94, Capital Shopping Centres PLC 1994–2005; Hon. Life Pres. Liberty Life; Hon. D.Econ.Sc. (Witwatersrand) 1991; Financial Mail Businessman of the Year 1965; Sunday Times Man of the Year 1969; Achiever of the Century in South Africa Financial Services (Financial Mail 1999); Business Statesman Award (Harvard Business School); London Entrepreneur of the Year 2000, Special Award for Lifetime Achievement 2001. *Leisure interests:* opera, ballet. *Website:* www.donaldgordon.org (office).

GORDON, Douglas Lamont, BA, MA; British artist; b. 20 Sept. 1966, Glasgow; s. of James Gordon and Mary Clements Gordon (née McDougall); ed Glasgow School of Art, Slade School of Art; works in video, film, photography and sculpture; Curator, The Vanity of Allegory, Deutsche Guggenheim, Berlin 2005, Palais des Papes, Avignon 2008; Visiting Prof. Fine Art, Glasgow School of Art, Glasgow Univ. 1999–; fmr Visiting Prof. and John Florent Stone Fellow, Edinburgh Coll. of Art; Int. Juror, 65th Venice Film Festival 2008; Dir Lost But Found Ltd 2010–; Ordre des Arts et des Lettres 2012; Turner Prize 1996, Premio 2000 1997, Hugo Bass Prize 1998, Roswitha Haftmann Prize 2008, London Award for Art and Performance 2011, Käthe Kollwitz Preis, Akademie der Künste, Berlin 2012. *Address:* Glasgow School of Art, 167 Renfrew Street, Glasgow, G3 6RQ, Scotland (office). *Website:* www.gsa.ac.uk (office).

GORDON, Ilene S., MSc, BSc; American business executive; *Chairman, President and CEO, Ingredion Inc.;* m.; two c.; ed Massachusetts Inst. of Tech.; served as Vice-Pres. of Operations, Tenneco Inc. 1994–97, Vice-Pres. and Gen. Man. Folding Carton Business 1997–99; Pres. Pechiney Plastic Packaging Inc. and Sr Vice-Pres. Pechiney Group 1999–2004; Pres. Food Packaging, Americas, Alcan Inc. 2004–06, Sr Vice-Pres. Alcan Inc. and Pres. and CEO Alcan Global Packaging 2006–07, Pres. and CEO Packaging, Rio Tinto Alcan 2007–09, mem. Exec. Cttee, Paris, France 2007–09; Chair., Pres. and CEO Corn Products International, Inc. (changed its name to Ingredion Inc. 2012) 2009–. *Address:* Ingredion Inc., 5 Westbrook Corporate Center, Westchester, IL 60154, USA (office). *Telephone:* (708) 551-2600 (office). *E-mail:* info@ingredion.com (office). *Website:* www.ingredion.com (office).

GORDON, Jeffrey Ivan, AB, MD; American biologist, physician and academic; *Director, The Edison Family Center for Genome Sciences and Systems Biology, Washington University, St Louis;* b. 4 Oct. 1947, New Orleans, La; ed Oberlin Coll., Univ. of Chicago; Intern, Jr Asst Resident, Medicine, Barnes Hosp., St Louis, Mo., later Sr Asst Resident, Medicine; Research Assoc., Lab. of Biochemistry, Nat. Cancer Inst., NIH; Fellow in Medicine (Gastroenterology), Washington Univ., St Louis, Asst Prof. 1981–84, Assoc. Prof. 1985–87, Prof. of Medicine and Biological Chem. 1987–90, Prof. and Head, Dept of Molecular Biology and Pharmacology 1991–2004, Dr Robert J. Glaser Distinguished Univ. Prof. 2002–, Dir The Edison Family Center for Genome Sciences and Systems Biology 2004–, Prof. of Pathology/Immunology 2008–, Chair. Exec. Council, Div. of Biology and Biomedical Sciences 1994–2003; Wellcome Visiting Prof. in the Basic Medical Sciences 1998; mem. Asscn of American Physicians 1989, NAS 2001, American Acad. of Arts and Sciences 2004, Inst. of Medicine, Nat. Inst. of Sciences 2008, American Philosophical Soc. 2014; Fellow, AAAS 1992, American Acad. of Microbiology 2001; Dr hc (Sahlgrenska Acad., Univ. of Gothenburg) 2011; Upjohn Achievement Award 1973, Young Investigator Award, American Fed. for Clinical Research 1990, NIDDK Young Scientist Award 1990, Distinguished Achievement Award, American Gastroenterology Asscn 1992, Distinguished Service Teaching Awards, Washington Univ. School of Medicine 1991–94, Marion Merrell Dow Distinguished Prize in Gastrointestinal Physiology 1994, Janssen Sustained Achievement Award in Digestive Sciences 2003, Sr Scholar Award in Global Infectious Diseases, The Ellison Medical Foundation 2003, ASM Lecturer, American Soc. of Microbiology 2005, Selman A. Waksman Award in Microbiology 2013, Robert Koch Prize 2013, King Faisal Int. Prize in Medicine 2015, Keio Medical Science Prize 2015, Steven C. Beering Award 2016, Massry Prize 2017, Sanofi-Institut Pasteur Int. Award for Biomedical Research 2017, Jacobaeus Prize, Novo Nordisk Foundation 2017, Louisa Gross Horwitz Prize 2017, Copley Medal, Royal Soc. 2018, Luminary Award, PMWC (Precision Medicine World Conf.) 2018, BBVA Foundation Frontiers of Knowledge Award in Biology and Biomedicine 2018. *Publications:* numerous papers in professional journals on gastrointestinal devt. *Address:* Room 5401, The Edison Family Center for Genome Sciences and Systems Biology, Campus Box 8510, 4523 Clayton Avenue, St Louis, MO 63110 (office); Couch Biomedical Research Building, 4515 McKinley Avenue, St Louis, MO 63110, USA (office). *Telephone:* (314) 362-7047 (office); (314) 362-5443 (Lab.) (office). *Fax:* (314) 362-7047 (Lab.) (office). *E-mail:* jgordon@wustl.edu (office). *Website:* gordonlab.wustl.edu (office).

GORDON, Jeff; American motor racing driver; b. 4 Aug. 1971, Vallejo, Calif.; s. of William Grinnell Gordon and Carol Ann Bickford; m. 1st Brooke Sealy 1994 (divorced 2002); m. 2nd Ingrid Vandebosch 2006; one s. one d.; current team: Hendrick Motorsports; United States Auto Club (USAC) Rookie of the Year 1989; youngest USAC National Midget Champion 1990 (aged 19); NASCAR racing driver; winner USAC Silver Crown and Busch Series Rookie of the Year 1991; three Busch Series victories 1992; Winston Cup debut 1992 (Atlanta Speedway); Darlington Raceway winner 1995, 1996, 1997, 1998, 2002, 2007; 69 Winston Cup victories including: Brickyard 400 1994, 1998, 2001, 2004, Southern 500 1995, 1996, 1997, 1998, 2002, Daytona 500 1997, 1999, 2009; Rookie of the Year 1993; Winston Cup Champion 1995, 1997, 1998, 2001; Winston Million Champion 1997; record seven career victories on road courses; youngest driver to achieve 50 career victories 2000; over US $50m. career winnings; f. Jeff Gordon Foundation charity for children 1999; launched Jeff Gordon Collection of Wines 2005; Co-founder Athletes for Hope 2007; Designer, Canadian Motor Speedway, Fort Erie, Ontario 2012; Global Business Advisor, Axalta 2015; Silver Buffalo Award 2009. *Films include:* Cars 2 (voice) 2011. *Publication:* (with Steve Eubanks) Jeff Gordon: Racing Back to the Front – My Memoir 2003. *Address:* Hendrick Motorsports, 4414 Pappa Joe Hendrick Blvd., POB 9, Harrisburg, NC 28075, USA. *Website:* www.jeffgordon.com (office); www.jeffgordonchildrensfoundation.org (office).

GORDON, Mark, BA; American politician; *Governor of Wyoming;* b. 14 March 1957, New York City, NY; m. 1st (died 1993); two d.; m. 2nd Jennie Muir Gordon (née Young) 2000; two s. two d.; ed Middlebury Coll.; Sec./Treasurer, Merlin Ranch, Wyo. 1988–; Partner, The Book Shop 1997–2006, Buffalo Movie Theater 2002–; Dir of Conservation/Stewardship, Apache Corpn 2006–07; Treasurer, State of Wyo. 2012–19; Gov. of Wyo. 2019–; mem. and Chair., Wyo. Environmental Quality Council 2003–07; mem. Bd of Dirs, Fed. Reserve Bank, Kansas City 2008–12; mem. Gordon Ranch 2010–, Financial Advisory Council; mem. Bd of Deposits and of Land Commrs; fmr mem. Advisory Bd, Sheridan Research and Extension Center, Coll. of Agriculture and Natural Resources, Univ. of Wisconsin; Excellence in Range Stewardship Award, Wyo. Section Soc. for Range Man. 2009. *Leisure interests:* fishing, hunting, climbing, skiing, kayaking, rodeo. *Address:*

Office of the Governor, Idelman Mansion, 2323 Carey Avenue, Cheyenne, WY 82002-0010, USA (office). *Telephone:* (307) 777-7434 (office). *Fax:* (307) 632-3909 (office). *Website:* www.governor.wyo.gov (office).

GORDON, Robert James, BA, AB, AM, PhD; American economist and academic; *Stanley G. Harris Professor in the Social Sciences, Northwestern University;* b. 3 Sept. 1940, Boston, Mass; s. of Robert A. Gordon and Margaret S. Gordon; m. Julie S. Peyton 1963; ed Harvard Univ., Univ. of Oxford, UK, Massachusetts Inst. of Tech.; Assoc. Prof. of Econs, Harvard Univ. 1967–68, Univ. of Chicago 1968–73; Prof. of Econs, Northwestern Univ. 1973–87, Stanley G. Harris Prof. in the Social Sciences 1987–, Chair. Dept of Econs 1992–96; mem. or Sr Advisor, Brookings Panel on Econ. Activity 1970–2007, Econ. Advisory Panel, Congressional Budget Office 1996–2010, Advisory Cttee, Bureau of Econ. Analysis 1999–, Tech. Panel on Assumptions and Methods of the Social Security Admin 2002–03, 2006–07; Fellow, Econometric Soc. 1977 (Treas. 1975–2005), American Acad. of Arts and Sciences 1997; John Simon Guggenheim Memorial Fellowship 1980–81, Lustrum Award, Erasmus Univ., Rotterdam 1999, Invited Lecturer, Australian Econs Asscn 2000, Swiss Econs Asscn 2001, European Cen. Bank 2001, IUI Stockholm 2001, AWH Phillips Lecturer, Australasian Econometric Soc. Meetings, Wellington, NZ 2008. *Publications include:* Milton Friedman's Monetary Framework: A Debate With His Critics 1977, Macroeconomics 1978 (12th edn 2012), Challenges to Interdependent Economies: The Industrial West in the Coming Decade (co-author) 1979, The American Business Cycle: Continuity and Change 1986, The Measurement of Durable Goods Prices 1990, The Economics of New Goods 1997, Inflation, Unemployment, and Productivity Growth 2004; more than 120 articles in professional journals. *Leisure interests:* photography, gardening, mil. history, airline man. *Address:* Department of Economics, 350 Arthur Andersen Hall, Northwestern University, 2001 Sheridan Road, Evanston, IL 60208-2600 (office); 202 Greenwood Street, Evanston, IL 60201-4714, USA (home). *Telephone:* (847) 491-3616 (office); (847) 869-3544 (home). *Fax:* (847) 491-7001 (office). *E-mail:* rjg@northwestern.edu (office). *Website:* economics.weinberg.northwestern.edu/robert-gordon/indexmsie.html (office).

GORDON-LEVITT, Joseph Leonard; American actor and director; b. 17 Feb. 1981, Los Angeles, Calif.; s. of Dennis Levitt and Jane Gordon; m. Tasha McCauley 2014; two s.; ed Van Nuys High School, Columbia Univ. School of General Studies, New York; joined a musical theatre group aged four and played the Scarecrow in a production of The Wizard of Oz; began career in commercials as a child before making his film debut in Beethoven 1992; f. and Dir online production co. hitRECord 2004; directed and edited short films Morgan M. Morgansen's Date with Destiny and Morgan and Destiny's Eleventh Date: The Zeppelin Zoo 2010; feature film directing and screenwriting debut with Don Jon 2013; Host, TV series HitRecord on TV 2014–; Primetime Emmy Award (Jtly) for Outstanding Creative Achievement in Interactive Media-Social TV Experience 2014. *Theatre includes:* a producer of the Broadway show Slava's Snowshow 2008. *Films include:* Beethoven 1992, A River Runs Through It 1992, Holy Matrimony 1994, Roadflower 1994, Angels 1994, The Juror 1996, Sweet Jane 1998, Halloween H20: 20 Years Later 1998, 10 Things I Hate About You 1999, Picking Up the Pieces 2000, Forever Lulu 2000, Manic 2001, Treasure Planet (voice) 2002, Latter Days 2003, Mysterious Skin 2004, Brick 2005, Havoc 2005, Shadowboxer 2005, The Lookout 2007, Stop-Loss 2008, Miracle at St. Anna 2008, Killshot 2008, 500 Days of Summer 2009, Uncertainty 2009, Women in Trouble 2009, G.I. Joe: The Rise of Cobra 2009, Hesher 2010, Elektra Luxx 2010, Inception 2010, 50/50 2011, The Dark Knight Rises 2012, Premium Rush 2012, Looper 2012, Lincoln 2012, Don Jon's Addiction 2013, Sin City: A Dame to Kill For 2014, The Walk 2015, Snowden 2016, Straight Outta Oz 2016. *Television includes:* Stranger on My Land (film) 1988, Settle the Score (film) 1989, Changes (film) 1991, Hi Honey – I'm Dead (film) 1991, Plymouth (film) 1991, The Powers That Be (series) 1992–93, Gregory K (film) 1993, Roseanne (series) 1993–95, The Great Elephant Escape (film) 1995, 3rd Rock from the Sun (series) 1996–2001, Numb3rs (series) – Sacrifice 2005, Comrade Detective (series) 2017. *Publications:* The Tiny Book of Tiny Stories Vol. 1 (book/CD/DVD package) 2011, Vol. 2 2012. *E-mail:* support@hitrecord.org (office). *Website:* www.hitrecord.org (office).

GORDON-REED, Annette, AB, JD; American lawyer, academic and writer; *Charles Warren Professor of American Legal History, Harvard Law School;* m. Robert Reed; one s. one d.; ed Dartmouth Coll., Harvard Law School; fmr Assoc., Cahill Gordon & Reindel (law firm); fmr Counsel to New York City Bd of Corrections; Prof. of Law, New York Law School 1992–2010; Prof. of History, Rutgers Univ. 2007–10; Charles Warren Visiting Prof. of American Legal History, Harvard Law School 2009, Prof. of Law 2010–, Carol K. Pforzheimer Prof., Radcliffe Inst. for Advanced Study 2010–, Prof. of History 2010–, Charles Warren Prof. of American Legal History 2012–; mem. Bd of Trustees, Dartmouth Coll. 2010–; MacArthur Fellowship 2010, National Humanities Medal 2010. *Publications:* Thomas Jefferson and Sally Hemings: An American Controversy 1997, Vernon Can Read!: A Memoir (co-author) 2001, The Hemingses of Monticello: An American Family (Nat. Book Award, Pulitzer Prize for History 2009) 2008, Race on Trial: Law and Justice in American History (essays, ed.) 2009, Andrew Johnson: The American Presidents Series: The 17th President, 1865–1869 2011. *Address:* Griswold Hall 405, Harvard Law School, Cambridge, MA 02138, USA (office). *Telephone:* (617) 495-3894 (office). *E-mail:* agordonreed@law.harvard.edu (office). *Website:* www.law.harvard.edu (office).

GORDY, Berry, Jr; American music industry executive and songwriter; b. 28 Nov. 1929, Detroit, Mich.; s. of Berry Gordy, Sr and Bertha Fuller Gordy; m. 1st Thelma Coleman (divorced 1959); m. 2nd Raynoma Mayberry Liles (divorced 1964); m. 3rd Grace Eaton 1990 (divorced 1993); eight c.; owned record store in Detroit 1955; composer and ind. producer during late 1950s; Founder, Jobete Music 1958, Tamla Records 1959, Motown Record Corpn 1961–88; fmr Chair. The Gordy Co.; Dr hc (Michigan State Univ., Occidental Coll.); American Music Award, Outstanding Contrib. to Music Industry 1975, inducted into Rock and Roll Hall of Fame 1990, Michigan Rock and Roll Legends Hall of Fame 2009, NARAS Trustees Award 1991, Songwriters Hall of Fame Pioneer Award 2013. *Films include:* Lady Sings The Blues (exec. producer) 1972, Mahogany (dir) 1975, The Last Dragon (exec. producer) 1985. *Play:* Motown: The Musical (co-producer) 2013. *Recordings include:* as composer/producer: Reet Petite (Jackie Wilson), Shop Around (The Miracles), Do You Love Me? (The Contours), Try It Baby (Marvin Gaye), Shotgun (Junior Walker and The All-Stars), I Want You Back and ABC (The Jackson 5), Compilation: The Music, The Magic, The Memories of Motown 1995. *Publication:* To Be Loved 1994 (autobiography). *Website:* www.berrygordy.com.

GORE, Albert (Al) Arnold, Jr; American financial services industry executive, academic and fmr politician; *Chairman, Generation Investment Management LLP;* b. 31 March 1948, Washington, DC; s. of Albert Gore, Sr and Pauline Gore (née LaFon); m. Mary E. Aitcheson 1970 (separated 2010); one s. three d.; ed Harvard and Vanderbilt Univs; served with US Army during Viet Nam war; investigative reporter, editorial writer, The Tennessean 1971–76; home-builder and land developer, Tanglewood Home Builders Co. 1971–76; livestock and tobacco farmer 1973–; Head of Community Enterprise Bd 1993–; mem. US House of Reps 1977–79; Senator from Tennessee 1985–93; Vice-Pres. of USA 1993–2001; Democratic cand. in presidential elections 2000; Lecturer, Middle Tennessee State Univ., Columbia Univ. 2001–, Visiting Prof., UCLA, Fisk Univ. 2001–; Vice-Chair. Metropolitan West Financial LLC 2001–; Sr Adviser, Google Inc. 2001–; Co-founder and Chair. Current TV (youth cable TV network) 2004–13; Co-founder and Chair. Generation Investment Management LLP (fund man. firm), Washington, DC and London, UK 2004–; Pnr, Kleiner, Perkins, Caulfield & Byers 2007–; mem. Bd of Dirs Apple Computer Inc.; Dr hc (Harvard) 1994, (New York) 1998; Webby Award 2005, UNEP Champion of the Earth Laureate 2007, Prince of Asturias Award for Int. Co-operation 2007, Nobel Peace Prize (shared with UN Intergovernmental Panel on Climate Change) 2007, Primetime Emmy Award for Current TV 2007, Dan David Prize 2008. *Film:* An Inconvenient Truth (Best Documentary Los Angeles Film Critics Asscn 2006, Nat. Soc. of Film Critics 2007, Acad. Award for Best Documentary Feature 2007) 2006. *Publications:* Earth in the Balance 1992, An Inconvenient Truth (Quill Award for History, Current Affairs or Politics) 2006, The Assault on Reason: How the Politics of Blind Faith Subvert Wise Decision-Making (Quill Award for History/Current Affairs/Politics 2007) 2007, Our Choice: A Plan to Solve the Climate Crisis 2009, Future 2013. *Address:* Generation Investment Management US LLP, 750 17th Street, 11th Floor, Washington, DC 20006, USA (office). *Telephone:* (202) 785-7400 (office). *Fax:* (202) 785-7401 (office). *Website:* (office); www.algore.com.

GORE, Elizabeth McKee, BS, MS; American UN official; *President and Chairwoman, Alice;* b. Tex.; m. James Gore; two c.; ed Texas A&M Univ.; Devt Assoc. A&M Foundation 1999–2001; Dir of Corp. Relations and Devt, Points of Light Foundation 2001–03; volunteer at US Peace Corps, served in Bolivia 2003–05; Vice-Pres. Global Partnerships, UN Foundation 2006–13 (f. grassroots efforts, including Nothing But Nets Girl Up and the Shot@Life global vaccines campaign), Resident Entrepreneur, UN Foundation 2013–15, fmr Chair. Global Entrepreneurs Council, managed partnerships with Fortune 100 cos and with the Bill and Melinda Gates Foundation; Entrepreneur in Residence Dell 2015–17; Co-Founder Circular Board (business advisory firm, now Alice) 2016–, Pres. and Chair. Alice 2017–; mem. leadership councils of Women's Philanthropy Inst. in The Center on Philanthropy at Indiana Univ., CLASSY Awards; mem. Advisory Bd SOMA (all-natural water filter co.). *Achievements include:* joined Summit on the Summit and climbed Mt Kilimanjaro to raise awareness for the global clean water crisis on behalf of the UN 2010. *E-mail:* alice@helloalice.com (office). *Website:* www.helloalice.com (office).

GOREGLYAD, Valery Pavlovich, DrEconSci; Russian economist and politician; *Chief Auditor, Bank Rossii—Central Bank of the Russian Federation;* b. 18 June 1958, Gluzk, Mogilev Region, Belarus; m. Yaketarina Goreglyad; two s.; ed Moscow Inst. of Aviation; fmrly with mil. space industry; Head Tourism Co. –1990; Peoples' Deputy, Russian Fed. 1990–93; mem. Council of Feds, Fed. Ass. 1994; Exec. Dir Cttee on Budget, Revenue and Banking Activity 1994–2000, Deputy Head 2001–04; elected mem. (for Sakhalin region) Fed Council 2001–02 (resgnd), Leader Parl. Grouping Fed. 2002–03 (resgnd); Auditor, Accounts Chamber 2004–13; Chief Auditor, Bank Rossii—Cen. Bank of Russian Fed. 2013–; mem. Supervisory Bd Sberbank Rossii OAO 2014. *Publications:* The Budget as a Financial Regulator of Economic Development 2002; five monographs and various scholarly articles on macro-econ. analysis, problems of regional econ. devt, and innovative economy. *Leisure interests:* reading historical literature, tennis, basketball, football. *Address:* Bank Rossii—Central Bank of the Russian Federation, 107016 Moscow, ul. Neglinnaya 12, Russia (office). *Telephone:* (495) 771-91-00 (office). *Fax:* (495) 771-48-30 (office). *E-mail:* webmaster@www.cbr.ru (office). *Website:* www.cbr.ru (office).

GORELICK, Jamie Shona, BA, JD; American lawyer and fmr government official; *Partner, WilmerHale;* b. 6 May 1950, New York City; m. Richard Waldhorn 1975; two c.; ed Harvard Coll., Harvard Law School; attorney, Miller, Cassidy, Larroca & Lewin, Washington, DC 1975–79, 1980–83; Asst to US Sec. of Energy and Counselor to Deputy Sec., Washington, DC 1979–80; Gen. Counsel, US Dept of Defense 1993–94, Vice-Chair. Task Force on the Audit, Inspection and Investigation Components; Deputy Attorney-Gen., US Dept of Justice 1994–97; Vice-Chair. Fannie Mae 1997–2003; Pnr, WilmerHale (law firm), Washington, DC 2003–, Co-Chair. Nat. Security and Govt Contracts Dept, Co-Chair. Public Policy and Strategy Practice, Pnr, Litigation Dept; Pres. DC Bar 1992–93, mem. Bd of Govs 1982–88; fmr Lecturer, Harvard Law School, fmr mem. Bd of Overseers, Overseers' Visiting Cttee; Raytheon Lecturer on Business Ethics, Bentley Coll. 2004; has served on numerous govt bds and comms including CIA Nat. Security Advisory Panel 1997–2005, Pres.'s Intelligence Review Panel 2001–02, Nat. Comm. on Terrorist Attacks upon the US 2002–04; mem. ABA, American Law Inst., Women's Bar Asscn, Council on Foreign Relations; mem. Bd of Dirs United Technologies Corpn 2000–, Schlumberger Ltd 2002–10, John D. and Catherine T. MacArthur Foundation (Vice-Chair.), Amazon 2012–, Washington Legal Clinic for the Homeless, Carnegie Endowment for Int. Peace; Counselor American Soc. of Int. Peace; Trustee Urban Inst.; Sec. of Energy Outstanding Service Award 1980, Women's Bar Asscn Woman Lawyer of the Year 1993, Sec. of Defense Distinguished Service Award 1994, Prominent Woman in Int. Law 1994, Equal Justice Works Outstanding Advocate of the Year 1997, Dir of Cen. Intelligence Award 1997, Radcliffe Coll. Alumnae Recognition Award 1997, Dept of Justice Edmund J. Randolph Award 1997, American Bar Asscn Margaret Brent Award 1997, Wickersham Award for Exceptional Public Service and Dedication to the Legal Profession 1998, American Jewish Cttee Judge Learned Hand Award 1999, NOW Legal Defense and Educ. Fund Aiming High Award 2002, DC Chamber of

Commerce's Corp. Leadership Award 2003, Women's Bar Assen Star of the Bar Award 2003. *Publications:* Destruction of Evidence (co-author) 1983. *Address:* Wilmer Hale, 1875 Pennsylvania Avenue NW, Washington, DC 20006, USA (office). *Telephone:* (202) 663-6500 (office). *Fax:* (202) 663-6363 (office). *E-mail:* jamie.gorelick@wilmerhale.com (office). *Website:* www.wilmerhale.com/jamie_gorelick (office).

GORENAK, Vinko; Slovenian politician; b. 15 Dec. 1955, Boharina, Zreče; m. Irena Gorenak; ed Pedagogical Acad., Maribor, State Univ. of Maribor, Kranj; began working as an educator in School for Militia Cadets, Tacen 1977; Asst Chief of Police, Celje 1982–84, Commdr of Police 1984–89, also Head of the Police Inspectorate in Celje; adviser in office of Minister of the Interior 1990–91, at Ministry of Interior dealing with problems of organization and development of the police from 1990, government adviser in Office of the Minister of the Interior –1995, led service organization and personnel of the Ministry of Interior 1995–99, co-chaired working group that prepared the Police Act (adopted 1998); Sr Lecturer in Organization and Police Work, Faculty of Organizational Sciences, State Univ. of Maribor, Kranj 1995–2003, Asst Prof. of Man. and Security orgs 2004–09; Assoc. Prof., Faculty of Criminal Justice, Univ. of Maribor 2009–; State Sec., Ministry of Interior on Police and Gen. Affairs 2000–04, Head of Dept of Security Analysis and Policy; State Sec., Ministry of Internal Affairs 2004–05; State Sec., Cabinet of Prime Minister Janez Janša 2008–11; mem. Slovenian Democratic Party (SDP) 1999–; Deputy in Nat. Ass. 2008–, Deputy for 7th constituency (Maribor) 2011–; Minister of Internal Affairs 2012–13. *Publications:* numerous scientific and professional articles on police management. *Address:* Slovenian Democratic Party (SDP), 1000 Ljubljana, Trstenjakova 8, Slovenia (office). *Telephone:* (1) 4345450 (office). *Fax:* (1) 4345452 (office). *E-mail:* tajnistvo@sds.si (office). *Website:* www.sds.si (office); www.vinkogorenak.net.

GORENSTEIN, Mark Borisovich; Russian conductor; b. 16 Sept. 1946, Odessa, Ukraine; m. 2nd; one s.; ed Chişinău State Conservatory as violinist, Novosibirsk State Conservatory as conductor; violinist with Bolshoi Theatre Orchestra 1973–75, State Academic Symphony Orchestra 1975–84; Chief Conductor and Artistic Dir MAV Orchestra, Budapest, Hungary 1985–88; Chief Conductor Pusan City Symphony Orchestra, S Korea 1989–91; Founder, Chief Conductor and Artistic Dir New Russia State Symphony Orchestra 1992–2002, State Academic Symphony Orchestra of Russia 2002–11; Order for Merit for the Fatherland 2006; People's Artist of Russia 2002, Honoured Art Worker of Russia. *Address:* Rublevskoye shosse 28, Apt 25, 121609 Moscow (home). *Telephone:* (495) 414-52-03 (home). *Fax:* (495) 414-52-03 (home). *E-mail:* vladedmanagement@gmail.com. *Website:* www.markgorenstein.com.

GORGHIU, Alina-Ştefania, MA; Romanian lawyer and politician; b. 16 Sept. 1978, Tecuci, Galaţi Co.; ed Vlaicu Vodă Nat. Coll., Curtea de Argeş, Dimitrie Cantemir Christian Univ., Univ. of Piteşti, Hyperion Univ., Nat. School of Admin and Political Science of Bucharest; interned as lawyer in Bucharest 2002–03, then at firm of Bogdan Olteanu 2003–04; Prin. Assoc. at business and man. consulting firm in Bucharest 2004–; Assoc., Gorghiu, Pop & Assocs 2005–07, 2009–; adviser to Pres. of Authority for State Assets Recovery 2007–08; arbitrator, Int. Court of Arbitration 2008; accred mediator and affiliated with Mediation and Arbitration Dept, Faculty of Law, Titu Maiorescu Univ. 2008–09; mem. Partidul Naţional Liberal (PNL—Nat. Liberal Party) 2002–, party spokeswoman June–Dec. 2014, Co-Pres. PNL 2014–16; local councillor on Sector 5 Council, Bucharest 2004–08; mem. Chamber of Deputies (Camera Deputaţilor) for Bucharest 2008–, Vice-Chair. Cttee for investigating abuses and corruption and for petitions, Chair. Cttee of inquiry for verifying amounts of money paid by Youth and Sports Ministry through documents signed by minister Monica Iacob-Ridzi for organizing 2009 Youth Day festival, Vice-Pres. Chamber of Deputies Sept.–Dec. 2012, mem. Judiciary Cttee, Jt Cttee tasked with revising the Constitution. *Address:* c/o Partidul Naţional Liberal (National Liberal Party), 011866 Bucharest 1, Bd Aviatorilor 86, Romania (office). *Telephone:* (21) 2310795 (office). *Fax:* (21) 2310796 (office). *E-mail:* dre@pnl.ro (office). *Website:* www.pnl.ro (office).

GORMAN, James P., BA, MBA; Australian/American lawyer and business executive; *Chairman and CEO, Morgan Stanley;* b. 14 July 1958; m. Penny Gorman; two c.; ed Univ. of Melbourne, Columbia Univ., New York, USA; began career as attorney, Phillips Fox & Masel, Melbourne 1982–85; Partner, McKinsey & Co. 1992–97, Sr Partner 1997–99; Chief Marketing Officer, Merrill Lynch Inc. 1999–2001, Pres. US Private Client Relationship Group 2001–02, Pres. Global Private Client Group 2002–05, Exec. Vice Pres. Acquisitions, Strategy and Research 2005; Pres. and COO of Global Wealth Man., Morgan Stanley 2006–08, Co-Head of Corp. Strategy 2007–09, also Co-Pres. 2007–10, Pres. and CEO 2010–12, Chair. and CEO 2012–, also Chair. Morgan Stanley Smith Barney (jt venture) 2009–, Morgan Stanley Wealth Management; Co-Chair. Business Cttee, Metropolitan Museum of Art; mem. Bd of Overseers Columbia Business School; mem. Bd of Dirs Partnership for New York City; fmr mem. Bd, Securities Industry and Financial Markets Asscn, Washington, DC, Chair. 2006; mem. Bd of Dirs Federal Reserve Bank of New York 2016–; mem. Business Roundtable, Business Council; mem. Bd Inst. of Int. Finance; mem. Int. Advisory Panel Monetary Authority of Singapore; mem. Council on Foreign Relations; mem. Econ. Club of New York; Trustee, Columbia Business School, Spence School. *Address:* Morgan Stanley, 1585 Broadway, New York, NY 10036, USA (office). *Telephone:* (212) 761-4000 (home). *Fax:* (212) 762-0575 (office). *E-mail:* mediainquiries@morganstanley.com (office). *Website:* www.morganstanley.com (office).

GORMLEY, Sir Antony Mark David, Kt, KBE, OBE, RA, MA, DFA, FRSA; British sculptor; b. 30 Aug. 1950, London; s. of Arthur J. C. Gormley and Elspeth Brauninger; m. Vicken Parsons 1980; two s. one d.; ed Ampleforth Coll., Trinity Coll., Cambridge, Cen. School of Arts and Crafts, London, Goldsmiths' Coll., Univ. of London and Slade School of Fine Arts, London; works in numerous collections, including Tate Gallery, London, Scottish Nat. Gallery of Modern Art, Moderna Museet, Stockholm, Neue Galerie, Kassel, Victoria and Albert Museum, London, British Council, Arts Council of Great Britain, Art Gallery of NSW, Sydney, Leeds City Art Galleries, Modern Art Museum of Fort Worth, Louisiana Museum of Modern Art, Humblebaek, Denmark, Irish Museum of Modern Art, Dublin, Sapporo Sculpture Park, Japan; Trustee, British Museum; Hon. Fellow, Goldsmith's Coll., Univ. of London 1998, RIBA 2001, Jesus Coll., Cambridge 2003, Trinity Coll., Cambridge 2003; Dr hc (Univ. of Central England) 1998, (Open Univ.) 2001, (Cambridge) 2003, (Newcastle) 2004, (Liverpool) 2006, (Univ. Coll., London) 2006; Turner Prize 1994, South Bank Art Award for Visual Art 1999, Bernhard Heiliger Award for Sculpture 2007, Praemium Imperiale Award for Sculpture 2013. *Publications include:* Antony Gormley 1995, Making an Angel 1998, Total Strangers 1999, Antony Gormley, Asian Field 2004, "A meeting of minds: art and archaeology" (with Colin Renfrew) in Material Engagements: Studies in Honour of Colin Renfrew 2004, Making Space 2005, Antony Gormley Inside Australia 2005, Asian Field: Makers & Made 2006, Antony Gormley 2007, Antony Gormley: Blind Light 2007, Antony Gormley: Bodies in Space 2007, Antony Gormley 2007, Antony Gormley: Between You and Me, Kunsthal Rotterdam 2008, Antony Gormley, Museo De Arte Contemporaneo 2008, Ataxia Ii, Galerie Thaddaeus Ropac 2009, Antony Gormley, Kunsthaus Bregenz 2009, Antony Gormley: Another Singularity, Galleria Continua Beijing 2009, Antony Gormley: Aperture, Xavier Hufkens 2010, Antony Gormley (Modern Artists Series) 2010, One and Other: Antony Gormley 2010, Antony Gormley: Drawing Space 2010, Still Standing 2011, Horizon Field Hamburg 2012, Still Being 2012, Vessel 2012, according to a given mean 2013, Firmament and Other Forms 2013, Model 2013, Meter 2013, Expansion Field 2014, Human 2015, Antony Gormley on Sculpture 2015, Event Horizon Hong Kong 2016, Cast 2016, Land 2016, Field for The British Isles 2016, Host 2016, Fit 2016, Living Room 2017. *Leisure interests:* walking, talking. *Address:* 15–23 Vale Royal (studio), London, N7 9AP, England (home). *E-mail:* admin-work@antonygormley.com. *Website:* www.antonygormley.com.

GORMLY, Allan Graham, CMG, CBE; British business executive and chartered accountant; b. 18 Dec. 1937, Paisley, Scotland; s. of William Gormly and Christina Swinton Flockhart; m. Vera Margaret Grant 1962; one s. one d.; ed Paisley Grammar School; with Peat Marwick Mitchell & Co. 1956–61, Rootes Group 1961–65; joined John Brown PLC, apptd. Chief Exec. 1983, Dir Trafalgar House PLC (when it acquired John Brown PLC) 1986–95, CEO 1992–94; Deputy Chair. Royal Insurance Holdings PLC 1992–93, Chair. 1994–96 (mem. Bd 1990–96), Deputy Chair. Royal and Sun Alliance Insurance Group PLC 1996–98; Chair. BPB PLC 1997–2004 (Dir 1995–2004); Chair. Overseas Projects Bd 1989–91; Deputy Chair. Export Guarantees Advisory Council 1990–92; Dir Brixton PLC 1994–2003 (Chair. 2000–03), European Capital Co. 1996–99, Bank of Scotland 1997–2001; Dir (non-exec.) Nat. Grid. Co. 1994–95; Chair. Q-One Group Ltd 1999–2003; mem. British Overseas Trade Bd 1989–91, Top Salaries Review Body 1990–92; Dir Bd of Man., FCO 2000–04. *Leisure interests:* golf, music. *Address:* 56 North Park, Gerrards Cross, Bucks., SL9 8JR, England (home). *Telephone:* (1753) 885079 (home).

GORSKY, Alex, BS, MBA; American business executive; *Chairman and CEO, Johnson & Johnson;* ed US Mil. Acad., West Point, NY, Wharton School, Univ. of Pennsylvania; spent six years in US Army, finished mil. career with rank of Capt.; began Johnson & Johnson career as sales rep. with Janssen Pharmaceutical Inc. 1988, held posts of increasing responsibility in sales, marketing and management, Pres. Janssen Pharmaceutical Inc. 2001–03, Co. Group Chair. Johnson & Johnson's pharmaceuticals business in Europe, Middle East and Africa 2003–04; joined Novartis Pharmaceuticals Corpn, served as head of co.'s pharmaceuticals business in North America 2004–08; returned to Johnson & Johnson as Co. Group Chair. for Ethicon 2008–09, Worldwide Chair. Surgical Care Group and mem. Exec. Cttee early 2009, Worldwide Chair. Medical Devices and Diagnostics Group Sept. 2009–11, Vice-Chair. Exec. Cttee 2011–12, mem. Bd of Dirs, CEO and Chair. Exec. Cttee Johnson & Johnson April 2012–, Chair. Bd of Dirs Dec. 2012–; represents Johnson & Johnson on Bd of AdvaMed (US trade asscn); Exec. Sponsor of two Johnson & Johnson affinity groups, Women's Leadership Initiative and Veteran's Leadership Council; mem. Bd of Dirs, International Business Machines Corpn (IBM) 2014–; mem. Pres. Trump's American Manufacturing Council 2017 (resgnd); mem. Bd Travis Manion Foundation; named Mentor of the Year by Healthcare Businesswomen's Asscn 2009. *Address:* Johnson & Johnson, 1 Johnson & Johnson Plaza, New Brunswick, NJ 08933, USA (office). *Telephone:* (732) 524-0400 (office). *Fax:* (732) 524-3300 (office). *E-mail:* info@jnj.com (office). *Website:* www.jnj.com (office).

GORSUCH, Neil McGill, BA, JD, DPhil; American lawyer and judge; *Associate Justice, Supreme Court of the United States;* b. 29 Aug. 1967, Denver, Colo; s. of David Gorsuch and Anne Gorsuch Burford; m. Louise Gorsuch 1996; two d.; ed Columbia Univ., Harvard Law School, Univ. Coll., Oxford, UK; began career as clerk for Judge David B. Sentelle, US Court of Appeals for DC Circuit 1991–92, then for Justice Byron White and Justice Anthony Kennedy, US Supreme Court 1993–94; Assoc., Sullivan & Cromwell 1991; Assoc., Kellogg, Huber, Hansen, Todd, Evans & Figel (private law firm) 1995–97, Partner 1998–2005; Deputy Assoc. Attorney Gen., US Dept of Justice 2005–06; Judge, US Court of Appeals for the Tenth Circuit 2006–17; Adjunct Prof., Univ. of Colorado Law School 2009 (also, Visiting Prof.); Assoc. Justice, Supreme Court 2017–; mem. Bd of Dirs Walden Group, LLC 2005–; mem. Bd of Trustees Colonial Williamsburg Foundation 2019–; Edmund J. Randolph Award, Stevens Award, Harry S. Truman Foundation 2007. *Publications include:* Will the Gentlemen Please Yield?—A Defense of the Constitutionality of State-Imposed Term Limitations (co-author) 1992, The Future of Assisted Suicide and Euthanasia 2006, The Law of Judicial Precedent (co-author) 2016. *Leisure interests:* hunting, fishing. *Address:* Supreme Court of the United States, 1 First Street, NE, Washington, DC 20543, USA (office). *Telephone:* (202) 479-3000 (office). *Website:* www.supremecourt.gov (office).

GORTON, Slade, BA, LLB; American politician and lawyer; *Of Counsel, Policy and Public Law, K&L Gates LLP;* b. 8 Jan. 1928, Chicago, Ill.; s. of Thomas Slade Gorton and Ruth Gorton (née Israel); m. Sally Clark 1958; one s. two d.; ed Evanston High School, Ill., Dartmouth Coll., Columbia Univ. Law School; served in US Army 1945–46, USAF 1953–56, retd with rank of Col, USAF Reserve; admitted to Bar, Wash. State 1953; mem. Wash. State House of Reps 1959–69, Majority Leader 1967–68; Wash. State Attorney-Gen. 1969–81; Senator from Wash. 1981–87, 1989–2001; Partner, Davis, Wright & Jones, Seattle 1987–89; with Preston, Gates & Ellis (now K&L Gates LLP) 2001–, currently Of Counsel; mem. Wash. State Law and Justice Comm. 1969–80 (Chair. 1969–70), State Criminal Justice Training Comm. 1969–80 (Chair. 1969–76), Pres.'s Consumer Advisory Council 1975–77, Nat. Asscn of Attorneys-Gen. 1969–80 (Pres. 1976–77), Nat. Comm. on Fed. Election Reform 2001–02, Nat. Comm. on Terrorist Attacks (9/11 Comm.) 2002–04; mem. Bd of Dirs Fred Hutchinson Cancer Research Center

1987–2002, Discovery Inst.; mem. War Powers Comm. 2006–08; Co-Chair. Nat. Transportation Policy Project, Bipartisan Policy Center 2008 Wash. State Redistricting Commr 2011–12; Counselor, Nat. Bureau of Asian Research; Republican; Wyman Award for Outstanding Attorney-Gen. in the US 1980, Citizen of the Year, Seattle-King Co. Realtors 2010. *Address:* K&L Gates LLP, 925 Fourth Avenue, Suite 2900, Seattle, WA 98104-1158 (office); 9435 NE 18th Street, Clyde Hill WA 98004, USA (home). *Telephone:* (206) 370-8339 (office); (425) 635-0829 (home). *Fax:* (206) 623-7022 (office). *E-mail:* slade.gorton@klgates.com (office); sladeg@msn.com (home). *Website:* www.klgates.com (office).

GORVY, Brett; British/American art dealer; *Chairman and International Head of Post-War and Contemporary Art and Deputy Chairman, Christie's International PLC;* b. London, England; m. Amy Gold 2001; one c.; began career as an arts journalist; joined Christie's auction house 1994, apptd, along with Amy Cappellazzo, Co-Head of Post-War Art and Contemporary Art 2001–11, Chair. and Int. Head 2011–; presided over sales of Warhol portrait of Mao for US $17.2m. 2006, sale of Andy Warhol's 'Green Car Crash (Green Burning Car I)' for $71.72m. 2007, currently Deputy Chair. Christie's International PLC. *Address:* Christie's, 8 King Street, St James's, London, SW1Y 6QT, England (office); Christie's International, 20 Rockefeller Plaza, New York, NY 10020, USA (office). *Telephone:* (20) 7839-9060 (London) (office); (212) 636-2000 (New York) (office). *Fax:* (20) 7839-1611 (London) (office); (212) 636-2399 (New York) (office). *E-mail:* info@christies.com (office). *Website:* www.christies.com (office).

GOSDEN, Roger Gordon, PhD, DSc; British/American professor of medical sciences (retd) and writer; b. 23 Sept. 1948, Ryde, Isle of Wight, England; s. of Gordon Conrad Jason Gosden and Peggy Gosden (née Butcher); four s.; m. 2nd Lucinda Leigh Veeck 2004; ed Chislehurst and Sidcup Grammar School, London, Univs of Bristol and Cambridge; MRC Research Fellow, Univ. of Cambridge 1973–76; Population Council Fellow, Duke Univ., USA 1974–75; Lecturer in Physiology, Univ. of Edin. 1976–84, Sr Lecturer 1984–94; Prof. of Reproductive Biology, Univ. of Leeds 1994–99, Visiting Prof. 1999–2002; Research Dir and Prof., McGill Univ., Canada 1999–2001, Adjunct Prof. 2001–09; Howard and Georgeanna Jones Prof. of Reproductive Medicine and Scientific Dir, Eastern Virginia Medical School, USA 2001–04, Adjunct Prof., Old Dominion Univ., Va 2002–04; Prof. of Reproductive Medicine and of Reproductive Medicine in Obstetrics and Gynecology, Dir of Research in Reproductive Biology, Weill Medical Coll., Cornell Univ., New York 2004–10; writer and lecturer, Jamestowne Bookworks; pioneer in fertility conservation tech.; scientific adviser to industry and govt bodies (UK, The Netherlands, Canada); radio and TV broadcaster; lecturer and educator, including founding online master's degree programmes; int. conf. organizer; Distinguished Scientist Lecture, American Soc. of Reproductive Medicine 2001, Patrick Steptoe Lecturer, British Fertility Soc. 2003, Anne McLaren Lecturer 2011 and other awards, prizes and lectureships. *Publications:* Biology of Menopause 1985, Cheating Time 1996, Designer Babies 1999, Biology and Pathology of the Oocyte (with A. O. Trounson) 2003 (second edn 2012), Preservation of Fertility (with T. Tulandi) 2004; numerous articles in academic journals, magazines and newspapers. *Leisure interests:* writing, natural history, gardening. *Address:* 107 Paddock Lane, Williamsburg, VA 23188, USA (home). *E-mail:* roger.gosden@cantab.net (home). *Website:* www.jamestownebookworks.com (office).

GOŠEV, Petar, MA; Macedonian politician and fmr central banker; b. 5 Sept. 1948, Pirava; m.; two s.; ed Univ. of Skopje; with 11 Oktomvri Bus Co. 1971–73; mem. Council Macedonian Trade Union Fed. 1973–87 (econ. adviser 1973–84, Chief, Office of the Union Pres. 1977, mem. Presidency 1982–87); mem. Presidency, Cen. Cttee Union of Communists of Macedonia (renamed SKM–PDP 1990, Social Democratic Alliance of Macedonia 1991) 1986–89, Pres. 1989–91; Chief of the Del. of the Nat. Ass. in the Ass. of the fmr Socialist Fed. Repub. of Yugoslavia 1990; mem. Parl. 1990–2002; f. Democratic Party 1993, Pres. 1993–97; mem. Council Nat. Bank of Repub. of Macedonia 1993–97; Pres. Liberal-Democratic Party–LDP (formed from merger of Liberal Party and Democratic Party) 1997–99; Vice-Pres. Parl. Group of the Nat. Ass. to the Inter-Parl. Union 1998–2002; Vice-Pres. of Fmr Yugoslav Repub. of Macedonia and Minister of Finance 2002–04; Gov. Nat. Bank of Repub. of Macedonia 2004–11; mem. Bd of Govs EBRD; mem. Supervisory Bd Center of Excellence in Finance; mem. Vienna Econ. Forum.

GOSLING, Ryan; Canadian actor and musician; b. 12 Nov. 1980; s. of Thomas Gosling and Donna Gosling; began acting at age 12 in The Mickey Mouse Club (American variety TV show); co-f. Dead Man's Bones (pop band). *Television includes:* Mickey Mouse Club 1993–95, Breaker High 1997–98, Young Hercules 1998–99, Hercules: The Legendary Journeys 1998–99, The Unbelievables 1999. *Films include:* Frankenstein and Me 1996, The Believer 2001, Murder by Numbers 2002, The Notebook 2004, Half Nelson (Independent Spirit Award for Best Male Lead, Nat. Bd of Review Award for Best Breakthrough Performance, Stockholm Film Festival Award for Best Actor) 2006, Lars and the Real Girl 2007, All Good Things 2010, Blue Valentine 2010, The Place Beyond the Pines 2012, Only God Forgives 2013, Gangster Squad 2013, The Big Short 2015, The Nice Guys 2016, La La Land (Golden Globe Award for Best Performance by an Actor in a Motion Picture 2017) 2016, Blade Runner 2049 2017. *Address:* c/o IFA Talent Agency, 8730 Sunset Blvd, Suite 490, Los Angeles, CA 90069, USA (office).

GOSS, Porter J., BA; American politician and government official; *Co-Chairman, Office of Congressional Ethics;* b. 26 Nov. 1938, Waterbury, Conn.; s. of Richard Wayne Goss and Virginia Holland Goss (née Johnston); m. Mariel Goss; four c.; ed Yale Univ.; served US Army 1960–66; Clandestine Services Officer CIA 1962–71; Co-founder and publisher Community Newspaper 1971–74; Sanibel, Fla, City Council 1974–82, apptd Mayor of Sanibel 1974–77; mem. Lee Co. Bd of Commr 1983–88; mem. US House of Reps 1989–2004, Chair. House Perm. Select Cttee on Intelligence, mem. House Rules Cttee, Select Cttee for Homeland Security; Dir CIA 2004–06 (resgnd); small business owner and co-founder of local newspaper, Sanibel, Fla 2006–08; Co-Chair. Office of Congressional Ethics, Washington, DC 2008–; mem. Book and Snake Soc., Ripon Soc.; Distinguished Service Award 2006. *Address:* Office of Congressional Ethics, US House of Representatives, 425 3rd Street, SW, Suite 1110, Washington, DC 20024, USA (office). *Telephone:* (202) 225-9739 (office). *Fax:* (202) 226-0997 (office). *Website:* oce.house.gov (office); www.portergoss.com.

GOSWAMI, Jhulan Nishit; Indian professional cricketer; b. 25 Nov. 1982, Chakdaha, Nadia, West Bengal; d. of Nishit Goswami and Jharna Goswami; right-handed batswoman; right-arm medium-pace bowler; plays for ACC Asia XI Cricket Team, Bengal Women's Cricket Team, East Zone Women's Cricket Team, India Women Green Cricket Team, Indian Women's Cricket Team; ODI debut: India vs England, Chennai 6 Jan. 2002; Test debut: India vs England, Lucknow 14 Jan. 2002; T20I debut: India vs England, Derby 5 Aug. 2006; played ten Tests (to Nov. 2015), scored 283 runs (average 25.72) with two fifties, best score of 69; played 177 ODIs (to 28 Feb. 2019), scored 1,061 runs (average 13.96) with one fifty, best score of 57; played 68 WT20Is (to 10 June 2018), scored 405 runs (average 10.94), best score of 37; Captain, Indian Women's Cricket Team (Tests 2008–15, ODI 2008–19, WT20I 2008–18); named ICC Women Cricketer of the Year 2007, Arjuna Award 2010, Padma Shri 2012, 5 Rupee postage stamp issued in her honour 2018. *Leisure interests:* listening to music, reading. *Address:* c/o Dunamis Sportainment, 303 Nilgiri Apartments, 9 Barakhamba Road, New Delhi 110 001, India (office); Board of Control for Cricket in India, 4th Floor, Cricket Centre, Wankhede Stadium, 'D' Road, Churchgate, Mumbai 400 020, Maharashtra, India (office). *Telephone:* 9560133099 (mobile) (office); (22) 22898800 (office). *E-mail:* info@dunamissportainment.com (office); office@bcci.tv (office). *Website:* dunamissportainment.com (office); www.bcci.tv (office). *Fax:* (22) 22898801 (office).

GOTCHEV, Dimitar Bonev; Bulgarian judge; b. 27 Feb. 1936, Sofia; s. of Maj.-Gen. Boncho Gotchev and Zdravka Gotchev; m. Jova Gotcheva-Cholakova 1976; one d.; ed Univ. of Sofia St Kliment Ochridsky; legal adviser 1959–66; Arbiter, State Court of Arbitration 1966–89; Judge, Supreme Court 1990, Judge, Head of Commercial Div. 1990, Deputy Chief Justice, Supreme Court 1993; Judge, Constitutional Court 1994–2004; Judge, European Court of Human Rights, Strasbourg 1992–98. *Leisure interests:* music, mountaineering, skiing.

GÖTHE, (Lars) Staffan; Swedish playwright, actor, director and academic; b. 20 Dec. 1944, Luleå; s. of Thorsten Göthe and Margit Grape-Göthe; m. Kristin Byström 1969; one s.; ed Acad. of Performing Arts, Gothenburg; actor and playwright, regional theatre of Växjö 1971, Folkteatern, Gothenburg 1974; Headmaster, Acad. of Performing Arts, Malmö 1976; actor, Folkteatern, Gävleborg 1983; Dir The RTC Co. 1986–95; actor and playwright, Royal Dramatic Theatre, Stockholm 1995–2003, actor 2011–; Prof., Malmö Theatre Acad., Univ. of Lund 2003–11; Royal Medal Litteris et Artibus, Award of Royal Swedish Acad. 2005. *Plays include:* En natt i februari 1972, Den gråtande polisen 1980, La strada dell'amore 1986, En uppstoppad hund 1986, Den perfekta Kyssen 1990, Arma Irma 1991, Boogie Woogie 1992, Blått Hus Med Röda Kinder 1995, Ruben Pottas Eländiga Salonger 1996, Ett Lysande Elände 1999, Temperance 2000, Byta Trottoar 2001, Stjärnan Över Lappland 2005, Kvart i fem-ekot 2010. *Publication:* Lysande Eländen (complete works) 2004. *Address:* Vindragarvägen 8, 117 50 Stockholm, Sweden (home). *Telephone:* (8) 668-38-18 (office). *Website:* staffangothe@gmail.com (office).

GOTT, Karel; Czech singer; b. 14 July 1939, Plzeň; two d.; ed Prague Conservatory (studied under Prof. Karenin); mem. Semafor Theatre, Prague 1963–65; mem. Apollo Theatre, Prague, 1965–67; freelance artist 1967–; numerous foreign tours; charity concerts with Eva Urbanová 1998; CD Rocky mého mládí (Rocks of My Youth) 1999; exhbn of paintings, Bratislava 1999; f. and Chair. Interpo Foundation 1993–96; concerts in Carnegie Hall, New York, Expo, Hanover, Kremlin Palace, Moscow 2000; charity concerts in Czech Repub. after 2002 floods; f. Karel Gott Agency 2015; Golden Nightingale trophy (annual pop singer poll 1963–66, 1968–81, 1983, 1989–90, 1997–2001), MIDEM Prize, Cannes 1967, MIDEM Gold Record 1969, Polydor Gold Record 1970, Supraphon Gold Record 1972, 1973, 1979, 1980, 1996, Music Week Star of the Year 1974 (UK) 1975, Artist of Merit 1982, Gold Aerial 1983, radio station BRT (Belgium) 1984, Nat. Artist 1985, Polydor Golden Pin (Germany) 1986, Czech Nightingale Trophy 1996, 1997, 1999, 2001, 2002 (28 times in total), Czech TV Prize 1997, 1999, Platinum Record (for duets with Lucia Bílá) 1998, Josef Jungmann Medal 2011, and many other awards. *Radio:* presenter, monthly show Radio Impuls 2002–. *Film appearance:* Luck from Hell. *Recordings include:* Vánoce ve zlaté Praze 1969, 42 největších hitů 1991, Věci blízké mému srdci 1993, Zázrak vánoční 1995, Belcanto 1996, Duety s Lucií Bílou 1997, Miluj 1997, Svátek svátků 1998, Rocky mého mládí 1999, Originálni nahrávky ze 70.let 2000, Originálni nahrávky ze 80.let 2000, Originálni nahrávky ze 90.let 2000, Pokaždé 2002, Gott & Vondaáčková 2003, Lásko má 2004, Můj strážný anděl 2004, K. Gott zpívá hity K. Svobody 2005, Jsou svátky 2006, Má pouť 2006, Každý má svůj sen 2007, Zlatá Kolekce 2007, Zmírám láskou 2008, Leben 2009, Oslava 70 narozenin 2009, Frohe Weihnacht 2010, Sentiment 2011, Dotek lásky 2012, S pomocí přátel 2013, Duety 1962–2015 2015, 40Slavíků 2016. *Publication:* Why Painting is Important for Me 2001. *Address:* Nad Bertramkou 18, 150 00 Prague 5, Czech Republic (home). *E-mail:* office@karelgott.com. *Website:* www.karelgott.com.

GOTTI, Irv; American music company executive and producer; b. (Irv Lorenzo), Hollis, Queens, New York; m. Debbie Gotti; began music career as DJ Irv; fmr producer, Island Def Jam Records, artists produced include Ashanti, Charli Baltimore, Toni Braxton, DMX, Ja Rule, Jay-Z; fmr CEO Murder Inc. Records, known as The Inc. Records 2003–12, launched Visionary entertainment co. 2013, also relaunched label Murder Inc. Records. *Recordings include:* Irv Gotti Presents… (series of albums). *Website:* www.murderinc-online.com.

GOTTLIEB, Robert Adams, BA; American editor and critic; b. 29 April 1931, New York; s. of Charles Gottlieb and Martha Gottlieb (née Kean); m. 1st Muriel Higgins 1952 (divorced); m. 2nd Maria Tucci 1969; two s. one d.; ed Columbia Coll., Univ. of Cambridge, UK; with Simon and Schuster 1955–65, Ed.-in-Chief 1965–68; Ed.-in-Chief Alfred A. Knopf 1968–87, Pres. 1973–87; Ed.-in-Chief The New Yorker 1987–92; now dance and book critic for New York Observer, New York Times, The New Yorker and New York Review of Books; mem. Bd of Dirs New York City Ballet; mem. Bd of Trustees Miami City Ballet. *Publications include:* Reading Jazz 1996, Reading Lyrics (co-author) 2000, George Balanchine – The Ballet Maker 2004, Reading Dance (ed.) 2008, Sarah: The Life of Sarah Bernhardt 2010, Great Expectations: The Sons and Daughters of Charles Dickens 2014, Avid Reader: A Life 2016. *Leisure interests:* ballet, movies, reading. *Address:* 237 East 48th Street, New York, NY 10017-1538, USA (home). *Website:* www.newyorker

.com/contributors/robert-gottlieb; www.nybooks.com/contributors/robert-gottlieb; observer.com/author/robert-gottlieb.

GOTTLIEB, Scott, BA, MD; American physician and government official; b. 11 June 1972, East Brunswick, New Jersey; s. of Stanley Gottlieb and Marsha Gottlieb; m. Allyson Nemeroff 2004; three d.; ed Wesleyan Univ., Mount Sinai School of Medicine, New York; began career as healthcare analyst, Alex Brown & Sons (investment bank), Baltimore; fmr Clinical Asst Prof. and Hosp. Physician, New York Univ. School of Medicine; Sr Advisor to Commr and to Dir of Medical Policy Devt, Food and Drug Admin (FDA) 2003–04, Deputy Commr for Medical and Scientific Affairs, FDA 2005–07, Commr of Food and Drugs 2017–19; Sr Advisor to Admin., Centers for Medicare and Medicaid Services 2004; Resident Fellow, American Enterprise Inst. (think tank) 2007–17, 2019–; Venture Partner, New Enterprise Assocs (venture capital fund) 2007–17; mem. Fed. Health Information Tech. Policy Cttee 2013; Man. Dir of Investment Banking, T.R. Winston & Co. 2016–17; fmr consultant to numerous pharmaceutical cos including GlaxoSmithKline PLC, Vertex Pharmaceuticals Inc., Daiichi Sankyo Inc., Novo Nordisk, Bristol-Myers Squibb, Valeant Pharmaceuticals International Inc., Pfizer Inc., AstraZeneca PLC, Baxter International Inc., Baxter Healthcare, Bristol-Myers Squibb, Takeda Pharmaceutical Co. and Millennium Pharmaceuticals Inc.; Republican. *Publications:* regular contributor to leading publications including The Wall Street Journal, New York Times and USA Today. *Address:* American Enterprise Institute, 1789 Massachusetts Avenue NW, Washington, DC 20036, USA (office). *Telephone:* (202) 862-5800 (office). *Fax:* (202) 862-7177 (office). *E-mail:* scott.gottlieb@aei.org (office). *Website:* www.aei.org (office).

GOTTSCHALK, Gerhard, Dr rer. nat; German microbiologist and academic; *Professor of Genome Research, Georg-August-University of Göttingen;* b. 27 March 1935, Schwedt/Oder; s. of Gerhard Gottschalk and Irmgard Gottschalk (née Ploetz); m. Ellen-Marie Hrabowski 1960; two s. one d.; ed Humboldt Univ., Berlin and Georg-August-Univ., Göttingen; Research Assoc., Dept of Biochemistry, Univ. of Calif., Berkeley, USA 1964–66, Visiting Prof. 1978–79; Docent, Georg-August-Univ. of Göttingen 1967–70, Prof. of Microbiology 1970–2003, Rector 1975–76, Vice-Pres. 1979–81, Prof. of Genome Research 2003–; Visiting Prof., Dept of Bacteriology, Univ. of Calif., Davis 1972–73; Vice-Pres. Acad. of Science, Göttingen 1996, Pres. 1998–2000; Pres. ALLEA (All European Acads) 1998–2000; Pres. Union of German Acads of Sciences and Humanities 2003–07; mem., Göttingen Acad. of Sciences 1976, Deutsche Akademie der Naturforscher; Fellow, American Acad. of Microbiology 2010; Hon. mem., Israel Soc. for Microbiology 1996, Vereinigung für Allgemeine und Angewandte Mikrobiologie (VAAM) 2012; Fed. Cross of Merit (Germany) 2005; Dr hc (Slovac Acad. of Sciences) 1999, (Univ. of Rostock) 2013; Philip Morris Prize 1992, Winogradsky Medal, Russian Soc. for Microbiology 1997, Emil von Behring Prize 2006, IBN Award, Industrial Biotechnology North Asscn 2010. *Publications:* Bacterial Metabolism 1986, Biotechnologie 1986, Göttinger Gelehrte (co-ed. with K. Arndt and R. Smend) 2001, World of Bacteria 2009, Bakterien rüsten auf 2012. *Address:* Institute of Microbiology and Genetics, University of Göttingen, Grisebachstrasse 8, 37077 Göttingen, Germany (office). *Telephone:* (551) 394041 (office). *Fax:* (551) 394195 (office); (5503) 999128 (home). *E-mail:* ggottsc@gwdg.de (office). *Website:* www.img.bio.uni-goettingen.de (office); wwwuser.gwdg.de/~ggottsc (home).

GOTTSCHALK, Helmut; German business executive; *Chairman of the Supervisory Board, DZ Bank AG;* b. 1951, Calw; mem. Supervisory Bd DZ Bank AG 2004–, Deputy Chair. 2008–10, Chair. 2010–, also Vice-Chair. Supervisory Bd DZ Beteiligungs GmbH & Co. KG (largest shareholder of DZ Bank); CEO Volksbank Herrenberg-Rottenburg eG 2003–17, Deputy Chair. 2008, Speaker of the Bd of Man. Dirs; Chair. of the Council, Baden-Württemberg Cooperative Asscn 2009–; Chair. Supervisory Bd Internationales Bankhaus Bodensee AG 2018–; mem. Bd of Dirs Fed. Asscn of German Cooperative Banks (BVR); Staufer Medal (Baden-Württemberg) 2010, Raiffeisen-Schulze-Delitzsch-Medaille (Gold) 2016. *Address:* Deutsche Zentral-Genossenschaftsbank AG, Platz der Republik, 60325 Frankfurt am Main, Germany (office). *Telephone:* (69) 7447-01 (office). *Fax:* (69) 7447-1685 (office). *E-mail:* mail@dzbank.de (office). *Website:* www.dzbank.de (office).

GÖTZ, Magdalena, PhD Habil; German geneticist and academic; *Director, Institute of Stem Cell Research, Helmholtz Zentrum München;* b. 1962; ed Bunsen Gymnasium, Heidelberg, Univs of Heidelberg and Tübingen; earned doctorate in research group of Jürgen Bolz, Friedrich Miescher Lab., Max Planck Soc. 1992; Postdoctoral Fellow, Nat. Inst. for Medical Research, London, UK 1993–94; Postdoctoral Scientist, Smith Kline Beecham, Harlow, UK 1994–96; Scientist, Max Planck Inst. of Biophysical Chem., Göttingen 1997; Research Group Leader, Max Planck Inst. of Neurobiology, Munich-Martinsried 1997–2003; Dir Inst. of Stem Cell Research of GSF (now Helmholtz Zentrum München), Neuherberg and Prof. of Physiological Genomics, Univ. of Munich 2004–, W3 Research Prof. 2011–; Assoc. Ed. Journal of Neuroscience 2006–12; Ed. Development 2010–; mem. Editorial Bd, Cell Stem Cell, Development, EMBO Journal, Genes and Development, Journal of Neuroscience, Glia, BMC Developmental Biology, Cell Adhesion and Migration, Frontiers in Neurogenesis, Current Opinion in Genetics and Development; mem. European Molecular Biology Org., Akad. Leopoldina 2007; External mem. Max Planck Soc. 2013; Fed. Cross of Merit on Ribbon 2010; Otto Hahn Medal, Max Planck Soc. for her dissertation 1992, Gottfried Wilhelm Leibniz Prize 2007, Hansen Prize 2007, Hans and Ilse Breuer Award 2008, Remedios Caro Almela Prize on Developmental Neurobiology 2013, ERC Advanced Grant 2013, Ernst Schering Prize (for basic scientific research) 2014, IRP Schellenberg Research Prize 2018. *Publications:* numerous papers in professional journals. *Address:* Helmholtz Zentrum München, German Research Centre for Environmental Health (GmbH), Institute of Stem Cell Research, Ingolstädter Landstrasse 1, 85764 Neuherberg (office); Department of Physiological Genomics, Ludwig-Maximilians-University, Schillertrasse 46, 80336 Munich, Germany (office). *Telephone:* (89) 31873750 (Neuherberg) (office); (89) 218075255 (Munich) (office). *Fax:* (89) 31873761 (Neuherberg) (office); (89) 218075216 (Munich) (office). *E-mail:* magdalena.goetz@helmholtz-muenchen.de (office). *Website:* www.mcn.uni-muenchen.de/members/regular/goetz/index.html (office); www.helmholtz-muenchen.de/isf (office).

GÖTZE, Wolfgang; German theoretical physicist and academic; b. 11 July 1937, Fürstenwalde; Prof. for Theoretical Physics, Munich Univ. of Tech. 1970–2003, Prof. Emer. 2003–; Max Planck Medal, German Physical Soc. 2006, Tomassoni Award, Univ. of Rome (La Sapienza) 2006. *Publications include:* Complex Dynamics of Glass-Forming Liquids 2009; numerous scientific papers in professional journals. *Address:* Room 3333, Institute for Theoretical Physics, Munich University of Technology 85748, Garching, Germany (office). *Telephone:* (89) 289-12360 (office). *Fax:* (89) 289-14641 (office). *E-mail:* wg@ph.tum.de (office). *Website:* www.physik.tu-muenchen.de/lehrstuehle/T37_wg/Welcome_e.html (office).

GOU, Terry Tai-Ming; Taiwanese electronics industry executive; *Chairman and CEO, Hon Hai Precision Industry Co. Ltd;* b. 8 Oct. 1950, Banqiao Township, Taipei Co.; m. 1st Serena Lin (died 2005); one s. one d.; m. 2nd Delia Tseng 2008; one s. one d.; ed China Marine Tech. Coll.; f. Hon Hai Precision Industry Co. Ltd (trading name Foxconn; world's largest contract electronics manufacturer) with ten workers to make plastic parts for TV sets in a rented shed in Tucheng suburb of Taipei 1974, opened first factory in Shenzhen, China 1988, customers included HP, IBM, Apple, Inc., now Chair. and CEO; f. educational charity with first wife 2000; Taiwan Dir, Taiwan Electrical Equipment Asscn; Pres. Mold Industry Asscn. *Address:* Hon Hai Precision Industry Co. Ltd, 2 Zihyou Street, Tucheng City, Taipei County 236, Taiwan (office). *Telephone:* (2) 2268-3466 (office). *Fax:* (2) 2268-6204 (office). *E-mail:* webadmin@foxconn.com (office). *Website:* www.foxconn.com (office).

GOUBET, Cédric; French civil servant; *Vice-President, Commercial Engines, Snecma SA;* b. 12 May 1971, Cambrai; served as Chief of Staff to prefects Claude Guéant, Franche-Comté 1998–2002, Jean-Marie Rebière and Thierry Klinger, Finistère 2000–02; Chief of Staff to Minister of the Interior, Nicolas Sarkozy 2004, Tech. Adviser 2005–07; Prin. Pvt. Sec. to Pres. Nicolas Sarkozy 2007–10; Deputy Dir Aerospace Propulsion Branch, Safran 2010–11; Exec. Dir CFM International, Snecma SA 2011–, also Dir CFM Programs, Vice-Pres. Commercial Engines 2015–. *Address:* Snecma SA, 10, allée du Brévent, CE1420 Courcouronnes, Cedex Evry 91019, France (office). *Website:* www.safran-aircraft-engines.com (office).

GOUDET, Olivier; French business executive; *Chairman, Anheuser-Busch InBev;* b. 1964; ed Ecole Centrale de Paris, ESSEC Business School; began career serving on finance team at Mars, Inc. 1990–96, returned 1998, Chief Financial Officer 2004–08, Exec. Vice-Pres. and Chief Financial Officer 2008–12, Adviser to Bd 2012–13; joined VALEO Group 1996, held several sr exec. positions 1996–98; Partner and CEO JAB Holding Co., LLC 2012–; Chair. Peet's Coffee & Tea Inc. 2013; Ind. Dir, Anheuser-Busch InBev, Chair. 2015–; mem. Bd of Dirs, Coty Inc., D.E. Master Blenders 1753. *Address:* Anheuser-Busch InBev, Brouwerijplein 1, Leuven 3000, Belgium (office). *Telephone:* (16) 27-61-11 (office). *Fax:* (16) 50-61-11 (office). *E-mail:* info@ab-inbev.com (office). *Website:* www.ab-inbev.com (office).

GOUGH, Barry Morton, MA, PhD, DLit, FRHistS; Canadian historian and biographer; *Professor Emeritus of History, Wilfrid Laurier University;* b. 17 Sept. 1938, Victoria, BC; s. of John Gough and Dorothy Mouncy Morton Gough; m. 1st B. Louise Kerr 1964 (divorced 1977); one s. one d.; m. 2nd Marilyn J. Morris 1981; two s.; ed Victoria High School, Victoria Coll., Univs of British Columbia and Montana, King's Coll., London, UK; Prof. of History, Western Washington Univ. and Wilfrid Laurier Univ. 1972–2004, Asst Dean of Arts and Sciences, Wilfrid Laurier Univ. 1999–2001, now Prof. Emer.; Adjunct Prof. of History and War Studies, Royal Mil. Coll. of Canada 1994–2007; historian, Nuu Chah Nulth Tribal Council in Meares Island Case; Founding mem. Asscn for Canadian Studies in the US and Co-Dir Archives Center for Pacific Northwest Studies, Western Washington Univ., Bellingham, Wash. 1968–72; Visiting Prof., Duke Univ., Univ. of British Columbia, Otago Univ., Natal Univ., ANU, and others; Pres. N American Soc. for Oceanic History, Canadian Nautical Research Soc.; Vice-Pres. Social Sciences Fed. of Canada; Ed. American Neptune: Maritime History and Arts 1995–2001; Fellow, King's Coll. London; twice Archives Fellow, Churchill Coll. Cambridge, UK; Curator, George Vancouver Exhibit, Vancouver Maritime Museum 2011, Hon. Research Assoc., Vancouver Island Univ.; Hon. Pres. British Columbia Historical Fed.; mem. Canadian Historical Asscn, Canadian Nautical Research Soc.; Life mem. Soc. for the History of Discoveries; Order of St John of Jerusalem; The Roderick Haig-Brown, Keith Matthews, John Lyman, K. Jack Bauer, British Columbia Historical Fed. and other book prizes, Clio Prize, Canadian Historical Asscn, Lt-Gov. of BC Medal for Historical Writing, SS Beaver Medal for Maritime Excellence, Maritime Museum of British Columbia, Mountbatten Literary Award of British Maritime Foundation, Captain Robert Gray Medal, Washington State History Soc., Queen's Golden Jubilee Medal 2002, Queen's Diamond Jubille Medal 2012. *Television:* historical consultant, Dive Detectives: Lost Schooners War of 1812, Drake Sixpence, Vancouver Island. *Publications include:* Royal Navy and the Northwest Coast 1971, Distant Dominion 1980, Gunboat Frontier 1984, Journal of Alexander Henry the Younger 1988, 1992, The Northwest Coast 1992, Falkland Islands/Malvinas 1992, First Across The Continent: Sir Alexander Mackenzie 1997, Historical Dictionary of Canada 1999 (second edn 2011), HMCS Haida: Battle Ensign Flying 2001, Fighting Sail on Lake Huron and Georgian Bay: War of 1812 and its Aftermath 1812 2002, Through Water, Ice and Fire: Schooner Nancy of the War of 1812 2006, Fortune's a River: Contest for Empire in Northwest America 2007, Historical Dreadnoughts: Arthur Marder, Stephen Roskill and Battles for Naval History 2010, Introduction to William Robert Broughton Voyage of Discovery to the North Pacific 2010, Juan de Fuca's Strait: Voyages in the Waterway of Forgotten Dreams 2012, Pax Britannica: Ruling the Waves and Keeping the Peace before Armageddon 2014, The Elusive Mr Pond 2014, From Classroom to Battlefield: Victoria High School and the First World War 2014, Britannia's Navy and the West Coast of North America 2016, Churchill and Fisher: Titans at the Admiralty 2017; numerous reviews and articles. *Leisure interests:* golfing, jazz clarinet. *Address:* PO Box 5037, Victoria, BC V8R 6N3, Canada (home); 107 Pall Mall, London, SW1Y 5ER, England (home). *Telephone:* (250) 592-0800 (Victoria) (home). *E-mail:* bgough@wlu.ca (home); barrygough@shaw.ca (home).

GOUGH, Douglas Owen, MA, PhD, FRS, FInstP, CPhys; British astrophysicist; *Professor Emeritus of Theoretical Astrophysics, University of Cambridge;* b. 8 Feb. 1941, Stourport; s. of Owen Albert John Gough and Doris May Gough (née Camera); m. Rosanne Penelope Shaw 1965; two s. two d.; ed Hackney Downs School, London, St John's Coll., Cambridge; Research Assoc., JILA, Univ. of Colorado, USA 1966–67, Fellow Adjoint 1986–; NAS Sr Postdoctoral Research Assoc., New York 1967–69; mem. Grad. Staff, Inst. of Theoretical Astronomy, Univ. of Cambridge 1969–73, Lecturer in Astronomy and Applied Math., Inst. of

Astronomy and Dept of Applied Math. and Theoretical Physics 1973–85, Reader in Astrophysics, Inst. of Astronomy 1985–93, Prof. of Theoretical Astrophysics 1993–2008, Prof. Emer. 2008–; Deputy Dir, Inst. of Astronomy, Univ. of Cambridge 1993–99, Dir 1999–2004; Leverhulme Emer. Fellow 2008–11, 2016–18; Astronome Titulaire, Associé des Observatoires de France 1977; Fellow, Churchill Coll. Cambridge 1972–; Hon. Prof. Astronomy, QMW London 1986–2009; Visiting Prof. of Physics, Stanford Univ., USA 1996–2010, Consulting Prof. of Experimental Physics 2011–15, Sr Visiting Research Assoc. in Experimental Physics 2016–17; Visiting Prof., Aarhus Universitet, Denmark 2006; Distinguished Visiting Prof., Univ. Mumbai, India 2015; Foreign mem. Royal Danish Acad. of Sciences and Letters 1998; James Arthur Prize, Harvard Univ. (USA) 1982, William Hopkins Prize, Cambridge Philosophical Soc. 1984, George Ellery Hale Prize, American Astronomical Soc. 1994, Mousquetaire d'Armagnac 2001, Eddington Medal, Royal Astronomical Soc. 2002, Gold Medal, Royal Astronomical Soc. 2010. *Publications:* Problems in Solar and Stellar Oscillations (ed.) 1983, Seismology of the Sun and the Distant Stars (ed.) 1986, Challenges to Theories of the Structure of Moderate-Mass Stars (co-ed. with J. Toomre) 1991, Equation-of-state and Phase-transition Issues in Models of Ordinary Astrophysical Matter (co-ed. with V. Čelebonović and W. Däppen) 2004, The Scientific Legacy of Fred Hoyle (ed.) 2005; more than 300 papers in the professional scientific literature. *Leisure interest:* cooking. *Address:* Institute of Astronomy, Madingley Road, Cambridge, CB3 0HA, England (office). *Telephone:* (1223) 337516 (office). *Fax:* (1223) 337523 (office). *E-mail:* douglas@ast.cam.ac.uk (office).

GOUGH, Piers William, CBE, RIBA, RA; British architect; *Partner, CZWG Architects LLP;* b. 24 April 1946, Brighton; s. of Peter Gough and Daphne Mary Unwin Banks; one s.; ed Architectural Asscn School of Architecture; Partner, CZWG Architects, London 1975–; Pres. Architectural Asscn 1995–97 (mem. Council 1970–72, 1991–99); Commr English Heritage 2000–07, Comm. for Architecture and Built Environment 2007–11; Prof. of Architecture, Royal Acad. 2013–17; mem. Bd Stonehenge 2002–04, Council of the Royal Acad. 2003–04, 2011–17; Trustee, Trinity Buoy Wharf, Artangel 1994–2003; mem. RIBA Gold Medal Panel 2000, Planning Cttee London Legacy Devt Corp. 2013; Hon. mem. Royal Incorporation of Architects in Scotland (RIAS); Hon. DUniv (Middlesex) 1999, (Queen Mary Coll.); Royal Fine Art Comm. Award, Building of the Year Award, British Sky Broadcasting 1998. *Television:* presenter, Shock of the Old (six-part series), Channel 4 2000. *Principal works include:* Phillips West 2, Bayswater 1976, Cochrane Square (Phase I), Glasgow 1987, China Wharf, Bermondsey 1988, Craft, Design and Tech. Bldg, Bryanston School 1988, Street-Porter House 1988, The Circle, Bermondsey 1990, Westbourne Grove Public Lavatories 1993, 1–10 Summers Street, Clerkenwell 1994, Leonardo Centre, Uppingham School 1995, Cochrane Square (Phase II), Glasgow 1995, 90 Wardour Street, Soho 1995, 19th and 20th Century Galleries, Nat. Portrait Gallery 1996, Suffolk Wharf, Camden Lock 1996–, Brindleyplace Café, Birmingham 1997, Bankside Lofts, London 1997, The Glass Building, Camden 1999, The Green Bridge, Mile End Park 2000, Office Edinburgh Park 2000, Tunnel Wharf Rotherhithe, London 2001, Allen Jones' Studio, Ledwell 2001, Samworth's Girls' Boarding House Uppingham School 2001, Bankside Cen. 2001, Suffolk Wharf, Camden Lock, London 2002, Fulham Island, London 2002, Queen Elizabeth Square and Crown Street Corner, Gorbals 2003–04, Regency Galleries, Nat. Portrait Gallery 2003, Bling Bling Bldg, Liverpool 2006, South Cen. Bldg 2006, Arsenal Masterplan 2000 including Vision 7 N7 2007, Drayton Park 2008, Canada Water Library 2009, Fortune Green, London 2010, Islington Square, London 2010, Queensland Road 2010, Maggie's Centre, Nottingham 2011, Queensland Road Housing, London 2015, Meridian Gate, Kidbrooke Village, London 2016, Pavilion Square, Royal Arsenal, Woolwich 2018. *Publication:* English Extremists 1988, CZWG Gazetteer2016. *Leisure interests:* throwing parties, swimming. *Address:* CZWG Architects LLP, 17 Bowling Green Lane, London, EC1R 0QB, England (office). *Telephone:* (20) 7253-2523 (office). *Fax:* (20) 7250-0594 (office). *E-mail:* p.gough@czwgarchitects.co.uk (office). *Website:* www.czwg.com (office).

GOULARD, Sylvie, lic. en droit; French lawyer and politician; b. (Sylvie Grassi), 6 Dec. 1964, Marseilles; m. Guillaume Goulard; three c.; ed Univ. of Aix-en-Provence, Inst. d'études politiques de Paris, École nat. d'admin; began career in legal affairs and policy planning depts, Ministry of Foreign Affairs 1989–99; worked at Conseil d'Etat 1993–96; researcher Int. Study and Research Centre (CERI) 1999–2001; Political Adviser to Romano Prodi, Pres. of the European Comm. 2001–04; Pres., French br. of European Movement 2006–10; mem. European Parl. for W France 2009–14, for SE France 2014–17; Minister of the Armed Forces May–June 2017; mem. Mouvement Démocrate 2009–17, La République en marche 2017; Bundesverdienstkreuz am Bande 2003, Chevalier, ordre nat. du Mérite français 2008, Bundesverdienstkreuz (First Class) 2014, Officier de l'Ordre fédéral du Mérite, Germany 2015. *Publications include:* Le Grand Turc et la République de Venise 2004, Le coq et la perle 2007, Il faut cultiver notre jardin européen 2008, Europe for Dummies (L'Europe pour les nuls) (European Book Prize 2009) 2009, De la démocratie en Europe: Voir plus loin (jtly with Mario Monti) 2012, Europe: amour ou chambre à part? 2013, Goodbye Europe 2016, 50 notions sur l'Europe 2016. *Address:* c/o Ministry of Defence, 14 rue Saint Dominique, 75007 Paris, France (office). *Website:* www.sylviegoulard.eu.

GOULD, Andrew F., BA, FCA; British business executive; *Non-Executive Chairman, BG Group PLC;* b. 17 Dec. 1946; ed Univ. of Wales, Cardiff; began career with Ernst & Young; joined Internal Audit Dept, Schlumberger Ltd, Paris 1975, various man. roles including Treas., Schlumberger Ltd, Pres. Sedco Forex, Wireline & Testing and Oilfield Services Products, Exec. Vice-Pres. Schlumberger Oilfield Services, later Pres. and CEO Schlumberger Ltd, mem. Bd of Dirs 2002–, Chair. and CEO 2003–11, Chair. 2011–12; Dir Rio Tinto PLC, Rio Tinto Ltd; Dir (non-exec.) BG Group PLC 2011–, Chair. 2012–, Interim Exec. Chair. 2014–15. *Address:* BG Group PLC, 100 Thames Valley Park, Reading, Berks., RG6 1PT, England (office). *Telephone:* (118) 935-3222 (office). *Fax:* (118) 935-3484 (office). *E-mail:* box.info@bg-group.com (office). *Website:* www.bg-group.com (office).

GOULD, Bryan Charles, CNZM, BCL, LLM, MA; New Zealand/British politician and academic; *Chairman, National Centre for Tertiary Teaching Research;* b. 11 Feb. 1939, Hawera, Taranaki, North Island, NZ; s. of Charles T. Gould and Elsie M. Gould (née Driller); m. Gillian A. Harrigan 1967; one s. one d.; ed Victoria and Auckland Univs, New Zealand and Balliol Coll., Oxford, UK; in diplomatic service, British Embassy, Brussels 1964–68; Fellow and Tutor in Law, Worcester Coll., Oxford 1968–74; MP for Southampton Test 1974–79, Dagenham 1983–94; presenter and reporter Thames TV 1977–83; Opposition Spokesman on Trade 1983–86, on Trade and Industry 1987–89, on the Environment 1989–92; mem. of Shadow Cabinet, Labour's Campaign Co-ordinator 1986–89; Shadow Heritage Sec. 1992 (resgnd); unsuccessful cand. for Labour Party leadership 1992; Vice-Chancellor Waikato Univ. 1994–2004; Visiting Fellow, Nuffield Coll., Oxford 2005–; Chair. Nat. Centre for Tertiary Teaching Excellence, NZ, Eastern Bay Primary Health Alliance; Companion, NZ Order of Merit; Hon. PhD (Waikato). *Publications include:* Monetarism or Prosperity? 1981, Socialism and Freedom 1985, A Future for Socialism 1989, Goodbye to All That (memoirs) 1995, The Democracy Sham 2006, Rescuing the New Zealand Economy 2008, Myths, Politicians and Money 2013. *Leisure interests:* food, wine, gardening. *Address:* 239 Ohiwa Beach Road, RD2, Opotiki 3198, New Zealand (office). *E-mail:* bgould@paradise.net.nz (office). *Website:* www.bryangould.com (office).

GOULD, Elizabeth, BA, MA, PhD; American psychologist and academic; *Professor of Psychology and of Neuroscience, Princeton University;* ed St John's Univ., Queens, NY, Univ. of California, Los Angeles; Postdoctoral Fellow in Neuroendocrinology, The Rockefeller Univ. 1989–92, Asst Prof. 1993–96; Asst Prof., Princeton Univ. 1997–2000, Prof. of Psychology 2000–, also Prof. of Neuroscience, Co-Dir Neuroscience Certificate Program 2006–, Dept Chair.; mem. NSF Learning and Intelligence Systems KDI-LIS Review Cttee 1998–2000, NJ Gov.'s Council on Autism Grants Review Panel 2000–01; ad hoc reviewer for NIH 2000–04, mem. LAM NIH study section 2002–06, ad hoc reviewer for NIH grants 2002–, for NIH Pioneer Award, New Innovator Award Panel, K99 Award Panel 2008–; mem. Editorial Bd, Journal of Neuroscience, Neurobiology of Learning and Memory, Biological Psychiatry, Cell Stem Cell; an early investigator of adult neurogenesis in the hippocampus; Nat. Research Service Award Individual Postdoctoral Fellowship 1989–91, WinstonTri-Institutional (Rockefeller, Cornell, Sloan-Kettering) Fellowship 1991–92, American Paralysis Asscn Fellowship 1992–93, NARSAD (now The Brain & Behavior Research Foundation) Young Investigator Award 1994–96, Nat. Inst. of Mental Health FIRST Award 1994–99, NAS Troland Award 2000, NARSAD Distinguished Investigator Award 2006, Benjamin Franklin Award, Royal Soc. of Arts 2009. *Publications:* Psychology Around Us 2010; numerous book chapters, reviews and papers in professional journals. *Address:* Psychology Department, Princeton University, Princeton, NJ 08540, USA (office). *Telephone:* (609) 258-4483 (office). *Fax:* (609) 258-1113 (office). *E-mail:* goulde@princeton.edu (office). *Website:* psych.princeton.edu/psychology/research/gould/index.php (office).

GOULD, Elliott; American actor; b. (Elliott Goldstein), 29 Aug. 1938, Brooklyn, New York; s. of Bernard Goldstein and Lucille Goldstein); m. 1st Barbra Streisand (q.v.) 1963 (divorced 1971); one s.; m. 2nd Jenny Bogart 1973 (divorced 1975, remarried 1978); one s. one d.; ed Professional Children's School; made Broadway début in Rumple 1957; other appearances include Say Darling 1958, Irma La Douce 1960, I Can Get It For You Wholesale 1962, Drat! The Cat 1965, Alfred in Little Murders 1967; toured in The Fantastiks with Liza Minnelli; mem. Nat. Bd of Dirs Screen Actors Guild; Hon. LLD (Univ. of West Los Angeles). *Films include:* The Confession 1966, The Night They Raided Minsky's 1968, Bob and Carol and Ted and Alice 1969, Getting Straight 1970, M*A*S*H 1970, The Touch 1971, Little Murders 1971, The Long Good-Bye 1972, Nashville 1974, I Will . . . I Will . . . For Now 1976, Harry and Walter Go to New York 1976, A Bridge Too Far 1977, Capricorn One (1978), The Silent Partner 1979, The Lady Vanishes 1979, Escape to Athens 1979, The Muppet Movie 1979, Falling in Love Again 1980, The Devil and Max Devlin 1981, Over the Brooklyn Bridge 1984, The Naked Face 1984, Act of Betrayal 1988, Dead Men Don't Die 1989, Secret Scandal 1990, Bugsy 1991, Wet and Wild Summer! 1992, Beyond Justice 1992, Hoffman's Hunger 1993, Amore! 1993, The Feminine Touch 1994, The Dangerous 1994, The Glass Shield 1994, Bleeding Hearts 1994, P.C.H. 1995, I Want Him Back! 1995, Cover Me 1995, Kicking and Screaming 1995, Let It Be Me 1995, Busted 1996, Amanda's Game 1996, A Boy Called Hate 1996, Johns 1996, Camp Stories 1997, The Big Hit 1998, American History X 1998, Playing Mona Lisa 2000, Picking Up the Pieces 2000, Boys Life 3 2000, Ocean's Eleven 2001, The Experience Box 2001, Puckoon 2002, Ocean's Twelve 2004, Open Window 2006, Ocean's Thirteen 2007, Saving Sarah Cain 2007, The Ten Commandments 2007, WordGirl 2007, The Deal 2008, The Caller 2008, Noah's Ark: The New Beginning 2009, Little Hercules in 3-D 2009, Expecting Mary 2010, Contagion 2011, Dorfman in Love 2011, The Encore of Tony Duran 2011, Switchmas 2012, Fred Won't Move Out 2012, Ruby Sparks 2012, Divorce Invitation 2012, Live at the Foxes Den 2013. *TV appearances include:* Doggin' Around (BBC TV), Once Upon a Mattress (CBC), Friends, Kim Possible (series) 2003–07, Uncorked (film) 2009, I'm Not Dead Yet (film) 2012, Listen to Grandpa, Andy Ling (film) 2012, Ray Donovan (series) 2013–15, Mulaney (series) 2014–15, Oscar's Hotel for Fantastical Creatures (mini-series) 2015.

GOULIAN, Mehran, AB, MD; American physician and academic; *Professor Emeritus, School of Medicine, University of California, San Diego;* b. 31 Dec. 1929, Weehawken, NJ; s. of Dicran Goulian and Shamiram Mzrakjian; m. Susan Hook 1961; three s.; ed Columbia Coll. and Columbia Univ. Coll. of Physicians and Surgeons, Washington Univ. School of Medicine, Yale Univ. School of Medicine; Medical Internship, Barnes Hosp. 1954–55; Medical Residency, Mass. Gen. Hosp. 1958–59, 1960; Fellow in Medicine (Hematology), Yale Univ. School of Medicine 1959–60; Research Fellow in Medicine (Hematology), Harvard Univ. July–Dec. 1960, 1962–63, Instructor in Medicine 1963–65; Clinical and Research Fellow in Medicine (Hematology), Mass. Gen. Hosp. July–Dec. 1960, 1962–63, Asst in Medicine, 1963–65; Fellow in Biochemistry, Stanford Univ. School of Medicine 1965–67; Research Assoc. in Biochemistry, Univ. of Chicago and Argonne Cancer Research Hosp. 1967–69, Assoc. Prof. of Medicine 1967–70, Assoc. Prof. of Biochemistry 1969–70; Prof. of Medicine, Univ. of Calif., San Diego 1970–94, now Prof. Emer. *Publications include:* numerous papers on biochemistry. *Leisure interest:* music. *Address:* 9500 Gilman Drive, La Jolla, CA 92093, USA (office). *Telephone:* (858) 459-0088 (office). *Website:* ucsd.edu (office).

GOULONGANA, Jean-Robert; Gabonese diplomatist and government official; *Managing Director, Caisse Nationale d'Assurance Maladie et de Garantie Sociale;* b. 30 April 1953, Lambarene; m.; three c.; ed Dakar Univ., Senegal, Aix-Marseille III Univ., France; Minister of Waters, Forests and the Environment 1990–91; Amb.

to Italy 1992, to Belgium 1996; fmr Head, Gabonese Mission to EU, Brussels; Sec.-Gen. African, Caribbean and Pacific States 2000–05; Man. Dir Caisse Nationale d'Assurance Maladie et de Garantie Sociale (Nat. Social Insurance and Social Security) 2007–; Officier, Ordre du Mérite Maritime Gabonais. *Address:* Caisse Nationale d'Assurance Maladie et de Garantie Sociale, Libreville, Gabon (office).

GOUNARIS, Elias, LLM; Greek diplomatist; b. 7 Sept. 1941, Athens; s. of Panayotis Gounaris and Christine Gounaris; one s.; ed Univ. of Athens; served in Greek Navy 1964–66; Attaché, Ministry of Foreign Affairs, Athens 1966, Consul, New York 1969–73, Head of Section, Turkey-Cyprus Dept, Ministry of Foreign Affairs 1973, Sec., Perm. Mission of Greece to Int. Orgs, Geneva 1975, Counsellor 1976, Deputy Chief Minister, Embassy in Belgrade 1979–83, Head of the American Desk, Ministry of Foreign Affairs 1983–87, Minister-Counsellor, then Minister, Embassy in Bonn 1987–88, Minister Plenipotentiary 1988, Amb. to USSR 1988 (also accred to Mongolia) 1989–93, to UK (also accred to Iceland) 1993–96, Dir Dept of Eastern and Western Europe and Deputy Dir-Gen. for Political Affairs, Ministry of Foreign Affairs 1996–97, Dir-Gen. for Political Affairs 1997–99, Perm. Rep. to UN, New York 1999–2002; Chair. Cttee for the Environment and Sustainable Devt, Ministry of Foreign Affairs 2002–04; mem. Bd of Dirs OTE SA (Hellenic Telecommunications Org.), M.I. Maillis, Packaging Materials; Hon. Amb.; decorations from Austria, Finland, Germany, Greece, Italy, Spain, Ukraine and Russian Orthodox Church. *Address:* Akadimias Street 1, 106 71 Athens, Greece.

GOURDAULT-MONTAGNE, Maurice, BA, MA; French diplomatist; *Secretary-General, Ministry of Europe and Foreign Affairs;* b. 16 Nov. 1953, Paris; ed Institut d'Etudes Politiques, Paris, Univ. of Paris Sorbonne IV, Univ. Paris-Assas, Institut Nat. des Langues et Civilisations Orientales (INALCO); joined Ministry of Foreign Affairs 1978, Desk Officer for Indian Affairs, Asia and Oceania Directorate 1979–81, First Sec., Embassy in New Delhi 1981–83, Special Adviser to Sec.-Gen., Ministry of Foreign Affairs 1984–86, Counsellor (Parl. and press) in pvt. office of Foreign Minister Jean-Bernard Raymond 1986–88, Counsellor (Political Affairs, Bilateral Relations), Embassy in Bonn 1988–91, Deputy Head of Press, Information and Communication Dept 1991–92, Deputy, then interim Spokesman, Ministry of Foreign Affairs 1992–93, Deputy Prin. Pvt. Sec. to Foreign Minister Alain Juppé 1993–95, Prin. Pvt. Sec. to Prime Minister Alain Juppé 1995–97, Personal Rep. of Pres. of France 1997–98, Amb. to Japan 1998–2002, Sr Diplomatic Counsellor to Pres. Chirac and G8 Sherpa 2002–07, Amb. to UK 2007–11, to Germany 2011–14, to People's Repub. of China 2014–17, Sec.-Gen., Ministry of Europe and Foreign Affairs 2017–; mem. Bd of Dirs EDF 2017–; Hon. LVO 1992; Chevalier, Ordre nat. du Mérite 1998, Légion d'honneur 2001, Officier 2014; Hon. CMG 2004, Grand Cross of the Order of Merit of the Federal Repub. of Germany, Grand Cross of the Order of the Sacred Treasure of Japan, Order of Friendship, Russia. *Address:* Ministry of Europe and Foreign Affairs, 37 quai d'Orsay, 75351 Paris Cedex 07, France (office). *Telephone:* 1-43-17-53-53 (office). *Fax:* 1-43-17-47-53 (office). *Website:* www.diplomatie.gouv.fr (office).

GOURGEON, Pierre-Henri, BSc, BEng, MSc; French airline executive and fmr civil servant; b. 28 April 1946; ed Ecole de Salon de Provence et de Tours, Ecole Polytechnique, Ecole Nationale Supérieure de l'Aéronautique, California Inst. of Tech., USA; held various positions in French Govt and French state-owned enterprises –1990; Dir-Gen. French Civil Aviation Authority 1990–93; CEO Servair and several of its subsidiaries 1993–96; Exec. Man. Dir Air France SA 1993–97, Exec. Vice-Pres., Devt and Int. Affairs 1997–2008, Deputy CEO Air France-KLM 2004–08, Deputy COO 1998–2004, CEO Air France-KLM and Air France (subsidiary) 2009–13; Chair. and CEO Amadeus France/Estrel 1996–97; mem. Bd of Dirs and Vice-Chair. Amadeus Technology Group SA (fmrly Amadeus Global Travel Distribution SA) 1996, later Chair.; mem. Bd of Dirs Stria, Autoroutes Du Sud de La France 2002–, Soderi SAS Steria SA; mem. Bd of Dirs and Supervisory Bd, Man. and Gen. Partner, Groupe Steria SCA 2000–. *Address:* c/o Groupe Air France, 45 rue de Paris, 95747 Roissy CDG Cedex, France.

GOUTARD, Noël; French business executive; b. 22 Dec. 1931, Casablanca, Morocco; s. of F. Antoine Goutard and M. Edmée Goutard (née Lespinasse); m. Dominique Jung 1964; one s. one d.; ed Lycée Louis le Grand, Paris, Univ. of Bordeaux and Pace Coll., New York; Vice-Pres. Frenville Co., New York 1954–60; Finance Exec., Warner Lambert Int., Morris Plains, NJ 1960–62; African Area Man. Pfizer Inc., New York 1962–66; Exec. Vice-Pres. Gevelot SA Paris 1966–71; Pres. and COO Compteurs Schlumberger SA, Paris 1971–76; Exec. Vice-Pres. and mem. Bd of Dirs Chargeurs SA, Paris 1976–83; Exec. Vice-Pres. and COO Thomson SA, Paris 1983–84, Dir-Gen. 1983–86; Pres.-Dir-Gen. Valéo SA 1987–2000, Hon. Pres. 2000–01; Partner, LBO France 2000–05; Pres. NG Investments 2000–11; mem. Supervisory Bd Riber SA; fmr mem. Bd of Dirs Thomson CSF, Banque Thomson, Thomson-Brandt Armements, Imétal, Alcatel-Alsthom 1997–2001; Officier, Légion d'honneur. *Publication:* L'outsider, The Outsider Chronicles of a Patron Outside the Norm 2005. *Leisure interests:* tennis, travel, golf.

GOUVEIA, Maria Teresa Pinto Basto Patrício de; Portuguese politician; *Executive Director and Member, Board of Trustees, Fundação Calouste Gulbenkian;* b. 18 July 1946, Lisbon; d. of Afonso Patrício de Gouveia and Maria Madalena d'Orey Ferreira Pinto Basto; m. Alexandre Manuel Vahia de Castro O'Neill de Bulhões 1971 (divorced 1981); one s.; ed Univ. of Lisbon; Sec. of State for Culture 1985–90; mem. Parl. 1987–2004; Sec. of State for Environment 1991–93, Minister for Environment 1993–95; mem. Bd of Govs and Exec. Cttee, European Cultural Foundation, Amsterdam 1996–2002; Vice-Pres. Foreign Affairs Parl. Cttee 2002–03; Minister of Foreign Affairs and Portuguese Communities Abroad 2003–04; fmr Pres. Cttee for Cultural Cooperation, Council of Europe, Strasbourg; mem. Gen. Council O Público newspaper 1990–91; Pres. Bd of Trustees Serralves Foundation, Oporto 2001–03; mem. Portuguese Nat. Orders Council 2001–11; Exec. Dir and mem. Bd of Trustees Calouste Gulbenkian Foundation 2004–; mem. Supervisory Cttee, Partex Oil and Gas (Holdings) Corpn; mem. ECFR-European Council on Foreign Relations (London), EFLG-European Former Leaders Group (France); Great Cross, Ordem de Cristo, Great Cross, Ordem Infante D. Henrique. *Address:* c/o Board of Trustees, Fundação Calouste Gulbenkian, Avenida da Berna 45A, 1067-001 Lisbon, Portugal (office). *Telephone:* (217) 823306 (office). *Fax:* (217) 823088 (office). *E-mail:* tpgouveia@gulbenkian.pt (office). *Website:* www.gulbenkian.pt (office).

GOUYOU BEAUCHAMPS, Xavier; French television industry executive; *President, Citizenside;* b. 25 April 1937, Paris; s. of Charles Gouyou Beauchamps and Anne-Marie Coulombeix; m. 2nd Geneviève Decugis 1986; two s. (from previous marriage); ed Ecole St Joseph, Sarlat, Inst. d'études politiques and Ecole nat. d'admin; Dir of Staff Loiret Pref. 1964–66; Asst Head of Staff, Minister of Agric. 1966–68, Minister of Educ. 1968–69; Official Staff Rep., Minister of Econ. and Finance 1969–74; Press Sec. to the Pres. 1974–76; Prefect of Ardèche 1976–77; Pres. and Dir-Gen. SOFIRAD 1977–81; Pres. Télédiffusion de France 1986–92, Pres. Asscn des organismes français de radiodiffusion et de télévision (OFRT) 1990–92; Pres. French broadcasters' group (GRF) of European Union of Radio and TV (UER) 1990, Vice-Pres. UER 1990; Pres. Admin. Council Nat. Park of Port Cros, Sofipost 1992–94; Dir-Gen. France 3 1994–96, Chair. Bd of Dirs. 1998; Pres., Dir-Gen. France 2 and France 3 cos. 1996–99; Founder and Man. XGB Conseil 1999–; Co-founder IAM; Founder, Pres. and Dir-Gen. Antalis-TV 2001–06; Pres. Asscn des employeurs du service public de l'audiovisuel 1998; Pres. Citizenside 2007–; Pres. Cap24 –2010; Chevalier, Légion d'honneur, Officier, Ordre nat. du Mérite, Chevalier du Mérite agricole, Croix de la Valeur militaire. *Publication:* Le ministère de l'économie et des finances, un Etat dans l'Etat? 1976. *Address:* 73 avenue Franklin D. Roosevelt, 75008 Paris, France (home). *Website:* www.citizenside.com (office).

GOVAN, Michael, BA; American museum curator; *Director and CEO, Los Angeles County Museum of Art;* b. 1963, Washington, DC; m. Katherine Ross; ed Williams Coll., Mass, Univ. of San Diego, studied Renaissance art in Italy; Acting Curator and Special Asst, Williams Coll. Museum of Art, organized Picasso and Rembrandt in 1986; Deputy Dir Solomon R. Guggenheim Museum, New York, Venice, Italy, Bilbao, Spain 1986–94; Pres. and Dir Dia Art Foundation, New York 1994–2006; Co-curator touring exhbn 'Dan Flavin: A Retrospective' organized by Dia Art Foundation in asscn with Nat. Gallery of Art, Washington, DC, which opened at Hayward Gallery, London, UK 2006; Wallis Annenberg Dir and CEO Los Angeles Co. Museum of Art 2006–; mem. Advisory Bd Eli and Edythe Broad Art Museum, Michigan State Univ.; Leo Award 2015. *Publication:* The Great Utopia: The Russian and Soviet Avant-Garde, 1915–1932. *Address:* Los Angeles County Museum of Art, 5905 Wilshire Blvd, Los Angeles, CA 90036, USA (office). *Telephone:* (323) 857-6000 (office). *Fax:* (323) 857-0098 (office). *E-mail:* publicinfo@lacma.org (office). *Website:* www.lacma.org (office).

GOVE, Ernesto Gouveia, MEconSc; Mozambican economist and central banker; *Governor, Banco de Moçambique;* b. 1957; m.; four c.; ed Eduardo Mondlane Univ., Maputo, Univ. of London, IMF and World Bank Insts, Swiss Central Bank Inst., Berne; joined Banco de Moçambique (central bank) 1976, various managerial positions in Foreign, Issuing and Treasury and Credit Depts and Documentation Centre, including Dir for Foreign Currency, Issuing and Treasury Operations –1991, apptd Exec. Dir and mem. Bd 1991, Deputy Gov. 1995–2006, Gov. 2006–; Chair. African Mobile Phone Financial Services Policy Initiative 2016–; Lecturer, Eduardo Mondlane Univ. 1990–94; Alt. Gov. Islamic Devt Bank; fmr Chair. Bd of Dirs Sociedade de Noticias; fmr Chair. Fiscal Cttee Açucareira de Mafambisse (Mafambisse Sugar Co.). *Address:* Banco de Moçambique, Av. 25 de Setembro 1695, CP 423, Maputo, Mozambique (office). *Telephone:* 21354600 (office). *Fax:* 21323247 (office). *E-mail:* gpi@bancomoc.mz (office). *Website:* www.bancomoc.mz (office).

GOVE, Rt Hon. Michael Andrew, PC; British journalist, author and politician; *Secretary of State for Environment, Food and Rural Affairs;* b. 26 Aug. 1967, Edinburgh, Scotland; adopted; m. Sarah Vine; one s. one d.; ed state school educated in Aberdeen, Robert Gordon's Coll. (scholarship), Lady Margaret Hall, Oxford; fmr Pres. Oxford Union; following graduation worked as journalist for local and nat. newspapers, radio and TV; joined The Times as a leader writer 1996, has been its Comment Ed., News Ed., Saturday Ed. and Asst Ed., has also written a weekly column on politics and current affairs for The Times and contributed to the Times Literary Supplement, Prospect magazine and The Spectator; fmr Chair. Policy Exchange (think tank); MP for Surrey Heath 2005–, mem. European Scrutiny Cttee 2005–07; Shadow Minister for Housing 2005–07, Shadow Sec. of State for Children, Schools and Families 2007–10, Sec. of State for Educ. 2010–14, Parl. Sec. to the Treasury and Chief Whip 2014–15, Lord Chancellor and Sec. of State for Justice 2015–16, Sec. of State for Environment, Food and Rural Affairs 2017–; Conservative. *Radio:* fmr regular panellist on BBC Radio 4's The Moral Maze. *Television:* has worked for BBC Today programme, On The Record, Scottish Television and Channel 4 monologue programme A Stab In The Dark; fmr regular panellist on Newsnight Review (BBC 2). *Publications include:* Michael Portillo: The Future of the Right 1995, The Price of Peace 2000, A Blue Tomorrow: New Visions for Modern Conservatives (co-ed. with Edward Vaizey and Nicholas Boles) 2001, Celsius 7/7 2006. *Address:* Department for Environment, Food and Rural Affairs, Nobel House, 17 Smith Square, London, SW1P 3JR (office); House of Commons, London, SW1A 0AA, England (office). *Telephone:* (20) 7238-6951 (office). *E-mail:* defra.helpline@defra.gsi.gov.uk (office). *Website:* www.gov.uk/government/organisations/department-for-environment-food-rural-affairs (office); www.michaelgove.com.

GOVORUN, Oleg Markovich; Russian government official; *Head, Presidential Directorate for Social and Economic Cooperation with the Commonwealth of Independent States Member Countries, the Republic of Abkhazia, and the Republic of South Ossetia;* b. 15 Jan. 1969, Bratsk, Irkutsk region; m.; three s. one d.; ed Moscow State Forest Univ.; served in mil. 1987–89; Man.'s Asst, then Project Man., then specialist in GR Dept., Rosprom 1995–97; Vice-Pres. Alfa Bank 1997–2000; First Deputy Chief of Presidential Main Territorial Directorate 2000–04, Deputy Chief, Presidential Domestic Policy Directorate 2004–06, Chief 2006–11; Deputy Chair. Presidential Council on Cossack Affairs 2009; apptd Presidential Envoy to Cen. Federal Okrug 2011; apptd mem. Security Council of Russia 2011; Minister of Regional Devt 2012; Head, Presidential Directorate for Social and Economic Cooperation with the Commonwealth of Independent States Member Countries, the Republic of Abkhazia, and the Republic of South Ossetia 2013–; mem. Council of Trustees, Moscow State Forest Univ. 2010; Order for Services to the Fatherland, IV degree, Medal of the Order for Services to the Fatherland, II degree. *Address:* Presidential Directorate for Social and Economic Cooperation with the Commonwealth of Independent States Member Countries, the Republic of Abkhazia, and the Republic of South Ossetia, Office of the

President, 103132 Moscow, Staraya pl. 4, Russia (office). *Website:* www.kremlin.ru (office).

GOWAN, David John, CMG, MA; British fmr diplomatist; b. 11 Feb. 1949, Oxford, England; s. of Ivor Lyn Gowan and Gwendoline Alice Gowan (née Pearce); m. Marna Gowan; two s.; ed Nottingham High School, Ardwyn Grammar School, Balliol Coll., Oxford; Home Civil Service 1970–75; joined FCO 1975, Desk Officer, Near East and N Africa Dept 1975–76, full-time language training 1976–77, Second, later First Sec. (Commercial, later Chancery), Moscow 1977–80, Desk Officer, S Asian Dept, FCO 1981–82, Desk Officer, Soviet Dept 1982–84, Consul and Head of Chancery, Brasilia 1985–88, on loan to Cabinet Office 1988–89, Asst Head of Soviet Dept, FCO 1989–90, on loan to Cabinet Office (Counsellor) 1990–91, Counsellor (Commercial and Know How Fund), Moscow 1992–95, Counsellor and Deputy Head of Mission, Helsinki 1995–99, UK War Crimes Co-ordinator, FCO 1999, Minister and Deputy Head of Mission, Moscow 2000–03, Amb. to Serbia and Montenegro 2003–06 (retd); Sr Assoc. mem. St Antony's Coll., Oxford 1999–2000, Guest mem. 2007–10; mem. Bishop's Council and Synod of Diocese in Europe 2007–18, Advisory Cttee Centre for East European Language-Based Area Studies 2007–, Council of Keston Inst. 2009–; Chair. Russian Booker Cttee 2012–15; Hon. Sr Research Fellow, Univ. of Birmingham 2008–11. *Publications include:* pamphlets and articles on Russia, Serbia and Kosovo. *Leisure interests:* reading, walking, travel, theatre, music. *Address:* 8 Blackmore Road, Malvern, Worcs., WR14 1QX, England (home). *Telephone:* (1684) 565707 (home). *E-mail:* david.gowan@btinternet.com.

GOWANS, Sir James Learmonth, Kt, CBE, MB, DPhil, FRS, FRCP, FRSA; British medical scientist and fmr administrator; b. 7 May 1924, Sheffield, Yorks., England; s. of John Gowans and Selma Josefina Ljung; m. Moyra Leatham 1956; one s. two d.; ed Trinity School, Croydon, King's Coll. Hosp. Medical School, Univ. of Oxford; Fellow, St Catherine's Coll., Oxford 1961–; Sec.-Gen. Human Frontiers Science Programme, Strasbourg 1989–93; Consultant, WHO Global Programme on AIDS 1987–88; Henry Dale Research Prof. of Royal Soc. 1962–77; Dir MRC Cellular Immunology Unit 1963–77, mem. MRC 1965–69, Sec. (Chief Exec.) 1977–87, Chair. MRC Biological Research Bd 1967–69; mem. Advisory Bd for the Research Councils 1977–87; mem. Council and Vice-Pres. Royal Soc. 1973–75; Dir Celltech PLC 1980–87; Chair. European Medical Research Councils 1985–87; mem. Academia Europaea 1991; Foreign Assoc. NAS (USA); Hon. ScD (Yale) 1966, Hon. DSc (Chicago) 1971, (Birmingham) 1978, (Rochester, New York) 1987, Hon. MD (Edinburgh) 1979, (Sheffield) 2000, Hon. LLD (Glasgow) 1988, Hon. DM (Southampton) 1987; Gairdner Award, Ehrlich Prize, Feldberg Award, Royal Medal of Royal Soc., Wolf Foundation Prize in Medicine 1980, Medawar Prize, Galen Medal. *Publications include:* articles in scientific journals. *Leisure interest:* old books. *Address:* 75 Cumnor Hill, Oxford, OX2 9HX, England (home). *Telephone:* (1865) 862304 (home). *E-mail:* jamesgowans@btinternet.com (home).

GOWARIKER, Ashutosh, BSc; Indian actor, film director, film producer and scriptwriter; *Founding Director, Ashutosh Gowariker Productions Pvt. Ltd;* b. 15 Feb. 1964, Mumbai; s. of Kishori Gowariker and Ashok Gowariker; m. Sunita Gowariker 1988; two s.; ed Mithibai Coll., Mumbai; began career as model for commercials by Govind Mihalani and Jenny Pinto for Lifebuoy soap and Close-Up toothpaste; film acting debut in Holi 1984; directed first film Pehla Nasha 1993; directed five commercials for Coca-Cola 2001; Founding Dir Ashutosh Gowariker Productions Pvt. Ltd; mem. Acad. of Motion Picture Arts and Sciences 2004; Filmfare Award 2001, 2008, IIFA Award 2001, 2008. *Film appearances include:* Naam 1986, West Is West 1987, Salim Langde Pe Mat Ro 1989, Goonj 1989, Gawahi 1989, Indrajeet 1991, Jaanam 1992, Chamatkar 1992, Kabhi Haan Kabhi Naa 1993, Vazir 1994, Sarkarnama 1998. *Films directed include:* Pehla Nasha 1993, Baazi 1995, Lagaan: Once Upon a Time in India 2001, Swades 2004, Jodhaa Akbar 2007, What's Your Rashee 2009. *Television includes:* Kachchi Dhoop 1987, Circus 1990, Woh 1998, CID 1999. *Address:* Ashutosh Gowariker Productions Pvt. Ltd, 201, Kum Kum, 16th Road, Bandra, Mumbai 400 050, Maharashtra, India (office). *Telephone:* (22) 26044236 (office); (22) 26004687 (home). *Fax:* (22) 26487164 (office). *E-mail:* info@agppl.com; ashgow@hotmail.com (home). *Website:* www.agppl.com; www.ashutoshgowariker.com.

GOWDA, D(everagunda) V(enkatappa) Sadananda, BSc, LLB; Indian lawyer and politician; *Minister of Statistics and Programme Implementation;* b. 18 March 1953, Dakshina Kannada, Karnataka; s. of Venkappa Gowda and Kamala Gowda; m. Datty Sadananda; one s.; ed St Philomena Coll., Putur, Udupi Vaikunta Baliga Coll. of Law; began practising law in Sullia and Puttur 1976; Pres. Karnataka Industries Staff Union 1977–82; Asst Public Prosecutor 1979–82; State Sec. Bharatiya Janata Party (BJP) Yuva Morcha, Karnataka 1983–88; mem. Staff Selection Cttee, State LD Bank 1989–90; Dir CAMPCO, Mangalore, Karnataka 1991–94; mem. Karnataka Legis. Ass. 1994–2004, Deputy Leader of Opposition 1999–2004, mem. Cttee for Energy, Fuel and Power 2001–02, mem. Public Undertaking Cttee 2002–03, Pres. Public Accounts Cttee 2003–04; State Sec., BJP Karnataka 2003–04, State Pres. 2006–; mem. 14th Lok Sabha 2004–06, 15th Lok Sabha 2009–14, 16th Lok Sabha 2014–; Chief Minister of Karnataka 2011–12; Minister of Railways May–Nov. 2014, of Law and Justice Nov. 2014–16, of Statistics and Programme Implementation 2016–. *Address:* Ministry of Statistics and Programme Implementation, Patel Chowk, Road Area, Sansad Marg, Sardar Patel Bhavan, New Delhi 110 001; Anugraha, K K Annex, Kumarakrupa Road, Bangalore 560 001, India. *Website:* www.mospi.nic.in.

GOWER, David Ivon, OBE; British journalist, broadcaster and fmr professional cricketer; *Presenter, International Cricket, BSkyB;* b. 1 April 1957, Tunbridge Wells, Kent, England; s. of Richard Hallam Gower and Sylvia Mary Gower (née Ford); m. Thorunn Ruth Nash 1992; two d.; ed King's School, Canterbury and Univ. Coll., London; left-hand batsman; played for Leicestershire 1975–89 (Capt. 1984–86), Hampshire 1990–93; played in 117 Tests for England 1978–92, 32 as Capt., scoring then England record 8,231 runs (average 44.25, highest score 215) with 18 hundreds; toured Australia 1978–79, 1979–80, 1982–83, 1986–87, 1990–91; scored 26,339 First-class runs (average 40.08, highest score 228) with 53 hundreds; played in 114 One-Day Ints, scoring 3,170 runs (average 30.77, highest score 158); Sunday Express Cricket Corresp. 1993–95; Public Relations Consultant for cricket sponsorship, NatWest Bank 1993–2000; columnist, Sunday Telegraph 1995–98, The Sun 2000–02, Sunday Times 2002–; commentator, Sky TV cricket 1993–, presenter, Int. Cricket, BSkyB 1999–; commentator and presenter, BBC TV 1994–99; Trustee, David Shepherd Conservation Foundation; Hon. MA (Southampton Inst., Nottingham Trent Univ., Univ. of Loughborough); Hon. Blue (Herriott Watt Univ., Edinburgh); Wisden Cricketer of the Year 1979, Int. Cricketer of the Year 1982/83. *Television:* Team Capt., They Think It's All Over 1995–2003. *Publications:* With Time to Spare 1979, Heroes and Contemporaries 1983, A Right Ambition 1986, On the Rack 1990, The Autobiography 1992. *Leisure interests:* Cresta run, skiing, tennis, photography, wildlife conservation. *Address:* c/o Diana van Bunnens, Jon Holmes Media Ltd, 3 Wine Office Court, London, EC4A 3BY, England (office). *Telephone:* (1582) 469233 (office). *E-mail:* diana@jonholmesmedia.com (office). *Website:* www.jonholmesmedia.com (office).

GOWERS, Andrew, MA; British journalist, communications executive and consultant; *Global Head of Corporate Affairs, Trafigura;* b. 19 Oct. 1957, Reading, Berks.; s. of Michael Gowers and Anne Gowers; m. Finola Gowers (née Clarke); one s. one d.; ed Trinity School, Croydon and Univ. of Cambridge; grad. trainee, Reuters 1980, Brussels Corresp. 1981, Zurich Corresp. 1982, joined Foreign Desk, Financial Times (FT), London 1983, Agric. Corresp. 1984, Commodities Ed. 1985, Middle East Ed. 1987, Foreign Ed. 1992, Deputy Ed. 1994, Acting Ed. 1997, Ed. FT Deutschland (German Language Business Paper) 1999, Ed. FT 2001–05; columnist, Evening Standard, Sunday Times 2005–06; Leader Gowers' Review of Intellectual Property for UK Government 2005–06; Head of Corp. Communications (Europe and Asia), Lehman Brothers 2006–07, Global Co-head of Corp. Communications, Marketing and Brand Man. 2007–08; Interim Head of External Relations, London Business School 2008–09, Head of Group Media, BP PLC 2009–10; Dir of External Relations, Asscn for Financial Markets in Europe 2011–12; Global Head of Corp. Affairs, Trafigura 2013–. *Publications include:* Arafat, The Biography (co-author) 1991, The Gowers Review of Intellectual Property 2006, Investing in Change (commissioning ed.) 2012. *Leisure interests:* film, opera, music, theatre, gastronomy, tennis. *Telephone:* (20) 7733-4125 (home). *E-mail:* andrew.gowers@trafigura.com (office).

GOWERS, Sir (William) Timothy, Kt, PhD, FRS; British mathematician and academic; *Royal Society 2010 Anniversary Research Professor, Department of Pure Mathematics and Mathematical Statistics, University of Cambridge;* b. 20 Nov. 1963, Marlborough, Wilts., England; s. of (William) Patrick Gowers and Caroline (Molesworth) Maurice; m. 1st Emily Joanna Thomas 1988 (divorced 2007); two s. one d.; m. 2nd Julie Barrau 2008; one s.; ed Eton Coll., Trinity Coll., Cambridge; Lecturer, Univ. Coll. London 1991–94, Reader 1994–95; Lecturer, Univ. of Cambridge 1995–98, Rouse Ball Prof. of Math. 1998–2010, Royal Soc. 2010 Anniversary Research Prof. 2010–, Fellow, Trinity Coll., Cambridge 1995–; Visiting Prof., Princeton Univ. 2000–02; Hon. Fellow, Univ. Coll. London 1999; Jr Whitehead Prize, London Math. Soc. 1995, European Math. Soc. Prize 1996, Fields Medal 1998, Sylvester Medallist, Royal Soc. 2016. *Publications include:* Mathematics: A Very Short Introduction 2002, The Princeton Companion to Mathematics (ed.) 2008; mathematical papers in various journals. *Leisure interest:* playing jazz piano. *Address:* Department of Pure Mathematics and Mathematical Statistics, Room C2.04, Centre for Mathematical Sciences, Wilberforce Road, Cambridge, CB3 0WB, England (office). *Telephone:* (1223) 337973 (office). *Fax:* (1223) 337920 (office). *E-mail:* w.t.gowers@dpmms.cam.ac.uk (office). *Website:* www.dpmms.cam.ac.uk/~wtg10 (office); gowers.wordpress.com.

GOWIN, Jarosław Adam; Polish editor and politician; *Deputy Prime Minister and Minister of Science and Higher Education;* b. 4 Dec. 1961, Kraków; m. Anna Gowin; three c.; ed Jagiellonian Univ., Univ. of Cambridge, UK; Founder and Rector, Tischner European Univ., Kraków; Ed.-in-Chief Znak (conservative Catholic magazine) 1994–2005; mem. Platforma Obywatelska (PO—Civic Platform) 2005–13, Polska Razem (Poland Together) 2013–; mem. Senate (PO) for Kraków 2005–07; mem. Sejm (Ass.—Parl.) for Kraków 2007–; Minister of Justice 2011–13; Deputy Prime Minister and Minister of Science and Higher Educ. 2015–. *Address:* Ministry of Science and Higher Education, 00-529 Warsaw, ul. Wspólna 1/3, Poland (office). *Telephone:* (22) 5292718 (office). *Fax:* (22) 5017865 (office). *E-mail:* ssekretariat.bm@nauka.gov.pl (office). *Website:* www.nauka.gov.pl (office); www.jgowin.pl.

GOWON, Gen. Yakubu, PhD; Nigerian army officer, organization official and fmr head of state; *President and Chairman, Board of Trustees, Yakubu Gowon Center for National Unity and International Co-operation;* b. 19 Oct. 1934, Garam, Pankshin Div., Plateau State; s. of Yohanna and Saraya Gowon; m. Victoria Hansatu Zakari 1969; one s. two d.; ed St Bartholomew's School, Wusasa, Zaria, Govt Coll., Barewa, Zaria, Royal Mil. Acad., Sandhurst, Staff Coll., Camberley and Jt Services Staff Coll., Latimer, UK; Adjutant, Nigerian Army 1960; with UN Peacekeeping Force, Congo 1960–61, Jan.–June 1963; promoted Lt-Col and apptd Adjutant-Gen. Nigerian Army 1963; Chief of Staff 1966; Maj.-Gen. 1967; promoted Gen. 1971; Head of Fed. Mil. Govt and C-in-C of Armed Forces of Fed. Repub. of Nigeria 1966–75 (deposed in coup); studying at Univ. of Warwick, UK 1975–83, postgraduate 1978–82; Chair. Ass. of Heads of State, OAU 1973–74; Chair. Nigerian Nat. Oil and Chemical Marketing Co. 1996; founder, Pres., Chair. Bd of Trustees Yadubu Gowon Center for Nat. Unity and Int. Co-operation; Chair. Nigeria Prays; Assoc. Research Prof., Centre for Devt Studies, Univ. of Jos; fmr Chair. Arewa Consultative Forum (ACF); Chair. Trustees, Commonwealth Human Ecology Foundation 1986; Chair. Bd of Dirs Industrial And Gen. Insurance Co. Ltd (IGI); Lifetime Achievement Award, THISDAY 2007. *Publication:* Faith in Unity 1970. *Leisure interests:* squash, tennis, photography, pen-drawings. *Address:* Yakubu Gowon Center for National Unity and International Co-operation, POB 3995, Garki, Abuja (office); c/o Board of Directors, IGI, Plot, 741 Adeola Hopewell Street, Victoria Island, Lagos, Nigeria. *Telephone:* (9) 3140613 (office). *E-mail:* ygc@inforweb.abs (office). *Website:* www.yakubugowoncentre.org (office).

GOWRIE, Rt Hon. Alexander Patrick Greysteil Hore-Ruthven (Grey), The Earl of Gowrie, PC, BA, AM, FRSL; British/Irish politician, business executive and writer; *Chairman, The Fine Art Fund;* b. (Alexander Hore-Ruthven), 26 Nov. 1939; s. of Hon. A. H. P. Hore-Ruthven and Pamela Margaret Fletcher; m. 1st Xandra Bingley 1962 (divorced 1973); one s.; m. 2nd Adelheid Gräfin von den Schulenburg 1974; ed Eton Coll., Balliol Coll., Oxford and Harvard Univ., USA; Fellow and Tutor, Lowell House, Harvard Univ. 1965–68; Asst Prof., Emerson Coll., Boston 1967–68; Lecturer in English and American Literature, Univ. Coll. London 1969–72; a UK del. to UN 1971; a Lord-in-Waiting to HM the Queen 1972–74; Govt

Whip, House of Lords 1972–74; Consultant, Thomas Gibson Fine Art 1974–79; Opposition Spokesman on Econ. Affairs and Adviser to Margaret Thatcher 1977–79; Minister of State, Dept of Employment 1979–81; Minister of State and Deputy to the Sec. of State, Northern Ireland Office 1981–83; Minister of State, Privy Council Office and Minister for the Arts 1983–84; mem. of Cabinet as Chancellor of the Duchy of Lancaster (retaining portfolio as Minister for the Arts) 1984–85; Chair. The Really Useful Group 1985–90, Sotheby's Europe 1985–94, Arts Council 1994–98, Magdi Yacoub Inst., Fine Art Fund 2002–; Dir Sotheby's Holdings Inc. 1985–98; Provost RCA 1986–95; Chair. Devt Securities 1995–99, Dir (non-exec.) 1995–2001; Dir (non-exec.) NXT PLC, ITG PLC 1998–2002. *Publications:* A Postcard from Don Giovanni (poems) 1972, The Genius of British Painting: The Twentieth Century 1975, Derek Hill: An Appreciation 1987, The Domino Hymn: Poems from Harefield 2005, Third Day: New and Selected Poems 2008. *Leisure interests:* the arts. *Address:* The Magdi Yacoub Institute, Science Centre, Harefield, Middx, UB9 6JH, England (office). *Telephone:* (20) 7828-4777 (office).

GOYAL, Amit, BTech, MS, PhD, MBA, FInstP; American (b. Indian) metallurgical engineer; *UT-Battelle Corporate Fellow, Battelle Distinguished Inventor and ORNL Distinguished Scientist, Oak Ridge National Laboratory;* b. Rajasthan, India; m.; two c.; ed Mayo Coll., India, Indian Inst. of Tech., Univ. of Rochester, Purdue Univ., Tilburg Univ., The Netherlands, Sloan School of Man., Massachusetts Inst. of Tech.; joined Oak Ridge Nat. Lab., Tenn. 1991, currently UT-Battelle Corp. Fellow, a Battelle Distinguished Inventor and an ORNL Distinguished Scientist, Chair. UT-Battelle-ORNL Corp. Fellow Council; mem. Advisory Bd, NanoTech Briefs, Journal of the Korean Institute of Applied Superconductivity, Recent Patents on Materials Science, Superconductor Science & Technology; mem. Editorial Bd, Journal of Materials Research, Journal of the American Ceramic Society; fmr Guest Ed. Journal of Minerals, Metals and Materials; Chair. Electronics Div., American Ceramic Soc.; Fellow, Materials Research Soc., World Innovation Foundation, AAAS 2004, ASM International 2005, American Ceramic Soc. 2007, American Physical Soc. 2008, World Technology Network 2009; MIT Technology Review TR100 Award 1999, Global Indus Technovator Award 2005, Pride of India Gold Award 2007, Distinguished Alumnus Award, Indian Inst. of Tech., Kharagpur 2009, Innovator of the Year Award, R&D Magazine 2010, inaugural E.O. Lawrence Award for Energy Science and Innovation 2011, MRS Fellow 2012, World Technology Award (Advanced Materials) 2012, R&D 100 Award 2013. *Publications:* 30 invited book chapters and papers, six co-edited books, more than 350 papers in professional journals and 80 patents. *Address:* Oak Ridge National Laboratory, PO Box 2008, Oak Ridge, TN 37831, USA (office). *Telephone:* (865) 574-1587 (office). *E-mail:* goyala@ornl.gov (office). *Website:* www.ornl.gov/our-people/corporate-fellows/amit-goyal (office).

GOYAL, Naresh, BCom; Indian airline executive; b. 23 Dec. 1950, Patiala, Punjab; s. of Chowdhury Jagdish Rai; m. Anita Goyal 1988; one s. one d.; ed Bikram Coll. of Commerce, Patiala; began career as ticketing and reservations clerk, Lebanese Int. Airlines 1967, various man. positions 1967–74; f. Jetair (Private) Ltd May 1974, f. Jet Airways (India) Private Ltd 1991, Chair. 1991–2019, Chair. JetLite 2007–19; Owner, Tailwinds Holding Co.; mem. Bd of Govs Int. Air Transport Asscn 2004–06, 2008–10; Order of Leopold II (Belgium) 2011; AIMO Visvesvaraya Entrepreneurship Award 1993, Bharat Sarathi Samman Award 1995, Priyadarshni Acad. Award 2000, Ernst & Young Entrepreneur of the Year for Services Award 2000, Distinguished Alumni Award 2000, Aerospace Laurels 2000, 2004, ITFT Chandigarh Award of Excellence 2001, Qimpro Gold Standard Award 2001, Outstanding Asian-Indian Award, American Centre for Political Awareness 2003, BML Munjal Award 2006, Travel Entrepreneur of the Year, Travel Trade Gazette Travel Awards 2007, Man of the Year Award, Aviation Press Club 2008, Business Person of the Year, UK Trade and Investment 2008, Int. Entrepreneurs of the Year, UK Sec. of State for Transport 2009, Lifetime Achievement Award, Travel Agents Asscn of India 2010, Amity Leadership Award for Business Excellence 2012. *Address:* c/o Jet Airways (India) Private Ltd, SM Centre, Andheri-Kurla Road, Andheri East, Mumbai 400 059, India (office). *Telephone:* (22) 56986111 (office). *Fax:* (22) 28501313 (office). *Website:* www.jetairways.com (office).

GOYDER, Richard J. B., AO, BCom; Australian business executive; *Chairman, Qantas;* b. 1960; ed Univ. of Western Australia, Advanced Man. Program at Harvard Business School, USA; held several positions with Tubemakers of Australia Ltd; joined Wesfarmers Ltd 1993, Gen. Man., Business Devt 1994–96, Finance Dir, Wesfarmers Landmark Ltd 1996–99, Man. Dir, Wesfarmers Dalgety Ltd (subsequently became Wesfarmers Landmark Ltd) 1999–2002, mem. Bd of Dirs, Wesfarmers Ltd 2002–, Finance Dir 2002–04, Deputy Man. Dir and Chief Financial Officer 2004–05, CEO and Man. Dir 2005–17, mem. Bd of Dirs, Gresham Partners Holdings Ltd and several Wesfarmers group subsidiaries and related cos; Chair. Scotch Coll. Council, Australian B20 (business advisory body to int. econ. forum that includes business leaders from all G20 economies) 2013–; Chair. Qantas 2018–; mem. Bd of Dirs Fremantle Football Club Ltd, Business Council of Australia, Univ. of Western Australia Business School Advisory Bd; Council mem. Australian Business Arts Foundation; Advisory Council mem. Juvenile Diabetes Research Foundation; Fellow, Australian Inst. of Co. Dirs. *Website:* www.qantas.com (office).

GOZON, Richard C., BS; American business executive; b. 9 Oct. 1938, Pittsburgh, Pa; m. Fran Gozon (neé Burmeister); three c.; ed Valparaiso Univ., Harvard Univ.; began career in paper industry at Nationwide Papers 1970–72; joined Alco Standard Group as Pres. Rourke-Eno Paper Co. 1972–78, Exec. Vice-Pres. Unisource Corpn 1978–79, Pres. 1979, Pres. and CEO Paper Corpn of America 1979–87, elected mem. Bd of Dirs Alco Standard Group 1984, Exec. Vice-Pres. and COO 1987–88, Pres. and CEO 1988–93; Exec. Vice-Pres. for Pulp, Paper and Packaging, Weyerhaeuser Co. 1994–2002; mem. Bd of Dirs, AmeriSource Health Corpn 1994–2001, AmerisourceBergen Corpn 2001–16, Chair. 2006–16 (retd); mem. Bd of Dirs UGI Corpn 1989–2011, AmeriGas Partners LP 1998–2011, Triumph Group, Inc.; mem. Bd of Trustees (Chair.), Thomas Jefferson Univ., Interim Pres. 2012–13. *Address:* c/o AmerisourceBergen Corporation, 1300 Morris Drive, Suite 100, Chesterbrook, PA 19087, USA. *E-mail:* info@amerisourcebergen.com.

GRAB, Christoph, PhD; Swiss physicist; *Senior Scientist, Institute for Particle Physics, Eidgenössische Technische Hochschule (ETH), Zürich;* Fellowships include at Univ. of California, Berkeley, USA, Stanford Univ. (SLAC), USA, CERN, Geneva, Switzerland, DESY, Hamburg, Germany, Paul Scherrer Inst., Switzerland; currently Sr Scientist, Inst. for Particle Physics, ETH, Zürich, Switzerland; Swiss Rep., High Energy Physics Computing Coordinating Cttee; mem. Particle Data Group, CMS Experiment, CERN, H1 Experiment, DESY. *Publications:* numerous publs in scientific journals. *Address:* ETH Zürich, Institute for Particle Physics, Hönggerberg HPK/E 25, Otto-Stern-Weg 5, 8093 Zürich, Switzerland (office). *Telephone:* (1) 6332022 (office). *Fax:* (1) 6331233 (office). *E-mail:* grab@phys.ethz.ch (office). *Website:* www.ipp.phys.ethz.ch (office).

GRABAR-KITAROVIĆ, Kolinda, MA; Croatian diplomatist, politician and head of state; *President;* b. 29 April 1968, Rijeka, Socialist Repub. of Croatia, Socialist Fed. Repub. of Yugoslavia; m. Jakov Kitarović; one s. one d.; ed Los Alamos High School, NM, USA, Univ. of Zagreb, Diplomatic Acad., Vienna, Austria, George Washington Univ., USA; lived in USA for part of her childhood; Asst, then Adviser, Dept for Int. Co-operation, Ministry of Science and Tech. 1992–93; Adviser, then Sr Adviser to Deputy Minister, Ministry of Foreign Affairs 1993–95, Head of Dept for N America 1995–97; Diplomatic Counsellor, Embassy in Ottawa, Canada 1997–98, Minister Counsellor 1998–2000; Minister Counsellor, Ministry of Foreign Affairs 2001–03; mem. Parl. 2003–08; Minister for European Integration 2003–05; Nat. Aid Co-ordinator 2004; Head Del. for negotiations on accession to EU 2005; Minister of Foreign Affairs and European Integration 2005–08; Amb. to USA 2008–11; Asst Sec.-Gen. for Public Diplomacy, NATO, Brussels 2011–14; Pres. of Croatia Feb. 2015–; mem. Hrvatska Demokratska Zajednica (Croatian Democratic Union) 1993–2015, Deputy Campaign Dir, Sec.-Gen. for European Integration, mem. Cen. Cttee, Nat. Council, Presidency; mem. Trilateral Comm.; Presidential Medal, George Washington Univ. *Leisure interests:* literature, educ. and protection of children, hiking and walks in nature, film. *Address:* Office of the President, 10000 Pantovčak 241, Zagreb, Croatia (office). *Telephone:* (1) 4565191 (office). *Fax:* (1) 4565299 (office). *E-mail:* ured@predsjednica.hr (office). *Website:* www.predsjednica.hr (office).

GRABINER, Baron (Life Peer), cr. 1999, of Aldwych in the City of Westminster; **Anthony Stephen Grabiner,** QC, LLM MA; British barrister and college principal; b. 21 March 1945, London; s. of Ralph Grabiner and Freda Grabiner (née Cohen); m. Jane Aviva Portnoy 1983; three s. one d.; ed Cen. Foundation Boys' Grammar School, London School of Econs; called to the Bar (Lincoln's Inn) 1968; Droop Scholar, Lincoln's Inn 1968; Jr Counsel to Dept of Trade 1976–81; QC 1981; Bencher 1989–; Treas. of Lincoln's Inn 2013; Deputy High Court Judge, Chancery and Queen's Bench Divs 1998–; Vice-Chair. Court of Govs LSE 1993–98, Chair. 1998–2007; Head of Chambers One Essex Court 1994–; Leader, HM Treasury Inquiry into Black Economy 1999–2000; Chair. (non-exec.) Taveta Investments 2002–17; mem. Bd of Dirs (non-exec.) Next PLC 2002; mem. (Labour), House of Lords 1999–; Master of Clare Coll., Cambridge 2014–; mem. Advisory Bd Best Lawyers; mem. Financial Services Law Cttee, Bank of England 2002–05; Hon. Fellow, LSE 2009. *Publications:* Sutton and Shannon on Contracts 1970, The Informal Economy 2000. *Leisure interests:* golf, theatre. *Address:* One Essex Court, Temple, London, EC4Y 9AR, England (office). *Telephone:* (20) 7583-2000 (office). *Fax:* (20) 7583-0118 (office). *E-mail:* agrabiner@oeclaw.co.uk (office). *Website:* www.oeclaw.co.uk (office).

GRACH, Eduard Davidovich; Russian violinist; b. 19 Dec. 1930, Odessa; s. of David Grach and Evelina Grach; m. 2nd Valentina Vasilenko 1990; one s. one d.; ed P. Stolyarsky Odessa School of Music, Moscow State Conservatory (pupil of A. Yampolsky); winner of int. competitions in Budapest (First Prize) 1949, J. Thibaud in Paris 1955, P. Tchaikovsky in Moscow 1962; solo performances since 1953 in most countries of Europe; performer of classical and contemporary concertos and sonatas for violin; participant in trio with pianist Y. Malinin and cellist N. Shakhovskaya 1960–70; first performer of a number of works by Russian composers dedicated to him, including concertos by A. Eshpai; Head of Violin Dept, Moscow State Conservatory; Founder and Artistic Dir Moskovia Chamber Orchestra 1994–; Hon. Prof., Shanghai Conservatory, Sichuan Conservatory, Yakutian High School of Music, Univ. of Indianapolis; Hon. mem. Italian Monti Azzuri Acad.; Order for Services to the Fatherland, IV degree 1999, III degree 2005, Order of National Merit 2011, Kt, Imperial Order of St Anna 2015; People's Artist of USSR 1987, 1990, Prize of Moscow 2004, Laureate of the State Prize, Republic of Sakha 2009, Medal of the Int. Fund for Eugène Ysaÿe. *Leisure interest:* football. *Address:* Moscow State Conservatory, 125009 Moscow, Bolshaya Nikitskaya str. 13/6 (office); 1st Smolensky per. 9, kv. 98, 121099 Moscow, Russia (home). *Telephone:* (495) 241-21-57 (home). *Fax:* (495) 241-21-57 (home). *E-mail:* spravka@mosconsv.ru (office). *Website:* www.mosconsv.ru (office).

GRACIAS, HE Cardinal Oswald Anthony Agnelo, DCL, DiplJur; Indian ecclesiastic; *Archbishop of Bombay;* b. 24 Dec. 1944, Bombay (now Mumbai); s. of Jervis Gracias and Aduzinda Gracias; ed St Michael's School Mumbai, St Xavier's Coll. Mumbai, Pontifical Urbanian Univ., Rome, Gregorian Univ., Rome; ordained priest of Bombay 1970; Chancellor Diocese of Jamshedpur and Sec. to Diocesan Bishop 1970–75; Auxiliary Bishop of Bombay and Titular Bishop of Bladia 1997–2000; Archbishop of Agra 2000–06, of Bombay 2006–; cr. Cardinal (Cardinal-Priest of San Paulo della Croce a 'Corviale') 2007; participated in Papal Conclave 2013; Sec.-Gen. Catholic Bishops' Conf. of India (CBCI) 1998–2002, Vice-Pres. 2008–10, Pres. 2010–, Chair. CBCI Comm. for Social Communication 2002–, CBCI Comm. for Law and Public Litigation 2002–; Sec.-Gen. Feds of Bishops' Conf. of Asia; Chair. Nat. Inst. of Social Communications, Research and Training, New Delhi 2002–; Pres. Canon Law Soc. of India 1987–91 and 1993–97; Vice-Chair. Vatican's Vox Clara Cttee (advises Congregation for Divine Worship and Sacraments on trans. of Latin liturgical texts into English) 2001–, consultor to Pontifical Council for Interpretation of Legis. Texts 1992–97, currently mem.; currently Pres. Catholic Bishops' Conf. of India; teaches Canon Law at Pius X Seminary, Mumbai and St Peter's Pontifical Inst., Bangalore. *Publications include:* Conciliation Code. *Address:* Archbishop's House, 21 Nathalal Parekh Marg, Mumbai 400 001, India (office). *Telephone:* (22) 22021093 (office); (22) 22021193 (office). *Fax:* (22) 22853872 (office). *E-mail:* diocesebombay@gmail.com (office). *Website:* www.archdioceseofbombay.org (office).

GRADE OF YARMOUTH, Baron (Life Peer), cr. 2011, of Yarmouth in the County of Isle of Wight; **Rt Hon. Michael Ian Grade,** CBE, FRTS; British broadcasting executive; b. 8 March 1943, London, England; s. of Leslie Grade; m. 1st Penelope

Jane Levinson 1967 (divorced 1981); one s. one d.; m. 2nd Hon. Sarah Lawson 1982 (divorced 1991); m. 3rd Francesca Mary Leahy 1998; one s.; ed Stowe House, Bucks., St Dunstan's Coll., London; trainee journalist, Daily Mirror 1960, sports columnist 1964–66; theatrical agent, Grade Org. 1966; Jt Man. Dir London Man. and Representation 1969–73; Deputy Controller of Programmes (Entertainment), London Weekend TV 1973–77, Dir of Programmes and mem. Bd 1977–81; Pres. Embassy TV 1981–84; Controller BBC One 1984–86, Dir of Programmes BBC TV 1986–87; CEO Channel 4 1988–97; Chair. VCI PLC 1995–98; Chair. and CEO First Leisure Corpn 1997–98 (Dir 1991–2000, Chair. (non-exec.) 1995–97); Chair. Ind. Inquiry into Fear of Crime 1989, Devt Council, Royal Nat. Theatre 1997–; Deputy Chair. Soc. of Stars 1995–; Pres. TV and Radio Industries Club 1987–88, Newspaper Press Fund 1988–89, Entertainment Charities Fund 1994–, Royal TV Soc. 1995–97; Vice-Pres. Children's Film Unit 1993–; mem. Bd of Dirs ITN 1989–93, Open Coll. 1989–97, Delfont Macintosh Theatres Ltd 1994–99, Charlton Athletic Football Club 1997–, Jewish Film Foundation 1997–, New Millennium Experience Co. 1997–99, Camelot Group 2000–04, Digitaloctopus 2000–; Chair. Octopus 2000–04, Pinewood Studio Ltd 2000–, Hemscott.NET 2000–06, BBC 2004–06; Exec. Chair. ITV 2006–09, Chair. (non-exec.) 2009; Chair. (non-exec.) Ocado Group PLC 2006–13; Chair. (non-exec.) James Grant Group Ltd 2010–; Dir (non-exec.) SMG 2003–06; mem. Council, London Acad. of Music and Dramatic Art 1981–93, BAFTA 1981–82, 1986–88, 2004– (Fellow 1994), Milton Cttee, British Screen Advisory Council 1986–97, Gate Theatre, Dublin 1990–2004, Int. Council Nat. Acad. of TV Arts and Sciences 1991–97, Cities in Schools 1991–95, Cinema and TV Benevolent Fund 1993–2004, Nat. Comm. of Inquiry into Prevention of Child Abuse 1994–96, Royal Acad. of Dramatic Art 1996–2004, Royal Albert Hall 1997–2004, 300 Group, Press Complaints Comm. 2011–; mem. Bd of Govs BANFF TV Festival 1997–99; Trustee, Band Aid, Nat. Film and TV School, Virgin Health Care Foundation; mem. (Conservative) House of Lords 2011–; Hon. Prof., Thames Valley Univ. 1994; Hon. Treas. Stars Org. for Spastics 1986–92; Hon. LLD (Nottingham) 1997; Royal TV Soc. Gold Medal 1997. *Publication:* It Seemed Like a Good Idea at the Time (autobiog.) 1999. *Leisure interests:* entertainment, Charlton Athletic Football Club. *Address:* James Grant Group Ltd, 94 Strand on the Green, Chiswick, London, W4 3NN (office); House of Lords, Westminster, London, SW1A 0PW, England. *Telephone:* (20) 8742-4950 (office); (20) 7219-5353. *E-mail:* enquiries@jgg.co.uk (office). *Website:* www.jg-group.co.uk (office); www.parliament.uk/biographies/lords/lord-grade-of-yarmouth/4228.

GRADIN, Anita; Swedish politician (retd); b. 12 Aug. 1933, Hörnefors, Västerbotten Co.; m. Bertil Kersfelt; one d.; ed Coll. of Social Work and Public Admin., Stockholm and in USA; journalist 1950, 1956–58, 1960–63; with Swedish Union of Forest Workers and Log Drivers 1952; with Social Welfare Planning Cttee and Municipal Exec. Bd Cttee on Women's Issues, Stockholm 1963–67; mem. Exec. Cttee, Nat. Fed. of Social Democratic Women 1964–93, Vice-Chair. 1975–93; mem. Stockholm City Council 1966–68; First Sec. Cabinet Office 1967–82; mem. SDP Exec. Cttee of Stockholm 1968–82; mem. Parl. 1968–92; Chair. Dist Br., Fed. of Social Democratic Women, Stockholm 1968–82; Chair. Swedish Union of Social Workers and Public Admin. 1970–81; Chair. Nat. Bd for Intercountry Adoptions 1973–80; del. Council of Europe 1973–82, Chair. Cttee on Migration, Refugees and Democracy 1978–82; Minister with responsibility for Migration and Equality Affairs 1982–86; Vice-Chair. Socialist International Women's Council 1983–86, Chair. Socialist International Women 1986–92, Vice-Chair. Socialist International 1986–92; Minister with responsibility for Foreign Trade and European Affairs 1986–91; Amb. to Austria, Slovenia and to UN insts including IAEA, UNIDO and UNRWA 1992–94; EC Commr for Migration, Home and Judicial Affairs 1995–99; Chair. Research Council of Social Science and Working Life 2001–04; Chair. of Stockholm Conf. on Viet Nam 1974–76, of Swedish Cttee for Viet Nam, Laos and Cambodia 1977–82, Sr Club, Foreign Office 2002; mem. Exec. Cttee of RFSU (Nat. Asscn for Sexual Enlightenment) and Otterfonden 1969–92; mem. EFTA del. 1991–92; mem. Bd Stockholm School of Econs, Women's Forum 2001–08, Comm. on Gene Medicine 2002–08; Cavalieri di Gran Croce (Italy) 1991, Das Grosse Goldene Ehrenzeichen am Bande (Austria) 1994, The King's Medal in the 12th Dimension with ribbon of the Royal Order of the Seraphim 1998, European of the Year 2007; Dr hc (Umeå Univ.) 2002; Marisa Bellizario European Prize (Italy) 1998; Pro Merito Medal, Council of Europe 1982, Wizo Woman of the Year 1986. *Leisure interests:* fishing, reading books, jazz music. *Address:* Fleminggatan 85, 11245 Stockholm, Sweden (home). *Telephone:* (8) 269872 (home). *Fax:* (8) 269872 (home). *E-mail:* gradin.kersfelt@telia.com (home).

GRADY, Monica Mary, CBE, BSc, PhD; British meteoritic scientist and academic; *Professor of Planetary and Space Sciences, Planetary and Space Sciences Research Institute, Open University;* b. Leeds, Yorks.; m. Dr Ian Wright; ed Univs of Durham and Cambridge; Head of Div., Petrology and Meteoritics, Natural History Museum, London, Leader, Meteorites and Micrometeorites Programme, Curator Meteorite Collection, Ed. Catalogue of Meteorites 1991–2005; Prof. of Planetary and Space Sciences, Planetary and Space Sciences Research Inst., Open Univ., Milton Keynes 2005–; mem. UK Astrobiology Panel, UK Planetary Forum; mem. Particle Physics and Astronomy Council's Science Cttee 2005–07; Fellow, Meteoritical Soc., Royal Astronomical Soc., Mineralogical Soc.; Hon. Reader in Geological Sciences, University Coll., London; Asteroid (4731) Monicagrady named after her; Royal Inst. Christmas Lecturer 2003. *Publications:* Meteorites: Flux with Time and Impact Effects 1998, Catalogue of Meteorites 2000, Search for Life 2001, Meteorites (co-author) (second edn) 2002, Atlas of Meteorites 2013. *Address:* Faculty of Science, Planetary and Space Sciences Research Institute, Walton Hall, Milton Keynes, MK7 6AA, England (office). *Telephone:* (1908) 659251 (office). *Fax:* (1908) 858022 (office). *E-mail:* m.m.grady@open.ac.uk (office). *Website:* www.open.ac.uk/science (office).

GRAF, Hans; Austrian conductor and music director; b. 15 Feb. 1949, Linz; m. Margarita Graf; one d.; ed Bruckner Conservatory, Linz, Acad. of Music, Graz, studied in Italy with Franco Ferrara and Sergui Celibadache and in Russia with Arvid Jansons; Music Dir Iraqi Nat. Symphony Orchestra 1975–76, Mozarteum Orchestra, Salzburg 1984–94, Calgary Philharmonic Orchestra 1995–2003 (Music Dir Laureate 2006–), Orchestre Nat. de Bordeaux-Aquitaine 1998–2004, Opéra de Bordeaux 1998–2004, Houston Symphony 2001–13 (Conductor Laureate 2013–); guest conductor with several orchestras including Vienna Symphony, Vienna Philharmonic, Orchestre Nat. de France, Leningrad Philharmonic, Pittsburgh Symphony, Boston Symphony, Royal Concertgebouw Orchestra, Deutsches Symphony Orchestra, Bavarian Radio Orchestra; Prof. of Orchestral Conducting, Univ. Mozarteum Salzburg 2013–15; Chevalier, Légion d'honneur 2002, Grand Honour in Gold (Austria) 2007; First Prize, Karl Böhm Conductors Competition, Salzburg 1979. *Recordings include:* Anton Bruckner: Symphony Nr. 4 2004, George Gershwin: An American in Paris 2007, Gustav Holst: The Planets 2010, Carl Orff: Carmina Burana 2014, Alban Berg: Wozzeck (ECHO Klassik Prize 2017, Grammy Award for Best Opera Recording 2018) 2017. *Leisure interests:* literature, fine wine, jazz. *Address:* CM Artists, 127 West 96th Street, 13B, New York, NY 10025, USA (office). *Telephone:* (212) 864-1005 (office). *Website:* www.cmartists.com/artists/hans-graf.htm (office).

GRAF, Stefanie (Steffi) M.; German fmr professional tennis player; b. 14 June 1969, Mannheim; d. of Peter Graf and Heidi Graf; m. Andre Agassi (q.v.) 2001; one s. one d.; coached by her father; won Orange Bowl 12s 1981, European 14-and-under and European Circuit Masters 1982, Olympic demonstration event, LA; winner German Open 1986, French Open 1987, 1988, 1993, 1995, 1996, 1999; Australian Open 1988, 1989, 1990, 1994; Wimbledon 1988, 1989, 1991, 1992, 1993, 1995, 1996, US Open 1988, 1989, 1993, 1995, 1996, won ATP Tour World Championship 1996, German Open 1989, numerous women's doubles championships with Gabriela Sabatini, Federation Cup 1992; Olympic Champion 1988; ranked No. 1 Aug. 1987; named Official World Champion 1988; Grand Slam winner 1988, 1989; youngest player to win 500 singles victories as a professional Oct. 1991; 118 tournament wins, 23 Grand Slam titles; announced retirement Aug. 1999; Amb. World Wildlife Fund 1984–; Founder and Chair. Children for Tomorrow (charitable foundation); Amb. of EXPO 2000; Olympic Order 1999, German Medal of Honour 2002. *Publication:* Wege Zum Erfolg 1999. *Leisure interests:* music, dogs, photography, art, reading. *Address:* Steffi Graf Ventures, 3883 Howard Hughes Pkwy, #8, Las Vegas, NV 89169, USA; Stefanie Graf Marketing GmbH & Co.KG, Gartenstrasse 1, 68723 Schwetzingen, Germany. *Website:* www.stefanie-graf.com; www.children-for-tomorrow.com.

GRAHAM, Sir Alexander Michael, Kt, GBE, KStJ, JP, DCL, CBIM, FCII, FCIS, FRSA; British chartered insurance broker; b. 27 Sept. 1938, London, England; s. of Dr Walter Graham and Suzanne Simon; m. Carolyn Stansfeld 1964; three d.; ed St Paul's School; nat. service with Gordon Highlanders 1957–59; broker, Frizzell Group Ltd 1957–67, Dir 1967–73, Man. Dir 1973–90, Deputy Chair. 1990–92; Alderman, City of London 1979–, Sheriff 1986–87, Lord Mayor 1990–91; Chair. Nat. Employers Liaison Cttee for TA and Reserve Forces 1992–97; Chair. First City Insurance Brokers Ltd 1993–98; Chair. Council, Order of St John, Herts. 1993–2001; Chair. Bd of Trustees, Morden Coll. 1995–2013; Chair. Folgate Insurance Co. Ltd 1995–2002, Employment Conditions Abroad Ltd 1993–2005, Euclidian PLC 1994–2001, United Response 1994–2002; Pres. British Insurance Law Asscn 1994–96; Underwriting mem. of Lloyd's; Fellow, Chartered Insurance Inst.; Liveryman, Mercers' Co. 1971–, Master 1983–84; Vice-Pres. Royal Soc. of St George 1999–; Hon. DCL, DLitt; Grand Cross, Order of Merit (Chile), Order of Wissam Alouite Class 3 (Morocco). *Leisure interests:* golf, swimming, wine, music, calligraphy. *Address:* Walden Abbotts, Whitwell, Hitchin, Herts., SG4 8AJ, England (home). *Telephone:* (1438) 871223 (home). *E-mail:* alexander66graham@gmail.com (office).

GRAHAM, Andrew Winston Mawdsley, MA; British economist and academic; b. 20 June 1942, Perranporth, Cornwall; s. of Winston Mawdsley Graham; m. Peggotty Fawssett 1970; ed Charterhouse, St Edmund Hall, Oxford; Econ. Asst, Nat. Econ. Devt Office 1964, with Dept of Econ. Affairs 1964–66, Asst to Econ. Adviser to Cabinet 1966–68, Econ. Adviser to Prime Minister 1968–69; Fellow and Tutor in Econs, Balliol Coll. Oxford 1969–97, Estates Bursar 1978, Investment Bursar 1979–83, Vice-Master 1988, 1992–94, Acting Master 1997–2001, Master 2001–11; Policy Adviser to Prime Minister (leave of absence from Balliol) 1974–76; mem. ILO/JASPA Employment Advisory Mission to Ethiopia 1982; Head of Commonwealth/Food Studies Group assisting Govt of Zambia 1984; Econ. Adviser to Shadow Chancellor of Exchequer 1988–92, to Leader of Opposition 1992–94; Tutor, Oxford Univ. Business Summer School 1971, 1972, 1973, 1976; Visiting Scholar, MIT 1994; Chair. St James Group (Econ. Forecasting) 1982–84, 1985–92; Dir, Scott Trust (owner of the Guardian and the Observer) 2005–; consultant, BBC 1989–92; mem. Bd Channel 4 TV 1998–2005; Founder and Acting Dir Oxford Internet Inst. (OII) 2001, Founding Chair. OII Advisory Bd 2001–11, Sr Fellow 2011–; mem. Media Advisory Cttee, Inst. for Public Policy Research 1994–97, Council of Man. Templeton Coll. Oxford 1990–96, Council of Oxford Univ. 2006–; Founder-mem. Editorial Bd Library of Political Economy 1982–94; mem. Bd Channel Four Television Ltd 1998–2005; Sr Fellow, Gorbachev Foundation of N America 1999–; Trustee, Foundation for Information Policy Research 1998–2001, Esmée Fairbairn Foundation 2003–05, Oxford Centre for Islamic Studies 2007–10; Hon. DCL (Oxon.) 2003. *Publications:* Government and Economies in the Postwar Period (ed.) 1990, Broadcasting, Society and Policy in the Multimedia Age (co-author) 1997; contribs to books on econs and philosophy. *Leisure interest:* windsurfing. *Address:* Oxford Internet Institute, 1 St Giles, Oxford, OX1 3JS, England (office). *Telephone:* (1865) 287210 (office). *E-mail:* enquiries@oii.ox.ac.uk (office). *Website:* www.oii.ox.ac.uk (office).

GRAHAM, Christopher (Chris) Forbes, MA, DPhil, FRS; British biologist and academic; b. 23 Sept. 1940; s. of Christopher Graham and Elizabeth Campbell Wilson; m. Grizeide George Harris 1975; one s. one d.; ed King's School, Canterbury, Univ. of Oxford; fmrly Jr Beit Memorial Fellow in Medical Research, Sir William Dunn School of Pathology; Lecturer, Dept of Zoology, Univ. of Oxford 1970–85, fmr Prof. of Animal Devt, Professorial Fellow, St Catherine's Coll., Oxford 1985; mem. British Soc. for Cell Biology, British Soc. for Developmental Biology, Soc. for Experimental Biology, Genetical Soc. *Publications include:* The Developmental Biology of Plants and Animals 1976 (co-ed.), Developmental Control in Plants and Animals 1984.

GRAHAM, Daniel Robert (Bob), BA, LLD; American academic and fmr politician; b. 9 Nov. 1936, Coral Gables, Fla; s. of Ernest R. Graham and Hilda Graham (née Simmons); m. Adele Khoury 1959; four d.; ed Univ. of Florida, Harvard Law School; Vice-Pres. Sengra Devt Corpn 1963–79; mem. Fla State House of Reps from Coral Gables 1966–70; mem. Fla State Senate from Coral Gables 1970–78; Gov. of Fla 1979–87, Senator from Fla 1986–2005, mem. Senate Select Cttee on Intelligence (Chair. 2001–02); unsucessful cand. for Democratic nomination for Pres. of US 2004; Sr Research Fellow, Belfer Center for Science and

Int. Affairs, John F. Kennedy School of Govt, Harvard Univ. 2005–06; fmr Commr, Financial Crisis Inquiry Comm.; Chair. Comm. on the Prevention of Weapons of Mass Destruction Proliferation and Terrorism 2007–08, Chair. WMD Center 2010–12; Co-Chair. Nat. Comm. on BP Deepwater Horizon Oil Spill and Offshore Drilling 2010–11; mem. Council of Advisors, Bob Graham Center for Public Service, Univ. of Fla 2008–; mem. Bd of Dirs ACT Inc.; mem. CIA External Advisory Bd, Poynter Foundation; Hon. mem. American Soc. of Landscape Architects; Dr hc (Pomona Coll.), (Nova Southeastern Univ.); Audubon Soc. Conservation Award 1974, Woodrow Wilson Inst. Award for Public Service, National Park Trust Public Service Award, LeRoy Collins Lifetime Leadership Award, Leadership Florida. *Publications include:* Intelligence Matters (with Jeff Nussbaum) 2004, America: The Owners Manual (with Chris Hand) 2011, Keys to the Kingdom 2011. *Leisure interests:* golf, tennis and reading. *Address:* Bob Graham Center for Public Service, 220 Pugh Hall, Gainesville, FL 32611-2030, USA (office). *Telephone:* (352) 846-1575 (office). *Website:* www.bobgrahamcenter.ufl.edu (office).

GRAHAM, Donald (Don) Edward, BA; American newspaper publisher; *Chairman and CEO, Graham Holdings Company;* b. 22 April 1945, Baltimore, Md; s. of Philip L. Graham and Katharine Meyer Graham; m. 1st Mary L. Wissler 1967 (divorced 2007); one s. three d.; m. 2nd Amanda Bennett 2012; ed Harvard Univ.; joined the Washington Post 1971, Asst Man. Ed. (Sports) 1974–75, Asst Gen. Man. 1975–76, Exec. Vice-Pres. and Gen. Man. 1976–79, Publr 1979–2000, Chair. 2000–08; CEO The Washington Post Co. 1991–2014, Chair. 1993–2014; Chair. and CEO Graham Holdings Company 2014–; fmrly reporter and writer for Newsweek. *Address:* Graham Holdings Company, 1300 North 17th Street, 17th Floor, Arlington, VA 22209, USA (office). *Telephone:* (703) 345-6300 (office). *E-mail:* contact@ghco.com (office). *Website:* www.ghco.com (office).

GRAHAM, James (see PATTERSON, Harry).

GRAHAM, Jorie, BFA, MFA; American poet and academic; *Boylston Professor of Rhetoric and Oratory, Harvard University;* b. 9 May 1950, New York City; d. of Curtis Bill Pepper and Beverly Stoll Pepper; m. 1st William Graham (divorced); 2nd James Galvin 1983 (divorced 1999); 3rd Peter M. Sacks 2000; ed New York Univ. and Univ. of Iowa; Poetry Ed. Crazy Horse 1978–81, The Colorado Review 1990–; Contributing Ed., Boston Review, Conjunctions, Denver Quarterly; Asst Prof., Murray State Univ. 1978–79, Humboldt State Univ. 1979–81; Instructor, Columbia Univ. 1981–83; Bunting Fellow, Radcliffe Inst. 1982; staff mem. Writers' Workshop and Prof. of English, Univ. of Iowa 1983–98; Chancellor, Acad. of American Poets 1997–2003; Boylston Prof. of Rhetoric and Oratory in the Dept of English and American Literature and Language, Harvard Univ. 1998–; mem. American Acad. of Arts and Letters 2009–; American Acad. of Poets Award 1977, Poetry Northwest Young Poets Prize 1980, Pushcart Prizes 1980, 1982, Ingram Merrill Foundation grant 1981, Great Lakes Colleges Asscn Award 1981, American Poetry Review Prize 1982, Guggenheim Fellowship 1983–84, John D. and Catherine T. MacArthur Foundation Fellowship 1990, Morton Dauwen Zabel Award, American Acad. of Arts and Letters 1992, Int. Nonino Prize 2013, Wallace Stevens Award, Acad. of American Poets 2017. *Publications:* Hybrids of Plants and of Ghosts 1980, Erosion 1983, The End of Beauty 1987, The Best American Poetry (ed. with David Lehman) 1990, Region of Unlikeness 1991, Materialism 1993, The Dream of the Unified Field (Pulitzer Prize in Poetry 1996) 1995, Errancy 1997, Swarm 1999, Never 2002, Overlord 2004, Sea Change 2008, Place (Forward Poetry Prize 2012) 2012, From the New World: Poems (LA Times Book Award Prize in Poetry 2016) 1976–2014 2015, Fast (Rebekah Johnson Bobbitt Nat. Prize for Poetry 2018) 2017. *Address:* Department of English, Harvard University, Barker Center 263, 12 Quincy Street, Cambridge, MA 02138, USA (office). *Telephone:* (617) 495-2533 (office). *Fax:* (617) 496-8737 (office). *E-mail:* engdept@fas.harvard.edu (office). *Website:* english.fas.harvard.edu/people/jorie-graham (office); www.joriegraham.com.

GRAHAM, Lindsay O., BA, JD; American lawyer and politician; *Senator from South Carolina;* b. 9 July 1955, Central, South Carolina; s. of Florence James Graham and Millie Graham; ed D.W. Daniel High School, Clemson, South Carolina, Univ. of South Carolina; served in USAAF 1982–88, assignments included in Operation Desert Shield and Desert Storm, served as Base Staff Judge Advocate, McEntire Air Nat. Guard Base, Eastover 1989–94; est. pvt. law practice 1988; Asst Attorney in Oconee Co.; mem. S Carolina House of Reps from 2nd Dist Oconee Co. 1992–94; mem. US Congress from 3rd Dist S Carolina 1994–2003; Senator from S Carolina 2003–; Col Air Force Reserves 1995–2015, Sr Instructor for Judge Advocate Gen. (JAG) Corps (retd); Republican. *Address:* 290 Russell Senate Office Building, Washington, DC 20510, USA (office). *Telephone:* (202) 224-5972 (office). *Fax:* (202) 224-3808 (office). *Website:* lgraham.senate.gov (office).

GRAHAM, Patricia Albjerg, PhD; American academic; *Warren Professor Emerita, Graduate School of Education, Harvard University;* b. (Patricia Parks Albjerg), 9 Feb. 1935, Lafayette, Ind.; d. of Victor L. Albjerg and Marguerite Hall Albjerg; m. Loren R. Graham 1955; one d.; ed Purdue and Columbia Univs; teacher, Deep Creek and Maury High Schools, Norfolk, Va 1955–58; Chair. History Dept, St Hilda's and St Hugh's School, New York 1958–60, part-time Coll. Adviser 1961–63, 1965–67; Lecturer, Indiana Univ., School of Educ., Bloomington 1964–65; Asst Prof., Barnard Coll. and Columbia Teacher's Coll., New York 1965–68, Assoc. Prof. 1968–72, Prof. 1972–74; Prof., Harvard Univ. Grad. School of Educ., Cambridge, Mass 1974–79, Warren Prof. 1979–2006, Prof. Emer. 2006–, Dean, Grad. School of Educ. 1982–91; Dean, Radcliffe Inst. and Vice-Pres. Radcliffe Coll., Cambridge, Mass 1974–77; mem. Bd of Dirs Josiah Macy Jr Foundation 1976–77, 1979–2010; Dir Nat. Inst. of Educ. 1977–79; mem. Bd of Dirs Carnegie Foundation for the Advancement of Teaching 2009–16, (Chair. 2009–13); Vice-Pres. for Teaching, American Historical Asscn 1985–89; Pres. Nat. Acad. of Educ. 1985–89; Dir Spencer Foundation 1983–2000, Pres. 1991–2000; Dir Johnson Foundation 1983–2001, Hitachi Foundation 1985–2004; mem. AAAS (mem. Council 1993–96, Vice-Pres. 1998–2001), American Philosophical Soc. 1999–; mem. Bd of Dirs Center for Advanced Study in the Behavioral Sciences 2001–07; Dir Northwestern Mutual Life 1980–2005, Apache Corpn 2002–13; Trustee, Cen. European Univ. 2002–16; 15 hon. degrees; John Simon Guggenheim Award 1972–73, Woodrow Wilson Center Fellow 1981–82. *Publications include:* Progressive Education: From Arcady to Academe, A History of the Progressive Education Association 1967, Community and Class in American Education, 1865–1918 1974, Women in Higher Education (co-ed. with Todd Furniss) 1974, S.O.S. Sustain Our Schools 1992, Accountability (with Richard Lyman and Martin Trow) 1995, Schooling America 2005. *Address:* Harvard University Graduate School of Education, Appian Way, Cambridge, MA 02138, USA (office). *Telephone:* (617) 496-4839 (office). *Fax:* (617) 496-3095 (office). *E-mail:* patricia_graham@harvard.edu (office).

GRAHAM, Shawn; Canadian politician; b. 22 Feb. 1968, Kent Co., NB; s. of Alan Graham; m. Roxanne Reeves; ed Univ. of New Brunswick, St Thomas Univ.; mem. (Riding of Kent) Legis. Ass. of NB 1998–2010; Caucas Chair. Liberal Party of NB 1998–2002, Leader 2002–10; Premier of NB, Pres. Exec. Council, Minister of Wellness, Culture and Sport, of Intergovernmental Affairs, Minister responsible for the Premier's Council on the Status of Disabled Persons 2006–10; Chair. Council of Fed. 2007; Hon. LLD (Univ. of New Brunswick) 2009; Intelligent Community Visionary of Year Award, Intelligent Community Forum 2010.

GRAHAM, Stuart E., BSc; American construction industry executive; *Chairman, Skanska AB;* b. 1946; ed Holy Cross Univ.; Asst Field Supt, Sordoni Construction Co. 1969, Pres. Sordoni Skanska 1990–95, Pres. and CEO Slattery Skanska 1995–97, Pres. Skanska USA Inc. 1997–2001, Pres. and CEO Skanska AB 2002–08, Chair. 2009–; mem. Bd of Dirs Securitas AB 2005–11, PPL Corpn 2008–15; mem. and fmr Dir Construction Industry Round Table; Dr hc (Czech Tech. Univ.). *Address:* Skanska AB, Warfvinges väg 25, 112 74 Stockholm, Sweden (office). *Website:* group.skanska.com/ (office).

GRAHAM, Rt Hon William (Bill), PC, CM, BA, LLB, DJur; Canadian lawyer, academic and fmr politician; *Chancellor, Trinity College, University of Toronto;* b. 17 March 1939, Montreal, PQ; m. Catherine Graham; one s. one d.; ed Upper Canada Coll., Trinity Coll., Univ. of Toronto, Univ. of Paris, France; lawyer, Fasken and Calvin, Partner 1983–; Prof. of Law, Univ. of Toronto, Dir Centre of Int. Studies, Chancellor, Trinity Coll. 2007–; Visiting Prof., Université de Montréal, McGill Univ.; fmr Pres. Alliance Française, Toronto; MP 1993–2007, Chair. Standing Cttee on Foreign Affairs and Int. Trade 1995–2002; Minister of Foreign Affairs 2002–04, of Nat. Defence 2004–06; Parl. Opposition Leader 2006; Chair. Atlantic Council of Canada 2007–12, Advisory Bd, Bill Graham Centre for Contemporary Int. History 2011–; Co-Chair. Advisory Bd, Creative Destruction Lab 2012–18; Founding Pres. Inter-Parl. Forum of the Americas; Chair. Canadian Int. Council 2013–; fmr Vice-Pres. and Treas., Parl. Asscn of OSCE; mem. Inter-Parl. Council Against Anti-Semitism; Patron, Liberal Int; Hon. Life mem. Canadian Council of Int. Law; Hon. Lt Col, Gov. Gen.'s Horse Guards 2007–12, Hon. Col 2012–18; Hon. Col Canadian Special Operations Forces Command 2018–; Chevalier, Légion d'honneur, Ordre de la Pléiade, Ordre du mérite de l'Asscn des juristes de l'Ontario, Order of Canada 2014; Hon. LLD (Siena) 2010, (Royal Military Coll., Toronto) 2010, (Univ. of Toronto) 2018; Global Citizen Award, UNA, Canada 2016, Vimy Award, Conference of Defence Asscns 2017, Prix Jean-Baptiste Rousseaux, Médaille d'argent de la ville de Paris, Médaille d'or de l'alliance française, Golden Jubilee Medal, Diamond Jubilee Medal. *Publications:* The Canadian Law and Practice of International Trade (co-author), International Law: Chiefly as Interpreted and Applied in Canada (co-ed.), New Dimensions in International Trade Law (co-author), The Call of the World (political memoir) 2016. *Address:* 610-151 Bloor Street West, Toronto, ON M5S 1S4, Canada (office). *Telephone:* (416) 920-2205 (home). *Fax:* (416) 920-5140 (home). *E-mail:* bill.graham@afai.ca (office).

GRAHAM-DIXON, Andrew, MA; British critic, writer and broadcaster; *Chief Art Critic, Sunday Telegraph;* b. 26 Dec. 1960, London; s. of Antony Philip Graham-Dixon and Suzanne Graham-Dixon (née Villar); m. Sabine Marie-Pascale Tilly 1986; one s. two d.; ed Westminster School, Christ Church Coll. Oxford, Courtauld Inst., London; Chief Arts Critic, The Independent 1986–98; arts writer and presenter, BBC TV 1992–, Presenter, The Culture Show, BBC 2 2006–14; Curator Broken English, Serpentine Gallery, London 1992; Chief Arts Writer, Sunday Telegraph Magazine and columnist, In the Picture 1999–, Chief Art Critic, Sunday Telegraph 2005–; Trustee Baltic Centre of Contemporary Art 2005–; BP Arts Writer of the Year 1988, 1989, 1990; First Prize Reportage, Montreal Film & TV Festival 1992; Hawthornden Prize 1992. *Television includes:* Gericault 1992; TV documentary series: A History of British Art (also writer) 1996, Renaissance 1999, 1,000 Ways of Getting Drunk in England 2001, Secret Lives of the Artists 2003, The Elgin Marbles 2004, The Secret of Drawing 2005, The Art of Eternity 2007, The Art of Spain 2008, The Medici: Makers of Modern Art 2009, The Art of Russia 2010, The Art of Germany 2011, The Art of America 2011, Treasures of Heaven: The Art of Relics 2011, I Never Tell Anybody Anything: The Life and Work of Edward Burra (also Exec. producer) 2011, Cash in China's Attic 2012, Art of China 2014, Art of France 2017; TV mini series documentary: Sicily Unpacked (with Giorgio Locatelli) 2012, Italy Unpacked 2013–15, The Art of Gothic: Britain's Midnight Hour 2014, The Art of France (also writer) 2017, Rome Unpacked 2018, Art, Passion and Power: The Story of Royal Collection 2018; TV documentary movies: Midsummer Night's Dreaming 2004, I, Samurai 2006, 100% English 2006, Travels with Vasari 2008, Treasures of Heaven 2011, Secret of Mona Lisa 2015, Stealing Van Gogh 2018. *Publications:* Howard Hodgkin: A Monograph 1994, A History of British Art 1996, Paper Museum 1996, Renaissance 1999, In the Picture 2002, Michelangelo and the Sistine Chapel 2008, Caravaggio: A Life Sacred and Profane 2010. *Leisure interests:* walking, snooker, football, existentialism, golf. *E-mail:* info@andrewgrahamdixon.com. *Website:* www.andrewgrahamdixon.com.

GRAHAM-SMITH, Sir Francis, Kt, PhD, FRS, FRAS; British professor of radio astronomy; *Professor Emeritus of Physics, University of Manchester;* b. 25 April 1923, Roehampton, Surrey; m. Elizabeth Palmer 1946; three s. one d.; ed Rossall School, Epsom Coll., Downing Coll., Cambridge; with Telecommunications Research Establishment 1943–46; Cavendish Lab. 1947–64; 1851 Exhbn 1951–52; Warren Research Fellow, Royal Soc. 1959–64; Prof. of Radio Astronomy, Univ. of Manchester 1964–74, 1981–87, Pro-Vice-Chancellor 1987, Dir Nuffield Radio Astronomy Labs 1981–88, Langworthy Prof. of Physics 1987–90, Prof. Emer. 1990–; Deputy Dir Royal Greenwich Observatory 1974–75, Dir 1976–81; Astronomer Royal 1982–90; Visiting Prof. of Astronomy, Univ. of Sussex 1975–81; Sec. Royal Astronomical Soc. 1964–71, Pres. 1975–77; Sec., Vice-Pres. Royal Soc. 1988–94; Fellow, Downing Coll., Cambridge 1953–64, Hon. Fellow 1970; Chair. Govs Manchester Grammar School 1987–98; Hon. DSc (Queens Univ., Belfast) 1986, (Keele) 1987, (Birmingham) 1989, (Nottingham) 1990, (Trinity Coll. Dublin)

1990, (Manchester) 1993, (Salford) 2003, (Liverpool) 2003; Royal Medal, Royal Soc. 1987, Glazebrook Medal, Inst. of Physics 1991. *Publications:* Radio Astronomy 1960, Optics (with J. H. Thomson) 1971, Pulsars 1977, Pathways to the Universe (with Sir Bernard Lovell) 1988, Introduction to Radioastronomy (with B. F. Burke) 1997, Pulsar Astronomy (with A. G. Lyne) 1990 (third edn 2006), Optics and Photonics (with T. A. King) 2000, (with T. A. King and D. Wilkins) 2007. *Leisure interests:* gardening, beekeeping. *Address:* Old School House, Henbury, Macclesfield, Cheshire, SK11 9PH, England (home). *Telephone:* (1477) 571321 (office); (1625) 612657 (home). *E-mail:* fgs@jb.man.ac.uk (office); fgsegs@talktalk.net (home).

GRAINGE, Sir Lucian Charles, Kt, CBE; British music industry executive; *Chairman and CEO, Universal Music Group;* b. 1960, London; m.; three c.; song promoter April Music/CBS, later Head Creative Dept 1979–82; Dir and Gen. Man. RCA Music Publishing 1982–84; Dir of A&R MCA Records 1984–86; est. PolyGram Music Publishing UK office 1986–93; Gen. Man. A&R and business affairs, Polydor 1993–97, Man. Dir 1997–2001, following merger of Polygram and Universal promoted to Deputy Chair. Universal Music UK 2001, Chair. and CEO 2001–05, Chair. and CEO Universal Music Group Int. 2005–10, CEO Universal Music Group 2010–; Co-Chair. BRITS Cttee 2003–05; Dir BPI; bd mem. Int. Fed. of Phonographic Industry; Music Industry Trusts Award 2008, Humanitarian Award, Foundation for Ethnic Understanding 2013, SAG-AFTRA American Scene Award 2013, Salute to Industry Icons Award, Recording Acad. 2013. *Address:* Universal Music Group, 2220 Colorado Avenue, Santa Monica, CA 90404, USA (office). *Telephone:* (310) 865-4000 (office). *Website:* www.universalmusic.com (office).

GRAMEGNA, Pierre, DEA; Luxembourg politician and fmr diplomatist; *Minister of Finance;* b. 22 April 1958, Esch-sur-Alzette; m.; two c.; ed Univ. Panthéon-Assas (Paris 2), France; began career as correspondent, Républicain Lorrain; joined Ministry of Foreign Affairs (MFA) 1983, Political and Econ. Counsellor, Embassy in Paris 1988–92, Consul Gen. and Dir, Luxembourg Bd of Econ. Devt, San Francisco 1992, Amb. to Japan and Repub. of Korea 1996–2002, Dir of Int. Econ. Relations, MFA 2002–03; Dir-Gen., Luxembourg Chamber of Commerce 2003–13; Minister of Finance 2013–; fmr Dir several cos including Cargolux Airlines International SA (Pres. 2004–08), Bourse de Luxembourg SA, Société Nationale de Crédit et d'Investissement, LuxExpo Luxembourg, BGL-BNP Paribas Luxembourg SA. *Address:* Ministry of Finance, 3 rue de la Congrégation, 1352 Luxembourg, Luxembourg (office). *Telephone:* 247-82600 (office). *Fax:* 247-5241 (office). *Website:* www.mf.public.lu (office).

GRAMM, (William) Philip, PhD; American investment banker and fmr politician; *Senior Advisor, US Policy Metrics;* b. 8 July 1942, Fort Benning, Ga; s. of Kenneth M. Gramm and Florence Gramm (née Scroggins); m. Wendy Lee Gramm 1970; two s.; ed Univ. of Georgia; mem. Faculty, Dept of Econs, Texas A&M Univ. 1967–78, Prof. 1973–78; Partner, Gramm & Assocs 1971–78; mem. US House of Reps, Washington, DC 1979–85; Senator from Texas 1985–2002, fmr Chair. Senate Steering Cttee, Banking, Housing and Urban Affairs Cttee; Vice-Chair. UBS Warburg LLC, Washington, DC 2003–11, now consultant; Sr Partner, US Policy Metrics (consultancy), Washington, DC 2012–; Visiting Scholar, American Enterprise Inst.; Republican. *Publications include:* The Economics of Mineral Extraction 1980, Role of Government in a Free Society 1982; articles in professional journals. *Address:* US Policy Metrics, 1333 New Hampshire Avenue, NW, Washington, DC 20036-1564, USA (office). *Telephone:* (202) 652-0037 (office). *Website:* www.uspolicymetrics.com (office).

GRAMMER, Kelsey; American actor and comedian; b. (Allen Kelsey Grammer), 21 Feb. 1955, St Thomas, US Virgin Islands; s. of Frank Allen Grammer, Jr and Sally Grammer (née Cranmer); m. 1st Doreen Alderman 1982 (divorced 1990); one d. and one d. with Barrie Buckner; m. 2nd Leigh-Anne Csuhany 1992 (divorced 1993); m. 3rd Camille Donatacci 1997 (divorced 2011); one s. one d.; m. 4th Kayte Walsh 2011; one s. one d.; ed Juilliard School; three-year internship with Old Globe Theatre, San Diego in late 1970s; worked at Guthrie Theater, Minneapolis, Minn. 1980; Broadway debut in Lennox in Macbeth 1981; Broadway musical debut playing role of Georges in revival of La Cage aux Folles 2010; American Comedy Award (Funniest Male Performer in a TV Series) 1995, 1996, Primetime Emmy Award (Outstanding Lead Actor in a Comedy Series) 1994, 1995, 1998, 2004, Golden Globe Award (Best Performance by an Actor in a TV-Series Comedy/Musical) 1996, 2001, Golden Globe Award (Best Performance by an Actor in a TV-Series Drama) 2012. *Films include:* Galaxies Are Colliding 1992, Down Periscope 1996, Anastasia (voice) 1997, The Real Howard Spitz 1998, New Jersey Turnpikes 1999, Standing on Fishes 1999, Toy Story 2 (voice) 1999, 15 Minutes 2001, The Big Empty 2003, Teacher's Pet (voice) 2004, The Good Humor Man 2005, Even Money 2006, X-Men: The Last Stand 2006, Swing Vote 2008, An American Carol 2008, Middle Men 2009, Fame 2009, Crazy on the Outside 2010, I Don't Know How She Does It 2011, Dorothy of Oz (voice) 2012, Legends of Oz: Dorothy's Return (voice) 2014, X-Men: Days of Future Past 2014, Transformers: Age of Extinction 2014, The Expendables 3 2014, Reach Me 2014. *Television includes:* Kennedy (mini-series) 1983, George Washington (mini-series) 1984, Cheers (series) 1984–93, Crossings (mini-series) 1986, Dance 'Til Dawn (film) 1988, Top of the Hill (film) 1989, 227 (series) 1989, The Simpsons (series) 1990–2010, Beyond Suspicion (film) 1993, Frasier (series) 1993–2004, The Innocent (film) 1994, London Suite (film) 1996, The Pentagon Wars (film) 1998, Just Shoot Me! (series) (narrator) 1998, Animal Farm (film) (voice) 1999, The Sports Pages (film) 2001, Mr. St. Nick (film) 2002, Benedict Arnold: A Question of Honor (film) 2003, Frasier: Analyzing the Laughter (film) 2004, A Christmas Carol (film) 2004, Kelsey Grammer Presents: The Sketch Show (series) 2005, The Kelsey Grammer Bill Zucker Comedy Hour (film) 2010, Hank (series) 2009–10, Boss (series) 2011, Partners 2014, Who Do You Think You Are? 2014; as exec. producer: Girlfriends 2000–08, Neurotic Tendencies (film) 2001, In-Laws 2002–03, The Soluna Project (film) 2004, The Game 2006–, Dash 4 Cash (film) 2007.

GRANDAGE, Michael, CBE; British theatre director; *Director, Michael Grandage Company;* b. 2 May 1962; ed Humphry Davy Grammar School, Cornwall, Cen. School of Speech and Drama; began theatre career as actor 1981–96; full-time dir 1996–, Assoc. Dir Sheffield Theatres (including Sheffield Crucible) 2000–05; Assoc. Dir Donmar Warehouse, London 2000–02, Artistic Dir 2002–12; Dir Michael Grandage Company 2012–; also Visiting Prof., Univ. of Sheffield; Pres. Central School of Speech and Drama; Dr hc (Univ. of Sheffield), (Sheffield Hallam Univ.); Best Dir (for As You Like It and Passion Play), Evening Standard Theatre Awards 2000, Best Dir (for As You Like It, Passion Play and Merrily We Roll Along), Critics Circle Awards; Theatre Award (for As You Like It), South Bank Show Awards, Best Dir (for Caligula), Laurence Olivier Awards 2004, Best Dir (for Don Carlos), Evening Standard Theatre Awards 2005, TMA Awards 2005, German-British Forum Award for promoting relations between England and Germany 2005, Sydney Edwards Award for Best Dir 2008, Managed Networks Best Dir, WhatsOnStage Awards 2014. *Plays directed include:* Almeida Theatre: The Jew of Malta (also nat. tour), The Doctor's Dilemma (also nat. tour); Sheffield Theatres: Don Carlos Carlos (Evening Standard Award Best Dir), Suddenly Last Summer (also Albery Theatre, London), A Midsummer Night's Dream, The Tempest (also Old Vic, London), Richard III, Don Juan, Edward II, The Country Wife, As You Like It (also Lyric Hammersmith), Twelfth Night, What the Butler Saw; Donmar Warehouse: Guys and Dolls (Olivier Award for Outstanding Musical Production), Good 1999, Passion Play (Evening Standard Award and Critics' Circle Award for Best Dir) 2000, Merrily We Roll Along (Evening Standard Award Best Dir) 2000, Privates on Parade 2001, The Vortex 2002, Caligula (Olivier Award Best Dir) 2003, After Miss Julie 2003, Pirandello's Henry IV 2004, Grand Hotel (Olivier Award for Outstanding Musical Production, Evening Standard Award Best Dir) 2004, The Wild Duck (Critics' Circle Awards for Best Dir) 2005, Don Juan in Soho 2006, Frost/Nixon (also Gielgud Theatre) 2006, The Cut 2006, John Gabriel Borkman 2007, Othello (Evening Standard and Critics' Circle Awards for Best Dir) 2008, The Chalk Garden (Evening Standard and Critics' Circle Awards for Best Dir) 2008, Red (Tony Award for Best Direction of a Play 2010, Drama Desk Award 2010) 2009, King Lear 2011, Luise Miller 2011, Richard II 2012; Adelphi Theatre: Evita 2006; Donmar at Wyndham's Theatre: Ivanov (Evening Standard and Critics' Circle Awards for Best Dir) 2008, Twelfth Night 2008, Madame de Sade 2009, Hamlet 2009; Royal Nat. Theatre: Danton's Death 2010; Michael Grandage Company: Privates on Parade 2012, Peter and Alice 2013, The Cripple of Inishmaan 2013 (also Broadway 2014), A Midsummer Night's Dream 2013, Henry V 2013. *Publication:* A Decade at the Donmar 2013. *Address:* Michael Grandage Company, Fourth Floor, Gielgud Theatre, Shaftesbury Avenue, London, W1D 6AR, England (office). *Telephone:* (20) 3582-7210 (office). *E-mail:* info@michaelgrandagecompany.com (office). *Website:* www.michaelgrandagecompany.com (office).

GRANDI, Filippo, BA; Italian UN official; *Commissioner, United Nations High Commissioner for Refugees;* b. 1957, Milan; ed Univ. di Venezia, Univ. degli Studi di Milano, Univ. Gregoriana; Field Coordinator for UNHCR and UN humanitarian activities in Democratic Repub. of the Congo 1996–97, worked in UNHCR Exec. Office, Geneva 1997–2001 as Special Asst, later Chief of Staff, UNHCR Chief of Mission 2001–04, Deputy Special Rep. of UN Sec.-Gen., UN Assistance Mission in Afghanistan (UNAMA) 2004–05, Deputy Commr-Gen., UN Relief and Works Agency for Palestine Refugees in the Near East (UNRWA) 2005–10, Commr-Gen., UNRWA 2010–14, UN High Commr for Refugees 2016–; Dr hc (Coventry). *Address:* United Nations High Commissioner for Refugees, Case Postale 2500, 1211 Geneva, Switzerland (office). *Telephone:* 227398111 (office). *Fax:* 227397377 (office). *Website:* www.unhcr.org (office).

GRANDMONT, Jean-Michel, LèsL, MSc, PhD; French economist and researcher; *Emeritus Director of Research, Centre de Recherche en Économie et Statistique;* b. 22 Dec. 1939, Toulouse; s. of Jancu Wladimir Grunberg and Paule Cassou; m. 1st Annick Duriez 1967 (divorced 1978); two d.; m. 2nd Josselyne Bitan 1979; ed Ecole Polytechnique, Paris, Ecole Nationale des Ponts et Chaussées, Paris, Université de Paris, Univ. of California, Berkeley, USA; Research Assoc., CNRS, Centre d'Etudes Prospectives d'Economie Mathématique Appliquées à la Planification (CEPREMAP) 1970–75, then Dir various research units, Dir of Research, CNRS and CEPREMAP 1987–96, Dir Research Unit, CNRS 928, Recherches Fondamentales en Economie Mathématique 1991–96, Dir of Research, CNRS and Centre de Recherche en Économie et Statistique 1996–, now Emer. Dir of Research; Assoc. Prof., Ecole Polytechnique, Palaiseau 1977–92, Prof. 1992–2004, Chair. Dept of Econs 1997–2000, 2003–04; Prof. (part-time), Yale Univ., USA 1987, 1989–91, 1994; Pres. Econometric Soc. 1990; mem. Academia Europaea, American Acad. of Arts and Sciences; Hon. mem. American Econ. Asscn, Hon. Fellow, Kobe Univ. 2012, Perm. Hon. mem. Ca Foscari, Venice, 2016; Chevalier, Légion d'honneur 2004; Officier des Palmes académiques 2004; Dr hc (Lausanne) 1990, (Keio Univ., Tokyo) 2007; Alexander von Humboldt Award 1992. *Publications:* Money and Value 1983, Nonlinear Economic Dynamics (ed.) 1987, Temporary Equilibrium (ed.) 1988; articles in scientific econ. journals. *Address:* CREST-CNRS, Université Paris-Saclay, 5 Avenue Henry Le Chatelier, 91120 Palaiseau Cedex (office); 55 Blvd de Charonne, Les Doukas 23, 75011 Paris, France (home). *Telephone:* 1-70-28-68-05 (office); 1-43-70-37-28 (home). *E-mail:* grandmon@ensae.fr (office). *Website:* www.crest.fr/ses.php?user=2958 (office).

GRANGE, Sir Kenneth Henry, Kt, CBE; British industrial designer; *Visiting Professor, Design Products, Royal College of Art;* b. 17 July 1929; s. of Harry Alfred Grange and Hilda Gladys Grange (née Long); m. 1st (divorced); m. 2nd Apryl Grange; ed Willesden School of Arts and Crafts, London; tech. illustrator, Royal Engineers 1948–50; design asst, Arcon Chartered Architects 1948; Bronek Katz & Vaughn 1950–51; Gordon Bowyer & Partners 1951–54; Jack Howe & Partners 1954–58; industrial designer, Kenneth Grange Design Ltd (pvt. practice) 1958–72; Founding Partner, Pentagram Design 1972–2000; solo shows, Victoria and Albert Museum 1974, Tokyo 1985, 'Those That Got Away', London 2003; Pres. Chartered Soc. of Designers 1987–88; Master of Faculty, RDI 1985–87; currently Visiting Prof., Design Products, Royal Coll. of Art; mem. Bd of Dirs Shakespeare Globe Centre 1997–2002; mem. Advisory Bd for Product Design, Design Council, Industrial Design Adviser 1971; Hon. Prof., Heriot-Watt Univ. 1987; Hon. DUniv (Heriot-Watt) 1986; Dr hc (RCA) 1985, (De Montfort Univ.) 1998, (Staffordshire Univ.) 1998; ten Design Council Awards, Duke of Edinburgh Award for Elegant Design 1963, Royal Designer for Industry, Royal Soc. of Arts 1969, Chartered Soc. of Designers Gold Medal 1996, Prince Philip Designers' Prize 2001. *Leisure interests:* building. *Address:* Design Products, Royal College of Art, Kensington Gore, London, SW7 2EU (office); 53 Christchurch Hill, London, NW3 1LG, England (home). *Telephone:* (20) 7590-4444 (office). *Fax:* (20) 7590-4500 (office). *E-mail:* design@rca.ac.uk (office). *Website:* www.rca.ac.uk (office).

GRANGER, Brig. (retd) David Arthur, BA, MScS; Guyanese politician, head of state and fmr army officer; *President;* b. 15 July 1945, Georgetown; m. Sandra Granger; two d.; ed Queen's Coll. Guyana, Army Command and Staff Coll., Nigeria, Mons Officer Cadet School, UK; joined Guyana Defence Force (GDF) as officer cadet 1965, rank of Second-Lt 1966, roles included Planning Officer for establishment of Guyana Nat. Service 1973–74 and Guyana People's Militia 1976–77, Commdr, GDF 1979–90, Nat. Security Adviser to Pres. 1990–92, retd from mil. service 1992; Founder and Man. Ed. Guyana Review (news magazine) 1992–; Hubert H. Humphrey/Fulbright Fellow, Philip Merrill Coll. of Journalism, Univ. of Maryland, USA 1995–96; mem. Nat. Ass. 2012–15, Leader of the Opposition 2012–15; People's Nat. Congress Reform cand. for Pres. 2011; Pres. of Guyana 2015–; fmr Chair. Cen. Intelligence Cttee; mem. Partnership for Nat. Unity (APNU); Mil. Efficiency Medal 1976, Mil. Service Medal 1981, Mil. Service Star 1985. *Publications:* has written extensively on nat. defence and public security issues. *Address:* Office of the President, New Garden Street, Bourda, Georgetown, Guyana (office). *Telephone:* 225-7051 (office). *Fax:* 226-3395 (office). *E-mail:* opmed@op.gov.gy (office). *Website:* www.op.gov.gy (office).

GRANHOLM, Jennifer Mulhern, BA, JD; American lawyer, academic, presenter and fmr politician; *Distinguished Practitioner of Law and Public Policy, Richard and Rhoda Goldman School of Public Policy, University of California, Berkeley;* b. 5 Feb. 1959, Vancouver, BC, Canada; d. of Victor Ivar Granholm and Shirley Alfreda Granholm (née Dowden); m. Daniel Mulhern 1986; one s. two d.; ed San Carlos High School, Calif., Univ. of California, Berkeley, Harvard Univ. Law School; won Miss San Carlos beauty pageant; abandoned efforts to launch acting career 1980; held jobs as tour guide at Universal Studios, within customer service for Los Angeles Times and was first female tour guide at Marine World Africa USA, Redwood City, piloting boats with 25 tourists aboard; became US citizen 1980; worked for John Anderson's ind. run for Pres. 1980; law clerk, Sixth Circuit Court of Appeals, Detroit 1987–88; Exec. Asst Wayne Co. Exec., Detroit 1988–89; Asst US Attorney, Dept of Justice, Detroit 1990–94; Corp. Counsel, Wayne Co. 1994–99, Gen. Counsel Detroit/Wayne Co. Stadium Authority 1996–98; Attorney-Gen. of Mich. 1999–2002; Gov. of Mich. (first female gov.) 2003–11; Distinguished Practitioner of Law and Public Policy, Goldman School of Public Policy, Univ. of California, Berkeley 2011–; mem. Bd of Dirs Dow Chemical Co. 2011, Marinette Marine Corpn 2011; Sr Advisor on clean energy policies, Pew Charitable Trusts 2011; mem. transition team for presidency of Pres. Barack Obama 2008–09; Vice-Pres. YWCA Inkster, Mich. 1995; fmr Commr, Great Lakes Comm.; fmr mem. Midwestern Govs Asscn (Vice-Chair. 2008–09, Chair. 2009); mem. Detroit Bar Asscn, Leadership Detroit, Womens' Law Asscn, Inc. Soc. of Irish Lawyers, Bd Cyberstate.org, YWCA; Democrat; Commdr, Royal Order of the Polar Star (Sweden) 2010; Public Servant of the Year, Mich. Asscn of Chiefs of Police, Michigander of the Year, Michigan Jaycees, Woman of Achievement Award, YWCA 1997, named by Politico as one of The 50 Politicos to Watch 2010. *Television:* fmr contestant on daytime game show The Dating Game, announced as host, The War Room with Jennifer Granholm, Current TV. *Publications:* numerous articles in professional journals. *Leisure interests:* running, family. *Address:* Richard and Rhoda Goldman School of Public Policy, University of California, Berkeley, 2607 Hearst Avenue, Berkeley, CA 94720-7320, USA (office). *Telephone:* (510) 642-4670 (office). *Fax:* (510) 643-9657 (office). *Website:* gspp.berkeley.edu (office).

GRANIĆ, Mate, DrSc; Croatian politician and physician; b. 19 Sept. 1947, Baska Voda; m. Jadranka Granic; one s. two d.; ed Zagreb Univ.; physician, Vuk Vrhovac Inst. for Diabetes Endocrinology and Metabolic Diseases, School of Medicine, Zagreb Univ. 1975–79; Head of Clinical Dept Vuk Vrhovac Inst. 1979–85; Prof., Deputy Dir 1985–89; Vice-Dean, Faculty of Medicine, Zagreb Univ. 1989, Dean 1990; mem. and Vice-Pres. Croatian Democratic Union (HDZ); Deputy Prime Minister 1991–99; concurrently Minister of Foreign Affairs 1993–2000; presidential cand. (HDZ) Jan. 2000; led splinter faction of HDZ to form Democratic Centre Party (Demokratski centar—DC) 2000, Pres. 2000–02, left DC and retd from public life 2003; arrested under corruption charges 2004, charges later dropped; foreign policy adviser to Croatian Party of Rights 2005; Dean, School of Journalism, Univ. of Zagreb 2007; f. MAGRA Ltd consulting co. 2004. *Publications:* papers and articles on diabetes.

GRANT, Audrey Joy, BCom, MBA; Belizean diplomatist, politician and central banker; *Governor, Central Bank of Belize;* b. 5 Feb. 1951, Belize City; ed Univ. of Alberta, Canada; Exec. Dir Programme for Belize (conservation org.) 1989–2001; Vice-Pres. and Man. Dir Atlantic Conservation Region, The Nature Conservancy 2001–05; Sr Dir Natural Capital Project 2005–08; Amb. to Belgium and EU (also accred to the Netherlands, France, Spain, and Germany) 2008–12; apptd Senator, Minister of Energy, Science and Tech. and Public Utilities 2012–15, Dir Financial Intelligence Unit Jan.–Oct. 2016; Gov. Cen. Bank of Belize 2016–, also currently Alt. Gov., IMF, World Bank; fmr Perm. Rep. to WTO and Counsellor and Deputy Head of Mission, Embassy in Washington, DC; worked on econ. devt projects for several Caribbean countries for Caribbean Devt Bank; apptd to Transitional Cttee to design Green Climate Fund under the UN Framework Convention on Climate Change 2011; numerous nat. and int. awards. *Address:* Central Bank of Belize, Gabourel Lane, POB 852, Belize City, Belize (office). *Telephone:* 223-6194 (office). *Fax:* 223-6226 (office). *E-mail:* info@centralbank.org.bz (office). *Website:* www.centralbank.org.bz (office).

GRANT, B. Rosemary, PhD, FRS; British evolutionary biologist and academic; *Senior Research Scholar and Professor Emeritus, Department of Ecology and Evolutionary Biology, Princeton University;* b. (Barbara Rosemary Matchett), 8 Oct. 1936, Arnside, Cumbria, England; m. Peter Raymond Grant; two d.; ed Univ. of Edinburgh, Uppsala Univ., Sweden; Research Assoc., Univ. of British Columbia, Canada 1960–64, Yale Univ. 1964–65, McGill Univ., Montréal, Canada 1973–77, Univ. of Michigan 1977–85; Research Scholar and Lecturer, Princeton Univ. 1985–96, Sr Research Scholar and Prof. 1997–, now Emer.; Visiting Prof., Univ. of Zurich, Switzerland 2002, 2003; Edward P. Bass Distinguished Visiting Prof., Yale Univ. 2010; Foreign Fellow, RSC 2004; mem. American Acad. of Arts and Sciences 1997, Gen. Ass. Charles Darwin Foundation 2002, American Philosophical Soc. 2010; carried out, with Peter R. Grant, extensive research into evolution, ecology and behaviour amongst Darwin's finches of the Galápagos Islands from 1973; Foreign mem. NAS 2008; mem. American Acad. of Arts and Sciences 1997, American Philosophical Soc. 2010; Foreign FRSC 2004; Hon. Fellow, Deutsche Ornithologen-Gesellschaft 2003; Dr hc (McGill Univ.) 2000, (Universidad San Francisco, Quito) 2005; Hon. PhD (Univ. of Zurich) 2008; Hon. DSc (Ohio Wesleyan Univ.) 2012; (with Peter Grant) Leidy Medal, Acad. of Natural Sciences of Philadelphia 1994, E.O. Wilson Prize, American Soc. of Naturalists 1998, Darwin Medal, Royal Soc. of London 2002, Loye and Alden Miller Award, Cooper Ornithological Soc. 2003, Grinnell Award, Univ. of California, Berkeley 2003, A.I.B.S Outstanding Scientist Award 2005, Balzan Prize in Population Biology 2005, Darwin-Wallace Medal (bestowed every 50 years by Linnean Soc. of London) 2008, B. R. Grant Professorship est. at Univ. of Michigan 2008, Rosemary Grant Award est. by Soc. for the Study of Evolution 2008, Kyoto Prize, Inamori Foundation (co-recipient) 2009, Rosemary and Peter Grant Lecture series, Univ. of Zurich, inaugurated 2011, Margaret Morse Nice Prize, Wilson Ornithological Soc. 2013, Brewster Medal, American Ornithologists' Union 2015. *Publications:* Evolutionary Dynamics of a Natural Population – The Large Cactus Finch of the Galápagos (with Peter R. Grant) (Wildlife Publication Award, The Wildlife Soc. 1991) 1989, How and Why Species Multiply – The Radiation of Darwin's Finches 2008, In Search of the Causes of Evolution – From Field Observations to Mechanisms (co-ed.) 2010, 40 Years of Evolution – Darwin's Finches on Daphne Major Island (co-author) 2014; more than 100 publs in scientific journals. *Address:* Department of Ecology and Evolutionary Biology, Room 106, Eno Hall, Princeton University, Princeton, NJ 08544-1003, USA (office). *Telephone:* (609) 258-6290 (office). *Fax:* (609) 258-1334 (office). *E-mail:* rgrant@princeton.edu (office). *Website:* www.princeton.edu/eeb (office).

GRANT, Hugh, MSc, MBA; British bioengineering industry executive; *Chairman, President and CEO, Monsanto Company;* b. 23 March 1958, Larkhall, Scotland; ed Univs of Glasgow and Edinburgh, Int. Man. Centre, Buckingham; joined Monsanto as product devt rep. for co.'s agricultural business in 1981, led Monsanto's marketing, sales and tech. orgs in Europe and North America, later Man. Dir all Monsanto business units in SE Asia, Australia and NZ, later Exec. Vice-Pres. and COO Monsanto Co. –2003, Chair., Pres. and CEO 2003–, Chair. Exec. Cttee; mem. Int. Advisory Bd Scottish Enterprise, Civic Progress, Pres.'s Advisory Group of CropLife Int.; mem. Bd of Dirs PPG Industries Inc., Biotechnology Industry Org.; mem. Bd of Commrs St Louis Science Centre; mem. Bd of Trustees Donald Danforth Plant Science Centre, Washington Univ., St Louis; mem. CEO Council; Dr hc (Webster Univ.) 2009. *Address:* Monsanto Company, 800 North Lindbergh Boulevard, St Louis, MO 63167, USA (office). *Telephone:* (314) 694-1000 (office). *Fax:* (314) 694-8394 (office). *Website:* www.monsanto.com (office).

GRANT, Hugh John Mungo, BA; British actor; b. 9 Sept. 1960, London; s. of James Murray Grant and Fynvola Susan Grant (née Maclean); partner 1st Elizabeth Hurley 1987–2000; partner 2nd Jemima Khan 2004–07; two s. two d.; ed Latymer Upper School, Hammersmith, New College, Oxford; acting in theatre, TV and films and producer for Simian Films; began career in theatre performing Jockeys of Norfolk (written with Chris Lang and Andy Taylor); Fellow, BFI 2016; Best Actor, Venice Film Festival (jtly with James Wilby) 1987, BAFTA Stanley Kubrick Britannia Award 2003. *Films include:* White Mischief 1987, Maurice 1987, Lair of the White Worm 1988, La Nuit Bengali 1988, Impromptu 1989, Bitter Moon 1992, Remains of the Day 1993, Four Weddings and a Funeral (Golden Globe Award and BAFTA Award for Best Actor 1995, Peter Sellers Award for Comedy, Evening Standard British Film Awards 1995) 1994, Sirens 1994, The Englishman Who Went up a Hill But Came down a Mountain 1995, Nine Months 1995, An Awfully Big Adventure 1995, Sense and Sensibility 1995, Restoration 1996, Extreme Measures (for Simian Films) 1996, Mickey Blue Eyes (for Simian Films) 1998, Notting Hill (Peter Sellers Award for Comedy, Evening Standard British Film Award 2000, Best British Actor, Empire Film Awards 2000) 1999, Small Time Crooks 2000, Bridget Jones' Diary (Peter Sellers Award for Comedy, Evening Standard British Film Awards 2002) 2001, About a Boy (Best British Actor, Empire Film Awards 2003, London Critics Circle Film Award Best British Actor 2003) 2002, Two Weeks' Notice 2002, Love Actually 2003, Bridget Jones: The Edge of Reason 2004, American Dreamz 2006, Music and Lyrics 2006, Did You Hear About the Morgans? 2009, The Boat that Rocked 2009, The Pirates! Band of Misfits (voice) 2012, Cloud Atlas 2012, The Rewrite 2014, The Man from U.N.C.L.E. 2015, Florence Foster Jenkins 2016, Paddington 2 2017. *Television includes:* A Very English Scandal (mini-series) 2018. *Leisure interest:* golf.

GRANT, Sir Ian D., Kt, CBE, FRAgS; British civil servant (retd) and business executive; farmed in Perthshire 1962–93; Vice-Pres. Nat. Farmers Union Scotland 1981–84, Pres. 1984–90; Scottish Commr, The Crown Estate 1996–2002, Chair. 2002–09; Chair. Scottish Exhbn Centre Ltd, Glasgow 2002–13; mem. Bd of Dirs East of Scotland Farmers 1976–2002, Clydesdale Bank PLC 1989–97, NFU Mutual Insurance Soc. 1990–2008 (Deputy Chair. 2003–08), Scottish & Southern Energy PLC 1992–2003 (Deputy Chair. 2000–03); Chair. Int. Fed. of Agricultural Producers Grains Cttee 1984–89, Scottish Tourist Bd 1990–98; Trustee, NFU Mutual Charitable Trust 2009–, Queen Elizabeth Castle of Mey Trust 2010–; Hon. DBA (Napier Univ., Edinburgh).

GRANT, Sir John Douglas Kelso, Kt, KCMG, BA; British diplomatist (retd); b. 17 Oct. 1954; s. of Douglas Marr Kelso Grant and Audrey Stevenson Grant (née Law); m. Anna Maria Lindvall; one s. two d.; ed Edinburgh Acad., St Catharine's Coll., Cambridge; joined FCO 1976, W African Dept 1976–77, Third Sec. (later Second Sec.), Chancery, British Embassy, Stockholm 1977–80, Russian Language Training 1980–81, First Sec., Commercial, British Embassy, Moscow 1982–84, Desk Officer, Soviet Dept, FCO, London 1984–85, Press Office, FCO 1986–89, Press Spokesman (later First Sec. External Relations), UK Rep. Office, Brussels 1989–93, European Secr., Cabinet Office 1993–94, Counsellor, External Relations, UK Rep. Office, Brussels 1994–97, Prin. Pvt. Sec., Sec. of State's Office, London 1997–99, Amb. to Sweden 1999–2003, Perm. Rep. to EU 2003–07; Morgan Grenfell and Co. Ltd 1985–86; Exec. Vice-Pres., BG Group PLC 2009–15. *Leisure interests:* walking, cross-country skiing.

GRANT, Keith Frederick, NDD, ARCA; British landscape painter, muralist and lecturer; b. (Frederick Nall), 10 Aug. 1930, Liverpool; adopted s. of Charles Grant and Gladys Emma Grant; m. 1st Gisèle Barka Djouadi 1964 (divorced 1999); one s. (deceased) one d.; m. 2nd Hilde Ellingsen 2000; one d.; ed Bootle Grammar School, Willesden School of Art and RCA, London; State Scholarship to Norway 1960; Head of Fine Art Dept, Maidstone Coll. of Art, Kent 1968–71; Gulbenkian Award

Artist-in-Residence, Bosworth Coll., Leics. 1973–75; mem. Fine Art Bd CNAA 1978–81; Head of Painting Dept, Newcastle Polytechnic 1979–81; Head of Dept of Art, The Roehampton Inst., London 1981–90, Artist-in-Residence 1990–95; Expedition Artist to Guyana 1991; Art Dir Operation Raleigh 1991–95; solo shows in London 1960– and shows in Iceland, Norway, France, Italy and Luxembourg; recorded volcanic eruption, Iceland 1973; painted launch of Ariane Rocket 1982; visited Soviet Union for Anglo-Soviet cultural exchange programme of the British Council 1979; other British Council tours to Cyprus 1976, Hungary, Cuba 1985 and Norway 1987; visited Sarawak 1984 and 1985; designed prints for use in Earthlife Foundation's Rainforest Campaign; designed book covers for 6 Peter Mattheissen works 1988–89; visited Greenland to study icebergs at Ilulissat (Jakobshavn); Guest Artist, Ben Gurion Univ. of the Negev and British Israel Art Foundation 1988; elected mem. Telemark Artists' Asscn, Norway 1996; mem. Royal Cambrian Acad. 2001; selected to inaugurate Artists' and Writers' Programme Antarctica 2001/2002 of the British Antarctic Survey; visited Antarctica as Artist-in-Residence arranged by Ice Tracks Expeditions 2017; Silver Medal for Mural Painting, RCA 1958. *Works include:* works in many public collections including Arts Council of Great Britain, Nat. Gallery of New Zealand, Nat. Gallery of S Australia, Hamilton Art Gallery, Ontario, Trondheim Art Gallery, Norway, Contemporary Art Soc., Fitzwilliam Museum, Cambridge, Abbot Hall Gallery, Kendal, British Council, All Souls Coll. Oxford, Imperial Coll. London, Victoria and Albert Museum, Richmond College, London, Univ. of East Anglia, Haugesund Art Gallery, Norway, Nat. Gallery of Iceland; mural/mosaics, stained glass window, Charing Cross Hosp., London, Gateshead Metro Station; painting, Guildhall School of Music and Drama, London, Avaldsnes triptych, Karmøy Kommune, Norway; sculpture, Shaw Theatre, London; commissioned to paint triptych for Church of Kopervik, Karmøy, Norway 2004. *Publications:* journals and sketchbooks 1960s–, archived in Fitzwilliam Museum, Cambridge. *Leisure interests:* walking, music, travel and writing; member of Chelsea Arts Club, London. *Address:* Holmenvegen 43, PO Box 7, 3834 Gvarv, Norway (home); c/o Chris Beetles Gallery, 8 & 10 Ryder Street, St James's, London SW1Y 6QB, England. *Telephone:* 35959795 (home); (20) 7839-7551. *Fax:* 35959795 (home). *E-mail:* kefreg@online.no (home); gallery@chrisbeetles.com. *Website:* www.chrisbeetles.com.

GRANT, Sir Malcolm John, Kt, CBE, MA, LLD, FAcSS; New Zealand/British university administrator, barrister, environmental lawyer, academic and public servant; b. 29 Nov. 1947, Oamaru, New Zealand; s. of Frank Grant and Vera Grant; m. Christine Grant (née Endersbee) 1974; three c.; ed Univ. of Otago; barrister and solicitor, NZ 1969–; barrister, Middle Temple 1998–, Bencher 2004–; Lecturer in Law, Univ. of Southampton 1972–86; Prof. of Law and Vice-Dean, Univ. Coll. London 1986–91, Pres. and Provost 2003–13; Prof. of Land Economy, Univ. of Cambridge 1991–2003, Head, Dept of Land Economy 1993–2001, Pro-Vice-Chancellor 2002–03, Fellow, Clare Coll. 1991–; Specialist Adviser, Parl. Jt Cttee on Pvt. Bill Procedure 1987–88; Chair. Asscn of London Govt's Ind. Panel on Remuneration of Councillors in London 1998–2005, Agric. and Environment Biotechnology Comm. 2000–05, UK Ind. Steering Bd for Public Debate on Genetic Modification 2002–03, The Russell Group of UK Research Univs 2006–09, Standards Cttee, Greater London Authority 2004–08 (Ind. mem. 2000–08, Deputy Chair. 2001–04); UK Business Amb. 2008–18; mem. Local Govt Comm. for England 1992–2002 (Deputy Chair. 1995–96, Chair. 1996–2002), Advisory Bd Environmental Law Foundation 1993–, The Ditchley Foundation 2003–11 (Gov. 2002–), Higher Educ. Funding Council for England 2008–14, Econ. and Social Research Council 2008–11, Univ. Grants Cttee Hong Kong 2007–15, Int. Council for Global Competitiveness of Russian Univs 2013–; Dir, Genomics England Ltd 2013–18; Chair. NHS Commissioning Bd 2011–13, NHS England 2013–18; Pres. Council for At-Risk Academics 2013–; consultant, Singapore Govt 1992–98, UNESCO 1993–94; Ed. Encyclopedia of Planning Law and Practice (seven vols) 1981–2006, Consultant Ed. 2006–; Consultant Ed. Encyclopedia of Environmental Law (eight vols) 1993–; Trustee, Somerset House 2014–; Academician, Acad. of Learned Socs for the Social Sciences 2000; Chancellor, Univ. of York 2015–; Chair. Global Advisory Bd, Plus Alliance 2016–; Chair. Sainsbury Wellcome Centre for Neural Circuits and Behaviour 2017–; Hon. mem. Royal Town Planning Inst. 1993–, Royal Inst. of Chartered Surveyors 1995–; Hon. Life mem. NZ Resource Man. Law Asscn 1999–; Hon. Fellow, Clare Coll., Cambridge 2016–, Hon. FRCP 2016; Officier, Ordre nat. du Mérite 2004; Hon. LLD (Otago) 2006, (Univ. Coll. London) 2013, (Cambridge) 2017. *Publications include:* Planning Law Handbook 1981, Urban Planning Law 1982, Rate Capping and the Law 1984, The Local Government Finance Act 1988, Permitted Development 1989, The Concise Lexicon of Environmental Terms (co-author) 1995, Singapore Planning Law 1999, The Environmental Court Project: Final Report 2000; numerous articles on planning and environmental law, regulation of biotechnology, local govt structures, finance and political man., central-local govt relations, human rights, property and participation, and environmental dispute resolution.

GRANT, Peter Raymond, PhD, FRS, FRSC, FLS, FAAS; British biologist and academic; *Class of 1877 Professor Emeritus of Zoology and Professor Emeritus of Ecology and Evolutionary Biology, Princeton University;* b. 26 Oct. 1936, London, England; s. of Frederick Thomas Charles Grant and Mavis Irene Grant; m. Barbara Rosemary Matchett 1962; two d.; ed Univ. of Cambridge and Univ. of British Columbia, Canada; Postdoctoral Fellowship, Yale Univ. 1964–65; Asst Prof. of Biology, McGill Univ., Canada 1965–68, Assoc. Prof. 1968–73, Prof. 1973–78; Prof., Univ. of Michigan 1978–85; Prof. of Biology, Princeton Univ. 1985–89, apptd Class of 1877 Prof., Dept of Ecology and Evolutionary Biology 1989, now Prof. Emer.; Visiting Prof., Univs of Uppsala and Lund, Sweden 1981, Univ. of Uppsala 1985; Edward P. Bass Distinguished Visiting Prof., Yale Univ. 2010; Assoc. Ed., Ecology 1968–70, Evolutionary Theory 1973–, Biological Journal of the Linnean Soc. 1984–, Philosophical Transactions of the Royal Soc. of London 1990–93; mem. American Philosophical Soc. 1991, American Acad. of Arts and Sciences 1997, American Soc. of Naturalists (Pres. 1999, Past Pres. 2000), Soc. for the Study of Evolution, Ecological Soc. of America, Soc. for Behavioral Ecology; Foreign mem. Royal Soc. of Sciences, Uppsala 1993, NAS 2007; Fellow, American Ornithologists' Union; Hon. mem. Nuttall Ornithological Soc. 2004, American Soc. of Naturalists 2008, Gen. Ass., Charles Darwin Foundation 2010, Hon. Fellow, Deutsche Ornithologen-Gesellschaft 2003, Hon. Citizen, Puerto Bacquerizo, I. San Cristóbal, Galápagos 2005; Hon. PhD (Uppsala) 1986, (Zurich) 2008, Hon. DSc (McGill) 2000, (Universidad San Francisco, Quito, Ecuador) 2005, (Ohio Wesleyan Univ.) 2012; Brewster Medal, American Ornithologists' Union 1983, S. Guggenheim Memorial Fellowship 1985–86, Sr Visiting Research Fellowship, Jesus Coll., Oxford 1986, Leidy Medal, Acad. of Natural Sciences of Philadelphia (with B. R. Grant) 1994, Alexander von Humboldt Foundation Sr Scientist Research Prize 1996, E.O. Wilson Prize, American Soc. of Naturalists (with B. R. Grant) 1998, Convocation Address, McGill Univ. 2000, Charles Darwin Foundation Millenial Medal for Conservation in Galápagos 2000, Uppsala Univ. official inauguration of the Evolutionary Biology Centre, Plenary Address 2000, Darwin Medal, Royal Soc. (with B. R. Grant) 2002, Loye and Alden Miller Award, Cooper Ornithological Soc. (with B. R. Grant) 2003, Grinnell Award, Univ. of California, Berkeley 2003, Nobel Conf. XXXIX, Gustavus Adolphus Coll. 2003, Outstanding Scientist Award, American Inst. of Biological Sciences (with B. R. Grant) 2005, Balzan Prize in Population Biology (with B. R. Grant) 2005, Municipality of Puerto Ayora Science Award, I. Santa Cruz, Galápagos (with B. R. Grant) 2006, Darwin-Wallace Medal, Linnean Soc. (with B. R. Grant) 2009, Kyoto Prize in Basic Sciences (with B. R. Grant) 2009, Rosemary and Peter Grant Lecture series, Univ. of Zurich, inaugurated 2011. *Publications include:* Ecology and Evolution of Darwin's Finches 1986, Evolutionary Dynamics of a Natural Population: The Large Cactus Finch of the Galápagos (with B. Rosemary Grant) (Wildlife Publ. Award, The Wildlife Soc. 1991) 1989, Molds, Molecules and Metazoa: Growing Points in Evolutionary Biology 1992, Evolution on Islands (ed.) 1998, How and Why Species Multiply (with B. Rosemary Grant) 2008, In Search of the Causes of Evolution. From Field Observations to Mechanisms (co-ed.) 2010, 40 Years of Evolution: Darwin's Finches on Daphne Major Island (co-ed.) 2014. *Leisure interests:* camping, hiking, music and reading. *Address:* Department of Ecology and Evolutionary Biology, Room 105, Eno Hall, Princeton University, Princeton, NJ 08544-003, USA (office). *Telephone:* (609) 258-5156 (office). *Fax:* (609) 258-1334 (office). *E-mail:* prgrant@princeton.edu (office). *Website:* www.princeton.edu/eeb (office).

GRANT, Richard E., BA; British actor; b. 5 May 1957, Mbabane, Swaziland (renamed Eswatini 2018); s. of Hendrick Grant and Leonie Grant (née Esterhuysen); m. Joan Washington 1986; one d.; ed S Africa; grew up in Swaziland. *Stage appearances include:* Man of Mode 1988, The Importance of Being Earnest 1993, A Midsummer Night's Dream 1994, Otherwise Engaged 2005, My Fair Lady (Sydney Opera) 2008, God of Carnage 2009. *Films include:* Withnail and I 1986, How to Get Ahead in Advertising 1989, Warlock 1989, Henry and June 1990, Mountains of the Moon 1990, LA Story 1991, Hudson Hawk 1991, Bram Stoker's Dracula 1992, The Player 1993, The Age of Innocence 1993, Prêt à Porter 1995, Jack and Sarah 1995, Portrait of a Lady 1995, Twelfth Night 1995, The Serpent's Kiss 1996, Food of Love 1996, All For Love 1997, Spice World – The Movie 1997, The Match 1998, A Christmas Carol 1999, Trial and Retribution 1999, Little Vampires 1999, Hildegarde 2000, Gosford Park (Screen Actors Guild Best Actor 2001) 2001, Monsieur 'N' 2002, Tooth 2002, Bright Young Things 2003, The Story of an African Farm 2003, Colour Me Kubrick: A True. . .ish Story 2004, Wah-Wah (dir and writer) 2005, Corpse Bride (voice) 2005, Bustin' Bonaparte (video) 2005, Garfield: A Tail of Two Kitties (voice) 2006, Penelope 2006, Jackboots on Whitehall (voice) 2007, Love Hurts 2008, Cosi 2009, Zambezia (voice) 2010, The Iron Lady 2011, Jackie 2016, Their Finest 2017, Logan 2017, The Hitman's Bodyguard 2017, Can You Ever Forgive Me? (New York Film Critics Circle Award for Best Supporting Actor 2018) 2018, The Nutcracker and the Four Realms 2018. *TV appearances include:* Honest, Decent, Legal and True 1986, Here is the News 1989, Suddenly Last Summer 1992, Hard Times 1993, Karaoke 1996, A Royal Scandal 1996, The Scarlet Pimpernel 1998, Hound of the Baskervilles 2002, Posh Nosh 2003, Frasier 2004, Patrick Hamilton: Words, Whisky and Women (video) 2005, Home Farm Twins (series) 2005, Above and Beyond (mini-series) 2005, Marple: Nemesis 2006, Dalziel & Pascoe 2006, The Secret Policeman's Ball 2006, Freezing 2007, Mumbai Calling 2008, Dear Diaries 2009, History of Safari 2010, Girls 2014, Downtown Abbey 2014, Dig 2015, Jekyll and hyde 2015, Game of Thrones 2016, A Series of Unfortunate Events 2019. *Publications:* With Nails: The Film Diaries of Richard E. Grant 1995, Twelfth Night 1996, By Design – A Hollywood Novel 1998, The Wah-Wah Diaries: The Making of a Film 2006. *Leisure interests:* scuba diving, building dolls' houses, photography. *Address:* c/o Independent Talent, Oxford House, 76 Oxford Street, London, W1N 0AX, England (office). *Telephone:* (20) 7636-6565 (office). *Fax:* (20) 7323-0101 (office). *Website:* www.independenttalent.com (office); www.richard-e-grant.com (office).

GRAPSAS, Gen. Dimitrios; Greek military officer; b. 1948, Ypati; m. Ismini Sionidou; two c.; ed Hellenic Army War Coll., Hellenic Nat. Defense Coll.; fmr Commdr Armored Reconnaissance Battalion, Chief of Staff of 96th Mil. Command, Asst Chief of Staff of Higher Mil. Command of Interior and Islands, Commdr XXV Armored Brigade, Army Corps Chief of Staff; Dir Training Div., then Training and Doctrine Directorate, Hellenic Army Gen. Staff 2002–03; Commdr XX Mechanized Infantry Div. 2003–04; promoted to Lt-Gen. 2004; Commdr Higher Mil. Command of Interior and Islands 2005–06; Chief of Hellenic Army Gen. Staff 2006–07, Chief of Defence Staff 2007–09; Golden Cross, Order of Phoenix, Order of Merit, Kt Commdr, Order of Phoenix, Order of Merit, High Cross of the Order of Phoenix, High Cross of the Order of Merit; Medal for Mil. Valor, C Class, Medal for Mil. Valor, B Class, Outstanding Command Commendation Medal, B Class, Staff Officer Service Commendation Medal, B Class, Medal for Mil. Valor, A Class, Formation/Maj. Unit Commendation Medal, C Class, Outstanding Command Commendation Medal, A Class, Staff Officer Service Commendation Medal, A Class, Commendation Medal for Merit and Valor.

GRAPSTEIN, Steven H., BS; American business executive; *Chairman (non-executive), Tesoro Corporation;* ed Brooklyn Coll.; fmr Man. with Laventhol & Horwarth; Vice-Pres. Kuo Investment Co. and Subsidiaries –1992, CEO 1992–; mem. Bd of Dirs Tesoro Corpn 1992–, Chair. (non-exec.) 2010–, mem. Audit Cttee, Governance Cttee. *Address:* Tesoro Corporation, 300 Concord Plaza Drive, San Antonio, TX 78216-6999, USA (office). *Telephone:* (210) 828-8484 (office). *Fax:* (210) 283-2045 (office). *E-mail:* info@tsocorp.com (office). *Website:* www.tsocorp.com (office).

GRASSER, Karl-Heinz, MBA; Austrian business executive and fmr politician; b. 2 Jan. 1969, Klagenfurt; m. Fiona Pacifico Griffini 2005; one d.; ed Univ. of Klagenfurt; mem. Freedom Party (FPÖ), Spokesperson for Tourism and European

Integration 1992, FPÖ Sec.-Gen. and Man. Dir Party Educational Centre 1993; Second Deputy Gov. Prov. of Carinthia 1994–98; Vice-Pres. for Human Resources and Public Relations, Magna Europe 1998; Man. Dir Sport Management International 1999; Fed. Minister of Finance 2000–07; mem. Karl Popper Foundation (mem. Man. Bd –1999); Dir Meinl Power Management Ltd. *Address:* c/o Mr M Wanless, Aztec Financial Services (Jersey) Limited, PO Box 730, 11–15 Seaton Place, St Helier, Jersey, JE4 0QH, Channel Islands.

GRASSLEY, Charles ('Chuck') Ernest, BA, MA, PhD; American farmer, teacher and politician; *Senator from Iowa;* b. 17 Sept. 1933, New Hartford, Ia; s. of Louis Arthur Grassley and Ruth Grassley (née Corwin); m. Barbara Ann Speicher 1954; three s. two d.; ed Univ. of Northern Iowa, Univ. of Iowa; Instructor, Political Science, Drake Community Coll. 1962, Charles City Coll. 1967–68; mem. Ia House of Reps 1959–75; mem. US House of Reps from 3rd Dist of Ia 1975–81; Senator from Iowa 1981–, Chair. Senate Finance Cttee Jan.–June 2001, 2003–06 (ranking mem. from 2007), mem. Judiciary (now Chair.), Finance, Budget, Agric., and Jt Tax Cttees, Senate Caucus on Int. Narcotics Control (Co-Chair.), Senate Caucus on Foster Youth (Co-Chair.), Pres. pro tempore 2019–; mem. Farm Bureau, Butler Co., State of Iowa Historical Societies, Int. Asscn of Machinists 1962–71; Lifetime Achievement Award, Nat. Whistleblower Center 2007, American Council for Capital Formation Arena Award, Health Policy Hero Award, Nat. Research Center for Women and Families 2009, American Legion Distinguished Public Service Award, Dr Harold D. Prior Award, Iowa Wind Energy Asscn 2015, and several other awards. *Address:* 135 Hart Senate Office Building, Washington, DC 20510-0001, USA (office). *Telephone:* (202) 224-3744 (office). *Fax:* (202) 224-6020 (office). *Website:* grassley.senate.gov (office).

GRASSO, Pietro; Italian judge and politician; *Leader, Liberi e Uguali;* b. 1 Jan. 1945, Licata (Agrigento); m. Maria Grasso 1970; one s.; began career as magistrate, Barrafranca 1971–72; Prosecutor, Palermo 1972–84; Assoc. Judge, Cosa Nostra Maxi Trial 1984–87; consultant to Anti-Mafia Parl. Comm. 1987–91; adviser to criminal affairs dept, Ministry of Justice 1991; Chief Prosecutor, Palermo 1999–2005; Head, Nat. Anti-Mafia Directorate 2005–13; mem. Senate for Lazio 2013–, Pres. 2013–18; Acting Pres. of Italy 14 Jan.–3 Feb. 2015; mem. Partito Democratico –2017; Leader, Liberi e Uguali 2017–. *Publications include:* La mafia invisibile: La nuova strategia di Cosa nostra 2001, Per non morire di mafia 2010, Soldi sporchi: Come le mafie riciclano miliardi e inquinano l'economia mondiale 2011, Liberi tutti: Lettera ad un ragazzo che non vuole morire di mafia 2012. *Address:* Senate (Senato), Piazza Madama, 00186 Rome, Italy (office). *Telephone:* (06) 67061 (office). *E-mail:* pietro.grasso@senato.it (office). *Website:* www.senato.it (office); www.pietrograsso.org.

GRASSO, Richard A., BS; American fmr stock exchange executive; b. 26 July 1946, Jackson Heights, New York; m. Lorraine Grasso; four c.; ed Pace and Harvard Univs; served in numerous positions with New York Stock Exchange 1968–2003, Dir Listing and Marketing 1973–77, Vice-Pres. Corp. Services 1977–81, Sr Vice-Pres. Corp. Services 1981–83, Exec. Vice-Pres. Marketing Group 1983–86, Exec. Vice-Pres. Capital Markets 1986–88, Pres., COO 1988–93, Exec. Vice-Chair., Pres. 1993–95, Chair. CEO 1994–2003; f. Gladiator Holdings LLC (investment co.), New Jersey; Pres. World Fed. of Exchanges, Paris 2003; fmr Chair. Econ. Club, New York; fmr mem. Bd of Dirs Nat. Italian American Foundation, Washington DC Police Foundation, New York State Business Council, Congressional Medal of Honor Foundation, Centurion Foundation, Lower Manhattan Devt Corpn, New York City Police Foundation, New York City Public Private Initiatives, New York Univ.; mem. Bd of Dirs Computer Associates 1994–2002, Home Depot 2002–04, McCain 2000; Trustee, Stony Brook Foundation; fmr mem. Advisory Bd Yale School of Man.; mem. Advisory Bd Delaware Bd of Trade, New Castle County Council 2015–. *Address:* 231 Piping Rock Road, Locust Valley, NY 11560-2504, USA.

GRATTAN, Michelle, AO, BA; Australian journalist, political commentator and academic; b. 30 June 1944, Melbourne; ed Univ. of Melbourne; Chief Political Corresp., The Age 1976–93, Political Ed. 1995–96, 2004–13, Political Commentator 2002–04; Ed. Canberra Times 1993–95; sr writer and columnist, Australian Financial Review 1996–98; Chief Political Corresp. Sydney Morning Herald 1999–2002, columnist 2002–04; Professorial Fellow, Univ. of Canberra 2013–; Assoc. Ed. (Politics) and Chief Political Corresp., The Conversation (website) 2013–; Adjunct Prof., School of Journalism and Communication, Univ. of Queensland; Fellow, Acad. of the Social Sciences in Australia 2002–; Hon. DLitt (Univ. of Sydney) 2017; Graham Perkin Australian Journalist of the Year Award 1988, Walkley Award for Journalism Leadership 2006. *Publications:* Can ministers cope? 1981, Reformers: shaping Australian society from the 60s to the 80s 1989, Australian Prime Ministers (ed.) 2000, Reconciliation (ed.) 2000, Back on the Wool Track 2004. *Address:* Institute for Governance, University of Canberra, Building 23, level B, University Drive South, Canberra ACT 2601 (office); 147 Mugga Way, Red Hill, Canberra, ACT 2603, Australia (home). *Telephone:* (2) 6201-2074 (office). *E-mail:* michelle.grattan@theconversation.edu.au (office). *Website:* www.governanceinstitute.edu.au (office); theconversation.com (office).

GRÄTZEL, Michael, PhD, FRSC; Swiss (b. German) photochemist and academic; *Professor, École polytechnique fédérale de Lausanne;* b. 11 May 1944, Dorfchemnitz, Sachsen; m. Carole Grätzel; one s. two d.; ed Technical Univ. of Berlin; Scientific Staff Mem., Hahn-Meitner Inst., Berlin, Germany 1968–72, 1974–76; currently Prof., École polytechnique fédérale de Lausanne, Head, Dept of Chemistry 1983–85, 1991–93, Dir Lab. of Photonics and Interfaces; Mary Upton Visiting Prof., Cornell Univ.; Distinguished Visiting Prof., Nat. Univ. of Singapore; Invited Prof., Univ. of California, Berkeley, École nationale de Chachan (Paris), Delft Univ. of Tech.; Visiting Prof., Solar Energy Research Inst., Golden, Colo 1981–82, Lawrence Berkeley Lab., Univ. of California, Berkeley 1988; mem. Scientific Advisory Cttee, IMDEA Nanoscience Inst.; mem. Swiss Chemical Soc., European Acad. of Science; Distinguished Hon. Prof., Chinese Acad. of Science (Changchun) 2009, Huazhong Univ. of Science and Tech. 2009; Hon. mem. Soc. Vaudoise des Sciences Naturelles, Bulgarian Acad. of Science; Dr hc (Univ. of Uppsala, Sweden) 1996, (Univ. of Turin, Italy) 2004, (Delft Univ. of Tech., The Netherlands) 2006, (Univ. of Hasselt, Belgium) 2009, (Univ. of Nova Gorica, Slovenia) 2010, (Univ. of Lund, Sweden) 2011, (Nangyang Tech. Univ., Singapore) 2011, (Huazhong Univ. of Science and Tech., China) 2011, (Univ. of Roskilde, Denmark) 2012, (Univ. of Liège, Belgium) 2013; McKinsey Venture Award 1998, 2002, Balzan Prize 2009, Galvani Medal, Faraday Medal, Royal Soc. 2001, Harvey Prize, Technion – Israel Inst. of Tech. 2007, Gerischer Award 2005, Dutch Havinga Award and Medal 2001, Int. Prize of Japanese Soc. of Coordination Chem., ENI-Italgas Energy Prize 2004, European Grand Prix of Innovation 2000, Millennium Tech. Grand Prize (Finland) 2010, Paul Karrer Gold Medal 2011, Gutenberg Research Award 2011, Wilhelm Exner Medal 2011, Albert Einstein World Award of Science 2012, Marcel Benoist Prize 2013, Samson Prime Minister Prize 2014, King Faisal Int. Prize in Chem. (co-recipient) 2015. *Achievements include:* co-invented the Grätzel cell 1988; pioneered the use of nanomaterials in lithium ion batteries. *Publications:* two books and more than 1,000 papers in professional journals on energy and electron transfer reactions in mesoscopic materials and their optoelectronic applications; more than 50 patents. *Address:* Room CH G1 526, Station 6, Laboratory of Photonics and Interfaces, École polytechnique fédérale de Lausanne, Institut des sciences et ingénierie chimiques EPFL SB ISIC LPI, 1015 Lausanne, Switzerland (office). *Telephone:* (21) 6933112 (office). *Fax:* (21) 6936100 (office). *E-mail:* michael.graetzel@epfl.ch (office). *Website:* lpi.epfl.ch/graetzel (office).

GRAUBNER, Most Rev. Jan; Czech ecclesiastic; *Archbishop of Olomouc and Moravia;* b. 29 Aug. 1948, Brno; s. of Oldrich Graubner and Ludmila Graubner; ed Univ. of Olomouc; ordained priest 1973; ordained Bishop 1990; Auxiliary Bishop of Olomouc 1990–92, Archbishop of Olomouc and Moravia 1992–; Vice-Chair. Czech Bishops' Conf. 1991–2000, Chair. 2000–10; Chair. Czech Catholic Charity 1991–; Chair. Palacky Univ., Olomouc; Sec. of Defense Meritorious Cross 2003, Order of St Floriana Fire Asscn (Bohemia, Moravia and Silesia) 2003, Order of TG Masaryk (Czech Republic) 2008. *Publications:* several books and articles. *Address:* Archdiocese of Olomouc, Wurmova 9, p. schr. 193, 77101 Olomouc, Czech Republic (office). *Telephone:* (58) 7405111 (office). *Fax:* (58) 5224840 (office). *E-mail:* arcibol@arcibol.cz (office). *Website:* www.ado.cz (office).

GRAUŽINIENĖ, Loreta; Lithuanian economist and politician; b. 10 Jan. 1963, Rokiškis; m.; two s.; ed Žiežmariai Secondary School (now Žiežmariai Gymnasium), Kaišiadorys Dist, Lithuanian Acad. of Agric. (now Aleksandras Stulginskis Univ.), Lithuanian Inst. of Accounting and Audit; accountant, Peat Devt Authority 1982–86; economist, Asscn of Public Utilities, accountant, Agricultural Machinery Asscn of Ukmergė, collective farm Žiburys, Ukmergė Dist 1986–92; Chief Accountant, several pvt. cos 1992–94; Lecturer, Vocational Agricultural School, Ukmergė (now Vocational Business School) 1994–2004; Owner, pvt. co. providing business operation analysis, accounting, audit and advisory services 1996–2004; mem. Darbo Partija (DP—Labour Party) 2003–, Chair. Cttee on Audit, mem. Cttee on Budget and Finance, Cttee on European Affairs, Comm. for Parl. Scrutiny of Operational Activities 2004–08, mem. DP Political Group 2008–12, mem. Cttee on Audit, on European Affairs, DP Political Group 2012–13, Chair. DP 2013–16; cand. in presidential election 2009; mem. Seimas (Parl.) 2004–, mem. Cttee on Social Affairs and Labour 2012–13, Cttee on Audit 2013, Cttee on European Affairs 2013, Chair. (Speaker) 2013–16, mem. Bd of the Seimas 2013–, mem. DP Political Group 2012–13, mem. Conf. of Chairs 2013–, Deputy Chair. Women's Parl. Group, Parl. Group for Welfare of the Child, mem. Parl. Group 'For Corruption-Free Lithuania', Parl. Group 'Aukštaitija', Parl. Group for Assisting Rural Communities and Farmers in Addressing Matters of Their Concern, Group for Inter-Parl. Relations with Georgia, Group for Inter-Parl. Relations with India, Group for Inter-Parl. Relations with Estonia, Chair. Seimas Del. to Ass. of Mems of the Seimas of Lithuania, the Sejm and Senate of Poland, and Verkhovna Rada of Ukraine 2013–; mem. Lithuanian Chamber of Auditors. *Leisure interests:* reading, outdoor leisure activities. *Address:* Seimas (Parliament), Gedimino pr. 53, 01109 Vilnius (office); Constituency office, Klaipėdos g. 7-43, 20130 Ukmergė m., Lithuania. *Telephone:* (5) 239-6001 (office). *Fax:* (5) 239-6330 (office). *E-mail:* loreta.grauziniene@lrs.lt (office). *Website:* www.lrs.lt (office).

GRAVEL, Mike, BS; American organization official and fmr politician; b. (Maurice Robert Gravel), 13 May 1930, Springfield, Mass.; s. of Alphonse Gravel and Maria Gravel (née Bourassa); m. 1st Rita Martin 1959; m. 2nd Whitney Gravel; one s. one d.; ed Columbia Univ.; served in US Army 1951–54, served as adjutant in Communications Intelligence Services and Special Agent in Counter Intelligence Corps; real estate developer; mem. Alaska House of Reps 1962–66, Speaker 1965; Senator from Alaska 1969–81; Founder Mike Gravel Resource Analysts, Anchorage 1981–; Founder Philadelphia II and Direct Democracy (non-profit orgs), merged to create Democracy Foundation 1989; mem. Bd of Counselors, Center for Econ. and Social Justice; mem. Bd of Dirs Cannabis Sativa Inc., CEO KUSH Inc. (subsidiary) 2014–; mem. Bd of Dirs Alexis de Tocqueville Inst. 2001, Chair. 2004; Hon. mem. Advisory Bd Student World Ass.; four hon. degrees. *Publications include:* Jobs and More Jobs, Citizen Power, The Pentagon Papers (ed.). *Address:* Cannabis Sativa, Inc., 1646 West Pioneer Blvd, Suite 120, Mesquite, NV 89024; The Democracy Foundation, PO Box 850433, New Orleans, LA 70185, USA. *Website:* www.mikegravel.us.

GRAVES, Jennifer (Jenny) Ann, AO, BSc, MSc, PhD, FAA; Australian geneticist and academic; *Distinguished Professor, Institute of Molecular Science, La Trobe University;* b. (Jennifer Ann Marshall), 24 Nov. 1941, Adelaide; d. of Theo John Marshall and Ann Nicholls; m.; two d.; ed Univ. of Adelaide, Univ. of California, Berkeley, USA; Lecturer in Genetics, La Trobe Univ. 1971–77, Sr Lecturer in Genetics 1978–87, Reader in Genetics 1988–91, Prof. of Genetics 1991–2011, Distinguished Prof., Inst. of Molecular Science 2011–, Vice-Chancellor's Fellow 2017–; Prof. of Comparative Genomics and Group Leader, Comparative Genomics Research Group, Research School of Biological Sciences, ANU 2001, now Prof. Emer., Dir ARC Centre for Kangaroo Genomics 2004–09; Research Fellow, NOAHS Center 1991–98; Foreign Sec., Australian Acad. of Sciences 2006–10, Sec. for Educ. and Public Awareness 2010–14, Fellow 1999; Thinker-in-Residence, Univ. of Canberra 2010; Professorial Fellow, Univ. of Melbourne 2001–; Distinguished Fellow, UCLA Centre for Soc. and Genetics 2005; Hon. Life Fellowship, Museums Victoria 2000; Sir Ronald A. Fisher Prize in Genetics 1962, Fulbright Travel Award 1965–71, Centenary Silver Medal 2001, L'Oréal-UNESCO Women in Science Award (Asia/Pacific Laureate) 2006, Macfarlane Burnet Medal for Biology 2006, Australian Thinker of the Year, Int. School of Thinking 2007, MJD White Medal, Genetics Soc. of Australasia 2009, Julian Wells Medal for contribs. to Molecular Biology 2017, Prime Minister's Prize for Science 2017. *Publications:* more than 400 scholarly works, including four edited books, three edited journal issues, 40 reviews and more than 300 research papers. *Leisure interests* choral singing, berry farming. *Address:* Level 4, BS1, La Trobe University, Melbourne, VIC 3086 (office); Building 10 level C, University of Canberra, University Drive, Bruce, ACT 2617, Australia (office). *Telephone:* (3) 9439-5109 (office). *E-mail:* J.Graves@latrobe.edu.au (office); jenny.graves@anu.edu.au (office). *Website:* www.latrobe.edu.au/scitecheng (office).

GRAVES, Robert John, BSIE, MSIE, PhD; American biomedical engineer, academic and business executive; *John H. Krehbiel Sr Professor for Emerging Technologies, Emeritus, Thayer School of Engineering, Dartmouth College;* b. 25 Sept. 1945, Buffalo, New York; ed Syracuse Univ., State Univ. of New York, Buffalo; Instructor. State Univ. of New York, Buffalo 1973–74; Asst Prof., Georgia Inst. of Tech., Atlanta 1974–79; Assoc. Prof. of Industrial Engineering, Univ. of Massachusetts, Amherst 1979–88, Co-Dir Flexible Assemby System Lab. in Manufacturing 1988–91; Prof. of Industrial Engineering, Rensselaer Polytechnic Inst., Troy, New York 1991–2003, Assoc. Dir Center for Integrated Electronics and Electronics Manufacturing 1994–97, Prof. Emer. 1994–; apptd John H. Krehbiel Sr Prof. for Emerging Technologies, Thayer School of Eng, Dartmouth Coll. 2003, now Prof. Emer., also Adjunct Prof. Emer., Tuck School of Business; Founder and Chief Technical Officer, Ve-Design Inc. 1999–; Assoc. Ed. Journal of Manufacturing Systems 1993–; mem. Tech. Review Bd, CAD/CAM, Robotics and Factories of the Future, Kluwer Publishing; Chair. Program Planning Cttee, Material Handling Inst. and NSF Research Colloquium on Material Handling 1998; mem. Inst. of Industrial Engineers 1966 (Fellow 1992), Soc. of Mfg Engineers 1986 (Fellow 1995), IEEE 2004, INFORMS (fmrly Inst. of Man. Sciences) 1973; IIE Dr David F. Baker Distinguished Research Award 1997, Reed-Apple Award, Material Handling Industry of America 2002, School of Eng Research Award, Renssalaer Polytechnic Inst. 2003, Bernard M. Gordon Prize, Nat. Acad. of Eng (co-recipient) 2014. *Publications:* numerous papers in professional journals; several patents. *Address:* Thayer School of Engineering, Dartmouth College, 14 Engineering Drive, Hanover, NH 03755, USA (office). *Telephone:* (603) 646-6475 (office). *Fax:* (603) 646-3856 (office). *E-mail:* robert.j.graves@dartmouth.edu (office). *Website:* engineering.dartmouth.edu (office).

GRAVES, Rupert; British actor; b. 30 June 1963, Weston-Super-Mare, Somerset, England; s. of Richard Harding Graves and Mary Lucilla Graves (née Roberts); m. Susannah Lewis 2001; three s. two d.; ed Wyvern Community School. *Theatre includes:* Killing Mr Toad, Sufficient Carbohydrates, Torch Song Trilogy, The Importance of Being Earnest, A Midsummer Night's Dream, Madhouse in Goa, Closer (Theatre World Award) 1999, The Elephant Man 2002. *Films include:* A Room With A View 1986, Maurice 1987, A Handful of Dust 1988, Where Angels Fear To Tread 1991, Damage 1992, Royal Celebration 1993, The Madness of King George 1994, The Innocent Sleep 1995, Intimate Relations (Best Actor, Montréal Film Festival 1996) 1996, Different for Girls 1996, Mrs Dalloway 1997, Dreaming of Joseph Lees 1998, Room to Rent 2000, The Extremists 2001, V for Vendetta 2006, Death at a Funeral 2007, Intervention 2007, The Waiting Room 2007, Made in Dagenham 2010, Fast Girls 2012, Bone in the Throat 2015, Sacrifice 2015. *Television includes:* Fortunes of War (mini-series) 1987, Open Fire (film) 1994, Doomsday Gun (film) 1994, The Tenant of Wildfell Hall (mini-series) 1996, The Blonde Bombshell (film) 1999, Cleopatra (mini-series) 1999, The Forsyte Saga (mini-series) 2002–03, The Forsyte Saga: To Let (mini-series) 2003, Charles II: The Power & the Passion (mini-series) 2003, A Waste of Shame: The Mystery of Shakespeare and His Sonnets (film) 2005, Son of the Dragon (mini-series) 2006, To Be First 2007, Clapham Junction (film) 2007, The Dinner Party (film) 2007, To Be First (film) 2007, Ashes to Ashes (series) 2008, Waking the Dead (series) 2008, Midnight Man (mini-series) 2008, God on Trial (film) 2008, Marple: A Pocket Full of Rye (film) 2008, Masterpiece Contemporary (series) 2008, The Good Times Are Killing Me (film) 2009, Garrow's Law (series) 2009–12, Wallander (series) 2010, Lewis (series) 2010, Law & Order: UK (series) 2010, New Tricks (series) 2010, Single Father (mini-series) 2010, Sherlock (series) 2010–15, Case Sensitive (series) 2011, Scott & Bailey (series) 2011, Death in Paradise (series) 2011, The Charles Dickens Show (series) 2012, Doctor Who (series) 2012, Secret State (series) 2012, Air Force One is Down (series) 2013, The White Queen (series) 2013, Last Tango in Halifax 2014. *Address:* c/o United Agents, 12–26 Lexington Street, London, W1F 0LE, England. *Telephone:* (20) 3214-0800. *Fax:* (20) 3214-0801. *E-mail:* info@unitedagents.co.uk. *Website:* unitedagents.co.uk.

GRAVES, William (Bill) Preston; American national organization official and fmr politician; *President and CEO, American Trucking Associations Inc.;* b. 9 Jan. 1953, Salina, Kan.; s. of William Graves and Helen Mayo; m. Linda Richey 1990; one d.; ed Kansas Wesleyan Univ., Univ. of Kansas; Deputy Asst Sec. of State, Kan. 1980–85, Asst Sec. of State 1985–87, Sec. of State 1987–95; Gov. of Kan. 1995–2003; Pres. and CEO American Trucking Asscns Inc. 2003–; Trustee Kan. Wesleyan Univ. 1987–; mem. Bd of Dirs Int. Speedway Corpn 2004–; Republican. *Leisure interests:* running, reading, travel. *Address:* American Trucking Associations Inc., 950 North Glebe Road, Suite 210, Arlington, VA 22203-4181, USA (office). *Telephone:* (703) 838-1700 (office). *Fax:* (703) 838-1994 (office). *Website:* www.trucking.org (office).

GRAY, Alasdair James; British writer and painter; b. 28 Dec. 1934, Glasgow, Scotland; s. of Alexander Gray and Amy Fleming; m. 1st Inge Sørensen (divorced); one s.; m. 2nd Morag McAlpine 1991 (died 2014); one s.; ed Glasgow School of Art; art teacher, Glasgow and Lanarkshire 1958–62; scene painter, Pavilion and Citizens' theatres 1962–63; freelance writer and painter 1963–76; artist recorder, People's Palace Local History Museum, Glasgow 1976–77; Writer-in-Residence, Univ. of Glasgow 1977–79; freelance writer and painter 1979–2001; Prof. of Creative Writing, Univ. of Glasgow 2001–03; painter of mural decorations in Oran Mor Leisure Centre, Glasgow 2003–; works in collections of People's Palace Local History Museum, Glasgow, Collin's Gallery, Strathclyde Univ., Hunterian Museum, Univ. of Glasgow; mural paintings in Palace Rigg Nature Reserve Exhibition Centre, New Cumbernauld, Abbot's House Local History Museum, Dunfermline, The Ubiquitous Chip Restaurant, Glasgow, Riverside Restaurant, Kirkfieldbank; mem. Soc. of Authors, Scottish Artists Union; Saltire Soc. Award 1981, Times Literary Supplement Award 1983, Whitbread and Guardian Awards 1992. *Radio plays include:* Quiet People 1968, The Trial of Thomas Muir 1970, Dialogue 1971, Homeward Bound 1973, The Loss of the Golden Silence 1973, McGrothy and Ludmilla 1993, Working Legs 1998. *Television plays include:* The Fall of Kelvin Walker 1967, The Man Who Knew about Electricity 1973, The Story of a Recluse 1987. *Works include:* has designed and illustrated several books including Shoestring Gourmet 1986, Songs of Scotland 1997. *Publications include:* The Comedy of the White Dog (short story) 1979, Lanark: A Life in Four Books (novel) 1981, Unlikely Stories Mostly 1982, Janine (novel) 1984, The Fall of Kelvin Walker (novel) 1985, Lean Tales (co-writer) 1985, Five Scottish Artists (catalogue) 1986, Saltire Self-Portrait 4 (autobiographical sketch) 1988, Old Negatives (four verse sequences) 1989, Something Leather (novel) 1990, McGrotty and Ludmilla (novel) 1990, Poor Things (novel) 1992, Why Scots Should Rule Scotland (polemic) 1992, Ten Tales Tall and True (Short Stories) 1993, A History Maker (novel) 1994, Mavis Belfrage (novel) 1996, Working Legs (play) 1997, The Book of Prefaces 2000, Sixteen Occasional Poems 2000, A Study in Classic Scottish Writing 2001, The Ends of Our Tethers: 13 Sorry Stories 2003, How We Should Rule Ourselves (polemic, with Adam Tomkins) 2005, Old Men in Love 2007, A Gray Playbook (plays), Collected Verses 2010, A Life in Pictures (autobiography) 2010, Every Short Story 1951–2012 2012, Of Me & Others: An Autobiography 2014. *Leisure interests:* reading, walking. *Address:* c/o Morag McAlpine, 2 Marchmont Terrace, Glasgow, G12 9LT, Scotland. *Telephone:* (141) 339-0093. *Website:* www.alasdairgray.info.

GRAY, Allan, MBA; South African accountant and business executive; *Founder, Allan Gray Proprietary Ltd;* b. 8 April 1938, East London; m. Gill Gray; ed Rhodes Univ., Harvard Business School, USA; financial analyst with Fidelity Management and Research, Boston, USA 1965–73, becoming Portfolio Man., Fidelity Capital Fund; returned to Cape Town 1973, est. Allan Gray Investment Counsel 1973 (later Allan Gray Ltd, now Allan Gray Proprietary Ltd, largest privately-owned investment man. firm in S Africa); est. Orbis (int. investment group) 1988, London and Bermuda, later renamed Orbis Investment Management; f. Allan Gray Orbis Foundation (educational charity) 2007; Dr hc (Univ. of Cape Town) 2012. *Address:* Allan Gray Proprietary Ltd, POB 51605, V&A Waterfront, Cape Town 8002, South Africa (office). *Fax:* (21) 4152492 (office). *E-mail:* info@allangray.co.za (office). *Website:* www.allangray.com (office).

GRAY, Hon. C. Boyden, BA, JD; American lawyer and diplomatist; *Founding Partner, Boyden Gray & Associates;* b. Winston-Salem, N Carolina; ed Harvard Univ., Univ. of North Carolina, Chapel Hill; Ed.-in-Chief the Law Review, Univ. of North Carolina, Chapel Hill; service in US Marine Corps; admitted to Bar, DC, NC (inactive), US Supreme Court, US Court of Fed. Claims; clerk for Earl Warren, Chief Justice of US Supreme Court 1968–69; Partner, Wilmer, Cutler, Pickering, Hale & Dorr (law firm), Washington, DC 1969–81, 1993–2005; Legal Counsel to US Vice-Pres. George Bush 1981–89, to Pres. George H. W. Bush 1989–93; Chair. Admin. Law and Regulatory Practice, ABA 2000–02; Amb. to EU, Brussels 2006–07, Special Envoy for EU Affairs Jan. 2008–09, Special Envoy for Eurasian Energy March 2008–09; Founding Partner, Boyden Gray & Assocs, PLLC; fmr mem. Cttee to Visit the Coll. and Cttee on Univ. Devt, Harvard Univ.; Vice-Chair. Int. Advisory Bd, Atlantic Council; mem. Bd of Dirs European Inst.; Presidential Citizen's Medal, Univ., Distinguished Alumnus Award, Univ. of North Carolina Law School. *Address:* Boyden Gray & Associates, PLLC, 1627 I Street NW, Suite 950, Washington, DC 20006, USA (office). *Telephone:* (202) 955-0620 (office). *E-mail:* info@boydengrayassociates.com (office). *Website:* boydengrayassociates.com (office).

GRAY, Harry Barkus, BS, PhD; American chemist and academic; *Arnold O. Beckman Professor of Chemistry and Founding Director, Beckman Institute, California Institute of Technology;* b. 14 Nov. 1935, Woodburn, Ky; m. Shirley Barnes 1957; two s. one d.; ed Western Kentucky Univ., Northwestern Univ., Univ. of Copenhagen, Denmark; Asst Prof. of Chem., Columbia Univ. 1961–63, Assoc. Prof. 1963–65, Prof. 1965–66; Prof. of Chem., California Inst. of Tech. 1966–, currently Arnold O. Beckman Prof. and Founding Dir Beckman Inst.; Distinguished Visiting Prof., Univ. of Hong Kong 2005; mem. NAS, American Acad. of Arts and Sciences, American Philosophical Soc. 2000; Foreign mem. Royal Soc. 2000, Royal Danish Soc. of Science and Letters, Accad. dei Lincei 2008; Hon. FRSC 2005; Hon. DSc (Carleton Univ., Ottawa) 2001, (Univ. of South Carolina) 2003, (Copenhagen) 2003, (Edinburgh) 2006; Franklin Award 1967, Fresenius Award 1970, ACS Award in Pure Chem. 1970, Harrison Howe Award 1972, MCA Award 1972, Guggenheim Fellow 1972–73, ACS Award in Inorganic Chem. 1978, Remsen Award 1979, Tolman Award 1979, Centenary Medal 1985, Nat. Medal of Science 1986, Pauling Medal 1986, Calif. Scientist of the Year 1988, Alfred Bader Award 1990, Gold Medal, American Inst. of Chemists 1990, Waterford Prize 1991, Priestley Medal 1991, Gibbs Medal 1992, Linderstrøm-Lang Prize 1992, Chandler Medal, Columbia Univ. 1999, Harvey Prize, Technion-Israel Inst. of Tech. 2000, ACS George C. Pimentel Award 2001, ACS Kosalopoff Award, Auburn Univ 2001, ACS Oesper Award, Univ. of Cincinnati 2001, Nichols Medal 2003, Wheland Award, Univ. of Chicago 2003, NAS Award in Chemical Sciences 2003, Dwyer Medal, Univ. of New South Wales, Australia 2003, Benjamin Franklin Medal in Chem. 2004, Wolf Prize in Chem. 2004, RSC Wilkinson Medal 2004, City of Florence Prize in Molecular Sciences 2006, Antonini Award, SPP, Univ. of Rome 2008, Pupin Medal, Columbia Univ. 2008, Schulich Award, Technion-Israel Inst. of Tech. 2008, ACS Fellow 2009, Welch Award in Chem. 2009, Creativity Award, Univ. of Oregon 2010, Int. Award, Japan Soc. of Co-ordination Chem. 2010, Othmer Gold Medal, Chemical Heritage Foundation 2013. *Publications include:* 17 books, including Electrons and Chemical Bonding 1965, Molecular Orbital Theory 1965, Ligand Substitution Processes 1966, Basic Principles of Chemistry 1967, Chemical Dynamics 1968, Chemical Principles 1970, Models in Chemical Science 1971, Chemical Bonds 1973, Electronic Structure and Bonding 1981, Molecular Electronic Structures 1980, Braving the Elements 1995; more than 730 research papers. *Leisure interests:* tennis, music. *Address:* Noyes Laboratory of Chemical Physics, 408 Beckman, California Institute of Technology, Mail Code 127-72, 1200 East California Blvd, Pasadena, CA 91125-0001 (office); 1415 East California Blvd, Pasadena, CA 91106-4101, USA (home). *Telephone:* (626) 395-6500 (office); (626) 793-1978 (home). *E-mail:* hbgray@caltech.edu (office). *Website:* www.cce.caltech.edu/faculty/gray (office).

GRAY, Robin Trevor, BAgrSc, DDA, CPM; Australian company director, agricultural consultant and fmr politician; b. 1 March 1940, Vic.; s. of Rev. W. J. Gray; m. Judith F. Boyd 1965; two s. one d.; ed Box Hill High School, Dookie Agric. Coll., Univ. of Melbourne; teacher, Victoria Educ. Dept 1961, Middx Co. Council,

UK 1964; agric. consultant, Colac, Victoria 1965, Launceston, Tasmania 1965–76; part-time Lecturer in Agric. Econs, Univ of Tasmania 1970–76; Deputy Leader of Opposition, Tasmania 1979–81, Leader of Opposition 1981–82, 1989–91, Premier 1982–89, Minister for Racing and Gaming 1982–84, for Energy 1982–88, for Forests 1984–86, for State Devt 1984–89, for Primary Industry and Sea Fisheries 1992–95, for Energy 1992–95, for TT-Line 1993–95; Chair. R. T. Gray and Assocs. Pty Ltd 1995; Partner, Evers Gray 1996–2005; Dir Gunns Ltd 1996–2010, Gunns Plantations Ltd 2009; Chair. Botanical Resources Australia Pty Ltd 1996; Dir AMC Search Ltd 1996. *Leisure interests:* cricket, golf, reading.

GRAY, Vincent C., BS; American politician; b. 8 Nov. 1942, Washington, DC; m. Loretta Gray 1998 (died 1998); one s. one d.; ed Dunbar High School, George Washington Univ.; began political career with DC Asscn for Retarded Citizens (Exec. Dir); Dir DC Dept of Human Services 1991–94; Founding Exec. Dir Covenant House Washington 1994–2004; mem. Council of DC for Ward 7 2005–11, Chair. 2007–11, served on Cttees on Health, on Econ. Devt, on Human Services, on Educ., Libraries and Recreation, also apptd to chair Special Cttee on Prevention of Youth Violence; Mayor of DC 2011–15; Democrat; Mayor's Distinguished Public Service Award, United Way Outstanding Service Community Award. *Address:* Democratic National Committee, 430 South Capitol Street SE, Washington, DC 20003, USA (office). *Telephone:* (202) 863-8000 (office). *Fax:* (202) 863-8174 (office). *Website:* www.democrats.org (office).

GRAYDON, Air Chief Marshal Sir Michael (James), Kt, GCB, CBE, FRAeS; British air force officer (retd), company director and consultant; *Chairman, The Charterhouse;* b. 24 Oct. 1938, Kew, London, England; s. of James Graydon and Rita Alkan; m. Margaret Clark 1963; ed Wycliffe Coll. and RAF Coll., Cranwell; qualified flying instructor No. 1, Flight Training School, Linton-on-Ouse 1960–62; No. 56 Squadron 1962–64; No. 226 Operational Conversion Unit (Queen's Commendation) 1965–67; Flight Command, No. 56 Squadron 1967–69; RAF Staff Coll., Bracknell 1970; Personal Staff Officer to Deputy C-in-C Allied Forces Cen. Europe, Brunssum 1971–73; Operations, Jt Warfare, Ministry of Defence 1973–75; Nat. Defence Coll. Latimer 1976; Officer Commdg No. 11 Squadron, Binbrook 1977–79; Mil. Asst to Chief of Defence Staff 1979–81; Officer Commdg RAF Leuchars 1981–83, RAF Stanley, Falkland Islands 1983; Royal Coll. of Defence Studies 1984; Sr Air Staff Officer, 11 Group, Bentley Priory 1985–86; Asst Chief of Staff, Policy, SHAPE 1986–89; Air Officer Commdg-in-Chief, RAF Support Command 1989–91, HQ Strike Command 1991–92; Chief of Air Staff 1992–97; Air ADC to HM The Queen 1992–97; Chair. Symbiotics Ltd 2006–15; Dir, Air Tanker 2001–09, Cassidian PLC 2010–15; Dir (non-exec.), Thales UK PLC 2006–11; Pres. Battle of Britain Memorial Trust 1999–2016, Cranwellian Asscn; Chair. Lincolnshire Br., English Speaking Union, Sutton's Hosp., Charterhouse 2006–, United Church Schools Group 2012–16; Vice-Pres. Wycliffe Coll. 2011–; Gov. English Speaking Union 2011–; Vice-Patron Air Cadet Council 1999–; mem. Council, Air League; Pres. Royal British Legion Kyrenia Br.; Freeman, City of London 1995. *Publications:* contribs to professional journals. *Leisure interests:* golf, birdwatching, reading, flying. *Address:* 85B Charlwood Street, Pimlico, London, SW1V 4PB, England (office). *E-mail:* mikegraydon@clara.net (office).

GRAYFER, Valery Isaakovich, CandTechSci; Russian oil industry executive; *Chairman, Lukoil;* b. 1929; ed I.M. Gubkin Moscow Oil Inst.; began career with Tatneft State Production Asscn 1952, various positions including Deputy Foreman, Chief Engineer, Deputy Head of Tatneft 1952–72; Head of Econ. Planning Directorate, USSR Ministry of Oil Industry 1972–85; Deputy Minister of Oil Industry and Head of Glavtyumenneftegaz State Production Asscn 1985–92; CEO OAO Russian Innovation Fuel and Energy Co. (RITEK) 1992–2009, Chair. 2010–; mem. Bd of Dirs and Chair. PJSC Lukoil 2000–, OOO Burovaya Kompaniya Eurasia 2009–; Prof., Gubkin Russian State Oil and Gas Univ.; mem. Acad. of Mining Sciences; Honoured Oil and Gas Industrialist of the Russian SSR, Honoured Scientist of the Tatar ASSR; Order of Lenin, Order of the Red Banner of Labour, Order of Int. Friendship, Order of Service Rendered to the Country IVth Grade, Badge of Honour; Merited Worker of Science and Eng, Merited Worker of the Oil and Gas Industry, Lenin Prize, Russian Govt Prize. *Address:* PJSC Lukoil, 11 Sretenski Boulevard, 101000 Moscow, Russia (office). *Telephone:* (495) 627-4444 (office). *Fax:* (495) 625-7016 (office). *E-mail:* pr@lukoil.com (office). *Website:* www.lukoil.com (office).

GRAYLING, Rt Hon. Christopher (Chris) Stephen, PC, BA; British politician and fmr television executive; *Secretary of State for Transport;* b. 1 April 1962, London; m. Susan Clare Dillistone 1987; one s. one d.; ed Royal Grammar School, High Wycombe, Sidney Sussex Coll., Cambridge; joined BBC News as a trainee 1985, Producer 1986–88, Business Devt Man., BBC Select 1991–93; Ed. on Business Daily programme, Channel 4 1988–91; ran several TV production cos, including managing corp. communications div. of Workhouse Ltd 1992–95, SSVC Group, Gerrards Cross 1995–97; Man. Consultant, Burson Marsteller 1997–2001; fmr mem. Social Democratic Party; contested Warrington South in gen. election as a Conservative 1997; Councillor, London Borough of Merton 1998–2002; MP for Epsom and Ewell 2001–10, for Epsom and Ewell (revised boundary) 2010–, Select Cttees: Transport, Local Govt and the Regions 2001–02, Transport, Local Govt and the Regions (Transport Sub-Cttee) 2001–02, Transport, Local Govt and the Regions (Urban Affairs Sub-Cttee) 2001–02, Transport 2002, Modernisation of the House of Commons 2005–06; Opposition Whip 2002; Shadow Spokesperson for Health 2002–03; Shadow Minister for Public Services, Health and Educ. 2003–04, for Higher Educ. 2004–05, for Health 2005; Shadow Leader of the House of Commons 2005; ex-officio mem. House of Commons' Comm. 2005; Shadow Sec. of State for Transport 2005–07, for Work and Pensions 2007–09; Shadow Home Sec. 2009–10; Minister of State for Employment, Dept for Work and Pensions 2010–12; Lord Chancellor and Sec. of State for Justice (first non-lawyer as Lord Chancellor since 1558) 2012–15, Sec. of State for Transport 2016–; Lord Pres. of the Council 2015–16; Leader of the House of Commons 2015–16. *Publications include:* The Bridgewater Heritage: The Story of Bridgewater Estates 1983, A Land Fit for Heroes: Life in England After the Great War 1985, Holt's: The Story of Joseph Holt 1985, Just Another Star?: Anglo-American Relations Since 1945 (with Christopher Langdon) 1987, Insight Guide Waterways of Europe (contrib.) 1989. *Leisure interest:* Manchester United Football Club. *Address:* Department of Transport, Great Minster House, 33 Horseferry Road, London, SW1P 4DR, England (office). *Telephone:* (300) 330-3000 (office). *Website:* www.gov.uk/government/organisations/department-for-transport (office); www.gov.uk/government/ministers/secretary-of-state-for-transport (office).

GRAZER, Brian; American film company executive and film producer; *Principal, Imagine Entertainment;* b. 12 July 1951, Los Angeles; s. of Thomas Grazer and Arlene Grazer; m. 1st Theresa McKay; m. 2nd Corki Corman Grazer; one s. one d.; m. 3rd Gigi Levangie (divorced 2007); two s.; ed Univ. of Southern California School of Cinema and TV; Co-Chair. Imagine Films Entertainment; David O. Selznick Lifetime Achievement Award 2001, Lifetime Achievement Award, ShoWest 2003. *Films produced include:* Night Shift 1982, Splash 1984, Real Genius 1985, Spies Like Us (jtly) 1985, Armed and Dangerous (jtly) 1986, Like Father, Like Son (jtly) 1987, Parenthood 1989, Cry Baby (jtly) 1990, Kindergarten Cop 1990, Closet Land (jtly) 1991, The Doors (jtly) 1991, Backdraft (jtly) 1991, My Girl 1991, Far and Away (jtly) 1992, Housesitter 1992, Boomerang 1992, CB4 (jtly) 1993, For Love Or Money 1993, The Paper (jtly) 1994, My Girl 2 1994, Greedy 1994, The Cowboy Way 1994, Apollo 13 (jtly) (Daryl F. Zanuck Motion Picture Producer of the Year Award 1995) 1995, Sergeant Bilko 1996, Ransom 1996, Bowfinger 1999, Curious George 2000, Nutty Professor II: The Klumps 2000, How the Grinch Stole Christmas 2000, A Beautiful Mind 2001 (Academy Award 2002, four Golden Globe Awards), 8 Mile 2002, Intolerable Cruelty 2003, The Cat in the Hat 2003, Friday Night Lights 2004, Inside Deep Throat 2005, Cinderella Man 2005, Curious George (Daytime Emmy Award) 2006, Inside Man 2006, American Gangster 2007, Frost/Nixon 2008, The Da Vinci Code, Angels and Demons 2010, Changeling, Robin Hood 2010. *Television includes:* Sports Night (series) 1998, Felicity (series) 1998, From the Earth to the Moon (mini-eries) 1998, Student Affairs 1999, Wonderland (series) 2000, 24 (series) (Emmy Award) 2001–, The Beast (series) 2001, Miss Match (series) 2003, Arrested Development (series) 2003–, The Big House (series) 2004. *Address:* Imagine Films Entertainment, 9465 Wilshire Boulevard, Floor 7, Beverly Hills, CA 90212, USA (office). *Website:* www.imagine-entertainment.com.

GRAZIANO DA SILVA, José, BA, PhD; Brazilian/Italian agro-economist and international organization official; *Director-General, United Nations Food and Agriculture Organization;* b. 17 Nov. 1949, Urbana, Illinois, USA; m. Paola Ligasacchi; two c.; ed Univ. of São Paulo, State Univ. of Campinas, Univ. Coll., London, Univ. of California, Santa Cruz, USA; Prof., State Univ. of Campinas 1978–, also Chair of Master's and Doctoral Program in Econ. Devt, Space, and Environment at Inst. for Econs; coordinated the formulation of the Zero Hunger Program (Fome Zero) in 2001; Extraordinary Minister for Food Security 2003–04; Special Adviser to the Presidency of the Repub. 2004–06; Prof., State Univ. of Campinas and Chair of Master's and Doctoral Program in Econ. Devt, Space and Environment; Regional Rep. for Latin America and the Caribbean and Asst Dir-Gen. FAO 2006–11, Dir-Gen. 2011– (re-elected 2015); Ordem de Rio Branco; Paulista Medal for Scientific and Technological Merit, Brazilian Soc. of Rural Econs Prêmio Sober. *Publications include:* 26 books including O que é a questão agrária (What is the Agrarian Question?), De boias frias a empregados rurais (From Bóias Frias to Rural Workers). *Address:* Food and Agriculture Organization, Viale delle Terme di Caracalla, 00153 Rome, Italy (office). *Telephone:* (06) 5705-1 (office). *Fax:* (06) 5705-3152 (office). *E-mail:* fao-hq@fao.org (office). *Website:* www.fao.org (office); www.grazianodasilva.org.

GRAŽINYTĖ-TYLA, Mirga; Lithuanian conductor; *Music Director, City of Birmingham Symphony Orchestra;* b. 29 Aug. 1986, Vilnius; d. of Romualdas Gražinis and Sigutė Gražinienė; one s.; ed Univ. of Music and Performing Arts, Graz, Austria, Music Conservatory Felix Mendelssohn-Bartholdy, Leipzig, Germany, Music Conservatory, Bologna, Italy, Music Conservatory, Zurich, Switzerland; began career as Asst to Kurt Masur, Orchestre Nat. de France; Opera debut with La traviata, Theater Osnabrück 2010; Second Kapellmeister (conductor), Theater Heidelberg 2011–12; First Kapellmeister, Bern Opera 2013–14; Dudamel Fellow, Los Angeles Philharmonic 2012–13, Asst Conductor 2014–15, Assoc. Conductor 2016–; Music Dir, Salzburg Landestheater 2015–17; Music Dir, City of Birmingham Symphony Orchestra (first female) 2016–; guest appearances with numerous int. orchestras including Gustav Mahler Youth Orchestra, Beethoven Orchestra Bonn, Danish Nat. Symphony Orchestra, Komische Oper Berlin, Kremerata Baltica, Metropolitan Opera Orchestra; debut at BBC Proms, London 2016; Salzburg Festival Young Conductors Award 2012. *Address:* c/o Stefana Atlas, Columbia Artists LLC, 5 Columbus Circle, 1790 Broadway, New York, NY 10019-1412, USA (office); CBSO Centre, Berkley Street, Birmingham B1 2LF, England (office). *Telephone:* (212) 841-9543 (office); (121) 616-6500 (office). *Fax:* (212) 841-9517 (office). *E-mail:* satlas@cami.com (office); information@cbso.co.uk (office). *Website:* ww.cami.com (office); www.stefanaatlas.com (office); mirgagrazinytetyla.com; cbso.co.uk (office).

GRCIC, Konstantin, MA; German product designer; *Chairman, Konstantin Grcic Industrial Design;* b. 1965, Munich; ed Parnham Coll., Beaminster, UK, Royal Coll. of Art, London, UK; apprenticeship as cabinet maker, Parnham Coll. 1985–87; worked in studio of Jasper Morrison 1990; Founder-Chair. Konstantin Grcic Industrial Design, Munich 1991–; designed products for Progetto Ogetto collection of objects commissioned for Cappellini by Jasper Morrison and James Irvine 1992; collections at Museum of Modern Art, New York, Centre Pompidou, Paris, Die Neue Sammlung, Munich; Compasso d'Oro 2001. *Address:* Konstantin Grcic Industrial Design, Schillerstr 40, 80336 Munich, Germany (office). *Telephone:* (50) 79995 (office). *Fax:* (50) 79996 (office). *E-mail:* press@konstantin-grcic.com (office). *Website:* www.konstantin-grcic.com (office).

GREAVES, Derrick, ARCA; British artist; b. 5 June 1927, Sheffield; s. of Harry Greaves and Mabel Greaves; m. Mary Margaret Johnson 1951 (divorced 1991); two s. one d.; m. 2nd Sally Butler 1994; ed RCA, London and British School at Rome; part-time teacher St Martins School of Art 1954–64, Maidstone Coll. of Art and Royal Acad. Schools 1960; Head of Printmaking, Norwich Coll. of Art 1983–91; first one-man exhbn, Beaux Arts Gallery 1953; subsequent one-man exhbns at Zwemmer Gallery 1958, 1960, 1962, 1963, Inst. of Contemporary Arts (ICA), London 1969, 1971, Bear Lane Gallery, Oxford 1970, 1973, Belfast 1972, Dublin 1972, Whitechapel Gallery 1973, Monika Kinley 1973, City Gallery, Milton Keynes 1975, Cranfield Inst. of Tech. 1978, Exposición Int. de la Plástica, Chile 1978, Gallerie Daniel Wahrenberger, Zurich, Switzerland 1996, James Hyman Fine Art, London 2003, 2005, 2007, 2008; group exhbns include Contemporary Arts Soc. 1956, Venice Biennale 1956, Pushkin Museum, Moscow 1957, Whitechapel Gallery

1963, Carnegie Int. Exhbn, Pa 1964, Haymarket Gallery 1974, Royal Acad. 1977, Graves Art Gallery, Sheffield 1980, Fischer Fine Art 1980, Mall Galleries, London 1981, Mappin Art Gallery 1986, Leeds Art Gallery 1986, Philadelphia Museum of Art 1986, Walker Art Gallery; Dr hc (Anglia Ruskin Univ.) 2008; Special Prize, John Moore's Exhbn 1957, Belfast Open Painting Exhbn Purchase Prize 1962. *Publications:* Derrick Greaves. Paintings 1958–80; numerous catalogues; Derrick Greaves – Kitchen Sink to Shangri-La (by James Hyman) 2008. *Address:* c/o James Hyman Gallery, 16 Savile Row, London, W1S 3PL, England. *E-mail:* info@jameshymangallery.com. *Website:* www.derrickgreaves.com.

GREAVES, Roger F., BA; American health care industry executive; *Chairman, Health Net Inc.;* b. 1947, Los Angeles, Calif.; m. Erika Greaves; ed California State Univ., Long Beach; held various man. positions at Allstate Insurance Co. 1962–68, at Blue Cross of Southern Calif. –1982; Co-founder Health Net of California 1982, Pres. Health Systems Int. (renamed Health Net Inc.), then Co-Chair., Pres. and CEO 1994–95, Chair. 2004–; Founding Chair. The Calif. Wellness Foundation (TCWF) 1992, mem. Bd of Dirs 1992–; mem. Leadership Conf. Advisory Council, Schering Plough Pharmaceuticals, Bd of Dirs Health Net of Calif.; Founding mem. Bd of Govs, Calif. State Univ., Long Beach; fmr mem. Bd of Dirs March of Dimes Birth Defects Foundation, Blue Cross, Southern Calif.; Hon. mem. Bd of Trustees, Calif. State Univ. *Address:* Health Net Inc., 21650 Oxford Street, Woodland Hills, CA 91367, USA (office). *Telephone:* (818) 676-6000 (office). *Fax:* (818) 676-8591 (office). *Website:* www.healthnet.com (office).

GREBENÍČEK, Miroslav, PhDr, CSc; Czech university lecturer and politician; b. 21 March 1947, Staré Město, Uherské Hradiště Dist; m.; one s. two d.; ed Masaryk Univ., Brno; worked as teacher at several schools; specialist with Regional Museum, Mikulov 1973–75; mem. CP of Czechoslovakia 1975; Lecturer, Masaryk Univ., Brno 1975–86, Reader 1986–89; Deputy to House of Nations (Fed. Ass. of ČSFR) 1990–92, mem. Presidium 1992; First Vice-Pres., Fed. of CP of Bohemia and Moravia and Party of the Democratic Left (following re-organization of former communist party) Aug.–Nov. 1991, Pres. 1991–92, Chair. Communist Party of Bohemia and Moravia (KSČM) 1993–2005; mem. Chamber of Deputies (Parl.) (KSČM) for Southern Moravia constituency 1996–, mem. Organizational Cttee of Parl. 1996, Parl. Cttee for Petitions 1996–98, for Culture, Youth and Physical Training 1998. *Publications:* monographs, articles and reviews focusing on the history of 19th and 20th centuries. *Address:* Poslanecká sněmovna, Sněmovní 4, 110 00 Prague 1 (office); Zlámalova 9, 692 01 Mikulov, Czech Republic (home). *E-mail:* grebenicekm@psp.cz (office).

GREBENNIKOV, Valery Vassil'yevich; Russian lawyer and politician; b. 14 Oct. 1946; ed Lumumba Univ. of Peoples' Friendship; elected Deputy Chief State Arbiter, Russian Fed. 1990–91, Chief State Arbiter; mem. State Duma 1995, mem. Our Home Russia Faction (Motherland – All Russia) 1999; Vice-Chair., then Chair. Cttee on State Construction; First Deputy Chair. Duma Cttee for Civil, Criminal, Arbitration and Procedural Legislation; Deputy Head of Russian Del. to Parl. Ass. of Council of Europe (PACE); Vice-Pres. OLBI co.; mem. Bd of Dirs Bank of Nat. Credit.

GREBENSHCHIKOV, Boris Borisovich; Russian singer, composer, poet and painter; b. 27 Nov. 1953, Leningrad; s. of Boris A. Grebenshchikov and Ludmila Grebenshchikova; m. Irina Grebenshchikova; one s. two d.; ed Leningrad Univ.; worked as a computer programmer 1977–80; lead singer and guitarist of rock group Akvarium (Aquarium) 1975–; music for films and sound track albums includes Assa 1988, Black Rose 1990; tours and recordings in USA, Canada, Great Britain, Israel, France, China, Japan, all-Russia tour 1991 (110 concerts in 68 cities); performances at Royal Albert Hall, London 2007, 2008, 2014, Beacon Theatre, New York 2017; recorded more than 50 albums; as a painter has taken part in various art exhbns throughout fmr USSR; Medal for Services to the Fatherland 2003; Triumph Prize (for outstanding achievements in Russian culture) 1998. *Radio:* presenter, Aerostat. *Recordings include:* albums: with Akvarium: Blue Album 1981, Triangle 1981, Electricity 1981, Acoustic 1982, Taboo 1982, Radio Africa 1983, Ichthyology 1984, Day Of Silver 1985, Children Of December 1986, Akvarium (USSR) 1987, Equinox 1988, Radio Silence 1989, Russian Album 1992, Favourite Songs of Rameses the 4th 1993, Kostroma Mon Amour 1994, Navigator 1995, Snow Lion 1996, Hyperborea 1997, Lilith 1998, Psi 1999, Sister Chaos 2002, Fisherman's Song 2003, Zoom, Zoom, Zoom 2005, Careless Russian Rover 2006, White Horse 2008, Pushkinskaya 10 2009, Archangelsk 2011, Aquarium + 2013, Salt 2014, Time N 2018. *Publications include:* Ivan and Danilo 1989, poetry and song lyrics, trans. of Indian and Tibetan religious works, four vols of Aerostat's Musical Encyclopedia. *Leisure interests:* music, painting, writing, religions, travelling. *Address:* 2 Marata Street, Apt. 3, 191025 St Petersburg, Russia. *Fax:* (812) 272-05-41. *E-mail:* bg@aquarium.ru. *Website:* www.aquarium.ru; www.aquariumband.com.

GRECEANÎI, Zinaida, MA; Moldovan economist and politician; *Leader, Partidul Socialiştilor din Republica Moldova;* b. 7 Feb. 1956; m.; two c.; ed Moldova State Univ.; various roles within finance and budget inspectorate 1974–91; Economist, then Prin. Economist, Dept of Int. Finance, Ministry of Finance 1995–97, various sr positions including Dir of World Bank Section 1997–2001; Vice-Minister of Finance 2001–02, Minister of Finance 2002–05, served as Gov. for Moldova to IMF; First Deputy Prime Minister 2006–08, Prime Minister 2008–09; mem. Parl. 2009–; mem. Partidul Socialiştilor din Republica Moldova (PSRM), Leader 2016–; Order of Honour, Order of the Repub. *Address:* Parlamentul (Parliament), 2073 Chişinău, bd. Ştefan cel Mare 105, (office); Partidul Socialiştilor din Republica Moldova (PSRM), 2005 Chişinău, str. S. Lazo 25, Moldova (office). *Telephone:* (22) 23-33-52 (Parliament) (office); (22) 81-78-77 (PSRM) (office). *Fax:* (22) 23-30-12 (office). *E-mail:* greceanii.zinaida@gmail.com (office); psrm.md@gmail.com (office). *Website:* www.parliament.md (office); socialistii.md (office).

GRECH, Joe Debono; Maltese politician; b. 17 Sept. 1941, B'Kara; s. of Carmelo Debono and Giovanna Grech; m. Edith Vella; two c.; ed St Aloysius Coll.; mem. Gen. Workers, Union Rep. for Gozo 1971; Sec. Petrol and Chemicals Section 1973–76; fmr Pres. Nat. Exec. Socialist Youth Movt, Gen. Sec. 1967–76; fmr mem. Nat. Exec. Labour Party, Propaganda Sec. 1971–88; Man. Nat. Cargo Handling Co., Interprint; MP 1976–; Minister of Parastatal and People's Investments May–Sept. 1983, of Agric. and Fisheries 1983–87, for Transport and Ports 1996–98; Delegation Leader, Parl. Ass. of the Council of Europe (PACE); Deputy Leader Labour Party 1988; mem. Socialist Bureau, Council of Europe 1998–; Hon. Pres. Santa Venera Band Club. *Leisure interests:* reading, farming. *Address:* House of Representatives, Parliament of Malta, Freedom Square, Valletta VLT1111, Malta (office). *Telephone:* 25596000 (office). *Fax:* 25596400 (office). *E-mail:* parlinfo@parlament.mt (office). *Website:* www.parlament.mt (office).

GRECH, HE Cardinal Stanley (Prospero), OSA, LicScript, DD, PhD; Maltese ecclesiastic and academic; b. 24 Dec. 1925, Vittoriosa (Birgu); ed Gregorian Univ., Rome, Pontifical Biblical Inst., Rome, Univs of Oxford and Cambridge, Merrimack Coll., Boston; professed mem. of the Order of St Augustine 1944, ordained priest 1950; served for many years in Rome, mostly as mem. of community of Collegio Santa Monica; Prof. of Sacred Scripture at various univs in Rome, including the Biblicum and the Lateran and Gregorian Univs; Co-founder and first Pres. Patristic Inst., the Augustinianum; collaborated with numerous dicasteries of the Holy See, especially Congregation for the Doctrine of the Faith; cr. Cardinal (non-voting) (Cardinal-Deacon of Santa Maria Goretti) 2012; Kt of Malta, Companian of Order of Merit. *Publications:* Lo spiritualite del NT 2015, I valori che contano 2015. *Leisure interest:* photography. *Address:* International College of St Monica, Via S. Uffizio 1, Rome (office); Order of St Augustine, Via Paolo VI 25, 00193 Rome, Italy. *Telephone:* (06) 680069. *Fax:* (06) 6834051. *E-mail:* prosperogrech@gmail.com. *Website:* www.augustinians.net.

GRECO, Mario; Italian business executive; *Group CEO, Zurich Insurance Group Limited;* b. 16 June 1959, Naples; ed Univ. of Rome, Rochester Univ., NY, USA; began career at McKinsey & Co. 1986, Partner 1992–94; Head of Claims Div., RAS 1995–96, Gen. Man. 1996–98, Man. Dir 1998–2000, CEO 2000–05; joined Allianz AG Vorstand 2004–05; CEO EurizonVita, Sanpaolo IMI Group 2005, CEO Eurizon Financial Group 2005–07; Deputy CEO of Global Life, Zurich Financial Services 2007–08, CEO and mem. Exec. Cttee 2008–10, CEO Gen. Insurance, Zurich Insurance Group Ltd 2010–12, Group CEO 2016–; Group CEO, Man. Dir and Gen. Man. Assicurazioni Generali SpA 2012–16; mem. Bd of Dirs, Gruppo Editoriale L'Espresso, Indesit, Saras; Insurance CEO of the Year 2004. *Address:* Zurich Insurance Group Ltd, Austrasse 46, 8045 Zurich, Switzerland (office). *Telephone:* (44) 625-25-25 (office). *Fax:* (44) 625-02-99 (office). *E-mail:* info@zurich.com (office). *Website:* www.zurich.com (office).

GREEHEY, William (Bill) E., CPA; American energy industry executive; *Chairman, NuStar Energy L.P.;* b. 1936, Fort Dodge, Ia; m. Louree Bruce; five c.; ed St Mary's Univ., San Antonio, Tex.; began career as accountant, Price Waterhouse; fmr accountant, Exxon; fmr accountant, Coastal Gas Corpn, becoming Vice-Pres. and Controller, Pres. and CEO LoVaca (subsidiary co., Valero from 1980) 1973, CEO Valero Energy Corpn 1980–2006, Chair. 1980–2007, Chair. NuStar Energy L.P. (formerly Valero L.P.) 2002–, Chair. NuStar GP Holdings, LLC 2006–; Founder Pres. Greehey Family Foundation 2004–; Chair. Haven for Hope; fmr Chair. San Antonio Econ. Devt Foundation; mem. Bd of Dirs Southwest Foundation for Biomedical Research; mem. Bd of Trustees United Way of San Antonio (fmr Chair.), Bexar County, St Mary's Univ., San Antonio; fmr mem. Nat. Exec. Bd Boy Scouts of America; Dr hc (St Mary's Univ.) 1998; Silver Beaver Award, Alamo Area Council 1987, Distinguished Alumnus, St. Mary's Univ. 1986, Entrepreneur of the Year Award 1993, Outstanding Philanthropist Award 1998, Int. Citizen of the Year Award, San Antonio World Affairs Council 1999, Horatio Alger Award 2000, Golden Plate Award, American Acad. of Achievement 2000, Good Scout Award 2001, Tex. Business Hall of Fame 2002, Outstanding Volunteer Fundraiser Award, Asscn of Fundraising Professionals 2009. *Address:* NuStar Energy L.P., 19003 IH-10 W, San Antonio, TX 78257, USA (office). *Website:* www.nustarenergy.com (office).

GREEN, Al; American soul singer and songwriter; b. 13 April 1946, Forrest City, Ark.; Founder, The Creations 1964; singer, Al Green and The Soul Mates; f. record label Hot Line Music Journal, 1967; purchased his own church, The Full Gospel Tabernacle in Memphis, Tenn. in late 1970s, became pastor; left secular music 1980, returned 1993; American Music Award, Favourite Soul/R&B Album 1974, Grand Prize, Tokyo Music Festival 1978, Al Green Day, Los Angeles 1978, Soul Train, Best Gospel Recording 1987, numerous Grammy awards include: Best Soul Gospel Performances 1982–85, 1988, 1990, Best Male Soul Performance 1987, Best R&B Performance by a Duo or Group (for Stay With Me with John Legend) 2009, Best Traditional R&B Vocal Performance (for You've Got All the Love I Need) 2009, Grammy Lifetime Achievement Award 2002, Kennedy Center Honor 2014. *Recordings include:* albums: Al Green Gets Next To You 1971, Let's Stay Together 1972, I'm Still In Love With You 1972, Green Is Blues 1973, Call Me 1973, Livin' For You 1974, Al Green Explores Your Mind 1975, Al Green Is Love 1975, Full of Fire 1976, Have A Good Time 1977, Truth 'n' Time 1978, The Belle Album 1978, Cream of Al Green 1980, The Lord Will Make A Way 1980, Higher Plane 1982, Precious Lord 1983, I''ll Rise Again 1983, White Christmas 1983, Going Away 1986, Soul Survivor 1987, I Get Joy 1989, Al 1992, Love and Happiness 2001, I Can't Stop 2003, Everything's OK 2005, Lay it Down 2008. *Address:* Full Gospel Tabernacle, 787 Hale Road, Memphis, TN 38116, USA. *Telephone:* (901) 396-9192.

GREEN, Anthony Eric Sandall, RA; British artist; b. 30 Sept. 1939, Luton; s. of Frederick Sandall and Marie Madeleine Green (née Dupont); m. Mary Louise Cozens-Walker 1961; two d.; ed Highgate School, Slade School of Fine Art, Univ. Coll. London; Asst Art Master, Highgate School 1961–67; Harkness Fellowship, USA 1967–69; Fellow, Univ. Coll. London 1991; elected mem. New English Art Club 2003; held over 100 solo exhbns; works in public and pvt. collections worldwide; French Govt Scholarship, Paris 1960; Hon. RBA, Hon. ROI Exhibit of the Year RA Summer Exhbn 1977, Featured Artist RA Summer Exhbn 2003. *Publication:* A Green Part of the World (with Martin Bailey) 1984. *Leisure interests:* family, travel. *Address:* Mole End, 40 High Street, Little Eversden, Cambridge, CB23 1HE, England (home). *Telephone:* (1223) 262292 (home). *Fax:* (1223) 265656 (home).

GREEN, Ben Joseph, BA, PhD, FRS; British mathematician and academic; *Waynflete Professor of Pure Mathematics, University of Oxford;* b. 27 Feb. 1977, Bristol, England; m.; two s.; ed Fairfield Grammar School, Trinity Coll., Cambridge; Fellow under Title A, Trinity Coll., Cambridge 2001–05; EU Postdoctoral Researcher, Alfréd Rényi Inst., Budapest 2003; PIMS Postdoctoral Fellow in Number Theory, Univ. of British Columbia, Canada 2003–04; Prof. of Math., Univ. of Bristol 2005–06; Research Fellow, Clay Math. Inst. 2005–07;

inaugural Herchel Smith Prof. of Pure Math., Univ. of Cambridge 2006–13; Waynflete Prof. of Pure Math., Univ. of Oxford 2013–; mem. Inst. of Advanced Study, Princeton 2007; Visiting Prof., MIT 2005–06; Radcliffe Fellow, Harvard Univ. 2009–10; Int. Ed. Glasgow Mathematical Journal; Man. Ed. Proceedings of Cambridge Philosophical Society; Ed. Journal de Théorie des Nombres de Bordeaux; Fellow, American Math. Soc. 2012; Senior Wrangler title 1998, Smith's Prize, Univ. of Cambridge 2001, Clay Research Award 2004, Salem Prize 2005, Ostrowski Prize (co-recipient) 2005, Whitehead Prize, London Math. Soc. 2005, ICM Section Lecturer 2006, Leverhulme Prize 2007, SASTRA Ramanujan Prize 2007, European Math. Soc. Prize (co-recipient) 2008, ICM Plenary Lecturer 2014, Sylvester Medal, Royal Soc. 2014. *Achievements include:* competed in Int. Math. Olympiad 1994, 1995. *Publications:* numerous papers in professional journals on combinatorics and number theory; contrib. of more than 160 reviews to MathSciNet Reviews. *Leisure interests:* orienteering, gardening. *Address:* Room N1.29, Mathematical Institute, University of Oxford, Andrew Wiles Building, Radcliffe Observatory Quarter, Woodstock Road, Oxford, OX2 6GG, England (office). *Telephone:* (1865) 273588 (office); (1865) 273525 (office). *E-mail:* ben.green@maths.ox.ac.uk (office). *Website:* www.maths.ox.ac.uk (office).

GREEN, Rt Hon. Damian Howard; British politician; b. 17 Jan. 1956, Barry, Wales; m. Alicia Collinson; two d.; ed Balliol Coll., Oxford; began career as journalist for BBC, Channel 4 and The Times; worked in Prime Minister's Policy Unit 1992–94; MP (Conservative) for Ashford 1997–, mem. Culture, Media and Sport Cttee 1997–98, Procedure Cttee 1997–98, Home Affairs Cttee 2004–05, Treasury Cttee 2005–06, European Scrutiny Cttee 2015–, Nat. Security Strategy (Jt Cttee) 2015–; Shadow Spokesperson for Work and Pensions and for Educ. 1998–99, for Environment, Food and Rural Affairs 1999–2001, Shadow Sec. of State for Educ. 2001–03, for Transport 2003–04, Shadow Minister (Home Affairs) 2005–10, Minister of State (Home Office) (Immigration) 2010–12, Minister of State (Policing) (Home Office jtly with Ministry of Justice) 2012–14, Sec. of State for Work and Pensions 2016–17, First Sec. of State and Minister for the Cabinet Office June–Dec. 2017 (resgnd). *Address:* House of Commons, London, SW1A 0AA, England (office). *E-mail:* damian.green.mp@parliament.uk (office). *Website:* www.damiangreen.co.uk.

GREEN, Dan, BA; American book publishing executive; *Literary agent, Pom Inc.;* b. 28 Sept. 1935, Passaic, NJ; s. of Harold Green and Bessie Roslow; m. Jane Oliphant 1959; two s.; ed Syracuse Univ.; Publicity Dir Dover Press 1957–58; Station WNAC-TV 1958–59; Bobbs-Merrill Co. 1959–62; joined Simon & Schuster Inc. 1962, Assoc. Publr 1976–80, Vice-Pres., Publr 1980–84; Pres. Trade Publishing Group 1984–85; Founder and Publr, Kenan Press 1979–80; CEO Grove Press and Weidenfeld & Nicolson, New York 1985–89; Pres. Kenan Books, New York 1989–; Literary agent, Pom Inc. (literary agency) 1989–. *Address:* Pom Inc., 18-15 215 Street, Bayside, NY 11360 (office); Kenan Books, 18-15 215 Street, Bayside, NY 11360, USA (home). *Telephone:* (516) 487-3441 (office). *E-mail:* dangreen@pomlit.com (office).

GREEN, David Gordon; American film director, film and television producer and screenwriter; b. 9 April 1975, Little Rock, Ark.; s. of Hubert Gordon Green, Jr and Jean Ann (née Hunter); ed Richardson High School, North Carolina School of the Arts; raised in Tex.; wrote and directed first feature film George Washington (New York Film Critics' Prize and several major int. festival awards) 2000; also directs commercial advertising campaigns. *Films directed include:* Pleasant Grove (short, also writer) 1997, Physical Pinball (short, also writer) 1998, George Washington (also producer and writer) 2000, All the Real Girls (also writer) 2003, Undertow (also screenplay) 2004, Snow Angels (also screenplay) 2007, Pineapple Express 2008, Your Highness 2011, The Sitter 2011, Prince Avalanche (also producer and writer) (Silver Bear for Best Dir, Berlin Int. Film Festival) 2013, Joe (also producer) 2013, Manglehorn (also producer) 2014, Our Brand Is Crisis 2015. *Films produced include:* Shotgun Stories 2007, Great World of Sound 2007, The Catechism Cataclysm 2011, The Comedy (exec. producer) 2012, Compliance (exec. producer) 2012, Nature Calls (exec. producer) 2012, See Girl Run (exec. producer) 2012, Camp X-Ray (exec. producer) 2014, Land Ho! (exec. producer) 2014. *Television includes:* dir: Eastbound & Down (series, also consulting producer) 2009–13, Black Jack (film, also exec. producer) 2011, Red Oaks (series, also creator) 2014; exec. producer: Good Vibes (series) 2011, Chozen (series) 2014. *Address:* c/o Chelsea Pictures, 5979 West 3rd Street, Suite 203, Los Angeles, CA 90036, USA (office). *Telephone:* (323) 935-8030 (office). *E-mail:* info@chelsea.com (office). *Website:* www.chelsea.com (office).

GREEN, Hon. Sir Guy Stephen Montague, Kt, AC, KBE, CVO, LLB; Australian administrator and judge; b. 26 July 1937, Launceston, Tasmania; s. of Clement Francis Montague and Beryl Margaret Jenour (née Williams) Green; m. Rosslyn Marshall 1963; two s. two d.; ed Launceston Church Grammar School and Univ. of Tasmania; admitted to Bar 1960; Partner Ritchie & Parker Alfred Green & Co. 1963–71; Pres. Tasmanian Bar Assen 1968–70; Magistrate 1971–73; Chief Justice of Tasmania 1973–95; Lt-Gov. of Tasmania 1982–95; Gov. of Tasmania 1995–2003; mem. Faculty of Law Univ. of Tasmania 1974–85; Chair. Council of Law Reporting 1978–85; Chair. Tasmanian Cttee, Duke of Edinburgh's Award in Australia 1975–80; Dir Winston Churchill Memorial Trust 1975–85, Deputy Nat. Chair. 1980–85; Chancellor, Univ. of Tasmania 1985–95; Deputy Chair. Australian Inst. of Judicial Admin. 1986–88; Pres. St John Council 1984–92; Priory Exec. Officer, Order of St John in Australia 1984–91, Chancellor 1991–95; Deputy Prior St John Ambulance Australia 1995; Administrator of the Commonwealth (Acting Gov.-Gen. of Australia) 2003; Hon. LLD (Univ. of Tasmania) 1996; Kt of Grace, Most Venerable Order of the Hosp. of St John of Jerusalem 1985. *Address:* 13 Marine Terrace, Battery Point, Tasmania 7004, Australia.

GREEN, Hamilton; Guyanese politician; b. 9 Nov. 1934, Georgetown; s. of Wilfred Amelius Green and Edith Ophelia Dorothy Green; m. 1st Shirley Field-Ridley 1970 (died 1982); five s. three d.; m. 2nd Dr Jennifer Veronica Basdeo 1990; two d.; ed Queen's Coll.; fmrly Gen. Sec., People's Nat. Congress, Minister of Works, Hydraulics and Supply, of Public Affairs, of Co-operatives and Nat. Mobilization, of Health, Housing and Labour; fmrly Vice-Pres. with responsibility for Public Welfare, Vice-Pres. with responsibility for Production; Vice-Pres. and Prime Minister of Guyana 1985–92; expelled from People's Nat. Congress 1992; f. political and environmental group Good And Green Guyana; Mayor of Georgetown 1994, 2004–16; unsuccessful presidential cand. 1997; mem. Presiding Council, Universal Peace Fed. *Publication:* From Pain to Peace – Guyana 1953–1964 (series of lectures at Cyril Potter Coll. of Educ. 1986). *Leisure interests:* reading (history and philosophy), table tennis, boxing and fitness training.

GREEN, Harriet, OBE, BA; British business executive; b. 12 Dec. 1961, Cheltenham; m. Graham Clarkson; one step-s. one step-d.; ed King's Coll. London; joined Macro Group as Man. Trainee 1985, becoming Man. Dir 1990; various roles with Arrow Electronics 1993–2006, including Man. Dir, N Europe, Head of Sales, China, Pres., Asia Pacific; CEO Premier Farnell (electronic parts distributor) 2006–12; CEO Thomas Cook Group PLC 2012–14, mem. Bd of Dirs 2014–; mem. Bd of Dirs Emerson Electric Co. 2008–, BAE Systems 2010–; mem. Prime Minister's Business Advisory Group; Founder-mem. and Trustee PeaceWorks Foundation; UK Nat. Business Awards Leader of the Year 2013, winner, Veuve Clicquot Business Woman Award 2014. *Leisure interests:* reading, yoga.

GREEN, Malcolm Leslie Hodder, BSc, MA (Cantab.), MA (Oxon.), DIC, PhD, FRS; British chemist and academic; *Professor Emeritus of Inorganic Chemistry and Emeritus Fellow of Balliol College, University of Oxford;* b. 16 April 1936, Eastleigh, Hants., England; s. of Leslie E. Green and Sheila Mary Green (née Hodder); m. Jennifer C. Bilham; three c.; ed Acton Tech. Coll., Univ. of London, Imperial Coll. of Science and Tech.; Postdoctoral Research Assoc. Fellow, Imperial Coll. of Science and Tech. 1959–60; Asst Lecturer in Inorganic Chem., Univ. of Cambridge 1960–63, Fellow, Corpus Christi Coll. 1961; Septcentuary Tutorial Fellow, Balliol Coll. Oxford 1963–89, Lecturer, Univ. of Oxford 1965–, Fellow St Catherine's Coll. 1989–, Prof. of Inorganic Chem. and Head of Dept 1989–2003, Prof. Emer. 2003–; Visiting Prof., Univ. of Western Ontario, Canada 1971, Ecole de Chimie and Inst. des Substances Naturelles, Paris, France 1972, Harvard Univ., USA (A.P. Sloan Visiting Prof.) 1973, Wuhan Univ., China 1985; Bert and Keggie Vallee Visiting Prof., Harvard Univ., USA 2004; Distinguished Visiting Prof., Hong Kong Univ. 2004–12; Sr Research Fellow, British Gas Royal Soc. 1979–84, 1984–86; Head, Chem. Dept Cttee, RSC 1989–; Chair. Editorial Bd, RSC Chemical Communication 1997–99; Co-founder Oxford Catalysts PLC (now called Velocys) 2004, mem. Bd of Dirs and mem. Scientific Advisory Panel 2006–08; mem. Editorial Bd several journals, including Topics in Chemica, Communications, Catalysis, Organometallics, Nouveau Journal de Chimie, Journal of Organometallic Chemistry; mem. Bd, Inst. of Applied Catalysis 1995–; mem. EUAS 2016; Hon. Prof., Wuhan Univ., China 2004; Dr hc (Lisbon, Portugal) 1997; Hon. DSc (Southampton) 2006, (Warwick) 2015; invited to present numerous hon. lectures at int. univs 1974; numerous awards, including RSC Corday-Morgan Medal 1974, Tilden Prize 1982, ACS Annual Award for Inorganic Chem. 1984, RSC Medal in Organometallic Chem. 1986, Gesellschaft Deutscher Chemiker Karl-Ziegler Prize 1992, Royal Soc. Davy Medal 1995, Frank Dyer Medal, Univ. of New South Wales 1997, Fred Basolo Medal, Northwestern Univ. 1998, RSC Sir Geoffrey Wilkinson Medal 2000, Prix Franco-Britannique, Soc. française de Chimie 2006. *Publications:* two books and more than 740 publs. *Leisure interest:* family. *Address:* Inorganic Chemistry Laboratory, University of Oxford, South Parks Road, Oxford, OX1 3QR, England (office). *Telephone:* (1865) 272600 (office). *E-mail:* malcolm.green@chem.ox.ac.uk (office). *Website:* research.chem.ox.ac.uk/malcolm-green.aspx (office); www.covalentbondclass.org.

GREEN, Martin Andrew, AM, BE, MEngSc, PhD, DEng, FRS, FAA, FTS, FIEEE; Australian scientist, academic and business executive; *Executive Research Director, Australian Centre for Advanced Photovoltaics;* b. 20 July 1948, Brisbane, Queensland; s. of Eric William Green and Gwendolyn Lorraine Green (née Horsfall); m.; two c.; ed Univ. of Queensland, McMaster Univ., Canada, Univ. of New South Wales; initiated Solar Photovoltaics Group at Univ. of New South Wales 1974–, currently Scientia Prof., School of Photovoltaic and Renewable Energy Eng, Dir Australian Centre for Advanced Photovoltaics; Hon. Prof. Fuzhou Univ., Beijing Inst. of Tech.; Pawsey Medal, Australian Acad. 1982, Award for Outstanding Achievement in Energy Research 1988, IEEE Cherry Award 1990, CSIRO External Medal 1992, IEEE Ebers Award 1995, Australia Prize 1999, Gold Medal, Spanish Eng Acad. 2000, Medal of Eng Excellence for Distinguished Achievement in the Service of Humanity, World Eng Fed., Hanover 2000, Millennium Award, World Renewable Congress 2000, Right Livelihood Award 2002, Karl Böer Solar Energy Medal of Merit Award, Univ. of Delaware 2003, World Tech. Award in Energy, The World Tech. Network 2004, SolarWorld Einstein Award 2007, ENI Renewable Energy Award 2009, Eureka Prize 2010; AuSES Global Leadership in Solar Research Award 2011, James Cook Medal 2014, Ian Wark Medal 2016, World Solar Congress Award, Shanghai 2017, Global Energy Prize 2018. *Publications include:* five books, nine book chapters, numerous reports, patents and conference papers, and more than 500 papers in int. refereed journals on semiconductors, micro-electronics and solar cells. *Address:* Room 108, School of Photovoltaic and Renewable Energy Engineering, Tyree Energy Technologies Building, University of New South Wales, Sydney, NSW 2052, Australia (office). *Telephone:* (2) 9385-4018 (office). *Fax:* (2) 9662-4240 (office). *E-mail:* m.green@unsw.edu.au (office). *Website:* www.pv.unsw.edu.au (office).

GREEN, Michael Boris, PhD, FRS; British physicist and academic; *Lucasian Professor of Mathematics, University of Cambridge;* b. 22 May 1946, London, England; s. of Absalom Green and Genia Green; m. Joanna Chataway; one d.; ed William Ellis School, London, Univ. of Cambridge; Post-doctoral Fellowship, Inst. for Advanced Study, Princeton, NJ, USA 1970–72, Univ. of Cambridge 1972–77; Science and Eng Research Council (SERC) Advanced Fellowship, Univ. of Oxford 1977–79; Lecturer, Queen Mary and Westfield Coll., London 1979–85, Prof. of Physics 1985–93; SERC Sr Fellowship 1986–91; John Humphrey Plummer Prof. of Theoretical Physics, Univ. of Cambridge 1993–2009, Lucasian Prof. of Math. 2009–; numerous fellowships at US and European Insts, including Distinguished Fairchild Fellowship, Calif. Inst. of Tech. 1990; Hon. Fellow, Clare Hall, Cambridge 2009, Churchill Coll., Cambridge 2010; Hon. FInstP 2013; Hon. DSc (Queen Mary, Univ. of London) 2004; Maxwell Medal, Inst. of Physics 1987, William Hopkins Prize, Cambridge Philosophical Soc. 1987, Dirac Medal, Int. Center for Theoretical Physics 1989, Dannie Heineman Prize, American Physical Soc. 2002, Dirac Medal and Prize, Inst. of Physics 2004, Naylor Prize, London Math. Soc. 2007, Breakthrough Prize in Fundamental Physics (co-recipient) 2014. *Publications:* Superstring Theory (two vols, with J. H. Schwarz and E. Witten) 1987; numerous publs in scientific journals. *Leisure interests:* pottery, music.

Address: DAMTP, Centre for Mathematical Sciences, University of Cambridge, Wilberforce Road, Cambridge, CB3 0WA, England (office). *Telephone:* (1223) 330884 (office). *Fax:* (1223) 765900 (office). *E-mail:* mbg15@damtp.cam.ac.uk (office). *Website:* www.damtp.cam.ac.uk (office).

GREEN, Michael Philip, MA, ADipPsy, UKCP; British psychotherapist; b. 2 Dec. 1947, London; s. of Cyril Green and Irene Green; m. 1st Hon. Janet F. Wolfson 1972 (divorced 1989); two d.; m. 2nd Theresa Buckmaster 1990; three s. one d.; ed Haberdashers' Aske's School; Dir and Co-Founder, Tangent Industries Ltd 1968–; Chief Exec. Carlton Communications PLC 1983–91, Chair. 1983–2004, Chair. Carlton TV Ltd 1991–94, Chair. ITV PLC 2003–04, fmr Chair. ITN; Founder Tangent Charitable Trust 1984; mem. Bd of Dirs GMTV Ltd 1992–2004, Reuters Holdings PLC 1992–99, Getty Communications PLC 1997–98; Chair. The Media Trust 1997–2006; Trustee, Sainsbury Centre for Mental Health 2001–05; mem. British Assen of Counselling and Psychotherapy; Hon. DLitt (City Univ.) 1999. *Leisure interests:* reading, bridge. *Address:* 21 South Street, London, W1K 2XB, England (office). *Telephone:* (20) 7663-6464 (office). *Fax:* (20) 7663-6364 (office). *Website:* www.21southstreet.com (office).

GREEN, Sir Philip, Kt; British retail executive; *Chairman, Arcadia Group Ltd;* b. 15 March 1952, Croydon; m. Tina Green; two c.; took over family property co. 1973; bought Jean Jeanie 1985 (sold to Lee Cooper), Owen Owen 1994, Sports Division (sold to JJB Sports), Mark One 1996, Shoe Express 1997, Sears 1999, British Home Stores (sold to Retail Acquisitions Ltd 2015) 2000, Arcadia Group (now Chair., includes Top Shop, Top Man, Miss Selfridge, Dorothy Perkins, Wallis, Evans and Burtons clothing chains) 2002; Chair. and CEO Amber Day (now What Everyone Wants) 1988–92; Owner, Taveta Investments; apptd to lead UK govt efficiency review 2010. *Address:* Arcadia Group Ltd, Colegrave House, 70 Berners Street, London, W1T 3NL, England (office). *Telephone:* (20) 7636-8040 (office). *Fax:* (20) 7927-0577 (office). *Website:* www.arcadiagroup.co.uk (office).

GREEN, William (Bill) D., BS (Econs), MBA; American management consultancy executive; *Chairman of the Board, BackOffice Associates;* b. Aug. 1953; m.; two c.; ed Dean Coll., Babson Coll.; joined Accenture Ltd 1977, various positions including Partner 1986, Head of Mfg Industry Group, Man.-Partner of New England Operations, Head of Resources Operating Group 1997–99, CEO Communications & High Tech. Group 1999–2003, Country Man.-Dir, USA 2000–03, Dir 2001–13, COO Client Services 2003–04, CEO 2004–10, Exec. Chair. 2006–13; Chair. of the Bd BackOffice Assocs. 2017–; Co-CEO and Co-Chair. of the Bd GTY Tech. Holdings Inc.; Co-Chair. Business Coalition for Student Achievement; mem. Nat. Govs Assen's Complete to Compete Nat. Advisory Group, Business Higher Educ. Forum, The Business Council, G100; mem. Bd of Dirs EMC Corpn 2013–16, The McGraw-Hill Cos (now S&P Global Inc.), Pivotal Software, Inc., Inovalon, Dell Techs.; Trustee, Dean Coll.; Hon. LLD (Babson Coll.). *Address:* BackOffice Associates, 75 Perseverance Way, Hyannis, MA 02601, USA (office). *Telephone:* (508) 430-7100 (office). *E-mail:* info@boaweb.com (office). *Website:* www.boaweb .com (office).

GREEN OF HURSTPIERPOINT, Baron (Life Peer), cr. 2010, of Hurstpierpoint in the County of West Sussex; **Stephen Keith Green,** MSc; British banking executive and fmr government official; *Chairman, Natural History Museum;* b. 7 Nov. 1948; m.; two d.; ed Univ. of Oxford, Massachusetts Inst. of Tech., USA; early career with Ministry of Overseas Devt; consultant, McKinsey & Co. 1977; joined Hongkong and Shanghai Banking Corpn (HSBC) 1982, responsible for Corp. Planning, Group Treas., HSBC Holdings PLC 1992–98, Dir HSBC Bank PLC 1995, Exec. Dir Corp., Investment Banking and Markets 1998–2003, Group Chief Exec. 2003–06, Group Chair. 2006–10; Minister of State for Trade and Investment 2011–13; Chair. British Bankers' Assen 2006–10, Prime Minister's Business Council for Britain 2009–10; Dir (non-exec.) BASF SE 2009–10; mem. House of Lords; mem. Bd of Trustees, British Museum 2005–10, Natural History Museum 2014– (Chair. 2014–); Non-stipendiary minister with the Anglican Church, deacon 1987, priest 1988; Trustee, Archbishop of Canterbury's Anglican Communion Fund; Hon. Trustee, Peking Univ. *Publication:* Serving God? Serving Mammon? Christians and the Financial Market 1996, Good Value: Reflections on Money, Morality and an Uncertain World 2009, Reluctant Meister: How Germany's Past is Shaping its European Future 2014. *Address:* House of Lords, London, SW1A 0PW, England (office). *Telephone:* (20) 7219-5353 (office). *Fax:* (20) 7219-5979 (office). *E-mail:* contactholmember@parliament.uk (office). *Website:* www.parliament.uk/biographies/lords/lord-green-of-hurstpierpoint/4191 (office).

GREENAWAY, Sir David, Kt, BSc, MCom, DLitt; British economist, academic and university administrator; *Professor Emeritus, University of Nottingham;* b. 20 March 1952, Glasgow, Scotland; s. of David Greenaway and Agnes Greenaway; m. Susan Elizabeth Hallam; two s.; ed Liverpool Polytechnic, Univs of Liverpool and Nottingham; Head of Dept of Econs, Univ. of Nottingham 1987, later Prof. of Econs, Dean Faculty of Law and Social Sciences 1991–94, Univ. Pro-Vice-Chancellor (Vice-Pres.) 1994–2001, 2004–08, Vice-Chancellor (Pres.) 2008–17, now Prof. Emer.; mem. Armed Forces Pay Review Body 1998–2010 (Chair. 2004–10), Sr Salaries Review Body 2004–10, Review of Uninsured Driving for Sec. of State for Transport 2005–06; Chair. Ind. Review of Postgraduate Medical Educ. and Training in the UK 2012–13, Case Europe Bd of Trustees 2014–, Russell Group of Univs 2015–; f. Leverhulme Centre for Research on Globalisation and Econ. Policy 1998; Gov. Nat. Inst. of Econ. and Social Research; Chair. Scientific Advisory Council, Institut für Weltwirtschaft, Kiel Univ.; mem. Scientific Cttee European Trade Study Group; Man. Ed. The World Economy (journal); DL of Notts. 2009–; mem. Council, Univ. of Cambridge 2017–, Nat. Inst. of Econ. and Social Research 2018–; Hon. Fellow, Liverpool John Moores Univ.; Hon. Citizen of Ningbo, China 2012; Hon. Col, East Midlands Univs Officers' Training Corps 2013–; Hon. Freeman, City of Nottingham 2017; Dr hc (Univ. of Liverpool) 2015, (Univ. of Western Ontario) 2017, (Glasgow Caledonian Univ.) 2017. *Publications:* author or ed. of 40 books; 160 articles in learned journals. *Leisure interests:* football, cycling, reading. *Address:* School of Economics, University of Nottingham, University Park, Nottingham, NG7 2RD, England (office). *Telephone:* (115) 951-5469 (office). *E-mail:* david.greenaway@nottingham.ac.uk (office). *Website:* www .nottingham.ac.uk/Economics/People/david.greenaway (office); www.nottingham .ac.uk/aEconomics/People/david.greenaway (office).

GREENAWAY, Peter, CBE; British film director, writer and painter; b. April 1942, Newport, Gwent, Wales; m.; two d.; ed Forest School and Walthamstow Coll. of Art; trained as painter and first exhibited pictures at Lord's Gallery 1964; film ed. Cen. Office of Information 1965–76; began making own films in 1966, numerous curatorial exhbns, one-man shows and group shows in Europe, USA, Australia and Japan 1988–; currently Prof. of Cinema Studies, European Graduate School, Saas-Fee, Switzerland; Officier, Ordre des Arts et Lettres; BAFTA Award for Outstanding British Contrib. to Cinema 2014. *Films include:* Train, Tree 1966, Revolution, Five Postcards from Capital Cities 1967, Intervals 1969, Erosion 1971, H is for House 1973, Windows, Water, Water Wrackets 1975, Goole by Numbers 1976, Dear Phone 1977, 1–100, A Walk Through H (Hugo Award, Chicago), Vertical Features Remake 1978, Zandra Rhodes (Hugo Award, Chicago 1981) 1979, The Falls (BFI Award, L'Age d'Or Brussels) 1980, Act of God (Melbourne Short Film Prize, Sydney Short Film Prize) 1981, The Draughtsman's Contract 1982, Four American Composers 1983, Making a Splash 1984, Inside Rooms: 26 Bathrooms 1985, A Zed & Two Noughts 1986, The Belly of An Architect (Best Actor Prize, Chicago) 1987, Drowning by Numbers (Best Artistic Contribution Prize), Fear of Drowning, Death in the Seine 1988, A TV Dante Cantos 1–8, Hubert Bals Handshake 1989, The Cook, The Thief, His Wife and Her Lover 1989, Prospero's Books, M is for Man, Music, Mozart 1991, Rosa (Dance Screen Prize), Darwin 1992, The Baby of Macon 1993, The Stairs, Geneva 1994, The Pillow Book (La Distinction Gervais, Cannes, Best Film and Best Cinematographer, Sitges, Spain) 1995, Flying over Water 1997, 8½ Women 1999, The Death of a Composer: Rosa, a Horse Drama 1999, The Man in the Bath 2001, The Tulse Luper Suitcases, Part 1: The Moab Story 2003, The Tulse Luper Suitcases, Part 3: From Sark to the Finish 2003, The Tulse Luper Suitcases, Part 2: Vaux to the Sea 2004, A Life in Suitcases 2005, Nightwatching 2007, Rembrandt's J'Accuse (documentary) 2008. *Opera:* Rosa, a Horse Drama 1994, Writing to Vermeer 1999. *Publications include:* A Zed and Two Noughts 1986, Belly of an Architect 1987, Drowning By Numbers, Fear of Drowning 1988, The Cook, The Thief, His Wife and Her Lover 1989, Papers 1990, Prospero's Books 1991, Prospero's Subjects (picture book) 1992, Rosa, The Falls, The Baby of Macon 1993, The Draughtsman's Contract 1994, The Pillow Book 1996. *Address:* c/o European Graduate School, Building Steinmatte, 3906 Saas Fee, Switzerland; c/o The Vue, 387B King Street, London, W6 9NJ, England. *Fax:* (20) 8748-3597. *E-mail:* info@petergreenawayevents.com. *Website:* www .petergreenawayevents.com; www.egs.edu/faculty/petergreenaway.html.

GREENBERG, E(verett) Peter, BS, MS, PhD; American microbiologist and academic; *Professor of Microbiology, University of Washington, Seattle;* b. 1948, New York, NY; ed Western Washington Univ., Univ. of Iowa, Univ. of Massachusetts; fmr Postdoctoral Fellow, Harvard Univ.; fmr Asst Prof., Cornell Univ.; Prof., Univ. of Iowa 1988–2005; Prof. of Microbiology, Univ. of Washington, Seattle 2005–; mem. NAS 2004; Fellow, American Acad. of Arts and Sciences, AAAS, American Acad. of Microbiology; Shaw Prize in Life Science and Medicine (co-recipient) 2015. *Achievements include:* widely credited for discovery of quorum sensing, a process by which bacterial cells communicate with each other. *Publications:* numerous papers in professional journals on sociomicrobiology, quorum sensing, biofilm biology and regulation of virulence genes. *Address:* Microbiology, Mail Box 357735, Health Sciences K-359A, University of Washington, 1705 NE Pacific Street, Seattle, WA 98195-7735, USA (office). *Telephone:* (206) 616-2881 (office). *Fax:* (206) 543-8297 (office). *E-mail:* epgreen@uw.edu (office). *Website:* microbiology.washington.edu (office); depts.washington.edu/epglab (office).

GREENBERG, Jack M., BSc, JD, CPA; American business executive; *Chairman and Presiding Director, Western Union Company;* b. 1942; s. of Edith S. Scher; m. Donna Greenberg; one s. two d.; ed Depaul Univ.; with Arthur Young & Co. 1964–82; Chief Finance Officer and Exec. Vice-Pres. McDonald's Corpn 1982, Vice-Chair. 1992, Pres., CEO 1997–99, Chair., CEO 1999–2002 (retd), also Dir; Chair. and Presiding Dir. Western Union Co. 2006–; mem. Bd of Dirs The Allstate Corpn, Hasbro, Inc., Innerworkings, Inc., Manpower Inc., DePaul University (fmr Chair.), Field Museum, Chicago Metropolis 2020; Trustee, Inst. of Int. Educ., Ronald McDonald House Charities, Chicago Symphony Orchestra, Chicago Bar Foundation, Chicago Community Trust; mem. American Inst. of Certified Public Accountants, ABA, Illinois CPA Soc., Council of the World Econ. Forum, Chicago Commercial Club, Chicago Bar Assen; Hon. Dir American-Israel Chamber of Commerce and Industry, Inc. of Metropolitan Chicago; Hon. DHumLitt (DePaul) 1999. *Address:* Western Union Company, 12500 East Belford Avenue, Englewood, CO 80112, USA (office). *Telephone:* (720) 332-1000 (office). *Fax:* (720) 332-4753 (office). *Website:* www.westernunion.com (office).

GREENBERG, Jeffrey W., AB, JD; American business executive; *CEO, Aquiline Holdings LLC;* b. 1952; s. of Maurice R. Greenberg and Corinne P. Zuckerman; m. 1st Nikki Finke (divorced 1982); m. 2nd Kimberly Greenberg; ed Brown Univ., Georgetown Univ. Law School; fmr Head of Property/Casualty, American Int. Group; joined Marsh & McLennan Risk Capital 1996, CEO Marsh and McLennan Cos 1999–2004, Chair. 2000–04 (resgnd); Founder Chair. Aquiline Holdings LLC, currently also CEO Aquiline Capital Partners LLC; Chair. Conning Holdings Corpn; mem. Bd of Dirs Futurity First Insurance Group, Validus Holdings Ltd; mem. Bd of Overseers Joan and Sanford I. Weill Graduate School of Medical Sciences, Cornell Univ.; Trustee, Brookings Inst., Spence School, New York Presbyterian Hospital, Brookings Institution, Metropolitan Museum of Art; mem. Trilateral Comm., Council on Foreign Relations, Brown Univ. Corpn, Assen of the Bar, New York. *Address:* Aquiline Holdings LLC, 535 Madison Avenue, 24th Floor, New York, NY 10022, USA (office). *Telephone:* (212) 624-9500 (office). *E-mail:* contact@aquiline-llc.com (office). *Website:* www.aquiline-llc.com (office).

GREENBERG, Maurice Raymond (Hank), LLB; American lawyer and business executive; *Chairman and CEO, C.V. Starr & Co.;* b. 4 May 1925; s. of Jacob Greenberg and Ada Greenberg (née Rheingold); m. Corinne Phyllis Zuckerman 1950; four c.; ed Univ. of Miami, New York Univ. Law School; service with US army in Second World War and Korean War, rising to rank of Capt.; admitted to NY Bar 1953; worked for Continental Casualty Co. 1952–60; joined American Int. Group (AIG) Inc. 1960, Pres. American Home Assurance Co. 1962–67, CEO AIG Inc. 1967–2005, Chair. 1989–2005; Vice-Pres., C.V. Starr & Co. 1960–65, Dir 1965–68, Pres. 1968–2005, CEO 1968–, Chair. 2005–; mem. The Business Roundtable, Pres.'s Advisory Cttee for Trade Policy and Negotiations; Chair. US–China

Business Council, US–ASEAN Council on Business and Tech., US–Philippine Business Cttee, The Starr Foundation; Vice-Chair. Center for Strategic and Int. Studies, Council on Foreign Relations; Chair. Emer. and Gov. Soc. of the NY Hosp.; hon. degrees from New England School of Law, NY Law School, Bryant Coll., Middlebury Coll., Brown Univ., Pace Univ. *Publication:* The AIG Story 2013. *Address:* C.V. Starr and Co., 399 Park Avenue, New York, NY 10022, USA (office). *Telephone:* (212) 230-5050 (office). *Fax:* (212) 230-5092 (office). *Website:* www.cvstarrco.com (office).

GREENBERG, Robert R., PhD; American chemist; *Research Chemist and Group Leader, Chemical Science and Technology Laboratory, National Institute of Standards and Technology;* b. Brooklyn, New York; ed Brooklyn Coll.; Research Chemist and Group Leader, Chemical Science and Tech. Lab., Nat. Inst. of Standards and Tech. (NIST) 1976–; Fellow, American Nuclear Soc. 1998, mem. Exec. Cttee Biology and Medicine Div. 2009; NIST Judson C. French Award 2003, NIST Bronze Medal 2007, Hevesy Medal, Journal of Radioanalytical and Nuclear Chemistry 2007. *Publications include:* numerous scientific papers in professional journals on the devt of high accuracy/high precision nuclear analytical methods and quality assurance procedures, and application of these methods to certification of standard reference materials. *Address:* Analytical Chemistry Division (839), National Institute of Standards and Technology, 100 Bureau Drive, Stop 8395, Gaithersburg, MD 20899-8395, USA (office). *Telephone:* (301) 975-6285 (office). *Fax:* (301) 208-9279 (office). *E-mail:* robert.greenberg@nist.gov (office). *Website:* www.nist.gov (office).

GREENBLATT, Stephen J., BA, PhD; American academic; *Cogan University Professor of the Humanities, Harvard University;* b. 7 Nov. 1943, Cambridge, Mass; s. of Harry Greenblatt and Mollie Brown; m. 1st Ellen Schmidt 1969 (divorced 1996); three s.; m. 2nd Ramie Targoff 1998; ed Yale Univ., Pembroke Coll., Cambridge, UK; Asst Prof. of English, Univ. of Calif., Berkeley 1969–74, Assoc. Prof. 1974–79, Prof. of English 1979–97; Prof. of English, Harvard Univ. 1997–, Cogan Univ. Prof. of Humanities 2000–; Founding Ed. journal Representations; numerous visiting professorships; mem. Int. Assen of Univ. Profs of English, Modern Language Assen of America (fmr Pres.), Renaissance Soc. of America; Fellow, American Acad. of Arts and Sciences, American Acad. of Arts and Letters, American Philosophical Soc., Wissenschaftskolleg zu Berlin; Guggenheim Fellow 1975, 1983; Porter Prize 1969, British Council Prize 1982, James Russell Lowell Prize 1989, Distinguished Teaching Award, Erasmus Inst. Prize 2001, Mellon Distinguished Humanist Award 2002, Wilbur Cross Medal 2010, Holberg Prize Laureate 2016. *Publications include:* Three Modern Satirists: Waugh, Orwell and Huxley 1965, Sir Walter Raleigh: The Renaissance Man and his Roles 1970, Renaissance Self-Fashioning: From More to Shakespeare 1980, Allegory and Representation (ed.) 1981, Power of Forms 1982, Representing the English Renaissance 1988, Shakespearean Negotiations: The Circulation of Social Energy in Renaissance England 1988, Learning to Curse: Essays in Early Modern Culture 1990, Marvelous Possessions: The Wonder of the New World 1991, Redrawing the Boundaries of Literary Study in English 1992, New World Encounters 1992, The Norton Shakespeare (Gen. Ed.) 1997, The Norton Anthology of English Literature (Gen. Ed.) 2000, Practising New Historicism 2000, Hamlet in Purgatory 2001, Will in the World: How Shakespeare Became Shakespeare 2004, Cultural Mobility: A Manifesto 2009, Shakespeare's Freedom 2010, The Swerve: How the World Became Modern (Pulitzer Prize 2012, National Book Award 2011) 2011, The Rise and Fall of Adam and Eve 2017, Tyrant: Shakespeare on Politics 2018; contribs to scholarly journals. *Address:* Department of English, Harvard University, Cambridge, MA 02138, USA (office). *Telephone:* (617) 495-2101 (office). *Fax:* (617) 496-8737 (office). *E-mail:* greenbl@fas.harvard.edu (office). *Website:* www.english.fas.harvard.edu (office); stephengreenblatt.com.

GREENBLATT, Terry; Israeli human rights activist; spent 20 years in Israel as women's rights and anti-occupation activist; Co-founder Kol Ha-Isha (The Women's Voice) Center, Jerusalem and Shani (Israeli Women Against the Occupation); mem. Founder's Council, Community School for Women's Studies and Econ. Devt, Kufr Kara, Israel; fmr Dir Bat Shalom (Israeli nat. women's peace org.), Jerusalem Link; Exec. Dir and CEO Urgent Action Fund for Women's Human Rights 2008–12; mem. Bd of Trustees, Sarvoyada Gandhi Foundation, India; Ms Magazine Woman of the Year Award 2002, Italian Archivio Disarmo Colombe d'Oro per la Pace 2002, 'Dialogue on Diversity' Liberty Award, Washington, DC 2003.

GREENE, Brian R., PhD; American physicist, writer and academic; *Professor of Mathematics and Physics, Columbia University;* b. 9 Feb. 1963, New York; s. of Alan Greene; m. Tracy Day; ed Harvard Univ., Univ. of Oxford, UK; Post-doctoral Fellow, Harvard Univ. 1987–90; Asst Prof., Cornell Univ. 1990, Assoc. Prof. 1995, later Prof.; currently Prof. of Math. and Physics, Columbia Univ., also Co-Dir Inst. for Strings, Cosmology, and Astroparticle Physics, Dir Theoretical Advanced Study Inst. 1996–; Co-founder World Science Festival, New York 2008; mem. Editorial Bd Physical Review D, Advance in Theoretical and Mathematical Physics. *Television:* The Theory of Everything 2003, The Fabric of the Cosmos 2011. *Publications include:* The Elegant Universe (Aventis Prize for Science Books 2000) 1999, The Fabric of the Cosmos: Space, Time and the Texture of Reality 2004, Icarus at the Edge of Time 2008, The Hidden Reality: Parallel Universes and the Deep Laws of the Cosmos 2011. *Address:* 910 Pupin, MC 5210, Box 10, 538 West 120th Street, New York, NY 10027, USA (office). *Telephone:* (212) 854-3349 (office); (212) 854-4347 (office). *E-mail:* bg111@columbia.edu (office). *Website:* www.iscap.columbia.edu (office); www.columbia.edu/cu/physics (office); www.briangreene.org.

GREENE, Jack Phillip, PhD; American historian and academic; *Andrew W. Mellon Professor Emeritus in the Humanities, Johns Hopkins University;* b. 12 Aug. 1931, Lafayette, Ind.; s. of Ralph B. Greene and Nellie A. Greene (née Miller); m. 1st Sue L. Nuenswander 1953 (divorced 1990); one s. one d.; m. 2nd Amy Turner Bushnell 1990; ed Univ. of North Carolina, Indiana Univ. and Duke Univ., Durham, NC; History Instructor, Michigan State Univ., East Lansing 1956–59; Asst Prof. of History, Western Reserve Univ., Cleveland, OH 1959–62, Assoc. Prof. 1962–65; Visiting Assoc. Prof. and Visiting Ed., William and Mary Quarterly, Coll. of William and Mary, Williamsburg, Va 1961–62; Assoc. Prof. of History, Univ. of Mich., Ann Arbor 1965–66; Visiting Assoc. Prof. of History, Johns Hopkins Univ., Baltimore, Md 1964–65, Prof. 1966–75, Chair. Dept of History 1970–72, Andrew W. Mellon Prof. in Humanities 1975–, now Prof. Emer.; Distinguished Prof., Univ. of California, Irvine 1990–92; Harmsworth Prof. of American History, Univ. of Oxford 1975–76; Visiting Prof., Hebrew Univ. of Jerusalem 1979, École des Hautes Études en Sciences Sociales 1986–87; Freeman Prof., Univ. of Richmond, Va 1996; Sweet Prof., Michigan State Univ. 1997; Gast Prof., Frei Universität, Berlin 2009; mem. Inst. for Advanced Study 1970–71, 1985–86, American Philosophical Soc., American Acad. of Arts and Sciences; Corresp. mem. British Acad.; Fellow, Woodrow Wilson Int. Center for Scholars 1974–75, Center for Advanced Study in Behavioral Sciences 1979–80, Churchill Coll., Cambridge 1986–, Nat. Humanities Center 1987–88, 2009–10, Guggenheim Fellow 1964–65; John Carter Brown Library Fellow 1999–2000; several awards, including American Historical Assen Award for Scholarly Distinction 2008. *Publications:* 32 books, including Quest for Power 1963, Diary of Colonel Landon Carter of Sabine Hall (two vols) 1965, Settlements to Society 1966, Colonies to Nation 1967, Reinterpretation of American Revolution 1968, All Men are Created Equal 1976, Colonial British America 1983, Encyclopedia of American Political History 1984, Peripheries and Center 1986, Political Life in Eighteenth Century Virginia 1986, Intellectual Heritage of the Constitutional Era 1986, Magna Carta for America 1986, American Revolution 1987, Pursuits of Happiness 1988, Selling the New World 1988, Encyclopedia of the American Revolution (co-ed.) 1991, Imperatives, Behaviors and Identities 1992, Intellectual Construction of America 1993, Negotiated Authorities 1994, Understanding the American Revolution 1995, Interpreting Early America 1996, Companion to the American Revolution 2000, Atlantic History: A Critical Appraisal 2009, Exclusionary Empire 2009, Constitutional Origins of the American Revolution 2010, Evaluating Empire and Confronting Colonialism in Eighteenth-Century Britain 2013, Creating the British Atlantic 2013, Exploring the Bounds of Liberty: Political Writings of Colonial British America from the Glorious Revolution to the American Revolution (co-ed.) 2018. *Leisure interests:* travel, cinema. *Address:* Department of History, The Johns Hopkins University, Baltimore, MD 21218 (office); 1974 Division Road, East Greenwich, RI 02898, USA (home). *Telephone:* (410) 516-7575 (office); (401) 884-5883 (home). *Fax:* (410) 516-7586 (office); (401) 884-5883 (home). *E-mail:* jpgreene@jhem.jhu.edu (office); jack_greene@brown.edu (home). *Website:* www.jhu.edu/~history (office).

GREENE, Mark I., MD, PhD, FRCP; Canadian pathologist and academic; *John Eckman Professor of Medical Science, University of Pennsylvania;* ed Univ. of Manitoba, Canada; MRC Fellow, Harvard Univ., Mass 1976–78, Asst Prof. of Pathology 1978–80, Assoc. Prof. 1980–85; Clinical Consultant in Medicine, Dana Farber Cancer Inst., Boston 1980–86; Head, Basic Research Unit of Immunology, Univ. of Pennsylvania 1986–, Asst Dir of Fundamental Research, Cancer Center 1987–, Vice-Chair. Dept of Pathology 1993–, currently Eckman Prof. of Medical Science; Newton Abraham Prof. of Biological Science, Univ. of Oxford 2002–03; Hon. DSc (Univ. of Manitoba) 2009; J. Allyn Taylor Int. Prize in Medicine, Robarts Research Inst. 2006, Adams County Breast Cancer Research Award 2007, Cotlove Award 2008. *Publications:* numerous scientific papers in professional journals on receptors, reoviruses, neu-growth factor receptors and T-cell receptors. *Address:* Immunology Graduate Group, University of Pennsylvania, 410 BRB II/III, Philadelphia, PA 19104-6160, USA (office). *Telephone:* (215) 898-2847 (office). *Fax:* (215) 746-5525 (office). *E-mail:* greene@reo.med.upenn.edu (office). *Website:* www.med.upenn.edu/immun/greene.shtml (office); www.uphs.upenn.edu/abramson/greene.html (office).

GREENE, Maurice; American professional athlete (retd); b. 23 July 1974, Kansas City, Kan.; s. of Ernest Greene and Jackie Greene; ed Schlage High School and Park Coll., Kansas City, Kan.; world record-holder indoor 60m, fmr world record-holder indoor 50m; silver medal US Championships 60m 1995; gold medal US Indoor Championships 60m 1997; gold medal US Championships 100m 1997; gold medal World Championships 100m 1997, 100m, 200m and 4×100m relay 1999, 100m 2001; Olympic gold medallist 100m and 4×100m 2000, bronze medal 100m 2004; set world record for 100m in Athens 1999 (9.79 seconds); retd 2008; f. Finish the Race Foundation; Amb. IAAF; track coach, UCLA 2012–13. *Television includes:* participant, Dancing With The Stars season 7 2008. *Address:* HSInternational, 9871 Irvine Center Drive, Irvine, CA 92618, USA (office). *E-mail:* emanuel@hsi.net (office). *Website:* hsi.net (office).

GREENE, Dame Moya, DBE, BA; Canadian civil servant and business executive; *Chief Executive, Royal Mail Group;* b. Newfoundland; one d.; ed Osgoode Hall Law School, Memorial Univ. of Newfoundland; joined Public Service of Canada as an immigration adjudicator, Ottawa 1979, later held positions in Dept of Labour and Privy Council Office, as Asst Deputy Minister for Transport Canada, oversaw privatization of Canadian Nat. Railway and deregulation of Canadian airline industry; Man. Dir of Infrastructure Finance and Public Pvt. Partnership, TD Securities 1996–2000; Sr Vice-Pres. and Chief Admin. Officer, Retail Products, Canadian Imperial Bank of Commerce 2000–03; Sr Vice-Pres., Operational Effectiveness, Bombardier 2003–04; Pres. and CEO EPO Inc.; Pres. and CEO Canada Post Corpn 2005–10; Chief Exec. Royal Mail Holdings PLC and Royal Mail Group PLC, UK 2010–; mem. Bd of Dirs Purolator Courier, Tim Hortons (coffee shop chain); named by the National Post amongst the 100 Most Influential Women in Canada 2003, named by the Ivey School of Business as one of the Top 40 Female Corp. Execs in Canada 2004, Leader of the Year, Nat. Business Awards 2014. *Address:* Royal Mail Group PLC, 148 Old Street, London, EC1V 9HQ, England (office). *Telephone:* (20) 7250-2888 (office). *Fax:* (20) 7250-2244 (office). *E-mail:* info@royalmailgroup.com (office). *Website:* www.royalmailgroup.com (office).

GREENE, Paul (Chet); Antigua and Barbuda politician and fmr sports administrator; *Minister of Foreign Affairs, International Trade and Immigration;* b. Liberta; s. of Joseph Greene and Areril Greene; m.; five c.; ed Univ. de Poitiers, France; worked at Ministry of Sport, becoming Commr of Sports; fmr Pres. Liberta Sports Club; fmr Capt., Liberta Parish Cricket League team; propr, bakery business in Liberta and Barbuda; mem. Senate (upper house of parl.) 2009; mem. House of Reps (lower house of parl.) (ABLP) for St Paul 2014–; Minister of Trade, Industry, Sports, Culture and Nat. Celebrations 2014; Minister of Foreign Affairs, Int. Trade and Immigration 2017–; Pres. Antigua and Barbuda Olympic Assen; fmr Pres. Antigua and Barbuda Football Assen; mem. Antigua and Barbuda Labour Party (ABLP), Vice-Chair. 2012–14, Chair. 2014–. *Address:* Ministry of Foreign Affairs, International Trade and Immigration, Queen Elizabeth Hwy, St

John's, Antigua and Barbuda (office). *Telephone:* 462-1052 (office). *Fax:* 462-2482 (office). *Website:* chetgreene.com.

GREENE, Sally, MBA; British impresario and producer; *Chief Executive, Old Vic Productions PLC;* b. 27 May 1954; d. of Basil Greene and Clare Tully; m. Robert Bourne; one s. one d.; ed St Maur's Convent, Weybridge and Guildhall School of Music and Drama; bought Richmond Theatre, Surrey 1986, programmed then restored theatre 1991; took over Criterion Theatre, Piccadilly 1992, restored theatre, re-opening it 1993; f. Criterion Productions PLC 1994; bought The Old Vic Theatre 1998, est. charitable trust to run it; Founder (with Kevin Spacey q.v.) and CEO Old Vic Productions PLC 2000; Club Owner Ronnie Scott's, London 2005–. *Productions include:* Jack 1993, Taking Sides, Criterion Theatre 1994, Hot House, Comedy Theatre 1994, Cyrano de Bergerac, RSC 1995, Car Man, Old Vic 2000, Medea 2001, Life x 3, Old Vic 2001, Vagina Monologues, Ambassador's Theatre 2001–02. *Leisure interests:* piano, skiing, singing. *Address:* Old Vic Productions PLC, Park House, 26 North End Road, London, NW11 7PT; The Old Vic, The Cut, London, SE1 8NB (office); Lindsay House, 100 Cheyne Walk, London, SW10 0DQ, England (home). *Telephone:* (20) 7401-3534 (office). *Fax:* (20) 7261-9161 (office). *E-mail:* s.greene@dial.pipex.com (home). *Website:* www.oldvicproductions.com (office).

GREENER, Sir Anthony Armitage, Kt, FCMA; British business executive; *Chairman, The Minton Trust;* b. 26 May 1940, Bowden; s. of William Greener and Diana Greener; m. Min Ogilvie 1974; one s. one d.; ed Marlborough Coll.; Marketing Man. Thames Board Mills 1969; Retail Controller, Alfred Dunhill Ltd (later Dunhill Holdings PLC) 1972, Dir 1974, Man. Dir 1975; Man. Dir United Distillers 1987–92; Dir Guinness PLC 1986–97, Jt Man. Dir 1989–91, Chief Exec. 1992–97, Chair. 1993–97; Co-Chair. Diageo PLC (after merger with Grand Metropolitan PLC) 1997–98, Chair. 1998–2000; Chair. University for Industry Ltd 2000–04, Qualifications and Curriculum Authority 2002–08; Deputy Chair. BT 2001–06; Chair. The Minton Trust (family trust), St Giles Trust 2009–16; mem. Bd of Dirs Louis Vuitton Moet Hennessy 1989–97, Reed Int. 1990–93, Reed Elsevier 1993–98, Robert Mondavi 2000–04, United Learning Trust 2005–16, Williams Sonoma 2007–, WNSGS 2007–15; Trustee, Marlborough Coll. Foundation –2016. *Leisure interests:* skiing, sailing, gardening. *Address:* The Minton Trust, 26 Hamilton House, Vicarage Gate, London, W8 4HL, England (office). *Telephone:* (20) 7937-2048 (office). *Fax:* (20) 7937-2048 (office). *E-mail:* greenera@mintontrust.com (office).

GREENFIELD, Jerry; American business executive; *Co-founder, Ben & Jerry's Homemade Inc.;* b. 14 March 1951, Brooklyn, New York; m. Elizabeth Greenfield 1987; one s.; ed Calhoun High School, Merrick, New York, Oberlin Coll.; employed as lab technician, New York and North Carolina –1976; Co-founder (with Ben Cohen) Ben & Jerry's Homemade Inc. 1977 (acquired by Unilever 2000), opened first ice cream parlour in Burlington, Vt 1978, est. Ben & Jerry's Foundation to oversee donation of 7.5% of corp. profits to non-profit orgs; Founding mem. Businesses for Social Responsibility (org. which promotes socially responsible business practices); mem. New England Futures Project; James Beard Humanitarians of the Year Award 1993. *Leisure interests:* basketball, volleyball, spending time with family and friends. *Address:* Ben & Jerry's Homemade Inc., 30 Community Drive, South Burlington, VT 05403-6828, USA (office). *Telephone:* (802) 846-1500 (office). *Website:* www.benjerry.com (office).

GREENFIELD OF OTMOOR, Baroness (Life Peer), cr. 2001, of Otmoor in the County of Oxfordshire; **Susan Adele Greenfield,** CBE, BA (Hons), MA, DPhil, FRSE; British neuroscientist and author; *Founder and CEO, Neuro-Bio Ltd;* b. 1 Oct. 1950, London; d. of Reginald Myer Greenfield and Doris Margaret Winifred Greenfield; m. Peter William Atkins 1991 (divorced 2005); ed Godolphin and Latymer School for Girls, St Hilda's Coll., Oxford; Dame Catherine Fulford Sr Scholarship, St Hugh's Coll., Oxford 1974–75, MRC Training Fellow, Univ. Lab. of Physiology, Oxford 1977–81, Jr Research Fellow, Green Coll., Oxford 1981–84, Prof. in Synaptic Pharmacology, Univ. of Oxford 1985–96, Prof. of Pharmacology 1996–2013, Tutorial Fellow in Medicine, Lincon Coll. 1985–98, Sr Research Fellow 1998–2016, Gresham Prof. of Physics, Gresham Coll., Oxford 1995–98, Sr Research Fellow Univ. Dept of Pharmacology, Oxford 2011–13; Royal Soc. Study Visit Award 1978; MRC-INSERM French Exchange Fellow 1979–80; Visiting Fellow, Inst. of Neuroscience, La Jolla, Calif., USA 1995; Distinguished Visiting Scholar, Queen's Univ., Belfast 1996; Adelaide Thinker-in-Residence 2004–06; Chancellor Heriot-Watt Univ. 2005–12; Co-founder Synaptica Ltd 1997, Brain-Boost Ltd 2002; Chair. Pantheon (real estate firm) 2009–; Pres. Headway (brain injury charity), Asscn for Science Educ. 2000; Vice-Pres. Asscn of Women in Science and Eng 2001; Dir Royal Inst. of Great Britain 1998–2010; Pres. Headway: Brain Injury Asscn 2002–, Classical Asscn 2003; Chancellor, Heriot Watt Univ. 2005–12; Gov., Florey Inst. for Neuroscience and Mental Health 2012; Founder and CEO Neuro-Bio Ltd 2013–; mem. Bd of Dirs Enkephala Ltd 2005–, Greenfield PPS Ltd 2007–, Mind Change 2011–; Chair of Innovation, Queen's Univ. Belfast; Fellow, Australian Davos Connection 2007, Science Museum 2010; mem. Council Weizman Foundation 2000–04; mem. Bd of Govs Weizmann Inst. of Science, Israel 2004–13; Trustee, Alexandria Library, Egypt 2006–, Royal Inst. Australia 2008–, Cyprus Research Inst., Carnegie Mellon Univ., Australia, John Porter Charitable Trust, Natural Justice, Science for Humanity, Science Museum, London 1998–2003; mem. Advisory Bd Australian Science Media Centre, Kusuma School of Biological Sciences, Indian Inst. of Technology, Delhi; Fellow, Royal Soc. of Edinburgh 2007–; Hon. Fellow, St Hilda's Coll., Oxford, Cardiff Univ. 2000, Royal Soc. S Australia 2008, The Science Museum 2010; Hon. FRCP 2000; 32 hon. doctorates; Chevalier, Légion d'honneur 2003; Michael Faraday Medal, Royal Soc. 1998, Woman of Distinction, Jewish Care 1998, Golden Plate Award, American Acad. of Achievement 2003, Hon. Australian of the Year 2006, Science and Tech. Award, British Inspiration Awards 2010, Australian Soc. for Medical Research Medal 2010. *Publications include:* numerous articles (approx. 200) in learned journals; Mindwaves (co-ed. with C. B. Blakemore) 1987, Journey to the Centres of the Brain (with G. Ferry) 1994, Journey to the Centres of the Mind 1995, The Human Mind Explained (ed.) 1996, The Human Brain: A Guided Tour 1997; Brainpower (ed.) 2000, Brain Story 2000, Private Life of the Brain 2000, Tomorrow's People: How 21st Century Technology is Changing the Way We Think and Feel 2003, ID: The Quest for Identity in the 21st Century 2008, You and Me: The Neuroscience of Identity 2011, 2121: A Tale from the Next Century 2014, Mind Change: How Digital Technologies are Leaving Their Mark on Our Brains 2014, A Day in the Life of the Brain 2016. *Leisure interests:* squash, dancing. *Address:* Building F5, Culham Science Centre, Abingdon, Oxon., OX14 3DB (office); House of Lords, London, SW1A 0PW, England. *Telephone:* (01235) 420 084 (office). *E-mail:* greenfieldsu@parliament.uk (office); sagpa@susangreenfield.com (home); susan.greenfield@neuro-bio.com (home). *Website:* www.susangreenfield.com; neuro-bio.com (home).

GREENGRASS, Paul; British film and television director; b. 13 Aug. 1955, Cheam, Surrey; began career as an investigative journalist and award-winning documentary film-maker; Pres. Directors UK 2008–; BAFTA Alan Clarke Award for Outstanding Creative Contrib. to Television 2005, British Independent Film Variety Award 2013. *Films directed include:* Resurrected (Interfilm and OCIC Jury Awards, Berlin Film Festival) 1989, Sophie's World, The Theory of Flight 1998, Bloody Sunday (also writer) (Golden Bear, Berlin Int. Film Festival) 2002, The Bourne Supremacy 2004, United 93 (Best Dir, Los Angeles Film Critics Asscn, Best Film, New York Film Critics' Circle Awards, Best Dir, Best British Producer, Best Film, London Film Critics' Circle Awards, BAFTA Award for Best Dir 2007) 2006, The Bourne Ultimatum 2007, Green Zone 2010, Captain Phillips 2013, Jason Bourne 2016. *Television work includes:* World In Action, Food and Trucks and Rock and Roll, U2 – Anthem for the Eighties, Moscow Week, Coppers, What Ever Happened to Woodward and Bernstein, When The Lies Run Out (Chicago Film Festival Silver Medal) 1993, Kavanagh QC 1994, Open Fire (writer) 1994, The One That Got Away (also writer) 1996, The Fix (also writer) 1997, The Murder of Stephen Lawrence (also writer) 1999, Omagh (writer and producer) (BAFTA Award for Best Single Drama 2005) 2004. *Publication:* Spycatcher (with Peter Wright). *Address:* c/o CAA, 2000 Avenue of the Stars, Los Angeles, CA 90067, USA.

GREENIDGE, Carl Barrington, BA, MPhil; Guyanese/British economist and politician; b. 3 March 1949, New Amsterdam, Berbice; s. of Cecil Cappel Greenidge and Stella Leonie Ruperta (Hoppie) Greenidge; one s. two d.; ed Univ. of Exeter, Birkbeck Coll., Univ. of London, UK; Research Asst and Tutor, Wye Coll., Univ. of London 1972–74; Lecturer in Econs, Univ. of Guyana 1974–78; Consultant Economist, Aubrey Barker Associates, Georgetown 1975–79; Chief Planning Officer, Sec. to State Planning Bd, State Planning Comm. 1978–80; Econ. Adviser, Office of Pres. 1981; Minister of Finance and Planning 1983–92; Co-Pres., Jt African, Caribbean & Pacific (ACP)-EU Council, Brussels 1989–90; Deputy Sec.-Gen., Sec.-Gen. ad interim, Secr. of ACP Group, Brussels 1992–2000, Dir ACP-EU Technical Centre for Agricultural and Rural Cooperation, Netherlands 2000–05; Second Vice-Pres. and Minister of Foreign Affairs 2015–19; Research Fellow, Inst. of Social and Econ. Research, Univ. of West Indies, Jamaica 1987; mem. Inter-Regional Network on Privatization, UNDP, New York 1991–; mem. Advisory Bd, Regulatory Policy Research Centre/Inst., Hertford Coll., Oxford 1993–; Vice-Chair. European Centre for Devt Policy Man. 1995–96, European Forum on Int. Cooperation 1997–2000; external examiner, Univ. of West Indies; Visiting Lecturer, Univ. of Stellenbosch, South Africa 2003; mem. Int. Inst. of Public Finance, Agricultural Econs Soc., American Econs Asscn. *Publications include:* Privatisation: A Global Perspective (co-author) 1993, Empowering a Peasantry in a Caribbean Context 2000; numerous academic articles on economics. *Leisure interests:* gliding, cricket, squash, music. *Address:* c/o Ministry of Foreign Affairs, 254 South Road and Shiv Chanderpaul Drive, Bourda, Georgetown, Guyana (office).

GREENING, Rt Hon. Justine, MBA; British politician; b. 30 April 1969, Rotherham, S Yorks.; ed Oakwood Comprehensive School, Univ. of Southampton, London Business School; Councillor, Epping Town Council 1998–2002; contested Ealing, Acton and Shepherd's Bush constituency 2001; trained as accountant and worked as Accountant/Finance Man. for, amongst others, Price Waterhouse Coopers, GlaxoSmithKline and Centrica PLC –2005; MP for Putney 2005–March 2015, May 2015–; Shadow Minister for the Treasury 2007–09, for Communities and Local Govt 2009–10; Econ. Sec., HM Treasury 2010–11; Sec. of State for Transport 2011–12, for Int. Devt 2012–16, for Educ. 2016–18, also Minister for Women and Equalities 2016–18; mem. The Bow Group 1998–, Political Officer 1999–2000; Vice-Chair. (Youth), Conservative Party 2005–10; mem. (Select Cttees), Work and Pensions 2005–07, Public Accounts 2010–11; Conservative; London Business School Fellowship 2017–18. *Address:* House of Commons, Westminster, London, SW1A 0AA (office); Constituency Office, 3 Summerstown, London, SW17 0BQ, England (office). *Telephone:* (20) 7219-8300 (Westminster) (office); (20) 8946-4557 (Constituency Office) (office). *E-mail:* greeningj@parliament.uk (office). *Website:* www.justinegreening.co.uk.

GREENSPAN, Alan, KBE, MA, PhD; American economist and central banker (retd) and business consultant; *President, Greenspan Associates LLC;* b. 6 March 1926, New York; s. of Herbert Greenspan and Rose Goldsmith; m. Andrea Mitchell 1997; ed New York and Columbia Univs; Pres., CEO Townsend-Greenspan & Co. Inc. 1954–74, 1977–87; mem. Nixon for Pres. Cttee 1968–69; mem. Task Force for Econ. Growth 1969, Comm. on an All-Volunteer Armed Force 1969–70, Comm. on Financial Structure and Regulation 1970–71; Consultant to Council of Econ. Advisors 1970–74, to US Treasury 1971–74, to Fed. Reserve Bd 1971–74; Chair. Council of Econ. Advisers 1974–77, Nat. Comm. on Social Security Reform 1981–83; Chair. Bd of Govs Fed. Reserve System 1987–2006; Founder and Pres. Greenspan Assocs (consulting firm), Washington, DC 2006–, advisor to Pimco (for fund man.) 2007–, to Deutsche Bank (for investment banking) 2007–; Advisor Paulson and Co., New York 2008–; mem. Sec. of Commerce's Econ. Comm.'s Cen. Market System Cttee 1972, GNP Review Cttee of Office of Man. and Budget, Time Magazine's Bd of Economists 1971–74, 1977–87, Pres.'s Econ. Policy Advisory Bd 1981–87, Pres.'s Foreign Intelligence Advisory Bd 1983–85, Exec. Cttee Trilateral Comm.; Sr Advisor, Brookings Inst. Panel on Econ. Activity 1970–74, 1977–87; Adjunct Prof., Grad. School of Business Man., New York 1977–87; mem. Bd of Dirs Council on Foreign Relations; Past Pres. and Fellow, Nat. Asscn of Business Economists; mem. Bd of Dirs Trans World Financial Co. 1962–74, Dreyfus Fund 1970–74, Gen. Cable Corpn 1973–74, 1977–78, Sun Chemical Corpn 1973–74, Gen. Foods Corpn 1977–86, J.P. Morgan & Co. 1977–87, Mobil Corpn 1977–87, Aluminum Co. of America (ALCOA) 1978–87; Hon. KBE 2002, Commdr, Légion d'honneur; Jefferson Award 1976, William Butler Memorial Award 1977, Presidential Medal of Freedom 2005, New York Univ. Eugene J. Keogh Award for Distinguished Public Service 2012. *Publications:* The Age of Turbulence: Adventures in a New World (memoirs) 2007, The Map and the Territory 2013. *Leisure interest:* golf. *Address:* Greenspan Associates LLC, 1133 Connecticut Avenue, Suite 810, NW, Washington, DC 20036, USA (office). *Telephone:* (202) 457-8250 (office).

GREENSPON, Edward B., BA, MA; Canadian journalist and editor; *President and CEO, Public Policy Forum;* b. 26 March 1957, Montréal; s. of Mortimer Greenspon and Rosalie Greenspon; m. Janice Neil 1984; three s.; ed Carleton Univ., Ottawa, London School of Econs, UK (Commonwealth Scholar); fmr paperboy for (now defunct) Montréal Daily Star; moved to London, UK to study; Business Reporter, The Globe and Mail 1986, European Business Corresp., London, returned to Canada 1989, Man. Ed. Report on Business section and Deputy Man. Ed. The Globe and Mail 1989–93, Ottawa Bureau Chief and Assoc. Ed. 1993–99, Exec. News Ed., Political Ed. and columnist for Ottawa region 1999–2002, Founding Ed. www.globeandmail.com, Ed.-in-Chief 2002–09; Chair. The GPS Project, Canadian Int. Council 2009–10; Vice-Pres. Strategic Investments and News Ventures, Toronto Star and Star Media Group 2010–14; Sr Ed. Bloomberg LP 2014–16; Pres. and CEO Public Policy Forum 2016–; mem. Advisory Bd, The Mark 2010–; mem. Bd of Govs Carleton Univ. 2010–; Hyman Soloman Award for Excellence in Public Policy Journalism. *Publications:* Double Vision: The Inside Story of the Liberals in Power (co-author) (Douglas Purvis Award for best public policy book 1996) 1995, Searching for Certainty: Inside the New Canadian Mindset (with Darrell Bricker) 2001. *Address:* Public Policy Forum, Suite 1400, 130 Albert Street, Ottawa, ON K1P 5G4, Canada (office). *Telephone:* (613) 238-7160 (office). *Fax:* (613) 238-7990 (office). *E-mail:* mail@ppforum.ca (office). *Website:* www.ppforum.ca (office).

GREENSTOCK, Sir Jeremy (Quentin), Kt, GCMG, MA; British diplomatist; *Chairman, Gatehouse Advisory Partners;* b. 27 July 1943, Harrow, Middx, England; s. of John Wilfrid Greenstock and Ruth Margaret Logan; m. Anne Derryn Ashford Hodges 1969; one s. two d.; ed Harrow School and Worcester Coll., Oxford; Asst Master, Eton Coll. 1966–69; entered diplomatic service 1969, studied Arabic at MECAS 1970–72, served in Dubai 1972–74, Pvt. Sec. to Amb., Washington, DC 1974–78, with FCO (Planning, Personnel Operations Dept, Near East and N African Dept) 1978–83; Commercial Counsellor, Jeddah 1983–85, Riyadh 1985–86; Head of Chancery, Embassy in Paris 1987–90; Asst Under-Sec. of State, FCO 1990–93; Minister, Embassy in Washington, DC 1994–95; Deputy Under-Sec. of State, FCO 1995; Political Dir, FCO 1996–98; Perm. Rep. to UN, New York 1998–2003, Chair. UN Security Council Counter-Terrorism Cttee 2001–03; UK Special Rep. for Iraq 2003–04; Dir The Ditchley Foundation 2004–10; Special Adviser to BP Group 2004–10, Forward Thinking 2008–; Dir (non-exec.) De La Rue PLC 2005–13; Dir Lambert Energy Advisory 2010–, Chair. 2011–; Chair. Gatehouse Advisory Partners 2010–, UN Asscn-UK 2011–16; Trustee, Int. Rescue Cttee (UK) 2006–12; mem. Chatham House Council of Man. 2012–18; Hon. Fellow, King's Coll. London, Worcester Coll. Oxford. *Publication:* Iraq: the Cost of War 2016. *Leisure interests:* reading, travel, golf, skiing, listening to music, watching sport. *Address:* Gatehouse Advisory Partners Ltd, 1 Tudor Street, London, EC4Y 0AH, England (office). *Telephone:* (20) 7099-5533 (office). *E-mail:* info@gatehouseap.com (office). *Website:* www.gatehouseadvisorypartners.com (office).

GREENWOOD, Sir Brian Mellor, Kt, CBE, FRCP, FRS; British physician, biomedical research scientist and academic; *Manson Professor of Clinical Tropical Medicine, London School of Hygiene and Tropical Medicine;* b. 11 Nov. 1938, Manchester, England; m. Alice Margaret Greenwood; two d.; ed St Edward's School, Oxford, Univ. of Cambridge, Middlesex Hosp., London; spent ten years working in Nigeria and 15 years as Head of MRC Laboratories in The Gambia researching malaria and infections caused by capsulated bacteria such as the meningococcus (*Neissera meningitidis*); currently Manson Prof. of Clinical Tropical Medicine, London School of Hygiene and Tropical Medicine; Chalmers Medal, Royal Soc. of Tropical Medicine and Hygiene 1977, McKay Prize, American Soc. of Tropical Medicine and Hygiene 1991, Adesuyi Prize, West African Health Community 1995, Manson Medal, Royal Soc. of Tropical Medicine and Hygiene 2001, inaugural recipient, Hideyo Noguchi Africa Prize (Medical Research category) 2008, Canada Gairdner Global Health Award 2012, MRC Millennium Medal 2016. *Publications:* numerous papers in professional journals. *Address:* London School of Hygiene and Tropical Medicine, Keppel Street, London, WC1E 7HT, England (office). *Telephone:* (20) 7299-4712 (office). *Fax:* (20) 7436-5389 (office). *E-mail:* brian.greenwood@lshtm.ac.uk (office). *Website:* www.lshtm.ac.uk (office).

GREENWOOD, Christopher John, GBE, CMG, QC, BA (Hons), MA, LLB (Hons); British lawyer, academic and judge; *Judge, International Court of Justice;* ed Wellingborough School, Northants., Magdalene Coll., Cambridge (Whewell Scholar in Int. Law); called to the Bar, Middle Temple, London 1978–79, Bencher 2003; in practice 1985–; QC 1999; Univ. Lecturer, Univ. of Cambridge 1981–96, Dir of Studies of Law, Magdalene Coll. 1981–96, Dean, Magdalene Coll. 1981–87, Tutor 1989–96, Fellow, Magdalene Coll. 1978–96; Prof. of Int. Law, LSE 1996–; Judge, Int. Court of Justice, The Hague 2009–; mem. Arbitration Tribunal, Perm. Court of Arbitration, Larsen v. Hawaiian Kingdom 2001, Panel of Arbitrators, Law of the Sea Convention, Panel of Arbitrators, Int. Centre for the Settlement of Investment Disputes; mem. Editorial Cttee British Year Book of International Law, Year Book of International Humanitarian Law, Journal of Conflict and Security Law; mem. Council, British Br., Int. Law Asscn; mem. American Soc. of Int. Law 1979, British Inst. of Int. and Comparative Law, Int. Inst. of Humanitarian Law, Soc. of Public Teachers of Law. *Publications:* several books and numerous articles and other publs on int. law. *Address:* International Court of Justice, Peace Palace, Carnegieplein 2, 2517 KJ The Hague, The Netherlands (office). *Telephone:* (70) 302-2323 (office). *Fax:* (70) 364-9928 (office). *E-mail:* info@icj-cij.org (office). *Website:* www.icj-cij.org (office).

GREER, Germaine, PhD; Australian feminist, author and broadcaster; b. 29 Jan. 1939, Melbourne, Vic.; d. of Eric Reginald Greer and Margaret May Greer (née Lafrank); ed Star of the Sea Convent, Vic., Melbourne, Sydney Univ., Univ. of Cambridge, UK; Sr Tutor in English, Sydney Univ. 1963–64; Asst Lecturer, then Lecturer in English, Univ. of Warwick, UK 1967–72, Prof. of English and Comparative Studies 1998–2003; lecturer throughout N America with American Program Bureau 1973–78, to raise funds for Tulsa Bursary and Fellowship Scheme 1980–83; Visiting Prof., Grad. Faculty of Modern Letters, Univ. of Tulsa 1979, Prof. of Modern Letters 1980–83, Founder-Dir of Tulsa Centre for the Study of Women's Literature, Founder-Ed. Tulsa Studies in Women's Literature 1981; Dir Stump Cross Books 1988–; Special Lecturer and Unofficial Fellow, Newnham Coll., Cambridge 1989–98; broadcaster/journalist/columnist/reviewer 1972–; Jr Govt Scholarship 1952, Diocesan Scholarship 1956, Sr Govt Scholarship 1956, Teacher's Coll. Studentship 1956, Commonwealth Scholarship 1964; numerous TV appearances and public talks including discussion with Norman Mailer in The Theatre of Ideas, New York; Dr hc (Univ. of Griffith, Australia) 1996, (Univ. of York, Toronto) 1999, (UMIST) 2000; hon. degrees (Melbourne) 2003, (Essex) 2003, (Anglia Polytechnic) 2003, (Sydney) 2005; Australian Living Treasure Nat. Trust Award Centenary Medal 2003. *Film appearance:* Rabbit Fever 2006. *Television:* Nice Time, The Late Review, Celebrity Big Brother. *Publications include:* The Female Eunuch 1969, The Obstacle Race: The Fortunes of Women Painters and Their Work 1979, Sex and Destiny: The Politics of Human Fertility 1984, Shakespeare (co-ed.) 1986, The Madwoman's Underclothes (selected journalism 1964–85) 1986, Kissing the Rod: An Anthology of 17th Century Women's Verse (co-ed.) 1988, Daddy, We Hardly Knew You (J. R. Ackerly Prize and Premio Internazionale Mondello) 1989, The Uncollected Verse of Aphra Behn (ed.) 1989, The Change: Women, Ageing and the Menopause 1991, The Collected Works of Katherine Philips, the Matchless Orinda, Vol. III: The Translations (co-ed.) 1993, Slip-Shod Sybils: Recognition, Rejection and The Woman Poet 1995, The Surviving Works of Anne Wharton (co-ed.) 1997, The Whole Woman 1999, John Wilmot, Earl of Rochester 1999, 101 Poems by 101 Women (ed.) 2001, The Boy 2003, Poems for Gardeners (ed.) 2003, Whitefella Jump Up The Shortest Way to Nationhood 2004, Shakespeare's Wife 2007, White Beech: The Rainforest Years 2014; articles for Listener, Spectator, Esquire, Harper's Magazine, Playboy, Private Eye and other journals. *Leisure interest:* gardening. *Address:* c/o Aitken Alexander Associates Ltd, 18–21 Cavaye Place, London, SW10 9PT, England (office).

GREF, Herman Oskarovich, PhD; Russian politician, jurist and banker; *Chairman of the Executive Board and CEO, Sberbank;* b. 8 Feb. 1964, Panfilovo, Pavlodar Region, Kazakh SSR, USSR; m. 1st Yelena; one s.; m. 2nd Yana 2004; one d.; ed Faculty of Law, F.M. Dostoevsky Omsk State Univ., Faculty of Law, Leningrad State Univ.; Soviet Army service 1982–84; legal adviser, Cttee for Econ. Devt and Property, Petrodvoretz Dist Admin, Petrodvoretz, St Petersburg 1991–92; Chair. Property Cttee, concurrently Deputy Head, Petrodvoretz, St Petersburg Mayor's Office 1992–94; Deputy Chair., Dir Dept of Real Estate, First Deputy Chair. Cttee on Man. of Municipal Property, St Petersburg Admin 1994–97; Vice-Gov., Chair. Municipal Property Cttee, St Petersburg Admin 1997–98; mem. Exec. Bd Ministry of State Property, Russian Fed. 1998, First Deputy Minister 1998–2000; Minister of Econ. Devt and Trade 2000–07; Chair. Exec. Bd and CEO Sberbank (Savings Bank of Russian Fed.) 2007–; serves on bds and supervisory bds of several jt stock corpns and cos; Order of Holy Prince Daniel of Moscow, Class I 2006, Order for Merit to the Fatherland (Class IV) 2007, Class III 2011, P.A. Stolypin Medal (Class II) 2009, Officier, Légion d'honneur 2010, Order of Alexander Nevsky 2014, Order of Honour 2014; Certificate of Honour of the Pres. of the Russian Fed. 2009. *Address:* Sberbank, 117997 Moscow, ul. Vavilova 19, Russia (office). *Telephone:* (495) 500-55-50 (office); (495) 974-66-77 (office). *Fax:* (495) 957-57-31 (office). *E-mail:* sbrf@sberbank.ru (office); sberbank@sberbank.ru (office). *Website:* www.sberbank.ru (office).

GREGAN, George Musarurwa, BE; Australian rugby union player (retd); b. 19 April 1973, Ndola, Zambia; m. Erica Gregan; three c.; ed St Edmund's Coll., Canberra, Univ. of Canberra; scrum half; plays for Randwick; has played for ACT Under-19s, ACT Under-21s, Australian Under-19s, Australian Under-21s, Australian Sevens, ACT Brumbies (120 state caps, 103 appearances in Super 12 competition) 1996–2007, RC Toulonnais 2007–08; 139 caps (world record) and 99 Test points for Australia (debut versus Italy in Brisbane) 1994–2007; won World Cup 1999 with Australia, Capt. nat. team 2002–07, took Australia to World Cup final 2003; sr tours to S Africa (for World Cup) 1995, Europe 1996, Argentina and UK 1996, France and England 1997, UK (for World Cup) 1999, UK and Europe 2001, 2002, 2003, 2004, 2005, 2006, 2007 (World Cup, France); Asst Coach, Brumbies 2012; f. George Gregan Foundation and launched epilepsy awareness campaign with slogan 'Get on the Team' 2004; Patron Brainwave Australia; Super 12 Player of the Tournament 1997, Int. Players' Asscn Player of the Year 2001, Australian Super 12 Player of the Year 2001, Wallaby Players' Player 2001, awarded the inaugural Rugby Medal for Excellence in 2001. *Leisure interests:* golf, skiing, good food and wine. *Address:* George Gregan Foundation, GPO Box 873, Sydney, NSW 2001, Australia (office). *Website:* www.georgegreganfoundation.com.au (office).

GREGER, Janet L., BS, MS, PhD; American academic and author; *Professor Emerita, University of Wisconsin;* b. 18 Feb. 1948, Illinois; d. of Harold Greger and Marjorie Greger; ed Univ. of Illinois, Urbana-Champaign and Cornell Univ.; Asst Prof., Purdue Univ. 1973–78; Asst Prof., then Assoc. Prof., Univ. of Wisconsin, Madison 1978–83, Prof. of Nutritional Sciences 1983–2003, Prof. Emer. 2003–, Assoc. Dean, Grad. School 1990–96, Assoc. Dean, Medical School 1996–98; Vice-Provost of Research and Grad. Educ. and Dean of Grad. School, Univ. of Connecticut 2002–05, Vice-Provost for Strategic Planning 2005–07, fmr Prof., Dept of Nutritional Sciences; AAAS Congressional Sciences Eng Fellow 1984–85; mem. Bd of Man. COGR 1993–99; mem. Bd of Dirs AAALAC 1992–2003, NIH Panel on Regulatory Burden 1999–2002; mem. Council Soc. of Experimental Biology and Medicine 2002–05, NAS/NRC Cttees 1991–94, 1996–2000, 2003–07; novelist 2008–; Fellow, American Soc. of Nutrition 2016–; AAAS Congressional Science and Eng Fellowship 1984–85; Excellence in Nutrition Educ. Award, American Soc. for Nutrition 2008, Public Safety Writers Award for unpublished novels 2015, 2016. *Publications include:* Nutrition for Living 1985, 1988, 1991, 1994; more than 150 papers in scientific journals and books; author of medical thrillers and mysteries since 2007, including Coming Flu (novel) 2012, Ignore the Pain (novel) 2013, Malignancy (novel) (winner, Public Safety Writers Asscn) 2014, I Saw You in Beirut (novel) 2015, Murder: A Way to Lose Weight (novel) (Public Safety Writers Asscn Award) 2016, The Good Old Days? (collection of Stories) 2016, Other People's Mothers (collection of stories) 2016, Riddled with Clues (novel) 2017, The Flu Is Coming (novel) 2018. *Leisure interests:* travel, reading, pet therapy. *Address:* 925 Desert Willow Court, Bernalillo, NM 87004, USA (home). *Telephone:* (505) 876-4832 (home). *E-mail:* janet.greger@comcast.net (home). *Website:* www.jlgreger.com (home).

GREGERSON, Peter K., BS, MD; American geneticist and academic; *Director, Robert S. Boas Center for Genomics and Human Genetics, Feinstein Institute for Medical Research;* ed Johns Hopkins Univ., Columbia Univ. Coll. of Physicians and Surgeons; originally trained as a rheumatologist; Prof. of Molecular Medicine, Hofstra North Shore-LIJ School of Medicine; Dir Robert S. Boas Center for Genomics and Human Genetics, The Feinstein Inst. for Medical Research; leads North American Rheumatology Consortium; mem. Asscn of American Physicians 2009; Pfizer Scholars Award for New Faculty 1988, Klemperer Medal, New York Academy of Medicine 2007, Distinguished Basic Investigator Award, American Coll. of Rheumatology 2007, Crafoord Prize, Royal Swedish Acad. of Sciences (co-recipient) 2013. *Publications:* numerous papers in professional journals. *Address:* The Feinstein Institute for Medical Research, 350 Community Drive, Manhasset, NY 11030, USA (office). *Telephone:* (516) 562-1542 (office); (516) 562-1134 (office). *E-mail:* peterg@nshs.edu (office). *Website:* www.feinsteininstitute.org/faculty/peter-k-gregersen-md (office).

GREGG, Judd, AB, JD, LLM; American lawyer and fmr politician; *Senior Advisor, New Mountain Capital;* b. 14 Feb. 1947, Nashua, NH; s. of Hugh Gregg and Catherine Warner Gregg; m. Kathleen MacLellan 1973; one s. two d.; ed Phillips Exeter Acad., Columbia and Boston Univs; admitted to NH Bar 1972; law practice, Nashua, NH; mem. NH Gov.'s Exec. Council 1978–80; mem. US House of Reps for 2nd NH Dist, Washington, DC 1981–89; Gov. of NH 1989–93; Senator from NH 1993–2011 (retd), Chair. Health, Educ., Labor and Pensions Cttee 2003–05, Budget Cttee 2005–07 (Ranking mem.); Sr Advisor, New Mountain Capital 2011–; CEO Securities Industry and Financial Markets Asscn May–Dec. 2013, now Sr Advisor; currently Chair. Public Advisory Bd New Hampshire Inst. of Politics, St Anselm Coll.; Distinguished Fellow, Center for Global Business and Government, Dartmouth Coll. 2013–; mem. Bd of Dirs Honeywell International Inc., Stroz Friedberg, LLC; Republican; Hon. LLD (Univ. of New Hampshire) 1990, (Saint Anselm Coll.) 2001, (Boston Coll.) 2005, (Dartmouth Coll.) 2006; Moakley-Chafee New Englander of the Year Award, New England Council 2001, Conservationist of the Year Award, Soc. for the Protection of New Hampshire Forests 2003, Conservation Champion Award, Appalachian Mountain Club 2003, Rough Rider Award, Americans for Our Heritage and Recreation 2003, National Leadership Award, Big Brothers/Big Sisters of America 2005, Founders Medal, Boston Coll. Law School 2006, Lifetime of Service Award, City Year New Hampshire 2005, Paul E. Tsongas Economic Patriot Award, Concord Coalition 2009. *Address:* Tuck School of Business, 100 Tuck Hall, Hanover, NH 03755; New Mountain Capital, 787 7th Avenue, 49th Floor, New York, NY 10019, USA. *Telephone:* (603) 964-1976 (Tuck) (office). *E-mail:* judd.a.gregg@tuck.dartmouth.edu (office). *Website:* www.tuck.dartmouth.edu (office); www.newmountaincapital.com (office).

GREGOIRE, Christine O'Grady, BA, JuD; American lawyer, politician and fmr state governor; b. 24 March 1947, Auburn, Wash.; m. Mike Gregoire; two d.; ed Univ. of Washington, Gonzaga Univ.; began career as law clerk in Spokane Office, Attorney-Gen. for State of Washington 1976, became Asst Attorney-Gen. working on child abuse and neglect cases 1977–81, Sr Asst Attorney-Gen. and Man. Spokane Office 1981–82, Deputy Attorney-Gen. (first woman) 1982–92, Attorney-Gen. (first woman) 1993–2005; Gov. of Washington 2005–13; Dir Wash. Dept of Ecology 1988–92; Inaugural Chair. Bd of Dirs The Legacy Foundation 1999–2002; Pres. Nat. Asscn of Attorneys-Gen. (NAAG) 1999–2000; Chair. Nat. Govs Asscn 2010–11; Democrat; Hon. DJur (Gonzaga Univ.) 1995; US Supreme Court Best Brief Award, Wash. ACORN Fair Lending Champion Award, Campaign for Tobacco-Free Kids Champion Award, Distinguished Alumna Award, Univ. of Wash. Coll. of Arts and Sciences, Friend of Children Award, Wash. State Parent-Teachers Asscn, Pathfinder Award, Tri-City Chamber of Commerce, Woman of Distinction Award, YWCA's 7th Annual Woman of Achievement Awards, Child Health Advocacy Award, American Acad. of Pediatrics, Distinguished Jurisprudence Award, Pacific Northwest Region of Anti-Defamation League, Excellence in Leadership Award, Nat. Leadership Conf. of Women Execs in State Govt, Woman in Govt Award, Good Housekeeping Magazine, Woman of the Year Award, American Legion Auxiliary, Award of Excellence, Wash. State Asscn of Local Public Health Officials, 2000 Special Recognition Award, Wash. State Nurses Asscn, selected by Working Mother Magazine as one of nation's 25 Most Influential Working Mothers, Myra Bradwell Award, Gonzaga Univ. School of Law, Wash. State Bar Asscn Bd of Govs' Award for Professionalism, NAAG Wyman Award, Gleitsman Award for Leadership in Public Health, Gov.'s Child Abuse Prevention Award.

GREGORIAN, Vartan, MA, PhD; American university administrator and professor of history; *President, Carnegie Corporation of New York;* b. 8 April 1934, Tabriz, Iran; s. of Samuel B. Gregorian and Shushanik G. Gregorian (née Mirzaian); m. Clare Russell 1960; three c.; ed Coll. Arménien, Stanford Univ.; Instructor, San Francisco State Coll., then Asst Prof. and Assoc. Prof. of History 1962–68; Assoc. Prof. of History, UCLA 1968, Univ. of Texas, Austin 1968–72 (Dir Special Programs 1970–72); Tarzian Prof. of Armenian and Caucasian History, Univ. of Pennsylvania 1972–80, Dean 1974–79, Provost 1978–80; Prof. of History and Near Eastern Studies, New York Univ. 1984–89; Prof., New School for Social Research, New York 1984–89; Pres. New York Public Library 1981–89; Pres. Brown Univ. 1989–97, mem. Nat. Humanities Faculty 1970–; Pres. Carnegie Corpn of New York 1997–; mem. Bd of Dirs National September 11 Memorial and Museum, American Academy in Berlin; fmr mem. Bd of Dirs J. Paul Getty Trust, Aga Khan Univ., Qatar Foundation, McGraw-Hill Companies, Brandeis Univ., Human Rights Watch, Museum of Modern Art, Bill and Melinda Gates Foundation; mem. Acad. of Arts and Letters 1989–, Historical Asscn, Asscn for Advancement of Slavic Studies, American Philosophical Soc.; John Simon Guggenheim Fellow 1971–72; Hon. mem., American Library Asscn 2000; numerous hon. degrees, including from Brown Univ. Dartmouth Coll., Drew Univ., Johns Hopkins Univ., Univ. of Pennsylvania, Jewish Theological Seminary, City Univ. of New York, Rutgers Univ., Tufts Univ., New York Univ., Univ. of Aberdeen, Juilliard School, Univ. of Illinois, Fordham Univ., San Francisco State Univ., Univ. of Notre Dame, Carnegie Mellon Univ., Keio Univ., Univ. of Miami, Univ. of St. Andrews; Silver Cultural Medal Italian Ministry of Foreign Affairs 1977, Gold Medal of Honour City and Province of Vienna 1976, Ellis Island Medal of Honor 1986, American Acad. and Inst. of Arts and Letters Gold Medal for Service to the Arts 1989, Nat. Humanities Medal 1998, Eleanor Roosevelt Val-Kill Award 1999, Medal of Freedom 2004, Africa-America Inst. Award for Leadership in Higher Educ. Philanthropy 2009, Henry Crown Leadership Award, Aspen Inst. 2010, Distinguished Service Award, Council on Foundations 2013. *Publications include:* The Emergence of Modern Afghanistan 1880–1946 1969; Islam: A Mosaic, Not a Monolith 2003, The Road to Home: My Life and Times 2003; numerous articles for professional journals. *Address:* Office of the President, Carnegie Corporation of New York, 437 Madison Avenue, New York, NY 10022, USA. *Telephone:* (212) 371-3200. *Fax:* (212) 223-8831 (office). *Website:* www.carnegie.org (office).

GREGORY, Joseph M., BA; American financial services industry executive; m. Niki Gregory; five c.; ed Hofstra Univ.; joined Lehman Brothers 1974, held various man. positions including in Fixed Income Div., Head, Mortgage Business 1980–91, Co-Head Fixed Income Div. 1991–96, Head Global Equities Div. 1996–2000, Chief Admin. Officer 2000–02, Co-COO 2002–04, Pres. and COO 2004–08, Chair. Lehman Brothers Foundation; fmr mem. Nat. Advisory Bd The Posse Foundation Inc.; fmr mem. Bd of Trustees Harlem Children's Zone; fmr Trustee and mem. Finance, Endowment and Investment Cttees, Hofstra Univ.

GREGURIĆ, Franjo, DSc; Croatian politician; b. 12 Oct. 1939, Lobor, Zlata Bistrica; m. Jozefina Gregurić (née Abramović); one s. one d.; ed Univ. of Zagreb; early jobs working in chemical factories; Tech. Dir Radonia at Sisak; Dir-Gen. Chromos factory, Zagreb; rep. of Foreign Trade Co. Astra in Moscow, Gen. Dir Astra-Int. Trade, Zagreb –1990; Vice-Dir, then Dir Chamber of Econs, Zagreb; mem. Christian Democratic Union (CDU); Deputy Premier of Croatia 1990; Prime Minister 1991–92; mem. Sabor (Croatian Parl.) 1990–; Adviser to Pres. of Croatia 1992–, apptd Special Del. (with rank of Amb.) to Croat-Bosnian Fed. and Bosnia and Herzegovina 1997; Pres. Supervisory Bd ELKA kabeli d.o.o. 2004–; fmr Dir INA Co., Zagreb; Pres. Croatian Firefighting Asscn 1993–2000; numerous nat. and int. awards for econs. *Leisure interests:* oenology, pomology. *Address:* ELKA kabeli d.o.o., 10000 Zagreb, Koledovčina 1 (office); 41000 Zagreb, Ilica 49, Croatia. *Telephone:* (1) 2482600 (office). *Fax:* (1) 2404898 (office). *E-mail:* elka-marketing@elka.hr (office). *Website:* www.elka.hr (office).

GREIČIUS, Vytautas, LLM; Lithuanian judge; *Justice, Constitutional Court;* b. 9 May 1949, Tauragė; m. Teresė Greičiuvienė; one d. two s.; ed Faculty of Law, Vilnius Univ.; judge, Ukmergė Dist People's Court 1976–90; Judge, Supreme Court of Lithuania 1990–94, Chair. Div. of Criminal Cases 1995–99, Pres. of Supreme Court 1999–2009, apptd Judge, Div. of Criminal Cases 2009, served as Judge until 2014; Justice, Constitutional Court 2014–.

GREIDER, Carolyn (Carol) Widney, BA, PhD; American molecular biologist and academic; *Bloomberg Distinguished Professor, Daniel Nathans Professor and Director, Molecular Biology and Genetics, School of Medicine, Johns Hopkins University;* b. 15 April 1961, San Diego, Calif.; ed Univ. of California, Santa Barbara, Univ. of California, Berkeley; Fellow, Cold Spring Harbor Lab. 1988–90, Asst Investigator 1990–92, Assoc. Investigator 1992–94, Investigator 1994–97; Assoc. Prof. of Molecular Biology and Genetics, Johns Hopkins Univ. School of Medicine 1997–99, Prof. of Molecular Biology and Genetics 1999–2003, Prof. of Oncology 2001–, Acting Dir Dept of Molecular Biology and Genetics 2002–03, Daniel Nathans Prof. and Dir 2003–, Bloomberg Distinguished Prof. 2014–, Dept of Molecular Biology and Genetics; mem. Editorial Bd Cancer Cell 2001–, Molecular Cancer Research 2003–05, Int. Journal of Cancer 2004–07, Biomedical Central (BMC) Molecular Biology 2004–, eLife 2012–; mem. American Assoc. for the Advancement of Science 1989–, American Soc. for Microbiology, American Assoc. for Cancer Research 1994– (also Fellow 2013), RNA Soc. 1995–, American Soc. for Cell Biology 1996–, NAS 2003, American Soc. for Biochemistry & Molecular Biology 2004–, American Soc. for Human Genetics 2006–, Inst. of Medicine 2010, American Philosophical Soc. 2016–; Fellow, American Acad. of Arts and Sciences 2003, AAAS 2003, American Acad. of Microbiology 2004, Royal Acad. of Medicine of Catalonia 2012, Alpha Omega Alpha Honor Medical Soc. 2013; mem. Advisory Cttee Cold Spring Harbor Lab., Passano Foundation 2009–, HHMI Medical Advisory Board (MAB) 2010–, Pres.'s Cttee on Nat. Medal of Science 2012–, ASCB Public Policy Cttee 2013–, Hastings Center Council, Brigham and Women's Hosp. 2014–, Shaw Prize Cttee 2015–; Regents Scholarship, Univ. of California 1981, Pew Scholar in the Biomedical Sciences 1990–94, Allied Signal Outstanding Project Award 1992, Gertrude Elion Cancer Research Award, American Asscn for Cancer Research 1994, Glenn Foundation Award, American Soc. for Cell Biology 1995, Cornelius Rhoads Award, American Asscn for Cancer Research 1996, Schering-Plough Scientific Achievement Award, American Soc. for Biochemistry and Molecular Biology 1997, Ellison Medical Foundation Sr Scholar 1998, Gairdner Foundation Award 1998, Passano Foundation Award 1999, Rosenstiel Award in Basic Medical Research 1999, Harvey Soc. Lecturer 2000, NAS Richard Lounsbery Award 2003, Lila Gruber Cancer Research Award 2006, The Wiley Prize in Biomedical Sciences 2006, Albert Lasker Award for Basic Medical Research (with Elizabeth Blackburn and Jack Szostak) 2006, Louisa Gross Horwitz Prize, Columbia Univ. 2007, Nobel Prize in Physiology or Medicine (with Elizabeth Blackburn and Jack Szostak) 2009, Paul Ehrlich and Ludwig Darmstaedter Prize (jtly), Pearl Meister Greengard Prize 2009, Cosmos Club Award 2015, Alma Dea Morani M.D., Renaissance Woman Award 2017. *Achievements include:* discovery of chromosomes protection by telomeres and enzyme telomerase. *Publications:* more than 90 scientific publs. *Address:* Department of Molecular Biology and Genetics, Johns Hopkins University School of Medicine, 617 Hunterian, 725 North Wolfe Street, Baltimore, MD 21205, USA (office). *Telephone:* (410) 614-6506 (office). *Fax:* (410) 955-0831 (office). *E-mail:* cgreider@jhmi.edu (office). *Website:* www.mbg.jhmi.edu (office); www.greiderlab.org (office).

GREIFELD, Robert, BA, MBA; American business executive and stock exchange official; *Chairman, Nasdaq Stock Market Inc.;* b. 18 July 1957, Queens, New York; m. Julia Greifeld; two s. one d.; ed Iona Coll., Stern School of Business, NY Univ.; Pres. and COO, Automated Securities Clearance Inc. (ASC) 1991–99; created BRUT, trading consortium; Exec. Vice-Pres. SunGard Data Systems Inc. 1999, then Corp. Vice-Pres. and Group CEO; Pres. and CEO NASDAQ Stock Market Inc. 2003–16, Chair. 2017–; Chair. USA Track and Field Foundation 2004–; Vice-Chair. Kennedy Center Corp. Fund Bd; mem. Bd of Dirs Partnership for New York City, Committee on Capital Markets Regulation, Financial Services Roundtable, Business Roundtable; Brother Arthur A. Loftus Award for Outstanding Achievement, Iona Coll. 2004. *Leisure interests:* running, golf. *Address:* Nasdaq Stock Market Inc., 1 Liberty Plaza, 165 Broadway, New York, NY 10006, USA (office).

Telephone: (212) 401-8700 (office). *Fax:* (212) 401-1024 (office). *Website:* www.nasdaq.com (office).

GREIG, Geordie Carron, MA, FRSA; British journalist; *Editor, The Mail on Sunday;* b. 16 Dec. 1960, London, England; s. of Sir Carron Greig and Monica Greig (née Stourton); m. Kathryn Elizabeth Terry 1995; one s. two d.; ed Eton Coll. and St Peter's Coll., Oxford; reporter, South East London and Kentish Mercury 1981–83, Daily Mail 1984–85, Today 1985–87; reporter, The Sunday Times 1987–89, Arts Corresp. 1989–91, New York Corresp. 1991–95, Literary Ed. 1995–99; Ed. of Tatler 1999–2009; Ed., London Evening Standard 2009–12, Editorial Dir 2010–12, Dir 2012–; Editorial Dir, The Independent 2010–12, Dir 2012–; Ed. The Mail on Sunday 2012–, Dir, Mail Newspapers 2012–. *Publications:* Louis and the Prince 1999, Breakfast with Lucian 2013. *Address:* The Mail on Sunday, Northcliffe House, 2 Derry Street, London, W8 5TT, England (office). *Telephone:* (20) 3361-3001 (office). *Fax:* (20) 7937-6721 (office). *E-mail:* geordie.greig@mailonsunday.co.uk (office). *Website:* www.mailonsunday.co.uk (office).

GREINER, Helen, BS, MS; American engineer and business executive; *Chief Technology Officer, CyPhy Works;* b. 6 Dec. 1967, London, England; ed Massachusetts Inst. of Tech.; emigrated with family to USA in 1972; several sr positions working in robotic tech. including at NASA's Jet Propulsion Lab. and MIT's Artificial Intelligence Lab.; f. California Cybernetics 1989; Co-founder iRobot Corpn 1990, Pres. 1990–2004, Chair. –2008; currently Founder and Chief Technology Officer, CyPhy Works; Chair. Robotic Tech. Consortium; mem. World Econ. Forum's Young Global Leaders; mem. Bd of Dirs Nat. Defense Industrial Asscn; mem. Bd of Trustees Mass Tech. Leadership Council, MIT, Boston Museum of Science; mem. Robotics Advisory Bd Worcester Polytechnic Inst.; Presidential Amb. for Global Leadership 2014; Entrepreneur of the Year, Ernst and Young 2003, Innovator for the Next Century, Technology Review magazine, Top Ten Innovator, Fortune magazine 2003, Pioneer Award, Asscn for Unmanned Vehicle Systems Int. 2006, inducted into Women in Technology International Hall of Fame 2007, Women of Vision Award, Anita Borg Inst. 2008. *Publications:* numerous papers and articles on robotics in professional journals. *Leisure interest:* kayaking. *Address:* CyPhy Works, Inc., 16C Electronics Avenue, Danvers, MA 01923, USA (office). *E-mail:* info@cyphyworks.com (office). *Website:* cyphyworks.com (office); www.irobot.com (office).

GREITENS, Eric Robert, MA, PhD; American politician and fmr naval officer; b. 10 April 1974, St Louis, Mo.; s. of Robert Greitens and Becky Greitens; m. Sheena Elise Chestnut 2011; two s.; ed Duke Univ., Univ. of Oxford (Rhodes and Truman Scholar), UK; joined USN, selected for SEALS 2001, served in Afghanistan, South-East Asia, Africa and Iraq, transferred to Navy Reserve 2005, currently Lt-Commdr; White House Fellow, US Dept of Housing and Urban Devt 2005–06; Founder and CEO The Mission Continues (charity), St Louis 2007–14; Gov. of Missouri 2017–18 (resgnd); fmr Sr Fellow, Harry S. Truman School of Public Affairs, Univ. of Missouri; fmr mem. Faculty, Olin School of Business, Washington Univ., St Louis; Republican; Dr hc (Tufts Univ.) 2012; Bronze Star, Purple Heart, Jt Service Commendation Medal, Navy Commendation Medal, Jt Service Achievement Medal, Mil. Outstanding Volunteer Service Medal, Pres.'s Volunteer Service Award 2008, Maj. George A. Smith Memorial Fund 2009, Naval Reserve Junior Officer of the Year 2011, Charles Bronfman Prize 2012, named one of The 100 Most Influential People in the World by TIME magazine 2013, Gleitsman Citizen Activist Award, Center for Public Leadership, Harvard Kennedy School 2014. *Achievements include:* won two Univ. of Oxford Boxing Blues and gold medal at British Universities Sports Asscn's Nat. Boxing Championships. *Publications:* Strength and Compassion: Photographs and Essays (New York Book Festival Grand Prize 2009) 2008, The Heart & the Fist: The Education of a Humanitarian, the Making of a Navy SEAL 2011, Resilience: Hard-Won Wisdom for Living a Better Life 2015.

GREMINGER, Thomas, PhD; Swiss diplomatist; *Secretary-General, Organization for Security and Co-operation in Europe;* b. 22 April 1961, Lucerne; ed Univ. of Zurich; joined Federal Dept of Foreign Affairs (FDFA) 1990, Diplomatic Asst for Devt Policy, Swiss Agency for Devt and Cooperation (SDC) 1992–94, Deputy Head of Devt Policy and Research Div. 1994–96, then Head 1996–98, Deputy Dir-Gen. SDC 2015–17, Charge d'affaires Swiss Embassy in Mozambique 1999–2001, also Country Dir Devt Cooperation Program, Deputy Head Political Affairs Div. IV, Human Security 2004–10; Perm. Rep. to OSCE, UN and Int. Orgs in Vienna 2010–15, Sec.-Gen. OSCE 2017–; Chair. Peacenexus Foundation; mem. Advisory Bd DCAF; OSCE White Ribbon for long-standing support for gender equality 2012. *Publications include:* Armed Forces and Civilians in Complex Multilateral Peace Operations 2007, An Expansion of Military Peacebuilding is Overdue 2009, The Development of Switzerland's Civilian Peacebuilding 2011, The Human Dimension Committee of the OSCE 2012. *Address:* OSCE Secretariat, Wallnerstrasse 6, 1010 Vienna, Austria (office). *Telephone:* (1) 514-36 (office). *Fax:* (1) 514-36-69-96 (office). *E-mail:* pm@osce.org (office). *Website:* www.osce.org (office).

GRENELL, Richard A., MPA; American diplomatist; *Ambassador to Germany;* b. 18 Sept. 1966, Jenison, Michigan; partner Matt Lashey; ed Evangel Univ., Harvard Univ.; fmr Policy and Communications Advisor and Spokesman; Dir of Communications and Public Diplomacy to US Perm. Rep. to UN 2001–08; Sr Vice-Pres. DaVita Inc. 2008–09; Founder Capitol Media Partners 2009–; Nat. Security and Foreign Affairs Spokesman of Presidential Cand. Mitt Romney 2012; Founding partner chemoWave 2017–; Amb. to Germany 2018–; mem. Advisory Bd Newsmax Media Inc., Langley Intelligence Group Network. *Publications include:* contrib. numerous articles to Wall Street Journal, Los Angeles Times, CBS News, CNN, Washington Times. *Address:* US Embassy Berlin, Clayallee 170, 14191 Berlin, Germany (office). *Telephone:* (30) 83050 (office). *E-mail:* feedback@usembassy.de (office). *Website:* de.usembassy.gov (office).

GRENFELL, Baron, (Life Peer), cr. 2000, of Kilvey in the County of Swansea; **Julian Pascoe Francis St Leger Grenfell,** BA (Hons); British politician; b. 23 May 1935, London; s. of the 2nd Baron Grenfell of Kilvey; m. 1st Loretta Reali 1961 (divorced 1970); one d.; m. 2nd Gabrielle Raab 1970 (divorced 1987); two d.; m. 3rd Elizabeth Scott Porter 1987 (divorced 1992); m. 4th Dagmar Langbehn Debreil 1993; ed Eton Coll., King's Coll., Cambridge; Second Lt, King's Royal Rifle Corps 1954–56; Pres. Cambridge Union 1959; Capt. Queen's Royal Rifles (Territorial Army) 1963; TV journalist 1960–64; with World Bank 1965–95, Chief of Information and Public Affairs in Europe 1969–72, Deputy Dir European Office, Paris 1973–74, Special Rep. to the UN Orgs, New York 1974–81, Adviser, HQ 1983–90, Head of External Affairs, European Office, Paris 1990–95; mem. UK del. to Council of Europe 1997–99; sat in House of Lords as Lord Grenfell of Kilvey 1976–99, cr. Life Peer 2000, Chair. House of Lords Sub-cttee on Econ. and Financial Affairs 1998, mem. Select Cttee on EU 1999, 2000–08, Chair. 2002–08, Prin. Deputy Chair. of Cttees 2002–08, Deputy Speaker 2002–08, retd 2014; Pres. Anglo-Belgian Soc. of the UK 2006–13; Chevalier, Légion d'honneur 2005; Commdr, Order of Merit (FRG) 2008; Commdr, Order of Crown of Belgium 2009; High Order of Merit (Croatia) 2010, Médaille d'honneur. *Publications:* novels: Margot 1984, The Gazelle 2004, The Widow of Honfleur 2016. *Leisure interests:* 20th-century European history, writing fiction. *Address:* 24 rue Chaptal, 75009 Paris, France (home). *Telephone:* (1) 48-74-08-55 (home). *E-mail:* 23grenfellj@gmail.com (home).

GRENON, Thomas; French mining engineer, civil servant and museum director; *Director-General, Muséum national d'Histoire naturelle;* began career in public service in Dept of Nuclear Energy and Raw Materials, Ministry of Industry 1989–91; with Foreign Econ. Relations Dept, Ministry of Finance 1991–93, responsible for relations with all countries arising from the dissolution of the Soviet Union, Head of Corp. Finance supervising financial institutions specializing in business financing: Nat. Credit CEPME (Credit Facilities for Small and Medium Enterprises) Sofaris French Soc. Guarantee financing SMEs), Regional Devt Cos) 1993–95; tech. adviser, Ministry of Culture and Communication, in charge of budget, social relations, large-scale works and new technologies 1995–97, projects completed include Nat. Library of France, the Grand Louvre and renovation of the Centre Pompidou; worked in private sector 1997–2002, successively Deputy CEO Financière Agache, Sec.-Gen. AXA France, Investment Dir, Royal Bank of Scotland; CEO Museum of Science and Industry 2003–05; Gen. Man. Réunion des Musées Nationaux 2005–10; Dir-Gen. Muséum nat. d'Histoire naturelle (Nat. Museum of Natural History) 2010–. *Address:* Muséum national d'Histoire naturelle, 57 rue Cuvier, 75005 Paris, France (office). *Telephone:* 1-40-79-30-00 (office). *E-mail:* info@mnhn.fr (office). *Website:* www.mnhn.fr (office).

GRENS, Elmars; Latvian molecular biologist and academic; *Scientific Adviser, Biomedical Research and Study Centre;* b. 9 Oct. 1935, Rīga; s. of Janis Grens and Melita Grene; m. Eva Stankevich 1957; one s. one d.; ed Latvian State Univ.; researcher, Head of Lab., Research Dir, Inst. of Organic Synthesis, Latvian Acad. of Sciences 1958–90, Dir Inst. of Molecular Biology 1991–93; Dir Biomedical Research and Study Centre 1993–2001, 2009–10, Research Dir 2001–09, Head, Scientific Council 2010–15, Scientific Adviser 2015–; mem. Latvian Acad. of Sciences, Academia Europaea, Russian Acad. of Sciences. *Publications include:* more than 180 scientific articles on molecular biology of viruses, fine biotechnology and genetic eng. *Leisure interest:* downhill skiing. *Address:* Biomedical Research and Study Centre, Ratsupites 1, Rīga 1067, Latvia (office). *Telephone:* 2922-6029 (office). *Fax:* 6744-2407 (office). *E-mail:* grens@biomed.lu.lv (office).

GRETZKY, Wayne; Canadian professional ice hockey player (retd), sports industry executive and ice hockey coach; *Vice-Chairman and Partner, Oilers Entertainment Group;* b. 26 Jan. 1961, Brantford, Ont.; s. of Walter Gretzky and Phyllis Gretzky; m. Janet Jones 1988; three s. two d.; joined Indianapolis Racers of World Hockey Asscn (WHA) 1978 at age 17, traded to Edmonton Oilers (WHA then merged with Nat. Hockey League—NHL), played 1979–88, traded to Los Angeles Kings, played 1988–96, traded to St Louis Blues 1996, signed as free agent NY Rangers, played 1996–99 (retd); NHL scoring records include 2,857 points, 894 goals, 1,963 assists; winner Stanley Cup with Edmonton (four times); winner Canada Cup 1984, 1987, 1991; mem. Canadian Olympic team 1998; Exec. Dir Team Canada Hockey Team 2002 (Olympics), 2004 (World Cup of Hockey); investor, Los Acros Sports LLC, Man. Pnr, Phoenix Coyotes 1999–2009, Coach 2005–09; Vice-Chair. and Partner, Oilers Entertainment Group 2016–; f. Wayne Gretzky Foundation 2002; Special Advisor, Men's Nat. Hockey Team, Vancouver Winter Olympics 2010; apptd NHL Centennial Amb. 2016; Owner, Wayne Gretzky Estates (winery); Hon. LLD (Univ. of Alberta) 2000; NHL Most Valuable Player (Hart Memorial Trophy) nine times 1980–88; NHL scoring champion (Art Ross Trophy) ten times 1981–87, 1990–91, 1994; Most Valuable Player Stanley Cup playoffs (Conn Smythe Trophy) 1985, 1988; Most Gentlemanly Player (Lady Byng Memorial Trophy) 1980, 1991, 1992, 1994, 1999, Lester Patrick Trophy for Outstanding Service to Hockey in US 1994, voted Greatest Player in NHL History 1997, elected Hockey Hall of Fame 1999, Olympic Order from Int. Olympic Cttee 2002, Amb. Award of Excellence 2010. *Films include:* The Flamingo Kid 1984, A Chorus Line 1985. *Publication:* Gretzky: An Autobiography (with Rick Reilly). *Address:* Oilers Entertainment Group, 11230-110 Street, Edmonton, AB T5G 3H7, Canada (office). *Website:* oilers.nhl.com (office); www.gretzky.com.

GREY, Dame Beryl Elizabeth, CH, DBE, CBE; British prima ballerina; *Patron, Royal Ballet Benevolent Fund;* b. (Beryl Elizabeth Groom), 11 June 1927, London, England; d. of Arthur Ernest Groom and Annie Elizabeth Groom; m. Sven Gustav Svenson 1950; one s.; ed Dame Alice Owens School, London, Madeline Sharp School, Royal Ballet School and de Vos School of Dance; debut at Sadler's Wells Co. 1941; Prima Ballerina with Royal Ballet until 1957; freelance int. prima ballerina from 1957; first full-length ballet Swan Lake on 15th birthday; appeared in leading roles of classical and numerous modern ballets including Giselle, Sleeping Beauty, Sylvia, Casse Noisette, Les Sylphides, Checkmate, Donald of the Burthens, Dante Sonata, Three Cornered Hat, Ballet Imperial, Lady and the Fool, Les Rendezvous; American, Continental, African, Far Eastern tours with Royal Ballet from 1945; guest artist European Opera Houses in Norway, Finland, Sweden, Denmark, Belgium, Romania, Germany, Italy, etc.; guest artist, South and Central America, Middle East, Union of South Africa, Rhodesia, Australasia; first foreign guest artist ever to dance with the Bolshoi Ballet in Russia 1957–58 (Moscow, Leningrad, Kiev, Tbilisi) and first to dance with Peking Ballet and Shanghai Ballet 1964; Dir-Gen. of Arts Educational Trust, London 1966–68; Artistic Dir London Festival Ballet 1968–79; produced and staged Giselle, Perth, Australia 1984, 1986, Sleeping Beauty, Royal Swedish Ballet, Stockholm 1985, 2002; Pres. Dance Council for Wales 1981–2004, East Grinstead Operatic Soc. 1986–2010, Keep-fit Soc. 1992–93; Vice-Pres. Fed. of Music Festivals 1985–, The Music Therapy Charity 1980–, Royal Acad. of Dancing 1981–, East Grinstead Music Arts Festival 1991–; Chair. Imperial Soc. Teachers of Dancing 1962–91, Pres. 1991–2001, Life

Pres. 2002–, Fellow; Gov. Royal Ballet 1993, Vice-Chair. 1995–2002; Pres. All England Dance Competitions 2005–, British Ballet Org. 2010–; a Dir Birmingham Royal Ballet 1995–99, Royal Opera House, Covent Garden 1999–2003; Trustee, Royal Ballet Benevolent Fund 1983–2011 (Chair. 1992–2011, Patron 2011–), Dance Teachers' Benevolent Fund (Vice-Chair. 1987–2004), Discs 1994–2009; Vice-Patron British School of Osteopathy 1992–; Patron and Trustee, Dancers Resettlement Trust; Patron Benesh Inst., Language of Dance Centre, Lisa Ullman Travelling Scholarship Fund 1986–, Friends of Sadler's Wells 1991–2010, Furlong Hip Replacement (renamed Furlong Research Charitable Foundation) 1993–2009 (Trustee 2005–09), Osteopathic Centre for Children 1992–, Sussex Opera and Ballet Soc. 2001–, Theatre Design Trust for Dance 1995–, Critics' Circle Dance Awards 2005–10, German Shepherd Dog Rescue 2010–, Council for Dance Educ. and Training 2011–, Roshe School 2015–; Hon. DMus (Leicester) 1970, (Univ. of London) 1996; Hon. DLit (City of London Univ.) 1974, (Buckingham) 1993; Hon. DEd (CNAA), 1989; Hon. DArt (Bedford) 2010, (Bath) 2018; Queen Elizabeth II Coronation Award, Royal Acad. of Dancing 1996, Critics Circle Service to Dance Award 2002, Lifetime Achievement Award Imperial Soc. of Teachers of Dancing 2004, Carl Alan Lifetime Achievement Award 2010. *Film:* Black Swan (stereoscopic) 1952. *Radio:* Desert Island Discs (twice); numerous programmes and interviews since 1950. *Television:* numerous appearances and interviews since early 1950s. *Publications:* Red Curtain Up 1958, Through the Bamboo Curtain 1965, My Favourite Ballet Stories (ed.) 1981, For the Love of Dance 2017. *Leisure interests:* piano playing, painting, swimming, opera.

GREY, Clare, BA (Hons), DPhil, FRS; British physical chemist and academic; *Geoffrey Moorhouse Gibson Professor, Department of Chemistry, University of Cambridge;* ed Univ. of Oxford; Royal Soc. Postdoctoral Fellow, Univ. of Nijmegen, The Netherlands 1991; Visiting Scientist, DuPont CR&D, USA 1992; Asst Prof. of Chem., State Univ. of NY, Stony Brook 1994–2001, Full Prof. 2001–09, Assoc. Dir Northeastern Chemical Energy Storage Center 2009; Full Prof., Univ. of Cambridge 2009–, currently Geoffrey Moorhouse Gibson Prof., Dept of Chem., Fellow, Pembroke Coll.; Vaughan Lecturer 2008, RSC John Jeyes Award 2010, Günther Laukien Prize 2013, Davy Medal, Royal Soc. 2014. *Publications:* numerous papers in professional journals on the applications of nuclear magnetic resonance and in particular using it to study lithium ion batteries. *Address:* Department of Chemistry, Lensfield Road, Cambridge, CB2 1EW, England (office). *Telephone:* (1223) 336509 (office). *E-mail:* cpg27@cam.ac.uk (office). *Website:* www.ch.cam.ac.uk/person/cpg27 (office); www.ch.cam.ac.uk/group/grey (office).

GREY-JOHNSON, Crispin, BA, MA, PGCE; Gambian diplomatist, government official, development consultant and business consultant; *Chairman and CEO, St Mary's Holding Company (Gambia) Ltd;* b. 7 Dec. 1946, Banjul; m.; several c.; ed Methodist Girls High School, Methodist Boys High School, Gambia High School, McGill Univ., Montreal, Canada, Univ. of Oxford, UK, George Washington Univ., USA; Master, Sr Master, Head of Dept, Gambia High School, Banjul 1968–77; Assoc. Econ. Affairs Officer, UN Econ. Comm. for Africa (ECA) 1977–81, Econ. Affairs Officer 1981–90, Sr Regional Adviser 1990–94, Coordinator, Multidisciplinary Regional Advisory Group, Addis Ababa, Ethiopia 1994–96; Man. Dir Galloryaa Farms Ltd, The Gambia 1996–97; High Commr to Canada and Amb. to USA, Brazil and Venezuela 1997–99; High Commr to Sierra Leone and Amb. to Côte d'Ivoire and Liberia 1999–2002; Perm. Rep. to UN, New York 2002–07; Sec. of State for Higher Educ., Research, Science and Tech. Feb.–Sept. 2007, 2008–11, for Foreign Affairs 2007–08; Chair. and CEO St Mary's Holding Co. (Gambia) Ltd 2011–, MCM Holding Co. (Sierra Leone) Ltd 2011–; involved in setting up African Inst. for Higher Tech. Training and Research, Kenya, Return of Skills Programme for Africa 1982–92; served as Vice-Pres. UN Gen. Ass. UN Exec. Bd on Comm. on Population and Devt; Chair Group of Friends of Guinea-Bissau, Group of Friends of Taiwan; served as Gen. Ass. Facilitator in negotiations on the resolution on the Prevention of Armed Conflict; served also on many UN Task Forces; mem. African Asscn for Public Admin and Man., African Adult Educ. Asscn, African Asscn for Training and Devt; Millennium Medal in recognition of Services for Peace and Security (Repub. of The Gambia) 2001, Hon. Diploma (Guinea Bissau) 2004; Govt of Canada Special Commonwealth African Aid Programme Scholarship 1965–68, Govt of UK Overseas Devt Agency Scholarship 1970–71, UN Fellowship for Research at African Inst. for Econ. Devt and Planning, Dakar, Senegal 1973, USAID Agency for Int. Devt Fellowship 1980. *Publications:* The Employment Crisis in Africa: Issues in Human Resources Development Policy 1990; book chapters and articles on human resources devt. *Address:* St Mary's Holding Co. (Gambia) Ltd, PO Box 26, Banjul (office); 30 2nd Street East, Fajara, Banjul, The Gambia (home). *Telephone:* 449-6090 (home). *E-mail:* cgreyjohnson@hotmail.com (home).

GREY-THOMPSON, Baroness (Life Peer), cr. 2010, of Eaglescliffe in the County of Durham; **Tanni Carys Davina Grey-Thompson,** DBE, BA; British athlete; b. 26 July 1969, Cardiff, Wales; d. of Peter Alexander Harvey Grey and Sulwen Davina Grey (née Jones); m. Dr Ian Thompson 1999; one d.; ed St Cyres Comprehensive School, Penarth, Loughborough Univ. of Tech.; bronze medal for 400m wheelchair races, Seoul Paralympics 1988; gold medals for 100m, 200m, 400m and 800m wheelchair races, Barcelona Paralympics 1988; gold medal for 800m and silver medals for 100m, 200m, 400m wheelchair races, Atlanta Paralympics 1996; gold medals for 100m, 200m, 400m and 800m wheelchair races, Sydney Paralympics 2000, 100m and 400m wheelchair races, Athens Paralympics 2004; gold medals, women's wheelchair race, London Marathon 1992, 1994, 1996, 1998, 2001, 2002, bronze medal 1993, silver medals 1997, 1999, 2000, 2003; three gold medals and one silver medal at European Championships 2003; broke over 20 world records; Devt Officer, UK Athletics 1996–2001; apptd Cross Bench Peer, House of Lords 2010–; TV and radio presenter, conf. and motivational speaker, also numerous guest appearances; Pres. Welsh Asscn of Cricketers with a Disability; Vice-Pres. Women's Sports Foundation, South Wales Region of Riding for the Disabled, Get Kids Going; Deputy Chair. UK Lottery Awards Panel (Sport); mem. The Sports Council for Wales's Nat. Excellence Panel, Sports Council for Wales Sportlot Panel, Minister of Sport Implementation Group for the Devt of Sport, Welsh Hall of Fame Roll of Honour 1992–, English Sports Council Lottery Awards Panel 1995–99, Sports Council for Wales 1996–2002, for UK Sport 1998–2003, Nat. Disability Council 1997–2000, Manchester Commonwealth Games Organising Council Asscn 2002; mem. Elect Laureus World Sports Acad. 2001, mem. 2002–; Patron British Sports Leaders, British Sport Trust, Durham Sport Millennium Youth Games, Regain, Youth Sport Trust, Nat. Sports Medicine Inst. of UK, Shelter Cymru 2003 London Marathon, Lady Taverners, Nat. Blood Service; Vice-Patron Helen Rollason Cancer Care Appeal, Jubilee Sailing Trust 2002–; Hon. Fellow, Univ. of Wales Coll., Cardiff 1997, Univ. of Wales Inst., Cardiff 2001, Univ. of Swansea 2001, Coll. of Ripon and York St John 2001, Inst. of Leisure and Amenity Man. 2001, Univ. of Wales Coll., Newport 2003; Freeman, City of Cardiff 2003; Hon. DUniv (Staffordshire) 1998, (Southampton) 1998; Hon. LLD (Exeter) 2003; Dr hc (Surrey) 2000, (Leeds Metropolitan) 2001, (Wales) 2002, (Loughborough) 2002, (Heriot-Watt) 2004; Hon. Masters degree (Loughborough) 1994, (Teesside) 2001; Hon. MSc (Manchester Metropolitan) 1998; BBC Wales Sports Personality of the Year (three times), Sunday Times Sportswoman of the Year 1992, 2000, (Third Place) 2004, Royal Mail Best Female Performance of the Paralympic Games 1992, Panasonic Special Award 1992, Variety Club Disabled Sportswoman of the Year 1992, Welsh Sports Hall of Fame 1993, Sports Writers' Asscn Female Disabled Athlete of the Year 1994, Sporting Ambassador 1998, Sportswriters Award 2000, Third Place, BBC Sports Personality of the Year 2000, Helen Rollason Award for Inspiration, BBC Sports Personality of the Year 2000, Welsh Woman of the Year 2001, Welsh Sportswoman of the Year 2001, Pride of Britain Special Award 2001, awarded title of UK Sporting Hero by Sport UK 2001, Chancellor's Medal, Univ. of Glamorgan 2001, Walpole Best British Sporting Achievement Award 2002, Commonwealth Games Sports Award for Best Female Disabled Athlete 2002, UK Sport Fair Play Award 2004, Sports Journalist UK Sport Award 2004. *Radio:* numerous appearances including as presenter The Rush Hour, BBC Radio Wales 1995–96, Sportfirst, BBC Radio 4, BBC Radio 5 Live 1995–96. *Television:* Presenter, From the Edge (BBC 2) 1998–2000, X-Ray (BBC Wales) 2002, BBC Manchester; guest appearances on BBC Question Time, Breakfast with Frost, The Weakest Link, Grandstand, A Question of Sport, Countryside; It's My Funeral, My Favourite Hymns, CBBC's Blue Peter, They Think It's All Over, and various lifestyle programmes such as Gloria Hunniford and GMTV. *Publication:* Seize the Day: My Autobiography 2001; contrib. to leading newspapers including Daily Mail and the Guardian and various magazines including Disability Now, Now Magazine, Woman's Realm, Hello, Best, Good Housekeeping, Ability Needs. *Leisure interests:* reading, IT. *Address:* House of Lords, London, SW1A 0PW (office); c/o Helen Williams, Creating Excellence, Equity House, 1st Floor, Knight Street, South Woodham Ferrers, Chelmsford, Essex, CM3 5ZL, England (office). *Telephone:* (1245) 328303 (office). *Fax:* (1245) 323512 (office). *E-mail:* helen@creatingexcellence.co.uk (office). *Website:* www.creatingexcellence.co.uk (office).

GRI, Françoise; French business executive; b. 21 Dec. 1957, Agen (Lot-et-Garonne); ed École nationale supérieure d'informatique et de mathématiques appliquées de Grenoble (ENSIMAG); joined IBM as engineer in 1981, various man. positions both in France and abroad, Dir Sales and Marketing, E-Business Solutions, IBM Middle East and Africa 1996–2000, Dir Logistics Devt 2000–01, Dir Commercial Operations Jan.–Aug. 2001, Pres. and Dir-Gen. IBM France 2001–07; Pres. and CEO Manpower France and S Europe, Paris 2007–12; Dir-Gen. Pierre et Vacances/Center Parcs 2013–14; mem. Supervisory Bd Rexel 2010–; mem. Bd Edenred (fmrly Accor Services) 2010–, Crédit Agricole 2012–; mem. Policy Bd Institut de l'Entreprise (Vice-Pres.), Bd SFIB (French asscn of IT cos, now part of Alliance TICS), Ethics Cttee Mouvement des entreprises de France, Bd of Dirs École Centrale, Paris; Chevalier, Ordre nat. du Mérite 2004, Légion d'honneur 2009. *Publication:* Plaidoyer pour un Emploi Responsable (Plea for Responsible Employment) 2009. *Leisure interests:* travelling, cooking, gardening. *Address:* c/o Pierre & Vacances-Center Parcs, L'Artois, Espace Pont de Flandre, 11, rue de Cambrai, 75947 Paris Cedex 19, France (office). *Telephone:* 1-58-21-58-21 (office). *Website:* www.francoisegri.com.

GRIECO, Maria Patrizia; Italian business executive; *Chairman, Enel SpA;* b. 1952, Milan; ed Univ. of Milan; began career at Legal and Gen. Affairs Directorate of Italtel 1977, later Head 1994, Gen. Man. Italtel 1999–2002, CEO 2002–03; CEO Siemens Informatica 2003–06, mem. Exec. Council; Partner, Value Partners and CEO Group Value Team (now NTT Data) 2006–08; CEO Olivetti 2008–13, Chair. 2011–14, Dir 2014–; Chair. Enel SpA 2014–; Dir, Fiat Industrial (now CNHI) 2012–16, Anima Holding 2014–, Ferrari 2016–, Amplifon 2016–; mem. Steering Cttee and Gen. Council, Assonime 2014–, Bd of Dirs, Bocconi Univ. 2014–. *Address:* Enel SpA, Viale Regina Margherita 137, 00198 Rome, Italy (office). *Telephone:* (06) 83057610 (office). *Fax:* (06) 83057954 (office). *E-mail:* maria.grieco@enel.com (office). *Website:* www.enel.com (office).

GRIER, Pam; American actress and writer; b. 26 May 1949, Winston-Salem, NC; d. of Clarence Ransom Grier and Gwendolyn (Sylvia) Samuels; mem. Acad. of Motion Picture Arts and Sciences. *Films:* The Big Doll House 1971, Women in Cages 1971, Big Bird Cage 1972, Black Mama, White Mama 1972, Cool Breeze 1972, Hit Man 1972, Twilight People 1972, Coffy 1973, Scream, Blacula, Scream! 1973, The Arena 1973, Foxy Brown 1974, Bucktown 1975, Friday Foster 1975, Sheba Baby 1975, Drum 1976, Greased Lightning 1977, Fort Apache: The Bronx 1981, Something Wicked This Way Comes 1983, Stand Alone 1985, The Vindicator 1986, On the Edge 1986, The Allnighter 1987, Above The Law 1988, The Package 1989, Class of 1999 1991, Bill and Ted's Bogus Journey 1991, Tough Enough, Posse 1993, Serial Killer 1995, Original Gangstas 1996, Escape from LA 1996, Mars Attacks! 1996, Strip Search 1997, Fakin' Da Funk 1997, Jackie Brown (San Diego Film Critics Soc. Award for Best Actress) 1997, No Tomorrow 1998, Jawbreaker 1999, Holy Smoke 1999, In Too Deep 1999, Fortress 2 1999, Snow Day 2000, Wilder 2000, 3 A.M. 2001, Love the Hard Way 2001, Bones 2001, John Carpenter's Ghosts of Mars 2001, Undercover Brother 2002, The Adventures of Pluto Nash 2002, Baby of the Family 2002, Back in the Day 2005, Just Wright 2010, Mafia 2011, Larry Crowne 2011, Woman Thou Art Loosed: On the 7th Day 2012, The Man with the Iron Fists 2012, Mafia 2012. *Television includes:* Roots: The Next Generations (mini-series) 1979, Badge of the Assassin 1985, A Mother's Right: The Elizabeth Morgan Story 1992, Feast of All Saints (mini-series) 2001, 1st to Die 2003, The L Word (series) 2004–09, Smallville 2010, Cleveland Abduction (film) 2015, Bad Grandmas 2017, Rose 2017. *Stage appearances:* Fool for Love, Frankie and Johnnie, In the Claire De Lune; Best Actress NAACP 1986. *Publication:* Foxy: My Life in Three Acts 2010. *Leisure interests:* skiing, scuba diving, western and English horseback riding, tennis.

GRIESINGER, Christian, BSc, PhD; German chemist and academic; *Director, Max-Planck Institute for Biophysical Chemistry;* b. 5 April 1960, Ulm; s. of Karl and Christa Griesinger; ed Univ. of Frankfurt; Research Fellow, Univ. of Frankfurt 1984–86; Research Fellow, ETH Zürich 1985, Postdoctoral Assoc. 1986–89; Co-founder MRPHARM GmbH, Frankfurt 1998; Prof., Univ. of Frankfurt 1999–2000; Scientific mem. and Dir Max-Planck Inst. for Biophysical Chem., Göttingen 1999–, Man. Dir Max Planck Inst. for Biophysical Chem. 2007–08; Co-founder MODAG 2012; Assoc. Ed. Journal of Magnetic Resonance 1997–, FEBS Letters 2004–; mem. Council ISMAR (Int. Soc. for Magnetic Resonance) 2001, EUROMAR, Russel Varian Prize Cttee 2002–11, DFG Study Section: Basics of Biology and Medicine 2004–12; mem. German Chemical Soc. 1983– (mem. Nuclear Magnetic Resonance Group Exec. Cttee 1994–96, Chair. 1997–2000), Acad. of Sciences, Göttingen, Nat. Acad. of Sciences Leopoldina, Göttingen Research Council 2007–11, European Molecular Biology Org. 2011; Hon. Prof. of Physical Chem., Univ. of Göttingen 2001–; Hon. mem. Nat. Magnetic Resonance Soc. (India) 2009; Fonds der Chemischen Industrie Young Investigator Award 1989, Literature Prize 1996, Bavarian Acad. of Science Sommerfeld Prize 1997, Deutsche Forschungsgemeinschaft Leibniz Prize 1998, Otto Bayer Prize 2003, ERC advanced grant 2008, Elhuyar-Goldschmidt Prize, Royal Soc. of Spain and Gesellschaft Deutscher Chemiker 2011, Theodor Bücher Award Lecturer, Fed. of European Biochemical Socs 2012. *Address:* Abteilung 030, Max Planck Institute for Biophysical Chemistry, Am Fassberg 11, 37077 Göttingen, Germany (office). *Telephone:* (551) 201-2201 (office). *Fax:* (551) 201-2202 (office). *E-mail:* cigr@nmr.mpibpc.mpg.de (office). *Website:* medusa.nmr.mpibpc.mpg.de (office).

GRIEVE, Rt Hon. Dominic Charles Roberts, PC, QC, BA; British barrister and politician; b. 24 May 1956, Lambeth, London; s. of Percy Grieve QC and Evelyn Raymonde Louise Mijouain; m. Caroline Hutton 1990; two s.; ed Lycée Français Charles de Gaulle, South Kensington, St Paul's Prep School Colet Court, Westminster School, Magdalen Coll., Oxford, Polytechnic of Cen. London (now Univ. of Westminster); Pres. Oxford Univ. Conservative Assn 1977; called to the Bar, Middle Temple 1980, Bencher 2005, QC 2008; Councillor, London Borough of Hammersmith and Fulham 1982–86; contested Norwood constituency 1987; MP for Beaconsfield, Bucks. 1997–2010, for Beaconsfield (revised boundary) 2010–, mem. (Select Cttees), Jt Cttee on Statutory Instruments 1997–2001, Environmental Audit 1997–2001, Chair. Intelligence and Security Cttee 2015–; Opposition Spokesperson for Constitutional Affairs and Scotland 1999–2001, for Criminal Justice 2001–08; Shadow Attorney-Gen. 2003–09; Shadow Home Sec. 2008–09; Shadow Sec. of State for Justice 2009–10; Attorney-Gen. for England and Wales and Advocate Gen. for NI 2010–14; Chair. Research Cttee, Soc. of Conservative Lawyers 1992–95, Finance and General Purposes Cttee 2006–; Vice-Chair. Franco British Council; Pres. Franco–British Soc., police station lay visitor 1990–96, Deputy Church Warden; mem. London Diocesan Synod of the Church of England 1994–2000, Select Cttee on Standards and Privileges 2014–, Council of Luxembourg Soc., Gov. of Ditchley Park; Conservative; Légion d'honneur 2016. *Leisure interests:* canoeing, boating on the Thames at weekends, mountain climbing, skiing, travel, fell-walking, scuba diving, architecture, art. *Address:* House of Commons, Westminster, London, SW1A 0AA (office); Constituency Office, Disraeli House, 12 Aylesbury End, Beaconsfield, Bucks., HP9 1LW, England. *Telephone:* (20) 7219-6220 (Westminster) (office); (1494) 673745 (Beaconsfield). *Fax:* (1494) 670428 (Beaconsfield). *E-mail:* dominic.grieve.mp@parliament.uk (office); office@beaconsfieldconservatives.co.uk. *Website:* www.gov.uk/government/organisations/attorney-generals-office (office); www.parliament.uk/biographies/commons/mr-dominic-grieve/16 (office); www.dominicgrieve.org.uk; www.beaconsfieldconservatives.co.uk.

GRIFFEY, George Kenneth (Ken), Jr; American professional baseball player (retd); b. 21 Nov. 1969, Donora, Pa; s. of Ken Griffey, Sr (fmr professional baseball player); m. Melissa Griffey; one s.; one d.; ed Moeller High School, Cincinnati, Ohio; outfielder; drafted by Seattle Mariners in first round (1st pick) of 1987 amateur draft, played 1987–2000, traded to Cincinnati Reds 2000–08, Chicago White Sox 2008, Seattle Mariners 2009–10 (retd), Special Consultant to the Franchise 2011–; became 20th player to hit 500 career home runs June 2004, 630 home runs upon retirement 2010; Hon. Co-Chair. Aircraft Owners and Pilots Assn Foundation's Hat in the Ring Soc.; mem. All Star team 1990–2000, 2004, 2007, Most Valuable Player in All-Star Game 1992, American League Gold Glove Award winner 1990–99, American League Most Valuable Player 1997, named to All-Century Team 1999, inducted into Seattle Mariners Hall of Fame 2013, Cincinnati Reds Hall of Fame 2014, Baseball Hall of Fame 2016. *Address:* Seattle Mariners, Safeco Field, 1250 First Avenue South, Seattle, WA 98134, USA.

GRIFFIN, Jasper, MA, FBA; British academic and writer; *Professor Emeritus of Classical Literature, Balliol College;* b. 29 May 1937, London; s. of Frederick William Griffin and Constance Irene Cordwell; m. Miriam Tamara Griffin (née Dressler) 1960; three d.; ed Balliol Coll., Oxford; Jackson Fellow, Harvard Univ. 1960–61; Dyson Research Fellow, Balliol Coll., Oxford 1961–63, Fellow and Tutor in Classics 1963–2004, Sr Fellow 2000–04, Univ. Reader 1989–2004, Public Orator 1992–2004, Prof. of Classical Literature 1992–2004, Prof. Emer. 2004–. *Publications:* Homer on Life and Death 1980, Snobs 1982, Latin Poets and Roman Life 1985, The Mirror of Myth 1985, Virgil 1986, Homer: The Odyssey 1987, The Art of Snobbery 1998, Homer 2002, Latin Poets and Roman Life 2008; Ed. The Oxford History of the Classical World 1986, The Iliad: Book Nine 1995, Sophocles Revisited: Essays Presented to Sir Hugh Lloyd-Jones 1999; contrib. to articles and reviews. *Leisure interests:* music, wine. *Address:* Balliol College, Oxford, OX1 3BJ, England (office). *Telephone:* (1865) 277777 (office). *Fax:* (1865) 277803 (office). *Website:* www.balliol.ox.ac.uk (office).

GRIFFIN, Michael D., BSc, MSc, MBA, PhD; American physicist, engineer and academic; *Chairman and CEO, Schafer Corporation;* b. 1 Nov. 1949, Aberdeen, Md; ed Johns Hopkins Univ., Catholic Univ. of America, Univ. of Maryland, Univ. of Southern California, Loyola Coll., George Washington Univ.; fmr Deputy for Tech., Strategic Defense Initiative Org.; Chief Engineer, Assoc. Admin. NASA 1990s; fmr Adjunct Prof. Univ. of Maryland, Johns Hopkins Univ., George Washington Univ.; fmrly with Orbital Sciences Corpn, positions including CEO Magellan Systems, Inc.; Pres. and COO In-Q-Tel –2004; Head Space Dept, Applied Physics Lab., Johns Hopkins Univ. 2004–05; Admin. NASA 2005–09; King-McDonald Eminent Scholar and Prof. of Mechanical and Aerospace Eng and Dir Center for System Studies, Univ. of Alabama, Huntsville 2009–12; Chair. and CEO Schafer Corporation 2012–; Fellow, American Inst. of Aeronautics and Astronautics (fmr Pres.); mem. Nat. Acad. of Eng, American Astronautical Soc., Int. Acad. of Astronautics; Co-owner Grumman Tiger; Hon. Chancellor, Florida Southern Coll. 2008; Hon. DrIng (Univ. of Notre Dame) 2011; NASA Exceptional Achievement Medal, AIAA Space Systems Medal, Dept of Defense Distinguished Public Service Medal, Goddard Astronautics Award, Goddard Trophy, Nat. Space Club 2009, Rotary Nat. Award for Space Achievement, Space Center Rotary Club of Houston. *Publications include:* Space Vehicle Design (co-author), numerous technical papers. *Leisure interests:* golf, flying, amateur radio, skiing, scuba diving. *Address:* Schafer Corporation, 3811 North Fairfax Drive, Suite 400, Arlington, VA 22203, USA (office). *Telephone:* (703) 516-6000 (office). *Fax:* (703) 516-6065 (office). *Website:* www.schafercorp.com (office).

GRIFFITH, Alan Richard, MBA; American banker; b. 17 Dec. 1941, Mineola, NY; s. of Charles E. Griffith and Amalie Guenther; m. Elizabeth Ferguson 1964; one s. one d.; ed Lafayette Coll. and City Univ. of New York; Asst Credit Officer, Bank of New York 1968–72, Asst Vice-Pres. 1972–74, Vice-Pres. 1974–82, Sr Vice-Pres. 1982–85, Exec. Vice-Pres. 1985–88, Sr Exec. Vice-Pres. 1988–90, Pres. 1990–94, Vice-Chair. 1994–2005; US Chair. British-North American Cttee, Atlantic Council; fmr Chair. ALS Assn, currently mem. Chair.'s Council; Chair. Bd of Trustees, Chesapeake Bay Foundation; mem. Bd of Govs Chesapeake Bay Maritime Museum, now Gov. Emer.; Trustee Emer., Lafayette Coll.; Hon. DJur 2001; Lafayette's George T. Woodring Volunteer of the Year Award 1999, inducted into Société d'Honneur 2005. *Address:* Chesapeake Bay Foundation, Philip Merrill Environmental Center, 6 Herndon Avenue, Annapolis, MD 21403, USA (office). *Telephone:* (410) 268-8816 (office). *Fax:* (410) 268-6687 (office). *Website:* www.cbf.org (office).

GRIFFITH, Gavan, AO, QC, LLM, DPhil; Australian barrister and international arbitrator; b. 11 Oct. 1941, Melbourne; s. of F. E. Griffith; one s. three d.; ed Melbourne Univ. and Magdalen Coll., Oxford, UK; barrister 1963; Lincoln's Inn 1969; QC 1981; Solicitor-Gen. of Australia 1984–97; del. to UN Int. Trade Law Comm. (UNCITRAL) 1984–, Vice-Chair. 1987–88, 1994–95; Agent and Counsel for Australia at Int. Court of Justice 1989–95; mem. Perm. Court of Arbitration, The Hague 1987–99; mem. Intelsat Panel of Legal Experts 1988–97, Chair. 1993–94; del. Hague Conf. of Pvt. Int. Law 1992–97; Arbitrator, Int. Comm. for Settlement of Int. Disputes (ICSID) 1994–; Consultant, Office of Legal Counsel, UN, New York 1994–95; Dir Australian Centre for Int. Commercial Arbitration 1997–; mem. Council, Nat. Gallery of Australia 1986–92; Visiting Fellow, Magdalen Coll. Oxford 1973–74, 1976, 1980, 1995; Order of the Repub. of Austria 1997. *Publications:* contribs to various legal journals and books. *Leisure interest:* real tennis. *Address:* 205 William Street, Melbourne, Vic. 3000, Australia (office); Essex Court Chambers, Lincolns Inn Fields, London, WC2A 3EG, England (office). *Telephone:* (3) 9225-7658 (Australia) (office); (20) 7813-8000 (London) (office); (4) 1925-0666 (Australia) (home). *Fax:* (3) 9225-8974 (Australia) (office). *E-mail:* ggqc@gavangriffith.com; Griffithqc@aol.com (office). *Website:* www.listd.com.au (office); www.essexcourt.net (office).

GRIFFITH, Melanie; American actress; b. 9 Aug. 1957, New York; d. of Tippi Hedren and Peter Griffith; m. 1st Don Johnson 1975 (divorced 1976, remarried 1989, divorced 1993); one d.; m. 2nd Steven Bauer 1981 (divorced 1989); m. 3rd Antonio Banderas 1996 (divorced 2015); one d.; ed Hollywood Professional School; co-founder (with Antonio Banderas) Green Moon Productions. *Films:* Night Moves 1975, Smile 1975, The Drowning Pool 1975, One on One 1977, Underground Aces 1979, Roar, Fear City, Body Double 1984, Something Wild 1986, Stormy Monday 1987, The Milagro Beanfield War 1988, Working Girl 1988, Pacific Heights 1990, Bonfire of the Vanities 1990, Shining Through 1991, Paradise 1991, A Stranger Amongst Us 1992, Close to Eden 1993, Born Yesterday 1993, Milk Money 1994, Nobody's Fool 1994, Now and Then, Two Much, Mulholland Falls 1996, Lolita 1996, Shadow of Doubt 1998, Celebrity 1998, Another Day in Paradise 1998, Crazy in Alabama 1999, Cecil B. Demented 2000, Forever Lulu 2000, Life with Big Cats 2000, Tart 2001, Stuart Little 2 (voice) 2002, The Night We Called It a Day 2003, Shade 2003, Tempo 2003, Have Mercy 2006, The Grief Tourist 2012, Automata 2014, Day Out of Days 2015, The Disaster Artist 2017, Dabka 2017. *Theatre:* Chicago (Broadway) 2003. *Television:* Once an Eagle (mini-series) 1976, Daddy, I Don't Like It Like This 1978, Steel Cowboy 1978, Carter Country (series) 1978–79, Starmaker 1981, She's in the Army Now 1981, Golden Gate 1981, Buffalo Girls 1995, Me & George (series) 1998, RKO 281 1999, Twins (series) 2005–06, Viva Laughlin 2007, Nip/Tuck 2010, Hawaii Five-0 2014–16, The X-Files 2016. *Address:* 501 Doheny Road, Beverly Hills, CA 90210; Green Moon Productions, 11718 Barrington Court, Los Angeles, CA 90041, USA. *Website:* www.melaniegriffith.com (office).

GRIFFITH-JONES, John; British business executive and banking regulator; b. 11 May 1954; s. of Mervyn Griffith-Jones and Joan Baker; m. Cathryn Mary Stone 1990; one s. one d.; ed Trinity Hall, Cambridge; worked at KPMG 1975–2012, spent 11 years in Audit and 15 years in Corp. Finance before becoming CEO of KPMG's UK firm and subsequently Chair. and Sr Partner of UK div. 2006–07, Jt Chair. KPMG Europe 2007–12; Dir (non-exec.), Financial Services Authority (FSA) and Deputy Chair. 2012–13, Chair. (non-exec.) Financial Conduct Authority (successor of FSA, along with Prudential Regulatory Authority) 2013–18; Chair. Payment Systems Regulator (PSR) 2014–18, Every Child a Chance Trust; Vice-Chair. Nat. Numeracy Trust; mem. Advisory Bd Cambridge Judge Business School 2008–16.

GRIFFITHS, Alan Gordon, BEcons, LLB; Australian trade union official, politician, entrepreneur and investment banker; b. 4 Sept. 1952, Melbourne; s. of Alan Griffiths and Joy Griffiths; m. Sandra Griffiths 1970; one s.; three d.; ed Traralgon High School, Victoria, Monash Univ.; with Maurice Blackburn and Co. solicitors 1979–82; trade union industrial officer, Federated Rubber and Allied Workers' Union of Australia 1982–83; Labor mem. House of Reps for Maribyrnong, Vic. 1983–96; Jt Parl. Cttee Nat. Crime Authority 1984–87; Chair. House Reps Standing Cttee, Legal and Constitutional Affairs 1987–90; Minister for Resources and Energy 1990–93, for Tourism 1991–93, for Industry, Tech. and Regional Devt 1993–94; Chair. Int. Pty Ltd 1996; Founder, Exec. Chair. and Prin. Quantm Ltd 1999. *Leisure interests:* the arts, sport, politics, travel, sailing.

GRIFFITHS, Martin, CBE; British fmr diplomatist, lawyer and UN official; *Special Envoy for Yemen;* b. 1951; m.; two c.; ed School of Oriental and African Studies, Univ. of London; joined FCO, worked for UNICEF, Dir Dept of Humanitarian Affairs, UN (now UN Office for the Coordination of Humanitarian Affairs) 1994–98, Deputy UN Emergency Relief Coordinator, New York 1998–99, also UN Regional Humanitarian Coordinator for Great Lakes, and in Balkans, Adviser to Special Envoy for Syria and Deputy Head UN Supervision Mission in Syria (UNSMIS) 2012–14, Special Envoy for Yemen 2018–; Founding Dir Centre for Humanitarian Dialogue in Geneva 1999–2010; Sr Int. Mediator and Exec. Dir European Peace Inst. 2014–18; Co-Founder and Strategic Adviser, Inter Mediate. *Address:* Office of the Special Envoy for Yemen, Department of Political Affairs, United Nations, 405 E 42nd Street, New York, NY 10017, USA (office). *Telephone:* (212) 963-1234 (office). *Fax:* (212) 963-4879 (office). *Website:* www.osesgy.unmissions.org (office).

GRIFFITHS, Phillip Augustus, IV, BS, PhD; American mathematician and academic; *Professor Emeritus of Mathematics, Institute for Advanced Study, Princeton;* b. 18 Oct. 1938, Raleigh, North Carolina; s. of Phillip Griffiths and Jeanette Griffiths (née Field); m. 1st Anne Lane Crittenden 1958 (divorced 1967); one s. one d.; m. 2nd Marian Jones; two d.; ed Wake Forest and Princeton Univs; Univ. of California, Berkeley, Miller Fellow 1962–64, 1975–76, mem. Faculty 1964–67; Visiting Prof., Princeton Univ. 1967–68, Prof. 1968–72; Prof., Harvard Univ. 1972–83, Dwight Parker Robinson Prof. of Math. 1983; Provost and James B. Duke Prof. of Math., Duke Univ. 1983–91; Guest Prof., Univ. of Beijing 1983; Dir Inst. for Advanced Study, Princeton 1991–2003, Prof. of Math. 2004–09, Prof. Emer. 2009–, Chair. Science Initiative Group 1999–; Sr Advisor, The Andrew W. Mellon Foundation 2001–; mem. Bd of Dirs Bankers Trust NY Corpn 1994–99, Oppenheimer Funds 1999–, GSI Group 2001–; Sec., Int. Math. Union 1999–2006; Carnegie Fellow, Carnegie Corpn of New York 2007; mem. Council on Foreign Relations 2002–; mem. Editorial Bd, Duke Mathematical Journal 1983–, Selecta Mathematica 1994–, Annals of Math Studies 2001–, Advances in Function Theory 2001–, MSRI and Nankai Book Series on Mathematics 2008–; mem. NAS 1979– (Distinguished Presidential Fellow for Int. Affairs 2002–), American Acad. of Arts and Sciences 1995, American Philosophical Soc. 1996; Foreign Assoc., Accad. Nazionale dei Lincei 2001, TWAS (Acad. of Sciences for the Developing World) 2001, Indian Acad. of Sciences 2003; Fellow, American Math. Soc. 2012; Ordem Nacional do Mérito Científico (Brazil) 2002; Hon. DSc (Duke Univ.) 2004; hon. degrees from Wake Forest, Angers, Oslo and Beijing Univs; Guggenheim Fellow 1980–82, Wolf Foundation Prize in Math. (co-recipient) 2008, Brouwer Prize 2008, Steele Prize for Lifetime Achievement, American Mathematical Soc. 2014, Chern Medal 2014 and other awards and distinctions. *Publications:* some 15 books and monographs, including Entire Holomorphic Mappings in One and Several Complex Variables 1976, Principles of Algebraic Geometry (co-author) 1978, Rational Homotopy Theory and Differential Forms (co-author) 1981, Exterior Differential Systems and the Calculus of Variations 1983, Topics in Transcendental Algebraic Geometry 1984, Introduction to Algebraic Curves 1989; more than 100 articles in professional journals. *Leisure interest:* sailing. *Address:* Fuld Hall 315, Institute for Advanced Study, Einstein Drive, Princeton, NJ 08540, USA (office). *Telephone:* (609) 734-8041 (office). *Fax:* (609) 951-4430 (office). *E-mail:* pg@math.ias.edu (office). *Website:* www.ias.edu/people/faculty-and-emeriti/griffiths (office).

GRIFFITHS, Rachel; Australian actress; b. 18 Dec. 1968, Melbourne; ed Univ. of Melbourne. *TV includes:* Secrets (series) 1993, The Feds 1993, Jimeoin (series) 1994, Since You've Been Gone 1998, Very Annie Mary 2001, Six Feet Under (series) 2001–05, After the Deluge (mini-series) 2003, Plainsong 2004, Angel 2005, Brothers & Sisters (series) 2006–11, Comanche Moon (mini-series) 2008, Camp 2018, House Husbands 2014, Barracuda 2016, When We Rise 2017. *Films include:* Muriel's Wedding 1994, Small Treasures 1995, Cosi 1996, Children of the Revolution 1996, Jude 1996, To Have and to Hold 1996, Welcome to Woop Woop 1997, My Best Friend's Wedding 1997, My Son the Fanatic 1997, Among Giants 1998, Divorcing Jack 1998, Amy 1998, Hilary and Jackie 1998, Me Myself I 1999, Blow Dry 2001, Blow 2001, The Rookie 2002, The Hard Word 2002, Ned Kelly 2003, Step Up 2006, Beautiful Kate 2009, Rake 2010, Burning Man 2011, Underground 2012, Saving Mr Banks 2013, Mammal 2016, Hacksaw Ridge 2016. *Address:* c/o William Morris Agency, One William Morris Place, Beverly Hills, CA 90212, USA.

GRIFFITHS, Terence (Terry) Martin, OBE; British snooker coach and fmr professional snooker player; b. 16 Oct. 1947, Llanelli, Wales; s. of Martin Griffiths and Ivy Griffiths; m. Annette Jones 1968; two s.; fmr postman, insurance salesman, miner and bus conductor; won Welsh Amateur Championship 1975, English Amateur Championship 1977, 1978; turned professional snooker player 1978; ranking title: Embassy World Championship 1979; non-ranking titles: Benson & Hedges Masters 1980, Benson & Hedges Irish Masters 1980, 1981, 1982, Classic 1982, UK Championship 1982, Pot Black 1984, Hong Kong Masters 1985, Belgian Classic 1986, Welsh Professional Championship 1985, 1986, 1988; team events: World Cup with Wales team 1979, 1980; Trickshot events: World Trickshot 1992, 1994; f. Terry Griffiths Matchroom 1987; Dir World Snooker 1999–2000; Coach: The Sportsmasters Network 2000–; regular snooker commentator on BBC TV. *Publications include:* Championship Snooker, Complete Snooker, Griff. *Leisure interests:* golf, music, playing snooker. *Address:* Terry Griffiths Matchroom, Waunlanyrafon, Llanelli, Carmarthenshire, SA15 3AA, Wales (office). *Website:* www.terrygriffithssnooker.com (office).

GRIFFITHS, Trevor, BA; British playwright; b. 4 April 1935, Manchester; s. of Ernest Griffiths and Anne Connor; m. 1st Janice Elaine Stansfield 1961 (died 1977); one s. two d.; m. 2nd Gillian Cliff 1992; ed Univ. of Manchester; taught English language and literature 1957–65; Educ. Officer, BBC 1965–72; Dir Saint Oscar 1990, The Gulf Between Us 1992, Who Shall be Happy...? 1995, Food for Ravens 1997; BAFTA Writer's Award 1981. *Film scripts:* Reds (with Warren Beatty q.v., Writers Guild of America Best Original Screenplay 1981) 1981, Fatherland 1986. *Plays include:* Occupations 1970, Apricots and Thermidor 1970, Sam Sam 1972, The Party 1974, Comedians 1976, The Cherry Orchard 1977, Oi for England 1981, Real Dreams 1984, Piano 1990, The Gulf Between Us 1992, Thatcher's Children 1993, Who Shall Be Happy 1994, Camel Station 2001, A New World: A Life of Thomas Paine 2009, Habaccuc Dreams 2011. *Television includes:* All Good Men 1974, Absolute Beginners 1974, Through the Night 1975, Bill Brand 1976, Country 1981, Sons and Lovers 1982, The Last Place on Earth 1985, Hope in the Year Two 1994, Food for Ravens 1997 (Royal Television Soc. Best Regional Programme 1998, Gwyn A. Williams Special Award, BAFTA Wales 1998). *Radio:* These Are The Times: A Life of Thomas Paine (BBC Radio) 2008. *Publications include:* Occupations, Sam Sam 1972, The Party 1974, Comedians 1976, All Good Men, Absolute Beginners, Through the Night, Such Impossibilities, Thermidor and Apricots 1977, Deeds (co-author), The Cherry Orchard (trans.) 1978, Country 1981, Oi for England, Sons and Lovers (TV version) 1982, Judgement Over the Dead 1986, Fatherland, Real Dreams 1987, Collected Plays for TV 1988, Piano 1990, The Gulf Between Us 1992, Hope in the Year Two, Thatcher's Children 1994, Plays One (Collected Stage Plays) 1996, Food for Ravens 1998, These Are The Times 2005, Theatre Plays One 2007, Theatre Plays Two 2007, Bill Brand 2010, March Time 2012. *Address:* c/o United Agents, 12-26 Lexington Street, London W1F 0LE, England (office); 104 High Street, Boston Spa, Wetherby, LS23 6DR, England (home). *Telephone:* (203) 214-0800 (office). *Fax:* (203) 214-0801 (office). *E-mail:* rkirby@unitedagents.co.uk (office); aelliott@unitedagents.co.uk (office); nstoddart@unitedagents.co.uk (office); TGriffPost@aol.com. *Website:* www.unitedagents.co.uk (office); www.trevorgriffiths.co.uk.

GRIFFITHS OF FFORESTFACH, Baron (Life Peer), cr. 1991, of Fforestfach in the County of West Glamorgan; **Brian Griffiths,** MSc; British banker; *Vice-Chairman, Goldman Sachs International;* b. 27 Dec. 1941, Swansea, Wales; s. of Ivor Winston Griffiths and Phyllis Mary Griffiths (née Morgan); m. Rachel Jane Jones 1965; one s. two d.; ed Dynevor Grammar School and London School of Econs; Asst Lecturer in Econs, LSE 1965–68, Lecturer 1968–76; Dir Centre for Banking and Int. Finance, City Univ., London 1977–82, Prof. of Banking and Int. Finance 1977–85, Dean, City Univ. Business School 1982–85; Dir Bank of England 1984–86, mem. Panel of Acad. Consultants 1977–86; Head of Prime Minister's Policy Unit 1985–90; Chair. Centre for Policy Studies 1991–2000; Head School Examinations and Assessment Council 1991–93; Vice-Chair. Goldman Sachs International 1991–; Dir Thorn-EMI 1991–96, Herman Miller 1991–2011, HTV 1991–93, Times Newspapers Ltd 1991–, Servicemaster 1992–2007, Telewest 1994–98, English, Welsh and Scottish Railway 1996–2006; Chair. Trillium 1998–2001, Westminster Health Care 1999–2002, Land Securities Trillium 2001–09, Lambeth Fund 1997–2012; mem. (Conservative), House of Lords 1991–; Hon. Fellow, Trinity Coll., Carmarthen 1997, Swansea Inst. of Higher Educ. 2003, Sarum Coll. 2006; Hon. DSc (City Univ.) 1999, (Univ. Coll. of Wales) 2004. *Publications include:* Is Revolution Change? (ed. and contrib.) 1972, Mexican Monetary Policy and Economic Development 1972, Invisible Barriers to Invisible Trade 1975, Inflation: The Price of Prosperity 1976, Monetary Targets (co-ed. with G. E. Wood) 1980, The Creation of Wealth 1984, Monetarism in the United Kingdom (co-ed. with G. E. Wood) 1984, Morality and the Market Place 1989, Globalization, Poverty and International Development 2007, Fighting Poverty Through Enterprise 2007. *Leisure interests:* the family, reading, ornithology. *Address:* House of Lords, Westminster, London, SW1A 0PW, England (office). *Telephone:* (20) 7219-5353 (office). *Fax:* (20) 7219-5979 (office). *E-mail:* contactholmember@parliament.uk (office).

GRIGGS, Natasha, BBA; Australian politician and head of government; *Administrator of Australian Indian Ocean Territories—Christmas Island and Cocos (Keeling) Islands;* b. 24 Jan. 1969, Adelaide; m. Paul Griggs; one s.; ed NT Univ. (now Charles Darwin Univ.); various NT govt positions 1990–99; Man., Dialog Information Technology 1999–2003, Fujitsu Australia 2005–07, SRA Information Technology 2007–09; Relationship Man. CSM Technology 2003–05; Project Man. NT Govt 2009–10; Alderman, City of Palmerston 2008–09, Deputy Mayor 2009–10; mem., House of Reps. for Solomon, NT 2010–16; Admin. Australian Indian Ocean Territories—Christmas Island and Cocos (Keeling) Islands 2017–. *Address:* Office of the Administrator, PO Box 868, Christmas Island, Indian Ocean, WA 6798, Australia (office). *Telephone:* (8) 9164-7960 (office). *Fax:* (8) 9164-7961 (office). *Website:* regional.gov.au/territories/indian_ocean/ (office).

GRIGOROVICH, Yuriy Nikolayevich; Russian ballet master; *Artistic Director, Grigorovich Ballet Company;* b. 2 Jan. 1927, Leningrad; s. of K. A. Grigorovich-Rozay and N. E. Grigorovich; m. Natalya Igorevna Bessmertnova; ed Leningrad Choreographic School and Lunarcharski Inst. of Theatrical Art, Moscow; soloist, Kirov (now Mariinsky) Theatre 1946–64, Ballet Master 1962–64; Chief Ballet Master, Bolshoi Theatre, Moscow 1964–95; Chief Choreographer, Artistic Dir Kremlin Palace of Congresses Ballet 1998; now works in various theatres in Russia and abroad; Ed.-in-Chief Soviet Ballet Encyclopaedia 1981; Founder and Artistic Dir Bolshoi Ballet Grigorovich Co. (now Grigorovich Ballet Co.) 1990–; Chair. Int. Choreography Asscn; mem. Vienna Music Soc.; Hon. Chair. Int. Theatre Inst., Ukrainian Dance Acad.; Order Merit to Fatherland Third Degree 2004, Order of Merit for the Fatherland, 1st class 2011; Lenin Prize 1970, People's Artist of USSR 1973, USSR State Prize 1985, Hero of Socialist Labour 1986, Soul of Dance Prize (magazine Ballet) 2001, Golden Mask for Honour and Dignity 2003. *Ballets include:* Stone Flower (Kirov-Mariinsky) 1957, Legend of Love (Kirov-Mariinsky) 1960, Sleeping Beauty (Bolshoi) 1963, Nutcracker (Bolshoi) 1966, Spartacus 1968, Swan Lake 1969, Ivan the Terrible 1975, Angara 1976, Romeo and Juliet (Paris) 1978, Giselle 1979, Golden Age (Bolshoi) 1982, Raymonda 1984, Bayaderka 1991, Elektra (Grigorovich Ballet co-produced with Melanin and Bobrov) 1992, La Fille Mal Gardée (Grigorovich Ballet) 1993, Le Corsaire (Bolshoi) 1994. *Address:* Sretenskii Blvd 6/1, Apt 9, Moscow, Russia (home). *Telephone:* (495) 925-6431 (home).

GRIGORYEV, Anatoly Ivanovich, DrMed; Russian biologist and space scientist; b. 23 March 1943, Zhitomir region, Ukraine; s. of Ivan Grigoryevich Grigoryev and Olga Isakovna Grigoryeva; m. Dorokhova Bella Radikovna; two s.; ed 2nd Moscow Medical Inst.; Researcher, Sr Researcher, Head of Lab., Head of Div., Deputy Dir State Research Centre of Inst. for Biomedical Problems, USSR (now Russian) Acad. of Sciences 1966, Dir 1988, apptd Vice-Pres. Inst. for Biomedical Problems 2007; Chief Medical Commr, Russian Space Agency 1988–96, apptd Chief Medical Officer 1996; Co-Chair. Jt Soviet-American Workgroup on Space Biology and Medicine 1989–92; Chair. Section on Sciences of Life, Int. Acad. of Astronautics 1989–93, Section of Space Medicine, Russian Acad. of Sciences 1991, Scientific Council on Space Medicine, Russian Acad. of Medicine 1993–; Co-Chair. Int. Space Station (ISS) Multilateral Medical Policy Bd 2000, Man. of Medical

Support in space flights on ISS 2001; Vice-Pres. Int. Acad. of Astronautics 1993–2003, Int. Astronautical Fed. 2004, Int. Astronomic Fed. 2006; mem. Co-ordination Council, Russian Fed. Ministry of Science and Tech. 1998, Presidential Council on Science and Technologies 2004; mem. Aerospace Medical Asscn, USA 1991, Int. Union of Physiological Sciences 1992, Russian Acad. of Medicine 1993, New York Acad. of Sciences 1994, Int. Acad. of Sciences 1995, Russian Acad. of Natural Sciences 1996–, Russian Acad. of Sciences 1997 (mem. Presidium 2001, Academician-Sec. Biology Dept 2002), Russian R. Tsyolkovsky Acad. of Cosmonautics 1997; Order, Sign of Hon. 1976, Labour Red Banner 1982, Banner of Labour (DDR) 1985, Order For Merits to Motherland (IV Degree) 2003, Officier de la Légion d'honneur 2004; Dr hc (Lyon Univ.) 1989; USSR State Prize 1989, Russian Acad. of Medicine Prize 1996, Bointon Prize, American Astronautics Asscn 1995, 1999, Struckhold Prize, American Aviacosmic Asscn 1996, Françoise Xavier Banier Prize, Michigan Univ., USA 1999, S. Korolev and Yu. Gagarin Medals, USSR Fed. of Cosmonautics, Merited Worker of Science of Russia 1996, State Award of Russian Fed. 2001, Louis H. Bauer Founders Award, AMA 2001, IAA Team Achievement Award 2001, Silver Snoopy Award, NASA 2002, Ikarus Stair Medal, Russian Space Agency 2003, Award of Russian Govt 2003, Triumf Prize for achievements in medicine 2006. *Publications:* more than 400 scientific publs including seven monographs and 22 patents. *Leisure interests:* music, theatre, historical literature.

GRIGORYEV, Vladimir Viktorovich; Belarusian politician and diplomatist; b. 5 April 1941, Mogilev; m.; one s.; ed Belarus Agricultural Acad., Acad. of Social Sciences; began career with local newspaper 1957–58; Second Sec., Komsomol (All-Union Lenin Communist Union of Youth/VLKSM) Dist Cttee, Mogilev Br. 1958–62, 1966–68, First Sec. 1968–70, Instructor, Political Dept, Mogilev 1962–65, Head of Div., Mogilev Regional VLKSM Cttee 1965–66, Sec. VLKSM 1970–72, First Sec. Minsk Regional Cttee 1974, Moscow Regional Cttee 1974–80, Second Sec. Brest Regional Cttee 1980–83; Chair. Exec. Cttee, Brest Prov. Soviet of People's Deputies (Ass.) 1983–85; First Sec., Vitebsk Regional Cttee, Communist Party of Belarus (KPB) 1986–90; Chair. Vitebsk Prov. Soviet of People's Deputies 1990–91; Dir-Gen. Dolomite Production Asscn, Vitebsk 1992–96; fmr mem. Supreme Soviet of BSSR (Parl.); Amb. to Russia and Perm. Rep.to Eurasian Econ. Community 1997–2006; Order of the Red Banner of Labour, Order of the Fatherland.

GRIGSON, Paul, BA; Australian diplomatist; m.; two c.; ed Univ. of Queensland, Australian Nat. Univ., Securities Inst. of Australia; joined Dept of Foreign Affairs and Trade (DFAT), served in various positions including Dir, Parl. Liaison and Freedom of Information Section 1992–93, Deputy Head of Mission Phnom Penh 1993–95, Sr Adviser, Int. Div., Dept of the Prime Minister and Cabinet 1997–2000, Chief Negotiator Peace Monitoring Group, Bougainville 2000, Asst Sec., Maritime South-East Asia Br. 2000–03, Amb. to Myanmar 2003–04, First Asst Sec., South-East Asia Div. 2004–07, Chief of Staff, Minister for Foreign Affairs 2007–08, Amb. to Thailand 2008–10, Deputy Sec., DFAT 2010–14, represents DFAT on Nat. Intelligence and Coordination Cttee, also Special Rep. for Afghanistan and Pakistan, Amb. to Indonesia 2015–18.

GRILLI, Vittorio Umberto, MEconSc, PhD; Italian economist and politician; *Chairman, J.P. Morgan Corporate & Investment Bank EMEA;* b. 19 May 1957, Milan; ed Univ. Luigi Bocconi, Milan, Rochester Univ., USA; Asst Prof., Dept of Econs,Yale Univ. 1986–90; Lecturer in Financial Econs, Birkbeck Coll., Univ. of London 1990–94; joined Ministry of Economy and Finance as mem. Council of Experts, Treasury Dept 1993, Dir-Gen., Dept of Econ. and Financial Analysis and Privatization 1994–2000, also Dir-Gen. of Public Debt and Treasury 1996–97, becoming Dir-Gen., Treasury Dept 2005–11; Deputy Minister of Finance 2011–12, Minister of Finance 2012–13; Vice-Pres. ECOFIN Econ. and Finance Cttee 2009, later Pres.; Chair. J.P. Morgan Corporate & Investment Bank EMEA 2014–; several fmr private sector roles including Man. Dir Credit Suisse First Boston, London, Pres. Istituto Italiano di Tecnologia, fmr Dir Cassa Depositi e Prestiti, Istituto Nazionale di Genetica Molecolare, Scuola Superiore Sant'Anna di Pisa, ENEL SpA, Alitalia, Artigiancassa SpA, CONSAP SpA, CONSIP SpA, WIND, European Investment Bank; mem. European Bruegel (think tank), Brussels, Aspen Inst. Italia; Cavaliere di Gran Croce, Ordine al merito della Repubblica Italiana 2011; several awards including Medaglia d'Oro dell'Università Luigi Bocconi 1981, Premio Saint Vincent per l'Economia 1992, Premio Ezio Tarantelli for best economic idea 2004, Premio Bocconiano dell'anno 2005, Premio Guido Carli for best new financial initiative 2010. *Publications include:* numerous articles and books on topics of national and international economic policy. *Address:* c/o J.P. Morgan Corporate & Investment Bank, 25 Bank Street, Canary Wharf, London E14 5JP, England (office). *Website:* www.jpmorgan.com/pages/jpmorgan/emea/business (office).

GRILLO, (Giuseppe Piero) Beppe; Italian comedian, actor and political activist; b. 21 July 1948, Genoa; s. of Enrico Grillo and Piera Grillo; originally trained as accountant; discovered as comedian and launched by Italian TV presenter Pippo Baudo; known for satirical monologues; presented several TV programmes until increasing level of political satire led to ostracism in press and on TV; numerous tours in Italy and abroad; increasingly involved with political activism 2005–; addressed European Parl., Brussels 2007; organized 'V' protest movt 2007; best known for blog beppegrillo.it; Founder Movimento 5 Stelle (Five Star Movt) 2010, Leader 2010–18. *Tours include:* Energy and Information (tour of over 60 Italian towns and cities) 1995–96, Brain 1997, Soft Apocalypse 1998, Time Out 2000, The Great Transformation 2001, All is Well 2002–03, Black-Out — Facciamo Luce 2003–04. *Television includes:* Secondo Voi 1977–78, Luna Park 1979, Fantastico 1979, Te la do io l'America (four episodes) 1982, Te lo do io il Brasile (six episodes) 1984, Grillometro (Grillometer), Domenica In, Festival di Sanremo, Beppe Grillo Show (RAI 1) 1993. *Films:* Cercasi Gesù 1982, Scemo di Guerra 1985, Topo Galileo 1987. *Website:* beppegrillo.it (office).

GRILLO, Ulrich; German business executive; *President, Federation of German Industries;* b. 1959, Cologne; m.; two c.; ed Westfälische Wilhelms Univ., Münster; began career as trainee, Deutsche Bank AG, Duisburg; worked for Arthur Andersen & Co. Ltd (accounting firm), Frankfurt am Main 1987–89; with A.T Kearney Ltd (man. consulting firm), Düsseldorf 1989–93; joined Rheinmetall Group 1993, eventually becoming Deputy Chair. Exec. Bd, Rheinmetall DeTec, Ratingen –2001, also Chair. STN ATLAS Elektronik, Bremen (subsidiary co.); mem. Exec. Bd Grillo-Werke AG (family-owned metal and chemicals co.), Duisburg 2001–, Chair. 2004–; Vice-Pres. Fed. of German Industries (BDI) 2011–12, Pres. 2013–; Pres. WirtschaftsVereinigung Metalle (German non ferrous-metals asscn) 2006–12; Deputy Chair. Exec. Bd UVM Unternehmerverband der Metallindustrie, Duisburg; mem. Advisory Council Mercator School of Man., Univ. of Duisburg/Essen, Commerzbank AG, Frankfurt; mem. Supervisory Bd Klöckner & Co. SE, Duisburg, IKB Deutsche Industriebank AG, Düsseldorf; Order of Merit of North Rhine-Westphalia 2008. *Address:* BDI, Breite Strasse 29, 10178 Berlin, Germany (office). *Telephone:* (0) 30 2028-0 (office). *E-mail:* info@bdi.eu (office). *Website:* www.bdi.de (office).

GRIMMEISS, Hermann Georg, Dr rer. nat, DiplPhys; Swedish physicist and academic; *Professor Emeritus of Solid State Physics, University of Lund;* b. 19 Aug. 1930, Hamburg, Germany; s. of Georg Grimmeiss and Franziska März; m. Hildegard Weizmann 1956; one s. one d.; ed Oberschule Nördlingen and Univ. of Munich; Prof. of Solid State Physics, Head of Dept Univ. of Lund 1965–96, Prof. Emer. 1996–, Dean for Research 1993–96; Chair. Int. Conf. of the Physics of Semiconductors, Stockholm 1986; Chair. Nobel Symposium on Hetrostructures in Semiconductors, Sweden 1996; mem. Programme Cttee for Physics-Math. Swedish Natural Science Research Council 1971–80; mem. Bd Swedish Nat. Cttee for Physics 1971–72, 1981–97; Prof. of Physics, Dir, Univ. of Frankfurt am Main 1973–74; mem. Cttee for Electronics, Swedish Bd for Tech. Devt 1978–80; mem. Bd Swedish-German Research Asscn 1980–2011; mem. Cttee, Univ. Frankfurt/Oder (Germany) 1991–93; mem. Cttee for Science and Research, Brandenburg (Germany) 1993–95; Vice-Pres. RIFA (mem. Ericsson Group) 1981–83; Visiting Miller Prof., Univ. of California, Berkeley 1990; Dir Inst. of Semiconductor Physics, Frankfurt (Oder), Germany 1991–93; mem. Bd Einstein Forum, Potsdam, Germany 1993–; mem. Exec. Cttee European Materials Research Soc. 2001–15, Pres. 2003–07; Vice-Pres. European Materials Forum 2004–; mem. Int. Prize Cttee Global Energy, Moscow 2002–09, Senat European Materials Research Soc. 2016–; Chair. Scientific Advisory Bd IHP GmbH Frankfurt/Oder 2003–12; ed. and co-ed. several int. journals; mem. Royal Physiographic Soc. Lund, Royal Swedish Acad. of Eng Sciences, Royal Swedish Acad. of Sciences, Societas Scéntarium Sennica, Leibniz-Sozietät der Wissenschaften zu Berlin; Fellow, American Physical Soc.; Hon. mem. Roland Eötvös Physical Soc. 1983, Ioffe Inst., St Petersburg, Russia 1998, Viadrina European Univ. 2008; Order of North Star 1969, Bundesverdienstkreuz 1 Klasse 1993, King's Medal of 8th Dimension with Blue Ribbon, Stockholm 1998; Ehrenurkunde, Potsdam, Germany 2009, Czochralski Award, Washaw 2009. *Publications include:* more than 250 scientific publs in int. journals and books. *Leisure interests:* tennis, classical music. *Address:* Division of Solid State Physics, University of Lund, Box 118, 221 00 Lund, Sweden (office). *Telephone:* (46) 2227675 (office); (46) 140980 (home). *Fax:* (46) 2227675 (office). *E-mail:* hermann.grimmeiss@ftf.lth.se (office). *Website:* www.ftf.lth.se/staff/emeriti (office).

GRIMSHAW, Sir Nicholas Thomas, Kt, CBE, RA, FCSD, RIBA; British architect; b. 9 Oct. 1939, Hove; s. of Thomas Cecil Grimshaw and Hannah Joan Dearsley; m. Lavinia Russell 1972; two d.; ed Wellington Coll., Edinburgh Coll. of Art, Architectural Asscn School, London; Chair. Nicholas Grimshaw & Partners Ltd 1980– (renamed Grimshaw Architects 2007); Pres. Architectural Asscn; mem. Royal Acad. of Arts 1994–, Pres. 2004–11; Assessor for British Construction Industry Awards, RIBA, Dept of Environment; Hon. FAIA; Hon. DLitt; Hon. BDA; awards and commendations include 19 RIBA awards 1975–2007; seven Financial Times Awards for Industrial Architecture 1977–95, 14 Structural Steel Design Awards 1969–2007, eight Civic Trust Awards 1978–96, eight British Construction Industry Awards 1988–2001, four Royal Fine Art Comm./Sunday Times Bldg of the Year Awards 1989–2004, five Concrete Soc. Awards 1995–2001, Constructa Preis for Industrial Architecture in Europe 1990, European Award for Steel Structures 1981, Quaternario Foundation Int. Awards for Innovative Tech. in Architecture, Gold Award 1993, Mies Van der Rohe Pavilion Award for European Architecture 1994, RIBA Bldg of the Year Award 1994, Design Innovation Award 1996, British Council for Offices Award 1996, Int. Brunel Award 1996, AIA (UK) Excellence in Design Award 2001, 2005, Leisure Property Award for Best Regeneration Scheme 2001, European Award for Aluminium in Architecture 2001, RIBA Lubetkin Prize for Outstanding Architecture outside the EU 2007. *Major projects include:* Channel Tunnel Terminal, Waterloo, London; British Pavilion for Expo '92, Seville, Berlin Stock Exchange and Communications Centre, British Airways Combined Operations Centre, Heathrow Airport, London, Financial Times Printing Plant, HQ for Igus GmbH, Cologne, Germany, head office and printing press for Western Morning News, Plymouth, BMW HQ, Bracknell, new satellite and piers, Heathrow Airport, Western Region HQ for RAC, Herman Miller Factory, Bath, Oxford Ice Rink, Gillingham Business Park, Research Centre for Rank Xerox, J. Sainsbury Superstore, Camden, London, redevelopment of Terminal One, Manchester Airport, New Teaching and Research Bldg, Univ. of Surrey, Regional HQ for Orange Telecommunications, Darlington, Railway Terminus, Pusan, Korea, redevelopment of Zürich Airport, restoration of Paddington Station 1996, Ijburg Bridges, Amsterdam 2002, HQ for Lloyds TSB, Gresham Street, London 2002, Caixa Galicia Foundation, La Coruña, Spain, Exhbn hall for Frankfurt Fair, Eden Project, Cornwall 2001, Nat. Space Science Centre, Leicester 2002, Rolls Royce Factory, Goodwood 2003, Experimental Media and Performing Arts Center for Rensselaer Polytechnic Inst., Troy, NY, USA, HQ for KPMG, Berlin, Thermae Spa, Bath 2006, Southern Cross Station, Melbourne, Australia 2007, Newport City Footbridge, Wales 2007, Fulton Street Station, New York, Stansted Airport Generation 2, New Acad. Building, 24 Kingsway, for LSE 2008, London Southbank Univ. New Building, New Galleries for Queen's Museum of Art, New York, Museo del Acero, Monterrey, Mexico, Earthpark, Iowa, USA, ExCel London Phase 2 Devt, Garibaldi Republica Fashion and Events Bldg, Milan, Nirah visitor destination and research centre, Adelaide Univ. Project 2, St Botolph's Office Bldg, London, New York Housing Project, New York Univ. Strategic Planning Initiative, Nyetimber Vineyard, Sussex, The Edge, Pulkovo Airport, St Petersburg 2007, Eco Hotel Concept, North America 2011, St Botolph Building, London 2011, Mobilizarte Mobile Pavilion, Brazil 2012, Cutty Sark conservation project, London 2012, Fulton Center, Manhattan 2014, Miami Science Museum 2017. *Publications:* Product and Process 1988, Structure, Space and Skin 1993, Architecture, Industry and Innovation 1995, Equilibium 2000, The Architecture of Eden 2003; articles for RSA Journal and RIBA Journal. *Leisure* *interests:* sailing, tennis. *Address:* Royal Academy of Arts, Burlington House, Piccadilly, London, W1J 0BD, England (office). *Telephone:* (20) 7300-8000 (office). *E-mail:* press.office@royalacademy.org.uk (office). *Website:* www.royalacademy.org.uk (office).

GRIMSON, Eric, BSc, PhD; Canadian engineer and academic; *Bernard Gordon Professor of Medical Engineering and Chancellor for Academic Advancement, Massachusetts Institute of Technology;* b. Regina, Sask.; ed Univ. of Regina, Massachusetts Inst. of Tech., USA; has worked for more than 30 years at MIT, positions include Assoc. Dir Artificial Intelligence Lab. 1998–2003, Educ. Officer, Dept of Electrical Eng and Computer Science 2001–04, Head of Dept of Electrical Eng and Computer Science 2005, Prof. of Computer Science and Eng, Bernard Gordon Prof. of Medical Eng 1998–, Chancellor 2011–14, Chancellor for Academic Advancement 2014–; Lecturer on Radiology, Harvard Medical School and Brigham and Women's Hosp.; Fellow, Asscn for Computing Machinery 2014, Asscn for the Advancement of Artificial Intelligence (AAAI), IEEE; Bose Award for Excellence in Teaching, School of Eng, MIT. *Address:* MIT CSAIL, Stata Center, 77 Massachusetts Avenue, 32-D524, Cambridge, MA 02139, USA (office). *Telephone:* (617) 253-5415 (office). *Fax:* (617) 253-1387 (office). *E-mail:* welg@csail.mit.edu (office). *Website:* people.csail.mit.edu (office).

GRÍMSSON, Ólafur Ragnar, PhD; Icelandic politician and fmr head of state; b. 14 May 1943, Isafjörður; s. of Grimur Kristgeirsson and Svanhildur Ólafsdóttir; m. 1st Guðrún Katrín Thorbergsdóttir 1974 (died 1999); two d. (twins); m. 2nd Dorrit Moussaieff 2003; ed Reykjavik Higher Secondary Grammar School, Univ. of Manchester, UK; Lecturer in Political Science, Univ. of Iceland 1970–88, Prof. 1973; involved in production of political TV and radio programmes 1966–70; mem. Bd Progressive Party Youth Fed. 1966–73, Exec. Bd Progressive Party 1971–73, Alt. mem. Althing representing East Iceland (Liberal and Left Alliance) 1974–75; Chair. Exec. Bd Liberal and Left Alliance 1974–75; mem. Althing for Reykjavík 1978–83; mem. People's Alliance, Chair. Parl. Group 1980–83, Leader 1987–95; Minister of Finance 1988–91; Pres. of Iceland 1996–2016; f. Arctic Circle 2013, Hon. Pres. 2013–16, Chair. 2016–; Chair. Cttee on Relocation of Public Institutes 1972–75, Icelandic Social Sciences Asscn 1975, Organizing Cttee Parl. Conf. of Council of Europe: 'North-South: Europe's Role' 1982-84, Parliamentarians for Global Action 1984–90 (also fmr Pres., mem. Bd 1990–96); Vice-Chair. Icelandic Security Comm. 1979–90; mem. Bd Icelandic Broadcasting Service 1971–75, Nat. Power Co. 1983–88; mem. Parl. Ass. Council of Europe 1980–84, 1995. *Address:* Arctic Circle Secretariat, Menntavegur 1, 101 Reykjavík, Iceland (office). *E-mail:* secretariat@arcticcircle.org (office). *Website:* www.arcticcircle.org (office).

GRIMSTONE, Sir Gerald Edgar (Gerry), Kt, MA, MSc; British banking executive; *Chairman, Standard Life PLC;* b. 27 Aug. 1949; ed Whitgift School, Merton Coll. and Wolfson Coll., Oxford; held sr positions with Dept of Health and Social Security and HM Treasury –1986; with Schroders Investment Bank 1986–99, London, Hong Kong and New York, becoming Vice-Chair. Schroders' worldwide investment banking activities; mem. Bd of Dirs Standard Life Assurance Co. 2003–, Deputy Chair. Standard Life PLC 2006–07, Chair. 2007–; Chair. TheCityUK 2012–; Dir (non-exec.) Dairy Crest 1999–2007, Candover Investments PLC 1999–2011 (Chair. 2006–11), Aggregate Industries 2000–04, F&C Global Smaller Companies PLC 2002–07 (Chair. 2004–07); Ind. Dir (non-exec.), Deloitte LLP 2011–; Lead Dir (non-exec.), Ministry of Defence 2011–; apptd as one of UK's Business Ambs by the Prime Minister 2009–10; Chair. Jt Audit Cttee, RAF Strike Command Bd 2001–07; mem. Horserace Totalisator Bd 1999–2006; Trustee, The Queille Trust, RAF Museum 2008–. *Address:* Standard Life House, 30 Lothian Road, Edinburgh, EH1 2DH, Scotland (office). *Telephone:* (131) 225-2552 (office). *Fax:* (131) 245-7990 (office). *E-mail:* info@standardlife.com (office). *Website:* www.standardlife.com (office).

GRIMWADE, Sir Andrew (Sheppard), Kt, CBE, BSc, MA, FAIM; Australian business executive; b. 26 Nov. 1930, Melbourne; s. of Frederick Grimwade and Gwendolen Grimwade; m. Barbara Gaerloch Kater 1959 (died 1990); one s.; ed Melbourne Grammar School, Trinity Coll., Melbourne Univ., Oriel Coll. Oxford, UK; Dir Commonwealth Industrial Gases Ltd 1960–90, Nat. Australia Bank Ltd 1965–85, IBM Australia 1975–82, Sony (Australia) 1975–82, Turoa Holdings Ltd 1975–82; Chair. Australian Consolidated Industries Ltd 1977–82; fmr Vice-Chair. Nat. Mutual Life 1988 (Dir 1970); mem. Australian Govt Remuneration Tribunal 1976–82; mem. First Australian Govt Trade Mission to China 1973; Pres. Walter and Eliza Hall Inst. of Medical Research 1978–92 (Bd mem. 1963–); Deputy Pres. Australiana Fund 1978–82; Trustee Nat. Gallery of Victoria (Pres. 1976–90), Trustee Emer. 1990–; mem. Felton Bequests Cttee 1973–, now Chair.; Trustee Victorian Arts Centre 1980–90; mem. Council for Order of Australia 1975–82; Fellow and Life mem., Royal Australian Chemical Inst.; Hon. mem., Royal Soc. of Victoria. *Publications include:* Involvement: The Portraits of Clifton Pugh and Mark Strizic 1969, Great Philanthropists on Trial 2006, Storied Windows: Casting Light on the Arts, Science & Life in Australia 1959–2011 2012. *Leisure interests:* skiing, Santa Gertrudis cattle breeding, Australian art.

GRINBERG, Ruslan Semyonovich, DrSc; Russian institute director and academic; b. 1946; Deputy Dir Inst. for Int. Econ. and Political Studies, Russian Acad. of Sciences, Moscow –2002, Dir 2002–05; Vice-Chair. ECAAR Russia (Economists Allied for Arms Reduction); mem. Russian-American Econ. Transition Group; Ed.-in-Chief The World of Transformations; Admin. Adviser to Gorbachev Foundation; Chair. Cttee of CIS, Nat. Investment Council, Expertise Council for CIS of Russian Fed. Trade and Industry Chamber; mem. Expertise Council Supreme Certifying Comm., Expertise Bd for Ministry of Economy; mem. Cultural Information and Research Centres Liaison in Europe (CIRCLE); Corresp. mem. Russian Acad. of Sciences. *Publications include:* Economic Sociodynamics (with Alexander Rubinstein) 2000, The New Russia – Transition Gone Awry 2001, Rational Behavior of the State 2003; more than 184 publs on econ. theory, credit and monetary policy in post-Socialist countries, integration and disintegration in post-Soviet states, the role of state in transformation economies. *Address:* c/o Institute for International Economic and Political Studies, Novocheryemushkinskaya 42A, Moscow 117418, Russia. *Telephone:* (495) 128-67-80. *Fax:* (495) 120-83-71. *E-mail:* imepi@transecon.ru. *Website:* www.imepi-eurasia.ru.

GRINDEANU, Sorin Mihai; Romanian academic and politician; b. 5 Dec. 1973, Caransebeş; s. of Nicholas Grindeanu; m. Mihaela Grindeanu; ed West Univ. of Timişoara, Univ. of Bologna, Italy; Asst, Faculty of Sociology and Psychology, West Univ. of Timişoara 1998–2000, Asst Prof. 2000–01; Dir of Sports Dept, Timiş County 2001–03; City Councillor, Timişoara 2004–08, Deputy Mayor of Timişoara 2008–12; Pres. Timiş County Council 2016–17; Deputy Gen. Dir Delpack Invest SRL 2005–08; Dir SC AHM Smartel SRL March–June 2008; mem. Camera Deputaţilor (lower house of parl.) for Timiş 2012–16; Minister of Communications and Information Society 2014–15; Prime Minister Jan.–June 2017 (removed by parl. motion of no confidence); mem. Partidul Social Democrat—PSD (Social Democratic Party) 1996–2017, Vice-Pres. PSD Timiş youth org. 1998, mem. PSD Nat. Council 2002–17. *Publication:* Introduction to Social Informatics 2000. *Website:* www.soringrindeanu.ro.

GRININ, Vladimir Mikhailovich; Russian diplomatist; b. 15 Nov. 1947, Moscow; m.; one d.; ed Moscow State Univ. for Int. Relations, Diplomatic Acad., USSR Ministry of Foreign Affairs; joined Ministry of Foreign Affairs 1971, served in Embassy of USSR in Bonn, FRG 1973–80, mem. Soviet del. at negotiations between USSR and USA on disarmament and arms control in Geneva 1982–86, Counsellor, Embassy of USSR in East Berlin, GDR 1986–90, Head of Embassy of USSR/Russian Fed. in Bonn, FRG 1990–92, Dir 4th European Dept, Ministry of Foreign Affairs 1994–96, Amb. to Austria 1996–2000, Sec.-Gen. (mem. Collegium), Ministry of Foreign Affairs 2000–03, Amb. to Finland 2003–06, to Poland 2006–10, to Germany 2010–17.

GRINSTEIN, Gerald (Jerry), LLB; American business executive; *Strategic Director, Madrona Venture Group;* b. 1932, Seattle, WA; m.; four c.; ed Yale Coll., Harvard Law School; Counsel to merchant marine and transport subcttees., Chief Counsel, US Senate Commerce Cttee 1958–67; Admin. Asst to US Senator Warren Magnuson 1967–69; Pnr, Preston, Thorgrimson, Ellis & Holman 1969–73; Chair. Bd Western Air Lines Inc. LA 1983–84, Pres. and COO 1984–85, CEO 1985–86, Chair. and CEO 1986–87; Vice-Chair. Burlington Northern Inc., Fort Worth 1987–88, Pres., CEO 1989–90, Chair. 1990–96, CEO 1990–95; Pres., CEO Burlington Northern R.R. Co. 1989–90, Chair. 1990–96, CEO 1990–95; Chair. Delta Airlines Inc. 1997–99, CEO 2004–07, currently CEO Emer.; Chair. (non-exec.) Agilent Techs. 1999–2002; Co-founder and Strategic Dir Madrona Investment Group, Seattle 1995–2003, 2007–; mem. Bd of Dirs Long Live the Kings, Univ. of Washington Foundation, Seattle Foundation, Foster School of Business, William D. Ruckelshaus Center; Founder mem. Bd of Dirs Foundation Bank 2000–; fmr mem. Bd of Dirs Seattle First Nat. Bank, Browning Ferris Industries Inc., Sundstrand Corpn, Expedia.com, Imperial Sugar Corpn, PACCAR Inc., The Brink's Co.; Trustee, Henry M. Jackson Foundation. *Address:* Madrona Venture Group, 1000 Second Avenue, Suite 3700, Seattle, WA 98104, USA (office). *Telephone:* (206) 674-3000 (office). *Fax:* (206) 674-8703 (office). *Website:* www.madrona.com (office).

GRINT, Rupert Alexander Lloyd; British actor; b. 24 Aug. 1988, Herefords.; s. of Nigel Grint and Joanne Parsons; ed Richard Hale School, Hertford; first performed in school plays and with Top Hat Stage School (local theatre group). *Films include:* Harry Potter and the Philosopher's Stone 2001, Harry Potter and the Chamber of Secrets 2002, Thunderpants 2002, Harry Potter and the Prisoner of Azkaban 2004, Harry Potter and the Goblet of Fire 2005, Driving Lessons 2006, Harry Potter and the Order of the Phoenix 2007, December Boys 2007, Harry Potter and the Half-Blood Prince 2009, Harry Potter and the Deathly Hallows: Part 1 2010, Cherrybomb 2010, Wild Target 2010, Harry Potter and the Deathly Hallows: Part 2 2011, Enemy of Man 2015. *Television:* Come Fly with Me (BBC) 2010. *Radio:* Baggy Trousers (series, BBC Radio 4) 2003. *Theatre includes:* Mojo (WhatsOnStage Award for the Dewynters London Newcomer of the year 2014) 2013–14, It's Only a Play (Gerald Schoenfeld Theatre, New York) 2014–15. *Address:* Hamilton Hodell, Fifth Floor, 66–68 Margaret Street, London, W1W 8SR, England (office). *Telephone:* (20) 7636-1221 (office). *Fax:* (20) 7636-1226 (office). *E-mail:* info@hamiltonhodell.co.uk (office). *Website:* www.hamiltonhodell.co.uk (office).

GRINVALD, Amiram, BSc, MSc, PhD; Israeli neuroscientist and academic; b. Kibbutz Ramat Hashofet; ed Weizmann Inst. of Science, Hebrew Univ., Hadassah School of Medicine, Yale Univ., USA; joined Dept of Neurobiology, Weizmann Inst. of Science 1978, fmr Prin. Investigator, Israel, Helen and Norman Asher Professorial Chair in Brain Research, Dir Murray H. & Meyer Grodetsky Center for Research of Higher Brain Functions 1991–2012, Dir Dominic Inst. for Brain Research 1996–2002; Foreign Dir Max Planck Inst. for Medicine, Heidelberg, Germany, External Scientific mem. 2000–; Guest Staff mem. Frontier Research Program, RIKEN, Japan; Visiting Prof., Lab. of Neurobiology, Rockefeller Univ. 1985–91; Research Staff mem. IBM Thomas J. Watson Research Center 1986–91; Alice and Joseph Brooks Int. Lecturer in Neurosciences, Harvard Medical School 2002; mem. Israel Acad. of Sciences and Humanities 1998; Koerber's Europe Prize 2000, Dan David Prize (co-recipient) 2004. *Publications:* numerous scientific papers in professional journals on functional optical imaging. *Address:* c/o Department of Neurobiology, Weizmann Institute of Science, PO Box 26, Rehovot 76100, Israel (office).

GRIRA, Ridha, DEA, LèsSc; Tunisian politician; b. 21 Aug. 1955, Sousse; m.; two c.; ed Univ. Paris I (Pantheon-Sorbonne), Institut d'études politiques, Ecole Nationale d'Administration, France; held several sr admin. positions at Prime Ministry including Special Adviser and Dir-Gen. of Public Service; CEO Banque Arabe Tuniso-Libyenne de Développement et de Commerce 1991; fmr Sec.-Gen., Ministry of Foreign Affairs; Sec.-Gen. of Govt 1992–99; Minister of State-Administered Properties and Land Affairs 1999–2010, Minister of Nat. Defence 2010–11 (resgnd); mem. Rassemblement constitutionnel démocratique (RCD), mem. Cen. Cttee and Chair. RCD El Manar 2 Tunis Div. 1994–2011; arrested 2011, released 2014; Grand Cordon, Ordre de la République, Grand Officier, Ordre du 7 Novembre.

GRISHAM, John, BS, JD; American writer and lawyer; b. (John Ray Grisham, Jr), 8 Feb. 1955, Jonesboro, Ark.; s. of John Grisham, Sr and Wanda Grisham (née Skidmore); m. Renée Jones 1981; one s. one d.; ed Mississippi State Univ., Univ. of Mississippi Law School; called to the Bar, Miss. 1981; attorney in Southaven, Miss. 1981–90; mem. Miss. House of Reps 1984–90; f. Rebuild The Coast Fund; Lifetime Achievement Award, British Book Awards 2007. *Film screenplay:* The Gingerbread Man 1998. *Publications:* novels: A Time to Kill 1989, The Firm 1991, The

Pelican Brief 1992, The Client 1993, The Chamber 1994, The Rainmaker 1995, The Runaway Jury 1996, The Partner 1997, The Street Lawyer 1998, The Testament 1999, The Brethren 2000, A Painted House 2001, Skipping Christmas 2001, The Summons 2002, The King of Torts 2003, Bleachers 2003, The Last Juror 2004, The Broker 2005, Playing for Pizza 2007, The Appeal 2008, The Associate 2009, Ford County 2009, Theodore Boone: Kid Lawyer 2010, The Confession (Harper Lee Prize for Legal Fiction 2011) 2010, The Litigators 2011, Theodore Boone: The Abduction 2011, Calico Joe 2012, Theodore Boone: The Accused 2012, The Racketeer 2012, Sycamore Row (Harper Lee Prize for Legal Fiction 2014) 2013, Gray Mountain 2014, Rogue Lawyer 2015, The Tumor: A Non-Legal Thriller 2016, The Whistler 2016, Camino Island 2017, The Rooster Bar 2017, The Reckoning 2018; short stories: Ford County 2009, The Tumor 2016, Partners 2016, Witness to a Trial 2016; non-fiction: The Wavedancer Benefit: A Tribute to Frank Muller (with Pat Conroy, Stephen King and Peter Straub) 2002, The Innocent Man: Murder and Injustice in a Small Town 2006, Don't Quit Your Day Job: Acclaimed Authors and the Day Jobs They Quit 2010. *Website:* www.jgrisham.com.

GRISHKOVETS, Yevgeny B.; Russian actor, stage director and playwright; b. 17 Feb. 1967, Kemerovo; m.; one s.; two d.; ed Kemerovo State Univ.; f. and artistic Dir Theatre Lozha 1990; Anti-Booker Prize 1999, Golden Mask Prize 2000, Nat. Triumph Prize 2000. *Films include:* The Stroll, Not by Bread Alone, The First Circle. *Stage productions include:* Winter, How I Have Eaten a Dog, Simultaneously, Notes of a Russian Traveller, Titanic, Po Po. *Publications include:* Gorod 2001, Kak ya syel sobaku 2003, Rubashka 2004, Reki 2005, Planka 2006. *Website:* grishkovets.com.

GROCHOLEWSKI, HE Cardinal Zenon, DCL; Polish ecclesiastic; *Prefect Emeritus, Congregation for Catholic Education (for Seminaries and Institutes of Study);* b. 11 Oct. 1939, Bródki; s. of Stanisław Grocholewski and Józefa Grocholewski (née Stawińska); ed Archbishop's Seminary, Poznań, Pontifical Gregorian Univ., Rome, Studio Rotale, Rome; ordained priest 1963, worked in Christ the Redeemer Parish, Poznań 1963–66; studies in Rome 1966–72; Official of Supreme Tribunal of Apostolic Signatura 1972–82, Sec. 1982–98, Prefect 1998–99; Lecturer (later Prof.) in Canon Law, Pontifical Gregorian Univ. 1975–99 (currently Grand Chancellor), Pontifical Lateran Univ. 1980–89 and Studio Rotale 1986–98; consecrated Titular Bishop of Agropoli 1982; mem. Pontifical Cttee for Int. Eucharistic Congresses 1989–2001; promoted to Archbishop 1991; Prefect Congregation for Catholic Educ. (for Seminaries and Insts of Study) 1999–2015, Prefect Emer. 2015–; Pres. Comm. for the Lawyers of the Holy See and Roman Curia 1988–99, Pontifical Soc. for Priestly Vocations, Permanent Interdicasterial Comm. for the formation of candidates for Holy Orders; mem. Disciplinary Comm. of the Roman Curia 1983–99, Congregation for Bishops 1999–, Pontifical Council for Interpretation of Legis. Texts 2000–, Special Council Oceania, Secr. Gen. (Synod of Bishops), Congregation for the Doctrine of the Faith 2001–, Congregation for Divine Worship, Congregation for Evangelization of Peoples, Supreme Tribunal of the Apostolic Signatura; cr. Cardinal (Cardinal-Priest of San Nicola in Carcere) 2001; participated in Papal Conclave 2005, 2013; Hon. Citizen of Trenton, NJ 1988, Princeton, NJ 1992, Agropoli, Italy 1992, Levoča, Slovakia 1997; Hon. mem. Pontifical Acad. of St Thomas Aquinas, Rome 2001; Grand Cross, Order of Merit, Chile 2003, Grand Cross of Merit with Star and Sash, Order of Merit of the Fed. Repub. of Germany 2005, Commdr's Cross with Star, Order of Polonia Restituta, Commdr, Ordre des Palmes Académiques, France 2009; Dr hc (Acad. of Catholic Theology, Warsaw) 1998, (Catholic Univ. of Lublin) 1999, (Passau) 2001, (Glasgow) 2001, (Bratislava) 2002, (Catholic Univ. of Buenos Aires) 2002; Polonia Semper Fidelis Medal 1998, Grand Medal of St Gorazd, Slovakia 2000, Missio Reconciliationis Medal 2010. *Publications:* De exclusione indissolubilitatis ex consensu matrimoniali eiusque probatione 1973, Documenta recentoria circa rem matrimonialem et processualem, Vol. I (with I. Gordon) 1977, Vol. II 1980; La filosofía del derecho en las enseñanzas de Juan Pablo II y otros escritos 2001; four books in Slovakian, Hungarian and Polish and co-author of numerous other books. *Leisure interest:* tourism. *Address:* Congregazione per l'Educazione Cattolica, Palazzo delle Congregazioni, Piazza Pio XII 3, 00193 Cittàdel Vaticano, Rome (office); Palazzo della Cancelleria 1, 00186 Rome, Italy (home). *Telephone:* (06) 69884167 (office); (06) 69887546 (home). *Fax:* (06) 69884172 (office). *Website:* www .vatican.va/roman_curia/congregations/ccatheduc (office).

GROENING, Matthew (Matt), BA; American writer, cartoonist and screenwriter; b. 15 Feb. 1954, Portland, Ore.; s. of Homer Philip Groening and Margaret Ruth Groening (née Wiggum); m. 1st Deborah Lee Caplan (divorced 1999); m. 2nd Agustina Picasso 2011; three c.; ed Evergreen State Coll.; cartoonist drawing and writing Life in Hell syndicated weekly comic strip, Sheridan, Ore. 1980–; Pres. Matt Groening Productions, Inc., Los Angeles 1988–, Bongo Entertainment, Inc., Los Angeles 1993–, also Publr; creator, Simpsons interludes, The Tracey Ullman Show 1987–89; creator and Exec. Producer The Simpsons TV show 1989–; Founder and Publr Bongo Comics Group; Founder and Publr Zongo Comics (including Jimbo 1995, Fleener 1996); cartoonist for TV cartoon Futurama 1999; mem. Int. Acad. of Digital Arts and Sciences 1998–; 11 Emmy Awards, Diamond Distribution Gem Award 1993; George Foster Peabody Award 1997, Reuben Award, Nat. Cartoonist Soc. 2002, British Comedy Award 2004. *Publications include:* Love Is Hell 1985, Work Is Hell 1986, School Is Hell 1987, Childhood Is Hell 1988, Akbar and Jeff's Guide to Life 1989, Greetings from Hell 1989, The Postcards That Ate My Brain 1990, The Big Book of Hell 1990, The Simpsons Xmas Book 1990, Greetings from The Simpsons 1990, With Love from Hell 1991, The Simpsons Rainy Day Fun Book 1991, The Simpsons Uncensored Family Album 1991, The Simpsons Student Diary 1991, How to Go to Hell 1991, Maggie Simpson's Alphabet Book 1991, Maggie Simpson's Counting Book 1991, Maggie Simpson's Book of Colors and Shapes 1991, Maggie Simpson's Book of Animals 1991, The Road to Hell 1992, The Simpsons Fun in the Sun Book 1992, Making Faces with the Simpsons 1992, Bart Simpson's Guide to Life 1993, The Simpsons Ultra-Jumbo Rain-Or-Shine Fun Book 1993, Cartooning with the Simpsons 1993, Bongo Comics Group Spectacular 1993, Binky's Guide to Love 1994, Love Is Hell 10th Anniversary Edition 1994, Simpsons Comics Extravaganza 1994, Simpsons Comics Spectacular 1994, Bartman: The Best of the Best 1994, Simpsons Comics Simps-O-Rama 1995, Simpsons Comics Strike Back 1995, Simpsons Comics Wing Ding 1997, The Huge Book of Hell 1997, Bongo Comics, Binky's Guide to Love: A Little Book of Hell 2006, The Simpsons Forever – And Beyond! 2006, Will and Abe's Guide to the Universe 2007. *Address:* Matt Groening Productions, 9720 Wilshire Blvd, 3rd Floor, Beverly Hills, CA 90212, USA (office). *Telephone:* (310) 586-9800 (office).

GROENINK, Rijkman W. J., MBS, DrIur; Dutch banking executive; *Senior Partner, Atlas NV;* b. 25 Aug. 1949, Den Helder; m. Irene Verboon; four c.; ed Utrecht Univ., Univ. of Manchester, UK; joined Amro Bank 1974, apptd Head of Syndicated Loans 1978, Head of Int. Corp. Accounts, Int. Div. 1980–82, Man. Dutch Special Credit Dept 1982–86, Exec. Sr Pres. of Corp. Business 1986–90, mem. Man. Bd 1988–90, mem. Man. Bd ABN AMRO (following merger with ABN) 1990–2007, Chair. Man. Bd 2000–07; currently Sr Partner, Atlas NV, Belgium; Officer, Order of Orange-Nassau; Hon. MBA (Trieste); European Banker of the Year, Frankfurt 2006. *Leisure interests:* skiing, horse riding, farming, tennis, golf. *Address:* Chaussée de la Hulpe 120, 1000 Brussels, Belgium (office); Oud Over 4, 3632 VD Loenen aan den Vecht, Netherlands (home). *Telephone:* (294) 230289 (office); (2) 663-17-56 (Brussels) (office). *Fax:* (294) 230276 (office); (2) 663-17-60 (Brussels) (office). *E-mail:* rg@atlasinvest.eu (office); rijkman.groenink@vrederijk .nl (home).

GROMOV, Aleksey Alekseyevich; Russian diplomatist and government official; *First Deputy Chief of Staff, Presidential Executive Office;* b. 31 May 1960; m.; two c.; ed Moscow State Univ.; joined staff, USSR Ministry of Foreign Affairs 1982, Attaché, Embassy in Prague 1985–88, Sec., Office of the Deputy Minister 1988–91, First Sec., Gen. Office 1991–92, Consul, Russian Consulate Gen., Bratislava, Slovakia 1992–93, Counsellor, Embassy in Bratislava 1993–96; Head of Press Service of Russian Pres. 1996–2000, Press Sec. 2000–08, Deputy Chief of Staff of Presidential Exec. Office 2008–12, First Deputy Chief of Staff 2012–. *Address:* Office of the President, Staraya pl. 4, 103132 Moscow, Russia (office). *Telephone:* (495) 910-07-38 (office). *Fax:* (495) 910-07-38 (office). *Website:* www.kremlin.ru (office).

GROMOV, Col-Gen. Boris Vsevolodovich; Russian army officer and politician; b. 7 Nov. 1943, Saratov; m. 2nd Faina Gromov; two s. two adopted d.; ed Leningrad Gen. Troops School, Frunze Mil. Acad., Gen. Staff Acad.; mem. CPSU 1966–91; Commdr of platoon, co., Bn, Regt, div. 1965–87, Commdr 40 Army in Afghanistan 1987–89, Commdr of troops Kiev Command 1989–90, First Deputy Minister of Internal Affairs of USSR 1990–91, First Deputy Commdr of Armed Forces of CIS 1991–92, First Deputy Minister of Defence of Russia 1992–95; Chief Mil. Expert and Deputy Minister of Foreign Affairs 1995–97; mem. State Duma 1996–99, Chair. Sub-Cttee on Arms Control and Int. Security; Gov. of Moscow Oblast 2000–12; f. war veterans' movt, Fighting Fraternity (later Honour and Homeland) 1997–; Hero of Soviet Union, Order in the Name of Russia 2004. *Publication:* Memoirs of the Afghan War 1994. *Leisure interests:* tennis, cycling. *Address:* Administration of Moscow Region, 103070 Moscow, Staraya Pl. 6, Russia (office). *Telephone:* (495) 623-24-13; (495) 206-68-62 (office); (495) 206-60-42 (office). *Fax:* (495) 928-98-12 (office). *E-mail:* amo@mosreg.ru (office). *Website:* www.mosreg.ru/ gubernator; www.bgromov.ru.

GROMOV, Mikhael Leonidovich (Misha), PhD; Russian/French mathematician and academic; *Professor Emeritus, Institut des Hautes Études Scientifiques (IHÉS);* b. 23 Dec. 1943, Boksitogorsk, USSR; s. of Leonid Gromov and Lea Rabinovitz; m. Margarita Gromov 1967; ed Univ. of Leningrad; Asst Prof., Univ. of Leningrad 1967–74; Prof., State Univ. of New York, Stony Brook, USA 1974–81; Prof., Univ. of Paris VI, France 1981–82; Perm. Prof., IHÉS 1982–, Prof. Emer. 2015–; Prof. of Math., Univ. of Maryland 1991–96; Jay Gould Prof. of Math., Courant Inst. of Math. Sciences, New York Univ. 1996–; Foreign Assoc. mem. NAS; Foreign mem. American Acad. of Arts and Sciences 1989, Norwegian Acad. of Science and Letters, Royal Soc. 2011; Foreign Assoc., Acad. des Sciences, Institut de France, mem. 1997; Hon. mem. London Mathematical Soc. 2008; Dr hc (Geneva) 1992; Moscow Math. Soc. Prize 1971, Oswald Veblen Prize for Geometry, American Math. Soc. 1981, Prix Elie Cartan, Acad. des Sciences, Paris 1984, Prix Union des Assurances de Paris 1989, Wolf Prize in Math. 1993, Leroy P. Steele Prize for Seminal Contrib. to Research 1997, Lobachevsky Medal 1997, Balzan Prize for Math. 1999, Kyoto Prize in Math. Sciences 2002, Frederic Esser Nemmers Prize in Math. 2004, Northwestern Univ., Bolyai Prize 2005, Abel Prize 2009. *Publications:* Structures métriques pour les variétés riemanniennes 1981, Manifolds of nonpositive curvature. Progress in Mathematics 61 (co-author) 1985, Partial differential relations. Ergebnisse der Mathematik und ihrer Grenzgebiete 1986; papers in mathematical journals. *Address:* Institut des Hautes Études Scientifiques, 35 route de Chartres, 91440 Bures-sur-Yvette, France (office); 91 rue de la Santé, 75013 Paris, France (home). *Telephone:* 1-60-92-66-00 (Paris) (office); 1-45-88-14-42 (home). *Fax:* 1-60-92-66-09 (office). *E-mail:* gromov@ihes.fr (office). *Website:* www.ihes.fr (office).

GROMYKO, Alexey Anatolievich, DSc; Russian political scientist; *Director, Institute of Europe, Russian Academy of Sciences;* b. 20 April 1969, Moscow; s. of Anatoly Gromyko and Valentina Gromyko; grandson of Andrei Gromyko (fmr Chair. of the Presidium of the Supreme Soviet); ed Lomonosov Moscow State Univ., Inst. of Comparative Politology, Russian Acad. of Sciences; Chair., Council of Profs, Russian Acad. of Sciences (RAS), Founder and Head, Centre for British Studies 2000–14, currently Dir, RAS Inst. of Europe, also mem. Bureau of RAS Dept of Global Problems and Int. Relations and Chair., Inst. of Europe Academic Council, Ed.-in-Chief Contemporary Europe (journal); Expert on European programmes, Russkiy Mir Foundation and Chair., Expert Cttee, Inst. of Linguistic, Civilization and Migration Processes; Pres. Russian Asscn of European Studies; mem. Russian Int. Affairs Council; mem. Presidium, Free Econ. Soc. of Russia; mem. Editorial Bd Observer, Messenger of St Petersburg Univ. (Int. Relations series); mem. Editorial Council, Messenger of Diplomatic Acad. of Ministry of Foreign Affairs (MFA), Russia and the World, Geopolitical Journal; mem. Dissertation Council, Diplomatic Acad. of MFA; Chair. Russian Movt for Democratic Int. Order and Support of the UN; mem. Bd of Dirs New Economic Asscn; mem. Council Bureau, Russian Foundation for Humanities; mem. Academic Council, Security Council of Russia, Academic Council of MFA; mem. Comm., Presidential Council on the Russian Language; Sr Assoc., St Antony's Coll., Oxford 2004, Sr Visitor 2007; Hon. mem. Academic Forum, Chernorizets Hrabar Varna Free Univ., Bulgaria; Dr hc (Paisii Hilendarski Univ., Plovdiv); Russian Science Support Foundation Award 2004, 2006. *Publications include:* over 150 publs including Political Reformism in Great Britain 2001, Modernizing the UK Political System 2007, Images of Russia and Great Britain: Reality and

Superstition 2008, Great Britain. Era of Reforms (ed. and co-author) 2007, Better Ten Years of Negotiations Than One Day of War. Reminiscences of Andrey Andreevich Gromyko (ed. and compiler) 2009, Lessons of WWII for Europe in the XXI Century (ed. and co–author) 2011, Building Good Relations with Neighbours. Russia in Europe 2013, Dilemmas of Britain. In Search of Routes for Development 2014. *Address:* Institute of Europe, Russian Academy of Sciences, 125993 Moscow, Mokhovaya Str., 11/3, Russia (office). *Telephone:* (495) 692-21-02 (office). *E-mail:* alexey@gromyko.ru (office). *Website:* en.instituteofeurope.ru (office); www.gromyko.ru.

GRONDIN, Jean, OC, OQ, BA, MA, PhD, FRSC; Canadian philosopher and academic; *Professor, Department of Philosophy, University of Montréal;* b. 1955; ed Univ. of Montréal, Univs of Heidelberg and Tübingen, Germany; taught at Université Laval, Québec City 1982–90, Univ. of Ottawa 1990–91; Prof., Dept of Philosophy, Univ. of Montréal 1991–; Guest Prof., Univs of Nice 1998, Lausanne 1998, 2000, Minsk 2001, 2003, Istituto Italiano per gli Studi Filosofici de Naples 2003, Universidad Centroamericana de San Salvador 2005, École Normale Supérieure de Port-au-Prince 2008, Universidad del Norte Santo Tomás de Aquino (UNSTA) de Tucumán, Argentina 2009; Étienne Gilson Chair of Metaphysics, Univ. of Paris Feb.–March 2013; Pres. Acad. of Arts and Humanities, RSC 2016–; mem. Editorial Bd Archives de philosophie, Etudes philosophiques, Graduate Faculty Philosophy Journal, Dialogue, Philosophiques 1986–92, Symposium, Ars interpretandi. Giornale di ermeneutica giuridica, Theoros, Divinatio, Internationale Zeitschrift für Philosophie, Phainomena, Internationales Jahrbuch für Hermeneutik, Heidegger Jahrbuch, Studia Phaenomenologica, Heidegger Studies, Science et Esprit, Analogia, Studium, Vox philosophiae, Analecta hermeneutica, Horizontes filosóficos, Bulletin heideggérien des Archives de philosophie; specialist in the thought of Immanuel Kant, Hans-Georg Gadamer and Martin Heidegger; principal advocate for the work of Gadamer and Paul Ricoeur; prominent in contemporary hermeneutics and metaphysics; has also worked extensively on German idealism, metaphysics and the hermeneutics of Wilhelm Dilthey and Ricoeur; mem. Acad. des lettres et des sciences humaines, RSC 1998; Founding mem. and Vice-Pres. Soc. francophone de Philosophie de la religion 2011; Hon. mem. Fundación Miguel Lillo de Tucumán 2008; Hon. Prof., Pontificia Universidad Católica Argentina Santa Maria de los Buenos Aires 2011; Dr hc (UNSTA de Tucumán) 2008, (Universidad Nacional de Santiago del Estero) 2011, (Universidad San Martin de Buenos Aires) 2016; bursary from Alexander von Humboldt Foundation 1988–89, from Killam Foundation 1994–96, Konrad Adenauer Prize, Humboldt Foundation and the RSC 2010, Prix du Québec Léon-Gérin 2011, Killam Prize (Humanities), Canada Council for the Arts 2012, Prix André-Laurendeau 2012, Molson Prize of the Canada Council for the Arts 2014. *Publications include:* Hermeneutische Wahrheit? Zum Wahrheitsbegriff Hans-Georg Gadamers 1982 (second edn 1994), Le tournant dans la pensée de Martin Heidegger 1987 (second edn 2011), Kant et le problème de la philosophie: l'a priori 1989, Emmanuel Kant avant-après 1991, L'universalité de l'herméneutique 1993, L'horizon herméneutique de la pensée contemporaine 1993, Sources of Hermeneutics 1995, Hans-Gerog Gadamer. Eine Biographie 1999 (second edn 2013, trans. as Hans-Gerog Gadamer, A Biography 2003), Introduction à Hans-Georg Gadamers 1999 (trans. as Einführung zu Gadamer 2000), Von Heidegger zu Gadamer 2001, Du sens de la vie 2003, L'herméneutique 2006 (fourth edn 2017), La philosophie de la religion 2009 (third edn 2015), À l'écoute du sens 2011, Einführung in die philosophische Hermeneutik (third edn) 2012, Introduction to Metaphysics 2012, Paul Ricœur 2013 (second edn 2016), Du sens des choses. L'idée de la métaphysique 2013, Der Sinn für Hermeneutik 2014; numerous papers in philosophical journals. *Address:* Department of Philosophy, University of Montréal, CP 6128, Succursale Centre-ville, Montréal, PQ H3C 3J7, Canada (office). *Telephone:* (514) 343-6464 (office). *Fax:* (514) 343-7899 (office). *E-mail:* jean.grondin@umontreal.ca (office). *Website:* www.philo.umontreal.ca/personnel/professeur/grondin-jean (office); jeangrondin.wordpress.com.

GRÖNEMEYER, Herbert; German actor, singer and composer; b. 12 April 1956, Goettingen; wrote first compositions for Bochum Schauspielhaus Theatre 1974; Musical Dir, actor Schauspielhaus 1975; European Hero 2005, eight ECHO Awards, Single of the Year Award 2003, Album of the Year Award 2008, Best Nat. Music Award 2014. *Film appearances include:* The Hostage 1975, Daheim unter Fremden 1979, Springtime Symphony 1983, Father and Sons 1988, Control 2007, The American 2010, A Most Wanted Man 2014. *Theatre appearances include:* John, Paul, George, Ringo and Bert 1974, Spring Awakening 1976, The Winter's Tale 1978, The Merchant of Venice 1979, Big and Little 1982. *Albums include:* Ocean Orchestra 1978, Grönemeyer 1979, Stand der Dinge 2000, Mensch 2002, Zeit dass sich was dreht (official 2006 FIFA World Cup Anthem) 2007, Was muss muss 2008, I Walk 2013, Dauernd Jetzt (Goldene Kamera Award for best German language album 2015, Echo Award 2015) 2014. *Address:* ZBF Agentur, 80802 Munich, Germany (office). *Telephone:* (30) 89355081 (office). *E-mail:* groenland@groenemeyer.de. *Website:* www.groenemeyer.de.

GRÖNHOLM, Marcus; Finnish racing driver; b. 5 Feb. 1968, Finland; s. of Ulf Uffe Grönholm; m. Teresa Grönholm; three c.; with team Peugeot 1999–2005, team Ford 2006–07 (retd), came out of retirement to drive in selected rallies; rally debut Finland 1988; Finnish junior champion 1988; World Rally Championship (WRC) debut Sweden 1995; Scandinavia Rally Champion 1989, won Finnish Rally Championship (Group N) 1991, (Group A) 1994, 1996, 1997, 1998; won Race of the Champions 2002, Nations' Cup Winner (with Heikki Kovalainen) 2006; 16 WRC victories include Sweden 2000, 2002, 2003, 2006, 2007, Australia 2000, 2001, 2002, Finland 2000, 2001, 2002, 2004, 2005, 2006, 2007, Great Britain 2001, 2006, Cyprus 2002, New Zealand 2000, 2002, 2003, 2006, 2007, Argentina 2003, Greece 2007; WRC winner 2000, 2002; total WRC points 259; mem. Mensa Finland. *Address:* Team MGR Finland, Santapellontie 1, Espoo 02780, Finland (office). *Website:* www.mgr.fi (office); www.mgronholm.com.

GRONKIEWICZ-WALTZ, Hanna, LLD, PhD; Polish banker, lawyer and politician; b. 4 Nov. 1952, Warsaw; m.; one d.; ed Warsaw Univ.; mem. of academic staff, Warsaw Univ. 1975–; mem. Solidarity Trade Union 1980; expert on public and econ. law, Polish Parl. 1989; mem. of academic staff, Univ. of Cardinal Wyszy 1990–; Pres. Nat. Bank of Poland 1992–2000; Chair. Faculty, Solidarity Br. 1989–92; ind. cand. in presidential election 1995; Vice-Pres. EBRD 2001–05; mem. of Sejm (Parl.), Platforma Obywatelska Party 2005–07; Mayor of Warsaw (first female) 2006–18; Prof. Univ. of Warsaw; Dr hc (Marie Curie-Skłodowska Univ., Lublin) 1999; Global Finance magazine Award for Best Chair. of a Cen. Bank 1994, 1997, 1998, 1999, The Central European Award 1995, 1998, Życie Gospodarcze Award 1995, The Warsaw Voice Award 1995. *Publications:* Central Bank from Planned to Market Economy: Legal Aspects 1993, Economic Law (co-author) 1996; over 50 works and articles in econ. and financial journals. *Leisure interests:* American literature, classical music. *Address:* c/o Office of the Mayor, pl. Defilad 1, 00-142 Warsaw, Poland (office).

GROS, François; French biochemist; *Honorary Permanent Secretary, Académie des sciences, Institut de France;* b. 24 April 1925, Paris; s. of Alexandre Gros and Yvonne Haguenauer; m. 1st Françoise Chasseigne (divorced 1963); m. 2nd Danièle Charpentier 1964; three s.; ed Lycée Pasteur, Neuilly, Univs of Toulouse and Paris, Rockefeller Inst., Univ. of Illinois, USA; joined CNRS 1947, Researcher, Lab. Prof. J. Monod 1955, Head of Research 1959–62, Scientific Dir 1962–; Head, Dept, Inst. de Biologie Physico-chimique 1963–69; Prof., Faculté des Sciences de Paris 1968, Inst. Pasteur 1972, Collège de France (Chair in Cellular Biochemistry) 1973–96; Dir Inst. Pasteur 1976–81, Dir of Biochemistry Unit 1981, Hon. Dir 1982–; Adviser to Prime Minister 1981–85; mem. EC's CODEST 1984–90; Pres. Asscn Franco-Israélienne pour la recherche scientifique et tech. 1983, Scientific Council of Asscn Française de lutte contre la myopathie 1987–; Scientific Council of Nat. Agency for Research into AIDS 1989–; Chief Ed. Bulletin de la Société de chimie biologique 1964; mem. Nat. Consultative Cttee on the Ethics of Life and Health Sciences 1990–94; mem. EU Ass. on Science and Tech. 1994–97; mem. Inst. de France 1979–, Perm. Sec. 1991–2000, Hon. Perm. Sec. 2001–; mem. Institut de France, Acad. des Sciences, Acad. of Athens, Indian Nat. Sciences Acad. 1990; Assoc. mem. Acad. Royale de Belgique, Russian Acad. of Sciences, Acad. of Medical Science, UK, American Acad. of Arts and Sciences; Grand Officier, Ordre nat. du Mérite 2013, Grand Officier, Légion d'honneur 2014; several foreign distinctions; Dr hc (Weizmann Inst., Israel); Gold Medal, Pontifical Acad. of Sciences 1964, Fondation Lacassagne Prize 1968, Charles Léopold Mayer Prize, Acad. des Sciences 1969, Alexander von Humboldt Prize 1990, Jawahalral Nehru Medal, Indian Nat. Science Acad. 1999. *Publications:* Initiation à la biochimie (with others); Sciences de la vie et société (with others) 1979, Les secrets du gène 1986, La civilisation du gène 1989, L'ingénierie du vivant 1990, Regard sur la biologie contemporaine 1992, Memoires scientifiques – un demi-siècle de Biologie 2003, Une biologie pour le développement 2009, Les mondes nouveaux de la biologie 2012; over 300 articles in scientific journals (molecular biology, gene regulation, cell differentiation). *Leisure interests:* music, drawing. *Address:* Académie des sciences, Institut de France, 23 quai Conti, 75006 Paris (office); 102 rue de la Tour, 75116 Paris, France (home). *Telephone:* 1-44-41-45-57 (office); 1-45-03-40-91 (home). *Fax:* 1-44-41-43-74 (office). *E-mail:* nathalie.zajdman@academie-sciences.fr (office); francois.gros@academie-sciences.fr (office).

GROS, Philippe, BSc, MSc, PhD, FRSC; Canadian biochemist and academic; *Professor of Biochemistry, Rosalind and Morris Goodman Cancer Centre, McGill University;* ed Univ. of Montréal, McGill Univ.; post-doctoral studies, Harvard Medical School and MIT, USA; James McGill Prof. in Biochemistry, Rosalind and Morris Goodman Cancer Centre, McGill Univ. 2003–10, currently Prof. of Biochemistry, also Prin. Investigator, Life Sciences Complex; Int. Scholar, Howard Hughes Medical Inst.; Scientific Dir Canadian Genetic Diseases Network; f. biotechnology firms Phagetech, RGS Genome, Emerillon Therapeutics; Distinguished Scientist, Canadian Inst. of Health Research; Hon. LLD (St Francis Xavier Univ.); Dr hc (Helsinki); Michael Smith Award of Excellence 1994, Prix Wilder-Penfield 2008, Canada Council for the Arts Killam Prize 2009. *Publications:* more than 300 scientific papers. *Address:* Francesco Bellini Life Sciences Building, 3649 promenade Sir-William-Osler, Montréal, PQ HG3 0B1, Canada (office). *Telephone:* (514) 398-7291 (office). *Fax:* (514) 398-2603 (office). *E-mail:* philippe.gros@mcgill.ca (office). *Website:* www.mcgill.ca/biochemistry/department/faculty/gros (office).

GROS-PIETRO, Gian Maria; Italian economist, academic and business executive; *Chairman, Intesa Sanpaolo SpA;* b. 1942, Turin; Chair. Man. Bd, Intesa Sanpaolo 2013–16, Chair. Bd of Dirs 2016–; also Chair. ASTM SpA; mem. Exec. Cttee, Italian Bankers' Asscn (ABI) (Vice-Pres. 2014–), Inst. for Int. Political Studies, Exec. Bd, Italian Banking, Insurance and Finance Fed. (FeBAF), Employers' Asscn of Turin; Chair. Scientific Cttee, Nomisma; mem. Nat. Council for Economy and Labour for ten years; mem. Bd of Dirs, Edison, Libera Università Internazionale degli Studi Sociali 'Guido Carli' (LUISS Univ.), Head of Dept of Econs and Business 2004–11; Full Prof. of Business Econs first at Turin Univ., then at Luiss Univ. 1974–95; Dir Inst. for Econ. Research on Firms and Growth (CERIS), Italian Nat. Research Council (CNR); Chair. Iri with task of privatizing its subsidiaries 1997–99; Chair. Eni 1999; Chair. Atlantia 2002–10. *Address:* Intesa Sanpaolo SpA, Piazza San Carlo 156, 10121 Turin, Italy (office). *Telephone:* (011) 5551 (office). *Fax:* (011) 5557007 (office). *E-mail:* info@intesasanpaolo.com (office). *Website:* www.group.intesasanpaolo.com (office).

GROSS, David Jonathan, BSc, PhD; American physicist and academic; *Chancellor's Chair Professor of Theoretical Physics, Kavli Institute for Theoretical Physics, University of California, Santa Barbara;* b. 19 Feb. 1941, Washington, DC; s. of Bertram Meyer Gross and Nora Faine Gross; m. Jacquelyn Savani; three d.; ed Hebrew Univ., Jerusalem, Israel, Univ. of California, Berkeley; Visiting Prof., CERN, Geneva, Switzerland 1968–69, 1993; Asst Prof., Princeton Univ. 1969–71, Assoc. Prof. 1971–73, Prof. 1973–86, Eugene Higgins Prof. of Physics 1986–95, Jones Prof. of Physics 1995–97, Jones Prof. of Physics Emer. 1997–; Visiting Prof. Ecole Normale Supérieure, Paris, France 1983, 1988–89, Hebrew Univ., Jerusalem, Israel 1984, Lawrence Radiation Lab., Berkeley, Calif. 1992; Dir Kavli Inst. for Theoretical Physics, Univ. of Calif., Santa Barbara 1997, also Prof. 1997–, Frederick W. Gluck Prof. of Theoretical Physics 2001–, Chancellor's Chair. Prof. of Theoretical Physics, Kavli Inst. for Theoretical Physics 2013–; Rothschild Prof., Univ. of Cambridge, UK 2007; Dir Jerusalem Winter School 1999–; Assoc. Ed. Nuclear Physics 1972–; mem. Advisory Bd Inst. for Theoretical Physics 1983–87 (Chair. 1986); Chair. Solvay Scientific Cttee for Physics 2006–; mem. numerous review cttees; Fellow, Alfred P. Sloan Foundation 1970–74, American Physical Soc. 1974–, American Acad. of Arts and Sciences 1985–, NAS 1986–, AAAS 1987–, Indian Acad. of Science 2007–, Indian Nat. Science Acad. 2007–, Third World Acad. of Sciences 2007–; Hon. PhD (Univ. of Montpellier) 2000,

(Hebrew Univ., Jerusalem) 2001, (São Paulo Univ.) 2006, (Ohio State Univ.) 2007, (Univ. of the Philippines) 2008, (De La Salle Univ., Manila) 2008; American Physical Soc. J. J. Sakurai Prize 1986, MacArthur Foundation Fellowship Prize 1987, Dirac Medal 1988, Technion-Israel Inst. of Tech. Harvey Prize 2000, European Physical Soc. High Energy and Particle Physics Prize 2003, Grande Médaille d'Or (France) 2004, Nobel Prize in Physics (co-recipient) 2004. *Publications include:* numerous articles in professional journals. *Address:* Kavli Institute for Theoretical Physics, University of California, Santa Barbara, Kohn Hall, 1219, Santa Barbara, CA 93106-4030, USA (office). *Telephone:* (805) 893-7337 (office). *Fax:* (805) 893-2431 (office). *E-mail:* gross@kitp.ucsb.edu (office). *Website:* www.physics.ucsb.edu (office); www.kitp.ucsb.edu (office).

GROSS, Mark, BA, PhD, FRS; American mathematician and academic; *Professor of Pure Mathematics, University of Cambridge;* b. 30 Nov. 1965, Ithaca, New York; s. of Leonard Gross and Grazyna Gross; m. Rachel Engler; ed Cornell Univ., Univ. of California, Berkeley; NSF-NATO Postdoctoral Fellow, Université de Paris VI, Spring and Summer 1991, Summer 1992; Asst Prof., Univ. of Michigan 1990–93; Postdoctoral Fellow, Math. Sciences Research Inst., Berkeley, Calif. 1992–93, Simons Visiting Prof. Autumn 2009; Tenure-track Asst Prof., Cornell Univ. Autumn 1993, Assoc. Prof. with tenure, Cornell Univ. 1997–; Visiting Scholar, Trinity Coll., Cambridge Summer 1996, Visiting Fellow in Common Autumn 1998; Lecturer, Univ. of Warwick 1998, Sr Lecturer 1999–2001, Reader 2001–02, Prof. 2002–03; Full Prof., Univ. of California, San Diego 2001–13; Sr Researcher, Univ. of Cambridge April–June 2002, Prof. of Pure Math. 2013–; Clay Research Award, Clay Math. Inst. (co-recipient) 2016. *Publications:* more than 50 papers in professional journals. *Address:* Room E1.08, Department of Pure Mathematics and Mathematical Statistics, Centre for Mathematical Sciences, University of Cambridge, Wilberforce Road, Cambridge, CB3 0WB, England (office). *Telephone:* (1223) 337925 (office). *E-mail:* m.gross@dpmms.cam.ac.uk (office). *Website:* www.dpmms.cam.ac.uk (office).

GROSS, William (Bill) H., MBA; American investment company executive; *Chief Investment Officer, Pacific Investment Management Company (PIMCO);* b. 1944, Middletown, Ohio; ed Duke Univ., Univ. of California, Los Angeles; served in USN; briefly played blackjack professionally in Las Vegas; Co-founder Pacific Investment Management (PIMCO), Newport Beach, Calif. 1971, currently Chief Investment Officer managing PIMCO's Total Return Fund and several smaller funds. *Achievements include:* prominent philatelist, became third person (after Robert Zoellner in 1990s and Benjamin K. Miller pre-1925) to form complete collection of 19th-century US postage stamps Nov. 2005; auctioned British, Scandinavian and Finnish philatelic collections to make various charitable donations 2005–08. *Publications:* Everything You've Heard About Investing Is Wrong! 1997, Bill Gross on Investing 1998. *Address:* Pacific Investment Management Company, LLC, 840 Newport Center Drive, Suite 100, Newport Beach, CA 92660, USA (office). *Telephone:* (949) 720-6000 (office). *Fax:* (949) 720-1376 (office). *E-mail:* presscenter@pimco.com (office). *Website:* www.pimco.com (office).

GROSSART, Sir Angus McFarlane McLeod, Kt, CBE, LLD, DLitt, D.L., FRSE; British merchant banker, lawyer and company director; *Chairman, Noble Grossart Ltd;* b. 6 April 1937; s. of William John White Grossart and Mary Hay Gardiner; m. Gay Thomson 1978; one d.; ed Glasgow Acad. and Gasgow Univ.; mem. Faculty of Advocates 1963; practised at Scottish Bar 1963–69; Chair. Noble Grossart Ltd Merchant Bankers, Edin. 1969–, Chair. 1990–; Chair. Scottish Investment Trust PLC 1975–2003; mem. Bd of Dirs of numerous cos including Royal Bank of Scotland PLC 1982– (Vice-Chair. 1996–), Scottish and Newcastle 1998–, Trinity Mirror PLC 1998–; Chair. Bd of Trustees Nat. Galleries of Scotland 1988–97; Deputy Chair. and Trustee Nat. Heritage Memorial Fund 1999–2005; Chair. Nat. Museum of Scotland 2006–12; Chair. Burrell Renaissance 2013–, and other public and charitable appointments; Hon. QC 2011; Hon. LLD (Glasgow) 1985, (Aberdeen) 2006, Hon. DBA (Strathclyde) 1998, Hon. DLitt (St Andrews) 2004; Livingstone Captain of Industry Award 1990, Lord Provost of Glasgow Award for public service 1994, Paolozzi Gold Medal 1997, Walpole Medal of Excellence 2003, Nat. Museum of Scotland Gold Medal. *Leisure interests:* golf, the applied and decorative arts, Scottish castle restoration. *Address:* Noble Grossart Ltd, 48 Queen Street, Edinburgh, EH2 3NR, Scotland (office). *Telephone:* (131) 226-7011 (office). *Fax:* (131) 226-6032 (office). *E-mail:* fionacairns@noblegrossart.co.uk (office).

GROSSER, Alfred; French academic, writer and journalist; *Professor Emeritus, Institut d'études politiques;* b. 1 Feb. 1925, Frankfurt, Germany; s. of Paul Grosser and Lily Grosser (née Rosenthal); m. Anne-Marie Jourcin 1959; four s.; ed Univs of Aix en Provence and Paris; Asst Dir UNESCO Office in Germany 1950–51; Asst Prof., Univ. of Paris 1951–55; Lecturer, later Prof., Inst. d'études politiques, Paris 1954, Prof. Emer. 1992–; Dir Studies and Research, Fondation nat. des Sciences politiques 1956–92; with Ecole des hautes études commerciales 1961–66, 1986–88, with Ecole Polytechnique 1974–95; Visiting Prof., Bologna Center, Johns Hopkins Univ. 1955–69, Stanford Univ. 1964–67; political columnist, La Croix 1955–65, 1984–, Le Monde 1965–94, Ouest-France 1973–, L'Expansion 1979–89; Pres. Centre d'information et de recherche sur l'Allemagne contemporaine 1982–, Eurocréation 1986–92 (Hon. Pres. 1992–); Vice-Pres. Int. Political Science Asscn 1970–73; mem. Bd L'Express 1998–2003; Grosses Verdienstkreuz mit Stern 1995 und Schulterband 2003; Grand Officier, Légion d'honneur 2001; Grand Croix, Ordre nat. du Mérite 2013; Dr hc (Univ. of Aston, UK) 2001, (European Univ. of Humanities, Belarus) 2001; Peace Prize, Union of German Publrs 1975, Grand Prix, Acad. des Sciences Morales et Politiques 1998, Prize "für das Lebenswerk", German newspapers asscn 2013. *Publications include:* L'Allemagne de l'Occident 1953, La démocratie de Bonn 1958, Hitler, la presse et la naissance d'une dictature 1959, La Quatrième République et sa politique extérieure 1961, La politique extérieure de la Ve République 1965, Au nom de quoi? Fondements d'une morale politique 1969, L'Allemagne de notre temps 1970, les Occidentaux: Les pays d'Europe et les Etats Unis depuis la guerre 1978, Affaires extérieures: la politique de la France 1944–84, 1984 (updated 1989), L'Allemagne en Occident 1985, Mit Deutschen streiten 1987, Vernunft und Gewalt. Die französische Revolution und das deutsche Grundgesetz heute 1989, Le crime et la mémoire 1989 (revised 1991), Mein Deutschland 1993, Les identités difficiles 1996, Une Vie de Français (memoirs) 1997, Deutschland in Europa 1998, Les fruits de leur arbre: regard athée sur les Chrétiens 2001, L'Allemagne de Berlin 2002, La France, semblable et différente 2005, Die Früchte ihres Baumes 2005, La Joie et la Mort – Bilan d'une vie 2011, Die Freude und der Tod. Eine Lebensbilanz 2011. *Leisure interest:* music. *Address:* 8 rue Dupleix, 75015 Paris, France (home). *Telephone:* 1-43-06-41-82 (home). *E-mail:* grosser.alfred@wanadoo.fr.

GROSSMAN, David, BA; Israeli writer; b. 25 Jan. 1954, Jerusalem; m. Michal Grossman; two s. (one deceased) one d.; ed Hebrew Univ., Jerusalem; Chevalier, Ordre des Artes et Lettres; Dr hc (KU Leuven) 2007; Children's Literature Prize, Ministry of Educ. 1983, Prime Minister's Hebrew Literature Prize 1984, Israeli Publishers' Asscn Prize for Best Novel 1985, Vallombrosa Prize (Italy) 1989, Nelly Sachs Prize (Germany) 1992, Prix Eliette von Karajan (Austria), Premio Grinzane (Italy), Premio Mondelo (Italy), Vittorio de Sica Prize (Italy), Marsh Award for Children's Literature in Translation (UK), Juliet Club Prize (Italy), Buxtehuder Bulle (Germany), Sapir Prize (Israel), Italian Critics Prize (Italy), Nelly Sachs Prize (Germany), Mane Sperber Prize (Austria), Bernstein Prize (Israel), Bialik Prize (Israel), Emet Prize (Israel) 2007, Friedenspreis des Deutschen Buchhandels (Germany) 2010, Prix Medicis (France) 2011, St Louis Literary Award 2015, Israel Prize for Hebrew Literature and Poetry 2018. *Publications:* Hiyukh ha-gedi (trans. as The Smile of the Lamb) 1983, 'Ayen 'erekh-ahavah (trans. as See Under: Love) 1986, Ha-Zeman ha-tsahov (non-fiction, trans. as The Yellow Wind) 1987, Gan Riki: Mahazeh bi-shete ma'arakhot (play, trans. as Rikki's Kindergarten) 1988, Sefer hakikduk hapnimi (trans. as The Book of Intimate Grammar) 1991, Hanochachim hanifkadim (non-fiction, trans. as Sleeping on a Wire: Conversations with Palestinians in Israel) 1992, The Zigzag Kid (in trans.) (Premio Mondelo, Premio Grinzane), Duel (in trans.), Be My Knife (in trans.) 2002, Someone to Run With (in trans.) 2003, Death as a Way of Life: Dispatches from Jerusalem (non-fiction, in trans.) 2003, Her Body Knows (novel, in trans.), Lovers and Strangers (novel, in trans.) 2005, Dvash Arayiot (trans. as Lion's Honey: The Myth of Samson) 2005, Writing in the Dark (essays in trans.) 2009, To the End of the Land (novel, in trans.) (Jewish Quarterly-Wingate Literary Prize 2011) 2010, Falling Out of Time (memoir) 2014, A Horse Walks into a Bar (Man Booker International Prize 2017) 2017; also short stories, children's books, contribs to periodicals. *Address:* c/o Deborah Harris Agency, PO Box 8528, Jerusalem 91083, Israel (office). *E-mail:* deborah@thedeborahharrisagency.com (office).

GROSSMAN, Marc, BA, MSc; American diplomatist, government official and business executive; *Vice-Chairman, Cohen Group;* b. Los Angeles, Calif.; ed Univ. of California, Santa Barbara, London School of Econs, UK; joined US Foreign Service 1976, overseas assignments included Political Officer, Mission to NATO, Brussels, Embassy in Budapest, various positions at Bureau of Near Eastern and South Asian Affairs, Dept of State; fmr Deputy Special Adviser to Pres. Carter; Deputy Dir of Pvt. Office of Sec.-Gen. of NATO Lord Carrington 1984–86; Exec. Asst to Deputy Sec. of State John C. Whitehead 1986–89; Prin. Deputy Asst Sec. of State for Political and Mil. Affairs 1989–93; Special Asst to Sec. of State and Exec. Sec. Dept of State 1993–94; Amb. to Turkey 1994–97; Asst Sec. of State for European Affairs 1997–2000; Dir-Gen. of Foreign Service and Dir of Human Resources 2000–01; Under-Sec. of State for Political Affairs 2001–05 (retd); Vice-Chair. The Cohen Group, Washington, DC 2005–11, 2013–; Special US Rep. for Afghanistan and Pakistan 2011–12. *Address:* The Cohen Group, 500 Eighth Street, NW, Suite 200, Washington, DC 20004, USA (office). *Telephone:* (202) 863-7248 (office). *Fax:* (202) 863-7809 (office). *E-mail:* mgrossman@cohengroup.net (office). *Website:* www.cohengroup.net (office).

GROSSMAN, Mindy F.; American business executive; m.; one d.; ed George Washington Univ.; began career in menswear industry 1977; Vice-Pres. of Sales and Merchandising, Tommy Hilfiger Corpn 1987–91, Sr Vice-Pres. of Menswear, Warnaco Inc. 1991–94, Vice-Pres. of New Business, Polo Ralph Lauren Corpn 1994–95, Pres. and CEO Polo Jeans Co. 1995–2000; Vice-Pres. and Head of Global Apparel Business, Nike Inc. 2000–06; CEO of Retailing Div., IAC 2006–08, mem. Bd of Dirs and CEO HSN Inc. (fmrly IAC Retailing) 2008–17; mem. Bd of Dirs Nat. Retail Fed., East Harlem School; Chair. Exec. Women in Fashion Advisory Bd, Fashion Inst. of Tech.; mem. Advisory Bd, J. Baker School of Retail at the Wharton School of Business; Ellis Island Medal of Honor 2017.

GROSSMANN, Jürgen R., MSc, Dr-Ing; German business executive; b. 4 March 1952, Mülheim an der Ruhr; m. Dagmar Grossmann Sikorski 1985; three c.; ed Tech. Univs of Clausthal and Berlin, Univ. of Göttingen, Univ. of Freiburg, Purdue Univ., USA; held various man. positions at Klöckner-Werke AG Group 1980–93, mem. Exec. Bd 1991–93; Owner, Man. Dir, Georgsmarienhütte GmbH 1993–97, Owner and Man. Dir Georgsmarienhütte Holding GmbH 1997–2006, Owner 2007–; Pres. and CEO RWE AG 2007–12; Chair. Supervisory Bd SURTECO AG; mem. Supervisory Bd British American Tobacco (Industrie) GmbH, British American Tobacco (Germany) GmbH, Deutsche Bahn AG, Hanover Acceptances Ltd, JPMorgan Chase Council; Bundesverdienstkreuz 1. Klasse; Dr hc (Purdue Univ., USA); Courage Award 1997, Prize of Lower Saxony 2001, Vernon A. Walter Award 2007. *Address:* Georgsmarienhütte Holding GmbH, Elbchaussee 189, 22605 Hamburg, Germany (office). *E-mail:* juergen.grossmann@gmh-holding.de (office). *Website:* www.gmh-gruppe.de (office).

GROTJAHN, Mark, BFA, MFA; American artist; b. 1968, Pasadena, California; s. of Michael Grotjahn; ed Univ. of Colorado, Univ. of Calif.; Artist in Residence, Skowhegan School of Painting and Sculpture 1995; Visiting Scholar, Calif. Coll. of the Arts, San Francisco 2011–12; ran a gallery called Room 702 in Hollywood 1996–98; full-time artist 1998–; Trustee, Museum of Contemporary Art, Los Angeles 2014; Honoree, Dallas Museum of Art TWO x TWO for AIDS and Art 2011; Penny McCall Foundation Award 2003. *Address:* c/o Anton Kern Gallery, 16 E 55th Street, New York, NY 10022, USA. *Telephone:* (212) 367-9663. *Fax:* (212) 367-8135. *Website:* www.antonkerngallery.com.

GROYS, Boris Efimovich, PhD; Russian art critic, philosopher and academic; *Professor of Russian and Slavic Studies, New York University;* b. 19 March 1947, Berlin, Germany; ed high school in Leningrad, Univ. of Leningrad, Univ. of Münster, Germany; worked as research fellow at various scientific insts in Leningrad from 1971; Research Fellow, Inst. of Structural and Applied Linguistics, Univ. of Moscow 1976–81; participated in unofficial cultural scenes of Moscow and Leningrad, publishing in '37', 'Chasy' and other samizdat magazines; published essay 'Moscow Romantic Conceptualism' in art magazine A-YA in which he coined the term 'Moscow Conceptualism' 1979; emigrated to FRG to pursue various scholarships 1981; currently Prof. of Russian and Slavic Studies, New York Univ.; Sr Research Fellow, Acad. of Design, Karlsruhe, Germany; Prof. of Aesthetics, Art History and Media Theory, Acad. of Design/Centre for Art and Media Tech. (HfG/ZKM), Karlsruhe; Visiting Prof. at several univs in USA and Europe, including Univ. of Pennsylvania and Univ. of Southern California; mem. Asscn Internationale des Critiques d'Art; fmr Fellow, Internationales Forschungszentrum Kulturwissenschaften, Harvard Univ. Art Museum, Univ. of Pittsburg; Rector Acad. of Fine Arts, Vienna 2001; headed research programme Post-Communist Condition, in co-operation with Univ. of Karlsruhe and Fed. Cultural Foundation of Germany 2003–04; Andrei Belyi Prize, Frank Jewett Mather Award for Art Criticism from the College Art Asscn 2009. *Publications include:* The Total Art of Stalinism 1992, Dream Factory Communism 2004, Ilya Kabakov: The Man Who Flew into Space from His Apartment 2006, The Total Enlightenment: Conceptual Art in Moscow 1960–1990 2008, Art Power 2008, Wait to Wait – A Conversation (with Andro Wekua) 2009, Going Public 2010, History Becomes Form: Moscow Conceptualism 2010, The Communist Postscript 2010, Introduction to Antiphilosophy 2012; video: Thinking in Loop: Three Videos on Iconoclasm, Ritual and Immortality 2008; more than 150 articles in several languages on modern and contemporary art and Russian art and intellectual history. *Address:* Department of Art History, New York University, 100 Washington Square East, Silver 303, New York, NY 10003, USA (office). *Telephone:* (212) 998-8180 (office). *E-mail:* groys@aol.com (office). *Website:* arthistory.as.nyu.edu/object/borisgroys .html (office); www.borisgroys.com.

GRUBBS, Robert H., PhD, FRSC; American chemist and academic; *Victor and Elizabeth Atkins Professor of Chemistry, California Institute of Technology;* b. 27 Feb. 1942, nr Possum Trot, Ky; s. of Henry Howard Grubbs and Faye Atwood; m. Helen O'Kane Grubbs; three c.; ed Univ. of Florida, Columbia Univ.; Faculty Fellow, Columbia Univ. 1965–66, NIH Trainee 1966–68; NIH Postdoctoral Fellow, Stanford Univ. 1968–69; Asst Prof., Michigan State Univ. 1969–73, Assoc. Prof. 1973–78; Prof. of Chem., Calif. Inst. of Tech. 1978–90, Victor and Elizabeth Atkins Prof. of Chem. 1990–; Christensen Visiting Fellow, St Catherine's Coll., Oxford, UK 1997, Rayson Huany Visiting Lectureship in Chem., Hong Kong 2001; Tarrant Visiting Prof. of Organic Chem., Univ. of Florida 2004; Scientific Advisor, Wyatt Technology Corpn, Materia, Inc.; mem. Advisory Bd, Center on Polymer Interfaces and Macromolecular Assemblies 1999–2000, Advanced Synthesis and Catalysis 2000–; Advisory Ed. Journal of Polymer Science, Polymer Chemistry 1999–; mem. Editorial Advisory Bd Catalysis Technology 1996–, Accounts of Chemical Research 2000–; mem. ACS 1964–, NAS 1989–, Nat. Acad. of Eng 2015–; Fellow, American Acad. of Arts and Sciences 1994; mem. Alexander von Humbolt Asscn of America 1999–2000; Hon. MRIA (Science Section) 1999; Hon. Prof., Shanghai Inst. of Organic Chem., Chinese Acad. of Sciences 2001; Alfred P. Sloan Fellow 1974–76, Alexander von Humbolt Fellowship 1975, Camille and Henry Dreyfus Teacher-Scholar Award 1975–78, ACS Nat. Award in Organometallic Chem. 1988, Arthur C. Cope Scholar Award 1990, George Willard Wheland Award, Univ. of Chicago 1992, ACS Award in Polymer Chem., Mobil Chemical Co. 1995, Nagoya Medal of Organic Chem. 1997, Fluka Prize – Reagent of the Year 1998, Mack Memorial Award, Ohio State Univ. 1999, Benjamin Franklin Medal in Chem., Franklin Inst. 2000, Herman F. Mark Polymer Chem. Award, ACS POLY-Dow Chemical Co. Foundation 2000, Cliff S. Hamilton Award, Univ. of Nebraska, Lincoln 2000, Herbert C. Brown Award for Creative Research in Synthetic Methods, ACS-Aldrich Chemical Co. and Purdue Borane Research Fund 2001, Prelog Lecturer, ETH, Zürich 2001, Werner E. Bachmann Memorial Lecturer, Univ. of Michigan 2002, Edward Frankland Prize and Lecturer, Royal Soc. of Chem. 2002, Arthur C. Cope Award, ACS Div. of Organic Chem. 2002, ACS Award for Creative Research in Homogenous or Heterogeneous Catalysis, Shell Oil Foundation 2003, Richard C. Tolman Medal, Southern Calif. Section of ACS 2003, Pauling Award Medal, Oregon, Portland, Puget Sound Sections of ACS 2003, ACS Tetrahedron Prize for Creativity in Organic Chem. 2003, Priestly Lecturer, Pennsylvania State Univ. 2003, Ralph Hirschmann Lecturer, Univ. of Wisconsin 2003, Linus Pauling Distinguished Lecturer, Oregon State Univ. 2003, Gilman Lecturer, Iowa State Univ. 2003, Karabatsos Lecturer, Michigan State Univ. 2003, Bristol-Myers Squibb Distinguished Achievement Award in Organic Synthesis 2004, Nobel Prize for Chem. (jtly) 2005, Paul Karrer Gold Medal, Kuratorium der Stiftung für die Paul Karrer-Vorlesung, Univ. of Zurich 2005, August-Wilhelm-von-Hofmann-Denkmünze, German Chemical Soc. 2005, American Inst. of Chemists Gold Medal 2010. *Publications include:* more than 350 publs in scientific journals on design, synthesis and mechanistic studies of complexes that catalyse useful organic transformations. *Address:* Division of Chemistry and Chemical Engineering, California Institute of Technology, 1200 East California Blvd, Pasadena, CA 91125, USA (office). *Telephone:* (626) 395-6003 (office). *Fax:* (626) 564-9297 (office). *E-mail:* rhg@caltech.edu (office). *Website:* www.cce.caltech.edu (office).

GRUBE, Rüdiger, BEng, DSci; German business executive; *Chairman of the Management Board and CEO, Deutsche Bahn AG;* b. 2 Aug. 1951, Hamburg; m. 1st; one s. one d.; m. 2nd Cornelia Poletto 2015; ed Hamburg Univ.; teaching post, Production and Eng. Dept, Univ. of Hamburg 1981–86; joined MMB (Messerschmitt-Bölkow-Blohm) GmbH (later Daimler-Benz Aerospace, DASA), Munich 1989, Head of Marketing, Sales and Int. Relations, Energy and Industrial Tech. Div. 1989–90, Head of Man. Office, Deutsche Airbus GmbH, Hamburg 1990–92, Head of Munich-Ottobrunn site, Daimler-Benz Aerospace AG, Munich 1992–94, Head of Aviation Staff Unit 1994–95, Dir of Corp. Planning and Tech., Deutsche Aerospace AG, Munich 1995, Sr Vice-Pres. and Head of Corp. Strategy, Daimler-Benz AG (later DaimlerChrysler AG) 1996–2000, mem. Man. Bd, responsible for corp. devt and all NE Asia activities and for group's entire global IT operations 2001–09, Sr Vice-Pres. for Corp. Devt 2000–09, also Chair. Supervisory Bd DaimlerChrysler Off-Highway GmbH, Chair. DaimlerChrysler China Ltd, Beijing, Vice-Chair. Beijing Benz DaimlerChrysler Automotive (BBDC-A), mem. Advisory Bd DaimlerChrysler Fleetboard, DaimlerChrysler Aviation, mem. Supervisory Bd DaimlerChrysler Financial Services AG; Chair. (non-exec.) European Aeronautic Defence and Space Co. (EADS) NV 2004–09, also Chair. EADS Participations BV; Chair. Man. Bd and CEO Deutsche Bahn AG 2009–, concurrently Chair. Man. Bd DB Mobility Logistics AG; fmr Chair. Supervisory Bd MTU Friedrichshafen GmbH (now Tognum AG); mem. Bd of Dirs McLaren Group Ltd; mem. Supervisory Bd Hamburg Port Authority (HPA GmbH); fmr mem. Admin. Bd Hyundai Motor Co., Seoul, S Korea, Mitsubishi Motors Corpn, Tokyo, Japan. *Address:* Deutsche Bahn AG, Potsdamer Platz 2, 10785 Berlin, Germany (office). *Telephone:* (30) 297-61131 (office). *Fax:* (30) 297-61919 (office). *E-mail:* info@deutschebahn.com (office). *Website:* www.deutschebahn.com (office); www.bahn.de (office).

GRUBEŠA, Josip, DrSc; Bosnia and Herzegovina academic and politician; *Minister of Justice;* b. 4 Nov. 1978, Prozor-Rama, Socialist Repub. of Bosnia and Herzegovina, Socialist Fed. Repub. of Yugoslavia; m.; three c.; ed Archbishop Classical Gymnasium, Zadar, Croatia, SFR Yugoslavia, Faculty of Arts, Univ. of Split, Croatia, SFR Yugoslavia, Univ. of Mostar; employed in Faculty of Philosophy, Univ. of Mostar 2003, Visiting Prof. of Medicine, Faculty of Law 2010–; mem. Presidency of Hrvatska Demokratska Zajednica Bosne i Hercegovine (Croatian Democratic Union of Bosnia and Herzegovina) 2011–; Minister of Justice 2015–. *Address:* Ministry of Justice, 71000 Sarajevo, trg Bosne i Hercegovine 1, Bosnia and Herzegovina (office). *Telephone:* (33) 223501 (office); (33) 223502 (office). *Fax:* (33) 223504 (office). *E-mail:* info@mpr.gov.ba (office). *Website:* www.mpr.gov.ba (office).

GRUBISICH, José Carlos, BEng, MBA; Brazilian business executive; *CEO and President, Eldorado Brasil Celulose e Papel;* b. 1957; m.; two s.; ed Escola Superior de Química Osvaldo Cruz, INSEAD, France; various man., marketing and advertising roles with Grupo Rhône Poulenc, Brazil and other countries, including Pres. Rhodia Brazil and Latin America 1997–2000, mem. Exec. Cttee and Global Vice Pres. 2000–02; Pres. Grupo Odebrecht 2002; CEO Braskem SA (fmrly Copene Petroquímica do Nordeste SA) 2002–08, ETH Bioenergia SA 2008–12; Pres. and CEO Eldorado Brasil Celulose e Papel 2012–; mem. Supervisory Bd Vallourec SA 2012–; mem. Bd of Dirs UNICA Brazilian Sugarcane Industry Asscn. *Address:* Eldorado Brasil Celulose e Papel, Av., Faria Lima, 2601, 01451-001 São Paulo, Brazil (office). *Telephone:* 3643-2700 (office). *Fax:* 3643-2843 (office). *Website:* www .eldoradobrasil.com.br (office).

GRUBJEŠIĆ, Suzana; Serbian politician; b. 29 Jan. 1963, Sombor; ed Faculty of Political Sciences, Belgrade; Project Man., European Movt in Serbia 1996–97; Co-founder and Project Man. G17 Plus 1997–2003, Exec. Dir G17 Plus 2003–08, Vice-Pres. and Whip 2007–; mem. (G17 Plus) Serbian Parl. 2003–12, mem. Admin. Cttee and Cttee for European Integration, Head of Serbian Del. to Parl. Ass. of OSCE, Deputy Whip of Parl. Group United Regions of Serbia 2011–12; Deputy Prime Minister, responsible for European Integration 2012–13. *Address:* c/o Office of the Prime Minister, 11000 Belgrade, Nemanjina 11, Serbia. *E-mail:* kabinetpremijera@gov.rs.

GRUDININ, Pavel Nikolayevich; Russian engineer, farm director and politician; *Chairman, Council of Deputies, Vidnoye Municipality;* b. 20 Oct. 1960, Moscow, Russian SFSR, USSR; s. of Nikolai Konstantinovich Grudinin and Serafima Zinoviyevna Grudinina (née Pishchik); m. Irina Igorevna Grudinina; two s.; ed Moscow State Agroengineering Univ., Russian Acad. of Public Admin; began career as head of mechanical workshop, Lenin State Farm (co-operative) 1982–89, Deputy Dir 1990–95; Gen. Dir, ZAO Lenin State Farm Co. (newly-formed private co.) 1995–; Deputy, Moscow Oblast Duma (legis. ass.) 1997–2011; Chair., Council of Deputies, Vidnoye Municipality 2017–; selected by Kommunisticheskaya Partiya Rossiiskoi Federatsii (KPRF—Communist Party of the Russian Fed.) as cand. in presidential election 2018; mem. Yedinaya Rossiya (United Russia) –2010; Honoured Worker of Agric. of the Russian Fed. 2001; 850th Anniversary of Moscow Commemorative Medal. *Address:* Council of Deputies, 142700 Moscow Oblast, Leninskii Municipal District, Vidnoye, ul. Lemeshko, 15, Russia (office). *Telephone:* (498) 547-34-29 (office). *Fax:* (498) 547-34-29. *E-mail:* vidnoe-sd@yandex.ru (office). *Website:* www.vidnoe-adm.ru (office).

GRUDZIŃSKI, Przemysław, PhD; Polish diplomatist, academic and writer; b. 30 Oct. 1950, Toruń; s. of Prof. Tadeusz Grudziński; m.; two d.; ed Univ. of Nicolaus Copernicus, Toruń, Inst. of History, Polish Acad. of Sciences, Warsaw; Lecturer then Reader, Inst. of History, Polish Acad. of Sciences 1976–96; Adviser to Deputy Minister of Nat. Defence 1990; Dir Bureau of Research and Dir-Gen. Sejm (Parl.) 1991–92; Deputy Minister of Nat. Defence 1992–93; Prof., Marshall European Centre for Security Studies, Garmisch, Germany 1994–97, Coll. of Int. and Security Studies 2005–08; Under-Sec. of State, Ministry of Foreign Affairs 1997–2000, 2008–09; Amb. to USA 2000–05, to Finland 2015–17; Perm. Rep. to OSCE, Vienna 2009–14; mem. Solidarity Movt 1980s; Founder-mem. Euro-Atlantic Asscn 1994, Council on Foreign Policy, Warsaw 1996; Fellow, American Council of Learned Socs 1978–80; Fulbright Fellow, Princeton Univ. 1988, Visiting Fellow 1978–80, 1988; Visiting Fellow, Univ. of Southern California, UCLA 1989. *Publications include:* The Future of Europe in the Ideas of Franklin D. Roosevelt 1933–1945 1987, Scientists and Barbarians: The Nuclear Policy of the United States 1939–45 1987, Theology of the Bomb: The Origins of Nuclear Deterrence Vols 1–3 1988, A Critical Approach to European Security: Identity and Institutions 1999, Państwo inteligentne. Polska w poszukiwaniu międzynarodowej roli 2008; numerous articles in professional journals. *Leisure interests:* walking, mountains.

GRUEVSKI, Nikola, BEcons, MSc; Macedonian lawyer, economist and politician; b. 31 Aug. 1970, Skopje, Socialist Repub. of Macedonia, Socialist Fed. Repub. of Yugoslavia; s. of Talo Gruevski and Nadezda Gruevski; m. Borkica Gruevska; two d.; ed SS Cyril and Methodius Univ., Skopje, St Clement Ohrid Univ., Bitola; with Credit Dept, Foreign Dept, then Currency Dealing, Balkanska Banka Skopje 1994–98, Liquidity, Plan, Analyses and Securities Dept 1995–96; with Metal Bank, Frankfurt, Germany 1996–97, MG Finance PLC, London, UK 1997, Flemings Private Asset Man. Ltd, London 1997–98; Minister without Portfolio, then Minister of Trade 1998–99; Minister of Finance 1999–2002; Pres. Econ. Council 2000–02; mem. Macedonian Parl. 2002–06; Adviser, Ministry of Finance, Serbia 2003; mem. Vnatrešno-Makedonska Revolucionerna Organizacija–Demokratska Partija za Makedonsko Nacionalno Edinstvo (Internal Macedonian Revolutionary Org.–Democratic Party for Macedonian Nat. Unity), Pres. 2003–17; Prime Minister of Macedonia 2006–16; Vice-Pres. Euro-Atlantic Council of the Repub. of Macedonia 2005–06; Pres. Broker's Asscn of Macedonia 1998, State Securities and Exchange Comm. 2000–02, Parl. Cttee for Co-operation with European Parl. 2002–04; financial affairs commentator, MTM TV, Skopje 1998; sentenced to two years' imprisonment (subject to appeal) for abuse of power May 2018; fled to Hungary and granted political asylum; Order St Nicholas, Štip 2014, Order of the Baptist (Preteca), St Jovan Bigorski Monastery 2015; Vienna Econ. Forum Award 2011. *Publications:* The Macedonian Economy at a Crossroads: On the Way to a

Healthier Economy 1998, The Way Out: Foreign Direct Investment, Economic Development and Employment 2007; numerous articles on econ. and political issues. *Leisure interests:* boxing, basketball, football, fitness, reading.

GRUNBERG, Arnon; Dutch writer; b. (Arnon Yasha Yves), 22 Feb. 1971, Amsterdam; ed Vossius Gymnasium; f. publishing company Kasimir at age 19; columnist, Volkskrant (daily newspaper), Belgian magazine Humo (The Mailbox of Arnon Grunberg), VPRO Gids magazine, Vrij Nederland magazine (Grunberg Helps), Wordt Vervolgd; writes reports, book reviews and essays for Dutch newspaper NRC Handelsblad; contrib. of essays and stories in literary magazine Hollands Maandblad; Hon. Fellow, Univ. of Amsterdam 2015; German NRW Literature Prize 2002, Constantijn Huygens Prize 2009, Frans Kellendonk Prize 2010. *Television:* anchor, RAM 2004–05. *Films include:* de Kut van Maria 1989. *Publications include:* Blauwe Maandagen (novel, trans. as Blue Mondays) (Anton Wachter-prijs) 1994, Figuranten 1997, De troost van de slapstick (essays) 1998, Het veertiende kippetje 1998, Liefde is business 1999, Fantoompijn (novel, trans. as Phantom Pain) (AKO-Literatuurprijs 2000) 2000, The Asylum Seeker (Bordewijk Prize 2004, AKO-Literatuurprijs 2004) 2003, Grunberg The Bible 2005, Tirza (Libris Prize 2007, Golden Owl 2007, Flemish KANTL Prize 2011) 2006, Amuse-Bouche (short stories, in trans.) 2008, Onze oom 2008, Huid en Haar 2010, De man zonder ziekte 2012, Buster Keaton lacht nooit (essays) 2013, Apocalypse (short stories) 2013, Het bestand (novella) 2015. *Address:* c/o Arnon Grunberg Agency, Singel 262, Amsterdam, Netherlands. *E-mail:* info@arnongrunberg.com. *Website:* www.arnongrunberg.com.

GRUNDHOFER, Jerry A.; American banker; b. 1944, Glendale, Calif.; m.; ed Loyola Marymount Univ.; began banking career in southern Calif. 1967; Dir, Pres. and CEO Security Pacific Nat. Bank 1992, also Dir Security Pacific Corpn; Vice-Chair. and Dir BankAmerica Corpn –1993; joined Star Banc Corpn 1993, becoming Chair., Pres. and CEO –1998; CEO Firstar Corpn 1998–2001, Pres. and CEO US Bancorp (following acquisition of Firstar) 2001–06, also Chair. 2003–07, Chair. Emer. 2007–; Chair. Citibank NA, New York 2009–11, mem. Bd of Dirs Citigroup Inc. (parent) 2009–11; Chair. Santander Holdings USA, Inc. 2011–14, Sovereign Bank 2011–14; fmr mem. Bd of Dirs Ecolab Inc., Bank of America NT&SA, Lehman Brothers Inc., The Midland Co.; Forbes Magazine Banker of the Year 1998, American Banker Magazine Banker of the Year 2000, American Banker's Lifetime Achievement Award 2008.

GRUNSFELD, John M., BSc, MSc, PhD; American scientist and fmr astronaut; *Associate Administrator, Science Mission Directorate, NASA;* b. 10 Oct. 1958, Chicago, Ill.; s. of Ernest A. Grunsfeld III and Sally Mace Grunsfeld; m. Carol E. Schiff; two c.; ed Massachusetts Inst. of Tech., Univ. of Chicago; Visiting Scientist, Univ. of Tokyo 1980–81; Grad. Research Asst, Univ. of Chicago 1981–85, NASA Grad. Student Fellow 1985–87, W. D. Grainger Postdoctoral Fellow in Experimental Physics 1988–89; Sr Research Fellow, Calif. Inst. of Tech. 1989–92; scientist and astronaut with NASA 1992–2009, positions included Chief Computer Support Branch, Instructor and Chief Extravehicular Activity Branch, Chief Scientist 2003–04, Deputy Dir Space Telescope Science Inst. Baltimore, Md 2010–12, Assoc. Admin., Science Mission Directorate 2012–; veteran of four space flights, having logged over 45 days in space; mem. American Astronomical Soc., American Alpine Club, Experimental Aircraft Asscn, Aircraft Owners and Pilots Asscn; Distinguished Alumni Award, Alumni Service Award, Univ. of Chicago, Komarov Diploma 1995, NASA Space Flight Medals 1995, 1997, 1999, 2002, Exceptional Service Medals 1997, 1998, 2000, Korolov Diploma 1999, 2002, Distinguished Service Medal 2002, Constellation Award 2004, Space Logistics Medal, Soc. of Logistics Engineers 2006. *Leisure interests:* mountaineering, flying, sailing, bicycling, music. *Address:* Office of Associate Administrator, Science Mission Directorate, NASA, 300 E Street, SW, Suite 5R30, Washington, DC 20546, USA. *Telephone:* (202) 358-0001 (office). *Fax:* (202) 358-4338 (office). *Website:* www.science.nasa.gov (office).

GRUSHKO, Alexander V.; Russian diplomatist and politician; *Deputy Minister of Foreign Affairs;* b. 25 April 1955, Moscow; ed Moscow State Inst. of Int. Relations (MGIMO); Adviser, Soviet embassy in Brussels 1980–90s; Head of Russian del. at disarmament negotiations between USSR and NATO within framework of jt consultative group under Treaty on Conventional Armed Forces in Europe (CFE Treaty); Chief Adviser to Dept of Security and Disarmament Affairs, Ministry of Foreign Affairs mid-1990s, Deputy Dir Dept of European Cooperation 2002–03, Dir 2003–05, mem. Bd Ministry of Foreign Affairs 2003, rank of Amb. 2004, Deputy Minister of Foreign Affairs with responsibility for pan-European and Euro-Atlantic orgs 2005–12, Perm. Rep. to NATO, Brussels 2012–18, Deputy Minister of Foreign Affairs 2018–; Lecturer, MGIMO; Order of Friendship 2004. *Address:* Ministry of Foreign Affairs, 119200 Moscow, Smolenskaya-Sennaya pl. 32/34, Russian Federation (office). *Telephone:* (499) 244-16-06 (office). *Fax:* (499) 244-34-48 (office). *E-mail:* ministry@mid.ru (office). *Website:* www.mid.ru (office).

GRYAZNOVA, Alla Georgiyevna, DEcon; Russian economist and academic; *President, Financial University under the Government of the Russian Federation;* b. 27 Nov. 1937, Moscow; m. Viktor Kononov; one s.; ed Moscow Finance Coll., Moscow Inst. of Finance; served in several teaching positions at Moscow Inst. of Finance (now Financial Univ. under the Govt of the Russian Federation) including Asst, Lecturer, Sr Lecturer and Docent, Prof. 1964–74, Pro-rector on int. relations and research 1976–85, Rector 1985–2006, Pres. 2006–; Ed.-in-Chief Banking System in Russia; mem. New Way Movt 1995; Deputy-Chair. State Comm. for Academic Degrees; First Vice-Pres. Guild of Financiers; Vice-Pres. Acad. of Man. and Market; Pres. Moscow Int. School of Finance and Banking; mem. Acad. of Econ. Sciences, Int. Acad. of Informatics, Int. Acad. of Eurasia, Asscn of Russian Banks, Int. Fiscal Asscn, Business Club of APEC; Hon. Prof., Moscow Int. Higher Business School (MIRBIS); Order for Services to the Motherland (4th degree) 2002, (3rd degree) 2006, Order of the President of Ingushetia 2004; Dr hc (Tsenov Acad. of Economy, Bulgaria) 1997, (Univ. of East London, UK) 2001; Russian Nat. Olympus Int. Award 2002, Nat. Award, Russian Acad. of Business 2003, Honoured Worker of Science of Russian Fed. *Publications:* Mikroekonomika: Teoriya i rossiyskaya praktika 2009; over 200 articles on econ. problems. *Leisure interests:* tennis, ballet, volleyball, poetry. *Address:* Financial University under the Government of the Russian Federation, 125993 Moscow, Leningradsky prosp. 49, Russia (office). *Telephone:* (495) 157-56-61 (office). *Fax:* (495) 157-70-70 (office). *E-mail:* academy@fa.ru (office). *Website:* en.fa.ru (office).

GRYBAUSKAITĖ, Dalia, PhD; Lithuanian politician, diplomatist and head of state; *President;* b. 1 March 1956, Vilnius, Lithuanian SSR, USSR; ed Leningrad (now St Petersburg) Univ., Russian SFSR, USSR, Edmund A. Walsh School of Foreign Service, Georgetown Univ., Washington, DC, USA; Head, Dept for Science, Inst. of Econs 1990–91; Programme Dir, Govt of Repub. of Lithuania, Prime Minister's Office 1991; Dir European Dept, Ministry of Int. Econ. Relations 1991–93; Dir Econ. Relations Dept, Ministry of Foreign Affairs 1993–94; Chair. Comm. for Aid Coordination (PHARE and G-24) 1993–94; Chief of Negotiations with EU on Free Trade Agreement 1993–94; Envoy Extraordinary and Minister Plenipotentiary, Mission of Lithuania to EU, Brussels 1994–95, Deputy Chief Negotiator on Europe Agreement with EU; Rep. of Nat. Aid Coordinator, Brussels 1994–95; Minister Plenipotentiary, Embassy in Washington, DC 1996–99; Deputy Minister of Finance 1999–2000, Chief Negotiator in Negotiations with IMF and World Bank; Deputy Minister of Foreign Affairs 2000–01; Deputy Head of Negotiations, Del. to EU; Minister of Finance 2001–04; EU Commr for Educ. and Culture 2004, for Financial Programming and the Budget 2004–09; Pres. of Lithuania 2009–; Commdr's Cross, Order of Grand Duke Gediminas 2003, Order of Vytautas the Great with the Golden Chain 2009, Commdr Grand Cross with Chain, Order of the Three Stars 2011, Kt Grand Cross, Royal Norwegian Order of St Olav 2011, Kt Grand Cross, Order of the Falcon (Iceland) 2011, Grand Officer, Order of Saint-Charles (Monaco) 2012; Kt Grand Cross, Order of the White Rose of Finland 2013; Kt Grand Cross, Order of the Cross of Terra Mariana (Estonia) 2013; Order of the Republic (Moldova) 2015; Kt, Order of the Seraphim (Sweden) 2015; Hon. DHumLitt (Georgetown Univ., USA) 2013; named Commissioner of the Year in the European Voice Europeans of the Year poll 2005, Glamour magazine Woman of the Year (USA) 2010, Charlemagne Prize (Germany) 2013. *Address:* Office of the President, S. Daukanto 3, Vilnius 01122, Lithuania (office). *Telephone:* (5) 266-4154 (office). *Fax:* (5) 266-4145 (office). *E-mail:* kanceliarija@prezidentas.lt (office). *Website:* www.lrp.lt (office).

GRYNSPAN, Rebeca, BS, MS; Costa Rican politician and UN official; *Secretary-General, Ibero-American Secretariat (SEGIB);* b. 1955; m.; one s. one d.; ed Univ. of Costa Rica, Hebrew Univ., Israel, Univ. of Sussex, UK; fmr Prof., Univ. of Costa Rica; fmr Researcher, Instituto de Investigaciones de Ciencias Económicas de Costa Rica; various ministerial level positions 1986–94; Vice-Pres., Repub. of Costa Rica 1994–98; joined UN, becoming Dir Mexican Div., ECLAC 2001–06, Asst Admin. and Regional Dir, UNDP Latin America and Caribbean Bureau 2006–09, Under-Sec.-Gen. and Assoc. Admin., UNDP 2010–14; Sec.-Gen., Ibero-American Secretariat (SEGIB), Madrid, Spain 2014–; fmr Vice-Pres. Int. Food Policy Research Inst. *Address:* SEGIB Secretariat General Iberoamericana, Paseo de Recoletos 8, 28001 Madrid, Spain (office). *Telephone:* (91) 5901980 (office). *Website:* www.segib.org (office).

GRYTSENKO, Anatoliy P., MPA; Ukrainian politician and government official; b. 21 Sept. 1958, Kerch (Autonomous Repub. of Crimea); m. Olga A. Grytsenko; one s. one d.; ed Kalinin Crimean Agricultural Inst., Simferopol and Kharkov Regional Inst. of Public Admin; began career 1976; held various positions, including Chair. Exec. Cttee Chistopolskiy Town Council of nat. deputies, Chair. Leninskaya Dist State Admin; Deputy, Verkhovna Rada (Parl.) of the Autonomous Repub. of Crimea 1994–; first Vice-Chair. Presidium of the Supreme Council, Autonomous Repub. of Crimea 1987–97, Chair. 1997–98, 2006–10; Chair. Verkhovna Rada Comm. on Local Self-Govt 1987–97; Order of Merit (Third Degree) of Ukraine, Order of Peter the Great (First Degree), Russia, Order of St Anthony and Feodosiy Pecherski, Ukrainian Orthodox Church. *Leisure interests:* hunting, sociopolitical journalism. *Address:* 295000 Simferopol, 18 K. Marksa Street, Republic of Crimea, Russian Federation (office). *Telephone:* (65) 254-42-55 (office). *Fax:* (65) 227-25-81 (office). *E-mail:* svr@crimea.gov.ru (office). *Website:* crimea.gov.ru (office).

GRYZLOV, Boris Vyacheslavovich, PhD; Russian engineer and politician; *Chairman of Supreme Council, United Russia (Yedinaya Rossiya);* b. 15 Dec. 1950, Vladivostok; s. of Vyacheslav Gryzlov; m. Ada Viktorovna Gryzlova; one s. one d.; ed Leningrad (now St Petersburg) Inst. of Electro-Tech. Communications; radio engineer, Heavy Duty Radio Industry Scientific Research Inst. (Comintern), took part in devt of communications systems –1977; Head of construction, later Dept Dir, Electron-pribor Production Co. 1977–96; Dir New Training Tech. Centre, Baltic State Tech. Univ. 1996–99; cand. in St Petersburg city elections; Pres. Interregional Business Co-operation Fund Devt of Regions 1999–; Chief of Staff for Leningrad Oblast Gov. cand. Viktor Zubkov 1999; Founder mem. Unity (Yedinstvo) Movt 1999, Head of St Petersburg Regional Br. 1999, Chair. Unity Political Council 2000, Chair. Supreme Council of United Russia (Yedinaya Rossiya) 2004–, Chair. United Russia 2005–08; mem. Gosudarstvennaya Duma (State Duma) 1999–2001, 2003–, Leader, Unity faction 2000–01, Chair. State Duma Dec. 2003–11; Minister of Internal Affairs 2001–03; Chair. Inter-Parl. Ass., Eurasian Econ. Community (Eurasec IPA); Perm. mem., Security Council of Russian Fed. *Leisure interests:* soccer and other sports. *Address:* United Russia (Yedinaya Rossiya), 129110 Moscow, Pereyaslavskii per. 4, Russia (office). *Telephone:* (495) 786-82-89 (office). *Fax:* (495) 975-30-78 (office). *E-mail:* portalrss@edinros.ru (office). *Website:* er.ru (office); www.gryzlov.ru.

GRYZUNOV, Sergey Petrovich; Russian academic and fmr journalist; *Professor, Department of Journalism, Moscow State Institute for International Relations;* b. 23 July 1949, Kuybyshev; m.; one s.; ed Moscow State Univ., Acad. of Public Sciences, Cen. Communist Party Cttee; worked for Ria-Novosti 1974–94, fmr ed. Novosti, then reviewer, then Deputy Head of Bureau, Yugoslavia; Deputy Chair. Cttee on Press April–Sept. 1994, Chair. 1994–95; mem. Pres. Yeltsin's election campaign March 1996; Vice-Pres. ICN Pharmaceutical Corpn 1996–2001; Vice-Pres. Moscow News Publrs 2001–03, Russian Asscn of Ind. Publishers 2004–05; fmr Deputy Gen. Dir Rumelco OOO; fmr Chair. Communications and Public Relations Cttee Novolipetsk Steel (NLMK); Ed.-in-Chief and Dir-Gen. Novoe Russkoe Slovo Publishing House; Prof., Dept of Journalism, Moscow State Inst. for Int. Relations 2009–. *Leisure interests:* cooking, fishing, underwater swimming. *Address:* Department of Journalism, Moscow State Institute for International Relations, 119454 Moscow, Prospekt Vernadskogo, 76, Russia (office). *Telephone:* (495) 434-90-66 (office). *Website:* english.mgimo.ru (office).

GRZEŚKOWIAK, Alicja, PhD (Habil.); Polish lawyer, politician and academic; *Assistant Professor of Econometrics and Operations Research, Wrocław University of Economics;* b. 10 June 1941, Świrz, Lvov Prov., Ukrainian SSR, USSR; (husband deceased); one d.; ed Nicolaus Copernicus Univ., Toruń; research worker, Faculty of Law and Admin of Nicolaus Copernicus Univ., Toruń 1966–96, Prof. 1990, 2000; staff mem. John Paul II Catholic Univ. of Lublin (KUL) 1990, apptd Prof. of Criminal Law 1991, now Prof. Emer., mem. Scientific Council of John Paul II Inst. –2010; Lecturer in Religious Law, Higher Ecclesiastic Seminary, Toruń 1994–2002; fmr Prof., Kujawy and Pomorze Univ., Bydgoszcz; currently Asst Prof. of Econometrics and Operations Research, Wrocław Univ. of Econs; mem. Solidarity Trade Union 1980; Senator 1989–2001, Vice-Marshal of Senate 1991–93, Marshal 1997–2001, del. Parl. Ass. of the Council of Europe 1989–97, mem. 1991–97, Vice-Chair. Group of Christian Democrats 1992–97; mem. Social Movt of Solidarity Election Action (RSAWS) 1998–2001; mem. Admin. Council of John Paul II Foundation, Vatican 1992–2002; consultant of Pontifical Council for the Family 1993; mem. Pontificia Academia Pro Vita; Founder Foundation of Assistance to Single Mothers, Toruń; Hon. mem. Asscn of Catholic Families; Dr hc (Acad. of Catholic Theology, Warsaw) 1995, (Holy Family Coll., Phila) 1998, (Int. Ind. Univ. of Moldova) 1999; Pro Ecclesia et Pontifice Medal 1991, Medal of 13th Jan. of Lithuanian Repub.; Dame of the Holy Sepulchre Friars of Jerusalem, Great Cross, Order of Crown (Belgium) 1999, Great Cross, Orden del Merito Civil (Spain) 2001, Cross of Freedom and Solidarity 2017. *Publications:* numerous scientific publs on penal law, human rights and family rights. *Leisure interests:* reading, listening to music. *Address:* Department of Econometrics and Operations Research, Room 623,Wrocław University of Economics, 53-345 Wrocław, ul. Komandorska 118/120, Poland (office). *Telephone:* (71) 3680478 (office). *Fax:* (71) 3672778 (office). *E-mail:* alicja.grzeskowiak@ue.wroc.pl (home). *Website:* www.ue .wroc.pl (office).

GU, Binglin, BEng, PhD; Chinese physicist, academic and fmr university administrator; *Professor of Physics and Director, Institute for Advanced Study, Tsinghua University;* b. 8 Oct. 1945, Harbin, Heilongjiang; ed Tsinghua Univ., Beijing, Univ. of Århus, Denmark; mem. Faculty, Tsinghua Univ. 1970–, Assoc. Prof. of Physics, 1983–88, Prof. of Physics 1988–, Head, Dept of Physics 1994–2000, Pres. Academic Degree Cttee 2001–, Vice-Pres. and Dean, Grad. School 2001–03, Pres. 2003–12, Dir, Inst. for Advanced Study 2012–; Visiting Prof., Tohoku Univ., Japan 1993–94; Sr Visiting Scholar, Notre Dame Univ., USA 1985–86; Dir Steering Cttee for Physics and Astronomy, Ministry of Educ.; Pres. Chinese Stereology Cttee; Vice-Pres. Chinese Physical Soc.; mem. and Dir of Physics and Astronomy Senate; mem. Academic Degree Cttee of the State Council, Nat. Science and Tech. Reward Cttee, Council of Asscn of Asia Pacific Physical Socs; Academician, Chinese Acad. of Science; Second Prize of Scientific Achievement, Ministry of Educ. 1988, 1990, 1994, 1998, Top Award for Excellent Teacher, Baosteel Educ. Fund 1998, First Prize, Chinese Univ. Nature Science 2000, Second Nat. Prize of Nature Science 2000, Second Prize of Scientific Achievement, City of Beijing 2002, Award for Scientific and Technological Progress, Ho Leung Ho Lee Foundation 2002, First LuXun Award, Tohoku Univ. 2004. *Publications:* more than 200 scientific papers in professional journals on the properties of complex materials and phenomena. *Address:* Department of Physics, Tsinghua University, School of Sciences Building2405, Beijing 100084, People's Republic of China (office). *Telephone:* (10) 62782773 (office). *Fax:* (10) 62781604 (office). *E-mail:* gubl@phys.tsinghua.edu.cn (office). *Website:* www.phys.tsinghua.edu.cn (office).

GU, Jianguo; Chinese steel industry executive; *Chairman and Executive Director, Masteel;* b. 1954; many years with Ma'anshan Iron and Steel Co. Ltd (Masteel), Chair. Masteel 1993–95, Gen. Man. Magang (Group) Holding and Chair. Masteel 1995–99, Pres. Magang (Group) Holding Co. Ltd 1999–2011, currently Chair. and Exec. Dir Masteel Processing and Distribution Co. Ltd. *Address:* c/o Magang (Group) Holding, 8 Hong Qi Zhong Road, Maanshan City 243003, People's Republic of China (office).

GU, Liji, BEng, MEng; Chinese engineer and business executive; *Chairman of the Supervisory Board, China Ping An Insurance Corporation;* ed Tsinghua Univ., Univ. of Science and Tech. of China, Harvard Business School, USA; Man. Dir China Merchants Shekou Industrial Zone Co. Ltd –2008, Hoi Tung Marine Machinery Suppliers Ltd (Hong Kong) –2008, China Merchants Technology Group –2008; Chair. China Merchants Technology Holdings Co. Ltd –2008, Exec. Dir 2008–10, Exec. Dir China Merchants Technology Investment Co. Ltd, Shenzhen 2008–10; Man. Dir China Int. Marine Containers Co. Ltd –2008; Chair. and Pres. China Merchants Shekou Port Services Co. Ltd –2008; Vice-Chair. China Ping An Insurance Co. –2008, Ind. Supervisor and Chair. Supervisory Bd China Ping An Insurance Corpn 2009–; Dir China Merchants Bank, China Merchants Group Ltd –2008, ERGO China Life Insurance Co. Ltd 2013–; Outside Dir Xiang Tan Electric Manufacturing Group Co. Ltd (XEMC) 2011–; expert on Applicable Electronics, Shenzhen Expert Asscn; Vice-Chair. Scientific Asscn of Shenzhen Nanshan Dist. *Address:* China Ping An Insurance Corporation, Ping An Building, Bagua No. 3 Road, Shenzhen 518029, Guangdong (office); Ping An Insurance (Hong Kong) Co. Ltd, 11th Floor, Dah Sing Financial Centre, 108 Gloucester Road, Wanchai, Hong Kong Special Administrative Region, People's Republic of China (office). *Telephone:* (755) 82262888 (Shenzhen) (office); 28271883 (Hong Kong) (office). *Fax:* (755) 82414817 (Shenzhen) (office); 28020018 (Hong Kong) (office). *E-mail:* IR@ paic.com.cn (office). *Website:* www.pingan.com.cn (office).

GU, Songfen; Chinese aeronautical engineer; b. 4 Feb. 1930, Suzhou, Jiangsu Prov.; ed Shanghai Jiaotong Univ.; engineer, Aeronautical Industry Admin. of Ministry of Heavy Industry; Group Leader Aerodynamic Group of Design Dept, Shenyang Aeroplane Mfg Factory; Vice-Chief Designer, Chief Designer, Vice-Pres. then Pres. Aviation Science and Tech. Research Inst.; mem. 4th Presidium of Depts 2000–; responsible for jet fighter design; Chief Designer Shenyang Aeroplane Mfg Co.; Vice-Chair. Science and Tech. Cttee, China Aviation Industry Corpn; joined CCP 1981; Deputy, 7th NPC 1988–93, mem. 8th Standing Cttee of NPC 1993–98 (mem. Educ., Science, Culture and Health Cttee 1993–98), 9th Standing Cttee of NPC 1998–2003; Fellow, Chinese Acad. of Sciences 1991– (Deputy Dir Div. of Technological Sciences 1996–); mem. Chinese Acad. of Eng 1994–; Nat. Model Worker 1988, Gold Nat. Aeronautical Award 1992, Scientific and Technological Progress Award, Ho Leung Ho Lee Foundation 1995.

GU, Xiulian; Chinese economist, politician and party and government official; b. 1936, Nantong, Jiangsu Prov.; ed public security cadre's school, Shenyang, Liaoning Prov., Public Security Bureau of Benxi City, Liaoning, Secondary Metallurgical School of Shenyang; joined CCP 1956; technician and cadre, Communist Youth League of China Metallurgical Corpn 1961–64; technician, Ministry of Textile Industry 1969; cadre, State Council 1970; Vice-Minister, State Planning Comm., State Council 1973–83; Alt. mem. Cen. Cttee, CCP 1977; Vice-Chair. Cen. Patriotic Sanitation Campaign Cttee, Cen. Cttee 1981–89; mem. 12th Cen. Cttee, CCP 1982–87, 13th Cen. Cttee CCP 1987–92, 14th Cen. Cttee CCP 1992–97, 15th Cen. Cttee CCP 1997–2002; Deputy Sec. CCP Prov. Cttee, Jiangsu 1982–89; Gov. of Jiangsu 1983–89; Minister of Chemical Industry 1989–98 (also Party Cttee Sec. at the Ministry); Deputy, 9th NPC 1998–2003, Vice-Chair. 10th NPC Standing Cttee 2003–; Vice-Pres. 7th, 8th and 9th Exec. Cttee, All-China Women's Fed. 1998–2003, Pres. 9th All-China Women's Fed. 2003–08; Vice-Pres. 3rd Council, China Women's Devt Fund 1999, Vice-Pres. China Women's Devt Fund 2001–. *Address:* c/o The All-China Women's Federation, 15 Jian Guo Men Nei Street, Beijing 100730, People's Republic of China. *Telephone:* (10) 65211639. *Fax:* (10) 65211156. *E-mail:* yzhch@women.org.cn; acwf@women.org.cn. *Website:* www.women.org.cn.

GU, Yingqi; Chinese politician; b. 1930, Xinmin, Liaoning; m.; two s. one d.; joined PLA 1948, CCP 1950; Vice-Minister of Public Health 1984–95; Chief Physician; Co-ordinator State Co-ordination of Control of Narcotics and Against Drugs 1987–90; Head of Del. to UN Int. Conf. on Drug Abuse and Illicit Trafficking 1987, to Signing of Sino-US Memorandum of Understanding on Co-operation and Control of Narcotic Drugs, Washington 1987, to UN Conf. for Adoption of a Convention Against Illicit Traffic in Narcotic Drugs and Psychotropic Substances 1988, to 17th Special Session of UN Gen. Ass. on Int. Co-operation against Drugs 1990, to 44th Gen. Ass. of WHO 1991, to Int. Conf. for Protection of War Victims, Geneva, Switzerland 1993, to 9th Session of Gen. Ass. of Int. Fed. of Red Cross and Red Crescent Socs, Birmingham, UK 1993; Conf. Chair. 15th Meeting of Nat. Drug Law Enforcement Agencies for Asia and Pacific 1990, 4th Asia and Pacific Red Cross and Red Crescent Conf., Beijing 1993; Head of Chinese Red Cross Del. to 26th Int. Conf. of Red Cross and Red Crescent, Geneva 1995; Pres. China Rural Hygiene Asscn 1986, Chinese Asscn of Rehabilitation Medicine 1985, Chinese Asscn of Hosp. Man.; Exec. Vice-Pres. Red Cross Soc. of China 1990; Vice-Pres. Int. Fed. of Red Cross and Red Crescent Socs 1991–93. *Address:* c/o Red Cross Society of China, 53 Ganmian Hutong, Beijing 100010, People's Republic of China.

GUAIDÓ MÁRQUEZ, Juan Gerardo; Venezuelan engineer and politician; *President, National Assembly; Acting President;* b. 28 July 1983, La Guaira; s. of Norka Márquez and Wilmer Guaidó; m. Fabiana Rosales 2013; one d.; ed Andres Bello Catholic Univ., George Washington Univ., Inst. of Advanced Management Studies, Caracas; substitute mem. for Vargas Dist (MUD), Asamblea Nacional (Nat. Ass., parl.) 2011–16, mem. for Vargas Dist (MUD) 2015–, Vice Pres. Domestic Policy Perm. Cttee 2017–18, mem. Culture and Recreation Perm. Cttee, Pres. Asamblea Nacional 2019–; Deputy to Latin American Parl. for Venezuela 2016–; Acting Pres. of Venezuela (contesting leadership of Nicolás Maduro) 2019– (recognized as acting Pres. of Venezuela by 54 govts); mem. Mesa de Unidad Democrática (MUD). *Address:* Asamblea Nacional, Federal Legislative Palace, Caracas, Venezuela (office). *Telephone:* (212) 778–3322 (office). *Website:* www.asambleanacional.gob.ve (office); juanguaido.com.

GUAINO, Henri; French civil servant and economist; b. 11 March 1957, Arles; ed Institut d'études politiques de Paris, École nationale d'admin.; economist, Crédit Lyonnais 1982–86; Course Dir, École supérieure de commerce de Paris and École normale supérieure de Saint-Cloud 1984–87; Chief of Staff to Treasury Dir 1987–88; Asst Sec.-Gen. Club de Paris 1987–88; worked on Jacques Chirac's presidential campaign 1988; Head of Lectures, Institut d'études politiques de Paris 1988–2003; Head of Finance Research, Louis Dreyfus Group 1989–90; Chief of Staff to Dir-Gen., Mutuelle d'assurance des artisans 1990–93; Chief of Staff to Pres. of Nat. Ass., Philippe Séguin 1993; adviser to Minister of the Interior, Charles Pasqua 1994–95; Chief of Staff, Gen. Planning Commissariat 1995–98; Planning and Devt Adviser to Charles Pasqua for Hauts-de-Seine, Paris 1999–2000; Scientific Adviser, Agence pour la diffusion de l'information technologique 2002–04; Admin., Agence de l'environnement et de la maîtrise de l'énergie 2003; Chief Adviser, Cour des Comptes 2006; Special Adviser, Pres. of the Repub., Nicolas Sarkozy 2007–12; Deputy of Nat. Ass. for Third Constituency of Yvelines 2012–. *Publications:* L'Étrange renoncement 1998, La France est-elle soluble dans l'Europe? (with Daniel Cohn-Bendit) 1999, La sottise des modernes 2002. *Address:* National Assembly, 126 rue de l'Université, 75355 Paris, France (office). *Telephone:* 1-40-63-91-21 (office). *E-mail:* hguaino@assemblee-nationale.fr (office). *Website:* www.guaino.fr.

GUAN, Qiao; Chinese engineer; b. 2 July 1935, Taiyuan, Shanxi Prov.; ed Moscow Bauman Eng Inst., USSR; organized Nat. Key Labs, Power Beam Processing, Aeronautical Joining Tech., China Friction Welding Center; Vice-Chair. Science and Tech. Cttee, Beijing Aeronautical Manufacturing Tech. Research Inst. 1987–; Adjunct Prof., Tsing Hua Univ. and Beijing Univ. of Aeronautics and Astronautics; Pres. Chinese Welding Soc. 1990–95; Vice-Pres. Int. Inst. of Welding 1992–95; Fellow, Chinese Acad. of Eng 1994–; Nat. Invention Prize (2nd Class) 1995, GuangHua Prize (lst Class) 1996, Int. Inst. of Welding Lifetime Achievement Award 1999. *Achievements include:* invented low-stress no-distortion welding method. *Publications:* more than 80 technical papers published in Chinese, 40 papers in English and Russian. *Address:* Beijing Aeronautical Manufacturing Technology Research Institute, PO Box 863, 100024 Beijing, People's Republic of China (office). *Telephone:* (10) 8570-1243.

GUAN, Qing, PhD; Chinese engineer and business executive; *Chairman and President, China State Construction Engineering Corporation;* Vice-Pres. China Southwest Architectural Design & Research Inst. Corpn Ltd 1998–2003, Pres. 2003–06, Deputy Sec. Party Cttee 2006–07; Vice-Pres. China State Construction Engineering Corpn 2007–09, Vice-Chair. and Pres. China Construction Engineering Design Group Corpn Ltd 2009–11, Pres. China State Construction Engineering Corpn April–May 2011, mem. Bd of Dirs May–July 2011, Chair. China Construction Engineering Design Group Corpn Ltd July–Sept. 2011, Dir and Pres. China State Construction Engineering Corpn Sept. 2011–, Chair. 2015–; Deputy Dir China Green Building Council. *Address:* China State Construction Engineering Corporation, CSCEC Mansion, 15 Sanlihe Road, Haidian District, Beijing 100037, People's Republic of China (office). *Telephone:* (10) 88082888 (office). *Fax:* (10) 88082888 (office). *E-mail:* info@cscec.com (office); ir@cscec.com.cn (office). *Website:* www.cscec.com (office); english.cscec.com (office).

GUARD, Mark Perrott, MA, RIBA; Irish architect; *Principal, Mark Guard Architects;* b. 22 May 1952, Dublin; s. of Wilson Perrott Guard and Ethena Joy Wallace; ed Avoca School, Dublin, Univ. of Toronto, Royal Coll. of Art, London; worked for architectural, film and textile design cos in Ireland and UK 1969–73; emigrated to Canada 1973; architect asst, Toronto and Vancouver 1973–76; worked for Richard Rogers Partnership, Rick Mather Architects, Eva Jiricna Architects, London 1982–86; started pvt. practice in modernist residential design and devt of transformable spaces 1986; Prin. Mark Guard Design 1986–88, Mark Guard Assocs 1988–93, Mark Guard Architects 1993–; Dir Mark Guard Ltd 1998–; Dir Guard Tillman Pollock Ltd 2002–; mem. Royal Inst. of British Architects (RIBA), Royal Inst. of the Architects of Ireland (RIAI), Chartered Soc. of Designers (CSD); RIBA Regional Award for New House, London, W2 1992, for house refurbishment, London, NW6 1995, CSD Commendation for transformable flat, London, EC2 1993, for house refurbishment, London, NW6 1995, RIAI Commendation for new house, Galway 1993, RIBA Award for Houses and Housing for penthouse apartment, Paris 1997. *Publications:* Walls and Boxes 2017. *Address:* 161 Whitfield Street, London, W1T 5ET, England (office). *Telephone:* (20) 7380-1199 (office). *Fax:* (20) 7387-5441 (office). *E-mail:* reception@guardtillmanpollock.com (office). *Website:* www.guardtillmanpollock.com (office).

GUARDADO, Facundo; Salvadorean politician; b. 27 Nov. 1954, Arcatao, Dept of Chalatenengo; s. of Sixto Guardado and Herlinda Guardado; m. Carmen Cristina Alvarez Basso 1993; one s. three d.; ed fellowship to econ. seminars at Cen. American Business Admin. Inst. and Heredia Nat. Univ. of Costa Rica; co-operative movt leader 1972; Sec.-Gen. Revolutionary Popular Bloc 1977; mem. Cen. Cttee Nat. Liberation Front (FMLN) in 1980s, mem. Political Comm. 1993, Campaign Man. 1997, Gen. Co-ordinator 1997–99; Counsellor at San Salvador Majorship 1997; presidential cand. 1999; Leader, Movimiento Renovador (split from FMLN 2002) 2002–03 (dissolved after elections 2003); mem. peace negotiations del. La Palma 1984, Ayagualo 1984, La Nunciatura 1987, Mexico 1991; Vice-Pres. Perm. Conf. of Political Parties of Latin America and the Caribbean; mem. Initiatives Group for Latin America; Pres. El Salvador XXI Century Foundation. *Publications:* Political and Social Struggles in El Salvador, Participation and Social Change, Evolution of the Democratic Process in El Salvador. *Leisure interests:* agriculture, football. *Address:* Paseo Miralvalle 155, Colonia Miralvalle, San Salvador (home); c/o Motocross #49, Colonia Monteverde, San Salvador, El Salvador. *Telephone:* 274-2104 (home).

GUARDIOLA I SALA, Josep (Pep); Spanish football manager and fmr professional footballer; *Manager, Manchester City FC;* b. 18 Jan. 1971, Santpedor, Barcelona, Catalonia; s. of Dolors and Valentí; m. Cristina Serra 2014; one s. two d.; played as defensive midfielder for Barcelona B 1990–92, FC Barcelona 1990–2001 (472 appearances, scored 10 goals, Capt. 1997–2001), mem. team that won La Liga 1990–91, 1991–92, 1992–93, 1993–94, 1997–98, 1998–99, Copa del Rey 1996–97, 1997–98, Supercopa de España 1991, 1992, 1994, 1996, mem. of team that won European Cup 1991–92 (Barcelona's first), UEFA Cup Winners' Cup 1996–97, UEFA Super Cup 1992, 1997; also played for Brescia Calcio 2001–02, A.S. Roma 2002–03, Al-Ahli (Qatar) 2003–05, Dorados de Sinaloa (Mexico) 2005–06 (while attending managing school); served four-month ban for positive drug test while playing in Italy 2001, cleared of all charges on appeal 2007 and again 2009; played internationally for Spain U21 1991–92, Spain 1992–2001 (won Olympic Gold Medal 1992), Catalonia 1995–2005; following retirement as player, became coach of FC Barcelona B 2007–08 (won Tercera División 2007–08), First Team Man. FC Barcelona 2008–12, in first season won treble of La Liga 2008–09, Copa del Rey 2008–09 and Champions League (youngest-ever UEFA Champions League winning man.) 2008–09, won Supercopa de España against Athletic Club Bilbao 2009, UEFA Super Cup against Shakhtar Donetsk 2009, 2011, FIFA Club World Cup against Estudiantes 2009 (first ever sextuple of six trophies in six competitions in one year) 2011, won La Liga 2009–10, 2010–11, Supercopa de España 2009, 2010, 2011, UEFA Champions League 2010–11 (a record 13 trophies in four seasons making him the most successful coach in the club's history); Man. FC Bayern Munich 2013–16, won Bundesliga 2013–14, 2014–15, DFB-Pokal 2013–14, UEFA Super Cup 2013–14, FIFA Club World Cup 2013–14; Man. Manchester City FC 2016–, won Premier League 2017–18, Carabao Cup 2017–18, 2018–19; Bravo Award 1992, UEFA Euro Team of the Tournament 1992, 2000, Spain's Best Player, Olympic Games 1992, IFFHS World's Best Club Coach of the Year 2009, 2011, Don Balon Award for Best Coach of the Year 2009, 2010, 2011, Onze d'Or Coach of the Year 2009, 2011, Miguel Muñoz Trophy for Best Coach of the Year 2009, 2010, World Soccer Magazine World Manager of the Year 2009, 2011, UEFA Team of the Year Best Coach 2008–09, 2010–11, La Liga Coach of the Year 2009, 2010, 2011, Catalan of the Year Award 2009, FIFA Ballon d'Or Best Coach 2011, Gold Medal of the Royal Order of Sporting Merit 2010, Gold Medal of the Catalan parliament 2011, FIFA World Coach of the Year 2011. *Address:* Manchester City FC, Etihad Stadium, Etihad Campus, Manchester, M11 3FF, England (office). *Telephone:* (16) 1444-1894 (office). *E-mail:* mancity@mancity.com (office). *Website:* www.mancity.com (office).

GUARGUAGLINI, Pier Francesco, PhD; Italian aerospace industry executive; b. 25 Feb. 1937, Castagneto Carducci, Livorno; m., three c.; ed Univ. of Pisa, Univ. of Pennsylvania, USA; Asst Lecturer in Nuclear Electronics, Univ. of Pisa 1961–63; Asst Lecturer in Radar Systems, Univ. of Rome 1963–78; joined Selenia SpA as Systems Analyst 1963, Dir of Research Devt 1970–74, Dir IT and Telecommunications Div. 1975–79, Dir and Man. Civil Div. 1979–81, Deputy Gen. Man. 1981–82, Co-Gen. Man. 1982; Gen. Man. Officine Galileo 1984–87, Man. Dir 1987–94; Man. Dir Oto Melara SpA and Breda Meccanica Bresciana SpA 1994–96; Head, Defence Sector Businesses, Finmeccanica SpA 1996–99, Chair. Alenia Marconi Systems NV (joint venture between Finmeccanica and BAE) 1998–2000, Chair. and CEO Finmeccanica SpA 2002–11, Chair. May–Dec. 2011 (resgnd); CEO Fincantieri Cantieri Navali Italiani 1999–2002; Lecturer, Univ. of Rome; Pres. AeroSpace and Defence Industries Asscn of Europe; mem. Shareholders' Steering Cttee IJVC Horizon Ltd; mem. IEEE; Aviation Week and Space Technology Person of the Year. *Address:* c/o Finmeccanica SpA, Piazza Monte Grappa 4, Rome 00195, Italy. *E-mail:* info@finmeccanica.it.

GUARINI, Kathryn Wilder, BS, PhD; American scientist and academic; *Vice-President and BLE System z Growth Initiatives & Linux, IBM;* ed Yale and Stanford Univs; Intern, Hewlett-Packard 1993–94, AMD 1995; joined IBM Research Div., IBM T.J. Watson Research Center, Yorktown Heights, NY, Research Staff mem. 1999–2005, Man. 45nm Front End Integration 2003–05, Facilitator, Tech. Evaluation Team 2005–06, Sr Man., System z Processor Devt 2006–07, Exec. Asst to Sr Vice-Pres. 2007–08, Dir Systems Tech. Devt 2008–10, Dir System z Processor Devt 2011–14, Vice-Pres. and BLE System z Growth Initiatives & Linux, IBM 2014–; mem. IEEE, AAAS, Asscn for Women in Science; World Tech. Award in Information Tech. (Hardware), The World Tech. Network (co-recipient) 2004. *Publications:* Scanning Probe Lithography (Microsystems, Vol. 7; with Hyongsok T. Soh and Calvin F. Quate) 2001; more than 45 tech. publs on CMOS device fabrication, three-dimensional integrated circuits, and novel nanofabrication techniques and applications; more than 15 US patents. *Address:* IBM Corporate Division, 294 Route 100, Somers, NY 10598, USA (office). *E-mail:* kwg@us.ibm.com (office). *Website:* www.watson.ibm.com (office).

GUARINI, Renato; Italian statistician, university rector and academic; b. 16 March 1932, Naples; ed Univ. of Naples; did research at Univ. of Cen. Bureau of Statistics 1957–75, held post of Head of Dept for Gen. Methodology and Econ. Statistics; fmr Prof. of Econ. Statistics, Univ. of Cagliari; Prof. of Econ., Univ. of Rome 'La Sapienza' 1976–, Pres. Course of Statistics and Econs 1988–95, Dean of Faculty of Statistics 1995–2004, Pro-Rector La Sapienza Univ. 1997–2004, Rector 2004–08; mem. Comm. for the Guarantee of Information Statistics at Presidency of Council of Ministers, Scientific Advisory Cttee of Nat. Research Council, Ministry of Educ., Univ. and Research for 'decrees area', Comm. for the Reform of the Nat. Statistical System which prepared DL 322/89; mem. Accad. Nazionale dei Lincei 2001; Kt Grand Cross, Order of Merit of the Italian Repub. 2006. *Publications:* numerous scientific papers in professional journals. *Address:* c/o Office of the Rector, Università degli Studi di Roma 'La Sapienza', Piazzale Aldo Moro 5, 00185 Rome, Italy (office). *Telephone:* (06) 49914180 (office). *E-mail:* info@uniroma1.it (office). *Website:* www.uniroma1.it (office).

GUBBAY, Hon. Mr Justice Anthony Roy, BA, MA, LLM; Zimbabwean judge; b. 26 April 1932, Manchester, England; m. Wilma Sanger 1962 (died 2002); two s.; ed Univ. of Witwatersrand, South Africa, Univ. of Cambridge, UK; admitted to practice 1957; advocate in Bulawayo, S Rhodesia 1958, Sr Counsel 1974; Pres. Matabeleland and Midlands Valuations Bds; Nat. Pres. Special Court for Income Tax Appeals, Fiscal Court and Patents Tribunal; Vice-Chair. Bar Asscn; Judge of the High Court, Bulawayo 1977–83, Judge of the Supreme Court 1983; Chair. Legal Practitioners' Disciplinary Tribunal 1981–87, Law Devt Comm., Judicial Service Comm.; Chief Justice of Zimbabwe 1990–2001, retd 2001; mem. Perm. Court of Arbitration; Pres. Oxford and Cambridge Soc. of Zimbabwe; Patron Commonwealth Magistrates and Judges Asscn; mem. Advisory Bd of Commonwealth Judicial Educ. Inst., Commonwealth Reference Group on the Promotion of the Human Rights of Women and the Girl Child through the Judiciary; Hon. Fellow, Jesus Coll. Cambridge; Hon. Bencher of Lincoln's Inn (UK); Hon. mem. The Soc. of Legal Scholars (UK) 2004; Great Cross, Rio Branco Order (Brazil) 1999; Dr hc (Essex) 1994; Hon. LLD (London) 2002, (Witwatersrand) 2005; Peter Gruber Foundation Justice Award 2001. *Leisure interests:* classical music, philately, watching all forms of sport, travel. *Address:* 26 Dacomb Drive, Chisipite, Harare, Zimbabwe (home). *Telephone:* (4) 496882 (home). *E-mail:* supreme-court@gta.gov.zw (office); gubbay@zol.co.zw (home).

GUBBAY, Raymond, CBE, FRSA; British music promoter; b. 2 April 1946, London; s. of David Gubbay and Ida Gubbay; m. Johanna Quirke 1972 (divorced 1988); two d.; ed Univ. Coll. School, Hampstead; concert promoter 1966–; Founder, Man. Dir and Chair. Raymond Gubbay Ltd 1966–; presents regular series of concerts at major London and regional concert halls including Royal Albert Hall, Royal Festival Hall, Barbican Centre, Symphony Hall Birmingham, Bridgewater Hall Manchester, Royal Concert Hall Glasgow and in Ireland, Belgium, Germany, Austria, Switzerland, Netherlands and Scandinavia; has presented productions of: (operas and operettas) The Ratepayer's Iolanthe 1984, Turandot 1991–92, La Bohème (centenary production) 1996, 2004, 2006, Carmen 1997, 2002, 2005, 2009, 2010, 2013, Madam Butterfly 1998, 2000, 2003, 2011, The Pirates of Penzance 1998–99, 2000, Tosca 1999, Aïda 2001, Cavalleria Rusticana and Pagliacci 2002; (ballets) Swan Lake 1997, 1999, 2002, 2004, 2007, 2010, 2013, Romeo and Juliet 1998, The Sleeping Beauty 2000; D'Oyly Carte Opera Co. seasons 2000–03, Follies 2003, On Your Toes 2004, Savoy Opera 2004, Showboat 2006, Carmen Jones 2007, Strictly Gershwin 2008, 2011, The King and I 2009, Aïda (new production) 2012; mem. Bd Royal Philharmonic Orchestra, Bd Govs Cen. School of Ballet; Hon. FRAM 1988, Hon. FTCL 2000, Gold Badge Award, British Acad. of Songwriters, Composers and Authors 2009. *Leisure interests:* living in France, reading. *Address:* Raymond Gubbay Ltd, Dickens House, 15 Tooks Court, London, EC4A 1LB, England (office). *Telephone:* (20) 7025-3750 (office). *E-mail:* info@raymondgubbay.co.uk (office). *Website:* www.raymondgubbay.co.uk (office).

GUBBINS, David, BA, PhD, FRS, FInstP, MMath; British geophysicist and academic; *Professor Emeritus of Geophysics, School of Earth and Environment, University of Leeds;* b. 31 May 1947, Southampton, Hants.; s. of Albert Edmund Gubbins and Joyce Lucy Gubbins (née Rayner); m. Margaret Stella McCloy 1972; one s. two d.; ed King Edward VI Grammar School, Trinity Coll., Cambridge; Visiting Research Fellow, Univ. of Colorado 1972–73; instructor, MIT 1973–74; Asst Prof., UCLA 1974–76; Asst Dir of Research, Dept of Geodesy and Geophysics, Univ. of Cambridge 1976–89; Fellow, Churchill Coll., Cambridge 1978–90; Head of Geophysics, Univ. of Leeds 1989–2001, Research Prof. of Earth Sciences, now Prof. Emer. of Geophysics; Ed. Geophysical Journal of the Royal Astronomical Soc. 1982–90, Physics of the Earth and Planetary Interior 1990–2002; Fellow, American Geophysical Union 1985; Foreign mem. Norwegian Acad. of Arts and Sciences 2005; Hon. mem. European Geosciences Union; Murchison Medal, Geological Soc. of London 1998, Gold Medal, Royal Astronomical Soc. 2003, John Adam Fleming Medal, American Geophysical Union 2004, Chree Medal, Inst. of Physics 2005, Augustus Love Medal, European Geophysical Union 2007, Arthur Holmes Medal, European Geophysical Union 2009. *Publications:* Seismology and Plate Tectonics 1990, Time Series Analysis and Inverse Theory for Geophysicists 2004, Encyclopedia of Geomagnetism and Paleomagnetism 2007; more than 150 articles in scientific journals. *Leisure interests:* sailing, walking. *Address:* School of Earth and Environment, University of Leeds, Leeds, LS2 9JT, England (office). *Telephone:* (113) 343-7181 (office). *Fax:* (113) 343-5259 (office). *E-mail:* d.gubbins@

see.leeds.ac.uk (office). *Website:* www.see.leeds.ac.uk/people/d.gubbins (office); homepages.see.leeds.ac.uk/~ear6dg (office).

GUBENKO, Nikolai Nikolayevich; Russian actor, theatrical director and politician; b. 17 Aug. 1941, Odessa; m. Jeanna Bolotova; ed All-Union Inst. of Cinema; mem. CPSU 1987–91, Cen. Cttee 1990–91, CP of Russian Fed. 1992–2002, expelled from party 2002, Ind. 2002–; actor at Taganka Theatre, Moscow 1964–, Artistic Dir 1987–89; Founder and Head of Concord of Taganka actors 1993–; dir several films including The Orphans (Soviet entry Cannes Film Festival 1977), The Life of Holidaymakers (based on story by Ivan Bunin), Life. . .Tears. . .Love, Restricted Area 1988; stage appearances include Boris Godunov; USSR Minister of Culture 1989–91; mem. State Duma (Parl.) 1995–2003; Deputy Chair. Cttee for Culture 1997–99, Chair. 1999–2003; mem. Moscow City Duma (Parl.) 2005–, Vice-Chair. 2014–; Pres. Int. Asscn of Help for Culture 1992; fmr mem. USSR Presidential Council; RSFSR People's Artist 1985. *Films include:* produced: Mne dvadtsat let 1964, Kogda uletayut aisty 1965, Parol ne nuzhen 1967, Nachalo nevedomogo veka 1967, Parviyat kurier 1968, Dvoryanskoe gnezdo 1969, Direktor 1969, Prishyol soldat s fronta 1971, Yesli khochesh byt schastlivym 1974, Proshu slova 1975, They Fought for Their Country 1975, Podranki 1977; directed: Nastasiya i Fomka 1970, Bratya Makarovy 1970, Iz zhizni otdykhayushchikh 1980, I zhizn, i slyozy, i lyubov 1984, Zapretnaya zona 1988. *Television:* Isayev 2008. *Address:* 110270 Moscow, Franzenskaya nab. 46, Apt. 65, Russia. *Website:* gubenko.mos.ru.

GUDANOV, Dmitry Konstantinovich; Russian ballet dancer; b. 1975, Moscow; ed Moscow Academic School of Choreography; joined Bolshoi Theatre Ballet Co. as a corps-de-ballet dancer 1994, soloist 1997, leading soloist 2000, currently Prin. Dancer; took part in Bolshoi Theatre project New Choreography Workshop 2004; 1st Prize and Gold Medal 7th Int. Moscow Ballet Competition 1998, 1st Prize Int. Ballet Competition Paris 1998, Soul of Dance Prize, Ballet Magazine 2000, Merited Artist of the Russian Fed. 2005. *Ballet:* leading roles in Sleeping Beauty, Nutcracker, Le Mégère Apprivoisée, La Sylphide, Fantasia on the Theme of Casanova, Giselle, Romeo and Juliet, Symphony C-major (production of G. Balanchine), Heir in Hamlet (production of B. Eifman), Chopiniana 2003. *Address:* Bolshoi Theatre, Teatralnaya pl. 1, Moscow, Russia (office). *Website:* www.bolshoi .org (office); mariinsky.ru/en/ballet/gudanov05.

GUÐFINNSON, Einar Kristinn; Icelandic politician; *President of Parliament;* b. 2 Dec. 1955, Bolungarvík; s. of Guðfinnur Einarsson (deceased) and María K. Haraldsdóttir; m. Sigrún J. Þórisdóttir; three c.; ed Coll. of Isafjorður, Univ. of Essex, UK; fmr journalist; fmr CEO fisheries co.; mem. Parl. 1991–, fmr Chair. Fisheries Cttee, Econs and Trade Cttee, fmr mem. Finance Cttee, Social Cttee, Agric. Cttee, Parls Cttee for Foreign Affairs, Pres. of Parl. 2013–; Minister of Fisheries 2005–09 (resgnd), of Agriculture 2007–09 (resgnd); fmr Chair. Icelandic Group, IPU; fmr Group Chair. Independence Party. *Address:* Parliamentary Office, 101 Reykjavik, Iceland (office). *Telephone:* 4567540 (office). *E-mail:* einarg@ althingi.is (office). *Website:* www.xd.is (office); www.althingi.is (office).

GUDMUNDSSON, Már, BA, MPh, PhD; Icelandic economist and central banker; *Governor, Central Bank of Iceland;* b. 1954; m.; three c.; ed Univs of Essex and Cambridge, UK, Univ. of Gothenburg, Sweden; joined Seðlabanki Íslands (Cen. Bank of Iceland) as economist 1980, later Head of Research and Man., Chief Economist 1994–2004, Gov. 2009–; Econ. Adviser to Minister of Finance 1988–91; IMF Adviser to Trinidad and Tobago 1998–99; Deputy Head, Monetary and Econ. Dept, BIS, Basel, Switzerland 2004–09. *Publications include:* several articles in books and econ. journals. *Address:* Office of the Governor, Central Bank of Iceland, Kalkofnsvegur 1, 150 Reykjavík, Iceland (office). *Telephone:* 5699600 (office). *Fax:* 5699605 (office). *E-mail:* sedlabanki@sedlabanki.is (office). *Website:* www .sedlabanki.is (office).

GUÉANT, Claude Henri; French civil servant, government official and lawyer; b. 17 Jan. 1945, Vimy; s. of Robert Guéant and Madeleine Guéant (née Leclercq); m. Rose-Marie Benoist 1969; two c.; ed Faculté de droit de Paris, Institut d'études politiques de Paris, École nationale d'admin, Paris; Cabinet Dir, Prefect of Finistère 1971–74; Sec.-Gen. for Econ. Affairs, Guadeloupe 1974–77; served in Ministry of the Interior 1977–81; apptd sous-préfet hors classe, worked in Centre region prefect 1981, then Sec.-Gen. Hérault Prefect, then Sec.-Gen. Hauts-de-Seine Prefect; Préfet Hautes-Alpes 1991–94; Dir-Gen. Nat. Police Force 1994–98; Préfet Franche-Comté region and Doubs 1998–2000, of Brittany region, Western defence zone and d'Ille-et-Vilaine 2000–02; Chief of Staff to Minister of the Interior Nicolas Sarkozy 2002–04, 2005–07; with Ministry of Finance 2004; campaign manager for presidential campaign of Nicolas Sarkozy 2007; Adviser, Secrétaire général de la Présidence de la République 2007–11; Minister of the Interior, the Overseas Possessions, the Territorial Collectivities and Immigration 2011–12; political adviser to Union for a Popular Movement (UMP); Chevalier, Légion d'honneur, Commdr, Ordre Nat. de Mérite. *Address:* 34 avenue Georges V, 75008 Paris (office); 3 rue Weber, 75116 Paris, France (home). *Telephone:* 1-47-20-57-11 (office); 6-08-26-44-04 (home). *Fax:* 1-47-20-57-98 (office). *E-mail:* cg@ gueantavocats.com (office).

GUEBRE SELLASSIE, Hiroute, BL; Ethiopian lawyer and UN official; *Special Envoy of the Secretary-General for Sahel and Head of Office for Sahel, United Nations;* m.; three c.; ed Univ. of Paris (Sorbonne), France; CEO African Women Cttee on Peace and Devt (est. jtly by ECA and African Union) 1998–2004; Oxfam Regional Peace Building and Conflict Man. Advisor for Horn, East and Central Africa 2005–07; Dir Political Affairs Div. and Head of Goma Regional Office, UN Stabilization Mission in the Democratic Republic of the Congo (MONUSCO) 2007–14; Special Envoy of UN Sec.-Gen. for Sahel and Head of Office for Sahel 2014–. *Address:* United Nations Office for West Africa (UNOWA), Lot 14, Ouest Almadies, BP 23851, Dakar, Senegal (office). *Telephone:* 33-869-8585 (office). *Fax:* 33-820-4638 (office). *Website:* www.unowa.unmissions.org (office).

GUEBUZA, Armando Emílio; Mozambican politician and fmr head of state; *President, Frente de Libertação de Moçambique (Frelimo);* b. 20 Jan. 1943, Murrupula, Nampula Prov.; m. Maria da Luz Guebuza; five c.; joined Frente de Libertação de Moçambique (Frelimo) 1963; elected to Cen. Cttee 1966–, to Politburo 1977–; guerrilla commdr during war with Portugal, rising to rank of Lt Gen.; Political Commissar 1970–; Minister of Home Affairs 1974–78, 1983–84, Deputy Minister of Defence 1978–81, Resident Minister 1981–84, Minister in the Office of the Pres. 1984–86, Minister of Transport and Communication 1986–94; Head of Frelimo Parl. Bench 1994–2002, Frelimo Sec.-Gen. 2002–04, Pres. 2005–; Pres. of Mozambique and C-in-C of the Armed Forces 2005–15; Head of Govt Del. to Rome peace talks 1992; Chair. two Comms for Burundi peace process under Julius Nyerere and Nelson Mandela. *Address:* Frente de Libertação de Moçambique (Frelimo), Rua Pereira do Lago 229, Maputo, Mozambique (office). *Telephone:* (21) 491928 (office). *E-mail:* sg@frelimo.org.mz (office). *Website:* www.frelimo.org.mz (office).

GUEDES, Paulo Roberto Nunes, BEcons, MEcons, PhD; Brazilian economist and politician; *Minister of the Economy;* b. 24 Aug. 1949, Rio de Janeiro; ed Federal Univ. of Minas Gerais, Univ. of Chicago; fmr Prof., Univ. of Chile; Co-founder, CEO and chief strategist, Banco Pactual (now BTG Pactual) 1983; Exec. Dir and Prof., Brazilian Inst. of Capital Markets (IBMEC) 1983–99; co-f. Instituto Millenium (think tank) 2005; fmr Prof. of Macroeconomics, Pontifical Catholic Univ. of Rio de Janeiro, Fundação Getúlio Vargas and Inst. of Pure and Applied Mathematics; fmr columnist for O Globo, Folha de São Paulo and Exame; Pnr, Bozano Investimentos; econ. advisor for presidential campaign of Jair Bolsonaro 2018; Minister of the Economy 2019–. *Address:* Ministry of the Economy, Esplanada dos Ministérios, Bloco P, 5° andar, 70048-900 Brasília, DF, Brazil (office). *Telephone:* (61) 3412-2000 (office). *Website:* www.fazenda.gov.br (office).

GUEDES DE CARVALHO, Luiz Nelson, BA, MA, PhD; Brazilian business executive; *Chairman, Petróleo Brasileiro SA (Petrobras);* ed Univ. of São Paulo Coll. of Econs, Business Admin and Accounting; Dir, Banco Fibra SA 2007–; mem. Bd of Dirs, Petróleo Brasileiro SA (Petrobras) April 2015–, Chair. Sept. 2015–. *Address:* Office of the Chairman, Petrobras, Av. República do Chile, n° 65 - Centro, Rio de Janeiro 20031-912, Brazil (office). *Telephone:* (21) 3224-1000 (office). *Website:* www.petrobras.com.br (office).

GUÉDIGUIAN, Robert; French film-maker, actor and screenwriter; b. 3 Dec. 1953, L'Estaque, Marseille; m. Ariane Ascaride; producer associated with AGAT Films & Cie; Officier, Ordre national du Mérite 2010, Chevalier, Légion d'honneur 2016. *Films include:* Fernand (writer) 1979, Le souffleur (writer, producer) 1985; writer, dir, producer: Dernier été (Prix Georges Sadoul) 1980, Rouge midi 1983, Ki lo sa? 1985, Dieu vomit les tièdes (TV) 1989, Marie-Jo et ses 2 amours 2002, Mon père est ingénieur 2004, Le Voyage en Arménie 2006, Ariane's Thread 2014, Don't Tell Me the Boy Was Mad 2015; writer, dir: L'argent fait le bonheur (Prix Michel Kuhn, Rencontres européennes de Reims) 1992, The Army of Crime 2009, The Snows of Kilimanjaro 2011; producer: Un tour de manège, Montalvo et l'enfant, Variétés 1989, Le cri du cochon 1990, Suzanne Linke, Bali, les couleurs du divin 1992, Marseille, la vieille ville indigne 1993, Baudelaire modernité 1986, Vittel Design 1987 (Grand Prix, Vidéo Festival de Biarritz), Le coupeur d'eau 1989, En direct de l'être humain 1991, C'est trop con (Prix du Jury, Festival européen d'Angers) 1992, Ça se passe en Equateur, Que la vie est belle 1993, A la vie à la mort, Marius et Jeannette, La ville est tranquille 2001, Dernier des fous 2006, Sous les toits de Paris 2007, Romances de terre et d'eau 2002, Les Fautes d'orthographe 2004, Le Dernier des fous 2006, Beneath the Rooftops of Paris 2007, Les Amants naufragés 2010, La Vie en miettes 2011, Notre monde 2013, Les Déferlantes 2013, Le Jeune Karl Marx 2016; producer, dir: Le Promeneur du champ de Mars 2005; actor: L'Ami Giono: Jofroi de la Maussan 1990, Lulu 2002, Rendezvous in Kiruna 2012. *Address:* c/o AGAT Films & Cie., 52 rue Jean-Pierre Timbaud, 75011 Paris, France (office).

GUÉGUINOU, Jean, GCVO; French diplomatist; *President, French Section, Franco-British Council;* b. 17 Oct. 1941; s. of Louis-Bernard Guéguinon and Jeanne-Rose Le Fur; ed Ecole Nat. d'Admin; with Press and Information Dept, Ministry of Foreign Affairs 1967–69; Second Sec., London 1969–71; Head of Mission, Ministry of State/Ministry of Defence 1971–73; Head of Cabinet and Counsellor 1973–76; Dir of Cabinet of Sec. of State reporting to Prime Minister 1976–77; Asst Dir for Southern Africa and Indian Ocean 1977–82; Consul-Gen., Jerusalem 1982–86; Dir Press and Information Service 1986–90; Amb. to Czechoslovakia 1990–92, to Czech Repub. 1993, to UK 1993–98, to the Holy See 1998–2000, Amb. to UNESCO 2003–07; Pres. French Section, Franco-British Council (Conseil Franco-Britannique); Pres. Culturesfrance 2009–10; Chair. Cttee de patronage, Franco-Scottish Asscn 2001; mem. Admin Council, Agence France-Presse 1986–90, Soc. of Friends of the Louvre 2000–, Arts florissants 2001–; Chevalier, Légion d'honneur, Ordre Nat. du Mérite; Commdr Order of St Gregory the Great. *Address:* Conseil franco-britannique, 66 rue de Bellechasse, Paris 75007, France (office). *Telephone:* 1-42-75-79-83 (office). *E-mail:* conseilfrancobritannique@wanadoo.fr (office). *Website:* www .conseilfrancobritannique.info (office).

GUÉHENNO, Jean-Marie; French diplomatist and fmr UN official; *Senior Adviser, Centre for Humanitarian Dialogue;* b. 30 Oct. 1949, Boulogne-sur-Seine (Hauts-de-Seine); s. of Jean Guéhenno and Annie Guéhenno (née Rospabé); m. Michèle Fahy Moss 1981; one d.; ed Lycée Montaigne and Lycée Louis-le-Grand, Paris, École Normale Supérieure, Inst. d'Études Politiques, École Nat. d'Admin, Paris; mem. Court of Auditors 1976–2000, Sr Auditor 1993–2000; Dir Cultural Affairs, French Embassy in Washington, DC 1982–86; Dir Policy Planning Staff, Ministry of Foreign Affairs 1989–93; Amb. to WEU 1993–95; UN Under-Sec.-Gen. for Peacekeeping Operations, New York 2000–08; Chair. Inst. for Higher Defence Studies, Paris 1998–2000; non-resident Sr Fellow, Brookings Inst., Washington, DC (now Distinguished Fellow), New York Univ. Center on Int. Co-operation; Arnold Saltzman Prof. of Professional Practice in Int. and Public Affairs and Dir Center for Int. Conflict Resolution, School of Int. and Public Affairs, Columbia Univ., New York 2012–14, Assoc. Dir Arnold A. Saltzman Inst. for War; UN Deputy to Kofi Annan in his mission in Syria March–July 2012; Chair. Comm. of White Paper on French Defense and National Security 2012–13; Chair. Ethics Cttee of BNP-Paribas; Pres. and CEO Int. Crisis Group 2014–17; Senior Adviser, Centre for Humanitarian Dialogue, Geneva 2018–; mem. Sec.-Gen.'s High-Level Advisory Bd on Mediation, UN 2017–; Officier, Légion d'honneur; Commdr, Bundesverdienstkreuz. *Publications:* La fin de la démocratie (English trans. The End of the Nation-State) 1993, L'avenir de la liberté – la démocratie dans la mondialisation 1999, Guide du maintien de la paix (co-author) 2006, The Fog of Peace 2015. *Leisure interests:* sailing, walking, tennis, reading, art museums. *Address:* Centre for Humanitarian Dialogue, 114 rue de Lausanne, CH-1202

Geneva, Switzerland (office). *Telephone:* 229081130 (office). *E-mail:* guehenno@hdcentre.org (office). *Website:* www.hdcentre.org (office).

GUELENGDOUKSIA OUAÏDOU, Nassour; Chadian politician; b. 1947, Gounou Gaya; ed Paris Demography Inst.; fmrly Sec.-Gen. in Office of the Pres.; Prime Minister of Chad 1997–99; Pres. Nat. Ass. 2002–11; Sec.-Gen. Econ. Community of Cen. African States (ECCAS) 2012–13. *Website:* www.ceeac-eccas.org.

GUELLEH, Ismaïl Omar; Djibouti head of state; *President and Commander-in-Chief of the Armed Forces;* b. 1947, Dire Dawa, Ethiopia; m. Kadra Mahamoud Haïd; joined gen. security dept, French police force 1968, rank of Police Insp. 1970; fmr Chief of Staff of Pres. Hassan Gouled Aptidon; mem. Rassemblement populaire pour le progrès (RPP), currently Pres.; Pres. of Djibouti and C-in-C of the Armed Forces May 1999–. *Address:* Office of the President, Djibouti, Republic of Djibouti (office). *E-mail:* sggpr@intnet.dj (office). *Website:* www.presidence.dj (home).

GUENIN, Marcel André, PhD; Swiss scientist, academic and company director; *Honorary Professor, University of Geneva;* b. 17 July 1937, Geneva; s. of Léandré André and Isabelle Guenin-Bontempo; m. Ingrid Marina Selbach 1962; three s.; ed Eidgenössische Technische Hochschule Zürich, Univ. of Geneva and Harvard Univ., USA; Asst and Master Asst, Univ. of Geneva 1960–64; Research Assoc., Princeton Univ. 1964–66; Lecturer, Grad. Programme, Univs. of Lausanne, Neuchâtel and Geneva 1966–68; Asst Prof., Univ. of Geneva 1968–70, Professeur extraordinaire 1970–73, Professeur ordinaire 1973–2000, Hon. Prof. 2000–, Dir Dept of Theoretical Physics 1974–77, Dir Group of Applied Physics (GAP) 1993–2000, Vice-Rector Univ. of Geneva 1980–83, Rector 1983–87; Pres. PBG Pvt. Bank, Geneva 1987–89; Chair. Bd COGITAS 1988–94, E. & L. Schmidheiny Foundation 1992–2007; mem. Bd BBC Brown Boveri Ltd 1987–96, Brunet 1990–93, Lasarray 1990–93, Soc. d'Instruments de physique 1998–2000; Sec.-Gen. European Physical Soc. 1974–79, Fellow 1980; Sec. Swiss Physical Soc. 1975–79; mem. Bd Soc. Financière de Genève 1988–89; Founding mem. Int. Asscn of Math. Physicists; mem. American Physical Soc. *Publications:* three books and about 40 scientific publs. *Leisure interests:* skiing, sailing, music. *Address:* Applied Physics Group, University of Geneva, 20 Ecole de Medicine, 1211 Geneva 4 (office); 2B chemin des Manons, 1218 Grand-Saconnex (GE), Switzerland (home).

GUÉRARD, Michel Etienne; French chef, restaurateur and hotelier; *President and Director-General, Compagnie Hôtelière et Fermière d'Eugénie les Bains;* b. 27 March 1933, Vétheuil; s. of Maurice Guérard and Georgine Guérard; m. Christine Barthelemy 1974; two d.; ed Lycée Pierre Corneille, Rouen; apprentice patissier, Mantes la Jolie; Head Patissier, Hotel Crillon, Paris; chef to brothers Clérico, Lido, Paris; created restaurant le Pot au Feu, Asnières (two Michelin stars); undertook complex renovation of hotel and thermal treatment centre Les Prés d'Eugénie (now three Michelin stars), Eugénie les Bains; consultant to Nestlé; opened first Comptoir Gourmand Michel Guérard; restored Chai de Bachen and produced a white Tursan, Baron de Bachen; Officier, Légion d'honneur, Ordre nat. du Mérite, Mérite Agricole, des Arts et des Lettres; Chevalier des Palmes académiques; Meilleur Ouvrier de France (MOF Patisserie) 1958. *Publications:* La Grande Cuisine Minceur 1976, La Cuisine Gourmande 1978, Mes Recettes à la TV 1982, Minceur Exquise 1989, Le Sud-Ouest Gourmand de Relais en Châteaux 1993, La Cuisine Gourmande des Juniors 1997, Le Jeu de l'Oie et du Canard 1998, La Cuisine à Vivre 2000, Comment Briller aux Fourneaux sans Savoir Faire Cuire un Oeuf 2010, Minceur Essentielle 2012. *Leisure interests:* antiques, painting, sketchbooks, food and wine. *Address:* Les Prés d'Eugénie, place de l'Impératrice, 40320 Eugénie les Bains, France (office). *Telephone:* (5) 58-05-06-07 (office). *Fax:* (5) 58-51-10-10 (office). *E-mail:* direction@michelguerard.com (office). *Website:* www.michelguerard.com (office).

GUERIN, Orla, MA; Irish journalist; *Egypt Correspondent, British Broadcasting Corporation;* b. May 1966; d. of Patrick James Guerin and Monica Guerin; m. Michael Georgy; ed Coll. of Commerce, Dublin, Univ. Coll. Dublin; newscaster, presenter and Foreign Corresp. with Irish State TV, RTÉ, Dublin 1987–94; joined BBC TV as news corresp. 1995, Southern Europe Corresp. covering the Balkans 1996–2000, Middle East Corresp. 2001–05, Africa Corresp. 2006–08, Pakistan Corresp. 2009–13, Egypt Corresp. based in Cairo 2013–; Hon. MBE 2004; Hon. DUniv (Essex) 2002; Dr hc (Dublin Inst. of Tech.) 2005, (Open Univ.) 2007, (Queen's Univ. Belfast) 2009, (Bradford) 2014; Hon. DLitt (Ulster) 2009; Jacobs Award for Broadcasters (Ireland) 1992, London Press Club Broadcaster of the Year Award 2002, News and Factual Award, Women in Film and Television (UK) 2003, David Bloom Award 2009. *Address:* c/o BBC News, Broadcasting House, Portland Place, London, W1A 1AA, England (office). *Website:* www.bbc.co.uk (office).

GUERRA ABUD, Juan José, MA; Mexican academic, politician, company director and diplomatist; *Ambassador to Italy;* b. 4 Jan. 1952, Toluca, Mexico State; m. Lourdes Macedo Sánchez; three s.; ed Universidad Anáhuac, Univ. of Southern California, USA; Prof. of Macroeconomics, Financial Math. and Differential Calculus, Autonomous Univ. of the State of Mexico and Instituto Tecnologico de Estudios Superiores de Monterrey/Toluca Campus; Dir, Krone Communications 1990–92, Unitec Bölhoff 1993–94; Pres. Nat. Asscn of Mfrs of Buses, Trucks and Tractors 2001–09; Dir-Gen. of Industry, State of Mexico 1988–90, Sec. of Econ. Devt 1994–99; mem. Ecologist Green Party of Mexico; Deputy of LXI Legislature of Mexican Congress representing Mexico State 2009–12, mem. Bd of Political Co-ordination, Chamber of Deputies; Sec. of Environment and Natural Resources, Fed. Govt 2012–15; Amb. to Italy (also accred to Albania, Malta and San Marino and as Perm. Rep. to FAO, IFAD and World Food Programme, Rome) 2016–; Dir, Centre Mario Molina AC 2010–; mem. Bd of Dirs Petroleos Mexicanos (PEMEX) 2014–15, Fed. Electricity Comm. 2014–15; Pres. (ex officio) Tech. Advisory Councils of: Nat. Water Comm., Nat. Forestry Comm., Nat. Inst. of Ecology and Climate Change, Nat. Comm. of Natural Protected Areas, Mexican Inst. of Water Tech. and Interministerial Comm. on Climate Change 2012–15; Chair. State Symphony Orchestra of Mexico; contrib. to El Economista newspaper. *Address:* Embassy of Mexico, Via Lazzaro Spallanzani 16, 00161 Rome, Italy (office). *Telephone:* (06) 4416061 (office). *Fax:* (06) 44292703 (office). *E-mail:* ofna.embajador@emexitalia.it (office); correo@emexitalia.it (office); fao-mx@fao.org (office). *Website:* embamex.sre.gob.mx/italia (office).

GUERRA PASTORA, José Adán, PhD; Nicaraguan politician; b. 28 Oct. 1952, Managua; trained as lawyer; Acting Minister of Foreign Affairs 2000; Minister of Nat. Defence 2001–05; Pres. of Demining Comm.; mem. Office of Nat. Security; mem. Exec., Nat. Comm. for Disaster Prevention, Nat. Council of the War on Drugs; Simón Bolívar Democracy and Human Rights Award, WHINSEC.

GUERRAOUI, Abdellatif; Moroccan business executive and fmr government official; *Chairman, Auto Hall Group;* b. 10 July 1939, Safi; s. of Abdeslam Guerraoui and Oumhani Benazzouz; m. Laila Iaoufir 1968; one s. two d.; ed École nationale supérieure d'électronique, d'électrotechnique, d'informatique, d'hydraulique et des télécommunications, Toulouse, France; Chief of Staff, Computer Systems, Cherifien Office of Phosphates (OCP) 1964–70, Chief of Personnel Admin. Div. 1970–71, Sec.-Gen. OCP 1971–90, mem. Bd of Dirs –2000; Admin., Gen. Man. Moroccan-Saudi Investment Co. (ASMA-INVEST) 1991–93; Minister of Energy and Mines 1993–97, of Social Affairs, Health, Youth and Sports, Nat. Mutual Aid 1997–98; Pres. Bd Tharwa Finance 1999–2001; Wali of the Region Laayoune Boujdour Sakiat El Hamra 2001–02; Gen. Dir Agency for Promotion of Econ. and Social Devt Southern Provs 2002–03; CEO Soc. Maroc Emirats Arabes Unis de Développement (SOMED) 2003–06; Chair. Auto Hall Group 2004–; fmr Vice-Chair. Supervisory Bd Credit du Maroc; Pres. Japan-Morocco Friendship Asscn; Trustee, Al Akhawayn Univ.; mem. Bd Three Cultures and Three Religions Foundation; Officier, Wissam El Arch Grade 1985, Commdr Nat. Order of Merit (Portugal) 2003; Throne Award from King of Morocco 1985, Prize of Japanese Foreign Minister 2016. *Leisure interests:* classical literature, history, management, economy, futurology. *Address:* Auto Hall SA, 64 Avenue Lalla yacout, Casablanca (office); 39 rue Ksar El Badii, Hay El Hana, Préfecture Ain Chock-Hay Hassani, Casablanca 20200, Morocco (home). *Telephone:* (522) 460304 (office); (522) 303041 (home). *Fax:* (522) 318915 (office); (522) 318803 (home). *E-mail:* dg@autohall.ma (office). *Website:* www.autohall.ma (office).

GUERRERO ORTIZ, Donald; Dominican Republic business executive, banker and government official; *Minister of Finance;* ed Instituto Tecnológico de Santo Domingo (INTEC), Univ. of Maryland, USA; several years with Chase Manhattan Bank, including as Credit Man., Second Vice-Pres. of Institutional Banking and Vice-Pres. of Corporate Banking; fmr Vice-Pres., Intercontinental Bank Credit; fmr Commercial Dir, Reid & Pellerano (automotive distribution group); fmr Exec. Vice-Pres., Listin Diario (daily newspaper); co-f. Títulos y Valores, SA (Tivalsa) (securities brokerage) 2013; fmr Pres., Autocentro Toyota and Autocentro Nissan, Puerto Rico; fmr Lecturer in Microeconomics and Business Econs, National Univ. Pedro Henriquez Urena and in Int. Corporate Finance, INTEC; fmr Prof. of Business Strategy, Pontificia Universidad Catolica Madre y Maestra; Minister of Finance 2016–; mem. Dominican Liberation Party, mem. Central Cttee 2014–. *Address:* Ministry of Finance, Avda México 45, esq. Leopoldo Navarro, Apdo 1478, Santo Domingo DN, Dominican Republic (office). *Telephone:* 687-5131 (office). *Fax:* 682-0498 (office). *E-mail:* info@hacienda.gov.do (office). *Website:* www.hacienda.gov.do (office).

GUERRERO PEÑARANDA, Ramiro; Bolivian lawyer and politician; *Attorney-General;* ed Universidad San Francisco Xavier de Chuquisaca; practised law for 20 years; worked with peasant orgs and indigenous peoples with la Fundación Tierra; adviser to Federación de Campesinos, Consejo de Capitanes y Guaraníes de Chuquisaca; mem. Movimiento Al Socialismo 2006–07, was part of the Comm. on Land and Territory; apptd Judge of the then Supreme Court (Corte Suprema de Justicia) by Pres. Evo Morales 2010–12; Attorney-Gen. 2012–. *Address:* Office of the Attorney-General, c/o Ministry of Justice, Avenida 16 de Julio (El Prado) 1769, La Paz, Bolivia (office). *Telephone:* (2) 212-4725 (office). *Fax:* (2) 231-5468 (office). *E-mail:* ministerio@justicia.gob.bo (office). *Website:* www.justicia.gob.bo (office).

GUERROUJ, Hicham al-; Moroccan professional athlete; b. 14 Sept. 1974, Berkane; set six world records indoors and outdoors 1997–99 (including 1500m, 3:26.00, Rome, July 1998, one mile, 3:43.12, Rieti, July 1999, 2,000m, 4:44.79, Berlin, Sept. 1999); bronze medal, World Jr Championships 5000m 1992; World Champion 1,500m 1997, 1999, 2001, 2003; Indoor World Champion 1500m 2001; silver medallist, 2000 Olympics, gold medallist 1500m 2004 Olympics; winner IAAF Grand Prix Final 1500m 2001, 2002; silver medallist World Championships 5000m 2003; holder of outdoor world record for 1500m, 2000m and one mile, of indoor record for 1500m and one mile; winner of 72 races from 75 starts 1996–2002; retd 2006; mem. IAAF Athletes Comm. 2003–, Int. Cttee Olympic Athletes Comm. 2004–, Culture and Olympic Educ. Comm. 2007–, Nominations Comm. 2010–; Cordon de Commandeur 2004, IAAF Male Athlete of the Year 2001, 2002, 2003, US Track and Field Male Athlete of the Year 2002, Prince of Asturias Award 2004.

GUESNERIE, Roger Sylvain Maxime Auguste, DèsSc (Econs); French economist and academic; *Professor of Economics, Collège de France;* b. 17 Feb. 1943, Ste Gemmes Le Robert; s. of Sylvain Guesnerie and Marie Chapelière; ed Lycée de Rennes, Ecole Polytechnique and Ecole Nat. des Ponts et Chaussées, Univ. of Toulouse; Research Assoc., Centre d'Études Prospectives et de Recherches en Économie Mathématique Appliquée à la Planification (CEPREMAP) 1967–81; Lecturer, École Nationale des Ponts et Chaussées 1970–83, Paris X Nanterre 1972–73, École Polytechnique 1974–86, Institut d'Études Politiques de Paris 1975–78, Paris IX-Dauphine 1974–76; Research Assoc., CNRS 1976, Research Dir 1978; Prof., École Nationale de la Statistique et de l'Admin Économique 1978–84; Dir of Studies, École des Hautes Études en Sciences Sociales (EHESS) 1979–; Dir Centre d'Études Quantitatives Comparatives (CEQC) 1981–82, Centre d'Études et de Recherches en Analyse Socio-économiques (CERAS) 1982–84, Asscn pour le Développement de la Recherche en Économie et Statistique (ADRES) 1989–94, Dir Delta (mixed research unit of CNRS-EHESS-ENS) 1988–2000, Fédération Paris Jourdan 2001–05; Prof., LSE 1990–94; Prof. of Econs, Collège de France 2000–; Vice-Pres. European Econ. Asscn 1992, Pres. 1994; Pres. Scientific Cttee CEPREMAP 1992–95, Select Cttee on Econ. and Social Sciences, Brussels 1992–95, Asscn of Applied Econometrics 1997–2001, Asscn Française de Science Économique 2002–03; Pres. of Bd, Paris School of Econs 2008–; mem. Scientific Council EHESS 1985–91, Nat. Cttee CNRS 1987–91, European Asscn of Science and Tech. 1994–97, Research Council of École Polytechnique 2000–02, Conseil d'Analyse Économique 2000–10, Nat. Cttee on Social and Scientific Co-ordination 2001–02, Scientific Cttee École Normale Supérieure 2001–05, Jury des Chaires Blaise Pascal 2002–11; Co-Ed. Econometrica 1984–89; Pres. Programme Bd, Journées d'Économie de Lyon 2009–, Scientific Bd, Économie et Statistique 2009–;

mem. Editorial Bd, Macroeconomic Dynamics 1996–, Journal of Public Economic Theory 1998–, Revue d'Économie Politique 2003–, Mathematics and Financial Economics 2007–10, New Palgrave Dictionary of Economics 2009–; Foreign Fellow, Churchill Coll., Univ. of Cambridge 1978; Fellow, Econometric Soc., Pres. 1996; Foreign mem. American Acad. of Arts and Sciences 2000–; Hon. Foreign mem. American Econ. Asscn 1997; Chevalier, Legion d'honneur, Ordre nat. du Mérite; Dr hc (École des Hautes Études Commerciales) 2001; Silver Medal, CNRS 1994. *Publications:* La documentation Française (two vols), (co-author), Modèles de l'économie publique 1980, A Contribution to the Pure Theory of Taxation 1995, L'Économie de marché 1996, Assessing Rational Expectations 1 2001, Assessing Rational Expectations 2 2005, L'Économie de marché 2006, Ethique et changement climatique (co-author) 2009, La santé, par quels moyens, à quel prix (co-author) 2010, Pour une politique climatique globale 2010; about 100 articles in econ. journals. *Leisure interests:* cycling, jogging, walking. *Address:* Office 202, Second Floor, Building A, Campus Jourdan, Collège de France, 48 boulevard Jourdan, 75014 Paris, France (office). *Telephone:* 1-43-13-63-15 (office). *Fax:* 1-43-13-63-10 (office). *E-mail:* guesnerie@pse.ens.fr (office); roger.guesnerie@ens.fr (office); roger.guesnerie@college-de-france.fr (office). *Website:* www.college-de-france.fr/site/roger-guesnerie/biographie__1.htm (office); www.pse.ens.fr/guesnerie (office); www.delta.ens.fr/annuaires/chercheurs/article/guesnerie-roger?lang=fr (office); www.parisschoolofeconomics.eu/en/guesnerie-roger (office).

GUEST, 5th Baron Haden-Guest; **Christopher;** American actor, film director and screenwriter; b. (Christopher Haden-Guest), 5 Feb. 1948, New York City; s. of Peter Haden-Guest, Baron of Saling in the Co. of Essex; m. Jamie Lee Curtis 1984; two c.; ed High School of Arts and Music, New York City, Bard Coll.; theatre debut in Room Service, Broadway 1970; writer and performer, Nat. Lampoon radio series 1970s; appeared as Tufnel on Lenny and the Squigtones (album) 1980; wrote script and music for film This is Spinal Tap (with Rob Reiner, Michael McKean and Harry Shearer) 1984, later toured as band Spinal Tap; writer and dir Morton & Hayes TV series 1991; mem. House of Lords 1996–99; mem. Bd of Trustees Berklee Coll. of Music 2008. *Television:* films: The TVTV Show 1977, It Happened One Christmas 1977, The Billion Dollar Bubble 1978, Million Dollar Infield 1982, A Piano for Mrs. Cimino 1982, Likely Stories, Vol. 1 1981, Close Ties 1983, I, Martin Short, Goes Hollywood 1989, Halloween Jam at Universal Studios 1992, A Spinal Tap Reunion: The 25th Anniversary London Sell-Out 1992, D.O.A. 1999; others: Blind Ambition (mini-series) 1979, Saturday Night Live (series) 1984–85. *Films include:* The Hot Rock 1972, Death Wish 1974, The Fortune 1975, Girlfriends 1978, The Last Word 1980, The Long Riders 1980, Heartbeeps 1981, Million Dollar Infield 1982, Blind Ambition 1982, This is Spinal Tap 1984, Little Shop of Horrors 1986, The Princess Bride 1987, Beyond Therapy 1987, Sticky Fingers 1988, The Big Picture 1989 (writer and dir), The Return of Spinal Tap 1992, Spinal Tap: Break Like the Wind 1992 (writer and dir), A Few Good Men 1992, Attack of the 50 Foot Woman 1993 (writer and dir), Waiting for Guffman (also writer and dir) 1996, Spinal Tap: The Final Tour 1998, Small Soldiers 1998, Almost Heroes (writer and dir) 1998, Catching Up with Marty DiBeri 2000, Best in Show (also writer and dir) 2000, A Mighty Wind (also writer and dir) 2003, Mrs Henderson Presents 2005, For Your Consideration (also writer and dir) 2006, Night at the Museum: Battle of the Smithsonian 2009, The Invention of Lying 2009, Mascots 2016 (also writer and dir). *Address:* c/o United Talent Agency Inc., 9336 Civic Center Drive, Beverly Hills, CA 90210, USA (office). *Telephone:* (310) 273-6700 (office). *Fax:* (310) 247-1111 (office).

GUEST, John Rodney, DPhil, FRS; British molecular geneticist and academic; *Professor Emeritus of Microbiology, University of Sheffield;* b. 27 Dec. 1935, Leeds, Yorks.; s. of Sidney R. Guest and D. Kathleen Guest (née Walker); m. Barbara M. Dearsley 1962 (died 2015); one s. two d.; ed Campbell Coll., Belfast, Univ. of Leeds, Trinity Coll., Oxford; Guinness Research Fellow, Univ. of Oxford 1960–65; Research Assoc. and Fulbright Scholar, Stanford Univ., USA 1963, 1964; Lecturer in Microbiology, Univ. of Sheffield 1965–68, Sr Lecturer and Reader 1968–81, Prof. of Microbiology 1981–2000, Prof. Emer. 2000–; Science and Eng Research Council Sr Fellowship 1981–86; Hon. mem. Microbiology Soc. 2000; Royal Soc. Leeuwenhoek Lecturer 1995. *Achievements include:* cloned and sequenced genes of the Citric Acid Cycle, Aspartase, and discovered and characterized an Oxygen-responding Gene Regulator (FNR) in bacteria. *Publications:* research papers in scientific journals. *Leisure interests:* hill walking, beekeeping, family history, science, natural history. *Address:* Department of Molecular Biology and Biotechnology, University of Sheffield, Western Bank, Sheffield, South Yorks., S10 2TN, England (office). *Telephone:* (114) 230-4192 (home). *E-mail:* j.r.guest@sheffield.ac.uk (office).

GUEVARA MANZO, Gloria, MBA; Mexican tourism industry executive and politician; *President and CEO, World Travel & Tourism Council;* b. 1967; ed Universidad Anáhuac, Kellogg School of Business, Northwestern Univ., USA; began career with NCR Corpn and AT&GIS Mexico; several years in tourism industry with Sabre Travel Network in Mexico and USA, including sales, training, customer service, operations and technology roles, becoming Technology Dir Customer Service and Operations, Sabre Travel Network Latin America and the Caribbean, later with Sabre Holdings, Southlake, Tex., Vice-Pres. and Gen. Dir Sabre Travel Network Mexico 2005–10; Sec. of Tourism, and Head of Mexican Tourism Bd 2010–12; Pres. and CEO World Travel & Tourism Council 2017–. *Address:* World Travel & Tourism Council, The Harlequin Building, 65 Southwark Street, London, SE1 0HR, England (office). *Telephone:* (20) 74818007 (office). *Fax:* (20) 74881008 (office). *Website:* www.wttc.org (office).

GUEVARA OBREGÓN, Alberto José, MSc; Nicaraguan politician, economist and fmr central banker; b. 1963; m.; three c.; ed Carlos Fonseca Amador Univ., Catholic Univ. of Chile and Nat. Univ. of Nicaragua; fmr Prof. of Economics and Public Finance; held various positions at Banco Central de Nicaragua (cen. bank) 1999–2006, Pres. 2012–14, also Gov. Inter-American Devt Bank; Minister of Finance and Public Credit 2007–12.

GUHA, Ramachandra, MA, PhD; Indian writer and historian; b. 29 April 1958, Dehradun; s. of Subramaniam Rama Das Guha; m. Sujata Keshavan; two c.; ed St Stephen's Coll., Delhi, Delhi School of Econs, Indian Inst. of Man., Calcutta; taught at Yale Univ. and Stanford Univ., USA; Fellow, Wissenschaftskolleg zu Berlin, Germany 1994–95; fmr Arné Naess Chair. Univ. of Oslo; fmr Indo-American Community Visiting Prof., Univ. of California, Berkeley, Sundaraja Visiting Prof. in the Humanities, Indian Inst. of Science, Bangalore 2003; Philippe Roman Chair in History and International Affairs, LSE 2011–12; fmr columnist, The Telegraph of Calcutta; currently full-time writer; Trustee, New India Foundation; Dr hc (Yale Univ.) 2014; MacArthur Fellowship, Leopold-Hidy Prize, American Soc. of Environmental History 2001, Daily Telegraph Cricket Soc. Book of the Year 2002, Malcolm Adideshiah Award, R. K. Narayan Prize 2003, Padma Bhushan 2009, Fukuoka Asian Culture Prize 2015. *Publications:* The Unquiet Woods: Ecological Change and Peasant Resistance in the Himalaya 1989, This Fissured Land: An Ecological History of India (co-author) 1992, Wickets in the East 1992, Social Ecology (co-ed.) 1994, Spin and Other Turns 1994, An Indian Cricket Omnibus (co-ed.) 1994, Ecology and Equity (co-ed.) 1995, Nature, Culture, Imperialism: Essays on the Environmental History of South Asia (co-author) 1996, Varieties of Environmentalism: Essays North and South (co-author) 1997, Savaging the Civilized – Verrier Elwin, his tribals and India 1999, An Anthropologist Among the Marxists, and other essays 2000, Environmentalism: A Global History 2000, Institutions and Inequalities: Essays in Honour of André Béteille (co-author) 2000, A Corner of a Foreign Field (Daily Telegraph Cricket Soc. Book of the Year 2002) 2001, The Picador Book of Cricket (ed.) 2001, An Indian Cricket Century (ed.) 2002, The Last Liberal and Other Essays 2004, The States of Indian Cricket 2005, How Much Should a Person Consume?: Thinking Through the Environment 2006, Nature's Spokesman: M. Krishnan and Indian Wildlife (ed.) 2007, India after Gandhi: The History of the World's Largest Democracy (Sahitya Akademi Award 2011) 2007, The Miracle That Is India 2007, Gandhi Before India 2014, Makers of Modern Asia (ed.) 2014, Democrats and Dissenters 2016, Gandhi: The Years That Changed the World, 1914–1948 2018; contrib. essays, articles and reviews to magazines. *Address:* 22A Brunton Road, Bangalore 560 025, India (home). *E-mail:* ramachandraguha@yahoo.in. *Website:* ramachandraguha.in.

GUHA, Subhendu, PhD; American (b. Indian) scientist and academic; *Senior Vice-President and Chairman, United Solar Ovonic LLC;* b. Calcutta, India; ed Presidency Coll., Univ. of Calcutta, Univ. of Sheffield, UK; worked on semiconductors at Tata Inst. of Fundamental Research 1970–82; Sr Vice-Pres. Photovoltaic Tech., Energy Conversion Devices, USA 1982–90, Pres. United Solar Ovonic LLC (wholly-owned subsidiary) 2000–03, Pres. and COO 2003–07, Sr Vice-Pres. and Chair. 2007–, Co-founder United Solar Systems (jt venture co. with Canon Inc. of Japan) 1990; mem. Advisory Bd Nat. Center for Photovoltaics; Grand Award (Best of What's New), Popular Science 1996, Discover Magazine's Tech. Innovation Award 1997, R&D Magazine's R&D 100 Award 1998, Bright Light Award, US Dept of Energy, World Tech. Award in Energy, The World Tech. Network 2005. *Achievements include:* noted for pioneering work with amorphous silicon; leading inventor of flexible solar shingles for converting sunlight to electricity. *Publications:* more than 200 publs and 30 US patents on the science and tech. of amorphous silicon alloy solar cells. *Leisure interests:* reading, listening to music. *Address:* United Solar Ovonic LLC, 2956 Waterview Drive, Rochester Hills, MI 48309, USA (office). *Telephone:* (248) 293-0440 (office). *Fax:* (248) 844-1214 (office). *E-mail:* info@uni-solar.com (office). *Website:* www.uni-solar.com (office).

GUICHOT FLIPO, Isabelle, MBA; French business executive; *President and CEO, Balenciaga SA- Gucci Group;* b. 1 Oct. 1964, Suresnes; m.; two c.; ed École des Hautes Études Commerciales School of Man., Paris; several sr positions over 19 years at Richemont SA including Commercial Sales Dir, Man. Dir Cartier SA, CEO Lancel, CEO Van Cleef & Arpels Int. 1999–2005; Dir of Business Devt, Gucci Group NV 2005–, Exec. Vice-Pres. 2007–, Pres. and CEO Sergio Rossi 2005–07, Balenciaga SA (subsidiary of PPR) 2007–; Chevalier, Légion d'honneur. *Address:* Balenciaga SA, 15 rue Cassette, 75006 Paris, France (office). *Telephone:* 1-56-52-17-17 (office). *Website:* www.guccigroup.com (office); www.balenciaga.com (office).

GUIG, Mohamed Lemine Ould, DIur; Mauritanian politician; *Secretaire General Adjoint, League of Arab States;* b. 1 July 1959, Oualata; fmr Dir of Higher Educ.; Prof., Nouakchott Univ. 1987–97, Dean, Faculty of Law and Econs 1990–92; Lecturer and Dir of Studies, Int. Inst. of Human Rights, Strasbourg 1989; Chargé de mission to Sec. of State in charge of Civil Affairs 1993–95; Dir of Higher Educ., Ministry of Nat. Educ. 1995–97; Prime Minister of Mauritania 1997–98; Pres. Cour des Comptes 1998–2001; Minister Sec.-Gen. of the Presidency 2001–03, 2008–; Commr for Food Security 2003–04; Secretaire Gen. Adjoint, League of Arab States 2015–; Pres. Int. Political Science, Rights and Liberties Foundation; mem. Nat. Ass., Chair. Human Resources Cttee; Founder-mem. Asscn internationale des enseignants et chercheurs des droits de l'homme, Strasbourg; mem. Institut de Droit d'expression française, Paris; Gen. Insp. of State. *Address:* League of Arab States, Tahrir Square, Cairo, Egypt (office); c/o Office of the Prime Minister, Nouackchott, Mauritania. *Telephone:* (2) 25742989 (Cairo) (office); (2) 25752966 (Cairo) (office); 45252317 (Nouackchott) (office); 45252581 (Nouackchott) (office); 45258518 (Nouackchott) (office). *Fax:* (2) 25761017 (Cairo) (office); 45293473 (Nouackchott) (office). *E-mail:* mloguig@yahoo.fr (office). *Website:* www.lasportal.org/en/Pages/default.aspx (office); ouldguig.skyrock.com.

GUIGNABODET, Lily (Liliane), LèsL; French writer; b. (Lily Lea Graciani), 26 March 1939, Paris; d. of Moïse Graciani and Olympia N. Graciani; m. Jean Guignabodet 1961; one s. two d.; ed primary school in Sofia, Bulgaria, Lycée Jules Ferry, Paris, Univ. of Paris (Sorbonne), Univ. of London, UK; Prof. of French, San José, USA 1961–62; Prof. of Literature, Arts and Culture, Ecole Technique d'IBM France 1966–69; began career as author 1977; mem. PEN Club Français, Soc. des Gens de Lettres, Acad. Européenne des Sciences, des Arts et des Lettres, Acad. Valentin; Cambridge Proficiency Certificate; Prix George Sand 1977, Grand Prix du Roman, Acad. Française 1983, Grand Prix du Roman, Ville de Cannes 1991. *Publications include:* L'écume du silence 1977, Le bracelet indien 1980, Natalia 1983, Le livre du vent 1984, Dessislava 1986, Car les hommes sont meilleurs que leur vie 1991, Un sentiment inconnu 1998. *Leisure interests:* travel, photography, piano. *Address:* 55 rue Caulaincourt, 75018 Paris, France. *Telephone:* 1-46-06-09-86.

GUIGOU, Élisabeth Alexandrine Marie, LèsL; French politician; b. (Élisabeth Vallier), 6 Aug. 1946, Marrakesh, Morocco; d. of Georges Vallier and Jeanne Flecchia; m. Jean-Louis Guigou 1966; one s.; ed Lycée Victor Hugo, Marrakesh, Lycée Descartes, Rabat, Facultés des Lettres, Rabat and Montpellier, Faculté des Sciences Economiques, Montpellier and Ecole Nat. d'Admin; joined Ministry of Finance 1974, served in Office of the Treasury 1974–75, Office of Banks 1976–78,

Office of Financial Markets 1978–79; Deputy Chair. Finance Cttee VIIth Plan 1975–78; Maître de Conférences, Inst. d'Etudes Politiques, Paris 1976; Financial Attaché, Embassy in London 1979–81; Head, Office for Europe, America and Asia, Treasury 1981; Tech. Counsellor, Office of Minister of Economy and Finance 1982–88; with Office of Pres. of Repub. 1988–90; Sec.-Gen. Interministerial Cttee on European Econ. Cooperation 1985–90; Minister Delegate for European Affairs 1990–93; mem. Regional Council of Provence Alpes Côte-d'Azur 1992–2001, European Parl. 1994–97; elected Deputy to Nat. Ass. for Vaucluse (Socialist Party) 1997–2002, for Seine-Saint-Denis (9ème circonscription) 2002–; Minister of Justice 1997–2000, of Employment and Solidarity 2000–02; Deputy Mayor of Noisy-le-Sec 2008–10. *Publications:* Pour les Européens 1994, Etre femme en politique 1997, Je vous parle d'Europe 2004, Pour une Europe juste 2011, L'Europe: les défis de la première puissance économique mondiale 2014. *Address:* Assemblée nationale, 126 rue de l'Université, 75355 Paris 07 SP, France (office). *E-mail:* elisabeth.guigou@assemblee-nationale.fr (office). *Website:* www.assemblee-nationale.fr/13/tribun/fiches_id/1579.asp (office).

GUILFOYLE, The Hon. Dame Margaret Georgina Constance, AC, DBE, LLB; Australian politician and accountant; b. 15 May 1926, Belfast, Northern Ireland; d. of William McCartney and Elizabeth Jane Ellis; m. Stanley Martin Leslie Guilfoyle 1952; one s. two d.; ed ANU; chartered sec. and accountant 1947–; Liberal mem. Senate for Victoria 1971–87; Minister for Educ. Nov.–Dec. 1975, for Social Security 1975–80, for Finance 1980–83; Deputy Chair. Mental Health Research Inst. 1988–2000, Infertility Treatment Authority 1996–2002; Chair. Judicial Remuneration Tribunal 1995–2001, Ministerial Advisory Cttee on Women's Health 1996–99, Australian Political Exchange Council 1996–2009; Dir Australian Children's TV Foundation 1989–2003; mem. Nat. Inquiry Concerning Human Rights of People with Mental Illness 1990–93; Fellow, Australian Soc. of Accountants; Fellow, Chartered Inst. of Secs and Administrators; mem. Review of the Australian Blood Banking and Plasma Product Sector 1999; Silver Jubilee Medal 1977, Centenary Medal 2003. *Leisure interests:* reading, opera. *Address:* 34/2 Malmsbury Street, Kew, Vic. 3101, Australia (home).

GUILIANI CURY, Hugo, BEcons; Dominican Republic journalist, banker, politician and diplomatist; b. 25 May 1940, Puerto Plata; ed Univ. of Miami, USA, Latin America Econ. Planning Inst., Chile, Man. Research Inst. of Admin. Science, Netherlands; fmr Minister of Industry and Commerce 2001–02, and of Finance 1984; fmr mem. Pres.'s Council of Econ. Advisers; currently Pnr, Guiliani Cury and Asociados, Santo Domingo; Dir Banco de Reservas de la Republica, Gov. Banco Central de la República Dominicana 1984–86; chief negotiator for Dominican Repub. agreements with IMF and World Bank 1985; fmr Tech. Dir Corpn of Enterprises; Prof. of Business and Econs, Univ. of Santo Domingo 1966–77; producer of weekly ¿Con los Guiliani Cury? TV programme 1997–2008; columnist, Hoy (daily newspaper) 1970–84; Amb. to USA 2002–04, to Qatar 2006–. *Publications:* nine books on econ. subjects. *Address:* POB 23545, Doha, Qatar (office). *Telephone:* 44113868 (office). *E-mail:* info@domrepemb-qatar.com (office). *Website:* www.domrepemb-qatar.com (office).

GUILLAUD, Adm. Édouard; French naval officer; b. 10 July 1953, Paris; s. of Jean-Louis Guillaud; m. Odile Dattin; ed Lycée Hector Berlioz, Vincennes, École Sainte Geneviève, Versailles, École navale, École supérieure de guerre navale, École des applications militaires de l'énergie atomique, Centre des hautes études militaires, Institut des hautes études de Défense nationale; following graduation, served on escort ship Paimpolaise monitoring nuclear trials in Mururoa 1976–78, on SNLE L'Indomptable 1978, on Le Redoutable 1978; took command of minesweeper Lobelia 1979; studies in gunnery and missiles 1980–81; exchange visit to USA early 1980s; served on aviso Amyot d'Inville and T47 class destroyers, Du Chayla and Kersaint, cruising off Iran and Lebanon 1981–84; worked on computer expert systems of nuclear aircraft carrier programme 1984–87; promoted to Capitaine de corvette 1985; took command of the BATRAL (Bâtiment de Transport Léger) Dumont d'Urville taking part in operations surrounding the Ouvéa cave hostage taking 1987–88; promoted to Capitaine de frégate 1989; obtained degree in nuclear eng 1990; served as manoeuvre officer on Clemenceau in Gulf War 1990–92; took command of light escort Enseigne de vaisseau Henry (F749) 1992–93; promoted to Capitaine de vaisseau 1996; Deputy then Programme Officer on nuclear aircraft carrier Charles De Gaulle 1993–97, Second Officer 1997–99, Capt. 1999–2001, supervised her trials and fittings; served as naval aid to Chief of the Personal Staff of Pres. of the Repub. 2002–04; Préfet maritime for the English Channel and North Sea 2004–06; promoted to Vice-Adm. 2006; Chief of Mil. Staff of Pres. of the Repub. 2006; promoted to Adm. 2007; Chief of Defence Staff (Chef d'État-Major des Armées) 25 Feb. 2010–14; commanded French forces enforcing Libyan no-fly zone March–Oct. 2011; mem. Yacht Club of France, Cercle de la Mer; Grand Officier, Légion d'honneur; Officier, Ordre nat. du Mérite, Ordre du Mérite maritime; Médaille d'Outre-Mer; Médaille de la Défense nationale échelon bronze; Médaille de reconnaissance de la Nation; Croix du Mérite, Ordre de Malte. *Leisure interests:* spending time with his grandchildren, reading, art, history. *Address:* c/o Office of the Chief of the Defence Staff, Ministry of Defence, 14 rue Saint Dominique, 75007 Paris, France (office).

GUILLAUME, Gilbert; French judge; *Judge ad hoc, International Court of Justice;* b. 4 Dec. 1930, Bois-Colombes; s. of Pierre Guillaume and Berthe Guillaume; m. Marie-Anne Hidden 1961; one s. two d.; ed Univ. of Paris, Paris Inst. of Political Studies and Ecole Nat. Admin; mem. Council of State 1957; Legal Adviser, State Secr. for Civil Aviation 1968–79; French Rep. Legal Cttee of ICAO 1968–69, Chair. of Cttee 1971–75; Chair. Conciliation Comm. OECD 1973–78; Dir of Legal Affairs, OECD 1979; French Rep. Cen. Comm. for Navigation of the Rhine 1979–87, Chair. 1981–82; Dir of Legal Affairs, Ministry of Foreign Affairs 1979–87; Conseiller d'Etat 1981–96; Judge, Int. Court of Justice 1987–2005, Pres. 2000–03, Judge ad hoc 2006–; First Vice-Pres. Institut de droit int.; Counsel/agent for France in int. arbitration proceedings, numerous cases before European Courts etc.; mem. Perm. Court of Arbitration 1980–; currently mem. Acad. des Sciences Morales et Politiques; Arbitrator, OSCE, ICSID etc.; del. to numerous int. legal and diplomatic confs; Prof., Inst. of Political Studies, Univ. of Paris and other lecturing appointments; mem. Bd Hon. Eds Chinese Journal of International Law; mem. various legal asscns, insts etc.; Grand Officier, Légion d'honneur; Commdr des Arts et des Lettres; Chevalier, Ordre nat. du Mérite, du Mérite agricole, du Mérite maritime. *Publications:* numerous books and articles on admin. and int. law, including Terrorisme et droit international 1989, Les grandes crises internationales et le droit 1994, La Cour Internationale de Justice à l'aube du XXIème siècle 2003. *Address:* International Court of Justice, Peace Palace, 2517 KJ, The Hague, Netherlands (office); 36 rue Perronet, 92200 Neuilly-sur-Seine, France (home). *Telephone:* (70) 302-24-60 (office); 1-46-24-25-67 (home). *Fax:* (70) 302-24-09 (office); 1-47-45-67-84 (home). *E-mail:* g.guillaume@icj-cij.org (office); g.ma.guillaume@orange.fr (home).

GUILLAUME JEAN JOSEPH MARIE, HRH Prince; b. 11 Nov. 1981; s. of HRH Grand Duke Henri and HRH Grand Duchess Maria Teresa of Luxembourg; m. Countess Stéphanie de Lannoy 2012; ed Lycée Robert Schuman, Collège Alpin Int. Beau Soleil and Institut Le Rosey, Switzerland, Royal Mil. Acad., Sandhurst and Durham Univ., UK; proclaimed Hereditary Grand Duke of Luxembourg 18 Dec. 2000; apptd army Lt by Grand-Ducal Decree 2002, apptd First Lt 2003; Chair. Kräizbierg Foundation 2000–; Hon. Pres. Bd of Econ. Devt 2001–; Kt, Order of the Gold Lion of the House of Nassau 1981, Grand Cross, Order of Adolphe of Nassau 1999, Grand Cross, Order of the Oak Crown; Grand Officer (or 2nd Class), Order of the White Double Cross (Slovakia) 2005, Kt Grand Cross, Order of Merit of the Italian Repub. 2009, Grand Cross, Order of Orange-Nassau (Netherlands) 2012. *Leisure interests:* playing piano, enjoys football, swimming and volleyball. *Address:* Grand Ducal Palace, 2013 Luxembourg, Luxembourg (office). *Website:* www.gouvernement.lu.

GUILLEM, Sylvie; French ballet dancer; b. 23 Feb. 1965, Le Blanc Mesnil; joined Ecole de Danse, Paris Opera 1976; Ballet de l'Opéra as Quadrille 1981, promoted to Coryphée 1982, to Sujet 1983, Première Danseuse, later Etoile 1984; Prin. Guest Artist, Royal Ballet, London 1988–2007; choreographer, Giselle, Nat. Ballet of Finland 1999; Assoc. Artist, Sadler's Wells Theatre 2006–; embarked on int. farewell tour Life in Progress 2015; mem. Advisory Bd Sea Shepherd Conservation Soc.; Hon. CBE 2003; Commandeur des Arts et Lettres 1988, Médaille de Vermeil de la ville de Paris 1993, Chevalier, Légion d'honneur 1994, Gente Dame d'Honneur des Hospitaliers de Pomerol 2000, Officier, Légion d'honneur 2009; Grand Prix national de danse, Grand Prix Pavlova 1989, Médaille de Vermeil de la Ville de Paris 1993, Prix Nijinski 2001, Golden Lion for Lifetime Achievement, Biennale Danza of Venice 2012, Praemium Imperiale, Tokyo, Prix Benois de la Danse, Laurence Olivier Award, Soc. of London Theatre 2015, De Valois Award for Outstanding Achievements, Critics' Circle Nat. Dance Award 2016. *Leading roles in:* Romeo and Juliet, Don Quixote, Raymonda, Swan Lake, Giselle, Notre Dame de Paris, Manon, Marguerite and Armand. *Created roles include:* Cendrillon, In the Middle, Somewhat Elevated, Magnificat, Le Martyre de Saint-Sébastien. *Created and produced:* Evidentia (TV) 1995; Prize for Excellence and Gold Medal, Varna Int. Dance Competition 1983, Prix Carpeau 1985, Hans Christian Andersen Award 1988, Arpège Prize (Lanvin perfumes) 1989. *Address:* c/o Sadler's Wells, Rosebery Avenue, London, EC1R 4TN, England (office). *Telephone:* (20) 7863-8198 (office). *Fax:* (20) 7863-8016 (office). *E-mail:* reception@sadlerswells.com (office). *Website:* www.sadlerswells.com (office); www.sylvieguillem.com.

GUILLEMIN, Roger Charles Louis, BA, BSc, MD, PhD; American professor of medicine; *Distinguished Professor, The Salk Institute;* b. 11 Jan. 1924, Dijon, France; s. of Raymond Guillemin and Blanche Guillemin; m. Lucienne Jeanne Billard 1951; one s. five d.; ed Univs of Dijon and Lyon, France, Univ. of Montréal, Canada; Prosector of Anatomy, Univ. of Dijon Medical School 1946–47; Research Asst, Inst. of Experimental Medicine and Surgery, Univ. of Montréal 1949–51, Assoc. Dir and Asst Prof. of Experimental Medicine 1951–53; Asst Prof. of Physiology, Coll. of Medicine, Baylor Univ., Houston, Tex. 1953, Assoc. Prof. 1957, Prof. of Physiology and Dir Labs for Neuroendocrinology 1963–70, Adjunct Prof. of Physiology 1970–; Consultant in Physiology, Veterans' Admin. Hosp., Houston 1954–60, 1967–70; Lecturer in Experimental Endocrinology, Dept of Biology, W. M. Rice Univ., Houston 1958–60; Assoc. Dir, Dept of Experimental Endocrinology, Coll. de France, Paris, as jt appointment with Coll. of Medicine, Baylor Univ. 1960–63; Resident Fellow and Research Prof., The Salk Inst. for Biological Studies, San Diego, Calif. 1970–89, Dean 1972–73, 1976–77, Adjunct Prof. 1989–97, Distinguished Prof. 1997–; Distinguished Scientist, Whittier Inst. for Diabetes and Endocrinology, La Jolla 1989–93, Medical and Scientific Dir 1993–94; Adjunct Prof. of Medicine, Univ. of Calif., San Diego 1995–97; mem. NAS 1974–, American Acad. of Arts and Sciences, American Physiological Soc., Soc. for Experimental Biology and Medicine, Int. Brain Research Org., Int. Soc. for Research in Biology and Reproduction, Swedish Soc. of Medical Sciences, Acad. Nat. de Médecine, France, Acad. des Sciences, France, Acad. Royale de Médecine de Belgique, Belgium; Pres. The Endocrine Soc. 1986; Citoyen d'honneur 1983, Officier, Légion d'honneur 1984; hon. degrees (Univ. of Rochester, NY) 1976, (Univ. of Chicago, Ill.) 1977, (Baylor Coll. of Medicine, Houston, Tex.) 1978, (Univ. of Ulm) 1978, (Univ. of Dijon) 1978, (Univ. Libre de Bruxelles) 1979, (Univ. de Montréal) 1979, (Univ. of Manitoba) 1984, (Univ. of Turin) 1985, (Kung Hee Univ., Seoul) 1986, (Univ. Paris VII) 1986, (Autónoma, Madrid) 1988, (McGill Univ.) 1988, (Barcelona, Spain) 1988, (Sherbrook Univ., Québec) 1997, (Univ. Franche-Conté) 1999; Bonneau and La Caze Awards in Physiology, Acad. des Sciences 1957, 1960, Ayerst-Squibb Award American Endocrine Soc. 1970, Gairdner Award (Toronto) 1974, Lasker Foundation Award 1975, co-recipient of Nobel Prize in Physiology or Medicine with Andrew V. Schally for discoveries relating to peptide hormones 1977, Dickinson Prize in Medicine 1976, Passano Award in Medical Sciences 1976, Nat. Medal of Science 1977, Barren Gold Medal 1979, Dale Medallist, UK Soc. for Endocrinology 1980; numerous int. awards and lectureships. *Publications:* ed. or co-ed. three books on neuroendocrinology and pharmacology; History of Medicine: Neural Modulation of Immunity (co-author); author or co-author of over 700 tech. publs and reviews in scientific journals in USA, France, UK, Canada, USSR, Japan. *Leisure interests:* computer art, music, fine wines. *Address:* The Salk Institute, 10010 North Torrey Pines Road, La Jolla, CA 92037, USA (office). *Telephone:* (858) 453-4100 (office). *Fax:* (858) 625-0688 (office). *E-mail:* guillemin@salk.edu (office). *Website:* www.salk.edu (office).

GUILLÉN, Héctor (Tito); Honduran agricultural engineer, academic and politician; m. Dinorah Arambarry; two s.; ed Mississippi State Univ., USA; worked for several years in the sugar industry; Founder, School of Agric. and first Dean and Prof., Universidad de San Pedro Sula; Mayor of San Pedro Sula 1990–94; fmr Dir Organizacion de Desarollo Empresarial Femenino (ODEF, credit programme); mem. Congreso Nacional (Parl.) for Cortes constituency 2009–, Pres.

Parl. Budget Comm.; Minister of Finance 2012–13 (resgnd); mem. Partido Nacional.

GUILLÉN SUÁREZ, Mario Alberto, MBA; Bolivian engineer, lawyer and politician; *General Manager, Banco Unión;* b. 23 March 1968, Tarija; ed Escuela Militar de Ingeniería, Univ. Mayor de San Andrés, Univ. Católica Boliviana; worked for Banco Mercanti 1995–99; worked for Pensions, Securities and Insurance Regulatory Agency 1999–2008; Deputy Minister of Pensions and Financial Services 2008–17; Minister of Economy and Public Finance 2017–19; Gen. Man. Banco Unión 2019–; fmr lecturer at several insts including Univ. de Los Andes, Fundación IDEA, European Business School, La Paz, Univ. Mayor de San Simón. *Address:* Banco Unión, SA, Calle Libertad 156, POB 4057, Santa Cruz, Bolivia (office). *E-mail:* info@bancounion.com.bo (office). *Website:* www.bancounion.com.bo (office).

GUIMARÃES, Eduardo Augusto, PhD; Brazilian economist, academic and banking executive; b. 9 Jan. 1946, Rio de Janeiro; ed Pontifícia Universidade Católica do Rio de Janeiro, Univ. of London, UK, Universidade Federal do Rio de Janeiro; Prof., Dept of Econs, Pontifícia Universidade Católica do Rio de Janeiro 1969–71; Prof., School of Econs and Business Administration, Fluminense Federal Univ. 1969–80; Full Prof., Inst. of Econs, Federal Univ. of Rio de Janeiro 1987–88; Pres. Brazilian Inst. Foundation of Geography and Statistics (IBGE) 1990–92; Sec. of the Treasury 1996–99; CEO Banco do Estado de Sao Paulo – Banespa 1999–2000; Pres. and CEO Banco do Brasil SA 2001–03; mem. Audit Cttee Unibanco–Uniao de Bancos Brasileiros SA 2004–08, Globex–Utilidades Domesticas SA 2008–09, Forbes magazine 2008–; mem. Bd of Dirs Fertibras SA 2005–07; currently mem. of Teaching Staff, Direito GV, São Paulo; mem. Advisory Bd Chamber of Arbitration. *Publications:* author of numerous articles on econs in scholarly and professional journals.

GUINDON, Yvan, PhD, CM, FRSC; Canadian scientist and academic; *Director, Bioorganic Chemistry Research Unit, Institut de Recherches Cliniques de Montréal;* ed Université de Montréal; joined Merck Frosst Canada as Sr Research Chemist 1979, Dir Medicinal Chem. 1984–85, Sr Dir 1985–87; joined Bio-Méga as Scientific Dir 1987, Vice-Pres. Bio-Méga/Boehringer Ingelheim Research Inc. 1987–94; apptd CEO Institut de Recherches Cliniques de Montréal, Scientific Dir Bioorganic Chemistry Research Unit 1994; Prof., Dept of Chem., Université de Montréal; Adjunct Prof., Dept of Chem., McGill Univ.; Pres. Royal Soc. of Canada 2007–09; mem. Asscn des diplômés de l'Université de Montréal 2006; Fellow, Chemical Inst. of Canada 1988, AAAS 2014; Chevalier, Ordre national du Québec 2012; Lionel-Boulet Award 2006, Alfred-Bader Award 2012. *Publications:* more than 100 papers in scientific journals. *Address:* Bioorganic Chemistry Research Unit, Institut de Recherches Cliniques de Montréal, 110 avenue des Pins Ouest, Montréal PQ H2W 1R7, Canada (office). *Telephone:* (514) 987-5785 (office). *Fax:* (514) 987-5789 (office). *Website:* www.guindonsgroup.weebly.com (office).

GUINGONA, Teofisto T., Jr; Philippine lawyer, politician and writer; b. 4 July 1928, San Juan, Rizal; s. of Teofisto Guingona, Sr; m. Ruthie de Lara; two s. one d.; ed Ateneo de Manila Univ.; fmr Gov. Devt Bank of the Philippines and Pres. Chamber of Commerce of the Philippines; served as human rights lawyer 1970s; Founder SANDATA and Hon. Chair. of BANDILA; jailed in 1972 and 1978 for his opposition to marital law; fmr Chair. Comm. on Audit; Senator 1980s, Senate Pres. Pro-tempore and Majority Leader, Chair. Blue Ribbon Cttee, Senator 1998, Minority Leader; fmr Dir Mindanao Devt Authority; fmr Chair. Mindanao Labor Man. Advisory Council; fmr Exec. Sec. to Pres.; fmr Justice Sec.; Vice-Pres. of the Philippines 2001–04; Sec. of Foreign Affairs 2001–02; Pres. Lakas-Christian Muslim Democrats (Lakas—CMD) –2003 (resgnd); fmr adviser to Fernando Poe, Jr.

GUION DE MÉRITENS, Maj.-Gen. Isabelle; French police officer and naval officer; *Head of the Coast Guard;* b. 1 Oct. 1962, Pau (Pyrénées-Atlantiques); m.; two c.; ed Écoles de Saint-Cyr Coëtquidan, École des officiers de la gendarmerie nationale, Collège interarmées de défense, Paris (now the École de guerre); officer of French Nat. Gendarmerie, first woman to join the officer corps of gendarmerie 1987, attained rank of Lt, assigned to 1st group of mobile armoured police in Versailles-Satory as Officer in Charge and became Commdr of Armoured Training Centre, assigned as Educ. Officer to School of Sub-officers of Gendarmerie in Montlucon for two years, took command of a co. for training 1993, then took command of a co. of departmental police in Montmorency, Head of the Officers section, Office of Training Br., Maisons-Alfort 1998–2001; became an Officer of Staff to the Gen. Inspection of Armies, Paris; Commdr and Chief of Staff of Gendarmerie School, Chaumont 2004–06; apptd Col of the Gendarmerie (first woman) 2006; took command of Gendarmerie in Yvelines; Head of the Coast Guard 2012–; first woman to be apptd to the rank of Gen. of Police 2013, apptd Maj.-Gen. of Gendarmerie nationale 2016, Inspector Gen. of Admin 2018, commanded l'École des Officiers de la Gendarmerie Nationale 2015–18 2018; Medal of Nat. Defence with Bronze Clip 1993, Chevalier, Ordre nat. du Mérite 2000, Officier 2012, Chevalier, Légion d'honneur 2005, Officier 2016. *Address:* Head of the Coast Guard, c/o Ministry of the Armed Forces, 60 blvd du Général Martial Valin, 75007 Paris Cedex 15, France (office). *Telephone:* 1-80-50-14-00 (office). *Fax:* 1-47-05-40-91 (office). *E-mail:* courrier-ministre@sdbc.defense.gouv.fr (office). *Website:* www.defense.gouv.fr/marine/organisation/les-forces/gendarmerie-maritime/la-gendarmerie-maritime (office).

GUJRAL, Satish; Indian painter and sculptor; b. 25 Dec. 1925, Jhelum, Pakistan; m. Kiran Gujral; one s. two d.; ed Palacio Nationale de Belles Artes, Mexico, Sir J. J. School of Arts, Mumbai, Mayo School of Arts, Lahore; Order of the Crown (Belgium) 1984; Dr hc (Vishakapatnam Univ.) 1996, (Visva Bharti Univ., Santiniketan) 2000; Nat. Award, Lalit Kala Akademi 1956, 1957, 1974, Desikottama, Santiniketan 1989, Da Vinci Award for Life Time Achievement, Mexico 1989, Padma Vibhushan 1998, Lalit Kala Ratna Puraskar, Lalit Kala Akademi 2004, Amity Lifetime Achievement Award, Amity School of Fine Arts 2010, NDTV Indian of the Year Award 2014. *Publication:* A Brush with Life (autobiography). *Address:* 16 Feroz Gandhi Road, New Delhi 110 024, India (home). *Telephone:* (11) 29832154 (home). *Fax:* (11) 29832093 (home). *E-mail:* mail@satishgujral.com; gujralalpna@gmail.com. *Website:* www.satishgujral.com.

GÜL, Abdullah, BA, PhD; Turkish politician and fmr head of state; b. 29 Oct. 1950, Kayseri Prov.; s. of Ahmet Hamdi Gül and Adviye Gül; m. Hayrünnisa Gül; three c.; ed Istanbul Univ., Univ. of London, UK; participated in the foundation of the Dept of Eng, Sakarya Univ., Lecturer in Econs 1980–83, Assoc. Prof. of Econs 1991–; economist with Islamic Devt Bank, Jeddah 1983–91; mem. Parl. representing the Welfare Party (now outlawed) 1991, later WP Deputy Head of Foreign Affairs; held numerous ministerial posts including Minister of State for Foreign Affairs 1996–97, Spokesman for Welfare Party Govt, also mem. European Council; Founder-mem. and Deputy Chair. AK Parti (Justice and Devt Party) 2001–; mem. NATO Parl. Ass. 2001–02; Prime Minister of Turkey Nov. 2002–March 2003; Deputy Prime Minister and Minister of Foreign Affairs 2003–07; President of Turkey 2007–14; Hon. mem., Council of Europe 2001–; numerous Turkish and foreign decorations including Kt Grand Cross, Order of the Bath (UK) 2008, Kt Grand Cross with Collar, Order of Merit of the Italian Repub. 2009, Kt Grand Cross, Order of the Netherlands Lion 2012; hon. doctorates (Bourgas Free, Bulgaria) 2003, (Exeter, UK) 2005, (Baku State, Azerbaijan) 2007, (Dimitrie Cantemir Christian, Romania) 2008, (Kazan State, Tatarstan) 2008, (North-eastern, China) 2009; Pro-Merito Medal of the Council of Europe 2001, Chatham House Prize (UK) 2010. *Address:* c/o President's Office, Cumhurbaşkanlığı Köşkü, Çankaya, Ankara, Turkey (office).

GULABZOI, Maj.-Gen. Sayed Muhammad; Afghan fmr army officer and politician; b. 1951, Paktia Prov.; fmr Communist gen.; mem. Khalq faction of CP, People's Democratic Party of Afghanistan, took part in overthrow of King Muhammad Zahir Shah 1973; close aide of Communist leader Nur Muhammad Taraki; served as Interior Minister and Commdr Sarandoy (Defenders of the Revolution—nat. gendarmerie) for many years during Soviet occupation; spent 17 years in exile in Russia, returned to run in parl. elections 2004; elected mem. Wolasi Jirga (House of the People—Lower House of Parl.) for Khost Province 2004, mem. Internal Security Cttee.

GULAMOV, Kadir Gafurovich, PhD; Uzbekistani nuclear physicist, academic and fmr government official; b. 17 Feb. 1945, Tashkent; m. two c.; Sr Scientific Researcher, Physical Tech. Inst., Tashkent, later Head of Lab. 1983–88; Prof. of Physics 1980–; Prof., Faculty of Physics, Tashkent State Univ.; Deputy Minister of Defence –2000, Minister of Defence 2001–05; apptd presidential adviser 2005; currently Dir-Gen. Scientific Asscn Physics, Uzbekistan Acad. of Sciences; Fellow, Islamic Acad. of Sciences 1995–; Corresp. mem. Uzbekistan Acad. of Sciences 1989–; Beruni State Prize (Uzbekistan) 1983, Independence Memorial Medal (Uzbekistan) 1992. *Publications:* over 250 publs in fields of high energy and nuclear physics. *Address:* c/o Uzbekistan Academy of Sciences, 70 Acad. Gulyamov str., 700047 Tashkent, Uzbekistan. *E-mail:* yuldashev@iae.tashkent.su. *Website:* www.uzsci.net/academy.

GULBINOWICZ, HE Cardinal Henryk Roman, DTheol; Polish ecclesiastic; *Archbishop Emeritus of Wrocław;* b. 17 Oct. 1923, Szukiszki (now Sukiškes in Lithuania); s. of Antoni Gulbinowicz and Waleria Gajewska; ed Metropolitan Higher Ecclesiastic Seminary, Vilnius and Białystok, Catholic Univ. of Lublin; ordained priest, Vilnius, Lithuania 1950; Titular Bishop of Acci and Apostolic Admin. Archdiocese of Białystok, Vilnius 1970–76, Archbishop of Wrocław 1976–2004, Archbishop Emer. 2004–; mem. Congregation for the Evangelization of Nations, Congregation for Eastern Churches, Congregation Clergy Affairs; mem. Main Council Polish Episcopate and several episcopate cttees; High Chancellor Pontifical Faculty Theology, Wrocław; cr. Cardinal (Cardinal-Priest of Immacolata Concezione di Maria a Grottarossa) 1985–; Hon. Citizen of Wrocław 1996; Commdr's Cross with Star, Order of Polonia Restituta; Dr hc (Pontifical Faculty of Theology, Wrocław) 1995, (Agricultural Acad., Wrocław) 2000. *Publications:* more than 240 works on moral theology, ethics, ecumenism and history of the Polish Eastern Territories. *Address:* Kuria Metropolitalna, ul. Katedralna 13, 50-328 Wrocław, Poland (office). *Telephone:* (71) 327-11-11 (office). *Fax:* (71) 322-82-69 (office). *Website:* www.archidiecezja.wroc.pl (office).

GULEGHINA, Maria; Belarusian/Armenian/Ukrainian/Russian singer (soprano); b. (Maria Meytargian), 9 Aug. 1959, Odessa, Ukraine; two c.; ed Odessa Conservatory (studied with Yevgeni Ivanov); professional debut at Minsk Opera Theatre 1986; has performed more than 160 times at Metropolitan Opera, New York, performing title roles in Aida, Tosca, Norma, Adriana Lecouvreur, also roles in Macbeth, Nabucco, Andrea Chenier, Pique Dame, etc. 1991–; frequently performs in all major opera houses world-wide, including Vienna State Opera, Covent Garden, Opera Bastille, Bavarian State Opera, Deutsche Opera Berlin, Mariinsky Theatre, Teatro Liceu, Teatro Colon, etc.; opera roles include title roles in Tosca, Aïda, Manon Lescaut, Norma, Fedora, Adriana Lecouvreur, Turandot, as well as Lady Macbeth in Macbeth, Abigaille in Nabucco, Leonora in Il Trovatore, Oberto in La Forza del Destino, Elvira in Ernani, Elisabetta in Don Carlo, Amelia in Simon Boccanegra, Un Ballo in Maschera, Lucrezia in I due Foscari, Desdemona in Otello, Santuzza in Cavalleria Rusticana, Maddalena in Andrea Chénier, Lisa in Pique Dame, Odabella in Attila, others; UNICEF Int. Goodwill Amb.; sang at Winter Paralympics opening ceremony, Sochi 2014; Hon. Bd mem. Int. Paralympic Cttee; Order of Holy Olga, from Patriarch Alexis of Russia; numerous prizes and awards, including First Prize All-Union Glinka Competition 1984, Giovanni Zanatello Prize for her debut at Arena di Verona 1997, Maria Zamboni Gold Medal, Gold Medal, Osaka Festival 1999, Bellini Prize 2001, Arte e Operosita nel Mondo Prize, Milan. *Television:* Nabucco (Vienna Met), Andrea Chenier, Tosca, Manon Lescaut, Macbeth (all at La Scala), Verdi Arias, Italian Arias (both for NHK), Macbeth and Il Trittico (the Met), Nabucco (Arena di Verona). *Recordings include:* albums include: Tabarro, Oberto, Francesca di Rimini, Pique Dame, Passion of Verismo (live concert recording), Passion of Rachmaninov; video-audio includes: Tosca, Manon Lescaut, Macbeth (all at La Scala, Milan), Andrea Chenier, Nabucco (both at Metropolitan Opera, New York), Andrea Chenier (DVD, Teatro Communale di Bologna), Macbeth (DVD, Liceu in Barcelona), Nabucco with James Levine (DVD, Metropolitan Opera). *Address:* c/o Impresario e.K., Herzog-Welf-Str. 94, 85604 Zorneding, Germany (office). *Telephone:* (8106) 248808 (office). *Fax:* (8106) 375960 (office). *E-mail:* impresarioek@gmail.com (office); info@mariaguleghina.com. *Website:* www.impresario-art.com (office); www.mariaguleghina.com.

GÜLER, Gen. Yaşar; Turkish army officer; *Chief of the General Staff of the Armed Forces;* b. 18 Sept. 1954, Ardahan; m. Demet Güler; one c.; ed Army War Coll.; Head of Operations, Regional Command of Turkey 1986–88, Plan Officer for Inspection and Evaluation, Dept of Land Forces 1988–91, Chief of Operations and of Training Branch, 12th Infantry Div. 1991–92, Internal Security Battalion Commdr, Silopi 1992–94, Deputy Commdr, Brigade of Bosnia-Herzegovina 1994–95, Project Officer, Office of Military Senior Counsellor 1995–97, Deputy Chief of Signals, NATO South Regional Command, Napels, Italy 1997–99, Commdr, Partnership for Peace (PfP) Training Center 1999–2000, Chief of Exercise Branch of the Gen. Staff 2000–01, apptd Branch Dir 2001, promoted to Brig.-Gen. 2001, Commdr, 10th Infantry Brigade 2001–03, Chief of the Communication, Dept of Electronics and Information Systems 2003–05, promoted to Maj.-Gen. 2005, Head of Gen. Staff Training Dept 2007–09, promoted to Lt-Gen. 2009, Gen. Commdr of the Map, 4th Corps Command 2010–11, Chief of Gen. Staff Intelligence 2011–13, promoted to Gen. 2013, Gendarmerie Gen. Commdr 2016–17, Land Forces Commdr Aug. 2017–July 2018, Chief of the Gen. Staff 2018–. *Address:* Office of the Chief of the General Staff, Turkish Armed Forces, Genelkurmay Başkanlığ, 06100 Bakanlıklar, Ankara, Turkey (office). *Telephone:* (312) 4026100 (office). *Website:* www.tsk.tr (office).

GULIYEV, Fuad Khalil-ogly; Azerbaijani engineer and politician; b. 6 July 1941, Baku; m.; two c.; ed Azerbaijani Inst. of Oil Chem.; worked in Belorussia in oil chemical industry; Chief Engineer, later Gen. Dir Air Conditioners Factory, Baku; First Deputy Prime Minister of Azerbaijan 1994–95; Prime Minister of Azerbaijan 1995–96; mem. Milli Majlis (Nat. Ass.) 1991–; mem. New Azerbaijan Party; Science and Technology Prize Azerbaijan 1986, Honoured Engineer of Azerbaijan 1991. *Address:* New Azerbaijan Party (YAP) (Yeni Azärbaycan Partiyası), 1000 Baku, Bül-Bül pr. 13, Azerbaijan (office). *Telephone:* (12) 493-84-25 (office). *Fax:* (12) 498-59-71 (office). *E-mail:* secretariat@yap.org.az (office); fkuliev@azintex.com. *Website:* www.yap.org.az (office).

GULLICHSEN, Johan Erik, MSc; Finnish professor of pulping technology and engineer; *President and Partner, Arhippainen, Gullichsen & Company;* b. 28 June 1936, Pihlava; s. of Harry Gullichsen and Maire Ahlström; m. Anna Ramsay 1958; one s. two d.; ed Abo Akademi, Helsinki Univ. of Tech.; Research Asst, FPPRI 1962–64; Project Engineer, EKONO 1964–70; Pres. and Partner, Arhippainen, Gullichsen & Co. 1970–; Prof. of Pulping Tech., Helsinki Univ. of Tech. 1989–2000; Chair. Bd A. Ahlstrom Corpn 1987–2007; fmr Chair. A. Ahlstrom Oy, Dir Kymmene Oy; Hon. DTech (Abo Akademi) 1988; Engineer of the Year in Finland 1984, Marcus Wallenberg Prize 1986. *Publications:* tech. and scientific papers on pulping tech., econs and environmental control. *Leisure interest:* yachting. *Address:* Arhippainen, Gullichsen & Co., Palikaistentie 167, 31460 Hirsjärvi, Finland (office). *Telephone:* (8) 4002-06198 (office). *E-mail:* Johan.Gullichsen@agco.fi (office). *Website:* www.agco.fi/homepage.htm.

GULLIT, Ruud; Dutch sports commentator and fmr professional footballer (retd) fmr football manager; b. (Ruud Dil), 1 Sept. 1962, Amsterdam; m. 1st Yvonne de Vries 1984–91; two d.; m. 2nd Christina Pensa 1994–2000; one s. one d.; m. 3rd Estelle Cruyff 2000; one s. one d.; defender/midfielder/striker; played for HFC Haarlem, Netherlands 1979–82 (won Eerste Divisie 1981), Feyenoord 1982–85 (won Eredivisie 1984, KNVB Cup 1984), PSV Eindhoven 1985–87 (won Eredivisie 1986, 1987), AC Milan, Italy 1987–93 (won Serie A 1988, 1992, 1993, Supercoppa Italiana 1988, 1992, UEFA Champions League 1989, 1990, UEFA Super Cup 1989, 1990, Intercontinental Cup 1989, 1990), 1994 (won Supercoppa Italiana 1994), Sampdoria 1993–94 (won Coppa Italia 1994, Lotto Cup 1993), 1994–95, Chelsea, UK 1995–98 (Man. 1996–98) (won FA Cup 1997); Man. Newcastle United 1998–99; Head Coach Feyenoord 2004–05, Los Angeles Galaxy, USA 2007–08 (resgnd); mem. coaching staff, Dutch men's national team 2016–; won four caps and scored one goal for Netherlands U21 team 1979, 66 caps and 17 goals for Netherlands sr team 1981–94, including one in European Championship final victory over Russia 1988, also won Nasazzi's Baton 1985, 1986; football pundit for BBC during Euro 96 tournament 1996, for ITV during FIFA World Cup 2006; currently presenter for Dutch TV and analyst for UEFA Champions League games on Sky Sports, UK; Kt, Order of Orange-Nassau 1988; Netherlands Player of the Year (Second Level) 1981, Dutch Footballer of the Year 1984, Netherlands Cup Top Scorer (nine goals) 1984, Dutch Footballer of the Year 1986, Dutch Golden Shoe Winner1 1986, Netherlands League Silver Top Scorer (24 goals) 1986, European Footballer of the Year 1987, World Footballer of the Year 1987, 1989, Dutch Sportsman of the Year 1987, FIFA World Player of the Year 1987, 1989, Onze d'Silver 1988, 1989, Silver, World Soccer Player of the Year 1988, Bronze, Best World Player of the Year, IFFHS 1988, Silver Ball, Boot European Championship (one goal) 1988, World Soccer Magazine World Footballer of the Year 1989, Silver, Best Player of the Year, UEFA 1989, Bronze, Best World Player of the Year, Int. Fed. of Football History and Statistics (IFFHS) 1989, Dream Team European Championship 1988, 1992, Bronze, World Soccer Magazine World Footballer of the Year 1993, Silver Ball, English League Player of the Year 1996, Best Player of the Year, Chelsea 1996, named in FIFA 100 2004. *Recordings:* modest hit in 1984 with the song Not the Dancing Kind 1984, No. 3 hit with anti-apartheid song South Africa in Dutch Top 40 together with the reggae band Revelation Time 1988. *Website:* www.onsoranje.nl (office).

GULLIVER, Stuart T.; British banking executive; *Group Chief Executive, HSBC Holdings;* ed Univ. of Oxford; joined HSBC 1980, has held several key roles in Group's operations world-wide, including in London, Hong Kong, Tokyo, Kuala Lumpur and UAE, Head of Treasury and Capital Markets in Asia-Pacific 1996–2002, Group Gen. Man. 2000–04, Head of Global Markets 2002–03, Co-Head Global Banking and Markets 2003–06, Head 2006–10, Group Man. Dir 2004–10, Chair. Europe, Middle East and Global Businesses April–Dec. 2010, Exec. Dir 2008–10, Chair. HSBC France 2009–, HSBC Bank Middle East Feb.–Dec. 2010, HSBC Private Banking Holdings (Suisse) SA 2010–, HSBC Bank PLC April–Dec. 2010, Group Chief Exec. and Chair. Group Man. Bd, HSBC Holdings 2011–, Dir, The Hongkong and Shanghai Banking Corpn Ltd (Chair. 2011–), Deputy Chair. and mem. Supervisory Bd HSBC Trinkaus & Burkhardt AG 2006–11. *Address:* HSBC Holdings, 8 Canada Square, London, E14 5HQ, England (office); The Hongkong and Shanghai Banking Corporation Ltd, GPO Box 64, 1 Queen's Road Central, Hong Kong Special Administrative Region, People's Republic of China (office). *Telephone:* (20) 7991-8888 (London) (office); 2822-1111 (Hong Kong) (office). *Fax:* (20) 7992-4880 (London) (office); 2810-1112 (Hong Kong) (office). *E-mail:* pressoffice@hsbc.com (office). *Website:* www.hsbc.com (office); www.hsbc.com.hk (office).

GULOIEN, Donald A., BCom; Canadian business executive; *President and CEO, Manulife Financial Corporation;* ed Univ. of Toronto; joined Manulife Financial Corpn as research analyst 1981, held several marketing roles in both the Canadian and US Divs, held leadership roles in both insurance and investment operations, Vice-Pres., US Individual Business 1990–91, led Manulife's Business Devt Unit 1994–2001, mem. Bd of Dirs, Sr Exec. Vice-Pres. and Chief Investment Officer 2001–09, Pres. and CEO 2009–, Chair. Exec. Cttee; mem. Bd of Dirs Canadian Life and Health Insurance Asscn, Geneva Asscn; mem. Mayor of Shanghai's Int. Business Leaders' Advisory Council, Canadian Council of Chief Execs, Young Presidents' Org.; fmr mem. Bd Children's Aid Soc. Foundation, ThinkFirst Foundation of Canada, LIMRA International; mem. Campaign Cabinet for the Rotman School of Man. and fmr mem. Governing Council, Dean's Advisory Cttee for School of Grad. Studies and Hart House Bd of Stewards, Univ. of Toronto; Arbor Award for contribs to Univ. of Toronto 1998, Int. Business Exec. of the Year, Canadian Chamber of Commerce 2012. *Address:* Manulife Financial Corpn, 200 Bloor Street East, Toronto, ON M4W 1E5, Canada (office). *Telephone:* (416) 926-3000 (office). *Fax:* (416) 926-5454 (office). *E-mail:* info@manulife.com (office). *Website:* www.manulife.com (office).

G'ULOMOV, Ravshan; Uzbekistani fmr central banker and government official; fmr Deputy Chair. Nat. Bank for Foreign Econ. Affairs of the Repub.; First Deputy Chair. Cen. Bank –2006, Alt. Gov. Islamic Devt Bank; Chair. Asaka State Jt Stock Commercial Bank 2006–09; Exec. Dir Fund for Reconstruction and Devt in Uzbekistan 2006–09, 2012–17; First Deputy Minister of Finance 2009–10; Minister of the Economy 2010–11, of Foreign Econ. Relations, Investments and Trade 2011–12; Chair. Cttee for Assistance to Privatized Enterprises and Competition Devt 2017–18.

GULOMOVA, Dilbar Mukhammadkhonovna; Uzbekistani politician; ed Tashkent Textile Inst.; Deputy Prime Minister and Chair. Women's Cttee 1995–2004; Chair. Asscn Business Women of Uzbekistan.

GULYAEV, Yury Vasilievich, DPhys-MathSc; Russian physicist; *Director, Institute of Radio-engineering and Electronics, Russian Academy of Sciences;* b. 18 Sept. 1935, Moscow; m.; two c.; ed Moscow Inst. of Physics and Tech.; jr researcher, sr researcher, Head of Lab., Vice-Dir Inst. of Radio-engineering and Electronics, USSR (now Russian) Acad. of Sciences 1960–87, Dir 1988–; Corresp. mem. USSR (now Russian) Acad. of Sciences 1979, mem. 1984–, mem. Presidium 1992–; Chair. Saratov br., Russian Acad. of Sciences 1981–; mem. Russian Acad. of Natural Sciences; USSR People's Deputy 1989–91; mem. Polish Acad. of Sciences; Vice-Pres. World Fed. of Eng Orgs (WFEO); Pres. Russian A.S. Popov Scientific and Technical Soc. of Radio-engineering, Electronics and Telecommunications; currently Pres. Int. Union of Scientific and Technical Socs and Unions of CIS; Fellow and Sr Mem. IEEE and Chair. IEEE Russian Section; Ed.-in-Chief Radiotekhnica i Electronica, Radio and Communications Technology, Photonics and Optoelectronics, Nonlinear Applied Dynamics; Hon. Prof., St Petersburg Electrotechnical Univ. LETI (ETU); Order of Merit for the Fatherland, 3rd and 4th Class; Hewlett-Packard Europhysics Prize of European Physical Soc. 1979, State Prize of the USSR 1974, 1984, Konstantinov Prize of Russian Acad. of Sciences 1992, State Prize of Russian Fed. 1993, A.S. Popov Gold Medal of Russian Acad. of Sciences 1995, State Prize of the Russian Federation 2006. *Publications:* more than 100 articles, mainly on acoustic electronics, acoustic optics and spin-wave electronics. *Address:* Institute of Radio-engineering and Electronics, 125009 Moscow, Mokhovaya ul. 11-7, Russia (office). *Telephone:* (495) 200-52-58 (office). *Fax:* (495) 203-84-14 (office). *E-mail:* gulyaev@cplire.ru (office). *Website:* www.cplire.ru (office).

GULYAS, Diane H., BS; American chemical engineer and business executive; *President, Performance Polymers, E. I. du Pont de Nemours and Company;* b. Chicago, Ill.; ed Univ. of Notre Dame, Advanced Management Program, Wharton School, Univ. of Pennsylvania; joined DuPont in 1978, held a variety of sales, marketing, tech. and systems devt positions, primarily in DuPont Polymers 1978–88, European Business Man., Geneva, Switzerland, for Engineering Polymers, and Plant Supt, Mechelen, Belgium 1988–92, Exec. Asst to Chair. of Bd 1993–94, Global Business Dir Nylon Fibers New Business Devt and Global Zytel Eng Polymers 1997–2001, Vice-Pres. and Gen. Man. DuPont Advanced Fiber Businesses, Spruance Plant, Richmond, Va 1997–2003, Group Vice-Pres. Electronic and Communication Technologies Platform 2003–04, Chief Marketing and Sales Officer 2004–06, Group Vice-Pres. Performance Materials 2006–09, Pres. Performance Polymers 2009–; mem. Bd of Dirs Viasystems; mem. Strategic Planning and Advocacy Cttees Delaware Nature Soc.; mem. Bd of Dirs Ministry of Caring; fmr mem. Bd of Dirs United Way of Richmond; fmr mem. Exec. Cttee Virginia Business Council. *Address:* DuPont Performance Materials, 1007 Market Street, Wilmington, DE 19898, USA (office). *Telephone:* (302) 774-1000 (office). *Fax:* (302) 999-4399 (office). *Website:* www2.dupont.com (office).

GULZAR; Indian film-maker, poet and lyricist; b. (Sampooran Singh Kalra), 18 Aug. 1936, Deena, Jhelum Dist (now in Pakistan); s. of Makhan Singh Kalra and Sujan Kaur; m. Rakhee Gulzar; one d.; came to Delhi following partition; started as poet and was associated with Progressive Writers Asscn; joined Bimal Roy Productions in 1961; first break as lyricist came when he wrote Mora Gora Ang Lai Lae for Bimal Roy's Bandini 1963; began writing for films for dirs Hrishikesh Mukherjee and Asit Sen; turned film-maker with first film Mere Apne 1971; began partnership with Sanjeev Kumar; Lifetime Hon. Fellowship, Indian Inst. of Advanced Studies 2001; five Nat. Film Awards, more than 17 Filmfare Awards, including eight for Best Lyricist, Filmfare Lifetime Achievement Award 2002, Padma Bhushan 2004, Dada Saheb Phalke Award 2013. *Films directed:* Shriman Satyawadi (Asst Dir) 1960, Kabuliwala (Chief Asst Dir) 1961, Bandini (Asst Dir) 1963, Mere Apne 1971, Parichay 1972, Koshish 1972, Achanak 1973, Mausam (Nat. Award for Best Dir, Filmfare The Best Dir Award) 1975, Khushboo 1975, Aandhi (Storm) 1975, Kitaab (also Producer) 1977, Kinara (also Producer) 1977, Meera 1979, Sahira 1980, Namkeen 1982, Angoor 1982, Suniye 1984, Aika 1984, Ek Akar 1985, Ijaazat (Guest) 1987, Ghalib (TV) 1988, Libaas 1988, Lekin… (But…) 1990, Ustad Amjad Ali Khan 1990, Pandit Bhimsen Joshi 1992, Maachis 1996, Hu Tu Tu 1999. *Film roles include:* Jallianwalla Bagh 1979, Grihapravesh (The Housewarming) (as himself) 1979, Wajood (guest appearance as himself) 1998, Raincoat (voice) 2004, Yuvraaj (special appearance) 2008. *Film dialogue or scripts:* Sangharsh 1968, Aashirwad (The Blessing) 1968, Khamoshi 1969, Anand

1970, Guddi (Darling Child) 1971, Mere Apne 1971, Koshish (Nat. Award for Best Screenplay) 1972, Bawarchi 1972, Namak Haraam (The Ungrateful) 1973, Achanak 1973, Mausam 1975, Khushboo 1975, Chupke Chupke 1975, Aandhi (Storm) 1975, Palkon Ki Chhaon Mein 1977, Meera 1979, Grihapravesh (The Housewarming) 1979, Khubsoorat (Beautiful) 1980, Basera 1981, Namkeen 1982, Angoor 1982, Masoom (Innocent) 1983, New Delhi Times 1986, Ek Pal (A Moment) 1986, Ijaazat (Guest) 1987, Mirza Ghalib (TV) 1988, Lekin... (But...) 1990, Rudaal (The Mourner) 1993, Maachis 1996, Chachi 420 1998, Hu Tu Tu 1999, Saathiya 2002, Dus Kahaniya 2007. *Film song lyrics:* Swami Vivekananda 1955, Shriman Satyawadi 1960, Kabuliwala 1961, Prem Patra (Love Letter) 1962, Bandini 1963, Purnima 1965, Sannata 1966, Biwi Aur Makan 1966, Do Dooni Char 1968, Aashirwad (The Blessing) 1968, Rahgir 1969, Khamoshi 1969, Anand 1970, Guddi (Darling Child) 1971, Anubhav (Experience) 1971, Seema 1971, Mere Apne 1971, Parichay 1972, Koshish 1972, Doosri Seeta 1974, Chor Machaye Shor 1974, Mausam 1975, Khushboo 1975, Aandhi (Storm) 1975, Shaque 1976, Palkon Ki Chhaon Mein 1977, Kinara 1977, Gharaonda (The Nest) 1977, Ghar (Home) 1978, Meetha (Sweet and Sour) 1978, Devata 1978, Gol Maal (Hanky Panky) 1979, Ratnadeep (The Jewelled Lamp) 1979, Grihapravesh (The Housewarming) 1979, Sitara 1980, Thodisi Bewafaii 1980, Swayamvar 1980, Khubsoorat (Beautiful India) 1980, Garam 1981, Basera 1981, Namkeen 1982, Angoor 1982, Sadma 1983, Masoom (Innocent) 1983, Ghulami 1985, Jeeva 1986, Ek Pal (A Moment) 1986, Ijaazat (Guest) (Nat. Award for Best Lyricist) 1987, Libaas 1988, Lekin... (But...) 1990, Maya Memsaab (Maya: The Enchanting Illusion) 1992, Rudaali (The Mourner) 1993, Mammo 1994, Daayraa (The Square Circle, USA) 1996, Maachis 1996, Aastha (Aastha in the Prison of Spring) 1997, Satya 1998, Dil Se... (From the Heart, USA) 1998, Chachi 420 1998, Hu Tu Tu 1999, Khoobsurat 1999, Fiza 2000, Aks 2001, Asoka (Ashoka the Great, USA) 2001, Filhaal... 2002, Leela 2002, Lal Salaam (Red Salute) 2002, Dil Vil Pyar Vyar 2002, Makdee (The Web of the Witch) 2002, Saathiya 2002, Chupke Se 2003, Pinjar (The Cage) 2003, Jaan-E-Mann 2006, Guru 2007, Slumdog Millionaire (Jai Ho) (Academy Award for Best Original Song 2009, Grammy Award for Best Song Written for Motion Picture, Television or Other Visual Media 2010) 2008, Kaminey 2009, Veer 2010, Ishqiya 2010, Striker 2010, Raavan 2010, 7 Khoon Maaf 2011, Chala Mussaddi... Office Office 2011, Teen Thay Bhai 2011, Jab Tak Hai Jaan 2012, Do Paise Ki Dhoop, Chaar Aane Ki Baarish 2012, Kya Dilli Kya Lahore 2012, Matru Ki Bijlee Ka Mandola 2013, Ek Thi Daayan 2013, Shoebite 2013, Dedh Ishqiya 2014. *Publications include:* poetry: Jaanam 1962, Kuch Aur Nazme 1980, Chand Pukhraj Ka 1995, Triveni 2001, Dhuan 2001, Raat Pashmine Ki 2002, Raat Chand Aur Main 2004, Selected Poems 2008, Yaar Julaahe 2009, 100 Lyrics 2009, Selected Poems 2012; short stories: Raavi Paar 1999, Dhuaan (Sahitya Acad. Award 2003) 2001, Kharaashein 2003, Meelo Se Din 2013, Half a Rupee Stories 2013, My Favourite Stories: Boskys Panchatantra 2013; 12 books for children, including Ekta (Nat. Council for Educ. Research and Training Award 1989). *Leisure interests:* reading, writing, tennis, cricket. *Address:* Boskiyana, Pali Hill, Bandra (W), Mumbai 400 050, India (home). *Telephone:* (22) 6498351 (home).

GUMBEL, Bryant Charles, BA; American broadcaster; b. 29 Sept. 1948, New Orleans, La; s. of Richard Dunbar Gumbel and Rhea Alice Gumbel (née LeCesne); m. 1st June C. Baranco 1973 (divorced 2001); one s. one d.; m. 2nd Hilary Quinlan 2002; ed Bates Coll.; writer, Black Sports (magazine), New York 1971, Ed. 1972; sportscaster, KNBC-TV, Burbank, Calif. 1972–76, Sports Dir 1976–81; sports host, NBC Sports 1975–82; co-host, Today Show, NBC 1982–97; host of Real Sports with Bryant Gumbel, Home Box Office (HBO) 1995–, Public Eye, CBS 1997, The Early Show 1999–2000, Flashpoints USA with Bryant Gumbel and Gwen Ifill PBS; play-by-play announcer, NFL Network 2006–08; mem. Bd of Dirs United Negro Coll. Fund, United Way of New York City, Xavier Univ., Bates Coll.; recipient of four Emmy Awards and two Golden Mike Awards (LA Press Club); Edward R. Murrow Award (Overseas Press Club) 1988, Frederick D. Patterson Award (United Negro Coll. Fund), Martin Luther King Award (Congress of Racial Equality), three NAACP Image Awards, International Journalism Award (TransAfrica), Africa's Future Award (US Cttee for UNICEF); Dr hc (Bates Coll., Xavier Univ., Holy Cross Univ., Providence Coll., Clark Atlanta Univ.). *Address:* c/o Home Box Office, Inc., 1100 Avenue of the Americas, New York, NY 10036, USA (office). *Website:* www.hbo.com/realsports (office).

GUMBS, Marcel Faustiano Augustin; St Maarten politician; b. 26 Feb. 1953, Curaçao; began political career as observer in Parl. of Netherlands Antilles for Democratic Party 1983; mem. Parl. of Netherlands Antilles 1986–98; Sec. of State for Justice and Gen. Affairs 1998–2002; retired from politics 2006; Owner, MGC & Assocs (man. consultancy) 2006–; mem. Advisory Council of St Maarten –2014; Prime Minister 2014–15; mem. United People's Party. *Address:* c/o Office of the Prime Minister, Clem Labega Square, POB 943, Philipsburg, St Maarten (office).

GUMBS, Walford Vincent, OBE, JP; Saint Kitts and Nevis politician and trade unionist; *Ombudsman of the Federation of Saint Kitts and Nevis;* b. 21 Dec. 1946; m.; two s. one d.; ed Basseterre Senior School, Ruppin Inst. of Agric., Israel, ILO Int. Training Centre, Turin, Italy; customs clerk, St Kitts Sugar Factory Ltd, Basseterre 1965–70; Accounts Officer and Acting Man. Sun Island Clothes Ltd 1973–77; field officer, St Kitts Nevis Trades and Labour Union 1970–73, Exec. Officer 1978–, Second Vice-Pres. 1979–89, First Vice-Pres. 1989–2000, Pres. 2000–05; Pres. Young Labour 1969–71, Vice-Chair. St Kitts-Nevis Labour Party 1992–96; apptd Senator (Labour Party) in Nat. Ass. 1989, Speaker Nat. Ass. 1995–2004; Ombudsman of the Fed. of Saint Kitts and Nevis 2008–; non-resident Amb.; Deputy Speaker, Org. of Eastern Caribbean State Ass. 2012. *Leisure interests:* sports, jogging, int. affairs. *Address:* Office of the Federal Ombudsman, West Independence Square Street, Basseterre (office); Shadwell Housing, Basseterre, Saint Kitts and Nevis (home). *Telephone:* 466-5697 (office); 466-9126 (office); 665-8230 (home). *Fax:* 466-2352 (office). *E-mail:* walfordgumbs@ymail.com (office).

GUMMER, Rt Hon. Benedict (Ben) Michael; British politician and business executive; b. 19 Feb. 1978, London; s. of John Selwyn Gummer and Penelope Jane Gardner; m. Sarah Gummer; two s.; ed Peterhouse, Cambridge; began career as Dir, ICWL (eng firm); Man. Dir, Sancroft International (environmental consultancy co.) 2005–10; MP (Conservative) for Ipswich 2010–17, mem. Regulatory Reform Cttee 2010–12, Justice Cttee 2010–12; Parl. Adviser to Lord Feldman 2012, Parl. Private Sec. to Minister of State for Int. Devt 2012–13, Parl. Private Sec. to Sec. of State for Educ. 2013–15, Parl. Under-Sec. (Dept of Health) 2015–16, Paymaster Gen. and Minister for the Cabinet Office 2016–17; Consultant 2018–; Fellow of Practice, Blavatnik School of Govt, Univ. of Oxford. *Publication:* The Scourging Angel: The Black Death in the British Isles 2009. *Leisure interest:* landscape restoration. *E-mail:* ben@bengummer.com.

GUNATHILAKA, Nandana; Sri Lankan politician; s. of M. D. S. Gunathilaka; ed Sri Sumangala Vidyalaya, Panadura, Univ. of Peradeniya; mem. Parl. for Kalutara Dist 2000–10; Chair. United People's Freedom Alliance (later People's Alliance) 2004–08; Gen. Sec. Nat. Freedom Front 2008–09; fmr mem. Politburo, mem. and presidential cand. Janatha Vimukthi Peramuna party (resgnd 2006); Minister of Tourism July–Nov. 2009; Mayor of Panadura 2011–14.

GUNATILLEKE, Air Marshal Kolitha A., MSc; Sri Lankan air force officer (retd); m. Roshani Gunatilleke; one c.; ed Air Force Acad., China Bay, General Sir John Kotalawala Defence Univ.; commissioned as Pilot Officer 1982, first tour of duty with No. 2 Transport Squadron where he flew DC3s, Riley Herons and Avros, apptd Flying Instructor, saw extensive action and participated in support of all ground operations against Liberation Tigers of Tamil Eelam (LTTE), also held appointment of Command Instrument Rating Examiner, commanded No. 1 Flying Training Wing and No. 2 Transport Squadron, served as Staff Officer (Operations), Air Force HQ, Base Commdr SLAF China Bay, Base Commdr SLAF Katunayake, apptd Dir of Training 2008 then Dir of Air Operations, Commdr of Sri Lankan Air Force 2014–15, Chief of Defence Staff 2015–17; Pres. National Rifle Asscn of Sri Lanka 2007–09; mem. Badminton National Pool, Chair. Selection Cttee–Badminton 2010, Chair. Nat. Selection Cttee 2011–16; Prin., Bishop's Coll.; Vadamarachchi Medal 1989, Armed Service Long Service Medal 1994, Riviresa Campaign Service Medal 1999, North and East Operation Medal 2000, SLAF 50th Anniversary 2001, Utthama Seva Padakkama 2003, Armed Service Long Service Clasp 2003, North and East Humanitarian Medal 2011, Vishishta Seva Vibushanaya 2011, Rana Wickrama Padakkama, Rana Sura Padakkama. *Leisure interests:* music, social dancing, reading.

GUND, Agnes, BA, MA; American art gallery administrator (retd) and philanthropist; *President Emerita, Museum of Modern Art;* b. 1938, Cleveland, Ohio; d. of George Gund Jr; m. 1st Albrecht Saalfield; one s. three d.; m. 2nd Daniel Shapiro 1987; ed Connecticut Coll., Harvard Univ.; Trustee, Museum of Modern Art (MOMA), New York 1976–, Pres. 1991–2002, now Pres. Emer., Chair. MOMA Int. Council, MOMA PS1 Contemporary Art Center; f. Studio in a School 1977; Chair. Mayor's Cultural Affairs Advisory Comm. of New York City; mem. Bd Chess in the Schools, Cleveland Museum of Art, Foundation for Contemporary Arts, Foundation for Art and Preservation in Embassies, Robert Rauschenberg Foundation, Socrates Sculpture Park; mem. Bd of Trustees of Nat. Council on the Arts 2011–, New York State Council on the Arts 2012–; fmr mem. Bd J. Paul Getty Trust; Founding Trustee, Agnes Gund Foundation; regular contrib. on the arts, Huffington Post; Hon. Trustee, Cleveland Museum of Art, Ind. Curators Int., Museum of Contemporary Art, Cleveland; Dr hc (Hamilton Coll.) 1994, (Case Western Reserve Univ.) 1995, (Brown Univ.) 1996, (Kenyon Coll.) 1996, (Univ. of Illinois) 2002, (CUNY Grad. Center) 2007, (Bowdoin Coll.) 2012; Nat. Medal of Arts 1997, Arts Educ. Award 1999, Carnegie Medal of Philanthropy 2005. *Address:* c/o Museum of Modern Art, 11 West 53rd Street, New York, NY 10019, USA (office). *Website:* www.moma.org (office).

GUNDOGDYYEV, Gen. Maj. Begench; Turkmenistani army officer and government official; *Minister of Defence;* m. Ayna Gundogdyyeva; fmr Defence and Mil. Attaché, Embassy in Washington, DC; Deputy Minister of Defence 2009–11, Minister of Defence 2011–15, 2018–; Garrison Commdr, naval forces 2015–; demoted in rank from Gen. Maj. to Col following munitions explosion in Abadan July 2011, promoted to Gen. Maj. again Jan. 2013. *Address:* Ministry of Defence, 744000 Aşgabat, Galkynyş köç. 4, Turkmenistan (office). *Telephone:* (12) 40-27-64 (office). *Fax:* (12) 39-19-44 (office).

GUNESEKERA, Romesh, FRSL; British (b. Sri Lankan) writer and poet; b. 1954, Colombo; m. Helen; two d.; Writer-in-Residence, Scottish Book Trust, Isle of Jura 2008, Somerset House, London 2009, Ateneo Univ., Manila 2015, First Story, Highgate Wood School; Int. Writer-in-Residence, Nanyang Technological Univ. 2013; Assoc. Tutor, Golsmiths Coll.; mem. Council, RSL 2010–13; Ranjana (Sri Lanka) 2005; Arts Council Writers' Bursary 1991, New York Times Notable Book of the Year 1993, 2003, Yorkshire Post Best First Work Award 1994, Premio Mondello 1997, BBC Asia Award 1998, Asian Achievers Award 2015. *Publications include:* Monkfish Moon (short stories) 1992, Reef (novel) 1994, The Sandglass (novel) 1998, Heaven's Edge (novel) 2002, The Match (novel) 2006, The Spice Collector (short stories), The Prisoner of Paradise (novel) 2012, Noontide Toll (novel) 2014, The Writers' & Artists' Companion to Novel Writing (non-fiction) (with A L Kennedy) 2015. *Address:* c/o Bill Hamilton, A.M. Heath Literary Agents, 6 Warwick Court, Holborn, London, WC1R 5DJ, England (office). *Telephone:* (20) 7242-2811 (office). *E-mail:* enquiries@amheath.com (office). *Website:* www.amheath.com (office); www.romeshg.com.

GUNGAADORJ, Sharavyn, PhD; Mongolian politician and diplomatist; b. 2 May 1935, Ikh Khet soum, Dornogobi Aimak (Prov.); ed Acad. of Agriculture, USSR; Chief Agronomist, Amgalan State farm; agronomist, Dept of State Farms 1959–67; Instructor, Mongolian People's Revolutionary Party (MPRP) Cen. Cttee 1967–68; Deputy Minister for Agric.; head of fodder farm in Zabhan Aimak Prov.; Head of group, Ministry of Agric. 1968–80; First Deputy Minister for State Farms 1980–81; First Sec. Party Cttee of Selenge Aimak Prov. 1981–86; Minister for Agric. 1986–90; Deputy Chair. Council of Ministers 1987–90; Alt. mem. MPRP Cen. Cttee 1981–86, mem. 1986–; Deputy to Great People's Hural (Ass.) 1981–89, Prime Minister (Chair. Council of Ministers) April–Sept. 1990, Counsellor to the Pres., Chair. of the Civic Council attached to the Pres. 1990–91; Amb. to Democratic People's Repub. of Korea and Kazakhstan 1991–96; fmr Pres. Co-operatives Asscn; Man. Dir Agropro Corpn; mem. Mongolian Acad. of Sciences; Hon. mem. Gentleman's Mil. Interest Club.

GUNN, James Edward, BS, PhD; American astrophysicist and academic; *Eugene Higgins Professor of Astrophysics, Princeton University;* b. 21 Oct. 1938, Livingstone, Tex.; s. of James Edward Gunn and Rhea Gunn (née Mason); m. Gillian Knapp; two c.; ed Rice Univ., Calif. Inst. of Tech.; served with CE US Army Reserve 1967; Sr Space Scientist, Jet Propulsion Lab., Pasadena, Calif. 1966–69;

Asst Prof., Princeton Univ. 1969–70, Eugene Higgins Prof. of Astrophysics 1980–; Asst Prof. then Prof. of Astrophysics, Calif. Inst. of Tech. 1970–80; taught at Univ. of Calif., Berkeley, Univ. of Wash., Univ. of Chicago, Rice Univ.; Deputy Prin. Investigator, Space Telescope Wide Field Camera/Planetary Camera, Hubble Space Telescope, NASA 1977; fmr Assoc. Dir Apache Point Observatory; fmr Project Scientist and Tech. Dir Sloan Digital Sky Survey; Fellow, Sloan Foundation 1972–76, MacArthur Foundation 1983; mem. Astronomical Survey Cttee; mem. NAS, American Astronomical Soc., American Philosophical Soc.; Dr hc (Univ. of Portsmouth) 2006; Heinemann Prize, American Astronomical Soc. 1988, Gold Medal, Royal Astronomical Soc. London 1994, Distinguished Alumni Award, Calif. Inst. of Tech. 2003, Cosmology Prize, Peter Gruber Foundation 2005, Crafoord Prize, Royal Swedish Acad. of Sciences 2005, Henry Norris Russell Lectureship, American Astronomical Soc. 2005, Nat. Medal of Science 2009, Bruce Medal, Astronomical Soc. of Pacific 2013. *Publications include:* numerous scientific papers in professional journals. *Address:* Department of Astrophysical Sciences, Princeton University, Peyton Hall, Room 113, Princeton, NJ 08544-0001, USA (office). *Telephone:* (609) 258-3802 (office). *Fax:* (609) 258-8226 (office). *E-mail:* jeg@astro.princeton.edu (office). *Website:* www.princeton.edu/astro (office).

GUNN, John Charles, CBE, MD, FRCPsych, FMedSci; British psychiatrist; *Professor Emeritus of Forensic Psychiatry, Institute of Psychiatry, King's College, London;* b. 6 June 1937, Hove; s. of Albert Gunn and Lily Hilda Gunn (née Edwards); m. Celia Willis 1959 (divorced 1986, died 1989); one s. one d.; m. 2nd Pamela Taylor 1989; ed Brighton, Hove and Sussex Grammar School, Reigate Grammar School, Birmingham Univ. Medical School; Consultant Psychiatrist, Bethlem Maudsley Hosp. 1971–2002; Dir Special Hosps Research Unit 1975–78; Prof. of Forensic Psychiatry, Inst. of Psychiatry, King's Coll., London 1978–2002, Prof. Emer. 2002–; Chair. Research Cttee, Royal Coll. of Psychiatrists 1976–80; fmr Chair. Faculty of Forensic Psychiatry; Chair. Academic Bd, Inst. of Psychiatry 1980–85; Chair. Forensic Specialist Cttee, Jt Cttee on Higher Psychiatric Training 1982–85; Consultant, European Cttee for Prevention of Torture 1993; Ed. Criminal Behaviour and Mental Health 1991; mem. Ont. Govt Enquiry in Oakridge, Ont., Canada 1984–85, UK Home Secretary's Advisory Bd on Restricted Patients 1982–91, Bethlem Maudsley Special Health Authority 1986–90, Royal Comm. on Criminal Justice 1991–93, Council, Royal Coll. of Psychiatrists 1997–2004; Foundation mem. Acad. of Medical Sciences 1998; Chair. Faculty of Forensic Psychiatry, Royal Coll. of Psychiatry 2000–04; mem. Royal Comm. on Criminal Justice, Parole Bd for England and Wales 2006–; Royal Mil. Police Asscn Bronze Medal 1970, H. B. Williams Travelling Professorship to Australasia 1985, Phillipe Pinel Award 1992. *Publications include:* Violence 1973, Epileptics in Prison 1977, Psychiatric Aspects of Imprisonment 1978, Current Research in Forensic Psychiatry and Psychology (Vols 1–3) 1982–85, Forensic Psychiatry: Clinical, Legal and Ethical Issues 1993. *Leisure interests:* theatre, cinema, opera, walking, photography. *Address:* POB 725, Bromley, BR2 7WF, England (home). *Telephone:* (20) 8462-1751 (home). *Fax:* (20) 8462-0490 (home). *Website:* www.johngunn.co.uk.

GUNNARSSON, Birgir Ísleifur; Icelandic politician, lawyer and central banker (retd); b. 19 July 1936, Reykjavík; s. of Gunnar Espólín Benediktsson and Jorunn Ísleifsdóttir; m. Sonja Backman 1956; one s. three d.; ed Univ. of Iceland; advocate to lower courts 1962, Supreme Court 1967; law practice 1963–72; Leader Heimdallur Youth Soc. 1959–62; Sec.-Gen. Youth Fed. of Independence Party 1959–62; mem. Reykjavík City Council 1962–82; Mayor of Reykjavík 1972–78; mem. Parl. for Reykjavík 1979–91; Second Deputy Speaker of Althing 1983–87; Minister for Culture and Educ. 1987–88; Chair. Cttee on Heavy Industry 1983–87; mem. Bd Nat. Power Co. 1965–91, Civil Aviation Bd 1984–87; Gov. Cen. Bank of Iceland 1991–2005, Chair. Bd of Govs 1994–2005; Commdr, Order of the Falcon, Order of Dannebrog (Denmark), Order of St Olav (Norway), Order of the White Rose (Finland), Grosse Verdienstkreuz (Germany). *Leisure interests:* music, the outdoor life. *Address:* Fjölnisvegur 15, 101 Reykjavík, Iceland (home). *Telephone:* 552-0628 (home). *E-mail:* birgirisl@simnet.is (office).

GUNNELL, Sally, OBE; British sports commentator, fmr professional athlete and motivational speaker; b. 29 July 1966, Chigwell, Essex; m. Jon Bigg 1992; three s.; ed Chigwell High School; specialized in hurdles; coached by Bruce Longdon; mem. Essex Ladies Athletic Club; competed 400m hurdles Olympic Games, Seoul 1988; second, 400m hurdles World Championship, Tokyo 1991; bronze medal, 400m relay, Olympic Games, Barcelona 1992; women's team capt., Olympic Games 1992–97; gold medal, 400m hurdles, Barcelona 1992; gold medal, 400m hurdles, World Championships 1993 (world record); gold medal, 400m hurdles European Championships, Helsinki 1994; gold medal, 400m hurdles, Commonwealth Games, Canada 1994; only woman in history to have held four gold medals concurrently – Olympic, World, European and Commonwealth (as at end of 2002); retd 1997; sports commentator BBC 1999–2006; launched healthy living programme for the workplace. *Publications:* Running Tall (with Christopher Priest) 1994, Be Your Best 2001. *Address:* Old School Cottage, School Lane, Pyecombe, W Sussex, England. *Telephone:* (1903) 815510. *Fax:* (1903) 813888. *E-mail:* sally@sallygunnell.com. *Website:* www.sallygunnell.com.

GUNNING-SCHEPERS, Louise J., PhD; Dutch medical scientist, academic and university administrator; *Chairman of the Supervisory Board, Royal Schiphol Group;* b. 1 July 1951; m. Jan Willem Gunning; two s.; ed Erasmus Univ.; worked at Univ. of Leuven and at Erasmus Univ.; served as policy staff mem. at Ministry of Health; apptd Prof. of Social Medicine, Academisch Medisch Centrum-Universiteit van Amsterdam (AMC-UvA) 1991, mem. Exec. Bd AMC-UvA 1997–2001, also Vice-Dean, Pres. Exec. Bd, AMC-UvA and Dean Faculty of Medicine 2001–10, Univ. Prof. of Health and Society 2010–, Pres. Exec. Bd, Univ. of Amsterdam 2012–15; Pres. Health Council of the Netherlands –2012; Chair. Supervisory Bd, Royal Schiphol Group 2014–, ONVZ 2017–; mem. Scientific Council for Govt Policy 1995–97, Bd Stichting Comité for Concertgebouw; Int. Adviser, Cambridge University Health Partners; Chair. Supervisory Bd Netherlands Genomics Initiative, Scientific Advisory Council Aids Fund; mem. Social Advisory Council of the Dutch Council for Secondary Educ.; Officer, Order of Orange-Nassau 2010; Silver Medal of the City of Amsterdam 2017. *Publications:* numerous papers in professional journals. *Address:* Royal Schiphol Group, Evert van de Beekstraat 202, 1118 CP Schiphol, The Netherlands (office). *Telephone:* (20) 794-0800 (office). *Website:* www.schiphol.nl (office).

GUNNLAUGSSON, Sigmundur Davíð, DPhil; Icelandic politician; b. 12 March 1975, Reykjavík; s. of Gunnlaugur Sigmundsson and Sigríður G. Sigurbjörnsdóttir; m. Anna Sigurlaug Pálsdóttir; one d.; ed Univ. of Copenhagen, Denmark, Univ. of Oxford, UK; early career as journalist with state broadcaster Ríkisútvarpið (RÚV) 2000–07; mem. Althingi (parl.) for Reykjavík North Constituency 2009–13, for North-East Constituency 2013–, mem. Foreign Affairs Cttee 2009–13, Working Group on European Affairs 2010–13, mem. Icelandic del. to EFTA and EEA Parl. Cttees 2009–13, EU–Iceland Jt Parl. Cttee 2010–13; Prime Minister 2013–16 (resgnd); mem. Progressive Party, Chair. 2009–. *Address:* c/o Prime Minister's Office, Stjórnarráðshúsinu við Lækjartorg, 150 Reykjavík, Iceland.

GUO, Gen. Boxiong; Chinese army officer (retd); b. 1942, Liquan Co., Shaanxi Prov.; ed Mil. Acad. of the Chinese PLA; worker, No. 408 Factory, Xingping Co., Shaanxi Prov. 1958–61; joined PLA 1961, CCP 1963; Squad Leader 164th Regt, 55th Div., Army (or Ground Force), PLA Services and Arms 1961–66, Platoon Commdr 8th Co. 1964–65, mem. staff Propaganda Group 1965–66, mem. staff HQ 164th Regt, 55th Div., Combat Training Section 1966–70, Leader HQ 164th Regt, 55th Div., Combat Training Section 1970–71, Staff Officer, Deputy Head, later Head, later Divisional Chief-of-Staff 1971–81; Deputy Dir Combat Dept (HQ), Lanzhou Mil. Area Command 1982–83; Army Chief-of-Staff 1983–85; Deputy Chief-of-Staff Lanzhou Mil. Area Command 1985–90; Army Group Commdr 1990–93; Deputy Commdr Beijing Mil. Area Command 1993–97; rank of Lt-Gen. 1995, Gen. 1999; Commdr Lanzhou Mil. Area Command 1997–99; Exec. Deputy Gen., PLA 1999–2001, Chief of Staff 1999–2002, Exec. Deputy Chief, HQ of Gen. Staff 2002–; mem. 15th CCP Cen. Cttee 1997–2002 (mem. Cen. Mil. Comm.), 16th CCP Cen. Cttee 2002–07 (Vice-Chair. Cen. Mil. Comm. 2002–07), 17th CCP Cen. Cttee 2007–12 (Vice-Chair. Cen. Mil. Comm. 2007–12), also mem. Politburo 2007–12; Deputy Sec. PLA HQ of Gen. Staff, CCP Party Cttee 1999–; charged with taking bribes and expelled from CCP July 2015; sentenced to life imprisonment for bribery July 2016.

GUO, Dongpo; Chinese politician; b. Aug. 1937, Jiangdu Co., Jiangsu Prov.; ed Beijing Inst. of Foreign Trade; joined CCP 1960; Deputy Div. Chief, China Council for the Promotion of Int. Trade 1972 (Sec. CCP Party Br.), Deputy Dir Printing House, Vice-Pres. China Council for the Promotion of Int. Trade (Sec. CCP Party Cttee) 1982, Pres. 1992; fmr Vice-Pres. China Chamber of Int. Commerce, Pres. 1995; Dir Macau Bureau of Xinhua News Agency 1990–95; Vice-Dir Drafting Cttee of the Basic Law of Macau Special Admin. Zone 1990; Pres. Econ. and Trade Coordination Cttee for the Two Sides of the Straits 1996; Dir Foreign Econ. and Trade Arbitration Comm. 1996; Dir Office of Overseas Chinese Affairs of the State Council 1997–2003; Vice-Pres. China Overseas Exchanges Asscn 1998–; mem. 7th CPPCC Nat. Cttee 1988–93, Standing Cttee, 8th CPPCC Nat. Cttee 1993–98, Chair. Sub-cttee for Hong Kong, Macao and Taiwan Compatriots and Overseas Chinese 2003–; Alt. mem. 14th CCP Cen. Cttee 1992–97; mem. 15th CCP Cen. Cttee 1997–2002. *Address:* Chinese People's Political Consultative Conference, State Council, 23 Taipingqiao Street, Beijing 100811, People's Republic of China (office). *Website:* www.cppcc.gov.cn (office).

GUO, Guangchang, BA, MBA; Chinese business executive; *Chairman, Fosun Group;* b. Feb. 1967, Zhejiang Prov.; m.; one c.; ed Fudan Univ.; Co-founder Guangxin Consulting Co. 1989 (renamed Fosun Holdings Ltd 1993), Chair. Fosun Group 1994–, also CEO Fosun International and Chair. Fosun Pharmaceutical and Forte Land; Deputy Chair. Shanghai Chamber of Commerce 2002; policy adviser to Shanghai Municipal Govt 2000; co-funded Chinese Private Enterprise Pavilion, Shanghai World Expo 2010; fmr Standing Commissary of Ninth Exec. Council of Greater China Fed. of Industry and Commerce Cttee; mem. China Democratic League; Deputy, 10th NPC 2003–08, 11th NPC 2009–12, 12th NPC 2013–; Vice Chair. China Glory Soc., China Social Entrepreneur Foundation, Youth Business China Foundation; several nat. awards, including Outstanding Pvt. Entrepreneur Award, Outstanding Youth Entrepreneurs of Shanghai 1997. *Address:* Fosun Group Head Office, No. 2 East Fuxing Road, Shanghai 200010, People's Republic of China (office). *Telephone:* (21) 63325858 (office). *Fax:* (21) 63325028 (office). *Website:* www.fosun.com (office).

GUO, Jinggang, BA, PhD; Chinese engineer and business executive; *Vice-Chairman and General Manager, Datong Coal Mine Group Company Limited;* b. July 1964, Zhongmu Co., Henan; ed Henan Polytechnic Univ.; technician, Lu'an Mining Bureau of Zhangcun Coal Mine 1987–89, Chief of Lu'an Mining Bureau of Zhangcun Coal Mine Man. Div. and Deputy Chief Asst 1989–93; Office Dir and Kaiyuan Co. Man., Ren Luan Mining Bureau of Zhangcun Coal Mine, Zhengzhou 1993–94, Deputy Dir Zhangcun Coal Mine, Luan Mining Bureau March–Dec. 1994, Deputy Dir Zhangcun Coal Mine and Lu'an Mining Bureau Chief Engineer 1994–96, Chief Engineer and Office Deputy Dir (Chair.), Ren Luan Mining Bureau 1996–98, mem. Party Cttee, Lu'an Mining Group Co. 1998–2006, Deputy Gen. Man. Lu'an Mining Group Co. 2006–11, mem. Standing Cttee of Party Cttee, Lu'an Mining Group Co. and Gen. Man. June–Sept. 2011, Vice-Chair. and Gen. Man. Datong Coal Mine Group Co. Ltd 2011–; mem. CCP 1994–. *Address:* Datong Coal Mine Group Co. Ltd, 11 Dongmen Street, Datong 037003, People's Republic of China (office). *Telephone:* (352) 7868200 (office). *Fax:* (352) 7868201 (office). *E-mail:* dtmkjt@dtcoalmine.com (office). *Website:* www.dtcoalmine.com (office).

GUO, Jinlong; Chinese politician; *Vice-Chairman, CCP Central Commission for Guiding Cultural and Ethical Progress;* b. July 1947, Nanjing, Jiangsu Prov.; ed Nanjing Univ.; technician, Hydropower Bureau, Zhongxian Co., Sichuan Prov. 1969–73; coach, Physical Culture and Sports Cttee, Zhongxian Co., Sichuan Prov. 1973–79; joined CCP 1979; teacher, Publicity Dept, CCP Co. Cttee 1979–80; Deputy Sec. then Sec. Cultural Bureau of Zhongxian Co., Sichuan Prov. 1980–83; Deputy Sec. CCP Zhongxian Co. Cttee then Magistrate of Zhongxian 1983–85; Deputy Dir Rural Policy Research Office, CCP Sichuan Prov. Cttee, Deputy Dir Sichuan Prov. Rural Econ. Comm. 1985–87; Deputy Sec. then Sec. CCP Leshan City Cttee 1987–92; Deputy Sec. CCP Sichuan Prov. Cttee 1992–93; Deputy Sec. then Exec. Deputy Sec. CCP Tibetan Autonomous Region Cttee 1993–2000, Sec. 2000–04; Alt. mem. 15th CCP Cen. Cttee 1997–2002, mem. 16th CCP Cen. Cttee 2002–07, 17th CCP Cen. Cttee 2007–12, 18th CCP Cen. Cttee 2012–17, 18th CCP Cen. Cttee Politburo 2012–17; Acting Mayor of Beijing 2007–08, Mayor 2008–12 (resgnd), also Deputy Sec., CCP Municipal Cttee, Beijing Municipality 2007–12, Sec. 2012–17; Chair. Beijing 2022 Winter Olympics Organizational Cttee

2015–17; Vice-Chair., Central Comm. for Guiding Cultural and Ethical Progress 2017–; Deputy 11th NPC. *Address:* c/o Chinese Communist Party Politburo, Quanguo Renmin Diabiao Dahui, Zhongguo Gongchan Dang, 1 Zhongnanhai, Beijing, People's Republic of China. *Website:* www.cppcc.gov.cn (office).

GUO, Ping, MA; Chinese business executive; *Deputy Chairman and Rotating CEO, Huawei Technologies Company Limited;* b. 1966; ed Huazhong Univ. of Science and Tech.; joined Huawei Technologies Co. Ltd 1988, served successively as an R&D project manager, Gen. Man. of Supply Chain, Dir of Huawei Exec. Office, Chief Legal Officer, Pres. Business Process & IT Man. Dept, Pres. Corp. Devt Dept, Chair. and Pres. Huawei Device, Corp. Exec. Vice-Pres. and Chair. Finance Cttee, Deputy Chair. and Rotating CEO, Huawei Technologies Co. Ltd Oct. 2012–March 2013, April–Sept. 2014. *Address:* Huawei Technologies Co. Ltd, Bantian, Longgang District, Shenzhen 518129, People's Republic of China (office). *Telephone:* (755) 28780808 (office). *E-mail:* hwtech@huawei.com (office). *Website:* www.huawei.com (office).

GUO, Shengkun; Chinese metallurgist and politician; *Secretary, Central Political and Legal Affairs Commission of Communist Party of China;* b. Oct. 1954, Jiangxi Prov.; ed Jiangxi Inst. of Metallurgy, Central South Univ., Hunan Prov.; joined CCP 1974; Technician and Section Chief, Machinery Dept, Ministry of Metallurgical Industry 1979–85, also Sec., CCP Party Br. 1979–85; Superintendent, China Nat. Nonferrous Metals Industry Corpn 1985–93, Deputy Man. 1997–98; Group Leader, Preparatory Group, Aluminium Corpn of China 2000–01, Gen. Man. 2001–04, also Sec., CCP Party Br. 2001–04; Deputy Sec., CCP Autonomous Regional Cttee, Guangxi Zhuang Autonomous Region 2004–07, Sec. 2007–12; Vice-Chair., Autonomous Region People's Govt, Guangxi Zhuang Autonomous Region 2004–07; Minister of Public Security 2012–17; Dir Nat. Anti-Terror Work Leading Group 2013; mem. State Council 2013–18; Sec. Cen. Political and Legal Affairs Comm. CCP 2017–; alt. mem. 16th CCP Cen. Cttee 2002–07, 17th CCP Cen. Cttee 2007–12, mem. 18th CCP Cen. Cttee 2012–17. *Website:* www.chinapeace.gov.cn (office).

GUO, Shuqing, BA, DJur; Chinese banking executive; *Chairman, Bank of China Insurance Supervision and Management Committee;* b. Aug. 1956; ed Nankai Univ., Acad. of Social Sciences; Deputy Dir Econ. Research Centre, State Planning Comm. 1988–93; Dir, Gen. Planning and Experiment Dept, State Comm. for Econ. Restructuring 1993–96, Sec.-Gen. State Comm. for Econ. Restructuring 1996–98; Deputy Gov. Guizhou Prov. 1988–2001; Dir State Admin of Foreign Exchange 2001–05; Deputy Gov. People's Bank of China 2001–03; Chair. Huijin 2003–05; Chair. and Exec. Dir China Construction Bank 2005–11; Chair. China Securities Regulatory Comm. 2011–13, also Sec. Party Cttee 2011–13; Gov. Shandong Prov. 2013–17; Chair. China Banking Regulatory Comm. (renamed Bank of China Insurance Supervision and Management Cttee 2018) 2017–; mem. 10th CPPCC Nat. Cttee; Alt. mem. 17th CCP Cen. Cttee 2007–12, mem. 18th CCP Cen. Cttee 2012–17, 19th CCP Cen. Cttee 2017–; Visiting Fellow, Univ. of Oxford, UK 1986–87. *Address:* Bank of China Insurance Supervision and Management Committee, Jia No. 15, Financial Street, Xicheng District, Beijing 100033, People's Republic of China (office). *Website:* www.cbrc.gov.cn (office).

GUO, Wenqing, BA, MBA; Chinese business executive; *President and Secretary, China Metallurgical Group Corporation;* b. Dec. 1964; ed Univ. of Science and Tech., Tsinghua Univ.; began career as teacher in Xinlong Co., Hebei Prov., then worked successively as a secretary of county's educational bureau, secretary of county's local govt, head of local govt secr., Deputy Admin. of Beiyingfang Co., Hebei Prov., Sec. of Admin. Office for Chengde Dist, Hebei Prov., Sec. of Admin. Office, Hebei Prov. Party Cttee; Deputy Dir-Gen. Hebei Prov. Highway Admin Comm. 1994–2002, served as Sec. CCP Cttee and Dir-Gen. (Chair. and Pres. Hebei Prov. Highway Devt Co. Ltd); Dir-Gen. Hebei Prov. Waterway Admin Comm. 2002; Sec. CCP Cttee, Exec. Dir and Vice-Pres. Road & Bridge International Co. Ltd 2002–08; Dir, Deputy CCP Cttee and Sec. Disciplinary Cttee, China Metallurgical Group Corpn 2009–12, Vice-Chair. and Gen. Man. China Metallurgical Group Corpn 2012–14, also Deputy Sec. CCP Cttee, Chair. 2014–, Gen. Man. and Deputy Sec. 2014–15, Pres. and Sec. 2015–; Chair. China Minmetals Corpn 2016–, also mem. Bd of Dirs. *Address:* China Metallurgical Group Corporation, 28 Shuguangxili, Chaoyang, Beijing 100028, People's Republic of China (office). *Telephone:* (10) 59869999 (office). *Fax:* (10) 59869988 (office). *E-mail:* mcc@mcc.com.cn (office). *Website:* www.mcc.com.cn (office).

GUO, You, PhD; Chinese economist and business executive; *Chairman of the Board of Supervisors, China Construction Bank;* ed Heihe Normal School, Inst. of American Studies of Yellow River Univ., Southwestern Univ. of Finance and Econs; served successively as Chief of Foreign Exchange Trading Dept, Foreign Reserve Operation Centre, State Admin of Foreign Exchange of China, Deputy Gen. Man. China Investment Corpn (Singapore), State Admin of Foreign Exchange of China and Deputy Dir-Gen. Foreign Financial Inst. Supervision Dept, People's Bank of China 1994–98; Exec. Vice-Pres., China Everbright Bank Co. Ltd 1998–99, CEO China Everbright Ltd 1999–2001, Exec. Dir and Deputy Gen. Man. China Everbright Group and CEO China Everbright Ltd 2001–04, Vice-Chair. China Everbright Group, Exec. Dir and Pres. China Everbright Bank Co. Ltd 2004–14; Chair. Bd of Supervisors, China Construction Bank 2014–. *Address:* China Construction Bank, 25 Finance Street, Beijing 100032, People's Republic of China (office). *Telephone:* (10) 6759-7114 (office). *Fax:* (10) 6360-3194 (office). *E-mail:* info@ccb.cn (office). *Website:* www.ccb.cn (office).

GUO, Zhengqian; Chinese party and government official; b. Feb. 1933, Loning Co., Henan Prov.; ed People's Univ. of China, Beijing; joined CCP 1949; Judicial Officer and Investigator, Public Security Bureau, Songxian Co., Henan Prov. 1947–49; fmr Deputy Section Chief, Commercial Dept, Hubei Prov.; Vice-Pres. Hubei Prov. Commercial School 1964–66; Deputy Dir then Dir Political Dept, Financial and Trade Office, Hubei Prov. 1964–66, Deputy Dir Financial and Trade Office 1980–83; Gov. Hubei Br., People's Construction Bank of China 1980–83; Deputy Gov. Hubei Prov. 1983–86, Acting Gov. Jan. 1986, Gov. May–Oct. 1986; Deputy Sec. Hubei Prov. CCP Cttee 1985–90; Gov. Hubei Provincial People's Govt 1986–90; Deputy Gov. People's Bank of China 1990–93; First Deputy Auditor-Gen. of People's Repub. of China 1993–94, Auditor-Gen. 1994–98; Sr Economist, concurrently Prof., People's Univ. of China; Del. 12th CCP Nat. Congress 1982–87, mem. 13th and 14th CCP Cen. Cttees 1987–97, Del. 15th CCP Nat. Congress 1997–2002; Deputy, 6th NPC 1983–88, 7th NPC 1988–93, mem. 9th Standing Cttee of NPC 1998–2003 (Vice-Chair. Financial and Econ. Cttee 1998–2003, Chair. Budgetary Work Cttee 1998–2003). *Leisure interests:* reading, swimming, tennis, table tennis.

GUO MUSUN, Mooson Kwauk, BS, MS; Chinese scientist and academic; *Director Emeritus, Institute of Process Engineering, Chinese Academy of Sciences;* b. 9 May 1920, Hangyang; s. of Zung-Ung Kwauk and Za-Nan Chow; m. Huichun Kwei Kwauk 1950; two s. one d.; ed Univ. of Shanghai, Princeton Univ., USA; Prof., Inst. of Chemical Metallurgy (now Inst. of Process Eng), Chinese Acad. of Sciences 1956, Dir 1982–86, Dir Emer. 1986–; Visiting Prof., Ohio State Univ. 1989; Vice-Pres. Chemical Industry and Eng Soc. of China 1978–; Visiting Prof. Virginia Polytechnic Inst. and State Univ. 1986–87; mem. Chinese Acad. of Sciences 1981–; Pres. Emer. Chinese Soc. of Particuology 1986–; Corresp. mem. Swiss Acad. of Eng Sciences 1997–; Distinguished Scholar, CSCPRC Program, US Nat. Acad. of Science 1984, Davis-Swindin Memorial Lecturer, Univ. of Loughborough, UK 1985, Danckwerts Memorial Lecturer, Inst. of Dirs, London 1989, Int. Fluidization Award 1989. *Publications:* Fluidization: Idealized and Bubbleless, with Applications 1992, Fast Fluidization 1994, Geometric Mobiles 1998. *Leisure interests:* kites, mobiles. *Address:* Institute of Process Engineering, Chinese Academy of Sciences, Beijing, 100080, People's Republic of China (office). *Telephone:* (10) 6255-4241 (office); (10) 6255-4050 (home). *Fax:* (10) 6255-8065 (office). *E-mail:* mooson@home.ipe.ac.cn (office). *Website:* english.ipe.cas.cn/pe/cm/200906/t20090612_6012.html (office).

GUPTA, Modadugu V., PhD; Indian aquaculture scientist; b. 17 Aug. 1939, Bapatla, AP; ed Univ. of Calcutta; Scientist, Indian Council of Agricultural Research 1962–76; Aquaculture and Breeding Expert, UN Econ. and Social Comm. for Asia and the Pacific (UN-ESCAP) 1977–86; Fish Culture Expert, FAO, Bangladesh 1986–89; Asst Dir-Gen. WorldFish Center 1989–2004 (retd), Sr Research Fellow 2005–08; Research Co-ordinator, Int. Network on Genetics in Aquaculture 1996–2004; mem. High-Level Panel of Experts of Cttee on World Food Security; consultant to FAO, UNDP, World Bank, Asian Devt Bank, USAID, Danish Int. Devt Agency (DANIDA), Commonwealth Secr., others; chaired and organized numerous global and regional confs; Hon. Fellow, Asscn of Aquaculturists, and numerous other scientific socs; Hon. DSc (Fisheries Univ., Mumbai), (G.B. Pant Univ. of Agric. and Tech., Pantnagar); World Food Prize Laureate 2005, Sunhak Peace Prize Laureate 2015, Nutra Lifetime Achievement Award 2015, Gold Medal, Asian Fisheries Soc., Life Time Award, World Aquaculture Soc., Medal of Indian Council of Agricultural Research, Eminent Agriculture Scientist Award, Govt of AP, India. *Publications include:* more than 150 papers in books, journals and conf. proceedings. *Address:* C502, Aditya Elite, B.S. Maktha, Begumpet, Hyderabad 500 016, India (office). *Telephone:* (40) 23400229 (office); 98-66508555 (mobile) (office). *Fax:* (40) 23400229 (office). *E-mail:* guptamo2000@yahoo.co.in (office).

GUPTE, Lalita Dileep, BEcons, MMS; Indian banking executive; b. 1948; m.; two c.; ed Univ. of Delhi, Univ. of Bombay, Jamnalal Bajaj Inst. of Man. Studies; joined ICICI Bank Ltd 1971, held various leadership positions in corp. and retail banking, strategy and resources, and int. banking depts, Exec. Dir Bd of Dirs ICICI Ltd 1994–96, Deputy Man. Dir 1996–99, Jt Man. Dir and COO 2001–06, Chair. (non-exec.) ICICI Venture Funds Management Co. Ltd 2006–; mem. Advisory Bd RAND Center for Asia-Pacific Policy; mem. Bd of Dirs Bharat Forge Ltd 2006–, Kirloskar Brothers Ltd 2007–13 (ind. non-exec. 2014–), FirstSource Solutions Ltd 2007–10, Godrej Properties Ltd 2008–, HPCL-Mittal Energy Ltd, Swadhaar FinServe Pvt Ltd, Nokia 2007–11, Alstom 2010–; Twenty-First Century for Banking Finance and Banking Award, Ladies Wing of Indian Merchants' Chamber 1997, Women Achievers Award, Women Grads Asscn 2001, Int. Women's Asscn Woman of the Year Award 2002. *Leisure interest:* looking after my family. *Address:* ICICI Bank Ltd, ICICI Bank Towers, Bandra Kurla Complex, Mumbai 400 051, India (office). *Telephone:* (22) 26531414 (office). *Fax:* (22) 26531167 (office). *Website:* www.icicibank.com (office).

GURASSA, Charles Mark, BEcons, MBA, FRSA, FRAeS; British business executive; *Chairman, Channel Four Television Corporation;* b. 1956, London; m.; c.; ed Christ's Coll., London, Univ. of York, Int. Man. Centre, Buckingham; joined Thomas Cook 1977, posts in New York, London, Hong Kong, Gen. Man. Retail Operations 1988–89; Sr Commercial Dir British Airways 1989–99; CEO Thomson Travel Group PLC 1999–2000; Chair. TUI N Europe and Airline Group 2000–03, Exec. Dir TUI AG 2000–03; Chair. (non-exec.) 7days Ltd 2003–10, Worldwide Excellerated Leasing Ltd 2004, Vanguard Car Rental 2004–06, Virgin Mobile PLC 2004–06, LOVEFiLM Int. 2006–11, Nat. Trust Enterprises Ltd 2006–13, MACH S.a.r.l. 2007–13, Phones 4u Ltd 2007–11, Net Names 2012–, Channel Four Television Corpn 2016–; Chair. Genesis Housing Asscn 2010–; mem. Bd of Dirs Whitbread PLC 2000–09, easyJet PLC 2011– (Deputy Chair. 2011, Sr Ind. Dir 2011–), Merlin Entertainments PLC 2013–; Trustee, Whizz-Kidz 2003–09, National Trust 2005–14 (Deputy Chair. 2013–14), Migration Museum Project 2014–, English Heritage 2015–; mem. Advisory Bd Alpitour, Univ. of York; fmr mem. Comparable Bd Neos SPA, Thomson Travel Group (Holdings) Ltd; Patron Royal Opera House; inducted into Travel Industry Hall of Fame 2003. *Leisure interests:* music, travel, theatre, sports. *Address:* Office of the Chairman, Channel 4, 124 Horseferry Road, London, SW1P 2TX, England (office). *Telephone:* (20) 7396-4444 (office). *Website:* www.channel4.com (office).

GURBANMYRADOV, Yolly; Turkmenistani politician and economist; b. 1960, Ashgabat; ed Turkmen State Inst. of Nat. Econ.; worker in construction co. 1977–82; Sr Econ., Deputy Head Ashgabat br. USSR State Bank 1982–87; Head of Div. of Banking Automation State Bank (Ashgabat) 1988; Deputy Head of Regional Dept, USSR Zhilsotsbank 1988–89; man. of div. Agroprombank 1989–90; Br. Man. USSR Vnesheconombank 1990–92; First Deputy Chair., then Chair. Bd of Dirs State Bank of Foreign Trade of Turkmenistan 1992–96; Dir Turkmenistan State Agency on Foreign Investments 1996–97; Deputy Chair. Turkmen Cabinet of Ministers, concurrently Chair. Interbanking Council 1997–99; Deputy Prime Minister of Turkmenistan 1999–2004; sentenced to 20 years in prison for embezzlement and corruption Oct. 2005; released Aug. 2007.

GURBANNAZAROV, Orazmyrat; Turkmenistani diplomatist and government official; *Chairman, Chamber of Commerce and Industry of Turkmenistan;* apptd

Amb. to UAE 2012; fmr Chair. State Asscn of Food Industry; Hakim (Gov.) of Daşoguz Velayat (Prov.) –2017; Deputy Chair. of the Govt, responsible for Trade and the Devt of the Non-govt Economy May 2017–18, also Acting Deputy Chairman of the Government, responsible for Economic Affairs, Banks, and International Financial Organizations Sept. 2017–18; Chair. Chamber of Commerce and Industry of Turkmenistan 2018–.

GURDON, Sir John Bertrand, Kt, DPhil, FRS; British cell biologist; b. 2 Oct. 1933, Dippenhall, Hants.; s. of W. N. Gurdon and E. M. Gurdon (née Byass); m. Jean Elizabeth Margaret Curtis 1964; one s. one d.; ed Edgeborough School, Eton Coll., Univ. of Oxford; Beit Memorial Fellow 1958–61; Gosney Research Fellow, California Inst. of Tech., USA 1961–62; Research Fellow, Christ Church, Oxford 1962–72, Departmental Demonstrator 1963–64, Lecturer, Dept of Zoology 1966–72; Visiting Research Fellow, Carnegie Inst., Baltimore, Md, USA 1965; mem. Scientific Staff, Medical Research Council, Molecular Biology Lab., Univ. of Cambridge 1973–83, Head of Cell Biology Div. 1979–83, John Humphrey Plummer Prof. of Cell Biology 1983–2001, Master Magdalene Coll. Cambridge 1995–2002, Fellow, Churchill Coll., Cambridge 1973–95; Fellow, Eton Coll. 1978–93; Fullerian Prof. of Physiology and Comparative Anatomy, Royal Inst. 1985–91; Pres. Int. Soc. for Developmental Biology 1990–94; Chair. Wellcome Cancer Campaign Inst., Univ. of Cambridge 1990–2001; Gov. The Wellcome Trust 1995–2000; Chair. Co. of Biologists 2001–; Foreign Assoc., NAS 1980, Belgian Royal Acad. of Science, Letters and Fine Arts 1984, French Acad. of Sciences 1990; Foreign mem. American Philosophical Soc. 1983, Inst. of Medicine (USA) 2003; Hon. Foreign mem. American Acad. of Arts and Sciences 1978; Hon. Student, Christ Church, Oxford 1985; Hon. Fellow, Magdalene Coll. Cambridge 2002, Churchill Coll. Cambridge 2007; Hon. DSc (Chicago) 1978, (Oxford) 1988, (Hull) 1998, (Glasgow) 2000, (Cambridge) 2007, (Bruxelles) 2010; Dr hc (Paris) 1982, (Santiago, Chile) 2012, (Rockefeller, USA) 2014; Albert Brachet Prize, Belgian Royal Acad. 1968, Scientific Medal of Zoological Soc. 1968, Dunham Lecturer, Harvard Medical School 1974, Feldberg Foundation Award 1975, Croonian Lecturer, Royal Soc. 1976, Paul Ehrlich Award 1977, Carter-Wallace Lecturer, Princeton Univ. 1978, Nessim Habif Prize, Univ. of Geneva 1979, CIBA Medal, Biochemical Soc. 1981, Comfort Crookshank Award for Cancer Research 1983, William Bate Hardy Triennial Prize, Cambridge Philosophy Soc. 1983, Charles Léopold Mayer Prize, Acad. des Sciences (France) 1984, Ross Harrison Prize, Int. Soc. for Devt Biology 1985, Royal Medal, Royal Soc. 1985, Emperor Hirohito Int. Biology Prize 1987, Wolf Prize for Medicine (jtly with Edward B. Lewis) 1989, Distinguished Service Award, Miami 1992, Jean Brachet Memorial Prize, Int. Soc. for Differentiation 2000, Conklin Medal, Soc. for Developmental Biology 2001, Copley Medal, Royal Soc. 2003, Rosenstiel Award 2009, Albert Lasker Basic Medical Research Award 2009, Nobel Prize in Physiology or Medicine (with Shinya Yamanaka) 2012, Royal Coll. of Physicians Harveian Oration 2014. *Publication:* Control of Gene Expression in Animal Development 1974. *Leisure interests:* skiing, horticulture, lepidoptera. *Address:* Whittlesford Grove, Whittlesford, Cambridge, CB2 4NZ, England (home). *Telephone:* (1223) 334090 (office); (1223) 832674 (home).

GURFINKEL, Viktor Semenovich; Russian physiologist; *Senior Scientist, Oregon Health and Science University;* b. 2 April 1922; ed Kyrgyz State Medical Inst.; during World War II head div. of blood transfusion 19th Army 1941–45, chief dr hospital 1946–48; sr researcher, head of lab., Inst. of Orthopaedics 1949–58; head of lab. Inst. of Experimental Biology and Medical Siberian br. USSR Acad. of Sciences 1949–58; head of lab. Inst. of Biophysics USSR Acad. of Sciences 1960–67; head of lab. Inst. for Information Transmission Problems, Russian Acad. of Sciences; currently Sr Scientist, Oregon Health and Science Univ., USA; corresp. mem. USSR (now Russian) Acad. of Sciences 1987, mem. 1994; research in physiology of movements, space physiology and medicine; resident in USA 1999–; Hon. mem. American Physiological Soc.; Dr hc (Univ. of Arizona 1995); USSR State Prize 1970, R. Dow Prize (USA) 1990, Humboldt Foundation Award 1990. *Publications:* three books and numerous articles in scientific journals. *Leisure interest:* fishing. *Address:* Neurological Sciences Institute, Oregon Health and Science University, West Campus, 505 NW 185th Avenue, Beaverton, OR 97006, USA.

GURG, Easa Saleh al-, KCVO, CBE; United Arab Emirates diplomatist, banker and business executive; *Chairman, Easa Saleh Al Gurg Group;* b. Dubai; m. Soraya Al Gurg; f. Easa Saleh Al Gurg Group 1960; Co-founder and Chair. Al Gurg Fosroc LLC 1975–; Dir Emirates Bank Group 1983; Chair. Easa Saleh Al Gurg Group, Al Gurg Leigh's Pants LLC, Gulf Metal Foundry LLC, Arabian E-Lever LLC; Deputy Chair. Nat. Bank of Fujairah Bank; Dir Investcorp Bank EC, Emirates Merchant Bank Ltd, Emirates Bank International; Amb. to UK (also accred to Ireland) 1991–2009; sponsorship for grad. students, Oxford Centre for Islamic Studies. *Publications:* The Wells of Memory: An Autobiography 1999. *Address:* Easa Saleh Al Gurg Group, Easa Saleh Al Gurg Building, Baniyas Street, Deira, PO Box 325, Dubai, UAE (office). *Telephone:* (4) 2279666 (office). *Fax:* (4) 2278620 (office). *E-mail:* esag@algurg.ae (office). *Website:* www.algurg.com (office).

GURG, Raja Easa al-; United Arab Emirates business executive; *Managing Director, Easa Saleh Al Gurg Group;* b. Dubai; d. of Easa Saleh al-Gurg; Man. Dir Easa Saleh Al Gurg Group (ESAG); Pres. Dubai Business Women's Council; Deputy Chair. Dubai Healthcare City Authority; mem. bd Dubai Chamber of Commerce & Industry, Dubai Women's Asscn; mem. Dubai Econ. Council, Arab Int. Women's Forum, Nat. Advisory Council, Coll. of Business Sciences; mem. bd HSBC Bank Middle East; mem. advisory bd Coutts Bank; head and mem. bd, Auditing Cttee, Federal Customs Authority; mem. Bd of Govs Hamdan Bin Mohammed Smart Univ.; involved in philanthropic, social and charitable activities, notably with Easa Saleh Al Gurg Foundation and Al Jalila Foundation (Chair.); World of Difference Award, Int. Alliance for Women (TIAW) 2009, Stevie Award for Women in Business 2011. *Address:* Easa Saleh Al Gurg Group, Al Gurg Tower I, Baniyas Street, Deira, PO Box 325, Dubai, United Arab Emirates (office). *Telephone:* (4) 2279666 (office). *Fax:* (4) 2278620 (office). *E-mail:* esag@algurg.ae (office). *Website:* www.algurg.com (office).

GURGENIDZE, Vladimer (Lado), MBA; Georgian/British banker and politician; *Executive Chairman, Liberty Bank;* b. 7 Dec. 1970, Tbilisi; m. Larissa Gurgenidze; four s.; ed Tbilisi State Univ., Middlebury Coll., Goizueta School of Business of Emory Univ., USA; began his investment banking career with CEE corp. finance arm of MeesPierson; Dir ABN AMRO Corp. Finance in Russia and CIS 1997–98, served in various sr capacities at ABN AMRO Corp. Finance, London, including as a Dir and Head of Mergers and Acquisitions in the Emerging European Markets 1998–2000 and as a Man. Dir and Head of Tech. Corp. Finance 2001–03; Man. Dir and Regional Man. for Europe, Putnam Lovell NBF (boutique investment banking firm) 2003–04; CEO Bank of Georgia 2004–06, Chair. Supervisory Bd 2006–07; Chair. Supervisory Bd Galt & Taggart Securities, Galt & Taggart Capital 2005–07; Prime Minister of Georgia 2007–08; Exec. Chair. Liberty Bank (fmrly People's Bank of Georgia), Tbilisi 2009–; Co-Chair. Emory Center for Alternative Investments 2009–10; Co-f. Liberty Capital 2009; Chair. Supervisory Bd, Bank of Kigali, Rwanda 2009–; fmr mem. Supervisory Bd Georgian Stock Exchange; St George's Victory Order 2008, Presidential Order of Excellence 2010; Sheth Distinguished International Alumni Award, Goizueta Business School of Emory Univ. 2010. *Television:* hosted a reality TV show The Candidate on Rustavi 2 (Georgian version of franchise The Apprentice) 2006. *Address:* Liberty Bank, 0162 Tbilisi, 74, Chavchavadze Avenue, Georgia (office). *Telephone:* (32) 255-55-00 (office). *E-mail:* lado.gurgenidze@libertybank.ge (office). *Website:* www.libertybank.ge (office).

GURGULINO DE SOUZA, Heitor, BSc, Lic Math.; Brazilian academic, scientist and international organization official; *President, World Academy of Art and Science;* b. 1 Aug. 1928, São Lourenço, Minas Gerais; s. of Arthur Gurgulino de Souza and Catarina Sachser de Souza; m. Lilian Maria Quilici; two s.; ed Mackenzie Univ., São Paulo, Aeronautics Inst. of Tech., Sao Jose dos Campos, Univ. of Kansas, USA, Univ. of São Paulo; Instructor and Asst Prof., Physics Dept, ITA, São José dos Campos, São Paulo, Brazil 1951–57; Prof. of Physics, State Univ. of São Paulo (UNESP), Rio Claro Campus 1958–90; Program Specialist, Inter-American Science Program, Pan American Union, Washington, DC 1962–64; Head, Unit of Educ. and Research, Dept of Scientific Affairs, OAS, Washington, DC 1964–69; Rector, Fed. Univ. of São Carlos, State of São Paulo 1970–74; Dir Dept of Univ. Affairs, Ministry of Educ. and Culture, Brasília 1972–74; Chair. Inter-American Cttee on Science and Tech. (CICYT), Council for Educ., Culture, OAS, Washington, DC 1974–77; Vice-Pres. Fed. Council of Educ. of Brazil 1972–87; Dir CNPq (Nat. Council for Scientific and Tech. Devt), Brasília 1975–78, Special Adviser to Pres. 1979–80; Vice-Pres. International Asscn of Univ. Pres. 1985–87, 1999–2002, Sec.-Gen. 2008–11, Sec.-Gen. Emer. 2012; Pres. Grupo Universitario Latinoamericano (GULERPE), Caracas 1985–87; Rector UN Univ., Tokyo 1987–97; Special Adviser for Higher Educ. to Dir-Gen., UNESCO, Paris 1997–99; Vice-Rector Unilegis-Universidade do Legislativo Brasileiro, Fed. Senate, Brasília 2003–05; Pres., Asscn Virtual Educ. Brasil 2003–, World Acad. of Art and Science (WAAS) 2014–; mem. American Physical Soc. 1956–, Club of Rome 1996– (Vice-Pres. 2008–12), Brazilian Acad. of Educ. 2004–, Council of Sr Advisors of Int. Asscn of Univ. Pres 2014–; mem. Nat. Order of Educational Merit, MEC, Brasília 1973, Commdr Order of Rio Branco, MRE, Brasília 1974, Commdr Order Infante Dom Henrique, Portugal 1990, Nat. Order of Scientific Merit, MCT 1996; Dr hc (Universidad Autnoma de Guadalajara) 1984, (Espírito Santo) 1986, (Universidade Federal de São Carlos, São Paulo) 2006, (IESB, Brasilia) 2008, Hon. DJur (California State Univ., USA) 1997, Great-Cross, MCT- MRE, Paris 2002, (Obirin Univ., Tokyo, Japan) 2010, (Osaka Univ. of Commerce, Japan) 2010; Tiradentes Medal, Govt of State of Minas Gerais, Brazil 2012. *Television:* producer, Educação Tesouro a Descobrir, Rêde Vida 2004–12; numerous interviews. *Publications include:* Gamma Rays from the Proton Bombardment of Natural Silicon 1957, Science Policy (co-ed.) 1974; author of chapter on Brazil in International Encyclopedia of Higher Education 1978; several articles. *Leisure interests:* sailing, swimming, music. *Address:* S.Q.S. 116 Bloco B, Apto 501, Asa Sul, Brasília, DF, CEP 70386-020, Brazil (home). *Telephone:* (61) 3346-1414 (home); (61) 8159-9091 (mobile). *Fax:* (61) 3346-0938 (home). *E-mail:* hgurgulino@aol.com; heitorgurgulino@gmail.com (office).

GURIB-FAKIM, (Bibi) Ameenah (Firdaus), BSc, PhD, FLS; Mauritian university administrator, botanist, academic and fmr head of state; b. 17 Oct. 1959; ed Univs of Surrey and Exeter, UK; Research Asst, Dow Chemical Co., UK 1981–82; Teaching Asst, Univ. of Exeter 1984–86; Lecturer, Faculty of Agric., Univ. of Mauritius 1987–91, Sr Lecturer, Faculty of Science 1991–95, Assoc. Prof., Faculty of Science 1995–2001, Head of Chem. Dept 1998–2000, Prof. with Personal Chair in Organic Chem. 2001–, Dean Faculty of Science 2004–06, Pro-Vice-Chancellor (Teaching and Learning Portfolio), Univ. of Mauritius 2006–; Pres. of Mauritius (first woman) 2015–18 (resgnd); Man. Research, Tech. and Devt, Mauritius Research Council 1995–97; Chef d'Equipe to PLARM Project, IOC/EU 1990–95; Nat. Co-ordinator for Commonwealth Secr. on Identification and Monitoring of Biodiversity in Small Island Developing States 1997–98, Université de l'Océan Indien Project for the Indian Ocean Univ. 1998–2000; Devt Man., CAERENAD Project (funded by Canadian Int. Devt Agency in collaboration with TELUC) 1998–2000; invited speaker at several int. confs; Project Leader European Devt Fund regional research project 'Inventory and Study of Aromatic and Medicinal Plants of the States of the Indian Ocean', created complete database of plants of Mauritius 1994–97; has created medicinal plants gardens in primary schools and at the Office of the Pres. of Mauritius; consultant for World Bank, EU and others; Co-Ed. (Medicinal Plants Volumes) Plant Resources of Tropical Africa Series (PROTA), Univ. of Wageningen, Netherlands; mem. editorial Bd Journal of Essential Oil Bearing Plants 1997–; mem. Rajiv Gandhi Science Foundation Trust, Ministry of Educ. and Scientific Research 2002–; Founding mem. and Exec. Sec. Asscn of African Medicinal Plants Standards 2005–; mem. Asscn of Univs and Colls of Canada 2006–; Scientific Adviser, Int. Foundation of Science of Sweden 2006–; mem. Third World Acad. of Science (now World Acad. of Science) 1996–; Commdr, Order of the Star and Key of the Indian Ocean 2008, Chevalier, Ordre des Palmes Academiques (France) 2009; L'Oréal-UNESCO 'For Women in Science' Award (co-recipient, Africa) 2007, African Union Award for Women in Science (Eastern African Region) 2009. *Publications:* Plantes Médicinales de l'Ile Rodrigues (co-author) 1994, Plantes Médicinales de Maurice Vol. 1 (Acanthaceae: Convolvulaceae) (co-author), Plantes Médicinales de Maurice Vol. 2 (Cucurbitaceae: Oxalidaceae) (co-author), Plantes Médicinales de Maurice Vol. 3 (Pandanaceae: Zygophyllaceae) (co-author), Natural Toxins and Poisonous Plants of Mauritius (co-author) 1999, Maurice par des Plantes Medicinales 2002, Mauritius Through its Medicinal Plants 2002, An Illustrated Guide to the Flora of Mauritius and the Indian Ocean Islands (ed.) 2003, Molecular and Therapeutic Aspects of Redox Biochemistry (co-ed.) 2004, Medicinal Plants of the Indian Ocean Islands (co-author) 2004, Guide Illustré de la Flore de Maurice et des Iles de l'Ocean Indien (ed.) 2004, 2006, Biodiversity Towards Drugs Development (co-ed.) 2005, Booklet on 'Medicinal Plants at the State House, Le Reduit' 2005, Lesser-known and Under-utilised Plant Resources (ed.) 2005, Ressources vegetales mé-connues et sous-utilisées (ed.) 2005; several book chapters and more than 75 papers in professional journals.

GUROV, Maj.-Gen. Aleksander Ivanovich, DJur; Russian civil servant and politician; b. 17 Nov. 1945, Shushkan-Olshanka, Tambov Dist; m. Yelena Nikolayevna Gurova; one s.; ed Moscow State Univ.; inspector, Div. of Criminal Investigation, Vnukovo Airport 1970–74; mem. of staff, Dept of Criminal Investigation, USSR Ministry of Internal Affairs 1974–78, Head of Dept for Struggle Against Organized Crime, Corruption and Drug Business; USSR People's Deputy 1990–93; First Deputy Head of Centre of Public Relations, Ministry of Security; Vice-Pres. Inform-Service; Head of Tepko-Bank (security service) 1994–98; Head of All-Russian Inst., Ministry of Internal Affairs 1998–99; Co-founder and Co.-leader Yedinstvo 1999; mem. State Duma 1999, Chair. Cttee on Security 2000. *Publications include:* Red Mafia; over 150 scientific articles on struggle against organized crime.

GÜRRAGCHAA, Maj.-Gen. Jügderdemidiin; Mongolian politician, army officer and fmr cosmonaut; served in Mongolian Armed Forces, rank of Maj.-Gen.; first Mongolian (and second Asian) to travel to space 1981; Minister of Defence 2000–04; Hero of the Nation, Contribution to Space Research Award, Russian Fund for Space Research 2000.

GURRÍA TREVIÑO, José Ángel, BA, MA; Mexican economist, diplomatist and international organization official; *Secretary-General, Organisation for Economic Co-operation and Development;* b. 8 May 1950, Tampico, Tamaulipas; m. Dr Lulu Quintana; three c.; ed Universidad Nacional Autónoma de México, Univ. of Leeds, UK, Harvard Univ., USA; Perm. Rep. of Mexico to Int. Coffee Org., London 1976–78; held various positions in Fed. Electricity Comm., Nat. Devt Bank (Nafinsa), Rural Devt Fund and Office of Mayor of Mexico City; at Finance Ministry 1978–92; Pres. and CEO Bancomext (export-import bank) 1992–93, Nacional Financiera (nat. devt bank) 1993–94; Minister of Foreign Affairs 1994–98, of Finance and Public Credit 1998–2000; Sec.-Gen. OECD 2006–; Commr, Global Comm. on Internet Governance 2014–; Chair. External Advisory Group, IDB; mem. UN Sec.-Gen. Advisory Bd for Water and Sanitation, fmr Chair. Int. Task Force on Financing Water; mem. Global Agenda Council on Water Security, World Econ. Forum, Int. Advisory Bd of Govs., Centre for Int. Governance Innovation, Royal Acad. of Econ. and Financial Sciences of Spain, Advisory Bd Global Green Growth Forum, Int. Forum on Genomics, Innovation and Econ. Growth; Grand Officier de la Légion d'honneur, Chevalier dans l'ordre du Mérite agricole, Orden Bernardo O'Higgins en el Grado de Gran Cruz; Dr hc (Universidad de Valle de México), (Rey Juan Carlos Univ.), (European Univ., Madrid), (Univ. of Leeds), (Univ. of Haifa), (Univ. of Bratislava); Globalist of the Year Award Canadian Int. Council 2007, Ridder Grootkruis in de Orde van Oranje-Naussau, Netherlands, Gwangwha Medal for Diplomatic Service, Korea, Medalla al Mérito Administrativo Internacional "Gustavo Martínez Cabañas", Instituto Nacional de Administración Pública, Ben Gurion Leadership Award, Award Isidro Fabela, Mexican Asscn of Int. Studies, Nueva Economía Award, Medalla Rectoral, Univ. of Chile. *Address:* OECD, 2 rue André Pascal, 75775 Paris Cedex 16, France (office). *Telephone:* 1-45-24-82-00 (office). *Fax:* 1-45-24-88-26 (office). *E-mail:* secretary.general@oecd.org (office). *Website:* www.oecd.org (office).

GURRY, Francis, LLB, LLM, PhD; Australian lawyer and international organization official; *Director-General, World Intellectual Property Organization;* b. 17 May 1951, Melbourne, Vic.; s. of Raymond Paul Gurry and Eileen Gurry (née Galbally); m.; three c.; ed Univ. of Melbourne, Univ. of Cambridge, UK; articled clerk, then attorney-at-law, Arthur Robinson & Co., Melbourne 1974–76; admitted barrister and solicitor, Supreme Court of Vic. 1975; Sr Lecturer in Law, Univ. of Melbourne 1979–83; Visiting Prof. of Law, Univ. of Dijon, France 1982–83; attorney-at-law, Freehills, Sydney 1984; joined WIPO 1985, held various positions, including Deputy Dir-Gen. 2003–08, Dir-Gen. 2008–; Sec.-Gen. Int. Union for the Protection of New Varieties of Plants (UPOV) 2008–; Chair. High-Level Cttee on Man., UN System Chief Execs Bd 2012–14; Fellow, Australian Inst. of Int. Affairs 2012; Sr Fellow, Grad. Inst. of Int. and Devt Studies, Geneva 2014; Hon. Professorial Fellow, Univ. of Melbourne 2001; Hon. Prof., Peking Univ. 2009, Eurasian Nat. Univ. 2012, East China Univ. of Political Science and Law 2015, Tongji Univ. 2015; Hon. mem. Univ. Council of the Arts, Univ. of Alcala 2012; Alawite Commdr Wissam (Morocco) 2013; Order of the Polar Star (Mongolia) 2015; Chevalier des Palmes académiques 2015; Dr hc (Univ. of World and Nat. Economy, Sofia, Bulgaria) 2009, (Nat. Tech. Univ. of Ukraine 'Kiev Polytechnic Inst.') 2010, (Haifa Univ.) 2010, (Renmin Univ.) 2010, (Univ. of Akron) 2011, (Acad. of Econ. Studies of Moldova) 2012, (Tokyo Univ. of Science) 2014, (Acad. of Public Administration, Azerbaijan) 2014, (Univ. of Dhaka) 2015, (Mongolian Univ. of Science and Tech.) 2015; Yorke Prize, Univ. of Cambridge 1980. *Publications include:* Breach of Confidence 1984, International Intellectual Property System: Commentary and Materials (with Frederick Abbott and Thomas Cottier) 1999, International Intellectual Property in an Integrated World Economy (with Frederick Abbot and Thomas Cottier) 2014; several book chapters and articles in professional journals. *Address:* World Intellectual Property Organization, PO Box 18, 34 chemin des Colombettes, 1211 Geneva 20, Switzerland (office). *Telephone:* 223389428 (office). *Fax:* 223388090 (office). *E-mail:* directorgeneral@wipo.int (office). *Website:* www.wipo.int (office).

GURSKY, Andreas; German photographer; b. 15 Jan. 1955, Leipzig; s. of Willy Gursky and Rosemarie Gursky; ed Folkwang School, Univ. of Essen, Düsseldorf Acad. of Art; studied under Hilla and Bernd Becher; known for highly textured feel in enormous photographs, often using a high point of view; Foreign Hon. mem. American Acad. of Arts and Letters 2007; Prof. for Liberal Arts, Düsseldorf Acad. of Art 2010–18; lives and works in Düsseldorf; Citybank Photography Prize 1998, Wilhelm-Loth-Prize 2003, The Imperial Ring Art Prize of the City of Goslar 2008. *Solo exhibitions include:* Johnen & Schöttle Gallery, Cologne 1988, Centre Genevois de Gravure Contemporaine, Geneva 1989, Museum Haus Lange, Krefeld 1990, 303 Gallery, New York 1991, 1995, Rüdiger Schöttle Gallery, Munich 1991, Kunsthalle Zürich 1992, Victoria Miro Gallery, London 1992, Monika Sprüth Galery, Cologne 1993, Deichtorhallen, Hamburg 1994, De Appel Foundation, Amsterdam 1994, Rooseum, Centre for Contemporary Art, Malmö 1995, Portikus, Frankfurt 1995, Galerie Rüdiger Schöttle, Munich 1997, Mai 36 Gallery, Zürich 1997, Mathew Marks Gallery, New York 1997, 2007, Kunstmuseum, Wolfsburg 1998, Kunsthalle, Düsseldorf 1998, Fotomuseum, Winterthur 1998, Milwaukee Art Museum 1998, Serpentine Gallery, London 1999, Scottish Gallery of Modern Art, Edinburgh 1999, Castello di Rivoli, Museo d'Arte Contemporanea, Rivoli 1999, nbk, neue bildende kunst, Berlin 1999, Busch-Reisinger Museum, Havard Univ. Art Museums 2000; Retrospective, New York, Chicago, Madrid, Paris 2001, Centre Nat. d'Art et de Culture Georges Pompidou, Paris 2002, White Cube Gallery, London 2007, Museum für Moderne Kunst, Frankfurt am Main 2008, PinchukArtCentre, Kiev 2008, Modernamuseet, Stockholm 2009, Vancouver Art Gallery, Vancouver 2009, Centre Pompidou, Paris 2010, Sprüth Magers, Berlin 2010, Kunstmuseum, Bonn 2010, Gagosian Gallery, New York 2011, Galeries Rudolfinium, Prague 2011, Gagosian, Hong Kong 2012, Louisiana Museum, Denmark 2012, Nat. Art Center, Tokyo 2013, Sprüth Magers, London 2014, White Cube Bermondsey, London 2014, Parrish Art Museum, New York 2015, Museum Frieder Burda, Baden-Baden 2015, Gagosian Gallery, New York 2016, Gagosian Gallery, Rome 2017, Hayward Gallery, London 2018, Gallery of the German Acad. Rome Villa Massimo, Rome 2019. *Group exhibitions include:* Künstlerwerkstätten Lothringer Straße, Munich 1985, Galerie Wittenbrink, Munich 1987, Galerie Johnen & Schöttle, Cologne 1988, Galerie Mosel & Tschechow, Munich 1988, Deutscher Photopreis '89 1989, Galerie Landesgirokasse, Stuttgart 1989, Internationale Foto-Triennale, Esslingen 1989, Photoart, Staatsgalerie, Stuttgart 1989, Power Plant Museum, Toronto 1989, Nat. Museum of Modern Art, Tokyo 1990, Kunstsammlung Nordrhein-Westfalen, Düsseldorf 1991, Sguardo di Medusa, Castello di Rivoli, Turin 1991, Museum Ludwig, Cologne 1992, Musée d'Art Moderne de la Ville de Paris 1992, Sprengel Museum, Hanover 1993, 2000, Museum Folkwang, Essen 1993, Deutsches Architekturmuseum, Frankfurt 1993, Museum Ludwig, Cologne 1993, Ruhrlandmuseum, Essen 1994, Kunsthaus, Zürich 1996, Schirn Kunsthalle, Frankfurt 1996, Berlinische Galerie, Berlin 1997, Galerie für Zeitgenössische Kunst, Leipzig 1998, Kunstraum, Innsbruck 1999, Kunstmuseum, Bonn 1999, Kunstverein, Freiburg 1999, galerie rot, Aachen 2000, Akad. der Künste, Berlin 2000, Museum Ludwig, Cologne 2000, MMK Museum für Moderne Kunst, Frankfurt 2000, Deichtorhallen, Hamburg 2000, Contemporary Art from Germany, Mumbai 2000, Museum Bochum/Galerie für Zeitgenössische Kunst, Leipzig 2000, Stadtgalerie, Saarbrücken 2000, Museum Ludwig, Köln 2000, Museum für Moderne Kunst, Frankfurt am Main 2001, Kunstmuseum Wolfsburg 2001, Kunsthalle Tiro 2001, Brandenburgische Kunstsammlungen Cottbus 2001, Kunsthalle Dominikanerkirche, Osnabrück 2001, Kunsthalle Emden 2002, Schirn Kunsthalle, Frankfurt am Main 2002, Staatgalerij Heerlen 2002, Deichtorhallen, Hamburg 2002, museum kunst palast, Düsseldorf 2002, Galerie 22, Hamburg 2002, Galerie Fahnemann, Berlin 2002, Städtische Galerie Haus Coburg, Delmenhorst 2002, Museum der bildenden Künste, Leipzig 2002, Solomon R. Guggenheim Museum, New York 2002, Tate Liverpool 2002, Tate Modern, London 2003, Martin-Gropius-Bau, Berlin 2003, Museum Ludwig, Cologne 2003, Inst. of Contemporary Art, Boston 2004, Museum Moderner Kunst, Vienna, Austria 2005, Galerie Emmanuel Perrotin, Paris 2005, Marlborough Gallery, New York 2005, Palais des Beaux-Arts, Brussels 2006, White Cube, London 2007, Musse d'Art Moderne, Paris 2008, Haus der Kunst, Munich 2008, Passage de Retz, Paris 2009, New Work' Matthew Marks, New York 2010, Galeries Rudolfinium, Prague 2011, Museum Weserburg, Bremen 2012, Stills Edinburgh and CCA Glasgow 2013, Kumu Art Museum, Tallinn 2013, Hiroshima City Museum of Contemporary Art, Hiroshima 2014, Turner Contemporary, Kent 2015, Hammer Museum, Los Angeles 2015, Mori Art Museum, Tokyo 2016, Grande Halle de la Vilette, Paris 2016, Kunsthaus Wien, Vienna 2017, The Broad, Los Angeles 2017, Kröller-Müller Museum, Otterlo 2018, Deichtorhallen, Hamburg 2018, Puschkin Museum, Moscow 2019, Zentrum Paul Klee, Bern 2019. *Address:* c/o Sprüth Magers, Oranienburger Stra.e 18, 10178 Berlin, Germany (office). *Telephone:* (30) 8884030 (office). *Fax:* (30) 288840352 (office). *Website:* www.spruethmagers.com (office); www.andreasgursky.com.

GURUNG, Lt-Gen. Chhatra Man Singh, BA; Nepalese army officer; b. 18 July 1952, Pulimarang VDC, Tanauhu dist; ed Tribhuvan Univ., Command and Gen. Staff Course in USA, Sr Command Course in India, Strategic Studies on Nat. Security and Mil. Command in China; joined army 1971, commissioned as 2nd Lt, has held various positions including Chief of Staff Western Div., Dir of Mil. Training and Quarter Master Gen. and Chief of Gen. Staff; served as Mil. Attaché in UK and France; served in UN Interim Force in Lebanon; Divisional Chief Mid-western Div. 2006–07; Chief of Army Staff 2009–12. *Leisure interest:* Taekwondo. *Address:* c/o Office of the Chief of Army Staff, Ministry of Defence, Singha Durbar, Kathmandu, Nepal. *E-mail:* mod@mos.com.np.

GUSAU, Lt-Gen. (retd) Mohammed Aliyu; Nigerian army officer and government official; b. 18 May 1943, Gusau, Zamfara State; ed Royal Coll. of Defence Studies, UK; Commdr, 9th Infantry Brigade, Abeokuta 1976–78, Adjutant Gen., 2nd Mechanised Div. 1978–79, Dir of Personnel Services, Army HQ Oct.–Nov. 1979, Dir of Mil. Intelligence 1979–83, Dir, Defence Intelligence Agency and Acting Dir-Gen., Nat. Security Org. 1985–86, Coordinator on Nat. Security 1986–89; Gen. Officer Commanding 2nd Mechanised Div., Ibadan 1989–90, Chief of Admin, Defence HQ, Lagos 1990–92, Commdr, Nigerian Defence Acad., Kaduna 1992–93, Nat. Security Adviser 1993, Chief of Army Staff Aug.–Sept. 1993, Nat. Security Adviser 1999–2006, March–Sept. 2010; Minister of Defence 2014–15; Chair. and CEO Alpha Public Affairs Consultancy 1993; mem. People's Democratic Party. *Address:* c/o Ministry of Defence, Ship House, Central Area, Abuja, Nigeria (office).

GUSENBAUER, Alfred, PhD; Austrian politician and business executive; *Chairman of the Supervisory Board, Strabag SE;* b. 8 Feb. 1960, Sankt Pölten, Lower Austria; ed High School in Wieselburg, Univ. of Vienna; Fed. Leader Sozialdemokratische Partei Österreichs (Social Democratic Party of Austria—SPÖ) Youth Wing, Socialist Youth (SJ) 1984–90, Chair. SPÖ in Ybbs an der Donau and mem. Lower Austria Party Exec. 1991, Chair. SPÖ 2000–08; Vice-Pres. Socialist Youth Int. (IUSY) 1985–89, Socialist Int. 1989; elected Deputy for Lower Austria to Bundesrat 1991, Chair. Cttee for Devt Co-operation 1996–99, Leader of SPÖ Group in Bundesrat 2000–07; Fed. Chancellor 2007–08; mem. Austrian del. to parl. meeting of Council of Europe 1991, Chair. Social Cttee of Council of Europe 1995–98; Sr Research Fellow, Econ. Policy Dept, Lower Austria Chamber of

Labour 1990–99; Visiting Prof., Brown Univ.; Leitner Global Fellow, Columbia Univ. School of Int. and Public Affairs, New York, USA 2009–; Chair. Advisory Bd Signa Holdings 2009–; Chair. Supervisory Bd Strabag SE 2010–; mem. Supervisory Bd Alpine Holding 2009–10; Pres. Dr Karl Renner Inst., Austrian Inst. for Int. Affairs, Austrian-Spanish Chamber of Commerce; Chair. Bd of Trustees of pvt. foundation est. by Strabag's CEO, Hans Peter Haselsteiner 2010–. *Address:* Strabag SE, Donau-City-Straße 9, 1220 Vienna, Austria (office). *Telephone:* (1) 22422-1000 (office). *Fax:* (1) 22422-1003 (office). *E-mail:* HPH@strabag.com (office). *Website:* www.strabag.com (office); www.alfred-gusenbauer.at.

GUSEV, Pavel Nikolayevich; Russian journalist and publisher; *Editor-in-Chief, Moskovsky Komsomolets;* b. 4 April 1949, Moscow; s. of Nikolai Gusev and Alla Guseva; m. Yevgeniya Valeryevna Yefimova; three d.; ed Moscow Inst. of Geological Survey, Maxim Gorky Inst. of Literature; First Sec. Komsomol Cttee of Krasnaya Presnya Region of Moscow 1975–80; Exec. Cen. Komsomol Cttee 1980–83; Ed.-in-Chief Moskovsky Komsomolets (newspaper) 1983–; Minister, Govt of Moscow, Head of Dept of Information and Mass Media Jan.–Oct. 1992; press adviser to Mayor of Moscow 1992–95; Chair. Comm. for the Politics of Information and Freedom of the Word of the Public Chamber, Public Council of Fed. Agency of Culture and Cinematography 2007–; Chair. Ministry of Defence Public Council 2013–; Pres. Moscow Confed. of Journalists 1991–; also Prof. of Journalism, International Univ., Moscow. *Plays:* I Love You, Constance (Moscow Gogol Theatre) 1993, Cardinal's Coat (Maly Theatre) 2002. *Leisure interests:* golf, books, trophy hunting. *Address:* Moskovsky Komsomolets, 1905 Goda 7, 123995 Moscow, Russia (office). *Telephone:* (499) 259-50-36 (office). *Fax:* (499) 259-46-39 (office). *E-mail:* info@mk.ru (office). *Website:* www.mk.ru (office).

GUSEV, Vladimir A., CandArts; Russian arts administrator; *Director, State Russian Museum;* b. 25 April 1945, Kalinin (now Tver); m. Mukhina Xenia Vladimizovna; one d.; ed U.E. Repin Inst. of Painting, Sculpture and Architecture, Leningrad; Exec. Sec. Leningrad br., Russian Fed. Union of Artists 1974–78; Sr Asst, Head of Dept, Deputy Dir for Science, State Russian Museum 1978–88, Dir 1988–; headed reconstruction of Mikhailovsky Castle, Marble Palace and Inzhenerny Castle in St Petersburg; mem. Comm. on State Prizes; Corresp. Mem. Russian Acad. of Fine Arts; Officier, Légion d'honneur 2004; Medal for Valiant Labour 1971, Honoured Cultural Worker of the Russian Fed. 1996, State Award in Literature and Art 2003, Commemorative medal for tricentenary of St Petersburg 2003. *Publications:* more than 60 contribs to various publs in Russian, English, German, French, Italian, Spanish 1986–2005. *Address:* State Russian Museum, 191186 St Petersburg, Inzhenernaya 4 (office); 197101 St Petersburg, Bolshaya Monetnaya Street, app. 9, Russia (home). *Telephone:* (812) 595-42-40 (office). *Fax:* (812) 314-41-53 (office). *E-mail:* info@rusmuseum.ru (office). *Website:* www.rusmuseum.ru (office).

GUSINSKII, Vladimir Aleksandrovich; Russian/Spanish banker; b. 6 Oct. 1952, Moscow; m. Yelena Gusinskaya; three s.; ed Moscow Gubkin Inst. of Oil and Chem., A. Lunacharskii State Inst. of Theatrical Art; Dir cultural programme, Moscow Festival of Youth and Students 1982–85; Dir cultural programme, Goodwill Games in Moscow 1985–86; f. co-operative Infex, later transformed into Holding Most, now comprising more than 40 enterprises in the field of construction, construction materials production, real estate and trade operations, also Most-Bank est. 1991; Owner major non-state TV co. NTV, Segodnya (newspaper) 1992, radio station Ekho Moskvy, Obshcheye Delo weekly, weekly TV programme 7 Days, Russian Television International (RTVi); Dir-Gen. Holding Group Most 1989–97, concurrently Pres. Most-Bank 1992–97, Pres. Media-Most co. 1997–2001; Vice Pres. Asscn of Russian Banks, Chair. Council of Authorized Banks of the Govt of Moscow; Pres. Jewish Congress of Russia 1995–2001; arrested in Spain on Russian prosecutor's request for extradition Jan. 2000–01, released after request rejected; took up residence in Israel April 2001; acquired Spanish citizenship Feb. 2007. *Address:* c/o Russian Television International (RTVi), 110 West 40th Street, New York, NY 10018, USA.

GUS'KOVA, Yelena Yuryevna, DHist; Russian historian and political scientist; *Head, Contemporary Studies, Institute of Slavic and Balkan Studies, Russian Academy of Sciences;* b. 23 Sept. 1949, Moscow; m.; two d.; ed Moscow State Univ.; Head Centre of Contemporary Studies, Inst. of Slavic and Balkan Studies, Russian Acad. of Sciences; leading scientific employee INION Russian Acad. of Sciences; mem. Presidium Russian Asscn of Co-operation with the UN; Political and Policy Analyst UN HQ of Peace-keeping Operations in fmr Yugoslavia; mem. Serbian Acad. of Sciences and Arts; Outstanding Scientist of Russia, Njegosha Award (Bosnia & Herzegovina) 1997, 850th Anniversary Medal, Moscow 1997, NATO Medal for peace-making operations in Kosovo 2002. *Publications:* over 340 works on the history of Yugoslavia and recent crises in the Balkans, including History of Yugoslavian Crisis (1990–2000) 2001 (Moscow), 2003 (Belgrade). *Address:* Institute of Slavic and Balkan Studies, Russian Academy of Sciences, 112334 Moscow, Leninsky prosp. 32A, Russia (office). *Telephone:* (495) 938-58-61 (office). *Fax:* (495) 938-00-96 (office); (495) 420-94-20 (home). *E-mail:* jelena@guskova.ru (office); info@guskova.ru (office); eguskova@com2com.ru (home). *Website:* www.inslav.ru (office); guskova.ru.

GUSMAN, Mikhail Solomonovich; Russian journalist; *First Deputy Director-General, ITAR-TASS News Agency;* b. 23 Jan. 1950, Baku, Azerbaijan; m.; one s.; ed Baku Higher CPSU School, Azerbaijan Inst. of Foreign Languages; Deputy Chair. Cttee of Youth Orgs, Azerbaijan 1973–86; Head of Information Dept, then Head of Press Centre, USSR Cttee of Youth Orgs 1986–91; Head of Gen. Admin. of Information Co-operation INFOMOL 1991–95; Vice-Pres. International Analytic Press Agency ANKOM-TASS 1995–98; Head of Chief, Dept of International Co-operation, Public Contacts and Special Projects, ITAR-TASS News Agency 1998–99, Deputy Dir-Gen., First Deputy Dir-Gen. 1999–; Co-founder World Congress of Russian Press 1999; Exec. Dir World Asscn of Russian Press; writer and producer, nationally syndicated TV show Formula of Power; Diploma of the USSR Supreme Soviet, numerous medals; Gold Medal for contrib. to devt of TV and radio, International Acad. of Radio and Television (Russia) 2007. *Leisure interests:* travelling, reading newspapers. *Address:* ITAR-TASS News Agency, 103009 Moscow, Tverskoy Blvd 10–12, Russia (office). *Telephone:* (495) 629-7925 (office). *Website:* www.itar-tass.com (office).

GUSMAN, Yuly S.; Russian film administrator, producer and scriptwriter; b. 8 Aug. 1943, Baku, Azerbaijan; s. of Solomon M. Gusman and Lola Yu. Barsuk; m. Valida Gusman; one d.; ed Baku State Medical Inst.; Artistic Dir Baku Theatre of Musical Comedy 1965–72; Dir Central House of Cinematographers, Azerbaijan State Theatre of Musical Comedy; Chair. Cinematography Centre 1988–2002; mem. State Duma 1993–95; Founder CEO Russian Jewish Congress 1996; Founder CEO Nika Award; Sec., Union of Cinematographers of Russia; mem. Bd of Dirs State Cttee on Cinematography; mem. Russian Union of Writers; Merited Worker of the Arts, Order of Friendship 2004. *Films include:* On One Fine Day 1977, Cottage for a Family 1978, Don't Be Afraid, I'm with You 1981, Nastya (actor) 1993, The Soviet Period Park 2006, Don't Be Afraid, I Am Here For You! 1919 2011. *Address:* 103473 Moscow, Delegatskaya str. 11, apt 10, Russia (home). *Telephone:* (495) 284-31-45 (home).

GUSMÃO, Kay Rala Xanana; Timor-Leste politician and fmr head of state; b. (José Alexandre Gusmão), 20 June 1946, Laleia, Manatuto; m. 1st Emilia Batista 1969 (divorced 2000); two c.; m. 2nd Kirsty Sword 2000; three c.; ed Nossa Senhora de Fátima seminary, Dare; fmr poet, teacher and chartered surveyor; joined pro-independence Fretilin (Revolutionary Front of the Independence of Timor Leste) 1974, Commdr 1978, now retd; C-in-C FALINTIL (Nat. Liberation Armed Forces of Timor Leste) 1981; arrested by Indonesian troops and sentenced to life imprisonment (later commuted to 20 years) 1992; released August 1999; Pres. Nat. Council of Timorese Resistance 1999–2001; Chair. Timor Leste Nat. Council 2000–01; Pres. of Timor-Leste 2002–07; Prime Minister of Timor-Leste 2007–Feb. 2015; Founder and Pres. Conselho Nacional de Reconstrução do Timor (Nat. Congress for Timorese Reconstruction, CNRT) 2007–; Hon. Citizen of Brasília (Brazil) 1995, São Paulo (Brazil) 1998, Lisbon, Portugal (awarded the Gold Key of Lisbon City) 2000, Eminent Mem. Sergio Vieira de Mello Foundation; Great Cross, Order of Liberty (Portugal) 1993, Hon. Companion, New Zealand Order of Merit 2000, Grande Colar da Ordem do Cruzeiro do Sul (Brazil) 2002, Grande Colar da Ordem de Dom Infante (Portugal) 2006, Hon. KCMG 2003; Dr hc (Lusíada Univ., Portugal) 1999, (Univ. of Oporto, Portugal) 2000, Hon. LLD (Victoria Univ.) 2003, (Suncheon Nat. Univ., South Korea) 2004, Hon. PhD (Univ. of Takushoku, Japan) 2006; Sakharov Prize for Freedom of Expression 1999, Medal of the Vice-Presidency of the Federative Repub. of Brazil 2000, Order of Merit José Bonifácio, Grau de Gran-Oficial, Univ. of the State of Rio Janeiro 2000, Sydney Peace Prize 2000, first Gwangju Prize for Human Rights 2000, North-South Prize, Council of Europe 2002. *Address:* Congresso Nacional da Reconstrução de Timor-Leste, Rua Nu Laran, Bairro dos Grilos, Dili, Timor-Leste (office). *Telephone:* 7358696 (office). *E-mail:* info@partidocnrt.com (office). *Website:* www.partidocnrt.com (office).

GUSTAFSON, Kathryn, RLA, ASLA; American landscape architect; *Director, Gustafson Guthrie Nichol Limited* and *Gustafson Porter Limited;* b. Yakima, Wash.; ed Univ. of Washington, Seattle, Fashion Inst. of Tech., New York, Ecole Nat. Supérieure du Paysage, Versailles, France; moved to France 1973; environmental artist and landscape designer 1980–; Co-founder and Dir, Gustafson Guthrie Nichol Ltd, Seattle 2000–; Co-founder and Dir, Gustafson Porter Ltd 1997–; Licensed Landscape Architect, Wash., NY, USA, France; Licensed and Chartered Landscape Architect, UK; Hon. FRIBA 1999; Hon. Royal Designer for Industry, Royal Soc. for the Encouragement of Arts, Manufactures & Commerce 2001; Architectural Medal, Acad. d'Architecture, Paris 1993, Jane Drew Prize, London 1998, Chrysler Design Award, Chrysler Design Inst. 2001, Club Laureate, Rainier Club, Seattle, Wash. 2008, Design Medal, American Soc. of Landscape Architects 2008, Sckell Ring Award, Bayerische Akad. der Kunste 2009, Arnold W. Brunner Memorial Prize for Architecture 2012. *Address:* Gustafson Porter, Linton House, 39–51 Highgate Road, London, NW5 1RS, England (office). *Telephone:* (20) 7267-2005 (office). *Fax:* (20) 7485-9203 (office). *E-mail:* enquiries@gustafson-porter.com (office). *Website:* www.gustafson-porter.com (office); www.ggnltd.com (office).

GUSTOV, Vadim Anatolyevich; Russian politician; b. 26 Dec. 1948, Kalinino, Vladimir Region; m.; two c.; ed Moscow State Inst. of Geological Prospecting, Leningrad Inst. of Politology; Head of uranium mines, Navoi Metallurgy Factory, Uzbekistan 1971–77; Head of mine, Phosphorite Kingisepp, Leningrad Region 1977–78; instructor, Head of Div., Kingisepp City CP Cttee 1978–86; First Deputy Chair. Kingisepp City Exec. Cttee 1986–87; Second Sec. Kingisepp City CP Cttee 1987–90; Chair. Kingisepp City Soviet 1990–91; Chair. Soviet of People's Deputies Leningrad Region 1991–93; mem. Council of Fed. of Russia, Chair. Cttee on CIS Cos 1993–98; Gov. Leningrad Region 1996–98; First Deputy Chair., Govt of Russian Fed. 1998–99; Rep. of Vladimir Region to Federation Council 2001; Chair. Cttee on CIS 2001; Order of Honour 1998. *Publications include:* Russia-CIS: The Path of Integration is Thorny but Tempting (co-author) 2002, Russia-CIS: Co-operation for Development and Progress 2007. *Leisure interests:* hunting, fiction, sports.

GUT, Rainer Emil; Swiss banker and business executive; *Honorary Chairman, Credit Suisse Group;* b. 24 Sept. 1932, Baar; s. of Emil Anton Gut and Rosa Gut (née Müller); m. Josephine Lorenz 1957; two s. two d.; ed Cantonal School of Zug; professional training in Switzerland, France and England; Gen. Pnr, Lazard Frères & Co., New York 1968–71; Chair. and CEO, Swiss American Corpn (Credit Suisse's US investment banking affiliate) 1971–73; mem. Exec. Bd Credit Suisse, Zürich 1973–77, Speaker of Exec. Bd 1977–82, Pres. Exec. Bd 1982–83, Chair. 1983–2000, Chair. Credit Suisse Group (fmrly CS Holding) 1986–2000, Chair. Credit Suisse First Boston, New York 1988–97, Chair. Credit Suisse First Boston Zürich 1997–2000, Hon. Chair. Credit Suisse Group 2000–; Chair. Nestlé SA 2000–05 (retd); Chair. and Del. Uprona (Canada) Ltd, Toronto 2000; Vice-Pres. Gesparal, Paris 2000; mem. Bd of Dirs L'Oréal, Paris, Pechiney SA, Paris, Sofina SA, Brussels.

GUTERRES, António Manuel de Oliveira; Portuguese politician and UN official; *Secretary-General, United Nations;* b. 30 April 1949, Lisbon; m. 1st Luísa Amélia Guimarães e Melo (died 1998); one s. one d.; m. 2nd Catarina de Almeida Vaz Pinto 2001; ed Instituto Superior Técnico, Lisbon; trained as electrical engineer; joined Socialist Party 1974; Chief of Staff to Sec. of State for Industry 1974–75; fmr asst to several cabinet ministers; Pres. Municipal Ass. of Fundão 1979–95; Deputy to Ass. of the Repub. 1976–2002, Pres. Socialist Parl. Group 1988–91, Leader of Socialist Party 1992–2002; Strategic Devt Dir, IPE (State Investment and Participation Agency) 1984–85; Prime Minister of Portugal 1995–2001; Vice-Pres. Socialist International 1992–99, Pres. 1999–2005; High

Commr, Office of the UN High Commr for Refugees 2005–15, Sec.-Gen. UN 2017–; Co-ordinator, Tech. Electoral Comm. 1980–87; Founder and Vice-Pres. Portuguese Asscn for the Defence of the Consumer 1973–74; mem. Asscn for Econ. and Social Devt 1970–96, Club of Madrid; Grand Cross, Order of the Southern Cross (Brazil) 1996, Grand Cross, Order of Merit of the Repub. of Poland 1997, Grand Officer, Order of the Oriental Repub. of Uruguay 1998, Sash of Special Category, Order of the Aztec Eagle (Mexico) 1999, Grand Cross, Order of Honour (Greece) 2000, Grand Cross, Order of Charles III (Spain) 2000, Grand Cordon, Order of Leopold (Belgium) 2000, First Degree, Order of Amílcar Cabral (Cape Verde) 2001, Grand Cross, Order of Merit (Chile) 2001, Grand Cross, Order of Merit of the Italian Repub. 2001, Grand Cordon, Order of the Repub. (Tunisia) 2002, Grand Cross, Order of the Southern Cross (Brazil) 2002, Grand Croix, Ordre nat. du Mérite 2002, Grand Cross, Order of Christ (Portugal) 2002, Collar, Order of Isabella the Catholic (Spain) 2002, Grand Cross, Order of Liberty (Portugal) 2016, Order of Friendship (Kyrgyzstan) 2017; Dr hc (Univ. of Beira Interior) 2010, (Meiji Univ.) 2014, (Univ. of Coimbra) 2016; Hon. LLD (Carleton Univ.) 2016; Personality of the Year, Associação de Imprensa Estrangeira em Portugal 2005, Freedom Award 2007, Calouste Gulbenkian Int. Prize (shared with Peace Research Inst. in the Middle East) 2009, W. Averell Harriman Democracy Award 2015, Nat. German Sustainability Award 2015. *Publications:* several books; articles for newspapers and magazines. *Leisure interests:* travel, history (especially Middle Ages), cinema, opera. *Address:* Office of the Secretary-General, United Nations, New York, NY 10017, USA (office). *Telephone:* (212) 963-1234 (office). *Fax:* (212) 963-4879 (office). *Website:* www.un.org/sg (office).

GUTERRES, Aurélio Sérgio Cristóvão, PhD; Timor-Leste economist and politician; b. 27 July 1966, Venilale; ed Massey Univ., New Zealand; over 25 years as univ. lecturer, becoming Prof., Nat. Univ. of East Timor (UNTL), Rector –2016; mem. Nat. Parl. 2005–07; mem. Exec. Council, East Timor Red Cross 2010–14; Minister of Foreign Affairs and Co-operation 2017–18; mem. Frente Revolucionária do Timor Leste Independente (Fretilin) (Revolutionary Front for an Independent East Timor).

GUTERRES, Francisco, (Lú-Olo); Timor-Leste lawyer, politician, head of state and fmr resistance fighter; *President;* b. 7 Sept. 1954, Ossu; s. of Felix Guterres and Elda da Costa Guterres; m. 1st Clotilde Maria de Fatima (died 1981); m. 2nd Cidália Lopes Nobre Mouzinho Guterres 2002; three s.; ed Nat. Univ. of Timor Lorosa'e; joined Associação Social Democrática Timorense (ASDT, independence movt) following Indonesian invasion 1975 (ASDT later renamed FRETILIN); took part in armed resistance in eastern coastal zone and Matebian, later becoming Vice-Sec. FRETILIN Leadership/Directive/Policy Comm. (CDF) (top political role in FRETILIN leadership) 1987–98, CDF Sec. 1998; Gen. Coordinator FRETILIN Presidential Council 1998; elected to Constituent Ass. Aug. 2001 (renamed Nat. Parl. May 2002), Pres. Nat. Parl. 2002–17; as Pres. of Nat. Parl., read proclamation of independence 20 May 2002; cand. in presidential elections 2007, 2012; Pres. of Timor-Leste 2017–; Pres. Revolutionary Front for an Independent East Timor (FRETILIN) 2001–. *Address:* Office of the President, Palácio das Cinzas, Caicoli, Dili, Timor-Leste (office). *Telephone:* 3339011 (office). *Website:* presidenttimorleste.tl (office).

GUTERRES, José Luis; Timor-Leste politician and diplomatist; b. 1954, Uato-Lari; m.; two c.; ed Univ. of Cambridge, UK, Univ. of the Western Cape, S Africa, Malaysia Inst. of Diplomacy and Foreign Relations, Inst. of Strategic and Int. Studies, Portugal; Founding mem. Frente Revolucionária do Timor Leste Independente (FRETILIN—Revolutionary Front for an Independent East Timor), mem. FRETILIN external del. 1974–, Rep. to Angola, also Perm. Rep. to Mozambique and FRETILIN Rep. to UN; Vice-Minister for Foreign Affairs and Co-operation 2002–03, Head of Timor-Leste del., Council of Ministers meeting, Comunidade dos Países de Língua Portuguesa, Brazil and ACP/EU meeting, Dominican Repub. July 2002, Timor-Leste Rep. to Sustainable Devt Summit, S Africa Aug. 2002; Amb. to USA and Perm. Rep. to UN, New York 2003–06; Minister of State and of Foreign Affairs and Co-operation 2006–07, 2012–15. *Address:* c/o Ministry of Foreign Affairs and Co-operation, Avenida Portugal, Praia dos Coqueiros, Dili, Timor-Leste.

GUTERSON, David, BA, MFA; American author; b. 4 May 1956, Seattle, Wash.; s. of Murray Guterson and Shirley Guterson (née Zak); m. Robin Ann Radwick 1979; three s. two d.; ed Univ. of Washington, Brown Univ. *Publications include:* The Country Ahead of Us, The Country Behind (short stories) 1989, Family Matters: Why Home Schooling Makes Sense 1992, Snow Falling on Cedars (PEN/Faulkner Award for Fiction 1994, Barnes & Noble Discovery Award, Pacific NW Booksellers Award 1995) 1994, East of the Mountains 1998, Our Lady of the Forest 2003, The Other 2008, Ed King 2011, Descent 2013, Songs for a Summons (poetry) 2014, Problems with People: Stories 2014. *Address:* c/o Georges Borchardt Inc., 136 East 57th Street, New York, NY 10020, USA (office). *E-mail:* georges@gbagency.com (office).

GUTFREUND, Herbert, PhD, FRS; British academic; *Professor Emeritus of Physical Biochemistry, University of Bristol;* b. 21 Oct. 1921, Vienna, Austria; s. of Paul Gutfreund and Clara Gutfreund; m. Mary Kathleen Davies 1958; two s. one d.; ed Univs of Vienna, Austria and Cambridge, UK; Research Fellow, Univ. of Cambridge 1947–57; with Agricultural Research Council, Univ. of Reading 1957–64; Visiting Prof., Univ. of Calif. 1965, Max Planck Inst., Germany 1966, Dir Molecular Enzymology Lab. and Prof. of Physical Biochemistry, Univ. of Bristol 1967–86, Prof. Emer. 1986–; part-time Scholar in Residence, NIH, Bethesda, USA 1986–89; Scientific mem. (external) Max Planck Inst. for Medical Research 1987–; Fogarty Scholar, NIH, Washington, DC 1987–89. *Publications:* An Introduction to the Study of Enzymes 1966, Enzymes: Physical Principles 1972, Molecular Evolution 1981, Biothermodynamics 1983, Kinetics for the Life Sciences: Receptors, Transmitters and Catalysts 1995. *Leisure interests:* hill walking, reading, cooking. *Address:* Somerset House, Upton, Oxon., OX11 9JL, England (home). *Telephone:* (1235) 851468 (home). *E-mail:* h.gutfreund@bristol.ac.uk (home).

GUTH, Alan Harvey, PhD; American theoretical physicist and academic; *Victor F. Weisskopf Professor of Physics, Massachusetts Institute of Technology;* b. 27 Feb. 1947, New Brunswick, NJ; s. of Hyman Guth and Elaine Cheiten; m. Susan Tisch 1971; one s. one d.; ed Massachusetts Inst. of Tech.; Instructor, Princeton Univ. 1971–74; Research Assoc. Columbia Univ. New York 1974–77, Cornell Univ. 1977–79, Stanford Linear Accelerator Center, Calif. 1979–80; Assoc. Prof. of Physics, MIT 1980–86, Prof. 1986–89, Jerrold Zacharias Prof. of Physics 1989–91, Victor F. Weisskopf Prof. of Physics 1992–, Margaret MacVicar Faculty Fellow; Physicist, Harvard-Smithsonian Center for Astrophysics 1984–89, Visiting Scientist 1990–91; Alfred P. Sloan Fellow 1981; Fellow, American Physics Soc. (Chair. Astrophysics Div. 1989–90), AAAS, American Acad. of Arts and Sciences; mem. NAS, American Astronomical Soc.; Rennie Taylor Award, American Tentative Soc. 1991, Julius E. Lilienfeld Prize, American Physical Soc. 1992, Benjamin Franklin Medal for Physics, Franklin Inst. 2001, Cosmology Prize, Peter Gruber Foundation 2004, Isaac Newton Medal, British Inst. of Physics 2009, Breakthrough Prize in Fundamental Physics (co-recipient) 2012, Kavli Prize (co-recipient) 2015. *Publications:* The Inflationary Universe: The Quest for a New Theory of Cosmic Origins 1997, Inflation and the New Era of High-Precision Cosmology 2002; numerous papers in professional journals. *Address:* Center for Theoretical Physics, Room 6-322, Massachusetts Institute of Technology, 77 Massachusetts Avenue, Cambridge, MA 02139-4307, USA (office). *Telephone:* (617) 253-6265 (office). *E-mail:* guth@ctp.mit.edu (office). *Website:* web.mit.edu/physics/people/faculty/guth_alan.html (office).

GUTH, Lawrence (Larry) David, BS, PhD; American mathematician and academic; *Professor of Mathematics, Massachusetts Institute of Technology;* b. 1977; s. of Alan Guth; ed Yale Univ., Massachusetts Inst. of Tech.; Samelson Fellow, Stanford Univ. 2005–06, Szego Asst Prof. 2006–08; Tenure-stream Asst Prof., Univ. of Toronto 2008–11; Prof., Courant Inst. of Math. Sciences, New York Univ. 2011–12; Prof. of Math., MIT 2012–; Simons Investigator, Simons Foundation 2014–; mem. Inst. for Advanced Study, Princeton, NJ 2010–11; NSF Grad. Fellowship 2001–03, NSF Postdoctoral Fellow 2006–08, Alfred P. Sloan Research Fellowship 2010–14, Invited Speaker, Int. Congress of Mathematicians, India 2010, Salem Prize 2013, Marston Morse Lecturer, IAS 2013, Namboodiri Lecturer, Univ. of Chicago 2015, Teaching Prize in Grad. Educ., School of Science, MIT 2015, Clay Research Award, Clay Math. Inst. (co-recipient) 2015. *Publications:* numerous papers in professional journals. *Address:* Room E17-314, Department of Mathematics, Massachusetts Institute of Technology, 77 Massachusetts Avenue, Cambridge, MA 02139-4307, USA (office). *Telephone:* (617) 253-4326 (office). *Fax:* (617) 253-4358 (office). *E-mail:* lguth@math.mit.edu (office). *Website:* math.mit.edu (office).

GUTHRIE, Michelle L., BA, BLL; Australian lawyer and business executive; b. 1965, Sydney; m. Darren Farr; two d.; ed Univ. of Sydney; fmr lawyer, Allen, Allen and Hemsley, Sydney and Singapore; joined News Corpn 1994, becoming Gen. Counsel, BSkyB and News International, London, later Dir of Legal and Business Affairs, FOXTEL, Sydney; joined Star TV 2000, Sr Vice-Pres. Business Devt 2001–03, Exec. Vice-Pres. Regional Distribution and Business Devt June–Nov. 2003, CEO Nov. 2003–07; Man. Dir Providence Equity Partners LLC, Hong Kong 2007–10; Partner, Business Solutions, APAC 2011–14; Dir of Strategic Business Devt for Japan and Asia Pacific, Google Inc., Singapore 2011–15; Man. Dir, Australian Broadcasting Corpn 2016–18; Chair. Plan International Hong Kong (charity); mem. Bd of Dirs Metro International SA; fmr mem. Bd of Dirs Phoenix Satellite Television, Hathway, China Network Systems, Balaji Telefilms Ltd (STAR joint venture cos); fmr mem. Council of Govs Cable and Satellite Broadcasting Asscn of Asia. Head of Jury, APAC Effie Awards 2016; named Young Global Leader by the World Econ. Forum 2005, Veuve Clicquot Business Woman of the Year Award 2005. *Address:* c/o Australian Broadcasting Corporation, 14th Floor, 700 Harris Street, Ultimo, Sydney, NSW 2007, Australia (office).

GUTHRIE, Roderick (Rod) I. L., BSc (Eng), PhD, ARSM, DIC, FRSC, FCAE, FCIM; British/Canadian metallurgist, engineer and academic; *Macdonald Professor and Director, McGill Metals Processing Centre, McGill University;* b. 12 Sept. 1941, Sutton Coldfield, West Midlands, England; s. of Lawrence Carr Guthrie and Norah Smith; two c.; ed Royal School of Mines, Imperial Coll., Univ. of London; currently Macdonald Prof. of Metallurgy, Dept of Mining and Materials Eng and Dir McGill Metals Processing Centre, McGill Univ., Montréal, Canada; Fellow, Canadian Acad. of Engineers, Canadian Inst. of Mining; research consultant to steel and aluminium industries; Hon. mem. Japan Iron and Steel Inst., AIME 2014; Distinguished mem. Iron and Steel Soc., Asscn for Iron and Steel Technologies; 24 Best Paper Awards, Queen's Golden and Diamond Jubilee Medals, 77th Howe Memorial Lecturer, Iron and Steel Soc., John Elliott Distinguished Lecturer, Iron and Steel Soc. 2003–04, Killam Prize for Eng 2006, NSERC Leo Derikx Award for collaborative research with industry. *Publications:* Engineering in Process Metallurgy, The Physical Properties of Liquid Metals, The Science and Practice of Steel making, and Steel Processing; more than 200 patents on topics ranging from metal delivery systems for high-speed strip casting processes, to improved aerodynamics for batch annealing furnaces and in-situ detection of inclusions in liquid aluminium, steel and magnesium; more than 450 scientific papers in professional journals. *Leisure interests:* long distance kayaking, running, cycling. *Address:* McGill Metals Processing Centre, 3610 University Street, M.H. Wong Building, 2M040, Montréal, PQ H3A 2B2, Canada (office). *Telephone:* (514) 398-1555 (office); (514) 398-5556 (office). *Fax:* (514) 398-4168 (office). *E-mail:* rod@mmpc.mcgill.ca (office). *Website:* www.mmpc.mcgill.ca (office).

GUTHRIE OF CRAIGIEBANK, Baron (Life Peer), cr. 2001, of Craigiebank in the City of Dundee; **Charles (Ronald Llewelyn) Guthrie,** GCB, LVO, OBE, DL; British army officer and business executive; b. 17 Nov. 1938, London; s. of Ronald Guthrie and Nina Llewelyn; m. Catherine Worrall 1971; two s.; ed Harrow School and Royal Mil. Acad. Sandhurst; commissioned Welsh Guards 1959; served in BAOR, Aden; 22 Special Air Service (SAS) Regt 1965–69; Staff Coll. 1972; Mil. Asst (GSO2) to Chief of Gen. Staff, Ministry of Defence 1973–74; Brigade Maj., Household Div. 1976–77; CO, 1st Bn Welsh Guards, Berlin and NI 1977–80; Col, Gen. Staff, Mil. Operations, Ministry of Defence 1980–82; Commdr British Forces, New Hebrides 1980; 4th Armoured Brigade 1982–84; Chief of Staff 1st (British) Corps 1984–86; Gen. Officer Commdg NE Dist and Commdr 2nd Infantry Div. 1986–87; Asst Chief of Gen. Staff, Ministry of Defence 1987–89; Commdr 1st (British) Corps 1989–91; Commdr Northern Army Group 1992–93 and C-in-C BAOR 1992–94; Col Commdt, Intelligence Corps 1986–96; ADC Gen. to HM the Queen 1993–, Gold Stick to HM the Queen 1999–; Chief of Gen. Staff 1994–97, of the Defence Staff 1997–2001; Special Envoy to Pakistan 2001; Dir (non-exec.) N. M. Rothschild & Sons 2001–11, Petropavlovsk Colt, Gulf Keystone Petroleum; Chair. Hospital of St John & St Elizabeth, St John's Hospice; Col of the Life Guards 1999–; Chancellor Liverpool Hope Univ. 2013–; Pres. Action Medical Research, London Fed. of Youth Clubs; Freeman, City of London; Kt, Sovereign Mil. Order of Malta 1999; Commdr, Legion of Merit (USA) 2001. *Publication:* Just War: The Just War Tradition: Ethics in Modern Warfare (co-author) 2007. *Leisure interests:* tennis, opera. *Address:* PO Box 25439, London, SW1P 1AG, England.

GUTIERREZ, Carl T. C.; American computer industry executive and politician; b. 15 Oct. 1941, Agana Heights, Guam; s. of Tomas Taitano Gutierrez and Rita Benavente Cruz; m. Geraldine Chance Torres; one s. two d.; ed S. San Francisco High School; service with USAF 1960–65; est. first data processing centre in Guam; f. Carltom Enterprises 1971; Propr Carltom Consulting; elected Senator 1972, Speaker of Legislature; Gov. of Guam 1994–98, 1998–2003, Chair. and Vice-Pres. Guam Visitors Bureau 1988–89; Pres. Asscn of Pacific Island Legislatures; Chair. Guam Tax Code Comm., Cttee on Ways and Means; Vice-Chair. Cttee on Rules, Cttee on Tourism and Transportation; f. People Helping People 1994; Hon. Citizen (Belau); Hon. DHumLitt (World Acad. of Art and Sciences) 1985, Hon. DJur (Univ. of Guam) 1996; Eagle Award, Nat. Guard Bureau. *Leisure interests:* tennis, fishing, hunting. *Address:* c/o PO Box 2950, Agana, GU 96932-2950, USA.

GUTIERREZ, Carlos M.; American (b. Cuban) business executive and fmr government official; *Co-Chairman, Albright Stonebridge Group;* b. 4 Nov. 1953, Havana, Cuba; m.; three c.; ed Monterrey Inst. of Tech.; joined Kellogg de Mexico as sales rep. 1975, Supervisor, Latin America Marketing Services, Kellogg HQ, Mich. 1982–83, Man. Int. Marketing Services 1983–84, Gen. Man. Kellogg de Mexico 1984–89, Pres. and CEO Kellogg Canada Inc. 1989–90, Corp. Vice-Pres. Product Devt at Kellogg HQ 1990, Vice-Pres. Kellogg Co. and Exec. Vice-Pres. Sales and Marketing, Kellogg USA 1990–93, Exec. Vice-Pres. Kellogg USA and Gen. Man. Kellogg USA Cereal Div. 1993–94, Exec. Vice-Pres. Kellogg Co. and Pres. Kellogg Asia-Pacific 1994–96, Exec. Vice-Pres. Business Devt 1996–98, Pres. and COO 1998–99, elected to Bd of Dirs Jan. 1999, apptd CEO April 1999, Chair. 2000–04; US Sec. of Commerce, Washington, DC 2004–09; Co-Chair. Global Political Strategies div., APCO Worldwide Inc. 2010–11; Vice-Chair., Institutional Clients Group, Citigroup Inc. 2011–13, also mem. Sr Strategic Advisory Group; Vice-Chair. Albright Stonebridge Group 2013–14, Co-Chair. 2014–; Founder and Chair. Republicans for Immigration Reform 2012–; Nat. Trustee Univ. of Miami, also Visiting Scholar, Inst. for Cuban and Cuban American Studies; Trustee Meridian International Center; mem. Bd of Dirs US-Mexico Foundation, Occidental Petroleum Corpn, Met Life, Inc., Time Warner, Inc. *Address:* Albright Stonebridge Group, 1101 New York Avenue, NW, Suite 900, Washington, DC 20005, USA (office). *Website:* www.albrightstonebridge.com (office).

GUTIÉRREZ, Gustavo, DTheol, OP; Peruvian ecclesiastic and academic; *John Cardinal O'Hara Professor of Theology, Department of Theology, University of Notre Dame;* b. 8 June 1928, Lima; ed Univ. Nacional Mayor de San Marcos, Lima, Univ. Catholique de Louvain, Univ. de Lyon, Univ. Gregoriana and Inst. Catholique de Paris; ordained priest 1959; Adviser, Nat. Union of Catholic Students 1960; Prof. Catholic Univ. of Lima 1960; mem. Pastoral-Theological team, Latin American Conf. of Catholic Bishops (CELAM) 1967–68; currently John Cardinal O'Hara Prof. of Theology, Univ. of Notre Dame, USA; mem. Bd of Dirs Inst. Bartolomé Las Casas-Rímac 1974–, Concilium; Assoc. Vicar, Rímac, Lima 1980–; fmr Prin. Prof. Pontifical Univ. of Peru; Visiting Prof. and lecturer at univs, colls and seminaries in USA and elsewhere; mem. EATWOT (Ecumenical Asscn of Third World Theologians), American Acad. of Arts and Sciences, Peruvian Acad. of Language; Legion of Honor 1993, Master of the Order, Order Of Preachers 2009; Dr hc (Nijmegen) 1979, (Tübingen) 1985, (King's Coll., USA) 1989, (Haverford Coll., USA) 1990, (Friburg, Germany) 1990, (San Marcos, Lima) 1991, (Montréal) 1993, (Universidad Nacional de Ingeniería, Peru) 1993, (State of NY) 1994, (Holy Cross, MA) 1994, (San Agustín Peru) 1995, (Catholic Theol. Union USA) 1995, (St Norbert Coll., USA) 1996, (St Michael, Canada) 1996, (Simón Bolívar, Peru) 1997, (Fribourg, Switzerland) 1998, (Southern Methodist, USA) 2000, (Brown, USA) 2000; Príncipe de Asturias Award 2003, Niebuhr Medal, Elmhurst Coll. 2009. *Publications:* A Theology of Liberation 1971, The Power of the Poor in History 1980, We Drink from Our Own Wells: the Spiritual Journey of a People 1983, On Job, God-talk and the Suffering of the Innocent 1986, La Verdad los hará libres 1986, Dios o el Oro en las Indias 1989, El Dios de la Vida 1989, Entre las Calandrias 1990, En Busca de los Pobres de Jesucristo 1992, Compartir la Palabra 1995, Essential Writings (with Nikoloff) 1996, Densidad del Presente 1996. *Leisure interests:* swimming, literature. *Address:* University of Notre Dame, Department of Theology, 331 Malloy Hall, Notre Dame, IN 46556, USA (office); Instituto Bartolomé Las Casas-Rímac, Apartado 3090, Lima 100, Peru. *Telephone:* (574) 631-5366 (office). *E-mail:* Gustavo.A.Gutierrez.30@nd.edu (office). *Website:* www.nd.edu/~theo (office).

GUTIERREZ, Lino, BA, MA; American diplomatist; *Executive Director, Una Chapman Cox Foundation;* b. 26 March 1951, Havana, Cuba; m. Miriam Gutierrez (née Messina); three d.; ed Univs of Miami and Alabama; social studies teacher, Dade County School System and Urban League, Miami 1973–75; joined US Foreign Service 1977, overseas assignments include at Embassies in Lisbon, Port-au-Prince, Grenada, Paris and Nassau, served as Officer-in-Charge of Nicaraguan Affairs, of Portuguese Affairs, Dir Office of Policy Planning, Coordination and Press, Bureau of Inter-American Affairs, Amb. to Nicaragua 1996–99, Prin. Deputy Asst Sec. for Western Hemisphere Affairs, Dept of State 1999–2001, Acting Asst Sec. 2001–02, Int. Affairs Advisor, Nat. War Coll. 2002–03, Amb. to Argentina 2003–06; Founder and CEO Gutierrez Global LLC (consultancy); Exec. Dir Una Chapman Cox Foundation 2010–; Adjunct Prof., Elliott School of Int. Affairs, George Washington Univ., School of Educ., Johns Hopkins Univ.; two Dept of State Distinguished Honour Awards, three Meritorious Honour Awards, US Army Award for Civilian Excellence. *Address:* Gutierrez Global LLC, 3424 Austin Court, Alexandria, VA 22310-3163 (office); Office of the Executive Director, Una Chapman Cox Foundation, 1200 18th Street, NW, Suite 902, Washington, DC 20036, USA (office). *Telephone:* (202) 331-3918 (Una Chapman Cox Foundation) (office); (703) 909-0290 (Gutierrez Global LLC) (office). *Fax:* (202) 833-4555(Una Chapman Cox Foundation) (office). *E-mail:* info@gutierrezglobal.com (office). *Website:* www.uccoxfoundation.org (office); www.gutierrezglobal.com (office).

GUTIERREZ BORBÚA, Lucio Edwin; Ecuadorean politician and fmr head of state; b. 23 March 1957, Quito; m. Ximena Bohórquez; two c.; ed Army Polytechnic School, Inter-American Defense Coll., Washington, DC, USA; fmr pentathelete; fmr Col in army; staged Indian uprising against Pres. Jamil Mahuad 2000, sentenced to six months in a mil. prison; Pres. of Ecuador 2003–05 (resgnd); cand. in presidential election 2009, 2013; Founder Partido Sociedad Patriótica 21 de Enero (PSP). *Address:* Partido Sociedad Patriótica 21 de Enero, Quito, Ecuador (office). *Website:* www.sociedadpatriotica.com (office).

GUTIÉRREZ FERNÁNDEZ, Gerónimo, BA, MPA; Mexican public servant, economist and diplomatist; b. Monterrey; ed Instituto Tecnológico Autónomo de México (ITAM), Harvard Univ. John F. Kennedy School of Govt; 15-year career in federal govt depts, including UnderSec. of Governance, Secretaría de Gobernación (Interior Ministry), positions with Secretaría de Economía (Commerce Dept), Secretaría de Hacienda y Crédito Público (Treasury Dept), Office of the Pres., Banobras (nat. public works bank), several roles in Secretaría de Relaciones Exteriores (State Dept), including UnderSec. for N America 2003–06, UnderSec. for Latin America and the Caribbean 2006–09; Deputy Sec. for Governance and Homeland Security 2009–10; Man. Dir North American Devt Bank (NADB) 2010–17; Amb. to USA 2017–18; worked as part of Pres.-elect Vicente Fox's transition team 2000; Dir Miguel Estrada Iturbide Foundation (think tank); mem. Partido Acción Nacional (PAN), fmr Chief of Staff, PAN Parl. Group. *Address:* c/o Mexican Embassy, 1911 Pennsylvania Avenue, NW, Washington, DC 20006, USA (office).

GUTIÉRREZ GIRÓN, Edgar Armando; Guatemalan politician; b. 27 July 1960, Guatemala City; m. María Elena Aiza Meade de Gutiérrez; two s. three d.; political and econ. analyst in Guatemala and Central America 1982–; consultant for various int. agencies in Europe and USA; Co-founder Asscn for the Advancement of the Social Sciences 1987, Coordinadora de ONG y Cooperativas 1992, Myrna Mack Foundation 1993; Co-ordinator-Gen. Interdiocesan Project 'Recuperación de la Memoria Histórica' 1995–98; Jt Ed. Periódico de Guatemala 1999; Sec. of Strategic Analysis 2000–02; Minister of Foreign Affairs 2002–04. *Publications include:* Centroamérica en el vórtice de la crisis 1986, Modelos heterogéneos en Centroamérica 1987, Guatemala: política exterior y estabilidad del Estado 1988, ¿Quién quiso asaltar el cielo? 1998, Sociedad civil y derechos humanos en la difícil transición guatemalteca 1998, Hacia un paradigma democrático del sistema de inteligencia en Guatemala 1999; poetry: Para conjurar su hechizo 1990, Al final de esta luna 1992, Memoria de la Muerte 1997.

GUTIÉRREZ IRIARTE, Waldo M.; Bolivian fmr government official; *Associated Consultant, International Institution for Economics and Business;* ed Univ. of Mayor Real y Pontificia de San Francisco Xavier de Chuquisaca, Univ. of New Mexico; fmr Deputy Minister of the Treasury; Minister of Finance 2005–06; Tax Policy Consultant, Int. Cooperation Agencies for Devt 2007–09; Public Finance Consultant, World Bank 2009; Consultant for Strengthening Capacities in Public Debt Man., CEMLA 2012–15; currently Associated Consultant, Int. Inst. for Econs and Business IIDEE. *Address:* International Institution for Economics and Business, Ed. Torre Ketal, Piso 3, Oficina 318 Calle 15, Calacoto, La Paz, Bolivia (office). *Telephone:* (2) 277-2170 (office). *Fax:* (2) 277-2170 (office). *Website:* www.iidee.net (office).

GUTIÉRREZ PEMBERTY, Javier Genaro, BEng, MEng; Colombian civil engineer, business executive and academic; b. 1951, Bogotá; m.; two c.; ed Universidad de los Andes in Bogotá, Int. Atomic Energy Agency, Argonne Nat. Lab., Illinois, USA, Escuela de Administración, Finanzas y Tecnología (EAFIT) Medellín; began career with Interconexión Eléctrica SA E.S.P. – ISA 1981, promoted to Man. of Planning Office, Gen. Man. ISA 1992–2007; Pres. and CEO Ecopetrol SA 2007–15; Prof. of Statistics and Operations Research, Universidad de los Andes and Prof. of Operations Research with emphasis on Dynamic Programming, EAFIT; mem. Bd of Dirs Empresas Públicas de Medellín E.S.P 2016; Portfolio Award (Best Corp. Leader category) 2002, Excellence Award (Internationalization category), América Economía Magazine 2005, acknowledged by Republica newspaper as one of the ten best executives of the year in Colombia 2005.

GUTIÉRREZ REINEL, Gonzalo Alfonso, BA, MA; Peruvian diplomatist, author and government official; b. 10 May 1955, Lima; ed Peruvian Diplomatic Acad., School of Advanced Int. Studies, Johns Hopkins Univ., Washington, DC, USA, London School of Econs, UK, Kennedy School of Govt, Harvard Univ., USA; joined Foreign Service 1978, fmr Prof., Peruvian Diplomatic Acad.; served at Perm. Mission to UN, New York, and at Embassies in Washington, DC and Santiago, fmr Deputy Perm. Rep. to UN Office and other Int. Orgs, Geneva, fmr Under-Sec. for Econ. Affairs, fmr Exec. Dir Bureau for Trade Promotion, fmr Acting Under-Sec. for the Americas and fmr Dir of South America, Ministry of Foreign Affairs, Deputy Sec.-Gen. for Foreign Affairs 2006–09, Amb. and Perm. Rep. to UN, New York 2009–11, Amb. to People's Repub. of China 2011–14, Minister of Foreign Affairs 2014–15; Chair. Sr Officials Meeting, APEC 2008; Vice-Pres. ECOSOC 2011; Prof. of Int. Politics, Peruvian Univ. of Applied Sciences; fmr Guest Prof., Catholic Univ. of Peru, Ricardo Palma Univ., San Martin de Porres Univ.; Grand Cross, Order of Merit for Distinguished Services, Grand Cross, Order 'José Gregorio Paz Soldan' (Paraguay), Grand Cross, Order of Merit (Chile); named Most Distinguished Public Officer by Perús Asscn of Exporters (ADEX) 2006. *Publications include:* Settlement of Disputes in the World Trade Organization: Peru in the Case against France and the European Community for the Commercial Designation of Scallops 1996, The Institutional Evolution of the Andean Integration Process 1996, The Pre-history of the WTO: The Creation of GATT and Peru's Membership 1999, Pisco: Arguments for the International Protection of the Peruvian Appellation of Origin 2003. *Address:* c/o Ministry of Foreign Affairs, Jirón Lampa 535, Lima 1, Peru.

GUTIONTOV, Pavel Semenovich; Russian journalist; b. 23 Jan. 1953; ed Moscow State Univ.; mem. staff, Moskovski Komsomolets 1970–75; fmr corresp., Komsomolskaya Pravda, then Head of Div. 1975–85; special corresp., Sovetskaya Rossiya 1985–87; political observer, Izvestia; Co-Chair. Liberal Journalists Club –1997; Chair. Cttee for Defence of Freedom of Speech and Journalists' Rights; Sec. Russian Journalists' Union; winner of numerous professional prizes. *Publications:* Games in the Fresh Air of Stagnation 1990, Fate of Drummers 1997 and numerous articles. *Address:* Russian Journalists' Union, 119021 Moscow, Zubovsky blvd 4, Russia (office). *Telephone:* (495) 637-21-59 (office). *E-mail:* gutiontov@mail.ru (office).

GUTMAN, Col Gen. (retd) Albin; Slovenian military officer; b. 17 Dec. 1947, Novo Mesto; m.; one s. one d.; ed Univ. of Ljubljana, Pedagogical Acad., Ljubljana; veteran of the Slovenian War 1991; previous posts include Territorial-Defence Municipal Staff, Novo Mesto, Defence Secr., Novo Mesto, Territorial-Defence Regional Staff, Dolenjska, Ministry of Defence; Chief of Armed Forces Gen. Staff 1993–98, 2006–09; Chief Defence Insp. 1998–2003; mil. adviser to Minister of Defence 2003–06; continued mil. career in Directorate of Defence Policy, Ministry of Defence 2009–10 (retd); Silver Order of Freedom; Order of Gen. Maister with Swords; Chevalier, Légion d'honneur 1998; Manoeuvre Structure of Nat. Defence (MSNZ) Badge 1990, Defended Slovenia Badge, Slovenian Armed Forces Gold Medal, Slovenian Armed Forces Gold Plaque. *Address:* Ministry of Defence, 1000 Ljubljana, Vojkova cesta 55, Slovenia (office). *Telephone:* (1) 4712211 (office). *Fax:* (1) 4712978 (office). *E-mail:* glavna.pisarna@mors.si (office). *Website:* www.mors.si (office).

GUTMAN, Natalia Grigorievna, FRAM; Russian/German cellist; b. 14 Nov. 1942; m. Oleg Kagan (deceased); three c.; ed Gnessin Music School, Moscow under R. Shaposhnikov, Moscow Conservatory under Prof. Kozolupova and postgraduate studies in Leningrad under Mstislav Rostropovich; tours include visits to Europe, USA and Japan, appearing with the Berlin Philharmonic Orchestra, Vienna Philharmonic Orchestra, London Symphony Orchestra, Orchestre Nat. de France and Orchestre de Paris; played chamber music in USSR and Europe with Eliso Virsaladze and Oleg Kagan; played sonatas, trios and quartets with Sviatoslav Richter; plays sonata and concerto written for her by Alfred Schnittke; solo tours include USA with USSR State Symphony Orchestra and Yevgeny Svetlanov, Italy with BBC Symphony and Yuri Temirkanov, USSR with Sir John Pritchard; performed with Royal Philharmonic Orchestra under Yuri Temirkanov, Royal Festival Hall, London, Concertgebouw, London Philharmonic, Munich Philharmonic, Berlin Philharmonic, Orchestre Nat. de France, Los Angeles Philharmonic under André Previn, Chicago Symphony under Claudio Abbado 1988–89; fmr teacher at Moscow Conservatory; Prof., Stuttgart Conservatory 1997–2004; f. Oleg Kagan Music Festival, Kreuth and Moscow; winner, Vienna Student Festival Competition, Dvořák Competition, Prague, ARD Competition, Munich, National Artist of the USSR 1991, State Prize of Russian Federation 2000, Shostakovich Prize 2002, 2013, Triumph Award 2002, Musikpreis des Verbandes der Deutschen Konzertdirektionen 2012, Premio NEM in Florence 2014. *Address:* Natalia Gutman's Office, c/o Tallafocs els Ferros 7, 46012 Valencia, Spain. *Telephone:* 6-9380483 (mobile). *E-mail:* cellogutman@gmail.com. *Website:* www.nataliagutman.com.

GUTMANN, Amy, BA, MSc, PhD; American academic and university president; *President, University of Pennsylvania;* b. 19 Nov. 1949, New York; m. Michael W. Doyle; one d.; ed Harvard-Radcliffe Coll., London School of Econs, UK, Harvard Univ.; Asst Prof. of Politics, Princeton Univ. 1976–81, Assoc. Prof. 1981–86, Dir of Grad. Studies 1986–88, Prof. 1987–2004, Andrew W. Mellon Professorship 1987–90, Laurance S. Rockefeller Prof. of Politics 1990–2004, Founding Dir Univ. Center for Human Values 1990–95, 1998–2001, Dean of Faculty 1995–97, Academic Adviser to Pres. 1997–98, Provost 2001–04; Pres. Univ. of Pennsylvania and Christopher H. Browne Distinguished Prof. of Political Science, School of Arts and Sciences, Annenberg School for Communication, Grad. School of Educ. and Dept of Philosophy 2004–; Visitor, Inst. for Advanced Study, Princeton 1981–82; Visiting Rockefeller Faculty Fellow, Center for Philosophy and Public Policy, Univ. of Maryland 1984–85; Visiting Prof., John F. Kennedy School of Govt, Harvard Univ. 1988–89; Pres. American Soc. for Political and Legal Philosophy 2001–04; Chair. US Presidential Comm. for the Study of Bioethical Issues 2009–, APSA Charles Merriam Award Cttee 2012–, Re-accrediting Cttee for Brown Univ. 2009; mem. Bd of Dirs Salzburg Seminar 1987–90, Center for Policy Research in Educ. 1987–95, Exec. Cttee Asscn of Practical and Professional Ethics 1990–2007, Bd and Exec. Cttee, Princeton University Press 1996–2004, Advisory Council, Kennedy School of Govt, Harvard Univ. 1996–2001, Bd and Exec. Cttee, Center for Advanced Study in the Behavioural Sciences, Stanford Univ. 1998–2005, Int. Advisory Bd Ethnicities 2000–, Academic Advisory Bd Inst. for Human Sciences, Vienna 2001, Advisory Bd Annenberg Public Policy Center Student Voices Project 2000–05, Bd of Govs Partnership for Public Service 2004–07, Service Nation Leadership Council 2008, Teach for America Champions' Bd 2010–, Exec. Cttee, Asscn of American Univs 2011–, Presidents Circle, Nat. Council for Research on Women 2011, Comm. on the Humanities and Social Sciences, American Acad. of Arts and Sciences 2011–, Int. Advisory Council, The Israel Democracy Inst. 2012–; Ed. Univ. Center for Human Values Series, Princeton University Press 1992–2004; mem. Editorial Bd Teachers' College Record 1990–95, Cambridge Studies in Philosophy and Public Policy 1991–, Raritan 1995–, Journal of Political Philosophy 1995–, Handbook of Political Theory 1999–, Annual Reviews 2001–05; Chair. Bd of Trustees, Whig-Cliosophic Soc. 1985–88; mem. Nat. Constitution Center Bd of Trustees 2007–; Fellow, American Acad. of Arts and Sciences 1997, Nat. Acad. of Educ. 1997, American Philosophical Soc. 2005; W.E.B. Du Bois Fellow, American Acad. of Political and Social Science 2001–; Hon. DIur (Kalamazoo Coll.) 1992; Hon. LLD (Rochester) 2005, (Columbia Univ.) 2012; Hon. DLitt (Wesleyan Univ.) 2005; Nat. Endowment for the Humanities Summer Fellowship 1977, American Council of Learned Socs Fellowship 1978–79, Bicentennial Preceptorship, Princeton 1979–82, N American Soc. for Social Philosophy Book Award 1996–97, American Asscn of Univ. Profs Betram Mott Award 1998, Kenneth Robinson Fellowship, Univ. of Hong Kong 1998–99, Spencer Foundation Sr Scholar Award 1999, Princeton Univ. Distinguished Teaching Award 2000, Harvard Univ. Centennial Award 2003, Carnegie Corpn Leadership Award 2009, Benjamin E. Mays Award, A Better Chance 2010. *Publications:* Liberal Equality 1980, Ethics and Politics: Cases and Comments (co-author) 1984, Democratic Education 1987, Democracy and the Welfare State (ed.) 1988, Multiculturalism and the Politics of Recognition (ed.) 1992, Democracy and Disagreement (co-author) 1996, Color Conscious: The Political Morality of Race (N American Soc. for Social Philosophy Book Award 1996–97, Gustavus Myers Center for the Study of Human Rights in N American Award 1997, Ralph J. Bunche Award, American Political Science Asscn 1997) 1996, A Matter of Interpretation: Federal Courts and the Law (ed.) 1997, Work and Welfare (ed.) 1998, Freedom of Association (ed.) 1998, The Lives of Animals (ed.) 1999, Goodness and Advice (ed.) 2001, Identity in Democracy 2003, Why Deliberative Democracy? 2004, The Spirit of Compromise: Why Governing Demands It and Campaigning Undermines It 2012; as Chair of the Presidential Commission for the Study of Bioethical Issues: New Directions: The Ethics of Synthetic Biology and Emerging Technologies 2010, Moral Science: Protecting Participants in Human Subjects Research 2011, Research Across Borders: Proceedings of the International Research Panel of the Presidential Commission for the Study of Bioethical Issues 2011, Ethically Impossible: STD Research in Guatemala from 1946–48 2011; numerous chapters in books and articles in professional journals. *Address:* Office of the President, University of Pennsylvania, 1 College Hall, Room 100, Philadelphia, PA 19104-6380 (office); The President's House, Eisenlohr, 3812 Walnut Street, Philadelphia, PA 19104, USA (home). *Telephone:* (215) 898-7221 (office). *Fax:* (215) 898-9659 (office). *E-mail:* presweb@pobox.upenn.edu (office). *Website:* president.upenn.edu (office).

GUTMANN, Francis Louis Alphonse Myrtil; French diplomatist; b. 4 Oct. 1930, Paris; s. of Robert Gutmann and Denise (née Coulom) Gutmann; m. Chantal de Gaulle 1964; two s. one d.; ed Lycée Pasteur, Neuilly-sur-Seine; Head of Dept, Ministry of Foreign Affairs 1951–57; Asst Head Office of Sec. of State for Econ. Affairs 1955, mem. French Del. to Econ. and Social Council and to UN Gen. Ass. 1952–55, to Common Market Conf., Brussels 1956–57; Adviser Pechiney Co. 1957–59, Sec.-Gen. 1963, Dir 1970–71; Sec.-Gen. Fria 1960–62; mem. Governing Bd Pechiney-Ugine-Kuhlmann group 1962–78, Pres.-Dir-Gen. Ugine-Kuhlmann 1971–76, in charge of social affairs 1975–78; Pres. Alucam 1968–72; Pres. Frialco and Vice-Pres. Friguia 1977–81; Dir-Gen. French Red Cross 1980–81; Sec.-Gen. Ministry for External Relations 1981–85; Admin. representing the State, Paribas 1982–84, Gaz de France 1984–85, St Gobain 1982–85; Amb. to Spain 1985–88; Pres. Admin. Council Gaz de France 1988–93, Hon. Pres. 1993–; Pres. Fondation Méditerranéenne d'Etudes Stratégiques 1989–2000, Assoc. Eurogas-Union 1990–94, (Admin. Council) Institut Français du Pétrole (IFP) 1993–96; Vice-Pres. Mémoire et espoirs de la Résistance 1994–2000; attached to Ministry of Foreign Affairs 1996–; Pres. Scientific Council for Defence, Ministry of Defence 1998–; Dir French Red Cross 1992–2000; Officier, Légion d'honneur, Commdr, Ordre nat. du Mérite, Grand croix de l'ordre du Merité (Spain); numerous foreign awards. *Publications:* Les chemins de l'effort 1975, Le nouveau décor international 1994, Demain est un autre monde 2008, Changer de politique: une autre politique étrangère pour un monde différent? 2011. *Address:* 1–4 avenue de Bois-Préau, 92500 Rueil-Malmaison, France (office). *Telephone:* 1-47-52-68-84 (office). *Fax:* 1-47-52-67-54 (office).

GUTZWILLER, Peter Max, LLM, DrIur; Swiss lawyer; *Counsel, Lenz & Staehelin;* b. 30 April 1941, Basle; s. of Max and Helly Gutzwiller; m. 1st Vreny Lüscher 1971 (divorced); one s.; m. 2nd Barbara Menzel; ed Univs of Basle and Geneva and Harvard Law School, USA; Assoc., Staehelin Hafter & Pnrs (now Lenz & Staehelin) 1970–76, Pnr 1977–2007, Counsel 2007–; mem. Bd of Int. Law Asscn (Swiss Br.) 1975–; Sec. Swiss Asscn of Int. Law 1976; Maj., Swiss Army 1979; Chair. Harvard Law School Foundation, Swiss Nat. Museum Foundation; mem. Bd of Dirs Beyer Chronometrie AG; mem. Soc. of Trust and Estate Practitioners, Chambers of Commerce China, Germany, GB, Munich, USA. *Publications:* Swiss International Divorce Law 1968, Von Ziel und Methode des IPR 1968, Arbeitsbewilligungen für Ausländer 1975, 1976, Grundriss des schweizerischen Privat- und Steuerrechtes (co-author) 1976, Schweizerisch-Deutsches Erbrecht (co-author) 2005, The Swiss Legal System, in: Switzerland Business and Investment Handbook 2006, Trusts für die Schweiz 2007, Über die Substanz der Urteilsfähigkeit 2008, Das schweizerische internationale Trustrecht im Lichte der Haager Trust-Konvention-eine Einführung 2008. *Leisure interests:* art collection (cartoons), music, travel. *Address:* Lenz & Staehelin, Bleicherweg 58, 8027 Zurich (office); Sonnenrain 15, 8700 Küsnacht, Switzerland (home). *Telephone:* 4508000 (office). *Fax:* 4508001 (office). *E-mail:* peter-max.gutzwiller@lenzstaehelin.com (office). *Website:* www.lenzstaehelin.com (office).

GUY, George (Buddy); American blues musician (guitar); b. 30 July 1936, Lettsworth, La; played with artists, including Slim Harpo, Lightnin' Slim; mem., Rufus Foreman Band; solo artist; mem. houseband, Chess Records, including sessions with Muddy Waters, Howlin' Wolf; musical partnership with Junior Wells; numerous live performances; numerous awards including 23 W.C. Handy Awards, Billboard Music Awards Century Award 1993, Nat. Medal of Arts 2003, Kennedy Center Honor 2012. *Recordings include:* albums: Blues From Big Bill's Copa Cobana 1963, A Man and The Blues 1968, This Is Buddy Guy 1968, Hold That Plane! 1972, I Was Walking Through The Woods 1974, Hot and Cool 1978, Got To Use Your House 1979, Dollar Done Fell 1980, DJ Play My Blues 1982, The Original Blues Brothers – Live 1983, Ten Blue Fingers 1985, Live At The Checkerboard, Chicago 1979 1988, Breaking Out 1988, Damn Right I Got The Blues (with Eric Clapton, Jeff Beck, Mark Knopfler) (Grammy Award 1992) 1991, My Time After Awhile 1992, Feels Like Rain (Grammy Award 1994) 1993, American Bandstand, Vol. 2 1993, Slippin' In (Grammy Award 1996) 1994, I Cry 1995, Live! The Real Deal 1996, As Good As It Gets 1998, Heavy Love 1998, Last Time Around 1998, The Real Blues 1999, 20th Century Masters – The Millennium Collection 2000, Sweet Tea 2001, Blues Singer (Grammy Award 2004) 2003, Bring 'Em In 2006, Skin Deep 2008, Living Proof (Grammy Award 2011) 2010, Rhythm & Blues 2013, Born to Play Guitar (Grammy Award for Best Blues Album 2016) 2015; with Junior Wells: Buddy and The Juniors 1970, Buddy Guy and Junior Wells Play The Blues 1972, Drinkin' TNT and Smokin' Dynamite 1982, Alone and Acoustic 1991, Alive in Montreux 1992. *Publications:* When I Left Home: My Story (autobiography) 2012. *Address:* Annie Lawlor, GBG Enterprises, 700 South Wabash Avenue, Chicago, IL 60605, USA (office). *Telephone:* (312) 427-0962 (office). *Fax:* (312) 427-5922 (office). *E-mail:* annie@buddyguy.com (office). *Website:* www.buddyguy.com.

GUYAUX, Joseph C., BS, MBA; American banking executive; ed Brown Univ., Univ. of Pittsburgh, Stonier Grad. School of Banking; joined PNC 1972, held several man. positions, Sr Vice-Pres. and Man. of Metropolitan Commercial Banking, Pittsburgh 1989–91, Pres. PNC's Northeast Pa 1991–93, Exec. Vice-Pres. and Retail Market Man. for the Pittsburgh market 1993–95, Sr Vice-Pres. and Man. PNC Private Bank 1995–97, Deputy Man. Consumer Banking business 1997, CEO 1997–2001, responsible for PNC's middle market, corp. finance, capital markets, asset-based lending, treasury man. and leasing businesses 2001–02,

Pres. PNC Financial Services Group 2002–05, Head of Retail Banking 2005–12, Sr Vice-Chair. and Chief Risk Officer 2012–15, Pres. and CEO PNC Mortgage 2015–16 (retd); Chair. Civic Light Opera, Carnegie Museum of Natural History, Pittsburgh (also Life Trustee); mem. Bd of Dirs DQE Holdings LLC, Pittsburgh Cultural Trust, Highmark, Inc., Private Export Funding Corpn; mem. Bd of Dirs Emer. Duquesne Univ. 2009–.

GUYTON, Wade, BA, MFA; American artist and sculptor; b. 1972, Hammond, Indiana; ed Univ. of Tenn., Hunter Coll.; worked at St Mark's Bookshop, Manhattan and Dia Art Foundation, Chelsea –2004; worked from a rented studio in East Village, New York 2004; currently lives and works in New York; Socrates Sculpture Park Emerging Artist Grant 2003; American Acad. of Arts and Letters Award in Art 2014. *Address:* c/o Whitney Museum of American Art, 99 Gansevoort Street, New York, NY 10014, USA. *Telephone:* (212) 570-3600.

GUZMÁN LAUGIER, Pablo, MA; Bolivian economist and international organization official; ed Centro de Docencia e Investigación Económica, Mexico, Universidad Autónoma Metropolitana Xochimilco; worked at Bolivia Centre for Labour and Agricultural Devt (CEDLA), Dir Inst. of Financial Planning Devt (IDEPRO); ind. consultant working on various projects 1994–2005; with Ministry of Foreign Affairs 2006–, positions included Head of Unit for Foreign Policy Analysis and Gen. Trade Negotiations, Deputy Minister of Foreign Trade and Integration –2013; Sec.-Gen. Andean Community 2013–16, also Prin. Rep. of Bolivia to Comm. of Andean Community; fmr Prof., CIDES-UMSA Devt Training Centre, Universidad Mayor de San Andrés, La Paz. *Address:* c/o Andean Community, Avenue Paseo de la República 3895, San Isidro, Lima 27, Peru (office).

GUZY, Carol; American photographer; b. 7 March 1956, Bethlehem, Pa; m. Jonathan Utz; ed Northampton Co. Area Community Coll., Art Inst. of Fort Lauderdale; attended nursing school; intern then staff photographer Miami Herald 1980–88; staff photograher, The Washington Post 1988–; notable assignments include coverage of volcanic eruption in Colombia, fall of communism, nomads in Mali, Rwandan exodus, famine in Ethiopia, civil war in Somalia, daily life in Haiti, and plight of Kosovo refugees; Pulitzer Prize 1986, 1995, 2000, 2011, Photographer of the Year (Nat. Press Photographers Asscn) 1990, 1993, 1997, Robert F. Kennedy Memorial Prize 1997, eight White House Press Photographers Asscn's Photographer of the Year, Leica Medal of Excellence, Overseas Press Club Citation of Excellence and numerous other awards. *Address:* The Washington Post, 1150 15th Street, NW, Washington, DC 20071-0002, USA. *Website:* www.washingtonpost.com/wp-dyn/photo/bestofthepost/guzycarol.

GUZZANTI, Corrado; Italian actor, director, writer and satirist; b. 17 May 1965, Rome; s. of journalist and Senator Paolo Guzzanti; brother of Sabina and Caterina Guzzanti; began career as writer for his sister Sabina; debut as actor in roles for himself in Avanzi, hosted by Serena Dandini; collaborated with her in TV shows, including Tunnel, Maddecheaò, Pippo Chennedy Show and L'ottavo nano; famous for his satirical imitations of Italian politicians and personalities; also cr. several characters, including the Quelo (comical version of a New Age guru) and the poet Brunello Robertetti (satire of a typical Italian alleged intellectual); debut as film dir with Fascisti su Marte 2006. *Films include:* I Cammelli (The Camels) (voice) 1988, Prima le donne e i bambini 1992, DeGenerazione 1994, Und1c1/8ttavi (also writer and dir) 2000, Fascisti su Marte (Fascists on Mars) (also writer, dir and producer) 2006, The Passion 2010, Ogni maledetto Natale 2014, A Bigger Splash 2015. *Television includes:* Scusate l'interruzione (series) 1990, Avanzi 1992 (series) 1991, L'ottavo nano 2000, Boris 2008, Dov'è Mario? 2016. *E-mail:* info@corradoguzzanti.it (office). *Website:* www.corradoguzzanti.it (office).

GVENETADZE, Koba, BA, MA (Econs); Georgian economist, international organization official and central banker; *President and Chairman of the Board, National Bank of Georgia;* b. 26 Dec. 1971; m. Irine Kokaia; three c.; ed Tbilisi State Univ., American Univ., USA; awarded Edmund S. Muskie Graduate Fellowship to study in USA; Financial Columnist, Iveria Express 1993–94; Sr Economist, Nat. Bank of Georgia 1994–96; Rep. in Georgia, IMF 1996–98; Deputy Finance Minister 2000–01, Deputy State Minister 2001–02; Resident Chief Economist, IMF Middle East and Cen. Asia Dept 2002–15; Econ. Adviser, Galt & Taggar (subsidiary of JSC Bank of Georgia) 2015–16; Pres. and Chair. of Bd, Nat. Bank of Georgia 2016–. *Publications include:* numerous articles published in IMF Azerbaijan Briefcase. *Address:* National Bank of Georgia, 0105 Tbilisi, Leonidze 3–5, Georgia (office). *Telephone:* (32) 240-64-06 (office). *Fax:* (32) 244-25-77 (office). *E-mail:* info@nbg.gov.ge (office). *Website:* www.nbg.gov.ge (office).

GVINDADZE, Dimitri, MPA/ID, MS; Georgian economist and politician; *Lead Economist, European Bank for Reconstruction and Development;* b. 23 Dec. 1973, Tbilisi; m. Maia Kvaliashvili; two d.; ed Tbilisi State Tech. Univ., Diplomatic Acad. of Paris, France, Int. Inst. of Social Studies, The Hague, The Netherlands, John F. Kennedy School of Govt, Harvard Univ. and Financial Programming and Policy course at Int. Monetary Fund Inst., Washington, DC, USA; served in various positions at Ministry of Foreign Affairs 1994–2003; Deputy Minister of Finance 2005–11, Minister of Finance 2011–12; First Deputy CEO JSC Partnership Fund 2012; Global Head of Research, Liberty Securities 2012–13; Int. Consultant UNDP 2013; Lead Economist, EBRD 2014–. *Address:* European Bank for Reconstruction and Development, 0105 Tbilisi, 6 Marjanishvili street, Green Building, IV–V Floor, Georgia (office). *Telephone:* (32) 24-47-400 (office). *Fax:* (32) 29-20-512 (office). *Website:* www.ebrd.com (office).

GVOZDENOVIĆ, Branimir (Brano), MSc; Montenegrin politician; *Minister of Sustainable Development and Tourism;* b. 1961, Bar; ed Univ. of Montenegro, Podgorica; Programmer, Republican Information Cttee 1986–89; Adviser for Devt of Information System, Republican Secr. for Devt 1989–90; Sr Adviser for Informatics 1990–91, Asst Dir 1991–95, Republican Devt Bureau; Asst Sec., Secr. for Devt 1995–99; Dir, Post of Montenegro Ltd 1999–2002; acting Minister of Maritime Affairs 2002, Deputy Prime Minister for Econ. Policy and Devt 2002–06, Minister of Econ. Devt 2006–09, of Urban Planning and Environment 2009–10, of Sustainable Devt and Tourism 2012–; Pres. of Bar Municipality 2002–03; Political Dir Democratic Party of Socialists of Montenegro (Demokratska Partija Socijalista Crne Gore) (DPS) 2011–12; Pres. Council of Montenegro Civil Aviation Agency 2012; Expo Italia Real Estate Award 2009. *Address:* Ministry of Sustainable Development and Tourism, 81000 Podgorica, St. 4. Proleterske 19, Montenegro (office). *Telephone:* (20) 446200 (office). *Fax:* (20) 446215 (office). *E-mail:* branimir.gvozdenovic@mrt.gov.me (office). *Website:* www.mrt.gov.me (office).

GWAIDER, Ageela Issa Salah; Libyan politician and lawyer; *President, Libyan House of Representatives;* b. 1 June 1942, Al Qubbah; mem. Rep. Govt of Al Qubbah; Pres. Libyan House of Reps. 2014–. *Address:* POB 9414, Tibesti Hotel, Benghazi. *Website:* www.libyan-parliament.org (office).

GWIN, Robert G., BS, MBA; American chartered financial analyst and business executive; *Chairman of the Supervisory Board, LyondellBasell Industries;* ed Univ. of Southern California, Fuqua School of Business at Duke Univ.; joined Prudential Capital in 1990, served at Prudential Capital Group (an asset management unit of The Prudential Insurance Co. of America) in merchant banking roles for ten years, including as its Man. Dir; joined Prosoft Learning Corpn (fmrly Prosoft training) in 2000, Consultant and Chief Financial Officer (CFO) 2000–04, Exec. Vice-Pres. 2001–04, Pres. and CEO 2002–04, Chair. 2002–06; CEO Community Broadband Ventures LP 2004–06; Vice-Pres. of Finance and Treas., Anadarko Petroleum Corpn 2006–08, Sr Vice-Pres. 2008–09, Exec. Vice-Pres. of Finance and CFO 2009–13; mem. Bd of Dirs Western Gas Holdings LLC (General Partner of Western Gas Partners LP) 2007–, Pres. 2007–09, CEO 2007–10, Chair. (non-exec.) 2009–13, Chair. Western Gas Equity Holdings, LLC 2012–; mem. Supervisory Bd, LyondellBasell Industries NV 2011–, Vice-Chair. (non-exec.) May–Aug. 2013, Chair. Aug. 2013–, Supervisory Dir of Lyondell Chemical Co. *Address:* LyondellBasell Industries, PO Box 2416, 3000 CK Rotterdam (office); LyondellBasell Industries, Groot Handelsgebouw – Entrance A, Stationsplein 45, 3013 AK Rotterdam, The Netherlands (office). *Telephone:* (10) 275-5500 (office). *Fax:* (10) 275-5599 (office). *E-mail:* info@lyondellbasell.com (office). *Website:* www.lyondellbasell.com (office).

GYAMTSHO, Pema, MAgrSc (Hons), PhD; Bhutanese agriculturalist and politician; *President, Druk Phuensum Tshogpa (DPT);* b. 15 Nov. 1961, Bumthang; m.; one s. four d.; ed Lincoln Univ., New Zealand, Eidgenössische Technische Hochschule (Swiss Fed. Inst. of Tech.), Switzerland; Research Officer, Grassland and Associated Fodder Research Centre, Bumthang 1983–86; Pasture Devt Officer, Dept of Animal Husbandry, Ministry of Agric., Thimphu 1986–90, Project Man. Nat. Sheep Devt Project, Bumthang 1990–92, Research Programme Coordinator, Ministry of Agric. 1992–96, Deputy Sec. and Head, Policy and Planning Div. 1997–2002; Head, Policy and Partnership Devt, Int. Centre for Integrated Mountain Devt (ICIMOD), Kathmandu 2002–06, Sr Natural Resources Policy Specialist 2005–06, Deputy Resident Coordinator of Helvetas 2006–07, resgnd to join politics; elected to Nat. Ass. for Druk Phuensum Tshogpa (DPT) party from Chhoekhor-Tang constituency, Bumthang 2008, Opposition Leader 2013–; Minister of Agriculture and Forests 2008–13; Pres. DPT party 2013–; Founding Co-Chair. Bhutan Water Partnership; Chair. Bhutan Trust Fund for Environment Conservation 2008; mem. Planning Comm. 1998–2002, Sustainable Devt Secr. 1998–2002, Forestry Devt Corpn Bd 1998–2002, South Asia Technical Advisory Cttee on Water 2000–02, Nat. Biodiversity Bd 2000–02. *Publication:* Securing Sustainable Livelihoods in the Hindu Kush-Himalayas: Directions for Future Research, Development, and Cooperation 2006. *Address:* National Assembly, Gyelyong Tshokhang, POB 139, Thimphu (office); Druk Phuensum Tshogpa (DPT), Chang Lam, Thimphu, Bhutan (office). *Telephone:* (2) 336337 (DPT) (office); (2) 336566 (office). *Fax:* (2) 335845 (DPT) (office). *E-mail:* pgyamtsho@nab.gov.bt (office); ol@nab.gov.bt (office). *Website:* www.nab.gov.bt (office); www.dpt.bt (office).

GYAMTSHO, Lyonpo Thinley, BA; Bhutanese politician; b. 1952; ed Trashigang High School, St Joseph's Coll., India, Wellington Univ., NZ; Jt Dir Dept of Educ. 1985, Dir Dept of Nat. Budget and Accounts 1986, Dir of Educ. 1987–90, Dir-Gen. 1990–94, Sec. 1994–96; Sec. Royal Civil Service Comm. 1996–98, Deputy Minister 1998; Minister of Home Affairs 1998–2003, of Educ. 2003–08; Red Scarf 1991, Orange Scarf 1998, Coronation Medal 1999. *Address:* c/o Education Division, Ministry of Health and Education, Tashichhodzong, PO Box 726, Thimphu, Bhutan. *Telephone:* (2) 325146. *Fax:* (2) 324823. *E-mail:* lyonpo_tg@hotmail.com. *Website:* www.education.gov.bt.

GYANENDRA BIR BIKRAM SHAH DEV, BA; Nepalese fmr ruler; b. 7 July 1947, Kathmandu; s. of King Mahendra Bir Bikram Shah and Crown Princess Indra Rajya Laxmi Devi Shah; brother of King Birendra Bir Bikram Shah Dev; m. Komal Rajya Laxmi Devi Shah 1970; one s. one d.; ed St Joseph's Coll., Darjeeling, India, Tribhuvan Univ. Kathmandu; King of Nepal 2001–08; Supreme Commdr Royal Nepalese Army –2006; made state visits to India 2002, China 2002; official visits to India 1976, Democratic People's Repub. of Korea 1978, Repub. of Korea 1987; other visits to India, Pakistan, China, Bhutan, Thailand, Myanmar, Singapore, USA, USSR, UK, The Netherlands, Denmark, Germany, France, Italy, Switzerland, Saudi Arabia, Turkey, Yugoslavia, Romania, Hungary, Bulgaria, Czechoslovakia, Australia, New Zealand, Belgium, Spain, UAE, Austria, Canada, Iran; Chair. (currently Patron) Lumbini Devt Trust 1986–1991, King Mahendra Trust for Nature Conservation 1982–2001; Founding mem. 1001–Nature Trust 1986; Patron, Pushupati Area Devt Trust; Chancellor Tribhuvan Univ. and Mahendra Sanskrit Univ.; special interest in conservation and preservation of natural and man-made heritage; declared state of emergency, took over as Chair. of Council of Ministers Feb. 2005, relinquished power April 2006, stripped of most constitutional powers 2006, monarchy abolished May 2008; Hon. mem. Worldwide Fund for Nature; Grand Cross of the House Order of Orange (Netherlands) 1967, Kt Grand Cordon of the Most Exalted Order of the White Elephant (Thailand) 1979, Grand Cross Ordre nat. du Mérite 1983, Kt Grand Cross of the Most Distinguished Order of St Michael and St George 1986, Grand Cross of Order of Isabel la Católica (Spain) 1987, His Holy Majesty, King of the Lands of the Nepalese People and Kt of the Holy and Most Majestic Order of the Rose of Jordan, Sovereign of all Orders of the Kingdom of Nepal. *Leisure interests:* nature, reading, writing poetry.

GYAWALI, Pradeep Kumar; Nepali writer and politician; *Minister of Foreign Affairs;* b. 13 Sept. 1962, Baletaxar-2 Chautara, Gulmi; s. of Narayan Dutta Gyawali and Punya Kala Gyawali; m. Saraswati Gyawali; three c.; involved in politics since 1970 through affiliation with Nepali Left Movement; mem. Communist Party of Nepal—Unified Marxist-Leninist (CPN—UML) 1978–, Cttee mem. Gulmi Dist 1979–89, Dist Sec., Arghakhanchi Dist 1989–93, Zonal Sec.

1994–95, mem. Cen. Cttee 1997–; mem. House of Reps (lower house of parl.) from Gulmi-2 1999–2008, from Gulmi-1 2017–, mem. State Affairs Cttee 1999–2012; Minister for Culture, Tourism and Civil Aviation 2006–07; Govt rep. during negotiations with rebel Maoists 2006–07; mem. Constituent Ass. from Gulmi-2 2008–12, also mem. Parl. Proceedings Advisory Cttee; Minister of Foreign Affairs 2018–. *Publications include:* Sahayatri (novel) 1990, Chita Jalirahechha (poetry) 1994, Marxvadko Srijanatmak Prayog (essays) 2000, Aastha o Mery Priya (poetry) 2002, Prachandpath (criticism) 2002, Kuhiro (short stories) 2003, Phoenix Panchi (criticism) 2003, Yuba: ... (essay) 2005, Rastriyata, Pahichan ra Samajik Rupantaran (essay) 2013, Samskritik Rupantaran: Ek Vimarsha (essay) 2015, Bina Salik Ka Nayakharu (poetry) 2016; more than 1,000 articles, work papers and research papers. *Address:* Ministry of Foreign Affairs, Singha Durbar, Kathmandu, Nepal (office). *Telephone:* (1) 4200182 (office). *Fax:* (1) 4200061 (office). *E-mail:* info@mofa.gov.np (office). *Website:* www.mofa.gov.np (office); www .pradeepgyawali.com.np.

GYLL, (John) Sören; Swedish business executive; b. 26 Dec. 1940, Skorped; s. of Josef Gyll and Gertrud Gyll; m. Lilly Margareta Hellman 1974; two s. one d.; Marketing Dir and Vice-Pres. Rank Xerox 1963–77; Pres. Uddeholms Sweden AB 1977–79, Exec. Vice-Pres. Uddeholms AB 1979–81, Pres. and CEO 1981–84; Pres. and CEO Procordia AB 1984–92; Pres. and CEO AB Volvo 1992–97, also Dir; fmr Chair. Pharmacia and Upjohn Inc.; fmr Chair. Gyttorp Cartridge Co.; Chair. Capedal AB, Genesis-IT AB; mem. Bd of Dirs Svenska Cellulosa Aktiebolaget SCA 1997–, Fenix Outdoor, SKF, Skanska, Topeja Holding, Scandinavian Touch, Medicover Holding, Askus AB, Oresa Ventures AB, Probi AB; mem. Bd of Dirs Junior Achievement and Young Entreprise Europe –2004; mem. European Advisory Bd, Schroder Salomon Smith Barney 2001; fmr Pres. Confederation of Swedish Enterprise; mem. Royal Acad. of Eng Sciences. *Leisure interests:* hunting, skiing.

GYLLENHAAL, Jake; American actor; b. 19 Dec. 1980, Los Angeles, Calif.; s. of Stephen Gyllenhaal and Naomi Foner Gyllenhaal; brother of Maggie Gyllenhaal; ed Columbia Univ.; Nat. Arts Award 2006, Int. Star of the Year Award, Variety Magazine 2015. *Films include:* City Slickers 1991, A Dangerous Woman 1993, Josh and S.A.M 1993, Homegrown 1998, October Sky 1999, Donnie Darko (Young Hollywood Award 2002, Chlotrudis Award 2003) 2001, Bubble Boy 2001, Lovely and Amazing 2001, The Good Girl 2002, Highway 2002, Moonlight Mile 2002, The Day After Tomorrow 2004, The Man Who Walked Between the Towers 2005, Brokeback Mountain (BAFTA Award for Best Actor in a Supporting Role 2006) 2005, Proof 2004, Jarhead 2005, Zodiac 2007, Rendition 2007, Brothers 2009, Prince of Persia: The Sands of Time 2010, Love and Other Drugs 2010, End of Watch 2012, Prisoners 2013, Enemy 2013, Nightcrawler 2014, Accidental Love 2015, Southpaw 2015, Everest 2015, Demolition 2015. *Plays include:* This Is Our Youth (New York and London) (Evening Standard Award). *Publication:* Between My Legs 2008. *Leisure interests:* woodworking, cooking. *Address:* WME, 9601 Wilshire Blvd, Beverly Hills, CA 90201, USA (office). *Website:* www.jakegyllenhaal .com.

GYLLENHAAL, Maggie, BA; American actress; b. 16 Nov. 1977, New York City; d. of Stephen Gyllenhaal and Naomi Foner Gyllenhaal; sister of Jake Gyllenhaal; m. Peter Sarsgaard 2009; two d.; ed Columbia Univ., Royal Acad. of Dramatic Arts, UK. *Films include:* Waterland 1992, A Dangerous Woman 1993, Homegrown 1998, The Photographer 2000, Cecil B. DeMented 2000, Donnie Darko 2001, Riding in Cars with Boys 2001, Secretary (several awards including Boston Soc. of Film Critics Award for Best Actress) 2002, 40 Days and 40 Nights 2002, Adaptation 2002, Confessions of a Dangerous Mind 2002, Casa de los babys 2003, Mona Lisa Smile 2003, The Pornographer: A Love Story 2004, Criminal 2004, Happy Endings 2005, The Great New Wonderful 2005, Trust the Man 2005, SherryBaby 2006, Paris, je t'aime 2006, Monster House 2006, World Trade Center 2006, Stranger Than Fiction 2006, High Falls 2007, The Dark Knight 2008, Crazy Heart 2009, Nanny McPhee and the Big Bang 2010, Hysteria 2011, Won't Back Down 2012, White House Down 2013, Frank 2014, River of Fundament 2014, The Deuce 2017–. *Television includes:* Shattered Mind 1996, Patron Saint of Liars 1998, Resurrection 1999, Shake, Rattle and Roll: An American Love Story 1999, Strip Search 2004, The Corrections (film) 2012, The Honorable Woman (Golden Globe Award for Best Actress in a TV Mini-series or Movie 2015) 2014. *Address:* c/o William Morris Endeavor Entertainment, 9601 Wilshire Blvd, Beverly Hills, CA 90210, USA (office).

GYLLENHAMMAR, Pehr Gustaf, BLL; Swedish business executive; *Vice-Chairman Europe, Rothschild;* b. 28 April 1935, Gothenburg; s. of Pehr Gustaf Victor Gyllenhammar and Aina Dagny Kaplan; m. 1st Eva Christina Engellau 1959 (died 2008); one s. three d.; m. 2nd Christel Sofia Behrmann 2010 (divorced 2012); m. 3rd Lee Welton Croll 2013; ed Univ. of Lund, studied int. law in England, vocational studies in maritime law, USA, Centre d'Etudes Industrielles, Geneva; employed by Mannheimer & Zetterlöf (solicitors), Gothenburg 1959, Haight, Gardner, Poor & Havens (Admiralty lawyers), New York 1960, Amphion Insurance Co., Gothenburg 1961–64; Asst Admin. Man. Skandia Insurance Co., Stockholm 1965–66, Vice-Pres. Corporate Planning 1966–68, Exec. Vice-Pres. 1968, Pres. and CEO 1970; joined AB Volvo, Gothenburg 1970, Man. Dir and CEO 1971–83, Chair. of Bd and CEO 1983–90, Exec. Chair. Bd of Dirs 1990–93; Chair. Bd MC European Capital SA 1994–96; Chair. Swedish Ships Mortgage Bank 1976–2007, Procordia AB 1990–92; Sr Adviser Lazard Frères & Co. 1996–99, Man. Dir 2000–03; Chair. Cofinec NV 1996–2000; fmr Chair. CGU PLC (fmr Chair. CGNU after merger of CGU PLC and Norwich Union PLC, co. changed name to Aviva 2002); Vice-Chair. Europe, Rothschild 2003–; Chair. Investment AB Kinnevik (formed by merger of Industriförvaltnings AB Kinnevik and Invik & Co. AB) 2004–08, Majid Al Futtaim Group 2005–09, Arise AB 2007–14; f. European Round Table of Industrialists 1982–93, European Financial Services Round Table 2003–06; Chair. London Philharmonic Trust 2006–11; mem. Int. Advisory Cttee, Chase Manhattan Bank 1972–95, Bd of Dirs, Skandinaviska Enskilda Banken 1979–94, United Technologies Corpn 1981–99, Kissinger Assocs, Inc. 1982–97, Pearson PLC 1983–97, Reuters Holdings PLC 1984–97, Philips Electronics NV 1990–96, Renault SA 1990–93 and numerous other cos and orgs; Trustee, Reuters (now Thomson Reuters) 1997–2012 (Chair. Trustees 1999–2012); mem. Royal Swedish Acad. of Eng Sciences 1974; Hon. Master, Bench of Inner Temple 2001; Officer (1st Class), Royal Order of Vasa 1973, Commdr, Order of the Lion of Finland 1977, Commdr, Ordre nat. du Mérite 1980, King's Medal (12th Size) with Ribbon, Order of the Seraphim 1981, Commdr, St Olav's Order 1984, Commdr, Order of the Lion of Finland (1st Class) 1986, Commdr, Légion d'honneur 1987, Kt Grand Officer, Order of Merit (Italy) 1987, Commdr, Order of Leopold 1989; Hon. DrMed (Gothenburg Univ.) 1981; Hon. DTech (Brunel) 1987; Hon. DrEng (Nova Scotia) 1988; Hon. DrScS (Helsinki) 1990; Hon. LLD (Vermont) 1993; Hon. Dr of Econs and Commercial Law (Gothenburg) 2003; Hon. DBA (Metropolitan Univ., London) 2004; Golden Award, City of Gothenburg 1981. *Publications:* Mot sekelskiftet på måfå (Towards the Turn of the Century at Random) 1970, Jag tror på Sverige (I Believe in Sweden) 1973, People at Work 1977, En industripolitik för människan (Industrial Policy for Human Beings) 1979, Fortsättning följer... (To Be Continued...) 2000, Oberoende är stark (Independent is Strong) 2014. *Leisure interests:* golf, music, sailing.

GYLYJOV, Chary, LLB; Turkmenistani lawyer and politician; *Deputy Chairman of the Government, responsible for Trade and the Development of the Non-Government Economy;* b. 1974, Sandykachi, Tagtabazar Dist, Mari Velayat, Turkmen SSR, USSR; ed Magtymguly Turkmen State Univ.; began career with various positions in Balkanabat City Prosecutor's Office 1996–97, in Balkan Velayat Prosecutor's Office 1999–2001; Prosecutor, later Sr Prosecutor, Information and Methodology Group, Supervisory Office (Legality of Judicial Decisions), Office of the Prosecutor-Gen., Aşgabat 2001–03, Acting Deputy Dept Head 2003–05; Deputy Prosecutor, Aşgabat 2005–12; Deputy Chair., Supreme Control Chamber 2012–16, Chair. 2016–18; Deputy Chair. of the Govt, responsible for Trade and the Devt of the Non-Govt Economy 2018–; Medal For Love of the Fatherland. *Address:* Office of the President and the Council of Ministers, 744004 Aşgabat, Galkynyş köç. 20, Turkmenistan (office). *Telephone:* (12) 35-45-34 (office). *Fax:* (12) 35-51-12 (office). *E-mail:* nt@online.tm (office). *Website:* www .turkmenistan.gov.tm (office).

GYLYS, Povilas, DSc (Econ); Lithuanian economist, academic and fmr politician; b. 14 Feb. 1948, Didžiokai, Molėtai Region; m. Nijole Rezaitė 1969; two s.; ed Molėtai Secondary School and Vilnius Univ.; Lecturer, later Prof. of Econs, Vilnius Univ. 1969–92, Head, Dept of Int. Econ. Relations 1992, Prof., Dept of Econ. Theory (fmr Chair.) 2003–12, mem. Univ. Senate; mem. Parl. (Seimas) 1992–2000, 2012–16, mem. Lithuanian Democratic Labour Party Parl. Group 1996–2000, Cttee on Foreign Affairs 1998–2000, Comm. on Econ. Crimes Investigation 1999–2000, Seimas Del. to Parl. Ass. of Council of Europe 1999–2000), Deputy Chair., Cttee on European Affairs 2012, Seimas Delegation to the Inter-Parliamentary Union 2012; Minister of Foreign Affairs 1992–96; Ed.-in-Chief Ekonomika; mem. Council, Lithuanian Social Research Inst.; Expert, Lithuanian State Science and Studies Foundation. *Publications:* Economy, Anti-economy and Globalization; numerous articles and monographs.

GYMNASTIAR, Abdullah, (Aa Gym); Indonesian religious speaker and business executive; b. 30 Feb. 1962, Bandung; m. 1st Teteh Nini Gym; m. 2nd Alfarini Eridani; six c.; fmr student military leader; Commdr Regiment Students Acad. of Eng 1982; f. Daarut Tauhiid ('Home of the One God') movt 1990; Man. Dir MQ Corpn; business interests include 15 media cos.; frequent TV appearances as Islamic preacher. *Publications include:* Berani karena Benar, Jujur Kunci Sukses, Memberi dengan Gembira, Pantang Mengeluh, Percaya Diri, Semangat Tanpa Henti, Sayang Orang Tua. *Leisure interests:* diving, shooting, parachuting, singing country songs, riding.

GYNGELL, Allan, AO; Australian research institute director; *National President, Australian Institute of International Affairs;* joined Ministry of Foreign Affairs 1969, overseas postings include Embassies in Rangoon, Singapore and Washington, DC; fmr First Asst Sec., Int. Div., Dept of Prime Minister and Cabinet; worked on Southeast Asian issues and Maj. Power relations, Office of Nat. Assessments; Foreign Policy Adviser, Office of Prime Minister Paul Keating 1993–96; consultant to numerous pvt. cos 1997–; Founding Exec. Dir Lowy Inst. for Int. Policy 2003–10, Contrib. 2010–; Dir-Gen. Australian Office of Nat. Assessments 2009–13; Nat. Pres. Australian Inst. of Int. Affairs 2017–; currently Dir Crawford Australian Leadership Forum; Adjunct Prof. Crawford School of Public Policy; mem. Australian Foreign Affairs Council; Hon. Prof., Australian Nat. Univ. *Publication:* Making Australian Foreign Policy (with Michael Wesley) 2003 (2nd edn 2007). *Address:* Lowy Institute for International Policy, PO Box H-159, Australia Square, Sydney, NSW 1215 (office); Australian Institute of International Affairs, Stephen House, 32 Thesiger Court, Deakin, ACT 2600, Australia (office). *Telephone:* (2) 8238-9000 (Lowy) (office); (2) 6282 2133 (AIIA) (office). *Fax:* (2) 8238-9005 (Lowy) (office); (2) 6285 2334 (AIIA) (office). *E-mail:* director@lowyinstitute.org (office); info@internationalaffairs.org.au (office). *Website:* www.lowyinstitute.org (office); www.internationalaffairs.org.au (office).

GYOHTEN, Toyoo; Japanese economist and fmr banker; b. 2 Jan. 1931, Yokohama; m.; one s. one d.; ed Univ. of Tokyo, Princeton Univ., USA; joined Ministry of Finance 1955; worked at Japan Desk, Asian Dept, IMF 1964–66; Special Asst to Pres. of Asian Devt Bank, Manila, Philippines 1966–69; Dir-Gen. Int. Finance Bureau 1984–86, Vice-Minister of Finance for Int. Affairs 1986–89; Visiting Prof., Grad. School of Business, Harvard Univ., USA 1990, Woodrow Wilson School, Princeton Univ. 1990–91, Univ. of St Gallen, Switzerland 1991; joined Bank of Tokyo Ltd (merged with Mitsubishi Bank Ltd 1996) 1991, Chair. 1992–96, Sr Adviser, Bank of Tokyo-Mitsubishi Ltd 1996, 2006–; Pres. Inst. for Int. Monetary Affairs 1995–2016; Chair. Working Party III, OECD, Paris 1988–90, Inst. of Int. Finance Inc., USA 1994–97; Special Adviser to Prime Minister Keizo Obuchi 1998, Special Adviser to the Cabinet as Special Envoy of the Prime Minister 2008–10, Special Adviser to Minister of Finance 2009–14; mem. Bd of Trustees, Princeton in Asia, USA 1989, Advisory Panel, E African Devt Bank, Kampala, Uganda 1990–, Asia Pacific Advisory Cttee, New York Stock Exchange (now NYSE Next) 1990–, Int. Council, The Asia Soc., New York 1991–, Exec. Cttee of Trilateral Comm. 1991–, Group of Thirty, Washington, DC 1992–2009 (now Emer.), Council of Inst. Aspen France, Banking Advisory Group of IFC, Washington, DC 1992–; Founding mem. Int. Advisory Bd of Council on Foreign Relations 1995–; Fulbright Scholar 1956–58. *Publication:* Changing Fortunes (with Paul Volcker) 1992. *Address:* c/o Institute for International Monetary Affairs, 12F, The Bank of Tokyo- Mitsubishi UFJ Ltd, Nihombashi Annex, 3-2 Nihombashi, Hongokucho, 1-Chome, Chuo-ku, Tokyo 103-0021, Japan (office). *E-mail:* admin@iima.or.jp (office). *Website:* www.iima.or.jp (office).

GYÖRKÖS ŽNIDAR, Vesna, LLM; Slovenian lawyer and politician; *Minister of the Interior;* b. 29 Dec. 1977, Ljubljana, Socialist Repub. of Slovenia, Socialist Fed. Repub. of Yugoslavia; ed Faculty of Law, Univ. of Maribor, London School of Econs, UK; began legal career at Maribor Higher Court and at a notary office; worked for Office for Money Laundering Prevention and apptd mem. Slovenian del. to Cttee of Experts on Evaluation of Anti-Money Laundering Measures and Financing of Terrorism; with Bank of Slovenia 2006–12; f. own legal practice 2012; Minister of the Interior 2014–; mem. Stranka Modernega Centra (Modern Centre Party). *Address:* Ministry of the Interior, 1501 Ljubljana, Štefanova 2, Slovenia (office). *Telephone:* (1) 4284721 (office). *Fax:* (1) 4284972 (office). *E-mail:* gp.mnz@gov.si (office); vesna.gyorkos@amis.net. *Website:* www.mnz.gov.si (office).

GYSI, Gregor; German lawyer and politician; b. 16 Jan. 1948, Berlin; s. of Klaus Gysi and Irene Gysi; m. 1st (divorced); two s.; m. 2nd; one d.; ed Humboldt Univ.; defence lawyer; elected Leader CP 1989, name changed to PDS (now known as Left Party), Parl. Leader; mem. Bundestag 1990–2002, 2005–, Group Chair. Die Linke (Left Party), Bundestag 2005–15; Deputy Mayor of Berlin and Senator for Econs, Labour and Women's Issues 2002; Founder-mem. Cttee for Justice. *Publications:* Das Waris: Noch Lange Nicht (biog. notes) 1999, Ein Blick Zürück: Ein Schritt Nachvorn 2001. *Address:* Bundestag, Pl. der Republik 1, 11011, Berlin, Germany (office). *Telephone:* (30) 2270 (office). *Fax:* (30) 22736979 (office). *E-mail:* mail@bundestag.de (office). *Website:* www.bundestag.de (office); www.gregorgysi.de.

GYURCSÁNY, Ferenc; Hungarian business executive and politician; *Chairman, Demokratikus Koalíció (DK—Democratic Coalition);* b. 4 June 1961, Pápa; m. 2nd Edina Bognár; two s.; m. 3rd Klára Dobrev; one s. one d.; ed Faculty of Economy, Janus Pannonius Univ. of Sciences, Pécs; Sec. Pécs City Cttee, Kommunista Ifjúsági Szövetség (KISZ—Communist Youth Alliance) 1984–88, Pres. Univ. and Coll. Council, Cen. Cttee 1988–89, Vice-Pres. Demokratikus Ifjúsági Szövetség (DEMISZ—Democratic Youth Alliance) 1989; Consultant, CREDITUM Financial Consultant Ltd 1990–92; Dir EUROCORP Int. Financial Inc. 1992; CEO ALTUS Investment and Assets Man. Inc. 1992–2002, Chair. 2002–03; Sr Adviser to Prime Minister Medgyessy 2002–03; mem. Nat. Exec. Cttee Magyar Szocialista Párt (MSzP—Hungarian Socialist Party) 2003–11, Chair. Győr-Moson-Sopron Co. Org. Feb.–Sept. 2004, Chair. MSzP 2007–09; Minister of Children, Youth and Sports 2003–04 (resgnd); Prime Minister of Hungary 2004–09 (resgnd); Chair. Demokratikus Koalíció (DK—Democratic Coalition) 2011–, with four other groups formed Összefogás (Unity) political alliance Jan.–April 2014. *Publication:* Útközben (On the Way, political essay) 2005. *Leisure interests:* running, skiing. *Address:* Demokratikus Koalíció (Democratic Coalition), 1132 Budapest, Victor Hugo u. 11–15, Hungary (office). *Telephone:* (21) 300-1000 (office). *E-mail:* info@dkp.hu (office). *Website:* web.dkp.hu (office).

H

HAACKE, Hans Christoph Carl, MFA; German artist and professor of art; *Professor Emeritus of Art, Cooper Union for the Advancement of Science and Art;* b. 12 Aug. 1936, Cologne; s. of Dr Carl Haacke and Antonie Haacke; m. Linda Snyder 1965; two s.; ed State Art Acad., Kassel; taught at Univ. of Washington, Rutgers Univ., Philadelphia Coll. of Art 1966–67; joined Cooper Union for the Advancement of Science and Art, New York 1967, Asst Prof. 1971–75, Assoc. Prof. 1975–79, Prof. 1979–2002, Prof. Emer. 2002–; Guest Prof., Hochschule für Bildende Künste, Hamburg 1973, 1994, Gesamthochschule, Essen 1979; Regents Lecturer, Univ. of California, Berkeley 1997; Hon. DFA (Oberlin Coll.) 1991, (San Francisco Art Inst.) 2008; Dr hc (Bauhaus-Universität, Weimar) 1998, (Maryland Inst. of Contemporary Art) 2016; numerous awards including Golden Lion, Venice Biennale 1993, Prize of Helmut-Kraft-Stiftung, Stuttgart 2001, Peter-Weiss-Preis, Bochum 2004, Roswitha Haftmann Foundation Prize 2017. *Works include:* perm. sculptural installation in Reichstag Bldg (German Parl.), Berlin 2000, Denkzeichen Rosa Luxemburg, Berlin 2006. *Publications:* solo exhbn catalogues: Werkmonographie (with Edward F. Fry) 1972, Framing and Being Framed (co-author) 1975, *Nach* allen Regeln der Kunst 1984, Unfinished Business (co-author) 1987, Artfairismes 1989, Bodenlos (co-author) 1993, Obra Social (co–author) 1995, AnsichtsSachen/ Viewing Matters 1999, Mia san mia (co-author) 2001, Hans Haacke (monograph, co-author) 2004, Hans Haacke – For Real, Works 1959–2006 2006; Libre-Echange (with Pierre Bourdieu) 1994; numerous articles and interviews in int. art magazines. *Address:* Cooper Union for the Advancement of Science and Art, Cooper Square, New York, NY 10003, USA (office). *Telephone:* (212) 353-4200 (office). *Website:* www.cooper.edu (office).

HAAK, Willem Elize (Pim), LLM; Dutch fmr chief justice; b. 19 April 1934, Haarlem; s. of Willem Adriaan Haak and Elisabeth Willemina H. ten Hooven; m. Cornelia Jacoba van Heek 1968; two s.; ed Univ. of Amsterdam; worked as advocate in Amsterdam until 1972; Dist Court Judge 1972–76; Justice, Amsterdam Court of Appeal 1976–79; Advocate Gen. to the Supreme Court 1979–81, Justice, Supreme Court 1981–92, Deputy Pres. 1992–99, Chief Justice 1999–2004; Chair. Advisory Bd Foundation of the Old Church Amsterdam 2004–09; Pres. Court of Appeals for the Gen. Comm. for the Navigation of the Rhine, Strasbourg 2004–07; Appointing Authority for the Iran-US Claims Tribunal, Perm. Court of Arbitration, The Hague 2009–13; mem. Advisory Bd Resolution Group (Effective Negotiation and Dispute Resolution), The Hague 2005–09; fmr Sec. Asscn of Dutch Lawyers; fmr Deputy Chair. Int. Law Inst.; fmr Pres. Appeals Tribunal, Dutch Inst. of Psychologists; fmr mem. Insurance Cos Supervisory Bd; fmr Pres. Bd Frits Lugt art collection; fmr Deputy Chair. Supervisory Bd, Institut Néerlandais, Paris; mem. Advisory Cttee on Endowed Chairs, Univ. of Amsterdam; mem. Perm. Appeals Tribunal of the Gen. Meeting of the Remonstrant Church; Kt, Order of the Dutch Lion 1991, Commdr, Order Oranje-Nassau 2004, Officier, Légion d'honneur 2004. *Publications include:* several articles and monographs on pvt. int. law, transport law, comparative law and criminal law. *Leisure interest:* mountain hiking. *Address:* Joh. Vermeerstraat 75, 1071 DN Amsterdam, The Netherlands (home). *Telephone:* (20) 6796935 (home). *E-mail:* pimhaak@xs4all.nl.

HAAKON, HRH Crown Prince (Haakon Magnus), BSc, MSc; b. 20 July 1973, Rikshospitalet, Oslo; s. of HM King Harald V and HM Queen Sonja; m. Mette-Marit Tjessem Høiby 2001; one s. one d. one step-s.; ed Kristelig Gymnasium, Officers' Cand. School/Navy, Horten, Royal Norwegian Naval Acad., Bergen, Univ. of California, Berkeley, USA, London School of Econs, UK; became Crown Prince when his father ascended the throne 1991; second-in-command, missile torpedo boat 1995–96; numerous official functions; rank of Adm. in Royal Norwegian Navy, Gen. in Norwegian Army and Royal Norwegian Air Force; Regent of Norway during the King's treatment for cancer and subsequent convalescence 2003–04, during the King's heart surgery and convalescence March–June 2005; est. Global Dignity org. with Pekka Himanen and John Hope Bryant 2006; Grand Cross with Collar, Royal Norwegian Order of St Olav, Grand Cross, Royal Norwegian Order of Merit, Defence Service Medal with Laurel Branch, Royal House Centenary Medal, Olav V's Commemorative Medal, Olav V's Jubilee Medal, Olav V's Centenary Medal, Royal Norwegian Navy Service Medal, Norwegian Reserve Officers Fed. Badge of Honour, Naval Soc. Medal of Merit in Gold, Oslo Mil. Soc. Badge of Honour in Gold; Grand Decoration of Honour in Gold with Sash (Austria) 2007, Grand Cross, Order of the Southern Cross (Brazil), Cordon of the Order of Stara Planina (Bulgaria), Kt, Order of the Elephant (Denmark) 1991, Grand Cross, Order of the Cross of Terra Mariana (Estonia), 2002, Commander, Grand Cross, Order of the White Rose of Finland, Grand Cross, Order of Merit of the FRG, Grand Cross, Order of Merit of the Italian Republic, Grand Cross, Order of the Chrysanthemum (Japan), Grand Cordon, Supreme Order of the Renaissance (Order of Al-Nahda, Jordan), Grand Cross, Order of the Three Stars (Latvia), Grand Cross, Order of Vytautas the Great (Lithuania), Grand Cross, Order of Adolph of Nassau (Luxembourg), Grand Cross with Swords, Order of Orange-Nassau (Netherlands), Grand Cross, Order of Merit (Poland), Grand Cross, Order of Infante Dom Henrique (Portugal), Grand Cross, Order of Charles III (Spain) 2006, Kt, Royal Order of the Seraphim (Sweden), King Harald V's Jubilee Medal 1991–2016; horse race bears his name, Kronprins Haakons Pokalløp, 14 August Cttee's Bridge Building Prize 2011. *Leisure interests:* skiing, cycling, paragliding, sailing, theatre. *Address:* The Royal Palace, 0010 Oslo, Norway. *Telephone:* (47) 2204-8700. *Fax:* (47) 2204-8790. *E-mail:* post@slottet.no. *Website:* www.royalcourt .no.

HAAKONSEN, Bent, LLB; Danish diplomatist (retd); b. 10 Jan. 1936; m. Kirsten Haakonsen; one d.; joined Ministry of Foreign Affairs 1961; served Bonn 1964–67, Perm. Rep. to EEC, Brussels 1972–74; Amb. to Czechoslovakia 1978–79; Head, Danish del. to CSCE, Madrid 1980–81; Under-Sec. for Trade Relations 1983–86; Perm. Under-Sec. of State 1986–91; Perm. Rep. to UN, New York 1991–95; Amb. to Germany 1995–2001, to Sweden 2001–04; Pres. Franz Schubert Soc., Denmark. *Address:* Provstevænget 10, 4000 Roskilde, Denmark (home).

HAARDE, Geir Hilmar, MA; Icelandic politician, economist and diplomatist; *Ambassador to USA;* b. 8 April 1951; m. Inga Jona Thordardottir; five c.; ed Brandeis Univ., Johns Hopkins Univ., Univ. of Minnesota, USA; teaching asst, Univ. of Minnesota, USA 1976–77; economist, Int. Dept, Cen. Bank of Iceland 1977–83; Lecturer, Econs Dept, Univ. of Iceland 1979–83; Special Asst to Minister of Finance 1983–87; mem. Althing (Parl.) 1987–2009; mem. Foreign Affairs Cttee 1991–98, Chair. 1995–98; Minister of Finance 1998–2005; Minister of Foreign Affairs 2005–06; Prime Minister 2006–09 (resgnd); Chair. Youth Org. of Independence Party 1981–85, Chair. Parl. Group 1991–98, Vice-Chair. 1999–2005, Party Chair. 2005–09; Pres. Icelandic Group Inter-Parl. Union 1988–98, mem. Exec. Cttee 1994–98, Vice-Pres. 1995–97; Amb. to USA (also accred to Argentina, Brazil, Chile, El Salvador, Guatemala, Mexico and Uruguay) 2015–; mem. Control Cttee Nordic Investment Bank 1991–95; mem. Presidium Nordic Council 1991–98, Pres. 1995, Chair. Conservative Party Group 1995–97; Chair. Standing Cttee of Parliamentarians of Arctic Region 1995–98; Hon. LLD (Univ. of Minnesota) 2007; Alumni of the Year Award, Brandeis Univ., USA 2006. *Address:* Embassy of Iceland, House of Sweden, Suite 509, 2900 K Street, NW, Washington, DC 20007-1704, USA (office). *Telephone:* (202) 265-6653 (office). *Fax:* (202) 265-6656 (office). *E-mail:* icemb.wash@utn.stjr.is (office). *Website:* www.iceland.org/us (office).

HAAS, Peter M., PhD; American political scientist and academic; *Professor of Political Science, University of Massachusetts, Amherst;* b. 23 Jan. 1955, Oakland; s. of Ernst B. Haas and Hildegarde Haas; m. Julie Zuckman; one s.; ed Univ. of Michigan, Massachusetts Inst. of Tech.; Visiting Asst Prof., Yale Univ. 1986; Marine Policy Research Fellow, Woods Hole Oceanographic Inst. 1986–87; Asst Prof. of Political Science, Univ. of Massachusetts, Amherst 1986–92, Assoc. Prof. 1992–98, Prof. 1998–; visiting positions, Univ. of Oxford, UK 2002, Brown Univ. 2002–03, Wissenschaftszentrum, Berlin 2009; Distinguished Scholar Award, Environmental Studies Section of Int. Studies Asscn 2014, UMASS Award for Outstanding Accomplishments in Research and Creative Activity 2015. *Publications include:* Saving the Mediterranean 1990, Institutions for the Earth 1993, Knowledge, Power and International Policy Co-ordination (ed.) 1997, The International Environment in the New Global Economy 2003, Emerging Forces in Environmental Governance 2004, Global Environmental Governance 2006, Controversies in Globalization 2012, Improving Global Environmental Governance 2013, Epistemic Communities, Constructivism and International Environmental Politics 2015; articles and chapters on int. environmental politics and int. relations. *Address:* Department of Political Science, University of Massachusetts, 216 Thompson Hall, Amherst, MA 01003, USA (office). *Telephone:* (413) 250-7246 (office). *Fax:* (413) 545-3349 (office). *E-mail:* haas@polsci.umass.edu (office). *Website:* www.umass.edu/polsci (office).

HAAS, Richard John, BS, MFA; American artist; b. 29 Aug. 1936, Spring Green, Wis.; s. of Joseph F. Haas and Marie N. Haas; m. 1st Cynthia Dickman 1963 (divorced 1970); m. 2nd Katherine Sokolnikoff 1980; one s.; ed Univ. of Wisconsin-Milwaukee and Univ. of Minnesota; Instructor of Art, Univ. of Minn. 1963–64; Asst Prof. of Art, Michigan State Univ. 1964–68; Instructor in Printmaking, Bennington Coll. 1968–80, Fine Arts Faculty, School of Visual Arts 1977–81; Commr New York City Art 1976–79; Bd mem. Public Art Fund 1980–84, New York State Preservation League 1983–90; Gov. Skowhegan School of Painting and Sculpture 1980–; mem. Bd of Trustees, Hudson River Museum 1989–; Pres. Nat. Acad. of Design, New York 2009–11, Dir Abbey Mural Fund 2000–11; AIA Medal of Honor 1977, Municipal Art Soc. Award 1977, Nat. Endowment for the Arts Fellowship 1978, Guggenheim Fellowship 1983, Doris C. Freedman Award 1989, Fellowship, MacDowell Colony 2003, Individual Artist Award, Westchester Arts Council 2003, Yonkers Friends of the Arts Public Art Honoree 2003, Jimmy Ernst Award, American Acad. of Arts and Letters 2005. *Publication:* Richard Haas: An Architecture of Illusion 1981. *Leisure interests:* tennis, film. *Address:* c/o Harmon Meek Gallery, 599 9th Street, North Suite 309, Naples, FL 34102, USA; 361 West 36th Street, 5A, New York, NY 10018, USA (office). *Telephone:* (239) 261-2637; (212) 947-9868 (office). *Website:* www.harmonmeekgallery.com; www.richardhaas .com (office). *E-mail:* haasnyc@aol.com (office).

HAAS, Robert Douglas, BA, MBA; American business executive; *Chairman Emeritus, Levi Strauss & Company;* b. 3 April 1942, San Francisco, Calif.; s. of Walter Haas and Evelyn Danzig; m. Colleen Gershon 1974; one d.; ed Univ. of California, Berkeley and Harvard Univ.; with US Peace Corps, Côte d'Ivoire 1964–66; Assoc., McKinsey and Co. 1969–72; joined Levi Strauss & Co., San Francisco 1973, Sr Vice-Pres. (Corp. Planning and Policy) 1978–80, Pres. New Business Group 1980, Pres. Operating Groups 1980–81, Exec. Vice-Pres. and COO 1981–84, Pres. and CEO 1984–89, CEO and Chair. 1989–99, Chair. 1989–2008, Chair. Emer. 2008–; mem. Bd of Dirs Levi Strauss Foundation, Calif. Business Roundtable, Stark County Veterans Service Comm.; White House Fellow 1968–69; mem. Advisory Bd Haas School of Business, Stanford Humanities and Sciences Council, Stanford Humanities and Sciences Council; fmr mem. Bd of Dirs American Apparel Asscn; mem. Trilateral Comm., Council on Foreign Relations; fmr mem. Nat. Advisory Cttee League of Women Voters Educ. Fund; Trustee, Ford Foundation, Evelyn & Walter Haas JR Fund; Hon. Trustee, Brookings Inst.; Hon. Dir San Francisco AIDS Foundation; Chancellor's Award 1968, Nat. Leadership Coalition on AIDS Edward N. Brandt, Jr Award 1991, Ron Brown Award 1998, Cal Alumnus of the Year Award 2009. *Address:* Levi Strauss & Co., 1155 Battery Street, San Francisco, CA 94111, USA (office). *Telephone:* (415) 501-6000 (office). *Fax:* (415) 501-7112 (office). *Website:* www.levistrauss.com (office).

HAASAN, Kamal; Indian actor, filmmaker and screenwriter; *Founder and President, Makkal Needhi Maiyyam;* b. 7 Nov. 1954, Paramakudi, Tamil Nadu; s. of D. Srinivasan and Rajalakshmi; m. 1st Vani Ganapathy 1978 (divorced 1988); m. 2nd Sarika 1988 (divorced 2002); partner Gouthami Tadimalla 2004; two c.; Owner, Rajkamal Int. (production co.); apptd Chair., Fed. of Indian Chambers of Commerce and Industry 2009; Amb. Tamil Thalaivas (Kabbadi Team) 2017–; f. and Pres., Makkal Needhi Maiyyam (People's Justice Centre) 2018–; Dr hc (Sathyabama Deemed Univ.) 2005; Kalaimamani Award 1979, Padma Shri 1990, Abraham Kovoor National Award for Humanist Activities 2004, Chevalier Sivaji Ganesan Award for Excellence in Indian Cinema 2006, Living Legend Award, FICCI 2009, CNN-IBN Indian of the Year 2010, Hon. Award, Govt of Kerela 2010,

Padma Bhushan 2014. *Films include:* Kalathur Kannamma (Nat. Film Award) 1960, Paadha Kannikkai 1962, Anandha Jodhi 1963, Mundram Pirai (Nat. Film Award) 1963, Maanavan 1969, Annai Velankanni 1971, Kanna Nalama 1972, Sollathaan Ninaikkiren 1973, Aval Oru Thodar Kathai 1974, Pattikkaattu Raja 1975, Moondru Mudichu 1976, Lalitha 1976, Oor Magal Marikkumo 1977, Satyavan Savithri 1977, Maro Charitra 1978, Madanolsavam 1978, Allaudinaum Arputha Vilakkum 1979, Azhiyadha Kolangal 1979, Maria, My Darling 1980, Natchathiram 1980, Thillu Mullu 1981, Kadal Meengal 1981, Do Dil Diwane 1981, Apoorva Raagangal (Filmfare Award), Agni Sakshi 1982, Moondram Pirai 1982, Moondram Pirai (Nat. Film Award) 1982, Sattam 1983, Thoongadhey Thambi Thoongadhey 1983, Sagara Sangamam (Filmfare Award, Nandi Award) 1983, Yeh Desh 1984, Raj Tilak 1984, Oru Kaidhiyin Diary 1984, Kaakki Sattai 1985, Mangamma Sabadham 1985, Dekha Pyar Tumhara 1985, Naanum Oru Thozhilali 1986, December Pookal 1986, Kadamai Kanniyam Kattupaadu 1987, Nayagan (Nat. Film Award) 1987, Pushpak (Filmfare Award) 1988, Sathya 1988, Daisy 1988, Indrudu Chandrudu (Filmfare Award for Best Actor, Nandi Award) 1989, Apoorva Sagodharargal (Filmfare Award) 1989, Chanakyan 1989, Michael Madhana Kamarajan 1990, My Dear Marthandan 1990, Guna 1991, Thevar Magan (also producer) (Filmfare Award, Nat. Film Award for Best Feature Film) 1992, Singaravelan 1992, Kalaignan 1993, Maharasan 1993, Nammavar 1994, Mahanadhi 1994, Kuruthipunal 1995, Sathi Leelavathi 1995, Avvai Shanmugi 1996, Indian (Nat. Film Award for Best Actor, Filmfare Award) 1996, Kaathala Kaathala 1998, Chachi 420 (also Dir) 1998, Hey Ram (also Dir and producer) (Filmfare Award for Best Actor) 2000, Aalavandhan 2000, Parthale Paravasam 2001, Panchathantiram Nala 2002, Pammal K. Sambandam 2002, Damayanthi 2003, Anbe Sivam 2003, Virumaandi (Best Asian Film Award, Puchon Int. Fantastic Film Festival) 2004, Mumbai Xpress 2005, Vettaiyaadu Vilaiyaadu 2006, Dasavathaaram (also writer) (Tamil Nadu State Film Award) 2008, Unnaipol Oruvan 2009, Four Friends 2010, Manmadan Ambu 2010, Vishwaroopam (also writer, dir and co-producer) (Nat. Film Award for Best Production Design and Best Choreography 2013) 2013, Vishwaroopam 2 2014. *Address:* Makkal Needhi Maiyyam, 4 Eldams Road, Alwarpet, Chennai 600 018 (office); 63, Luz Church Road, Mylapore, Chennai 600 004, India (home). *Telephone:* (44) 24358718 (office). *E-mail:* feedback@maiam.com (office). *Website:* www.maiam.com (office).

HAASE, Barry Wayne; Australian politician, government official and business executive; b. 19 Nov. 1945, Southern Cross, WA; served as a co. dir before entering politics; mem. House of Reps (Liberal Party of Australia) for Kalgoorlie 1998–2010, for Durack 2010–13 (retd); Admin. Australian Indian Ocean Territories—Christmas Island and the Cocos (Keeling) Islands 2014–17.

HAASIS, Heinrich; German banking executive and politician; b. 21 April 1945, Balingen-Streichen (Baden-Wurttemberg); m.; two c.; ed Balingen Gymnasium, Albstadt-Ebingen Commercial Coll.; Mayor of Bisingen Dist 1971–81; mem. State Parl. (Landtag) for Zollernalb Dist 1976–2001, also Chair. Christian Democratic Union (CDU) Parl. Group and Head CDU Regional Party Group for Baden-Württemberg; mem. State Senate (Zollernalb Dist) 1981–91; Pres. Baden-Württemberg Asscn of Savings Banks 1991–2001, German Savings Banks and Giro Asscn, Berlin 2006–12; Chair. Supervisory Bd Landesbank Baden-Württemberg (LBBW) –2008; Pres. European Savings Bank Group 2006–09; Chair. DekaBank 2007–12; Chair. Supervisory Bd Deutsche Sparkassen Leasing AG Man. 2006, Supervisory Bd Foundation Schloss Neuhardenberg GmbH 2006–, Supervisory Bd Landesbank Berlin Holding AG 2007; Chair. Bd of Trustees Savings Bank Foundation for Int. Cooperation Asscn 2006; mem. Bd of Dirs Kreditanstalt for Wiederaufbau; mem. Bd of Gov. Fed. Financial Supervisory Authority (BaFin); Chair. Higher Council of Univ. of the Sparkassen finance group; Dist Chair. German Red Cross; mem. Bd Donors' Asscn for German Science, Bd of Trustees of German Sports Aid Foundation, Bd of Trustees of Cultural Foundation of countries eV, and numerous bds in other social and cultural orgs; Hon. Senator, Albstadt-Ebingen Univ. for Applied Science, Hon. Citizen of Bisingen; Verdienstkreuz am Bande des Verdienstordens der Bundesrepublik Deutschland 1983, Verdienstkreuz 1. Klasse 1988, Großes Verdienstkreuz 1999; AMSEL-Landesverband Prize 2002.

HAASS, Christian, Dr rer. nat; German biochemist and academic; *Professor of Neurobiochemistry, Ludwig Maximilians University of Munich;* b. 19 Dec. 1960, Mannheim; ed Univ. of Heidelberg; Postdoctoral Fellow, Center for Neurologic Diseases, Harvard Medical School, Boston, Mass, USA, Asst Prof. 1993–95; Assoc. Prof. of Molecular Biology, Cen. Inst. of Mental Health, Mannheim 1995–99; Prof. of Neurobiochemistry, Dept of Biomedicine I, Ludwig Maximilians Univ. of Munich 1999–, Head Lab. for Alzheimer's and Parkinson's Disease Research, German Center for Neurodegenerative Diseases, Prin. Investigator, Collaborative Research Center SFB 596 Molecular Mechanisms of Neurodegeneration; mem. Center for Integrated Protein Science Munich; Dr hc (Univ. of Zurich) 2010; awards from Heidelberg Soc. for Molecular Biology for diploma thesis 1986, doctoral thesis 1989, Organon Research Award, Award of Heidelberg Acad. of Sciences, Award of German Brain League, Int. Alois Alzheimer Award, Family Hansen Award, Ernst Jung Prize for Medicine 2002, Gottfried Wilhelm Leibniz Prize 2002, Potamkin Prize, American Acad. of Neurology 2002, MetLife Foundation Award for Medical Research 2006, Sheik Hamdan Award for Medical Sciences 2006, ERC Advanced Grant 2013, MetLife Award 2015. *Publications:* Molecular Biology of Alzheimer's Disease: Genes and Mechanisms Involved in Amyloid Generation 1998; numerous articles in scientific journals. *Address:* Adolf-Butenandt-Institut, Lehrstuhl für Stoffwechselbiochemie, Ludwig-Maximilians-Universität, Schillerstraße 44, 80336 Munich, Germany (office). *Telephone:* (89) 218075-472 (office). *Fax:* (89) 218075-415 (office). *E-mail:* chaass@med.uni-muenchen.de (office). *Website:* www.med.uni-muenchen.de/haass (office).

HAASS, Richard N., BA, DPhil; American fmr government official and fmr diplomatist; *President, Council on Foreign Relations;* m.; two c.; ed Oberlin Coll., Ohio, Univ. of Oxford, UK; fmr legis. aide, US Senate; various posts in Dept of Defense 1979–80, Dept of State 1981–85, Special Asst to Pres. and Sr Dir for Near East and S Asian Affairs, Nat. Security Council 1989–93; Vice-Pres. and Dir of Foreign Policy Studies, Sydney Stein Jr Chair in Int. Security, Brookings Inst. –2001; Dir of Policy Planning, Dept of State 2001–03, US Co-ordinator for Afghanistan policy; fmr Special Envoy of Pres. George W. Bush to NI Peace Process; fmr Sr Fellow and Dir of Nat. Security Programs, Council on Foreign Relations, Pres. Council on Foreign Relations 2003–; mem. IISS (fmr Research Assoc.), Trilateral Comm.; Sr Assoc., Carnegie Endowment for Int. Peace; fmr Sol. M. Linowitz Visiting Prof. of Int. Studies, Hamilton Coll.; fmr Lecturer in Public Policy, Harvard Univ. Kennedy School of Govt; fmr consultant, NBC News; Presidential Citizen's Medal 1991, Dept of State Distinguished Honor Award 2003. *Publications:* The Reluctant Sheriff: The United States after the Cold War 1998, Economic Sanctions and American Diplomacy 1998, The Bureaucratic Entrepreneur: How to Be Effective in Any Unruly Organization 1998, Intervention: The Use of American Military Force in the Post-Cold War World 1999, The Opportunity: America's Moment to Alter History's Course 2005, War of Necessity, War of Choice: A Memoir of Two Iraq Wars 2009, Foreign Policy Begins at Home: The Case for Putting America's House in Order 2013; frequent contribs to foreign affairs journals. *Address:* Council on Foreign Relations, 58 East 68th Street, New York, NY 10021, USA (office). *Telephone:* (212) 434-9540 (office). *Fax:* (212) 434-9880 (office). *E-mail:* president@cfr.org (office). *Website:* www.cfr.org (office).

HAAVISTO, Heikki Johannes, MSc, LLM; Finnish politician; b. 20 Aug. 1935, Turku; s. of Johan Haavisto and Alli Svensson; m. Maija Rihko 1964; three s.; Head of Dept, Oy Vehnä Ab 1963–66; Sec.-Gen. Cen. Union of Agricultural Producers and Forest Owners in Finland (MTK) 1966–75, Pres. 1976–94; Vice-Pres. Int. Fed. of Agricultural Producers 1977–80, 1986–90, mem. Bd of Dirs 1984–86; mem. Cen. Council of Nordic Farmer Orgs (NBC), Pres. 1977, 1985–87; Chair. Del. of Finn Cooperative Pellervo (Confed. of Finnish Cooperatives) 1979–2000; mem. Admin. Council, Osuuskunta Metsäliitto, Vice-Chair. 1976–82, Pres. 1982–93; Vice-Chair. Admin. Council, OKO (Cen. Union of Cooperative Credit Banks) 1985–93; mem. Bd of Dirs Metsä-Serla Oy 1986–93; Pres. Admin. Council, Raisio Group 1987–96, Pres. Bd of Dirs 1997–2000; mem. Int. Policy Council on Agric. and Trade 1988–2000; Minister for Foreign Affairs 1993–95, for Devt Co-operation 1994–95; three hon. doctorates. *Address:* Hintsantie 2, 21200 Raisio, Finland (home). *Telephone:* (2) 4383020 (home). *Fax:* (2) 4383499 (home).

HABASHI, Wagdi George, BEng, MEng, PhD; Canadian (b. Egyptian) engineer, academic and entrepreneur; *Professor, Department of Mechanical Engineering, McGill University;* b. 29 June 1946, Egypt; s. of Georges Habashi and Iris Banoub; one s. two d. two step-d.; ed McGill Univ., Cornell Univ., USA; Asst Prof., Dept of Mechanical Eng, Concordia Univ., Montreal 1975–79, Assoc. Prof. 1979–84, Prof. 1984–2000; Prof., Dept of Mechanical Eng, McGill Univ. 2000–, also Dir Computational Fluid Dynamics Lab.; Aerodynamics Consultant, Pratt & Whitney Canada 1977–2001, Research Fellow 2000–; Pres. and CEO Newmerical Technologies International (now ANSYS-Montreal) 2000–15; NSERC-Bombardier-Bell 2002–07, NSERC- Bombardier-Bell Helicopter- CAE Industrial Research Chair of Multidisciplinary CFD 2008–12; NSERC-Lockheed Martin-Bell Helicopter Industrial Research Chair for Multi-physics Analysis and Design of Aerospace Systems 2014–20; Pres. CERTIF-ICE Inc. 2015–; Ed.-in-Chief, International Journal of Computational Fluid Dynamics; mem. Ordre des ingénieurs du Québec 1975; Fellow, ASME 1996, Canadian Acad. of Eng 2002, Acad. of Science Royal Soc. 2009, AIAA 2009; Hon. Prof., Tongji Univ., Shanghai, People's Repub. of China; Chevalier, Ordre nat. du Québec 2012, Queen's Diamond Jubilee Medal 2012; British Asscn Medal for Great Distinction in Mechanical Eng, E.W.R. Steacie Fellowship, Nat. Sciences and Eng Research Council (NSERC), Tech. Partnership Award, Pratt & Whitney Canada, Sr Research Fellow Award, Concordia Univ., Cray Gigaflop Performance Award, Computerworld Smithsonian Award, named by Canadian Foundation for Innovation as one of Canada's top 25 scientists, featured by NSERC as one of 12 Great Canadian Stories, Achievement Awards, Hon. Pioneer Award, Pratt & Whitney Canada, Killam Prize for Eng, Canada Council for the Arts, James C. Floyd Award for Recent Canadian Aerospace Achievement, McCurdy Award, Canadian Aerospace & Space Inst., selected by Jury of Innovation-Inspiration as one of the five most innovative persons in the aerospace sector of the Greater Montreal area, Engineering awarded him its first Christophe Pierre Award for Research Excellence, McGill Univ. Faculty of Eng. *Publications include:* selected by Canadian Foundation for Innovation to write 'Essays by Leading Canadian Researchers' 2002; more than 400 publs in refereed scientific journals and at confs. *Address:* CFD Laboratory, Department of Mechanical Engineering, McGill University, 680 Sherbrooke Street West, Suite 717, Montreal, QC H3A 2S6, Canada (office). *Telephone:* (514) 398-3747 (office). *E-mail:* wagdi.habashi@mcgill.ca (office). *Website:* people.mcgill.ca/wagdi.habashi (office); www.cfdlab.mcgill.ca/wordpress (office).

HABER, Emily, PhD; German diplomatist; *Ambassador to USA;* b. 1956, Bonn; d. of Dirk Oncken; m. Hansjörg Haber; two s.; worked in the Soviet Union Dept, as Dir, OSCE Div., Embassy of Germany, Berlin 2002–06, Commr, SE Europe and Turkey 2006–09, Political Dir, Federal Foreign Office 2009–11, State Sec. 2011, also as Deputy Head of the Cabinet and Parl. Liaison Div., Deputy Dir-Gen., Western Balkans, Head, Econ. Affairs Dept, Embassy of Germany, Moscow, Head, Political Affairs Dept, Cultural Affairs Officer, Embassy of Germany, Ankara; State Sec. Federal Ministry of the Interior 2014–18; Amb. to USA 2018–. *Address:* Embassy of Germany, 4645 Reservoir Road, NW, Washington, DC 20007, USA (office). *Telephone:* (202) 298-4000 (office). *Fax:* (202) 298-4249 (office). *Website:* www.germany.info (office).

HABERMAS, Jürgen, DPhil (Habil.); German philosopher, sociologist and writer; *Professor Emeritus of Philosophy, University of Frankfurt;* b. 18 June 1929, Düsseldorf; m. Ute Habermas-Wesselhoeft 1955; one s. two d.; ed Univs of Bonn and Göttingen; Research Asst, Inst. für Soziale Forschung, Frankfurt 1956; apptd Prof. of Philosophy, Univ. of Heidelberg 1961, of Philosophy and Sociology, Univ. of Frankfurt 1964; Dir Max Planck Inst., Starnberg, Munich 1971; Prof. of Philosophy, Univ. of Frankfurt 1983–94, Prof. Emer. 1994–; mem. Academia Europaea; Foreign mem. American Acad. of Arts and Sciences 1984, British Acad. of Science 1994; Hon. DD (New School for Social Research) 1984; hon. degrees from Hebrew Univ. (Jerusalem), Univs of Hamburg, Buenos Aires, Evanston (Northwestern), Utrecht, Athens, Bologna, Paris, Tel-Aviv, Cambridge, Harvard; Hegel Prize 1972, Sigmund Freud Prize 1976, Adorno Prize 1980, Geschwister Scholl Prize 1985, Leibniz Prize 1986, Sonning Prize 1987, Jaspers Prize 1997, Culture Prize of the State of Hesse 1999, Friedenspreis des deutschen Buchhandels 2001, Prince of Asturias Award for Social Science 2003, Kyoto Prize for Philosophy 2004, Holberg Int. Memorial Prize 2005, Bruno Kreisky Prize 2006, Staatspreis des landes Nordheim-Westfalen 2006, Int. Brunet Prize, Pamplona 2008, Ulysses Medal, Dublin 2010, Heinrich Heine Prize 2012, Erasmus Prize 2013, John W. Kluge Prize for Lifetime Achievement in the Study of Humanity, Library of Congress (co-recipient) 2015. *Publications include:* Strukturwandel der Öffentlichkeit 1962, Theorie und Praxis 1963, Erkenntnis und Interesse 1968, Legitimationsprobleme im Spätkapitalismus 1973, Theorie des kommunikativen Handelns 1981, Moralbewüsstsein und Kommunikatives Handeln 1983, Der Philosophische Diskurs ober Moderne 1985, Eine Art Schadensabwicklüng 1987, Nachmetaphysisches Denken 1988, Nachholende Revolution 1990, Texte und Kontexte 1991, Erläuterungen zur Diskursetnik 1991, Faktizität und Geltung 1992, Vergangenheit als Zukunft 1993, Die Normalität einer Berliner Republik 1995, Die Einbeziehung des Anderen 1996, Vom sinnlichen Eindruck zum symbolischen Ausdruck 1997, Die postnationale Konstellation 1998, Wahrheit und Rechtfertigung 1999, Zeit und Übergänge 2001, Kommunikatives Handeln und Detranszendentalisierte Vernunft 2001, Die Zukunft der Menschlichen Natur 2001, Zeitdiagnosen 2003, Der gespaltene Westen 2004, Ach Europa 2008, Philosophische Texte (five vols) 2009, Zür Verfassung Europas 2011, Nachmetaphysisches Denken II 2012. *Address:* Department of Philosophy, University of Frankfurt, Grüneburgplatz 1, 60629 Frankfurt am Main (office); Ringstrasse 8B, 82319 Starnberg, Germany (home). *Telephone:* (8151) 13537 (home). *Fax:* (8151) 13537 (home).

HABGOOD, Sir Anthony John, Kt, MA, MS; British business executive and banking executive; *Chairman, Court of Bank of England;* b. 8 Nov. 1946; m. Nancy Atkinson; three c.; ed Gresham's School, Gonville and Caius Coll., Cambridge, Carnegie Mellon Univ., USA; joined Boston Consulting Group as Man. Consultant 1970, Dir 1977–86; CEO Tootal Group PLC 1986–91; CEO Bunzl PLC 1991–2005, Chair. 2005–09; Chair. Whitbread PLC 2005–14; Chair. Reed Elsevier PLC 2009–; Chair. Court of Bank of England 2014–; Chair. Mölnlycke Healthcare (UK) Ltd 2006–07, Preqin Holding Ltd 2011, Norwich Research Park 2013–; mem. Bd of Dirs Geest PLC 1989–93, SVG Capital PLC 1996–2009, Schroder Ventures International Investment Trust PLC 1996–2004, Marks & Spencer Group PLC 2004–05, National Westminster Bank PLC, Powergen PLC, Norfolk and Norwich Univ. Hospitals Trust 2006–13; Visiting Fellow, Oxford Univ. *Address:* Bank of England, Threadneedle Street, London, EC2R 8AH, England (office). *Telephone:* (20) 7601-4444 (office). *Fax:* (20) 7601-5460 (office). *E-mail:* enquiries@bankofengland.co.uk (office). *Website:* www.bankofengland.co.uk (office).

HABIB, Irfan, MA, DPhil; Indian historian and academic; *Professor Emeritus, Aligarh Muslim University;* b. 1931; s. of Mohammad Habib and Sohaila; ed Aligarh Muslim Univ., New College Oxford, UK; Prof. of History, Aligarh Muslim Univ. 1969–91, Dir Centre for the Advanced Study of History 1975–77, 1984–94, Prof. Emer. 2007–; Jt Ed. Cambridge Economic History of India (journal); Radhakrishnan Lecturer, Oxford 1991; Jawaharlal Nehru Fellow 1968; Fellow, British Royal Historical Soc. 1997; Pres. Indian History Congress 1981; Chair. Indian Soc. for Historical Research 1987–93; mem. Indian Inst. of Advanced Studies, Shimla; Hon. DLitt, Banaras Hindu Univ. 2008; Watumull Prize, American Historical Asscn 1982, Padma Bhushan 2005, Muzaffar Ahmad Memorial Prize 2006, Yash Bharti 2016. *Publications include:* The Agrarian System of Mughal India 1556–1707 1963, An Atlas of the Mughal Empire 1982, Essays in Indian History: Towards a Marxist Perception 1995, The Economic History of Medieval India: A Survey 2001, Confronting Colonialism: Resistance and Modernization Under Haidar Ali and Tipu Sultan 2002, Mauryan India 2004, The Cambridge Economic History of India 2005, Karl Marx on India 2006, Indian Economy, 1858–1914 2006, Medieval India: The Study of a Civilization 2008, Class, Caste and Colony: India from the Mughal Period to the British Raj 2010. *Address:* Badar Bagh, Civil Lines, Aligarh 202 992, India (home). *Telephone:* (571) 2702620 (home).

HABIB, Adm. Muhammad Farid; Bangladeshi naval officer; b. 1959, Tangail; joined Bangladesh Navy 1979, commands held include Cdre Commdg BN Flotilla (COMBAN), Cdre Commdg Khulna (COMKHUL), Naval Admin. Authority Dhaka (Admin Dhaka), Asst Chief of Naval Staff (Personnel), Asst Chief of Naval Staff (Operations), Chief of Naval Staff 2013–15.

HABIB, Rafiq M.; Pakistani business executive; *Group Chairman, House of Habib;* b. 18 Oct. 1937; ed Life Insurance Man. Inst., New York; Group Chair. House of Habib, includes Agriauto Industries Ltd, AuVitronics Ltd, Habib Insurance Co. Ltd, Indus Motor Co. Ltd, Makro Habib Pakistan Ltd, Metro Habib Cash & Carry Pakistan, Noble Computer Services (Pvt.) Ltd, Shabbir Tiles & Ceramic Ltd, Thal Ltd, Thal Ltd–Corp. Office, Thal Ltd–Eng Divs; Chancellor Habib Univ., currently Chair. Habib Univ. Foundation; Life mem. Fed. of Pakistan Chambers of Commerce and Industry; multiple awards for leadership and industry innovation. *Address:* House of Habib, 2nd Floor, Jinnah C.H. Society, Sharea Faisal, Karachi 75350, Pakistan (office). *Telephone:* (21) 3431-2030 (office). *Fax:* (21) 3431-2314 (office). *E-mail:* hoh@hoh.net (office). *Website:* www.hoh.net (office).

HABIB, Randa, MA; Lebanese/French journalist; *Director and Head, Middle East and North Africa, Agence France Presse Foundation;* b. 16 Jan. 1952, Beirut, Lebanon; d. of Farid Habib; m. Adnan Gharaybeh 1973; one s. one d.; ed French Lycée, Rio de Janeiro and Univ. Saint Joseph of Beirut; corresp., Agence France Presse (AFP) 1980, Dir and Head of AFP Office, Amman 1987–2012, Dir and Head, Middle East and North Africa, AFP Foundation 2012–; corresp., Radio Monte Carlo 1988–2006, columnist for local Jordanian papers, corresp. also for several int. publs and TV; Chair. Foreign Press Club, Jordan; mem. Bd of Dirs, Jordan Media Inst.; Chevalier, Ordre nat. du Mérite 2001, Légion d'honneur 2008; Médaille du Travail (France) 2000. *Publications include:* Hussein père et fils, 30 années qui ont changé le Moyen-Orient 2007, Hussein and Abdullah Inside the Jordanian Royal Family 2010. *Leisure interests:* reading, swimming, painting. *Address:* Agence France Presse, Jebel Amman, 2nd Circle, PO Box 3340, Amman 11181, Jordan (office). *Telephone:* (6) 4642976 (office). *Fax:* (6) 4654680 (office). *E-mail:* randa.habib@afp.com (office); randa.habib@gmail.com. *Website:* www.afp.com (office).

HABIBI, Gen. Abdullah Khan, MA; Afghan military commander and government official; b. 1952, Kunar Prov.; s. of Ghulam Habibi; m.; five c.; ed Nat. Mil. Acad. of Afghanistan; Artillery Officer, Corps 88 1972, Lecturer, Nat. Mil. Acad. 1974, Commdr, Brigade 28, Div. 17 1980, Operations Officer, Border Protection Forces 1985, Deputy Intelligence Officer, Border Protection Forces (rank of Maj.-Gen.) 1987–88, First Deputy Commdr, Border Protection Forces 1988, Gen. Commdr, Border Protection Forces (rank of Lt-Gen.) 1988, First Deputy, Educ. Dept, Ministry of Defence 1996, Audit Head of Chief of Gen. Staff (after formation of Afghan Transitional Govt and of nat. army) 2004–06, Personnel Officer of Chief of Gen. Staff 2006–09, 2013–16, Mil. Asst to Minister of Defence 2009–11, Commdr, 201st Selab Corps 2011–13; Minister of Defence 2016–17; Red Flag Medal, Baryal Medal (grade 3), Ghazi Mohammad Ayub Khan Higher Govt Medal.

HABIBIE, Bacharuddin Jusuf, DEng; Indonesian aviation engineer, politician and fmr head of state; b. 25 June 1936, Pare-Pare, South Sulawesi; m. H. Hasri Ainun Besari 1962 (died 2010); two s.; ed Bandung Inst. of Tech., Technische Hochschule, Aachen; Head of Research at Messerschmitt-Boelkow-Blohm, Hamburg, Germany 1966; Govt Adviser 1976; Chair., CEO, Pres. Indonesian State Aircraft Industry 1976–98; Minister of State for Research and Tech. 1978–98; Head of Agency for Tech. Evaluation and Application 1978–98; Chair., CEO, Pres. Indonesian Shipbuilding Industry 1978–98; Chair. Batam Industrial Devt 1978–98; mem. Indonesian Parl. 1982–99; Vice-Pres. of Indonesia March–May 1998, Pres. 1998–99; Chair. Team for Defence Security Industrial Devt 1980–99; Chair., CEO, Pres. Small Arms and Munitions Industry 1983–98; Chair. Nat. Research Council 1984; Vice-Chair. Bd of Patrons, Indonesian Strategic Industries 1988; Chair. Agency for Strategic Industries 1989–98; Head of Indonesian Muslim Intellectuals Asscn 1990; Founder and Chair. Indonesian Aeronautics and Astronautics Inst.; Founder and Chair. Bd of Trustees, Habibie Center 1999–; mem. Royal Swedish Acad. of Eng Sciences, Acad. Nat. de l'Air et de l'Espace (France); Fellow, Royal Aeronautical Soc.; Gran Cruz del Mérito Aeronáutico con Distintivo Blanco (Spain) 1980, Grosses Bundesverdienstkreuz 1980, Dwidya Sistha Medal 1982, Grand Cross of the Order of Orange Nassau 1983, Grand Officier, Ordre nat. du Mérite; Dr hc (Univ. of Indonesia) 2010. *Publications:* Detik-Detik Yang Menentukan: Jalan Panjang Indonesia Menuju Demokrasi 2006; numerous scientific and tech. papers. *Address:* Habibie Centre, Jl. Kemang Selatan No. 98, South Jakarta 12560, Indonesia. *Telephone:* (21) 7817211. *Fax:* (21) 7817212. *E-mail:* thcasean@habibiecenter.or.id. *Website:* thcasean.org/about/thc.

HABICHT, Werner, DPhil; German academic; *Professor Emeritus of English, University of Würzburg;* b. 29 Jan. 1930, Schweinfurt; s. of Wilhelm Habicht and Magda Habicht (née Müller); ed Univ. of Munich, Johns Hopkins Univ., Baltimore, USA, Univ. of Paris, France; Asst, Freie Universität, Berlin 1957–60, Univ. of Munich 1960–65; Prof. of English, Univ. of Heidelberg 1966–70, Univ. of Bonn 1970–78, Univ. of Würzburg 1978–95, Prof. Emer. 1995–; Visiting Prof., Univ. of Tex. at Austin 1981, Univ. of Colo 1987, Ohio State Univ. 1988, Univ. of Cyprus 1995–96; mem. Akad. der Wissenschaften und der Literatur, Mainz, Bayerische Akad. der Wissenschaften; Pres. Deutsche Shakespeare-Gesellschaft West 1976–88, Vice-Pres. 1988–93; Hon. Vice-Pres. Int. Shakespeare Asscn 1996–. *Publications include:* Die Gebärde in englischen Dichtungen des Mittelalters 1959, Studien zur Dramenform vor Shakespeare 1968, Shakespeare and the German Imagination 1994, Texte und Kontexte der englischen Literatur im Jahr 1595 1995, English and American Studies in German (ed.) 1968–82, Jahrbuch, Deutsche Shakespeare-Gesellschaft West (ed.) 1982–95, Literatur Brockhaus (three vols) (co-ed.) 1988; numerous articles on English literature and drama and on the reception of Shakespeare in Germany. *Address:* Allerseeweg 14, 97204 Höchberg, Germany (home). *Telephone:* (931) 49267 (home). *E-mail:* whabicht@t-online.de.

HABRAKEN, Nicolaas John; Dutch architect; *Professor Emeritus of Architecture, Massachusetts Institute of Technology;* b. 29 Oct. 1928, Bandung, Indonesia; s. of J. W. L. Habraken and J. L. S. Heyting; m. E. Marleen van Hall 1958; one s. one d.; ed Delft Tech. Univ.; architect, Lucas & Niemeyer (architects), Voorburg 1961–65; Dir Stichting Architecten Research, Voorburg 1965–66, Eindhoven 1966–75; Prof. and First Chair. Dept of Architecture, Eindhoven Tech. Univ. 1966–70, Prof. of Architecture 1966–75; Head, Dept of Architecture, MIT, USA 1975–81, Prof. of Architecture 1975–89, Prof. Emer. 1989–; Partner, Infill Systems, Delft 1986–99; Hon. mem. Architectural Inst. of Japan 1994; Kt, Order of the Dutch Lion 2003; Dr hc (Tech. Univ. Eindhoven) 2005; David Roell Prize 1979, King Fahd Award for Design and Research in Islamic Architecture 1985, ACSA Creative Achievement Award 1989, BKVB Nat. Architecture Award 1996, BNA (Dutch Architects' Asscn) Kubus Award of Merit 2003. *Publications include:* Supports: An Alternative to Mass Housing 1962, Transformations of the Site 1983, The Appearance of the Form 1985, The Structure of the Ordinary 1998, Palladio's Children 2005, Conversations with Form (co-author) 2014; research reports and numerous articles and chapters in book. *Address:* 63 Wildernislaan, 7313 BD Apeldoorn, Netherlands (home). *Telephone:* (55) 355-6354 (home). *E-mail:* habraken@xs4all.nl (office). *Website:* www.habraken.com (office); thematicdesign.org (office).

HABTOUR, Abdul Aziz bin-, MEcons, DEcon; Yemeni politician; b. 8 Aug. 1955, Shabwah Governorate; ed Univ. of Aden, Berlin School of Econs and Law, Leipzig Univ.; Pro-Rector, Univ. of Aden 1994–2001; Deputy Minister of Educ. 2001–08; Gov. of Aden 2014–15; apptd Chair., Nat. Salvation Govt (Prime Minister) by al-Houthi Movt (in Houthi-led parallel govt) Oct. 2016–April 2017; mem. Gen. People's Congress. *E-mail:* gpc@y.net.ye (office). *Website:* www.almotamar.net (office).

HACHIGO, Takahiro; Japanese engineer and automotive executive; *President and CEO, Honda Motor Company Limited;* b. 19 May 1959; m.; joined Honda Motor Co. Ltd as chassis design engineer 1982, worked as Asst Chief Engineer for second-generation Odyssey minivan in 1999 and Chief Engineer for second-generation CR-V crossover in 2001, Operating Officer, Honda R&D Co. Ltd 2006–07, Man. Officer 2007–08, Gen. Man., Automobile Purchasing Div. II, Honda Motor Co. Ltd April–June 2008, Operating Officer, Honda Motor Co. Ltd 2008–10, Gen. Man., Purchasing Div. II, Honda Motor Co. Ltd 2010–11, Gen. Man., Suzuka Factory, Production Operations 2011–12, Vice-Pres. and Dir, Honda Motor Europe Ltd April–Sept. 2012, Man. Officer, Honda R&D Co. Ltd 2012–13, also Pres. and Dir, Honda R&D Europe (UK) Ltd 2012–13, Rep. of Devt, Purchasing and Production (China), Honda Motor Co. Ltd 2013–15, also Vice-Pres., Honda Motor (China) Investment Co. Ltd 2013–15, Vice-Pres., Honda Motor Technology (China)

Co. Ltd 2013–15, Man. Officer, Honda Motor Co. Ltd 2013–15, Pres. and CEO 2015–. *Leisure interests:* building model cars and collecting toy cars. *Address:* Honda Motor Co. Ltd, 2-1-1, Minami-Aoyama, Minato-ku, Tokyo 107-8556, Japan (office). *Telephone:* (3) 3423-1111 (office). *Fax:* (3) 5412-1515 (office). *E-mail:* info@honda.com (office). *Website:* www.honda.com (office); world.honda.com (office).

HACKETT, Grant George, BCom, BL, MBA; Australian swimmer; b. 9 May 1980, Southport, Queensland; s. of Neville Hackett and Margaret Hackett; m. Candice Alley 2007; ed Merrimac State High School, Bond Univ., Gold Coast; mem. Miami Swim Club; Olympic Games, Sydney 2000: Gold Medal 1500m freestyle, 4×200m freestyle relay (heat swim); World Championships, Fukuoka 2001: Gold Medal 4×200m freestyle relay (world record), 1500m freestyle (world record time of 14:34.56), Silver Medal 400m freestyle, 800m freestyle; Commonwealth Games, Manchester 2002: Gold Medal 1500m freestyle, 4×200m freestyle relay, 4×100m freestyle relay (heat swim), Silver Medal 800m freestyle, 400m freestyle; Pan Pacific Games 2002: Gold Medal 1500m freestyle, 800m freestyle, 4×200m freestyle relay, 4×100m freestyle relay, Silver Medal 400m freestyle, 200m freestyle; World Championships, Barcelona 2003: Gold Medal 1500m freestyle, 800m freestyle, 4×200m freestyle relay, Silver Medal 400m freestyle; Olympic Games, Athens 2004: Gold Medal 1500m freestyle (Olympic record), Silver Medal 400m freestyle, 4×200m freestyle relay; Telstra Australian Swimming Championships 2005: Gold Medal 1500m freestyle, 800m freestyle, 400m freestyle, 200m freestyle; World Championships, Montreal 2005: Gold Medal 1500m freestyle, 800m freestyle (world record time of 7:38.65), 400m freestyle, Silver Medal 200m freestyle; World Championships, Melbourne 2007: Bronze Medal 400m freestyle; Olympic Games, Beijing 2008: Silver Medal 1500m freestyle (Olympic record, heat swim), Bronze Medal 4×200m freestyle relay; unbeaten at 1500m freestyle 1996–2007, first to swim under 15 minutes for the distance; won his first Nat. Championship 10km Open Water race 2007; Order of Australia Medal 2001; Australian Swimming Male Distance Swimmer of the Year 1998, 2002, 2003, 2004, Australian Sports Medal 2000, Centenary Medal 2000, Goodwill Games Ambassador 2001, Swimmer of the Year 2003, Telstra People's Choice Award 2004, Telstra Swimmer of the Year (with Ian Thorpe) 2004, Australian Export Awards Special Achievement Award 2004, World Swimmer of the Year 2005, Pacific Rim Swimmer of the Year 2005, Telstra Swimmer of the Year 2005, Telstra Swimmers' Swimmer of the Year 2005, Telstra Middle and Distance Swimmer of the Year 2005, 'The Don' Award, Sport Australia Hall of Fame 2005, Telstra Dolphins Australian Swim Team Captain 2005. *Leisure interests:* surfing, fast cars, playing drums and guitar. *Address:* c/o Lisa Stallard, International Quarterback Pty Ltd, 24/76 Doggett Street, Newstead, Queensland 4006, Australia (office). *Telephone:* (7) 3252-2311 (office). *Fax:* (7) 3252-3411 (office). *E-mail:* lisa@iqsport.com.au (office). *Website:* www.iqsport.com.au (office).

HACKETT, James (Jim) Patrick; American business executive; *President and CEO, Ford Motor Company;* b. 22 April 1955, Columbus, Ohio; m. Kathy Hackett; two s.; ed Univ. of Michigan; began career with various sales and man. positions at Procter & Gamble, Detroit 1977–81; CEO Steelcase 1981–2014, Vice Chair. 2014–15; mem. Bd of Dirs Ford Motor Co. 2013–, mem. Audit and Nominating and Governance Cttees, Chair. Ford Smart Mobility LLC 2016–17, Pres. and CEO, Ford Motor Co. 2017–; Interim Dir of Athletics, Univ. of Michigan 2014–16; mem. Bd of Dirs Northwestern Mutual Life, Steelcase Foundation; mem. Exec. Cttee Nat. Center for Arts and Tech.; mem. Bd of Advisors Gerald R. Ford School of Public Policy, Univ. of Michigan Life Sciences Inst.; fmr Pres. Bd of Overseers, Illinois Inst. of Tech. Inst. of Design. *Address:* Ford Motor Company, 1 American Rd, Dearborn, MI 48126, USA (office). *Telephone:* (313) 322-3000 (office). *Fax:* (313) 337-1764 (office). *Website:* corporate.ford.com (office).

HACKING, Ian MacDougall, CC, PhD, FRSC, FBA; Canadian academic; *Professor Emeritus, Collège de France;* b. 18 Feb. 1936, Vancouver, BC; s. of Harold Eldridge Hacking and Margaret Elinore MacDougall; m. 1st Laura Anne Leach 1962; m. 2nd Judith Polsky Baker 1983; one s. two d.; ed Univ. of British Columbia, Univ. of Cambridge, UK; Asst then Assoc. Prof., Univ. of British Columbia 1964–69; Univ. Lecturer in Philosophy, Univ. of Cambridge, UK and Fellow of Peterhouse 1969–74; Prof., then Henry Waldgrave Stuart Prof. of Philosophy, Stanford Univ., USA 1975–82; Prof., Univ. of Toronto 1983–2003, Univ. Prof. 1991–2003, Prof. Emer. 2003–; Prof., Chair of Philosophy and History of Scientific Concepts, Collège de France, Paris 2000–06, Prof. Emer. 2006–; Fellow, American Acad. of Arts and Sciences 1991; Hon. Fellow, Trinity Coll., Cambridge 2000, Peterhouse, Cambridge 2002; Hon. LLD (Univ. of British Columbia) 2001, (McMaster Univ.) 2008, (Toronto) 2010; Hon. PhD (Univ. of Córdoba, Argentina) 2007; Molson Prize, Canada Council 2001, Killam Prize, Canada Council 2002, Holberg Int. Memorial Prize 2009. *Publications include:* Logic of Statistical Inference 1965, Why Does Language Matter to Philosophy? 1975, The Emergence of Probability 1975, Representing and Intervening 1983, The Taming of Chance 1991, Le plus pur nominalisme 1993, Rewriting the Soul: Multiple Personality and the Sciences of Memory 1995, Mad Travelers 1998, The Social Construction of What? 1999, Probability and Inductive Logic 2001, Historical Ontology 2002, Scientific Reason 2009. *Leisure interests:* walking, canoeing. *Address:* Philosophy Department, University of Toronto, 170 St George Street, Toronto, ON M5R 2M8, Canada (office). *E-mail:* ian.hacking@college-de-france.fr (office). *Website:* www.ianhacking.com.

HACKMAN, Gene; American actor and writer; b. 30 Jan. 1930, San Bernardino, Calif.; s. of Eugene Ezra Hackman; m. 1st Fay Maltese 1956 (divorced 1985); m. 2nd Betsy Arakawa; one s. two d.; studied acting at the Pasadena Playhouse; Cecil B. DeMille Award, Golden Globes 2003. *Films include:* Lilith 1964, Hawaii 1966, Banning 1967, Bonnie and Clyde 1967, The Split 1968, Downhill Racer 1969, I Never Sang For My Father 1969, The Gypsy Moths 1969, Marooned 1970, The Hunting Party 1971, The French Connection (Acad. Award for Best Actor, New York Film Critics' Award, Golden Globe Award for Best Actor, BAFTA Award for Best Actor in a Leading Role) 1971, The Poseidon Adventure 1972, The Conversation 1973, Scarecrow 1973, Zandy's Bride 1974, Young Frankenstein 1974, The French Connection II 1975, Lucky Lady 1975, Night Moves 1976, Domino Principle 1977, Superman 1978, Superman II 1980, All Night Long 1980, Target 1985, Twice in a Lifetime 1985, Power 1985, Bat 21, Superman IV 1987, No Way Out 1987, Another Woman 1988, Mississippi Burning (Silver Bear for Best Actor, Berlin Int. . Film Festival) 1988, The Package 1989, The Von Metz Incident 1989, Loose Connections 1989, Full Moon in Blue Water 1989, Postcards from the Edge 1989, Class Action 1989, Loose Canons 1990, Narrow Margin 1990, Necessary Roughness 1991, Company Business 1991, The William Munny Killings 1991, The Unforgiven (Acad. Award for Best Supporting Actor, BAFTA Award for Best Actor in a Supporting Role, Golden Globe for Best Supporting Actor) 1992, The Firm 1992, Geronimo, Wyatt Earp 1994, Crimson Tide, The Quick and the Dead 1995, Get Shorty, Birds of a Feather, Extreme Measures 1996, The Chamber 1996, Absolute Power 1996, Twilight 1998, Enemy of the State 1998, Under Suspicion 2000, Heist 2001, The Royal Tenenbaums (Golden Globe for Best Actor in a Musical or Comedy) 2001, Runaway Jury 2003, Welcome to Mooseport 2004. *Stage plays include:* Children From Their Games 1963, Cass Henderson in Any Wednesday 1964, Poor Richard, 1964, Death and the Maiden 1992. *Television includes:* many guest appearances on US series; also My Father, My Mother, CBS Playhouse 1968 and Shadow on the Land 1971, Under Suspicion 1999. *Publications:* Wake of the Perdido Star (with David Lenihan) 2000, Justice for None (co-author) 2004, Escape from Andersonville (co-author) 2009, Payback at Morning Peak 2011, Pursuit 2013. *Address:* c/o Fred Specktor, Creative Artists Agency, 9830 Wilshire Boulevard, Beverly Hills, CA 90212; c/o Barry Haldeman, 1900 Avenue of the Stars, Suite 2000, Los Angeles, CA 90067, USA.

HACKNEY, Roderick (Rod) Peter, PhD, PRIBA; British architect; *Managing Director, Rod Hackney and Associates Limited;* b. 3 March 1942, Liverpool, England; s. of William Hackney and Rose Hackney (née Morris); m. Christine Thornton 1964; one s.; ed John Bright's Grammar School, Llandudno, School of Architecture, Univ. of Manchester; Job Architect, Expo '67, Montreal, for monorail stations 1967; Housing Architect for Libyan Govt, Tripoli 1967–68; Asst to Arne Jacobsen, working on Kuwait Cen. Bank, Copenhagen 1968–71; est. practice of Rod Hackney Architect, Macclesfield 1972, architectural practices in Birmingham, Leicester, Belfast, Cleator Moor, Workington, Carlisle, Millom, Clitheroe, Manchester, Stirling, Burnley, Chesterfield and Stoke on Trent 1975–88, Man. Dir Rod Hackney and Assocs Ltd; Jt Dir with Tia Kansara, Kansara Hackney Ltd 2009–; Council mem. RIBA, including Vice-Pres. for Public Affairs and Vice-Pres. for Overseas Affairs 1978–84, Pres. 1987–89, mem. of Council 1991–, Vice-Pres. Int. Affairs 1992–94, Hon. Librarian 1998–2001; Council mem. Int. Union of Architects 1981–85, 1991–, Pres. 1987–90; Patron Llandudno Museum and Art Gallery 1988–2000; Pres. Snowdonia Nat. Park Soc. 1987–2003; Pres. North Wales Centre of The Nat. Trust 1990–2009; mem. Editorial Bd, UIA Journal of Architectural Theory and Criticism; Chair. Times/RIBA Community Enterprise Scheme 1985–89, Trustees of Inner City Trust 1986–97, British Architecture Library Trust 1999–2001; Special Prof. in Architecture, Univ. of Nottingham 1987–91; Int. Adviser, Univ. of Manchester School of Architecture Centre for Int. Architectural Studies 1992–2000; adviser on regeneration and inner city problems in Sweden, Italy, UAE, Germany, Denmark, Libya, Canada and USA 1990–; consultant, World Architecture Review Agency 1992–; Adviser, Centre for Human Settlements Int. 1994–, Habitat Centre News Journal, India 1996; Chair. UN Habitat Award 2004–05, UN Habitat Awards, UAE 2004; Jt Chair., with Tia Kansara, Sustainability for Life 2009–; mem. Chartered Inst. of Building 1987–, Asscn of Planning Supervisors 1996–2006; Adviser, UN Int. Council for Caring Communities 1995–, World Habitat Awards, Social Housing Foundation, Coalville, UK 2003–; RIBA Sr Conservation Architect 2011–; Hon. FAIA; Hon. Fellow, Fed. de Colegios de Arquitectos de la República Mexicana, United Architects of the Philippines, Royal Architectural Inst. of Canada, Indian Inst. of Architects, Architectural Soc. of China; Hon. Fellow, nat. architectural soc. in Spain; Hon. DLitt (Keele) 1989; Dept of Environment Good Design in Housing Award 1975, 1980, First Prize, for St Ann's Hospice, Manchester 1976, Prix Int. d'Architecture de l'Institut Nat. du Logement 1979–80, RICS/Times Conservation Award 1980, Civic Trust Award of Commendation 1980, 1981, 1984, Sir Robert Matthews Award (Honourable Mention), Int. Union of Architects 1981, Manchester Soc. of Architects Pres.'s Award 1982, Otis Award 1982, Gold Medal, Bulgarian Inst. of Architects 1983, Gold Medal, Young Architect of the Year, Sofia 1983, Grand Medal of Federación de Colegios de Arquitectos (Mexico) 1986, Commendation, Business Enterprise Award for Housing 1993, Citation for World Habitat Awards 1996, Stone Award 1996. *Plays include:* Good Golly Miss Molly, Augustus Welby Northmore Pugin versus Charles Barry. *Films include:* The Hackney Way, BBC Tomorrow's World – Rod Hackney Community and Sustainability. *Dance includes:* Walking Towards the Hackney Way, It's a Climb, The Architect and the Child, Ganbappe Iwaki with Tia Kansara. *Musicals include:* Good Golly Miss Molly – Sustainability and Community, The Child is the Architect, with G. Uis (Italy). *Radio includes:* panellist on Any Questions (BBC Radio 4), contrib. to Woman's Hour (BBC Radio 2), Today (BBC Radio 4), Newsnight (BBC Radio 4). *Television includes:* Consultant to Chapman Clarke Films' Forever England, Central TV 1995; TV features: Build Yourself a House 1974, Community Architecture (RAI, Italy) 1977, BBC Omnibus 1987, The Hackney Way, Tomorrow's World – Rod Hackney Community and Sustainability Sustainability, The Man Who Led an Entire Street to Take Control (BBC). *Publications include:* Highfield Hall, A Community Project 1982, The Good, the Bad and the Ugly 1990, Good Golly Miss Molly (musical play) 1991. *Leisure interests:* outdoor pursuits, walking, fossils, geology, travelling, ballooning, looking at buildings, talking at conferences, go-carting, painting, writing. *Address:* Rod Hackney and Assocs Ltd, St Peter's House, Windmill Street, Macclesfield, Cheshire, SK11 7HS (office); Kansara Hackney Ltd, St Peter's House, Windmill Street, Macclesfield, Cheshire, SK11 7HS, England (office). *Telephone:* (1625) 431792 (Rod Hackney and Assocs) (office); (1625) 431792 (Kansara Hackney) (office). *E-mail:* roderick.hackney@gmail.com (home); kansarahackney@gmail.com (home). *Website:* www.kansarahackney.com (office).

HACON, Christopher, BA, MS, PhD; American (b. British) mathematician and academic; *Distinguished Professor of Mathematics, University of Utah;* b. 14 Feb. 1970, Manchester; m.; two s. one d.; ed Univ. of Pisa, Italy, Univ. of California, Los Angeles; Research Fellowship, CNR 1998; Math. Instructor, Univ. of Utah 1998–2000, Asst Prof. 2002–05, Assoc. Prof. 2005–08, Prof. 2008–10, Distinguished Prof. 2010–, McMinn Presidential Endowed Chair in Mathematics 2017–; Asst Prof., Univ. of California, Riverside 2000–02; Sloan Fellowship 2003, American Math. Soc. Centennial Fellowship 2006; Clay Research Award, Clay Math. Inst. 2007, Cole Prize in Algebra (jtly), American Math. Soc. 2009, Antonio Feltrinelli Prize in Math., Mechanics, and Applications 2011, Moore Prize, American Math.

Soc. 2015, Breakthrough Prize in Mathematics 2017. *Publications:* more than 40 papers in professional journals. *Address:* JWB 233, Department of Mathematics, University of Utah, 155 South 1400 East, Salt Lake City, UT 84112-0090, USA (office). *Telephone:* (801) 581-7429 (office). *Fax:* (801) 581-4148 (office). *E-mail:* hacon@math.utah.edu (office). *Website:* www.math.utah.edu (office).

HADAWAL, Khan Afzal, BA, LLB, MA, MSc; Afghan banker; *First Deputy Governor, Da Afghanistan Bank;* ed Int. Islamic Univ., Islamabad, Univ. Coll. London, UK; Project Devt Officer, Sanayee Devt Foundation, Kabul June–Aug. 2001; Legal Consultant, Islamic Foundation for Rehabilitation of Afghanistan Jan.–March 2002; Legal Adviser, Counter Narcotic Directorate, Nat. Security Council 2002; Head of Licensing and Regulations, Bearing Point Inc., USAID Da Afghanistan Bank (Cen. Bank) in Reformation Project 2002–03, Head of Legis. and Regulatory Section, Bearing Point Inc., USAID Da Afghanistan Bank Reformation Project 2003–05, Adviser to Gov. and Sec.-Gen. Supreme Council of Da Afghanistan Bank 2005–09, Acting Gov. Da Afghanistan Bank –2009, First Deputy Gov. 2011–; Pres. and CEO Bank-e-Millie Afghan 2009–11; participated in numerous nat. and int. confs and headed several dels of Afghanistan. *Achievements include:* played key role in establishment of Financial Intelligent Unit in Afghanistan and in developing the legal framework for the country's banking sector. *Address:* Da Afghanistan Bank, Ibne Sina Wat, Kabul, Afghanistan (office). *Telephone:* (20) 2100302 (office). *Fax:* (20) 2100305 (office). *E-mail:* info@centralbank.gov.af (office); khan.afzal@centralbank.gov.af (office). *Website:* www.centralbank.gov.af (office).

HADDAD-ADEL, Gholam-Ali, MSc, PhD; Iranian politician and institute director; *Director, Academy of Persian Language and Literature;* b. 4 May 1945, Tehran; m.; four c.; ed Univs of Tehran and Shiraz; Prof. of Literature and Philosophy, Univ. of Tehran; fmr Deputy Minister of Educ. and Training, of Culture and Islamic Guidance; fmr Exec. Dir Islamic Encyclopaedia Foundation; Dir Acad. of Persian Language and Literature 1995–2004, 2008–; mem. Majilis-e-Shura-e Islami (Parl.) for Tehran 2004–16, Speaker, Majilis-e-Shura-e Islami 2004–08; mem. Supreme Cultural Revolutionary Council, Iranian Acad. of Persian Language and Literature, Expediency Discernment Council; helped start nat. scientific olympiads in Iran. *Publications include:* Farhang-e Berahnegi va Berahnegi-e Farhangi 1981, Daaneshnaame-ye Jahaan-e Eslam 1996–2001, Haj: Namaaz-e Bozorg 2000, Still Again (poetry) 2016. *E-mail:* president@persianacademy.ir. *Website:* www.persianacademy.ir.

HADDOCK, Michael Kenneth; British diplomatist; m. Irene Haddock; one s. one d.; Research Asst, Research Dept, FCO 1973–78, Third Sec. (Comprehensive Test Ban Del.), Geneva 1978–80, Third Sec. (Commercial), Moscow 1981–83, Third Sec. (Chancery), Kuwait 1983–84, language training (Arabic), SOAS 1984–86, Second Sec. and Vice-Consul (Head of Commercial Section), Damascus 1986–88, Second Sec. (Commercial), Prague 1988–91, First Sec. (Head of Commercial Section), Abu Dhabi 1991–94, S Asian Dept, FCO 1994–97, First Sec. (Head of Press and Public Affairs), Moscow 1997–2001, Whitehall Liaison Dept, FCO 2001–03, Deputy Head of WMD (Weapons of Mass Destruction) Review Unit 2004, Head of Int. Orgs Bill Unit 2004–05, Amb. to Belarus 2007–08.

HADDON, Mark, MSc; British writer and illustrator; b. 26 Sept. 1962, Northampton; m. Sos Eltis; two s.; ed Merton Coll., Oxford, Edinburgh Univ.; positions at Mencap and other charity orgs; illustrator and cartoonist; painter; television work. *Screenplays include:* Microsoap (Royal Television Soc. Best Children's Drama) 1998, episodes of Starstreet, Fungus and Bogeyman (adaptation). *Publications include:* fiction: Gilbert's Gobstopper 1988, A Narrow Escape for Princess Sharon 1989, Toni and the Tomato Soup 1989, Agent Z Meets the Masked Crusader 1993, Gridzbi Spudvetch! 1993, In the Garden 1994, On Holiday (aka On Vacation) 1994, At Home 1994, At Playgroup 1994, Titch Johnson 1994, Agent Z Goes Wild 1994, Agent Z and the Penguin from Mars 1995, Real Porky Philips 1995, The Sea of Tranquillity 1996, Secret Agent Handbook 1999, Ocean Star Express 2001, Agent Z and the Killer Bananas 2001, The Ice Bear's Cave 2002, The Curious Incident of the Dog in the Night Time (Booktrust Teenage Prize 2003, Guardian Children's Fiction Prize 2003, South Bank Show Best Book Prize 2004, Whitbread Best Novel and Book of the Year 2004, Commonwealth Writers Prize for best first book 2004, Soc. of Authors McKitterick Prize 2004, WHSmith Children's Book of the Year 2004, Waterstone's Literary Fiction award 2004) 2003, A Spot of Bother 2006, Boom! 2009, The Red House 2012, The Pier Falls: And Other Stories 2016; poetry: The Talking Horse and the Sad Girl and the Village Under the Sea 2005. *Address:* c/o Clare Alexander, Aitken Alexander Associated Ltd, 291 Gray's Inn Road, Kings Cross, London, WC1X 8QJ, England (office); 4 Farndon Road, Oxford, OX2 6RS, England. *Telephone:* (20) 7373-8672 (office). *E-mail:* reception@aitkenalexander.co.uk (office). *Website:* www.literature.britishcouncil.org (office); www.markhaddon.com.

HADEMINE, Yahya Ould, BEng; Mauritanian engineer and politician; *Minister of Defence;* b. 31 Dec. 1953, Timbedra; m.; four c.; ed École polytechnique de Montréal, Canada; Head of Dept, Société nationale industrielle et minière (SNIM, state-owned steel mill) 1979–85, Head of Procurement Dept 1985–88, Dir-Gen. SAFA (subsidiary steel co.) 1989–2003, Dir-Gen. ATTM (transport, cleaning and maintenance co.) 2003–10; Minister of Equipment and Transport 2010–14, Prime Minister 2014–18 (resgnd), Minister of Defence 2019–; mem. Union pour la République (UPR). *Website:* www.primature.gov.mr (office).

HADI, Field Marshal Abd ar-Rabbuh Mansur al-; Yemeni politician, army officer and head of state; *President;* b. 1 Sept. 1945, Al-Wadhee'a Region, Governorate of Abyan; m.; three s. two d.; ed Supreme Acad. of Nasser, Egypt, Sandhurst Mil. Acad., UK, Frunze Acad., fmr USSR; mem. staff, Armoured Brigades, Mil. Acad.; Dir of Combat Training, of Supply and Provisions; Deputy Chief of Staff, Supply and Provisions; apptd Adviser to Presidential Council 1990; Minister of Defence May–Oct. 1994; Vice-Pres. 1994–2012, Acting Pres. 4 June–23 Sept. 2011, 23 Nov. 2011–24 Feb. 2012, Pres. of Yemen 25 Feb. 2012–; rank of Gen. 1994, Lt-Gen. 1997, later Field Marshal; mem. Gen. People's Congress, fmr Vice-Chair.; Order of the First Grade Badge 1995; numerous medals including Medal of Honour of Mil. Service 1980. *Leisure interests:* reading, current affairs, public folklore, local and classical music, swimming.

HADLEE, Sir Richard John, Kt, MBE; New Zealand fmr professional cricketer; *Director, New Zealand Cricket;* b. 3 July 1951, St Albans, Christchurch; s. of W. A. Hadlee (New Zealand cricketer); m. Dianne Hadlee; ed Christchurch Boys High School; middle-order left-hand batsman, right-arm fast-medium bowler; played for Canterbury 1971–72 to 1988–89, NZ 1972–90, Nottinghamshire 1978–87, Tasmania 1979–80; played in 86 Tests 1972/73–90, scoring 3,124 runs (average 27.16, highest score 151 not out) and taking then world record 431 wickets (average 22.29); first to take 400 Test wickets (at Christchurch in Feb. 1990 in his 79th Test); took five or more wickets in an innings a record 36 times in Tests; highest Test score 151 against Sri Lanka, Colombo 1987; best Test bowling performance 9/52 against Australia, Brisbane 1985–86; toured England 1973, 1978, 1983, 1986, 1990; scored 12,052 First-class runs (average 31.71, highest score 210 not out) including 14 hundreds, and took 1,490 wickets, including five or more in an innings 102 times; achieved Double (1,179 runs and 117 wickets) 1984; Level III Coach, Christchurch; NZ Cricket (NZC) Selection Man. 2000–08, Chair. of Selectors, NZC 2000–08, Life mem. NZC 2010, Dir 2013–; NZC World Cup Project Man. for 2007 World Cup in West Indies; consultant, APL (American Premier Cricket League) 2009; Public Relations Amb. for Bank of New Zealand 1991–2007; Brand Amb. for Christchurch Int. Airport, Ecoglo, Shelter Box, Pingar, Domain Consulting, FernRidge; Founder and Patron The Sir Richard Hadlee Sports Trust 1990; Patron, Kidz Zipper, India New Zealand Business Council 2009–; int. after-dinner, seminar and conf. speaker; Hon. DLitt (Nottingham) 2008; Wisden Cricketer of the Year 1982, Winner, Winsor Cup on 13 occasions (including 12 consecutive years) for the most meritorious bowling performance of the season, NZ Sportsperson of the Year (Supreme Award) 1980, 1986, NZ Sportsman of the Year 1987, NZ Sportsman of the last 25 years (shared with Sir John Walker) 1987, NZ Sportsperson of the Decade 1989, chosen by Wisden as second greatest Test bowler of all time 2002, Bert Sutcliffe Medal for Services to New Zealand Cricket 2008, commemorated as one of the Twelve Local Heroes, and a bronze bust of him unveiled outside Christchurch Arts Centre 2009, inducted into ICC (Int. Cricket Council) Cricket Hall of Fame 2009, 12th Best Cricketer of all time in ESPN Legends Of Cricket, inducted into ICC/FICA World Cricket Hall of Fame 2009, Altiora Peto Medal, High School Old Boys Asscn (Christchurch Boys High School) 2009, inducted as a Canterbury Sporting Legend 2010. *Achievement:* aged 56, played in NZ Cricket Beach team that defeated England in the final against Australia 2008. *Publications include:* Hadlee on Cricket – The Essentials of the Game 1982, Rhythm and Swing (autobiog.) 1989, Soft Deliveries – A Century of Cricket Years 1996, Hard Knocks – A Selection of Cricket Capers 1997, Caught Out – Tales from The Pavilion 1998, Cricket – The Essentials of the Game 2000, Howzat! – Hadlee's Tales from the Boundary 2002, Changing Pace – A Memoir 2009. *Leisure interests:* movies, golf, gardening. *Address:* Box 78-061, Pegasus 7648, North Canterbury 7648, New Zealand (office). *Telephone:* (3) 920-0220 (office). *Fax:* (3) 920-0220 (office). *E-mail:* hadleerj@clear.net.nz (office). *Website:* www.hadlee.co.nz (office); www.hadlee.org.nz (office).

HADLEY, Stephen John, BA, JD; American lawyer and fmr government official; *Principal, RiceHadleyGates LLC;* b. 13 Feb. 1947, Toledo, Ohio; m. Ann Simon; two d.; ed Cornell Univ., Yale Law School; worked as an analyst for Comptroller, US Dept of Defense 1972–74; mem. Nat. Security Council staff 1974–77; Pnr, Shea and Gardner (law firm), Washington, DC 1977–2001; fmr Prin. The Scowcroft Group Inc. (consulting firm), Washington, DC; Counsel, Tower Comm. Special Review Bd 1986–87; Asst US Sec. of Defense for Int. Security Policy 1989–93; sr foreign policy and defence policy adviser to George W. Bush during his first presidential campaign, Deputy Nat. Security Advisor 2001–05, Nat. Security Advisor 2005–09; Co-f. and Prin. RiceHadley Group (consulting firm, now RiceHadleyGates LLC) 2009–; Sr Advisor, Int. Affairs, United States Inst. of Peace 2009, Chair. Bd of Dirs 2014–; mem. Bd of Dirs Raytheon 2009–, Atlantic Council of US, Bessemer Group Inc.; mem. Bd of Mans., John Hopkins Univ. Applied Physics Lab.; Chair. Advisory Bd, RAND Centre for Middle East Public Policy. *E-mail:* info@ricehadleygates.com (office). *Website:* www.ricehadleygates.com (office).

HAEFLIGER, Andreas; Swiss pianist; b. Berlin, Germany; m. Marina Piccinini; ed Juilliard School, USA, studied with Herbert Stessin; has appeared with numerous orchestras in N America, Europe and Japan; numerous recital appearances including Great Performers Series, Lincoln Center, New York, Wigmore Hall, London and in Germany, Austria, France and Italy; has performed regularly at BBC Proms, London; performs in USA with Takacs String Quartet; performs frequently with baritone Matthias Goerner; twice won Gina Bachauer Memorial Scholarship, Preis der Deutschen Schallplattenkritik (for recording of Schubert's Goethe Lieder). *Recordings include:* Mozart Piano Sonatas, Schumann's Davidsbündlertanze and Fantasiestücke, Schubert's Impromptus, music by Sofia Gubaidulina, Schubert's Goethe Lieder (with Matthias Goerne), Perspectives I–IV (including works by Schubert, Adès, Mozart and Beethoven), Schubert: Erlkönig (Int. Classical Music Award for Vocal Recital 2014). *Address:* c/o Susie McLeod, Intermusica Artists Management Ltd, Crystal Wharf, 36 Graham Street, London, N1 8GJ, England (office). *Telephone:* (20) 7608-9920 (office). *Fax:* (20) 7490-3263 (office). *E-mail:* smcleod@intermusica.co.uk (office). *Website:* www.andreashaefliger.com (office).

HÆKKERUP, Nick, LLM, PhD; Danish politician; *Minister for Health and Prevention;* b. 3 April 1968, Fredensborg; s. of Klaus Hækkerup and Irene Hækkerup; m. Petra Freisleben Hækkerup; four c.; ed Univ. of Copenhagen; mil. service, Auderød Naval Coll.; Head of Section, Nat. Income Tax Tribunal 1994; mem. Hillerød Town Council 1994–2007, Mayor of Hillerød 2000–07; Lecturer, Univ. of Copenhagen 1998–2000; mem. Folketing (Parl.) for Nordsjællands Storkreds constituency 2007–, mem. Finance Cttee 2007–11, Fiscal Affairs Cttee 2007–11, Standing Orders Cttee 2009–10, Nat. Tax Bd 2007–09; Minister of Defence 2011–13, Minister for European Affairs 2013–14, Minister for Health and Prevention 2014–; Chair. Man. Cttee Danish Atlantic Treaty Asscn 2004–09; mem. Socialdemokraterne (Social Democrats), Vice-Chair. 2005–. *Publications include:* Udvikling i EU siden 1992 på de områder, der er omfattet af de danske forbehold (co-author) 2000, Controls and Sanctions in the EU Law 2001. *Address:* Ministry of Health, Holbergsgade 6, 1057 Copenhagen K, Denmark (office). *Telephone:* 72-26-90-00 (office). *Fax:* 72-26-90-01 (office). *E-mail:* sum@sum.dk (office). *Website:* www.sum.dk (office).

HAENNI, Tatjana; Swiss sports organization executive; Responsible Women's Football, Union of European Football Asscns (UEFA) 1994–98; Ed. Sat.1 1998–99; Man. Dir of Women's Football, FIFA 2001–07, Head of Women's Competitions

2008–17; Chair. FC Zürich Frauen. *Address:* FC Zürich Frauen, PO Box 3375, 8021 Zurich, Switzerland (office). *Telephone:* (43) 5211212 (FC Zürich Frauen) (office). *Fax:* (43) 5211213 (FC Zürich Frauen) (office). *E-mail:* haenni@fcz-frauen.ch (office). *Website:* www.fcz.ch (office).

HAFEN, Ernst, PhD; Swiss geneticist and academic; *Professor, Institute of Molecular Systems Biology, Eidgenössische Technische Hochschule (ETH) Zürich;* b. 1956, St Gallen; ed Univ. of Basel; Research Asst, Biocenter Basel 1983; Postdoctoral Research Asst, Dept of Biochemistry, Univ. of California, Berkeley, USA 1984–86; Asst Prof. for Developmental Genetics, Univ. of Zürich 1987–94, Assoc. Prof. 1994–97, Full Prof. 1997–2005, Dir Zoological Inst. 2005; Dir ETH Zürich 2005–06, now Prof. Inst. of Molecular Systems Biology; fmr mem. Nat. Research Council; fmr rep. profs at Council of Univ. of Zürich; mem. editorial bds of several major journals, including The EMBO Journal; helped develop jt centres of ETH and Univ. of Zürich, including SystemsX, Life Science Zurich, Life Science Learning Center Zürich; Co-founder and Scientific Advisor, The Genetics Co.; Ernst Jung Prize for Medicine, Jung-Stiftung für Wissenschaft und Forschung (co-recipient) 2005. *Publications:* numerous scientific papers in professional journals on developmental and cell biology. *Address:* Institute for Molecular Systems Biology, ETH Zürich, Wolfgang-Pauli-Strasse 16, 8093 Zürich, Switzerland (office). *Telephone:* (44) 633-36-88 (office). *Fax:* (44) 633-10-51 (office); (44) 633-11-41 (office). *E-mail:* hafen@imsb.biol.ethz.ch (office); ernst.hafen@imsb.biol.ethz.ch (office). *Website:* www.zool.uzh.ch (office).

HAFEZ, Suleiman al-, BA; Jordanian economist and politician; *Chairman, Royal Jordanian Airlines;* b. 1941; ed Beirut Arab Univ. (br. of Alexandria Univ., Egypt); fmr Minister of Posts and Communications, Minister of Energy 2010–12, Minister of Finance 2012–13; Chief Commr Electricity Regulatory Comm.; Chair. Royal Jordanian Airlines 2014–; mem. Bd of Dirs of several orgs, including Jordan Electricity Authority, Civil Aviation Authority, Jordan Phosphate Mines Co., Jordan Cement Factories, Agricultural Credit Corpn. *Address:* Royal Jordanian Airlines, POBox 302, Amman 11118, Jordan (office). *Website:* www.rj.com (office).

HAFFAR AL-HASSAN, Raya, BBA, MBA; Lebanese politician; b. 1967; m.; three c.; ed American Univ. of Beirut, George Washington Univ., USA; Reform Implementation Specialist, UNDP/Ministry of Finance 1993–98; Adviser to Minister of Economy and Trade 2000–03; Project Director/Manager for EU and UNDP reform projects, Presidency of the Council of Ministers 2003–09; Minister of Finance 2009–11; mem. Bd of Dirs BankMed 2011–; mem. March 14 Alliance, Future Movt.

HÁFOSS, Kristina, Cand.jur; Faroese economist, lawyer and politician; *Minister of Finance;* b. 26 June 1975; d. of John P. Danielsen and Anna Helena Danielsen (neé Zachariasen); m. Ronnie Háfoss; four c.; ed Univ. of Copenhagen, Denmark; worked at Danish Ministry of Foreign Affairs 1998–99, Ministry of Finance 1999–2000; worked at Prime Minister's Office, Faroe Islands summer 1999 and 2000; Econ. Adviser, Action Plan for Útoyggjar Islands 2000–01; Deputy Dir, Suðurstreymoyar Tjóðveldisfelag (regional publisher) 2001–02; mem. Løgting (parl.) for Suðurstreymoy constituency 2002–04, 2011–, mem. Finance Cttee 2002–04 (Deputy Chair. 2011–15); Minister of Culture Feb.–Aug. 2008, of Finance 2015–; Economist, Landsbanki Føroya 2004–05; Project Man. and Investment Adviser, Føroya Banki 2006; Head of Dept, Tryggingarfelagið Føroyar (insurance co.) 2007. *Address:* Ministry of Finance, Kvíggjartún 1, POB 2039, 165 Argir, Faroe Islands (office). *Telephone:* 352020 (office). *E-mail:* fmr@fmr.fo (office). *Website:* www.fmr.fo (office); kristinahafoss.fo.

HAFTAR, Gen. Khalifa; Libyan military commander; *Chief of Staff, Libyan National Army;* b. 1943, Ajdabiya; ed Benghazi Mil. Acad., mil. training in Soviet Union and Egypt; served in Libyan army under Mu'ammar al-Gaddafi, took part in coup which brought Gaddafi to power in 1969; mem. Revolutionary Command Council (est. to govern Libya following 1969 coup); commanded Libyan contingent against Israel in Yom Kippur War 1973; Chief officer in command of mil. forces in Chad during Chadian–Libyan conflict 1986 until being taken prisoner of war 1987; during imprisonment formed a group with fellow officers hoping to overthrow Gaddafi; released around 1990 in a deal with US govt, spent two decades in exile in USA; returned to Libya to support Libyan Civil War 2011, becoming commdr of ground forces with rank of Lt-Gen. 2011, rank of Gen. 2015; apptd Chief of Staff of Libyan Nat. Army 2015. *Address:* General Headquarters, Libyan National Army, Tobruk, Libya (office).

HAGAN, Kay Ruthven, BA, JD; American lawyer and politician; b. 26 March 1953, Shelby, N Carolina; m. Charles T. (Chip) Hagan, III; one s. two d.; ed Florida State Univ., Wake Forest Univ.; served in pvt. law practice as attorney for North Carolina Nat. Bank (now Bank of America) 1978–88; mem. N Carolina State Senate 1999–2003, Co-Chair. Pensions, Retirement and Aging Cttee, mem. Cttees on Appropriations and Base Budget, on Commerce, Small Business and Entrepreneurship, on Educ., on Finance, on Health Care; Senator from N Carolina 2009–15; Democrat.

HAGEDORN, Jürgen, Dr rer. nat; German academic; *Professor Emeritus of Geography, University of Göttingen;* b. 10 March 1933, Hankensbüttel; s. of Ernst Hagedorn and Dorothea Schulze; m. Ingeborg A. Carl 1965; one d.; ed Hermann-Billung-Gymnasium, Celle, Tech. Hochschule Hanover and Univ. of Göttingen; Asst Lecturer, Univ. of Göttingen 1962–69, Dozent 1969–70, Prof. 1970–72, Prof. of Geography and Dir Inst. of Geography 1972–2001, now Prof. Emer.; mem. Göttingen Acad., Akad. Leopoldina. *Publications:* Geomorphologie des Uelzener Beckens 1964, Geomorphologie griechischer Hochgebirge 1969, Late Quaternary and Present-Day Fluvial Processes in Central Europe (ed.) 1995. *Address:* Jupiterweg 1, 37077 Göttingen, Germany (home). *Telephone:* (551) 21323 (home). *E-mail:* jhagedo@gwdg.de (office); a.j.hagedorn@arcor.de (home).

HAGÈGE, Claude, LèsL, TH; French linguist, author and academic; b. 1 Jan. 1936, Carthage, Tunisia; s. of Edmond Hagège and Liliane Taïeb-Hagège; ed Lycée Carnot, Tunisia, Lycée Louis-le-Grand, Ecole Normale Supérieure, Ecole Nationale des Langues Orientales, Harvard Univ. and Massachusetts Inst. of Tech., USA; teacher, Lycée Carnot, Tunis 1959–61, Lycées Victor Duruy et Saint-Louis, Paris 1963–66; Prof. of Linguistics, Univ. of Poitiers 1971–87; Chief of Confs, Univ. of Paris XII Val-de-Marne 1971–74, Univ. of Paris IV 1976–78, Univ. of Paris III 1977–78; Dir of Linguistic Studies, Ecole Pratique des Hautes Etudes 1977; Prof., Collège de France 1988–96, now Hon. Prof.; Hon. Dir of Studies, Ecole Pratique des Hautes Etudes, Paris; Officier, Ordre des Palmes académiques 1995, Chevalier, Ordre des Arts et des Lettres 1995, Officier, Légion d'honneur 2005; Prix Volney, Acad. des Inscriptions et Belles-Lettres 1981, CNRS Médaille d'or 1995, Prix du Mot d'or des langues 2003. *Publications include:* La Structure des langues 1982, L'Homme de paroles (English trans.: The Dialogic Species 1990) (Grand Prix de l'Essai, Soc. des Gens de Lettres 1986, Prix de l'Académie Française 1986) 1985, Le Français et les siècles 1987, Le Souffle de la langue 1992, The Language Builder, An Essay on the Human Signature in Linguistic Morphogenesis 1993, L'Enfant aux deux langues 1996, Le Français, histoire d'un combat 1996, Halte à la mort des langues 2001 (English trans.: On the Death and Life of Languages 2009), Combat pour le français 2006, Dictionnaire amoureux des langues 2009, Contre la pensée unique 2012, Les religions, la parole, la violence 2017. *Fax:* 1-44-27-13-29 (home). *E-mail:* claude-hagege@wanadoo.fr (home). *Website:* www.college-de-france.fr/site/claude-hagege/biographie.htm; claude.hagege.free.fr.

HAGEL, Charles (Chuck) T., BA; American politician; b. 4 Oct. 1946, North Platte, Neb.; m. Lilibet Hagel (née Ziller); one s. one d.; ed Brown Inst. of Radio and Television, Univ. of Nebraska at Omaha; served in US Army 1967–68; Chief of Staff to Neb. Congressman John Y. McCollister; Deputy Admin. Virginia 1981–82; Pres. and CEO World United Service Org. 1987–90; Pres. McCarthy & Co. 1991–96; Senator from Nebraska 1996–2009, mem. numerous Senate cttees including Chair. Senate Sub-cttee on Int. Econ. Policy, Export and Trade Promotion; Distinguished Prof. in the Practice of Nat. Governance, Edmund A. Walsh School of Foreign Service, Georgetown Univ. 2009–13; Prof., Univ. of Nebraska at Omaha 2009–13; Chair. Atlantic Council 2009–13; Sec. of Defense 2013–14 (resgnd); Co-Chair. Pres.'s Intelligence Advisory Bd; Founder-Dir Vanguard Cellular Systems Inc.; fmr mem. Bd of Dirs Public Broadcasting Service (PBS), Chevron Corpn, Zurich Holding Co. of America; fmr mem. Advisory Bd, Deutsche Bank Americas, Corsair Capital, M.I.C. Industries, Kaseman LLC; fmr Sr Advisor, McCarthy Capital Corpn (investment bank); mem. American Legion, Veterans of Foreign Wars; Trustee, Omaha Chamber of Commerce; Republican; numerous awards including Cordell Hull Award 2003, Award for Distinguished Int. Leadership, Atlantic Council 2004, Woodrow Wilson Int. Center for Scholars Public Service Award 2005, Marlin Fitzwater Excellence in Public Communication Award 2005, US Chamber of Commerce 'Spirit of Enterprise' Award 2007, Millard E. Tydings Award for Courage and Leadership in American Politics, Univ. of Maryland 2008, Aspen Strategy Group Leadership Award 2008. *Publication:* America: Our Next Chapter 2008. *Address:* c/o Office of the Secretary of Defense, Department of Defense, 1400 Defense Pentagon, Washington, DC 20301-1400, USA.

HAGEN, Carl I.; Norwegian politician; b. 6 May 1944, Oslo; s. of Ragnar Hagen and Gerd Gamborg Hagen; m. 1st Nina Aamodt 1970; m. 2nd Eli Engum Hagen 1983; one s. one d.; ed Inst. of Marketing, London; CEO Tate and Lyle 1970–74; Sec., Anders Lange Party 1973–74; mem. Stortinget (Parl.) 1974–77, 1981–2009, Deputy Speaker 2005–09; Communication Consultant, Burson-Marsteller 2009–10; unsuccessful cand. for Mayor of Oslo 2011; consultant, Finansanalyse 1977–79; consultant on econ. policy 1979–81; Leader of Fremskrittspartiet (Progress Party) and Parl. Group 1978–2006; mem. Bd British Business Forum 1972, Norske Agenters Landsforbund 1972–74. *Publication:* Ærlighet Varer Lengst (autobiog.) 1984, Ærlig talt 2007, Klar tale 2010. *Leisure interests:* tennis, family, golf. *Address:* c/o Fremskrittspartiet (Progress Party), Karl Johans gt. 25, 0159 Oslo, Norway.

HAGERTY, William (Bill), IV, BA, JD; American business executive and diplomatist; *Ambassador to Japan;* b. 14 Aug. 1959, Nashville, Tennessee; m. Chrissy Hagerty; four c.; ed Vanderbilt Univ., Vanderbilt Univ. Law School; Int. Man. Consultant, Boston Consulting Group (global man. consultancy) 1984–91; White House Fellow 1991–93; Private Equity Investor, Trident Capital LP 1993–94; Co-Founder and Man. Dir, Hagerty Peterson & Co. (private equity investment firm) 1997–2017; mem. Advisory Bd Hall Capital (private investment co.) 2016–17; mem. Gov.'s Cabinet and Commr, Dept of Econ. and Community Devt, State of Tenn. 2011–15; Organizer, Nashville NLS Organizing Cttee 2016–17; Dir of Presidential Appointments for Trump Presidential Transition Team 2016–17; Amb. to Japan 2017–; mem. Bd of Dirs Pinnacle Bank 2015–17, RenaissanceRe 2015–17; Dir and mem. Audit Cttee, Ryman Hospitality Properties 2016–17; Republican. *Address:* Embassy of the USA, 1-10-5, Akasaka, Minato-ku, Tokyo, 107-8420, Japan (office). *Telephone:* (3) 3224-5000 (office). *Fax:* (3) 3505-1862 (office). *Website:* tokyo.usembassy.gov (office).

HAGGIS, Paul; Canadian screenwriter, film director and film producer; b. 10 March 1953, London, Ont.; s. of Ted Haggis and Mary Haggis; m. 1st Deborah Rennard; m. 2nd Diane Christine Gettas; four c.; ed Fanshawe Coll.; directed and wrote plays for parents' Gallery Theatre, London, Ontario 1970s; co-founder Artists for Peace and Justice; Chair. of Film Programs, Canadian Film Centre, Toronto 2011–; mem. Bd of Dirs Environmental Media Assn, Pres.'s Council of Defenders of Wildlife; mem. Advisory Bd Centre for the Advancement of Non-Violence; Valentine Davies Award, Writers' Guild of America 2001. *Films include:* Red Hot (screenwriter) 1993, Million Dollar Baby (screenwriter and producer) 2004, Crash (writer, dir and producer) (Acad. Award for Best Film 2006, Humanitas Prize 2006) 2005, Last Kiss (screenwriter) 2006, Flags of Our Fathers (screenwriter) 2006, Casino Royale (screenwriter) 2006, Letters from Iwo Jima (story) 2006, In the Valley of Elah (screenwriter, producer and dir) 2007, Quantum of Solace (writer) 2008, Next Three Days (screenwriter, producer and dir) 2010. *Television includes:* Due South (exec. producer and writer), creator Walker, Texas Ranger, Family Law (exec. producer and writer), EZ Streets (exec. producer and writer), creator The Black Donnellys 2007, Speechless 2008, Crash (exec. producer) 2008–09; writer numerous episodes in series. *Address:* c/o CAA, 9830 Wilshire Blvd., Beverly Hills, CA 90212-1825, USA.

HÄGGLUND, Gen. (retd) Gustav, MS (Pol.Sc.); Finnish army officer (retd); *Chancellor, The Order of the Cross of Liberty;* b. 6 Sept. 1938, Wyborg; m. Ritva Ekström; one s. two d.; ed Finnish Mil. Acad., Univ. of Helsinki, Finnish War Coll., Command and General Staff Coll., USA; nat. mil. service 1957–58; commanded Finnish Bn UNEF II, Sinai 1978–79, Nyland Brigade, Finland 1984–85, UNDOF, Golan Heights 1985–86, UN Interim Force in Lebanon (UNIFIL), Lebanon 1986–88, South East Mil. Area Finland 1988–90; Chief of Defence Staff 1990–94,

Chief of Defence 1994–2001; Chair. EU Mil. Cttee, Brussels 2001–04; US Army Command and Gen. Staff Coll. 1972–73; currently Chancellor, The Order of the Cross of Liberty; Fellow, Harvard Univ. Center for Int. Affairs 1981–82; Legion of Merit (twice); Commdr, Légion d'honneur, and about 50 others. *Publications include:* Peace-making in the Finnish Winter War 1969, Northern Europe in Strategic Perspective 1974, US Strategy for Europe 1974, Parliamentary Defence Committees in Finland 1981, Modern US Cruise Missiles, an Evaluation 1982, Peace-keeping in a Modern War Zone 1990, Defence of Finland 2001, European Defence 2004, The Lion and the Dove (autobiog.) 2006, We Were Young Soldiers 2009, The Lucky Hunter 2010, Colorful Generals 2011, An Utopia of Peace 2014. *Leisure interests:* hunting, shooting, roaming in the wilderness. *Address:* Ylänkötie 3N, 00650 Helsinki, Finland (home). *Telephone:* (9) 7242192 (office).

HAGIWARA, Toshitaka, LLM; Japanese business executive; *Senior Adviser, Komatsu Ltd;* b. Tokyo; ed Waseda Univ.; joined Komatsu Ltd 1969, mem. Bd of Dirs 1990–2007, Man. Dir 1995–97, Exec. Man. Dir 1997–99, Rep. Dir 1999–2007, Exec. Vice-Pres. 1999–2003, Chair. 2003–07, Sr Adviser 2007–; Pres. Financial Accounting Standards Foundation; Chair. Int. Financial Reporting Standards Council; Chair. Jt Cttee on Econ. Regulation, Nippon Keidanren; Co-Chair. Japan Business Fed.'s Econ. Law Cttee; mem. Bd of Dirs Yamato Holdings Co. Ltd 2009–, Zensho Holdings Co. Ltd 2010–; mem. Legislative Council, Ministry of Justice; Integrity Award 2010. *Address:* Komatsu Ltd, 2-3-6 Akasaka, Minato-ku, Tokyo 107-8414, Japan (office). *Website:* www.komatsu.com (office).

HAGUE OF RICHMOND, Baron (Life Peer), cr. 2015, of Richmond in the County of Yorkshire; **Rt Hon. William Jefferson Hague,** PC, MA, MBA, FRSL; British fmr politician and writer; b. 26 March 1961, Rotherham, Yorks., England; s. of Timothy N. Hague and Stella Hague; m. Ffion Jenkins 1997; ed Wath-upon-Dearne Comprehensive School, Magdalen Coll. Oxford, Institut Européen d'Admin des Affaires (INSEAD), France; made nat. news aged 16 by speaking at Conservative Party's nat. conf. 1977; Pres. Oxford Union 1981; man. consultant, McKinsey & Co. 1983–88; political adviser, HM Treasury 1983; MP (Conservative) for Richmond, Yorks. 1989–2015; Parl. Pvt. Sec. to Chancellor of Exchequer 1990–93; Parl. Under-Sec. of State, Dept of Social Security 1993–94; Minister for Social Security and Disabled People, Dept of Social Security 1994–95; Sec. of State for Wales 1995–97; Leader of Conservative Party and Leader of the Opposition 1997–2001; Chair. Int. Democratic Union 1999–2001, now Deputy Chair.; Shadow Foreign Sec. and Sr mem. of the Shadow Cabinet 2005–10; Sec. of State for Foreign and Commonwealth Affairs 2010–14; First Sec. of State and Leader of the House of Commons 2014–15; mem. (Conservative), House of Lords 2015–; Econ. and Political Adviser, JCB PLC 2001–; Dir (non-exec.), AES Eng PLC 2001–; mem. Political Council of Terra Firma Capital Partners 2001–; Vice-Pres. Friends of the British Library; mem. Conservative Friends of Israel 1976–; apptd Visiting Prof. in Practice, Centre for Women, Peace and Security, LSE 2016; The Spectator Parliamentarian of the Year Award 1998, Channel 4 Politician of the Year 2001, The Spectator Speech of the Year Award 2007, Trustees Award, Longman/History Today Awards 2008. *Publications:* William Pitt the Younger (biog.) (British Book Award for History Book of the Year 2005) 2004, William Wilberforce: The Life of the Great Anti-Slave Trade Campaigner 2007. *Leisure interests:* walking, judo, playing the piano. *Address:* House of Lords, Westminster, London, SW1A 0PW, England (office). *Telephone:* (20) 7219-4611 (office). *E-mail:* william.hague.mp@parliament.uk (office). *Website:* www.parliament.uk/biographies/lords/lord-hague-of-richmond/379 (office).

HAHN, Carl Horst, Dr rer. pol; Austrian business executive; b. 1 July 1926, Chemnitz; m. Marisa Traina 1960; three s. one d.; Chair. of Bd, Continental Gummi-Werke AG 1973–81, Saurer AG 1983–99; Chair. Man. Bd, Volkswagen AG 1981–92, currently Chair. Emer., Volkswagen Group; mem. Supervisory Bd HAWESKO, Hamburg, Perot Systems 1993–, Dallas; mem. Int. Supervisory Bd Indesit Co., Fabriano; mem. Int. Advisory Bd, Textron, Wichity, Inst. de Empresa, Madrid; mem. Int. Advisory Cttee, Salk Inst., Calif.; Chair. Bd of Trustees, Kunstmuseum Wolfsburg; mem. Bd Mayo Clinic, Stiftung, Frankfurt, Lauder-Inst., Wharton School, Pa; Pres. German-Czech Chamber of Commerce 1993–99; several hon. doctorates. *Publication:* Meine Jahre mit Volkswagen. *Address:* Hollerplatz 1, 38440 Wolfsburg, Germany (office). *Telephone:* (5361) 26680 (office). *Fax:* (5361) 266815 (office). *E-mail:* carl.hahn@volkswagen.de (office). *Website:* www.carl-hahn.de.

HAHN, James (Jim) Kenneth, BA, JD; American politician, lawyer, business executive and judge; *Judge, Los Angeles County Superior Court;* b. 3 July 1951, Los Angeles, Calif.; s. of Kenneth Hahn and Ramona Hahn (née Fox); divorced; one s. one d.; ed Lutheran High School, South LA, Pepperdine Univ.; pvt. law practice in Marina del Rey, Calif. 1979–81; Deputy City Prosecutor, LA City Attorney's Office 1975–79, City Controller of LA 1981–85, City Attorney of LA 1985–2001; Mayor of LA 2001–05; Man. Dir Chadwick Saylor and Co. Inc., LA 2005–07; CEO Los Angeles Devt Partners, LP 2006–08; Judge, Los Angeles County Superior Court 2008–; Democrat. *Address:* Santa Monica Courthouse, 1725 Main Street, Santa Monica, CA 90401, USA (office). *Telephone:* (310) 255-1847 (office). *Website:* www.lacourt.org (office).

HAHN, Johannes; Austrian politician and EU official; *Commissioner for European Neighbourhood Policy and Enlargement Negotiations, European Commission;* b. 2 Dec. 1957, Vienna; m. Marina Hahn; one s.; ed Univ. of Vienna; various man. posts in different business sectors in Austria 1985–92; Bd mem., later Chair. Novomatic AG 1997–2003; mem. Austrian People's Party (ÖVP), Chair. Viennese group, Youth Austrian People's Party 1980–85, Man. Dir ÖVP Vienna 1992–97, mem. Vienna City Council and Health Policy Spokesman of ÖVP Vienna 1996–2003, Deputy Chair. ÖVP Vienna 2002–04, Acting Chair. 2004–05, Chair. 2005–10; mem. Vienna City Govt 2003–07; Fed. Minister for Science and Research 2007; Commr for Regional Policy, EC, Brussels 2010–14, for European Neighbourhood Policy and Enlargement Negotiations 2014–. *Address:* European Commission, 200 Rue de la Loi/Wetstraat 200, 1049 Brussels, Belgium (office). *Telephone:* (2) 299-11-11 (switchboard) (office). *Website:* ec.europa.eu/commission/2014-2019/hahn_en (office).

HAI, Musharaf; Pakistani business executive; *Managing Director, L'Oreal Pakistan;* ed London School of Econs, UK, Boston Univ., USA; joined Unilever 1983, several man. positions including Marketing Man., Co-ordinator for Detergents in East Asia-Pacific and Africa/Middle East regions, Unilever HQ, London 1993–96, responsible for Unilever Pakistan Ice Cream Div. 1996, later Dir Home & Personal Care Div., Sales Dir –2001, Chair. Unilever Pakistan 2001–06; Country Business Man. Citibank NA Pakistan, Karachi 2006, also Head of Consumer Banking Pakistan; Man. Dir L'Oreal Pakistan 2009–; mem. Bd of Govs Lahore Univ. Man. Sciences 2003; mem. Bd LEAD Pakistan 2003–09; mem. Nat. Council Duke of Edinburgh's Award Programme Pakistan; mem. Man. Cttee Overseas Investors' Chamber of Commerce and Industry, Bd of Investment, Govt of Pakistan 2002–03. *Address:* L'Oréal Pakistan, The Forum, Floor 6 Office 603 & 604, G-20 Block 9, Clifton, Karachi, Pakistan (office).

HAIDALLA, Lt-Col Mohamed Khouna Ould; Mauritanian politician and army officer (retd); b. 1940, La Güera; ed École Spéciale Militaire de Saint-Cyr; Chair. Mil. Cttee for Nat. Recovery (now Cttee for Nat. Salvation) 1978–84; Chief of Staff of Mauritanian Army 1978–79; Minister of Defence April–May 1979, 1980, Prime Minister 1979–80, Pres. of Mauritania 1980–84 (overthrown in coup); stood as unsuccessful cand. in presidential election 2003, 2007; arrested and charged with treason Nov. 2003, trial suspended Dec. 2003, acquitted 2005.

HAIDAR, Shoukria, MA, PhD; French/Afghan human rights activist and teacher; *President, NEGAR—Support Women of Afghanistan Association;* b. 11 Nov. 1957, Kabul; m.; ed Univ. of Nice, France; fmr ping-pong champion, Kabul; worked for IOC 1979–80; exile in France 1980–; various jobs in a bakery, dress-making workshop, Paris; Founding Pres. NEGAR—Support Women of Afghanistan Asscn 1996–; obtained French citizenship 1998; currently Prof. of Physical Educ., Collège d'Aulnay-sous-Bois; organiser and Speaker, Women on the Road to Afghanistan Conf., Dushanbe, Tajikistan 2000; Prix de la laïcité 2014. *Address:* Negar—Soutien aux Femmes d'Afghanistan, BP 10, 25770 Franois, France (office). *Telephone:* 1-48-35-07-56 (office). *Fax:* 1-48-35-07-56 (office). *E-mail:* negar@wanadoo.fr (office); negarafghanwomen@yahoo.fr (office). *Website:* www.negar-afghanwomen.org (office).

HAIDER, Maximilian, PhD; Austrian physicist and business executive; *Managing Director, Corrected Electron Optical Systems (CEOS) GmbH;* b. 23 Jan. 1950, Freistadt; ed Univ. of Kiel, Darmstadt Univ. of Tech.; Group Leader, Physical Instrumentation Program, European Molecular Biology Lab. (EMBL), Heidelberg 1989; co-f. CEOS (Corrected Electron Optical Systems) GmbH, Heidelberg 1996, Man. Dir 1996–; Hon. Prof., Karlsruher Institut für Technologie 2008, Hon. Fellow, Royal Microscopical Soc. 2015; several awards, including Innovation Award of the State of Baden Württemberg (Rudolf Eberle Award) (jtly) 2005, Karl Heinz Beckurts Prize (jtly) 2006, Honda Prize (jtly) 2008, Wolf Prize in Physics (jtly) 2011, Foundation Frontiers of Knowledge Award (shared with Harald Rose and Knut Urban) 2013, NIMS Award 2015. *Address:* CEOS GmbH, Englerstr. 28, 69126 Heidelberg, Germany (office). *Telephone:* (6221) 89467-0 (office). *Fax:* (6221) 89467-29 (office). *E-mail:* info@ceos-gmbh.de (office). *Website:* www.ceos-gmbh.de (office).

HAIDUC, Ionel, MSc, PhD; Romanian chemist and academic; b. 9 May 1937, Cluj; m. Iovanca Haiduc; two c.; ed Babes-Bolyai Univ., Inst. of Fine Chemicals Tech., Moscow, Iowa State Univ., Univ. of Georgia, USA; Lab. Asst, Dept of Chem., Babes-Bolyai Univ. 1959–62, Asst 1962–64, Lecturer 1964–69, Reader 1969–73, Prof. 1979–, Pro-Rector 1976–84, Rector 1990–93; NSF Visiting Scientist, Dept of Chem., Univ. of Georgia, USA 1992; EC Visiting Scientist, Univ. of Santiago de Compostela, Spain 1993; Visiting Scientist, Nat. Univ. of Singapore 2002; Visiting Prof., Instituto de Quimica, Universidad Nacional Autonoma de Mexico 1993–94, Instituto de Quimica, Universidade Federal de Sao Carlos, Brazil 1994, 2000, Univ. of Santiago de Compostela 1998, Univ. of Texas, El Paso 2000–01, 2004, Göttingen Univ., Germany 1998–99, 2002; Consultant Dept of Chem., Univ. of Texas, El Paso 1997, 2005; Visiting Lecturer, Columbia Univ., New York 2003; UNESCO Expert, Consulting Mission to Moldova 1999; Corresp. mem. Romanian Acad. 1990–, mem. 1991–, Pres. Transylvania Br. 1995, Vice-Pres. 1998–2000, Pres. 2006–14; Bd mem. Nat. Council for Academic Research 1992, Nat. Council for Academic Titles and Diplomas 1992, Nat. Council for Academic Reform 1998; Pres. Consultative Coll., Nat. Agency for Research, Devt and Innovation 1998–2003; mem. Bd of Dirs Alliance of Univs for Democracy 1991–93; Founding mem. Nat. Foundation for Science and Arts; mem. Accad. Europaea 2002–; mem. Editorial Bd Synthesis and Reactivity in Inorganic and Metal-organic Chemistry, Main-Group Metal Chemistry, Metal-Based Drugs, Science and Engineering Ethics, Revue Roumaine de Chimie, Revista de Chimie; Hon. Citizen of Cluj-Napoca 1999, Hon. mem. Moldavian Acad. of Sciences 2002, Hon. mem. Hungarian Acad. of Sciences 2007; Star of Romania 2000, Order of Honour (Moldova) 2006; Dr hc (Moldavian Acad. of Sciences) 1999, (Gh. Assachi Tech. Univ.) 2002, (Polytechnic Univ. of Timisoara) 2004; Fulbright Fellowship 1966, G. Spacu Prize, Romanian Acad. 1974, Pro Colaboratione Award, Hungarian Acad. of Sciences 1999, Romanian Chemical Soc. Prize 2004, Patriarchal Cross, Romanian Acad. 2011. *Publications:* Chemistry of Inorganic Ring Systems 1970, Basic Organometallic Chemistry (with J.J. Zuckerman) 1985, Chemistry of Inorganic Homo and Heterocycles 1987, Organometallics in Cancer Chemotherapy (with C. Silvestru) 1990, Supramolecular Organometallic Chemistry (with F.T. Edelmann) 1999; numerous contribs to academic journals. *Address:* Romanian Academy, 125 Calea Victoriei, sector 1, 010071 Bucharest, Romania (office). *Telephone:* (21) 28640 (office). *Fax:* (21) 16608 (office). *E-mail:* ihaiduc@chem.ubbcluj.ro (office). *Website:* www.academiaromana.ro (office).

HAIGNERÉ, Claudie, MD, PhD; French politician, astronaut, physician and rheumatologist; *Senior Adviser to the Director-General, European Space Agency;* b. (Claudie André), 13 May 1957, Le Creusot (Saône-et-Loire); m. Jean-Pierre Haigneré; one d.; ed Faculté de Médecine, Dijon and Paris-Cochin, Faculté des Sciences, Paris-VII; physician, rheumatologist and researcher, Rheumatology Clinic and Rehab Dept, Cochin Hosp., Paris 1984–92; postgraduate researcher, Neurosensory Physiology Lab., CNRS 1985–90; cand. astronaut, French Space Agency (CNES) 1985; responsible for French and int. space physiology and medicine programmes, CNES Life Sciences Div., Paris 1990–92; French Rep. Starsem, Moscow 1997; backup astronaut for Perseus mission, Crew Interface Co-ordinator, Mission Control Centre 1998–99; mem. European Astronaut Corps, ESA, Cologne 1999–; trainee Soyuz flight engineer for Andromède mission to Int. Space Station (first European woman on space station) 2001–; Minister for Research and New Technologies, Ministry of Youth, Nat. Educ. and Research

2002–04; Minister-Del. attached to the Ministry of Foreign Affairs, responsible for European Affairs 2004–05; Sr Adviser to Dir-Gen. ESA 2005–09, 2015–; Pres. and CEO Universcience, Science Centre, Palais de la Decouverte-Cité des Sciences et de l'Industrie 2009–15; fmr Vice-Pres. Int. Acad. of Astronautics; Perm. mem. French Acad. of Tech., French Sport Acad.; mem. Bd, Sanofi, Fondation L'Oréal, Fondation CGénial; mem. Acad. de l'Air et de l'Espace, Acad. des Sports, Acad. des Technologies, Acad. des Sciences de l'Outre-Mer, Acad. des Sciences de Belgique; Hon. mem. Asscn Aéronautique et Astronautique de France, Soc. Française de Médecine Aéronautique et Spatiale; Grand Officier, Légion d'honneur, Chevalier, Ordre nat. du Mérite, Medaille Aeronautique, Russian Order of Friendship, Bundesverdienstkreuz; Dr hc (École Polytechnique Fédérale de Lausanne, Faculté Polytechnique de Mons, Beihang Univ., Université catholique de Louvain); Russian Medal for Personal Valour. *Leisure interests:* contemporary art, reading, golf. *Address:* European Space Agency, 24 rue du Général Bertrand, 75007 Paris, France (office). *Telephone:* 1-53-69-74-48 (office). *Fax:* 1-53-69-73-69 (office). *E-mail:* claudie.haignere@esa.int (office). *Website:* www.esa.int (office).

HAILEMICHAEL, Maj.-Gen. Tesfay Gidey, MPH; Ethiopian army officer and UN official; b. 1965; m.; three c.; ed Ethiopian Defence Command and Staff Coll., Siddartha HIV Research Inst., Addis Ababa; 33 years with Ethiopian Armed Forces, becoming Brigade Commdr 1997–98, Division Commdr 2003–07, Deputy Army Corps Commdr 2009–11, Corps Commdr 2011–14, Head, Defence Logistics Dept 2014–17; rank of Maj.-Gen. 2013; mem. Defence Council 2011–; Head of Mission and Force Commdr, UN Interim Security Force for Abyei (UNISFA) 2017–18.

HAIN, Baron (Life Peer), cr. 2015, of Neath in the County of West Glamorgan; **Rt Hon. Peter Gerald Hain,** PC, BSc, MPhil; British politician; b. 16 Feb. 1950, Nairobi, Kenya; s. of Walter Hain and Adelaine Hain; m. 1st Patricia Western 1975; two s.; m. 2nd Elizabeth Haywood 2003; ed Pretoria Boys High School, Emanuel School, Queen Mary Coll., London, Univ. of Sussex; noted anti-apartheid campaigner 1970s; Head of Research, Communication Workers' Union 1976–91; MP (Labour) for Neath 1991–2015; Labour Party Foreign Affairs Whip 1995–96; Shadow Employment Minister 1996–97; Parl. Under-Sec. of State, Welsh Office 1997–99; Minister of State, FCO 1999–2001; Minister for Energy and Competitiveness in Europe 2001; Minister of State for Europe, FCO 2001–02; Sec. of State for Wales 2002–08, 2009–10; Leader of the House of Commons 2003–05; Lord Privy Seal 2003–05; Sec. of State for Northern Ireland 2005–07, for Work and Pensions 2007–08; Shadow Sec. of State for Wales and Chair. of the Nat. Policy Forum 2010–12; mem. (Labour), House of Lords 2015–; Founding mem. Anti-Nazi League 1970s; Chair. Tribune magazine 1993–97; mem. GMB Union, Friends of the Earth, Fabian Soc., Unite Against Fascism, Action for Southern Africa, Advisory Council for the Coll. of Medicine; fmr Hon. Vice-Pres. Campaign for Homosexual Equality 1972–73. *Publications include:* Ayes to the Left: A Future for Socialism 1995, Sing the Beloved Country: Struggle for the New South Africa 1996, Outside In (memoir) 2012, Back to the Future of Socialism 2015, Mandela: His Essential Life 2018. *Leisure interests:* football, cricket, rugby, motor racing. *Address:* House of Lords, Westminster, London, SW1A 0PW, England (office). *Telephone:* (20) 7219-3000 (office). *E-mail:* peter.hain@parliament.uk (office). *Website:* www.parliament.uk/biographies/lords/lord-hain/567 (office); www.peterhain.org.uk.

HAIRER, Martin, FRS, BSc, MSc, PhD; Austrian mathematician and academic; *Regius Professor of Mathematics, University of Warwick;* b. 14 Nov. 1975, Geneva, Switzerland; s. of Ernst Hairer; m. Xue-Mei Li; ed Univ. of Geneva, Switzerland; Lecturer/Asst Prof., Math. Dept, Univ. of Warwick 2004–06, Assoc. Prof. 2006–07, Reader 2007–09, Full Prof. 2010–14, Regius Prof. of Math. 2014–; Assoc. Prof., New York Univ. (Courant Inst.) 2009–10; Assoc. Ed. several journals including Probability Theory and Related Fields 2008–, Electronic Journal of Probability 2010–, Journal of Mathematical Analysis and Applications 2010–11, Journal of Functional Analysis 2013–; also writes computer software (creator of Amadeus, award-winning sound-editing program); Whitehead Prize, London Math. Soc. 2008, Philip Leverhulme Prize 2008, Fermat Prize (with C. de Lellis) 2013, Fröhlich Prize, London Math. Soc. 2014, Fields Medal 2014. *Leisure interests:* reading, cooking, skiing. *Address:* Mathematics Department, University of Warwick, Coventry, CV4 7AL, England (office). *Telephone:* (24) 7652-8335 (office). *E-mail:* martin@hairer.org (office). *Website:* www.hairer.org (office).

HAJDU, Patricia (Patty) A., PC, MP, BA; Canadian graphic designer and politician; *Minister of Status of Women;* two s.; ed Lakehead Univ., Univ. of Victoria; Customer Service Rep., Cantel (telecoms co.) 1985–87; Desktop Publishing Coordinator, Thunder Bay Literacy Group 1990–99; Graphic Designer, Wrightsell Advertising 1999–2003; Designer, Bayview Magazine 2002–14; Health Planner/Drug Strategy Coordinator, Thunder Bay District Health Unit 2003–12; Course Content Developer and Instructor, Confederation Coll. 2008–10; Exec. Dir, Shelter House (homeless shelter) 2012–15; mem. House of Commons (Parl.) for Thunder Bay–Superior North 2015–; Minister of Status of Women 2015–; Chair. Drug Awareness Cttee of Thunder Bay 2004–09; mem. Bd of Dirs Alpha Court Mental Health Services 2011–12; fmr mem. Bd of Dirs Ontario Literacy Coalition; fmr mem. Community Advisory Bd, Homelessness Partnering Strategy; mem. Liberal Party of Canada. *Address:* Status of Women Canada, McDonald Bldg, 10th Floor, 123 Slater Street, Ottawa, ON K1P 1H9, Canada (office). *Telephone:* (613) 420-6905 (office). *Fax:* (819) 420-6906 (office). *E-mail:* communications@swc-cfc.gc.ca (office). *Website:* www.swc-cfc.gc.ca (office); pattyhajdu.liberal.ca.

HAJI-FAQI, Abdihakim Mohamoud; Somali diplomatist and politician; fmr diplomat, served in New York; Minister of Defence and Second Deputy Prime Minister 2010–14. *Address:* c/o Ministry of Defence, Mogadishu, Somalia.

HAJI-IOANNOU, Sir Stelios, Kt, BSc (Econ), MSc; British/Cypriot entrepreneur; *Founder and Chairman, easyGroup;* b. 14 Feb. 1967, Athens, Greece; s. of Loucas Haji-Ioannou and Nedi Haji-Ioannou; ed Doucas School, Athens, London School of Econs and Political Science, Cass Business School, UK; joined father's co., Troodos Maritime 1988, CEO –1991; Founder, Cyprus Marine Environment Protection Asscn (CYMEPA) 1992; Founder and Chair. Stelmar Tankers, Athens and London 1992; Founder easyJet, London 1995 (Chair. 1995–2002), Founder and Chair. easyGroup 1998, Founder, easyCar 2000, easyBus 2004, easyHotel 2005, easyProperty 2012; Founder, Stelios Philanthropic Foundation 2009; lives in Monaco; Hon. Gen. Consul of Cyprus to the Principality of Monaco; Dr hc (Liverpool John Moores Univ.), (Cass Business School), (Cranfield Univ.), (Newcastle Business School). *Leisure interest:* yachting. *Address:* easyGroup Holdings Ltd, Le Ruscino, 14 Quai Antoine 1er, 98000 Monaco (office). *Telephone:* 98-80-10-10 (office). *Fax:* 97-97-37-88 (office). *E-mail:* chairmansoffice@easygroup.co.uk (office); mlb@stelios.com (office). *Website:* www.easy.com (office); www.stelios.com (office).

HAJJAJ, Emad, BA; Palestinian cartoonist; b. 1967, Ramallah; ed Yarmouk Univ.; first cartoon published in Yarmouk Univ. newspaper (Sahafat Al Yarmouk) 1987, later worked for several newspapers including Akher Khabar, Al Ahali, Al Raseef, Al Bilad, Al Mustaqbal, Al Dustour, Al Rai; worked for Al Quds Al Arabi newspaper, London 1992; currently with Al Gahd, Amman; mem. Jordan Press Union 1999–, Cartoonists and Writers Syndicate, USA; Best Published Cartoon in the Arabic Media (for 'The Crying Arabic Camel') 2005, winner Arabic Press Award (Dubai Press Club) 2006. *Website:* www.hajjajcartoons.com.

HAJJAR, Bandar bin Mohammed As'ad, BSc, MA, PhD; Saudi Arabian government official and banker; *President, Islamic Development Bank;* b. 1955, Medina; m.; four c.; ed King Sa'ud Univ., Indiana Univ., USA, Loughborough Univ., UK; Lecturer, King Abdul Aziz Univ. 1989–2005, Deputy Dean, Coll. of Economy and Admin 1995–98; mem. Shura Council 1998–2008, Chair. Foreign Affairs Cttee 2000, apptd Vice-Speaker 2008; represented Shura Council at Arab Parl. Union 2001–02; Minister of Hajj 2011–15; Pres. Islamic Development Bank 2016–; mem. Admin Council, King Abdulaziz Endowment (Al Ain Al Aziziyah), also Chair. Investment Cttee 2003–09; Chair. Nat. Soc. for Human Rights 2005–08, Nat. Council for Election Control 2005–; mem. Islamic Int. Foundation for Econs & Finance; Chief Ed. Money and Markets magazine. *Address:* Islamic Development Bank, POB 5925, Jeddah 21432, Saudi Arabia (office). *Telephone:* (2) 636-1400 (office). *Fax:* (2) 636-6871 (office). *E-mail:* info@isdb.org (office). *Website:* www.isdb.org (office).

HAJJRI, Abdulwahab Abdulla al-, LLM; Yemeni diplomatist; b. 1958; m.; three c.; ed Sana'a Univ., American Univ., Washington DC, USA, Al Azhar Univ., Cairo, Egypt; joined Ministry of Foreign Affairs 1980, Diplomatic Attaché, Political Dept, Sana'a 1980–82, Cultural Attaché, Cairo 1982–87, Washington, DC 1987–92, Counsellor, Cairo 1992–95, Minister Plenipotentiary, Embassy in Washington, DC 1995–97, Amb. to USA (also accred to Mexico and Venezuela) and Perm. Observer of Yemen to OAS 1997–2012.

HAJRAF, Nayef Falah al-, BS, MS, PhD; Kuwaiti academic and politician; *Minister of Finance;* ed Kuwait Univ., Univ. of Illinois at Urbana-Champaign, USA, Univ. of Hull, UK; Curriculum Co-ordinator, Coll. of Business Admin, Gulf Univ. for Science & Tech. 2002–04, Head of Accounting Dept 2004–07, later Prof. of Accounting and Asst Vice-Pres. for Academic Services; Financial Adviser, Kuwait Stock Exchange 2003–04; Financial Adviser to UN Devt Programme, Ministry of Planning 2003–04, 2007–08; CEO First Abu Dhabi Co. for Real Estate Devt 2009; Commr, Kuwait Capital Markets Authority 2011; Minister of Finance, of Educ. and Acting Minister of Higher Educ. 2012–13, Minister of Educ. and of Higher Educ. 2013, of Finance 2017–; Chair. Kuwait Public Authority for Applied Educ. and Training; mem. Bd of Govs., Islamic Devt Bank. *Address:* Ministry of Finance, POB 9, 13001 Safat, al-Morkab St, Ministries Complex, Kuwait City, Kuwait (office). *Telephone:* 22480000 (office). *Fax:* 22404025 (office). *E-mail:* minister@mof.gov.kw (office). *Website:* www.mof.gov.kw (office).

HÄKÄMIES, Jyri Jukka, MSSc; Finnish business executive and politician; *Director General, Confederation of Finnish Industries (Elinkeinoelämän Keskusliitto);* b. 30 Aug. 1961, Karhula; s. of Erkki Häkämies and Pirkko Häkämies; m. Tuija Arhosola; two s.; Communications Man. Kymen Viestintä Oy (newspaper publr) 1989–91; Sales Man. Kymen Sanomat (newspaper) 1991–94; Man. Dir Kymenlaakso Chamber of Commerce 1994–99; mem. Suomen Eduskunta (Parl.) (Nat. Coalition Party—NCP) 1999–, mem. NCP Communications Sec., Parl. Group 1987–89, Vice-Chair. (Parl. Group) 2003–06, Chair. 2006–; Minister of Defence 2007–11, also Minister at the Prime Minister's Office (ownership steering) 2007–11, Minister of Econ. Affairs 2011–12; Dir-Gen. Confed. of Finnish Industries (Elinkeinoelämän Keskusliitto) 2012–; mem. Kotka City Council 2005–, Regional Council of Kymenlaakso Ass. (Chair. 2005–); mem. Supervisory Bd Port of Kotka Ltd (Chair. 2005–07), Sitra, The Finnish Innovation Fund 2006–07, Kymen Puhelin Oy 1998–2007; Vice-Pres. European People's Party 2003–06; mem. Council, Finland-Russia Soc. 2006–. *Leisure interests:* jogging, tennis, golf, skiing, reading. *Address:* Elinkeinoelämän Keskusliitto, PO Box 30, Eteläranta 10, 00131 Helsinki, Finland (office). *Telephone:* (9) 4202-2400 (office). *E-mail:* etunimi.sukunimi@ek.fi (office); ek@ek.fi (office). *Website:* ek.fi/en (office).

HAKEEM, Abdul Rauff, LLB, LLM; Sri Lankan lawyer and politician; *Minister of City Planning, Water Supply and Higher Education;* b. 13 April 1960, Nawalapitiya, Kandy Dist; m. Shanaz Hakeem; two d.; ed Royal Coll. Colombo, Univ. of Colombo; enrolled as a solicitor by British Law Soc. 1984; joined Sri Lanka Muslim Congress (SLMC) as prin. aide of party Founder-Leader M. H. M. Ashraff 1987, held several positions including First Sec., Working Cttee, Deputy Sec.-Gen., then Sec.-Gen. 1992, Leader SLMC 2001–; mem. Parl. for Kandy, Deputy Chair. of Cttees 1994–2000; Minister of Internal and Int. Trade and Commerce, of Shipping Devt and of Muslim Religious Affairs 2000–01, of Port Devt and Shipping and of Eastern Devt and Muslim Religious Affairs 2001–04, of Posts and Telecommunications 2007–08, of Justice 2010–14, of City Planning and Water Supply 2015–18, of City Planning, Water Supply and Higher Educ. 2018–; Chair. Public Accounts Cttee, Parl. 2001–04, 2006–08; apptd as an intermediary between Pres. of Sri Lanka and Tamil Nat. Alliance 2012; Sir Ponnambalam Ramanathan Oratory Award, Royal Coll. Colombo 1977. *Leisure interests:* Tamil poetry, cricket. *Address:* Ministry of City Planning, Water Supply and Higher Education, Room 18, Ward Place, Colombo 7 (office); Sri Lanka Muslim Congress, Dharussalam, 53 Vauxhall Lane, Colombo 2, Sri Lanka (office). *Telephone:* (11) 2685268 (office); (11) 2697721 (office); (74) 717720 (SLMC) (office). *Fax:* (11) 2682612 (office); (74) 717722 (SLMC) (office). *E-mail:* hakeem_r@parliament.lk (office); minister@mohe.gov.lk (office). *Website:* www.mohe.gov.lk (office); slmc.lk (office); rauffhakeem.lk.

HAKEEM, Mohammed Ali al-, BA, MSc, PhD; Iraqi politician and diplomatist; *Minister of Foreign Affairs;* b. 1952, Najaf; ed Al-Mustansiriya Univ., Univ. of Birmingham, Univ. of Southern California; Deputy Sec.-Gen., Iraqi Governing Council 2003–04; Minister of Communications 2004–05, also Acting Minister of

Finance 2004–05; mem. Transitional Nat. Ass. 2005–06, mem. Foreign Relations Cttee 2005–06; various sr positions with Ministry of Foreign Affairs, including in Dept of European Affairs and Dept of Arab Affairs 2006–10; Perm. Rep. of Iraq to UN, Geneva 2010–13, to UN, New York 2013–17; UN Under-Sec.-Gen. and Exec. Sec., Econ. and Social Comm. for Western Asia (ESCWA) 2017–18; Minister of Foreign Affairs 2018–. *Address:* Ministry of Foreign Affairs, opp. State Organization for Roads and Bridges, Karradat Mariam, Baghdad, Iraq (office). *Telephone:* (1) 537-0091 (office). *E-mail:* press@iraqmfamail.com (office). *Website:* www.mofa.gov.iq (office).

HAKIM, Nadey S., MD, PhD, FRCS, FACS; British surgeon and fmr international organization official; *Max Thorek Professor, International College of Surgeons;* b. 9 April 1958, Beirut, Lebanon; m. Nicole Hakim; four c.; ed René Descartes Univ., Paris, Mayo Clinic, Univ. of Minnesota, USA; Consultant Surgeon and Surgical Dir Transplant Unit, Hammersmith Hosp., London; Fellow, Int. Coll. of Surgeons 1987, Max Thorek Prof. 2008–, fmr European Fed. Sec., fmr Sec. UK Section, WHO Rep., Pres. 2004–; Surgical Dir Transplant Unit, Imperial Coll. Healthcare NHS Trust London 1995–2015, Pres.'s Envoy 2017; Special Advisor Nat. Inst. of Clinical Excellence 2010–; Vice Pres. Royal Soc. of Medicine 2014–16 (mem. Council 2009–12, Hon. Sec. 2011–14); Ed.-in-Chief Emer. Journal of International Surgery; Registered Sculptor, Royal Soc. of British Sculptors, American Soc. for Bariatric and Metabolic Surgery; mem. Int. Bariatric Surgery Review Cttee 2010; Hon. Fellow Asscn of Surgeons of India 2010, Hon. Visiting Prof. Faculty of Medicine, Univ. of Belgrade 2018, Hon. Prof. of Surgery, Univ. of São Paolo, Ricardo Palma Peru Univ., Univ. of Bashkent; Hon. Prof., Univ. of Lyon, Hon. Fellow, Int. Coll. of Surgeons, Int. Medical Sciences Acad., Int. Napoleonic Soc.; Hon. Sec., Royal Soc. of Medicine; Grand Cross, Order of St John of Jerusalem, Bailiff of the Order of St John of Jerusalem, Kt of the Order of the Cedars (Lebanon), Chevalier de l'Ordre national de la Légion d'honneur; Makhzoumi Prize of Medical Excellence, Laureate, Faculty of Medicine, Paris 1984, J. Wesley Alexander Prize for Outstanding Research in Transplantation 2007. *Music:* six Music Recordings (clarinet), USA. *Television:* Presenter, Insider programme (Channel 4) 2007. *Publications include:* author or editor of more than 20 textbooks; Transplantation Surgery (co-ed.), Introduction to Organ Transplantation (ed.), History of Organ and Cell Transplantation (co-ed.), Pancreas and Islet Transplantation (co-ed.), Haemostasis in Surgery (co-ed.), Composite Tissue Allograft (co-ed.), Atlas of Transplantation, Bariatric Surgery State of the Art, Hernias, Artificial Organs; more than 150 peer-reviewed papers. *Leisure Interests:* music, sculpture. *Address:* 10 Harley Street, London, W1G 7LG, England (office). *Telephone:* 7850-503297 (mobile) (office). *Fax:* (20) 7431-8497 (home). *E-mail:* nadey@globalnet.co.uk (home). *Website:* www.icsglobal.org (office).

HAKIMI, Eklil Ahmad; Afghan diplomatist and politician; b. 1968, Kabul; m. Sultana Hakimi; three d.; ed Kabul Polytechnic Inst., California State Univ., Long Beach, USA; joined Ministry of Foreign Affairs 1992, served in various positions including policy formation and strategic planning 1998–2002; Adviser, Ind. Admin. Reform and Civil Service Comm., Office of the Vice-Pres. 2002–05; Chair. and Founding mem. Afghanistan Civil Service and Administrative Reform Comm. 2003; Amb. to People's Repub. of China (also accred to Mongolia and Viet Nam) 2005–09, to Japan (also accred to Philippines and Singapore) 2009–10, Deputy Foreign Minister for Political Affairs 2010, Amb. to USA (also accred to Mexico, Brazil, Argentina and Colombia) 2011–15; Minister of Finance 2015–18; fmr Chair. Govt High Econ. Comm., Co-Chair. Jt Coordination and Monitoring Bd; fmr Coordinator, Brussels Int. Conf. on Afghanistan; mem. Bd of Govs. Asian Infrastructure Investment Bank, Multilateral Investment Guarantee Agency, World Bank. *Address:* c/o Ministry of Finance, Pashtunistan Wat, Kabul, Afghanistan (office).

HÄKKÄNEN, Matti Klaus Juhani, LLM; Finnish diplomatist (retd); b. 21 July 1936, Helsinki; s. of Klaus Häkkänen and Kaiju Broms; m. Pirkko Hentola 1962; two s.; ed Univ. of Helsinki; served in Finnish Foreign Service Helsinki, Paris, New York, Moscow and Peking 1960–76; Amb. to Romania (also accred to Albania) 1976–80; Under-Sec. of State 1980–83; Amb. to Netherlands (also accred to Ireland) 1983–87, to Argentina (also accred to Chile and Uruguay) 1987–88, to France 1988–93, to Italy (also accred to Malta and San Marino) 1993–97, to Portugal (also accred to Morocco) 1997–2001, mem. Selection and Training Bd Finnish Foreign Ministry 2004–07; mem. Bd French-Finnish Chamber of Commerce 2005–08; First Lt, Finnish Naval Forces; Kt Commdr, Order of Lion of Finland, Grand Cross, Orange Nassau of the Netherlands, Officer, Black Star of France, Grand Cross, Nat. Merit of Italy, Kt Commdr, Ordre nat. du Mérite (France), Mil. Medal of Finland, Grand Cross, Order of Infante Dom Henrique (Portugal). *Publications include:* Marshal Mannerheim in Portugal 1945, Mannerheimiana 2004. *Leisure interest:* tennis. *Address:* Töölönkatu 9, 00100 Helsinki, Finland (home). *Telephone:* (9) 497515 (home); 50-5497895 (mobile). *E-mail:* matti.hakkanen@welho.com.

HÄKKINEN, Mika; Finnish fmr professional racing driver; *Brand Ambassador and Driver Manager, Aces Management Group;* b. 28 Sept. 1968, Helsinki; s. of Harri Häkkinen and Aila Häkkinen; five c.; fmrly go-kart driver, Formula Ford 1600 driver, Finnish, Swedish and Nordic Champion 1987; Formula 3 driver, British Champion with West Surrey Racing 1990; Formula One driver Lotus 1991–93, McLaren 1993–2001; Grand Prix wins: European 1997, Australia 1998, Brazil 1998, 1999, Spain 1998, 1999, 2000, Monaco 1998, Austria 1998, 2000, Germany 1998, Luxembourg 1998, Japan 1998, 1999, Canada 1999, Malaysia 1999, Hungary 1999, 2000, Belgium 2000; Formula One World Champion 1998, 1999; took sabbatical at end of 2001, then announced retirement from Formula 1; driver for Mercedes in German Touring Car Championship 2004–07; Brand Amb. and Driver Man., Aces Management Group; mem. Laureus World Sports Acad.; Laureus Media Award 2009, Best Amb. for Sports (Finland). *Leisure interests:* karting, golf, music. *Address:* c/o Didier Coton, Aces Management Group, 23 Boulevard des Moulins, MC 98000 Monte Carlo, Monaco (office). *Telephone:* 93-50-08-80 (office). *Fax:* 93-50-08-90 (office). *E-mail:* didier.coton@aces-management.com (office).

HAKOPIAN, Vilen Paruirovich; Armenian university rector and neuropharmacologist; b. 1 May 1938, Garnahovit, Talin; s. of Paruir Hakopian and Inthizar Hakopian; m. Rosa Hovhannes Gasparian; one s. one d.; ed Yerevan Medical Inst.; Jr research worker, Biochem. Inst., Nat. Acad. of Sciences of Armenia 1961–65; Sr research worker and Asst, Dept of Pharmacology, Yerevan State Medical Univ. (YSMU) 1965–80, Prof. 1980–94, Dean of Foreign Students 1972–79, Dean of Medical Faculty 1979–83, Vice-Rector of Educational Affairs 1986–87, Rector of YSMU 1987–2006, Head Dept of Pharmacology 1994; mem. Nat. Acad. of Sciences of Armenia, NAS (USA), Int. Union of Pharmacology (Belgium), Int. Pharmaceutical Fed. (Netherlands), Int. Information Acad., Moscow, Int. Higher Educ. Acad. of Sciences, Moscow, Int. Acad. of Ecology and Life Protection Sciences, St Petersburg; Fellow Scientific Council of Int. Coll. of Angiology, New York; Ed.-in-Chief Medical Science of Armenia; mem. Editorial Bd Experimental and Clinical Pharmacology (Moscow) 1993, Int. Asscn of Pathophysiology (Moscow) 1991 and many other scientific bodies. *Publications:* nearly 200 works, including nine monographs. *Leisure interests:* chess, reading, geology, apiculture. *Address:* c/o Department of Pharmacology, Yerevan State Medical University, 2 Koryun Street, 0025 Yerevan (office); Apt. 33, 28 Orbelli Street, Yerevan 375012, Armenia (home).

HALAIQA, Mohammad al-, BSc, PhD; Jordanian government official; b. 20 May 1951, Al Shioukh; m.; ed Univ. of Jordan, Univ. of Leeds, UK; Gen. Man. of industrial co., Jordan 1981–87; Dir-Gen. Jordan Chamber of Industry 1990–92; Dir Industry and Mineral Resources Sector, Higher Council for Science and Tech. 1992–93, Asst Sec.-Gen. Higher Council for Science and Tech. 1993–94; Dir-Gen. Jordanian Export Devt and Commercial Centres Corpn (JEDCO) 1994–97; Sec.-Gen. Ministry of Trade and Industry 1997–2000; Deputy Prime Minister and Minister Admin. Devt 2003–05, Minister of Industry and Commerce 2003–04; currently mem. Senate; Pres. Jordan Chemical Soc. 1983–91, Union of Arab Chemists 1985–86, Jordanian Soc. for Quality 1997–99; fmr Pres. Arab Acad. for Banking and Financial Sciences.; led Jordanian del. to Free Trade Agreement negotiations with USA and to negotiations for Jordan's accession to WTO; mem. Bd of Dirs Jordan Valley Authority 1997–2000, Aqaba Region Authority 1997–2000, Social Security Corpn 1997–2000, Jordan Cement Factories Co. 1997–2000, Industrial Estates Corpn 1997–2000; mem. Bd of Trustees (fmr Chair.) Al Quds Coll.; mem. Econ. Consultative Council, Hashemite Royal Court; mem. Bd Trustees Princess Sumayya Coll. 1995–99, Faculty of Sciences, Hashemite Univ., Faculty of Sciences, Univ. of Jordan; mem. Higher Advisory Bd Talal Abu Ghazaleh Coll. of Business; Independence Medal of the First Order (Jordan), Al-Kawkab Medal of the Second Order. *Address:* The Senate, POB 72, Amman 11101, Jordan (office). *Telephone:* (6) 5664121 (office). *Fax:* (6) 5689313 (office). *E-mail:* M_halaiqa@hotmail.com; info@senate.jo (office). *Website:* www.senate.jo (office).

HALANE, Hussein Abdi; Somali economist and politician; fmr exec. with UN Children's Fund; various roles with Save the Children including Country Dir for Sudan 2007, Emergency Adviser in Haiti 2010; Minister of Finance 2010–11, 2014–15. *Address:* c/o Ministry of Finance, 1 Villa Somalia, 2525 Mogadishu, Somalia.

HALAS, Naomi J., BA, MA, PhD, DSc; American scientist and academic; *Stanley C. Moore Professor in Electrical and Computer Engineering and Professor of Biomedical Engineering, Chemistry, Physics and Astronomy, Rice University;* ed La Salle Coll., Bryn Mawr Coll., La Salle Univ.; Grad. Research Fellow, IBM T.J. Watson Research Center, Yorktown, NY 1983–86; Postdoctoral Assoc., Vanderbilt Univ. 1987, AT&T Bell Laboratories, Holmdel, NJ 1987–89; Asst Prof., Rice Univ. 1989–94, Assoc. Prof. 1994–99, Prof., Dept of Electrical and Computer Eng 1999–2001, Prof., Dept of Chem. 1999–, Stanley C. Moore Prof. in Electrical and Computer Eng 2001–, Founder and Dir Lab. for Nanophotonics 2004–, Prof., Dept of Biomedical Eng 2006–, Prof., Dept of Physics and Astronomy 2009–; Visiting Prof., Inst. of Physics, Chinese Acad. of Sciences; Co-founder Nanospectra Biosciences, Inc; Prin. Investigator of NSF-funded integrative grad. educ. and research training grant (IGERT) in Nanophotonics; Co-Chair. Gordon Research Conf. on Plasmonics 2008; Chair. Plasmonics Gordon Research Conf. 2010; mem. Advisory Bd Center for Integrated Nanotechnologies, Los Alamos Nat. Lab., Sandia Nat. Laboratories; mem. Keck Center for Gene Therapy, Univ. of Texas M.D. Anderson Cancer Center, Houston, Tex.; mem. Nanophotonics Program Cttee, IQEC 2009, Scientific Advisory Cttee, SPP4 (Int. Conf. on Plasmonics) 2009; mem. Editorial Advisory Bd Laser and Photonics Reviews 2009–, Nano Letters 2006–08 (Assoc. Ed. 2009–); Fellow, American Physical Soc. 2001, Optical Soc. of America 2003, AAAS 2005, Int. Soc. for Optical Eng (SPIE) 2007; Sr mem. IEEE 2004, Fellow 2008; mem. American Acad. of Arts and Sciences 2009, ACS; NSF Young Investigator 1992, Hershel M. Rich Invention Award: C60 Purification Method 1993, Hershel M. Rich Invention Award: Metal Nanoshells 1998, Hershel M. Rich Invention Award: Photothermal Nanoshell-Polymer Drug Delivery Material 2001, Hershel Rich Invention Award: Optically Active Nanoparticles for use in Therapeutic and Diagnostic Methods 2003, Chevy Trucks' 'Lone Star Hero' week of 10 Nov. 2003, Breast Cancer Research Program Innovator Award, US Army Medical Research and Material Command, Congressionally Funded Medical Research Programs, Dept of Defense (DoD) 2003, Nanotechnology Now's "Best Discovery of 2003" 2004, Woman of Achievement, YWCA, Houston 2005, Nanotech Brief's Nano 50 Innovator Award 2006, Esquire's Best and Brightest, Dec. 2006, NBIC Research Excellence Award, Univ. of Pennsylvania 2008, DoD Nat. Security Science and Eng Faculty Fellow 2009, ACS Award in Colloid Chemistry 2019. *Achievements include:* best known in the field of plasmonics as the inventor of tunable nanoparticles with resonances spanning the visible and infrared regions of the spectrum. *Publications:* several book chapters and tech. reports and more than 200 papers in professional journals on the design and fabrication of optically responsive nanostructures, nanophotonics and plasmonics; 15 issued and pending patents. *Address:* Abercrombie Lab A237, Department of Electrical and Computer Engineering, Rice University, 6100 Main Street, MS 366, Houston, TX 77005-1892, USA (office). *Telephone:* (713) 348-5611 (office). *Fax:* (713) 348-5686 (office). *E-mail:* halas@rice.edu (office). *Website:* halas.rice.edu (office).

HALBERT, David D., BS, BBA; American business executive; *Chairman and CEO, Caris Life Sciences;* m. Kathryn Ann Halbert; three c.; ed Abilene Christian Univ.; f. Halbert & Assocs Inc.; f. AdvancePCS, Chair., Pres. and CEO 1987–2004 (after merger with Caremark Rx); Founder and Chair. Caris, Ltd (investment partnership) 2004, now Chair. and CEO Caris Life Sciences, Co-founder Caris Foundation, Chair. Pathology Partners Inc. (now Caris Diagnostics) 2005; fmr Ind. Dir Herbalife Ltd, fmr Chair. of Nutrition and Scientific Advisory Bd. *Leisure* *interest:* baseball. *Address:* Caris Life Sciences, 5215 North O'Connor Boulevard, Irving, TX 75039, USA (office). *Telephone:* (866) 771-8946 (office). *Fax:* (214) 294-5690 (office). *Website:* www.carislifesciences.com (office).

HALBRON, Jean-Pierre; French business executive; b. 31 Aug. 1936; ed Ecole Polytechnique, Paris, Corps des Mines, Inst. Français du Pétrole; various posts with Compagnie Financière 1963–82, including Gen. Man. 1968–74, CEO 1974–82; Finance Dir Rhône-Poulenc SA 1983, Deputy Man. Dir 1984–87; Gen. Man. CdF Chimie (later Orkem) 1987–90; Finance Dir Total SA 1990–92; Man. Dir Wasserstein Perella Corpn and Chair. Wasserstein Perella France 1992–95; Dir of Strategy and Finance, Alcatel SA 1995–97, Co-Dir-Gen. 1997–99, Financial Dir 1997–2001, Dir-Gen. 2000–02, mem. Exec. Cttee 2002, also CEO Electro Banque SA (Alcatel bank); fmr mem. Bd of Dirs Alstom SA; mem. Strategic Cttee Agence France Trésor.

HALDANE, F(rederick) Duncan Michael, BA, PhD, FRS, FInstP; American (b. British) physicist and academic; *Eugene Higgins Professor of Physics, Princeton University;* b. 14 Sept. 1951, London, England; m. Odile Belmont; ed St Paul's School, London and Christ's Coll., Cambridge, UK; worked as physicist at Institut Laue–Langevin, France 1977–81; mem. Faculty, Univ. of Southern California 1981–84; Alfred P. Sloan Foundation Research Fellow 1984–88; joined Faculty, Princeton Univ. 1990, currently Eugene Higgins Prof. of Physics; Distinguished Visiting Research Chair, Perimeter Inst. for Theoretical Physics; Lorentz Chair, Lorentz Inst. Leiden 2008; Fellow, American Physical Soc. 1986, American Acad. of Arts and Sciences 1992, AAAS 2001; Dr hc (Université de Cergy-Pontoise) 2015; Oliver E. Buckley Condensed Matter Physics Prize, American Physical Soc. 1993, Dirac Medal (co-recipient) 2012, Simons Fellow in Theoretical Physics 2013–14, Nobel Prize in Physics (co-recipient with David Thouless and J. Michael Kosterlitz) 2016. *Publications:* numerous papers in professional journals. *Address:* 330 Jadwin Hall, Princeton University, Princeton, NJ 08544-0708, USA (office). *Telephone:* (609) 258-5856 (office). *Fax:* (609) 258-1549 (office). *E-mail:* haldane@princeton.edu (office). *Website:* physics.princeton.edu (office).

HALDEMAN, Charles Edgar (Ed), Jr, AB, MBA, JD; American business executive; *Chairman, KCG Holdings Inc.;* b. 29 Oct. 1948, Philadelphia, Pa; s. of Charles Edgar Haldeman, Sr and Betty Jane Haldeman; m. Barbara Haldeman; one s. two d.; ed Dartmouth Coll., Harvard Business School (Baker Scholar), Harvard Law School; Chartered Financial Analyst; began career at Cooke & Bieler, Inc. (affiliate of United Asset Management Corpn—UAM) 1974, held a series of sr exec. positions; Chair. and CEO Delaware Investments, and Pres. and COO UAM 2000–02; Co-Head of Investment Div., Putnam Investments 2002–03, Pres. and CEO Putnam Investments 2003–08, led sale of Putnam Investments to Power Financial Corpn Jan. 2007, mem. Putnam Funds' Board of Trustees 2004–09, Pres. Putnam Funds 2007–09, Chair. Putnam Investment Man., LLC (investment adviser for the Putnam Funds) 2008–09; CEO Freddie Mac (Federal Home Loan Mortgage Corpn) 2009–11 (retd); Chair. KCG Holdings Inc. 2013–, McGraw Hill Financial Inc. 2015–; Chair. Bd of Trustees, Dartmouth Coll. 2007–10; mem. Bd of Dirs DST Systems Inc. 2014–; fmr mem. Bd of Govs Investment Company Inst., Investment Counsel Asscn of America; Trustee Emer., Abington Memorial Hosp. *Address:* KCG Holdings Inc., 545 Washington Boulevard, Jersey City, NJ 07310, USA (office). *Website:* www.kcg.com (office).

HALE OF RICHMOND, Baroness (Life Peer), cr. 2004, of Easby in the County of North Yorkshire; **Rt Hon. Brenda Marjorie Hale,** DBE, PC, MA; British judge and barrister; *President, The Supreme Court;* b. 31 Jan. 1945, Leeds, Yorks., England; d. of Cecil Frederick Hale and Marjorie Hale (née Godfrey); m. 1st Anthony John Christopher Hoggett 1968 (divorced 1992); one d.; m. 2nd Julian Thomas Farrand 1992; ed Richmond High School for Girls, Yorks., Girton Coll., Cambridge and Gray's Inn, London; Asst Lecturer, Faculty of Law, Univ. of Manchester 1966–68, Lecturer 1968–76, Sr Lecturer 1976–81, Reader 1981–86, Prof. 1986–89; Prof., King's Coll., London 1989–90; practice, Manchester Bar 1969–72; Asst Recorder 1982–89, Recorder 1989–94; Law Commr 1984–93; Judge of the High Court, Family Div. 1994–99; Lord Justice of Appeal 1999–2004, Lord of Appeal in Ordinary (first female Law Lord) 2004–09; Justice of the Supreme Court 2009–, Deputy Pres. 2013–17, Pres., The Supreme Court (first female) 2017–; Visiting Fellow, Nuffield Coll., Oxford 1997–2005; Chancellor Univ. of Bristol 2004–16; Visitor, Girton Coll., Cambridge 2004–, Hon. Fellow 1996–2004; Pres. Asscn of Women Barristers 1998–2005, UK Asscn of Women Judges 2003–, Int. Asscn of Women Judges 2010–12; Ed. Journal of Social Welfare Law 1978–84; mem. Mental Health Review Tribunal for the North-West 1979–80, Council on Tribunals 1980–84; Chair. Nat. Family Conciliation Council 1989–93; mem. Judicial Studies Bd Civil and Family Cttee 1990–94, Human Fertilization and Embryology Authority 1990–93; Gov. Centre for Policy on Ageing 1990–93; Pres. Nat. Family Mediation 1994–; Man. Trustee Nuffield Foundation 1987–2002; Hon. FBA 2004; Hon. FRCPsych 2007; Hon. LLD (Sheffield) 1989, (London Guildhall) 1996, (Manchester) 1997, (Bristol) 2002, (Cambridge) 2005, (Hull) 2006, (King's Coll. London) 2007, (Oxford) 2007, (City) 2007, (Reading) 2007, (Coll. of Law) 2008, (West of England) 2009, (Huddersfield) 2009, (Sussex) 2009, (Salford) 2010, (Westminster) 2011; Hon. DUniv (Essex) 2005. *Publications:* Women and the Law (co-author) 1984, Parents and Children (fourth edn) 1993, From the Test Tube to the Coffin: Choice and Regulation in Private Life 1996, The Family Law and Society: Cases and Materials (sixth edn, co-author) 2009, Mental Health Law (fifth edn) 2010. *Leisure interests:* bridge, theatre, home. *Address:* The Supreme Court, Parliament Square, London, SW1P 3BD, England (office). *Telephone:* (20) 7960-1936 (office). *Fax:* (20) 7960-1961 (office). *E-mail:* justices@supremecourt.gsi.gov.uk (office). *Website:* www.supremecourt.gov.uk (office).

HALES, Antony John (Tony), CBE, BSc; British business executive; b. 25 May 1948, Blackpool, Lancs., England; s. of S. A. Hales and M. J. Hales; m. Linda Churchlow 1975; three s. one d.; ed Repton School, Univ. of Bristol; Marketing Man. Cadbury Schweppes 1969–79; joined Allied Domecq 1979, Marketing Dir Joshua Tetley 1979–83, Man. Dir Hall's Oxford SW 1983–85, Man. Dir Taylor Walker 1985–87, Man. Dir Ansells 1987–89, Dir Allied Breweries, Chair. and CEO Allied Domecq Spirits and Wine (fmrly Hiram Walker Group) 1995; CEO J. Lyons 1989–91, Dir Allied Domecq (fmrly Allied-Lyons) PLC 1989–99, CEO 1991–99; Dir Hyder PLC 1994–97, Midland Bank PLC (now HSBC Bank) 1994–2001, Aston Villa PLC 1997–2006, David Halsall International 2000–06, Tempo Holdings Ltd 2000–01, Reliance Security Group 2001–05, Satellite Information Services Holdings 2002–10, IPF Group PLC 2006–19, Welsh Nat. Opera 2010–19, Capital and Regional plc 2011–; Chair. Naati 2001–08, Workspace Group PLC 2002–11, British Waterways 2005–12, NAAFI Pension Fund Trustees 2010–, Canal and River Trust 2012–15, Greenwich Foundation 2014–, Associated Bd of Royal Schools of Music 2018–. *Leisure interests:* football, theatre, opera. *Address:* Belvoir House, Edstone Court, Wooton Wawen, Henley in Arden, Warwicks., B95 6DD (home); Greenwich Foundation, 2 Cutty Sark Gardens, Greenwich, London, SE10 9LW, England (office). *E-mail:* thales_uk@yahoo.com (office). *Website:* www.ornc.org (office).

HALEY, Nimrata (Nikki) Randhawa, BS; American business executive, politician, state governor and diplomatist; b. (Nimrata Randhawa), 20 Jan. 1972, Bamberg, S Carolina; d. of Dr Ajit Randhawa and Raj Randhawa; m. Michael Haley 1996; one s. one d.; ed Clemson Univ., S Carolina; Accounting Supervisor, FCR Corpn (waste man. and recycling co.) 1994–96; joined her mother's business, Exotica International (clothing firm) as Chief Financial Officer 1996–2004; mem. Bd of Dirs Orangeburg Co. Chamber of Commerce 1998, Lexington Chamber of Commerce 2003; Treas. Nat. Asscn of Women Business Owners 2003–04, Pres. 2004 (also Pres. S Carolina Chapter); Chair. Friends of Scouting Leadership Div. campaign 2006; mem. SC House of Reps for 87th Dist 2005–10, Majority Whip 2006–10; Gov. of South Carolina 2011–17); Perm. Rep. to UN 2017–18; mem. Bd Lexington Medical Foundation 2004, Lexington Co. Sheriff's Foundation 2004–06, West Metro Republican Women, Lexington Rotary Club, Mount Horeb United Methodist Church, Nat. Rifle Asscn; Republican; Hon. DH (Clemson Univ.) 2018. *Address:* c/o United States Mission to UN, 799 United Nations Plaza, New York, NY 10017, USA.

HALÍK, Mgr Tomáš, PhDr, ThD; Czech philosopher, academic, ecclesiastic and writer; *Professor, Department of Philosophy of Religion, Charles University;* b. 1 June 1948, Prague; s. of Miroslav Halík and Marie Halík; ed Charles Univ., Pontifical Lateran Univ., Vatican City; psychologist, Inst. of Ministry of Industry 1972–89; clandestinely ordained priest, Erfurt, GDR 1978; psychotherapist, Prague 1984–90; involved in 'underground' RC Church as close co-worker with Cardinal Tomášek; Gen. Sec. Czech Bishops' Conf. 1990–93; consultant, Pontifical Council for Dialogue with non-believers, Vatican 1990–93; Prof. Faculty of Philosophy, Charles Univ., Rector Univ. Church, mem. Scientific Bd Centre for Theoretical Study Charles Univ. 1992–; Visiting Fellow, St Edmund's Coll. Cambridge, UK 2003; lectures in univs world-wide, including Oxford and Cambridge, UK and Harvard, USA; Pres. Czech Christian Acad.; adviser to Pres. Havel; mem. Academic Bd Palacký Univ. Olomouc 1994–, European Acad. of Sciences and Arts, Cttee of Wise Persons, COMECE (Commissio Episcopatuum Communitatis Europensis—Comm. of the Bishops' Confs of the EC), Brussels 2006–08; Hon. mem. Church Law Soc., Hon. Prelate of His Holiness 2009; Kt's Cross, Order of Merit 2012; Hon. DD (Oxford Univ.) 2016; Hon. DTheol (Univ. Erfurt, Germany); Konrad Adenauer Silver Medal 1995, Masaryk's Arts Acad. Prize 1997, Andrew Elias SVU Human Tolerance Award 2002, Communio et Progressio Cardinal König Prize (Austria) 2003, Prize for Literature 2006, Czech Soc. for Science and Art 2007, Polish Fenix Prize for the best work by a foreign author 2008, Truth and Justice Award 2009, Romano Guardini Prize 2010, Man of Reconciliation, Soc. of Christians and Jews 2010, Prize for the best theological book of Europe, European Soc. for Catholic Theology 2010, Golden Medal of St Adalbert 2010, Templeton Prize 2014, Pontifice Award (Warsaw) 2016. *Television:* 18 TV films on the world's religions 2006–07. *Publications include:* books in 18 languages: O přítomnou církev a společnost 1992, Sedm úvah o slubě nemocným a trpícím 1993, Du wirst das Angesicht der erde erneuern: Kirche und Gesellschaft an der Schwelle zur Freiheit 1993, Víra a kultura 1995, Un proyecto de renovación espiritual 1996, Ptal jsem se cest 1997, Wyzwoleni, jesze nie wolni 1997, Mistica, anima della filosofia? 1999, Radzilem sie dróg 2001, Co je bez chvění, není pevné 2002, Oslovit Zachea 2003, Co nie jest chwiejne, jest nietrwałe 2004, Vzýván i nevzýván 2004, Noc zpovědník 2005, Prolínání světů 2006, Wzywany czy niewzywany 2006, Premówic do Zacheusza 2006, Zacheuszu! 2006, Vzdáleným nablízku 2007, Dotkni se ran 2008, Blizu pola: Molk na Antarktiki 2008, Stromu zbývá naděje 2009, Cierpliwosc wobec Boga 2009, Divadlo pro anděly 2010, Dotknij ran 2010, A gyóntató éjszakája 2010, Drzewo ma jescze nadzieje 2010, Patience with God 2009, Geduld mit Gott 2010, Dotakni se ran 2010, Smířená různost 2011, Uvahy na prahu tisíciletí 2011, Nič zpovidnika 2011, Night of the Confessor 2012, Nachtgedanken eines Beichtvaters 2012, Chci, abys byl 2012, Przenikanie światów 2012, Vicino ai lontani 2012, Blizu oddaljenim 2012, Těplelivist z Bogom 2012, Blizu oddaljenim 2012, Berühre die Wunden 2013, La Notte del Confessore 2013; more than 300 articles (some distributed secretly in Czechoslovakia before 1989). *Address:* Univerzita Karlova, ÚFaR FF UK, nám. Jana Palacha 2, 110 00 Prague 2 (office); Naprstkova 2, 110 00 Prague 1, Czech Republic (home). *E-mail:* tomas.halik@gmail.com (home). *Website:* www.halik.cz.

HALILI, Festim, BSc, MSc, PhD; Macedonian computer scientist, academic and politician; b. 5 May 1984, Tetovo; ed South East European Univ., Tech. Univ. Munich, Germany, Royal Holloway Univ. of London, UK, Tirana Univ.; with IT Office, Tetovo State Univ. 2005–05, 2009–13, Head of Project Office, Rectorat 2014–16; consultant, INACON GmbH, Karlsruhe, Germany 2008–10; Jr Asst, Informatics Dept, South East European Univ. 2009, Asst 2012, Docent 2014; Researcher, Royal Holloway Univ. of London 2013; Docent, Int. Balkan Univ. 2014; Software Engineer, Scopic Software, USA 2010; IT expert, Public Procurement Bureau 2014; Deputy Prime Minister responsible for the implementation of the Ohrid Framework Agreement 2016–17. *Address:* c/o Office of the Prime Minister, 1000 Skopje, Ilindenska b.b. 2, North Macedonia (office). *Telephone:* (2) 3118022 (office). *Fax:* (2) 3112561 (office). *E-mail:* primeminister@primeminister.gov.mk (office). *Website:* www.vlada.mk (office).

HALILOVIĆ, Safet, PhD; Bosnia and Herzegovina political scientist, academic and politician; *Professor, Department of Political Science, University of Sarajevo;* b. 3 April 1951, Orahova, Bosanska Gradiška; ed Univ. of Sarajevo; Pres. Renaissance (Bosniak cultural asscn) 1990–92, Bosniak Cultural Centre, Sarajevo 1995–98; entered politics as a mem. Stranka Demokratske Akcije— (SDA—Party of Democratic Action), Chair. Municipal Bd SDA, Sarajevo 1994–96; left to join Party for Bosnia and Herzegovina, Sec.-Gen. 1996; mem. House of Reps of Fed. of Bosnia and Herzegovina 1996–2001; Vice-Pres. Fed. of Bosnia and Herzegovina 2001–02, Pres. 2002–03; Minister of Civil Affairs 2003–07, of Human Rights and Refugees 2007–12; Prof., Dept of Political Science, Univ. of Sarajevo 2012–.

Address: Department of Political Science, University of Sarajevo, 71000 Sarajevo, Skenderija 72, Bosnia and Herzegovina (office). *Telephone:* (33) 203562 (ext. 188) (office). *Fax:* (33) 666884 (office). *E-mail:* halilovics@fpn.unsa.ba (office). *Website:* fpn.unsa.ba (office).

HALIM, Abdul Sayed Yusuf, BA; Afghan government official and judge; *Chief Justice of the Supreme Court;* b. 1959, Nangarhar Prov.; s. of Said Hussain; ed Kabul Univ., Univ. of Afghanistan; joined Ministry of Justice 1985, mem. Criminal Law Dept, Inst. of Legis. Affairs 1985–90, Deputy Dir of Law Study Dept 1990–92, Asst Dir Law Study Dept 1992–96, Deputy Head of Inst. of Legis. Affairs 1997–99, mem. Int. Law Dept 1998–2000, Gen. Dir of Legislation 2000–08, Deputy Admin. Minister 2009–10, Deputy Minister of Justice for Legal Affairs 2010–14, Acting Minister of Justice 2015; Chief Justice of the Supreme Court 2015–. *Address:* Supreme Court, Masood Square, Kabul, Afghanistan (office). *Telephone:* (20) 2300359 (office). *E-mail:* info@supremecourt.gov.af (office). *Website:* www.supremecourt.gov.af (office).

HALIMAN, Trihatma Kusuma; Indonesian real estate industry executive; *President Director, Agung Podomoro Group JL;* b. 6 Jan. 1952, Jakarta; s. of Anton Haliman; m.; two c.; ed Trier Univ., Germany; joined family real estate co. (now Agung Podomoro Group JL) 1973, Pres. Dir 1986–. *Address:* Agung Podomoro Group JL, Danau Sunter Blok M2 No. 7, Kompleks Podomoro, Sport Centre Sunter Agung, Jakarta Utara 14350, Indonesia (office). *Telephone:* (21) 6511435 (office). *Fax:* (21) 6511496 (office). *Website:* www.agungpodomoro.com (office).

HALL, Aleksander, MA; Polish historian, academic and fmr politician; *Professor, Wyższa Szkoła Informatyki i Zarządzania;* b. 20 May 1953, Gdańsk; m. Katarzyna Hall; ed Gdańsk Univ.; history teacher, Secondary School No 6, Gdańsk 1977; active in Acad. Pastoral Cure, Gdańsk in early 1970s; mem. Movt for Defence of Human and Civic Rights (ROPCIO) 1977–79; Ed. Bratniak 1977–81; Co-Founder and Leader, Young Poland Movt 1979; mem. Solidarity Trade Union 1980–; co-f. Cttee for Defence of Persons Imprisoned because of their Opinions, attached to Solidarity Trade Union 1980; mem. Regional Co-ordinative Comm. of Solidarity Trade Union, Gdańsk 1981–84; publicist, Przegląd Katolicki (Catholic Review) 1984–89, Polityka Polska (Polish Politics) 1982–89; mem. Primatial Social Council 1986–; mem. Civic Cttee attached to Lech Wałęsa, Chair. Solidarity Trade Union 1988–90, Vice-Pres., Dziekania Political Thought Club 1988–89; participant in Round Table debates, mem. group for political reforms Feb.–April 1989; Minister-mem. Council of Ministers (for co-operation with political orgs and Asscns) 1989–90; Deputy to Sejm (Parl.) 1991–93, 1997–2001; Vice-Chair. Solidarity Election Action Parl. Caucus 1997–2000; Leader, Democratic Right Forum 1990–92; Co-founder and Leader Conservative Party 1992–96, mem. Conservative Peasant Party (SKL) 1996– (Conservative Peasant Party-New Poland Movt, SKL-RNP from 2002), mem. Bd and Political Council; Prof., Wyższej Szkoły Informatyki i Zarządzania, Rzeszowie 2002–; Commander Cross, Order of the Rebirth of Polish 2006, Order of the White Eagle 2010, Officier, Légion d'Honneur 2015; Medal of Honor of Merit 2015. *Publications include:* Refleksje i polemiki, Wybór publicystyki politycznej 1989, Spór o Polskę 1993, Zanim bęclzie za późno 1994, Polskie patriotyzmy 1997, Pierwsza taka dekada 2000, Widziane z prawej strony 2000, Charles de Gaulle 2002, Jaka Polska? 2004, Naród i państwo w myśli politycznej Charles'a de Gaulle'a 2005, Francja i wielcy Francuzi 2007, Historia francuskiej prawicy 2009, W przededniu wielkiej zmiany 2010, Osobista historia III Rzeczypospolitej (Nagrody Historycznej POLITYKI 2012) 2011; numerous articles in Polish periodicals. *Leisure interests:* reading, history, politics, political thought and history of ideas, culture and history of France. *Address:* Wyższa Szkoła Informatyki i Zarządzania, mjr. Henryka Sucharskiego 2, 35-225 Rzeszów,, Poland (office). *Website:* wsiz.rzeszow.pl/pl/Uczelnia/kadra/ahall/Strony/default.aspx.

HALL, Andrew Rotely, OBE, BA (Hons), PhD; British diplomatist (retd); b. 3 May 1950, Bromley, Kent, England; s. of David Roteley Hall and Sheila Mary Stephens; m. Kathleen Wright; two d.; ed Univ. of Keele, Staffs., Univ. of London, School of Oriental and African Studies; Sr Research Officer (S Asia), Research Dept, FCO 1980–84; First Sec. (Political), New Delhi 1984–87; Prin. Research Officer, Research and Analysis Dept, FCO 1987–91; First Sec. and Consul and Deputy Head of Mission, Kathmandu 1991–94; Sr Prin. Research Officer, later Research Counsellor, S and SE Asia Research Group, FCO 1995–2003; Deputy High Commr (Eastern India), Kolkata 2003–06; Amb. to Nepal 2006–10 (retd).

HALL, Brian, BSc, PhD, DSc, FAAA, FRSC; Australian/Canadian biologist and academic; *George S. Campbell Professor Emeritus of Biology and University Research Professor Emeritus, Dalhousie University;* b. 28 Oct. 1941, Port Kembla, NSW; s. of Harry Hall and Dorris Garrad; ed Univ. of New England, Armidale, NSW; Asst Prof., Dalhousie Univ., Halifax, NS, Canada 1968–75, Full Prof. of Biology 1975–96, Chair. of Biology 1978–85, Faculty of Science Killam Prof. of Biology 1996–2001, then George S. Campbell Prof. of Biology, Killam Research Fellow 2003–05, George S. Campbell Prof. Emer. of Biology and Univ. Research Prof. Emer. 2007–; Visiting Distinguished Prof., Arizona State Univ. 2008–12; Fellow, Centre for Human Biology, Univ. of Western Australia, Perth 1993; Hon. mem. St Petersburg Soc. of Naturalists, Golden Key Int. Honor Soc. 2003, Foreign Hon. Mem. American Acad. of Arts and Sciences 2002; Hon. LLD (Univ. of Calgary) 2014; Fry Medal, Canadian Soc. of Zoologists 1994, Int. Craniofacial Biology Distinguished Scientist Award 1996, Alexander Kowalevsky Medal St Petersburg Soc. of Naturalists 2001, Killam Prize for Natural Sciences 2005, Thomas S. Hall Lecturer in the History of Science, Washington Univ. in St Louis 2013. *Publications:* has written more than 350 scientific articles and more than 16 books including Evolutionary Development Biology (textbook), Neural Crest in Development and Evolution (1999), Homology: Hierarchical Basis of Comparative Biology 2000, Evolution and Development 2000. *Leisure interest:* gardening. *Address:* 15/6770 Jubilee Road, Halifax, NS B3H 2H8, Canada (office); Department of Biology, Life Science Center, Dalhousie University, 1355 Oxford Street, PO Box 15000, Halifax, NS B3H 4R2, Canada (office). *Telephone:* (902) 494-3522 (office). *Fax:* (902) 494-3736 (office). *E-mail:* bkh@dal.ca (office). *Website:* www.dal.ca/faculty/science/biology (office).

HALL, Sir David Michael Baldock, Kt, MB, BS, BSc, FRCP, FRCPCH; British paediatrician and academic; *Professor of Community Paediatrics, University of Sheffield;* b. 4 Aug. 1945; s. of Ronald Hall and Ethel Gwen Hall (née Baldock); m. Susan M. Luck 1966; two d.; ed Reigate Grammar School, St George's Hosp., Univ. of London; Sr Medical Officer, Baragwanath Hosp., Johannesburg, South Africa 1973–76; Sr Registrar, Charing Cross Hosp., London 1976–78; Consultant Paediatrician, St George's Hosp. 1978–93; Prof. of Community Paediatrics, Univ. of Sheffield 1993–; Fellow, Royal Coll. of Paediatrics and Child Health 1996–, Pres. 2000–03; retd 2005; Hon. FRCPE 1999; Hon. Prof. of Paediatrics, Univ. of Cape Town 2007–; Univ. of London Gold Medal. *Publications include:* Child with a Disability 1996, Health for All Children (fourth edn) 2003, Child Surveillance Handbook 2006; numerous articles and chapters in scientific journals and books. *Leisure interests:* horses, travel. *Address:* Storrs House Farm, Storrs Lane, Stannington, Sheffield, S Yorks., S6 6GY, England (home). *E-mail:* d.hall@sheffield.ac.uk (office).

HALL, Jeffrey C., PhD; American geneticist, biologist and academic; *Part-time Faculty Member, University of Maine;* b. 1945, Brooklyn, New York; ed Amherst Coll., Univ. of Washington, Seattle; Postdoctoral Researcher, California Inst. of Tech. –1974; apptd Faculty mem., Brandeis Univ., Waltham, Mass 1974; currently Part-time Faculty mem., Univ. of Maine; Louisa Gross Horwitz Prize 2011, Gairdner Int. Award 2012, Shaw Prize in Life Science and Medicine (co-recipient) 2013, Nobel Prize in Physiology or Medicine (co-recipient with Michael Rosbash and Michael W. Young) 2017. *Achievements include:* cloned, with Michael Rosbash, the Period gene in *Drosophila melanogaster* controlling its biological rhythms 1984; also discovered that the mRNA and protein encoded by this gene show circadian oscillations. *Publications:* numerous papers in professional journals. *Address:* School of Biology and Ecology, 5751 Murray Hall, Orono, ME 04469, USA (office). *Telephone:* (207) 581-2540 (office). *Fax:* (207) 581-2537 (office). *Website:* www.umaine.edu (office).

HALL, Jerry; American model and actress; b. 2 July 1956, Gonzales, Tex.; d. of John P. Hall and Marjorie Sheffield; m. 1st Mick Jagger (q.v.) 1990 (divorced 1999); two s. two d.; m. 2nd Rupert Murdoch 2016; ed The Actors' Studio, New York, Nat. Theatre, London and Open Univ., UK; moved to Paris aged 16, began modelling career in 1970s; numerous TV appearances, USA; stage debut in William Inge's Bus Stop, Lyric Theatre, London 1990; Contributing Ed. Tatler 1999–; contracts include Yves Saint Laurent, Revlon Cosmetics, L'Oréal Hair, Thierry Mugler; Judge, Whitbread Book Awards and WH Smith Travel Book Awards; mem. Leadership Group for Amnesty International; Amb. for Prince's Trust, Caldicott Foundation, Breast Cancer; Patron Richmond Theatre, Tate Museum, Campaign for Stowe School, Pink Ribbon Foundation, Frontline Homeopathy, WELLBEING, UNICEF, Human Rights Centre for Amnesty International; Patron and Spokesperson for Nat. Soc. for Prevention of Cruelty to Children; Vice-Pres. Kingston Theatre Trust; Trustee, Tate Modern; Hon. Chair. British Red Cross London Ball. *Plays include:* The Graduate, Gielgud Theatre, London 2000 (US tour 2003), Picasso's Women 2001, The Play What I Wrote 2002, The Vagina Monologues 2002 (US tour 2003), Benchmark, New End Theatre, Hampstead 2003, UK tour 2007, Bus Stop, Snow White and the Seven Dwarves, Richmond Theatre 2014. *Films include:* Merci Docteur Rey, Willie and Phil 1980, Urban Cowboy 1980, Topo Galileo 1987, Let's Spend the Night Together, Running Out of Luck 1987, Hysteria! 2 (TV) 1989, The Emperor and the Nightingale, Batman 1989, 25 × 5: The Continuing Adventures of the Rolling Stones 1989, The Wall: Live in Berlin (TV) 1990, Bejewelled (TV) 1991, Freejack 1992, Princess Caraboo 1994, Savage Hearts 1995, Vampire in Brooklyn 1995, Diana and Me 1997, R.P.M. 1997, Being Mick (TV) 2001, Comic Relief: Say Pants to Poverty 2001, Tooth 2004, Enchantement (short) 2004, Gangster Kittens 2011. *Television includes:* Married with Children, Just Shoot Me, Saturday Night Live (host), The Clive James Show, French and Saunders, Jerry Hall's Gurus, Popetown, Art Deco, Annie Proulx, Way Out West, The Holiday Show, Lenny Goes to Town, Cluedo (six-part series) 2004, Kept 2005, Popetown (series) 2006, The Children's Party at the Palace (special) 2006, Hotel Babylon (series) 2007, The All Star Impressions Show (film) 2009, Money (series) 2010, contestant on Strictly Come Dancing (BBC) 2012. *Radio:* The Magic Flute (Classic FM), The Betty Grable Story (BBC Radio 3). *Publications:* Tall Tales 1985, Jerry Hall's Gurus 2004. *Leisure interests:* riding, swimming, reading, playing piano, travelling. *Address:* c/o Elite Model Management Ltd, 3–5 Islington High Street, London, N1 9LQ (office); 12 Macklin Street, Covent Garden, London, WC2B 5EZ, England.

HALL, John L., BS, MS, PhD; American physicist and academic; *Professor Adjoint, Physics Department, University of Colorado;* b. 21 Aug. 1934, Denver, Colo; s. of John Ernest Hall and Elizabeth Rae Hall (née Long); m. Marilyn Charlene Robinson; two s. one d.; ed Carnegie Inst. of Tech. (now Carnegie-Mellon Univ.); NRC Postdoctoral Fellow, Nat. Bureau of Standards (now Nat. Inst. of Standards and Tech.) 1961–62, Physicist 1962–71, apptd Sr Scientist 1971, currently Scientist Emer.; Lecturer, Physics Dept, Univ. of Colorado 1961–, Prof. Adjoint 2007–; Fellow, Jt Inst. for Lab. Astrophysics (now JILA) 1964–, American Physical Soc., Optical Soc. of America; Sr Fellow Emer., Nat. Inst. of Standards and Tech. (NIST); mem. Acad. of Science; Légion d'honneur 2004; Dr hc (Université Paris Nord) 1989; Hon. DSc (Carnegie Mellon) 2006, (Glasgow) 2007, (Ohio State) 2008; Dept of Commerce Gold Medal 1969, (group) 1974, 2002, Samuel W. Stratton Award 1971, E. U. Condon Award 1979, Optical Soc. of America Charles Hard Townes Award (co-recipient) 1984, American Physical Soc. Davisson-Germer Prize 1988, Optical Soc. of America Frederic Ives Medal 1991, American Physical Soc. Arthur L. Shawlow Prize 1993, Allen V. Astin Measurement Science Award 2000, Optical Soc. of America Max Born Award 2002, Office of Personnel Man. Presidential Rank Award 2002, IEEE Soc. for Ultrasonic, FerroElectricity and Frequency Control I. I. Rabi Prize 2004, Nobel Prize in Physics (co-recipient) 2005. *Publications:* numerous articles in peer-reviewed journals, and 11 patents. *Leisure interests:* music, photography, electronic design, travel. *Address:* JILA, University of Colorado, 440 UCB, Boulder, CO 80309-0440, USA (office). *Telephone:* (303) 492-7789 (office). *Fax:* (303) 492-5235 (office). *E-mail:* jhall@jila.colorado.edu (office). *Website:* jila.colorado.edu (office); www.hallstablelasers.com.

HALL, Most Hon. Sir Kenneth O., Kt, BA, MA, PhD, GCMG, OJ; Jamaican academic, university administrator and government official; b. 24 April 1941, Hanover; m. Rheima Holding; one d.; ed Univ. of the West Indies, Mona, Inst. of Int. Relations, Univ. of the West Indies, St Augustine, Trinidad, Queen's Univ., Canada; Prof. of History, State Univ. of NY (SUNY), Oswego, becoming Adjunct Prof. of Caribbean Studies, SUNY, Albany, also Prof. of American Studies, SUNY,

Old Wesbury, also Vice-Pres., Academic Affairs; Deputy Sec.-Gen. Caribbean Community (CARICOM) Secr. 1994–96; Pro-Vice-Chancellor and Prin. Univ. of the West Indies, Mona campus 1996–2006, later Prof. Emer.; Gov.-Gen. of Jamaica 2006–09; Chancellor, Univ. Coll. of the Caribbean 2011–12 (resgnd); mem. Univ. Council of Jamaica; mem. Bd Dirs Bank of Jamaica; Chair. Caribbean Examinations Council 2003–07; Order of the Nation 2004, Grand Cross, Order of Civil Merit (Spain) 2008.

HALL, Michael N., BS, PhD; Swiss molecular biologist and academic; *Professor, Biozentrum, University of Basel;* b. 12 June 1953, Puerto Rico; ed St Mark's School, Southborough, Mass, Univ. of North Carolina, Harvard Univ.; grew up in Venezuela and Peru; Research Asst, Dept of Bacteriology and Immunology, Univ. of North Carolina 1975–76; NIH Training Grant Fellow, Nat. Research Service Award, Dept of Microbiology and Molecular Genetics, Harvard Medical School 1976–79; Travelling Scholar, NCI Cancer Biology Program, Frederick Cancer Research Center, Frederick, Md 1979–81; Asscn pour le Développement de l'Institut Pasteur (ADIP) Fellow, Unité de Génétique Moléculaire, Institut Pasteur, Paris, France 1981; Helen Hay Whitney Fellow, Dept of Biochemistry and Biophysics, Univ. of California, San Francisco 1981–84, Asst Research Biochemist/Prin. Investigator 1984–87; Asst Prof., Biozentrum, Univ. of Basel 1987–92, Full Prof. 1992–, Chair. Div. of Biochemistry 1995–98, 2002–08, Deputy Dir of Biozentrum 2002–09; Univ. Visiting Professorship, The Hebrew Univ., Jerusalem 2014; mem. European Molecular Biology Org. 1995, Swiss Acad. of Medical Sciences 2013, NAS 2014; Fellow, AAAS 2009; Dr hc (Univ. of Geneva) 2016; Litton Advanced Tech. Achievement Award 1982, Cloëtta Prize for Biomedical Research 2003, Louis-Jeantet Prize for Medicine 2009, Marcel Benoist Prize for Humanities or Science 2012, Christian de Duve Lecture (Inaugural), The de Duve Institute and Université Catholique de Louvain, Brussels, Belgium 2013, Sir Hans Krebs Medal, Fed. of European Biochemical Socs 2014, Breakthrough Prize in Life Sciences (co-recipient) 2014, Synergy Grant, European Research Council 2014, Canada Gairdner Int. Award for Biomedical Research 2015, Debrecen Award for Molecular Medicine, Hungary 2016, Szent-Györgyi Prize for Progress in Cancer Research 2017, Albert Lasker Basic Medical Research Award 2017, Lelio Orci Award for Advances in Cell Biology 2017, Genome Valley Excellence Award, India 2018, Brupbacher Prize for Cancer Research 2019. *Publications:* numerous papers in professional journals. *Address:* Room 512, Biozentrum, University of Basel, Klingelbergstrasse 50–70, 4056 Basel, Switzerland (office). *Telephone:* (61) 2672150 (office). *Fax:* (61) 2070759 (office). *E-mail:* m.hall-at-unibas.ch (office). *Website:* www.biozentrum.unibas.ch/research/researchgroups/overview/unit/hall/ (office).

HALL, Nigel John, MA, RA; British sculptor; b. 30 Aug. 1943, Bristol; s. of Herbert John Hall and Gwendoline Mary Hall (née Olsen); m. Manijeh Yadegar 1986; ed Bristol Grammar School, West of England Coll. of Art, Royal Coll. of Art, London; Harkness Fellowship to USA 1967–69; first solo exhbn, Galerie Givaudan, Paris 1967; represented in the following collections: Tate Gallery, London, Musée Nat. d'Art Moderne, Paris, Nat. Galerie, Berlin, Museum of Modern Art, New York, Australian Nat. Gallery, Canberra, Art Inst. of Chicago, Kunsthaus, Zurich, Tokyo Metropolitan Museum, Musée d'Art Moderne, Brussels, Louisiana Museum, Denmark, Nat. Museum of Art, Osaka, Museum of Contemporary Art, Sydney, Tel-Aviv Museum, others; sculpture commissioned for Thameslink Tunnel, London 1993, Bank of America, London 2003, Said Business School, Univ. of Oxford 2005, Bank for Int. Settlements, Basel 2006, Kirkpatrick Oil, USA 2011, Kensington Leisure Centre 2015; Dr. hc (Univ. of Arts, London); Jack Goldhill Prize for Sculpture, RA, London 2002. *Publications:* Nigel Hall: Other Voices, Other Rooms, Galerie Scheffel, Bad Homburg, Germany 2007, Nigel Hall: Sculpture and Works on Paper, Royal Acad. of Arts 2008, Nigel Hall: Artists' Laboratory 3 2011. *Address:* 11 Kensington Park Gardens, London, W11 3HD, England (home). *Telephone:* (20) 7727-3162 (home). *E-mail:* info@nigelhallartist.com (office); nigelhallra@gmail.com (home). *Website:* www.nigelhallartist.com.

HALL, Philip David; British journalist and public relations consultant; *Chairman, PHA Media;* b. 8 Jan. 1955; s. of Norman Philip Hall and Olive Jean Hall; m. Marina Thomson 1997; two c.; ed Beal Grammar School, Ilford; reporter, Dagenham Post 1974–77, Ilford Recorder 1977–80; Sub-Ed. Newham Recorder 1980–84, Weekend Magazine 1984–85; reporter, The People 1985–86, Chief Reporter 1986–89, News Ed. 1989–92; News Ed. Sunday Express 1992–93; Asst Ed. (Features) News of the World 1993–94, Deputy Ed. 1994–95, Ed. 1995–2000; with Max Clifford Assocs 2000–01; Ed.-in-Chief Hello! 2001–02; Founder and Chair. Phil Hall Assocs. (public relations firm, now PHA Media) 2004–; fmr mem. Press Complaints Comm.; mem. Council, Public Relations Consultants Asscn. *Leisure interests:* golf, cinema, theatre, football. *Address:* PHA Media, 117 Wardour Street, London, W1F 0UN, England (office). *Telephone:* (20) 7025-1350 (office). *Fax:* (20) 7025-1351 (office). *E-mail:* info@pha-media.com (office). *Website:* www.pha-media.com (office).

HALL, Sir Wesley (Wes) Winfield, Kt; Barbadian church leader, politician, public relations consultant and fmr cricketer; b. 12 Sept. 1937, Glebe Land, Station Hill, St Michael; m. (divorced); four c.; ed Combermere School and Industrial Soc. London (personnel man.); right-arm fast bowler and lower-order right-hand batsman; took 192 wickets (average 26.38) in 48 Tests, best bowling (innings) 7/69, (match) 11/126; took 546 First-class wickets (average 26.14), best bowling (innings) 7/51; played amateur and professional cricket in England, Australia, NZ, India, Sri Lanka and throughout West Indies including 48 Test matches in which he took 192 wickets and first hat-trick by a West Indian 1961–69; Man. West Indies Cricket Team throughout West Indies and abroad 1983–85; Pres. West Indies Cricket Bd 2001–03; trainee telegraphist, Cable and Wireless, Barbados 1955–60; Public Relations Consultant, Esso, Queensland, Australia 1960–63, British American Tobacco Co. Ltd (Trinidad and Tobago) 1968–78; Personnel and Public Relations Man., Banks Barbados Breweries Ltd 1975–85; Ind. Senator, Barbados Senate 1971–76, Opposition Senator 1981–86; Minister of Employment, Labour Relations and Community Devt 1986–88, of Tourism and Sports 1988–93, of Industrial Relations, Community Devt and Sports 1993–94; Minister, Christian Pentecostal Church; fmr mem. Bd of Dirs Stanford 20/20 Cricket Project; Life mem. MCC; Hon. Life mem. Barbados Football Asscn; Humming Bird Gold Medal 1987, inducted into Int. Cricket Council Cricket Hall of Fame 2015. *Publications:* Secrets of Cricket 1962, Pace Like Fire 1965.

HALL OF BIRKENHEAD, Baron (Life Peer), cr. 2010, of Birkenhead in the County of Cheshire; **Anthony (Tony) William Hall,** CBE, MA, FRSA; British business executive; *Director-General, British Broadcasting Corporation;* b. 3 March 1951, Birkenhead, Merseyside, England; s. of Donald William Hall and Mary Joyce Hall; m. Cynthia Lesley Davis 1977; one s. one d.; ed King Edward's School, Birmingham, Birkenhead School, Merseyside, Keble Coll., Oxford; joined BBC as a news trainee 1973, News Ed. 1987–90, Dir News and Current Affairs 1990–93, Man. Dir News and Current Affairs 1993–96, Chief Exec. BBC News 1996–2001, Dir-Gen., BBC 2013–; Chief Exec. Royal Opera House, London 2001–13; mem. Council Brunel Univ. 1999–2002; Fellow, Vice-Chair. Royal TV Soc. (Chair. 1998–2000); Dir (non-exec.) Customs and Excise 2002–05, Channel 4 TV (Deputy Chair. 2012–13); Chair. Sector Skills Council for the Creative and Cultural Industries 2004–09, Theatre Royal Stratford East, Cultural Olympiad 2009–, Mayor of London's Cultural Forum; Dir (non-exec.), London Organising Cttee of the Olympic Games 2009–12, Paul Hamlyn Foundation; Trustee, High House Production Park Ltd, British Council 2008–; Patron Newsworld 1999–2000; mem. (Crossbench), House of Lords 2010–; Hon. Visiting Fellow, City Univ. 1999–2000. *Publications include:* King Coal: A History of the Miners 1981, Nuclear Politics: The History of Nuclear Power in Britain 1986, articles in various periodicals. *Leisure interests:* reading, writing, church architecture, opera, walking in Dorset. *Address:* Office of the Director-General, Broadcasting House, Portland Place, London, W1A 1AA (office); House of Lords, Westminster, London, SW1A 0PW, England. *Telephone:* (20) 7580-4468 (office). *Fax:* (20) 7637-1630 (office). *E-mail:* tonyhallandpa@bbc.co.uk (office); halla@parliament.uk. *Website:* www.bbc.co.uk (office); www.parliament.uk/biographies/lords/lord-hall-of-birkenhead/3765.

HALLBERG, Anders, BScEd, MSc, PhD; Swedish chemist, academic and fmr university vice-chancellor; *Professor Emeritus of Medicinal Chemistry, Uppsala University;* b. 29 April 1945; ed Lund Univ.; teacher/Research Asst, schools in Sweden/Lund Univ. 1970–73; Asst Research Fellow, The Chemical Centre, Lund 1973–79; Research Scientist, Nobel Kemi, Karlskoga 1980; Research Assoc., Univ. of Arizona, Tucson 1980, Asst Prof. (Pharmacy) 1981–82; Assoc. Prof. (forskare, NFR grant), The Chemical Centre, Lund 1983–86; Assoc. Dir, Astra (now AstraZeneca), Lund 1986–88, Dir, Head of Medicinal Chem. 1988–90, Scientific Adviser, AstraZeneca Lund 1990–99, Scientific Adviser, AstraZeneca Mölndal 2000–06; Prof. of Medicinal Chem., Uppsala Univ. 1990, now Emer., Head, Dept of Organic Pharmaceutical Chem. 1991–2006, Dean for Research, Faculty of Pharmacy 1996–2002, Deputy Vice-Pres. (Medicine/Pharmacy) 2002–05, Deputy Vice-Chancellor Uppsala Univ. 2005–06, Vice-Chancellor 2006–11; Visiting Researcher and Prof. at univs in USA; Section Ed., European Journal of Pharmaceutical Sciences 1998–2005; mem. Bd Åbo Akademi Univ. Finland 2009–, Forskningsberedningen (Scientific Advisory Bd of the Govt) 2011–, Bd Baltic Sea Foundation 2012–, Bd Medivir AB 2012–, Bd Beijer Foundation 2012–; mem. Royal Soc. of Sciences, Uppsala 1994, Royal Soc. of Arts and Sciences, Uppsala 2004, Royal Physiographic Soc., Lund 2005, Royal Swedish Acad. of Sciences (KVA, class IV chemistry) 2006, Royal Swedish Acad. of Eng Sciences (IVA, class IV chemistry) 2007, Royal Patriotic Soc.; Hon. mem. Småland Student Nation, Upland Student Nation, Uppsala, Allmänna Sången, Uppsala Univ. Jazz Orchestra, Orpheus Drängar, Royal Academic Orchestra, Rotary International; Order of the Cross of Terra Mariana (Estonia) 2011; Dr hc (Univ. of Sherbrooke, Canada) 2009; Fabian Gyllenberg Award, Royal Physiographic Soc. for best PhD thesis 1981, Sr Individual Grant Award to Outstanding Sr Scientist 1998, first recipient of Nat. Swedish Prize in Organic Chem. (The Holmquist Prize) 2004, Oscar Carlsson Medal for Excellence, Swedish Chemical Soc. 2005, Best Teacher Prize, Pharmacy Student Union, Uppsala Univ. 2006, HM the King's Medal for Distinguished Achievements in Educ. and Research 2008, Gustav Adolf Medal (of the year 1924), Uppsala Univ. 2011, Hon. Medal (Förtjänstmedaljen) of Kuratorskonventet, Curator curatorum 2011, Hon. Medal of Uppsala County (Förtjänstmedaljen) from the Gov. 2011, Rudbeck Medal for Outstanding Achievements in Science, Uppsala Univ. 2013. *Publications:* more than 240 scientific papers on organic synthesis and the devt of new pharmaceuticals against infectious diseases such as HIV/AIDS, HCV and malaria. *Address:* Department of Medicinal Chemistry, BMC, Box 574, 751 23 Uppsala, Sweden (office). *Telephone:* (18) 471-42-84 (office). *Fax:* (18) 471-44-74 (office). *E-mail:* anders.hallberg@orgfarm.uu.se (office). *Website:* www.farmfak.uu.se/organisk (office).

HALLBERG, Paul Thure, Fil Lic; Swedish fmr library director; b. 10 Dec. 1931, Gothenburg; s. of Severin Hallberg and Eva Hallberg (née Theorell); m. Elisabeth Löfgren 1958; one s.; ed Göteborg Univ., Yale Univ., USA; Asst Teacher, Dept of English Language and Literature, Göteborg Univ. 1958–59; Librarian, Göteborg Univ. Library 1960–68, Head of Dept 1968–77, Dir 1977–96; Sec. Main Cttee for Scandia Plan 1964–65; Sec., Scandinavian Fed. of Research Librarians 1966–69, mem. Bd 1979–84; mem. Royal Soc. of Arts and Sciences in Göteborg 1977–99, Librarian and Publications Officer 1977–2005, Hon. mem. 1999–; mem. Nat. Bibliographic Council 1983–96; Chair. Swedish Cataloguing Cttee 1979–85; Chair. Steering Group of Swedish LIBRIS system 1992–96; mem. of Bd Nordic Council for Scientific Information and Research Libraries (NORDINFO) 1986–88; mem. Standing Cttee, International Fed. of Library Asscns and Insts, Section on Acquisition and Exchange 1977–85, mem. Standing Cttee, Section of Univ. Libraries and other Gen. Research Libraries 1985–93, Sec. 1985–89; Dr hc (Göteborg) 1997. *Publications include:* A Passage to China: Colin Campbell's Diary of the First Swedish East India Company Expedition to Canton 1732–33 (co-ed.) 1996, En ostindiefarande fältskärs berättelse. Carl Fredrik Adlers journal från skeppet Prins Carl 1753–56 (co-ed.) 2013; author and ed. of numerous books and articles on bibliography and librarianship. *Leisure interests:* music, gardening. *Address:* Orangerigatan 34, 412 66 Göteborg, Sweden (home). *Telephone:* (31) 40-23-18 (home). *E-mail:* paul.hallberg@ub.gu.se (office).

HALLIER, Hans-Joachim, DIur; German diplomatist; b. 25 April 1930, Offenbach; s. of Christian L. Hallier and Sophie Heberer; m. Almuth H. Frantz 1966; two s.; ed Lessing Gymnasium, Frankfurt and Univs of Frankfurt and Heidelberg, Western Reserve Univ., Cleveland, Ohio, USA; attaché, German NATO Del. Paris 1960–61; Second Sec., Djakarta 1962–66; First Sec., Tokyo 1966–69; Dir Cabinet of Foreign Minister, Bonn 1970–74; Amb. to Malaysia 1974–76, to Indonesia 1980–83, to Japan 1986–90, to the Holy See 1990–95; Dir-Gen. Foreign Office, Bonn 1983–86. *Publications:* Völkerrechtliche Schiedsinstanzen für Einzelpersonen und ihr Verhältnis zur innerstaatlichen Gerichtsbarkeit 1962, Zwischen Fernost und Vatikan (memoirs) 1999, Das Dorf – eine mecklenburgische Chronik 2001; books and research papers on int. law. *Address:* Eifelblick 11, 53619 Rheinbreitbach, Germany (home). *Telephone:* (2224) 5931 (home). *Fax:* (2224) 70183 (home). *E-mail:* poreta91@aol.com (home).

HALLIWELL, Geraldine (Geri) Estelle; British singer; b. 7 Aug. 1972, Watford; one s. one d.; mem. (with Victoria Adams, Melanie Brown, Emma Bunton and Melanie Chisholm) Touch, later renamed The Spice Girls 1993–98, as 'Ginger Spice', reunion tour 2007–08, 2018–; UN Goodwill Amb. 1998–; Prince's Trust Amb.; Patron Breast Cancer Care; solo artist 1998–; two Ivor Novello songwriting awards 1997, Smash Hits Award for Best British Band 1997, BRIT Award for Best Single (for Wannabe, with The Spice Girls) 1997, BRIT Award for Best Video (for Say You'll Be There, with The Spice Girls) 1997, for Best Performance of the last 30 years 2010, three American Music Awards 1998, Special BRIT Award for Int. Sales 1998. *Films include:* Spiceworld The Movie 1997, Fat Slags 2004. *Television appearances:* judge on Popstars – The Rivals (ITV 1) 2002, appearance in Sex and the City (HBO) 2003, Australia's Got Talent (series judge) 2013. *Recordings include:* albums: with The Spice Girls: Spice 1996, Spiceworld 1997, Greatest Hits 2007; solo: Schizophonic 1999, Scream If You Wanna Go Faster 2001, Passion 2005. *Publications include:* If Only (autobiography) 1999, Just for the Record (autobiography) 2002; Ugenia Lavender children's series: Ugenia Lavender 2008, Ugenia Lavender and the Terrible Tiger 2008, Ugenia Lavender and the Burning Pants 2008, Ugenia Lavender: Home Alone 2008, Ugenia Lavender and the Temple of Gloom 2008, Ugenia Lavender the One and Only 2008. *E-mail:* jamesfox@astonfoxproductions.com. *Website:* gerihalliwell.com.

HALLSTRÖM, Lasse; Swedish film director; b. 2 June 1946, Stockholm; m. 1st Malou Hallström (divorced), one s.; m. 2nd Lena Olin, one d. *Films include:* A Lover and his Lass 1975, Abba – The Movie 1977, Father-to-be 1979, The Rooster 1981, Happy We 1983, My Life as a Dog 1985 (Film of the Year 1985), The Children of Bullerby Village 1986, More about the Children of Bullerby Village 1987, Once Around 1991, What's Eating Gilbert Grape (also co-exec. producer) 1993, Something to Talk About 1995, Lumière and Company 1995, The Cider House Rules 1999, Chocolat 2000, The Shipping News 2002, An Unfinished Life 2004, Casanova 2005, The Hoax 2006, Hachiko: A Dog's Story 2009, Dear John 2010, The Danish Girl 2010, Salmon Fishing in the Yemen 2011, Safe Haven 2013, The Hundred Foot Journey 2014, A Dog's Purpose 2017, The Nutcracker and the Four Realms 2018. *Promotional films include:* music videos for Abba including Waterloo 1974, Mamma Mia 1974, Money, Money, Money 1976, Summer Night City 1978, The Winner Takes It All 1980, When All Is Said and Done 1981, Head Over Heels 1982. *Address:* c/o David Nochimson, Ziffren, Brittenham, Branca, Fischer, Gilbert-Lurie, Stiffelman & Cook LLP, 1801 Century Park West, Los Angeles, CA 90067-6406; c/o United Talent Agency, 9336 Civic Center Drive, Beverly Hills, CA 90210, USA.

HALLÚ, Rubén Eduardo, BSc; Argentine veterinarian, academic and university administrator; *President, Centro de Estudios de Políticas Universitarias (CEPU), University of Buenos Aires;* b. 16 Jan. 1951; ed Univ. of Buenos Aires; fmr Assoc. Teacher and Dir of Basic Science, Faculty of Veterinary Sciences, Nat. Univ. of La Pampa, Santa Rosa; fmr Lecturer in Pharmacology, Nat. Univ. of Rosario; Assoc. Prof., later Prof. of Pharmacology, Univ. of Buenos Aires, also Sec. of Admin Supervision, Vice-Dean, Faculty of Veterinary Sciences 1994–2002, apptd Dean 2002, mem. Univ. of Buenos Aires Superior Bd 2002–, Rector Univ. of Buenos Aires 2006–14, Pres. Centro de Estudios de Políticas Universitarias (Center for Univ. Policy Studies) 2014–; mem. Comisión Nacional de Evaluación y Acreditación Universitaria (CONEAU) 2014–. *Publications:* more than 50 research papers. *Address:* Centro de Estudios de Políticas Universitarias (CEPU), University of Buenos Aires, 430/444 Viamonte, 1053 Buenos Aires, Argentina (office).

HALONEN, Tarja Kaarina, LLM; Finnish politician, lawyer and fmr head of state; b. 24 Dec. 1943, Helsinki; d. of Vieno Olavi Halonen and Lyyli Elina Loimola; m. Pentti Arajärvi 2000; one d. from previous relationship with Kari Pekkonen; ed Univ. of Helsinki and Univ. of Kent at Canterbury, UK; lawyer, Lainvalvonta Oy 1967–68; social welfare officer, organizing Sec. Nat. Union of Finnish Students 1969–70; lawyer, Cen. Org. of Finnish Trade Unions 1970–2000; mem. Social Democratic Party 1971–2000; Parl. Sec. to Prime Minister Sorsa 1974–75; mem. Helsinki City Council 1977–96; mem. Parl. 1979–2000, Chair. Parl. Social Affairs Cttee 1984–87; Second Minister, Ministry of Social Affairs and Health 1987–90, for Nordic Co-operation 1989–91, of Justice 1990–91, for Foreign Affairs 1995–2000; Pres. of Finland (first woman) 2000–12; Chair. Int. Solidarity Foundation 1991–2000 (mem. Bd of Dirs), TNL Theatre Org., Council of Women World Leaders 2009–14; Co-Chair. World Comm. on the Social Dimension of Globalization, ILO 2002–04; mem. Rep. Body of the Cooperative Retail Co. Elanto 1975–2000 (mem. Supervisory Bd 1980–96), UNCTAD Panel of Eminent Persons 2005–06, Bd Oslo Centre for Peace and Human Rights 2009–, UN High-level Panel on Global Sustainability (co-Chair.) 2012–, Leadership Council UN Sustainable Development Solutions Network 2014–, mem. Sec.-Gen.'s High-Level Advisory Bd on Mediation 2017–; Chair. Bd of Trustees WWF Finland; 17 hon. degrees from (Univ. of Helsinki) 2000, (Helsinki School of Econs) 2001, (Ewha Womens Univ., Repub. of Korea) 2002, (Univ. of Kent) 2002, (Eötvös Loránd Univ., Budapest) 2002, Chinese Acad. of Forestry) 2002, (Finlandia Univ., USA) 2003, (Univ. of Turku) 2003, (Univ. of Bluefiels, Nicaragua) 2004, (Univ. of Tartu, Estonia) 2004, (State Univ. of Yerevan, Armenia) 2005, (Helsinki Univ. of Tech.) 2008, (Univ. of Minnesota, Duluth) 2008, (Theatre Acad., Helsinki) 2009, (Umeå Univ.) 2009, (Univ. of Helsinki) 2010, (Univ. of Kazan, Russia) 2010. *Leisure interests:* art history, drawing, painting, the theatre, swimming. *Address:* c/o Office of the President, Mariankatu 2, 00170 Helsinki, Finland.

HALPERIN, Bertrand Israel, PhD; American physicist and academic; *Hollis Professor of Mathematicks and Natural Philosophy, Harvard University;* b. 6 Dec. 1941, Brooklyn, New York; s. of Morris Halperin and Eva Halperin; m. Helena Stacy French 1962; one s. one d.; ed George Wingate High School, Brooklyn, Harvard Coll. and Univ. of California (Berkeley); NSF Postdoctoral Fellow, Ecole Normale Supérieure, Paris 1965–66; mem. tech. staff, Bell Labs 1966–76; Prof. of Physics, Harvard Univ. 1976–, Chair. Dept of Physics 1988–91, Hollis Prof. of Mathematicks and Natural Philosophy 1992–; Assoc. Ed. Reviews of Modern Physics 1974–80; mem. NAS, American Acad. of Arts and Sciences, American Philosophical Soc.; Fellow, American Physical Soc.; Oliver Buckley Prize for Condensed Matter Physics 1982, Lars Onsager Prize 2001, Wolf Prize in Physics (jt recipient) 2003, Goettingen Akademie der Wissenschaften Dannie Heineman Prize 2007, Lars Onsager Medal and Lecture, Norwegian Univ. of Science and Tech. 2009. *Publications include:* about 250 articles in scientific journals. *Address:* Lyman Laboratory of Physics, Harvard University, 17 Oxford Street, Cambridge, MA 02138, USA (office). *Telephone:* (617) 495-4294 (office). *E-mail:* halperin@physics.harvard.edu (office). *Website:* www.physics.harvard.edu/people/facpages/halperin.html (office); cmtw.harvard.edu (office).

HALPERN, Sir Ralph (Mark), Kt, CBIM, FID; British business executive; *Principal, Halpern Consulting;* b. 24 Oct. 1938, London; s. of Bernard Halpern and Olga Halpern; m. Joan Halpern (divorced); one s. one d.; ed St Christopher School, Letchworth; fmr trainee Selfridges; joined Burton Group PLC 1961, Chief Exec. and Man. Dir 1978–90, Chair. 1981–90; Co-Founder Top Shop 1970; Chair. Halpern Assocs; Chair. CBI Marketing and Common Affairs Cttee 1984; Chair. Police and Community Partnership Group, E Surrey; Prin., Halpern Consulting 2005–; mem. CBI City-Industry Task Force 1986; mem. Pres.'s Cttee, Chair. British Fashion Council 1990–94; mem. Advisory Council Prince's Youth Business Trust 1991–92; fmr Hon. Prof., Univ. of Warwick; Retailer of the Year, London. *Leisure interest:* country pursuits. *E-mail:* Knightfirstk@gmail.com.

HALQI, Wael Nader al-, MD; Syrian physician and politician; b. 1964, Jasim, Dar'a Governorate; m.; four c.; ed Univ. of Damascus; Dir of primary health care, Jasim 1997–2000; Pres. Syrian Doctors' Syndicate 2010; Minister of Health 2011–12; Prime Minister 2012–16; mem. Baath Arab Socialist Party, Sec.-Gen., Dar'a Br. 2000–04. *Address:* c/o Office of the Prime Minister, rue Chahbandar, Damascus, Syria.

HALSBAND, Frances, BA, MArch, FAIA; American architect; *Partner, Kliment Halsband Architects;* b. 30 Oct. 1943, New York City; m. Robert Kliment 1971; one s.; ed Swarthmore Coll., Columbia Univ., New York; worked at Mitchell & Giurgola Architects, New York 1968–72; Founding Pnr (with Robert Kliment), Kliment Halsband Architects, New York 1972–; fmr Dean School of Architecture, Pratt Inst.; Guest Lecturer, Ball State Univ., Univ. of California, Berkeley, Univ. of Cincinnati, Columbia Univ., Harvard Univ., Univ. of Illinois, North Carolina State Univ., Univ. of Maryland, Univ. of Pennsylvania, Rice Univ. and Univ. of Virginia; fmr Pres. New York Chapter, AIA, Architectural League of New York; fmr Commr New York City Landmarks Preservation Comm.; Chair. Cttee on Design, AIA 1999; mem. Architectural Review Bd of Fed. Reserve Bank; Architect Advisor, Corpn at Brown Univ.; fmr mem. Architectural Advisory Bd US Dept of State; AIA NY State Award of Merit, Interfaith Forum on Religion, Art and Architecture Design Award, Gen. Services Admin Design Award Citation, AIA New York Chapter Medal of Honour. *Architectural works include:* Roth Center for Jewish Life, Hanover, New Hampshire, Long Island Railroad Entrance Pavilion to Pennsylvania Station, New York. *Publications include:* articles in professional journals. *Address:* Kliment Halsband Architects, 322 Eighth Avenue, New York, NY 10001, USA (office). *Telephone:* (212) 243-7400 (office). *Fax:* (212) 633-9769 (office). *E-mail:* info@kliment-halsband.com (office). *Website:* www.kliment-halsband.com (office).

HALSE, Bengt Gösta, DEng; Swedish business executive; b. 2 Feb. 1943, Gothenburg; ed Chalmers Inst. of Tech., Gothenburg, Linköping Univ.; with Ericsson Group 1974–95; Pres. and CEO Saab AB 1995–2003; Chair. Comhem AB, Flexlink AB, IFK Gothenburg 2003–06; mem. Bd of Dirs Omhex AB, Teleca AB, TietoEnator 2004–09, Denel Ltd; fmr Chair. ACARE (Advisory Council for Aeronautical Research in Europe; mem. Advisory Bd Tracab; mem. Royal Swedish Acad. of Engineering Sciences, Royal Swedish Acad. of War Sciences; Hon. DrIng (Linköping Univ.) 1999; Hon. mem. Royal Swedish Soc. of Naval Sciences 2002; Hon. Fellow, Royal Aeronautical Soc., London 2001, Hon. Consul, Gothenburg 2008; King's Medal of the 12th Dimension with Ribbon, Order of the Seraphim 2004. *Address:* c/o Comhem AB, POB 43, 871 21, Härnösand, Sweden. *Telephone:* (734) 187105. *Fax:* (31) 930926.

HALSTEAD, Sir Ronald, Kt, CBE, MA, CBIM, FRSC, FRSA; British business executive; *President, Engineering Industries Association;* b. 17 May 1927, Lancaster, Lancs., England; s. of Richard Halstead and Bessie Harrison Halstead; m. 1st Yvonne Cecile de Monchaux 1968 (deceased); two s.; m. 2nd Susanne Eugenie Stoessl (died 2013); ed Queens' Coll., Cambridge; Research Chemist H.P. Bulmer & Co. 1948–53; Mfg Man. Macleans Ltd 1954–55; Factory Man. Beecham Products Inc., USA 1955–60, Asst Man. Dir Beecham Research Lab. Ltd 1960–62, Pres. Beecham Research Labs, Inc. (USA) 1962–64, Vice-Pres. Marketing, Beecham Products, Inc. (USA) 1962–64, Chair. Food and Drink Div. Beecham Group 1964–67; Chair. Beecham Products 1967–84, Man. Dir (consumer products) Beecham Group 1973–84, Chair. and Chief Exec. Beecham Group PLC 1984–85; Dir The Otis Elevator Co. Ltd 1978–83, Burmah Oil 1983–89; Dir (non-exec.) American Cyanamid Co. 1986–94, Davy Corpn PLC 1986–91, Gestetner Holdings PLC 1986–95; Dir Laurentian Financial Group PLC 1991–95; Chair. CAB Int. 1995–98; Deputy Chair. Tech. Colls Trust 1993–2006; Vice-Chair. Proprietary Asscn of GB 1968–77; Pres. Nat. Advertising Benevolent Soc. 1978–80; Vice-Pres. Inst. of Packaging 1979–81, Pres. 1981–83; Dir British Steel Corpn 1979–86, Deputy Chair. 1986–94; Gov. Ashridge Man. Coll. 1970–2007, Vice-Chair. 1977–2007; Pres. Inc. Soc. of British Advertisers 1971–73; Chair. British Nutrition Foundation 1970–73, Council mem. 1967–79; Vice-Chair. Advertising Asscn 1973–81; Vice-Chair. Food & Drink Industries Council 1973–76; Pres. Food Mfrs Fed. 1974–76; mem. CBI 1970–86, BIM 1972–77, Cambridge Univ. Appointments Bd 1969–73, Agric. Research Council 1978–84; Dir Nat. Coll. of Food Tech. 1977–78, Chair. of Bd 1978–83; Chair. Knitting Sector Working Group, NEDO 1978–90, Textile and Garment Working Group, 1991–93; Fellow, Inst. of Grocery Distribution 1979–, Marketing Soc. 1981–99; Trustee, Inst. of Econ. Affairs 1980–93; mem. Monopolies and Mergers Comm. Newspaper Panel 1980–92; mem. Industrial Devt Advisory Bd Dept of Trade and Industry 1983–93, Chair. 1984–93; Hon. Treas. and Dir, Centre for Policy Studies 1984–93; mem. Priorities Bd for Research and Devt in Agric. and Food, Ministry of Agric. Fish and Food 1984–87; Chair. Bd of Food Studies Univ. of Reading 1983–86; Pres. Eng Industries Asscn 1991–; mem. Monopolies and Mergers Comm. 1993–99; Council mem. European Policy Forum 1993–; Council mem. Univ. of Buckingham 1973–95, Univ. of Reading 1978–98; Council and Exec. Cttee mem., Imperial Soc. of Kts Bachelor

1985–2003; Chair. Conservative Foreign and Commonwealth Council 1995–; Gov. De Montfort Univ. (fmrly Leicester Polytechnic) 1989–97; Fellow, Inst. of Marketing 1975–, Vice-Pres. 1980–99; mem. Council, Food Mfrs Fed. Inc. 1966–85; Hon. Fellow, Inst. of Food Science and Tech., Inst. of Marketing, Queens' Coll. Cambridge 1985; Hon. DSc (Reading) 1982, (Univ. of Lancaster) 1987. *Leisure interests:* sailing, squash racquets, skiing. *Address:* Engineering Industries Association, 62 Bayswater Road, London, W2 3PS (office); 37 Edwardes Square, London, W8 6HH, England (home). *Telephone:* (20) 7298-6455 (office); (20) 7603-9010 (home). *Fax:* (20) 7298-6456 (office); (20) 7371-2595 (home). *E-mail:* head.office@eia.co.uk (office). *Website:* www.eia.co.uk (office).

HALVORSEN, Kristin; Norwegian politician; *Director, Centre for International Climate and Environmental Research;* b. 2 Sept. 1960; m. Charlo Halvorsen; two c.; mem. Stortinget (Parl.) for Oslo 1989–, mem. Standing Cttee on Finance 1989–97, on Scrutiny and Constitutional Affairs 1997–2001, on Foreign Affairs 2001–05, mem. Parl. Del. in Connection with European Parl. 2001–05; Leader, Socialist Left Party of Norway 1997–2012; Minister of Finance 2005–09, of Educ. 2009–13; Dir Centre for Int. Climate and Environmental Research (CICERO) 2014–; Head Bioteknologirådet 2014–; Observer UN Gen. Meeting 1985; Chair. Natural History Museum; Deputy mem. Cttee on Ex-Gratia Payment of Compensation 1996; mem. Consulting Agency Regarding EEC Matters 1997–2001. *Publications include:* Rett Fra Hjertet (co-authored with Ingolf Håkon Teigene) 2004, Gjennomslag (co-authored with Lilla Sølhusvik) 2012. *Address:* Centre for International Climate Research, Gaustadalleen 21, 0349, Oslo, Norway (office). *Telephone:* 22-00-47-00 (office). *E-mail:* kristin.halvorsen@cicero.oslo.no (office).

HALYLOV, Muhammetnur; Turkmenistani geologist and government official; Dir Inst. of Geology, State Geological Co., TurkmenGeology –2013; Minister of the Petroleum and Gas Industry and Mineral Resources 2013–16. *Address:* c/o Ministry of the Petroleum and Gas Industry and Mineral Resources, 744000 Aşgabat, Arçabil Saýoly 56, Turkmenistan. *E-mail:* ministryoilgas@online.tm.

HAMÁČEK, Jan; Czech politician; *First Deputy Prime Minister and Minister of the Interior;* m. Camilla Hamáček; two s.; ed Univerzita Karlova v Praze (Charles Univ., Prague); Chair. Young Social Democrats 2002–06; Sec. Česka Strana Sociálně Demokratická (ČSSD—Czech Social Democratic Party) faction, Ass. of Cen. Bohemia (Středočeský) Region 2001–04, Head of Int. Dept of Social Democrats 2004–06; adviser to the Prime Minister, especially on foreign policy 2005–06; Vice-Pres. World Org. of Socialist Youth 2006–08; mem. ČSSD, Chair. 2018–; mem. Chamber of Deputies (Poslanecká Sněmovna) for the Cen. Bohemia (Středočeský) Region 2006–Aug. 2013, Oct. 2013–, Deputy Chair. Foreign Affairs Cttee 2006–10, Chair. 2010–13, Head of Czech Del. to NATO Parl. Ass., Shadow Minister of Defence and Deputy Chair. Chamber of Deputies 2012–13, Chair. Nov. 2013–17; Minister of the Interior 2018–, also First Deputy Prime Minister 2018–, Acting Minister of Foreign Affairs June–Oct. 2018. *Publications:* articles on defence and world affairs in the Harvard International Review, US Atlantic Council, Europe's World. *Address:* Ministry of the Interior, Nad Štolou 3, POB 21, 170 34 Prague 7, Czech Republic (office). *Telephone:* 974811111 (office). *Fax:* 974833582 (office). *E-mail:* posta@mvcr.cz (office). *Website:* www.mvcr.cz (office).

HAMAD, Abdulatif Yousef al-, BA (Hons); Kuwaiti banker, politician and international organization official; *Director General and Chairman, Arab Fund for Economic and Social Development;* b. 1936; m.; four c.; ed Claremont Coll., Calif. and Harvard Univ., USA; mem. Kuwaiti del. to UN 1962; Dir-Gen. Kuwait Fund for Arab Econ. Devt 1963–81; Dir The South & Arabian Gulf Soc. 1963–81, Assistance Authority for the Gulf and Southern Arabia 1967–81; Dir, then Man. Dir Kuwait Investment Co. 1963–71; Man. Dir Kuwait Investment Co. 1965–74; Chair. Kuwait Prefabricated Bldg Co. 1965–78, United Bank of Kuwait Ltd, London 1966–84; Exec. Dir Arab Fund for Econ. and Social Devt 1972–81, Dir-Gen. and Chair. 1985–; Chair. Compagnie Arabe et Internationale d'Investissements, Luxembourg 1973–81; Chair. Devt Cttee Task Force on Multilateral Devt Banks; mem. Bd of Trustees, Corporate Property Investors, New York 1975–; mem. Governing Body Inst. of Devt Studies, Sussex, UK 1975–87; mem. Ind. Comm. on Int. Devt Issues (Brandt Comm.) 1976–79; mem. Bd Int. Inst. for Environment and Devt, London 1976–80; Minister of Finance and Planning 1981–83; Gov. for Kuwait, World Bank and IMF 1981–83; mem. UN Cttee for Devt Planning 1982–91, Chair. 1987; mem. IFC Banking Advisory Bd Group 1987–, Advisory Group on Financial Flows for Africa (UN) 1987–88, South Comm. 1987–89, Group of Ten (African Devt Bank) 1987–, World Bank's Pvt. Sector Devt Review Group 1988–, UN Panel for Public Hearings on Activities of Transnational Corpns in S Africa and Namibia 1989–92, Bd Trustees of Stockholm Environment Inst. 1989–92, Comm. on Global Governance 1992–, Int. Finance Corpn, Banking Advisory Bd Group (World Bank), Bd of Kuwait Investment Authority, Group of Thirty Consultative Group on Int. Econ. and Monetary Affairs, Inc., Washington, DC; Trustee, Arab Planning Inst. *Address:* Arab Fund for Economic and Social Development, PO Box 21923, Safat 13080, Kuwait (office). *Telephone:* 24959000 (office). *Fax:* 24959390 (office). *E-mail:* hq@arabfund.org (office). *Website:* www.arabfund.org (office).

HAMAD, Seif Sharif, BA; Tanzanian politician and political scientist; *Vice-President of Zanzibar;* b. 22 Oct. 1943, Pemba; s. of Sharif Hamad Shehe and Time Seif Haji; m. 1st Furtunah Saleh Mbamba 1971; m. 2nd Aweinah Sanani Massoud 1977; one s. four d.; ed King George VI Secondary School, Zanzibar, Univ. of Dar es Salaam; teacher, Lumumba Coll., Fidel Castro Coll. 1964–72; Asst to Pres. of Zanzibar 1975–77, Minister of Educ., Zanzibar 1977–80; mem. Tanzanian Parl. 1977–80; mem. Zanzibar House of Reps 1980–99; mem. Cen. Cttee Chama Cha Mapinduzi (CCM) Party 1977–88, Head Econ. and Planning Dept of CCM 1982–88; Chief Minister of Zanzibar 1984–88; political prisoner in Zanzibar 1989–91; apptd Nat. Vice-Chair. Civic United Front 1992, now Sec.-Gen.; unsuccessful presidential cand. in Zanzibar elections 2000, 2010, Vice-Pres. of Zanzibar 2010–; Chair. Gen. Ass. Unrepresented Nations and Peoples' Org. (UNPO) 1997. *Leisure interests:* reading, swimming. *Address:* Civic United Front, Mtendeni Street at Malindi, PO Box 3637, Zanzibar (office); PO Box 10976, Dar es Salaam, Tanzania. *Telephone:* (24) 2237446 (office). *E-mail:* headquarters@cuftz.org (office). *Website:* www.cuf.or.tz (office).

HAMADA, Hiroshi; Japanese business executive; b. 28 April 1933, Kagoshima Pref.; m.; three c.; ed Tokyo Univ.; Pres. Ricoh Co. Ltd 1983–96, Chair. 1996–2004, now Supreme Adviser; Chair. Keidanren Cttee on Human Resources Devt 2000; fmr Vice-Chair. Japan Business Fed.; Pres. Japan Business Machines and Information System Industries Asscn 1992–93; Dir UFJ Holdings; mem. Council, Japan Productivity Centre for Socio-Econ. Devt; Counselor, Sasakawa Peace Foundation; Officer, Légion d'honneur 1998; Blue Ribbon Medal 1991. *Address:* c/o Ricoh Company Limited, 15–5 Minami Aoyama 1–chome, Minato-ku, Tokyo 107–8544, Japan.

HAMADA, Junichi, BA, MA, PhD; Japanese academic and university administrator; b. 14 March 1950, Akashi, Hyōgo Prefecture; ed Faculty of Law, Univ. of Tokyo; has been closely connected with the Inst. of Journalism and Communication Studies (renamed the Inst. of Socio-Information and Communication Studies) at Univ. of Tokyo (Todai) throughout his career, Research Assoc. and Inst. Dir 1995–99, Dean of Interfaculty Initiative in Information Studies and Grad. School of Interdisciplinary Information Studies 2000–02, Man. Dir and Exec. Vice-Pres. Univ. of Tokyo 2005–09, Pres. Univ. of Tokyo 2009–15; served as a govt adviser; Dr hc (Shanghai Jiaotong Univ.) 2015. *Publications:* numerous papers in professional journals.

HAMADA, Rick, BS; American business executive; b. 1958; m. Michele Hamada; ed San Diego State Univ.; joined Hamilton/Avnet Electronics as technical specialist in San Diego 1983, roles included sales and marketing, including serving as field sales rep., computer sales manager, sales unit dir, regional sales manager, Area Vice-Pres. and Vice-Pres. of Business Devt for Open Systems, Corp. Vice-Pres. Avnet, Inc. 1999–2002, Sr Vice-Pres. 2002–03, Global Pres. Avnet Computer Marketing 2003, Global Pres. Avnet Tech. Solutions (formed from integration of Avnet Computer Marketing and Avnet Applied Computing) 2003–06, COO Avnet, Inc. 2006–10, Pres. and COO 2010–11, mem. Bd of Dirs and CEO 2011–16; apptd Chair. Global Tech. Distribution Council 2012 (fmrly Vice-Chair.); mem. Advisory Bd Coll. of Business Admin, San Diego State Univ. 2009; mem. Bd of Dirs Keysight Technologies 2014–; mem. Bd of Trustees Nat. Univ. 2018–; Avnet Chair.'s Award, twice named to Computer Reseller News' Top 25 Most Influential Channel Executives. *Leisure Interests:* bonsai gardening.

HAMAGUCHI, Michinari, BMed, MD, PhD; Japanese physician, academic and university administrator; *President, Japan Science and Technology Agency;* b. 19 Feb. 1951, Ise, Mie Prefecture; ed Nagoya Univ.; Research Assoc., Cancer Research Facility, School of Medicine, Nagoya Univ. 1980–83, Research Assoc., Pathological Control Research Facility 1983–84, Assoc. Prof., Pathological Control Research Facility 1984–93, Prof., Pathological Control Research Facility 1993–97, Dir Radioisotope Research Centre 1997–2001, Prof. 2001–02, Dir Pathological Control Research Facility, Grad. School of Medicine 2002–03, Dir Research Inst. for Disease Mechanism and Control 2002–03, Prof. Div. of Cancer Biology, Graduate School of Medicine 2003–, Prof., Centre for Neural Disease and Cancer 2003–04, Vice-Dir Grad. School of Medicine 2004–05, Dir Centre for Medical Educ. Research and Support, Grad. School of Medicine 2004–05, Dean, Grad. School of Medicine and School of Medicine 2005–09, Pres. Nagoya Univ. 2009–15, apptd Special Advisor to Pres., Nagoya Univ. 2015; Pres. Japan Science and Tech. Agency 2015–; Chair. Council for Science and Technology, MEXT 2015–; Councillor, Japanese Cancer Asscn, Japanese Biochemical Soc., Japanese Soc. of Virology; mem. Japanese of Virology, Japanese Biochemical Soc., Japanese Cancer Asscn, American Soc. for Cell Biology, American Asscn of Cancer Research; Royal Order of Sahametrei Officer Class, Cambodia 2015; Dr hc (Sungkyunkwan Univ.) 2009, (Mongolian Nat. Univ. of Science and Tech.) 2010, (Poland Gdansk Univ.) 2011; Polar Star Medal of Mongolia 2014, Award for Justice Cause, Ministry of Justice, Vietnam 2015. *Publications:* numerous papers in professional journals on the molecular mechanism in cancer invasion and metastasis. *Leisure interests:* music appreciation, drawing, gardening. *Address:* Japan Science and Technology Agency, 5-3 Yonbancho, Chiyoda-ku, Tokyo 102-8666, Japan (office). *Telephone:* (52) 789-5111 (office). *Website:* www.jst.go.jp/EN/ (office).

HÄMÄLÄINEN, Sirkka Aune-Marjatta, DSc (Econ); Finnish banker and economist; b. 8 May 1939, Riihimäki; d. of Martti Hinkkala and Aune Hinkkala; m. 1st Arvo Hämäläinen 1961; one s. one d.; m. 2nd Bo Lindfors 1999; ed Helsinki School of Econs and Business Admin.; Economist, Econs Dept, Bank of Finland 1961–72, Head of Office, Econs Dept 1972–79, Head of Dept 1979–81, Dir 1982–91, mem. Bd 1991–92, Gov. and Chair. Bd 1992–98; Dir Econs Dept, Ministry of Finance 1981–82; Chair. Financial Supervision Authority 1996–97; mem. Exec. Bd, European Cen. Bank, Frankfurt 1998–2003, mem. Single Supervisory Bd 2014–16; Docent, Adjunct Prof. of Econs Helsinki School of Econs and Business Admin 1991–2006; Dir Investor AB 2004–11, Sanoma Corpn 2004–14; Chair. Finnish Nat. Opera 2007–16; Vice-Chair. KONE Corpn 2004–15; Foreign Academian, Real Academia de Ciencias Económicas y Financieras, Barcelona; Commdr, First Class, Order of the White Rose; Merit Medal, First Class, Order of the White Star (Estonia); Dr hc (Turku School of Econs and Business Admin.) 1995. *Publications include:* books, numerous articles, speeches. *Leisure interests:* travelling, literature, music. *Telephone:* 50-5021831 (mobile). *E-mail:* sam.hamalainen@kolumbus.fi.

HAMARI, Julia; Hungarian/German singer (mezzo-soprano); b. 21 Nov. 1942, Budapest; d. of Sándor Hamari and Erzsébet Dokupil; ed Franz Liszt Music Acad. of Budapest, Hochschule für Musik, Stuttgart, Germany; debut as soloist, Bach's St Matthew Passion in Vienna under Karl Richter 1966; specializes in Rossini, Mozart, Bellini; lieder recitalist and oratorio performer; has appeared world-wide with conductors including Herbert von Karajan, Sergiu Celibidache, Rafael Kubelik, Georg Solti, Karl Böhm, Pierre Boulez, Carlo M. Giulini, Nikolaus Harnoncourt, Claudio Abbado, Riccardo Muti and Mariss Jansons; debut in USA as soloist with Chicago Symphony Orchestra 1967; opera debut at Salzburg Festival as Mercedes in Bizet's Carmen 1967 and as Carmen in Stuttgart 1968; has appeared with Deutsche Oper am Rhein in various baroque and classical operas; has appeared at major opera houses including La Scala, Covent Garden, Vienna State Opera, Metropolitan Opera; opera roles include Celia in La fedeltia premiata (J. Haydn), Orpheus (Gluck), Dorabella and Despina (Così fan tutte), Angelina in La Cenerentola (Rossini), Rosina in Il Barbiere di Siviglia (Rossini), Sesto in La clemenza di Tito (Mozart), Cherubino in Le Nozze di Figaro (Mozart), Sinaide in Mosé in Egitto (Rossini), Romeo in I Capuleti ed I Montecchi (Bellini), Farnace in Mitridate (Mozart); Prof., Staatliche Hochschule für Musik, Stuttgart 1989–2009; performed in festivals of Edinburgh, Glyndebourne, Florence (Maggio Musicale),

Netherlands (Schleswig-Holstein Musik, Schwetzingen); Offizierskreuz (Hungary) 2002; prizewinner, Erkel Int. Singing Competition, Budapest 1964, Kodály Prize 1987. *Recordings include:* Bach's St John and St Matthew Passion 2006, Bach's Mass in B Minor, Oratorios, Cantatas, Oberon by Weber, Il matrimonio segreto by Cimarosa, Giulio Cesare by Handel, Roméo et Juliette by Berlioz, Mozart's Requiem, Mass in C major by Beethoven, Ernani by Verdi, Tito Manlio, Cavalleria rusticana, Juditha Triumphans by Vivaldi, I Puritani by Bellini, Beethoven's 9th Symphony, Mahler's Second and Eighth Symphonies, Orpheus by Gluck, Stabat Mater by Haydn and Pergolesi, Don Sanche by F. Liszt, Mosé in Egitto by Rossini, Prima la musica by A. Salieri, Eugen Onegin (also video), Meistersinger, Zigeunerlieder 1967, Lieder 1969, Bartók Songs 1973, Nausikaa Lieder Recital 1982, Lieder der Romantik 1982–94, Handel German Arias 1990, Julia Hamari Operatic Recital 1983–2000. *Address:* Max Brod-Weg 14, 70437 Stuttgart, Germany (office). *Fax:* (711) 8403625 (home). *E-mail:* julia.hamari@live.de (home).

HAMBAYASHI, Toru; Japanese business executive; b. 7 Jan. 1937; joined Nichimen Co. Ltd (now Sojitz Corpn) 1959, Pres. Nichimen Corpn 2001–03, Chair. and Co-CEO, Nissho Iwai-Nichimen Holding Corpn (following merger) April 2003–04, now Special Corp. Adviser; Int. Sr Econ. Consultant, The People's Govt of Shaanxi Prov. 2002; Econ. Adviser, Heilongjiang Prov. 2004; mem. Bd of Dirs Fast Retailing Co. Ltd 2005–, Maeda Corpn 2007–, Daikyo Inc. 2011–, Unitika Ltd 2015– (External Auditor 2004); Adviser, Asscn for Promotion of Int. Trade 2009–; mem. Bd World Forestry Center 2001; mem. Japan and Tokyo Chambers of Commerce and Industry. *Address:* c/o Board of Directors, Fast Retailing Company Limited, 717-1 Sayama, Yamaguchi City, Yamaguchi 754-0894, Japan.

HAMBLING, Maggi, CBE, OBE, Higher Diploma in Fine Art; British artist; b. 23 Oct. 1945, Sudbury, Suffolk; d. of Harry Leonard Hambling and Marjorie Rose Hambling; ed Hadleigh Hall School and Amberfield School, Suffolk, Ipswich School of Art, Camberwell School of Art, London, Slade School of Fine Art, London; studied painting with Lett Haines and Cedric Morris 1960–; tutor, Morley Coll., London; First Artist in Residence, Nat. Gallery, London 1980–81; Oscar Wilde memorial, Adelaide St, London 1998; Scallop-Benjamin Britten memorial, Aldeburgh, Suffolk (Marsh Award for Excellence in Public Sculpture 2005) 2003; The Brixton Heron, London SW4 2010; Boise Travel Award 1969, Arts Council Award 1977, Jerwood Prize (jtly) 1995. *Publications:* Maggi and Henrietta 2001, Father 2001, Maggi Hambling – The Works and Conversations with Andrew Lambirth 2006, George Always 2009, The Sea 2009, You are the Sea 2009, The Aldeburgh Scallop 2010, War Requiem & Aftermath 2015. *Leisure interest:* tennis. *Address:* Morley College, 61 Westminster Bridge Road, London, SE1 7HT, England (office). *Telephone:* (20) 7928-8501 (office); (20) 7450-1856 (office). *Fax:* (20) 7928-4074 (office). *Website:* www.maggihambling.com (office).

HAMBRECHT, Jürgen, Dr rer. nat; German chemical industry executive; *Chairman of the Supervisory Board, BASF SE;* b. 1946, Reutlingen; m.; four c.; ed Univ. of Tübingen; joined BASF AG Polymer Lab. 1976, Head of Research and Purchasing, Lacke und Farben AG, Münster 1985–90, Pres. Eng Plastics Div. 1990–95, Pres. E Asian Div., Hong Kong 1995, mem. Bd of Exec. Dirs 1997–2011, Chair. BASF AG (renamed BASF SE Jan. 2008) 2003–11, Chair. Supervisory Bd 2014–; Chair. Supervisory Bd Fuchs Petrolub SE, Trumpf GmbH & Co. KG; mem. Supervisory Bd, Daimler AG; Pres. German Chemical Industry Asscn 2003–; Vice-Pres. Fed. of German Industries (BDI); Chair. Asia Pacific Cttee of German Business (APA). *Address:* BASF SE, Carl-Bosch Strasse 38, 67056 Ludwigshafen, Germany (office). *Telephone:* (621) 60-20916 (office). *Fax:* (621) 60-92693 (office). *E-mail:* presse.kontakt@basf.com (office). *Website:* www.basf.com (office).

HAMBRO, Rupert Nicholas, CBE, FRSA; British private investor; *Chairman, J.O. Hambro Limited and Hambro Perks Limited;* b. 27 June 1943, London, England; s. of Jocelyn Olaf Hambro and Anne Silvia Muir; m. Mary Robinson Boyer 1970; one s. one d.; ed Eton Coll., Aix-en-Provence Univ., France; with Peat Marwick Mitchell & Co. 1962–64; joined Hambros Bank 1964, Dir 1964–86, Deputy Chair. 1980–83, Chair. 1983–86; Chair. J.O. Hambro Magan Ltd 1988–96, Chair. J.O. Hambro Ltd 1986–, Founding Partner, Robinson Hambro Ltd 2010–, Co-founder and Chair. Hambro Perks Ltd 2012–; Chair. Asscn of Int. Bond Dealers 1979–82, Wiltons (St James's) Ltd 1987–2003, Fenchurch PLC 1993–97, Longshot PLC 1996–2007, Woburn Golf & Country Club Ltd 1998–2003, Roland Berger and Partners Ltd 2000–02, Jermyn Street Asscn 2000–03, The Walpole Cttee Ltd 2000–05, Cazenove & Loyd 2004–17, Theo Fennell PLC 2009–13, Sipsmith Ltd 2009–17, Seenit Ltd 2015–18; mem. Bd of Dirs, Anglo-American Corpn of SA Ltd 1981–97, Chatsworth House Trust Ltd 1982–2004, Mayflower Corpn PLC 1988–2004, Racecourse Holdings Trust Ltd 1985–94, Telegraph Group Ltd 1986–2003, Sedgwick Group PLC 1987–92, Triton Europe PLC 1987–90, Hamleys PLC 1988–96 (Chair. 1989–94), Pioneer Concrete Holdings Plc 1989–99, CTR Group 1990–97, KBC Peel Hunt Ltd 2000–03; Treas., Business for Sterling Ltd 2002–07; mem. Supervisory Bd, Bank Gutmann AG 2000–17; mem. Advisory Bd, Open Europe Ltd 2006–; mem. Int. Advisory Bd, Montana AG, Vienna 1988–2000, Third Space Group Ltd 1999–2007, Woburn Enterprises Ltd 2003–11, Lovedean Ltd 2008–11; mem. Council and Chair. Devt Bd, RCA 2010–18, Chair. Angel Club 2015–18; Chair. Devt and Strategy Bd, Zoological Soc. of London 2013–; Chair. Soc. of Merchants Trading to the Continent 1995–2009; Chair. of Trustees, Silver Trust 1987– (Patron 2005–08, Pres. 2008–), Boys' Club Trust 1991–2000, Old Etonian Trust 2001–, Henry VI Trust 2001–, Chiswick House and Gardens Trust 2005–11; Treas., Nat. Art Collections Fund 1991–2003; Deputy Pres. Anglo-Danish Soc. 1987–; Vice-Pres. Royal Soc. of British Sculptors 1997–; Chair. of Govs, Museum of London 1998–2005, Co-Chair. Museum in Docklands 2003–05; Chair. Kraydel Ltd 2017–; mem. Court of the Co. of Goldsmiths, Freeman Fishmongers' Co. 1969–; Trustee, Wallace Collection 2013–17; Patron Asscn of British Designer Silversmiths 2006–; Hon. Fellow, Univ. of Bath 1998; Liveryman, Court of Goldsmiths 1998– (Prime Warden 2009–10); Order of the Falcon (Iceland) 1986; Walpole Award for British Excellence 2005. *Leisure interests:* country pursuits. *Address:* Hambro Perks, 8 Greencoat Place, London, SW1P 1PL, England (office). *Telephone:* (20) 3653-0329 (office); (20) 7259-0101 (home). *E-mail:* rnhambro@joh.co.uk (office). *Website:* www.hambroperks.com (office).

HAMBURG, Margaret A., MD; American physician, scientist and government official; b. Chicago, Ill.; d. of Dr David Hamburg and Dr Beatrix Hamburg; m.; two c.; ed Harvard Medical School; completed residency in internal medicine at what is now New York-Presbyterian Hosp./Weill Cornell Medical Center; conducted research on neuroscience at Rockefeller Univ.; studied neuropharmacology at Nat. Inst. of Mental Health; later focused on AIDS research as Asst Dir Nat. Inst. of Allergy and Infectious Diseases; Commr New York City Dept of Health and Mental Hygiene 1991–97; Asst Sec. for Policy and Evaluation, US Dept of Health and Human Services 1997–2001; Founding Vice-Pres. for Biological Programs, Nuclear Threat Initiative 2001–05, Sr Scientist 2005–09; Commr Food and Drug Admin, Silver Spring, Md 2009–15; mem. Inst. of Medicine 1994. *Address:* c/o Food and Drug Administration, 10903 New Hampshire Avenue, Silver Spring, MD 20993-0002, USA (office). *Telephone:* (888) 463-6332 (office).

HAMDALLAH, Rami, BA, MA, PhD; Palestinian academic and politician; b. 10 Aug. 1958, Anabta, West Bank; m.; three c. (deceased); ed Univ. of Jordan, Manchester Univ., UK, Lancaster Univ., UK; Instructor, Dept of English, An-Najah Nat. Univ. 1982–85, Chair., Dept of English 1988–92, Dean, Faculty of Arts 1992–95, Vice-Pres. for Academic Affairs, Colls of Humanities 1995–98, Pres. An-Najah Nat. Univ. 1998–; Sec.-Gen. Palestinian Central Elections Comm. 2002–13, Deputy Chair. 2011; Prime Minister 3–20 June 2013 (resgnd), Interim Prime Minister 2013–14, Prime Minister and Minister of the Interior 2014–19; mem. Fatah Movt. *Address:* c/o Ministry of the Interior, POB 641, Ramallah, Palestinian Territories.

HAMDAN, Mohammed Ahmed, BSc, MSc, PhD; Jordanian engineer and academic; *Advisor, Engineering Sector, Higher Council for Science and Technology;* b. 5 Aug. 1952; m.; two s. one d.; ed Univ. of Wales, Cardiff and Univ. of Leeds, UK, Washington State Univ., USA; Lecturer, Mechanical Engineering Dept, Univ. of Jordan 1979–80, Asst Prof. 1985–90, Assoc. Prof. 1990–95, Chair. Mechanical Engineering Dept 1991–93, 1995–97, Dean of Faculty of Engineering and Technology 1997–2001; Research Asst, Washington State Univ. 1981–83, Teaching Asst 1983–84; Chair. Engineering Dept, Philadelphia Univ., Amman (while on sabbatical from Univ. of Jordan) 1993–94; Dean of Faculty of Engineering, Hashmite Univ. 2001–03; Advisor, Engineering Sector, Higher Council for Science and Technology 1995–; Dean of Faculty of Engineering, Al-Zaytoonah Univ. 2009–; Visiting Prof., Friedrich-Alexander-Universität Erlangen-Nürnberg, Germany 2006, 2007, 2008, 2010; mem. Islamic Acad. of Sciences, mem. Council 1994–99. *Publications:* numerous tech. papers. *Address:* Faculty of Engineering and Technology, University of Jordan, Amman 11942 (office); The Higher Council for Science and Technology, PO Box, 36 Jubaiha, Amman, Jordan (office). *Telephone:* (6) 5355000 (University of Jordan) (office); (6) 5536636 (home). *E-mail:* mashamdan@yahoo.com. *Website:* engineering.ju.edu.jo (office).

HAMDI, Mongi, PhD; Tunisian international organization official and government official; b. 23 April 1959, Sidi Bouzid; m.; three c.; ed Ecole Nat. d'Ingénieurs, Tunis, Univ. of Southern California, Harvard Univ., USA; with UN Secr., New York 1988–98, Head, Science, Tech. and ICT Div., UN Comm. on Science and Tech. for Devt (CSTD), Geneva 2001–13, Head of Cabinet of Sec.-Gen., UN Conf. on Trade and Devt (UNCTAD), Geneva 2012–13, Special Rep. of the Sec.-Gen. and Head, UN Multidimensional Integrated Stabilization Mission in Mali (MINUSMA) 2015–16; Minister of Foreign Affairs 2014–15; Commdr, Ordre nat. du Mali 2016. *Address:* c/o MINUSMA, Bamako, Mali (office).

HAMED FRANCO, Alejandro; Paraguayan academic, diplomatist and government official; b. 26 Feb. 1934, Asunción; of Syrian descent; ed Universidad de la República, Montevideo, Universidad Nacional de Asunción; fmr Prof., Universidad Católica, Universidad Nacional de Ciudad del Este; Asunción; fmr Docent, Universidad Nacional en Asunción; Amb. to Lebanon (also accred to Qatar, Syria and Kuwait) –2008; Minister of Foreign Affairs 2008–09; Amb. to Venezuela 2009–10. *Publications include:* El Islán Diferente 2001, La Intifad Palestina an y su Poesía 2002, Los Árabes y sus Descendientes en el Paraguay 2002. *Address:* Ministry of Foreign Affairs, Edif. Benigno López, Palma, esq. 14 de Mayo, Asunción, Paraguay (office). *Telephone:* (21) 49-3928 (office). *Fax:* (21) 49-3910 (office). *E-mail:* sistemas@mre.gov.py (office). *Website:* www.mre.gov.py (office).

HAMELIN, Louis-Edmond, OC, MA, PhD, DèsSc, FRSC; Canadian researcher and consultant in polar affairs; b. 21 March 1923, St Didace; m. Colette Lafay 1951; one s. one d.; ed Laval Univ. and Univs of Grenoble and Paris, France; Prof., Laval Univ. 1951–78, Dir Inst. of Geography 1955–61, Founding Dir Centre for Northern Studies 1962–72; mem. Legis. Ass., Yellowknife, NWT 1971–75; Rector Université de Québec, Trois-Rivières 1978–83; Gov. Int. Devt Research Centre, Ottawa 1984–88; Corresp., Inst. de France, Paris 1989; Ordre des francophones d'Amérique 1994, Grand Officier, Ordre nat. du Québec 1998; Dr hc (McGill, Ottawa, Waterloo, Sherbrooke, Montreal, Trois-Rivières); Léo-Pariseau Prize 1972, Pierre Chauveau Medal 1972, Gov.-Gen.'s Award 1976, Massey Medal 1976, Grand Prix Geography (Paris) 1977, Gloire de l'Escolle Medal 1982, Molson Foundation Prize 1982, Human Sciences Prize (Québec) 1987, Léon-Gérin Prize 1987. *Publications include:* Illustrated Glossary of Periglacial Phenomena 1967, Atlas du Monde 1967, Canada: A Geographical Perspective 1973, Canadian Nordicity 1979, The Canadian North 1988, Obiou 1990, Le rang d'habitat 1993, Écho des pays froids 1996, Le Québec par des mots 2000–03 (electronic and printed versions, three vols), L'âme de la terre 2006. *Leisure interests:* writing, walking, sightseeing. *Address:* 1244 Rue Albert Lozeau, Sillery, PQ G1T 1H4, Canada (home). *Telephone:* (418) 683-0386 (home). *E-mail:* louis-edmond.hamelin@sittel.ca. *Website:* www.lehamelin.sittel.ca.

HAMERS, R.A.J.G. (Ralph); Dutch banking executive; *CEO and Chairman of the Executive Board, ING Groep NV;* b. 1966, Simpelveld; m.; twins; ed Tilburg Univ.; Relationship Man., Structured Finance in the Global Clients Div., ING Groep NV 1991–95, Head of Media Finance Group 1995–97, Deputy Gen. Man., Global Lending Risk Man. 1997–99, Gen. Man. ING Romania 1999–2002, Gen. Man. ING Bank br. network 2002–05, CEO ING Bank Netherlands 2005–07, Global Head of Commercial Banking network 2007–10, Head of Network Man. for Retail Banking Direct & International 2010–11, CEO ING Belgium and Luxembourg 2011–13, mem. Exec. Bd, ING Groep May 2013–, CEO and Chair. Exec. Bd, ING Group, Chair. Man. Bd Banking and Man. Bd NN Group Oct. 2013–. *Address:* ING Groep NV, PO Box 1800, 1000 BV Amsterdam, The Netherlands (office). *Telephone:* (20) 563-91-11 (office). *E-mail:* info@ing.com (office). *Website:* www.ing.com (office).

HAMID, Abdul, BA, LLB; Bangladeshi lawyer, politician and head of state; *President;* b. 1 Jan. 1944, Kamalpur, Mithamain, Kishoreganj, Bengal Presidency, British India; s. of Hazi Md. Tayebuddin and Tomiza Khatun; m. Rashida Hamid; three s. one d.; ed Cen. Law Coll. under Univ. of Dhaka; imprisoned by Pakistan Govt for taking part in student movt 1961; Gen. Sec. Student Union, Gurudayal Coll., Kishoreganj 1963, Vice-Pres. 1965; Founder-Pres. Student League Kishoreganj Sub-Div. 1964, Vice-Pres. Student League, Mymensingh Dist 1966–67; imprisoned by Pakistan Govt 1968; joined Awami League 1969; mem. Nat. Ass. of Pakistan from Mymensingh 18 constituency 1970; Chair. recruiting camp in Meghalaya, India, during liberation war 1971, Commdr Sub-Sector Kishoreganj, Bangladesh Liberation Force; mem. Constitutent Ass., Bangladesh 1972; mem. Jatiya Sangsad (Parl.) from Kishoreganj-5 constituency 1973–2013, Deputy Speaker 1996–2001, Deputy Leader of the Opposition 2001–06, Speaker July–Oct. 2001, 2009–13; Acting Pres. of Bangladesh (following death of Zillur Rahman) March–April 2013, Pres. 2013–; Pres. Kishoreganj Bar Asscn several times; Swadhinata Padak 2013. *Address:* President's Secretariat, Old Sansad Bhaban, Dhaka (office); Jatiyo Sangshad Bhaban, Dhaka, Bangladesh (office).

HAMID, Milud Ahmed Khalifa; Libyan politician; Minister of Finance June 2014. *Address:* c/o Ministry of Finance, Tripoli, Libya (office).

HAMIDI, Dato' Seri Ahmad Zahid, PhD; Malaysian business executive and politician; *President, United Malays National Organization;* b. 4 Jan. 1953, Kampung Sungai Nipah Darat; s. of Raden Hamidi Abdul Fatah and Tuminah Abdul Jalil; m. Hamidah Khamis; two c.; ed Universiti Putra Malaysia, Seri Kembangan, Univ. of Malaya, Kuala Lumpur; Banker, Oversea-Chinese Banking Corpn Ltd 1976–77; Marketing Exec., Amanah Saham Nasional Berhad 1979–84; Exec. Dir Scandinavian Motors Sdn Bhd; CEO Kretam Holding Berhad; Chair. Tekala Corpn Berhad, Chair. Seng Hup Berhad, Chair. Pengerusi Ramatex Berhad, Chair. Bank Simpanan Nasional 1995–98, apptd Chair. Syarikat Perumahan Negara Berhad 1999; fmr Senator Dewan Negara (Upper House); Minister of Defence 1990–95, 2009–13; apptd Youth Chief United Malays Nat. Org. (UMNO) 1996, Pres. 2018– (on leave since Dec. 2018); Deputy Tourism Minister 2004–08, Deputy Minister of Information 2006–08, Home Sec. 2013–18, Deputy Prime Minister 2015–18, Leader of the Opposition 2018–; mem. Parl. of Malaysia for the Bagan Datok constituency in Perak. *Address:* UMNO Malaysia, Tingkat 38, Menara Dato' Onn, Jalan Tun Ismail, Chow Kit, 50480 Kuala Lumpur, Malaysia (office). *Telephone:* (3) 40429511 (office). *E-mail:* media.umnomalaysia@gmail.com (office). *Website:* www.umno-online.my (office).

HAMIDI, Mohammad Farid, BA, MPA; Afghan lawyer and government official; *Attorney-General;* b. 24 Aug. 1967, Nengarhar; ed Acad. of Police, Kabul, Faculty of Law and Political Sciences, Univ. of Kabul, Azad Islamic Univ., Pakistan, Harvard Univ., USA; as a student was active in anti-Taliban political underground in the late 1990s and early 2000s; mem. Emergency Loya Jirga, developed electoral rules to elect the transitional admin 2002; Co-founder Free and Fair Election Foundation of Afghanistan 2004; apptd Commr, Ind. Electoral Complaints Comm. 2005; apptd Commr, Afghanistan Ind. Human Rights Comm. in charge of Monitoring and Investigation Unit, apptd Deputy Dir 2013, also chaired Advisory Bd to the Pres. of Afghanistan on Sr Appointments, also adviser to Policy and Man. Unit of the Pres.'s office; mem. Treaty Reporting Cttee; Attorney-Gen. 2016–; mem. Bd of Dirs Foundation for Cultural and Civil Soc.; mem. Asia Pacific Forum for Human Rights. *Address:* Attorney-General's Office, District 10, Qala-i-Fatullah, Kabul, Afghanistan (office). *Telephone:* (20) 2200017 (office). *E-mail:* ago.afg@gmail.com (office). *Website:* ago.gov.af (office).

HAMIDY, Abdulrahman Al-, PhD; Saudi Arabian economist; *Chairman and Director-General, Arab Monetary Fund;* b. 19 Dec. 1960, Zolfi; ed Univ. of Oregon, USA; Deputy Gov. of Tech. Affairs, Saudi Arabian Monetary Agency 2004–09, Vice-Gov. 2009–13; mem. Bd of Exec. Dirs Arab Monetary Fund (AMF) 2003–, Chair. and Dir-Gen. 2014–, Chair. and CEO Arab Trade Financing Programme (AMF subsidiary) 2014–; mem. Bd of Dirs Saudi Stock Exchange (Tadawul) Co.; has rep. Saudi Arabia in deputies' meetings of IMF and G20. *Address:* Office of the Chairman and Director-General, Arab Monetary Fund, Arab Monetary Fund Building, Corniche Street, PO Box 2818, Abu Dhabi, UAE (office). *Telephone:* (2) 6171400 (office). *Fax:* (2) 6326454 (office). *Website:* www.amf.org.ae (office).

HAMIED, Yusuf K., PhD; Indian pharmaceuticals industry executive; *Chairman (non-executive), Cipla Ltd;* b. 25 July 1936, Vilnius, Lithuania; s. of Khwaja Abdul Hamied; m.; ed Cathedral and John Connon School, Bombay (now Mumbai), Univ. of Cambridge, UK; raised in Bombay; began career as research officer, Cipla Ltd 1960, Man. Dir 1976–2013, Chair. 1989–2013, Chair. (non-exec.) 2013–; Fellow, Christ's Coll., Cambridge; known outside India for defying large Western pharmaceutical cos in order to provide generic AIDS drugs and treatments for other ailments primarily affecting people in poor countries; Two Chemexcil Awards 1979, 1982, Sir P. C. Ray Award for Development Of Indigenous Technology 1983, Nat. Award, Dept of Science and Tech., Lifetime Achievement award, Express Pharma Pulse 2002, Padma Bhushan 2005, Indian of The Year in (Business category) CNN-IBN 2012. *Leisure interest:* Western classical music. *Address:* Cipla Ltd, Mumbai Central, 289 J. B. B. Marg, Mumbai 400 008, India (office). *Telephone:* (22) 23095521 (office). *Fax:* (22) 23070013 (office). *Website:* www.cipla.com (office).

HAMILTON, Andrew David, BSc MSc, PhD, FRS; British chemist, academic and university administrator; *President, New York University;* b. 3 Nov. 1952, Guildford, Surrey, England; m. Jennifer Hamilton; two s. one d.; ed Royal Grammar School, Guildford, Univ. of Exeter, Univ. of British Columbia, Canada, St John's Coll., Cambridge; post-doctoral researcher, Université Louis Pasteur, Strasbourg 1980–81; Asst Prof., Dept of Chem., Princeton Univ. 1981–88; Assoc. Prof., Dept of Chem., Univ. of Pittsburgh 1988–92, Prof. 1992–97, Chair. Dept of Chem. 1994–97; Irénée duPont Prof. of Chem., Yale Univ. 1997–2004, Chair. Dept of Chem. 1999–2003, Benjamin Silliman Prof. of Chem. 2004–09, Deputy Provost for Science and Tech., Yale Univ. 2003–04, Provost Yale Univ. 2004–08; Vice-Chancellor Univ. of Oxford 2009–15, Hon. Fellow, Harris Manchester Coll., Kellogg Coll.; Pres. New York Univ. 2016–; mem. American Acad. of Arts and Sciences 2010; Fellow, AAAS 2004; ACS Arthur C. Cope Scholar Award 1999, Int. Izatt Christiansen Award in Macrocyclic Chem. 2011. *Leisure interest:* football. *Address:* Office of the President, New York University, 70 Washington Square South, New York, NY 10012, USA (office). *Telephone:* (212) 998-2345 (office). *Fax:* (212) 995-4790 (office). *Website:* www.nyu.edu/about/leadership-university-administration/office-of-the-president.html (office).

HAMILTON, Hon. Lee H., BA, JD; American research institute director and fmr politician; *Professor of Practice, School of Public and Environmental Affairs, Indiana University;* b. 20 April 1931, Daytona Beach, Fla; m. Nancy Ann Hamilton (née Nelson); one s. two d.; ed DePauw Univ., Goethe Inst., Germany, Indiana Univ. School of Law; practised law in Chicago and Columbus, Ind. –1965; mem. US House of Reps from Ind. 9th Dist 1965–99, served as Chair., ranking mem. Cttee on Int. Relations, Chair. and Vice-Chair. Jt Econ. Cttee, Chair. Perm. Select Cttee on Intelligence, Chair. Jt Cttee on Org. of Congress, Chair. Oct. Surprise Task Force, Chair. Select Cttee to Investigate Covert Arms Transactions with Iran, Chair. Sub-Cttee on Europe and Middle East 1970–93, mem. House Standards of Official Conduct Cttee; Dir Woodrow Wilson Int. Center for Scholars 1999–2010; has served on numerous panels and comms including Commr US Comm. on Nat. Security in the 21st Century (Hart-Rudman Comm.), Co-Chair. Baker-Hamilton Comm. to Investigate Certain Security Issues at Los Alamos, Commr Carter-Baker Comm. on Fed. Election Reform, Vice-Chair. Nat. Comm. on Terrorist Attacks Upon the US (9-11 Comm.); mem. US Dept of Homeland Security Advisory Council; Co-Chair. Ind. Task Force on Immigration and America's Future, Nat. Advisory Cttee to Campaign for Civic Mission of Schools, Dept of Energy Blue Ribbon Comm on America's Nuclear Future, Pres.'s Foreign Intelligence Advisory Bd; Co-Chair. Iraq Study Group, US Inst. of Peace 2006–07; currently Prof. of Practice, School of Public and Environmental Affairs, Indiana Univ., Dir Center on Congress 1999–2015, Distinguished Scholar, School of Global and Int. Studies; Chevalier, Légion d'honneur 1984, Grosses Verdienstkreuz 1985, Bundesverdienstkreutz 1999; Dr hc (DePauw Univ.), (Hanover Coll.), (Detroit Coll. of Law), (Ball State Univ.), (Univ. of Southern Ind.), (Wabash Coll.), (Union Coll.), (Marian Coll.), (American Univ.), (Ind. Univ.), (Suffolk Univ.), (Ind. State Univ.), (Anderson Univ.), (Franklin Coll.), (Shenandoah Univ.), (Bellarmine Univ.), (Georgetown Univ. School of Law), (St Joseph's Coll.), (Illinois Coll.), (Manchester Coll.), (Univ. of Evansville); Defense Intelligence Agency Medallion 1987, CIA Medallion 1988, Indiana Univ. Inst. for Advanced Study Distinguished Citizen Fellow 1994, Indiana Univ. Pres.'s Medal for Excellence 1996, Center for Nat. Policy Edmund S. Muskie Distinguished Public Service Award 1997, American Political Science Asscn Hubert H. Humphrey Award 1998, ABA CEELI Award 1998, Center for Civic Educ. Civitas Award 1998, US Dept of Defense Medal for Distinguished Public Service 1998, Paul H. Nitze Award for Distinguished Authority on Nat. Security Affairs 1999, Eisenhower Nat. Security Series Award 2003, Franklin and Eleanor Roosevelt Inst. Freedom from Fear Award (co-recipient) 2005, Dwight D. Eisenhower Medal for Leadership and Service 2007, George C. Marshall Foundation Award 2007, Gerald R. Ford Medal for Distinguished Public Service 2007, Churchill Award for Statesmanship 2007, World Affairs Councils of America Chair.'s Award for Lifetime Achievement 2008, Benjamin Harrison Presidential Site Advocating American Democracy Award 2011, 9/11 Tenth Anniversary Summit Distinguished Public Service Award 2011, Chicago Council on Global Affairs Nat. Leadership Award 2012, Distinguished Service Award, US Asscn of Former Members of Congress 2014, Presidential Medal of Freedom 2016. *Publications include:* A Creative Tension: The Foreign Policy Roles of the President and Congress (with Jordan Tama) 2002, How Congress Works and Why You Should Care 2004, Without Precedent: The Inside Story of the 9/11 Commission (with Thomas H. Kean) 2006, Strengthening Congress 2009, Congress, Presidents, and American Politics: Fifty Years of Writings and Reflections 2016. *Address:* School of Public and Environmental Affairs, 355 N Jordan Avenue, Room 4062, Bloomington, IN 47405-1701, USA (office). *Telephone:* (812) 856-4700 (office). *Website:* spea.indiana.edu (office).

HAMILTON, Lewis Carl Davidson, MBE; British racing driver; b. 7 Jan. 1985, Stevenage, Herts., England; ed John Henry Newman School; took up Karting 1993, Cadet 1993–97, Super One British Champion 1995, STP Champion 1995, Sky TV Kart Masters Champion 1996, Five Nations Champion 1996, Jr Yamaha 1998, Super One British Champion 1998, Jr Intercontinental A 1999, Italian Industrials Champion 1999, Vice European Champion 1999, winner Trophy de Pomposa 1999, Formula A 2000, European Champion 2000, World Cup Champion 2000, Karting World Number 1, Formula Super A 2001, European Champion 2000; signed to McClaren F1 Driver Devt Program 1998; participated in British Formula Renault Winter Series 2001, Formula Renault 2002–03, Champion 2003, Third 2002; competed for Manor Motorsport in Formula 3 Euroseries Championship 2004, for ASM Formula 3 2005, Drivers' Champion 2005, Fifth 2004; joined ART Grand Prix team and competed in GP2 Series 2006, Drivers' Champion 2006, Formula 1 debut, Australian Grand Prix 2007, Formula 1 World Drivers' Champion Runner-up 2007, 2016, Champion (youngest Formula 1 Drivers' Champion) 2008, 2014, 2015 (first British driver to win consecutive F1 titles and the second to win three titles after Jackie Stewart) 2017, 2018; associated with McLaren Mercedes Formula 1 team 2007–12, Mercedes AMG Petronas Formula 1 Team 2013–; British Club Driver of the Year 2003, Rookie Of The Year 2006–07, Hawthorn Memorial Trophy 2007, 2008, British Competition Driver 2007, Int. Racing Driver Award 2007, German GQ magazine Man of the Year 2007, UK Sportsman of the Year 2007, BRDC Gold Star Award 2007, Walpole Award for British Excellence 2007, Laureus World Breakthrough of the Year 2008, BBC Sports Personality of the Year 2014. *Publication:* Lewis Hamilton: My Story 2007. *Address:* Mercedes AMG Petronas Formula 1 Team, Operations Centre, Brackley, NN13 7BD, England (office). *E-mail:* enquiries@mercedesamgf1.com (office). *Website:* www.mercedesamgf1.com (office); www.lewishamilton.com.

HAMILTON, Linda; American actress; b. 26 Sept. 1956, Salisbury, Md; m. 1st Bruce Abbott (divorced); m. 2nd James Cameron (q.v.) 1996 (divorced); one d. *Stage appearances:* Looice 1975, Richard III 1977. *Films include:* T.A.G.: The Assassination Game 1982, Children of the Corn 1984, The Stone Boy 1984, The Terminator 1984, Black Moon Rising 1986, King Kong Lives! 1986, Mr Destiny 1990, Terminator 2: Judgment Day 1991, Silent Fall 1994, The Shadow Conspiracy 1997, Dante's Peak 1997, The Secret Life of Girls 1999, Skeletons in the Closet 2000, Wholey Moses 2003, Jonah 2004, Smile 2005, Missing in America 2005, In Your Dreams 2008, Holy Water 2009, Refuge 2010, Bad Behavior 2012. *Television includes:* Reunion 1980, Rape and Marriage: The Rideout Case 1980, The Secrets of Midland Heights (series) 1980–81, King's Crossing (series) 1982, Country Gold

1982, Secrets of a Mother and Daughter 1983, Secret Weapons 1985, Club Med 1986, Beauty and the Beast (series) 1987–90, Go Toward the Light 1988, The Way to Dusty Death 1995, A Mother's Prayer 1995, On the Line 1998, Point Last Seen 1998, The Color of Courage 1999, Sex & Mrs X 2000, A Girl Thing (mini-series) 2001, Bailey's Mistake 2001, Silent Night 2002, Take 3 2006, Home by Christmas 2006, The Line (series) 2008–09, Chuck (series) 2010–12, Lost Girl 2013, Defiance 2014–15. *Address:* United Talent Agency, 5th Floor, 9560 Wilshire Boulevard, Beverly Hills, CA 90212, USA.

HAMILTON, Richard Streit, BA, PhD; American mathematician and academic; *Davies Professor of Mathematics, Columbia University;* b. 19 Dec. 1943, Cincinnati, Ohio; ed Yale and Princeton Univs; has taught at Univ. of California, Irvine, Univ. of California, San Diego and Cornell Univ.; currently Davies Prof. of Math., Columbia Univ.; mem. NAS 1999, American Acad. of Arts and Sciences 2003; Oswald Veblen Prize in Geometry 1996, Clay Research Award 2003, Leroy P. Steele Prize for a Seminal Contrib. to Research, American Math. Soc. 2009, Shaw Prize in Math. Sciences (co-recipient) 2012. *Publications:* numerous papers in professional journals. *Address:* Mathematics Department, Columbia University, Room 522, MC 4424, 2990 Broadway, New York, NY 10027, USA (office). *Telephone:* (212) 854-4755 (office). *Fax:* (212) 854-8962 (office). *E-mail:* hamilton@math.columbia.edu (office). *Website:* www.math.columbia.edu (office).

HAMM-GARCIAPARRA, Mariel Margret (Mia); American fmr professional footballer; b. 17 March 1972, Selma, Ala; m. 1st Christian Corry 1994 (divorced 2001); m. 2nd Nomar Garciaparra 2003; twin d. one s.; ed Lake Braddock Secondary School, Burke, Va, Notre Dame High School, Wichita Falls, Tex., Univ. of North Carolina; centre forward; with Washington Freedom 1987–2003; played for US nat. team (youngest player aged 15) 1987–2004, represented USA at World Cup 1991 (gold medal), 1995 (bronze medal), 1999 (gold medal), 2003 (bronze medal), Olympic Games 1996 (gold medal), 2000 (silver medal), 2004 (gold medal), CONCACAF Cup 2002 (gold medal); US coll. football's leading scorer (103 goals); 276 int. caps (third highest total), 158 goals (world record); retd 2004; apptd Amb. FIFA 2005, Int. Amb. FIFA Women's World Cup 2011; f. Mia Hamm Foundation (supports young female athletes and bone marrow research) 1999. Co-f. Athletes for Hope 2007; Co-owner, Los Angeles Football Club; Global Amb. Futbol Club Barcelona; mem. Bd of Dirs Associazione Sportiva Roma 2014; mem. Bd Nat. Soccer Hall of Fame 2014; won four NCAA Championships with Univ. of North Carolina 1989, 1990, 1992, 1993, Most Valuable Player (MVP) at Chiquita Cup 1994, US Soccer Athlete of the Year 1994, 1995, 1996, MVP at World Cup 1995, Women's Sports Foundation Athlete of the Year 1997, ESPN Outstanding Female Athlete 1998, FIFA Female Player of the Year 2001, 2002, inducted into Nat. Soccer Hall of Fame 2007, World Football Hall of Fame (first women). *Publications:* (with Aaron Heifetz) Go for the Goal: A Champions Guide to Winning in Soccer and Life 1999, Winners Never Quit! 2006. *Leisure interests:* golf, basketball, reading, cooking. *Address:* c/o Mia Hamm Foundation, 5315 Highgate Drive, Suite 204, Durham, NC 27713, USA. *Telephone:* (919) 544-9848. *Fax:* (919) 544-9878. *E-mail:* michelle@miafoundation.org. *Website:* www.miafoundation.org.

HAMM, Jonathan (Jon) Daniel; American actor; b. 10 March 1971, St Louis, Mo.; s. of Daniel Hamm and Deborah Hamm; partner Jennifer Westfeldt 1997–2015; ed John Burroughs School, Univ. of Missouri; fmr drama teacher, John Burroughs School, Mo.; f. Points West Pictures (production co.) 2009; named among Entertainers of the Year, Entertainment Weekly 2008. *Films include:* Space Cowboys 2000, Kissing Jessica Stein 2001, We Were Soldiers 2002, Ira and Abby 2006, The Ten 2007, The Day the Earth Stood Still 2008, A Single Man 2009, Stolen 2009, Howl 2010, The Town 2010, Shrek Forever After 2010, Sucker Punch 2011, Friends with Kids 2012, The Congress 2013, Million Dollar Arm 2014, Minions (voice) 2015, Baby Driver 2017, Nostalgia 2018, Beirut 2018, Tag 2018. *Television includes:* The Hughleys 2000, The Trouble with Normal 2000, Providence 2000, Early Bird Special 2001, Gilmore Girls 2002, The Division 2002, Charmed 2005, Point Pleasant 2005, CSI: Miami 2005, Related 2006, What About Brian 2006, The Unit 2006, The Sarah Silverman Program 2007, Mad Men (Golden Globe Award for Best Actor in TV Series Drama 2008, Golden Nymph Award 2009, Screen Actors Guild Award for Outstanding Performance by an Ensemble in a Drama Series 2009, 2010, Primetime Emmy Award for Outstanding Lead Actor in a Drama Series 2015, Golden Globe Award for Best Actor in TV Series Drama 2016) 2007–15, 30 Rock (guest actor) 2009–10, Children's Hospital (series) 2010–16, The Increasingly Poor Decisions of Todd Margaret 2012, 7 Days in Hell 2015, Wet Hot American Summer: First Day of Camp (mini-series) 2015, TripTank (series) 2015. *Leisure interests:* ice hockey, baseball. *Address:* c/o Viewpoint, Inc. 8820 Wilshire Blvd, Suite 220, Beverly Hills, CA 90211-2618, USA (office). *Website:* www.jonhamm.net.

HAMM, Paul; American gymnast (retd); b. (Paul Elbert Hamm), 24 Sept. 1982, Washburn, Wis.; s. of Sandy Hamm and Cecily Hamm; ed Univ. of Wisconsin; took up gymnastics in 1989, int. debut 1999; fifth place in team event Olympic Games, Sydney 2000; team silver medal World Championships 2001; team silver medal, bronze medal floor exercise World Championships 2002; gold medal horizontal bar World Cup 2002; gold medals floor exercise and individual all-round (first US male gymnast to win all-round gold medal at World Championships), team silver medal World Championships 2003; gold medal floor exercise World Cup 2003; gold medals vault and horizontal bar, silver medal floor exercise, bronze medals parallel bars and pommel horse World Cup 2004; gold medal individual all-round (first US male to win all-round Olympic gold medal), silver medals horizontal bar and team event Olympic Games, Athens 2004; American Cup 2007, 2008, Pacific Rim Championship 2008; retd 2012; James E. Sullivan Award 2004. *Leisure interests:* playing tennis, cards, chess.

HAMMAMI, Hamma; Tunisian politician; *Leader, Parti communiste des ouvriers tunisiens (PCOT);* b. 8 Jan. 1952, El Aroussa; m. Radhia Nasraoui 1981; three d.; Co-founder and Leader, Parti communiste des ouvriers tunisiens (PCOT) (banned communist party); Dir El Badil (The Alternative) banned newspaper, fmr ed.; imprisoned for participation in student movt 1972–74, for membership in El Aamel Ettounsi (The Tunisian Worker) 1974–80, exiled in France, sentenced in absentia May 1987, returned to Tunisia, numerous arrests 1989–91, went into hiding Oct. 1992, tried in absentia Dec. 1992, arrested Feb. 1994, imprisoned June 1994–Nov. 1995, went into hiding, sentenced in absentia July 1999, emerged from hiding and imprisoned March–Sept. 2002, released a few months later. *E-mail:* pcot@albadil.org. *Website:* www.albadil.org.

HAMMEL, Eugene Alfred, AB, PhD; American demographer and academic; *Professor Emeritus, Department of Demography, University of California, Berkeley;* b. 18 March 1930, New York, NY; s. of William Hammel and Violet Brookes; m. Joan Marie Swingle 1951; ed Univ. of California, Berkeley; field work in archaeology and linguistics, Calif. 1947–51, in ethnography, Peru 1957–58, in archaeology and ethnography in New Mexico 1959–61, in ethnography in Mexico 1963, in Yugoslavia and Greece 1963, 1965–66; Asst Prof., Univ. of New Mexico 1959–61; Asst Prof., Univ. of Calif., Berkeley 1961–63, Assoc. Prof. 1963–66, Prof. 1966–93, Prof. of Anthropology and Demography 1978–93, Prof. Emer. 1993–, Dir Quantitative Anthropology Lab. 1974–90, Chair., Demography 1978–88, Admin. Exec. Cttee for Information Systems and Tech. 1987–88; archival research in Yugoslavia, Hungary, Austria 1983–; mem. NAS; Fellow, AAAS 1963; Guggenheim Fellow 1965–66; American Acad. of Arts and Sciences Award 1991. *Publications include:* Wealth, Authority and Prestige in the Ica Valley, Peru 1962, Ritual Relations and Alternative Social Structures in the Balkans 1968, The Pink Yoyo: Occupational Mobility in Belgrade c. 1915–65 1969, Statistical Studies of Historical Social Structure (with Wachter and Laslett) 1978, Population Dynamics and Political Stability (with Erik Smith) 2002; approximately 180 articles. *Leisure interests:* hiking, guitar, carpentry, photography. *Address:* Department of Demography, University of California, 2232 Piedmont Avenue, Berkeley, CA 94720-2120, USA (office). *Telephone:* (510) 642-9800 (office). *E-mail:* gene@demog.berkeley.edu (office). *Website:* www.demog.berkeley.edu/~gene (office).

HAMMER, Bonnie, BA, MA; American television executive; *Chairman, Cable Entertainment and Cable Studios, NBCUniversal;* b. Queens, NY; m.; two c.; ed Boston Univ. Coll. of Communication and School of Educ.; began TV career at WGBH, Boston, produced This Old House and ZOOM series; later executive producer of Good Day! for Boston's ABC affiliate, WCVB; programming exec. at Lifetime Television, New York, oversaw production of award-winning series of documentaries; Pres. Cable Entertainment and Cable Studios, NBCUniversal –2010, exec. responsibility for Syfy, USA Network 2004–, Chiller 2008–, Cloo 2008–, Universal HD 2008–, Universal Cable Productions 2008–, Chair. Cable Entertainment and Cable Studios, NBCUniversal 2011–, added exec. responsibility for E! Entertainment, E! Studios and G4. *Address:* NBCUniversal Media LLC, 30 Rockefeller Plaza, New York, NY 10112, USA (office). *Telephone:* (212) 664-4444 (office). *Fax:* (212) 664-4085 (office). *E-mail:* info@nbcuni.com (office). *Website:* www.nbcuni.com (office).

HAMMERGREN, John H., BA, MBA; American pharmaceuticals industry executive; *Chairman, President and CEO, McKesson Corporation;* b. 1959; ed Univ. of Minnesota, Xavier Univ., Cincinnati, Ohio; Vice-Pres. McKesson Health Systems 1996–97, Group Pres. 1997–99, Exec. Vice-Pres. McKesson Corpn Jan.–July 1999, Dir, Co-Pres. and Co-CEO 1999–2001, Pres. and CEO 2001–, Chair. 2002–, CEO Supply Man. Business Jan.–July 1999; Chair. Supervisory Bd, Celesio AG; mem. Bd of Dirs, Hewlett Packard, Nadro SA de CV (Mexico); mem. Business Council, Business Roundtable, Healthcare Leadership Council (Chair. 2009–10), Bd of Trustees, Center for Strategic & Int. Studies. *Publication:* Skin in the Game: How Putting Yourself First Today Will Revolutionize Health Care Tomorrow (co-author) 2008. *Address:* McKesson Corporate Headquarters, One Post Street, San Francisco, CA 94104, USA (office). *Telephone:* (415) 983-8300 (office). *Fax:* (415) 983-7160 (office). *E-mail:* corp.communications@mckesson.com (office). *Website:* www.mckesson.com (office).

HAMMES, Gordon G., PhD; American biochemist, academic and fmr university administrator; *Professor Emeritus and University Distinguished Service Professor Emeritus of Biochemistry, Medical Center, Duke University;* b. 10 Aug. 1934, Fond du Lac, Wis.; s. of Jacob Hammes and Betty Hammes (née Sadoff); m. Judith Ellen Frank 1959; one s. two d.; ed Princeton Univ., Univ. of Wisconsin; Postdoctoral Fellow, Max Planck Inst. für physikalische Chemie, Göttingen, FRG 1959–60; instructor, subsequently Assoc. Prof., MIT, Cambridge, Mass. 1960–65; Prof., Cornell Univ. 1965–88, Chair. Dept of Chem. 1970–75, Horace White Prof. of Chem. and Biochemistry 1975–88, Dir Biotechnology Program 1983–88; Prof., Univ. of Calif., Santa Barbara 1988–91, Vice-Chancellor for Academic Affairs 1988–91; Prof., Duke Univ., Durham, North Carolina 1991–96, Univ. Distinguished Service Prof. of Biochemistry 1996–2008, Prof. Emer. and Univ. Distinguished Service Prof. Emer. of Biochemistry 2008–, Vice-Chancellor Duke Univ. Medical Center 1991–98; mem. Physiological Chem. Study Section, Physical Biochemistry Study Section, Training Grant Cttee, NIH; mem. Bd of Counsellors, Nat. Cancer Inst. 1976–80, Advisory Council, Chem. Dept, Princeton Univ. 1970–75, Polytechnic Inst., New York 1977–78, Boston Univ. 1977–85; mem. Nat. Research Council, US Nat. Comm. for Biochemistry 1989–95; mem. ACS, American Soc. of Biochemistry and Molecular Biology (Pres. 1994–95), NAS, American Acad. of Arts and Sciences; Ed. Biochemistry 1992–2003; ACS Award in Biological Chem. 1967, William C. Rose Award, American Soc. of Biochemistry and Molecular Biology 2002. *Achievements include:* ACS est. the Gordon G. Hammes Lecture annual award 2008. *Publications include:* Principles of Chemical Kinetics, Enzyme Catalysis and Regulation, Chemical Kinetics: Principles and Selected Topics (with I. Amdur), Thermodynamics and Kinetics for the Biological Sciences 2000, Spectroscopy for the Biological Sciences 2005, Physical Chemistry for the Biological Sciences 2007; numerous learned articles. *Leisure interests:* music, tennis. *Address:* 7515 Pelican Bay, Boulevard #7A, Naples, FL 34108, USA (home). *Telephone:* (239) 593-0346 (home). *E-mail:* gordon.hammes@duke.edu (office). *Website:* medschool.duke.edu (office); www.biochem.duke.edu (office).

HAMMES, Michael Noel, BS, MBA; American business executive; *Chairman, James Hardie Industries SE;* b. 25 Dec. 1941, Evanston, Ill.; s. of Ferdinand Hammes and Winifred Hammes; m. Lenore Lynn Forbes 1964; three s. two d.; ed Georgetown Univ., New York Univ.; Asst Controller, Ford Motor Ass. Div. 1974, Plant Man., Ford Wixom Assembly Plant 1975, Man. Program Planning, Ford Automotive Ass. Div. 1976, Dir Int. Business Planning, Int. Operations, Ford 1977, Man. Dir and Pres., Ford Motor Co. of Mexico 1979, Vice-Pres. Truck Operations, Ford of Europe 1983–86; Vice-Pres., Int. Operations, Chrysler Motors Corpn 1986–90; Pres. Worldwide Consumer Product Operations, Black and Decker Corpn 1990–93; Chair. and CEO Coleman Co. 1993–97; CEO Guide Corpn 1998–2000;

Chair. and CEO Sunrise Medical Inc., Carlsbad, Calif. 2000–07, Chair. 2000–08; Chair. James Hardie Industries SE 2008–, Joerns Healthcare Inc.; mem. Bd of Dirs Navistar Int. Corpn 1996–, DynaVox Mayer-Johnson 2010–; mem. Bd of Visitors, Georgetown Univ. School of Business. *Leisure interests:* skiing, tennis, golf, antique cars. *Address:* Office of the Chairman, James Hardie Industries SE, Second Floor, Europe House, Harcourt Centre, Harcourt Street, Dublin 2, Ireland (office). *Telephone:* (1) 4116924 (office). *Fax:* (1) 4791128 (office). *Website:* www.jameshardie.com (office).

HAMMOND, Aleqa; Greenlandic politician; b. 23 Sept. 1965, Narsaq; ed in Ellekilde, Denmark, Arctic Coll., Iqaluit; Regional Co-ordinator for Greenland Tourism, Diskobugten 1993–95; Information Officer, Landsstyre Secr. 1995–96; worked for Nuuk Tourism 1996–99; Commr Inuit Circumpolar Conf. 1999–2003; Culture Co-ordinator Arctic Winter Games 2002; worked in Tourism and Culture, Sulisartut Højskoliat, Qaqortoq 2002–03; Head of Tourism, Qaqortoq 2004–05; mem. Parl. for the Social Democratic Siumut (Forward) party 2005–, Leader 2009–14 (resgnd); Minister for Family Affairs and Justice 2005–07, of Finance and Foreign Affairs 2007–08 (resgnd); Prime Minister (first female), responsible for Foreign Affairs 2013–14; mem. Folketing (Danish Parl.) (Siumut) 2015–. *Address:* Siumut (Forward) Party, PO Box 357, 3900 Nuuk, Greenland (office).

HAMMOND, Norman David Curle, MA, Dip. Class. Arch., PhD, ScD, FSA, FBA; British archaeologist and journalist; *Senior Fellow, McDonald Institute for Archaeological Research, University of Cambridge;* b. 10 July 1944, Brighton, Sussex, England; s. of William Hammond and Kathleen Jessie Howes; m. Jean Wilson 1972; one s. one d.; ed Varndean Grammar School, Peterhouse, Cambridge; Research Fellow, Centre of Latin American Studies, Cambridge 1967–71, Leverhulme Research Fellow 1972–75; Research Fellow, Fitzwilliam Coll., Cambridge 1973–75; Sr Lecturer, Univ. of Bradford 1975–77; Visiting Prof., Univ. of Calif., Berkeley 1977; Visiting Prof., Rutgers Univ. 1977–78, Assoc. Prof. 1978–84, Prof. of Archaeology 1984–88; Prof. of Archaeology, Boston Univ. 1988–2011, Prof. Emer. 2011–; Assoc. in Maya Archaeology, Peabody Museum, Harvard Univ. 1988–; Sr Fellow, McDonald Inst. for Archaeological Research, Univ. of Cambridge 2009–; Archaeology Corresp., The Times 1967–, Archaeology Ed. Times Literary Supplement 2009–11; Ed. South Asian Archaeology 1970–73, Afghan Studies 1976–79, International Congress of Americanists Archaeology Proceedings 1982–84; Consulting Ed. Library of Congress, USA 1977–89; Archaeological Consultant, Scientific American 1979–95; Acad. Trustee, Archaeological Inst. of America 1990–93; mem. Council, Soc. of Antiquaries of London 1996–99; excavations and surveys in Libya and Tunisia 1964, Afghanistan 1966, Belize 1970–2002, Ecuador 1972–84; Fellow, Dumbarton Oaks, Washington, DC; Visiting Fellow, Worcester Coll., Oxford 1989, Peterhouse, Cambridge, 1991, 1996, All Souls Coll., Oxford 2004, Clare Hall, Cambridge 2004; De Carle Distinguished Prof., Univ. of Otago 2013, Visiting Prof. 2016; Hon. Sackler-Hammond Distinguished Lecturer in Archaeology, Boston Univ. 2010–, Cambridge Univ. 2015–; Hon. DSc (Bradford) 1999; Curl Lecturer, Royal Anthropological Inst. 1985, British Archaeological Press Award 1994, 1998, Bushnell Lecturer, Univ. of Cambridge 1997, Stone Lecturer, Archaeological Inst. of America 1998, Willey Lecturer, Harvard Univ. 2000, Sackler Distinguished Lecturer, Metropolitan Museum of Art 2001, Soc. of Antiquaries Medal, London 2001, Reckitt Lecturer, British Acad. 2006, Aronui Lecturer, Royal Soc. of New Zealand 2011. *Publications include:* South Asian Archaeology (ed.) 1973, Mesoamerican Archaeology (ed.) 1974, Lubaantun: A Classic Maya Realm 1975, Social Process in Maya Prehistory (ed.) 1977, The Archaeology of Afghanistan (co-ed. with F. R. Allchin) 1978, 2019, Ancient Maya Civilisation 1982, Nohmul: Excavations 1973–83, 1985, Cuello: An Early Maya Community in Belize 1991, The Maya 2000; Archaeology Proc. 44th Congress of Americanists (Gen. Ed.) 1982–84; contribs to learned and other journals. *Leisure interests:* heraldry, genealogy, wine. *Address:* McDonald Institute for Archaeological Research, University of Cambridge, Downing Street, Cambridge, CB2 3ER (office); Wholeway, Harlton, Cambridge, Cambs., CB23 1ET, England (home). *Telephone:* (1223) 262376 (home). *E-mail:* ndch1@cam.ac.uk (office). *Website:* www.mcdonald.cam.ac.uk (office); www.bu.edu/archaeology/people/hammond (office).

HAMMOND, Rt Hon. Philip, PC, BA; British politician; *Chancellor of the Exchequer;* b. 4 Dec. 1955, Epping, Essex; m. Susan Carolyn Williams-Walker 1991; one s. two d.; ed Shenfield School (now Shenfield High School), Brentwood, Univ. Coll., Oxford; joined medical equipment mfrs Speywood Laboratories Ltd 1977, Dir Speywood Medical Ltd 1981–83; Dir, Castlemead Ltd 1984–93; Partner, CMA Consultants 1993–95; Dir, Castlemead Homes 1994; various business interests, including house building and property, manufacturing, healthcare and oil and gas; various consulting assignments in Latin America for the World Bank, Washington, DC; consultant to Govt of Malawi 1995–97; contested Newham North-East by-election 1994; MP for Runnymede and Weybridge 1997–, mem. (Select Cttees), Unopposed Bills (Panel) 1997–2004, Environment, Transport and Regional Affairs 1998, Environment, Transport and Regional Affairs (Transport Sub-Cttee) 1998, Trade and Industry 2002, Opposition Spokesperson for Health and Social Services 1998–2001, for Trade and Industry 2001–02, Shadow Minister for Local and Devolved Govt Affairs 2002–05, Shadow Chief Sec. to the Treasury May–Dec. 2005, 2007–10, Shadow Sec. of State for Work and Pensions 2005–07, Sec. of State for Transport 2010–11, for Defence 2011–14, for Foreign and Commonwealth Affairs 2014–16, Chancellor of the Exchequer 2016–; Chair. East Lewisham Conservative Asscn 1989–96; mem. Greater London Area Exec. Council 1989–96; mem. Transport, Telecommunications and Energy Council, Home Affairs Cttee 2011–14, Nat. Security Council 2011–, Economic Affairs Cttee 2014–, European Affairs Cttee 2014–; Foreign Affairs Council of the European Union 2014–. *Address:* HM Treasury, 1 Horse Guards Road, London, SW1A 2HQ (office); Constituency Office, Runnymede, Spelthorne and Weybridge, Conservative Association, 55 Cherry Orchard, Staines, TW18 2DQ, England (office). *Telephone:* (20) 7270-5000 (office); (1784) 453544 (Constituency Office) (office). *Fax:* (1784) 466109 (Constituency Office) (office). *E-mail:* public.enquiries@hmtreasury.gsi.gov.uk (office); office@runnymedeweybridgeconservatives.com (office). *Website:* www.hm-treasury.gov.uk (office); www.runnymedeweybridgeconservatives.com (office).

HAMMONDS, Bruce L., BS; American business executive (retd); b. 25 April 1948; m.; two c.; ed Univ. of Baltimore; began career as Br. Man. Pacific Finance Co.; COO MBNA Corpn 1991–2002, Pres. and CEO 2003–05, Chair. and CEO 2002–05; Pres. Global Card Services, Bank of America Corpn 2006–08; fmr Dir Financial Services Roundtable; Dir Delaware Business Roundtable, Chair. Roundtable's Educ. Cttee; mem. Bd of Trustees, Goldey-Beacom Coll.; mem. Advisory Council, Univ. of Baltimore.

HAMNETT, Katharine Eleanor, CBE; British fashion designer; b. 16 Aug. 1947; d. of Group Capt. James Appleton; two s.; ed Cheltenham Ladies' Coll. and St Martin's School of Art; co-f. Tuttabankem (with Anne Buck) 1969–74; designed freelance in New York, Paris, Rome and London 1974–76; f. Katharine Hamnett Ltd 1979; launched Choose Life T-Shirt collection 1983; involved in Fashion Aid 1985; opening of first Katharine Hamnett shop, London 1986, followed by two more shops in 1988; production moved to Italy 1989; Visiting Prof., London Inst. 1997–; Hon. Prof., Cen. St Martin's Coll. of Art; Designer of the Year, Int. Inst. of Cotton 1982, British Fashion Industry Designer of the Year 1984, Menswear Designer of the Year Award, Bath Costume Museum 1984, Award for Export, British Knitting and Clothing Export Council 1988. *Publications:* various publs in major fashion magazines and newspapers. *Leisure interests:* travel, photography, gardening, archaeology. *Address:* Katharine E. Hamnett Head Office, Unit 3D, Aberdeen Studios, 22–24 Highbury Grove, London, N5 2EA, England (office). *E-mail:* info@katharinehamnett.com (office). *Website:* www.katharinehamnett.com (office).

HAMPE, Michael, DPhil; German stage and television director, actor and academic; *Professor, Hochschule für Musik und Tanz, Cologne;* b. 3 June 1935, Heidelberg; s. of Hermann Hampe and Annemarie Hampe; m. 1st Sibylle Hauck 1971 (divorced 2014); one d.; m. 2nd Iwamitsu Sai 2015; ed Falckenberg Schule, Munich, Univs of Vienna and Munich, Syracuse Univ., USA; Deputy Dir Schauspielhaus, Zürich 1965–70; Dir Nat. Theatre, Mannheim 1972–75, Cologne Opera 1975–95, Salzburg Festival 1984–90, Dresden Music Festival 1992–2000; has directed opera at La Scala, Milan, Covent Garden, London, Paris Opera, Salzburg and Edin. Festivals, Munich, Stockholm, Cologne, Geneva, San Francisco, Sydney, Los Angeles, Buenos Aires, Tokyo; has directed drama at Bavarian State Theatre, Munich Schauspielhaus, Zürich, etc; dir and actor in film and TV; Prof., State Music Acad., Cologne and Cologne Univ.; mem. Bd European Acad. of Music, Vienna; theatre-bldg consultant; Prof., Hochschule für Musik und Tanz, Cologne; teaches at Vienna Univ., UCLA, Univ. of Southern California and Yale Univ., USA, Kunitachi Coll. of Music and Studio, New Nat. Theatre, Tokyo, Universität der Künste, Berlin; Bundesverdienstkreuz, Commendatore Ordine al Merito (Italy), Goldenes Ehrenzeichen des Landes Salzburg; Olivier West End Award 1983. *Productions include:* Don Giovanni, Così fan tutte, le Nozze di Figaro, Il Ritorno d'Ulisse in Patria, La Cenerentola for Salzburg Festival, Andrea Chénier for Royal Opera House, Covent Garden 1984, Il Barbiere di Siviglia for Royal Opera House, Covent Garden 1985, La Gazza Ladra for Cologne Opera 1987, L'Italiana in Algeri 1987, Die Meistersinger von Nürnberg 1988, Il Barbiere di Siviglia 1988, Così fan tutte 1989, La Cenerentola for Royal Opera House, Covent Garden 1990, Don Giovanni 1991, Falstaff at Schwetzingen Festival 1996, world premiere of Farinelli, oder die Macht des Gesangs at Karlsruhe 1998, Così fan tutte in Santiago and in Genoa, Fidelio for San Francisco Opera 2005, Die Zauberflöte at Megaron, Athens, Die Frau ohne Schatten for Helsinki Opera, Die Zauberflöte at New Nat. Theatre, Toyko, Dallas and San Diego, La clemenza di Tito for Washington Opera 2006, Così fan tutte at Teatro Colón, Buenos Aires 2006, Maometto II at Pesaro 2008, Trovatore at Semperoper, Dresden, Elektra, Aïda, Teatro Municipal, Santiago, etc. *Publications include:* 20 Jahre Kölner Oper 1995, Alles Theater, Reden und Aufsätze 2000, Oper-Spiel ohne Regel 2012, Opernschule-für Liebhaber, Macher und Verächter des Musiktheaters 2015, Über Theater 2015; articles in newspapers and periodicals. *Address:* Carl Spitieler Strasse 105, 8053 Zürich, Switzerland (home). *Telephone:* 443801833 (office).

HAMPEL, Sir Ronald Claus, Kt, MA; British business executive; b. 31 May 1932, Shrewsbury; s. of Karl Victor Hugo Hampel and Rutgard Emil Klothilde Hauck; m. Jane Bristed Hewson 1957; three s. one d.; ed Canford School, Wimborne, Dorset, Corpus Christi Coll., Cambridge; 2nd Lt in Royal Horse Artillery 1950–51; joined ICI 1955, Vice-Pres. ICI Agrochemicals USA 1973–75, ICI Latin America 1975–77, ICI Gen. Man. Commercial 1977–80, Chair. ICI Paints 1980–83, ICI Agrochemicals 1983–85, Dir ICI 1985–99, COO ICI 1991–93, CEO ICI 1993–95, Chair. 1995–99; Chair. United News and Media (now United Business Media) 1999–2002; mem. Bd of Dirs Powell Duffryn 1983–88, Commercial Union 1987–95, British Aerospace 1989–2002, ALCOA 1995–, Teijin 1999–2004, TI Automotive 2007–09; Chair. Templeton Emerging Markets Investment Trust 2003–07, Int. Stadia Group (ISG) Holdings Ltd 2010–16, Overseas Services Ltd 2012–; Dir American Chamber of Commerce 1985–90; mem. Exec. Cttee British North America Cttee 1989–96, Listed Companies Advisory Cttee, London Stock Exchange 1996–99, Nomination Cttee, NY Stock Exchange 1996–99; mem. European Round Table 1995–99, UK Advisory Bd INSEAD 1994–99, Advisory Cttee Karlpreis Aachen 1997–2001; Vice-Pres. All England Lawn Tennis Club, mem. Exec. Cttee 1994–2007; Chair. Cttee on Corp. Governance 1995–97; Chair. Bd of Trustees Eden Project 2000–07; Hon. Fellow, Corpus Christi Coll. Cambridge 1997. *Leisure interests:* tennis, golf, skiing. *Telephone:* (44) 1798-861351 (home). *E-mail:* rch@hampelrc.com.

HAMPSHIRE, Susan, CBE, OBE; British actress and writer; b. 12 May 1937; d. of George Kenneth Hampshire and June Hampshire; m. 1st Pierre Granier-Deferre 1967 (divorced 1974); one s. one d. (deceased); m. 2nd Sir Eddie Kulukundis (q.v.) 1981; ed Hampshire School, Knightsbridge; Hon. DLitt (City Univ., London) 1984, (St Andrews) 1986, (Exeter) 2001, Hon. DArts (Pine Manor Coll., Boston, USA) 1994, Dr hc (Kingston) 1994; Emmy Award, Best Actress for The Forsyte Saga 1970, for The First Churchills 1971, for Vanity Fair 1973, E. Poe Prize du Film Fantastique, Best Actress for Malpertius 1972. *Stage roles include:* Expresso Bongo 1958, Follow that Girl 1960, Fairy Tales of New York 1961, Marion Dangerfield in Ginger Man 1963, Kate Hardcastle in She Stoops to Conquer 1966, On Approval 1966, Mary in The Sleeping Prince 1968, Nora in A Doll's House 1972, Katharina in The Taming of the Shrew 1974, Peter in Peter Pan 1974, Jeannette in Romeo and Jeannette 1975, Rosalind in As You Like It 1975, Miss Julie 1975, Elizabeth in The Circle 1976, Ann Whitefield in Man and Superman 1977, Siri Von Essen in Tribades 1978, Victorine in An Audience Called Edouard 1978, Irene in The Crucifer of Blood 1979, Ruth Carson in Night and Day 1979, Elizabeth in The Revolt 1980, Stella Drury in House Guest 1981, Elvira in Blithe Spirit 1986, Marie Stopes in Married Love, The Countess in A Little Night

Music 1989, Mrs Anna in The King and I 1990, Gertie in Noel and Gertie 1991, The Countess of Marshwood in Relative Values 1993, Suzanna Andler in Suzanna Andler, Alicia Christie in Black Chiffon 1995–96, Sheila Carter in Relatively Speaking 2000–01, Felicity Marshwood in Relative Values 2002, Miss Shepherd in The Lady in the Van 2004–05, The Fairy Godmother in Cinderella, Wimbledon 2005–06, The Bargain 2007, Lady Kitty in The Circle 2008, Mrs Bennet in Pride and Prejudice 2009–10. *Television roles include:* Andromeda in The Andromeda Breakthrough (series) 1962, Katy (series) 1962, Fleur Forsyte in The Forsyte Saga (mini-series) 1967, Becky Sharp in Vanity Fair (mini-series) 1967, Dr. Jekyll and Mr. Hyde 1973, Glencora Palliser in The Pallisers 1974, The Story of David 1976, Kill Two Birds 1976, Lady Melford in Dick Turpin 1981, Madeline Neroni in The Barchester Chronicles (mini-series) 1982, Going to Pot 1985, Don't Tell Father (series) 1992, Esme Harkness in The Grand 1996–98, Miss Catto in Coming Home 1998–99, Miss Catto in Nancherrow 1999, Molly in Monarch of the Glen 1999–2005, Lucilla Drake in Sparkling Cyanide 2003, The Circle 2008, The Royal 2008–09, Bridge Celebrity Grand Slam 2009, Casualty 2011, 2013. *Films include:* The Woman in the Hall 1947, Upstairs and Downstairs 1959, The Long Shadow 1961, During One Night 1961, The Three Lives of Thomasina 1964, Night Must Fall 1964, Wonderful Life 1964, Paris in August 1965, The Fighting Prince of Donegal 1966, Monte Carlo or Bust 1969, Malpertuis 1971, A Time for Loving 1971, Le fils 1973, Another Mother's Son 2016, Midsomer Murders 2017. *Publications:* Susan's Story (autobiographical account of dyslexia) 1981, The Maternal Instinct, Lucy Jane at the Ballet 1985, Lucy Jane on Television 1989, Trouble Free Gardening 1989, Every Letter Counts 1990, Lucy Jane and the Dancing Competition 1991, Easy Gardening 1991, Lucy Jane and the Russian Ballet 1993, Rosie's First Ballet Lesson 1997. *Leisure interests:* gardening, music. *Address:* c/o Chatto & Linnit Ltd, 123A Kings Road, London, SW3 4PL, England (office). *Telephone:* (20) 7352-7722 (office).

HAMPSON, Christopher, CBE, BEng, MBA; Canadian/British business executive; b. 6 Sept. 1931, Montreal; s. of Harold Ralph Hampson and Geraldine Mary Hampson (née Smith); m. Joan Margaret Cassils Evans 1954; two s. three d.; ed Ashbury Coll. School, Ottawa, McGill Univ., CEI Geneva, Switzerland; joined Canadian Industries Ltd (subsidiary of ICI) 1956, Vice-Pres., Dir 1973; seconded to ICI PLC as Gen. Man. Planning 1978, Sr Vice-Pres. Canadian Industries Ltd 1982, fmr CEO, Dir ICI Australia Ltd, Exec. Dir, mem. Bd ICI 1987–94; Chair. Yorks. Electricity Group 1995–97, RMC Group 1996–2002, British Biotech PLC 1998–2002; mem. Bd The Environment Agency 1994–, Deputy Chair. 2000–01. *Leisure interests:* gardening, tennis, skiing. *Address:* 77 Kensington Court, London, W8 5DT, England. *Telephone:* (20) 7937-0325. *Fax:* (20) 7376-1906.

HAMPSON, Sir Stuart, Kt, MA; British civil servant and business executive; *Chairman and First Commissioner, The Crown Estate;* b. 7 Jan. 1947; s. of Kenneth Hampson and Mary Hampson; m. Angela McLaren 1973; one s. one d.; ed Royal Masonic School, Bushey, St John's Coll., Oxford; with Board of Trade 1969–72; FCO Mission to UN, Geneva 1972–74; Dept of Prices and Consumer Protection 1974–79; Dept of Trade 1979–82; with John Lewis Partnership PLC 1982–, Dir of Research and Expansion 1986, Deputy Chair. 1989–93, Chair. and CEO 1993–2007; Chair. and First Commr The Crown Estate 2010–; Founding Deputy Chair. London First; Pres. Royal Agricultural Soc. of England 2005–06, Employee Ownership Asscn; chaired team tackling econ. renewal in deprived communities, one of Prince of Wales's Ambs in this area; Hon. DBA (Kingston Univ.) 1998. *Address:* The Crown Estate, 16 New Burlington Place, London, W1S 2HX, England (office). *Telephone:* (20) 7851-5000 (office). *E-mail:* enquiries@thecrownestate.co.uk (office). *Website:* www.thecrownestate.co.uk (office); www.stuarthampson.co.uk.

HAMPSON, (Walter) Thomas, BA; American singer (baritone); b. 28 June 1955, Elkhart, Ind.; s. of Walter Hampson and Ruthye Hampson; one d.; ed Eastern Washington Univ., Fort Wright Coll., Music Acad. of West; with Düsseldorf Ensemble 1981–84; title role in Der Prinz von Homburg, Darmstadt 1982; debut in Cologne, Munich, Santa Fé 1982–84, Metropolitan Opera, New York, Vienna Staatsoper, Covent Garden 1986, La Scala, Milan, Deutsche Oper, Berlin 1989, Carnegie Hall, San Francisco Opera 1990; Artist-in-Residence, New York Philharmonic; has performed with Vienna Philharmonic, New York Philharmonic, London Philharmonic and Chicago Symphony orchestras; Special Advisor to the Study and Performance of Music in America, US Library of Congress; f. The Hampsong Foundation 2003; mem. American Acad. of Arts and Sciences 2010–; Hon. mem. RAM 1996, Freunde der Wiener Staatsoper 2004, Wiener Konzerthausgesellschaft 2005, Hon. Prof., Univ. of Heidelberg; Chevalier des Arts et des Lettres, Officer of the Order Pro Merito Melitensi (Malta) 2006; Dr hc (Whitworth Coll., Washington, San Francisco Conservatory, Manhattan School of Music); Edison Prize, Netherlands 1990, 1992, Grand Prix du Disque 1990, 1996, Cannes Classical Award 1994, Echo Klassik 1995, EMI Artist of the Year 1997, Deutsche Schallplattenkritik Award 1999, Cecilia Award 2000, Diapason d'Or Award 2000; Citation of Merit, Vienna Kammersänger 1999, Edison Award for Life Achievement 2005, Grammy Award for Best Opera Recording 2006, Deutsche Schallplatten Prize 2008, Distinguished Artistic Leadership Award, Atlantic Council 2009, Award for Distinguished Achievement in the Arts, Third Street Music School Settlement 2009, Living Legend Award, Library of Congress 2010, Concertgebouw Prize 2011, Venetian Heritage Award 2013, inducted into Hall of Fame by Gramophone 2013. *Recordings include:* Schubert's Winterreise 1997, Das Lied von der Erde 1997, Belshazzar's Feast 1998, Operetta Album with London Philharmonic 1999, No Tenors Allowed: Opera Duets (with Samuel Ramey) 1999, Verdi Arias with Orchestra of the Age of Enlightenment 2001, Wagner's Tannhäuser 2002, Cole Porter's Kiss Me Kate 2002, Forbidden and Banished 2006, I Hear America Singing 2006, Simon Boccanegra 2006, Don Giovanni 2006, Doktor Faust 2007, Athanaël 2008, Mozart Gala From Salzburg 2008, Wondrous Free—Song of America II 2009, Mahler: Des Knaben Wunderhorn 2011, Brahms: Ein Deutsches Requiem 2011, Schubert: Winterreise 2011, Puccini: Tosca 2011, Verdi: La Traviata 2011. *Address:* Centre Stage Artist Management, Stralauer Allee 1, Raum 1.11, 10245 Berlin, Germany (office); 1841 Broadway, Suite 1204, New York, NY 10023, USA (office). *Telephone:* (30) 520071762 (office); (212) 767-0074 (office). *Fax:* (20) 87425682 (office). *E-mail:* jonathan.letts@umusic.com (office); judith.neuhoff@umusic.com (office); office@thomashampson.com (office). *Website:* www.thomashampson.com (office); www.hampsong.com.

HAMPTON, Christopher James, CBE, MA, FRSL; British playwright; b. 26 Jan. 1946, Fayal, The Azores, Portugal; s. of Bernard Patrick Hampton and Dorothy Patience Hampton (née Herrington); m. Laura Margaret de Holesch 1971; two d.; ed Lancing Coll., New Coll., Oxford; wrote first play When Did You Last See My Mother? 1964; Resident Dramatist, Royal Court Theatre 1968–70; freelance writer 1970–; Officier, Ordre des Arts et des Lettres 1998; Evening Standard Award for Best Comedy 1970, 1983, for Best Play 1986, Plays and Players London Critics' Award for Best Play 1970, 1973, 1985; Los Angeles Drama Critics' Circle Award 1974, Laurence Olivier Award for Best Play 1986, New York Drama Critics' Circle Award for Best Foreign Play 1987, Prix Italia 1988, Writers' Guild of America Screenplay Award 1989, Academy Award for Best Adapted Screenplay 1989, BAFTA Award for Best Screenplay 1990, Special Jury Award, Cannes Film Festival 1995, Tony Awards for Best Original Score (lyrics) and Best Book of a Musical 1995, Scott Moncrieff Prize 1997. *Plays include:* When Did You Last See My Mother? 1964, Total Eclipse 1969, The Philanthropist 1970, Savages 1973, Treats 1976, Able's Will (TV) 1978, Tales from Hollywood 1983, Les Liaisons Dangereuses 1985, The Ginger Tree (adaptation) 1989, The Philanthropist/Total Eclipse/Treats 1991, White Chameleon 1991, Sunset Boulevard 1993, Alice's Adventures Underground (adaptation) 1995, Carrington 1995, The Secret Agent/Nostromo (adaptation) 1996, The Talking Cure 2002. *Translations include:* Marya (Babel) 1967, Uncle Vanya, Hedda Gabler 1970, A Doll's House 1971 (film 1974), Don Juan 1972, Tales from the Vienna Woods 1977 (film 1979), Don Juan Comes Back from the War 1978, The Wild Duck 1980, Ghosts 1983, Tartuffe 1984, Faith, Hope and Charity 1989, Art 1996, An Enemy of the People 1997, The Unexpected Man 1998, Conversations After a Burial 2000, Life × Three 2001, Three Sisters 2005, Embers 2006. *Films as writer include:* The Honorary Consul 1983, Dangerous Liaisons 1988, Total Eclipse 1995, Mary Reilly 1996, The Secret Agent 1996, The Quiet American 2002. *Films directed:* Carrington 1995, The Secret Agent 1996, Imagining Argentina 2003. *Opera libretto:* Waiting for the Barbarians (music by Philip Glass) 2005. *Publications include:* Hampton on Hampton 2005. *Leisure interests:* travel, cinema. *Address:* c/o Jenne Casarotto, Casarotto Ramsay and Associates Ltd., Waverley House, 7–12 Noel Street, London, W1F 8GQ, England (office). *E-mail:* jenne@casarotto.co.uk (office). *Website:* www.casarotto.co.uk (office).

HAMPTON, Sir Philip Roy, Kt, MA, MBA; British business executive; b. 5 Oct. 1953; ed Lincoln Coll. Oxford, Institut Européen d'Admin des Affaires (INSEAD), Fontainebleau, France; qualified as chartered accountant 1978; began career as Auditor, Coopers & Lybrand, London and W Africa 1975–81; various positions in Mergers and Acquisitions, Business Restructurings and Capital Markets, Lazard Brothers 1981–86; seconded to Lazard Freres, New York and Paris 1986–90; Group Finance Dir British Steel plc 1990–95, British Gas plc 1995–97, BG Group plc 1997–2000, British Telecommunications (BT) plc 2000–02, Lloyds TSB plc 2002–04; Chair. J Sainsbury plc 2004–09; Deputy Chair. Royal Bank of Scotland Group plc Jan.–Feb. 2009, Chair. 2009–15; Chair. GlaxoSmithKline plc 2015–19; Dir (non-exec.) RMC Group plc 2002–05, Belgacom SA (Belgian telecom group) 2004–, Anglo American plc 2009–; led Treasury review on govt red tape 2004–05; fmr Chair. UK Financial Investments Ltd (co. est. to manage UK Govt's shareholding in banks subscribing to its recapitalization fund); Assoc., Inst. of Chartered Accountants. *Address:* c/o GlaxoSmithKline plc, 980 Great West Road, Brentford, London, TW8 9GS, England.

HAMRAWI, Habib Chawki; Algerian broadcasting executive, international organization executive and diplomatist; b. 1 Aug. 1962; m.; four c.; ed Univ. of Algiers; Minister of Communication and Culture 1992, 1997–99, also Govt Spokesman 1997–99; journalist with Algerian Television (ENTV) 1997, Dir-Gen. 1999–2008; Pres. High Coordination Cttee of Arab Satellite Channel 2000–; Chair. Conférence Permanente de l'Audiovisuel Méditerranéen (CoPeAM) 2002–06; Pres. Exec. Council, Arab States Broadcasting Union (ASBU) 2004–08; Pres. Festival International du Film Arabe, Oran 2007–; Amb. to Romania 2009–14; mem. Bd European Broadcasting Union. *Address:* c/o Embassy of Algeria, 010663 Bucharest, Bd. Lascăr Catargiu 29, Sector 1, Romania (office).

HAMUD, Maj.-Gen. Mohamed Sheikh Hassan; Somali army officer and politician; fmr Dir, Somali Nat. Intelligence and Security Service; Minister of Defence 2014–15. *Address:* c/o Ministry of Defence, Mogadishu, Somalia.

HAMUD, Muhammad Ali; Somali politician; Minister for Foreign Affairs and Int. Co-operation 2007–08, of Finance and Planning 2008–10.

HAMZA, Ahmed Amin, MSc, PhD; Egyptian physicist, academic and university administrator; *President, British University, Cairo;* b. 8 March 1941, Giza; s. of Amin Hamza and Hanim Abdel Meguid; m. Sahar Khalil 1968; three d.; ed Saaidiya Secondary School, Giza and Ain Shams Univ. Cairo; Head of Printing Dept, Cairo Dyeing & Finishing Co. 1962–72; Lecturer in Physics, Mansoura Univ. 1972–76, Assoc. Prof. 1994–99, Prof. of Experimental Physics 1999, Head of Dept of Physics 1984–86, Vice-Dean, Faculty of Science 1986–92, Vice-Pres. Univ. for Community and Environmental Devt 1992–94, now Prof. Emer.; Pres. Univ. of Mansoura 1994–2001; Vice-Pres. British Univ. 2005–08, Pres. 2008–; Scientific Consultant, Thebes Acad.; Assoc. Prof., Sana'a Univ., Yemen 1989–91; Assoc. Prof., UAE Univ. 1991–94; Postdoctoral Research Fellow, Univ. of Leeds 1976–77; Fellow, Royal Microscopical Soc. (Oxford) 1977–, Inst. of Physics (London) 1982–, African Acad. of Sciences 1995–; mem. Bd of Dirs Acad. of Scientific Research and Tech., Head Cttee of Pure and Applied Physics 2001–; mem. Nat. Cttee UNESCO, Advisory Cttee for Minister of Higher Educ. and Scientific Research; mem. Bd of Devt of Higher Educ. Supreme Council of Egyptian Univs; mem. Int. Soc. for Optical Eng 1989, New York Acad. of Sciences 1995, Egyptian Acad. of Sciences 1995, AAAS 1995–, Basic Science Council; Dr hc (Tech. Univ. of Liberec, Czech Repub.) 2000; Egyptian Nat. Award in Physics 1987, Sr Academic Prize and Certificate Distinction of the Univ. of Mansoura in Basic Sciences 1992, First-Class Medal for Distinction 1995, State Prize of Merit in Basic Sciences 1997, Certificate of Merit, Faculty of Science Ain Shams Univ., Mubarak Prize in Advanced Tech. Science 2005. *Publications:* Interferometry of Fibrous Materials (co-author) 1990; numerous publs in fields of interferometry, fibre optics, colour measurement and polymer physics. *Leisure interest:* playing football. *Address:* British University, Suez Desert Road, El Sherouk City, Cairo (office); Mansoura University, Faculty of Science, 60 El-Gomhoria Street, Mansoura (office); 6 Korash Street, 6th District, Nasr City, Cairo, Egypt (home). *Telephone:* (2) 26875892 (office); (50) 2259427 (office); (2) 22462549 (home). *Fax:* (2) 26875889 (office); (50) 247900. *E-mail:* ahamza@bue.edu.eg (home); scimphydept@mum.mans.eun.eg (office); hamzaaa@idsc.net.eg (home). *Website:* www.bue.edu.eg (office); www.mans.eun.eg (office).

HAMZA, Bedri, MBA; Kosovo accountant, politician and fmr central banker; *Minister of Finance;* b. 8 Nov. 1963, Klina e Epërme, Skënderaj/Srbica Municipality; m. Remzie Hamza; one s. two d.; ed Prishtina Univ., Tirana Univ., Albania; Head of Accounting and Finance, Lead Metallurgy Dept, KXMK Trepça Mining Complex 1987–90; engaged in pvt. business 1990–98; Dir of Public Services, Mitrovica Municipal Ass. 2000–03; Deputy Minister of Economy and Finance 2008–11, Minister of Finance 2011–13, 2017–; Gov. Central Bank of the Republic of Kosovo 2013–17; mem. Democratic Party of Kosovo (DPK), fmr Deputy Pres. DPK Mitrovica br. *Address:* Ministry of Finance, 10000 Prishtina, Sheshi Nënë Terezë, Kosovo (office). *Telephone:* (38) 20034101 (office). *Fax:* (38) 213113 (office). *E-mail:* muharrem.shahini@mf-rks.org (office). *Website:* mf.rks-gov.net (office).

HAMZAH, Tengku Tan Sri Datuk Razaleigh (see Razaleigh).

HAMŽÍK, Pavol, JUDr; Slovak academic, politician and diplomatist; *Ambassador at Large for Energy Security;* b. 20 Aug. 1954, Trenčín; s. of Pavol Hamžík and Júlia Hamžíková; m. Dagmar Hamžíková (née Kiššová) 1976; two d.; ed Komensky Univ., Bratislava, Diplomatic Acad., Moscow; lawyer 1978–84; joined Czechoslovak Foreign Ministry 1984, Consul, Embassy in Copenhagen 1985–89; studied at Diplomatic Acad., Moscow 1989–91; Vice-Chair. del. to int. disarmament negotiations, Vienna 1991; mem. del. to CSCE 1991–92, Pres. CSCE Steering Group on crisis in Yugoslavia 1992, Head of Slovak del. to CSCE 1993, Head of Slovak Perm. Mission to CSCE 1993–94; Amb. to Germany 1994–96; Foreign Minister 1996–97; f. Party of Civic Understanding (SOP) 1998, Chair. 1999–2003; mem. Parl. 1998–2002, mem. Defence and Security Cttee 2001–02; Vice-Prime Minister 1998–2001; mem. Convention for the Slovak Repub. on the Future of the EU 2001–02; Rep. of the Prime Minister during discussion of Lisbon Treaty 2007–08; Amb. to Ukraine 2009–13; Amb. at Large for Energy Security, Ministry of Foreign and European Affairs 2013–; fmr Lecturer and mem. Scientific Bd, Faculty of Political Sciences and Int. Relations, Matej Bell Univ.; Golden Biatec, Informal Econ. Forum 2000. *Leisure interests:* history, skiing, literature, tennis. *Address:* Ministry of Foreign and European Affairs, Hlboká cesta 2, 833 36 Bratislava (office); Žilinská 1, 81105 Bratislava, Slovak Republic (home). *Telephone:* (2) 5978-1111 (office); (2) 9079-09011 (home). *Fax:* (2) 5978-3333 (office). *E-mail:* info@mzv.sk (office). *Website:* www.mzv.sk (office).

HAN, Chang-woo; South Korean business executive; *Chairman and CEO, Maruhan Corporation;* b. 15 Feb. 1931, Samcheonpo City, Gyeongsangnam-do; ed Hosei Univ., Japan; moved to Japan 1947; Pres. Maruhan Corpn 1972–99, Chair. and CEO 1999–; Admin. Dir Han Tetsu Foundation; Dir Kyoto UNESCO Asscn; Admin Officer, Kyoto Chapter, UN Asscn of Japan; mem. R.I.D. 2650 Rotary Club of Kyoto Heian (Chair. 2006–07), Advisory Council on Democratic and Peaceful Unification; Chair. World Fed. of Korean Asscn of Commerce; Hon. Dir Kyungnam Univ., S Korea; Hon. Citizen of Mineyama-town, Kyoto where Maruhan was founded 1995, of Los Angeles, Calif. for contrib. to amity of Japan, USA and S Korea 1995; Cheongryong Medal (Order of Sports Merit, S Korea) 1987, Mugunghwa Medal (Order of Civil Merit, S Korea) 1995, Order of the Sacred Treasure, Gold Rays with Neck Ribbon (Japan) 1999, Medal for the Most Distinguished Service (Marshall Islands) 2004, Royal Order of Cambodia, Grand Cross with First Style Ribbons 2008; Hon. DEcon (Kyungnam Univ., S Korea) 1996, Hon. DBA (Pusan Nat. Univ., S Korea) 2006; Medal with Dark Blue Ribbon, Prime Minister of Japan 1972, Presidential Citation (18th Commerce and Industry Day, S Korea) 1991, 6th Korean Overseas Compatriots' Prize, KBS (S Korea) 1998, Goodwill Amb. of Arkansas (USA) 2003. *Address:* Maruhan Corporation, 231 Seiryu-cho, Demachi, Imadegawa, Kamigyo-ku, Agaru, Kyoto 602-0822, Japan (office). *Telephone:* (75) 252-0011 (office). *Fax:* (75) 252-0018 (office). *E-mail:* info@maruhan.co.jp (office). *Website:* www.maruhan.co.jp (office).

HAN, Changfu; Chinese politician; *Minister of Agriculture;* b. 1954, Heilongjiang Prov.; ed Renmin Univ. of China; joined CCP 1974, mem. Communist Youth League of China 1986–2001, mem. Cen. Cttee Standing Cttee 1990–2001; Deputy Dir, State Council Research Office 2003–06; Deputy Sec., CCP Jilin Prov. Cttee 2006–09; Acting Gov. Jilin Prov. 2006–07, Gov. 2007–09; Exec. Vice-Minister of Agric. 2001–03, Minister of Agric. 2009–; mem. 16th CCP Cen. Cttee Cen. Comm. for Discipline Inspection 2002–07; mem. 17th CCP Cen. Cttee 2007–12, 18th CCP Cen. Cttee 2012–17, 19th CCP Cen. Cttee 2017–. *Address:* Ministry of Agriculture, 11 Nongzhanguan Nanli, Chao Yang Qu, Beijing 100125, People's Republic of China (office). *Telephone:* (10) 59193366 (office). *Fax:* (10) 59192468 (office). *E-mail:* webmaster@agri.gov.cn (office). *Website:* www.agri.gov.cn (office).

HAN, Duk-soo, MA, PhD; South Korean politician and diplomatist; *Chairman and CEO, Korea International Trade Association;* b. 18 June 1949, Jeonju, N Jeolla Prov.; ed Seoul Nat. Univ., Harvard Univ., USA; Dir Policy Coordinate Div., Econ. Planning Bd 1980–82; Dir Bureau of Int. Trade Promotion, Ministry of Trade and Industry 1982–85, Dir Bureau of Industry Policy 1985–87, Dir Bureau of Machinery Industry 1987–89, Dir-Gen. Small and Medium Enterprise Bureau 1989–90, Dir-Gen. Industrial Policy Bureau 1990–92, Dir-Gen. Electronics and Information Industry Bureau 1992–93; Presidential Sec. for Econ. Affairs 1993; Asst Minister for Planning and Man., Ministry of Trade and Industry 1994; Asst Minister, Int. Trade Affairs Bureau, Ministry of Trade, Industry and Energy (MOTIE) 1995–96, Vice-Minister MOTIE 1997–98; Commr Korean Industrial Property Office 1996; Minister for Trade Affairs, Ministry of Foreign Affairs and Trade 1998–2000; Amb. to OECD 2001; Sr Presidential Sec. for Policy and Planning 2001, for Econ. Affairs Jan.–July 2002; Minister, Office for Govt Policy Co-ordination 2004–05; Deputy Prime Minister and Minister of Finance and the Economy 2005–06 (resgnd); Prime Minister of South Korea 2007–08; Amb. to USA 2009–13; Pres. Korea Inst. for Industrial Econs and Trade 2003; Chair. and CEO Korea Int. Trade Asscn 2012–. *Address:* Korea International Trade Association, 511 Yeongdongdae-ro, Gangnam-gu, Seoul, Republic of Korea (office). *Telephone:* (2) 1566-5114 (office). *E-mail:* kitainfo@kita.net (office). *Website:* www.kita.org (office).

HAN, Joon-ho, BA, PhD; South Korean energy industry executive; ed Seoul Nat. Univ., Kyung Hee Univ.; Asst Minister, Ministry of Trade, Industry and Energy 1997–98; Admin. Korean Small and Medium Business Admin 2000–04; Chair., Pres. and CEO Korea Electric Power Corpn (KEPCO) 2004–06; fmr Chair. and CEO Samchully Co., Ltd; fmr Chair. Korean Productivity Centre (KPC); Chief of Presidential Comm. on Small & Medium Enterprise 2003; mem. Bd of Dirs Daelim Industrial Co., Ltd, POSCO; mem. Pacific Basin Econ. Council.

HAN, Kwang-bok; North Korean politician; b. 18 March 1946; ed Kim Chaek Univ. of Tech.; worked as an instructor and Chief Instructor at Comm. for the Metal Industry and Construction Equipment; Deputy Minister for the Electronics Industry –2009, Minister for the Electronics Industry 2009–12; Vice-Premier 2010–12; mem. Korean Workers' Party Cen. Cttee 2012–. *Address:* Ministry of the Electronics Industry, Pyongyang, Democratic People's Republic of Korea (office).

HAN, Mingzhi, MA; Chinese economist and business executive; *Chairman of the Board of Supervisors, China Merchants Group Limited;* ed Johns Hopkins Univ., USA; Exec. Dir, China Soc. for Finance and Banking; China Exec. Dir, IMF 1996–98; Deputy Dir, Int. Dept, People's Bank of China 1999–2003; Dir, Int. Dept, China Banking Regulatory Comm. 2003–10; Chair. Bd of Supervisors, China Merchants Group Ltd 2010–. *Address:* China Merchants Group Ltd, 40th Floor, China Merchants Building, 168–200 Connaught Road, Central, Hong Kong Special Administrative Region (office); China Merchants Bank Co. Ltd, 7088 Shen Nan Road, Futian District, Shenzhen 518040, Guangdong, People's Republic of China (office). *Telephone:* 25428288 (Hong Kong) (office); (755) 83198888 (Shenzhen) (office). *Fax:* 25448851 (Hong Kong) (office); (755) 83195109 (Shenzhen) (office). *E-mail:* cmhk@cmhk.com (office). *Website:* www.cmhk.com (office); www.cmbchina.com (office).

HAN, Myong-sook, BA, MA; South Korean politician; b. 24 March 1944, Pyeongyang; m. Park Sung-jun; ed Ewha Womans Univ.; mem. staff, Korea Christian Acad. 1974–79; jailed as a prisoner of conscience, Christian Acad. Case 1979–81; Lecturer, Dept of Women's Studies, Ewha Womans Univ. 1986–97, Visiting Researcher, Asian Center for Women's Studies 1996–2003; Lecturer, Dept of Women's Studies, Sungsim Womans Univ. 1988–94; Chair. of Special Cttee on Revision of Family Law, Korea Women's Asscns United Jan.–Dec. 1989, Co-rep. 1993–96; Pres. Korean Womenlink 1990–94; Chief Dir Korea Inst. for Environmental and Social Policies 1992; fmr Head, Presidential Comm. on Women's Affairs; mem. Nat. Ass. 2000–01, 2004–, mem. Unification, Foreign Affairs and Trade Cttee; Minister of Gender Equality 2001–03, of the Environment 2003–04; Prime Minister (first woman) 2006–07 (resgnd); Pres. Korean Parl. League on Children, Population and Environment 2004–06, Korea-Singapore Parliamentarians' Friendship Asscn June 2004; Pres. Exec. Cttee Asia-Pacific Parliamentarians' Conf. on Environment and Devt 2004–06; Vice-Pres. Korea–Japan Parl. League 2006–; mem. Exec. Cttee Seoul and Pyongyang on Symposium Peace in Asia and Women's Role 1992–96; Co-rep., Viewers Alliance for Fair Broadcasting Policy Advisor 1993–94, Cttee for Interchange and Cooperation, Ministry of Unification 1993–94, Citizens' Asscn for Broadcasting Reform 1994–95; mem. Environmental Reservation Cttee, Ministry of Environment 1993–95, Anti-Corruption Cttee, Bd of Audit and Inspection 1993–95; fmr mem. Uri Party, mem. Cen. Standing Cttee April–Nov. 2005, Nat. Ass. Environment and Labour Cttee 2006–; currently mem. Democratic Party (fmrly United New Democratic Party), unsuccessful campaign to become party cand. for Pres. of South Korea 2007; Civil Merit Medal 1998; Order of Service Merit Medal (Blue Stripes) 2005. *Address:* c/o Democratic Party, 133-6, Youngdeungpo-dong, Youngdeungpo-gu, Seoul 150-036, Republic of Korea. *Website:* www.minjoo.kr.

HAN, Sang-beom, PhD; South Korean business executive; *Representative Director, President and CEO, LG Display Company Ltd;* b. 18 June 1955; ed Stevens Inst. of Tech.; fmr Head of IT Business Unit, LG.Philips LCD Co. Ltd, Vice-Pres. Panel 5 Factory and Manufacturing Tech. Centre 2001–06, Exec. Vice-Pres. LG.Philips LCD Co. Ltd 2006–09, Head of TV Business Div. 2009–12, Rep. Dir, Pres. and CEO LG Display Co. Ltd 2012–; Vice-Pres. Hynix Semiconductor Inc. *Address:* LG Display Co. Ltd, 65-228 Hangang-ro 3-ga, Seoul 140-716, Republic of Korea (office). *Telephone:* (2) 3777-1010 (office). *E-mail:* info@lgdisplay.com (office). *Website:* www.lgdisplay.com (office).

HAN, Seung-soo, PhD; South Korean politician, economist, diplomatist and international organization official; *Special Envoy on Disaster Risk Reduction and Water, United Nations;* b. 28 Dec. 1936, Chunchon, Kangwon Prov.; m. Hong Soja; two c.; ed Yonsei Univ., Seoul Nat. Univ. and Univ. of York, UK; taught econs at Univ. of York 1965–68, Univ. of Cambridge 1968–70; Prof. of Econs, Seoul Nat. Univ. 1970–88; Sr Fulbright Scholar, Dept of Econs, Harvard Univ., USA 1985–86; Visiting Prof., Univ. of Tokyo, Japan 1986–87; fmr Distinguished Visiting Prof., Yonsei Univ.; served as advisor to Bank of Korea, Korea Export–Import Bank, Korea Industrial Bank, Korea Chamber of Commerce and Industry, Fed. of Korea Industries and Korea Int. Trade Asscn; consultant to World Bank and UN Econ. Comm. for Asia and the Pacific (ESCAP), seconded by World Bank as Financial Adviser to Govt of Jordan 1974–76; Pres. Korea Int. Econ. Asscn 1983–84; first Chair. Korea Trade Commr 1987–88; elected mem. of Nat. Ass., Repub. of Korea 1988–2004; Minister of Trade and Industry 1988–90; Amb. to USA 1993–94; Chair. Council of the Repub. of Korea Group of the Inter-Parl. Union (IPU); Chief of Staff to Pres. of Repub. of Korea 1994–95; Deputy Prime Minister and Minister of Finance and Economy 1996–97; Minister of Foreign Affairs and Trade 2001–02; Pres. 56th Session of UN Gen. Ass. 2001–02; Pres. Korean Water Forum 2004; UN Special Envoy for Climate Change 2007–08; Prime Minister of South Korea 2008–09; Chair. Global Green Growth Inst. 2010–12; apptd Special Envoy of UN Sec.-Gen. on Climate Change 2007; Founding Chair. UN High-Level Expert Panel on Water and Disaster/UNSGAB, mem. Sec.-Gen.'s High-Level Panel on Global Sustainability; Special Envoy of UN Sec.-Gen. for Disaster Risk Reduction and Water 2013–; f. Korean Acad. of Industrial Tech. (KAITEC) 1989; Pres. Korea-Britain Soc., Korea-UK Forum for the Future, Alumni Asscn of the Grad. School of Public Admin, Seoul Nat. Univ.; mem. Bd of Dirs Standard Chartered PLC 2010–; mem. Royal Econ. Soc., Korean Econ. Asscn, Int. Inst. of Public Finance, Seoul Forum for Int. Affairs, Korean Council on Foreign Relations, Korean Soc. for Future Studies, Korean Asscn of Public Admin, Bretton Woods Club, Club de Madrid; Hon. Prof., Univ. of York; Order of Public Service Merit (First Class, Blue Stripes), Order of Industrial Merit (Bronze Tower), Order of Nat. Security Merit (Cheonsu Medal); Hon. KBE 2004; Sixth European Communities Prize 1971, Columbia Law School/Parker School Award for Distinguished Int. Service 1997. *Publications include:* Taxes in Britain and the EEC: The Problem of Harmonization (co-author) 1968, Britain and the Common Market (co-author) 1971, The Growth and Function of the European Budget 1971, The Health of Nations 1985; numerous articles in learned journals and press commentaries in both Korean and English. *Address:* Office of the Secretary-General, United Nations, New York, NY 10017, USA (office). *Telephone:* (212) 963-1234 (office). *Fax:* (212) 963-4879 (office). *Website:* www.un.org (office).

HAN, Shao Gong; Chinese writer; b. 1 Jan. 1953, Chang Sha; s. of Han Ke Xian and Zhang Jing Xing; m. Liang Yu Li 1980; one d.; ed Hunan Teacher's Univ.; Council mem. Chinese Writers' Asscn 1984; Vice-Chair. Hunan Youth Union 1985; Chief Ed. of Hainan Review 1988; Pres. Hainan Literature Correspondence Coll. 1988; Chair. Hainan Writers Asscn 1995; mem. Standing Cttee CPPCC Hainan Prov. 1988; Chair. Hainan Artists' Asscn 2000; mem. Council Chinese Artists' Union 2001; Prize for Best Chinese Stories 1980, 1981, Newman Prize for Chinese Literature 2011. *Film:* The Deaf and Mute 1983. *Publications:* Biography of Ren Bi Shi 1979; (collections of short stories): Yue Nan 1981, Flying Across the Blue Sky 1983, New Stories 1986, Fondness for Shoes 1994, Red Apple is an Exception 1994; To Face the Mystical and Wide World (selection of articles) 1985, The Other Shore (selection of prose pieces) 1988, The Murder 1990, Pa Pa Pa and Seduction and Femme Femme Femme 1990–91, Homecoming 1992, The Play and Holy War 1993, Raving of a Pedestrian in the Night 1994, The Thought of the Sea 1994, Dictionary of Ma-Bridge (novel) 1995, Ma Qiao ci Dian 1997, Gui Qu Lai 2008; trans: The Unbearable Lightness of Being (Kundera) 1987, The Book of Disquiet (F. Pessoa) 1999, Collected Works (10 vols) 2001. *Leisure interest:* Chinese calligraphy. *Address:* Room 2-602, Hainan Teachers' University, Haikou 571100, Hainan (home); 1st Building, Hainan Plaza, 69 Guoxing Road, Haikou, People's Republic of China (office). *Telephone:* (898) 5882748 (home); (898) 5336231 (office). *Fax:* (898) 53328034 (office). *E-mail:* hanshaog@public.hk.hi.cn (home).

HAN, Sung-joo, PhD; South Korean academic and fmr politician; *President Emeritus, Seoul Forum for International Affairs;* b. 1940; ed Seoul Nat. Univ. and Univ. of California, Berkeley; taught at CUNY, New York 1970–78, Columbia Univ., New York 1986–87, Stanford Univ., Calif. 1992; Distinguished Fellow, Rockefeller Brothers Fund 1986–87; fmr Vice-Chair. Int. Political Science Asscn; int. columnist, Newsweek 1984–93; Adviser to Govt on foreign affairs, nat. defence and unification since late 1970s; Minister of Foreign Affairs 1993–95; Prof. of Political Science and Pres. Ilmin Int. Relations Inst., Korea Univ. 1995–, fmr Acting Pres. Korea Univ.; UN Sec.-Gen.'s Special Rep. for Cyprus 1996–97; mem. UN Inquiry Comm. on the 1994 Genocide in Rwanda 1999; Amb. to USA 2003–05; Freeman Foundation Visiting Prof. in Asian Affairs, Claremont McKenna Coll., USA 2006; fmr Pres. Seoul Forum for Int. Affairs, currently Pres. Emer.; Chair. for Asia Pacific, Trilateral Comm.; Chair. East Asia Vision Group 2000–01; Co-Chair. Council for Security Co-operation in the Asia-Pacific; mem. Int. Panel on Democracy and Devt, Int. Bd of Govs The Peres Center for Peace; fmr mem. Bd Asia Pacific Foundation of Canada, Hon. Advisers of New Zealand's Asia 2000. *Publications include:* The Failure of Democracy in South Korea 1974, The US-South Korean Alliance 1983, The Division and Unification of Korea 1992, Choice for Korea in a World in Transition 1992, Korean Diplomacy in an Era of Globalization 1995, Korea in a Changing World 1995, Changing Values in Asia: Their Impact on Governance and Development (ed.). *Address:* Ilmin International Research Institute, Korea University, 5th Floor, Inchon Memorial Building, 5-1 Anam-dong, Seongbuk-Gu, Seoul 136-701, Republic of Korea (office). *Telephone:* (2) 923-2416/7 (office). *Fax:* (2) 927-5265 (office). *E-mail:* irikor@unitel.co.kr (office). *Website:* www.korea.ac.kr/~ilmin (office).

HAN, Wan-sang; South Korean professor of sociology, university administrator and fmr government official; b. 18 March 1936; s. of Han Young-Jik; m. 1966; three d.; Asst Prof., Coll. of Eng, Univ. of Tenn. 1967–69, E Carolina Univ. 1969–70; Assoc. Prof. of Sociology, Seoul Nat. Univ. 1970–76, Prof. 1984–93; adviser to Kim Young Sam; Deputy Prime Minister and Minister of Unification 1993; Pres. Korea Nat. Open Univ. 1994–98; Pres. Sangji Univ. 1999–2001; First Deputy Prime Minister and Minister of Educ. and Human Resource Devt 2001–02; Pres. Hansung Univ. 2002–05; Pres. Korea Nat. Red Cross (KNRC) 2004–07; Dr hc (Emory Univ.) 1999; Sheth Int. Alumni Award, Emory Univ. 2009. *Leisure interest:* tennis.

HAN, Zhaoshan; Chinese business executive; *Chairman and General Manager, Panpan Group Limited;* b. 1949, Yingkou, Liaoning Prov.; Vice-Dir Shuiyuan Township Agric. Machinery Factory, Yingkou 1970–83; founded Yingkou Great Wall Metal Product Factory 1983–92; Chair. and Gen. Man. Panpan Group Ltd 1992–, Panpan Security Industries Co. Ltd; took part as torchbearer during Olympic flame relay, Shenyang, Liaoning Prov. July 2008. *Leisure interest:* basketball. *Address:* Panpan Group Ltd, Yingkou, Liaoning Province, People's Republic of China (office).

HAN, Zheng, MA; Chinese economist and politician; *First Vice Premier;* b. April 1954, Cixi Co., Zhejiang Prov.; ed East China Normal Univ.; joined CCP 1979; served successively as Sec. CYLC Shanghai Chemical Industry Bureau Cttee 1982–86, Deputy Party Sec. Shanghai Chemical Eng School 1986–87, Party Sec. and Deputy Dir Shanghai No. 6 Rubber Shoes Factory 1987–88, Party Sec. and Deputy Dir Dazhonghua Rubber Factory 1988–90, Sec. Communist Youth League of China Shanghai Cttee 1991–92, Gov. Shanghai Luwan Dist 1992–93, Deputy Sec.-Gen. Shanghai Municipality 1995–97; Dir Shanghai Devt Planning Comm. –1998; mem. Standing Cttee CCP Shanghai Cttee and Vice-Mayor of Shanghai 1997–2002, Vice-Sec. CCP Shanghai Cttee May 2002, Exec. Vice-Mayor Oct. 2002, mem. 16th CCP Cen. Cttee 2002–07, Deputy Sec. CCP Shanghai Cttee and Mayor of Shanghai 2003–12, Acting Sec. CCP Shanghai Cttee 2006–07, Sec. 2012–17; mem. State Council 2018–; First Vice Premier 2018–; mem. 17th CCP Cen. Cttee 2007–12, 18th CCP Cen. Cttee 2012–17, 18th CCP Cen. Cttee Politburo 2012–17; mem. 19th CCP Cen. Cttee 2017–, also mem. 19th CCP Cen. Cttee Politburo 2017– and Politburo Standing Cttee 2017–. *Leisure interest:* dancing. *Address:* Chinese Communist Party, Quanguo Renmin Diabiao Dahui, Zhongguo Gongchan Dang, 1 Zhongnanhai, Beijing, People's Republic of China. *Website:* cpc.people.com.cn (office).

HAN, Zhubin; Chinese politician and lawyer (retd); b. Feb. 1932, Harbin, Heilongjiang Prov.; ed Beijing Econs Corresp. Univ.; train captain, Railway Admin, Harbin City 1946–50; joined CCP 1950; Dir Railway Admin, Liuzhou City, Guangxi Zhuang Autonomous Region, Railway Admin, Shanghai 1983–90; fmr Vice-Sec., then Sec. Communist Youth League, Liuzhou Railway Bureau Cttee, Dir 1975–83; Vice-Sec. CCP Group and Sec. CCP Cttee for Discipline Inspection, Ministry of Railways 1990–92; Minister of Railways 1993–98; Deputy Head Leading Group for Beijing-Kowloon Railway Construction 1993; Procurator-Gen., Supreme People's Procuratorate 1998–2003; Pres., Chinese Asscn of Prosecutors 1998–2003, China Law Society 2003–13; mem. 14th Cen. Cttee CCP 1992–97, 15th Cen. Cttee CCP 1997–2002 (Deputy Sec. Cen. Comm. for Discipline Inspection 1997–2002); Deputy, 8th NPC 1993–98.

HANANIA, Daoud Anastas, MBBS, FRCS, FRSM, FRCSE; Jordanian surgeon and fmr army officer; *Consultant Cardiovascular Surgeon, Hanania Medical Center;* b. 1934, Jerusalem; m. Nada Pio; two c.; ed St Mary's Hosp. Medical School, Univ. of London, UK; joined Royal Jordanian Army 1951, Head of Royal Medical Services of Jordanian Armed Forces 1976–88, retd from army with rank of Lt-Gen. 1989; House Surgeon and Surgical Registrar, Royal Northern Hosp., London 1959–61; Fellow in Thoracic and Cardiovascular Surgery, Baylor Univ. Coll. of Medicine, Texas in 1960s; Dir King Hussein Medical Centre (KHMC), Jordan 1973–76, Chief of Cardiovascular Surgery 1973–92 (performed first heart transplant in the Arab world 1985); Dir-Gen. Nat. Medical Inst., Amman 1987–89; Clinical Prof. of Surgery, Jordan Univ. of Science and Tech. 1989; mem. Senate 1989–97, 2007–13; f. Arab Centre for Heart and Special Surgery (now Arab Medical Centre), Dir 1991–99; f. pvt. clinic, Hanania Medical Center, Amman; mem. Bd of Trustees, King Hussein Foundation 1999, Al Quds Univ.; elected Pres. for Life, Jordan Cardiothoracic Soc. 2005; Fellow, American Coll. of Surgeons 1971, American Coll. of Cardiology 1977, Int. Coll. of Angiology 1979; Hon. Fellow, Royal Coll. of Surgeons in Ireland 1980, Royal Coll. of Physicians and Surgeons of Glasgow 1988; Hon. KBE 1984, Légion d'honneur 1984, Nile Medal First Class (Sudan) 1986, Commdr (First Class), Royal Swedish Order 1989, Medal of the Banner/Bright Star of Taiwan; Ben Qurrah Award for Excellence in Medicine, Arab-American Medical Asscn-Houston 1998. *Leisure interests:* tennis, motor racing. *Address:* Hanania Medical Center, 13 Khalil Maz'al Street, Amman, Jordan (office).

HANCE, James Henry, Jr, BA, MBA; American accountant and business executive; *Operating Executive, The Carlyle Group LP;* b. 16 Sept. 1944, St Joseph, Mo.; ed Westminister Coll., Washington Univ.; Partner, Price Waterhouse, Charlotte, NC 1968–85; Chair. Consolidated Coin Caterers Corpn 1985–86; Exec. Vice-Pres. and Chief Accounting Officer NCNB Corpn 1987–88; Chief Financial Officer, Bank of America Corpn 1988–2004, Vice-Chair. 1993–2005 (retd); mem. Bd of Dirs Sprint Nextel Corpn 2005–13, Chair. 2007–13; Sr Advisor, The Carlyle Group LP 2005–, Operating Exec. 2012–; mem. Bd of Dirs, Summit Properties Inc. 1994–, Caraustar Industries Inc. 1995–2003, Lance Inc. 1995–2003, Fon Group, Enpro Industries Inc. 2002–, Rayonier Inc. 2004–, Cousins Properties Inc. 2005–, Duke Energy Corpn 2005–, Morgan Stanley 2009–12, Ford Motor Co. (Ind. Dir) 2010–, Duke Energy Carolinas, LLC, American City Business Journals Inc., ACE Guaranty RE, ACE Capital RE Corpn; mem. Bd of Visitors, Duke Univ. Fuqua School of Business, Johnson C. Smith Univ.; Chairman of Trustees at North Carolina Blumenthal Performing Arts Center; Dir, United Negro College Fund, Foundation for Univ. of N Carolina at Charlotte; mem., Soc. of Int. Business Fellows; mem. Washington Univ. Nat. Council for John M. Olin School of Business; Trustee, Washington Univ.; fmr Co-Chair. Advantage Carolina. *Address:* The Carlyle Group LP, 520 Madison Avenue, New York, NY 10022, USA (office). *Telephone:* (212) 813-4900 (office). *Fax:* (212) 813-4901 (office). *E-mail:* info@carlyle.com (office). *Website:* www.carlyle.com (office).

HANCHARYK, Uladzimir; Belarusian economist, politician and trade union official; m. Lilia Hancharyk; one s. one d.; ed Belarusian Inst. of Nat. Economy; head of Belarusian Fed. of Trade Unions 1990–2001; mem. Supreme Council –1996; Co-Founder Consultative and Coordinating Council of Democratic Forces (alliance of opposition parties cr. to contest Presidential elections) 2000; cand. in Presidential elections 2001, requested opening of criminal case to investigate malpractice during election, rejected by Supreme Court 2001; denied registration as candidate in Chamber of Reps election 2004.

HANCOCK, Herbert (Herbie) Jeffrey, BA; American jazz pianist and composer; b. 12 April 1940, Chicago, Ill.; s. of Wayman Edward Hancock and Winnie Griffin; m. Gudrun Meixner 1968, one d.; ed Grinnell Coll., Roosevelt Univ., Manhattan School of Music, New School for Social Research; Owner and Publr Hancock Music Co. 1962–; Founder Hancock and Joe Productions 1989–; Pres. Harlem Jazz Music Center, Inc.; Creative Chair for Jazz, Los Angeles Philharmonic Orchestra 2010–; has performed with Chicago Symphony Orchestra 1952, Coleman Hawkins, Chicago 1960, Donald Byrd 1960–63, Miles Davis Quintet 1963–68; recorded with Chick Corea; mem. Nat. Acad. of Recording Arts and Sciences, Jazz Musicians Asscn, Nat. Acad. of TV Arts and Sciences, Broadcast Music; apptd UNESCO Goodwill Ambassador 2011; Prof., UCLA 2013–; Inst. Chair., Thelonious Monk Inst. of Jazz; Co-founder International Committee of Artists for Peace; Commdr des Arts et des Lettres 1985; numerous awards including Citation of Achievement, Broadcast Music, Inc. 1963, Jay Award, Jazz Magazine 1964, several awards from Black Music Magazine 1967–71, 5 MTV Awards, Grammy Award for Best Rhythm and Blues Instrumental Performance 1984, 1985, for Best Jazz Instrumental Composition 1988 (as co-composer), 1997, for Best Instrumental Arrangement Accompanying Vocals 1999, for Best Jazz Instrumental Solo 2003, 2005, for Best Improvised Jazz Solo 2011, for Best Pop Collaboration with Vocals 2011, Jazz Journalists Asscn Lifetime Achievement in Jazz Award 2014, San Francisxo Jazz Lifetime Achievement Award 2014, Jazz Foundation of America Lifetime Achievement Award 2014. *Albums include:* Takin' Off 1963, Succotash 1964, Maiden Voyage 1965, Speak Like a Child 1968, Fat Albert Rotunda 1969, Mwandishi 1971, Crossings 1972, Sextant 1972, Headhunters 1973, Thrust 1974, The Best of Herbie Hancock 1974, Man-Child 1975, The Quintet 1977, V.S.O.P. 1977, Sunlight 1978, An Evening with Herbie Hancock and Chick Corea In Concert 1979, Feets Don't Fail Me Now 1979, Monster 1980, Greatest Hits 1980, Lite Me Up 1982, Future Shock 1983, Sound System 1984, Perfect Machine 1988, Jamming 1992, Cantaloupe Island 1994, A Tribute to Miles (Grammy Award for Best Jazz Instrumental Performance 1995) 1994, Dis Is Da Drum 1995, The New Standard 1996, Gershwin's World (Grammy Award for Best Jazz Instrumental Performance 1999) 1998, Night Walker 2000, Future 2 Future

2001, Directions in Music (with others) (Grammy Award for Best Jazz Instrumental Album 2003) 2002, River: The Joni Letters (Grammy Awards for Best Album and Best Contemporary Jazz Album 2008) 2007, The Imagine Project 2010; with Miles Davis Quartet: Miles in the Sky, Nefertiti, Sorcerer, ESP, Miles Davis In Concert (My Funny Valentine), In A Silent Way, Jack Johnson, Seven Steps to Heaven; contrib. to Colour and Light – Jazz Sketches On Sondheim 1995. *Films:* composed film music for Blow Up 1966, The Spook Who Sat by the Door 1973, Death Wish 1974, A Soldier's Story 1984, Jo Jo Dancer, Your Life is Calling 1986, Action Jackson 1988, Colors 1988, Harlem Nights 1989, Livin' Large 1991; wrote score and appeared in film Round Midnight 1986 (Acad. Award Best Original Score 1986). *Publications include:* A Tribute to Miles 1994, Dis is Da Drum 1994, The New Standard 1996, I H with Wayne Shorter 1997, Gershwin's World 1998, Possibilities (co-author) 2014. *Address:* c/o Melinda Murphy, Hancock Music Company, 1250 North Doheny Drive, Los Angeles, CA 90069, USA (office). *Telephone:* (310) 273-3321 (office). *E-mail:* hhmusicco@herbiehancock.com (office). *Website:* www.herbiehancock.com (office).

HANCOCK, Matthew (Matt) John; British politician; *Secretary of State for Health and Social Care;* b. 2 Oct. 1978; m. Martha Hancock; three c.; ed Exeter Coll., Oxford, Christ's Coll., Cambridge; began career working for family computer software co.; fmr economist, Bank of England; econ. adviser to Shadow Chancellor of the Exchequer George Osborne 2005, later becoming Chief of Staff to George Osborne; mem. House of Commons for West Suffolk (Conservative) 2010–; Parl. UnderSec. of State for Skills 2012–13, Minister of State for Skills and Enterprise 2013–14, Minister of State for Portsmouth 2014–15, Minister for Small Business, Industry and Enterprise 2014–15, Minister of State for Energy 2014–15, Minister for the Cabinet Office 2015–16, Paymaster Gen. 2015–16, Minister for Digital and the Creative Industries 2016–18, Sec. of State for Digital, Culture, Media and Sport Jan.–July 2018, for Health and Social Care July 2018–; mem. Conservative Party 1999–. *Leisure interests:* horse racing, cricket. *Address:* Department of Health, Richmond House, 79 Whitehall, London, SW1A 2NS (office); House of Commons, Westminster, London, SW1A 0AA, England. *Telephone:* (20) 7210-5202 (Dept) (office). *Website:* www.dh.gov.uk (office); www.matt-hancock.com.

HANCOCK, Peter Douglas, BA; American banking executive; *President and CEO, American International Group (AIG), Inc.;* ed Univ. of Oxford, UK; raised in Hong Kong; joined Corp. Finance Unit, J.P. Morgan & Co., London, England 1980, Man. Dir J.P. Morgan Guaranty Trust Co., New York 1990–95, est. Global Derivatives Group, J.P. Morgan & Co. 1991, ran the Global Fixed Income business and Global Credit portfolio 1995–99, Chair. Risk Man. Cttee and Chief Financial Officer 1999–2000; Co-founder and Pres. Integrated Finance Ltd 2002–07; Man. Dir Trinsum Group Inc. 2007–08; Vice-Chair., responsible for Key National Banking, KeyCorp 2008–10; Exec. Vice-Pres. Finance, Risk and Investments, American International Group, Inc. (AIG), 2010–11, Exec. Vice-Pres., Finance, Risk, and Investments and CEO AIG Property Casualty 2011–14, Pres. and CEO AIG 2014–; mem. Bd Japan Soc.; mem. Int. Advisory Bd British American Business; mem. The Business Council, Financial Services Forum, The Geneva Asscn, Int. Advisory Bd, BritishAmerican Business; William Pitt Fellow, Pembroke Coll., Cambridge, UK; Corp. Citizenship Award, BritishAmerican Business 2014. *Address:* American International Group, Inc., 180 Maiden Lane, New York, NY 10038, USA (office). *Telephone:* (212) 770-7000 (office). *Fax:* (212) 509-9705 (office). *Website:* www.aig.com (office).

HANDLER, Chelsea Joy; American television presenter, stand-up comedian, actress, model and author; *Host, Chelsea Lately;* b. 25 Feb. 1975, Livingston, NJ; d. of Melvin Handler and Sylvia Handler; moved from NJ to Los Angeles to pursue acting career 1984, became stand-up comic 1986; has performed nationwide as a stand-up comedian, appeared as regular on the Oxygen Network series Girls Behaving Badly and on other shows, including Weekends at the D.L., The Bernie Mac Show, My Wife and Kids, and The Practice; regular commentator on E! and Scarborough Country as well as a corresp. on The Tonight Show; hosted The Chelsea Handler Show April 2006 (two seasons); guest on Red Eye with Greg Gutfeld and The View; hosts own late night talk show Chelsea Lately on E! Cable Television Network 2007– (only second woman in TV history to host late-night talk show); host of MTV Video Music Awards 2010; writes column in Cosmopolitan and UK celebrity magazine NOW; production co., Borderline Amazing Productions, produces Chelsea Lately; Bravo A-List Award for A-List Funny 2009. *Films include:* National Lampoon Presents Cattle Call 2006, Hop 2011, This Means War 2012. *Television includes:* Spy TV 2001, The Plotters 2001, The Practice 2002, My Wife and Kids 2002, Girls Behaving Badly 2002, The Bernie Mac Show 2004, Weekends at the D.L. 2005, Dirty Famous (unsold pilot) 2005, Totally High 2005, The Chelsea Handler Show 2006, Red Eye with Greg Gutfeld 2007, Chelsea Lately 2007–, Comedy Central Presents (stand-up), In The MotherHood (webseries) 2007–08, The Good Wife 2009, Pretty Wild (producer) 2010, After Lately 2011–13, Whitney 2011, 2013, Are You There, Chelsea? 2012, Web Therapy 2013. *Publications:* three books on New York Times Best Seller List: My Horizontal Life: A Collection of One-Night Stands (memoir), Are You There, Vodka? It's Me, Chelsea (collection of humorous essays), Chelsea Chelsea Bang Bang 2010. *E-mail:* chelsea@chelseahandler.com (office). *Website:* www.eonline.com/on/shows/chelsea (office); www.borderlineamazingcomedy.com (office); chelseahandler.com.

HANDLEY, Joseph (Joe); Canadian politician and consultant; *Special Advisor, VersaBank;* b. 9 Aug. 1943, Meadowlake, Saskatchewan; m. Theresa Handley; two c.; Asst Prof., Univ. of British Columbia and Univ. of Manitoba –1985; moved to NWT to assume position of Deputy Minister of Educ. with Govt of NWT 1985; Deputy Minister for Govt of NWT –1999; MLA for Weledeh 1999–2007, Minister of Finance, Chair. Financial Man. Bd and Minister Responsible for Workers' Compensation Bd 2000, Minister of Transportation and Minister Responsible for NWT Power Corpn 2001, Premier of NWT (retd) 2003–07; Special Advisor, Pacific & Western Bank of Canada (now VersaBank) 2007–; fmr Official Trustee and Chief Supt Frontier School Div., Manitoba; Queen's Golden Jubilee Medal 2002, Saskatchewan Medal for outstanding achievement 2005, Aboriginal Achievement Award 2008. *Address:* VersaBank, 410–121 Research Drive, Saskatoon, Sask. S7N 1K2, Canada (office). *Telephone:* (306) 244-1868 (office). *Fax:* (306) 244-4649 (office). *Website:* www.versabank.com (office).

HANDOVER, Richard, CBE; British retail executive; b. 1946; joined W H Smith Group 1964, numerous man. posts within the group including Man. Dir, Our Price Music Ltd 1989, Man. Dir W H Smith News 1995, mem. Bd, W H Smith PLC 1995–2004, CEO 1997–2003, Chair. 2003–04; Chair. Alexon Group plc (now Irisa Group Ltd) 2008–11; Chair. Adult Learning Inspectorate 2001–07, Chair. Strategy Board that merged three inspectorates and cr. OFSTED 2008; Chair. Power to Change 2014–; Dir (non-exec.) Nationwide Building Soc. 2000–07, Royal Mail Holdings PLC 2003–11, Kids Company 2005–15 (fmr Vice-Chair.); mem. Bd of Trustees, Community Foundation for Wiltshire and Swindon. *Address:* Power to Change, The Clarence Centre, 6 St George's Circus, London, SE1 6FE, England.

HANDS, Terence David (Terry), CBE, BA; British theatre director; *Director, Clwyd Theatr Cymru;* b. 9 Jan. 1941, Aldershot; s. of Joseph Ronald and Luise Bertha Hands (née Köhler); m. 1st Josephine Barstow 1964 (divorced 1967); m. 2nd Ludmila Mikael 1975 (divorced 1980); one d.; partner Julia Lintott; two s.; m. 3rd Emma Lucia 2002; ed Woking Grammar School, Birmingham Univ., Royal Acad. of Dramatic Art (RADA), London; Founder-Dir Everyman Theatre, Liverpool 1964–66; Artistic Dir Theatreground, RSC 1966; Assoc. Dir RSC 1967–77, Jt Artistic Dir 1978–86, Artistic Dir and Chief Exec. 1986–91, Dir Emer. 1991; Dir Clwyd Theatr Cymru 1997–; Consultant Dir Comédie Française 1975–80; Hon. Fellow Shakespeare Inst. 1990, Welsh Coll. of Music and Drama 2002, Glyndwr Univ. 2002, Bangor Univ. 2010; Chevalier, Ordre des Arts et Lettres; Hon. DLit (Birmingham) 1988, (Liverpool); Hon. LLD (Middx) 1997; Meilleur Spectacle de l'Année for Richard III 1972, for Twelfth Night 1976; Plays and Players Award for Henry VI 1977, Society of West End Theatre Award 1978 and 1984, Pragnell Shakespeare Award 1991, Evening Standard Best Dir Award 1993. *Productions:* over 50 plays with RSC, five with Comédie Française, two with Burgtheater, Vienna, one opera at Paris Opera House, one at Covent Garden, London, one at Bremen, 40 at Clwyd Theatr Cymru; Women Beware Women, Teatro Stabile di Genova, Italy; Arden of Faversham, Schauspielhaus, Zürich; Hamlet, Paris 1994, Merry Wives of Windsor, Oslo 1995, Kongsemnerne 1996, The Seagull 1998; recording: Murder in the Cathedral 1976; trans. (with Barbara Wright): The Balcony (Genet) 1971, Pleasure and Repentance 1976, Henry V (ed. Sally Beauman) 1976, Cyrano de Bergerac (TV). *Translation:* Hamlet, into French. *Address:* Clwyd Theatr Cymru, Mold, Flintshire, CH7 1YA, N Wales (office). *Telephone:* (1352) 756331 (office). *Fax:* (1352) 701558 (office). *E-mail:* terryhands@clwyd-theatre-cymru.co.uk (office). *Website:* www.clwyd-theatr-cymru.co.uk (office).

HANEDA, Katsuo; Japanese airline industry executive; b. 1943; m. Teiko Haneda; ed Faculty of Econs, Keio Univ.; joined Japan Airlines Co. Ltd 1965, apptd mem. Bd of Dirs 1995, Man. Dir and Sr Vice-Pres., Passenger Marketing 2001–02, Vice-Pres. 2002–03, Pres. 2003–04, Exec. Vice-Pres. Japan Airlines Corpn (holding co. cr. following merger of Japan Airlines and Japan Air Systems 2004) 2004–06, Japan Airlines Int. Co. 2004–06, Japan Airlines Domestic Co. Ltd 2004–06; mem. Bd of Dirs Ishiyama Gateway Holdings Inc. 2013–. *Address:* 2-22-8 Yakumo, Meguro-ku, Tokyo, Japan.

HANEGBI, Tzahi, BA, LLB; Israeli lawyer and politician; b. 26 Feb. 1957, Jerusalem; m. Randi Hanegbi; four s.; ed Hebrew Univ. of Jerusalem; served in an Israeli Defence Forces paratroopers unit 1974–77; Pres. Hebrew Univ. Student Union 1979–80, Nat. Union of Israeli Students 1980–82; Asst to Minister of Transport 1983–84; Adviser to Minister of Foreign Affairs 1984–86; Bureau Dir, Prime Minister's Office 1986–88; mem. Knesset (Parl.) 1988–2005, 2006–, Chair. Foreign Affairs and Defence Cttee 2006–10, 2015–, Chair. Likud faction and Coalition Chair. 2015–; Minister of Health 1996–97, of Justice 1997–2001, of the Environment 2001–03, of Transport 2002–03, of Public Security 2003–04, Minister in Prime Minister's Office 2004–06, Deputy Minister of Foreign Affairs 2014–15, Deputy Minister of Health 2014–; resigned from Likud party to join Kadima party Dec. 2005, resigned from Kadima and rejoined Likud 2010; cleared of bribery and fraud charges 2010. *Address:* Knesset, Kiryat Ben-Gurion, Jerusalem 91950, Israel (office). *Telephone:* (2) 6408394 (office). *Fax:* (2) 6408351 (office). *E-mail:* tzhanegbi@knesset.gov.il (office). *Website:* www.knesset.gov.il (office); hanegbi.org.il/english.

HANEKE, Michael; Austrian (b. German) film director and screenwriter; b. 23 March 1942, Munich, Germany; s. of Fritz Haneke and Beatrix von Degenschild; ed Univ. of Vienna; fmr film critic; ed. and dramaturg, Südwestfunk (German TV) 1967–70; directed several stage productions in German, including Strindberg, Goethe and Heinrich von Kleist in Berlin, Munich and Vienna; debut as TV dir in 1973; directed first opera, Mozart's Don Giovanni, Paris 2006; currently Prof. of Directing, Univ. of Music and Performing Arts, Vienna; Ordre des Arts et des Lettres 2010, Chevalier, Légion d'honneur 2012, Goldenes Komturkreuz des Ehrenzeichens für Verdienste um das Bundesland Niederösterreich 2013; Prince of Asturias Award for the Arts 2013, Sonning Prize 2014. *Films include:* writer and dir: Der siebente Kontinent (The Seventh Continent) 1989, Benny's Video 1992, 71 Fragmente einer Chronologie des Zufalls (71 Fragments of a Chronology of Chance) 1994, Lumière et compagnie (Lumière and Company, segment 'Michael Haneke/Vienne') 1995, Funny Games 1997, Das Schloß (The Castle) 1997, Code inconnu: Récit incomplet de divers voyages (Code Unknown: Incomplete Tales of Several Journeys) 2000, La pianiste (The Piano Teacher) (Grand Prize, Best Actor and Actress Awards, Cannes Film Festival 2001) 2001, Le temps du loup (The Time of the Wolf) 2003, Caché (Hidden) 2005, Funny Games (remake) 2007, Das weiße Band (The White Ribbon) (Palme d'Or, Cannes Film Festival 2009) 2009, Amour 2012 (Palme d'Or, Cannes Film Festival 2012); actor: Charms Zwischenfälle (Charm's Incidents) 1996. *Television includes:* writer and dir: After Liverpool 1974, Sperrmüll 1976, Drei Wege zum See 1976, Lemminge, Teil 1 Arkadien 1979, Lemminge, Teil 2 Verletzungen 1979, Variation 1983, Wer war Edgar Allan? 1984, Fraulein 1986, Nachruf für einen Mörder 1991, Die Rebellion 1993. *Address:* Universität für Musik und darstellende Kunst Wien, Anton-von-Webern-Platz 1, 1030 Vienna, Austria.

HANEKOM, Derek; South African politician; *Minister of Tourism;* b. 13 Jan. 1953, Cape Town; m. Trish Hanekom; mem. African Nat. Congress (ANC); arrested 1977 for protesting against detentions, imprisoned for ANC activities 1983–86; in exile in Zimbabwe 1987–90; fmr ANC Co-ordinator of Land and Agricultural Devt; MP 1994–; Minister of Land Affairs 1994–99, of Agric. 1996–99; Chair. Man. Cttee Nat. Rural Devt Forum; Deputy Minister of Science and Tech. 2004–14; Minister of Tourism 2014–17, 2018–; mem. Bd of Dirs Land and Agric. Policy Centre; mem. Bd SEED; mem. Bd of Trustees Ahmed Kathrada Foundation;

mem. Nat. Exec. Cttee African Nat. Congress; Free Market Award 2002. *Address:* Ministry of Tourism, Tourism House, 17 Trevenna St, Sunnyside, Pretoria 0001, South Africa (office). *Telephone:* (12) 4446000 (office). *Fax:* (12) 4447000 (office). *Website:* www.tourism.gov.za (office).

HANGST, Jeffrey Scott, SB, SM, PhD; American physicist and academic; *Professor of Physics, University of Århus;* b. Pa; ed Massachusetts Inst. of Tech., Univ. of Chicago; Assoc. Prof., later Prof. Dept of Physics and Astronomy, Univ. of Århus; Physics Co-ordinator ATHENA Experiment, CERN, Geneva, Switzerland, Spokesperson, ALPHA Experiment 2004–; Fellow, American Physical Soc. 2005; European Physical Soc. Accelerator Prize 1996, John Dawson Award for Excellence in Plasma Physics Research, American Physical Soc. 2011. *Address:* Department of Physics and Astronomy, University of Århus, New Munkegade 120, Building 1520, 427, 8000 Århus C, Denmark (office). *Telephone:* 89-42-37-51 (office). *Fax:* 86-12-07-40 (office). *E-mail:* hangst@phys.au.dk (office). *Website:* www.phys.au.dk (office).

HANIEL, Franz Markus; German engineer and business executive; *Chairman of the Supervisory Board, Franz Haniel & Cie. GmbH;* b. 1955; career in family-owned co. Franz Haniel & Cie. GmbH, Chair. Supervisory Bd 2003–04, 2007–; mem. Bd of Dirs, Giesecke & Devrient GmbH; mem. Supervisory Bd BMW AG 2004–, Security Networks (Secunet) AG 2004–, Heraeus Holding GmbH; mem. Supervisory Bd, Metro AG 2007–16, Chair. 2007–10, 2012–16; Vice-Chair. Supervisory Bd, DELTON AG; mem. Bd of Dirs, TBG Ltd, St Julian's, Malta 2014–. *Address:* Franz Haniel & Cie. GmbH, Franz-Haniel-Platz 1, 47119 Duisberg, Germany (office). *Telephone:* (203) 806-0 (office). *Fax:* (203) 806-622 (office). *E-mail:* jstolle@haniel.de (office). *Website:* www.haniel.de (office).

HANINGTON, Sandra, BASc, MBA; Canadian business executive; *Master, Royal Canadian Mint;* m. Eric Windeler; three c. (one deceased); ed Univ. of Waterloo, Univ. of Toronto; began career as Consultant with Andersen Consulting (now Accenture) 1985–87; Marketing Specialist and Sr Operations Research Analyst, Suncor Inc./Sunoco Group 1987–88; joined Royal Trustco Ltd 1988 as Asst Vice-Pres. for Affinity Markets, North American Life/Manulife Financial; Vice-Pres., Insurance, Personal and Commercial Client Group, BMO Financial Group 1999, progressively sr exec. roles in Canada and USA, becoming Exec. Vice-Pres., BMO Financial Group 2009–11; Master (Pres. and CEO) Royal Canadian Mint 2015–; Co-founder, Bd Dir and fmr Chair. Jack.org (org. dedicated to mental health wellness for Canadian youth, in memory of her late son); mem. Bd of Dirs Canada Mortgage and Housing Corpn 2014–; Ind. Dir Extendicare Inc. 2014–; fmr Dir Kids Help Phone, Symcor Corpn; mem. Inst. of Corporate Dirs; named by Women's Exec. Network (WXN) as one of Canada's Top 100 Most Powerful Women 2007–09. *Address:* Royal Canadian Mint, 320 Sussex Drive, Ottawa, ON K1A 0G8, Canada (office). *Telephone:* (613) 993-8990 (office). *Fax:* (613) 998-4130 (office). *E-mail:* info@mint.ca (office). *Website:* www.mint.ca (office).

HANIYA, Ismail Abd as-Salam Ahmad, BA; Palestinian politician; b. 1962, Gaza; m.; 12 c.; ed Islamic Univ. of Gaza; jailed by Israelis for three years, released 1992 and deported to Lebanon; returned to Gaza 1993; Dean, Islamic Univ. of Gaza 1993–97; Head of Office of Sheikh Ahmed Yassin (Hamas spiritual leader) 1997–2004; Prime Minister, Palestinian Nat. Authority (Hamas) 2006–07 (resgnd), March–June 2007 (under unity govt), also Minister of the Interior May–June 2007; self-declared as Prime Minister of Palestinian Nat. Authority (disputed); Leader Political Bureau, Hamas 2017–. *Address:* c/o Islamic Resistance Movement (Hamas: Harakat al-Muqawama al-Islamiyya), Gaza Palestinian Autonomous Areas.

HANKEN, James, AB, PhD; American zoologist and academic; *Alexander Agassiz Professor of Zoology, Curator in Herpetology and Director, Museum of Comparative Zoology, and Professor of Biology, Department of Organismic and Evolutionary Biology, Harvard University;* b. 14 July 1952, New York City, NY; s. of William Hanken and Miriam Gertz; one s. one d.; ed Univ. of California, Berkeley; Postdoctoral studies at Dalhousie Univ., Canada; then Faculty position, Univ. of Colorado, Boulder; Prof. of Biology, Dept of Organismic and Evolutionary Biology and Faculty mem., Center for Health and the Global Environment, Harvard School of Public Health, Harvard Univ. 1999–, currently Alexander Agassiz Prof. of Zoology, Curator in Herpetology and Dir Museum of Comparative Zoology; Past Pres. Int. Soc. of Vertebrate Morphologists, American Soc. of Ichthyologists and Herpetologists; fmr Chair. Int. Bd of Dirs Declining Amphibian Populations Task Force; fmr Co-Chair. Scientific Advisory Bd Consortium for the Barcode of Life; mem. Soc. for Study of Evolution, Soc. for Integrative and Comparative Biology, Herpetologists League; Fellow, AAAS; von Hofsten Lecturer, Uppsala Univ., Sweden, Gompertz Lecture in Integrative Biology, Univ. of California, Berkeley, Chief Guest, Int. Peradeniya Univ. Research Sessions (iPURSE), Univ. of Peradeniya, Sri Lanka. *Achievements include:* nature and scientific photographer whose photographs appear in several books, field guides and magazines, including Natural History, Geo, Audubon and National Geographic World. *Publications include:* Skull, Vol. 1: Development 1993, Skull, Vol. 2: Patterns of Structural and Systematic Diversity 1993, Skull, Vol. 3: Functional and Evolutionary Mechanisms 1993; has edited four books and published more than 125 scientific papers in professional journals on the evolutionary morphology, development and systematics of vertebrates, especially amphibians. *Address:* Museum of Comparative Zoology, 26 Oxford Street, Cambridge, MA 02138, USA (office). *Telephone:* (617) 495-2496 (office). *Fax:* (617) 495-5667 (office). *E-mail:* hanken@oeb.harvard.edu (office). *Website:* www.oeb.harvard.edu/faculty/hanken/hanken-oeb.html (office); www.oeb.harvard.edu/faculty/hanken/public_html/index.html (office); eol.org/info/bio_jhanken (home).

HANKES, Sir Claude, KCVO; British macro-strategist and adviser; b. 8 March 1949; with Manufacturers Hanover 1968–72, with Robert Fleming & Co. Ltd 1972–77, Dir 1974–77; Chair. Man. Cttee Price Waterhouse and Partners 1983–89, Action Resource Centre 1986–91; Adviser to the Bd Corange (Boehringer Mannheim) 1988–94; Deputy Chair. Leutwiler and Partners Ltd 1992–96; Chair. Shaw & Bradley 1993–; Interim Chair. Roland Berger Strategy Consultants Ltd 2003–05; Chair. Advisory Cttee to Jordan on Strategic Econ. Policy Matters 1993–94; Adviser to Iraq 2003, to Iraq Governing Council 2003–04, to Iraq (on macro-strategic issues) 2005–06; Sr Adviser to Trade Bank of Iraq 2007–11; Trustee, Windsor Leadership Trust 1998–2007 (Chair. 2000–07), Hawthornden Int. Retreat for Writers 2008–10; Trustee and Adviser, St George's House, Windsor Castle 2000–06; Hon. Fellow, Corpus Christi Coll., Oxford, Coll. of St George, Windsor Castle 2006 (Hon. mem. 2006, Hon. Fellow and Adviser 2002–06), Hon. Life Mem. of the Council, St George's House, Windsor Castle, 2006. *Publications include:* The Dangers of the Banking System: Funding Country Deficits 1975, Nobel Industrier Independent Report, Stockholm 1991. *Leisure interests:* gardening, art.

HANKS, Tom; American actor and film producer; b. 9 July 1956, Concord, Calif.; m. 1st Samantha Lewes 1978 (divorced 1985); two c.; m. 2nd Rita Wilson 1988; two s.; ed California State Univ.; began acting career with Great Lakes Shakespeare Festival; mem. Acad. of Motion Picture Arts and Sciences, mem. Bd of Govs 2001–, Vice-Pres. 2005–09, First Vice-Pres. 2009–; American Film Inst. Lifetime Achievement Award 2002, BAFTA Award for Excellence in Film 2004, People's Choice Award 1995–96, 1999, 2002, 2004, Kennedy Center Honor 2014, Presidential Medal of Freedom 2016, Icon Award, Palm Springs Int. Film Festival 2016. *Films include:* He Knows You're Alone 1980, Splash 1984, Bachelor Party 1984, The Man with One Red Shoe 1985, Volunteers 1985, The Money Pit 1986, Nothing in Common 1986, Every Time We Say Goodbye 1986, Dragnet 1987, Big 1988, Punchline 1988, The 'Burbs 1989, Turner & Hooch 1989, Joe Versus the Volcano 1990, The Bonfire of the Vanities 1990, Radio Flyer (uncredited) 1992, A League of Their Own 1992, Sleepless in Seattle 1993, Philadelphia (Acad. Award for Best Actor 1994) 1993, Forrest Gump (Acad. Award for Best Actor 1995) 1994, Apollo 13 1995, Toy Story (voice) 1995, That Thing You Do (also dir) 1996, Turner & Hooch 1997, Saving Private Ryan 1998, You've Got Mail 1998, The Green Mile 1999, Toy Story 2 (voice) 1999, Cast Away (also producer) 2000, Road to Perdition 2002, My Big Fat Greek Wedding (producer) 2002, Catch Me If You Can 2003, The Ladykillers 2004, Connie and Carla (producer) 2004, The Terminal 2004, Elvis Has Left the Building 2004, The Polar Express (also exec. producer) 2004, Magnificent Desolation: Walking on the Moon 3D (documentary short) (voice) 2005, Da Vinci Code 2006, Cars (voice) 2006, Neil Young: Heart of Gold (producer) 2006, The Ant Bully (producer) 2006, Starter for Ten (producer) 2006, Charlie Wilson's War 2007, The Great Buck Howard 2008, Angels & Demons 2009, Beyond All Boundaries (short) (voice) 2009, Where the Wild Things Are (producer) 2009, Toy Story 3 (voice) 2010, Hawaiian Vacation (short) (voice) 2011, Larry Crowne 2011, Small Fry (short) (voice) 2011, Extremely Loud & Incredibly Close 2011, Cloud Atlas 2012, Captain Phillips 2013, Saving Mr. Banks 2013, Bridge of Spies 2015, Ithaca 2015, A Hologram for the King 2015, Sully: Miracle on the Hudson 2016, Inferno 2016, The Circle 2017, The Post 2017. *Television includes:* Bosom Buddies (series) 1980–82, From the Earth to the Moon (mini-series, also exec. producer) 1998, West Point (series, producer) 2000, We Stand Alone Together (exec. producer) 2001, Scene by Scene (series) 2001, Band of Brothers (Emmy Award for Outstanding Mini-series 2002, also exec. producer) 2001, My Big Fat Greek Life (exec. producer) 2003, Freedom: A History of Us (series documentary) 2003, We're with the Band (producer) 2005, Big Love (exec. producer) 2006–07, The Pacific (mini-series) (exec. producer) 2010, 30 Rock 2011, Killing Lincoln 2013, Toy Story of Terror! 2013, The Sixties 2014, Olive Kitteridge (exec. producer), Toy Story That Time Forgot 2014, The Seventies (exec. producer) 2015, The Eighties (exec. producer) 2016. *Plays:* Lucky Guy (Broadway) 2013. *Address:* 8383 Wilshire Blvd, Suite 500, Beverly Hills, CA 90211 (office); c/o Creative Artists Agency, 2000 Avenue of the Stars, Los Angeles, CA 90067, USA (office). *Telephone:* (424) 288-2000 (office). *Fax:* (424) 288-2900 (office). *Website:* www.caa.com (office).

HANLEY, Rt Hon. Sir Jeremy James, KCMG, PC, FCA, FCIS, FCCA; British business executive, politician and chartered accountant; b. 17 Nov. 1945, Amersham, Bucks.; s. of Jimmy Hanley and Dinah Sheridan; m. 1st Helene Mason 1968 (divorced 1973); one s.; m. 2nd Verna, Viscountess Villiers (née Stott) 1973; one s. one step d.; ed Rugby School; with Peat Marwick Mitchell & Co. 1963–66; Dir Anderson Thomas Frankel (ATF) 1969, Man. Dir ATF (Jersey and Ireland) 1970–73; Deputy Chair. The Financial Training Co. Ltd 1973–90; Sec. Park Place PLC 1977–83; Chair. Fraser Green Ltd 1986–90; Parl. Adviser to ICA 1986–90; Conservative MP for Richmond and Barnes 1983–97; Parl. Under-Sec. of State, Northern Ireland Office 1990–93; Minister for Health, Social Security and Agric. 1990–92, for Political Devt, Community Relations and Educ. 1992–93; Minister of State for the Armed Forces, Ministry of Defence 1993–94; Cabinet Minister without Portfolio 1995; Chair. Conservative Party 1994–95; Foreign Office Minister of State for the Middle East and Hong Kong 1995–97; Chair. AdVal Group PLC, Int. Trade and Investment Missions Ltd 1998–2002; Dir ITE Group PLC 1996–2010, GTECH Corpn, USA 2001–06; fmr Chair. Financial Reporting Council UK Corporate Governance Cttee; Dir Lottomatica SpA, Arab-British Chamber of Commerce 1998–2012, European Advisory Bd 2004–05, Calyon (fmrly Crédit Lyonnais) 2000–05, Nymex Europe Ltd 2005–08, Blue Hackle Ltd 2006–10, Willis Group Holdings Inc. 2006–; Chair. British Iran Chamber of Commerce 2000 (Vice-Pres. 2001–06), Brain Games Network PLC 2000–01; Deputy Chair. Langbar International 2006–; mem. British-American Parl. Group 1983–97, Anglo-French Parl. Group 1983–97, CPA 1983–97, IPU 1983–97, British-Irish Inter-Parl. Body 1990, Advisory Bd Talal Abu-Ghazaleh Int.; Vice-Chair. Nat. Anglo-West Indian Conservative Soc. 1982–83; Chair. Conservative Cands Asscn 1982–83; mem. Bow Group 1974–97, European Movement 1974–97, Mensa 1968–; mem. Court of Assts, Worshipful Co. of Chartered Accountants, Master 2005–06; mem. Dyers' Co.; mem. Brixham Rotary Club, Brixham Yacht Club; Fellow, Asscn of Chartered Certified Accountants; Freeman of the City of London 1989. *Leisure interests:* cookery, chess, cricket, languages, theatre, cinema, music. *Address:* Berry Head House, Victoria Road, Brixham, Devon, TQ5 9AR (home); 6 Butts Mead, Northwood, Middx, HA6 2TL, England (home). *Telephone:* (1803) 882317 (Devon) (home); (1923) 826675 (Middx) (home). *E-mail:* jeremy@hanley.com (home).

HANLON, Lt-Gen. Edward, BS, MS; American military officer (retd); *President, Raytheon International, Inc. Europe;* ed Southeastern Oklahoma Univ., Pepperdine Univ., Univ. of Minnesota, Officer Candidates School, Quantico; commissioned Second Lt 1967; posts have included Exec. Officer and Fire Direction Officer 1st Bn, 13th Marines, Vietnam 1968–69, Asst S-3 Legal Officer and Public Affairs Officer, Marine Corps HQ 1969–72, Bn S-4 2nd Bn, later CO E Battery, 12th Marines 1973–74, Exec. Officer Training Support Co., CO Enlisted Instructor Co. and Exec. Officer Company M, The Basic School, Quantico 1974–77, Marine Officer Instructor and Exec. Officer, Naval Reserve Officers Training Course Unit,

Univ. of Minn. 1977–80, Bn S-4 2nd Bn, Exec. Officer 3rd Bn and Div. Staff Sec., 1st Marine Div., Camp Pendleton 1981–84, CO 3rd Bn, 12th Marines 1984–85, Dir of Personal Services Marine Corps Recruit Depot, San Diego 1985–86, Asst Chief of Staff for Plans and Operations, HQ Fleet Marine Force Europe, London 1987–90, Atlantic Fleet Marine Officer 1990–92, CO 10th Marines, 2nd Marine Div. 1992–93, promoted to Brig.-Gen. 1993, Deputy Commdr Naval Striking and Support Forces Southern Europe, Naples, Italy 1993–96, promoted to Maj.-Gen. 1996, Dir Expeditionary Warfare Div. 1996–98, Commanding Gen. Marine Corps Base, Camp Pendleton 1998–2001, promoted to Lt-Gen. 2001, Commanding Gen. Marine Corps Combat Devt Command, Quantico and Deputy Commandant Combat Devt, Marine Corps HQ 2001–04; Mil. Rep. to NATO 2004–06; Pres. Raytheon International Inc. Europe, Brussels 2007–; Defense Superior Service Medal with oak leaf, Legion of Merit with two gold stars, Defense Meritorious Service Medal, Meritorious Service Medal, Navy and Marine Corps Commendation Medal with Combat "V" and gold star, Combat Action Ribbon. *Address:* Raytheon International Inc., avenue Ariane 5, Arianelaan, 1200 Brussels, Belgium (office). *Website:* www.raytheon.com (office).

HANLON, Philip J., AB, PhD; American college administrator and mathematician; *President, Dartmouth College;* b. 10 April 1955, New York; m. Gail Gentes; three c.; ed Dartmouth Coll., California Inst. of Tech.; Instructor of Applied Math., Massachusetts Inst. of Tech. 1981–83; Bantrell Fellow in Math., California Inst. of Tech. 1983–86; Assoc. Prof., Univ. of Michigan 1986–90, Prof. 1990–2013, Arthur F. Thurnau Prof. 1992–2013, Donald J. Lewis Prof. of Math. 2001–13, Assoc. Dean for Planning and Finance, Coll. of Literature, Science and the Arts 2001–04, Assoc. Provost for Academic and Budgetary Affairs 2004–07, Vice-Provost for Academic and Budgetary Affairs 2007–10, Provost and Exec. Vice-Pres. for Academic Affairs 2010–13, mem. Exec. Cttee, Coll. of Literature, Science and the Arts 1994–97, mem. Univ. of Michigan Presidential Comm. on Undergraduate Studies 2000–01; Pres. Dartmouth Coll. 2013–; visiting positions: Center for Communications Research, Princeton 1984, 1986, 1990, Univ. of Oxford, UK 1988, Univ. of Strasbourg, France 1988, 1993, Institut des Hautes Études Scientifiques, Bures-sur-Yvette, France 1988, Mittag-Leffler Inst., Stockholm, Sweden 1992, Isaac Newton Inst., Univ. of Cambridge, UK 2001; Founder and Exec. Dir Michigan Math Scholars Program 1996–99, Chair. Planning Cttee 1997–99; Prin. Organizer of six-month programme on Symmetric Functions at Isaac Newton Inst., Univ. of Cambridge 2001; Chair. Presidential Task Force on Multidisciplinary Learning and Team Teaching, Univ. of Michigan 2004–05, mem. Bd of Dirs Univ. of Michigan Hosps and Health Centers 2010–, Bentley Historical Library 2010–12; mem. Nat. Security Agency Advisory Bd 1994–2007, mem. Math. Sub-panel 1994–, Chair. 1994–2006; Chair. Mathematical Reviews Editorial Cttee 1992–95; mem. Editorial Bd Transactions of the American Mathematical Society 1992–2000, Journal of Algebraic Combinatorics 1993–, Electronic Journal of Combinatorics 1996–; mem. Council of American Math. Soc. 1992–95, FOCUS Advisory Cttee 1989–93, 2007; mem. Bd of Dirs Consortium on Financing Higher Educ. (COFHE); NSF Presidential Young Investigator Award 1987–92, Alfred P. Sloan Fellowship 1986–88, Prin. Speaker, American Math. Soc. 1988, Henry Russel Award 1990, Plenary Speaker, Canadian Math. Soc. 1992, John Simon Guggenheim Fellowship 1992, Michigan Soc. of Fellows 1993–96, Literature, Science and the Arts Excellence in Educ. Award 1997. *Publications include:* more than 60 papers in professional journals on algebraic combinatorics, discrete probability, bioinformatics and theoretical computer science. *Address:* Office of the President, Dartmouth College, 207 Parkhurst Hall, Hanover, NH 03755, USA (office). *Telephone:* (603) 646-2223 (office). *Fax:* (603) 646-8264 (office). *E-mail:* president's .office@dartmouth.edu (office). *Website:* www.dartmouth.edu/~president (office).

HANNAH, Daryl; American actress; b. 3 Dec. 1960, Chicago, Ill.; d. of Donald Christian Hannah and Susan Jeanne Metzger; m. Neil Young 2018; ed Univ. of California, Los Angeles; studied with Stella Adler; studied ballet with Marjorie Tallchief; appeared on TV in Paper Dolls. *Films include:* The Fury 1978, The Final Terror, Hard Country, Blade Runner, Summer Lovers, Splash, The Pope of Greenwich Village, Reckless, Clan of the Cave Bear, Legal Eagles, Roxanne, Wall Street, High Spirits, Steel Magnolias, Crazy People, At Play in the Fields of the Lord, Memoirs of an Invisible Man, Grumpy Old Men, Attack of the 50 ft Woman, The Tie That Binds, Grumpier Old Men 1995, Two Much 1996, The Last Days of Frankie the Fly 1996, Wild Flowers 1999, My Favorite Martian 1999, Dancing at the Blue Iguana 2000, Cord 2000, Speedway Junky 2001, Jackpot 2001, A Walk to Remember 2002, Hard Cash 2002, Northfork 2002, Kill Bill Vol. I 2003, Kill Bill: Vol. 2 2004, Yo puta 2004, Silver City 2004, Careful What You Wish For 2004, Love is the Drug 2006, Keeping Up with the Steins 2006, Olé 2006, The Poet 2007, Vice (also producer) 2008, Shannon's Rainbow 2009, The Cycle 2009, A Closed Book 2010, S.O.S Love! The Million Dollar Contract 2011, The Hot Flashes 2013, 2047: Sights of Death 2014, I Am Michael 2015, Skin Traffik 2015, Awaken 2015, Sicilian Vampire 2015, The American Connection 2017, The Slider 2017, Papa 2018; Dir, Writer, Producer: The Last Supper (Berlin Int. Film Festival Jury Award for Best Short) 1994; Dir: A Hundred and One Nights 1995, Strip Notes 2001; Dir and Screenwriter: Paradox 2018. *Television:* Sense 8 (lead role) 2015–18. *Play:* The Seven Year Itch 2000. *Address:* c/o Chuck Binder, Binder and Associates, 1465 Lindacrest Drive, Beverly Hills, CA 90210, USA. *Telephone:* (310) 274-9995. *Website:* darylhannah.com.

HANNAH, John; British actor; b. 23 April 1962, East Kilbride, Scotland; s. of John Hannah and Susan Hannah; m. Joanna Roth; two c.; ed Royal Scottish Acad. of Music and Drama; fmrly electrician; worked with Workers' Theatre Co. *Television includes:* Bookie 1987, Brond 1987, Paul Calf's Video Diary 1993, Milner 1994, Faith 1994, Pauline Calf's Wedding Video 1994, McCallum (series) 1995, Out of the Blue (series) 1995, Truth or Dare 1996, Circles of Deceit: Kalon 1996, The Love Bug 1997, Rebus: Black and Blue 2000, Rebus: The Hanging Garden 2000, Rebus: Dead Souls 2001, Dr. Jekyll and Mr. Hyde 2002, MDs (series) 2002, Amnesia 2004, Rebus: Mortal Causes 2004, Marple: 4.50 from Paddington 2004, Cold Blood 2005, Ghost Son 2006, New Street Law 2006–07, Kidnap and Ransom 2011, Spartacus: Gods of the Arena 2011, Touch of Cloth 2012, Widower (mini-series) 2014. *Films include:* Harbour Beat 1990, Four Weddings and a Funeral 1994, The Final Cut 1995, Madagascar Skin 1995, The Innocent Sleep 1996, The James Gang 1997, Sliding Doors 1998, Resurrection Man 1998, So This Is Romance? 1998, The Mummy 1999, The Hurricane 1999, The Intruder 1999, Circus 2000, Pandaemonium 2000, The Mummy Returns 2001, Before You Go 2002, I'm with Lucy 2002, I Accuse 2003, Male Mail 2004, The Last Legion 2007, The Mummy: Tomb of the Dragon Emperor 2008, The Wee Man 2013, Ping Pong Summer 2014.

HANNAY OF CHISWICK, Baron (Life Peer), cr. 2001, of Chiswick, of Bedford Park in the London Borough of Ealing; **David Hugh Alexander Hannay,** CMG, KCMG, GCMG, CH, MA, DLitt; British diplomatist; b. 28 Sept. 1935, London; s. of Julian Hannay and Eileen Hannay; m. Gillian Rosemary Rex (deceased) 1961; four s.; ed Craigflower School, Torryburn, Fife, Scotland, Winchester Coll. and New Coll. Oxford; Second Lt, King's Royal Irish Hussars 1954–56; Persian language student, Foreign Office and British Embassy, Tehran 1959–61; Oriental Sec., British Embassy, Kabul 1961–63; Second Sec., Eastern Dept, Foreign Office, London 1963–65; Second, then First Sec., UK Del. to EC, Brussels 1965–70, First Sec. UK Negotiating Team 1970–72; Chef de Cabinet to Sir Christopher Soames, Vice-Pres. EC Comm. 1973–77; Counsellor, Head of Energy, Science and Space Dept, FCO, London 1977–79, Counsellor, Head of Middle East Dept 1979, Asst Under-Sec. of State (EC) 1979–84; Minister, Embassy in Washington, DC 1984–85; UK Perm. Rep. to EC 1985–90, to UN 1990–95; British Govt Special Rep. for Cyprus 1996–2003; Prime Minister's Personal Envoy to Turkey and EU Special Rep. for Cyprus 1998; Life Peer (Ind.), House of Lords 2001–; mem. UN Sec. Gen.'s High Level Panel on Threats, Challenges and Change 2003–04, House of Lords EU Select Cttee 2002–06, 2008–14, House of Lords Inter-Governmental Orgs Cttee 2007–08, House of Lords Cttee on the Arctic 2014–15, House of Lords Sexual Violence in Conflict Cttee 2015–, International Relations Cttee 2016–; Chair. Int. Advisory Bd EDHEC 2003–09, UN Asscn of the UK 2006–11; Vice-Chair. All Party Parl. Group on Europe 2006–, Chair. on UN 2011–; Jt Convenor, All-Party Parl. Group on Global Security and Non-Proliferation 2007–; Dir (non-exec.) Chime Communications 1996–2006, Aegis 2000–03; mem. Court and Council, Univ. of Birmingham 1998–2006, Pro-Chancellor 2001–06; mem. Council of Britain in Europe 1999–2005; mem. Council Univ. of Kent 2009–15; mem. Advisory Bd Centre for European Reform 1997–; mem. Top Level Group on Nuclear Disarmament and Nonproliferation 2011–; mem. Bd Salzburg Seminar 2002–05, TANGGUH Ind. Advisory Panel 2002–09, Advisory Bd Judge Business Schools 2004, GPW & Co. 2011–; Gov. Ditchley Foundation 2005–; Hon. Fellow, New Coll. Oxford; Hon. DLitt (Birmingham) 2003. *Publications include:* Britain's Entry into the European Community: Report on the Negotiations (ed.) 1970–72, Cyprus: The Search for a Solution 2004, A More Secure World: Our Shared Responsibility (UN Panel Report) 2004, New World Disorder: The UN After the Cold War 2008, Britain's Quest for a Role: a Diplomatic Memoir from Europe to the UN 2012. *Leisure interests:* gardening, travel, photography. *Address:* 3 The Orchard, London, W4 1JZ (home); House of Lords, London, SW1A 0PW, England (office). *Telephone:* (20) 8987-9012 (home); (20) 7219-5353 (office). *Fax:* (20) 8987-9012 (home); (20) 7219-5979 (office).

HANNIBALSSON, Jón Baldvin, MA (Econ); Icelandic politician, diplomatist and academic; b. 21 Feb. 1939, Ísafjörður; s. of Hannibal Valdimarsson and Sólveig Ólafsdóttir; m. Bryndís Schram 1959; one s. three d.; ed Menntaskólinn í Reykjavik, Univ. of Edinburgh, UK, Nationalökonomiska Inst., Sweden, Univ. of Iceland and Harvard Univ., USA; teacher in secondary school, Reykjavik 1964–70; journalist, Frjáls thjóð (Free Nation), Reykjavik 1964–67; Founder and Rector Ísafjörður Coll. 1970–79; Chief Ed. Althýðublaðið (People's Daily), Reykjavik 1979–82; mem. Althingi (Parl.) 1982–98; Chair. SDP 1984–96; Minister of Finance 1987–88, for Foreign Affairs and External Trade 1988–95, led negotiations with EU on European Econ. Area 1989–94; mem. North Atlantic Council, NATO 1988–95; Amb. to USA (also accred to Canada, Mexico, Brazil, Chile and Argentina) 1998–2002, to Finland (also accred to Estonia, Latvia, Lithuania and Ukraine) 2002–05; Visiting Lecturer at the univs of Iceland and Univ. of Bifrost 2006–09; Visiting Scholar and Research Assoc., Univ. of Vilnius, Lithuania 2013, Univ. of Tartu, Estonia 2014; writer and frequent commentator on current affairs; Hon. Citizen of Vilnius, Lithuania 1996; Hon. mem. Bd Baltic Devt Forum; Order of Terra Marina, Estonia 1996, Order of Grand Duke Gediminas, Lithuania 1996, Order of Pres. of Latvia 1996, Order of Prince Trpimir and Croatian Morning Star 2001, Presidential Order of Merit (Slovenia); Dr hc (Univ. of Vilnius) 2016, (Univ. of Lithuania) 2016. *Film:* Those Who Dare (documentary on Iceland's role in support of the restored independence of the Baltic States) 2015. *Television:* Dialogue with Jón Baldvin (Stod 2) 1997, Hans Kristján Árnason: Iceland and the Surrounding World through the Eyes of Jón Baldvin Hannibalsson 2001. *Publications include:* Who Owns Iceland? 1985, Economic Strategy for Social-Democrats (co-author) 1986, The Icelandic Tax Reform 1987, The Age of Extremes – Reflections of 22 Icelanders at the Dawn of a New Millennium (co-ed. with Gunnar G. Schram) 2000, Iceland and the Baltic Nations' Struggle for the Restoration of Independence 1988–91 2001, Iceland in the New Century (co-author) 2001, Expectations and Disappointments of the 20th Century 2001, Tilhugalíf (Honeymoon; political memoirs) 2002, The Welfare State and Its Enemies 2004, The Baltic Road to Freedom: The Western Response to The Restoration of Independence of the Baltic States 2005, Iceland and the Current Economic Crisis – Political Implications and the Way Forward 2009, Iceland and the European Union 2009, Iceland's Triple Crisis – Are There Lessons to be Learned? 2010, The Solidarity of Small Nations 2010, The Future of Enlargement, European Strategy Forum 2010, The First Decade of the 21st Century in Retrospect: To Be or Not to Be – A Republic at a Crossroads 2011, The Baltic Road to Freedom – Revisited 2015, The Transition from Totalitarianism to Democracy: What Can We Learn from the Post-Independence Baltic Experience 2015. *Leisure interests:* reading, swimming, travel. *Address:* Álfhóll v/ Engjaveg, 270 Mosó, Iceland. *Telephone:* 566-6362; 895-6362. *E-mail:* jbhannibalsson@gmail .com. *Website:* www.jbh.is.

HANOOMANJEE, Hon. Santi Bai; Mauritian politician and civil servant; *Speaker of the National Assembly;* b. 15 Nov. 1952, Vacoas; m.; three d.; ed Queen Elizabeth Coll., Univ. of Mauritius; worked in Electoral Commrs' Office, Ministry of Educ. and Cultural Affairs, Ministry of Employment, Ministry of Internal Communications, Prime Minister's Office, Ministry for Women's Rights, Child Devt and Family Welfare, Ministry of Civil Service Affairs, Ministry of Agric. and Natural Resources, Ministry of Finance and Econ. Devt; retd as Perm. Sec. 2005; joined MSM Party 2005; mem. of Nat. Ass. for Constituency No. 14 Savanne- Black River 2005–10; Minister of Health and Quality of Life 2010–11; Speaker of the Nat. Ass. 2014–; Chair. Farmers' Service Corpn 1996–2005, Sugar Planters' Mechanical

Pool Corpn 1996–2001, Tea Bd 1996–2005, Mauritius Sugar Authority 2001–05; First Chair. Mauritius Revenue Authority 2004–05; Chair. Parliamentary Asscn, Indian Ocean Comm. 2016–, also Pres. Africa Region 2015–16; elected mem. Standing Cttee, Speakers and Presiding Officers of the Commonwealth 2018; mem. Nat. Women's Council, Nat. Children's Council, Mauritius Sugar Industry Research Inst., Film Devt Corpn, Mauritius Sugar Bulk Terminal Corpn; Grand Commdr, Order of the Star and Key of the Indian Ocean 2015. *Leisure interests:* social work, promoting women's interests, reading, cooking, jogging. *Address:* National Assembly, Parliament House, Place d'Armes, Port Louis (office); 15 Gold Coast Complex, Kalimay Road, Flic en Flac, Mauritius (home). *Telephone:* 201-2306 (office). *Fax:* 212-3232 (office). *E-mail:* shanoomanjee@govmu.org (office). *Website:* mauritiusassembly.govmu.org (office).

HANRAHAN, Paul T., BS, MBA; American energy industry executive; *CEO, Energy and Infrastructure, American Capital Ltd;* b. 1957; ed Harvard Business School, US Naval Acad.; active service in USN; various man. roles with AES Corpn in USA, Europe and Asia including Gen. Man. AES Transpower Inc. 1990–93, Exec. Vice-Pres., CEO and Sec. AES China Generating Co. (Chigen) 1993–95, Pres. and CEO 1995–98, Vice-Pres. AES 1994–97, Sr Vice-Pres. 1997, CEO and Exec. Vice-Pres. 1997–2002, Pres. and CEO 2002–11; Co-founder and CEO, Energy and Infrastructure, American Capital Ltd 2012–; mem. Bd of Dirs Arch Coal, Ingredion Inc. 2006–, Great Point Energy, LLC, AquaVentures Holdings, LLC, Seven Seas Water Corpn 2012–. *Address:* American Capital Ltd, Energy and Infrastructure, 180 Main Street 2/F, Annapolis, MD 21401, USA (office). *Telephone:* (443) 214-7070 (office). *E-mail:* info@acei.com (office). *Website:* www.acei.com (office).

HANS-ADAM II, HSH Prince of Liechtenstein Johannes (Hans) Adam Ferdinand Alois Josef Maria Marco d'Aviano Pius Fürst von und zu Liechtenstein, Duke of Troppau and Jägerndorf, Count of Rietberg; b. 14 Feb. 1945, Zurich, Switzerland; s. of Prince Franz Josef II and Countess Georgina von Wilczek; m. Countess Marie Aglaë Kinsky von Wchinitz und Tettau 1967; three s. (including Hereditary Prince Alois Philipp Maria) one d.; ed Schottengymnasium, Vienna, School of Econs and Social Sciences, St Gallen, Switzerland; Chief Exec. of Prince of Liechtenstein Foundation 1970–84; took over exec. authority of Liechtenstein Aug. 1984; transferred exec. power to Hereditary Prince Alois Aug. 2004; Kt, Order of the Golden Fleece (House of Habsburg) 1961; Commemorative Medal on the Occasion of the 70th Birthday of HSH Prince Franz Joseph II 1976; Grand Master, Order of Merit of the Principality of Liechtenstein 1989; Great Star of Honour for Services to the Repub. of Austria 1991. *Address:* Schloss Vaduz, 9490 Vaduz, Principality of Liechtenstein. *E-mail:* office@fuerstenhaus.li (office). *Website:* www.fuerstenhaus.li/en/princely-house/prince-hans-adam-II.

HÄNSCH, Theodor Wolfgang, MSc, PhD; German physicist and academic; *Carl Friedrich von Siemens Professor of Physics and Director, Max-Planck-Institut für Quantenoptik, Ludwig-Maximilians-Universität Munich;* b. 30 Oct. 1941, Heidelberg; s. of Karl Hänsch and Marta Hänsch; ed Helmholtz-Gymnasium, Heidelberg, Univ. of Heidelberg; Asst Prof. Inst. of Applied Physics, Univ. of Heidelberg 1969–70; NATO Postdoctoral Fellow, Stanford Univ. 1970–72, Assoc. Prof. of Physics 1972–75, Prof. of Physics 1975–86; Dir Max-Planck-Institut für Quantenoptik 1986– (Exec. Dir 1993–96, 2003–04), Carl Friedrich von Siemens Prof. of Physics, Ludwig-Maximilians-Universität Munich 1986–, Chair. Physics Dept 2001–02; Chair. Int. Science Council, King Abdullah Inst. of Nanotechnology; Visiting Prof., College de France 1978, Univ. of Kyoto 1979, Univ. of Florence 1979, 1995, Fudan Univ. 1982, Ecole Normale Superieure, Paris 1992; Gordon Moore Distinguished Scholar 2001; Qatar Foundation Distinguished Lecturer, Texas A&M Univ.; Consultant, Scientific Advisory Bd Cold Quanta Inc. 2007; Fellow, American Physical Soc., Optical Soc. of America; mem. Editorial Bd Applied Physics B, Physics in Perspective, Springer Series in Optical Sciences, Laser Physics Review; mem. American Acad. of Arts and Sciences, Bavarian Acad. of Arts and Sciences, Berlin-Brandenburg Acad. of Sciences; Hon. Citizen, City of Garching 2006, City of Florence, Italy 2007; Hon. mem. Optical Soc. of America 2008, German Physical Soc. 2011; Hon. Prof., Nat. Chiang Tung Univ., Hsinchu, Taiwan 2010; Hon. Chair. Prof., Univ. System of Taiwan 2010; Bayerischer Maximiliansorden, Grand Officer Cross (Order of Merit) 2006, Grosses Bundesverdienstkreuz mit Stern 2007; Dr hc (Univ. of St Andrews) 2006, (Free Univ., Berlin) 2006, (Bar-Ilan-Univ.) 2008; Calif. Museum of Science and Industry Calif. Scientist of the Year 1973, Alexander von Humboldt Sr US Scientist Award 1977, Freie Universität Berlin Otto Klung Prize 1980, NAS Cyrus B. Comstock Prize 1983, American Physical Soc. Herbert P. Broida Prize 1983, Optical Soc. of America William F. Meggers Award 1985, Franklin Inst. Michelson Medal 1986, Italgas Prize for Research and Innovation 1987, Deutsche Forschungsgemeinschaft Gottfried Wilhelm Leibniz Preis 1988, King Faisal Int. Prize for Science 1989, Einstein Medal for Laser Science 1995, American Physical Soc. Arthur L. Schawlow Prize for Laser Science 1996, Philip Morris Research Prize 1998, 2000, Deutsche Physikalische Gesellschaft Stern-Gerlach Medal 2000, Laser Inst. of America Arthur L. Schawlow Award 2000, European Physical Soc. Quantum Electronics and Optics Prize 2001, Int. Union of Pure and Applied Physics SUNAMCO Medal 2001, Italian Nat. Acad. of Sciences Matteucci-Medal 2002, Alfried Krupp Prize for Science 2002, IEEE I. I. Rabi Award 2005, Optical Soc. of America Frederic Ives Medal 2005, Otto-Hahn-Prize for Chem. and Physics 2005, Nobel Prize in Physics (jtly) 2005, De Scientia et Humanitate Meritis Medal 2007, Carl Friedrich von Siemens Prize and Chair 2007, Ioannes Marcus Marci Medal, Czech Spectroscopic Soc. 2007, Garbsen Ring, City of Garbsen 2007, Rudolf Diesel Gold Medal, German Inst of Interventions 2007, Orden Pour Le Mérite für Wissenschaften und Künste (Germany) 2008, James Joyce Award 2009, Sayling Wen Excellent Lecture Award, Nat. Central Univ., Taiwan 2010, Bavarian Constitution Medal in Gold, Order of Merit 2010, Advanced Grant, European Research Council 2010. *Publications:* more than 620 scientific articles. *Address:* c/o G. Gschwendtner, Schellingstr. 4/III, 80799 Munich, Germany (office). *Telephone:* (89) 2180-3212 (office). *Fax:* (89) 285192 (office). *E-mail:* t.w.haensch@physik.uni-muenchen.de (office). *Website:* www.mpq.mpg.de/~haensch (office).

HANSEID, Einar; Norwegian journalist (retd); b. 19 Nov. 1943, Sandefjord; m. Mari Onsrud 1977; two s.; reporter, Sandefjords Blad 1965; Sub-Ed. Bondebladet 1966–68; News Ed. Dagbladet 1974; Chief Ed. Hjem & Fritid 1982; Man. Ed. Verdens Gang 1984, Chief Ed. 1987–93; Chief Ed. Aftenposten 1994–2003; Counselor, Schibsted Group.

HANSEN, Barbara C., PhD; American professor of physiology and university administrator; *Director, Obesity, Diabetes and Aging Research and Center for Preclinical Research and Professor of Internal Medicine and Pediatrics, University of South Florida;* b. 24 Nov. 1941, Boston, Mass; d. of Reynold Caleen and Dorothy Richardson Caleen; m. Kenneth D. Hansen 1976; one s.; ed Univ. of California, Los Angeles, Univ. of Pennsylvania and Univ. of Washington, Seattle; Research Fellow, Univ. of Pennsylvania Inst. of Neurosciences 1966–68; Asst and Assoc. Prof., Univ. of Washington 1971–76; Prof. and Assoc. Dean, Univ. of Michigan, Ann Arbor 1977–83; Assoc. Vice-Pres. of Academic Affairs and Research and Dean of Grad. School, Southern Illinois Univ., Carbondale 1983–85; Vice-Pres. for Grad. Studies and Research, Univ. of Maryland, Baltimore 1986–90, Prof. of Physiology 1990, Dir Obesity and Diabetes Research Center 1990, also Dir Obesity, Diabetes and Aging Animal Resource and Dir of Research, Joslin Clinic; currently Dir Obesity, Diabetes and Aging Research and Center for Preclinical Research and Prof. of Internal Medicine and Pediatrics, Univ. of South Florida, Tampa 2005–; Pres. Int. Asscn for Study of Obesity 1987–90, N American Asscn for Study of Obesity 1984–85, American Soc. of Clinical Nutrition 1995–96; mem. NAS Inst. of Medicine 1981–, Chair. Section 3 Membership Cttee 2012–14. *Publications include:* Controversies in Obesity (ed.) 1983, The Commonsense Guide to Weight Loss for People with Diabetes 1998, The Metabolic Syndrome X 1999; book chapters and articles in learned journals. *Leisure interests:* sailing, scuba diving, golf, reading. *Address:* Center for Preclinical Research, Morsani College of Medicine, University of South Florida, 12901 Bruce B Downs Blvd . Tampa, FL 33612-4799, USA (office). *Telephone:* (703) 589-7112 (office). *E-mail:* bhansen@health.usf.edu (office). *Website:* health.usf.edu/medicine/internalmedicine/index.htm (office).

HANSEN, James E., BA, MS, PhD; American scientist, academic and research institute director; *Adjunct Professor, Department of Earth and Environment Sciences, Columbia University;* b. 29 March 1941, Denison, Ia; ed Univ. of Iowa; NASA Grad. Traineeship 1963–66; NAS-NRC Resident Research Assoc., Goddard Inst. for Space Studies (GISS), New York 1967–69, Staff mem./Space Scientist, GISS, Man. GISS Planetary and Climate Programs 1972–81, Dir NASA Goddard Inst. for Space Studies 1981–2013; NSF Postdoctoral Fellow, Leiden Observatory, Netherlands 1969; Research Assoc., Columbia Univ., New York 1969–72, Adjunct Assoc. Prof., Dept of Geological Sciences 1978–85, Adjunct Prof. of Earth and Environmental Sciences 1985–; Co-Prin. Investigator, AEROPOL Project (airborne terrestrial infrared polarimeter) 1971–74; Co-Investigator, Voyager Photopolarimeter Experiment 1972–85; Prin. Investigator, Pioneer Venus Orbiter Cloud-Photopolarimeter Experiment 1974–78, Co-Investigator 1974–94; Prin. Investigator, Galileo (Jupiter Orbiter) Photopolarimeter Radiometer Experiment 1977–2000, Earth Observing System Interdisciplinary Investigation: Interannual Variability of Earth's Carbon, Energy and Water Cycles 1989–2000; mem. NAS 1996; Fellow, American Geophysical Union 1992; Goddard Special Achievement Award (Pioneer Venus) 1977, NASA Group Achievement Award (Voyager, Photopolarimeter) 1978, NASA Exceptional Service Medal (Radiative Transfer) 1984, Nat. Wildlife Fed. Conservation Achievement Award 1989, NASA Presidential Rank Award of Meritorious Exec. 1990, Alumni Achievement Award, Univ. of Iowa 1991, NASA Group Achievement Award (Galileo, Polarimeter/Radiometer) 1993, William Nordberg Achievement Medal, Goddard Space Flight Center 1996, Editor's Citation for Excellence in Refereeing for Geophysical Research Letters 1996, NASA Presidential Rank Award of Meritorious Exec. 1997, Alumni Fellow, Univ. of Iowa 2000, GISS Best Scientific Publication (peer vote): 'Global warming – alternative scenario' 2000, John Heinz Environment Award 2001, Roger Revelle Medal, American Geophysical Union 2002, GISS Best Scientific Publication (peer vote): 'Soot climate forcing' 2004, GISS Best Scientific Publication (peer vote): 'Earth's Energy Imbalance' 2005, Duke of Edinburgh Conservation Medal, World Wildlife Fund (WWF) 2006, Laureate, Dan David Prize 2007, Leo Szilard Lectureship Award, American Physical Soc. 2007, Carl-Gustaf Rossby Research Medal, American Meteorological Soc. 2009, Stephen H. Schneider Award for Outstanding Climate Science Communications, Commonwealth Club of Calif. 2012, Joseph Priestley Award, Dickinson Coll. 2013, Tang Prize in Sustainable Devt (co-recipient) 2018. *Publications:* Storms of My Grandchildren 2009; also numerous scientific papers in professional journals on radiative transfer in planetary atmospheres and interpretation of remote sounding of atmospheres, devt of global climate models, analysis of climate change, current climate trends, and projections of man's impact on climate. *Address:* Climate Science, Awareness and Solutions Program, Earth Institute, Columbia University, 475 Riverside Drive, New York, NY 10115, USA (office). *E-mail:* jeh1@columbia.edu (office). *Website:* csas.ei.columbia.edu (office).

HANSEN, John Mark, BA, MPhil, PhD; American political scientist, academic and university dean; *Charles L. Hutchinson Distinguished Service Professor, Department of Political Science, University of Chicago;* ed Univ. of Kansas, Yale Univ.; Asst Prof. in Political Science, Univ. of Chicago 1986–92, Assoc. Prof. 1992–94, Prof. 1994–, Chair. Dept of Political Science 1995–98, Assoc. Provost for Educ. and Research 1998–, William R. Kenan Jr Prof. in Political Science –2001, currently Charles L. Hutchinson Distinguished Service Prof. and Sr Advisor to Pres. of Univ. of Chicago, Chair. Confucius Inst.; Prof. of Govt, Harvard Univ. 2001; Fellow, American Acad. of Arts and Sciences 2003; fmr Chair. Bd of Overseers, American Nat. Election Studies; Heinz Eulau Award, American Political Science Asscn for the Best Article Published in the American Political Science Review in 1998, 1999. *Publications:* Mobilization, Participation and Democracy in America (with Steven Rosenstone) (Outstanding Book Award, Nat. Conf. of Black Political Scientists 1995) 1993, Gaining Access: Congress and the Farm Lobby, 1919–1981 1991; numerous papers and articles on interest groups, citizen activism, public opinion, public budgeting and politicians' inferences from the outcomes of elections. *Address:* Department of Political Science, University of Chicago, Pick Hall 401, 5828 South University Avenue, Chicago, IL 60637, USA (office). *Telephone:* (773) 702-5476 (office). *Fax:* (773) 702-1689 (office). *E-mail:* jhansen@midway.uchicago.edu (office). *Website:* political-science.uchicago.edu (office).

HANSEN, Kai Aaen, MSc(Econ); Danish central banker and international civil servant; b. 26 Nov. 1942, Hadsten; s. of Hans Helge Hansen and Kathrine Elisabeth Hansen; m. Ann Marie Skovløv 1970; ed Univ. of Århus; economist, Danmarks Nationalbank (Cen. Bank of Denmark) 1972–77, Asst Head of Dept

1980–82, Head of Dept 1985–91, Dir 1992–97, 2000–11, Consultant 2011–; economist, OECD, Paris 1977–80; Econ. Adviser, IMF, Washington, DC 1983–85, Exec. Dir 1998–2000; Deputy Chair. Nordic Comm. on Money Transmission 1981–83; mem. UN Informal Group on Money Transmission 1981–83, Govt Comm. on Money Transmission 1982–83, Econ. Ministry Cttee on Econ. Policies 1987–91, on Econ. and Monetary Union Issues 1996–97; Alt. mem. EU Comm. of Cen. Bank Govs 1991–94, European Monetary Comm. 1987–93; Alt. Council mem. European Monetary Inst. 1994–97; Chair. Nordic-Baltic Monetary and Financial Alt. Cttee 2000–04, Nordic-Baltic Cttee on IMF Governance 2005–06; mem. Int. Relations Cttee, European Cen. Bank 2000, Sub-cttee on Int. Monetary and Finance Insts, EU/EFC 2000; Asst Prof. (part-time), Copenhagen School of Econs 1974–77, 1980–83; Kt, First Degree, Order of Dannebrog. *Publications:* The International Monetary System, an Essay in Interpretation (with Erik Hoffmeyer) 1991, Pengepolitiske Problem-stillinger (with Erik Hoffmeyer) 1993. *Leisure interest:* history.

HANSEN, Lars Peter, BS, PhD; American economist and academic; *David Rockefeller Distinguished Service Professor in Economics, Statistics, Department of Economics, University of Chicago;* b. 26 Oct. 1952; m. Grace Tsiang; one c.; ed Univ. of Minn., Utah State Univ.; Asst Prof., Carnegie-Mellon Univ. 1978–80, Assoc. Prof., Grad. School of Industrial Admin 1980–81; Visiting Assoc. Prof., Univ. of Chicago 1981–82, Prof. 1984–90, Homer J. Livingston Prof. in Econs 1990–97, Homer J. Livingston Distinguished Service Prof., Dept of Econs 1997–2008, David Rockefeller Distinguished Service Prof. in Econs, Statistics, Dept of Econs 2008–, Dir of Grad. Studies, Dept of Econs 1988–94, Chair. Dept of Econs 1998–2002, Research Dir Becker Friedman Inst.; Visiting Assoc. Prof., MIT 1983; Visiting Prof., Dept of Econs, Harvard Univ. 1986, Stanford Univ. 1989–90, Univ. of Chicago Grad. School of Business 2003–05; Project Dir, Macroeconomic Modeling and Systemic Risk Research Initiative; fmr Co-Ed. Econometrics, Journal of Political Economy; Research Assoc., Econs Research Center, N.O.R.C. 1984–; mem. Bd Govs, The Stevanovich Center for Financial Math.; mem. American Acad. of Arts and Sciences; Fellow, Sloan Foundation 1982, Econometric Soc. 1985 (First Vice-Pres. 2006), NAS; Distinguished Fellow, Macro Finance Soc.; Guggenheim Fellow, Frisch Prize (co-winner), Econometric Soc. 1984, Faculty Award for Excellence in Grad. Teaching, Univ. of Chicago 1997–98, Erwin Plein Nemmers Prize in Econs 2006, CME Group-MSRI Prize in Innovative Quantitative Applications 2008, Nobel Prize in Econs (with Eugene Fama and Robert Shiller) 2013. *Achievements include:* inventor of statistical technique GMM or Generalized Method of Moments 1982. *Publications:* author or co-author of numerous articles and books, including Robust Control and Economic Model Uncertainty (with Thomas J. Sargent); co-ed. Handbook of Financial Econometrics. *Address:* Department of Economics, University of Chicago, 1126 East 59th Street, Chicago, IL 60637, USA (office). *Telephone:* (773) 702-8170 (office); (773) 702-3908 (Asst) (office). *Fax:* (773) 702-8490 (office). *E-mail:* lhansen@uchicago.edu (office). *Website:* larspeterhansen.org (office).

HANSEN, Mogens Herman, DPhil; Danish reader in classical philology; *Emeritus Associate Professor, The SAXO Institute, University of Copenhagen;* b. 20 Aug. 1940, Copenhagen; s. of Herman Hansen and Gudrun Maria (née Heslet) Hansen; m. Birgitte Holt Larsen; one s.; ed Univ. of Copenhagen; Research Fellow, Inst. of Classics, Univ. of Copenhagen 1967–69, Lecturer in Classical Philology 1969–88, Reader in Greek 1989–, currently Emer. Assoc. Prof., The SAXO Inst.; Dir The Copenhagen Polis Centre 1993–2005; Visiting Fellow, Wolfson Coll., Cambridge, UK 1974; Visiting Prof., Univ. of Melbourne, Australia 1988, Univ. of British Columbia, Canada 2001; mem. Inst. for Advanced Study, Princeton, NJ, USA 1983; Corresp. Fellow, Deutsches Archaeologisches Institut 1995, British Acad. 1997; Fellow, Royal Danish Acad. of Sciences and Letters 1987; Kt of the Dannebrog; Chrysos Stauros tou tagmatos tes times (Greece); Dr hc (Athens) 2012; Einar Hansen Stipendium 2000, Fordyce Mitchel Memorial Lecturer 2004, Gad Rausing Prize for outstanding research in the humanities 2007, Royal Swedish Acad. 1997; Fellow, Royal Danish Acad. of Sciences and Letters 1987 1987, British Acad. Lecturer 2010. *Publications include:* The Sovereignty of the People's Court in 4th Century Athens 1974, Eisangelia 1975, Aspects of Athenian Society 1975, Apagoge, Endeixis and Ephegesis 1976, The Athenian Ecclesia I 1983, II 1989, Demography and Democracy 1985, The Athenian Assembly 1987, The Athenian Democracy in the Age of Demosthenes 1991, Acts of the Copenhagen Polis Centre I 1993, II 1995, III 1996, IV 1997, V 1998, VI 1999, VII 2005, Papers from the Copenhagen Polis Centre I 1994, II 1995, III 1996, IV 1997, V 2000, VI 2002, VII 2004, VIII 2007, A Comparative Study of Thirty City-State Cultures 2000, A Comparative Study of Six City-State Cultures 2002, An Inventory of Archaic and Classical Poleis 2004, The Tradition of Ancient Greek Democracy and Its Importance for Modern Democracy 2005, The Shotgun Method – The Demography of the Ancient Greek City-State 2006, Polis – An Introduction to the Ancient Greek City-State 2007, Démocratie Athénienne – démocratie moderne: Tradition et influences. Fondation Hardt Entretiens sur l'Antiquité Classique 2009, Reflections on Aristotle's Politics 2013, Political Obligation in Ancient Greece and in the Modern World 2015; more than 170 articles in int. journals on Athenian democracy and ancient Greek constitutional history. *Leisure interests:* playing the flute, writing poetry, book binding. *Address:* Videnskabernes Selskab, H.C. Andersens Boulevard 35, 1553 Copenhagen V (office); Wilhelm Marstrandsgade 15, 2100 Copenhagen Ø, Denmark (home). *Telephone:* 21-38-20-08 (office); 35-26-15-88 (home). *E-mail:* mhh@hum.ku.dk (office). *Website:* saxoinstitute.ku.dk (office).

HANSENNE, Michel, DenD; Belgian politician; b. 23 March 1940, Rotheux-Rimiere; ed Univ. of Liège; Researcher, Univ. of Liège 1962; MP 1974–89; Minister of French Culture 1979–81, of Employment and Labour 1981–88, for Civil Service 1988–89; Dir-Gen. Int. Labour Org., Geneva 1989–98; MEP 1999–2004. *Publications include:* Emploi, les scénarios du possible, Un garde-fou pour la mondialisation: le BIT dans l'après-guerre froide 1999.

HANSO, Hannes, BA, MA; Estonian politician, government official and translator; b. 6 Oct. 1971, Tartu; ed Univ. of Tartu, Sichuan Univ., China, Univ. of London, UK; English teacher, Sichuan Univ. 1996–98; UK Corresp., Estonian Radio 1998–2005; London Corresp., Radio Free Europe 2002–04; Adviser to Ministry of Defence 2005–07, to Ministry of Finance 2007–08; mem. EU Del., Beijing 2008–11; mem. Sotsiaaldemokraatlik Erakond (SDE—Estonian Social Democratic Party) 2009–; Mayor of Kuressaare 2013–15; mem. Riigikogu (Parl.) 2015–; Minister of Defence 2015–16; Fellow, Int. Centre for Defence Studies 2011–. *Radio:* host, Välismääraja (Kuku Radio). *Address:* c/o Ministry of Defence, Sakala 1, Tallinn 15094, Estonia. *E-mail:* info@kaitseministeerium.ee.

HANSON, Margus, PhD; Estonian politician and academic; b. 6 Jan. 1958, Tartu; m.; two s. one d.; ed Tartu Secondary School No. 2, Leningrad Inst. of Financial Economy, Tartu State Univ.; engineer, Lab. of Educational Sociology, Tartu Univ. 1981–84, Asst to Chair of Finance and Credit 1984–87, Sr Lecturer 1990–91, Lecturer and Assoc. Prof. of Public Finance, Inst. of Econ. Policy and Public Economy 1992–94; Chair. Bd Estonian Commercial Bank of Industry and Construction 1995–96; Head of Tartu Br., Tallinn Bank 1996–97; mem. Tartu City Council 1996, 1999, 2002; Deputy Mayor of Tartu 1997–2003; mem. Riigikogu (Parl.) 2004–13, mem. Nat. Defence Cttee; Minister of Defence 2003–04 (resgnd); professional training courses with Bank of Finland 1990–91, World Bank and Soros Foundation 1992, Austrian Bankers Club 1995, Estonian Banking Asscn, Barcelona 1996; mem. Eesti Reformierakond (Estonian Reform Party), Tartu Rotary Club.

HANSSON, Ardo Hillar, BA (Hons), MA, PhD; Estonian academic and central banker; *Governor, Bank of Estonia;* b. 15 July 1958, Chicago, Ill., USA; m.; two s.; ed Semiahmoo Senior Secondary School and Univ. of British Columbia, Canada, Harvard Univ., USA; Research Asst, Univ. of British Columbia 1980–82, Lecturer, Dept of Econs 1987–90; Research Asst, Harvard Univ. 1984–87; Researcher, WIDER Inst./Jeffrey D. Sachs & Assocs, United Nations Univ. 1990–92; short-term econ. adviser to the govts and central banks of Poland, Slovenia, Mongolia and Ukraine 1990–96; Adviser to Minister of Foreign Affairs 1991–92; Alt. mem. Monetary Reform Cttee of the Repub. of Estonia 1992; Econ. Adviser to the Prime Minister of Estonia 1992–94, 1997; Researcher, Stockholm School of Econs 1992–96; Head of Working Group on Econ. Co-operation, Council of the Baltic Sea States 1993–94; mem. Supervisory Bd Eesti Pank (Bank of Estonia) 1993–98, Gov. 2012–; Economist for Poland and the Baltic States, World Bank 1998–99, Sr Economist for Lithuania 1999–2000, Sr Economist for Yugoslavia 2000–02, Lead Economist for Serbia and Montenegro 2002–03, Lead Economist for the Western Balkans 2003–08, Chief of Econ. Policy Unit in China 2008–12; Order of the White Star (Third Class) 1998, Grand Cross of Commdr, Order for Merit to Lithuania 2013. *Address:* Bank of Estonia (Eesti Pank), Estonia pst. 13, Tallinn 15095, Estonia (office). *Telephone:* 668-0810 (office). *Fax:* 668-0836 (office). *E-mail:* info@eestipank.ee (office). *Website:* www.eestipank.ee (office).

HANWAY, H. Edward, BA, MBA, CPA; American insurance executive; *Chairman Emeritus, CIGNA Corporation;* b. 1951; m. Ellen Hanway; three c.; ed Loyola Coll. of Baltimore, Widener Univ.; joined CIGNA Corpn 1978, Pres. CIGNA Int. 1989–96, mem. Bd of Dirs 1992–, Pres. CIGNA HealthCare 1996–99, Pres. Cigna Corpn 1999–2008, COO 1999–2000, CEO 2000–09, Chair. Dec. 2000–09, now Chair. Emer.; mem. Bd of Dirs Philadelphia Orchestra, Council for Affordable Quality Healthcare 2000– (Treas. 2000–01, Chair. 2001–02), Alliance for Health Reform, Marsh & McLennan Companies, Inc. (Ind. Dir) 2010–; fmr mem. Bd of Dirs America's Health Insurance Plans, Alliance for Health Reform; mem. Bd of Advisors March of Dimes Foundation; mem. Pennsylvania and American Insts of Certified Public Accountants; Trustee, Loyola Coll. of Baltimore, Eisenhower Exchange Fellowships; Outstanding Alumnus Award, Loyola Coll. of Baltimore 2002.

HAOMAE, William Ni'i; Solomon Islands politician; b. 26 Nov. 1960, Mou Village, Small Malaita; m. Filistas T. Haomae; two s. two d.; ed East-West Centre, Honolulu; early govt posts include Information Officer, Prime Minister's Office, Press Sec. to the Prime Minister, Foreign Affairs Information Officer, Ministry of Foreign Affairs, Dir of Information Dept, Prime Minister's Office; mem. Parl. from Small Malaita, Malaita Prov. 1993–, mem. Parl. House Cttee July–Dec. 2007, Foreign Relations Cttee 2006–07; Minister for Culture, Tourism and Aviation 1994–97, for Police and Justice 2000–01; Deputy Prime Minister and Caretaker Minister for Nat. Unity, Reconciliation and Peace Aug.–Dec. 2001; Minister for Police and Nat. Security April–May 2006; Minister of Foreign Affairs, External Trade and Immigration 2007–10. *Leisure interests:* reading, gardening, fishing, soccer. *Address:* National Parliament, POB G19, Honiara, Solomon Islands (office). *Telephone:* 28520 (office). *Fax:* 24272 (office). *Website:* www.parliament.gov.sb (office).

HAQ, Ameerah, BA, MA, MBA; Bangladeshi UN official; *Co-Chair, High-Level Independent Panel on Peace Operations, United Nations;* d. of A. R. M Inamul Haq and Nazera Begum; one s. one d.; ed Viqarun Nisa Noon School, Holy Cross Coll., Dhaka, Western Coll. for Women, Oxford, Ohio, Columbia Univ., New York Univ., USA; Jr Professional Officer, Jakarta 1976; UNDP Asst Resident Rep., Afghanistan 1978, Coordinator of Round Table Meetings and Area Officer, Regional Bureau for Asia and the Pacific, Chief UNIFEM Asia and the Pacific Unit 1987–88, UN Resident Coordinator and UNDP Resident Rep., Laos 1991–94, Malaysia 1994–97, Assoc. Dir UN Devt Group Office –2002, Deputy Asst Admin. and Deputy Dir, UNDP Bureau for Crisis Prevention and Recovery 2002–04, Deputy Special Rep. of the UN Sec.-Gen. in Afghanistan, responsible for Recovery and Reconstruction, UN Assistance Mission for Afghanistan (UNAMA), also UN Resident Coordinator, Humanitarian Coordinator, UNDP Resident Rep. 2004–07, Deputy Special Rep. of UN Sec.-Gen. for Sudan, also UN Resident Co-ordinator and Humanitarian Co-ordinator 2007–09, Under-Sec.-Gen., Special Rep. of UN Sec.-Gen. for Timor-Leste and Head of UN Integrated Mission in Timor-Leste (UNMIT) 2009–12, Under-Sec.-Gen. Dept of Field Support 2012–14; Co-Chair. UN High-Level Ind. Panel on Peace Operations 2014–. *Address:* High-Level Independent Panel on Peace Operations, Room S-3727B, United Nations, New York, NY 10017, USA (home).

HAQ, Gen. Ehsan-ul-; Pakistani army officer; b. 22 Sept. 1949, Mardan, Khyber Pakhtunkhwa; ed Command and Staff Coll., Quetta, Nat. Defence Coll., Islamabad; first commissioned Army Air Defence Regt 1969, fmr Head of Mil. Intelligence, promoted to Lt-Gen. 2001, to Gen. 2004, Dir-Gen. Inter-Services Intelligence 2001–04, Chair. Jt Chiefs of Staff Cttee 2004–07; Hilal-e-Imtiaz (Mil.), Nishan-e-Imtiaz.

HAQ, Maulvi Anwar ul-; Pakistani lawyer and judge; practising lawyer of High Court and Supreme Court for many years; served as judge of Lahore High Court for 10 years; Deputy Attorney-Gen. during premiership of Mian Nawaz Sharif

1990s; one of judges of Lahore High Court who took oath on Provisional Constitutional Order of Gen. Pervez Musharraf in violation of Supreme Court verdict of 3 Nov. 2007, received notice of court contempt and tendered his resignation following Supreme Court verdict declaring 3 Nov. steps as extra-constitutional; Attorney-Gen. 2010–12.

HAQ, Siraj-ul, BA, MA; Pakistani politician; *Chief Leader, Jamaat-e-Islami Pakistan;* b. 5 Sept. 1962, lower Dir Dist; ed Univ. of Peshawar; Chief, Islami Jamiat-e-Talaba 1988–91; elected to Khyber Pakhtunkhwa Ass. 2002; Finance Minister 2002–06, 2013–14, Sr Minister 2013–14; Deputy Leader, Jamaat-e-Islami Pakistan 2009–14, Chief Leader 2014–; mem. Senate 2015–; Baba-e-Jamhooriyat Award 2014. *Address:* Jamaat-e-Islami Pakistan, Mansoorah Multan Road, Lahore, Pakistan (office). *Telephone:* (42) 35419520 (office). *Fax:* (42) 35432194 (office). *Website:* www.jamaat.org (office).

HAQQANI, Husain, BA, MA; Pakistani journalist and diplomatist; *Senior Fellow and Director for South and Central Asia, Hudson Institute;* b. 1 July 1956, Karachi; m. Farahnaz Ispahani 2000; one s. three d.; ed Univ. of Karachi; started career as journalist 1980–88, wrote numerous articles on nat. and int. politics published by Pakistan's leading newspapers Jang (Urdu) and Dawn (English); worked in Hong Kong as East Asian Corresp. for London-based Arabia – the Islamic World Review 1980–84; wrote extensively on Muslims in China and East Asia and Islamic political movts in aftermath of Iranian Revolution of 1979; Pakistan and Afghanistan Corresp. for Far Eastern Economic Review 1984–88; covered Pakistani politics, India-Pakistan relations and war in Afghanistan; contributed to Voice of America radio 1984–86; syndicated columnist for The Indian Express, Gulf News, Oman Tribune, Daily Star (Bangladesh) and The Nation (Pakistani newspaper); Special Asst to Chief Minister, Punjab 1988–90; served as main Opposition Spokesman, represented Opposition at int. forums, including in negotiations with US Govt; organized parl. election campaign for IJI alliance led by Nawaz Sharif 1988; Special Asst to Prime Minister Ghulam Mustafa Jatoi 1990, Special Asst and Prin. Spokesman of Prime Minister Nawaz Sharif 1990–92, represented Prime Minister in talks with US Govt over imposition of sanctions in retaliation for Pakistan's nuclear programme; Amb. to Sri Lanka 1992–93; worked in parl. election campaign for Peoples Democratic Front led by Mohtarma Benazir Bhutto 1993, Spokesman for Prime Minister Benazir Bhutto with rank of Minister of State, and Fed. Sec. for Information and Broadcasting 1993–95; Chair. House Building Finance Corpn 1995–96; Assoc. Prof. for Int. Relations, Boston Univ. 2004–08; Co-Chair. Project on Islam and Democracy, Hudson Inst., Washington, DC 2004–08, Ed. Current Trends in Islamists Ideology (journal) 2004–08, Prof., Practice of Int. Relations 2012–14, Dir Center for Int. Relations 2012–14, currently Sr Fellow and Dir for South and Cen. Asia; Visiting Scholar, Carnegie Endowment for Int. Peace, Washington DC 2002–05; Professional Lecturer, School of Advanced Int. Studies, Johns Hopkins Univ., Washington, DC 2003–04; Amb. to USA 2008–11 (resgnd); mem. South Asia Council, Asscn of Asian Studies 2007; Resident Fellow, Univ. of Chicago Inst. of Politics. *Publications include:* Pakistan Between Mosque and Military 2005, Magnificent Delusions: Pakistan, the United States, and an Epic History of Misunderstanding 2013, India vs Pakistan 2016; numerous book chapters and articles and more than 390 op-ed articles in newspapers and magazines 2000–; articles have been published in The Wall Street Journal, The New York Times, Boston Globe, Financial Times, International Herald Tribune, South China Morning Port, Indian Express, The Hindu, Toronto Globe and Mail, The Ottawa Citizen, Arab News, The New Republic, Gulf News and Le Monde. *Address:* Hudson Institute, 1201 Pennsylvania Avenue, NW, Suite 400, Washington, DC 20004, USA (office). *Telephone:* (202) 974-2400 (office). *Fax:* (202) 974-2410 (office). *E-mail:* haqqani@bu.edu (office). *Website:* www.hudson.org (office).

HARA, Hiroshi, BA, MA, DArch; Japanese architect and academic; *Professor Emeritus, University of Tokyo;* b. 9 Sept. 1936, Kawasaki, Kanagawa Pref.; ed Univ. of Tokyo; mem. generation of avant-garde New Wave architects; developed unique anthropological approach and theories of design from studies of vernacular architecture and indigenous settlements; conducted research trips in Europe, Asia and Africa; Asst Prof., then Prof., Inst. of Industrial Science, Univ. of Tokyo 1969–97, Prof. Emer. 1997–; cr. so-called 'reflection houses' in 1970s; began receiving commissions for large public bldgs 1980s; developed style of 'architecture of modality' whereby bldgs became metaphors of 'cities with the city' late 1980s; began designing 'modal spaces of consciousness' inspired by electronic and information technologies 1990s; began designing futuristic spaceship-like urban-scale projects late 1990s; Victor L. Regnier Chair in Architecture, Dept of Architecture, Kan. State Univ., USA 2004–05; Murano Togo Prize 1986, Suntory Arts and Science Prize 1988. *Publications:* Hiroshi Hara (co-author) 1993, The Floating World of Architecture (co-author) 2001; numerous monographs, chapters in books and articles in professional journals.

HARA, Kazuo; Japanese film director; b. 8 June 1945, Yamaguchi; m. Sachiko Kobayashi; known for creating films that blur the distinction between documentary films and fiction films, so-called 'action documentaries'; co-f. Shissō Productions 1971. *Films include:* Sayonara CP (Goodbye, CP) 1972, Gokushiteki erosu: Renka 1974 (Extreme Private Eros: Love Song 1974) 1974, Umi to dokuyaku (The Sea and Poison: Asst Dir) 1986, Yuki Yukite shingun (The Emperor's Naked Army Marches On: KNF Award, Director's Guild of Japan New Director's Award 1986, Caligari Film Award, Berlin Film Festival 1987) 1986, Sen no Rikyu (Death of a Tea Master: Asst Dir) 1989, Shikibu monogatari (Mount Aso's Passions: Chief Asst Dir) 1989, Zenshin shosetsuka (A Dedicated Life) 1994, Fukai kawa (Deep River: Second Unit Dir) 1995, Watashi no Mishima 1999, Mata no hi no Chika 2005, Kaitei Mikan no Kawa Mairu 2009, Shin Godzilla 2016, Nippon Asbest Village (Documentary) 2016, Godzilla Resurgence (Actor) 2016. *Television includes:* National Kid 1960, Air in Summer Kôhen: Ametsuchi-Universe 2005, ETV Tokushû 2007. *Publication:* Camera Obtrusa: The Action Documentaries of Hara Kazuo 2009. *Address:* Shisso Productions, 1-15-16-202 Shinjuku, Shinjuku-ku, Tokyo 160-0022, Japan.

HARABIN, Štefan, DJur; Slovak judge and politician; b. 4 May 1957, Ľubica; m.; four c.; ed Univ. of Pavel Jozef Šafárik, Košice; Judge, Dist Court, Poprad 1983–90, Regional Court, Košice 1990–91; Judge of the Supreme Court 1991–98, Pres. of the Supreme Court 1998–2003, 2009–14, Chair. Criminal Panel 2003–06; Head of Penal Dept, Section of Justice Admin., Ministry of Justice 1991–92; Pres. of Senate and Penal Bd 1996–98; Pres. Judicial Council 2002–03; Deputy Prime Minister and Minister of Justice 2006–09; cand. in presidential election 2019. *Address:* c/o Supreme Court of the Slovak Republic, Župné nám. 13, 814 90 Bratislava, Slovakia (office). *Website:* www.harabin.sk.

HARAD, George Jay, BA, MBA; American business executive; b. 24 April 1944, Newark, NJ; s. of Sidney Harad and Irma Harad; m. Beverly Marcia Harad 1966; one s. one d.; ed Franklin & Marshall Coll., Harvard Business School; Admin. Asst to Sr Vice-Pres. Housing Group, Boise Cascade Corpn 1971–72, Finance Man. Boise Cascade Realty Group 1972–76; Man. Corp. Devt, Boise Cascade Corpn 1976–80, Dir Retirement Funds 1980–82, Vice-Pres. Controller 1982–84, Sr Vice-Pres., Chief Financial Officer 1984–89, Exec. Vice-Pres., Chief Financial Officer 1989–90, Exec. Vice-Pres. Paper 1990–91, Pres., COO 1991–94, Pres., CEO 1994–95, Chair. Bd and CEO 1995–2004; Chair. Harad Capital Management LLC 2004–; Exec. Chair. OfficeMax Inc. 2004–05 (retd); mem. Bd of Dirs Clorox Co. 2006–, Ind. Chair 2015–16; George F. Baker Scholar, Harvard Univ. 1970–71; Frederick Roe Fellow, Harvard Univ. 1971; Patron Surel's Place (Art Community Centre in Boise, ID); mem. Advisory Council Boys & Girls Clubs of Ada County; Executive Papermaker of the Year Award, PaperAge Magazine 2001. *Leisure interests:* golf, skiing.

HARADA, Minoru; Japanese religious leader; *President, Soka Gakkai;* b. 8 Nov. 1941, Tokyo; s. of Eiji Harada and Yuriko Harada; m. Kimie Harada 1968; two s.; ed Univ. of Tokyo; with Soka Gakkai (Buddhist network), Japan 1953–, Head of Student Div. 1973–76, Head of Youth Div. 1976–77, Vice-Pres. 1977–2001, Sec.-Gen. 1984–2006, Vice-Gen. Dir 2001–06, Pres. 2006–; Vice-Pres. Soka Gakkai Int. 1997–07, Deputy Pres. 2007–. *Leisure interests:* reading, watching sports. *Telephone:* (3) 3353-7111 (office). *Website:* www.sgi.org (office).

HARADINAJ, Ramush, MBA; Kosovo politician and fmr guerrilla leader; *Prime Minister;* b. 3 July 1968, Gllogjan/Glođane, nr Deçan/Dečani, Socialist Autonomous Province of Kosovo, Socialist Repub. of Serbia, Socialist Fed. Repub. of Yugoslavia; m. 1st, one s.; m. 2nd Anita Haradinaj; two s. one d.; ed High School, Gjakovë/Đakovica, Faculty of Law, Univ. of Prishtina, American Univ. of Kosovo (associated with Rochester Inst. of Tech.); nat. mil. service in Yugoslav People's Army 1987; emigrated to Switzerland 1991; returned to Kosovo 1998; Commdr Kosovo Liberation Army 1998–99; Co-founder and Pres. Aleanca për Ardhmërinë e Kosovës (Alliance for the Future of Kosovo) 2001–; Prime Minister of Kosovo Dec. 2004–05 (resgnd); acquitted of war crimes by Int. War Crimes Tribunal, The Hague 3 April 2008; asked by Ugandan Rebel Group 'Allied Democratic Forces' to mediate peace talks with Cen. Govt in Kampala Feb. 2009; re-arrested to face a partial retrial 21 July 2010, trial began 2011, acquitted for a second time 29 Nov. 2012; Prime Minister 2017–. *Address:* Office of the Prime Minister, 10000 Prishtina, Rruga Nënë Terezë, Kosovo (office). *Telephone:* (38) 211202 (office). *E-mail:* izkp.zkm@rks-gov.net (office). *Website:* www.kryeministri-ks.net (office).

HARAGUCHI, Kazuhiro; Japanese politician; *Vice-President, Democratic Party of Japan;* b. 2 July 1959, Saga Pref.; m. Naoko Haraguchi; one c.; ed Tokyo Univ., Matsushita Inst. of Govt and Man., Chigasaki; elected mem. Saga Prefectural Ass. (LDP) 1987, served two terms; mem. House of Reps for Saga No. 1 constituency 1996–, Sr Dir Parl. Cttee on Internal Affairs and Communications; mem. Shinshinto (New Frontier Party) –1998, mem. Democratic Party of Japan (DPJ) 1998–, currently Vice-Pres.; Minister of Internal Affairs and Communications and Minister of State for Promotion of Regional Sovereignty 2009–10. *Address:* Democratic Party of Japan, #307, 1st Members' Office Building, 1-11-1 Nagata-cho Chiyoda-ku, Tokyo 100-0014, Japan (office). *Telephone:* (3) 3508-7238 (office). *Fax:* (3) 3508-3238 (office). *Website:* www.dpj.or.jp/english (office); haraguti.com.

HARALD V, HM The King of Norway, KG, GCVO; b. 21 Feb. 1937, Skaugum; s. of King Olav V and Crown Princess Märtha; m. Sonja Haraldsen 1968 (now HM Queen Sonja); one s. (HRH Crown Prince Haakon) one d.; ed Oslo Katedralskole, Cavalry Officers' Cand. School, Mil. Acad. and Balliol Coll., Oxford, UK; lived in Washington, DC, USA 1940–45; has participated in numerous int. sailing competitions, representing Norway at Olympic Games several times; undertook frequent official visits abroad while Crown Prince; succeeded his father, King Olav V 17 Jan. 1991; final Col-in-Chief, Green Howards (UK); Patron, Anglo-Norse Soc., London and numerous other orgs; Grand Master, Royal Norwegian Order of St Olav, Royal Norwegian Order of Merit; Hon. Fellow, Balliol Coll., Oxford; Hon. Col, British Royal Marines; Hon. Freedom of Newcastle upon Tyne; Hon. Fellow, Balliol Coll., Oxford; Freedom of the City of Cork; Key of Honour to the City of Lisbon 2008; Grand Cross with Collar, Royal Norwegian Order of St Olav; Grand Cross, Royal Norwegian Order of Merit, St Olav's Medal, Defence Service Medal with Laurel Branch, The Royal House Centenary Medal, Haakon VII's Commemorative Medal 1957, Haakon VII's Jubilee Medal 1905–55, Haakon VII's Centenary Medal, Olav V's Commemorative Medal 1991, Olav V's Jubilee Medal, Olav V's Centenary Medal, Defence Service Medal with Three Stars, Army Nat. Service Medal with Three Stars, Krigsdeltakerforbundet Badge of Honour, Norwegian Red Cross Badge of Honour, Norwegian Reserve Officers Fed. Badge of Honour, The Naval Soc. Medal of Merit in Gold, Norwegian Shooting Soc. Badge of Honour, The Norwegian Confed. of Sports Centenary Medal, Norwegian Shooting Soc. Commemorative Medal in Gold, Oslo Mil. Soc. Badge of Honour in Gold; Royal Victorian Chain, and numerous other foreign decorations; Hon. LLD (Univ. of Strathclyde, UK) 1985, (Waseda Univ., Japan) 2001; Hon. DCL (Univ. of Oxford) 2006; Dr hc (Pacific Lutheran Univ., Tacoma, Wash.) 2015; Spirit of Luther Award, Luther Coll., Decorah, Ia, a 230,000 km^2 area in Antarctica is named Prince Harald Coast in his honour, Holmenkollen Medal (co-recipient) 2007, a 6,500 km^2 area in Svalbard was named Harald V Land 2013. *Achievements include:* world's first reigning monarch to visit Antarctica 2015. *Address:* The Royal Palace, 0010 Oslo, Norway. *Telephone:* 22-04-87-00. *Fax:* 22-04-87-90. *E-mail:* post@slottet.no. *Website:* www.royalcourt.no.

HARARI, Yuval Noah, BA, MA, PhD; Israeli historian and writer; *Professor of History, Hebrew University of Jerusalem;* b. 24 Feb. 1976, Kiryat Ata; partner Itzik Yahav; ed Hebrew Univ. of Jerusalem, Jesus Coll., Oxford, UK; Adjunct Lecturer, Dept of History, Hebrew Univ. of Jerusalem 2002–05, Lecturer 2005–08, apptd Sr Lecturer 2008, now Prof. of History, Coordinator, World History programme 2003–12; Adjunct Lecturer, Ofakim Program for Outstanding Students, Univ. of Haifa 2005–06; mem. Young Scholars Forum, Israeli Acad. of Sciences 2011–, Young Israeli Acad. of Sciences 2012; Moncado Award, Soc. for Military History

2011. *Publications include:* Renaissance Military Memoirs: War, History and Identity, 1450–1600 2004, Special Operations in the Age of Chivalry, 1100–1550 2007, The Ultimate Experience: Battlefield Revelations and the Making of Modern War Culture, 1450–2000 (Polonsky Prize for Creativity and Originality 2009) 2008, A Brief History of Mankind (in Hebrew) (Polonsky Prize for Creativity and Originality 2012) 2011, Sapiens: A Brief History of Humankind (adaptation of A Brief History of Mankind) 2014, Homo Deus: A Brief History of Tomorrow 2016. *Address:* Department of History, Room 6523, Hebrew University of Jerusalem, Jerusalem, 91905, Israel (office). *Telephone:* 02-5883780 (office). *E-mail:* ynharari@mscc.huji.ac.il (office); Info@ynharari.com (office). *Website:* www.hum.huji.ac.il/english (office); www.ynharari.com (office).

HARASZTI, Miklós; Hungarian writer, journalist, human rights advocate, international organization official and academic; b. 2 Jan. 1945, Jerusalem, Israel; m. Antónia Szenthe; ed Univ. of Budapest; co-f. Hungarian Democratic Opposition Movt 1976; Ed. samizdat periodical Beszélo 1980; participated in roundtable negotiations on transition to free elections 1989; mem. Hungarian Parl. 1990–94; fmr Lecturer, Budapest Study Centre, Univ. of California; fmr Adjunct Prof., School of Int. and Public Affairs, Columbia Law School, New York; Visiting Prof., Dept of Public Policy, Central European Univ.; Rep. on Freedom of the Media, OSCE 2004–10; apptd UN Special Rapporteur on the human rights situation in Belarus 2012; Dr hc (Northwestern Univ., USA) 1996. *Publications:* A Worker in a Worker's State, The Velvet Prison (both translated into several languages); several essays have been published in The New York Times and The Washington Post. *Address:* Budapest Study Centre KHT, Eötvös Loránd University, Pazmany Peter setany 1/A, 1117 Budapest, Hungary (office).

HARBERGER, Arnold C., PhD; American economist and academic; *Professor, Department of Economics, University of California, Los Angeles;* b. 27 July 1924, Newark, NJ; s. of Ferdinand C. Harberger and Martha L. Bucher; m. 1958; two s.; ed Univ. of Chicago; Asst Prof., Johns Hopkins Univ., Baltimore, Md 1949–53; Assoc. Prof., Univ. of Chicago 1953–59, Prof. 1959–76, Gustavus F. and Ann M. Swift Distinguished Service Prof. 1976–91, Prof. Emer. 1991–; Prof. of Econs, UCLA 1984–; Pres. Western Econ. Assen 1988–89, American Econ. Asscn 1997; consultant to numerous econ. govt depts and int. orgs; Fellow, Econometric Soc. 1967, American Acad. of Arts and Sciences 1969; mem. NAS 1989. *Publications include:* Project Evaluation 1972, Taxation and Welfare 1974, World Economic Growth 1984. *Address:* 8283 Bunche Hall, University of California at Los Angeles, 405 Hilgard Avenue, Los Angeles, CA 90095 (office); 136 Buckskin Road, Bell Canyon, CA 91307, USA (home). *Telephone:* (310) 825-1011 (office). *Fax:* (310) 825-9528 (office). *E-mail:* harberger@econ.ucla.edu (office). *Website:* www.econ.ucla.edu/harberger (office).

HARBI, Mohammed; Algerian politician, historian and academic; b. 16 June 1933, El-Arrouch; s. of Brahimi Harbi; m. (divorced); c.; ed Sorbonne, France; joined Parti du people algérien 1948; various posts with Front de Libération Nationale (FLN) 1954–62, including Leader, French Div. 1957, Dir FLN cabinet 1959, FLN Rep. in Cairo 1960, Del. Evian Accord negotiations 1961; Adviser to Pres. Ahmed Ben Bella 1963; Founding mem. Organisation de la résistance populaire 1965; imprisoned 1964–71, house arrest 1971; fled to France 1973; Lecturer in Sociology, Univ. de Paris-V, Prof. of History, Paris-VII 1974. *Publications include:* Aux origines du Front de libération nationale 1975, FLN: Mirage et réalité 1980, L'Algérie et son destin, La guerre commence en Algérie; Mémoires politiques Tome 1: 1945–1962 (first volume of his political memoirs) 2001.

HARBINSON, Stuart Wreford, OBE, JP; British lawyer and international organization official; *Senior Fellow, European Centre for International Political Economy;* b. 1948; m.; one s.; ed Univ. of Cambridge; Perm. Rep. to WTO, Geneva 1994–2002, Chair. Gen. Council 2001–02, Chair. Special Sessions of WTO Cttee on Agric. 2002–03, Chief of Staff, Office of the Dir-Gen. 2002–05, Special Adviser to Dir-Gen. 2005–07, fmr Chair. special sessions of negotiations on agriculture, working party on Tonga accession; consultant on projects with UNCTAD Secr., Geneva; Sr Fellow, European Centre for Int. Political Economy; fmr Adviser, Winston & Strawn LLP (law firm), Geneva; Special Adviser Fipra 2012–; fmr Chair. Int. Textiles and Clothing Bureau; Gold Bauhinia Star 2002. *Address:* European Centre for International Political Economy, Rue Belliard 4–6, 1040 Brussels, Belgium, 1040 Brussels, Belgium (office). *Telephone:* (2) 289-1350 (office). *Website:* www.ecipe.org/person/stuart-harbinson/ (office).

HARBISON, Peter, MA, DPhil, MRIA, FSA; Irish archaeologist, art historian and editor; *Honorary Academic Editor, Royal Irish Academy;* b. 14 Jan. 1939, Dublin; s. of Dr James Austin Harbison and Sheelagh Harbison (née McSherry); m. Edelgard Soergel 1969 (died 2008); three s.; ed St Gerard's School, Bray, Glenstal, Univ. Coll. Dublin and Univs of Marburg, Kiel and Freiburg, Germany; awarded travelling scholarship by German Archaeological Inst. 1965; archaeological officer, Irish Tourist Bd 1966–84, editorial publicity officer 1984–86, Ed. Ireland of the Welcomes (magazine) 1986–95; Sec. Friends of the Nat. Collections of Ireland 1971–76; mem. Council, Royal Irish Acad. 1981–84, 1993–96, 1998–2001, 2004–, Vice-Pres. 1992–93, 2006–07, Hon. Academic Ed. 1997–; Prof. of Archaeology, Royal Hibernian Acad. of Arts; Chair. Nat. Monuments Advisory Council 1986–90, Dublin Cemeteries Cttee 1986–89, 1996–2002, Bunratty Castle Ownership and Furniture Trusts 2004–; Vice-Pres. for Leinster, Royal Soc. of Antiquities of Ireland 2005–07; Guest Prof., Univ. of Vienna summer 2004; Corresp. mem. German Archaeological Inst.; Hon. mem. Royal Hibernian Acad. of Arts 1998, Royal Inst. of Architects of Ireland; Hon. Fellow, Trinity Coll., Dublin 2000. *Publications include:* Guide to National Monuments of Ireland 1970, The Archaeology of Ireland 1976, Irish Art and Architecture (co-author) 1978, Pre-Christian Ireland (Archaeological Book of the Year Award 1988) 1988, Pilgrimage in Ireland 1991, Beranger's Views of Ireland 1991, The High Crosses of Ireland 1992, Irish High Crosses 1994, Ancient Ireland (with Jacqueline O'Brien) 1996, Ancient Irish Monuments 1997, Beranger's Antique Buildings of Ireland, L'Art Médiéval en Irlande 1998, Spectacular Ireland 1999, The Golden Age of Irish Art 1999, The Crucifixion in Irish Art 2000, Cooper's Ireland 2000, Our Treasure of Antiquities 2002, Treasures of the Boyne Valley 2003, Ireland's Treasures 2004, Beranger's Rambles in Ireland 2004, A Thousand Years of Church Heritage in East Galway 2005, William Burton Conyngham and his Irish Circle of Antiquarian Artists 2012; articles in books and journals. *Leisure interests:* music, travel, wining, dining, cruising. *Address:* 5 St Damian's, Loughshinny, Skerries, Co. Dublin (home); Royal Irish Academy, 19 Dawson Street, Dublin 2, Republic of Ireland (office). *Telephone:* (1) 8490940 (home); (1) 6762570 (office). *Fax:* (1) 6762346 (office). *E-mail:* p.harbison@ria.ie (office). *Website:* www.ria.ie (office).

HARCOURT, Geoffrey Colin, AO, PhD, LittD, FASSA, AcSS; Australian/British economist and academic; b. 27 June 1931, Melbourne, Vic.; s. of Kenneth Harcourt and Marjorie Harcourt (née Gans); m. Joan Bartrop 1955; two s. two d.; ed Univ. of Melbourne, Univ. of Cambridge, UK; Lecturer in Econs, Univ. of Adelaide 1958–62, Sr Lecturer 1962–65, Reader 1965–67, Prof. (Personal Chair) 1967–85, Prof. Emer. 1988–; Lecturer in Econs and Politics, Univ. of Cambridge 1964–66, 1982–90, Reader in the History of Econ. Theory 1990–98, Reader Emer. 1998–, Dir of Studies in Econs and Fellow, Trinity Hall, Cambridge 1964–66, Fellow and Lecturer in Econs, Jesus Coll., Cambridge 1982–98, Fellow Emer. 1998, Pres. 1988–92; Leverhulme Exchange Fellow, Keio Univ., Tokyo 1969–70; Visiting Fellow, Clare Hall, Cambridge 1972–73; Visiting Prof., Univ. of Toronto, Canada 1977, 1980, Univ. of Melbourne 2002; Visiting Fellow, ANU 1997; Visiting Professorial Fellow, Univ. of New South Wales 2010–16; Pres. Econ. Soc. of Australia and New Zealand 1974–77; mem. Council Royal Econ. Soc. 1990–95, Life mem. 1998–; Distinguished Fellow, Econ. Soc. of Australia 1996, 2015, History of Econs Soc., USA 2004, European Soc. for the History of Econ. Thought 2004, History of Econ. Thought Soc. of Australia 2012, Alumni Soc., Univ. of Adelaide 2015; Academician, now Fellow, Acad. of Learned Socs for the Social Sciences 2003; Fellow, Acad. of the Social Sciences in Australia 1971 (Exec. Cttee mem. 1974–77), Jubilee Fellow 2015; Fellow, Royal Soc. of New South Wales 2016, 2018; Hon. Fellow, Queen's Coll., Melbourne 1998, Sugden Fellow 2002, Hon. Prof., Univ. of NSW 1997, 1999, 2016–19; Hon. LittD (De Montfort Univ.) 1997, Hon. DCom (Melbourne) 2003, Hon. Dr rer. pol (Fribourg) 2003; Wellington Burnham Lecturer, Tufts Univ., Medford, Mass 1975, Edward Shann Memorial Lecturer, Univ. of Western Australia 1975, Newcastle Lecturer in Political Economy, Univ. of Newcastle 1977, Acad. Lecturer, Acad. of the Social Sciences in Australia 1978, G.L. Wood Memorial Lecturer, Univ. of Melbourne 1982, John Curtin Memorial Lecturer, ANU 1982, Special Lecturer in Econs, Univ. of Manchester 1984, Lecturer, Nobel Conf. XXII, Gustavus Adolphus Coll., Minn. 1986, Laws Lecturer, Univ. of Tennessee at Knoxville 1991, Donald Horne Lecturer 1992, Sir Halford Cook Lecturer, Queen's Coll., Univ. of Melbourne, Kingsley Martin Memorial Lecturer, Cambridge 1996, Colin Clark Memorial Lecturer, Brisbane 1997, Bernard Hesketh Lecturer, Univ. of Minn., Kansas City 2006, Veblen-Commons Award, Asscn for Evolutionary Econs (USA) 2010, Distinguished Alumni Award, Univ. of Adelaide 2015. *Publications include:* Economic Activity (with P. H. Karmel and R. H. Wallace) 1967, Readings in the Concept and Measurement of Income (co-ed.) 1969 (second edn with R. H. Parker and G. Whittington 1986), Capital and Growth, Selected Readings (co-ed.) 1971, Some Cambridge Controversies in the Theory of Capital 1972, The Microeconomic Foundations of Macroeconomics (ed.) 1977, The Social Science Imperialists, Selected Essays (ed. Prue Kerr) 1982, Keynes and his Contemporaries (ed.) 1985, Controversies in Political Economy, Selected Essays of G. C. Harcourt (ed. Omar Hamouda) 1986, International Monetary Problems and Supply-Side Economics: Essays in Honour of Lorie Tarshis (co-ed.) 1986, On Political Economists and Modern Political Economy, Selected Essays of G. C. Harcourt (co-ed.) 1992, Post-Keynesian Essays in Biography: Portraits of Twentieth Century Political Economists 1993, The Dynamics of the Wealth of Nations. Growth, Distribution and Structural Change: Essays in Honour of Luigi Pasinetti (co-ed.) 1993, Income and Employment in Theory and Practice. Essays in Memory of Athanasios Asimakopulos (co-ed.) 1994, Capitalism, Socialism and Post-Keynesianism. Selected Essays of G. C. Harcourt 1995, A 'Second Edition' of The General Theory (two vols, co-ed.) 1997, 50 Years a Keynesian and Other Essays 2001, Selected Essays on Economic Policy 2001, L'Economie rebelle de Joan Robinson (ed.) 2001, Joan Robinson: Critical Assessments of Leading Economists (five vols, co-ed.) 2002, Editing Economics: Essays in Honour of Mark Perlman (co-ed.) 2002, Capital Theory (three vols, co-ed.) 2005, The Structure of Post-Keynesian Economics: The Core Contributions of the Pioneers 2006, Joan Robinson (with Prue Kerr) 2009, On Skidelsky's Keynes and Other Essays 2012, The Making of a Post-Keynesian Economist 2012, Cambridge Harvest 2012, The Oxford Handbook of Post-Keynesian Economics (two vols, co-ed.) 2013, Financial Crises and the Nature of Capitalist Money. Critical Developments from the Work of Geoffrey Ingham (co-ed.) 2013, Post-Keynesian Essays from Down Under: Theory and Policy from an Historical Perspective (four vols, co-author) 2016; more than 400 articles, chapters and reviews, including 13 volumes of selected essays. *Leisure interests:* bike riding, politics, reading, watching cricket, gossip.

HARDADÓTTIR, Oddný G.; Icelandic teacher and politician; b. 9 April 1957; began career as math. teacher, Akureyri Jr Coll. and later Suðurnesja Comprehensive, Keflavík 1994, Prin. 2005; Project Man., Ministry of Educ. 2001–03; Mayor of Garði 2006–09; mem. Althingi (Parl.) for South Constituency 2009–, mem. Educ. and Gen. Affairs Cttee, Special Cttee on Standing Orders of Althingi; Minister of Finance 2011–12; mem. Icelandic Del. to IPU (apptd Vice-Chair. 2011); mem. Social Democratic Alliance, Chair. SDA Parl. Group 2011–13, 2016–. *Address:* Social Democratic Alliance—SDA, Hallveigarstíg 1, 101 Reykjavík, Iceland (office). *Telephone:* 4142200 (office). *Fax:* 4142201 (office). *E-mail:* samfylking@samfylking.is (office). *Website:* www.samfylking.is (office).

HARDCASTLE, Jack Donald, CBE, MA, MChir, FRCS, FRCP; British surgeon and academic; *Emeritus Professor of Surgery, University of Nottingham;* b. 3 April 1933, Yorks.; s. of Albert Hardcastle and Bertha Hardcastle (née Ellison); m. Rosemary Hay-Shunker 1965; two c.; ed Emmanuel Coll., Cambridge; House Physician, London Hosp. 1959–60; House Surgeon, Hammersmith Hosp., London 1961–62; Research Asst London Hosp. 1962, Lecturer in Surgery 1963, Registrar in Surgery 1964, Registrar in Surgery, Thoracic Unit 1965, Sr Registrar 1965, Sr Lecturer 1968; Sr Registrar St Mark's Hosp., London 1968; Prof. of Surgery, Univ. of Nottingham 1970–98, Prof. Emer. 1998–; Lead Clinician, Mid-Trent Cancer Network 1998–2005; Sir Arthur Sims Commonwealth Travelling Prof., Royal Coll. of Surgeons 1985; Mayne Visiting Prof., Univ. of Brisbane, Australia 1987, Univ. of Melbourne 2001; Dir of Educ. Royal Coll. of Surgeons 1993–98, mem. Council 1987–99, Vice-Pres. 1995–97, Dir of Overseas Office 1996–99; Pres. Surgical Section Royal Soc. Medicine 1981, Pres. Coloproctology Section, Royal Soc. 1983, Pres. Asscn of Surgical Oncology 1992–93; Pres. Surgical Research Soc. 1995–96;

Hon. Fellow, Royal Coll. of Physicians and Surgeons (Glasgow), Asscn of Coloproctology; Huntarian Orator 1998, Royal Coll. of Surgeons (England) Gold Medal 1999. *Publications include:* Isolated Organ Perfusion (with H. D. Ritchie) 1973; articles in professional journals. *Leisure interests:* golf, gardening. *Address:* Field House, 32 Marlock Close, Fiskerton, Notts., NG25 0UB, England (home). *Telephone:* (1636) 830316 (home). *Fax:* (1636) 830316 (home). *E-mail:* hardcastlejdr@aol.com.

HARDIE, (Charles) Jeremy (Mawdesley), CBE, BPhil (Econs), ACA; British business executive; b. 9 June 1938; s. of Sir Charles Hardie; m. 1st Susan Chamberlain 1962 (divorced 1976); two s. two d.; m. 2nd Xandra, Countess of Gowrie 1978 (divorced 1994); one d.; m. 3rd Kirsteen Margaret Tait 1994; ed Winchester Coll. and New Coll., Oxford; Nuffield Coll., Oxford 1966–67; Jr Research Fellow, Trinity Coll., Oxford 1967–68; Fellow and Tutor in Econs Keble Coll., Oxford 1968–75; Partner, Dixon Wilson & Co. 1975–82; Deputy Chair. Monopolies and Mergers Comm. –1975; Dir (non-exec.) W. H. Smith Group 1988 (Deputy Chair. 1992–94, Chair. 1994–99); Chair. Nat. Provident Inst. 1980–89, Alexander Syndicate Man. Ltd 1982–95, Radio Broadland Ltd 1983–85; fmr Chair. David Mann Underwriting Agency Ltd; mem. Bd of Dirs Alexanders Discount Co. Ltd 1978–87, John Swire and Sons Ltd 1982–98, Alexanders Laing & Cruickshank Gilts Ltd 1986–87, Butler Foundation 1988–94, Northdor Holdings 1989–93; Chair. Centre for Econ. Policy Research 1984–89, Blanc Brasseries PLC, China Dialogue, Esmée Fairbairn Foundation 2003–07; currently Commr and Trustee, UK Drug Policy Comm.; also currently Research Assoc. Centre for Philosophy of Natural and Social Science, LSE; other business and public appointments; parl. cand. Norwich South, (SDP) 1983, (SDP/Alliance) 1987; Trustee, Somerset House, Int. House, Butler Foundation 1988–94; Hon. Fellow, Keble Coll. *Publication:* Evidence Based Policy: A Practical Guide to Doing It Better (with Nancy Cartwright) 2012. *Leisure interests:* sailing, skiing.

HARDIE BOYS, Rt Hon. Sir Michael, GNZM, GCMG, QSO, PC; New Zealand judge and fmr Governor-General; b. 6 Oct. 1931, Wellington; s. of Justice Reginald Hardie Boys and Edith May Hardie Boys (née Bennett); m. Edith Mary Zohrab 1957; two s. two d.; ed Wellington Coll., Victoria Univ. of Wellington; barrister, solicitor with pvt. practice 1950–80; Councillor, then Pres., Wellington Dist Law Soc. 1974–79; Judge, High Court 1980–89, Court of Appeal 1989–95; Gov.-Gen. of New Zealand 1996–2001; mem. Legal Aid Bd (Chair.); Hon. Bencher of Gray's Inn; Hon. Fellow, Wolfson Coll., Cambridge; KStJ; Hon. LLD (Victoria Univ., Wellington) 1997. *Leisure interest:* the outdoors. *Address:* 387A Te Moana Road, Waikanae 5036, New Zealand (home).

HARDING, James; British editor and journalist; *Co-founder and Editor, Tortoise Media;* ed St Paul's School, London, Trinity Coll., Cambridge; learnt Japanese and moved to Japan, worked as speechwriter in office of Chief Cabinet Sec. Koichi Kato early 1990s; worked in Japan unit of EC; joined Financial Times (FT) 1994, posted to Shanghai bureau (first European newspaper since 1949 revolution) 1996–99, returned to UK as Media Ed. 1999–2002, Chief of Washington, DC bureau 2002–05, Business and City Ed. The Times 2006–07, Ed. The Times 2007–12 (resgnd); Dir of News and Current Affairs, BBC 2013–18; Co-founder and Ed. Tortoise Media 2018–; est. justdosomething.net jtly with Common Purpose civic action group (online service that links professionals with non-exec. positions in local schools, prisons, hosps and nat. charities). *Publication:* Alpha Dogs: How Spin became a Global Business 2008.

HARDING, Marshal of the RAF Sir Peter Robin, GCB, DSc, FRAeS, FRSA; British air force officer (retd) and business executive (retd); b. 2 Dec. 1933, London; s. of Peter Harding and Elizabeth Kezia Harding (née Clear); m. Sheila Rosemary May 1955; three s. one d.; ed Chingford High School; joined RAF 1952; pilot, numerous appointments in fighter, light bomber, strike/attack, reconnaissance and helicopters; Air Officer Commanding Number 11 Group 1981–82; Vice-Chief Air Staff 1982–84, of Defence Staff 1985; Air Officer Commdg-in-Chief, RAF Strike Command and C-in-C UK Air Forces (NATO) 1985–88; Chief of Air Staff 1988–92, Chief of Defence Staff 1993–94; ADC to HM the Queen 1975, Air ADC to HM the Queen 1988–92; Deputy Chair. GEC-Marconi Ltd 1995–98; Chair. Thorlock Int. Ltd 1998–2000, Merlyn Int. Assocs Ltd 1995–2002, Sienna Cancer Diagnostics Ltd 2003–05; Council mem. Winston Churchill Memorial Trust 1990–2008; Cttee mem. Leonard Cheshire Conflict Recovery Centre 1996–2005; Vice-Pres. The Guild of Aviation Artists 1994; Vice-Patron, UK Nat. Defence Asscn; mem. Pilgrims Soc. of GB; Liveryman Guild of Air Pilots and Navigators; Fellow and Hon. Companion, Royal Aeronautical Soc. 1989; Commdr, Legion of Merit (USA); CB 1980, KCB 1982, GCB 1988; Hon. DSc (Cranfield Inst. of Tech.) 1990. *Leisure interests:* grandchildren, swimming, piano, bridge, birdwatching and shooting (normally separately), the Beefsteak and Garrick clubs. *E-mail:* alice_merlyn@btinternet.com (home).

HARDOUVELIS, Gikas A., BA, MSc, PhD; Greek economist, academic and government official; *Professor of Finance and Economics, Department of Banking and Financial Management, University of Piraeus;* b. 8 Oct. 1955; ed Harvard Univ. and Univ. of California, Berkeley, USA; Asst Prof., Barnard Coll., Columbia Univ. 1983–89; Assoc. Prof., then Full Prof., Rutgers Univ. 1989–93; banking experience includes with Fed. Reserve Bd, New York 1987–93, Bank of Greece 1994–95, also served as Second Alt. to Gov. at European Monetary Inst.; Chief Economist, Nat. Bank of Greece 1996–2000; played role in establishment of Athens Derivatives Exchange as an original mem. Bd of Dirs 1997–2000; Dir Econ. Office of the Prime Minister 2000–04, 2011–12; Chief Economist and Dir of Research, Eurobank Group SA 2005–13; currently Prof. of Finance and Econs, Dept of Banking and Financial Man., Univ. of Piraeus; Minister of Finance 2014–15; mem. Cyprus Int. Inst. of Man. Academic Council, Bd of Dirs Foundation for Econ. and Industrial Research, Academic Council of the Hellenic Banks Asscn (and its Econ. and Monetary Affairs Cttee-European Banking Fed. Rep.); Research Fellow, Centre for Econ. Policy Research and Centre for Money, Banking and Insts, Univ. of Surrey; Trustee, Anatolia Coll.; included in Hall of Fame of the top 50 individual publishers world-wide in applied econometrics 1989–95. *Publications:* articles in journals including American Economic Review, Journal of Finance, Quarterly Journal of Economics, Journal of Monetary Economics. *Address:* Krinon 18, Paleo Psychico, 15452 Athens (home). *Telephone:* (210) 414-2323 (office). *E-mail:* gikas.hardouvelis@gmail.com (office). *Website:* www.hardouvelis.gr.

HARDY, Sir David William, Kt, CBIM, FCA, FILT; British business executive; b. 14 July 1930, Wilmslow, Cheshire; s. of Brig. John H. Hardy; m. Rosemary Collins 1957; one s. one d.; ed Wellington Coll. and Harvard Business School, USA; with Funch Edye Inc. and Imperial Tobacco, USA 1954–70; HM Govt Coordinator of Industrial Advisers 1970–72; Group Finance Dir Tate & Lyle Ltd 1972–77; Dir Ocean Transport & Trading PLC 1977–83; Dir Globe Investment Trust PLC 1976–90, Exec. Chair. 1983–90; Chair. Ocean Inchcape 1980–83, London Park Hotels 1983–87, Docklands Light Railway 1984–87, Swan Hunter 1986–88, MGM Assurance 1986–99, London Docklands Devt Corpn 1988–92, Europa Minerals 1991–94, Bankers Trust Investment Man. Ltd 1992–94, Burmine 1992–96, James Fisher 1992–93, Y. J. Lovell 1994–99; Dir (non-exec.) Imperial Tobacco Group 1996–2001, Milner Estates 1996–99, Sons of Gwalia 1996–98, Hanson 1991–2001, Ciba Geigy 1991–96, J. Devenish 1991–93; mem. Financial Services Practitioner Forum 2001–; numerous other directorships, professional appointments etc.; Chair. of Trustees Nat. Maritime Museum 1995–2005; Chair. Transport Research Foundation 1996–2007; Fellow, Chartered Inst. of Transport; Hon. LLD (Greenwich) 2003. *Address:* Crowthorne House, Nine Mile Ride, Wokingham, Berks., RG40 3GA, England (home). *Telephone:* (1344) 773131 (home). *Fax:* (20) 7584-0086 (home). *E-mail:* seahardy@aol.com (office).

HARDY, Françoise; French singer, writer and astrologer; b. 17 Jan. 1944, Paris; m. Jacques Dutronc 1981; one s.; ed Inst. La Bruyère, Faculté des Lettres de Paris; solo recording artist 1962–; lyricist for musicians, including Diane Tell, Julien Clerc, Khalil Chahine, Guesch Patti and composer-arranger Alain Lubrano; also worked as model and actor; presents Horoscope RTL. *Films include:* Château en suède 1963, I Ragazzi dell'hully-gully 1964, Questo pazzo, pazzo mondo della canzone 1965, What's New, Pussycat 1965, Altissima pressione 1965, Une balle au coeur 1966, Europa canta 1966, Grand Prix 1966, Le Lapin de Noël (TV) 1967, Les Colombes 1972, Émilie Jolie (TV) 1980. *Recordings include:* albums: Françoise Hardy 1965, The Yeh-Yeh Girl from Paris 1965, Ma jeunesse fout le camp 1967, Comment te dire adieu 1968, Françoise Hardy en anglais 1969, Je vous aime 1969, Soleil 1970, La Question 1971, Et si je m'en vais avant toi 1972, Love Songs 1972, Message personnel 1973, Star 1977, J'écoute de la musique saoûle 1978, Gin Tonic 1980, Vingt ans vingt titres 1993, Blues 1995, Le Danger 1996, Maison ou j'ai grandi 1996, Clair obscur 2000, En Resume 2000, If You Listen 2000, Ce petit coeur 2004, Tant de Belle Choses 2005, Parenthèses 2006, La Pluie sans parapluie 2010, L'Amour fou 2012, Message personnel 2013. *Publications include:* Le Grand livre de la vierge (with B. Guenin), Entre les lignes, entre les signes (with Anne-Marie Simond) 1986, Françoise Hardy présente L'Astrologie universelle 1986, Notes secrètes (with E. Dumont) 1991, 35 Succès 1992, Les Rythmes du Zodiaque 2003, Le Désespoir des Singes et Autres Bagatelles 2008, Entre les lignes entre les signes 2009. *Leisure interest:* reading, especially books dealing with spirituality. *Address:* c/o VMA, 20 avenue Rapp, 75007 Paris (office); 13 rue Hallé, 75014 Paris, France (office). *E-mail:* info@vma.fr (office). *Website:* www.francoise-hardy.com (office).

HARDY, John Anthony, BSc (Hons), PhD, FRS, FMedSci; British geneticist, molecular biologist and academic; *Professor of Neuroscience, University College London;* b. 9 Nov. 1954; ed Univ. of Leeds, Imperial Coll., London; postdoctoral training at MRC Neuropathogenesis Unit, Newcastle upon Tyne; further postdoctoral work at Swedish Brain Bank, Umeå, Sweden; Asst Prof. of Biochemistry, St Mary's Hosp., Imperial Coll., London 1985–89, Assoc. Prof. 1989–92; Pfeiffer Endowed Chair of Alzheimer's Research, Univ. of South Florida, USA 1992–96; Consultant and Prof. of Neuroscience, Mayo Clinic, Jacksonville, Fla 1996–2000, Chair. of Dept of Neuroscience 2000–01; Chief of Lab. of Neurogenetics, Nat. Inst. of Ageing, Bethesda, Md 2001–07; Prof. of Molecular Biology of Neurological Disease, Reta Lila Weston Inst. of Neurological Studies, Univ. Coll. London 2007–; Fellow, Inst. of Biology 2011, European Molecular Biology Org. 2015; Hon. DSc (Newcastle) 2010; Hon. MD (Univ. of Umeå) 2008; Peter Debje Prize, Univ. of Limburg, Belgium 1991, IPSEN Prize 1992, Potamkin Prize, American Acad. of Neurology 1993, Allied Signal Prize 1995, MetLife Prize 1995, Kaul Prize 2002, Anne Marie Oprecht Int. Prize 2008, Dan David Prize 2014, Thuduchum Medal, Biochemistry Soc. 2014, Pritzker, MJ Fox Award 2014, Breakthrough Prize in Life Sciences (co-recipient) 2016. *Publications:* numerous papers in professional journals on research into Alzheimer's disease. *Address:* 10–12 Russell Square House, Room 232, London, WC1B 5EH (office); Department of Molecular Neuroscience, Queen Square House, Queen Square, London, WC1N 3BG, England (office). *Telephone:* (20) 3108-7466 (office); (20) 3448-4722 (office); 7768-027039 (mobile). *Fax:* (20) 7833-1016 (office). *E-mail:* j.hardy@ucl.ac.uk (office). *Website:* www.ucl.ac.uk/rlweston-inst (office); www.ucl.ac.uk/ukpdc (office).

HARDY, John Philips, MA, DPhil; Australian fmr professor of English; b. 1 Jan. 1933, Brisbane, Qld; s. of E. A. Hardy and N. A. Hardy (née Philips); m. 1st 1961 (divorced); three s. one d.; m. 2nd 1992; ed Church of England Grammar School, Brisbane, Univ. of Queensland and Univ. of Oxford, UK; Fellow, Magdalen Coll. Oxford 1962–65; Asst Prof., Univ. of Toronto, Canada 1965–66; Prof. of English, Univ. of New England, Armidale, New South Wales, Australia 1966–72, ANU 1972–87; Foundation Prof. of Humanities and Social Sciences, Bond Univ. 1988–94; Sec. Australian Acad. of the Humanities 1981–88; Harold White Hon. Fellow, Nat. Library of Australia 1992; Australian Centenary Medal; Queensland Rhodes Scholar 1957. *Publications include:* Reinterpretations: Essays on Poems by Milton, Pope and Johnson 1971, Samuel Johnson 1979, Jane Austen's Heroines 1984, Stories of Australian Migration (ed.) 1988, Terra Australis to Australia (co-ed.) 1989, European Voyaging towards Australia (co-ed.) 1990. *Leisure interests:* films. *Address:* 26 Rawson Street, Deakin, ACT 2600, Australia (home).

HARDY MEICHTRY, Jessica Adele; American swimmer; b. 12 March 1987, Long Beach, Calif.; d. of George Hardy and Denise Robinson; m. Dominik Meichtry; one d.; ed Wilson Classical High School, Long Beach, Univ. of California, Berkeley; competed for two years at Univ. of California, Berkeley, four-time NCAA Champion; turned professional 2007; World Championships (long course): Montreal 2005: silver medal, 4×100m medley, 50m breaststroke, 100m breaststroke; Melbourne 2007: gold medal, 50m breaststroke, silver medal, 4×100m medley; Shanghai 2011: gold medal, 50m breaststroke, silver medal, 4×100m freestyle; Barcelona 2013: gold medal, 4×100m medley, bronze medal, 50m breaststroke, 100m breaststroke; World Championships (short course): Manchester 2008: gold medal, 50m breaststroke, 100m breaststroke, 4×100m medley;

Shanghai 2006: silver medal, 4×100m medley, bronze medal, 50m breaststroke; Dubai 2010: silver medal, 4×100m freestyle, 4×100m medley; Pan Pacific Championships: Victoria 2006: gold medal, 4×100m medley, 50m breaststroke, 50m freestyle, 4×100m freestyle, 4×100m medley; California 2010: gold medal, 50m breaststroke, 4×100m freestyle relay, 50m freestyle; Queensland 2014: gold medal, 100m breaststroke, silver medal, 4x100m medley relay; withdrew from US Olympic Team for Beijing Olympics and suspended for one year following a failed drugs test 2008, resumed swimming 2009; Olympic Games: London: gold medal, 4x100m medley (swam in heats), bronze medal 2012 4×100m freestyle relay; coach: Dave Salo; voted Capt. 2014 Pan Pacific USA team, 2015 World Championships team; Brand Amb., BSN Sports 2019–; Female High School Swimmer of the Year, Swimming World magazine 2004, 2005, Female World Cup Overall Winner 2009. *Leisure interests:* surfing, scuba diving, water polo. *Telephone:* (562) 260-3923. *E-mail:* swimhardy@gmail.com. *Website:* www.jessicahardy.net.

HARE, Sir David, Kt, MA, FRSL; British playwright and theatre director; b. 5 June 1947, Hastings, Sussex; s. of Clifford Theodore Rippon Hare and Agnes Cockburn Gilmour; m. 1st Margaret Matheson 1970 (divorced 1980); two s. one d.; m. 2nd Nicole Farhi 1992; ed Lancing Coll., Jesus Coll., Cambridge; Literary Man. and Resident Dramatist, Royal Court 1969–71; Resident Dramatist, Nottingham Playhouse 1973; f. Portable Theatre 1968, Joint Stock Theatre Group 1975, Greenpoint Films 1983; Assoc. Dir Nat. Theatre 1984–88, 1989–; UK/US Bicentennial Fellowship 1978; Hon. Fellow, Jesus Coll. Cambridge 2001; Officier, Ordre des Arts et des Lettres 1997; Evening Standard Drama Award 1970, John Llewellyn Rhys Prize 1974, BAFTA Best Play of the Year 1978, New York Critics' Circle Awards 1983, 1990, 1997, 1999, Golden Bear Award for Best Film 1985, Evening Standard Drama Award for Best Play 1985, Plays and Players Best Play Awards 1985, 1988, 1990, City Limits Best Play 1985, Drama Magazine Awards Best Play 1988, Laurence Olivier Best Play of the Year 1990, 1996, Time Out Award 1990, Dramalogue Award 1992, Time Out Award for Outstanding Theatrical Achievement 1998, Outer Critics' Circle Award 1999, Drama League Award 1999, Drama Desk Award 1999, Joan Cullman Award 1999, PEN Pinter Prize 2011. *Plays include:* Slag, Hampstead 1970, Royal Court 1971, New York Shakespeare Festival (NYSF) 1971, The Great Exhibition, Hampstead 1972, Brassneck (with Howard Brenton), Nottingham Playhouse 1973 (also Dir), Knuckle, Comedy Theatre 1974, Fanshen, Inst. of Contemporary Arts 1975, Hampstead 1975, Nat. Theatre 1992, Teeth 'n' Smiles, Royal Court 1975 (also Dir), Wyndhams 1976 (also Dir), Plenty, Nat. Theatre 1978 (also Dir), NYSF and Broadway 1982 (also Dir), Albery 1999, A Map of the World, Nat. Theatre 1983 (also Dir) NYSF 1985 (also Dir), Pravda: A Fleet Street Comedy (with Howard Brenton), Nat. Theatre 1985 (also Dir), The Bay at Nice, Nat. Theatre 1986 (also Dir), The Secret Rapture, Nat. Theatre 1988, NYSF and Broadway 1989 (also Dir), Racing Demon, Nat. Theatre 1990, 1993, Broadway 1995, Murmuring Judges, Nat. Theatre 1992, 1993, The Absence of War, Nat. Theatre 1993, Skylight, Nat. Theatre 1995, Wyndhams and Broadway 1996, Vaudeville 1997, Amy's View, Nat. Theatre 1997, Aldwych 1998, Broadway 1999, The Judas Kiss, Almeida and Broadway 1998 (Dir on radio only), Via Dolorosa, Royal Court 1998 (also acted), Almeida and Broadway 1999 (also acted), My Zinc Bed, Royal Court 2000 (also Dir), The Breath of Life, Theatre Royal, Haymarket 2002, The Permanent Way, Nat. Theatre 2003, Stuff Happens, Nat. Theatre 2004, The Vertical Hour (Music Box Theatre, Broadway) 2006, Gethsemane, Nat. Theatre 2009, Behind the Beautiful Forevers (Royal Nat. Theatre) 2014, The Moderate Soprano 2015, The Red Barn 2016. *Plays adapted:* The Rules of the Game, Nat. Theatre 1971, Almeida 1992, The Life of Galileo, Almeida 1994, Mother Courage and Her Children, Nat. Theatre 1995, Ivanov, Almeida and Broadway 1997 (Dir on radio only), The Blue Room, Donmar and Broadway 1998, Theatre Royal 2000, Platonov, Almeida 2001, The House of Bernarda Alba, Lorca 2005. *Plays directed:* Christie in Love, Portable Theatre 1969, Fruit, Portable Theatre 1970, Blowjob, Portable Theatre 1971, England's Ireland, Portable Theatre 1972 (Co-Dir), The Provoked Wife, Palace, Watford 1973, The Pleasure Principle, Theatre Upstairs 1973, The Party, Nat. Theatre 1974, Weapons of Happiness, Nat. Theatre 1976, Devil's Island, Joint Stock 1977, Total Eclipse, Lyric 1981, King Lear, Nat. Theatre 1986, The Designated Mourner, Nat. Theatre 1996, Heartbreak House, Almeida 1997. *Radio play:* Murder in Samarkand 2010. *TV screenplays include:* Man Above Men (BBC) 1973, Licking Hitler (BBC) 1978 (also Dir), Dreams of Leaving (BBC) 1979 (also Dir), Saigon: Year of the Cat (Thames) 1983 (also Assoc. Producer), Heading Home (BBC) 1991 (also Dir), The Absence of War (BBC) 1995, Page Eight (also Dir) 2011, Turks & Caicos (also Dir) 2014, Salting the Battlefield (also Dir) 2014, Collateral (BBC) 2018. *Film screenplays include:* Wetherby 1985 (also Dir), Plenty 1985, Paris by Night 1989 (also Dir), Strapless 1990 (also Dir), Damage 1992, The Secret Rapture 1993 (also assoc. producer), Via Dolorosa 2000 (also actor), The Hours (adaptation of Michael Cunningham's novel) 2001, Lee Miller 2003, The Corrections (adaptation of Jonathan Franzen's novel) 2005, Denial 2016. *Film directed:* The Designated Mourner 1996 (also Producer). *Opera libretto:* The Knife, New York Shakespeare Festival 1988 (also Dir). *Publications include:* Writing Lefthanded 1991, Asking Around 1993, Acting Up: A Diary 1999, Obedience, Struggle and Revolt (collection of speeches) 2005, The Blue Touch Paper: A Memoir 2015. *Address:* c/o Casarotto Ramsay & Associates Ltd, Waverley House, 7–12 Noel Street, London, W1F 8GQ, England (office). *Telephone:* (20) 7287-4450 (office). *Fax:* (20) 7287-9128 (office). *E-mail:* info@casarotto.co.uk (office). *Website:* www.casarotto.co.uk (office).

HARGROVE, Basil (Buzz), OC; Canadian trade union official (retd); *Distinguished Visiting Professor, Ted Rogers School of Management, Ryerson University;* b. 8 March 1944, Bath, NB; s. of Percy Hargrove and Eileen Doucet; m. Denise Small 2007; three c.; mem. Canadian Auto Workers (CAW) Cttee Chrysler Canada 1965–75, Nat. Rep. 1975–78, Asst to Pres. and Dir CAW 1978–92, Nat. Pres. CAW 1992–2008 (retd); Vice-Pres. Exec. Cttee Canadian Labour Congress; Ombudsman Nat. Hockey League Players Assn Feb.–Nov. 2009; currently Distinguished Visiting Prof., Ted Rogers School of Man., Ryerson Univ., Toronto, also Co-Dir Centre for Labour Man. Relations; Fellow, Centennial Coll.; Dr hc (Brock Univ.) 1998, (Univ. of Windsor) 2003, (Wilfred Laurier Univ.) 2004, (Ryerson Univ.) 2006, Univ. of New Brunswick) 2008, (Queen's Univ.) 2009. *Publications include:* Labour of Love 1998, Laying It on the Line: Driving a Hard Bargain in Challenging Times 2009. *Address:* Ted Rogers School of Management, Ryerson University, 350 Victoria Street, Toronto, ON M5B 2K3, Canada (office). *Telephone:* (416) 979-5000 (office). *Fax:* (416) 979-5001 (office). *Website:* www.ryerson.ca/tedrogersschool (office).

HARIB, Mohammed Saeed; United Arab Emirates animator; *Founder, Lammtara Pictures;* b. 1978, Dubai; s. of Saeed Harib; ed Northeastern Univ., Boston, USA; began career as Art Dir, Tech. and Media Free Zone Authority, Dubai 2005; f. Lammtara Pictures Sept. 2005; created Freej (Middle East's first computer animated TV series), first broadcast Sept. 2006; Young CEO of the Year, CEO Magazine 2008, Dubai Int. Film Festival Muhur Award for Best UAE Talent 2008, Majid Bin Mohammed Youth Media Award 2011. *Films include:* The Prophet (segment dir) 2015. *Address:* Lammtara Pictures, Dubai Media City, PO Box 502274, Dubai, United Arab Emirates (office). *Telephone:* (4) 3757478 (office). *Fax:* (4) 4290949 (office). *E-mail:* info@lamtarapictures.com (office). *Website:* www.lammtarapictures.com (office).

HARIHARAN, BSc, LLB; Indian singer; b. 3 April 1955, Mumbai; s. of Ananthasubramani Iyer ('H. A. S. Mani') and Alamelu Mani; m. Lalita 1994; two s.; ed SIES Coll., trained in Hindustani music with Ustad Ghulam Mustafa Khan; signed by the late music dir Jaidev to sing for Hindi film Gaman following success in singing competition 1977; toured concert circuit and performed on TV for several serials, e.g. Junoon; recorded several successful ghazal albums for which he wrote the scores; sang in several Hindi movies such as Sahibaan, Lamhe, Raam Nagari, Dard Ke Rishte, Zamana, Sindoor, Rangeela, Bombay, Pardes, Traffic Signal, Muukhbir; debut singing in Tamil in film Roja 1993; sang more than 1000 Tamil songs; All-India Sur Singaar Competition Prize 1977, UP State Award 1977, Best Male Playback Singer, Tamil Nadu State Govt Film Awards 1995, 2004, Nat. Award for Best Male Playback Singer 1998, 2009, Padma Shri 2004, Yesudas Award 2004, Dinanath Mangeshkar Award 2010, Kerala State Film Award for Best Singer 2011, Asianet Film Award for Best Male Playback Singer 2011, Filmfare South Award for Best Male Playback Singer 2011, Nat. Lata Mangeshkar award 2013. *Albums include:* Shamakhana, Horizon 1983, Sukoon 1983, Aabshar-e-Ghazal 1985, Reflections 1987, Dil Nasheen 1988, The Very Best of Hariharan (compilation) 1989, Hariharan In Concert 1989, Dil Ki Baat 1989, My Favourite Hits (compilation) 1990, Hazir 1992, Gulfam (Double Platinum) (Diva Award for Best Album of the Year 1994) 1994, Saptarishi 1995, Paigham 1995, Intoxicating Hariharan 1996, Qaraar 1996, Visaal 1996, Halka Nasha 1996, Jashn 1996, Colonial Cousins (first Indian act to be featured on MTV Unplugged, also won MTV Indian Viewers' Choice Award and US Billboard Award) 1996, Paigham 1997, Aathwan Sur – The Other Side of Naushad 1998, 2009, The Way We Do It 1998, Kaash (Screen Videocon Award for Best Non-film Album 2000) 2000, Aatma 2001, Swar Utsav 2001, Lahore Ke Rang Hari Ke Sang 2005, Dil Aisa Kisi Ne Mera Toda 2006, Waqt Par Bolna 2007, Lafzz... 2008, Nandagopalam 2013. *Films include:* Power of Women. *Leisure interests:* film, travel, antique collecting, football. *Address:* c/o Tarsame Mittal Talent Management, Bungalow no. 181, 1st Floor, Aram Nagar Part 2, Versova, Andheri (W), Mumbai 400 061, India (office); 101 (1st Floor), Legacy Tower, Powai Vihar Complex, Powai, Mumbai 400 076, India (home). *Telephone:* (22) 26358498 (office); (22) 25701673 (office). *E-mail:* info@tmtalentmanagement.com (office); singerhari@gmail.com (office). *Website:* www.tmtalentmanagement.com (office); www.singerhariharan.co (office). *Fax:* (22) 25704619 (office).

HARIRI, Ayman Rafik; Lebanese business executive; *CEO, Vero;* b. 16 May 1978; s. of Rafik Hariri (assassinated fmr Prime Minister) and Nazek Hariri; brother of Saad ed-Din Hariri (Prime Minister); m.; one c.; ed Georgetown Univ., Washington, DC, USA; began career with Intelsat (satellite provider); currently mem. Bd of Dirs, Vice-Chair. and Deputy CEO Saudi Oger Ltd; Chair. Epok (software co.); Co-Founder and CEO Vero (social media co.) 2013–; Dir Cell C, South Africa (mobile telephone co.). *Website:* www.vero.co (office).

HARIRI, Nazek; Lebanese foundation executive; b. (Nazek Audeh), widow of Rafik Hariri (fmr Prime Minister of Lebanon); four s. one d. three step-c.; supports Lebanese fashion designers and works for several charitable causes, including Children's Cancer Center of Lebanon, Int. Osteoporosis Foundation, Chronic Care Center, Muslim Inst. for Orphanages; fmr Pres. Hariri Foundation; Amb. of Int. Osteoporosis Foundation 2003; unanimously chosen to head all social and charitable orgs est. by her husband in Lebanon following his assassination 2005; campaigned for step-son Saad in Lebanese elections. *Address:* c/o Hariri Foundation, Beirut, Lebanon (office). *E-mail:* info@rafichariri.org (office); m.i.s@hariri-foundation.org.lb (office). *Website:* www.nazekhariri.net; www.hariri-foundation.org.lb (office).

HARIRI, Saad ed-Din; Lebanese business executive and politician; *Prime Minister;* b. 18 April 1970, Riyadh, Saudi Arabia; s. of Rafik Hariri and Nidal al-Bustani; m. Lara Bashir Al Adem 1998; two s. one d.; ed McDonough School of Business, Georgetown Univ., Washington, DC, USA; Marketing Man. Sipco Saudi Industrial Paints Co., Riyadh 1993; fmr Chair. Exec. Cttee Oger Telecom, also Gen. Man. Saudi Oger Ltd and Dir Oger International Entreprise de Travaux Internationaux; Chair. Omnia Holdings; Dir and Chair. Saraya Holdings, UAE; returned to Lebanon 2005; Leader, Tayyar al-Mustaqbal (Movement of the Future) 2005–; Prime Minister 2009–11, 2016– (anounced intention to resign 4 Nov. 2017, but suspended resignation 22 Nov.). *Address:* Office of the Prime Minister, Riad El-Solh Square, Beirut, Lebanon (office). *Telephone:* (1) 746800 (office). *Fax:* (1) 746805 (office). *Website:* www.pcm.gov.lb (office); www.almustaqbal.org (office).

HARISH, Michael, BA; Israeli economist and politician; b. 28 Nov. 1936, Romania; s. of Joseph Harish and Esther Harish; m. Edith Normand 1963; three s. one d.; ed Hebrew Univ.; Sec.-Gen. Labour Party's Student Org. 1961–63; Dir and Chair. Int. Dept Israel Labour Party 1967–82, Sec.-Gen. Israel Labour Party 1989–92, Temp. Chair. Labour Party's Political Cttee 2011; Minister of Industry and Trade 1992–96; mem. Knesset 1974–96, Deputy Chair. Defence and Foreign Affairs Cttee 1984–88, Chair. Finance Cttee 1988–89, Co-Chair. Jt Science and Tech. Cttee; Chair. Israel Centre for Energy Policy; mem. several ministerial cttees including Econ. Affairs, Immigrants' Absorption, Devt Areas, Jerusalem Affairs; mem. Cttee for co-ordinating activities between Govt and the Jewish Agency and the Zionist Org.; fmr Pres. Me Harish Enterprises Ltd; mem. Public Council for Soviet Jewry. *Leisure interests:* sport, music. *Address:* 5 Mishmar

Hayarden Street, Givatayim, 53582, Israel (home). *Telephone:* (3) 571-5233 (home). *Fax:* (3) 571-5233 (home). *E-mail:* meharish@internet-zahav.net.il.

HARKIN, Thomas (Tom) R., JD; American lawyer and politician; b. 19 Nov. 1939, Cumming, Ia; s. of Patrick Harkin and Frances Harkin; m. Ruth Raduenz 1968; two d.; ed Iowa State Univ. and Catholic Univ. of America Law School; admitted to Iowa bar 1972; served in USN 1962–67, Naval Reserve 1968–74; Attorney, Polk Co., Ia Legal Aid Soc. 1973; mem. US House of Reps, Washington, DC 1975–85; Senator from Iowa 1985–2015, Chair. Cttee on Agric., Nutrition, and Forestry 2001–03, Cttee on Health, Educ., Labor and Pensions 2009–15; fmr mem. Bd of Dirs Iowa Consumers League; mem. Small Business Cttee, Democratic Steering Cttee; Democrat. *Publication:* Five Minutes to Midnight 1990. *Address:* c/o 731 Hart Senate Office Building, Washington, DC 20510, USA.

HARLEY, Ian, MA; British finance executive; b. Falkirk, Scotland; ed Univ. of Edinburgh; articled clerk, Touche Ross & Co. 1972; later with Corp. Planning Dept, Morgan Crucible Ltd; joined Abbey Nat. Building Soc. (later Abbey Nat. PLC) 1977, Financial Analyst then various Sr Man. posts with Finance, Treasury and Retail Divs., Reg. Man. for the SE, Retail Operations Div. 1984–86, Commercial Man. for Business Devt 1986, Group Financial Controller 1986–88, Asst Gen. Man. of Finance 1988–91, Finance Dir of Retail Operations 1991–92, Operations Dir Jan.–Oct. 1992, Group Treas. and Chief Exec. Abbey Nat. Treasury Services PLC 1992–98, Finance Dir and mem. Bd 1993–2002, CEO 1998–2002; mem. Bd of Dirs British Energy Group PLC and British Energy Holdings PLC 2004–09, Rentokil Initial plc, Remploy; Gov. Whitgift Foundation (Chair. Court of Govs 2007–15); Vice-Pres. Nat. Deaf Children's Soc.; fmr Chair. Asscn for Payment Clearing Services; Bd Mentor, Criticaleye; Fellow, Inst. of Chartered Accountants, Inst. of Bankers.

HARLIN, Renny; Finnish film director, producer and screenwriter; b. 15 March 1959, Helsinki; m. Geena Davis (q.v.) (divorced 1998); one s.; ed Univ. of Helsinki Film School; f. Midnight Sun Pictures (production co.). *Films include:* Born American (debut) 1986, Prison, A Nightmare on Elm Street IV: The Dream Master, Die Hard 2, The Adventures of Ford Fairlane, Rambling Rose (producer only), Cliffhanger, Speechless (co-producer only), Cutthroat Island (also producer), The Long Kiss Goodnight (also producer) 1996, Deep Blue Sea 1999, Blast from the Past (producer) 1999, Exorcist: The Beginning 2004, Mindhunters (also producer) 2004, The Covenant 2006, Cleaner 2007, 12 Rounds 2009, 5 Days of War 2011, Devil's Pass 2013, The Legend of Hercules 2014, Skiptrace 2016. *Films for television include:* Freddy's Nightmares 1990, T.R.A.X. 2000, Burn Notice 2011–12, White Collar 2012, Graceland 2013. *E-mail:* renny@rennyharlin.com. *Website:* www.midnightsunpictures.com (office); www.rennyharlin.com.

HÄRMÄLÄ, Jukka, BSc; Finnish business executive; *Chairman, Delta Motor Group Oy;* b. 15 Oct. 1946; m. Marjatta Härmälä; three c.; ed Helsinki School of Econs; joined Enso-Gutzeit Oy 1970, Dir of Finance 1981–83, Vice-Pres. and Gen. Man., Sawmill Div. 1983–84, Pres. and COO Enso Oyj 1988–92, Chair., Pres. and CEO 1992–98, CEO Stora Enso Oyj (following merger) 1999–2007; Chair. Delta Motor Group Oy 2014–; mem. Bd Finnish Forest Industries Fed.; fmr Vice-Chair. Finnlines; mem. European Round Table of Industrialists. *Leisure interests:* skiing, tennis, hunting, fishing. *Address:* Delta Motor Group Oy, Vaisalantie 6, 02130 Espoo, Finland (office). *Telephone:* (7) 408111 (office). *Website:* www.deltamotorgroup.fi (office).

HARMAN, Gilbert Helms, BA, PhD; American academic and writer; b. 26 May 1938, East Orange, New Jersey; s. of William H. Harman, Jr and Marguerite Page; m. Lucy Newman 1970; two d.; ed Swarthmore Coll., Harvard Univ.; mem. Faculty, Dept of Philosophy, Princeton Univ. 1963, apptd Stuart Prof. of Philosophy 1971, Co-Dir Cognitive Science Lab. 1986–2000, James S. McDonnell Distinguished Univ. Prof. of Philosophy –2017; mem. American Philosophical Asscn, Philosophy of Science Asscn, Soc. for Philosophy and Psychology, American Psychological Soc., Linguistic Soc. of America, American Acad. of Arts and Sciences 2005; Fellow, Cognitive Science Soc. 2002, Asscn for Psychological Science 2011; Jean Nicod Prize 2005, Behrman Award 2009. *Publications include:* Semantics of Natural Language (co-ed. with Donald Davidson) 1971, Thought 1973, On Noam Chomsky (ed.) 1974, The Logic of Grammar (ed. with Donald Davidson) 1975, The Nature of Morality: An Introduction to Ethics 1977, Change in View: Principles of Reasoning 1986, Skepticism and the Definition of Knowledge 1990, Conceptions of the Human Mind (ed.) 1993, Moral Relativism and Moral Objectivity (with Judith Jarvis Thomson) 1996, Reasoning, Meaning and Mind 1999, Explaining Values and other Essays in Moral Philosophy 2000, Reliable Reasoning: Induction and Statistical Learning Theory 2007, An Elementary Introduction to Statistical Learning Theory (with Sanjeev Kulkarni) 2011; contrib. to scholarly journals.

HARMAN, Rt Hon. Harriet Ruth, PC, QC; British solicitor and politician; b. 30 July 1950, London, England; d. of John Harman and of Anna Spicer; m. Jack Dromey 1982; two s. one d.; ed St Paul's Girls' School and Univ. of York; Brent Community Law Centre 1975–78; Legal Officer, Nat. Council for Civil Liberties 1978–82; MP for Peckham 1982–97, for Camberwell and Peckham 1997–; Shadow Chief Sec. to Treasury 1992–94; Shadow Spokesperson on Employment 1994–95, on Health 1995–96, on Social Security 1996–97; Sec. of State for Social Security 1997–98; Solicitor-Gen., Law Officers Dept 2001–05; Minister of State, Dept of Constitutional Affairs 2005–07; Leader, House of Commons, Lord Privy Seal, Minister for Women and Sec. of State for Equalities 2007–10; Deputy Leader and Chair. Labour Party 2007–10, Interim Leader and Chair. Labour Party and Leader of the Opposition May–Sept. 2010; Deputy Leader of the Opposition 2010–15, Shadow Sec. of State for Int. Devt 2010–11, for Culture, Media and Sport 2011–15; Interim Leader and Chair. Labour Party and Leader of the Opposition May–Sept. 2015. *Publications:* Sex Discrimination in Schools 1977, Justice Deserted: The Subversion of the Jury 1979, The Century Gap 1993, A Woman's Work (Best Memoir by a Parliamentarian, Parliamentary Book Awards 2017) 2017. *Address:* House of Commons, Westminster, London, SW1A 0AA (office); Labour Party, Labour Central, Kings Manor, Newcastle upon Tyne, NE1 6PA, England (office). *Telephone:* (20) 7219-3000 (Westminster) (office); (870) 590-0200 (Labour) (office). *Fax:* (20) 7802-1234 (Labour) (office). *E-mail:* harriet.harman.mp@parliament.uk (office); info@new.labour.org.uk (office). *Website:* www.parliament.uk/biographies/commons/ms-harriet-harman/150 (office); www.labour.org.uk (office); www.harrietharman.org.

HARMAN, Sir John, Kt, BSc; British teacher, lecturer and civil servant; *Chairman, Institute for European Environment Policy;* b. 30 July 1950, Leeds, Yorks., England; s. of John Edward Harman and Patricia Josephine Harman (née Mullins); m. Susan Harman; one s. three d.; ed St George's Coll., Weybridge, Univ. of Manchester and Huddersfield Coll. of Educ.; teacher and lecturer –1997; elected to W Yorks. Metropolitan Co. Council 1981–86; elected to Kirklees Metropolitan Co. Council 1986, Leader 1986–99; first Leader Regional Ass. for Yorks. and Humberside 1999–2000; mem. Bd Environment Agency 1996, later Deputy Chair., Chair. 2000–08; Co-Chair. Sustainable Building Task Group 2004–05; Vice-Chair. Asscn of Metropolitan Authorities 1992–97; Deputy Leader Labour Group and Chair. Local Govt Asscn Urban Comm. 1997–2000; Local Govt Adviser to UK Del. to the Earth Summit, Rio de Janeiro 1992; Founder-Chair. UK Local Agenda 21 Steering Group; Chair. Kirklees Stadium Devt Ltd, Inst. for European Environmental Policy; Dir Nat. House Building Council, Aldersgate Group; mem. Math. Asscn; Trustee, Nat. Coal Mining Museum for England, One Community Foundation; Hon. FICE; Hon. Fellow, Chartered Inst. of Waste Man., Chartered Inst. of Water and Environmental Mans, Soc. for the Environment; Hon. DCL. *Leisure interests:* music, gardening, Huddersfield Town Football Club.

HARMOKO, Haji; Indonesian politician and journalist; *Co-ordinator of Advisers, Partai Golongan Karya;* b. 7 Feb. 1939, Kertosono, E Java; ed Sr High School, Kediri, E Java and Inst. of Nat. Defence (LEMHANAS), Jakarta; journalist, Merdeka (magazine and daily) 1960–65; Ed. Api (daily); Man. Ed. Merdeka and Chief Ed. Merdiko 1966–68; Chief Ed. Mimbar Kita 1968–69; Gen. Man., Chief Ed. Pos Kota (daily); mem. Bd of Film Censors 1974; mem. Press Council 1975; Chief Ed. Warna Sari 1976–83; mem. House of Reps and People's Consultative Ass. and Head of Information and Mass Media Div. of Functional Group (GOLKAR) 1978, Pres. and Chair. Partai Golongan Karya 1993–98, Co-ordinator of Advisers 1998–; Head of Advisory Bd of Newspaper Publrs Asscn 1979–84; mem. Exec. Bd Press and Graphics Asscn 1980–84; Minister of Information 1983–97; Speaker, People's Consultative Ass. and House of Reps 1997–2004. *Publications:* Mengabdi pada professi: sebuah buku Kenangan terhadap reken Harmoko dari Ketua-Ketua cabang dan anggota BPK-PWI se Indonesia 1983, Ceramah, pidato sambutan Menteri Penerangan Haji Harmoko 1984, Himpunan pengumuman pers Menteri Penerangan RI 1987, Pemerataan informasi meningkatkan peranserta masyarakat dalam pembangunan: himpunan pidato, sambutan, pengarahan, dan ceramah Menteri Penerangan 1987, Peranan pers Pancasila menuju era masyarakat informasi 1988, Non-aligned Movement in the Era of Globalization 1992, Information Strategy in the Era of Globalization 1993, Kopi pagi bersama Harmoko 2008, Nasihat Harmoko untuk anak-anak dan cucu-cucu 2009, Zaman edan: kopi pagi bersama Harmoko 2010. *Address:* c/o People's Consultative Assembly, Jalan Gatot Subroto 6, Jakarta, Indonesia.

HARNEY, Mary, BA; Irish fmr politician and company director; b. 1953, Ballinasloe, Co. Galway; ed Presentation Convent, Clondalkin, Co. Dublin and Trinity Coll. Dublin; mem. Seanad Éireann 1977–81; mem. Dublin Co. Council 1979–91; TD 1981–2011, Co-founder Progressive Democrats 1985, Deputy Leader Progressive Democrats 1993, then Leader and Spokesperson on Justice, Equality and Law Reform; Minister for Environmental Protection 1989–92; Tánaiste (Deputy Prime Minister) and Minister for Enterprise, Trade and Employment 1997–2004, Tánaiste 2004–07, Minister for Health and Children 2004–11; mem. bd Euro Insurances 2012–.

HARNISH, Reno L., III, MA, MIS; American academic and fmr diplomatist; b. 21 Jan. 1949, Norman, Okla; m. Leslie Harnish; one s. one d.; ed San Diego State Univ., American Univ., Massachusetts Inst. of Tech.; worked as research asst at American Enterprise Inst., as int. economist at US Dept of Treasury and as clerk for US Congressman Dave Martin of Neb.; served as Environment, Science and Tech. Counselor, Embassy in Rome, Econ. and Commercial Counselor, Embassy in GDR, in Office of Developed Country Trade, US State Dept, as Econ. Officer, Embassy in Vienna, as Political Officer, Status Liaison Office, Saipan and as Econ. Commercial Officer, Embassy in Lagos; led US policy on Cen. Asian politics and scientific cooperation with New Independent States, US State Dept 1992–95; fmr Deputy Chief of Mission, Stockholm, then Cairo, fmr Chief of Mission, US Office, Pristina, Amb. to Azerbaijan 2004–06, Gen. Chair. WIREC 2008 Interagency Leadership Group 2006, Prin. Deputy Asst Sec. of State, Bureau of Oceans and Int. Environmental and Scientific Affairs 2006–09; Dir Center for Environment and Nat. Security, Scripps Inst. of Oceanography, San Diego 2009–17; mem. Threat Reduction Advisory Cttee, Dept of Defense; Order of Malta; twice honoured for Presidential Meritorious Service and once for State Dept Distinguished Service, multiple Sr Performance Pay Awards, Meritorious Honor Award, two Superior Honor Awards. *Leisure interests:* golf, tennis, skiing, reading, gardening. *Address:* 1439 Monitor Road, San Diego, CA 92110, USA (home). *Telephone:* (619) 892-7255 (home). *E-mail:* rlharnish@hotmail.com.

HAROCHE, Serge, PhD; French physicist and academic; *Administrator, Collège de France;* b. 11 Sept. 1944, Casablanca, Morocco; s. of Albert Haroche and Valentine Haroche (née Roublev); m. Claudine Haroche (née Zeligson); two c.; ed École Normale Supérieure and Université Pierre et Marie Curie, Paris; left Morocco and settled in France 1956; worked at CNRS, Paris as research scientist 1967–71, Chargé de recherches 1971–73, Maître de recherches 1973–75; Visiting Scholar, Stanford Univ., USA 1972–73, 1976, 1979; Maître de conferences, École Polytechnique, Paris 1973–84; apptd Prof., Paris VI Univ. 1975; Visiting Scientist, MIT, USA 1979; Visiting Prof., Harvard Univ., USA 1981; Prof. (part-time), Yale Univ., USA 1984–93; Professeur de Physique, Université Pierre et Marie Curie 1975–2001; Prof., École Normale Supérieure 1982–2001, mem. Institut Universitaire de France 1991–2001, Head of Dept of Physics 1994–2000; Prof., Collège de France and holder of the Chair of Quantum Physics 2001–15, Admin. 2012–; mem. Soc. Française de Physique, European Physical Soc., Acad. des Sciences 1993, European Acad. of Sciences 2009; Foreign Assoc., Brazilian Acad. of Sciences 2009, NAS 2010; mem. American Physical Soc. 1988, Fellow 1990; Officier, Légion d'honneur, Gra Cruz Ordem Nacional Do Merito Cientifico (Brazil) 2007; Prix Aimé Cotton, Soc. Française de Physique 1971, Loeb Lecturer, Harvard Univ. 1980, Grand Prix de Physique Jean Ricard, Soc. Française de Physique 1983, Einstein Prize for Laser Science (Industrial and Univ. Research Affiliates) 1988,

Humboldt Award (Germany) 1992, Michelson Medal, Franklin Inst., Philadelphia 1993, EPS travelling lecturer 1993–94, Manne Siegbahn Lecture, Stockholm 2000, Tomassoni Award, La Sapienza Univ., Rome 2001, Quantum Electronics Prize, European Physical Soc. 2002, Quantum Communication Award, Int. Org. for Quantum Communication, Measurement and Computing and Tamagawa Univ. (Japan) 2002, Charles Hard Townes Award, Optical Soc. of America 2007, CNRS Gold Medal 2009, Advanced Research Grant, European Research Council 2009, Herbert Walther Award, German Physical Soc. and Optical Soc. of America 2010, Nobel Prize in Physics (jtly with David J. Wineland) for "ground-breaking experimental methods that enable measuring and manipulation of individual quantum systems" 2012. *Achievements include:* principally known for proving quantum decoherence by experimental observation, while working with colleagues at École Normale Supérieure 1996. *Publications include:* Laser Spectroscopy, Proceedings of the Second International Conference, Megève (co-ed.) 1975, Frontiers in Laser Spectrscopy, Proceedings of Les Houches Summer School, Session XXVII (co-ed.) 1977, Atomic Physics 11, Proceedings of the 11th International Conference in Atomic Physics (co-ed.) 1989, La physique quantique 2004, Exploring the Quantum: Atoms, Cavities and Photons (with Jean-Michel Raimond) 2006; more than 240 papers in professional journals. *Address:* Collège de France, 11 place Marcelin Berthelot, 75231 Paris Cedex 05, France (office). *Telephone:* 1-44-32-34-20 (office). *Fax:* 1-44-32-34-94 (office). *E-mail:* haroche@lkb.ens.fr (office). *Website:* www.college-de-france.fr/site/en-serge-haroche (office).

HAROON, Abdullah Hussain; Pakistani diplomatist and politician; b. 21 Oct. 1950, Karachi; ed Karachi Grammar School, Univ. of Karachi; began career in public service as Election Co-ordinator for Pakistan Muslim League 1970; Councillor, Karachi Metropolitan Corpn 1979–85; Trustee, Karachi Port Trust 1980–82; mem. Prov. Ass. of Sindh 1985–88, Speaker 1985–86, Leader of Opposition 1986–88; consultant, Pakistan Herald Publication Ltd 1988–89; fmr del. to UN Gen. Ass.; Amb. and Perm. Rep. to UN, New York 2008–12; Minister of Defence and of Foreign Affairs (in caretaker govt June–Aug. 2018; mem. Bd of Govs, Inst. of Business Admin, Karachi 1996–99; mem. Bd of Dirs, Karachi Electric Supply Corpn 1997–99; Chair. Griffith Coll., Karachi 1999–2005; Pres. Pakistan-China Business Forum 1999–2004, English Speaking Union of Pakistan, Sindh Club (youngest pres.).

HAROUN, Mahamat-Saleh; Chadian film director, former journalist and government official; *Minister of Culture, Tourism and Crafts;* b. 1961, Abéché; ed Conservatoire Libre du Cinéma, Paris, Institut Technique de Bordeaux; mem. jury, Cannes Film Festival 2011; Minister of Culture, Tourism and Crafts 2017–. *Films include:* Maral Tanié 1994, Goi Goi 1995, A Tea in the Sahel, Bord'Africa 1995, Soitgui Kouyate 1996, Un griot moderne, Bye Bye Africa (film prizes in Venice 1999, Zanzibar 2000, M-Net All African Awards 2000) 1999, Abouna (Best Cinematography Award, FESPACO) 2002, Dry Season 2006, Sexe, gombo et beurre salé 2008, A Screaming Man (Grand Prix du Jury, Cannes Film Festival) 2010, Grigris 2013, Hissein Habré, une tragédie tchadienne (documentary) 2016. *Address:* Ministry of Culture, Tourism and Crafts, N'Djamena, Chad.

HAROUTUNIAN, Michael; Armenian army officer and government official; b. 10 Feb. 1946, Sagiyan village, Shemakhin; m.; three c.; ed Frunze Mil. Acad. and Mil. Acad. of the Soviet Armed Forces; early career in Soviet Army, posts included CO of reconnaissance unit, Deputy Chief of Staff, Head of Reconnaissance Dept; Sr Instructor of Reconnaissance Unit, Military Acad. of the Soviet Armed Forces 1988–92; enlisted in Armed Forces of Armenia 1992; Head of Operations Dept and Deputy Head, Chief of Staff 1992–93; First Deputy Head, Chief of Staff of Armed Forces 1993–94, Chief of Staff of Armed Forces and First Deputy Minister of Defence 1994–2007, Minister of Defence 2007–08; 'For Service to the Motherland', Second Degree (USSR), Combat Cross, Second Degree (Armenia), Vardan Mamikonyan (Armenia), Combat Cross, Second Degree (NKR), Legion of Honor (USA), Combat Service, First Degree (Armenia), 'For Service to the Motherland', First Degree (Armenia), Marshal Baghramyan decoration, Ministry of Defence, 'For Perfect Service', First and Second Degrees, Ministry of Defence, Andranik Ozanyan decoration, Ministry of Defence, 'Coat of Arms', Ministry of Defence, Nominal Weapon, Ministry of Defence, 'For Strengthening Combat Collaboration', Ministry of Defence, Russian Fed.

HARPER, Judson Morse, BS, MS, PhD; American academic administrator (retd), consultant and academic; b. 25 Aug. 1936, Lincoln, Neb.; s. of Floyd Harper and Eda Harper; m. Patricia A. Kennedy 1958; three s.; ed Iowa State Univ.; with General Mills 1963–70, latterly Man. for New Business Ventures in Research Div.; Prof. of Chemical and Bioresource Eng, Colorado State Univ. 1970–2002, Prof. Emer. 2004–, Vice-Pres. for Research and Information Tech. 1982–2000, Interim Pres. 1989–90, Special Asst to Pres. 2000–04; consultant 1974–2010; Fellow, Inst. of Food Technologists 1992, AAAS 1995; Fulbright-Hayes Scholar 1978–79; Food Eng Award 1983, Int. Award, Inst. of Food Technologists 1990, Charles A. Lory Public Service Award, Colorado State Univ. 1993, Professional Achievement Award, Iowa State Univ. 1986; named Harper Research Complex, Colorado State Univ. 2000. *Publications include:* Extrusion of Foods 1981, Extrusion Cooking 1989; 91 refereed publs; holder of six US patents. *Leisure interests:* walking, gardening, reading. *Address:* 1818 Westview Road, Fort Collins, CO 80524, USA (home). *Telephone:* (970) 222-0357 (office); (970) 493-1191 (office). *Fax:* (970) 493-1191 (office). *E-mail:* judson.harper@colostate.edu (office).

HARPER, Sarah, CBE, FRSA, MA, DPhil; British gerontologist; *Director, The Royal Institution of Great Britain;* ed Girton Coll., Cambridge, St Catherine's Coll., Oxford; trained with BBC as News and Current Affairs Reporter and Producer, worked in TV and radio for BBC News and Newsnight; fmr Lecturer, Univ. of London; Visiting Prof., Univ. of Utah 1987; Irving B Harris Visiting Chair, Univ. of Chicago –1997; Prof. of Gerontology, Univ. of Oxford, also Co-Dir, Oxford Inst. of Population Ageing; Int. Chair in Old Age Financial Security, Univ. of Malaya 2009–10; Dir The Royal Inst. of Great Britain 2017–; mem. Prime Minister's Council for Science and Tech. 2014; Gov., Pensions Policy Inst.; mem. Editorial Advisory Panel, Nature Sustainability; frequent speaker at literary and scientific festivals, including World Econ. Forum, TED talks, Hay, Cheltenham and Edinburgh Festivals; Fellow, Royal Anthropology Inst.; Royal Soc. for Public Health Arts and Health Research Award 2011. *Publications include:* Families in Ageing Societies 2004, Ageing Societies: Myths, Challenges and Opportunities 2006, Ageing in Asia (with Roger Goodman) 2008, How Population Change will Transform our World 2016. *Address:* The Royal Institution of Great Britain, 21 Albemarle Street, London, W1S 4BS, England (office). *Telephone:* (20) 7409-2992 (office). *Website:* www.rigb.org (office).

HARPER, Rt Hon Stephen, PC MA; Canadian politician and economist; *Chairman, International Democrat Union;* b. 20 April 1959, Toronto; m. Laureen Teskey; one s. one d.; ed Richview Collegiate Inst., Univ. of Calgary; Chief Aide to Jim Hawkes MP 1985; Exec. Asst to Deborah Grey MP 1989, Chief Adviser and Speech Writer –1993; Founding mem. Reform Party 1987–97; mem. House of Commons (Calgary West) 1993–97, (Calgary Southwest) 2002–16 (resgnd), Leader of the Opposition 2002–06, Prime Minister of Canada 2006–15; Vice-Pres. Nat. Citizens Coalition 1997, later Pres.; Leader, Canadian Alliance 2002; Co-founder Conservative Party of Canada 2003, Leader 2004–15; Co-founder Harper & Associates Consulting Inc. (consultancy) 2015; Chair. Int. Democrat Union 2018–. *Address:* Harper & Associates Consulting Inc., 495 Richmond Road, Ottawa, ON K2A 4B2, Canada (office). *Website:* www.idu.org (office).

HARRACH, Péter, JCB; Hungarian politician; b. 2 Nov. 1947, Budapest; m. Csilla Harrach 1973; three c.; ed Catholic Univ. of Budapest; joined Christian Democratic People's Party (KDNP) 1989, specialist on church policy, Pres. KDNP Budapest Zugló district 1990–97, Pres. Budapest co-ordinating org. 1993–94, Nat. Vice-Pres. 1995–97 (resgnd), Parl. Group Deputy Leader 2006, Leader 2010–; mem. Parl. 1998–; Vice-Pres. Hungarian Christian Democratic Alliance (MKDSZ) 1997–2000, Co-Pres. 2000–04, Pres. 2004–; pastoral assistant at several parishes –1990; official in charge of secular affairs Secr. of Hungarian Catholic Bishops' Conf. 1990–98; mem. Budapest Zugló (District XIV) Ass. 1990–98; mem. Budapest Municipal Ass. 1994–98; Minister for Social and Family Affairs 1998–2002; Deputy Speaker Nat. Ass. 2002–10, mem. (as MKDSZ del.) Exec. of Alliance of Young Democrats (FIDESZ); Pres. Szob constituency FIDESZ-Hungarian Civic Alliance 2004–06. *Address:* Hungarian National Assembly, 1357 Budapest, Kossuth tér 1–3, Hungary (office). *Telephone:* (1) 441-4000 (office); (1) 441-4408 (office). *Fax:* (1) 441-4414 (office). *Website:* www.parlament.hu (office); harrachpeter.kdnp.hu.

HARRELL, Lynn; American cellist and academic; b. 30 Jan. 1944, New York; s. of Mack Harrell and Marjorie Fulton; m. 1st Linda Blandford-Kate; one s. one d.; m. 2nd Helen Nightengale; one s. one d.; ed Juilliard School of Music, Curtis Inst. of Music; Prin. Cellist, Cleveland Orchestra (under George Szell) 1963–71; now appears as soloist with various orchestras; Piatigorsky Prof. of Cello, Univ. of Southern California 1987–93; Prof. of Int. Cello Studies, RAM, London 1988–93, 1993–95; Artistic Dir LA Philharmonic Inst. 1988–92; Music Advisor, San Diego Symphony Orchestra 1988–89; soloist, Memorial Concert for Holocaust Victims, Vatican 1994; Prof. of Cello, Shepherd School of Music, Rice Univ. 2002–09; collaborations with Anne-Sophie Mutter, André Previn; f. HEARTbeats Foundation (charity) 2010; two Grammy Awards, Avery Fisher Award 1975, Piatigorsky Award, Ford Foundation Concert Artists' Award, others. *Recordings include:* works by J. S. Bach, Beethoven, Bloch, Boccherini, Brahms, Bruch, Debussy, Dutilleux, Dvořák, Elgar, Fauré, Haydn, Herbert, Hindemith, Lalo, Mendelssohn, Prokofiev, Rachmaninov, Rosza, Saint-Saëns, Schoenberg, Schubert, Schumann, Shostakovich, Strauss, Tchaikovsky, Villa-Lobos, Vivaldi, Walton. *Leisure interests:* chess, fishing, golf, writing. *Address:* R. Douglas Sheldon, Columbia Artists Management, 1790 Broadway at 5 Columbus Circle, New York, NY 10019, USA (office). *E-mail:* rdsheldon@cami.com (office). *Website:* www.lynnharrell.com; www.heartbeatsforchildren.org.

HARRELSON, Woodrow (Woody) Tracy, BA; American actor; b. 23 July 1961, Midland, Tex.; m. Laura Louie 2008; three d.; ed Hanover Coll.; Founder, Voice Yourself (website). *Theatre includes:* The Boys Next Door, Two on Two (author, producer, actor), The Zoo Story (author, actor), Brooklyn Laundry, Furthest from the Sun (also playwright), On An Average Day (Comedy Theatre, London) 2002, Night of the Iguana (Lyric Theatre, London) 2005–06. *Television includes:* Cheers (series) 1985–93, Bay Coven 1987, Killer Instinct 1988, Mother Goose Rock 'n' Rhyme 1990, Will & Grace (series) 2001, Game Change (film) 2012, True Detective (series) 2014. *Films include:* Wildcats 1986, Cool Blue 1988, Doc Hollywood 1991, Ted and Venus 1991, White Men Can't Jump 1992, Indecent Proposal 1993, I'll Do Anything 1994, The Cowboy Way 1994, Natural Born Killers 1994, Money Train 1995, The Sunchaser 1996, The People vs Larry Flynt 1996, Kingpin 1996, Wag the Dog 1997, Welcome to Sarajevo 1997, The Thin Red Line 1998, Palmetto 1998, The Hi-Lo Country 1998, EdTV 1999, Play It to the Bone 1999, American Saint 2001, Scorched 2003, Anger Management 2003, She Hate Me 2004, After the Sunset 2004, The Big White 2005, North Country 2005, The Prize Winner of Defiance, Ohio 2005, A Prairie Home Companion 2006, Free Jimmy (voice) 2006, A Scanner Darkly 2006, The Grand 2007, The Walker 2007, No Country for Old Men 2007, Battle in Seattle 2007, Transsiberian 2008, Sleepwalking 2008, Semi-Pro 2008, Surfer, Dude 2008, Management 2008, Seven Pounds 2008, The Messenger 2009, Zombieland 2009, 2012 2009, Defendor 2010, Bunraku 2010, The Hunger Games 2012, Seven Psychopaths 2012, Now You See Me 2013, Out of the Furnace 2013, The Hunger Games: Catching Fire 2013, Lost in London 2017, Three Billboards Outside Ebbing, Missouri 2017. *Leisure interests:* sports, juggling, writing, chess. *Address:* c/o Creative Artists Agency, 9830 Wilshire Boulevard, Beverly Hills, CA 90212, USA. *Website:* www.voiceyourself.com.

HARRIES OF PENTREGARTH, Baron (Life Peer), cr. 2006, of Ceinewydd in the County of Dyfed; **Richard Douglas Harries,** DD, FKC, FRSL, FLSW; British ecclesiastic and academic; *Honorary Professor of Theology, King's College London;* b. 2 June 1936, Eltham, London; s. of Brig. W. D. J. Harries and G. M. B. Harries; m. Josephine Bottomley 1963; one s. one d.; ed Wellington Coll., Royal Mil. Acad., Sandhurst, Selwyn Coll., Cambridge, Cuddesdon Coll., Oxford; Lt, Royal Corps of Signals 1955–58; Curate, Hampstead Parish Church 1963–69; Chaplain, Westfield Coll. 1966–69; Lecturer, Wells Theological Coll. 1969–72; Warden, Salisbury and Wells Theological Coll. 1971–72; Vicar, All Saints, Fulham, London 1972–81; Dean, King's Coll., London 1981–87, Fellow and Hon. Prof. of Theology; Bishop of Oxford 1987–2006; Prof. of Divinity, Gresham Coll., London 2008–12, Prof. Emer. 2012–; Vice-Chair. Council of Christian Action 1979–87, Council for Arms Control 1982–87; Chair. Southwark Ordination Course 1982–87, Shalom, End Loans to South Africa (ELSTA) 1982–87, Christian Evidence Soc.; Chair. Church of England Bd of Social Responsibility 1996–2001; Consultant to the Archbishops on Jewish-Christian Relations 1986–92; Chair. Council of Christians and Jews

1993–2001, House of Lords Select Cttee on Stem Cell Research 2001–02; Visiting Prof., Liverpool Hope Coll. 2002; mem. (Crossbench) House of Lords 2006–; mem. Home Office Advisory Cttee for Reform of Law on Sexual Offences 1981–85, Bd Christian Aid 1994–2001, Royal Comm. on Lords Reform 1999–, Nuffield Council of Bioethics 2002–06, Human Fertilisation and Embryology Authority 2003–09, Parl. Select Cttee on Privacy and Superinjunctions 2012, Parl. Select Cttee on Charities 2016, Parl. Select Cttee on Citizenship and Democratic Engagement 2017; Trustee, Multi-Faith School Trust, Woolf Inst., Cambridge; Fellow, Learned Soc. of Wales 2011; Hon. Fellow, Selwyn Coll., Cambridge, St Anne's Coll. Oxford, Hon. FMedSci 2004, Hon. Fellow, Soc. of Biology 2009; Hon. DD (London) 1996, (Grad. Theological Foundation) 2012; Hon. DUniv (Oxford Brookes) 2001, (Open Univ.), (Huddersfield) 2008; Sir Sigmund Steinberg Award 1989, Pres.'s Medal, British Acad. 2012. *Radio:* regular broadcaster, particularly on BBC Radio 4's Today Programme. *Publications include:* Prayers of Hope 1975, Turning to Prayer 1978, Prayers of Grief and Glory 1979, Being a Christian 1981, Should Christians Support Guerrillas? 1982, The Authority of Divine Love 1983, Praying Round the Clock 1983, Seasons of the Spirit (co-ed.) 1984, Prayer and the Pursuit of Happiness 1985, Reinhold Niebuhr and the Issues of Our Time (ed.) 1986, Christianity and War in a Nuclear Age 1986, C. S. Lewis: The Man and His God 1987, Is There a Gospel for the Rich? 1992, Art and the Beauty of God 1993, The Value of Business and its Values (co-author) 1993, Questioning Faith 1995, A Gallery of Reflections 1995, In the Gladness of Today 2000, Christianity: Two Thousand Years (co-ed.) 2000, God Outside the Box: Why Spiritual People Object to Christianity 2002, After the Evil: Christianity and Judaism in the Shadow of the Holocaust 2003, The Passion in Art 2005, The Re-Enchantment of Morality 2008, Faith in Politics? – Rediscovering the Christian Roots of Our Political Values 2010, 2014, Questions of Life and Death 2010, Reinhold Niebuhr and Contemporary Politics (co-ed.) 2010, The Image of Christ in Modern Art 2013, The Beauty and the Horror: Searching for God in a Suffering World 2016, Haunted by Christ: Modern Writers and the Struggle for Faith 2018; contrib. to several books; numerous articles. *Leisure interests:* theatre, literature, sport. *Address:* House of Lords, Westminster, London, SW1A 0PW, England (office). *E-mail:* harriesr@parliament.uk (office). *Website:* www.parliament.uk/biographies/lords/lord-harries-of-pentregarth/3813 (office).

HARRINGTON, Anthony Stephen, BA, JD; American lawyer, consultant and fmr diplomatist; *Chair of the Managing Board and Head of the Brazil and Latin America practice, Albright Stonebridge Group;* b. 9 March 1941, Taylorsville, NC; s. of Atwell Lee Harrington and Louise Harrington (née Chapman); m. Hope Reynolds 1971; two s.; ed Univ. of North Carolina, Duke Univ.; Sr Pnr, Hogan & Hartson (law firm), Washington, DC, then Sr Advisor; Amb. to Brazil 2000–01; fmr Pres. and CEO Stonebridge Int. LLC (now Albright Stonebridge Group after 2009 merger with Albright Group) 2001, currently Chair. of the Man. Bd and Head of Brazil and Latin America practice; mem. Man. Bd Civitas Group LLC (investment and consulting group); fmr mem. Bd of Dirs PRE Holdings, Inc.; fmr Chair. Pres.'s Intelligence Oversight Bd; Vice-Chair. Pres.'s Foreign Intelligence Advisory Bd 1994–99; Chair. Advisory Council Brazil Inst. of Woodrow Wilson Int. Center for Scholars; Chair. Emer. Brazil-US Business Council; mem. Bd of Dirs Center for Democracy; mem. Bd of Trustees, Kenan Inst. for Pvt. Enterprise; fmr mem. Comm. on the Roles and Capabilities of the US Intelligence Community; Co-founder Telecom USA; Co-founder and Dir Ovation (arts television network); Order of Rio Branco, Grand Cross (Brazil); Distinguished Service Medal, Univ. of North Carolina General Alumni Asscn 2008. *Leisure interests:* politics, tennis, gardening, reading. *Address:* Albright Stonebridge Group, 601 Thirteenth Street, NW, 10th Floor, Washington, DC 20005, USA (office). *Telephone:* (202) 759-5100 (office). *Website:* www.albrightstonebridge.com (office).

HARRINGTON, Padraig; Irish professional golfer; b. 31 Aug. 1971, Dublin; s. of Patrick Harrington and Breda Harrington; m. Caroline Harrington 1997; two s.; turned professional 1995, joined European Tour 1996, PGA Tour 2005; European Tour wins include Spanish Open 1996, Brazil Sao Paulo 500 Years Open 2000, BBVA Turespana Masters de Madrid 2000, Volvo Masters 2001, Dunhill Links Championship 2002, 2006, BMW Asian Open 2003, Deutsche Bank Open 2003, Omega Hong Kong Open 2004, Linde German Masters 2004, Irish Open 2007; major tournament wins include the Open Championship 2007, 2008, PGA Championship 2008; PGA Tour wins include Honda Classic 2005, 2015, Barclay's Classic 2005; other wins include World Cup of Golf (with Paul McGinley) 1997, Irish PGA Championship 1998, 2004, 2005, 2007, 2008, 2009, Target World Challenge 2002, Dunlop Phoenix Tournament 2006, Hassan II Trophy, Morocco 2007, Iskandar Johor Open 2010, PGA Grand Slam of Golf 2012; represented Europe in Ryder Cup 1999, 2002 (winners), 2004 (winners), 2006 (winners), 2008, 2010 (winners), Vice-Capt. 2014 (winners); f. Padraig Harrington Charitable Foundation 2005; Amb. for Setanta Coll. (distance learning); Texaco Ireland Sportstar Golf Award 1996, 1999, 2001, 2002, (with Darren Clarke and Paul McGinley) 2004, 2005, 2006, 2007, 2008, RTÉ Sports Person of the Year 2002, 2007, 2008, European Tour Order of Merit 2006, European Tour Golfer of the Year 2007, 2008, Irish Golf Writers Professional of the Year Award 2008, European Tour Shot of the Year 2008, AGW Trophy 2007, 2008, Asscn of Golf Writers Player of the Year 2007, 2008, PGA Player of the Year 2008, PGA Tour Player of the Year 2008, Golf Writers Asscn of America Player of the Year 2008, European Tour Shot of the Year 2008. *Address:* c/o IMG, McCormack House, Burlington Lane, Chiswick, London, W4 2TH, England (office). *Telephone:* (20) 8233-5300 (office). *Fax:* (20) 8233-5268 (office). *E-mail:* katie.powell@imgworld.com (office). *Website:* www.padraigharrington.com.

HARRIS, Edward Allen (Ed), BFA; American actor; b. 28 Nov. 1950, Englewood, NJ; s. of Bob L. Harris and Margaret Harris; m. Amy Madigan; one c.; ed Columbia Univ., Univ. of Oklahoma, Calif. Inst. of Arts; Saturn Award for Best TV Supporting Actor 2017. *Stage appearances include:* A Streetcar Named Desire, Sweet Bird of Youth, Julius Caesar, Hamlet, Camelot, Time of Your Life, Grapes of Wrath, Present Laughter, Fool for Love (Obie Award 1983), Prairie Avenue (LA Drama Critics Circle Award 1981), Scar 1985 (San Francisco Critics Award), Precious Sons 1986 (Theater World Award), Simpatico 1994, Taking Sides 1996, Wrecks 2005. *Films include:* Coma 1978, Borderline 1978, Knightriders 1980, Creepshow 1981, The Right Stuff 1982, Swing Shift 1982, Under Fire 1982, A Flash of Green 1983, Places in the Heart 1983, Alamo Bay 1984, Sweet Dreams 1985, Code Name: Emerald 1985, Walker 1987, To Kill a Priest 1988, Jacknife 1989, The Abyss 1989, State of Grace 1990, Paris Trout 1991, Glengarry Glen Ross 1992, Needful Things 1993, The Firm 1993, China Moon 1994, Milk Money 1994, Apollo 13 1995, Just Cause 1995, Eye for an Eye 1995, The Rock 1996, Absolute Power 1997, Stepmom 1998, The Truman Show 1998, The Third Miracle 1999, Waking the Dead 2000, The Prime Gig 2000, Pollock (also producer and dir) 2001, Enemy at the Gates 2001, Buffalo Soldiers 2001, A Beautiful Mind 2001, Just a Dream (voice) 2002, The Hours 2002, Masked and Anonymous 2003, The Human Stain 2003, Radio 2003, Dirt Nap 2005, Winter Passing 2005, A History of Violence (Nat. Film Critics Supporting Actor Award) 2005, Copying Beethoven 2006, Gone Baby Gone 2007, Cleaner 2007, National Treasure Book of Secrets 2007, Touching Home 2008, Appaloosa (also dir) 2008, Once Fallen 2010, The Way Back 2010, Virginia 2010, Salvation Boulevard 2011, That's What I Am 2011, Man on a Ledge 2012, Sweetwater 2013, Phantom 2013, Snowpiercer 2013, Pain & Gain 2013, Look of Love 2013. *Television includes:* Gibbsville – Trapped 1976, The Amazing Howard Hughes 1977, The Seekers 1979, The Aliens are Coming 1980, The Last Innocent Man 1987, Running Mates 1992, The Stand 1994, Riders of the Purple Sage 1996, Empire Falls 2005, Game Change (film) (Golden Globe Award for Best Performance by an Actor in a Supporting Role in a Series, Mini-Series or Motion Picture Made for Television 2013) 2012. *Address:* c/o Rick Kurtzman, CAA, 15260 Ventura Blvd, Suite 940, Sherman Oaks, CA 91403, USA (office).

HARRIS, Emmylou; American singer; b. 2 April 1947, Birmingham, Ala; m. 1st Brian Ahern; m. 2nd Paul Kennerley 1985; two d.; ed Univ. of North Carolina; singer 1967–, toured with Fallen Angels Band in USA and Europe; Pres. Country Music Foundation 1983–; Fellow, American Acad. of Arts and Sciences 2009–; Grammy Awards 1976, 1977, 1980, 1981, 1984, 1987, 1992, 1996, Country Music Asscn Female Vocalist of the Year 1980, Grammy Award for Best Female Country Vocal Performance (for The Connection) 2006, Polar Music Prize 2015. *Recordings include:* albums: Gliding Bird 1969, Pieces of the Sky 1975, Elite Hotel 1976, Luxury Liner 1977, Quarter Moon in a Ten-Cent Town 1978, Blue Kentucky Girl 1979, Light of the Stable 1979, Roses In The Snow 1980, Evangeline 1981, Cimarron 1981, Last Date 1982, White Shoes 1983, The Ballad of Sally Rose 1985, Thirteen 1986, Trio (with Dolly Parton and Linda Ronstadt) (Acad. of Country Music Album of the Year 1988) 1987, Angel Band 1987, Bluebird 1989, Brand New Dance 1990, Duets (with Nash Ramblers) 1990, At The Ryman 1992, Cowgirl's Prayer 1993, Songs of the West 1994, Wrecking Ball 1995, Portraits 1996, Nashville 1996, Spyboy 1998, Red Dirt Girl 2000, Singin' with Emmylou Harris (vol. I) 2000, Anthology 2001, Stumble Into Grace 2003, All the Roadrunning (with Mark Knopfler) 2006, Neil Young Heart of Gold 2006, All I Intended to Be 2008, Hard Bargain 2011, Old Yellow Moon (with Rodney Crowell) (Grammy Award for Best Americana Album 2014) 2013, The Travelling Kind (with Rodney Crowell) 2015. *Address:* 1025 16th Ave South, Suite 202, Nashville, TN 37212-2328, USA (office).

HARRIS, Adm. Harry; American retd naval officer and diplomatist; *Ambassador to South Korea;* b. (Harry Binkley Harris Jr), 4 Aug. 1956, Yokosuka, Japan; s. of Harry Binkley Harris Sr and Fumiko Harris; m. Brunhilde Kempf Bradley; ed US Naval Acad., Harvard Univ., Georgetown Univ.; joined USN as Naval Flight Officer (NFO) 1979; CO Jt Task Force Guantanamo, Cuba 2004, Dir of Operations US Southern Command 2007–08, Deputy Chief Naval Operations for Communication Networks and Deputy Dept of Navy Chief Information Officer –2009, CO US 6th Fleet and Striking and Support Forces NATO 2009, concurrently Deputy Commdr US Naval Forces Europe, and Africa, Jt Force Maritime Component Commdr (for Operation Odyssey Dawn) 2011, Asst to Chair. of Jt Chief of Staffs 2011–13, promoted to Adm. 2013, CO US Pacific Fleet 2013–15, Commdr US Pacific Command (USPACOM) 2015–18; Amb. to South Korea 2018–; Hon. Chief Petty Officer, Master Chief Petty Officer of Navy Steven S. Giordano 2017; Agency Seal Medal, CIA, Navy League's Stephen Decatur Award, Ellis Island Medal of Honor, Asian Pacific American Inst. for Congressional Studies Lifetime Achievement Award, among others. *Address:* US Embassy, 188, Sejong-no, Jongno-gu, Seoul 03141, Republic of Korea (office). *Telephone:* (2) 397-4114 (office). *Fax:* (2) 397-4080 (office). *E-mail:* embassyseoulpa@state.gov (office). *Website:* seoul.usembassy.gov (office).

HARRIS, Isaiah (Ike), Jr; American business executive; *Chairman, CIGNA Corporation;* b. 27 Nov. 1952, West Memphis, AR; Pres. BellSouth Enterprises, Inc. 2004–05; Pres. and CEO AT&T Advertising & Publishing – East (fmr BellSouth Advertising and Publishing Group) 2005–07; mem. Bd of Dirs CIGNA Corpn 2005–, Vice-Chair. July–Dec. 2009, Chair. 2009–; mem. Bd of Dirs Deluxe Corpn 2004–11; Ind. Trustee, Wells Fargo Advantage Funds 2008–. *Address:* CIGNA Corpn, 2 Liberty Place, 1601 Chestnut Street, Philadelphia, PA 19192, USA (office). *Telephone:* (215) 761-1000 (office). *Fax:* (215) 761-5515 (office). *E-mail:* info@cigna.com (office). *Website:* www.cigna.com (office).

HARRIS, Jeff, CA; British business executive; *Chairman, Essentra PLC;* b. 1948; began career as accountant with two auditing firms; Chief Accountant, Alliance UniChem PLC 1985, Finance Dir 1986, then Deputy CEO then CEO, Chair. 2001–05; Chair. Filtrona PLC (now Essentra PLC) 2005–, Cookson Group plc (now Vesuvius plc) 2010; mem. Bd of Dirs Bunzl PLC –2010, Andreae-Noris Zahn 1999–2007, Associated British Foods May 2003–07; Hon. DBA (Kingston Univ.). *Address:* Essentra PLC, Avebury House, 201–249, Avebury Boulevard, Milton Keynes, MK9 1AU, England (office). *Telephone:* (1908) 359100 (office). *E-mail:* enquiries@essentra.com (office). *Website:* www.essentraplc.com (office).

HARRIS, Jeremy Andrew (Drew), OBE; British/Irish police officer; *Garda Commissioner;* b. 1965, Belfast, Northern Ireland; m.; four c.; ed Univ. of Cambridge; joined Royal Ulster Constabulary as Police Officer 1983; worked with Police Service of Northern Ireland for 34 years, was responsible for Crime Operations Dept, fmr Asst Chief Constable, Deputy Chief Constable 2014–18; Superintendent, Her Majesty's Inspectorate of Constabulary, Scotland 2000–02; apptd High Level Expert, European Parl. Cttee reporting on organised crime and corruption 2013; Garda Commr, An Garda Síochána, Repub. of Ireland 2018–; held Hate Crime portfolio of Asscn of Chief Police Officers, UK (replaced by Nat. Police Chiefs' Council 2015). *Address:* An Garda Síochana Headquarters, Phoenix Park, Dublin 8, Ireland (office). *Telephone:* (1) 6660000 (office). *Website:* www.garda.ie.

HARRIS, Kamala Devi, JD; American lawyer and politician; *Senator from California;* b. 20 Oct. 1964, Oakland, Calif.; d. of Donald Harris and Shyamala

Gopalan; ed Howard Univ., Univ. of California, Hastings Coll. of Law; spent several years in Prosecutor's Office, including Deputy Dist Attorney, Alameda Co., Calif. 1990–98, Man. Attorney, Career Criminal Unit, San Francisco Dist Attorney's Office 1998–2000, Chief of Community and Neighborhood Div., Office of San Francisco City Attorney 2000–04, Dist Attorney of San Francisco 2004–10, Attorney-Gen. of Calif. 2011–17; Senator from California 2017–. *Publications include:* Smart on Crime: A Career Prosecutor's Plan to Make Us Safer 2009. *Address:* B40B, Dirksen Senate Office, United States Senate, Washington, DC 20510, USA (office). *Telephone:* (202) 224-3553 (office). *Website:* www.senate.gov (office).

HARRIS, Sir Martin Best, Kt, CBE, PhD, DL; British administrator and fmr university vice-chancellor; b. 28 June 1944, Ruabon, Wales; s. of William Best Harris and Betty Evelyn Harris (née Martin); m. Barbara Mary Daniels 1966; two s.; ed Devonport High School, Plymouth, Queens' Coll., Cambridge, School of Oriental and African Studies, Univ. of London; Lecturer in French Linguistics, Univ. of Leicester 1967–72; Sr Lecturer in French Linguistics, Univ. of Salford 1972–76, Prof. of Romance Linguistics 1976–87, Pro-Vice-Chancellor 1981–87; Vice-Chancellor, Univ. of Essex 1987–92, Univ. of Manchester 1992–2004; Chair. Cttee of Vice-Chancellors and Prins 1997–99; mem. Univ. Grants Cttee 1984–87, Chair. Northern Ireland Sub-Cttee 1985–87; Chair. Northern Ireland Cttee, Univs Funding Council 1987–91, Nat. Curriculum Working Group on Modern Languages 1989–90, HEFCE/CVCP Review of Postgraduate Educ. 1995–96, Clinical Standards Advisory Group 1996–99, North West Univs Assen 1999–2001, Higher Educ. Careers Advisory Services Review 2000–01, Manchester: Knowledge Capital 2003–08; Deputy Chair. Northwest Devt Agency 2002–08; Pres. Clare Hall, Cambridge Univ. 2008–13; mem. Bd Universities' Superannuation Scheme Ltd 1991–2015, Deputy Chair. 2004–06, Chair. 2006–15; Dir Office of Fair Access 2004–12; Chair. of Govs, Centre for Information on Language Teaching 1990–96; Crown Gov. SOAS 1990–93; Gov. Anglia Polytechnic Univ. 1989–93; mem. High Council, European Univ. Inst., Florence 1992–97, Comm. for Health Improvement 1999–2002; DL (Greater Manchester) 1997; Hon. mem. Royal Northern Coll. of Music 1996; Hon. Fellow, Queens' Coll., Cambridge 1992, Bolton Inst. 1996, Univ. of Central Lancashire 1999; Hon. LLD (Queen's Univ., Belfast) 1992; Hon. DUniv (Essex) 1993; Hon. DLitt (Salford) 1995, (Manchester Metropolitan) 2000, (Leicester) 2003, (Lincoln) 2003, (Ulster) 2004, (Manchester) 2004, (UMIST) 2004, (Keele) 2006, (Exeter) 2008, (Plymouth) 2009, (London) 2013. *Publications include:* The Evolution of French Syntax 1978, The Romance Languages (with N. Vincent) 1988; numerous articles in anthologies and professional journals. *Leisure interests:* gardening, walking.

HARRIS, Michael, BSc, PhD; American mathematician and academic; *Professor of Mathematics, Université de Paris 7 Denis Diderot;* ed Princeton Univ. and Harvard Univ; held positions at Brandeis Univ. 1977–94, Prof. 1989–94; Prof. Institut de Math de Jussieu, Université de Paris 7 Denis Diderot 1994–; mem. Institut Universitaire de France 2001; Sloan Fellowshiop 1982, Grand Prix Sophie Germain de l'Acad. des Sciences 2006, Clay Research Award, Clay Math. Inst. (co-recipient) 2007. *Publications:* more than 60 publs in professional journals. *Address:* Institut de Mathématiques de Jussieu, Université Paris 7 Denis Diderot, Tour 15-25, 4ème étage, bureau 420, 4 place Jussieu, 75252 Paris Cedex 05, France (office). *Telephone:* 1-44-27-86-78 (office). *E-mail:* michael.harris@imj-prg.fr (office). *Website:* webusers.imj-prg.fr (office).

HARRIS, Michael (Mike) Deane, ICD.D; Canadian business executive, consultant and fmr politician; *Senior Business Advisor, Fasken Martineau DuMoulin LLP;* b. 23 Jan. 1945, Toronto, Ont.; s. of Deane Harris and Hope Harris; m. Laura Marie Harris; two s.; ed Inst. of Corp. Dirs; fmr school teacher, School Bd Trustee and School Bd Chair. Nipissing Bd of Educ.; began career in tourism and recreation industry owning ventures including tourist resort and ski centre; first elected to Ont. Prov. Legislature as MPP for Nipissing 1981, Minister of Natural Resources and Energy 1985, Premier of Prov. of Ont. 1995–2002; Leader of Conservative Party 1990–2002; fmr Sr Business Advisor, Cassels Brock & Blackwell LLP; currently Sr Business Advisor, Fasken Martineau DuMoulin LLP; mem. Bd of Dirs, Chartwell Retirement Residences 2003– (Chair.), Canaccord Genuity Inc. 2004–, Colliers International Group Inc. 2006–, Route1 Inc. 2009– (Chair.); Sr Fellow, Fraser Inst., Vancouver; Hon. DLitt (Nipissing Univ.) 2010; Nat. Citizens' Coalition Freedom Medal 1996, E.P. Taylor Award of Merit, Standardbred Canada 2000, Tax Fighter of the Year Award, Canadian Taxpayer's Fed. 2000, Paul Harris Award, Rotary Club of North Bay 2008, Harris Learning Library, Nipissing Univ. 2011. *Leisure interests:* golf, skiing, bridge. *Address:* Fasken, 2400-333 Bay Street, Toronto, ON M5H 2T6, Canada (office). *Telephone:* (416) 865-4535 (office). *Fax:* (416) 364-7813 (office). *E-mail:* mharris@fasken.com (office). *Website:* www.fasken.com (office).

HARRIS, Naomie Melanie, OBE; English actress; b. 6 Sept. 1976, Islington, London; d. of Carmen Harris; ed Pembroke Coll., Cambridge. *Plays include:* The Witch of Edmonton 2000, Frankenstein 2011. *Films include:* Crust 2001, Living In Hope 2002, Anansi 2002, 28 Days Later 2002, Trauma 2004, After the Sunset 2004, Pirates of the Caribbean: Dead Man's Chest 2006, Miami Vice 2006, A Cock and Bull Story 2006, Pirates of the Caribbean: At World's End 2007, Street Kings 2008, Explicit Ills 2008, August 2008, Morris: A Life with Bells On 2009, Ninja Assassin 2009, Sex & Drugs & Rock & Roll 2009, My Last Five Girlfriends 2009, The First Grader 2010, Skyfall 2012, Mandela: Long Walk to Freedom 2013, Southpaw 2015, Spectre 2015, Our Kind of Traitor 2016, Moonlight 2016, Collateral Beauty 2016. *Television includes:* Simon and the Witch (series) 1987–88, Erasmus Microman (series) 1989, Runaway Bay (series) 1992–93, The Tomorrow People (series) 1992–95, Trial & Retribution (series) 2002, White Teeth (mini-series) 2002, The Project (film) 2002, Dinotopia (series) 2002–03, Poppy Shakespeare (film) 2008, Small Island (film) 2009, Blood and Oil (film) 2009, Accused (series) 2010. *Address:* c/o Tavistock Wood, 45 Conduit Street, London W1S 2YN, England (office). *Telephone:* (20) 7494-4767 (office). *E-mail:* info@tavistockwood.com (office). *Website:* www.tavistockwood.com (office).

HARRIS, Patricia (Patti), BA; American foundation executive and fmr public servant; *CEO, Bloomberg Philanthropies;* b. 1 Sept. 1955, New York; d. of Walter E. Harris; m. Mark Denis Lebow; three c.; ed Franklin and Marshall Coll.; Asst to Rep. Edward Koch, US House of Reps, Washington, DC 1977–79; Asst to Deputy Mayor, New York City 1979–83; Exec. Dir, New York City Art Comm. 1983–90; Vice-Pres. of Corp. and Cultural Marketing, Rogers & Cowan 1990–92; Vice-Pres. of Public Relations, Serino Coyne Advertising 1992–94; Man., Corp. Communications, Bloomberg LP 1994–2002; First Deputy Mayor, New York City 2002–13; CEO, Bloomberg Philanthropies 2010–; mem. Bd of Trustees, Franklin and Marshall Coll. 2006–; mem. Bd of Dirs Nat. September 11 Memorial and Museum, World Trade Center. *Address:* Bloomberg Philanthropies, 800 Third Avenue, New York, NY 10022, USA (office). *Telephone:* (212) 205-0100 (office). *E-mail:* info@bloomberg.org (office). *Website:* www.bloomberg.org (office).

HARRIS, Robert Dennis, FRSL; British journalist and writer; b. 7 March 1957, Nottingham; s. of Dennis Harris and Audrey Harris; m. Gill Hornby 1988; two s. two d.; ed Univ. of Cambridge; Pres. Cambridge Union; Dir and reporter, BBC 1978–86; Political Ed. Observer 1987–89; columnist, Sunday Times 1989–92, 1996–97. *Publications include:* non-fiction: A Higher Form of Killing (with Jeremy Paxman) 1982, Gotcha! 1983, The Making of Neil Kinnock 1984, Selling Hitler 1987, Good and Faithful Servant 1990; novels: Fatherland 1992, Enigma 1995 (film 2001), Archangel 1998, Pompeii 2003, Imperium 2006, The Ghost 2007, Lustrum 2009, Conspirata 2010, The Fear Index 2011, An Officer and a Spy (Popular Fiction Book of the Year, Specsavers Nat. Book Awards) 2013, Dictator 2015, Conclave 2016. *Leisure interests:* collecting books, walking. *Address:* Old Vicarage, Church Street, Kintbury, RG17 9TR, England (home). *Website:* www.robert-harris.com.

HARRIS, Stephen E., BS, MS, PhD; American physicist and academic; *Kenneth and Barbara Oshman Professor Emeritus, Department of Applied Physics, Stanford University;* b. 29 Nov. 1936, Brooklyn, New York; s. of Henry Harris and Anne Alpern Harris; m. Frances J. Greene 1959; one s. one d.; ed Rensselaer Polytechnic, Troy, New York and Stanford Univ.; Prof. of Electrical Eng, Stanford Univ. 1963–79, of Electrical Eng and Applied Physics 1979–88, Kenneth and Barbara Oshman Prof. 1988, now Prof. Emer., Dir Edward L. Ginzton Lab. 1983–88, Chair. Dept of Applied Physics 1993–96; Stephen E. Harris Endowed Prof., Texas A&M Univ. 2005; Guggenheim Fellowship 1976–77; Fellow, Optical Soc. of America 1968, IEEE 1972, American Physical Soc. 1975, American Acad. of Arts and Sciences 1995; mem., Nat. Acad. of Eng, NAS; Hon. mem. Optical Soc. of America 2013–; A. Noble Prize 1965, McGraw Research Award 1973, Sarnoff Award 1978, Davies Medal 1984, C. H. Townes Award 1985, Einstein Prize 1991, Quantum Electronics Award 1994, Frederic Ives Medal 1999, Arthur L. Schawlow Prize in Laser Science 2002, Harvey Prize 2007, inducted into Rensselaer Polytechnic Alumni Hall of Fame 2015. *Achievements include:* holds 16 US patents. *Publications:* articles in professional journals. *Leisure interests:* skiing, jogging, hiking. *Address:* Edward L. Ginzton Laboratory, Stanford University, 350 Via Palou, Mall Room 204, Stanford, CA 94305-4088, USA (office). *Telephone:* (650) 725-2248 (office). *Fax:* (650) 725-2666 (office). *E-mail:* seharris@stanford.edu (office). *Website:* ginzton.stanford.edu (office).

HARRIS, Thomas; American writer; b. 11 April 1940, Jackson, Tenn.; s. of William Thomas Harris, Jr and Polly Harris; m. (divorced); one d.; ed Baylor Univ.; worked on news desk at Waco News-Tribune newspaper; mem. staff, Associated Press, New York City 1968–74. *Publications include:* Black Sunday 1975, Red Dragon 1981, The Silence of the Lambs (Bram Stoker Best Novel Award) 1988, Hannibal 1999, Hannibal Rising 2007. *Address:* c/o Janklow & Nesbit Associates, 445 Park Avenue, New York, NY 10022, USA. *Website:* www.randomhouse.com/features/thomasharris.

HARRIS, Timothy Sylvester, BSc, MSc, PhD; Saint Kitts and Nevis politician; *Prime Minister and Minister of Finance;* b. 6 Dec. 1964, Tabernacle; two d.; ed Cayon High School, Basseterre Sr High School, Univ. of the West Indies, Cave Hill and Sr Augustine, Concordia Univ., Montreal, Canada; worked at Social Security Office, Wellington Ltd and S. L. Horsford & Co. Ltd; mem. Labour Party –2013, Constituency Sec. and Constituency Rep. on Nat. Exec. Bd, mem. Young Labour Advisory Cttee, and Youth Co-ordinator, fmr Chair. St Kitts-Nevis Labour Party; Leader, People's Labour Party 2013–; mem. Parl. 1993–; Minister of Agric., Lands and Housing 1995–2000, of Foreign Affairs and Educ. 2000–04, of Foreign Affairs, Int. Trade, Industry, Commerce and Consumer Affairs 2004–10, of Int. Trade, Industry, Commerce, Agric., Marine Resources, Consumer Affairs and Constituency Empowerment 2010–13; Prime Minister and Minister of Finance 2015–; Chair. Caribbean Devt Bank 2015; Chair. Org. of Eastern Caribbean States 2016–; Victor Cooke Prize, Univ. of W Indies, Post Graduate Award, Cen. Bank of Trinidad and Tobago, Concordia/UWI Post Graduate Award. *Publications:* St Kitts and Nevis: A Portrait of a Nation Celebrating 25 Years of Independence 2008; several articles in journals. *Leisure interests:* cricket, tennis, swimming, basketball, dominoes, travel. *Address:* Office of the Prime Minister, Government Headquarters, Church Street, PO Box 186, Basseterre, Saint Kitts and Nevis (office); Ministry of Finance, Finance Building, Golden Rock, Basseterre, Saint Kitts and Nevis (office). *Telephone:* 465-0299 (office); 467-1092 (Ministry of Finance) (office); (869) 465-7768 (home). *Fax:* 465-1001 (office); 465-1532 (Ministry of Finance) (office). *E-mail:* timskb@yahoo.co.uk (home). *Website:* www.gov.kn (office); mof.govt.kn (office).

HARRISON, (William) Alistair, CMG, CVO, MA, DipEcon; British diplomatist and government official; *Marshal of the Diplomatic Corps;* b. 14 Nov. 1954, Guisborough, North Yorks., England; m. Sarah Wood 1996; one s. two d.; ed Newcastle Royal Grammar School, Univ. Coll., Oxford, Univ. of London; joined Defence Dept, FCO 1977, Third, then Second Sec., Embassy in Warsaw 1979–82, First Sec. Cyprus/Malta Desk, FCO 1982–84, Pvt. Sec. to Parl. Under-Sec. 1984–87, First Sec., Perm. Mission to UN, New York 1987–92, Deputy Head of Middle East Dept, FCO 1992–95, Deputy Head of Mission, Embassy in Warsaw 1995–98, Foreign Policy Adviser, European Comm. 1998–2000, Counsellor and Head of Chancery, Perm. Mission to UN, New York 2000–03, Head of UN Dept, then Head of Int. Orgs Dept 2003–05, High Commr to Zambia 2005–08, Head of Zimbabwe Unit, FCO 2008, Gov. of Anguilla 2009–13, Marshal of the Diplomatic Corps 2014–. *Leisure interests:* music, skiing, sailing, tennis, bridge, golf. *Address:* The Lord Chamberlain's Office, Royal Household, Buckingham Palace, London, SW1A 1AA, England. *Website:* www.royal.gov.uk.

HARRISON, Sir David, Kt, CBE, ScD, FREng, FRSC, FIChemE, CCMI, FRSA, FRSCM; British chemist and academic; b. 3 May 1930, Clacton-on-Sea, Essex, England; s. of Harold David Harrison and Lavinia Wilson; m. Sheila Rachel Debes

1962; one s. one d. (one s. deceased); ed Bede School, Sunderland, Clacton County High School, Selwyn Coll., Univ. of Cambridge; Lecturer in Chemical Eng, Univ. of Cambridge 1956–79, Fellow, Selwyn Coll. 1957–, Sr Tutor 1967–79, Master of Selwyn Coll. 1994–2000, Chair. Faculty of Eng 1994–2001, mem. Council, Univ. of Cambridge 1967–75, 1995–2000, Chair. Faculty Bd of Educ. 1976–78, Deputy Vice-Chancellor 1995–2000, Pro-Vice-Chancellor 1997; Vice-Chancellor Univ. of Keele 1979–84, Univ. of Exeter 1984–94; Visiting Prof. of Chemical Eng, Univ. of Delaware, USA 1967, Univ. of Sydney, Australia 1976; Hon. Ed. Transactions, Inst. of Chemical Engineers 1972–78; Chair. Bd Trustees, Homerton Coll., Cambridge 1979–2010, Council Ely Cathedral 2001–, Univs' Cen. Council for Admissions 1984–91, Church & Associated Colls Advisory Cttee of the Polytechnics and Colls Funding Council 1989–91, Cttee of Vice-Chancellors and Prins of UK 1991–93, Shrewsbury School 1989–2003, Advisory Cttee on Safety of Nuclear Installations 1993–99, Eastern Arts Bd 1994–98, Arts Council of England 1996–98; Dir Salters' Inst. of Industrial Chem. 1993–; Vice-Pres. Inst. of Chemical Engineers 1989, Pres. 1991–92; Fellow, Royal Acad. of Eng, Royal School of Church Music; Liveryman, Salters' Co. 1998; Hon. DUniv (Keele) 1992, (York) 2008; Hon. DSc (Exeter) 1995; George E. Davis Medal, Inst. of Chemical Engineers 2001. *Publications include:* Fluidized Particles (with J. F. Davidson) 1963, Fluidization (with J. F. Davidson) 1971, Fluidization (with J. F. Davidson and R. Clift) 1985. *Leisure interests:* music, tennis, hill walking, good food. *Address:* 7 Gough Way, Cambridge, Cambs., CB3 9LN, England (home). *Telephone:* (1223) 359315 (home). *E-mail:* sirdavidharrison@yahoo.co.uk (home).

HARRISON, Patricia De Stacy, MA; American government official and broadcast executive; *President and CEO, Corporation for Public Broadcasting;* b. Brooklyn, New York; m. Emmett Bruce Harrison; three c.; ed American Univ.; mem. Pres.'s Export Council 1990, fmr mem. Exec. Cttee; mem. US Trade Rep.'s Service Policy Advisory Council 1992; Co-Chair. Republican Nat. Cttee 1997–2001; Asst Sec. for Educ. and Cultural Affairs, US Dept of State, Washington, DC 2001–05, Acting Under-Sec. for Public Diplomacy and Public Affairs 2004; Pres. and CEO Corpn for Public Broadcasting, Washington, DC 2005–; Founding Pnr, E. Bruce Harrison Co. (public relations agency) 1973–96; Founder and Pres. Nat. Women's Econ. Alliance; fmr Pres. Capital Press Women; fmr Chair. Guest Services Inc., Int. Cttee, Small Business Advisory Council, Small Business Admin; Visiting Fellow John F. Kennedy School of Govt 1992, Inst. for Public Service, Annenberg Public Policy Center 2000; est. Partnerships for Learning initiative; Dr hc (American Univ. of Rome) 2002; Entrepreneur of the Year, Arthur Young Co. and Venture Magazine 1988, Northwood Inst. Distinguished Woman Award 1989, Hispanic Heritage Leadership Award 1998, Global Women's Leadership Award 1999, Woman of the Year Award, New York Black Republican Council 1999, Ellis Island Medal of Honor, Nat. Ethnic Coalition of Organizations 2017, Sec. of State's Distinguished Service Award. *Publications:* A Seat at the Table: An Insider's Guide for America's New Women Leaders, America's New Women Entrepreneurs 1986. *Address:* Corporation for Public Broadcasting, 401 Ninth Street, NW, Washington, DC 20004-2129, USA (office). *Telephone:* (202) 879-9600 (office). *Website:* www.cpb.org (office).

HARRISON, Stephen Coplan, AB, PhD; American biochemist, pharmacologist, professor of paediatrics and academic; *Professor of Biological Chemistry and Molecular Pharmacology and of Pediatrics and Giovanni Armenise-Harvard Professor in Basic Biomedical Sciences, Harvard Medical School;* b. New Haven, Conn.; ed Harvard Coll. and Harvard Univ.; Henry Fellow, Univ. of Cambridge and MRC Lab. of Molecular Biology, Cambridge, UK 1964–65; Resident Tutor and Tutor in Biology, Lowell House, Harvard Univ. 1965–68; Helen Hay Whitney Postdoctoral Research Fellow, Children's Cancer Research Foundation, Boston, Mass 1967–68, Research Assoc. in Pathology 1969–71; Research Fellow in Biophysics, Harvard Univ. 1967–68, Jr Fellow, Soc. of Fellows 1968–71, mem. Faculty 1971–, Asst Prof. of Biochemistry 1971–75, Non-resident Tutor, Lowell House 1971–, Chair. Bd of Tutors in Biochemical Sciences 1971–96, Assoc. Prof. of Biochemistry 1975–77, Prof. of Biochemistry and Molecular Biology 1977–88, Chair. Dept of Biochemistry and Molecular Biology (Faculty of Arts and Sciences) 1988–92, Higgins Prof. of Biochemistry 1998–2002, Acting Head Tutor in Biochemical Sciences 2000–02, Prof. of Biological Chem. and Molecular Pharmacology and Prof. of Pediatrics, Harvard Medical School 1996–, Dir Center for Structural Biology 1996–2002, Dir Center for Molecular and Cellular Dynamics, Harvard Medical School 2002–, Giovanni Armenise-Harvard Prof. in Basic Biomedical Sciences 2007–, Acting Chair. Dept of Biological Chem. and Molecular Pharmacology, Harvard Medical School 2009–12, Head of Lab. of Molecular Medicine, Boston Children's Hosp. 1996–, Investigator, Howard Hughes Medical Inst., Harvard Univ. 1987–; Visiting Research Assoc. in Biophysics, Max-Planck Inst. 1971–72; Visiting Prof., Faculty of Biology, Univ. of Heidelberg, Germany 1971–72; Visiting Fellow Commoner, Trinity Coll., Cambridge 1977; Visiting Scientist, MRC Lab. of Molecular Biology, Cambridge 1977; Vice-Pres. and Chair. Scientific Advisory Bd, Helen Hay Whitney Foundation 2000–; mem. Scientific Advisory Bd, Novartis Foundation 2000–; mem. Editorial Bd, Structure 1993–, Cell 2001–05; mem. NAS 1991, American Philosophical Soc. 1997, American Crystallographic Asscn, American Soc. for Microbiology, American Soc. for Virology; Foreign mem. European Molecular Biology Org. 2001, Royal Soc. 2014; Fellow, American Acad. of Arts and Sciences 1989, AAAS 2005; Ledlie Prize, Harvard Univ. 1982, Sumner Lecturer, Cornell Univ. 1984, John T. Edsall Lecturer, Harvard Univ. 1987, Wallace P. Rowe Award, Nat. Inst. of Allergy and Infectious Diseases 1988, Shipley Symposium Lecturer, Harvard Medical School 1988, Harvey Lecturer, The Harvey Soc., New York 1990, Louisa Gross Horwitz Prize, Columbia Univ. (co-recipient) 1990, E.J. Cohn Lecturer, Harvard Medical School 1991, Stein Memorial Lecturer, Rockefeller Univ., NY 1992, Searle Distinguished Lectureship, Northwestern Univ. 1995, ICN Int. Prize in Virology 1998, Klaus Hoffman Lectureship, Univ. of Pittsburgh 2000, Paul Ehrlich and Ludwig Darmstaedter Prize (co-recipient) 2001, Bristol Myers Squibb Distinguished Achievement Award in Infectious Disease Research 2005, Gregori Aminoff Prize in Crystallography, Royal Swedish Acad. of Sciences 2006, Univ. of California, San Diego/Merck Life Sciences Achievement Award 2007, Hans Neurath Lecturer, Univ. of Washington, Seattle 2007, Harland Wood Memorial Lecturer, Case Western Reserve Univ. 2011, William Silen Lifetime Achievement in Mentoring Award 2011, Pauling Lectureship, Stanford Univ. 2012, Welch Award in Chem., Welch Foundation 2015. *Publications:* numerous papers in professional journals on structural biology, in particular the structures of viruses and viral proteins. *Address:* Harrison Laboratory, BCMP, Harvard Medical School, Seeley G. Mudd 130, 250 Longwood Avenue, Boston, MA 02115 (office); 19R Sparhawk Street, Boston, MA 02135, USA (home). *Telephone:* (617) 432-5609 (office); (617) 432-5601 (Lab.) (office). *Fax:* (617) 432-5600 (office). *E-mail:* schadmin@crystal.harvard.edu (office). *Website:* crystal.harvard.edu/pages/StephenHarrison (office); www.hhmi.org/scientists/stephen-c-harrison (office).

HARRISON, Sir Terence, Kt, BSc, DL, FREng, FIMechE, FIMARE; British business executive (retd); b. 7 April 1933; s. of Roland Harrison and Doris Wardle; m. June Forster 1956; two s.; ed A. J. Dawson Grammar School, Co. Durham, West Hartlepool and Sunderland Tech. Colls. and Univ. of Durham; marine eng apprenticeship, Richardson's Westgarth, Hartlepool 1949–53; mil. service, Nigeria 1955–57; Clarke Chapman Ltd, Gateshead 1957–77, Man. Dir 1976–77; Northern Eng Industries 1977, Chief Exec. 1983–86, Exec. Chair. 1986–89; Dir Rolls-Royce PLC 1989–96, Chief Exec. 1992–96; fmr Chair. Newcastle United PLC; Dir (non-exec.) Alfred McAlpine PLC 1995–2002, Chair. 1996–2002; Hon. DEng (Newcastle) 1991; Hon. DTech (Sunderland) 1995; Hon. DSc (Durham) 1996. *Publications:* technical papers. *Leisure interests:* golf, fell walking. *Address:* 2 The Garden Houses, Whalton, Northumberland, NE61 3HB, England (home). *Telephone:* (1670) 775400 (home). *Fax:* (1670) 775291 (home).

HARRISON, Tony; British poet, dramatist and director; b. 30 April 1937, Leeds, Yorks.; s. of Harry Ashton Harrison and Florence Horner (née Wilkinson); m. Sian Thomas; ed Leeds Grammar School and Univ. of Leeds; Dramatist, Nat. Theatre 1977–78; Northern Arts Literary Fellow 1967–68, 1976–77; Hon. DPhil (Athens); Hon. DLitt (Leeds); Cholmondeley Award for Poetry, Geoffrey Faber Memorial Award, European Poetry Translation Prize, Whitbread Poetry Prize 1993, Mental Health Award 1994, Prix Italia 1994, Northern Rock Foundation Writers' Award 2004, PEN/Pinter Prize 2009, Wilfred Owen Award for Poetry 2008, European Prize for Literature (Strasbourg) 2011, David Cohen Prize for Literature 2015. *Plays include:* Aikin Mata (with J. Simmons) 1965, The Misanthrope (version of Molière's play) 1973, Phaedra Britannica (version of Racine's Phèdre) 1975, The Passion 1977, Bow Down 1977, The Bartered Bride (libretto) 1978, The Oresteia (trans.) 1981, The Mysteries 1985, The Trackers of Oxyrhynchus 1990, The Common Chorus 1992, Square Rounds 1992, Poetry or Bust 1993, The Kaisers of Carnuntum 1995, The Labourers of Herakles 1995, The Prince's Play 1996, Fire and Poetry 1999, Hecuba 2005, Fram 2008. *Writing for TV and film includes:* Yan Tan Tethera 1983, The Big H 1984, 'V' 1987, Loving Memory 1987, The Blasphemers' Banquet 1989, The Gaze of the Gorgon 1992, Black Daisies for the Bride 1993, A Maybe Day in Kazakhstan 1994, The Shadow of Hiroshima 1995, Prometheus 1998, Crossings 2002. *Publications include:* poetry: Earthworks 1964, Newcastle is Peru 1969, The Loiners 1970, Poems of Palladas of Alexandria (ed. and trans.) 1973, From the School of Eloquence and Other Poems 1978, Continuous 1981, A Kumquat for John Keats 1981, US Martial 1981, Selected Poems 1984, Fire-Gap 1985, 'V' 1985, Dramatic Verse, 1973–1985 1985, 'V' and Other Poems 1990, A Cold Coming: Gulf War Poems 1991, The Gaze of the Gorgon and other poems 1992, The Shadow of Hiroshima and other film/poems 1995, Permanently Bard 1995, Laureate's Block and other poems 2000, Under the Clock 2005, Collected Poems 2007, Collected Film Poetry 2007; collections of plays: Plays 1 1985, Theatre Works 1973–1985 1986, Plays 2 2002, Plays 3 1996, Plays 4 2002, Plays 5 2004, Hecuba 2005, Fram 2008. *Address:* c/o Emma Cheshire, Faber & Faber Ltd, Bloomsbury House, 74–77 Great Russell Street, London, WC1B 3DA, England (office).

HARRISON, Wayne David, BA, AM; Australian theatre director and producer; *Head of Creation, Spiegelworld International;* b. 7 March 1953, Melbourne; s. of Lindsay Graham Harrison and Florence Rosina Cannell; ed Christian Brothers' Coll., Melbourne, Univ. of Melbourne, Univ. of New South Wales; Dramaturge, Sydney Theatre Co. 1981–86; Asst Dir Northside Theatre Co., NSW 1987–89; Artistic Dir Sydney Theatre Co. 1990–99; Creative Dir Back Row Int., London and Clear Channel Entertainment Europe 1999–2001; Creative Dir New Year's Eve celebration, Sydney 2005–07, Closing Ceremony 2006 Melbourne Commonwealth Games, Helpmann Awards for Live Performance 2007; Dir 2 Weeks with the Queen, Adelaide's Windmill Theatre Arts, End of the Rainbow, Sydney, Melbourne, Edinburgh Festival; currently Head of Creation, Spiegelworld Int.; mem. Advisory Bd Alex Buzo Co. *Plays directed include:* Alone it Stands, Mum's The Word for Mollison Productions 2002, The Return of Houdini for City Theatre, Reykjavik 2005, Sunset Boulevard for The Production Company, Melbourne 2005, End of The Rainbow for Ensemble Theatre, Sydney Opera House and MTC, Melbourne 2005, Just Macbeth for Bell Shakespeare Co. 2008, Absinthe and Desir for Spiegelworld Productions 2008, The Normal Heart, A Little Night Music, Shadowlands, Into the Woods, The Gift of the Gorgon, Much Ado About Nothing, Two Weeks with the Queen, Dead White Males, Heretic, Medea, Amy's View. *Address:* Spiegelworld International, 4625 S. Polaris Avenue, Suite 110, Las Vegas, NV 89103, USA (office). *Telephone:* (702) 749-5881 (office). *E-mail:* info@spiegelworld.com (office); wayne@wayneharrison.com. *Website:* www.spiegelworld.com (office); www.wayneharrison.com.

HARRISON, William Burwell, Jr, AB; American banker; b. 12 Aug. 1943, Rocky Mount, NC; s. of William Burwell and Katherine Spruill; m. Anne MacDonald Stephens 1985; two d.; ed Univ. of North Carolina; trainee, Chemical Bank, New York 1967–69, Mid-South Corpn and corresp. banking group 1969–74, West Coast corp. and corresp. banking group 1974–76, Dist Head and Western Regional Co-ordinator San Francisco 1976–78, Regional Co-ordinator and Sr Vice-Pres. London 1978–82, Sr Vice-Pres. and Divisional Head, Europe 1982–83, Exec. Vice-Pres. US corp. div. New York 1983–87, Group Exec., banking and corporate finance group 1987–90, Vice-Chair. institutional banking 1990–2000; Vice-Chair. Global Bank 1992–2000; Vice-Chair. Manhattan Corpn (then Chase Manhattan Corpn) New York 1995–2000, Pres. and CEO 1999–2000, Chair. and CEO 2000, Pres. JPMorgan Chase (following merger) 2000–04, CEO 2000–05, Chair. 2001–06; mem. investment advisory cttee, Aurora Capital Partners 2008–; mem. Bd of Dirs Merck & Co., Cousins Properties, Inc.; mem. The Business Council. *Leisure interests:* athletics, travel. *Address:* c/o Aurora Capital Partners, 10877 Wilshire Boulevard, Suite 2100, Los Angeles, CA 90024, USA (office).

HARRY, Deborah (Debbie) Ann; American singer and actress; b. 1 July 1945, Miami, Fla; d. of Richard Smith and Catherine Harry (Peters); ed Centenary Coll.;

singer and songwriter, rock group Blondie 1975–83, group reformed 1997. *Singles include:* Heart of Glass, Call Me, Tide is High, Rapture. *Recordings include:* albums: with Blondie: Blondie 1976, Plastic Letters 1977, Parallel Lines 1978, Eat to the Beat 1979, Autoamerican 1980, The Hunter 1982, Rapture 1994, No Exit 1999, Livid 2000, The Curse of Blondie 2003, Panic of Girls 2011, Ghosts of Download 2014, Pollinator 2017; solo: Koo Koo 1981, Rockbird 1986, Def, Dumb and Blonde 1989, Debravation 1993, Virtuosity (with the Heads) 1995, Necessary Evil 2007, Ghosts of Download 2014. *Film appearances include:* The Foreigner 1978, Unmade Beds 1980, Union City 1980, New York Beat Movie 1981, Videodrome 1983, Forever, Lulu 1987, Satisfaction 1988, Hairspray 1988, New York Stories 1989, Tales from the Darkside: The Movie 1990, Dead Beat 1994, Drop Dead Rock 1995, Heavy 1995, Cop Land 1997, Six Ways to Sunday 1997, Joe's Day 1998, Zoo 1999, Red Lipstick 2000, Deuces Wild 2000, Spun 2002, Try Seventeen 2002, My Life Without Me 2003, A Good Night to Die 2003, Tulse Luper Suitcases, Part 1: The Moab Story 2003, Patch 2005, I Remember You Now 2005, Elegy 2008, River of Fundament 2014. *Theatre includes:* Teaneck Tanzi, The Venus Flytrap. *Address:* Tenth Street Entertainment, 6420 Wilshire Blvd, #950, Los Angeles, CA 90048, USA (office). *E-mail:* info@10thst.com (office). *Website:* www.blondie.net; www.deborahharry.com.

HART, Ann Weaver, MA, PhD; American professor of educational administration and university administrator; *President, University of Arizona;* b. Salt Lake City, Utah; m. Randy B. Hart; four d.; ed Univ. of Utah; began career teaching math., English and history at Cottonwood High School and Bonneville Jr High, Salt Lake City 1971–74; Prin. Farrer Jr High School, Provo, Utah 1983–84; Asst Prof., Educational Admin Dept, Univ. of Utah 1984, held various positions including Prof. of Educational Leadership, Assoc. Dean, then Dean of Grad. School of Educ., Accreditation Liaison Officer and Special Asst to Pres. –1998; Provost, Vice-Pres. for Academic Affairs and Faculty mem., Claremont Grad. Univ., Calif. 1998–2002; Pres. Univ. of New Hampshire 2002–06; Pres. Temple Univ., Phila 2006–12; Pres. Univ. of Arizona 2012–, also Prof. of Educational Policy Studies and Practice, College of Educ.; fmr Pres. Western Asscn of Grad. Schools; fmr Chair. Research Cttee Grad. Record Examination, Educational Testing Service; fmr Ed. Educational Administration Quarterly; mem. Asscn of American Universities, Asscn of Public Land Grant Universities, Arizona State Bd of Educ., Campus Research Corporation, Greater Phoenix Leadership, Southern Arizona Leadership Council, Tucson Regional Economic Opportunities, Chairman's Circle, Udall Foundation; fmr mem. Bd of Dirs Citizens Bank of New Hampshire; awards from Univ. Council for Educational Admin 1992, Business and Professional Women's Foundation 1995, Utah Women's Forum, Univ. of Utah Distinguished Alumna Humanities 2004, Business New Hampshire Magazine (Ten Most Powerful People in NH) 2006, Jack Culbertson Award in Educational Admin, Univ. Council for Educational Admin, Outstanding Professional Award, Business and Professional Women's Foundation, PoWeR Award, Professional Women's Roundtable, Champion of Diversity and Access Award, Urban STEM Strategy Group 2009, Outstanding Community Service Award, Network for Teaching Entrepreneurship. *Publications:* The Principalship: A Theory of Professional Learning and Practice (co-author) 1996, Designing and Conducting Research (co-author) 1996; more than 85 refereed journal articles and book chapters, five books and edited vols and numerous articles in publs on leadership succession and development, work redesign and organizational behaviour in educational organizations, and academic freedom. *Leisure interests:* cross-country hiking, camping in Wind River Range, Wyo., kayaking, bicycling. *Address:* Office of the President, University of Arizona, Administration Building, Room 712, 1401 East University Boulevard, PO Box 210066, Tucson, AZ 85721-0066, USA (office). *Telephone:* (520) 621-5511 (office). *Fax:* (520) 621-9323 (office). *E-mail:* president@email.arizona.edu (office). *Website:* president.arizona.edu (office).

HART, Gary, BA, BD, JD, DPhil, LLB; American politician and lawyer; *Founder and Chairman, American Security Project;* b. 28 Nov. 1936, Ottawa, Kan.; m. Lee Ludwig 1958; one s. one d.; ed Bethany Coll., Okla, Yale Univ.; assisted in John F. Kennedy Presidential Campaign 1960; called to Bar 1964; Attorney, US Dept of Justice and Special Asst to Sec., US Dept of Interior 1964–67; voluntary organizer, Robert F. Kennedy Presidential Campaign 1968; legal practice, Denver, Colo 1967–70, 1972–74; Nat. Campaign Dir, George McGovern Democratic Presidential Campaign 1970–72; Senator for Colorado 1975–86; with Davis, Graham & Stubbs, (law firm) Denver 1985; Of Counsel, Coudert Brothers LLP 1988–2003; co-Chair. US Comm. on Nat. Security for the 21st Century (Hart-Rudman Comm.) 1998–2000; Chair. Council for a Livable World 2006–09, mem. Bd of Dirs; Founder, American Security Project 2007–; Vice-Chair. Homeland Security Advisory Council 2008–11; US Special Envoy for Northern Ireland, United States Department of State 2014–17; Sr Strategic Advisor and Ind. Consultant-Denver, McKenna Long & Aldridge LLP 2012–15; Wirth Chair Prof., Univ. of Colorado; fmr mem. Bd of Commrs, Denver Urban Renewal Authority; fmr mem. Park Hill Action Cttee. *Publications include:* Right From the Start, A New Democracy 1983, The Double Man (with W. S. Cohen,) 1985, America Can Win 1986, The Strategies of Zeus 1987, Russia Shakes the World 1991, The Minutemen: Restoring an Army of the People 1998, The Fourth Power: An Essay Concerning A Grand Strategy for the United States in the 21st Century 2004, The Thunder and the Sunshine: Four Seasons in a Burnished Life 2010; novels: The Double Man (with William Cohen) 1984, The Strategies of Zeus 1985, Sins of the Fathers 1999, I, Che Guevara 2000, The Shield and The Cloak: The Security of the Commons 2006, The Courage of Our Convictions: A Manifesto for Democrats by Gary Hart 2006, Under The Eagle's Wing: A National Security Strategy of the United States for 2009 2008, The Thunder and the Sunshine: Four Seasons in a Burnished Life 2010, Durango 2012. *Address:* 1100 New York Avenue, NW West Tower, 7th floor, Washington, DC 20005 USA. *Telephone:* (202) 347-4267 (office). *Website:* www.americansecurityproject.org (office).

HART, Graeme, MBA; New Zealand business executive; b. 1955; m.; two c.; ed Univ. of Otago; f. Rank Group Australia Pty Ltd (pvt. investment co.), Auckland, has acquired several cos including Burns, Philp & Co. Ltd (food products), Carter Holt Harvey (forest products), Evergreen Packaging Inc. (packaging equipment co.), SIG Holding (drink carton manufacturer), Alcoa Packaging & Consumer Group (now Reynolds Packaging Group). *Address:* Rank Group Ltd, Level 12, 132 Quay Street, Auckland 1001, New Zealand (office).

HART, Michael, CBE, PhD, DSc, FRS, FInstP; British physicist and academic; b. 4 Nov. 1938, Bristol; s. of Reuben H. V. Hart and Phyllis M. Hart (née White); m. Susan M. Powell 1963; three d.; ed Cotham Grammar School, Bristol and Univ. of Bristol; Research Assoc., Dept of Materials Science and Eng, Cornell Univ. 1963–65; Dept of Physics, Univ. of Bristol 1965–67, Lecturer in Physics 1967–72, Reader 1972–76; Sr Resident Research Assoc., Nat. Research Council, NASA Electronics Research Center, Boston, Mass 1969–70; Special Adviser, Cen. Policy Review Staff 1975–77; Wheatstone Prof. of Physics, King's Coll. London 1976–84; Prof. of Physics, Univ. of Manchester 1984–93, Prof. Emer. of Physics 1993–; Visiting Prof. of Applied Physics, De Montfort Univ. 1993–98, Hon. Prof. in Eng, Univ. of Warwick 1993–95; Science Programme Co-ordinator (part-time), Daresbury Lab. Science and Eng Research Council 1985–88; Chair. Nat. Synchrotron Light Source, Brookhaven Nat. Lab., USA 1995–2000; apptd Visiting Prof. of Physics, Univ. of Bristol 2000; Bertram Eugene Warren Award, American Crystallographic Asscn 1970, Charles Vernon Boys Award, Inst. of Physics 1971. *Publications:* contribs to learned journals. *Leisure interests:* flying kites, cookery. *Address:* 2 Challoner Court, Merchants Landing, Bristol, BS1 4RG, England (home). *Telephone:* (117) 921-5291 (home). *E-mail:* michael.hart8@btopenworld.com (home).

HART, Oliver D'Arcy, BA, MA, PhD; British/American economist and academic; *Andrew E. Furer Professor of Economics, Harvard University;* b. 9 Oct. 1948, London, England; s. of Philip D'Arcy Hart and Ruth Meyer; m. Rita B. Goldberg 1974; two s.; ed Univs of Cambridge and Warwick, Princeton Univ., USA; Lecturer in Econs, Univ. of Essex 1974–75; Asst Lecturer, then Lecturer in Econs, Univ. of Cambridge 1975–81; Prof. of Econs, LSE 1981–85, BP Centennial Visiting Prof. 1992–93, 1997–; Prof. of Econs, MIT 1984–93; Prof. of Econs, Harvard Univ. 1993–97, Andrew E. Furer Prof. of Econs 1997–; mem. NAS 2016–; Fellow, American Finance Asscn 2016–, American Acad. of Arts and Sciences; Corresp. Fellow, British Acad. 2000; Hon. DPhil (Basle) 1994, Hon. DSc (Econ) (London Business School) 2011, Hon. LLD (Warwick) 2012, Dr hc (Free Univ. of Brussels) 1992, (Copenhagen Business School) 2009, (Paris-Dauphine) 2009, Sveriges Riksbank Prize in Econ. Sciences in Memory of Alfred Nobel (co-recipient) 2016. *Publications include:* Firms, Contracts, and Financial Structure 1995; numerous articles in professional journals. *Leisure interest:* listening to music. *Address:* Department of Economics, Littauer 220, Harvard University, Cambridge, MA 02138, USA (office). *Telephone:* (617) 496-3461 (office). *E-mail:* ohart@harvard.edu (office). *Website:* economics.harvard.edu/faculty/hart (office).

HART, Stanley Robert, BS, MS, PhD; American geochemist and academic; *Scientist Emeritus, Woods Hole Oceanographic Institution;* b. 20 June 1935, Swampscott, Mass; s. of Robert W. Hart and Ruth M. Hart; m. 1st Joanna Smith 1956 (divorced 1976); m. 2nd Pamela Shepherd 1980; one s. two d.; ed Massachusetts Inst. of Tech., California Inst. of Tech.; Fellow, Carnegie Inst. of Washington 1960–61, mem. staff 1961–75; Visiting Prof., Univ. of Calif., San Diego 1967–68; Prof. of Geology and Geochemistry, MIT 1975–89; Sr Scientist, Woods Hole Oceanographic Inst. 1989–2007, Scientist Emer. 2007–; mem. NAS; Fellow, American Geophysical Union, Geological Soc. of America, European Asscn of Geochemistry, Geochemical Soc., European Union of Geosciences, American Acad. of Arts and Sciences; Dr hc (Paris) 2005; Goldschmidt Medal, Geochemical Soc. 1992, Hess Medal, American Geophysical Union 1997, Columbus O'Donnell Iselin Chair for Excellence in Oceanography, NAS Arthur L. Day Prize and Lectureship 2007, William Bowie Medal, American Geophysical Union 2016. *Publications:* more than 235 articles in scientific journals. *Leisure interests:* woodworking, fishing, running. *Address:* Woods Hole Oceanographic Institution, Woods Hole, MA 02543 (office); 4671 East Madera Vista Road, Green Valley, AZ 85614, USA (home). *Telephone:* (508) 524-2019 (office); (520) 625-4543 (office). *Fax:* (508) 457-2175 (office). *E-mail:* shart@whoi.edu (office). *Website:* www.whoi.edu/science/GG/people/shart (office).

HART OF CHILTON, Baron (Life Peer), cr. 2004, of Chilton in the County of Suffolk; **Garry Richard Rushby Hart,** LLB, FRSA; British solicitor; b. 29 June 1940, London; s. of Dennis George Hart and Evelyn Mary Hart; m. 1st Paula Lesley Shepherd 1966 (divorced 1986); two s. one d.; m. 2nd Valerie Elen Mary Davies 1986; two d.; ed Northgate Grammar School, Ipswich, Univ. Coll., London; solicitor, Herbert Smith 1966–70, Partner 1970–98, Head of Property Dept 1988–97; Special Expert Adviser to Sec. of State for Constitutional Affairs and Lord Chancellor 1998–2007; Chancellor Univ. of Greenwich 2008–14; mem. House of Lords Select Cttee on Merits of Statutory Instruments, House of Lords Select Cttee on the Constitution, Leaders Group Rules of Conduct for Mems of the House of Lords (The Eames Group) 2009, House of Lords Appointments Comm. 2010–; mem. Hon. Degrees and Fellowships Cttee and Research Governance Cttee, Univ. Coll. London, Project & Devt Cttee, Victoria & Albert Museum, Devt Council of Almeida Theatre; Trustee, Architecture Foundation 1997–2005 (Deputy Chair. 2000–05), Almeida Theatre 1997–2004 (Chair. 1997–2002), British Architectural Library Trust 2000–; Fellow, Univ. Coll., London 2001; Hon. FRIBA 2000; Hon. LLD (Greenwich Univ.) 2014. *Publications include:* Blundell & Dobry's Planning Applications Appeals and Procedures (co-ed. 4th and 6th edns) 1990, 1996. *Leisure interests:* travel, conservation, talking. *Address:* House of Lords, Westminster, London, SW1A 0PW, England (office). *Telephone:* (20) 7226-5431 (office). *E-mail:* hartofchilton@btinternet.com (office).

HÄRTER, Hans-Georg; German engineer and business executive; *Chairman, Deutz AG;* b. 2 May 1945, Bensheim; m.; two s.; ed Berlin Tech. School, Meersburg Acad.; trained as machine fitter; certified as state-approved mechanical engineer (industrial production); joined ZF Passau GmbH, Passau 1973, Head of Dept, Value Analysis/Methods 1982–87, Head of Specialist Dept, Value Analysis/Methods 1987–90, Sr Head of Tech. Cost Budgeting 1990, Deputy Group Vice-Pres., ZF Passau GmbH, Passau 1990–91, Group Vice-Pres. 1991–94, mem. Bd of Man. ZF Group Off-Road Driveline Tech. and Axle Systems Div., Marine Propulsion Systems Business Unit and Production Tech. 1994–2002, mem. Bd of Man., ZF Group Powertrain and Suspension Components, Div. Business Unit Aftermarket Trading, Asian Pacific Region and CEO ZF Sachs AG, Schweinfurt 2002–06, Exec. Vice-Pres., ZF Group 2006–07, CEO 2007–12; Chair. Deutz AG 2015–; mem. Supervisory Cttee, Kiekert AG, Knorr-Bremse AG; mem. Supervisory Bd Klingelnberg AG, Zurich; mem. Bd of Dirs Saurer AG, Jiangsu; Hon. Senator, Univ. of Passau 2007, Hon. Chair., European Festival Passau 2007; Bavarian

Order of Merit 2002; Civil Medal of the City of Passau 2005. *Address:* Deutz AG, Ottostr 1, 51149 Köln-Porz, Eil, Germany (office). *Telephone:* (2218) 22-0 (office). *Fax:* (2218) 22-5850 (office). *E-mail:* info@deutz.com (office). *Website:* www.deutz.com (office).

HARTERY, Nicky, CEng, MBA, FIEI; Irish engineer and business executive; *Chairman, CRH plc;* fmr Pres. and CEO Verbatim Corpn, USA; Exec. Vice-Pres., Eastman Kodak –2000; Vice-Pres. of Manufacturing and Business Operations, Europe, Middle East and Africa operations, Dell Inc. 2000–08; Dir (non-exec.) CRH plc 2004–, Chair. 2012–; Chief Exec. Prodigium (consulting co.); Dir (non-exec.), Musgrave Group plc 2010–, Chair. 2017–; Dir Eircom Ltd; Fellow, Inst. of Engineers of Ireland. *Address:* CRH plc, Belgard Castle, Clondalkin, Dublin 22, Ireland (office). *Telephone:* (1) 4041000 (office). *Fax:* (1) 4041007 (office). *E-mail:* mail@crh.com (office). *Website:* www.crh.com (office).

HARTHY, Khalifa bin Ali Issa al-; Omani diplomatist; *Permanent Representative to United Nations;* b. 21 Aug. 1963; m.; four c.; ed American Int. Univ., Univ. of London; worked for Econ. and Tech. Cooperation Dept, Ministry of Foreign Affairs 1996–97; Amb. to India 1998–2005, to Germany 2005–09, to Egypt 2009–16, also Perm. Rep. to Arab League 2009–16; Perm. Rep. to UN 2016–; Adviser to Sultan for Econ. Affairs 1997–98. *Address:* Permanent Mission of Oman, 3 Dag Hammarskjöld Plaza, 305 E t 47th Street, 12th Floor, New York, NY 10017, USA (office). *Telephone:* (212) 355-3505 (office). *Fax:* (212) 644-0070 (office). *E-mail:* oman@un.int (office). *Website:* www.un.int/oman (office).

HARTL, Franz-Ulrich, MD, DrMed (Habil.); German biochemist and academic; *Professor of Cellular Biochemistry and Managing Director, Max Planck Institute for Biochemistry;* b. 10 March 1957, Essen; ed Univs of Heidelberg and Munich; Postdoctoral Fellow, Inst. of Physiological Chem., Univ. of Munich 1985–86, Group Leader Inst. of Physiological Chem. 1987–89, 'Akademischer Rat', Inst. of Physiological Chem. 1990–91; Postdoctoral Fellow, UCLA and Fellow, Deutsche Forschungsgemeinschaft (German Research Council) 1989–90; Assoc. mem. Program in Cellular Biochemistry and Biophysics, Sloan-Kettering Inst., New York 1991–92, mem. (with tenure) 1993–97, William E. Snee Chair of Cellular Biochemistry 1995; Assoc. Prof. of Cell Biology and Genetics, Grad. School of Medical Science, Cornell Univ., NY 1991–92, Prof. 1993–97; Assoc. Investigator, Howard Hughes Medical Institute 1994–97; Prof. of Cellular Biochemistry and Dir, Max Planck Inst. for Biochemistry, Martinsried 1997–, Man. Dir 2002; mem. European Molecular Biology Org. 1998, German Acad. of Sciences Leopoldina 2002, Bavarian Acad. of Sciences 2004; Foreign mem. Acad. of Science of Nordrhein-Westfalen 1997; Fellow, AAAS 2010, American Acad. of Microbiology 2012; Hon. Prof., Univ. of Munich 1997; Foreign Hon. mem. American Acad. of Arts and Sciences 2000; Hon. mem. Japanese Biochemical Soc. 2008; Order of Merit 2011; Dr hc (La Trobe University, Melbourne) 2014; Vinci Award, LVMH Science for Art competition 1996, Lipmann Award, American Soc. of Biochemistry and Molecular Biology 1997, Academy Prize, Acad. of Science of Berlin-Brandenburg 1999, Wilhelm Vaillant Research Prize 2000, Gottfried Wilhelm Leibniz-Prize, Deutsche Forschungsgemeinschaft 2002, Feldberg Prize 2003, Gairdner Foundation Int. Award 2004, Ernst Jung Prize for Medicine, Jung-Stiftung für Wissenschaft und Forschung (co-recipient) 2005, Stein and Moore Award, Protein Soc. 2006, Koerber European Science Award 2006, Wiley Prize in Biomedical Sciences 2007, Lewis S. Rosenstiel Award 2008, Louisa Gross Horwitz Prize 2008, Otto Warburg Medal, German Soc. for Biochemistry and Molecular Biology (GBM) 2009, van Gysel Prize for Biomedical Research in Europe 2010, Dr H.P. Heineken Prize for Biochemistry and Biophysics, Royal Netherlands Acad. of Arts and Sciences 2010, Albert Lasker Basic Medical Research Award 2011, Massry Prize 2011, Heinrich Wieland-Prize, Boehringer Ingelheim Foundation 2011, Shaw Prize in Life Science and Medicine 2012, Tabor Research Award 2013, Biochemical Analytic Prize, German Soc. for Clinical Chem. and Lab. Medicine 2013, Linacre Lecturer, St John's Coll., Cambridge 2014, Sigman Lecture Award, UCLA 2015, Wenner-Gren Distinguished Lecturer, Wenner-Gren Foundation, Stockholm 2015, IUBMB Lecture Award, FOABMB, Hyderabad 2015, Ernst Schering Prize 2016, Debrecen Award for Molecular Medicine, Univ. of Debrecen 2017, Wilson Medal, American Soc. of Cell Biology 2017, Paul Ehrlich and Ludwig Darmstaedter Prize (co-recipient) 2019. *Publications:* numerous scientific papers in professional journals. *Address:* c/o Evelyn Frey-Royston, Max Planck Institute of Biochemistry, Department of Cellular Biochemistry, Am Klopferspitz 18, 82152 Martinsried, Germany (office). *Telephone:* (89) 8578-2244 (office). *Fax:* (89) 8578-2211 (office). *E-mail:* uhartl@biochem.mpg.de (office); efrey@biochem.mpg.de (office); office-hartl@biochem.mpg.de (office). *Website:* www.biochem.mpg.de/en/rd/hartl (office).

HARTLAND, Michael (see James, Michael Leonard).

HARTLEY, Frank Robinson, DSc, FRSC, CCMI; British chemist, academic and university administrator (retd); *Professor Emeritus, Cranfield University;* b. 29 Jan. 1942, Epsom, Surrey; s. of Sir Frank Hartley and Lydia May England; m. 1st Valerie Peel 1964 (died 2005); three d.; m. 2nd Charmaine Jasmine Harvey 2009; ed King's Coll. School, Wimbledon, Magdalen Coll., Oxford; Post-doctoral Fellow, Commonwealth Scientific and Industrial Research Org., Div. of Protein Chem., Melbourne, Australia 1966–69; ICI Research Fellow and Tutor in Physical Chem., Univ. Coll., London 1969–70; Lecturer in Inorganic Chem., Univ. of Southampton 1970–75; Prof. of Chem. and Head of Dept of Chem. and Metallurgy, Royal Mil. Coll. of Science, Shrivenham 1975–82, Acting Dean 1982–84, Prin. and Dean 1984–89; Vice-Pres. Cranfield Trust 1989–; fmr Man. Dir CIT Holdings Ltd; Dir (non-exec.), T&N PLC 1989–98, Nat. Westminster Bank Eastern Region Advisory Bd 1990–92, Kalon PLC 1994–99, Kenwood PLC 1995–99; Vice-Chancellor Cranfield Univ. 2000–06, currently Prof. Emer.; Asscn of Commonwealth Univs Sr Travelling Fellow 1986; Special Adviser on Defence Systems to the Prime Minister 1988–90; Specialist Adviser to House of Lords Select Cttee on Science and Tech. 1993–94; Chair. AWE Academic Council 1998–2001; Chair. Sr Council for Devon, Teignmouth 2008–13, Teignmouth and Dawlish Ramblers 2010–16; fmr mem. Int. Advisory Bd Kanazawa Acad. of Science and Tech., Japan; Dir Shuttleworth Trust 1994–97; Trustee, Lorch Foundation 1994–2006; fmr mem. Advisory Panel AWE Corp.; fmr DL Beds.; Hon. FRAeS; Hon. Life mem. Cranfield Students Asscn. *Publications include:* The Chemistry of Platinum and Palladium (Applied Science) 1973, Elements of Organometallic Chemistry (Chemical Soc.) 1974, Solution Equilibria (with C. Burgess and R. M. Alcock) 1980; The Chemistry of the Metal Carbon Bond (Vols 1–5) 1983–89, Supported Metal Complexes 1985, Brassey's New Battlefield Weapons Systems and Technology series 1988– (Ed.-in-Chief), The Chemistry of Organophosphorus Compounds Vols 1–4 1990–96, Chemistry of the Platinum Group Metals 1991; papers in inorganic, co-ordination and organometallic chem. in major English, American and Australian journals. *Leisure interests:* rambling, travel, swimming, gardening.

HARTLEY, Hal, (Ned Rifle), BA; American film director, producer and scriptwriter; b. 3 Nov. 1959, Lindenhurst, NY; s. of Harold Hartley and Eileen Hartley (nee Flynn); m. Miho Nikaido 1996; ed Massachusetts Coll. of Art, State Univ. of New York-Purchase Film School; worked with Action Productions; f. True Fiction Pictures 1984 (now Possible Films); Visiting Lecturer, Harvard Univ. 2001–04; Fellow, American Acad., Berlin 2004; Chevalier, Ordre des Arts et des Lettres 1996. *Films:* Kid 1984, Home of The Brave 1986, The Cartographer's Girlfriend 1987, Dogs 1988, The Unbelievable Truth 1990, Trust 1991, Simple Men 1992, From a Motel 6 1993, Iris 1993, The Only Living Boy in New York 1993, Flirt 1993, Amateur (Young Filmmakers Award 1994) 1994, Henry Fool (Best Screenplay Award, Cannes Film Festival 1998) 1997, The Book of Life 1998, Monster 2000, Kimono 2000, No Such Thing 2001, The Girl from Monday 2004, Fay Grim 2006. *Television films:* Surviving Desire 1989, Achievement 1991, Ambition 1991, Flirt 1993, Opera No. 1 1994, NYC 3/94 1994, The New Math(s) 2000, Kimono 2001, The Girl from Monday (Premi Noves Visions Award, Sitges Int. Film Festival 2005) 2005, Fay Grim (RiverRun Int. Film Festival Audience Choice Award 2006) 2006, Accomplice 2010, Meanwhile 2011, Ned Rifle 2014. *Address:* Possible Films, LLC, 779 Riverside Drive, New York, NY 10032, USA (office); c/o Stephen Gates & Sekka Scher. Ellipsis Entertainment Group, 175 Varick Street, New York, NY 10014, USA (office). *Telephone:* (646) 998-4261 (office); (646) 561-6791 (office). *E-mail:* info@possiblefilms.com (office); dpatack@ellipsisentgroup.com (office). *Website:* www.possiblefilms.com (office).

HARTLEY, Jane D., BA; American government official, diplomatist and fmr media executive; ed Boston Coll. (Newton Coll.); held various sr man. positions in media industry, including Vice-Pres. Group W Cable, Westinghouse Broadcasting (CBS), MCA (Universal) and as Vice-Pres. and Station Man. of WWOR-TV, NJ; fmr CEO Observatory Group (advisory firm), New York; CEO G7 Group (research firm) 1994–2007; extensive career in public service, including serving as Dir of Congressional Relations, Dept of Housing and Urban Devt and later as Pres. Carter's Assoc. Asst in Office of Public Liaison; Amb. to France (also accred to Monaco) 2014–17; fmr mem. Bd of Dirs Heidrick & Struggles, Corpn for Nat. and Community Service, Memorial Sloan Kettering Cancer Center; fmr Vice-Chair. and mem. Exec. Cttee, Econ. Club of New York; fmr mem. Exec. Cttee, John F. Kennedy School of Govt, Harvard Univ.; fmr mem. Wall Street Council of Boston Coll., Women's Council of Boston Coll., Pres.'s Leadership Council of Dartmouth Coll.; mem. Council on Foreign Relations; fmr Dir Parsons School of Design, The New School; fmr Trustee, Nightingale-Bamford School, Sesame Workshop.

HARTMAN, George Eitel, BA, MFA, FAIA; American architect; *Principal Emeritus, Hartman-Cox Architects;* b. 7 May 1936, Fort Hancock, NJ; s. of George E. Hartman and Evelyn Ritchie; m. 1st Ann Burdick 1965 (divorced 2000); one s. one d.; m. 2nd Ian Cigliano 2001; ed Princeton Univ.; with Keyes Lethbridge & Condon Architects 1960–64; own pvt. practice George E. Hartman 1964–65, Hartman-Cox Architects 1965–, currently Prin. Emer.; mem. US Comm. of Fine Arts 1990–93, Architectural Advisory Bd, Foreign Bldg Office, Dept of State 1991–; taught in Catholic Univ., North Carolina State Univ., Univ. of Maryland; fmr Pres. Washington Chapter AIA; mem. Bd of Dirs Arthur C. Clarke Foundation; Fellow, American Acad. Rome; Co-publr Acad. Press; mem. Comm. of Fine Arts; AIA Nat. Honor Awards 1970, 1971, 1981, 1988, 1989, 2005 and numerous other awards. *Buildings include:* US Embassy, Kuala Lumpur 1979, 1001 Pennsylvania Avenue, Washington, DC 1979, HEB HQ, San Antonio, Tex. 1982, Chrysler Museum, Norfolk, NJ 1984, Georgetown Univ. Law Library 1989, Market Square, Washington, DC 1990, 800 N Capital Street, Washington, DC 1990, 1200 K Street and 154 K Street, Washington, DC 1991. *Leisure interest:* sailing. *Address:* Hartman Cox Architects, 1074 Thomas Jefferson Street, NW, Washington, DC 20007 (office); 1657 31st Street, Washington, DC 20007, USA (home). *Telephone:* (202) 333-6446 (office); (202) 333-1657 (home). *E-mail:* inquiries@hartmancox.com (office). *Website:* www.hartmancox.com (office).

HARTMANN, Peter C., DPhil; German historian and academic; *Professor Emeritus of General and Modern History, University of Mainz;* b. 28 March 1940, Munich; s. of Alfred Hartmann and Manfreda Knote; m. Beate Just 1972; two s. two d.; ed Univs of Munich and Paris; Research Assoc. Deutsches Historisches Institut, Paris 1970–81; Privatdozent, Munich 1979; Prof. Univ. of Passau 1982; Prof. of Gen. and Modern History, Univ. of Mainz 1988–2005, currently Prof. Emer.; held Chair of Educ. and Modern History, Johannes Gutenberg Univ. of Mainz; mem. Bd Franco-German Cultural Foundation; mem. Historical Comm. of Bavarian History, Bavarian Acad. of Sciences; Sr Phili. KDStV Aenania, Munich 2005–; Chevalier des Palmes académiques 2001, Bundesverdienstkreuz a. Bande 2012; Hon. DUniv (Paris); Strasbourg Int. Prize, Buchpreis d. Bayer. Clubs. *Publications include:* Pariser Archive, Bibl. u. Dok.zentren 1976, Geld als Instrument europäischer Machtpolitik im Zeitalter des Merkantilismus 1978, Das Steuersystem der europäischen Staaten am Ende der Ancien Regime 1979, Karl Albrecht-Karl VII: Glücklicher Kurfürst, Unglücklicher Kaiser 1985, Französische Geschichte 1914–1945, Französische Verfgeschichte der Neuzeit (1450–1980), Ein Überblick 1985 (second edn 2003), Bayerns Weg in die Gegenwart: Vom Stammesherzogtum bis zur Freistaat heute 1989 (third edn 2012), Der Jesuitenstaat in Südamerika 1609–1768 1994, Franz. Könige u. Kaiser der Neuzeit 1994, Regionen in der Frühen Neuzeit 1994 (second edn 2006), Der Mainzer Kurfürst als Reichskanzler 1996, Der Bayerische Reichskreis (1500–1803) 1997, Kurmainz, das Reichskanzleramt und der Reich 1998, Geschichte Frankreichs 1999 (fourth edn 2007), Geschichte aktuell, hg. v.K. Amann 2000, Reichskirche, Kurmainz und Reichserzkanzleramt 2001, Die Jesuiten 2001 (second edn 2008), Kulturgeschichte des Heiligen Römischen Reiches 1648 bis 1806 Verfassung, Religion und Kultur 2001 (second edn 2011), Die Mainzer Kurfürsten d. Hauses Schönborn 2002, Religion und Kultur im Europa d.17 u.18 Jahrhunderts 2004 (second edn 2006), Das Heilige Römische Reich deutscher Nation in der Neuzeit 1485–1806 2005, Kleine Mainzer Stadtgeschichte 2005 (second edn 2011), Das Hl Röm. Reich u. sein Ende 2006,

Münchens Weg in d. Gegenwart 2008, Bayer.-cgines. Beziehungen 2008, Der Dreißigjähr. Krieg 2010, Bayern in Lateinamerika 2011. *E-mail:* peterclaushartmann@gmx.de.

HARTONO, Michael (Bambang), (Oei Wie Siang); Indonesian business executive; *Joint Chief Executive, PT Djarum;* s. of Oei Wie Gwan; brother of Robert Budi Hartono; m.; four c.; joined family co. PT Djarum (clove cigarette mfr) 1981, now Co-Propr and CEO (with brother); major shareholder (via FarIndo Investments, Mauritius Ltd) PT Bank Central Asia Tbk (BCA) 1998–. *Address:* PT Djarum, Jl Aipda K. S. Tubun 2C/57, Jakarta, Indonesia (office). *Telephone:* (21) 5346901 (office). *Fax:* (21) 5346892 (office). *Website:* www.djarum.co.id (office).

HARTONO, Robert Budi, (Oei Wie Tjhong); Indonesian business executive; *Joint Chief Executive, PT Djarum;* s. of Oei Wie Gwan; brother of Michael (Bambang) Hartono; m.; three s.; joined family co. PT Djarum (clove cigarette mfr) 1981, now Co-Propr and CEO (with brother); major shareholder (via FarIndo Investments, Mauritius Ltd) PT Bank Central Asia Tbk (BCA) 1998–. *Leisure interest:* badminton. *Address:* PT Djarum, Jl Aipda K. S. Tubun 2C/57, Jakarta, Indonesia (office). *Telephone:* (21) 5346901 (office). *Fax:* (21) 5346892 (office). *Website:* www.djarum.co.id (office).

HARTUNG, Harald; German poet, academic and critic; b. 29 Oct. 1932, Herne; s. of Richard Hartung and Wanda Hartung; m. Freia Schnackenburg 1979; two s.; secondary school teacher 1960–66; Prof., Pädagogische Hochschule Berlin 1971–80, Tech. Univ. Berlin 1971–98 (retd); mem. Akad. der Künste, Berlin, Akad. der Wissenschaften und der Literatur, Mainz, Deutsche Akad. für Sprache und Dichtung, Darmstadt, PEN; Literature Promotion Prize of the Berlin Art Prize 1979, Annette von Droste-Hulshoff Prize 1987, Int. Poetry Prize Chianti Ruffino Antico Fattore 1999, Prize of the Frankfurt anthology 2002, Würth Prize for European Literature 2004, Johann Heinrich Merck Prize 2009, Literatur Prize Ruhr 2012. *Publications:* Experimentelle Literatur und Konkrete Poesie 1975, Das Gewöhnliche Licht 1976, Augenzeit 1978, Deutsche Lyrik seit 1965 1985, Traum im Deutschen Museum 1986, Luftfracht 1991, Jahre mit Windrad 1996, Masken und Stimmen 1996, Jahrhundertgedächtnis.Deutsche Lyrik im 20.Jahrhundert 1998, Machen oder Entstehenlassen 2001, Langsamer träumen 2002, Aktennotiz meines Engels 2005, Ein Unterton von Glück – Über Dichter und Gedichte 2007, Wintermalerei. Gedichte 2010, Der Tag vor dem Abend 2012, Die Launen der Poesie 2014. *Address:* Rüdesheimer Platz 4, 14197 Berlin, Germany.

HARTWELL, Leland (Lee) H., BS, PhD; American geneticist and academic; *Virginia G. Piper Chair in Personalized Medicine and Chief Scientist, Center for Sustainable Health, Arizona State University;* b. 30 Oct. 1939, Los Angeles, Calif.; s. of Ernest Hartwell and Marjorie Taylor Hartwell; m. Theresa Naujack-Hartwell; ed California Inst. of Technology, Massachusetts Inst. of Tech., Salk Inst. for Biological Studies; Assoc. Prof., Univ. of Calif. 1965–68; Assoc. Prof., then Prof., Univ. of Washington 1968–2010; Pres. and Dir Fred Hutchinson Cancer Research Center, Seattle, Wash. 1997–2010, Pres. and Dir Emer. 2010–; Virginia G. Piper Chair of Personalized Medicine, Arizona State Univ. 2009–, Chief Scientist, Center for Sustainable Health, Biodesign Inst. 2010–, Prof., Ira A. Fulton School of Eng 2010–; Prof., American Cancer Soc.; Chair. Scientific Advisory Bd Canary Foundation; mem. Nat. Advisory Bd BioLab 2000–; mem. Bd of Sponsors Fed. of American Scientists; mem. Editorial Bd Molecular and Cellular Biology, Journal of Cell Biology 1988–91, Molecular Biology of the Cell 1991–93; mem. Bd of Scientific Advisors, Nat. Cancer Inst. 2006–09; mem. NAS 1987–, American Soc. of Microbiology, American Acad. of Microbiology, Genetics Soc. of America, American Soc. for Cell Biology, American Asscn for Cancer Research, American Acad. of Arts and Sciences; Hon. Prof., Tsinghua Univ. China 2004, Peking Union Medical Coll., Beijing 2004; Hon. Academician, Academica Sinica 2008; Hon. DrSc (Arizona State Univ.) 2007; numerous awards including General Motors Sloan Award 1991, Gairdner Foundation Int. Award 1992, Genetics Soc. of America Medal 1994, Louisa Gross Horwitz Prize 1995, Albert Lasker Basic Medical Research Award 1998, Nobel Prize in Medicine (jtly) 2001, Medal of Merit 2003, Komen Brinker Award for Scientific Distinction. *Publications:* co-author of several books. *Leisure interests:* health care. *Address:* Center for Sustainable Health, Biodesign Institute, Arizona State University, 1001 South McAllister Avenue, Tempe, AZ 85287-6701 USA (office). *Telephone:* (480) 727-0779 (office). *Fax:* (480) 727-9296 (office). *E-mail:* Lee.Hartwell@asu.edu (office). *Website:* www.sustainablehealth.org (office).

HARTWIG, John F., AB, PhD; American chemist and academic; *Henry Rapoport Professor of Chemistry, University of California, Berkeley;* b. 7 Aug. 1964, Elmhurst, Ill.; ed Princeton Univ., Univ. of California, Berkeley; American Cancer Soc. Postdoctoral Fellow, MIT 1990–92; Asst Prof., Yale Univ. 1992–96, Assoc. Prof. 1996–98, Prof. 1998–2004, Irénée P. duPont Prof. of Chem. 2004–06; Kenneth L. Rinehart Jr Prof. of Chem., Univ. of Illinois, Urbana-Champaign 2006–11; Henry Rapoport Prof. of Chem., Univ. of California, Berkeley 2011–, also Sr Faculty Scientist, Lawrence Berkeley Nat. Lab.; mem. NAS 2012; Dreyfus Foundation New Faculty Award 1992, DuPont Young Professor Award 1993, NSF Young Investigator Award 1994, Union Carbide Innovative Recognition Award 1995, 1996, Alfred P. Sloan Research Fellow 1996–98, Camille Dreyfus Teacher-Scholar Award 1997, Eli Lilly Grantee 1997, A.C. Cope Scholar 1997, Leo Hendrik Baekeland Award 2003, Thieme-IUPAC Prize in Synthetic Organic Chem. 2004, ACS Award in Organometallic Chem. 2006, Raymond and Beverly Sackler Prize in the Physical Sciences 2007, Tetrahedron Young Investigator Award in Organic Synthesis 2007, Mukaiyama Award, Soc. of Synthetic Organic Chem. of Japan 2008, Paul N. Rylander Award, Organic Reactions Catalysis Soc. 2008, Int. Asscn of the Catalysis Socs Award 2008, Joseph Chatt Award, RSC 2009, Mitsui Chemicals Catalysis Science Award (Japan) 2009, Edward Mack Jr Memorial Award, Ohio State Univ. 2009, NIH MERIT Award 2009, GlaxoSmithKline Scholars' Award 2010, Einstein Fellowship, Berlin 2011, Herbert C. Brown Award for Creative Research in Synthetic Methods 2013, ACS Catalysis Lectureship for the Advancement of Catalytic Science 2013, Nagoya Gold Medal Award 2014, Tetrahedron Chair, Belgium Symposium on Organic Synthesis 2014, Distinguished Chemist Award, Sierra Nevada Section of the ACS 2014, Janssen Pharmaceutica Prize for Creativity in Organic Synthesis 2014, Organometallics Sr Fellowship 2014, J. Willard Gibbs Medal Award, Chicago Section of the ACS 2015. *Publications:* numerous papers in professional journals on new reactions catalysed by transition metal complexes. *Address:* Department of Chemistry, University of California, 718 Latimer Hall MC #460, Berkeley, CA 94720-1460, USA (office). *Telephone:* (510) 642-2038 (office). *Fax:* (510) 642-2049 (office). *E-mail:* jhartwig@berkeley.edu (office). *Website:* www.cchem.berkeley.edu/jfhgrp (office).

HARTZENBERG, Ferdinand, DSc; South African fmr politician; b. 8 Jan. 1936, Lichtenburg; s. of Ferdinand Hartzenberg; m. Magdalena Judith de Wet 1962; two s.; ed Sannieshof, Hoër Volkskool, Potchefstroom and Univ. of Pretoria; mem. Parl. for Lichtenburg; Leader, Conservative Party of SA (CPSA) 1993–2004; Deputy Minister of Devt 1976; Minister of Educ. and Training 1979–82.

HARUTYUNYAN, Arayik; Armenian economist and politician; *Chairman, Azat Hayrenik;* b. 14 Dec. 1973, Stepanakert (Xankändi), Nagornyi Karabakh Autonomous Oblast, Azerbaijan SSR, USSR; m.; three d.; ed Physics and Math. School, Stepanakert, Inst. of Nat. Economy, Yerevan, Artsakh State Univ.; entered defence forces of 'Nagornyi Karabakh Repub.' (NKR) 1992, active participation in several operations; Asst to the Minister of Finance and Economy (NKR) 1995–97; banking exec., Askeran br. of Hayagrobank 1997–99, Stepanakert br. of Hayagrobank 1999–2004; head of Hayrenik (Fatherland) faction of NKR Nat. Ass. 2005–07; co-Chair. Azat Hayrenik (AH—Free Fatherland) party 2005–06, Chair. 2006–07, 2009–Exec. Dir Karabakh Gold, CJSC 2006–07; Prime Minister of the 'Nagornyi Karabakh Repub.' (Artsakh) 2007–17; Minister of State 2017–18; Advisor to the President of 'Nagornyi Karabakh Repub.' (Artsakh) July 2018–Feb. 2019; Order of Martial Cross, II degree, Order of Grigor Lusavorich 2016; For liberation of Shushi medal 2003. *Address:* Azat Hayrenik, 75000 Stepanakert, National Assembly (Azgayin Zhoghov), Nagornyi Karabakh, Azerbaijan (office). *Telephone:* (47) 94-85-15 (office).

HARUTYUNYAN, Gagik G., DL; Armenian politician and lawyer; *Chairman, Supreme Judicial Council;* b. 1948, Geghashen; three c.; ed Yerevan State Univ.; Lecturer, Yerevan Inst. of Industry 1975–77; in Yugoslavia 1977–78; on staff Cen. Cttee Armenian CP 1982–88; Head of Dept 1988–90; joined nationalist opposition 1990; Deputy Chair. Armenian Parl. 1990–91; Vice-Pres. of Armenia 1991–95; Acting Chair. Council of Ministers (Prime Minister) 1991–92; Chair. Constitutional Court 1996–2018; Chair. Supreme Judicial Council 2018–; Council Pres. Centre of Constitutional Law 1996–2009; Pres. Int. Conf. of Constitutional Control Organs of New Democracy States 1997; mem. Comm. for Democracy Through Law, Council of Europe 1997–, Int. Asscn of Constitutional Law 1998–, Bureau of the World Conference on Constitutional Justice 2009– (Chair. 2014–15), Bureau of the Venice Comm. 2014–17; The High Judicial Qualification of a Judge 1998. *Publications:* 35 monographs, including Constitutional Review (with A. Mavčič) 1999, 2002; 150 scientific works. *Address:* c/o Constitutional Court, Marshal Baghramian Avenue 10, 0019 Yerevan (office); Avan, Quchak Quarter, Apt 11, Yerevan, Armenia (home).

HARVEY, Caroline (see TROLLOPE, Joanna).

HARVEY, HE Cardinal James Michael, DCL; American ecclesiastic and diplomatist; *Archpriest of the Basilica di San Paolo fuori le Mura;* b. 20 Oct. 1949, Milwaukee, Wis.; ed St Francis Seminary, Pontifical North American Coll., Rome, Pontifical Ecclesiastical Acad.; ordained priest, Archdiocese of Milwaukee 1975; entered diplomatic service of the Holy See 1980, served as attaché in Apostolic Nunciature in Dominican Repub. 1980–81, Sec. 1981–82, worked at Secr. of State 1982–97, Assessor of Secr. of State 1997–98; Titular Bishop of Memphis (Egypt) 1998–2003, Titular Archbishop of Memphis 2003–; Prefect of the Papal Household 1998–2012; Archpriest of Basilica di San Paolo fuori le Mura 2012–; cr. Cardinal (Cardinal-Deacon of San Pio V a Villa Carpegna) 2012; mem. Congregation for Causes of Saints 2012–, Admin of Patrimony of the Apostolic See 2013–, Congregation for Evangelization of Peoples 2013–; Hon. mem. Circolo San Pietro; Kt Grand Cross, Order of Merit of the Italian Rep. 1999. *Address:* Roman Curia, 00120 Città del Vaticano, Rome, Italy (office). *Telephone:* (06) 69880800 (office); (06) 69880802 (office). *Fax:* (06) 69880803 (office). *E-mail:* info@basilicasanpaolo.org (office); spbasilica@org.va (office). *Website:* www.vatican.va/various/basiliche/san_paolo/index_en.html (office).

HARVEY, Richard, FIA; British insurance industry executive; *Chairman, PZ Cussons PLC;* b. 1951, Gloucestershire; m. Kay Harvey; joined Norwich Union 1992, various sr man. posts in NZ and UK, fmr Dir, Group CEO 1998–2000, Deputy Group CEO Aviva PLC (following merger) 2000–01, CEO 2001–07; Chair. (non-exec.) PZ Cussons PLC 2010–; Dir Asscn of British Insurers 2001–05; mem. Bd of Dirs Jardine Lloyd Thompson PLC 2009–; mem. Audit, Nominations and Remuneration Cttees. *Address:* PZ Cussons, Manchester Business Park, 3500 Aviator Way, Manchester, M22 5TG, England (office). *Telephone:* (16) 1435-1000 (office). *E-mail:* pzweb.general@pzcussons.com (office). *Website:* www.pzcussons.com (office).

HARWIT, Martin Otto, BA, MA, PhD; American (b. Czechoslovak) astrophysicist, academic and fmr museum director; *Professor Emeritus of Astronomy, Cornell University;* b. 9 March 1931, Prague, Czechoslovakia; s. of Felix Michael Haurowitz and Regina Hedwig Haurowitz (née Perutz); m. Marianne Mark; three c.; ed English High School for Boys, Istanbul, Bronx High School of Science, New York, Oberlin Coll., Univ. of Michigan, Massachusetts Inst. of Tech.; moved with family to Istanbul, Turkey aged eight, to USA aged 15; served in US Army 1955–57; carried out postdoctoral research on theoretical astrophysical problems with Fred Hoyle at Univ. of Cambridge, UK 1960–61; postdoctoral researcher, Cornell Univ. 1961, mem. astronomy faculty 1962, visited Naval Research Lab. with Herbert Friedman's group 1963–64, returned to Cornell 1964, worked with Aerobee rockets to conduct infrared astronomy from space, built several rocket payloads with liquid nitrogen, helium-cooled telescopes and infrared detectors; went into airborne infrared astronomy working on NASA's Learjet and Kuiper flying observatories, co-f. and co-directed doctoral programme in the history and philosophy of science and tech. at Cornell Univ., Prof. Emer. of Astronomy 1988–; one of original planners of NASA's Great Observatories programme; NAS/Czechoslovak Acad. of Sciences Exchange Fellow, Prague 1969–70; Mission Scientist, ESA Infrared Space Observatory 1985, ESA Herschel Space Observatory; Science Team mem., NASA Submillimeter Wave Astronomy Satellite Project and Vision Mission Far-Infrared and Submillimeter Interferometer study; Dir Smithsonian Nat. Air and Space Museum, Washington, DC 1987–95; External mem. Max Planck Inst. for Radioastronomy, Germany 1979; Adriaan Blaauw Visiting Prof., Univ. of Groningen, Netherlands 2002; Distinguished Fellow, Inst.

of Advanced Study, Durham Univ., UK 2007; Hon. DSc (Oberlin Coll.) 2011; Alexander von Humboldt Sr US Scientist Award (Germany) 1976–77, Bruce Medal, Astronomical Soc. of the Pacific 2007. *Films:* Blue Planet 1990, Destiny in Space 1994, Cosmic Voyage 1996. *Achievements include:* co-pioneered infrared spectroscopy and made near- and far-infrared observations culminating in discovery of several strong far-infrared astronomical fine-structure emission lines; developed the Hadamard Transform technique of multislit spectroscopic imaging; Solar System Asteroid 12143 named Harwit, Int. Astronomical Union (IAU). *Publications include:* Astrophysical Concepts 1973 (translated into Chinese) (fourth edn 2006), Hadamard Transform Optics (with Neil J. A. Sloane) 1979, Cosmic Discovery: The Search, Scope and Heritage of Astronomy 1981 (translated into German and French), Treasures of the National Air and Space Museum 1995, An Exhibit Denied – Lobbying the History of Enola Gay (translated into Japanese) 1996, The Extragalactic Background and its Cosmological Implications (with M. G. Hauser) 2001, In Search of the True Universe: The Tools, Shaping and Cost of Cosmological Thought 2013. *Address:* 511 H Street, SW, Washington, DC 20024, USA (office). *Telephone:* (202) 479-6877 (office). *E-mail:* harwit@verizon.net (office). *Website:* astro.cornell.edu (office).

HARWOOD, Sir Ronald, Kt, CBE, FRSL; British author and playwright; b. (Ronald Horwitz), 9 Nov. 1934, Cape Town, South Africa; s. of Isaac Horwitz and Isobel Pepper; m. Natasha Riehle 1959 (died 2013); one s. two d.; ed Sea Point Boys' High School, Cape Town and Royal Acad. of Dramatic Art; actor 1953–60; author 1960–; Artistic Dir Cheltenham Festival of Literature 1975; presenter, Kaleidoscope, BBC Radio 1973, Read All About It, BBC TV 1978–79, All The World's A Stage, BBC TV; Chair. Writers' Guild of GB 1969; Visitor in Theatre, Balliol Coll. Oxford 1986; Pres. PEN (England) 1989–93, Int. PEN 1993–97; Gov. Cen. School of Speech and Drama; mem. Council Royal Soc. of Literature 1998–2001, Chair. 2001–04; Trustee, Booker Foundation 2002; Chevalier des Arts et Lettres 1996; Hon. DLitt (Keele) 2002; New Standard Drama Award 1981, Drama Critics Award 1981, Molière Award for Best Play, Paris 1993. *TV plays include:* The Barber of Stamford Hill 1960, Private Potter (with Casper Wrede) 1961, The Guests 1972, Breakthrough at Reykjavik 1987, Countdown to War 1989. *Screenplays include:* A High Wind in Jamaica 1965, One Day in the Life of Ivan Denisovich 1971, Evita Perón 1981, The Dresser 1983, Mandela 1987, The Browning Version 1994, Cry, Beloved Country 1995, Taking Sides 2002, The Pianist 2002 (Acad. Award for Best Adapted Screenplay 2003), The Statement 2003, Being Julia 2004, Oliver Twist 2005, Le Scaphandre et le Papillon (BAFTA Award for Best Adapted Screenplay 2008) 2007, Love in the Time of Cholera 2007, The Diving Bell and the Butterfly 2007, Australia 2008, Quartet 2012. *Plays include:* Country Matters 1969, The Good Companions (musical libretto) 1974, The Ordeal of Gilbert Pinfold 1977, A Family 1978, The Dresser 1980, After the Lions 1982, Tramway Road 1984, The Deliberate Death of a Polish Priest 1985, Interpreters 1985, J. J. Farr 1987, Ivanov (from Chekhov) 1989, Another Time 1989, Reflected Glory 1992, Poison Pen 1994, Taking Sides 1995, The Handyman 1996, Equally Divided 1998, Quartet 1999, Mahler's Conversion 2002, An English Tragedy 2007. *Publications include:* fiction: All the Same Shadows 1961, The Guilt Merchants 1963, The Girl in Melanie Klein 1969, Articles of Faith 1973, The Genoa Ferry 1976, César and Augusta 1978, Home 1993; non-fiction: Sir Donald Wolfit, CBE: His Life and Work in the Unfashionable Theatre (biog.) 1971; editor: A Night at the Theatre 1983, The Ages of Gielgud 1984, Dear Alec: Guinness at Seventy-Five 1989, The Faber Book of the Theatre 1994; vols of essays and short stories. *Leisure interest:* cricket. *Address:* Judy Daish Associates, 2 St Charles Place, London, W10 6EG, England (office). *Telephone:* (20) 8964-8811 (office).

HASAN, Abdulkasim Salad; Somali fmr head of state; b. 1 Jan. 1941, Galdogob, Italian Somaliland; ed Lomonosov Moscow State Univ., USSR; Co-founder Suhl (reconciliation) group; held several positions in Somali Govt, including Minister of Industry, of Trade, of Labour, of Information and of the Interior 1973–90; fled to Cairo for a few months following outbreak of Somali Civil War 1991; Pres. of Somalia 2000–04; now takes part in numerous rallies and events in and around Somalia. *Address:* c/o Office of the President, 1 Villa Baidao, Baydhabo 2525, Somalia. *E-mail:* president@president.somaligov.net. *Website:* www.president.somaligov.net.

HASAN, Khandaker Mahmud-ul, MA, LLM; Bangladeshi international organisation official, fmr judge and diplomatist; b. 27 Jan. 1939; s. of Khandaker Mohammed Hasan; enrolled as Supreme Court advocate 1963, Judge of the High Court 1991–2002, Appellate Div. 2002, apptd Chief Justice, Supreme Court 2003; Amb. to Iraq 1980–82; mem. Arbitral Tribunal Commonwealth Secr. 2005–08, apptd Pres. 2009; fmr Chair. Fed. Insurance Co.; fmr Int. Assoc. American Bar Asscn; fmr part-time Lecturer, Dhaka Univ.; fmr mem. Governing Body Cen. Law Coll.; fmr mem. Bangladesh Bar Council; mem. Del. Islamic Foreign Ministers Conf. Baghdad, Iraq 1981, Non-Aligned Labour Ministers Conf. Baghdad, Iraq 1981; Hon. Sec., Bangladesh Inst. of Law and Int. Affairs 1975–80, Hon. Dir 1982–85. *Publications include:* several articles.

HASAN, Masuma, MA, PhD; Pakistani diplomatist and academic; *Chair, Pakistan Institute of International Affairs;* ed Univ. of Cambridge, UK, Univ. of Karachi; mem. Faculty, Nat. Inst. of Public Admin, Karachi 1967–81, Dir 1991–94, 1997–99; Dir Public Admin Research Centre, Govt of Pakistan, Islamabad 1981–84, Dir-Gen., Man. Services Div., Islamabad and Karachi 1984–90; Perm. Rep. to UN, IAEA, UNIDO and other int. orgs, Vienna 1994–97, Chair., Group of 77, UN in Vienna 1996, Amb. to Australia (also accred to Slovenia and Slovakia) 1994–97; Goodwill Amb. World NGO Day 2014; Cabinet Sec., Islamabad 2000–01; currently Chair. Pakistan Inst. of Int. Affairs; Pres. Aurat Foundation. *Publication:* Pakistan in a Changing World 1978. *Address:* Pakistan Institute of International Affairs, Aiwan-e-Sadar Road, PO Box 1447, Karachi 74200, Pakistan (office). *Telephone:* (21) 35686069 (office). *Fax:* (21) 35686069 (office). *E-mail:* masumahasan@hotmail.com; info@piia.org.pk (office). *Website:* www.piia.org.pk (office).

HÄSÄNLI, Cämil Poladxan oğlu, PhD; Azerbaijani historian, academic and politician; b. 15 Jan. 1952, Ağalikänd, Bilasuvar Rayon, Azerbaijan SSR, USSR; ed Azerbaijan State Univ., Southern Illinois Univ., USA; worked as history teacher in Tazakend village, Cëlilabad Rayon; Lecturer, Baku br. of Cen. Lenin Museum 1976–77; entered doctoral courses at Baku State Univ. 1977, Docent 1990–, Dean of New and Modern History of Europe and Americas Dept 1992–94, now Prof.; Adviser to Pres. of Azerbaijan April–Sept. 1993; mem. Pres.'s Expert Council of High Accreditation Comm. of Azerbaijan 1994–2004; elected Deputy to Nat. Ass. 2000; Deputy Chair. Azerbaijan Popular Front Party; unsuccessful cand. (Nat. Council of Democratic Forces bloc) in presidential election Oct. 2013; participated in research projects at Humboldt Univ. of Berlin 2013; mem. Azerbaijan Nat. Acad. of Sciences, North American Soc. for Middle Eastern Studies 1998. *Publications include:* Black Shadow of White Dots: Soviet Totalitarism in Azerbaijan in 1920–1930 1991, Azerbaijan Republic in the International Relations System 1993, History of Azerbaijan (co-author) 1995, Azerbaycan Tarihi: Türkiye Yardımından Rusya İşgaline Kadar (1918–1920) 1998, History of Azerbaijan: From Turkey's Help to Russian Occupation (1918–1920) 1998, South Azerbaijan: Between Tehran, Baku and Moscow 1998, History: From the Past to the Future 1998, South Azerbaijan: Place of Beginning of the Cold War 1999, Soviet-American-British Confrontation in South Azerbaijan 2001, South Azerbaijan: Beginning of the Cold War 2003, USSR–Turkey: Cold War Arena 2005, Soğuk Savaşın İlk Çatışması: İran Azerbaycanı 2005, First Confrontation of the Cold War: Iranian Azerbaijan 2005, At the Dawn of the Cold War: The Soviet-American Crisis over Iranian Azerbaijan, 1941–1946 2006, USSR-Iran: Azerbaijani Crisis and the Beginning of the Cold War 2006, USSR-Turkey: From Neutrality to Cold War 2008, National Question in Azerbaijan: Political Leadership and Intelligence 2008, Khrushchev's Thaw and the National Question in Azerbaijan, 1954–1959 2009, Diplomatic History of the Azerbaijan Republic (in three vols), Vol. 1 The Foreign Policy of the Azerbaijan Democratic Republic (1918–1920) 2010, Stalin and the Turkish Crisis of the Cold War, 1945–1953 2011, Azerbaijan and the Russian Revolution: A Difficult Path to Independence, 1917–1920 2011, Sovet dövründä Azärbaycanın Xarici Siyasäti (1920–1939) 2012, Foreign Policy of the Republic of Azerbaijan, 1918–1920: The Difficult Road to Western Integration 2014. *Address:* c/o Azärbaycan Xalq Cabhasi Partiyası (Azerbaijan Popular Front Party), 1152 Baku, Milli Mäclis, Mehti Hussein küç. 2, Azerbaijan (office). *Telephone:* (12) 498-07-94 (office). *E-mail:* faiq73@mail.ru (office). *Website:* www.camilhasanli.com.

HASANOV, Ramiz Ayvaz oglu; Azerbaijani government official and fmr diplomatist; *Chairman, State Committee on Standardization, Metrology and Patents;* b. 20 Aug. 1961; m.; two c.; ed Faculty of Int. Law, Moscow State Inst. of Int. Relations, USSR; worked in various Govt ministries responsible for foreign trade issues; First Deputy Chair. Azcontrakt Open Jt Stock Co. 1983–2004; Amb. to Georgia 2004–05; Chair. State Cttee on Standardization, Metrology and Patents 2005–; Co-Chair. EuroAsian Interstate Council for Standardization, Metrology and Certification. *Address:* State Committee on Standardization, Metrology and Patents, Mardanov Gardashlary str. 124, 1147 Baku, Azerbaijan (office). *Telephone:* (12) 449-99-59 (office). *Fax:* (12) 440-52-24 (office). *E-mail:* azs@azstand.gov.az (office). *Website:* (office).

HÄSÄNOV, Col Gen. Zakir Äsgär oğlu; Azerbaijani politician and fmr army officer; *Minister of Defence;* b. 6 June 1959, Astara, Azerbaijan SSR, USSR; m.; two c.; ed Baku High Army Commanders School; served in Soviet Armed Forces units in Germany 1980–85; worked in Altai Mil. Registration and Enlistment Office, Siberia Mil. Okrug of USSR Ministry of Defence 1985–93; served in Main Office of Border Troops, Nat. Ministry of Security, Azerbaijan 1993–2003, Chief of Office of Int. Relations of State Border Service 2003; Deputy Minister of Interior and Commdr of Internal Troops 2003–13; Minister of Defence 2012–; attained rank of Maj.-Gen. 2003, Col-Gen. 2013; Order of Azerbaijan Flag 2004; Medal for Distinguished Service in the Border 1998, Medal for Distinguished Services 2002. *Address:* Ministry of Defence, 1073 Baku, Parlament pr. 3, Azerbaijan (office). *Telephone:* (12) 439-41-89 (office). *Fax:* (12) 492-92-50 (office). *E-mail:* pressmd@mod.gov.az (office). *Website:* www.mod.gov.az (office).

HASEEB, Khair El-Din, BA, MSc, PhD; Iraqi economist and statistician; *Director-General, Centre for Arab Unity Studies;* b. 1 Aug. 1929, Mosul; m. 1955; one s. two d.; ed Univ. of Baghdad, London School of Econs and Univ. of Cambridge, UK; civil servant, Ministry of Interior 1947–54; Head of Research and Statistics Dept, Iraqi Oil Co. 1959–60; Full-time Lecturer, Univ. of Baghdad 1960–61, Part-time 1961–63; Dir-Gen. Iraqi Fed. of Industries 1960–63; Gov. and Chair. Cen. Bank of Iraq 1963–65; Pres. Gen. Org. for Banks 1964–65; Acting Pres. Econ. Org., Iraq 1964–65; Assoc. Prof., Dept of Econs, Univ. of Baghdad 1965–71, Prof. of Econs 1971–74; mem. Bd of Dirs Iraq Nat. Oil Co. 1967–68; Chief, Programme and Co-ordination Unit and Natural Resources, Science and Tech. Div. UN Econ. Comm. for Western Asia, then Lebanon and Iraq 1974–76 and 1976–83; Acting Dir-Gen. Centre for Arab Unity Studies, Lebanon 1978–83, Dir-Gen. 1983–; Chair. Bd of Trustees and Dirs Arab Cultural Foundation, London 1987; Chair. Bd of Trustees Arab Org. for Translation, Lebanon 1999–. *Publications:* The National Income of Iraq 1953–1961, 1964, Workers' Participation in Management in Arab Countries (in Arabic) 1971, Sources of Arab Economic Thought in Iraq 1900–71 (in Arabic) 1972, Arab Monetary Integration (co-ed.) 1982, Arabs and Africa (ed.) 1985, The Future of the Arab Nation 1991, Arab-Iranian Relations (ed.) 2002, The Future of Iraq: Occupation, Resistance, Liberation and Democracy 2004, Planning Iraq's Future: A Detailed Project to Rebuild Post-Liberation Iraq (ed.) 2006, An Overview of Arab Concerns: Arab Nationalism, Arab Unity; The Centre for Arab Unity Studies; The Arab Intellectual and Democracy 2008, The Future of the Arab Nation: Challenges and Options 2012; numerous articles. *Leisure interests:* swimming, tennis. *Address:* Centre for Arab Unity Studies, 'Beit Al-Nahda' Bldg, Basra Street, PO Box 113-6001, Hamra, Beirut 2034 2407, Lebanon (office). *Telephone:* (1) 750084 (office); (1) 740631 (home). *Fax:* (1) 750088 (office). *E-mail:* info@caus.org.lb (office). *Website:* www.caus.org.lb (office).

HASEGAWA, Itsuko; Japanese architect; *Founder, Itsuko Hasagawa Atelier;* b. 1941, Shizuoka Pref.; ed Kanto Gakuin Univ., Tokyo Inst. of Tech.; worked for Kiyonori Kikutate 1964–69; researcher Dept of Architecture, Tokyo Inst. of Tech. 1969–71, Asst to Prof. Kazuo Shinohara 1971–78; est. Itsuku Hasagawa Atelier 1979; Lecturer, Waseda Univ. 1988, Tokyo Inst. of Tech. 1989, Niigata Univ. 1993, Tokyo Denki Univ. 1995; Visiting Prof., Grad. School of Design, Harvard Univ., USA 1992, Kanto Gakuin Univ. 2001; Hon. FRIBA 1997; Hon. FAIA 2006; hon. degree (Univ. Coll. London) 2001; Japan Inter-Design Forum Award 1986, Japan Cultural Design Award 1986, First Prize, Competition for Sumida Cultural Centre 1990, First Prize, Competition for Shiogama City Town Centre 1995, Int. Young Generation Award 1998, Avon Arts Award, Japan Art Academy Award 2000, RA of

Arts Architecture Prize 2018. *Architectural works include:* Tokumaru children's clinic, Ehime 1979, House in Kuwahara, Matsuyama 1980, Aono Bldg, Matsuyama 1982, Bizan Hall (Architectural Inst. of Japan Prize for Design) 1984, Sugai Internal Clinic, Ehime 1986, Shonandai Cultural Centre, Fujisawa, Kanagawa (BCS Award, Bldg Constructors Soc. 1992) 1987–90, STM House, Shibuya-ku, Tokyo 1991, Sumida Culture Factory 1994, Oshima-Machi Picture Book Museum, Toyama (Public Building Award 2000) 1994, Yamanashi Fruit Garden 1995, Imai Newtown Housing, Nagano (Olympic Village) 1998, Niigata City Performing Arts Centre (Japan Art Acad. Award 2000, BCS Award, Bldg Constructors Soc. 2001, Public Bldg Award 2004) 1998, Fukuroi Workshop Centre, Shizuoka 2001, Centre in Shizuoka 2004, Taisei Jr High and High School, Shizuoka 2004, Ohota Project 2005, Suzu Performing Arts Center, Ishikawa 2006, Shizuoka Univ. of Welfare 2006, Techno Plaza Ota 2008, K House 2009, Hayashi Kindergarten 2010, Kira Messe Numadu 2013. *Publications include:* "The Age of Dwellers", A Dialogue with Takamasa Yoshizawa 1979, The Complete Works of Itsuko Hasegawa 1985, Architectural Monographs No.31: Itsuko Hasegawa 1993, The Complete Works of Itsuko Hasegawa: 1985-1995 1995, Itsuko Hasegawa 1997, New Wave of Waterfront Process City 1998, The Equipment of Life 1999, Island Hopping 2000, Details of Garando and Harappa 2003, Design Studio of Itsuko Hasegawa 2004 2006, Of Seas and Nature and Architecture 2012; articles in professional journals. *Address:* Itsuku Hasegawa Atelier, 1-9-7 Yushima, Bunkyo-ku, Tokyo 113-0034, Japan (office). *Telephone:* (3) 3818-5470 (office). *Fax:* (3) 3818-1821 (office). *E-mail:* ihasegawa@ihasegawa.com (office). *Website:* www.ihasegawa.com (office).

HASEGAWA, Toru; Japanese automotive industry executive; *Corporate Vice-President, Nissan Motor Company Limited;* joined Yamaha Motor Co. Ltd 1960, various positions including export agent, Dir of Procurement 1970s, Dir of European Operations, Netherlands 1990, Sr Man. Dir –2001, Pres. and Rep. Dir, Yamaha Motor Co. Ltd 2001–04, fmr Chair. and Dir; Man. Dir Nissan Middle East F Z E from 2005, Pres. Nissan Motor Co. Ltd Thailand, Regional Vice-Pres. Asia and Oceania Operations –2012, Corp. Vice-Pres. Nissan Motor Co. Ltd 2012–, also Corp. Vice-Pres. for Africa, Middle East and Indian Operations, Nissan Motor India Pvt. Ltd, Pres. Dir, PT Nissan Motor Indonesia –2014; fmr mem. Bd of Dirs Int. Business Dept Fuji Kiko Co. Ltd, Euroland.com AB. *Address:* Nissan Motor Co. Ltd, 1-1, Takashima 1-chome, Nishi-ku, Yokohama 220-868, Kanagawa, Japan (office). *Telephone:* (45) 523-5523 (office). *Website:* www.nissan-global.com (office).

HASELSTEINER, Hans Peter, MA, PhD; Austrian business executive and fmr politician; b. 1 Feb. 1944, Wörgl; m. Ulrike Haselsteiner; ed Vienna Univ. of Econs and Business Admin; mil. service 1963–64; univ. studies 1964–70; worked for auditing and tax consultancy firm, Perfekta GmbH, Vienna 1970–74; joined ILBAU AG as mem. Supervisory Bd 1972, mem. Man. Bd and CEO group parent co. 1974–94, Chair. Man. Bd Bauholding Strabag AG (Bauholding Strabag SE from 2004, Strabag SE from 2006) 1998–2013; Co-owner, RAIL Holding AG 2008; mem. Parl. and Vice-Chair. Liberal Forum 1994–98; Chair. Fachverband der Bauindustrie (Austrian Construction Industry Asscn), Vienna 2002; Ehrenzeichen des Landes Tirol 2012.

HASELTINE, William A., BA, PhD; American scientist, academic and business executive; *Chairman and President, Access Health International, Inc.;* b. 17 Oct. 1944, St Louis, Mo.; s. of William R. Haseltine and Jean Adele Ellsberg; m. 1st Patricia Gercik; m. 2nd Gale Hayman 1991; two c.; ed Univ. of California, Harvard Univ.; Prof., Dana-Farber Cancer Inst., Harvard Medical School and Harvard School of Public Health 1976–93, fmr Chair. Div. of Cancer Pharmacology, Div. of Human Retrovirology; f. Human Genome Sciences Inc. (HGS) 1992, Chair. and Chief Exec. 1993–2004; Chair. and CEO Haseltine Associates Ltd; Chair. Haseltine Global Health LLC; currently Chair. and Pres. Access Health International, Inc.; also currently Chair. Haseltine Foundation for Science and the Arts; adviser and Bd mem. of several healthcare cos; mem. Advisory Bd, IE University, Madrid, Advisory Council for Koch Inst. of MIT, Advisory Bd of Ragon Inst. of Harvard Univ. and MIT, Advisory Council of the Council of Scientific and Industrial Research of India, Innovation Council of Reliance Industries (India), Advisory Council on Creativity and Innovation of NYU-Shanghai Univ., Council on Foreign Relations, Bd of AID for AIDS International; Lifetime Gov., New York Acad. of Sciences; Trustee, Lee Berger Trust for Paleoanthropology (South Africa), Brookings Inst., FXB Center for Health and Human Rights at Harvard School of Public Health; Dir, Int. China Ageing Industry Asscn; Chair. US-China Health Summit; mem. Bd of Dirs, Young Concert Artists, Youth Orchestra of the Americas, China Arts Foundation; Patron Metropolitan Opera, Metropolitan Museum, Guggenheim Museum, Museum of Modern Art, Patron's Circle of the Asia Soc.; Hon. mem. Bd of Trustees, Brookings Inst.; numerous awards. *Achievement:* well known for his pioneering work on cancer, HIV/AIDS and genomics. *Publications:* several books and more than 200 scientific publs; more than 50 patents. *Address:* Access Health International, Inc., 1016 5th Avenue, Suite 11A/C, New York, NY 10028, USA (office). *E-mail:* william.haseltine@accessh.org (office). *Website:* accessh.org (office).

HASHEL, Mohammad Y. al-, BSc, MBA, PhD; Kuwaiti economist and central banker; *Governor and Chairman, Central Bank of Kuwait;* b. 28 April 1974; ed Kuwait Univ., Emory Univ., Georgia, Old Dominion Univ., Virginia; fmr Prof., Coll. of Business Admin, Kuwait Univ.; Deputy Gov., Central Bank of Kuwait 2009–12, Gov. and Chair. Bd of Dirs 2012–; Alt. Gov. of Kuwait at IMF and Arab Monetary Fund; Chair. Exec. Cttee Int. Islamic Liquidity Man. (ILM) 2013–16, also mem. Governing Bd and Deputy Chair. 2019; Chair. Bd of Dirs, Kuwait Inst. of Banking Studies; Co-Chair. Financial Stability Bd Regional Consultative Group for Middle East and N Africa; mem. Kuwait Stock Exchange Cttee 2008–11; mem. Council Islamic Financial Services Bd; mem. Higher Council of Planning and Devt, Higher Petroleum Council; mem. Bd of Dirs Kuwait Investment Authority 2012–, Gulf Monetary Council; mem. Financial Stability Bd (FSB), Regional Consultative Group for Middle East and North Africa (MENA); Visionary Award Central Bank Gov. of the Year, Union of Arab Banks 2015. *Address:* Office of the Governor, Central Bank of Kuwait, POB 526, 13006 Safat, Abdullah al-Salem Street, Kuwait City, Kuwait (office). *Telephone:* 1814444 (office). *Fax:* 22443354 (office). *E-mail:* cbk@cbk.gov.kw (office). *Website:* www.cbk.gov.kw (office).

HASHEMI BAHREMANI (Rafsanjani), Faezeh, MA; Iranian politician and sports administrator; b. 7 Jan. 1962, Qum; d. of Ali Akbar Hashemi Bahremani (fmr Pres. of Iran) and Effat Marashi Ali-abadi; m. Hamid Lahouti Oshkevari 1980; one s. one d.; ed Al-Zahra Univ. and Islamic Azad Univ., Tehran; mem. Majlis-e-Shura e Islami (Parl.) 1996–2000; Vice-Pres. Nat. Olympic Cttee 1990–; Founder and Pres. Islamic Countries Women Sports Solidarity Council (ICWSSC) 1991–; mem. Cen. Council of the Communications Network of Women's NGOs 1995–; Man. Dir Zanan (women's journal). *Publication:* The First Meeting 1993. *Leisure interests:* study, sport, cinema, music. *Address:* 10 Simin Alley, Asef Street, Vali Asr Ave Zaferanieh, Tehran 19879, Iran. *Telephone:* (21) 8019934. *Fax:* (21) 8019906.

HASHIM, Abdelrahman Hassan Abdelrahman, BSc; Sudanese banking executive and central banker; *Governor, Central Bank of Sudan;* b. 1957, Barber; ed Univ. of Khartoum; fmrly with Faisal Islamic Bank; Gen. Man., Omduran Nat. Bank 2006–13, also Gen. Man. Saving and Social Devt Bank; Gov. and Chair. Cen. Bank of Sudan 2013–; also currently Vice-Pres. Bank of Sahel and Sahara Community, Tripoli, Libya; mem. Union of Arab Banks, Nat. Congress Party. *Publications include:* numerous articles on financial issues. *Address:* Central Bank of Sudan, Gamhoria Street, POB 313, Khartoum, Sudan (office). *Telephone:* (183) 782246 (office). *Fax:* (183) 787226 (office). *E-mail:* sudanbank@sudanmail.net (office). *Website:* www.cbos.gov.sd (office).

HASHIM, Ali; Maldivian business executive and politician; ed Australian Nat. Univ.; Consultant Program Officer, UNDP 1995–99; helped establish Maldives Stock Exchange 2007, Man. Dir 2007–08; Minister of Finance and Treasury 2008–10; Dir Lintel Investments and Man. Services Pvt. Ltd 2010; mem. Maldivian Democratic Party, fmr Vice-Chair.

HASHIM, Fawzia; Eritrean politician; *Minister of Justice;* women's rights campaigner; fought as soldier in Eritrean wars of independence in 1970s; Minister of Justice 1991–. *Address:* Ministry of Justice, POB 241, Asmara, Eritrea (office). *Telephone:* (1) 127739 (office). *Fax:* (1) 126422 (office).

HASHIMI, Tariq al-, BA, MA; Iraqi politician; b. 1942, Baghdad; s. of Yassin al-Hashimi; ed Al-Mustansiriyah Univ.; attended Mil. Acad. 1959–62, pursued mil. career –1975; instructor, Leadership Acad. 1975; Iraq Br. Man., Arab Shipping Co. 1979–81, moved to Kuwait, served as Dir-Gen., Arab Shipping Co. –1990; returned to Iraq 1990; mem. Iraqi Islamic Party, fmr mem. Planning Cttee and Shura Council, Sec.-Gen. –2009; Second Vice-Pres. of Iraq 2006–11, First Vice-Pres. 2011, currently living in exile in Istanbul, Turkey, faced trial in absentia 2012. *E-mail:* info@alhashimi.org (office). *Website:* alhashimi.org (office).

HASHIMOTO, Toru; Japanese lawyer and politician; b. 29 June 1969, Hatagaya, Shibuya; m. Noriko Hashimoto; three s. four d.; ed Waseda Univ.; mem. Osaka Bar Asscn 1996–; f. Hashimoto Law Office 1998, currently Partner; became well-known giving legal advice on local radio and TV programmes in Kansai area, including programmes Super Morning (TV Asahi) and Gyōretsu no Dekiru Hōritsu Sōdanjo (The Legal Advisory Office that People Queue Up For, NTV); Gov. Osaka Pref. 2008–11 (youngest gov. in Japan); Mayor of Osaka 2011–15; Founding Pres. Osaka Restoration Asscn ('One Osaka') 2010–; Founder Japan Restoration Asscn 2012–14. *Television includes:* Panel, Gyōretsu no Dekiru Hōritsu Sōdanjo, NTV 2003–07. *Address:* Osaka Restoration Association, Chuo-ku, Osaka Shimanouchi 1-17-16, Sanei Nagahori Building 2F, Yubinbango 542-0082, Japan. *Telephone:* (6) 6120-5581. *Fax:* (6) 6120-5582. *Website:* www.oneosaka.jp.

HASHMI, (Aurangzeb) Alamgir, MA, DLit; Pakistani academic, poet, writer, editor and translator and broadcaster; b. 15 Nov. 1951, Lahore; s. of Syed Sharif Ahmed Hashmi and Nasim Akhtar Hashmi; two s. one d.; ed Univ. of Louisville, USA, Univ. of Punjab; Instructor and Tutor in English, Govt Coll., Lahore 1971–73; Lecturer, Forman Christian Coll., Lahore 1973–74; Davidson Int. Visiting Scholar, Univ. of North Carolina 1974–75; Lecturer in English, Univ. of Louisville 1975–78, Univ. of Zürich and Volkshochschule, Zürich 1980–85; Asst Prof. of English, Univ. of Bahawalpur, Pakistan 1979–80; Lecturer in English, Univ. of Basel, Univ. of Bern 1982; Prof. of English and Commonwealth Literature, Univ. of Geneva, Univ. of Fribourg 1985; Assoc. Prof. of English, Int. Islamic Univ., Islamabad 1985–86; Foundation Chair, Prof. of English and Head, Dept of English, Univ. of Azad Jammu and Kashmir, Muzaffarabad 1986–87; Visiting Prof. of English, Govt Postgraduate Coll., Islamabad 1986; Research Prof. of English, American, African and Comparative Literature, Quaid-i-Azam Univ., Islamabad 1986–2000; Prof./Ed., PIDE, Quaid-i-Azam Univ. Campus, Islamabad 1988–2011; Course Dir, Foreign Service Training Inst. and Acad., Islamabad 1988–; Prof. of English and Comparative Literature, Univ. of Iceland 2000; Founder and Chair. Standing Int. Cttee on English in S Asia 1989–; Founder and Chair. Townsend Poetry Prize Cttee 1986–; Judge, Commonwealth Writers Prize 1990, nat. literature prizes, Pakistan Acad. of Letters 1998–; jury mem., Neustadt Int. Prize for Literature 1996; Ed., Advisory Ed., Editorial Adviser and referee for numerous int. scholarly and literary journals and book series; thesis supervisor and external examiner for many univs world-wide; broadcaster, lecturer, scriptwriter, translator, ed. for Radio Pakistan and Pakistan TV 1968–; adviser, Nat. Book Council of Pakistan 1989–95, Nat. Book Foundation 1993–; Judge, Prime Minister's Award for Literature 1999; Founding Pres. The Literature Podium; mem. Council Asscn for Commonwealth Studies 2005–07, Bd of Govs Pakistan Acad. of Letters 2009–12; mem. Poetry Soc., Associated Writing Programs, Asscn for Asian Studies, Syndicate, Univ. of the Punjab, New York Acad. of Sciences, Council on Nat. Literatures, Asscn for Commonwealth Literature and Language Studies, Int. Asscn of Univ. Profs of English, Modern Language Asscn of America; Fellow, Int. Centre for Asian Studies, Int. PEN; Rockefeller Foundation Fellow; Life Fellow, Pakistan Acad. of Letters; Hon. LittD (Luxembourg, San Francisco); First Prize, All Pakistan Creative Writing Contest 1972, Patras Bokhari Award, Pakistan Acad. of Letters 1985, Roberto Celli Memorial Award 1994, Pres. of Pakistan's Award for Pride of Performance (Medal for Literature); numerous other academic and literary distinctions, prizes and citations from different countries. *Publications include:* poetry: The Oath and Amen: Love Poems 1976, America is a Punjabi Word 1979, An Old Chair 1979, My Second in Kentucky 1981, This Time in Lahore 1983, Neither This Time/Nor That Place 1984, Inland and Other Poems 1988, The Poems of Alamgir Hashmi 1992, Sun and Moon and Other Poems 1992, Others to Sport with Amaryllis in the Shade 1992, A Choice of Hashmi's Verse 1997, The Ramazan Libation: Selected Poems 2003; other: Pakistani Literature (two vols; ed., second edn as Pakistani Literature: The Contemporary English Writers) 1978, Ezra Pound 1983, Commonwealth Literature 1983, The Worlds of Muslim

Imagination (ed.) 1986, The Commonwealth, Comparative Literature and the World 1988, Pakistani Short Stories in English (ed.) 1992, Encyclopedia of Post-Colonial Literatures in English (ed.) 1994, 2005, Post-independence Voices in South Asian Writings (co-ed.) 2001, Your Essence, Martyr (ed.) 2011; contrib. to numerous books, anthologies, journals, periodicals and festschrift. *Leisure interests:* walking, cricket, music, theatre, films. *Address:* 1542 Service Road West, G-11/2, Islamabad, Pakistan (home). *E-mail:* alamgirhashmi@yahoo.co.uk (home).

HASHMI, Makhdoom Javed; Pakistani politician; b. 1 Jan. 1948, Multan; m.; two d.; mem. Parl. 1985–88, 1990–99, 2008–11 (resgnd), 2013–14 (resgnd); fmr Fed. Minister for Labour, Minister for Health and Population Welfare 1997–99; fmr mem. Pakistan Muslim League (Nawaz), apptd Parl. Leader 1999, fmr Acting Pres.; mem. Alliance for the Restoration of Democracy 2003; arrested Oct. 2003, sentenced to 23 years in prison for inciting mutiny in the army, forgery and defamation April 2004, released Aug. 2007; Pres. Pakistan Tehreek-e-Insaf 2012–14. *Address:* House No.50, Muhallah Qasim Multan Cantt, Multan, Punjab, Pakistan (home).

HASHMI, Moneeza, MEd, MA; Pakistani television executive; *General Manager, International Relations, HUM TV Eye Television Network;* b. (Moneeza Gul Faiz), 22 Aug. 1946, Simla; d. of Faiz Ahmad Faiz; m. Humair Hashmi; two s.; ed Univ. of Hawaii, USA, Punjab Univ., Lahore; Program Man., Pakistan TV (PTV), Lahore 1974–81, Man. Educational TV 1982–88, Gen. Man. 1988–2003, Director of Programmes 2003–04; Gen. Man. Int. Relations, HUM TV Eye Television Network, Lahore 2005–; Chair. Asia-Pacific Media AIDS Initiative; Co-founder Himmat Soc. (charity); mem. Bd of Govs Omar Asghar Khan Devt Foundation; Grad. Award 2000, 2001, Commonwealth Broadcasting Award Citation 2002, Pres. of Pakistan's Pride of Performance 2002, Fatima Jinnah Award 2004. *Television includes:* Khwateen Time (Exec. Producer). *Leisure interests:* travelling, reading. *Address:* HUM TV, Office #102, 1st Floor, Siddique Centre, Gulberg, Lahore; 102-H Model Town, Lahore, Pakistan (home). *Telephone:* (42) 5884324 (home). *Fax:* (42) 5782007 (office); (42) 5884866 (home). *E-mail:* moneezahashmi@yahoo.co.uk (office).

HASHWANI, Sadruddin; Pakistani business executive; *Chairman, Hashoo Group;* b. 19 Feb. 1940, Karachi; s. of Mukhi Varas Hussain and Varasiani Zaverba; m. Noori Hashwani; two s. three d.; business ventures in cotton, petroleum, hotel industry, real estate, trading, information technology, minerals, ceramics pharmaceuticals, travel and tourism, commodity trading business and property devt 1950–; f. Hashwani Hotels Ltd, Net 21; Founder and Chair. Hashoo Group. *Publication:* Truth Always Prevails: A Memoir 2014. *Address:* Hashoo Group, PEC Building Ataturk Avenue G-5/2, POB 1670, Islamabad, Pakistan (office). *Telephone:* (51) 2272890 (office). *Fax:* (51) 2274812 (office). *E-mail:* info@hashoogroup.com (office); hashwani@net21pk.com (office). *Website:* www.hashoogroup.com (home).

HASKINS, Baron (Life Peer), cr. 1998; of Skidby in the County of the East Riding of Yorkshire; **Christopher Robin Haskins,** BA; Irish business executive; b. 30 May 1937, Dublin; s. of Robert Brown Haskins and Margaret Elizabeth Haskins (née Mullen); m. Gilda Susan Horsley 1959; three s. two d.; ed St Columba's Coll., Dublin, Trinity Coll., Dublin; with Ford Motor Co. 1960–62; joined Northern Foods PLC 1962, Chair. 1986–2002 (retd); mem. Culliton Irish Industrial Policy Review Group 1991–92, Ind. Comm. Social Justice 1992–94, UK Round Table on Sustainable Devt 1995–98, CBI's Pres. Cttee 1996–99, Hampel Cttee on Corp. Governance 1996–97; Chair. Better Regulation Task Force 1997–2002, Express Dairies 1998–2002, DEFRA (Dept for Environment, Food and Rural Affairs) Review Group 2002–03; Dir Lawes Agricultural Trust, Yorkshire TV 2002–; Dir Yorkshire and Humber Regional Devt Agency 1998–; mem. New Deal Task Force 1997–2001, Yorkshire Forward 1998–; Co-ordinator Rural Recovery 2001–03; fmr Chair. European Movement; Chair. of Council and Pro-Chancellor, Open Univ. 2005–14; hon. degrees (Leeds Metropolitan Univ., Dublin, Essex, Nottingham, Hull, Huddersfield, Lincoln, Cranfield, Bradford). *Leisure interests:* farming, watching cricket, writing, politics. *Address:* Quarryside Farm, Main Street, Skidby, nr Cottingham, East Yorks., HU16 5TG, England (home). *Telephone:* (1482) 842692 (home). *Fax:* (1482) 845249 (home). *E-mail:* gshaskins@aol.com (home).

HASLAM, William Edward (Bill), BA; American business executive, politician and fmr state governor; b. 23 Aug. 1958, Knoxville, Tenn.; s. of Jim Haslam and Cynthia Haslam (née Allen); m. Crissy Garrett 1981; two s. one d.; ed Webb School of Knoxville, Emory Univ.; began working as teenager part-time in family business, Pilot Corpn (petroleum co. f. by his father), Knoxville, following graduation returned to Knoxville to work for Pilot, later became Pres. and Dir –2003; Mayor of Knoxville 2003–10; Gov. of Tenn. 2011–19; fmr CEO SAKS Direct 1999–2001; Co-owner Tennessee Smokies (minor league baseball team); mem. Bd Advisory Council on Historical Preservation 2008–, Tennessee Tech. Devt Corpn 2008–; Chair. East Tennessee Center for Non-Profit Man.; Chair. and Pres. Project GRAD; Chair. Exec. Cttee Young Life of Knoxville; Campaign Chair. Foothills Land Conservancy; Chair. Republican Govs. Asscn 2014–15, 2017–18; Vice-Chair. Knoxville Museum of Art; fmr mem. Bd Cornerstone Foundation and World Vision, Emerald Avenue Youth Foundation, Diversity Task Force of Nine Counties, One Vision; mem. Salvation Army (Chair.), United Way of Greater Knoxville; Elder, Cedar Springs Presbyterian Church; mem. Mayors Against Illegal Guns Coalition –2009 (resgnd), Nat. Rifle Asscn; Republican. *Leisure interests:* bicycling, running. *Address:* c/o Office of the Governor, 1st Floor, State Capitol, Nashville, TN 37243-0001, USA (office). *E-mail:* bill.haslam@tn.gov (office).

HASLER, Adrian; Liechtenstein economist and politician; *Prime Minister and Minister of General Government Affairs and of Finance;* b. 11 Feb. 1964; m. Gudrun Hasler-Elkuch; two s.; ed Univ. of St Gallen, Switzerland; Dir, Control Dept, Balzers AG 1992–96; Head of Finance Group and Deputy Dir Verwaltungs- und Privat-Bank AG, Vaduz 1996–2004; Chief of Nat. Police Force 2004–13; mem. Landtag (Parl.) (FBP) 2001–04, mem. Finance Cttee 2001–04; Prime Minister and Minister of Gen. Govt Affairs and of Finance 2013–; mem. Progressive Citizens' Party (FBP). *Address:* Regierungsgebäude, Peter-Kaiser-Pl. 1, Postfach 684, 9490 Vaduz, Liechtenstein (office). *Telephone:* 2366111 (office). *Fax:* 2366022 (office). *E-mail:* info@regierung.li (office). *Website:* www.liechtenstein.li (office).

HASLER, Otmar; Liechtenstein politician; b. 28 Sept. 1953, Vaduz; m. Traudi Hasler-Hilti; two s. two d.; ed secondary school-teaching diploma from Fribourg Univ.; teacher, Realschule, Eschen 1979–2001; Pres. Progressive Citizens' Party of Liechtenstein (FBP) 1993–95, mem. Exec. Cttee 1993–; mem. Parl. 1989–2001, Vice-Pres. 1993–94, 1996–2001, Pres. 1995; Prime Minister of Liechtenstein, also responsible for Govt Affairs, Finance, Construction and Public Works 2001–09 (resgnd); Pres. newly founded Liechtenstein Sr Citizens' Org. 1999; mem. Historical Soc., Liechtenstein Art Soc., Liechtenstein Senior Educational Asscn; Grand Gold Decoration with Ribbon (Austria) 2004. *Leisure interests:* reading, music, hiking.

HASNEDL, Jerry, AA; American business executive; b. Thief River Falls, Minn.; m. Ruth Hasnedl 1971; two c.; ed Northland Coll., Thief River Falls, Minn.; served in the US Air Force; mem. Bd of Dirs CHS 1995, served as Sec.-Treas., chaired Capital Cttee and served as mem. Govt Relations Cttee, Chair. CHS 2011–12, also Chair. Exec. Cttee and Chair. CHS Foundation; mem. Minn. Farmers Union; mem. and fmr Dir Northwest Grain (CHS retail business); mem. Bd of Dirs Agricultural Utilization Research Inst. 2016–, Cooperative Network. *Address:* c/o Agricultural Utilization Research Institute, 510 County Road 71, Suite 120, Crookston, MN 56716, USA. *Telephone:* (218) 281-7600. *Fax:* (218) 281-3759. *E-mail:* news@auri.org. *Website:* www.auri.org.

HASPEL, Gina; American intelligence officer and government official; *Director, Central Intelligence Agency;* b. (Gina Walker), 1956, Ashland, Kentucky; m. Jeff Haspel (divorced); ed Univ. of Louisville; began career as contractor for US Army's 10th Special Forces Group; joined Central Intelligence Agency (CIA) as reports officer 1985, becoming Deputy Dir, Nat. Resources Div., moved into counter-terrorism 2001, assigned to oversee secret CIA prison in Thailand, Oct.–Dec. 2002, Chief of Staff to Dir of Nat. Clandestine Service 2005, fmr Operations Officer, Counterterrorism Center near Washington, DC, CIA Station Chief in London, in New York 2011, fmr Deputy Dir, Nat. Clandestine Service and Nat. Clandestine Service for Foreign Intelligence and Covert Action, Acting Dir, Nat. Clandestine Service 2013, Deputy Dir, CIA 2017–18, Dir, CIA (first female) 2018–; George H. W. Bush Award for excellence in counterterrorism, Donovan Award, Intelligence Medal of Merit, Presidential Rank Award. *Address:* Central Intelligence Agency, Office of Public Affairs, Washington, DC 20505, USA (office). *Telephone:* (703) 482-0623 (office). *Fax:* (571) 204-3800 (office). *Website:* www.cia.gov (office).

HASQUIN, Hervé, PhD; Belgian historian, academic and politician; *Permanent Secretary, Académie Royale des Sciences, des Lettres et des Beaux-Arts de Belgique;* b. 31 Dec. 1942, Charleroi; s. of René-Pierre Hasquin and Andrée Jacquemart; m. Michèle Nahum 1986; one s.; Dean, Faculty of Arts and Philosophy, Université Libre de Bruxelles 1979–82, Rector 1982–86, Chair. Bd of Dirs 1986–95, Pres. Inst. for Religious and Secular Studies 1987–; Head French-speaking network Scientific Information and Technological Devt 1986–87; Vice-Pres. Parti Réformateur Libéral (PRL) 1986–89, Gen. Sec. 1990–92, Head PRL Group, Council of Brussels, Capital Region 1991–; Senator 1988–95; Regional Deputy, Brussels 1989–99; Minister of Environmental Planning, Town Planning and Transport, Brussels Capital Region 1995–99; Minister-Pres. of French-speaking Community of Belgium responsible for Int. Relations 1999–2004; Prés. de la Fédération MR du Hainaut 2000–04; Fed. Deputy 2003–07; Perm. Sec. Acad. Royale des Sciences, des Lettres et des Beaux-Arts de Belgique 2008–; Chair. Centre de l'Egalité des Chances et Contre le racisme 2008–11; mem. Acad. Royale de Belgique 2002, Academia Toscana Di Scienze e Lettre 'La Colombaria'; Sociétaire hc, Acad. des Sciences et des Arts 2000; Chevalier, Légion d'honneur 1989, Commdr, Order of Leopold II 1984, Order of the Lion (Senegal) 1987, Grand Officer, Order of Leopold 1999, Grand Cross, Order of the Crown 2004; Dr hc (Cluj, Romania); Royal Acad. of Belgium Prize 1990, Literary Prize of French-speaking Community Council 1981, Prix ALUMNI Fondation universitaire and other prizes. *Publications:* Dictionnaire d'histoire de Belgique: Vingt siècles d'institutions. Les hommes. Les faits 1988, La Wallonie: Le Pays et les Hommes, Histoire de la Laïcité principalement en Belgique et en France, La Wallonie, son histoire 1999, Dictionnaire d'histoire de Belgique: Les Hommes, les institutions, les faits, le Congo Belge et le Ruanda-Urundi 2000, Les séparatistes wallons et le gouvernement de Vichy (1940–43), Acad. royale de Belgique lecture 2003, Louis XIV: Face à l'Europe du Nord 2005, Joseph II: Catholique anticlerical et réformateur impatient 2007, Population, commerce et religion au siècle des lumières 2008, Les catholiques belges et la franc-maconnerie. De la 'rigidite Ratzinger' a la transgression 2011, Les pays d'islam et la Franc-maçonnerie 2013; about 150 articles and papers in Belgian and foreign learned journals. *Leisure interests:* writing, teaching, football, cycling, cinema. *Address:* Académie royale des sciences, des lettres et des beaux-arts de Belgique, Palais des Académies, 1 rue Ducale, 1000 Brussels (office); Rue du Long Bois 1, 7830 Graty Silly, Belgium (home). *Telephone:* (2) 550-22-12 (office). *Fax:* (2) 550-22-05 (office). *E-mail:* herve.hasquin@cfwb.be (office). *Website:* www.academieroyale.be (office); www.hasquin.be.

HASSAN, Az-Zobeir Ahmed al-; Sudanese politician; Minister of Finance and Nat. Economy –2008; Sec.-Gen. Islamic Movt (IM) 2012.

HASSAN, Fred, BSc, MBA; American (b. Pakistani) business executive; *Managing Director, Warburg Pincus LLC;* b. 12 Nov. 1945, Multan, Pakistan; m. Noreen Hassan; one s. two d.; ed Imperial Coll. of Science and Tech., Univ. of London, UK, Harvard Business School; joined Sandoz Pharmaceuticals (now Novartis) in 1972, Head, US Pharmaceuticals 1984; Exec. Vice-Pres. Pharmaceutical and Medical Products, Wyeth (fmrly American Home Products), Head, Genetics Inst. (wholly-owned subsidiary), mem. Bd of Dirs 1995–97; CEO and mem. Bd of Dirs Pharmacia & Upjohn 1997–2001, Chair. and CEO Pharmacia Corpn (formed following merger of Monsanto and Pharmacia & Upjohn cos) 2001–03; Chair. and CEO Schering-Plough Corpn 2003–09; apptd Sr Advisor Warburg Pincus LLC 2009, Man. Dir 2011–, Chair. Bausch & Lomb (Warburg Pincus is majority owner) 2010–13; Pres. Int. Fed. of Pharmaceutical Mfrs Asscns; Chair. Pharmaceutical Research and Mfrs of America; mem. Bd of Dirs Avon Products, Inc. 1999–2013, CIGNA Corpn, TimeWarner Inc. 2009, Amgen, Inc. 2015–, Intrexon Corpn 2016–; mem. Investor Advisory Bd Caerus Ventures; fmr Chair. Bd of Dirs HealthCare Inst. of New Jersey; CEO-of-the-Year in the Global Pharmaceutical Industry, Financial Times 1999. *Publication:* Reinvent: A Leader's Playbook for Serial Success 2013. *Address:* Warburg Pincus LLC, 450

Lexington Avenue, New York, NY 10017, USA (office). *Telephone:* (212) 878-0600 (office). *Fax:* (212) 878-9351 (office). *Website:* www.warburgpincus.com (office).

HASSAN, Jafar Abed A., MSc, PhD; Jordanian diplomatist and politician; *Director, The Royal Hashemite Court;* b. 1968, Khreibet al Souq; ed Grad. Inst. of Int. and Devt Studies, Univ. of Geneva, Switzerland, Boston Univ., Harvard Business School, USA, American Coll., Paris, France; joined Foreign Service 1991; fmr Head of Human Rights Issues and Humanitarian Affairs, Perm. Mission to UN, Geneva 1995–99; fmr Personal Asst to Dir of Nat. Security, Royal Palace, Jordan; Dir Israel Section, Ministry of Foreign Affairs –2001, Deputy Chief of Mission, Embassy in Washington, DC 2001–06; Dir Int. Affairs Dept, Royal Hashemite Court 2006–09, Dir, Royal Hashemite Court 2012–; Minister of Planning and Int. Co-operation 2011–12. *Address:* Royal Hashemite Court, Royal Palace, Amman 11118, Jordan (office). *Telephone:* (6) 4630617 (office). *Fax:* (6) 4634641 (office). *Website:* www.kinghussein.gov.jo/royal_offices.html (office).

HASSAN, Jean-Claude Gaston; French banker and public servant; *State Councillor;* b. 11 Nov. 1954, Tunis, Tunisia; s. of Charles Hassan and Yvonne Lellouche; m. Françoise Benhamou 1981; two s. one d.; ed Lycée de Mutuelleville, Tunis, Lycée Louis-le-Grand, Paris, École normale supérieure, École nat. d'admin; mem. Conseil d'Etat, Auditeur 1981, Counsel 1985; Tech. Adviser to Office of Minister of Social Affairs and Nat. Solidarity 1984–85; Deputy Dir-Gen. Banque Stern 1986–89, Dir-Gen. 1989–92; Dir-Gen. Banque Worms 1992–94; rejoined Conseil d'État 1994–2000, 2002, Conseiller d'État (State Councillor) 2005–; Conseiller pour l'euro de Laurent Fabius, Ministry of the Econ., Finance and Industry 2000–02; mem. Cttee de règlement des différends de la CRE, Comm. de Régulation de l'Énergie from 2006, Enforcement Cttee of Autorité des marchés financiers 2008–, Comm. of the Supervisory Authority 2011–. *Address:* Conseil d'État, 1 place du Palais-Royal, 75100 Paris Cedex 01, France (office). *Telephone:* 1-40-20-80-00 (office). *E-mail:* lise.ardhuin@conseil-etat.fr. *Website:* www.conseil-etat.fr (office).

HASSAN, M. A.; Bangladeshi pharmaceuticals industry executive; *Chairman and Managing Director, Aristopharma Ltd;* f. Aristopharma Ltd 1986, currently Chair. and Man. Dir; apptd Vice-Pres. Bangladesh Asscn of Pharmaceutical Industries 2007. *Address:* Aristopharma Ltd, 7 Purana Paltan Line, Dhaka 1000, Bangladesh (office). *Telephone:* (2) 93516913 (office). *Fax:* (2) 8317005 (office). *E-mail:* apl@aristopharma.com (office). *Website:* www.aristopharma.com (office).

HASSAN, Maggie, BA, JD; American lawyer, politician, state governor and business executive; *Senator from New Hampshire;* b. 27 Feb. 1958, Boston, Mass; m. Thomas Hassan; two c.; ed Brown Univ., Northeastern Univ. School of Law; attorney, Palmer & Dodge (law firm) 1985–92; Assoc. Gen. Counsel for Brigham and Women's Hosp./Partners Healthcare 1993–96; attorney, Sullivan, Weinstein & McQuay (law firm) 1996–; apptd by Gov. Jeanne Shaheen as citizen adviser to Advisory Cttee to Adequacy in Educ. and Finance Comm. 1999; unsuccessful cand. for New Hampshire Senate 2002; mem. New Hampshire Senate from 23rd Dist 2005–10, served as Asst Democratic Whip, Pres. Pro Tempore and Majority Leader; Gov. of New Hampshire 2013–17; Senator from New Hampshire 2017–; Democrat. *Address:* United States Senate, B85 Russell Senate Office Building, Washington, DC 20510 (office); PO Box 298, Concord, NH 03302, USA (office). *Telephone:* (202) 224-3324 (office). *Website:* www.maggiehassan.com; www.senate.gov (office).

HASSAN, Mohamed Hag Ali, BSc, MSc, PhD; Sudanese mathematician, academic and international organization official; b. 21 Nov. 1947, Elgetina; m.; three c.; ed Univ. of Newcastle-upon-Tyne, Univ. of Oxford, UK; Sr Lecturer, Dept of Math. Sciences, Univ. of Khartoum 1974, Assoc. Prof. 1979, Prof. –1986, Dean of Math. Sciences 1985–86; Fulbright Research Fellow 1984; Exec. Dir Third World Acad. of Sciences (now World Acad. of Sciences) Trieste, Italy 1983–2011, Treas. 2011–15, Interim Dir 2016–; Sec.-Gen. Third World Network of Scientific Orgs 1988–2006; Pres. Network of African Science Acads 2001; Dir of Secr., InterAcademy Panel 2001, Co-Chair. 2010–; Chair. Co-ordinating Council Comm. on Science and Tech. for Sustainable Devt in the South 1995, Hon. Presidential Advisory Council for Science and Tech. (apptd by Pres. of Nigeria) 2001, Advisory Bd UN Univ./Inst. of Natural Resources in Africa 2003; currently Special Advisor, Org. for Women in Science for Developing World (OWSD); fmr Chair. Council of the United Nations Univ., Tokyo mem. Bd of Dirs Int. Science Programs 1998, Science Initiative Group 2004; mem. Bd of Trustees Future Univ.; Fellow, Third World Acad. of Sciences 1985, African Acad. of Sciences 1985 (Pres. 2000), Islamic Acad. of Sciences 1992 (mem. Council 1999); Corresp. mem. Académie Royale des Sciences d'Outre, Belgium 2001; Foreign Fellow, Pakistan Acad. of Sciences 2002; Foreign mem. Lebanese Acad. of Sciences 2006–; Hon. mem. Colombian Acad. of Exact Sciences 1996, Palestine Acad. of Science and Tech. 2005; Comendator, Ordem Nacional de Mérito Cientifico, Brazil 1996; Cavaliere Ufficiale dell'Ordine al Merito della Repubblica Italiana, Italy 2003; Classe da Grã-Cruz na Ordem Nacional do Mérito Cientifico, Brazil 2005. *Publications includes:* over 40 scientific papers and over 30 articles on applied math. *Address:* World Academy of Sciences, ICTP Enrico Fermi Building, Room 108, Strada Costiera 11, 34151 Trieste, Italy. *Telephone:* (40) 2240327 (office). *Fax:* (40) 224559 (office). *E-mail:* edoffice@twas.org (office). *Website:* www.twas.org (office).

HASSAN, Tan Sri Mohamed Sidek bin Haji, BEcon, MBA; Malaysian civil servant (retd) and business executive; *Chairman, Petroliam Nasional Berhad (PETRONAS);* b. 24 June 1951, Pekan, Pahang; ed Univ. of Malaya, New Hampshire Coll., USA; began career in Admin. and Diplomatic Service as an Asst Dir, Int. Trade Div., Ministry of Trade and Industry 1974–77, Asst Trade Commr, Embassy in Tokyo 1977–80, served in Implementation Coordination Unit of Prime Minister's Dept, initially as Prin. Asst Dir, later promoted to Deputy Dir, Project Analysis Sector and subsequently as Deputy Dir of Research in same dept 1980–84, held positions in Ministry of Int. Trade and Industry including Malaysia's Trade Commr in Sydney, Deputy Dir in Policy and Research, Deputy Dir (Operations) in Int. Trade Div., Minister Counsellor of Econ. Affairs at Malaysian Trade Commr's Office, Washington, DC, Dir of Multilateral Relations Div., Deputy Sec.-Gen. (Trade), Ministry of Int. Trade and Industry 2001–04, Sec.-Gen. 2004–06, Chief Sec. to the Govt 2006–12; mem. Bd of Dirs and Chair. Petroliam Nasional Berhad (PETRONAS) 2012–; Pres. Int. Islamic Univ. Malaysia 2008–. *Address:* Petroliam Nasional Berhad (PETRONAS), Tower 1, Petronas Twin Towers, Kuala Lumpur City Centre, Kuala Lumpur 50088, Malaysia (office). *Telephone:* (3) 20515000 (office). *Fax:* (3) 20265050 (office). *E-mail:* webmaster@petronas.com.my (office). *Website:* www.petronas.com.my (office).

HASSAN, Sheikh Najamul, LLB; Pakistani judge; *Chief Justice, Federal Shariat Court;* b. 15 March 1952, Lahore; s. of Sheikh Jan Hussain; ed Forman Christian Coll., Punjab Univ.; enrolled as Advocate 1977, Advocate of High Court 1980, Advocate of Supreme Court 2003, Judge Lahore High Court 2009; Chair. Punjab Bar Council Tribunal, Lahore, Election Tribunal, Punjab; Judge, Special Appellate Court, Prov. of Punjab; Sr Judge, Bahawalpur and Multan Benches of Lahore High Court; Acting Chief Justice, Lahore High Court; Chair. Punjab Environmental Tribunal; Judge, Federal Shariat Court 2014–, Chief Justice 2017–; mem. Admin. Cttee, Lahore High Court, Punjab Judicial Acad.; mem. Bd of Govs and mem. Bd of Trustees, National Coll. of Arts, Lahore. *Address:* Federal Shariat Court, G-5/2, Constitution Avenue, Islamabad, Pakistan (office). *Telephone:* (51) 9208679 (office). *E-mail:* registrar@federalshariatcourt.gov.pk (office). *Website:* www.federalshariatcourt.gov.pk (office).

HASSAN, Sabir Muhammad, BSc, MA, PhD; Sudanese fmr central banker; b. 1 Jan. 1945, Dongola; ed Univ. of Khartoum, Syracuse Univ., NY, USA; Financial Insp., Export Section Exchange Control Dept, Bank of Sudan, Khartoum 1968–71, Deputy Man., Export Section 1972–76, Chair. and Gov., Bank of Sudan 1993–96, Gov. Cen. Bank of Sudan 1998–2011; Teaching Asst, Econs Dept Syracuse Univ. 1978–81; part-time Lecturer, Econs Dept, Islamic Univ. of Omdurman 1982–83, The Bank Inst., Khartoum 1982–83, Econs Dept, Univ. of Khartoum 1992–93; consultancy work, including Financial Analysis and Project Evaluation 1982–83; Advisor to Exec. Dir of IMF, Washington, DC 1983–90; State Minister, Ministry of Finance 1996–98; Chair. Commercial Bank's Portfolio for Agricultural Schemes, Commercial Bank Cttee for Exchange Rate Determination; Sec.-Gen. Islamic Soc. of Upstate NY 1978; Pres. Dar Al-Higra Mosque, Washington, DC 1985–86; mem. Bd of Dirs North American Islamic Trust 1986–. *Publication:* Money Supply and Inflation in the Sudan (co-author) 1970–1981.

HASSAN, Syed Munawar, MScS; Pakistani politician; b. Aug. 1944, Delhi, British India; ed Karachi Univ.; migrated with his family from Delhi to Karachi following Partition 1947; Ed. coll. magazine; joined Nat. Students Fed., elected Pres. 1959; became acquainted with activists of Islami Jamiat-e-Talaba (IJT) Pakistan and studied writings of Mawlana Sued Abul A'ala Mawdudi, joined IJT 1960, elected Pres. of its Karachi Univ. Unit, Karachi City Unit and became mem. Cen. Exec. Council, became all-Pakistan Pres. 1964–67; Research Asst, Islamic Research Acad., Karachi 1963, Sec.-Gen. 1969; Man. Ed. monthlies The Criterion, The Universal Message, Karachi; mem. Jamaat-e-Islami Pakistan 1967–, served in Karachi unit as Asst Sec., Sec., Deputy Amir and Amir of the city, elected to Cen. Shura and Exec. Council, Asst Sec.-Gen. Jamaat-e-Islami Pakistan 1992–93, Sec.-Gen. 1993–2009, represented Jamaat at several platforms, including United Democratic Front and Pakistan Nat. Alliance, heads several planning and research bodies within Jamaat, Amir (Pres.) Jamaat-e-Islami Pakistan 2009–14; cand. in Nat. Ass. elections 1977. *Address:* c/o Jamaat-e-Islami Pakistan, Mansoorah, Multan Road, Lahore 54570, Pakistan.

HASSAN, Tayem; Syrian actor; b. 17 Feb. 1976, Tartous; m. Dima Bayaa 2004 (divorced); two c.; ed Higher Inst. of Dramatic Arts, Damascus; debut appearance in TV series Kan yama kan (Once Upon a Time) 1999; has since appeared in several Arabic series, with particular success in Egypt. *Television series:* Al-Zir Salem (The Philanderer Salem) 2000, Nizar Qabbani (Best Actor's Award, Cairo Festival for Arab Media) 2005, Al-Malek Farouq (King Farouk) (Best Actor's Award, Cairo Festival for Arab Media) 2007, Zaman al A'ar (Time of Disgrace), Al Intizar 2008, Conflict on the Sand 2008, Abid Karman 2010, Cello 2015, Nos Youm 2016–. *Films include:* Molouk el Tawa'ef, Rabie'Qortoba, Saladin 2001, Taifas 2005, The Waiting 2006, Meccano 2009.

HASSAN BIN TALAL, HRH Prince, BA, GCVO, MA; b. 20 March 1947, Amman; s. of Talal of Jordan and Zein al Sharaf Talal; m. Sarvath Khujista Akhter Banu 1968; one s. three d.; ed Harrow School, England, Christ Church, Univ. of Oxford; brother of the late Hussein ibn Talal, King of Jordan and heir to the throne until the changes in succession announced by the late King Hussein Jan. 1999; fmrly acted as Regent during absence of King Hussein; Ombudsman for Nat. Devt 1971–; Founder Royal Scientific Soc. of Jordan 1970, Royal Acad. for Islamic Civilization Research (Al AlBait) 1980, Arab Thought Forum 1981, Forum Humanum (now Arab Youth Forum) 1982, Royal Inst. for Inter-Faith Studies 1994; Co-Chair. Independent Comm. on Int. Humanitarian Issues; Founder, Pres. Higher Council for Science and Tech.; Pres. Club of Rome 1999–2007, Fed. for Martial Arts, Polo and Squash; currently Pres. Emer., World Conf. of Religions for Peace; Co-Patron Islamic Acad. of Sciences; joined Soldiers of Peace project 2003; Amb. Islamic Educational, Scientific and Cultural Org. 2006; co-f. Int. Cultures Foundation; Founder, Pres. Foundation for Inter-religious and Intercultural Research and Dialogue, Foundation for Interreligious and Intercultural Research and Dialogue; Chair. Arab Thought Forum; mem. Bd of Dirs Nuclear Threat Initiative 2002–; Co-Pres. Int. Tolerance Foundation for Humanities and Social Studies 2006; Co-founder Parliament of Cultures 2002, Partners in Humanity 2003; Int. Patron, Rights and Humanity; Chair. water and sanitation (UNSGAB) 2013–; mem. Advisory Council Research of the Center for Democracy and Community Devt 2010; mem. Int. Bd, Council on Foreign Relations; Hon. Gen. of Jordan Armed Forces, Hon. Fellow, Royal Soc. of Edinburgh 2008, Hon. Pres. Euro-Mediterranean Asscn for Cooperation and Devt 2012; Kt of Grand Cross of Order of Merit (Italy) 1983, Order of Al Hussein bin Ali 1987, Grand Decoration of Honour in Gold with Sash 2004; Hon. PhD (Econ.) (Yarmouk) 1980, Hon. DSc (Bogazici Univ., Turkey) 1981, Hon. Dr Arts and Sciences (Jordan) 1987, Hon. DCL (Univ. of Durham) 1990, Dr hc (Ulster) 1996, (Moscow State Inst. for Int. Relations) 1997, (Bilkent Univ.) 1999, (Univ. of York) 2002, (Faculdades Metropolitanas Unidas) 2006, (Eötvös Loránd Univ.) 2007, Hon. LLB (Univ. of Hertfordshire) 2000, Hon. DTheol (Eberhard-Karls-Univ.) 2001, Hon. DIur Int. Islamic Univ. of Islamabad) 2005, (Univ. of Calgary) 2008, (Hasanuddin Univ., Indonesia) 2012; Medal of Pres. of Italian Repub. 1982, Gandhi/King/Ikeda Community Builders Medal and Torch of Nonviolence 2001, Distinguished Foreign Visitor Award 2002, Rabbi Marc H. Tanenbaum Award 2003, Abraham Fund Pioneer of Co-existence Award 2003, Eternal Flame Award 2005, Abraham Geiger

Award 2008, Peace Prize 2008, inducted into Académie des Sciences Morales et Politiques of Institut de France 2008, Four Freedoms Award 2014. *Publications:* A Study on Jerusalem 1979, Palestinian Self-Determination 1981, Search for Peace 1984, Christianity in the Arab World 1994, Continuity, Innovation and Change 2001, To be a Muslim 2003, In Memory of Faisal I: The Iraqi Question 2003, El Hassan bin Talal Collected Works: Volume One 2007. *Leisure interests:* polo, squash, scuba diving, mountaineering, archaeology, karate, taekwondo, helicopter piloting, skiing. *Address:* The Royal Palace, Amman, Jordan. *Telephone:* 64649186 (office). *Fax:* 64634755 (office). *E-mail:* majlis@majliselhassan.org (office). *Website:* www.elhassan.org (office).

HASSAN MARICAN, Tan Sri Dato Sri Mohamed, FCA; Malaysian oil industry executive; *President and CEO, Petroliam Nasional Berhad (PETRONAS);* b. 1952, Sungai Petani, Kedah; m. Puan Sri Datin Sri Noraini Mohd Yusoff; ed Sekoleh Rendah Ibrahim, Malay Coll., Kuala Kangsar; began career as articled clerk, Touche Ross & Co., London 1972, later becoming Audit Man.; Accountant, Tetuan Hanfiah Raslan & Mohamed/Touche Ross & Co., Kuala Lumpur 1980, Pnr 1981–89; Sr Vice-Pres., Finance, Petroliam Nasional Berhad (PETRONAS) 1989, Pres. and CEO 1995–; Chair. Engen Ltd; Dir Pergaanan Kemajuan Negeri Kedah 1986–94; Dir Malaysia-Thailand Jt Authority; mem. Int. Investment Council for Repub. of SA, Commonwealth Business Council, World Econ. Forum Council of 100 Leaders; fmr mem. council Majlis Amanah Rakyat, Malaysian Accounting Standards Bd, Kumpulan Wang Amanah Pencen Investment Panel; Darjah Sultan Mahmud Terengganu Yang amat Terpuji 1992, Bintang Darjah Seri Paduka Mahkota Terengganu 1996, Panglima Setia Mahkota 1997, Panglima Negara Bintang Sarawak 2003; Commdr Légion d'honneur (France) 2000; DEng hc (Univ. Malaya) 2001; Vietnamese Govt Friendship Medal 2001. *Address:* Petroliam Nasional Berhad (PETRONAS), Tower 1, PETRONAS Twin Towers, 50088 Kuala Lumpur, Malaysia (office). *Telephone:* (603) 20265000 (office). *Fax:* (603) 20265050 (office). *Website:* www.petronas.com.my (office).

HASSANI, Hajim al-, PhD; Iraqi politician; b. 1954, Kirkuk; ed Mosul Univ., Univs of Nebraska and Conn., USA; moved to USA 1979; Researcher, Dept of Agricultural and Resource Econs, Univ. of Conn. 1990; Head of American Investment and Trading Co., Claremont, Calif. 1991–2003; active mem. of Iraqi Islamic Party (IIP) in exile; returned to Iraq following invasion 2003; worked for Iraqi Interim Governing Council 2003; Leader IIP 2003–04; involved in negotiating unsuccessful cease-fire between US forces and insurgents in Fallujah April 2004; Minister of Industry and Minerals 2004; Speaker, Transitional Nat. Ass. 2005–07; Sr Aide to Prime Minister Nouri al-Maliki.

HASSANOV, Hassan Aziz Oglu, PhD; Azerbaijani politician and diplomatist; *Ambassador to Poland;* b. 20 Oct. 1940, Tbilisi, Georgia; s. of Aziz Hassanov and Ruhsara Adjalova; m. 1964; one s. one d.; ed Azerbaijan Polytech. Inst., Higher Party School, Azerbaijan State Pedagogical Univ.; mem. various student groups 1958–61; Chair. Baku Student Council 1960–63; with Lenin Young Communists League (Komsomol) Orgs of Yasamal region of Baku 1961–66; with Komsomol Cen. Cttee, Moscow, 1967–69; with Construction Section, Cent. Cttee, Azerbaijan CP 1971–75; First Sec. CP, Sabail region, then of Communist Party of Sumgayit and Gandja cities 1975–81; mem. Azerbaijan Supreme Soviet (Parl.) 1977–95, USSR Supreme Soviet 1979–84; Sec., Cent. Cttee Communist Party, Azerbaijan (Ideology) 1981, (Construction and Transport) 1983–90, (Econ.) 1989; first Prime Minister of the Repub. of Azerbaijan 1990–92; Perm. Rep. to UN 1992–93; Minister of Foreign Affairs 1993–98; mem. of Mili Mejlis (Parl.) 1995–2000; Amb. to Hungary 2004–10, to Poland 2010–; mem. Security Council 1993–98. *Play:* Letter from Brussels (Azerbaijan State Drama Theatre) 2001. *Publications:* more than 100 articles on Azerbaijani economy, policies, diplomacy and history. *Leisure interests:* art, music, history, politics, chess. *Address:* Azerbaijani Embassy, 03-941 Warsaw, ul. Zwycięców 12, Poland (office); Gendjler Meydani 3, Baku 370001; Apt. 36, 9 Istiglad Str., Baku 370001 Azerbaijan (home). *Telephone:* (22) 6162188 (office); (12) 4927744 (home); (12) 4929114. *Fax:* (22) 6161949 (office); (12) 4651038; (12) 4988480. *E-mail:* warsaw@mission.mfa.gov.az (office); Ggassuhov@hotmail.com. *Website:* www.azembassy.pl (office).

HASSELL, Michael Patrick, CBE, MA, PhD, DSc, FRS; British professor of insect ecology; *Honorary Distinguished Research Fellow, Imperial College, London;* b. 2 Aug. 1942, Tel-Aviv, Israel; s. of Albert Hassell and Ruth Hassell; m. 1st Glynis M. Everett 1966; m. 2nd Victoria A. Taylor 1982; three s. one d.; ed Whitgift School, Croydon, Clare Coll., Cambridge and Oriel Coll., Oxford; Visiting Lecturer, Univ. of California, Berkeley 1967–68; NERC Research Fellowship, Hope Dept of Entomology, Oxford 1968–70; Lecturer, Dept of Zoology and Applied Entomology, Imperial Coll., London 1970–75, Reader 1975–79, Prof. of Insect Ecology, Dept of Biology 1979–, Deputy Head, Dept of Biology 1984–92, Head 1993–2001; Prin. Faculty of Life Sciences 2001–04; Dir Imperial Coll., Silwood Park 1988–2007, Dean 2004–07, Hon. Distinguished Research Fellow 2007–; Storer Life Sciences Lecturer, Univ. of California, Davis 1985; Pres. British Ecological Soc. 1998–99; Chair. Nat. Biodiversity Network 2011–19; Ed.-in-Chief, Proceedings B of the Royal Soc. 2008–14; Pres. Royal Entomological Soc. 2016–18; Assoc. Ed. Researches in Population Ecology; mem. Editorial Bd Journal of Theoretical Biology; mem. Bd of Reviewing Eds Science; mem. Council of Zoological Soc. of London, Chair. Awards Cttee; Trustee, Natural History Museum 1999–2004; Fellow, Academia Europaea 1998; Hon. mem. British Ecological Soc. 2012; Scientific Medal, Zoological Soc. 1981, Gold Medal, British Ecological Soc. 1994, Weldon Prize, Univ. of Oxford 1995. *Publications include:* Insect Population Ecology (with G. C. Varley and G. R. Gradwell) 1973, The Dynamics of Competition and Predation 1975, The Dynamics of Arthropod Predator-Prey Systems 1978, The Spatial and Temporal Dynamics of Host-Parasitoid Interactions 2000; numerous publs on population ecology. *Leisure interests:* walking, natural history. *Address:* Biology, Silwood Park, Ascot, Berks., SL5 7PY (office); Barnside, Buckland Brewer, Bideford, Devon, EX39 5NF, England (home). *E-mail:* m.hassell@imperial.ac.uk (office).

HASSI, Omar al-; Libyan politician; fmr Lecturer in Political Science, Univ. of Benghazi; elected Prime Minister by Gen. Nat. Congress 2014 (now disputed).

HASSINK, Martinus J.; St Maarten accountant and politician; Asst Accountant, Moret & Limperg (later Ernst & Young), Amsterdam 1974–77, Curaçao 1977–81; Accountant, Van Dien+Co (later PriceWaterhouseCoopers) 1981; Dir Dat-Acc NV 1986; Dir KPMG Accountants 1989; Vice-Pres. USFilter Enerserve Group 1998; fmr Pnr, Hassink & Roos Accounting and Financial Advisory Services; Dir and freelance consultant Baker Tilly St Maarten BV 2012; Interim Dir of Resources, Island Govt of St Maarten 2000; Minister of Finance 2013–15. *Leisure interests:* gardening, photography, writing, drawing. *Address:* c/o Ministry of Finance, Government Administration Building, POB 943, Clem Labega Square, Philipsburg, St Maarten.

HASSON, Maurice; French/Venezuelan violinist; b. 6 July 1934, Berck-Plage, Pas de Calais; m. Jane Hoogesteijn 1969; one s. three d.; ed Conservatoire Nat. Supérieur de Musique, Paris, further studies with Henryk Szeryng; concert artist in major concert halls worldwide, also in TV and radio performances; Prof. of Violin, RAM, London 1986–2015; Hon. mem. RAM; Orden Andrés Bello, First Class, Orden Tulio Febres Cordero, First Class (Venezuela), refused Orden Francisco de Miranda, First Class as a political statement against Pres. Hugo Chavez of Venezuela, Médaille de Vermeil de la Ville de Paris; First Prize Violin, Prix d'Honneur and First Prize Chamber Music, Conservatoire Nat. Supérieur de Musique, Paris 1950, Int. Prize Long Thibaut 1951, Int. Prize, Youth Festival, Warsaw 1955, Grand Prix Musique de Chambre 1957. *Recordings include:* Concerto No. 1 (Paganini), Concerto No. 2 (Prokofiev), Debussy Sonatas, Fauré Sonatas, Concerto No. 1, Scottish Fantasy (Bruch), Concerto for 2 and 4 violins (Vivaldi), Double Concerto (Bach), Concerto (Brahms), Brilliant Showpieces for the Violin, Tzigane (Ravel), Rondo Capriccioso (Saint Saëns), Poème (Chausson), Gypsy Airs (Sarasate), Violin Concerto (Castellanos-Yumar), Sonata (Franck), virtuoso pieces. *Leisure interests:* reading, painting, politics. *Address:* 18 West Heath Court, North End Road, London, NW11 7RE, England. *Telephone:* (20) 8458-3647. *E-mail:* jdehasson@btinternet.com.

HASTE, Andy; British insurance executive; *Chairman, Wonga Group;* b. 1962; m.; three c.; fmrly with National Westminster (NatWest) Bank, Head Consumer Loans Products Div., NatWest US operations 1992–95, Pres. US consumer credit business 1995–99; Pres. and CEO Global Consumer Finance Europe, GE Capital; CEO AXA Sun Life (also Exec. Dir AXA UK) 1999–2003; Group CEO Royal & Sun Alliance Group (also mem. Main Bd Dirs Royal & Sun Alliance) 2003–12; Chair. Wonga Group 2014–; Deputy Chair. Lloyd's 2012–; mem. Bd Dirs Asscn of British Insurers 2003–11, ITV PLC 2008–. *Address:* Wonga Group, 88 Crawford Street, London, W1H 2EJ, England (office). *Website:* about.wonga.com/leadership/andy-haste (office).

HASTINGS, Sir Max Macdonald, Kt, FRSL, FRHistS; British writer and broadcaster; b. 28 Dec. 1945, London; s. of Macdonald Hastings and Anne Scott-James (Lady Lancaster); m. 1st Patricia Edmondson 1972 (divorced 1994); one s. (and one s. deceased) one d.; m. 2nd Penelope Grade 1999; ed Charterhouse and Univ. Coll., Oxford; reporter, London Evening Standard 1965–67, 1968–70; Fellow, US World Press Inst. 1967–68; reporter, current affairs, BBC Television 1970–73; freelance journalist, broadcaster and author 1973–; columnist, Evening Standard 1979–85, Daily Express 1981–83, Sunday Times 1985–86; Ed. Daily Telegraph 1986–95, Dir 1989–95, Ed.-in-Chief 1990–95; Ed. Evening Standard 1996–2002; Dir Evening Standard Ltd 1996–2002; columnist Daily Mail 2002–; book reviewer Sunday Times 2006–; mem. Press Complaints Comm. 1990–92; Trustee Liddell Hart Archive, King's Coll. London 1988–2004, Nat. Portrait Gallery 1995–2004; Pres. Council for the Protection of Rural England 2002–07; Trustee, Nat. Portrait Gallery 1995–2004; Hon. Fellow, King's Coll. London 2004; Hon. DLitt (Leicester) 1992, (Nottingham) 2005; Journalist of the Year 1982, Reporter of the Year 1982, Somerset Maugham Prize for Non-fiction 1979, Ed. of the Year 1988, Royal United Services Inst. Westminster Medal 2008, Pritzker Mil. Library Literature Award for Lifetime Achievement 2012, èStoria Festival Friuladria Prize 2014. *Television:* documentaries: Ping-Pong in Peking 1971, The War About Peace 1983, Alarums and Excursions 1984, Cold Comfort Farm 1985, The War in Korea (series) 1988, We Are All Green Now 1990, Spies (in series Cold War) 1998, Churchill and His Generals (series) 2003, The Falklands Legacy 2012, The Necessary War 2014. *Publications:* America 1968: The Fire, The Time 1968, Ulster 1969, The Struggle for Civil Rights in Northern Ireland 1970, Montrose: The King's Champion 1977, Yoni: Hero of Entebbe 1979, Bomber Command 1979, The Battle of Britain (with Lee Deighton) 1980, Das Reich 1981, Battle for the Falklands (with Simon Jenkins) 1983, Overlord: D-Day and the Battle for Normandy 1984, Victory in Europe 1985, The Oxford Book of Military Anecdotes (ed.) 1985, The Korean War 1987, Outside Days 1989, Scattered Shots 1999, Going to the Wars 2000, Editor (memoir) 2002, Armageddon: The Battle for Germany 1944–45 2004, Warriors: Extraordinary Tales from the Battlefields 2005, Country Fair 2005, Nemesis: The Battle for Japan 1944–45 2007, Finest Years: Churchill as Warlord, 1940–45 2009, Did You Really Shoot the Television? A Family Fable 2010, All Hell Let Loose 2011, Catastrophe 1914: Europe Goes to War 2013, The Secret War: Spies, Codes And Guerrillas, 1939–45 2015, Vietnam: An Epic Tragedy 1945–1975 2018. *Leisure interests:* shooting, fishing. *Address:* c/o PFD, Drury House, 34–43 Russell Street, London, WC2B 5HA, England (office). *Telephone:* (20) 7344-1000 (office). *Fax:* (20) 7836-9539 (office). *E-mail:* info@pfd.co.uk (office). *Website:* www.pfd.co.uk (office); www.maxhastings.com.

HASTINGS, Reed, BA, MS; American business executive; *Chairman and CEO, Netflix;* b. 8 Oct. 1960, Boston, Mass; s. of Wilmot Reed Hastings and Joan Amory (née Loomis); m. Patrician Ann Quillin 1991; two c.; ed Bowdoin Coll., US Marine Corps Officer Cand. School, Quantico, Stanford Univ.; joined Peace Corps 1983, stationed in Swaziland, taught high school math. 1983–85; mem. Tech. Staff, Schlumberger Palo Alto Research 1988–89; Software Engineer, Coherent Thought 1989–90; Software Engineer, Network Equipment Technologies 1990–91; f. Pure Software 1991, CEO 1991–97, CEO Pure Atria (after merger with Atria Software) 1996, Chief Tech. Officer (after acquisition of Pure by Rational Software) 1997; co-f. (with Marc Randolph) Netflix 1997, Chair. and CEO 1997–; Pres. State Bd of Educ. 2001–2004; mem. Bd of Dirs Microsoft Corpn 2007–12, Technology Network (also CEO for one year), KIPP Foundation 2007–, California Charter Schools Asscn 2008–16, DreamBox 2010–, Pahara Inst. 2011–, Facebook 2011–, Hispanic Foundation of Silicon Valley 2014–, Giving Pledge; Founding mem. NewSchools.org, Aspire Public Schools, Pacific Collegiate School, EdVoice.net. *Address:* Netflix Corporate Headquarters, 100 Winchester Circle, Los Gatos, CA 95032, USA (office). *Telephone:* (866) 716-0414 (office). *E-mail:* reed.hastings@netflix.com (office). *Website:* www.netflix.com (office).

HASUMI, Shigehiko, MA, PhD; Japanese film critic, academic and fmr university administrator; b. 29 April 1936, Tokyo; s. of Shigeyasu Hasumi; m. Marie Chantal Hasumi; one c.; ed Dept of Literature, Univ. of Tokyo, Univ. of Paris, France; began publishing film criticism in Cinema 69 1968; work influenced by Cahiers du Cinéma and post-structuralism; Ed.-in-Chief Lumiére 1985–88; began academic career as Asst Lecturer, Univ. of Tokyo, held positions successively as Asst Prof., fmr Prof. of Pedagogics, now Prof. Emer., Head of Pedagogics Dept 1993–95, Vice-Chancellor 1995–97, Chancellor 1997–2001; fmr Vice-Chair. Asscn of East Asian Research Univs; fmr Asst Prof., Rikkyo Univ.; Hon. Founder Sino-Japanese Cultural Research Centre Nanjing Univ. 2001; Dr hc (Asian Inst. of Tech.). *Publications include:* Hihyō Aruiwa Kashi No Saiten 1974, Han Nihongo Ron 1977, Natsume Sōseki Ron 1978, Eiga no Shinwagaku 1979, Eiga: Yūwaku No. Ekurichūru 1983, Hihan Josetsu Monogatari 1985, Kanbotsu Chitai 1986, Bonyo na Geijutsuka No. Shōzō 1988, Shosetsu Hanarete Toku Kara 1989, Teikoku no Inbo 1991, Hollywood Eigashi Kogi 1993, Zettai Bungei Jihyo Sengen 1994, Tamashii no Yuibutsuronteki na Yogo no Tame no 1994, Watakushi Daigaku ga ni tsuite Shitteiru Ni San Kotogara No. 2001, Supōtsu Hihyō Sengen 2004, Miserarete: Sakka Ronshū 2005, Hyōshō No. Naraku 2006, Aka no Yūwaku 2007, Eigaron Kogi 2008, Zuisō 2010, Eiga Jihyo 2009-2011 2012; Portrait of a Common Artist, The Argument Against Japanese, Statement of Superficial Critique, Maxime Du Camp: The Invention of Mediocrity, The Director Yasujirou Ozu; chapters in books.

HATAB, Abdul Karim Mahoud al-, (Abu Hattem); Iraqi guerrilla leader; b. 1958, Amara; ed religious school; fmr fighter with peshmerga (Kurdish guerrilla group); imprisoned, Abu Ghraib prison, Baghdad 1980–86; guerrilla leader 1990, leader Hizbullah of Iraq. *Address:* Hizbullah of Iraq, Amara, Iraq.

HATAMI, Brig.-Gen. Amir; Iranian army officer and politician; *Minister of Defence;* ed Supreme Nat. Defence Univ.; long career in army, took part in Iran–Iraq war including Operation Mersad 1988; roles include Head of Army's Int. Relations Office, Deputy Chief of Staff in Gen. Staff of the Armed Forces –2013; Deputy Minister of Defence 2013–17, Minister of Defence 2017–. *Address:* Ministry of Defence, Shahid Yousuf Kaboli Street, Sayed Khandan Area, Tehran, Iran (office). *Telephone:* (21) 26126988 (office). *E-mail:* info@mod.ir (office). *Website:* www.mod.ir (office).

HATANO, Yoshio, BA; Japanese university administrator and fmr diplomatist; b. 3 Jan. 1932, Tokyo; s. of Keizo Hatano and Tatsuko Hatano; m. Sumiko Shimazu 1961; one s. one d.; ed Tokyo Univ., Princeton Univ., USA; joined Foreign Ministry 1953, held various positions including Dir Econ. Affairs, Asian Affairs and Treaties Bureaux, Personnel Div., Gen. Co-ordination Div.; First Sec., Embassy, London 1970; Counsellor, Embassy, Jakarta 1971; Minister, Embassy, Washington, DC 1979, Envoy Extraordinary and Minister Plenipotentiary 1981; Dir-Gen. Middle Eastern and African Affairs Bureau, Dir-Gen. for Public Information and Cultural Affairs, Ministry of Foreign Affairs 1982–87; Perm. Rep. to int. orgs in Geneva 1987–90; Perm. Rep. to UN, New York 1990–94; Pres. Foreign Press Center 1994; Pres. Gakushuin Women's Coll. 2003–06, Chancellor 2006–14, now Hon. Chancellor. *Television:* regular mem. of Wake Up panel, Yomiuri TV. *Leisure interests:* golf, opera. *Address:* 3-20-1 Toyama, Shinjuku-ku, Tokyo (office); 2-14-13 Hiroo, Shibuya-ku, Tokyo, Japan (home). *Telephone:* (3) 3203-1906 (office); (3) 3407-0463 (home). *Fax:* (3) 3203-8373 (office); (3) 3407-0463 (home). *E-mail:* gwc-off@gakushuin.ac.jp (office). *Website:* www2.gwc.gakushuin.ac.jp (office).

HATCH, Marshall Davidson, AM, BSc, PhD, FRS, FAA; Australian research scientist (retd); b. 24 Dec. 1932, Perth; s. of Lloyd D. Hatch and Alice Dalziel; m. 2nd Lyndall Langman 1983; two s.; ed Newington Coll., Sydney Univ., Univ. of California, USA; Research Scientist, CSIRO 1955–59; Post-doctoral Fellow, Univ. of California 1959–61; Research Scientist, Colonial Sugar Refining Co. Ltd 1961–70; Chief Research Scientist, Div. of Plant Industry, CSIRO, Canberra 1970–98; Pres. Australian Soc. of Plant Physiologists 1980–81; Foreign Assoc. NAS 1990; Hon. Research Fellow, CSIRO 1998–2008; Dr hc (Göttingen) 1993, (Queensland) 1997; Clark Medal, Royal Soc. of North South Wales 1973, Lemberg Medal, Australian Biochemical Soc. 1974, Charles Kettering Award for Photosynthesis, American Soc. of Plant Physiologists 1980, Rank Award, Rank Foundation 1981, Int. Prize for Biology, Japan Soc. for Promotion of Science 1991. *Publications include:* Historical Records of Australian Science (co-author); over 165 review articles, chapters in books and research papers in scientific journals relating to the mechanism and function of c-4 photosynthesis. *Leisure interests:* reading, skiing, cycling, hiking. *Address:* 34 Dugdale Street, Cook, ACT 2614, Australia. *Telephone:* (2) 6251-5159. *E-mail:* halhatch@bigpond.com.

HATCH, Orrin Grant, BS, JD; American lawyer and politician; b. 22 March 1934, Homestead Park Pa; s. of Jesse Hatch and Helen Kamm Hatch; m. Elaine Hansen 1957; three s. three d.; ed Brigham Young Univ., Univ. of Pittsburgh; journeyman metal lather; Pnr, Thomson, Rhodes & Grigsby (law firm) 1962–69; Sr Vice-Pres. and Gen. Counsel, American Minerals Man. and American Minerals Fund Inc., Salt Lake City, Utah 1969–71; Pnr, Hatch & Plumb (law firm), Salt Lake City 1976; Senator from Utah 1977–2019, mem. Senate Labor and Human Resources Cttee 1981, Senate Judiciary Cttee 1995–2001, Jt Cttee on Taxation 2016–17, 2018–19, Cttee on Indian Affairs, Sub Cttee on Taxation, Chair. Senate Cttee on Finance, Senate Cttee on Intelligence 1977–2019; Co-Chair. Federalist Soc., pres. pro tempore 2015–19; mem. Bd of Dirs Holocaust Memorial Museum; mem. Bd of Advisors Becket Fund for Religious Liberty, Close Up Foundation, Defenders of Property Rights; mem. Nat. Bd of Advisors Washington Legal Foundation; Band Man. Free Agency; Republican; Hon. Co-Chair. Afghanistan Relief Cttee; numerous hon. degrees; 111th Congress Tax Fighter Award, Nat. Tax-Limitation Cttee 2010, Presidential Medal of Freedom 2018. *Recording:* album: My God Is Love (with Janice Kapp Perry) 1997. *Publications include:* ERA Myths and Realities 1983, Good Faith under the Uniform Commercial Code, Higher Laws: Understanding the Doctrines of Christ 1995, Square Peg: Confessions of a Citizen Senator (autobiography) 2002, articles in legal journals. *Leisure interests:* wrestling, basketball, music. *Address:* c/o Hart Senate Office Building, 120 Constitution Avenue NE, Washington, DC 20002, USA.

HATHAWAY, Anne; American actress; b. 12 Nov. 1982, Brooklyn, NY; d. of Gerald Hathaway and Kate McCauley; m. Adam Shulman 2012; one s.; ed Vassar Coll., New York Univ., American Acad. of Dramatic Arts; apptd UN Women's Goodwill Amb. *Films include:* The Princess Diaries 2001, The Other Side of Heaven 2001, The Cat Returns 2002, Nicholas Nickleby 2002, Ella Enchanted 2004, The Princess Diaries 2: Royal Engagement 2004, Hoodwinked! 2005, Havoc 2005, Brokeback Mountain 2005, The Devil Wears Prada 2006, Becoming Jane 2007, Get Smart 2008, Passengers 2008, Rachel Getting Married (Austin Film Critics Award for Best Actress 2008, Nat. Bd of Review Award for Best Actress, SE Film Critics Award for Best Actress) 2008, Bride Wars 2009, Valentine's Day 2010, Alice in Wonderland 2010, Love and Other Drugs 2010, The Dark Knight Rises (Saturn Award for Best Supporting Actress 2013) 2012, Les Misérables (Austin Film Critics Award for Best Supporting Actress 2012, Golden Globe Award for Best Supporting Actress in a Motion Picture 2013, EDA Award for Best Supporting Actress 2013, BAFTA Award for Best Supporting Actress 2013, Acad. Award for Best Supporting Actress 2013) 2012, Don Jon 2013, Song One 2014, Interstellar 2014, The Intern 2015, Alice Through the Looking Glass 2016, Colossal 2016. *Television:* Get Real (series) 1999–2000, The Simpsons (two episodes) (Outstanding Voice-Over Performance 2010) 2009–10. *Address:* c/o Creative Artists Agency, 2000 Avenue of the Stars, Los Angeles, CA 90067, USA (office). *Telephone:* (424) 288-2000 (office). *Fax:* (424) 288-2900 (office). *Website:* www.caa.com (office).

HATOYAMA, Yukio, PhD; Japanese politician; *Senior Consultant and Honorary Chairman, Hoifu Energy Group Ltd;* b. 11 Feb. 1947, Tokyo; s. of Iichirō Hatoyama; brother of Kunio Hatoyama; m. Miyuki Hatoyama 1975; one c.; ed Tokyo Univ., Stanford Univ., USA; Asst Prof., Senshyu Univ. 1981; Pvt. Sec. to Iichiro Hatoyama, House of Councillors 1983; elected to House of Reps as mem. Parl. for Hokkaido 9th Dist 1986–2012, Parl. Vice-Minister, Hokkaido Devt Agency 1990, Vice-Chief Sec. to Hosokawa Cabinet 1993; mem. New Party Sakigake 1993, Chief Sec. New Party Sakigake Perm. Cttee 1994; Jt Leader Democratic Party of Japan (DPJ) 1996–97, Sec.-Gen. 1997, Deputy Sec.-Gen. 1998–99, Pres. of DPJ 1999–2002, fmr Sec.-Gen.; Prime Minister of Japan 2009–10 (resgnd); Sr Consultant and Hon. Chair. Hoifu Energy Group Ltd 2013–; Vice-Chair. Japan-Russia Soc.; Chair. Touch Football Asscn of Japan; Hon. DrIur (Maharishi Univ. of Man.) 2015; Sustainable Devt Leadership Award 2010. *Leisure interests:* touch football, tennis, karaoke, computers. *Website:* www.hoifuenergy.com (office).

HATTERSLEY, Baron (Life Peer), cr. 1997, of Sparkbrook in the County of West Midlands; **Roy Sydney George Hattersley,** PC, BSc (Econ.), FRSL; British politician, writer and broadcaster; b. 28 Dec. 1932; s. of Frederick Roy Hattersley and Enid Hattersley (née Brackenbury); m. 1st Molly Loughran 1956 (divorced); m. 2nd Maggie Pearlstine 2013; ed Sheffield City Grammar School, Univ. of Hull; journalist and health service exec. 1956–64; mem. Sheffield City Council 1957–65; MP for Sparkbrook Div. of Birmingham 1964–97; Parl. Pvt. Sec. to Minister of Pensions and Nat. Insurance 1964–67; Dir Campaign for European Political Community 1965; Jt Parl. Sec. Dept of Employment and Productivity 1967–69; Minister of Defence for Admin 1969–70; Opposition Spokesman for Defence 1970–72, for Educ. 1972–74, for the Environment 1979–80, for Home Affairs 1980–83, on Treasury and Econ. Affairs 1983–87, on Home Affairs 1987–92; Minister of State for Foreign and Commonwealth Affairs 1974–76; Sec. of State for Prices and Consumer Protection 1976–79; Deputy Leader of the Labour Party 1983–92; Pres. Local Govt Group for Europe 1998–; Public Affairs Consultant, IBM 1971, 1972; columnist, Punch, The Guardian, The Listener 1979–82; Visiting Fellow, Inst. of Politics, Harvard Univ. 1971, 1972, Nuffield Coll., Oxford 1984–; Labour; Hon. LLD (Hull) 1985; Dr hc (Aston) 1997. *Publications include:* Nelson – A Biography 1974, Goodbye to Yorkshire – A Collection of Essays 1976, Politics Apart – A Collection of Essays 1982, Press Gang 1983, A Yorkshire Boyhood 1983, Choose Freedom: The Future for Democratic Socialism 1987, Economic Priorities for a Labour Government 1987, The Maker's Mark (novel) 1990, In That Quiet Earth (novel) 1991, Skylark's Song (novel) 1994, Between Ourselves (novel) 1994, Who Goes Home? 1995, Fifty Years On 1997, Buster's Diaries: As Told to Roy Hattersley 1998, Blood and Fire: The Story of William and Catherine Booth and their Salvation Army 1999, A Brand from the Burning: The Life of John Wesley 2002, The Edwardians 2004, Borrowed Time: The Story of Britain Between the Wars 2007, David Lloyd George: The Great Outsider 2010; contrib. to newspapers and journals. *Leisure interests:* watching cricket and football, writing. *Address:* House of Lords, Westminster, London, SW1A 0PW, England (office). *Telephone:* (20) 7219-3000 (office).

HATTON, Stephen Paul, BComm; Australian politician; b. 28 Jan. 1948, Sydney; s. of Stanley J. Hatton and Pauline Hatton (née Taylor); m. 1st Deborah J. Humphreys 1969 (divorced 1993); three s. one d.; m. 2nd Cathy Huyer 1995; one d.; ed Univ. of New South Wales; Personnel Officer, James Hardie & Co. Pty Ltd 1965–70; Industrial Officer Nabalco Pty Ltd 1970–75; Exec. Dir NT Confed. of Industries and Commerce Inc. 1975–83; elected NT Legislative Ass. (Nightcliff) 1984, Minister for Lands, Conservation, Ports and Fisheries, Primary Production 1983–84, for Mines and Energy, Primary Production 1986, for Health and Community Services 1989, for Conservation 1989, for Industries and Devt and for Trade Devt Zone and Liquor Comm. 1990–91, for Lands, Housing and Local Govt and Minister for Aboriginal Devt 1992, for Constitutional Devt 1994, Attorney-Gen., Minister for Educ. for Constitutional Devt 1995–96, for Sport and Recreation 1995–97, for Correctional Services 1996–97, for Parks and Wildlife 1996–97, for Ethnic Affairs 1996–97; Chief Minister for NT 1986–88. *Leisure interest:* sport.

HAU DO SUAN, BA, MA; Myanma diplomatist; *Permanent Representative to United Nations;* b. 1 Nov. 1954, Tiddim, Chin State; m.; two c.; ed Nat. Univ. of Singapore; Jr Staff Ministry of Foreign Affairs 1979–81, Deputy Asst Dir Political Dept 1983–84, Third Sec. Perm. Mission to UN, New York 1984–86, Deputy Asst Dir, Legal Div. and Admin. and Personal Div. Oct. 1986–April 1987, Third Sec. Perm. Mission to UN, Geneva 1987–91, Head of Branch Int. Orgs Div. 1991–96, Second Sec. to Counsellor, Deputy Head of Mission and Chargé d'affaires, Myanma Embassy, Canberra 1996–99, Deputy Dir East Asia and Pacific Div., Political Dept 1999–2003, Counsellor/Minister Counsellor, Myanma Embassy, Beijing 2003–06, Acting Consul-Gen., Myanma Consulate-Gen. in Kunming, China Dec. 2004–Aug. 2005, Dir Middle East and Africa Div., Political Dept 2006–09, Deputy Dir-Gen. 2009–11, Dir-Gen. 2011–13; Amb. to Canada 2013–16, Perm. Rep. to UN 2016–; Personal Asst to Deputy Minister of Educ. 1981–83; Public Service Medal, State Peace and Tranquility Medal, Law and Order and Rule of Law Medal. *Address:* Permanent Mission of Myanmar, 10 E 77th Street, New York, NY 10075, USA (office). *Telephone:* (212) 744-1271 (office). *Fax:* (212) 744-1290 (office). *E-mail:* myanmarmission@verizon.net (office). *Website:* www.un.int/myanmar (office).

HAUB, Christian; American retail executive; *CEO, Tengelmann Group;* b. 1964, Tacoma, Washington; s. of the late Erivan Haub; ed Vienna Univ. of Econs and Business Admin; joined Great Atlantic & Pacific Tea Co. Inc. 1998, Pres. and CEO 1998–2000, Exec. Chair. 1991–2010, Interim Pres. and CEO 2009–10, Chair. (non-exec.) 2010–12; Partner and Co-CEO Tengelmann Warenhandelsgesellschaft KG (Tengelmann Group) 2001–18, CEO 2018–; Chair. and Pres., Emil Capital Partners 2011–; mem. Bd of Dirs Metro Inc. 2006–, BrightFarms 2015–; fmr Trustee, St Joseph's Univ.; mem. Bd of Trustees, Boston Coll.; mem. Advisory Bd, Schulich School of Business, York Univ.; Grand Marshal 2009. *Address:* Tengelmann Warenhandelsgesellschaft, Wissollstrasse 5-43, Mülheim an der Ruhr 45478, Germany. *Telephone:* (208) 5806-0 (office). *Website:* tengelmann.de (office).

HAUER, Rutger; Dutch actor; b. 23 Jan. 1944, Amsterdam; s. of Arend Hauer and Teunke Hauer (née Mellema); m. 1st Heidi Merz (divorced); m. 2nd Ieneke Hauer 1985; one d.; f. Rutger Hauer Starfish Asscn; Order of the Netherlands Lion 2013; Golden Heron 2004, Career Achievement Award, Golden Calf Culture Award 2008. *Films include:* Turkish Delight 1973, The Wilby Conspiracy 1975, Keetje Tippel 1975, Max Havelaar 1976, Mysteries 1978, Soldier of Orange 1978, Woman Between Dog and Wolf 1979, Spetters 1980, Nighthawks 1981, Chanel Solitaire 1981, Blade Runner 1982, Eureka 1982, Outsider in Amsterdam 1983, The Osterman Weekend 1983, A Breed Apart 1984, Ladyhawke 1984, Flesh and Blood 1985, The Hitcher 1986, Wanted Dead or Alive 1986, The Legend of the Holy Drinker 1989, Salute of the Juggler, Ocean Point, On a Moonlit Night, Split Second, Buffy the Vampire Slayer, Past Midnight, Nostradamus, Surviving the Game, The Beans of Egypt Maine, Angel of Death, New World Disorder 1999, Wilder 2000, Lying in Wait 2000, Partners in Crime 2000, Jungle Juice 2001, Flying Virus 2001, I Banchieri di Dio 2002, Scorcher 2002, Warrior Angels 2002, Confessions of a Dangerous Mind 2002, In the Shadow of the Cobra 2004, Tempesta 2004, Never Enough 2004, Sin City 2005, Batman Begins 2005, Mirror Wars: Reflection One 2005, Minotaur 2006, Mentor 2006, Goal II: Living the Dream 2007, 7eventy 5ive 2007, Moving McAllister 2007, Spoon 2008, Magic Flute Diaries 2008, Bride Flight 2008, The Rhapsody 2008, Dazzle 2009, Barbarossa 2009, Happiness Runs 2009, The 5th Execution 2010, Life's a Beach 2010, Hobo With a Shotgun 2011, The Rite 2011, Dracula 3D 2012, Real Playing Game 2013, 2047: Sights of Death 2014, WAX: We Are the X 2015, Beyond Valkyrie: Dawn of the 4th Reich 2016. *TV films include:* Angel of Death 1994, Menin 1998, The 10th Kingdom 2000, Salem's Lot 2004, The New Poseidon Adventure 2005, The Prince of Motor City 2008, Michelangelo - Il cuore e la pietra 2012, Wilfred 2014, Francesco 2014, Galavant 2015, The Last Kingdom 2015. *Publications include:* All Those Moments 2007. *Address:* Rutger Hauer Starfish Association, Via Tulipani, 2, 20146 Milan, Italy (office). *E-mail:* rhinfo1@rutgerhauer.org (office). *Website:* www.rutgerhauer.org (office).

HAUFF, Volker, Dr rer. pol; German politician and business consultant; b. 9 Aug. 1940, Backnang; s. of Richard Hauff and Ilse Hauff (née Dieter); m. Ursula Irion 1967; two s.; ed Free Univ. of Berlin; with IBM Deutschland, Stuttgart 1971–72; Sec. of State to Fed. Minister for Research and Tech. 1972–78; Fed. Minister for Research and Tech. 1978–80, of Transport 1980–82; mem. Bundestag 1969; mem. Social Democratic Party (SPD) 1959, Vice-Pres. Parl. Group 1983; Mayor of Frankfurt 1989–91; with Axel Springer Verlag AG 1992–94; with KPMG Deutsche Treuhand-Gesellschaft AG 1995–98, mem. Bd KPMG Germany 1999–2001; Sr Vice-Pres. Bearing Point GmbH 2003–08, mem. Supervisory Bd 2005–08; Chair. German Council for Sustainable Devt 2001–10; fmr mem. UN World Comm. on Environment and Devt; Bundesverdienstkreuz mit Stern und Schulterband. *Publications:* Wörterbuch der Datenverarbeitung 1966, Programmierfibes – Eine verständliche Einführung in das Programmieren digitaler Automaten 1969, Für ein soziales Bodenrecht 1973, Modernisierung der Volkswirtschaft 1975, Politik als Zukunftsgestaltung 1976, Damit der Fortschritt nicht zum Risiko wird 1978, Sprachlose Politik 1979, Global Denken – Lokal Handeln 1992. *Leisure interests:* modern art, cooking. *Address:* c/o German Council for Sustainable Development, GTZ Potsdamer Platz 10, 10785 Berlin, Germany.

HÄUPL, Michael, DPhil; Austrian politician; *Mayor and Governor of Vienna;* b. 14 Sept. 1949, Altlengbach; m. 1st Helga Häupl; two c.; m. 2nd Barbara Hörnlein 2011; ed Bundesrealgymnasium, Krems a.d. Donau, Univ. of Vienna; scientific worker, Natural History Museum, Vienna 1975–83; mem. SPÖ (Austrian Socialist Party), Chair. VSSTÖ (Asscn of Austrian Socialist Students) 1975–77, mem. Ottakring Party Cttee 1978–, various appointments in SPÖ Youth Div. (JG) 1978–84, elected Chair. Vienna JG and fmr Vice-Chair. Nat. JG; mem. Vienna Regional Legislature 1983–88; City Councillor for Environment and Sport 1988–94; fmr Chair. SPÖ Regional Cttee; Mayor and Gov. of Vienna 1994–; Chair. Council of European Municipalities and Regions 2004–10; Pres. Austrian Asscn of Cities and Towns; Dir Austria Vienna Football Club. *Leisure interest:* football. *Address:* Rathaus, Rathausplatz 1, Stiege 5, 1 Vienna 1010, Austria (office). *Telephone:* (1) 4000-8111 (office). *Fax:* (1) 4000-8111 (office). *E-mail:* buergermeister@magwien.gv.at (office); michael.haeupl@wien.gv.at (office). *Website:* www.wien.gv.at (office).

HAUSER, Claude, Lic. Oec., MBA; Swiss business executive; b. 1942, Casablanca, Morocco; ed Collège Calvin, Geneva, Univ. of Geneva, Univ. of Lausanne, Columbia Univ., New York and Stanford Univ., Calif., USA; Controlling Montres Universal, Geneva 1966–67; various roles at Migros, Geneva 1967–76, Man.-Dir 1976–2000, Chair. Migros-Genossenschafts-Bund and Fed. of Migros Cooperatives, Zürich 2000–12; Chair. Clinique G-Beaulieu SA, Migros Beteiligungen AG; mem. Bd of Dirs CIES/CGF (Consumer Goods Forum), Paris, Fondation Signal de Bougy. *Address:* c/o Federation of Migros Cooperatives, Limmatstrasse 152, 8005 Zürich, Switzerland. *E-mail:* media@migros.ch.

HAUSIKU, Marco Mukoso; Namibian politician; *Deputy Prime Minister;* b. 25 Nov. 1953, Kapako; m.; ed Bunya Roman Catholic Mission School, Rundu Secondary School, Dobra Training Coll., Augustineum Training Coll.; teacher, Katutura Secondary School 1977–89; mem. SWAPO Windhoek Br. Exec. Cttee 1977–89, mem. Cen. Cttee and Polit-Bureau 1991; Election Dir Kavango and Tsumkwe Area 1989; Minister of Lands, Resettlement and Rehabilitation 1990, of Works, Transport and Communication 1992, of Prisons and Correctional Services 1995, of Labour 2002, of Foreign Affairs 2004–10; Deputy Prime Minister 2010–; Founding mem. and Pres. Namibia Nat. Teachers Union 1988. *Leisure interests:* reading, watching television, listening to music. *Address:* Office of the Prime Minister, Robert Mugabe Avenue, P/Bag 13338, Windhoek, Namibia (office). *Telephone:* (61) 2872191 (office). *Fax:* (61) 230648 (office). *E-mail:* lamathila@opm.gov.na (office). *Website:* www.opm.gov.na (office).

HÄUSLER, Gerd; German business executive; *CEO, Bayerische Landesbank;* ed Univ. of Frankfurt, Univ. of Geneva, Switzerland; with Deutsche Bundesbank 1978–96, mem. Exec. Bd and Cen. Bank Council 1994–96; mem. Bd of Man. Dirs Dresdner Bank AG, Frankfurt 1996–2000; Chair. Dresdner Kleinwort Benson, London, UK 1997–2000; Counsellor and Dir of Int. Capital Markets Dept, IMF 2001–06, credited with creation of Global Financial Stability Report, represented the Fund at the Financial Stability Forum; Vice-Chair. and Man. Dir Financial Insts Group and Sovereign Debt Advisory practice, Lazard 2006–08; joined RHJ International as a Bd Dir and Sr Adviser 2008; Deputy Chair. Supervisory Bd Bayerische Landesbank 2008–10, CEO Bayerische Landesbank 2010–; Chair. Supervisory Bd DKB Deutsche Kreditbank AG 2013–; served as outside dir on bds of various cos (Airbus Germany, RWE Solutions, ARBED SA and ESSO Germany); mem. Group of Thirty (think tank) 1996–. *Address:* Bayerische Landesbank Girozentrale, Briennerstrasse 18, 80333 Munich, Germany (office). *Telephone:* (89) 2171-01 (office). *Fax:* (89) 2171-23-578 (office). *E-mail:* info@bayernlb.de (office). *Website:* www.bayernlb.de (office).

HAUSMAN, Jerry Allen, AB, BPhil, DPhil; American economist and academic; *John and Jennie S. MacDonald Professor, Massachusetts Institute of Technology;* b. 5 May 1946, Weirton, W Va; s. of Harold Hausman and Rose Hausman; m. Margaretta Stone; one s. one d.; ed Brown Univ., Univ. of Oxford, UK; served in US Army Corps of Engineers 1968–70; Visiting Scholar, Dept of Econs, MIT 1972–73, Asst Prof. 1973–76, Assoc. Prof. 1976–79, Prof. 1979–, John and Jennie S. MacDonald Prof. 1992–; numerous visiting positions including Visiting Prof., Harvard Univ. 1982–83, Harvard Business School 1986–87, univs of Washington, Oxford, Sydney, Wuhan, Beijing, Xiamen, Uppsala, ANU, Ecole Normale Superieure, Univ. of West Australia, Univ. Coll. London, Sorbonne; Research Assoc., Nat. Bureau of Econ. Research 1979–; Assoc. Ed. numerous journals including Bell Journal of Economics 1974–83, Journal of Public Economics 1982–98, Journal of Applied Econometrics 1985–93, 2009–; Advisory Ed., Economics Research Network and Social Science Research 1998–, Journal of Sports Economics 1999–, Journal of Competition Law & Economics 2004–, Journal of Applied Economics 2005–; mem. Cttee on Nat. Statistics 1985–90, Nat. Acad. of Social Insurance 1990, FTC Panel on Merger Evaluation 2005; Fellow, Econometric Soc. 1979, American Acad. of Arts and Sciences 1991; Advisor, New Zealand Commerce Comm. 2010; mem. Hon. Advisory Bd, ChangMai Univ., Thailand 2009–; Hon. Prof., Xiamen Univ. 2005; Hon. Fellow, Nuffield Coll., Oxford 2008;Dr hc (ChangMai Univ., Thailand) 2010; Econometric Soc. Frisch Medal 1980, Biennial Medal, Modeling and Simulation Soc. of Australia and New Zealand 2005, MIT Undergraduate Economics Asscn Teaching Award 2009. *Publications:* numerous papers on econometrics and applied microeconomics. *Address:* MIT Department of Economics, 50 Memorial Drive Building E52, Room 271D, Cambridge, MA 02142-1347, USA (office). *Telephone:* (617) 253-3644 (office). *Fax:* (617) 253-1330 (office). *E-mail:* jhausman@mit.edu (office). *Website:* economics.mit.edu (office).

HAUSNER, Jerzy, PhD; Polish politician, economist and academic; b. 6 Oct. 1949, Swinovjście; m. Maria Hausner; two d.; ed Kraków Econ. Acad.; Lecturer on Econs, Kraków Econ. Acad. 1972–94, Head, Dept of Public Economy and Admin 1993, Prof. of Econs 1994–; Sec., Regional Kraków Cttee, Polish United Workers' Party 1986–89; Dir-Gen. Office of the Prime Minister and Adviser to Deputy Prime Minister 1994–96; Commr for Social Security Reform 1997–2001; Minister of Labour and Social Policy 2001–03; Deputy Prime Minister and Minister of the Economy, Labour and Social Policy 2003–04; Deputy Prime Minister and Minister of the Economy and Labour 2004–05; mem. Monetary Policy Council, Nat. Bank of Poland 2010–16; mem. Polish Econ. Asscn, Scientific Asscn of Org. and Man., European Asscn for Evolutionary Political Economy; Hon. Prof., Copenhagen Business School 1997; Cross of Merit 1996, Kt's Cross of Polonia Restituta Order 1996; Nat. Educ. Comm. Medal 1996, 75th Anniversary Medal of Kraków Econ. Acad. 2001, Kisiel Prize 2004. *Publications include:* numerous articles in scientific journals, 38 chapters in books. *Leisure interests:* mountain walking, music, soccer. *Address:* Kraków University of Economics, 31-510 Kraków, 27 Rakowicka, Poland (office). *Telephone:* (12) 2935731 (office). *Fax:* (12) 2935051 (office). *E-mail:* hausnerj@uek.krakow.pl (office). *Website:* www.uek.krakow.pl (office).

HAUSSLER, David, BA, MS, PhD; American computer scientist and academic; *Distinguished Professor of Biomolecular Engineering and Director, Center for Biomolecular Science and Engineering, University of California, Santa Cruz;* ed Connecticut Coll., New London, Conn., California Polytechnic State Univ. at San Luis Obispo, Univ. of Colorado at Boulder; Asst Prof. of Math. and Computer Science, Univ. of Denver, Colo 1982–86; Asst Prof. of Computer Science, Univ. of California, Santa Cruz (UCSC) 1986–89, Assoc. Prof. 1989–93, Prof. 1993–2004, Dir Center for Biomolecular Science and Eng 1999–, Adjunct Prof. 2000–, Distinguished Prof. of Biomolecular Eng 2004–, Dir Training Program in the Systems Biology of Stem Cells 2005–, mem. Chancellor's Millennium Cttee 1997–98, Dir, Inst. for the Biology of Stem Cells 2008–12, UCSC Cancer Genomics Hub 2011–; Consulting Prof., Stanford Univ. School of Medicine 2000–; Investigator, Howard Hughes Medical Inst. 2000–; Affiliate, Crown Coll.; mem. Univ. of California System-Wide Life Science Informatics Working Group 1998–; Scientific Co-Dir California Inst. for Quantitative Biosciences (QB3) 2000–; Co-founder, Genome 10K Project 2009–; Assoc. Ed. Machine Learning 1988–97, Journal of Computational Biology 1996–, Public Library of Science Computational Genomics 2005–; mem. Editorial Bd, Journal of Artificial Intelligence Research 1993–95, Journal of Neurocomputing 1995–2002, Neural Computing Surveys 1996–2002, Drug Discovery Today 2001–; mem. NAS 2006, American Asscn for Cancer Research 2008–, Cancer Genome Atlas Steering Cttee, Nat. Cancer Inst. 2008–, American Genetic Asscn 2009–, Soc. of Immunotherapy of Cancer 2015–; Fellow, American Asscn of Artificial Intelligence 1992, California Acad. of Sciences 2001, AAAS 2003, American Academy of Arts and Sciences 2006, Int. Soc. for Computational Biology 2009–; Julia Bower Math. Award, Connecticut Coll.

1975, Math. Award, California Polytechnic State Univ. at San Luis Obispo 1979, Grad. Student Research Award, Univ. of Colorado at Boulder 1982, Univ. of California Presidential Chair of Computer Science 2000–03, Scientist of the Year, Research and Development Magazine 2001, Featured Scientist, Incyte Genomics 2001, UCSC Faculty Research Lecturer 2001–02, Distinguished Scientist of the Year Award, Boston Biomedical/Clinical Ligand Assay Soc. 2003, Tech Award Laureate, San Jose Tech Museum of Innovation 2003, Allen Newell Award, Asscn for Computing Machinery (ACM) and American Asscn for Artificial Intelligence (AAAI) 2004, Distinguished Eng Alumni Award, Univ. of Colorado, Boulder 2005, AAAI Classic Paper Award, for "Quantifying the inductive bias in concept learning" 1986 2005, World Tech. Award in Information Tech. (Software), The World Tech. Network 2005, Dickson Prize in Science, Carnegie Mellon Univ. 2006, Sr Scientist Accomplishment Award, Int. Soc. for Computational Biology 2008, Curt Stern Award, American Soc. of Human Genetics 2009, Weldon Memorial Prize, Univ. of Oxford 2011, Innovation in Networking Award, Corpn for Educ. Network Initiatives in Calif. (Cenic) 2013, Dan David Prize, Tel Aviv Univ. 2015. *Publications:* Proceedings of the First Workshop on Computational Learning Theory (co-ed.) 1988, Proceedings of the Second Workshop on Computational Learning Theory (co-ed.) 1989, Proceedings of the Fifth ACM Workshop on Computational Learning Theory (co-ed.) 1992; numerous scientific papers in professional journals. *Address:* University of California, Santa Cruz, 1156 High Street, MS: CBSE/ITI Engineering 2 Building, Suite 501, Santa Cruz, CA 95064, USA (office). *Telephone:* (831) 459-2105 (office). *Fax:* (831) 459-1809 (office). *E-mail:* haussler@soe.ucsc.edu (office). *Website:* www.cbse.ucsc.edu/staff/haussler .shtml (office).

HAUSSMANN, Helmut, DEcon, Dr rer. pol; German politician; *Honorary Professor of International Management, University of Erlangen-Nürnberg;* b. 18 May 1943, Tübingen; s. of Emil Haussmann and Elisabeth Rau; m. Dr Margot Scheu 1980; ed Univ. of Hamburg, Univ. of Tübingen; business exec. 1968–71; Research and Academic Asst, Univ. of Erlangen-Nuremberg 1971–75; joined FDP 1969; mem. Bad Urach Town Council, FDP Dist Chair., Reutlingen 1975–80; mem. Deutscher Bundestag 1976–2002; Econ. Cttee 1977–88; mem. FDP Fed. Exec. Cttee 1978; Ombudsman FDP Econs Cttee 1980; Econ. Spokesman, FDP Parl. Party 1980–84; Vice-Chair. FDP in Land Baden-Württemberg 1983–88, 1995; Sec.-Gen. FDP 1984–88; Fed. Minister of Econ. Affairs 1988–91; mem. Foreign Affairs Cttee and Spokesman on EC Policy 1991–2002; Hon. Prof. of Int. Man., Univ. Erlangen-Nürnberg 1996–; Adjunct Prof., Dept of Int. Business, Univ. of Tübingen 2010–; Chair. Asia-Europe Foundation 1997–98; Chair. Advisory Bd Gemini Exec. Search GmbH; Order of Merit 1983. *Leisure interests:* reading, tennis, golf. *Address:* Department of International Business, University of Tübingen, Melanchthonstr 30, 72074 Tübingen, Germany (office). *Telephone:* (7071) 2978179 (office). *Fax:* (7071) 295534 (office). *E-mail:* internationales .management@wiso.uni-erlangen.de (office); ib@wiwi.uni-tuebingen.de (office). *Website:* www.helmut-haussmann.de.

HAVIGHURST, Clark Canfield, JD; American legal scholar; *William Neal Reynolds Professor Emeritus of Law, Duke University;* b. 25 May 1933, Evanston, Ill.; s. of Harold Canfield and Marion Clay Havighurst (née Perryman); m. Karen Waldron 1965; one s. one d.; ed Princeton and Northwestern Univs; Research Assoc., Duke Univ. School of Law 1960–61; pvt. practice, Debevoise, Plimpton, Lyons & Gates, New York 1958, 1961–64; Assoc. Prof. of Law, Duke Univ. 1964–68, Prof. 1968–86, William Neal Reynolds Prof. 1986–2005, Prof. Emer. 2005–; Interim Dean Duke Univ. School of Law 1999; numerous other professional appointments; mem. Inst. of Medicine, NAS. *Publications:* Deregulating the Health Care Industry 1982, Health Care Law and Policy 1988 (second edn 1998), Health Care Choices: Private Contracts as Instruments of Health Reform 1995; articles on regulation in the health services industry, the role of competition in the financing and delivery of health care and anti-trust issues arising in the healthcare field. *Address:* 1109 Fearrington Post, Pittsboro, NC 27707, USA (home). *Telephone:* (919) 542-5084 (home). *E-mail:* hav@law.duke.edu (office). *Website:* www.law.duke.edu (office).

HAWASS, Zahi, PhD; Egyptian archaeologist and Egyptologist; b. 28 May 1947, Damietta; ed Alexandria Univ., Cairo Univ., Univ. of Pennsylvania, USA; Inspector of Antiquities of Middle Egypt, Tuna El-Gebel and Mallawi 1969, Italian Expedition, Sikh Abada, Minia 1969, Edfu-Esna, Egypt 1969, Pennsylvania Yale Expedition at Abydos 1969, Western Delta at Alexandria 1970, Embaba, Giza 1972–74, Abu Simbel 1973–74, Pennsylvania Expedition, Malkata, Luxor 1974, Giza Pyramids (for Boston Museum of Fine Arts) 1974–75; First Inspector of Antiquities, Embaba and Bahariya Oasis 1974–79, Chief Inspector 1980, Gen. Dir 1987–98; Gen. Dir Saqqara and Bahariya Oasis 1987–98; apptd Archaeological Site Man. Memphis 1991; Under-Sec. of State for Giza Monuments 1998–2002; apptd Sec.-Gen. of the Supreme Council of Antiquities 2002; Goodwill Amb. to Japan 2008; Minister of State for Antiquities Affairs Jan.–July 2011; Dir of numerous excavations, conservation projects and discoveries including tombs of the pyramid builders at Giza and the Valley of the Golden Mummies in Bahariya; mem. Bd Egyptian Nat. Museum 1996–; Trustee, Egyptian Nat. Museum; Sound and Light Co. 1990; mem. German Archaeological Inst. 1991–, Russian Acad. of Natural Sciences 2001–, Austrian Archaeological Inst.; Explorer-in-Residence Nat. Geographic 2001; Officier, Ordre des Arts et des Lettres 2007, Commdr, Order of Merit (Italy) 2008, Grand Decoration of Honour in Silver with Star (Austria), Order of the Sun (Peru); Hon. PhD (American Univ., Cairo) 2005, Dr hc (Catholic Univ. of Santo Domingo, Dominican Republic) 2009, (Bansomdejchaopraya Rajabhat Univ., Thailand) 2009, (Univ. of Veliko Tarnovo, Bulgaria) 2010, (New Univ. of Lisbon) 2011; Grantee Mellon Fellowship, Univ. of Pennsylvania, Presidential Medal 1988, Golden Plate Award, American Acad. of Achievement 2000, Distinguished Scholar of the Year Asscn of Egyptian-American Scholars 2000, Silver Medal Russian Acad. of Natural Sciences 2001, Achievement Award Mansoura Univ. 2002, named one of Five Distinguished Egyptians Egyptological Soc. of Spain 2002, Paestum Archaeology Award 2006, Emmy Award Nat. Acad. of Television Arts and Sciences 2006, World Tourism Award 2008, Medal of the Spanish Order of Arts and Culture 2009, Cape Breton Univ./Canadian International Coll. Special Award 2010. *Television:* numerous appearances in documentaries and features on Egypt including BBC, CNN, Discovery Channel, History Channel, National Geographic, The Learning Channel. *Publications:* Valley of the Golden Mummies 2000, Silent Images: Women in Pharaonic Egypt 2000, Secrets from the Sand 2003, Hidden Treasures of Ancient Egypt 2004, The Curse of the Pharaohs (children's book), Tutankhamun and the Golden Age of the Pharaohs 2005, Mountains of the Pharaohs 2006, The Great Book of Ancient Egypt: In the Realm of the Pharaohs 2006, The Royal Tombs of Egypt 2006, The Archeaeology and Art of Ancient Egypt: Essays in Honor of David B. O'Connor 2007, Pyramids: Treasures, Mysteries, and New Discoveries in Egypt 2007, Treasures of Ancient Egypt 2007, King Tutankhamun: The Treasures of the Tomb 2007, Tutankhamun: The Golden King and the Great Pharaohs 2008, Royal Mummies: Immortality in Ancient Egypt 2008, Wonders of the Horus Temple: The Sound and Light of Edfu 2011; numerous papers on Egyptology and archaeology. *Address:* 42 Aden Street, Mohandiseen, Cairo, Egypt (home). *E-mail:* pyramiza2004@yahoo.com. *Website:* www.drhawass.com.

HAWK, Tony; American professional skateboarder; b. 12 May 1968, San Diego, Calif.; s. of Frank Hawk and Nancy Hawk; m. 1st Cindy Dunbar 1990 (divorced 1994); one s.; m. 2nd Erin Lee 1996 (divorced 2004); two s.; m. 3rd Lhotse Merriam 2006 (divorced 2011); one d.; m. 4th Catherine Goodman 2015; finished in top five in Van's/Offshore Amateur State Finals (Calif.) in boys 11–13 div. 1980; turned professional aged 14, mem. Powell Peralta's Bones Brigade; pioneered modern vertical skateboarding; entered an estimated 103 professional contests, won 73, placed second in 19; est. children's skate clothing co. Hawk Clothing 1998, acquired by Quiksilver 2000; has accomplished numerous historic tricks including ollie 540, kickflip 540, varial 720 and first 900 degree spin (at 1999 X Games after 11 failed attempts, winning the Best Trick competition); retd from competitive skateboarding 1999; launched Boom Boom HuckJam, a 24-city arena tour featuring world's best skateboarders, BMX bike riders and Motocross riders performing choreographed routines 2002, YouTube channel, RIDE Channel 2012; owner, Birdhouse; est. Tony Hawk Foundation 2002; voted Best Vert Skater by readers of Transworld Skateboarding magazine. *Film roles in:* Thrashin' 1986, Police Academy 4: Citizens on Patrol 1987, Gleaming the Cube 1989, Destroying America (video) 2001, CKY 3 (video) 2001, Collage (video) (stunts) 2001, xXx 2002, Haggard: The Movie 2003, Lords of Dogtown 2005, Jackass Number Two 2006, Parental Guidance 2012. *Television includes:* The Contest 1989, MTV Sports & Music Festival 3: Skate Trick 1999, Reunion X 2004, The Suite Life of Zack & Cody 2008, Kick Buttowski: Suburban Daredevil (voice) 2011, Hell's Kitchen (reality show) 2013, Comedy Bang! Bang! 2014, Skylanders Academy 2017; cameo roles in Cyberchase, Rocket Power, The Simpsons, Max Steel, Sifl and Olly and CSI: Miami, and in films such as Jackass: The Movie, The New Guy, Max Keeble's Big Move, and Dogtown and Z-Boys; hosted documentary, Video Game Invasion. *Publication:* Hawk–Occupation: Skateboarder (autobiog.) 2000, Tony Hawk: Professional Skateboarder 2002, Between Boardslides and Burnout: My Notes from the Road 2002, How Did I Get Here? 2010. *Address:* THI, 1611-A South Melrose Drive, #362, Vista, CA 92081; c/o Terra McGibbon, Tony Hawk Foundation, 1611-A South Melrose Drive, #360, Vista, CA 92081, USA. *Telephone:* (760) 477-2479. *E-mail:* info@tonyhawk.com; questions@tonyhawkfoundation.org; tony@clubtonyhawk.com. *Website:* www.tonyhawk.com.

HAWKE, Allan, BS, PhD; Australian diplomatist, business executive and university chancellor; b. 18 Feb. 1948, Canberra; m. Maria Michele Senti 1977; one c.; ed Australian Nat. Univ.; with Australian Public Service 1974–91; Deputy Sec. Dept of Defence 1991–93; Chief of Staff to Prime Minister 1993–94; Deputy Sec. Dept of Prime Minister and Cabinet 1994; Sec. Dept of Veterans' Affairs 1994–96; Sec. Dept of Transport and Regional Services 1996–99; Sec. of Defence 1999–2001; Head of Secr. for Review of Aboriginal and Torres Strait Islander Comm. 2001–03; Amb. to New Zealand 2003–06; Chancellor ANU, Canberra 2006–10; currently Chair. Civil Aviation Safety Authority Bd; Dir Canberra Raiders; Fellow, Australian Inst. of Public Administration 1998, Australian Inst. of Management 1999, mem. Royal Canberra Golf Club; AC 2010; Centenary Medal 2003. *Address:* CASA Board Secretariat, PO Box 2005, Canberra, ACT 2601, Australia (office). *Telephone:* (7) 3144-7400 (office). *E-mail:* brian.calder@casa.gov .au (office). *Website:* www.casa.gov.au (office).

HAWKE, Ethan; American actor, writer and director; b. 6 Nov. 1970, Austin, Tex.; s. of James Steven Hawke and Leslie Carole Hawke; m. 1st Uma Thurman (q.v.) 1998 (divorced 2005), one s. one d.; m. 2nd Ryan Shawhughes 2008; two d.; ed New York Univ.; co-f. Malaparte Theatre Co.; Co-Founder and Sponsor New York Public Library Young Lions Fiction Award; inducted into Tex. Film Hall of Fame 2004; Michael Mendelson Award for Outstanding Commitment to the Theater. *Theatre appearances include:* Casanova 1991, A Joke, The Seagull 1992, Sophistry, Henry IV (Broadway) 2003, Hurlyburly 2005, The Coast of Utopia 2006, The Cherry Orchard 2009, The Winter's Tale 2009, A Lie of the Mind (dir) 2010. *Films include:* Explorers 1985, Dead Poets Society 1989, Dad 1989, White Fang 1991, Mystery Date 1991, A Midnight Clear 1992, Waterland 1992, Alive 1993, Rich in Love 1993, Straight to One 1993 (dir), Reality Bites 1994, Quiz Show 1994, Floundering 1994, Before Sunrise 1995, Great Expectations, Gattaca, Joe the King 1999, Hamlet 2000, Tape 2001, Waking Life 2001, Training Day 2001, The Jimmy Show 2001, Before Sunset 2004, Taking Lives 2004, Assault on Precinct 13 2005, Lord of War 2005, The Hottest State (also writer and dir) 2006, Fast Food Nation 2006, Before the Devil Knows You're Dead 2007, What Doesn't Kill You 2008, New York, I Love You 2009, Daybreakers 2009, Brooklyn's Finest 2010, The Woman in the Fifth 2011, Sinister 2012, Before Midnight (also writer) (Hollywood Film Award for Screenwriter of the Year 2013) 2013, Boyhood 2014, Seymour: An Introduction (also dir) 2014, The Magnificent Seven 2016, First Reformed (Gotham Independent Film Award for Best Actor 2018, New York Film Critics Circle Award for Best Actor 2018, Georgia Film Critics Asscn Award for Best Actor 2018) 2017, 24 Hours to Live 2018, Juliet, Naked 2018, Blaze (also writer and dir) 2018, The Kid 2019. *Television:* Moby Dick 2010. *Publication:* The Hottest State 1996, Ash Wednesday 2002. *Address:* c/o Erwin Stoff, 3 Arts Entertainment, Inc., 27 West 24th Street, New York, NY 10010, USA. *Telephone:* (310) 888-3200. *E-mail:* estoff@ 3arts.com. *Website:* www.3arts.com.

HAWKE, Gary Richard, CNZM, DPhil, FRSNZ; New Zealand economic historian and academic; *Professor Emeritus, Victoria University of Wellington;* b. 1 Aug. 1942, Napier; s. of Vyvyan Nesbitt Hawke and Jean Avis Hawke (née Carver); m. Helena Joyce Powrie 1965; two s.; ed Victoria Univ. of Wellington, Balliol and Nuffield Colls, Oxford, UK; Lecturer, Victoria Univ. of Wellington 1968–70, Reader 1971–73, Prof. of Econ. History 1974–2008, Prof. Emer. 2008–, Head, School of

Govt 2003–08; Dir Inst. of Policy Studies 1987–97; visiting appointments at Stanford Univ., USA 1972–73, All Souls Coll., Oxford, UK 1977–78, Japan Foundation 1993, Japan Soc. for Promoting Knowledge 1994; Chair. NZ Planning Council 1986–91; Fellow, Inst. of Public Admin of NZ 2008; Sr Fellow, NZ Inst. of Econ. Research (NZIER); Distinguished Fellow, New Zealand Asscn of Economists 2005; Companion, NZ Order of Merit 2009; NZIER-QANTAS Award for Econs 1998, Inaugural Minister of Education's Award for Lifetime Contrib. to Raising Educational Achievement 2014. *Publications include:* Railways and Economic Growth 1970, Between Governments and Banks 1973, Economics for Historians 1980, The Making of New Zealand 1985, The Thoroughbred Among Banks (co-author) 1997, Innovation and Independence: The Reserve Bank of New Zealand 1973–2002 2006. *Leisure interests:* classical music, armchair criticism. *Address:* New Zealand Institute of Economic Research, PO Box 3479, Wellington 6140 (office); 7 Voltaire Street, Karori, Wellington, New Zealand (home). *Telephone:* (4) 470-1806 (office); (4) 476-9109 (home); 27-5635794 (mobile). *E-mail:* gary.hawke@vuw.ac.nz (office). *Website:* www.vuw.ac.nz (office).

HAWKE, Robert (Bob) James Lee, AC, BA, LLB, BLitt; Australian politician and fmr trade union official; b. 9 Dec. 1929, Bordertown, S Australia; s. of A. C. Hawke; m. 1st Hazel Masterson 1956 (divorced 1995); one s. two d.; m. 2nd Blanche d'Apulget 1995; ed Univs of Western Australia and Oxford; Rhodes scholar 1953; Research Officer, Australian Council of Trade Unions 1958–70, Pres. 1970–80; Sr Vice-Pres. Australian Labor Party 1971–73, Pres. 1973–78, Leader 1983–91; MP for Wills, Melbourne 1980–92; Prime Minister 1983–91, mem. Nat. Exec. 1971–91; reporter 1992; Business Consultant 1992; Adjunct Prof. Research School of Pacific Studies and Social Sciences, ANU 1992–95; Hon. Visiting Prof. in Industrial Relations Sydney Univ.; mem. Advisory Council of Inst. for Int. Studies, Stanford Univ., Calif.; Chair. Cttee of Experts on mem. of Educ. Int. 1993–, Sydney City Mission Fundraising Task Force; Dir Quantum Resources Ltd 1996–; mem. Bd Reserve Bank of Australia 1973–83, Governing Body ILO 1972–80; mem. Australian Council for Union Training, Australian Population and Immigration Council; mem. Australian Manufacturing Council 1977, Nat. Labour Consultative Council 1977–92, Australian Refugee Advisory Council; Patron Australia-China Sports Friendship Cttee 2000; Hon. Fellow, Univ. Coll., Oxford 1984; Dr hc (Nanjing) 1986; Hon. DPhil (Hebrew Univ. of Jerusalem) 1987; Hon. LLD (Univ. of NSW) 1987; UN Media Peace Prize 1980. *Publication:* The Hawke Memoirs 1994. *Leisure interests:* tennis, golf, cricket, reading. *Address:* Suite 1, Level 13, 100 Williams Street, Sydney, NSW 2001, Australia.

HAWKEN, Paul; American environmental activist, entrepreneur, journalist and author; *Executive Director, Project Drawdown;* b. 8 Feb. 1946; f. or co-f. cos or software cos specializing in proprietary content man. tools, including Smith & Hawken (garden and catalogue retailer) 1979, and several first natural food cos in USA relying solely on sustainable agricultural methods; Head of PaxIT, PaxTurbine, PaxFan (three cos associated with Pax Scientific, a research and devt co. focused on energy-saving technologies that apply biomimicry to fluid dynamics); Founder and Exec. Dir Natural Capital Inst., Sausalito, Calif.; Co-founder and Exec. Dir Project Drawdown 2014–; fmr mem. Bd numerous environmental orgs, including Point Foundation (publr of Whole Earth Catalogs), Center for Plant Conservation, Trust for Public Land, Friends of the Earth, Nat. Audubon Soc.; six hon. doctorates; Esquire Magazine Award for the Best 100 People of a Generation 1984, California Inst. of Integral Studies Award 'For Ongoing Humanitarian Contributions to the Bay Area Communities', Cine Golden Eagle Award in video for the PBS programme 'Marketing' from Growing a Business, Metropolitan Home Design 100 Editorial Award for the 100 best people, products and ideas that shape our lives, American Horticultural Soc. Award for commitment to excellence in commercial horticulture, Corp. Conscience Award, Council on Econ. Priorities 1990, Small Business Admin Entrepreneur of the Year 1990, Design in Business Award for environmental responsibility, American Center for Design, Creative Visionary Award, Int. Soc. of Industrial Design, World Council for Corp. Governance 2002, Green Cross Millennium Award for Individual Environmental Leadership 2003, named one of the three Pioneers of Sustainability (with Professors Peter Senge and Michael Porter) 2014. *Achievements include:* has given keynote addresses to Liberal Party of Canada, King of Sweden at his inaugural Environmental Seminar, American Booksellers' Asscn, Urban Land Inst., SRI International, Harvard Univ., Stanford Univ., Wharton School, Cornell Univ., Prime Minister of NZ's Conf. on Natural Capitalism, US Dept of Commerce, Australian Business Council, Yale Univ. and Yale Univ. Commencement, Univ. of California, Berkeley Commencement, French Ministry of Agric., AAAS, Prince of Wales Conf. on Business and the Environment at Univ. of Cambridge, Commonwealth Club, Herman Miller, Nat. Wildlife Fed., State of Washington, American Soc. of Landscape Architects, AIA, American Inst. of Graphic Arts, American Solar Energy Asscn, Apple Computer, World Business Council for Sustainable Devt, Cleveland City Club, Conf. Bd, US Forest Service, Ontario Hydro, Environment Canada, Environmental Protection Agency, and several hundred others. *Television:* host and producer of 17-part PBS series based on his book Growing a Business, shown in 115 countries. *Publications include:* author or co-author of numerous articles, op-eds, papers, as well as seven books, including The Next Economy 1983, Growing a Business 1987, The Ecology of Commerce 1993, Natural Capitalism: Creating the Next Industrial Revolution (with Amory Lovins) 1999, Blessed Unrest: How the Largest Movement in the World Came Into Being, and Why No One Saw it Coming 2007, Drawdown: The Most Comprehensive Plan Ever Proposed to Roll Back Global Warming 2017; writings have appeared in Harvard Business Review, Resurgence, New Statesman, Inc., Boston Globe, Christian Science Monitor, Mother Jones, Utne Reader, Orion, and more than 100 other publs. *Address:* Project Drawdown, 27 Gate 5 Road, Sausalito, CA 94965, USA (office). *Telephone:* (415) 332-2860 (office). *Fax:* (415) 331-6242 (office). *E-mail:* info@paulhawken.com (office). *Website:* www.drawdown.org (office); www.paulhawken.com.

HAWKER, Graham Alfred, CBE, CIMgt, FCCA, FRSA; British business executive; b. 12 May 1947; s. of Alfred Hawker and Sarah Rebecca Bowen; m. Sandra Ann Evans 1967; one s. one d.; ed Bedwelty Grammar School; trainee accountant, Caerphilly Dist Council 1964–66; accountant, Abercarn Dist Council 1966–67, Chief Accountant 1967–68, Deputy Treas. 1968–70; Chief Auditor, Taf Fechan Water Bd 1970–74; Audit Man. Welsh Water Authority 1974–78, Div. Finance Man. 1978–84, Chief Accountant 1984–86, Dir Planning and Devt 1986–87, Finance 1987–89; Dir Finance Welsh Water PLC 1989–91, Group Man. Dir 1991–93, Chief Exec. Hyder (fmrly Welsh Water) PLC 1993–2000; Chair. Dwr Cymru Ltd 1993–2000, Hyder Consulting (fmrly Acer) 1993–2000, Swalec 1996–2000; Dir (non-exec.) Bank of England 1998–2000; Chair. BITC (Wales) 1994–2000; fmr Dir Welsh Devt Agency, Deputy Chair. 1998–2000, CEO 2000–04; Chair. New Deal Task Force Advisory Cttee (Wales) 1997–98; mem. New Deal Advisory Cttee (UK) 1997–98; mem. CBI Council, Wales 1994–97, Prince of Wales Review Cttee on Queen's Awards 1999; Fellow, Inst. of Certified Accountants; Hon. Fellow, Univ. of Wales, Cardiff 1999; Dr hc (Univ. of Glamorgan) 1996, Hon. DL (Gwent) 1998; Prince of Wales Ambassador's Award for Corp. Social Responsibility 1999. *Leisure interests:* family, walking, wine, career.

HAWKES, John; American actor; b. (John Marvin Perkins), 11 Sept. 1959, Alexandria, Minn.; s. of Pete Perkins and Patricia Perkins. *Television includes:* Wings 1994, Shaughnessy 1996, ER 1997, Buffy the Vampire Slayer 1998, The X-Files 1999, The Practice 2000, 24 2001, Taken 2002, Deadwood 2004–06, CSI: Crime Scene Investigation 2007, Eastbound & Down 2009–13, Lost 2010. *Films include:* Future-Kill 1985, Scary Movie 1989, From Dusk Till Dawn 1996, Rush Hour 1998, The Perfect Storm 2000, Buttleman 2002, Me and You and Everyone We Know 2005, American Gangster 2007, Wasteland 2009, Small Town Saturday Night 2010, Winter's Bone (several awards including San Diego Film Critics Soc. Award for Best Supporting Actor, San Francisco Film Critics Circle Award for Best Supporting Actor) 2010, Lincoln 2012, The Sessions (Film Ind. Spirit Award for Best Male Lead 2013) 2012, The Pardon 2013, Life of Crime 2013, Low Down 2014, The Driftless Area 2015, Everest 2015, Small Town Crime 2017, Three Billboards Outside Ebbing, Missouri 2017, Unlovable 2018.

HAWKINS, Jeff, BS; American business executive, computer scientist and inventor; b. 1 June 1957, Long Island, Huntingdon, New York; s. of Robert Hawkins; m.; two d.; ed Cornell Univ.; served in various tech. positions with Intel Corpn 1979–82; Vice-Pres. of Research, GriD Systems Corpn 1982–92; f. Palm Computing 1994, invented PalmPilot (hand held computer) 1994; Co-founder, Handspring Inc., fmr Chair. and Chief Product Officer and fmr Chief Tech. Officer, Palm Inc. (after Handspring merger with Palm Inc.); Founder Redwood Neuroscience Inst. (now Redwood Center for Theoretical Neuroscience) 2002, fmr Exec. Dir and Chair., now mem. Advisory Bd; Co-founder Numenta Inc. (medical tech. firm) 2005–; mem. Scientific Bd of Dirs Cold Spring Harbor Lab., New York; mem. Advisory Bd Secular Coalition for America; mem. Nat. Acad. of Eng 2003–; PC Magazine Lifetime Achievement Award for Tech. Excellence 2000, Cornell Univ. Entrepreneur of the Year 2000. *Publications include:* On Intelligence: How a New Understanding of the Brain will Lead to the Creation of Truly Intelligent Machines 2004. *Leisure interests:* sailing, music, family. *Address:* Numenta, Inc., 791 Middlefield Road, Redwood City, CA 94063, USA (office). *Telephone:* (650) 369-8282 (office). *Fax:* (650) 369-8283 (office). *Website:* www.numenta.com (office).

HAWLEY, Christine, CBE, AADipl, RIBA, FRSA; British architect; *Dean, The Bartlett School;* began career with Dept of the Environment, UK Govt; worked for Pearson Int. Architects, London; fmr Pnr Yorke Rosen Cook & Hawley Architects; f. Christine Hawley Architects, London 1998; fmrly Lecturer, Architectural Asscn and Head School of Architecture, Univ. of E London; currently Dean The Bartlett School, Head Faculty of the Built Environment and Prof. of Architectural Studies, Univ. Coll. London; Visiting Chair. of Design, Tech. Univ. of Vienna, Austria and Univ. of Oslo, Norway; currently Adviser UK Govt Comm. for Architecture and the Built Environment; lectured extensively throughout USA, Europe and Far East; RIBA Teaching Award. *Architectural works include:* Social Housing for Int. Bau Austellung, Berlin, Canteen, Städel Acad., Frankfurt, Osaka Folly, Japan, Exhbn Pavilions at Osaka and Nagoya Expo, Pfaffenberg Museum Ext., Bad Deutsch-Altenberg, Austria, Kitagata Housing Reconstruction, Gifu, Japan, Museum for Roman Remains, Carnuntum, Austria, Congress Centre, Rome, Federation Square, Melbourne, Turin Library. *Publications include:* chapters in books The Architect: Reconstructing Her Practice 1996, The Architect: Women in Contemporary Architecture 2001; numerous articles in professional journals. *Address:* The Bartlett School, Wares House, 22 Gordon Street, London, WC1H 0QB (office); Christine Hawley Architects, 10 Lyndhurst Square, London, SE15 5AR, England (office). *Telephone:* (20) 7679-7505 (office). *Fax:* (20) 7679-7453 (office). *E-mail:* c.hawley@ucl.ac.uk (office). *Website:* www.bartlett.ucl.ac.uk (office); christinehawleyarchitects.co.uk.

HAWLEY, John F., BA, PhD; American astronomer, astrophysicist and academic; *Professor and Associate Dean for the Sciences, College of Arts and Sciences, University of Virginia;* b. 23 Aug. 1958, Annapolis, MD; ed Haverford Coll., Univ. of Illinois; Bantrell Fellow, California Inst. of Tech. 1984–87; Asst Prof., Univ. of Virginia 1987–93, Assoc. Prof. 1993–99, Prof. 1999–, Chair. Dept of Astronomy 2006–12, Assoc. Dean for the Sciences, Coll. of Arts and Sciences 2012–; Helen B. Warner Prize, American Astronomical Soc. 1993, Shaw Prize in Astronomy (co-recipient) 2013. *Publications:* Foundations of Modern Cosmology 2005; numerous papers in professional journals on accretion disks and related phenomena. *Address:* Associate Dean's Office, PO Box 400772, University of Virginia, Charlottesville, VA 22904-4775 (office); Astronomy Main Office, PO Box 400325, University of Virginia, Charlottesville, VA 22904-4325, USA. *Telephone:* (434) 982-2381 (Dean's Office) (office); (434) 924-7494 (Astronomy Main Office) (office). *E-mail:* jh8h@virginia.edu (office). *Website:* www.astro.virginia.edu/~jh8h (office).

HAWLEY, Josh, AB, JD; American lawyer and politician; *Senator from Missouri;* b. 31 Dec. 1979, Springdale, Ark.; m. Erin Morrow; two s.; ed Stanford Univ., Yale Law School; Judicial Clerk, US Court of Appeals, 10th Circuit 2006–07, US Supreme Court 2007–06; Attorney, Hogan Lovells 2008–11; Of Counsel, Becket Fund for Religious Liberty 2011–15; Assoc. Prof., Univ. of Missouri School of Law 2011–; Founder and Pres., Mo. Liberty Project 2014–15; Attorney-Gen., State of Mo. 2017–19; Senator from Missouri 2019–; mem. Cttees on Judiciary, Armed Services, Homeland Security and Governmental Affairs, Small Business and Entrepreneurship; Republican. *Address:* United States Senate, B40A Dirksen Senate Office Building, Washington, DC 20510, USA (office). *Telephone:* (202) 224-6154 (office). *Website:* www.hawley.senate.gov (office); www.joshhawley.com.

HAWLEY, Robert, CBE, PhD, DSc, CEng, CPhys, FRSE, FREng, FInstP, FIMechE, FIEE; British business executive and engineer; b. 23 July 1936,

Wallasey, The Wirral; s. of William Hawley and Eva Hawley; m. 1st Valerie Clarke 1961 (divorced); one s. one d.; m. 2nd Pamela Swan; ed Wallasey Grammar School, Wallasey Tech. Coll., Birkenhead Tech. Coll. and King's Coll., Univ. of Durham; joined C.A. Parsons 1961, Electrical Designer, Generator Dept 1964, Chief Electrical Eng 1970, Dir of Production and Eng 1973–74; Dir of Production and Eng NEI Parsons 1974, Man. Dir 1976; Man. Dir Power Eng Group, NEI PLC 1984–88, Man. Dir Operations 1989–92; Main Bd Dir Rolls Royce PLC 1989–92; Chief Exec. Nuclear Electric PLC 1992–95, British Energy PLC 1995–97; Chair. Taylor Woodrow PLC 1999–2003; mem. Bd of Dirs Colt Telecom 1998–; Chair. Eng Council 1999–2002, Particle Physics and Astronomy Research Council 1999–2002, Rocktron 2001; Pres. IEE 1996–97; Adviser, HSBC Investment Bank PLC; Chair. Council Univ. of Durham; Master Worshipful Co. of Engineers 2005–06; Order of Diplomatic Service Gwanghwa Medal 1999, IEE Honorary Fellowship 2003. *Publications:* Dielectric Solids (co-author) 1970, Conduction and Breakdown in Mineral Oil 1973, Fundamentals of Electromagnetic Field Theory 1974, Vacuum as an Insulator. *Leisure interests:* philately, gardening. *Address:* Summerfield, Rendcomb, nr Cirencester, Glos., GL7 7HB (home); 823 Whitehouse Apartments, 9 Belvedere Road, London, E1 9AT, England (home). *Telephone:* (20) 7265-2340 (office); (1285) 831610 (Cirencester) (home); (20) 7620-3145 (London) (home). *Fax:* (20) 7265-2341 (office); (1285) 831801 (Cirencester) (home); (20) 7620-3144 (London) (home). *E-mail:* robert.hawley@btinternet.com.

HAWLY, Mustafa Yousef; Sudanese politician; Minister of State, Ministry of Finance and Econ. Planning –Feb. 2019, Minister of Finance and Econ. Planning Feb.–March 2019; mem. Nat. Congress Party. *Address:* c/o Ministry of Finance and Economic Planning, POB 735, Khartoum, Sudan (office).

HAWN, Goldie; American actress and film producer; b. 21 Nov. 1945, Washington, DC; d. of Edward Rutledge Hawn and Laura Hawn; m. 1st Gus Trikonio 1969 (divorced); m. 2nd Bill Hudson (divorced); one s. one d. (Kate Hudson); pnr, Kurt Russell, one s.; ed American Univ., Washington, DC; began career as chorus-line dancer, World's Fair, New York 1964; Pnr, Hawn/Sylbert Movie Co. with Anthea Sylbert 1984–95; Co-founder Cosmic Entertainment (production co., fmrly Cherry Alley Productions) 2003; f. Goldie Hawn Inst., Bright Light Foundation 2003 (renamed Hawn Foundation 2005). *Stage appearances include:* Romeo and Juliet (Williamsburg), Kiss Me Kate, Guys and Dolls (New York). *Television series include:* Good Morning World (series) 1967, Rowan and Martin's Laugh-In 1968–70, Goldie and Kids—Listen to Us. *Films include:* Cactus Flower 1969, There's a Girl in My Soup 1970, $ 1971, Butterflies are Free 1972, The Girl from Petrovka 1974, The Sugarland Express 1974, Shampoo 1975, The Duchess and the Dirtwater Fox 1976, Foul Play 1978, Viaggio con Anita 1979, Private Benjamin (also producer) 1980, Seems Like Old Times 1980, Best Friends 1982, Swing Shift 1984, Protocol (also producer) 1984, Wildcats (also producer) 1986, Overboard 1987, Bird On A Wire 1990, Deceived 1991, CrissCross 1992, Housesitter 1992, Death Becomes Her 1992, The First Wives Club 1996, Everybody Says I Love You 1996, The Out Of Towners 1999, Town and Country 2001, The Banger Sisters 2003, Snatched 2017. *Publications:* A Lotus Grows in the Mud (with Wendy Holden) 2005, 10 Mindful Minutes 2011. *Address:* c/o Alan Nevins, Renaissance Literary & Talent, PO Box 17379, Beverly Hills, CA 90209, USA. *Telephone:* (323) 848-8305. *E-mail:* Alan@RenaissanceMgmt.Net. *Website:* thehawnfoundation.org.

HAWTHORNE, M(arion) Frederick, BA, PhD; American chemist and academic; *Director, International Institute of Nano and Molecular Medicine, University of Missouri;* b. 1928, Fort Scott, Kan.; ed Missouri School of Mines and Metallurgy, Pomona Coll., Univ. of California, Los Angeles; began career as Postdoctoral Assoc. in Physical-Organic Chem., Iowa State Univ.; Sr Research Chemist, Rohm & Haas Co., Huntsville, Ala, Head of Lab. –1962; Prof., Univ. of California, Riverside 1962–69; Prof., UCLA 1969–98, Univ. Prof. of Chem. 1998–2006; Founder-Dir Int. Inst. of Nano and Molecular Medicine, Univ. of Missouri 2006–, Curators' Distinguished Prof. 2010; Visiting Lecturer at several int. univs, including Distinguished Visiting Prof., Ohio State Univ. 1990; Assoc. Ed. Inorganic Chemistry 1966–69, fmr Ed.-in-Chief; mem. Editorial Advisory Bd Bioconjugate Chemistry; mem. NAS 1973, American Acad. of Arts and Sciences 1975; Fellow, AAAS 1980, Japan Soc. for the Promotion of Science 1986, ACS 2009, Nat. Acad. of Inventors 2016; Hon. DSc (Pomona Coll.) 1974; numerous awards, including Alfred P. Sloan Research Fellowship 1963, Univ. of California, Riverside Chancellor's Award for Research 1968, UCLA McCoy Award for Contribs to Chem. 1972, ACS Award in Inorganic Chem. 1973, USAF Meritorious Civilian Service Medal 1986, ACS Richard C. Tolman Medal 1986, Boron USA Award 1988, Alexander von Humboldt Foundation Award for Sr US Scientists 1990, Bailar Medal 1991, Chemical Pioneer Award 1994, Willard Gibbs Medal 1994, Seabord Medal 1997, Basolo Medal 2001, King Faisal Int. Prize for Science (co-recipient) 2003, Monie A. Ferst Award 2003, ACS Priestley Medal 2009, Senate of the State of Missouri Resolution of Appreciation for Scientific Achievements 2009, Boron in the Americas Pioneer Award 2012, Nat. Medal of Science 2012. *Publications:* 10 book chapters, more than 500 research papers, 30 patents. *Address:* International Institute of Nano and Molecular Medicine, University of Missouri, 1514 Research Park Drive, Columbia, MO 65211-3450, USA (office). *Telephone:* (573) 882-7016 (office). *Fax:* (573) 884-6900 (office). *E-mail:* hawthornem@health.missouri.edu (office). *Website:* www.nanomed.missouri.edu (office).

HAXHINASTO, Edmond; Albanian politician and diplomatist; *Minister of Transport and Infrastructure;* b. 16 Nov. 1966, Tirana; ed Univ. of Tirana, Int. Devt Exec. Center, Brdo, Slovenia, Woodrow Wilson School of Public and Int. Affairs, Princeton Univ., NJ, USA; Head of Foreign Relations, Kuvendi Popullor (Parl.) 1991–92; worked in pvt. sector 1993–97; Head of Co-ordination Dept, Office of the Prime Minister 1997–99, Diplomatic Adviser to Prime Minister 2000–01; Chargé d'affaires a.i., Embassy in Belgrade, Yugoslavia 2001–02; Chief of Cabinet, Ministry of Foreign Affairs 2002–03; Adviser to Ilir Meta (mem. Int. Comm. on the Balkans) 2004–05; Co-founder Inst. for Peace, Devt and Integration, Tirana 2004; mem. Socialist Movt for Integration, becoming Int. Sec., Head of Nat. Cttee and Vice-Chair. 2004–09; Deputy Minister of Public Works and Transport 2009–10, Minister of Foreign Affairs 2010–12, Deputy Prime Minister 2011–13, Minister of Economy, Trade and Energy 2012–13, Minister of Transport and Infrastructure 2013–. *Address:* Ministry of Transport and Infrastructure, Sheshi Skënderbej 5, Tirana, Albania (office). *Telephone:* (4) 2380833 (office). *E-mail:* www.transporti.gov.al (office).

HAY, John, AC, PhD; Australian university administrator; m. Barbara Hay; three s. one d.; ed Univ. of Western Australia, Univ. of Cambridge, UK; fmr Chair of English, Head of Dept, Deputy Chair. Academic Bd, Univ. of Western Australia; fmr Dean of Arts, Chair. Nat. Key Centre, Sr Deputy Vice-Chancellor Monash Univ.; Vice-Chancellor and Pres. Deakin Univ. 1992–95; Vice-Chancellor and Pres. Univ. of Queensland 1996–2008, now Prof. Emer.; Chair. Group of Eight 2002–03, Universitas 21 2003, Carrick Inst. for Learning and Teaching in Higher Educ., Australian Learning and Teaching Council, Queensland Inst. of Medical Research, Springfield Health City, Martin Inst.; Chair. Bd of Trustees, Queensland Art Gallery; Deputy Chair. Library Council Nat. Library of Australia; Fellow, Australian Coll. of Educators, Australian Inst. of Man., Australian Acad. of Humanities, Australian Coll. of Educators; mem. Judging Panel Prime Minister's Literary Awards 2010; mem. Higher Educ. Review Reference Group 2002, City Planning and Econ. Devt; Hon. DLitt (Deakin, Univ. of Western Australia), Hon. LLD (Univ. of Queensland); Centenary Medal 2003.

HAY, Lewis, III, BS, MS; American business executive; *Advisor, Clayton, Dubilier & Rice, LLC;* b. 1955, Pennsylvania; m. Sherry Hay; three c.; ed Lehigh Univ., Carnegie Mellon Univ.; Man. Trainee US Steel Corpn, Pittsburgh 1977–80; Pnr Strategic Planning Assocs (later Mercer Man. Consulting) 1982–91; Chief Financial Officer US Foodservice Inc. 1991–99; joined NextEra Energy as Vice-Pres., Finance and Chief Financial Officer 1999, Pres. NextEra Energy Resources LLC 2000–01, Pres. and CEO NextEra Energy, Inc. 2001–06, Chair. 2002, Exec. Chair. –2013, also Chair. Florida Power & Light Company and NextEra Energy Resources, LLC (subsidiaries), Chief Financial Officer Florida Power & Light Co. (FPL) Inc. 1999–2000, Pres. FPL Energy 2000–01, Pres. FPL Group 2001–06, Chair. and CEO 2002–08; Advisor, Clayton, Dubilier & Rice LLC 2014–; fmr Chair. Edison Electric Inst., Inst. of Nuclear Power Operations; mem. Bd of Dirs Capital One Financial Corpn, Harris Corpn, WellPoint, Inc.; mem. Business Bd of Advisors, Tepper School of Business, Carnegie Mellon Univ., Presidential Consultation Cttee, Carnegie Mellon Energy Futures Inst., President's Council on Jobs and Competitiveness 2011–12; Ernst & Young Florida Lifetime Achievement Award 2010, CEO of the Year, Energy Biz Magazine 2011. *Address:* Clayton, Dubilier & Rice, LLC, 375 Park Avenue, 18th Floor, New York, NY 10152, USA (office). *Website:* www.cdr-inc.com (office).

HAY, Marianne, BSc, DipEd; British banking executive and private equity consultant; *Advisory Board Member, RiverPeak Wealth;* ed Univ. of Edinburgh; completed qualification of Inst. of Bankers in Scotland; began career as an analyst with Bank of Scotland, Edinburgh; later Portfolio Manager, Ivory & Sime; later Dir of Martin Currie; joined Morgan Stanley, New York in institutional investment man. business 1993, Co-Head of Global Emerging Markets 1995–99, Chief Investment Officer, Pvt. Wealth Man. 1999, later Head of Pvt. Wealth Man. Europe and the Middle East, fmr mem. European Exec. Cttee, Dir, Morgan Stanley International Ltd, Morgan Stanley Quilter, fmr Chair. Morgan Stanley Iberia, fmr mem. Bd of Dirs Morgan Stanley's UK and Swiss Banks; fmr CEO Citi Global Wealth Man., Europe; Head of Pvt. Banking, Europe, Americas and MENA (Middle East and North Africa), Standard Chartered Private Bank 2007–10; consultant 2010–; mem. Advisory Bd RiverPeak Wealth 2014–; fmr mem. European Diversity Council, Court and Finance Cttee, Univ. of Greenwich 2007–. *Address:* c/o RiverPeak Wealth, Suite 1, 53 Perrymount Road, Haywards Heath, West Sussex, RH16 3BN, England (office). *Telephone:* (1444) 810845 (office).

HAYASHI, Fumiko; Japanese business executive and politician; *Mayor of Yokohama;* ed Aoyama High School, Tokyo; began career working for Toray and Matsushita Electric; salesperson, Honda 1977–87; joined BMW Japan as Br. Man. 1987, Sales Man. –1999, Pres. BMW Tokyo 2003–05; Pres. Fahren Tokyo, Volkswagen Group Japan 1999–2003; CEO Daiei Inc. 2005–07, Chair. 2005–07, Adviser 2005–07, Vice-Chair. 2007; Chair. Tonichi Carlife Group Inc. and Pres. Tokyo Nissan Auto Sales Co. Ltd 2008; Mayor of Yokohama 2009–. *Website:* www.city.yokohama.lg.jp/ex/mayor (office).

HAYASHI, Keiichi; Japanese diplomatist; m.; several adult c.; ed Kyoto Univ., English language school, Folkestone, UK; entered Ministry of Foreign Affairs 1974, overseas postings include Moscow and Washington, DC, Dir Second SE Asia Div., Asian Affairs Bureau 1991–93, Dir Treaties Div. 1993–96, Political Counsellor, subsequently Political Minister, Embassy in London 1996–98, Deputy Dir-Gen. Treaties Div., Ministry of Foreign Affairs 2000–02, Dir-Gen. 2002–04, Amb. to Ireland 2005–08, Deputy Vice-Minister for Foreign Affairs 2008, Asst Chief Cabinet Sec. in the Prime Minister's Office 2008–10, Minister Plenipotentiary (Deputy Head of Mission) to UK 2010–11, Amb. to UK 2011–16.

HAYASHI, Motoo; Japanese politician; b. 3 Jan. 1947, Chiba Pref.; m.; one s. one d.; ed Univ. of Nihon; elected to Chiba Prefectural Ass. 1983; mem. House of Reps (10th Electoral Dist of Chiba Pref.) 1989–; Parl. Sec. Vice-Minister of Transport 1998–2003; Vice-Minister of Land 2003–05, Chair. Ministry of Land, Infrastructure and Transport 2005–08; Minister of State, Chair. Nat. Public Safety Comm., and Minister of State in charge of Okinawa and Northern Territories and Disaster Man. 2008–09, Minister of Economy, Trade and Industry 2015–16; First Deputy Sec.-Gen. LDP 2007, Vice-Chair. Gen. Council 2013, Chair. 2014; Visiting Prof., Univ. of Nihon 2008. *Publication:* Pursuing Dreams – The Near Future of a Metropolitan Area Airport. *Leisure interests:* walking, reading. *Address:* House of Representatives, 1-7-1 Nagatacho, Chiyoda-ku, Tokyo 100-0014, Japan (office). *Telephone:* (3) 3581-3111 (office). *E-mail:* webmaster@shugiin.go.jp (office). *Website:* www.shugiin.go.jp/internet/index.nsf/html/index_e.htm (office).

HAYASHI, Naoki, BA; Japanese business executive; ed Keio Univ.; joined AEON Co. Ltd 1970, Gen. Man. Gen. Affairs 1990–96, Gen. Man. Kanto Regional Operations, Jusco Co. Ltd 1996–98, Gen. Man. Exec. Sec. Office 1996–98, Man. Dir from 1998, Exec. Vice-Pres. AEON Co. Ltd (fmrly Jusco Co. Ltd) 1998–2008, Sr Exec. Officer 2004–06, Exec. Vice-Pres. Shopping Centre Devt Business 2006–08, CEO Shopping Centre Devt Business, Exec. Officer and Vice-Pres. AEON Co. Ltd 2008–11, Dir, AEON Mall Co. Ltd 2007–14, Chair. 2008–11, Chair. AEON Co. Ltd 2011–14; Pres. and CEO Yozo Tai; Chair. Diamond City Co. Ltd 2006–; Vice-Chair. Japan Council of Shopping Centres 2008–; Non-Ind. and Dir (non-exec.), AEON

Co. (Malaysia) Berhad 2009–14. *Address:* c/o AEON Co. Ltd, 1-5-1 Nakase, Mihama-ku, Chiba-shi, Chiba 261-8515, Japan. *E-mail:* info@aeon.info.

HAYASHI, Yoshimasa, LLB, MPA; Japanese lawyer and politician; *Minister of Education, Culture, Sports, Science and Technology;* b. 19 Jan. 1961; s. of Yoshiro Hayashi; m.; one d.; ed Univ. of Tokyo, Kennedy School of Govt, Harvard Univ., USA; Asst to US Congressman Steve Neal, Washington, DC 1991, also Int. Affairs Intern at Office of US Senator William Roth; worked in pvt. for Mitui & Co. Ltd, Tokyo, Sanden Koutsu Co., Yamaguchi, Yamaguchi Godo Gas Co., Keefe Co., Washington, DC; mem. House of Councillors, Liberal Democratic Party (LDP) for Yamaguchi Pref. 1995–, Leader Pro-Whaling League; Sec., Ministry of Finance 1999–2000; Deputy Minister, Cabinet Office 2006–07; Minister of Econ. and Fiscal Policy 2008–09; Minister of Agriculture, Forestry and Fisheries 2012–14; Minister of Education, Culture, Sports, Science and Technology 2017–, Minister in charge of Education Rebuilding 2017–. *Address:* Ministry of Education, Culture, Sports, Science and Technology, 3-2-2, Kasumigaseki, Chiyoda-ku, Tokyo 100-8959 (office); House of Councillors, Nagatacho 1-7-1, Chiyoda-ku, Tokyo, Japan (office). *Telephone:* (3) 5253-4111 (office). *Fax:* (3) 3595-2017 (office). *Website:* www.mext.go.jp (office); www.sangiin.go.jp/eng (office).

HAYASHI, Yujiro, PhD, DEng; Japanese university administrator and academic; Lecturer, Kanazawa Univ. 1970–71, Asst Prof. 1971–81, Prof. of Mechanical Systems Eng 1981–99, fmr Pres. Kanazawa Univ.; mem. Science Council of Japan; fmr Auditor, Japan Inst. of Science and Tech.; fmr mem. Bd of Dirs Asscn of Nat. Univs.

HAYAT, Sardar Sikander; Pakistani lawyer and politician; *Senior Vice-President, Pakistan Muslim League Nawaz;* b. 1 June 1934, Karela Majhan; s. of Sardar Fateh Mohammad Khan Karelvi; ed Gordon Coll., Rawalpindi, Univ. Law Coll., Lahore; practised law in Kotli 1958; mem. Kolti local council for eight years; elected to first Azad Jammu and Kashmir Legis. Ass. 1970; Minister of Revenue, Forests and Finance 1972–74; Pres. All Pakistan Jammu and Kashmir Conf. 1976–88; Prime Minister Azad Jammu and Kashmir 1985–89, 2001–05; Pres. Azad Jammu and Kashmir 1991–96; fmr Pres. Bar Asscn Kotli; Sr Vice-Pres. Pakistan Muslim League Nawaz (PML-N) 2011–. *Address:* Pakistan Muslim League Nawaz, House 20-H, Street 10, F-8/3, Islamabad, Pakistan (office). *Website:* www.pmln.org (office).

HAYAT, Makhdoom Syed Faisal Saleh, MA; Pakistani politician; b. 21 July 1952, Lahore; m.; one s. one d.; ed Aitchison Coll., FC Govt Coll., Lahore, King's Coll. London, UK; elected to Nat. Ass. 1977–2012; Sr mem. Cen. Exec. Cttee, Pakistan People's Party 1987; fmr Sr Minister for Home and Services and Gen. Admin., Punjab Cabinet; Minister of Commerce, Industries and Local Govt –2002, of the Interior, Narcotics Div., Control and Capital Admin. and Devt Divs 2002–04, Minister of the Environment 2006–07; mem. Nat. Security Council; currently Pres. Pakistan Football Fed. *Leisure interests:* squash, cricket, riding. *Website:* www.pff.com.pk (office).

HAYAT, Gen. Zubair Mahmood; Pakistani army officer; *Chairman, Joint Chiefs of Staff Committee;* s. of Maj-Gen Mahmood Aslam Hayat; ed Fort Sill Oklahoma, USA, Staff Coll., Camberley, UK, National Defence Univ., Islamabad; commissioned in Artillery Regiment 1980; fmr Prin. Staff Officer to the then army chief; served as Gen. Officer Commanding Sialkot and led Staff Duties Directorate; apptd Lt-Gen. and Corps Commdr Bahawalpur 2013–, apptd Dir-Gen. Strategic Plans Div. 2013; Chief of Gen. Staff 2015–16, Chair. Joint Chiefs of Staff Cttee 2016–; apptd Col Commdt of Regiment of Artillery 2015; Hilal-i-Imtiaz, Nishan-e-Imtiaz 2016. *Address:* Ministry of Defence, Pakistan Secretariat II, Rawalpindi, Pakistan (office). *Telephone:* (51) 9271107 (office). *Fax:* (51) 9221596 (office). *Website:* www.mod.gov.pk (office).

HAYDEN, Matthew Lawrence, AO; Australian fmr professional cricketer; b. 29 Oct. 1971, Kingaroy, Queensland; m. Kellie Hayden; left-hand opening batsman; teams: Queensland 1991–2009, Hampshire 1997, Northamptonshire 1999–2000, Australia 1993–2009 (Capt. Australia A 2000–01, Australia 1993–2009), Chennai Super Kings 2008–10, Brisbane Heat 2011–12; First-class debut: 1991/92; Test debut: Australia vs S Africa, Johannesburg 4–8 March 1994; One-Day Int. (ODI) debut: Australia vs England, Manchester 19 May 1993; T20I debut: England vs Australia, Southampton 13 June 2005; played 103 tests for Australia, scored 8,625 runs (average 50.73) with 30 centuries and 29 fifties, highest score 380 (fmr world record) against Zimbabwe, Perth, Australia 9–10 Oct. 2003; played 161 ODIs, scored 6,133 runs (average 43.80) with ten centuries and 36 fifties, highest score 181 not out against Zealand, Hamilton 2007; played 295 First-class matches, scored 24,603 runs (average 52.57) with 79 centuries and 100 fifties; first Australian to score 1,000 runs in debut season 1991/92; six centuries in seven consecutive innings in 1993/94; shared in Queensland record 2nd wicket partnership (with Martin Love) vs Tasmania 1995/96; second highest run-scorer for Australia in a calendar year 2001 (1,391 runs); ranked World No. 1 Batsman 2003; four consecutive double century first-wicket partnerships (with Justin Langer) for Australia (world record); Queensland's most prolific century-maker (24); mem. Australia's World Cup winning side 2003; Founder, The Hayden Way; Amb., Australian Indigenous Education Foundation; Mercantile Mutual Cup Player of the Year 1998/99, 1999/2000, Allan Border Medal 2002, Wisden Cricketer of the Year 2003, ODI Player of the Year 2007, QLD Sportsman of the Year 2007. *Address:* The Hayden Way, PO Box 4134, Gumdale, Queensland 4154, Australia (office). *Telephone:* (7) 3245-1765 (office). *Fax:* (7) 3245-3392 (office). *E-mail:* team@thehaydenway.com (office). *Website:* www.thehaydenway.com (office).

HAYDEN, Michael R., CM, MB, ChB, PhD, FRCP(C), FRSC; South African geneticist and academic; *Killam Professor, Department of Medical Genetics, University of British Columbia;* b. 21 Nov. 1951, Cape Town; m.; four c.; ed Harvard Univ., USA, Univ. of Cape Town; began scientific career with investigations of Huntington disease and discovery of neuroendocrine abnormalities; later work contributed to understanding and gene identification of atherosclerosis, Huntington disease and inherited lipid disorders; currently Prin. Investigator and Univ. Killam Prof., Dept of Medical Genetics, Univ. of British Columbia, also Canada Research Chair in Human Genetics and Molecular Medicine; fmr Dir, now Sr Scientist and Prin. Investigator, Centre for Molecular Medicine and Therapeutics; Pres. Global R&D, Teva Pharmaceutical Industries Ltd 2012–, Chief Scientific Officer 2012–; Founder of biotechnology cos NeuroVir, Aspreva Pharmaceuticals, Xenon Pharmaceuticals Inc. (Chief Scientific Officer 2000–12); mem. Bd of Dirs Med Biogene Inc. 2010–11; Order of British Columbia 2009; Hon. DSc (Univ. of Gottingen) 2014; Prix Galien (Canada) 2007, Canada's Health Researcher of the Year: Canadian Insts of Health Research Michael Smith Prize in Biomedical and Clinical Research 2008, Canada Gairdner Wightman Award for leadership in medical science in Canada 2011, Killam Prize in Health Sciences, Canada Council for the Arts 2011, Diamond Jubilee Medal 2012, Luminary Award 2014. *Publications include:* numerous papers in professional journals. *Address:* Room 3025, Centre for Molecular Medicine and Therapeutics, 950 West 28th Avenue, Vancouver, BC V5Z 4H4 (office); Department of Medical Genetics, University of British Columbia, C201-4500 Oak Street, Vancouver, BC V6H 3N1, Canada (office). *Telephone:* (604) 875-3535 (office). *Fax:* (604) 875-3819 (office). *E-mail:* mrh@cmmt.ubc.ca (office). *Website:* www.cmmt.ubc.ca (office); www.ubc.ca (office); www.tevapharm.com (office).

HAYDEN, Gen. Michael Vincent, BA, MA; American air force officer (retd) and fmr government official; *Principal, Chertoff Group;* b. 17 March 1945, Pittsburgh, Pa; s. of Harry Hayden, Sr and Sadie Hayden; m. Jeanine Hayden; three c.; ed Duquesne Univ., Academic Instructor School, Squadron Officer School, Air Command and Staff Coll., Air War Coll., Maxwell AF Base, Ala, Defense Intelligence Agency, Bolling AF Base, Washington DC, Armed Forces Staff Coll., Norfolk, Va; rank of Second Lt 1967–70; Analyst and Briefer, Strategic Air Command HQ, Offnut AF Base, Neb. 1970–72; promoted to First Lt 1970, to Capt. 1971; Chief Current Intelligence Div., 8th AF HQ, Andersen AF Base, Guam 1972–75; Academic Instructor and Commdt of Cadets, ROTC Program, St Michael's Coll., Winooski, Vt 1975–79; promoted to Maj. 1980; Chief of Intelligence, 51st Tactical Fighter Wing, Osan Air Base, S Korea 1980–82; Air Attaché, Embassy in Sofia, Bulgaria 1984–86; promoted to Lt–Col 1985; Politico-Mil. Affairs Officer, Strategy Div., USAF HQ, Washington, DC 1986–89, Chief, Sec. of AF Staff Group 1991–93; Dir for Defense Policy and Arms Control, Nat. Security Council 1989–91; promoted to Col 1990; Dir Intelligence Directorate, US European Command HQ, Stuttgart, Germany 1993–95; promoted to Brig. Gen. 1993; Special Asst to Commdr, Air Intelligence Agency HQ, Kelly AF Base Oct.–Dec. 1995, Commdr 1996–97, Dir Jt Command and Control Warfare Center 1996–97; Deputy Chief of Staff, UN Command and US Forces Korea, Yongsan Army Garrison, S Korea 1997–99; promoted to Lt Gen. 1999; Dir Nat. Security Agency 1999–2005, Chief, Cen. Security Service, Fort George G. Meade, Md 1999–2005; promoted to Gen. 2005; Prin. Deputy Dir, Nat. Intelligence, Washington, DC 2005–06; Dir CIA 2006–09; Prin., Chertoff Group (security consulting firm) 2009–; mem. Bd of Dirs Motorola Solutions 2011–; Distinguished Visiting Prof., School of Public Policy, George Mason Univ.; Dr hc (Inst. of World Politics in Washington DC) 2009; Defense Distinguished Service Medal, Defense Superior Service Medal with oak leaf cluster, Legion of Merit, Bronze Star Medal, Meritorious Service Medal with two oak leaf clusters, AF Commendation Medal, AF Achievement Medal, Air Force Reserve Officer Training Corps Distinguished Alumni 2011. *Address:* Chertoff Group, 1399 New York Avenue, NW, Suite 900, Washington, DC 20005, USA (home). *Telephone:* (202) 552-5280 (office). *Fax:* (202) 330-5505 (office). *Website:* www.chertoffgroup.com (office).

HAYDEN, Hon. William (Bill) George, AC, BEcons; Australian fmr politician, fmr police officer and farmer; b. 23 Jan. 1933, Brisbane, Queensland; m. Dallas Broadfoot 1960; one s. three d. (one deceased); ed Brisbane State High School, Queensland Secondary Correspondence School, Univ. of Queensland; Queensland State Public Service 1950–52; mem. Queensland Police Force 1953–61; mem. Fed. Parl. for Oxley 1961–88; Parl. Spokesman on Health and Welfare 1969–72, Treas. 1975; Minister for Social Security 1972–75, for Foreign Affairs 1983–88, for Foreign Affairs and Trade 1987–88; Gov.-Gen. Commonwealth of Australia 1989–96 (retd); Leader Parl. Labor Party (Opposition) 1977–83; Adjunct Prof., Queensland Univ. of Tech. 1996; Chair. Editorial Cttee Quadrant Journal 1998–2004; Resident Visiting Fellow, Jane Franklin Hall, Univ. of Tasmania 2000; mem. The Gen. Sir John Monash Foundation Asscn of Fmr Mems of the Parl. of Australia, Queensland Retd Police Asscn Inc.; Patron Australian Inst. of Int. Affairs (Queensland Br.), Australian Fabian Soc. (Queensland Br.); Hon. FRACP 1995; KStJ; Commdr, Order of the Three Stars (Latvia); Gwanghwa Medal (Korean Order of Diplomatic Merit); Hon. LLD (Queensland) 1990; Hon. DUniv (Central Queensland) 1992; Hon. DLitt (Southern Queensland) 1997; Dr hc (Griffith) 1990; Australian Humanist of the Year 1996. *Publication:* Hayden: An Autobiography 1996. *Address:* Level 13, Waterfront Place, 1 Eagle Street, Brisbane, Queensland (office); GPO Box 7829, Waterfront Place, Brisbane, Queensland 4001, Australia. *Telephone:* (7) 3229-3500 (office). *Fax:* (7) 3229-3499 (office). *E-mail:* wdhayden@bigpond.net.au (office).

HAYEK, Nayla; Swiss/Lebanese business executive and horse breeder; *Chairman, Swatch Group Ltd;* b. 1951, Switzerland; d. of Nicolas Hayek, Chair. Swatch Group Ltd; m. Roland Weber (divorced); one s.; Adviser, Swatch Group Middle East, Dubai, then hired as employee, est. Tiffany Watch Co. Ltd 2008, mem. Bd of Dirs Swatch Group 1995–, Vice-Chair. May–June 2010, Chair. 2010–; CEO Harry Winston, Inc. 2013–; mem. Bd of Dirs Belenos Clean Power Holding Ltd, Hayek Group, Rivoli Investments LLC, Dubai; mem. World Arabian Horse Org.; Owner, Hanaya Stud, Schleinikon, Switzerland; serves as int. Arabian horse judge; Dr hc (European Univ., Montreux). *Address:* Swatch Group Limited, Seevorstadt 6, PO Box 2501, 2501 Biel, Switzerland (office). *Telephone:* 3436811 (office). *Fax:* 3436911 (office). *Website:* www.swatchgroup.com (office); www.hanaya.ch.

HAYEK, Salma; Mexican actress; b. (Salma Valgarma Hayek-Jimenez), 2 Sept. 1966, Coatzacoalcos, Veracruz; m. François-Henri Pinault 2009; one d.; Pres. and Chief Exec. Ventanazul (production co.) 2007–; Chevalier, Ordre national de la Légion d'honneur 2012; Bambi Award 2012. *Films include:* Mi vida loca 1993, Miracle Alley 1995, Desperado 1995, Four Rooms 1995, Fair Game 1995, From Dusk Till Dawn 1996, Fled 1996, Fools Rush In 1997, Breaking Up 1997, Follow Me Home 1997, The Velocity of Gary 1998, 54 1998, Wild Wild West 1999, Dogma 1999, Frida 2002 (also producer), Death to Smoochy 2002, Once Upon a Time in Mexico 2003, Hotel 2003, After the Sunset 2004, Ask the Dust 2006, Lonely Hearts 2006, Across the Universe 2007, Cirque Du Freak: The Vampire's Assistant 2009, Grown Ups 2010, Americano 2011, La chispa de la vida 2011, Puss in Boots (voice) 2011, The Pirates! Band of Misfits (voice) 2012, Savages 2012, Here Comes the Boom 2012, Grown Ups 2 2013, Kahlil Gibran's The Prophet (voice, producer)

2014, Everly 2014, How to Make Love Like an Englishman. *Television appearances include:* The Hunchback 1997, In the Time of the Butterflies 2001, The Maldonado Miracle (Daytime Emmy Award for Outstanding Directing in a Children/Youth/Family Special 2004) 2003, 30 Rock 2006, Ugly Betty (also exec. producer) 2006–07, Ferite a morte (documentary) 2014. *Address:* William Morris Agency, 1325 Avenue of the Americas, New York, NY 10019-6047, USA.

HAYES, Gregory J., BA; American certified public accountant and business executive; *Chairman, President and CEO, United Technologies Corporation;* b. 1961; ed Purdue Univ.; held several leadership positions with Sundstrand Corpn 1989–99 (merged with United Technologies Corpn), Sr Vice-Pres. and Chief Financial Officer, United Technologies Corpn 2008–14, Pres. and CEO 2014–, also Chair. 2016–; mem. Pres. Trump's American Manufacturing Council Jan.–Aug. 2017; mem. Bd of Dirs, Nucor Corpn. *Address:* United Technologies Corpn, 1 Financial Plaza, Suite 22, Hartford, CT 06103-2608, USA (office). *Telephone:* (860) 728-7000 (office). *Fax:* (860) 728-7979 (office). *E-mail:* invrelations@corphq.utc.com (office). *Website:* www.utc.com (office).

HAYES, Roger Peter, BSc (Econ), MA, DBA; British public relations executive, company director, lecturer and trainer; *Senior Counsellor, APCO Worldwide;* b. 15 Feb. 1945, Hampton, Richmond upon Thames; s. of Peter Hall and Patricia Hall; m. Margaret Jean Eales 1974 (deceased); one s.; ed Isleworth Grammar School, Univ. of London, Univ. of Southern California, USA, Henley Business School; Reuters Corresp., Paris and London 1967–72; Vice-Pres. and Dir Buson-Marsteller 1972–79; Man. P.A. Consulting Group 1979–83; Dir Corp. Communications, Thorn-EMI PLC 1983–87; Chair. Hayes-MacLeod; Sec.-Gen. Int. Public Relations Asscns (Bd mem. 1984–88); Dir (non-exec.) IT World 1985–; fmr Int. Dir Perception Man., Perception International; Chair. Int. Foundation for Public Affairs Studies 1986–89; Dir-Gen. British Nuclear Industry Forum 1993–97; Vice-Pres. (Public Affairs and Govt Relations) Ford of Europe 1991–93; Pres. Int. Public Relations Asscn 1997, now mem. Emer.; Dir Int. Inst. of Communications 1997–; Dir (non-exec.), Echo Communications Research Group 1999–2009, Communications Ethics Ltd; Group CEO British Amusements Catering Trades Asscn 2004–, Amusements Trades Exhbns Ltd 2004–; currently Sr Counsellor, APCO Worldwide, postings to S Africa and India; Assoc. Faculty mem. Henley Business School; Lecturer, Greenwich Univ. Business School, London; Assoc. Prof., Lee Kuan Yew School of Public Policy, Nat. Univ. of Singapore; Fellow, Chartered Inst. of Public Relations; Adviser, Consortium for Street Children NGO. *Publications:* co-author: Corporate Revolution 1986, Experts in Action 1988, Systematic Networking 1996, Reframing the Leadership Landscape 2015. *Leisure interests:* books, music, cinema, politics, tennis, travel. *Address:* 9 Alder Lodge, 73 Stevenage Road, London, SW6 6NP, England (home). *Telephone:* (20) 7526-3600 (office); (20) 7731-1255 (home). *Fax:* (20) 7323-9623 (office). *E-mail:* roger_p_hayes@yahoo.co.uk (home); rhayes@apcoworldwide.com (office).

HAYES, William, MA, PhD, DPhil; Irish physicist and fmr university administrator; b. 12 Nov. 1930, Killorglin, Co. Kerry; s. of Robert Hayes and Eileen Tobin; m. Joan Ferriss 1962 (died 1996); two s. one d.; ed Univ. Coll., Dublin and St John's Coll., Oxford; Official Fellow, St John's Coll. Oxford 1960–87, Prin. Bursar 1977–87, Pres. 1987–2001; Univ. Lecturer in Physics, Univ. of Oxford 1962–87; Dir Clarendon Lab. Oxford 1985–87; Pro-Vice-Chancellor, Univ. of Oxford 1990–2001; Chair. Curators of Oxford Univ. Chest 1992–2000; Sr Foreign Fellow, NSF, Purdue Univ., USA 1963–64; Visiting Prof., Univ. of Ill., USA 1971; mem. Tech. Staff, Bell Labs, New Jersey, USA 1974; Hon. MRIA 1998, Hon. Fellow, St John's Coll. Oxford 2001–; Hon. DSc (Nat. Univ. of Ireland) 1988, (Purdue Univ.) 1996. *Publications include:* Scattering of Light by Crystals (with R. Loudon) 1978, Defects and Defect Processes in Non-Metallic Solids (with A. M. Stoneham) 1985; research papers in professional journals. *Leisure interests:* walking, reading, listening to music. *Address:* 91 Woodstock Road, Oxford, OX2 6HL, England (home). *E-mail:* bill.hayes@physics.ox.ac.uk (office).

HAYMAN, Baroness (Life Peer), cr. 1996, of Dartmouth Park in the London Borough of Camden; **Rt Hon. Helene Valerie Hayman,** GBE, PC, MA; British politician; b. 26 March 1949, Wolverhampton, West Midlands, England; d. of Maurice Middleweek and Maude Middleweek; m. Martin Heathcote Hayman 1974; four s.; ed Wolverhampton Girls' High School, Newnham Coll., Cambridge; Pres. Union, Newnham Coll. Cambridge 1969; with Shelter: Nat. Campaign for the Homeless 1969–71; mem. staff, Social Services Dept, London Borough of Camden 1971–74; MP for Welwyn and Hatfield 1974–79 (Baby of the House 1974–79); Deputy Dir Nat. Council for One Parent Families 1974; Jr Minister, Dept for Environment, Transport and the Regions and Dept of Health 1997–99; Minister of State in the House of Lords for Agric., Fisheries and Food 1999–2001; mem. (Crossbench), House of Lords 1996–, elected first ever Lord Speaker of the House of Lords 2006–11, Pres. America Group 2007–; mem. Royal Coll. of Gynaecologists Ethics Cttee 1982–97, Univ. Coll. London/Univ. Coll. Hosp. Cttee on Ethics of Clinical Investigation 1987–97 (Vice-Chair. 1990–97), Univ. Coll. London 1992–97, Human Fertilisation and Embryology Authority, Gen. Medical Council; Chair. Whittington Hosp. NHS Trust 1992–97, Cancer Research UK 2001–04, Specialised Health Care Alliance 2004–06, Human Tissue Authority 2005; mem. Bd Roadsafe 2001–05 (Patron 2006–), Review Cttee of Privy Counsellors of the Anti-terrorism, Crime and Security Act 2002–04; Pres. Commonwealth Parl. Asscn (UK Br.) 2006–11; Chair. Cambridge Univ. Health Partners 2014–, Ethics & Governance Council, UK Biobank; Trustee, Royal Botanical Gardens, Health and Educ. Trust; mem. Bd, Disasters Emergency Cttee 2013–; mem. Exec. Cttee Commonwealth Parl. Asscn; Hon. Pres. British Group, Inter-Parl. Union 2006–11; Copy of the Key of the City of Tirana on the occasion of her state visit to Albania 2010; Hon. Fellow, Newnham Coll., Cambridge; several hon. degrees from British univs. *Address:* House of Lords, Westminster, London, SW1A 0PW, England (office). *Telephone:* (20) 7219-5083 (office). *E-mail:* haymanh@parliament.uk (office). *Website:* www.parliament.uk/biographies/lords/baroness-hayman/1649 (office).

HAYMAN, Walter Kurt, MA, ScD, FRS; British mathematician and academic; *Professor Emeritus and Senior Research Fellow, Department of Mathematics, Imperial College London;* b. 6 Jan. 1926, Cologne, Germany; s. of Franz Samuel Haymann and Ruth Therese Hensel; m. 1st Margaret Riley Crann 1947 (died 1994); three d.; m. 2nd Wafícka Katifi 1995 (died 2001); m. 3rd Marie Jennings 2007; ed Gordonstoun School and Univ. of Cambridge; Lecturer, King's Coll., Newcastle and Fellow, St John's Coll., Cambridge 1947; Lecturer 1947–53 and Reader, Univ. of Exeter 1953–56; Visiting Lecturer, Brown Univ., USA 1949–50, Stanford Univ. summer 1950, 1955, American Math. Soc. 1961; first Prof. of Pure Math., Imperial Coll. of Science and Tech., London 1956–85, Dean Royal Coll. of Science 1978–81, Prof. Emer. 1985–, Sr Research Fellow 1995–; Prof. Univ. of York 1985–93, Prof. Emer. 1993–; mem. London Math. Soc.; mem. Cambridge Philosophical Soc.; Fellow, Imperial Coll. 1989; Foreign mem. Finnish Acad. of Science and Letters, Accad. dei Lincei; Corresp. mem. Bavarian Acad. of Science; first organizer (with Margaret Hayman) of British Math. Olympiad 1964–68; Hon. DSc (Exeter) 1981, (Birmingham) 1985, (Giessen) 1992, (Uppsala) 1992, (Nat. Univ. of Ireland) 1997; First Smiths Prize 1948, shared Adams Prize, Univ. of Cambridge 1949, Junior Berwick Prize 1955, Sr Berwick Prize 1964, de Morgan Medal, London Math. Soc. 1995. *Publications:* Multivalent Functions 1958, 1994, Meromorphic Functions 1964, Research Problems in Function Theory 1967, Subharmonic Functions I 1976, II 1989; and over 200 articles in various scientific journals. *Leisure interests:* music, television, poetry, languages. *Address:* Department of Mathematics, Room 6M43, Imperial College, London, SW7 2AZ (office); Cadogan Grange, Bisley, Stroud, Glos., GL6 7AT, England (home). *Telephone:* (20) 7594-8535 (office); (1452) 770545 (home). *Fax:* (20) 7594-8517 (office). *Website:* www.ma.ic.ac.uk (office).

HAYMET, A. D. J. (Tony), BSc, PhD, DSc; Australian/American chemist, environmental scientist, academic, research institute director and business executive; *Distinguished Professor and Director and Vice-Chancellor Emeritus, Scripps Institution of Oceanography;* ed Sydney Grammar School, Univ. of Sydney, Univ. of Chicago, USA; Postdoctoral Research Fellow, Lyman Lab. of Physics, Harvard Univ. 1981–83; Asst Prof. of Chem., Univ. of California, Berkeley 1983–88; Assoc. Prof. of Chem., Univ. of Utah 1988–91, Prof. of Chem. 1991, Adjunct Prof. of Chem. 1991–95; Deputy Dir for Physical Sciences, UniServe Science, CAUT Center for Educational Software in Science, Univ. of Sydney, Australia 1994–97, Prof. of Chem. (Established Chair of Theoretical Chem.), Univ. of Sydney 1991–98, Visiting Prof. in School of Chem. 1998–99; Affiliated Faculty mem. W. M. Keck Center for Computational Biology 1998–2002; Affiliate Staff Scientist, Pacific Northwest Nat. Lab., PASS 1996–2002; Chair. Physical Chem. Div., Univ. of Houston, Tex. 1998–2001, Founder Univ. of Houston Environmental Modeling Inst. 2000–02, Distinguished Univ. Prof. of Chem. 1998–2002; mem. Advisory Bd Environmental Inst. of Houston 2001–02; mem. Founding Group, WA Marine Science Inst. 2005–06; mem. Bd of Dirs CRC for Antarctic Climate and Ecosystems 2003–06, Western Australian Marine Science Inst.; seconded as CSIRO Dir of Science and Policy 2005–06, Chief of CSIRO Marine Research, then Marine & Atmospheric Research 2006; Dir Scripps Inst. of Oceanography, Univ. of California, San Diego 2006–12, Vice-Chancellor for Marine Sciences and Dean of Grad. School of Marine Sciences, Univ. of California, San Diego 2006–12, now Emer.; Co-founder, mem. Bd and fmr Chair. CleanTECH, San Diego 2007–; Strategic Advisor (part time), Pegasus Capital Advisors 2010–; Special Counsel (part time), Phillips & Assocs 2012–; Visiting Research Fellow, ANU Research School of Chem. 1993; Australian Acad. of Science Fellowship to Japan 1994; Visiting Prof. of Chemical Eng and Petroleum Refining, Colorado School of Mines, Golden, Colo, USA 1997; Chair. Partnership for the Observation of Global Oceans (POGO); Chair. Ocean Global Agenda, Council Ocean Council, World Econ. Forum 2012–13, Vice-Chair. 2013–14; Vice-Chair. VCAT, Nat. Inst. of Standards and Tech. 2008–13; mem. Chemical Educ. Sub-cttee Australian Acad. of Science 1997–98, Advisory Editorial Bd PhysChemComm 1998–2001; Fellow, Royal Australian Chemical Inst. 1992; Hon. Research Prof. of Chem., Univ. of Tasmania 2002–06; Sr Knox Prize, Sydney Grammar School 1973, Levey Scholarship for Chem. I and Physics I and Iredale Prize for Chem. II 1974–75, C.S.R. Chemicals Prize for Chem. and Union Carbide Prize for Chem. 3 1976–77, Univ. Medal and First Class Honours in Theoretical Chem. 1977, Masson Medal, Royal Australian Chemical Inst. 1977, NSF Presidential Young Investigator 1985–90, Alfred P. Sloan Research Fellow 1986–89, Rennie Medal, Royal Australian Chemical Inst. 1988, Student Distinguished Service Award, Univ. of Utah 1990, Antarctic Service Medal, US Dept of Navy and NSF 1994, Distinguished Young Chemist Award, Fed. of Asian Chemical Socs 1997, Woolmers Lecturer in Chemical Educ., Univ. of Tasmania 1997, Excellence Award in Oceanography, Werner Petersen Foundation 2013. *Publications:* more than 173 scientific papers in professional journals; numerous op-ed pieces in leading newspapers. *Leisure interests:* bushwalking, tennis. *Address:* Integrative Oceanography Division, Scripps Institution of Oceanography, University of California, San Diego, MC 0209, 9500 Gilman Drive, La Jolla, CA 92093-0209, USA (office). *Telephone:* (858) 534-2083 (office). *Fax:* (858) 453-0167 (office). *E-mail:* haymet@ucsd.edu (office). *Website:* scripps.ucsd.edu/profiles/thaymet (office).

HAYNES, Desmond Leo; Barbadian politician and fmr professional cricketer; b. 15 Feb. 1956, Holders Hill, St James; m. Dawn Haynes 1991; ed Fed. High School, Barbados; right-hand opening batsman, teams: Barbados 1976–95 (Capt. 1990–91), Scotland (Benson & Hedges Cup) 1983, Middx 1989–94, W Prov. 1994–97; played in 116 Tests for West Indies 1977–94 (four as Capt.), scoring 7,487 runs (average 42.29, highest score 184) including 18 hundreds; played in 238 One-Day Ints, scoring record 8,648 runs (average 41.37, highest score 152 not out) including record 17 hundreds; scored 26,030 First-class runs (average 45.90, highest score 255 not out) including 61 hundreds; formed partnership with Gordon Greenidge for West Indies cricket team in Test cricket during 1980s, between them they made 16 century stands, four in excess of 200, 6,482 runs while batting together in partnerships, the highest total for a batting partnership in Test cricket history; toured England 1979 (World Cup), 1980, 1983 (World Cup), 1984, 1988, 1991; Chair. Barbados Cricket Asscn Sr Selection Panel 1999–2001; elected Senator in Parl. 2001; fmr Chair. Nat. Sports Council; fmr Pres. Carlton Cricket Club; fmr Sec. West Indies Players' Asscn; Special Adviser, Cricket Cttee, West Indies Cricket Bd; Wisden Cricketer of the Year 1991. *Leisure interest:* playing golf.

HAYRIKYAN, Paruyr, PhD; Armenian lawyer and politician; *President, Union for National Self-Determination party;* b. 5 July 1949, Yerevan; s. of Arshavir Hayrikyan and Zaruhi Abrahamyan; m. Susanna Avakian; one s. five d.; ed Yerevan State Univ.; founder and leader of democracy movts in USSR; leading role in Nat. United Party of Armenia (reformed on principle of independence through referendum and renamed Union for Nat. Self-Determination (UNSD) 1987) 1968–; sentenced to imprisonment for various nationalist activities 1969–73, 1974–87, with latest arrest after mass demonstrations in Yerevan in 1988; deprived of Soviet citizenship 1989, deported from USSR, citizenship restored 1990; elected to Parl. 1990; cand. for Presidency of Armenia Oct. 1991; fmrly Chair. Union for Nat. Self-Determination (also 1991–96), now Pres. UNSD; Adviser to Pres. of Armenia 1998–99; Chair. Comm. on Human Rights in Presidential Admin. 1998–2002; Pres. Constitutional Reform Comm. 1998–99; Prefect of Goris and Goris Region 1992; elected Pres. int. org. Democracy and Independence, Paris 1989, Prague 1990; has also written nationalistic, freedom-fighting and lyrical songs; Nat. Council to Support Democracy Movements in the USSR Democracy Award (USA) 1990, First Prize (Lyrical Category) for 'The Bird of Love', Pan-Armenian Sayat Nova Song Competition 2001, Conservative Political Action Conf. Honoree and Guest Speaker, Hagop Megapart Medal, Nat. Library of Armenia 2009, Parl. Club (Geragun Horurt) First Medal for Democracy and Human Rights 2010. *Compositions:* albums: Zimvori Avotka (Soldier's Prayer) album (composer, performer, producer) 1988, Hayastan (Armenia) 2002. *Publications include:* Independence (weekly newspaper) 1987, Knight of Freedom 1989; collection of articles, songs, poems, interviews and memoirs 1989; poetry collections: Freedom Songs 1996, And Thus Until Death 1997, Three Annals on the Road to Independence, The Human Rights Point of View of the Election Committee of the Armenian Republic 2000, The Representative Coefficient of the Voters or the True Equality of the Voters 2002, Democracy by Word and Act 2002, The Strategically Victorious National Organization 2002, Formula of States' Democracy 2003, Armenian People on the Border of 2003–2004 2004, Cooperation for the Main Issues of Democracy 2004, On the Quest of Light (autobiog.) 2004, With Faith and Love (filmscript) 2004, Complete Democracy 2008. *Address:* Union for National Self-Determination, Grigor Lusavorichi Street 15, 375013 Yerevan (office); Tpagrichneri 9, Apt 102, Yerevan, Armenia (home). *Telephone:* (10) 36-94-46 (office); (10) 58-94-85 (home). *Fax:* (10) 57-38-70 (office). *E-mail:* aim@aimusd.org (office). *Website:* www.aimusd.org (office).

HAYS, Hon. Daniel (Dan), BA, LLB; Canadian lawyer, politician and business executive; *Partner, Norton Rose Canada LLP;* b. 24 April 1939, Calgary; s. of Harry Hays; m. Kathy Hays; three d.; ed Univ. of Alberta and Univ. of Toronto; Senator for Alberta 1984–2007, Deputy Leader of the Govt in the Senate 1999–2001, Speaker of the Senate 2001–06, Leader of the Opposition 2006–07; mem. Liberal Party of Canada, Pres. 1994–98; currently Partner Norton Rose Canada LLP; Chair. Canada-Japan Inter-Parl. Group 1994–99, Asia-Pacific Parl. Forum 1994–99; fmr Pres. Canadian Hays Converter Asscn; fmr mem. Bd of Dirs CBC, Calgary Dist Foundation, Rotary Club of Calgary; mem. Advisory Council Canadian Defence and Foreign Affairs Inst.; mem. Law Soc. of Alberta, Bar Asscn, Canadian Tax Foundation; mem. Rotary Club, Trustee, Rotary Challenger Park Soc.; Hon. Col King's Own Calgary Regt; Grand Cordon, Order of the Sacred Treasure (Japan), Ordre de la Pléiade. *Leisure interests:* downhill skiing, horseback riding, films. *Address:* Norton Rose Canada LLP, Suite 3700, 400 3rd Avenue SW, Calgary, T2P 4H2, Canada (office). *Telephone:* (403) 267-8338 (office). *Fax:* (403) 264-5973 (office). *E-mail:* dan.hays@nortonrose.com (office). *Website:* www.nortonrose.com (office).

HAYSOM, Nicholas; South African lawyer and UN official; b. 21 April 1952, Johannesburg; m.; five c.; ed Univ. of KwaZulu-Natal, Univ. of Cape Town; Assoc. Prof., Univ. of the Witwatersrand and Deputy Dir, Centre for Applied Legal Studies 1981–94; Founding Partner, Cheadle Thompson and Haysom, Attorneys 1981–94; Professional Mediator, Independent Mediation Service of S Africa 1985–95; Chief Legal Adviser, Office of the Pres. (Nelson Mandela) 1995–99; Chair., Constitutional Principles Negotiations Cttee (Burundi Peace Negotiations) 1998–2001; Sr Adviser, Sudan Peace Process 2002–05; several sr positions with UN including Dir, Office of Constitutional Support, UN Assistance Mission in Iraq 2005–07, Dir, Political, Peacekeeping, Humanitarian and Human Rights Affairs, Office of Sec.-Gen. 2007–12, Asst Sec.-Gen. and Deputy Special Rep. of Sec.-Gen. for Political Affairs, UN Assistance Mission to Afghanistan (UNAMA) 2012–14, UnderSec.-Gen., Special Rep. of the Sec.-Gen. and Head, UNAMA 2014–16, Special Envoy for Sudan and South Sudan 2016–18, Special Rep. of the Sec.-Gen. and Head, UN Assistance Mission to Somalia (UNAMS), Special Envoy for Somalia Sept. 2018 – Jan. 2019; Trustee Nelson Mandela Foundation, Forum of Federations. *Address:* c/o Office of the Secretary-General, United Nations, New York, NY 10017 (office); 222 East 34th Street, Apt 1502, New York, NY 10016, USA (home). *Telephone:* (212) 963-1234 (office). *Fax:* (212) 963-4879 (office). *Website:* www.un.org (office).

HAYTHORNTHWAITE, Richard (Rick), SM, MA; British business executive; *Chairman, Centrica plc;* b. Dec. 1956; m.; one s. one d.; ed Colston's School, Bristol, Queen's Coll., Oxford; joined British Petroleum 1978, exploration geologist, then Man. Magnus Oilfield, Pres. Venezuela and other group posts until 1995; Corp. and Commercial Dir Premier Oil PLC 1995–97; joined Blue Circle Industries PLC 1997, CEO Heavy Bldg Materials Asia and Europe, CEO 1999–2001; CEO Invensys PLC 2001–05; mem. Bd of Dirs, MasterCard Inc. 2006–, currently Chair.; Chair. Network Rail Ltd 2009–12; Dir (non-exec.), Centrica plc 2013–, Chair. 2014–, Chair. Nominations Cttee; Chair. Centre for Creative Communications, Almeida Theatre, Southbank Centre; mem. Bd of Dirs Cookson Group 1999–2003, Imperial Chemical Industries PLC, Lafarge SA 2001–03, Land Securities Group PLC 2008–09, British Council; fmr Gen. Man. BP Exploration Inc.; fmr Pres. PetroSaudi International Ltd; fmr Pres. Almeida Theatre; Trustee, Nat. Museum of Science and Industry; Sloan Fellow, MIT, USA; Adviser and Partner, Star Capital Partners Ltd 2006–08. *Leisure interests:* travel, tennis, skiing, theatre, visual arts. *Address:* Centrica plc, Millstream, Maidenhead Road, Windsor, Berks., SL4 5GD, England (office). *Telephone:* (1753) 494000 (office). *Fax:* (1753) 494001 (office). *E-mail:* info@centrica.co.uk (office). *Website:* www.centrica.co.uk (office).

HAYWARD, Anthony Bryan (Tony), BSc, PhD, CCMI, FRSE; British business executive; *Non-Executive Chairman, Glencore plc;* b. 21 May 1957, Slough, Berks., England; m. Maureen Hayward; one s. one d.; ed Univs of Edinburgh and Birmingham; joined BP plc 1982, various tech. and commercial posts with BP Exploration, London, Aberdeen, France, China and Glasgow, later Exploration Man., Colombia, Pres. BP Exploration Venezuela 1995–97, Dir BP Exploration, London 1997–99, Group Vice-Pres. and mem. Upstream Exec. Cttee 1999–2000, Group Treas. 2000–02, Exec. Vice-Pres. and CEO Exploration and Production 2003–07, Exec. Dir BP 2003–07, Group Chief Exec. 2007–10 (resgnd), Dir (non-exec.) TNK-BP, Moscow 2010–13; Sr Ind. Dir (non-exec.), Corus Group plc 2002–; Sr Ind. Dir (non-exec.), Glencore International plc 2011– (merged with Xstrata plc to form Glencore Xstrata plc May 2013, now called Glencore plc), Interim Chair. 2013–14, Chair. (non-exec.) 2014–; Chair. CompactGTL 2013–; Dir (non-exec.) Tata Steel; mem. Advisory Bd Citibank 2000–03, Tsinghua, MIT Energy; mem. Business Council of Britain; Chair. GLOBE CEO Forum for Climate Change; Trustee, Emirates Foundation; Companion, Chartered Man. Inst. 2005; Dr hc (Univs of Edinburgh, Aston, Birmingham); hon. degree from Robert Gordon Univ. 2013; honoured as a "distinguished leader" by Univ. of Birmingham 2013. *Leisure interests:* sailing, skiing, triathlons, watching sport. *Address:* Glencore plc, Baarermattstrasse 3, 6340 Baar, Switzerland (office). *Telephone:* (41) 7092000 (office). *Fax:* (41) 7093000 (office). *E-mail:* info@glencore.com (office). *Website:* www.glencore.com (office).

HAZ, Hamzah, BA, MA, PhD; Indonesian politician; b. 15 Feb. 1940, Ketapang, W Kalimantan; m. (two wives Asmaniah and Titin Kartini); twelve c.; ed Sr Econ. High School, Ketapang, Tanjungpura Univ.; newspaper journalist, Pontianak; teacher of econs, Tanjungpura Univ.; mem. W Kalimantan Prov. Legis. Council 1968–71; mem. Nahdlatul Ulama (NU; later amalgamated into United Devt Party – PPP), Chair. 1998–2007; elected House of Reps 1971; fmr State Minister of Investment, Co-ordinating Minister for People's Welfare and Eradication of Poverty; Vice-Pres. of Indonesia 2001–04. *Leisure interest:* music. *Address:* Jalan Tegalan No. 27, Matraman, Jakarta Timur, Indonesia (home). *Telephone:* (21) 8581327 (home).

HAZANAVICIUS, Michel, (L'Impavide); French film director and screenwriter; b. 29 March 1967, Paris; m. Bérénice Bejo; two c.; two c. (with Virginia Lovisone); ed École nationale supérieure d'arts, Cergy-Pontoise; joined Canal+ Channel as Dir 1988; Award for Best Director, Alliance of Women Film Journalists 2012. *Films include:* as co-writer: Delphine 1, Yvan 0 1996, Le clone 1998, Les Dalton 2004; as screenwriter and dir: Mes amis 1999, OSS 117: Cairo, Nest of Spies 2006, OSS 117: Lost in Rio 2009, The Artist (Academy Award for Best Dir and Best Picture 2012, BAFTA Awards for Best Dir, and for Best Original Screenplay 2012, Australian Acad. of Cinema and TV Arts Award for Best Direction –Int. 2012, César Award for Best Dir 2012, Directors Guild Award for Outstanding Achievement in Directing in a Theatrical Release 2012) 2011, The Players 2012, The Search 2014. *Television includes:* Derrick contre Superman 1992, Ca détourne 1992, La Classe américaine 1993, C'est pas le 20 heures 1994, Les films qui sortent le lendemain dans les salles de cinema 1996. *Address:* c/o La Petite Reine, 20 rue de Saint Pétersbourg, 75008 Paris, France (office). *Telephone:* (1) 44-90-73-90 (office). *Fax:* (1) 44-90-73-99 (office). *E-mail:* thomas.langmann@lapetitereine.fr (office); ombeline.marchon@lapetitereine.fr (office).

HAZARE, Anna; Indian social worker; b. (Kisan Baburao Hazare), 15 June 1937, Bhingar, Ahmednagar, Maharashtra; s. of Baburao Hazare and Laxmibai Hazare; served in Indian Army 1963–78, posted to Sikkim, Bhutan, Jammu-Kashmir, Assam, Mizoram, Leh and Ladakh, posted to Khemkaran border with Pakistan 1965; worked on Ralegan Siddhi model village rural devt project 1975–; began new venture Bhrashtachar Virodhi Jan Aandolan or public movt against corruption 1991, went on indefinite hunger strike in Alandi in protest at corruption of govt officials, and in Azad Maidan in protest at govt inaction over Right To Information Act 2003; known for his contrib. to Watershed Devt Programme; prominent leader in Indian Anti-Corruption Movt 2011; Dr hc (Gandhi Gram Rural Inst. Deemed Univ. Tamil Nadu) 2005, (Vijayanagar Sri Krishnadevaraya Univ., Bellary) 2014; Indira Priyadarshini Award 1986, Man of the Year Award 1988, Padmashri Award 1990, Krushibhushan Award, Maharashtra Govt Padmabhushan Award 1992, Swami Vivekanand Seva Award, Kolkata 1994, Young India Award 1997, Mahaveer Award 1997, Rotary Manav Seva Award 1998, Care International Award 1998, Sat Paul Mittal Nat. Award 2000, Transparency Int. Integrity Award 2003, Maharana Udaysinh Award 2004, Mother Theresa Nat. Award 2006, Samajprabodhan Award 2007, Jit Gill Memorial Award 2007, Jeevan Sadhna Gaurav Award, Pune University 2008, Allard Prize Award, Univ. of British Columbia, Canada 2013, Dinanath Mangeshkar Jeevan Gaurav Award 2014. *Publications include:* Right to Information Act 2005, Gramsabha, My Village My Pilgrimage, Ration Sarvanchya Hakkache. *Address:* Ralegan Siddhi Pariwar, Ralegan Siddhi, Parner, Ahmednagar 414 302, India (office). *Telephone:* (24) 88240401 (office); 98-50200090 (mobile). *Fax:* (24) 88240581 (office). *E-mail:* annahazareoffice@gmail.com (home); annahazareoffice1@gmail.com (office). *Website:* www.annahazare.org; www.joinannahazare.org.in.

HAZARIKA, A. K., BE; Indian engineer and business executive; ed Assam Eng Coll.; grad. trainee, Oil and Natural Gas Corpn (ONGC) 1976, first assignment was as driller (cementing) in Assam, then transferred to Mumbai 1995, Head of Multidisciplinary Team, Mumbai High Redevelopment Projects, Head of Well Services, Mumbai 2002, Exec. Dir and Chief of Well Services 2003, Dir (Onshore) 2004–12, Chair. and Man. Dir Feb.–Oct. 2011, also Dir (Exploration); Chair. Mangalore Refinery and Petrochemicals Ltd Feb.–Nov. 2011, also Dir (Onshore); apptd Chair. ONGC TERI Bio-technology Ltd, Exhibition Cttee Petrotech 2010; Chair. Working Group for Underground Coal Gasification, Office of Principal Scientific Adviser, Govt of India; mem. Bd of Dirs ONGC Videsh Ltd 2004–12, Jindal Saw Ltd 2016–, Tripura Power Co.; Rep., Oil and Gas Sub-cttee, Int. M2M (Methane to Market) Partnership, US Environmental Protection Agency; mem. Soc. of Petroleum Engineers, New Delhi; mem. Governing Council, Petroleum Fed. of India; Drilling Engineer of the Year 1990, Soc. of Petroleum Engineers Pres.'s Award, Greening of Oil and Gas Business Award 2010.

HAZELTINE, Richard Deimel, MS, PhD; American physicist and academic; *Professor, Department of Physics, College of Natural Sciences, University of Texas;* b. 12 June 1942, Jersey City, NJ; s. of Alan Hazeltine and Elizabeth Barrett Hazeltine; m. Cheryl Pickett 1964; one s. one d.; ed Harvard Coll. and Univ. of Michigan; mem. Inst. for Advanced Study 1969–71; Research Scientist, Univ. of Texas 1971–82, then Prof. of Physics 1986–, Asst Dir Inst. for Fusion Studies 1982–86, Acting Dir 1987–88, 1991, Dir 1991–2002, fmr Chair. Dept of Physics, Coll. of Natural Sciences; fmr Assoc. Ed. Reviews of Modern Physics; fmr Ed. Physical Review, Physics of Fluids; Fellow, American Physical Soc., AAAS, Atomic Energy Research Foundation; mem. Fusion Energy Sciences Cttee US Dept of Energy; mem. Bd of Physics and Astronomy, NRC. *Publications include:* Plasma Confinement (with J. D. Meiss) 1992, Framework of Plasma Physics (with F.

Waelbroeck) 1998; more than 140 articles in scientific journals. *Address:* University of Texas, Institute for Fusion Studies, 1 University Station C1500, Austin, TX 78712-0262, USA (office). *Telephone:* (512) 471-4307 (office). *Fax:* (512) 471-6715 (office). *E-mail:* rdh@physics.utexas.edu (office). *Website:* www.physics.utexas.edu (office).

HAZEN, Paul Mandeville, BS, MBA; American banker and business executive; *Chairman, Accel-KKR;* b. 29 Nov. 1941, Lansing, Mich.; m.; ed Univ. of Arizona, Univ. of California, Berkeley; Asst Man., Security Pacific Bank 1964–66; Vice-Pres. Union Bank 1966–70; Chair. Wells Fargo Realty Advisors 1970–76; with Wells Fargo Bank, San Francisco 1979–98, Exec. Vice-Pres. and Man. Real Estate Industries Group 1979–80, mem. Exec. Office 1980, Vice-Chair. 1980–84, Pres. and COO 1984–94, Chair. 1995–98, also Dir; Pres. and Treas. Wells Fargo Mortgage & Equity Trust 1977–84; with Wells Fargo & Co. (parent), San Francisco 1978–2001, Exec. Vice-Pres., then Vice-Chair., Pres., COO and Dir 1978–95, CEO 1995–98, Chair. 1998–2001; currently Chair. Accel-KKR, KKR Financial Corpn, Sr Advisor, Kohlberg Kravis Roberts; Deputy Chair. and Lead Ind. Dir Vodafone Group plc 2000–06; mem. Bd of Dirs Applied Predictive Technologies, Safeway, Inc., Xstrada AG, Prosper Marketplace Inc., Blackhawk Network Holdings Inc.; Trustee, Wells Fargo Mortgage and Equity Trust. *Address:* Accel-KKR, 2500 Sand Hill Road, Suite 300, Menlo Park, CA 94025, USA (office). *Telephone:* (650) 289-2460 (office). *Fax:* (650) 289-2461 (office). *E-mail:* inquiries@accel-kkr.com (office). *Website:* www.accel-kkr.com (office).

HE, Chunlin; Chinese politician; b. Aug. 1933, Wuxi City, Jiangsu Prov.; ed Northeast China Agricultural Coll.; joined CCP 1951; technician, engineer, then Deputy Section Chief and Section Chief, Chinese Acad. of Agricultural Mechanization Sciences 1962–66; clerk, Org. Dept, CCP Hebei Prov. Cttee 1966–67; Deputy Chief, Science and Tech. Div., Agricultural Machinery Research Inst., First Ministry of Machine-Building Industry 1972–78; Chief, Comprehensive Div., Survey and Research Section, Ministry of Agricultural Machinery 1979–80, Dir, Gen. Office and of Survey and Research Section 1980–82; Dir Special Econ. Zones Office of State Council 1984–93; Deputy Sec.-Gen. State Council 1988–98 (Deputy Sec. CCP Leading Party Group 1988–91); Head, Nat. Leading Group for Suppressing Smuggling 1993; mem. State Leading Group for Science and Tech. 1996; mem. Hong Kong Special Admin. Region Preparatory Cttee, Govt Del. at Hong Kong Hand-Over Ceremony 1997; Sec.-Gen. 9th Standing Cttee of NPC 1998–2003, Chair. Internal and Judicial Affairs Cttee of 10th NPC 2003–08, Chair. Credentials Cttee 2003–08; mem. 14th CCP Cen. Cttee 1992–97, 15th CCP Cen. Cttee 1997–2002.

HE, Guangwei; Chinese civil servant; Deputy Dir China Nat. Tourism Admin. 1986–95, Dir 1995. *Address:* China National Tourism Administration, 9A Jian Guo Men Nei Dajie, Beijing 100740, People's Republic of China. *Telephone:* (10) 65138866. *Fax:* (10) 65122096.

HE, Guangyuan; Chinese state official; b. 1930, Anxin Co., Hebei Prov.; ed No. 9 Middle School, Hebei Mil. Dist, PLA Beijing Mil. Region; joined CCP 1945, PLA 194; Deputy Dir Forging Sub-Plant, Changchun No. 1 Motor Vehicle Plant, Changchun City, Jilin Prov. 1956–66, Dir 1966; criticized and denounced in Cultural Revolution 1966–70; Vice-Mayor of Changchun City 1980–82; Vice-Minister of Agricultural Machinery 1980 (Deputy Sec. CCP Leading Party Group); Vice-Minister of Machinery and Electronics Industry 1982–88, Minister 1988–93, of Machine-Building Industry 1993–96; Alt. mem. 12th CCP Cen. Cttee 1982–87, 13th Cen. Cttee 1987–92; mem. 14th CCP Cen. Cttee 1992–97; mem. Standing Cttee, 8th CPPCC 1993–98, 9th CPPCC 1998–2003, Chair. Motions Cttee 9th CPPCC Nat. Cttee 1998–2003.

HE, Guoqiang; Chinese politician; b. Oct. 1943, Xiangxiang Co., Hunan Prov.; ed Beijing Chemical Eng Inst.; joined CCP 1966; fmr technician, later Dir Synthesizing Workshop, Lunan Chemical Fertilizer Plant, Shandong Prov. (Sec. CCP Party Br. 1967–78), later Deputy Dir Lunan Chemical Fertilizer Plant, Deputy Chief Engineer 1978–80; Dir Control Office, People's Govt, Shandong Prov. 1980–82; Deputy Dir-Gen. and CCP Sec. Shandong Petro-Chemical Dept 1982–84, Dir-Gen. 1984–86; mem. of the Standing Cttee of CCP Shandong Provincial Cttee, Vice-Sec., Sec. CCP Ji'nan City Cttee 1986; Vice-Minister of Chemical Industry 1991–96; Vice-Sec. CCP Fujian Provincial Cttee, Acting Gov. Fujian Prov. 1996–97, Gov. 1997–99; Sec. CCP Chongqing Municipal Cttee 1999–2002; mem. 12th CCP Cen. Cttee 1982–87, 13th CCP Cen. Cttee 1987–92, 14th CCP Cen. Cttee 1992–97, 15th CCP Cen. Cttee 1997–2002, 16th CCP Cen. Cttee 2002–07 (Head of Org. Dept and mem. Secr. of Politburo 2002–07), 17th CCP Cen. Cttee 2007–12, Politburo Standing Cttee 2007–12 (Sec. Cen. Comm. for Discipline Inspection 2007–12).

HE, Jiaying; Chinese painter; b. 1957, Tianjin; ed Tianjin Acad. of Fine Arts; Prof. Tianjin Acad. of Fine Arts 1980–; Council mem. Contemporary Gongbi Painting Asscn, Chinese Artists' Asscn. *Address:* Tianjin Academy Of Fine Arts4 Tianwei Road, Hebei, Tianjin 300141, People's Republic of China (office). *Telephone:* (22) 26241505 (office). *Fax:* (22) 26241505 (office).

HE, Jiuchang; Chinese business executive; *General Manager, Shaanxi Yanchang Petroleum (Group) Company Limited;* fmr Deputy Dir Gen., Devt and Reform Comm. of Shaanxi Prov.; Dir, Gen. Man. and Deputy Sec. of Party Cttee, Shaanxi Yanchang Petroleum (Group) Co. Ltd 2013–. *Address:* Shaanxi Yanchang Petroleum (Group) Co. Ltd, 75 Keji Road, Xi'an 710075, Shaanxi, People's Republic of China (office). *Telephone:* (29) 88899666 (office). *Fax:* (29) 88899669 (office). *E-mail:* webmaster@sxycpc.com (office). *Website:* www.sxycpc.com (office).

HE, Kang, BSc; Chinese politician; b. 26 Feb. 1923, Hebei Prov.; m. Miao Shixia 1945; two s.; m. 2nd Yu Junmin 1993; ed Agric. Coll. of Guangxi Univ.; Chief Dir of Agric. and Forestry under Shanghai Mil. Control Cttee 1949–50; Deputy Head Dept of Agric. and Forestry under E China Mil. and Political Cttee 1950–52; Dir Dept of Special Forestry of Ministry of Forestry 1952–54; Dir Dept of Tropical Plants, Ministry of Agric. 1955–57; Dir S China Tropical Crop Science Research Inst. and Tropical Crop Coll. 1957–72; Deputy to 3rd NPC 1965–75; Deputy Dir-Gen. Bureau of Land Reclamation, Guangdong Prov. 1972–77; Vice-Minister of Agric., Deputy Dir Nat. Planning Comm., Deputy Dir Nat. Comm. on Agric. 1978–82; mem. 12th CCP Cen. Cttee 1982–87, 13th Cen. Cttee 1987–93; mem. 8th NPC Standing Cttee 1993–98; Minister of Agric. 1983–90; Vice-Chair. Nat. Cttee, China Asscn for Science and Tech. 1986–96; Vice-Chair. Nat. Agric. Regional Planning Cttee 1979–90; Pres. Chinese Village & Township Enterprises Asscn 1990–2000, Chair. China-Bangladesh Friendship Asscn 1993–; Vice-Chair. Zhongkai Inst. of Agric. Tech.; Hon. DUniv (Maryland, USA) 1986; World Food Prize 1993. *Publications:* Agricultural Reform and Development in China, Rubber Culture in Northern Tropical Area (ed. and writer). *Leisure interests:* photography, listening to music, reading.

HE, Lifeng; Chinese politician; *Chairman, National Development and Reform Commission;* b. Feb. 1955, Xingning, Guangdong Prov.; ed Xiamen Univ.; sent to work in rural area during Cultural Revolution; joined CCP 1981; Deputy Dir, later Dir, Finance Dept, Xiamen City, Fujian Prov. 1985–90; Sec., CCP Dist Cttee, Xinglin Dist, Xiamen City 1990–92; Vice-Mayor, Xiamen City 1992–96; Mayor, Quanzhou City 1996–98; Sec., CCP City Cttee, Quanzhou City 1998–2000, Fuzhou City 2000–05, Xiamen City 2005–09; Deputy Sec., Tianjin CCP Municipal Cttee 2009–13; Deputy CCP Branch Sec., Nat. Devt and Reform Comm. (NDRC) 2014–, Deputy Chair. NDRC 2014–17, Chair. 2017–; alt. mem. 17th CCP Cen. Cttee 2007–12, 18th CCP Cen. Cttee 2012–17. *Address:* National Development and Reform Commission, 38 South Yuetan Street, Beijing 100824, People's Republic of China (office). *Website:* en.ndrc.gov.cn (office).

HE, Luli; Chinese politician and paediatrician; b. 7 June 1934, Jinan, Shandong Prov.; d. of He Siyuan and He Yiwen; m. Rong Guohuang 1958 (died 1989); two s.; ed Beijing Coll. of Medicine; paediatrician, Beijing Children's Hosp. 1957–, Beijing No. 2 Hosp. 1988–96; Deputy Head, People's Govt, Xicheng Dist, Beijing 1984–88; Vice-Mayor Beijing Municipality 1988–96; Vice-Chair. Cen. Cttee, 7th Revolutionary Cttee of the Chinese Kuomintang (RCCK) 1988–92, Vice-Chair. Women and Youth Cttee, RCCK 1988–96, Chair. Beijing Municipal Cttee 1988–93, Chair. Cen. Cttee of 8th RCCK 1992–97, Chair. Cen. Cttee of 9th RCCK 1997–2002; Pres. Cen. Acad. of Socialism 1999–; mem. CPPCC 8th Nat. Cttee 1993–98, Vice-Chair. 1996–98; Vice-Chair. Standing Cttee of 9th NPC 1998–2003, of 10th NPC 2003–08; elected Vice-Pres. Exec. Cttee of All China Women's Fed. 1993; apptd Pres. China Population Welfare Foundation 2000; mem. Govt Del. at Macao Hand-Over Ceremony, Macao Special Admin. Region Preparatory Cttee 1999; Hon. Vice-Pres. Red Cross Soc. of China 1999; honoured as Nat. March 8 Red-Banner Bearer 1994. *Address:* Central Academy of Socialism, Beijing 100081, People's Republic of China.

HE, Ping; Chinese news agency executive; *Editor-in-Chief, Xinhua News Agency;* b. 1957; ed Beijing Univ.; Deputy Ed.-in-Chief, Xinhua News Agency 1982–2007, Vice-Pres. 1993–2007, Ed.-in-Chief 2007–; mem. 18th CCP Central Cttee Central Comm. for Discipline Inspection 2012–17, 19th CCP Central Cttee Central Comm. 2017–. *Address:* Xinhua, 20F Dacheng Plaza, 127 Xhuanwumen Street West, Beijing 100031, People's Republic of China (office). *E-mail:* xxp69@xinhuanet.com (office). *Website:* (office).

HE, Maj.-Gen. Qizong; Chinese army officer; b. 1943, Yingshan Co., Sichuan Prov.; joined PLA 1961; joined CCP 1965; Deputy Commdr Kunming Mil. Region 1979–85; Chief of Staff of Div. 1982–83, Div. Commdr 1983, Deputy Commdr of Army 1983–84, Commdr 1984–85, Deputy Chief of Gen. Staff, PLA 1985; Alt. mem. 13th CCP Cen. Cttee 1987–92; Alt. mem. 14th Cen. Cttee 1992–97; Deputy Commdr Nanjing Mil. Region 1993; rank of Maj.-Gen. 1988.

HE, Wenbo, EMBA; Chinese engineer and business executive; *Chairman and President, China Minmetals Corporation;* ed Northeast Univ., China Europe Int. Business School; joined Baosteel 1982, Dir, Vice-Pres. and mem. CCP Cttee of Shanghai Baosteel Group Corpn 1998, Dir Baoshan Iron & Steel Co. Ltd 2000–01, Dir, Vice-Pres. and Standing mem. CCP Cttee of Shanghai Baosteel Group Corpn and Dir of Baoshan Iron & Steel Co. Ltd 2001–05, Vice-Pres. and Standing mem. CCP Cttee of Baosteel Group Corpn and Dir of Baoshan Iron & Steel Co. Ltd 2005–06, Standing mem. CCP Cttee of Baoshan Iron & Steel Co. Ltd 2006–08, Dir, Pres., Standing mem. CCP Cttee of Baosteel Group Corpn and Dir and Standing mem. CCP Cttee of Baoshan Iron & Steel Co. Ltd 2008–14, Vice-Chair. Baoshan Iron & Steel Co. Ltd 2009–14, Chair. and Sec. CCP Cttee of Baoshan Iron & Steel Co. Ltd 2010–14; Pres. China Minmetals Corpn –2015, Chair. and Pres. 2015–; Exec. Dir Chinese Soc. for Metals 2011–. *Address:* China Minmetals Corporation, Building B, 5 Sanlihe Road, Haidian District, Beijing 100044, People's Republic of China (office). *Telephone:* (10) 68495888 (office). *Fax:* (10) 68335570 (office). *E-mail:* zc@minmetals.com.cn (office). *Website:* www.minmetals.com (office).

HE, Xiangjian; Chinese business executive; *Chairman, Midea Investment Holding Co. Ltd;* b. 5 Oct. 1941, Guangdong Prov.; m.; three c.; co-founded with 23 neighbours (fmr rice-farmers and fishermen) Beijiao Neighbourhood Plastic Production Team 1968 (renamed Midea 1981), Chair. and CEO Guangdong Midea Electric Appliances Co. Ltd 2001–12, currently Chair. Midea Investment Holding Co. Ltd. *Address:* Guangdong Midea Electric Appliances Co. Ltd, Midea Industrial City, Shunde District, Foshan 528311, Guangdong, People's Republic of China (office). *Telephone:* (757) 26338823 (office). *Fax:* (757) 26651991 (office). *E-mail:* inquiry@midea.com.cn (office). *Website:* www.midea.com.cn (office).

HE, Yong; Chinese politician; b. Oct. 1940, Qianxi Co., Hebei Prov.; ed Tianjin Univ.; joined CCP 1958; technician, Metering Office, No. 238 Factory 1968–70, Production Sec., Head Office 1970–75, Dir Political Dept 1975–78 (mem. Standing Cttee of CCP Party Cttee 1975–78), Dir No. 238 Factory 1978–83 (Deputy Sec. CCP Party Cttee 1978–83); Deputy Dir Office of Science, Tech. and Industry for Nat. Defence, Hubei Prov. 1983–85; Dir-Gen. Personnel Dept, Ministry of Ordinance Industry 1985–86; Deputy Head, Org. Dept of CCP Cen. Cttee 1986–87, Dir Bureau of Party and Govt Personnel Engaged in Foreign Affairs 1986–87; Vice-Minister of Supervision 1987–98, Minister 1998–2002; mem. Standing Cttee of 14th CCP Cen. Comm. for Discipline Inspection 1992–97, mem. 15th CCP Cen. Cttee 1997–2002 (Deputy Sec. Cen. Comm. for Discipline Inspection 1997–2002), 16th CCP Cen. Cttee 2002–07 (mem. Politburo Secr. 2002–07, Deputy Sec. Standing Cttee of Cen. Comm. for Discipline Inspection 2002–07); mem. 17th CCP Cen. Cttee 2007–12, Deputy Sec. Cen. Comm. for Discipline Inspection 2007–12.

HE, Zuoxiu; Chinese physicist; *Peofessor, Institute of Theoretical Physics, Chinese Academy of Sciences;* b. 27 July 1927, Shanghai; m. Qing Chengrui 1962; one s.; ed Shanghai Jiaotong Univ., Tsinghua Univ.; researcher, Beijing Modern Physics Inst. and Atomic Energy Inst., Academia Sinica 1951–80; Deputy

Dir Theoretical Physics Inst., Academia Sinica 1978–84, mem. Dept of Math. and Physics, Academia Sinica 1980–; mem. Chinese Acad. of Sciences 1980, currently Prof. Inst. of Theoretical Physics; fmr mem. Standing Cttee CPPCC; Nat. Natural Sciences Prize. *Publications:* A New Possible Quantum Field Theory of Composite Particles, (with Falung Gong), From Theory of Elementary Chi to Particle Physics, Wind Power – the most realistic and best choice for sustainable devt of China 2004; more than 200 published papers. *Address:* Institute of Theoretical Physics, Chinese Academy of Sciences, Zhong Guan Cun East Street 55 #, PO Box 2735, Beijing 100190, People's Republic of China (office). *Telephone:* (10) 62569352 (office). *Fax:* (10) 62562587 (office). *E-mail:* qcr@itp.ac.cn (office); lijing@itp.ac.cn. *Website:* itp.ac.cn.

HEAD, Tim David, BA; British artist; b. 22 Oct. 1946, London, England; s. of Percy Head and Muriel Head; m. Vivian Katz 1973; two d.; ed Dept of Fine Art, Univ. of Newcastle-upon-Tyne, St Martin's School of Art, London; Lecturer, Goldsmith's Coll. School of Art, London 1971–79; Lecturer, Slade School of Fine Art, Univ. Coll. London 1976–; Fellowship at Clare Hall and Kettle's Yard, Cambridge 1977–78; Gulbenkian Foundation Visual Arts Award 1975, First Prize, John Moores Liverpool Exhbn 15, Walker Art Gallery, Liverpool 1987, Wellcome Trust Artist's Residency, Dept of Biochemistry, Univ. of Oxford 2006–07. *Commissions:* Sculpture, Nat. Museum of Photography, Film and TV, Bradford, Yorks. 1985, Floor Design, Science Museum, London 1995 Installation, Chatham Historic Dockyard, Rochester, Kent, Sculpture, Dance Performance with Laurie Booth Co. 1997–98, Light Rain, Artezium Arts and Media Centre, Luton 1998, A Hard Day's Night (CD ROM) 2000 www.eyestorm.com; Artistic Dir Eurythmics Peace Tour 1999. *Address:* c/o The Slade School of Fine Art, UCL, Gower Street, London WC1E 6BT, England. *E-mail:* info@timhead.net (home). *Website:* www.timhead.net (home).

HEAL, (Barbara) Jane, PhD, FBA; British academic; *Professor Emerita and Fellow, St John's College, University of Cambridge;* b. 21 Oct. 1946, Oxford, England; d. of William Calvert Kneale and Martha Kneale (née Hurst); m. John Gauntlett Benedict Heal 1968 (divorced 1987); one s. one d.; ed Oxford High School for Girls, New Hall, Cambridge; Research Fellow, Newnham Coll., Cambridge 1971–74; Harkness Fellow of the Commonwealth Fund, Visiting Fellow, Princeton Univ. and Univ. of Calif., Berkeley, USA 1974–76; Lecturer in Philosophy, Univ. of Newcastle upon Tyne 1976–86, Univ. of Cambridge 1986–96, Reader in Philosophy 1996–99, Prof. 1999, now Prof. Emer. and Fellow, St John's Coll., Pres. St John's Coll. 1999–2003; mem. Aristotelian Soc., Pres. 2001–02. *Publications include:* Fact and Meaning 1989, Mind, Reason and Imagination 2003. *Address:* St John's College, Cambridge, CB2 1TP, England (office). *Telephone:* (1223) 338668 (office); (1223) 314317 (home). *E-mail:* jane.heal@phil.cam.ac.uk (office). *Website:* www.phil.cam.ac.uk (office).

HEALD, Sir Oliver, PC, QC; British barrister and politician; *Minister of State for Justice;* b. 15 Dec. 1954, Reading, Berks.; m. Christine Whittle; one s. two d.; ed Reading School, Pembroke Coll., Cambridge; called to the Bar, Middle Temple 1977; practising barrister in London and East Anglia 1979–95; contested Southwark and Bermondsey constituency in Gen. Election 1987; MP for N Hertfordshire 1992–97, for NE Hertfordshire 1997–2010, for NE Hertfordshire (revised boundary) 2010–, mem. several select cttees; Parl. Pvt. Sec. to Sir Peter Lloyd as Minister of State, Home Office 1994, to William Waldegrave as Minister of Agric., Fisheries and Food 1994–95; sponsored Pvt. Mem.'s Bill Insurance Companies (Reserves) Act 1995; Parl. Under-Sec. of State, Dept of Social Security 1995–97; Opposition Whip 1997–2000; Opposition Spokesperson for Home Affairs 2000–01, for Health 2001–02; Shadow Minister for Work and Pensions 2002–03; Shadow Leader of the House 2003–05; mem. House of Commons' Comm. 2003–05; Shadow Sec. of State for Constitutional Affairs 2004–07; Shadow Chancellor of the Duchy of Lancaster 2005–07; Solicitor-Gen. for England and Wales 2012–14; Minister of State for Justice 2016–; Chair. North Hertfordshire Conservative Asscn 1984–86; mem. Southwark and Bermondsey Conservative Asscn, Pres. 1993–98, Patron 1998–; Chair. Exec. Soc. of Conservative Lawyers 2008–12, Exec. Parl. Resources Unit; mem. Cttee on Standards in Public Life 2008–; mem. Council of Europe 2008–; mem. Ind. High Level Int. Oxfam Comm. on Sexual Misconduct 2018–; Conservative. *Publication:* An Executive Decision: Military Action. *Address:* House of Commons, Westminster, London, SW1A 0AA, England (office). *Telephone:* (20) 7219-6354 (office); (1763) 247640 (constituency) (home). *Fax:* (1763) 247640 (constituency) (home). *E-mail:* oliver.heald.mp@parliament.uk (office). *Website:* www.oliverhealdmp.com.

HEALEY, Rt Hon. John, PC, BA; British politician; b. 13 Feb. 1960, Wakefield, West Yorks.; m. Jackie Bate 1993; one s.; ed Lady Lumley's Comprehensive School, Pickering, St Peter's School, York, Christ's Coll., Cambridge; worked in voluntary sector at MIND, Royal Nat. Inst. for the Deaf, Royal Asscn for Disability and Rehabilitation 1984–90; journalist, Issue Communications (public relations co.) 1990–92; Head of Communications, MSF (trade union) 1992–94; Campaigns Dir TUC 1994–97; fmr part-time tutor, Open Univ. Business School; MP (Labour) for Wentworth 1997–2010, for Wentworth and Dearne 2010–, mem. Employment Select Cttee, Parl. Pvt. Sec. to Chancellor of the Exchequer, Parl. Under-Sec. of State for Adults Skills, Dept for Educ. and Skills, Financial Sec. to Treasury 2005–07, Local Govt Minister, Dept for Communities and Local Govt 2007–09, Minister of State for Housing and Planning 2009–10; Shadow Minister for Housing May–Oct. 2010, Shadow Sec. of State for Health Oct. 2010–11, Shadow Minister for Housing and Planning 2015–16; Vice-Pres. Local Govt Asscn 2010–11. *Address:* House of Commons, Westminster, London, SW1A 0AA (office); Wentworth and Dearne Parliamentary Office, 79 High Street, Wath upon Dearne, Rotherham, S63 7QB, England. *Telephone:* (1709) 875943 (Rotherham). *Fax:* (1709) 874207 (Rotherham). *E-mail:* john.healey.mp@parliament.uk (office). *Website:* www.parliament.uk/biographies/commons/john-healey/400 (office); www.johnhealeymp.co.uk (office).

HEALEY, Melanie L., BS; American business executive; *Group President, North America and Global Hyper-Super-Mass Channel, Procter & Gamble Company;* b. 5 April 1961, Rio de Janeiro, Brazil; m.; two c.; ed Univ. of Richmond, Va; Asst Brand Man. S.C. Johnson & Sons 1983–86, Brand Man. and Marketing Man. Johnson & Johnson 1987–90; Brand Man. for Phebo Soap, Procter & Gamble, Brazil 1990–92, Marketing Man. for Pampers 1992–93, for Personal Cleansing and Fabric Softeners, Procter & Gamble, Mexico 1993–95, Marketing Dir for Health Care, Procter & Gamble, Brazil 1995–97, for Health and Hair Care 1997–98, Feminine Care 1998, Gen. Man. Feminine Care Latin America 1998–2001, Feminine Care N America 2001, Vice-Pres. and Gen. Man. 2001–05, Pres. Global Feminine Care 2005–06, Global Feminine Care and Adult Care 2006–07, Group Pres. Global Feminine and Health Care 2007–09, Group Pres., North America 2009–11, Group Pres., North America and Global Hyper-Super-Mass Channel 2011–, fmr Chair. P&G Fine Arts Fund Corp. Campaign; mem. Bd of Dirs Verizon Communications Inc.; fmr mem. Bd of Dirs Bacardi Ltd; mem. Bd Grocery Mfrs Asscn, Cincinnati-Northern Kentucky Int. Airport; mem. Bd of Trustees Univ. of Richmond; mem. Women's Capital Club of Cincinnati; Founding mem. Women's Leadership Initiative, United Way of Greater Cincinnati, Cincinnati Women's Exec Forum; fmr mem. Bd of Dirs Fine Arts Fund of Greater Cincinnati, Univ. of Richmond Alumni Asscn; YWCA Career Woman of Achievement Award 2007. *Address:* Procter & Gamble Co., 1 Procter & Gamble Plaza, Cincinnati, OH 45202, USA (office). *Telephone:* (513) 983-1100 (office). *Website:* www.pg.com (office).

HEALY, Thomas William, AO, MSc, PhD, FAA; Australian chemist and academic; *Professorial Fellow and Chairman of the Science Board, Particulate Fluids Processing Centre, Department of Chemical and Biomolecular Engineering, University of Melbourne;* b. 1 June 1937; s. of W. T. Healy and C. M. Healy; m. Beverley Healy 1960; four s.; ed St Kilda, Univ. of Melbourne and Columbia Univ., New York, USA; Lecturer in Materials Science, Univ. of California, Berkeley 1963–65, Visiting Assoc. Prof. 1970; Queen Elizabeth II Fellow, Univ. of Melbourne 1965–67, Sr Lecturer in Physical Chem. 1967–75, Reader 1976–77, Prof. 1977–98, Prof. Emer. 1998–, Professorial Fellow 1999–, Deputy Chair. School of Chem. 1979–81, Assoc. Dean (Research and Grad. Studies), Faculty of Science 1983–84, Dean 1985–90, also currently Chair. Science Bd, mem. Council Univ. of Melbourne 1985–88, Dir Advanced Mineral Products Special Research Centre 1991–99, Vice-Pres. Academic Bd 1994–96, and Pro-Vice-Chancellor 1997–98, Deputy Dir Particulate Fluids Processing Centre (ARC), Dept of Chemical and Biomolecular Eng 2000–04 (Chair. Scientific Bd 2005), mem. Bd Ian Potter Museum of Art 2004; Sr Visiting Research Fellow, Univ. of Bristol, UK 1975; Visiting Sr Research Scientist, ICI Corp. Colloid Group, Runcorn, Cheshire, UK 1981; Fulbright Sr Scholar, Inst. of Colloid and Surface Science, Clarkson Univ., Potsdam, NY, USA 1981; Visiting Prof., Columbia Univ., New York 2001; mem. Council Australian Research Council (ARC) 1993, Chair. Institutional Grants Cttee 1995–96, mem. Planning and Review Cttee ARC-ANU Review of the Inst. of Advanced Studies 1994–95, Research Grants Appeals Cttee 1998–2004; Vice-Pres. Victorian Br. Royal Australian Chemical Inst. (RACI) 1983, Pres. 1984, mem. Cttee 1972–74, 1976, 1982–85, mem. Exec. Council RACI 1984; Deputy Chair. Victorian Univs and Schools Examination Bd Science Standing Cttee 1977–79, Course Advisory Cttee, Bendigo, Victorian Inst. of Colls of Advanced Educ.; mem. numerous review bds; Dir UniMelb Ltd 1990–92; part-time consultant to Geopeko Pty Ltd, Australia Mt Morgan Mines Pty Ltd, Australia Peko Wallsend Pty Ltd, BHP Co. Ltd Australia, Monier Ltd, ICI (Australia) Ltd, Tioxide (Australia) Pty Ltd, Burnie, Tasmania and Tioxide International Ltd, Teeside, UK, ICI UK Ltd, ICI Glidden Paints USA, Orica Pty Ltd, Lachlan Resources Pty Ltd NSW, Davies Ryan & De Boos, Corr Pavey Whiting & Byrne, Kitchener Mines Pty Ltd, Supreme Court of NSW, Mallesons, Brisbane, Sienna, NSW; Gov. Ian Potter Foundation 1990–; Chair. Australian Landscape Trust 1995–; mem. Australasian Inst. of Mining and Metallurgy, Royal Soc. of Chem. (Faraday Div.), Soc. of Sigma XI, Council Victorian Inst. of Marine Sciences 1986; mem. and Founding Cttee mem. Int. Asscn of Colloid and Interface Scientists 1979–, Div. of Colloid and Surface Chem., Chemical Soc. of Japan; mem. Editorial Advisory Bd Journal of Colloid and Interface Science 1969–74, Advances in Colloid and Interface Science 1975; Founding Ed. and Regional Ed. Colloids and Surfaces 1979–83, mem. Editorial Advisory Bd 1979–; mem. Editorial Bd Langmuir 1987–96, Current Opinion in Colloid and Interface Science 1995; Fellow, Australian Acad. of Science 1975, RACI 1975, Australian Acad. of Technological Sciences and Eng; Foreign Assoc., US Nat. Acad. of Eng 2008; Hon. DSc (Melbourne) 1999, Hon. LLD (Melbourne); ACS Certificate of Merit 1967, RACI Rennie Medal 1968, Grimwade Prize, Univ. of Melbourne 1974, RACI Hartung Youth Lecturer 1979, Chemical Soc. (London) Lecturer 1980, Freundlich Centennial Lecturer, ACS 55th Colloid Symposium 1981, Liversidge Lecturer, Australia and NZ Asscn for the Advancement of Science Festival of Science 1985, RACI-ICI (Australia) Inaugural Bicentennial Lectureship 1988, Plenary Lecturer, Papua New Guinea Inst. of Chem., Fifth Congress 1988, Plenary Lecturer IACIS Conf., Hakone, Japan 1989, Plenary Lecturer, R.K. Her Symposium, ACS, Washington DC 1990, A.E. Alexander Lectureship, RACI and Univ. of Sydney 1991, Royal Soc. of Vic. Medallist 1992, Plenary Lecturer XVIth Int. Minerals Processing Congress, Sydney 1993, Plenary and Foreign Guest Lecturer, 46th Nat. Colloid Symposium, Japanese Chemical Soc., Tokyo, Japan 1993, Plenary and Foreign Guest Lecturer, Mineral Processing: Recent Advances and Future Trends, Kanpur, India 1995, Plenary and Foreign Guest Lecturer, NEPTIS-5 Conf., Kyoto, Japan 1996, Plenary and Foreign Guest Lecturer, 5 Australian Japan Symposia on Colloid and Surface Chem., Fukuoka, Japan 1998, Ian Wark Medal and Lecture, Australian Acad. of Science 1999, T.G.H. Jones Memorial Lecturer, Univ. of Queensland 2001, T.H. Healy Award est. by School of Chem., Univ. of Melbourne to commemorate his distinguished career 2002, Impact Faraday Partnership Annual Lecture, Royal Chemical Inst. of GB 2003, Australian Centenary Medal 2003, RACI 40 Year Membership Award 2003, Sr Australian of the Year (Victorian Finalist) 2004, Australasian Inst. of Mining and Metallurgy 40 Year Membership Award 2005, Sir Eric Rideal Medal, RSC-UK Soc. of Chemical Industry Jt Award 2010. *Publications include:* more than 200 research papers in physical chem., colloid and surface science, process eng and mineral processing. *Leisure interests:* sailing, golf, reading. *Address:* Particulate Fluids Processing Centre, Department of Chemical and Biomolecular Engineering, Room 1.20, Building 167, University of Melbourne, Melbourne, Vic. 3010 (office); 9 Vine Street, Heidelberg, Vic. 3084, Australia (home). *Telephone:* (4) 1713-4430 (office). *E-mail:* tomhealy@unimelb.edu.au (office). *Website:* www.pfpc.unimelb.edu.au (office).

HEALY, Tom; Irish stock exchange executive; *CEO, Abu Dhabi Securities Exchange;* ed Trinity Coll., Dublin; early career with Export Board and Industrial Devt Agency; Chief Exec. Irish Stock Exchange 1987–2007 (retd), oversaw Irish Stock Exchange's de-merger from London Stock Exchange 1995; CEO Abu Dhabi Securities Exchange 2007–; int. consultancy and advisory assignments included

IBRD, EU, USAID; active involvement with World Fed. of Exchanges and Fed. of European Securities Exchanges; mem. Securities Inst., UK. *Address:* Abu Dhabi Securities Exchange, Al Ghaith Tower, Hamdan Street, POB 54500, Abu Dhabi, UAE (office). *Telephone:* (2) 627-7777 (office). *Fax:* (2) 627-0300 (office). *Website:* www.adsm.ae (office).

HEAP, Sir Robert Brian, Kt, KBE, CBE, BSc, MA, PhD, ScD, FRS, CChem, FRSC, FRSB; British research scientist and academic; *Research Associate, Centre of Development Studies, University of Cambridge;* b. 27 Feb. 1935, Derbyshire; s. of Bertram Heap and Eva M. Melling; m. Marion P. Grant 1961; two s. one d.; ed New Mills Grammar School, Univ. of Nottingham and King's Coll., Cambridge; Univ. Demonstrator, Cambridge 1960; Lalor Research Fellow, ARC Babraham, Cambridge, staff mem. 1964, Head, Dept of Physiology 1976, Head Cambridge Research Station 1986; Dir of Research, Agricultural and Food Research Council Inst. of Animal Physiology and Genetics Research, Cambridge and Edinburgh 1989–93, Dir of Science, Biotechnology and Biological Sciences Research Council 1991–94, Dir of Research, Babraham Inst. 1993–94; UK Rep., NATO Science Cttee, Brussels 1997–2005; Visiting Prof., Univ. of Nairobi 1974; Visiting Research Fellow, Murdoch Univ. 1976; Visiting Prof., Univ. of Guelph, Canada 1990; Visiting Sr Fellow, School of Clinical Medicine, Univ. of Cambridge 1994–2002, Babraham Inst. 1995; Master St Edmund's Coll., Cambridge 1996–2004; Research Assoc., Centre of Devt Studies, Univ. of Cambridge 2013–, also Distinguished Fellow; Chief Scientific Adviser, Cambridge Malaysian Education and Development Trust; fmr Ed. Philosophical Transactions of the Royal Society, Series B; Pres. Inst. of Biology 1996–98, Int. Soc. of Science and Religion 2006–08, European Acads Science Advisory Council 2010–13; Co-leader, Biosciences for Farming in Africa 2011–14; Sr Advisor, Smart Villages-New Thinking For Off-Grid-Communities Worldwide 2014–17; Chair. of Trustees, Academia Europaea; mem. Council Royal Soc. 1994–2001 (Foreign Sec. and Vice-Pres. 1996–2001), Nuffield Council on Bioethics 1997–2001; Trustee, China Cambridge Devt Trust; Fellow, Royal Soc. of Biology, World Acad. of Art and Science; other professional appointments and distinctions; Hon. Prof., Univ. of Nottingham 1988–2008; Hon. FZS; Hon. Fellow, Royal Agricultural Soc. of England 1995, Green-Templeton Coll., Oxford, St Edmund's Coll., Cambridge, Korean Acad. of Science; Hon. DSc (Nottingham) 1994, (St Andrews) 2007; Hon. DUniv (York) 2001. *Publications:* papers on reproductive biology, endocrinology, growth, lactation, science policy and biotechnology in biological and medical journals. *Leisure interests:* music, walking, travel. *Address:* St Edmund's College, Cambridge, CB3 0BN (office); Lincoln House, 8 Fendon Road, Cambridge, CB1 7RT, England (home). *Telephone:* (1223) 248509 (home). *E-mail:* rbh22@cam.ac.uk (office). *Website:* www.b4fa.org (office).

HEARN, Loyola; Canadian politician and diplomatist; b. Renews, Newfoundland; m. Maureen Hearn; one s. one d.; ed Memorial Univ., Univ. of New Brunswick; elected mem. Newfoundland House of Ass. for St Mary's the Capes, Newfoundland 1982–93; Minister of Educ. for Newfoundland and Labrador 1985–89; left politics and returned to teaching in Renews 1993–2000; MP 2000–08 (re-elected for new riding of St John's South-Mount Pearl 2004), House Leader for Progressive Conservative Party (later first House Leader for new Conservative Party of Canada following merger with Canadian Alliance parties), also held several critic roles, including lead critic for Fisheries and Oceans; Minister of Fisheries and Oceans and Regional Minister for Newfoundland and Labrador 2006–08; Amb. to Ireland 2010–14.

HEARNE, Sir Graham James, Kt, CBE; British business executive and solicitor; *Chairman, Catlin Group Limited;* b. 23 Nov. 1937, Birmingham; s. of Frank Hearne and Emily Hearne (née Shakespeare); m. Carol Jean Brown 1961; one s. three d.; ed George Dixon Grammar School, Birmingham; admitted solicitor 1959; with Pinsent & Co. Solicitors 1959–63, Fried, Frank, Harris, Shriver & Jacobson Attorneys, New York 1963–66, Herbert Smith & Co., Solicitors 1966–67, Industrial Reorganization Corpn 1967–68, N. M. Rothschild & Sons Ltd 1968–77 (mem. Bd of Dirs 1991–98); Finance Dir Courtaulds Ltd 1977–81; Chief Exec. Tricentrol 1981–83; Group Man. Dir Carless, Capel & Leonard 1983–84; Chair. Catlin Group Ltd 2003–; Chair. Braemar Seascope Group PLC; Deputy Chair. Gallaher Group PLC; Chief Exec. Enterprise Oil PLC 1984–91, Chair. 1991–2002; Deputy-Chair. (non-exec.) Gallaher Group PLC 1997; Chair. (non-exec.) Braemar Seascope Group PLC 1999–2002, Novar PLC 1999–2005; mem. Bd of Dirs Courtaulds PLC 1991–98, Invensys (fmrly BTR) PLC 1998–2003, Novar (fmrly Caradon) PLC 1999–2005, Rowan Companies Inc. 2004–, Stratic Energy Corpn 2005–; High Sheriff of Greater London 1995–96. *Address:* Catlin Group Limited, 3 Minster Court, Mincing Lane, London, EC3R 7DD, England (office). *Telephone:* (20) 7626-0486 (office). *Fax:* (20) 7623-9101 (office). *E-mail:* catlininfo@catlin.com (office). *Website:* www.catlin.com (office).

HEARNS, Thomas; American fmr professional boxer; b. 18 Oct. 1958, Grand Junction, Tenn.; s. of John Hearns and Lois Hearns; m. Rena Hearns; four c.; as amateur won 147 of 155 fights, Amateur Athletic Union (AAU) national and Golden Gloves 147–pound championships 1977; turned professional Nov. 1977 winning 28 straight fights before winning World Boxing Asscn (WBA) welterweight championship knocking out Pepino Cuevas 1980; lost title on technical knockout to Sugar Ray Leonard 1981; won World Boxing Council (WBC) super welterweight championship beating Wilfred Benitez 1982, beat Roberto Duran to win WBA version 1984; as middleweight lost to Marvin Hagler for world middleweight championship 1985; won WBC world light-heavyweight championship from Dennis Andries and WBC middleweight championship beating Juan Roldan 1987; won World Boxing Org. (WBO) super-middleweight championship by beating James Kinchen 1988; rematch with Leonard ending in draw 1989; won WBA light-heavyweight championship 1991, lost it to Ivan Barkley 1992; won North American Boxing Fed. (NABF) cruiserweight title 1995, won Int. Boxing Org. (IBO) version 1999, lost IBO title to Uriah Grant 2000; in professional career won 59 of 64 fights (46 by knockout) with one draw; Ring Magazine Fighter of the Year 1980, 1984, Boxing Writers Asscn of America Fighter of the Year 1980, 1984. *Website:* thomashitmanhearns.net.

HEATHER-LATU, Brenda Patricia, LLB, BA; Samoan/New Zealand barrister and solicitor; *Partner, Latu Lawyers, Barristers & Solicitors;* b. 23 Dec. 1961, Wellington, New Zealand; d. of Cuthbert Stanley Heather and Winnie Anesi Heather; m. George Latu; one s. one d.; ed Wellington Girls Coll., Victoria Univ. of Wellington, John F. Kennedy School of Govt, Harvard Univ.; solicitor, Dept of Educ., New Zealand 1987–88; Asst Crown Counsel, Crown Law Office, Wellington, New Zealand 1988–91, Crown Counsel 1991–96; Prin. State Solicitor, Office of the Attorney-Gen., Apia, Samoa 1996–97; Attorney-Gen. of Samoa 1997–2006; currently Partner and Legal Consultant, Latu Lawyers, Barristers & Solicitors; Hon. Consul for Great Britain and Nothern Ireland to Samoa, Foreign and Commonwealth Office 2014–. *Publications include:* Pacific Islands AIDS Trust Education Prevention Programme 1993. *Leisure interests:* Samoan culture and traditions, pacific migration, genealogy, corporate and good governance. *Address:* Latu Lawyers, Barristers & Solicitors, Ground Floor, ANZ House, PO Box 3619, Apia, Samoa (office). *Telephone:* 30364 (office). *Fax:* 30365 (office). *E-mail:* heather-latu@latulaw.com (office); latu@latulaw.com (office).

HEATON, Brian Thomas, DPhil, DSc, CChem, FRSC; British chemist and academic; *Professor Emeritus, University of Liverpool;* b. 16 Feb. 1940, Broughton-in-Furness, Cumbria; s. of William Edwin Heaton and Mabel Heaton (née Benson); m. Wendy Janet Durrant 1964; three d.; ed Ulverston Grammar School, Hatfield Polytechnic, Univ. of Sussex; Lecturer in Chem., Univ. of Kent at Canterbury 1968–81, Sr Lecturer 1981–84, Reader 1984, Prof. 1984–85; Grant Prof. of Inorganic Chem., Univ. of Liverpool 1985–2004, Prof. Emer. 2005–, Head of Dept of Chem. 1988–97; Chair. SERC Inorganic Cttee 1990–93; Sec. and Treas. Dalton Div., RSC 1990–93; Leverhulme Foundation Research Fellowship 1997; Visiting Prof., Univ. Louis Pasteur, Strasbourg 2001, Univ. of Heidelberg, Germany 2003; consultant, Inst. of Chemical and Eng Sciences, Singapore 2007–10, Nat. Univ. of Singapore 2008; Nuffield Foundation Research Fellowship 1981–82, RSC Tilden Lectureship and Prize 1986, Japanese Soc. for Promotion of Science Fellowship 1989, First Prize, Dept of Trade and Industry 1996, Leverhulme Foundation Research Fellowship 1997–98, RSC Award for research on platinum metals 2002. *Publications:* several books, including Mechanisms in Homogeneous Catalysis (ed.) 2005; numerous articles in professional journals. *Leisure interests:* rugby, walking, listening to and playing music, eating and drinking (especially wine). *Address:* 44 Graham Road, West Kirby, CH48 5DW, England (home). *Telephone:* (151) 632-3206 (home). *E-mail:* bth@liv.ac.uk (office). *Website:* www.liv.ac.uk/chemistry (office).

HEATON, Frances Anne, BA, LLB; British barrister and financial services industry executive; b. (Frances Anne Whidborne), 11 Aug. 1944, Winchester, Hants.; d. of John Ferris Whidborne and Marjorie Annie Maltby; m. Martin Heaton 1969; two s.; ed Trinity Coll., Dublin; with Dept of Econ. Affairs 1967–70; joined HM Treasury 1970, Asst Sec. 1979–80; seconded to S. G. Warburg & Co. Ltd 1977–79; with Corp. Finance Div., Lazard Bros & Co. Ltd 1980–2001, Exec. Dir 1987–2001, apptd Chair. Lazard London Dirs' Pension Scheme 2006; Chair. Schroders Pension Trustee Ltd 2008–14; Dir (non-exec.) W.S. Atkins PLC 1990–2003 (Deputy Chair. (non-exec.)) 1996–2003, BUPA 1998–2001, World Pay Group PLC 2000, Fountain GB Ltd 2001, Legal & General Group plc 2001–10, AWG PLC 2002–07, Jupiter Primadona Growth Trust 2005–14, BMT Ltd 2007–14, Bank of England 1993–2001; Dir-Gen. Take-overs and Mergers Panel 1992–94; mem. Cttee on Standards in Public Life 1997–2005. *Leisure interests:* bridge, gardening, riding. *Telephone:* (7831) 099539 (home). *E-mail:* fah@carillon.co.uk (office).

HEBEISH, Ali Ali, BSc, MSc, PhD, DSc; Egyptian chemist and academic; *Professor Emeritus, National Research Centre, Cairo;* b. 21 Dec. 1936, Mehalla El-Kubra, Gharbia; m.; two c.; ed Cairo Univ., Gujarat Univ.; Research Fellow, Nat. Research Centre, Cairo 1960–61, other research positions 1962–74, Assoc. Prof. 1974–79, Prof. 1979–84, Prof. Emer. 1996–, mem. Research and Devt Council; Under-Sec. of State, Office of the Pres., Acad. of Scientific Research and Tech., Cairo 1985–88, Vice-Pres. 1988–91, Pres. 1992–96; Pres. Egyptian Asscn for Scientific Culture 1993–96, Egyptian Textile Soc. 1993–; Chair. Egyptian Syndicate for Science Professions 1994–2011; Pres. Egyptian Science Unions; mem. Bd of Egyptian Acad. of Science, IFSTAD Council 1992–96, Shura Council 2012–13; mem. African Acad. of Sciences, Third World Acad. of Sciences, Islamic Acad. of Science; Fellow, Alexander von Humboldt Foundation 1973–75; Order of Science and Art, First Class 1974; Order of the Repub., Second Class 1983; Dr hc (Leberec Univ., Czech Repub.) 1995; State Prize for Chem. 1972, Production Prize in Chem. 1985, 1990, TWNSO First Prize in Tech. 1990, State Merit Prize 1995, The Nile Prize 2004, A.U. Kwame Nkrumah Continental Scientific Award 2016. *Publications:* 22 books, more than 580 scientific papers and 14 patents. *Address:* 26 El-Basra Street, Mohandseen, Dokki, Cairo (home); National Research Centre, Tahrir Street, Dokki, Giza, Egypt (office). *Telephone:* 3357807 (office); 37499125 (home). *Fax:* 33363261 (office). *E-mail:* alihebeish@hotmail.com (office).

HECHE, Anne; American actress; b. 25 May 1969, Aurora, Ohio; d. of Donald Heche and Nancy Heche; m. Coleman Laffoon 2001; one s. *Films include:* An Ambush of Ghosts 1993, The Adventures of Huck Finn 1993, A Simple Twist of Fate 1994, Milk Money 1994, I'll Do Anything 1994, The Wild Side 1995, Pie in the Sky 1995, The Juror 1996, Walking and Talking 1996, Donnie Brasco 1997, Volcano 1997, Subway Stories, Wag the Dog 1997, Six Days Seven Nights 1998, A Cool Dry Place 1998, Psycho 1998, The Third Miracle 1999, Auggie Rose 2001, John Q 2002, Prozac Nation 2003, Birth 2004, Sexual Life 2005, Suffering Man's Charity 2006, Toxic Skies 2008, The Other Guys 2010, Cedar Rapids 2011, That's What She Said 2012, Black November 2012, Arthur Newman 2012, Nothing Left to Fear 2013, Wild Card 2015. *Television includes:* (series) Another World; (films) O Pioneers! 1992, Against the Wall 1994, Girls in Prison 1994, Kingfish: A Story of Huey P. Long 1995, If These Walls Could Talk 1996, If These Walls Could Talk 2 (dir and screenwriter), One Kill 2000, Gracie's Choice 2004, The Dead Will Tell 2004, True 2005, Everwood (series) 2004–05, Silver Bells 2005, Fatal Desire 2006, Men in Trees (series) 2006–07, Hung 2009–10, Blackout 2012, Save Me (series) 2013, Adventure Time (episode) 2013, The Michael J Fox Show (series) 2013–14, One Christmas Eve (film) 2014, The Legend of Korra (series) 2014, Dig (series) 2015. *Publication:* Call Me Crazy: A Memoir 2001. *Address:* c/o United Talent Agency 9560 Wilshire Blvd, Beverly Hills, CA 90212, USA (office). *Website:* www.anneheche.com.

HECHTER, Daniel; French couturier; b. 30 July 1938, Paris; s. of Raymond Hechter and Rosy Mendelsohn; m. 1st Marika Stengl Diez Deaux (deceased); one d.; m. 2nd Jennifer Chambon 1973; ed Lycées Voltaire and Chaptal, Paris; designer, House of Pierre d'Alby 1959–62, first women's collection 1962, first men's collection 1968, first perfume line 1989; sold label to Miltenberger Otto Aulbach 1999; Founder and Dir-Gen. Vêtements Hechter 1962–; Co-founder Paris Saint-Germain football club, Chair. 1974–78; Pres. Fed. Française du Pret-à-Porter Féminin 1984–87; Pres. Festival de la Mode 1987; Pres. Strasbourg Racing Club 1987; fmr Vice-Pres. Etoile-Carouge football club; creator of Pret-a-Porter or ready-to-wear fashion. *Publications include:* Le Boss 2000. *Leisure interests:* football, tennis, swimming, skiing, curling, golf. *Website:* www.daniel-hechter.com.

HECKER, Zvi, BArch; Israeli architect; b. 31 May 1931, Kraków, Poland; m. Deborah Houchman 1957; one s. one d.; ed Kraków Polytechnic School of Architecture, Poland, Israel Inst. of Tech., Avni Acad.; worked in office of Arieh Sharon and Benjamin Idelson, Tel-Aviv 1957–58; in partnership with Eldar Sharon, Tel-Aviv 1959–65, with Alfred Neumann, Tel-Aviv 1960–68; Visiting Prof., Laval Univ., Québec, Canada 1968–69, Adjunct Prof. 1969–72; Visiting Lecturer, McGill Univ., Montreal and Univ. of Pennsylvania 1969–72; pvt. practice, Tel-Aviv 1972–, Berlin 1991–; work includes housing projects, synagogues, public bldgs etc.; Hon. Fellow, AIA 2013; 1996, Deutscher Kritikerpreis für Architektur; 1998, Rechter Architecture Prize for the Spiral House Apartment, Israel, Merentibus Medal, Scientific Council of Krakow Polytechnic 2016. *Publications:* exhbn catalogues, articles in professional journals. *Address:* Fehrbelliner Street 34, 10119 Berlin, Germany (office). *Telephone:* (30) 275-82-670 (office). *Fax:* (30) 275-82-677 (office). *E-mail:* berlin@zvihecker.com (office). *Website:* www.zvihecker.com (office).

HECKMAN, James Joseph, PhD; American economist and academic; *Henry Schultz Distinguished Service Professor of Economics, University of Chicago;* b. 19 April 1944, Chicago, Ill.; s. of John Heckman and Bernice Heckman; m. Lynne Pettler Heckman; one s. one d.; ed Colorado Coll. and Princeton Univ.; systems engineer, Martin-Marietta Aerospace 1965; Jr Economist, Council of Econ. Advisors 1967; Adjunct Asst Prof., New York Univ. 1972; Asst Prof., Columbia Univ. 1970–73, Assoc. Prof. 1973–74; Assoc. Prof. of Econs, Univ. of Chicago 1973–77, Prof. of Econs 1977–, Henry Schultz Prof. of Econs 1985–95, Henry Schultz Distinguished Service Prof. of Econs 1995–, Prof., Irving Harris School of Public Policy 1990–, Dir Center For Evaluation of Social Programs 1991–; A. Whitney Griswold Prof. of Econs, Yale Univ. 1988–90, Irving Fisher Prof. 1984, Prof. of Statistics 1990–, Lecturer, Yale Law School 1989–90, Alfred Cowles Distinguished Visiting Prof., Cowles Foundation 2008–; Research Assoc., Nat. Bureau of Econ. Research 1971–85, 1987–, Harry Scherman Fellow 1972–73; consultant, RAND Corpn 1975–76; Social Science Research Council Training Fellow 1977–78; Guggenheim Fellow 1978–79; Fellow, Center for Advanced Study in the Behavioral Sciences, Stanford Univ. 1978–79; Research Assoc., Nat. Opinion Research Center: Econs Research Center 1979–; Sr Research Fellow, American Bar Foundation 1991–; Pres.-elect Midwest Econs Asscn 1996–97, Pres. 1998; Fellow, Econometric Soc. 1980, American Acad. of Arts and Sciences 1985, American Statistical Asscn 2001; mem. NAS 1992–; Co-Ed. Journal of Political Economy 1981–87; Assoc. Ed. Journal of Econometrics 1977–83, Journal of Labor Economics 1982–, Review of Economic Studies 1982–85, Econometric Reviews 1987–, Journal of Economic Perspectives 1989–96; mem. Editorial Bd Review of Economics and Statistics 1994–; Dir Econs Research Center, Univ. of Chicago 2001–; Pres. Western Econs Asscn 2005–06; Lifetime mem. Irish Econ. Asscn 2009; Fellow, Int. Statistical Inst. 2007, AAAS 2009; Hon. Prof., Univ. of Tucuman 1998, Huazhong Univ., China 2001, Huazhong Univ. 2001, Univ. of Chile 2002, Wuhan Univ. 2003, Universidad Autónoma del Estado de México 2003, Bard Coll., Univ. of Montreal 2004, Pontifical Univ. of Chile 2009; Hon. mem. Latin and Caribbean Econ. Asscn 1999; Gold Medal, Pres. of Italian Repub. 2008, Frisch Medal 2014, Spirit of Erikson Award 2014; Hon. MA (Yale) 1989; Hon. PhD (Colo Coll.) 2001; Hon. DUniv (Chile) 2002, (UAEM, Mexico) 2003; John Bates Clark Medal, American Econs Asscn 1983, First Annual Louis T. Benezet Distinguished Alumnus Award, Colo Coll. 1985, Nobel Prize in Econs 2000, Statistician of the Year, Chicago Chapter, American Statistical Asscn 2002, Jacob Mincer Award, Soc. of Labour Econs 2005, Dennis Aigner Award 2005, 2007, Distinguished Contrib. Public Policy for Children, Soc. for Research in Child Devt 2009. *Publications include:* Longitudinal Analysis of Labor Market Data (co-ed.) 1985, Performance Standards in A Government Bureaucracy (ed collection), Lecture Notes on Longitudinal Data Analysis (co-author) 1997, Inequality in America: What Role for Human Capital Policy? (co-ed.) 2003, Law and Employment: Lessons From Latin America and the Caribbean (co-author) 2003, Handbook of Econometrics (co-ed.), Vol. 5 2001, Vol. 6 2007, Global Perspectives on the Rule of Law (co-ed.) 2010; more than 260 articles in professional journals. *Address:* Department of Economics, University of Chicago, 1126 East 59th Street, Chicago, IL 60637, USA (office). *Telephone:* (773) 702-0634 (office). *Fax:* (773) 702-8490 (office). *E-mail:* j-heckman@uchicago.edu (office); hiraic@uchicago.ed (office). *Website:* jenni.uchicago.edu (office).

HECKMANN, Fritz-Jürgen; German lawyer and business executive; m.; two c.; ed Univ. of Konstanz, Univ. of St Gallen, Switzerland; lectured in commercial law at Univ. of Konstanz; worked in tax advice office –1983; with Kees Hehl Heckmann commercial law firm, Stuttgart 1983–, Partner 1985–; Chair. Supervisory Bd HeidelbergCement 2005–14; holds mandates in supervisory and advisory bodies, including Hübner GmbH, Kassel, Infoman AG, Stuttgart, Drews Holding AG, Schrozberg, Neue Pressegesellschaft mbH & Co. KG (Südwestpresse Group), Ulm, LTG Holding GmbH & Co. KG, Stuttgart, Paul Hartmann AG, Heidenheim, SWMH Südwestdeutsche Medien Holding GmbH (Stuttgarter Zeitung/Stuttgarter Nachrichten Group), Stuttgart.

HEDEGAARD, Connie, MA; Danish journalist, politician and EU official; b. 15 Sept. 1960, Copenhagen; m. Jacob Andersen; two c.; ed Holbæk Pvt. Lower Secondary School, Stenhus Upper Secondary School, Univ. of Copenhagen; mem. Folketing (Det Konservative Folkeparti—Conservative Party) for Copenhagen Co. constituency 1984–90, 2005–07, for Greater Copenhagen constituency 2007–, Spokeswoman on Defence Policy 1987–89; journalist, Berlingske Tidende newspaper 1990–94; Head of News Bulletin Service, Radioavisen, Danish Broadcasting Corpn 1994–98, Anchorwoman with DR 2 1998–2004; regular columnist, Politiken daily newspaper 1998–2004; Minister for the Environment 2004–07, for Nordic Co-operation 2005–07, of Climate and Energy 2007–10, for the UN Climate Change Conf. in Copenhagen 2009; Commr for Climate Action, EC, Brussels 2010–14; Chair. Conservative Students in Metropolitan Region 1981–82, Centre for Cultural Co-operation with the Developing Countries 1998–2001, Man. Cttee Ministry of Culture's Devt Fund 2001–02, Man. Cttee BUSTER children's film festival 2002–; Nat. Chair. Denmark's Conservative Students 1983–84; Pres. Atlantic Asscn of Young Political Leaders 1985–87; mem. Council of Reps of Danish Atlantic Treaty Asscn 1986–, Bd Democracy Foundation 1990–95, Man. Cttee Centre for Tech. Supported Teaching (Center for Teknologistøttet Undervisning) 1995–98, Cttee on Public Information Policy 1996–97, Year 2000 Foundation (År 2000-Fonden) 1999–2000; KLF/Kirke & Mediers Scholarship Grant 2001, Culture Prize, Popular Educ. Asscn 2002, Nat. Press Club of Denmark Prize 2003, Ebbe Munck Award 2003, Publicist Award 2003. *Publications:* contrib. to various books. *Address:* European Commission, 200 Rue de la Loi, 1049 Brussels, Belgium (office); Høyrups Alle 24, 2900 Hellerup, Denmark (home). *Telephone:* (2) 299-11-11 (office). *Fax:* (2) 298-86-06 (office). *E-mail:* kirsten.winther@ec.europa-eu (office). *Website:* ec.europa.eu/commission_2010-2014/hedegaard (office); www.conniehedegaard.dk.

HEDELIUS, Tom Christer, MBA; Swedish banker; b. 3 Oct. 1939, Lund; s. of Curt Hedelius and Brita (Påhlsson) Hedelius; m. Ulla Marianne Ericsson 1964; three s.; ed Univ. of Lund; industrial expert, Svenska Handelsbanken 1967–69, Credit Man. 1969–74, Head, Regional Unit (Stockholm City) 1974–76, Head, Cen. Credit Dept 1976–78, Pres. 1978–91, Chair. 1991–2001, Hon. Chair. 2001–; Chair. AB Industrivärden, Bergman & Beving AB, Svenska AB Le Carbone, Anders Sandrews Stiftelse, Addtech. AB, Lagercrantz Group AB; mem. Bd of Dirs Svenska Cellulosa AB, AB Volvo; Hon. DEcon (Umeå) 1989. *Address:* Sturegatan 38, 11436 Stockholm, Sweden (home).

HEDGES, Lucas; American actor; b. 12 Dec. 1996, New York; s. of Peter Hedges and Susan Bruce; ed Saint Ann's School. *Films include:* Dan in Real Life 2007, Moonrise Kingdom 2012, Arthur and Mike 2012, Labor Day 2013, The Zero Theorem 2013, The Grand Budapest Hotel 2014, Kill the Messenger 2014, Anesthesia 2015, Manchester by the Sea 2016. *Television includes:* The Corrections (film) 2012, The Slap (series) 2015.

HEDGES, Robert Ernest Mortimer, PhD; British archaeologist and academic; *Professor of Archaeological Science, University of Oxford;* b. 9 June 1944; ed High Wycombe Royal Grammar School, Univ. of Cambridge; Fellow, St Cross Coll., Univ. of Oxford, now Emer., Lecturer in Archaeology 1994–, Deputy Dir Research Lab. for Archaeology and the History of Art –2009, now Prof. of Archaeological Science, School of Archaeology; Royal Medal, Royal Soc. 2008. *Publications:* numerous papers in professional journals. *Address:* School of Archaeology, University of Oxford, 1 South Parks Road, Oxford, OX1 3TG, England (office). *Telephone:* (1865) 285230 (office). *Fax:* (1865) 278254 (office). *E-mail:* robert.hedges@rlaha.ox.ac.uk (office). *Website:* www.arch.ox.ac.uk (office).

HEEGER, Alan J., PhD; American physicist and academic; *Professor of Physics and Materials Engineering, University of California, Santa Barbara;* b. 22 Jan. 1936, Sioux City, Ia; m. Ruth Heeger; two s.; ed Univ. of California, Berkeley; Prof. of Physics, Univ. of Calif., Santa Barbara 1982–, Dir Inst. for Polymers and Organic Solids 1982–2000, Prof. of Physics and Materials Engineering 1987–; Adjunct Prof. of Physics, Univ. of Utah 1988–, Chief Scientist 1999–; Pres. UNIAX Corpn 1990–94, Chair. 1990–99, Chief Tech. Officer 1999–; Co-founder and Chair. Brite Inc.; Co-founder and Vice-Chair. Cynvenio, Cytomx Therapeutics; Venture Partner, NGEN LLC; mem. Bd of Dirs Konarka Techs Inc., QTL Biosystems; mem. Advisory Bd Science and Eng Festival, Clipper Windpower PLC; Foreign mem. Korean Acad. of Science and Tech. 2001; mem. Russian Acad. of Sciences, American Physical Soc. 1968; Fellow, Alfred P. Sloan Foundation 1963–65, Guggenheim Foundation 1968–69; Hon. DrSc (Univ. of Mons) 1992, (Abo Akademie Univ.) 1998; Hon. DTheol (Univ. of Linköping) 1996; Oliver E. Buckley Prize 1983, John Scott Medal 1989, Balzan Prize for Science of Non-Biological Materials 1995, Nobel Prize for Chem. (co-recipient) for pioneering work on conductive polymers 2000, World Technology Award (Materials) 2013. *Achievements include:* holds several patents. *Address:* Department of Physics, Broida 4415, University of California, Santa Barbara, CA 93106-9530 (office); UNIAX Corporation, 6780 Cortona Drive, Santa Barbara, CA 93117, USA. *Telephone:* (805) 893-3184 (office). *Fax:* (805) 893-4755 (office). *Website:* www.cpos.ucsb.edu (office).

HEFFER, Simon James, MA, PhD; British journalist and writer; b. 18 July 1960, Chelmsford, Essex; s. of James Heffer and Joyce Mary Clements; m. Diana Caroline Clee 1987; two s.; ed King Edward VI School, Chelmsford and Corpus Christi Coll., Cambridge; medical journalist 1983–85; freelance journalist 1985–86; Leader Writer, Daily Telegraph 1986–91, Deputy Political Corresp. 1987–88, political sketch writer 1988–91, political columnist 1990–91, Deputy Ed. 1994–96; Deputy Ed. The Spectator 1991–94; columnist, Evening Standard 1991–93, Daily Mail 1993–94, 1995–2005; Assoc. Ed. Daily Telegraph 2005–11; Ed. Mail Comment Online 2011–, columnist, Daily Mail 2011–; Fellow Commoner, Corpus Christi Coll., Cambridge 2010; Charles Douglas-Home Prize 1993. *Publications include:* A Tory Seer (co-ed. with C. Moore) 1989, A Century of County Cricket (ed.) 1990, Moral Desperado: A Life of Thomas Carlyle 1995, Power and Place: The Political Consequences of King Edward VII 1998, Like the Roman: The Life of Enoch Powell 1998, Nor Shall My Sword; The Reinvention of England 1999, Vaughan Williams 2000, The Great British Speeches 2007, Strictly English: The Correct Way to Write and Why It Matters 2010, A Short History of Power 2011. *Leisure interests:* cricket, music, ecclesiology, bibliophily. *Address:* The Daily Mail, 2 Derry Street, London, W8 5TT, England (office). *Telephone:* (20) 7938-6000 (office). *E-mail:* simon.heffer@dailymail.co.uk (office). *Website:* www.dailymail.co.uk (office).

HEGARTY, (Anthony) Francis (Frank), PhD, DSc, MRIA, FRSC, FICI; Irish chemist and academic; *Professor Emeritus of Organic Chemistry, University College Dublin;* b. 5 Aug. 1942, Cork; s. of Daniel F. Hegarty and Patricia Doyle; m. Ann M. Fleming 1967; two s. two d.; ed Univ. Coll. Cork (Nat. Univ. of Ireland) and Univs of Paris, France and California, USA; Lecturer in Chem., Univ. Coll. Cork 1970–79; Prof. and Chair. of Organic Chem., Univ. Coll. Dublin (UCD) 1980–2007, Prof. Emer. 2007–, Head of Dept 1980–83, 1986–89, 1996–99, Dean of Postgraduate Studies 1989–96, mem. Governing Body of UCD 1990–2005, Chair. Bd for Funded Research and Research and Scholarship Bd 1995–2004, Vice-Pres. for Research at UCD 1998–2004; Visiting Prof., Brandeis Univ. 1975, Kuwait Univ.

1983, Univ. of Paris VII 1987; Chair. Nat. Trust for Ireland 1984–87, Royal Soc. of Chem. in Ireland 1987–90; Deputy Chair. Irish Research Council for Science, Eng and Tech. 2001–12; mem. Senate Nat. Univ. of Ireland 1992–2007; Council mem. Royal Irish Acad. 1982–96, 2003–11, Sec. for Science 1986–88, Treas. 1988–96; Dir, Topchem Laboratories 2002–, Topchem Pharmaceuticals 2002–; mem. Panel of the Chief Science Advisor to the Govt of Ireland 2009–; Fellow, Inst. of Chem. in Ireland; Boyle-Higgins Medal, Inst. of Chem. in Ireland 2011. *Publications:* 187 papers in int. journals in area of organic reaction mechanisms and bioorganic chem. *Leisure interests:* sailing, walking, classical music. *Address:* School of Chemistry and Chemical Biology, University College Dublin, Belfield, Dublin 4 (office); 2 Belgrave Square, Monkstown, Co. Dublin, Ireland (home). *Telephone:* 87-2201014 (mobile) (home); (1) 2806631 (home). *Fax:* (1) 7161178 (office). *E-mail:* f.hegarty@ucd.ie (office).

HEGAZI, Al-Mursi al-Sayid, MEconSc, PhD; Egyptian economist, academic and government official; ed Univ. of Alexandria, Univ. of Connecticut, USA; Asst Prof., Dept of Public Finance, Univ. of Alexandria 1986–96, Chair. Dept of Public Finance 2003–08, Prof. Emer. 2008–; Asst, later Assoc. Prof., Dept of Econs, King Abdul-Aziz Univ., Qassim, Saudi Arabia 1990–95, Chair. Dept of Econs 1995–96; Chair. Dept of Public Finance, Beirut Arab Univ., Lebanon 1997–99, Dean, Faculty of Commerce 1999–2001; Minister of Finance Jan.–May 2013. *Address:* c/o Ministry of Finance, Ministry of Finance Towers, Cairo, Egypt.

HEHR, Kent, PC, BA, LLB; Canadian lawyer, community leader and politician; *Minister of Veterans Affairs, and Associate Minister of National Defence;* b. 16 Dec. 1969, Calgary; s. of Richard Hehr and Judy Hehr; partner Deanna Holt; ed Univ. of Calgary; lawyer with Fraser Milner Casgrain 2001–08; mem. Legis. Ass. of Alberta for Calgary-Buffalo 2008–15; mem. House of Commons (Parl.) for Calgary Centre 2015–; Minister of Veterans Affairs, and Assoc. Minister of Nat. Defence 2015–; mem. City of Calgary Accessability Advisory Cttee 1998–2006; mem. Canadian Paraplegic Asscn (Alberta) 2000–; mem. Liberal Party of Canada. *Address:* Veterans Affairs Canada, 161 Grafton Street, POB 7700, Charlottetown, PEI C1A 8M9, Canada (office). *Telephone:* (866) 522-2122 (office). *Fax:* (902) 566-8508 (office). *E-mail:* information@vac-acc.gc.ca (office). *Website:* www.vac-acc.gc.ca (office); kenthehr.liberal.ca.

HEIDE, Ola Mikal, MSc, DrAgr; Norwegian botanist and academic; *Professor Emeritus of Botany, Norwegian University of Life Sciences;* b. 26 April 1931, Trondenes; s. of Hans Kr. Heide and Marit Heide; m. Gerd Lillebakk 1955; three s. two d.; ed Agricultural Univ. of Norway, Univ. of Wisconsin; Research Fellow, Agric. Univ. of Norway 1961–70; Prof. of Plant Sciences, Makerere Univ. of Kampala, Uganda 1970–72; Prof. of Plant Physiology, Univ. of Tromsö 1972–76; apptd Prof. of Botany, Agric. Univ. of Norway (renamed Norwegian Univ. of Life Sciences 2005) 1976, now Prof. Emer.; Head, Dept of Biology and Nature Conservation 1990–95, Rector 1978–83; Vice-Chair. Agric. Research Council of Norway 1979–84; mem. Norwegian Acad. of Sciences, Royal Soc. of Sciences of Uppsala 1991, Finnish Acad. of Science and Letters 1994; Pres. Scandinavian Soc. of Plant Physiology 1976–82, 1988–94, Fed. of European Socs of Plant Physiology 1988–90; Kellogg Foundation Fellowship 1965; Norsk Varekrigsforsikrings Fund Science Prize 1968. *Publications include:* more than 150 primary scientific publs in the fields of plant physiology and ecophysiology. *Leisure interests:* sport, especially cross country skiing and running. *Address:* Norwegian University of Life Sciences, Department of Ecology and Nature Resource Management, 1432 Ås (office); Skogvegen 34, 1430 Ås, Norway (home). *Telephone:* 64-96-53-86 (office); 64-94-16-01 (home). *Fax:* 64-96-58-01 (office). *Website:* www.nmbu.no (office).

HEIDEN, Eric A., MD; American orthopaedic surgeon, fmr speed skater and fmr professional cyclist; b. 14 June 1958, Madison, Wis.; m. Karen Drews 1995; ed Univ. of Wis., Stanford Medical School; competed in Winter Olympics, Innsbruck, Austria 1976, Lake Placid, New York 1980 (five gold medals for men's speed skating, became first athlete ever to win five gold medals in a single Winter Olympics); winner, three consecutive World Speed Skating Championships 1977–79 (set new world records for 3,000m 1978, 1,000m 1978); retd from speed skating 1980; became professional cyclist 1981, winner US Professional Cycling Championships 1985; took part in Tour de France 1986; Asst Prof., Univ. of Calif., Davis Sports Medicine Clinic, Sacramento, Calif. –2006, Co-founder Sports Performance Program; Co-founder Heiden Davidson Orthopedics 2006; also affiliated with LDS Hospital, Salt Lake Regional Medical Center, Park City Medical Center; US speed skating team physician, Winter Olympics 2002, 2006, 2010, 2014; fmr team physician, Sacramento Kings professional basketball team; Fellow, American Sports Medicine Inst. 1996–97; Team Doctor, BMC Racing Team 2012–; mem. American Acad. of Orthopedic Surgeons; Sullivan Award for Best US Amateur Athlete 1980, UPI Int. Athlete of the Year 1980, USOC Sportsman of the Year 1980, inducted into Olympic Hall of Fame 1983, Bicycling Hall of Fame 1999. *Publication:* Faster, Better, Stronger 2008. *Address:* Heiden Davidson Orthopedics, 2200 North Park Avenue, Building D, Suite 100, Park City, UT 84060, USA (office). *Telephone:* (435) 615-8822 (office). *E-mail:* Eric@heidendavidsonortho.com (office). *Website:* www.heidendavidsonortho.com (office).

HEIFETZ, Zvi; Israeli lawyer and diplomatist; *Ambassador to Russia;* b. USSR; m. Sigalia Heifetz; seven c.; ed Tel-Aviv Univ.; family exiled from Latvia to Siberia during World War II; following high school, served in army for seven years in Intelligence, now a Maj. in Reserves; est. law practice in Tel-Aviv; went to USSR in 1989; fmr legal advisor to Prime Minister's Office on Soviet matters; Vice-Chair. Ma'ariv (publishing group) 1999, Chair. Tower Records 2001; Hon. Consul of Latvia to Israel –2004, Amb. to UK 2004–07, to Russia 2015–; adviser and spokesman for Defense Ministry dealing with Russian-language media; mem. Bd of Dirs Hadera Paper Ltd 2012–, Clal Industries and Investments Ltd 2012–; mem. Israel Bar Asscn. *Address:* Israeli Embassy, 119017 Moscow, ul. B. Ordynka 56, Russia (office). *Telephone:* (495) 660-27-00 (office). *Fax:* (495) 660-27-68 (office). *E-mail:* info@moscow.mfa.gov.il (office). *Website:* moscow.mfa.gov.il (office).

HEIGHTON, Steven, MA; Canadian author; b. 14 Aug. 1961, Toronto, Ont.; ed Silverthorn Coll. Inst., Queen's Univ.; Ed. Quarry magazine 1988–94; Writer-in-Residence, Concordia Univ. 2002–03; Jack McLelland Writer-in-Residence, Massey Coll., Univ. of Toronto 2004; participating author, American Movements II course, Univ. of New Orleans 2006; instructor, Summer Literature Seminars, Herzen Univ., Russia 2007; Writer-in-Residence, Univ. of Ottawa 2009, Royal Mil. Coll., Kingston 2010; Mordecai Richler Writer-in-Residence, McGill Univ. 2013; Fellow, Cambridge Literary Seminars 1997; Ed. Quarry Magazine 1988–94; Gerald Lampert Award for Best First Book of Poetry 1990, Air Canada Award 1990, Gold Medal for Fiction, Nat. Magazine Awards 1992, 2007, 2009, Petra Kenney Prize 2002, Gold Medal for Poetry, Nat. Magazine Awards 2003, K. M. Hunter Award (Literature Category) 2010, P.K. Page Founders Award for Poetry 2011. *Publications include:* Stalin's Carnival (poetry) 1989, Foreign Ghosts (travelogue/poetry) 1989, Flight Paths of the Emperor (stories) 1992, The Ecstasy of Skeptics (poetry) 1994, On earth as it is (stories) 1995, The Admen Move on Lhasa: Writing and Culture in a Virtual World (essays) 1997, The Shadow Boxer (novel) 2000, Musings: An Anthology of Greek-Canadian Literature (co-ed.) 2003, The Address Book (poetry) 2004, Afterlands (novel) 2006, Patient Frame (poetry) 2010, Every Lost Country (novel) 2010, Workbook: Memos & Dispatches on Writing 2011, The Dead Are More Visible (short stories) 2012, The Waking Comes Late (Gen.-Gov.'s Award for Poetry 2016) 2016, The Nightingale Won't Let You Sleep (novel) 2017; poetry, fiction and critical articles in various periodicals and anthologies, including London Review of Books, Poetry, Tin House, New York Times Book Review, Best English Stories, Best Canadian Stories, Poetry London, Brick. *Address:* c/o Anne McDermid Agency, 320 Front Street W, Suite 1105, Toronto, ON M5V 3B6, Canada (office). *Telephone:* (647) 788-4016 (office). *E-mail:* anne@mcdermidagency.com (office); sheighton@kos.net (office). *Website:* www.mcdermidagency.com (office); www.stevenheighton.com.

HEILBRONNER, François; French government official and business executive; b. 17 March 1936, Paris; s. of Paul Heilbronner and Elsie Schwob; m. Nathalie Ducas 1966; two s. two d.; ed Lycée Charlemagne, Paris, Inst. d'Etudes Politiques, Paris and Ecole Nat. d'Admin; Insp. des Finances 1964; apptd to Secr. of Interministerial Cttee on Questions of European Econ. Cooperation 1966, Deputy Sec.-Gen. 1969–72; Adviser to Minister of Foreign Affairs 1968–69; Deputy Dir Office of Minister of Agric. 1972–73, Dir 1973–74; Econ. and Financial Adviser to Prime Minister Jacques Chirac 1974, Deputy Dir of Office of Prime Minister Chirac 1975–76, 1986; Insp.-Gen. des Finances 1983; Pres. Groupe des assurances nationales (Gan) 1986, Banque pour l'industrie française, Phénix Soleil SpA (Italy) (now Gan Italia SpA) 1986–94; consultant, FH Conseil 1995; Pres. HL Gestion 1997–99; Man. Dir REFCO HL Securities 1999–2000; Chair. and CEO Arbel 2001–04; mem. Bd of Dirs Fondation Médecins sans Frontières; Chevalier, Légion d'honneur, du Mérite maritime, Officier, Ordre nat. du Mérite, Commdr du Mérite agricole.

HEIMANN, John G.; American investment banker; *Senior Advisor, Financial Stability Institute, Bank for International Settlements;* NY State Supervisor of Banking 1975–76; NY Commr of Housing and Community Devt 1976–77; Comptroller of the Currency 1977–81; also served as first Chair. Fed. Financial Insts Examination Council and Acting Chair. Fed. Deposit Insurance Corpn; joined Warburg Paribas Becker-AG Becke 1981; Founding Chair. Financial Stability Inst. (jt initiative of BIS and Basel Cttee on Banking Supervision) 1999–2000, Sr Advisor 2002–; mem. Emer. Group of Thirty Consultative Group on Int. Econ. and Monetary Affairs, Inc. (G-30), Washington, DC. *Address:* Financial Stability Institute, Bank for International Settlements, 4002 Basel, Switzerland (office). *Telephone:* (61) 280-99-89 (office). *Fax:* (61) 280-91-00 (office). *E-mail:* fsi@bis.org (office). *Website:* www.bis.org (office).

HEIN, Christoph; German novelist and playwright; b. 8 April 1944, Heinzendorf, Schlesien; ed Gymnasium Berlin, Univ. of Leipzig, Humboldt Univ.; dramatist and playwright, Volksbühne Berlin 1971–79; Chevalier, Ordre des Arts et des Lettres; Heinrich Mann-Preis der Akad. der Künste Berlin 1982, (westdeutscher) Kritikerpreis für Literatur Berlin 1983, Literaturpreis Hamburg 1985, Lessing Prize 1989, Stefan Andres Prize, Schweich 1989, Erich Fried Prize, Vienna 1990, Ludwig Mülheims Prize 1992, Berliner Literaturpreis der Stiftung Preussische Seehandlung 1992, Norddt. Literaturpreis 1998, Peter-Weiss-Preis 1998, Solothurner Literaturpreis 2000, Premio Grinzane Cavour Turin 2002, State Prize for European Literature Austria 2002, Schiller-Gedächtnispreis 2004, Verdi Literaturpreis 2004, Ver.di-Literaturpreis Berlin-Brandenburg 2004, Walter-Hasenclever-Literaturpreis 2008, Eichendorff-Literaturpreis 2010, Gerty-Spies-Literaturpreis 2011, Uwe-Johnson-Preis 2012, Internationaler Stefan-Heym-Preis 2013. *Plays:* Schlötel oder Was solls 1974, Cromwell 1980, Lassalle fragt Herrn Herbert nach Sonja 1981, Die wahre Geschichte des Ah Q 1983, Passage 1987, Die Ritter der Tafelrunde 1989, Randow 1994, Bruch 1998, Himmel auf Erden 1998, In Acht und Bann 1998, Mutters Tag 2000, Noach (opera) 2001, Zur Geschichte des menschlichen Herzens 2002. *Publications:* fiction: Einladung zum Lever Bourgeois (stories) 1980, Nachfahrt und früher Morgen (juvenile) 1980, Der fremde Freund (novel) (trans. as The Distant Lover) 1982, Horns Ende (novel) 1985, Das Wildpferd unterm Kachelofen (juvenile) 1985, Der Tangospieler (novel) (trans. as The Tango Player) 1989, Die Vergewaltigung (stories) 1991, Matzeln 1991, Das Napoleonspiel (novel) 1993, Exekution eines Kalbes und andere Erzählungen 1994, Von allem Anfang an (novel) 1997, Willenbrock (novel) 2000, Mama ist gegangen (juvenile) 2003, Landnahme (trans. as Settlement) 2004, In seiner frühen Kindheit ein Garten (novel) 2005, Frau Paula Trosseau (novel) 2007, Weiskerns Nachlass (novel) 2011; non-fiction: Die wahre Geschichte des Ah Q (plays/essays) 1984, Schlötel oder Was solls (essays) 1986, Öffentlich arbeiten. Essays und Gespräche 1987, Die fünfte Grundrechenart. Aufsätze und Reden 1986–1989 1990, Als Kind habe ich Stalin gesehen (essays/speeches) 1990, Die Mauern von Jerichow 1996.

HEINÄLUOMA, Eero; Finnish politician; b. 4 July 1955, Kokkola; s. of Heimo Olavi Heinäluoma and Aino Maria Heinäluoma; m. Satu Orvokki Siitonen-Heinäluoma; mem. Eduskunta (Parl.) for Uusimaa constituency 2003–07, for Helsinki constituency 2007–, Vice-Chair. and mem. Parl. Supervisory Council 2003–05, Chair. Social Democratic Parl. Group 2010–11, Speaker of Parl. 2011–15; Minister of Finance 2005–07, Deputy Prime Minister 2006–07; Sec. Finnish Social Democratic Party 2002–05, Chair. 2005–08; Speaker Forum for Int. Affairs 2011–15 (also mem. 2015–); Vice-Chair. NATO Parliamentary Ass. 2015– (also mem. 2011–15); mem. Auditors Bank of Finland 2007–10, Helsinki City Council 2008–; Deputy mem. Finnish Del. to Nordic Council Sept. 2007–Feb. 2008, 2008–11. *Address:* Parliament of Finland, Eduskunta, 00102 Helsinki, Finland (office). *Telephone:* (9) 432-3058 (office). *E-mail:* eero.heinaluoma@parliament.fi (office). *Website:* www.eduskunta.fi (office).

HEINDORFF, Michael, MA; German artist; b. 26 June 1949, Braunschweig; s. of Hans Heindorff and Sigrid Bootz (née Hampe); m. Monica Buferd 1983 (died 2002); one s. one d.; ed Art Coll. and Univ. of Braunschweig, Royal Coll. of Art, London, UK; has been represented in numerous group exhbns internationally 1976–, also numerous solo exhbns 1977–; Sr Tutor in Painting, RCA 1980–99, Hon. Fellow 2001; various comms 1986–; Life mem. Chelsea Arts Club 1988–; John Moore's Liverpool Award 10 1976, Schmidt-Rotluff Prize 1981, Villa Massimo Prize 1981. *Art exhibitions include:* Drawn to Seeing, London 1995, Drawn to Seeing II, touring Germany 1999–2001, Guildhall Art Gallery, London 2002, Deutsche Bank, London 2003. *Leisure interests:* gardening, walking. *Address:* 2 Shrubland Road, London, E8 4NN, England (home). *Telephone:* 7773-429774 (mobile) (home). *E-mail:* heindorff@aol.com. *Website:* www.londonartscafe.org.uk/shows/mh/index.htm.

HEINE, Volker, MSc, PhD, FRS, FInstP; British theoretical physicist and fmr academic; b. 19 Sept. 1930, Germany; m. Daphne Hines 1955; one s. two d.; ed Wanganui Collegiate School, Otago Univ., New Zealand, Univ. of Cambridge; Demonstrator, Lecturer and Reader, Univ. of Cambridge 1958–76, Prof. in Theoretical Physics 1976–97; Visiting Prof., Univ. of Chicago 1965–66; Visiting Scientist, Bell Labs, USA 1970–71; Fellow, Clare Coll. Cambridge 1960–; Foreign mem. Max Planck Gesellschaft; Fellow, American Physical Soc.; Maxwell Medal, Inst. of Physics, Royal Medal, Royal Soc., Dirac Medal, Inst. of Physics, Max Born Medal, Inst. of Physics and German Physical Soc. 2001. *Publications include:* Group Theory in Quantum Mechanics 1960, Solid State Physics (Vol. 24) 1970, (Vol. 35) 1980; articles in Journal of Physics, Physical Review etc. *Address:* Cavendish Laboratory, JJ Thomson Avenue, Cambridge, CB3 0HE, England (office). *Telephone:* (1223) 768151 (office).

HEINEMAN, David (Dave) Eugene, BS; American politician fmr army officer and state governor; b. 12 May 1948, Falls City, Neb.; s. of Jean Heineman and Irene Heineman; m. Sally Ganem 1977; one s.; ed US Mil. Acad., West Point; fmr Capt. in US Army; fmr Chief of Staff for Congressman Hal Daub; fmr Fremont Area Office Man. for Congressman Doug Bereuter; Neb. State Treas. 1995–2001; Lt Gov. of Neb. 2001–05, Dir of Homeland Security for Neb. (mem. Homeland Security Advisory Council 2004), Chair. Neb. Information Comm., Presiding Officer Neb. Legislature; US Sec. of Agric., Washington, DC 2005; Gov. of Nebraska 2005–Jan. 2015; Chair. Nat. Govs Asscn 2011–12; Republican. *Address:* Republican National Committee, 310 First Street, SE, Washington, DC 20003, USA (office). *Telephone:* (202) 863-8500 (office). *Fax:* (202) 863-8820 (office). *E-mail:* info@gop.com (office). *Website:* www.gop.com (office).

HEINONEN, Olavi Ensio, LLD; Finnish judge; b. 12 Sept. 1938, Kuopio; s. of Eino Ensio Heinonen and Aili Vesa; m. Marjatta Rahikainen 1962; two s. two d.; ed Univ. of Helsinki; Asst Prof. of Law, Univ. of Helsinki 1969–70; Justice, Supreme Court of Finland 1970–86; Parl. Ombudsman 1986–89; Chief Justice, Supreme Court of Finland 1989–2001 (retd); Grand Cross, Order of White Rose of Finland; Hon. LLD (Turku). *Publications include:* books and articles on criminal justice and criminal policy. *Leisure interests:* cycling, basketball.

HEINRICH, Martin Trevor, BS; American politician; *Senator from New Mexico;* b. 17 Oct. 1971, Fallon, Nev.; s. of Peter C. Heinrich and Shirley A. Heinrich (née Bybee); m. Julie Heinrich; two c.; ed Univ. of Missouri, Univ. of New Mexico; served as Exec. Dir Cottonwood Gulch Foundation; f. public affairs consulting firm; mem. Albuquerque City Council 2003–07, City Council Pres. 2006; apptd by Gov. Bill Richardson to be state's Natural Resources Trustee 2006; mem. US House of Reps for 1st Congressional Dist of NM 2009–13, mem. Cttee on Armed Services, Cttee on Natural Resources; Senator from New Mexico 2013–; Democrat. *Address:* 303 Hart Senate Office Building, Washington, DC 20510, USA (office). *Telephone:* (202) 224-5521 (office). *Website:* www.heinrich.senate.gov (office).

HEINRICHER, Arthur C., BS, PhD; American mathematician and academic; *Professor of Mathematical Sciences and Dean of Undergraduate Studies, Worcester Polytechnic Institute;* b. 24 Feb. 1956, St Louis, Mo.; m.; ed Univ. of Missouri-St Louis, Carnegie-Mellon Univ.; fmr Asst Prof., Univ. of Kentucky; fmr Visiting Asst Prof., Univ. of Tennessee; joined Faculty of Math. Sciences, Worcester Polytechnic Inst. 1992, Harold J. Gay Professorship in Math. 1996, served as Dir Center for Industrial Math. and Statistics, Co-Dir Research Experiences for Undergraduates program in industrial math. and statistics 1998–2006, currently Prof. of Math. Sciences and Dean of Undergraduate Studies; Gordon Prize, Nat. Acad. of Eng (co-recipient) 2016. *Address:* Boynton Hall, 1st Floor, Worcester Polytechnic Institute, 100 Institute Road, Worcester, MA 01609-2280, USA (office). *Telephone:* (508) 831-5397 (office). *E-mail:* heinrich@wpi.edu (office). *Website:* www.wpi.edu/people/faculty/heinrich (office).

HEINRICHT, Frank, DrIng; German business executive; *Chairman of the Board of Management, Schott AG;* b. 1962, Berlin; m.; three c.; ed Tech. Univ. of Berlin; trainee programme, TEMIC Semiconductors 1992, held several man. positions, including Project Man. and Plant Man., apptd Gen. Man. for Integrated Circuits 1995, later Head of Integrated Circuits Div., responsible for subsidiaries in Germany, France, UK and USA, CEO TEMIC Semiconductor Group 1998–2003; Chief Operating and Tech. Officer and mem. Bd of Man., Heraeus Holding GmbH 2003–13, Chair. Bd of Man. 2008–13; Chair. Bd of Man. Schott AG 2013–; mem. Supervisory Bd Würth Group, Sennheiser Electronic GmbH & Co. KG; First Deputy Chair. German Materials Soc. (DGM). *Address:* Schott AG, Hattenbergstraße 10, 55122 Mainz, Germany (office). *Telephone:* (6131) 66-0 (office). *Fax:* (6131) 66-2000 (office). *E-mail:* info@schott.com (office). *Website:* www.schott.com (office).

HEINS, Thorsten, MSc; German telecommunications executive; b. 29 Dec. 1957, Gifhorn; ed Univ. of Hanover; CEO of various business divs in the communication business, Chief Tech. Officer and mem. Group Bd Siemens Communications Group, Siemens AG –2007; Sr Vice-Pres., Handheld Business Unit, Research In Motion (name changed to BlackBerry 2013) 2007–09, COO Product Eng 2009–11, COO Product and Sales 2011, mem. Bd of Dirs, Pres. and CEO 2012–13; Chair. and CEO Powermat Technologies 2013–16; mem. Bd of Dirs Canadian German Chamber of Industry and Commerce Inc.

HEISBOURG, François; French/Luxembourg academic and business executive; *Special Adviser, Fondation pour la Recherche Stratégique;* b. 24 June 1949, London, England; s. of Georges Heisbourg and Hélène Pinet; m. Elyette Levy 1989; two s.; ed Coll. Stanislas, Paris, Inst. d'Etudes Politiques, Cycle Supérieur d'Aménagement et d'Urbanisme, Ecole Nat. d'Admin; Asst to Dir of Econ. Affairs, Ministry of Foreign Affairs 1977–78; policy planning staff, Ministry of Foreign Affairs 1978–79; First Sec. Perm. Mission of France to UN 1979–81; Int. Security Adviser to Minister of Defence 1981–84; Vice-Pres. Thomson–CFS 1984–87; Dir IISS, London 1987–92, Chair. Council 2001–; Sr Vice-Pres. Matra Défense Espace 1992–98; Head, French Interministerial Group on teaching of and research in, strategic and int. affairs 1999–2000; Prof., Sciences-Po, Paris 1999–2001; Chair. Geneva Centre for Security Policy 1998–; Dir Fondation pour la Recherche Stratégique, Paris 2001–05, Special Adviser 2005–; mem. Royal Soc. for Encouragement of Arts, Manufacture and Commerce; Officier, Légion d'honneur; Chevalier, Ordre nat. du Mérite; Grosses Verdienstkreuz (FRG); Commdr, Ordre de la Couronne de Chêne (Luxembourg), Merito Militar (Spain). *Publications:* La puce, les Hommes et la bombe (with P. Boniface) 1986, Les volontaires de l'an 2000 1995, The Future of Warfare 1997, European Defence: Making It Work 2000, Hyperterrorisme: La nouvelle guerre 2001, La fin de l'Occident? – L'Amérique, l'Europe et le Moyen Orient 2005, Le terrorisme en France (with J. L. Marret) 2006, L'Epaisseur du monde 2007, L'Iran, le choix des armes? 2007, Après Al Qaïda 2008, Vainqueurs et vaincus, lendemains de crise 2009, Espionnage et renseignement 2012, La fin du rêve européen 2013, Secrètes histoires 2015; numerous articles in int. media and scholarly journals. *Leisure interests:* hiking, chess, collecting atlases. *Address:* Fondation pour la Recherche Stratégique, 27 rue Damesme, 75013 Paris, France (office). *Telephone:* 1-43-13-77-80 (office). *Fax:* 1-43-13-77-78 (office). *E-mail:* f.heisbourg@frstrategie.org (office); heisbour@noos.fr (home). *Website:* www.frstrategie.org (office).

HEITKAMP, Mary Kathryn (Heidi), BA, JD; American lawyer and politician; b. 30 Oct. 1955, Mantador, North Dakota; m. Dr Darwin Lange; two s.; ed Univ. of North Dakota, Lewis and Clark Coll.; attorney, US Environmental Protection Agency 1980–81; attorney, Office of ND State Tax Commr 1981–86; Tax Commr of North Dakota 1986–92; Attorney Gen. of ND 1993–2000; unsuccessful cand. on Democratic-NPL ticket for State Gov. 2000; Dir Great Plains Synfuels Plant, Dakota Gasification Co. 2001–12; Senator from North Dakota 2013–19; Democrat. *Address:* c/o United States Senate, Washington, DC 20510, USA (office).

HEITSCH, Ernst, DPhil; German classicist and academic; *Professor of Classical Linguistics, University of Regensburg;* b. 17 June 1928, Celle; s. of Ernst Heitsch and Luise Meineke; m. Paula Sötemann 1961; two s. one d.; ed Univ. of Göttingen; Univ. Lecturer in Classical Linguistics, Univ. Göttingen 1960–66, Prof. 1966–67; Prof. of Classical Linguistics, Univ. of Regensburg 1967–; mem. Akad. der Wissenschaften und der Literatur zu Mainz, Akad. der Wissenschaften zu Göttingen, Deutsches Archäologisches Institut. *Publications:* Die griechischen Dichterfragmente der römischen Kaiserzeit I und II 1963–65, Epische Kunstsprache und Homer 1968, Parmenides 1974, 1995, Parmenides und die Anfänge der Erkenntniskritik und Logik 1979, Xenophanes 1983, Antiphon aus Rhamnus 1984, Willkür und Problembewusstsein in Platons Kratylos 1984, Platon über die rechte Art zu reden und zu schreiben 1987, Überlegungen Platons im Theaetet 1988, Wege zu Platon 1992, Platon Phaidros 1993, 1997, Geschichte und Situationen bei Thukydides 1996, Gesammelte Schriften I 2001, II 2002, III 2003, Platon Apologie 2002, 2004, Dialoge Platons vor 399? 2002, Platon und die Aufänge seines dialektischen Philosophierens 2004, Geschichte und Personen bei Thukydides 2007, Platon Hippias Major 2011, Eine Episode aus der Geschichte des Wahrheitsbegriffs 2011, Vision als Offenbarüng? 2012, Die drei frühesten Dialoge Platons 2014; numerous articles in periodicals. *Leisure interest:* sailing. *Address:* Mattinger Strasse 1, 93049 Regensburg, Germany (home). *Telephone:* (941) 31944 (home).

HEKMATYAR, Gulbuddin; Afghan politician and fmr guerrilla leader; b. 26 June 1947, Imam Saheb, Kunduz Prov.; s. of Ghulam Qader; ed Kabul Univ.; mem. Muslim Youth 1970; imprisoned 1972–73; fled to Pakistan 1973; Leader, Hizb-i Islami Mujahidin Movt against Soviet-backed regime; Prime Minister of Afghanistan 1993–94, 1996–97; returned from exile in Iran 1998; Leader, Hizb-i Islami Gulbuddin; returned to Afghanistan from exile 2017.

HELBLE, Joseph J., BS, PhD; American chemical engineer and academic; *Professor of Engineering and Dean, Thayer School of Engineering, Dartmouth College;* b. 12 April 1960, Paterson, New Jersey; ed Lehigh Univ., Massachusetts Inst. of Tech.; Research Scientist and Man., Physical Sciences Inc., Andover, Mass 1987–95; AAAS Science and Policy Fellow, US Environmental Protection Agency (EPA), Washington, DC 1993; Assoc. Prof., Dept of Chemical Eng, Univ. of Connecticut 1995–2003, Grad Program Chair. 1996–99, Chair chemical engineering department 1999–2004, Prof., Dept of Chemical Eng 2003–05; Prof. of Eng, Dartmouth Coll. 2005–, Dean, Thayer School of Eng 2005–; Conf. Organizer and Program Chair., Eng Foundation Conf. on Nanoparticles and Nanostructures by Vapor Phase Synthesis, Barga Italy 2002; mem. EPA Science Advisory Bd, reviews of 'Air Toxics Research Strategy' and 'EPA Draft Report on the Environment 2003' 2003–05; mem. Chemical Eng Advisory Bd, Coll. of Eng, Brown Univ. 2005–, Bd of Advisors, Coll. of Eng and Math., Univ. of Vermont 2005–; Nat. Meetings Program Chair., Div. of Fuel Chem., ACS 2007; mem. Editorial Bd, Fuel Processing Technology 2002–, Environmental Engineering Science 2004–; mem. Connecticut Acad. of Science and Eng, AAAS (Roger Revelle Fellow 2004–05), ACS, American Inst. of Chemical Engineers, Combustion Inst., American Asscn Aerosol Research; Hon. Advisor Prof., Huazhong Univ. of Science and Tech., China 2004; AAAS Barnard Award 1994, NSF CAREER Award 1998, inaugural Environmental Leadership Faculty Award, Univ. of Connecticut 2005, R.A. Glenn Award, American Inst. of Chemical Engineers 1989, Gordon Prize, Nat. Acad. of Eng (co-recipient) 2014. *Publications:* more than 100 papers in professional journals on air pollution, aerosols, nanoscale ceramics and air quality; several US patents. *Address:* Thayer School of Engineering, Dartmouth College, 14 Engineering Drive, Hanover, NH 03755, USA (office). *Telephone:* (603) 646-2238 (office). *Fax:* (603) 646-3856 (office). *E-mail:* joseph.j.helble@dartmouth.edu (office). *Website:* engineering.dartmouth.edu (office).

HELD, Heinz Joachim, DrTheol; German theologian and fmr bishop; b. 16 May 1928, Wesseling/Rhein; s. of Heinrich Held and Hildegard Röhrig; m. Anneliese Novak 1959 (died 2002); one s. three d.; m. Barbara Mauritz 2003; ed Wuppertal, Göttingen, Heidelberg, Bonn and Austin, Tex.; Research Asst, Wuppertal Theological Seminary 1952, 1953–56; parish pastor, Friedrichsfeld/Niederrhein 1957–64; Prof. of Theology, Buenos Aires Lutheran Seminary 1964–68; Pres. River Plate Evangelical Church, Buenos Aires 1968–74; mem. Cen. Cttee World Council of Churches 1968–91, Moderator of Cen. Cttee and Exec. Cttee 1983–91; Pres. Dept of Ecumenical Relations and Ministries Abroad of the Evangelical Church in Germany 1975–93; Bishop 1991; Chair. Council of Christian Churches, FRG 1982–88, 1992–95; Hon. DrTheol (Lutheran Theological Univ., Budapest) 1985; Hon. DD (Acad. of Ecumenical Indian Theology and Church Admin., Chennai) 1988. *Publications include:* Matthew as Interpreter of the Miracle Stories 1960 (English trans. 1963), Von Nairobi nach Canberra.EKD und ÖRK im Dialog 1975–1991 1994/1996, Den Reichen wird das Evangelium gepredigt 1997, Ökumene im Kalten Krieg 2000, Der Ökumenische Rat der Kirchen im Visier der Kritik 2001, Einsichten und Ausblicke 2008. *Leisure interests:* stamp collecting, amateur music (piano), photography. *Address:* Bussilliatweg 32, 30419 Hanover, Germany (home). *Telephone:* (511) 2714308 (home). *E-mail:* heijo.held@htp-tel.de (home).

HELENIUS, Ari, PhD; Finnish biochemist and academic; *Professor Emeritus, Institute of Biochemistry, Eidgenössische Technische Hochschule Zürich;* b. 3 Sept. 1944, Oulu; ed Univ. of Helsinki; fmr Staff Scientist, European Lab. for Molecular Biology, Heidelberg, Germany, later Assoc. Prof.; Prof., Dept of Cell Biology, Yale Univ., New Haven, Conn., USA 1983–97 (Chair. Dept 1992–97); apptd Prof., Inst. of Biochemistry, ETH, Zürich, Switzerland 1997, now Prof. Emer.; mem. American Soc. for Cell Biology, Finnish Soc. of Sciences and Letters, European Molecular Biology Org.; Komppa Prize 1973, Ernst Prize for Medicine 2003, The Schleiden Medal in Cell Biology 2003, Marcel Benoist Prize 2007, Govt Medal 2007, Van Deenen Medal 2008, Otto Warburg Medal 2010, Loeffler Frog Medal 2016. *Publications include:* numerous publs in scientific journals on membrane biology, virology and protein chem. *Leisure interests:* literature, hiking. *Address:* Institute of Biochemistry, Department of Biology, ETH, MPM, E 14.2, Otto-Stern-Weg 3, 8093 Zürich, Switzerland (office). *Telephone:* (44) 6326817 (office). *Fax:* (44) 6321269 (office). *E-mail:* ari.helenius@bc.biol.ethz.ch (office). *Website:* www.bc.biol .ethz.ch (office).

HELETEY, Col Gen. Valeriy V.; Ukrainian police officer and government official; *Head of State Security Administration;* b. 28 Aug. 1967, Mukacheve Raion, Transcarpathian Oblast; ed Ukrainian Acad. of Internal Affairs (Higher Police Acad.), Kyiv; worked briefly as an electrical mechanic at a local truck co. 1985; drafted into army 1985, served as a border guard 1985–88; began career in the police, Ministry of Internal Affairs 1988, worked for HUBOZ (police dept specializing in the fight against organized crime) for the City of Kyiv 1994–2006; employed by Presidential Admin heading its service on issues of law enforcement agencies Oct. 2006; promoted to special rank of Maj. Gen. of Police Dec. 2006; Chief of State Security Admin (UDO) specializing in security of govt officials 2007–09, March–July 2014, Head of State Security Admin Oct. 2014–; mil. rank of Maj. Gen. June 2007, Lt-Gen. Aug. 2007, Col Gen. 2008; Minister of Defence July–Oct. 2014 (resgnd). *Address:* Ministry of Defence, 01021 Kyiv, vul. M. Hrushevskoho 30/1, Ukraine (office). *Telephone:* (44) 253-04-71 (office). *Fax:* (44) 226-20-15 (office). *E-mail:* admou@mil.gov.ua (office). *Website:* www.mil.gov.ua (office).

HELFT, Jorge Santiago; Argentine arts foundation director; b. 10 June 1934, France; s. of Jacques Helft and Marianne Loevi; m. Mariana Eppinger 1955; three s.; ed New York Univ. and Columbia Univ., USA; lived in Paris until 1940, New York 1940–47, Buenos Aires 1947–; business exec. with Continental Grain Co. 1956–74, Vesuvio SA 1974–82; Trustee and Dir Fundación Antorchas 1985–93, Fundación Lampadia, Vaduz, Liechtenstein; Pres. Fundación San Telmo 1980; Founding mem. and mem. Bd of Dirs Fundación Teatro Colón 1978; fmr mem. Int. Council of Museum of Modern Art; Oficial, Ordem de Rio Branco (Brazil). *Leisure interests:* arts and music. *Address:* Defensa 1364 (1143), Buenos Aires, Argentina (home).

HELINSKI, Donald Raymond, PhD, FAAS; American biologist and academic; *Professor Emeritus, Section of Molecular Biology, University of California, San Diego;* b. 7 July 1933, Baltimore, Md; s. of George L. Helinski and Marie M. Helinski; m. Patricia M. Doherty 1962; one s. one d.; ed Univ. of Maryland, Case Western Reserve Univ., Cleveland, Ohio, Stanford Univ.; US Public Health Service Postdoctoral Fellow, Stanford Univ., Calif. 1960–62; Asst Prof., Princeton Univ., New Jersey 1962–65; Assoc. Prof., Dept of Biology, Univ. of California, San Diego 1965–70, Prof. 1970 then Research Prof., Chair. Dept of Biology 1979–81, Dir Center for Molecular Genetics 1984–95, Assoc. Dean of Natural Sciences 1994–97, now Prof. Emer., Section of Molecular Biology; Public Health Service Predoctoral Fellow, Western Reserve Univ. 1957–59; Fellow, American Soc. of Microbiology; mem. NIH Advisory Cttee on DNA Recombinant Research 1975–78; mem. NAS, AAAS, American Acad. of Microbiology; Assoc. mem. European Molecular Biology Org. *Publications include:* more than 180 publs and 50 review articles in the fields of biochemistry, molecular genetics and microbiology. *Address:* Department of Biology, Division of Biological Sciences, University of California, San Diego, 9500 Gilman Drive, La Jolla, CA 92093-0322 (office); 8766 Dunaway Drive, La Jolla, CA 92037, USA (home). *Telephone:* (858) 534-3638 (office); (858) 453-2758 (home). *E-mail:* dhelsinki@ucsd.edu (office). *Website:* biology.ucsd.edu (office).

HELL, Stefan W., Dr rer. nat; German (b. Romanian) chemist and academic; *Director, Department of NanoBiophotonics, Max Planck Institute for Biophysical Chemistry;* b. 23 Dec. 1962, Arad, Romania; m. Anna Hell; two s.; ed Univ. of Heidelberg; worked at European Molecular Biology Lab., Heidelberg 1991–93; Sr Researcher, Univ. of Turku, Finland 1993–96; Visiting Scientist, Univ. of Oxford, UK 1994; apptd to Max Planck Inst. for Biophysical Chemistry, Göttingen 1997, Dir Dept of NanoBiophotonics 2002–; Dir High Resolution Optical Microscopy Research Group, German Cancer Research Centre; mem. German Nat. Acad. Leopoldina 2013; Hon. mem. Romanian Acad. 2012; several hon. doctorates; Prize of the Int. Comm. in Optics 2000, Carl Zeiss Research Award 2002, Innovation Award of the German Fed. Pres. 2006, Julius Springer Award for Applied Physics 2007, Leibniz Prize 2008, Lower Saxony State Award 2008, Otto-Hahn-Prize in Physics 2009, Ernst Hellmut Vits Prize 2010, Hansen Family Award 2011, Körber European Science Prize 2011, Gothenburg Lise Meitner Prize 2010–11, Meyenburg Prize 2011, Science Prize, Fritz Behrens Foundation 2012, Carus Medal of the Leopoldina 2013, Kavli Prize 2014, Nobel Prize in Chem. (co-recipient with Eric Betzig and William Moerner for the development of super-resolved fluorescence microscopy) 2014. *Publications:* more than 100 publs in refereed journals. *Address:* Department of NanoBiophotonics, Max Planck Institute for Biophysical Chemistry, Am Faßberg 11, 37077 Göttingen, Germany (office). *Telephone:* (551) 2012501 (office). *Fax:* (551) 2012505 (office). *E-mail:* shell@mpibpc.mpg.de (office); shell@gwdg.de (office). *Website:* www3.mpibpc.mpg.de/groups/hell (office).

HELLAWELL, Keith, QPM, LLB, MSc, LLD; British business executive and fmr police officer; b. 18 May 1942, Yorks.; s. of Douglas Hellawell and Ada Alice Hellawell; m. Brenda Hey 1963; one s. two d.; ed Kirkburton Secondary Modern School, Dewsbury Tech. Coll., Cranfield Inst. of Tech. and London Univ.; worked for five years as a miner before joining Huddersfield Borough Police; progressed within W Yorks. Police to Asst Chief Constable; Deputy Chief Constable of Humberside 1985–90, Chief Constable of Cleveland Police 1990–93, Chief Constable of W Yorks. Police 1993–98; first UK Anti-Drugs Co-ordinator 1998–2001; Adviser to Home Sec. on Int. Drug Issues 2001; Asscn of Police Officers Spokesman on Drugs; mem. Advisory Council on the Misuse of Drugs, Bd Community Action Trust; Chair. Catapult Presentations Ltd, Airshelter 2009; Chair. Goldshield Group PLC 2006–09, Dynamic Change 2006–10, Sports Direct Int. PLC 2009–18; mem. Bd of Dirs Universal Vehicles Group Ltd, Evans PLC 1998–99, Dalkia PLC 2006–09, Mortice PLC 2008–; fmr Trustee, Nat. Soc. for the Prevention of Cruelty to Children; mem. Editorial Advisory Bd Journal of Forensic Medicine; Dr hc (Leeds Metropolitan Univ.) 1997, (Huddersfield Univ.) 1998, Hon. LLD (Univ. of Bradford) 1998. *Publication:* The Outsider (autobiog.) 2002. *Leisure interests:* gardening, design, reading.

HELLBERG, Klaus; Finnish politician and business executive; b. 29 Aug. 1945, Porvoo; s. of Edvard Raul Hellberg and Karin Evi Wäyrynen; m. Kaaru Regina Hellberg; mem. Eduskunta (Finnish Parl.) for Uusimaa constituency (Suomen Sosialidemokraatinen Puolue/Finnish Social Democratic Party) 1995–2007; elected Chair. Supervisory Bd Neste Oil Oyj 2007; mem. Supervisory Bd Fortum Corpn; mem. Finnish Council for Environment and Natural Resources.

HELLER, Dean A., BBA; American stockbroker and politician; b. 10 May 1960, Castro Valley, Calif.; s. of Charles Alfred 'Jack' Heller and Janet Heller (née MacNelly); m. Lynne Heller; four c.; ed Carson High School, Univ. of Southern California; moved to Carson City, Nev. 1961; worked as stockbroker and broker/trader on Pacific Stock Exchange; moved back to Carson City; Chief Deputy Nev. State Treas. 1988–91; mem. Nev. State Ass. representing Carson City 1991–95; consultant, Bank of America 1990–95; Sec. of State of Nev. 1995–2007; mem. US House of Reps for 2nd Congressional Dist of Nev. 2007–11, mem. House Ways and Means Cttee, Vice-Chair. Western Caucus; apptd Senator from Nevada by Gov. Brian Sandoval to a vacant seat created by the resignation of John Ensign 2011–19; Founding Bd mem. Boys and Girls Club of Western Nevada, Western Nevada Community Coll. Foundation; Advisory Bd mem. Nevada's Foster Grandparent programme; Republican. *Address:* c/o United States Senate, Washington, DC 20510, USA (office). *Website:* www.deanheller.com.

HELLER, Jeffrey M. (Jeff), BBA; American information technology industry executive (retd); m. Carol Heller; one s. one d.; ed Univ. of Texas; served in US Marine Corps as jet pilot 1960–66, attained the rank of Capt.; joined Electronic Data Systems Corpn's Systems Eng Devt Program 1968, worked as systems engineer in medicare field in Pa, Calif., Ia, Ind., New York and Boston, worked on a New York Stock Exchange sales study 1970, man. of a regional data center, Dallas 1972, Regional Man. of Healthcare, eastern USA 1973–74, Corp. Vice-Pres. 1974–79, Head of Tech. Services 1979–84, led a project for General Motors, Detroit 1984–87, Sr Vice-Pres. 1987–96, Pres. and COO 1996–2000, Vice-Chair. 1996–2002, 2006–08, Pres. 2003–06; mem. Bd of Dirs Principal Solar, Inc. 2013–; fmr mem. Bd of Dirs Mutual of Omaha, Dallas Symphony Asscn, Trammell Crow Co., Cotton Bowl Athletic Asscn, Temple-Inland; Trustee, Southwestern Medical Foundation; mem. Men's Athletics Council, Univ. of Tex.; fmr mem. Chancellor's Council, Eng Foundation Advisory Council, McCombs School of Business Advisory Council, Devt Bd; mem. Longhorn Foundation.

HELLER, Margot, OBE; British gallery curator; *Director, South London Gallery;* Dir South London Gallery 2001–, five exhbns each year profile the work of est. int. figures, including Tom Friedman, Mark Dion, Rivane Neuenschwander, Alfredo Jaar and Superflex, as well as that by younger and mid-career British artists, including Eva Rothschild and Ryan Gander, gallery's live art and film programme has included presentations by Rachel Gomme, Nathaniel Mellors, Gail Pickering, OMSK and Gisele Vienne, and occasional large scale off-site projects have included those by On Kawara in Trafalgar Square 2004 and Chris Burden at Chelsea Coll. of Art Parade Ground 2006, presented Omer Fast, Ryan Gander, Tatiana Trouvé and Alfredo Jaar 2010, Julia Crabtree and William Evans 2014. *Publications include:* Incommunicado (with Tom McCarthy). *Address:* South London Gallery, 65 Peckham Road, Camberwell, London, SE5 8UH, England (office). *Telephone:* (20) 7703-6120 (office). *E-mail:* mail@southlondongallery.org (office). *Website:* www .southlondongallery.org (office).

HELLER, Michał Kazimierz, PhD; Polish professor of philosophy of science and ecclesiastic; b. 12 March 1936, Tarnów; ed Inst. of Theology, Tarnów, Catholic Univ. of Lublin; ordained priest 1959; Catholic Univ. of Lublin, Pontifical Acad. of Theology, Kraków, Extraordinary Prof. 1985, Ordinary Prof. 1990, Prof. of Cosmology and Philosophy of Science; Jt mem. Vatican Astronomical Observatory; Rector Inst. of Theology, Tarnów; Ordinary mem. Pontifical Acad. of Sciences, Rome 1991; mem. Petersburg Acad. of Sciences 1997, Int. Astronomical Union, Int. Soc. for General Relativity and Gravitation, European Physical Soc., Int. Soc. of the Study of Time, Polish Physical Soc., Polish Astronomical Soc., Science Soc. of Catholic Univ. of Lublin; Dr hc (Acad. of Mining and Metallurgy, Kraków) 1996; Templeton Prize 2008. *Publications include:* The Singular Universe – An Introduction to the Classical Singularity Theory 1991, Theoretical Foundations of Cosmology – Introduction to the Global Structure of Space-Time 1992, Physics of Space-Time and Motion 1993, The New Physics and a New Theology 1996, To Catch Passing Away 1997, Quantum Cosmology 2001, The Beginning is Everywhere 2002, and over 600 publs on relativistic physics, cosmology, history and philosophy of science and relations between science and theology and articles in journals.

HELLMAN, Martin Edward, BE, MS, PhD; American electrical engineer, cryptologist and academic; *Professor Emeritus of Electrical Engineering, Stanford University;* b. 2 Oct. 1945, New York, NY; m. Dorothie Hellman; ed Bronx High School of Science, New York Univ., Stanford Univ.; mem. staff, IBM Watson Research Center 1968–69; Asst Prof. of Electrical Eng, MIT 1969–71; Asst Prof. of Electrical Eng, Stanford Univ. 1971–75, Assoc. Prof. of Electrical Eng 1975–79, Prof. of Electrical Eng 1979–96, Prof. Emer. 1996–, Assoc. Dept Chair. 1978–80, Dir Information Systems Lab. 1988–89, Acting Assoc. Dean of Grad. Studies (Minority Student Affairs) 1989–90, Assoc. Dept Chair. for Grad. Admissions 1989–90; mem. Nat. Acad. of Eng 2002; Fellow, IEEE 1980, Int. Eng Consortium 1998, Int. Asscn for Cryptologic Research 2006, Computer History Museum 2011; Arnold Award, New York Univ. 1966, NSF Grad. Fellow 1966–68, First Prize, New York Section, Second Prize, Region 1, IEEE Student Paper Contest 1966, Calif. State Psychological Asscn Award for Distinguished Contribs to Consumer Protection 1978, IEEE Information Theory Group Award for Best Paper Published in the Preceding Two Years (New Directions in Cryptography, with Whitfield Diffie) 1978, IEEE Donald G. Fink Award 1981, IEEE Centennial Medal 1984, Stanford Univ. Tau Beta Pi Award for Undergraduate Teaching 1987, Outstanding Prof. Award, Stanford Soc. of Black Scientists and Engineers 1987, Outstanding Prof. Award, Stanford Soc. of Chicano and Latino Engineers and Scientists 1989, Outstanding Prof. Award, Stanford Soc. of Black Scientists and Engineers 1989, Pioneer Award, Electronic Frontier Foundation 1994, Security Award, Nat. Computer Systems 1996, Louis E. Levy Medal, The Franklin Inst. 1997, Kanellakis Award, Asscn for Computing Machinery (ACM) 1997, Golden Jubilee Award, IEEE Information Theory Soc. 1998, IEEE Kobayashi Computers and Communications Award 1999, Marconi Int. Fellow Award 2000, IEEE Richard W. Hamming Medal 2010, inducted into Nat. Inventors Hall of Fame 2011, RSA Lifetime Achievement Award 2012, inducted into Nat. Acad. of Inventors Hall of Fame 2012, Nat. Cyber Security Hall of Fame 2012, Stanford Eng Hero 2012, inducted into Information Systems Security Asscn Hall of Fame 2013, Silicon Valley Hall of Fame 2013, A.M. Turing Award, Asscn for Computing Machinery (with Whitfeld Diffie) 2015. *Achievements include:* collaborated with Whitfiled Diffie and Ralph Merkle, introduced radically new method of distributing cryptographic keys (Diffie–Hellman key exchange) 1976. *Publications include:* Breakthrough: Emerging New Thinking (with Anatoly Gromyko; published in Russian and English) 1987, A New Map for Relationships: Creating True Love at Home & Peace on the Planet (with his wife) 2016; more than 70 papers in professional journals; 12 US patents. *Leisure interests:* soaring, speed skating, hiking. *Address:* Department of Electrical Engineering, Stanford University, David Packard Building, 350 Serra Mall, Mail Code: 9505, Stanford, CA 94305-9505, USA (office). *Telephone:* (650) 723-3931 (office). *Fax:* (650) 723-1882 (office). *E-mail:* martydevoe@gmail.com (office). *Website:* www-ee.stanford.edu/~hellman (office).

HELLMAN, Peter S., MBA, BEcons; American business executive; b. 16 Oct. 1949, Cleveland, Ohio; s. of Arthur Cerf Hellman and Joan Alburn; m. Alyson Dulin Ware 1976; one s. one d.; ed Hobart Coll. and Case Western Reserve Univ.; with The Irving Trust Co., New York 1972–79; Financial Planning Assoc., BP America 1979–82, Man. Financial Planning 1982–84, Dir, Operations Analysis 1984–85, Asst Treas. 1985–86, Corp. Treas. 1986–89; Vice-Pres. and Treas. TRW Inc. 1989–91, Exec. Vice-Pres. and Chief Financial Officer 1991–94, Exec. Vice-Pres. and Asst Pres. 1994–95, Pres. and COO 1995–2000; Exec. Vice-Pres. and Chief Financial Officer Nordson Corpn, Ohio 2000–04, Pres. and Chief Financial and Admin. Officer 2004–08; mem. Bd of Dirs Qwest Communications 2000–, Baxter Int. 2005–, Owens-Illinois Inc. 2007–, Goodyear Tire and Rubber Co. 2010–, Nordson Corpn 2001–08; mem. Cleveland Clinic Foundation Urological Inst. Advisory Cttee; Trustee, Baxter Int., Case Western Reserve Univ., Lifebank Lorain Co. Community Coll. Foundation, Western Reserve Acad. *Address:* c/o Board of Directors, Baxter International, One Baxter Parkway, Deerfield, IL 60015-4625, USA.

HELLSTRÖM, Mats, MA; Swedish politician and diplomatist; b. 12 Jan. 1942, Stockholm; m. Elisabeth Hellström; two c.; ed Univ. of Stockholm; Lecturer in Econs, Univ. of Stockholm 1965–69; mem. Parl. 1968, 1969–96, mem. Exec. Cttee Social Democratic Party Youth League 1969–72; mem. Bd Social Democratic Party 1969–96; Special Adviser, Ministry of Labour 1973–76; Minister of Foreign Trade at Ministry of Foreign Affairs 1983–86; Minister of Agric. 1986–91, for Foreign Trade and European Union Affairs 1994–96; Amb. to Germany 1996–2001; Gov. Stockholm Co. 2002–06; Chair. Nordic Folk High School Biskops-Arnö; mem. High Level Advisory Group of Global Subsidies Initiative 2005–, Advisory Bd Globe Forum 2008–; Sr Advisor, Plantagon 2009–, Magnusson (Baltic Sea region law firm) 2010–, GAIA Leadership 2010–. *Publications include:* A Seamless Globe? A Personal Story of the Uruguay Round in GATT 1999, Östersjömat 2005. *Address:* Nytorgsgatan 19A, 116 22 Stockholm, Sweden (home). *Telephone:* (70) 610-41-43 (office); (8) 640-80-50 (home). *E-mail:* mats.hellstrom@bfrex.se (office).

HELLYER, Hon. Paul Theodore, PC, BA; Canadian politician; b. 6 Aug. 1923, Waterford, Ont.; s. of Audrey S. Hellyer and Lulla M. Anderson; m. 1st Ellen Jean Ralph (died 2004); two s. one d.; m. 2nd Sandra Bussiere (née Meades) 2005; ed Waterford High School, Curtiss Wright Tech. Inst., California and Univ. of Toronto; Fleet Aircraft Manufacturing Co., Fort Erie 1942–44; RCAF 1944–45; Owner, Mari-Jane Fashions, Toronto 1945–56; Treas. Curran Hall Ltd 1950, Pres. 1951–62; Pres. Trepil Realty Ltd 1951–62; Pres. Hendon Estates Ltd 1959–62; mem. House of Commons 1949–57, 1958–74, Parl. Asst to Minister of Nat. Defence 1956–57, Assoc. Minister April–June 1957, Minister of Nat. Defence 1963–67, of Transport 1967–69, responsible for Central Mortgage and Housing Corpn 1968–69; Chair. Task Force on Housing and Urban Devt 1968; Acting Prime Minister 1968–69; joined Progressive Conservative Party July 1972; rejoined Liberal Party 1982; Leader Canadian Action Party 1997–2004; Opposition Spokesman on Industry, Trade and Commerce 1973; Distinguished Visitor, Faculty of Environmental Studies, York Univ. 1969–70; Founding Chair. Action Canada 1971; syndicated columnist, Toronto Sun 1974–84; Exec. Dir Canada UNI Asscn 1991–95; Fellow, Royal Soc. for Encouragement of the Arts. *Publications:* Agenda – A Plan for Action 1971, Exit Inflation 1981, Jobs For All – Capitalism on Trial 1984, Canada at the Crossroads 1990, Damn the Torpedos 1990, Funny Money – A Common Sense Alternative to Mainline Economics 1994, Surviving the Global Financial Crisis – The Economics of Hope for Generation X 1996, Arundel Lodge – A Little Bit of Old Muskoka 1996, The Evil Empire: Globalization's Darker Side 1997, Stop – Think 1999, Goodbye Canada 2001, One Big Party – To Keep Canada Independent 2003. *Leisure interests:* swimming, skin and scuba diving, stamp collecting. *Address:* Suite 506, 65 Harbour Square, Toronto, ON M5J 2L4, Canada (home). *Telephone:* (416) 850-1375 (office); (416) 366-4092 (home). *Fax:* (416) 850-1486 (office). *E-mail:* phellyer@sympatico.ca (office). *Website:* www .paulhellyerweb.com.

HELME, Mart; Estonian diplomatist and politician; *Minister of the Interior;* b. 31 Oct. 1949, Parnu; m. 1st Sirje Helmega Helme (divorced); one s. two d.; m. 2nd Helle-Monika Helme; two c.; ed Tartu Univ.; with Eesti Raamat Publishing House 1973–75; reporter Harju Elu (newspaper) 1975–77; Sr Ed. Literature section Pioneer magazine 1977–86; farmer 1986–89; publisher 1989–91; Acting Dir Union of Publishers of Estonia, political observer Paeveleht (daily) 1991–93; Head, Fourth Bureau (Asia, Africa, S America) Political Dept, Ministry of Foreign Affairs Feb.–May 1994; Head of Third Bureau (Russia, CIS, E and Cen. Europe) Political Dept, Ministry of Foreign Affairs 1994–95; Amb. to Russian Fed. 1995–2000; apptd Vice-Chancellor Ministry of Foreign Affairs 1999; fmr Counsellor to Minister of Agric.; Minister of the Interior 2019–; fmr Dir Research Center Free Europe; Chair. Nat. Conservative Party-Farmers' Ass.; cand. for People's Union in elections for European Parl. 2004; Adviser to Tunne Kelam 2005–09; Chair. Estonian Conservative People's Party (Eesti Konservatiivseks Rahvaerakonnaks) 2013–; cand. in presidential election 2016; Lecturer, International University Audentes (now merged with Tallinn School of Econs and Business Admin) 2001–. *Publications include:* Two Swords: a collection of Chinese stories 2009, Lembitu: Estonians' Uncrowned King 2010. *Address:* Ministry of the Interior, Pikk 61, Tallinn 15065 (office); Estonian Conservative People's Party (Eesti Konservatiivseks Rahvaerakonnaks), Pärnu mnt. 30–5, Tallinn 10141, Estonia (office). *Telephone:* 612-5008 (ministry) (office); 616-1790 (office). *Fax:* 616-1791 (office). *E-mail:* info@siseministeerium.ee (ministry) (office); erl@erl.ee (office). *Website:* www.siseministeerium.ee (ministry) (office).

HELØE, Leif Arne; Norwegian dentist and fmr politician; *Senior Researcher, Norwegian Institute for Urban and Regional Research;* b. 8 Aug. 1932, Harstad; m. Berit Heløe; two s. one d.; ed Univ. of Oslo; school and dist dentist, Harstad region 1957; Prof. of Community Dentistry, Univ. of Oslo 1975; mem. Harstad City Council 1960–69, mem. Municipal Exec. Bd 1968–69, Mayor of Harstad 1968–69; proxy mem. Storting (Parl.) 1965–73; Minister of Health and Social Affairs 1981–86; Dir-Gen. Norwegian Research Council for Science and Humanities 1988–91; Co-Gov. of Troms 1991–2000; Prof. (part-time), Norwegian Inst. for Urban and Regional Research 2000, Sr Researcher 2013–; Commdr, Order of the Finnish Lion 1996, Order of St Olav 2014; Hon. Dr of Dentistry (Kupio) 1982, (Lund) 1984. *Address:* Rosenborggaten 5, 0356 Oslo, Norway (home). *Telephone:* 22-95-89-64 (office); 23-36-75-99 (home). *Fax:* 22-60-77-74 (office). *E-mail:* leif .heloe@nibr.no (office); arn-helo@online.no.

HELTAU, Michael; Austrian actor and singer; *Kammerschauspieler, Burgtheater, Vienna;* b. 5 July 1933, Ingolstadt; s. of Georg Heltau and Jakobine Heltau; ed gymnasium and Reinhardt Seminar; appeared at Würzburg and Bayerische Staatstheater, Munich 1953, Schillertheater, Berlin and Hamburg Schauspielhaus 1964–68, Theater in der Josefstadt, Vienna 1957–69, Volkstheater, Vienna 1970, Salzburg Festival 1965–75, Théâtre du Châtelet, Paris 1986; Kammerschauspieler, Burgtheater, Vienna 1972–, Doyen of the Burgtheater; noted for appearances in Shakespearean roles including Hamlet, Romeo, Richard II, Henry VI, Schnitzler's Anatol, von Hofmannsthal's Der Schwierige, Schiller's Wallenstein, etc.; second career as singer, especially songs of Jacques Brel (in German) and Viennese songs; numerous one-man shows on stage and TV; Hon. mem. Vienna Burgtheater 2003, Vienna Volksoper 2004; Austrian Cross of Honour (First Class) for Science and Art, Order of Merit (Germany) 2006; Karl Skraup Prize, Kainz Medal/Goldener Rathausmann, Gold Award of City of Vienna Nestroy Life Achievement Award 2005. *Films include:* Verlobung Am Wolfgangsee 1956, Der Letzte Mann 1956, Die Liebe Familie 1957, Lemkes Sel. Witwe 1957, Wiener Luft 1958, Das Weite Land 1970, Reigen 1974. *Publication:* Auf d'Nacht Herr Direktor! Momente aus dem Milieu (co-author) 2012. *Leisure interests:* reading, swimming. *Address:* Sulzweg 11, 1190 Vienna, Austria.

HELY-HUTCHINSON, Timothy Mark, MA; British publisher; *Group Chief Executive, Hachette UK;* b. 26 Oct. 1953, London; s. of Earl of Donoughmore and Countess of Donoughmore (née Parsons); ed Eton Coll., Univ. of Oxford; Man. Dir Macdonald & Co. Ltd (publrs) 1982–86, Headline Book Publishing PLC (Founder) 1986–93, Group Chief Exec. Hodder Headline Ltd 1993–, Dir W. H. Smith PLC 1999–, Chair. W. H. Smith News Ltd 2002–04, Group Chief Exec. Hachette Livre UK Ltd 2004–, mem. International Bd Hachette Livre and Dir Hachette Book Group USA; Venturer of the Year (British Venture Capital Asscn) 1990, Publr of the Year (British Book Awards) 1992. *Leisure interests:* opera, racing, bridge. *Address:* Hachette UK, 338 Euston Road, London, NW1 3BH, England (office). *Telephone:* (20) 7873-6011 (office). *Fax:* (20) 7873-6012 (office). *Website:* www .hachette.co.uk (office).

HEMINGER, Gary R., BA, MBA; American oil company executive; *Chairman, President and CEO, Marathon Petroleum Corporation;* ed Tiffin Univ., Univ. of Dayton, Ohio, Wharton School Advanced Man. Program, Univ. of Pennsylvania; joined Marathon Petroleum 1975, spent five years in various financial and admin. roles, three years in London, UK as Audit Supervisor of the Brae Project, Pres. Marathon Pipe Line Co. 1995–96, Man., Business Devt and Jt Interest, Marathon Oil Co. 1996–98, Vice-Pres. Business Marathon Ashland Petroleum LLC (Marathon Petroleum Co. LLC from 2005, Marathon Petroleum Co. LP from 2010) 1998–99, Sr Vice-Pres., Business Devt 1999–2001, Exec. Vice-Pres., Supply, Transportation and Marketing 2001, Pres. Marathon Petroleum Co. LLC (Marathon Petroleum Co. LP from 2010, wholly owned subsidiary of Marathon) and Exec. Vice-Pres., Downstream, Marathon Oil Corpn 2001–11, mem. Exec. Cttee, Pres. and CEO 2011–, Chair. 2016–; Chair. and CEO MPLX GP LLC (Gen. Partner of MPLX LP) 2012–; worked with Emro Marketing for eight years in several marketing and commercial roles, Vice-Pres. Western Div. Emro Marketing (Speedway SuperAmerica LLC) 1991; Chair. Bd of Trustees, Tiffin Univ.; Past Chair. American Petroleum Inst. Downstream Cttee, Louisiana Offshore Oil Port; mem. Bd of Dirs Fifth Third Bancorp; mem. Bd of Dirs and Exec. Cttee Nat. Petrochemical and Refiners Asscn; mem. Oxford Inst. for Energy Studies, US-

Saudi Arabian Business Council Exec. Cttee. *Address:* Marathon Petroleum Corporation, Corporate Headquarters, 539 South Main Street, Findlay, OH 45840, USA (office). *Telephone:* (419) 422-2121 (office). *Fax:* (419) 425-7040 (office). *E-mail:* info@marathonpetroleum.com (office). *Website:* www.marathonpetroleum.com (office).

HEMINGFORD, 3rd Baron of Watford in the County of Hertford (cr. 1943); **(Dennis) Nicholas Hemingford,** (Nicholas Herbert), MA, FRSA; British fmr journalist; b. (Dennis Nicholas Herbert), 25 July 1934, Watford, Herts., England; s. of Dennis George Ruddock Herbert, 2nd Baron Hemingford and Elizabeth McClare (née Clark); m. Jennifer Mary Toresen Bailey 1958; one s. three d.; ed Oundle School, Clare Coll., Cambridge; Sports Desk, Reuters 1956–57, Diplomatic Desk 1957–60, Washington, DC Bureau 1960–61; Asst Washington Corresp., The Times 1961–65, Middle East Corresp. 1965–69, Deputy Features Ed. 1969–70; Ed. Cambridge Evening News 1970–74; Editorial Dir Westminster Press 1974–91, Deputy Chief Exec. 1991–95; Pres. Guild of British Newspaper Eds 1980–81, Media Soc. 1982–84; Hon. Sec. Asscn of British Eds 1985–95; mem. E Anglian Regional Cttee, Nat. Trust 1983–2000, Chair. 1990–2000; Gov. Bell Educational Trust 1985–90; mem. Council Europa Nostra 1999–2005, Culture Cttee, UK Comm., UNESCO 1999–2003; Pres. Huntingdonshire Family History Soc.; mem. Council Friends of the British Library 2005–11, 2013–; Hon. mem. Soc. of Eds 1999; Hon. Sr mem. Wolfson Coll., Cambridge; Liveryman, Grocers' Co.; Jt Self-Publisher of the Year Award, Self-Publishing Awards 2010. *Publications:* Jews and Arabs in Conflict 1969, Press Freedom in Britain (with David Flintham) 1991, Successive Journeys (First Prize for Non-Fiction, Nat. Self-Publishing Awards 2010) 2008. *Leisure interests:* Egyptian War 1882, family history, computers, sport. *Address:* The Coach House, 4 Common Lane, Hemingford Abbots, Huntingdon, Cambs., PE28 9AN, England (home). *Telephone:* (1480) 466234 (home). *Website:* nicholas-herbert.co.uk (home).

HEMINGWAY, Wayne, MBE, BSc, FRSA; British designer; *Partner, Hemingway Design;* b. 19 Jan. 1961, Morecambe, Lancs., England; s. of Billy Two Rivers (Mohawk Indian chief) and Maureen Hemingway; m. Gerardine Hemingway; two s. two d.; ed Univ. Coll., London; together with wife started in business with market stall in Camden, London; cr. footwear, clothing and accessory label Red or Dead 1992 (now non-exec. Chair.); collection retailed through eight Red or Dead shops in UK and three Red or Dead shops in Japan and wholesaled to int. network of retailers; jt venture with Pentland Group PLC 1996–; Founder and Partner, hemingwaydesign 1999–; designed new wing for Inst. of Dirs 2001; current design and consultancy projects include an award-winning 800-unit housing estate, urban design, student accommodation, regeneration, branding, marketing design, interiors, product design; Trustee, Design Council; Fellow, Blackburn Coll.; Hon. Prof., Univ. of Northumbria, Univ. of Wolverhampton, Lancaster Univ., Leeds Met Univ.; Hon. MA (Surrey); Dr hc (Wolverhampton), (Stafford); Street Designers of the Year, British Fashion Awards 1996, 1997, 1998, Housing Development of the Year 2005, Hero to Animals Award 2010, various regeneration and design awards. *Television:* appeared in various TV programmes, including The Art Show (Channel 4), The Noughties… Was That It? 2009, Late Review 2010, Newsnight, Question Time etc. *Publications:* Red or Dead: The Good, the Bad and the Ugly (with Gerardine Hemingway) 1998, Kitsch Icons 1999, Just Above the Mantelpiece 2000, Mass Market Classics The Home 2003, Vintage Fashion Bible 2015; articles in newspapers and journals. *Address:* Hemingway Design, 15 Wembley Park Drive, Wembley, Middx, HA9 8HD, England (office). *Telephone:* (20) 8903-1074 (office). *E-mail:* wayne@hemingwaydesign.co.uk (office). *Website:* www.houseofhemingway.co.uk (office).

HEMMING, John Henry, CMG, MA, DLitt, FSA; British/Canadian writer and publisher; b. 5 Jan. 1935, Vancouver, BC; s. of H. Harold Hemming, OBE, MC and Alice L. Hemming, OBE; m. Sukie Babington-Smith 1979; one s. one d.; ed Eton Coll., UK, McGill Univ. and Univ. of Oxford, UK; Dir and Sec. Royal Geographical Soc. 1975–96; Jt Chair. Hemming Group Ltd 1976–2015; Chair. Brintex Ltd, Newman Books Ltd; explorations in Peru and Brazil 1960, 1961, 1971, 1972, 1986–88, led Maracá Rainforest Project, Brazil (largest ever Amazon research programme by a European country) 1987–88; Hon. Fellow, Magdalen Coll. Oxford 2004; Commdr, Order of Southern Cross (Brazil) 1998, Grand Cross, Order of Merit (Peru) 2007; Hon. DLitt (Oxford) 1981, Dr hc (Warwick) 1989, (Stirling) 1991; Pitman Literary Prize 1970, Christopher Award (USA) 1971, Founder's Medal, Royal Geographical Soc. 1989, Bradford Washburn Medal, Boston Museum of Science 1989, Mungo Park Medal, Royal Scottish Geographical Soc. 1988, Special Award, Instituto Nacional de Cultura (Peru) 1996, Citation of Merit, Explorers' Club (New York) 1997. *Publications:* The Conquest of the Incas 1970, Tribes of the Amazon Basin in Brazil (with others) 1973, Red Gold: The Conquest of the Brazilian Indians 1978, The Search for El Dorado 1978, Machu Picchu 1982, Monuments of the Incas 1983, Change in the Amazon Basin (two vols) (ed.) 1985, Amazon Frontier: The Defeat of the Brazilian Indians 1987, Maracá 1988, Roraima, Brazil's Northernmost Frontier 1990, The Rainforest Edge (ed.) 1993, Royal Geographical Society Illustrated (ed.) 1997, The Golden Age of Discovery 1998, Die If You Must: Brazilian Indians in the Twentieth Century 2003, Tree of Rivers: The Story of the Amazon 2007, Naturalists in Paradise: Wallace, Bates and Spruce in the Amazon 2015. *Leisure interests:* travel, writing. *Address:* 10 Edwardes Square, London, W8 6HE (home). *Telephone:* (20) 7602-6697 (home).

HEMMINGSEN, Ralf, MD, DrMed; Danish psychiatrist, academic and university rector; b. 12 Oct. 1949; ed Univ. of Copenhagen; research training and clinical training as consultant in psychiatry 1975–76; Sr Lecturer in Psychiatry, Univ. of Copenhagen 1978–80, 1984–95, Prof. of Psychiatry 1995–, Dean of Faculty of Health Sciences 2002–05, Rector Univ. of Copenhagen 2005–17, Chair. Faculty Jt Cttee 2002–05, Faculty Occupational Health Cttee 2002–05, Man. Forum, Copenhagen Univ. Hosp. (KUHL) 2002–05, Copenhagen Tech Transfer Consortium 2003–05, mem. Main Jt Cttee 2002–05, Steering Group for Univ. of Copenhagen's Value Process 2003–05, Human Resources Policy Cttee 2004–05; Consultant in Psychiatry, Frederiksberg Hosp. 1986; Medical Dir Bispebjerg Hosp. 1986–2002; Chair. Danish Soc. for Biological Psychiatry 1997–2000; mem. Danish Medicolegal Council 1992–; mem. Bd The Medical Soc. in Copenhagen 1991–97; mem. Danish Psychiatric Soc. (Chair. 1986–90); mem. European Soc. for Clinical Investigation (Pres. 1983–87); Kt of the Dannebrog 2007; Gold Medal, Univ. of Copenhagen. *Publications:* more than 150 papers in scientific journals. *Address:* Department of Clinical Medicine, University of Copenhagen, Region Hovedstadens Psykiatri, Edel Sauntes Allé 10, 2100 Copenhagen Ø, Denmark (office). *Telephone:* 38-64-73-00 (office). *E-mail:* (office). *Website:* www.ku.dkcuris.ku.dk (office).

HEMSLEY, Stephen J.; American business executive; *CEO, UnitedHealth Group;* ed Fordham Univ.; fmr Man. Partner, Chief Financial Officer and Head of Strategy, Tech., and Operating Professional Service Lines, Arthur Andersen and Co.; Sr Exec. Vice-Pres. UnitedHealth Group 1997–98, COO 1998–2006, Pres. 1999–2014, mem. Bd of Dirs 2000–, CEO 2006–. *Address:* UnitedHealth Group, PO Box 1459, Minneapolis, MN 55440-1459, USA (office). *Telephone:* (952) 936-1300 (office). *E-mail:* info@unitedhealthgroup.com (office). *Website:* www.unitedhealthgroup.com (office).

HEN, Józef, (Korab); Polish writer and playwright; b. (Józef Henryk Cukier), 8 Nov. 1923, Warsaw; s. of Rubin Cukier and Ewa Cukier; m. Irena Hen 1946; one s. one d.; Lecturer, Univ. of Paris (Sorbonne), France 1993, Univ. of Warsaw 1995–96; mem. Acad. des Sciences, Belles Lettres et des Beaux Arts, Bordeaux, France; mem. Polish PEN Club; Order of Merit of the Republic of Poland, 2nd class; Great Literary Prize of Warsaw, Pen Club Award. *Film screenplays include:* Krzyż walecznych (Cross of Valour) 1959, Kwiecień (April) 1961, Nikt nie woła (Nobody's Calling) 1961, Bokser i śmierć (The Boxer and Death), Prawo i pięść (Law and the Fist) and Don Gabriel. *Screenplays for TV serials:* Zycie Kamila Kuranta (The Life of Kamil Kurant) 1983, Crimen and Królewskie Sny (Royal Dreams) 1987. *Theatre plays:* Ja, Michał z Montaigne (I, Michel de Montaigne) 1984, Justyn! Justyn!, Popołudnie kochanków (Lovers' Afternoon) 1994. *Publications include:* Skromny chłopiec w haremie (A Modest Boy in a Harem) 1957, Kwiecień (April) 1960 (Book of the Year 1961), Teatr Heroda (Herod's Theatre) 1966, Twarz pokerzysty (Pokerface) 1970, Oko Dajana (Dayan's Eye, as Korab) 1972, Yokohama 1973, Crimen 1975, Bokser i śmierć (The Boxer and Death) 1975, Ja, Michał z Montaigne (I, Michel de Montaigne) 1978, Milczące między nami (Silent between Us) 1985, Nie boję się bezsennych nocy (I'm Not Afraid of Sleepless Nights), 3 books 1987, 1992, 2001, Królenskie sny (Royal Dreams) 1989, Nikt nie woła (Nobody's Calling) 1990, Nowolipie 1991, Odejście Afrodyty (Aphrodite's Departure) 1995, Najpiękniejsze lata (The Most Beautiful Years) 1996, Niebo naszych ojcow (Sky of Our Fathers 1997, Błazen – wielki mąż (Jester – The Great Man) (ZAiKS Book of the Year Award 1999) 1998, Mój Przyjaciel Król (My Friend the King) (Booker's Club Book of the Year Award 2005) 2003, Bruliony profesora T. (The Bloch-notes of Professor T.) 2006, Ping-pomgista (The Ping-pongist) 2008, Dziennik na nowy wiek (A Diary for the New Age) 2009, Szóste, najmlodsze (The Sixth, The Youngest) 2012, Dziennika Ciąg Dalszy (Journal, Continued) 2014, Powrót Do Bezsennych Nocy (Return to Sleepless Nights) 2016. *Leisure interests:* historical and literary monographs, watching sports programmes on television, films.

HENARE, Tau; New Zealand politician (retd); b. 29 Sept. 1960, Auckland; m. Ngaire Elisabeth Brown 2012; five c.; ed Hillary Coll.; Advisory Officer in Maori Devt, Waitakere City Council 1988–90; Youth Educ. Co-ordinator, Race Relations Conciliator, Advisory Officer, Dept of Internal Affairs 1990–94; MP for Northern Maori (now Te Tai Tokerau) 1993–99, 2005–14; Minister of Maori Affairs 1997–99, for Racing, Assoc. Minister for Sport, Fitness and Leisure; New Zealand First Party 1993–98, Deputy Leader, Spokesperson on Cultural Affairs and Treaty of Waitangi Negotiations; mem. Bd of Dirs Te Pataka Ohanga Ltd 2004–05; Host, Newstalk ZB; mem. Clerical Workers' Union 1984–88.

HENAULT, Gen. (retd) Raymond (Ray) Roland, CD, BA, LLD, MSc; Canadian business executive and fmr armed forces officer; *Chairman of the Advisory Council and Chief Strategic Advisor, ADGA Group Consultants Inc.;* b. 26 April 1949, Winnipeg, Manitoba; s. of Roland Henault and Sylvia Henault; m. Loraine Anne Henault; ed Univ. of Man., Nat. Defence Coll., Kingston, Ontario, École Supérieure de Guerre Aérienne, Paris, France; began career in Canadian Armed Forces 1968; training at Canadian Force Base (CFB) Borden, Ontario and Gimili, Man.; CF-101 Voodoo Pilot, 425 Squadron, CFB Bagotville, Québec 1971; Flying Instructor, Musketeer, CFB Portage la Prairie 1972–74; Air Traffic Controller, CFB Bagotville 1974–76; Twin Huey Helicopter Pilot, 408 Squadron, CFB Edmonton, Alberta 1976–80; Staff Officer Aviation, 5 Canadian Brigade Group HQ, CFB Valcartier 1980–81; Twin Huey Flight Commdr, 430e Escardon, CFB Valcartier 1981–83; Ecole supérieure de Guerre aérienne, Paris, France, 1983–85; Head of Doctrine and Int. Programs, Directorate of Land Aviation, Nat. Defence HQ, Ottawa 1985; Project Dir Canadian Forces Light Helicopter Project, Ottawa 1985–87; Commdg Officer 444(CA) Tactical Helicopter Squadron, CFB Lahr, Germany 1987–89; Sr Staff Officer Requirements, Air Command HQ, Winnipeg 1989–90; Base Commdr, CFB Portage la Prairie 1990–92; Deputy Commdr 10 Tactical Air Group, CFB Montreal 1992–93, Commdr 1994–95; Chief of Staff Operations, Air Command HQ 1995–96; Chief of Staff J3 and Dir-Gen. Mil. Plans and Operations, Nat. Defence HQ 1996–97; Acting Deputy Chief of Defence Staff 1997, Asst Chief of Air Staff 1997–98, Deputy Chief of Defence Staff 1998–2001, Chief of Defence Staff 2001–05; Chair. Mil. Cttee NATO 2005–08 (retd); promoted to Brigadier-Gen. 1994, Maj.-Gen. 1997, Lt-Gen. 1998, Gen. 2001; Chair. Advisory Council and Chief Strategic Advisor, ADGA Group Consultants Inc. 2008–; Pres. Canadian Defence Asscns Inst.; mem. Minister's Advisory Panel, Canadian Defence Policy Review 2016–17; Hon. Prof., Univ. of Pécs, Hungary; Commdr Order of Mil. Merit, Canadian Meritorious Service Cross, Commdr Légion d'honneur, Most Venerable Order of St John of Jerusalem, US Legion of Merit, Czech Cross of Merit, NATO Meritorious Service Medal, Ukrainian Medal of Honour, Commdr's Cross, Hungarian Order of Merit, Commdr, Belgian Order of the Grand Croix; Hon. LLD (Univ. of Man.), Hon. PhD (Royal Military Coll. of Canada) 2005. *Leisure interests:* flying private aircraft, golf. *Address:* ADGA Group Consultants Inc., 110 Argyle Avenue, Ottawa, ON K2P 1B4, Canada (office). *Telephone:* (613) 237-2930 (office). *Fax:* (613) 237-5359 (office). *E-mail:* rhenault@adga.ca (office). *Website:* www.adga.ca (office).

HENDE, Csaba, PhD; Hungarian lawyer and politician; b. 5 Feb. 1960, Szombathely; m.; twin d.; ed Nagy Lajos Secondary Grammar School, Szombathely, Eötvös Loránd Univ.; worked as attorney trainee at Attorneys' Asscn, Szombathely 1984–91; Parl. Sec., Head of Legal Dept and Cabinet Sec., Ministry of Defence 1991–94; worked as attorney in Szombathely 1994–98; mem. Gen. Ass. of Szombathely 1990; mem. Parl. (Magyar Demokrata Fórum—MDF) 1993–96, (Country List) 2002–06, for Vas Co. 2006–; Political State Sec., Ministry of Justice

1998–2002; asked by Pres. Viktor Orbán to be Nat. Coordinator of the Civic Circles 2002–05; Notary for Legislation during inaugural session of Parl. 2005–10; mem. Nat. Security Cttee 2009–; Minister of Defence 2010–15; mem. MDF 1988–2004, Pres. MDF org. in Szombathely 1990–91, Nat. Commr for Ethics 1993–96, mem. party presidency 1996–2002, Nat. Vice-Pres., then Gen. Vice-Pres. 1999–2002; ind. June–Dec. 2004; mem. Fidesz—Hungarian Civic Alliance (Fidesz—Magyar Polgári Szöevetség) 2004–; mem. Apáczai Csere János Foundation Advisory Bd 1990–97; col in army reserve. *Leisure interest:* cycling.

HENDERSON, Frederick A. (Fritz), BBA, MBA; American business executive; *Principal, Hawksbill Group;* b. 29 Nov. 1958, Detroit, Mich.; m. Karen Henderson; two d.; ed Lake Orion High School, Mich., Ross School of Business, Univ. of Michigan, Harvard Business School, Harvard Univ.; joined General Motors (GM) 1984, Group Vice-Pres. of Finance, GMAC Financial Services (fmrly General Motors Acceptance Corpn), Detroit 1992–97, GM Vice-Pres. and Man. Dir GM do Brasil (covering GM operations in Brazil, Argentina, Paraguay and Uruguay) 1997–2000, Group Vice-Pres. and Pres. GM-LAAM (Latin America, Africa and Middle East) 2000–02, Pres. GM Asia Pacific, Singapore 2002–04, Chair. GM Europe, Zurich, Switzerland 2004–06, Vice-Chair. and Chief Financial Officer 2006–09, Pres. and CEO General Motors Corpn (following Chapter 11 bankruptcy reorganization) 2009, Consultant, General Motors LLC Feb.–Sept. 2010; Chair. and CEO SunCoke Energy Inc. 2010–17, Pres. 2015–17; Prin. Hawksbill Group 2018–; mem. Bd of Dirs Ally Credit Canada Ltd 2006–, Compuware Corpn 2011–, Marriott International Inc. 2013–, Suzuki Motor Corpn; Trustee, Alfred P. Sloan Foundation. *Achievements include:* pitched for Univ. of Michigan Wolverines baseball team. *Address:* Hawksbill Group, 1050 Connecticut Avenue, NW, Suite 500, Washington, DC 20036, USA (office). *Telephone:* (202) 772-1128 (office). *E-mail:* info@hawksbillgroup.com (office). *Website:* www.hawksbillgroup.com (office).

HENDERSON, Richard, CH, PhD, FRS, FMedSci; British molecular biologist; *Programme Leader, Laboratory of Molecular Biology, Medical Research Council;* b. 19 July 1945, Edinburgh, Scotland; s. of John W. Henderson and Grace S. Henderson (née Goldie); m. 1st Penelope Fitzgerald 1969 (divorced 1988); one s. one d. (one d. deceased); m. 2nd Jade Li 1995; ed Hawick High School, Boroughmuir Secondary School, Univs of Edinburgh and Cambridge; professional interest in structure and function of protein molecules, especially in biological membranes; Helen Hay Whitney Postdoctoral Fellow, Yale Univ., USA 1970–73; Fellow, Darwin Coll. Cambridge 1982–2012; mem. research staff, MRC Lab. of Molecular Biology 1973–, Dir 1996–2006, Programme Leader 2006–; Scientific Founder, Heptares Therapeutics 2007; Foreign Assoc., NAS; Fellow, Microscopy Soc. of America 2005; Helen Hay Whitney Postdoctoral Fellowship 1970–73; Hon. mem. British Biophysical Soc. 2003, Hon. Fellow, Corpus Christi Coll., Cambridge 2003; Hon. DSc (Edinburgh) 2008, Isaac Newton Undergraduate Scholarship, Edinburgh 1963–65, Neil Arnott Scholarship in Experimental Physics Undergraduate 1965–66, MRC Scholarship for training in research methods 1966–69; William Bate Hardy Prize, Cambridge Philosophical Soc. 1978, Ernst Ruska Prize for Electron Microscopy 1981, Lewis S. Rosenstiel Award, Brandeis Univ. 1991, Louis Jeantet Award 1993, Gregori Aminoff Prize for Crystallography, Royal Swedish Acad. 1999, Distinguished Scientist Award, Microscopy Soc. of America 2005, Copley Medal, Royal Soc. 2016, Nobel Prize in Chemistry (with Jacques Dubochet and Joachim Frank) 2017. *Publications include:* numerous scientific articles in books and journals. *Leisure interests:* canoeing, wine. *Address:* MRC Laboratory of Molecular Biology, Francis Crick Avenue, Cambridge, CB2 0QH, England (office). *Telephone:* (1223) 267065 (office). *Fax:* (1223) 268305 (office). *E-mail:* rh15@mrc-lmb.cam.ac.uk (office). *Website:* www2.mrc-lmb.cam.ac.uk/group-leaders/h-to-m/richard-henderson (office); www2.mrc-lmb.cam.ac.uk/groups/rh15 (office).

HENDRICKS, Barbara Ann, BSc, BMus; Swedish (b. American) singer (soprano); b. 20 Nov. 1948, Stephens, Ark., USA; d. of M. L. Hendricks and Della Hendricks; m. Ulf Englund 1978; one s. one d.; ed Univ. of Nebraska-Lincoln, Juilliard School of Music, studying with Jennie Tourel; operatic debut, San Francisco Opera (L'Incoronazione di Poppea) 1976; has appeared with opera companies of Boston, Santa Fe, Glyndebourne, Hamburg, La Scala (Milan), Berlin, Paris, Los Angeles, Florence and Royal Opera, Covent Garden (London), Vienna; recitals in most major centres in Europe and America; toured extensively in USSR and Japan; concert performances with leading European and US orchestras; has appeared at numerous music festivals including Edinburgh, Osaka, Montreux, Salzburg, Dresden, Prague, Aix-en-Provence, Orange and Vienna; apptd Goodwill Amb. for Refugees at UNHCR 1987; Founder Barbara Hendricks Foundation for Peace and Reconciliation 1998; f. record label Arte Verum 2006; Artist-in-Residence, Pitea, Sweden 2008; Hon. mem. Inst. of Humanitarian Law, San Remo, Italy 1990; Commdr des Arts et des Lettres 1986, Chevalier, Légion d'honneur 1993; Hon. DMus (Nebraska Wesleyan Univ.) 1988; Dr hc (Univ. of Louvain, Belgium) 1990, 1993, (Dundee) 1992, (Univ. of Paris VIII) 1999, (Juilliard School) 2000, (Liege) 2004; Laurent Perrier Champagne Award for Service to the Community and to French Culture 1988, Prince of Asturias Foundation Award 2000, Lions Club International Award for the Defense of Human Rights 2001, Premio Internacional Xifra Heras, Univ. of Gerona, Spain 2004, La Medaille D'Or de la ville de Paris 2004, Creu de Sant Jordi, Catalunya, Spain 2006, Medal of the City of Sarajevo 2007, Save the Children Prize, Spain 2009. *Film appearances:* La Bohème 1988, The Rake's Progress 1994. *Recordings:* nearly 90 recordings. *Leisure interest:* reading. *Address:* B H Office, Fondberg Produktion, Dalagatan 48, 11324, Stockholm, Sweden (office). *E-mail:* aino.turtiainen@fazerartists.fi (office); bh.office@bluewin.ch (office). *Website:* www.fazerartists.fi (office); www.barbarahendricks.com (office).

HENDROPRIYONO, Lt-Gen. (retd) Abdullah Mahmud; Indonesian politician; *Chairman, Indonesian Justice and Unity Party;* b. 7 May 1945, Jakarta; two c.; ed AMN Military Acad.; mil. career with Kopassus Unit, including several tours of combat duty in Kalimantan 1960s and 1970s, in East Timor 1975; sr positions in Bais (Indonesian mil. intelligence agency) 1990s, Jakarta Area Commdr 1993–94; Minister of Transmigration and Resettlement 1998–99; Head of Nat. Intelligence Agency (BIN) 2001–04; currently Chair. Indonesian Justice and Unity Party (Partai Keadilan dan Persatuan Indonesia); also owner of a law firm; Bintang Mahaputera Indonesia Adipradana, Bintang Kartika Eka Paksi Nararya Prestasi, Satya Lencana Bhakti. *Address:* Indonesian Justice and Unity Party, JL. Diponegoro 63, Menteng, Jakarrta 10310, Indonesia (office). *Telephone:* (21) 31922733 (office). *Fax:* (21) 31922822 (office). *E-mail:* info@pkpi.or.id (office). *Website:* www.pkpi.info (office).

HENDRY, Sir David Forbes, Kt, MA, PhD, FBA, FRSE; British economist and academic; *Professor of Economics, University of Oxford;* b. 6 March 1944, Nottingham; ed London School of Econs; Lecturer, then Reader, later Prof. of Econs, LSE –1982; Prof. of Econs, Univ. of Oxford 1982–, Head of Dept of Econs 2001–07, Professorial Fellow, Nuffield Coll. Oxford, Dir Economic Modelling, Inst. for New Economic Thinking, Oxford Martin School; Fellow, Econometric Soc., Journal of Econometrics; Hon. Vice-Pres. Royal Econ. Soc.; Hon. Fellow, Int. Inst. of Forecasters; Foreign Hon. mem. American Acad. of Arts and Sciences, American Econ. Asscn, Academician, Acad. of Social Sciences 2012–; Dr hc (Aarhus Univ.) 2013; Celebrating Impact Lifetime Achievement Award, Economic and Social Research Council 2014. *Publications include:* Econometrics and Quantitative Economics (co-ed.) 1984, PC-NAIVE, An Interactive Program for Monte Carlo Experimentation in Econometrics. Version 6.0 (co-author) 1991, PcGive 7: An Interactive Econometric Modelling System (co-author) 1992, Econometrics: Alchemy or Science? 1993, 2001, Co-integration, Error Correction and the Econometric Analysis of Non-Stationary Data (co-author) 1993, Dynamic Econometrics 1995, The Foundations of Econometric Analysis (co-author) 1995, Forecasting Economic Time Series (co-author) 1998, Forecasting Non-stationary Economic Time Series (co-author) 1999, Nonlinear Econometric Modeling in Time Series. Proceedings of the Eleventh International Symposium in Economic Theory (co-ed.) 2000, Automatic Econometric Model Selection (co-author) 2001, Empirical Econometric Modelling Using PcGive Volumes I, II and III (co-author) 2001, GiveWin: An Interface to Empirical Modelling (2nd edn) (co-author) 2001, Interactive Monte Carlo Experimentation in Econometrics Using PcNaive (co-author) 2001, Understanding Economic Forecast (co-author) 2001, A Companion to Economic Forecasting (co-author) 2002, General to Specific Modelling (co-author) 2004, Econometric Modeling: A Likelihood Approach (co-author) 2007; numerous papers in professional journals on time series econometrics and the econometrics of the demand for money, the theory of forecasting and on automated model building. *Address:* Eagle House, Jericho, Oxford, OX2 6ED, England (office). *Telephone:* (1865) 281485 (office). *E-mail:* david.hendry@economics.ox.ac.uk (office); david.hendry@nuffield.ox.ac.uk (office). *Website:* www.nuff.ox.ac.uk/users/hendry (office); www.economics.ox.ac.uk (office).

HENDRY, Stephen Gordon, MBE; British professional snooker player; b. 13 Jan. 1969, South Queensferry, Edinburgh, Scotland; s. of Gordon J. Hendry and Irene Anthony; m. Amanda Elizabeth Teresa Tart 1995; two s.; ed Inverkeithing High School; began playing snooker aged 12; won Scottish U-16 Championship 1983; appeared on BBC's Junior version of Pot Black 1983; won Scottish Amateur Championship 1984, 1985; youngest ever entrant in World Amateur Championship 1984; turned professional 1985 (youngest ever); winner of 74 titles (36 ranking, 38 non-ranking), including Scottish Professional 1986, 1987, 1988, Grand Prix 1987, 1990, 1991, 1995, Australian Masters 1987, British Open 1988, 1991, 1999, 2003, New Zealand Masters 1988, Masters 1989, 1990, 1991, 1992, 1993, 1996, Scottish Masters 1989, 1990, 1995, UK Championship 1989, 1990, 1994, 1995, 1996, Dubai Duty Free Classic 1989, 1990, 1993, Continental Airlines London Masters 1989, 1990, Embassy World Championship 1990, 1992, 1993, 1994, 1995, 1996, 1999, Pontins Professional 1990, 1991, Indian Challenge 1991, Matchroom League 1991, 1992, Irish Masters 1992, 1997, 1999, Regal Welsh 1992, 1997, 2003, Scottish Open 1993, 1997, 1999, European Challenge 1992, 1993, European Open 1993, 1994, 2001, European League 1994, 1995, Top Rank Classic 1994, Charity Challenge 1995, 1997, Thailand Masters 1998, Red Bull Super Challenge 1998, Malta Grand Prix 1998, 2001, Champions Cup 1999, Premier League Snooker 2000, 2004, Malta Cup 2005, Legends of Snooker 2009; team events: World Doubles (with Mike Hallett) 1987, Mita/Sky World Masters Men's Doubles (with Mike Hallett) 1991, World Cup (with team Scotland) 1996, Nations Cup (with team Scotland) 2001; holds the most world ranking titles (36) and most competitive century breaks (762); second only to Ronnie O'Sullivan for the most competitive 147 breaks with 10 in total; announced retirement May 2012; Dr hc (Stirling) 2000; World Professional Billiards and Snooker Asscn (WPBSA) Young Player of the Year 1988, BBC Scotland Sports Personality of the Year 1987, 1996, WPBSA Player of the Year 1990, 1991, 1992, 1993, 1995, 1996, WPBSA Performance of the Year 1995, MacRoberts Trophy 2001. *Publication:* Snooker Masterclass 1994. *Leisure interests:* golf, poker, music, Formula 1, Heart of Midlothian (Hearts) Football Club. *Address:* Stephen Hendry Snooker Club, 275 Brook Street, Preston, PR1 7NH, England (office). *Telephone:* (1772) 824861 (office). *E-mail:* info@stephenhendrysnookerclub.co.uk (office). *Website:* www.stephenhendrysnookerclub.co.uk (office).

HENFIELD, Lt-Commdr (retd) Darren Allen, LLB, MA; Bahamian lawyer, politician and fmr naval officer; *Minister of Foreign Affairs;* b. 15 May 1962, Spring City, Abaco Islands; s. of Clifford Henfield and Evelyn Henfield; m. Deirdre Edgecombe; three s.; ed Univ. of the W Indies, Britannia Royal Naval Coll., Dartmouth, US Naval Postgraduate School, Monterrey; 36-year career with Royal Bahamas Defence Force (navy) 1981–2017, including six months with UN peacekeeping service in CARICOM Bn, Haiti 1995, retd from RBDF 2017; called to the Bar, Bahamas 2011; Jr Counsel, Office of the Attorney-Gen. 2011–14; Sr Assoc. Pastor, Calvary Deliverance Church 2012–; mem. House of Ass. (lower house of parl.) (FNM) for North Abaco, New Providence 2017–; Minister of Foreign Affairs 2017–; mem. Free Nat. Movt. *Leisure interests:* travelling, meeting people. *Address:* Ministry of Foreign Affairs, Goodman's Bay Corporate Centre, 2nd Floor, West Bay Street, POB N-3746, Nassau, Bahamas (office). *Telephone:* 356-5960 (office); 356-5956 (office). *Fax:* 328-8212 (office). *E-mail:* mofabahamas@bahamas.gov.bs (office). *Website:* www.bahamas.gov.bs/foreignaffairs (office).

HENG, Swee Keat, MA, MPA; Singaporean government official, politician and fmr central banker; *Minister of Finance;* b. 1 Nov. 1961; ed Univ. of Cambridge, UK, Kennedy School of Govt, Harvard Univ., USA; fmr Sr Police Officer; Dir of Higher Educ., Ministry of Educ. –1997; served in Prime Minister's Office as Prin. Pvt. Sec., then Sr Minister Lee Kuan Yew 1997–2000; Deputy Sec. (Trade), Ministry of Trade and Industry 2000–01, concurrently CEO Trade Devt Bd 2001, Perm. Sec. 2001–05; Man. Dir Monetary Authority of Singapore 2005–11; mem.

People's Action Party 2011–, Asst Sec.-Gen. 2018–; mem. of Parl. 2011–; Minister of Educ. 2011–15, of Finance 2015–; Overseas Singapore Police Force Scholar, Gold Medal in Public Admin 2001, Meritorious Service Medal 2010, Asia-Pacific Central Bank Governor of the Year Award, The Banker magazine 2011. *Address:* Ministry of Finance, The Treasury 100 High Street, #10-01, Singapore 179434 (office). *Telephone:* 63322717 (office). *Fax:* 63367001 (office). *E-mail:* tharman_s@mof.gov.sg (office). *Website:* www.mof.gov.sg (office).

HENG SAMRIN; Cambodian politician; *Chairman, National Assembly of Cambodia;* b. 25 May 1934, Prey Veng Prov.; m. Sao Ty; four c.; Political Commissar and Commdr of Khmer Rouge 4th Infantry Div. 1976–78; led abortive coup against Pol Pot and fled to Viet Nam 1978; Pres. Nat. Front for Nat. Salvation of Kampuchea 1978; Pres. People's Revolutionary Council 1979 (took power after Vietnamese invasion of Kampuchea); Chair. Council of State of Cambodia 1991; Sec.-Gen. People's Revolutionary Party of Kampuchea (KPRP) 1981–91, Vice-Chair. 1998–2006; Chair. Nat. Ass. of Cambodia 2006–; mem. Politburo of Cambodia 1991–; Hon. Chair. Cambodian People's Party 1993. *Address:* National Assembly of Cambodia, Rathasaphea Street, Tonle Bassac, Khan Chamcar Morn, Phnom Penh, Cambodia (office). *Telephone:* (23) 213535 (office). *Fax:* (23) 220629 (office). *E-mail:* sg@nac.org.kh. *Website:* en.nac-kh.org/httpdocs/naweb/english.

HENIN, Justine; Belgian professional tennis player (retd); b. 1 June 1982, Liège; d. of José Henin and Françoise Henin; m. Pierre-Yves Hardenne 2002 (divorced 2007); one d.; right-handed, one-handed backhand; winner, French Open Jr Championship 1997; turned professional 1 Jan. 1999; semi-finalist, French Open 2001, winner 2003, 2005, 2006, 2007; finalist, Wimbledon 2001, 2006, semi-finalist 2002, 2003; semi-finalist, Australian Open, 2003, winner 2004, finalist 2010; winner, US Open 2003, 2007; winner, WTA Championships 2006, 2007; Gold Medal, Olympic Games, Athens 2004; retd from professional tennis 14 May 2008; returned from retirement Jan. 2010, retd again 2011; 503 career singles wins, 109 defeats, 47 career doubles wins, 35 defeats; 43 singles WTA titles, two doubles titles; highest ranking (singles): World No. 1 20 Oct. 2003; commentator; f. tennis acad. *Address:* c/o Vincent Stavaux, Place Riva Bella 12/5, 1420 Braine L'Alleud, Belgium.

HÉNIN, Pierre-Yves, PhD; French academic, university administrator and economist; *Professor Emeritus, Université Paris I (Panthéon Sorbonne);* b. 11 April 1946, St-Aubin, Saône et Loire; m.; four c.; ed Faculté de Droit et de Sciences Economiques de Paris, Université Paris I (Panthéon Sorbonne); Research Dir ISEA, CNRS 1967–71; Prof. Université d'Orléans 1972–75; Founder and Dir Macroéconomie et Analyse des Déséquilibres research centre, Université Paris I (Panthéon Sorbonne) 1974–90, Prof. Université Paris I (Panthéon Sorbonne) 1975–2009, Dir UER 1978–82, 1985–90, Vice-Pres. Scientific Council 1982–89, 1993–2004, Pres. Université Paris I (Panthéon Sorbonne) 2004–09, Prof. Emer. 2009–; Consultant to Ministry of Research and Tech. 1985–86; Dir CEPREMAP 1991–2004; mem. Scientific Council Ecole Nationale des Statistiques et de l'Admin Economique 1980–86; Vice-Pres. Asscn Française de Sciences Economiques 1994–95, Pres. 1995–97; Chevalier, Ordre Nationale du Mérite 1993, Chevalier des Palmes Académiques 1998, Chevalier, Légion d'Honneur 2002; AFSE Thesis Prize 1970, Le Nouvel Economiste Economist of the Year 1996. *Publications include:* Macrodynamics: Fluctuations And Growth 1986, Advances in Equilibrium Business Cycles Research 1995, Should we Rebuild Built-in Stabilizers? 1997 and several other books and articles.

HENKEL, Hans-Olaf; German business executive and politician; b. 14 March 1940, Hamburg; m. 1st Marlene Henkel –2004; m. 2nd Bettina Hannover 2005; four c.; joined Int. Business Machines (IBM), Germany 1962, Pres. IBM Germany 1987–89, Vice-Pres. IBM Corpn 1989–95, CEO IBM Europe 1993–95; Pres. Bundesverband der Deutschen Industrie 1995–2000; Pres. Leibniz Gemeinschaft 2001–05; mem. European Parl. 2014–, currently Vice-Chair. Cttee on Industry, Research and Energy, European Conservatives and Reformists Group, mem. Subcommittee on Human Rights; mem. Supervisory Bd Altira, Bayer AG, Continental AG, Daimler Luft- und Raumfahrt Holding AG, SMS GmbH, Ringier AG; mem. Amnesty Int.; Co-founder Konvent für Deutschland; mem. European Conservatives and Reformists; Hon. Prof. of Int. Man., Univ. of Mannheim 2000–; Dr hc (Tech. Univ. of Dresden) 1991; Commdr, Légion d'honneur; WWF Environmental Manager of the Year 1991, Wirtschaftswoche magazine Innovation Award, Corine Writers' Award, Ludwig-Erhard Award, Cicero 'Best Business Speaker' Award, Deutscher Mittelstandspreis 2006, Hayek Medal 2007. *Publications include:* Jetzt oder nie 1998, Die Macht der Freiheit 2000, Die Ethik des Erfolgs 2002, Die Kraft des Neubeginns 2004, Der Kampf um die Mitte 2006, Die Abwracker 2009, Rettet unser Geld 2010, Die Euro-Lügner: Unsinnige Rettungspakete, vertuschte Risiken – so werden wir getäuscht 2013, Deutschland gehört auf die Couch 2016. *Leisure interests:* sailing, jazz. *Address:* European Parliament, Bât. Altiero Spinelli, 60 rue Wiertz, 1047 Brussels, Belgium (office). *Telephone:* (2) 284-21-11 (office). *Fax:* (2) 284-69-74 (office). *Website:* www.europarl.europa.eu (office).

HENKELMAN, R. Mark, PhD, FRSC; Canadian biophysicist and academic; *University Professor, Department of Medical Biophysics and Medical Imaging, University of Toronto;* Prof., Dept of Medical Biophysics and Medical Imaging, Univ. of Toronto, Univ. Prof. 2005–, also Canada Research Chair Imaging Technologies in Human Disease and Preclinical Models; Sr Scientist and Dir Mouse Imaging Centre (MICe), The Hosp. for Sick Children; Sr Scientist in Translational Medicine, SickKids; Researcher CP-NET; Gold Medal, Int. Soc. of Magnetic Resonance in Medicine 1998, Killam Prize in Health Sciences, Canada Council for the Arts 2010. *Publications:* co-author on over 350 papers in professional journals. *Address:* Mouse Imaging Centre, The Hospital for Sick Children, Toronto Centre for Phenogenomics, 25 Orde Street, Toronto, ON M5T 3H7, Canada (office). *Telephone:* (416) 813-7654 (office). *Fax:* (647) 837-5832 (office). *E-mail:* mhenkel@mouseimaging.ca (office); mark.henkelman@sickkids.ca (office). *Website:* medbio.utoronto.ca/faculty/henkelman.html (office).

HENLEY, Jeffrey O., BA, MBA; American computer software industry executive; *Vice-Chairman, Oracle Corporation;* b. 1945; ed Univ. of California, Santa Barbara, Univ. of California, Los Angeles; fmr Controller of Int. Operations, Fairchild Camera and Instruments; fmr Dir of Finance, Memorex Corpn; fmr Exec. Vice-Pres., Chief Financial Officer, Saga Corpn, Pacific Holding Co.; Exec. Vice-Pres. and Chief Financial Officer, Oracle Corpn 1991–2004, mem. Bd Dirs 1995–, Chair. 2004–14, Vice-Chair. 2014–, mem. Exec. Man. Cttee; Chair. Mid-Pacific Region Trustees, Boys & Girls Clubs of America; mem. Bd Dirs CallWave Inc.; mem. Bd Govs Boys and Girls Clubs of America; mem. Chancellor's Advisory Council and Int. Advisory Council, Eng Coll., Univ. of California, Santa Barbara; mem. Advisory Bd InTouch Technologies; UCLA Anderson School's Outstanding Alumnus Award 2004. *Address:* Oracle Corpn, 500 Oracle Parkway, Redwood City, CA 94065, USA (office). *Telephone:* (650) 506-7000 (office). *E-mail:* info@oracle.com (office). *Website:* www.oracle.com (office).

HENNEKENS, Charles H., MD, DrPH; American epidemiologist and academic; *Sir Richard Doll Research Professor, College of Medicine, Florida Atlantic University;* ed Cornell Univ. Medical Coll. and Harvard School of Public Health; Epidemic Intelligence Officer, US Public Health Service, Dada Co., Fla 1969–71; Asst Prof. of Epidemiology, Univ. of Miami School of Medicine 1972–74; Asst Prof. of Medicine, Harvard Univ. 1975–81, Assoc. Prof. of Medicine and Clinical Epidemiology 1981–88, Prof. of Medicine and Preventive Medicine 1990–99; Physician, Brigham and Women's Hosp. 1982–92, Sr Physician 1992–93, Prof. of Medicine and Head of Div. of Preventive Medicine 1993–99; Visiting Epidemiologist, Univ. of Oxford, UK 1978–79; Prof. of Medicine & Epidemiology and Public Health, Univ. of Miami School of Medicine, Fla 1999; Co-Dir Cardiovascular Research, Mount Sinai Medical Center-Miami Heart Inst., Miami Beach, Fla 2001–04; currently Sir Richard Doll Research Prof., Charles E. Schmidt Coll. of Biomedical Science, Florida Atlantic Univ.; Clinical Prof., Nova Southeastern Univ.; fmr Pres. Soc. for Epidemiologic Research; Pres. American Epidemiological Soc.; Visiting Fellow, Green Coll. Univ. of Oxford 2000–; Fellow, American Coll. of Preventive Medicine, American Coll. of Epidemiology; mem. Asscn of American Physicians, Food and Nutrition Bd; fmr Ed.-in-Chief American Journal of Preventive Medicine; Founding Ed.-in-Chief Annals of Epidemiology; mem. Preventive Medicine Residency Advisory Cttee Health Dept, External Advisory Bd Cardiovascular Research Inst. 2003–; Hon. FACC; Hon. DSc (Univ. of Medicine and Dentistry) 1996, (City Univ.) 1997; Bruce Award, American Coll. of Physicians, Lilienfeld Award American Coll. of Epidemiology, Duncan Clark Award, Lewis Atterbury Conner Lectureship Award, Jan J. Kellermann Memorial Award, Sr Int. Aspirin Award, First Public Health Physician of the Year Award, inducted into Hall of Fame, American Asscn of Clinical Chemistry 2007, Fries Prize, Centers For Disease Control and Prevention (CDC) 2014. *Publications:* Epidemiology in Medicine (co-author) 1987, Clinical Trials in Cardiovascular Disease: A Companion to Braunwald's Heart Disease (co-author) 1999 and several other books. *Address:* Charles E. Schmidt College of Medicine, Florida Atlantic University, 777 Glades Road, Boca Raton, FL 33431, USA (office). *Telephone:* (561) 297-4074 (office). *Fax:* (561) 297-3843 (office). *E-mail:* chenneke@health.fau.edu (office). *Website:* www.med.fau.edu (office).

HENNEKINNE, Loïc; French diplomatist and business executive; b. 20 Sept. 1940, Caudéran, Gironde; s. of Michel Hennekinne and Elisabeth Declemy; m. 2nd Marie Bozelle 1987; one d.; two s. (by first m.); ed Ecole Nat. d'Admin; First Sec., embassies in Viet Nam 1969–71, Chile 1971–73; Minister-Counsellor, Japan 1979–81; Del. for External Action, Ministry of Industry 1981–82; Dir of Cabinet of Minister of Research and Industry 1982; Dir of Personnel and Admin Ministry of Foreign Affairs 1983–86; Amb. to Indonesia 1986–88; Gen. Sec. summit conf. of Western industrialized nations, Paris 1989; Diplomatic Adviser to Pres. Mitterrand 1989–91; Amb. to Japan 1991–93; Inspector-Gen. of Foreign Affairs 1993–96; Amb. to Canada 1997–98; Sec.-Gen. Ministry of Foreign Affairs (with rank of Amb. of France) 1998–2002; Amb. to Italy 2002–05; Adviser to Pres. PlaNet Finance France 2007–12, also Head of Confs; numerous int. decorations, including Officier, Ordre nat. du Mérite, Commdr, Légion d'honneur, Grand' Ufficiale Ordine Naz. al Merito della Repub. Italiana, Ordine Bernardo O'Higgins. *Leisure interest:* tennis. *Address:* 15 avenue Frochot, 75009 Paris, France. *Telephone:* 1-42-82-03-38; 6-74-76-65-25 (mobile). *E-mail:* loic.hennekinne@laposte.net.

HENNEQUIN, Denis, BA, MA; French business executive; *Founding Partner, French Food Capital;* b. 8 June 1958; m.; three c.; ed Université Panthéon-Assas, Paris; began career at McDonald's as Asst Dir of a Paris-based restaurant, promoted to Restaurant Man. Dir, later held numerous positions within the co., including Training and Recruitment Consultant, Field Service Consultant, Dir of Franchising, Dir of Operations and Regional Man. for Paris and the surrounding suburbs, Pres. and Man. Dir McDonald's France 1996–2005, Pres. McDonald's Europe Ltd (first non-American) 2005–10; joined Bd of Accor (hotels group) as Ind. Dir 2009, Exec. Dir Accor SA 2010–11, Chair. and CEO 2011–13; Partner Cojean Int. 2014–16; Founding Partner French Food Capital 2017–; mem. Bd of Dirs Eurostar 2012–, SSP Group PLC 2014–, John Lewis Partnership 2014–17, Bakkavor Group Ltd 2017–. *Leisure interests:* motorcycles, rock music. *Address:* French Food Capital, 2 Avenue de Messine, 75008 Paris, France (office). *Telephone:* 1-70-81-04-45 (office). *E-mail:* contact@frenchfoodcapital.com (office).

HENNESSEY, Keith, BAS, MPP; American economist, government official and academic; *Lecturer, Graduate School of Business and School of Law, Stanford University;* ed Stanford Univ., John F. Kennedy School of Govt, Harvard Univ.; Program Designer, Symantec Corpn, Cupertino, Calif. 1990–92; Research Asst, Bipartisan Comm. on Entitlement and Tax Reform 1994–95; Health Economist, Budget Cttee, US Senate 1995–97, Policy Dir for Senate Majority and Senator Trent Lott 1997–2002; Deputy Asst to US Pres. for Econ. Policy and Devt and Deputy Dir Nat. Econ. Council 2002–07, Asst to US Pres. for Econ. Policy and Devt and Dir Nat. Econ Council 2007–09; Lecturer, Graduate School of Business, Stanford Univ. 2010–, Stanford Law School 2011–, Public Policy Program 2013, Research Fellow, Hoover Inst. *Address:* Stanford Graduate School of Business, 655 Knight Way, Stanford, CA 94305, USA (office). *Telephone:* (202) 669-5107 (office). *E-mail:* keith.hennessey@stanford.edu (office). *Website:* www.gsb.stanford.edu (office).

HENNESSY, Edward Lawrence, Jr, BS; American business executive (retd); b. 22 March 1928, Boston, Mass; s. of Edward L. Hennessy and Celina Mary Doucette; m. Ruth F. Schilling 1951; one s. one d.; ed Fairleigh Dickinson Univ., Rutherford, NJ and New York Univ. Law School; Asst Controller, Textron 1950–55; Group Controller, Eastern Electronics Group, Lear Siegler Inc. 1956–60; Controller, Int. Electronic Corpn, Int. Telephone & Telegraph Corpn (ITT) 1960–61, Controller, Corporate Staff 1961–62, Controller, ITT Europe 1962–64;

Dir of Finance, Europe, Middle East and Africa, Colgate Palmolive Co. 1964–65; Vice-Pres. Finance, Heublein Inc. 1965–68, Sr Vice-Pres. Admin. and Finance 1969–72; Dir United Technologies Corpn 1972–79, Sr Vice-Pres. Finance and Admin. 1972–77, Exec. Vice-Pres., Group Vice-Pres. Systems & Equipment Group and Chief Financial Office 1977–79; Chair. and CEO AlliedSignal Corpn (now Honeywell) 1979–93 (retd); mem. Bd of Dirs Bank of New York, Wackenhut Corpn, Avanir Pharmaceuticals, Automatic Data Processing, Northeast Utilities, Lockheed Martin Corpn, Coast Guard Foundation, Powertrusion 2000; Trustee, Fairleigh Dickinson Univ. (fmr chair.), Catholic Univ. of America; Officier Légion d'honneur 1991, Kt of Malta (Vatican) 1981, Kt of St Gregory (Vatican) 1984, Hilal-i-Quaid-i-Azam (Pakistan) 1985, Kt of the Holy Sepulchre (Vatican) 1986. *Leisure interests:* sailing, tennis, reading, golf. *Address:* PO Box 3000 R, Morristown, NJ 07960 (office); 500 Island Drive, Palm Beach, FL 33480, USA (home). *Telephone:* (973) 455-4811 (office); (561) 655-0107 (home). *Fax:* (973) 455-2973 (office).

HENNESSY, Helen (see VENDLER, Helen Hennessy).

HENNESSY, John L., BE, MS, PhD; American computer scientist and university administrator; b. 1953; ed Villanova Univ., State Univ. of New York at Stony Brook; apptd Asst Prof. of Electrical Eng, Stanford Univ. 1977, Full Prof. 1986–, inaugural Willard R. and Inez Kerr Bell Prof. of Electrical Eng and Computer Science 1987–2004, Dir Computer Systems Lab. 1983–93, Chair. Computer Science 1994–96, Dean, School of Eng 1996–99, Provost, Stanford Univ. 1999–2000, Pres. 2000–16, inaugural holder of Bing Presidential Professorship 2005; a pioneer in computer architecture, particularly RISC (Reduced Instruction Set Computer); Co-founder MIPS Computer Systems (now MIPS Technologies) 1984; mem. Bd of Dirs Atheros Communications 1998– (currently Chair.), Cisco Inc. 2002–, Google Inc. 2004–, Daniel Pearl Foundation; mem. Bd of Govs Partnership for Public Service; First Int. Advisor, Trinity Coll./Univ. Coll. Dublin; mem. Academic Advisory Council Coll. of Eng Cornell Univ., Computer Science Dept Princeton Univ.; mem. Cttee on Research Univs Nat. Research Council; mem. NAS, Nat. Acad. of Eng, American Philosophical Soc. 2008; Fellow, American Acad. of Arts and Sciences, Asscn for Computing Machinery, IEEE, Computer History Museum 2007; Hon. Fellow, Foreign Policy Asscn 2010; several Hon. degrees; IEEE John von Neumann Medal 2000, ASEE Benjamin Garver Lamme Award 2000, ACM Eckert-Mauchly Award 2001, Seymour Cray Computer Eng Award 2001, NEC C&C Prize for lifetime achievement in computer science and eng 2004, Founders Award, American Acad. of Arts and Sciences 2005, Lifetime Achievement Award, Silicon Valley Leadership Group 2009, Ulysses Medal, Univ. Coll. Dublin 2009, Morris Chang Exemplary Leadership Award, Global Semiconductor Alliance 2010, IEEE Medal of Honor 2012, A.M. Turing Award, Asscn for Computing Machinery 2018. *Publications include:* Computer Organization and Design: The Hardware/Software Interface, Computer Architecture: A Quantitative Approach. *Address:* Stanford University, Stanford, CA 94305-2061, USA (office). *E-mail:* hennessy@stanford.edu (office). *Website:* www.stanford.edu/~hennessy (office).

HENNESSY, Patrick; Irish diplomatist; b. 1952; m. Pauline Hennessy; ed Trinity Coll. Dublin, Univ. of Reading; joined Dept of Foreign Affairs (DFA) as Third Sec., HQ Econ. Div. 1974, Third Sec., Embassy in Luxembourg 1975, First Sec., HQ Anglo-Irish Div. 1977, Embassy in London 1980–85, Perm. Mission to UN, New York 1988–91, Counsellor, Embassy in Washington, DC 1995, Amb. to Israel 2001, Dir-Gen., DFA 2005–09, Amb. to Italy 2009–13, Amb. to UAE 2013–17.

HENNIS-PLASSCHAERT, Jeanine Antoinette; Dutch politician; b. 7 April 1973, Heerlen; m. Erik-Jan Hennis; one s.; ed St Antonius Coll., Gouda, European Secretarial Acad., Utrecht; began career with Directorate-Gen. for Enlargement, EC, Brussels, including two years working for EC in Rīga, Latvia; consultant for KPMG, Amstelveen 2000–02; Political Asst to Amsterdam Municipal Exec. Bd 2002–04; MEP (VVD—People's Party for Freedom and Democracy) 2004–10; mem. House of Reps (VVD) 2010–12, 2017–; Minister of Defence 2012–17. *Address:* People's Party for Freedom and Democracy (VVD), Binnenhof 1A, PO Box 20018, 2500 EA The Hague, Netherlands (office). *Telephone:* (70) 3183036 (office). *E-mail:* vvdvoorlichting@tweedekamer.nl (office). *Website:* www.vvd.nl (office).

HENRETTA, Deborah (Deb) A., BA, MA; American business executive; *Group President, Global Beauty Care, The Procter & Gamble Company;* b. 1 May 1961, Rochester, NY; two d. one s.; ed St Bonaventure Univ., Syracuse Univ.; intern, WXXI Channel 21, Rochester, NY 1982, WOKR Channel 13, Rochester, NY 1982–85; brand asst, Procter & Gamble 1985–86, Asst Brand Man. Bold/Dawn 1986–88, Brand Man. Cheer 1988–91, Assoc. Advertising Man. Tide 1991–93, Marketing Dir Laundry Products, Procter & Gamble North America 1993–96, Gen. Man. Fabric Conditioners, Procter & Gamble North America 1996–98, Gen. Man. Fabric Conditioners and Bleach, Procter & Gamble Worldwide 1998–99, Vice-Pres. Global Strategic Planning and Design, Laundry Fabric Conditioners/Bleach 1999, Vice-Pres. North America Baby Care 1999–2001, Pres. Global Baby Care 2001–04, Pres. Global Baby and Adult Care 2004–05, Pres. ASEAN/Australasia/India 2005–07, Group Pres., Asia 2007–11, Group Pres., Asia and Global Speciality Channel 2011–12, Group Pres., Skin Care, Cosmetics and Personal Care 2012, Group Pres., Global Beauty Care 2012–; mem. Bd of Dirs WCET/Channel 48 1997–2001, Chair. Strategic Planning Cttee 1998–2001; mem. Conf. Cincinnati Women 1988–90, Advisory Cttee Newhouse School, Syracuse Univ. 1998–, Advisory Council for Children's Day Care Center 1999–2002, Oversight Cttee for Children's Day Care Center 1999–, Strategy and Marketing Cttee Children's Hosp. of Cincinnati 2000–, Bd of Trustees for Children's Hosp. 2001–, YWCA Career Women of Achievement Steering Cttee 2002–, The Committee of 200 2003–, Bd of Trustees St Bonaventure Univ. 2003–; mem. Alexis de Tocqueville Soc. of the United Way 2001–; led P&G's Advancement of Women effort (which won P&G the Catalyst Award 1998) 1994–2000; YWCA Career Women of Achievement Award 2002, YWCA Acad. of Career Women 2002. *Address:* The Procter & Gamble Co., 238A Thomson Road, #21- 09/10, Novena Square, Tower A, Singapore City 307684, Singapore (office). *Telephone:* 6824-5800 (office). *Fax:* 6824-6309 (office). *E-mail:* henretta.da@pg.com (office). *Website:* www.pg.com (office).

HENRI ALBERT FÉLIX MARIE GUILLAUME, HRH Grand Duke of Luxembourg, LèsScPol; b. 16 April 1955, Château de Betzdorf; s. of Jean Benoît Guillaume Marie Robert Louis Antoine Adolphe Marc d'Aviano, HRH fmr Grand Duke of Luxembourg and Princess Josephine-Charlotte of Belgium; m. María Teresa Mestre y Batista-Falla 1981; four s. (including Prince Guillaume Jean Joseph Marie) one d.; ed Royal Mil. Acad. Sandhurst, Univ. of Geneva; mem. State Council 1980–98; apptd Lt Rep. of Grand Duke March 1988; succeeded father as Grand Duke of Luxembourg Oct. 2000; Chair. Bd of Econ. Devt, Galapagos Darwin Trust Luxembourg; Pres. Organizing Cttee, Int. Trade Fairs of Luxembourg; mem. Mentor Foundation, Int. Olympic Cttee; Hon. Maj., Parachute Regt; Co-Grand Master, Order of the Gold Lion of the House of Nassau, Grand Master, Mil. and Civil Order of Adolphe of Nassau, Grand Master, Order of the Oak Crown, Grand Master, Order of Merit of the Grand Duchy of Luxembourg, Grand Collier of the Fondation du Mérite européen; Grand Star of the Decoration of Honour for Services to the Repub. of Austria, Kt, Order of the Elephant (Denmark), Kt Grand Cross, Royal Victorian Order (UK), Kt with the Collar, Order of Pope Pius IX (Vatican), Bailiff Grand Cross of Honour and Devotion, Sovereign Mil. Order of Malta, Kt, Supreme Order of the Most Holy Annunciation (House of Savoy), Kt, Order of the Seraphim (Sweden) 1983, Grand Cordon, Order of Leopold (Belgium) 1994, Kt Grand Cross with Collar, Order of St Olav (Norway) 1996, HM King Carl XVI Gustaf 50th Anniversary Medal (Sweden) 1996, Grand Cross, Order of the Redeemer (Greece) 2001, Kt Grand Cross with Collar, Order of Charles III (Spain) 2001, Grand Cross (or First Class), Order of the White Double Cross (Slovakia) 2002, Collar of the Order of the Cross of Terra Mariana (Estonia) 2003, Kt Grand Cross with Collar, Order of Merit of the Italian Repub. 2003, Collar of the Order of the Star of Romania 2004, Grand Collar of the Order of Prince Henry (Portugal) 2005, Grand Cross, Nat. Order of Mali 2005, Commdr Grand Cross with Chain, Order of the Three Stars (Latvia) 2006, Kt Grand Cross, Order of the Netherlands Lion 2006, Grand Collar, Order of the Southern Cross (Brazil) 2007, Kt, Order of the Golden Fleece (Spain) 2007, Grand Cross with Collar, Order of the White Rose of Finland 2008, Grand Collar, Order of St James of the Sword (Portugal) 2010, Mem. Order of the State of Repub. of Turkey 2013, Kt, Order of the White Eagle (Poland) 2014; Hon. Dr rer. pol (Trier); Hon. DHumLitt (Sacred Heart); Hon. LLD (Miami), Hon. DEcon (Khon Kaen). *Leisure interests:* reading, listening to classical music, skiing, swimming, water skiing, tennis, hunting. *Address:* Grand Ducal Palace, 2013 Luxembourg, Luxembourg (office). *Website:* www.gouvernement.lu.

HENRICH, Dieter, DrPhil; German philosopher and academic; *Professor Emeritus of Philosophy, University of Munich;* b. 5 Jan. 1927, Marburg; s. of Hans Harry Henrich and Frieda Henrich; m. Dr Bettina von Eckardt 1975; two d.; ed Univ. of Heidelberg; Prof., Freie Univ. Berlin 1960–65, Univ. of Heidelberg 1965–81; Prof., then Prof. Emer. of Philosophy, Univ. of Munich; Visiting Prof., Columbia Univ. 1968–72, Univ. of Mich. 1969, Harvard Univ. 1973–86, Tokyo Univ. 1979, Yale Univ. 1987; mem. Heidelberg and Bavarian Acads; Hon. Prof., Humboldt Univ., Berlin 1997; Hon. Foreign mem. American Acad. of Arts and Sciences; Maximilians Orden für Kunst und Wissenschaft 2007; Hon. DTheol (Münster) 1999, (Marburg) 2002; Hon. DrPhil (Jena) 2005; Hoelderlin Prize 1995, Hegel Prize 2003, Kant Prize 2004, German Language Award 2006, Leopold Lucas Prize 2008, Kuno Fischer Prize, Univ. of Heidelberg 2008. *Publications:* Der ontologische Gottesbeweis 1960, Fichtes ursprüngliche Einsicht 1967, Hegel im Kontext 1971, Identität und Objektivität 1976, Fluchtlinien 1982, Der Gang des Andenkens 1986, Konzepte 1987, Ethik zum nuklearen Frieden 1990, Konstellationen 1991, Der Grund im Bewusstsein 1992, The Moral Image of the World 1992, The Unity of Reason 1994, I. C. Diez 1997, Bewusstes Leben 1999, Versuch über Kunst und Leben 2001, Fixpunkte 2003, Between Kant and Hegel 2003, Grundlegang aus dem Ich 2004, Die Philosophie im Prozess der Kultur 2006, Denken und Selbstsein 2007, Die Philosophie in der Sprache 2007, Endlichkeit und Sammlung des Lebens 2009, Werke im Werden 2011. *Address:* Gerlichstrasse 7A, 81245 Munich, Germany (home). *Telephone:* (89) 8119131 (home). *E-mail:* dieter.henrich@lrz.uni-muenchen.de.

HENRIKSON, C(arl) Robert (Rob), BA, JD; American insurance industry executive; b. 1947; m. Mary Henrikson; two s.; ed Univ. of Pennsylvania, Emory Univ., Wharton School Advanced Management Program; joined MetLife Inc. as life insurance agent, held numerous sr man. positions, including apptd Vice-Pres. of Pensions—Nat. Accounts 1983, Sr Vice-Pres. 1991, head of all pension operations 1993, Exec. Vice-Pres. and mem. MetLife's Corp. Man. Office 1995, head of Institutional Business 1996, Sr Exec. Vice-Pres. 1997, Exec. Officer responsible for MetLife Bank 2001, Pres. US Insurance and Financial Services 2002, COO 2004–06, Pres. 2004–11, mem. Bd of Dirs 2005–11, Chair. and CEO 2006–11, Chair. June–Dec. 2011; mem. Bd of Dirs Swiss Re AG 2012–, Invesco Ltd 2012–; apptd by Pres. Obama to President's Export Council 2010; Bd mem. Emer. American Benefits Council; mem. Bd and fmr Chair. Financial Services Forum, American Council of Life Insurers; mem. Nat. Bd of Advisors, Morehouse School of Medicine; Chair. S.S. Huebner Foundation for Insurance Educ., Emory Univ.; mem. Emory Law School Council, Emory Campaign Steering Cttee; mem. Bd The New York Botanical Garden, New York Philharmonic, Partnership for New York City; Trustee, American Museum of Natural History; fmr mem. Cttee on Econ. Devt's Subcommittee on Social Security Reform; fmr adviser and consultant various Congressional and US Dept of Labor hearings; fmr del. Nat. Summit on Retirement Savings; Alumni Trustee, Emory Law School's Bd of Trustees 2007; Distinguished Alumni Award, Emory Law School 2006, Best CEO in the Life Insurance Industry, Institutional Investor 2010.

HENRÍQUEZ, Roberto C.; Panamanian business executive and politician; *Minister of the Presidency;* b. 4 Dec. 1950, Panamá City; ed Universidad Santa Maria La Antigua; Co-owner Compañía Atlas SA (co. with interests in commercial, industrial and real estate sectors) 1972–; mem. Cámara de Comercio, Industrias y Agricultura de Panamá, Sr Vice-Pres. 1990–91, Chair. Econ. Research Centre 1989; Deputy Minister of Foreign Trade 2000, Minister of Trade and Industry 2009–11, Minister of Foreign Affairs 2011–12, of the Presidency 2012–; mem. Asociación Panameña de Ejecutivos de Empresas, Pres. 1984, 1985; Vice-Pres. Nat. Council of Private Enterprise 1985; mem. Cambio Democrático. *Address:* Ministry of the Presidency, Palacio de Las Garzas, Corregimiento de San Felipe, Apdo 2189, Panamá 1, Panama (office). *Telephone:* 527-9600 (office). *E-mail:* ofasin@presidencia.gob.pa (office). *Website:* www.presidencia.gob.pa (office).

HENRY, André Armand; French teacher, trade union official and politician; b. 15 Oct. 1934, Fontenoy-le-Château; s. of Alice Henry; m. Odile Olivier 1956; one s. one d.; ed Cours Complémentaire de Bains-les-Bains, Ecole normale d'instituteurs,

Mirecourt; teacher, Fontenoy-le-Château 1955–56, Thaon-les-Vosges 1956–69; began trade union career with Syndicat Nat. des Instituteurs (SNI), Training Coll. Rep. (Vosges) 1954, mem. Exec. Comm. (Vosges) 1955–69, Asst Sec.-Gen. 1960–63, Sec.-Gen. 1963–69, mem. Nat. Council, SNI 1965–74, Perm. Sec. 1969–74; in charge of youth, then gen. admin. section of SNI; mem. Fed. Council, in charge of culture, youth and leisure sections, Fédération de l'education nationale (FEN) 1971, Perm. Sec. and Sec.-Gen. 1974–81; Minister for Free Time 1981–83; Délégué Général à l'économie sociale 1983; Chair. and Man. Dir Caisse Nat. de l'Energie 1984–87; Inspecteur Général de l'administration de l'education nat. 1989–95; Nat. Vice-Pres. Asscn laïque pour l'éducation, la formation, la prévention et l'autonomie (ALEFPA) 1995–2001, Pres. 2001–06; Délégué départemental de l'education nationale; Vice-Pres. Mission Laïque française 1997–2002; Hon. Pres. ALEFPA 2006; Commdr, Ordre du Mérite; Chevalier, Légion d'honneur, Chevalier des Palmes académiques. *Publications include:* Dame l'école 1977, Serviteurs d'idéal (two vols) 1988, Conquérir l'avenir 1992, Le Ministre qui voulait changer la vie 1996. *Leisure interests:* football, volleyball, photography, flying light aircraft. *Address:* 1 bis rue de l'Espérance, 94000 Créteil, France (home). *Telephone:* 1-48-99-37-79 (office); (6) 11-87-30-51 (home). *E-mail:* andre.h@cegetel.net (home).

HENRY, Charles Bradford (Brad), BA, JD; American lawyer and fmr politician; *Of Counsel, Lester, Loving & Davies, PC;* b. 10 July 1963, Shawnee, Okla; s. of Charles Henry; m. Kimberley Blain; three d.; ed Shawnee High School, Univ. of Oklahoma; econs teaching asst, Univ. of Oklahoma, Norman 1983–85; staff researcher, Oklahoma State Senate, Oklahoma City 1984, mem. 1992–2002; legal asst, Henry Henry & Henry, Shawnee 1985; Okla/Cleveland Co. Coordinator Robert Henry for Attorney General campaign 1986; law clerk, Andrews Davis Legg Bixler Milsten & Murrah, Oklahoma City 1987; legal intern, Cleveland Co. Legal Aid Office, Norman 1987–88; Pres. Brad Henry Oil Co., Inc., Shawnee 1987–89; Commr, Univ. of Oklahoma Election Comm. 1987–88; called to Okla Bar 1988, US Dist Court (We. Dist) Okla, US Court of Appeals (10th Circuit); assoc. attorney, Andrews Davis Legg Bixler Milsten & Price 1988–89; attorney, City of Shawnee 1989–2002; est. law firm Henry, Canavan & Hopkins PLLC; mem. Okla State Senate 1992–2002, Chair. Senate Judiciary Cttee; Gov. of Okla 2003–11; of Counsel, Lester, Loving & Davies, PC, Edmond, Okla 2011–; Co-founder Henry Adams Cos LLC, Norman, Okla; mem. Bd of Dirs Gateway to Prevention and Recovery, Inc.; mem. Asscn of Trial Lawyers of America, ABA, American Inns of Court, Pottawatomie Co. Bar Asscn (Pres. 1991), Okla Bar Asscn, Shawnee Chamber of Commerce, Jaycees, Lions, Norman Chamber of Commerce; mem. Bd Govs, Univ. Oklahoma 1982–84, Bd of Trustees, St Gregories Coll., Govs' Council, Health Project, Bipartisan Policy Center, Washington, DC 2011–; Democrat; Letzeiser Gold Medal, Univ. of Oklahoma, Outstanding Young Oklahoman 1997, Charles Dick Medal of Merit, Nat. Guard Asscn of US 2010. *Address:* Lester, Loving & Davies, PC, 1701 South Kelly Avenue, Edmond, OK 73013-3018, USA (office). *Telephone:* (405) 844-9900 (office). *Fax:* (405) 844-9958 (office). *E-mail:* info@lldlaw.com (office). *Website:* www.lldlaw.com (office).

HENRY, Graham, KNZM, BEd; New Zealand professional rugby union coach; b. 8 June 1946, Christchurch; m. Raewyn Henry; two s. one d.; ed Christchurch Boys High School, Univ. of Otago, Massey Univ.; played rugby union for Canterbury and cricket for Otago in the Plunket Shield; became a secondary school geography and physical education teacher 1969; taught at Auckland Grammar School 1973–81, coached first XV; Deputy Headmaster, Kelston Boys' High School 1982–87, Headmaster 1987–96, coached first XV; first major role as coach of Auckland prov. rugby team 1992–97, won Nat. Prov. Championship 1993, 1994, 1995, 1996; also coached the Blues in the Super 12, won title 1996, 1997, runner-up 1998, won title again as technical adviser 2003; left NZ to coach Wales (first ever Lions' coach from outside Home Nations) 1998–2002, became highest paid rugby union coach in the world, coached team to 11 consecutive victories; apptd coach of British and Irish Lions for their unsuccessful tour to Australia 2001; left Wales following record defeat to Ireland (54–10) in Six Nations 2002; returned to NZ and apptd defensive coach of the Blues during Super 12 season 2003; coach of New Zealand rugby team (All Blacks) 2004–11, began career with wins over Rugby World Cup 2003 winners England in NZ in both Tests 2004, coached All Blacks in 3–0 series defeat of British and Irish Lions 2005, to Tri-Nations victories 2005, 2006, 2007, 2008, 2010, to second ever Grand Slam over the four Home Nations 2005, lost to France (20–18) in World Cup quarterfinal 2007, coached All Blacks to win Rugby World Cup defeating France 8–7 in final 2011, coached All Blacks to 88 wins in 103 Tests (140 matches); announced retirement as coach of New Zealand 1 Nov. 2011; Asst Coach, Argentina Rugby Team 2012–13; Consultant, Leinster Rugby Team 2016–; Int. Rugby Bd (IRB) Int. Coach of the Year 2005, 2006, 2008, 2010, 2011. *Address:* Leinster Rugby Office, Newstead Building A UCD, Belfield, Dublin 4, Ireland (office). *Telephone:* (1) 2693224 (office). *Fax:* (1) 2693142 (office). *E-mail:* information@leinsterrugby.ie (office). *Website:* www.leinsterrugby.ie (office).

HENRY, Sir Lenworth (Lenny) George, Kt, CBE, BA (Hons); British comedian, actor, writer and television presenter; b. 29 Aug. 1958; m. Dawn French (q.v.) (divorced 2010); one d.; Monaco Red Cross Award, The Golden Nymph Award (for Alive and Kicking) 1992, BBC Personality of the Year, Radio and Television Industry Club 1993, Golden Rose of Montreux Award for Lenny in Pieces (Christmas Special) 2000, Lifetime Achievement Award for Ongoing Performance UK Comedy Awards 2003. *Tours include:* Loud!, UK and Australia 1994, 1995, Large!, UK, Australia and NZ 1998, Have You Seen This Man tour 2001, So Much Things to Say, Wyndhams Theatre 2003, tour 2004, Where You From? tour 2007–08, Othello regional tour and West End (London Evening Standard Theatre Award for Outstanding Newcomer 2009) 2009. *Films include:* The Suicide Club 1988, Work Experience 1989, True Identity 1991, Famous Fred 1997, Mirrormask 2004, Harry Potter and the Prisoner of Azkaban 2004, MirrorMask 2005, Penelope 2008, The Pirates! in an Adventure with Scientists 2012, Postman Pat: The Movie 2014. *Radio:* Lenny and Will Acts 1 & 2 2006, Anansi Boys 2007, Rudy's Rare Records series 2008–12, Bad Faith 2008, What's So Great About? 2008. *Television includes:* New Faces (debut) 1975, Tiswas 1978–81, Three of a Kind 1981–83, The Lenny Henry Show 1984–85, 1987–88, Comic Relief 1985–, Lenny Henry Tonite! 1986, Coast to Coast 1990, Alive and Kicking 1991, Bernard and the Genie 1991, In Dreams 1992, The Real McCoy 1992, Chef (title role) (three series) 1993–96, Lenny Hunts the Funk, New Soul Nation, White Goods 1994, Funky Black Shorts 1994, Comic Relief, Lenny Go Home 1996, British Acad. Awards (host) 1997, Lenny's Big Amazon Adventure 1997, Lenny Goes to Town 1998, The Man 1999, Hope and Glory 1999–2000, Lenny's Atlantic Adventure 2000, Lenny in Pieces (Christmas Special) 2000, Lenny in Pieces (Christmas Special) 2001, Lenny Henry – This is My Life 2003, Lenny Henry in Pieces series 2 2003, The Lenny Henry Show 2004, Berry's Way 2006, Lenny's Britain 2007, Lennyhenry.tv 2008, Big & Small 2008–11, Happy Birthday OU 2009, Live at the Apollo 2009, 2011, The Teaching Awards (presenter) 2010–, The Magicians (presenter) 2011, Famous, Rich and in the Slums 2011, Operation Health for Comic Relief 2015, The Olivier Awards (presenter) 2015, The Syndicate 2015. *Videos:* Lenny Henry Live and Unleashed 1989, Lenny Henry Live and Loud 1994. *Publications:* The Quest for the Big Woof (autobiog.) 1991, Charlie and the Big Chill (children's book) 1995. *Leisure interests:* R'n'B, HipHop, Funk, reading, tennis, comics, family. *Address:* c/o PBJ Management Ltd, 5 Soho Square, London, W1D 3QA, England (office). *Telephone:* (20) 7287-1112 (office). *Fax:* (20) 7287-1191 (office). *E-mail:* general@pbjmgt.co.uk (office). *Website:* www.pbjmgt.co.uk (office).

HENRY, Thierry Daniel; French professional footballer (retd); b. 17 Aug. 1977, Les Ulis, Essonne, Paris; s. of Antoine Henry and Maryse Henry; m. Nicole Merry 2003 (divorced 2007); one s. one d.; Partner Andrea Rajacic 2008; striker/winger; signed as schoolboy player, Versailles football club; youth player, CO Les Ulis 1983–89, US Palaiseau 1989–90, Viry-Châtillon 1990–92, Clairefontaine 1992, Monaco 1992–94; sr player, Monaco 1994–99 (won Ligue 1 1996–97, French Super Cup 1997), Juventus, Italy 1999, Arsenal, England 1999–2007 (winner FA Cup 2002, 2003, 2005, Premiership 2002, 2004, Community Shield 2002, 2004, Capt. of team 2005–07), 2012 (on loan), Barcelona, Spain 2007–10 (won La Liga 2008/09, 2009/10, Copa del Rey 2008/09, UEFA Champions League 2008/09, Supercopa de España 2009, UEFA Super Cup 2009, FIFA Club World Cup 2009); with New York Red Bulls 2010–11, 2012–14 (won MLS Eastern Conf. 2010, Atlantic Cup 2011, Walt Disney World Pro Soccer Classic 2010, Emirates Cup 2011), apptd Capt. 2011; mem. French nat. team 1997–2010 (winner FIFA World Cup 1998, UEFA European Football Championship 2000, FIFA Confederations Cup 2003), Capt. 2008–10; retd 2014; Second Asst Man., Belgium Nat. Football Team 2016; mem. UNICEF-FIFA squad; Chevalier, Légion d'honneur 1998; Premier League 10 Seasons Awards 1992/93–2001/02, UNFP Ligue 1 Young Player of the Year 1996–97, PFA Players' Player of the Year 2002–03, 2003–04, PFA Team of the Year 2000–01, 2001–02, 2002–03, 2003–04, 2004–05, 2005–06, FWA Footballer of the Year 2002–03, 2003–04, 2005–06, Premier League Golden Boot 2001–02, 2003–04, 2004–05, 2005–06, Golden Boot Landmark Award 10 2004–05, Golden Boot Landmark Award 20 2004–05, Premier League Goal of the Season 2002–03, UEFA Team of the Year 2001, 2002, 2003, 2004, 2006, MLS Best XI 2011, Onze d'Or 2003, 2006, European Golden Boot 2003–04, 2004–05, French Player of the Year 2000, 2003, 2004, 2005, 2006, IFFHS World's Top Goal Scorer of the Year 2003, FIFA FIFPro World XI 2006, FIFA World Cup All-Star Team Germany 2006, FIFA Confederations Cup Golden Ball France 2003, FIFA Confederations Cup Golden Shoe France 2003, UEFA European Football Championship Team of the Tournament 2000, FIFA 100 2004, Time 100 Heroes & Pioneers No. 16 2007, inducted into English Football Hall of Fame 2008, MLS Best XI 2011. *Website:* www.newyorkredbulls.com.

HENRYSSON, Haraldur; Icelandic judge; b. 17 Feb. 1938, Reykjavik; s. of Henry Alexander Hálfdanarson and Gudrun Thorsteinsdottir; m. Elisabet Kristinsdóttir 1972; one s.; ed Reykjavik High School, Univ. of Iceland; Asst Judge 1964–73; Judge, Criminal Court, Reykjavik 1973–89; fmr Judge Supreme Court, Pres. 1996–97; Chair. Cttee Investigating Accidents at Sea 1973–83; Pres. Nat. Life Saving Asscn 1982–90; Vice-mem. Althing 1967–71; Kt Grand Cross of Icelandic Falcon. *Leisure interest:* outdoor sports.

HEPPELL, (Thomas) Strachan, CB; British public service official; b. 15 Aug. 1935, Teesside; s. of Leslie Heppell and Doris Potts; m. Felicity Rice 1963; two s.; ed Acklam Hall Grammar School, Middlesbrough and Queen's Coll. Oxford; Asst Prin. Nat. Assistance Bd (NAB) 1958; Prin. NAB, Cabinet Office, Dept of Health and Social Security (DHSS) 1963; Asst Dir of Social Welfare, Hong Kong 1971–73; Asst Sec. DHSS 1973, Under-Sec. 1979; Deputy Sec. DHSS, Dept of Health 1983–95; Chair. Man. Bd European Medicines Agency 1994–2000, Chair. Audit Advisory Cttee 2005–12; Chair. European Inst. for Health 2007–10; Consultant Dept of Health 1995–2000; Chair. Family Fund Trust 1997–2003; Visiting Fellow, LSE 1996–2000; mem. Broadcasting Standards Comm. 1996–2002. *Publications:* contribs to publs on social security, social welfare, health and pharmaceuticals. *Address:* 61 Tor Bryan, Ingatestone, CM4 9HN, England.

HERAEUS, Jürgen, PhD; German business executive; *Chairman of the Supervisory Board, Heraeus Holding GmbH;* b. 2 Sept. 1936, Hanau; m.; five d.; ed Univ. of Munich; joined family firm Heraeus Holding GmbH 1964, lived in USA for two years and worked for several Heraeus subsidiaries, mem. Bd of Man. 1970–, Head of Finance 1970, Vice-Chair. Bd of Man. 1977–83, Chair. 1983–2000, Chair. Supervisory Bd 2000–, Chair. Shareholders' Cttee 2000–; Chair. TEUTONIA Zementwerk AG, Lafarge Roofing GmbH; mem. Supervisory Bd Messer Group GmbH 2001–, Chair. 2004–; Chair. Supervisory Bd MG Technologies AG (now GEA Group AG) 2003–16; Chair. Business 20 (B20) 2017–; mem. Admin. Bd Argor-Heraeus SA, Switzerland; Special Adviser CVC Capital Partners; Sr Adviser to WTO Cttee in Shanghai and Chair. Working Group on China, Asia Pacific Cttee of German Business (APA), Berlin 1998–; mem. Bd of Dirs Buderus AG, EPCOS AG, Heidelberger Druckmaschinen AG, IKB Deutsche Industriebank, Schmalbach-Lubeca AG; mem. Presidium, Bundesverbandes der Deutschen Industrie (Fed. of German Industries) 1990–; mem. Advisory Bd Technische Universität, Darmstadt 2001–, Chair. 2007–; Chair. German UN Children's Fund, UNICEF 2008–18; Chair. Kathinka Platzhoff Foundation; mem. Int. Advisory Bd and Joint Advisory Council, Allianz SE –2015; Fed. Cross of Merit, First Class 2000; Hon. Chair. German UN Children's Fund, UNICEF inducted into Manager Magazine Hall of Fame 2009, German Founders' Award for Lifetime Achievement 2012. *Address:* Heraeus Holding GmbH, Postfach 1561, 63405 Hanau (office); Heraeus Holding GmbH, Heraeusstrasse 12–14, 63450 Hanau, Germany (office). *Telephone:* (6181) 35-0 (office). *Fax:* (6181) 35-35-50 (office). *E-mail:* info.electro-nite.de@heraeus.com (office). *Website:* www.heraeus.com (office).

HERBEN, Mathieu (Mat); Dutch politician; b. 15 July 1952, The Hague; m. 1975; one d.; journalist for internal publications, Ministry of Defence 1977–87, Chief Ed. 1990–2002; Ed.-in-Chief, Manna (catholic newspaper) 1987–90; various roles with Orde van Vrijmetselaren (freemasons' lodge) 1993–97; Leader, Lijst Pim

Fortuyn (LPT) May–Aug. 2002, Parl. Leader May 2002, Leader LPF Advisory Council Aug. 2002–06; Owner, Consultancy Media and Politics Consult 2007; Sr Adviser, NIDV 2007. *Publications include:* De Luchtstrijdkrachten van het Warschaupact en neutraal Europa 1982, Vijftig jaar vrijmetselaarij, Vrij denken. Over religie, politiek en vrijmetselarij 2005. *Leisure interests:* classical music, reading, nature.

HERBERT, Adam, BA, MPA, PhD; American university administrator and professor of public administration; *Professor Emeritus, Indiana University;* b. Muskogee, Okla; m. Karen Herbert; ed Univs of Southern Calif. and Pittsburgh; White House Fellow in Ford Admin 1974, served as Special Asst to US Sec. of Health, Educ. and Welfare; Special Asst to US Under-Sec. of Housing and Urban Devt 1975; academic positions at Univ. of Southern Calif., Howard Univ., Va Polytechnic Inst. and State Univ., Univ. of Pittsburgh; fmr Dean School of Public Affairs and Services and Vice-Pres. for Academic Affairs, Fla Int. Univ.; fmrly Regents Prof. and Founding Exec. Dir, The Fla Center for Public Policy and Leadership, Univ. of N Fla, also Univ. Pres. 1989–98; Chancellor of State Univ. System of Fla 1998–2000; Prof. of Public Admin and Political Science, and Pres. Indiana Univ. 2003–07, currently Prof. Emer.; Sr Consultant Michael L. Buckner Law Firm 2009–; led transition team for Gov.-Elect Jeb Bush 1998; Co-Chair. Gov. Bush's Reading Priority Transition Team 2002; fmr Pres. Nat. Asscn of Schools of Public Affairs and Admin; Chair. Jacksonville Chamber of Commerce 1993; served as Fla Commr, Comm. on Educ.; mem. Bd of Dirs Indiana Univ. Foundation –2010, St Joe Corpn; mem. Nat. Acad. of Public Admin (NAPA), Knight Foundation Comm. on Intercollegiate Athletics, Fla Fed. Judicial Nominating Comm. *Address:* c/o Indiana University, 107 South Indiana Avenue, Bloomington, IN 47405-7000, USA (office).

HERBERT, Rt Rev. Christopher William, BA, MPhil, PhD; British ecclesiastic (retd); b. 7 Jan. 1944, Lydney, Glos.; s. of Walter Herbert and Hilda Dibben; m. Janet Turner 1968; two s.; ed Monmouth School, Univ. of Wales, Lampeter, Univ. of Bristol, Wells Theological Coll., Univ. of Leicester; Curate, St Paul's, Tupsley, Hereford 1967–71; Adviser in Religious Educ., Diocese of Hereford 1971–76, Dir of Educ. 1976–81; Vicar, St Thomas on the Bourne, Diocese of Guildford 1981–90, Dir of Post-Ordination Training 1984–90; Archdeacon of Dorking 1990–95; Bishop of St Albans 1995–2009; Visiting Prof. of Christian Ethics, Univ. of Surrey 2016–; Hon. Citizen, Fano, Italy; Hon. DLitt (Hertfordshire), Hon. DArts (Bedfordshire). *Publications include:* Be Thou My Vision 1985, This Most Amazing Day 1986, The Question of Jesus 1987, Alive to God 1987, Ways Into Prayer 1987, Help in Your Bereavement 1988, Prayers for Children 1993, Pocket Prayers 1993, The Prayer Garden 1994, Words of Comfort 1994, A Little Prayer Diary 1996, Pocket Prayers for Children 1999, Pocket Prayers for Commuters 2009, Health 2012, Foreshadowing the Reformation: Art and Religion in the 15th Century Burgundian Netherlands 2016; contrib. to Edinburgh Companion to the Bible and the Arts 2014. *Leisure interests:* cycling, reading, writing, walking, art history. *Address:* 1 Beacon Close, Farnham, Surrey, GU10 4PA, England (home). *Telephone:* (1252) 795600 (home). *E-mail:* cwherbert7@gmail.com (home). *Website:* www.threeabbeys.me.uk.

HERBERT, Gary Richard; American business executive, politician and state governor; *Governor of Utah;* b. 7 May 1947, American Fork, Utah; s. of Paul Peters and Carol Peters; adopted s. of Duane Barlow Herbert; m. Jeanette Snelson; three s. three d.; ed Orem High School, served two-year mission for the Church of Jesus Christ of Latter-day Saints in Eastern Atlantic States Mission, later attended Brigham Young Univ.; served for six years as mem. Utah Army Nat. Guard, becoming a staff sergeant; est. real estate firm, Herbert & Assocs Realtors in Orem, and a child-care service with his wife, The Kids Connection; Commr on Utah Co. Comm. 1990–2004; fmr Pres. Utah Asscn of Counties, Utah Asscn of Realtors; campaigned for Republican nomination for Gov. of Utah Nov. 2003, running mate of Jon Huntsman April 2004, Lt-Gov. of Utah 2005–09, served as Chair. of 13 statewide comms, including Comm. on Volunteers and Comm. on Civic and Character Educ. and the Emergency Man. Admin. Council, Gov. of Utah 2009–; Vice-Chair. Nat. Governors Asscn 2014–15, Chair. 2015–16; mem. Bd Provo Orem Chamber of Commerce, Utah Water Conservancy Dist; Republican. *Address:* Office of the Governor, Utah State Capitol Complex, 350 North State Street, Suite 200, PO Box 142220, Salt Lake City, UT 84114-2220, USA (office). *Telephone:* (801) 538-1000 (office). *Fax:* (801) 538-1528 (office); (801) 538-1557 (office). *Website:* www.utah .gov/governor (office).

HERBISH, Suleiman Jasir Al-, BA, MEconSc; Saudi Arabian international organization official; b. 6 Nov. 1942, Ar-Rass; m. Dr May Al-Jasser; four c.; ed Trinity Univ., San Antonio, Tex., USA, Univ. of Cairo, Egypt; fmr Dir Saline Water Conversion Corpn, Saudi Co. for Precious Metals; Asst Deputy Minister 1982–90; fmr Chair. Nat. Shipping Co. of Saudi Arabia, Saudi Arabian Oil Texaco Ltd (later renamed Saudi Arabian Chevron Co.), Arabian Drilling Co.; Gov. for Saudi Arabia, OPEC, Vienna 1990–2003; Dir-Gen. OPEC Fund for Int. Devt 2003–18; Commdr, Ordre Nat. Ivoirien (Côte d'Ivoire) 2009, Commdr, Order of Wissam Al Alaoui (Morocco) 2009, Chevalier, Ordre Nat. (Burkina Faso) 2011, Medal of Nat. Recognition (Mauritania) 2012, Golden Medal of Merit and Excellence (Palestine) 2013, Order of the Two Niles, First Degree (Sudan) 2013, Golden Medal of Merit and Excellence (Palestine) 2013, Grand Decoration of Honor in Silver with Sash (Austria) 2013, Nat. Order of Merit (Côte d'Ivoire) 2013, Grand Decoration of Honor in Gold (Austria) 2015; Congressional Medal of Achievement (Philippines) 2005, Prix de la Fondation, Crans Montana Forum 2007, Anania Shirakatsi Medal (Armenia) 2009. *Address:* c/o OPEC Fund for International Development, Parkring 8, 1010 Vienna, Austria.

HERBST, John Edward; American diplomatist (retd); *Director, Atlantic Council Dinu Patriciu Eurasia Center;* b. 1952; m. Nadezda Christoff Herbst.; five c.; ed School of Foreign Service, Georgetown Univ., Fletcher School of Law and Diplomacy; worked in embassies in Moscow and Saudi Arabia; Dir Office of Ind. States and Commonwealth Affairs; Dir Office of Regional Affairs, Near East Asia Bureau; Political Counsellor, Embassy in Tel-Aviv; Deputy Dir for Econs, Office of Soviet Union Affairs; Dir for Policy, Nat. Security Council; Prin. Deputy to Amb.-at-Large for the New Ind. States; Consul-Gen. Jerusalem 1997–2000; Amb. to Uzbekistan 2000–03, to Ukraine 2003–06; Coordinator, Office for Reconstruction and Stabilization, US State Dept 2006–10; Dir, Atlantic Council Dinu Patriciu Eurasia Center 2014–. *Address:* Atlantic Council, 1030 15th Street, NW, 12th Floor, Washington, DC 20050 (office); 8355 Thompson Road, Annandale, VA 22003, USA (home). *Telephone:* (202) 463-7226 (office). *Fax:* (202) 463-7241 (office). *E-mail:* info@AtlanticCouncil.org (office). *Website:* www.atlanticcouncil.org/about/experts/list/john-e-herbst (office).

HERCUS, Dame (Margaret) Ann, DCMG, BA, LLB; New Zealand politician, diplomatist and international consultant; b. 24 Feb. 1942, Hamilton; d. of Horace Sayers and Mary Sayers (née Ryan); m. John Hercus; two s.; ed Univs of Auckland and Canterbury; Lawyer and Staff Training Officer, Beath & Co., Christchurch 1969–70; mem. Price Tribunal and Trade Practices Comm. 1973–75; Deputy Chair. Commerce Comm. 1975–78; Chair. Consumer Rights Campaign 1975; MP for Lyttelton 1978–87, Opposition Spokesperson on Social Welfare, Consumer Affairs and Women's Affairs 1978–84; Minister of Social Welfare, Police and Women's Affairs 1984–87; Perm. Rep. to UN, New York 1989–90; int. consultant 1991–98; Chief of Mission, UN Force in Cyprus 1998–99; mem. Bd of Dirs Television New Zealand Ltd 2002–05 (resgnd); Labour. *Leisure interests:* collecting original New Zealand prints, theatre, reading. *Address:* 209 Collingwood Street, Nelson 7010, New Zealand. *E-mail:* ajhercus@clear.net.nz.

HERFKENS, Eveline L.; Dutch diplomat, politician and UN official; b. 1952, The Hague; ed Leiden Univ.; Policy Officer for Devt Cooperation, Ministry of Foreign Affairs 1976–81; mem. Lower House of Parl. 1981–90; Treasurer and mem. Cttee of Parliamentarians for Global Action 1985–96; mem. Econ. Cttee, Parliamentary Ass. of Council of Europe 1986–89, also Jt Organiser North-South Campaign; Exec. Dir World Bank, Washington, DC 1990–96; Amb. and Perm. Rep. to UN, Geneva 1996–98; Minister for Devt Co-operation 1998–2002; Exec. Coordinator Millennium Devt Goals Campaign, UN, NY 2002–06, Special Adviser 2006–; fmr Chair. Evert Vermeer Foundation, Dutch Fair Trade Org.; fmr mem. Council of the Labour Party (PvdA), Devt Cttee of Netherlands Council of Churches; mem. Bd of Dirs International Partnership for Microbicides 2008–. *Address:* c/o Board of Directors, International Partnership for Microbicides, 8401 Colesville Road, Suite 200, Silver Spring, MD 20910, USA.

HÉRIARD DUBREUIL, Dominique; French business executive; b. 6 July 1946, Paris; d. of André Hériard Dubreuil and Anne-Marie Hériard Dubreuil (née Renaud); m. Alain-Pierre Jacquet 1975; one d.; ed Univ. of Paris II (Panthéon-Assas) and Inst. des Relations Publiques; press attaché, Havas Conseil 1969–72; est. public relations dept for Ogilvy & Mather 1972; Programme Head, Hill & Knowlton 1973–75; est. public relations dept for McCann-Erickson France 1975–77; Founder, Chair. and Man. Dir Agence Infoplan 1978–87; Man. Dir E. Rémy Martin & Cie SA 1988–, Chair. 1990–, CEO Rémy Cointreau 1998–2004, Chair. 2001–12; currently Chair. Cointreau SAS; Pres. Fed. of Wine and Spirit Exporters of France 1992–94; Pres. Comite Colbert 1994–98, Vinexpo 1998; mem. Supervisory Bd Vivendi; Chevalier, Légion d'honneur, Officier, Ordre nat. du Mérite. *Leisure interest:* visual arts. *Address:* Rémy Cointreau, 21 boulevard Haussman, 75009 Paris, France (office). *Telephone:* 1-44-13-44-13 (office). *Fax:* 1-44-13-44-66 (office); 1-45-62-82-52 (office). *E-mail:* dominique.heriard.dubreuil@remy-cointreau.com (office). *Website:* www.remy-cointreau.com (office).

HERING, Jürgen; German librarian; b. 15 Sept. 1937, Chemnitz; s. of Karl Hering and Margot Hering (née Schubert); m. Inge Rich 1961; one s. two d.; ed Univs of Stuttgart, Munich and Tübingen; Library Asst Stuttgart Univ. Library 1968, Library Adviser 1971, Sr Library Adviser 1972, Librarian 1974, Chief Librarian 1975–96; Chief Librarian Sächsische Landesbibliothek–Staats and Dresden Univ. Library 1997–2003 (retd); Chair. Verein Deutscher Bibliothekare 1979–83, First Deputy Chair. 1983–85; Geschäftsführer Max-Kade-Stiftung Stuttgart 1982–, Wissenschaftlicher Beirat Bibliothek für Zeitgeschichte, Stuttgart 1986–99, Kuratorium Deutsches Biblioteksinstitut Berlin 1990–95; mem. Exec. Cttee German Libraries Asscn 1992–95 (Chair. 1989–92); Adviser, Stiftung Preussischer Kulturbesitz 1999–2003; Hon. Prof., School of Eng, Econs and Culture 1999; Verdienstorden des Freistaates Sachsen 2003, Cross of Merit (Germany) 2009, Verdienstkreuz am Bande des Verdienstordens der Bundesrepublik Deutschland 2009; Dr Josef Bick Ehrenmedaille (Austria) 1992, Saxon Merit Award 2003. *Leisure interests:* photography, travel. *Address:* Eichenparkstrasse 34, 70619 Stuttgart, Germany (home). *Telephone:* (711) 473944 (home). *Fax:* (711) 47059770 (home). *E-mail:* juergen.k.hering@web.de.

HERKERT, Craig R., BS, MBA; American business executive; b. 1959; ed St Francis Coll., Northern Illinois Univ.; first job as teenager at Jewel-Osco; spent 23 years with Albertsons and American Stores, held positions including Exec. Vice-Pres., Marketing, and Pres., Acme Markets; Pres. and CEO The Americas, Wal-Mart 2007–09; Pres. and CEO Supervalu Inc. 2009–12; Vice-Pres. Distribucion y Servicio SA; mem. Exec. Cttee Minnesota Business Partnership; mem. Bd and Exec. Cttee Food Marketing Inst.; mem. The Business Council (nat. org. of CEOs), Bd of the Council of the Americas.

HERKSTRÖTER, Cornelius Antonius Johannes, BSc; Dutch business executive; b. 21 Aug. 1937, Venlo; m. Regina Maria Haske 1959; two s. one d.; ed Erasmus Univ. Rotterdam; qualified as chartered accountant; joined Billiton as business economist 1967, following acquisition of Billiton by Shell Petroleum, apptd. Head Dept Financial and Econ. Affairs 1971, various sr posts in Billiton cos, Switzerland and Netherlands 1972–80, Area Co-ordinator SE Asia, Shell Int. Petroleum Co. Ltd 1980, Vice-Pres. (Finance) Shell Française SA 1982, Chair. Bd of Man. Deutsche Shell AG 1985, Regional Co-ordinator Europe, Dir Shell Internationale Petroleum Mij. BV 1988, Man. Dir The Shell Petroleum Co. Ltd, Chair. Supervisory Bd Shell Nederland BV, Group Man. Dir 1989, Chair. Supervisory Bd Deutsche Shell AG 1990, Dir Shell UK Ltd; Chair. Bd of Dirs Billiton Int. Metals BV 1991; Pres. NV Koninklijke Nederlandsche Petroleum Maatschappij (Royal Dutch Petroleum Co.) 1992–98; mem. Supervisory Bd ING Groep N.V. 1998–2007, Chair. 1999–2007; fmr Chair. Public Advisory Council Tinbergen Inst.; fmr Chair. Supervisory Council Erasmus Univ.; Prof. Int. Man. Amsterdam Univ.; Trustee, Int. Accounting Standards Cttee; mem. Supervisory Bd DSM Special Products BV, Hollandsche Beton Group NV; mem. Int. Advisory Bd CNOOC Ltd; mem. Advisory Council Robert Bosch GmbH; Verdienstkreuz (First Class) (Germany), Kt Order of Netherlands Lion. *Leisure interests:* reading, music, photography.

HERMAN, Alexis M.; American politician and administrator; *Chairman and CEO, New Ventures LLC;* b. 16 July 1947, Mobile, Ala; m. Dr Charles Franklin 2000; ed Xavier Univ.; with Recruitment and Training Program Inc., US Dept of

Labor, New York City 1971–72, Consulting Supervisor 1973–74; Nat. Dir Minority Women's Employment Program 1974–77; Dir Women's Bureau, US Dept of Labor 1977–81, Washington, DC 1977–81; Founder A.M. Herman & Assocs, Washington, DC 1981, Pres. and CEO 1985–93; Chief of Staff and Deputy Chair. Democratic Nat. Convention Cttee –1991, CEO 1991–92; Deputy Dir Clinton-Gore Presidential Transition Office 1992–93; Asst to Pres. of USA; Public Liaison Dir White House 1993–96; Sec. of Labor 1997–2000; Chair. and CEO New Ventures LLC (corp. consulting firm) 2001–; Chair. and mem. North America Advisory Bd of Sodexo Inc. (formerly Sodexo Marriot Inc.) 2004–; mem. Toyota Advisory Bd on Diversity 2001–; mem. Bd of Dirs Cummins Inc. 2001–, MGM Resorts International 2002–, Entergy Corpn 2003–, Coca-Cola Company 2007–; mem. Nat. Council of Negro Women, Ron Brown Foundation; Sara Lee Front Runner Award 1999. *Address:* New Ventures LLC, 1333 H Street, NW, Washington, DC 20005, USA.

HERMANN, Valerie; French business executive; *President, Luxury Collections, Ralph Lauren;* three d.; Gen. Man. John Galliano –2005; CEO Yves Saint Laurent (acquired by the Gucci Group, the luxury div. of the PPR Group, in 1999) 2005–11; CEO Reed Krakoff 2011–14; Pres. Luxury Collections, Ralph Lauren 2014–. *Address:* Ralph Lauren Corpn, 625 Madison Avenue, New York, NY 10022, USA (office). *Telephone:* (212) 318-7000 (office).

HERMANS, Christopher, MA; Botswana banker; b. 23 Dec. 1936, Cape Town, South Africa; s. of Henry Hodgson Hermans and Marjorie Stanhope Hermans; m. 1st Janet Gallagher 1960 (divorced 1987); one s. two d.; m. 2nd Vonna Deulen 1987; two d.; ed Diocesan Coll., Rondebosch, Cape Town, Trinity Coll., Oxford, UK, Howard Univ. and Vanderbilt Univ., USA; Asst Sec. for Devt, Bechuanaland Protectorate Admin. 1961–66; Perm. Sec., Ministry of Devt Planning, Botswana Govt 1966–70, Ministry of Finance and Devt Planning 1970–75; Gov. Bank of Botswana 1975–77, 1987–99; Sr Planning Adviser/Loan Officer, World Bank 1977–82, CEO Thailand and Indonesia Programs Div., 1982–84; CEO World Bank Regional Mission, Bangkok 1984–87; Presidential Order of Meritorious Service. *Leisure interests:* tennis, wildlife, windsurfing, gardening.

HERMASZEWSKI, Gen. (retd) Mirosław; Polish astronaut and air force officer (retd); b. 15 Sept. 1941, Lipniki (now Ukraine); s. of Roman Hermaszewski and Kamila Hermaszewska; m. Emilia Hermaszewska 1965; one s. one d.; ed Air Force Officers School, Dęblin, Karol Sverchevski Mil. Acad., Gen. Staff Acad., Warsaw, Voroshilov Mil. Acad., Moscow; served in Nat. Air Defence 1964–76, 1st class pilot 1966, supersonic MiG-21 pilot 1967, flight leader 1971–72, Deputy Squadron Leader 1972–75, Regt Commdr 1975–76, master's class pilot in Cosmonauts' Training Centre, Zvezdnoy Gorodok, nr Moscow 1976–78, space flight on board Soyuz-30 and space-station Salyut-6 June–July (7 days 22 hours 2 minutes and 59 seconds) 1978, service in HQ of Nat. Air Defence 1978–80, Chief of Shkola Orlyat High Aviation School 1982–85, Second-in-Command, Air Forces and Air Defence of Polish Repub. 1990–91, Commdr Air Force Officers' School, Dęblin 1984–90, Adviser for Polish Sec. of Defence 2009; apptd mem. Space Research Cttee of Polish Acad. of Sciences 1978, Asscn of Space Explorers 1985; Pres. Gen. Bd Polish Astronautical Soc. 1983–87; Pres. Nat. Council of Aviation 1998–2000; Hon. Citizen, Frombork 1983, Wołów 2011; Gold Cross of Merit 1976, Cross of Grunwald Order (1st Class) 1978, Gold Star of Hero of USSR 1978, Order of Lenin 1978, Mil. Champion Pilot 1978, Cosmonaut of Polish People's Repub. 1978, Int. Order of Smile 1991, Order of Polonia Restituta 2003, Gold Order of Merit of Lower Silesia 2013; Gold Medal, Silver Medal and Bronze Medal of Armed Forces in the Service of the Fatherland, Gold Medal, Silver Medal and Broze Medal of Merit for Nat. Defense. *Leisure interests:* science fiction novels, sailing, hunting, sports, dogs. *Website:* www.hermaszewski.com.

HERNÁDI, Zsolt, BEcons; Hungarian business executive; *Chairman and CEO, MOL Group;* b. 1960; ed Budapest Univ. of Econ. Sciences; various posts with Kereskedelmi és Hitelbank Rt. 1989–94, becoming Deputy Gen. Man. 1992–94; CEO Cen. Bank of Hungarian Savings Cooperatives 1994–2001, Dir 1994–2002; Dir MOL Group 1999–, Chair. 2000–, CEO 2001–, mem. Corp. Governance and Remuneration Cttee; Dir Hungarian Banking Asscn 1995–2001, Panrusgas; mem. European Round Table of Industrialists 2001–; mem. Nat. Competitiveness Council 2017–; Hon. Citizen of Corvinus Univ. of Budapest 2009. *Address:* MOL Hungarian Oil and Gas Plc, 1117 Budapest, Október huszonharmadika u. 18, Hungary (office). *Telephone:* (1) 209-0000 (office). *Website:* www.mol.hu (office).

HERNÁNDEZ ALCERRO, Jorge Ramón; Honduran lawyer, politician and diplomatist; *Coordinator General of the Government;* b. 29 Aug. 1948; m.; two c.; ed Inst. Européen de Hautes Etudes Internationales, France, Univ. of Nice and Universidad Nacional Autónoma de Honduras; fmr attorney and lecturer at Univ. Nacional Autónoma de Honduras; fmr Judge, Inter-American Court of Human Rights; fmr Gen. Sec. Inovación y Unidad Party, Deputy to Nat. Ass. and Deputy to Nat. Congress; fmr Deputy Foreign Minister; Amb. and Perm. Rep. to UN, New York 1987–89; Amb. on Special Assignment in Latin America, USA and at UN Gen. Ass. 1990–94; Minister of the Interior and Justice 2002–06; Amb. to USA 2010–13; Coordinator Gen. of the Govt, Honduras 2014–. *Address:* Centro Cívico Gubernamental, Bulevar Fuerzas Armada, contiguo a Chiminike, Tegucigalpa, Honduras (office). *Telephone:* 2230-7000 (office). *Website:* www.scgg.gob.hn (office).

HERNÁNDEZ ALVARADO, Juan Orlando; Honduran lawyer, business executive, politician and head of state; *President;* b. 28 Oct. 1968, Gracias; s. of Juan Hernández Villanueva and Elvira Alvarado Castillo; m. Ana García Carías; one s. three d.; ed Universidad Nacional Autónoma de Honduras, State Univ. of New York, USA; business interests include coffee production in Gracias, hotels and broadcasting cos; Asst to First Sec. of Congreso Nacional (Parl.) 1990–94; Lecturer in constitutional law, Universidad Nacional Autónoma de Honduras –1999; mem. Congreso Nacional for Lempira 1998–2014, Pres. 2010–13; Pres. of Honduras 2014–; mem. Partido Nacional. *Address:* Office of the President, Palacio José Cecilio del Valle, Boulevard Francisco Morazán, Tegucigalpa, Honduras (office). *Telephone:* 2290-5010 (office). *Fax:* 2231-0097 (office). *E-mail:* diseloalpresidente@presidencia.gob.hn (office).

HERNÁNDEZ DE COS, Pablo, PhD; Spanish banker and economist; *Governor, Banco de España;* b. 21 Jan. 1971, Madrid; ed Univ. Coll. of Financial Studies (CUNEF), Univ. of Madrid, Complutense Univ. of Madrid, IESE Business School; Economist, DG Econs, Statistics and Research, Banco de España 1997–2004, Head of Econ. Policy Analysis Div. 2007–15, Dir-Gen. 2015–18, Gov. 2018–; mem. Public Finances Working Group, European Central Bank 1998–2004, then Chair. 2010–15, Adviser to the Exec. Bd 2004–07, Alternate to the Gov. 2015–18, also mem. Governing and Gen. Council 2018–; Assoc. Lecturer of Econs, Univ. of Madrid 2000–04, Instituto de Empresa 2011–14; mem. Working Group on Ageing and Sustainability 1998–2014, Econ. Policy Cttee of ECOFIN Council, EU 2008–14, Econ. and Financial Cttee 2017–18; Vice-Chair. Bd, Macroprudential Authority Financial Stability Bd 2019–; mem. Experts' Cttee, Reform of Spanish Tax System 2013–14; mem. Consejo Superior de Estadística de España 2015–18, Consejo de Estado 2018–, BIS Group of Govs and Heads of Supervision 2018–, Financial Stability Bd 2018–; mem. Bd, Int. Center for Monetary and Banking Studies 2016–19; mem. Bd of Govs, Center for Latin American Monetary Studies 2018–; mem. Gen. Bd of European Systemic Risk 2018–; mem. Bd of Trustees, Centro de Estudios Monetarios y Financieros 2015– (Pres. 2018–), Exec. Bd of Foundation for Applied Econ. Studies 2015–18. *Address:* Banco de España, Calle de Alcalá, 48, 28014, Madrid, Spain (office). *Telephone:* (91) 3385000 (office). *E-mail:* bde@bde.es. *Website:* www.bde.es (office).

HERODOTOU, Constantinos, BSc, MBA; Cypriot economist and central banker; *Governor, Central Bank of Cyprus;* ed Univ. Coll. London and London Business School, UK; Exec. Dir UBS Investment Bank 2001–12; Man. Dir Sentaris Capital Partners 2012–13; Lead Advisory, Ernst & Young Oct. 2013–June 2014; Exec. Dir and Bd mem., Cen. Bank of Cyprus 2017–, Gov. 2019–; Commr of Privatizations of the Repub. of Cyprus 2014–17. *Address:* Central Bank of Cyprus, 80, Kennedy Avenue, POB 25529, 1076 Nicosia, Cyprus (office). *Telephone:* 22714100 (office). *Fax:* 22714959 (office). *Website:* www.centralbank.cy (office).

HERRERA, Juan Felipe; American poet, writer and academic; b. 27 Dec. 1948, Fowler, Calif.; ed Univ. of California, Los Angeles, Stanford Univ., Univ. of Iowa; Instructor, Stanford Univ. 1979–80, De Anza Community Coll. 1986–88, New Coll. of California 1987–88; Teaching Fellow, Univ. of Iowa Writers' Workshop 1988–90; Assoc. Prof. of English, Univ. of Southern Illinois at Carbondale 1992–93; Prof. of Culture Studies and Creative Writing, California State Univ., Fresno 1990–2005; Prof. of Creative Writing, Univ. of California, Riverside 2005–15, Prof. Emer. 2015–; Visiting Prof., Dept of American Ethnic Studies, Univ. of Washington-Seattle 2015; Poet Laureate of California 2012–15; Poet Laureate of US 2015–17. *Publications include:* Rebozos of Love 1974, Exiles of Desire 1985, Facegames 1987, Akrilika 1989, Memoria(s) from an Exile's Notebook of the Future 1993, The Roots of a Thousand Embraces 1994, Night Train to Tuxtla 1994, Calling the Doves 1995, Love After the Riots 1996, Mayan Drifter: Chicano Poet in the Lowlands of America 1997, Border Crosser with a Lamborghini Dream 1999, Loteria Cards and Fortune Poems 1999, Crashboomlove: A Novel in Verse 1999, The Upside Down Boy 2000, Thunderweavers 2000, Giraffe on Fire 2001, Grandma and Me at the Flea 2002, Notebooks of a Chile Verde Smuggler 2002, Cilantro Girl 2003, 187 Reasons Mexicanos Can't Cross the Border: Undocuments 1971–2007 2008, Half of the World in Light (Nat. Book Critics Circle Award in Poetry) 2008, Senegal Taxi 2013, Notes on the Assemblage 2015. *Address:* Department of Creative Writing, University of California, College of Humanities, Arts and Social Sciences, Riverside, CA 92521, USA (office). *Telephone:* (951) 827-5027 (office). *E-mail:* juan.herrera@ucr.edu (office). *Website:* www.creativewriting.ucr.edu/herrera (office); www.loc.gov/poetry.

HERRERA, Paloma; Argentine ballet dancer; b. 21 Dec. 1975, Buenos Aires; d. of Alberto Herrera and Marisa Herrera; ed Teatro Colón, Buenos Aires, Minsk Ballet School, School of American Ballet; joined American Ballet Theater (ABT) corps de ballet; roles in Sleeping Beauty, Don Quixote and La Bayadère; soloist, ABT 1992, prin. dancer 1995–; leading role in How Near Heaven (cr. for her by (Twyla Tharp q.v.), 1994); other notable roles include Clara in The Nutcracker, Medora in Le Corsaire, Kitri in Don Quixote, Juliet in Romeo and Juliet 1995; Int. Prize Gino Tani 1997, Top Ten Dancers of the Twentieth Century, Dance Magazine 1999, Leader of the Millennium, Time Magazine and CNN 1999, Konex Platinum Prize, Ballerina of the Decade 1989–99, Buenos Aires, Argentina 1999, Maria Ruanova Award 2000, NY Immigrant Achievement Award 2001. *Address:* American Ballet Theater, 890 Broadway, New York, NY 10003 (office); One Lincoln Plaza, 20 West 64th Street, Apt F, New York, NY 10023, USA (home); Billinghurst 2553, 10 Piso Dto, CP 1425 Buenos Aires, Argentina. *Website:* www.palomaherrera.com; www.abt.org.

HERRERA ARAYA, Marvin; Costa Rican politician and international organization executive; Deputy Minister of Public Educ. 1978–81; mem. Inter-American Cttee on Educ., OAS 1980–82; Deputy to Legis. Ass. 1982–86; Minister of Public Educ. 1990–94; mem. Higher Council of Educ. 1999–2003; apptd Sec.-Gen. Coordinación Educativa y Cultural Centroamericana 2003.

HERRERA FLORES, Jordy Hernán; Mexican economist and politician; b. 24 Jan. 1974; ed Universidad Iberoamericana; subject teacher in Dept of Econs, Universidad Iberoamericana 1996–2003; Dir-Gen. Liaison H. Congress of the Social Devt Secr. Jan.–Nov. 2001; Sec. to Dir-Gen. of Banobras April–Sept. 2003; Pvt. Sec. to the Sec. of Energy 2003–04; Dir-Gen. Investment Promotion Unit, Ministry of Energy 2004–05; Undersecretary of Energy Planning and Technological Devt, Ministry of Energy 2006–10; Sec. of State for Energy 2011–12; CEO Pemex Gas and Basic Petrochemicals 2010–11, CEO Petróleos Mexicanos (PEMEX) 2011–12; mem. Partido Acción Nacional. *Address:* Partido Acción Nacional (PAN), Avenida Coyoacán 1546, Col. del Valle, Del. Benito Juárez, 03100 México DF, Mexico (office). *Telephone:* (55) 5200-4000 (office). *E-mail:* correo@cen.pan.org.mx (office). *Website:* www.pan.org.mx (office).

HERRERA NICOLALDE, Fausto Eduardo, MBA; Ecuadorean economist and government official; ed Pontificia Universidad Católica del Ecuador, INCAE Business School, Costa Rica; Jr Consultant, Inter-American Devt Bank 2002–03; several roles within Ministry of Economy and Finance including Coordinator of Studies and Macroeconomic Programming 2003–06, Asst Sec. for Econ. Policy 2005–06, Asst Sec. for Fiscal Consistency 2007–08, Adviser to Nat. Sec., Nat. Secr. for Planning and Devt (SENPLADES) 2009, Adviser to Minister of Finance 2010, Asst Sec. for Fiscal Relations 2012, Vice-Minister of Finance 2012–13, Minister of Finance 2013–16.

HERRERA NIETO, Gen. (retd) Nelson; Ecuadorean government official, fmr diplomatist and fmr army officer; fmr Dir of Educ. for the Army; fmr Dir Instituto de Altos Estudios Nacionales; fmr Commdr Aerial Brigade of the Army; fmr Amb. to Mexico; fmr Pres. INVEREC; Minister of Nat. Defence 2004–05; fmr mem. Instituto Panamericano de Geografía e Historia.

HERRERO ACOSTA, Fernando, MA, PhD; Costa Rican government official and academic; *Professor, Universidad Nacional de Costa Rica;* b. 15 Dec. 1952, San José; s. of Fernando Herrero Acosta Serrano and Isabel Sanchez Flor; m. Isabel Flor Rodríguez Céspedes 1975; ed Univ. of New York, Univ. of Costa Rica; Prof., Cen. American and the Caribbean Nat. Univ. 1975–2005; Adviser to Minister of Nat. Planning and Econ. Policy 1984; Consultant and Dir of Devt Alternatives, Oikos Economic Advisers 1984–87; Econ. Adviser to the Pres. of Costa Rica 1988, Deputy Minister of Nat. Planning and Econ. Policy 1988–89, Deputy Minister of Finance 1989–90, Minister of Finance 1994–96, 2010–12; Amb. to OAS 1996–98, also Amb. to American Council for Integral Devt; Exec. Dir PROCESOS (research and consulting group concerned with devt of democracy in Cen. America and the Caribbean) 1998–2005; Prof., Universidad Nacional 2000–05, 2015–; Gov. Gen. Public Services Regulatory Authority 2006–10; mem. Consultant Bd Cen. American Inst. for Fiscal Studies. *Publications include:* several books and articles. *Address:* Universidad Nacional de Costa Rica, Campus Omar Dengo, Avenida 1, 9 Street, PO Box 86-3000, Heredia, Costa Rica. (office). *Telephone:* 2277-3000 (office). *Website:* www.una.ac.cr (office).

HERRERO RODRIGUEZ DE MIÑON, Miguel, BA, LPh, PhD, JD; Spanish politician and barrister; *Permanent Councillor of State;* b. 18 June 1940; s. of Miguel Herrero and Carmen Rodríguez de Miñon; m. Cristina de Jáuregui 1975; one s. two d.; ed Univs of Madrid, Oxford, Luxembourg, Geneva, Paris and Louvain; Lecturer in Int. Law, Univ. of Madrid 1963–65; Sr Legal Adviser to Spanish Admin 1966; Gen. Sec. Ministry of Justice 1976; mem. Parl. 1977–93; Leader, Parl. Group of Unión de Centro Democrático in Govt 1980–81; Deputy Leader of Parl. Group of AP, major opposition group in Parl. 1982–87; Magistrate, Constitutional Court, Andorra 2001–08; Perm. Councillor of State 2009–; mem. Trilateral Comm. 1982–2004, State Council of Spain; mem. Real Academia de Ciencias Morales y Políticas 1991–; Gran Cruz de Isabel la Católica, Gran Cruz de San Raimundo de Peñafort, Orden Mérito Constitucional, Creu San Jordi, G. Off. Merito (Italy), Collar Merito Civil; Dr hc (UNED, Leon); Blanquerna Prize of Generalitat of Catalonia, Sabino Arana 1998, Pelayo Lawyers Legal Award 2007, Gold Medal, Community of Madrid, Madrid City Council, Medal of King, Juan Carlos Univ, Medal of Andalusian Parl. *Publications include:* several books on constitutional law and int. relations. *Leisure interests:* collecting old books, hunting. *Address:* Calle Mayor 79, 28013 Madrid, Spain (office). *Telephone:* (91) 5166262 (office). *E-mail:* miguel.herrerominon@consejo-estado.es (office). *Website:* www.racmyp.es (office).

HERRMAN, Ernie L.; American business executive; *CEO and President, The TJX Companies, Inc.;* b. 1961; ed Boston Coll.; joined TJX as a buyer 1989, held a series of sr merchandising positions of increasing responsibility, Exec. Vice-Pres. of Merchandising at Marmaxx 2001–04, COO Marmaxx of TJX Companies 2004–05, Exec. Vice-Pres. TJX 2004–05, Pres. and COO T.J. Maxx, Pres. The Marmaxx Group 2005–08, Sr Exec. Vice-Pres. TJX 2007–11, Group Pres. 2008–11, Pres. The TJX Companies, Inc. 2011–, Dir 2015–, CEO 2016–; mem. Bd of Trustees, Save the Children 2014–. *Address:* The TJX Companies, Inc., 770 Cochituate Road, Framingham, MA 01701, USA (office). *Telephone:* (508) 390-1000 (office). *E-mail:* info@tjx.com (office). *Website:* www.tjx.com (office).

HERRMANN, Wolfgang A., Dipl. Chem. Univ., Dr rer. nat; German chemist, academic and university administrator; *Professor of Chemistry and President, Technische Universität München;* b. 18 April 1948, Kehlheim/Donau, Bavaria; ed Donau-Gymnasium Kelheim, Bavaria, Technische Hochschule München, Univ. of Regensburg; Research Fellow, Penn State Univ., USA 1975–76; Assoc. Prof., Univ. of Regensburg 1979–81; Prof., Univ. of Frankfurt 1982–85; Prof. of Chem., Technische Universität München 1985–, Dean of Science Faculty 1988–90, Univ. Pres. 1995–; Chair. Scientific Council, VIAG AG, Bonn 1991–96; fmr Visiting Prof. at numerous int. univs, including Strasbourg, Bordeaux, Rennes and Toulouse, France, Rijksuniversiteit Utrecht, Netherlands, Texas A&M Univ., USA; mem. Editorial Bd numerous publs, including Journal of Cluster Science 1988–94, Journal of Molecular Catalysis 1994–2000, Angewandte Chemie 1999–, Catalysis Letters 1999–; Chair. Supervisory Bd Deutsches Museum, Munich 1998–, Bayerische Rektorenkonferenz (Bavarian Univ. Rectors Conf.) 2002–04, Global Alliance of Technological Univs. 2015–; Founding Chair. Universität Bayern e.V. 2004–05; mem. Int. Advisory Council, King Abdullah Univ. of Science and Tech., Saudi Arabia 2007–, Governing Bd European Inst. of Innovation and Tech. 2008–14,Advisory Bd, Univ. of Music and Performing Arts Munich 2011–, Catholic Univ. of Eichstätt-Ingolstadt 2015–; mem. Supervisory Bd Evonik Industries AG 2008–; mem. Acad. of Science and Literature, Mainz 1990–, Deutsche Akad. der Naturforscher 1995–, Royal Swedish Acad. of Eng Science 2011–; mem. Zukunftsrat (Future Council of the Bavarian Govt) 2010–12, Chair. 2014–; Exec. Bd mem. Econ. Advisory Council of Bavaria 2008–, Int. Academic Advisory Panel, Ministry of Educ., Singapore 2014–, Senate of the Max Planck Soc. 2017–; mem. Bd of Trustees, American Acad. in Berlin 2013–, TÜV SÜD Foundation 2014– (Chair. 2018–), Bertelsmann Stiftung 2016–; Fellow, Japanese Soc. for Promotion of Science 1992; Hon. Citizen, Burghausen 2016; Fed. Cross of Merit 1997, Chevalier, Légion d'honneur 2000, Bavarian Order of the Constitution 2005, Bavarian Order of Merit 2006, Bavarian Maximilian Order of Science and Art 2012; Hon. DrSc (Univ. Claude Bernard, Lyon) 1990, (Univ. Veszprém, Hungary) 1995, (Univ. of South Carolina, USA) 1999, (Lisbon) 2002, (Rennes) 2003, (Nanjing Univ., China) 2003, (Univ. of Timişoara, Romania) 2005, (Frankfurt) 2006, (Texas A&M Univ.) 2006, (Baumann Univ., Moscow) 2006, (Tiflis Univ., Georgia) 2009; Otto-Klung Award for Chem. 1982, Gottfried Wilhelm Leibniz Prize, German Research Foundation 1987, Alexander von Humboldt Award 1989, Otto Bayer Award 1990, Max Planck Research Award (co-recipient) 1991, Pino Medal, Italian Chemical Soc. 1994, Wilhelm Klemm Award, German Chemical Soc. 1995, Luigi Sacconi Medal 2000, Werner Heisenberg Medal 2000, ACS Award in Organometallic Chemistry 2004, Univ. Manager of the Year, Financial Times Deutschland, Centrum für Hochschulentwicklung 2009, Goldene Bürgermedaille of Freising 2010, President of the Year, Deutscher Hochschulverband 2012, Graf Maximilian Montgelas Prize 2018, Golden Ring of Honor from the county of Altötting 2018. *Address:* Hochschulpräsidium, Technische Universität München, Arcisstr. 21 80333 München (office); Lehrstuhl für Anorganische Chemie, Technische Universität München, Lichtenbergstrassse 4, Garching bei München 85747, Germany (office). *Telephone:* (89) 28922200 (office); (89) 28913080 (office). *Fax:* (89) 28923399 (office); (89) 28913473 (office). *E-mail:* wolfgang.herrmann@ch.tum.de (office); praesident@tum.de (office). *Website:* portal.mytum.de/tum/praesident/index_html (office); aci.anorg.chemie.tu-muenchen.de/wah (office).

HERSCHBACH, Dudley Robert, BS, MS, AM, PhD, FRSC; American chemist and academic; *Professor Emeritus, Harvard University;* b. 18 June 1932, San José, Calif.; s. of Robert Dudley Herschbach and Dorothy Edith Beer; m. Georgene Lee Botyos 1964; two d.; ed Stanford and Harvard Univs; Asst Prof., Univ. of Calif., Berkeley 1959–61, Assoc. Prof. 1961–63; Prof. of Chem., Harvard Univ. 1963–76, Frank B. Baird, Jr Prof. of Science 1976–2003, Chair. Chemical Physics Program 1964–77, Chair. Dept of Chem. 1977–80, mem. Faculty Council 1980–83, Co-Master of Currier House 1981–86, now Prof. Emer.; Prof. Texas A&M Univ. 2005–; Assoc. Ed., Journal of Physical Chemistry 1980–88; Scientific Advisor, Aerodyne Corpn; Chair. Soc. for Science and the Public 1992–2010; mem. Bd of Dirs, Council for a Livable World, Center for Arms Control and Non-Proliferation, Benjamin Franklin Creativity Fed., Benjamin Franklin Papers, Yale Univ.; mem. Bd of Sponsors, Fed. of American Scientists, Bulletin of Atomic Scientists; mem. Advisory Bd, USA Science and Eng Festival; Jr Fellow, Harvard Soc. of Fellows 1957–59; Fellow, American Acad. of Arts and Sciences, NAS, American Philosophical Soc.; Hon. Life mem. Asscn for Women in Science, New York Acad. of Sciences; Hon. FRSC; Hon. DSc (Univ. of Toronto) 1977, (Charles Univ., Prague) 1982, (Adelphi Univ., USA) 1990, (Harvard Univ.) 2011, (Univ. of Edinburgh) 2016, and others; Guggenheim Fellowship 1968, Nobel Prize for Chem. (co-recipient) 1986, ACS Pure Chem. Prize 1965, ACS Pauling Medal 1978, RSC Polanyi Medal 1981, Langmuir Prize, American Physical Soc. 1983, Nat. Award of Science 1991, Sierra Nevada Distinguished Chemist Award 1993, Kosolapoff Medal 1994, William Walker Prize 1994, Pres.'s Award, Council of Scientific Soc. 1999, Distinguished Eagle Scout Award, Gold Medal, Chem. Inst. 2011. *Television:* guest voice on The Simpsons; host of PBS programme on Nobel Legacy. *Publications:* Dimensional Scaling in Chemical Physics; more than 500 research papers. *Leisure interests:* viola, running. *Address:* Department of Chemistry and Chemical Biology, Harvard University, 12 Oxford Street, Cambridge, MA 02138, USA (office). *Telephone:* (617) 495-3218 (office). *Fax:* (617) 495-4723 (office). *E-mail:* herschbach@chemistry.harvard.edu (home). *Website:* www.chem.harvard.edu/herschbach (office).

HERSH, Seymour Myron, BA; American journalist and writer; b. 8 April 1937, Chicago; m. Elizabeth Sarah Klein 1964; two s. one d.; ed Univ. of Chicago; Chicago City News Bureau 1959; corresp., United Press International 1962–63, Associated Press 1963–67, The New Yorker 1992–; mem. of staff, New York Times 1972–79; nat. corresp. Atlantic Monthly 1983–86; Pulitzer Prize for Int. Reporting 1970, George Polk Memorial Awards 1970, 1973, 1974, 1981, 2004, Scripps-Howard Public Service Award 1973, Sidney Hillman Award 1974, John Peter Zenger Freedom of the Press Award 1975, Los Angeles Times Book Prize 1983, Nat. Book Critics Circle Award 1983, Investigative Reporters and Editors Prizes 1983, 1992, Nat. Magazine Award 2004, George Orwell Award 2004. *Publications include:* Chemical and Biological Warfare: America's Hidden Arsenal 1968, My Lai 4: A Report on the Massacre and Its Aftermath 1970, Cover-Up: The Army's Secret Investigation of the Massacre at My Lai 1972, The Price of Power: Kissinger in the Nixon White House (Nat. Book Critics Circle Award, Los Angeles Times Book Prize) 1983, The Target is Destroyed: What Really Happened to Flight 007 and What America Knew About It 1986, The Samson Option: Israel's Nuclear Arsenal and America's Foreign Policy 1991, The Dark Side of Camelot 1997, Against All Enemies: Gulf War Syndrome: The War Between America's Ailing Veterans and Their Government 1999, Chain of Command: The Road from 9/11 to Abu Ghraib 2004; contribs to various magazines. *Address:* 3214 Newark Street, NW, Washington, DC 20008-3345, USA (home).

HERSHEY, Barbara; American actress; b. 5 Feb. 1948, Hollywood, Calif.; d. of William H. Herzstein; one s.; m. Stephen Douglas 1992 (divorced 1995); ed Hollywood High School; debut in TV series The Monroes. *Films include:* With Six You Get Eggroll 1968, Heaven with a Gun 1969, The Last Summer 1969, The Liberation of L.B. Jones 1970, The Baby Maker 1970, The Pursuit of Happiness 1971, Dealing: Or the Berkeley-to-Boston Forty-Brick Lost-Bag Blues 1972, Boxcar Bertha 1972, Love Comes Quietly 1973, The Crazy World of Julius Vrooder 1974, You and Me 1975, Diamonds 1975, Trial by Combat 1976, The Last Hard Men 1976, The Stuntman 1980, The Entity 1981, Americana 1981, Take This Job and Shove It 1981, The Right Stuff 1983, The Natural 1984, Hannah and Her Sisters 1986, Hoosiers 1986, Tin Men 1987, Shy People 1987 (Best Actress, Cannes Film Festival), The Last Temptation of Christ 1988, A World Apart 1988 (Best Actress, Cannes Film Festival), Beaches 1988, Tune in Tomorrow 1990, Paris Trout 1990, The Public Eye 1991, Defenseless 1991, Swing Kids 1993, Splitting Heirs 1993, Falling Down 1993, A Dangerous Woman 1994, Last of the Dogmen 1995, Portrait of a Lady 1996, The Pallbearer 1996, A Soldier's Daughter Never Cries 1998, Frogs for Snakes 1999, Drowning on Dry Land 1999, Breakfast of Champions 1999, Lantana 2001, 11:14 2003, Riding the Bullet 2004, The Bird Can't Fly 2007, Love Comes Lately 2007, Childless 2008, Black Swan 2010, Insidious 2010, Answers to Nothing 2011, Insidious 2 2013, Sister 2014. *Television includes:* Just a Little Inconvenience, A Killing in a Small Town (Emmy and Golden Globe Awards 1990), The Bible 1993, Return to Lonesome Dove 1993, Portrait of a Lady 1996, A Soldier's Daughter Never Cries 1998, Frogs for Snakes 1998, The Staircase 1998, Breakfast of Champions 1999, Passion 1999, Chicago Hope (series) 1999–2000, Daniel Deronda 2002, Hunger Point 2003, The Stranger Beside Me 2003, Paradise 2004, The Mountain (series) 2004–05, Anne of Green Gables: A New Beginning 2008, Agatha Christie: Poirot 2010, Left to Die (film) 2012, Once Upon a Time in Wonderland 2014. *Address:* c/o Suzan Bymel, Bymel O'Neill Management, N Vista, Los Angeles, CA 90046 (office); c/o Jenny Rawlings, CAA, 9830 Wilshire Boulevard, Beverly Hills, CA 90212, USA.

HERSHKO, Avram, MD, PhD; Israeli biochemist and academic; *Distinguished Professor, Faculty of Medicine, Technion-Israel Institute of Technology;* b. 31 Dec. 1937, Karcag, Hungary; s. of Moshe Hershko and Shoshana Margit Hershko; m. Judith Leibowitz Hershko 1963; three s.; ed Hebrew Univ. of Jerusalem; prisoner in Nazi concentration camp; emigrated to Israel with parents 1950; mil. service as physician in Israeli army 1965–67; postdoctoral fellowship in San Francisco 1969–71; Research Prof., Faculty of Medicine, Technion-Israel Inst. of Tech. 1980, now Distinguished Prof., B. Rappaport Faculty of Medicine; studied protein degradation at biochemical level with Aaron Ciechanover (q.v.) and Irwin Rose 1977–90; studies roles of protein degradation in the control of cell division 1990–; mem. Scientific Advisory Bd Oramed Pharmaceuticals; Dr hc (Hebrew Univ.) 2009; Weizmann Prize for Sciences 1987, Israel Prize in biochemistry 1994, Gairdner Int. Award, Canada 1999, Albert Lasker Basic Medical Research Award 2000, Louisa Gross Horwitz Prize, Columbia Univ. 2001, Wolf Prize for Medicine (with Alexander Varshavsky q.v.) 2001, Nobel Prize in Chemistry (with Aaron Ciechanover and Irwin Rose) 2004. *Publications include:* co-author of several books. *Address:* Faculty of Medicine, 6th Floor, Technion-Israel Institute of Technology, Haifa 31096, Israel (office). *Telephone:* (4) 8295344 (office). *Fax:* (4) 8535230 (office). *E-mail:* hershko@tx.technion.ac.il (office). *Website:* www1.technion.ac.il (office); md.technion.ac.il.

HERSOV, Basil Edward, DMS, BA (Hons), MA, FRSA, FID, FSAIM; South African business executive (retd); b. 18 Aug. 1926, Johannesburg; s. of Abraham Sundel (Bob) Hersov and Gertrude Hersov (née Aronson); m. Antoinette Herbert 1957; two s. two d.; ed Michaelhouse, Natal, Christ's Coll., Cambridge, UK; pilot in S African Air Force 1944–46; joined Anglovaal Ltd as Learner Official on gold mine 1949, later holding a number of sr positions with Anglovaal Group: Deputy Chair. 1970, Chair. and Man. Dir 1973–98; Chair. Hartebeestfontein Gold Mining Co. Ltd, Anglovaal Industries Ltd, The Associated Manganese Mines of SA Ltd; mem. bd of many other cos within and outside Anglovaal Group; Dir Mutual and Fed. Insurance Co. Ltd; Pres. and Fellow, Inst. of Dirs (SA); Hon. Pres., mem. Council, South Africa Foundation; Gov. Rhodes Univ. Bd of Trustees, Business South Africa, Nat. Business Initiative; Fellow, S African Inst. of Man., S African Inst. of Mining and Metallurgy; Hon. Col, 21 Squadron, SAAF, Doyen, SAAF Hon. Cols 1980, Hon. Liveryman, Hon. Co. of Pilots and Navigators 2009; Decoration for Meritorious Service; Hon. LLD (Rhodes); Witwaterstand Univ. Award for Business Excellence 1984, Brig. Stokes Memorial Award, S African Inst. of Mining and Metallurgy 1996. *Leisure interests:* skiing, horse racing, tennis, flying, sailing, polo. *Address:* Springwaters, Box 65097, Benmore 2010, South Africa (home). *E-mail:* basilh@hersov.co.za (home).

HERTELEER, Adm. (retd) Willy Maurits; Belgian naval officer (retd); *President, Koninklijk Werk IBIS;* b. 1 Oct. 1941, Assenede; m. Jacqueline Liekens 1962 (deceased); one s. three d.; ed Royal Cadet School, Brussels, Merchant Navy Acad., Belgian Staff Coll., Brussels, École Supérieure de Guerre Navale, Paris; commissioned Belgian Navy 1962, as ensign served on minesweepers and a supply/command ship 1963-68, became mine warfare specialist 1969–70, Staff Officer, Mine Countermeasures, Operational Command 1970–72; Commdr coastal minesweeper 1975, ocean minesweeper/hunter 1978, (instructor Belgian-Dutch School for Mine Warfare, Ostend between these postings); rank of Lt-Commdr 1979; apptd to Planning section, Belgian Naval Staff, also mem. Naval Bd, NATO Mil. Standardization Agency 1979–82; Second-in-Command frigate Westdiep 1982–84, CO 1984–85; Asst Chief of Staff Operations, Naval Operations Command 1986, Chief of Staff 1986–87; Head Belgian-Dutch School for Mine Warfare 1987–89; mem. Audit Team, Belgian Naval Staff, Brussels 1989, Staff Officer, Operations 1990, Commdr Naval Operations 1990–92; rank of Rear-Adm. 1992; joined Gen. Staff HQ, Brussels 1992, Chief of Naval Staff 1993–95; rank of Vice-Adm. 1995; Chief of the Gen. Staff 1995–2002; retd 2003; Pres. Koninklijk Werk IBIS (school for boys) 2005–, EuroDefense Belgium 2008–; promoted to Aide to King Albert II 1999; Belgische Nationale Orden – Grootkruis in de Kroonorde, Commdr in de Leopoldorde, Belgische Militaire Eretekens, Militair Kruis 1ste Klasse, Buitenlandse Orden, Commdr, Légion d'honneur, Commdr, Legion of Merit (USA), Grand Officier, Ordre de Mérite du Grand-Duché de Luxembourg, Commdr, Order of Merit of the Repub. of Poland, Commdr, Ordre Nat. du Benin, Grootofficier 'Merito Naval' (Brazil), La Medaille du Mérite Naval (France), Grand Cross (Repub. of Hungary), Liberation Medal, Third Degree (Kuwait), Liberation Medal with Palm (Saudi Arabia). *Address:* Koninklijk Werk IBIS, 1 Prinses Elisabethlaan, 8450 Bredene, Belgium (office). *Telephone:* (2) 742-62-09 (IBIS) (office); (59) 50-86-39 (EuroDefense Belgium) (office). *Fax:* (59) 32-69-47 (home). *E-mail:* willy@herteleer.eu (office). *Website:* www.ibisschool.be (office); eurodefense-belgium.eu (office).

HERTRICH, Rainer, BCom; German fmr aerospace industry executive; b. 6 Dec. 1949, Ottengrün; m.; two c.; ed Tech. Univ. of Berlin, Univ. of Nuremberg; apprenticeship and business training, Siemens AG 1969–71; Information Processing Supervisor controlling Dept, Mil. Aircraft Div., Messerschmitt-Bölkow-Blohm (MBB) GmbH 1977, Head Controlling Dept MBB Service Div., Ottobrunn 1978–83, Chief Financial Officer 1983–84, Head Controlling and Finance Dept, MBB Dynamics Div. 1984–87, Chief Financial Officer and mem. Div. Man., MBB Marine and Special Products Div. 1987–90; Head Divisional Controlling, Cen. Controlling Section, Deutsche Aerospace AG, Dasa (now European Aeronautic Defence and Space Co.—EADS) 1990–91, Sr Vice-Pres., Corp. Controlling, Dasa 1991–96, Head Aeroengines Business Unit, Dasa, Pres. and CEO Motoren- und Turbinen-Union München (MTU München) GmbH, mem. Exec. Cttee Dasa 1996–2000, Pres. and CEO DaimlerChrysler Aerospace (Dasa) AG 2000, Co-CEO EADS 2000–05 (Head of Aeronautic Div. 2004–05); Pres. BDLI (German aerospace industries asscn) 2001–05; Officier, Légion d'honneur.

HERTZ, Noreena, BA, MBA, PhD; British economist, academic and writer; *Honorary Professor, Centre for the Study of Decision-Making Uncertainty, University College London;* b. 24 Sept. 1967, London; ed Univ. Coll., London, Univ. of Cambridge, Wharton School of Univ. of Pennsylvania, USA; helped establish first Leningrad (now St Petersburg) stock exchange 1991; Int. Finance Corpn adviser to Russian Govt on econ. reforms 1992; fmr head of research team working on prospects for regional econ. co-operation in the Middle East; fmr Distinguished Fellow and Assoc. Dir Centre for Int. Business and Man., Judge Inst. of Man. Studies, Univ. of Cambridge, Fellow, Judge Business School 2000–15; also Duisenberg Prof. of Globalization, Sustainability and Finance, Duisenberg School of Finance 2010–13, Erasmus Univ. 2009–14; Belle van Zuylen Chair of Global Political Economy, Utrecht Univ. April–Sept. 2005; Hon. Prof., Centre for the Study of Decision-Making Uncertainty, Univ. Coll., London 2014–; mem. Bd of Dirs Warner Music Group 2014–; mem. Citigroup Politics and Economics Global Advisory Board 2007–08; mem. Advisory Group, McKinsey CEO Dominic Barton's Inclusive Capitalism Taskforce 2012–13; Trustee Inst. for Public Policy Research (think-tank); Adviser, Centre for the Analysis of Social Media. *Television:* documentary film of her book The Silent Takeover (UK Channel 4) 2001. *Publications include:* Russian Business in the Wake of Reform (doctoral thesis) 1996, The Silent Takeover: Global Capitalism and the Death of Democracy 2001, IOU: The Debt Threat and Why We Must Defuse It 2004, Eyes Wide Open: How to Make Smart Decisions in a Confusing World 2013; contribs to New Statesman, Observer, Guardian, Washington Post, among others. *Address:* Centre for the Study of Decision-Making Uncertainty, Faculty of Brain Sciences, University College London, Gower Street, London, WC1E 6BT, England (office). *Website:* www.ucl.ac.uk/csdu (office); www.noreena.com.

HERTZBERGER, Herman; Dutch architect and academic; *Architect and Adviser, Architectuurstudio HH/AHH b.v.;* b. 6 July 1932, Amsterdam; m. J. C. Van Seters 1959; one s. two d.; ed Delft Tech. Univ.; pvt. practice, Architectuurstudio HH/AHH b.v., Amsterdam 1958–; Co-Ed. (Dutch) Forum 1959–63; teacher, Acad. of Architecture, Amsterdam 1965–69; Prof. of Architectural Design, Tech. Univ. of Delft 1970–99; Prof., Univ. of Geneva 1986–93; Chair. Berlage Inst., Amsterdam 1990–95; guest teacher at univs/architectural insts in Argentina, Austria, Belgium, Brazil, Croatia, Cyprus, Denmark, France, Germany, Greece, Ireland, Israel, Italy, Japan, Mexico, the Netherlands, Norway, Slovenia, S Korea, Spain, Switzerland, Taiwan, UK, USA; Hon. mem. Acad. Royale de Belgique 1975, Bund Deutscher Architeckten 1983, Akad. der Künste 1993, Accad. delle Arti del Disegno, Florence 1995, Acad. d'Architecture de France 1997, Bond van Nederlandse Architecten 2002, Architectural Asscn, London 2013; Hon. FRIBA 1991; Hon. Fellow, Royal Incorporation of Architects in Scotland 1996; Hon. FAIA 2004; Kt, Order of Oranje Nassau 1991, Companion, Order of the Dutch Lion; Hon. DUniv (Geneva) 2001; numerous prizes and awards, including Architectural Award of the Town of Amsterdam 1968, Eternit Award 1974, Fritz Schumacher Award 1974, Architecture Award of the City of Amsterdam 1985, Premio Europa 1991, BNA Award 1991, Concrete Award 1991, Prix Rhénan 1993, Architecture Award, City of Breda 1998, Premios Vitruvio 98 Trayectoria Internacional 1998, Dutch School Bldg Award 2000, Leone d'oro (Venice) 2002, Architecture Award, City of Apeldoorn 2004, Oeuvre Award for Architecture of the Netherlands Foundation for Visual Arts, Design and Architecture 2004, Dutch School Building Award 2004, Arie Keppler Award 2005, Architecture Award of the Citizens of Apeldoorn 2006, RIBA Royal Gold Medal 2012, Andreas Penning Amsterdam 2012, Thomas Jefferson Foundation Medal in Architecture 2015, Rietveld Award 2015. *Major works include:* 14 primary schools, six extended school complexes and four secondary schools in the Netherlands since 1966, office bldg, 'Centraal Beheer', Apeldoorn 1972, housing for old and disabled people 'De Drie Hoven', Amsterdam 1974, music centre 'Vredenburg', Utrecht 1978, urban renewal 'Haarlemmer Houttinen', Amsterdam 1982, office bldg Ministry of Social Welfare and Employment, The Hague 1990, Theatre Centre Spui, The Hague 1993, library and art and music centre, Breda 1993, Chassé Theater, Breda 1995, Theater Markant, Uden 1996, residential bldgs, Haarlem 1996, Düren, Germany 1996, Berlin 1997, extension to Vanderveen Department Store, Assen 1997, YKK Dormitory Guesthouse, Kurobe City, Japan 1998, Bijlmer Monument (with Georges Descombes) 1998, residential area 'Merwestein Noord', Dordrecht 1999, Waterhouse, Middelburg 2002, Il Fiore office bldg, Maastricht 2002, MediaPark office bldgs and residential complex, Cologne 2004, CODA museum, library and municipal archives, Apeldoorn 2004, Theatre and Congress Centre ORPHEUS, Apeldoorn 2004, Head Office, Waternet, Amsterdam 2005, Faculty, FNWI Univ. of Amsterdam 2009, NHL Univ., Leeuwarden 2009, Faculty of Science, Univ. of Utrecht 2011, Primary and Junior School, Rome, Italy 2012, ABC School De Bron, Arnhem 2012, Multi Renovation MFC Geitenkamp, Arnhem 2012, Tivoli Vredenburg Music Centre, Utrecht 2014, FLUX Faculty, Tech. Sciences Univ., Eindhoven 2014, Multi-Functional Centre with Schools Omnibus, Arnhem 2015, Twickel College Hengelo 2016. *Publications include:* Homework for More Hospitable Form (Dutch) Forum XXIV 1973, Herman Hertzberger 1959–86 Bauten und Projekte/Buildings and Projects/Bâtiments et Projets (co-author) 1987, Lessons for Students in Architecture 1991 (edns in Chinese, German, Japanese, Italian, Portuguese, Korian, Persian, Greek, French, Czech 1991–2015), Herman Hertzberger Projekte/Projects 1990–1995 1995, Chassé Theater 1995, Herman Hertzberger: View of Projects of 1960–1997 (co-author) 1997, Space and the Architect: Lessons for Students in Architecture Part II 2000 (Chinese and other edns 2000–14), Articulations 2002, Cultuur onder Dak: Shelter for Culture – Herman Hertzberger and Apeldoorn 2004, De theaters van Herman Hertzberger 2005, Waternet Doubeltower 2006, Hertzberger's Amsterdam 2007, Space and Learning 2008, The Schools of Herman Hertzberger 2009, The Future of Architecture 2013, Architecture and Structuralism 2015. *Leisure interest:* music. *Address:* Architectuurstudio HH/AHH b.v., Gerard Doustraat 220, 1073 XB Amsterdam, Netherlands (office). *Telephone:* (20) 6765888 (office). *E-mail:* office@ahh.nl (office). *Website:* www.ahh.nl (office); www.hertzberger.nl.

HERVÉ, Edmond; French politician; b. 3 Dec. 1942, La Bouillie, Côtes du Nord; s. of Marcel Hervé and Renée Hervé Baudet; m. Jeannine Le Gall 1978; two s. one d.; Prof. of Constitutional Law, Rennes Univ.; Conseiller Général, Ille-et-Vilaine 1973–82; Mayor of Rennes 1977–2008, Hon. Mayor 2008; Pres. regional hosp. centre and univ. hosp. centre, both in Brittany 1977; fmr Minister of Health; Minister Del. to Minister of Industry for Energy 1981–83; Sec. of State for Health 1983–86; Regional Councillor, Brittany 1986–88; Deputy for Ille-et-Vilaine to Nat. Ass. 1986–2002; Pres. Dist Urbain de l'agglomeration rennaise (Audiar) 1989, Conf. permanente du tourisme urbain 1989–95, Hon. Pres. 1995–; apptd Chair. Conf. de villes de l'arc atlantique 2000; Senator 2008–14; mem. Conseil de Surveillance du Crédit local de France 1990, City Scientific Cttee on Science and Industry of La Villette 1990, Nat. Council on Towns and Urban Social Devt 1991, Parti Socialiste.

HERZ, Robert (Bob) H., BEcons, CPA, CA, FCA; American financial executive; *President, Robert H. Herz LLC;* ed Univ. of Manchester, UK; accountant, Price Waterhouse 1974–96, Pricewaterhouse Coopers 1998–2002, becoming Sr Partner 1998 and mem. Global and US Bds; Chair. Financial Accounting Standards Bd 2002–10 (retd); Pres. Robert H. Herz LLC (financial consulting firm) 2010–; Sr Tech. Partner, Coopers & Lybrand 1996; Sr Advisor Workiva Inc. 2011–14, mem. Bd of Dirs 2014–; currently Exec. in Residence, Columbia Business School, Columbia Univ.; fmr Chair. AICPA SEC Regulations Cttee, Transnational

Auditors Cttee, Int. Fed. of Accountants; mem. Int. Accounting Standards Bd (IASB) 2001–02; mem. Bd of Dirs Fed. Nat. Mortgage Asscn (Fannie Mae) 2011–, Paxos Trust Co., LLC; fmr mem. Emerging Issues Task Force, American Accounting Asscn Financial Accounting Standards Cttee. *Publications:* The Value Reporting Revolution: Moving Beyond the Earnings Game (jt author) 2001, Accounting Changes: Chronicles of Convergence, Crisis, and Complexity in Financial Reporting 2013. *Address:* 211 Uris, Columbia Business School, Columbia University, 3022 Broadway, New York, NY 10027, USA (office). *Telephone:* (212) 854-6100 (office). *E-mail:* rh2551@gsb.columbia.edu (office). *Website:* www.gsb.columbia.edu/cbs-directory/detail/rh2551 (office).

HERZOG, Jacques, DipArch; Swiss architect; b. 1950, Basel; ed Swiss Federal Tech. Univ. (ETH), Zurich; Asst to Prof. Dolf Schnebli, ETH, Zurich 1977; f. architectural practice Herzog & De Meuron (with Pierre de Meuron, q.v.) 1978; Prof. of Architecture and Design, ETH 1999–; Visiting Prof., Harvard Univ., Cambridge, Mass, USA 1989, Tulane Univ., New Orleans 1991; (all jtly with Pierre de Meuron q.v.) Architecture Prize, Berlin Acad. of Arts 1987, Andrea Palladio Int. Prize for Architecture, Vicenza, Italy 1988, Pritzker Architecture Prize 2001, Praemium Imperiale 2007. *Principal works include:* Blue House, Oberwil 1979–80, Photostudio Frei, Weil am Rhein 1981–82, Sperrholz Haus, Bottmingen 1984–85, Apartment Bldg, Hebelstr. 11, Basel 1984–88, Wohn- und Geschäftshaus Schwitter, Basel 1985–98, Goetz Art Gallery, Munich 1989–92, Wohn- und Geschäftshaus Schützenmattstr., Basel 1992–93, Dominus Winery, Napa Valley, Yountville, Calif. 1995–97, Tate Gallery Extension (Tate Modern), Bankside, London (RIBA Gold Medal 2007) 1995–99, Cultural Centre and Theatre, Zurich 1996, Ricola Marketing Bldg, Laufen 1998, Laban Centre for Dance, London (Stirling Prize) 2003, M. H. de Young Memorial Museum, San Francisco 2005, Walker Art Center expansion, Minneapolis, Minnesota 2005, Beijing Nat. Stadium, China ('The Bird's Nest', Lubetkin Prize 2009) 2008, Pérez Art Museum Miami 2013, Messe Basel 2014, Blavatnik School of Govt, Univ. of Oxford, UK 2015, Tate Modern Switch House, London 2016, Elbe Philharmonic Hall, Hamburg. *Works in progress include:* Prada Headquarters, New York, São Paulo Companhia de Dança Brazil, Kolkata Museum of Modern Art, India, National Library of Israel, as well as projects in UK, France, Germany, Italy, Spain and Japan. *Address:* Herzog & de Meuron Architekten, Rheinschanze 6, 4056 Basel, Switzerland (office). *Telephone:* (61) 3855757 (office). *Fax:* (61) 3855758 (office). *E-mail:* info@herzogdemeuron.com (office).

HERZOG, Werner; German film director; b. 5 Sept. 1942, Munich; f. Werner Herzog Filmproduktion 1963. *Films include:* Signs of Life 1967, Even Dwarfs Started Small 1970, Fata Morgana 1971, The Land of Darkness and Silence 1971, Aguirre Wrath of God 1973, The Enigma of Kaspar Hauser 1974, The Great Ecstasy of Woodcutter Steiner 1974, How Much Wood Would a Woodchuck Chuck 1976, Heart of Glass 1976, Stroszek 1976–77, Woyzeck 1979, Nosferatu 1979, Le pays du silence et de l'obscurité 1980, Fitzcarraldo 1982, Where the Green Ants Dream 1984, Cobra Verde 1987, Les Gauloises 1988, Echos aus einem düstern Reich 1990, Scream from Stone 1991, Lektionen in Finsternis 1992, Glocken aus der Tiefe 1993, Little Dieter Needs to Fly 1997, Wings of Hope 1998, Mein liebster Feind - Klaus Kinski 1999, Pilgrimage 2001, Invincible 2001, Ten Minutes Older: The Trumpet 2002, Wheel of Time 2003, The White Diamond 2004, Grizzly Man (Dirs Guild of America Best Dir Documentary 2006) 2005, The Wild Blue Yonder 2005, Rescue Dawn 2006, Mister Lonely 2006, Encounters at the End of the World 2008, Bad Lieutenant: Port of Call New Orleans 2009, My Son, My Son, What Have Ye Done 2009, Happy People: A Year in the Taiga (co-dir), Cave of Forgotten Dreams 2010, Ode to the Dawn of Man (short) 2011, Into the Abyss 2011, Queen of the Desert 2015, Lo and Behold, Reveries of the Connected World (documentary) 2016, Salt and Fire 2016. *Television includes:* On Death Row (series documentary) 2012–13. *Opera directed includes:* Lohengrin (Bayreuth Festival) 1987, Tannhäuser (Houston Grand Opera) 2001, Die Zauberflöte (Baltimore Opera) 2001, Parsifal (Palau de les Arts, Valencia) 2008. *Publications:* Conquest of the Useless: Reflections from the Making of Fitzcarraldo, Of Walking In Ice 2007. *Address:* Werner Herzog Filmproduktion, Türkenstrasse 91, 80799 Munich, Germany.

HESELTINE, Colin S., BEcons; Australian diplomatist and international organization official; *Co-Chairman, Asia Pacific Exchange and Co-operation Foundation;* b. 1947; m.; two d.; ed Monash Univ.; joined Dept of External Affairs, Canberra 1969, served in Embassy in Santiago, Chile 1970–75, in Madrid 1975–80, Chinese language training 1981–82, Minister and Deputy Head of Mission, Embassy in Beijing 1982–85, Dir, China Investment Project, Dept of Industry, Tech. and Resources, Victorian Govt 1985–87, Minister and Deputy Head of Mission, Embassy in Beijing 1988–92, Rep. (Head of Mission), Australian Commerce and Industry Office, Taipei 1992–97; Asst Sec., Maritime South East Asia Br. (covering Indonesia, Malaysia, Singapore, Philippines), Dept of Foreign Affairs and Trade 1997–98, First Asst Sec., North Asia Div. 1998–2001; Amb. to South Korea 2001–05; Deputy Exec. Dir APEC Secr. 2006, Exec. Dir 2007–08; Co-Chair. Asia Pacific Exchange and Co-operation Foundation 2011–. *Address:* Asia Pacific Exchange and Co-operation Foundation, 01-01, Section A, Liangmaqiao DRC, 22 Dongfang East Road, Chaoyang District, Beijing 100600, People's Republic of China (office). *Telephone:* (10) 85322403 (office). *Fax:* (10) 85322405 (office). *E-mail:* contact@apecf.org (office). *Website:* www.apecf.org (office).

HESELTINE, Baron (Life Peer), cr. 2001, of Thenford in the County of Northamptonshire; **Rt Hon. Michael Ray Dibdin Heseltine,** PC, CH; British politician and publisher; *Chairman, Haymarket Group;* b. 21 March 1933, Swansea, Wales; s. of Col Rupert Heseltine and Eileen Ray Heseltine; m. Anne Edna Harding Williams 1962; one s. two d.; ed Shrewsbury School, Pembroke Coll., Oxford; Pres. Oxford Union 1954; Dir Bow Publs 1961–65; Chair. Haymarket Press 1966–70; MP for Tavistock 1966–74, for Henley 1974–2001; Parl. Sec. Ministry of Transport 1970; Parl. Under-Sec. of State, Dept of the Environment 1970–72; Minister of Aerospace and Shipping 1972–74; Opposition Spokesman for Industry 1974–76, for the Environment 1976–79; Sec. of State for the Environment 1979–83, 1990–92, for Defence 1983–86, Sec. of State for Industry and Pres. of the Bd of Trade 1992–95; Deputy Prime Minister and First Sec. of State 1995–97; Dir Haymarket Group 1997, Chair. 1999–; Pres. Asscn of Conservative Clubs 1982–84, Chair. Conservative Mainstream 1998–2006; Pres. Quoted Companies Alliance Int. Advisory Council 2000–05, Anglo-China Forum 1998–2001; Pres. Conservative Group for Europe 2001–04; Vice-Pres. Royal Horticultural Soc. 2009–; Chair. Regional Growth Fund Advisory Cttee 2010–17, Thames Estuary 2050 Growth Comm. 2016–17; Co-Chair. Estate Regeneration Advisory Panel 2016–17; mem. Nat. Infrastructure Comm. 2015–17; Fellow, Chartered Inst. of Man. 1998, The 48 Group Club 2003; Hon. Fellow, Pembroke Coll. Oxford 1986, Leeds Metropolitan Univ. 1988, Univ. of Wales (Swansea) 2001, John Moore's Univ., Liverpool 2013, Univ. of Northampton 2013; Hon. FRIBA 1991; Freedom of the City of Liverpool 2012, City of London 2012; Hon. LLD (Liverpool) 1990; Hon. DBA (Bedfordshire) 2003; Dr hc (Univ. of South Wales) 2013, (Aston) 2013, (Birmingham City Univ.) 2014; Pres.'s Medal, Inst. of Public Relations 1998, Gold Medal, Inst. of Sheet Metal Eng 1999, PPA Marcus Morris Award 2003, Lifetime Achievement Award, Nat. Business Awards 2005, Publicity Club of London Cup 2005, Golden Oldie of the Year Award 2013. *Publications include:* Reviving the Inner Cities 1983, Where There's a Will 1987, The Challenge of Europe: Can Britain Win? (Bentinck Prize 1989) 1988, Life in the Jungle (memoirs) 2000, No Stone Unturned 2012, Thenford: The Creation of an English Garden (with Lady Heseltine) 2016, Industrial Strategy (pamphlet) 2017. *Address:* House of Lords, Westminster, London, SW1A 0PW, England. *Telephone:* (20) 8267-4213 (External Office) (office). *Website:* www.thenfordarboretum.com.

HESS, John B., BA, MBA; American energy industry executive; *CEO, Hess Corporation;* b. 5 April 1954; s. of Leon Hess and Norma Hess; m. Susan Elizabeth Kessler; ed Harvard Univ.; joined Amerada Hess Corpn (now Hess Corpn) 1977, mem. Bd of Dirs 1978–, Sr Vice-Pres. –1986, Sr Exec. Vice-Pres. 1986–95, Chair. and CEO 1995–2013, CEO 2013–; mem. US Sec. of Energy's Advisory Bd 1999–2002, Nat. Petroleum Council at US Dept of Energy; Vice-Chair. Lincoln Center for the Performing Arts, Inc., Dir 2007–; Dir, Nat. Advisory Board of J.P. Morgan Chase & Co. 1991–, Deerfield Acad. 2004–, The Dow Chemical Company 2006–13, Trilateral Comm. 2009–, NYC2012, Inc, Kohlberg Kravis Roberts & Co. 2011–, KKR Management LLC 2011–; mem. Bd of Trustees, Wildlife Conservation Soc./New York Zoo 1991–, United Cerebral Palsy Research and Educational Foundation; Trustee, The Mount Sinai Hosp. 1988–, New York Public Library 2008–, Center for Strategic and Int. Studies, Inc.; mem. Dean's Advisors of Harvard Business School 2001–, The Business Council of the Council of Foreign Relations 2003–. *Address:* Hess Corporation, 1185 Avenue of the Americas, New York, NY 10036, USA (office). *Telephone:* (212) 997-8500 (office). *Fax:* (212) 536-8390 (office). *E-mail:* info@hess.com (office). *Website:* www.hess.com (office).

HESS, Ortwin, PhD, FInstP; German theoretical physicist and academic; *Leverhulme Chair in Metamaterials, Imperial College London;* b. 1966; ed Univ. of Erlangen and Tech. Univ. of Berlin; postdoctoral studies at Univ. of Edinburgh, UK and Univ. of Marburg 1995–2003; mem. Faculty, Inst. of Tech. Physics, Stuttgart 1997, Adjunct Prof., Dept of Physics 1998; subsequently also Docent of Photonics, Finnish Tampere Univ. of Tech.; currently Leverhulme Chair in Metamaterials, Imperial Coll., London, UK, Co-Dir Centre for Plasmonics and Metamaterials and Deputy Head of Condensed Matter Theory Group, Academic mem. Thomas Young Centre; Visiting Prof., Stanford Univ. 1997–98, Univ. of Munich 1999–2000, Abbe School of Photonics, Jena 2012; mem. Quantum Electronics Group, Inst. of Physics 2008–13, Scientific Advisory Bd, A*STAR Inst. for High Performance Computing 2014–; Fellow, Optical Soc. of America 2013; Rumford Medal, Royal Soc. 2016. *Publications:* more than 300 papers in peer-reviewed journals on theoretical condensed matter quantum photonics. *Address:* Room 806, Blackett Laboratory, Department of Physics, Imperial College London, South Kensington Campus, London, SW7, England (office). *Telephone:* (20) 7594-7586 (office). *E-mail:* o.hess@imperial.ac.uk (office). *Website:* www.imperial.ac.uk/physics (office).

HESSE, Daniel (Dan) Ryan, BA, MS, MBA; American telecommunications executive; b. 18 Oct. 1953, Fort Belvoir, Va; s. of Richard Joseph Hesse and Ellen Louise Hesse (née Seidell); m. Diane Yvette Canaday 1990; ed Univ. of Notre Dame, Cornell Univ., Massachusetts Inst. of Tech.; worked for 23 years with AT&T Corpn, becoming Sales Vice-Pres. 1990–91, Pres. and CEO AT&T Network Systems International 1991–95, Sr Vice-Pres. Online Services Group 1996, Exec. Vice-Pres. 1997–2000, Pres. and CEO AT&T Wireless Services Inc. 1997–2000; Chair., Pres. and CEO Terabeam Corpn 2000–04; CEO Local Telecommunications Div., Sprint Nextel Corpn 2005–06, CEO Sprint Nextel Corpn 2007–14 (renamed Sprint Corpn 2013); Chair., Pres. and CEO Embarq Corpn 2006–07; mem. Bd Dirs Nokia Inc. 2005–07, VF Corpn 2001–08, Better Business Bureau Online, CTIA (Wireless Asscn), Clearwire Corpn; Gov. Boys & Girls Club of America, Akamai Technologies, Technology Subcommittee, PNC Financial Services Group, Inc. 2016–; mem. Business Advisory Council, Mendoza Coll. of Business, Univ. Notre Dame; mem. MIT's Soc. of Sloan Fellows, Univ. of Notre Dame's E.F. Sorin Soc., Cornell Univ. Dean's Soc.; appointed by President Obama to Nat. Security Telecommunications Advisory Cttee; Brooks Thesis Prize, MIT 1990, Ellis Island Medal of Honor, named Most Influential Person in Mobile Technology by LAPTOP magazine, RCR Magazine Wireless Industry Person of theYear, Wireless Business and Tech. Magazine Exec. of the Year, Wireless Week magazine's Leadership Award, named by Junior Achievement of Middle America to Greater Kansas City Business Hall of Fame 2010, recognized by Ingram's magazine as Kansas City's Best CEO 2010, John J. Sullivan, Jr Foundation Humanitarian Award of The Irish Museum and Cultural Center of Kansas City 2010. *Website:* www.danhesse.com (office).

HESSELS, Jan-Michiel, LLM, MA; Dutch business executive; *Chairman, Supervisory Board, Royal Boskalis Westminster NV;* b. 21 Dec. 1942, The Hague; m. Elisabeth Hillen; three c.; ed Univ. of Leiden, London School of Econs, UK, Wharton School of Finance, Univ. of Pennsylvania, USA; with S.G. Warburg & Co., London, Overseas Devt Bank, Geneva, McKinsey & Co. Inc., New York and Amsterdam 1967–73; Corp. Treas., Akzo NV 1973–77, Pres. Akzo Ltda (Brazil and Argentina), São Paulo 1977–82, Exec. Vice-Pres. Akzona Inc., Asheville, NC, USA 1982–85; CEO NV Deli Universal, Rotterdam 1985–90; CEO Vendex International NV/Royal Vendex KBB NV 1990–2000; Chair. Dutch Retail Asscn (RND) 1991–98; mem. Supervisory Bd Royal Philips Electronics 1999–, fmr Chair.; Chair. Election Platform Cttee, CDA 2002–03; Chair. Supervisory Bd Euronext NV 2000–07, Chair. NYSE Euronext Inc. (following merger with NYSE Group) 2007–14; Chair. Supervisory Bd Royal Boskalis Westminster NV 2011–; Special Advisor, Gen. Atlantic LLC 2014–; mem. Bd of Dirs Amsterdam Airport Schiphol Group NV, Schiphol Airport Devt Corpn (Chair.), SC Johnson Europlant NV (Chair.); mem.

Supervisory Bd BAM 1988–93, Dillards Department Stores Inc. 1990–98, Barnes & Noble Inc. 1990–2000, Yule Catto PLC 1991–98, Royal Vopak NV 1993–2005, Amsterdam Exchange 1997, Laurus 1998–2004, B&N Com, Inc. 1999–2003, Heineken NV; mem. Int. Advisory Bd Morgan Stanley –2006, The Blackstone Group, SC Johnson Corpn; mem. Bd of Trustees and Chair. Rijksmuseum, Amsterdam 1996–2003; Chair. Medisch Centrum, Haaglanden 1992–2003. *Address:* Royal Boskalis Westminster N.V., PO Box 43, 3350 AA Papendrecht, Netherlands (office). *Telephone:* (78) 6969000 (office). *Fax:* (78) 6969555 (office). *Website:* www.boskalis.com (office).

HESTER, Ronald Ernest, PhD, DSc, FRSC; British chemist and academic; *Professor Emeritus of Chemistry, University of York;* b. 8 March 1936, Slough, Bucks.; s. of Ernest Hester and Rhoda Lennox; m. Bridget Maddin 1958; two s. two d.; ed Royal Grammar School, High Wycombe, Univs of London and Cambridge and Cornell Univ., USA; Asst Prof., Cornell Univ. 1962–65; Lecturer, Sr Lecturer, Reader, Univ. of York 1965–85, Prof. of Chem. 1985–2001, Prof. Emer. 2001–; European Ed. Biospectroscopy 1994–2005; Jt Ed. Issues in Environmental Science and Technology 1994–; mem. Council and various bds, Science and Eng Research Councils. *Publications:* Physical Inorganic Chemistry 1964, Advances in Spectroscopy (26 vols) 1975–98, Understanding Our Environment 1986, Spectroscopy of Biological Molecules 1991, Issues in Environmental Science and Technology 1994–; more than 300 research papers in int. journals. *Leisure interests:* skiing, tennis, golf, travel. *Address:* Department of Chemistry, University of York, York, YO10 5DD, England (office). *Website:* www.york.ac.uk/chemistry/staff/academic/emeritus/rhester (office).

HESTER, Stephen, BA; British banking executive; *Group Chief Executive, RSA Insurance Group plc;* b. 14 Dec. 1960, Yorkshire; s. of Ronald Hester and Dr Bridget Hester; m. 1st Barbara Abt 1991 (divorced 2010); two c.; m. 2nd Suzy Neubert 2012; ed Lady Margaret Hall, Univ. of Oxford; worked for Credit Suisse First Boston, holding various Investment Banking roles until becoming Chief Financial Officer 1996, then Global Head of Fixed Income Div. 2000–02; Finance Dir, later COO Abbey National plc 2002–04; mem. Bd of Dirs and Chief Exec. The British Land Company PLC 2004–08; Group Chief Exec. and Exec. Dir Royal Bank of Scotland Group plc 2008–13; Group Chief Exec. RSA Insurance Group plc 2014–; apptd Deputy Chair. of Northern Rock Plc by UK Treasury on its nationalization Feb.–Oct. 2008; mem. Bd of Dirs Centrica plc 2016–; Trustee, The Foundation and Friends of the Royal Botanic Gardens, Kew Foundation. *Leisure interests:* tennis, running, shooting, skiing, horse riding. *Address:* RSA Insurance Group plc, 20 Fenchurch Street, London, EC3M 3AU, England (office). *Telephone:* (14) 0323-2323 (office). *E-mail:* stephen.hester@gcc.rsagroup.com (office). *Website:* www.rsagroup.com (office).

HETFIELD, James Alan; American singer and musician (guitar); b. 3 Aug. 1963, Downey City, Calif.; s. of Virgil Hetfield and Cynthia Hetfield; fmr mem. Obsession, Leather Charm; mem. and lead singer heavy rock group, Metallica 1981–; world-wide tours and concert appearances; nine Grammy Awards, including Grammy Award for Best Metal Performance (for My Apocalypse) 2009, two American Music Awards, including American Music Award for Favorite Heavy Metal Artist (with Metallica) 1993, multiple MTV Video Music Awards, inducted into Rock and Roll Hall of Fame and Museum 2009. *Film:* Some Kind Of Monster (Independent Spirit Award for Best Documentary 2005) 2004. *Recordings include:* albums: Kill 'Em All 1983, Ride The Lightning 1984, Master Of Puppets 1986, ...And Justice For All 1988, The Good, The Bad And The Live 1990, Metallica 1991, Load 1996, Reload 1997, Early Days 1997, S&M (live) 1999, St Anger 2003, Death Magnetic 2008, Hardwired...To Self Destruct (Billboard Music Award for Top Rock Album 2017) 2016; singles: Whiplash 1985, Garage Days Revisited 1987, Creeping Death 1990, Harvester Of Sorrow 1988, One (Grammy Award for Best Heavy Metal Performance) 1989, Stone Cold Crazy (Grammy Award for Best Heavy Metal Performance) 1991, Jump In The Fire 1991, The Unforgiven (Grammy Award for Best Heavy Metal Performance 1992) 1991, Enter Sandman 1991, Nothing Else Matters 1992, Wherever I May Roam 1992, Sad But True 1992, Until It Sleeps 1996, Hero Of The Day 1996, Mama Said 1996, King Nothing 1997, The Memory Remains 1997, Fuel 1998, Turn The Page 1998, Whisky In The Jar (Grammy Award for Best Hard Rock Performance 2000) 1999, Die Die My Darling 1999, No Leaf Clover 2000, I Disappear 2000, Call Of The Ktulu (Grammy Award for Best Rock Instrumental Performance) 2001. *Achievements include:* performed concert in Antarctica 2013, becoming first act to ever play all seven continents all within a year, earning a spot in Guinness Book of World Records. *Address:* Q-Prime Inc., 729 Seventh Avenue, 16th Floor, New York, NY 10019, USA (office). *Telephone:* (212) 302-9790 (office). *Fax:* (212) 302-9589 (office). *E-mail:* newyork@qprime.com (office). *Website:* www.metallica.com.

HEUER, Rolf-Dieter, PhD; German physicist; *President, Deutsche Physikalische Gesellschaft;* b. 24 May 1948, Boll; ed Univ. of Stuttgart, Univ. of Heidelberg; worked on OPAL experiment, CERN, Geneva 1984–98, Dir-Gen. CERN 2009–15; Prof., Univ. of Hamburg 1998; worked on JADE experiment, Deutsches Elektronen-Synchrotron (DESY), Hamburg, Research Dir for high-energy physics, DESY 2004–09; Pres., Deutsche Physikalische Gesellschaft 2016–; mem. Deutsche Akademie der Naturforscher Leopoldina 2011; hon. degrees from Univs of Victoria 2011, Liverpool 2011, Birmingham 2011, Glasgow 2012; Edison Volta Prize 2012, Niels Bohr Medal 2013. *Address:* Deutsche Physikalische Gesellschaft e.V., Magnus-Haus, Am Kupfergraben 7, 10117 Berlin, Germany (office). *Telephone:* (30) 20-17-48-0 (office). *Fax:* (30) 20-17-48-50 (office). *E-mail:* dpg@dpg-physik.de (office). *Website:* dpg-physik.de (office).

HEUSGEN, Christoph, PhD; German diplomatist; *Permanent Representative to UN;* b. 17 March 1955, Düsseldorf-Heerdt; m. Ina Heusgen; four c.; ed Georgia Southern Univ., Panthéon-Assas Univ., Paris; joined German Foreign Service 1980, trained in Foreign Office, Bonn 1980–82, Consulate-Gen. (Press and Econ. Affairs) in Chicago 1983–86, Deputy Head of Del. to COCOM, Embassy in Paris 1986–88, Private Sec. to Coordinator for German-French Relations 1988–99, Deputy Head of Special Section, in-charge of negotiations of Treaty of Maastricht 1990–92, Deputy Prin. Private Sec. in Private Office of Foreign Minister Klaus Kinkel (in-charge of European Affairs) 1993–97, Deputy Dir-Gen., European Affairs 1997–99, Dir of Policy-Planning and Early Warning Unit, Secr. of Council of EU 1999–2005, Foreign Policy and Security Adviser to Fed. Chancellor and Dir-Gen. 2005–17, Perm. Rep. to UN 2017–; mem. Hon. Advisory Council, Dag Hammarskjöld Fund for Journalists 2017–; mem. Council German Inst. for Int. and Security Affairs; Grand Decoration of Honour in Gold for Services to Republic of Austria 2006, Grand Officer of the Order of Merit (Portugal) 2009, Nat. Order of the Legion of Honour (France) 2010, Badge of Honour of the Bundeswehr in Gold 2015. *Address:* Permanent Mission of the Federal Republic of Germany, 871 United Nations Plaza, New York, NY 10017, USA (office). *Telephone:* (212) 940-0400 (office). *Fax:* (212) 940-0402 (office). *E-mail:* info@new-york-un.diplo.de (office). *Website:* www.new-york-un.diplo.de (office).

HEWAGE, Thosapala; Sri Lankan civil servant, diplomatist and business executive; *Chairman, LB Finance Plc;* b. 19 Feb. 1949, Kalawana; s. of U. Hewage; m. Thilaka Hewage; one s. one d.; ed Univ. of Ceylon, Univs of Wales and Cambridge, UK; Sec., Ministry of Environment and Natural Resources 1999, Ministry of Urban Devt and Water Supply *c.* 2005, to Ministry of Enterprise Devt and Investment Promotion *c.* 2007, to Ministry of Ports and Aviation *c.* 2008; Amb. to Nepal 2009–12; Chairman and Non Executive Director of LB Finance Plc 2013–. *Leisure interests:* sports. *Address:* Office of the Chairman, LB Finance Plc, No. 20, Dharmapala Mawatha, Colombo 03, Sri Lanka (office). *Website:* www.lbfinance.com (office).

HEWISH, Antony, PhD, FRS, FRAS; British radio astronomer and academic; *Professor Emeritus of Radio Astronomy, University of Cambridge;* b. 11 May 1924, Fowey, Cornwall; s. of Ernest W. Hewish and Grace F. L. Hewish (née Pinch); m. Marjorie E. C. Richards 1950; one s. one d.; ed King's Coll., Taunton and Gonville and Caius Coll., Cambridge; war service 1943–46; Research Fellow, Gonville and Caius Coll., Cambridge 1951–54, Supernumerary Fellow 1956–61; Univ. Asst Dir of Research 1953–61, lecturer 1961–69; Fellow, Churchill Coll. Cambridge 1962–; Reader in Radio Astronomy, Univ. of Cambridge 1969–71, Prof. 1971–89, Prof. Emer. 1989–; Prof. Royal Inst. 1977; Vikram Sarabhai Prof., Ahmedabad 1988; Head, Mullard Radio Astronomy Observatory, Cambridge 1982–88; mem. Belgian Royal Acad. of Arts and Sciences 1989; mem. Emer. Academia Europaea 1996; Foreign Fellow, Indian Nat. Science Acad.; Foreign Hon. mem. American Acad. of Arts and Sciences 1977, Hon. Fellow, Indian Inst. of Electronics and Telecommunication Engineers 1985, Hon. Citizen of Kwangju, S Korea 1995; Hon. ScD (Leicester) 1976, (Exeter) 1977, (Manchester) 1989, (Santa Maria, Brazil) 1989, (Cambridge) 1996, (Univ. Teknologi Malaysia) 1997; Hamilton Prize (Cambridge) 1951, Eddington Medal, Royal Astronomical Soc. 1968, Boys Prize, Inst. of Physics 1970, Dellinger Medal, Int. Union of Radio Science 1972, Hopkins Prize, Cambridge Philosophical Soc. 1972, Michelson Medal 1973, Franklin Inst. 1973, Holweck Medal and Prize, Soc. Française de Physique 1974, Nobel Prize for Physics (jtly with Sir Martin Ryle) 1974, Hughes Medal, Royal Soc. 1977, Vainu Bappu Prize, Indian Nat. Science Acad. 1998. *Achievements:* discovery of pulsars, first ground-based measurements of the solar wind, and discovery of enhanced speed from the solar pole. *Publications:* Seeing Beyond the Invisible, Pulsars as Physics Laboratories (ed.), numerous papers in scientific journals. *Leisure interests:* listening to good music, gardening, cliff walking. *Address:* Cavendish Laboratory, Madingley Road, Cambridge, CB3 0HE (office); Pryor's Cottage, Kingston, Cambridge, CB3 7NQ, England (home). *Telephone:* (1223) 337299 (office); (1223) 262657 (home). *Fax:* (1223) 354599 (office). *E-mail:* ah120@mrao.cam.ac.uk (office). *Website:* www.mrao.cam.ac.uk (office).

HEWITT, Lleyton Glynn; Australian fmr professional tennis player; b. 24 Feb. 1981, Adelaide, S Australia; s. of Glynn Hewitt and Cherilyn Rumball; m. Bec Cartwright 2005; one s. two d.; turned professional 1998; became youngest-ever season-ending World No. 1 following Masters Cup victory over Pete Sampras (q.v.) 2001; winner, Davis Cup 1999, 2003, finalist 2000, 2001; winner, 30 singles titles (including US Open 2001, Wimbledon 2002), three doubles titles (including US Open 2000), Tennis Masters Cup (now called the ATP World Tour Finals) 2001, 2002, Indian Wells 2002, 2003, Queen's Club Championship 2006, BMW Open 2009, Gerry Weber Open 2010, Brisbane International 2014, Hall of Fame Tennis Championships 2014; finalist, Australian Open 2005; quarterfinalist, French Open 2001, 2004; coached by Peter Smith 1997–98, Darren Cahill 1998–2001, Jason Stoltenberg 2001–03, Roger Rasheed 2003–07, Scott Draper Jan. 2007, Tony Roche 2007–09, Nathan Healey 2009–10, Brett Smith Aug.–Nov. 2010, Tony Roche Nov. 2010–16, Peter Luczak 2013–16; retd following Australian Open Jan. 2016; ATP Player of the Year Award 2001, 2002, Most Popular South Australian Award 2001, Australia's Athlete of the Year Award 2002, ESPY Best Male Tennis Player 2002, Young Australian of the Year 2003, Vogue Australia Sportsman of the Year Award 2003, Most Popular South Australian Award 2003, Young Australian of the Year Award 2003, Newcombe Medal (most outstanding Australian player) 2013, Davis Cup Commitment Award. *Leisure interests:* Australian Rules football, golf. *Address:* Lleyton Hewitt Marketing, Suite 35, 209 Toorak Road, South Yarra, Vic. 3141, Australia. *Website:* www.lleytonandbechewitt.com.

HEWITT, Patricia Hope, MA (Cantab.), MA (Oxon.); British/Australian company director and fmr politician; *Chair, UK India Business Council;* b. 2 Dec. 1948, Canberra, ACT, Australia; d. of Sir (Cyrus) Lenox (Simson) Hewitt and Alison Hope Hewitt; m. William Birtles 1981; one s. one d.; ed Church of England Girls' Grammar School, Canberra, Australia, Australian Nat. Univ., Newnham Coll. Cambridge; Public Relations Officer, Age Concern 1971–73; Women's Rights Officer, Nat. Council for Civil Liberties (now Liberty) 1973–74, Gen. Sec. 1974–83; Labour Party cand. Leicester E, gen. elections 1983; Press and Broadcasting Sec. to Leader of Opposition 1983–88, Policy Co-ordinator 1988–89; Sr Research Fellow, Inst. for Public Policy Research 1989, Deputy Dir 1989–94; Visiting Fellow, Nuffield Coll. Oxford 1992–; Head, then Dir of Research, Andersen Consulting (now Accenture) 1994–97; Labour MP for Leicester W 1997–2010, mem. Select Cttee on Social Security 1997–98; Econ. Sec. to the Treasury 1998–99, Minister of State, Dept of Trade and Industry 1999–2001, Sec. of State for Trade and Industry 2001–05; Minister for Women 2001–05; Sec. of State for Health 2005–07; Chair. UK India Business Council 2010–; mem. Bd of Dirs BT Group plc 2008–14 (fmr Sr Ind. Dir), Eurotunnel Group (now Getlink) 2010–; mem. Asia Pacific Advisory Cttee, Barclays Group plc 2010–12; mem. Global Advisory Bd, Sutherland Global Services 2012–; Sr Adviser, FTI Consulting 2015–; mem. UK India Round Table 2009–15, Asia Task Force 2010–15; Hon. Fellow, London Business School 2004; Dr hc (De Montfort Univ.) 2011. *Publications include:* Civil Liberties, the NCCL Guide (co-ed.) 1977, The Privacy Report 1977, Your Rights at Work 1981, The Abuse of Power 1981, Your Second Baby (co-author) 1990, About Time: The

Revolution in Work and Family Life 1993. *Leisure interests:* reading, theatre, music, gardening. *Address:* UK India Business Council, 12th Floor, Millbank Tower, 21–24 Millbank, London, SW1P 4QP, England (office). *Telephone:* (20) 7592-3040 (office). *E-mail:* patricia.hewitt@ukibc.com (office). *Website:* www.ukibc.com (office).

HEWSON, John Robert, AO, BEcons, MA, PhD; Australian academic, business executive and fmr politician; *Chairman, The John Hewson Group Proprietary;* b. 28 Oct. 1946, Sydney, NSW; s. of Donald Hewson and of Eileen Isabella Hewson (née Tippett); m. 1st Margaret Hewson; two s. one d.; m. 2nd Carolyn Judith Hewson 1988; m. 3rd Jessica Wilson 2007; one d.; ed Univ. of Sydney, Univ. of Saskatchewan, Canada and Johns Hopkins Univ. USA; Research Officer, Bureau of Census and Statistics, Treasury 1967–68; Teaching Fellow, Dept of Econs, Univ. of Saskatchewan 1968–69; Teaching Asst, Dept of Political Economy, Johns Hopkins Univ. 1969–71; Consultant and Economist IMF 1969–74; Research Economist Reserve Bank of Australia 1975–76; Econ. Adviser to Fed. Treas. 1976–77, 1978–81, Chief of Staff 1981–82; Prof. of Econs, Univ. of NSW 1978–87, Head School of Econs 1983–87; MP for Wentworth, Fed. Parl. 1987–95; Shadow Minister for Finance 1988–89, Shadow Treas. 1989–90; Leader of the Liberal Party and Leader of the Opposition 1990–94; Shadow Minister for Industry, Commerce, Infrastrucuture and Customs 1994–95; Dean, Grad. School of Man., Macquarie Univ. 2002–04; Consultant Hill Samuel Australia 1982–85; mem. Advisory Council ABN AMRO Australia Ltd 1998–2004 (Chair. 1995–98); Chair. The John Hewson Group Pty Ltd 1995–, Network Entertainment Ltd 1996–97, Chair. Churchill Funds Man. 1996–99, subsequently GRD 2000–04, Australian Bus Mfg Co. Ltd (now Universal Bus Co. Pty Ltd) 1999–, Global Renewables Ltd 2000–04, Strategic Capital Man. Pty Ltd 2000–04, Belle Property Pty Ltd 2000–03, Investment Advisory Cttee Australian Olympic Foundation 2001, RepuTex Advisory Cttee 2003–04, X Capital Health 2004–, The Freehand Group 2004–; Special Advisor to Under-Sec. UN 2006; Chair. Pisces Group; Chair. Osteoporosis Australia Council 1997–, Arthritis Research Taskforce 2003–, Business Leaders Forum on Sustainable Devt 2003–, Gen. Security Australia Insurance Brokers Pty Ltd; Foundation Dir Macquarie Bank Ltd 1985–87; Dir and Vice-Chair. TV Shopping Network Ltd 1996–98; Deputy Chair. Miniproc Ltd 1998–2000; Pres. Arthritis Foundation of Australia 1997–2002; mem. Bd of Dirs Moran Health Care Group 1998–2001; mem. Bd of Dirs Positive Ageing Foundation 1999–2003; Patron, Australian Corp. Games; mem. Trilateral Comm. 2005–, External Advisory Group, Group Training Australia; weekly columnist, Australian Financial Review 1998–; Fellow, Australian Inst. of Co. Dirs, Hong Kong Man. Asscn; Hon. Trustee, Cttee of Econ. Devt of Australia; Centenary Medal. *Television:* Frontline 2004, Enough Rope with Andrew Denton 2006, The Gruen Transfer 2010. *Publications:* Liquidity Creation and Distribution in the Eurocurrency Market 1975, The Eurocurrency Markets and their Implications: A New View of International Monetary Problems and Monetary Reform (jtly) 1975, Offshore Banking in Australia 1981, innumerable articles in professional journals. *Leisure interests:* gardening, jazz, theatre, sport, cars, motor sports. *Address:* Level 10, 1 Market Street, Sydney, NSW 2000, Australia (office). *Telephone:* (2) 9372-9764 (office). *Fax:* (2) 9372-0364 (office). *E-mail:* john.hewson@horwath.com (office).

HEWSON, Marillyn A., BS, MEcons; American business executive; *Chairman, President and CEO, Lockheed Martin Corporation;* b. Junction City, Kan.; m. James Hewson; two s.; ed Univ. of Alabama, Columbia Business School and Harvard Business School Exec. Devt Programs; joined Lockheed Martin 1983, held several corp. exec. roles, including Sr Vice-Pres. Corp. Shared Services, Vice-Pres. Global Supply Chain Man. and Vice-Pres. Corp. Internal Audit, Pres. and Gen. Man. Kelly Aviation Center, LP (affiliate of Lockheed Martin) 2004–07, Pres. Lockheed Martin Logistics Services Jan.–Feb. 2007, Exec. Vice-Pres. Global Sustainment for Lockheed Martin Aeronautics 2007–08, Pres. Lockheed Martin Systems Integration, Owego, NY 2008–09, Exec. Vice-Pres. Electronic Systems, Lockheed Martin Corpn 2010–12, Pres. and COO Lockheed Martin Corpn 2012, mem. Bd of Dirs 2012–, Chair., Pres. and CEO 2013–; Chair. Sandia Corpn 2010–13; mem. Bd of Dirs Carpenter Technology Corpn 2002–06, DuPont; mem. Pres. Trump's American Manufacturing Council Jan.–Aug. 2017; mem. USO Bd Govs, Economic Club of Washington, DC, Univ. of Alabama's Culverhouse Coll. of Commerce and Business Administration Bd of Visitors, Congressional Medal of Honor Foundation; Chair. Steering Cttee, Defense Industry Initiative. *Address:* Lockheed Martin Corporation, 6801 Rockledge Drive, Bethesda, MD 20817-1877, USA (office). *Telephone:* (301) 897-6000 (office). *Fax:* (301) 897-6704 (office). *E-mail:* info@lockheedmartin.com (office). *Website:* www.lockheedmartin.com (office).

HEWSON, Paul (see BONO).

HEY, John Denis, MA, MSc; British economist, statistician and academic; *Professor Emeritus of Economics and Statistics, University of York;* b. 26 Sept. 1944, Tynemouth, N Tyneside, England; s. of G. B. Hey and E. H. Hey; m. Marlene Bissett 1968 (divorced 1997); one s. two d.; ed Univs of Cambridge and Edinburgh; econometrician, Hoare & Co. London 1968–69; Lecturer in Econs, Univ. of Durham 1969–74, Univ. of St Andrew's 1974–75; apptd Lecturer in Econ. Statistics, Univ. of York 1975, Sr Lecturer, Prof. of Econs and Statistics 1984–16 (part-time 1998–16), Co-Dir Centre for Experimental Econs 1986–2005, Prof. Emer. 2016–; Prof. Ordinario, Univ. of Bari 1998–2005, LUISS, Rome, Italy 2005–10; Hon. Prof. of Econs and Econometrics, Univ. of Vienna. *Publications:* Statistics in Economics 1974, Uncertainty in Microeconomics 1979, Economics in Disequilibrium 1981, Data in Doubt 1984, Experiments in Economics 1991, Experimental Economics (ed.) 1995, Economics of Uncertainty 1997, Intermediate Microeconomics 2003. *Leisure interests:* walking, opera, music. *Address:* Department of Economics and Related Studies, University of York, Heslington, York, YO1 5DD, England (office). *Telephone:* (1904) 433786 (office). *Fax:* (1904) 433759 (office). *E-mail:* john.hey@york.ac.uk (office). *Website:* sites.google.com/a/york.ac.uk/john-hey/home (office).

HEYMAN, Bruce Alan, BA, MBA; American business executive and diplomatist; m. Vicki Simons; one s. two d.; ed Vanderbilt Univ.; with Goldman Sachs 1980–2013, Regional Man. Dir Midwest Pvt. Wealth Man. Group 1999–2013; Amb. to Canada 2014–17; mem. Econ. Club of Chicago, Execs Club of Chicago, Facing History and Ourselves Chicago Advisory Bd; Past Pres. Alumni Bd, Vanderbilt Univ., fmr mem. Bd of Visitors, Owen Grad. School of Man.; fmr mem. Bd Chicago Council on Global Affairs, Northwestern Memorial Hosp. Foundation; fmr adviser to Fix the Debt CEO Council, Cttee for a Responsible Fed. Budget.

HEYMAN, David; British film producer; b. 26 July 1961; ed Hill House London, Westminster School, London, Harvard Univ., USA; began career as production runner for film producers Milos Forman and David Lean; Creative Exec. Warner Bros, Los Angeles 1986–89, Vice-Pres. United Artists 1989; now working as ind. producer; returned to UK 1997, f. Heyday Films 1997; Showest Producer of the Year 2003. *Films produced include:* Juice, The Daytrippers, Harry Potter and the Philosopher's Stone 2001, Harry Potter and the Chamber of Secrets 2002, Harry Potter and the Prisoner of Azkaban 2004, Harry Potter and the Goblet of Fire 2005, Harry Potter and the Order of the Phoenix 2007, I Am Legend 2007, The Boy in the Striped Pyjamas 2008, Harry Potter and the Half-Blood Prince 2009, Harry Potter and the Deathly Hallows Part 1 2010, Part 2 2011, Gravity 2013, Paddington 2014, Testament of Youth 2015, Fantastic Beasts and Where to Find Them 2016, Paddington 2 2017, Fantastic Beasts: The Crimes of Grindelwald 2018. *Address:* Heyday Films, 5 Denmark Street, London, WC2H 8LP, England (office). *Telephone:* (20) 7836-6333 (office). *Fax:* (20) 7836-6444 (office). *E-mail:* office@heydayfilms.com (office).

HEYMAN, Pascal; Belgian diplomatist; *Permanent Representative of Belgium to NATO;* ed Univ. of Leuven, Univ. of Antwerp; Asst to Prof. Dr Eric Suy for Public Int. Law, Univ. of Leuven 1990–91; started diplomatic career 1991, Sec. of Embassy, Perm. Delegation of Belgium to EU 1993, Dept of Peace and Security 1994–97, First Sec., Perm. Delegation to NATO 1997–2002, Counsellor of Embassy and Deputy Perm. Rep. to OSCE in Vienna 2001–08; Deputy Dir and Head of Policy Support Service, OSCE Conflict Prevention Centre 2008–13; Counsellor of Embassy, Dept of Security Policy of the Fed. Public Service of Foreign Affairs, Foreign Trade and Devt Cooperation of Belgium 2014; Perm. Rep. of Belgium to NATO 2018–; Diplomatic Dir, Cabinet of the Minister of Defence and Public Service 2014–18, Defence Policy Dir 2015–18. *Leisure interest:* photography. *Address:* Permanent Representation of Belgium to NATO (BELOTAN), Blvd Leopold III, 1110 Brussels, Belgium (office). *Telephone:* (2) 707-60-11 (office). *Fax:* (2) 707-60-90 (office). *E-mail:* BrusselsNATO@diplobel.fed.be (office). *Website:* nato.diplomatie.belgium.be/en (office); www.leicapages.com.

HEYMANN, Daniel, PhD; Argentine economist and academic; *Professor of Economics and Director, Instituto Interdisciplinario de Economía Política de Buenos Aires (IIEP BAIRES), University of Buenos Aires;* b. 30 Dec. 1949, Buenos Aires; s. of Gunther Heymann and Marta Weil; m. Cristina Bramuglia 1976; two s.; ed Coll. Français de Buenos Aires, Univ. of Buenos Aires and Univ. of Calif. Los Angeles; Asst Prof., Univ. of Buenos Aires 1973–75, Prof. of Econs 1987–, Dir Instituto Interdisciplinario de Economía Política de Buenos Aires (IIEP BAIRES) 2012–; Research Asst, ECLAC, Buenos Aires 1974–78, Sr Economist 1987–2010; Prof. of Econs, Instituto Torcuato Di Tella, Buenos Aires 1982–2003; Prof. of Econs, Univ. of La Plata 2004–; Prof. of Econs, Univ. of San Andres 2010–; Pres. Argentine Political Economy Asscn 2008–10; mem. Argentine Acad. of Econ. Sciences; Academic Distinction Prize in Econs, Univ. of Buenos Aires 2009. *Publications:* Fluctuaciones de la Industria Manufactturera Argentina 1980, Tres Ensayos sobre Inflación y Políticas de Estabilzacion 1986, The Austral Plan 1987, Distributive Conflict and the Fiscal Deficit: Some Inflationary Games (co-author) 1991, Fiscal Inconsistencies and High Inflation (co-author) 1994, On the Interpretation of the Current Account 1994, High Inflation (co-author) 1995, Business Cycles from Misperceived Trends (co-author) 1998, Price Setting in a Schematic Model of Inductive Learning (co-author) 1999, Learning about Trends: Spending and Business Fluctuations in Open Economies (co-author) 2001, Great Expectations and Hard Times: The Argentine Convertibility (co-author) 2003, Land-Rich Economies, Education and Economic Development (co-author) 2008, Macroeconomics of Broken Promises 2009, Economía de Fronteras Abiertas: Exploraciones en Sistemas Sociales Complejos (co-author) 2013, Behavioral Heuristics and Market Patterns in a Bertrand Edgeworth Game (co-author) 2014, Life After Debt: The Origins and Resolutions of Debt Crisis (co-ed.) 2014. *Address:* Faculty of Economics, Universidad de Buenos Aires, Avenida Córdoba 2122, CP 1120 AAQ, Buenos Aires, Argentina (office). *Telephone:* (11) 4725-6969 (office); (11) 4374-4448 (office). *E-mail:* dheymann@udesa.edu.ar (office); dheymann@econ.uba.ar (office). *Website:* iiep-baires.econ.uba.ar (office).

HEYMANN, Klaus; German business executive; *CEO, Naxos;* b. 22 Oct. 1936, Frankfurt; m. Takako Nishizaki; one s.; Export Advertising and Promotion Man., Max Braun AG 1961–62; with The Overseas Weekly, Frankfurt 1962–67, ran Hong Kong Office 1967–69; f. Pacific Mail-Order System 1969; organized classical concerts in Hong Kong; mem. Bd Hong Kong Philharmonic Orchestra, later Chair. Fund-Raising Cttee; Founder and CEO Naxos; Chair. HNH Int. Ltd 1987; Co-Founder and Dir Artaria Edns; Hon. Gen. Man. Hong Kong Philharmonic Orchestra; Int. Classical Music Award for Special Achievement 2017. *Address:* Naxos Rights International Ltd, Level 11, Cyberport 1, 100 Cyberport Road, Hong Kong Special Administrative Region (office); HNH International Ltd, 6/F, Sino Industrial Plaza, 9 Kai Cheung Road, Kowloon Bay, Hong Kong Special Administrative Region, People's Republic of China (office). *Telephone:* 27607818 (office). *Fax:* 27601962 (office). *E-mail:* info@naxos.com.hk (office). *Website:* www.naxos.com (office).

HEYZER, Noeleen, PhD; Singaporean UN official; m.; two d.; ed Univ. of Singapore, Univ. of Cambridge, UK; Fellow and Research Officer, Inst. of Devt Studies, Univ. of Sussex, UK 1979–81; with Social Devt Div., ESCAP, Bangkok, Thailand early 1980s; Dir Gender and Devt Programme, Asian and Pacific Devt Centre, Kuala Lumpur, Malaysia 1984–94; Co-ordinator for the Asia-Pacific NGO Working Group for the UN Fourth World Conf. on Women, Beijing, People's Repub. of China; Exec. Dir UN Devt Fund for Women (UNIFEM) 1994–2007; Exec. Sec. ESCAP 2007–14; Special Adviser of the Sec.-Gen. for Timor-Leste, UN 2013–15, mem. Sec.-Gen.'s High-Level Advisory Bd on Mediation 2017–; Convener Int. Women's Comm. for a Just and Sustainable Palestinian-Israeli Peace; mem. Bd Pres. Ahtisaari's Crisis Man. Initiative; mem. High-Level Commonwealth Comm. on Respect and Understanding; New Millennium Distinguished Visiting Scholar, Columbia Univ.; Chair. Consortium Advisory Group, Research Programme on Women's Empowerment in Muslim Contexts; has served on bds of several humanitarian orgs including Devt Alternatives with Women for a New Era, the Global South, ISIS, Oxfam, Panos and Soc. for Int. Devt; Global Tolerance

Award for Humanitarian Service, Friends of the UN 2000, Lifetime Achievement Award, Inst. for Leadership Devt 2000, Woman of Distinction Award, UN NGO Cttee 2003, Leadership Award, Mount Sinai Hosp., New York 2004, Leadership Award, UN Asscn Greater Boston 2004, Dag Hammarskjöld Medal 2004, NCRW Women Who Make a Difference Award 2005, Univ. of Groningen Aletta Jacobs Prize 2014. *Publications include:* Working Women in South-East Asia 1986, Gender, Economic Growth and Poverty (with Gita Sen) 1994, The Trade in Domestic Workers (with Geertje Lycklama A'Nieholt and Nedra Werakoon) 1994, Women, War and Peace 2004. *Address:* United Nations, New York, NY 10017, USA (office). *Telephone:* (212) 963-1234 (office). *Fax:* (212) 963-4879 (office). *Website:* www.un.org (office); www.noeleenheyzer.com.

HIATT, Fred, BA; American journalist; *Editorial Page Editor, The Washington Post;* b. 30 April 1955, Washington, DC; s. of Howard Haim Hiatt and Doris Bieringer; m. Margaret Shapiro; three c.; ed Harvard Univ.; City Hall reporter, Atlanta Journal-Constitution 1979–80; reporter, The Washington Star 1981; Virginia Reporter, The Washington Post 1981–83, Pentagon Reporter 1983–86, NE Asia Co-Bureau Chief 1987–90, Moscow Co-Bureau Chief 1991–95, Editorial Page Ed. 1996–. *Publications:* The Secret Sun: A Novel of Japan 1992 (novel), If I Were Queen of the World 1997 (children's book), Baby Talk 1999, Nine Days 2013. *Address:* The Washington Post, 1150 15th Street, NW, Washington, DC 20071, USA (office). *Telephone:* (202) 334-6000 (office). *E-mail:* twpcoreply@washpost.com (office). *Website:* www.washingtonpost.com/people/fred-hiatt (office); www.fredhiatt.com.

HIBRI, Fuad el-, BA, MA; American/Lebanese business executive; *Executive Chairman, Emergent BioSolutions Inc.;* b. 2 March 1958, Hildesheim, Germany; s. of Ibrahim el-Hibri and Liane el-Hibri; ed Yale Univ., Stanford Univ., USA; Man., Mergers and Acquisitions dept, Citibank, New York and Jeddah, Saudi Arabia; Chair. East West Resources Corpn 1990–2004, Pres. 1990–2004; Founder Emergent BioSolutions Inc. 1998, CEO 1998–2012, now Exec. Chair., Chair. and CEO BioPort Corpn 1998–2004 (co. acquired by Emergent); Chair. Digicel Holdings Ltd (telecommunications co.) 2000–06, Pres. 2000–05; Chair. El-Hibri Charitable Foundation; mem. Bd of Dirs US Chamber of Commerce; mem. Bd of Trustees International Biomedical Research Alliance, National Health Museum, American Univ.; mem. Advisory Bd Yale Healthcare Conference; f. El Hibri Peace Educ. Prize; Rene Moawad Foundation Distinguished Community Service and Achievement Award 2007, Ernst & Young Entrepreneur of the Year for Greater Washington 2009, Int. Leadership Award, World Trade Center Inst. 2010, Biotech CEO of the Year, World Vaccine Congress 2011, Exec. of the Year, Tech Council of Maryland 2012, Shining Stars Award, Dar Al-Aytam 2012, Citation for Public Service by Hon. US Senator Barbara A. Mikulski 2012. *Address:* Office of the Chairman, Emergent BioSolutions, 2273 Research Boulevard, Suite 400, Rockville, MD 20850, USA (office). *Telephone:* (301) 795-1800 (office). *Fax:* (301) 795-1899 (office). *Website:* ebsi.com (office).

HICK, Graeme Ashley, MBE; British (b. Zimbabwean) cricket coach and fmr professional cricketer; *Batting Coach, Australia National Cricket Team;* b. 23 May 1966, Salisbury (now Harare); s. of John Hick and Eve Hick; ed Banket Primary School, Prince Edward Boys' High School; right-hand batsman, off-break bowler, slip fielder; teams: Zimbabwe 1983–86, Worcs. 1984–2008 (Capt. 2000–02), Northern Dists 1987–89, Queensland 1990–91, Chandigarh Lions (Indian Cricket League) 2008; scored his first hundred when aged six (for Banket primary school); youngest player (aged 17) to appear in 1983 World Cup and youngest to rep. Zimbabwe; 65 Tests for England 1991–2001, scoring 3,383 runs (average 31.32, highest score 178), including six hundreds, and took 23 wickets; played in 120 One-Day Ints for 3,846 runs (average 37.33, highest score 126 not out); played in 526 First-class matches, scoring 41,112 runs (average 52.23, highest score 405 not out) including 136 hundreds and 709 catches; youngest to score 2,000 First-class runs in a season (1986); scored 1,019 runs before June 1988, including a record 410 runs in April; fewest innings for 10,000 runs in county cricket (179); youngest (24) to score 50 First-class hundreds; toured Australia 1994–95; mem. England World Cup Squad 1996, 1999; scored 315 not out against Durham June 2002 – highest championship innings of the season; surpassed Graham Gooch's record for the most matches in all forms of the game combined 2008; retd from county cricket at end of 2008 season; apptd Coach, Malvern Coll. 2008; later coach for cricket at Barbados 2009 Sports Camp; High Performance Coach, Cricket Australia's Centre of Excellence 2013–16, Batting Coach, Australia Nat. Cricket Team 2016–; Wisden Cricketer of the Year 1987, Walter Lawrence Trophy 1988, Indian Cricket Cricketer of the Year 1993. *Publication:* My Early Life (autobiog.) 1992. *Leisure interests:* golf, tennis, squash, indoor hockey, cinema, television, listening to music. *Address:* c/o Cricket Australia Public Enquiries, 60 Jolimont St, Jolimont, Vic. 3002, Australia (office). *Website:* www.cricket.com.au (office).

HICKENLOOPER, John Wright, BA, MS; American business executive, politician and fmr state governor; b. 7 Feb. 1952, Narberth, Pa; m. 1st Helen Thorpe 2002 (divorced 2015); one s.; m. 2nd Robin Pringle 2016; ed Wesleyan Univ.; exploration geologist, Buckhorn Petroleum, Denver, Colo 1981–86; turned entrepreneur, owned restaurants in lower downtown area of Denver, Colo (LoDo) late 1980s; Co-founder The Wynkoop Brewing Co. microbrewery 1988–98; Mayor of Denver 2003–11; Gov. of Colorado 2011–19; fmr mem. Mayors Against Illegal Guns Coalition; Co-founder CultureHaus, Chinook Fund; mem. Bd of Dirs Colorado Business Cttee for the Arts, Denver Metro Convention and Visitors Bureau, Denver Art Museum, Denver Civic Ventures, Volunteers for Outdoor Colorado; Democrat. *Address:* c/o Office of the Governor, 136 State Capitol, Denver, CO 80203-1792, USA (office).

HICKEY, John; Papua New Guinea politician; mem. Parl. (Nat. Alliance Party) 2002–, Chair. Public Accounts Cttee 2003–05; Minister of Finance and Nat. Planning and Monitoring 2005–07, of Agric. and Livestock 2007–11. *Address:* National Parliament, Parliament House, Waigani, NCD, Papua New Guinea.

HICKS, Kenneth C., MBA; American retail executive; ed US Mil. Acad., Harvard Business School; worked for McKinsey and Co. (man. consultancy firm) for five years; joined May Department Stores 1987, held several exec. positions including Sr Vice-Pres. and Gen. Merchandise Man. –1998; Exec. Vice-Pres. and Gen. Merchandise Man. Home Shopping Network 1999; Pres. Payless Shoes Inc. 1999–2002; Pres. and COO Stores and Merchandise Operations, J.C. Penney Co. Inc. 2002–05, Pres. and Chief Merchandising Officer 2005–09; CEO and Pres. Foot Locker Inc. 2009–14, Exec. Chair. 2010–15; mem. Bd of Dirs Avery Dennison Corpn 2007–.

HIDALGO, Anne, DEA; French (b. Spanish) politician and fmr civil servant; *Mayor of Paris;* b. 19 June 1959, San Fernando, Andalusia, Spain; m. Jean-Marc Germain; ed Univ. Jean Moulin Lyon 3, Univ. Paris Ouest Nanterre La Défense; worked as civil servant 1984–2011, including in Inspection du travail (Labour Inspectorate) 1984–93, Professional Training Div., Dept of Labour 1993–95, Mission to ILO, Geneva 1995–96; Officer, Human Resources Directorate, Compagnie générale des eaux (later renamed Vivendi then Vivendi Universal) 1996–97; Adviser to cabinet office of Minister of Employment and Solidarity 1997–98; Technical Adviser to cabinet office of Sec. of State for Women's Rights and Vocational Training 1998–2000, to cabinet office of Minister of Justice 2000–02; mem. Conseil de Paris for 15th arrondissement 2001; First Deputy Mayor of Paris 2001–14, Mayor of Paris 2014–; mem. Conseil régional d'Île-de-France 2004–; mem. Parti socialiste 1994–; Commdr, Order of Isabella the Catholic 2010; Chevalier, Légion d'honneur 2012. *Address:* Hôtel de Ville, 29 rue de Rivoli, 75004 Paris, France (office). *Telephone:* 1-42-76-40-40 (office). *Website:* www.paris.fr (office); www.anne-hidalgo.net (office).

HIDAYAT, Bambang, PhD, FAAS, FRAS; Indonesian astronomer and academic; *Professor Emeritus, Bandung Institute of Technology (ITB);* b. 18 Sept. 1934, Kundus, Cen. Java; s. of Soedirgo Dhonomidjojo; m. Estiti Bambang Hidayat (died 1995); two s.; ed Case Inst. of Tech., Cleveland; Dir Bosscha Observatory 1968–83; Asst Prof. of Astronomy, Bandung Inst. of Tech. (ITB) 1968, Assoc. Prof. 1974, Prof. 1976–2004, Prof. Emer. 2004–; fmr Chair. Indonesian–Dutch Astronomy Programme; Chair. Indonesian–Japan Astronomy Programme 1980–94, Consortium of Science and Mathematics; Vice-Pres. Int. Astronomical Union 1994–2000; f. Indonesian Astronomical Soc. 1978, co-f. Indonesian Physics Soc.; mem. American Astronomical Soc., Royal Astronomical Soc., Indonesian Inst. of Sciences 1991, Nat. Research Council, Indonesian Nat. Acad. of Sciences, Royal Comm. Al Albait Univ., Jordan 1993; Fellow, Islamic Acad. of Sciences 1992; Hon. mem. AAAS 2000, Indian Inst. of Science; Habibie Award 2003. *Publications include:* several astronomy textbooks and more than 40 scientific papers. *Address:* Institut Teknologi Bandung (ITB), Jalan Tamansari 64, Bandung 40116 (office); Indonesian Institute of Sciences, Jl. Jendral Gatot Subroto no. 10, PO Box 250, Jakarta, Indonesia (office). *Telephone:* (22) 2500935 (office); (21) 5251542 (office). *Fax:* (22) 2500935 (office); (21) 5207226 (office). *E-mail:* info-center@itb.ac.id (office); bhidayat@as.itb.ac.id; hidayatbambang@yahoo.com; bhidayat07@hotmail.com. *Website:* www.itb.ac.id (office).

HIDAYAT, Taufik; Indonesian badminton player (retd); b. 10 Aug. 1981, Bandung, West Java; s. of Aries Harris and Enok Dartilah; m. Armidianti Gumelar 2006; one d.; winner Djarum Indonesia Open 1999, 2000, 2002, 2003, 2004, Singapore Open 2005; Gold Medal Athens Olympics 2004, XIV World Championships, Anaheim 2005, Asian Games, Busan 2002, Doha 2006; Gold Medal, French Open BWF Superseries 2010, Grand Prix Gold, Macau Open 2008, India Open 2009, Indonesian Masters 2010, Syed Modi Int. 2011, Grand Prix, US Open 2009, Canada Open 2010; Owner, Taufik Hidayat Arena 2012; Bintang Jasa Utama (First Class Merit Star). *Leisure interests:* travelling, football. *Address:* Taufik Hidayat Arena, JL. PKP, No. 8, Kiwi Raya Kelapa Dua Wetan, RT 7/RW 12 Kel Cibubur, Kec Ciracas, Jakarta, Indonesia (office). *Telephone:* (21) 87715959 (office). *E-mail:* marketing@taufikhidayatarena.com (office). *Website:* www.taufikhidayatarena.com (office).

HIDE, Rodney, QSO, MSc; New Zealand politician; b. 1956, Oxford, North Canterbury; ed Univs of Canterbury and Lincoln, Montana State Univ., USA; fmrly rig worker on North Sea oil rig, truck driver; fmr Lecturer, Centre for Resource Man. and Dept of Econs, Univ. of Lincoln, UK; Founding Chair. Asscn of Consumers and Taxpayers 1993; Founding Chair. and first Pres. ACT New Zealand 1994, Vice-Pres. 2000–04, Leader 2004–11; elected list MP 1996, ACT Spokesman for Finance 1996–, ACT Rep., Finance and Expenditure Select Cttee 1996–; ACT cand. for Epsom 1998, 2002; MP for Epsom 2005–11 (retd); Minister of Local Govt 2008–11, of Regulatory Reform 2008–11, Assoc. Minister of Commerce 2008–11; 'Backbencher of the Year' New Zealand Herald 2001, 'Opposition MP of the Year' Dominion 2001, 'Leader of the Opposition' North and South 2002, 'Politician of the Year' Dominion 2003. *Publications:* The Power to Destroy 1999; HideSight column for Nat. Business Review 1989–99; HideSight email newsletter published by rodneyhide.com 2003–, My Year of Living Dangerously 2007.

HIÉGEL, Catherine; French actress; b. 10 Dec. 1946, Montreuil; d. of Peter Hiégel; partner Richard Berry; one d.; ed Conservatoire nat. supérieur d'art dramatique; as a child, sang with André Claveau in Viens danser avec papa (Come and Dance with Dad) 1956; studied with Charon Jacques and Jean Darnel and began stage career at Théâtre des Bouffes-Parisiens; joined Comédie-Française 1969, worked with directors including Philippe Adrien, Patrice Chéreau, Dario Fo, Jorge Lavelli, Joel Jouanneau, Jacques Lassalle, Jean-Paul Roussillon in the classical and contemporary repertoire; Assoc. mem. Comédie-Française 1976, Dean (Doyen) 2008–09, Hon. mem. 2010–; Prof., Conservatoire nat. supérieur d'art dramatique 1998–. *Plays at Comédie-Française include:* Le Dépit amoureux (Molière) 1969, Le Jeu de l'amour et du hasard (Marivaux) 1969, Le Malade imaginaire (Molière) 1969, 1971, 1972, 1973 (toured to USSR) 2001, 2006, Dom Juan (Molière) 1970 (toured to USA, Canada and London), 1971, George Dandin (Molière) 1970, 1972, 1973, L'Impromptu de Versailles (Molière) 1971, 1973, Les Femmes savantes (Molière) 1971, 1973, Cœur à deux (Foissy 1972 (toured in Italy)), Les Fausses Confidences (Marivaux) 1972, Électre (Giraudoux) 1972, Amphitryon (Molière) 1973, L'Île des esclaves (Marivaux) 1973, Les Précieuses ridicules (Molière) 1973, 2007, 2009, Henri IV (Pirandello) 1974, Maître Puntila et son valet Matti (Brecht) 1976, Cyrano de Bergerac (Rostand) 1976, Les Acteurs de bonne foi (Marivaux) 1977, Les Trois Sœurs (Chekhov) 1979, Le roi se meurt (Ionesco) 1980, La locandiera (Goldoni) 1981, 1983, Le Bourgeois gentilhomme (Molière) 1985, Le Médecin malgré lui (Molière) 1990, Maman revient pauvre orphelin (Grumberg) 1994, Le Shaga (Duras) 1995, Les Bonnes (Genet) 1997, Mère Courage et ses enfants (Brecht) 1998, Savannah bay (Duras) 2002, 2003, 2004, Les Papiers d'Aspern (Jean Pavans after Henry James) 2003, 2004, Tartuffe (Molière) 2005, Il Campiello (Goldoni) 2007, 2009, Une confrérie de farceurs (Faivre) 2007, Les Joyeuses Commères de Windsor (Shakespeare) 2009, Mystère Bouffe et fabulages (Fo) 2010, Les Oiseaux (Aristophanes) 2010. *Other plays include:* Quai Ouest (Koltès), Théâtre Nanterre-Amandiers 1986, Une visite inopportune (Copi), Théâtre nat. de la Colline, Nouveau Théâtre d'Angers 1988, La Veillée (Norén), Théâtre nat. de la Colline (Prix du Syndicat de la critique for Best Comedienne 1989) 1989, Arloc (Kribus), Théâtre nat. de la Colline 1996, Les Présidentes (Schwab), Théâtre nat. de Chaillot 1998, J'étais dans ma maison et j'attendais que la pluie vienne (Lagarce), Théâtre de la Cité internationale (Prix du Syndicat de la critique for Best Comedienne 2005) 2005, Objet perdu (Keene), Théâtre de la Commune 2006, La Mère (Zeller), De beaux lendemains (Banks), Théâtre des Bouffes du Nord 2011, Tout doit disparaître (Pessani), Festival d'Avignon 2011, Moi je crois pas! (Grumberg), Théâtre du Rond-Point 2012, Whistling psyche, Théâtre Gérard-Philipe 2013, Anna et Martha, Théâtre Nat. de Nice 2014, Le Retour au désert, Théâtre de la Ville 2015, Votre maman, Théâtre de l'Atelier 2017, La Nostalgie des blattes, Théâtre du Petit Saint-Martin 2018. *Plays directed at Comédie-Française:* Le Misanthrope (Molière) (co-directed with Jean-Luc Boutté) 1975, Les Femmes savantes (Molière), Comédie-Française au Théâtre de la Porte Saint-Martin 1987, Purgatoire (Minyana) 1994, La Demoiselle de la poste (Pokas) 1996, L'Âge d'or (Feydeau) 1998, George Dandin (Molière) 1999, Le Retour (Pinter) 2000, L'Avare (Molière) 2009. *Other plays directed:* Je danse comme Jésus Christ sur le vaste océan (after Alfred de Musset), Conservatoire nat. supérieur d'art dramatique 2011, Le Bourgeois gentilhomme (Molière), CADO 2011, Je danse comme Jésus Christ sur le vaste océan 2011, Dramuscules 2013, Les Femmes savantes 2016, Le Jeu de l'amour et du hasard 2018. *Films include:* L'état de grâce 1986, Life is a Long Quiet River 1988, Widow's Walk 1988, La petite amie 1988, My Life Is Hell 1991, Gazon maudit 1995, La serva amorosa 1996, Fred 1997, L'autre côté de la mer 1997, Hygiène de l'assassin 1999, Les après-midi de Laura (short) 2000, Les côtelettes 2003, Secret défense 2008, He Is My Girl 2009, Un baiser papillon 2011, Adieu Berthe 2012, Violette 2013. *Television includes:* films: Spéciale dernière 1967, Le bourgeois gentilhomme 1968, Les précieuses ridicules 1972, Georges Dandin 1973, Chez les Titch 1974, La confession d'un enfant du siècle 1974, Ondine 1975, Le roi se meurt 1978, Les acteurs de bonne foi 1979, La folle de Chaillot 1980, Les trois soeurs 1980, Une page d'amour 1980, Créanciers 1981, La locandiera 1982, La corruptrice 1994, Le mangeur de lune 1994, Youth Without God 1996, Mylène 1996, Le malade imaginaire 2002, Les précieuses ridicules 2009; series: Le théâtre de la jeunesse – L'homme qui a perdu son ombre 1966, Au théâtre ce soir – Aux quatre coins 1970, Ferbac – Ferbac et le festin de miséricorde 1994, Julie Lescaut – Le secret des origines 1996, Le Malade imaginaire 2002, Neuf jours en hiver 2015. *Address:* c/o Comédie-Française, 1er Arrondissement, 75001 Paris, France. *Telephone:* 1-44-58-13-16. *E-mail:* informations@comedie-francaise.org. *Website:* www.comedie-francaise.fr.

HIERRO LÓPEZ, Luis; Uruguayan politician, teacher and journalist; b. 6 Jan. 1947, Montevideo; s. of Luis Hierro Gambardella and Celia Lopez; m. Ligia Armitran; four c.; journalist 1965–84; history teacher 1968–73; researcher, Museo Histórico Nacional 1974–84; mem. Nat. Exec. Cttee Colorado Party and Nat. Convention 1982–98, Chamber of Deputies (Pres. 1989) 1985–94; Chair. Cttees on the Constitution, Gen. Legislation and Admin and Human Rights, Special Cttee dealing with proposed anti-corruption legislation, Uruguayan Section of Jt Parl. Cttee of MERCOSUR; Senator, Colorado Party 1995–97, Deputy Gen. Sec. 2005–09; Vice-Pres. of Uruguay 2001–05. *Publications include:* Diario del Uruguay (co-author) 1975, Battle y la Reforma del Estado 1978, Thresholds and Locks 1993, The People Said NO: A Chronicle of the 1980 Plebiscite 2005.

HIESINGER, Heinrich, Dr-Ing; German business executive; b. 25 May 1960, Bopfingen; ed Tech. Univ. of Munich; Research Asst, Tech. Univ. of Munich 1986–92; held various positions in various countries in the Power Transmission and Distribution Group of Siemens 1992–2000, Pres. Power Transmission and Distribution Group 2000–03, Pres. and CEO Siemens Building Technologies AG, Zug, Switzerland 2003–07, mem. Man. Bd Siemens AG 2007–10, CEO Industry Sector of Siemens and Head of Cen. Dept Corp. Information Tech. 2008–10; Vice-Chair. Exec. Bd ThyssenKrupp AG 2010–11, Chair. 2011–18. *Address:* c/o ThyssenKrupp AG, ThyssenKrupp Allee 1, 45143 Essen, Germany (office).

HIGASHIHARA, Toshiaki, MSc; Japanese business executive; *Representative Executive Officer, President and CEO, Hitachi Limited;* b. 16 Feb. 1955; ed Univ. of Tokushima, Boston Univ., USA; joined Hitachi Ltd 1977, Sr Man. Transportation Systems Design Dept, Omika Industrial Systems Div., Power & Industrial System Group 1999–2000, Sr Man. Public Utility and Energy Industry Information Systems Design Dept, Information & Control Systems Div. 2000–01, Gen. Man. Public Utility and Energy Industry Information Systems Div., Information & Control Systems Div., System Solutions Group 2001–04, Gen. Man. Information & Control Systems Div., Information & Telecommunication Systems Group 2004–06, COO Information & Telecommunication Systems Group 2006–07, Vice-Pres. and Exec. Officer, COO Power Systems Group 2007–08, Pres. Hitachi Power Europe GmbH 2008–10, Rep. Exec. Officer, Pres. and CEO Hitachi Plant Technologies Ltd 2010, Rep. Dir and Pres. 2010–11, Vice-Pres. and Exec. Officer, in charge of Industrial & Social Systems Business 2011–12, Vice-Pres. and Exec. Officer, Vice-Pres. and Exec. Officer of Infrastructure Systems Group, Gen. Man. Water Environment Solutions Div. 2012–13, Sr Vice-Pres. and Exec. Officer, Pres. and CEO Infrastructure Systems Group and Infrastructure Systems Co. 2013–14, Rep. Exec. Officer, Pres. and COO Hitachi Ltd 2014–16, Rep. Exec. Officer, Pres. and CEO 2016–, also Gen. Man. Smart Transformation Project Initiatives Div., Dir and mem. Compensation Cttee. *Address:* Hitachi Ltd, 6-6 Marunouchi 1-chome, Chiyoda-ku, Tokyo 100-8280, Japan (office). *Telephone:* (3) 3258-1111 (office). *Fax:* (3) 3258-2375 (office). *E-mail:* ir@hdq.hitachi.co.jp (office). *Website:* www.hitachi.com (office).

HIGGINS, Chester, Jr, BS; American photographer; b. Nov. 1946, Lexington, Ky; s. of Varidee Loretta Young Higgins Smith and step-s. of Johnny Frank Smith; m. 1st Renelda Walker (divorced); one s. one d.; m. 2nd Betsy Kissam; ed Tuskegee Inst. (now Tuskegee Univ.); became photographer 1967; photographer for Look magazine 1970; part-time photography instructor, New York Univ. School of Fine Arts 1975–78; staff photographer, New York Times 1975–; photographs have appeared in ARTNews, Look, New York Times Magazine, Life, Newsweek, Fortune, Ebony, Essence, Archaeology; Fellow, Int. Center for Photography, Ford Foundation, Nat. Endowment for the Arts, Rockefeller Foundation, Andy Warhol Foundation; collections, The Museum of Modern Art (MoMA), New York; UN Award, Graphics Magazine Award, American Graphic Design Award, Art Dirs of New York Award. *Publications include:* Student Unrest at Tuskegee Institute 1968, Black Woman 1970, Drums of Life 1974, Some Time Ago: A Historical Portrait of Black Americans 1850–1950 1980, Feeling the Spirit: Searching the World for the People of Africa 1994, Elder Grace: The Nobility of Aging 2000, Echo of the Spirit: A Visual Journey 2004, Ancient Nubia: African Kingdoms on the Nile 2012; numerous reviews and articles in journals. *Address:* Peter Fetterman Gallery, 2525 Michigan Avenue, Santa Monica, CA 90404, USA. *Website:* www.peterfetterman.com; www.chesterhiggins.com.

HIGGINS, Christopher Francis, BSc (Hons), PhD, FRSE, FRSA, FMedSci; British geneticist, biochemist, academic and fmr university administrator; *Professor Emeritus, Durham University;* b. 24 June 1955, Cambridge, England; s. of Prof. Philip J. Higgins; pnr; five d.; ed Raynes Park Comprehensive, London, Royal Coll. of Music, London, Durham Univ., Univ. of California, Berkeley, USA; Lecturer, then Reader in Molecular Genetics, Univ. of Dundee 1981–88, Prof. 1988–89; Dir of Research Labs, Imperial Cancer Research Fund (now Cancer Research UK), Inst. of Molecular Medicine 1989–94, Nuffield Prof. and Head, Dept of Clinical Biochemistry 1994–98; Dir Clinical Science Centre, MRC 1998–2007; Head of Div., Faculty of Medicine, Imperial Coll. London 1998–2007; Scientific Advisor, House of Lords Select Cttee on Stem Cells 2001–02; Vice-Chancellor and Warden, Durham Univ. 2007–14, Pro-Chancellor 2014–15, Prof. Emer. 2015–; Chair. Spongiform Encephalopathy Advisory Cttee; mem. Exec. Bd Asscn of Medical Research Charities; fmr Council mem. Acad. of Medical Sciences, Biotechnology and Biological Sciences Research Council, North East Regional Devt Agency; mem. Human Genetics Comm.; Trustee, Kennedy Inst. for Rheumatology; Chair. of Trustees, Nat. Youth Choirs of GB 2011–; Vice-Chair. Govs., West Suffolk Coll. 2015–; Vice-Chair. Suffolk Academies Trust 2016–; DL, Co. Palatine of Durham 2011–15; Fellow, European Molecular Biology Org.; Trustee, Suffolk Philharmonic Orchestra 2015–, Britten-Pears Foundation 2017–; Hugh Bean Prize, Royal Coll. of Music, CIBA Medal, British Biochemical Soc., Fleming Award, Soc. for Gen. Microbiology, Howard Hughes Int. Scholar. *Publications include:* numerous articles in academic journals. *Leisure interests:* opera and classical music, medieval buildings, five daughters, writing. *E-mail:* chris.higgins@durham.ac.u; chrishigginsxx@yahoo.com.

HIGGINS, Desmond G., PhD; Irish biologist/biochemist and academic; *Professor of Bioinformatics and Principal Investigator, Conway Institute of Biomolecular and Biomedical Research, University College Dublin;* ed Trinity Coll. Dublin; Postdoctoral Researcher, Sharp Lab., Dept of Genetics, Trinity Coll. Dublin 1985–90; Staff Scientist, European Molecular Biology Lab. (EMBL), Heidelberg, Germany 1990–94, Staff Scientist and Group Leader, EMBL/EBI, Hinxton, UK 1994–96; Statutory Lecturer, Dept of Biochemistry, Univ. Coll. Cork 1997–2003; Prof. of Bioinformatics and Prin. Investigator, Conway Inst. of Biomolecular and Biomedical Research, Univ. Coll. Dublin 2003–, Conway Fellow; mem. Royal Irish Acad. 2007. *Publications:* numerous articles in scientific journals. *Address:* Bioinformatics Department, Conway Institute of Biomolecular and Biomedical Research, University College Dublin, Belfield, Dublin 4, Ireland (office). *Telephone:* (1) 7166833 (office). *Fax:* (1) 7166701 (office). *E-mail:* des.higgins@ucd.ie (office). *Website:* www.ucd.ie/conway (office); bioinf.ucd.ie (home).

HIGGINS, Jack (see PATTERSON, Harry).

HIGGINS, John, MBE; British professional snooker player; b. 18 May 1975, Wishaw, N Lanarkshire, Scotland; m. Denise Higgins; two s. one d.; winner, Mita/Sky World Masters – Junior (Under 16) 1991; turned professional 1992; won first tournament by defeating Dave Harold 9–6 in final of Grand Prix 1994; first teenager to win three ranking events in a season 1994–95; winner (ranking tournaments), Grand Prix 1994, 1999, 2005, 2008, British Open 1995, 1998, 2001, 2004, Int. Open 1995, 1996, German Open 1995, 1997, European Open 1997, World Snooker Championship 1998, 2007, 2009, 2011, UK Championship 1998, 2000, 2010, China Int. 1999, Welsh Open 2000, 2010, 2011, 2015, Shanghai Masters 2012, Australian Goldfields Open 2015, Int. Championship 2015; runner-up (ranking tournaments), Welsh Open 1995, 1998, Grand Prix 1995, 1997, British Open 1996, UK Championship 1996, 2009, Scottish Open 1998, World Snooker Championship 2001, 2017, Irish Masters 2003, LG Cup 2003, Malta Cup, 2006, China Open 2006, 2009, Wuxi Classic 2013; winner (non-ranking tournaments), Charity Challenge 1998, 1999, Masters 1999, 2006, Premier League Snooker 1999, Irish Masters 2000, 2002, Scottish Masters 2001, Champions Cup 2001, Euro-Asia Masters Challenge 2007, Scottish Open Championship 2008, Hainan Classic 2011, Scottish Professional Championship 2011; winner (minor ranking tournaments), Ruhr Championship 2010, Kay Suzanne Memorial Trophy 2012, Bulgarian Open 2013; winner (Pro-am tournaments), World Series of Snooker – Tournament in Saint Helier 2008, World Series of Snooker – Tournament in Moscow 2008; winner (team events), World Cup (with Team Scotland) 1996, Nations Cup (with Team Scotland) 2001; has won 24 ranking titles and made more than 400 competitive century breaks, including five maximum 147 breaks; ninth player to win World Championship title three or more times; ranked World No. 1 1998–99, 1999–2000, 2007–08, 2010–11; Patron, The Dalziel Centre hospice 2010; World Snooker Player of the Year, World Snooker Awards 2011, Snooker Journalists Player of the Year, World Snooker Awards 2011. *Leisure interests:* Celtic Football Club, Everton Football Club, playing poker, playing golf, enjoys gourmet food and cooking.

HIGGINS, Dame Julia Stretton, DBE, BA, DPhil, FRS, FREng; British polymer scientist and academic; *Professor of Polymer Science and Senior Research Investigator, Department of Chemical Engineering and Chemical Technology, Imperial College London;* b. 1 July 1942, London, England; d. of George Stretton Downes and Sheilah Stretton Downes; ed Ursuline Convent School, Wimbledon, Somerville Coll., Oxford; physics teacher, Mexborough Grammar School 1966–68; Research Assoc., Univ. of Manchester 1968–72, Centre de Recherche sur les Macromolécules, Strasbourg, France 1972–73; physicist, Institut Laue-Langevin, Grenoble, France 1973–76; Lecturer, Chemical Eng Dept, Imperial Coll., London 1976–85, Reader in Polymer Science 1985–89, Prof. of Polymer Science and Sr Research Investigator 1989–, Dir Grad. School in Eng and Physical Sciences 2002–06, Prin. Faculty of Eng 2006–; Dean City and Guilds Coll. 1993–97; Chair. UK Eng and Physical Sciences Research Council 2003–07; Pres. BAAS; Foreign Sec. and Vice-Pres. Royal Soc. 2001–; Foreign mem. Nat. Acad. of Eng, USA. *Publications:* more than 200 articles in scientific journals. *Leisure interests:*

theatre, opera, travel. *Address:* Department of Chemical Engineering and Chemical Technology, ACE Building, Room 510, Imperial College, London, SW7 2BY, England (office). *Telephone:* (20) 7594-5565 (office). *Fax:* (20) 7594-5638 (office). *E-mail:* j.higgins@imperial.ac.uk (office); j.higgins@ic.ac.uk (office). *Website:* www3.imperial.ac.uk/people/j.higgins (office).

HIGGINS, Michael D., BComm, MA; Irish politician, writer and head of state; *President;* b. 18 April 1941, Limerick; m. Sabina Coyne; three s. one d.; ed Univ. Coll. Galway, Indiana Univ., USA and Univ. of Manchester, UK; fmr Lecturer in Sociology and Politics, Univ. Coll. Galway; Senator 1973–77; mem. Galway Co. Council 1974–85; Alderman, Galway Borough Council 1974–85, Mayor of Galway 1982–83; mem. Galway City Council 1985–93; TD 1981–82, 1987–2011; Chair. The Labour Party 1978–87, Pres. 2003–11, Spokesperson on Foreign Affairs; Minister for Arts, Culture and the Gaeltacht 1994–97; Pres. of Ireland 2011–; Pres. European Council of Culture Ministers 1996, Council of Broadcasting Ministers 1996, Galway United Football Club; fmr Visiting Prof., Univ. of Southern Illinois; mem. Sociological Asscn of Ireland, American Sociological Asscn, PEN, Irish Writers' Union; Patron, Amnesty Int; Hon. Adjunct Prof., Univ. Coll. Galway; Dr hc (Vytautas Magnus Univ.) 2018; Sean McBride Peace Prize, Int. Peace Bureau, Helsinki 1992, Robert Adams Medal 1993, Kilkenny Award for Contrib. to Arts 1997. *Television:* The Other Emerald Isle. *Publications:* Poetry: Betrayal 1990, The Season of Fire 1993, An Arid Season 2004; numerous papers on cultural and political issues. *Leisure interests:* sports, writing. *Address:* Office of the President, Aras an Uachtaráin, Phoenix Park, Dublin 8 (office); Aimhirgin, Circular Road, Rahoon, Galway; Letteragh, Rahoon, Galway, Ireland (home). *Telephone:* (1) 6171000 (office); (1) 528500 (home). *Fax:* (1) 6171001 (office); (1) 528501 (home). *E-mail:* webmaster@president.ie (office). *Website:* www.president.ie (office).

HIGGINS, Baroness; **Rosalyn,** DBE, JSD, QC, FBA; British judge and fmr professor of international law; b. 2 June 1937; d. of Lewis Cohen and Fay Inberg; m. Rt Hon. Sir Terence L. (now Lord) Higgins 1961; one s. one d.; ed Burlington Grammar School, London, Girton Coll., Cambridge and Yale Law School, USA; UK Intern, Office of Legal Affairs, UN 1958; Commonwealth Fund Fellow 1959; Visiting Fellow, Brookings Inst. Washington, DC 1960; Jr Fellow in Int. Studies, LSE 1961–63; staff specialist in int. law, Royal Inst. of Int. Affairs 1963–74; Visiting Fellow, LSE 1974–78; Prof. of Int. Law, Univ. of Kent at Canterbury 1978–81; Prof. of Int. Law, LSE 1981–95; Judge (first woman), Int. Court of Justice 1995–2009, Pres. 2006–09; mem. UN Cttee on Human Rights 1985–95; Visiting Prof., Stanford Univ. 1975, Yale Univ. 1977; Vice-Pres. American Soc. of Int. Law 1972–74, British Inst. of Int. and Comparative Law 2002–; Ordre des Palmes académiques 1988; Dr hc (Paris XI); Hon. DCL (Dundee) 1992, (Durham, LSE) 1995, (Cambridge, Sussex, Kent, City Univ., Greenwich, Essex) 1996, (Birmingham, Leicester, Glasgow) 1997, (Nottingham) 1999, (Bath, Paris II, Sorbonne) 2001, (Oxford) 2002, (Reading) 2003; Yale Law School Medal of Merit 1997, Manley Hudson Medal (ASIC) 1998, Harold Weig Medal, New York Univ. 1995, Prize of Int. Balzan Foundation 2007. *Publications include:* The Development of International Law Through the Political Organs of the United Nations 1963, Conflict of Interests 1965, The Administration of the United Kingdom Foreign Policy Through the United Nations 1966, Law in Movement – Essays in Memory of John McMahon (co-ed., with James Fawcett) 1974, UN Peacekeeping: Documents and Commentary: (Vol. I) Middle East 1969, (Vol. II) Asia 1971, (Vol. III) Africa 1980, (Vol. IV) Europe 1981, Problems and Process – International Law and How We Use It 1994; articles in law journals and journals of int. relations. *Leisure interests:* sport, cooking, eating. *Address:* c/o International Court of Justice, Peace Palace, 2517 KJ The Hague, Netherlands. *Telephone:* (70) 302-2415.

HIGGINS, Stuart; British journalist; *Managing Director, Stuart Higgins Media;* b. 26 April 1956; m. Jenny Higgins; one s. one d.; ed Chase School for Boys, Filton Tech. Coll., Arblaster's of Bristol, Cardiff Coll. of Food, Tech. and Commerce; Dist reporter, The Sun, Bristol 1979, fmr New York corresp., Royal reporter, Features Ed., Exec. News Ed., Deputy Ed. 1991–93, Ed. 1994–98; public relations consultant 1998–; Founder and Man. Dir Stuart Higgins Media 1999–; Acting Ed. News of the World 1993–94; mem. Bd of Dirs Project Associates; Vincent Fairfax Fellow, St James Ethics Centre. *Television:* Grow Your Own (produced), Bush Telegraph Water Challenge (produced). *Address:* Stuart Higgins Media, Southside, 6th Floor, 105 Victoria Street, London, SW1E 6QT, England (office). *Telephone:* (20) 7096-5814 (office). *E-mail:* contact@stuarthigginsmedia.com (office); hannah@stuart-higgins.com (office). *Website:* www.stuarthigginsmedia.com (office).

HIGGS, Matthew; British artist and curator; *Director, White Columns Gallery;* b. 1964, Wakefield, W Yorks.; m. Anne Collier; ed Blackburn School of Art, Newcastle-upon-Tyne Polytechnic; began career with advertising agency, London 1988; f. Imprint 93 (publishing imprint) 1993; fmr teacher, RCA and Goldsmiths Coll., London; Curator, Wattis Inst. for Contemporary Arts, California Coll. of Arts and Crafts, San Francisco, USA 2001–04; Dir White Columns Gallery, New York 2004–; collaborator, Creative Growth Art Center, Oakland; Assoc. Dir of Exhbns, Inst. of Contemporary Art, London; mem. jury, Turner Prize 2006; mem. New Art Dealers Alliance; Wingate Artists Award 1996. *Address:* White Columns Gallery, 320 West 13th Street, New York, NY 10014, USA (office). *Telephone:* (212) 924-4212 (office). *Fax:* (212) 645-4764 (office). *E-mail:* info@whitecolumns.org (office). *Website:* www.whitecolumns.org (office).

HIGGS, Peter Ware, CH, PhD, FRS, FRSE; British theoretical physicist; *Professor Emeritus of Theoretical Physics, University of Edinburgh;* b. 29 May 1929, Newcastle-upon-Tyne, England; s. of Thomas W. Higgs and Gertrude M. Higgs (née Coghill); m. Jo Ann Williamson 1963; two s.; ed Cotham Grammar School, Bristol and King's Coll., London; Sr Research Fellow, Univ. of Edinburgh 1955–56; ICI Research Fellow, Univ. Coll. London 1956–57, Imperial Coll. London 1957–58; Lecturer in Math., Univ. Coll. London 1958–60; Lecturer in Math. Physics, Univ. of Edinburgh 1960–70, Reader 1970–80, Prof. of Theoretical Physics 1980–96, Prof. Emer. 1996–; Fellow, King's Coll. London 1998; Hon. FInstP 1998; Hon. Fellow, Univ. of Swansea 2008; Hon. DSc (Bristol) 1997, (Edin.) 1998, (Glasgow) 2002, (King's Coll., London) 2009, (Univ. Coll., London) 2010, (Cambridge) 2012, (Heriot-Watt) 2012, (Durham) 2013, (Manchester) 2013; Hughes Medal, Royal Soc. 1981, Rutherford Medal, Inst. of Physics 1984, James Scott Prize, Royal Soc. of Edin. 1994, Paul Dirac Medal and Prize, Inst. of Physics 1997, High Energy and Particle Physics Prize, European Physical Soc. 1997, Royal Medal, Royal Soc. of Edin. 2000, Wolf Prize in Physics 2004, Oskar Klein Medal, Swedish Royal Acad. of Sciences 2009, Sakurai Prize, American Physical Soc. 2010, Edinburgh Award 2011, Prince of Asturias Award for Technical & Scientific Research 2013, Nonino Prize 2013, Edinburgh Medal 2013, Nobel Prize in Physics (with François Englert) 2013, Copley Medal, Royal Soc. 2015. *Publications include:* numerous papers in scientific journals. *Leisure interests:* walking, swimming, listening to music. *Address:* 2 Darnaway Street, Edinburgh, EH3 6BG, Scotland. *Telephone:* (131) 225-7060; (131) 650-5248. *E-mail:* p.w.higgs@ed.ac.uk (office). *Website:* www.ph.ed.ac.uk/higgs (office).

HIGUCHI, Takeo; Japanese business executive; *Representative Director, Chairman and CEO, Daiwa House Industry Company Ltd;* b. 1938; joined Daiwa House Industry 1963, Dir 1984–, Pres. Daiwa Danchi 1993–2001, Pres. Daiwa House Industry Co. Ltd 2001–04, Rep. Dir, Chair. and CEO 2004–; mem. Bd of Dirs Kansai Int. Public Relations Promotion Office (KIPPO) 2004–; fmr Dir Konica Minolta Holdings Inc., now Outside Dir Konica Minolta Business Solutions USA Inc.; Chair. Osaka Symphoniker Soc. 2006, Japan Fed. of Housing Orgs 2009; Vice-Chair. Osaka Chamber of Commerce and Industry 2005. *Address:* Daiwa House Industry Company Ltd, 3-3-5 Umeda, Kita-ku, Osaka 530-8241, Japan (office). *Telephone:* (6) 6346-2111 (office). *Fax:* (6) 6342-1419 (office). *E-mail:* info@daiwahouse.com (office). *Website:* www.daiwahouse.com (office); www.daiwahouse.co.jp (office).

HIGUCHI, Teruhiko, MD, PhD; Japanese psychiatrist, neurologist and academic; *President, National Center of Neurology and Psychiatry;* ed Univ. of Tokyo; residency, Tokyo Univ. Hosp.; fmr Lecturer in Psychiatry, Saitama Medical School; worked as postdoctoral researcher at Univ. of Manitoba, Canada, specialized in neuroendocrinology; fmr Prof., Gunma Univ. and Showa Univ., Yokohama; cr. Nat. Center for Neurology and Psychiatry by merging six nat. inst., first Dir, now Pres.; Golden Kraepelin Medal, Max-Planck-Gesellschaft (co-recipient) 2014. *Publications:* numerous papers in professional journals. *Address:* National Center of Neurology and Psychiatry, 4-1-1 Ogawa-Higashi, Kodaira, Tokyo, 187-8551, Japan (office). *E-mail:* webadmin@ncnp.go.jp (office). *Website:* www.ncnp.go.jp (office).

HIGUCHI, Tomio; Japanese insurance executive; joined Nichido Fire & Marine Insurance Co. Ltd 1965, various sr positions include Dir 1993–95, Man.-Dir 1995–98, Sr Man.-Dir 1998–2000, Vice-Pres. 2000–01, Pres. and Sr Gen. Man. of Marketing and Sales Promotion HQ 2001–02, Chair. and Pres. 2002–04; Chair. Millea Holdings Inc. (following merger between Nichido Fire & Marine Insurance Co. and Tokio Marine 2004) 2004–07; fmr mem. Bd of Dirs Transatlantic Holdings Inc.

HIJAB, Riyad Farid; Syrian politician; b. 1966, Deir ez-Zor; m.; four c.; Gov. of Quneitra Governorate 2008–11, of Latakia Governorate 2011; Minister of Agric. 2011–12; Prime Minister June–Aug. 2012; mem. al-Baath Arab Socialist Party; Leader of Opposition 2015–17.

HILAIRE, Alvin, PhD; Trinidad and Tobago economist, international organization official and central banker; *Governor, Central Bank of Trinidad and Tobago;* ed Columbia Univ., USA, Univ. of the West Indies, St Augustine; worked for IMF for 11 years including as Sr Economist, Resident Rep. to Guinea and Sierra Leone; fmr Chair. CARICOM Devt Fund; worked for Central Bank of Trinidad and Tobago for 21 years including as Sr Economist, Chief Economist and Dir of Research, Deputy Gov. 2013–15, Gov. 2015–. *Address:* Central Bank of Trinidad and Tobago, Eric Williams Plaza, Brian Lara Promenade, POB 1250, Port of Spain, Trinidad and Tobago (office). *Telephone:* 625-4835 (office). *Fax:* 627-4696 (office). *E-mail:* info@central-bank.org.tt (office). *Website:* www.central-bank.org.tt (office).

HILBORN, Ray, BA, PhD, FRSC; Canadian/American marine biologist and academic; *Professor, School of Aquatic and Fishery Sciences, University of Washington, Seattle;* b. 31 Dec. 1947; ed Grinnell Coll., USA, Univ. of British Columbia; Research Scholar, Int. Inst. for Applied Systems Analysis, Laxenburg, Austria 1974–75; Policy Analyst, Depts of Environment and Fisheries, Govt of Canada 1975–80; Hon. Lecturer, Inst. of Animal Resource Ecology, Univ. of British Columbia 1975–80, Adjunct Assoc. Prof. 1980–85; Sr Fisheries Scientist, Tuna and Billfish Program, South Pacific Comm., Noumea, New Caledonia 1985–87, Prof., School of Aquatic and Fishery Sciences, Univ. of Washington, Seattle 1987–; Guest Ed Proceedings of Nat. Acad. of Sciences 2010; mem. Bd of Reviewing Eds, Science 2006–13; mem. Editorial Bd, Natural Resource Modeling 1993–, Natural Resource Modeling 2007–, Reviews in Fish Biology and Fisheries 1993–, Fish and Fisheries 1999–, New Zealand Journal of Marine and Freshwater Research 2003–10; Assoc. Ed. Canadian Journal of Fisheries and Aquatic Sciences 2002–13; mem. External Advisory Bd, Nat. Socio-Environmental Synthesis Center, Univ. of Maryland 2011–13; mem. Washington State Acad. of Sciences 2010; Fellow, American Acad. of Arts and Sciences 2010; Award of Excellence, American Fisheries Soc. 2005, Volvo Environment Prize, Volvo Environment Foundation (co-recipient) 2006, Outstanding Achievement Award, American Inst. of Fisheries Research Biologists 2008, Ecological Soc. of America Sustainability Science Award 2011, American Fisheries Soc. Carl Sullivan Conservation Award 2012. *Publications include:* Adaptive Environmental Assessment and Management (co-author) 1978, Quantitative Fisheries Stock Assessment: Choice, Dynamics and Uncertainty (co-author) 1992 (also translated into Russian), Biomass Dynamics Models. FAO Computerized Information Series (Fisheries). No. 10 (co-author) 1996, The Ecological Detective: Confronting Models with Data (co-author) 1997, Bayesian Stock Assessment Methods in Fisheries. FAO Computerized Information Series (Fisheries) No. 12 (co-author) 2002, Overfishing: What Everyone Needs to Know 2012; numerous scientific papers in professional journals. *Address:* School of Aquatic and Fishery Sciences, 352B, University of Washington, Box 355020, Seattle, WA 98195-5020, USA (office). *Telephone:* (206) 543-3587 (office). *Fax:* (206) 685-7471 (office). *E-mail:* rayh@uw.edu (office). *Website:* fish.uw.edu (office).

HEINE, Hilda, EdD; Marshall Islands politician, educator and head of state; *President;* b. 6 April 1956, Jaluit Atoll; d. of Rev. Bourne Heine and Kathy Heine; m. Thomas (Tommy) Kijiner Jr; three c.; ed Univ. of Oregon, Univ. of Hawaii, Univ. of Southern Calif.; classroom teacher and counsellor, Marshall Islands High School 1975–82; Scholar, Dir of Policy and Capacity Bldg, FAS Education 1995–2006; f. Women United Together Marshall Islands 2000; Program Dir of Pacific Resources for Educ. and Learning, Pacific Comprehensive Assistance Center 2006–11; Pres. of Marshall Islands 2016–; fmr Minister of Educ. *Leisure interests:* reading, music, cooking. *Address:* Office of the President, Government of the Republic of the Marshall Islands, PO Box 2, Majuro, MH 96960, The Marshall Islands (office). *Telephone:* (692) 625-2233 (office). *Fax:* (625) 3649 (office). *E-mail:* rmiop.press@gmail.com (office). *Website:* www.rmigov.com (office).

HILDEBRAND, Philipp M., BA, MA, DPhil; Swiss financial services industry executive and fmr central banker; *Vice-Chairman, BlackRock Inc.;* b. 19 July 1963, Bern; m. Kashya Hildebrand (divorced); one d.; Partner Margarita Louis-Dreyfus; two d.; ed Univ. of Toronto, Canada, Grad. Inst. of Int. Studies, Geneva, Univ. of Oxford, UK; raised in Switzerland and USA; worked as a bellhop at a hotel in Davos, Switzerland, where he met many leading European bankers; began career at World Econ. Forum, Geneva 1994; joined Moore Capital Management, London, UK 1995, Partner 1997–2000; Chief Investment Officer, Vontobel Group 2000–01; mem. Exec. Cttee and Chief Investment Officer, Union Bancaire Privée, Geneva 2001–03; apptd mem. Governing Bd and Head of Dept III (Financial Markets, Banking Operations, Information Tech.), Swiss Nat. Bank 2003, Vice-Chair. Governing Bd and Head of Dept II (Finance, Cash, Financial Systems, Security) 2007–10, Chair. Governing Bd and Head of Dept I (Econ. Affairs, Int. Affairs, Legal and Property Services), Zurich 2010–11 (resgnd), also Vice-Chair., Financial Stability Bd 2011–12, mem. Bd of Dirs BIS, Basel 2010–12, Gov., IMF; Vice-Chair. BlackRock Inc. 2012–, also oversees BlackRock Investment Inst.; Visiting Prof. of Econs, Grad. Inst. of Int. Studies 2002–; Chair. of the Deputies of the Group of Ten (G10) 2006–07; Pres. Foundation Bd of Int. Centre for Monetary and Banking Studies, Geneva; Strategic Cttee of French Debt Man. Office (Agence France Trésor) 2006–09; mem. Group of Thirty Consultative Group on Int. Econ. and Monetary Affairs, Inc. (G-30), Washington, DC 2008–; Hon. Fellow, Lincoln Coll., Oxford; Visiting Fellowships at European Univ. Inst., Florence, Italy 1992, Center for Int. Affairs, Harvard Univ., USA 1993. *Achievements include:* fmr mem. Swiss nat. swimming team. *Address:* BlackRock, Bahnhofstrasse 39, 8001 Zurich, Switzerland (office). *Telephone:* 442977373 (office). *Website:* www.blackrock.com (office).

HILDENBERG, Humphrey; Suriname economist and government official; ed Univ. of Groningen, The Netherlands; with Nationale Ontwikkelings Bank (NOB) 1981–92, 1996–2000; Minister of Finance 1992–96, 2000–10.

HILDENBRAND, Werner, PhD Habil.; German economist, mathematician and academic; *Professor Emeritus of Economics, University of Bonn;* b. 25 May 1936, Göttingen; ed Univ. of Heidelberg; Lecturer, Univ. of Heidelberg 1964–66; Visiting Asst Prof., Univ. of California, Berkeley, USA 1966–67, Visiting Assoc. Prof. 1967–68, Visiting Prof. of Econs 1970, 1973–74, Visiting Ford Prof. 1985–86, Visiting Prof. of Econs 2001; Research Prof., Univ. of Louvain, Belgium 1968–76; Prof. of Econs and Dir Wirtschaftstheoretisches Institut, Univ. of Bonn 1969–2001, Prof. Emer. 2001–; Visiting Prof. of Econs, Stanford Univ. 1970, 2001; Visiting Ford Prof., European Univ. Inst., Florence 1989–, Univ. of California, San Diego 1986–91; European Chair., Collège de France 1993–94; Assoc. Ed. Journal of Economic Theory 1971–78, International Economic Review 1972–84; Ed. Journal of Mathematical Economics 1974–85; mem. Rhein-West Akad. der Wissenschaften 1981, Academia Europaea 1985, Berlin-Brandenburgischen Akad. der Wissenschaften 1993; Fellow, Econometric Soc. 1971, mem. Council 1973–78, 1982–84, 1986–91, 1993–95; Foreign Hon. mem. American Acad. of Arts and Sciences 2005; Dr hc (Univ. Louis Pasteur, Strasbourg) 1988, (Bern) 2002, (Manchester) 2007; Leibniz Prize Deutsche Forschungsgemeinschaft 1987, Max Planck Forsch Prize 1995, Alexander von Humboldt Prize 1997, Gay Lussac Prize 1997. *Publications:* Core and Equilibria of a Large Economy 1974, Lineare ökonomische Modelle (co-author) 1975, Introduction to Equilibrium Analysis (co-author) 1976, Equilibrium Analysis (co-author) 1988, Market Demand: Theory and Empirical Evidence 1994; numerous papers. *Address:* Department of Economics, University of Bonn, Lennéstr. 37, 53113 Bonn (office); Königstr. 86, 53115 Bonn, Germany (home). *Telephone:* (228) 733754 (office); (228) 91254578 (home). *Fax:* (228) 737940 (office). *E-mail:* FgHildenbrand@uni-bonn.de (office). *Website:* www.econ2.uni-bonn.de/members-of-the-chair/hildenbrand (office).

HILDNER, Rolf; German banking executive (retd); b. 16 Nov. 1945, Wiesbaden; joined Wiesbadener Volksbank eG 1964, mem. Bd of Dirs 1977, Chair. Bd of 1987–2010 (retd); mem. Supervisory Bd SGZ Bank (now DZ Bank AG) 1990–2010, Chair. 1995–2001, Vice-Chair. Supervisory Bd DZ Bank AG 2001–08, Chair. 2008–10; apptd Vice-Pres. IHK Wiesbaden 1985; mem. Supervisory Bd R+V Leben and R+V Versicherung AG 1989–2010; mem. Fed. Council, Co-operative Asscn, Frankfurt 1989–, Bd mem. 1994–2010, Chair. 1997–2010; mem. Fed. Council, Fed. Asscn of German Co-operative Banks (BVR) 1989–2010, Bd mem. 1994–2010. *Address:* c/o Wiesbadener Volksbank eG, Schillerplatz 4, 65185 Wiesbaden, Germany. *E-mail:* angelika.menager@wvb.de.

HILFIGER, Tommy; American fashion designer; b. (Thomas Jacob Hilfiger), 24 March 1951, Elmira, NY; m. 1st Susie Hilfiger (divorced); four c.; m. 2nd Dee Ocleppo 2008; one s.; ed Elmira Free Acad.; opened first store, People's Place, Elmira, NY 1969; owned ten clothes shops throughout NY by 1978; moved to NY City to became full-time designer 1979; launched own sportswear label 1984; acquired fashion business from Mohan Muranji, cr. Tommy Hilfiger Inc. 1989, Pres. 1982–89, Vice-Chair. 1989–94, Hon. Chair. 1994–2003, now Prin. Designer; mem. Bd Fresh Air Fund, Race to Erase Multiple Sclerosis; f. Tommy Hilfiger Corp. Foundation 1995; From the Catwalk to the Sidewalk Award, VH-1 Fashion and Music Awards 1995, Menswear Designer of the Year, Council of Fashion Designers of America 1995, Parsons School of Design, Designer of the Year Award 1998, Individual Achievement Award, Hispanic Federation 2006, UNESCO Support Award 2009, Marie Claire Lifetime Achievement Award 2009, Legends Award, Pratt Inst. 2010, Geoffrey Beene Lifetime Achievement Award, Council of Fashion Designers of America 2012. *Publications include:* New England: Icons, Influences and Inspirations from the American Northeast 2004, Iconic America: A Roller-Coaster Ride through the Eye-Popping Panorama of American Pop Culture (with George Lois) 2007. *Leisure interests:* fishing, scuba diving, skiing. *Address:* Tommy Hilfiger USA Inc., 601 West 26th Street, New York, NY 10001, USA (office). *Telephone:* (212) 549-6000 (office). *Website:* www.tommy.com (office).

HILL, (Hugh) Allen (Oliver), PhD, FRS, FRSC; British chemist and academic; *Professor Emeritus of Bioinorganic Chemistry, University of Oxford;* b. 23 May 1937; ed Queen's Univ., Belfast; moved to Oxford 1962, Fellow, The Queen's Coll. 1965–, now Prof. Emer. of Bioinorganic Chem., Univ. of Oxford, Hon. Fellow, The Queen's Coll. and Wadham Coll.; Interdisciplinary Award, Chemistry and Electrochemistry of Transition Metals Medal, RSC Robinson Award, Breyer Medal, Royal Australian Chemical Inst., Mullard Award and Royal Medal, Royal Soc. "for his pioneering work on protein electrochemistry, which revolutionised the diagnostic testing of glucose and many other bioelectrochemical assays" 2010, Landmark blue plaque in Oxford 2012. *Publications:* numerous papers in professional journals. *Address:* Inorganic Chemistry Laboratory, South Parks Road, Oxford, OX1 3QR, England (office). *Telephone:* (1865) 272639 (office). *Fax:* (1865) 272690 (office). *E-mail:* allen.hill@chem.ox.ac.uk (office); allen.hill@oxford-biosensors.com (office). *Website:* research.chem.ox.ac.uk/allen-hill.aspx (office).

HILL, Anita F., BS, JD; American legal scholar and academic; *Professor of Social Policy, Law and Women's Gender and Sexuality Studies, Heller School for Social Policy and Management, Brandeis University;* b. 30 July 1956, Lone Tee, Okla; d. of Albert Hill and Emma Hill; ed Oklahoma State Univ., Yale Univ. Law School; admitted to DC Bar 1980; Assoc., Wald, Harkrader & Ross, Washington, DC 1980–81; Special Counsel to Asst Sec., Office for Civil Rights, US Dept of Educ. 1981–82; Adviser to Chair. of Equal Employment Opportunity Comm. 1982–83; Asst Prof., Oral Roberts Univ. 1983–86; Prof., Coll. of Law, Univ. of Oklahoma 1986–97; Visiting Prof., Univ. of California Inst. for the Study of Social Change 1997; Prof. of Social Policy, Law and Women's Gender and Sexuality Studies, Heller Grad. School, Brandeis Univ. 1997–, also Sr Advisor to the Provost; Visiting Scholar, Wellesley Coll., Newhouse Center for the Humanities and Wellesley Centers for Women 2007; mem. Bd of Trustees, Southern Vermont Coll.; Dr hc (Simmons Coll.) 2001, (Dillard Univ.) 2001, (Smith Coll.) 2003, (Lasell Coll.) 2007, (Massachusetts Coll. of Liberal Arts) 2010, (Mount Ida Coll.) 2013; Hon. LLM (Wesleyan Univ.) 2018; Alphonse Fletcher Sr Fellowship Award 2005, Ford Hall Forum First Amendment Award 2008, Alice and Clifford Spendlove Prize in Social Justice, Diplomacy and Tolerance 2016, Lifetime Leadership DVF Award 2019. *Publications include:* Race, Gender and Power in America: The Legacy of the Hill-Thomas Hearings 1995, Speaking Truth to Power (on her testimony of sexual harassment during US Senate confirmation hearings of Supreme Court nominee Clarence Thomas 1991) 1997, Reimagining Equality: Stories of Gender, Race and Finding Home 2011; articles on int. commercial law, bankruptcy and civil rights. *Address:* Heller 374, Heller School for Social Policy and Management, Brandeis University, 415 South Street, Waltham, MA 02454-9110, USA (office). *Telephone:* (781) 736-3896 (office). *E-mail:* ahill@brandeis.edu (office). *Website:* heller.brandeis.edu (office).

HILL, Anthony, (Achill Redo); British artist; b. 23 April 1930, London; s. of Adrian Hill and Dorothy Whitley; m. Yuriko Kaetsu 1978; ed Bryanston School, St Martin's School of Art, Cen. School of Arts and Crafts; works in nat. collections in UK, USA, France, Israel, Denmark, Brazil; Leverhulme Fellowship, Dept of Math., Univ. Coll. 1971–72, Hon. Research Assoc. 1972–; mem. The London Math. Soc. 1979–; First Prize, Norwegian Print Biennale 1999. *Publications:* Data: Directions in Art, Theory and Aesthetics (ed.) 1968, Duchamp: Passim 1994; numerous articles in art and math. journals. *Leisure interest:* erotology. *Address:* 24 Charlotte Street, London, W1T 2ND, England (office). *Telephone:* (20) 7436-8820 (office). *E-mail:* achillredo@tiscali.co.uk.

HILL, Bonnie Guiton, BA, MS, EdD; American business executive; *President, B. Hill Enterprises LLC;* b. 30 Oct. 1941, Springfield, Ill.; d. of Henry Frank Brazelton and Zola Elizabeth Brazelton (née Newman); m. Walter Hill, Jr; one d.; ed Mills Coll., California State Univ., Hayward, Univ. of California, Berkeley; Admin. Asst to Presidential Special Asst, Mills Coll., Oakland, Calif. 1970–71, Admin. Asst to Asst Vice-Pres. 1972–73, Student Services Counsellor, Adviser to Resuming Students 1973–74, Asst Dean of Students, Interim Dir Ethnic Studies, Lecturer 1975–76; Exec. Dir Marcus A. Foster Educational Inst. 1976–79; Admin. Man. Kaiser Aluminium & Chemical Corpn 1979–80; Vice-Pres. and Gen. Man. Kaiser CTR, Inc. 1980–84; Vice-Chair. Postal Rate Comm., Washington, DC 1985–87; Asst Sec. for Vocational and Adult Educ., US Dept of Educ. 1987–89; Special Adviser to Pres. Bush for Consumer Affairs 1989–90; Pres. and CEO Earth Conservation Corps, Washington, DC 1990–91; Sec., State and Consumer Services Industry, State of Calif. 1991–92; Dean McIntire School of Commerce, Univ. of Virginia, Charlottesville 1992–97; Vice-Pres. The Times Mirror Co. Ltd 1997–2000; Co-founder and COO Icon Blue, Inc. (marketing consultancy) 2001–; Sr Vice-Pres. Communications and Public Affairs, LA Times newspaper 1998–2001, Pres. and CEO The Times Mirror Foundation 1997–2001; Pres. B. Hill Enterprises LLC (consulting firm) 2001–; mem. Bd of Dirs, Hershey Foods Corpn 1993–2007, AK Steel Holding Corpn 1994–2014, Choice Point, Inc. 2001–14, Albertsons, Inc. 2001–, The Nat. Grid Group PLC 2002–03, Yum! Brands 2003, California Water Service Group 2003–17, The Home Depot Co. 2008–14; mem. Nat. Advisory Panel, Inst. for Research on Women and Gender, Stanford Univ.; mem. LA Urban League, United Way of Greater LA, Goodwill Industries of Southern Calif.; Nat. Women's Econ. Alliance Foundation Dirs' Choice Award, YWCA Tribute to Women in Int. Industry Award, Angeles Girl Scouts Council Grace Award, Anti-Defamation League Deborah Award. *Address:* Icon Blue, 5055 Wilshire Boulevard, Suite 305, Los Angeles, CA 90036, USA (office). *Telephone:* (323) 634-5301 (office). *Fax:* (323) 634-5314 (office). *E-mail:* info@iconblue.com (office). *Website:* iconblue.com (office).

HILL, Rt Rev. Christopher John, BD, MTh; British ecclesiastic; *Bishop of Guildford;* b. 10 Oct. 1945; s. of Leonard Hill and Frances Hill; m. Hilary Ann Whitehouse 1976; three s. one d.; ed Sebright School, Worcs., King's Coll., London; ordained (Diocese of Lichfield) 1969; Asst Chaplain to Archbishop of Canterbury for Foreign Relations 1974–81, Sec. for Ecumenical Affairs 1981–89; Anglican Sec. Anglican-Roman Catholic Int. Comm. I and II 1974–91; Anglican-Lutheran European Comm. 1981–82; Chaplain to Queen 1987–96; Canon Residentiary of St Paul's Cathedral, London 1989–96; Area Bishop of Stafford, Diocese of Lichfield 1996–2004, Hon. Canon, Lichfield Cathedral 1996–2004; Bishop of Guildford 2004–; Clerk of Closet, Royal Household 2005–; mem. Gen. Synod 1999–, House of Bishops 1999–; mem. Church of England-German Churches Conversations 1987–89, Church of England-Nordic-Baltic Conversations 1989–93, Church of England Legal Advisory Comm. 1991–, Faith and Order Advisory Group of Gen. Synod 1997–2010 (Vice-Chair. 1998–2010); mem. Council for Christian Unity 1992–97 (Chair. 2008–), Faith and Order Comm. 2010–, Anglican-Roman Catholic

Int. Comm. III 2011–; Co-Chair. London Soc. of Jews and Christians 1991–96, Church of England-French Protestant Conversations 1993–98; Vice-Chair. Ecclesiastical Law Soc. 1993–2002, Chair. 2002–; Chair. Cathedrals' Precentors Conf. 1994–96, Women Bishops' Group 2005–06; Anglican Co-Chair. Meissen Theological Conf. 1999–2001; Vice-Pres. Conf. of European Churches 2009–; mem. London Soc. for the Study of Religion 1990–2000, Working Party on Women in the Episcopate 2001–04 (Vice-Chair. 2003–04), Liturgical Comm. 2003–, Clergy Discipline Comm. 2004–06, Theological Group 2006; Assoc., King's Coll. London, mem. Council 2010–; Lay mem. Council King's Coll.; mem. House of Lords 2010–; Hon. Canon, Canterbury Cathedral 1982–89; Relton Prize for Theology 1967. *Publications:* Anglicans and Roman Catholics: the Search for Unity (co-ed.), The Documents in the Debate. A Retrospect on the Papal Decision on Anglican Orders 1896 (co-ed.) 1996; ecumenical articles. *Leisure interests:* music, walking, reading. *Address:* Willow Grange, Woking Road, Guildford, Surrey, GU4 7QS, England (home). *Telephone:* (1483) 590500 (home). *Fax:* (1483) 590501 (home). *E-mail:* bishop.christopher@cofeguildford.org.uk (office). *Website:* www.cofeguildford.org.uk (office).

HILL, Christopher R., MA; American university administrator and fmr diplomatist; *Chief Advisor to Chancellor for Global Engagement, University of Denver;* b. 1952, Little Compton, RI; m. 1st Patty Whitelaw (divorced); three c.; m. 2nd Julie Ann Ryczek; ed Bowdoin Coll., Maine, Naval War Coll.; with Peace Corps in Cameroon 1974; joined Foreign Service 1977, overseas assignments in Yugoslavia, Albania, S Korea and Poland; Sr Country Officer for Polish Affairs, Dept of State; Amb. to Macedonia 1996–99; Special Envoy to Kosovo 1998–99; Special Asst to Pres. and Sr Dir, Nat. Security Council 1999–2000; Amb. to Poland 2000–04, to S Korea 2004–05; Asst Sec. Bureau of E Asian and Pacific Affairs 2005–09; Amb. to Iraq 2009–10; Head of US del. to Six-Party Talks on N Korean nuclear issue 2005; fmr Sr Dir Southeast European Affairs, Nat. Security Council; Dean, Josef Korbel School of Int. Studies, Univ. of Denver 2010–17, Chief Advisor to Chancellor for Global Engagement 2017–, Prof. of the Practice in Diplomacy 2017–; mem. Bd, International Relief and Development Inc.; adviser, Albright Stonebridge Group; Hon. Citizen of Macedonia; Hon. mem., New Zealand Order of Merit 2013; several State Dept awards, including Robert S. Frasure Award and Distinguished Service Award, Distinguished Grad. Leadership Award, Naval War Coll. 2005, Building Bridges Award, Pacific Century Inst. 2008. *Publication:* The Geopolitical Implications of Enlargement. In Jan Zielonka (ed.), Europe Unbound – Enlarging and Reshaping the Boundaries of the European Union 2002. *Address:* Josef Korbel School of International Studies, University of Denver, 2201 South Gaylord Street, Denver, CO 80208 (office); University of Denver, 2199 South University Blvd, Denver, CO 80208, USA (office). *Telephone:* (303) 871-2539 (office). *Fax:* (303) 871-2456 (office). *E-mail:* christopher.r.hill@du.edu (office). *Website:* www.du.edu/korbel/about/dean (office).

HILL, Damon Graham Devereux, OBE; British fmr racing driver, company director and television presenter; b. 17 Sept. 1960, Hampstead, London; s. of Graham Hill (fmr Formula One world champion) and Bette Hill; m. Georgie Hill 1988; two s. two d.; ed Haberdashers' Aske's School, London; first drove a car aged five; first drove in motorcycle racing 1979; driver with Canon Williams team 1993, Rothmans Williams Renault team 1994–96, Arrows Yamaha team 1997, Benson and Hedges Jordan team 1998–99; first motor racing victory in Formula Ford 1600, Brands Hatch 1984; first Formula One Grand Prix, Silverstone 1992; winner, Italian Grand Prix 1993, 1994, Belgian Grand Prix 1993, 1994, 1998, Hungarian Grand Prix 1993, 1995, Spanish Grand Prix 1994, British Grand Prix 1994, Portuguese Grand Prix 1994, Japanese Grand Prix 1994, 1996, Argentine Grand Prix 1995, 1996, San Marino Grand Prix 1995, 1996, Australian Grand Prix 1995, 1996, French Grand Prix 1996, Brazilian Grand Prix 1996, German Grand Prix 1996, Canadian Grand Prix 1996; third place, Drivers' World Championship 1993, second place 1994, 1995, Formula One World Champion 1996; 84 Grand Prix starts, 22 wins, 20 pole positions, 19 fastest laps, 42 podium finishes; retd end of 1999 season; Co-founder and Chair. P1 International 2000–; Pres. British Racing Drivers' Club 2006–11; Dir, Hill Sport Ltd; analyst for Sky F1 HD channel 2012–; British Competition Driver of the Year Autosport Awards 1995, BBC Sports Personality Award 1994, 1996, numerous racing awards. *Publications:* Damon Hill Grand Prix Year 1994, Damon Hill: My Championship Year 1996, F1 Through the Eyes of Damon Hill. *Leisure interests:* family, reading. *Address:* c/o British Racing Drivers' Club, Silverstone Circuit, Towcester, Northants. NN12 8TN, England. *E-mail:* enquiries@brdc.co.uk.

HILL, David Rowland; British government adviser; b. 1948, Birmingham; partner Hilary Coffman; ed King Edward's School, Birmingham, Brasenose Coll., Oxford; began career as industrial relations officer, Unigate Dairies, Birmingham; fmr press aide to Labour MP Roy Hattersley; Dir of Communications and Chief Media Spokesperson, Labour Party 1991–98; Labour cand. for Burton-on-Trent (unsuccessful), Sr Labour Party Press Spokesman during 2001 election campaign; Dir of Communications, Prime Minister's Office 2003–07; mem. Bd of Dirs Good Relations (public relations co.) 1998–2003, Bell Pottinger Group 2007. *Leisure interest:* football.

HILL, Jay, PC; Canadian politician (retd); b. 27 Dec. 1952, British Columbia; m. Leah Murray Hill; fmr Pres. BC Grain Producers Asscn and Dir for Grain, BC Fed. of Agric.; mem. Parl. for Prince George–Peace River 1993–2010; mem. Reform Party of Canada 1993–2000, Canadian Alliance 2000–03, Conservative Party of Canada 2003–10; Chief Govt Whip 2006–08; Leader of the Govt in the House of Commons 2008–10.

HILL, John (see KOONTZ, Dean Ray).

HILL, Jonah; American actor, comedian, screenwriter and producer; b. (Jonah Hill Feldstein), 20 Dec. 1983, Los Angeles, Calif.; s. of Richard Feldstein and Sharon Lyn; ed Crossroads School, Santa Monica, New School Univ., New York; wrote and performed plays in East Village, New York. *Films include:* I Heart Huckabees 2004, The 40-Year-Old Virgin 2005, Grandma's Boy 2006, Click 2006, Accepted 2006, 10 Items or Less 2006, Knocked Up 2007, Evan Almighty 2007, Rocket Science 2007, Superbad 2007, Strange Wilderness 2008, Forgetting Sarah Marshall 2008, Just Add Water 2008, Emerson Park 2008, Funny People 2008, The Invention of Lying 2008, Get Him to the Greek 2010, Cyrus 2010, Megamind (voice) 2010, Moneyball 2011, Dragons: Gift of the Night Fury (short) 2011, The Sitter 2011, 21 Jump Street 2012, The Watch 2012, Django Unchained 2012, This Is the End 2013, The Wolf of Wall Street 2013, The Lego Movie 2014, True Story 2014, 22 Jump Street 2014, How to Train Your Dragon 2 (voice) 2014; as producer: Brüno 2008. *Television includes:* NYPD Blue 2004, Campus Ladies 2006, Clark and Michael 2007, Human Giant 2007, Reno 911 2009, The Simpsons (guest voice) 2009, Legend of the Boneknapper Dragon (short) 2010, Allen Gregory (series co-creator, exec. producer, voice artist) 2011–12. *Address:* c/o WME Entertainment, 9601 Wilshire Boulevard, Beverly Hills, CA 90210-5213, USA. *Telephone:* (310) 285-9000. *Fax:* (310) 285-9010. *Website:* www.wma.com.

HILL, Lynn, BS; American rock climber; b. (Carolynn Marie Hill), 1961, Detroit, Mich.; one s.; ed Staffs. State Univ. of NY, New Paltz, NY; began climbing aged 14; won over 30 int. climbing titles during 1980s; f. Lynn Hill Rock Climbing Camps; first person to free climb Nose route on El Capitan, Yosemite Valley, Calif. 1993, later free climbed the route in 23 hours in 1994, feat not repeated by any other climber until 2005; winner Survival of the Fittest TV competition (four times). *Main achievements:* competition winner, Troubat 1987, 1988, 1989, Worldwide indoor competition, Grenoble 1987, Arco Rock Master 1987, 1990, 1992, Bercy 1988, 1990, World Cup (jt winner) 1991, Stopped Competition 1993. *Film appearances include:* Extreme, Free Climbing the Nose, La Maitresse du Vide (French version). *Publications:* Climbing Free: My Life in the Vertical World (autobiography) 2002. *Address:* Lynn Hill Rock Climbing Camps, PO Box 383, Eldorado Springs, CO 80025, USA (office). *Telephone:* (303) 919-3223. *E-mail:* lynn@lynnhillblogs.com. *Website:* www.lynnhillclimbs.com; lynnhillblogs.com.

HILL, Michael William, MA, MSc, MRSC, FIInfSc, FCILIP, FRSA; British fmr information consultant, research chemist and library director; b. 27 July 1928, Ross-on-Wye, Herefords.; s. of Geoffrey Hill and Dorothy Hill; m. 1st Elma Jack Forrest (died 1967); one s. one d.; m. 2nd Barbara Joy Youngman; ed King Henry VIIIth School, Coventry, Nottingham High School, Lincoln Coll., Oxford; Research Chemist, Laporte Chemicals Ltd 1953–56; Tech. and Production Man., Morgan Crucible Group 1956–64; Asst Keeper, British Museum 1964–68, Deputy Librarian Nat. Reference Library of Science and Invention (NRLSI) 1965–68, Keeper 1968–73; Dir, Science Reference Library, British Library 1973–86; Assoc. Dir Science, Tech. and Industry, British Library 1986–88; fmr Chair. Circle of State Librarians; fmr Vice-Pres. Int. Asscn of Tech. Univ. Libraries; Co-founder European Council of Information Asscns; Hon. Pres. Fed. Int. d'Information et de Documentation 1985–90 (Hon. Fellow 1992–), Hon. Fellow, European Council of Information Asscns 1996–. *Publications include:* Patent Documentation (with Wittmann and Schiffels) 1979, Michael Hill on Science, Technology and Information 1988, National Surveys of Library and Information Services: 2: Yugoslavia (with Tudor Silovic), National Information Policies and Strategies 1994, The Impact of Information on Society 1998; Jt Series Ed. Saur Guides to Information Sources. *Leisure interests:* golf, theatre, music, Scottish dancing. *Address:* Jesters, 137 Burdon Lane, Cheam, SM2 7DB, England. *Telephone:* (20) 8642-2418.

HILL, Robert Murray, AC, BA, BLL, LLM; Australian politician and diplomatist; *Commissioner, Global Ocean Commission;* b. 25 Sept. 1946, Adelaide, S Australia; m. Diana Hill; four c.; ed Scotch Coll., Univ. of Adelaide, London School of Econs and Univ. of London, UK; barrister and solicitor 1970–; Liberal Party Campaign Chair. 1975–77, Chair., Constitutional Cttee 1977–81; Vice-Pres. Liberal Party, S Australian Div. 1977–79, State Pres. of S Australia Div. 1985–87; mem. Fed. Exec. of Liberal Party 1985–87, 1990–2006; Senator for S Australia 1981–2006; shadow portfolios in opposition include Foreign Affairs –1993, Defence 1993–94, Public Admin 1993–94, Educ., Science, Tech. 1994–96, Leader of Opposition in Senate 1993–96, Leader of Govt in Senate 1996–2006; Fed. Minister for Environment 1996–98, for Environment and Heritage 1998–2001, of Defence 2001–06; Head of Australian del. which negotiated Kyoto Protocol to the International Framework Convention on Climate Change 1997, Australian del. International Whaling Comm. 1996–2002; Amb. and Perm. Rep. to UN, New York 2006–09; Adjunct Prof. in Sustainability, US Studies Centre, Univ. of Sydney 2009–16, also Co-Dir Alliance 21 project; apptd Chair. Australian Carbon Trust 2009; Chancellor, Univ. of Adelaide 2010–14; Commr Global Ocean Comm.; mem. Bd of Dirs Karrkad-Kandji Ltd, supporting Indigeneous Protected Areas in West and Central Arnhem Land; mem. Law Soc. of S Australia; Hon. DJur (Univ. of Adelaide) 2015. *Leisure interests:* law reform, Australian and Asian history, legal and environmental educ., the arts. *Address:* Global Ocean Commission, Somerville College, Woodstock Road, Oxford OX2 6HD, England (office). *Website:* www.some.ox.ac.uk/research/global-ocean-commission (office).

HILL OF OAREFORD, Baron (Life Peer), cr. 2010, of Oareford in the County of Somerset; **Rt Hon. Jonathan Hopkin Hill,** PC, CBE; British politician, business executive and fmr EU official; b. 24 July 1960; s. of Rowland Louis Hill and Paddy Marguerite Henwood; m. Alexandra Jane Nettelfield 1988; one s. two d.; ed Highgate School, London, Trinity Coll., Cambridge; worked in Conservative Party Research Dept 1985–86; special adviser to Kenneth Clarke at Dept of Employment, Dept of Trade and Industry and Dept of Health 1986–89; worked for Lowe Bell Communications 1989–91; worked at the Number 10 Policy Unit 1991–92, Political Sec. to Prime Minister John Major 1992–94; Sr Consultant, Bell Pottinger Group 1994–98; Co-founding Dir, Quiller Consultants 1998; Parl. Under-Sec. of State for Schools and Govt Spokesperson, Dept for Educ. 2010–13; mem. (Conservative), House of Lords 2010–, Leader of the House of Lords and Chancellor of the Duchy of Lancaster 2013–14; Commr for Financial Stability, Financial Services and Capital Markets Union, European Comm. (EC), Brussels 2014–16 (resgnd). *Address:* House of Lords, Westminster, London, SW1A 0PW, England (office). *Telephone:* (20) 7219-5353 (office). *Fax:* (20) 7219-5979 (office). *E-mail:* contactholmember@parliament.uk (office). *Website:* www.parliament.uk/biographies/lords/lord-hill-of-oareford/4144 (office).

HILL WELLS, Susan Elizabeth, (Susan Hill), CBE, BA, MA, FRSL; British writer and playwright; b. 5 Feb. 1942, Scarborough, Yorks.; d. of R. H. Hill and Doris Hill; m. Prof. Stanley W. Wells 1975; two d. (and one d. deceased); ed grammar schools in Scarborough and Coventry and King's Coll. London; literary critic, various journals 1963–; numerous plays for BBC 1970–; Fellow, King's Coll. London 1978; presenter, Bookshelf, BBC Radio 1986–87; Founder and Publr Long Barn Books 1996–. *Publications include:* The Enclosure 1961, Do Me a Favour 1963, Gentleman and Ladies 1969, A Change for the Better 1969, I'm the King of the Castle (Somerset Maugham Award) 1970, The Albatross (John Llewellyn Rhys

Prize) 1971, Strange Meeting 1971, The Bird of the Night (Whitbread Novel Award) 1972, A Bit of Singing and Dancing 1973, In the Springtime of the Year 1974, The Cold Country and Other Plays for Radio 1975, The Ramshackle Company (play) 1981, The Magic Apple Tree 1982, The Woman in Black 1983 (stage version 1989, film 2012), One Night at a Time (for children) 1984, Through the Kitchen Window 1984, Through the Garden Gate 1986, Mother's Magic (for children) 1986, The Lighting of the Lamps 1987, Lanterns Across the Snow 1987, Shakespeare Country 1987, The Spirit of the Cotswolds 1988, Can it be True? (for children) 1988, Family (autobiog.) 1989, Susie's Shoes (for children) 1989, Stories from Codling Village (for children) 1990, I've Forgotten Edward (for children) 1990, I Won't Go There Again (for children) 1990, Pirate Poll (for children) 1991, The Glass Angels 1991, Beware! Beware! 1993, King of Kings 1993, Reflections from a Garden (with Rory Stuart) 1995, Contemporary Women's Short Stories (co-ed. with Rory Stuart) 1995, Listening to the Orchestra (short stories) 1996, The Second Penguin Book of Women's Short Stories 1997, The Service of Clouds 1998, The Boy Who Taught the Beekeeper to Read and Other Stories 2003, The Various Haunts of Men 2004, The Pure in Heart 2005, The Risk of Darkness 2006, The Man in the Picture 2007, Desperate Diary of a Country Housewife (non-fiction) 2007, The Battle for Gullywith (for children) 2008, The Beacon 2008, The Man in the Picture 2008, The Vows of Silence 2008, Howards End is on the Landing 2009, The Small Hand 2010, The Shadows in the Street 2010, The Betrayal of Trust 2011, A Kind Man 2011, A Question of Identity 2012, Black Sheep 2013, The Soul of Discretion 2014, Printer's Devil Court 2014, From the Heart 2017, Jacob's Room is Full of Books. *Address:* c/o Sheil Land, 52 Doughty Street, London, WC1N 2LS, England (office). *E-mail:* vgreen@sheilland.co.uk (office); mail@susan-hill.com. *Website:* www.susan-hill.com.

HILLE, Bertil, BS, PhD; American physiologist, neurobiologist, biophysicist and academic; *Professor of Physiology and Biophysics, School of Medicine, University of Washington;* b. 10 Oct. 1940, New Haven, Conn.; s. of Einar Hille and Kirsti Ore Hille; m. Merrill Burr Hille; two s.; ed Yale Univ., The Rockefeller Univ.; Asst Prof., Dept of Physiology and Biophysics, Univ. of Washington School of Medicine 1968–71, Assoc. Prof. 1971–74, Prof. 1974–; mem. NAS 1986–, AAAS, Physiological Soc., Soc. for Neuroscience; Fellow, American Acad. of Arts and Sciences 1998–, Acad. of Medicine 2002–, Biophysical Soc.; Dr hc (Rockefeller Univ.) 2008; Louisa Gross Horwitz Prize for Biology or Biochemistry, Columbia Univ. (co-recipient) 1996, Albert Lasker Award for Basic Medical Research (co-recipient) 1999, Gairdner Int. Award, Gairdner Foundation (Canada) (co-recipient) 2001. *Publications:* Ion Channels of Excitable Membranes 1984, 1991, 2001; more than 200 publs in scientific journals on cell signalling by ion channels, neurotransmitters and hormones acting through G-protein coupled receptors and intracellular calcium, phosphoinositide messengers. *Address:* Department of Physiology and Biophysics, University of Washington School of Medicine, 1705 NE Pacific Street, G-424 HSB, Box 357290, Seattle, WA 98195-7290, USA (office). *Telephone:* (206) 543-8639 (office). *Fax:* (206)-685-0619 (office). *E-mail:* hille@uw.edu (office). *Website:* depts.washington.edu/pbiopage (office).

HILLEL, Daniel, BA, MA, PhD; Israeli (b. American) water and soil scientist and academic; *Adjunct Senior Scientist, NASA Goddard Institute for Space Studies;* b. 1930, Los Angeles, Calif.; ed American univs, Hebrew Univ. of Jerusalem; family emigrated to Palestine 1931; worked for Israeli Ministry of Agric.; Founding mem. Sde Boker kibbutz in Negev desert, where he worked as a surveyor; began developing the concept behind drip irrigation late 1950s; undertook missions to Burma 1956 and later to arid regions in Africa, Asia, S America and Australia; served as Head of Agricultural Research Service, Soil and Water Inst. of Israel, later consulted with governmental agencies in various countries; fmr Prof., Hebrew Univ. of Jerusalem, Univ. of Massachusetts, Columbia Univ.; also worked with int. orgs including World Bank, FAO, US Agency for Int. Devt, IAEA; currently Adjunct Sr Research Scientist, NASA Goddard Inst. for Space Studies, The Earth Inst. at Columbia Univ., New York; Hon. DSc (Guelph Univ., Canada) 1992; Chancellor's Medal, Univ. of Massachusetts 1982, Guggenheim Fellowship and grant 1993, World Food Prize 2012. *Publications:* 21 books, including Soil and Water: Physical Principles and Processes 1971, Computer Simulation of Soil-Water Dynamics: A Compendium of Recent Work 1977, Applications of Soil Physics 1980, Fundamentals of Soil Physics 1980, Negev, Land, Water, and Life in a Desert Environment 1982, Introduction to Soil Physics 1982, Efficient Use of Water in Irrigation: Principles and Practices for Improving Irrigation in Arid and Semiarid Regions 1987, Out of the Earth: Civilization and the Life of the Soil 1992, The Rivers of Eden: The Struggle for Water and the Quest for Peace in the Middle East 1994, Environmental Soil Physics: Fundamentals, Applications, and Environmental Considerations 1998, Climate Change and the Global Harvest: Potential Impacts of the Greenhouse Effect on Agriculture 1998, Salinity Management for Sustainable Irrigation: Integrating Science, Environment, and Economics 2000, Introduction to Environmental Soil Physics 2003, Soil in the Environment: Crucible of Terrestrial Life 2007, The Natural History of the Bible: An Environmental Exploration of the Hebrew Scriptures 2007, Climate Variability and the Global Harvest: Impacts of El Niño and Other Oscillations on Agroecosystems 2008; more than 200 papers in professional journals. *Address:* NASA Goddard Institute for Space Studies, 2880 Broadway, New York, NY 10025, USA (office). *Telephone:* (212) 678-5508 (office). *E-mail:* dh244@columbia.edu (office). *Website:* www.giss.nasa.gov (office).

HILLEL, Shlomo; Israeli politician and fmr diplomatist; *President, The Society for the Preservation of Heritage Sites in Israel;* b. (Selim Hillel), 9 April 1923, Baghdad, Iraq; s. of Aharom Hillel and Hanini Hillel; m. Tmima Rosner 1952; one s. one d.; ed Herzliah High School, Tel-Aviv and Hebrew Univ., Jerusalem; mem. Ma'agan Michael Kibbutz 1942–58; Jewish Agency for Palestine—mission to countries in Middle East 1946–48, 1949–51; Israel Defence Forces 1948–49; Prime Minister's Office 1952–53; mem. of Knesset 1953–59, 1974–; Amb. to Guinea 1959–61, to Côte d'Ivoire, Dahomey, Upper Volta and Niger 1961–63; mem. Perm. Mission to UN with rank of Minister 1964–67; Asst Dir-Gen. Ministry of Foreign Affairs 1967–69; Minister of Police 1969–77; Co-ordinator of political contacts with Arab leadership in administered territories 1970–77; Minister of the Interior June–Oct. 1974, 1996–97; Chair. Ministerial Cttee for Social Welfare 1974–77, Cttee of the Interior and Environment 1977–81, of Foreign Affairs and Defence 1981–84; Perm. Observer to Council of Europe 1977–84; Speaker of the Knesset 1984–88; Chair. Sephardi Fed. 1976–; World Chair. Keren Hayesod United Israel Appeal 1989–98; Pres. Soc. for Preservation of Historical Sites in Israel 1996–; Chair. Zalman Shazar Center, Jerusalem; Commdr Nat. Order of Repubs of Ivory Coast, Upper Volta and Dahomey; Dr hc (Hebrew Univ.) 1995, (Ben-Gurion Univ.) 1997, (Tel-Aviv) 1998; Israel Prize for Life Achievement 1998. *Publication:* Operation Babylon 1988. *Leisure interests:* tennis, gardening. *Address:* 4 Shalom Aleichem str., Ra'anana 43368, Israel (home). *Telephone:* (9) 7741789 (home). *Fax:* (9) 7741788 (home). *E-mail:* s-t-h@zahav.net.il (home).

HILLEN, Johannes Stefanus Joseph (Hans), MA; Dutch politician and fmr journalist; b. 17 June 1947, The Hague; m.; three c.; ed State Univ. of Utrecht; spent 14 years as journalist with Nederlandse Publieke Omroep (Netherlands Public Broadcasting), including as Desk Ed., NOS Studio Sport 1969–73, Foreign Ed., NOS Journaal (nat. TV news broadcast) 1973–77, Political Journalist, NOS Journaal, The Hague 1977–83; worked as social studies teacher in secondary schools in Hilversum and Bussum 1973–77; Dir of Information, Ministry of Finance 1983; mem. Tweede Kamer (House of Reps, lower house of Parl.) 1990–2002; mem. Eerste Kamer (Senate, upper house) 2007–10; Minister of Defence 2010–12; mem. Christian Democratic Alliance (CDA), Parl. Party Sec. 1998–2001; fmr Chair. Health Care Insurance Bd; fmr columnist, Elsevier Weekblad, Katholiek Nieuwsblad; mem. Exec. Bd VNO-NCW (Confed. of Netherlands Industry and Employers); Chair. Centrum voor Merk en Communicatie (Centre for Brands and Communication); Special mem. Research Council for Security 2006–08; Chair. Friends of the Metropole Orchestra Foundation 2007–; Kt, Order of Orange-Nassau 2002. *Address:* c/o Ministry of Defence, Plein 4, PO Box 20701, 2500 ES The Hague, The Netherlands. *E-mail:* defensievoorlichting@mindef.nl.

HILLEN, John, BA, MA, MBA, PhD; American consultant, fmr diplomatist and army officer (retd); *Executive-in-Residence and Professor of Practice, School of Business, George Mason University;* ed Duke Univ., King's Coll. London and Univ. of Oxford, UK, Cornell Univ.; served 12 years as US Army officer; Defense Analyst, Heritage Foundation 1995–97; Fellow, Nat. Security Council on Foreign Relations 1997–98; Sr Fellow and Asst to the Pres., Center for Strategic and Int. Studies 1999; COO Island ECN Inc. 2000–02; Sr Vice-Pres. and Head of Defense and Intelligence Group, American Man. Systems 2003–04; Pres. CGI Federal 2005; Asst Sec. for Political-Military Affairs, US Dept of State 2005–07; CEO and Pres. Sotera Defense Solutions Inc. 2008–13, Vice-Chair. Advisory Bd 2013–15; Chair. Applied Communication Sciences 2012–13; Exec.-in-Residence and Prof. of Practice, School of Business, George Mason Univ. 2013–; Chair. CygnaCom Solutions 2014–; Sr Operating Advisor and Operating Partner, LLR Partners Inc. 2014–; fmr CEO and Pres. GTEC Cyber Solutions Inc.; Pres. Global Strategies Group (USA) LLC 2007; fmr Contributing Ed., Nat. Review magazine, Chair. 2010–; mem. Bd of Dirs Software AG Government Solutions, Inc. 2013–, Atkins Nuclear Solutions US 2014–, IAP Worldwide Services 2014–; mem. US Comm. on Nat. Security/21st Century 1999–2000; Chair. Bd of Advisors, SOS Int. Ltd 2013–; mem. Exec. Cttee Professional Services Council 2008–; mem. Council, IISS 2012–15, Pres. US Friends for the IISS 2014–; mem. Young Pres.s' Org. (YPO) 2005–15; mem. Council of Foreign Relations 1996–, Veterans of Foreign Wars; Founding Henry Crown Fellow, Aspen Inst. 1997–2000; Trustee Hampden-Sydney College 2014–; Trustee and Treasurer, Foreign Policy Research Inst. 2007–; fmr Consultant, ABC News; Bronze Star, Operation Desert Storm 1991, Fed100 Award 2011, GovCon Contractor of the Year 2012. *Publications:* Blue Helmets: The Strategy of UN Military Operations 1998, Future Visions for US Defense Policy (ed.) 2001; numerous articles in leading journals and newspapers. *Address:* George Mason University School of Business, 4400 University Drive, Fairfax, VA 22030, USA (office). *Telephone:* (703) 993-1880 (office). *Website:* business.gmu.edu (office).

HILLER, István, PhD; Hungarian academic and politician; *President, Hungarian Socialist Party;* b. 7 May 1964, Sopron; m. Julianna Hillerné Farkas; two c.; ed Eötvös Loránd Univ., Karls-Ruprecht Univ., Germany; Researcher, Historical Inst., Univ. of Vienna 1995, 1997; Asst Lecturer, Eötvös Loránd Univ. 1989–94, Sr Lecturer 1994–2001, Prof. 2001–02; Founding mem. Hungarian Socialist Party (MSZP) 1989, Deputy Pres. MSZP Nat. Bd 1998, Vice-Pres. MSZP 2003–04, Pres. 2005–07, 2016–; mem. Parl. 2002–, Vice-Pres. 2014, currently Chair. Asscn of Social Platform for Values; Parl. State Sec., Ministry of Educ. 2002–03; Minister of Cultural Heritage 2003–05, of Educ. and Culture 2006–10; Chevalier, Ordre des Arts et des Lettres, Cavaliere di Gran Croce (Italy), Große Verdienstkreuz (Germany); Prof. of the Year, Eötvös Loránd Univ. 1999. *Address:* Hungarian Socialist Party, 1055 Budapest, Kossuth tér 1-3, Hungary (office). *E-mail:* istvan.hiller@parlament.hu (office). *Website:* mszp.hu (office).

HILLIER, Gen. (retd) Rick J., BSc, OC; Canadian army officer (retd); b. 1955, Newfoundland and Labrador; m.; two s.; ed Memorial Univ. of Newfoundland; posted to 8th Canadian Hussars 1976, Royal Canadian Dragoons 1979, staff officer, Army HQ, Montréal, Nat. Defence HQ, Ottawa, Canadian Deputy Commdg Gen. 1998–2000, Commdr Multinational Div. (Southwest), Bosnia-Herzegovina, Asst Chief of the Land Staff –2003, Chief of the Land Staff 2003–05, Commdr Int. Security Assistance Force, Kabul, Afghanistan Feb.–Aug. 2004, Chief of Defence Staff 2005–08 (retd); apptd Chancellor, Memorial Univ. of Newfoundland 2008, co-f. Project Hero (scholarship programme) 2009; Chair. TELUS Atlantic Canada Community Bd 2008; Strategic Advisor, Gowling Lafleur Henderson LLP, (law firm), Ottawa 2009; Order of Newfoundland and Labrador 2014, Commdr of the Order of Military Merit, Meritorious Service Cross; Lincoln Alexander Outstanding Leader Award, Univ. of Guelph. *Publications include:* Good News Bible: Canadian Forces Edition 2004, A Soldier First: Bullets, Bureaucrats and the Politics of War 2009, Leadership: 50 Points of Wisdom For Today's Leaders 2010. *Leisure interests:* running, hockey, golf. *Website:* www.generalhillier.com.

HILLS, Carla Anderson, AB, LLD; American lawyer and fmr government official; *Chairman and CEO, Hills and Company;* b. 3 Jan. 1934, Los Angeles, Calif.; d. of Carl Anderson and Edith Anderson (née Hume); m. Roderick Maltman Hills 1958; one s. three d.; ed Stanford Univ., Calif., St Hilda's Coll., Oxford, UK, Yale Law School; Asst US Attorney, Civil Div., LA, Calif. 1958–61; Pnr, Munger, Tolles, Hills & Rickershauser (law firm) 1962–74; Adjunct Prof., School of Law, UCLA 1972; Asst Attorney-Gen. Civil Div., US Dept of Justice 1974–75; Sec. of Housing and Urban Devt 1975–77; Partner, Latham, Watkins & Hills (law firm) 1978–86, Weil, Gotshal and Manges, Washington 1986–88, Mudge Rose Gutherie Alexander & Ferdon 1994; US Trade Rep., Exec. Office of the Pres. 1989–93;

Chair., CEO Hills & Co. (consulting firm) 1993–; Co-Chair. Alliance to Save Energy 1977–89; Vice-Chair. Bar of Supreme Court of the US, Calif. State and DC Bars, Council Section of Anti-trust Law, ABA 1974, American Law Inst. 1974–, Fed. Bar Asscn (LA Chapter, Pres. 1963), Women Lawyers Asscn (Pres. 1964), LA Co. Bar Asscn, Chair. of various cttees including Standing Cttee on Discipline, Calif. 1970–74; mem. Bd Dirs American Int. Group (AIG), Lucent Technologies Inc., Bechtel Enterprises, Trust Co. of the West Group Inc., AOL Time-Warner Inc. 1993–2006, Chevron Corp. 1993–; mem. Carnegie Comm. on the Future of Public Broadcasting 1977–78, Sloan Comm. on Govt and Higher Educ. 1977–79, Advisory Cttee Woodrow Wilson School of Public and Int. Affairs 1977–80, Yale Univ. Council 1977–80, Fed. Accounting Standards Advisory Council 1978–80, Trilateral Comm. 1977–82, 1993–, American Cttee on East–West Accord 1977–79, Int. Foundation for Cultural Cooperation and Devt 1977, Editorial Bd, Nat. Law Journal 1978, Calif. Gov.'s Council of Econ. Policy Advisers 1993–, Council on Foreign Relations 1993–; Co-Chair. Int. Advisory Bd, Center for Strategic and Int. Studies; Chair. Nat. Cttee on US-China Relations 1993–; Contributing Ed., Legal Times 1978–88; Fellow, American Bar Foundation 1975; Trustee, Pomona Coll. 1974–79, Norton Simon Museum of Art 1976–80, Brookings Inst. 1977, Univ. of Southern Calif. 1977–79; Advisor, Annenberg School of Communications, Univ. of Southern Calif. 1977–78; Chair. Urban Inst. 1983; Dir Time Warner 1993–2006, AIG –2006; Vice-Chair. Interamerican Dialogue 1997–; mem. Bd Trustees Asia Soc., Inst. for Int. Econs, Americas Soc.; Dr hc (Pepperdine Univ.) 1975, (Washington Univ., St Louis, Mo.) 1977, (Mills Coll., Calif.) 1977, (Lake Forest Coll.) 1978, (Williams Coll.), (Notre Dame Univ.), (Wabash Coll.). *Publications:* Federal Civil Practice (co-author) 1961, Antitrust Adviser (ed. and co-author) 1971. *Leisure interest:* tennis. *Address:* Hills & Company, 1120 20th Street, NW, Suite 200 North, Washington, DC 20036 (office); 3125 Chain Bridge Road, NW, Washington, DC 20016, USA (home). *Telephone:* (202) 822-4700 (office). *Fax:* (202) 822-4710 (office). *E-mail:* CAHills@hillsandco.com (office). *Website:* www.hillsandco.com (office).

HILLY, Hon. Francis Billy, BA, CMG, KCMG; Solomon Islands business executive and politician; b. 20 July 1948, Emu Harbour, Rannoga; ed King George VI Secondary School, Univ. of the South Pacific; joined pre-independence govt working under Solomon Mamaloni; later worked for a pvt. co. in Gizo; mem. Parl. for Ranogga/Simbo Constituency 1976–84, 1993–, Chair. Public Accounts Cttee 2004–05, Parl. House Cttee 2006–07; fmr Premier of Western Prov.; Prime Minister of the Solomon Islands 1993–94; Leader of the Opposition 1994–95, 2004–06; govt-nominated cand. for position of Prime Minister June 2000; Minister for Commerce, Industry and Employment May–Aug. 2006 (dismissed), 2007–10, for Finance and Treasury May–Aug. 2010; also served for periods as Minister for Home Affairs and as Minister for Health and Medical Services and Deputy Prime Minister; Head Melanesian Spearhead Group, Observer Mission to Vanuatu's Snap Elections 2016. *Address:* National Parliament of Solomon Islands, PO Box G19, Vavaya Ridge, Honiara, Solomon Islands (office). *Telephone:* 28520 (office). *Fax:* 24272 (office). *Website:* www.parliament.gov.sb (office).

HILMER, Frederick George, AO, LLB, LLM, MBA; Australian academic, business executive and fmr university administrator; *Professor Emeritus, University of New South Wales;* b. 2 Feb. 1945; ed Sydney Univ., Univ. of Pennsylvania, Wharton School of Finance, USA; mem. Higher Educ. Council 1987–93; Dean and Prof. of Man., Australian Grad. School of Man., Univ. of New South Wales 1989–98, Pres. and Vice-Chancellor Univ. of New South Wales 2006–15, Prof. Emer. 2015–; Deputy Chair. Westfield Group 1991–; CEO John Fairfax Holdings Ltd 1998–2005; fmr Chair. Commonwealth Higher Educ. Council; Chair. Nat. Competition Policy Review Cttee 1992–93, Group of Eight (Go8, coalition of Australia's leading research univs) 2011–, U21 (global network of research-intensive univs) 2013–; fmr Joseph Wharton Fellow, Wharton School of Finance; Hon. mem. CPA Australia 2010; Hon. DSc (Univ. of New South Wales) 2015; John Storey Medal, Australian Inst. of Man. 1991. *Publications include:* several books, including When The Luck Runs Out: The Future for Australians at Work 1985, New Games/New Rules: Work in Competitive Enterprises 1989, Strictly Boardroom: Improving Governance to Enhance Company Performance 1993, Management Redeemed: Debunking the Fads that Undermine Our Corporations (co-author) 1996, The Fairfax Experience – What the Management Texts Didn't Teach Me 2007; articles in the fields of gen. man., industrial relations, and competition law and policy. *Address:* AGSM, University of New South Wales, Sydney, NSW 2052, Australia (office). *Telephone:* (2) 9385-2788 (office). *Fax:* (2) 9385-1949 (office). *E-mail:* f.hilmer@unsw.edu.au (office). *Website:* www.unsw.edu.au (office).

HILSKÝ, Martin, PhD; Czech translator, writer and academic; *Professor of English Literature, Charles University;* b. 8 April 1943, Prague; s. of Václav Hilský and Vlasta Hilská; m. Kateřina Hilská; two s. one d.; ed Charles Univ., Prague, Univ. of Oxford, UK; Asst Prof., Charles Univ., Prague 1965, Prof. of English Literature 1993–, Dir Inst. of English & American Studies 1988–98; Jr Research Fellow, Univ. of Oxford 1968–69; mem. Czech Modern Language Asscn (Chair. 1993–96), European Soc. for Study of English, PEN Club; also performer at Czech Radio 3, Vltava, Czech TV; Hon. MBE 2002; IREX grant, USA 1985, Jungmann Translation Prize 1997, Tom Stoppard Award 2003, State Prize for Translation 2011. *Achievements:* Shakespeare translations performed throughout the Czech Repub. *Publications:* Současný britský román (Contemporary British Fiction) (Rector's Prize) 1991, Modernisté (The Modernists 1995), Od Poea k postmodernismu (essays) (From Poe to Postmodernism 1993), Od slavíka k papouškovi (co-author, essays) (Nightingales and Parrots 2003), Když ticho mluví (Languages of Silence 2007), Rozbité zrcadlo (The Broken Mirror 2009), Shakespeare a jeviště svět (Shakespeare and Theatrum Mundi 2011); over 80 papers on English and American literature; translations of Shakespeare (plays and poems), Thornton Wilder's Our Town 1978, Peter Shaffer's Amadeus 1981, James Goldman's Lion in Winter 1988, Peter Barnes's Red Noses 1991, J.M. Synge's The Playboy of the Western World 1996; Complete Works of Shakespeare (in Czech) 2011; Ed. dual language edn of Shakespeare plays and poems (six vols). *Leisure interests:* literature, theatre, arts, good wine, skiing, jogging, gardening. *Address:* Room 110, Department of English and American Studies, Faculty of Philosophy and Arts, Charles University, Jana Palacha 2, 116 38 Prague (office); Tychonova 10, 160 00 Prague 6, Czech Republic (home). *Telephone:* (2) 221619341 (office); (2) 607560926 (home). *E-mail:* hilsky@volny.cz (office). *Website:* ualk.ff.cuni.cz/staff/martin-hilsky.

HILSUM, Cyril, CBE, PhD, FRS, FREng, SFIEE; British research scientist and academic; b. 17 May 1925, London; s. of Ben Hilsum and Ada Hilsum; m. Betty Hilsum 1947 (died 1987); one d. (one d. deceased); ed Raines School, London and Univ. Coll., London; HQ Admiralty 1945–47; Admiralty Research Lab., Teddington 1947–50; Services Electronics Research Lab., Baldock 1950–64; Royal Signals and Radar Establishments, Malvern 1964–83; Visiting Prof., Univ. Coll., London 1988–; Chief Scientist, Gen. Electric Co. (GEC) Research Labs 1983–85; Dir of Research, GEC PLC 1985–92, Corp. Research Adviser 1992–; Pres. Inst. of Physics 1988–90; mem. Science and Eng Research Council 1984–88; Hon. FInstP; Hon. DEng (Sheffield) 1992, (Nottingham Trent) 1998; recipient of several awards from UK and Int. Inst. *Publications:* Semiconducting III-V Compounds 1961; over 100 scientific and tech. papers. *Leisure interests:* chess. *Address:* 12 Eastglade, Pinner, Middx, HA5 3AN, England (home). *Telephone:* (20) 8866-8323 (home). *E-mail:* cyrilhilsum@aol.com (home).

HILSUM, Lindsey, BA (Hons); British journalist; *International Editor, Channel 4 News (UK);* b. 3 Aug. 1958, Hitchin; d. of Cyril Hilsum and Betty Hilsum; ed Univ. of Exeter; joined Oxfam working in Guatemala and Haiti 1979; began journalism career freelance reporting from Mexico and the Caribbean 1980; worked for three years as Information Officer for UNICEF, Nairobi; covered events in E Africa for BBC and The Guardian newspaper 1986–89; Sr Producer, BBC World Service 1990–93, reported from Rwanda, Middle East, Mexico, S Africa, S Pacific; Diplomatic Corresp., Channel 4 News 1996–2003, Int. Ed. 2003–, China Corresp. 2006–08; regular contrib. to Granta, Observer, Sunday Times, New York Review of Books; Dr hc (Essex) 2004, (Leeds Metropolitan) 2009, (Exeter) 2017; Amnesty International Awards 1997, 2004, TV News Award 2004, Royal TV Soc. Specialist Journalist of the Year 2003, Emmy Award for coverage of fall of Saddam Hussein (co-recipient) 2004, Royal Television Soc. TV Journalist of the Year Award 2005, James Cameron Award 2005, Women in Film and TV Award 2005, Foreign Press Asscn Award 2010, Charles Wheeler Award 2011, One World Journalist of the Year 2011, Political Studies Asscn Award 2011, Mungo Park Medal, Royal Scottish Geographical Soc. 2015, BAFTA 2016, Patron's Medal, Royal Geographical Soc. 2017. *Publication:* Sandstorm: Libya in the Time of Revolution 2012. *Leisure interests:* bird watching, horse riding. *Address:* c/o Knight Ayton Management, 35 Great James Street, London, WC1N 3HB, England (office); Channel 4 News, 200 Grays Inn Road, London, WC1X 8XZ, England (office). *Telephone:* (20) 7831-4400 (office); (20) 7430-4606 (office). *Fax:* (20) 7831-4455 (office); (20) 7430-4607 (office). *E-mail:* sueayton@knightayton.co.uk (office); c4foreign@itn.co.uk (office). *Website:* knightayton.co.uk (office); www.channel4.com/news (office).

HILTON, Janet, ARNCM, FRCM; British clarinettist and academic; *Professor of Clarinet, Royal College of Music;* b. 1 Jan. 1945, Liverpool; d. of H. Hilton and E. Hilton; m. David Richardson 1968; two s. (one deceased) one d.; ed Belvedere School, Liverpool, Royal Northern Coll. of Music, Vienna Konservatorium; BBC concerto debut 1963; appearances as clarinet soloist with major British orchestras including Royal Liverpool Philharmonic, Scottish Nat., Scottish Chamber, City of Birmingham Symphony Orchestra (CBSO), Bournemouth Symphony, Bournemouth Sinfonietta, City of London Sinfonia, BBC Scottish and Welsh Symphony, BBC Philharmonic; guest at Edinburgh, Aldeburgh, Bath, Cheltenham, City of London Festivals, BBC Henry Wood Promenade concerts; appearances throughout Europe and N America; Prin. Clarinet Scottish Chamber Orchestra 1974–80, Kent Opera 1984–88; teacher Royal Scottish Acad. of Music and Drama 1974–80, Royal Northern Coll. of Music 1983–87; Head of Woodwind, Birmingham Conservatoire 1992–; Prof. of Clarinet, Royal Coll. of Music, London 1998–, Head of Woodwind 1998–2010; Prof., Univ. of Central England 1993; Dir Camerata Wind Soloists; works composed for her by Iain Hamilton, John McCabe, Edward Harper, Elizabeth Maconchy, Alun Hoddinott, Malcolm Arnold; Reger Clarinet Sonatas with Jakob Fichert, piano 2009; int. master classes in Paris, Vienna, Wrocław, Singapore, Hong Kong, USA (Chicago, Indiana and Michigan), Australia (Sydney and Melbourne); Pres. Clarinet and Saxophone Soc. of GB; Hon. Fellow, Birmingham Conservatoire 2009. *Recordings include:* several recordings for Chandos, including all of Weber's music for clarinet with the CBSO, Lindsay Quartet and Keith Swallow, the Nielsen and Copland Concertos with the Scottish Nat. Orchestra, Stanford Clarinet Concerto with Ulster Orchestra, Mozart Clarinet Quintet with the Lindsay Quartet 1998; Dedications—concertos by McCabe, Harper, Maconchy and Hoddinott with BBC Scottish Symphony Orchestra, Reger Clarinet Sonatas with Jakob Fichert, piano 2010. *Leisure interests:* cookery, reading. *Address:* Royal College of Music, Prince Consort Road, London, SW7 2BS (office); Holte End, Whitehall Lane, Checkendon, Oxon., RG8 0TN, England (home). *Telephone:* (1491) 682853 (home). *E-mail:* jhilton@rcm.ac.uk (office). *Website:* www.impulse-music.co.uk/hilton.htm.

HILZINGER, Kurt J., BBA; American certified public accountant and business executive; *Chairman, Humana Incorporated;* ed Univ. of Michigan; with AmerisourceBergen and AmeriSource Corpn from 1991, Treas. 1995–97, Vice-Pres. 1995–97, Chief Financial Officer 1995–99, Sr Vice-Pres. 1997–2000, Pres. AmeriSource Health Corpn 2000–01, Exec. Vice-Pres. and COO AmerisourceBergen Corpn 2001–02, Pres. and COO 2002–07, mem. Bd of Dirs 2004–07; mem. Bd of Dirs, Humana Inc. 2003–, Lead Dir 2010–14, Chair. 2014–; Partner, Court Square Capital Partners, LP (ind. pvt. equity firm) 2007–; Dir, Physiotherapy Assocs, Western Dental; fmr Chair. Healthcare Distribution Man. Asscn. *Address:* Humana Inc., 500 West Main Street, Louisville, KY 40202, USA (office). *Telephone:* (502) 580-1000 (office). *Fax:* (502) 580-3677 (office). *E-mail:* info@humana.com (office). *Website:* www.humana.com (office).

HIMELFARB, Alexander (Alex), PhD; Canadian sociologist, academic and fmr diplomatist; *Director, The Glendon School of Public and International Affairs, York University;* b. 1947; m. Frum Himelfarb; ed Univ. of Toronto; Prof. of Sociology, Univ. of New Brunswick 1972–81; Head, Unified Family Court Project, Dept of Justice 1979–81; joined Dept of Solicitor-Gen. 1981, held several positions including Dir-Gen. Planning and Systems Group; other public service posts have included Exec. Dir Nat. Parole Bd, Asst Sec. to Cabinet for Social Policy Devt, Privy Council Office, Assoc. Sec. Treasury Bd, Head, Fed. Task Force on Social Union; Deputy Minister of Canadian Heritage 1999–2002; Clerk of Privy Council and Sec. to Cabinet 2002–06; Amb. to Italy 2006–09 (also accred to Albania and San Marino and as High Commr to Malta); Dir The Glendon School of Public and

Int. Affairs, York Univ. 2009–. *Address:* The Glendon School of Public and International Affairs, York University, 2275 Bayview Avenue, Toronto, ON M4N 3M6, Canada (office). *Telephone:* (416) 487-6706 (office). *E-mail:* publicaffairs@glendon.yorku.ca (office). *Website:* www.glendon.yorku.ca (office); www.alexsblog.ca.

HIMID, Lubaina, CBE, BA, MA, MBE, FRSA; British (b. Tanzanian) artist and curator; *Professor of Contemporary Art, University of Central Lancashire;* b. 1954, Zanzibar; ed Wimbledon Coll. of Art, Royal Coll. of Art; pioneer of the British black arts movement since the 1980s; Dir The Elbow Room, London 1986–90; Artist-in-residence, Tate St Ives 1998–2000; currently Prof. of Contemporary Art, Univ. of Central Lancashire; works are displayed in numerous public collections including Tate, Victoria & Albert Museum, The Whitworth Art Gallery, Arts Council England, Manchester Art Gallery, The Int. Slavery Museum Liverpool, The Walker Art Gallery, Birmingham City Art Gallery, Bolton Art Gallery, New Hall Cambridge, Ferens Art Gallery, Hull, Harris Museum and Art Gallery Preston; mem. Council, Tate Liverpool 2000–05; Trustee, Lowry Arts Centre Manchester 2013–; elected Royal Academician, Royal Acad. of Arts 2019; mem. Greater London Arts Asscn, Visual Arts Panel Soc.; named Artist of the Year by Apollo Magazine 2017, Turner Prize 2017. *Documentaries:* (as producer, in collaboration with Tate Liverpool): Open Sesame 2005, The Point of Collection 2007. *Solo exhibitions include:* A Fashionable Marriage, Pentonville Gallery, London 1986, The Ballad of the Wing, Chisenhale Gallery, London 1989, African Gardens, Black Art Gallery, London 1993, Inside The Invisible, St Jørgens Museum, Bergen, Norway 2001, Fabrications, C.U.B.E, Manchester 2002, Tailor Striker Singer Dandy, Platt Hall Museum of Costume, Manchester Galleries 2011, Moments that Matter/ Cultural Olympiad, Harris Museum & Art Gallery 2012, Navigation Charts, Spike Island, Bristol 2017, Invisible Strategies, Modern Art Oxford, Oxford 2017, Our Kisses are Petals, Baltic Centre for Contemporary Art, Gateshead 2018. *Address:* School of Art Design and Fashion, Faculty of Culture and the Creative Industries, University of Central Lancashire, 37 St Peters Street, Preston, PR1 2HE, England (office). *Telephone:* (1772) 893991 (office). *E-mail:* lhimid@uclan.ac.uk (office). *Website:* www.uclanfcci.co.uk (office); lubainahimid.uk.

HINAULT, Bernard; French fmr professional cyclist; b. 14 Nov. 1954, Yffiniac, Côtes du Nord; s. of Joseph Hinault and Lucie (Guernion) Hinault; m. Martine Lessard Hinault 1974; two s.; competitive cycling début 1971; French jr champion 1972; French champion 1978; world champion 1980, third 1981; winner, Tour de France 1978, 1979, 1981, 1982, 1985, Tour d'Italie 1980, 1982, 1985, Tour d'Espagne 1978, 1983, Grand Prix des Nations 1978, 1982, 1984, Luis Puig Trophy 1986, Coors Classic, USA 1986 and many other int. racing events; retd from racing 1986; fmr Technical Adviser, fmr External Relations Dir Tour de France; fmr Sports Dir French team; fmr Dir-Gen. Ouest Levure; Chevalier, Légion d'honneur, Ordre Nat. du Mérite. *Publications include:* Moi, Bernard Hinault (with others) 1979, Le Pentolou des souvenirs, Cyclisme sur route, technique, tactique, entraînement, Vélo tout terrain, découverte, technique et entraînement.

HINCH, (Edward) John, PhD, FRS; British academic; *Professor of Fluid Mechanics, University of Cambridge;* b. 4 March 1947, Peterborough; s. of Joseph Edward Hinch and Mary Grace Hinch (née Chandler); m. Christine Bridges 1969; one s. one d.; ed Univ. of Cambridge; Fellow, Trinity Coll., Cambridge 1971–, Asst Lecturer, Univ. of Cambridge 1972–75, Lecturer 1975–94, Reader in Fluid Mechanics 1994–98, Prof. 1998–; Fellow, American Physical Soc. 1997–; Assoc. Ed. Letters of Physics of Fluids; mem. Editorial Bd Physics of Fluids, Journal of Non-Newtonian Fluid Mechanics, Granular Matter; Trustee, Isaac Newton Trust 2000–07; mem. Int. Science Cttee 2006, 2008, 2010; mem. EPSRC Coll. in Mathematics, Francqui Prize Cttee 2006; Chevalier, Ordre nat. du Mérite 1997; Dr hc (l'INP Toulouse) 2010; APS Fluid Dynamaics Prize 2010, Euromech Fluid Mechanics Prize 2010. *Publications:* Perturbation Methods 1991; various papers in learned journals on fluid mechanics and its application. *Address:* Department of Applied Mathematics and Theoretical Physics, Centre for Mathematical Sciences, Wilberforce Road, Cambridge, CB3 0WA (office); Trinity College, Cambridge, CB2 1TQ, England. *Telephone:* (12) 2333-7864 (office); (12) 2333-8427. *Fax:* (12) 2333-8564; (12) 2376-5900 (office). *E-mail:* e.j.hinch@damtp.cam.ac.uk (office); ejh1@cam.ac.uk (office). *Website:* www.damtp.cam.ac.uk (office); www.damtp.cam.ac.uk/user/hinch (office).

HINCHCLIFFE, Peter Robert Mossom, CVO, CMG, MA; British diplomatist (retd) and academic; b. 9 April 1937, Mahableshwar, India; s. of Peter Hinchcliffe and Jeannie Hinchcliffe; m. Archbold Harriet Siddall 1965; three d.; ed Radley Coll., Trinity Coll., Dublin; British Army 1955–57; HMOCS, Aden Protectorate 1961–67; First Sec., FCO 1969–71; mem. UK Mission to UN 1971–74; Head of Chancery, British Embassy, Kuwait 1974–76, FCO 1976–78, Deputy High Commr, Dar es Salaam 1978–81, Consul Gen., Dubai 1981–85; Head of Information Dept, FCO 1985–87, Amb. to Kuwait 1987–90; High Commr in Zambia 1990–93; Amb. to Jordan 1993–97; Chair. Hutton and Paxton Community Council 2001–07; Adjunct Fellow, Curtin Univ., Perth, WA 2001–04; Sr Reseach Fellow, Queens Univ., Belfast 1997–2002; Hon. Fellow, Univ. of Edinburgh 1997–2009. *Publications:* Time to Kill Sparrows (anthology of diplomatic verse) 1999, History of Conflicts in the Middle East Since 1945 (third edn) 2007, Without Glory in Arabia: End of British Rule in Aden 1960–67 2006, Jordan: A Hashemite Legacy (2nd edn) 2009. *Leisure interests:* golf, cricket, hill walking, writing poetry. *Address:* Old Bakery, Willis Wynd, Duns, Scottish Borders, TD11 3AD, Scotland. *Telephone:* (1361) 883315.

HINDERY, Leo Joseph, Jr, MBA; American business executive; *Managing Partner, InterMedia Partners, LLP;* b. 31 Oct. 1947, Springfield, Ill.; s. of Leo Joseph Hindery and E. Marie Whitener; m. 1st Deborah Diane Sale 1980; one d.; m. 2nd Patti Wheeler; one s.; ed Seattle Univ. and Stanford Univ. Business School; US Army 1968–70; Asst Treas., Utah Int., San Francisco 1971–80; Treas. Natomas Co., San Francisco 1980–82; Exec. Vice-Pres. Finance Jefferies and Co., LA 1982–83; Chief Finance Officer, AG Becker Paribas, New York 1983–85; Chief Officer, Planning and Finance, Chronicle Publishing Co., San Francisco 1985–88; Man. Gen. Pnr, Intermedia Partners, San Francisco 1988–97; Pres. TCI Cable Vision 1998–2000; Chair. and CEO Global Crossing Ltd March–Sept. 2000; Chair. The YES Network 2001–04; currently Man. Pnr, InterMedia Partners, LLP (investment firm); currently Exec.-in-Residence, Columbia Business School, Columbia Univ.; Chair. Economy/ Smart Globalization Initiative New America Foundation; Pres. HL Capital Inc.; fmr Chair. Nat. Cable TV Asscn; fmr Pres. and CEO Tele-Communications Inc. (now AT& T Broadband); Vice-Chair. HELP Comm. 2003–07; Sr Econ. Policy Advisor to presidential cand. John Edwards 2006–08; Econ. Advisor to Pres. Barack Obama; Co-Chair. Task Force on Jobs Creation; mem. Bd of Dirs Library of Congress Trust Fund, Minority Media & Telecommunications Council, Paley Center for Media and Teach for America, Daniels Fund, Global Business Council on HIV/AIDS, Milano School of New School Univ., Teach for America, Victory Junction Gang Camp, West Virginia Media Holdings LLC; mem. Bd of Visitors, Grad. School of Journalism, Columbia Univ.; Founder Jobs First 2012; mem. Bd Huffington Post Investigative Fund; mem. Council on Foreign Relations; Hon. mem. Bd of Dirs The Cable Center; Chapel of Four Chaplains Legion of Honor Award 2004; Hon. DHumLitt (Emerson Coll.), (Rabbinical Coll. of America); Foundation Award, Int. Radio and TV Soc. 1998, Executive Achievement Award, Nat. Asscn of Minorities in Cable 1998, President's Award 1998, Joel A. Berger Award 1998, Distinguished Vanguard Award for Leadership, Nat. Cable TV Asscn 1999, inducted into the Hall of Fame, Minority Media and Telecom Council 2002, Oates-Shrum Leadership Award, Gay and Lesbian Victory Fund 2002, Man of the Year Award, Kidney and Urology Foundation of America 2004, Chapel of Four Chaplains Legion of Honor Award 2004, Founders Award, Asia Society 2005. *Publications:* The Biggest Game of All 2003, It Takes a CEO 2005. *Leisure interest:* golf, racing. *Address:* InterMedia Advisors, LLC, 405 Lexington Avenue, 48th Floor, New York, NY 10174, USA (office). *Telephone:* (212) 503-2850 (office). *Website:* www.intermediaadvisors.com (office).

HINDLIP, 6th Baron of Hindlip in the County of Worcester and of Alsop-en-le-Dale in the County of Derby (cr. 1886); **Charles Henry Allsopp;** British business executive; b. 5 April 1940; s. of Baron Hindlip and Cecily Valentine Jane Borwick; m. Fiona Victoria Jean Atherley McGowan 1968; one s. three d.; ed Eton Coll.; served in Coldstream Guards 1959–62; joined Christie's 1962, Gen. Man. New York 1965–70, Chair. 1996–2002; mem. House of Lords 1993–99; fmr mem. Bd of Dirs Christie Manson & Wood, Deputy Chair. 1985–86, Chair. 1986–96; fmr Chair. Christie's Int; Chevalier, Légion d'honneur 1998. *Leisure interests:* painting, shooting, skiing. *Address:* 32 Maida Avenue, London, W2 1ST; Lydden House, King's Stag, Sturminster Newton, Dorset, DT10 2AU, England.

HINDS, Damian, BA; British politician; *Secretary of State for Education;* b. 27 Nov. 1969, London; m. Jacqui Morel; three c.; ed Trinity Coll., Oxford; Analyst/ Consultant, Mercer Management Consulting 1992–95; various positions in eCommerce and Brand Management with InterContinental Hotels Group in Brussels, London and Windsor 1995–2001, Commercial Vice Pres., InterContinental Hotels Group 2001–03; Strategy Dir, Greene King PLC 2005–07; mem. House of Commons (Conservative) for East Hampshire 2010–, mem. Educ. Select Cttee 2010–12; Asst Govt Whip 2014–15; Exchequer Sec. to the Treasury 2015–16; Minister of State, Dept of Work and Pensions 2016–18; Sec. of State for Educ. 2018–; Conservative. *Address:* Department for Education, Sanctuary Bldgs, Great Smith Street, London, SW1P 3BT, England (office). *Telephone:* (870) 000-2288 (office). *Website:* www.gov.uk/government/organisations/department-for-education (office); www.damianhinds.com.

HINDS, Samuel Archibald Anthony, BSc; Guyanese chemical engineer, politician and fmr head of state; b. 27 Dec. 1943, Mahaicony, E Coast, Demerara, British Guiana; m. Yvonne Zereder Burnett 1967; three c.; ed Queen's Coll., Georgetown, Univ. of New Brunswick, Canada; various positions with Bauxite Co., Linden, Guyana 1967–92; mem. Science and Industry Cttee Nat. Science Research Council 1973–76; fmr Chair. Guyanese Action for Reform and Democracy (GUARD); Prime Minister of Guyana 1992–97, 1997–99, 1999–2015, also Minister of Parl. Affairs and Energy; Pres. of Guyana March–Dec. 1997; Leader CIVIC (special political movt of business people and execs); Order of Excellence 2011. *Address:* c/o Office of the Prime Minister, Shiv Chanderpaul Drive, Bourda, Georgetown (office); CIVIC, New Garden Street, Georgetown, Guyana. *E-mail:* info@opm.gov.gy (office).

HINDUJA, Gopichand Parmanand; British (b. Indian) business executive; *Co-Chairman, Hinduja Group;* b. 29 Feb. 1940; s. of Parmanand Deepchand Hinduja and Jamuna Parmanand Hinduja; brother of Srichand Hinduja; m. Sunita Hinduja; two s. one d.; ed Jai Hind Coll., Mumbai; joined family business 1958; Pres. Hinduja Foundation and Hinduja Group of Cos 1962, now Co-Chair., Chair. Hinduja Automotive Limited, UK, Head of Hinduja Group Operations in Iran –1978; Chair. of Gurnanank Trust, Tehran; mem. Advisory Council, Hinduja Cambridge Trust 1991, Advisory Cttee Prince's Trust, Duke of Edin. Fellowship; Patron Balaji Temple, Swaminaryan Hindu Mission, London; Hon. LLD (Univ. of Westminster) 1996; Hon. DEcon (Richmond Coll.). *Leisure interests:* music, trekking, swimming. *Address:* Hinduja House, 171, Dr. Annie Besant Road, Worli, Mumbai 400 018 India (office). *Telephone:* (22) 24960707 (office). *E-mail:* gph@hindujagroup.com (office). *Website:* www.hindujagroup.com (office).

HINDUJA, Srichand Parmanand; Indian business executive; *Chairman, Hinduja Group;* b. 28 Nov. 1935, Shikarpur, Sindh (now in Pakistan); s. of Parmanand Deepchand Hinduja and Jamuna Parmanand Hinduja; brother of Gopichand Hinduja; m. Madhu Srichand Hinduja; two d.; ed Nat. Coll., Mumbai, Davar Coll. of Commerce, Mumbai; joined family business 1952, Chair. Hinduja Group of Cos 1962–, Chair. Hinduja Bank of Switzerland, Hinduja Foundations; Global Co-ordinator IndusInd 1962; Pres. IndusInd Int. Fed. 1996; mem. Advisory Council, Dharam Hinduja Indic Research Centres in Columbia, USA and UK, Advisory Council, Hinduja Cambridge Trust, Corpn of Mass. Gen. Hosp., Duke of Edinburgh's Award Fellowship; patron Centre of India–US Educ., Asia Soc.; Hon. LLD (Univ. of Westminster) 1996; Hon. DEcon (Richmond Coll.) 1997. *Publications include:* Indic Research and Contemporary Crisis 1995, Conceptualiser of Series of Paintings Theorama 1995, The Essence of Vedic Marriage For Success and Happiness 1996. *Leisure interests:* tennis, volleyball, cricket, Indian classical music. *Address:* Hinduja Group, Hinduja House, 171, Dr. Annie Besant Road, Worli, Mumbai 400 018, India (office). *Telephone:* (22) 24960707 (office). *Website:* www.hindujagroup.com (office).

HINE, Air Chief Marshal Sir Patrick Bardon, (Paddy), Kt, GCB, GBE, FRAeS, CIMgt; British air force officer (retd); b. 14 July 1932, Chandlers Ford, Hants.; s. of Eric Graham Hine and Cecile Grace Hine (née Philippe); m. Jill Adèle

Gardner 1956; three s.; ed Peter Symonds School, Winchester; fighter pilot and mem. RAF 'Black Arrows' and 'Blue Diamonds' Formation Aerobatic Teams 1957–62; Commdr No. 92 Squadron 1962–64 and 17 Squadron 1970–71, RAF Germany Harrier Force 1974–75; Dir RAF Public Relations 1975–77; Asst Chief of Air Staff for Policy 1979–83; C-in-C RAF Germany and Commdr NATO's 2nd Allied Tactical Air Force 1983–85; Vice-Chief of the Defence Staff 1985–87; Air mem. for Supply and Org., Air Force Bd 1987–88; Air Officer Commdg-in-Chief, Strike Command, C-in-C UK Air Forces 1988–91; Jt Commdr British Forces in Gulf Conflict, Aug. 1990–April 1991; with RAFVR, rank of Flying Officer 1991–97; Mil. Adviser to British Aerospace 1992–99; defence and aerospace consultant 1999–2005; mem. Royal and Ancient Golf Club St Andrews 1995–, Capt. 2010–11; Pres. Brokenhurst Manor Golf Club 2014–, RAF and Aero Golfing Socs; mem. Sr Golfers Soc., RAF Club; Air Aide de Camp to HM The Queen 1988–91; Kt Grand Cross, Order of Bath 1989, Kt Grand Cross, Most Excellent Order of British Empire 1991, King of Arms of the Order of British Empire 1997–2010; England Boy Int. Golf 1948, 1949, Hampshire Co. Championship 1949, Carris Trophy 1949, Brabazon Trophy 1949, Award of Honour, Hon. Company of Air Pilots 2017. *Television:* The Gulf War 1996. *Leisure interests:* golf, mountain walking, skiing, photography, caravanning, travel. *Address:* Royal and Ancient Golf Club, St Andrews, Fife, KY16 9JD, Scotland (office). *Telephone:* (13) 34460000 (office). *Website:* www.randa.org (office).

HINGIS, Martina; Swiss professional tennis player; b. 30 Sept. 1980, Košice, Czechoslovakia; d. of Karol Hingis and Mélanie Molitor; m. Thibault Hutin 2010; competed in first tennis tournament 1985; family moved to Switzerland aged eight; winner French Open Jr championship 1993, Wimbledon Jr Championship 1994; turned professional and won first professional tournament Filderstadt (Germany) 1996; winner Australian Open 1997 (youngest winner of a Grand Slam title), 1998, 1999 (singles and doubles), beaten finalist 2000, 2001, 2002, winner Mixed Doubles (with Leander Paes) 2015; winner US Open 1997, beaten finalist 1998, 1999; winner Wimbledon Singles 1997, Wimbledon Doubles (with Sania Mirza) 2015, Wimbledon Mixed Doubles (with Leander Paes) 2015, US Open Doubles (with Sania Mirza) 2015; Swiss Fed. Cup Team 1996–98; semifinalist US Open 2001; won 92 tournament titles, including five Grand Slam singles, 11 doubles titles and three mixed doubles titles; elected to WTA Tour Players' Council 2002; retd 2002, returned to WTA Tour 2006, came out of retirement July 2013; won Italian Open 2006; won Qatar Ladies Open, Doha 2007; retd 2007; with Lindsay Davenport, won Wimbledon Ladies' Invitation Doubles title 2011, 2012, 2013; won women's doubles with Sabine Lisicki, Sony Open, Miami 2014 (first title win since Doha 2007), won women's doubles with Sania Mirza, BNP Paribas Open, Indian Wells 2015; spent a total of 209 weeks as World No. 1; WTA Tour Most Impressive Newcomer 1995, Most Improved Player 1996, Player of the Year 1997, Associated Press Female Athlete of the Year 1997, selected as Player of the Year by WTA Tour, Int. Tennis Fed. and Tennis magazine 1997, BBC Overseas Sports Personality of the Year 1997, WTA Tour Doubles Team of the Year with Jana Novotná 1998, WTA Tour Doubles Team of the Year with Anna Kournikova 1999, WTA Tour Diamond ACES Award 2000, elected to Tour Players' Council 2002, World Comeback of the Year Award, Laureus World Sports Awards 2006, Meredith Inspiration Award, Family Circle Cup/Family Circle magazine 2007, inducted into Int. Tennis Hall of Fame 2013. *Leisure interests:* horse-riding, roller-blading, skiing, swimming, going to musicals. *Website:* www.facebook.com/MartinaHingisOfficial; www.wtatennis .com/players/player/3491.

HINGORANI, Narain G., PhD, DSc; Indian/American engineer and consultant; b. 15 June 1931, Pakistan; m. Joyce Hingorani; ed Baroda Univ., Univ. of Manchester Inst. of Science and Tech.; worked for Bombay Electricity Bd 1953–55; moved to UK to study 1955; Lecturer, Univs of Loughborough and Salford, UK 1960s; Sr Scientist, Bonneville Power Admin 1968–74; mem., later Vice-Pres. Electrical Systems Div., Electric Power Research Inst., Palo Alto, Calif. 1974–94; ind. consultant; Chair. CIGRE Study Cttee 1988–96; mem. Nat. Acad. of Eng; Life Fellow, IEEE; considered father of flexible alternating current transmission systems (FACTS) and custom power innovations; IEEE Lamme Medal, Uno Lamm Award, IEEE Power Eng Soc., IEEE Power Eng Soc. renamed its FACTS and Custom Power Awards as the Nari Hingorani FACTS Award and the Nari Hingorani Custom Power Award 2004, Benjamin Franklin Inst. Bower Award and Prize for Achievement in Science 2006, Franklin Inst. Laureate 2006. *Publications include:* HVDC Transmission (co-author) 1960, Understanding FACTS Flexible AC Transmission (co-author) 2000. *Telephone:* (650) 941-5240 (home). *E-mail:* nhingorani@aol.com.

HINSHAW, Virginia S., BS, MS, PhD; American medical researcher, academic and university administrator; *Chancellor Emeritus and Professor of Tropical Medicine, Infectious Diseases and Pharmacology, University of Hawaii at Manoa;* m. Bill Hinshaw; two s.; ed Auburn Univ.; Clinical and Research Microbiologist, Medical Coll. of Virginia 1967–68; Research Virologist, Univ. of California, Berkeley 1974; Research Assoc., Div. of Virology, St Jude Children's Research Hosp., Memphis, Tenn. 1974–83, 1984–85; one year sabbatical, Harvard Medical School 1983–84; Assoc. Prof. of Virology, Dept of Pathobiological Sciences, School of Veterinary Medicine, Univ. of Wisconsin 1985–88, Prof. 1988–92, Interim Assoc. Dean, Research and Grad. Studies 1992–93, Assoc. Vice-Chancellor 1994–95, Vice-Chancellor, Research, Dean of Grad. School 1995–2001; Provost and Exec. Vice-Chancellor, Univ. of California, Davis 2001–07, also Prof. of Virology, Dept Internal Medicine, School of Medicine 2001–07, Prof. of Virology, Dept of Pathology, Microbiology, Immunology, School of Veterinary Medicine 2001–07; Chancellor, Univ. of Hawaii at Manoa 2007–12, Chancellor Emer. and Prof. of Tropical Medicine, Infectious Diseases and Pharmacology 2012–. *Address:* Department of Tropical Medicine, Medical Microbiology and Pharmacology, John A. Burns School of Medicine, 651 Ilalo Street, BSB 402F, Honolulu, HI 96813, USA (office). *Telephone:* (808) 692-1215 (office). *E-mail:* vhinshaw@hawaii .edu (office). *Website:* blog.hawaii.edu/tropicalmedicine (office).

HINSON, David R.; American aviation industry executive; b. 2 March 1933; m. Ursula Hinson; three c.; ed Univ. of Washington, Stanford Univ.; fighter pilot, USN 1956–60, airline and eng pilot 1960–72; f. Hinson-Mennella 1973; Pres. Flightcraft, Inc. –1984; Co-founder and Dir Midway Airlines Inc. 1979–91, Chair. and CEO 1985–91; Exec. Vice-Pres. McDonnell Douglas Aircraft 1991–93; Admin., US Fed. Aviation Admin (FAA), Washington, DC 1993–96; currently Chair. Int. Aerospace Solutions (aviation consulting firm); Chair. Bd of Visitors, Air Safety Foundation, Aircraft Owners and Pilots Asscn (AOPA); mem. Bd of Dirs Nat. Air and Space Museum; mem. Nat. Aeronautic Asscn; Hon. mem. Advisory Bd, Flight Safety Foundation; Operations Award, Aviation Week and Space Technology 1997, Pathfinder Award, Museum of Flight 2005. *Leisure interests:* aviation history, collecting aviation art. *Address:* International Aerospace Solutions, 3639 East Harbor Blvd, Suite 210, Ventura, CA 93001, USA (office). *Telephone:* (805) 644-1105 (office).

HINTERHÄUSER, Markus; Austrian conductor; *Artistic Director, Wiener Festwochen and Salzburg Festival;* b. 30 March 1958, La Spezia, Italy; ed Vienna Conservatory with Elisabeth Leonskaja, Mozarteum Univ. of Salzburg with Oleg Maisenberg; has performed as pianist in orchestral concerts, as recitalist and also in chamber concerts in major concert halls including Carnegie Hall, New York, the Muiskverein and Konzerthaus, Vienna, La Scala, Milan; festival appearances including Salzburg Festival, Schubertiade in Hohenems, Lucerne Festival, Wien Modern, Festival d'Automne, Holland Festival, Berlin Festival; performed with Arditti Quartet; worked with Brigitte Fassbaender as lied accompanist; known for interpretation of Second Viennese School and 20th century works, especially works by Luigi Nono, Karlheinz Stockhausen, Morton Feldman, John Cage, Galina Ustwolskaja and György Ligeti; worked with Christoph Marthaler, Johan Simons and Klaus Michael Grüber on music theatre productions; Co-founder (with Tomas Zierhofer-Kin) Zeitfluss series as part of Salzburg Festival 1993–2001; fmr Artistic Dir Zeit-Zone Project, Vienna Festival; Concert Dir Salzburg Festival 2006–11, Interim Artistic Dir 2011, Artistic Dir 2016–; apptd Dir Wiener Festwochen (Vienna Festival). *Recordings include:* several radio and TV recordings and CDs of entire piano works of Schoenberg, Berg and Webern as well as compositions by Feldman, Nono, Scelsi, Ustvolskaya and Cage. *Address:* Wiener Festwochen, Lehárgasse 11/1/6, 1060 Vienna, Austria. *Telephone:* (1) 589-22-0. *E-mail:* festwochen@festwochen.at. *Website:* www.festwochen.at/en.

HINTON, Geoffrey E., CC, BA, PhD, FRS, FRSC; British/Canadian computer scientist and academic; *Emeritus University Professor, Department of Computer Science, University of Toronto;* b. 6 Dec. 1947, London; m. Ros Hinton (died 1994); ed Univs of Cambridge and Edinburgh, UK; Research Fellow, Cognitive Studies Program, Univ. of Sussex, UK 1976–78; Visiting Scholar, Program in Cognitive Science, Univ. of California, San Diego, USA 1978–80, Visiting Asst Prof., Psychology Dept Jan.–June 1982; Scientific Officer, MRC Applied Psychology Unit, Cambridge 1980–82; Asst Prof. then Assoc. Prof., Computer Science Dept, Carnegie-Mellon Univ., Pittsburgh, USA 1982–87; Prof., Computer Science Dept, Univ. of Toronto, Canada 1987–98, 2001–06, Univ. Prof. 2006–14, Emer. Univ. Prof. 2014–; Founding Dir Gatsby Computational Neuroscience Unit, University Coll., London 1998–2001; Chief Scientific Adviser, Vector Inst. Oct. 2016–Jan. 2017; fmr mem. Editorial Bd Neural Computation, The Journal of Machine Learning Research; mem. Editorial Bd Artificial Intelligence, Cognitive Science, Machine Learning; Fellow, Canadian Inst. for Advanced Research 1987–98, 2004–14, Asscn for the Advancement of Artificial Intelligence 1991, Cognitive Science Soc. 2003; Eng Fellow, Google, Inc. 2013–16; Hon. Foreign mem. American Acad. of Arts and Sciences 2003; Hon. DSc (Edinburgh) 2001, (Sussex) 2011, Dr hc (Sherbrooke) 2013; David Marr Memorial Lecturer, King's Coll., Cambridge 1986, Weigand Lecturer, Univ. of Toronto 1987, Sun Annual Lecturer, Univ. of Manchester (eight lectures) 1989, Fourth Annual Hebb Lecturer, Dalhousie Univ., Halifax, NS 1989, St Andrews Easter Lecturer, Univ. of St Andrews (six lectures) 1991, Benjamin Meaker Lecturer, Univ. of Bristol (five lectures) 1992, Broadbent Lecturer, London 1993, Herzberg Lecturer, Ottawa 1993, Rockwood Memorial Lecture, Univ. of California, San Diego 1995, 1998, 2010, David E. Rumelhart Prize Lecturer, Edinburgh 2001, Pinkel Lecturer, Univ. of Pennsylvania 2003, Graham Lecturer, Univ. of Toronto 2006, Ian Howard Lecturer, York Univ. 2009, Ed Posner Lecturer, NIPS-09, Vancouver 2009, 'Big Thinkers' Lecturer, Yahoo, San Jose 2010, Hans-Lukas Teuber Lecturer, MIT 2010; Sr Award, IEEE Signal Processing Soc. 1990, ITAC/NSERC Award for Academic Excellence 1992, IEEE Neural Networks Pioneer Award 1998, The David E. Rumelhart Prize 2001, IJCAI Research Excellence Award 2005, Gerhard Herzberg Canada Gold Medal 2011, Killam Prize (co-recipient), Canada Council for the Arts 2012, BBVA Foundation Frontiers of Knowledge Award 2017, Toronto Region Builder Award 2019, ACM Turing Award (co-recipient) 2019. *Publications:* Parallel Models of Associative Memory 1981 (revised second edn 1989), Proceedings of the Connectionist Models Summer School (co-ed.) 1988, Proceedings of the Connectionist Models Summer School (co-ed.) 1990, Connectionist Symbol Processing (special issue of the Journal of Artificial Intelligence issued as a book) 1991, Unsupervised Learning: Foundations of Neural Computation (co-ed.) 1999; numerous papers in professional journals. *Address:* Department of Computer Science, University of Toronto, 10 King's College Road, Toronto, ON M5S 3G4, Canada (office). *E-mail:* hinton@cs.toronto.edu (office); geoffrey.hinton@ gmail.com. *Website:* www.cs.toronto.edu/~hinton (office).

HINZPETER KIRBERG, Rodrigo; Chilean lawyer and politician; b. 27 Oct. 1965, Santiago; m. Joyce Ventura Nudman; three s.; ed Pontifical Catholic Univ. of Chile; fmr Prof. of Civil Law, Pontifical Catholic Univ. of Chile; fmr consultant and dir of several cos; served as lawyer with Simpson Thacher & Bartlett, New York, USA; fmr Partner, Bofill Mir & Alvarez Jana Hinzpeter Abogados, Santiago; campaign manager for presidential cand. Sebastián Piñera 2005–06; Minister of the Interior 2010–11, of Interior and Public Security 2011–12, of Nat. Defence 2012–14; Founding-mem. Renovación Nacional, Nat. Sec. and First Vice-Pres. 2001–04, mem. Political Comm.; mem. Chilean Bar Asscn. *Publication:* La hipoteca 1993. *Address:* c/o Ministry of National Defence, Edif. Diego Portales 22°, Villavicencio 364, Santiago, Chile (office).

HIRAI, Kazuo (Kaz), BLibArts; Japanese entertainment industry executive; *Chairman, Sony Corporation;* b. 22 Dec. 1960, Tokyo; ed Int. Christian Univ., Tokyo; hired at CBS/Sony Inc. (now Sony Music Entertainment (Japan) Inc.) 1984, involved in marketing int. music within Japan, promoted until Head of Sony Computer Entertainment (int. business affairs office), joined Sony Computer Entertainment America 1995, Vice-Pres. Corp. Exec. Group 2006–07, Pres. Sony Computer Entertainment Inc. (SCEI) 2006–07, also COO SCEI 2006–07, Pres. and Group CEO SCEI 2007–11, Corp. Exec. Officer and Exec. Vice-Pres. Sony Corpn (following reorganization of electronics and game businesses into Consumer

Products & Devices Group (CPDG) and Networked Products & Services Group (NPSG) 2009), concurrently Pres. NPSG 2009–11, Rep. Corp. Exec. Officer and Exec. Deputy Pres. Sony Corpn (following reorganization of consumer electronics, game and networked service businesses into Consumer Products & Services Group 2011) 2011–12, Rep. Corp. Exec. Officer, mem. Bd of Dirs, Pres. and CEO Sony Corpn 2012–18, also Pres. Consumer Products & Services Group and Chair. SCEI; Chair. Sony Corpn 2018–; noted by Entertainment Weekly as one of the most powerful executives in the world 2006. *Address:* Sony Corporation, 1-7-1 Konan, Minato-ku, Tokyo 108-0075, Japan (office). *Telephone:* (3) 6748-2111 (office). *Fax:* (3) 6748-2244 (office). *E-mail:* info@sony.net (office). *Website:* www.sony.net (office); www.sony.com (office).

HIRANO, Hirofumi; Japanese politician; b. 19 March 1949, Wakayama Pref.; ed Chuo Univ., Tokyo; joined Matsushita Electric Industrial Co. (now Panasonic Corpn) 1971, becoming Exec. mem. Matsushita Electric Union 1988–94; fmr Chief Sec. to Masao Nakamura (Socialist House of Reps mem.); Adviser to Japanese Electrical Electronic and Information Union; mem. House of Reps for Osaka No. 11 constituency 1996–, Sr Dir Parl. Cttee on Fundamental Nat. Policies; mem. Democratic Party of Japan (DPJ) 1998–, Chief Cabinet Sec. 2009–10; Minister of Educ., Culture, Sports, Science and Tech. Jan.–Oct. 2012; Vice-Chair. Chuo Univ. 2013, Dir Osakafuren Special Representative of School Corpn 2014; Visiting Prof., Grad. School, Takushoku Univ. *Website:* www.hhirano.jp.

HIRANO, Nobuyuki; Japanese business executive; *Representative Corporate Executive Officer, President and Group CEO, Mitsubishi UFJ Financial Group, Inc.;* joined The Mitsubishi Bank Ltd 1974, Non-Bd mem. Dir, The Bank of Tokyo-Mitsubishi Ltd (BTM) 2001–04, Exec. Officer, Mitsubishi Tokyo Financial Group, Inc. (MTFG) 2004–05, Non-Bd mem. Man. Dir BTM May–June 2005, Man. Dir BTM and Dir of MTFG June–Oct. 2005, Dir of Co. Oct. 2005–06, Man. Dir Bank of Tokyo-Mitsubishi UFJ Ltd (BTMU) 2006–08, Sr Man. Dir BTMU 2008–09, Deputy Pres. BTMU and Managing Man. of Co. 2009–10, Dir of Co. 2010–, Deputy Pres. of Co. 2010–12, Pres. BTMU and Dir of Co. 2012–13, Pres. and CEO Mitsubishi UFJ Financial Group, Inc. (MUFG) 2013–15, Dir, Rep. Corp. Exec. Officer, Pres. and Group CEO MUFG 2015–, Chair. BTMU 2016–. *Address:* Mitsubishi UFJ Financial Group, Inc., 7-1, Marunouchi 2-chome, Chiyoda-ku, Tokyo 100-8330, Japan (office). *Telephone:* (3) 3240-8111 (office). *Fax:* (3) 3240-8203 (office). *E-mail:* info@mufg.jp (office). *Website:* www.mufg.jp (office).

HIRANO, Shin-ichi, BEng, MEng, DEng; Japanese university administrator; b. 7 Aug. 1942, Aichi Pref.; ed Nagoya Univ.; Research Assoc., Research Lab. of Eng Materials, Tokyo Inst. of Tech. 1970–76, Assoc. Prof. 1976–78; Assoc. Prof., School of Eng, Nagoya Univ. 1978–83, Prof. 1983–97, Prof., Grad. School of Eng 1997–2004, Dir Research Center for Advanced Energy Conversion 1999–2002, Dir Center for Cooperative Research in Advanced Science and Tech. 2002–03, Dean Grad. School of Eng and School of Eng 2003–04, Pres. Nagoya Univ. 2004–09; apptd Pres. Nat. Inst. for Academic Degrees and Univ. Evaluation 2009; Zhiyuan Prof., Special Pres. Advisory, Shanghai Jiao Tong Univ.; Einstein Chair Prof., Chinese Acad. of Sciences 2008; fmr Adjunct Prof. of Materials Science and Eng, Pennsylvania State Univ.; mem. Man. Council Nat. Insts of Natural Sciences; mem. World Acad. of Ceramics; Pres. Int. Ceramic Fed. 1997–99; fmr Pres. Asia-Oceania Ceramic Fed.; fmr Pres. Ceramic Soc. of Japan; Trustee, Japan Univ. Accreditation Asscn; Fellow, American Ceramic Soc. 1989, Distinguished Life mem. 2006–; Dr hc (Shanghai Jiao Tong Univ.); Soc. Award, Tokai Chemical Industry Soc. 1982, Soc. Award, Powder and Powder Metallurgy Soc. of Japan 1984, Academic Award, Ceramic Soc. of Japan 1986, Academic Award, Chemical Soc. of Japan 1989, Richard M. Fulrath Award, American Ceramic Soc. 1989, Memorial Award, Ceramic Soc. of Japan 1991, Int. Prize, Japanese Fine Ceramic Asscn 2000. *Publications include:* numerous scientific papers in professional journals on inorganic materials chem.

HIRANO, Toshio, MD, PhD; Japanese medical scientist, academic and university administrator; ed Osaka Univ.; Visiting Fellow, NIH, USA 1973–76; mem. Medical Staff, Dept of Internal Medicine, Osaka Prefectural Habikino 1978–80; Assoc. Prof., Dept of Biochemistry, Inst. for Medical Immunology, School of Medicine, Kumamoto Univ. 1980–84; Assoc. Prof., Div. of Immunology, Inst. for Molecular and Cellular Biology, Osaka Univ. 1984–89, Prof., Div. of Molecular Oncology, Biomedical Research Centre, Faculty of Medicine 1989–2001, Dir Biomedical Research Centre 1997–99, Prof., Dept of Molecular Oncology (Lab. of Developmental Immunology), Grad. School of Medicine 2001–11, Prof., Lab. of Developmental Immunology, Grad. School of Frontier Biosciences 2002–11, mem. Council, Osaka Univ. 2003–04, 2007–08, Dean, Grad. School of Frontier Biosciences 2004–06, Prof., Lab. of Developmental Immunology, WPI Immunology Frontier Research Centre 2007–11, Dean, Grad. School of Medicine 2008–11, Pres. Osaka Univ. 2011–15; mem. Science Council of Japan 2011–; Exec. mem. Council for Science and Tech. Policy, Cabinet Office 2012–14; Sandoz (now Novartis) Prize for Immunology (Switzerland) 1992, Osaka Science Prize (Japan) 1997, Academic Award, Mochida Memorial Foundation (Japan) 1998, Fujihara Award 2004, Medical Award, Japan Medical Asscn 2005, The Emperor's Purple Ribbon Medal 2006, The Crafoord Prize 2009, Japan Prize 2011. *Achievements include:* discovery of the interleukin-6 (IL-6) gene 1986, clarification of the role of this gene in chronic inflammatory and auto-immune diseases. *Publications:* Signal Transducers and Activators of Transcription (STATs): Activation and Biology (co-ed.) 2003; several book chapters and more than 250 papers in peer-reviewed journals.

HIRANUMA, Takeo; Japanese politician; b. 3 Aug. 1939, Shibuya, Tokyo; s. of Hiranuma Kiichirō; three c.; ed Keio Univ.; fmr Parl. Vice-Minister of Finance; Deputy Chair. LDP Policy Research Council, Chair. LDP Nat. Org. Cttee; mem. House of Reps; Minister of Transport 1995–96; Minister of Int. Trade and Industry 2000–01, of Economy, Trade and Industry 2001–03; f. Party for Future Generations 2014, left party 2015 to rejoin LDP. *E-mail:* info@hiranuma.org. *Website:* www.hiranuma.org.

HIRAOKA, Hideo; Japanese lawyer and politician; b. 14 Jan. 1954, Iwakuni, Yamaguchi Prefecture; m.; two s.; ed Univ. of Tokyo; held various positions in Ministry of Finance 1976–88, including Section Chief Nat. Tax Agency Corp. Tax Dept, Dir-Gen. Tokai Finance Bureau, Dir-Gen. Tokyo Regional Taxation Bureau; fmr Counsellor, Cabinet Legislation Bureau; fmr First Sec., Embassy in Delhi; admitted to the bar 1998; mem. House of Reps (Democratic Party of Japan) for Yamaguchi No 2 Dist 2000–; fmr Sr Vice Minister of Internal Affairs, Sr Vice Minister for Cabinet Office 2010, Sec. of State for Internal Affairs and Communications 2010–11, Minister of Justice 2011–12. *Leisure interest:* Igo (traditional board game).

HIROKAZU, Kore-eda; Japanese film director, producer and screenwriter; b. 6 June 1952, Tokyo; ed Waseda Univ.; began career as Asst Dir on documentaries; Donostia Award, San Sebastián Int. Film Festival 2018. *Films include:* as dir: Lessons from a Calf (documentary) 1991, However ... (documentary) 1991, August without Him (documentary) 1994, Maborosi (Golden Osella for Best Dir, Venice Film Festival 1995) 1995, Without Memory (documentary) 1996, After Life (also screenwriter and ed.) (Best Film and Best Screenplay, Buenos Aires Int. Festival of Independent Cinema 1999) 1998, Distance (also screenwriter and ed.) 2001, Nobody Knows (also screenwriter and producer) (Blue Ribbon Award for Best Film and Best Dir 2004) 2004, Hana (also screenwriter) 2006, Still Walking (also screenwriter and ed.) (Best Film, Mar del Plata Int. Film Festival 2008, Asian Film Award for Best Dir 2009) 2008, Daijōbu Dearu Yō ni: Cocco Owaranai Tabi (documentary) 2008, Air Doll (also screenwriter, producer and ed.) 2009, I Wish (also screenwriter) 2011, Like Father, Like Son (also screenwriter and ed.) (Jury Prize, Cannes Film Festival 2013) 2013, Our Little Sister (also screenwriter and ed.) (Best Dir, Yokohama Film Festival 2015) 2014, After the Storm (also screenwriter and ed.) (Best Film, Films from the South 2016) 2016, The Third Murder (also screenwriter and ed.) (Japan Acad. Awards for Best Film and Best Dir 2018) 2017, Shoplifters (also screenwriter and ed.) (Palme d'Or, Cannes Film Festival) 2018.

HIROKI, Shigeyuki; Japanese diplomatist; *Ambassador to South Africa;* m. Mamiko Hiroki; two d.; ed Vanderbilt Univ., USA; AFS exchange student at a Milwaukee high school in Wis., later served as Chair. 29th Japan–America Student Conf.; joined Ministry of Foreign Affairs (MFA) 1979, held various responsibilities at Ministry and abroad, including planning Japan's security policy, developing Japan–Korea relations, managing MFA budgetary affairs and overseeing Japan's foreign policy towards Europe, overseas assignments include at Embassies in The Hague and London 1990s, Consul in New York 1990s, fmr Head of 9/11 Crisis Man. Team, MFA, Amb. to Afghanistan 2009–11, Consul-Gen. in New York 2011–13, Chief of Protocol, MFA 2013–15, Amb. to South Africa 2015–. *Leisure interests:* tennis, practising the tea ceremony in his spare time. *Address:* Embassy of Japan, 259 Baines Street, corner Frans Oerder Street, Groenkloof, Pretoria 0181 (office); Embassy of Japan, Private Bag X999, Pretoria 0001, South Africa (office). *Telephone:* (12) 4521500 (office). *Fax:* (12) 4521633 (office). *E-mail:* info@pr.mofa.go.jp (office). *Website:* www.za.emb-japan.go.jp (office).

HIRONAKA, Heisuke, PhD; Japanese mathematician and academic; b. 9 April 1931, Yamaguchi-ken; m. Wakako Hironaka; two c.; ed Kyoto Univ. and Harvard Univ., USA; mem. staff, Harvard Univ. following graduation, later Prof. of Math., currently Prof. Emer.; Dir Research Inst. for Math. Sciences, Kyoto Univ. 1983–85, Visiting Scholar 1991–92; Prof. of Math. Seoul Nat. Univ. South Korea; Pres. Yamaguchi Univ. 1996–2002, Univ. of Creation, Art, Music and Social Work; Foreign Assoc. Acad. des sciences 1981–; mem. Japan Acad.; f. Japan Asscn for Mathematical Sciences 1984; active in fund-raising for math. educ.; Order of Culture (Japan) 1975; Fields Medal, Int. Congress of Mathematicians, Nice, France 1970, Japan Acad. Award 1970. *Publications include:* Formal Functions and Formal Imbeddings (co-author) 1967, Introduction to the Theory of Infinitely Near Singular Points 1974, The Theory of the Maximal Contact (co-author) 1975, Desingularization Theorems (co-author) 1977, Geometric Singularity Theory (co-ed.) 2004, numerous articles in math. journals on complex analysis and singularity theory. *Leisure interest:* music.

HIRONO, Mazie Keiko, BA, JD; American (b. Japanese) lawyer and politician; *Senator from Hawaii;* b. 3 Nov. 1947, Fukushima Pref., Japan; d. of Hirono Matabe and Sato Laura Chie; m. Leighton Kim Oshima; one d.; ed Kaimuki High School, Univ. of Hawaii, Manoa, Georgetown Univ.; came to US 1955, naturalized 1959; Deputy Attorney Gen., State of Hawaii (Anti-Trust Div.) 1978–80; mem. Hawaii House of Reps from the 12th Dist 1981–83, from the 20th Dist 1983–85, from the 32nd Dist 1985–93, from the 22nd Dist 1993–95; with Shim, Tam, Kirimitsu & Naito (law firm) 1984–88; Lt Gov. of Hawaii 1994–2002; cand. for Office of Gov. 2002; mem. US House of Reps for the 2nd Congressional Dist of Hawaii 2007–13, mem. Cttee on Educ. and the Workforce, Cttee on Ethics, Cttee on Transportation and Infrastructure; Senator from Hawaii (first female Senator from HI, first Asian-American woman elected to the Senate, first US Senator born in Japan, first Buddhist US Senator) 2013–; Chair. Consumer Protection and Commerce Cttee 1987–92, Hawaii Policy Group, Nat. Comm. on Teaching and America's Future, Gov.'s Task Force on Science and Tech., Nuuanu YMCA, Honolulu 1982–84, Moiliili Community Center, Honolulu 1984; Deputy Chair. Democratic Nat. Cttee 1997; Co-Chair. Susan G. Komen Race for the Cure; Co-founder University Connections; Leader Pre-Plus (public–pvt. partnership providing opportunities for pre-school children); mem. US Supreme Court Bar, Hawaii Bar Asscn, Hawaii Public Television Bd, Japanese American Nat. Museum Bd, Women's Health Hawaii Advisory Bd; Democrat; Legislator of the Year 1984, Georgetown Univ. Law Center Alumni Achievement Award 2001. *Address:* United States Senate, Washington, DC 20510, USA (office). *Telephone:* (202) 224-3121 (switchboard) (office). *Website:* www.senate.gov (office).

HIROSE, Hiroshi; Japanese business executive; *President and CEO, East Nippon Expressway Company Ltd;* served as Man. Exec. Officer, Gen. Affairs Dept and Head of Investor Relations and Public Relations Dept, Sumitomo Chemical Co. Ltd, Dir and Pres. Sumitomo Chemical Co. Ltd –2011, Vice-Chair. and Chair. Internal Control Cttee 2011; Outside Dir Inabata & Co. Ltd; Pres. and CEO East Nippon Expressway Co. Ltd 2012–. *Website:* www.e-nexco.co.jp/english.

HIROSE, Naomi; Japanese energy industry executive; *President, Tokyo Electric Power Company (TEPCO), Inc.;* spent most of career in Sales, Tokyo Electric Power Co. (TEPCO), Inc., served as Chief of Kanagawa br. and its Marketing and Customer Relations Dept, later in charge of compensating victims of the accident at Fukushima No. 1 nuclear power plant that occurred in March 2011, fmr Gen. Man. Marketing & Customer Relations Dept, TEPCO, Man. Dir TEPCO 2011–12, Pres. 2012–, Pres. and Gen. Man. Man. Restructuring Div. 2012–, Chief of Nuclear Reform Special Task Force 2013–, Dir Social Communication Office 2012–, Chief of

The New Growth Task Force 2013–; Exec. Dir, Japan Nuclear Fuel Ltd. *Address:* Tokyo Electric Power Co., Inc., 1-1-3 Uchisaiwai-cho, Chiyoda-ku, Tokyo 100-8560, Japan (office). *Telephone:* (3) 4216-1111 (office). *Fax:* (3) 4216-2539 (office). *E-mail:* info@tepco.co.jp (office). *Website:* www.tepco.co.jp (office).

HIRSCH, Georges-François; French opera administrator and government official; b. 5 Oct. 1944, Paris; s. of Georges Hirsch; stage-hand, Théâtre des Capucines 1960; later stage man. Théâtre de la Culture de l'Ile de France; Dir Théâtre de Limoges 1969–74; directed various productions especially in USA 1974–79; Lyric Arts Prof. Int. Summer Acad. of Nice 1974–80; Dance Admin. Paris Opéra 1979–82; mem. directing team, RTLN 1982–83; Dir Théâtre des Champs-Elysées 1983–89; Gen. Admin. Opéra Bastille 1989–92, Opéra de Paris (Garnier Bastille) 1991–92; mem. council CSA 1993–96; Dir-Gen. Orchestre de Paris 1996–2008; Chair. Syndicat nat. des orchestres et théâtres lyriques subventionnés de droit privé 1999–2008; Vice-Chair. French Asscn of Orchestras 2000–08; Dir Music, Theatre, Dance and Entertainment, Ministry of Culture 2008–10, Dir Gen., Artistic Creation 2010–12; consultant, GFH Consultants, Paris 2013–; Officier, Légion d'honneur, Chevalier, Ordre nat. du Mérite, Commdr des Arts et Lettres. *Address:* GFH Consultants, 26 rue Vaneau, 75007 Paris, France.

HIRSCH, Judd, BS; American actor; b. 15 March 1935, Bronx, New York; s. of Joseph S. Hirsch and Sally Kitzis; m. 1st Elissa 1956 (divorced 1958); m. 2nd Bonni Sue Chalkin 1992 (divorced 2005); two s. one d.; ed City Coll. of New York; has appeared in numerous TV plays, series, films etc.; mem. Screen Actors Guild, AEA, AFTRA. *Stage appearances include:* Barefoot in the Park 1966, Knock Knock 1976 (Drama Desk Award), Scuba Duba 1967–69, King of the United States 1972, Mystery Play 1972, Hot L Baltimore 1972–73, Prodigal 1973, Chapter Two 1977–78, Talley's Folly 1979 (Obie Award), The Seagull 1983, I'm Not Rappaport 1985–86 (Tony Award), Conversations with My Father (Tony Award) 1992, A Thousand Clowns 1996, Below the Belt 1996, Death of a Salesman 1997, Art 1998, I'm Not Rappaport (revival) 2002, Sixteen Wounded 2004. *Films include:* King of the Gypsies 1978, Ordinary People 1980, Without a Trace 1983, Teachers 1984, The Goodbye People 1984, Running on Empty 1988, Independence Day 1996, Man on the Moon 1999, A Beautiful Mind 2002, Zeyda and the Hitman 2004, Brother's Shadow 2006, Polish Bar (Beverly Hills Film Festival Award for Best Actor 2011) 2010, Tower Heist 2011, This Must Be the Place 2011, The Red Robin 2013, Wild Oats 2015. *Television appearances include:* Delvecchio (series) 1976–77, Taxi (series) 1978–83 (Emmy Award 1981, 1983, Medallion Award 2007), Dear John (series) 1988–92 (Golden Globe Award 1989), George and Leo (series) 1997, Regular Joe (series) 2003, Who Killed the Federal Theatre 2003, Street Time (series) 2003, Law and Order: Criminal Intent (series) 2003, Numbers (series) 2005–10, Studio 60 on the Sunset Strip (series) 2006, Tom Goes to the Mayor (series) 2006, American Dad! (series) 2009, The Whole Truth (series) 2010, Warehouse 13 (series) 2010, Sharknado 2: The Second One (film) 2014, Forever (series) 2014, numerous appearances in TV episodes and movies. *Address:* c/o J. Wolfe Provident Financial Management, 2850 Ocean Park Blvd, Santa Monica, CA 90405, USA.

HIRSCH, Leon C.; American business executive; b. 20 July 1927, Bronx, New York; s. of Roslyn Hirsch and Isidor Hirsch; m. 2nd Turi Josefsen 1969 (divorced); two s. one d. from 1st m.; ed Bronx School of Science; Chair. and CEO US Surgical Corpn 1964–2000; Founder JHK Investments, LLC, invested in Jarvik Heart, Inc., Chair. 2001–; inventor and developer of Auto Suture surgical staplers; Chair. Advisory Bd American Soc. of Colon and Rectal Surgeons Research Foundation; mem. American Business Conf.; fmr mem. Bd of Dirs Americans for Medical Progress; Trustee Emer., Boston Univ.; Gordon Grand Fellow, Yale Univ. 1993; Hon. DSc (Univ. of Illinois) 1994, Hon. DHumLitt (Quinnipiac Coll.) 1998; Michelangelo D'Oro Children of the World Award 1994, Surgery Award Nessim Habif, Univ. of Geneva. *Leisure interests:* fishing, horseback riding, skiing, tennis. *Address:* JHK Investments, LLC, 1 Gorham Island Road, Westport, CT 06880-3212, USA.

HIRSCH, Sir Peter Bernhard, Kt, MA, PhD, FRS; British scientist and academic; *Professor Emeritus of Metallurgy, University of Oxford;* b. 16 Jan. 1925, Berlin, Germany; s. of Ismar Hirsch and Regina Meyersohn; m. Mabel A. Kellar (née Stephens) 1959; one step-s. one step-d.; ed Univ. of Cambridge; Lecturer in Physics, Univ. of Cambridge 1959–64, Reader 1964–66; Fellow, Christ's Coll., Cambridge 1960–66; Isaac Wolfson Prof. of Metallurgy, Univ. of Oxford 1966–92, Prof. Emer. 1992–, Fellow, St Edmund Hall 1966–92, Fellow Emer. 1992–; Chair. Metallurgy and Materials Cttee, SRC 1970–73; mem. Council, Inst. of Physics 1968–72, Inst. of Metals 1968–73, Electricity Supply Research Council 1969–82, Council for Scientific Policy 1970–72, Metals Soc. Council 1978–82, Council Royal Soc. 1977–79; Royal Soc. UK-Canada Lecture 1992; mem. Bd (part-time) UKAEA 1982–94, Chair. 1982–84; mem. Tech. Advisory Cttee Advent 1982–89; Dir Cogent 1985–89, Rolls-Royce Assocs 1994–98; mem. Bd of Dirs OMIA 2000–01; mem. Tech. Advisory Cttee Monsanto Electronic Materials 1985–88; Chair. Isis Innovation Ltd 1988–96, Tech. Advisory Group on Structural Integrity 1993–2002, Materials and Processes Advisory Bd Rolls-Royce PLC 1996–2000; Fellow, Imperial Coll., London 1988; Assoc. mem. Royal Acad. of Sciences, Letters and Fine Arts of Belgium 1996; Foreign Assoc. Nat. Acad. of Eng, USA 2001; Hon. Fellow, St Catharine's Coll., Cambridge 1982, Royal Microscopical Soc. 1977, Christ's Coll., Cambridge 1978, Japan Soc. of Electron Microscopy 1979, Japan Inst. of Metals 1989, Inst. of Materials 2002, Hon. mem. Spanish Electron Microscopy Soc., Materials Research Soc., India 1990, Chinese Electron Microscopy Soc. 1992, Foreign Hon. mem. American Acad. of Arts and Sciences 2005; Hon. DSc (Newcastle Univ.) 1979, (City Univ.) 1979, (Northwestern Univ.) 1982, (East Anglia Univ.) 1983, Hon. DEng (Liverpool) 1991, (Birmingham) 1993; Dr hc (York Univ.) 2013; Rosenhain Medal, Inst. of Metals 1961, Boyes' Prize, Inst. of Physics and Physical Soc. 1962, Clamer Medal, Franklin Inst. 1970, Wihuri Int. Prize 1971, Hughes Medal of the Royal Soc. 1973, Platinum Medal of the Metals Soc. 1976, Royal Medal of Royal Soc. 1977, A. A. Griffith Medal, Inst. of Materials 1979, Arthur Von Hippel Award, Materials Research Soc. 1983, Wolf Prize in Physics (jtly) 1984, Distinguished Scientist Award, Electron Microscopy Soc. of America 1986, Holweck Prize, Inst. of Physics and French Physical Soc. 1988, Gold Medal, Japan Inst. of Metals 1989, Acta Metallurgica Gold Medal 1997, Heyn Medal of German Soc. for Materials Science 2002, Lomonosov Gold Medal, Russian Acad. of Sciences 2006. *Publications include:* Electron Microscopy of Thin Crystals (co-author) 1965, The Physics of Metals, 2, Defects (ed.) 1975, Progress in Materials Science, Vol. 36 (co-ed.) 1992, Topics in Electron Diffraction and Microscopy of Materials (ed.) 1999, Fracture, Plastic Flow and Structural Integrity (co-ed.) 2000, Methods for the Assessment of the Structural Integrity of Components and Structures (co-ed.) 2003; and numerous articles in learned journals. *Leisure interest:* walking. *Address:* Department of Materials, University of Oxford, 16 Parks Road, Oxford, OX1 3PH (office); 104A Lonsdale Road, Oxford, OX2 7ET, England (home). *Telephone:* (1865) 273676 (office); (1865) 559523 (home). *Fax:* (1865) 273789 (office). *E-mail:* peter.hirsch@materials.ox.ac.uk (office). *Website:* www.materials.ox.ac.uk (office).

HIRSCH BALLIN, Ernst M. H., LLM, PhD; Dutch lawyer, judge, politician and academic; *President, Asser Institute for International and European Law, The Hague;* b. 15 Dec. 1950, Amsterdam; s. of Ernst D. Hirsch Ballin and Maria Koppe; m. Pauline van de Grift 1974; two c.; ed Univ. of Amsterdam; Researcher, Faculty of Law, Amsterdam Univ. 1974–77; Legal Expert, Ministry of Justice 1977–81; Prof. of Constitutional and Admin. Law, Tilburg Univ. 1981–89, Prof. of Int. Law 1994–2006, Prof. of Dutch and European Constitutional Law 2011–16, Distinguished Univ. Prof. 2016–; Minister of Justice and Netherlands Antillean and Aruban Affairs 1989–94, Minister of the Interior 1994, Minister of Justice 2006–10, of the Interior and Kingdom Relations 2010; mem. Parl. (Christian Democrat; Lower House) 1994–95, (Upper House) 1995–2000; Councillor of State 2000–06; Pres. Admin. Jurisdiction Div. Council of State 2003–06; Prof., Human Rights Law, Faculty of Law, Univ. of Amsterdam 2011–; Pres. Asser Inst. for Int. and European Law, The Hague 2015–; fmr Vice-Pres. Supervisory Bd, Anne Frank Stichting, Pres. 2017–; Pres. Premium Erasmianum 2017–; mem. Royal Netherlands Acad. of Science 2005–, Scientific Council for Govt Policy 2014–; mem. Advisory Council for Int. Relations 2014–; Kt, Order of the Dutch Lion, Grand Cross, Order of the Chest Crown (Luxembourg), Grand Cross, Orden del Libertador (Venezuela), Grand Cross, Bundesverdienstkreuz (Germany), Officier, Légion d'honneur, Kt Order of Holy Sepulchre of Jerusalem; G.A. van Poelje Prize 1980, NJV-prijs, Dutch Lawyers Asscn 2015. *Publications include:* Publiekrecht en beleid 1979, Rechtsstaat en beleid 1992, De Koning (2nd Edn 2014) 2013, Citizens' Rights and the Right to Be a Citizen 2015, Dynamiek in de bestuursrechtspraak 2015, Tegen de stroom 2016; 300 other publs on int. and comparative law, legal theory, constitutional and admin. law. *Leisure interests:* Brazilian music, philosophy, hiking. *Address:* Asser Institute for International and European Law, PO Box 30461, 2500 GL The Hague (office); Tilburg University, Law School, PO Box 90153, 5000 LE Tilburg, Netherlands. *Telephone:* (70) 3420300 (office). *E-mail:* ballin@asser.nl (office). *Website:* www.tilburguniversity .edu (office).

HIRSCHHORN, Thomas; Swiss artist; b. 16 May 1957, Bern; ed Schule für Gestaltung, Zurich; moved to France and joined Grapus, Parisian collective of communist graphic designers 1984; first solo exhbn at Bar Floréal, Paris 1986; influenced by Kurt Schwitters and Andy Warhol; translates leftist ideals into sculptural displays combining everyday materials such as aluminium foil, tape, board, plastic, and paper with wide array of cultural references; represented Switzerland at the Venice Biennale 2011; lives and works in Paris; Preis für Junge Schweizer Kunst 1999, Marcel Duchamp Prize 2000, Rolandpreis für Kunst im öffentlichen Raum 2003, Joseph Beuys Prize 2004, Beaux-Arts magazine Art Award 2005, Prix Aica 2006. *Major works include:* FlugplatzWelt/World Airport, Venice Biennale 1999, 2011, Battle Monument, Documenta XI, Kassel 2002, Gramsci Monument 2013, Flamme éternelle, Palais de Tokyo, Paris 2014; works on display in Kunstsammlung Nordrhein-Westfalen, Dusseldorf, S.M.A.K. (Stedelijk Museum voor Actuele Kunst), Ghent, Tate Modern, London, Walker Art Center, Minn., Art Inst. of Chicago, La Caixa, Barcelona, Centre Pompidou, Paris, Musée Précaire Albinet Aubervilliers 2004; and in major contemporary art museums in LA, Miami, New York, Philadelphia, Boston, Amsterdam, Porto, Basel, Munich, Marseille, Bordeaux, Paris, Santiago de Compostela, Zurich. *Publications:* Parkett #57 (co-author) 2000, Material: Public Works – The Bridge 2000 2001, Bataille Maschine (with M. Steinweg) 2003. *Address:* c/o Stephen Friedman Gallery, 25–28 Old Burlington Street, London, W1S 3AN, England. *Telephone:* (20) 7494-1434. *Fax:* (20) 7494-1431. *E-mail:* info@stephenfriedman .com. *Website:* www.stephenfriedman.com.

HIRST, Damien; British artist; b. 1965, Bristol; m. Maia Norman; three s.; ed Goldsmiths Coll., London; became well-known with Young British Artists movement 1990s; his work Lullaby Spring (2007) set European record for most expensive work of art by a living artist when sold at Sothebys for $19.2m.; Beautiful Inside My Head Forever auction sale broke single-artist record again, raising £111m. at Sothebys in 2008; his representation of the Union Jack formed backdrop for London 2012 Summer Olympics closing ceremony; designed BRIT Awards statue 2013; winner Turner Prize 1995; various other awards. *Television:* Channel 4 documentary about Damien Hirst and Exhbn at Gagosian Gallery, directed by Roger Pomphrey 2000. *Publication:* I Want to Spend the Rest of My Life Everywhere, One to One, Always, Forever 1997, Theories, Models, Methods, Approaches, Assumptions, Results and Findings 2000. *Leisure interests:* losing myself, pub lunches. *Address:* c/o White Cube, Hoxton Square, London, N1 6PB, England. *Telephone:* (20) 7930-5373. *E-mail:* enquiries@science.ltd.uk (office). *Website:* www.damienhirst.com/.

HIRST, Paul Heywood, MA; British academic; *Emeritus Professor of Education, University of Cambridge;* b. 10 Nov. 1927, Huddersfield; s. of Herbert Hirst and Winifred Hirst (née Michelbacher); ed Huddersfield Coll., Trinity Coll., Cambridge and Univ. of London; school teacher of math. 1948–55; Lecturer and Tutor, Dept of Educ., Univ. of Oxford 1955–59; Lecturer in Philosophy of Educ., Inst. of Educ., Univ. of London 1959–65; Prof. of Educ., King's Coll., Univ. of London 1965–71; Prof. of Educ. and Head Dept of Educ., Univ. of Cambridge 1971–88, Emer. Prof. 1988–; Fellow, Wolfson Coll., Cambridge 1971–88, Fellow Emer. 1988–; Visiting Prof., Univs of British Columbia, Alberta, Malawi, Otago, Melbourne, Sydney, Puerto Rico, London 1988–; Vice-Chair. Cttee for Educ., CNAA 1975–81, Chair. Cttee for Research 1988–92; Chair. Univs Council for Educ. of Teachers 1985–88; Pres. Philosophy of Educ. Soc. 2012; mem. Swann Cttee on Educ. of Children of Ethnic Minorities 1981–85; Hon. DEd (CNAA) 1992; Hon. DPhil (Cheltenham and Gloucester Coll. of Higher Educ.) 2000; Hon. DLitt (Huddersfield) 2002. *Publications:* The Logic of Education (with R. S. Peters) 1970, Knowledge and the

Curriculum 1974, Moral Education in a Secular Society 1974, Educational Theory and its Foundation Disciplines (ed.) 1983, Initial Teacher Training and the Role of the School (with others) 1988, Philosophy of Education: Major Themes in the Analytic Tradition (four vols) (co-ed.) 1998; numerous articles in educational and philosophical journals. *Leisure interest:* music (especially opera). *Address:* Flat 3, 6 Royal Crescent, Brighton, BN2 1AL, England (home). *Telephone:* (1273) 684118 (home).

HISLOP, Ian David, BA (Hons); British editor, writer and broadcaster; *Editor, Private Eye magazine;* b. 13 July 1960; s. of David Atholl Hislop and Helen Hislop; m. Victoria Hamson 1988; one s. one d.; ed Ardingly Coll. and Magdalen Coll., Oxford; joined Private Eye (satirical magazine) 1981, Deputy Ed. 1985–86, Ed. 1986–; columnist, The Listener magazine 1985–89, The Sunday Telegraph 1996–2003; TV critic, The Spectator 1994–96; Violet Vaughan Morgan Scholarship, BAFTA Award for Have I Got News for You 1991, Editors' Editor, British Soc. of Magazine Eds 1991, Magazine of the Year, What the Papers Say 1991, Editor of the Year, British Soc. of Magazine Eds 1998, Award for Political Satire, Channel 4 Political Awards 2004, Award for Political Comedy, Channel 4 Political Awards 2006. *Radio includes:* The News Quiz (BBC Radio 4) 1985–90, Fourth Column 1992–96, Lent Talk 1994, Gush (scriptwriter, with Nick Newman) 1994, Words on Words 1999, The Hislop Vote (BBC Radio 2) 2000, A Revolution in 5 Acts (BBC Radio 4) 2001, The Real Patron Saints (BBC Radio 4) 2002, The Choir Invisible 2003, A Brief History of Tax (BBC Radio 4) 2003, Blue Birds over the White Cliffs of Dover (BBC Radio 4) 2004, Are We Being Offensive Enough? (BBC Radio 4) 2004, Looking for Middle England (BBC Radio 4) 2006. *TV scriptwriting includes:* Spitting Image (with Nick Newman; ITV) 1984–89, The Stone Age (with Nick Newman) 1989, Briefcase Encounter (with Nick Newman) 1990, Harry Enfield's Television Programme (with Nick Newman) 1990–92, Harry Enfield and Chums (with Nick Newman) 1994–98, Mangez Merveillac (with Nick Newman) 1994, Dead on Time (with Nick Newman) 1995, Gobble (with Nick Newman; BBC 1) 1996, Sermon from St Albions (ITV Granada) 1998, Songs and Praise from St Albions (with Nick Newman; ITV Granada) 1999, Confessions of a Murderer (with Nick Newman) 1999, My Dad's the Prime Minister (with Nick Newman; BBC) 2003, 2004. *TV performer includes:* Have I Got News for You (BBC 2) 1990–2000, (BBC 1) 2000–. *TV presenter includes:* Canterbury Tales (Channel 4) 1996, School Rules (Channel 4) 1997, Pennies from Bevan (Channel 4) 1998, Great Railway Journeys East to West (BBC) 1999, Who Do You Think You Are? (BBC 2) 2004, Not Forgotten (Channel 4) 2005, Not Forgotten: Shot at Dawn (Channel 4) 2007, Scouting for Boys (BBC 4) 2007, Ian Hislop Goes Off the Rails (BBC 4) 2008, Changing of the Bard (BBC 4) 2009, Age of the Do-Gooders (BBC 2) 2010, When Bankers Were Good (BBC 2) 2011, Stiff Upper Lip – An Emotional History of Britain (BBC 2) 2012, Olden Days (BBC 2) 2014. *Publications include:* various Private Eye collections 1985–, contribs to newspapers and magazines on books, current affairs, arts and entertainment. *Address:* Private Eye, 6 Carlisle Street, London, W1D 3BN, England (office). *Telephone:* (20) 7437-4017 (office). *Website:* www.private-eye.co.uk (office).

HITAM, Tun Musa, BA, MA; Malaysian politician (retd) and international organization official; *Chairman, World Islamic Economic Forum Foundation;* b. 18 April 1934, Johor; m. Toh Puan Zulaikha Sheardin; one s.; ed English Coll., Johor Baharu Univ. of Malaya and Univ. of Sussex, UK; held a resident Fellowship at Harvard Univ., USA; Assoc. Sec. Int. Student Conf. Secr. (COSEC), Leiden 1957–59; civil servant 1959–64; Political Sec. to Minister of Transport 1964; mem. Parl. 1968–90; Asst Minister to Deputy Prime Minister 1969; studied in UK 1970, subsequently lectured at Univ. of Malaya; Chair. Fed. Land Devt Authority 1971; Deputy Minister of Trade and Industry 1972–74; Minister of Primary Industries 1974–78, of Educ. 1978–81; Deputy Prime Minister and Minister of Home Affairs 1981–86; Deputy Pres. UMNO 1981–86; Special Envoy to UN 1990–91; Malaysia's Chief Rep. to UN Comm. on Human Rights 1993–98; Special Envoy of the Prime Minister to Commonwealth Ministerial Action Group 1995–; Chair. World Islamic Econ. Forum Foundation; Chair. Suhakam (Malaysian Human Rights Comm.) 1999–2002; Chair. Lion Industries Corpn Berhad, UMLand Bhd, Sime Darby Berhad, Synergy Drive Berhad 2007–; mem. Int. Advisory Council, Brookings Doha Centre; Seri Setia Mahkota 2006. *Publication:* Frankly Speaking 2016. *Address:* Office of the Chairman, World Islamic Economic Forum Foundation, A-9-1, Level 9, Hampshire Place Office, 157 Hampshire, 1 Jalan Mayang Sari, 50450 Kuala Lumpur, Malaysia (office). *Telephone:* (3) 2163-5500 (office). *Fax:* (3) 2163-5504 (office). *E-mail:* enquiry@wief.org (office). *Website:* wief.org (office).

HITCHCOCK, Karen R., BS, PhD; American biologist, academic and university administrator; ed St Lawrence Univ., Univ. of Rochester; fmr Postdoctoral Fellow, Webb-Waring Inst. for Medical Research, Univ. of Colo Medical Centre; fmr George A. Bates Prof. of Histology and Chair Dept of Anatomy and Cellular Biology, Tufts Univ.; Assoc. Dean for Basic Sciences, Research and Grad. Studies, School of Medicine, Tex. Tech Health Sciences Center 1985–87; fmr Vice-Chancellor for Research, Dean of Grad. Coll., Prof. of Anatomy and Cell Biology, of Biological Sciences, Univ. of Ill. at Chicago; Vice-Pres. of Academic Affairs, Univ. of Albany, State Univ. of NY 1991–95, Pres. 1996–2004; Prin. and Vice-Chancellor Queen's Univ., Kingston, Ont., Canada 2004–08; Special Advisor, Park Strategies, LLC 2010–; Nat. Science Foundation Professorship for Women in Science and Eng 1983–84; fmr Pres. American Asscn of Anatomists; fmr mem. Nat. Bd of Medical Examiners; Dr hc (Albany Medical Coll., St Lawrence Univ.); Marketer of Excellence Award, New York Capital Region Chapter, American Marketing Asscn 2002, Capital Region Business Hall of Fame 2004, Woman in the Media Award, Women's Press Club of New York State 2004. *Publications:* numerous works on cell and developmental biology. *Address:* Park Strategies LLC, 101 Park Avenue, Suite 2506, New York, NY 10178, USA (office). *Telephone:* (212) 883-5608 (office). *Website:* www.parkstrategies.com (office).

HITCHIN, Nigel, BA (Hons), DPhil, FRS; British mathematician and academic; *Emeritus Savilian Professor of Geometry, University of Oxford;* b. 2 Aug. 1946, Holbrook, Derbyshire; s. of Eric Hitchin and Bessie Hitchin (née Blood); m. Nedda Hitchin 1973; ed Ecclesbourne School, Duffield, Derbyshire, Jesus Coll., Oxford, Wolfson Coll., Oxford; Research Asst, Inst. for Advanced Study, Princeton, NJ, USA 1971–73; Instructor, Courant Inst., New York Univ., USA 1973–74; SRC Research Asst, Univ. of Oxford and Jr Research Fellow, Wolfson Coll. 1974–77, SRC Advanced Research Fellow, Univ. of Oxford and Research Fellow, Wolfson Coll. 1977–79, Fellow and Tutor in Math. and CUF Lecturer, St Catherine's Coll., Oxford 1979–90, Savilian Prof. of Geometry, Univ. of Oxford and Professorial Fellow, New Coll. 1997–2016, now Emer. Prof.; Prof. of Math., Univ. of Warwick 1990–94; Rouse Ball Prof. of Math., Univ. of Cambridge, Professorial Fellow, Gonville and Caius Coll. 1994–97; visiting positions, Institut des Hautes Etudes Scientifiques, Bures-sur-Yvette 1975, 1979, 1987, 1990, 1994, 1997, Ecole Normale Superieure, Paris 1979, SFB 40, Univ. of Bonn 1979, Inst. for Advanced Study, Princeton 1982, State Univ. of NY, Stony Brook 1983–84, Ecole Polytechnique, Palaiseau 1988, Catedra BBV, Universidad Autónoma, Madrid 2001, Simons Center for Geometry and Physics, Stony Brook 2011; mem. Editorial Bd, Annals of Global Analysis and Geometry, Journal of Differential Geometry, International Mathematics Research Notices; Pres. London Math. Soc. 1994–96; Chair. RAE Assessment Panel, Pure Math. 1999–2001, Scientific Steering Cttee, Isaac Newton Inst. 1999–2001, RAE 2008 Main Panel F 2005–08; mem. Scientific Cttee, Max Planck Inst., Bonn 2000–16, Council of the Royal Soc. 2002–04, Program Cttee, Int. Congress of Math. 2006 2004–06; mem. Scientific Advisory Bd, Erwin Schrödinger Inst., Vienna 2005–12, Nominating Cttee, Int. Math. Union 2008–10, Steering Cttee, String-Math Biennial Conf. Series, Univ. of Pennsylvania 2010–; Trustee, Simons Inst. for Geometry and Physics, Stony Brook 2008–16, Nigel Hitchin Laoboratory, ICMAT Madrid 2011–; mem. Academia Europea (mem. Math. Cttee 2008–), American Math. Soc., European Math. Soc., London Math. Soc.; Hon. Fellow, Jesus Coll., Oxford 1998, Gonville and Caius Coll., Cambridge 2008, St Catherines Coll., Oxford 2014; Hon. DSc (Bath) 2003, (Warwick) 2014; Jr Math. Prize, Univ. of Oxford 1968, Jr Whitehead Prize, London Math. Soc. 1981, Schlumberger Lecturer, Rice Univ. 1983, Phillips Lecturer, Haverford Coll. 1989, Sr Berwick Prize, London Math. Soc. 1990, Clifford Lecturer, Tulane Univ. 1992, Marston Morse Memorial Lecturer, Inst. for Advanced Study, Princeton 1993, Coble Lecturer, Univ. of Illinois, Urbana 1995, Namboodiri Lecturer, Univ. of Chicago 1995, D'Atri Lecturer, Rutgers Univ. 1998, A.T. Brauer Lecturer, Univ. of North Carolina 1999, Sylvester Medal, Royal Soc. 2000, Bergman Lecturer, Stanford Univ. 2000, Simons Lecturer, Stony Brook 2001, Polya Prize, London Math. Soc. 2002, Andrejewski Lecturer, Göttingen 2002, Ritt Lecturer, Columbia Univ. 2003, Coxeter Lecturer, Fields Inst., Toronto 2004, Simons Lecturer, MIT 2005, Plücker Lecturer, Bonn 2006, Chern Lecturer, Berkeley 2013, Santalo Lecturer, Universidad Complutense de Madrid 2013, Rademacher Lecturer, Univ. of Pennsylvania 2014, Chen-Jung Hsu Lecturer, Academia Sinica, Taipei 2014, S.S. Chern Distinguished Lecturer, Tsinghua Univ., Beijing 2014, Shaw Prize in Math. 2016. *Publications:* numerous papers in professional journals on differential and algebraic geometry and their relationship to the equations of mathematical physics. *Address:* Mathematical Institute, Andrew Wiles Building, University of Oxford, Radcliffe Observatory Quarter, Woodstock Road, Oxford, OX2 6GG, England (office). *Telephone:* (1865) 273515 (office). *Fax:* (1865) 273583 (office). *E-mail:* hitchin@maths.ox.ac.uk (office). *Website:* www.maths.ox.ac.uk (office).

HITE, Shere D., MA, PhD; German cultural historian, writer and researcher; b. 2 Nov. 1942, St Joseph, Mo.; d. of Paul Gregory and Shirley Hurt Gregory; m. Friedrich Höericke 1985 (divorced 1999); ed Univ. of Florida, Columbia Univ., Nihon Univ., Japan; Dir feminist sexuality project NOW, New York 1972–78; Dir Hite Research Int., New York 1978–; Researcher, The Hite Reports, 1976, 1981, 1987, 1996, 2006; fmr instructor in female sexuality, New York Univ.; lecturer Harvard Univ., McGill Univ., Columbia Univ., also numerous women's groups, int. lecturer 1977–89, currently Visiting Prof. of Gender and Culture, Nihon Univ., Japan; renounced American citizenship 1995; mem. Advisory Bd Foundation of Gender and Genital Medicine, Johns Hopkins Univ.; Consultant Ed. Journal of Sex Education and Therapy, Journal of Sexuality and Disability; mem. NOW, American Historical Asscn, American Sociological Asscn, AAAS, Acad. of Political Science, Women's History Asscn, Soc. for Scientific Study of Sex, Women's Health Network; Prof., Maimonides Univ. 2003; f. Nike Prize for Women's Non-Fiction Writing, Frankfurt 1997; Hon. Prof. Chongqing Medical Univ., China 2004; Award for Distinguished Contribs, American Asscn of Sex Educators, Counsellors and Therapists 1988. *Publications:* Sexual Honesty: By Women For Women 1974, The Hite Report: A Nationwide Study of Female Sexuality 1976, The Hite Report on Male Sexuality 1981, Hite Report on Women and Love: A Cultural Revolution in Progress 1987, Good Guys, Bad Guys (with Kate Colleran) 1989, Women as Revolutionary Agents of Change: The Hite Reports and Beyond 1993, The Hite Report on the Family: Growing Up Under Patriarchy 1994, The Divine Comedy of Ariadne and Jupiter 1994, The Hite Report on Hite: A Sexual and Political Autobiography 1996, How Women See Other Women 1998, Sex and Business 2000, Shere Hite Reader 2004, Oedipus Revisited: Sexual Behaviour in the Human Male Today 2005, Shere Hite Reader: Sex, Globalisation and Private Life 2006. *Leisure interests:* answering e-mails, writing weekly columns for int. newspapers. *Website:* www.hiteresearchfoundation.org.

HIYALI, Erfan al-; Iraqi politician and fmr army officer; *Minister of Defence;* b. 8 Oct. 1956, Haditha, Anbar; m.; seven c.; ed Iraqi Mil. Coll.; served in Iraqi army during presidency of Saddam Hussein until discharged for attempting to overthrow Ba'athist regime; went into exile; returned to Iraq and served in Golden Division (1st Brigade counter terrorism force) under command of Prime Minister Nuri al-Maliki; Minister of Defence 2017–. *Address:* Ministry of Defence, Baghdad, Iraq (office). *Telephone:* (1) 548-5228 (office). *E-mail:* shakawa@mod.mil.iq (office). *Website:* www.mod.mil.iq (office).

HJELM-WALLÉN, Lena, MA; Swedish politician; b. 14 Jan. 1943, Sala; d. of Gustaf Hjelm and Elly Hjelm; m. Ingvar Wallén 1965; one d.; ed Uppsala Univ.; teacher in Sala 1966–69; active in Social Democratic Youth League; mem. Parl. 1969–2002; elected to 2nd Chamber of Parl. 1968; mem. Exec. Cttee Västmanland br. of Socialdemokratiska Arbetarepartiet (Social Democratic Labour Party—SDLP) 1968, mem. SDLP Parl. Exec. 1976–82, SDLP Spokeswoman on Schools, mem. Bd SDLP 1978–87, SDLP Spokeswoman on Educ. 1991–94; Minister without Portfolio, with responsibility for schools 1974–76; Minister of Educ. and Cultural Affairs 1982–85, of Int. Devt Co-operation 1985–91, of Foreign Affairs 1994–98; Deputy Prime Minister of Sweden 1998–2002; Govt Rep. to EU Convention on Future of Europe; Chair. European Forum for Democracy and Solidarity, Olof Palme International Center; fmr Chair. Int. Inst. for Democracy and Electoral Assistance (IDEA); Trustee Raoul Wallenberg Inst. 2003–, International Crisis Group. *Leisure interests:* nature, books, gardening, family. *Address:* c/o International IDEA, Strömsborg, 103 34 Stockholm, Sweden (office).

HJÖRNE, Peter Lars; Swedish newspaper editor, publisher and media executive; b. 7 Sept. 1952, Gothenburg; s. of Lars Hjörne and Anne Gyllenhammar; m. 2nd Karin Linnea Tufvesson Hjörne 1995; five d.; ed Göteborgs Högre Samskola and Univ. of Gothenburg; Man. Trainee John Deere Co., USA 1978–79; Exec. Asst Göteborgs-Posten 1979–82, Deputy Man. Dir 1983–85, Man. Dir 1985–93, Owner, Publr and Ed.-in-Chief 1993; prin. owner, Skärleja AB, Stampen Media Group. *Leisure interests:* sailing, literature, music, art. *Address:* Stampen Media Group, Polhemsplatsen 5, 405 02 Gothenburg, Sweden (office). *Telephone:* 31-62-40-00 (office). *Fax:* 31-15-76-92 (office). *E-mail:* peter.hjorne@gp.se (office). *Website:* www.stampen.com (office).

HLA, Maj.-Gen. Tun; Myanma army officer (retd) and politician; b. 11 July 1951, Yangon; s. of U Tin Ngwe and Daw Khin Kyi; m. Daw Khin Than Win; two c.; ed Defence Services Acad., Pyin-Oo-Lwin; fmr Deputy Dir-Gen. Myanmar Police Force; attained rank of Maj.-Gen. in Myanmar Army, retd 2010; Minister of Finance and Revenue 2003–11, mem. of Pres.'s Office 2012–; General Service Medal, People's War Medal, State Peace and Tranquility Medal, Maing Yan/Me Tha Waw Battle Star, Distinguished Service Medal, Service Medal. *Leisure interests:* golf, painting. *Address:* No. 28, Pan Wah Street, Kamayut Tsp., Yangon, Myanmar (home).

HLAWITSCHKA, Eduard, Dr Habil.; German academic; *Professor, University of Munich;* b. 8 Nov. 1928, Dubkowitz; s. of Ernst Hlawitschka and Emilie Tschwatschal; m. Eva-Marie Schuldt 1958; one s. one d.; ed Univs of Rostock, Leipzig, Freiburg and Saarbrücken; Prof., Univ. of Düsseldorf 1969, Univ. of Munich 1975–; Pres. Sudetendeutsche Akad. der Wissenschaften und Künste 1991–94; Sudetendeutscher Kulturpreis für Wissenschaft 1987, Prix de Liechtenstein, Conf. Int. de Généalogie et d'Héraldique 1991. *Publications:* Franken, Alemannen, Bayern und Burgunder in Oberitalien 1960, Studien zur Äbtissinnenreihe von Remiremont 1963, Lotharingien und das Reich an der Schwelle der deutschen Geschichte 1968, Die Anfänge des Hauses Habsburg-Lothringen 1969, Libri memoriales I 1970, Vom Frankenreich zur Formierung der europäischen Staaten- und Völkergemeinschaft 840–1046 (1986), Untersuchungen zu den Thronwechseln der ersten Hälfte des 11. Jahrhunderts und zur Adelsgeschichte Süddeutschlands 1987, Stirps Regia 1988, Dubkowitz im Böhmischen Mittelgebirge 1997 (3rd edn 2009), Andechser Anfänge 2000, Konradiner-Genealogie, unstatthafte Verwandtenehen und spätottonisch-frühsalische Thronbesetzungspraxis 2003, Die Ahnen der hochmittelalterlichen deutschen Könige, Kaiser und ihrer Gemahlinnen Bd I (Vols 1 & 2) 2006, Bd II 2009, Bd III 2013. *Address:* Panoramastrasse 25, 82211 Herrsching/Ammersee, Germany. *Telephone:* (70) 81524991.

HO, Ching, BEng, MSc; Singaporean business executive; *Executive Director and CEO, Temasek Holdings (Private) Ltd;* b. 1953, d.-in-law of Lee Kuan Yew (fmr Prime Minister of Singapore); m. Brig.-Gen. (retd) Lee Hsien Loong (Prime Minister of Singapore) 1985; four c.; ed Nat. Univ. of Singapore, Stanford Univ., USA; began career as engineer at Ministry of Defence with System Integration Man. Team –1986; Pres. and CEO Singapore Technologies (state defence contractor) –2002; Exec. Dir and CEO Temasek Holdings (has stakes in more than 40 cos, including Singapore Airlines, SingTel, DBS Bank, SMRT Corpn, Neptune Orient Lines, Keppel Corpn, SembCorp Industries, Singapore Technologies, PSA Corpn, Singapore Power) 2002–; Hon. Fellow, Inst. of Engineers, Singapore; Distinguished Engineering Alumnus Award, Nat. Univ. of Singapore 1995; Public Admin Silver Medal 1985, Public Service Star 1996, Medal of Commendation (Gold) Award for her support of the work of unions and for safeguarding workers' interests in Singapore 2009. *Address:* Temasek Holdings (Private) Ltd, 60B Orchard Road, #06–18, Tower 2, The Atrium, Singapore 238891 (office). *Telephone:* (65) 6828-6828 (office). *Fax:* (65) 6821-1188 (office). *E-mail:* enquiry@temasek.com.sg (office). *Website:* www.temasek.com.sg (office).

HO, Daisy Chiu Fung, (Daisy Ho), MBA; Hong Kong business executive; *Chairman and Executive Director, SJM Holdings Limited;* d. of Stanley Ho; ed Univs of Toronto and Southern California; joined Shun Tak Group 1994, Exec. Dir 1994, Deputy Man. Dir and Chief Financial Officer 1999–; Dir MGM Grand Paradise Ltd –2010; Chair. Univ. of Toronto (Hong Kong) Foundation 2007–, also Chair. Scholarship Cttee; Chair. Hong Kong Ballet 2013– (mem. Bd 2008); Chair. and Exec. Dir SJM Holdings Ltd 2018– (mem. Bd of Dirs 2017–); mem. Gov.'s Council, Canadian Chamber of Commerce in Hong Kong; mem. Dean's Advisory Bd Rotman School of Man.; mem., Hong Kong Inst. of Real Estate Administrators, Macao Chamber of Commerce; mem. Bd of Dirs Shun Tak Shipping Co. Ltd, Innowell Investments Ltd. *Address:* SJM Holding Limited, Suites 3001–3006, 30th Floor, One International Finance Centre, 1 Harbour View Street, Central, Hong Kong Special Administrative Region, People's Republic of China (office). *Telephone:* 39608000 (office). *Fax:* 39608111 (office). *E-mail:* pr@sjmholdings.com (office). *Website:* www.sjmholdings.com (office).

HO, Edmund H. W. (Hau Wah), BA; Chinese business executive and politician; b. 13 March 1955; s. of Ho Yin and Chan Keng; m.; one s. one d.; ed York Univ., Canada; chartered accountant and certified auditor 1981–; worked for accounting firm in Toronto, Ont. 1981–82; Gen. Man. Tai Fung Bank 1983, CEO 1999; mem. CPPCC 1986–; elected Deputy to NPC 1988, elected to 8th and 9th Standing Cttees; mem. Legis. Ass. of Macao 1988–, Vice-Pres. 1988–99; Vice-Pres. Macao Chamber of Commerce; Chair. Macao Asscn of Banks 1985–; Chief Exec. Macao Special Admin. Region (MSAR) May 1999–2009; Vice-Chair. 11th CPPCC 2010–13, 12th CPPCC 2013–18, 13th CPPCC 2018–; Vice-Chair. All-China Fed. of Industry and Commerce, Econ. Council of the Macao Govt, Kiang Wu Hosp. Bd of Charity, Tung Sin Tong Charitable Inst.; Vice-Pres. Drafting Cttee of the Basic Law of the MSAR 1988, Consultative Cttee of the Basic Law of the MSAR 1989, Preparatory Cttee of the MSAR 1998; Convenor of Land Fund Investment Comm. of the MSAR; Chair. Bd of Dirs Univ. of Macao; Vice-Chair. Bd of Dirs Jinan Univ., Guangzhou; Pres. Exec. Cttee Macao Olympic Cttee; Pres. Macao Golf Asscn; Founding mem. Macau Management Asscn. *Website:* www.cppcc.gov.cn.

HO, Pansy, BA; Hong Kong business executive; *Managing Director, Shun Tak Holdings;* b. 1962; d. of Dr Stanley Ho; ed Univ. of Santa Clara, USA; fmrly with high soc. events promotion co.; joined Shun Tak Group (cr. by father Stanley Ho in 1972) 1995, Exec. Dir 1995–99, Man. Dir Shun Tak Holdings (oversaw establishment of Macau Tower Convention and Entertainment Centre 2001) 1999–, also CEO Shun Tak-China Travel Shipping Investments Ltd (oversaw merger between shipping operations of Shun Tak and China Travel Services 1999) 1999–; CEO and Dir Melco Int. Devt Ltd; Dir Air Macau Corpn, Asia TV Ltd, Sociedade de Turismo e Diversões de Macau; entered into jt venture with MGM MIRAGE of Las Vegas, Nev. to build and operate MGM Grand Macau hotel and casino resorts 2005–; mem. Cttee CPPCC of Guangdong Prov.; Founding Hon. Adviser and Bd Dir Univ. of Hong Kong Foundation for Educational Devt and Research; mem. Advisory Council The Better Hong Kong Foundation. *Address:* Shun Tak Holdings Ltd, Penthouse 39/F, West Tower, Shun Tak Centre, 200 Connaught Road Central, Hong Kong Special Administrative Region, People's Republic of China (office). *Telephone:* (852) 2859-3111 (office). *Fax:* (852) 2857-7181 (office). *E-mail:* enquiry@shuntakgroup.com (office). *Website:* www.shuntakgroup.com (office).

HO, Stanley Hung Sun, OBE; Chinese (Hong Kong) business executive; *Chairman Emeritus, Sociedade de Jogos de Macao, SA;* b. 25 Nov. 1921, Hong Kong; m.; 17 c.; ed Univ. of Hong Kong; Group Exec. Chair. Shun Tak Holdings Ltd (operator of world's largest jetfoil fleet) –2017; Founder and Man. Dir Sociedade de Turismo e Diversões de Macao, (SARL—tourism and entertainment, banking, property, airport and airline); Man. Dir Sociedade de Jogos de Macao, SA 2001–10, Chair. and Exec. Dir 2006–18, Chair. Emer. 2018–; Pres. Real Estate Developers' Asscn 1984–; Chair. Univ. of Hong Kong Foundation for Educational Devt and Research 1995–; mem. Court of Univ. of Hong Kong 1982–, Council 1984–; Vice-Patron Community Chest 1986–; Vice-Chair. Basic Law Drafting Cttee, Macao Special Admin. Region (MSAR) 1988–93, Vice-Chair. Preparatory Cttee, MSAR 1988–99; mem. Selection Cttee for First Govt of Hong Kong Special Admin. Region 1996–97; mem. Standing Cttee 9th CPPCC Nat. Cttee 1998–2003; Co-Chair. Int. Cttee Franklin Delano Roosevelt Memorial Comm. 1994–97; mem. Econ. Council of Macao SAR 2000–; Hon. Citizen of Beijing 2001; Comendador da Ordem de Benemerência (Portugal) 1970; Comendador da Ordem de Infante Dom Henrique (Portugal) 1981; CStJ 1983; Chevalier, Légion d'honneur 1983, Grande-Oficial da Ordem do Infante Dom Henrique (Portugal) 1985, Order of the Sacred Treasure (Japan) 1987, Equitem Commendatorem Ordinis Sancti Gregorii Magni 1989, Darjah Dato Seri Paduka Mahkota Perak (Malaysia) 1990, Grã-Cruz, Ordem do Mérito (Portugal) 1990, Medalha Naval de Vasco da Gama (Portugal) 1991, Cruz de Plata de la Medalla de la Solidaridad (Spain) 1993, Grã-Cruz, Ordem do Infante Dom Henrique (Portugal) 1995, Hon. Order of the Crown of Terengganu Darjah Seri' Paduka Mahkota Terengganu (Malaysia) 1997, Nuno Gonçalo Vieira Matias (Portugal) 1999; Hon. DScS (Univ. of Macao) 1984, (Univ. of Hong Kong) 1987; Global Award for Outstanding Contrib. for the Devt of Int. Trade and Relations, Priyadashni Acad. (India) 2000, Gold Medal of Merit in Tourism (Portugal) 2001. *Leisure interests:* ballroom dancing, swimming, playing tennis. *Address:* Suites 3001–06, 30th Floor, One Int. Finance Centre, 1 Harbour View Street, Central, Hong Kong Special Administrative Region, People's Republic of China (office). *Telephone:* 39608000 (office). *Fax:* 39608111 (office). *E-mail:* pr@sjmholdings.com (office). *Website:* www.sjmholdings.com (office).

HO LAU YUNG, Lawrence, BA; Canadian (b. Hong Kong Chinese) business executive; *Chairman and CEO, Melco International Development Ltd;* b. 1977; s. of Stanley Ho; m. Sharen Lo; ed Univ. of Toronto; fmrly worked for Jardine Fleming, Citibank and iAsia (online stock trader); bought Melco (family-held firm) 2001, Chief Man. Dir Melco International Development Ltd 2001–06, Chair. and CEO 2006–, also Co-Chair. and CEO Melco PBL Entertainment (Macao) Ltd; mem. Nat. Cttee CPPCC; Chair. Macao Int. Volunteers Asscn, Bd of Govs Canadian Chamber of Commerce in Hong Kong, The Chamber of Hong Kong Listed Cos; mem. Bd of Dirs, mem. Exec. Cttee, Vice-Patron, The Community Chest of Hong Kong; mem. Science and Tech. Council of Macao Special Admin. Region Govt; mem. All China Youth Fed., Macao Basic Law Promotional Asscn; Hon. Lifetime Dir Chinese Gen. Chamber of Commerce of Hong Kong, Hon. Patron Macao Canadian Chamber of Commerce, Hon. Pres. Asscn of Property Agents and Real Estate Developers of Macao; Dr hc (Edinburgh Napier Univ., Scotland) 2009; named Best CEO, Institutional Investor 2005, Leader of Tomorrow, Hong Kong Tatler 2005, Dir of the Year, Hong Kong Inst of Dirs 2005, Fifth China Enterprise Award for Creative Businessmen. *Address:* Melco International Development Limited, 38th Floor, The Centrium, 60 Wyndham Street, Central, Hong Kong Special Administrative Region, People's Republic of China (office). *Telephone:* 31513777 (office). *E-mail:* info@melco-group.com (office). *Website:* www.melco-group.com (office).

HOAGLAND, Edward, AB; American author; b. 21 Dec. 1932, New York; s. of Warren Eugene Hoagland and Helen Kelley Morley; m. 1st Amy J. Ferrara 1960 (divorced 1964); m. 2nd Marion Magid 1968 (died 1993); one d.; ed Harvard Univ.; mem. Faculty, New School for Social Research, New York 1963–64, Rutgers Univ. 1966, Sarah Lawrence Coll. 1967, 1971, CUNY 1967, 1968, Univ. of Iowa 1978, 1982, Columbia Univ. 1980, 1981, Brown Univ. 1988, Bennington Coll. 1987–2005, Univ. of California, Davis 1990, 1992, Beloit Coll. 1995; Gen. Ed. Penguin Nature Library 1985–2004; Houghton Mifflin Literary Fellow 1954; American Acad. of Arts and Letters Travelling Fellow 1964; Guggenheim Fellow 1964, 1975; mem. American Acad. of Arts and Letters, American Acad. of Arts and Sciences; Longview Foundation Award 1961, O. Henry Award 1971, Brandeis Univ. Citation in Literature 1972, New York State Council on Arts Award 1972, American Acad. of Arts and Letters Harold D. Vursell Memorial Award 1981, Nat. Endowment for the Arts Award 1982, NY Public Library Literary Lion Award 1988, Nat. Magazine Award 1989, Lannan Foundation Literary Award 1993, Boston Public Library Literary Lights Award 1995, John Burroughs Medal 2012. *Publications include:* Cat Man 1956, The Circle Home 1960, The Peacock's Tail 1965, Notes from the Century Before: A Journal from British Columbia 1969, The Courage of Turtles 1971, Walking the Dead Diamond River 1973, The Moose on the Wall: Field Notes from the Vermont Wilderness 1974, Red Wolves and Black Bears 1976, African Calliope: A Journey to the Sudan 1979, The Edward Hoagland Reader 1979, The Tugman's Passage 1982, City Tales 1986, Seven Rivers West 1986, Heart's Desire 1988, The Final Fate of the Alligators 1992, Balancing Acts 1992, Tigers and Ice 1999, Compass Points 2001, Hoagland on Nature 2003, Early in the Season 2008, Sex and the River Styx 2011, Alaskan Travels: Far-Flung Tales of Love and Adventure 2012, Children Are Diamonds (novel) 2013, The Devil's Tub (short stories) 2014, On Nature: Selected Essays 2014. *Address:* POB 51, Barton, VT 05822 (office); POB 615, Edgartown, MA 02539, USA (home). *Telephone:* (508) 627-8803 (office). *Website:* www.edwardhoagland.com.

HOAGLAND, Richard Eugene, AB, MA, MFA; American diplomatist; b. Fort Wayne, Ind.; ed Univ. of Virginia, Univ. of Grenoble, France; taught English as a foreign language in Zaïre 1974–76, and African literature at Carter-Woodson Inst. of African and Afro-American Studies, Univ. of Virginia; joined Foreign Service 1985, now career mem. Sr Foreign Service with rank of Minister-Counselor, foreign assignments have included Russia (Press Spokesman for the Embassy), Uzbekistan, Pakistan (twice), has also served in State Dept's Bureau of Intelligence and Research (Lead Analyst for Afghanistan 1989–91), US Deputy Special Envoy for Afghanistan 1991–92, Dir Office of Public Diplomacy, Bureau of S Asian Affairs and Special Adviser to Nat. Security Council for public diplomacy on Afghanistan 1999–2001, Dir Office of Caucasus and Cen. Asian Affairs, Bureau of Europe and Eurasian Affairs 2001–03, Amb. to Tajikistan 2003–06, Chargé d'affaires a.i., Embassy in Ashgabat, Turkmenistan 2007–08, Amb. to Kazakhstan 2008–11, Deputy Chief of Mission, Embassy in Islamabad 2011–13; two Meritorious Honor Awards, three Superior Honor Awards, several Group Honor Awards, Presidential Performance Awards.

HOARE, Sir Charles Antony Richard, Kt, MA, FRS, FREng; British computer scientist; *Consultant Principal Researcher, Microsoft Research Ltd;* b. 11 Jan. 1934, Colombo, Ceylon (now Sri Lanka); s. of Henry S. M. Hoare and Marjorie F. Hoare; m. Jill Pym 1962; two s. one d.; ed Dragon School, Oxford, King's School, Canterbury, Merton Coll., Oxford, Unit of Biometry, Oxford and Moscow State Univ.; with Elliott Brothers (London) Ltd 1960–68; Prof. of Computing Science, Queen's Univ., Belfast 1968–77; Prof. of Computation, Univ. of Oxford 1977–93; James Martin Prof. of Computing 1993–99, Prof. Emer. 1999–; Sr Researcher, Microsoft Research Ltd 1999–, now Consultant Prin. Researcher; Fellow, Wolfson Coll. 1977–99; mem. Academia Europea; Foreign mem. Accad. dei Lincei, Italy; Corresp. mem. Bavarian Acad. of Sciences; Assoc. mem. US Nat. Acad. of Eng; Distinguished Fellow, British Computer Soc.; Fellow, Royal Acad. of Eng; Fellow, Royal Soc.; Hon. Fellow, Kellogg Coll. Oxford 1998, Darwin Coll. Cambridge 2001, Merton Coll. Oxford; Hon. DSc (Univ. of Southern Calif., Warwick, Pennsylvania, Queen's, Belfast, ITMO St Petersburg); Hon. DUniv (York) 1989, (Essex) 1991, (Bath) 1993, (Oxford Brookes) 2000, (Queen Mary & Westfield Coll., London) 2005, (Heriot Watt) 2007, (Athens) 2007, (Warsaw) 2012, (Madrid) 2013; A.M. Turing Award 1980, Harry Goode Memorial Award, Faraday Medal 1985, Kyoto Prize 2000, John von Neumann Medal 2011, Sigplan Distinguished Achievement Award 2011. *Publications:* Structured Programming (co-author) 1972, Communicating Sequential Processes 1985, Essays in Computing Science 1989, Unifying Theories of Programming (co-author) 1998. *Leisure interests:* walking, music, jigsaws, reading, gardening. *Address:* Microsoft Research Ltd, 21 Station Road, Cambridge, CB1 2FB, England (office). *Telephone:* (1223) 479800 (office). *Fax:* (1223) 479999 (office).

HOBBS, Franklin (Fritz) W., BA, MBA; American business executive; *Chairman, Ally Financial Inc.;* ed Harvard Coll., Harvard Univ. Business School; competed as rower as mem. of US eight-oared shell in 1968 and 1972 Summer Olympics; joined Dillon, Read & Co. 1972, served as Head of Corp. Finance and Mergers and Acquisitions, Pres. and CEO Inc. 1994–97, Chair. 1999–2001, then Chair. UBS Warburg (after Dillon Read merger with UBS); CEO Houlihan Lokey Howard & Zukin (investment bank) 2002–03; adviser to One Equity Partners LLC (manages investments for JPMorgan Chase & Co.) 2004–; Chair. GMAC Financial Services (renamed Ally Financial Inc. 2010) 2009–; Chair. Supervisory Bd Bawag PSK Bank AG 2013–; mem. Bd of Dirs Last Mile Connections Inc. 2004–, Lord Abbett & Co., Adolph Coors Co. (now Molson Coors Brewing Co.) 2001–, US Fund for UNICEF; mem. Advisory Bd Freeman & Co.; fmr mem. Bd of Overseers, Harvard Coll.; Trustee The Frick Collection 2007–; fmr Pres. Bd of Trustees, Milton Acad. *Address:* Ally Financial Inc., 200 Renaissance Center, Detroit, MI 48243, USA (office). *Website:* www.ally.com (office).

HOBBS, Helen Haskell, BA, MD; American medical geneticist and academic; *Professor, Departments of Internal Medicine and Molecular Genetics, University of Texas Southwestern Medical Center;* b. 5 May 1952, Boston, Mass; m. Dennis Keith Stone, MD; two s.; ed Univ. of Pennsylvania, Stanford Univ., Case Western Reserve Univ. School of Medicine; Intern, Internal Medicine, Columbia Presbyterian Medical Center, New York 1979–80; Resident, Internal Medicine, Parkland Memorial Hosp., Dallas, Tex. 1980–82; Chief Resident, Dept of Internal Medicine, Univ. of Texas Southwestern Medical Center at Dallas 1982–83, Postdoctoral Fellow, Dept of Molecular Genetics, and Subspecialty Training in Endocrinology 1983–87, Asst Prof., Depts of Internal Medicine and Molecular Genetics, and Chief, Div. of Medical Genetics 1987–91, Assoc. Prof., Depts of Internal Medicine and Molecular Genetics, and Chief, Div. of Medical Genetics 1991–95, Prof., Depts of Internal Medicine and Molecular Genetics, and Chief, Div. of Medical Genetics 1995–, Dir McDermott Center for Human Growth and Devt 2000–, Dallas Heart Ball Chair in Cardiology Research, Philip O'Bryan Montgomery Jr, MD, Distinguished Chair in Developmental Biology, Eugene McDermott Distinguished Chair for the Study of Human Growth and Devt, Eugene McDermott Center for Human Growth and Devt, Internal Medicine, Molecular Genetics; Investigator, Howard Hughes Medical Inst. 2002–; mem. Scientific Advisory Bd, Metabolism, Pfizer Co. 2009–; consultant, Regeneron 2011–; Consulting Ed., Journal of Clinical Investigation 1993–96, 1997–; mem. Editorial Bd, Cell Metabolism 2004–; mem. American Soc. of Clinical Investigation 1991, Inst. of Medicine, NAS 2004, Asscn of American Physicians 1997, American Acad. of Arts and Sciences 2006, NAS 2007, American Soc. of Human Genetics, American Soc. for Biochemistry and Molecular Biology, Arteriosclerosis, Thrombosis and Vascular Disease Council of the American Heart Asscn; Hon. Degree in Medicine (Univ. of Ferrara, Italy) 2003; Alfred S. Maschke Award for Excellence in the Art and Practice of Medicine, Case Western Reserve Univ. School of Medicine 1979, Syntex Scholar 1987–90, Established Investigator, American Heart Asscn 1990–95, Bristol Myers Squibb Metabolism Freedom to Discover Research Grant 2002–07, Heinrich Wieland Prize 2005, Clinical Research Prize, American Heart Asscn 2005, Distinguished Alumnus Award, Case Western Reserve Univ. School of Medicine 2006, Distinguished Scientist Award, American Heart Asscn 2007, Glorney-Raisbeck Award, New York Acad. of Medicine 2007, Carl Landsteiner Lecturer, Austrian Acad. of Science, Vienna 2010, Distinguished Physician-Scientist Lecturer, Univ. of North Carolina 2011, Breakthrough Prize in Life Sciences (co-recipient) 2016, Passano Award (co-recipient) 2016, Schottenstein Prize in Cardiovascular Sciences 2017, Gerald D. Aurbach Award for Outstanding Translational Research 2018. *Publications:* several book chapters and more than 150 papers in professional journals; five US patents. *Address:* Department of Molecular Genetics, University of Texas Southwestern Medical Center at Dallas, 5323 Harry Hines Boulevard, Dallas, TX 75390-9046, USA (office). *Telephone:* (214) 648-6724 (office). *Fax:* (214) 648-7539 (office). *E-mail:* helen.hobbs@utsouthwestern.edu (office). *Website:* www.utsouthwestern.edu/education/medical-school/departments/molecular-genetics/index.html (office).

HOBERMAN, Brent Shawzin, CBE, MA; British entrepreneur and business executive; b. 25 Nov. 1968; m.; one s. two d.; ed Eton Coll. and New Coll., Oxford; Sr Consultant, Media and Telecoms Spectrum Strategy Consultants, LineOne; Gen. Man., Head of Business Devt and Founder-mem. QXL; co-f. with Martha Lane Fox (q.v.) and CEO lastminute.com 1998–2006, Chair. and Chief Strategy Officer 2006–07, Consultant 2007–; Chair. (non-exec.) Wayn.com (travel and social networking site) 2007–09; Exec. Chair. mydeco.com (home design website) 2007–; co-f. PROfounders Capital 2009; Advisor, Twitter Partners 2009–; Dir (non-exec.), Guardian Media Group 2007–, TalkTalk, Time Out Group; Dir, easyCar.com, Shazam; investor in several Internet cos, including Viagogo, erepublik, wayn.com, academia.edu; mem. The Business Council for Britain 2009–, Council of Inst. of Contemporary Arts; UK Business Trade Amb.; Gov. Univ. of the Arts, London; Fellow, Eton Coll.; selected as one of the World Econ. Forum's Global Young Leaders for the UK 2009. *Address:* Guardian Media Group plc, Kings Place, 90 York Way, London, N1 9GU, England (office). *Telephone:* (20) 3353-2000 (office). *Website:* www.gmgplc.co.uk (office).

HOBSON, Mellody, BA; American investment management executive; *President, Ariel Investments LLC;* b. 3 April 1969, Chicago, Ill.; m. George Lucas 2013; one d.; ed St Ignatius Coll. Prep., Woodrow Wilson School of Int. Relations and Public Policy, Princeton Univ.; joined Ariel Capital Man. LLC (now Ariel Investments) 1991, Pres. 2000–, also Chair. Bd of Trustees Ariel Investment Trust; financial analysis contrib., Good Morning America, ABC; appearances on CNN, WGN-TV; mem. Bd of Dirs Field Museum, Chicago Public Library, Chicago Public Educ. Fund, Sundance Inst., Tellabs Inc., DreamWorks Animation SKG Inc., Estée Lauder Cos Inc., Starbucks Corpn, Groupon 2011–; term mem. New York Council on Foreign Relations; mem. Econ. Club of Chicago, Commercial Club of Chicago, Young Pres.'s Org.; Trustee Princeton Univ.; Global Leader of Tomorrow, World Econ. Forum, Davos 2001. *Address:* Ariel Investments LLC, 200 East Randolph Drive, Suite 2900, Chicago, IL 60601, USA (office). *Telephone:* (312) 726-0140 (office). *Fax:* (312) 726-7473 (office). *E-mail:* email@arielinvestments.com (office). *Website:* www.arielinvestments.com (office).

HOCH, Orion, PhD; American business executive; b. 21 Dec. 1928, Canonsburg, Pa; m. 1st Jane Lee Ogan 1952 (died 1978); one s. two d.; m. 2nd Catherine Nan Richardson 1980; one s.; ed Carnegie Mellon Univ., UCLA and Stanford Univ.; engaged in research and devt Hughes Aircraft 1952–54; various positions, Electron Devices Div. Litton Industries Inc. 1957–68, Vice-Pres. Litton Components Group 1968–70, Corp. Vice-Pres. Litton Industries Inc. 1970, Sr Vice-Pres. 1971, Deputy Head, Business Systems and Equipment Group 1973–74, Pres. Advanced Memory Systems (later Intersil Inc.) 1974–81, Pres. Litton Industries Inc. 1982–88, Dir and COO 1982, CEO 1986–93, Chair. 1988–94, Chair. Emer. 1994–; mem. Bd of Dirs UNOVA Inc. 1982–2001; fmr mem. Bd of Dirs Bessemer Group Inc., Honeywell Measurex Corpn; Chair. Exec. Cttee Western Atlas Inc. 1994–98; Trustee, Carnegie Mellon Univ. *Address:* 55 Melanie Lane, Atherton, CA 94027, USA.

HOCHHUTH, Rolf; German playwright; b. 1 April 1931; m.; three s.; fmr publisher's reader; Resident Municipal Playwright, Basel 1963; mem. PEN of FRG. *Publications include:* plays: Der Stellvertreter: Ein christliches Trauerspiel (The Deputy, a Christian Tragedy) 1963, The Employer 1965, The Soldiers 1966, Anatomy of Revolution 1969, The Guerrillas 1970, The Midwife 1972, Lysistrata and NATO 1973, The Survivor 1981, Alan Turing 1987, Judith 1984, The Immaculate Conception 1989, Wessis in Weimar 1993, McKinsey is Coming 2004, Livia and Julia 2005, Death of a Hunter 2018; novel: A Love in Germany 1980; poetry: Vorbeugehaft (Protective Custody) 2008. *Address:* Agentur Hegmann, Essener Str. 32, 45529 Hattingen, Germany (office). *Telephone:* (23) 2443157 (office). *E-mail:* ahegmann@web.de (office). *Website:* www.hegmann.de.tt (office); www.rolf-hochhuth.de.

HOCHMAIR, Erwin, Dipl.-Ing., DTech; Austrian electrical engineer, academic and entrepreneur; *Professor, Institute of Experimental Physics, University of Innsbruck;* b. 1940, Vienna; m. Ingeborg J. Hochmair-Desoyer; ed Technical Univ. of Vienna; joined Inst. for Physical Electronics, Technical Univ. of Vienna 1965, taught courses on linear integrated circuits and circuit design; Research Assoc., Marshall Space Flight Center, USA 1970–72; Visiting Assoc. Prof., Stanford Univ., USA 1979; Prof., Inst. of Experimental Physics, Univ. of Innsbruck 1986–; Co-founder and Owner MED-EL (medical device co.), Vienna 1989–; Hon. DrMed (Technical Univ. of Munich) 2004; Best Paper Award, Int. Solid-State Circuits Conf. 1977, Erwin Schrödinger Prize, Austrian Acad. of Sciences 2003, Holzer-Prize, Vienna Technical Univ., Russ Prize, Nat. Acad. of Eng (USA) (co-recipient) 2015. *Publications:* more than 100 papers in professional journals and approx. 50 patents. *Address:* MED-EL GmbH, Fürstengasse 1, 1090 Vienna, Austria (office). *Telephone:* (1) 317-24-00 (office). *Fax:* (1) 317-24-00-14 (office). *E-mail:* office@at.medel.com (office). *Website:* www.medel.com (office).

HOCHMAIR-DESOYER, Ingeborg J., PhD; Austrian electrical engineer and entrepreneur; *CEO and Chief Technology Officer, MED-EL GmbH;* b. 17 Jan. 1953, Vienna; d. of Kurt Desoyer and Elisabeth Desoyer; m. Erwin Hochmair; four c.; ed Vienna Univ. of Tech.; spent a semester abroad in Karlsruhe, then worked as an Asst at Inst. of Gen. Electrical Eng and Electronics, Vienna; Fulbright Scholar, Stanford Univ. 1979; partnered with 3M 1981–88; Co-founder, CEO and Chief Tech. Officer, MED-EL GmbH 1989–; Dr hc (Innsbruck Medical Univ.) 2010; Holzer-Prize, Vienna Tech. Univ. 1979, Leonardo da Vinci Award 1980, Sandoz Prize 1984, Entrepreneur of the Year 1995, Veuve Clicquot Business Woman of the Year 1995, Wilhelm Exner Medal 1996, Lasker-DeBakey Clinical Medical Research Award (co-recipient) 2013, Russ Prize, Nat. Acad. of Eng (co-recipient) 2015. *Achievements include:* co-developed, with Erwin Hochmair, the first multi-channel microelectronic cochlear implant 1977. *Publications:* more than 100 scientific publs. *Address:* MED-EL GmbH, Fürstengasse 1, 1090 Vienna, Austria (office). *Telephone:* (1) 317-24-00 (office). *Fax:* (1) 317-24-00-14 (office). *E-mail:* office@at.medel.com (office). *Website:* www.medel.com (office).

HOCHSCHILD, Eduardo; Peruvian mining industry executive; *Executive Chairman, Hochschild Mining plc;* s. of Luis Hochschild and Ana Navarro; m. Mariana Correa Sabogal; ed Tufts Univ., USA; joined Hochschild Mining Group as Safety Asst, Arcata Unit 1987, Head of Group 1998–2006, Exec. Chair. 2006–, oversaw listing of co. on London Stock Exchange 2006; Vice-Chair. Cementos Pacasmayo SAA; Dir Banco de Credito del Peru 2003; mem. Bd of Dirs COMEX Peru, Banco de Crédito del Perú, Sociedad Nacional de Minería y Petróleo, Asian Pacific Econ. Council Business Advisory Cttee, Conferencia Episcopal Peruana, Pacífico Peruano Suiza, TECSUP, Universidad Nacional de Ingeniería, Universidad de Ciencias Aplicadas. *Address:* Hochschild Mining Corporation, Calle La Colonia No. 180, Urb. El Vivero, Santiago de Surco, Lima, 33, Peru (office). *Telephone:* (1) 3172000 (office). *Fax:* (1) 4375009 (office). *E-mail:* info@hocplc.com. (office). *Website:* www.hochschildmining.com (office).

HOCKEY, Joseph (Joe) Benedict, BA, LLB; Australian lawyer and politician; *Ambassador to USA;* b. 2 Aug. 1965, Sydney, NSW; m. Melissa Babbage; two s. one d.; ed Univ. of Sydney; fmr banking and finance lawyer, Corrs Chambers Westgarth; fmr Dir of Policy to Premier of NSW; mem. House of Reps (Parl.) for N Sydney 1996–2015, Man. of Opposition Business in the House 2007–09; Minister for Financial Services and Regulation 1998–2001, for Small Business and Tourism 2001–04, for Human Services 2004–07, also Minister assisting Minister for Workplace Relations 2006–07, Minister for Employment and Workplace Relations and Minister assisting Minister for Public Service Jan.–Dec. 2007; Shadow Minister for Health and Ageing 2007–08, for Finance, Competition Policy and Deregulation 2008–09, Shadow Treas. 2009–13, Treas. 2013–15; Amb. to USA 2016–; mem. Liberal Party of Australia. *Address:* Embassy of Australia, 1601 Massachusetts Avenue NW, Washington, DC 20036-2273, USA (office). *Telephone:* (202) 797-3000 (office). *Fax:* (202) 797-3331 (office). *Website:* www.usa.embassy.gov.au (office).

HOCKFIELD, Susan, BA, PhD; American neuroscientist, academic and fmr university administrator; *Professor of Neuroscience and President Emerita, Massachusetts Institute of Technology;* b. 24 March 1951; m. Prof. Thomas N. Byrne 1991; one d.; ed Horace Greeley High School, Chappaqua, NY, Univ. of Rochester, Georgetown Univ. School of Medicine; Postdoctoral Fellow, Univ. of California, San Francisco 1979–80; Jr Staff Investigator, Cold Spring Harbor Lab. 1980–82, Sr Staff Investigator 1982–85, Dir Summer Neurobiology Program 1985–97; Asst Prof., Section of Neurobiology, Yale Univ. School of Medicine 1985–89, Dir of Grad. Studies, Section of Neurobiology 1986–94, Assoc. Prof. 1989–94, Prof. 1994–2004, Dean Grad. School of Arts and Sciences 1998–2002, William Edward Gilbert Prof. of Neurobiology 2001–04, Provost 2003–04; Prof. of Neuroscience, MIT 2004–, Pres. (first woman) MIT 2004–12, Pres. Emer. 2012–; Marie Curie Visiting Prof., John F. Kennedy School of Govt, Harvard Univ. 2012–13, now mem. Bd of Dirs Belfer Center for Science and International Affairs; mem. Editorial Bd Learning and Memory 1993–, NeuroImage 1994–; mem. Bd of Dirs General Electric Co. 2006–, Lord Foundation of Massachusetts 2005–, Nat. Math and Science Initiative 2007–, World Econ. Forum 2008–; mem. Leadership Council, The Climate Group 2009–; mem. Bd of Overseers Boston Symphony Orchestra 2006–; Trustee Carnegie Corpn of New York 2006–; Corpn mem. Woods Hole Oceanographic Inst. 2006–; mem. Soc. for Neuroscience, NIH Nat. Advisory Neurological Disorders and Stroke Council 2002–04; Trustee, Cold Spring Harbour Lab.; Life mem. Council on Foreign Relations 2007; Fellow, American Acad. of Arts and Sciences 2004, AAAS 2005; Affiliated Fellow, American Acad. of Rome 2012; Hon. MRIA 2010; Hon. mem. Asscn of Alumni and Alumnæ of the Massachusetts Inst. of Tech. 2010; Hon. DSc (Cold Spring Harbor Lab., Watson School of Biological Sciences) 2006, (Brown Univ.) 2006, (Mount Sinai School of Medicine, New York Univ.) 2009, (Univ. of Edinburgh) 2009; Dr hc (Tsinghua Univ.) 2006, (jtly by New Univ. of Lisbon, Technical Univ. of Lisbon and Univ. of Porto, Portugal) 2009, (Univ. Pierre and Marie Curie, Paris) 2010; Charles Judson Herrick Award, American Asscn of Anatomists 1987, Wilbur Lucius Cross Medal, Yale Univ. 2003, Meliora Citation for Career Achievement, Univ. of Rochester 2003, Sheffield Medal, Yale Univ. 2004, Golden Plate Award, Acad. of Achievement 2005, Amelia Earhart Award, Women's Union 2005, Citation Award, Midwest Research Inst. 2009, America's Best Leaders honoree, U.S. News & World Report and the Center for Public Leadership, John F. Kennedy School of Govt 2009, Edison Achievement Award 2010, Pinnacle Award for Lifetime Achievement, Greater Boston Chamber of Commerce 2013. *Publications:* Molecular Probes of the Nervous System – Selected Methods for Antibodies and Nucleic Acid Probes (co-author) 1993; numerous book chapter and scientific papers and reviews in professional journals and articles for the Boston Globe; six US patents 1997–2009. *Address:* Department of Brain and Cognitive Sciences, Massachusetts Institute of Technology, Building 3-207, Cambridge, MA 02139-4307, USA (office). *E-mail:* hockfield@mit.edu (office). *Website:* bcs.mit.edu (office).

HOCKING, John, BSc, LLM; Australian lawyer and UN official; b. 6 Aug. 1957; one c.; ed Monash Univ., Univ. of Sydney, London School of Econs and Political Science, UK; fmr Legal and Policy Adviser, OECD, Special Broadcasting Service (nat. multi-cultural TV and radio broadcaster), British Film Inst., Australian Film Comm.; served as Legal Assoc. to Justice Michael Kirby (fmr Pres. of Court of Appeal, Judge of High Court); joined Int. Criminal Tribunal for the fmr Yugoslavia (ICTY) 1997, served as Sr Legal Officer for Appeals Chambers of both ICTY and Int. Criminal Tribunal for Rwanda, Deputy Registrar, ICTY 2004–09, Asst Sec.-Gen. and Registrar 2009; Registrar, Mechanism for Int. Criminal Tribunals (MICT), UN, The Hague 2012–16; barrister, Lincoln's Inn, UK, Supreme Court of Victoria, Supreme Court of NSW.

HOCKNEY, David, OM, CH, RA; British artist, stage designer and photographer; b. 9 July 1937, Bradford, Yorks.; s. of Kenneth Hockney and Laura Hockney; ed Bradford Grammar School, Bradford Coll. of Art, Royal Coll. of Art, London; taught at Maidstone Coll. of Art 1962, Univ. of Iowa 1964, Univ. of Colorado 1965, UCLA 1966 (Hon. Chair. of Drawing 1980), Univ. of California, Berkeley 1967; has travelled extensively in Europe and USA; many works now housed in Salts Mill, Saltaire, nr Bradford; has painted hundreds of portraits, still lifes and landscapes using the Brushes iPhone and iPad application since 2009; mem. Advisory Bd Standpoint (political magazine) 2008–; Assoc. mem. Royal Acad. 1985; Foreign Hon. mem. American Acad. of Arts and Sciences 1997; Freedom of the City of Bradford 2000; Hon. PhD (Aberdeen) 1988, (Royal Coll. of Art) 1992; Hon. DLitt (Oxford) 1995, (Leeds) 2000, (Cambridge) 2007; hon. degree from Acad. of Fine Arts, Florence 2003; Guinness Award 1961, Graphic Prize, Paris Biennale 1963, First Prize 8th Int. Exhbn of Drawings and Engravings, Lugano 1964, prize at 6th Int. Exhbn of Graphic Art, Ljubljana 1965, Cracow 1st Int. Print Biennale 1966, First Prize, 6th John Moores Exhbn 1967, Hamburg Foundation Shakespeare Prize 1983, Progress Medal, Royal Photographic Soc. 1988, Praemium Imperiale, Japan Art Asscn 1989, Fifth Annual Gov.'s Award for Visual Arts in Calif. 1994, Kulturpreis, Deutsche Gesellschaft für Photographie E.V. 1997, Mario Tamayo Award for Outstanding Dedication in the Visual Arts, Los Angeles Contemporary Exhbns 1998, Charles Wollaston Award, Royal Acad. of Arts, Summer Exhbn, London 1999, Commendation by the Gov. of Calif., Gray Davis, for Efforts on Behalf of People Living with HIV/AIDS 1999, Centenary Medal, Royal Photographic Soc. 2003, Lorenzo De' Medici Lifetime Career Award, Florence Biennale 2003, Orthopaedic Ward at The Yorkshire Clinic, W Yorks. named 'The Hockney Ward' 2003, La Rosa D'Oro Award, Palermo, Italy 2004, Bannister Fletcher Award 2004, San Francisco Opera Medal 2017, Queen Sonja Print Lifetime Achievement Award 2018. *Film:* A Bigger Splash (autobiographical documentary) 1974. *Stage design:* set: Ubu Roi, Royal Court Theatre, London 1966, Rake's Progress, Glyndebourne 1975, Die Zauberflöte, Glyndebourne 1978, La Scala 1979, Nightingale, Covent Garden 1983, Varii Capricci, Metropolitan Opera House, New York 1983, Tristan and Isolde, LA Music Centre Opera, LA 1987, Turandot, Lyric Opera 1992–, San Francisco 1993, Die Frau Ohne Schatten, Covent Garden, London 1992, LA Music Centre Opera 1993, The Performing Arts Museum, Melbourne (Green Room Award for Stage Design in Opera 1997) 1997; costume and set: Les Mamelles de Teresias, Metropolitan Opera House, New York 1980, L'Enfant et les sortilèges, Metropolitan Opera House, New York 1980, Parade, Metropolitan Opera House, New York 1980, Oedipus Rex, Metropolitan Opera House, New York 1981, Le Sacre du Printemps, Metropolitan Opera House, New York 1981, Le Rossignol, Metropolitan Opera House, New York 1981. *Radio:* guest ed., Today programme (BBC Radio 4) 2009. *Publications include:* Hockney by Hockney 1976, David Hockney, Travel with Pen, Pencil and Ink (autobiog.) 1978, Paper Pools 1980, Photographs 1982, China Diary (with Stephen Spender), 1982, Hockney Paints the Stage 1983, David Hockney: Cameraworks 1984, Hockney on Photography: Conversations with Paul Joyce 1988, David Hockney: A Retrospective 1988, Hockney's Alphabet (ed. by Stephen Spender) 1991, That's the Way I See It (autobiog.) 1993, Off the Wall: Hockney Posters 1994, David Hockney's Dog Days 1998, Hockney on Art: Photography, Painting and Perspective 1999, Hockney on 'Art': Conversation with Paul Joyce 2000, Secret Knowledge: Rediscovering the Lost Techniques of the Old Masters (British Book Design and Production Award 2002) 2001, Hockney's Pictures 2004; illustrated Six Fairy Tales of the Brothers Grimm 1969, The Blue Guitar 1977, Hockney's Alphabet 1991; contributed original sketches to launch edn of Standpoint magazine June 2008. *Website:* www.hockneypictures.com.

HODDLE, Glenn; British football manager and fmr professional footballer; b. 27 Oct. 1957, Hayes, Middx; s. of Derek Hoddle and Teresa Roberts; m. Christine Anne Stirling (divorced 1999); one s. two d.; ed Burnt Mill School, Harlow; attacking midfielder; played for Tottenham Hotspur 1975–87 (won UEFA Cup 1984, FA Cup 1981, 1982, FA Community Shield 1981), AS Monaco, France 1988–91 (won Ligue 1 Title 1987–88, French Cup 1991), Swindon Town (also Man.) 1991–93, Chelsea (also Man.) 1993–95; won 12 Under-21 caps and 53 full caps on England nat. team 1979–88, played in World Cup 1982 and 1986, Man. 1996–99 (won Tournoi de France 1997); Man. Chelsea 1996, Southampton 2000–01, Tottenham Hotspur 2001–03, Wolverhampton Wanderers 2004–06; Team Coach, Queens Park Rangers 2015; Founder and Dir The Glenn Hoddle Acad. (first ind., professional football acad. offering alternative to professional club system), Spain 2008–11, Bisham Abbey, Bucks., UK 2011–; Co-founder Zap Sportz (sports website); football pundit for Sky TV, for BT Sport 2015–. *Publications:* Spurred to Success (autobiography), Glenn Hoddle: The 1998 World Cup Story 1998. *Leisure interests:* tennis, golf, reading. *Website:* zapsportz.com.

HODEL, Donald Paul, JD; American lawyer (retd) and fmr government official; *Chairman Emeritus, Summit Power Group Inc.;* b. 23 May 1935, Portland, Ore.; s. of Philip E. Hodel and Theresia R. (Brodt) Hodel; m. Barbara B. Stockman 1956; two s. (one deceased); ed Harvard Coll. and Univ. of Oregon; admitted to Ore. Bar 1960 (retd 2008); Attorney, Davies, Biggs, Strayer, Stoel & Boley 1960–63; Georgia Pacific Corpn 1963–69; Deputy Admin., Bonneville Power Admin. 1969–72, Admin. 1972–77; Pres. Nat. Elec. Reliability Council, Princeton, NJ 1978–80; Pres. Hodel Assocs. Inc. 1978–81; Under-Sec. Dept of Interior 1981–83; Sec. of Energy 1982–85, of the Interior 1985–89; Founder and Chair. Summit Power Group Inc. 1989–, currently Chair. Emer.; Pres. Christian Coalition 1997–99; Pres. and CEO Focus on the Family 2003–05; Republican; Dir Columbia Gas System Inc., Hart Publications Inc., Integrated Electrical Services Inc. *Address:* c/o Summit Power Group, LLC, 83 South King Street, Suite 200, Seattle, WA 98104, USA (office). *Telephone:* (206) 780-3551 (office). *E-mail:* info@summitpower.com (office). *Website:* www.summitpower.com (office).

HODGE, Daniel Robert; Curaçao banker and politician; *Chairman, Curaçao Bankers' Association;* b. 23 Oct. 1959; ed Erasmus Universiteit Rotterdam, Netherlands; Man. Dir Curaçaose Postspaarbank (PSB Bank) NV 2002–12; Prime Minister 2012–13; Leader, Partido Alternativo Real (PAR, Real Alternative Party) June–Sept. 2013; Chair. Curaçao Bankers' Asscn (CBA) 2015–. *Address:* Curaçao Bankers' Association, A.M. Chumaceiro Boulevard 3, Willemstad, Curaçao (office).

HODGE, Sir James William, KCVO, CMG, MA; British diplomat; *Chairman, Society of Pension Consultants;* b. 24 Dec. 1943; s. of William Hodge and Catherine Hodge (née Carden); m. Frances Margaret Coyne 1970; three d.; ed Holy Cross Acad., Edin., Univ. of Edin.; entered FCO 1966, Rhodesia Political Dept 1966–67, Second Sec. (Information), Tokyo 1967–72, FCO Marine and Transport Dept 1972–73, UN Dept 1973–75, First Sec. (Devt and later Chancery), Lagos 1975–78, FCO Personnel Operations Dept 1978–81, First Sec. (Econ.) and later Counsellor (Commercial), Tokyo 1981–86, Head of Chancery, Copenhagen 1986–90, FCO Security Dept 1990–93, attached to Royal Coll. of Defence Studies 1994; Minister Consular Gen. and Deputy Head of Mission, Beijing 1995–96; Amb. to Thailand 1996–2000; Consul-Gen. to Hong Kong Special Admin. Region, People's Repub. of

China (concurrently non-resident Consul-Gen. to Macao) 2000–03; Chair. Soc. of Pension Consultants 2007–, Foreign and Commonwealth Office Asscn; Deputy Chair. Asia House; mem. Cen. Council of Royal Over-Seas League; Advisor to Mansion House Scholarship Scheme; Hon. DIur (Univ. of Liverpool) 2004. *Leisure interests:* books, music. *Address:* Foreign and Commonwealth Office Association, Room KG/117, King Charles Street, London, SW1A 2AH; Society of Pension Consultants, St Bartholomew House, 92 Fleet Street, London, EC4Y 1DG, England (office). *Telephone:* (20) 7353-1688 (office). *Fax:* (20) 7353-9296 (office). *E-mail:* info@spc.uk.com (office). *Website:* www.spc.uk.com (office); www.fcoa.org.uk (office).

HODGE, Patricia Ann, OBE; British actress; b. 29 Sept. 1946, Grimsby, Lincs.; d. of Eric Hodge and Marion Phillips; m. Peter Owen 1976; two s.; ed Wintringham Girls' Grammar School, Grimsby, St Helen's School, Northwood, Middx, Maria Grey Coll. (now West London Inst. of Higher Educ.), Brunel Univ., Twickenham, London Acad. of Music and Dramatic Art (LAMDA); Eveline Evans Award for Best Actress LAMDA, Olivier Award for Best Supporting Actress 1999, Spoken Word Award for Female Performer of the Year 2003; Hon. DLitt (Hull) 1996, (Brunel) 2001, (Leicester) 2003. *Stage appearances include:* No-one Was Saved, All My Sons, Say Who You Are, The Birthday Party, The Anniversary, Popkiss, Two Gentlemen of Verona, Pippin, Maudie, Hair, The Beggar's Opera, Pal Joey, Look Back in Anger, Dick Whittington, Happy Yellow, The Brian Cant Children's Show, Then and Now, The Mitford Girls, As You Like It, Benefactors, Noel and Gertie, Separate Tables, The Prime of Miss Jean Brodie, A Little Night Music (Royal Nat. Theatre), Heartbreak House 1997, Money (Royal Nat. Theatre) (Laurence Olivier Theatre Award for Best Supporting Actress 2000) 1999, Summer-folk (Royal Nat. Theatre) 1999, Noises Off (Royal Nat. Theatre and tour) 2000–01, His Dark Materials (Royal Nat. Theatre) 2004, Boeing Boeing 2007, The Country Wife 2008, The Clean House 2008, Calendar Girls 2008, Relative Values 2014. *Film appearances:* The Disappearance 1977, Rosie Dixon – Night Nurse 1978, The Waterloo Bridge Handicap 1978, The Elephant Man 1980, Heavy Metal 1981, Betrayal 1983, Sunset 1988, Just Ask for Diamond 1988, The Secret Life of Ian Fleming 1990, The Leading Man 1996, Prague Duet 1996, Jilting Joe 1997, Before You Go 2002. *Television appearances:* Jackanory Playhouse 1972, Valentine 1973, The Girls of Slender Means 1975, Night of the Father 1975, Great Big Groovy Horse 1975, The Naked Civil Servant 1975, Softly, Softly 1976, Act of Rape 1977, Crimewriters 1978, Rumpole of the Bailey 1978–92, Target 1978, The One and Only Mrs Phyllis Dixey 1978, Edward and Mrs Simpson 1978, Disraeli 1978, Rumpole of the Bailey 1980, The Professionals 1980, Holding the Fort 1980–82, The Other 'Arf 1980–81, Jemima Shore Investigates 1983, Hay Fever 1984, Time for Murder 1985, O.S.S. 1985, Robin of Sherwood 1986, The Return of Sherlock Holmes 1986, Hotel du Lac 1986, The Life and Loves of a She Devil 1986, The Death of a Heart 1987, Rich Tea and Sympathy 1991, The Cloning of Joanna May 1991, The Legacy of Reginald Perrin 1996, The Moonstone 1996, The People's Passion (film) 1999, The Falklands Play (film) 2002, Waking the Dead (series) 2002, Sweet Medicine (series) 2003, Agatha Christie Marple: The Sittaford Mystery (film) 2006, Hustle (series) 2007, Maxwell 2007, Miranda 2009–15, Poirot 2014. *Address:* c/o Independent Talent Group Ltd, 40 Whitfield Street, London, W1T 2RH, England (office). *Telephone:* (20) 7636-6565 (office). *Fax:* (20) 7323-0101 (office). *Website:* www.independenttalent.com (office).

HODGES, James (Jim) H., BA, JD; American consultant and fmr state governor; *Partner, McGuireWoods LLP;* b. 19 Nov. 1956, Lancaster, SC; m. Rachel Gardner; two s.; ed Davidson Coll., Univ. of South Carolina; Lancaster Co. Attorney 1983–87; Pnr, Thomas, Goldsmith, Folks and Hodges 1983–90; mem. South Carolina House of Reps 1986–97; Gen. Counsel, Springs Co. 1990–98; Gov. of South Carolina 1999–2002; Founder, CEO and Man. Dir Hodges Consulting Group 2003–09; Pnr, Covington Lobdell and Hickman LLP 2003–08; currently Pnr, McGuireWoods LLP, Sr Advisor, McGuire Woods Consulting LLC; Nat. Co-Chair. for Obama Pres. Campaign 2008; Chair. Southern Growth Policies Bd; Chair. Southern Tech. Council; Chair. Business Partnership School of Business, Univ. of South Carolina; mem. Bd of Dirs Park City Center for Public Policy; mem. Bd of Advisors, Imadgen, Strategic Partnerships LLC, Public Insight LP; Dr hc (Univ. of South Carolina), (South Carolina State Univ.), (Winthrop Univ.), (Francis Marion Univ.); Legislator of the Year, SC Chamber of Commerce 1993, Compleat Lawyer Silver Medallion 1994, Guardian of Small Business Award, Nat. Fed. of Ind. Businesses 1996, Special Service Award, Common Cause 1998. *Address:* McGuire-Woods LLP, 1301 Gervais Street, Suite 1050, Columbia, SC 29201, USA. *Telephone:* (803) 251-2301 (office). *Fax:* (803) 251-2315 (office). *E-mail:* jhodges@mcguirewoods.com (office). *Website:* www.mcguirewoods.com (office).

HODGKINSON, Sir Mike, Kt, BA; British business executive; *Chairman, Keolis UK;* b. 7 April 1944, Berkhamsted, Herts.; m.; three c.; ed Hornchurch Grammar School, Univ. of Nottingham; Ford Grad. Training Programme 1965; Finance and Admin. Dir Leyland Cars (Eng Div.) 1973–77; Man. Dir Land Rover 1978–82; Man. Dir Express Dairy Group 1985; CEO GM Foods Europe, Grand Metropolitan Group 1986–91; Group Airports Dir BAA 1992–99, CEO 1999–2003; Chair. The Post Office 2003–07, Keolis UK 2011–; Deputy Chair. Tui Travel plc 2007–14, Tui Group 2014–; mem. Bd of Dirs Bank of Ireland plc 2004–06, Dublin Airport Authority plc –2011, Crossrail Limited –2012, Transport for London –2012. *Leisure interests:* golf, theatre. *Address:* Keolis UK, Evergreen Building North, 160 Euston Road, London, NW1 2DX, England (office); TUI Group, Karl-Wiechert-Allee 4, 30625 Hanover, Germany (office). *E-mail:* comms@keolis.co.uk (office). *Website:* www.keolis.co.uk (office); www.tuigroup.com (office).

HODGMAN, William Edward Felix (Will), BA, BL; Australian politician; *Premier of Tasmania;* b. 20 April 1969, Hobart, Tasmania; s. of Michael Hodgman; m. Nicky Hodgman; two s. one d.; ed Univ. of Tasmania; Barrister and Solicitor of Supreme Court of Tasmania 1994–95, Prosecutor, Wiltshire County Council, UK 1995–2001; elected Liberal Member for Franklin, Tasmanian House of Assembly 2002–, Deputy Leader of Opposition 2002–06, Leader State Opposition 2006–; Leader Liberal Party 2006–; Premier of Tasmania 2014–, currently Minister for Tourism, Hospitality and Events, Minister for Parks, Minister for Heritage and Minister for Trade. *Address:* Level 11, 15 Murray Street, Hobart, TAS 7000, Australia (office). *Telephone:* (3) 6165-7650 (office). *Fax:* (3) 6234-1572 (office). *E-mail:* will.hodgman@parliament.tas.gov.au (office). *Website:* www.premier.tas.gov.au (office).

HODGSON, George Wilson, MA; British diplomatist; *Ambassador to Senegal;* m.; three c.; ed Woodrow Wilson School of Public and Int. Affairs, Princeton Univ.; joined FCO 2002, Desk Officer, Enlargement and Wider Europe Team 2002–03, Second Sec., Embassy in Kabul 2004, Second Sec., Representation to EU, Brussels 2005–06, First Sec. (Political), Embassy in Islamabad 2008–10, Political Counsellor, Embassy in Kabul 2010–11, Sr Adviser, Office of Special Rep. for Afghanistan and Pakistan, US Dept of State, Washington, DC 2011–12, Head of Parl. and Communications Dept, Europe Directorate 2012–14, Head of Ebola Taskforce, Africa Directorate 2014–15, Amb. to Senegal (also accred to Cabo Verde and Guinea-Bissau) 2015–. *Address:* British Embassy, BP 6025, Dakar, Senegal (office). *Telephone:* 33-823-7392 (office). *Fax:* 33-823-2766 (office). *E-mail:* britembe@orange.sn (office). *Website:* www.gov.uk/government/world/organisations/british-embassy-dakar (office); www.gov.uk/government/world/senegal (office).

HODGSON, Pete; New Zealand politician (retd); b. 13 June 1950, Whangarei; m.; two s.; ed Massey Univ.; fmrly worked as Veterinary Surgeon in New Zealand and UK; mem. New Zealand Labour Party 1976; MP for Dunedin N 1990–2011; Minister of Energy, Fisheries, Forestry, Research Science and Tech. 1999–2004, Minister for Crown Research Insts, Assoc. Minister of Econ., Industry and Regional Devt and Assoc. Minister of Foreign Affairs and Trade 1999–2005; Minister of Transport, of Commerce, for Land Information, of Statistics and Assoc. Minister of Health 2004–05, Minister of Health 2005–07, of Econ. Devt, Tertiary Educ. and Minister of Research, Science and Tech. 2007–08; mem. Representation Comm. 2013.

HODGSON, Thomas R., BS, MS, MBA; American business executive; *Chairman, Idenix Pharmaceuticals, Inc.;* b. 17 Dec. 1941, Lakewood, Ohio; s. of Thomas J. Hodgson and Dallas L. Hodgson; m. Susan Cawrse 1963; one s. two d.; ed Purdue Univ., Univ. of Michigan and Harvard Univ. Business School; Devt Engineer, DuPont 1964; Assoc., Booz-Allen & Hamilton 1969–72; with Abbott Labs 1972–99, Gen. Man. Faultless Div. 1976–78, Vice-Pres. and Gen. Man. Hosp. Div. 1978–80, Pres. Hosp. Div. 1980–83, Group Vice-Pres. and Pres. Abbott Int. Ltd 1983–84, Exec. Vice-Pres. 1985–80, Pres. and COO Abbott Labs Oct. 1990–99 (retd); mem. Bd of Dirs Idenix Pharmaceuticals Inc. 2002–, Chair. 2012–; Visiting Prof., Purdue Univ. 1996; mem. Bd of Dirs The St. Paul Travelers Inc. 1997–, Intermune, Inc. 2003–; Dr hc (Purdue Univ.). *Leisure interests:* skiing, scuba, wind-surfing, racquetball, tennis, kayaking. *Address:* Idenix Pharmaceuticals, Inc., 320 Bent Street, 4th Floor, Cambridge, MA 02141-2025, USA (office). *Telephone:* (617) 995-9800 (office). *Website:* www.idenix.com (office).

HOEFDRAAD, Gillmore; Suriname economist, central banker and government official; *Minister of Finance;* b. 1962; coordinator of Caribbean Programme, Center for Latin American Monetary Studies, Mexico –1999; Sr Economist with IMF 1999–2010; Gov. Centrale Bank van Suriname 2010–15; Minister of Finance 2015–. *Achievements include:* fmr champion chess player, represented Suriname at Chess Olympiad, Lucerne 1982. *Address:* Ministry of Finance, Tamarindelaan 3, Paramaribo, Suriname (office). *Telephone:* 472610 (office). *Fax:* 476314 (office). *E-mail:* secmin@finance.gov.sr (office). *Website:* www.gov.sr/sr/ministerie-van-financien.aspx (office).

HØEG, Peter, MA; Danish writer and teacher; b. 17 May 1957, Copenhagen; m.; four c.; ed Univ. of Copenhagen; worked as sailor, ballet dancer, athlete and actor before becoming full-time writer; f. Lolwe Foundation 1996; currently Resident, Vækstcentret, Nørre Snede; Co-founder and teacher, Børns Livskundskab 2007–. *Publications include:* Forestilling om det Tyvende århundrede (trans. as The History of Danish Dreams) 1988, Fortællinger om natten (trans. as Tales of the Night; short stories) 1990, Frk. Smillas fornemmelse for sne (trans. as Miss Smilla's Feeling for Snow) 1992, De måske egnede (trans. as Borderliners) 1994, Kvinden og aben (trans. as The Woman and the Ape) 1996, Den stille pige (trans. as The Quiet Girl) 2006, Elefantpassernes børn (The Elephant Keepers' Children) 2010, Det drejer sig om kærlighed (ed.) 2013, Effekten af Susan (trans. as The Susan Effect) 2014, Gennem dine øjne (trans. as Through Your Eyes) 2018. *Address:* c/o Rosinante & Co., Købmagergade 62, 3rd Floor, 1150 Copenhagen K, Denmark (office). *Telephone:* 33-41-18-00 (office). *E-mail:* info@rosinante-co.dk (office). *Website:* www.rosinante-co.dk (office); www.vaekstcenteret.dk (office); www.bornslivskundskab.dk (office).

HOEKSTRA, Peter, BSc, MBA; American politician and diplomatist; *Ambassador to the Netherlands;* b. 30 Oct. 1953, Groningen, Netherlands; m. Diane Hoekstra; three c.; ed Hope Coll., Univ. of Michigan; immigrated to USA with parents as child; worked at Herman Miller, Inc. (office furniture maker), Zeeland, Michigan 1997–2002, becoming Vice Pres. of Marketing; mem. House of Reps for Michigan 2nd Dist 1993–2011, Chair. House Perm. Select Cttee on Intelligence 2004–11; Amb. to the Netherlands 2018–; fmr Distinguished Fellow, The Heritage Foundation; Shillman Sr Fellow, Investigative Project on Terrorism; fmr mem. Bd of Dirs Gentex Corpn; mem. Exec. Cttee Netherlands American Foundation; Republican; Dr hc (Grand Valley State Univ.); Officer, Order of Orange-Nassau 2008; Nat. Intelligence Distinguished Public Service Medal, CIA Agency Seal Medal. *Publication:* Architects of Disaster: The Destruction of Libya 2015. *Address:* Embassy of the USA, Lange Voorhout 102, 2514 EJ The Hague, Netherlands (office). *Telephone:* (70) 3102209 (office). *Fax:* (70) 3102207 (office). *E-mail:* ircthehague@state.gov (office). *Website:* nl.usembassy.gov (office).

HOEKSTRA, Wopke, MBA; Dutch politician; *Minister of Finance;* b. 30 Sept. 1975, Bennekom; m.; four c.; ed Univ. of Leiden, INSEAD; with Sales Dept, Royal Dutch Shell PLC, Berlin, Hamburg and Rotterdam 2002–04; Partner, McKinsey Consulting 2006–17; mem. States Gen. First Chamber (upper house of parl.) 2011–17; Minister of Finance 2017–; mem. Christen Democratisch Appèl (CDA) (Christian Democratic Appeal), Chair. CDA Electoral Programme Cttee 2017; fmr columnist, Het Financieele Dagblad (financial daily); Chair. Bd of Supervisors, Scheepvaartmuseum (Nat. Maritime Museum); mem. Bd of Dirs Friends of Hubrecht; mem. (ex-officio) Bd of Govs., European Stability Mechanism 2017–, EIB 2017–, EBRD 2017–, Multilateral Investment Guarantee Agency 2017–, World Bank 2017–; Amb., Princess Maxima Centre for Child Conscience. *Address:* Ministry of Finance, Korte Voorhout 7, POB 20201, 2500 EE The Hague, Netherlands (office). *Telephone:* (70) 3428000 (office). *Fax:* (70) 3427900 (office).

E-mail: webmaster@minfin.nl (office). *Website:* www.rijksoverheid.nl/ministeries/ministerie-van-financien (office).

HOEVEN, John, BA, MBA; American banker and politician; *Senator from North Dakota;* b. 13 March 1957, Bismarck, N Dakota; m. Mical (Mikey) Laird; one s. one d.; ed Dartmouth Coll., Northwestern Univ. Business School; Exec. Vice-Pres. First Western Bank, Minot 1986–93; Pres. and CEO Bank of North Dakota 1993–2000; Gov. of N Dakota 2000–10; Senator from N Dakota 2011–, mem. Appropriations Cttee 2011–, Energy and Natural Resources Cttee 2011–; mem. Souris Valley Humane Soc.; Chair. Interstate Oil & Gas Compact Comm., Govs' Ethanol Coalition, Midwestern Govs Asscn, Health and Human Services Cttee, and Ntural Resources Cttee, Nat. Govs Asscn, Minot Area Devt Corpn; Trustee, Bismarck State Coll.; mem. Bd of Dirs First Western Bank & Trust, North Dakota Bankers Asscn, North Dakota Small Business Investment Co., North Dakota Econ. Devt Asscn, Bismarck YMCA, Harold Schafer Leadership Center; Dir Minot Kiwanis Club; Republican. *Address:* 120 Russell Senate Office Building, Washington, DC 20510, USA (office). *Telephone:* (202) 224-2551 (office). *Fax:* (202) 224-7999 (office). *Website:* hoeven.senate.gov (office).

HOFER, Norbert Gerwald; Austrian politician; b. 2 March 1971, Vorau; s. of Gerwald Julius Hofer; m. Verena Elfriede Maria Malus; four c. from previous marriage; ed Eisenstadt Higher Tech. School; served on Hungarian border during mil. service 1990–91; worked as aeronautical engineer at Lauda Air Engineering 1991–94; Burgenland Provincial Party Sec., FPÖ 1996–2007, Deputy Regional FPÖ Chair. 2006–; mem. council, City of Eisenstadt 1997–2007; mem. Nationalrat (Nat. Council, lower house of parl.) for Burgenland 2006–, Third Pres. 2013–; unsuccessful FPÖ cand. in presidential election April–May 2016; mem. Bd of Dirs Eurosolar Austria, Mapjet AG 2010–11, International Sky Services AG 2011–12; Exec. Chair. PAF (private trust) 2011–12; Vice-Pres. for Burgenland, Österreichischer Zivilinvalidenverband 2008–12; Jt Acting Pres. of Austria July 2016–Jan. 2017 (following annulment by Constitutional Court of presidential election result 1 July 2016); unsuccessful cand. in re-run presidential election Dec. 2016; mem. Freiheitliche Partei Österreichs (FPÖ, Freedom Party of Austria); Kt, Order of St George. *Address:* Freiheitliche Partei Österreichs, Friedrich Schmidt-Pl. 4/3a, 1080 Vienna, Austria (office). *Telephone:* (1) 512-35-35-0 (office). *Fax:* (1) 512-35-35-9 (office). *E-mail:* bgst@fpoe.at (office). *Website:* www.fpoe.at (office).

HOFFALT, Josua; French ballet dancer; *Star Dancer (Étoile), Ballet de l'Opéra National de Paris;* b. 1984; ed Dance School of the Paris Opera, Nanterre; began dancing aged eight, took private lessons with Colette Armand, then with Dir of Nat. Ballet of Marseille, aged ten; mem. Ballet of Paris Opera 2002–, promoted to Prin. Dancer 2009–, named Star Dancer (Étoile) by Dir Nicolas Joel 2012–; Silver Medal (Junior category), Int. Ballet Competition, Varna 2003, (Senior category, pas de deux with Mathilde Froustey) 2004, Prix du Cercle Carpeaux 2004, Prix de l'AROP 2009. *Ballet roles include:* Drosselmeyer in The Nutcracker, title role in Romeo and Juliet, Gaston Rieux in The Lady of the Camellias, the Prince in The Sleeping Beauty, Beranger in Raymonda, Frederick Lemaître and Lacenaire in Les Enfants du Paradis, Solor in La Bayadère, Frantz in Coppélia. *Address:* Ballet de l'Opéra National de Paris, Palais Garnier, 8 rue Scribe, 75009 Paris, France. *E-mail:* info@operadeparis. *Website:* www.operadeparis.fr.

HOFFMAN, Alan Jerome, AB, PhD; American mathematician and educator; *IBM Fellow Emeritus, T.J. Watson Research Center, IBM;* b. 30 May 1924, New York; s. of Jesse Hoffman and Muriel Hoffman; m. 1st Esther Walker 1947 (died 1988); two d.; m. 2nd Elinor Hershaft 1990 (divorced 2014); ed George Washington High School, Columbia Univ.; mem. US Army Signal Corps 1943–46; mem. Inst. for Advanced Study 1950–51; Mathematician, Nat. Bureau of Standards 1951–56; Scientific Liaison Officer, Office of Naval Research, London 1956–57; Consultant, Gen. Electric Co. 1957–61; Adjunct Prof., CUNY 1965–75; Research Staff mem. T.J. Watson Research Center, IBM 1961–2002, IBM Fellow 1977–2002, IBM Fellow Emer. 2002–; Visiting Prof., Yale Univ. 1975–80, Rutgers Univ. 1990–96, Georgia Inst. of Tech. 1992–93; Consulting Prof., Stanford Univ. 1981–91; Founding Ed., Linear Algebra and Its Applications; mem. NAS; Fellow, New York Acad. of Sciences, American Acad. of Arts and Sciences, INFORMS; Hon. DSc (Technion) 1986; Von Neumann Prize, Operations Research Soc. and Inst. of Man. Science 1992, Founders Award, Math. Programming Soc. 2000. *Publications:* Selected Papers of Alan Hoffman 2003; numerous articles in math. journals. *Address:* T.J. Watson Research Center, IBM, Box 218, Yorktown Heights, NY 10598, USA (office). *E-mail:* ajh@us.ibm.com (office). *Website:* www.research.ibm.com/people/a/ajh (office).

HOFFMAN, Darleane Christian, BS, PhD; American nuclear chemist and academic; *Faculty Senior Scientist, Nuclear Science Division, Lawrence Berkeley National Laboratory;* b. 8 Nov. 1926, Terril, Ia; d. of Carl Christian and Elverna Christian; m. Marvin Hoffman 1951; one s. one d.; ed Iowa State Univ., Ames; Researcher, Oak Ridge Nat. Lab. 1952–53; Researcher, Los Alamos Nat. Lab. 1953–84, becoming Assoc. Group Leader and later Leader, Nuclear Chem. Div., Isotope and Nuclear Chem. Div.; Prof. of Chem., Univ. of California, Berkeley 1984–91, Prof. Emer. 1991–93, Prof., Grad. School 1993–, now Emer.; Faculty Sr Scientist and Group Leader, Heavy Element, Nuclear and Radiochemistry Group, Lawrence Berkeley Nat. Lab. 1984–96, Faculty Sr Scientist and Co-Group Leader 1996–2001, Faculty Sr Scientist, Nuclear Science Div. 2002–; Dir Seaborg Inst. for Transactinium Science 1991–96; Fellow, Norwegian Acad. of Science and Letters 1990, American Acad. of Arts and Sciences 1998; Hon. Int. mem. Japan Soc. of Nuclear and Radiochemistry 2004; Dr hc (Clark Univ.) 2000, (Univ. of Bern) 2001; Alumni Citation Merit, Iowa State Univ. 1978, Guggenheim Fellow 1978–79, ACS Award for Nuclear Chem. 1983, Distinguished Achievement Award, Iowa State Univ. 1988, ACS Garvan Medal 1991, US Nat. Medal of Science 1997, ACS Priestley Medal 2000, Women in Science and Tech. Hall of Fame 2000, Alpha Chi Sigma Hall of Fame 2002, Sigma Xi Procter Prize 2003, Lifetime Achievement Award, Radiochemistry Soc. 2003, Hevesy Medal Award 2011, Invited Lecturer, organizer of Symposia celebrating 100th Anniversary of Marie Curie's 1911 Nobel Prize in Chem. 2011, ACS Western Regional Meeting Symposium Honoree 2013. *Publications:* The Transuranium People: The Inside Story (co-author) 2000; more than 280 articles in books and scientific journals. *Leisure interests:* swimming, music. *Address:* Nuclear Science Division, MS70R0319, Lawrence Berkeley National Laboratory, One Cyclotron Road, Berkeley, CA 94720, USA (office). *Telephone:* (510) 486-4474 (office). *Fax:* (510) 486-7444 (office). *E-mail:* dchoffman@lbl.gov (office). *Website:* chem.berkeley.edu/faculty/emeriti/hoffman/index.php (office).

HOFFMAN, Dustin Lee; American actor; b. 8 Aug. 1937, Los Angeles, Calif.; s. of Harry Hoffman; m. 1st Anne Byrne 1969 (divorced); two d.; m. 2nd Lisa Gottsegen 1980; two s. two d.; ed Santa Monica City Coll.; worked as an attendant at a psychiatric inst.; demonstrator, Macy's toy dept; first stage role in Yes is for a Very Young Man (Sarah Lawrence Coll., Bronxville, NY); Broadway debut in A Cook for Mr. General 1961; Founder Punch Productions; Fellow, American Acad. of Arts and Sciences 2009–; Officier, Ordre des Arts et des Lettres; Britannia Award (BAFTA) 1997, Golden Globe Lifetime Achievement Award 1997, American Film Inst. Lifetime Achievement Award 1999, Kennedy Center Honor 2012. *Other stage appearances in:* Harry, Noon and Night 1964, Journey of the Fifth Horse (Obie Award) 1966, Star Wagon 1966, Fragments 1966, Eh? (Drama Desk, Theatre World, Vernon Rice Awards) 1967, Jimmy Shine 1968, Death of a Salesman 1984, The Merchant of Venice 1989; Asst Dir A View from the Bridge; Dir All Over Town 1974. *Films include:* The Tiger Makes Out 1966, Madigan's Millions 1966, The Graduate 1967, Midnight Cowboy 1969, John and Mary 1969, Little Big Man 1970, Who is Harry Kellerman...? 1971, Straw Dogs 1971, Alfredo Alfredo, Papillon 1973, Lenny 1974, All the President's Men 1975, Marathon Man 1976, Straight Time 1978, Agatha 1979, Kramer vs. Kramer (Acad. Award 1980, New York Film Critics Award) 1979, Tootsie (New York Film Critics Award, Nat. Soc. of Film Critics Award) 1982, Ishtar 1987, Rain Man (Acad. and Golden Globe Awards) 1988, Family Business 1989, Dick Tracy 1990, Hook 1991, Billy Bathgate 1991, Hero 1992, Outbreak 1995, American Buffalo, Sleeper 1996, Wag the Dog 1997, Mad City 1997, Sphere 1997, The Messenger: the Story of Joan of Arc 1999, Being John Malkovich 1999, Moonlight Mile 2002, Confidence 2003, Runaway Jury 2003, Finding Neverland 2004, I Heart Huckabees 2004, Meet the Fockers 2004, Racing Stripes (voice) 2005, The Lost City 2005, Perfume: The Story of a Murderer 2006, Stranger Than Fiction 2006, Mr. Magorium's Wonder Emporium 2007, Kung Fu Panda (voice) 2008, Last Chance Harvey 2009, Little Fockers 2010, Kung Fu Panda 2 (voice) 2011, Chef 2014, Boychoir 2014, The Cobbler 2014, The Program 2015, Kung Fu Panda 3 (voice) 2016, The Meyerowitz Stories (New and Selected) 2017. *TV appearance in:* Death of a Salesman 1985, Liberty's Kids: Est. 1776 2002–03, Luck 2011–12, Roald Dahl's Esio Trot (film) 2015, Medici: Masters of Florence 2016. *Leisure interests:* tennis, piano, photography, reading. *Address:* Punch Productions, 1926 Broadway, Suite 305, New York, NY 10023; PO Box 492359, Los Angeles, CA 90049-8359; c/o The Endeavor Agency, 9601 Wilshire Blvd., 10th Floor, Beverly Hills, CA 90212, USA. *Telephone:* (212) 595-8800 (Punch Productions).

HOFFMAN, Jerzy; Polish film director; b. 15 March 1932, Kraków; s. of Siegmund Hoffman and Maria Schmelkes; m. 1st Walentyna (deceased 1998); m. 2nd Marlena (divorced); one d.; m. 3rd Jagoda Pradzynska; ed All-Union State Inst. of Cinematography, Moscow; has directed 27 documentaries with Edward Skórzewski including Remembrance of Kalwaria (Oberhausen and Florence Film Festival awards), Two Aspects of God, and others 1955–62; Vice-Pres. Asscn of Polish Filmakers 1983–87; mem. Acad. of Fine Arts, Ukraine; Great Cross with Star, Order of Polonia Restituta; numerous Polish and int. film prizes including Minister of Culture and Arts Prize (four times). *Films include:* Gangsters and Philanthropists (feature film debut with Edward Skórzewski) 1962, Colonel Wolodyjowski (also wrote screenplay) 1969, Mazowsze 1971, The Deluge 1973, Leper 1976, The Quack 1981, Medicine Man, Beautiful Stranger 1993, With Fire and Sword (also wrote screenplay) (Polish Eagles for Best Film Producer 2000) 1999, Army of Valhalla 2003, Sienkiewicz Trilogy 2004, Battle of Warsaw 1920 2011; documentary: Ukraine 2005. *Leisure interests:* historical books, bridge, cooking, swimming. *Address:* Zodiak Jerzy Hoffman Production, ul. Puławska 61, 02-595 Warsaw, Poland (office). *Telephone:* (22) 845-20-47 (office). *Website:* www.zodiakfilm.pl.

HOFFMAN, Mat; American professional BMX rider; b. 9 Jan. 1972, Edmond, Okla; entered Freestyle BMX circuit as amateur aged 13, quickly rose to top of amateur class and turned professional aged 16; considered the greatest vert-ramp rider in history of BMX; Founder and Owner Hoffman Bikes, Hoffman Sports Asscn/Hoffman Promotions and Hoffman Enterprises, Inc.; first rider to perform 900 degree spin in competition and take backflip to vert; came out of retirement to compete in Summer X-Games 2002 and won Bronze Medal, also landed no-handed 900 for first time in competition resulting in Silver Medal; set record for highest air jump 26 feet 6 inches (8.07m) on 24-foot (7.31m) ramp (jump listed in 2004 Guinness Book of World Records as High Air World Record holder for BMX bike) 2002; creator of Mat Hoffman's Crazy Freakin Stunt Show for Universal Studios, Orlando, Fla 2003, 2005; involved in several film projects, including Keep Your Eyes Open, IMAX film Ultimate X, xXx, Jackass – The Movie; host of series of behind-the-scenes segments for Tomb Raider 2 2003; appeared in video games such as Mat Hoffman BMX, Mat Hoffman BMX 2, and Tony Hawk Pro Skater 4; participated in Tony Hawk's (q.v.) Boom Boom Huck Jam 2002, 2003, 2005; Vice-Pres. Int. BMX Freestyle Fed., US BMX Freestyle Fed.; Lifetime Achievement Award, ESPN Action Sports and Music Awards 2002. *Television:* has produced, directed and hosted several TV series for ESPN including Kids in the Way, HBtv, Mat's World, a nine-episode segment on X-2day and the CFB Series; mem. cast of MTV's Trippin' 2005. *Publications:* The Ride of My Life (autobiog.) 2002. *Address:* c/o Brian Dubin, William Morris Agency, 1325 Avenue of the Americas, New York, NY 10019, USA. *Telephone:* (212) 903-1184. *E-mail:* bd@wma.com. *Website:* www.mathoffman.com.

HOFFMAN, Reid Garrett, BS, MSt (Oxon.); American business executive; *Executive Chairman, LinkedIn;* b. 5 Aug. 1967, Stanford, CA; s. of William Parker Hoffman, Jr and Deanna Ruth Rutter; m. Michelle Yee; ed The Putney School, Coll., Stanford Univ., Univ. of Oxford, UK; Sr User Experience Architect, Apple Computer 1994–96; Dir of Product Man. and Devt, Fujitsu Software Corpn 1996–97; Co-founder, Bd mem. and Vice-Pres., Product Socialnet.com 1997–2000; Exec. Vice-Pres. PayPal 2000–02; Co-founder, Chair. and CEO LinkedIn 2003–07, Chair. and Pres., Products, LinkedIn 2007–08, Chair. and CEO 2008–09, Exec. Chair. 2009–; Angel Investor, Aufklarung LLC 2000–09; Chair. Westcoast Advisory Bd, Questbridge 2008–; Partner, Greylock, Menlo Park, Calif. 2009–; mem. Bd of Dirs PayPal 1998–2000, Grassroots 2003–09, Vendio 2003–10, Six Apart 2003–10, Tagged 2005–10, Mozilla Corpn 2005–16, Kiva.org 2006–, Zynga

2008–14, Edmodo 2011–, Microsoft 2017–; mem. Bd of Advisors, Lulan LLC 2003–09, Center for Citizen Media 2006–07; mem. Provost Council, College Eight, Univ. of California, Santa Cruz 2006–; Hon. Fellow Wolfson Coll, Oxford 2016–; Hon. DJur 2012; Marshall Scholarship and Dinkelspiel Award, Stanford Univ., Matthew Arnold Memorial Prize (Proxime Accessit), SD Forum Visionary Award, Henry Crown Fellowship, shared the Ernst and Young US Entrepreneur of the Year Award 2011, honoured by the World Affairs Council and Global Philanthropy Forum 2012, David Packard Medal of Achievement Award, TechAmerica 2012. *Publication:* The Startup of You: Adapt to the Future, Invest in Yourself, and Transform Your Career (with Ben Casnocha) 2012. *Address:* LinkedIn, 2029 Stierlin Court, Mountain View, CA 94043, USA (office). *Telephone:* (650) 687-3600 (office). *E-mail:* press@linkedin.com (office). *Website:* www.linkedin.com/reidhoffman (office).

HOFFMANN, Claus Dieter; German business executive; *Chairman, Supervisory Board, Energie Baden-Württemberg AG;* b. 1942; fmrly with Robert Bosch GmbH, becoming Chief Financial Officer –2002; Founder and Man. Partner, H + H Senior Advisors GmbH 2002–; Chair. Supervisory Bd Energie Baden-Württemberg AG 2006–; mem. Supervisory Bd ING Group from 2003, Bauerfeind AG, Jowat AG, De Boer Group; Chair. Charlottenklinik Foundation; Chair. Bd of Trustees (Vereinigung der Freunde), Stuttgart Univ.; mem. Foundation Council Japanisch-Deutsches Zentrum Berlin. *Leisure interest:* golf. *Address:* Energie Baden-Württemberg AG, Durlacher Allee 93, 76131 Karlsruhe, Germany (office). *Telephone:* (721) 6312750 (office). *Fax:* (721) 6312672 (office). *E-mail:* info@enbw.com (office). *Website:* www.enbw.com (office).

HOFFMANN, Gleisi Helena; Brazilian lawyer and politician; b. 6 Sept. 1965, Curitiba, Paraná; d. of Júlio Hoffmann and Getúlia Agda; m. Paulo Bernardo; one s. one d.; fmr Sec. of State, Mato Grosso do Sul State; fmr Muncipal Sec., City of Londrina; mem. Pres. Lula da Silva's transition team 2002; Dir of Finance, Itaipu (hydroelectric dam) 2003–06; unsuccessful cand. for Mayor of Curitiba 2008; mem. Senate for Paraná Feb.–June 2011; Cabinet Chief June 2011–14; mem. Partido dos Trabalhadores 1989–, fmr Pres. Paraná Regional Br. *Address:* c/o Partido dos Trabalhadores, SCS, Quadra 2, Bloco C, Edif. Toufic, Sala 256, 70302-000 São Paulo, Brazil.

HOFFMANN, Jules A., PhD; French (b. Luxembourg) biologist and academic; *Professor and Chair of Integrative Biology, University of Strasbourg Institute for Advanced Study (USIAS);* b. 2 Aug. 1941, Echternach, Luxembourg; m. Daniele Hoffmann; two c.; ed Louis Pasteur Univ., Strasbourg, France, Philipps Univ., Marburg, Germany; Research Asst, CNRS 1964–68, Research Assoc. 1969–74, Research Dir 1974–2009, Dir, CNRS Immune Response and Devt in Insects Lab. 1978–2005, Dir, Inst. of Molecular and Cellular Biology 1994–2006, now Emer. Distinguished Class Research Dir, also mem. CNRS Bd of Admin; Researcher, Gen. Biology Lab., Univ. of Strasbourg 1975–, Dir 1978, also currently Prof. and Chair. of Integrative Biology, Univ. of Strasbourg Inst. for Advanced Study (USIAS); Pres. Acad. des Sciences 2007–08; mem. German Acad. of Sciences Leopoldina, Acad. française 1992–, Academia Europaea 1993–, European Molecular Biology Org. (EMBO) 1995–; Foreign Assoc. American Acad. of Arts and Sciences 2003, Russian Acad. of Sciences 2006; Chevalier, Légion d'honneur 2012; Dr hc (Munich) 2006, (Padova) 2013, (Liege) 2014; numerous awards, including William B. Coley Award 2003, Robert Koch Prize in Immunology 2004, Lewis S. Rosenstiel Award (jtly) 2010, Keio Medical Science Prize (with Shizuo Akira) 2011, Gairdner Award for Medical Research 2011, Shaw Prize in Life Science and Medicine (jtly) 2011, CNRS Gold Medal 2011, Nobel Prize in Physiology or Medicine (jtly) 2011. *Publications:* author or co-author of 250 publs, ed of numerous vols. *Address:* Institute of Advanced Study, University of Strasbourg, 5 allée du Général Rouvillois, 67083 Strasbourg, France (office). *Telephone:* 3-88-71-70-77 (office). *E-mail:* j.hoffmann@unistra.fr (office). *Website:* www.usias.fr (office).

HOFFMANN, Baron (Life Peer), cr. 1995, of Chedworth in the County of Gloucestershire; **Rt Hon. Leonard Hubert Hoffmann,** Kt, MA, PC; British judge; b. 8 May 1934, Cape Town, South Africa; s. of B. W. Hoffmann and G. Hoffmann; m. Gillian Sterner 1957; two d.; ed South African Coll. School, Cape Town, Univ. of Cape Town and Queen's Coll. Oxford; Advocate, Supreme Court of S Africa 1958–60; called to the Bar, Gray's Inn, London 1964, Bencher 1984; QC 1977; Judge, Courts of Appeal of Jersey and Guernsey 1980–85; Judge, High Court of Justice, Chancery Div. 1985–92; Lord Justice of Appeal 1992–95; a Lord of Appeal in Ordinary 1995–2009; Judge, Court of Final Appeal, Hong Kong Special Admin. Region 1997–; Chair. Financial Markets Law Cttee, Bank of England; Law Prof. and Consultant, Queen Mary Coll., Univ. of London; Arbitrator and Mediator, Brick Court Chambers, London; Dir ENO 1985–90, 1991–94; Stowell Civil Law Fellow, Univ. Coll. Oxford 1961–73, now Hon. Fellow; Pres. British-German Jurists Asscn 1991–; Hon. Fellow, Queen's Coll. Oxford 1992; Hon. Prof. of Intellectual Property Law, Centre for Commercial Law Studies, Queen Mary, Univ. of London 2009; Gold Bauhinia Star, Order of the Bauhinia Star (Hong Kong) 2010; Hon. DCL (City) 1992, (Univ. of the West of England) 1995. *Publication:* The South African Law of Evidence 1963 (second edn 1970). *Address:* Centre for Commercial Law Studies, 67-69 Lincoln's Inn Fields, London, WC2A 3JB (office); Surrey Lodge, 23 Keats Grove, London, NW3 2RS, England (home). *Telephone:* (20) 7882 8061 (office). *E-mail:* hoffmannl@parliament.uk (office).

HOFFMANN, Maja; Swiss art collector, art patron, filmmaker, impresario and entrepreneur; *President, Kunsthalle Zürich;* b. 1956; d. of Luc Hoffmann and Daria Hoffmann-Razumovsky; ed New School and New York Univ., USA; Founder LUMA Foundation, Arles France 2004, supports initiatives in Switzerland and around the world, including Center for Curatorial Studies at Bard Coll. and New Museum of Contemporary Art in New York (mem. Bd); also supports several art-based int. initiatives and institutional projects, including Kunsthalle Basel and Kunst-Werke Berlin, Fotomuseum Winterthur, Palais de Tokyo in Paris, Venice Biennale, Artangel and Serpentine Gallery, London; Pres. Kunsthalle Zürich; Vice-Pres. Council of Emanuel Hoffmann Foundation, Basel; Trustee, Tate Gallery, London. *Film:* produced documentary film Jean-Michel Basquiat: The Radiant Child 2010. *Address:* Kunsthalle Zürich, Limmatstrasse 270, 8005 Zürich, Switzerland (office). *Telephone:* (44) 272-15-15 (office). *Fax:* (44) 272-18-88 (office). *E-mail:* info@kunsthallezurich.ch (office). *Website:* www.kunsthallezurich.ch (office).

HOFFMANN, Roald, MA, PhD; American chemist and academic; *Frank H.T. Rhodes Professor Emeritus of Humane Letters, Department of Chemistry and Chemical Biology, Cornell University;* b. (Roald Safran), 18 July 1937, Złoczów, Poland; s. of Hillel Safran and Clara Rosen, step-s. of Paul Hoffmann; m. Eva Börjesson 1960; one s. one d.; ed Columbia and Harvard Univs; Jr Fellow, Soc. of Fellows, Harvard Univ. 1962–65; Assoc. Prof., Dept of Chem. and Chemical Biology, Cornell Univ. 1965–68, Prof. 1968–74, John A. Newman Prof. of Physical Science 1974–96, currently Frank H.T. Rhodes Prof. Emeritus of Humane Letters; mem. NAS, USSR (now Russian) Acad. of Sciences, Societas Scientarum Fennica 1986, Int. Acad. of Quantum Molecular Science; Foreign mem. Royal Soc. 1984, Royal Swedish Acad. of Sciences 1985, Indian Nat. Acad. of Sciences; Fellow, American Acad. of Arts and Sciences 1971, American Philosophical Soc. 1984; Hon. DTech (Royal Inst. of Technology, Stockholm) 1977, Hon. DSc (Yale) 1980, (Columbia) 1982, (Hartford) 1982, (City Univ. of New York) 1983, (Puerto Rico) 1983, (Uruguay) 1984, (La Plata) 1984, (Colgate) 1985, (State Univ. of New York at Binghamton) 1985, (Ben Gurion Univ. of Negev) 1989, (Lehigh) 1989, (Carleton) 1989, (Maryland) 1990, (Arizona) 1991, (Bar-Ilan Univ.) 1991, (Central Florida) 1991, (Athens) 1991, (Thessaloniki) 1991, (St Petersburg) 1991, (Barcelona) 1992, (Northwestern Univ.) 1996, (The Technion) 1996, (Durham) 2000 and others; ACS Award 1969, Fresenius Award 1969, Harrison Howe Award 1969, Annual Award of Int. Acad. of Quantum Molecular Sciences 1970, Arthur C. Cope Award, ACS 1973, Linus Pauling Award 1974, Nichols Medal 1980, Nobel Prize in Chem. (shared with Kenichi Fukui) 1981, Inorganic Chem. Award, ACS 1982, Nat. Medal of Science 1984, Nat. Acad. of Sciences Award, in Chemical Sciences 1986, Priestley Medal 1990, Pimentel Award in Chemical Educ. 1996, Lomonosov Gold Medal, Russian Acad. of Sciences 2011, Linus Pauling Legacy Award 2012, Harvard Centennial Medal, James T. Grady-James H. Stack Award for Interpreting Chem., and several others. *Plays:* Oxygen (with Carl Djerassi) 2001, Should've 2006, Something That Belongs To You 2009. *Publications:* Conservation of Orbital Symmetry 1970, The Metamict State (poetry) 1987, Solids and Surfaces: A Chemist's View of Bonding in Extended Structures 1988, Gaps and Verges (poetry) 1990, Chemistry Imagined (co-author) 1993, The Same and Not the Same 1995, Old Wine, New Flasks (co-author) 1997, Memory Effects (poetry) 1999, Soliton (poetry) 2002, Catalísta (poetry) 2002, Roald Hoffmann Izbrannie Stichotvorenia (poetry) 2010. *Address:* Department of Chemistry and Chemical Biology, Cornell University, Baker Laboratory, Room 226, Ithaca, NY 14853-1301, USA (office). *Telephone:* (607) 255-3419 (office). *Fax:* (607) 255-5707 (office). *E-mail:* rh34@cornell.edu (office). *Website:* chemistry.cornell.edu (office); www.roaldhoffmann.com.

HOGAN, Joseph M., BS, MS (Business Admin); American business executive; *President and CEO, Align Technology Inc.;* b. 7 May 1957; m. Lisa Hogan; three c.; ed Geneva Coll., Robert Morris Univ.; Sales, Marketing and Product Devt roles with GE Plastics, USA 1985–90, Business Leader, Lexan Europe, GE Plastics, Netherlands 1990–93, Gen. Man. Americas Marketing, GE Plastics, USA 1994–96, Staff Exec., GE Corpn, USA 1996–98, Pres. and CEO, GE Fanuc Automation N America 1998–2000, Exec. Vice-Pres. and COO GE Medical Systems, USA 2000, Pres. and CEO GE Healthcare, USA and UK 2000–08; CEO ABB Group worldwide and ABB Ltd, Switzerland 2008–13; Pres. and CEO Align Tech. Inc. 2015–, also mem. Bd of Dirs; mem. Bd of Dirs Multiple Myeloma Research Foundation Inc.; mem. Bd Centres for Disease Control and Prevention. *Address:* Align Technology Incorporated, 2560, Orchard Parkway, San Jose, CA 95134, USA (office). *Telephone:* (408) 470-1000 (office). *Fax:* (408) 470-1010 (office). *Website:* www.aligntech.com (office).

HOGAN, Lawrence (Larry) J., Jr, BA; American real estate executive and politician; *Governor of Maryland;* b. 25 May 1956, Washington, DC; s. of Lawrence Joseph Hogan and Ilona Hogan (née Modly); m. Yumi Kim 2004; three d.; ed Florida State Univ.; f. Hogan Cos (real estate firm), Md 1985, Pres., CEO; Cabinet Sec. to Gov. of Maryland Bob Ehrlich 2003–07; Founder and Chair. Change Maryland 2011–; Gov. of Maryland 2015–; Republican. *Address:* Office of the Governor, State House, 100 State Circle, Annapolis, MD 21401-1925, USA (office). *Telephone:* (410) 974-3901 (office). *Fax:* (410) 974-3275 (office). *Website:* www.governor.maryland.gov (office).

HOGAN, Mark T., BSc, MBA; American automobile industry executive; *President, Dewey Investments LLC;* b. 15 May 1951, Chicago; ed Univ. of Ill., Harvard Univ.; joined General Motors (GM) 1973, Factory Analyst, Electro-Motive Div., Chicago 1973–77, several analytical and supervisory positions, GM Financial Staff 1977–81, Sr Admin. for Forward Business Planning, Fisher Body Div. 1981–82, Dir of Material, Labour and Forecast Section, Comptroller's Staff 1982–83, Dir Treasurer's Office, Detroit 1983–84, Group Dir Public Affairs Staff, Chevrolet-Pontiac-Canada Group 1984–86, Gen. Man. and Comptroller, New United Motor Mfg Inc. 1986–88, Group Dir of Business Planning, Truck and Bus Group 1988–92, Exec. Dir of Planning, N American Operations (NAO) 1992–94, Exec. Dir NAO Planning and Corp. Information Man. 1994, Pres. and Man.-Dir GM do Brasil, Group Vice-Pres. e-GM 1999–2004, Group Vice-Pres. for Advanced Vehicle Devt 2001–04; Pres. Magna Int. Inc. 2004–07; Pres. and CEO Vehicle Production Group, LLC 2008–10; Pres. Dewey Investments LLC 2010–; Advisor, Toyota Motor Corpn 2010–; mem. Bd of Dirs Visteon Corpn 2010–. *Address:* Dewey Investments LLC, 39533 Woodward Ave., Bloomfield Hills, MI 48304-5095, USA.

HOGAN, Paul, AO; Australian film actor; b. 8 Oct. 1940, Lightening Ridge; m. 1st Noelene Hogan (divorced 1989); five c.; m. 2nd Linda Kozlowski 1990 (divorced 2012); one s.; ed Parramatta High School; fmr rigger on Sydney Harbour Bridge; filmed TV specials on location in England 1983; commercials for Australian Tourist Comm., Fosters Lager; Australian of the Year 1985, Longford Lyell Award for Outstanding Contribution, Australian Acad. of Cinema and Television Arts 2016. *Films:* Crocodile Dundee (Golden Globe Award) 1986, Crocodile Dundee II 1989, Almost An Angel 1993, Lightning Jack 1994, Flipper 1996, Sorrow Floats 1997, Crocodile Dundee in Los Angeles 2001, Strange Bedfellows 2004, Charlie & Boots 2009. *TV:* The Paul Hogan Show 1973, Hogan in London 1975, Anzacs (miniseries) 1985, Floating Away 1998, Open Slather 2015.

HOGAN, Phil, BA, H Dip in Ed; Irish politician and EU official; *Commissioner for Agriculture and Rural Development, European Commission;* b. 4 June 1960, Kilkenny; separated; one s.; ed St Joseph's Coll., Freshford, St Kieran's Coll., Kilkenny, Univ. Coll. Cork; est. Hogan Campion Auctioneers, Urlingford 1980s;

mem. Kilkenny Co. Council 1982–2003, Chair. 1985–86, 1989–90; mem. South-Eastern Health Board 1991–99; unsuccessful cand. in gen. election 1987; Senator (Fine Gael) in Seanad Éireann 1987–89, Fine Gael spokesman on Justice and Industry and Commerce; TD (mem. Dáil) for Carlow-Kilkenny constituency 1989–, Opposition Spokesperson on the Food Industry 1989–91, Consumer Affairs 1991–93, Regional Affairs and European Devt 1993–94, Chair. Fine Gael Parl. Party 1995–2001; Minister of State, Dept of Finance with special responsibility for Office of Public Works 1994–95 (resgnd); Dir of Organisation, Fine Gael 2002, unsuccessful cand. in leadership election 2002, apptd Spokesperson for Enterprise, Trade and Employment 2002, Dir of Organisation for gen. election 2007; Minister for the Environment, Community and Local Govt 2011–14; Commr for Agric. and Rural Devt, European Comm. (EC), Brussels Nov. 2014–. *Address:* European Commission, 200 Rue de la Loi/Wetstraat 200, 1049 Brussels, Belgium (office). *Telephone:* (2) 299-11-11 (office). *E-mail:* philip.hogan@oireachtas.ie (office). *Website:* ec.europa.eu (office); www.philhogan.ie.

HOGE, James Fulton, Jr, BA, MA; American academic and editor; b. 25 Dec. 1935, New York, NY; m. Kathleen Lacey Hoge; ed Yale Univ., Univ. of Chicago, Harvard Univ.; Ed. Foreign Affairs (journal) 1992–2010, Peter G. Peterson Chair 1997–2010; fmr Ed.-in-Chief Chicago Sun-Times newspaper, then Publr and Pres. NY Daily News; fmr Dir Council on Foreign Relations; Chair. Human Rights Watch 2010–13; mem. Bd of Dirs Int. Center for Journalists (ICFJ) 1992–, currently Chair.; mem. Bd of Dirs Center for Global Affairs, New York Univ.; Congressional Fellow, American Political Science Asscn 1962; Fellow, John F. Kennedy School of Govt Harvard Univ. 1991; Sr Fellow, Freedom Forum Media Studies Columbia Univ. 1992; Dir Foundation for Civil Society; mem. American Council on Germany, Program Cttee of American Ditchley Foundation; Dr hc (Columbia Coll.) 1985; Public Service Award, Univ. of Chicago 1973, Award for Contributions to Journalism, The Better Govt Asscn of Chicago 1975, Public Service Award, The Citizens Cttee for New York City 1985, six Pulitzer Prizes (to Chicago Sun Times while Ed. and Publr), Pulitzer Prize (to New York Daily News while Publr). *Television:* The Threat of Terrorism (documentary writer and narrator). *Publications include:* The American Encounter: The United States and the Making of the Modern World (co-ed.) 1997, How Did This Happen? Terrorism and the New War (co-ed.) 2001; numerous articles, reviews and chapters in journals, newspapers and books. *Address:* c/o Human Rights Watch, 350 Fifth Avenue, 34th Floor, New York, NY 10118-3299, USA.

HOGG, Sir Christopher Anthony, Kt, MA, MBA, FCGI (Hon.); British business executive; b. 2 Aug. 1936, London; s. of Anthony Wentworth Hogg and Monica Mary Gladwell; m. 1st Anne Patricia Cathie 1961 (divorced 1997); two d.; m. 2nd Dr Miriam Stoppard 1997; ed Marlborough Coll., Trinity Coll., Oxford and Harvard Business School, USA; Nat. Service, Parachute Regt 1955–57; Research Assoc. Institut pour l'Etude des Méthodes de Direction de l'Entreprise (business school), Lausanne, Switzerland 1962–63; with Philip Hill, Higginson, Erlangers Ltd (later Hill Samuel & Co. Ltd) 1963–66; staff mem. Industrial Reorganisation Corpn 1966–68; joined Courtaulds Group 1968, Man. Dir 1971, Dir (non-exec.) British Celanese Ltd 1971–72, Chair. 1972–75, Dir Courtaulds Ltd 1973–96, a Deputy Chair. 1978–80, Chief Exec. 1979–91, Chair. Courtaulds PLC 1980–96, Courtaulds Textiles PLC 1990–95; Deputy Chair. Allied Domecq 1995–96, Chair. 1996–2002; Dir (non-exec.) Reuters Group PLC 1984–2004 (Chair. 1985–2004), SmithKline Beecham PLC 1993–2000, GlaxoSmithKline 2000–04 (Chair. 2002–04); Air Liquide SA 2000–05; Chair. Financial Reporting Council 2006–10; Chair. (non-exec.) Royal Nat. Theatre 1995–2004; Trustee, Ford Foundation 1987–99; mem. Dept of Industry Industrial Devt Advisory Bd 1976–81, Cttee of Award for Harkness Fellowships 1980–86, Int. Council J.P. Morgan 1988–2003, Court, Bank of England 1992–96; Hon. Fellow, Trinity Coll. Oxford 1982, London Business School 1992, City and Guilds of London Inst. 1992; Hon. FCSD 1987; Foreign Hon. mem. American Acad. of Arts and Sciences 1991; Hon. mem. ICAEW 2013; Hon. DSc (Cranfield Inst. of Tech.) 1986, (Aston) 1988; BIM Gold Medal 1986, Centenary Medal, Soc. of Chemical Industry 1989, Hambro Businessman of the Year 1993. *Publication:* Masers and Lasers 1962. *Leisure interests:* theatre, reading, walking.

HOGG, James C., OC, FRSC, MD, MSc, PhD; Canadian pathologist and academic; *Professor Emeritus of Pathology, University of British Columbia;* b. 3 Dec. 1935, Winnipeg; ed Univ. of Manitoba, McGill Univ., Montreal; Medical Officer, Royal Canadian Air Force 1963–66; specialist training in pathology, Mass Gen. Hosp., Boston and Royal Victoria Hosp., Montreal; Asst Prof. of Pathology, McGill Univ. 1971, Miranda Fraser Prof. of Comparative Pathology 1975–77; joined Univ. of British Columbia (UBC) and St Paul's Hosp., Vancouver 1977 (first full-time prof. based at St Paul's), co-f. pulmonary research lab. (later renamed UBC James Hogg Centre for Cardiovascular and Pulmonary Research), Prin. Investigator, UBC James Hogg Research Centre, currently Prof. Emer. of Pathology, UBC; Canadian Medical Hall of Fame 2010, American Soc. for Investigative Pathology Chugai Award 2003, Canada Gairdner Wightman Award 2013. *Publications:* more than 300 papers in peer-reviewed literature. *Address:* UBC James Hogg Research Centre, St Paul's Hospital, Room 166, 1081 Burrard Street, Vancouver, BC V6Z 1Y6, Canada (office). *Telephone:* (604) 806-8346 (office). *Fax:* (604) 806-8351 (office). *Website:* www.hli.ubc.ca (office).

HOGG, Baroness (Life Peer), cr. 1995, of Kettlethorpe in the County of Lincolnshire; **Sarah Elizabeth Mary Hogg;** British economist; b. 14 May 1946; d. of Lord Boyd-Carpenter; m. Rt Hon. Douglas M. Hogg QC, MP 1968; one s. one d.; ed St Mary's Convent, Ascot and Lady Margaret Hall, Oxford Univ.; staff writer, The Economist 1967, Literary Ed. 1970, Econs Ed. 1977; Econs Ed. Sunday Times 1981; Presenter, Channel 4 News 1982–83; Econs Ed. and Deputy Exec. Ed. Finance and Industry, The Times 1984–86; Asst Ed. and Business and City Ed. The Independent 1986–89; Econs Ed. The Daily Telegraph 1989–90; Head Policy Unit, 10 Downing Street (rank Second Perm. Sec.) 1990–95; Chair. London Econs 1997–99 (Dir 1995–97), Frontier Econs 1999–; mem. Int. Advisory Bd, Nat. Westminster Bank 1995–97, Advisory Bd, Bankinter 1995–98, House of Lords Select Cttee on Science and Tech. 1995–98, House of Lords Select Cttee on Monetary Policy 2000, Council, Royal Econ. Soc. 1996–, Council, Hansard Soc. 1995–99; Dir London Broadcasting Co. 1982–90, Royal Nat. Theatre 1988–91, Foreign & Colonial Smaller Cos Investment Trust 1995–2002 (Chair. 1997–2002), Nat. Provident Inst. 1996–99, GKN 1996– (Deputy Chair. 2003–), 3i Group 1997–2010 (Deputy Chair. 2000, Chair. 2002–10), P&O 1999–2000, P&O Princess Cruises 2000–03, Carnival Corpn & Carnival PLC 2003–, Martin Currie Portfolio Investment Trust 1999–02; Gov. BBC 2000–04, Centre for Econ. Policy Research 1985–92, London Business School 2004–, Financial Reporting Council 2004–; Fellow, Eton Coll. 1996–; Hon. Fellow, Lady Margaret Hall, Oxford 1994; Hon. MA (Open Univ.) 1987; Hon. DPhil (Loughborough Univ.) 1992; Hon. DL (Lincoln) 2001; Hon. DSc (City Univ.) 2002; Wincott Foundation Financial Journalist of the Year 1985. *Publication:* Too Close to Call (with Jonathan Hill) 1995. *Address:* House of Lords, Westminster, London, SW1A 0PW, England.

HOGGETT, Dame Brenda Marjorie (see HALE, Rt Hon. Dame Brenda Marjorie).

HOGNESS, David Swenson, BS, PhD; American geneticist and academic; *Rudy J. and Daphne Donohue Munzer Professor Emeritus in the School of Medicine, Stanford University;* b. 17 Nov. 1925, Oakland, Calif.; ed California Inst. of Tech.; Post-doctoral fellowship, Institut Pasteur, France 1952–54; Nat. Foundation Fellow, New York Univ. 1954–55; Instructor of Microbiology, Washington Univ. School of Medicine, St. Louis 1955–57, Asst Prof. of Microbiology 1957–59; Asst Prof., Dept of Biochemistry, Stanford Univ. 1959–61, Assoc. Prof. 1961–66, apptd Prof. 1966, Chair. Dept of Biochemistry 1986–89, Prof. of Development Biology and of Biochemistry 1989–99, Rudy J. and Daphne Donohue Munzer Professorship 1991, Prof. Emer. 1999–; mem., NAS 1976, American Academy of Arts and Sciences 1976; Assoc. mem. European Molecular Biology Org. 1992; Hon. mem. Japanese Biochemical Soc. 1987; Dr hc (Univ. of Crete, Greece), (Univ. of Basel, Switzerland) 1986; Genetics Soc. of America Medal 1984, Newcomb Cleveland Prize of the American Asscn for the Advancement of Science 1966, 1988, Rickets Award, Univ. of Chicago 1977, Humboldt Research Award, Germany 1995, Darwin Prize, Univ. of Edinburgh 1995, March of Dimes Prize in Developmental Biology (shared with W. Ghering) 1997, Lifetime Achievement Award of the Society for Developmental Biology 2002, Int. Prize for Biology, Japan Soc. for the Promotion of Science 2007, Warren Alpert Foundation Prize 2013. *Publications:* numerous scientific papers in professional journals on the study of gene structure in higher eukaryotes, the developmental genetics of the fruit fly *Drosophila melanogaster* and how the hormone ecdysone acts to regulate metamorphosis in *Drosophila*. *Address:* Stanford University School of Medicine, 291 Campus Drive, Palo Alto, CA 94305, USA (office). *Telephone:* (650) 721-2656 (office). *E-mail:* tran@cmgm.stanford.edu (office). *Website:* med.stanford.edu (office).

HOHLER, Erla Karine Bergendahl, DPhil, FSA; Norwegian archaeologist, art historian and academic; *Professor Emerita, Institute of Archaeology, Art History and Numismatics, Oslo University;* b. 20 Nov. 1937, Oslo; m. Christopher Hohler 1961; three c.; ed Univ. of Oslo, Courtauld Inst., UK; Asst Prof., Inst. of Art History, Univ. of Oslo 1975, Prof., Inst. of Archaeology, Art History and Numismatics 1993, now Prof. Emer.; Keeper, Medieval Dept, Univ. Museum of Nat. Antiquities, Oslo 1987; Prof. of Art History, Univ. of Tromsø 1994; mem. Soc. of Antiquaries of London 1986, Det Norske Videnskaps-akademi 1994. *Publications:* The Capitals of Urnes Church 1975, Stavkirkene 1981, Stilentwicklung in der Holzkirchen Architektur 1981, Norwegian Stave Church Carving 1989, Norwegian Stave Church Sculpture I-II 1999, Catalogue Raisonné 1999, Painted Altar Frontals of Norway I-III 2004. *Address:* Lyder Sagens Gt. 23, 0358 Oslo (home); Universitetets Kulturhistoriske Museer, Frederiks Gt. 3, 0164 Oslo, Norway (office). *Telephone:* 22-46-57-32 (home); 22-85-95-36 (office). *E-mail:* hohler@extern.uio.no (office). *Website:* www.khm.uio.no (office).

HOI, Dato Lim Jock, BSc; Brunei government official and international organization official; *Secretary-General, Association of Southeast Asian Nations;* b. 5 Dec. 1951; m.; two s.; ed City of London Polytechnic; Educ. Officer, Dept of Educ. 1977, Asst Dir of Educ., Perm. Sec.'s Office, Ministry of Educ. 1986–89; Special Duties Officer, Int. Relations and Trade Devt, Ministry of Industry and Primary Resources 1989–96, Dir 1996–2001, Dir-Gen. 2001–05, Deputy Perm. Sec. Ministry of Foreign Affairs and Trade 2005–06, Perm. Sec. 2006–18; Chair. Governing Bd, Econ. Research Inst., ASEAN 2011–17, Sec.-Gen. ASEAN 2018–; fmr Chief Negotiator Trans-Pacific Partnership Agreement (TPP); Order of Seri Paduka Mahkota Brunei 2007. *Address:* ASEAN Secretariat, Jl. Sisingamangaraja 70A, Jakarta 12110, Indonesia (office). *Telephone:* (21) 7262991 (office). *Fax:* (21) 7398234 (office). *E-mail:* public@asean.org (office). *Website:* www.asean.org (office).

HØJ, Peter, MSc, PhD, FTSE; Danish scientist, academic and university administrator; *Vice-Chancellor and President, University of Queensland;* b. 29 April 1957, Hundested; ed Univ. of Copenhagen; Man. Dir Australian Wine Research Inst., Adelaide 1997–2004; CEO Australian Research Council 2004–07; Vice-Chancellor and Pres. Univ. of South Australia 2007–12; Vice-Chancellor and Pres. Univ. of Queensland 2012–; Deputy Chair. Universities Australia 2011–13, Lead Vice-Chancellor Research 2010–13; pvt. mem. Prime Minister's Science Eng and Innovation Council 1999–2005, ex-officio mem. 2006–07; mem. Bd CSIRO 2011–14, Medical Research Future Fund 2016–; Foreign mem. (Natural Sciences Class) Royal Danish Acad. of Sciences and Letters; Fellow, Australian Acad. of Technological Sciences and Eng; Hon. DUniv (Copenhagen), (South Australia); Centenary Medal 2002. *Address:* Office of the Vice-Chancellor, Level 4, Brian Wilson Chancellery, University of Queensland, Brisbane, Qld 4072, Australia (office). *Telephone:* (7) 3365-1300 (office). *Fax:* (7) 3365-1266 (office). *E-mail:* vc@uq.edu.au (office). *Website:* www.uq.edu.au (office).

HOJABERDYYEV, Guychgeldy; Turkmenistani politician and government official; Rector of Turkmen Nat. Inst. of Sport and Tourism –2007; apptd Chair. State Cttee for Tourism and Sport 2007; Minister of Nat. Security 2015–16. *Address:* c/o Ministry of National Security, 744000 Aşgabat, Magtymguly Şaýoly 93, Turkmenistan.

HOJAMAMMEDOV, Byashimmyrat; Turkmenistani politician and government official; Deputy Minister of Econs and Devt –2008, Minister of Econs and Devt 2008–13; Gov. Balkan Prov. 2013–15; Deputy Chair. of the Govt, responsible for Econ. Affairs 2015–17, also responsible for Mari Velayat (Prov.) 2017; Rep. of Turkmenistan to Econ. Council of CIS 2015–. *Address:* c/o Office of the President and the Council of Ministers, 744000 Aşgabat, Galkynyş köç. 20, Turkmenistan (office). *Telephone:* (12) 35-45-34 (office). *Fax:* (12) 35-51-12 (office). *E-mail:* nt@online.tm (office). *Website:* www.turkmenistan.gov.tm (office).

HOJAMUHAMMEDOV, Baymyrat; Turkmenistani hydrogeologist and government official; b. 15 Nov. 1961, Aşgabat, Turkmen SSR, USSR; s. of Geldymyrat Hojamuhammedov and Aynagozel Hojamuhammedov; m.; two s. two d.; ed Ordzhonikidze Moscow Geology Inst.; Hydrogeologist, Turkmen Research Inst. 1984–86; Sr Scientist, Turkmenistan Geology Scientific Research Inst. 1991–93; Sr Hydrogeologist, Turkmengeologiya 1993–97; Head of Gas Export Dept, Turkmenneftgas State Trade Corpn 1997, later Deputy Chair. Nat. Clearing Center; Head of Gas Export Dept, Turkmengas 2006–07; Head of Investments and Mineral Resources, Ministry of Petroleum 2007, Minister of Petroleum, Natural Gas and Mineral Resources 2007–09, Deputy Chair. of Govt 2009–, responsible for Petroleum and Natural Gas 2009–11, for the Oil and Gas Sector and Fisheries 2011–16. *Address:* c/o Office of the President and the Council of Ministers, 744000 Aşgabat, Galkynyş köç. 20, Turkmenistan. *E-mail:* nt@online.tm.

HOLBOROW, Leslie Charles, QSO, BPhil, MA; New Zealand fmr university vice-chancellor; *Professor Emeritus, Victoria University of Wellington;* b. 28 Jan. 1941, Auckland; s. of George Holborow and Ivah V. Holborow; m. Patricia L. Walsh 1965 (died 2012); one s. two d.; partner Elizabeth McLeay 2013–; ed Henderson High School, Auckland Grammar School, Univ. of Auckland and Univ. of Oxford, UK; Jr Lecturer, Univ. of Auckland 1963; Lecturer, Sr Lecturer, Univ. of Dundee (until 1967 Queen's Coll. Univ. of St Andrew's) 1965–74; Prof. of Philosophy, Univ. of Queensland, Brisbane 1974–85, Pres. Professorial Bd 1980–81, Pro-Vice-Chancellor (Humanities) 1983–85; Vice-Chancellor, Victoria Univ. of Wellington 1985–98, Prof. Emer. 1998–; Chair. NZ Vice-Chancellors' Cttee 1990, 1996; Council mem. Asscn of Commonwealth Univs 1990–91, 1996; Pres. Australasian Asscn of Philosophy 1977; Nat. Pres. NZ Inst. of Int. Affairs 1987–90, Standing Cttee 2002–13; Chair. NZ Univs Acad. Audit Unit 2003–09, Lilburn Residence Trust, Mahara Gallery 2016–; mem. NZ Cttee for Pacific Econ. Co-operation 1986–94, Educ. Sub-cttee of NZ Nat. Comm. for UNESCO 1996–99; Trustee, NZ String Quartet 1990–2011; mem. Bd, NZ School of Dance 2010–16; Hon. LLD (Victoria Univ. of Wellington) 1998. *Publications:* articles in philosophical journals and on New Zealand foreign policy. *Leisure interests:* golf, tramping, listening to music. *Address:* 16 Ames Street, Paekakariki 5034, New Zealand (home). *Telephone:* (4) 905-9886 (home); 27-7338728 (mobile) (home). *E-mail:* holborowles@gmail.com (home).

HOLBROOK, Harold (Hal) Rowe, Jr; American actor; b. 17 Feb. 1925, Cleveland, Ohio; s. of Harold Rowe Holbrook, Sr and Aileen Holbrook (née Davenport); m. 1st Ruby Holbrook 1945 (divorced 1965); one s. one d.; m. 2nd Carol Eve Rossen 1966 (divorced 1983) one d.; m. 3rd Dixie Carter 1984 (died 2010); ed Culver Academies, Denison Univ.; served in US Army in World War II, stationed in Newfoundland; performed a one-man show as Mark Twain 1954; mem. Valley Players, Holyoke, Mass 1941–62, performed at Mountain Park Casino Playhouse, Mountain Park, and performed Mark Twain Tonight to open the season 1957; sent by State Dept on a European tour, which included appearances behind the Iron Curtain; first played role of Mark Twain Off-Broadway 1959; Tony Award, Drama Desk Award. *Films include:* The Group 1966, Wild in the Streets 1968, The People Next Door 1970, The Great White Hope 1970, They Only Kill Their Masters 1972, Jonathan Livingston Seagull (voice) (uncredited) 1973, Magnum Force 1973, The Girl from Petrovka 1974, All the President's Men 1976, Battle of Midway 1976, Julia 1977, Rituals 1977, Capricorn One 1977, Natural Enemies 1979, The Fog 1980, The Kidnapping of the President 1980, Creepshow 1982, Girls Nite Out 1982, The Star Chamber 1983, Wall Street 1987, The Unholy 1988, Fletch Lives 1989, The Firm 1993, Acts of Love 1996, Cats Don't Dance (voice) 1997, Hercules (voice) 1997, Eye of God 1997, Hush 1998, Walking to the Waterline 1998, Judas Kiss 1998, Rusty: A Dog's Tale 1998, The Florentine 1999, The Bachelor 1999, Waking the Dead 2000, Men of Honour 2000, The Life and Adventures of Santa Claus (voice) 2000, The Majestic 2001, Purpose 2002, Seventh Day Documentary 2002, Country Music: The Spirit of America IMAX 2003, Shade 2003, Into the Wild 2007, Killshot 2008, That Evening Sun 2009, Flying Lessons 2010, Good Day for It 2011, Water for Elephants 2011, Lincoln 2012, Promised Land 2012, Savannah 2012. *Television includes:* The Brighter Day (series) 1954–59, Mr. Citizen (series) 1955, Preview Tonight (series) – The Cliff Dwellers 1966, The Glass Menagerie (film) 1966, Mark Twain Tonight (series) 1967, Coronet Blue (series) 1967, Off to See the Wizard (series) – Wild World (narrator) 1968, The F.B.I. (series) – The Fraud 1969, The Bold Ones: The Lawyers (series) – The Whole World Is Watching 1969, The Name of the Game (series) – The Perfect Image 1969, Disneyland (series) – The Wacky Zoo of Morgan City: Part 1, Part 2 1970, The Bold Ones: The Senator (series) (Outstanding Lead Actor – Drama Series, Primetime Emmy Awards 1971) 1970–71, Travis Logan, D.A. (film) 1971, Suddenly Single (film) 1971, Goodbye, Raggedy Ann (film) 1971, Appointment with Destiny (series) – Surrender at Appomattox (narrator) 1972, That Certain Summer (film) 1972, Pueblo (film) (Primetime Emmy Awards: Outstanding Lead Actor in a Miniseries or a Movie 1974, Actor of the Year 1974) 1973, Lincoln (mini-series) (Primetime Emmy Awards Outstanding Lead Actor in a Miniseries or a Movie 1976) 1974–75, Great Performances (series) 1975–77, 33 Hours in the Life of God (film) 1976, Our Town (film) 1977, Tartuffe (film), Host (uncredited) 1978, The Awakening Land (mini-series) 1978, Murder by Natural Causes (film) 1979, The Legend of the Golden Gun (film) 1979, When Hell Was in Session (series) 1979, Off the Minnesota Strip (film) 1980, Omnibus (series) 1980, The Killing of Randy Webster (series) 1981, Celebrity (mini-series) 1984, George Washington (mini-series) 1984, The Three Wishes of Billy Grier (film) 1984, North and South Part 1 (mini-series) 1985, Behind Enemy Lines (film) 1985, Under Siege (film) 1986, Dress Gray (film) 1986, North and South Part 2 (mini-series) 1986, Designing Women (series) 1986–89, Plaza Suite (film) 1987, The Fortunate Pilgrim (mini-series) 1988, Emma: Queen of the South Seas (mini-series) 1988, I'll Be Home for Christmas (film) 1988, Day One (film) 1989, Sorry, Wrong Number (film) 1989, Evidence of Love (film) 1990, Evening Shade (series) 1990–94, Bonds of Love (film) 1993, A Perry Mason Mystery: The Case of the Lethal Lifestyle (film) 1994, A Perry Mason Mystery: The Case of the Grimacing Governor (film) 1994, A Perry Mason Mystery: The Case of the Jealous Jokester (film) 1995, She Stood Alone: The Tailhook Scandal (film) 1995, Innocent Victims (film) 1996, The Battle of the Alamo (documentary) (narrator) 1996, Great Soldiers (film) 1997, All the Winters That Have Been (film) 1997, The Third Twin (film) 1997, My Own Country (film) 1998, Beauty (film) 1998, A Place Apart (film) 1999, The Outer Limits (series) – Final Appeal 2000, Family Law (series) – One Mistake 2000, The Legend of the Three Trees (film) (voice) 2001, Haven (film) 2001, The West Wing (series) 2001–02, Becker (series) 2002, The Street Lawyer (film) 2003, Hope & Faith (series) – A Room of One's Own 2005, The Cultivated Life: Thomas Jefferson and Wine (film) (voice) 2005, Captain Cook's Extraordinary Atlas (film) 2009, Sons of Anarchy (series) 2010, The Event (series) 2010–11, Rectify (series) 2012–13. *Address:* c/o Abrams Artists Agency L.A., 9200 Sunset Blvd, 11th Floor, Los Angeles, CA 90069, USA (office).

HOLBROOK, Karen A., BS, MS, PhD; American biologist, academic and university administrator; *Regional Chancellor, University of South Florida Sarasota-Manatee;* b. 6 Nov. 1942, Des Moines, IA; m. Jim Holbrook; one s.; ed Univ. of Wisconsin in Madison, Univ. of Washington, Seattle; Teaching Asst, Zoology, Univ. of Wisconsin 1963–66; Instructor of Biology, Ripon Coll. 1966–69, Instructor, Upward Bound Program 1967; Instructor, NSF Summer Inst. 1969; Teaching Asst, Biological Structure, Univ. of Washington 1969–72, Instructor, Biological Structure, School of Medicine 1972–75, Asst Prof., Biological Structure, Adjunct Asst Prof., Dermatology 1975–79, Assoc. Prof., Biological Structure, Adjunct Assoc. Prof., Dermatology 1979–84, Assoc. Chair. Biological Structure 1981–85, Prof., Biological Structure, Adjunct Assoc. Prof., Dermatology 1984–93, Assoc. Dean, Scientific Affairs 1985–94; Prof. of Anatomy and Dermatology, Vice-Pres. for Research and Dean Grad. School, Univ. of Florida 1993–98; Prof. of Cell Biology, Sr Vice-Pres. for Academic Affairs and Provost Univ. of Georgia 1998–2002, Medical Coll. of Georgia Adjunct Prof. of Anatomy, Cell Biology and Medicine 1998–2002; Prof. of Internal Medicine—Dermatology, Ohio State Univ. 2002–07, Prof. of Physiology and Cell Biology 2002–07, Pres. Ohio State Univ. 2002–07; Sr Vice-Pres. for Research, Innovation and Global Affairs 2007–10, Sr Vice-Pres. for Global Affairs and Int. Research 2010–12, Sr Advisor to Pres., Univ. of South Florida 2013–16, 2017–; Exec. Vice-Pres. Univ. of South Florida Sarasota-Manatee, Regional Chancellor 2018–, mem. Bd of Dirs Health Byrd Alzheimer's Inst.; Interim Pres. Embry-Riddle Aeronautical University 2016–17; Dir Bio-Techne Corpn 2007–18; Sr Fellow, Dermatology, Univ. of Wash. 1976–79, Distinguished Fellow, Global Fed. of Competitiveness Councils; fmr mem. of Advisory Cttee to the Dir of NIH; Assoc. Ed. Journal of Investigative Dermatology 1987–92, Journal of Investigative Dermatology 1997–; mem. Editorial Bd Journal of Investigative Dermatology 1978–82, Journal of Pediatric Dermatology 1982–89, American Journal of Anatomy 1983–92, Medicine Northwest 1985–87, Journal of Investigative Dermatology 1992–97, The Anatomical Record 1993–96; mem. Editorial Advisory Bd University Business magazine 2003–; mem. AAAS, American Soc. for Cell Biology, American Asscn of Anatomists, Soc. for Investigative Dermatology, Soc. for Pediatric Dermatology, American Civilization Seminar, Univ. of Florida; Hon. Mem. Epsilon Lambda Chi Alpha Engineering Leadership Circle, Nat. Bd Medical Coll. of Pennsylvania; Distinguished Mem. Nat. Soc. for Collegiate Scholars; Hon. DSc (Punjab Agricultural Univ.) 2006; Kung Sun Oh Memorial Prize, Yonsei Medical College, Seoul, S Korea 1994, 34th Annual Marion Spencer Fay Nat. Bd Award to a Distinguished Woman Physician/Scientist, Medical Coll. of Pennsylvania 1996, Pinkus Award, American Soc. of Dermatopathology 1997, Distinguished Contrib. to Research Admin Award, Soc. of Research Admins Int. 2002, Director's Award, Ohio Dept of Alcohol and Drug Addiction Services 2003, The Women's Center Leadership Award 2004, Acad. for Leadership Award, Harding-Evans Foundation 2004, Pres.'s Leadership Group Award, US Dept of Educ., Higher Educ. Center for Alcohol and Other Drug Abuse and Violence Prevention 2004, Women in Higher Educ. Award, Nat. Panhellenic Conf. Foundation, Inc. 2005, YWCA Women of Achievement Award 2006, Sixth Annual Empowered Woman Award, Columbus Women Pres.'s Org. 2006. *Films:* Prenatal Diagnosis of Inherited Skin Disease, Video Journal of Dermatology 1990, Fetal Skin Sampling, Dialogs in Dermatology 1994. *Publications:* more than 30 book chapters and more than 150 scientific papers in professional journals. *Address:* University of South Florida Sarasota-Manatee, 8350 N Tamiami Trail, Sarasota, FL 34243, USA (office). *Telephone:* (941) 359-4340 (office). *E-mail:* kholbrook@usf.edu (office). *Website:* sar.usfsm.edu/dr-karen-holbrook (office).

HOLCOMB, Eric, BA; American politician; *Governor of Indiana;* b. 2 May 1968; m. Janet Holcomb; ed Hanover Coll.; served in USN 1990–96; unsuccessful cand. for Indiana House of Reps 2000; Adviser to Gov. of Indiana Mitch Daniels 2003; Chair. Indiana Republican Party 2011–13; Chief of Staff to US Senator from Indiana Dan Coats 2013–15; apptd Lt-Gov. of Indiana March 2016, Gov. of Indiana 2017–; Chair., Republican Govs. Public Policy Cttee 2019–; mem. Indiana Farm Bureau, Nat. Fed. of Independent Business, American Legion; mem. Bd of Dirs Benjamin Harrison Presidential Site; Republican. *Publication:* Leading the Revolution 2012. *Address:* Office of Governor, State House Room 206, 200 West Washington Street, Indianapolis, IN 46204, USA (office). *Telephone:* (317) 232-4567 (office). *Fax:* (317) 232-3443 (office). *Website:* www.in.gov/gov (office).

HOLDEN, Bob, BS; American fmr politician; b. 26 Aug. 1949, Kansas City, Mo.; m. Lori Hauser; two s.; ed Southwest Missouri State Univ. (now Missouri State Univ.), Harvard Univ.; mem. Mo. House of Reps. 1983–89; Admin. Asst to Congressman Richard Gephardt, St. Louis 1989–91; Mo. State Treas. 1993–2001; Gov. of Mo. 2001–04; f. Holden Group, St Louis 2005; Adjunct Prof., Webster Univ. 2005–, Founder Holden Public Policy Forum 2005–; Vice-Chair. Mo. Cultural Trust; Chair. Midwest US–China Asscn 2011–; mem. Bd of Dirs Missouri Energy Initiative 2012–. *Address:* Midwest US–China Association, Willis Tower, Suite 7800, 233 South Wacker Drive, Chicago, IL 60606, USA (office). *Telephone:* (314) 246-7423 (office). *Website:* www.midwestuschina.org (office).

HOLDER, Eric Himpton, Jr, BA, JD; American lawyer, judge and government official; b. 21 Jan. 1951, Bronx, New York, NY; s. of Eric Himpton Holder, Sr and Miriam R. Yearwood; m. Dr Sharon Malone; one s. two d.; ed Stuyvesant High School, Manhattan, Columbia Coll. and Columbia Law School; worked for NAACP Legal Defense and Educational Fund during first summer and for US Attorney during second summer; Trial Attorney, Public Integrity Section, US Dept of Justice 1976–88, US Attorney 1993–97, US Deputy Attorney-Gen. 1997–2001, Attorney-Gen. 2009–14; Assoc. Judge, Superior Court, Washington, DC 1988–93; Partner, Covington & Burling (law firm), Washington, DC 2001–09; joined Senator Barack Obama's presidential campaign as a senior legal adviser 2007, served on Obama's vice-presidential selection cttee; Hon. LLD (Boston Univ.) 2010. *Leisure interest:* watching basketball. *Address:* c/o Department of Justice, 950 Pennsylvania Avenue NW, Washington, DC 20530-0001, USA. *E-mail:* askdoj@usdoj.gov.

HOLDER, Rt Rev. John Walder Dunlop, BA, STM, PhD; Barbadian ecclesiastic; *Bishop of Barbados;* b. 16 Feb. 1948, Barbados; m. Betty Lucas-Holder; one s.; ed Codrington Coll., Barbados, Univ. of the West Indies, The School of Theology (Univ. of the South), King's Coll., London, UK; ordained priest 1975; tutor in Biblical Studies, Codrington Coll. 1977–81, Lecturer 1984–93, Acting Prin. Sept.–Dec. 1988, Sr Lecturer 1993–99, Deputy Prin. 1999–; Visiting Lecturer in Religious Studies, Erdiston Teacher Training Coll., Barbados; Lecturer in Biblical Studies, Lay Training Programme, Diocese of Barbados 1984–90; Visiting Lecturer, Barbados Community Coll. 1985; Visiting Sabbatical Prof., Gen. Theological Seminary, New York March–May 1988; Chair. Ministry of Educ. Cttee on Religious and Moral Educ. Syllabus for the primary schools of Barbados 1992–94; Visiting Lecturer, Bucknell Univ. Summer Programme 1996–98; Curate St George's Cathedral, St Vincent, West Indies 1975–77; Asst Priest, St John's Parish Church, Barbados 1977–81, Priest-in-Charge 1990–92; Hon. Chaplain, Univ. Church of Christ the King, London 1981–84; Asst Priest, St Michael's Cathedral, Barbados 1984–86, St Augustine 1986–89, Priest-in-Charge 1989–90; Priest-in-Charge, St Mark and St Catherine, Barbados 1992–93, St Mark 1993–94, Holy Trinity 1994–95, Holy Cross 1995–2000; Hon. Canon, Diocese of Barbados 1996; Bishop of Barbados 2000–; mem. Advisory Bd Anglican Observer, UN 2003–06; Long and Dedicated Service Award, Codrington Coll. 1994, Errol Barrow Award 2005. *Television:* Religion in Barbados During the First Twenty-Five Years of Independence 1966–91 CBC 1990, CBC presentation on professions 1994. *Publications include:* Christian Commitment 1985, Set the Captives Free: The Challenge of the Biblical Jubilee 1987, A Layman's Guide to the Bible (Vols I & II) 1989, The Intertestamental Period 1994, Biblical Reflections on the Book of Hosea 1999. *Address:* Diocesan Office, Mandeville House, Henry's Lane, St Michael (office); Leland, Philip Drive, Pine Gardens, St Michael, Barbados (home). *Telephone:* 426-2761 (office); 435-0466 (home). *Fax:* 426-0871 (office). *E-mail:* bishop_holder@sunbeach.net (office).

HOLDGATE, Sir Martin Wyatt, Kt, CB, MA, PhD, FSB; British biologist and academic; b. 14 Jan. 1931, Horsham, Sussex, England; s. of Francis W. Holdgate and Lois M. Holdgate (née Bebbington); m. Elizabeth M. Weil (née Dickason) 1963; two s.; ed Arnold School, Blackpool and Queens' Coll., Cambridge; Research Fellow, Queens' Coll., Cambridge 1953–56; Jt Leader, Gough Island Scientific Survey 1955–56; Lecturer in Zoology, Univ. of Manchester 1956–57, Univ. of Durham 1957–60; Leader, Royal Soc. Expedition to Southern Chile 1958–59; Asst Dir of Research, Scott Polar Research Inst., Cambridge 1960–63; Chief Biologist, British Antarctic Survey 1963–66; Deputy Dir (Research), The Nature Conservancy (UK) 1966–70; Dir Central Unit on Environmental Pollution, Dept of Environment 1970–74; Dir Inst. of Terrestrial Ecology 1974–76; Dir-Gen. of Research, Dept of Environment 1976–81; Chief Scientist and Deputy Sec. (Environment Protection), Dept of Environment and Chief Scientific Adviser, Dept of Transport 1981–88; Dir-Gen. Int. Union for Conservation of Nature and Natural Resources 1988–94; Pres. Zoological Soc. of London 1994–2004; Co-Chair. Intergovernmental Panel on Forests, UN Comm. on Sustainable Devt 1995–97; mem. Royal Comm. on Environmental Pollution 1994–2002; Chair. Int. Inst. for Environment and Devt 1994–2000, Governing Council, Arnold School 1997–2004; Pres. Freshwater Biological Asscn 2002–10; Fellow, Soc. of Biology (UK); Hon. mem. British Ecological Soc. 1996, Int. Union for the Conservation of Nature and Natural Resources 2000; Commdr, Order of the Golden Ark 1991; Hon. DSc (Durham) 1991, (Sussex) 1993, (Lancaster) 1995, (Queen Mary, London) 2006; Bruce Medal, Royal Soc. of Edinburgh and Royal Scottish Geog. Soc. 1964, Silver Medal, UNEP 1983, UNEP Global 500 1988, Patrons Medal, Royal Geographical Soc. 1992, Livingstone Medal, Royal Scottish Geographical Soc. 1993, Int. Conservationist of the Year Award, Nat. Wildlife Fed. (USA) 1992. *Publications include:* Mountains in the Sea: The Story of the Gough Island Expedition 1958, A Perspective of Environmental Pollution 1979, From Care to Action: Making a Sustainable World 1996, The Green Web: A Union for World Conservation 1999, Penguins and Mandarins 2003, The Story of Appleby in Westmoreland 2006, Arnold: The Story of a Blackpool School 2009. *Leisure interests:* natural history, local history. *Address:* Fell Beck, Hartley, Kirkby Stephen, Cumbria, CA17 4JH, England (home). *Telephone:* (1768) 372316 (home). *E-mail:* martin@holdgate.org.

HOLDREN, John Paul, SB, SM, PhD; American environmental scientist, academic and government official; b. 1 March 1944, Sewickley, Pa; s. of Raymond Andrew Holdren and Virginia June Holdren (née Fuqua); m. Cheryl Edgar 1966; one s. one d.; ed Massachusetts Inst. of Tech., Stanford Univ.; Assoc. Engineer, Performance Analysis, Lockheed Missiles and Space Co., Sunnyvale, Calif. Summer 1965, Sr Assoc. Engineer, Re-Entry Aerodynamics Summer 1966, Consultant in Re-Entry Physics 1966–67; Research Asst, Inst. for Plasma Research, Stanford Univ. 1969–70; Physicist, Theory Group, Magnetic Fusion Energy Div., Lawrence Livermore Nat. Lab. 1970–73 (on leave 1972–73); Sr Research Fellow, Div. of Humanities and Social Sciences and Environmental Quality Lab., California Inst. of Tech. 1972–73; Asst Prof. of Energy and Resources, Univ. of California, Berkeley 1973–75, Assoc. Prof. 1975–78, Acting Chair. Energy and Resources Group 1982–83, Fall 1990, Vice-Chair. 1983–96 (on leave 1987–88), Chair. of Grad. Advisors, Energy and Resources Group 1988–96, Prof. of Energy and Resources 1978–96, Class of 1935 Prof. of Energy 1991–96, Prof. Emer. of Energy and Resources 1996–; Teresa and John Heinz Prof. of Environmental Policy and Dir Science, Tech. and Public Policy Program, Belfer Center for Science and Int. Affairs, Kennedy School of Govt, Harvard Univ. 1996–2008, also Prof. of Environmental Science and Policy, Dept of Earth and Planetary Sciences, mem. Bd of Tutors, undergraduate concentration in Environmental Science and Public Policy; Asst to Pres. Obama for Science and Tech. and Dir Office of Science and Tech., Exec. Office of the Pres. 2009–17; Visiting Scholar, Woods Hole Research Center 1992–94, Distinguished Visiting Scientist and Vice-Chair Bd of Trustees 1994–2005, Dir-Designate 2004–05, Dir 2005–08; Guest Prof., Tsinghua Univ., Beijing, People's Repub. of China 2008; Pres.-elect AAAS 2005, Pres. 2006, Chair. 2007; Chair. Exec. Cttee Pugwash Conf. on Science and World Affairs 1987–97, NAS Cttee on Int. Security and Arms Control 1994–2005 (mem. 1993–2005); mem. Pres. Clinton's Cttee of Advisors on Science and Tech. 1994–2001; Co-Chair. Nat. Comm. on Energy Policy 2002–07; mem. NAS, Nat. Acad. of Eng, American Acad. of Arts and Sciences, Council on Foreign Relations; Foreign mem. Royal Soc. of London; Dr hc (Univ. of Puget Sound, Colorado School of Mines, Clark Univ., Univ. of Rome, Univ. of the Dist of Columbia); MacArthur Prize Fellowship 1981–86, Volvo Environment Prize 1993, Tyler Prize for Environment 2000, John Heinz Prize for Public Policy 2001, gave acceptance speech for Nobel Peace Prize on behalf of Pugwash Conf. on Science and World Affairs 1995. *Publications:* numerous scientific papers in professional journals on global environmental change, energy technology and policy, nuclear proliferation, and science and technology policy. *Address:* c/o Office of Science and Technology Policy, NEOB 5230, The White House, Washington, DC 20502, USA (office). *Telephone:* (202) 456-6064 (office). *Fax:* (202) 456-6021 (office).

HOLE, (Christopher Charles) Maximilian (Max), CBE; British music industry executive; b. 26 May 1951, London, England; m. Jan Ravens 1999; three s.; began career in music industry as Co-founder (with Geoff Jukes) Gemini Artists (agency) 1972; Man., Artists and Repertoire Dept, Warner Music Group 1982–98, Man. Dir East West Records 1990; Sr Vice-Pres. for Marketing and A&R, Universal Music Group International 1998–2004, Exec. Vice-Pres. 2004, also assumed responsibility for Universal's Asia/Pacific business, COO Universal Music Group International 2010–13, Chair. and CEO 2013–15.

HOLENDER, Ioan; Romanian opera house director; b. 18 July 1935, Timisoara; m.; two s. one d.; ed Timisoara Polytechnic Inst., Vienna Conservatory, Austria; expelled from Romanian higher educ. system on political grounds 1956; worked as tennis trainer and stage dir's asst 1956–59; moved to Vienna and began singing studies 1960; opera singer, Vienna and Klagenfurt 1962–66; joined Starka Theater Agency 1966, later took control of agency and renamed it Holender Opera Agency; Gen. Sec. Vienna Staatsoper and Vienna Volksoper 1988–92, Dir Vienna Volksoper 1992–96, Gen. Dir Vienna Staatsoper 1992–2010; Guest Lecturer, Univ. of Vienna, Donau-Universität Krems 2008–; Artistic Adviser, Teatro Massimo Bellini, Catania 2008–; Artistic Consultant, Metropolitan Opera 2010–, Spring Festival Tokyo; Artistic Dir and Pres. George Enescu Music Festival, Bucharest 2005–15; Host, kulTOUR with Holender (ServusTV); Hon. mem. Romanian Acad., Hon. Citizen of Timisoara; Vienna Municipality Golden Medal of Merit, Golden Medal for Services to Vienna Community, Grand Golden Hon. Medal of Austrian Repub., Austrian Hon. Cross for Science and Art, First Class, Officier, Ordre des Artes et des Lettres, Großes Verdienstkreuz des Verdienstordens der Bundesrepublik Deutschland 2011; Dr hc (Gheorge Dima Music Acad.); Vienna Philharmonic Franz Schalk Gold Medal. *Publications:* Ioan Holender: Der Lebensweg des Wiener Staatsoperndirektors (autobiog.) 2001, Ioan Holender: Ich bin noch nicht fertig 2010. *Website:* www.holender.at.

HOLGATE, Stephen T., CBE, BSc, MB BS, MD, DSc, FRCP, FRCPE, FRCPath, FIBMS, FSB, FMedSci; British immunologist, physician and academic; *Medical Research Council Clinical Professor of Immunopharmacology and Honorary Consultant Physician within Medicine, University of Southampton;* b. 1947, Manchester; ed Univ. of London, Charing Cross Hosp. Medical School, Univ. of Southampton; House Physician, Charing Cross Hosp., London 1971–72; Sr House Officer (Neurology), Nat. Hosp. for Nervous Diseases, London 1972–73; Sr House Officer (Respiratory Medicine and Cardiology), Brompton Hosp., London 1973–74; Registrar (Gen. Medicine), Gen. Infirmary, Salisbury and Southampton Gen. Hosp., 1974–75; Lecturer and Hon. Sr Registrar in Medicine, Southampton Gen. and Western Hosps 1975–80; MRC and Wellcome Trust Overseas Research Fellow, Harvard Univ., Boston, USA 1978–80; Lecturer in Medicine and Hon. Sr Registrar, Univ. of Southampton Hosps 1975–80; Sr Lecturer, Reader, then Prof. of Medicine and Hon. Consultant Physician 1980–86, MRC Clinical Prof. of Immunopharmacology and Hon. Consultant Physician, Southampton Univ. and Foundation Trust 1987–; Hurst Brown Visiting Professorship, Univ. of Toronto, Canada 1991; Visiting Prof., Ontario Thoracic Soc., Canada 1995, Vanderbilt Univ., USA 1996, Visiting Professor, Harvard Univ., USA 1997, Univ. of Rochester, USA 1998, Harvard Medical School 2001, Thomas Jefferson Medical Coll., Philadelphia, USA 2001, Yale Univ. School of Medicine 2001, Univ. of Cincinnati Medical Center, USA 2002, Univ. of Michigan, Ann Arbor, USA 2004, Wake Forest Univ., Winston-Salem, N Carolina, USA 2004, Univ. of British Columbia, Canada 2005, Univ. of California, San Francisco and the Sandler Asthma Foundation, USA 2005, John Hopkins Bloomberg School of Public Health, Baltimore, USA 2007, Harvard Medical School, Boston and Ohio State Univ. 2007; Jeffrey Drazen Visiting Prof., Harvard Medical School 2010; Sr Investigator, Nat. Inst. for Health Research 2011; The K Frank Austen Visiting Prof., Harvard Univ. 2014; Pres. British Soc. of Allergy and Clinical Immunology –1993, British Thoracic Soc. 2006; Chair. Main Panel A (Medicine, Health and Life Sciences), UK Research Excellence Framework 2014, UK Nat. Centre for the Replacement, Refinement and Reduction of Animals in Research, British Lung Foundation Research Cttee, Hazardous Substances Advisory Cttee, European Respiratory Soc. Scientific Cttee; Treas. World Allergy Org.; mem. Medical Science Cttee of Science Europe, Science and Innovation Strategy Bd of Natural Environment Research Council 2014–; fmr Chair. MRC Population and Systems Medicine Bd; co-f. Synairgen 2003; mem. Council of the Acad. of Medical Sciences 2009; Overseas mem. American Asscn of Physicians 2005; Overseas Fellow, Polish Acad. of Science 2001; Hon. mem. Nordic Soc. of Allergology 1996, Germany Soc. for Pulmonology 2000, Asscn of Physicians of GB and Ireland 2004, Biochemical Soc. 2004, German Soc. of Allergy and Clinical Immunology 2006; Hon. Fellow, South African Pulmonology Soc. 1996, American Coll. of Asthma, Allergy and Immunology 2004, Inst. of Biomedical Science 2009; Hon. Chartered Scientist (CSci), Science Council 2009; Hon. Life Mem., Primary Care Respiratory Soc. UK 2011; Alec Sehon Distinguished Professorship in Allergy, Univ. of Manitoba, Canada 2000; Hon. Visiting Professorship, Univ. of Manchester (renewed 2012); Miegunyah Distinguished Visiting Fellowship, Univ. of Melbourne 2012, Hon. Visiting Research Professorship 2013; MRC Dorothy Temple Cross & Wellcome Trust Travel Fellowship 1978, ISI Most Highly Cited Researcher for Publications 1980–2011, Philip Ellman Lecturer, Royal Coll. of Physicians 1990, Altounyan Lecturer, British Thoracic Soc. 1991, Cournand Lecturer, European Respiratory Soc. 1992, James-Parkinson Memorial Lecturer, Soc. of Occupational Medicine 1993, Thomas Young Medal, St George's Hosp., London 1993, Graham Bull Prize for Clinical Research, Royal Coll. of Physicians 1993, Lilly Lecturer, Royal Coll. of Physicians of Edinburgh 1994, CIBA Foundation Lecturer, Science Festival, Edinburgh 1994, Jack Pepys Lecturer, British Soc. for Allergy and Clinical Immunology 1994, Scientific Achievement Award, Int. Asscn of Allergy and Clinical Immunology, Stockholm 1994, Robert Cooke Memorial Lecturer, American Acad. of Allergy and Immunology 1995, Rhône-Poulenc Rorer World Health Award 1995, Priscilla Piper

Memorial Lecturer, Royal Coll. of Surgeons 1996, Evening Discourse, Royal Inst. of GB 1996, Brian Sproule Lecturer, Univ. of Alberta, Canada 1998, King Faisal Int. Prize in Medicine 1999, Medal for Scientific Achievement, Rijksuniversiteit, Gent, Belgium 1999, ranked eighth in UK Citations in Biomolecular Subjects (ISI) 1990–2000, Lumleian Lecturer, Royal Coll. of Physicians 2000, Robert Cooke Memorial Lecturer, American Acad. of Allergy, Asthma and Immunology 2000, The Hon. Fellow Award, American Acad. of Allergy, Asthma and Immunology 2001, Czech Repub. Medical Soc. Medal for Scientific Achievement, Prague 2001, Norman Sterrie Lecturer, Univ. of Minnesota, USA 2002, Highly Cited Researcher, ISI 2002, Sir William Osler Lecturer, Asscn of Physicians of GB and Ireland 2003, Ellison-Cliffe Medal, Royal Soc. of Medicine 2003, G.B. West Memorial Lecturer, European Histamine Research Soc. 2003, Scientific Achievement Award, Int. Asscn of Asthmology (Interasma) 2003, Health and Life Sciences Gold Medal, Rijksuniversiteit, Gent 2004, Quintiles Prize in Immunopharmacology, British Pharmacological Soc. 2004, Hosp. Doctor Academic Medicine Team of the Year Award 2004, Sir Anthony Dawson Lecturer, Royal London and St Bartholomew's Hosps 2005, The Huxley Lecturer, Imperial Coll., London 2006, Burns Lecturer, Royal Coll. of Physicians, Glasgow 2006, Paul Ehrlich Award for Research, European Acad. of Allergy, Asthma and Clinical Immunology 2008, Opening Plenary Lecturer, Keystone Conf. on Asthma and Allergy 2009, Almroth Wright Lecturer, Imperial Coll., London 2009, David W. Talmage Lectureship, Aspen Allergy Jack Selner Conf., Colo, USA 2010, second most cited European author 1998–2009 in Respiratory Research 2011, Recognition Award for Scientific Accomplishments, American Thoracic Soc. 2012, Alain De Weck Hon. Lecturer, VI World Asthma and COPD Forum, New York 2012, Longdagen Lecturer, Longdagen Scientific Conf., Utrecht, The Netherlands 2013, The Annual Wade Lecturer, Faculty of Medicine, Univ. of Southampton 2013, Keynote Lecturer, Keystone Conf. on Biologics 2014, J. Allyn Taylor Int. Prize in Medicine (co-recipient) 2016. *Publications:* Allergy (third edn) (BMA Medical Book of the Year Award, Royal Soc. of Medicine Book Commendation) 2007; 60 book editorships, 453 book chapters and reviews, 48 editorials, 76 official and govt reports and more than 980 peer-reviewed publications in professional journals. *Address:* Room SGH/LF102/MP810, University of Southampton, University Road, Southampton, SO17 1BJ, England (office). *Telephone:* (23) 8120-6960 (office). *Fax:* (23) 8070-1771 (office). *E-mail:* sth@southampton.ac.uk (office). *Website:* www.southampton.ac.uk/medicine (office).

HOLIDAY, Eugene Bernard; St Maarten economist and government official; *Governor;* b. 14 Dec. 1962, Philipsburg; s. of Eugene Bernard Holiday Sr and Leone Cassandra Holiday-Marsham; m. Marie Louise Holiday-Hasell; ed Oranje School, Philipsburg, Milton Peters Coll., Catholic Univ. Brabant, The Netherlands; analyst and policy adviser, Cen. Bank of the Netherlands Antilles 1987–89, Head of Research and Monetary Policy Dept 1989–91, Co-ordinator Monetary and Econ. Affairs 1991–94, Deputy Dir Monetary and Econ. Affairs 1994–95; Man. Dir Windward Island Airways International Ltd 1995–98; Pres. Princess Juliana Int. Airport Exploitatiemaatschappij NV, Sint Maarten 1998–2010; Gov. of Sint Maarten (first Gov. following dissolution of Netherlands Antilles) Oct. 2010–. *Leisure interests:* sports, especially NBA basketball, tennis and golf. *Address:* Cabinet of the Governor, Falcon Drive 3, Philipsburg, Sint Maarten (office). *Telephone:* 542-1199 (office). *Fax:* 542-1187 (office). *E-mail:* kabinet@kabgsxm.com (office). *Website:* www.kabgsxm.com (office).

HOLLÁN, R. Susan, MD; Hungarian professor of haematology; *Consultant, National Institute of Haematology and Blood Transfusion;* b. 26 Oct. 1920, Budapest; d. of Dr Henrik Hollán and Dr Malvin Hornik; m. Dr György Révész; one s. one d.; ed Univ. Medical School, Budapest; intern, Rokus Hosp., Budapest 1945–50; Research Fellow, Univ. Medical School, Budapest 1950–54; Science Adviser, Inst. for Experimental Medical Research 1954–91; Dir Nat. Inst. of Haematology and Blood Transfusion 1959–85, Dir-Gen. 1985–90, Consultant 1990–; Prof. of Haematology, Postgraduate Medical School 1970–90; Corresp. mem. Hungarian Acad. of Sciences 1973, mem. 1982– (mem. of Presidium 1976–84); fmr Pres. Int. Soc. of Haematology and Vice-Pres. Int. Soc. of Blood Transfusion; mem. WHO Global AIDS Research Steering Cttee; mem. WHO Expert Cttee on Biological Standardization; mem. Clinical and Immunological Work Cttee of Hungarian Acad. of Sciences; Pres. Bd of Special Cttee for Clinical Sciences; Exec. mem. Hungarian Medical Research Council; Ed.-in-Chief Hungarian Medical Encyclopaedia and Haematologia (quarterly); mem. HSWP Cen. Cttee 1975–89; Foreign Corresp. mem. Soc. de Biologie, Collège de France, Paris; Vice-Pres. Nobel Prize Award, Int. Physicians Prevention of Nuclear War 1983–89; Hon. mem. American Soc. of Hematology, Polish Soc. of Haematology, German Soc. of Haematology (FRG), Purkinje Soc. (Czechoslovakia), Turkish Soc. of Haematology, All-Union Scientific Soc. of Haematology and Blood Transfusion (USSR); Hon. Pres. Hungarian Soc. of Human Genetics; Hungarian Academic Award 1970, State Prize 1974, Socialist Hungary Medal. *Publications:* Basic Problems of Transfusion 1965, Haemoglobins and Haemoglobinopathies 1972, Genetics, Structure and Function of Blood Cells 1980, Management of Blood Transfusion Services 1990; over 300 papers in Hungarian and int. medical journals. *Leisure interests:* fine arts, sport. *Address:* Daróczi ut 24, 1113 Budapest (office); Palánta u. 12, 1025 Budapest, Hungary (home). *Telephone:* (1) 372-4210 (office); (1) 326-0619 (home). *Fax:* (1) 372-4352. *E-mail:* hollan@ella.hu (office).

HOLLAND, Agnieszka; Polish film director and screenwriter; b. 28 Nov. 1948, Warsaw; m. Laco Adamik (divorced); one d.; ed FAMU film school, Prague; Asst to Krzysztof Zanussi in filming of Illumination 1973; mem. production group 'X' led by Andrzej Wajda in Warsaw 1972–81; Dir first TV film 1973; subsequently worked in theatre in Kraków; Co-Dir (with Jerzy Domaradzki and Paweł Kędzierski) film Screen Test 1977; co-scripted Wajda's film Rough Treatment 1978; also worked with Wajda on A Love in Germany, Man of Marble, Man of Iron, The Orchestra Conductor, Korczak, Danton 1982; wrote screenplay for Yurke Bocayevicz's Anna; has also made documentaries for French TV; directs plays for TV theatre (with Laco Aolamik); mem. Polish Film Asscn, European and American Acad. Award; Robert L. Hess Scholar in Residence, Brooklyn Coll. 2005; Chair. European Film Acad. Bd 2014; Officer's Cross, Order of Polonia Restituta 2001; Las Vegas Film Festival Award 1999, Viadrina Prize, European Univ. Viadrina 2019. *Achievements include:* retrospective of films held at Museum of Modern Art, New York 2008–09. *Films directed include:* Provincial Actors (Critics' Award, Cannes 1980) 1979, The Fever (Gdańsk Golden Lions 1981) 1980, The Lonely Woman 1981, Angry Harvest (Germany) 1985, To Kill a Priest (France) 1987, Europa, Europa (Germany, France) 1990, (Golden Globe 1991), Olivier, Olivier (France) 1992, The Secret Garden (USA) 1993, Red Wind (USA) 1994, Total Eclipse (England, France) 1995, Washington Square (USA) 1996, The Third Miracle (USA) 1999, Golden Dreams 2001, Julie Walking Home (Poland–Canada–Germany) 2002, Prawdziwa historia Janosika i Uhorcika (co-dir) 2005, Copying Beethoven 2006, Janosik: A True Story 2009, In Darkness 2011. *Television includes:* Shot in the Heart (USA) 2001, Veronica Mars (series) 2004, A Girl Like Me: The Gwen Araujo Story (film) 2006, Burning Bush (mini-series) 2013, Spoor (Silver Bear Alfred Prize 2017) 2017; directed several episodes of series The Wire, Cold Case, The Killing, Treme. *Play:* Dybuk (Polish TV) 1999, Rosemary's Baby (TV mini–series) 2014. *Publications:* Magia i pieniadze (Magic & Money): Conversations with Maria Komatowska 2002.

HOLLAND, Julian (Jools) Miles, OBE; British musician (piano, keyboard) and broadcaster; b. 24 Jan. 1958, London; s. of Derek Holland and June Rose Lane; one s. two d.; m. Christabel McEwen 2005; ed Invicta Sherington School, Shooters' Hill School; pianist 1975–78; Founder-mem. Squeeze 1974–81, 1985–90; regular tours and concerts; formed The Jools Holland Big Band 1987, later renamed The Rhythm and Blues Orchestra 1991–; BBC Radio 2 Jazz Artist of the Year 2006. *Films:* Spiceworld: The Movie 1997, Milk (wrote score) 1999. *Radio:* presenter BBC Radio 2 1997–. *Television:* The Tube (presenter) 1982–87, Walking to New Orleans (writer, producer and presenter, documentary) 1985, The Groovy Fellas (actor and writer) 1988, Juke Box Jury (presenter) 1989–90, Saturday Night (co-presenter New York NBC music show with David Sanborn) 1989, The Happening 1990, Mr Roadrunner (writer and producer, film) 1991, Later with Jools Holland (presenter) 1992–, Hootenanny (presenter) 1993–, Don't Forget Your Toothbrush 1994–95, Name That Tune 1997, Beat Route (writer and producer, film) 1998, Jools Meets The Saint (writer and producer) 1999, Jools' History of the Piano 2002, Jools Holland: London Calling 2012. *Recordings include:* albums: with Squeeze: Squeeze 1978, Cool for Cats 1979, Argy Bargy 1980, East Side Story 1981, Cosi Fan Tutti Frutti 1985, Babylon and On 1987, Frank 1989; solo: A World of his Own 1990, Full Complement 1991, A–Z of the Piano 1992, Live Performance 1994, Solo Piano 1994, Sex and Jazz and Rock and Roll 1996, Lift the Lid 1997, Sunset Over London 1999, Hop the Wag 2000, Small World, Big Band – Friends 2001, Small World, Big Band Vol. 2 – More Friends 2002, Small World, Big Band Vol. 3 2003, Tom Jones and Jools Holland 2004, Swinging the Blues, Dancing the Ska 2005, Moving Out to the Country (with Rhythm & Blues Orchestra) 2006, The Informer 2008, Rocking Horse (with Rhythm & Blues Orchestra) 2010, The Golden Age of Song 2012, Sirens of Song 2014, Piano 2016, As You See Me Now (with José Feliciano and Rhythm & Blues Orchestra) 2017, A Lovely Life to Live (with Marc Almond and Rhythm & Blues Orchestra) 2018. *Publications include:* Beat Route 1998, The Hand That Changed Its Mind 2004, Barefaced Lies and Boogie-Woogie Boasts (autobiog.) 2007. *Leisure interests:* sketching, giving advice. *Address:* One-Fifteen, 1 Globe House, Middle Lane Mews, London, N8 8PN, England (office); Helicon Mountain Ltd, Helicon Mountain, Station Terrace Mews, London, SE3 7LP, England (office). *Telephone:* (20) 8442-7560 (office); (20) 8858-0984 (office). *Fax:* (20) 8442-7561 (office); (20) 8293-4555 (office). *E-mail:* enquiries@onefifteen.com (office); contact@joolsholland.com (home). *Website:* www.onefifteen.com (office); www.joolsholland.com (home).

HOLLANDE, François Gérard Georges; French politician and fmr head of state; b. 12 Aug. 1954, Rouen (Seine-Maritime); fmr partner Valerie Trierweiler; three s. one d. with fmr partner Ségolène Royal; ed École des Hautes Études Commerciales de Paris, Institut d'Études Politiques de Paris, École Nat. d'Admin, Strasbourg; fmr Councillor, Cour des comptes; mem. Ussel City Council 1983–89; Deputy for Corrèze (1ère) in Nat. Ass. 1988–93, 1997–2012, mem. Defence Comm.; Deputy Mayor of Tulle 1989–95, mem. Tulle City Council 1995–2001, Mayor of Tulle 2001–08; mem. Limousin Regional Council March 1992, 1998–2001; Pres. Conseil Gen. Corrèze 2008–; First Sec. Parti socialiste (PS) 1997–2008; mem. European Parl. July–Dec. 1999; Pres. of France 2012–17, Co-Prince of Andorra 2012–17. *Address:* Parti Socialiste, 10 rue de Solférino, 75333 Paris Cedex 07, France (office). *Telephone:* 1-45-56-77-00 (office). *Fax:* 1-47-05-15-78 (office). *E-mail:* interps@parti-socialiste.fr (office). *Website:* www.parti-socialiste.fr (office).

HOLLANDER, Samuel, OC, PhD, FRSC; British/Canadian/Israeli economist and academic; *University Professor Emeritus, University of Toronto;* b. 6 April 1937, London; s. of Jacob Hollander and Lily Bernstein; m. Perlette Kéroub 1959; one s. one d.; ed Gateshead Talmudical Acad., Hendon Tech. Coll., Kilburn Polytechnic, London School of Econs, Princeton Univ., USA; emigrated to Canada 1963; Asst Prof., Univ. of Toronto 1963–67, Assoc. Prof. 1967–70, Prof. 1970–84, Univ. Prof. 1984–98, Univ. Prof. Emer. 1998–; Research Dir, Univ. of Nice (CNRS) 1999–2000; Visiting Prof., Florence Univ., Italy 1973–74, Univ. of London 1974–75, Hebrew Univ., Jerusalem 1979–80, 1988, La Trobe Univ., Melbourne, Australia 1985, Auckland Univ., NZ 1985, 1988, Sorbonne, Paris 1997, Nice Univ., France 2001, Ben Gurion Univ., Israel 2000–06; several guest lectureships; emigrated to Israel 2000; Fellow, Canadian Econs Asscn 2015; Hon. LLD (McMaster) 1999; Fulbright Fellowship 1959; Guggenheim Fellowship 1968–69; Social Science Fed. of Canada 50th Anniversary Book Award 1990, Thomas Guggenheim Prize in History of Economic Thought 2011. *Publications include:* The Sources of Increased Efficiency 1965, The Economics of Adam Smith 1973, The Economics of David Ricardo 1979, The Economics of J. S. Mill 1985, Classical Economics 1987, Ricardo – The New View: Collected Essays I 1995, The Economics of T. R. Malthus 1997, The Literature of Political Economy: Collected Essays II 1998, John Stuart Mill on Economic Theory and Method: Collected Essays III 2000, Jean-Baptiste Say and the Classical Canon in Economics 2005, The Economics of Karl Marx 2008, Friedrich Engels and Marxian Political Economy 2011, Essays on Classical and Marxian Political Economy: Collected Essays IV 2013, John Stuart Mill: Political Economist 2015. *Address:* 2 Rehov Sapir, 8906627 Arad, Israel (home). *Telephone:* 54-9474846 (mobile). *E-mail:* shollande@gmail.com (home). *Website:* www.samuel-hollander.com.

HOLLEIN, Max; Austrian fine arts administrator, curator and director; *Director, Metropolitan Museum of Art;* b. 7 July 1969, Vienna; s. of Hans Hollein; m. Nina Hollein; ed Wirtschaftsuniversität Wien, Universität Wien; Project Dir for Exhbns, Solomon R. Guggenheim Museum, New York 1995, Exec. Asst to the Dir 1996–98, Chief of Staff and Man. of European Relations 1998–2000; Commr and Curator American Pavilion, Seventh Biennale of Architecture, Venice 2000;

Dir Schirn Kunsthalle Frankfurt 2001–06, Städel Museum, Frankfurt 2006–16, Liebieghaus-Museum alter Plastile, Frankfurt 2006–16; Dir, Fine Arts Museums of San Francisco 2016–18, Metropolitan Museum of Art 2018–; Commr Austrian Pavilion, Biennale of Visual Art, Venice 2005; mem. Bd of Dirs Kulturveranstaltungen des Bundes in Berlin GmbH; mem. Bd of Trustees Neue Galerie, New York; Chevalier, Ordre des Arts et des Lettres 2009, Medal of Honour for Science and Arts 2010, Binding-Kulturpreis 2015. *Publications include:* Zeitgenössische Kunst und der Kunstmarktboom (Contemporary Art and the Boom on the Art Market) 1999, Unternehmen Kunst: Entwicklungen und Verwicklungen (The Business of Art) 2006, Cut-Out Fun with Matisse 2014. *Address:* Metropolitan Museum of Art, 1000 Fifth Avenue, New York, NY 10028, USA (office). *Telephone:* 212-535-7710 (office). *Website:* www.metmuseum.org (office).

HÖLLER, Carsten, DHabil; Belgian artist; b. Dec. 1961, Brussels; ed Univ. of Kiel, Germany; began his artistic career in 1988; uses his training as a scientist in his work as an artist, concentrating particularly on the nature of human relationships and demanding viewer participation; rejected any specific artistic identity, creating works that range from films, drawings, architectural plans and photographs to performances, sculptures and installations; works are most frequently devoted to chemically analysing the nature of human emotions; has collaborated with many other artists, notably with German artist Rosemarie Trockel, with whom, for Documenta X, they together created A House for Pigs and People 1997, in which people and pigs share the same physical space; works include: Addina 1997, Valerio I and II 1998, The Forest, Light Wall 2000, Solandra Greenhouse (garden filled with the Solandra maxima vine); lives and works in Fasta, Sweden.

HOLLICK, Baron (Life Peer), cr. 1991, of Notting Hill in the Royal Borough of Kensington and Chelsea; **Clive Richard Hollick,** BA; British business executive; b. 20 May 1945, Southampton, Hants., England; s. of Leslie George Hollick and Olive Mary Hollick (née Scruton); m. Susan Mary Woodford 1977; three d.; ed Univ. of Nottingham; joined Hambros Bank 1968, Dir 1973; CEO MAI PLC (fmrly Mills & Allen Int. PLC) 1974–96, Shepperton Studios 1976–84, Garban Ltd (USA) 1983–97, United Business Media PLC 1996–2005; Partner, Kohlberg Kravis Roberts UK 2005–10, GP Bullhound 2011–18; mem. Int. Advisory Bd Jefferies 2011–17; mem. Bd of Dirs Logica PLC 1987–91, Meridian Broadcasting 1991–96, British Aerospace 1992–97, Anglia TV Ltd 1994–97, TRW Inc. 2000–03, Diageo PLC 2001–11, Honeywell Int. 2003–, Pro Siebensat1 AG 2007–10, BMG Music Rights Management 2009–13; mem. Nat. Bus Co. 1984–91, Applied Econs Dept Advisory Cttee Univ. of Cambridge 1989–97, Financial Law Panel 1993–97; Special Adviser to Dept of Trade and Industry 1997–98; mem. (Labour), House of Lords 1991–, Chair. Select Cttee on Econ. Affairs 2010–17; Chair. South Bank Centre, London 2002–08; Chair. SBS NV 2005–07; Founder and Trustee, Inst. for Public Policy Research 1988–; Hon. LLD (Nottingham) 1993. *Leisure interests:* cinema, countryside, reading, golf, theatre. *Address:* House of Lords, Westminster, London, SW1A 0PW, England (office). *Telephone:* (20) 7219-6746 (office). *E-mail:* hollickrc@parliament.uk (office). *Website:* www.parliament.uk/biographies/lords/lord-hollick/2732 (office).

HOLLIDAY, Charles Otis (Chad), Jr, BS; American engineer and business executive; *Chairman, Royal Dutch Shell plc;* b. 9 March 1948, Nashville, Tenn.; s. of Charles O. Holliday, Sr and Ann Hunter; m. Ann Holliday; two s.; ed Univ. of Tennessee; joined DuPont Fibers Dept as engineer, Old Hickory, Tenn. 1970, Business Analyst, Wilmington, Del. 1974, later product planner, Asst Plant Man., Seaford, Del. 1978, joined DuPont Corp. Planning Dept 1984, Global Business Man. for Nomex 1986, Global Business Dir for Kevlar 1987, Dir of Marketing DuPont Chemicals and Pigments Dept 1988, Vice-Pres., then Pres. DuPont Asia-Pacific 1990, Chair. 1995, Sr Vice-Pres. DuPont 1992, Exec. Vice-Pres. and mem. Office of Chief Exec., E.I. du Pont de Nemours & Co. 1995, Dir 1997–2009, Pres. 1997–2009, CEO 1998–2008, Chair. 1999–2009 (retd); Chair. Bank of America Corpn 2009–14; Dir (non-exec.), Royal Dutch Shell plc 2010–, Chair. 2015–; Chair. Catalyst; mem. Bd of Dirs, DuPont Photomasks Inc., Deere & Co. 2007–; Chair. Emer. US Council on Competitiveness; fmr Chair. Business Roundtable's Task Force for Environment, Tech. and Economy, World Business Council for Sustainable Devt, The Business Council, Soc. of Chemical Industry (American Section); Founding mem. Int. Business Council; mem. Chancellor's Advisory Council for Enhancement, Univ. of Tennessee, Knoxville; Sr mem. Inst. of Industrial Engineers; mem. Nat. Acad. of Eng; Dr hc (Polytechnic Univ., Brooklyn, NY, Washington Coll., Chestertown, Md). *Publication:* Walking the Talk (co-author). *Address:* Royal Dutch Shell plc, PO Box 162, 2501 AN The Hague (office); Royal Dutch Shell plc, Carel van Bylandtlaan 30, 2596 HR The Hague, The Netherlands (office). *Telephone:* (70) 3779111 (office). *Fax:* (70) 3773115 (office). *Website:* www.shell.com (office).

HOLLIDAY, Steven J., BSc; British business executive; b. 26 Oct. 1956; s. of Michael J Holliday and Jean I Holliday (née Day); m. Katharine Patterson 1996; three c.; ed Univ. of Nottingham; 19 years with Exxon Group; fmrly Exec. Dir British Borneo Oil & Gas PLC; Group Dir, UK and Europe, Nat. Grid PLC 2001–02, Head of Electricity and Gas Transmission Businesses 2002–03, Group Dir responsible for UK Gas Distribution and Business Services 2003–06, Deputy CEO April–Dec. 2006, Chief Exec. 2007–16; fmr Chair. UK Business Council for Sustainable Energy, Technician Council; mem. Bd of Dirs (non-exec.) Marks & Spencer Group PLC 2004–14; Chair. Bd of Trustees Crisis (homeless charity); mem. Bd of Trustees, Dirs for Business in the Community, Infrastructure UK; Fellow, Royal Acad. of Eng 2010. *Leisure interests:* sports, rugby, skiing, arts.

HOLLIGER, Heinz; Swiss oboist, composer and conductor; b. 21 May 1939, Langenthal; m. Ursula Holliger; ed in Berne, Paris and Basel under Emile Cassagnaud (oboe) and Pierre Boulez (composition); Prof. of Oboe, Freiberg Music Acad. 1965–; has appeared at major European music festivals and in Japan, USA, Australia, Israel, etc.; conducted Chamber Orchestra of Europe, London 1992, London Sinfonietta 1997; Composer-in-Residence, Lucerne Festival 1998; Hon. mem. American Acad. of Arts and Sciences 2016; Frankfurter Musikpreis 1988, Ernst von Siemens Music Award 1991, Prix de Composition Musicale de la Fondation Prince Pierre de Monaco 1994, Zurich Festival Award 2007, Rheingau Musikpreis 2008, among others. *Compositions include:* Der magische Tänzer, Trio, Siebengesang, Wind Quintet, Dona nobis pacem, Pneuma, Psalm, Cardiophonie, Kreis, String Quartet, Atembogen, Die Jahreszeiten, Come and Go, Not I. *Recordings:* numerous recordings, mainly for Philips and Deutsche Grammophon; Koechlin's Vocal works with orchestra (Midem Classical Award for Vocal Recitals 2006), Machaut-Transkriptionen 2015. *Address:* Colbert Artists Management, 307 Seventh Avenue, Suite 2006, New York, NY 10001, USA (office). *Telephone:* (212) 757-0782 (office). *Website:* www.colbertartists.com/heinz-holliger (office).

HOLLINGHURST, Alan James, BA, MLitt, FRSL; British novelist, poet, short story writer and translator; b. 26 May 1954, Stroud, Glos.; s. of James Kenneth Hollinghurst and Elizabeth Lilian Hollinghurst (née Keevil); ed Canford School, Dorset, Magdalen Coll., Oxford; Asst Ed., Times Literary Supplement 1982–84, Deputy Ed. 1985–90, Poetry Ed. 1991–95; Visiting Prof., Univ. of Houston, USA 1998; Old Dominion Fellow, Princeton Univ., USA 2004; Hon. Fellow, Magdalen Coll., Oxford 2013; Hon. DLit (Univ. Coll. London) 2012; Newdigate Prize 1974, Stonewall Writer of the Year 2011, Bill Whitehead Award for Lifetime Achievement, Publishing Triangle 2011. *Publications include:* Confidential Chats with Boys (poems) 1982, The Swimming-Pool Library (novel) (Somerset Maugham Award 1989, American Acad. of Arts and Letters E.M. Forster Award 1989) 1988, Bajazet, by Jean Racine (trans.) 1991, The Folding Star (novel) (James Tait Black Memorial Prize) 1994, New Writing 4 (co-ed. with A. S. Byatt) 1995, The Spell (novel) 1998, Three Novels, by Ronald Firbank (ed.) 2000, A. E. Housman: Poems Selected by Alan Hollinghurst (ed.) 2001, The Line of Beauty (novel) (Man Booker Prize for Fiction) 2004, The Stranger's Child (novel) (Galaxy Nat. Book Award for UK Author of the Year 2011, Prix du meilleur livre étranger) 2011, Bérénice, by Jean Racine (trans.) 2012, The Sparsholt Affair (novel) 2017. *Leisure interests:* music, architecture. *Address:* c/o Antony Harwood Ltd, 103 Walton Street, Oxford, OX2 6EB, England (office).

HOLLINGWORTH, Rt Rev. Peter, AC, AO, OBE, BA, MA, DipSocialStudies, ThL, FAIM; Australian ecclesiastic; b. 10 April 1935, Adelaide; m. Kathleen Ann Turner 1960; three d.; ed Trinity Coll. Univ. of Melbourne; Deacon-in-Charge then Priest-in-Charge, St Mary's, N Melbourne 1960–64; Chaplain to the Brotherhood of St Laurence 1964–90, Assoc. Dir 1970, later Dir of Social Services, Exec. Dir 1980–90; Hon. Curate, St Silas's, North Balwyn, later Hon. Curate at St Faith's, Burwood and Priest-in-Charge, St Mark's, Fitzroy; recipient of travelling bursary 1967; elected Canon, St Paul's Cathedral 1980; Bishop of the Inner City 1985–90, Archbishop of Brisbane 1990–2001; Gov.-Gen. of the Commonwealth of Australia 2001–03; Prior to Order of St John of Jerusalem; Chair. Int. Year of Shelter for the Homeless, Nat. Cttee of Non-Governmental Orgs 1986–88, Anglican Social Responsibilities Comm. of Gen. Synod 1990–98, Anglicare in diocese of Brisbane; Pres. Victorian Council of Social Services 1969; mem., Hon. Chair. Centenary of Fed. Council, Constitutional Convention (as non-parl. Rep.); Fellow, Trinity Coll. Melbourne; Hon. LLD (Monash Univ.) 1986, (Melbourne) 1990; Hon. DUniv (Griffith Univ.) 1993, (Queensland Univ. of Tech.) 1994, (Cen. Queensland) 1995; Hon. DLitt (Univ. of Southern Queensland) 1999; Victorian Rostrum Award of Merit 1985, Advance Australia Award 1988, Paul Harris Fellowship, Rotary Club 1989, Australian of the Year 1992, Nat. Living Treasure of Australia (Nat. Trust) 1997, Centenary Medal 2001. *Publications include:* The Powerless Poor 1972, The Poor: Victims of Affluence? 1974, Australians in Poverty 1979, Kingdom Come 1991, Public Thoughts of an Archbishop 1996, Memories of Bush Ministry and the Challenge of the Future 1999. *Leisure interests:* swimming, Australian Rules football, theatre, reading, music. *Address:* POB 18081, Collins Street East, Melbourne, Victoria, 8003, Australia (office). *Telephone:* (3) 8633-3990 (office). *Fax:* (3) 9671-3954 (office). *E-mail:* amanda.dinsdale@pmc.gov.au (office).

HOLLIS, Brenda Joyce, JD; American lawyer and UN official; ed Bowling Green State Univ., Ohio, Univ. of Denver; Sr Trial Attorney, Int. Criminal Tribunal for the Fmr Yugoslavia (ICTY) 1994–2001; Expert Legal Consultant on int. law and criminal procedure 2001–07, trained judges, prosecutors and investigators at courts and int. tribunals in Indonesia, Iraq and Cambodia, also assisted victims of int. crimes in Democratic Repub. of the Congo and in Colombia to prepare submissions requesting investigations by Int. Criminal Court in The Hague; consultant to Office of the Prosecutor 2002–03, 2006, Prin. Trial Attorney, Office of the Prosecutor 2007–10, responsible for leading legal team prosecuting fmr Liberian Pres. Charles Taylor; Chief Prosecutor, Special Court for Sierra Leone, UN 2010–13, Prosecutor, Residual Special Court for Sierra Leone 2014–15; Reserve Int. Co-Prosecutor, Extraordinary Chambers in the Courts of Cambodia 2015. *Address:* c/o Office of the Co-Prosecutors, Extraordinary Chambers in the Courts of Cambodia, National Road 4, Chaom Chau Commune, Dangkao District, PO Box 71, Phnom Penh, Cambodia (office).

HOLLOWAY, Bruce William, AO, PhD, DSc, FAA, FTSE; Australian geneticist and academic; *Professor Emeritus, Monash University;* b. 9 Jan. 1928, Adelaide, S Australia; s. of Albert Holloway and Gertrude C. Walkem; m. Brenda D. Gray 1952; one s. one d.; ed Scotch Coll., Adelaide, Univ. of Adelaide, California Inst. of Tech., USA, Univ. of Melbourne; Lecturer in Plant Pathology, Waite Agric. Research Inst. 1949–50; Research Fellow in Microbial Genetics, John Curtin School of Medicine, ANU 1953–56; Sr Lecturer 1956–60, then Reader in Microbial Genetics, Univ. of Melbourne 1956–67; Foundation Prof. of Genetics, Monash Univ. 1968–93, Head, Dept of Genetics and Developmental Biology 1968–93, Prof. Emer. 1993–, Chair. Bd CRC for Vertebrate Biological Control 1994–99; Dir, Master Classes, Crawford Fund 1994–2004; Visiting Lecturer in Microbiology and Fellow, MIT, USA 1962–63; Sec. Biological Sciences, Australian Acad. of Science 1982–86; Visiting Prof., Univ. of Newcastle-upon-Tyne 1977–78; Chair. Nat. Biotechnology Program Research Grants Scheme 1983–86; mem. Industry and Research Devt Bd 1986–89; Kathleen Barton-Wright Lecturer, Soc. for Gen. Microbiology, UK 1998; Fellow, Australian Acad. of Science 1979, Australian Acad. of Technological Sciences and Eng 1993; Hon. Professorial Fellow, Monash Univ. 1994–2001; 50th Anniversary Research Award, Monash Univ. 2008. *Publications:* more than 190 papers on genetics and microbiology in scientific journals and conf. proceedings. *Leisure interests:* music, reading, tennis. *Telephone:* (3) 9836-5515 (home). *E-mail:* hollowab@ozemail.com.au (home).

HOLLOWAY, Rt Rev. Richard Frederick, BD, STM, FRSE; British ecclesiastic (retd); b. 26 Nov. 1933, Glasgow, Scotland; s. of Arthur Holloway and Mary Holloway; m. Jean Holloway 1963; one s. two d.; ed Kelham Theological Coll., Edinburgh Theological Coll., Univ. of London (External), Union Theological Seminary, New York, USA; Curate, St Ninian's, Glasgow 1959–63; Priest-in-Charge, St Margaret's and St Mungo's, Gorbals, Glasgow 1963–68; Rector, Old St

Paul's, Edin. 1968–80, Church of the Advent, Boston, Mass 1980–84; Vicar, St Mary Magdalen's, Oxford 1984–86; Bishop of Edinburgh 1986–2000; Primus, Scottish Episcopal Church 1992–2000; Prof. of Divinity, Gresham Coll., London 1997–2001; Chair. Scottish Arts Council, Scottish Screen 2006–10; mem. Human Fertilisation and Embryology Authority 1991–97, Broadcasting Standards Comm. 2001–04; Hon. DUniv (Strathclyde) 1994, (Open Univ.), (Stirling) 2010; Hon. DD (Aberdeen) 1994, (Glasgow) 2001; Hon. DLitt (Napier) 2001, (St Andrews) 2017; Hon. LLD (Dundee) 2008; Dr hc (Royal Conservatoire of Scotland) 2012. *Radio:* Cover Stories (BBC) 2003, 2004, Divine Comedy (BBC) 2003, Sunday Morning with Richard Holloway (BBC). *Television:* Holloway's Road (BBC) 2000, The Sword and the Cross (BBC) 2003, Art and Soul (BBC) 2005. *Publications include:* Beyond Belief 1981, The Killing (Winifred M. Stanford Award) 1984, Paradoxes of Christian Faith and Life 1984, The Sidelong Glance 1985, The Way of the Cross 1986, Seven to Flee, Seven to Follow 1986, Crossfire 1988, Another Country, Another King 1991, Who Needs Feminism? 1991, Anger, Sex, Doubt and Death 1992, The Stranger in the Wings 1994, Churches and How To Survive Them 1994, Behold Your King 1995, Limping Towards the Sunrise 1996, Dancing on the Edge 1997, Godless Morality 1999, Doubts and Loves 2001, On Forgiveness 2002, Looking in the Distance 2004, Between the Monster and the Saint: Reflections on the Human Condition 2008, Leaving Alexandria: A Memoir of Faith and Doubt 2012 (PEN Ackerley Award 2013), A Little History of Religion 2016, Waiting for the Last Bus: Reflections on Life and Death 2018. *Leisure interests:* walking, movies, reading, cooking. *Address:* 6 Blantyre Terrace, Edinburgh, EH10 5AE, Scotland (home). *Telephone:* (131) 446-0696 (home). *E-mail:* richard@dochollowayorg.uk (home).

HOLLOWAY, Robin Greville, PhD, DMus; British composer, writer and fmr academic; b. 19 Oct. 1943, Leamington Spa; s. of Robert Charles Holloway and Pamela Mary Holloway (née Jacob); ed St Paul's Cathedral Choir School, King's Coll. School, Wimbledon, King's Coll., Cambridge, New Coll., Oxford; Lecturer in Music, Univ. of Cambridge 1975, Reader in Musical Composition 1999, Prof. of Musical Composition 2001–11; Fellow, Gonville and Caius Coll., Cambridge 1969. *Compositions include:* Garden Music (Opus 1) 1962, First Concerto for Orchestra 1969, Scenes from Schumann (Opus 13) 1970, Evening with Angels (Opus 17) 1972, Domination of Black (Opus 23) 1973, Clarissa (opera) (Opus 30) 1976, Second Concerto for Orchestra (Opus 40) 1979, Brand (dramatic ballad) (Opus 48) 1981, Women in War (Opus 51) 1982, Seascape and Harvest (Opus 55) 1983, Viola Concerto (Opus 56) 1984, Peer Gynt 1985, Hymn to the Senses for chorus 1990, Serenade for strings 1990, Double Concerto (Opus 68), The Spacious Firmament for chorus and orchestra (Opus 69), Violin Concerto Opus 70 1990, Boys and Girls Come Out To Play (opera) 1991, Winter Music for sextet 1993, Frost at Midnight (Opus 78), Third Concerto for Orchestra (Opus 80) 1994, Clarinet Concerto (Opus 82) 1996, Peer Gynt (Opus 84) 1984–97, Scenes from Antwerp (Opus 85) 1997, Gilded Goldberg for two pianos 1999, Symphony 1999, Missa Caiensis 2001, Cello Sonata 2001, Spring Music (Opus 96) 2002, String Quartet No. 1 2003, String Quartet No. 2 2004, Six Quartettini 2006, Suite en Saga 2008, Hommage to Haydn 2009, Gold on Bronze 2010, String Quartet no. 4 2011, Suite in Baroque Style 2012, On a Drop of Dew 2013, String Quartet No. 5 2014, Thou Art There 2015. *Recordings include:* Fantasy Pieces (Opus 16) 1971, Sea Surface Full of Clouds chamber cantata, Romanza for violin and small orchestra (Opus 28) 1974–75, Second Concerto for Orchestra (Opus 40) 1978–79, Horn Concerto (Opus 43) 1979–80, Third Concerto for orchestra (Opus 80) 1981–90, Violin Concerto (Opus 70) 1990, Gilded Goldberg (Opus 86) 1992–97, Missa Caiensis, Organ Fantasy 1993–2001, Woefully Arrayed 1999, Fourth Concerto for Orchestra 2003–05, Reliquary – Scenes from the life of Mary Queen of Scots enclosing an instrumentation of Robert Schumann's 'Gedichte der Königin Maria Stuart' 2009–10, Andante and Variations 2010, Fifth Concerto for Orchestra (Opus 107) 2011, Trio for Oboe, Violin, Piano 2011, String Quartet No. 4 2011, C'est l'extase (after Debussy) for soprano and orchestra 2012, Europa and the Bull for tuba and orchestra 2013. *Publications include:* Debussy and Wagner 1978, On Music: Essays and Diversions 1963–2003 2004; numerous articles and reviews. *Leisure interests:* cities, architecture, books. *Address:* Finella, Queen's Road, Cambridge, CB3 9AH, England (home). *Telephone:* (1223) 335424. *E-mail:* rgh@robinholloway.info. *Website:* www.robinholloway.info.

HOLM, Erik, MA, PhD; Danish foundation director and political economist; b. 6 Dec. 1933, Hobro; s. of Carl Holm and Anne Margrethe Holm (née Nielsen); m. Annie Jacoba Kortleven 1960 (died 1984); two s. two d.; ed Univ. of Copenhagen; economist, Cen. Statistical Office, Copenhagen 1961–65; Lecturer in Econs, Univ. of Copenhagen 1962–65, in Political Science 1971–81; economist, IMF, Washington, DC 1965–69; Sr Economist, Ministry of Econ. Affairs, Copenhagen 1969–72; Adviser on European Affairs to Prime Minister 1972–82; Prin. Adviser (econ. and financial affairs), EC Comm., Brussels 1982–87; Visiting Scholar, Inst. of Int. Studies, Univ. of Calif., Berkeley 1987–89; Dir Eleni Nakou Foundation, London 1989–2003; Kt of the Dannebrog. *Publications:* Stabilitet og Uligevagt 1986, Money and International Politics 1991, Union eller Nation 1992, Europe, a Political Culture? Fundamental Issues for the 1996 IGC 1994, The European Anarchy: Europe's Hard Road into High Politics 2001; articles in Danish and int. publs on European econ. and political affairs. *Address:* Vester Søgade 24, 1601 Copenhagen (home); Xylografensvej 4, 3220 Tisvildeleje, Denmark (Summer) (home). *Telephone:* 40-46-37-75 (home). *E-mail:* erik-holm@mail.dk (home).

HOLM, Sir Ian, Kt, CBE; British actor; b. 12 Sept. 1931, Ilford, Essex; s. of Dr James Harvey Cuthbert and Jean Wilson Cuthbert; m. 1st Lynn Mary Shaw 1955 (divorced 1965); two d.; one s. one d. (with Bee Gilbert); m. 2nd Sophie Baker 1982 (divorced 1986); one s.; m. 3rd Penelope Wilton 1991 (divorced); one step-d.; ed Chigwell Grammar School, Essex, RADA (Royal Acad. of Dramatic Art); joined Shakespeare Memorial Theatre 1954; Worthing Repertory 1956; on tour with Lord Olivier in Titus Andronicus 1957; mem. RSC 1958–67; Laurence Olivier Award 1998, Evening Standard Award for Best Actor 1993 and 1997. *Roles include:* Puck, Ariel, Lorenzo, Henry V, Richard III, The Fool (in King Lear), Lennie (in The Homecoming); appeared in Moonlight 1993, King Lear 1997, Max in The Homecoming 2001. *Films include:* Young Winston, Oh! What a Lovely War, Alien, All Quiet on the Western Front, Chariots of Fire, The Return of the Soldier, Greystoke 1984, Laughterhouse 1984, Brazil (Boston Society of Film Critics Award for Best Supporting Actor) 1985, Wetherby 1985, Dance with a Stranger 1985, Dreamchild 1985, Henry V 1989, Another Woman 1989, Hamlet 1990, Kafka 1991, The Hour of the Pig 1992, Blue Ice 1992, The Naked Lunch 1992, Frankenstein 1993, The Madness of King George 1994, Loch Ness 1994, Big Night 1995, Night Falls on Manhattan 1995, A Life Less Ordinary 1996, The Sweet Hereafter (Genie Award for Best Performance by an Actor in a Leading Role) 1997, The Fifth Element 1997, eXistenZ 1998, Simon Magus 1998, Esther Kahn 1999, Joe Gould's Secret 1999, Beautiful Joe 1999, From Hell 2000, The Emperor's New Clothes 2000, The Lord of the Rings – The Fellowship of the Ring 2001, The Lord of the Rings – The Return of the King 2003, Garden State 2004, The Day After Tomorrow 2004, The Aviator 2004, Strangers with Candy 2005, Chromophobia 2005, Lord of War 2005, Renaissance (voice) 2006, O Jerusalem 2006, The Treatment 2006, Ratatouille (voice) 2007, The Hobbit: An Unexpected Journey 2012, The Hobbit: The Battle of the Five Armies 2014. *Television appearances include:* The Lost Boys 1979, We, the Accused 1980, The Bell 1981, Strike 1981, Inside the Third Reich 1982, Mr. and Mrs. Edgehill 1985, The Browning Version 1986, Game, Set and Match 1988, The Endless Game 1989, The Last Romantics 1992, The Borrowers 1993, The Deep Blue Sea 1994, Landscape 1995, Little Red Riding Hood 1996, King Lear (Critics' Circle Theatre Award for Best Actor, Laurence Olivier Award for Best Actor) 1997, Alice Through the Looking Glass 1998, Animal Farm (voice) 1999, The Miracle Maker (voice) 2000, The Last of the Blonde Bombshells 2000, D-Day 6.6.1944 (voice) 2004. *Publication:* Acting My Life (autobiog.) 2004. *Leisure interests:* tennis, walking. *Address:* The Peggy Thompson Office, 296 Sandycombe Road, Kew, Richmond, Surrey, TW9 3NG (office); c/o Markham & Froggatt Ltd, Julian House, 4 Windmill Street, London, NW1T 2HZ, England (office).

HOLM, Richard H., BS, PhD; American academic and chemist; *Higgins Professor Emeritus of Chemistry, Harvard University;* b. 24 Sept. 1933, Boston, Mass; m. Florence L. Jacintho 1958; four c.; ed Univ. of Massachusetts, Amherst and Massachusetts Inst. of Tech.; Asst Prof. of Chem., Harvard Univ. 1960–65; Assoc. Prof. of Chem., Univ. of Wisconsin 1965–67; Prof. of Chem., MIT 1967–75, Stanford Univ. 1975–80; Prof. of Chem., Harvard Univ. 1980–83, Higgins Prof. of Chem. 1983–2006, Higgins Research Prof. of Chem. 2006–13, Chair. Dept of Chem. 1983–86, Prof. Emer. 2013–; mem. American Acad. of Arts and Sciences, NAS; several hon. degrees; Chemical Sciences Award 1993, NAS Award in Chemical Sciences 1993, F.A. Cotton Medal for Excellence in Chemical Research, ACS 2005, Bailar Medal, F. P. Dwyer Medal, Pauling Medal (Stanford Univ.), Harrison Howe Award, Polyhedron (Wilkinson) Prize, Centenary Medal of Royal Society of Chemistry, Chatt Medal, Richards Medal, NAS Award in the Chemical Sciences, Welch Award in Chem. (co-recipient) 2016; several ACS awards for research in inorganic chem. *Publications:* numerous research papers in professional journals in the fields of inorganic chem. and biochemistry. *Address:* Holm Group, Department of Chemistry, Harvard University, 12 Oxford Street, Cambridge, MA 02143 (office); 483 Pleasant Street, #10, Belmont, MA 02418, USA (home). *Telephone:* (617) 495-0853 (office). *Fax:* (617) 496-9289 (office). *E-mail:* holm@chemistry.harvard.edu (office). *Website:* faculty.chemistry.harvard.edu/holm (office).

HOLM, Stefan Christian; Swedish high jumper (retd); b. 25 May 1976, Forshaga; s. of Johnny Holm and Elisabeth Holm; m. Anna; one s.; Silver Medal, Swedish Championships 1994–96, European Indoor Championships 2002, European Championships 2002, World Championships 2003; Gold Medal, Swedish Indoor Championships 1997–2004, Swedish Championships 1998–2005, Goodwill Games 2001, World Indoor Championships 2001, 2003, 2004, Athens Olympics 2004, European Indoor Championships 2005; winner IAAF Grand Prix 2002, World Athletics Final 2004; ranked No. 1, Athletics Ints World Ranking 2002, 2004, Track & Field News World Ranking 2001, 2002, 2004; mem. Kils AIK Friidrottsklubb, IOC 2013. *E-mail:* stefan.holm@scholm.com. *Website:* www.scholm.com.

HOLM-NIELSEN, Kt ; Lauritz Broder, MSc; Danish botanist, academic and university administrator; *Chairman, DenDanske Naturfond;* b. 8 Nov. 1946, Nordby; s. of Jens Gregers Holm-Nielsen and Bodil Holm-Nielsen (née Arctander); m. Helle Holm-Nielsen; two s. one d.; ed Aarhus Univ.; Asst Prof. of Botany, Aarhus Univ. 1972–75, Assoc. Prof. 1975–86, Dir Botanical Inst. 1983–85, Rector 2005–13, Special Adviser to the Sr Man. 2013–17; Prof., Universidad Católica, Quito, Ecuador 1979–81; Rector Danish Research Acad. 1986–93; Lead Higher Educ. Specialist, The World Bank 1993–2005; Exec. Dir Sino Danish Center for Educ. and Research (SDC-UCAS), Beijing 2014–17; Chair. Danish Science Research Council 1985–87, Danish Council for Devt Research 1990–93, Danish Strategic Environment Research Programme 1991–2004, Den Danske Naturfond 2015–; Vice-Chair. Danish Research Comm. 2000–01; Pres. Nordic Acad. for Advanced Study 1991–93, Euroscience 2012–18; Vice-Pres. European Univ. Asscn 2012–15; Commr Africa Comm. 2008–09; mem. Danish Prime Minister's Growth Forum 2009–11, Nordic Univs Asscn 2008–12; mem. The Learned Soc.; Fellow, London, Danish Acad. of Natural Sciences, Acad. of Tech. Sciences; Hon. mem. Instituto Ecuatoriano de Ciencias Naturales; Commdr, Star of the Order of Dannebrog, Gran Oficial del Orden Gabriela Mistral (Chile), Commdr, Order of the Dannebrog 2012; Lime Prize 1984, Outstanding Performance Award, World Bank 2000, Educational Merit Medal, World Cultural Council 2012. *Publications:* more than 130 research publs. *Address:* Valdemarsgade 42, DK 8000 Aarhus, Denmark (office). *Telephone:* 23-38-21-26 (mobile) (office). *E-mail:* lhn@au.dk (office). *Website:* www.ddnf.dk (office).

HOLMES, Andrew S., BA, AM, PhD, FRS, FIET, MIEEE; British electronics engineer and academic; *Professor of Micro-Electro-Mechanical Systems, Imperial College London;* ed Univ. of Cambridge, Imperial Coll. London; Research Assoc., Dept of Electrical and Electronic Eng, Imperial Coll. London 1991–93, Jt Research Fellowship in Microengineering with Imperial Coll. and Rutherford Appleton Lab. 1993–95, apptd Lecturer, Imperial Coll. London 1995, currently Prof. of Micro-Electro-Mechanical Systems (MEMS); Co-founder and Dir, Microsaic Systems plc (Imperial Coll. spin-off) 2001–; mem. IEEE; Fellow, Inst. of Eng and Tech.; Royal Medal, Royal Soc. 2012. *Publications include:* more than 150 journal and conference papers. *Address:* Optical and Semiconductor Devices Research Group, Department of Electrical and Electronic, Room 701, South Kensington Campus, London, SW7 2AZ, England (office). *Telephone:* (20) 7594-6239 (office). *Fax:* (20) 7594-6308 (office). *E-mail:* a.holmes@imperial.ac.uk (office). *Website:* www.imperial.ac.uk/people/a.holmes (office).

HOLMES, Sir John Eaton, Kt, GCVO, KBE, CMG; British fmr diplomatist and UN official; *Chair, UK Electoral Commission;* b. 29 April 1951, Preston, Lancs.; s. of Leslie Holmes and Joyce Holmes; m. Penelope Morris 1976; three d.; ed Preston Grammar School, Balliol Coll., Oxford; joined FCO 1973; with Embassy, Moscow 1976–78; First Sec. FCO 1978–82; Asst Pvt. Sec. to Foreign Sec. 1982–84; First Sec. Embassy, Paris 1984–87; Asst Head Soviet Dept, FCO 1988–89; seconded to Thomas De La Rue & Co. 1989–91; Counsellor, British High Comm., New Delhi 1991–95; Prin. Pvt. Sec. to Prime Minister 1996–99; Amb. to Portugal 1999–2001, to France 2001–07; Under-Sec.-Gen. for Humanitarian Affairs and Emergency Relief Co-ordinator, UN Office for Co-ordination of Humanitarian Affairs, New York 2007–10; Dir Ditchley Foundation 2010–16; Chair. Int. Rescue Cttee (UK), UK Electoral Comm. 2017–, Advisory Bd, Cargo Logic Air; Council mem. Radley Coll.; mem. Exec. Cttee, The Pilgrims. *Publication:* The Politics of Humanity: The Reality of Relief Aid 2013. *Leisure interests:* reading, music, sport. *Address:* Electoral Commission, 3 Bunhill Row, London, EC1Y 8YZ (office); International Rescue Committee, 3 Bloomsbury Place, London, WC1A 2QL, England (office). *Telephone:* (20) 7692-2727 (IRC) (office). *E-mail:* info@electoralcommission.org (office). *Website:* www.electoralcommission.org (office); www.rescue-uk.org (office).

HOLMES, John T., BA, LLB; Canadian diplomatist; *Ambassador to Turkey;* m. Carol Bujeau; one s. one d.; ed McGill Univ.; joined Dept of External Affairs 1982, positions in Bridgetown, Accra and Perm. Mission to UN, New York, fmr Dir Legal Advisory Div., Dir UN Human Rights and Econ. Law Div. 2002–03, Amb. to Jordan 2003–06 (also accred to Iraq 2005–06), to Indonesia (also accred to Timor Leste and ASEAN) 2006–09, Dir-Gen. of Middle East and Maghreb Bureau 2009–11, Amb. to Turkey (also accred to Azerbaijan, Georgia and Turkmenistan) 2011–. *Address:* Embassy of Canada, Cinnah Caddesi 58, 06690, Çankaya, Ankara, Turkey (office). *Telephone:* (312) 4092700 (office). *Fax:* (312) 4092712 (office). *E-mail:* ankra@international.gc.ca (office). *Website:* www.canadainternational.gc.ca/turkey-turquie (office).

HOLMES, Dame Kelly, DBE, MBE (Mil); British fmr athlete and business executive; *President, Commonwealth Games England;* b. 19 April 1970, Pembury, Kent; d. of step-father Michael Keith Norris and Pamela Thomson (née Norman); ed Hugh Christie Comprehensive School, Tonbridge, Kent; mem. Tonbridge, Ealing, Southall and Middlesex Athletics Clubs; competes primarily in 800m. and 1,500m events; won English Schools' titles then Recreation Asst 1986–87, Nursing Asst 1987–88; joined Army as Physical Training Instructor 1988–97; 12 major championship medals include silver medal, 1,500m European Championships 1994, gold medal, 1,500m Commonwealth Games 1994, bronze medal, 800m, silver medal, 1,500m World Championships 1995, silver medal, 1,500m Commonwealth Games 1998, bronze medal, 800m. Olympic Games, Sydney 2000, bronze medal, 800m European Championships 2002, gold medal, 1,500m Commonwealth Games 2002, silver medal, 1,500m World Indoor Championships 2003, silver medal, 800m World Championships 2003, gold medal, 800m, gold medal, 1,500m Olympic Games, Athens 2004; 1,500m, European Cup results include second 1994, first 1995, first 1997; 800m European Cup results include second 1996, fourth 2002; third 1,500m World Cup 2003; Amateur Athletics Asscn titles include 800m 1993, 1995, 1996, 1999, 2000, 2001, indoors 800m 2001, UK 800m 1993, 1997, 1,500m 1994, 1996, 2002; Founder and Dir Double Gold Enterprises Ltd 2004–; Dir Nat. School Sport Champion 2006–08; Pres. Commonwealth Games England 2009–; Chair. Dame Kelly Holmes Trust 2008–; Owner, Cafe 1809 2014–; 12 hon. degrees including Brunel, Kent, Leeds Metropolitan, London South Bank; European Athlete of the Year 2004, BBC Sports Personality of the Year 2004, winner, Performance of the Year Award, IAAF Gala 2004, Laureus World Sports Woman of the Year Award 2005, Pride of Sport Life Time Achievement Award 2016. *Publications include:* My Olympic Ten Days (with Richard Lewis) 2004, Black, White and Gold 2006, Get Your Kids Fit 2007, Katy the Shooting Star 2008, Just Go for It 2011. *Address:* Double Gold Enterprises Ltd (office). *E-mail:* info@doublegold.co.uk (office). *Website:* www.kellyholmes.co.uk.

HOLMES, Kenneth Charles, MA, PhD, FRS; British research biophysicist and academic (retd); b. 19 Nov. 1934, London, England; s. of Sidney C. Holmes and Irene M. Holmes (née Penfold); m. Mary Lesceline Scruby 1957; one s. three d.; ed Chiswick Co. School, St John's Coll., Cambridge and Birkbeck Coll., London; Research Asst, Birkbeck Coll., London 1955–59; Research Assoc., Children's Hosp., Boston 1960–62; mem. scientific staff, MRC Lab. of Molecular Biology, Cambridge 1962–68; Dir Dept of Biophysics, Max-Planck-Inst. for Medical Research, Heidelberg 1968–2003; Prof. of Biophysics, Univ. of Heidelberg 1972–99; mem. European Molecular Biology Org. 1968, Heidelberger Akad. der Wissenschaften 1994; Corresp. mem. Nordrhein-Westfälische Akad. der Wissenschaften, Düsseldorf; Gabor Medal, Royal Soc. of London 1997, European Latsis Prize 2000, Gregori Aminoff Prize, Royal Swedish Acad. of Sciences 2001. *Publications:* articles in scientific books and journals. *Leisure interests:* rowing, singing. *Address:* Max-Planck-Institute for Medical Research, Abt. Biophysik, Jahnstrasse 29, 69120 Heidelberg (office); Mühltalstrasse 117B, 6900 Heidelberg, Germany (home). *Telephone:* (6221) 486270 (office); (6221) 471313 (home). *E-mail:* holmes@mpimf-heidelberg.mpg.de (office). *Website:* homes.mpimf-heidelberg.mpg.de/~holmes (office).

HOLMES, Larry; American fmr boxer; b. 3 Nov. 1949, Cuthbert, Ga; s. of John Holmes and Flossie Holmes; m. Diana Holmes; one s. four d.; amateur boxer 1970–73; 22 amateur fights, 19 wins; lost by disqualification to Duane Bobick in finals of American Olympic trials 1972; won World Boxing Council (WBC) version of world heavyweight title from Ken Norton June 1978; made nine defences, all won inside scheduled distance (breaking previous record held by Joe Louis); became first man to stop Muhammad Ali Oct. 1980; stripped of WBCl version 1983; lost Int. Boxing Fed. version to Michael Spinks 1985, beaten again by Spinks 1986; defeated by Mike Tyson (q.v.) in attempts to win World Boxing Asscn, WBC and Int. Boxing Fed. heavyweight titles 1988; beaten by Evander Holyfield (q.v.) for World Boxing Asscn, WBC and Int. Boxing Fed. heavyweight titles 1992, by Oliver McCall for WBC heavyweight title 1995; was undefeated for record 13 years; career record 69 wins, (44 KOs), six defeats; runs an Internet casino business. *Leisure interests:* food, sport and self-education. *Address:* Larry Holmes Enterprises Inc., 91 Larry Holmes Drive, Suite 200, Easton, PA 18042, USA (office). *Telephone:* (610) 253-6905 (office). *E-mail:* larryholmes@larryholmes.com (office). *Website:* www.larryholmes.com (office).

HOLMES, Richard Gordon Heath, OBE, MA, FBA, FRSL; British writer, poet and academic; b. 5 Nov. 1945, London; s. of Dennis Patrick Holmes and Pamela Mavis Gordon; partner Rose Tremain; ed Downside School, Churchill Coll., Cambridge; literacy features writer, The Times 1967–92; Visiting Fellow, Trinity Coll., Cambridge 2000; Prof. of Biographical Studies, Univ. of East Anglia 2001–07; Hon. DLitt (East Anglia) 2000, (Tavistock Inst.) 2001, (Kingston Univ.) 2008; Somerset Maugham Award 1977, James Tait Black Memorial Prize 1994, Whitbread Book of the Year Prize 1989, Duff Cooper Prize 1998. *Radio:* BBC Radio: Inside the Tower 1977, To the Tempest Given 1992, The Nightwalking (Sony Award) 1995, Clouded Hills 1999, Runaway Lives 2000, The Frankenstein Project 2002, A Cloud in a Paper Bag 2007. *Publications:* Thomas Chatterton: The Case Re-Opened 1970, One for Sorrows (poems) 1970, Shelley: The Pursuit 1974, Shelley on Love (ed.) 1980, Coleridge 1982, Nerval: The Chimeras (with Peter Jay) 1985, Footsteps: Adventures of a Romantic Biographer 1985, Mary Wollstonecraft and William Godwin (ed.) 1987, Kipling: Something Myself (ed. with Robert Hampson) 1987, Coleridge: Early Visions 1989, Dr Johnson and Mr Savage 1993, Coleridge: Selected Poems (ed.) 1996, The Romantic Poets and Their Circle 1997, Coleridge: Darker Reflections 1998, Sidetracks: Explorations of a Romantic Biographer 2000, Classic Biographies (series) 2004–, Insights: The Romantic Poets and Their Circle 2005, The Age of Wonder (Nat. Book Critics' Circle Award for General Nonfiction 2009, Royal Soc. Prize for Science Books 2009) 2008, Falling Upwards: How We Took to the Air 2013. *Address:* c/o HarperCollins, 77–85 Fulham Palace Road, Hammersmith, London, W6 8JB, England.

HOLMES, Roger; British business executive; *Partner, Change Capital Partners;* m. Kate Holmes; one s. one d.; ed Bristol Univ.; began career with McKinsey & Co.; joined Kingfisher Group 1994, Finance Dir B&Q (subsidiary co.) 1994, becoming Man. Dir Woolworths and later CEO Kingfisher Electrical Retailing Div. –2000; joined Marks & Spencer Group PLC as Head of UK Retail Sales 2001–02, CEO 2002–04; Dir Change Capital Pnrs (pvt. equity firm) 2004–, currently Partner; Hon. LLD (Bristol) 2013. *Address:* Change Capital Partners, 2nd Floor, College House, 272 Kings Road, London, SW3 5AW, England (office). *Telephone:* (20) 7808-9110 (office). *Fax:* (20) 7808-9111 (office). *E-mail:* rholmes@changecapitalpartners.com (office). *Website:* www.changecapitalpartners.com (office).

HOLMES À COURT, Janet Lee, AC BSc, FAHA, HFAIB; Australian business executive and arts patron; b. 29 Nov. 1943, Perth; m. Robert Holmes à Court (died 1990); three s. one d.; ed Perth Modern School and Univ. of Western Australia; fmr science teacher; Exec. Chair. Heytesbury Pty Ltd (family-owned co. which includes Heytesbury Beef Ltd, Vasse Felix (Vineyards), Heytesbury Thoroughbreds, John Holland Group and Key Transport) 1990–2005 (retd); Chair. John Holland Group 1991–, West Australian Symphony Orchestra, Australian Children's Television Foundation, Australian Urban Design Research Centre of WA; mem. Bd of Dirs Vision 2020 Australia, Rio Tinto WA Future Fund, Australian Nat. Acad. of Music, Australian Chamber Orchestra, Australian Major Performing Arts Group, Chamber of Arts and Culture WA; f. Holmes à Court Gallery, Cowaramup 2000; Pro-Chancellor, Univ. of Western Australia 1990–94; fmr mem. Senate, Murdoch Univ., Univ. of Western Australia; mem. Bd Man. Festival of Perth; Founding Patron, Black Swan Theatre Company; Patron, Parks Forum, Manning Clark House; Hon. Fellow, Australian Inst. of Building, Australian Acad. of the Humanities; six hon. doctorates; British Business Woman of the Year 1996, Corporate Citizenship Award, Woodrow Wilson Int. Center for Scholars 2009. *Leisure interest:* the arts. *Website:* www.heytesbury.com.au; www.holmesacourtgallery.com.au.

HOLMES TRUJILLO, Carlos; Colombian lawyer, diplomatist and politician; *Minister of Foreign Affairs;* b. 23 Sept. 1951, Cartago; m. Alba Lucía Anaya; four s.; ed Univ. del Cauca, Sofia Univ., Tokyo; Consul and Chargé d'affaires, Embassy in Tokyo 1976–82; Pres., Fedemetal (metallurgical asscn) 1983–85; Mayor of Cali 1988–90; mem. Nat. Constituent Ass. 1991; Minister of Nat. Educ. 1992–93; Perm. Rep. to OAS, Washington 1995–97; Minister of the Interior 1997–98; Amb. to Austria (also accred to int. orgs in Vienna) 1998–99, to Russia 1999–2001, to Sweden 2004–06, to Belgium and EU 2006–11; Minister of Foreign Affairs 2018–; mem. Centro Democrático (CD). *Address:* Ministry of Foreign Affairs, Palacio de San Carlos, Calle 10a, No 5-51, Bogotá, DC, Colombia (office). *Telephone:* (1) 282-7811 (office). *Fax:* (1) 341-6777 (office). *Website:* www.minrelext.gov.co (office).

HOLMSTRÖM, Bengt Robert, BSc, MSc, PhD; Finnish economist and academic; *Paul A. Samuelson Professor of Economics, Massachusetts Institute of Technology;* b. 18 April 1949; m. Anneli Kuusakoski; one s.; ed Univ. of Helsinki, Stanford Univ., USA; corp. planner, A. Ahlstrom Ltd 1972–74; Asst Prof. of Systems and Operations Research, Swedish School of Econs and Business Admin 1978–79; Asst Prof. of Managerial Econs, Northwestern Univ., USA 1979–80, J.L. Kellogg Research Professorship 1980–81, Assoc. Prof. of Managerial Econs 1980–83, IBM Research Professorship 1982–83; Research Assoc. (Labor Studies), Nat. Bureau of Econ. Research 1984–86, Research Assoc. (Corp. Finance Program) 1996–; Prof. of Econs, Yale Univ., USA 1983–94, Prof. of Econs and Org. 1983–85, Edwin J. Beinecke Prof. of Man. Studies 1985–94; Prof. of Econs and Man., Dept of Econs (jt appointment with Sloan School of Man.), MIT 1994–, Paul A. Samuelson Prof. of Econs 1997–, Chair. Dept of Econs 2003–06; Sr Research Fellow, Inst. for Policy Reform 1991–95; Visiting Research Fellow, CORE, Université Catholique de Louvaine, Belgium 1977–78; Visiting Assoc. Prof. of Econs, Univ. of Chicago Spring 1982; Visiting Prof. of Research, Stanford Univ. 1985–86; Visiting Prof. of Man., Helsinki School of Econs 1991–92; Visiting Prof. (recurring), Stockholm School of Econs 1996–99; Visiting Prof., Univ. of Helsinki Spring 1999; Visiting Prof., Univ. of Chicago, Initiative on Global Markets Fall 2006; Visiting Prof., Hanken School of Econs, Helsinki Spring 2007; Mark and Sheila Wolfson Distinguished Visiting Prof., Stanford Inst. of Econ. Policy Research, Stanford Univ. Spring 2010; mem. Bd of Dirs, Nokia 1999–2012; mem. Bd, Aalto Univ.; Chair. Advanced Research Grants Panel, European Research Council 2009–11; mem. Cttee, Alfred P. Sloan Foundation Dissertation Fellowship 1988–94; mem. Advisory Bd, Financial and Econs Network, SSRN 1995–, CIRANO 1997–98, SITE, Stockholm School of Econs 1998–, School of Econs and Man., Tsinghua Univ. 1999–2002; mem. Research Council, Finnish Nat. Foundation for Research and Devt 1996–99, Law, Econs and Financial Inst. Centre, Copenhagen Business School 2001–06, Legatum Center, MIT 2007–13, Dept of Econs, Univ. of Zurich 2011–; mem. Exec. Cttee, Centre for Econ. Policy Research 2000–; mem. Exec. Bd,

European Corp. Governance Inst. 2000–05, Nomination Cttee, American Econ. Asscn 2001–02; mem. Int. Advisory Bd, New Econ. School, Moscow 2006–09, Baltic Action Group 2008–10; mem. Scientific Council, Barcelona Grad. School of Econs 2006–, Foundation J.J. Laffont-Toulouse Sciences Economiques 2006–13; mem. Foundation for the Advancement of Research in Financial Econs 2010; Foreign Ed., Review of Economic Studies 1982–85; Assoc. Ed., Journal of Economic Theory 1983–93, Econometrica 1984–2000, Rand Journal of Economics 1986–89, Finnish Economic Papers 1988–, Journal of Law, Economics and Organization 1989–, Journal of Financial Intermediation 1989–95, Journal of Economics and Management Strategy 1990–98; mem. Advisory Bd, Journal of Institutional and Theoretical Economics 1992–, Journal of Economic Perspectives 2003–06; mem. Editorial Bd, Review of Economic Design 1993–, MIT Press 1996–97, Finnish Economy and Society 2001–; Trustee, SNS – Center for Business and Policy Studies 2010–12; Foreign mem. Royal Swedish Acad. of Sciences 2001, Royal Swedish Acad. of Eng 2005, Finnish Acad. of Sciences and Letters 2007; Fellow, Econometric Soc. 1983, mem. Council 1994–2000, mem. Exec. Cttee 1998–2000, 2009–12, Second Vice-Pres. 2009, First Vice-Pres. 2010, Pres. 2011; Fellow, European Corp. Governance Inst. 2000, European Econ. Asscn (EEA) 2004, Financial Theory Group 2012, Soc. for the Advancement of Econ. Theory 2013; Year 2013 Fellow, American Finance Asscn; Foreign Fellow, Finnish Soc. of Sciences and Letters 1992, American Acad. of Arts and Sciences 1993; numerous lectureships at int. univs; Dr hc (Univ. of Vaasa, Finland) 1988, (Stockholm School of Econs) 1998, Swedish School of Econs and Business Admin) 2004; NSF Grant, 'Dynamic Models of Employment' 1981–83, 1984–87, Finnish Expatriate of the Year, The Finnish Soc. 2008, Alumni of the Year, Helsinki Univ. 2009, Inauguration Lecturer, Universitat Politecnica de Catalunya 2009, Lifetime Achievement Award, Financial Intermediation Research Soc. 2010, Arrow Lecturer, Univ. of Jerusalem 2011, Presidential Address, Econometric Soc., Seoul, Oslo, Santiago 2011, Chicago 2012, Banque de France-TSE Senior Prize in Monetary Econs and Finance 2012, OP-Pohjola Econs Prize, Helsinki 2012, Froystein Gjesdal Lecturer, NHH, Bergen 2013, Stephen A. Ross Prize in Financial Econs (with Jean Tirole) 2013, CME Group-MSRI Prize in Innovative Quantitative Applications 2013, Yrjö Jahnsson Foundation Science Prize 2014, Sveriges Riksbank Prize in Econ. Sciences in Memory of Alfred Nobel (co-recipient) 2016. *Publications:* numerous papers in professional journals. *Address:* Department of Economics, Massachusetts Institute of Technology, E18-220, Cambridge, MA 02142 (office); 108 Mt Vernon Street, Boston, MA 02108, USA (home). *Telephone:* (617) 253-0506 (office); (781) 888-5672 (home). *Fax:* (617) 253-1330 (office). *E-mail:* bengt@mit.edu (office). *Website:* economics.mit.edu (office).

HOLNESS, Andrew Michael, BSc, MSc; Jamaican politician; *Prime Minister;* b. 22 July 1972, Spanish Town; m. Juliet Holness; two s.; ed Univ. of the West Indies; Exec. Dir Voluntary Org. for Uplifting Children (non-govt org.) 1994–96; Personal Asst to Leader of the Opposition Edward Seaga 1995–97; MP for West Central St Andrew 1997–, Opposition Spokesperson on Land and Devt 1999–2002, on Housing 2002–05, on Educ. 2005–07; Minister of Educ. 2007–11, Minister with responsibility for Electoral Matters and Leader of Govt Business in Parl. 2008–11, Prime Minister and Minister of Defence and of Educ. 2011–12, Leader of the Opposition and Shadow Minister of Defence, Devt and OPM Operations and Shadow Minister of Educ. 2012; Prime Minister 2016–; mem. Jamaica Labour Party, Leader 2011–. *Leisure interests:* chess, jogging, cycling, table tennis. *Address:* Jamaica House, 1 Devon Road, POB 272, Kingston 6, Jamaica (office). *Telephone:* 927-9941 (office). *Fax:* 968-8229 (office). *E-mail:* pmo@opm.gov.jm (office). *Website:* www.opm.gov.jm (office).

HOLOMISA, Maj.-Gen. Bantubonke Harrington, (Bantu); South African politician and army officer; *President, United Democratic Movement;* b. 25 July 1955, Mqandull, Transkei; s. of Chief B. Holomisa; m. Tunyelwa Dube 1981; one s. one d.; ed Army Coll. of South Africa; joined Transkei Defence Force 1976, Lt Platoon Commdr 1978–79, Capt. Training Wing Commdr 1979–81, Lt-Col Bn Command 1981–83, Col SS01 Operations and Training 1984–85, rank of Brig., Chief of Staff, Transkei Defence Force 1985–87, Commdr 1987–94; Leader of Transkei 1987–94; mem. African Nat. Congress Nat. Exec. Cttee 1994; Deputy Minister of Environmental Affairs, Govt of Nat. Unity 1994–96; Pres. United Democratic Movt 1997–; several mil. medals. *Publications:* Future Plan for South Africa, Comrades in Corruption (booklet). *Leisure interests:* soccer, rugby, cricket, athletics, wildlife gaming resorts. *Address:* PO Box 15, Parliament, Cape Town 8000 (office); PO Box 26290, Arcadia 0007, South Africa (home). *Telephone:* (21) 4033921 (Cape Town) (office); (12) 3210010 (Pretoria) (office); (82) 5524156 (Pretoria) (home). *Fax:* (21) 4032525 (Cape Town) (office); (12) 3210014 (Pretoria) (home). *E-mail:* holomisa@udm.org.za (home); bholomisa@holomisa.org.za (office). *Website:* www.udm.org.za (office).

HOLONYAK, Nick, Jr, MS, PhD; American physicist and academic; *John Bardeen Endowed Chair in Electrical and Computer Engineering and Physics, University of Illinois;* b. 3 Nov. 1928, Zeigler, Ill.; ed Univ. of Illinois, Urbana-Champaign; Researcher, Bell Labs 1954–55; Soldier (draftee), US Army Signal Corps 1955–57; Consulting Scientist, General Electric Co., Syracuse, NY 1957–63; Prof., Dept of Electrical and Computer Eng, Univ. of Illinois, Urbana-Champaign 1963–, John Bardeen Endowed Chair Prof. of Electrical and Computer Eng and Physics 1993–, Prof. Emer.; mem. NAS 1984, Nat. Acad. of Eng, IEEE, American Physical Soc.; Foreign mem. Russian Acad. of Sciences 1999; Fellow, American Acad. of Arts and Sciences 1984, Int. Eng Consortium 1995, AAAS 2003; Charter Fellow, Nat. Acad. of Inventors 2013; Hon. mem. Ioffe Physical-Tech. Inst., Petersburg 1992, Optical Soc.; Hon. DSc (Northwestern Univ.) 1992; Hon. DEng (Notre Dame Univ.) 1994; Cordiner Award, General Electric 1962, IEEE Morris N. Liebmann Award 1973, John Scott Award, City of Philadelphia 1975, GaAs Symposium Award with Welker Medal 1976, IEEE Jack A. Morton Award 1981, Solid State Science and Tech. Award, Electrochemical Soc. 1983, IEEE Edison Medal 1989, Nat. Medal of Science 1990, Charles Hard Townes Award, Optical Soc. of America 1992, NAS Award for the Industrial Application of Science 1993, ASEE Centennial Medal 1993, 50th Anniversary Award ('Inventing America's Future'), American Electronics Asscn 1993, John Bardeen Award, The Minerals, Metals, and Materials Soc. 1995, Japan Prize 1995, Optical Soc. of America Nick Holonyak, Jr Award est. in his honour 1997, IEEE Third Millennium Medal 2000, Frederic Ives Medal, Optical Soc. of America 2002, Global Energy Int. Prize 2003, IEEE Medal of Honor 2003, Nat. Medal of Tech. 2003, Washington Award, Western Soc. of Engineers 2004, Lemelson-MIT Prize 2004, MRS Von Hippel Award 2004, Energy Conservation Award, Izaak Walton League of America Ill. Div. 2004, Laureate, Lincoln Acad. of Illinois 2005, inducted into US Consumers Electronics Hall of Fame 2006, US Inventors Hall of Fame 2008, The Eng at Illinois Hall of Fame 2010, Eng and Sciences Hall of Fame (Dayton) 2011, Chancellor's Medallion, Univ. of Illinois, Urbana-Champaign 2012, LED Pioneer Awards of Strategies Unlimited 2013, Outstanding Achievement for Global SSL Devt, Beijing, People's Repub. of China 2013, Charles Stark Draper Prize, Nat. Acad. of Eng (co-recipient) 2015, Achievement Award, Univ. of Illinois Alumni Asscn 2015, Benjamin Franklin Medal in Electrical Eng, Franklin Inst. 2017, Progress Award, Photographic Soc. of America 2017. *Achievements:* inventor of the light emitting diode (LED); co-inventor (with Milton Feng) of the transistor laser; holder of 56 patents, inventor of shorted-emitter symmetrical switch (TRIAC). *Publications:* Semiconductor Controlled Rectifiers 1964, Physical Properties of Semiconductors 1989; more than 580 papers in scientific journals. *Address:* 2113 Micro and Nanotechnology Lab, University of Illinois at Urbana-Champaign, 208 N. Wright Street, Urbana, IL 61801, USA (office). *Telephone:* (217) 333-4149 (office). *E-mail:* nholonya@illinois.edu (office); feng5@illinois.edu (office). *Website:* www.ece.illinois .edu (office).

HOLROYD, Sir Michael de Courcy Fraser, Kt, CBE, CLit; British writer; *President Emeritus, Royal Society of Literature;* b. 27 Aug. 1935, London; s. of Basil Holroyd and Ulla Holroyd (née Hall); m. Margaret Drabble 1982; ed Eton Coll.; Chair. Soc. of Authors 1973–74, Nat. Book League 1976–78; Pres. English Centre of PEN 1985–88; Chair. Strachey Trust 1990–95, Public Lending Right Advisory Cttee 1997–2000, Royal Soc. of Literature 1998–2001 (Pres. 2003–10, Pres. Emer. 2010–); Vice-Pres. Royal Literary Fund 1997–; mem. Arts Council (Chair. Literature Panel) 1992–95; Gov. Shaw Festival Theatre, Niagara-on-the-Lake 1993–2010; Pres. Stephen Spender Trust 1998–; Trustee Laser Foundation 2001–03; Hon. DLitt (Ulster) 1992, (Sheffield, Warwick) 1993, (East Anglia) 1994, (LSE) 1998, (Sussex) 2009; Saxton Memorial Fellowship 1964, Bollingen Fellowship 1966, Winston Churchill Fellowship 1971, Irish Life Arts Award 1988, Heywood Hill Prize 2001, David Cohen Prize for Literature 2005, Golden Pen Award 2006, The Sheridan Morley Prize 2009. *Publications include:* Hugh Kingsmill: A Critical Biography 1964, Lytton Strachey: A Critical Biography 1967–68 (new edn 1994, Prix du Meilleur Livre Etranger 1996), A Dog's Life (novel, new edn 2014) 1969, The Best of Hugh Kingsmill (ed) 1970, Lytton Strachey by Himself: A Self-Portrait (ed) 1971, Unreceived Opinions (essays) 1973, Augustus John 1974–75 (new edn 1996), The Art of Augustus John (with Malcolm Easton) 1974, The Genius of Shaw (ed) 1979, The Shorter Strachey (ed with Paul Levy) 1980, William Gerhardie's God's Fifth Column (ed with Robert Skidelsky) 1981, Peterley Harveset: The Private Diary of David Peterley (ed) 1985, Bernard Shaw: Vol. 1: The Search for Love 1988, Vol. II: The Pursuit of Power 1989, Vol. III: The Lure of Fantasy 1991, Vol. IV: The Last Laugh 1992, Vol. V: The Shaw Companion 1992, Bernard Shaw 1997 (one-vol. biog.), Basil Street Blues 1999, Works on Paper: The Craft of Biography and Autobiography 2002, Mosaic: Portraits in Fragments 2004, A Strange Eventful History: The Dramatic Lives of Two Remarkable Families (James Tait Black Memorial Prize for Biography) 2008, A Book of Secrets 2010, On Wheels 2012, The Good Bohemian: Letters of Ida John (co-ed with Rebecca John) 2017, Ancestors in the Attic 2017. *Leisure interests:* music, stories. *Address:* c/o AP Watt at United Agents LLP, 12–26 Lexington Street, London, W1F 0LE, England (office). *Telephone:* (20) 3214-0800 (office). *Fax:* (20) 3214-0801 (office). *E-mail:* info@unitedagents.co.uk (office). *Website:* www .apwatt.co.uk (office).

HOLST, Carl; Danish politician; b. 29 April 1970; s. of Peter Holst; m. Lone Holst; three c.; ed Haderslev State Training Coll.; Chair. Venstre Ungdom (youth org. of Venstre, Liberal Party) 1993–95; teacher, Povlsbjerg Primary School, Vojens 1996–2000; mem. S Jutland (Sønderjylland) County Council 1994–2006, Mayor of S Jutland 2000–06; Chair. Team Denmark (sports promotion org.) 2004–12; Regional Council Chair., S Danish Region 2006–15, Vice-Chair. of Danish Regions 2010–15; mem. Folketing (Parl.) (Venstre, Liberal Party) for S Jutland constituency 2015–; Minister of Defence and Nordic Co-operation June–Sept. 2015; mem. Venstre, mem. Central Bd, mem. Exec. Cttee 2010–. *Address:* Folketinget, Christiansborg, 1240 Copenhagen K, Denmark (office). *Telephone:* 33-37-55-00 (office). *Website:* www.thedanishparliament.dk (office).

HOLST, Per; Danish film producer; b. 28 March 1939, Copenhagen; s. of Rigmor Holst and Svend Holst; m. 1st Anni Møller Kjeldsen 1962–72; m. 2nd Kristina Holst 1976; four s.; joined Nordisk Film 1957; film man. and copywriter, WA Advertising Agency 1962; returned to Nordisk Film 1965; f. Per Holst Filmproduktion ApS 1965; numerous film awards including Palme d'Or and Cannes Film Festival. *Films:* Afskedens Time 1967, Benny's Bathtub 1967, Kaptajn Klyde og Hans Venner vender tilbage 1981, The Tree of Knowledge 1982, Zappa 1983, Beauty and the Beast 1983, The Boy Who Disappeared 1984, Twist and Shout 1984, Element of Crime 1984, Up on Daddy's Hat 1985, Coeurs Flambés 1986, Pelle the Conqueror (Acad. Award 1988) 1987, The Redtops 1988, Aarhus by Night 1989, Sirup 1990, War of the Birds 1990, Cassanova 1990, The Hideaway 1991, Pain of Love 1992, Jungle Jack 1993, All Things Fair 1995, Barbara 1998, Let's Get Lost 1998, Bornholms Stemme 2000, I Am Dina 2002, Ondskan 2003, Evergreen 2007, Max Embarrassing 2008, Brotherhood 2009, Max Pinlig 2-sidste skrig 2011, Max Pinlig 3-på Roskilde 2012, Walk with Me 2016, Cykelmyggens far (documentary) 2016. *Leisure interest:* golf. *Address:* Nordisk Film, Mosedalvej 14, 2500 Valby, Denmark. *Website:* www.nordiskfilm.com.

HOLT, Dame Denise Mary, DCMG, CMG, BA; British banking executive and fmr diplomatist; *Chairman, M&S Bank;* b. 1 Oct. 1949, Vienna, Austria; d. of William Dennis Mills and Mary Johanna Shea; m. David Holt 1987; one s.; ed New Hall School, Chelmsford, Univ. of Bristol; grew up in Russia, Japan, Lebanon, the Netherlands, Iran and Bulgaria; joined British Diplomatic Service 1970; Desk Officer for Spain, Portugal and Gibraltar, FCO; First Sec., Embassy in Dublin 1984–88; Head of Section, Dept of Cen. America and Mexico 1988–90; First Sec., Embassy in Brasilia 1990–93; Deputy Dir Dept of Cen. Asia 1993–94; Deputy Dir of Personnel 1996–98, Dir 2001–02; Counsellor, Embassy in Dublin 1998–2001; Amb. to Mexico 2002–05, to Spain (also accred to Andorra) 2007–09; Dir Migration and Overseas Territories 2005–07; Chair. Anglo-Spanish Soc. (now the British-Spanish Soc.) –2013; Chair. M&S Bank 2013–, Dir, Marks & Spencer Savings and

Investments Ltd 2013–, Marks & Spencer Unit Trust Management Ltd 2013–; mem. Bd of Dirs Ofqual; Dir (non-exec.), HSBC Bank plc 2011–, Scottish Power Renewables 2011–; mem. NHS Pay Review Body, Office of Manpower Econs; Ind. Chair. Nominations Cttee, Alzheimer's Soc.; mem. Man. Council, Canada Blanch Centre for Contemporary Spanish Studies, LSE; Robin Humphrey Fellow, School of American Studies, Univ. of London; Hon. LLD (Bristol) 2012. *Leisure interests:* spending time with family and friends, reading, cooking. *Address:* M&S Bank, Kings Meadow, Chester, CH99 9FB, England (office). *Telephone:* (1244) 879080 (office). *E-mail:* ddpholt@aol.com (home); info@marksandspencer.com (office). *Website:* bank.marksandspencer.com (office).

HOLTEN, Kasper Bech; Danish theatre, opera and film director; *CEO, Royal Danish Opera;* b. 29 March 1973, Copenhagen; ed Univ. of Copenhagen; worked as an Asst Dir to John Cox, David Pountney and Harry Kupfer; mem. Danish Music Council 1995–99, Danish Radio and TV Council 2000–08; Artistic Dir Århus Sommeropera Festival 1997–2000; Artistic Dir Royal Danish Opera 2000–11, CEO 2018–; production of Wagner's Ring in Copenhagen 2003–06, other productions include Le nozze di Figaro, Theater an der Wien, Tannhäuser, Copenhagen, A Clockwork Orange, Stockholm, My Fair Lady, Copenhagen and Die Tote Stadt, Helsinki, Don Giovanni, Covent Garden 2014, led move into Copenhagen's new opera house 2005; apptd Assoc. Prof., Copenhagen Business School 2007; Dir of Opera, The Royal Opera, Covent Garden 2011–17, directorial debut with Eugene Onegin in 2013, has also directed Don Giovanni, L'Ormindo, Król Roger, Die Meistersinger von Nürnberg; mem. Bd European Acad. of Music Theatre; Knight of Dannebrog; Ingenio et Arti 2011. *Film:* Juan (writer and dir) 2010. *Address:* c/o Ian Stones, Harrison/Parrott Ltd, The Ark, 201 Talgarth Road, London, W6 8BJ, England. *Telephone:* (20) 7313-3504. *Fax:* (20) 7221-5042. *E-mail:* ian.stones@harrisonparrott.co.uk. *Website:* www.harrisonparrott.com.

HOLTON, A. Linwood, Jr, BA, LLB; American lawyer and fmr politician; *Partner, McCandlish Holton, PC;* b. 21 Sept. 1923, Big Stone Gap, Va; s. of Abner Linwood Holton and Edith Holton (née Van Gorder); m. Virginia Harrison Rogers 1953; two s. two d.; ed public schools in Big Stone Gap, Washington and Lee Univ. and Harvard Law School; fmr Pnr, Eggleston, Holton, Butler and Glenn (law firm); served submarine force during Second World War; fmr Chair. Roanoke City Republican Cttee; Vice-Chair. Va Republican State Cen. Cttee 1960–69; del. to Republican Nat. Convention 1960, 1968, 1972; mem. Nat. Nixon for Pres. Cttee 1967, Regional Co-ordinator for Nixon for Pres. Cttee; Gov. of Va 1970–74; Asst Sec. of State for Congressional Relations, US Dept of State, Washington, DC 1974–75; Pnr, Hogan and Hartson (law firm) 1975–78; Vice-Pres. and Gen. Counsel American Council Insurance, Washington, DC 1978–84; Chair. Burket Miller Center for Public Affairs, Univ. of Va 1979–; Pres. Supreme Court Historical Soc. 1980–89; Chair. Metropolitan Washington Airports Authority 1987–93; Pnr, McCandlish Holton PC (law firm), Richmond 1994–; Pres. Center for Innovative Tech., Herndon, Va 1988–94. *Address:* McCandlish Holton PC, PC, 1111 East Main Street, Suite 1500, PO Box 796, Richmond, VA 23218 (office); 3883 Black Stump Road, Weems, VA 22576, USA (home). *Telephone:* (804) 775-3817 (office); (804) 435-0604. *Fax:* (804) 775-3800 (office). *E-mail:* lholton@lawmh.com (office). *Website:* www.lawmh.com (office).

HOLTON, Gerald, PhD; American physicist, historian of science and academic; *Mallinckrodt Professor of Physics and Professor of the History of Science Emeritus, Harvard University;* b. 23 May 1922, Berlin, Germany; s. of Dr Emanuel Holton and Regina Holton; m. Nina Rossfort 1947; two s.; ed Harvard Univ.; Harvard Univ. staff, officers' radar course and Lab. for Research on Electro-Acoustics 1943–45, various faculty posts 1945–, Mallinckrodt Prof. of Physics and Prof. of History of Science 1975–2011, Emer. 2011–; Visiting Prof., MIT 1976–94; NSF Faculty Fellow, Paris 1960–61; Exchange Prof., Leningrad Univ., USSR 1962; Founder and Ed.-in-Chief, Daedalus 1958–61; mem. Council, History of Science Soc. 1959–61, Pres. 1982–84; Visiting mem. Inst. for Advanced Study, Princeton, NJ 1964, 1967; mem. NAS Cttee on Communication with Scholars in the People's Repub. of China 1969–72, US Nat. Comm. on IUHPS 1982–88 (Chair. 1988); mem. German-American Acad. Council Kuratorium 1997–2000; mem. Bd Govs, American Inst. of Physics 1969–74; Fellow, Center for Advanced Study in Behavioral Sciences, Stanford, Calif. 1975–76; mem. US Nat. Comm. on UNESCO 1975–80, Library of Congress Council of Scholars 1979–98, US Nat. Comm. on Excellence in Educ. 1981–83, Advisory Bd Nat. Humanities Center 1989–93; mem. Editorial Bd Collected Papers of Albert Einstein; Nat. Assoc., NAS; Fellow, American Physical Soc. (Chair. Div. of History of Physics 1992–93), American Acad. of Arts and Sciences (mem. Council 1991–95), American Philosophical Soc., AAAS, Acad. Internationale d'Histoire des Sciences (Vice-Pres. 1982–89), Deutsche Akad. der Naturforscher Leopoldina, Acad. Internationale de Philosophie des Sciences; Ehrenkreuz 1. Klasse (Repub. of Austria); eight hon. degrees; Robert A. Millikan Medal 1967, Herbert Spencer Lecturer, Univ. of Oxford 1979, Jefferson Lecturer 1981, Oersted Medal 1980, Guggenheim Fellowship 1980–81, McGovern Medal 1985, Andrew Gemant Award 1989, George Sarton Medal 1989, Bernal Prize 1989, Joseph Priestley Award 1994, Joseph H. Hazen Prize of the History of Science Soc. 1998, Abraham Pais Prize, American Physical Soc. 2008. *Film:* People and Particles (co-producer), The Life of Enrico Fermi (co-producer). *Publications:* Introduction to Concepts and Theories in Physical Science 1952, Project Physics Course (co-author) 1970, 1981, Thematic Origins of Scientific Thought 1973, 1988, Scientific Imagination 1978, Limits of Scientific Inquiry (ed.) 1979, Albert Einstein, Historical and Cultural Perspectives (ed.) 1982, The Advancement of Science and its Burdens 1986, Science and Anti-Science 1993, Einstein, History and Other Passions 1995, Gender Differences in Science Careers (co-author) 1995, Who Succeeds in Science? The Gender Dimension (co-author) 1995, The Scientific Imagination 1998, Physics, the Human Adventure (co-author) 2001, Ivory Bridges: Connecting Science and Society (co-author) 2002, Understanding Physics (co-author) 2002, Victory and Vexations in Science 2005, What Happened to the Children Who Fled Nazi Persecution (co-author) 2006, Helping Young Refugees and Immigrants Succeed (co-author) 2010. *Leisure interests:* music, kayaking. *Address:* 64 Francis Avenue, Cambridge, MA 02138 (home); Jefferson Physical Laboratory, Harvard University, Cambridge, MA 02138, USA (office). *Telephone:* (617) 868-9003 (home); (617) 495-4474 (office). *Fax:* (617) 495-0416 (office). *E-mail:* holton@physics.harvard.edu (office). *Website:* www.physics.harvard.edu/people/facpages/holton.html (office).

HOLUM, John D., BS, JD; American lawyer and fmr government official; b. 4 Dec. 1940, Highmore, S Dak; m. Barbara P. Pedersen; one d.; ed Northern State Teachers Coll., George Washington Univ.; on staff of Senator George McGovern, US Senate Foreign Relations Cttee 1965–79; mem. Policy and Planning Staff, US State Dept 1979–81; attorney, O'Melveny & Myers 1981–93; defence and foreign policy adviser to Gov. Bill Clinton during 1992 presidential campaign; Exec. Dir 1992 Democratic Nat. Convention; Dir Arms Control and Disarmament Agency 1993–98, Sr Advisor for Arms Control and Int. Security Affairs 1998–2000; Under-Sec. of State for Arms Control and Int. Security 2000–01; Vice-Pres. Int. and Govt Affairs, Atlas Air Inc. 2000–03; mem. Center for Nonproliferation Studies Int. Advisory Bd. *Leisure interests:* flying, scuba diving, playing bluegrass and country music.

HOLYFIELD, Evander; American professional boxer (retd); b. 19 Oct. 1962, Atlanta, Ga; s. of Anna Laura Holyfield; won Bronze Medal at 1984 Olympic Games; won World Boxing Asscn (WBA) cruiserweight title 1986, Int. Boxing Fed. cruiserweight title 1987, World Boxing Council (WBC) cruiserweight title 1988; world heavyweight champion 1990–92, 1993–94, 1996–99 (following defeat of Mike Tyson q.v. Nov. 1996), defended title against Tyson 1997 (Tyson disqualified); defended IBF heavyweight title against Michael Moorer 1997; defended WBA and IBF titles and contested WBC title, against Lennox Lewis (q.v.) March 1999, bout declared a draw; lost to Lennox Lewis Nov. 1999; 2000–01 WBA heavyweight champion; suspended by New York State Boxing Comm. after defeat by Larry Donald Nov. 2004; comeback match against Jeremy Bates (defeated by TKO) 2006; retd with 44 wins, 10 losses, 1 draw, 1 no contest 2014; f. Real Deal Record Label 1999; f. Holyfield Foundation to help inner-city youth; Espy Boxer of the Decade 1990–2000, inducted into Nevada Boxing Hall of Fame 2014. *Leisure interests:* all kinds of music, American football. *Address:* Holyfield Management, 794 Evander Holyfield Highway, Fairburn, GA 30213, USA (office). *Telephone:* (770) 460-6807 (office). *Fax:* (770) 460-5381 (office). *E-mail:* info@EvanderHolyfield.com (office). *Website:* www.evanderholyfield.com (office).

HOLZER, Jenny, BFA, MFA; American artist; b. 29 July 1950, Gallipolis, Ohio; d. of Richard Vornholt Holzer and Virginia Beasley Holzer; m. Michael Andrew Glier 1984; one d.; ed Ohio Univ., Rhode Island School of Design, Whitney Museum of American Art Ind. Study Program; became working artist in New York 1977; special projects and comms since 1978 include Green Table, Univ. of Calif., San Diego 1993, Lustmord, Süddeutsche Zeitung Magazin, No. 46, Germany, Black Garden, Nordhorn, Germany 1994, Allentown Benches, Allentown, Pa 1995, Erlauf Peace Monument, Erlauf, Austria 1995, installation at Schiphol Airport, Amsterdam, Netherlands 1995, Biennale di Firenze, Florence, Italy 1996, installation for Hamburger Kunsthalle, Hamburg, Germany 1996, perm. installation at Guggenheim Museum, Bilbao, Literaturhaus Munich, Germany, Oskar Maria Graf Memorial 1997, Kunsthalle Zürich, Switzerland, Telenor HQ, Norway 2002, Univ. of Pennsylvania 2003, Paula Hodersohn—Becker Museum 2005, Lawrence Convention Center, Pittsburgh 2005, SDtora Torget, Karlstad 2005; Fellow American Acad., Berlin 2000; Resident, American Acad. Rome 2003–04; Hon. DFA (Ohio Univ.) 1994, (Williams Coll.) 2000, (Rhode Island School of Design) 2003, (New School Univ.) 2005, (Smith Coll.) 2009, (Montserrat Coll. of Art) 2009; Golden Lion Award for Best Pavilion, 44th Venice Biennale, Italy 1990, Gold Medals for Title and Design, Art Directors' Club of Europe 1993, Skowhegan Medal for Installation, New York 1994, Crystal Award, for outstanding contrib. to cross-cultural understanding, World Econ. Forum, Switzerland 1996, Kaiserring, City of Goslar 2002, Urban Visionaries Award, The Cooper Union 2006, LA MOCA Award for Distinguished Women in the Arts 2010, Medal of Distinction, Barnard Coll., Outstanding Contributions to the Arts Award, Americans for the Arts 2011; Chevalier, Ordre des Arts et Lettres 2002. *Publications:* A Little Knowledge 1979, Black Book 1980, Eating Through Living 1981, Truisms and Essays 1983, The Venice Installation 1990, Die Macht des Wortes 2006. *Leisure interests:* reading, riding. *Address:* c/o Sprüth Magers, 5900 Wilshire Blvd, Los Angeles, CA 90036, USA. *Telephone:* (323) 634-0600. *Fax:* (323) 634-0602. *Website:* www.spruethmagers.net; www.jennyholzer.com. *E-mail:* jh@jennyholzer.com.

HOMBACH, Bodo; German business executive and fmr politician; *Managing Director, WAZ Media Group;* b. 19 Aug. 1952, Mülheim; m. 1977; ed Düsseldorf Polytechnic, Duisberg Comprehensive Univ., Hagen Correspondence Univ.; fmrly trainee telecommunications worker, youth affairs spokesman and youth worker; Personal Asst to Chair. of German TU Confed. (DGB) North Rhine Westphalia 1974; Educ. Policy Sec. Educ. and Science TU North Rhine Westphalia 1976, Regional Dir 1977; Deputy Regional Dir German Social Democratic Party (SPD) North Rhine Westphalia 1979, Regional Dir 1981–91, Sr Election Campaign Man., 1979–91; Deputy Chair. Mülheim Dist 1993, Deputy Chair. Niederrhein Dist 1998; Fed. Minister Without Portfolio and Head Fed. Chancellery 1998–99; mem. North Rhine Westphalia Landtag 1990–98, Chair. Parl. Inquiry Comm. 1992–94, Parl. Econ. Affairs Spokesman 1994–98, State Minister for Econ. SMEs, Tech. and Transport 1998; Dir Marketing, Org. and Corp. Strategy Preussag Handel GmbH (fmrly Salzgitter Stahl AG) 1991, Man. Dir Preussag Trade Ltd 1992–98, mem. Bd Preussag Int. GmbH 1995–98; Special Co-ordinator of the Stability Pact for S Eastern Europe 1999–2001; Man. Dir WAZ (Westdeutschen Allgemeine Zeitung) Media Group 2002–; Chair. Initiativkreis Ruhr 2011–. *Publications include:* Die SPD von innen (with Horst Becker) 1983, Die Zukunft der Arbeit, Aufruf für eine Geschichte des Volkes in Nordrhein-Westfalia, Die Lokomotive in voller Fahrt der Räder wechseln, Anders Leben, Sozialstaat 2000, Die Kraft der Region: Nordrhein-Westfalia in Europa, The Politics of the New Centre 2002; numerous articles in books. *Address:* Zeitungsverlagsgesellschaft E. Brost und J. Funke GmbH & Co., Friedrichstr. 34-38, 45123 Essen, Germany (office). *Telephone:* (201) 804-0 (office). *Website:* www.waz-mediengruppe.de (office).

HOME, 15th Earl of, cr. 1605; **David Alexander Cospatrick Douglas-Home,** Kt, CVO, CBE, MA; British banker; *Chairman, Coutts & Company Limited;* b. 20 Nov. 1943, Coldstream, Scotland; s. of Rt Hon. Alexander Frederick, Lord Home of the Hirsel and Elizabeth Hester Alington; m. Jane Margaret Williams-Wynne; one s. two d.; ed Eton Coll., Christ Church, Oxford; Dir Morgan Grenfell & Co. Ltd (now Deutsche Securities Ltd) 1974–99; Chair. Coutts & Co. 1999–2013; Chair. Coutts Bank (Switzerland) Ltd (now Coutts & Co. Ltd) 2000–15; Chair. MAN Ltd 2000–10, Grosvenor Group Ltd 2007–10; Pres. British Malaysian Soc. 2001–; mem. Bd of Dirs Dubai Financial Services Authority 2005–10; Adviser, Southern

Capital, Singapore; Trustee The Grosvenor Estate 1993–2010; Opposition Frontbench Spokesperson for Trade, House of Lords 1997–98, for the Treasury 1997–98. *Leisure interest:* outdoor activities. *Address:* House of Lords, London, SW1A 0PW (office); Coutts & Co., 440 Strand, London, WC2R 0QS (office); 43 Chelsea Towers, Chelsea Manor Street, London, SW3 5PN, England (home). *Telephone:* (20) 7753-1000) (office); (20) 3730-1696 (home). *Fax:* (20) 7753-1066 (office). *Website:* www.coutts.com (office).

HOMER-DIXON, Thomas F., BA, PhD; Canadian political scientist, academic and writer; *Centre for International Governance Innovation Chair of Global Systems, Balsillie School of International Affairs, University of Waterloo;* b. 1956, Victoria, BC; m. Sarah Wolfe; one s. one d.; ed Carleton Univ., Ottawa, Massachusetts Inst. of Tech., USA; jobs in construction, forestry and petroleum industries in western Canada and as leader of nat. student org. based in Ottawa 1975–83; research position with Project Athena, MIT, Cambridge, Mass 1983–89; consultant, World Resources Inst., Washington, DC 1983–89; Prin. Investigator, Univ. of Toronto 1990–93, Dir Peace and Conflict Studies Program, Univ. Coll. 1990–2001, Asst Prof. of Political Science, Univ. of Toronto 1993–98, Assoc. Prof. 1998–2006, Prof. 2006–08, George Ignatieff Chair of Peace and Conflict Studies 2007–08, Dir Trudeau Centre for Peace and Conflict Studies 2001–07; Prof., Faculty of Arts, and Centre for Environment and Business, Faculty of Environment, Univ. of Waterloo, Ont. 2008–, Centre for Int. Governance Innovation Chair of Global Systems, Balsillie School of Int. Affairs 2008–, Prof. in Faculty of Environment 2008–, Assoc. Dir Waterloo Inst. for Complexity and Innovation 2009–; Adjunct Research Fellow, Center of Science and Int. Affairs, Kennedy School of Govt, Harvard Univ. 1986–88; SSRC/MacArthur Foundation Dissertation Fellowship in Int. Peace and Security 1986–88; Visiting Scholar, Aspen Inst. 1994; Assoc. Fellow, Canadian Inst. for Advanced Research 1995–; Postdoctoral Fellowship, Social Sciences and Humanities Research Council of Canada 1989–90, Northrop Frye Award, Univ. of Toronto 1999, Outstanding Performance Award, Univ. of Waterloo 2010. *Publications:* Science in Society: Its Freedom and Regulation (co-ed.) 1982, Ecoviolence: Links Among Environment, Population, and Security (co-ed.) 1998, Environment, Scarcity, and Violence (Lynton Keith Caldwell Prize, American Political Science Asscn 2000) 1999, The Ingenuity Gap (Gov.-Gen.'s Non-fiction Award, Canada Council for the Arts 2001) 2000, The Upside of Down: Catastrophe, Creativity, and the Renewal of Civilization (Nat. Business Book Award 2007) 2006, Carbon Shift: How the Twin Crises of Oil Depletion and Climate Change Will Define the Future (co-ed.) 2009; numerous book chapters, and articles in learned journals and newspapers. *Address:* Room 312, Balsillie School of International Affairs, 67 Erb Street West, Waterloo, ON N2L 6C2, Canada (office). *Telephone:* (226) 772-3092 (office). *E-mail:* tad@homerdixon.com (office). *Website:* www.balsillieschool.ca (office); www.homerdixon.com.

HOMMELHOFF, Peter, DrIur; German lawyer, accountant and fmr university rector; *Partner, KPMG AG;* b. 13 Sept. 1942, Hamburg; m. Margret Hommelhoff (née Middelschulte); two c.; ed law studies in Berlin, Tübingen and Freiburg Univs, Univ. of Bochum; in-house legal adviser, Preußen Elektrizitäts AG, Hanover 1972; Academic Research Asst, Univ. of Bochum (Chair for German and European Commercial and Econ. Law) 1974; Chair of Civil Law, Commercial and Econ. Law, Univ. of Bielefeld 1981; part-time judge, Higher Regional Court (Oberlandesgericht), mem. Special Div. for Commercial and Co. Law 1983, Hamm –1990, Karlsruhe 1993–98; Dean Faculty of Law, Univ. of Heidelberg 1993–95, Partnership Commr Exchange Relations between Univ. of Heidelberg and Jagiellonian Univ. of Kraków –2002, Chair. Company Law Asscn (Gesellschaftsrechtliche Vereinigung) 1998–2001, mem. and Deputy Chair. Heidelberg Univ. Council 2000–01, Rector Ruprecht-Karls Univ. of Heidelberg 2001–07; Partner, KPMG AG, Frankfurt 2007–; mem. Bd of Examiners for Chartered Accountants, Ministry of Econ. Affairs, North Rhine-Westphalia –2001, Ministry of Econ. Affairs, Baden-Württemberg 1986, Extended Bd in Asscn of Profs of Civil Law 1995; Expert for Civil, Econ. and Labour Law, German Research Asscn (Deutsche Forschungsgemeinschaft) 1996–2001; fmr Deputy Chair. Professional Bd of Advisors, Max Planck Inst. for Intellectual Property, Competition and Tax Law, Munich; Vice-Pres. Council of Acad. Pres (Hochschulrektorenkonferenz); Speaker for the Univs 2002; mem. Scholarly Bd of Advisors, German Railway Corpn (Deutsche Bahn AG) and of its Strategic Council 1999, Speaker of Legal Bd of Advisors 2006; mem. Professional Bd of Advisors, Max Planck Inst. for Foreign and Int. Pvt. Law, Hamburg; mem. Editorial Bd Journal for Business and Corporate Law (Zeitschrift für Unternehmens- und Gesellschaftsrecht, ZGR), Man. Ed. 1997; First Class Order of Merit 2007; Hon. DrIur (Jagiellonian Univ. of Kraków) 2002, (Univ. of Montpellier I) 2005; Max Planck Research Prize for Int. Cooperation 1997, Medal of Honour, Jagiellonian Univ. of Kraków 1999, Leo Baeck Prize, Cen. Council of Jews in Germany 2005. *Publications include:* more than 300 publs in professional journals. *Address:* KPMG AG, Marie-Curie-Straße 30, 60439 Frankfurt am Main, Germany (office). *Telephone:* (69) 9587-3311 (office). *E-mail:* phommelhoff@kpmg.com (office). *Website:* www.kpmg.de (office).

HOMMEN, Jan H. M.; Dutch business executive; *Chairman of the Supervisory Board, Royal Ahold NV;* b. 29 April 1943, 's-Hertogenbosch; Controller, Alcoa Nederland BV, Drunen 1970–74, Financial Dir 1974–78, Corp. Finance Man. Aluminum Co. of America (Alcoa), Pittsburgh 1978–79, Asst Treas. 1979–86, Vice-Pres. and Treas. 1986–91, Exec. Vice-Pres. and Chief Financial Officer 1991–97; Vice-Chair., Chief Finance Officer and mem. Bd of Man. Koninklijke Philips Electronics NV 1997–2005; mem. Supervisory Bd ING Group NV 2005–09, Chair. 2008–09, Chair. Exec. Bd (CEO) 2009–13, also fmr Chair. Man. Bds Banking and Insurance; mem. Supervisory Bd TNT NV 1998–2009, Chair. 2005–09; Chair. Supervisory Bd Reed Elsevier 2005–09, Royal Ahold NV 2013–, Academisch Ziekenhuis Maastricht, TiasNimbas Business School; Chair. MedQuist, USA –2006; mem. Bd of Dirs Campina BV, Voya Financial, Inc. 2011–13; mem. Bd Royal Concertgebouw Orchestra; Officer, Order of Orange-Nassau 2005, Commdr 2013. *Address:* Royal Ahold NV, Piet Heinkade 167–173, 1019 GM Amsterdam, Netherlands (office). *Telephone:* (20) 509-51-00 (office). *Fax:* (20) 509-51-10 (office). *E-mail:* info@ahold.com (office). *Website:* www.ahold.com (office).

HONARDOOST, Mehdi; Iranian diplomatist; *Ambassador to Pakistan;* over 30 years working in Ministry of Foreign Affairs (MFA), including as fmr Consul-Gen., Mumbai, Deputy Head of Mission, Embassy in Beijing, fmr Amb. to Greece, with W Europe Directorate, MFA –2015, Amb. to Pakistan 2015–. *Address:* Embassy of Iran, Plot No. 222–238, St 2, F-5/1, Islamabad, Pakistan (office). *Telephone:* (51) 8318901 (office). *Fax:* (51) 8318906 (office). *E-mail:* info@iranembassy.pk (office). *Website:* islamabad.mfa.ir (office).

HONDA, Katsuhiko, LLB; Japanese tobacco industry executive; b. 12 March 1942, Kagoshima Pref.; ed Univ. of Tokyo; joined Japan Tobacco and Salt Public Corpn 1965, Vice-Pres. Corp. Planning Div. 1989–92, Man. Dir Human Resources Div. 1992–94, Exec. Dir Personnel and Labor Relations 1994–95, Exec. Dir Tobacco Business 1995–96, Exec. Vice-Pres. Tobacco Business 1996–98, Sr Exec. Vice-Pres., Japan Tobacco Inc. 1998–2000, Pres., Rep. Dir and CEO 2000–06, mem. Bd of Dirs 2006.

HONDA, Keiko, BA, MBA; Japanese international organization official and consultant; *Executive Vice-President and CEO, Multilateral Investment Guarantee Agency, World Bank Group;* ed Ochanomizu Univ., Univ. of Pennsylvania, USA; fmr consultant, Bain and Co., Financial Analyst, Lehman Brothers; joined McKinsey and Co. 1989, mem. Bd of Dirs McKinsey and Co., Japan 1989–2013; Exec. Vice-Pres. and CEO Multilateral Investment Guarantee Agency, World Bank 2013–; Visiting Assoc. Prof. of Corp. Finance, Hitotsubashi Univ. 2002–03; Lecturer, Chuo Business School 2002–05; Vice-Chair. Cttee on Promotion of EPAs/FTA, Keizai Doyukai (Japan Asscn of Corp. Execs); mem. Bd of Dirs Japanese Foundation for Cancer Research; mem. Council for Promotion of Regulatory Reform 2004–10, Business Accounting Council 2012–; mem. jury, Cartier Women's Initiative Award. *Publications include:* M&A and Strategic Alliances 1998, Turnaround 2004, Valuation. *Address:* Multilateral Investment Guarantee Agency, 1818 H Street, NW, Washington, DC 20433, USA (office). *Telephone:* (202) 458-2538 (office). *Fax:* (202) 522-0316 (office). *Website:* www.miga.org (office).

HONG, Guofan, PhD; Chinese molecular biochemist; *Professor and Principal Investigator, Shanghai Institute of Biochemistry and Cell Biology, Chinese Academy of Sciences;* b. 24 Dec. 1939, Ningbo, Zhejiang Prov.; s. of Xiangxin Hong and Deyi Hong (née Chen); m. Renying Zhu 1968; two c.; ed Fudan Univ., Shanghai, Chinese Acad. of Sciences; researcher, Shanghai Inst. for Biochemistry and Cell Biology, Chinese Acad. of Sciences 1964–78, Prof. and Prin. Investigator 1983–, apptd Dir Nat. Genetics Research Centre 1992, Fellow 1997–; researcher, MRC Molecular Biological Lab., UK 1979–83; fmr Prof., Coll. of Pharmaceuticals and Biotechnology, Tianjin Univ.; coordinated Chinese Rice Genome Program 1992–98; Vice-Pres. Chinese Bio-Chemical Soc. 1987–90; mem. Editorial Bd DNA Sequence 1990–; mem. UNESCO, Third World Acad. of Sciences, New York Acad. of Sciences; Fellow, Rockefeller Foundation 1985–, Acad. of Sciences for the Developing World 1993–; Ho Leung Ho Lee Foundation Life Sciences Award 2006. *Leisure interests:* music, english literature. *Address:* Institute of Biochemistry and Cell Biology, Shanghai Institutes for Biological Sciences, 320 Yue Yang Road, Shanghai 200031, People's Republic of China. *Telephone:* (21) 54920000 (office). *Fax:* (21) 54921011 (office). *E-mail:* gfhong@sibcb.ac.cn. *Website:* www.sibcb.ac.cn.

HONG, Hu; Chinese politician; b. June 1940, Jinzhai Co., Anhui Prov.; ed Beijing Eng Inst.; joined CCP 1965; fmr technician, later Deputy Chief, Dye Plant, Jilin Chemical Industry Co.; fmr Workshop Chief, Liming Chemical Industry Factory, Qinghai Prov. (Vice-Chair. CCP Revolutionary Cttee); fmr Head, Comprehensive Planning Div., 2nd Bureau, Ministry of Chemical Industry; fmr Div. Chief, Planning Bureau, State Machine-Building Industry Comm.; Deputy Sec.-Gen., Sec.-Gen. State Comm. for Econ. Restructuring 1982–91; Vice-Minister, State Comm. for Econ. Restructuring 1991–98; Vice-Gov. Jilin Prov. (also Acting Gov.) 1998–99, Gov. 1999–2004; mem. Comm. of Securities of the State Council 1992–98; mem. CCP Cen. Cttee for Discipline Inspection 1992; mem. 15th CCP Cen. Cttee 1997–2002, 16th CCP Cen. Cttee 2002–07; Del., 10th NPC 2003–08, Vice-Chair. 10th NPC Law Cttee 2005; Outstanding CCP Mem. at State Organs Level 2002–.

HONG, Jae-hyong; South Korean politician; b. Cheongju, N Chungcheong Prov.; ed Seoul Nat. Univ.; joined Foreign Exchange Bureau, Ministry of Finance 1963; later worked at IBRD, Washington, DC; Admin., Korean Customs Admin.; Pres. Export-Import Bank of Korea, Korea Exchange Bank; Minister of Finance 1993; Deputy Prime Minister, Minister of Finance and Econs 1994–96; elected mem. Kuk Hoe (Nat. Ass.) (Democratic Party) for Cheongju, N Chungcheong Prov. 2000, apptd Vice-Speaker 2010; Partner, Northeast Asia Econ. Forum.

HONG, Nam-ki, BA, MA, MBA; South Korean civil servant and politician; *Deputy Prime Minister and Minister of Economy and Finance;* b. 29 July 1960, Chuncheon; ed Hanyang Univ., Univ. of Salford, UK; Dir, Budget Standards Div., Ministry of Planning and Budget 2003–04, also Sec. to Minister of Planning and Budget 2003–04; Asst Sec. to the Pres. for Policy Planning, Office of the Pres. 2004–06, Sr Asst Sec. to the Pres. for Econ. Policy 2006–07, Sec. to the Pres. for Planning 2013–16; Minister Counselor, Embassy in Washington, DC 2007–10; Sec. Gen., Korea Lottery Comm., Ministry of Strategy and Finance 2010–11, Spokesperson, Ministry of Strategy and Finance 2011–12, Dir Gen., Policy Coordination Bureau, Ministry of Strategy and Finance 2012–13; First Vice Minister of Science, ICT and Future Planning 2016–17; Minister, Office for Govt Policy Coordination 2017–18; Deputy Prime Minister for Econ. Affairs and Minister of Economy and Finance 2018–. *Address:* Ministry of Economy and Finance, Sejong Government Complex, 477, Galmae-ro, Sejong City, Seoul 30109, Republic of Korea (office). *Telephone:* (44) 215-2114 (office). *Fax:* (44) 215-8033 (office). *E-mail:* fppr@korea.kr (office). *Website:* www.moef.go.kr (office).

HONG, Qi, PhD; Chinese economist and business executive; *Chairman, China Minsheng Banking Corporation Limited;* b. 1957; fmr Man. Dir Beihai Br. of Bank of Communications; fmr Deputy Dir Securities Research Inst. of Renmin Univ. of China; fmr Section Chief, Head Office of the People's Bank of China; fmr Vice-Pres. and Gen. Man. Beijing Admin. Dept, China Minsheng Banking Corpn Ltd, Vice-Chair., Pres. and Sec. CCP Cttee –2015, Chair. 2015–. *Address:* China Minsheng Banking Corporation Ltd, 2 Fuxingmennei Avenue, Beijing 100873, People's Republic of China (office). *Telephone:* (10) 68946790 (office). *E-mail:* webmaster@cmbc.com.cn (office). *Website:* www.cmbc.com.cn (office).

HONG, Xiaoyong; Chinese diplomatist; *Ambassador to Singapore;* b. March 1961, Jiangsu Prov.; ed Peking Univ.; joined Dept of Asian Affairs, Ministry of Foreign Affairs 1984, Third and Second Sec. 1989–94, Second and First Sec., Deputy Div. Chief, and Div. Chief 1998–2004, Counsellor and Div. Chief 2005–07,

Deputy Dir-Gen. Dept of General Affairs 2008–11, also, Asst to Foreign Minister; Deputy Commr Hong Kong Special Admin. Region 2011–14; Attaché, Chinese Embassy in Japan 1985–89, Second Sec. 1994–98; Counsellor, Chinese Mission to UN 2004–05; Minister Counsellor, Chinese Embassy in Singapore 2007–08; Ambassador to Vietnam 2014–18, to Singapore 2018–. *Address:* Embassy of People's Republic of China, 150 Tanglin Road, Singapore 247969 (office). *Telephone:* 64180252 (office). *Fax:* 64180250 (office). *E-mail:* chinaemb_sg@mfa.gov.cn (office). *Website:* www.chinaembassy.org.sg (office).

HONGJOO, Hahm, PhD; South Korean UN official and economist; *Deputy Executive Secretary, United Nations Economic and Social Commission for Asia and the Pacific (ESCAP);* ed London School of Econs, Harvard Business School, Univ. of Cambridge, New York Univ.; Economist Asian Devt Bank (ADB), Manila 1989–91; Sr Economist World Bank Group 1991–2000, Sr Advisor 2005–15, Country Man., Head of Infrastructure Unit, Jakarta; Exec. Dir Goldman Sachs 2000–05; Deputy Exec. Sec. ESCAP 2016–. *Address:* ESCAP, The United Nations Building, Rajadamnern Nok Avenue, Bangkok 10200, Thailand (office). *Telephone:* (2) 288-1234 (office). *Fax:* (2) 288-1000 (office). *E-mail:* escap-scas@un.org (office). *Website:* www.unescap.org (office).

HONJO, Tasuku, MD, PhD; Japanese molecular biologist and academic; *Professor, Department of Immunology and Genomic Medicine, Graduate School of Medicine, Kyoto University;* b. 27 Jan. 1942, Kyoto; s. of Shoichi Honjo and Ryu Honjo; m. Shigeko Kotani 1969; one s. one d.; ed Ube High School and Kyoto Univ.; Fellow, Carnegie Inst. of Washington, Baltimore, Md, USA 1971–73; Visiting Fellow and Assoc., Lab. of Molecular Genetics, NIH 1973–74; Asst Prof., Dept of Physiological Chem. and Nutrition, Faculty of Medicine, Univ. of Tokyo 1974–79; Prof., Dept of Genetics, Osaka Univ. School of Medicine 1979–84; Prof., Dept of Immunology and Genomic Medicine, Grad. School of Medicine, Kyoto Univ. 1984–, Dir Center for Molecular Biology and Genetics 1988–97, Dean, Faculty of Medicine, Kyoto Univ. 1996–2000, 2002–04; Science Adviser, Ministry of Educ., Culture, Sports, Science and Tech. (MEXT) 1999–2003; Dir Japan Soc. for the Promotion of Science, Research Centre for Science Systems 2004–06; Exec. mem. Council for Science and Tech. Policy, Cabinet Office 2006–12; Chair. Shizuoka Prefectural Univ. Corpn 2012–; mem. Leopoldina German Acad. of Natural Sciences 2003, Japan Acad. 2006; Foreign Assoc., NAS 2001; Hon. mem. American Asscn of Immunologists; Order of Culture from the Emperor of Japan 2013; Noguchi Hideyo Memorial Award for Medicine 1981, Asahi Award 1981, Erwin von Baelz Prize 1985, Takeda Medical Prize 1988, Behring-Kitasato Prize 1992, Imperial Prize and Japan Acad. Prize 1996, Person of Cultural Merit Award by Japanese Govt 2000, Robert Koch Prize 2012, Kyoto Prize, Inamori Foundation (jt winner) 2016, Nobel Prize in Physiology or Medicine (jt winner) 2018. *Publications:* Molecular Biology of B Cell 2003; numerous papers in scientific journals. *Leisure interest:* golf. *Address:* Department of Immunology and Genomic Medicine, Graduate School of Medicine, Kyoto University, Yoshida, Sakyo-ku, Kyoto 606-8501, Japan (office). *Telephone:* (75) 753-4371 (office). *Fax:* (75) 753-4388 (office). *E-mail:* honjo@mfour.med.kyoto-u.ac.jp (office). *Website:* www2.mfour.med.kyoto-u.ac.jp/en/index.html (office).

HONKAPOHJA, Seppo Mikko Sakari, DSocSc; Finnish economist, academic and banker; b. 7 March 1951, Helsinki; m. Sirkku Anna-Maija Honkapohja 1973; one s. one d.; ed United World Coll. of the Atlantic, UK, Univ. of Helsinki; Scientific Dir Yrjö Jahnsson Foundation 1975–87; Prof. of Econs, Turku School of Econs and Business Admin 1987–91, Prof.-at-Large (Docent) 1992–; Prof.-at-Large (Docent) of Econs, Univ. of Helsinki 1981–91, Acting Prof. of Econs (Econometrics) 1985–87, Prof. of Econs 1992–; Visiting Lecturer and Scholar, Harvard Univ., USA 1978–79; Visiting Assoc. Prof. of Econs, Stanford Univ., USA 1982–83; Sr Fellow, Acad. of Finland 1982–83, Acad. Prof. 1989–95, 2000–04; Prof. of Int. Macroeconomics, Univ. of Cambridge, UK 2004–08, Professorial Fellow, Clare Coll. 2004–08; mem. Bd, Bank of Finland 2008–; Man. Ed. Scandinavian Journal of Economics 1984–88; Ed. European Economic Review 1993–98; mem. Bd Finnish Econ. Asscn 1989–91, Finnish Soc. for European Studies 1994–2000; mem. Council, European Econ. Asscn 1985–86, 1999–2003, mem. Exec. Cttee 2004–06; Vice-Chair. Kansallis Foundation for Financial Research 1989–96; mem. Governing Body, The Finnish Cultural Foundation 1994–2001, Chair. 1997–2001, mem. Supervisory Bd 2003–09; mem. Supervisory Bd, Okopankki Ltd 1996–2007, Chair. 1997–2007; Vice-Chair. Bd, Univ. of Helsinki 2014–; mem. Academia Europaea 1990, Finnish Acad. of Science and Letters 1991; Fellow, Econometric Soc. 1999, European Econ. Asscn 2004; Commdr, Finnish White Rose; Hon. DSc (Turku School of Econs) 2010; Jaakko Honko Medal, Helsinki School of Econs and Business Admin 1998, Yrjo Jahnsson Foundation Anniversary Prize 2004. *Publications include:* Limits and Problems of Taxation (co-author) 1985, Frontiers of Economics (co-author) 1985, Information and Incentives in Organizations 1989, The Crisis of the Finnish Economy 1990, Learning and Expectations in Macroeconomics 2001, Economic Prosperity Recaptured: The Finnish Path from Crisis to Rapid Growth 2009; ed. several books, including The State of Macroeconomics 1990, Macroeconomic Modelling and Policy Implications 1993; numerous articles in professional journals. *Leisure interest:* fishing. *Address:* Bank of Finland, PO Box 160, 00101, Helsinki, Finland (office). *Telephone:* (10) 8312015 (office). *E-mail:* seppo.honkapohja@bof.fi (office). *Website:* www.bof.fi (office).

HONOHAN, Patrick, BA, MA, MSc, PhD, MRIA; Irish economist, academic and fmr central banker; *Honorary Professor of Economics, Trinity College Dublin;* b. 9 Oct. 1949, Dublin; m.; one s.; ed Univ. Coll., Dublin, London School of Econs, UK; Sec.'s Dept, IMF 1971–73, Visiting Scholar, Research Dept 1996, European Dept 2016; Temporary Lecturer in Econs, LSE, UK 1974; Economist, Research and Int. Relations Dept, Cen. Bank of Ireland 1976–80, Sr Economist 1980–84; Econ. Advisor to the Taoiseach (Prime Minister), Dr Garret FitzGerald 1981–82, 1984–86; Visiting Asst Prof., Dept of Econs, Univ. of California, San Diego, USA 1982–83; Coll. Lecturer, Dept of Political Economy, Univ. Coll. Dublin 1986–87; Visiting Fellow, Dept of Statistics, ANU, Australia 1987; Sr Economist, World Bank, Washington, DC, USA 1987–90, Lead Economist, Devt Research Group 1998–2002, Advisor, Financial Policy and Strategy Dept 2001–02, Sr Advisor, Financial Sector Policy 2002–07; Research Prof. and Dir Banking Research Centre, Econ. and Social Research Inst., Dublin 1990–98; Research Assoc., Inst. for Int. Integration Studies, Trinity Coll. Dublin 2003–15, Prof. of Int. Financial Econs and Devt, Dept of Econs and Inst. for Int. Integration Studies, 2007–09, Professorial Fellow 2008–09, Hon. Prof. of Econs 2010–; Gov. Cen. Bank of Ireland 2009–15; Sr Fellow (non-resident), Peterson Inst. for Int. Econs, Washington, DC 2016–; Research Fellow, Centre for Econ. Policy Research, London 1992, mem. Bd of Trustees 2016–; Council mem. Irish Econ. Asscn 1993–2002 (Pres. 1998–2000), Econ. and Social Research Inst., Foundation for Fiscal Studies, Statistical and Social Inquiry Soc. of Ireland; mem. Sr Council, Cen. Bank Research Asscn 2016–; mem. Nat. Econ. and Social Council 1995–98; mem. Royal Irish Acad. 2002–; Hon. Fellow, Societies of Actuaries in Ireland 2013–; Cunningham Medal, Royal Irish Acad. 2014. *Address:* 11 Cowper Gardens, Dublin 6, Ireland (home). *E-mail:* phonohan@tcd.ie (office). *Website:* people.tcd.ie/Profile?Username=phonohan (office); piie.com/experts/senior-research-staff (office).

HONORÉ, Sandra; Trinidad and Tobago diplomatist and UN official; b. 1955, Tunapuna; m.; one c.; ed Univs of Besançon and Bordeaux, France; several years' service with Ministry of Foreign Affairs (MFA) including postings to Brazil 1983–88, USA 1997–2000, Special Asst to Chief of OAS Electoral Observation Mission to Haiti 1995–96, Chief of Staff, Office of OAS Asst Sec.-Gen. 2000–05, Dir CARICOM and Caribbean Affairs Div. 2005, Chief of Protocol, MFA 2007, Amb. to Costa Rica –2012; Special Rep. of the UN Sec.-Gen. and Head of UN Stabilization Mission in Haiti (MINUSTAH) 2013–17.

HONSCHEID, Klaus, PhD; German particle physicist and academic; *Professor, Department of Physics, Ohio State University;* b. Eschweiler; ed Univ. of Bonn, Germany; Research Assoc., Univ. of Bonn 1988–89; Research Assoc., Cornell Univ., USA 1990–92; Asst Prof., Ohio State Univ. 1993–96, Assoc. Prof. 1996–2000, Prof. of Physics 2000–; mem. Center of Cosmology and Astro Particle Physics (CCAPP) Science Bd 2006–, Dark Energy Survey Project (DES) Man. Cttee 2007–, IEEE Computer Applications in Nuclear and Plasma Sciences (CANPS) Tech. Cttee 2008–; Co-Founder and Pres., Ohio Chapter, Alexander von Humboldt Asscn of America; Alexander von Humboldt Foundation Lynen Fellow 1990–92; Alfred P. Sloan Research Fellow 1995–97; Fellow, American Physical Soc. 2005; Coll. of Arts and Sciences PhD Award (Univ. of Bonn) 1989, Alfred P. Sloan Foundation Fellowship 1995–96, Alumni Award for Distinguished Teaching, Ohio State Univ. 2004. *Publications include:* numerous publs in scientific journals on particle and high-energy physics. *Address:* 3054 Physics Research Building, Ohio State University, 191 West Woodruff Avenue, Columbus, OH 43210, USA (office). *Telephone:* (614) 292-3287 (office). *Fax:* (614) 292-8261 (office). *E-mail:* kh@mps.ohio-state.edu (office). *Website:* www.physics.ohio-state.edu (office).

HONTAREVA, Valeriya O., MA (Econs); Ukrainian fmr central banker; b. 20 Oct. 1964, Dnipropetrovsk, Ukrainian SSR, USSR; m.; two s.; ed Kyiv Polytechnic Inst., Kyiv Nat. Econ. Univ.; Jr Research Fellow, Ukrainian Centre for Standardization and Metrology 1987–89; Design Engineer, Hiprostrommashyna Inst. 1989–93; Chief Economist at the Ukrainian Interbank Currency Exchange 1993–96; mem. Bd and Dir of Resource Man., JSCB Société Générale Ukraine 1996–2001; First Deputy Chair. and Head of Financial Markets Dept, JSB ING Bank Ukraine 2001–07; Chair. Investment Capital Ukraine 2007–14; Gov. Nat. Bank of Ukraine 2014–17; medal and diploma of the Cabinet for contrib. to the devt of Ukraine stock market 2008.

HOOD, Amy, BA, MBA; American business executive; *Chief Financial Officer, Microsoft Corporation;* m.; several d.; ed Duke Univ., Harvard Univ.; worked at Goldman Sachs & Co. in various roles including investment banking and capital markets groups; joined Microsoft 2002, held positions in Server and Tools Business and Corp. Finance Org., Vice-Pres. and Chief Financial Officer, Microsoft Business Div. –2013, Chief Financial Officer, Microsoft Corpn 2013–. *Address:* Microsoft Corporation, 1 Microsoft Way, Redmond, WA 98052-8300, USA (office). *Telephone:* (425) 882-8080 (office). *Fax:* (425) 936-7329 (office). *E-mail:* info@microsoft.com (office). *Website:* www.microsoft.com (office).

HOOD, Brenda; Grenadian social worker and politician; *Minister of Culture;* ed York Univ., Canada; fmr Chair. Nat. Coalition on the Rights of the Child, Grenada Adoption Bd; fmr Exec. Dir Grenada Save the Children Fund; mem. Parl. 1999–2003, Senator 2003–, Minister of State for Housing, Women's Affairs and Social Security 1999, Minister of Social Security, Nat. Insurance Scheme, Gender and Family Affairs 1999–2003, Minister of Tourism, Civil Aviation, Culture and the Performing Arts 1999–2007, Minister of Communications, Works and Transport 2007–08; Parliamentary Sec., Ministry of Tourism, Culture, and Civil Aviation with responsibility for Culture 2013–14, Minister of Culture 2014–; mem. Exec. Cttee Inter-Parl. Forum of the Americas (FIPA); mem. New Nat. Party. *Address:* Ministry of Tourism, Civil Aviation and Culture Ministerial Complex, 4th Floor, Botanical Gardens, Tanteen, St George's, Grenada (office). *Telephone:* 440-0366 (office). *Fax:* 440-0443 (office). *E-mail:* tourism@gov.gd (office). *Website:* www.grenada.mot.gd (office).

HOOD, Hon. (Ignatius Joachim) Karl; Grenadian politician and diplomatist; *High Commissioner to UK;* b. 27 Oct. 1954, Happy Hill, St George's; s. of Anthony Percival Hood and Constance Hood (née Antoine); divorced; two c.; ed West Indies School of Theology, Trinidad, Nyack Coll., NY, USA; trained as optician and Minister of Religion; mem. House of Reps for St George South East; fmr Minister for Labour, Social Security and Ecclesiastical Affairs; fmr Minister of Health; Minister of Foreign Affairs 2010–12; Amb. to People's Repub. of China 2013–15, High Commr to UK (also accred to South Africa), Perm. Rep. to IMO, London 2016–; mem. Nat. Democratic Congress; Hon. DBA. *Address:* Ministry of Foreign Affairs, Ministerial Complex, Fourth Floor, Botanical Gardens, Tanteen, St George's, Grenada (office); High Commission for Grenada, The Chapel, Archel Road, West Kensington, London, W14 9QH, England (office). *Telephone:* 440-2640 (St George's) (office); (20) 7385-4415 (London) (office). *Fax:* (20) 7381-4807 (London) (office). *E-mail:* office@grenada-highcommission.co.uk (office). *Website:* www.grenadahclon.co.uk (office).

HOOD, Sir John, BE, MPhil PhD, KNZM; New Zealand engineer, foundation executive and fmr university administrator; *President and CEO, The Robertson Foundation;* b. 2 Jan. 1952, Napier; one s. two d.; ed Univ. of Auckland, Univ. of Oxford, UK; held various sr positions with Fletcher Challenge Ltd, including Head of Paper, Bldg and Construction Divs 1980–98; Vice-Chancellor Univ. of Auckland 1998–2004, Univ. of Oxford 2004–09; Pres. and CEO The Robertson Foundation 2010–; fmr NZ Sec., The Rhodes Trust, Chair. 2011–; Chair. Global Private Educ. Provider Study Group 2012–; Chair. TeachForAll, Inc., Urenco Ltd, Study Group

Ltd, Matakina Ltd; fmr Chair. Tonkin & Taylor Ltd; fmr Visiting Lecturer, Dept of Civil Eng, Univ. of Auckland; Chair. NZ Vice-Chancellors Cttee, The Knowledge Wave Trust, Universitas 21 Ltd 2002–04; fmr mem. Prime Minister's Growth and Innovation Advisory Bd, Prime Minister's Enterprise Council; Chair. Prime Minister's Think Tank on High Performance Sport 1996; fmr Gov. and mem. Exec. Bd, NZ Sports Foundation; mem. Bd of Dirs BG Group PLC, WPP PLC; fmr Dir Universitas 21 Global, ASB Bank Ltd, ASB Group, Fonterra Cooperative Group Ltd fmr Trustee Asia 2000 Foundation, King's School (also Gov.); Rhodes Scholarship. *Address:* 101 Park Avenue, 48th Floor, New York, NY 10178 (office); The Robertson Foundation, 300 Maynard Street, Ann Arbor, MI 48104-2212, USA (office). *Telephone:* (734) 663-8088 (office). *E-mail:* john.hood@robertstonfoundation.org (office). *Website:* www.robertsonfoundation.org (office).

HOOD, Leroy Edward, MD, PhD; American biologist, academic and entrepreneur; *President, Institute for Systems Biology;* b. 10 Oct. 1938, Missoula, Mon.; s. of Thomas Edward Hood and Myrtle Evylan Wadsworth; m. Valerie A. Logan 1963; one s. one d.; ed California Inst. of Tech. and Johns Hopkins School of Medicine; NIH Predoctoral Fellowship, California Inst. of Tech. 1963–64, NIH Postdoctoral Fellowship 1964–67; Sr Investigator, Immunology Branch, GL&C, NCI, NIH, Bethesda, Md 1967–70; Asst Prof. of Biology, California Inst. of Tech. 1970–73, Assoc. Prof. 1973–75, Prof. 1975–77, Bowles Prof. of Biology 1977–92, Chair. Div. of Biology 1980–89, Dir Cancer Center 1981; Gates Prof. and Chair of Molecular Biotechnology, Univ. of Washington 1992–99; Dir NSF Science and Tech. Center for Molecular Biotechnology 1989–2000; Founder and Pres. Inst. for Systems Biology 1999–; Co-founder P4 Medicine Inst. (P4Mi) 2010; mem. IOM, NAS, Nat. Acad. of Eng, American Acad. of Arts and Sciences, AAAS, American Asscn of Immunologists, American Philosophical Soc., American Soc. for Clinical Investigation, American Soc. of Biological Chemists, Asscn of American Physicians, Int. Soc. of Molecular Evolution, Soc. for Integrative and Comparative Biology; Fellow, American Acad. of Microbiology; Hon. DSc (Montana State) 1986, (Mount Sinai School of Medicine, CUNY) 1987, (Univ. of British Columbia) 1988, (Univ. of Southern California) 1989, (Wesleyan) 1992, (Whitman Coll.) 1995, (Bates Coll.) 1999, (Penn State) 2001, (Zhejiang Univ., Tsinghua Univ., China) 2004, (Medical Coll. of Wisconsin) 2005, (Coll. of Wooster) 2007; Hon. DHumLitt (Johns Hopkins) 1990, (Loyola) 2005, (Yale) 2010; Albert Lasker Basic Medical Research Award 1987, Commonwealth Award of Distinguished Service 1989, Cetus Award for Biotechnology 1989, American Coll. of Physicians Award 1990, Ciba-Geigy/Drew Award 1993, Lynen Medal 1994, Distinguished Alumnus Award, Johns Hopkins Univ. 1994, Beckman Lecturer Award 1998, Distinguished Service Award, American Asscn for Clinical Chem. 1998, Koyoto Prize in Advanced Technologies 2002, Economists Award for Innovation in Biosciences 2002, Lemelson-MIT Prize 2003, World Tech. Award for Biotechnology 2003, American Asscn for Pathology Award for Excellence in Clinical Diagnosis 2004, Heinz Award for Tech. and Econ. Devt 2006, Inventors Hall of Fame 2007, Kistler Prize 2010, Fritz J. and Dolores H. Russ Prize, Nat. Acad. of Eng 2011, Nat. Medal of Science 2011, IEEE Medal for Innovations in Healthcare Technology 2014. *Publications:* co-author of six books on immunology, biochemistry, molecular biology, genetics and the human genome project and of more than 750 papers in learned journals. *Leisure interests:* mountaineering, running, exercise, photography, reading. *Address:* Institute for Systems Biology, 401 Terry Avenue North, Seattle, WA 98109, USA (office). *Telephone:* (206) 732-1202 (office). *Fax:* (206) 732-1254 (office). *E-mail:* lhood@systemsbiology.org (office). *Website:* www.systemsbiology.org (office).

HOODA, Bhupinder Singh, BA, LLB; Indian politician, agriculturist and lawyer; b. 15 Sept. 1947, Sanghi, Rohtak Dist; s. of Choudhary Ranbir Singh; m. Asha Hooda 1976; one s. one d.; ed Punjab Univ., Chandigarh, Univ. of Delhi; Pres. Block Congress Cttee, Kiloi, Haryana 1972–77; Sr Vice-Pres. Haryana Pradesh Youth Congress 1982–83, Pres. 1982–83; Chair. Panchayat Samiti, Rohtak 1983–87, Panchayat Parishad, Haryana 1984–87; mem. Lok Sabha for Rohtak constituency 1991–99, 2004–05; mem. All India Congress Cttee 1992–; mem. Exec. Congress Parl. Party 1994–; Convenor Haryana Congress Parl. Group 1994–96; Pres. Haryana Pradesh Congress Cttee 1997–2002; mem. Consultative Cttee Ministry of Communication 1998–99, Cttee on Subordinate Legislation; mem. Haryana Vidhan Sabha 2000–, Leader of the Opposition 2002–04; Leader Haryana Legislature Party 2005–; Chief Minister of Haryana 2005–14; Pres. All India Young Farmers Asscn, Haryana, Khadi and Village Industries Comm. Employees Union; Dir, New Bank of India 1989–92; Patron Nat. Khadi and Village Industries Bd Employees Fed.; Founder-mem. and Working Pres. All India Freedom Fighters' Successors' Org.; Working Pres. Nat. Fed. of Railway Porters, Vendors and Bearers; Sec. Jat Educ. Soc., Rohtak, Farmers' Parl. Forum 1991–; mem. Man. Cttee, D.A.V. Educational Soc., Hasangarh, Haryana; National Law Day Award 2009. *Leisure interests:* reading, sports. *Address:* Haryana Vidhan Sabha Bhawan, Sector 1, Chandigarh 160 001 (office); Matu Ram Bhawan, Model Town, Delhi Road, Rohtak, India (home). *Telephone:* (1262) 42283 (home). *Fax:* (1262) 212030 (home). *Website:* www.haryana.nic.in/government/cmbio (office); www.haryanaassembly.gov.in.

HOOGENDOORN, Piet; Dutch business executive; b. 1946; ed Netherlands Inst. of Register Accountants; worked as public auditor; Man. Partner, Deloitte & Touche Netherlands 1990–2001, Vice-Chair. Deloitte Touche Tohmatsu Global Bd 1999–2000, Chair. 2000–07; Pres. Royal NIvRAm (professional org. of Dutch accountants); mem. Supervisory Bd ING Groep NV 2007–10, ING Bank NV –2010, Groene Hart Ziekenhuis Gouda (hosp.) –2010, Nyenrode Univ.; mem. Bd Rabobank Group, Netherlands Foundation for Annual Reporting. *Address:* c/o ING House, Amstelveenseweg 500, 1081 Amsterdam, The Netherlands.

HOOKER, (Charles Raymond) Charlie, BA (Hons); British sculptor, artist, musician and academic; *Professor of Sculpture, University of Brighton;* b. 1 June 1953, London; s. of Raymond C. Hooker and Daphne Hooker; Partner Margery Jane Forest Taylor; ed Purley Grammar School, Croydon Coll. of Art and Brighton Polytechnic; Founder-mem. The Artistics (music ensemble) 1972–75, 2B Butlers Wharf (art space) 1974–75; Visiting Lecturer, Chelsea, Croydon, Winchester, Trent, Cardiff, Central, Brighton, Newport, Newcastle, Camberwell Schools of Art/Polytechnics 1977–; part-time Lecturer, Brighton Polytechnic 1990–92; External Examiner, Chelsea School of Art, Camberwell Coll. of Art, Slade School of Fine Art, Univ. of Reading, UCA Canterbury, Coventry Univ., Manchester Metropolitan Univ. 1995–; Sr Lecturer, Camberwell Coll. 1990–92; Sr Lecturer, Univ. of Brighton 1992–, Prof. of Sculpture 2005–, Subject Leader for Sculpture and Critical Fine Art Practice, currently Course Leader, MA in Fine Art and Research Initiative Leader, Coll. of Arts and Humanities; Leader of The Spring Group Art/Science research group, linking the Univs of Brighton, Sussex, Reading, Exeter and Bergen 2005–; Visiting Prof., Univ. of Chichester 2013–; Artist in Residence, Amherst Jr and Hatcham Wood Secondary Schools 1985; Co-ordinator, Artists' Open Week, Camberwell School of Art 1989; works in Arts Council collection and pvt. collections and perm. public outdoor work in UK; numerous exhbns; Art/Science projects with Science Museum, London and Herstmonceux Science Centre 1995; Visiting lectures and installations, Bjerknes Centre for Climate Research 2005–; Leader of The Art Cell research group 2013–. *Films:* Two Views, Nat. Review of Live Art 2009, Bangs, Thumps, Taps & Rattles 2010, Cosmic Drums 2010. *Audio recordings:* Restricted Movement 1982, Transitions 1984, Charlie Hooker and Performers 1987, Wave-Wall/Dust and a Shadow 1991 for Audio Arts, Separate Elements 1992, Night Sky Series 2002, North Atlantic Oscillation 2004, Mindscape 2004, Stroll On 2005, Audio Accompaniment 2011. *Radio:* cosmic ray activity interview (BBC Radio NI) 2013. *Leisure interests:* walking, drumming. *Address:* School of Arts, University of Brighton, Grand Parade, Brighton, BN2 0JY, England (office). *Telephone:* (1273) 643068 (office); (1273) 643041 (office). *E-mail:* charlie.hooker234@btinternet.com (home). *Website:* www.charliehooker.co.uk.

HOOKER, Morna Dorothy, MA, PhD, DD; British theologian and academic; *Lady Margaret's Professor Emerita of Divinity, University of Cambridge;* b. 19 May 1931, Surrey; d. of P. F. Hooker and L. Hooker (née Riley); m. Rev. Dr W. D. Stacey 1978 (died 1993); one step-s. two step-d.; ed Univs of Bristol and Manchester; Research Fellow, Durham Univ. 1959–61; Lecturer in New Testament, King's Coll., London 1961–70, Fellow 1979–; Lecturer in Theology, Univ. of Oxford 1970–76, Keble Coll., Oxford 1972–76; Fellow, Linacre Coll., Oxford 1970–76, Hon. Fellow 1980–; Visiting Fellow, Clare Hall, Cambridge 1974; Lady Margaret's Prof. of Divinity, Univ. of Cambridge 1976–98, Prof. Emer. 1998–, Fellow, Robinson Coll. 1977–; Jt Ed. Journal of Theological Studies 1985–2005; Visiting Prof., McGill Univ., Canada 1968, Duke Univ., USA 1987, 1989, York St John Univ. 2008–12; Pres. Studiorum Novi Testamenti Societas 1988–89; Ed. Black Series of Commentaries 1999–; Hon. DLitt (Bristol) 1994; Hon. DD (Edinburgh) 1997; Burkitt Medal 2004. *Publications:* Jesus and the Servant 1959, The Son of Man in Mark 1967, Pauline Pieces 1979, Studying the New Testament 1979, The Message of Mark 1983, Continuity and Discontinuity 1986, From Adam to Christ 1990, A Commentary on the Gospel According to St Mark 1991, Not Ashamed of the Gospel 1994, The Signs of a Prophet 1997, Beginnings: Keys that Open the Gospels 1997, Paul: A Short Introduction 2003, Endings 2003. *Leisure interests:* molinology, music, walking. *Address:* Robinson College, Cambridge, CB3 9AN, England (office). *Telephone:* (1223) 339100 (office). *Fax:* (1223) 351794 (office). *E-mail:* mdh1000@cam.ac.uk (office).

HOOKER, Steven; Australian fmr athlete; b. 16 July 1982, Melbourne, Vic.; s. of Bill Hooker (represented Australia in 800m and 4×400m at 1974 Commonwealth Games) and Erica Hooker (1972 Olympian and Commonwealth Games long jump silver medallist 1978); pole vaulter; finished fourth at World Jr Championships, Santiago, Chile 2000; Gold Medal, Commonwealth Games, Melbourne 2006, New Delhi, India 2010; finished fifth at World Athletics Final, Stuttgart 2006; finished first at World Cup, Athens 2006; Bronze Medal, World Athletics Final, Stuttgart 2007, World Indoor Championships, Valencia 2008; set personal best of 6.00m in Perth, WA Jan. 2008; Gold Medal, Olympic Games, Beijing 2008 (set new Olympic record of 5.96m), first Australian male track and field gold medallist since 1968; Gold Medal, World Championships, Berlin, Germany 2009; Gold Medal, World Indoor Championships, Doha 2010; retd 2014; Medal of the Order of Australia 2009.

HOON, Rt Hon. Geoffrey William, PC, MA; British lawyer and politician; b. 6 Dec. 1953; s. of Ernest Hoon and June Hoon; m. Elaine Ann Dumelow 1981; one s. two d.; ed Jesus Coll., Cambridge; labourer at furniture factory 1972–73; Lecturer in Law, Univ. of Leeds 1976–82; Visiting Prof. of Law, Univ. of Louisville, USA 1979–80; called to the Bar, Gray's Inn 1978; in practice in Nottingham 1982–84; MEP for Derbyshire 1984–94, mem. Legal Affairs Cttee 1984–94; MP for Ashfield 1992–2010; Opposition Whip 1994–95, Opposition Spokesman on Information Tech. 1995–97; Parl. Sec., Lord Chancellor's Dept 1997–98, Minister of State 1998–99, Sec. of State for Defence 1999–2005, Leader of the House of Commons 2005–06, Minister for Europe, FCO 2006–07, Parl. Sec. to the Treasury and Chief Whip 2007–08, Sec. of State for Transport 2008–09; Consultant, TaylorHoon Strategy May 2010–April 2011; Man. Dir for Int. Business, AgustaWestland (helicopter manufacturer) 2011–; Vice-Chair. and Gov. Westminster Foundation 1994–97; mem. Labour Party; US Dept of Defense Distinguished Public Service Award 2004. *Leisure interests:* cinema, cricket, football, music. *Address:* 8 Station Street, Kirkby-in-Ashfield, Notts., NG17 7AR, England (home). *Telephone:* (1623) 720399 (home). *Fax:* (1623) 720398 (home). *Website:* www.agustawestland.com (office).

HOOPER, Thomas (Tom) George; British television and film director; b. 1 Oct. 1972, London, England; s. of Richard Hooper and Meredith Hooper; ed Westminster School, London, University Coll., Oxford; early experience as dir whilst student as mem. Oxford Univ. Dramatic Soc.; began directing TV commercials, later directed episodes of various series for BBC and Granada TV. *Films:* Red Dust (IFFI Special Jury Award Special Award) 2004, Elizabeth I (Emmy Award for Outstanding Directing for a Miniseries, Movie or Dramatic Special) 2005, The Damned United 2009, The King's Speech (Dir's Guild of America Award for Outstanding Directorial Achievement in Motion Pictures 2010, London Film Critics' Circle Award for British Director of the Year 2010, Academy Award for Best Dir 2011) 2010, Les Misérables 2012, The Danish Girl 2015. *Television:* Painted Faces (short) (Channel 4) 1992, four episodes of Byker Grove (Children's BBC series) 1997, EastEnders (BBC One) 1998–2000, Cold Feet (Granada TV) 1999, Love in a Cold Climate (mini-series) 2001, Daniel Deronda (mini-series) 2002, Prime Suspect 6: The Last Witness (Granada TV) 2003, Elizabeth I (mini-series) (Primetime Emmy Award for Outstanding Directing for a Miniseries, Movie or Dramatic Special 2006) 2005, Longford (film) (BAFTA for Best Single Drama 2007) 2006, John Adams (mini-series) 2008. *Address:* c/o Independent Talent Group, 40 Whitfield Street, London, W1T 2RH,

England (office). *E-mail:* info@independenttalent.com (office). *Website:* www.independenttalent.com (office).

HOPE, Christopher David Tully, BA, MA, FRSL; South African writer; b. 26 Feb. 1944, Johannesburg; s. of Dudley Mitford Hope and Kathleen Mary Hope; m. Eleanor Marilyn Margaret Klein 1967 (divorced 1992); two s.; ed Natal Univ., Univ. of the Witwatersrand; Founder Franschhoek Literary Festival 2007; Co-founder Hermanus Fynarts Festival 2012; Fellow, Stellenbosch Inst. for Advanced Study 2017; mem. Soc. of Authors; Cholmondeley Award 1972, David Higham Award 1981, Int. PEN Award 1983, Whitbread Award 1986, CNA Literary Award (S Africa) 1989, Travelex Travel Writer of the Year 1997. *Music:* librettist, A Distant Drum, Carnegie Hall 2014. *Publications include:* A Separate Development 1981, Private Parts 1982, The King, the Cat and the Fiddle (with Yehudi Menuhin) 1983, Kruger's Alp (Whitbread Prize for Fiction 1985) 1984, The Dragon Wore Pink 1985, The Hottentot Room 1986, Black Swan 1987, White Boy Running 1988, My Chocolate Redeemer 1989, Moscow! Moscow! 1990, Serenity House 1992, The Love Songs of Nathan J. Swirsky 1993, Darkest England 1996, Me, the Moon and Elvis Presley 1997, Signs of the Heart 1999, Heaven Forbid 2002, Brothers Under the Skin 2003, My Mother's Lovers 2006, The Garden of Bad Dreams 2008, Shooting Angels 2011, A Distant Drum (libretto) 2014, Jimfish 2015, The Café de Move-On Blues 2018; poetry: Cape Drives 1974, In the Country of the Black Pig 1981, Englishmen 1985; contrib. to TLS, London Magazine, Les Temps Modernes, BBC, Guardian. *Leisure interest:* getting lost. *Address:* c/o Rogers, Coleridge & White Ltd, 20 Powis Mews, London, W11 1JN, England (office). *Telephone:* (20) 7221-3717 (office). *Fax:* (20) 7229-9084 (office). *E-mail:* christopher1hope@gmail.com (home).

HOPE OF CRAIGHEAD, Baron (Life Peer), cr. 1995, of Bamff in the District of Perth and Kinross; **Rt Hon. James Arthur David Hope,** Kt, PC, BA, LLB, FRSE; British judge (retd); b. 22 June 1938, Edinburgh, Scotland; s. of Arthur Henry Cecil Hope and Muriel Ann Neilson Hope; m. Katharine Mary Kerr 1966; two s. one d.; ed The Edinburgh Acad., Rugby School, St John's Coll., Cambridge, Univ. of Edinburgh; nat. service, Seaforth Highlanders 1957–59; admitted to Faculty of Advocates, to practise at Scottish Bar 1965; Standing Jr Counsel to Bd of Inland Revenue in Scotland 1974–78; apptd QC in Scotland 1978; Advocate-Depute, Crown Office, Edinburgh 1978–82; Chair. and Legal Chair. Medical Appeal Tribunals 1985–86; Dean Faculty of Advocates 1986–89; Lord Justice Gen. of Scotland and Lord Pres. of Court of Session 1989–96; mem. (Cross-Bench), House of Lords 1995–; a Lord of Appeal in Ordinary 1996–2009; Deputy Pres. The Supreme Court 2009–13; Chair. Sub-cttee E (Law and Insts), House of Lords Select Cttee on the EU 1998–2001; Pres. Stair Soc. 1993–2013, Int. Criminal Lawyers Asscn 2000, Commonwealth Magistrates' and Judges' Asscn 2003–06; Chancellor Univ. of Strathclyde 1998–2013, Prof. Emer. of Law 2013–; Hon. Prof. of Law, Univ. of Aberdeen 1994–; Hon. Fellow, St John's Coll., Cambridge 1995, American Coll. of Trial Lawyers 2000; Hon. LLD (Aberdeen) 1991, (Strathclyde) 1993, (Edin.) 1995, (Glasgow) 2013; Hon. DUniv (Strathclyde) 2013. *Publications:* Gloag & Henderson's Introduction to the Laws of Scotland (co-ed.) 1968, (asst ed.) 1980, 1987, 2001, Armour on Valuation for Rating (co-ed.) 1971, 1985, The Rent (Scotland) Act (co-author) 1984, 1986, Stair Memorial Encyclopedia of Scots Law (contrib.). *Leisure interests:* walking, ornithology, music. *Address:* House of Lords, Westminster, London, SW1A 0PD, England (office); 34 India Street, Edinburgh, EH3 6HB, Scotland (home). *Telephone:* (20) 7219-8308 (office); (131) 225-8245 (home). *E-mail:* hopejad@parliament.uk (office). *Website:* www.parliament.uk/biographies/lords/lord-hope-of-craighead/2004 (office).

HOPE OF THORNES, Baron (Life Peer), cr. 2005, of Thornes in the County of West Yorkshire; **Rt Rev. and Rt Hon. David Michael Hope,** KCVO, PC, BA, DPhil; British ecclesiastic (retd); b. 14 April 1940, Wakefield, Yorks.; s. of Jack Hope and Florence Hope; ed Wakefield Grammar School, Univ. of Nottingham, Linacre Coll., Oxford; Curate, St John's, Tuebrook, Liverpool 1965–70; Chaplain, Church of Resurrection, Bucharest 1967–68; Vicar, St Andrew's, Warrington 1970–74; Prin. St Stephen's House, Oxford 1974–82; Warden, Community of St Mary the Virgin, Wantage 1980–87; Vicar, All Saints', Margaret Street, London 1982–85; Bishop of Wakefield 1985–91, of London 1991–95; Archbishop of York 1995–2005; Vicar of St Margaret's, Ilkley, W Yorks. 2005–06 (retd); Prelate of the Order of the British Empire 1991–95; Dean of the Chapels Royal 1991–95; mem. (Crossbench), House of Lords 2005–15; Trustee, Skipton Building Society Charitable Foundation; Hon. Asst Bishop, Diocese of Bradford 2006, Hon. Fellow, Linacre Coll., Oxford; Hon. DD (Nottingham, Hull). *Publications include:* The Leonine Sacramentary 1971, Living the Gospel 1993, Signs of Hope 2001. *Address:* 35 Hammerton Drive, Hellifield, Skipton, N Yorks., BD23 4LZ, England (home). *E-mail:* dmhhellifield@gmail.com (home).

HOPFIELD, John Joseph, AB, PhD; American scientist and academic; *Howard A. Prior Professor Emeritus of Molecular Biology, Princeton University;* b. 15 July 1933, Chicago, Ill.; s. of John Joseph Hopfield and Helen Staff Hopfield; m. Mary Waltham; three c.; ed Swarthmore Coll., Cornell Univ.; mem. tech. staff, Bell Labs 1958–60, 1973–89; Research Physicist, École Normale Supérieure, Paris 1960–61; Asst/Assoc. Prof. of Physics, Univ. of California, Berkeley 1961–64; Prof. of Physics, Princeton Univ. 1964–80, Eugene Higgins Prof. of Physics 1979–80, Prof., Dept of Molecular Biology 1997–2008, Howard A. Prior Prof. of Molecular Biology 2001–08, now Emer.; Roscoe Gilkey Dickinson Prof. and Prof. of Chem. and Biology, Calif. Inst. of Tech. 1980–97; Chair. NAS Cttee on Publication 1995–98, Selection Cttee, Burroughs-Wellcome Fund Interfaces Program 1997–99; mem. NASA Tycho Study Group on the nature of the lunar surface 1965–67, Strategic Mil. Panel of PSAC 1971–73, American Physical Soc. (APS) Study on Solar Photoelectricity 1977–78, Neurosciences Research Program 1978–89, Solar Photovoltaic Energy Advisory Cttee 1980–82, Advisory Council, Keck Grad. Inst. of Applied Life Sciences 1997–2001, NAS Cttee Bio 2010: Undergraduate Biology Educ. for Future Scientists 2000–02; Pres. APS 2006; Visiting Prof. of Natural Sciences, Inst. for Advanced Study 2010–13; mem. NAS 1973–, American Acad. of Arts and Sciences 1976–, American Philosophical Soc. 1988–; Trustee, Battelle Memorial Inst. 1982–2006, Neuroscience Research Inst. 1986–87, Harvey Mudd Coll. 1990–96, Huntington Medical Research Inst. 1991–96; Hon. DSc (Swarthmore Coll.) 1992, (Univ. of Chicago) 2009, Hon. Alumnus, Caltech 2017–; Alfred Sloan Fellow 1962–64, Guggenheim Fellow, Univ. of Cambridge, UK 1969, APS Oliver E. Buckley Prize 1969, John and Catherine T. MacArthur Award 1983–88, APS Prize in Biophysics 1985, Michelson-Morley Award, Case-Western Univ. 1988, The Wright Prize, Harvey Mudd Coll. 1989, California Scientist of the Year, California Museum of Science and Industry 1991, IEEE Neural Network Pioneer Award 1997, Helmholtz Award, Int. Neural Network Soc. 1999, Dirac Medal and Prize, Int. Centre for Theoretical Physics, Trieste 2001, Pender Award, Moore School of Eng, Univ. of Pennsylvania 2002, Albert Einstein World Award of Science, World Cultural Council 2005, IEEE Rosenblatt Award 2009, Swarz Prize for Theoretical and Computational Neuroscience, Soc. for Neuroscience 2012, Benjamin Franklin Medal in Physics 2019, among others. *Achievements include:* most widely known for his invention of the associative neural network, the Hopfield Model 1982. *Publications:* more than 190 scientific papers in professional journals. *Address:* 150 Princeton Neuroscience Institute, Princeton University, Princeton, NJ 08544, USA (office). *Telephone:* (609) 258-1239 (office). *E-mail:* hopfield@princeton.edu (office). *Website:* pni.princeton.edu/john-hopfield (office).

HOPKINS, Sir Anthony, Kt, CBE; American (b. British) actor; b. (Philip Anthony Hopkins), 31 Dec. 1937, Margam, Port Talbot, Wales; s. of Richard Hopkins and Muriel Hopkins; m. 1st Petronella Barker 1967 (divorced 1972); one d.; m. 2nd Jennifer Lynton 1973 (divorced 2002); m. 3rd Stella Arroyave 2003; ed Cowbridge Grammar School, S Wales, Welsh Coll. of Music and Drama, Cardiff, Royal Acad. of Dramatic Art; mil. training and service: clerk Royal Artillery Unit, Bulford 1958–60; joined Manchester Library Theatre, Asst Stage Man. 1960; then at Nottingham Repertory Co.; joined Phoenix Theatre, Leicester 1963; then Liverpool Playhouse, then Hornchurch Repertory Co.; joined Nat. Theatre Co. 1967; Film debut The Lion in Winter 1967; film, TV, stage actor in UK and USA 1967–, in USA 1974–84; Hon. RAM 1979; Hon. Fellow, St David's Coll., Lampeter 1992; BAFTA Fellowship 2008; Hon. DLitt (Univ. of Wales) 1988; Commdr, Ordre nat. des Arts et Lettres; US Film Advisory Bd Special Career Achievement Award for US Work 1994, BAFTA (US) Britannia Award for Outstanding Contrib. to the Int. Film and TV Industry 1995, Golden Globe Cecil B. DeMille Award 2006, and numerous others world-wide. *Stage appearances include:* title role in Macbeth, Nat. Theatre 1972, Dr Dysart in Equus, Plymouth Theatre, New York 1974, 1975, Huntingdon Hartford Theatre, Los Angeles (also Dir) 1977, Prospero in The Tempest, Los Angeles 1979, Old Times, New York 1983, The Lonely Road, Old Vic Theatre, London 1985, Pravda, Nat. Theatre Stage Actor of the Year, Soc. of West End Theatres Award, The Observer Award) 1985, King Lear (title role), Nat. Theatre 1986, Antony and Cleopatra (title role), Nat. Theatre 1987, M. Butterfly 1989, August (also Dir) 1994. *Films include:* The Lion in Winter 1967, The Looking Glass War 1967, Claudius in Hamlet 1969, When Eight Bells Toll 1969, Torvald in A Doll's House 1972, The Girl from Petrovka 1973, Juggernaut 1974, A Bridge Too Far 1976, Audrey Rose 1976, International Velvet 1977, Magic 1978, The Elephant Man 1979, A Change of Seasons 1980, Capt. Bligh in The Bounty 1983, The Good Father 1985, 84 Charing Cross Road (Best Actor, Moscow Film Festival) 1987, The Old Jest 1987, A Chorus of Disapproval 1988, The Tenth Man 1988, Desperate Hours 1989, The Silence of the Lambs (BAFTA Award and Acad. Award for Best Actor) 1990, Spotswood 1990, One Man's War 1990, Howard's End 1991, Freejack 1991, Bram Stoker's Dracula 1991, Chaplin 1992, The Trial 1992, The Innocent 1992, The Remains of the Day (BAFTA Award for Best Actor) 1992, Shadowlands 1993, Legends of the Fall 1993, The Road to Wellville 1993, August (also Dir) 1994, Nixon 1995, Surviving Picasso 1995, The Edge 1996, The Mask of Zorro 1997, Meet Joe Black 1998, Amistad 1998, Instinct 1999, Titus 1999, Mission Impossible 2, Hannibal 2001, Hearts in Atlantis 2001, The Devil and Daniel Webster 2001, Bad Company 2002, Red Dragon 2002, Human Stain 2003, Alexander 2004, Proof 2004, The World's Fastest Indian 2005, All the King's Men 2006, Bobby 2006, Slipstream 2007, Fracture 2007, Beowulf (voice) 2007, The City of Your Final Destination 2007, Where I Stand: The Hank Greenspun Story (documentary) (voice) 2008, Immutable Dream of Snow Lion (short) 2008, The City of Your Final Destination 2009, The Wolfman 2010, The Third Rule (short) 2010, You Will Meet a Tall Dark Stranger 2010, Bare Knuckles 2010, The Rite 2011, Thor 2011, 360 2011, Hitchcock 2012, Bare Knuckles 2013, RED 2 2013, Noah 2014, Blackway 2015, Misconduct 2016, Collide 2016. *Television includes:* A Heritage and its History, A Company of Five 1968, The Three Sisters, The Peasants Revolt 1969, title roles in Dickens, Danton, Astrov in Uncle Vanya, Hearts and Flowers 1970, Pierre in War and Peace (BAFTA TV Actor Award 1972) 1971–72, title role in Lloyd George 1972, QB VII 1973, A Childhood Friend, Possessions, All Creatures Great and Small, The Arcata Promise 1974, Dark Victory, The Lindbergh Kidnapping Case (Emmy Award) 1975, Victory at Entebbe 1976, title role in Kean 1978, The Voyage of the Mayflower 1979, The Bunker (Emmy Award), Peter and Paul 1980, title role in Othello, Little Eyolf, The Hunchback of Notre Dame 1981, A Married Man 1982, Strangers and Brothers 1983, Old Times, The Arch of Triumph, Mussolini and I, Hollywood Wives, Guilty Conscience 1984, Blunt (role of Guy Burgess) 1987, Heartland 1989, Across the Lake (Donald Campbell) 1989, Great Expectations (Magwitch) 1989, To Be the Best 1990, A Few Selected Exits (Gwyn Thomas) 1993, Big Cats 1993, American Masters (series documentary) – Tony Bennett: The Music Never Ends (narrator) 2007, The Dresser 2015, Westworld 2016. *Leisure interests:* music, playing the piano, reading philosophy and European history. *Address:* c/o Creative Artists Agency, 2000 Avenue of the Stars, Los Angeles, CA 90067, USA. *Telephone:* (424) 288-2000. *Fax:* (424) 288-2900. *Website:* www.caa.com.

HOPKINS, Bernard; American professional middleweight boxer; b. 15 Jan. 1965, Philadelphia; ed Germantown High School; 95 victories and four defeats as an amateur; spent four years in jail for armed robbery when 17; turned professional on 11 Oct. 1988 (defeated by Clinton Mitchell); suffered second defeat versus Roy Jones, Jr, in world title bout on 22 May 1993; won Int. Boxing Fed. world title defeating Segundo Mercado on 29 April 1995; added World Boxing Council belt defeating Keith Holmes on 14 April 2001 and World Boxing Asscn title defeating Felix Trinidad on 29 Sept. 2001; undisputed middleweight champion of the world with 19 title defences (middleweight record), defeating Oscar de la Hoya on 19 Sept. 2004 in Las Vegas; light heavyweight champion of the world after defeating Antonio Tarver in Atlantic City on 10 June 2006; defeated Ronald Wright 2007, lost to Joe Calzaghe 2008, defeated Kelly Pavlik 2008, defeated Enrique Ornelas 2009, defeated Roy Jones Jr 2010, drew to Jean Pascal 2010, fought and defeated Pascal 2011, won Int. Boxing Fed. (IBF) light heavyweight championship defeating Tavoris Cloud 2013, defeated Karo Murat 2013, Beibut Shumenov 2014, lost his titles to Sergey Kovalev 2014; won 55 fights, including 32 knockouts, seven defeats, two draws, two no contest. *Address:* c/o Swanson Communications,

1425 K Street, NW, Suite 350, Washington, DC 20005, USA (office). *Telephone:* (202) 783-5500 (office). *Fax:* (202) 783-5516 (office). *E-mail:* contact@swansonpr.com (office). *Website:* www.swansonpr.com (office).

HOPKINS, Sir Michael John, Kt, CBE, RA, FRIBA; British architect; *Founding Partner, Hopkins Architects Partnership LLP;* b. 7 May 1935, Poole, Dorset; s. of Gerald Hopkins and Barbara Hopkins; m. Patricia Wainwright 1962; one s. two d.; ed Sherborne School, Architectural Asscn and RIBA; partnership with Norman Foster 1969–75; Founding Pnr, Michael Hopkins & Partners (now Hopkins Architects Partnership LLP), London 1976–; Consultant Architect, Victoria & Albert Museum 1985; Vice-Pres. Architectural Asscn 1987–93, Pres. 1997–99; mem. Royal Fine Art Comm. 1986–99; Trustee Thomas Cubitt Trust 1987–, British Museum 1993–; mem. RIBA Council, London Advisory Cttee to English Heritage, Architectural Advisory Group, Arts Council; Hon. mem. Bund Architekten; Hon. FAIA 1996; Hon. Fellow, Royal Incorporation of Architects of Scotland 1996; Hon. DLitt (Nottingham) 1995; Hon. DTech (London Guildhall); RIBA Award 1977, 1980, 1988, 1989, 1994, 1996; Civic Trust Award 1979, 1988, 1990, 1997; Financial Times Award 1980, 1982; Structural Steel Award, 1980, 1988; Royal Acad. Architectural Award 1982, co-winner (with wife Patricia Hopkins) RIBA Gold Medal for Architecture 1994. *Major works include:* Patera Bldg System 1984, Research Centre for Schlumberger, Cambridge 1984, Bicentenary Stand, Lord's Cricket Ground 1987, redevelopment of Bracken House for Ohbayashi Corpn 1987–91, R&D Centre, Solid State Logic 1988, Glyndebourne Opera House 1987–94, Portcullis House, Westminster 1989–2000, Westminster Underground Station 1990–99, The William Younger Centre 1990–99, Office Bldg for IBM at Bedfont Lakes, The Queen's Bldg, Emmanuel Coll., Cambridge 1993–95, Dynamic Earth, Edinburgh 1990–99, Jubilee Campus, Nottingham 1996–99, Saga Group Headquarters 1994–99, Hampshire Co. Cricket Club 1994–2001, Wildscreen@-Bristol 2000 1996–99, Goodwood Racecourse 1997–2001, Haberdashers' Hall 1996–2002, The Forum, Norwich 1996–2001, Manchester City Art Gallery 1994–, Nat. Coll. of School Leadership, Nottingham 2000–02, London 2012 Velodrome 2011, Siemens Headquarters, Munich 2011, WWF-UK Headquarters, Woking 2013, Univ. of East London: Stratford Library 2013, Dubai Int. Finance Centre 2014, etc. *Leisure interests:* sailing, Catureglio, Blackheath. *Address:* Hopkins Architects, 27 Broadley Terrace, London, NW1 6LG (office); 49A Downshire Hill, London, NW3 1NX, England (home). *Telephone:* (20) 7724-1751 (office); (20) 7435-1109 (home). *Fax:* (20) 7723-0932 (office); (20) 7794-1494 (home). *E-mail:* mail@hopkins.co.uk (office). *Website:* www.hopkins.co.uk (office).

HOPKINS, Patricia (Patty) Anne, Lady Hopkins; British architect; *Partner, Hopkins Architects Partnerships LLP;* b. 7 April 1942, Staffs.; d. of Denys Wainwright; m. (now Sir) Michael Hopkins 1962; one s. one d.; ed Wycombe Abbey School, Architectural Asscn, London; Founding Pnr, Michael Hopkins and Pnrs (now Hopkins Architects Partnership LLP) 1976–; Assessor for Civic Trust Award Schemes 1993–2000; Gov. Queen's Coll., Harley St 1998–; mem. Arts Council Nat. Lottery Advisory Bd 1994–99, Architectural Asscn 150 Campaign Bd 1994–99; Trustee Nat. Gallery, London 1998–; Hon. Fellow, Royal Inst. of Architects in Scotland 1996, American Inst. of Architects; Hon. DTech (London Guildhall) 1996. *Architectural works include:* Hopkins House, Hampstead (RIBA Award 1997) 1996, Hopkins Office, Marylebone 1985, Fleet Velmead School, Hants (RIBA Award, Civic Trust Award 1988) 1986, Victoria and Albert Museum (Consultant Architect and Masterplan) 1988, Glyndebourne Opera House (RIBA Award, Royal Fine Art Comm. Award 1994, Civic Trust Award, FT Award 1995) 1994, Queen's Bldg, Emmanuel Coll. Cambridge (RIBA Award, Royal Fine Art Comm. Award 1996) 1995, Jewish Care Home for the Elderly 1996, Preacher's Court, Charterhouse 2000, Wildscreen at Bristol (Civic Trust Award, DTLR Urban Design Award 2001) 2001, Manchester Art Gallery 2002, Haberdasher's Hall 2002. *Leisure interests:* family and friends at Catureglio and Blackheath. *Address:* Hopkins Architects, 27 Broadley Terrace, London, NW1 6LG (office); 49A Downshire Hill, London, NW3 1NX, England (home). *Telephone:* (20) 7724-1751 (office); (20) 7794-1494 (home). *Fax:* (20) 7723-0932 (office); (20) 7794-1494 (home). *E-mail:* patty.h@hopkins.co.uk (office). *Website:* www.hopkins.co.uk (office).

HOPKINS, Paul Jeffrey, BA, PhD; American academic; *Founder and President, UMA Institute for Tibetan Studies;* b. 30 Sept. 1940, Providence, RI; s. of Charles E. Hopkins and Ora Adams; m. 1st Elizabeth S. Napper 1983 (divorced 1989); m. 2nd Hong-Ming Chen 2014; ed public school in Barrington, RI, Pomfret School, Conn., Harvard Univ., Univ. of Wisconsin and Lamaist Buddhist Monastery of America; Asst Prof. of Religious Studies, Univ. of Virginia 1973–77, Assoc. Prof. 1977–89, Prof. 1989–2005, Prof. Emer. of Tibetan Buddhist Studies 2005–, Dir Center for South Asian Studies 1979–82, 1985–94; Founder and Pres. UMA Inst. for Tibetan Studies 1973–, Inst. for Asian Democracy 1994–2015; Visiting Prof., Univ. of British Columbia 1983–84; Yehan Numata Distinguished Visiting Prof. of Buddhist Studies, Univ. of Hawaii 1995; Chief Interpreter to Dalai Lama (q.v.) on overseas tours 1979–89, 1996; Fulbright Scholar, India and Germany 1971–72, India 1982, Taiwan 2002–03; Leverett Poetry Prize 1963. *Achievements include:* organized and directed the Nobel Peace Laureates Conf., Univ. of Virginia 1998. *Publications include:* Meditation on Emptiness 1973, Emptiness Yoga 1987, Fluent Tibetan 1993, Emptiness in the Mind-Only School of Buddhism 1999, Mountain Doctrine: Tibet's Fundamental Treatise on Other-Emptiness and the Buddha Matrix 2006; Tantric Techniques 2009; author, ed. or trans. of 47 other books, including 15 in collaboration with the Dalai Lama; 29 articles. *Leisure interests:* meditation, walking in woods, video, films. *Website:* uma-tibet.org (office).

HOPP, Dietmar, MS; German software industry executive; m.; two c.; ed Univ. of Karlsruhe; fmrly with IBM; co-f. SAP AG (software co.), CEO 1988–98, Chair. Supervisory Bd 1998–2003, mem. 2003–05; f. Dietmar Hopp Stiftung (charitable foundation) 1996. *Leisure interests:* beer, golf. *Address:* Dietmar Hopp Stiftung, Raiffeisenstraße 51, 68789 St Leon-Rot, Germany. *Telephone:* (6227) 8608550. *Fax:* (6227) 8608571. *E-mail:* info@dietmar-hopp-stiftung.de. *Website:* www.dietmar-hopp-stiftung.de.

HOPPE, Dominique; French international organization official; *President, Assemblée des fonctionnaires francophones des organisations internationales;* b. 24 Nov. 1959, Longwy; ed Lycée Alfred Mézières, Univ. of Nancy, Institut d'études politiques de Paris (Sciences Po), Stanford Univ. and Harvard Business School, USA; began career as int. civil servant at European Patent Office, Munich, Germany 1984, later Admin.; Vice-Pres. Asscn des Fonctionnaires Internationaux Français des Pays-Bas since its creation, Pres. 2006–07; Pres. Assemblée des fonctionnaires francophones des organisations internationales (Org. of French-speaking int. civil servants) 2007–; Pres. Superior Council of Int. Civil Servants in the Netherlands 2008; Vice-Pres. Defense of the French Language; mem. MENSA Int. 1994–; gives confs and courses on Management of Multicultural Environments at Harvard Business School and Sciences Po, Paris to several multilateral insts, including the UN, Int. Court of Justice, Int. Criminal Court, OPCW, European Space Agency, Europol and Eurojust, amongst others; elected, with Abdou Diouf, Francophone of the Year 2011, Gusi Peace Prize 2014. *Publications include:* articles in the French press for Le Monde and Le Post; technical reviews. *Address:* Assemblée des fonctionnaires francophones des organisations internationales, Sir Winston Churchilllaan 289F39, 2288 DB Rijswijk, Belgium (office). *E-mail:* affoimonde@gmail.com (office). *Website:* www.affoi.org (office).

HOPWOOD, Sir David Alan, Kt, MA, PhD, DSc, FRS, FIBiol; British geneticist and academic; *Fellow Emeritus, John Innes Centre;* b. 19 Aug. 1933, Kinver, Staffs.; s. of Herbert Hopwood and Dora Grant; m. Joyce Lilian Bloom 1962; two s. one d.; ed Purbrook Park County High School, Hants., Lymm Grammar School, Cheshire, St John's Coll., Cambridge; John Stothert Bye-Fellow, Magdalene Coll., Cambridge 1956–58, Research Fellow, St John's Coll. 1958–61, Univ. Demonstrator 1957–61; Lecturer in Genetics, Univ. of Glasgow 1961–68; Prof. of Genetics, Univ. of E Anglia, Norwich 1968–98, Prof. Emer. 1999–; Head of Genetics Dept, John Innes Centre 1968–98, Fellow Emer. 1999–; fmr Pres. Genetical Soc. of GB; Foreign Fellow, Indian Nat. Science Acad.; Pres. Soc. for Gen. Microbiology 2000–03; Hon. Prof., Chinese Acad. of Medical Science, Inst. of Microbiology and Plant Physiology, Chinese Acad. of Sciences, Huazhong Agricultural Univ., Wuhan, China, Jiaotong Univ., Shanghai, Guangxi Univ., Nanning; Hon. mem. Hungarian Acad. of Sciences, Soc. for Gen. Microbiology, Spanish Soc. of Microbiology; Hon. Fellow, UMIST, Magdalene Coll. Cambridge, St John's Coll. Cambridge; Dr hc (ETH, Zurich), (Univ. of East Anglia, Norwich), (Athens); Medal for Research in New Bioactive Compounds, Kitasato Inst. (Japan) 1988, Hoechst Award for Research in Antimicrobial Chemotherapy, American Soc. for Microbiology 1988, Chiron Biotech. Award, American Soc. for Microbiology 1992, Mendel Medal, Czech Acad. of Sciences 1995, Gabor Medal, Royal Soc. 1995, Stuart Mudd Prize Int. Union of Microbiological Sciences 2002, Ernst Chain Medal Imperial Coll., London 2003, Andre Lwoff Prize, Fed. of European Microbiology Socs 2003, Prize Lecturer, Soc. for Gen. Microbiology 2011. *Publications include:* Genetics of Bacterial Diversity (co-ed. with K. F. Chater) 1989, Streptomyces in Nature and Medicine: The Antibiotic Makers 2007; 270 articles and chapters in scientific journals and books. *Leisure interests:* gardening, cooking, natural history. *Address:* John Innes Centre, Norwich Research Park, Colney, Norwich, NR4 7UH (office); 244 Unthank Road, Norwich, NR2 2AH, England (home). *Telephone:* (1603) 450000 (office). *Fax:* (1603) 450778 (office). *E-mail:* david.hopwood@jic.ac.uk (office). *Website:* www.jic.ac.uk (office).

HOR, Nam Hong, LLB, ML; Cambodian diplomatist and politician; *Deputy Prime Minister;* b. 15 Nov. 1935, Phnom-Penh; m.; five c.; ed Univ. of Phnom-Penh, Univ. of Paris, L'Ecole Royale d'Admin, France; Embassy in Paris 1967–73; Amb. to Cuba 1973–75; Khmer Rouge prisoner 1975–79; Vice-Minister of Foreign Affairs 1980–82; Amb. to fmr USSR 1982–89; Minister of Foreign Affairs 1990–93; Amb. to France 1993–98; Minister of Foreign Affairs and Int. Co-operation 1998–2016, Deputy Prime Minister 2003–; mem. Nat. Ass. 1998–; mem. Supreme Nat. Council of Cambodia 1991–93; mem. Cambodian People's Party (CPP); Grand Officer of Monisaraphon, Grand Cross, Royal Order of Cambodia, Grand Collier, Royal Order of Cambodia, Grand Officier, Ordre nat. du Mérite, Grand Cross of the Most Exalted Order of the White Elephant (Thailand). *Leisure interests:* reading, swimming, gymnastics. *Address:* Office of the Council of Ministers, 41 blvd Confédération de la Russie, Sangkat Toeuk Thla, Khan Sen Sok, Phnom-Penh, Cambodia (office). *Telephone:* (12) 804442 (office). *Fax:* (23) 880624 (office). *E-mail:* ocm@cambodia.gov.kh (office). *Website:* www.pressocm.gov.kh (office).

HORBULIN, Volodymyr Pavlovych, DTech; Ukrainian politician and space scientist; b. 17 Jan. 1939, Zaporozhya; ed Dniepropetrovsk State Univ.; fmr engineer and mechanic Pivdenne construction co., then jr researcher 1962–76; took part in devt of Cosmos space rockets; mem. Cen. Cttee CP 1977; Head Rocket, Space and Aviation Tech. Sector 1980; Head of Defence Complex Section, Cabinet of Ministers 1990–92; Dir-Gen. Ukrainian Nat. Space Agency 1992–94; Sec. Council on Nat. Security 1994–96, Council on Nat. Security and Defence 1996–99; apptd Head of Supreme Econ. Council 1997; Deputy Chair. Council on Problems of Science and Tech. Policy 1999; Chair. State Cttee of Defence-Industrial Complex 1999; Pres. Ukrainian Basketball Fed.; Head Interagency Commission for Political Conflict Resolution, Transdniestria region, Moldova 2000–01; Chair. State Comm. for Defence and Industrial Complex 2000–02; Asst to Pres. of Ukraine for Nat. Security Issues 2002–03; Chair. Nat. Centre of Euro-Atlantic Integration 2003; Head, Working Group of the State Comm. for Reformation and Devt of Armed Forces 2003–05; Adviser to Pres. of Ukraine 2005, 2006, 2014; Founder and Pres. Council for Foreign and Security Policy, Kiev 2009–; Dir Nat. Institute for Strategic Studies 2014–18; Ed.-in-Chief Strategic Panorama; apptd Special Rep., Trilateral Contact Group on Ukraine 2015; mem. Ukrainian Nat. Acad. of Sciences 1997–, also mem. of the Presidium; Order of Red Banner of Labour 1976, 1982, First Class Order of Yaroslav the Wise 1997; Ukrainian Nat. Acad. of Sciences Prize 1988, USSR State Prize 1990. *Publications include:* Road to Security: Ukrainian Fata Morgana (co-author) 2010. *Leisure interests:* music, playing cards, literature, theatre. *Address:* Council for Foreign and Security Policy, 13 Chokolivsky Blvd, Kiev 03186, Ukraine (office). *Telephone:* (44) 229-13-21 (office). *Website:* www.cfsp.org.ua (office).

HORCHANI, Farhat, lic. en droit, DEA; Tunisian lawyer and politician; b. 20 Jan. 1953, Tunis; m.; two c.; ed Univ. of Tunis, Univ. of Dijon, France; fmr Assoc. Prof., Faculty of Law and Political Sciences, Univ. of Tunis, Vice-Dean, Faculty of Law and Political Science 1993–96; Judge, Arab Court of Investment, League of Arab States 2004–, Pres. of Court 2005–07; Minister of Nat. Defence 2015–17; adviser to several UN and int. bodies on foreign direct investment policy, including UNCTAD, Econ. and Social Comm. for Western Asia, WTO, UNDP, World Bank; Pres. Tunisian Asscn of Constitutional Law; mem. Int. Econ. Law Asscn, Belgium, French Soc. for Int. Law; mem. Scientific Council, Int. Acad. of Constitutional Law.

Publications include: Les sources du droit international public, Bilan d'un système, Où va le droit de l'investissement?. *Address:* c/o Ministry of National Defence, blvd Bab Menara, 1008 Tunis, Tunisia (office).

HORGAN, John, BA, MA; Canadian politician; *Premier of British Columbia;* b. 7 Aug. 1959, Victoria, BC; m. Ellie Horgan; two s.; ed Trent Univ., Ont., Univ. of Sydney; spent four years as Legis. Asst to MPs Jim Manly and later Lynn Hunter, Ottawa 1987–91; Ministerial Asst to MLA Dave Zirnhelt, Victoria 1991–93; Analyst, Policy Coordination Br., BC Ministry of Govt Services 1993–96; Dir, Cabinet Policy and Communications Secr., BC Ministry of Finance and Corp. Relations 1996, Dir, Crown Corpns Secr. 1998; Chief of Staff, Office of BC Premier Dan Miller 1999; f. IdeaWorks (consultancy) 2001; mem. BC Legis. Ass. for Malahat-Juan de Fuca 2005–09, for Juan de Fuca 2009–17, for Langford-Juan de Fuca 2017–; Opposition Energy Critic 2011–14, also Official Opposition House Leader 2011–14, Leader of the Opposition 2014–17; Premier of BC 2017–; Leader, BC New Democratic Party 2014–. *Address:* Office of the Premier, POB 9041, STN PROV GOVT, Victoria, BC, V8W 9E1, Canada (office). *Telephone:* (250) 387-1715 (office). *Fax:* (250) 387-0087 (office). *E-mail:* premier@gov.bc.ca (office). *Website:* news.gov.bc.ca/office-of-the-premier (office).

HORI, Kosuke; Japanese politician; b. 23 Sept. 1934, Tokyo; ed Keio Univ.; mem. House of Reps 1979–, fmr Chair. LDP Diet Affairs Cttee, Parl. Vice-Minister for Agric., Forestry and Fisheries; fmr Minister for Educ.; Minister of Home Affairs, Chair. Nat. Public Safety Comm. 1999–2000; Chair. LDP Policy Research Council 2008–. *Address:* House of Representatives, 1-7-1 Nagatacho, Chiyoda-ku, Tokyo 100-0014, Japan (office). *E-mail:* koho@ldp.jimin.or.jp (office). *Website:* www.shugiin.go.jp/internet/index.nsf/html/index_e.htm (office); www.jimin.jp (office).

HORN, Paul M., PhD; American physicist, academic and electronics industry executive; *Senior Vice-Provost for Research, New York University;* b. New York; ed Clarkson Coll. of Tech., Univ. of Rochester; trained as solid state physicist; Asst, then Assoc. Prof., Dept of Physics, James Franck Inst., Univ. of Chicago 1973–79; joined IBM Corpn 1979, various positions including Vice-Pres. and Lab. Dir of Almaden Research Centre, San Jose, Sr Vice-Pres. and Dir of Research 1996–2007; Distinguished Scientist in Residence, New York Univ. 2007–09, Sr Vice-Provost for Research 2009–, also Sr Vice-Dean for Strategic Initiatives and Entrepreneurship, Tandon School of Eng, Chair. Advisory Bd NYU Innovation Venture Fund; fmr Assoc. Ed. Physical Review Letters; mem. Bd of Dirs Virtual Personalities Inc.; mem. Council on Competitiveness, Govt Univ. Industry Research Roundtable, Univ. of Calif., Berkeley Industrial Advisory Bd, Gallaudet Univ. Advisory Bd; Fellow, American Physical Soc., Grad. Fellow, Nat. Science Foundation; mem. Bd of Trustees, Clarkson Univ. 1998–, New York Hall of Science, Cttee for Econ. Devt; mem., Nat. Academy of Eng; Alfred P. Sloan Research Fellowship 1974–78, Bertram Eugene Warren Award, American Crystallographic Asscn 1988, Distinguished Leadership Award, NY Hall of Science 2000, Hutchison Medal, Univ. of Rochester 2002, Pake Prize, American Physical Soc. 2002, Golden Kt Award, Clarkson Univ. 2004. *Publications:* over 85 scientific and technical papers. *Address:* Office of the Senior Vice Provost for Research, Bobst Library, 70 Washington Square South, 1224, New York, NY 10012, USA (office). *Telephone:* (212) 998-3228 (office). *Fax:* (212) 995-4121 (office). *E-mail:* paul.horn@nyu.edu (office).

HORNBY, Andrew (Andy) H., MA, MBA; British business executive; *Chief Operating Officer, Gala Coral Group;* b. 21 Dec. 1967, Scarborough, North Yorks.; m. Cathy Hornby; ed St Peter's Coll., Oxford, Harvard Business School, USA; worked for Boston Consulting Group for three years; held sr line man. posts with Blue Circle; worked at ASDA plc 1996–99, held posts of Dir of Corp. Devt, Retail Man. Dir, Man. Dir of George, ASDA's clothing business; Chief Exec. Halifax Retail 1999–2001, Chief Exec. Retail Div., HBOS plc (after merger between Halifax and Bank of Scotland) 2001–05, COO Retail Div. 2005–06, Chief Exec. HBOS plc 2006–08 (resgnd); Group Chief Exec. Alliance Boots 2009–11; COO Gala Coral Group 2011–; Chair. (non-exec.) Pharmacy2U 2012–; mem. Bd of Dirs (non-exec.) GUS/Home Retail Group 2002–09. *Address:* Gala Coral Group, 2nd Floor, 34 St James's Street, London, SW1A 1HD, England (office). *Telephone:* (20) 7484-1370 (office). *Fax:* (20) 7930-8929 (office). *Website:* www.galacoral.co.uk (office); www.pharmacy2u.co.uk (office).

HORNBY, Nick; British journalist and novelist; b. 17 April 1957, Redhill, Surrey; ed Univ. of Cambridge; co-f. Treehouse Trust 1997, Ministry of Stories 2010; Vice-Pres. Ambitious about Autism (charity); William Hill Sports Book of the Year Award 1992, Writers' Guild Best Fiction Book Award 1995, American Acad. of Arts and Letters E. M. Forster Award 1999, WHSmith Fiction Award 2002, London Award 2003, British Sports Book Award for Outstanding Contribution to Sports Writing 2012. *Recordings:* wrote lyrics for Ben Folds album, Lonely Avenue 2010. *Publications include:* Contemporary American Fiction (essays) 1992, Fever Pitch (memoir) 1992, (screenplay) 1997, My Favourite Year: A Collection of New Football Writing (ed.) 1993, High Fidelity (novel) 1995, Speaking With the Angel (ed.) 2000, About a Boy (novel) 2000, How to be Good (novel) 2001, 31 Songs (non-fiction) 2003, A Long Way Down 2005, The Complete Polysyllabic Spree (collected columns) 2006, Slam (juvenile fiction) (ALA Best Books for Young Adults 2008) 2007, Juliet, Naked 2009, More Baths, Less Talking (non-fiction) 2012, Funny Girl (novel) 2014; contrib. to Sunday Times, TLS, Literary Review, New York Times, New Yorker, the Believer, Vogue, Elle. *Address:* c/o Jeanette Casarotto, Casarotto Ramsay & Associates Limited, Waverley House, 7–12 Noel Street, London, W1F 8GQ, England (office). *Telephone:* (20) 7287-4450 (office). *E-mail:* jenne@casarotto.co.uk (office). *Website:* www.casarotto.co.uk (office); www.ambitiousaboutautism.org.uk; www.ministryofstories.org; www.nickhornbyofficial.com.

HORNE, Marilyn; American singer (mezzo-soprano); b. 16 Jan. 1934, Bradford, Pa; d. of Bentz Horne and Berneice Horne; m. 1st Henry Lewis (divorced); one d.; ed Univ. of Southern California with William Vennard; debut as Hata in The Bartered Bride, Guild Opera Co. 1954; performed with several German opera cos in Europe 1956; has since appeared at Covent Garden, London, San Francisco Opera, Chicago Lyric Opera, La Scala, Milan, Metropolitan Opera, New York; repertoire includes Eboli in Don Carlo, Marie in Wozzeck, Adalgisa in Norma, Jane Seymour in Anna Bolena, Amneris in Aida, Carmen, Rosina in Il Barbiere di Siviglia, Fides in Le Prophète, Mignon, Isabella in L'Italiana in Algeri, Romeo in I Capuletti ed i Montecchi, Tancredi in Tancredi, Orlando in Orlando Furioso, Malcolm in La Donna del Lago, Calbo in Maometto II; retd from singing 1999, with galas in New York and San Francisco 1998; f. Marilyn Horne Foundation to coach and encourage young singers 1993 (now part of Weill Music Inst. at Carnegie Hall); mem. Faculty, Music Acad. of the West 1995–, Dir Voice Program 1997–; Fellow, American Acad. of Arts and Sciences 2009–; regular master-classes; Commdr, Ordre des Arts et des Lettres; numerous hon. doctorates, including Hon. DMus (Univ. of Pittsburgh) 2005; Nat. Medal of Arts 1992, Kennedy Center Honor 1995, Musical American Musician of the Year 1995, Classic FM Gramophone Award for Lifetime Achievement 2005, Opera News Award 2008, Nat. Endowment for the Arts Opera Award 2009. *Publications:* My Life (autobiography with Jane Scovell), The Song Continues (autobiography with Jane Scovell) 2005. *Leisure interests:* needlepoint, swimming, reading, sightseeing. *Address:* Voice Program, Music Academy of the West, 1070 Fairway Road, Santa Barbara, CA 93108, USA (office). *E-mail:* info@musicacademy.org (office). *Website:* www.musicacademy.org (office).

HORNER, Christian, OBE; British sports executive and fmr racing car driver; *Team Principal, Red Bull Racing;* b. 16 Nov. 1973, Leamington Spa, Warwicks.; partner Beverley Allen 2010–14; one c.; m. Geri Halliwell 2015; one s.; began career in motorsport after winning a Formula Renault scholarship 1991; competed in British Formula Renault Championship with Manor Motorsport 1992, finished season as a race winner and highest placed rookie; moved up to British Formula Three, debut with the Fortec team 1994; moved to Alan Docking Racing team 1995, to TOM'S team 1996; also raced in British Formula Two 1996; moved up to Formula 3000 and f. Arden team 1997, Team Prin. for GP2 Series team Arden Motorsport; stayed in F3000 for 1998, retired from active racing at end of season; continued with team in F3000 as the owner, signed Viktor Maslov and Marc Goossens for 1999 season, signed Tomáš Enge and Björn Wirdheim 2002, Enge replaced by Townsend Bell, Wirdheim won title 2003; won both drivers' and constructors' championship titles in F3000 with Vitantonio Liuzzi and Robert Doornbos 2004; team leader Red Bull Racing Formula One team 2005–, team's first podium finish at Monaco Grand Prix 2006, team won Constructors' Championship 2010, 2011, 2012, 2013. *Address:* Red Bull Racing, Bradbourne Drive, Tilbrook, Milton Keynes, Bucks., MK7 8BJ, England (office). *E-mail:* info@redbullracing.com (office). *Website:* www.redbullracing.com (office).

HORNHUES, Karl-Heinz, Dr rer. pol; German international organization official and fmr politician; *Honorary President, Deutsche Afrika Stiftung e.V.;* b. 10 June 1939, Stadtlohn; m. Ellen Buss 1965; two s.; ed Univ. of Münster; adviser, Catholic Adult Educ. Centre, Ludwig-Windthorst-Hause, Holthausen 1966–71, Dir 1970–71; Educ. and Teaching Dir Hofmann-La Roche AG, Grenzbach 1971; Assoc. Prof. of Social Econs and Political Science 1974, Prof. 1977; mem. Bundestag 1972–2002; Deputy Chair. of CDU/CSU Parl. Party in Bundestag in charge of foreign policy, defence policy and European affairs 1989–94; Chair. Foreign Affairs Cttee 1994–98; Chair. German Del., Ass. of WEU 1998–2002; Pres. Deutsche Afrika Stiftung e.V. (German Africa Foundation) 1987–2010, Hon. Pres. 2010–; Kommendeurkreuz 1999. *Address:* Deutsche Afrika Stiftung e.V., Ziegelstraße 30, 10117 Berlin, Germany (office). *Telephone:* (30) 28094727 (office). *Fax:* (30) 28094728 (office). *Website:* www.deutsche-afrika-stiftung.de (office).

HORNSBY, Claude (Chip) A. S., BA; American business executive; *Chief Executive Officer, MORSCO Inc.;* m. Lynn Hornsby, three c.; ed Virginia Polytechnic and State Univ.; joined Ferguson Enterprises Inc. as man. trainee 1982 (bought by Wolseley PLC), Pres. and CEO 2001–05, CEO US Plumbing and Heating Div., Wolseley PLC, which incorporated Ferguson, Familian Northwest and US operations of Westburne, acquired in 2001, CEO, North America, Wolseley PLC 2006–09, mem. Bd of Dirs Wolseley PLC 2001–09, Group Chief Exec. 2006–09; CEO MORSCO Inc. 2011–; Dir (non-exec.) Virginia Co. Bank 2005–, Univar Inc. 2010–; mem. Visitors Bd, Christopher Newport Univ. 2001; mem. Nat. Asscn of Wholesaler-Distributors (Chair. 2007), Southern Wholesalers Asscn, American Supply Asscn, Virginia Tech. Pamplin Advisory Council; Rector for Christopher Newport Univ. *Address:* MORSCO Inc., 100 East 15th Street, Suite 200, Fort Worth, TX 76102, USA (office). *Telephone:* (877) 709-2227 (office). *E-mail:* customerservice@morsco.com (office). *Website:* www.morsco.com (office).

HOROVITZ, Joseph, MA, BMus, FRCM; British composer and conductor; *Professor of Composition, Royal College of Music;* b. 26 May 1926, Vienna, Austria; ed New Coll., Oxford and Royal Coll. of Music (RCM), London and studied with Nadia Boulanger, Paris; resident in UK 1938–; Music Dir Bristol Old Vic 1949–51; Conductor Festival Gardens Orchestra and open-air ballet, London 1951; Co-Conductor Ballets Russes, English season 1951–52; Assoc. Dir Intimate Opera Co. 1952–63; Asst Conductor Glyndebourne Opera 1956; Prof. of Composition, RCM 1961–; mem. Council, Composers' Guild 1970–, Performing Right Soc. 1969–96; Pres. Int. Council of Composers and Lyricists, Int. Fed. of Socs of Authors and Composers 1981–89; Cross of Honour for Science and Art, First Class (Austria) 2007; Commonwealth Medal Composition 1959, Leverhulme Music Research Award 1961, Gold Order of Merit of Vienna 1996, Nino Rota Prize (Italy) 2002, Cobbett Medal for services to chamber music, Worshipful Co. of Musicians 2008. *Compositions include:* 12 ballets including Alice in Wonderland, Les Femmes d'Alger, Miss Carter Wore Pink, Concerto for Dancers; opera: Ninotchka; one-act operas: The Dumb Wife, Gentlemen's Island; concertos for violin, trumpet, jazz-piano (harpsichord), oboe, clarinet, bassoon, percussion, tuba; other orchestral works include Horizon Overture, Jubilee Serenade, Sinfonietta for Light Orchestra, Fantasia on a Theme of Couperin, Toy Symphony; brass band music includes a euphonium concerto, Sinfonietta, Ballet for Band, Concertino Classico, Theme and Co-operation, The Dong with a Luminous Nose; music for wind band includes a divertimento Bacchus on Blue Ridge, Windharp, Fête Galante, Commedia dell'Arte, Dance Suite and Ad Astra in commemoration of the Battle of Britain; choral music includes Samson, Captain Noah and his Floating Zoo (Ivor Novello Award for Best British Music for Children 1976), Summer Sunday, Endymion, Sing Unto the Lord a New Song, three choral songs from As You Like It; vocal music includes Lady Macbeth (mezzo-soprano and piano) and works for the King's Singers (e.g. Romance); chamber music includes five string quartets, oboe sonatina, oboe quartet and clarinet sonatina; contribs to Hoffnung Concerts: Metamorphoses on a Bed-Time Theme and Horrortorio for chorus, orchestra and soloists; numerous scores for theatre productions, films and TV series (Ivor Novello Award for Best TV Theme of 1978 for the series Lillie); productions of Son et Lumière include St Paul's Cathedral, Canterbury Cathedral, Brighton Pavilion,

English Harbour, Antigua, Bodiam Castle, Chartwell. *Address:* Royal College of Music, Prince Consort Road, London, SW7 2BS, England (office). *Website:* www.rcm.ac.uk (office).

HORROCKS, Jane; British actress; b. 18 Jan. 1964, Lancs.; d. of John Horrocks and Barbara Horrocks; partner Nick Vivian; one s. one d.; ed Royal Acad. of Dramatic Art, London. *Stage appearances include:* The Rise and Fall of Little Voice, Cabaret, Absurd Person Singular 2007, The Good Soul of Szechuan 2008, Aunt Dan and Lemon 2009, Annie Get Your Gun 2009, East is East 2014–15. *Films include:* The Dressmaker 1988, Getting It Right 1989, The Wolves of Willoughby Chase 1989, The Witches 1990, Memphis Belle 1990, Life is Sweet (Best Supporting Actress, LA Critics Award) 1990, Deadly Advice 1994, Second Best 1994, Some Kind of Life 1995, Combination Skin (short) (voice) 1996, Bring Me the Head of Mavis Davis 1997, Little Voice 1998, Faeries (voice) 1999, Lion of Oz (voice) 2000, Discover Spot (video) (voice) 2000, Chicken Run (voice) 2000, Born Romantic 2000, Christmas Carol: The Movie 2001, Last Rumba in Rochdale (short) 2002, Wheeling Dealing (short) 2004, Look I'm Talking (video short) 2005, Corpse Bride (voice) 2005, Brothers of the Head 2005, Garfield 2 (voice) 2006, Tinker Bell (video) (voice) 2008, Tinker Bell and the Lost Treasure (voice) 2009, Tinker Bell and the Mysterious Winter Woods 2010, The Itch of the Golden Nit (short) (voice) 2011, Sunshine on Leith 2012 Ab Fab: The Movie 2016. *Television includes:* Screenplay (series) 1987–92, First Sight (series) 1987, The Storyteller (series) 1988, The Ruth Rendell Mysteries (series) 1988, The Fifteen Streets (film) 1989, Heartland (film) 1989, The Jim Henson Hour (series) 1989, Victoria Wood (series) 1989, Smith & Jones (series) 1990, Boon (series) 1990, Came Out, It Rained, Went Back in Again (film) 1991, Screen One (series) 1991, Nona (film) 1991, Red Dwarf (series) 1992, Absolutely Fabulous 1992–2012, Bad Girl 1992, Roots (film) 1992, Cabaret (film) 1993, Suffer the Little Children (film) (Royal TV Soc. Award) 1994, Butter (short) 1994, Self Catering (film) 1994, Performance (series) 1995, Crapston Villas (series) 1995–98, Nightlife (film) 1996, Tales from the Crypt (series) 1996, Never Mind the Horrocks (special) 1996, Wyrd Sisters (mini-series) 1997, The Blobs (series) 1997, Hunting Venus (film) 1999, Foxbusters (series) 1999, The Flint Street Nativity (film) 1999, Hooves of Fire (short) 1999, Watership Down (series) 1999–2000, Mirrorball (short) 2000, Little Big Mouth (series) 2001, Ivor the Invisible (film) 2001, Linda Green (series) 2002, Legend of the Lost Tribe (short) 2002, Monkey Trousers (film) 2004, Who Do You Think You Are 2005, Happy Birthday, Peter Pan (special documentary) 2005, Jericho (series) 2005, Fifi and the Flowertots (series) 2005–06, The Street (series) 2006, Little Princess (series) 2006, The Amazing Mrs Pritchard (series) 2006, Robbie the Reindeer in Close Encounters of the Herd Kind (short) 2007, Gracie! (film) 2009, The Road to Coronation Street (film) 2010, Coming Up (series) 2011, This is Jinsy (series) 2011, Trollied (series) 2011–13, 2015, True Love (series) 2011, Inside No 9 (series) 2014. *Address:* c/o United Agents, 12–26 Lexington Street, London, W1F 0LE, England (office). *Telephone:* (20) 3214-0800 (office). *Fax:* (20) 3214-0801 (office). *E-mail:* info@unitedagents.co.uk (office). *Website:* www.unitedagents.co.uk (office).

HORTA DOS SANTOS, Henrique; Guinea-Bissau banker and politician; ed Martin Luther Univ. of Halle-Wittenberg, Germany; fmr Sr Official with Banque Centrale des Etats de l'Afrique de l'Ouest (BCEAO); fmr Nat. Dir, Banque Régionale de Solidarité Guinea-Bissau; apptd Sec. of State in the Treasury 2016, Minister of the Economy and Finance June–Dec. 2016. *Address:* c/o Ministry of the Economy and Finance, Av. dos Combatentes da Liberdade da Pátria, CP 67, Bissau, Guinea-Bissau (office).

HORTA-OSÓRIO, António, MBA; Portuguese banking executive and academic; *Executive Director and Group Chief Executive, Lloyds Banking Group;* m.; three c.; ed Universidade Católica Portuguesa, Institut Européen d'Admin des Affaires (INSEAD), France, Harvard Business School, USA; began career at Citibank Portugal, later Head of Capital Markets; also Asst Prof., Universidade Catolica Portuguesa; then worked for Goldman Sachs in New York and London; joined Grupo Santander as Chief Exec. Banco Santander de Negocios Portugal 1993, later CEO Banco Santander Brazil –2000, CEO Santander Totta 2000–06, Chair. 2006–11, also Exec. Vice-Pres. Grupo Santander and mem. Man. Cttee, Dir (non-exec.) Santander UK 2004–10, Chief Exec. 2006–10; Exec. Dir Lloyds Banking Group plc Jan. 2011–, Group Chief Exec. March 2011–; Dir (non-exec.), Fundação Champalimaud, Sociedade Francisco Manuel dos Santos (Portugal); fmr Dir (non-exec.) Court of the Bank of England; Gov., London Business School; Henry Ford II Prize, INSEAD. *Leisure interests:* tennis, scuba diving. *Address:* Lloyds Banking Group plc, 25 Gresham Street, London, EC2V 7HN, England (office). *Telephone:* (20) 7626-1500 (office). *Fax:* (20) 7356-2049 (office). *E-mail:* info@lloydsbankinggroup.com (office). *Website:* www.lloydsbankinggroup.com (office).

HORTEFEUX, Brice, LenD; French politician; b. 11 May 1958, Neuilly-sur-Seine; s. of Claude Hortefeux and Marie-Claude Hortefeux (née Schuhler); m. Valérie Dazzan 2000; three c.; ed Inst. of Political Studies, Paris, Univ. Paris X–Nanterre; Territorial Admin. 1986–94; mem. Regional Council, Auvergne 1992–2007; Chief of Cabinet of Minister for Budget and Communications 1993–95; Govt Spokesperson 1993–95; fmr mem. Political Cttee Rassemblement pour la République 1998–2002; mem. Union pour un Mouvement Populaire (UMP), mem. Political Cttee 2002; MEP 1999–2005; Adviser to Minister of Interior and Security, later to Minister of Finance, Economy and Industry 2002–04; Minister-Del. for Territorial Collectivities 2005–07; Minister of Immigration, Integration, Nat. Identity and Co-Devt 2007–09, of Labour, Social Relations, the Family, Solidarity and Urban Affairs 2009, of the Interior, the Overseas Possessions and Territorial Collectivities and of Immigration 2009–11; Political Adviser to Nicolas Sarkozy 2014. *Publications include:* Jardin à la française, plaidoyer pour une république de proximité 2003. *Leisure interest:* tennis.

HORTON, Donald R.; American real estate executive; *Chairman, D. R. Horton Inc.;* m. Marty Horton; two s.; ed Univ. of Central Arkansas, Univ. of Oklahoma; took over father's Marshall, Ark. real estate business 1971; f. D. R. Horton Inc., Fort Worth, Tex. 1978, Pres. 1991–98, Chair. 1991–; Distinguished Alumni Award, Univ. of Cen. Ark. 2004. *Address:* D.R. Horton, Inc., 301 Commerce Street, Suite 500, Fort Worth, TX 76102-4140, USA (office). *Telephone:* (817) 390-8200 (office). *Fax:* (817) 390-8249 (office). *Website:* www.drhorton.com (office).

HORTON, Frank Elba, BS, MS, PhD; American academic and university administrator; *President and Professor Emeritus, University of Toledo;* b. 19 Aug. 1939, Chicago, Ill.; s. of Elba E. Horton and Mae P. Prohaska; m. Nancy Yocom 1960; four d.; ed Western Illinois Univ, Northwestern Univ; mem. Faculty, Univ. of Iowa 1966–75, Prof. of Geography 1966–75, Dir Inst. of Urban and Regional Research 1968–72, Dean of Advanced Studies 1972–75; Vice-Pres. for Acad. Affairs and Research, Southern Illinois Univ. 1975–80; Chancellor Univ. of Wisconsin, Milwaukee 1980–85; Pres. Univ. of Oklahoma 1985–88; Pres. and Prof. of Geography and Higher Educ., Univ. of Toledo 1988–98, Pres. and Prof. Emer. 1999–; Prin. Horton and Assocs 1999; Interim Pres. Southern Illinois Univ. 2001; Interim Dean School of Biological Sciences, Univ. of Missouri 2002–03, Exec. Consultant to the Provost, Univ. of Missouri, Kansas City 2003–04; Vice-Chair. Toledo Chamber of Commerce 1991–93; mem. Bd Dirs Inter-State Bakeries, GAC Corpn; Trustee Toledo Symphony Orchestra 1989, Toledo Hosp. 1989, Public Broadcasting Foundation, NW Ohio 1989–93, Soc. Bank and Trust 1990–. *Publications:* Geographic Perspectives on Urban Systems with Integrated Readings (with B. J. L. Berry) 1970, Urban Environmental Management Planning for Pollution Control 1974. *Leisure interests:* hiking, skiing, golf, jogging. *Address:* 288 River Ranch Circle, Bayfield, CO 81122, USA (home). *Telephone:* (970) 884-2102 (office); (970) 884-2102 (home). *E-mail:* fehorton@attglobal.net (office).

HORTON, Richard C., BSc, MB, FRCP, FMedSci; British physician and editor; *Editor, The Lancet;* b. 29 Dec. 1961, London; ed Univ. of Birmingham; Visiting Prof., London School of Hygiene and Tropical Medicine; Asst Ed., The Lancet (medical journal) 1990, North American Ed. 1993, Ed. 1995–; Chair. Royal Coll. of Physicians' Working Party on Physicians and Pharmaceutical Industry; fmr Pres. World Asscn of Medical Editors; Pres. US Council of Science Editors 2005–06; Co-Chair. Expert Review Group, WHO; Sr Assoc., Nuffield Trust; Foreign Assoc., Inst. of Medicine (US) 2011–; Bd mem. Health Metrics Network; Hon. Prof., London School of Hygiene and Tropical Medicine, Univ. Coll. London, Univ. of Edinburgh; Dr hc (Univ. of Birmingham), (Univ. of Umea, Sweden); Edinburgh Medal for professional achievements 2007, Dean's Medal, Johns Hopkins School of Public Health 2009. *Publications include:* non-fiction: Preventing Coronary Artery Disease (with Martin Kendall) 1997, How to Publish in Biomedicine 1997, Second Opinion: Doctors and Diseases 2003, Health Wars: On the Global Front Lines of Modern Medicine 2003, MMR: Science and Fiction 2004; contrib. to New York Review of Books, London Review of Books, The Lancet, journals. *Address:* The Lancet, 32 Jamestown Road, London, NW1 7BY, England (office). *Telephone:* (20) 7424-4910 (office). *Fax:* (20) 7424-4911 (office). *E-mail:* richard.horton@lancet.com (office). *Website:* www.lancet.com (office).

HORTON, Thomas W., BBA, MBA; American business executive; b. 24 May 1961, Hampton, Va; ed Baylor Univ., Cox School of Business, Southern Methodist Univ.; joined AMR Corpn (parent co. of American Airlines) 1985, held several sr financial positions, including Vice-Pres. and Controller, Vice-Pres. responsible for airline's Europe business, based in London, UK 1998–2000, Sr Vice-Pres. and Chief Financial Officer (CFO) AMR 2000–06, Exec. Vice-Pres., Finance and Planning, and CFO AMR and American Airlines 2006–10, Pres. AMR Corpn and American Airlines 2010–13, Chair. and CEO 2011–13, Chair. American Airlines Group, Inc. (following merger with US Airways Group) and American Airlines 2013–14; joined AT&T Corpn as CFO 2002, Vice-Chair. and CFO –2006; Chair. oneworld® Alliance 2012–14; mem. Bd of Dirs, Qualcomm, Inc., Walmart 2014–, W; mem. Exec. Bd Cox School of Business, Southern Methodist Univ. *Address:* Walmart, 702 SW 8th Street, Bentonville, AR 72716-8611, USA (office). *Telephone:* (479) 273-4000 (office). *Fax:* (479) 277-1830 (office); (479) 277-4053 (office). *Website:* www.walmart.com (office); corporate.walmart.com (office).

HORVAT, Darko, MSc; Croatian engineer, business executive and politician; *Minister of the Economy, Small and Medium-sized Enterprises and Crafts;* b. 28 Sept. 1970, Čakovec, Socialist Repub. of Croatia, Socialist Fed. Repub. of Yugoslavia; m. Petra Horvat; ed Univ. of Maribor, Zagreb Faculty of Electrical Eng and Computing; began career with HEP Group (state-owned power utility), including with Koprivnica HEP Distribution 1996–2006, becoming Dir, Elektra Čakovec (HEP-Operator Distribution System Ltd) 2006; Founder and Owner, Aktiva Group (financial corpn), currently Pres.; mem. Man. Bd Croatian Agency for Small Business 2008–11; several roles with Ministry of Economy, Labour and Entrepreneurship, including mem. Comm. for Off-set Programs 2008–11, Dir, Crafts Directorate 2008, Dir of Energy 2009; Chair. Supervisory Bd Hrvatska Elektroprivreda DD 2009–11; Chair. Supervisory Bd Plinacro 2009–11; Head of Working Group appointed for the adaptation of Croatian Energy Legislation III (EU energy package) 2010–11; Chair. Expert Cttee for Monitoring the Regular Supply of Petroleum and Petroleum Products Market 2010–11; mem. Supervisory Bd Hrvatska banka za obnovu i razvitak d.d., Deputy Chair., Supervisory Bd 2018–; mem. Man. Bd, EnergyPlus d.o.o (electronics co.), Ludbreg 2012; Minister of Entrepreneurship and Crafts Jan.–Oct. 2016; Minister of the Economy, Small and Medium-sized Enterprises and Crafts 2018–; mem. Hrvatska Demokratska Zajednica (HDZ—Croatian Democratic Union), currently Vice-Pres., also Pres., HDZ County Org., Međimurje County. *Address:* Ministry of the Economy, Small and Medium-sized Enterprises and Crafts, 10000 Zagreb, ul. grada Vukovara 78, Croatia (office). *Telephone:* (1) 6106111 (office). *Fax:* (1) 6109110 (office). *E-mail:* ministar@mingo.hr (office). *Website:* www.mingo.hr (office).

HORVATH, Philippe, PhD; French molecular biologist; *Senior Scientist, E. I. du Pont de Nemours and Company (DuPont);* b. 17 April 1970; ed Univ. Louis-Pasteur, Strasbourg; Research Engineer in Molecular Biology, Rhodia Food SAS, Dangé-Saint-Romain 2000–04 (Rhodia Food acquired by Danisco 2004), Sr Scientist, Danisco 2006– (Danisco acquired by E. I. du Pont de Nemours and Company (DuPont) 2011); Assoc., DuPont Fellows Forum 2014; DuPont Nutrition and Health Technical Fellow 2015; Danisco Innovation Award 2008, Bolton/Carothers Innovative Science Award 2013, Massry Prize 2015, Canada Gairdner Int. Award 2016. *Achievements include:* research on CRISPR adaptive immune system in the field of food technology. *Publications include:* co-author of 95 patents and/or patent applications, co-author of 31 peer-reviewed articles and four book chapters. *Address:* Danisco France SAS, Zone d'Activite de Buxières, 86220 Dangé-Saint-Romain, France (office). *Telephone:* (5) 49-19-71-00 (office). *Website:* www.dupont.com (office).

HORVITZ, H. Robert, MA, PhD; American biologist and academic; *David H. Koch Professor of Biology, Massachusetts Institute of Technology;* b. 8 May 1947, Chicago, Ill.; s. of Oscar Freedom Horvitz and Mary R. Horvitz; ed Harvard Univ.;

Asst Prof. of Biology, MIT 1978, Assoc. Prof. 1981, Prof. 1986, now David H. Koch Prof.; Investigator, Howard Hughes Medical Inst. 1988–, McGovern Inst. for Brain Research; also currently Neurobiologist and Geneticist, Mass Gen. Hosp., Boston; mem. NAS 1991–, Nat. Acad. of Medicine 2003–, Inst. of Medicine; Fellow, American Acad. of Arts and Sciences, American Acad. of Microbiology, American Philosophical Soc., Physiological Soc., London, Royal Soc.; numerous awards and honours including Spencer Award in Neurobiology 1986, US Steel Foundation Award in Molecular Biology 1988, Hans Sigrist Award 1994, Gairdner Foundation Int. Award 1999, Segerfalk Award 2000, Bristol-Myers Squibb Award for Distinguished Achievement in Neuroscience 2001, Genetics Soc. of America Award 2001, Nobel Prize in Physiology or Medicine (jtly) 2002. *Publications include:* numerous articles in professional journals. *Address:* Department of Biology, Room 68-425, Massachusetts Institute of Technology, 77 Massachusetts Avenue, Cambridge, MA 02139, USA (office). *Telephone:* (617) 253-4671 (office). *Fax:* (617) 253-8126 (office). *E-mail:* horvitz@mit.edu (office). *Website:* biology.mit.edu (office); web.mit.edu/horvitz/www (office); www.hhmi.org/research/investigators/horvitz_bio.html.

HORWICH, Arthur L., AB, MD; American biologist and academic; *Eugene Higgins Professor of Genetics and Pediatrics, Yale School of Medicine;* b. 1951, Oak Park, Ill.; ed Brown Univ.; postdoctoral research, Salk Inst. for Biological Studies, La Jolla, Calif.; Intern and Resident, Pediatrics, Yale Univ. School of Medicine 1975–78, Postdoctoral Fellow 1981–84, Asst Prof., Dept of Genetics 1984–87, Eugene Higgins Prof. of Genetics and Pediatrics 1995–; Investigator, Howard Hughes Medical Inst. 1990–; mem. NAS 2003; Dr hc (Brown Univ.) 2014; Hans Neurath Award, Protein Soc. 2001, Gairdner Int. Award 2004, Stein and Moore Award, Protein Soc. 2006, Wiley Prize in Biomedical Science 2007, Rosenstiel Award 2008, Louisa Gross Horwitz Prize 2008, Massry Prize, Keck School of Medicine, Univ. of Southern California 2011, Albert Lasker Basic Medical Research Award 2011, Shaw Prize 2012, Herbert Tabor Research Award, American Soc. for Biochemistry and Molecular Biology 2013, Albany Prize in Medicine and Biomedical Research 2016, Paul Ehrlich and Ludwig Darmstaedter Prize (co-recipient) 2019. *Publications include:* numerous papers in professional journals. *Address:* Yale School of Medicine, 145 Boyer Center for Molecular Medicine, 295 Congress Avenue, New Haven, CT 06510, USA (office). *Telephone:* (203) 737-4431 (office). *Fax:* (203) 737-1761 (office). *E-mail:* arthur.horwich@yale.edu (office). *Website:* bbs.yale.edu (office); medicine.yale.edu (office).

HOSEIN, Mainul, BA; Bangladeshi barrister, newspaper executive and politician; b. Jan. 1940, Pirojpur (then Barisal) Dist; s. of Tafazzal Hossain; ed Dhaka Univ., studied law in London, UK; joined Middle Temple, London; called to Bar 1965; represented The Daily Ittefaq (f. by his father), Ed. 1969–73, Chair. Editorial Bd 1973–2010; mem. Commonwealth Press Union, London; practised law at Dhaka High Court 1965; mem. official del. to China on occasion of Nat. Day 1969; attended CPU Conf., Zimbabwe 1988; MP for village constituency at Bhandaria, Pirojpur (Barisal) 1973–75, resgnd in protest over changes to electoral system; Pres. Bangladesh Sangbadpatra Parishad (asscn of newspaper owners); mem. Press Council; Deputy Head Press Comm. 1984; Pres. Bangladesh Supreme Court Bar Asscn 2000–01; Hon. Adviser to Caretaker Govt, in charge of Ministry of Law, Justice and Parl. Affairs, of Parl. Secr., of Ministry of Housing and Public Works, of Ministry of Land and of Ministry of Information 2007–08.

HOSKING, Geoffrey Alan, OBE, PhD, FBA, FRHistS; British historian and academic; *Professor Emeritus of Russian History, School of Slavonic and East European Studies, University College London;* b. 28 April 1942, Troon, Ayrshire, Scotland; s. of Stuart Hosking and Jean Smillie; m. Anne Lloyd Hirst 1970; two d.; ed Maidstone Grammar School, Moscow State Univ., Kings Coll., Cambridge, St Antony's Coll., Oxford; Lecturer in Govt, Univ. of Essex 1966–71, Lecturer in History 1972–76, Sr Lecturer and Reader in History 1976–84; Prof. of Russian History, School of Slavonic and East European Studies, Univ. Coll. London 1984–99, 2004–07, Prof. Emer. of Russian History 2007–, Leverhulme Research Prof. 1999–2004, Deputy Dir School of Slavonic and East European Studies 1996–98; Visiting Prof. in Political Science, Univ. of Wisconsin, USA 1971–72, Slavisches Institut, Univ. of Cologne, Germany 1980–81; mem. Inst. for Advanced Studies, Princeton, USA 2006–07; mem. Booker Prize Jury for Russian Fiction 1993; co-f. Nightline; Dr hc (Russian Acad. of Sciences) 2000; LA Times History Book Prize 1986, US Ind. Publrs History Book Prize 2001, Alex Nove Book Prize 2008. *Radio:* BBC Reith Lectures 1988. *Publications include:* The Russian Constitutional Experiment 1973, Beyond Socialist Realism 1980, The First Socialist Society: A History of the Soviet Union from Within 1985, The Awakening of the Soviet Union 1990, The Road to Post-Communism: Independent Political Movements in the Soviet Union 1985–91 (with J. Aves and P. Duncan) 1992, Russia: People and Empire (1552–1917) 1997, Myths and Nationhood (co-ed. with George Schöpflin) 1997, Russian Nationalism Past and Present (co-ed. with Robert Service) 1998, Reinterpreting Russia (co-ed. with Robert Service) 1999, Russia and the Russians: A History 2001, Rulers and Victims: The Russians in the Soviet Union 2006, Trust: Money, Markets and Society 2010, Russian History: A Very Short Introduction 2012, Trust: A History 2014. *Leisure interests:* music, walking, chess. *Address:* School of Slavonic and East European Studies, University College London, Gower Street, London, WC1E 6BT (office); Flat 15, Julian Court, 150 Camden Road, London, NW1 9HU, England (home). *Telephone:* (20) 7267-5543 (home). *E-mail:* geoffreyhosking@mac.com (home).

HOSODA, Hiroyuki, LLB; Japanese politician; b. 5 April 1944, Matsue City, Shimane Pref.; ed Faculty of Jurisprudence, Tokyo Univ.; joined Ministry of Int. Trade and Industry (MITI) 1967, Dir Price Policy Div., Industrial Policy Bureau 1985–86; Dir Washington Office, Japan Nat. Oil Corpn, USA 1983–85; elected mem. House of Reps for Shimane Constituency 1990–; Parl. Vice-Minister for Econ. Planning 1994–97; Dir Transport Div., Liberal Democratic Party (LDP) 1997–98, Dir Foreign Affairs Div. 1998–99, Deputy Sec.-Gen. LDP 2001, Dir-Gen. Election Bureau 2001–02, Sec.-Gen. 2008–09; Parl. Sec. for Int. Trade and Industry 1999–2001, Acting Exec. Deputy Sec.-Gen., Chair. LDP Gen. Council 2016–17, Head LDP panel promoting constitutional reform 2017–; Minister of State for Okinawa and Northern Territories Affairs, for Science and Tech. Policy, and for Information Tech. Policy 2002–03; Deputy Chief Cabinet Sec. 2003; Minister of State for Gender Equality and Chief Cabinet Sec. 2004–05; currently Pres., Japan Contract Bridge League. *Leisure interest:* bridge. *Address:* Liberal-Democratic Party–LDP (Jiyu-Minshuto), 1-11-23, Nagata-cho, Chiyoda-ku, Tokyo 100–8910, Japan (office). *Telephone:* (3) 3581-6211 (office). *E-mail:* koho@ldp.jimin.or.jp (office). *Website:* www.jimin.jp (office).

HOSOI, Susumu; Japanese business executive; *Representative Director and Chairman, Isuzu Motors Ltd;* b. 9 Aug. 1949, Tokyo; joined Isuzu Motors Ltd 1973, has led operations in USA and Asia, has overseen divs including Corp. Planning, Finance, and Supplier Relations, Rep. Dir 2002, Vice-Pres. 2006, Exec. Vice-Pres. 2006–07, Pres. 2007–15, Chair. 2015–. *Address:* Isuzu Motors Ltd, 26-1 Minami 6-chome, Shinagawa-ku, Tokyo 140-8722, Japan (office). *Telephone:* (3) 5471-1141 (office). *Fax:* (3) 5471-1043 (office). *E-mail:* info@isuzu.com (office). *Website:* www.isuzu.co.jp (office).

HOSONO, Hideo, PhD; Japanese materials scientist and academic; *Professor of Materials Science, Tokyo Institute of Technology;* b. 7 Sept. 1953, Kawagoe, Saitama Pref.; ed Tokyo Metropolitan Univ.; Prof. of Materials Science, Tokyo Inst. of Tech. 1999–; Medal of Honor (Purple Ribbon) 2009; Jan Rajchaman Prize, Soc. for Information Displays, James C. McGroddy Prize for New Materials, Research Achievement Award, Japanese Soc. of Applied Physics, W.H. Zachariasen Award, Journal of Non-Crystalline Solids, Otto-Schott Research Award, Ernst Abbe Foundation, Bernd T. Matthias Prize for Superconductivity 2009, Nishina Memorial Prize 2012, Japan Prize, Thomson Reuters Citation Laureates 2013, Imperial Prize, Japan Acad. 2015, Japan Prize Foundation 2016. *Achievements include:* known for the discovery of iron-based superconductors and for developing transparent oxide semiconductors. *Publications:* numerous papers in professional journals. *Address:* Materials and Structures Laboratory, Department of Materials Science and Engineering, Tokyo Institute of Technology, 4259 Nagatsuta-cho, Midori-ku, Yokohama 226-8503, Japan (office). *Telephone:* (45) 924-5359 (office). *Fax:* (45) 924-5339 (office). *E-mail:* hosono@msl.titech.ac.jp (office). *Website:* www.materia.titech.ac.jp/English/LaboratoryProfile/Hosono.html (office); www.khlab.msl.titech.ac.jp (office).

HOSPITAL, Janette Turner, (Alex Juniper), MA; Australian/American writer and academic; *Carolina Distinguished Professor Emerita of English, University of South Carolina;* b. 12 Nov. 1942, Melbourne, Vic.; d. of Adrian Charles Turner and Elsie Turner; m. Clifford Hospital 1965; one s. one d.; ed Univ. of Queensland and Queen's Univ., Canada; high school teacher, Queensland 1963–66; librarian, Harvard Univ. 1967–71; Lecturer in English, St Lawrence Coll., Kingston, Ont., in maximum and medium-security fed. penitentiaries for men 1971–82; professional writer 1982–; Writer-in-Residence and Lecturer, Writing Program, MIT 1985–86, 1987, 1989, Writer-in-Residence, Univ. of Ottawa, Canada 1987, Univ. of Sydney, Australia 1989, Queen's Univ. at Herstmonceux Castle, UK 1994; Adjunct Prof. of English, La Trobe Univ., Melbourne 1990–93; Visiting Fellow and Writer-in-Residence, Univ. of East Anglia, UK 1996; O'Connor Chair. in Literature, Colgate Univ., Hamilton, NY 1999; apptd Carolina Distinguished Prof. of English and Distinguished Writer-in-Residence, Univ. of South Carolina 1999, now Prof. Emer.; Hon. DUniv (Griffith Univ., Qld) 1995; Hon. DLitt (Univ. of Queensland) 2003; Gold Medal, Nat. Magazine Awards (Canada) 1991 (for travel writing), First Prize, Magazine Fiction, Foundation for the Advancement of Canadian Letters 1982, Patrick White Award for lifetime literary achievement (Australia) 2003, Russell Research Award for Humanities and Social Sciences, Univ. of South Carolina 2003. *Publications include:* The Ivory Swing (Seal First Novel Award 1982) 1982, The Tiger in the Tiger Pit 1983, Borderline 1985, Charades 1988, The Last Magician 1992, Oyster 1996, Due Preparations for the Plague (Qld Premier's Literature Award 2003, Davitt Award for Best Crime Novel by an Australian Woman 2003) 2003, The Claimant 2014; short story collections: Dislocations (Fellowship of Australian Writers Fiction Award 1988) 1986, Isobars 1990, Collected Stories 1995, North of Nowhere, South of Loss 2003, Forecast: Turbulence (Steele Rudd Award for Best Collection of Short Stories 2012) 2011; as Alex Juniper: A Very Proper Death 1991, Orpheus Lost 2007. *Leisure interests:* hiking, music, opera, gardening. *Address:* c/o Barbara Mobbs, PO Box 126, Edgeclif, Sydney, NSW 2027, Australia; c/o Elaine Markson, Literary Agent, 44 Greenwich Avenue, New York, NY 10011, USA (office). *Telephone:* (803) 777-2186 (office). *Website:* www.janetteturnerhospital.com.

HOSS, Nina; German actress; b. 7 July 1975, Stuttgart; d. of Willi Hoss (co-founder German Green Party) and Heidemarie Rohweder; ed Drama School 'Ernst Busch', Berlin; stage debut aged 14; first major success in title role of Bernd Eichinger's A Girl Called Rosemarie 1996; close collaboration with dir Christian Petzold; ensemble mem. Deutsches Theater, Berlin 1998–, appeared as Medea; mem. jury, Locarno Int. Film Festival 2009, Berlin Int. Film Festival 2011; Amb. of Terre des Femmes, fighting against female genital cutting, supports the Make Poverty History campaign; Shooting Stars Award, European Film Promotion at Berlin Int. Film Festival 2000. *Films include:* And Nobody Weeps for Me 1996, Feuerreiter 1998, Der Vulkan (Best Actress, Montréal World Film Festival) 1999, Naked 2002, Epstein's Night 2002, Something to Remind Me (Adolf Grimme Award) 2003, Wolfsburg (Adolf Grimme Award in Gold 2005) 2003, The White Massai (Bavarian Film Award for Best Actress 2005) 2005, Atomised 2006, Leben mit Hannah 2006, Yella (Silver Bear for Best Actress, Berlin Int. Film Festival 2007, German Film Award 2008) 2007, Das Herz ist ein dunkler Wald 2007, The Anarchist's Wife 2008, Jerichow 2008, We Are the Night 2010, Summer Window 2011, Barbara 2012, Gold 2013, A Most Wanted Man 2014, Phoenix 2014. *Television includes:* The Girl Rosemarie (film) 1996, Liebe deine Nächste! 1998, Die Geiseln von Costa Rica (film) 2000, Toter Mann (film) 2001, Emilia Galotti (film) 2002, Leonce und Lena (film) 2003, Bloch (series) 2004, History (series) 2008, Kinotipp (series) 2008, Eine Frau in Berlin – Anonyma (series) 2010, Die Akte Kleist (film) (voice) 2011, Homeland 2014.

HOSS, Selim al-, MBA, PhD; Lebanese professor of economics and fmr politician; b. 20 Dec. 1929; s. of Ahmad El-Hoss and Wadad Hoss; m. Leila Hoss (died 1990); one d.; ed American Univ. of Beirut, Indiana Univ., USA; teacher, later Prof. of Business, American Univ. of Beirut 1955–69; Financial Adviser, Kuwait Fund for Arab Econ. Devt, Kuwait 1964–66; Pres. Banking Supervision Comm. 1967–73; Chair. and Gen. Man. Nat. Bank for Industrial Devt 1973–76; Prime Minister 1976–80, remaining as Prime Minister in caretaker capacity July–Oct. 1980, Minister of the Econ. and Trade and Information 1976–79, of Industry and Petroleum 1976–77, of Labour, Fine Arts and Educ. 1984–85 (resgnd); Adviser to Arab Monetary Fund, Abu Dhabi, UAE 1983; Chair. Banque Arabe et Int.

d'Investissement, Paris 1982–85; Head, Arab Dinar Study Group, Arab Monetary Fund 1984–85; Minister of Educ. 1985–87; Head, Arab Experts Team commissioned by Arab League 1986–87; Prime Minister 1987–90, also Minister of Foreign and Expatriate Affairs; elected Deputy to Parl. 1992–2000; Pres. of Council of Ministers (Prime Minister of Lebanon) 1976–80, 1987–90, 1998–2000; mem. Bd of Trustees, American Univ. of Beirut 1991; mem. Consultative Council, Int. Bank for the Middle East and North Africa 1992; Higher Nat. Decoration of Lebanon; Jamal Abdul Nasser Award. *Publications:* The Development of Lebanon's Financial Markets 1974, Lebanon: Agony and Peace 1982 and 17 books in Arabic; numerous articles on econs and politics. *Leisure interest:* reading. *Address:* Aisha Bakkar, Beirut, Lebanon (office). *Telephone:* 736000 (office); 736001 (home). *Fax:* 354929 (office). *E-mail:* amirhamawi@salimelhoss.com (office). *Website:* www.salimelhoss.com (office).

HOSSAIN, Muzammel, MA, LLB, LLM; Bangladeshi lawyer, academic and judge; b. 17 Jan. 1948; s. of Alhaz Ahmed Hossain and Asia Akther Khatun; ed Univ. of Dhaka, Sheffield Univ., UK; Advocate, Dist Court 1971, High Court Div., Supreme Court 1978, apptd Judge 1998, Judge of Appellate Div. 2009, Chief Justice of Supreme Court 2011–15; Chair. Judicial Service Pay Comm. 2010; Lecturer, Faculty of Law, Univ. of Miadiguri, Nigeria; Prof. (part-time), City Law Coll., Dhanmandi Law Coll., Bhuiyan Acad., Dhaka.

HOSSAIN, Shah Moazzem, MA; Bangladeshi politician; b. 10 Jan. 1939, Munsigonj Dist; m. Begum Saleha Hossain (died 2009); one s. one d.; ed Dhaka Univ.; Gen. Sec. East Pakistan Students League 1959–60, Pres. 1960–63; Chair. the All-Party Action Cttee 1962; political prisoner for several years between 1953 and 1978; Chief Whip, Bangladesh Parl. 1972–73; co-f. Democratic League 1976, Gen. Sec. 1977–83; Minister of Land Admin. and Land Revenue 1973–75, in charge of Ministry of Labour and Manpower 1984–85, of Information 1985–86, of Local Govt, Rural Devt and Co-operatives 1986–88, of Labour and Manpower 1988–90, of Food 1990; Deputy Prime Minister 1987–90; mem. Bangladesh Jatiyatabadi Dal (Bangladesh Nationalist Party). *Publication include:* Nitta Keragarey 1976.

HOSSAIN, Suhrab; Bangladeshi diplomatist; *High Commissioner to Pakistan;* ed Univ. of Dhaka; joined Foreign Service 1973, held numerous posts including Amb. to Uzbekistan, to Thailand, High Commr to Canada, also served in diplomatic missions in Bangkok, Birmingham, Dakar, Ottawa, Paris, High Commr to Pakistan 2010–. *Address:* Bangladesh High Commission, House No. 1, Street No. 5, F-6/3, Islamabad, Pakistan (office). *Telephone:* (51) 2279260 (office). *Fax:* (51) 2279266 (office). *E-mail:* mission.islamabad@mofa.gov.bd (office). *Website:* www.bdhcpk.org (office).

HOSSEIN, Robert; French actor and director; b. 30 Dec. 1927, Paris; s. of Amin Hossein and Anna Mincovschi; m. 1st Marina de Poliakoff 1955 (divorced); two s.; m. 2nd Caroline Eliacheff 1962 (divorced); one s.; m. 3rd Candice Patou 1976; one s.; stage actor, dir and playwright, film dir and producer, scriptwriter and actor; Chair. and Man. Dir Sinfonia Films 1963–; founder and Dir Théâtre Populaire de Reims and of Théâtre-Ecole de Reims 1971; Artistic Dir Théâtre de Paris-Théâtre Moderne 1975–, Théâtre Marigny 2000–08; Commdr, Ordre nat. du Mérite, Officier, Légion d'honneur, Commdr des Arts et des Lettres; Prix Orange 1963, Médaille de Vermeil de la Ville de Paris, Molière d'honneur 1995, Prix Grand siècle Laurent Perrir 2000. *Plays include:* La neige était sale, Haute surveillance, Les voyous (writer), La P. respectueuse, Huis-Clos, Vous qui nous jugez (writer), Les six hommes en question (co-writer with Frédéric Dard and producer), La moitié du plaisir (producer), Crime et châtiment, Les bas-fonds, Roméo et Juliette, Pour qui sonne le glas, La maison des otages, Hernani (produced for the Comédie Française) 1974, La maison de Bernada (produced at the Odéon) 1975, Le cuirassé Potemkine (dir at Palais des Sports) 1975, Des souris et des hommes, Shéhérazade (ballet) 1975, Procès de Jeanne d'Arc (producer) 1976, Pas d'orchidées pour Miss Blandish (producer and actor) 1977, Notre-Dame de Paris (producer) 1978, Le cauchemar de Bella Manningham (producer) 1978, Danton et Robespierre (producer) 1979, Lorna et Ted 1981, Un grand avocat 1983, Les brumes de Manchester 1986, Liberty or Death and the Heritage of the French Revolution (Dominique Prize for Best Dir) 1988, Dans la nuit la liberté (producer) 1989, Cyrano de Bergerac (producer) 1990, Jésus était son nom 1991, Les bas-fonds 1992, Je m'appelais Marie-Antoinette 1993, La nuit du crime (producer and actor) 1994, Angélique, Marquise des anges (director and actor) 1995, Ouragan sur le Caine 1997, La Vie en bleu 1997, Surtout ne coulez pas (producer) 1997, De Gaulle, celui qui a dit non (producer) 1999, Jésus, la Résurrection 2000, Coupable ou non coupable 2001, Lumières et ténèbres 2002. *Films include:* Quai des blondes, Du rififi chez les hommes, Crime et châtiment, Toi le venin (script-writer and producer), Le jeu de la vérité (writer), Le goût de la violence (script-writer and producer), Le repos du guerrier, Le vice et la vertu, Les yeux cernés, Angélique marquise des anges, Banco à Bangkok, Le vampire de Düsseldorf, Le tonnerre de Dieu, La seconde vérité, J'ai tué Raspoutine (writer and producer), Indomptable Angélique, Don Juan 1973, Prêtres interdits, Le protecteur, Le faux cul 1975, Les uns et les autres, Le professionnel 1981, Les Misérables (producer) 1982, Un homme nommé Jésus (director) 1983, Jules César 1985, Les brumes de Manchester 1986, Un homme et une femme, vingt ans déjà 1986, Les Enfants du désordre 1989, L'Affaire 1994, la Nuit du Crime 1994, L'Homme au masque de cire 1996, Vénus beauté 1999, Gialloparma 1999, San Antonio 2004. *Television includes:* Les Uns et les autres (miniseries) 1983, Le Juge (miniseries) 2005. *Publications:* La sentinelle aveugle 1978, Nomade sans tribu 1981, En désespoir de cause (memoirs) 1987, La Nostalgie (autobiog.) 2001. *Leisure interest:* skiing. *Address:* c/o Mme Ghislaine de Wing, 10 rue du Docteur Roux, 75015 Paris, France.

HOSSEINI, Sayed Shamseddin, PhD; Iranian politician; b. 1967, Mazandaran; ed Islamic Azad Univ.; fmr lecturer, Islamic Azad Univ., Payame Noor Univ. and Allameh Tabatabai Univ.; fmr Dir-Gen. for Econ. Studies, Ministry of Commerce; fmr Deputy Minister of Welfare and Social Security; Sec., Working Group for Econ. Transformation –2008; Minister of Econ. Affairs and Finance 2008–13; Vice-Pres., Iranian Univ. 2013–. *Address:* c/o Ministry of Economic Affairs and Finance, Sour Esrafil Avenue, Nasser Khosrou Street, Tehran 11149-43661, Iran (office).

HOSSEINI, Seyed Safdar, BA, PhD; Iranian politician and academic; *Professor, Department of Agricultural Economics, University of Tehran;* b. 1954, Khuzestan; ed Shiraz Univ., Univ. of Saskatchewan, Canada; Minister of Labour and Social Affairs 2001–04; Minister of Econ. Affairs and Finance 2004–05, Chair. Nat. Devt Fund 2013–16; currently Prof., Dept of Agricultural Econs, Univ. of Tehran. *Address:* Department of Agricultural Economics, University of Tehran, Karaj, Iran (office). *Telephone:* (261) 2247783 (office). *Fax:* (261) 2247783 (office). *E-mail:* hosseini_Safdar@yahoo.com (office). *Website:* can.ut.ac.ir/member/shosseini.aspx.

HOSTETTER, Amos Barr, Jr, BA, MBA; American media executive; *Chairman, Pilot House Associates, LLC;* b. 12 Jan. 1937, New York; s. of Amos Barr Hostetter and Leola Hostetter (née Conroy); m.; three c.; ed Amherst Coll., Harvard Univ.; Asst to Vice-Pres. of Finance, American and Foreign Power Co., New York 1958–59; investment analyst, Cambridge Capital Corpn 1961–63; Co-founder and Exec. Vice-Pres. Continental Cablevision Inc., Boston, Mass 1963–80, Pres. and CEO 1980–85, Chair. and CEO (co. renamed MediaOne) 1985–96, CEO MediaOne Inc. 1996–2000, returned as Bd mem.; Chair. AT&T Broadband and Internet Services 1999–2003; Chair. Pilot House Assocs LLC 1997–, GlobalPost, LLC; Co-founder and mem. Bd of Dirs and Exec. Cttee, Cable-Satellite Public Affairs Network (C-SPAN) 1979 (fmr Chair.); Co-founder (with wife) Barr Foundation 1997; Founding Chair. and mem. Exec. Cttee, Cable in the Classroom; mem. Bd of Dirs Commodities Corpn, Corpn for Public Broadcasting 1975–79, Walter Kaitz Foundation 1981; Corporator, Perkins School for the Blind, Watertown, Mass 1982; fmr mem. Bd of Overseers, Museum of Fine Arts, Boston; mem. Nat. Cable TV Asscn (Dir 1965–75, 1982, Nat. Chair. 1973–74), Int. Radio and TV Soc.; Chair. Emer. Amherst Coll., WGBH-TV; fmr Trustee Children's TV Workshop, New England Medical Center Hosp., Nantucket Conservation Foundation, Colonial Williamsburg Foundation; named Cablevision Magazine Man of the Year 1972, Nat. Cable TV Asscn Larry Boggs Award 1975, named to Broadcasting magazine's Hall of Fame 1991, Cable Television Public Affairs Asscn Beacon Award 1991, Cable Television Admin and Marketing Soc. 'Grand TAM Award' 1993, Walter Kaitz Foundation Award 1993, Harvard Business School Alumni Achievement Award 1994, Mass Telecommunications Council Hall of Fame 2000. *Address:* Pilot House Assocs LLC, 2 Atlantic Avenue, Boston, MA 02110, USA (office). *Telephone:* (617) 742-9500 (office). *Website:* www.barrfoundation.org.

HOTI, Abdullah, BA, PhD; Kosovo economist and politician; b. 4 Feb. 1976; m.; two s.; ed Univ. of Prishtina, Staffordshire Univ. Business School, UK; Part-time Asst Lecturer, Faculty of Econs, Univ. of Prishtina 1998–2001, Lecturer in Macroeconomics and Econs of Labour 2002–, Asst Prof. 2008–12, Assoc. Prof. 2012–; Researcher, Riinvest Inst. for Devt Research 1999–2004; Consultant and Chief Magazine Ed., Soc. of Certified Accountants and Auditors of Kosovo 2003–04; Dir Integra Consulting, Prishtina 2004; Political Adviser to Minister of Educ., Science and Tech. 2006–07; Adviser on Econs to Mayor of Prishtina 2008–09; Deputy Mayor of Prishtina 2010–13; mem. Kosovo Ass. (Parl.) 2014–; Minister of Finance 2014–17; mem. Lidhja Demokratike e Kosovës (LDK—Democratic League of Kosovo), mem. LDK Gen. Council 2006–.

HOTOVELY, Tzipi, LLB, LLM; Israeli lawyer and politician; *Deputy Minister of Foreign Affairs;* b. 2 Dec. 1978, Rehovot; m. Or Alon; one d.; ed Bar-Ilan Univ., Tel-Aviv Univ.; Ed., Bar-Ilan Univ. Journal of Law 2003–05; Contrib. (opinion pieces), Maariv (daily newspaper) 2006–; regular Contrib., Judaism section of nrg (news website) 2007–; mem. Knesset (Likud) 2009–, Chair. Cttee on Status of Women; Deputy Minister of Transportation and Road Safety 2013–15, also Deputy Minister of Science and Tech. 2014–15, Deputy Minister of Foreign Affairs 2015–. *Address:* Ministry of Foreign Affairs, 9 Yitzhak Rabin Blvd, Kiryat Ben-Gurion, Jerusalem 91950, Israel (office). *Telephone:* 2-5303111 (office). *Fax:* 2-5303367 (office). *E-mail:* ssar@mfa.gov.il (office). *Website:* www.mfa.gov.il (office).

HÖTTGES, Timotheus; German business executive; *Chairman of the Management Board (CEO), Deutsche Telekom AG;* b. 1962; ed Univ. of Cologne; spent three years with a business consulting co., latterly as a project man.; moved to VIAG Group, Munich 1992, div man. 1997, later mem. extended man. bd responsible for controlling, corp. planning, and mergers and acquisitions, played role in merger of VIAG AG and VEBA AG to form E.ON AG 2000; Man. Dir, Finance and Controlling, later Chair. Man. Bd T-Mobile Deutschland 2000–04, headed European operations as mem. Bd of Man., T-Mobile International 2005–06, mem. Bd of Man. responsible for T-Home unit 2006–09, mem. Group Bd of Man. responsible for Finance and Controlling 2009–14, Chair. Man. Bd (CEO) Deutsche Telekom AG 2014–. *Address:* Deutsche Telekom AG, Friedrich-Ebert-Allee 140, 53113 Bonn, Germany (office). *Telephone:* (228) 1814949 (office). *Fax:* (228) 18194004 (office). *E-mail:* info@deutschetelekom.com (office). *Website:* www.deutschetelekom.com (office); www.telekom.com (office).

HOU, Hsiao-hsien; Taiwanese film director, screenwriter, producer and actor; b. 8 April 1947, Meixian, Guangdong Prov.; ed Taipei Nat. Acad. of Arts Film and Drama Dept; worked as an electronic calculator salesman; entered film industry in 1973; asst to several dirs from 1974; Chair. Asian Film Soc. *Films include:* Chiu shih liu-liu-te t'a (Cute Girl) 1980, Feng-erh t'i-t'a-ts'ai (Cheerful Wind) 1981, Tsai na ho-pan ch'ing-ts'ao-ch'ing (Green Grass of Home) 1982, Erh-tzu-te ta wan-ou (The Sandwich Man) 1983, Feng-kuei-lai-te jen (The Boys from Fengkuei/All the Youthful Days) 1983, Tung-tung-te chia-ch'i (A Summer at Grandpa's) 1984, T'ung-nien wang-shih (The Time to Live and the Time to Die) 1985, Ni-lo-ho nü-erh (Daughter of the Nile) 1987, Lien-lien feng-ch'en (Dust in the Wind/Rite of Passage) 1987, Pei-ch'ing ch'eng-shih (A City of Sadness) (Golden Lion, Venice Film Festival) 1989, The Puppetmaster 1993, Good Men, Good Women 1995, Goodbye, South, Goodbye 1996, Flowers of Shanghai 1998, Millennium Mambo 2001, Café Lumière 2003, Three Times 2005, Flight of the Red Balloon 2007, To Each His Own Cinema (segment: The Electric Princess House) 2007, 10+10 (segment: La Belle Epoque) 2011, Nie Yinniang (The Assassin) (Award for Best Dir, Cannes Film Festival) 2015.

HOU, Jianguo, BS, MS, PhD; Chinese chemist, academic, university administrator and politician; *Professor, Department of Chemical Physics, University of Science and Technology of China;* b. 29 Oct. 1959, Fujian; ed Univ. of Science and Technology of China; Visiting Scientist, Lab. of Electron Microscopy, Inst. of Crystallography, USSR Acad. of Sciences 1988; Post-doctor, Material Science Div., Lawrence Berkeley Lab. and Dept of Physics, Univ. of California at Berkeley, USA 1991–93; Research Assoc., Dept of Chem., Oregon State Univ., USA 1993–95; Prof., Dept of Chemical Physics, Univ. of Science and Tech. of China 1995–, Univ. Vice-Pres. 1999–2005, Pres. 2008–15, also currently Deputy Dir Hefei Nat. Lab. for Physical Sciences; Vice-Minister of Science and Tech. 2014–; Deputy Party Sec.,

CPC (Guangxi Zhuang Autonomous Region) 2016–17; Head of Gen. Admin of Quality Supervision, Inspection and Quarantine 2017–; mem. Chinese Acad. of Sciences 2003–; mem. 11th NPC Standing Cttee 2008–13, 19th CCP Cen. Cttee 2017–; Fellow, Third World Acad. of Science 2004–; Natural Science Award (First-Class), Chinese Acad. of Sciences 1997, US Overseas Chinese Physics Asscn Achievement in Asia Award 2002 (co-winner), Holeung Ho Lee Advancement Prize 2007, Tan Kah Kee Science Prize in Chem. 2008, China Asscn for Instrumental Analysis Distinguishing Research Award 2013. *Publications:* more than 20 research papers on nanomaterials, nanostructures and molecular orientations. *Address:* Hefei National Laboratory for the Physical Sciences at the Microscale, University of Science and Technology of China, Hefei 230026, People's Republic of China (office). *Telephone:* (551) 63600456 (office). *Fax:* (551) 63606266 (office). *E-mail:* jghou@ustc.edu.cn (office). *Website:* physics.ustc.edu.cn (office).

HOUENIPWELA, Rick, (Rick Hou); Solomon Islands banker and politician; b. 8 Aug. 1958; with Cen. Bank of Solomon Islands 1983–2008, beginning as Internal Auditor, Gov. –2008; Chair. Solomon Airlines 2007–08; Sr Adviser to Exec. Dir, World Bank Group, Washington, DC 2008; MP (Democratic Party) for Small Malaita constituency 2010–, mem. Bills and Legislation Cttee, Public Accounts Cttee; Shadow Minister for Finance and the Treasury 2010; Minister for Public Service April–Nov. 2011, for Finance and Treasury 2011–17, Prime Minister 2017–19. *Address:* National Parliament of Solomon Islands, PO Box G19, Vavaya Ridge, Honiara, Solomon Islands. (office). *Telephone:* 28520 (office). *Fax:* 24272 (office). *Website:* www.parliament.gov.sb (office).

HOU, Yifan; Chinese chess player; b. 27 Feb. 1994, Xinghua, Taizhou; d. of Hou Xuejian; ed Nat. Chess Centre, Beijing; started playing chess aged six; first major tournament at Chinese Team Chess Championship (Men's), Tianjin 2003; first Fédération Int. des Échecs (FIDE, World Chess Fed.) rating of 2168 2004; took part aged 12 in FIDE Women's World Championship, Yekaterinburg 2006 and Chess Olympiad, Turin 2006; China Nat. Women's Champion 2007; other titles include Woman FIDE Master 2004, Woman Grandmaster 2007, Int. Master 2008, Women's World Chess Champion (after winning Women's World Championship in Hatay, Turkey aged 16) 2010–11, lost in 2012, regained title 2013–, FIDE Women's Grand Prix 2013–14; Best Sportsperson of the Year in China (non-Olympic category) 2011.

HOU, Yunde, DMSc; Chinese virologist; b. 13 July 1929, Changzhou, Jiangsu Prov.; ed Tongji Univ. Medical Coll., Russian Inst. of Medical Sciences; Fellow Chinese Acad. of Eng; Dir Inst. of Virology, Chinese Acad. of Preventive Medicine 1985–; Dir WHO Virus Research Centre, researching para-influenza and the structure and function of virus gene; Vice-Pres. Chinese Acad. of Eng 1994–98; Dir Nat. Key Research Lab. for Virogenetic Eng 1998–; Dir Nat. Eng Research Center for Viro Bio-technology 1998–; now Dir Inst. of Virology, Chinese Acad. of Preventive Medicine; Chair. Bd of Tri-Prime Gene 1998–; Dir of Expert Cttee of Defense and Control Mechanism during H1N1 flu outbreak in 2009; Assoc. Chief Ed. Chinese Medical Sciences Journal; 21 prizes including one First Prize and two Second Prizes of Nat. Science and Tech. Advancement Award, He Liang & He Li Medical Prize 1994, China Medical Science Award 1996, Highest Science and Tech. Award 2017. *Publications:* nine monographs and over 400 scientific treatises. *Address:* Virology Research Institute, Chinese Academy of Preventative Medical Science, 100 Yingxin Street, Xuanwu District, Beijing 100052, People's Republic of China (office). *Telephone:* (10) 63529224 (office). *Fax:* (10) 63532053 (office). *E-mail:* engach@mail.cae.ac.cn (office).

HOUBEN, Francine M. J., MSc; Dutch architect, company director and academic; *Creative Director, Mecanoo Architecten;* b. 2 July 1955, Sittard; m.; one s. two d.; ed Delft Univ. of Tech.; Founding Partner, Döll-Houben-Steenhuis architecten 1980–84; Creative Dir Mecanoo Architecten, Delft 1984–; Prof. in Architecture and Aesthetics of Mobility, Delft Univ. of Tech. 2000–; Visiting Prof., Philadelphia Univ., USA 1990, Univ. of Calgary, Canada 1992, Berlage Inst., Amsterdam 1994, Univ. of Oxford, UK 1994, Università della Svizzera Italiana, Mendrisio, Switzerland 2000–01, Harvard Univ., USA 2007; Dir/Curator First Int. Architecture Biennale Rotterdam 1997–2000; columnist, Het Financieele Dagblad 2006–; mem. Bd Netherlands Architecture Inst. 1990–92, Int. Design Cttee, London, UK 1990–92, Fine Art, Design and Architecture Fund 1990–2006, Forum for Urban Renewal 2003–, Int. Film Festival, Rotterdam 2005–; mem. Supervisory Bd Kröller Museum, Otterlo 2005–; jury mem. for awards in Netherlands, Turkey, Germany, USA, UK, Canada; appeared in TV documentaries; Hon. FRIBA 2001, Hon. FRAIC 2007; numerous awards include Rotterdam-Maaskant Prize for Young Architects 1987, Nieuwe Maas Prize for Housing Hillekop, Rotterdam 1990, Berlagevlag Award for Offices for Gravura Lithographers, The Hague 1993, Auszeichnung Guter Bauten and Hugo Häring Prize Bund Deutscher Architekten for Experimental Housing Int. Gartenbau Ausstellung, Stuttgart, Germany 1993/1994, Jhr Victor de Stuerspenning for Herdenkingsplein housing project, Maastricht 1994, Scholenbouwprijs 1996, 2003, Nat. Staalprijs and Corus Construction Award for the Millennium for Library at Delft Tech. Univ. 1996/2000, Bouwkwaliteitsprijs, Rotterdam 2000, TECU Architecture Award and Dutch Building Prize for Nat. Museum of Heritage, Arnhem 2000/2003, Gezichtsbepalend 3 Culture Award Prov. of South Holland 2005, Building Quality Award for Montevideo Rotterdam 2006, Amsterdam Architecture Prize for Amsterdam Univ. Coll. 2013, Architects Journal Building of the Year 2013 and RIBA Nat. Award 2014 for Library of Birmingham, RIBA Nat. Award for HOME, Manchester 2016, Boston Soc. of Architects Harleston Parker Medal for Bruce C. Bolling Municipal Building, Boston 2017. *Publications include:* Mecanoo architecten (with P. Volland and L. Waaijers) 1998, Maliebaan, een huis om te werken 2000, Composition, Contrast, Complexity 2001, Mobility – A Room with a View 2002. *Address:* Mecanoo architecten, Postbus 3277, 2601 DG Delft, Netherlands (office). *Telephone:* (15) 279-81-00 (office). *Fax:* (15) 279-81-11 (office). *E-mail:* francine.houben@mecanoo.nl (office). *Website:* www.mecanoo.nl (office).

HOUELLEBECQ, Michel, DipAgr; French novelist, poet and film director; b. 26 Feb. 1958, Réunion; s. of René Thomas and Lucie Ceccaldi; m. 1st 1980 (divorced); one s.; m. 2nd Marie-Pierre Gauthier 1998; ed Institut Nat. Agronomique Paris-Grignon; fmr Admin. Sec., French Nat. Ass.; first works (poetry) published in Nouvelle Revue de Paris 1986; Chevalier, Légion d'honneur 2019; Grand Prix Nat. des Lettres Jeune Talent 1998. *Music:* Présence Humaine 2000. *Films include:* Cristal de souffrance 1978, Déséquilibres 1982, La rivière 2001, La Possibilité d'une île 2008, The Kidnapping of Michel Houellebecq 2014, Near Death Experience 2014, Saint-Amour 2016, To Stay Alive: A Method 2016. *Publications include:* H.P. Lovecraft (Contre le monde, contre la vie) 1991, Rester vivant: méthode 1991, La poursuite de bonheur (Prix Tristan Tzara) 1992, Extension du domaine à la lutte 1994, Le sens du combat (Prix de Flore) 1996, Interventions, Les Particules élémentaires (Prix Novembre, Int. Impac Dublin Literary Prize) 1998, Renaissance 1999, Lanzarote 2000, Plateforme 2002, La Possibilité d'une île (Prix Interallié) 2005, Ennemis Publics (with Bernard-Henri Lévy) 2008, La Carte et le Territoire (Prix Goncourt 2010) 2010, Configuration du dernier rivage 2013, Soumission 2015, En présence de Schopenhauer 2017, Sérotonine 2019. *Address:* c/o Editions Flammarion, 87, Panhard-et-Levassor, 75006 Paris Cedex 13, France. *Telephone:* 1-40-51-31-00.

HOUGH, Stephen Andrew Gill, CBE, MMus, GMus, FRNCM, PPRNCM; British pianist, composer and writer; b. 22 Nov. 1961, Heswall, Cheshire; ed Chetham's School of Music, Royal Northern Coll. of Music, Juilliard School, USA; guest performer with Berlin Philharmonic, London Symphony, New York Philharmonic, Cleveland, Philadelphia, Los Angeles Philharmonic, Boston Symphony, NHK Symphony, Chicago Symphony, Philharmonia, Royal Philharmonic and London Philharmonic Orchestras; Visiting Prof., Juilliard School and RAM; Int. Chair of Piano, RNCM; regular appearances with other orchestras and as recitalist in USA, Europe, Australia, Far East and at int. music festivals including Verbier, Salzburg, Aldeburgh, Edinburgh, BBC Proms, Mostly Mozart, Ravinia, Blossom, Tanglewood, Hollywood Bowl, La Roque d'Anthéron; Hon. RAM, Hon. Fellow, Guildhall School of Music and Drama, Hon. mem. Royal Philharmonic Soc.; Hon. DMus; Dayas Gold Medal, RNCM, Terence Judd Award 1982, Naumburg Int. Piano Competition 1983, Gramophone Record of the Year 1996, 2002, MacArthur Foundation Fellowship 2001, Jean Gimbel Lane Prize 2007, Gramophone Gold Disc 2008, Royal Philharmonic Soc. Award for Best Instrumentalist 2010. *Compositions include:* Transcriptions, Suite R-B and Other Enigmas, Piano Album, songs and choral works 2005, Viola Sonata 2000, Piano Pieces, The Loneliest Wilderness: Elegy for Cello and Orchestra 2005, Mass of Innocence and Experience 2006, Missa Mirabilis 2007, The Bible as Prayer 2007, Un Piccolo Sonatina, Threnody for Guitar, Three Grave Songs, Was mit den Tranen Geschieht: trio for flute or piccolo, bassoon or contrabassoon and piano, Herbstlieder for baritone and piano, Requiem Aeternum (after Victoria) for string sextet, Other Love Songs for SATB solo voices and piano duet, Sonata for piano (Broken Branches) 2011, Piano Sonata No. 2 (Notturno Luminoso), Bridgewater for bassoon and piano, Missa Mirabilis (orchestral version) 2012, Sonata for cello and piano (Les Adieux) 2013, Dappled Things for baritone and piano 2014, Piano Sonata III (Trinitas) 2015, Piano Sonata No. 4 (Vida Breve) 2016, Hallowed for SATB 2017. *Recordings include:* complete Beethoven violin sonatas (with Robert Mann), Hummel piano concertos, recitals of Liszt and Schumann, Brahms concerto Nos 1 and 2, The Piano Album Vols I, II, Britten Music for One and Two Pianos, Scharwenka and Sauer concertos, Grieg, Liszt, Rubinstein cello sonatas (with Steven Isserlis), Brahms violin sonatas (with Robert Mann), York Bowen piano music, Franck piano music, Mompou piano music, Liebermann piano concertos, Mendelssohn piano and orchestral works, Schubert sonatas and New York Variations, Brahms clarinet trio, The New Piano Album, Liszt sonata, Mozart piano and wind quintet, Brahms F minor sonata, Saint-Saëns Complete Music for Piano and Orchestra (Gramophone Gold Disc Award and CD of the Year), English Piano Album, Hummel piano sonatas, Chopin ballades and scherzos, Rachmaninov and Franck cello sonatas (with Steven Isserlis), Rachmaninov piano concertos (with Dallas Symphony and A. Litton) (Classical BRIT Critics' Award 2005, Classic FM Gramophone Editor's Choice Award 2005) 2004, Brahms, Dvořák and Suk 2005, Liszt Années de Pèlerinage (Suisse), Brahms cello sonatas with Stephen Isserlis, Children's Cello with Steven Isserlis, Beethoven and Mozart piano and wind quintets with the Berlin Philharmonic Wind Quintet, Stephen Hough's Spanish Album, Tsontakis Man of Sorrows, Brahms piano quintet with the Takacs Quartet, complete Tchaikovsky works for piano and orchestra with Minnesota Orchestra and Osmo Vanska, Stephen Hough in Recital, Chopin: Late Masterpieces, Chopin Complete Waltzes (Diapason d'Or de l'Année 2011), Liszt and Grieg Concertos 2011, Broken Branches (compositions by Stephen Hough) 2011, Stephen Hough's French Album 2012, Two Brahms Piano Concertos 2013, In the Night recital 2014, Grieg, Mendelssohn and Hough Cello Sonatas (with Steven Isserlis) 2014, Grieg Lyric Pieces 2015, Scriabin and Janacek recital 2015, Dvorak and Schumann piano concertos (with City of Birmingham Symphony Orchestra and Andris Nelsons) 2016, Debussy solo recital 2018, Dream Album 2018. *Publications:* contrib. to The Times, Guardian, Daily Telegraph, Evening Standard and others; regular blog for The Telegraph website 2010–15, The Final Retreat: a novel. *Leisure interests:* reading, writing, painting. *Address:* c/o Harrison Parrott, The Ark, 201 Talgarth Road, London, W6 8BJ, England (office). *Telephone:* (20) 7229-9166 (office). *Fax:* (20) 7221-5042 (office). *E-mail:* info@harrisonparrott.co.uk (office); houghwebsite@gmail.com (office). *Website:* www.harrisonparrott.co.uk (office); www.stephenhough.com.

HOUGHTON, James Richardson, AB, MBA; American business executive; b. 6 April 1936, Corning, NY; s. of Amory Houghton and Laura Richardson Houghton; m. May Kinnicutt 1962; one s. one d.; ed St Paul's School, Concord, NH, Harvard Coll. and Harvard Univ. Grad. Business School; worked for Goldman, Sachs and Co., New York 1959–61; worked for Corning Glass Works, Danville, Ky and Corning, New York 1962–64, Vice-Pres. and Area Man., Corning Glass Int., Zurich and Brussels 1964–68, Vice-Pres. and Gen. Man. Consumer Products Div., Corning Glass Works (named Corning Inc. 1989–) 1968–71, Vice-Chair. of Bd 1971–83, Chair. and CEO 1983–96, 2002–05, Chair. 2005–07 (retd), now Chair. Emer.; elected Trustee, Metropolitan Museum of Art 1982, Vice-Chair. 1984–98, Chair. 1998–2011; fmr Chair. Business Council of New York State; fmr mem. Bd of Dirs Exxon Mobil, Metropolitan Life Insurance Co., J. P. Morgan; fmr Trustee Corning Glass Works Foundation, Corning Museum of Glass, Metropolitan Museum of Art, Pierpont Morgan Library; mem. Harvard Corpn 1995–2010 (fmr Chair.); mem. Council on Foreign Relations, The Business Council.

HOUGHTON, Sir John T., Kt, CBE, MA, DPhil, FRS; British physicist; *Honorary Scientist, Hadley Centre, Meteorological Office;* b. 30 Dec. 1931, Dyserth, Clwyd, Wales; s. of Sidney Houghton and Miriam Houghton (née Yarwood); m. 1st Margaret E. Broughton 1962 (died 1986); one s. one d.; m. 2nd Sheila Thompson

1988; ed Rhyl Grammar School and Jesus Coll., Oxford; Research Fellow, Royal Aircraft Establishment. Farnborough 1954–57; Lecturer in Atmospheric Physics, Univ. of Oxford 1958–62, Reader 1962–76, Prof. 1976–83, Fellow, Jesus Coll. 1960–83, Hon. Fellow 1983–; Dir Appleton, Science and Eng Research Council 1979–83; Chair. Earth Observation Advisory Cttee, ESA 1980–93; Chair. Jt Scientific Cttee, World Climate Research Prog. 1981–83; Dir-Gen. Meteorological Office 1983–90, Chief Exec. 1990–91; mem. Exec. Cttee WMO 1983–91, Vice-Pres. 1987–91; Pres. Royal Meteorological Soc. 1976–78; Chair. (or Co-Chair.) Scientific Assessment Working Group, Intergovernmental Panel on Climate Change 1988–2002, Royal Comm. on Environmental Pollution 1992–98, Jt Scientific and Tech. Cttee, Global Climate Observing System 1992–95; mem. UK Govt Panel on Sustainable Devt 1994–2000; Chair. The John Ray Initiative 1997–2007, Pres. 2007–; Hon. Scientist, Rutherford Appleton Lab. 1992–, Hadley Centre 2002–; Trustee, Hadley Centre 2000–; mem. Academia Europaea; Fellow, Optical Soc. of America, Learned Soc. of Wales; Hon. FRIBA 2001; Hon. mem. Royal Meteorological Soc., American Meteorological Soc.; Hon. DSc (Univ. of Wales) 1991, (Stirling) 1992, (East Anglia) 1993, (Leeds) 1995, (Heriot-Watt) 1997, (Greenwich) 1997, (Glamorgan) 1998, (Reading) 1999, (Birmingham) 2000, (Gloucestershire) 2001, (Hull) 2002, (Oxford) 2006; Hon. LLD (Dalhousie, Canada) 2010; Charles Chree Medal and Prize, Inst. of Physics 1979, Rank Prize for opto-electronics (jt recipient) 1989, Glazebrook Medal, Inst. of Physics 1990, Symonds Gold Medal, Royal Meteorological Soc. 1991, Bakerian Lecturer, Royal Soc. 1991, Global 500 Award, UNEP 1994, Gold Medal, Royal Astronomical Soc. 1995, Int. Meteorological Org. Prize 1998, Japan Prize 2006, Albert Einstein Science Award, World Cultural Council 2009. *Publications:* Infra Red Physics (with S. D. Smith) 1966, The Physics of Atmospheres 1977 (revised edn 2003), Remote Sounding of Atmospheres (with F. W. Taylor and C. D. Rodgers) 1984, Does God Play Dice? 1988, The Search for God: Can Science Help? 1995, Global Warming: The Complete Briefing 1997 (revised edn 2003). *Address:* 6 Bryn y Paderau, Tywyn, Gwynedd, LL36 9LA, England (office).

HOUGHTON, Michael, PhD; American virologist and academic; *Director, Li Ka Shing Applied Virology Institute, University of Alberta;* ed Kings Coll. London, UK; Vice-Pres. Hepatitis C Research, Chiron Corpn, Emeryville, Calif. 1982–2007; Chief Scientific Officer, Epiphany Biosciences, Calif. 2007–10; Canada Excellence Research Chair in Virology, Univ. of Alberta 2010–17, currently Dir, Li Ka Shing Applied Virology Inst., also Prof., Dept of Medical Microbiology and Immunology; Karl Landsteiner Memorial Award 1992, Robert Koch Award 1993, William Beaumont Prize 1994, Beatrice Vitiello Award 1994, Int. Hepatitis Foundation Award 1998, Hans Popper Award 1999, Lasker Award for Clinical Medical Research 2000, Dale A. Smith Memorial Award 2005, William H. Prusoff HEP DART Lifetime Achievement Award 2009. *Achievements include:* headed research team that discovered Hepatitis C virus in 1987 and cloned it in 1989. *Publications:* numerous articles in scientific journals. *Address:* Faculty of Medicine & Dentistry, 7-126, Li Ka Shing Centre for Health Research Innovation, University of Alberta, Edmonton, AB T6G 2E1, Canada (office). *Telephone:* (780) 248-5816 (office). *Fax:* (780) 492-3592 (office). *E-mail:* michael.houghton@ualberta.ca (office). *Website:* www.ualberta.ca/medicine/about/people/michael-houghton (office).

HOUK, Kendall N., AB, MS, PhD, FRSC; American chemist and academic; *Saul Winstein Chair in Organic Chemistry, University of California at Los Angeles;* b. 27 Feb. 1943, Nashville, Tenn.; ed Harvard Univ.; Instructor, Harvard Extension School 1966–68; Asst Prof., Louisiana State Univ. 1968–72, Assoc. Prof. 1972–75, Prof. 1975–80; Visiting Prof., Princeton Univ. 1974–75; Prof., Univ. of Pittsburgh 1980–85; Prof. of Chem., UCLA 1986–87, Distinguished Prof. of Chem. 1987–, Chair. 1991–94, Saul Winstein Chair in Organic Chem. 2009–, mem. UCLA Molecular Biology Inst. 2010–; Dir NSF Chem. Div. 1988–90; Visiting Lecturer at numerous univs, including Lady Davis Fellow and Visiting Prof., Technion (Israel Inst. of Tech.) 2000; Sr Ed. Accounts of Chemical Research 2005–; mem. Int. Acad. of Quantum Molecular Science 2003–, NAS 2010; mem. Editorial Advisory Bd of several learned journals including Central European Journal of Chemistry, Chinese Journal of Chemistry, Chemical and Engineering News; Fellow, AAAS 1988, American Acad. of Arts and Sciences 2002; Hon. Dr rer. nat (Essen) 1999; ACS Akron Section Award 1983, Arthur C. Cope Scholar Award 1988, James Flack Norris Award 1991, Schroedinger Medal 1998, Richard C. Tolman Medal 1999, ACS Award for Computers in Chemical and Pharmaceutical Research 2003, ACS Arthur C. Cope Award 2010, RSC Robert Robinson Award 2012, UCLA Soc. of Postdoctoral Scholars Mentoring Award 2013, UCLA Glenn T. Seaborg Medal 2013. *Leisure interest:* cycling. *Address:* Department of Chemistry and Biochemistry, UCLA, 607 Charles E. Young Drive East, Box 951569, Los Angeles, CA 90095-1569, USA (office). *Telephone:* (310) 206-0515 (office). *Fax:* (310) 206-1843 (office). *E-mail:* houk@chem.ucla.edu (office). *Website:* www.chem.ucla.edu/houk (office).

HOUNGBÉDJI, Adrien; Benin lawyer and politician; *Leader, Parti du renouveau démocratique;* b. 5 March 1942, Aplahoué; ed Univ. of Paris; legal practice in Cotonou 1968–75; sentenced to death in absentia March 1975 after alleged involvement in attempted coup; in exile in France, Gabon and Senegal (returned after amnesty 1989); mem. Nat. Ass. 1991–, Speaker 1991–96, 1999–2003, 2015–; Prime Minister 1996–98; cand. in presidential elections 1991, 1996, 2001, 2006, 2011; Co-Pres. Africa Caribbean Pacific-European Union (ACP-EU) Jt Parl. Ass. 2001; Mayor of Porto Novo Feb.–June 2003; mem. Académie des Sciences d'Outre Mer; Founder and Leader, Parti du renouveau démocratique (PRD) 1990–. *Publication:* Il n'y a de richesse que d'hommes 2005. *Address:* Parti du renouveau démocratique, Immeuble Babo Oganla, 01 BP 1157, Porto-Novo, Benin (office). *Telephone:* 21-30-07-57 (office).

HOUNGBO, Gilbert Fossoun, BA; Togolese politician and international organization official; *President, International Fund for Agricultural Development;* b. 4 Feb. 1961, Agbandi; ed Université de Lomé, Univ. of Quebec-Trois Rivières; worked at Price Waterhouse Canada; mem. UNDP Strategic Man. Team and Dir of Finance and Admin, then Chief of Staff UNDP, New York 2003–05; Asst Sec.-Gen., Asst Admin. of UNDP and Dir of UNDP's Regional Bureau for Africa 2005–08; Prime Minister of Togo 2008–12 (resgnd); Deputy Dir-Gen. for Field Operations and Partnerships, ILO 2013–17; Pres. Int. Fund for Agricultural Devt 2017–; mem. Canadian Inst. of Chartered Accountants. *Address:* International Fund for Agricultural Development, Via Paolo di Dono, 44, 00142 Rome, Italy (office). *Telephone:* (06) 54591 (office). *Fax:* (06) 5043463 (office). *E-mail:* ifad@ifad.org (office). *Website:* www.ifad.org (office).

HOUNSOU, Djimon; Benin actor and fmr fashion model; b. 24 April 1964, Cotonou; m. Kimora Lee Simmons; one c. *Films include:* Without You I'm Nothing 1990, Unlawful Entry 1992, Stargate 1994, The Small Hours 1997, Amistad (NAACP Image Award 1998)1997, Ill Gotten Gains 1997, Deep Rising 1998, Gladiator 2000, The Middle Passage Narrator 2000, The Tag 2001, Dead Weight 2002, The Four Feathers 2002, In America (Independent Spirit Award 2004, Black Reel Award 2004) 2002, Heroes 2002, Biker Boyz 2003, Lara Croft Tomb Raider: The Cradle of Life 2003, Blueberry 2004, Constantine 2005, Beauty Shop 2005, The Island 2005, Blood Diamond (Black Reel Award 2007, NAACP Image Award 2007, Nat. Bd of Review 2006) 2006, Eragon 2006, Never Back Down 2008, Push 2009, Elephant White 2011, Baggage Claim 2013, Guardians of the Galaxy 2014, Furious 7 2015, The Legend of Tarzan 2016. *Television includes:* ER (series) 1999, Alias (series) 2003–04, Black Panther (series) 2010, Wayward Pines (series) 2016.

HOUSE, Karen Jo Elliott, BJ; American publishing executive, journalist and academic; *Senior Fellow, Belfer Center for Science and International Affairs, Kennedy School of Government, Harvard University;* b. (Karen Jo Elliott), 7 Dec. 1947, Matador, Tex.; d. of Ted Elliott and Bailey Elliott; m. 1st Arthur House 1975 (divorced 1983); m. 2nd Peter Kann 1984; one s. three d.; ed Univ. of Texas at Austin and Harvard Univ. Inst. of Politics, Cambridge, Mass; Educ. Reporter, Dallas Morning News 1970–71, with Washington, DC bureau 1971–74; Regulatory Corresp., Wall Street Journal 1974–75, Energy and Agric. Corresp. 1975–78, Diplomatic Corresp. 1978–83, Asst Foreign Ed. 1984, Foreign Ed. 1984–89; Vice-Pres. Dow Jones Int. Group 1989–95, Pres. 1995–2006, Vice-Pres. and mem. Exec. Cttee Dow Jones & Co. 2002, Sr Vice-Pres. 2002–06, Publr The Wall Street Journal 2002–06; Sr Fellow, Belfer Center for Science and Int. Affairs, Kennedy School of Govt, Harvard Univ. 2006–; Public Del., US Mission to UN 2008; Dir German-American Council 1988–, Council on Foreign Relations 1987–98, Cttee to Protect Journalists; Trustee, Boston Univ.; Chair. Bd of Trustees, RAND Corpn 2013–; Fellow, American Acad. of Arts and Sciences; Dr hc (Lafayette Coll., Pa) 1992, (Boston Univ.) 2003, (Pepperdine Univ.) 2013; Georgetown Univ. Edward Weintal Award 1980, Nat. Press Club Edwin Hood Award 1982, Univ. of Southern California Distinguished Achievement Award 1983, Pulitzer Prize in Int. Reporting for coverage of Middle East 1984, Overseas Press Club Bob Considine Award 1984, 1988, Pulitzer Prize for International Reporting 1984, Univ. of Texas Distinguished Alumnus Award 1992. *Publications include:* On Saudi Arabia: Its People, Past, Religion, Fault Lines – and Future 2012. *Leisure interest:* tennis. *Address:* Belfer Center, Kennedy School of Government, 79 John F. Kennedy Street, Cambridge, MA 02138, USA (office). *Telephone:* (609) 921-8923 (home). *Fax:* (609) 921-2041 (home). *E-mail:* karenehouse@gmail.com (home).

HOUSER, Sam; British/American computer games industry executive; *President, Rockstar Games;* b. 24 May 1971, London; s. of Walter Houser and Geraldine Moffat; ed Univ. of London, Univ. of Cambridge; started career as in-house music video dir BMG Entertainment; Head int. product devt BMG Interactive Div. –1998; Co-Founder and Pres. Rockstar Games 1998–, also Vice-Pres. Worldwide Product Development, Take-Two Interactive Software Inc. *Address:* Rockstar Games, 622 Broadway, New York, NY 10012, USA (office). *Telephone:* (646) 536-2842 (office). *Fax:* (646) 536-2926 (office). *Website:* www.rockstargames.com (office).

HOUSHIARY, Shirazeh, BA; British (b. Iranian) sculptor; b. 15 Jan. 1955, Shiraz, Iran; ed Tehran Univ., Chelsea School of Art and Cardiff Coll. of Art; sculptor at the Lisson Gallery, London; Jr Fellow, Cardiff Coll. of Art 1979–80; Prof., London Inst. 1997–; comms include Art for the World with UNICEF 2000; lives and works in London. *Address:* c/o Lisson Gallery London Ltd, 67 Lisson Street, London, NW1 5DA, England; c/o Lehmann Maupin Gallery, 540 West 26th Street, New York, NY 10001, USA. *Telephone:* (20) 7724-2739 (London); (212) 255-2923 (New York). *Fax:* (20) 7724-7124 (London). *E-mail:* info@lehmannmaupin .com. *Website:* www.lehmannmaupin.com.

HOUSLAY, Miles, BSc, PhD, FRSE, FMedSci, CBiol; British biochemist, molecular pharmacologist and academic; *Chief Scientific Officer, Mironid Ltd;* b. 20 June 1950; m. Rhian Houslay; ed The Grammar School, Brewood, Staffs., Univ. Coll., Cardiff, King's Coll., Cambridge; ICI Postdoctoral Research Fellow, Univ. of Cambridge 1974–76, Research Fellow, Queen's Coll. 1975–76; Lecturer in Biochemistry, UMIST 1976–82, Reader 1982–84; Prof., Gardiner Chair of Biochemistry, Univ. of Glasgow 1984–2011; Prof. (part time), Chair of Pharmacological Innovation, King's Coll. London 2011–; Prof. (part time), Strathclyde Inst. of Pharmacology and Biomedical Sciences, Univ. of Strathclyde 2012–15; Burroughs Wellcome Fund Visiting Prof. (USA) in Basic Medical Sciences 2000; CEO, BioGryffe Consulting Ltd 2011–; Chief Scientific Officer, Mironid Ltd 2015–; Co-founder BioTheryX Inc., USA, Chair. Scientific Advisory Bd 2009–15; Ed.-in-Chief, Cellular Signalling 1987–2014; Deputy Chair. Editorial Bd Biochemical Journal 1983–86; mem. Editorial Bd Progress in Growth Factor Research 1988–93; external assessor, Univ. of Malaysia 1991–95; Pres. Conferences Jacques Monod (France) 1998; Chair. Gordon Research Conf. on Cyclic Nucleotide Phosphodiesterases 1998; mem. Cttee Biochemical Soc. 1982–86; mem. MRC Cell Bd 1989–94, Chair. MRC Cell Bd Research Grant Cttee A 1990–92, British Heart Foundation Research Grant Panel 1996–98; mem. Scottish Home and Health Dept Research Cttee 1991–94, Wellcome Trust Biochemistry Cell Biology Grant Panel 1996–2000, Scientific Advisory Bd Celgene Corpn, USA 2002–05, Scientific Advisory Bd Fission Pharmaceuticals, USA 2007–11; Selby Fellow, Australian Royal Soc. 1984; Trustee, British Heart Foundation 1996–2000; Fellow, Royal Soc. of Biology; Hon. Sr Research Fellow, California Metabolic Research Foundation, La Jolla, USA 1980–91; Colworth Medal, Biochemical Soc. 1985, Joshua Lederberg Society Prize, Celgene Corpn 2012. *Publications:* Dynamics of Biological Membranes; more than 450 scientific articles. *Leisure interests:* walking, music, driving. *E-mail:* miles .houslay@glasgow.ac.uk (office). *Website:* www.mironid.com/management (office).

HOUTHI, Muhammad Ali al-; Yemeni military officer; *President, Revolutionary Committee of Yemen;* b. 14 July 1979, Sa'dah; part of group of mil. field commdrs which seized control of Yemeni capital Sana'a, Sept. 2014; apptd Pres. Revolutionary Cttee of Yemen 2015–. *Address:* Revolutionary Committee of Yemen, Sana'a, Yemen (office).

HOVE, Andrew C. (Skip), Jr, BS; American banker and financial services industry executive; *Chairman, Great Western Bancorp, Inc.;* b. 9 Nov. 1934, Minden, Neb.; s. of Andrew C. Hove and Rosalie Vopat; m. Ellen Matzke 1956; one s. two d.; ed Univ. of Nebraska and Univ. of Wisconsin Grad. School of Banking; served in USN 1956–60, Neb. Nat. Guard 1960–63; Officer, Minden Exchange Bank & Trust Co. 1960–81, Chair. and CEO 1981–90, Vice-Chair. then Acting Chair. 1990–2001; Treas., City of Minden 1962–74, Mayor of Minden 1974–82; Vice-Chair. Federal Deposit Insurance Corpn 1990–2001 (Acting Chair. three times); apptd Sr Advisor to Chair. and CEO, Promontory Financial Group LLC 2009, now mem. Advisory Bd; mem. Bd of Dirs Great Western Bancorp, Inc. 2014–, Chair. 2015–; mem. Bd of Dirs Federal Home Loan Bank of Topeka. *Address:* Great Western Bancorp, Inc., 100 North Phillips Avenue, Sioux Falls, SD 57104, USA (office). *Telephone:* (605) 334-2548 (office). *Website:* www.greatwesternbank.com (office).

HOVERS, Joannes Coenradus Maria, PhD; Dutch business executive; b. 29 July 1943, Beek; m. Ineke van der Heijde 1971; three s.; ed Michiel Lyceum, Geleen, Tilburg Univ.; with Océ NV 1967–76, Chair. Bd of Exec. Dirs 1998; Chair. Man. Bd Teewen Group (bldg materials), later Chair. Man. Bd Synres (synthetic resins) 1976–83; fmr Chair. of Exec. Bd Nederlandsche Apparatenfabriek NV; mem. Man. Bd Stork NV 1983–88, Exec. Vice-Pres. Man. Bd 1988–89, CEO Man. Bd 1989–98; Chair. Comm. of Int. Econ. Relations; Supervisory Dir De Nederlandsche Bank NV, Hoechst AG, Koninklijke Grolsch NV, Ericsson Telecommunicatie BV; Dir Asiarim Corpn July–Oct. 2011; mem. Supervisory Bd TIAS Training Inst., Gooi-Noord Regional Hosp.; Asscn of European Man. Publrs Award 1973.

HOVHANNISYAN, Raffi K. Richardi, BA, MALD, JD; Armenian (b. American) politician; *Chairman, Zharangutyun Kusaktsutyun (ZhK—Heritage Party);* b. 20 Nov. 1959, Fresno, Calif., USA; eldest s. of Prof. Richard Hovhannisyan and Dr Vartiter Hovhannisyan; m. Armenouhi Hovhannisyan; four s. one d.; ed Georgetown Univ. Law Center, Univ. of California, Berkeley and Los Angeles, Fletcher School of Law and Diplomacy, Tufts Univ., USA; Lecturer in Armenian History, Tufts Univ. 1981–82; fmr Int. Lawyer and Civil Litigator, Hill, Farrer and Burrill, Whitman & Ransom, Stroock & Stroock & Lavan, and Coudert Brothers 1985–89; Founder and Dir Armenian Bar Asscn 1989–90; Project Dir, Armenian Ass. of America Earthquake Relief 1990–91; first Minister of Foreign Affairs, Repub. of Armenia 1991–92; Founding Dir Armenian Centre for Nat. and Int. Studies, Yerevan 1993–; Chief, Dept of Information and Publications March–April 1998; Exec. Chair. 'Hayastan' All-Armenian Fund 1998; mem. Parl. and Chair. Zharangutyun Kusaktsutyun (ZhK—Heritage Party) 2007–; took part in public hunger strike in Freedom Square, Yerevan in protest against Pres. Serzh Sargsyan and his govt March 2011; runner-up cand. in presidential election Feb. 2013; relinquished US citizenship to be eligible to become an Armenian citizen 2001; Justin Turner Prize for Outstanding Honours Thesis. *Publications:* numerous treatises, monographs, essays and articles in Armenian, Russian, American, European and Middle Eastern publs. *Address:* Zharangutyun Kusaktsutyun (Heritage Party), 0002 Yerevan, Moskovyan poghots 31, Armenia (office). *Telephone:* (10) 53-69-13 (office). *Fax:* (10) 53-26-97 (office). *E-mail:* office@heritage.am (office). *Website:* www.heritage.am (office).

HOWAI, Larry, BSc; Trinidad and Tobago accountant and politician; m. Anu Howai; ed Univ. of the West Indies; CEO First Citizens Bank 1996–2012; Minister of Finance and the Economy 2012–15; fmr Chair. Nat. Gas Co.; fmr Pres. Bankers Asscn of Trinidad and Tobago; fmr Dir of numerous cos including Trinidad and Tobago Unit Trust Corpn, Home Mortgage Bank, Nat. Energy Corpn of Trinidad and Tobago, St Lucia Electricity Co. Man. Authority, Commonwealth Business Council Ltd; Dir United Way of Trinidad and Tobago, Habitat for Humanity, Guardian Media Ltd (fmrly Trinidad Publishing Co. Ltd) –2011; mem. Bd of Dirs ANSA Merchant Bank Ltd 2017, Caribbean Airlines Ltd –2013; fmr mem. Finance and General Purposes Cttee, Univ. of the West Indies; fmr Dir and Chair. of Audit Cttee, Guardian Media Ltd; Fellow, Inst. of Banking of Trinidad and Tobago; Caribbean Banking Excellence Award.

HOWARD, Sir David Howarth Seymour, Bt , MA, DSc; British business executive; *Chairman, Charles Stanley & Company, Stockbrokers;* b. 29 Dec. 1945, Lincoln; s. of Sir Edward Howard, Bt and Elizabeth Howarth Ludlow; m. Valerie Picton Crosse 1968; two s. two d.; ed Radley Coll., Worcester Coll., Oxford; joined Charles Stanley & Co., Stockbrokers 1967, apptd Man. Partner 1971, Man. Dir 1988, Chair. 1999, CEO –2014, Chair. (non–exec.) 2014–; Pro-Chancellor and Chair. City Univ. 2003–08; Pres., Chartered Man. Inst. 2008–10; mem. Bd of Dirs WMA (pvt. client stockbrokers trade asscn); mem. EUI Settlements Appeals Panel; mem. Sutton London Borough Council 1974–78; Common Councilman, City of London 1972–86, Alderman 1986–, Sheriff 1997–98, Lord Mayor of London 2000–01; Master, Gardeners' Co. 1990–91; Hon. Fellow, Chartered Inst. for Securities and Investment; Grand Cordon of the Order of Independence of Jordon 2001. *Leisure interest:* gardening. *Address:* Office of the Chairman, Charles Stanley & Co. Ltd, 25 Luke Street, London, EC2A 4AR, England (office). *Telephone:* (20) 7739-8200 (office). *Fax:* (20) 7739-7798 (office). *E-mail:* info@charles-stanley.co.uk (office). *Website:* www.charles-stanley.co.uk (office).

HOWARD, James Kenneth (Ken), OBE, RA, RWS, RWA, ARCA, PPNEAC; British painter; *Professor of Perspective, Royal Academy of Arts;* b. 26 Dec. 1932, London; s. of Frank Howard and Elizabeth Howard; m. 1st Ann Popham (divorced 1974); m. 2nd Christa Gaa (née Köhler; died 1992); m. 3rd Dora Bertolutti 2000; ed Kilburn Grammar School, Hornsey School of Art, Royal Coll. of Art; British Council Scholarship to Florence 1958–59; taught in various London art schools 1959–73; Official Artist for Imperial War Museum, NI 1973, 1978; painted for British Army in NI, Germany, Cyprus, Oman, Hong Kong, Brunei, Nepal, Canada, Norway, Belize, Beirut 1973–83; Prof. of Perspective, Royal Acad. of Arts 2004–; works in public collections including Plymouth City Art Gallery, Ulster Museum, Imperial War Museum, Nat. Army Museum, Hove City Art Gallery, Guildhall Art Gallery; comms for UN, BAOR, Stock Exchange, London, States of Jersey, Banque Paribas, Drapers Co., Royal Hosp. Chelsea, Richard Green 2003; Pres. NEAC 1998–2003; Hon. mem. Royal Inst. of Oil Painters, Royal Soc. of British Artists, Soc. of Graphic Artists 2011; First Prize Lord Mayor's Art Award 1965, Hunting Group Award 1982, Sparkasse Karlsruhe 1983, Prizewinner John Moores 1978, Annual Critics' Prize, New English Art Club 2000. *Publications:* The Paintings of Ken Howard 1992, Ken Howard: A Personal Viewpoint 1998 (revised 2014), Light and Dark: an Autobiography 2011, Ken Howard: Switzerland 2013. *Leisure interests:* opera, cinema. *Address:* St Clements Studio, Paul Lane, Mousehole, Cornwall, TR19 6TR; 8 South Bolton Gardens, London, SW5 0DH, England (home); 6262 Canareggio, Venice, Italy (home). *Telephone:* (1736) 731596 (Cornwall) (home); (20) 7373-2912 (London) (home); (41) 5202277 (Italy) (home). *Fax:* (20) 7244-6246 (home).

HOWARD, Hon. John Winston, AC, LLB; Australian lawyer and fmr politician; b. 26 July 1939, Sydney, NSW; s. of Lyall Falconer Howard and Mona Jane Howard; m. Alison Janette Parker 1971; two s. one d.; ed Univ. of Sydney; solicitor to Supreme Court, NSW 1962; Partner, Sydney solicitors' firm 1968–74; Liberal MP for Bennelong, NSW, Fed. Parl. 1974–2007; Minister for Business and Consumer Affairs 1975–77, Minister Assisting Prime Minister 1977, Fed. Treas. 1977–83; Deputy Leader of Opposition 1983–85, Leader 1985–89; Shadow Minister for Industrial Relations, Employment and Training, Shadow Minister Assisting the Leader on the Public Service and Chair. Manpower and Labour Market Reform Group 1990–95; Prime Minister of Australia 1996–2007; mem. State Exec., NSW Liberal Party 1963–74; Vice-Pres., NSW Div., Liberal Party 1972–74; Fed. Parl. Leader Liberal Party 1985–89, 1995–2007; Order of Merit 2012, Grand Cordon, Order of the Rising Sun (Japan) 2013; US Presidential Medal of Freedom 2009. *Leisure interests:* reading, cricket, tennis. *Address:* GPO Box 36, Sydney, NSW 2001, Australia.

HOWARD, Sir Michael Eliot, Kt, OM, CH, CBE, MC, MA, DLitt, FBA, FRHistS; British historian and academic; *Regius Professor Emeritus of Modern History, University of Oxford;* b. 29 Nov. 1922, London; s. of Geoffrey Eliot Howard and Edith Howard (née Edinger); civil pnr Mark James; ed Wellington Coll., Christ Church, Oxford; served in army 1942–45; Asst Lecturer, Lecturer in History, King's Coll., London 1947–53; Lecturer, Reader in War Studies, Univ. of London 1953–63; Prof. of War Studies, Univ. of London 1963–68; Fellow in Higher Defence Studies, All Souls Coll., Oxford 1968–77; Chichele Prof. of the History of War, Univ. of Oxford 1977–80; Regius Prof. of Modern History, Univ. of Oxford 1980–89, Prof. Emer. 1989–; Robert A. Lovett Prof. of Mil. and Naval History, Yale Univ. 1989–93; Leverhulme Lecturer 1996; Lee Kuan Yew Distinguished Visitor, Nat. Univ. of Singapore 1996; Founder and Pres. Emer. Int. Inst. for Strategic Studies; mem. The Literary Soc. (Pres. –2004); Foreign mem. American Acad. of Arts and Sciences; Hon. Fellow, Oriel Coll., Oxford 1990; Hon. Student Christ Church 1990; Order of Merit; Hon. LittD (Leeds) 1979; Hon. DLitt (London) 1988; Duff Cooper Memorial Prize 1961, Wolfson Foundation History Award 1972, NATO Atlantic Award 1989, Chesney Memorial Gold Medal, Royal United Services Inst., Samuel Eliot Morison Prize, Soc. for Mil. History 1992, Paul Nitze Award, Center for Naval Analysis 1994, Political Book Prize, Friedrich Ebert Stiftung 2002. *Publications include:* The Coldstream Guards 1920–1946 (with John Sparrow) 1951, Disengagement in Europe 1958, Wellingtonian Studies 1959, The Franco-German War 1961, The Theory and Practice of War 1965, The Mediterranean Strategy in the Second World War 1967, Studies in War and Peace 1970, Grand Strategy, Vol. IV (in UK History of Second World War) 1972, The Continental Commitment 1973, War in European History 1976, Clausewitz on War (trans. with Peter Paret) 1976, War and the Liberal Conscience 1978, Restraints on War (ed.) 1979, The Causes of Wars 1983, Clausewitz 1983, Strategic Deception: British Intelligence in the Second World War 1990, The Lessons of History (essays) 1991, The Oxford History of the Twentieth Century (co-ed. with W. R. Louis) 1998, The Invention of Peace 2000, The First World War 2001, Captain Professor: A Life in War and Peace 2006, Liberation or Catastrophe?: Reflections on the History of the Twentieth Century 2007. *Leisure interests:* music, gardening. *Address:* The Old Farm, Eastbury, Hungerford, Berks., RG17 7JN, England (home). *Telephone:* (1488) 71387 (home). *Fax:* (1488) 71387 (home). *E-mail:* michaelhoward@xlninternet.co.uk (home).

HOWARD, Adm. Michelle Janine, MS; American naval officer; *Vice-Chief of Naval Operations;* b. 30 April 1960, March Air Force Base, Riverside County, Calif.; d. of Nick Howard and Philippa Howard; m. Wayne Cowles; ed US Naval Acad., US Army Command and General Staff Coll.; served aboard USS Hunley 1982–87, USS Lexington 1987–90, Chief Engineer, USS Mount Hood 1990–92, served in Operations Desert Shield and Desert Storm, Persian Gulf War, First Lt, USS Flint 1992–95, Exec. Officer, USS Tortuga 1996–98, Commdr, USS Rushmore 1999–2001 (first African-American woman to command a ship in US Navy), Action Officer J-3, Global Operations, Readiness on Jt Staff 2001–03, Exec. Asst to Jt Staff Dir of Operations 2003–04, Commdr, Amphibious Squadron Seven 2004–05, Deputy Dir N3 on OPNAV Staff 2005–06, promoted to Rear Adm. (lower half) 2007, Sr Mil. Asst to Sec. of the Navy 2007–09, Commdr, Expeditionary Strike Group Two 2009–10, Maritime Task Force Commdr for BALTOPS 2010, promoted to Rear Adm. 2010, Chief of Staff to Dir for Strategic Plans and Policy, J-5, Jt Staff 2010–12, promoted to Vice-Adm. 2012, Deputy Commdr, US Fleet Forces Command 2012–13, Vice-Chief of Naval Operations 2014–, promoted to Adm. 2014 (first woman to be apptd four-star adm. in USN history); fmr Action Officer and USN Liaison to Defense Advisory Cttee on Women in Military Services Bureau of Personnel; Capt. Winifred Collins Award, Sec. of the Navy/Navy League 1987, Women of Color STEM Career Achievement Award 2008, Dominion Power Strong Men and Women Excellence in Leadership Award 2009, USO Military Woman of the Year 2011, NAACP Chairman's Award 2013. *Address:* Office of the Vice-Chief of Naval Operations, 2000 Navy Pentagon, Washington, DC 20350-1200, USA (office). *Website:* www.navy.mil/cno (office).

HOWARD, Ron; American film director, film producer and actor; *Principal, Imagine Entertainment;* b. 1 March 1954, Duncan, Okla; s. of Rance Howard and Jean Howard; m. Cheryl Alley 1975; two s. two d.; ed Univ. of Southern Calif. and Los Angeles Valley Coll.; Co-founder and Prin. Imagine Entertainment 1986–; National Medal of Arts 2003, American Soc. of Cinematographers Board of Governors Award 2007, Milestone Award, Producers Guild of America (with Brian Grazer) 2009. *Films directed include:* Night Shift 1982, Splash 1984, Cocoon 1985, Gung Ho 1986, Return to Mayberry 1986, Willow 1988, Parenthood 1989, Backdraft 1991, Far and Away (also co-producer) 1992, The Paper 1994, Apollo 13 1995 (Outstanding Directorial Achievement in Motion Picture Award from Directors' Guild of America (DGA) 1996), How the Grinch Stole Christmas 2000, A Beautiful Mind (Acad. Awards for Best Dir and Best Film (producer) 2002, DGA Best Dir Award 2002) 2001, The Missing 2003, Cinderella Man 2005, The Da Vinci

Code 2006, Frost/Nixon 2008, Angels & Demons 2009, The Dilemma 2011, Rush 2013, Made in America (documentary) 2013, In the Heart of the Sea 2015, The Beatles: Eight Days a Week - The Touring Years (documentary) 2016, Inferno 2016. *Film appearances include:* The Journey 1959, Five Minutes to Live 1959, Music Man 1962, The Courtship of Eddie's Father 1963, Village of the Giants 1965, Wild County 1971, Mother's Day, American Graffiti 1974, The Spikes Gang, Eat My Dust 1976, The Shootist 1976, More American Graffiti 1979, Leo and Loree (TV), Act of Love 1980, Skyward 1981, Through the Magic Pyramid (Dir, exec. producer) 1981, When Your Lover Leaves (co-exec. producer) 1983, Return to Mayberry 1986, Ransom 1996, Ed TV 1999. *Television includes:* The Andy Griffith Show (series) 1960–68, The Smith Family (series) 1971–72, Happy Days (series) 1974–80, Arrested Development (series narrator) 2003–13, and many other TV appearances. *Address:* Imagine Entertainment, 9465 Wilshire Blvd, Beverly Hills, CA 90212 (office); Creative Artists Agency, 2000 Avenue of the Stars, Los Angeles, CA 90067, USA (office). *Website:* www.imagine-entertainment.com (office).

HOWARD OF LYMPNE, Rt Hon. Baron (Life Peer), cr. 2010, of Lympne in the County of Kent; **Michael Howard,** PC, CH, QC; British politician and barrister; b. (Michael Hecht), 7 July 1941, Gorseinon, NW Swansea, Wales; s. of Bernard Howard (originally Hecht, name anglicized from Romanian 1947) and Hilda Howard (née Kershion); m. Sandra Clare Paul 1975; one s. one d. one step-s.; ed Llanelli Grammar School, Peterhouse Coll., Cambridge; Pres. Cambridge Union 1962; called to Bar, Inner Temple 1964, Master of the Bench of Inner Temple 1992; Jr Counsel to the Crown (Common Law) 1980–82; a Recorder 1986–; Conservative Parl. cand., Liverpool (Edge Hill) 1966, 1970; Chair. Bow Group 1970–71; MP for Folkestone and Hythe 1983–2010; Parl. Pvt. Sec. to Solicitor-Gen. 1984–85; Under-Sec. of State, Dept of Trade and Industry, Minister for Corp. and Consumer Affairs 1985–87; Minister of State, Dept of the Environment 1987–88, Minister of Water and Planning 1988–90; Sec. of State for Employment 1990–92, for the Environment 1992–93, Home Sec. 1993–97; Opposition Front-Bench Spokesman on Foreign and Commonwealth Affairs 1997–99; Shadow Chancellor of the Exchequer 2001–03; Leader of the Conservative Party and Leader of the Opposition 2003–05; mem. House of Lords Appointments Comm. 2010–; Chair. Advisory Bd Diligence, Europe 2006–; Chair. (non-exec.) Northern Racing Ltd, Luup Ltd; Deputy Chair. (non-exec.) Entrée Gold Inc.; Dir, Luup International Ltd; Dir (non-exec.) Helphire Group PLC, Orca Exploration Group Inc., Global Switch (UK) Ltd; Hon. Patron Univ. Philosophical Soc. 2007–. *Leisure interests:* watching football and films, reading, walking. *Address:* House of Lords, Westminster, London, SW1A 0PW (office); Diligence, Inc., 10th Floor, One Canada Square, Canary Wharf, London, E14 5AB, England (office). *Telephone:* (20) 7219-5353 (office); (20) 7516-0007 (office). *Fax:* (20) 7516-0004 (office); (20) 7219-5979 (office). *E-mail:* london@diligence.com (office); howardm@parliament.uk (office); webcontact@michaelhoward.org. *Website:* www.diligence.com (office); www.parliament.uk/biographies/lords/lord-howard-of-lympne/82; www.michaelhoward.org.

HOWARTH, Elgar, ARAM, DMus, FRCM, FRNCM; British musician (trumpet), conductor and composer; b. 4 Nov. 1935, Cannock, Staffs.; s. of Oliver Howarth and Emma Wall; m. Mary Bridget Neary 1958; one s. two d.; ed Eccles Grammar School and Manchester Univ./Royal Northern Coll. of Music (jt course); orchestral player 1958–70; Chair. Royal Philharmonic Orchestra 1968–70; Prin. Guest Conductor, Opera North 1985–88; freelance orchestral conductor 1970–; Musical Adviser and Conductor, Grimethorpe Colliery Brass Band 1972–; apptd Dir of Brass Ensembles, Royal Acad. of Music 2011, now Consultant in Brass Chamber Music; Fellow, Welsh Coll. of Music and Drama; Hon. FRNCM 1999; Hon. FRCM 2001, Univ. Coll. Salford; Hon. DUniv (Cen. England, York); Hon. DMus (Keele) 1996, (York) 2000; Hon. DLitt (Salford) 2003; Eddison Award 1977, Olivier Award for Outstanding Achievement in Opera 1997. *Compositions include:* Trombone Concerto 1962, Trumpet Concerto 1968, Music for Spielberg 1984, Songs for BL for brass band. *Leisure interests:* hypochondria, cricket, football. *Address:* Brass Department, Royal Academy of Music, Marylebone Road, London, NW1 5HT, England (office). *Website:* www.ram.ac.uk (office).

HOWATCH, Susan, LLB; British writer; b. 14 July 1940, Leatherhead, Surrey; d. of G. S. Sturt and Ann Sturt; m. Joseph Howatch 1964 (separated 1975); one d.; ed Sutton High School, King's Coll., London; emigrated to USA 1964, lived in Ireland 1976–80, returned to UK 1980; first book published 1965; Fellow, King's Coll. London 1999–; f. Starbridge Lectureship in Theology and Natural Science Univ. of Cambridge 1992; Winifred Mary Stanford Memorial Prize 1991; Hon. DLit (Hope Coll., Mich., USA) 2012. *Publications:* novels: The Dark Shore 1965, The Waiting Sands 1966, Call in the Night 1967, The Shrouded Walls 1968, April's Grave 1969, The Devil on Lammas Night 1970, Penmarric 1971, Cashelmara 1974, The Rich are Different 1977, Sins of the Fathers 1980, The Wheel of Fortune 1984, Glittering Images 1987, Glamorous Powers 1988, Ultimate Prizes 1989, Scandalous Risks 1991, Mystical Paths 1992, Absolute Truths 1994, A Question of Integrity (revised title: The Wonder Worker) 1997, The High Flyer 1999, The Heartbreaker 2003. *Leisure interest:* theology. *Address:* Aitken Alexander Associates Ltd, 18–21 Cavaye Place, London, SW10 9PT, England (office). *Telephone:* (20) 7373-8672 (office). *Fax:* (20) 7373-6002 (office). *E-mail:* reception@aitkenalexander.co.uk (office). *Website:* www.aitkenalexander.co.uk (office).

HOWDEN, Timothy Simon; British business executive; b. 2 April 1937, London; s. of Phillip Alexander Howden and Rene Howden; m. 1st Penelope Mary Howden 1958 (divorced 1984); two s. one d.; m. 2nd Lois Chesney 1999; ed Tonbridge School; 2nd Lt, RA 1955–57; Factory Man., Floor Treatments, SA, then Sales, UK 1957–62; on staff of Reckitt & Colman in France, FRG and UK, ending as Dir Reckitt & Colman Europe 1962–73; Dir RH.M. Flour Mills 1973–75, Man. Dir RH.M. Foods Ltd 1975–80, Chair. and Man. Dir British Bakeries Ltd 1980–85, Planning Dir RH.M. PLC 1985–89, Man. Dir RH.M. PLC 1989–92; Group Chief Exec. for Europe, The Albert Fisher Group 1992–96, CEO for N America 1996–97; Chair. Zwetshoot Ltd 2001–04, Benchmark Dental Holdings Ltd 2001–04; Dir (non-exec.) SSL International PLC 1994–2004, Finning International Inc. 1998–2007, Hyperion Insurance Group Ltd 2000–10; Assoc. Dir Mahendra British Telecom Ltd 2000–03. *Leisure interests:* skiing, scuba diving, tennis, sailing, opera. *Address:* Flat 72, Berkeley House, Hay Hill, London, W1J 8NT, England (home). *Telephone:* (20) 7355-1608 (home). *E-mail:* timlwe@btinternet.com (office).

HOWE, Brian Leslie, AO, AM, MA; Australian politician and academic; b. 28 Jan. 1936, Melbourne; s. of John Percy Howe and Lilian May Howe; m. Renate Morris 1962; one s. two d.; ed Melbourne Univ., McCormick Theological Seminary, Chicago; worked as Uniting Church Minister, Melbourne and Morwell, Victoria; fmr Sr Lecturer in Sociology and Chair. Dept of Social and Political Studies, Swinburne Inst. of Tech., Melbourne; joined Australian Labor Party 1961; MP for Batman 1977–96; Minister for Defence Support 1983–84, for Social Security and assisting the Prime Minister for Social Justice 1984–90, for Health, Housing and Community Services and assisting the Prime Minister for Social Justice 1990–93, for Housing, Local Govt and Community (now Human) Services 1993–94, for Housing and Regional Devt 1994–96; Deputy Prime Minister 1991–95; Minister assisting the Prime Minister for Commonwealth Relations 1991–93; Professorial Assoc. Centre for Public Policy and Dept of Social Work, Univ. of Melbourne 1996; Visiting Research Fellow, Woodrow Wilson School of Public Policy and Int. Affairs 1997, 1998; Fellow, Queen's Coll., Univ. Melbourne 2000; mem. Patrons Council of Epilepsy Foundation of Victoria. *Leisure interests:* Australian Rules football, tennis, films, reading. *Address:* 6 Brennand Street, North Fitzroy, Vic. 3068, Australia (home). *Telephone:* (3) 9489-4787 (home). *Fax:* (3) 9482-3202 (home).

HOWE, Geoffrey Michael Thomas, MA; British solicitor and business executive; b. 3 Sept. 1949, Cambridge, Cambs.; s. of Michael Edward Howe and Susan Dorothy Howe (née Allan); m. Karen Mary Webber (née Ford); two d.; ed Manchester Grammar School, St John's Coll., Cambridge; with Stephenson Harwood law firm 1971–75 (qualified as solicitor 1973); joined Clifford Chance 1975, apptd Partner, Corp. Dept 1980, Man. Partner 1989–97; Dir and Gen. Counsel, Robert Fleming Holdings Ltd 1998–2000; Dir J.P. Morgan, Fleming Overseas Investment Trust PLC 1999–2008; Chair. Railtrack Group PLC March–Oct. 2002; Dir Jardine Lloyd Thompson Group PLC 2002–, Jt Deputy Chair. 2004–06, apptd Chair. 2006, currently Chair. Nominations Cttee; Dir (non-exec.) Investec PLC 2003–10, Close Brothers Group PLC 2011– (Sr Ind. Dir 2014–); mem. Bd of Dirs Nationwide Building Society 2005–15, Chair. 2007–15. *Leisure interests:* opera, wine, paintings. *E-mail:* geoffreymt.howe@lineone.net (home).

HOWELL OF GUILDFORD, Baron (Life Peer), cr. 1997, of Penton Mewsey in the County of Hampshire; **David Arthur Russell Howell,** PC, BA; British journalist, economist and politician; b. 18 Jan. 1936, London, England; s. of Col Arthur Howell and Beryl Howell; m. Davina Wallace 1967; one s. two d.; ed Eton Coll., King's Coll., Cambridge (Foundation Scholar); Lt Coldstream Guards 1954–56; Econ. Section, HM Treasury 1959, resgnd 1960; Leader-writer, The Daily Telegraph 1960; Chair. Bow Group 1961–62; fmr Crossbow; MP for Guildford 1966–97; a Lord Commr of Treasury 1970–71; with Civil Service Dept 1970–72; Parl. Under-Sec. Dept of Employment 1971–72; Minister of State, NI Office 1972–74, Dept of Energy Jan.–Feb. 1974; Sec. of State for Energy 1979–81, for Transport 1981–83; Chair. House of Commons Foreign Affairs Cttee 1987–97, One Nation Group of Conservative MPs 1987–97, European Cttee on Common Foreign and Security Policy 1999–2000; Opposition Spokesman on Foreign and Commonwealth Affairs 2000–10, Deputy Leader of the Opposition 2005–10, Minister of State and Govt Spokesperson, FCO 2010–12; Chair. UK–Japan 2000 Group 1989–2001; Dir Conservative Political Centre 1964–66; Dir Monks Investment Trust 1992–2005, John Laing Investments PLC 1997–2002; Advisory Dir UBS-Warburg 1996–2000; Sr Adviser, Japan Central Railway Co. 2001–; European Adviser, Mitsubishi Electric BV; Adviser to Kuwait Investment Office; apptd Pres. The Royal Commonwealth Soc. 2013, Energy Industries Council 2012–15; Chair. House of Lords Int. Relations Cttee; Chair. Council of Commonwealth Socs; mem. Governing Bd Centre for Global Energy Studies; Visiting Fellow, Nuffield Coll., Oxford 1993–2001; Gov. Sadler's Wells Trust 1995–98; Trustee, Shakespeare's Globe Theatre 2000–06, Duke of Edinburgh's Commonwealth Study Conf.; Grand Cordon of the Order of the Sacred Treasure (Japan) 2001; Richards Prize 1959. *Publications include:* Principle in Practice (co-author) 1960, The Conservative Opportunity 1965, Freedom and Capital 1981, Blind Victory 1986, The Edge of Now 2000, Out of the Energy Labyrinth 2008, Old Links and New Ties 2013, Energy Empires in Collision 2016. *Leisure interests:* family life, writing. *Address:* House of Lords, Westminster, London, SW1A 0PW, England (office). *E-mail:* howelld@parliament.uk (office). *Website:* www.lorddavidhowell.com (office).

HOWELLS, Rt Hon. Kim Scott, PC, BA, PhD; British broadcaster, writer, painter and fmr politician; b. 27 Nov. 1946, Merthyr Tydfil, Wales; s. of Glanville James Howells and Joan Glenys Howells (née Edwards); m. Eirlys Howells; three c.; ed Mountain Ash Grammar School, Hornsey Coll. of Art, Cambridge Coll. of Art and Tech., Univ. of Warwick; lecturer 1975–79; Official Research Officer, Coalfield History Project, Nat. Union of Miners (NUM) 1979–82, research officer and journal ed., NUM S Wales Area 1982–89; writer and broadcaster 1986–89; Labour MP for Pontypridd 1989–2010, Opposition Spokesman on Devt and Co-operation 1993–94, for Home Affairs 1994–95, for Foreign and Commonwealth Affairs 1994–95, for Trade and Industry 1995, Parl. Under-Sec. of State for Lifelong Learning, Dept for Educ. and Employment 1997–98; Minister for Consumers and Corp. Affairs, Dept for Trade and Industry 1998–2001; Minister for Tourism, Broadcasting and Media, Dept of Culture, Media and Sport 2001–03; Minister of State for Transport 2003–04, for Further and Higher Educ. and Lifelong Learning 2004–05, for the Middle East and South Asia, FCO 2005–08; mem. Welsh Affairs Select Cttee 1989–90, mem. Environmental Select Cttee 1990–92, mem. Public Accounts Cttee 1992–93, 1993–94, Chair. Intelligence and Security Cttee 2008–10; mem. British Mountaineering Council; Hon. Fellow, Univ. of Wales Inst. Cardiff; Dr hc (Anglia Ruskin Univ.), (Univ. of Glamorgan). *Television:* Framing Wales: History of Art in Wales in the 20th Century (BBC 2) 2011. *Leisure interests:* painting, mountaineering, cycling, jazz, gardening. *Address:* 16 Tyfica Road, Pontypridd, Wales (home). *Telephone:* (1443) 402551 (home). *E-mail:* kim.howells@hotmail.co.uk (office).

HOWIE, Archibald (Archie), CBE, PhD, FRS; British research physicist and academic; *Fellow, Churchill College, University of Cambridge;* b. 8 March 1934, Kirkcaldy, Scotland; s. of Robert Howie and Margaret Marshall McDonald; m. Melva Jean Scott 1964; one s. (deceased), one d.; ed Kirkcaldy High School, Univ. of Edinburgh, California Inst. of Tech., USA, Univ. of Cambridge; ICI Research Fellow, Cavendish Lab. and Research Fellow, Churchill Coll., Cambridge 1960–61, Demonstrator in Physics, Cavendish Lab. 1961–65, Teaching Fellow and Dir of

Studies in Physics, Churchill Coll. 1961–86, Lecturer 1965–79, Reader 1979–86, Professorial Fellow 1986–2001, Pensioner Fellow 2001–, Head of Dept of Physics 1989–97; part-time consultant, Union Carbide Corpn 1977–78, World Bank China Univ. Devt Programme 1984, Norwegian Research Council 1986; Dir (non-exec.) NPL Man. Ltd 1995–2001; Pres. Royal Microscopical Soc. 1984–86, Int. Fed. of Socs for Electron Microscopy 1999–2002; Hon. FRSE 1995; Hon. Fellow, Royal Microscopical Soc. 1978, Japanese Microscopy Soc. 2003; Hon. FInstP 2015; Hon. mem. Electron Microscopy Soc. of America 1991, Chinese Electron Microscopy Soc. 2000; Hon. Prof., Univ. of York 2009–; Hon. Dr of Physics (Bologna) 1989, (Thessaloniki) 1995, (York) 2011; C.V. Boys Prize (co-recipient), Guthrie Medal, Inst. of Physics 1992, Hughes Medal (co-recipient), Royal Soc. 1988, Distinguished Scientist Award, Electron Microscopy Soc. of America 1991, Royal Medal, Royal Soc. 1999. *Publications:* Electron Microscopy of Thin Crystals (co-author) 1965 and numerous articles on electron microscopy and related subjects in scientific journals. *Leisure interest:* making wine. *Address:* Cavendish Laboratory, J J Thomson Avenue, Cambridge, CB3 0HE (office); 194 Huntingdon Road, Cambridge, CB3 0LB, England (home). *Telephone:* (1223) 337335 (office); (1223) 570977 (home). *Fax:* (1223) 363263 (office). *E-mail:* ah30@cam.ac.uk (office). *Website:* www.phy.cam.ac.uk (office).

HOXHA, Dhurata; Kosovo politician; *Minister of European Integration;* m. Visar Hoxha; two c.; ed Graceland Univ., Iowa, USA, Georgetown Univ., Washington, DC, USA; fmrly employed in Political Section, US Office (now US Embassy) in Prishtina and as Project Man. at British Embassy in Prishtina; Adjunct Prof., Coll. ESLG and American Univ. in Kosovo 2008–; Adviser to Minister of Interior 2008–11; Political Adviser to Prime Minister 2011–15; Political Adviser to Speaker of Kosovo Ass. (Parl.) 2015–16; Minister of Justice 2016–17; Minister of European Integration 2017–; mem. Partia Demokratike e Kosovës (PDK—Democratic Party of Kosovo), mem. PDK Central Presidency; mem. Women in Int. Security (WIIS), Washington, DC. *Address:* Ministry of European Integration, 10000 Prishtina, Rruga Nënë Terezë 14, Ndërtesa e Qeverisë, Kati 9, Kosovo (office). *Telephone:* (38) 20027001 (office). *E-mail:* mei@rks-gov.net (office). *Website:* www.mei-ks.net (office).

HOXHAJ, Enver; Kosovo political scientist, academic and politician; *Deputy Prime Minister;* b. 22 Feb. 1967, Prizren, Socialist Autonomous Province of Kosovo, Socialist Repub. of Serbia, Socialist Fed. Repub. of Yugoslavia; m. Remzie Hoxhaj; one s. one d.; ed Univ. of Prishtina, Univ. of Vienna, Austria; Scientific Researcher, Univ. of Vienna and Head of Research Team on the Balkans, Ludwig Boltzmann Inst. für Menschenrechte, Vienna 1996–2000; Fellow, LSE Centre for Study of Global Governance 2003–04; Founder Kosovar Research and Documentation Inst. –2004 (resgnd); mem. Partia Demokratike e Kosovës (Democratic Party of Kosovo) 2004–; mem. Kosovo Del. to negotiations on Comprehensive Settlement of Kosovo's Status 2005–07; Assoc. Prof., Dept of Political Science, Univ. of Prishtina 2006–; Minister of Educ., Science and Tech. 2008, also Head, Parl. Comm. for Educ., Culture and Youth; Minister of Foreign Affairs 2011–14, 2016–17, Deputy Prime Minister 2017–; guest lecturer at many int. univs including Univ. of Oxford, Univ. Coll. London, Johns Hopkins Univ., Columbia Univ. *Address:* Office of the Prime Minister, 10000 Prishtina, Rruga Nënë Terezë, Kosovo (office). *Fax:* (38) 211202 (office). *E-mail:* izkp.zkm@rks-gov.net (office). *Website:* www.kryeministri-ks.net (office).

HOY, Sir Christopher Andrew (Chris), Kt, MBE, BSc (Hons); British cyclist; b. 23 March 1976, Edinburgh, Scotland; m. Sarra Kemp 2010; ed George Watson's Coll., Edinburgh, Univ. of St Andrews, Univ. of Edinburgh; track cyclist representing GB team at four Olympic Games 2000, 2004, 2008, 2012, World and European Championships 1996–2012, World Cup Team 1997–2012, and Scotland Team at three Commonwealth Games, Kuala Lumpur 1998, Manchester 2002, Melbourne 2006; most successful Scottish Olympian ever; multiple World and Olympic Champion; first Briton to win three medals in a single Olympic games since Henry Taylor in 1908; most successful Olympic male cyclist of all time; raced BMX (Scotia BMX 1984–86, GT Factory BMX Team 1986–91) and was ranked 2nd in Britain, 5th in Europe and 9th in the world; sponsored by Slazenger and Kwik-Fit and competed in GB, Europe and USA; also rowed for Scottish jr team, coming second in British Championships with Grant Florence in coxless pairs 1993; also played rugby as part of his school's team; joined his first cycling club, Dunedin Cycling Club 1992–94; joined City of Edinburgh Racing Club and began concentrating on track cycling 1994–2001; set sea-level kilometre record of 1:00.711 seconds by winning gold at Athens Olympics 2004; set second fastest time ever (58.880) in attempt on world record for the kilometre May 2007; set record of 24.758 seconds for 500m flying start; World Championships: Silver Medal, Team sprint, Berlin 1999, Manchester 2000, Bronze Medal, Team sprint, Antwerp 2001, Gold Medals, 1km time trial and Team sprint, Copenhagen 2002, Bronze Medal, Team sprint, Stuttgart 2003, Gold Medal, 1km time trial, Bronze Medal, Team sprint, Melbourne 2004, Gold Medal, Team sprint, Bronze Medal, 1km time trial, Los Angeles 2005, Gold Medal, 1km time trial, Silver Medal, Team sprint, Bordeaux 2006, Gold Medals, Keirin and 1km time trial, Silver Medal, Team sprint 2007, Gold Medals, Sprint and Keirin, Silver Medal, Team sprint, Manchester 2008, Gold Medal, Keirin, Copenhagen 2010, Bronze Medal, Team sprint, Copenhagen 2010, Gold Medal, Keirin, Silver Medal, Team Sprint and Silver Medal, Sprint, Apeldoorn, Netherlands 2011, Gold Medal, Keirin and Bronze Medal, Sprint, Melbourne 2012; Commonwealth Games: Gold Medal, 1km time trial, Bronze Medal, Team sprint (with Craig MacLean and Ross Edgar), Manchester 2002, Bronze Medal, 1km time trial, Gold Medal, Team sprint (with Craig MacLean and Ross Edgar), Melbourne 2006; Olympic Games: Silver Medal, Team sprint (with Craig MacLean and Jason Queally), Sydney 2000, Gold Medal, 1km track time trial, Athens 2004, Gold Medal, Team sprint (with Jason Kenny and Jamie Staff), Gold Medal, Keirin, Gold Medal, Sprint, Beijing 2008, Gold Medal, Team sprint (with Jason Kenny and Philip Hindes), London 2012; raced for Team Athena 2001–03, Team Persil 2004, Team Wolfson Microelectronics/Miller 2005–07, Team Sky+ HD 2008–13; Amb. for 2012 Summer Olympics in London; announced retirement from competitive cycling April 2013; Hon. PhD (Edinburgh) 2005, (Heriot-Watt) 2005, (St Andrews) 2009; BBC Sports Personality Team of the Year 2000, 2008, Glenfiddich Scottish Sports Personality 2002, Edinburgh City Council Civic Reception 2002, 2007, Commonwealth Games Council Scottish Sports Personality 2003, 2004, 2005, 2007, BBC Scottish Sports Personality of the Year 2003, Radio Forth Sports Personality 2004, cyclingnews.com Track Cyclist of the Year 2005, Glasgow Sportsperson of the Year 2007, BBC Sports Personality of the Year 2008, inducted into Univ. of Edinburgh's Sports Hall of Fame 2009, The Sir Chris Hoy Velodrome built for the 2014 Commonwealth Games in Glasgow is named in his honour, BBC Lifetime Achievement Award 2014. *Publication:* Chris Hoy: The Autobiography 2009. *Address:* c/o British Cycling, Stuart Street, Manchester, M11 4DQ, England. *Telephone:* (161) 274-2000. *Fax:* (161) 274-2001. *E-mail:* info@britishcycling.org.uk; admin@chrishoy.com. *Website:* www.britishcycling.org.uk; www.chrishoy.com.

HØYBRÅTEN, Dagfinn, Cand.Polit; Norwegian politician and international organization official; b. 2 Dec. 1957, Oslo; s. of Per Høybråten and Åse Margrethe Hallen; m. Jorun Høybråten; four c.; ed Univ. of Oslo; Chair. Youth Div., Christian People's Party 1979; Political Adviser to Minister for Church and Educ. Kjell Magne Bondevik 1983–86; mem. Akershus Co. Council 1984–91; Under-Sec., Ministry of Finance 1989–90; mem. Council, Oppegård 1994–97; mem. Storting (Parl.) for Rogaland 2005–13; Leader Christian Democratic Party 2004–11; Dir Nat. Insurance Admin 1997; Minister of Health and Social Affairs 1997–2000, of Health 2001–04, of Labour and Social Affairs 2004–05; Sec.-Gen. Nordic Council of Ministers 2013–19; Commdr, Order of St Olav. *Publications include:* Pengene eller livet: Livskvalitet for alle 2009, Drivkraft 2012. *Address:* c/o Nordic Council of Ministers, Ved Stranden 18, 1061 Copenhagen K, Denmark.

HØYEM, Tom, MA; Danish politician, teacher, journalist and business executive; b. 10 Oct. 1941, Nykøbing, Falster; s. of Ove Charles Høyem and Karen Høyem; m. 1st Inge-Lise Bredelund 1969 (died 2000); one s. one d.; m. 2nd Gerlinde Martin 2002; ed Univ. of Copenhagen, Univ. of Bergen, Norway; schoolteacher 1960–64; teacher, Skt Jørgens Gymnasium 1964–80; Sr Master, Foreningen Norden, Sweden 1967–68; business exec. 1968–; co-founder, Chair. Centre Democratic Party 1973; Asst Prof. of Danish Language and Literature, Univ. of Stockholm 1975–79; Foreign corresp., Berlingske Tidende, Sweden 1975–80; headmaster Høng Gymnasium 1979; Sec. of State for Greenland 1982–87; Headmaster European School, Culham 1987–94, Munich 1994–2000, Karlsruhe 2000–15; mem. (Liberal) Karslruhe Town Council 2004–15; Co-founder European Folk High School, Møn, Denmark and of similar insts in Sicily, Austria, Ireland and Luxembourg; Leader of European Movt West Zeeland, Denmark 1980–82; election observer in Albania and Bosnia 1996; Goodwill Amb. for Copenhagen; mem. Ausländerbeirat, Munich 1997–2000; OSCE observer of elections in Bosnia, Albania, Montenegro, Ukraine and Palestine; Hon. Pres. European Inst., Luxembourg 1983; Order of Merit (Germany) 2014, Kt of the Dannebrog. *Publications include:* Avisens spiseseddel-avisens ansigt 1975, Tabloidetik i Norden 1976, Mulighedernes Samfund (co-author) 1985, Laegaest 1985, Dagens Grønland 1986, There is Something Wonderful in the State of Denmark 1987, Gud, Konge, Faedreland 1987, Nordisk i Europa 1988, From My Office 1999, Danmark 2020 (co-author) 2004. *Leisure interests:* politics, reading, golf, walking.

HOYER, Steny Hamilton; American politician; b. 14 June 1939, New York City; s. of Steen Hoyer; m. Judy Pickett (died 1997); three d.; ed Suitland High School, Md, Univ. of Maryland, College Park, Georgetown Univ. Law Center, Washington, DC; fmr intern for US Senator Daniel Brewster from Md; mem. Md State Senate for Prince George's Co. 1966–81, Pres. State Senate 1975–81 (youngest in state history); mem. Bd of Higher Educ. 1978–81; mem. US House of Reps for Md 5th Congressional Dist 1981–, Deputy Majority Whip 1987–89, Chair. Democratic Caucus 1989–94, fmr Co-Chair. (and current mem.) Democratic Steering Cttee, Chief Cand. Recruiter for House Democrats 1995–2000, House Democratic Minority Whip 2002–06, 2011–; Sr mem. House Appropriations Cttee, mem. Transportation, Treasury and Housing Sub-cttee, Labor, Health and Human Services, Educ., and Related Agencies Sub-cttee, House Majority Leader 2007–11; mem. Bd of Trustees St Mary's Coll. of Md; Democrat; Congressional Leadership Award, Epilepsy Foundation 2002. *Address:* 1705 Longworth House Office Building, Washington, DC 20515, USA (office). *Telephone:* (202) 225-4131 (office). *Fax:* (202) 225-4300 (office). *Website:* www.hoyer.house.gov (office).

HRDLIČKOVÁ, Ivana, JUDr, PhD; Czech judge; *President, Special Tribunal for Lebanon, United Nations;* ed Charles Univ.; Judge, Hradec Kralove Dist Court 1990–95, Appellate Court 1996–2003, High Court of Pardubice 2003; legal expert, Council of Europe 1992–2012; Judge of the Appeals Chamber, UN Special Tribunal for Lebanon, The Netherlands 2012–, Pres. 2015–; mem. Man. Bd CEELI Inst., Prague; mem. Int. Asscn of Women Judges. *Address:* Special Tribunal for Lebanon, POB 115, 2260 AC Leidschendam, Netherlands (office). *Telephone:* (70) 800-3400 (office). *E-mail:* ivana@hrdlickova.com (office). *Website:* www.stl-tsl.org (office); www.hrdlickova.com.

HRISTOV, Kalin, MEconSc; Bulgarian economist and politician; b. 1971, Pleven; ed Univ. of Nat. and World Economy (UNWE), Sofia; Asst Prof., Econs Dept, UNWE 1977–2000, Chief Asst Prof., Finance Dept 2001–04; Researcher, Exchange Rate Issues Project, Bank of England Sept.–Dec. 2001; Expert, Econ. Research and Forecasting Directorate, Bulgarian Nat. Bank (BNB) 1997–2001, mem. BNB Investment Cttee 2002–, Adviser to Deputy Gov. in charge of Issue Dept 2002–03, Adviser to BNB Gov. 2003–09, mem. BNB Governing Council and Deputy Gov. in charge of Issue Dept 2009–13; Minister of Finance (in caretaker govt) March–May 2013; mem. Monetary Policy Cttee, European Central Bank 2005–; Chair. Governing Council, Bulgarian Macroeconomics Asscn; mem. Governing Council, Inst. of Market Economy. *Publications:* several publs in Bulgaria and abroad on macroeconomics, monetary policy, currency and adoption of the euro. *Address:* c/o Ministry of Finance, 1040 Sofia, ul. G. S. Rakovski 102, Bulgaria.

HROISMAN, Volodymyr Borysovych; Ukrainian politician; *Prime Minister;* b. 20 Jan. 1978, Vinnytsya, Ukrainian SSR, USSR; m.; one s. two d.; ed Interregional Acad. of Personnel Man., Nat. Acad. of State Admin; locksmith, Shkoliar MP, Vinnytsya 1992–94; Commercial Dir, OKO PMP Aug.–Nov. 1994; Commercial Dir, Yunist PP pvt. enterprise 1994–2005; mem. Vinnytsya City Council from 29th electoral Dist 2002–06, Vice-Chair. Deputies' Standing Cttee on Human Rights, Rule of Law, Parl. Activity and Ethics 2002–06, Sec. of City Council and Acting Mayor Nov. 2005–March 2006, Mayor of Vinnytsya 2006–14; mem. (Blok Petra Poroshenka—Petro Poroshenko Bloc), Parl. (Verkhovna Rada), Chair. (Speaker) 2014–16; Deputy Prime Minister for Regional Policy and Minister of Regional Devt, Construction and Housing and Communal Services Feb.–Nov. 2014; Prime Minister of Ukraine 2016–; Vice-Pres. Asscn of Ukrainian Cities and Communities for Housing and Utility Infrastructure 2006–, Legal Issues Soc.; mem. Nat. Security and Defence Council of Ukraine; Order of Merit (Third Degree) 2008, (Second Degree) 2012; Kt's Cross, Order of Merit (Poland) 2011. *Address:* Office of the Cabinet of Ministers, 01008 Kyiv, vul. M. Hrushevskoho 12/2, Ukraine (office). *Telephone:* (44) 256-63-33 (office). *E-mail:* shustenko@kmu.gov.ua (office). *Website:* www.kmu.gov.ua (office).

HRUBY, Jill M., BS, MS; American engineer and laboratory director; *President and Laboratories Director, Sandia National Laboratories;* b. 16 March 1959, Defiance, Ohio; d. of Thomas J. Hruby and Joan Marie Fisher; m. Stewart Griffiths; ed Purdue Univ., Univ. of California, Berkeley; began career at Lawrence Berkeley Nat. Lab.; joined Sandia Nat. Labs 1983, held technical leadership positions in polymer and electrochemical technologies, materials synthesis, and inorganic and physical chemistry for eight years, becoming Sr Man. responsible for weapon components, micro-technologies, and materials processing, Dir Materials and Eng Sciences 2003–05, Dir Homeland Security Programs 2005–10, Vice-Pres. 2010–15, Pres. and Labs Dir (first woman to lead a nat. security lab.) 2015–, mem. Exec. Diversity Council; mem. Dept of Defense Threat Reduction Advisory Cttee; mem. NAS Bd of Chemical Science and Tech.; fmr Campus Exec. Georgia Inst. of Tech.; Distinguished Engineering Alumna Award, Purdue Univ. 2014. *Address:* Sandia National Laboratories, New Mexico, PO Box 5800, Albuquerque, NM 87185, USA (office). *Telephone:* (505) 284-2000 (office). *Fax:* (505) 844-1120 (office). *E-mail:* jmhruby@sandia.gov (office). *Website:* www.sandia.gov (office).

HRUŠOVSKÝ, Pavol, JUDr; Slovak politician; b. 9 June 1952, Veľká Maňa, Nové Zámky Dist; ed Comenius Univ., Bratislava; worked in various econ. orgs as a lawyer 1980s; Head of the Legal Dept, Jednota SD co-operative, Nitra 1989; Head of Dist Council, Nitra 1992; mem. Christian Democratic Movt (Krestanskodemokratické hnutie) 1989–, Leader 2000–09; co-opted as a Deputy of Fed. Ass. (Parl.) of Czechoslovakia 1989, elected as a Deputy of the Ass. 1990, mem. Constitutional, Foreign Relations and Mandate and Immunity Cttees; mem. Nat. Council of the Slovak Republic (Parl.) 1992–, mem. Constitutional and Mandate and Immunity Cttees, Deputy Speaker 1998–2002, 2010–11, Speaker 2002–06, 2011–12; parl. cand. for Slovak Democratic Coalition 1998, mem. of coalition 1998–99, Deputy Leader of the movt for Domestic Politics 1999–2000. *Address:* National Council of the Slovak Republic (Národná rada Slovenskej republiky), Námestie Alexandra Dubčeka 1, 812 80 Bratislava, Slovakia (office). *Telephone:* (2) 5972-1111 (office). *Fax:* (2) 5441-9529 (office). *E-mail:* pavol_hrusovsky@nrsr.sk (office). *Website:* www.nrsr.sk (office).

HRYSHCHENKO, Kostyantyn Ivanovich; Ukrainian politician and diplomatist; b. 28 Oct. 1953, Kyiv; m. Nataliya Ihorivna Hryshchenko; one d.; ed Moscow State Inst. of Int. Relations, USSR; staff mem., UN Secr., New York, USA 1976–80; various positions in Ministry of Foreign Affairs, USSR 1981–91; various positions in Arms Control and Disarmament Directorate, Ministry of Foreign Affairs, Kyiv 1992–95; Deputy Foreign Minister 1995–98; Amb. to Belgium, the Netherlands and Luxembourg, Head of Mission to NATO and Perm. Rep. to OPCW, The Hague, Netherlands 1998–2000; Amb. to USA 2000–03; Minister of Foreign Affairs 2003–05, 2010–12; Counsellor of Prime Minister 2006–07; First Deputy, Nat. Security and Defence Council (RNBO) 2008; Amb. to Russia 2008–10; Chair. UN Advisory Bd on Disarmament Matters 2003; Co-founder Republican Party of Ukraine 2004, Vice-Chair. 2004–; Vice-Prime Minister 2012–14 (resgnd); mem. Foundation Council, Geneva Centre for Security Policy 1995–98; fmr mem. Coll. of Commrs of UN Monitoring, Verification and Inspection Comm. (UNMOVIC); Order of Merit, Third Class 1998, Second Class 2003, several foreign decorations. *Address:* c/o Office of the Cabinet of Ministers, 01008 Kyiv, vul. M. Hrushevskoho 12/2, Ukraine. *E-mail:* web@kmu.gov.ua.

HRYTSENKO, Anatoliy Stepanovych, DTechSci; Ukrainian government official and political analyst; b. 1957, Cherkasy Oblast; ed Kyiv School of Higher Mil. Aviation Eng and Acad. of Armed Forces; Lecturer, Kyiv Higher School of Mil. Aviation Eng; fmr Head, Problem-Analytical Dept, Science-Research Centre, Armed Forces of Ukraine; fmr Head, Dept for Mil. Security and Construction, Nat. Scientific Research Centre for Defence Techs; Head, Analytical Apparatus, Nat. Security and Defence Council 1997–99; Pres. Center for Econ. and Political Studies 1999–2005; Minister of Defence 2005–07; cand. in presidential election 2014; mem. People's Union Our Ukraine party. *Address:* People's Union Our Ukraine, 04070 Kyiv, vul. Borychiv Tik 22A, Ukraine (office). *Telephone:* (44) 206-60-95 (office). *E-mail:* tak@ua.org.ua (office). *Website:* www.razom.org.ua (office).

HSIAO, Hsin-Huang Michael, BA, MA, PhD; Taiwanese academic; *Director, Institute of Sociology, Academia Sinica, Taiwan;* b. (Hsiao Hsin-Huang), 26 Dec. 1948, Taipei; m. Yu-Hyang Lee Hsiao; two s.; ed Nat. Taiwan Univ., State Univ. of New York at Buffalo; Assoc. Research Fellow, Inst. of Ethnology, Academia Sinica 1979–83, Research Fellow 1983–95, Distinguished Research Fellow 2011–, Chair. 1980–82, Deputy Dir 1989–94; Dir Program for SE Asian Area Studies 1996–2001; Dir Asia-Pacific Research Program 2001–02; Exec. Dir Centre for Asia-Pacific Area Studies, Academia Sinica 2003–09, Dir Inst. of Sociology 2009–; Assoc. Prof., Dept of Sociology, Nat. Taiwan Univ. 1980–84, Prof. 1984–; Sr Prof., Grad. Inst. of Sociology, Nat. SYS Univ., Kaohsiung City 2009–; Chair Prof., Coll. of Hakka Studies, Nat. United Univ. 2007–09, Coll. of Hakka Research, Nat. Cen. Univ. 2010–11, Visiting Chair Prof., Leiden Univ., The Netherlands; Visiting Prof., Ritsumeikan Univ., Japan; Int. Assoc., Inst. on Culture, Religion and World Affairs, Boston Univ. 1990–; Nat. Policy Adviser to Pres. of Taiwan 1996–2006; Hon. Sr Research Fellow, Hong Kong Inst. of Asia-Pacific Studies, Chinese Univ. of Hong Kong 1999–; Pres. Taiwanese Sociological Asscn 1992–93, Taiwan Asscn of Southeast Asian Studies 2004–09; mem. Bd of Dirs Public TV Service 1998–2001, Nat. Culture and Art Foundation 1998–2001, 2007–; mem. Nat. Unification Council 1997–2000; Councillor Nat. Council on Sustainable Devt, Exec. Yuan of Taiwan 1999–2008; Pres. Inst. of Nat. Devt 2000–02, Adviser 2002–; Councillor, Govt Reform Council, Office of the Pres. of Taiwan 2002–03; Man. Dir Asia Foundation in Taiwan 2003–; standing supervisor, Taiwan Foundation for Democracy 2003–09; mem. editorial bd several Taiwanese and int. journals; Fulbright Sr Visiting Scholar, Center for Asian Devt Studies, Boston Univ. and Fairbank Center for East Asian Research, Harvard Univ. 1983–84; Visiting Prof., Dept of Sociology and Center for Int. Studies, Duke Univ. 1988; Dr Hu Shi Visiting Chair Prof. Sinological Inst., Leiden Univ., Netherlands 1994; Distinguished Research Award, Nat. Science Council, Exec. Yuan of Taiwan 1990–91, 1992–94, Distinguished Int. Alumni Award, State Univ. of New York at Buffalo 2005. *Publications include:* more than 100 books, including Exploration of the Middle Classes in Southeast Asia (ed.) 2003, Chinese Enterprise, Transnationalism and Identity (co-ed.) 2003, Sustainable Taiwan 2011 (co-ed.) 2003, Taiwan and Southeast Asia: Go-South Policy and Vietnamese Brides (ed.) 2004, Green Blueprint: Toward Local Sustainable Development in Taiwan (in Chinese, co-ed.) 2005, Taiwan's New Paradigms (in Chinese, co-author) 2006, Asian New Democracies: The Philippines, South Korea and Taiwan Compared (ed.) 2006, Capital Cities in Asia-Pacific: Primacy and Diversity (co-ed.) 2007, Asia-Pacific Peace Watch 2008, Non-Profit Sector: Organization and Practice 2009, 2011, Rise of China: Beijing's Strategies and Implications for the Asia-Pacific 2009, Cross-Border Marriages with Asian Characteristics (co-ed.) 2009, Changing Faces of Hakka in Southeast Asia: Singapore and Malaysia (ed.) 2011, The Social History of Ethnic Groups in Taiwan (in Chinese, co-author) 2011, The Social History of Surnames and Lineages in Taiwan (in Chinese, co-author) 2011; 150 book chapters and more than 144 journal articles in the fields of sociology of devt, civil society and democracy, environmental sociology, and the middle classes in Asia-Pacific. *Leisure interests:* gardening, classical music, travel, film. *Address:* Institute of Sociology, Academia Sinica, Nankang, Taipei, Taiwan (office). *Telephone:* (2) 2652-5140 (office); (2) 2652-5068 (office); (2) 2691-3880 (home). *Fax:* (2) 2788-8911 (office); (2) 2652-5060 (office); (2) 2691-3895 (home). *E-mail:* michael@gate.sinica.edu.tw (office). *Website:* www.ios.sinica.edu.tw (office).

HSIEH, Frank Chang-ting, LLB, LLM; Taiwanese politician and diplomatist; *Representative, Taipei Economic and Cultural Representative Office in Japan;* b. 18 May 1946, Taipei; m. Yu Fang-chih; ed Nat. Taiwan Univ., Kyoto Univ., Japan; practised as attorney 1969–81; Defence Counsel in Kaohsiung Incident 1990; mem. Taipei City Council 1981–88; Co-Founder and mem. Cen. Standing Cttee, Democratic Progressive Party (DPP) 1986–96, Legislator 1989–96, Chair. Cen. Review Cttee 1996–98, DPP Vice-Presidential cand. 1996, Chair. DPP 2000–02, Jan.–March 2008; Mayor of Kaohsiung 1998–2005; Premier of Taiwan 2005–06; cand. for Mayor of Taipei 2006; DPP Presidential cand. 2008 elections; Rep., Taipei Econ. and Cultural Rep. Office in Japan 2016–. *Address:* Taipei Economic and Cultural Representative Office in Japan, No.20-2 Shirokanedai, 5-chome, Minato-ku, Tokyo 108-0071, Japan (office). *Telephone:* (3) 3280-7811 (office). *Website:* www.taiwanembassy.org/jp (office).

HSIEH, Hsiang-chuan, BS, MS, PhD; Taiwanese academic and politician; b. 12 Dec. 1944; ed Nat. Taiwan Univ., Univ. of Wisconsin, USA; Postdoctoral Fellow, Dept of Biochemistry, Florida State Univ. 1974–77; Investigator, Inst. of Dental Research, Univ. of Alabama 1977–82; Visiting Specialist, Nat. Science Council, Exec. Yuan 1982–84, Dir-Gen. Dept of Planning and Evaluation 1984–86, Dept of Life Sciences 1986, Deputy Dir-Gen. Hsinchu Science-based Industrial Park Admin 1989–96, Deputy Minister 1996–2001, Convener, Economy and Tech. Div., Nat. Policy Foundation 2003–08, Sec.-Gen. Exec. Yuan 2008–09, Gov. Fujian Prov. 2008–09; Chair. Taiwan Lottery Corpn 2010–.

HSIUNG, Ming-Ho, MA; Taiwanese business executive; *General Manager, Cathay Life Insurance Company Limited;* b. Feb. 1960; ed Univ. of Iowa, USA; apptd Pres. and Co-CEO Cathay Life Insurance Co. Ltd 2008, Vice Chair. 2017–, also, currently Dir and Gen. Man., mem. Bd of Dirs Cathay Financial Holdings Co. Ltd 2007– (fmr Exec. Vice Pres.), Cathay United Bank Co. Ltd. *Address:* Cathay Life Insurance Co. Ltd, 296 Jen Ai Road, Section 4, Taipei 106, Taiwan (office). *Telephone:* (2) 2755-1399 (office). *Fax:* (2) 2704-1485 (office). *E-mail:* service@cathaylife.com.tw (office). *Website:* www.cathaylife.com.tw (office).

HSÜ, Kenneth Jinghwa, MA, PhD; Swiss scientist, inventor and writer; *President, Kenneth Hsü IHC Technology Ltd; Professor Emeritus, ETH Zürich; Director, Kenneth Center for ZHC Development, Beijing National Institute of Geosciences;* b. (Jinghwa Hsü), 28 June 1929, China; s. of Sin-wu Hsü and Su-lan; m. 1st Ruth Grunder 1958 (deceased); two s. one d.; m. 2nd Christine Eugster 1966; one s.; m. 3rd Susan Milan 2005; ed Chinese Nat. Univ., Nanking, Ohio State Univ., Univ. of California, Los Angeles, USA and ETH, Zürich; Research Geologist and Research Assoc., Shell Devt Co., Houston, Tex. 1954–63; Assoc. Prof., State Univ. of New York, Binghamton, NY 1963–64; Assoc. Prof., Univ. of Calif., Riverside 1964–67; Prof., Swiss Fed. Inst. of Tech. (ETH), Zürich 1967–94, Prof. Emer. 1994–; Pres. Kenneth Hsü IHC Tech. Ltd, Beijing 2004–; Prof., Nanjing Univ. 2004–; Pres. Int. Asscn of Sedimentologists 1978–82; Chair. Int. Marine Geology Comm. 1980–89; Dir Kenneth Center for ZHC Devt, Beijing Nat. Inst. of Geosciences 2004–; Foreign assoc. mem. NAS, Acad. Sinica, Taiwan; Fellow, Inst. of Advanced Studies, Berlin, Germany 1995–96; Assoc. Fellow, Third World Acad. of Sciences; Hon. Prof., Chinese Acad. of Sciences, Univ. Coll. London; Hon. mem. Int. Asscn of Sedimentologists; Dr hc (Nanjing Univ.) 1994; Wollaston Medal, Geological Soc. of London; Twenhofel Medal, American Sedimentological Soc., Penrose Medal, Geological Soc. of America, President's Award, American Asscn of Petroleum Geologists, Alumnus of the Century, Nanjing Univ., Int. Writer of the Year, IBC 2003. *Publications:* Ein Schiff revolutioniert die Wissenschaft 1982, The Mediterranean was a Desert 1984, The Great Dying 1986, Challenger at Sea 1994, Geology of Switzerland 1995, Tectonic Facies Map of China 1996, Geologic Atlas of China 1998, Klima macht Geschichte 2000, Mozart in Love (in Chinese) 2003, Physics of Ledimen trilogy 2004; other books and more than 400 scientific articles. *Leisure interest:* Chinese aerophilately. *Address:* Oakcombe, Marley Common, Haslemere, Surrey, GU27 3PT, England (home). *Telephone:* (1) 3621462 (office); (1428) 641457 (home). *E-mail:* kenjhsu@aol.com (home).

HSU, Li-Teh, LLM, MPA; Taiwanese politician and business executive; *Chairman, Global Investment Holdings Co., Ltd;* b. 6 Aug. 1931, Loshan County, Honan; m.; two s.; ed Taiwan Prov. Coll. of Law and Commerce, Nat. Chengchi Univ. and Harvard Univ.; Dir Fifth Dept Exec. Yuan 1972–76; Admin. Vice-Minister of Finance 1976–78; Commr Dept of Finance, Taiwan Prov. Govt 1978–81; Minister of Finance 1981–84, of Econ. Affairs 1984–85; Chair. Lien-ho Jr Coll. of Tech., Global Investment Holding Co. Ltd 1986–88; Chair. Finance Comm. Cen. Cttee Kuomintang 1988–93; Deputy Sec.-Gen. and Exec. Sec. Policy Coordination Comm. Cen. Cttee Kuomintang 1990–93; Vice-Premier of Taiwan 1993–97; Founder and Chair. Global Investment Holdings Co., Ltd 1988–, also Chair. Prudence Venture Investment Corpn. *E-mail:* info@gih.com.tw. *Website:* www.cidc.com.tw.

HSU, Sheng-Hsiung (Rock); Taiwanese business executive; *Chairman, Compal Electronics;* ed Nat. Taiwan Normal Univ.; Chair. Compal Electronics, Inc. 1984–; Chair., Exec. Dir, Man. Dir, Gen. Man. and other sr positions in more than 30 technological cos in Taiwan, including Kinpo Electronics Inc., AcBel Polytech Inc., Cal-Comp Electronics & Communications Co., Vibo Telecom Inc. as well as China Productivity Center; Vice-Chair. Straits Exchange Foundation; Deputy Dir-Gen. Chinese Nat. Fed. of Industries; Nat. Policy Advisor under the Office of the Pres.; Chair. Chinese National Federation of Industries; Advisor, Exec. Yuan; Hon. Dir-Gen. Taiwan Electrical & Electronic Mfrs' Asscn, Importers & Exporters Asscn of Taipei; Hon. PhD (Nat. Taiwan Normal Univ.) 2008; Nat. Quality Award (Individual), Ministry of Econ. Affairs 1999, named as one of Nat. Taiwan Normal Univ.'s Outstanding Alumni for 2005, Exceptional Accomplishment Award, 7th Industrial Sustainable Excellence Awards 2006. *Address:* Compal Electronics Inc., 581 Burghardt Road, Neihu District, Taipei 11492, Taiwan (office). *Telephone:* (2) 87978588 (office). *Fax:* (2) 26585001 (office). *E-mail:* info@compal.com (office). *Website:* www.compal.com (office).

HSU, Shui-Teh, MA; Taiwanese politician; b. 1 Aug. 1931, Kaohsiung City; m. Yang Shu-hua; two s.; ed Nat. Taiwan Normal Univ., Nat. Chengchi Univ. and Japan Univ. of Educ.; official, Pingtung County Govt 1968–70, Kaohsiung City Govt 1970–75; Commr Dept of Social Affairs, Taiwan Provincial Govt 1975–79; Dir Dept of Social Affairs, Cen. Cttee, Kuomintang 1979, fmr Sec.-Gen.; Sec.-Gen. Kaohsiung City Govt 1979–82; Mayor of Kaohsiung 1982–85, of Taipei 1985–88; Minister of the Interior 1988–91; Rep. Taipei Econ. and Culture Rep. Office in Japan 1991–93; Pres. Examination Yuan 1996–2002; Hon. LLD (Lincoln Univ.) 1985. *Publications include:* The Childhood Education of Emile, My Compliments—Recollections of Those Days Serving as Kaohsiung Mayor, A Thousand Sunrises and Midnights, My Scoopwheel Philosophy, A Study of Welfare Administration for the Aged, several works on psychology and educ.

HTIN, Kyaw, MEcon; Myanma fmr teacher, writer and fmr head of state; b. 20 July 1946, Kungyangon, Hanthawaddy Prov.; s. of Min Thu Wun and Kyi Kyi; m. Su Su Lwin; ed Rangoon Arts and Science Univ., Univ. of London, UK, Arthur D. Little School of Man., Cambridge, Mass, USA; began career as teacher; worked as programmer/system analyst, Yangon Univ. Computer Centre 1970; fmr univ. teacher; held positions in Ministry of Industry, late 1970s and 1980s, becoming Deputy Dir, Foreign Econ. Relations Dept –1992 (resgnd in opposition to mil. junta); childhood friend and sr aide to democracy leader Aung San Suu Kyi (worked closely with her at offices of Nat. League for Democracy); imprisoned in Insein prison for four months for assisting Aung San Suu Kyi to travel outside Yangon 2000; Sr Exec., Daw Khin Kyi Foundation (f. by Aung San Suu Kyi) 2012; nominated as Pres. in her place by Aung San Suu Kyi (who is barred from taking up the post by the constitution); Pres. of Myanmar 2016–18 (resgnd). *Publications:* several publs under pen name Dala Ban. *Address:* c/o President's Office, Bldg 18, Nay Pyi Taw, Myanmar (office).

HU, Chunhua, BA; Chinese politician; *Vice Premier;* b. 1963, Wufeng Co., Hubei Prov.; ed Beijing Univ., CCP Cen. Cttee Central Party School; joined CCP 1983; Man., Ministry of Human Resources and Social Security, Tibet Lhasa Hotel, Tibet Autonomous Region 1985–87; Deputy Commr, Admin Office, Nyingchi, Tibet Autonomous Region 1992–95; Deputy Sec., CCP Autonomous Prefectural Cttee, Lhokha Pref., Tibet Autonomous Region 1995–97; Vice-Chair. All-China Youth Fed. 1997–2001; Commr, Standing Cttee, CCP Autonomous Regional Cttee, Tibet Autonomous Region 2001–07; First Sec., Communist Youth League of China Cen. Cttee 2007–08; Gov. Hebei Prov. (China's youngest gov.) 2008–09; Deputy Sec., Hebei CCP Provincial Cttee 2009; Sec., Inner Mongolia Autonomous Regional CCP Cttee 2009–12, Chair., Standing Cttee, Regional People's Congress, Inner Mongolia Autonomous Region 2010–12; Sec., CCP Provincial Cttee, Guangdong Prov. 2012–17; mem. State Council 2018–; Vice Premier 2018–; mem. 17th CCP Cen. Cttee 2007–12, 18th CCP Cen. Cttee 2012–17, mem. 18th CCP Cen. Cttee Politburo 2012–17; mem. 19th CCP Cen. Cttee 2017–, also mem. 19th CCP Cen. Cttee Politburo 2017–. *Address:* Chinese Communist Party Politburo, Quanguo Renmin Diabiao Dahui, Zhongguo Gongchan Dang, 1 Zhongnanhai, Beijing, People's Republic of China. *Website:* cpc.people.com.cn (office).

HU, Fuguo; Chinese politician and engineer; b. Oct. 1937, Changzi Co., Shanxi Prov.; m. Chang Genxiu; two s.; ed Fuxin Mining Coll.; Dir Xishan Coal Mining Admin. of Shanxi Prov., 1978–82, Gov. (a.i.) of Shanxi Prov. 1992–93; Sec. CCP 6th Shanxi Prov. Cttee 1993–99; Chair. CCP 7th Shanxi Prov. Cttee 1994; Vice-Minister of Coal Industry 1982–88; Vice-Minister of Energy 1988; mem. State Econ. Examination Cttee 1983; mem. 14th CCP Cen. Cttee 1992–97, 15th CCP Cen. Cttee 1997–2002; Pres. China Asscn of Poverty Alleviation & Devt.

HU, Houkun, (Ken Hu), BSc; Chinese business executive; b. 1967; ed Huazhong Univ. of Science and Tech.; joined Huawei 1990, served successively as Pres. of Marketing and Sales Dept in China, Pres. of Latin America Region, Pres. of Global Sales Dept, Chief Sales and Service Officer, Chief Strategy and Marketing Officer, Chair. Corp. Global Cyber Security Cttee, Chair. Huawei USA, Corp. Exec. Vice-Pres., Chair. Human Resources Cttee, Deputy Chair. and Rotating CEO, Huawei Technologies Co. Ltd April–Sept. 2013, Oct. 2014–March 2015. *Address:* Huawei Technologies Co. Ltd, Bantian, Longgang District, Shenzhen 518129, People's Republic of China (office). *Telephone:* (755) 28780808 (office). *E-mail:* hwtech@huawei.com (office). *Website:* www.huawei.com (office).

HU, Huaibang, PhD; Chinese economist and banking executive; *Chairman, China Development Bank Corporation;* b. Sept. 1955, Henan Prov.; ed Shaanxi Inst. of Finance and Econs; worked at Shaanxi Inst. of Finance and Econs 1982–97; successively Vice-Prin. and Prin. China Finance Coll. 1997–2000; Deputy Gen. Man. People's Bank of China (PBC), Chengdu Br., Gen. Man. PBC, Xi'an Br. and concurrently Deputy Dir of State Admin of Foreign Exchange, Shaanxi Br. 2000–03; Dir, Working Dept of Supervisory Cttee and Commr of Discipline Inspection, China Banking Regulatory Comm. (CBRC) 2003–07; Chair. Bd of Supervisors China Investment Corpn 2007–08; Exec. Dir and Chair. Bank of Communications 2008–13; Chair. China Development Bank Corpn 2013–; Alt. mem. 18th CCP Cen. Cttee 2012–17. *Address:* China Development Bank Corpn, 29 Fuchengmenwai Street, Xicheng District, Beijing 100037, People's Republic of China (office). *Telephone:* (10) 6830-6688 (office). *Fax:* (10) 6830-6699 (office). *E-mail:* info@bcdb.com.cn (office). *Website:* www.cdb.com.cn (office).

HU, Jason Chih-chiang, DPhil; Taiwanese politician and academic; *Vice-President, Kuomintang;* b. 15 May 1948, Yungchi Co., Kirin Prov., China; m. Shirley S. Hu; one s. one d.; ed Nat. Chengchi Univ., Univ. of Southampton, Univ. of Oxford; Exec. Sec. Nat. Union of Students 1966–68; led del. to UN World Youth Asscn 1970; fmr instructor Inst. of Int. Studies, Univ. of SC, USA; taught Oxford Overseas Studies Programme 1982–83, Research Fellow, St Antony's Coll., Oxford, UK 1985; Assoc. Prof., Nat. Sun Yat-sen Univ. 1986–90; Deputy Dir Sun Yat-sen Centre for Policy Studies 1986–90; Deputy Dir First Bureau, Office of the Pres., concurrently Presidential Press Sec. 1991; Dir-Gen. Govt Information Office and Govt Spokesman 1991–96; Rep. of Taipei Econ. and Cultural Office, Washington, DC; Minister of Foreign Affairs 1997–99; Presidential Campaign Man., Kuomintang 1999–2000, Dir Cultural and Communication Affairs Cen. Comm. 2000–01, Deputy Sec.-Gen. 2001, Vice-Pres. 2014–; Mayor of Taichung City 2001–14; Dr hc (Southampton) 1997; Best Govt Spokesman Award 1993, Top Ten Chinese Award 1994, Outstanding Professional Achievement Award 1996. *Publications include:* Say Yes to Taiwan! 1997, Quiet Revolution (in Chinese) 1996; many other books in Chinese. *Address:* Kuomintang, 232–234 Bade Rd, Sec. 2, Taipei 10492, Taiwan (office). *Telephone:* (2) 87711234 (office). *Fax:* (2) 23434561 (office). *Website:* www.kmt.org.tw (office).

HU, Jia; Chinese platform diver (retd); b. 10 Jan. 1983, Wuhan, Hubei Prov.; m. Luo Xi 2013; one s.; joined Guangdong prov. team 1994, nat. team 1998; winner 10m. Platform Synchronized, World Championships, Fukuoka 2001, Grand Prix, Southern Cross 2003; winner 10m. Platform, Grand Prix, Bangkok 2000, Grand Prix, USA Diving 2001; Silver Medal 10m. Platform, Platform Synchronized, Sydney Olympics 2000; Gold Medal 10m. Platform, Athens Olympics 2004; retd from diving 2009. *Leisure interests:* music, computers, travelling.

HU, Jiangchao; Chinese business executive; *Chairman, Zhejiang Materials Industry Group Corporation;* Legal Rep., Zhejiang Southeast Electric Power Co. Ltd; Chair. Zhejiang Provincial Energy Group Corpn, currently Chair. Zhejiang Materials Industry Group Corpn. *Address:* Zhejiang Materials Industry Group Corporation, 56 West Huancheng Road, Hangzhou 310006, Zhejiang Prov., People's Republic of China (office). *Telephone:* (571) 87054509 (office). *Fax:* (571) 87054509 (office). *E-mail:* office@zjmi.com (office). *Website:* www.zjmi.com (office).

HU, Jintao; Chinese engineer and fmr head of state; b. 21 Dec. 1942, Jixi, Anhui Prov.; m. Liu Yongqing; two c.; ed Tsinghua Univ., Beijing; joined CCP 1964; postgraduate and political instructor, Water Conservancy Eng Dept, Tsinghua Univ. 1964–65, researcher 1965–68; Sec. Gansu Prov. Construction Cttee, Deputy Dir 1974–75, Vice-Chair. 1980–82; Chair. All-China Youth Fed. 1982–84; Sec. Gansu Prov. Br. Communist Youth League 1982; Sec. Communist Youth League 1982–84, First Sec. 1984–85; mem. Standing Cttee, 6th NPC, mem. Presidium and mem. Standing Cttee, CPPCC 6th Nat. Cttee 1983–98; Sec. CCP Prov. Cttee, Guizhou 1985–88, Tibet 1988–92; Vice-Pres. of People's Repub. of China (PRC) 1998–2003, Pres. 2003–13; Gen. Sec. CCP 2002–12; Vice-Chair. Cen. Mil. Comm. of PRC 1999–2002, Chair. 2005–; mem. 12th CCP Cen. Cttee 1982–87, 13th CCP Cen. Cttee 1987–92, 14th CCP Cen. Cttee 1992–97 (mem. Secr. and Standing Cttee of Politburo 1992–97), 15th CCP Cen. Cttee 1997–2002 (mem. Secr. and Standing Cttee of Politburo 1992–97, Vice-Chair. Cen. Mil. Comm. 1997–2002), 16th CCP Cen. Cttee 2002–07 (Gen. Sec. 2002–07, Vice-Chair. Cen. Mil. Comm. 2002–05, Chair. 2005–07, mem. Standing Cttee of Politburo 2002–07); Gen. Sec. 17th CCP Cen. Cttee 2007–12 (mem. Standing Cttee of Politburo 2007–12, Chair. CCP Cen. Mil. Comm. 2007–12); Pres. Cen. Party School 1993–2002. *Address:* c/o Office of the President, Great Hall of the People, West Edge, Tiananmen Square, Beijing, People's Republic of China (office). *Website:* www.gov.cn (office).

HU, Kehui; Chinese lawyer; b. Feb. 1944, Anshun, Guizhou Prov.; ed Southwest Univ. of Political Science and Law; joined CCP 1971; Chief Procurator of Guizhou Prov. People's Procuratorate 1993–98; Deputy Procurator-Gen., Supreme People's Procuratorate 1998–2009; Vice-Pres. Chinese Asscn of Public Prosecutors. *Address:* c/o Supreme People's Procuratorate, Beijing, People's Republic of China.

HU, Maoyuan; Chinese automobile industry executive; b. April 1951, Shanghai; ed Fudan Univ.; began career in automotive industry 1968; mem. CCP 1980–; Man. Dir Shanghai Tractor Factory 1983; served as Deputy Gen. Man. and Asst to Gen. Man. of Shanghai Automotive and Tractor Industry Jt Business Co., Asst to Gen. Man., Deputy Gen. Man., Vice-Pres. Shanghai Automotive Industry Corpn (SAIC), Deputy Gen. Man. Shanghai Automotive Co. Ltd and Gen. Man. Shanghai General Motors Automotive Co. Ltd, Vice-Pres. 1991–99, later Pres., Vice-Sec. Party Cttee of Shanghai SAIC (Group), Chair. and Sec. Party Cttee of SAIC (Group) 2008–14, also fmr Chair. and Sec. Party Cttee of SAIC Motor Corpn Ltd and Chair. HUAYU Automotive Systems Co. Ltd; State Model Worker, State Advanced Individual in Quality Man., Excellent Party Mem. of Shanghai Municipality, Master of Operation and Man. in Machinery Industry, CCTV Award for People of Economy. *Publication:* Dialogue with the World. *Address:* c/o SAIC Motor Corporation Ltd, 487 Weihai Road, Shanghai 200041, People's Republic of China. *E-mail:* info@saicgroup.com.

HU, Ping; Chinese government official; b. 1930, Jiaxing Co., Zhejiang Prov.; ed Jiangsu Industry Inst.; joined CCP 1950; Vice-Gov. of Fujian 1981–83; Sec. CCP Prov. Cttee Fujian 1982; Deputy Sec. CCP Prov. Cttee, Fujian 1982; Dir Fujian Cttee for Econ. Reconstruction 1983; Alt. mem. 12th CCP Cen. Cttee 1982–87; mem. 13th CCP Cen. Cttee 1987–92; Sec. CCP Prov. Cttee 1982–83; Acting Gov. of Fujian 1983, Gov. 1983–87 (removed from post); Vice-Minister, State Planning Comm. 1987–88; Minister of Commerce 1988–93; Dir Special Econ. Zones Office 1993–96; Chair. Bd of Regents, Overseas Chinese Univ. 1986.

HU, Qiheng; Chinese scientist and public official; b. 15 June 1934, Beijing; d. of Shu Wei Hu and Wen Yi Fan; m. Yuan Jian Lian 1959; one s. one d.; ed Moscow Inst. of Chemical Machinery, USSR; Dir Inst. of Automation, Academia Sinica 1980–89; Vice-Pres. Chinese Acad. of Sciences 1988–96; mem. Nat. Cttee, 8th and 9th CPPCC 1993–2003; Vice-Pres., China Asscn for Science and Tech. 1996–; Chair. Internet Soc. of China 2001–13; mem. UN Working Group on Internet Governance 2004; Visiting Research Prof., Case Western Reserve Univ., USA 1980–82; mem. Chinese Acad. of Eng; Outstanding Woman of China 1984, Award for contrib. to Nat. Hightech. Programme 863 1996. *Publications:* book chapters in Advances in Information Systems Science 1986; Processing of Pattern-Based Information, Parts I and II (with Yoh Han Pao). *Leisure interests:* reading novels, growing flowers, pets (kittens and guinea-pigs), bicycling, computer drawing. *Address:* Internet Society of China, No.13, West Chang'an Avenue, Beijing 100804, People's Republic of China. *Telephone:* (10) 66068552 (office). *Fax:* (10) 68512458 (office); (10) 66418201 (office). *E-mail:* isc@isc.org.cn (office).

HU, Qili; Chinese politician; b. Oct. 1929, Yulin Co., Shaaxi Prov.; m.; one s. one d.; ed Beijing Univ.; joined CCP 1948; Sec. Communist Youth League (CYL) Cttee, Beijing Univ. 1954; Vice-Chair. Students' Fed. 1954; mem. Standing Cttee, Youth Fed. 1958; Sec. CYL 1964, 1978; Vice-Chair. Youth Fed. 1965; purged 1967; Vice-Pres. Tsinghua Univ., Beijing 1976; Sec. CYL 1978; Chair. Youth Fed. 1979–80; mem. Standing Cttee, 5th CPPCC 1979–83; Mayor, Tianjin 1980–82; Sec. CCP Cttee, Tianjin 1980–82; Dir-Gen. Office Cen. Cttee CCP 1982–87; Vice-Chair. Cen. Party Consolidation Comm. 1983–89; mem. Presidium, 1st session 7th NPC; Vice-Minister of Electronics Industry and Machine-Building Industry 1991–93; Minister of Electronics Industry 1993–98; Deputy Head, State Leading Group for Information 1996; Chair. Song Qingling Foundation 1998; mem. 12th CCP Cen. Cttee 1982–87, 13th CCP Cen. Cttee 1987–92 (mem. Politburo 1982–89, Politburo Standing Cttee 1987–89, Sec. Secr. CCP 1982–89), mem. 14th CCP Cen. Cttee 1992–97; Vice-Chair. 9th Nat. Cttee of CPPCC 1998–2003. *Leisure interests:* tennis, cycling. *Address:* c/o Song Qingling Foundation, A12F, Zhejiang Plaza, No. 29 Anzhen Xili, Chaoyang District, Beijing, People's Republic of China (office).

HU, Shuli; Chinese journalist and media executive; *Editor-in-Chief, Caixin Media Co Ltd and Caixin Century Weekly;* b. 1953, Beijing; d. of Cao Qifeng and Hu Lingsheng; m. Miao Di 1982; ed Renmin Univ. of China; began career as Asst Ed., Reporter and Int. Ed., Worker's Daily 1982; Int. Ed. China Business Times 1992–95, Chief Reporter 1995; Founding Ed. Caijing (finance and econs magazine) 1998–2009 (resgnd); Ed.-in-Chief Caixin Media Co. Ltd and Caixin Century Weekly 2009–; Dean, School of Communication and Design, Sun Yat-sen Univ. 2009–; Knight Journalism Fellow, Stanford Univ. 1994; Fellow, China Media Project, Univ. of Hong Kong; World Press Review Int. Ed. of the Year 2003, Harvard Univ. Nieman Foundation Louis Lyons Award for Conscience and Integrity in Journalism 2007. *Publications include:* New Financial Time, Reform Bears No Romance, The Scenes Behind American Newspapers. *Address:* Caixin Media Company Limited, Floor 15/16, Tower A, Winterless Center, No.1 Xidawanglu, Chaoyang District, Beijing 100026, People's Republic of China (office). *Website:* english.caixin.com (office).

HU, Xiaolian; Chinese central banker; *Deputy Governor, People's Bank of China;* b. 1958; ed People's Bank of China Grad. School; held various positions at State Admin of Foreign Exchange, including Deputy Dir then Dir Policy Research Office, Deputy Dir Law and Regulation Dept, Deputy Dir Reserves and Man. Dept, Deputy Dir State Admin of Foreign Exchange 2001–07, Dir 2007–09; Deputy Gov. People's Bank of China 2009–; Alt. mem. 17th CCP Cen. Cttee 2007–12, 18th CCP Cen. Cttee 2012–17. *Address:* People's Bank of China, 32 Chengfang Jie, Xicheng Qu, Beijing 100800, People's Republic of China (office). *Telephone:* (10) 66194114 (office). *Fax:* (10) 66195370 (office). *E-mail:* master@pbc.gov.cn (office). *Website:* www.pbc.gov.cn (office).

HU, Heping, MEng; Chinese engineer and politician; *Governor and Communist Party Secretary, Shaanxi Province;* b. Oct. 1962, Linyi, Shandong Prov.; ed Tsinghua Univ., Univ. of Tokyo; joined CCP 1982; Assoc. Prof., Dept of Water Resources and Hydraulic Eng, Tsinghua Univ. 1996–2015, also Vice Dean, Dept of Hydraulic Eng and Head, Inst. of Water Resources, Dean, Office of Academic Affairs 2003, Vice Pres., Tsinghua Univ. 2006–07, also CCP Sec. 2008–13; Head, Org. Dept, Zhejiang Prov. CCP Cttee 2013–15; Deputy CCP Sec., Shaanxi Prov. 2015–16, CCP Sec. 2017–; Gov. of Shaanxi 2016–; alt. mem. 18th CCP Cen. Cttee 2012–17, mem. 19th CCP Cen. Cttee 2017–. *Address:* CPC Provincial Committee, Shaanxi Province, Xi'an 710000, People's Republic of China (office). *Website:* www.xa.gov.cn (office).

HU TSU TAU, Richard, PhD; Singaporean politician and business executive; *Chairman, CapitaLand Ltd;* b. 30 Oct. 1926; m. Irene Tan Dee Leng; one s. one d.; ed Anglo-Chinese School, Univ. of California, Berkeley, USA, Univ. of Birmingham, UK; Lecturer in Chemical Eng, Univ. of Manchester, UK 1958–60; joined Shell (Singapore and Malaysia) 1960, Dir Marketing and Gen. Man. Shell (KL) 1970, with Shell Int. Petroleum Co., Netherlands 1973, Chief Exec. Shell Cos (Malaysia) 1974, Chair. and Chief Exec. Shell Cos (Singapore) 1977, Chair. 1982; Man. Dir The Monetary Authority of Singapore and Man. Dir Govt of Singapore Investment Corpn Pte. Ltd 1983–84, Chair. The Monetary Authority of Singapore, Chair. Bd of Commrs of Currency 1985; elected MP (People's Action Party) 1984; Minister for Trade and Industry Jan.–May 1985, for Health 1985–87, for Finance 1985–2001, of Nat. Devt 1992; Chair. CapitaLand Ltd 2004–, Fullerton Financial Holdings Pte Ltd; mem. Bd of Dirs Govt of Singapore Investment Corpn (GIC) Real Estate Pte Ltd (fmr Chair.), Buildfolio; Chancellor, Singapore Management Univ. 2002–10. *Leisure interests:* golf, swimming. *Address:* CapitaLand Ltd, 168 Robinson Road, #30-01, Capital Tower, Singapore 068912 (office). *Telephone:* 68233200 (office). *Fax:* 68202202 (office). *E-mail:* ask-us@capitaland.com (office). *Website:* www.capitaland.com (office).

HUA, Junduo; Chinese diplomatist and government official; b. 5 April 1942; m. Zhao Shuyun; mem. staff, Foreign Affairs Office of State Council, Beijing 1965–69; mem. staff, Friendship Asscn with Other Countries, Beijing 1969–72; mem. staff, Foreign Affairs Inst. 1972–76; attaché, Embassy in Australia 1976–80, counsellor 1986–89; Deputy Chief, later Chief of Division, Ministry of Foreign Affairs 1980–86, Deputy Head of Dept 1986–89; Amb. to Fiji 1991; Amb. to India 2001–04; Commr-Gen. World Expo 2010 Shanghai China 2006.

HUA, Qingshan, MEng; Chinese economist and banking executive; ed Hunan Univ.; served successively at Nat. Gen. Labour Union, Dept of Labour and Gen. Office of State Council 1979–94; Asst to Pres. of Bank of China 1994–98, Deputy Pres. 1998–2007, Exec. Dir 2004–07, Dir (non-exec.) Bank of China Hong Kong (Holdings) Ltd 2002–07; joined Bank of Communications June 2007, Chair. Bd of Supervisors Aug. 2007–14. *Address:* c/o Bank of Communications, 188 Yin Cheng Zhong Lu, Shanghai 200120, People's Republic of China. *E-mail:* info@bankcomm.com.

HUANACUNI MAMANI, Fernando, LLB, PhD; Bolivian lawyer, broadcaster and politician; b. 29 May 1966, La Paz; ed Univ. of San Andrés, La Paz, Zambuling Inst., Washington, DC; Producer and Co-Host Pacha Ajayu weekly programme (Channel 4 RTP) 2004–10; Dir and Presenter Taypi Uta programme (Channel 4 RTP) 2005–10; Prof., Univ. Mayor de San Andrés 2008; Lecturer, AGRUCO Univ. Center, Univ. Mayor San Simon 2010; fmr Lecturer, Simon Bolivar Andean Univ.; Chief of Protocol and Dir of Ceremonies, Ministry of Foreign Affairs (rank of amb.) 2008–14, Minister of Foreign Affairs and Worship 2017–18; Columnist, Cambio (nat. newspaper) 2012–13; mem. Movimiento al Socialismo. *Publications:* Vivir Bien/Buen Vivir Filosofía, Políticas, Estrategias y Experiencias Regionales 2010, Visión Cósmica de los Andes, Llatunka: La Sabiduría Ancestral. *Address:* c/o Ministry of Foreign Affairs and Worship, Plaza Murillo, Calle Ingavi, esq. Calle Junín, La Paz, Bolivia (office). *Telephone:* (2) 240-8900 (office). *Fax:* (2) 240-8905 (office). *E-mail:* mreuno@rree.gob.bo (office). *Website:* www.cancilleria.gob.bo (office).

HUANG, Chih-Fang, BA; Taiwanese diplomatist and politician; b. 14 Sept. 1958; ed Nat. Taiwan Univ.; Officer, Taipei Rep. Office, UK 1985–86; Officer, Dept of N American Affairs, Ministry of Foreign Affairs (MoFA), Exec. Yuan 1986–91; Sec. Congressional Liaison Div., Taipei Econ. and Cultural Rep. Office in USA 1991–96; Chief, Section 1, Dept of N American Affairs (DNAA), MoFA 1996–99; Sr Specialist, and concurrently Chief of Section 1, DNAA 1999; Sr Specialist, Dept of Policy Planning, Mainland Affairs Council (MAC), Exec. Yuan 1999, Sr Researcher, MAC 1999, Deputy Dir Dept of Information and Liaison, MAC 2001–02; Dir-Gen. Dept of Public Affairs, Office of the Pres. 2002–04, Deputy Sec.-Gen., Office of the Pres. 2004–06; Minister of Foreign Affairs 2006–08; mem. Democratic Progressive Party. *Address:* Democratic Progressive Party, 10/F, 30 Beiping East Road, Taipei 10051, Taiwan (office). *E-mail:* foreign@dpp.org.tw (office). *Website:* www.dpp.org.tw (office).

HUANG, Da, MA; Chinese economist and academic; b. 22 Feb. 1925, Tianjin; s. of Shu-ren and Gao Huang; m. Shu-zhen Luo 1952; two s.; ed Northern China United Univ.; Dir Finance Dept Renmin Univ. of China 1978–83, Vice-Pres. 1983–91, Pres. 1991–94, now Prof., School of Finance; mem. NPC, NPC Cttee on Finance & Econ. 1993–98; mem. and head of econ. group, Academic Degrees Cttee of the State Council 1988–; apptd mem. Monetary Policy Cttee of People's Bank of China 1997; Dir Expert Advisory Cttee on Humanities and Social Sciences Studies, State Educ. Comm. 1997–; in charge of Eighth 5-Year Plan 1991–95; Vice-Chair. Chinese Soc. for Finance and Banking 1984–95 (Chair. 1995), Chinese Soc. for Public Finance 1983, Chinese Soc. for Prices 1986, Chinese Soc. for Materials Circulation 1990; Vice-Pres. China Enterprise Man. Asscn and the Securities Asscn of China 1987; Council mem., Chinese Asscn for Int. Understanding 1982; Chair. Chinese Cttee on Econs Educ. Exchange with USA 1985; Hon. Dir China Financial Policy Research Center (FRC), Hon. Chair. Chinese Soc. for Finance and Banking. *Publications:* Money and Money Circulation in the Chinese Socialist Economy 1964, Socialist Fiscal and Financial Problems 1981, Introduction to the Overall Balancing of Public Finance and Bank Credit 1984, The Price Scissors on the Price Parities Between Industrial and Agricultural Products 1990, The Economics of Money and Banking 1992, Macro-economic Control and Money Supply 1997. *Leisure interest:* calligraphy. *Address:* School of Finance, Renmin University of China, 59 Zhongguancun Street, Haidian District, Beijing 100872P, People's Republic of China. *Website:* sf.ruc.edu.cn/en.

HUANG, Daren; Chinese mathematician, academic and university administrator (retd); b. April 1945, Zhejiang Prov.; ed Zhejiang Univ.; Visiting Scholar, Dept of Math., Univ. of South Carolina, USA 1985–86; Vice-Pres., Zhejiang Univ. 1992–98; Vice-Pres. Zhongshan Univ. (Sun Yat-sen Univ.) 1998–99, Pres. 1999–2010; Progress in Science and Tech. Award, Nat. and Prov. Awards for Excellence in Teaching. *Publications:* over 100 research papers on math. *Address:* c/o Office of the President, Sun Yat-sen University, 135 Xingang Xi Road, Guangzhou 510275, Guangdong Province, People's Republic of China (office).

HUANG, Guangyu, (Wong Kwong Yu); Chinese business executive; b. 24 June 1969, Shantou, Guangdong Prov.; brother of Huang Junqin; m. Du Juan; two c.; left high school 1987, moved to Beijing with older brother Huang Junqin, took out small bank loan and began selling household appliances; Founder and Chair. GOME Appliances (fmrly China Eagle Group Co. Ltd, name changed to GOME 1993) 2002–2009; convicted of bribery, insider trading and illegal foreign exchange dealings, sentenced to 14 years in prison 2010.

HUANG, Jack; Taiwanese editor and newspaper executive; s. of Y. P. Huang and Nancy Huang, co-founders of The China Post; Publr and Ed. The China Post. *Address:* The China Post, 5F-1, 88 Yanchang Rd, Xinyi District, Taipei, Taiwan. *Telephone:* (2) 6639-6890. *Fax:* (2) 6639-6890. *E-mail:* webmaster@mail.chinapost.com.tw. *Website:* www.chinapost.com.tw.

HUANG, James C. F., BA; Taiwanese government official; b. 14 Sept. 1958, Tainan City; m. Charlene Ting; one s. two d.; ed Nat. Taiwan Univ.; Officer, Dept of North American Affairs, Ministry of Foreign Affairs 1986, Officer, Secr. 1989, Section Chief, First Section 1996, Asst Deputy-Gen. and Section Chief, First Section 1999; Sec., Congressional Liaison Div., Taipei Econ. and Cultural Rep. Office, USA 1991; Asst Deputy-Gen. Dept of Policy and Planning, Mainland Affairs Council, Exec. Yuan 1999, Sr Researcher, Mainland Affairs Council 2000, Deputy Dir-Gen. Dept of Information and Liaison, Mainland Affairs Council 2001; Dir-Gen. Dept of Public Affairs, Office of the Pres. 2002, Deputy Sec.-Gen. to the Pres. 2004; Minister of Foreign Affairs 2006–08 (resgnd).

HUANG, Jianxin; Chinese film director; b. 14 June 1954, Shenxian, Hebei Prov.; ed Northwest Univ., Beijing Motion Picture Acad. *Films include:* as director: The Black Cannon Incident (Golden Rooster Best Director Award 1986) 1985, Samsara, Lun Hui (Golden Rooster Best Director Award) 1989, Stand Straight, Don't Collapse 1993, Back to Back, Face to Face 1994, Signal Left, Turn Right 1996, Surveillance 1997, Shuibuzhao (Can't Fall Asleep) 1998, Shei Shuo Wo Bu Zaihu (Who Says I Don't Care?) 2001, Gimme Kudos 2005, The Founding of a Republic 2009, The Founding of a Party 2011; as producer: 2 Young 2005, A Battle of Wits 2006, All About Women 2008, Qian Xuesen 2012, Little Tigers 2013, Angry Kid 2013, The White Haired Witch of Lunar Kingdom 2014, The Taking of Tiger Mountain 2014, Operation Mekong 2016, WuKong 2017, Iceman: The Time Traveller 2018. *Address:* Xian Film Studio, Xian, People's Republic of China.

HUANG, Junqin, (Wong Chung-yam); Chinese business executive; b. Shantou, Guangdong Prov.; brother of Huang Guangyu; moved to Beijing with younger brother Huang Guangyu, took out small bank loan and began selling household appliances; f. GOME brand for their electronics business 1987; moved into real estate industry, two brothers later separated and Junqin obtained assets of real estate business; f. Towercrest Group, later Chair.; Chair. Shandong Jintai Group Co. 2002; convicted of fraud and insider dealing, served three and a half years in prison 2010–12.

HUANG, Pi-twan, BA, MA, PhD; Taiwanese academic and politician; b. 14 Nov. 1945; ed Nat. Taiwan Univ., Univ. of Wisconsin, USA; Assoc. Prof. and Chair. Dept of Foreign Languages and Literature, Nat. Sun Yat-sen Univ. 1980–92; Deputy Dir Nat. Chiang Kai Shek Cultural Center 1992–95, Artistic Dir 2010–13; Chair. Dept of Foreign Languages and Literature, Nat. Chi Nan Univ. 1995–97, Dean, Coll. of Humanities 2000; Dir Dept of Higher Educ., Ministry of Educ., Exec. Yuan 1997–2000; Pres. Tainan Nat. Univ. of the Arts 2000–06; Minister of the Council for Cultural Affairs 2008–12; Nat. Policy Adviser to the Pres. 2011–12; Political Deputy Minister, Ministry of Educ. 2013–14; Hon. Fellow, Univ. of Wisconsin 1989–90. *Address:* c/o Council for Cultural Affairs, 30-1 Beiping East Road, Taipei 10051, Taiwan (office).

HUANG, Shuxian; Chinese politician; *Minister of Civil Affairs;* b. 1955, Yangzhong; ed Nanjing Univ.; began career as jr cultural official and CCP Party Sec. in Yangzhong County, Jiangsu Prov.; Chinese Communist Youth League Prov. Sec., Jiangsu Prov. 1985; Minister of Supervision 2013–16, of Civil Affairs 2016–; Dir Nat. Bureau of Corruption Prevention 2013–16; Deputy Sec., 17th CCP Cen. Cttee Cen. Comm. for Discipline Inspection 2007–12, 18th CCP Cen. Cttee Cen. Comm. for Discipline Inspection 2012–17; mem. 18th CCP Cen. Cttee 2012–17, 19th CCP Cen. Cttee 2017–. *Address:* Ministry of Supervision, 2 Guanganmen Nan Jie, Xuanwu Qu, Beijing 100053, People's Republic of China (office). *Telephone:* (10) 58123114 (office). *Website:* www.mca.gov.cn (office).

HUANG, Tiao-kuei, MA; Taiwanese insurance industry executive; *Vice-Chairman, Cathay Life Insurance Co. Ltd;* ed Nat. Tsing Hua Univ., Swiss Insurance Training Centre, Switzerland; fmrly Exec. Vice-Pres. Cathay Life Insurance Co. Ltd, Pres. 2005–08, also fmr Pres. Cathay Financial Holdings, Vice-Chair. 2011–; fmr Man. Dir Life Insurance Asscn of Repub. of China, Chair. 2003; mem. Int. Insurance Soc. *Address:* Cathay Life Insurance Company Ltd, 296 Jen Ai Road, Section 4, Taipei 10639, Taiwan (office). *Telephone:* (22) 755-1399 (office). *Fax:* (22) 704-1485 (office). *Website:* www.cathaylife.com.tw (office).

HUANG, Zhendong; Chinese politician; b. 1941, Dafeng Co., Jiangsu Prov.; ed Nanjing Navigation Eng School, Shanghai Shipping Inst.; Sr Engineer at Research Fellow level, Nanjing Navigation Eng School 1962; entered workforce, Admin. Bureau, Qinhuangdao Harbour, Hebei Prov. 1963, Deputy Chief of Planning Div. and Deputy Dir Admin. Bureau 1963–82, Dir 1982; joined CCP 1981; Vice-Minister of Communications 1985–88, Minister 1991–2003 (Sec. CCP Leading Party Group, Ministry of Communications 1991); Gen. Man. State Communications Investment Co. 1988–91; Chair. China Merchants' Steam Navigation Group Ltd 1991; mem. 14th CCP Cen. Cttee 1992–97, 15th Cen. Cttee 1997–2002, 16th CCP Cen. Cttee 2002–07; Sec. Chongqing CCP Municipal Cttee 2002–05; Chair., Standing Cttee Chongqing Municipal People's Congress 2003–06, Credentials Cttee of the 11th NPC 2008–13, Internal and Judicial Affairs Cttee of the 11th NPC 2008–13.

HUANG, Zhiquan; Chinese politician; b. Feb. 1942, Tongxiang, Zhejiang Prov.; ed Zhejiang Agricultural Univ.; joined CCP 1979; Div. Head and Deputy Dir Jiangxi Prov. Planning Comm. 1984–91, Dir 1991–93; Asst Gov. Jiangxi Prov. 1991–93, Vice-Gov. 1993–2001, Gov. 2001–06; Deputy Sec. CCP Jiangxi Prov. Cttee 1995–98, 2001–; mem. 15th CCP Cen. Cttee 1997–2002, 16th CCP Cen. Cttee 2002–07.

HUBBARD, Allan (Al) Brooks, BA, MA, JD MBA; American business executive and fmr government official; *Partner and Chairman, E&A Industries Inc.;* b. 8 Sept. 1947, Jackson, Tenn.; m. Kathryn Hubbard (née Fortune) 1979; three c.; ed Vanderbilt Univ., Harvard School of Business Admin, Harvard Law School; Co-founder and CEO E&A Industries Inc., Indianapolis, Ind. 1977, now Partner and Chair.; Deputy Chief of Staff to Vice-Pres. Dan Quayle 1990–92, fmr Dir Pres.'s Council on Competitiveness; Asst to Pres. for Econ. Policy and Dir Nat. Econ. Council 2005–07 (resgnd); Trustee Emer., Hudson Inst.; mem. Bd of Dirs Simon Property Group, Acadia Healthcare, Lumina Foundation, Economic Club, Central Indiana Corp. Partnership, Indiana Chamber Commerce. *Address:* E&A Industries Inc., 101 West Ohio Street, Suite 1350, Indianapolis, IN 46204, USA (office). *Telephone:* (317) 684-3150 (office). *Fax:* (317) 681-5068 (office). *Website:* ea-companies.com (office).

HUBBARD, Richard (Dick), ONZM, B Tech; New Zealand business executive and fmr politician; b. 18 Nov. 1946, Paeroa; s. of Colin Hubbard and Margaret Hubbard (née Syme); m. Diana Reader 1970; two c.; f. Hubbard Foods Ltd 1990; Mayor of Auckland 2004–07; Founding Chair. NZ Businesses for Social Responsibility (now The Sustainable Business Network); Dir Outward Bound NZ; councillor, Massey Univ.; Trustee, NZ Nat. Parks and Conservation Foundation; Fellow, NZ Inst. of Food Science and Tech., NZ Inst. of Man.; Dr hc (Massey Univ.) 1999. *Leisure interests:* climbing, motorcycling, photography.

HUBBARD, R(obert) Glenn, PhD; American economist, academic and fmr government official; *Russell L. Carson Professor of Finance and Economics and Dean, Graduate School of Business, Columbia University;* b. 4 Sept. 1958, Apopka, Fla; m. Constance Pond Hubbard; two s.; ed Univ. of Cen. Florida, Harvard Univ.; Asst Prof. of Econs, Northwestern Univ. 1983–88; Prof. of Finance and Econs, Grad. School of Business, Columbia Univ. 1988–, Russell L. Carson Prof. of Finance and Econs 1994–, Sr Vice-Dean 1994–97, Co-Dir Entrepreneurship Program 1998–2004, Dean 2004–; Deputy Asst Sec. for Tax Policy, US Treasury Dept, Washington, DC 1991–93; Chair. Pres. Council of Econ. Advisers, White House 2001–03; Visiting Scholar, American Enterprise Inst., Washington, DC; econ. advisor to Mitt Romney campaign for Republican nomination for Pres. 2008; Visiting Prof. of Business Admin, Harvard Business School 1997–98; mem. Bd of Dirs ADP Inc. 2004–, KKR Financial Corpn 2004–, BlackRock Closed-End Funds 2004–, MetLife 2007–; Chair. Econ. Policy Cttee OECD 2001–03, Econ. Club of New York 2008–; Co-Chair. Cttee on Capital Markets Regulation 2006–; Life Mem. Council on Foreign Relations 2007–; mem. Advisory Bd Nat. Center for Addiction and Substance Abuse 2004–; mem. Panel of Econ. Advisors, Fed. Reserve Bank of New York 1993–2001, 2007–, Panel of Academic Advisors, Tax Foundation 2003, American Council for Capital Formation 2003–; Fellow, Nat. Asscn of Business Economists 2005; Nat. Soc. of Professional Engineers Award, Univ. of Cen. Florida, Northwestern Univ. Associated Student Govt Teaching Awards 1985, 1986, 1987, John M. Olin Fellowship, Nat. Bureau of Econ. Research 1987–88, Distinguished Alumnus Award, Univ. of Cen. Florida 1991, Exceptional Service Award, US Treasury Dept 1992, Best Paper Award for Corp. Finance, Western Finance Asscn 1998, Alumni Hall of Fame, Univ. of Cen. Florida 2000, Michelle Akers Award for Distinguished Service, Univ. of Cen. Florida 2001, Exceptional Service Award, The White House 2002; William F. Butler Memorial Award, New York Asscn of Business Economists 2005. *Television:* commentator, Nightly Business Report (PBS) 2003–. *Radio:* commentator, Marketplace, Nat. Public Radio 2003–. *Publications:* as co-author: Healthy, Wealthy and Wise: Five Steps to a Better Health Care System 2005, Principles of Economics 2006, The Aid Trap: Hard Truths About Ending Poverty 2009; commentator for press titles including Business Week, Wall Street Journal, New York Times, Financial Times, Washington Post, Nikkei, Daily Yomiuri; books: Money, the Financial System and the Economy 1994; over 100 scholarly articles. *Address:* Graduate School of Business, Columbia University, 3022 Broadway, New York, NY 10027, USA (office). *Telephone:* (212) 854-2888 (office). *Fax:* (212) 932-0545 (office). *E-mail:* rgh1@columbia.edu (office). *Website:* www.columbia.edu (office).

HUBBARD, Thomas C.; American business executive and fmr diplomatist; *Senior Director for Asia, McLarty Associates;* b. 1943, Ky; m. Joan Magnusson Hubbard; two c.; ed Univ. of Ala; joined Foreign Service 1965, Political/Econ. Officer, Embassy in Santo Domingo 1966, Econ./Commercial Officer, Fukuoka, Japan, with Political Section, Embassy in Tokyo 1971, Econ. Officer, Japan Desk, Dept of State 1973–75, Exec. Sec. to Del., then Energy Advisor, Perm. Mission to OECD, Paris 1975–78, with Political Section, Embassy in Tokyo 1978–81, Dir Training and Liaison Staff, Bureau of Personnel, State Dept, Deputy Dir, Philippine Desk 1984–85, Country Dir 1985–87, Deputy Chief of Mission, Embassy in Kuala Lumpur 1987, Minister-Counsellor, Sr Foreign Service 1989, Minister and Deputy Chief of Mission, Embassy in Manila 1990–93, Deputy Asst Sec., East Asian and Pacific Affairs, Dept of State 1993–96, Amb. to Philippines 1996–2000, Prin. Deputy Asst Sec. of State for E Asian and Pacific Affairs 2000–01, Amb. to Repub. of Korea 2001–04, Sr Advisor, Akin Gump Strauss Hauer & Feld LLP, Washington, DC 2004; currently Sr Dir for Asia, McLarty Associates; Chair. Korea Soc. 2009–; mem. Advisory Council Korea Econ. Inst.; Dr hc (Univ. of Maryland), (Univ. of Alabama). *Address:* McLarty Associates, 900 Seventeenth Street, NW, Suite 800, Washington, DC 20006, USA (office). *Telephone:* (202) 419-1420 (office). *E-mail:* info@maglobal.com (office). *Website:* www.maglobal.com (office).

HUBBELL, Stephen Philip, BA, PhD; American ecologist and academic; *Distinguished Professor of Ecology and Evolutionary Biology, University of California, Los Angeles;* b. 17 Feb. 1942, Gainesville, Fla; m. Patricia Adair Gowaty; ed Carleton Coll., Univ. of California, Berkeley; Asst Prof. of Zoology, Univ. of Michigan 1969–74, Assoc. Prof. of Zoology 1974–75; Asst Prof. of Zoology, Univ. of Iowa 1975–80, Prof. of Zoology 1980–88; Staff Scientist, Smithsonian Tropical Research Inst., Panama 1982–88, Research Assoc. 1990–2000, Staff Scientist 2000–02, Sr Staff Scientist 2002–; Prof. of Ecology and Evolutionary Biology, Princeton Univ. 1988–99; Prof. of Plant Biology, Univ. of Georgia 1999–2002, Distinguished Research Prof. of Plant Biology 2003–07; Distinguished Prof. of Ecology and Evolutionary Biology, UCLA 2007–; Visiting Distinguished Prof., Univ. of Texas, Austin 1980; Summer Faculty mem., Univ. of Minnesota Forestry and Biological Station, Itasca, Minn. 1978, 1979, 1980; Visiting Distinguished Prof., Forest Research Inst., Kuala Lumpur, Malaysia 1986; Research Assoc., Arnold Arboretum, Harvard Univ. 1985–; Visiting Distinguished Prof., Univ. of Turku, Finland 1995, Univ. of Amsterdam, The Netherlands 2001; mem. Bd of Dirs, Org. for Tropical Studies 1979–81; mem. Selection Cttee, Cosmos Environmental Prize, Kyoto, Japan 1998–; Assoc. Ed., Theoretical Population Biology 1976–1978, Tropical Biology Series, Cambridge Univ. Press 1983–; Co-Ed., Monographs in Population Biology, Princeton Univ. Press 1989–96; mem. Bd of Eds, Ecology 1989–90; mem. American Soc. of Naturalists, Ecological Soc. of America, Asscn of Tropical Biology; Fellow, AAAS 1982, American Acad. of Arts and Sciences 2003; Faculty Scholar, Univ. of Iowa 1980–83; Hon. DSc (Carleton Coll.) 2006; Guggenheim Fellow 1984–85, Pew Scholar Award in Conservation and the Environment, 1990–93, Distinguished Service Medal, Soc. of Conservation Biology 1992, Marsh Global Ecology Prize, British Ecological Soc. 2004, Lamar Dodd Creative Research Award 2006, W.S. Cooper Award in Plant Ecology, Ecological Soc. of America 2006, Kempe Global Ecology Award (Sweden) 2008, Thomson Reuters Citation Laureate 2009, Eminent Ecologist Award, Ecological Soc. of America 2009, Scientific Achievement Award, Int. Union of Forestry 2014, Int. Prize for Biology 2016. *Publications include:* The National Institute for the Environment: A Proposal for Improving the Scientific Basis of Environmental Decision-making (co-author) 1993, Distribution of Tree Species in the Fifty Hectare Research Plot at Pasoh Forest Reserve (co-author) 1993, The Unified Neutral Theory of Biodiversity and Biogeography 2001, The Dynamics of a Neotropical Forest: Theoretical and Empirical Studies 2002; numerous papers in professional journals. *Address:* Botany 114C, Department of Ecology and Evolutionary Biology, University of California, 612 Charles E. Young Drive South, Los Angeles, CA 90095-7246, USA (office). *E-mail:* shubbell@eeb.ucla.edu (office). *Website:* www.eeb.ucla.edu (office).

HUBER, Bernd, DHabil; German economist, university president and academic; *President, Ludwig Maximilian University (LMU), Munich;* b. 20 May 1960, Wuppertal; m.; two c.; ed Univs of Giessen and Würzburg; Lecturer in Econs, Univ. of Würzburg 1985–89, Akademischer Rat 1989–94, on leave of absence 1993–; Visiting Prof., Univ. of Bochum 1993–94, Univ. of Dresden April–July 1994, Univ. of Munich April–July 1994; currently Prof. of Econs, Ludwig Maximilian Univ. (LMU), Munich, Pres. 2002–; Chair. League of European Research Univs 2008–14; mem. Bd of Dirs Venice Int. Univ.; mem. Strategic Orientation Cttee, Paris-Sorbonne Univ.; mem. Scientific Council, Ministry of Finance; Bavarian Order of Merit 2007. *Publications include:* Staatsverschuldung und Allokationseffizienz – Schriften zur öffentlichen Verwaltung und öffentlichen Wirtschaft 1990, Optimale Finanzpolitik und zeitliche Inkonsistenz, Studies in Contemporary Economics

1996, Die Einwohnergewichtung auf Länderebene im Länderfinanzausgleich – ifo Beiträge zur Wirtschaftsforschung (co-author) 2000; numerous articles on public finance, govt and debt, European fiscal and monetary integration, int. taxation and labour markets. *Address:* University Executive Board, Ludwig-Maximilians-Universität München, Leopoldstr. 3, 80802 Munich, Germany (office). *Telephone:* (89) 2180-2412 (office). *Fax:* (89) 2180-3656 (office). *E-mail:* huber.sekretariat@lrz.uni-muenchen.de (office); presidium@lmu.de (office). *Website:* www.uni-muenchen.de (office); www.en.uni-muenchen.de/about_lmu/index.html (office).

HUBER, Erwin; German politician; b. 26 July 1946, Reisbach, Lower Bavaria; m.; two c.; ed Univ. of Munich; started career at Bavarian state finance office 1963; joined Bavarian State Ministry of Finance 1970; fmr Borough and Dist Chair., Junge Union (Young Conservative Party); mem. Borough Council and Cttee, Dingolfing-Landau 1972–78; mem. Bavarian Landtag (Parl.) 1978–, Chair. Parl. Cttee on Devt and Environmental Affairs 1986–87; State Minister and Head of State Chancellery 1994–95, 1998–2005, State Minister of Finance 1995–98, 2007–08, Minister of State for Fed. Matters and Admin. Reform 2003–05, for Economy 2005–07; Deputy Sec.-Gen. CSU party 1987–88, Sec.-Gen. 1988–94, Dist Chair., Lower Bavaria 1993–2007, Party Leader 2007–08 (resgnd). *Website:* www.erwin-huber.de (office).

HUBER, Robert, Dr rer. nat, FRS; German biochemist and academic; *Director Emeritus, Max-Planck-Institut für Biochemie;* b. 20 Feb. 1937, Munich; s. of Sebastian Huber and Helene Huber; m. Christa Huber 1960; two s. two d.; ed Tech. Univ. Munich; Dir Max-Planck-Inst. für Biochemie 1972–2005, Dir Emer. 2006–; fmr External Prof. then Assoc. Prof., Munich Tech. Univ. 1976; Visiting Prof., Univs of Barcelona, Singapore, Duisburg-Essen, Cardiff; Ed. Journal of Molecular Biology 1976–; Emeriti of Excellence, Technische Universität München 2013–; Scientific mem. Max-Planck-Gesellschaft; mem. Bavarian Acad. of Sciences, Accad. Nazionale dei Lincei, Gesellschaft für Biologische Chemie, Deutsche Chemische Gesellschaft, Deutsche Akademie der Naturforscher, Leopoldina and numerous socs; Corresp. mem. Academia Mexicana de Ciencias, Croatian Acad. of Sciences and Arts; Fellow, American Acad. of Microbiology; Assoc. Fellow, Third World Acad. of Sciences, Trieste, Italy; Foreign Assoc. NAS; Foreign Fellow, Indian Nat. Science Acad.; numerous hon. professorships; Hon. mem. Real Academia Sevillana de Ciencias, Spain, Sociedad Espanola de Bioquimica y Biologia Molecular, Japanese Biochemical Soc., Swedish Soc. for Biophysics, American Soc. of Biological Chemists; Hon. Pres. and Chief Scientific Advisor, Tianjin Int. Joint Acad. of Biotechnology & Medicine, China 2012; Grosse Verdienstkreuz mit Stern und Schulterband 1997, Cross Commdr of Order for Merits to Lithuania 2017; mem. Orden pour le Merite für Wissenschaften und Künste; Dr hc (Louvain) 1987, (Ljubljana) 1989, (Tor Vergata, Rome) 1990, (Lisbon) 2000, (Barcelona) 2000, (Tsinghua Univ., Beijing) 2003, (Universidad de Buenos Aires, Argentina) 2010, (Universitas Vilnensis, Lithuania) 2011, (Bulgarian Acad. of Sciences) 2012, (Jagiellonian Univ., Poland) 2014, (Universidad Nacional, Costa Rica) 2016, (Jessore Univ. of Science and Tech., Bangladesh) 2018, (Shiraz Univ., Iran) 2018; E.K. Frey Prize, German Surgical Soc. 1972, Otto Warburg Medal, Soc. for Biological Chem. 1977, Emil von Behring Prize, Univ. of Marburg 1982, Keilin Medal, Biochemical Soc., London, Richard Kuhn Medal, Soc. of German Chemists 1987, Nobel Prize in Chemistry (jtly) 1988, E.K. Frey-E. Werle Medal 1989, Kone Award, Asscn of Clinical Biochemists 1990, Sir Hans Krebs Medal 1992, Bayerischer Maximiliansorden für Wissenschaft und Kunst 1993, Linus Pauling Medal 1993, Distinguished Service Award, Miami Winter Symposia 1995, Max Tishler Prize, Harvard Univ. 1997, Max Bergmann Medal, Max-Bergmann-Kreises zur Förderung der peptidchemischen Forschung 1997, Röntgenplakette der Stadt Remscheid-Lennep 2004, Premio Citta di Firenze sulle Scienze Molecolari 2004, Erice Prize-Premio Ettore Majorana 2009, National Medal of the Order 'Manuel Amador Guerrero', Panama 2011, Xu Guangqi Medal, SIBS, Shanghai,China 2014, Panama Science Award 2016. *Leisure interests:* hiking, biking, skiing. *Address:* Max-Planck-Institut für Biochemie, Am Klopferspitz 18, 82152 Martinsried, Germany (office). *Telephone:* (89) 85782678 (office). *Fax:* (89) 85783516 (office). *E-mail:* huber@biochem.mpg.de (office). *Website:* www.biochem.mpg.de/xray (office).

HUBER-HOTZ, Annemarie; Swiss politician; b. 16 Aug. 1948, Baar, Canton Zug; m.; three c.; ed Univ. of Geneva, Swiss Fed. Inst. of Tech., Zürich; fmr Head Secr. Dept for German Law, Faculty of Law, Univ. of Geneva; translator, ILO, Geneva 1973–75; mem. staff Regional Planning Office, Canton of Zug 1976–77; Asst to Sec.-Gen. Fed. Ass. 1978–81, Dir Scientific Services 1989–99, Sec.-Gen. 1992–99; Chancellor of the Swiss Confed. 2000–07; mem. Swiss Red Cross (SRC) Ass. 2007–, re-elected 2011, Vice-Pres. SRC 2007–11, Pres. 2011–; mem. Radical Free Democratic Party. *Address:* Swiss Red Cross, Postfach 3001, Berne, Switzerland (office). *Telephone:* (31) 3877111 (office).

HUBERT, Jean-Paul, BA, BCL, MIA, DPolSci, PhD; Canadian lawyer, diplomatist, international organization executive and academic; b. 16 Dec. 1941, Grand-Mère, QC; s. of Jean-Paul Hubert and Cécile Hubert (née Laperrière); m. 1st Mireya Melgar 1967 (divorced 1995); two s. one d.; m. 2nd Florence Fournier 1995; ed Laval Univ., McGill Univ., Columbia Univ., New York, Univ. of the Sorbonne, Paris, Moncton (New Brunswick) Univ.; with Dept of Foreign Relations and Int. Trade, Canadian Diplomatic Service, Ottawa 1971–72, Second Sec., Vice-Consul for Spain and Morocco, Madrid 1972–74, Legal Affairs Div., Ottawa 1974–76, Personnel Div. 1976–78, First Sec. and Consul, Havana 1978–81, Political Counsellor and Rep., Agency for Cultural and Tech. Co-operation, Paris 1991–95, Econ. and Treaty Law Div., Ottawa 1985–86, Fed. Co-ordinator for La Francophonie 1986–88, Amb. to Mauritania, Guinea, Guinea-Bissau, Cape Verde and Senegal 1988–90, High Commr to the Gambia 1988–90, Prime Minister's Personal Rep. for La Francophonie 1988–90, Embassy in Dakar 1988–90, first Amb. and Perm. Rep. of Canada to OAS, Washington, DC 1990–93, Sr Advisor, Commonwealth La Francophonie/Hemispheric Affairs, Ottawa 1993–94, Prime Minister's Personal Rep. for La Francophonie, Ottawa, Brussels 1994–98, Amb. to Belgium and Luxembourg 1994–98, to Argentina and Paraguay 1998–2001, to Switzerland and Liechtenstein 2001–05, Amb. and Perm. Observer of Canada to the Council of Europe 2001–05; elected mem. Inter-American Juridical Cttee, OAS 2004–12, Pres. 2005–07; Interim Pres. Int. Centre for Human Rights and Democratic Devt (Rights & Democracy) 2007–08; Designated Order of la Pleiade, Int. Asscn of French-Speaking Parliamentarians 1989. *Leisure interests:* genealogy, trekking.

HÜBNER, Danuta, PhD; Polish politician and economist; *Chairman, Committee on Regional Policy, European Parliament;* b. 8 April 1948, Nisko; two d.; ed Warsaw School of Econs; researcher, Main School of Planning and Statistics, Warsaw (now Warsaw School of Econs) 1971–, Deputy Dir Research Inst. for Developing Countries, Warsaw School of Econs 1981–87, Deputy Dir Inst. for Devt and Strategic Studies 1991–94; Deputy Ed.-in-Chief Ekonomista (bi-monthly) 1991–97; Ed.-in-Chief Gospodarka Narodowa (monthly) 1994–97; Under-Sec. of State Ministry of Industry and Trade 1994–96; Sec. Cttee for European Integration 1996–97, 2001–04; Sec. of State for European Integration 1996–97; Head, Chancellery of the Pres. of Poland 1997–98; Econ. Adviser to Pres. of Poland 1998–2001; Deputy Exec. Sec. UN Econ. Comm. for Europe 1998–2000, Exec. Sec. 2000–01, UN Under-Sec.-Gen. 2000–01; Sec. of State, Ministry of Foreign Affairs 2001–04; Minister for European Affairs 2003–04; EU Commr without Portfolio 2004, for Regional Policy 2004–09; mem. European Parl. 2009–, Chair. Cttee on Regional Policy; Chair. Council for Social Planning 1996–98; mem. Exec. Cttee European Asscn of Devt Research and Training Insts 1987–96, Nat. Statistics Council 1995–97, Scientific Bd Econ. Sciences Inst., Polish Acad. of Science 1996–98; Hon. LLB (Univ. of Sussex) 2005; Dr hc (Univ. of Nat. and World Economy, Sofia) 2007, (Univ. of Poznań) 2010. *Address:* European Parliament, Rue Wiertz 60, 1047 Brussels, Belgium (office). *Telephone:* (2) 283-71-92 (office). *E-mail:* danuta.huebner@ep.europa.eu (office). *Website:* www.danuta-huebner.pl.

HUCKABEE, Michael Dale, BA; American politician and ecclesiastic; b. 24 Aug. 1955, Hope, Ark.; m. Janet McCain 1974; three s. one d.; ed Ouachita Baptist Univ., Southwestern Baptist Theological Seminary; ordained to ministry 1974; pastor, various Baptist churches 1974–, Beech St 1st Baptist Church, Texarkana, Ark. 1986–; Lt Gov. State of Ark. 1994–96, Gov. of Arkansas 1996–2007; Founder, Past-Pres. American Christian TV System, Pine Bluff; Pres. Ark. Baptist Convention 1989–91; columnist, weekly newspaper Positive Alternatives; unsuccessful cand. for Republican nomination for Pres. of US 2007–08; host, Huckabee (Fox News Channel) 2008–15; host, The Mike Huckabee Show (daily radio show) 2012–13; unsuccessful candidate for Republican nomination for Pres. of US 2016. *Address:* 1800 Center Street, Little Rock, AR 72206, USA (home).

HUCKLE, Alan, MA; British diplomatist (retd); b. 15 June 1948, Penang, Malaya; s. of Albert Huckle and Ethel Huckle; m. Helen Huckle 1973; one s. one d.; ed Rugby School, Univ. of Warwick; with Civil Service Dept (CSD) 1971–74; Asst Pvt. Sec. to Sec. of State for NI, Belfast 1974–75, Machinery of Govt Div., CSD 1975–78; Political Affairs Div., NI Office 1978–80; with FCO 1980–83; Exec. Dir British Information Services, New York, USA 1983–87; Head of Chancery, Manila 1987–90; Deputy Head, Arms Control and Disarmament Dept, FCO 1990–92; Counsellor and Head of Del. to CSCE, Vienna 1992–96; Head, Dept Territories Regional Secr., Bridgetown 1996–98; Head, OSCE/Council of Europe Dept, FCO 1998–2001; Head, Overseas Territories Dept, FCO and Commr (non-resident) British Antarctic Territory and British Indian Ocean Territory 2001–04; Gov. of Anguilla 2004–06; Gov. of Falkland Islands and Commr S Georgia and S Sandwich Islands 2006–10; apptd Research Analyst, FCO 2012; Chair. Chagos Conservation Trust 2011–13, Falkland Islands Asscn 2011–18; Leverhulme Trust Scholar, British School at Rome Scholar 1971. *Leisure interests:* armchair mountaineering, hill-walking.

HUCKNALL, Michael (Mick) James, BA; British singer and songwriter; b. 8 June 1960, Manchester; m. Gabriella Wesberry; one d.; ed Manchester Polytechnic; fmrly with own punk band, Frantic Elevators 1979; founder mem. and lead singer, Simply Red 1984–2010, 2015–; numerous world tours; co-f. reggae music label, Blood and Fire 1992; mem. Govt Task Force on the Music Industry 1997–; founded record label, Simplyred.com 2003–; solo artist 2009–; Hon. MSc (UMIST) 1997; BRIT Award for Best British Band 1991, 1992, Best Male Solo Artist 1992, Ivor Novello Songwriter of the Year Award 1992, MOBO Award for Outstanding Achievement 1997, Manchester Making it Happen Award 1998. *Recordings include:* albums: with Simply Red: Picture Book 1985, Early Years 1987, Men and Women 1987, A New Flame 1989, Stars 1991, Life 1995, Blue 1997, Love and the Russian Winter 1999, It's Only Love 2000, Home 2003, Simplified 2005, Stay 2007, Simply Red 25 2008, Songs of Love 2010, Big Love 2015; solo: Tribute to Bobby 2008, American Soul 2012. *Address:* c/o Quietus Management, The Phoenix Brewery, 13 Bramley Road, London, W10 6SP, England (office). *E-mail:* info@quietusmanagement.com (office); info@simplyred.com (office). *Website:* www.quietusmanagement.com (office); www.simplyred.com; www.mickhucknall.com.

HUDA, A. T. M. Shamsul, BA, MA, MPA, PhD; Bangladeshi civil servant; b. 10 July 1943; ed Univ. of Dhaka, Syracuse Univ., USA; Asst Commr, Cadre of the Civil Service of Pakistan 1966–68; Sub-Div. Officer, in sub-dist in present Bangladesh and Pakistan 1968–71; Deputy Dir (Food), Punjab, West Pakistan 1971; Additional Deputy Commr 1971–72; Deputy Sec., Establishment Div. 1972–75, 1979–82; Research Asst, World Bank, Washington, DC, USA 1978–79, Maxwell School, Syracuse Univ. 1978–79; Deputy Sec., Ministry of Agric. and Forests 1981–82, Jt Sec. 1982–84, Project Coordinator, Bangladesh Jute Seed Project 1982–84, Project Dir, Agricultural Man. Devt Programme 1981–84; mem. Directing Staff, Bangladesh Public Admin Training Centre 1984–88; Jt Sec., Ministry of Irrigation, Water Devt and Flood Control 1988–91, Additional Sec. and Chair. Bangladesh Water Devt Bd 1991–92; Man. Dir Bangladesh Agricultural Devt Bank 1992–94; Sec., Banking Div., Ministry of Finance 1994–96; Sec., Ministry of Water Resources 1996–2000 (retd); Chief Election Commr 2007–12; Pres. Gulshan Soc. 2016–. *Publications include:* The Small Farmer and the Problem of Access 1983, Co-ordination in Public Administration in Bangladesh 1987, Sustainability of Projects for Higher Agricultural Education: A Case Study of Bangladesh Agricultural University 1988, Sustainable Agricultural Development Strategies: The Case of Bangladesh 1996, Flood Management Issues: The Bangladesh Experience 2000, Constraints and Opportunities for Co-operation towards Development of Water Resources in the Ganges Basin 2001. *Address:* Gulshan Society, House 7/B, Flat A-1 Road 103, Gulshan-2, Dhaka 1212 (office); House 10, Apartment 401, Road 59 Gulshan-2, Dhaka 1212, Bangladesh (home). *Telephone:* (2) 9881375 (office); 1715882117 (mobile) (office); 1711599998 (mobile) (home); (2) 8813802 (home). *E-mail:* gulshansociety@gmail.com (office). *Website:* www.gulshansociety.com (office).

HUDA, K.M. Nurul; Bangladeshi civil servant and fmr government official; *Chief Election Commissioner, Bangladesh Election Commission;* b. 30 April 1948, Patuakhali; s. of Abdur Rashid Khan and Mehen Nega Khanom; m. Hosne Ara Huda; one s. two d.; ed Dhaka Univ., Univ. of Manchester, UK; fought war of liberation 1971; joined Bangladesh Civil Service 1973, fmr Deputy Dir Local Govt of Dhaka Div., Jt Sec. Parl. Secr., Nat. Project Dir Strengthening Nat. Parl., Jt Sec. Ministry of Forest and Environment, CEO Dhaka City Corpn, retd 2006; Head of Admin and Human Resources, Gemcon Ltd 2005–08; Man. Dir Bangladesh Municipal Devt Fund 2010–15; Chief Election Commr, Bangladesh Election Comm. 2017–; mem. Int. Advisory Bd, Int. Environmental Tech. Center, UN Environment Programme 2012–15; mem. Nat. Cttee of Bangladesh Paribesh Andolon. *Publication:* Municipal Solid Waste Management: Bangladesh Perspective 2008; 80 articles published in English—language dailies and periodicals. *Address:* Bangladesh Election Commission, Nirbachan Bhaban, Agargaon, Dhaka 1207, Bangladesh (office). *Website:* www.ec.org.bd (office).

HUDEČEK, Václav; Czech violinist; b. 7 June 1952, Rozmital pod Třemšínem; m. Eva Trejtnarova 1977; ed Acad. of Performing Arts, Prague, studied with David Oistrakh in Moscow; debut with Royal Philharmonic Orchestra in London 1967; soloist with Czech Philharmonic Orchestra 1984–90, Royal Philharmonic Orchestra, London, Berlin Philharmonic, Leipzig Gewandhaus Orchestra, NHK Orchestra of Tokyo; concert tours in Europe, Japan and USA since London debut, and tours in Europe, USA, Japan and Australia; f. Akademie Václava Hudečka; Cavaliere delle Ordine della Stella d'Italia 2015; Award for Outstanding Labour 1978, Artist of Merit of Czechoslovakia 1980, Supraphon Gold Record Prize 1994, recognized by Pres. Vaclav Klaus through Nat. Award for Achievement in Area of Culture and the Arts 2007, Award of City of Prague 2012. *Recordings include:* Bach: Concertos, Bravo Vivaldi, Czech Christmas – Eva Urbanová, Drdla/Sarasate/Hubay/Lehár/Ravel, Dvorák: Compositions for Violin and Piano, Dvorák: Concerto for Violin and Orchestra in A minor, Op. 53, Guitar: Prague Guitar Concertos, Haydn: Sitkovetsky, Davidovich, Hudeček play Haydn, Mendelssohn-Bartholdy/Sibelius: Violin Concertos, Mozart: The Famous Violin Concertos, Music for Weddings, P.I. Tchaikovsky, J. Sibelius: Violin Concertos, Paganini: Hudeček and Brabec play Paganini, Prokofjev/Tchaikovsky, Souvenir, Václav Hudeček – Violin Recital, Supraphon Stars 2000, Tartini/Paganini/Gragnani/Giuliani, Triny – Gipsy Streams, Trojan: Suites from the Films, Violin: Hudeček Il Giardino di Musica, Vivaldi: Concertos for Various Instruments, Vivaldi: Le Quattro Stagioni (Record of the Year 1992). *Address:* Akademie Václava Hudečka, Kvítková 4703, 760 03 Zlín (office); Londynskà 83, 120 00 Prague 2, Czech Republic. *Telephone:* (571) 117130 (office). *E-mail:* violin@vaclav-hudecek.cz. *Website:* www.vaclav-hudecek.cz; www.akademievhudecka.cz (office).

HUDES, Quiara Alegría, BA, MFA; American playwright and teacher; m. Ray Beauchamp; one d.; ed Yale Univ., Brown Univ.; raised in W Philadelphia; resident writer, New Dramatists; Visiting Writer, Theater Dept, Wesleyan Univ., Middletown, Conn., teacher of advanced intensive course in playwriting 2011–12; mem. Bd Philadelphia Young Playwrights; United States Artists Fellow 2010, Roe Green Award 2012. *Plays include:* Yemaya's Belly (Clauder Prize 2003, Paula Vogel Award in Playwriting 2003, Kennedy Center/ACTF Latina Playwriting Award 2003), Elliot, a Soldier's Fugue 2007, In the Heights (book for musical) (Tony Award for Best Musical 2008, Lucille Lortel Award 2008, Outer Critics Circle Award for Best Musical 2008) 2008, 26 Miles 2009, Barrio Grrrl! 2009, Water by the Spoonful (Pulitzer Prize for Drama 2012) 2011, Miss You Like Hell (co-author) (musical) 2016. *Publications include:* Yemaya's Belly 2008, Welcome to My Neighborhood! A Barrio ABC (co-author) 2010, 26 Miles 2011, Water by the Spoonful 2012, Elliot, A Soldier's Fugue 2012. *Address:* c/o John Buzzetti, William Morris Endeavor Entertainment, 1325 Avenue of the Americas, New York, NY 10019, USA (office). *Telephone:* (212) 903-1166 (office). *E-mail:* jbuzzetti@wmeentertainment.com (office). *Website:* www.wmeentertainment.com (office).

HUDON, Isabelle; Canadian diplomatist; *Ambassador to France;* b. 18 Feb. 1967, Montreal; Pres., Chambre de commerce du Montréal métropolitain 2004–08 (also, CEO 2004–08), Marketel 2008–10, Sun Life Financial, Québec 2010–14; Exec. Chair. Sun Life Financial 2014–17, Vice-Pres. of Canada 2014–17; Co-f. L'effet A 2015; Amb. to France 2017–; fmr mem. Bd, Holt Renfrew, Hydro Québec, Mount Royal Club, Groupe Marcelle; Hon. DJur (Concordia Univ.) 2017 Prix Femmes d'affaires du Québec 2014, Medal of the Nat. Ass. 2016, Queen Elizabeth II Diamond Jubilee Medal. *Address:* Embassy of Canada, 130 rue du Faubourg Saint-Honoré, 75008 Paris 8e, France (office). *Telephone:* 1-44-43-29-00 (office). *Website:* www.canadainternational.gc.ca/france (office).

HUDSON, Hugh; British film director and producer; b. 25 Aug. 1936, London; s. of Michael Donaldson-Hudson and Jacynth Ellerton; m. 1st Susan Caroline Michie 1977; one s.; 2nd Maryam d'Abo 2003; ed Eton Coll.; numerous awards and prizes. *Films include:* The Tortoise and the Hare 1967, Chariots of Fire 1980 (five BAFTA Awards, four Acad. Awards, other awards), Greystoke: The Legend of Tarzan (also producer) 1984, Revolution 1985 (BFI Anthony Asquith Award for Music), Lost Angels 1989, Lumière et compagnie 1996, A Life So Far 1999, I Dreamed of Africa 2000, Revolution Revisited 2008, Altamira 2016; numerous documentaries, political films (for Labour Party) and over 600 advertisements. *Address:* Hudson Film Ltd, 24 St Leonard's Terrace, London, SW3 4QG, England (office). *Telephone:* (20) 7730-0002 (office). *Fax:* (20) 7730-8033 (office). *E-mail:* hudsonfilm@aol.com (office).

HUDSON, Jennifer Kate; American singer and actress; b. 12 Sept. 1981, Chicago, Ill.; one s.; ed Dunbar Vocational Career Acad.; solo artist and actress 2003–; American Idol contestant 2004; Co-f. Julian D. King Gift Foundation 2009; Soul Train Sammy Davis Jr Award for Entertainer of the Year 2007, Samsung Galaxy Impact Award 2013. *Television includes:* American Idol (contestant) 2004, Smash 2013. *Films:* Dreamgirls (Satellite Award for Best Actress in a Supporting Role 2006, NYFCC Award for Best Supporting Actress 2006, Screen Actors Guild Award for Outstanding Performance by a Female in a Supporting Role 2007, Image Award for Outstanding Supporting Actress in a Motion Picture 2007, Golden Globe for Best Performance by an Actress in a Supporting Role in a Motion Picture 2007, Critics Choice Award for Best Supporting Actress 2007, BET Award for Best Actress 2007, BAFTA Award for Best Actress in a Supporting Role 2007, Academy Award for Best Performance by an Actress in a Supporting Role 2007) 2006, Sex and the City 2008, Winged Creatures (aka Fragments) 2008, The Secret Life of Bees 2008, Winnie 2011, The Three Stooges 2012, The Inevitable Defeat of Mister and Pete 2013, Black Nativity 2013, Lullaby 2014. *Recordings include:* albums: Jennifer Hudson (Grammy Award for Best R&B Album 2009) 2008, I Remember Me 2011, JHUD 2014, The Color Purple (Grammy Award for Best Musical Theater Album 2017) 2016. *Publication:* I Got This: How I Changed My Ways, Found Myself and Lost Everything that Weighed Me Down (memoir) 2012. *Website:* www.jenniferhudson.com.

HUDSON, Linda Parker, BS; American business executive; *President and CEO, BAE Systems, Inc.;* b. 22 Aug. 1950; ed Univ. of Florida; began career at Harris Corpn, Melbourne, Fla as research and devt engineer 1972–76; joined Ford Aerospace and Communications Corpn, Newport Beach, Calif. 1976, led reliability engineering and quality assurance orgs and was programme man. on a multi-billion dollar production programme; held a variety of sr man. positions in production operations, programme man. and business devt in the defence industry 1985–99, beginning with Martin Marietta, led orgs through the Lockheed Martin merger and a subsequent divestiture to General Dynamics; served for seven years as an officer and Vice-Pres. of General Dynamics Corpn, later Pres. General Dynamics Armament and Tech. Products, Charlotte, NC; Pres. Land and Armaments operating group, BAE Systems, Inc. 2007–10, Pres. and CEO BAE Systems, Inc. (US-based, wholly owned subsidiary of BAE Systems plc, London, UK) 2010–, Exec. Dir BAE Systems, Inc. Bd and BAE Systems plc Bd and mem. Exec. Cttee BAE Systems plc; mem. United Service Orgs Worldwide Bd Govs, Asscn of the US Army Council of Trustees, Blue Star Families Bd of Dirs, Univ. of Florida Foundation Bd, Advisory Bd for the Women in Eng Program at the Univ. of Maryland; mem. N Carolina and Washington, DC chapters of the Int. Women's Forum and C200 (global org. of women business leaders); mem. Alumni and Athletic Asscns of Univ. of Florida and mem. Advisory Bd Coll. of Eng; Dr hc (Worcester Polytechnic Inst.) 2011; Distinguished Alumnus, Univ. of Florida and mem. Industrial and Systems Eng Hall of Fame, Woman of the Year Distinguished Service Award, United Service Orgs 2011. *Address:* BAE Systems, Inc., 1101 Wilson Blvd, Suite 2000, Arlington, VA 22209, USA (office). *Telephone:* (301) 838-6000 (office); (703) 312-6100 (office). *Fax:* (301) 838-6925 (office). *E-mail:* baesystemsinfo@baesystems.com (office). *Website:* www.baesystems.com/WorldwideLocations/UnitedStates (office).

HUE, Robert Georges Auguste; French politician and nurse; b. 19 Oct. 1946, Cormeilles-en-Parisis, Val-d'Oise; s. of René Hue and Raymonde Gregorius; m. Marie-Edith Solard 1973; one s. one d.; ed Coll. d'Enseignement Technique and Ecole d'Infirmier; mem. Young Communists 1962; mem. French CP 1963–, mem. Secr. Fed. of Val-d'Oise 1970–77, mem. Cen. Cttee 1987, mem. Politburo 1990, Nat. Sec. 1994–2001, Pres. 2001, Chair. 2001–03, Senator for Val-d'Oise (Île-de-France) 2004–; CP cand. in presidential election 1995, 2002; Mayor of Montigny-les-Cormeilles 1977–; Conseiller-Général Val d'Oise 1988–97; Deputy for Argenteuil-Bezons 1997–; mem. European Parl. 1999–2000; Pres. Nat. Asscn of Communist and Republican elected mems 1991–94, Fondation Gabriel Péri 2003–. *Publications:* Histoire d'un village du Parisis des origines à la Révolution 1981, Du village à la ville 1986, Montigny pendant la Révolution 1989, Communisme: la mutation 1995, Il faut qu'on se parle 1997, Communisme: un nouveau projet 1999, Qui êtes-vous? 2001. *Leisure interests:* reading, painting, cinema, music (jazz and rock), walking, judo. *Address:* Senat, Palais du Luxembourg, 15 rue de Vaugirard, 75291 Paris Cedex 06, France (office). *Telephone:* 1-42-34-20-00 (switchboard) (office). *E-mail:* robert.hue-senat@wanadoo.fr (office); fondation@gabrielperi.fr (office). *Website:* www.senat.fr/senateur/hue_robert04078q.html (office).

HUERTA, Dolores C.; American trade union official; *First Vice-President Emerita, United Farm Workers of America;* b. 10 April 1930, New Mexico; d. of Juan Fernandez and Alicia Chavez; 11 c.; ed Delta Community Coll., Univ. of the Pacific; fmr teacher at grammar school; Founding mem. Stockton Chapter, Community Service Org. (campaigned against segregation and police brutality) 1955–62; Founder Agricultural Workers Asscn 1960; est. (with Cesar Chavez) Nat. Farm Workers Asscn 1962; during Delano Grape Strike 1965–70, merger of Nat. Farm Workers Asscn and Agricultural Workers Organizing Cttee to form United Farm Workers Organizing Cttee (UFWOC) 1966; negotiated UFWOC contract with Schenley Wine Co. (first time a negotiating cttee comprised of farmworkers negotiated collective bargaining agreement with agric. corpn in USA) 1966; co-f. (with Cesar Chavez) Robert F. Kennedy Medical Plan, Juan De La Cruz Farm Worker Pension Fund, Farm Workers Credit Union, Nat. Workers Service Center, Inc.; currently First Vice-Pres. Emer. United Farm Workers of America (AFL–CIO), Vice-Pres. Coalition for Labor Union of Women, Vice-Pres. AFL–CIO Calif.; mem. Bd Fund for the Feminist Majority, Democratic Socialists of America, Latinas for Choice, Fairness in Media Reporting, Center for Voting and Democracy; Founder and Pres. Dolores Huerta Foundation 2002–; Hon. PhD (New Coll. of San Francisco) 1990, (San Francisco State Univ.) 1993, (SUNY New Palz Univ.) 1999; Dr hc (California State, Northridge) 2003, (Wayne State) 2004, (SUNY School of Law) 2004, (North Texas) 2005, (Princeton) 2006; Calif. State Senate Outstanding Labor Leader Award 1984, inducted into Nat. Women's Hall of Fame 1993, American Civil Liberties Union Roger Baldwin Medal of Liberty Award 1993, Eugene V. Debs Foundation Outstanding American Reward 1993, Ellis Island Medal of Freedom Award 1993, Consumers Union Trumpeter's Award, Eleanor Roosevelt Human Rights Award 1998, Community of Christ Int. Peace Award (jtly) 2007. *Achievements include:* instrumental in passage of legislation allowing voters right to vote in Spanish language 1961; lobbied for end to 'captive labour' Bracero Programme 1962; instrumental in securing Aid For Dependent Families for un- and under-employed, and disability insurance for farm workers in Calif. 1963; negotiated contracts to establish first health and benefit plans for farmworkers; led consumer boycotts resulting in enactment of Agricultural Labor Relations Act 1974; lobbied against fed. guest worker programmes resulting in Immigration Act 1985. *Address:* c/o Dolores Huerta Foundation, PO Box 2087, Bakersfield, CA 93303, USA (office). *Website:* www.doloreshuerta.org (office).

HUERTA TORRES, José Modesto, BSc; Peruvian government official and fmr army officer; *Minister of Defence;* ed Chorrillos Mil. School, Centro de Altos Estudios Nacionales (CAEN), Nat. Defense Univ., Washington DC; joined Peruvian Army 1969, more than 35 years' service, becoming Aide-de-camp to the Pres. 1984–85; Visiting Prof., School of the Americas, Fort Benning, Georgia 1988–89; Chief of Staff, Huallaga Front (emergency zone) 1993; Mil. Attaché,

Embassy in Caracas 1995; Gen. Commdr, 31st Infantry Brigade, VRAEM emergency zone 1996–97; Dir, Army War Coll. 1998; Gen. Commdr, Central Mil. Region 2000; Inspector Gen. of the Army 2001–02; Mil. Attaché, Embassy in Washington DC 2003; retd from army 2004 (rank of Gen.); Dir-Gen. of Policy and Strategy, Ministry of Defence 2004–05, Inspector Gen., Ministry of Defence 2016–18, Minister of Defence 2018–; Exec. Dir, South American Defense Council (CDS) 2011–12; consultant, prof. and lecturer on security and defence topics; Grand Cross, Order of Ayacucho, Commdr, Merit Award for Distinguished Services, Medal of Commendation for Meritorious Service (US Army), José María Córdova Medal (Colombia), Cross of the Venezuelan Land Forces and Honor to Merit (Venezuela). *Address:* Ministry of Defence, Edif. Quiñones, Avda de la Peruanidad s/n, Jesús María, Lima 1, Peru (office). *Telephone:* (1) 2098530 (office). *E-mail:* despacho@mindef.gob.pe (office). *Website:* www.gob.pe/mindef (office).

HUERTAS MEJÍAS, Antonio, BA; Spanish insurance executive; *Chairman and CEO, MAPFRE SA;* b. 18 Jan. 1964, Villanueva de la Serena (Badajoz); ed Univ. of Salamanca; joined MAPFRE SA (insurance co.) as intern 1988, subsequent roles include Man. IT Trames, MAPFRE Mutualidad Functional Area 1990–94, Regional Dir MAPFRE Mutualidad in Asturias and Extremadura 1994–98, Exec. Vice-Chair. MAPFRE Praico 1998–2000, Gen. Man. 2000–04, Chair. and CEO 2001–04, Gen. Man. MAPFRE Mutualidad and Chief Exec. MAPFRE's Motor Unit 2005–06, Chair. Exec. Cttee MAPFRE Mutualidad 2005–06, Exec. Vice-Chair. MAPFRE Agricultural 2006–08, Chair. MAPFRE Box Health 2006–08, Chair. MAPFRE Automotive 2006–08, Chair. MAPFRE Seguros Generales SA 2006–08, Car Chair. MAPFRE SA 2006–08, Chair. MAPFRE Familiar SA 2006–10, mem. Bd of Dirs and Steering Cttee 2006–11, mem. Bd of Dirs MAPFRE Vida SA 2007–12, mem. Exec. Cttee 2009–12, Chair. Ascat General Insurance 2010–11, mem. Bd of Dirs and Exec. Cttee MAPFRE Familiar SA 2011–12, Chair. MAPFRE Domestic Insurance Div. 2011–12, Chair. and CEO MAPFRE SA 2012–, First Vice-Chair. UNESPA 2011–, CEO Int. Insurance and Global Business Divs 2012–; mem. Bd of Dirs Spanish Insurance Compensation Consortium 2012–; mem. Bd of Trustees, Fundación MAPFRE 2006–14, currently Pres.; mem. Advisory Bd Spanish Gen. Directorate for Insurance and Pension Funds 2011–, Business Council for Competitiveness 2012–17. *Address:* MAPFRE SA, Carretera de Pozuelo-Majadahonda 52, 28220 Majadahonda, Madrid, Spain (office). *Telephone:* (91) 581-11-00 (office). *Fax:* (91) 581-11-34 (office). *E-mail:* info@mapfre.com (office). *Website:* www.mapfre.com (office).

HUFFINGTON, Arianna, MA; Greek/American editor and internet industry executive; *Founder and CEO, Thrive Global;* b. (Arianna Stassinopoulou), 15 July 1950, Athens, Greece; d. of Konstantinos Stassinopoulos and Elli Stassinopoulou (née Georgiadi); m. Michael Huffington 1986 (divorced 1997); two d.; ed Girton Coll., Cambridge, UK; moved to England aged 16; fmr Pres. Cambridge Union 1971; moved to London and lived with journalist and broadcaster Bernard Levin; moved to USA 1980; nationally syndicated columnist and author; provided political coverage of Nat. Elections for Comedy Central 1996; co-f. Americans for Fuel Efficient Cars; spokesperson Detroit Project 2003; ind. cand. for Gov. in Calif. recall election 2003; Founder and Ed.-in-Chief The Huffington Post (news website) 2005–11, Pres. and Ed.-in-Chief Huffington Post Media Group 2011–16 (after acquisition of Huffington Post by AOL); Founder and CEO Thrive Global 2016–; mem. Bd Points of Light Foundation, A Place Called Home; mem. Bd Trustees Archer School for Girls; mem. Advisory Bd Council on American Politics, George Washington Univ.; mem. Bd Reform Inst. *Publications include:* The Female Woman 1973, After Reason 1978, Maria Callas: The Woman Behind the Legend 1981, Pablo-Picasso: Creator and Destroyer 1988, The Gods of Greece 1993, The Fourth Instinct 1994, Greetings from the Lincoln Bedroom 1998, How to Overthrow the Government 2000, Pigs at the Trough: How Corporate Greed and Political Corruption are Undermining America 2003, Fanatics and Fools 2004, On Becoming Fearless... In Love, Work, and Life 2007, Right is Wrong: How the Lunatic Fringe Hijacked America, Shredded the Constitution, and Made Us All Less Safe 2008, Third World America: How Our Politicians Are Abandoning the Middle Class and Betraying the American Dream 2010, Thrive: The Third Metric to Redefining Success and Creating a Life of Well-Being, Wisdom, and Wonder 2014, The Sleep Revolution: Transforming Your Life, One Night at a Time 2016. *E-mail:* info@thriveglobal.com (office). *Website:* www.thriveglobal.com (office).

HUG, Michel, PhD; French civil engineer; b. 30 May 1930, Courson; s. of René Hug and Marcelle Hug (née Quenee); m. Danielle Michaud; one s. two d.; ed Ecole Polytechnique, Ecole Nationale des Ponts et Chaussées, Univ. of Iowa; joined Electricité de France 1956, various positions at the Chatou Research and Test Centre 1956–66, Regional Man. (Southern Alps) 1967–68, Research and Devt Man. 1969–72, Planning and Construction Man. 1972–82; Gen. Man. Charbonnages de France (French Coal Bd) 1982–86; Prof. of Fluid Mechanics, Ecole Nationale des Ponts et Chaussées 1963–80; Chair. Bd Ecole Nationale Supérieure d'Electrotechnique, d'Electronique, d'Informatique et d'Hydraulique de Toulouse 1980–90; Chair. Bd CdF Chimie 1985–86; Deputy Admin. Org. des Producteurs d'Energie Nucléaire (OPEN) 1992–2000; mem. Applications Cttee of Acad. des Sciences 1987; Foreign mem. US Nat. Acad. of Eng 1979–; mem. American Nuclear Soc.; Hon. mem. Int. Assoc. of Hydraulics Research; Lauréat de l'Institut (Prix des Laboratoires) 1964; Commdr Ordre nat. du Merite 1980; Officier, Légion d'honneur 1977; Officier des Palmes académiques (Ministry of Educ.) 1986; Chevalier des Arts et Lettres 1981, du Mérite agricole. *Publications include:* Mécanique des fluides appliquée aux problèmes d'aménagement et d'énergétique 1975, Organiser le changement dans l'entreprise—une expérience à E.D.F. 1975. *Leisure interests:* tennis, shooting, swimming, flying. *Address:* Design Stratégique, BP 2, 78290 Croissy-sur-Seine, France (office). *E-mail:* michel.hug@neuf.fr (office).

HUGHES, Anthony Vernon, MA; Solomon Islands banking executive and civil servant; b. 29 Dec. 1936, England; s. of Henry Norman Hughes and Marjorie Hughes; m. 1st Carole Frances Robson 1961 (divorced 1970); one s.; m. 2nd Kuria Vaze Paia 1971; one s. one d. two adopted d.; ed Queen Mary's Grammar School, Walsall, England, Pembroke Coll., Oxford and Bradford Univ.; Commr of Lands, Registrar of Titles, Solomon Islands 1969–70, Head of Planning 1974–76, Perm. Sec. Ministry of Finance 1976–81, Gov. Cen. Bank 1982–93; Devt Sec., Gilbert and Ellice Islands 1971–73; Regional Econ. Adviser UN Econ. and Social Comm. for Asia and the Pacific 1994–99; freelance econ. man. consultant; Cross of Solomon Islands 1981. *Publications include:* numerous articles on land tenure, econ. planning, devt admin, foreign investment, expecially jt ventures, with special emphasis on small countries. *Leisure interests:* working outside, squash, rowing, sculling, sailing. *Address:* PO Box 486, Honiara, Solomon Islands (home).

HUGHES, Rev. Gerard Joseph, MA, STL, PhD; British ecclesiastic and academic; *Tutor in Philosophy, Campion Hall, University of Oxford;* b. 6 June 1934, Wallington, Surrey; s. of Henry Hughes and Margaret Hughes; ed St Aloysius Coll. Glasgow, London Inst. of Educ., Campion Hall, Univ. of Oxford, Heythrop Coll., Oxford and Univ. of Michigan, USA; Chair. Dept of Philosophy, Heythrop Coll., Univ. of London 1973–96, Vice-Prin. 1986–98; mem. Senate and Academic Council, Univ. of London 1987–96; Vice-Prov. British Prov. of SJ 1982–88; Austin Fagothey Prof. of Philosophy, Univ. of Santa Clara, Calif. 1988, 1992; Master, Campion Hall, Oxford 1998–2005, Tutor in Philosophy 2005–; Hon. DLit (London) 2009. *Publications:* Authority in Morals 1978, Moral Decisions 1980, The Philosophical Assessment of Theology (ed.) 1987, The Nature of God 1995, Aristotle on Ethics 2001, Is God to Blame? 2007, Fidelity without Fundamentalism 2010. *Leisure interests:* music, crosswords, walking, gardening. *Address:* University of Oxford, Faculty of Philosophy, Radcliffe Humanities, Radcliffe Observatory Quarter, Woodstock Road, Oxford, OX2 6GG, England. *Telephone:* (1865) 276926. *Fax:* (1865) 276932. *E-mail:* enquiries@philosophy.ox.ac.uk. *Website:* www.philosophy.ox.ac.uk.

HUGHES, H. Richard, FRIBA; British architect; b. 4 July 1926, London; s. of Maj. Henry Hughes and Olive Hughes (née Curtis); m. 1st Anne Hill 1951 (died 2006); one s. two d.; m. 2nd Anna Kavya (née Strouts) 2009; ed Kenton Coll., Nairobi, Kenya, Hilton Coll., Natal, SA, Architectural Asscn School of Architecture, London; Corporal in Kenya Regt attached to Royal Engineers 1945–46; Asst Architect, Kenya and Uganda 1950–51; Architect, Hartford, Conn., USA 1953–55, Nairobi, Kenya 1955–57; Prin. Richard Hughes and Partners 1957–86; Chair. Kenya Br., Capricorn Africa Soc. 1958–61, Environment Liaison Cen. 1976–78, Lamu Soc. 1977–79; UNEP Consultant on Human Settlements 1978; UN Cen. for Human Settlements Consultant on bldg materials, construction tech. in developing countries 1979; Ed., Fireball Int. 1986–92; mem. Exec. Cttee, Friends of the Elderly, London 1987–92; mem. Zebra Housing Asscn Bd, London 1988–98, Trustee, Zebra Trust, London 1988–2012 (Vice-Chair. 1994); Voluntary Guide, Tate Britain and Tate Modern, London 1987–; NADFAS Lecturer 1995–2006. *Publications include:* Habitat Handbook (co-author with Graham Searle) 1982, In the Frame 1989, Living Paintings Trust Albums of Architecture for the Blind (ed.) 1991, 1994, Capricorn – David Stirling's Second African Campaign 2003; contribs to books on architecture and articles in New Commonwealth, Architectural Review, Architects Journal and Modern Painters. *Leisure interests:* collecting modern art, dinghy sailing. *Address:* 47 Chiswick Quay, London, W4 3UR, England. *E-mail:* richard@cquay.f9.co.uk.

HUGHES, Hubert Benjamin; Anguillan politician; b. 15 Oct. 1933; m.; mem. House of Ass. for Dist 6, Road South constituency; Chief Minister of Anguilla 1994–2000, 2010–15, also Minister of Finance, Econ. Devt and Tourism 2010–15; Leader, Anguilla United Movt. *Address:* c/o Office of the Chief Minister, The Secretariat, POB 60, The Valley, Anguilla (office).

HUGHES, John Lawrence, BA; American publisher (retd); b. 13 March 1925, New York; s. of John C. Hughes and Margaret Kelly; m. Rose M. Pitman 1947; three s. one d.; ed Yale Univ.; reporter, Nassau Review Star, Rockville Centre, Long Island, NY 1949; Asst Sr Ed., Pocket Books, Inc. New York 1949–59; Vice-Pres. Washington Square Press 1958; Sr Ed., Vice-Pres. and Dir William Morrow & Co. 1960–65, Pres. and CEO 1965–85; Pres. and CEO The Hearst Book Group 1985–87, Chair. and CEO 1988–90, Ed.-at-Large, Group Adviser 1990–99; Consultant and Ed.-at-Large HarperCollins Publrs, New York 1999–2001; Trustee, Yale Univ. Press, Pierpont Morgan Library and Museum, Library of America, Acad. of American Poets; mem. Bd Asscn of American Publishers 1986–90 (Chair. 1988–90); mem. Bd Nat. Book Awards 1982–94 (Chair. 1988–89); mem. Publrs Hall of Fame 1989. *Leisure interest:* golf. *Address:* 1 Church Street, Southport, CT 06890, USA (home). *Telephone:* (203) 257-9004 (home). *Fax:* (203) 259-8142 (home). *E-mail:* lawrencehughes@earthlink.net (home).

HUGHES, Karen, BA, BFA; American communications consultant, fmr political adviser and fmr diplomatist; *Worldwide Vice-Chairman, Burson-Marsteller;* b. 27 Dec. 1956, Paris, France; d. of Harold Parfitt and Patricia Parfitt; m. Jerry Hughes; one s. one step-d.; ed Southern Methodist Univ.; TV news reporter, KXAS-TV, Dallas/Fort Worth, Tex. 1977–84; press coordinator for Reagan-Bush presidential campaign 1984; fmr Exec. Dir Republican Party of Tex.; Communications Dir for George W. Bush (while Gov. of Tex. and for presidential campaign) 1995–2000, Counselor to the President 2001–02, left Bush admin to return to Tex. July 2002, Sr Advisor to White House 2003–04, returned to full-time service with Bush campaign Aug. 2004; Under-Sec. of State for Public Diplomacy and Public Affairs with rank of Amb., US State Dept 2005–07 (resgnd); Worldwide Vice-Chair. Burson-Marsteller (communications consultancy), Austin, Tex. 2008–; mem. West Point Bd of Visitors 2008–. *Publication:* Ten Minutes from Normal 2004. *Address:* Burson-Marsteller, 98 San Jacinto, Suite 1450, Austin, TX 78701-3232, USA (office). *Telephone:* (512) 879-0990 (office). *Fax:* (512) 879-0999 (office). *Website:* www.burson-marsteller.com (office).

HUGHES, Louis R., BS, MBA; American business executive; *Chairman, InZero Systems;* b. 10 Feb. 1949, Cleveland, Ohio; m. Candice Ann Hughes 1972; two c.; ed Gen. Motors Inst., Flint, Mich. and Harvard Univ.; began career with Gen. Motors on financial staff in New York; Asst Treas 1982; Vice-Pres. of Finance, Gen. Motors of Canada 1985–86; Vice-Pres. for Finance, Gen. Motors (Europe), Zürich 1987–89; Chair., Man. Dir Adam Opel AG 1989–92; Exec. Vice-Pres. Gen. Motors Corpn (responsible for int. operations) 1992–2000; Pres. Gen. Motors (Europe) AG 1992–94; Chair. Bd Saab Automobile AB 1992; Pres. Gen. Motors Int. Operations, Inc., Switzerland 1994–98; Exec. Vice-Pres. New Business Strategies, Gen. Motors Corpn, Detroit 1998–2000; Pres. and COO Lockheed Martin 2000; Chair. Maxager Technology Inc. 2000–08; Chief of Staff, Afghanistan Reconstruction Group, US State Dept 2004–05; Chair. and CEO InZero Systems, Herndon, Va 2005–10, CEO 2010–11, Chair. 2011–; Exec. Advisor Partner, Wind Point Partners; mem. Bd of Dirs ABB 2003–, Akzo Nobel (Netherlands), Sulzer (Switzerland), Alcatel-Lucent (France); mem. Supervisory Bd Deutsche Bank 1993–2000; Pres. Swiss-American

Chamber of Commerce; Chair. European Council of American Chambers of Commerce; mem. British Telecom US Advisory Bd; Order of Merit (Germany); Vernon A. Walters Award 1993. *Leisure interests:* skiing, mountain climbing, antiques. *Address:* InZero Systems, 13755 Sunrise Valley Drive, Suite 750, Herndon, VA 20171, USA (office). *Telephone:* (703) 636-2048 (office). *Website:* www.workplaytechnology.com (office).

HUGHES, Mervyn Gregory; Australian fmr professional cricketer; b. 23 Nov. 1961, Euroa, Vic.; s. of Ian Hughes and Freda Hughes; m. Sue Hughes 1991; one d.; right-arm fast bowler and right-hand lower-order batsman; played for Victoria 1981–95, Essex 1983; played in 53 Test matches for Australia 1985–94, taking 212 wickets (average 28.38) and scoring 1,032 runs (average 16.64, highest score 72 not out), took hat-trick v. W Indies, Perth 1988; toured England 1989, 1993; played in 33 One-Day Ints, taking 38 wickets (average 29.34), best bowling (innings) 4/44; played in 165 First-class matches, taking 593 wickets (average 29.39), best bowling (innings) 8/87 and scoring 2,649 runs (average 17.54); replaced Allan Border as a selector for Australian cricket team June 2005–10; Host, Merv Hughes Fishing (TV series) 2015; Wisden Cricketer of the Year 1994. *Film:* has done some acting, portraying Ivan Milat in comedy movie, Fat Pizza. *Leisure interests:* golf, relaxing at home, going to the beach, Australian Rules, basketball, fishing. *Address:* c/o Bravo Management, Level 5, 111 Coventry Street, Southbank, Vic. 3006, Australia (office). *Telephone:* (3) 8825-6641 (office). *E-mail:* admin@bravotalentmgmt.com (office). *Website:* www.bravotalentmgmt.com (office).

HUGHES, Sean Patrick Francis, MS, FRCS, FRCSEd (Orth.), FRCSI; British surgeon and academic; *Professor Emeritus of Orthopaedic Surgery, Imperial College London;* b. 2 Dec. 1941, Farnham, Surrey; s. of Patrick Hughes and Kathleen E. Hughes; m. Felicity M. Anderson 1971; one s. two d.; ed Downside School and St Mary's Hosp. Medical School, Univ. of London; Asst Lecturer in Anatomy, St Mary's Hosp. Medical School 1969; Research Fellow, Mayo Clinic, USA 1975; Sr Registrar in Orthopaedics, Middlesex Hosp., London 1977; Sr Lecturer in Orthopaedics, Royal Postgraduate Medical School, London 1979, Prof. of Orthopaedic Surgery, Royal Postgraduate Medical School (became part of Imperial Coll. School of Medicine) 1991–96, Prof. of Orthopaedic Surgery, Imperial Coll. London 1996–2006, Prof. Emer. 2006–, Head of Div. Surgery, Anaesthetics and Intensive Care 1996–2004, Hon. Consultant, Imperial Coll. Health Care Trust 2007–; Prof. of Orthopaedic Surgery, Univ. of Edinburgh 1979–91; Hon. Consultant, Orthopaedic Surgeon Hammersmith Hosps 1991–2006; Clinical Dir Surgery and Anaesthetics, Hammersmith Hosps NHS Trust 1998–2002; Medical Dir, Ravenscourt Park Hosp., Hammersmith Hosps NHS Trust 2002–07; Rahume Darwood Prof., E Africa 1993, Patrick Kelly Visiting Prof., Mayo Clinic 2000; Vice-Pres. Royal Coll. of Surgeons of Edinburgh 1994–97; Fellow, Royal Coll. of Surgeons in Ireland; Hon. Civilian Consultant to RN, Hon. Consultant 1994–; Aris and Gale Lecturer, Royal Coll. of Surgeons 1976, Walter Mercer Medal, British Orthopaedic Asscn 2004. *Publications:* textbooks and scientific publications on orthopaedics, particularly bone blood flow, musculoskeletal infection, fractures and management of spinal disorders. *Leisure interests:* swimming, walking, skiing, opera, ballet, supporting Tottenham Hotspur, running. *Address:* Department of Surgery and Cancer, 1st Floor, B-Block, Imperial College London, Hammersmith Hospital, Hammersmith Campus, London, SW7 2AZ (office); 5 Meadow Place, Edensor Road, London, W4 2SY, England (home). *Telephone:* (20) 8995-7708 (home). *E-mail:* seanfrancishughes@imperial.ac.uk (office). *Website:* www1.imperial.ac.uk/surgeryandcancer (office).

HUGHES, Sir Simon Henry Ward, Kt, PC, MA; British politician and barrister; b. 17 May 1951, Cheshire; s. of James Henry Annesley Hughes and Sylvia Hughes (née Ward); ed The Cathedral School, Llandaff, Christ Coll., Brecon, Selwyn Coll., Cambridge, Inns of Court School of Law; called to the Bar, Inner Temple 1974; trainee, EEC, Brussels 1975–76; trainee and mem. Secr., Directorate and Comm. on Human Rights, Council of Europe, Strasbourg 1976–77; practising barrister 1978–; Vice-Chair. Bermondsey Liberal Asscn 1981–83; MP for Southwark and Bermondsey 1983–97 (Liberal 1983–88, Liberal Democrat 1988–97), for Southwark N and Bermondsey 1997–2010, for Bermondsey and Old Southwark 2010–15; Vice-Chair. Parl. Youth Affairs Lobby 1984–2015; Vice-Pres. Southwark Chamber of Commerce 1987–, Pres. 1984–87; Liberal Spokesman on the Environment 1983–87, 1987–88; Alliance Spokesman on Health Jan.–June 1987; Liberal Democrat Spokesperson on Educ. and Science 1988–90, on Environment 1988–94, on Natural Resources 1992–94, on Community and Urban Affairs and Young People 1994–95, on Social Welfare 1995–97, on Health 1995–99, on Home Affairs 1999–2003, on Constitutional Affairs and Attorney-Gen. 2006–07, on the House of Commons 2007–08, on Energy and Climate Change 2009–10, cand. for London Mayor 2004, Deputy Leader Liberal Democrat Party 2010–15; Minister of State for Justice 2013–15; Chair. Liberal Party Advisory Panel on Home Affairs 1981–83; mem. Accommodation and Works Select Cttee 1992–97; mem. Southwark Area Youth Cttee, Anti-Apartheid Movt; mem. Liberal Democrat Party, (Pres. 2004–08); Hon. Fellow, South Bank Univ. *Publications:* Across the Divide 1986, Pathways to Power 1992. *Leisure interests:* music, sport, theatre, the outdoors. *Address:* 6 Lynton Road, Bermondsey, London, SE1 5QR, England (home). *Telephone:* (20) 7237-8444 (office). *E-mail:* simon@simonhughes.org.uk (home). *Website:* www.simonhughes.org.uk.

HUGHES OF STRETFORD, Baroness (Life Peer), cr. 2010, of Ellesmere Port in the County of Cheshire; **Rt Hon. Beverley Hughes,** PC, MSc; British politician; b. 30 March 1950; d. of Norman Hughes and Doris Hughes; m. Tom McDonald 1973; one s. two d.; ed Ellesmere Port Girls' Grammar School, Univs of Manchester and Liverpool; Probation Officer, Merseyside –1976; Research Assoc., Univ. of Manchester 1976–81, Lecturer 1981–93, Sr Lecturer and Head of Dept 1993–97; Councillor, Trafford Metropolitan Borough Council 1986–97, Council Leader 1995; MP (Labour) for Stretford and Urmston 1997–2010, mem. Select Cttee on Home Affairs 1997–98; Parl. Pvt. Sec. to Hilary Armstrong, Minister for Local Govt and Housing 1998–99, Parl. Under-Sec. of State, Dept of the Environment, Transport and the Regions 2000–02; Minister of State for Immigration, Citizenship and Counter-Terrorism 2002–04, for Children, Young People and Families 2005–07, for Children and Youth Justice 2007–09 (resgnd); mem. (Labour), House of Lords 2010–, Shadow Spokesperson for Children and Educ. 2010–15, mem. EU Justice Sub-cttee 2015–. *Leisure interests:* walking, jazz. *Address:* House of Lords, Westminster, London, SW1A 0PW, England (office). *Telephone:* (20) 7219-0956 (office). *E-mail:* hughesb@parliament.uk (office). *Website:* www.parliament.uk/biographies/lords/baroness-hughes-of-stretford/459 (office).

HUH, Chang-soo, BBA, MBA; South Korean business executive; *Chairman, GS Holdings Corporation;* b. 6 Oct. 1948, Jinju; m.; two c.; ed Korea Univ., St Louis Univ., USA; joined LG Group strategic planning office 1977, worked in LG International and LG Chemical, Man. Dir LG International Hong Kong and Tokyo offices 1982–86, Exec. Vice-Pres. LG Industrial Systems 1992–95, Chair. LG Cable 1995–2001, with LG Engineering and Construction 2002–04, Chair. GS Holdings Corpn (conglomerate of 59 affiliate cos spun off from LG Group in 2004) 2004–, mem. Exec. Bd; f. J.K. Huh Foundation (charity); Chair. Fed. of Korean Industries 2010–; Dr hc (St Louis Univ.) 2007. *Leisure interest:* football fan. *Address:* GS Holdings Corporation, GS Tower 508, Nonhyeon Ro, Gangnam Gu, Seoul, Republic of Korea (office). *Telephone:* (2) 2500-5300 (office). *Fax:* (2) 2500-5301 (office). *Website:* www.gsgcorp.com (office).

HUH, Jin-soo, BBA, MBA; South Korean business executive; *Vice-Chairman and CEO, GS Caltex Corporation;* b. 1953, Busan; ed Korea Univ., George Washington Univ., USA; joined GS Caltex Corpn in 1986, has held positions of increasing responsibility in the co., Vice-Chair. and CEO 2013–. *Address:* GS Caltex Corporation, 679 Yeoksam-dong, Seoul 135-985, Republic of Korea (office). *Telephone:* (2) 2005-1114 (office). *Fax:* (2) 2005-8181 (office). *E-mail:* info@gscaltex.com (office). *Website:* www.gscaltex.com (office).

HUHNE, Christopher (Chris) Murray Paul-, BA (Hons); British economist, politician, journalist and author; *Consultant, Chris Huhne & Associates Limited;* b. 2 July 1954, Westminster, London; s. of Peter Paul-Huhne and Ann Murray; m. Vicky Pryce 1984 (divorced 2011); two s. one d. two step-d.; ed Westminster School, Magdalen Coll., Oxford (Demy Scholar), Univ. of Paris (Sorbonne); edited Isis student magazine at Oxford; served on Exec. of Oxford Univ. Labour Club; financial and econ. journalist at the Guardian, Independent and the Economist for 19 years, also Business Ed. The Independent and The Independent on Sunday; undercover freelance reporter in India during Prime Minister Indira Gandhi's emergency when western journalists had been expelled; also worked for Liverpool Daily Post and Liverpool Echo and The Economist; f. Sovereign Ratings IBCA 1994; Man. Dir Fitch IBCA 1997, Vice-Chair. Fitch Ratings 1999–2003; contested Reading East constituency (Social Democratic Party-Liberal Alliance) 1983, Oxford West and Abingdon 1987; MEP for SE England 1999–2005; MP for Eastleigh, Hants. 2005–10, for Eastleigh (revised boundary) 2010–13 (resgnd); Liberal Democrat Shadow Chief Sec. to the Treasury 2005–06, Shadow Sec. of State for Environment, Food and Rural Affairs 2006–07, Shadow Home Sec. 2007–10, Shadow Sec. of State for Justice and Lord Chancellor 2008–09; Sec. of State for Energy and Climate Change 2010–12; charged with perverting the course of justice for speeding offence 2012, served nine weeks in prison 2013; European Chair., Zilkha Biomass Energy 2013–; currently Consultant, Chris Huhne & Assocs. Ltd; Chair. Press and Broadcasting Policy Panel 1994–95; Econ. Adviser, Gen. Election 1997; mem. Econ. Policy Comm. 1998; apptd Advisory Bd mem. Centre for Reform 1998; Jt Chair. Policy Panel on Global Stability, Security and Sustainability 1999–2000; Chair. Expert Comm. of Britain's Adoption of the Euro 1999–2000, Comm. on Public Services 2001–02; contested Liberal Democrat leadership 2006, 2007; currently Co-Chair. ET Index Research; mem. Council of the EU, Environment Council 2010–13, Transport, Telecommunications and Energy Council 2010–13, European Movt, Green Lib Dems, Asscn of Liberal Democrat Trade Unionists, Nat. Union of Journalists; Liberal Democrat; Jr and Sr Wincott Awards for Financial Journalist of the Year 1980, 1989, respectively. *Publications include:* Debt and Danger (with Lord Lever of Manchester) 1985, Real World Economics 1990, Both Sides of the Coin (with James Forder) 1999; contrib.: Orange Book 2004, The City in Europe and the World 2005; articles for the Financial Times, The Guardian, The Independent and New Statesman. *Address:* 48a Britton Street, London, EC1M 5UL, England (home). *E-mail:* chris@chrishuhne.org.uk (home). *Website:* www.chrishuhne.org.uk.

HUI, Ann; Chinese film director; b. 23 May 1947, Anshan, Liaoning Prov.; ed Hong Kong Univ., London Film School; moved to Hong Kong aged five; fmr asst to film director Hu Jingquan; joined TVB and began career making TV documentaries and features; joined Ind. Comm. for Anti-Corruption 1977, made seven TV episodes for drama series (two of which were banned); joined RTHK (Govt TV network) 1978, directed three segments of Beneath the Lion Rock (series); acted in The River 1998, 2001; Lifetime Achievement Award, Asian Film Awards 2012. *Films include:* The Secret 1979, The Spooky Bunch 1980, Boy From Vietnam (TV feature), The Story of Woo Viet (TV feature) 1981, The Boat People (TV feature) (Official Selection at Cannes Film Festival, Best Film, Hong Kong Film Awards) 1982, Love in a Fallen City 1984, The Romance of Book and Sword/Princess Fragrance 1987, Starry is the Night 1988, Song of the Exile (Best Film, Asian Pacific Film Festival and Rimini Film Festival) 1990, Zodiac Killers 1991, My American Grandson 1991, A Boy and His Hero 1993, The Day the Sun Turned Cold (exec. producer) (Best Film, Tokyo Int. Film Festival) 1994, Ah Kam 1996, Opium War (assoc. producer) 1997, Ordinary Heroes 1999, Black Mask (screenwriter) 1999, Summer Show (Silver Bear Award, Berlin Film Festival), Ordinary Heroes, Visible Secret 2002, July Rhapsody 2002, Jade Goddess of Mercy 2003, The Postmodern Life of My Aunt 2006, The Way We Are (Hong Kong Film Award 2009) 2008, Night and Fog 2009, All About Love 2010, A Simple Life 2011, The Golden Era 2014. *Publications include:* The Secret 1979, Boat People 1982, Romance of Book and Sword 1987, Yakuza Chase 1991, Summer Snow 1995.

HUI, Liangyu; Chinese politician and economist; b. 29 Oct. 1944, Yushu Co., Jilin Prov.; ed Jilin Agricultural School, Party School of CCP Jilin Prov. Cttee; clerk, Agricultural Bureau and Personnel Supervision Bureau, Yushu Co. 1964–68; joined CCP 1966; clerk and Deputy Head, CCP Revolutionary Cttee (Political Dept), Yushu Co. 1969–72; Deputy Dir Org. Dept, CCP Yushu Co. Cttee 1972–74; Deputy Sec. CCP Yushu Co. Cttee 1974–77; Deputy Dir Jilin Prov. Agricultural Bureau, Prov. Agricultural and Animal Husbandry Dept; Deputy Sec. CCP Leading Group 1977–84; Deputy Sec. CCP Baichengzi Prefectural Cttee, Commr Baichengzi Admin. Office 1984–85; elected mem. Standing Cttee CCP Jilin Prov. Cttee 1985; Dir Rural Policy Research Office, Dir Rural Work Dept CCP Jilin Prov. Cttee 1985–87; apptd Vice-Gov. Jilin Prov. 1987; Deputy Dir CCPCC Policy Research Office 1990; Deputy Sec. CCP Hubei Prov. Cttee 1992; Chair. 1993 Hubei Prov. CPPCC Cttee, Deputy Sec. CCP Anhui Prov. Cttee and Acting Gov. Anhui

Prov. 1994–95, Gov. 1995–98; Sec. CCP Anhui Prov. Cttee 1998, Sec. CCP Jiangsu Prov. Cttee 1999–2002; Rep. 15th CCP Congress; Alt. mem. 14th CCP Cen. Cttee, mem. 15th CCP Cen. Cttee 1997–2002, 16th CCP Cen. Cttee 2002–07, 17th CCP Cen. Cttee 2007–12, also mem. Politburo 2007–12; Rep. of 7th, 8th and 9th NPC; Vice-Premier, State Council 2003–13.

HUI SI-YAN, Rafael, BA, MPA; Hong Kong government official; b. 8 Feb. 1948; m. Teresa Lo Mei-mei 1974; ed Queen's Coll., Univ. of Hong Kong, Harvard Univ., USA; joined Civil Service 1970, Admin. Officer 1971, with Ind. Comm. Against Corruption 1977–79, Deputy Sec.-Gen. Unofficial Mems of the Exec. and Legis. Councils Office 1985–86, Deputy Sec. for Econ. Services 1986–90, for Works 1990–91, Dir New Airport Projects Co-ordination Office 1991, Commr for Transport 1992–95, Sec. for Financial Services 1995–2000; Man. Dir Mandatory Provident Fund Schemes Authority 2000–03; Dir Kowloon Motor Bus Holdings Ltd 2004–05; Chief Sec. for Admin, Hong Kong Special Admin. Region 2005–07; Vice-Chair. Hong Kong Arts Festival Soc. 2001–05; Chief Sec. for Admin, Central People's Govt of People's Repub. of China 2005–07, unofficial mem. Exec. Council 2007–09; mem. Exec. Cttee Hong Kong Philharmonic Soc. Ltd 2004–05; Steward, Hong Kong Jockey Club 2002; sentenced to seven and a half years in prison for corruption 2014; Justice of the Peace 1986, Hon. Sec. Hong Kong Int. Film Festival Soc. Ltd 2004–05; Gold Bauhinia Star 1998.

HUILLARD, Xavier; French construction industry executive; *Chairman and CEO, Vinci;* b. 27 June 1954; ed École Polytechnique, École Nationale des Ponts et Chaussées; served as civil servant in a local Public Works and Planning Dept and in Ministry for Infrastructure's Dept of Int. Business; joined SGE as Dir of Int. Business at SOGEA 1996, Chair. 1997–2000; Chair. Vinci Construction 2000–02, Sr Exec. Vice-Pres. Vinci and Chair. Vinci Energies 2002, mem. Bd of Dirs and CEO Vinci 2006–, Chair. 2010–, also Chair. VINCI Concessions 2006–; Chair. Institut de l'Entreprise 2011–. *Address:* Vinci, 1 cours Ferdinand de Lesseps, 92851 Rueil-Malmaison Cedex France (office). *Telephone:* 1-47-16-35-00 (office). *Fax:* 1-47-51-91-02 (office). *E-mail:* contact.internet@vinci.com (office). *Website:* www.vinci.com (office).

HUISGEN, Rolf, PhD; German chemist and academic; *Professor Emeritus of Organic Chemistry, University of Munich;* b. 13 June 1920, Gerolstein, Eifel; s. of Edmund Huisgen and Maria Flink; m. Trudl Schneiderhan 1945 (died 2010); two d.; ed Univs of Bonn and Munich; Lecturer, Univ. of Munich 1947–49, Full Prof. of Organic Chem. 1952–88, Prof. Emer. 1988–; Assoc. Prof., Univ. of Tübingen 1949–52; Rockefeller Fellow, USA 1955; numerous guest professorships, USA, Israel, Japan, Spain and Switzerland; mem. Bavarian Acad. of Science, Deutsche Akad. der Naturforscher Leopoldina; Foreign Assoc. NAS, Washington; Corresp. mem. Real Acad. de Ciencias Exactas, Madrid, Heidelberg Acad. of Sciences, Polish Acad. of Sciences, Chemical Soc. of Japan; Hon. FRSC, London; Hon. mem. American Acad. of Arts and Sciences, Soc. Chimique de France, Pharmaceutical Soc. of Japan, Gesellschaft Deutscher Chemiker, Accad. Nazionale dei Lincei (Italy), Istituto Lombardo, Polish Acad. Sciences; Hon. Prof., Univ. of St Petersburg; Bavarian Order of Merit 1982, Bavarian Maximilian Order for Science and Art 1984; Hon. Dr rer. nat (Freiburg) 1977, (Erlangen-Nuremberg) 1980, (Würzburg) 1984, (Regensburg) 1985, (Tech. Inst., St Petersburg) 1993, (Freie Univ., Berlin) 2010; Dr hc (Univ. Complutense de Madrid) 1975; Liebig Medal, Gesellschaft Deutscher Chemiker 1961, Médaille Lavoisier, Soc. Chimique de France 1965, ACS Roger Adams Award in Organic Chem. 1975, Otto Hahn Award for Chem. and Physics 1979, Adolfo Quilico Medal, Italian Chemical Soc. 1987 and other awards. *Publications:* The Adventure Playground of Mechanisms and Novel Reactions (autobiog.) 1994; more than 600 research papers on organic reaction mechanisms and cycloadditions. *Leisure interests:* modern art, archaeology. *Address:* Kaulbachstr. 10, 80539 Munich (home); Department Chemie, Universität München, Butenandtstr. 5–13, 81377 Munich, Germany (office). *Telephone:* (89) 218077712 (office); (89) 281645 (home). *E-mail:* rolf.huisgen@cup .uni-muenchen.de (office). *Website:* www.cup.uni-muenchen.de (office).

HUITFELDT, Anniken; Norwegian politician; b. 29 Nov. 1969, Bærum; d. of Iver Huitfeldt and Sidsel Scharning; m. Ola Petter Flem; three c.; ed London School of Econs, Univ. of Oslo; Pres. Labour Youth League, Ullensaker municipality 1985–88; mem. Bd Labour Youth League, Akershus Co. 1986–90, Sec. 1988–89, mem. Bd Labour Youth League 1990–94, Vice-Pres. 1994–96, Pres. 1996–2000; Student Rep., Akershus Co. School Bd 1986–88; Pres. Nordic Socialist Youth League 2000; Vice-Pres. Int. Union of Socialist Youth 2000–01; mem. Housing Comm. 2000–02; Researcher, Inst. for Applied Social Science 2000–05; mem. Cen. Exec. Cttee Det norske Arbeiderparti (DnA—Norwegian Labour Party) 2002–; mem. Stortinget (Parl.) (DnA) for Akershus Co. 2005–; First Deputy Chair. Standing Cttee for Educ., Research and Church Affairs 2005–08; Head of DnA women's network 2007–; Minister of Children and Equality 2008–09, of Culture 2009–12, of Labour and Social Inclusion 2012–13; mem. Foreign and Defense Cttee 2013–; mem. Cen. Exec. Cttee, Norwegian School Students' Union 1987–88, Comm. for Gen. Educ. Subjects 1987–89, Gender Equality Cttee, Ullensaker municipality 1987–91, School Cttee, Akershus Co. 1989–95, Falstad Memorial and Human Rights Centre 2000–05, Save the Children Norway 2001–07, Comm. on Quality in Basic Educ. 2001–03, Bd of Norwegian Org. for Asylum Seekers 2003–05. *Address:* c/o Utenriks-og forsvarskomiteen, Stortinget, PO Box 1700 Sentrum, 0026 Oslo, Norway (office). *Telephone:* 23-31-35-13 (office). *E-mail:* anniken.huitfeldt@stortinget.no (office). *Website:* www.stortinget.no.

HULCE, Thomas (Tom) Edward; American actor and producer; b. 6 Dec. 1953, Detroit, Mich.; ed North Carolina School of Arts. *Plays include:* Broadway: The Rise and Rise of Daniel Rocket 1982, Eastern Standard 1988, A Memory of Two Mondays, Equus, A Few Good Men 1990, Spring Awakening (producer) (Tony Award) 2007; London: The Normal Heart, Hamlet. *Films include:* September 30th 1955, National Lampoon's Animal House, Those Lips Those Eyes, Amadeus 1985, Echo Park 1985, Slam Dance 1987, Nicky and Gino 1988, Parenthood 1989, Shadowman, The Inner Circle, Fearless, Mary Shelley's Frankenstein 1994, Wings of Courage 1995, The Hunchback of Notre Dame (voice) 1996, Home at the End of the World (producer) 2004, Stranger Than Fiction 2006, Jumper 2008. *Television includes:* Emily Emily, St Elsewhere, Murder in Mississippi 1990, Black Rainbow, The Heidi Chronicles (Emmy Award) 1995.

HULL, Brett; American (b. Canadian) professional ice hockey player (retd); b. 9 Aug. 1964, Belleville, Ont., Canada; s. of Bobby Hull; ed Univ. of Minnesota-Duluth; right-winger; played two seasons for Univ. of Minn.-Duluth; began professional career with Calgary Flames of National Hockey League (NHL) 1986, traded to St Louis Blues, played 1988–98, signed as free agent Dallas Stars, played 1998–2001 (team won Stanley Cup 1999), signed as free agent for Detroit Red Wings, played 2001–04 (team won Stanley Cup 2002), signed as free agent for Phoenix Coyotes 2004–05 (retd); All-Star games appearances 1989, 1990, 1991, 1992, 1993, 1994, 1995, 1997, 2001, All-Star First Team 1990, 1991, 1992; led the NHL in goals with 72 1989/90, with 86 1990/91 (2nd highest total, record for a right-winger); 3rd highest goal total in NHL history (741); 3rd fastest to 600 goals (900 games); 494 goals in 1990s (record); record 17 consecutive seasons of 20 goals or more, including 13 seasons of 30 or more; represented USA at Canada Cup 1991–92, World Cup 1996–97, 2004, Winter Olympics 1998, 2002; Exec. Dallas Stars 2006–07, Co-Gen. Man. 2007–09, Exec. Vice-Pres. 2009–; studio analyst NHL on NBC TV 2006; WCHA Freshman of the Year 1984/85, NHL Lady Byng Trophy 1989/90, NHL Most Valuable Player 1990/91, NHL Lester B. Pearson Award 1990/91, Gold Medal at World Cup 1996 (and named in All-Tournament Team), USA Hockey Distinguished Achievement Award 2003, inducted into Hockey Hall of Fame 2009. *Address:* Dallas Stars, L.P., 2601 Avenue of the Stars, Frisco, TX 75034, USA (office). *Telephone:* (214) 387-5500 (office). *Fax:* (214) 387-5610 (office). *Website:* www.dallasstars.com (office).

HULOT, Nicolas; French broadcaster, environmental campaigner, writer and politician; b. 30 April 1955, Lille; s. of Philippe Hulot and Monique Hulot (née Moulun); m. 1st Isabelle Patissier 1993 (divorced 1996); m. 2nd Florence Lasserre 2002; two s.; photographer, SIPA Presse (news agency) 1973–78; TV journalist and producer, France Inter 1978–87; f. Fondation Ushuaïa 1990 (renamed Fondation Nicolas Hulot pour la Nature et l'Homme 1995); Ed.-in-chief VSD Nature (magazine) 1992–95; cand. in 2012 presidential election; Minister of the Environment 2017–18 (resgnd); Officier, ordre nat. du Mérite, Chevalier des Arts et Lettres, Officier, ordre du Lion du Sénégal, Commdr, Légion d'honneur 2015. *Television includes:* Les Visiteurs du mercredi 1980, Les Pieds au mur 1982–83, Ushuaïa, le magazine de l'Extrême (producer and presenter) 1987–95, Opération Okavango (producer and presenter) 1996–97. *Publications include:* Tabarly: 45 ans de défi 1976, Ces enfants qui souffrent 1978, Les Chemins de traverse 1990, Pour que la Terre reste humaine 1999, Écologuide de A à Z: pour les juniors 2004, La Terre en partage: éloge de la biodiversité 2005, Pour un pacte écologique 2006, Nos années Ushuaïa: 25 ans d'émerveillement 2012, Mon écologuide de A à Z 2015. *Address:* Fondation Nicolas Hulot pour la Nature et l'Homme, 6 rue de l'Est, 92100 Boulogne-Billancourt, France (office). *Telephone:* 1-41-22-10-70 (office). *Website:* www.fondation-nicolas-hulot.org (office).

HULSE, Russell Alan, BS, PhD; American research physicist; *Regental Professor and Associate Professor for Strategic Initiatives, University of Texas at Dallas;* b. 28 Nov. 1950; s. of Alan Earle Hulse and Betty Joan Wedemeyer; ed The Cooper Union, New York and Univ. of Massachusetts; worked at Nat. Radio Astronomy Observatory 1975–77; researcher at Plasma Physics Lab., Princeton Univ. 1977–80, Prin. Research Physicist 1992–2007, Head of Advanced Modelling Sciences Lab. 1994–2007; Assoc. Vice-Pres. for Research and Econ. Devt, Univ. of Texas at Dallas 2004–07, Regental Prof. and Assoc. Prof. for Strategic Initiatives 2007–; Distinguished Resident Fellow, Princeton Univ. 1994; Fellow, American Physical Soc. 1993, AAAS, Inst. of Physics; mem. Bd of Dirs Battelle Memorial Inst. 2006–; mem. American Astronomical Soc.; Hon. DS (Univ. of Massachusetts); Nobel Prize in Physics (jt winner) 1993, Gano Dunn Alumni Award for Achievement in Science, The Cooper Union. *Publications include:* numerous papers in professional journals and conf. proceedings in fields of pulsar astronomy, controlled fusion plasma physics and computer modelling. *Leisure interests:* cross-country skiing, canoeing, nature photography, bird watching, other outdoor activities, target shooting, music. *Address:* Office of the President-Strategic Initiatives, University of Texas at Dallas, 800 West Campbell Road, Richardson, TX 75080-3021, USA (office). *Telephone:* (972) 883-2111 (office); (972) 883-4573 (office). *E-mail:* rah043000@utdallas.edu (office). *Website:* www.utdallas.edu (office).

HULTQVIST, (Carl Anders) Peter; Swedish politician; *Minister for Defence;* b. 31 Dec. 1958; journalist 1977–89; Chair. Municipal Exec. Cttee, Borlänge 1989–2006; mem. (Social Democrats) Riksdag (Parl.) 2006–, mem. Exec. Cttee 2009–, Chair. Cttee on Defence 2011–14; Minister for Defence 2014–; Grand Cross, Order for Merit (Lithuania), Commdr, Order for Merit (Palestine). *Address:* Ministry of Defence, Jakobsgatan 9, 103 33 Stockholm, Sweden (office). *Telephone:* (8) 405-10-00 (office). *Fax:* (8) 723-11-89 (office). *E-mail:* peter.hultqvist@gov.se (office). *Website:* www.government.se/government-of-sweden/ministry-of-defence (office); www.socialdemokraterna.se.

HUMAIDHI, Badr Mishari al-, BA; Kuwaiti economist and government official; b. 23 Oct. 1948; ed Kuwait Univ.; Lecturer of Econs, Kuwait Univ. 1972–74; Econ. Expert, Operations Dept, Kuwait Fund for Arab Econ. Devt 1974–78, Deputy Dir-Gen. 1981–86, Dir-Gen. 1986–2005; Minister of Finance 2006–08; Bd mem. Arab Gulf Program for Supporting UN Devt Orgs 1981, Arab Fund for Social and Econ. Devt 1986, Arab Planning Institute; fmr Deputy Gov. World Bank, Int. Fund for Agricultural Devt for Kuwait.

HUMALA TASSO, Lt Col (retd) Ollanta Moisés, BA, MA; Peruvian army officer (retd), politician and fmr head of state; b. 27 June 1962, Lima; m. Nadine Heredia; three c.; ed Chorrillos Mil. School, Colegio Franco Peruano, Pontifical Catholic Univ. of Peru; began mil. career 1982, officer 1984; formed clandestine group within army called Militares etnocaceristas 1989; rank of Capt. 1991, Maj. 1996, Lt Col 2000; led uprising against then Pres. Alberto Fujimori in Tacna 2000, imprisoned but pardoned; Exec. Dir of Mobilization, Ministry of Nat. Defence, Sedena 2001; Mil. Attaché, Embassy in Paris 2003, in Seoul 2004; retd from army 2005; Founder and Leader Partido Nacionalista Peruano 2005–, unsuccessful presidential cand. Unión por el Perú 2006; Leader Gana Perú (Peru Wins) 2010–; Pres. of Peru 2011–16; Pres. *pro tempore* Union of South American Nations 2012–13; Officer, Cross of Mil. Merit 1996, Commdr 2001. *Address:* c/o Office of the President, Presidential Palace, Plaza Mayor, Lima (office); Partido Nacionalista Peruano, Avda Arequipa 3410, Lima 27, Peru (office).

HUMAM, Muhammad Awad bin, BSc; Yemeni economist and fmr central banker; b. 26 Dec. 1944, Hadramout; ed American Univ. of Beirut, Lebanon; Dir of Research and Statistics, Nat. Bank of Yemen 1978–90; joined Central Bank of Yemen 1990, Deputy Gov., Foreign Operations and Research Dept –2003, Gov. Central Bank of Yemen 2010–16.

HUME, Cameron R.; American lawyer and diplomatist; *Adjunct Professor, Georgetown University;* b. 1947; m.; four d.; ed Princeton Univ., American Univ. School of Law; joined Foreign Service 1970, early assignments included Vice-Consul in Palermo, Advisor on Human Rights, US Mission to UN, mem. planning staff, Sec. of State, Desk Officer for South Africa; Political Counsellor in Damascas and Beirut; Dir Foreign Service Inst. field school, Tunis –1986; Advisor on Middle East, Mission to UN 1986–90, Sr Advisor 1990–91; Deputy Chief of Mission, Holy See and US Rep. to Mozambique Peace Talks 1991–94; Minister Counsellor for Political Affairs, Mission to UN 1994–97; Amb. to Algeria 1997–2000; Special Advisor to Perm. Rep. to UN 2000–01; Amb. to South Africa 2001–05, Chargé d'affaires a.i., Embassy in Khartoum 2005–07; Amb. to Indonesia 2007–10; ind. business consultant to various interests in Indonesia, including Sinar Mas Group 2010–; Adjunct Prof., Georgetown Univ., 2014–; mem. Ocean Exploration Advisory Bd, Nat. Oceanic and Atmospheric Admin 2014–; Fellow, Council on Foreign Relations 1975–76, Harvard Univ. Center for Int. Affairs 1989–90; Guest Scholar, US Inst. of Peace 1994. *Publications include:* The United Nations, Iran and Iraq: How Peacemaking Changed 1994, Ending Mozambique's War 1994, Mission to Algiers: Diplomacy by Engagement 2006; numerous articles on diplomacy. *Address:* Georgetown University, 37th and O Streets NW, Washington, DC 20057, USA (office). *Telephone:* (202) 687-0100 (office). *Website:* www.georgetown.edu (office).

HUME, Gary, RA; British artist; b. 9 May 1962, Tenterden, Kent; ed Goldsmiths Coll., Univ. of London; mem. RA Summer Exhbn Selection Cttee 2002; Jerwood Painting Prize 1997. *Publications:* Gary Hume: Carnival 2005, Gary Hume: Yardwork 2009, Gary Hume: Other Criteria 2009, Gary Hume: The Wonky Wheel 2013. *Address:* c/o Matthew Marks Gallery, 522 West 22nd Street, New York, NY 10011, USA (office). *Telephone:* (212) 243-0200 (office). *Fax:* (212) 243-0047 (office). *E-mail:* info@matthewmarks.com (office). *Website:* matthewmarks.com (office).

HUME, Sir John, Kt, MA; British teacher and fmr politician; *Professor and Tip O'Neill Chair, University of Ulster;* b. 18 Jan. 1937, Londonderry, N Ireland; s. of Samuel Hume and Anne Hume (née Doherty); m. Patricia Hone 1960; two s. three d.; ed St Colomb's Coll., Londonderry, St Patrick's Coll., Maynooth, Nat. Univ. of Ireland; Research Fellow, Trinity Coll.; Assoc. Fellow, Centre for Int. Affairs, Harvard Univ., USA; Founder mem. Credit Union in NI, Pres. 1964–68; non-violent civil rights leader 1968–69; rep. Londonderry in NI Parl. 1969–72, in NI Ass. 1972–73; Minister of Commerce, Powersharing Exec. 1974; rep. Londonderry in NI Convention 1975–76; MEP 1979–2004; Leader, Social Democratic and Labour Party (SDLP) 1979–2001; mem. NI Ass. 1982–86; MP for Foyle 1983–98; mem. for Foyle, NI Ass. 1998–2005 (Ass. suspended 2002–07); currently Prof. and Tip O'Neill Chair, Univ. of Ulster; mem. SDLP New Ireland Forum 1983–84, Irish Transport and Gen. Workers Union, Bureau of European Parl. Socialist Group 1979, Regional Policy and Regional Planning Cttee 1979, EEC, Socialist Co-Chair. Intergroup on Minority Cultures and Languages; Co-Leader Int. Democratic Observers for 1986 Philippines Election; mem. Advisory Cttee on Pollution of the Sea (ACOPS) 1989; Sponsor, Irish Anti-Apartheid Movt; Club Pres. Derry City FC; Freedom, City of Cork 2004, Hon. Patron, Univ. Philosophical Soc., Trinity Coll. Dublin; Légion d'honneur; Dr hc (Massachusetts) 1985, (Catholic Univ. of America) 1986, (St Joseph's Univ., Phila) 1986, (Univ. of Mass., Catholic Univ. of America, Washington, DC, Tusculum Coll., Tenn.); Hon. LLD (Queen's) 1995, (Wales) 1996; Hon. DLitt (Ulster) 1998; shared Nobel Peace Prize 1998; Martin Luther King Award 1999, Gandhi Peace Prize 2002. *Publication:* Politics, Peace and Reconciliation in Ireland 1996. *Address:* Faculty of Social Sciences, University of Ulster, Magee Campus, Room MD 115, Derry, BT48 7JL, Northern Ireland (office). *Telephone:* (28) 71675575 (office). *E-mail:* j.hume@ulster.ac.uk (office). *Website:* www.ulster.ac.uk/socialsciences (office).

HUMER, Franz B., LLD, MBA; Swiss/Austrian pharmaceutical industry executive; *Chairman, International Centre for Missing and Exploited Children;* b. 1 July 1946; ed Univ. of Innsbruck, Institut Européen d'Admin des Affaires (INSEAD), Paris; ICME, Zurich 1971–73; Asst to Vice-Pres., Schering-Plough Corpn 1973–81; Area Man., S Europe, Glaxo Holdings PLC 1981, later becoming Dir of Marketing Devt, Man. Dir Glaxo Pharmaceutical Ltd, UK Dir Glaxo Holdings PLC –1995; joined F. Hoffman-La Roche Ltd 1995, Dir Roche Holding Ltd 1995–, Head of Pharmaceuticals Div. 1995–, COO 1996–98, CEO Roche Holding Ltd 1998–2008, Chair. 2001–14; Chair. (non-exec.) Diageo Plc 2008–17; currently Chair. Int. Centre for Missing and Exploited Children mem. Bd Dirs Chugai Pharmaceuticals, Japan (Roche subsidiary); mem. Int. Advisory Bd Allianz SE; Vice-Chair. Swiss Business Fed., EFPIA (trade asscn); Dir Project Hope (charity); mem. European Round Table of Industrialists (ERT), JPMorgan Int. Council, Int. Business Leaders' Advisory Council for the Mayor of Shanghai, Bd Univ. of Salzburg, Int. Advisory Bd Nat. Centre for Missing and Exploited Children (also Vice-Chair.); Chair. Friends of Phelophepa Foundation, Switzerland, Humer Stiftung, INSEAD; Dr hc (Basel), Hon. DSc (London School of Pharmacy). *Address:* International Centre for Missing and Exploited Children, 2318 Mill Road, Suite 1010, Alexandria, VA 22314, USA (office). *Telephone:* (703) 837-6313 (office). *Fax:* (703) 549-4504 (office). *E-mail:* information@icmec.org (office). *Website:* www.icmec.org (office).

HUMMES, HE Cardinal Cláudio, OFM; Brazilian ecclesiastic; *Prefect Emeritus, Congregation for the Clergy;* b. 8 Aug. 1934, Montenegro; s. of Pedro Adão Hummes and Maria Frank Hummes; ordained priest of Order of Friars Minor 1958; Titular Bishop of Carcabia 1975; Coadjutor Bishop of Santo André, São Paulo March–Dec. 1975, Bishop of Santo André 1975–96, Archbishop of Fortaleza, Ceara 1996–98, of São Paulo 1998–2006; cr. Cardinal (Cardinal-Priest of Sant'Antonio da Padova in Via Merulana) 2001; participated in Papal Conclave 2005, 2013; Prefect for the Congregation for the Clergy 2006–10, Prefect Emer. 2010–. *Address:* c/o Palazzo delle Congregazioni, Piazza Pio XII, 3, 00193 Rome, Italy (office).

HUMPHRIES, (John) Barry, AO, CBE; Australian entertainer and author; b. 17 Feb. 1934, Kew, Melbourne, Vic.; s. of J. A. E. Humphries and L. A. Brown; m. 1st Brenda Wright 1955 (divorced 1957); m. 2nd Rosalind Tong 1959 (divorced 1970); two d.; m. 3rd Diane Millstead 1979 (divorced 1989); two s.; m. 4th Lizzie Spender 1990; ed Melbourne Grammar and Univ. of Melbourne; repertory seasons at Union Theatre, Melbourne 1953–54, Phillip Street Revue Theatre, Sydney 1956, Demon Barber Lyric, Hammersmith 1959, Oliver, New Theatre 1960; one-man shows (author and performer): A Nice Night's Entertainment 1962, Excuse I 1965, Just a Show 1968, A Load of Olde Stuffe 1971, At Least You Can Say That You've Seen It 1974, Housewife Superstar 1976, Isn't It Pathetic at His Age 1979, A Night with Dame Edna 1979, An Evening's Intercourse with Barry Humphries 1981–82, Tears Before Bedtime 1986, Back with a Vengeance, London 1987–88, Look at Me When I'm Talking to You 1993–94, Edna: The Spectacle 1998, Dame Edna: The Royal Tour, San Francisco 1998, Remember You're Out 1999, My First Last Tour 2008, All About Me (Broadway) 2010, Eat, Pray, Laugh (farewell tour) 2012; numerous plays, films and broadcasts, including The Hobbit: An Unexpected Journey 2012; best-known for his comic characterizations of Dame Edna Everage, Sir Les Patterson and Sandy Stone; Pres. Frans de Boewer Soc. (Belgium); Vice-Pres. Betjeman Soc. 2001–; Dr hc (Melbourne Univ.), (Griffith Univ.) 1994, Hon. LLD (Melbourne) 2003; Douglas Wilkie Medal 1975, Comedy Performance of the Year, Soc. of West End Management, London (now known as the Laurence Olivier Awards) 1979, TV Personality of the Year 1990, Golden Rose of Montreux, Sir Peter Ustinov Award for Comedy, Banff World Television Festival 1997, Honoured Artists Award, Melbourne City Council 1997, British Comedy Awards – Lifetime Achievement Award 1999, Special Tony Award for a live theatrical event at the 55th Annual Tony Awards for Dame Edna: The Royal Tour 2000, Special Achievement Award by the Outer Critics Circle for The Royal Tour 2000, Best Play, National Broadway Theatre Awards for The Royal Tour 2000, J.C. Williamson Award for his life's work in the live performance industry 2007, Oldie of the Year for "his wonderful split personality which has entertained us for so many years" 2011, WhatsOnStage Award for Best Solo Performance (for Eat Pray Laugh!) 2014. *Films include:* Bedazzled 1967, Percy's Progress 1974, The Great Macarthy 1975, Side by Side 1975, The Getting of Wisdom 1977, Dr Fischer of Geneva 1985, Napoleon 1995, Finding Nemo (Voice) 2003, Salvation 2008, The Hobbit: An Unexpected Journey (Voice) 2012, Justin and the Knights of Valour (voice) 2013, Blinky Bill the Movie (Voice) 2015, Absolutely Fabulous 2016. *Television includes:* Not Only... But Also 1965, Barry Humphries' Scandals 1970, An Audience with Dame Edna Everage (TV film) 1980, The Dame Edna Experience 1987–89, A Night on Mount Edna (TV film) 1990, The Life and Death of Sandy Stone 1991, Ally McBeal 2001, The Jubilee Girl (TV film) 2002, Da Kath & Kim Code (TV film) 2005, The Dame Edna Treatment 2007, Parkinson 2007, The Tonight Show with Jay Leno 2001–11, Jack Irish: Dead Point (TV film) 2014, You've Got to Love Christmas (TV film) 2014. *Publications include:* Bizarre 1964, Innocent Austral Verse 1968, The Wonderful World of Barry McKenzie (with Nicholas Garland) 1970, Bazza Holds his Own (with Nicholas Garland) 1972, Dame Edna's Coffee Table Book 1976, Les Patterson's Australia 1979, Treasury of Australian Kitsch 1980, A Nice Night's Entertainment 1981, Dame Edna's Bedside Companion 1982, The Traveller's Tool 1985, The Complete Barry McKenzie 1988, My Gorgeous Life: The Autobiography of Dame Edna Everage 1989, The Life and Death of Sandy Stone 1991, More Please: An Autobiography (J.R. Ackerley Prize for Autobiography 1993) 1992, Women in the Background (novel) 1996, My Life As Me (autobiog.), Handling Edna (biog.) 2010. *Leisure interests:* reading second-hand booksellers' catalogues in bed, inventing Australia. *Address:* c/o Claire Nightingale, PBJ Management, 22 Rathbone Street, London, W1T 1LA, England (office). *Telephone:* (20) 7287-1112 (office). *Fax:* (20) 7287-1191 (office). *E-mail:* general@pbjmgt.co.uk (office). *Website:* www.pbjmgt.co.uk (office).

HUMPHRY, Richard George, AO, FCA, FCPA, FAICD, A Fin, MACS; Australian business executive and fmr stock exchange official; *Advisor, Morgan Stanley Australia Ltd;* b. 24 Feb. 1939, Perth; s. of Arthur D. Humphry and Enid G. Humphry; m. Rose Friel 1961; one s. one d.; ed Univ. of Western Australia; computer programmer in public service 1967–77; Asst Sec. Supply Computer Systems Br. 1978–79, Accounting Devt Br. 1979–81; Asst Sec. Defence Br. Commonwealth Dept of Finance 1981–82; First Asst Sec. Financial Man. and Accounting Policy Div. 1982–85; Deputy Sec. Commonwealth Dept of Aboriginal Affairs 1985; Auditor-Gen., Victoria 1986–88; Dir-Gen. Premier's Dept of NSW 1988–94; Chair. Audit and Compliance Cttee, State Super Financial Services 1992–2001; Dir State Super Financial Services 1992–2001; Chair. NSW Financial Institutes Comm. 1994–99; Man. Dir and CEO Australian Stock Exchange 1994–2004; currently Advisor to Morgan Stanley Australia Ltd; Chair. Australian Financial Insts Comm. 1996–2000 (Dir 1992–96); Dir Garvan Medical Research Foundation 1997; Pres. Commonwealth Remuneration Tribunal 1998; Ind. Reviewer Govt Information Tech. Outsourcing Initiative 2000; mem. Bd of Dir UGL Ltd 2004–, HSBC Bank Australia Ltd, BUPA Australia Pty Ltd, BUPA Australia Holdings Pty Ltd, BUPA Australia Health Pty Ltd, MBF Alliances Pty Ltd, MBF Travel Pty Ltd, MBF Foundation Ltd, O'Connell Street Associates Pty Ltd; Deputy Chair. Taronga Conservation Soc. Australia; Deputy Chair. Zoological Parks Bd, NSW 1998; mem. Advisory Bd Nat. Office for Information Economy 1997–98, Financial Sector Advisory Cttee Taskforce 1998–, Foreign Affairs Council 2000; Business Council of Australia 2000; mem. Australian Computing Soc., Australasian Inst. of Banking and Finance; Fellow, Australian Soc. of Certified Practising Accountants, Australian Inst. of Co. Dirs; Int. Fed. of Accountants Award 1988, Accountant of the Year (Public Sector Div.) 1989, Best Financial Services Exec. (Australian Banking and Finance Awards) 2000. *Leisure interests:* bush walking, reading, scuba diving. *Address:* Morgan Stanley Australia Ltd, Level 39, Chifley Tower, 2 Chifley Square, Sydney, NSW 2000, Australia (office). *Telephone:* (2) 9770-1111 (office). *Fax:* (2) 9770-1101 (office). *Website:* www.morganstanley.com/about/offices/australia.html (office).

HUMPHRYS, John; Welsh broadcaster; b. 17 Aug. 1943, Cardiff; s. of Edward George Humphrys and Winifred Matthews; m. 1st Edna Wilding 1942 (divorced); m. 2nd Valerie Sanderson (divorced); two s. one d.; ed Cardiff High School; Washington Corresp., BBC TV 1971–77, Southern Africa Corresp. 1977–80, Diplomatic Corresp. 1981; presenter, BBC Nine O'Clock News 1981–87; presenter, Today Programme, BBC Radio 4 1987–2019, On the Record, BBC TV 1993–2002, The John Humphrys Interview (Radio 4) 1995, On the Ropes (Radio 4), Mastermind (TV) 2003–; Hon. Fellow, Cardiff Univ. 1998; Hon. DLitt (Dundee) 1996; Hon. MA (Univ. of Wales) 1998; Hon. LLD (St Andrews) 1999; Sony Gold for

News Journalist of the Year 2007, Sony Radio Acad. Award for Radio Journalism of the Year 2013. *Publications:* Devil's Advocate 1999, The Great Food Gamble 2002, Lost for Words: The Mangling and Manipulation of the English Language 2004, Beyond Words 2006, In God We Doubt: Confessions of an Angry Agnostic 2007 The Welcome Visitor: Living Well, Dying Well (co-author) 2009. *Leisure interests:* cello, trees, books, farming, music. *Address:* c/o Kruger Cowne Ltd, Unit 7C, 15 Lots Road, Chelsea Wharf, London, SW10 0QJ, England (office); c/o Radio 4, BBC Broadcasting House, London, W1A 1AA, England. *Telephone:* (20) 3962-2186 (office). *E-mail:* hello@krugercowne.com (office). *Website:* www.krugercowne.com (office).

HUN SEN, Samdech, BA, PhD; Cambodian politician; *Prime Minister;* b. (Hun Bunal), 5 Aug. 1952, Stoeung Trang Dist, Kompang-Cham Prov.; s. Hun Neang and Dee Yon; m. Bun Rany 1976; three s. three d. (one c. deceased); ed Lycée Indra Devi, Phnom Penh, Univ. of Phnom Penh, Nat. Political Acad., Hanoi; joined Khmer Rouge 1970, rising to Commdt; in Viet Nam with pro-Vietnamese Kampucheans 1977, returned to Kampuchea (now Cambodia) after Vietnamese-backed takeover; Founding mem. United Front for the Nat. Salvation of Kampuchea 1978; Minister for Foreign Affairs 1979–86, 1987–90; Deputy Prime Minister 1981–85; Chair. Council of Ministers of Cambodia (Prime Minister) 1985–91, Second Prime Minister, Royal Govt of Cambodia 1993–98, Prime Minister of Cambodia 1998–; Vice-Pres. Cambodian People's Party (CPP) 1991–; mem. Parl. for Kandal 1993–; Chair. East Asia Summit 2012; mem. Russian Acad. of Sciences 2002, Bar Asscn of Cambodia 2004; Hon. mem. ASEAN Eng Fed. 2002; Grand Order of Nat. Merit; awarded title Samdech by the King of Cambodia; Hon. PhD (Southern California Univ.) 1995, (Iowa Wesleyan Coll.) 1996; Dr hc (Dankook Univ., S Korea) 2001, (Ramkhamhaeng, Thailand) 2001, (Irish Int. Univ.) 2004, (Univ. of Cambodia) 2004, (Soon Chun Hyang Univ., S Korea) 2006, (Rajabhat Univ., Thailand) 2006, (Hanoi Nat. Univ. of Educ.) 2007; World Peace Award, 'Lifting Up the World with a Oneness-Heart' Award, Int. Peace Center 2001, Medal of Excellence, Irish Int. Univ. 2004, U Thant Peace Award 2005. *Address:* Office of the Council of Ministers, 41 boulevard Confédération de la Russie, Sangkat Toeuk Thla, Khan Sen Sok, Phnom Penh, Cambodia (office). *Telephone:* (12) 804442 (office). *Fax:* (23) 880624 (office). *E-mail:* ocm@cambodia.gov.kh (office). *Website:* www.ocm.gov.kh (office).

HUNAIDI, Rima Khalaf, MA, PhD; Jordanian foundation executive, fmr government official and fmr UN official; *CEO, Mohammed bin Rashid Al Maktoum Foundation;* ed American Univ. of Beirut, Lebanon and Portland State Univ., Ore., USA; started career as Lecturer, Dept of Econs, Portland State Univ. 1979; Dir-Gen. Jordan Export Devt and Commercial Centers Corpn and Dir-Gen. for Investment Promotion Dept, Amman 1990–93; Minister of Industry and Trade 1993–95, of Planning 1995–98; Senator, Jordanian Upper House 1997–2000; Deputy Prime Minister 1999–2000; mem. Jordanian Econ. Consultative Council; Asst Sec.-Gen. and Dir UNDP Regional Bureau for the Arab States 2000–07; CEO Mohammed bin Rashid Al Maktoum Foundation, Dubai 2008–; mem. Bd of Dirs Centre for Global Devt; mem. Advisory Bd UN Democracy Fund; Grand Cordon of the Order of Al-Kawkab Al-Urduni (The Star of Jordan) 1995. *Address:* Mohammed bin Rashid Al Maktoum Foundation, PO Box: 214444, Building No. 26, 7th Floor, Dubai Healthcare City, Dubai, United Arab Emirates (office). *Telephone:* (4) 3299999 (office). *Fax:* (4) 3687777 (office). *Website:* www.mbrfoundation.ae (office).

HUNAITI, Abdelrahim A., BSc, MSc, PhD; Jordanian biochemist, academic and fmr university administrator; *Professor, University of Jordan;* b. Feb. 1952, Abu Alanda; m.; four c.; ed Univ. of Jordan, California State Univ., Washington State Univ., USA; Teaching Asst Wash. State Univ. 1980–81, Research Asst 1981–83; Asst Prof., Yarmouk Univ. 1983–87, Assoc. Prof. 1987–92, Chair. Dept of Biological Sciences 1989–91, Prof. 1992–93; Visiting Prof., Gar Younis Univ. 1991–92; Dean of Academic Research and Grad. Studies, Mu'tah Univ. 1993–94, Asst to Univ. Pres. for Admin. Affairs 1993–94, Foundation Dean Faculty of Agric. 1994–95, Vice-Pres. for Admin. Affairs and Projects 1994–96, for Academic Affairs 1996–98, for Faculties of Sciences Affairs 1998–2000; Vice-Pres. for Academic Affairs, Philadelphia Univ. 2000–04; Pres. Univ. of Jordan 2004–07, now Prof.; Pres. Higher Educ. Accreditation Comm. 2007–08; Pres. Hashemite Univ. 2008–12; Pres. Mutah Univ. 2012–15; mem. Higher Educ. Accreditation Council 1997–2004, Dir-Gen. Nov.–Dec. 2004; mem. Editorial Bd Yarmouk Applied and Engineering Scientific Journal 2000–; mem. Jordanian Biological Sciences Soc., Jordanian Environmental Pollution Soc., Int. Soc. for Free Radical Research in Medicine, Biology and Chem., Arab Biophysics Union, New York Acad. of Sciences; Von Humboldt Fellow 1992; Abdel Hamid Shouman Prize for Young Arab Scientists 1990. *Publications:* Laboratory Manual for Experimental Biochemistry 1986, Biochemistry (Arabic) (co-author) 1993, General Science (Arabic) (co-author) 1993, Science and Technology in the Arab World (co-author) 2002. *Address:* Department of Biological Sciences, University of Jordan, Amman, Jordan (office). *Telephone:* (6) 535000 (ext. 22241) (office). *E-mail:* hunaiti2001@yahoo.com (office). *Website:* www.ju.edu.jo (office).

HÜNER, Tomáš, DipEng; Czech business executive, engineer and government official; *Director, Division of Energy Management, Siemens AG;* b. 26 June 1959, Ostrava; s. of Julius Hüner and Olga Hüner; m. Katerina Trnková; two d.; ed Brno Univ. of Tech.; engineer at power station Dětmarovice 1984–94; Chair. and CEO Severomoravská energetika, a.s. 1994–2004; consultant for AP&P 2002; CEO ČEZ Group distribution cos in Bulgaria (following merger between Severočeská energetika, Severomoravská energetika, Středočeská energetická, Východočeská energetika and Západočeská energetika) 2004–06, fmr Vice-Chair.; Vice-Minister of Industry and Trade and Manager of Industry and Energy Sector 2006–11; Chair. Supervisory Bd CEPS, OTE 2006–14; Dir Div. of Energy Man., Siemens AG 2015–; Chair. Supervisory Bd Aliatel a.s.; Chair. Energetika Vítkovice a.s., ePRIM, a.s.; Vice-Chair. Supervisory Bd Union Group a.s. *Publications include:* Chronicle of Corporate Heads, Historica Prague (Publr); papers in specialist journals. *Leisure interests:* skiing, tennis, surfing, hiking, motorsports. *Address:* Siemens AG, Wittelsbacherplatz 2, 80333 Munich, Germany (office). *E-mail:* siemens.cz@siemens.com (office). *Website:* www.siemens.com (office).

HUNG, Huang; Chinese magazine publisher, television presenter and writer; *CEO, China Interactive Media Group;* b. 1961, Beijing; d. of Hong Junyan and Zhang Hanzhi; m. Chen Kaige 1989 (divorced); ed Vassar Coll., USA; returned to Beijing following educ. in USA 1983; began career as investment consultant; Chief Rep., Metallgesellschaft AG, Beijing 1986–96; Exec. Dir Standard International Management Ltd 1996–2000; currently CEO China Interactive Media Group, magazines published include iLook (relaunched 2006), Time Out Beijing, Chinese-language Seventeen; began writing China Chic (English-language column) in China Daily 2009–, also now writes column for Daily Beast website; author of popular blog on Sina.com; launched retail venture with BNC (Brand New China), Sanlitun, Beijing 2010. *Film:* co-wrote and starred in ind. film Perpetual Motion 2005. *Publications:* My Abnormal Life as a Publisher (autobiog), Conversation with Mom. *Address:* China Interactive Media Group, 2 Jiuxian Qiao Lu, PO Box 80, Beijing 100015, People's Republic of China (office). *Telephone:* (10) 6436 2098 (office). *Fax:* (10) 9437 2837 (home).

HUNGERFORD, John Leonard, MA, MB, MD, BChir, FRCS, FRCOphth; British ophthalmologist and ocular oncologist; *Consultant Ophthalmic Surgeon, St Bartholomew's Hospital;* b. 12 Sept. 1944; s. of Leonard Harold Hungerford and Violet Miriam Hungerford (née Bickerstaff); m. Yvonne Carole Rayment 1987; one d.; ed The Glyn School, Epsom, Gonville and Caius Coll., Cambridge, Charing Cross Hosp. Medical School; consultant surgeon, Moorfields Eye Hosp. 1983–; Consultant Ophthalmic Surgeon, St Bartholomew's Hosp. 1983–; Vice-Pres. Int. Soc. for Ocular Oncology 2001; Ridley Medal 1998, Gregg Medal 2001. *Publications:* several publs on ocular cancer. *Leisure interests:* travel, reading, music, gardening, architecture. *Address:* Department of Ophthalmology, St Bartholomew's Hospital, West Smithfield, London, EC1A 7BE (office); 114 Harley Street, London, W1N 1AG, England (office). *Telephone:* (20) 7601-7158 (St Bartholomew's Hospital) (office); (20) 7935-1565 (office). *Fax:* (20) 7601-7863 (St Bartholomew's Hospital) (office); (20) 7224-1752 (office). *E-mail:* john.hungerford@moorfields.nhs.uk (office); john.hungerford@btopenworld.co.uk (home). *Website:* www.bartsandthelondon.nhs.uk/ourservices/ophthalmology.asp (office).

HUNKAPILLER, Michael W., BS, PhD; American scientist and business executive; *Chairman, President and CEO, Pacific Biosciences of California Inc.;* b. 1949; ed Oklahoma Baptist Univ., California Inst. of Tech.; joined Research and Devt Dept, Applied Biosystems Inc. 1983, Exec. Vice-Pres. 1995, Gen. Man. 1995–97; Vice-Pres. PE Corpn 1995–97, Sr Vice-Pres. and Pres. of Applied Biosystems Div. 1997–98, Pres. Appled Biosystems Group 1998–2004 (retd); Gen. Partner, Alloy Ventures (investment capital firm) 2004–; mem. Bd of Dirs Pacific Biosciences of Calif., Inc. 2005–, Exec. Chair. 2011–, Pres. and CEO 2012–; mem. Bd of Dirs Fluidigm Corpn 2005, NuGen Techs., RainDance Techs.; mem. Nat. Acad. of Eng 2008–; Takeda Award, Techno-Entrepreneurial Achievements for Individual/Humanity Well-Being 2001 and numerous other awards. *Publications include:* more than 100 publs. *Address:* Pacific Biosciences, 1380 Willow Road, Menlo Park, CA 94025, USA (office). *Telephone:* (650) 521-8000 (office). *Website:* www.pacb.com (office).

HUNKIN, John S., BA, MBA; Canadian banking executive (retd); ed Univ. of Manitoba, York Univ.; joined Canadian Imperial Bank of Commerce (CIBC) 1969, various man. positions becoming Pres. Investment and Corp. Banking Div. (known as CIBC World Markets from 1997), Dir 1993–2005, Pres. and CEO CIBC 1999–2004, CEO 2004–05 (retd); fmr Gov. Council for Canadian Unity, York Univ., mem. Exec. Cttee 2012–, mem. Bd of Dirs York Univ. Foundation, St Michael's Hosp. Foundation, Centre for Addiction and Mental Health Foundation, mem. Advisory Council, Schulich School of Business, now Chair.; mem. Conf. Bd of Canada; Trustee, Li Ka Shing [Canada] Foundation, Centre for Addiction and Mental Health; Hon. LLD (York Univ.) 2004; Queen's Golden Jubilee Award 2002, Outstanding Volunteer, Asscn of Fundraising Professionals 2009. *Address:* York University Secretariat, 1050 Kaneff Tower, York University, 4700 Keele Street, Toronto, ON M3J 1P3, Canada (office). *Telephone:* (416) 736-5310 (office). *E-mail:* info.univsec@yorku.ca (office).

HUNT, Helen Elizabeth; American actress; b. 15 June 1963, Los Angeles, Calif.; d. of Gordon Hunt and Jane Hunt; m. Hank Azaria 1999 (divorced); f. Hunt-Tavel Productions (production co.). *Stage appearances include:* Been Taken, Our Town, The Taming of the Shrew, Methusalem. *Films include:* Rollercoaster 1977, Girls Just Want to Have Fun 1985, Peggy Sue Got Married 1986, Trancers 1985, Waiting to Act 1985, Project X 1987, Stealing Home 1988, Miles from Home 1988, The Frog Prince 1988, Next of Kin 1989, Trancers II 1991, The Waterdance 1992, Only You 1992, Bob Roberts 1992, Mr Saturday Night 1992, Sexual Healing 1993, Kiss of Death 1995, Twister 1996, As Good As It Gets (Acad. Award for Best Actress) 1997, Pay It Forward 2000, Dr. T and the Women 2000, Cast Away 2000, What Women Want 2000, The Curse of the Jade Scorpion 2001, A Good Woman 2004, Bobby 2006, Then She Found Me (also dir) 2007, Every Day 2009, The Sessions 2012, Decoding Annie Parker 2013, Ride 2014. *Television includes:* Swiss Family Robinson 1975, St Elsewhere (series) 1984–86, Mad About You (series, Emmy Award 1996, 1997, Golden Globe Award 1997) 1992–99, Empire Falls 2005, Shots Fired 2017. *Address:* Hunt-Tavel Productions, 10202 West Washington Blvd., Astaire 2410, Culver City, CA 90232, USA. *Telephone:* (310) 244-3144.

HUNT, James Baxter, Jr, BS, MS, JD; American lawyer and fmr politician; *Partner Emeritus, Womble, Carlyle, Sandridge & Rice PLLC;* b. 16 May 1937, Greensboro, North Carolina; s. of James Baxter Hunt and Elsie Hunt (née Brame); m. Carolyn Joyce Leonard 1958; one s. three d.; ed North Carolina State Univ., Univ. of North Carolina; called to Bar of North Carolina 1966; Econ. Adviser to Govt of Nepal for Ford Foundation 1964–66; Partner, Kirby, Webb and Hunt (law firm) 1966–72, Poyner and Spruill, Raleigh, NC 1985–93; Lt-Gov. of North Carolina 1973–77, Gov. of North Carolina 1977–85, 1993–2001; Attorney, Womble, Carlyle, Sandridge & Rice PLLC 2001, now Partner Emer.; Founder and Chair. Hunt Inst. for Educational Leadership and Policy, Univ. of North Carolina, Chapel Hill 2001, Inst. for Emerging Issues; fmr Chair. Nat. Bd for Professional Teaching Standards; Democrat; numerous awards, including 1st Annual Harry S. Truman Award, Nat. Young Democrats 1975, Outstanding Govt Leader in US Conservation, Nat. Wildlife Fed. 1983, James Bryant Conant Award, Education Commission of the States 1984, Soil Conservation Honors Award 1986, Harold W. McGraw Prize in Education, Innovations in American Government Award, Ford Foundation. *Address:* Womble, Carlyle, Sandridge & Rice PLLC, 150 Fayetteville Street Mall, Suite 2100, Raleigh, NC 27601, USA (office). *Telephone:* (919) 755-8165 (office). *Fax:* (919) 755-6755 (office). *E-mail:* info@wcsr.com (office). *Website:* www.wcsr.com (office).

HUNT, Jay; British (b. Australian) broadcasting executive; *Chief Creative Officer, Apple, Inc.;* b. 20 Jan. 1967, Sydney; m. Ian Blandford; one s. one d.; ed Lady Eleanor Holles School, Hampton, Middx, St John's Coll., Cambridge; joined BBC as researcher on Breakfast News 1989, becoming Output Ed., later Producer Newsnight –1998, Sr Producer Panorama 1998, Ed. One O'Clock News and Six O'Clock News 1999, Exec. Producer for Daytime TV 2002–03, BBC Controller Daytime and Early Peak –2007, Controller BBC One 2008–11; Dir of Programmes, Channel Five 2007; Chief Creative Officer, Channel 4 2011–17, Apple, Inc. 2017–. *Address:* Apple, Inc., 1 Hanover Street, London W1S 1YZ, England (office). *Website:* www.apple.com (office).

HUNT, Rt Hon. Jeremy Richard Streynsham, PC, BA (Hons); British politician; *Secretary of State for Foreign and Commonwealth Affairs;* b. 1 Nov. 1966, Godalming, Surrey; s. of Adm. Sir Nicholas Hunt and Meriel Eve Givan; m. Lucia Guo 2009; one s. two d.; ed Charterhouse School, Godalming, Magdalen Coll., Oxford; Pres. Oxford Univ. Conservative Assen 1987; worked for a man. consultancy firm before going to Japan for two years to teach English and learn Japanese; co-f. Profile PR (public relations agency); co-f. Hotcourses (educational publishing business); set up a charity to help AIDS orphans in Africa; MP for SW Surrey 2005–10, for SW Surrey (revised boundary) 2010–, mem. Int. Devt Select Cttee 2005–06; Shadow Minister for Disabled People 2005–07; Shadow Sec. of State for Culture, Media and Sport 2007–10; Sec. of State for Culture, Olympics, Media and Sport 2010–12, for Health 2012–18, for Health and Social Care Jan.–July 2018, for Foreign and Commonwealth Affairs July 2018–; mem. Educ., Youth, Culture and Sport Council, Council of the EU 2010–; Conservative. *Address:* Foreign and Commonwealth Office, King Charles St, London, SW1A 2AH (office); House of Commons, Westminster, London, SW1A 0AA; SW Surrey Conservative Association, 2 Royal Parade, Tilford Road, Hindhead, Surrey, GU26 6TD, England. *Telephone:* (20) 7008-1500 (FCO) (office); (20) 7219-6813 (Westminster); (1428) 609416 (Hindhead). *Fax:* (1428) 607498 (Hindhead). *E-mail:* fcocorrespondence@fco.gov.uk (office); huntj@parliament.uk. *Website:* www.gov.uk/government/organisations/foreign-commonwealth-office (office); www.parliament.uk/biographies/commons/mr-jeremy-hunt/1572; www.hotcourses.com; www.hotcoursesfoundation.org; www.jeremyhunt.org.

HUNT, Rt Hon. Jonathan Lucas, ONZ, PC, BA, MA; New Zealand politician and diplomatist; b. 2 Dec. 1938, Lower Hutt; s. of H. Lucas Hunt and A. Z. Hunt; m.; ed Auckland Grammar School, Auckland Univ.; teacher, Kelston Boys' High School 1961–66; tutor, Univ. of Auckland 1964–66; MP for New Lynn 1966–2005; Jr Govt Whip 1972, Chair. of Cttees and Deputy Speaker of House of Reps 1974–75, Acting Speaker 1975; Labour Opposition Spokesman on Health 1976–79, Constitution and Parl. Affairs 1978–81; Sr Opposition Whip 1980–84; Shadow Minister of Broadcasting 1982; Minister of Broadcasting and Postmaster-Gen. 1984–87, Minister of State 1987–89, Leader of the House 1987–90, Minister of Broadcasting 1988–90, for Tourism 1988–89, of Housing 1989, of Communications Jan.–Oct. 1990; Sr Opposition Whip 1990–96, Shadow Leader of the House 1996–99; Speaker, House of Reps 1999–2005; High Commr to UK and Nigeria and Amb. to Ireland 2005–08. *Leisure interests:* music, int. affairs, cricket, literature.

HUNT, Linda; American actress; b. 2 April 1945, Morristown, NJ; ed Interlochen Arts Acad., Mich. and Goodman Theater and School of Drama, Chicago; has appeared on Broadway and in films 1975–. *Plays include:* Down by the River 1975, A Metamorphosis in Miniature (Obie Award) 1982, Top Girls (Obie Award) 1983, Little Victories 1983, Aunt Dan and Lemon 1985, Cherry Orchard 1988; Broadway appearances: Ah, Wilderness! 1975, End of the World 1984. *Films include:* Popeye 1980, The Year of Living Dangerously (Acad. Award for Best Supporting Actress) 1983, Dune 1984, The Bostonians 1984, Eleni 1985, Silverado 1985, Waiting for the Moon 1987, She-Devil 1989, Kindergarten Cop 1990, If Looks Could Kill 1991, Rain Without Thunder 1993, Twenty Bucks. 1993, Younger and Younger 1993, Prêt-a-Porter 1994, Pocahontas (voice) 1995, Eat Your Heart Out 1997, Amazon (voice) 1997, The Relic 1997, Out of the Past 1998, Pocahontas II: Journey to a New World (voice) 1998, The Century (narrator) 1999, Dragonfly 2002, Yours, Mine & Ours 2005, Stranger Than Fiction 2006, Once Upon a Tide (narrator) 2008, The Crooked Eye (narrator) 2009. *Address:* c/o WME Entertainment, One William Morris Place, Beverly Hills, CA 90212, USA (office). *Telephone:* (310) 859-4000 (office). *Fax:* (310) 859-4462 (office). *Website:* www.wmeentertainment.com (office).

HUNT, Sir Richard Timothy (Tim), Kt, PhD, FRS; British biologist and academic; b. 19 Feb. 1943, Neston, Wirral; s. of Richard William Hunt and Kit Rowland; m. Dr Mary Collins; two d.; ed Dragon School, Oxford, Magdalen Coll. School, Oxford, Clare Coll., Cambridge; Instructor in Embryology, Marine Biological Lab., Woods Hole, USA 1977, 1979, Instructor in Physiology 1980–83; Postdoctoral Fellow, Dept of Medicine, Albert Einstein Coll. of Medicine, New York 1968–70; Research Fellow, Clare Coll., Cambridge 1967–74, Research Fellow, Dept of Biochemistry, Univ. of Cambridge 1971–81, Official Fellow, Clare Coll. 1975–2001, Hon. Fellow 2001, Univ. Lecturer, Dept of Biochemistry 1981–90; Prin. Scientist, London Research Inst., Cancer Research UK 1990–2010, now Group Leader Emer.; Foreign Assoc. NAS 1999–; mem. Royal Soc. Biological Sciences Awards Cttee –2015 (resgnd); mem. EMBO 1979–, American Acad. of Arts and Sciences 1997–, Academia Europaea 1998–; Hon. mem. Physiological Soc. 2009, Hon. Prof., Faculty of Life Sciences, Univ. Coll. London –2015 (resgnd); Officier, Légion d'honneur 2002; Dr hc (Univ. of Cambridge) 2002, (Univ. of Hertfordshire) 2002, (Univ. of Exeter) 2002, (Univ. of Dundee) 2002, (Univ. of Liverpool) 2003, (Univ. Coll. London) 2003, (Univ. of Brno) 2003, (Keio Univ.) 2008; Abraham White Scientific Achievement Award, George Washington Univ. Dept of Biochemistry and Molecular Biology 1993, Nobel Prize in Physiology or Medicine (with Paul Nurse and Leland H. Hartwell) 2001, Royal Medal of Royal Soc. 2007, Capo d'Orlando Prize, Vico Equense 2010; numerous lectureships. *Publications include:* DNA makes RNA makes Protein (ed.) 1983, Molecular Biology of the Cell: Problems Book (co-author) 1989, The Cell Cycle: An Introduction (co-author) 1993; papers in cell and molecular biology. *Address:* Rose Cottage, Ridge, Herts., EN6 3LH, England (home). *Telephone:* (1707) 646484 (home).

HUNT, Swanee, MA, PhD; American research institute director, diplomatist and academic; *Director, Women and Public Policy Program, Harvard University;* b. Dallas, Tex.; d. of H. L. Hunt; m. Charles Ansbacher; three c.; civic leader and philanthropist; led community efforts on public educ., mental health services and affordable housing in Denver, Colo; Founder Women's Foundation of Colo; co-dir half-way house for the mentally ill; Founder Hunt Alternatives (pvt. foundation addressing issues of poverty and discrimination), Chair. Inclusive Security: Women Waging Peace; Amb. to Austria 1993–97; hosted negotiations and int. symposia on efforts to secure peace in Balkans; launched Vienna Women's Initiative 1997; Dir Women and Public Policy Program (WAPPP), John F. Kennedy School of Govt, Harvard Univ. 1997–, also Adjunct Eleanor Roosevelt Lecturer in Public Policy; mem. Council on Foreign Relations; Contrib. Ed. The American Benefactor; syndicated columnist Scripps Howard news service; awards and hons from Anti-Defamation League, Inst. for Int. Educ., American Mental Health Assen, Nat. Women's Forum, named Woman of Peace, Together for Peace Foundation, Rome, Italy. *Publications include:* This Was Not Our War: Bosnian Women Reclaiming the Peace 2004, Half Life of a Zealot 2006; articles in professional journals and US and int. newspapers. *Leisure interests:* photography, music (composed The Witness Cantata, performed in Washington DC), poetry, hiking, running marathons. *Address:* Women and Public Policy Program (WAPPP), John F. Kennedy School of Government, Harvard University, 79 JFK Street, Cambridge, MA 02138 (office); Inclusive Security: Women Waging Peace, 2040 S Street, NW, Washington, DC 20009, USA (office). *Telephone:* (617) 995-1950 (office); (202) 403-2000 (office). *Fax:* (617) 496-6154 (office); (202) 299-9520 (office). *E-mail:* swanee_hunt@huntalternatives.org (office); information@womenwagingpeace.net (office). *Website:* www.ksg.harvard.edu/wappp (office); www.womenwagingpeace.net (office).

HUNT, Tristram Julian William, BA, PhD, FRHistS; British historian, writer, museum director and fmr politician; *Director, Victoria and Albert Museum;* b. 31 May 1974, Cambridge; s. of Julian, Baron Hunt of Chesterton, and Marylla Shephard; m. Juliet Thornback; one s. two d.; ed Trinity Coll., Cambridge, Univ. of Chicago; Special Adviser to Science Minister Lord Sainsbury 1997–2000; Assoc. Fellow, Centre for History and Econs, King's Coll., Cambridge 2001–02; Sr Fellow, Inst. for Public Policy Research 2001; Lecturer in British History, Queen Mary, Univ. of London 2003–08, Sr Lecturer 2008–10; MP for Stoke-on-Trent Central (Labour) 2010–17, mem. Select Cttee on Political and Constitutional Reform, Chair. All-Party Parl. Group on Energy Intensive Industries, Shadow Sec. of State and Shadow Minister for Educ. 2013–15; Dir, Victoria and Albert Museum (V&A) 2017–; Founder, Stoke-on-Trent Literary Festival; Patron, British Ceramics Biennial; fmr Trustee, Heritage Lottery Fund, Nat. Heritage Memorial Fund; fmr Curator, Mayor of London's History Festival; fmr Lecturer on British and int. culture, Centre for European Studies, Univ. of California, Berkeley, Centre for European Studies, Harvard Univ., Princeton Univ. and Nat. Univ. of Singapore; regular writer for The Guardian and The Observer. *Television includes:* Sir Isaac Newton 2002, The English Civil War 2002, The Protestant Revolution 2008. *Publications include:* The English Civil War: At First Hand 2002, Building Jerusalem: The Rise and Fall of the Victorian City 2004, The Frock-coated Communist: The Revolutionary Life of Friedrich Engels 2009, Ten Cities That Made an Empire 2014. *Address:* Victoria and Albert Museum, Cromwell Road, London, SW7 2RL, England (office). *Telephone:* (20) 7942-2000 (office). *E-mail:* contact@vam.ac.uk (office). *Website:* www.vam.ac.uk (office).

HUNT OF KINGS HEATH, Baron (Life Peer), cr. 1997, of Birmingham in the County of West Midlands; **Philip Alexander Hunt,** OBE, BA, PC; British politician; *Deputy Leader of Opposition, House of Lords;* b. 19 May 1949, Birmingham; m.; five c.; ed City of Oxford High School, Oxford School and Univ. of Leeds; joined Oxford Regional Hosp. Bd 1972; with Nuffield Orthopaedic Centre 1974; Sec. Edgware and Hendon Community Health Council 1975–79; joined Nat. Assen of Health Authorities 1978, Dir 1990; mem. House of Lords 1997–, apptd Govt Whip and Spokesman on Educ. and Employment and Health 1998, Deputy Leader, House of Lords 2008–10, Deputy Leader of Opposition 2010–; Parl. Under-Sec. of State, Dept of Health 1999–2003, 2007, Dept for Work and Pensions 2005–07, Ministry of Justice 2007–08; Minister of State, Dept for the Environment, Food and Rural Affairs 2008–09; Minister of State, Dept of Energy and Climate Change 2008–10; mem. Oxford City Council 1973–79, Birmingham City Council 1980–82; Jt Chair. All Party Care and Public Health Group 1997–98; Vice-Chair. All Party Group on AIDS 1997–98; Chair. Heart of England NHS Foundation Trust 2011; Dr hc (Birmingham) 2005. *Leisure interests:* swimming, Birmingham City Football Club, music. *Address:* House of Lords, Westminster, London, SW1A 0PW, England (office). *Telephone:* (20) 7238-0681 (office).

HUNT OF WIRRAL, Baron (Life Peer), cr. 1997, of Wirral in the County of Merseyside; **Rt Hon. David James Fletcher Hunt,** PC, MBE; British lawyer, politician and business executive; b. 21 May 1942; ed Liverpool Coll., Univ. of Bristol; practising solicitor and Partner, Beachcroft Wansbroughs (now Beachcroft LLP) 1968–, Sr Partner 1996–2005, currently Chair. Financial Services Div.; contested Bristol South constituency 1970, Kingswood 1974; MP (Conservative) for Wirral 1976–83, for Wirral W 1983–97; Opposition Spokesperson for Shipping and Shipbuilding 1977–97; Parl. Pvt. Sec. to John Nott as Sec. of State for Trade 1979–81, for Defence 1981; Asst Whip 1981–83; Govt Whip 1983–84; Parl. Under-Sec. of State, Dept of Energy 1984–87; Deputy Chief Whip (Treas. of HM Household) 1987–89; Minister for Local Govt and Inner Cities 1989–90; Sec. of State for Wales 1990–93, 1995, for Employment 1993–94; Chancellor of the Duchy of Lancaster and Minister for Public Service and Science 1994–95; Opposition Spokesperson for Business, Enterprise and Regulatory Reform/Business, Innovation and Skills, House of Lords 2008–10; Chair. Press Complaints Comm. 2011–14; Vice-Chair. Bristol Conservative Assen 1970; Chair. Nat. Young Conservatives 1972–73; Vice-Pres. European Conservative and Christian Democratic Youth Community 1974–76; Vice-Chair. Conservative Party 1983–84; Pres. Tory Reform Group 1991–97, Patron 1997–; Chair. British Youth Council 1971–74; mem. South West Econ. Planning Council 1972–76, Govt Advisory Cttee on Pop Festivals 1972–75; Pres. British Youth Council 1978–80; Gov., English Speaking Union 1998–, Deputy Chair. 2000–05, Chair. 2005–11, Int. Chair. 2008–11; Chair. Professional Standards Bd, Chartered Insurance Inst. 2004–06, Pres. 2007–08; Chair. (non-exec.) McDonald's Education Co. 2009–, Lending Standards Bd 2011–; Gov., European Youth Foundation, Strasbourg 1972–75; Chair. British Atlantic Group of Young Politicians 1979–81; Pres. Atlantic Assen for Young Political Leaders 1981–83; Dir, Assen of Conservative Clubs, Parl. Cttee against Anti-Semitism; Dir, Case Management Soc.; Vice-Pres. Holocaust Educational Trust; Deputy Pres. Royal Soc. for the Prevention of Accidents (RoSPA); Trustee and Churchwarden, St Mary Magdalene Church, Chewton Mendip, Somerset; mem.

(Conservative) House of Lords 1997–; Hon. LLD (Bristol) 2008; jt winner The Observer Mace debating competition for Univ. of Bristol 1995. *Address:* House of Lords, Westminster, London, SW1A 0PW, England (office). *Telephone:* (20) 7219-6688 (House of Lords) (office).

HUNTE, Julian Robert, OBE; Saint Lucia politician, diplomatist and sport administrator; *President, West Indies Cricket Board;* b. 14 March 1940, Castries; Mayor of Castries 1970–71; joined St Lucia Labour Party 1978, Leader 1984–96; mem. Parl. 1987–96; fmr Chair. Standing Conf. of Popular Democratic Parties of the Eastern Caribbean; Perm. Rep. to UN, New York –2001, 2004–06 (resgnd); currently Chair. and CEO The Julian R. Hunte Group of Cos; Minister of Foreign Affairs, Int. Trade and Civil Aviation 2001–04; Pres. of 58th Session, UN Gen. Ass. 2003–04; fmr Pres. St Lucia Cricket Asscn, Windward Islands Cricket BD; Pres. W Indies Cricket Bd 2007–; Knight of the Grand Cross Pian Order from Pope John Paul II 2004. *Address:* West Indies Cricket Board Inc., PO Box 616 W, St John's, Antigua. *Telephone:* 481-2450 (office). *Fax:* 481-2498 (office). *E-mail:* wicb@windiescricket.com (office). *Website:* www.windiescricket.com (office).

HUNTER, Anthony (Tony) Rex, MA, PhD, FRS, FRSA; British/American molecular biologist and cell biologist; *Renato Dulbecco Chair in Cancer Research, The Salk Institute;* b. 23 Aug. 1943, Ashford, Kent; s. of Ranulph Rex Hunter and Nellie Ruby Elsie Hitchcock; m. 1st Philippa Charlotte Marrack 1969 (divorced 1974); m. 2nd Jennifer Ann Maureen Price 1992; two s.; ed Felsted School, Essex, Gonville and Caius Coll., Cambridge; Research Fellow, Christ's Coll., Cambridge 1968–71, 1973–75; Research Assoc., Salk Inst., San Diego, Calif. 1971–73, Asst Prof. 1975–78, Assoc. Prof. 1978–82, Prof. 1982–, American Cancer Soc. Prof. 1992–2008, Dir Salk Cancer Center 2008–16 (then Deputy Dir), Renato Dulbecco Chair. in Cancer Research 2011–; Adjunct Assoc. Prof., Div. of Biology, Univ. of Calif., San Diego 1979–82, Adjunct Prof. 1982–; mem. Inst. of Medicine 2004–, American Philosophical Soc. 2006–; Assoc. mem. European Molecular Biology Org. 1992; Foreign Assoc. mem. NAS 1998; Fellow, American Acad. of Arts and Sciences 1992, American Asscn for Cancer Research Acad. 2013; American Business Foundation for Cancer Research Award 1988, Katharine Berkan Judd Award (Memorial Sloan-Kettering Cancer Center) 1992, Hopkins Medal (Biochemical Soc.) 1994, Gairdner Foundation Int. Award 1994, General Motors Cancer Research Foundation Mott Prize 1994, Feodor Lynen Medal 1999, J. Allyn Taylor Int. Prize in Medicine 2000, Keio Medical Science Prize 2001, Sergio Lombroso Award in Cancer Research 2003, City of Medicine Award 2003, American Cancer Soc. Medal of Honor 2004, Kirk A. Landon Prize for Basic Cancer Research, American Asscn for Cancer Research 2004, Prince of Asturias Award for Scientific and Tech. Research 2004, Louisa Gross Horwitz Prize 2004, Daniel Nathans Memorial Award 2005, Wolf Foundation Prize in Medicine 2005, Pasarow Award in Cancer Research 2006, American Soc. of Biochemistry and Molecular Biology, Herbert Tabor Award 2007, Clifford Prize for Cancer Research 2007, Hon. Medal, Signal Transduction Soc. 2011, Einstein Prof., Chinese Acad. of Sciences 2013, Royal Medal, Royal Soc. (jtly) 2014, Pezcoller-AACR Int. Award for Extraordinary Achievement in Cancer Research 2018, Tang Prize in Biopharmaceutical Science (co-recipient) 2018. *Publications include:* more than 525 papers and journal articles. *Leisure interests:* white-water rafting, desert camping. *Address:* Molecular and Cell Biology Laboratory, The Salk Institute, 10010 North Torrey Pines Road, La Jolla, CA 92037-1099 (office); 4578 Vista de la Patria, Del Mar, CA 92014-4150, USA (home). *Telephone:* (858) 453-4100 (ext. 1385) (office); (858) 792-1492 (home). *Fax:* (858) 457-4765 (office). *E-mail:* hunter@salk.edu (office). *Website:* www.salk.edu/scientist/tony-hunter (office).

HUNTER, Holly, BFA; American actress; b. 20 March 1958, Conyers, Ga; d. of Charles Hunter and Opal M. Catledge; m. Janusz Kaminski (q.v.) 1995; two c. (twins) with Gordon MacDonald; ed Carnegie-Mellon Univ.; Dir Calif. Abortion Rights Action League; Emmy Award for TV production Roe vs. Wade 1989; Best Actress Award, American TV Awards, for cable TV production of The Positively True Adventures of the Alleged Texas Cheerleader Murdering Mom 1993; Best Actress Award, Cannes Film Festival Award 1993 and Acad. Award 1994 for role in The Piano. *Theatre:* on Broadway: Crimes of the Heart, The Wake of Jamey Foster, The Miss Firecracker Contest; other: A Weekend Near Madison, The Person I Once Was, Battery (all in New York), A Lie of the Mind (Los Angeles), By the Bog of Cats (Wyndham's Theatre, London) 2004 and regional productions. *Films include:* The Burning 1981, Swing Shift 1984, Broadcast News 1987, Raising Arizona 1987, End of the Line 1988, Miss Firecracker 1989, Always 1989, Animal Behavior 1989, Once Around 1990, The Piano 1993, The Firm 1993, Home for the Holidays 1995, Copycat 1995, Crash 1996, A Life Less Ordinary 1997, Living Out Loud 1998, Jesus' Son 1999, Timecode 2000, Things You Can Tell Just by Looking at Her 2000, Woman Wanted 2000, O Brother, Where Art Thou? 2000, Moonlight Mile 2002, Thirteen 2003, Levity 2003, The Incredibles (voice) 2004, Little Black Book 2004, Nine Lives 2005, The Big White 2005, Won't Back Down 2012, Paradise 2013, Manglehorn 2014, Batman V. Superman: Dawn of Justice 2016, Strange Weather 2016, Breakable You 2017, The Big Sick 2017, Song to Song 2017. *Television includes:* Roe vs. Wade 1989, The Positively True Adventures of the Alleged Texas Cheerleader-Murdering Mom 1993, Harlan County War 2000, When Billie Beat Bobby 2001, Saving Grace (series) 2007–09, Top of the Lake (mini-series) 2013, Bonnie and Clyde (mini-series) 2013. *Address:* c/o International Creative Management, 8942 Wilshire Blvd, #219, Beverly Hills, CA 90211, USA.

HUNTER, Howard O., AB, JD; American lawyer, academic and university administrator; *Professor of Law, Singapore Management University;* m. Susan Frankel 1971; one d.; ed Yale Univ.; admitted to the Bar of Ga 1971; joined Faculty of Law, Emory Univ. 1976, Asst Prof. 1976–79, Assoc. Prof. 1979–82, Prof. 1982–2004, Dean, School of Law 1989–2001, Interim Provost and Exec. Vice-Pres. for Academic Affairs 2001–03, Prof. of Law and Dean Emer. 2005–; Pres. Singapore Man. Univ. 2004–10, Prof. of Law 2010–; Fulbright Sr Scholar, Univ. of Sydney Law School 1988, Visiting McWilliam Prof. of Commercial Law, Univ. of Sydney 2004; Recurring Visiting Prof. of Law, Cen. European Univ., Budapest 1999–; mem. Int. Academic Advisory Bd, Alliance Univ. Bangalore 2012–; mem. Bd of Dirs Workforce Devt Authority of Singapore 2005–07, Singapore Int. Chamber of Commerce 2005–10, Enterprise Challenge of Singapore 2005–07, Nat. Research Foundation of Singapore 2006–10, American Arbitration Asscn 2006–, Building and Construction Authority 2009–11; mem. Bd of Dirs Ga Volunteer Lawyers for the Arts Inc. 1975–89 (Pres. 1985–87, mem. Bd of Advisers 1997); mem. Chief Justice's Comm. on Professionalism 1990–2004; mem. Ga Supreme Court Comm. on Indigent Defense 2000–04; mem. Editorial Bd Journal of Contract Law 1988; mem. American Law Inst. 2005–, ABA 1972–, Asscn of American Law Schools 1976–, Cttee on the Legal Profession, Singapore Int. Chamber of Commerce 2011–; Hon. Prof. of Law, Hong Kong Univ. 1986; Bar and Media Award 1980, Supreme Court of Georgia Amicus Curiae Award 1998. *Publications include:* Recent Reforms in Swedish Higher Education (co-author) 1980, Universities and Community Service: Concepts and Problems 1980, Modern Law of Contracts, Law in Perspective: The Integrative Jurisprudence of Harold J. Berman (ed.) 1996, numerous journal articles. *Address:* School of Law, Singapore Management University, 60 Stamford Road, Level 4, 178900, Singapore (office). *Telephone:* 68085180 (office). *Fax:* 68280805 (office). *E-mail:* howardhunter@smu.edu.sg (office). *Website:* www.smu.edu.sg (office).

HUNTER, Larry D.; American television executive; *Executive Vice-President and General Counsel, The DIRECTV Group;* Corp. Vice-Pres. The DIRECTV Group, Inc. 1998–2001, Chair. and CEO DIRECTV Japan 1998–2001, Sr Vice-Pres., The DIRECTV Group, Inc. 2001–04, Assoc. Gen. Counsel 2001–02, Gen. Counsel 2002–, Exec. Vice-Pres. and Gen. Counsel 2004–09, 2009–, Interim CEO 2009. *Address:* The DIRECTV Group, Inc., 2230 East Imperial Highway, El Segundo, CA 90245, USA (office). *E-mail:* info@directv.com (office). *Website:* www.directv.com (office).

HUNTER, Robert John, AM, PhD, FAA; Australian research chemist and academic; *Honorary Associate Professor, School of Chemistry, University of Sydney;* b. 26 June 1933, Abermain, NSW; s. of Ronald Hunter and Elizabeth Dixon; m. Barbara Robson 1954 (divorced 1995); one s. one d.; ed Cessnock High School, New South Wales, New England Univ. Coll., Univ. of Sydney; secondary school teacher 1953–54; Tech. Officer, CSIRO 1954–57, Research Officer 1960–64; Lecturer, Univ. of Sydney 1964, Assoc. Prof. of Physical Chem. 1972–90, Head, School of Chem. 1987–90, Hon. Research Assoc. 1990–94, Hon. Assoc. Prof. 1994; Dir Colloidal Dynamics Pty Ltd 1988–96; Chair. Nat. Science and Industry Forum 1991–93; Pres. Int. Asscn of Colloid and Interface Scientists 1992–94; Nat. Pres. Scientists for Global Responsibility (fmrly Scientists Against Nuclear Arms) 1986–88, 1990–92, 1996–2008; Archibald Olle Prize 1982, 1993, Alexander Memorial Lecturer 1987, Liversidge Lecturer, Royal Soc. of New South Wales 1988, to Australia and New Zealand Acad. for Advancement of Science 2001. *Publications include:* Chemical Science 1976, Zeta Potential in Colloid Science 1981, Foundations of Colloid Science, (Vol. I) 1987, (Vol. 2) 1989, (second edn) 2001, Introduction to Modern Colloid Science 1993; author or co-author of about 100 research papers. *Leisure interests:* music, drama, reading, lawn bowls. *Address:* Room 146, School of Chemistry, Building F11, University of Sydney, Sydney, NSW 2006 (office); 26/20A Austin Street, Lane Cove, NSW 2066, Australia (home). *Telephone:* (2) 9427-6261 (home). *E-mail:* robert.hunter@sydney.edu.au (office); rjh33@iprimus.com.au (home). *Website:* sydney.edu.au/science/chemistry/about-us/honorary-staff.shtml (office).

HUNTSMAN, Jon Meade, Jr, BA; American business executive, politician and diplomatist; *Ambassador to Russia;* b. 26 March 1960, Redwood City, Calif.; s. of Jon Huntsman, Sr and Karen Huntsman (née Haight); m. Mary Kaye Cooper; two s. three d. two adopted d.; ed Univs of Utah and Pennsylvania; served as missionary for Church of Jesus Christ of Latter-day Saints (Mormon) in Taiwan; fmr White House Staff Asst to Pres. Ronald Reagan; served as Deputy Asst Sec. of Commerce for Trade Devt, then Deputy Asst Sec. of Commerce for E Asian and Pacific Affairs, then US Amb. to Singapore under Pres. George H. W. Bush; served as Deputy US Trade Rep./US Trade Amb. for Asia, South Asia and Africa under Pres. George W. Bush; currently Chair. and CEO Huntsman Family Holdings Co. LLC (holding co. for Huntsman Corpn, fmr Chair. Exec. Cttee); Gov. of Utah 2005–09 (resgnd); Amb. to People's Repub. of China 2009–11 (resgnd); unsuccessful cand. for Republican nomination for US Pres. 2012; Pres. and CEO Huntsman Cancer Foundation, Univ. of Utah, Chair. 2012–; Amb. to Russia 2017–; mem. Bd of Dirs Ford Motor Co. 2012–, Caterpillar Inc. 2012–, Hilton Worldwide, US Naval Acad. Foundation, fmr mem. Bd of Dirs Intermountain Health Care, ARUP Laboratories, Brookings Inst. Asia Policy Board, Asia Soc., New York, Nat. Bureau of Asian Research; fmr Br. Dir San Francisco Fed. Reserve Bank Bd; Founding Dir Pacific Council on Int. Policy; Visiting Fellow, Harvard's John F. Kennedy School of Govt; Distinguished Lecturer, Stanford School of Public Policy; fmr mem. Int. Advisory Council, Singapore Econ. Devt Bd, Nat. Bd, Juvenile Diabetes Foundation; fmr Chair. KSL's Family Now Campaign, Envision Utah, Utah Opera; fmr Vice-Chair. Coalition for Utah's Future; fmr mem. Advisory Bd, Univ. of Utah School of Business, Nat. Govs Asscn; fmr Chair. Western Govs Asscn; Distinguished Fellow, Brookings Inst., Washington, DC 2012; Trustee, Carnegie Endowment for Int. Peace, Reagan Presidential Foundation; fmr Trustee, Univ. of Pennsylvania; mem. American Academy of Diplomacy; Hon. Dr of Public Service (Snow College) 2005, Hon. DSc (Westminster College) 2008, Hon. DHumLitt (Univ. of Utah) 2010, Hon. LLD (Univ. of Pennsylvania) 2010, Hon. Dr of Law (Southern New Hampshire Univ.) 2011; Distinguished Eagle Scout Award, Boy Scouts of America 2007. *Address:* 121099 Moscow, B. Devyatinskii per. 8, Russia (office). *Telephone:* (495) 728-50-00 (office). *Fax:* (495) 728-50-90. *E-mail:* consulmo@state.gov (office). *Website:* ru.usembassy.gov (office); www.jon2012.com.

HUO, Lianhong, BEng; Chinese economist and business executive; ed Cen.-South Inst. of Mining and Metallurgy; Deputy Man. Insurance Dept, Hainan br., Bank of Communications –1993; joined China Pacific Insurance (Group) Co. Ltd 1993, held numerous positions, including Gen. Man. Hainan and Beijing brs, Exec. Vice-Pres. China Pacific Insurance (Group) Co. Ltd –2000, mem. Bd of Dirs, Gen. Man. and Pres. 2000–17, Dir 2017–, fmr Chair. China Pacific Property Insurance Co. Ltd, China Pacific Asset Management Co. Ltd. *Address:* China Pacific Insurance (Group) Co. Ltd, 190 Yincheng Zhong Road, Shanghai 200120, Shanghai Province, People's Republic of China (office). *Telephone:* (21) 58776688 (office). *Fax:* (21) 68870922 (office). *E-mail:* info@cpic.com.cn (office). *Website:* www.cpic.com.cn (office).

HUPPERT, Herbert Eric, MA, MSc, MS, PhD, ScD, FRS; Australian scientist and academic; *Professor Emeritus of Theoretical Geophysics and Director, Institute of Theoretical Geophysics, University of Cambridge;* b. 26 Nov. 1943, Sydney, NSW; s. of Leo Huppert and Alice Huppert (née Neumann); m. Felicia Ferster

1966; two s.; ed Sydney Boys High School, Univ. of Sydney, Australian Nat. Univ. and Univ. of California, San Diego, USA; ICI Research Fellow, Univ. of Cambridge 1968–69, Asst Dir Research Dept Applied Math. and Theoretical Physics 1970–81, Univ. Lecturer 1981–88, Reader in Geophysical Dynamics 1988–89, Prof. of Theoretical Geophysics and Dir Inst. of Theoretical Geophysics 1989–2011, Prof. Emer. 2011–, Fellow, King's Coll., Cambridge 1970–; Prof. of Math., Univ. of New South Wales 1991–95, 2012–; Prof. of Science, Univ. of Bristol 2012–; BP Venture Unit Sr Research Fellow 1983–89; fmr Visiting Research Scientist, Univ. of California, USA, Univ. of Canterbury, NZ, Univ. of New South Wales, ANU, MIT, USA, Univ. of Western Australia, Woods Hole Oceanographic Inst., USA, California Inst. of Tech., USA; Vice-Chair. Scientists for the Release of Soviet Refuseniks 1985–88, Co-Chair. 1988–92; mem. Council NERC 1993–98, Scientific Council, The Earth Centre 1995–, Council Royal Soc. 2001–03; Ed. Journal of Soviet Jewry 1986–92; Assoc. Ed. Journal of Fluid Mechanics 1971–90; mem. Editorial Bd Philosophical Transactions of the Royal Soc. A 1994–99, Reports on Progress in Physics 1997–2000, Proceedings of the Royal Soc. A 2016–; Fellow, American Geophysical Union 2002, American Physical Soc. 2004, Academia Europaea 2011; Evnin Lecturer, Princeton Univ. 1995, Mid-West Mechanics Lecturer 1996–97, Henry Charnock Distinguished Lecturer 1999, Smith Industries Lecturer, Univ. of Oxford 1999, Nat. Acad. of America's Arthur L Prize and Lectureship 2005, Distinguished Israel Pollak Lecturer of Technion 2005, William Hopkins Prize, Cambridge Philosophical Soc. 2005, Murchison Medal, London Geological Soc. 2007, Bakerian Lecturer, Royal Soc. 2011. *Achievement:* played squash for Cambridgeshire 1970–72. *Publications:* more than 250 papers on fluid motions associated with the atmosphere, oceans, volcanoes and the interior of the Earth. *Leisure interests:* his children, squash, mountaineering, lawn tennis, music, travel. *Address:* Institute of Theoretical Geophysics, Department of Applied Mathematics and Theoretical Physics, University of Cambridge, Centre for Mathematical Sciences, Wilberforce Road, Cambridge, CB3 0WA (office); 46 De Freville Avenue, Cambridge, CB4 1HT, England (home). *Telephone:* (1223) 337853 (office). *Fax:* (1223) 765900 (office). *E-mail:* heh1@damtp.cam.ac.uk (office); heh1@cam.ac.uk (office). *Website:* www.itg.cam.ac.uk/people/heh (office).

HUPPERT, Isabelle Anne Madeleine; French actress; b. 16 March 1953, Paris; d. of Raymond Huppert and Annick Beau; m. Ronald Chammah 1982; two s. one d.; ed Lycée de St-Cloud, Ecole nat. des langues orientales vivantes; Pres. Comm. d'avances sur recettes 1994–; several theatre appearances including Mary Stuart (London) 1996, 4.48 Psychose (Paris) 2002; Pres. Cannes Film Festival Jury 2009; BFI Fellowship 2011; Chevalier, Légion d'honneur 1999, Officier 2009; Chevalier, Ordre nat. du Mérite 1994, Officier 2005; Stanislavsky Award 2008, Outstanding European Achievement in World Cinema 2009, Excellence Award, Locarno Int. Film Festival 2011, Lifetime Achievement Award, Munich Film Festival 2014, Dilys Powell Award, London Film Critics' Circle 2016, UniFrance French Cinema Award 2017. *Theatre:* 4.48 Psychosis (New York) 2005. *Films include:* Le bar de la fourche 1972, César et Rosalie 1972, Les valseuses 1974, Aloïse 1975, Dupont Lajoie 1975, Rosebud 1975, Docteur Françoise Gailland 1976, Le juge et l'assassin 1976, Le petit Marcel 1976, Les indiens sont encore loin 1977, La dentellière (BAFTA for Most Promising Newcomer) 1978, Violette Nozière (Cannes Film Festival Best Actress Award 1978) 1978, Les soeurs Brontë 1978, Loulou 1980, Sauve qui peut (la vie), Les Héritières 1980, Heaven's Gate 1980, Coup de Torchon 1981, La Dame aux Camélias 1981, Les Ailes de la Colombe 1981, Eaux Profondes 1981, Passion, travail et amour, La Truite 1982, Entre Nous 1984, My Best Friend's Girl 1984, La Garce 1984, Signé Charlotte, Sac de noeuds 1985, Cactus 1986, Sincerely Charlotte 1986, The Bedroom Window 1986, The Possessed 1988, Story of Women 1989, Milan Noir 1990, Madame Bovary 1991, Malina 1991, Après l'amour 1992, La Séparation 1994, Amateur 1994, L'Inondation 1994, La Cérémonie (César Best Actress Award) 1995, Les Affinités électives 1996, Rien ne va plus 1997, Les Palmes de M. Schutz 1997, L'Ecole de la chair 1998, Merci pour le chocolat 2000, Les Destineées sentimentales 2000, La Fausse suivante et Saint-Cyr 2000, La Pianiste (Best Actress, Cannes Film Festival) 2001, 8 Femmes 2002, Deux 2002, La Vie promise 2002, Le Temps du loup 2003, Ma Mère 2004, I Heart Huckabees 2004, Les Soeurs fâchées 2004, Gabrielle (Venice Film Festival Special Lion) 2005, L'Ivresse du pouvoir, Nue Propriété 2006, L'Amour caché 2007, Médée miracle 2007, Home 2008, The Sea Wall 2008, Villa Amalia 2009, White Material 2009, Copacabana 2010, Sans queue ni tête 2010, Special Treatment 2010, My Little Princess 2011, My Worst Nightmare 2011, Dubaï Flamingo (voice, uncredited) 2012, Captive 2012, Amour 2012, In Another Country 2012, Lines of Wellington 2012, Dormant Beauty 2012, The Nun 2013, The Scapegoat (uncredited) 2013, Dead Man Down 2013, The Disappearance of Eleanor Rigby: Him 2013, The Disappearance of Eleanor Rigby: Her 2013, Tip Top 2013, Abuse of Weakness 2013, The Disappearance of Eleanor Rigby: Them 2014, Paris Follies 2014, Elle (Golden Globe Award for Best Performance by an Actress in a Motion Picture 2017, Lumières Award for Best Actress 2017) 2016, Tout de suite maintenant 2016, Souvenir 2016, Madame Hyde (Locarno Awards for Best Actress 2017) 2017. *Television:* Law & Order: Special Victims Unit (series) 2010, As Linhas de Torres Vedras (mini-series) 2012, Le tourbillon de Jeanne (series) 2013, Les fausses confidences 2016. *Publication:* Madame Deshoulières 2001. *Address:* c/o VMA, 20 avenue Rapp, 75007 Paris, France. *Telephone:* 1-43-17-37-00. *E-mail:* info@vma.fr. *Website:* www.vma.fr.

HÜPPI, Rolf; Swiss financial services industry executive; b. 25 April 1943, Uznach; joined Zurich Financial Services 1963, Man. India Office 1964–70, Zurich Office 1970–72, Regional Man. US Office, Pittsburgh 1972–74, mem. Group Exec. Bd 1983, CEO for US Br. 1983–87, Deputy COO 1987–88, COO 1988–91, Pres. and CEO 1991–98; mem. Bd of Dirs Zurich Insurance Co. 1993–2002, Chair. 1995–2002; Chair. and CEO Zurich Financial Services Group (following merger) 1998–2002 (resgnd); f. Rolf Hüppi AG, Zurich 2002; Founder, Pres. and CEO ParaLife Holding AG (micro-insurance co. operating in developing countries) 2006–; Chair. Advisory Bd The Peninsula Group LLC; Int. Counselor, Center for Strategic and Int. Studies, Washington, DC; Batten Fellow, Darden Business School, Univ. of Va 2004; Dr hc (Universidad Autonoma de Guadalajara). *Address:* Rolf Hüppi AG, Gartenstrasse 33, 8002 Zürich, Switzerland (office). *Website:* www.paralife.com (office).

HUQ, Lt-Gen. Abu Belal Mohammad Shafiul; Bangladeshi army officer; *Chief of Army Staff;* b. Dec. 1958, Brahmanbaria; m. Shoma Huq; one s. one d.; ed Dhaka Univ., National Univ., Bangladesh Univ. of Professionals, Defence Services Command and Staff Coll., Mirpur, Command and General Staff Coll., USA; commissioned in Armoured Corps, Bangladesh Army 1978, has held a range of command, staff and instructional positions, including command of two Armour Units, three Brigades (one Armour and two Infantry) and two Divs, ADC to Pres. of Bangladesh, Chief Instructor, Defence Services Command and Staff Coll., Mirpur, served as Mil. Sec. and Adjutant Gen., Bangladesh Army, Commdt, Bangladesh Mil. Acad. and Armoured Corps Centre, Dir-Gen. Bangladesh Inst. of Int. and Strategic Studies, Mil. Observer, UN Iran-Iraq Military Observer Group (UNIIMOG) 1988–89, Deputy Force Commdr, UNMEE (Ethiopia and Eritrea) 2007, Commdt, Defence Services Command and Staff Coll. –2013, Prin. Staff Officer, Armed Forces Div. 2013–15, Chief of Army Staff 2015–, Vice-Chair. Governing Body, Nat. Defence Coll.; Chair. Trust Bank Ltd; Sword of Honour as Best Officer Cadet, Bangladesh Mil. Acad. *Leisure interest:* golf. *Address:* Army Headquarters, Dhaka Cantonment, Dhaka, Bangladesh (office). *Website:* www.army.mil.bd (office).

HUR, Dong-soo, BS, MS, PhD; South Korean chemical engineer and business executive; *Chairman, GS Caltex Corporation;* b. 13 July 1943; ed Bosung Senior High School, Yonsei Univ., Univ. of Wisconsin, USA; mil. service 1961–63; Research Engineer, Chevron Research Co., USA 1971–73; joined GS Caltex Corpn 1973, Special Asst to Jt Rep. Dirs 1973–78, Vice-Pres. and Deputy Refinery Man. 1978–81, Vice-Pres., Planning/Project and Construction 1981–84, Exec. Vice-Pres., Corp. Planning/Crude Oil/Supply and Distribution 1984–87, Exec. Vice-Pres., Planning and Manufacturing 1987–91, Pres. and COO GS Caltex Corpn 1991–93, Pres. and CEO 1994–97, Vice-Chair. and CEO 1998–2002, Chair. and CEO 2003–12, Chair. 2013–, Chair. GS Caltex Foundation 2006–; Chair. Korea Petroleum Asscn 1994–95, Korea Baduk Asscn 2001–, Korea Business for Sustainable Devt 2002–, Cttee on Consumer Complaints Man. System 2005–, Korea Cttee on the Korea-China-Japan Business Forum 2005–, Korea-Oman Friendship Asscn 2007–; Head of Business Dialogue, Presidential Cttee on Green Growth 2009–; Auditor, Global Green Growth Inst. 2010–; Order of Industrial Service Merit, Bronze Tower 1995, Order of Industrial Service Merit, Gold Tower 2000, Order of Civil Merit, Mugunghwa Medal 2005, Order of Culture Merit, Geumgwan 2012; Industrial Service Medal 1985, Award for Energy Entrepreneur, Korea Resource Econs Asscn 2003. *Address:* GS Caltex Corporation, 679 Yeoksam-dong, Seoul 135-985, Republic of Korea (office). *Telephone:* (2) 2005-1114 (office). *Fax:* (2) 2005-8181 (office). *E-mail:* info@gscaltex.com (office). *Website:* www.gscaltex.com (office).

HUR, Won-joon, BSc; South Korean business executive; *Vice-Chairman, Hanwha Chemical Corpn;* b. 19 May 1956; ed Pusan High School, Yonsei Univ., Seoul; joined Hanwha Chemical 1968, Head of Research, Hanwha Group Research Centre, 1982–89, Head of Business Devt Div., Hanwha Chemical Corpn, 1989–92, Head of Tech. Planning Div. 1992–97, Head of New Business Devt Div. 1997–98, Head of Restructuring Team 1998–2001, Chief Planning, Tech. and Information Officer 2001, Pres. and CEO 2002–09, Vice-Chair. 2009–; Chair. Korea Petrochemical Industry Asscn 2007–10, Korea Responsible Care Council 2004–06; Order of Industrial Service Merit, Ivory Tower 2000. *Address:* Hanwha Chemical Corpn, Hanwha Building, 1 Changgyo-Dong, Chung-Ku, Seoul 100-797, Republic of Korea (office). *Telephone:* (2) 729-2700 (office).

HURD, Mark Vincent, BBA; American computer industry executive; *Co-CEO, Oracle Corporation;* b. 1 Jan. 1957, Flushing, NY; m. Paula Kalupa; ed Baylor Univ.; held various positions with NCR Corpn 1980–2005, including Vice-Pres. Worldwide Marketing and Americas Professional Services Div., Sr Vice-Pres. Teradata Solutions Group 1998–2000, COO Teradata Div., Pres. NCR 2001–05, COO 2002–03, CEO 2003–05; CEO and Pres. Hewlett-Packard Co. 2005–10 (resgnd), Exec. Dir 2005–10, Chair. 2006–10; Co-Pres. Oracle Corpn 2010–14, Co-CEO 2014–; mem. Bd of Dirs News Corpn; mem. Computer Systems Policy Project; mem. Bd of Regents, Baylor Univ.; CEO of the Year, San Francisco Chronicle 2008, Meritorious Achievement Award, Baylor Univ. 2012–13. *Address:* Oracle Corporation, 500 Oracle Parkway, Redwood Shores, CA 94065, USA (office). *Telephone:* (650) 506-7000 (office). *Fax:* (650) 506-7200 (office). *E-mail:* info@oracle.com (office). *Website:* www.oracle.com (office); markhurd.com.

HURD OF WESTWELL, Baron (Life Peer), cr. 1997, of Westwell in the County of Oxfordshire; **Douglas Richard Hurd,** CH, CBE, PC, BA (Hons); British politician, diplomatist, banker and author; b. 8 March 1930, Marlborough, Wilts.; s. of Anthony Hurd, Baron Hurd and Stephanie Corner; m. 1st Tatiana Elizabeth Michelle Eyre 1960 (divorced 1982); three s.; m. 2nd Judy Smart 1982 (died 2008); one s. one d.; ed Eton Coll., Trinity Coll., Cambridge; fmr Pres. Cambridge Union Soc.; joined diplomatic service 1952; served in Beijing 1954–56, UK Mission to UN 1956–60, Pvt. Sec. to Perm. Under-Sec. of State, Foreign Office 1960–63, in British Embassy, Rome 1963–66; joined Conservative Research Dept 1966, Head of Foreign Affairs Section 1968; Pvt. Sec. to Leader of the Opposition 1968–70, Political Sec. to the Prime Minister 1970–74; MP for Mid-Oxon 1974–83, for Witney 1983–97; Opposition Spokesman on European Affairs 1976–79, Minister of State, FCO 1979–83, Home Office 1983–84; Sec. of State for NI 1984–85; Home Sec. 1985–89; Sec. of State for Foreign and Commonwealth Affairs 1989–95; mem. Constitutional Comm. 1998–99, Royal Comm. on the Reform of the House of Lords 1999–2001, House of Lords Appointments Comm. 2000–10; Deputy Chair. NatWest Markets 1995–98; Dir NatWest Group 1995–99; Chair. British Invisibles 1997–2000; Deputy Chair. Coutts and Co. 1998–2010; cand. for Conservative Leadership 1990; Chair. Prison Reform Trust 1997–2001 (Pres.), Booker Prize Cttee 1998, Archbishop of Canterbury's Review 2000–01, Council for Effective Dispute Resolution 2001–04; Sr Adviser to Hawkpoint Partners Ltd 1999–; Pres. Montrose Strategic Consultancy, London; Chair. Advisory Council, FIRST Magazine (Forum For Decision Makers) (int. affairs org.), London; High Steward Westminster Abbey 2000–10; Pres. German-British Forum; Co-Pres. Royal Inst. Int. Affairs 2002–10; Vice-Pres. Falkland Islands Asscn 1996–2000 (Pres. 2000–), Commonwealth Parl. Asscn (UK Br.); mem. Global Leadership Foundation, Top Level Group of UK Parliamentarians for Multilateral Nuclear Disarmament and Non-proliferation 2009–; f. charity, Crime Concern 1988 (merged with young people's charity Rainer to become Catch22 2008); Fellow, Nuffield Coll. Oxford; Hon. DLitt (Aston) 2009, (Brunel) 2009; Spectator Award for Parliamentarian of the Year 1990. *Publications:* non-fiction: The Arrow War 1967, An End to Promises 1979, The Search for Peace 1997, Memoirs 2003, Robert Peel, a Biography 2007,

Choose Your Weapons: The British Foreign Secretary (with Edward Young) 2010, Disraeli: Or, the Two Lives (with Edward Young) 2013; fiction: Send Him Victorious (with Andrew Osmond) 1968, The Smile on the Face of the Tiger 1969, Scotch on the Rocks (with Andrew Osmond) 1971, Truth Game 1972, Vote to Kill 1975, War Without Frontiers (with Andrew Osmond) 1982, Palace of Enchantments (with Stephen Lamport) 1985, The Last Day of Summer 1992, The Shape of Ice 1998, Ten Minutes to Turn the Devil (short stories) 1999, Image in the Water 2001. *Leisure interests:* writing, broadcasting. *Address:* House of Lords, Westminster, London, SW1A 0PW, England (office).

HURLEY, David John, AC, DSC, KStJ; Australian public servant and fmr army officer; *Governor-General;* b. 26 Aug. 1953, Wollongong; m. Linda Hurley; three c.; ed Royal Mil. Coll., Duntroon Univ.; served in Australian Army 1972–2014, including service with 1st Battalion, Royal Australian Regt 1991–93, deployed on Operation Solace, Somalia 1993, later becoming Land Commdr Australia 2002–03, Chief of Capability Devt Group 2003–07, Chief of Jt Operations 2007–08, Vice Chief of Defence Force 2008–11, Chief of Defence Force 2011–14; retd from army with rank of Gen. June 2014; Gov. of New South Wales 2014–19; Gov.-Gen. of Australia June 2019–; Hon. Fellow, Australian Acad. of Tech. and Eng; Officer, Ordre nat. de la Légion d'honneur (France) 2012, Commdr, Legion of Merit (USA) 2012, Gold Medal of the Order of the Crown of Thailand 2014, Gold Decoration of Merit (Netherlands) 2014; Australian Active Service Medal, Australian Service Medal, Australian Defence Medal. *Address:* Government House Sydney, Macquarie Street, Sydney, NSW 2000, Australia (office); Government House, Canberra, ACT 2600, Australia (office). *Telephone:* (2) 9228 4111 (office); (02) 6283 3533 (office). *Fax:* (2) 9228 4509 (home); (02) 6281 3760 (office). *Website:* www.governor.nsw.gov.au (office); www.gg.gov.au (office).

HURLEY, Elizabeth Jane; British model, actress and fashion designer; b. 10 June 1965; d. of Roy Leonard Hurley and Angela Mary Hurley; m. Arun Nayar 2007 (divorced); one s. (from previous relationship); produced several films starring Hugh Grant under their jointly-owned production co. Simian Films; represents Estée Lauder as 'spokesmodel' 1994–; toured USA and other countries with the late Evelyn Lauder, raising funds and awareness for The Breast Cancer Research Foundation; owns 400-acre organic farm in Glos.; launched Elizabeth Hurley Beach fashion collection 2005; honoured by Landmark Foundation and awarded the Humanitarian Award for fundraising efforts 2009. *Films include:* Aria 1987, The Skipper 1990, The Long Winter of 39 1992, Passenger 57 1992, Mad Dogs and Englishmen 1995, Austin Powers: International Man of Mystery (ShoWest Award for Best Supporting Actress 1997) 1997, My Favourite Martian 1999, Austin Powers: The Spy Who Shagged Me 1999, The Weight of Water 2000, Bedazzled 2000, Double Whammy 2001, Dawg 2002, Method 2004, The Last Guy on Earth 2006. *Television:* title role in Christabel (film) 1988, Rumpole of the Bailey (series) 1988, Inspector Morse 1988, Act of Will (series) 1989, Death Has a Bad Reputation (film) 1990, The Orchid House (series) 1991, The Good Guys (series) 1992, The Young Indiana Jones Chronicles (series) 1992, Sharpe's Enemy (film) 1994, The Shamrock Conspiracy (film) 1995, Harrison: Cry of the City (film) 1996, Samson and Delilah (film) 1996, Wonder Woman (film) 2011, Gossip Girl (series) 2011. *E-mail:* ducotyG@unitedtalent.com (office); office@elizabethhurley.com (office). *Address:* PO Box 16, Cirencester, Glos., GL7 9GH, England. *Website:* www.elizabethhurley.com.

HURN, David; British photographer and lecturer; b. 21 July 1934, Redhill, Surrey, England; s. of Stanley Hurn and Joan Maynard; m. Alita Naughton 1964 (divorced 1971); one d.; ed Hardy's School, Dorchester and Royal Mil. Acad., Sandhurst; Asst Photographer to Michael Peto and George Vargas, Reflex Agency, London 1955–57; freelance photographer for The Observer, Sunday Times, Look, Life, etc. 1957, working from Wales 1971; mem. Magnum Photos co-operative agency, New York, Paris, London and Tokyo 1967–; Editorial Adviser Album Photographic magazine, London 1971; Head, School of Documentary Photography, Gwent Coll. of Higher Educ., Newport, Gwent 1973–90; Distinguished Visiting Artist and Adjunct Prof., Arizona State Univ., USA 1979–80; mem. Photographic Cttee, Arts Council of GB 1972–77, Arts Panel 1975–77, CNAA 1978–87; works in collections of Welsh Arts Council, Arts Council of GB, British Council, Bibliothèque Nationale, Paris, Int. Center of Photography, New York, San Francisco Museum of Modern Art, Museum of Modern Art, New York, Nat. Museum of Wales and others; Hon. Fellow, Univ. of Wales 1997, Royal Photographic Soc. 2016; Welsh Arts Council Award 1971, Imperial War Museum Arts Award 1987–88, Kodak Photographic Bursary 1975, UK/USA Bicentennial Fellowship 1979–80, Bradford Fellow 1993–94, Arts Council of Wales Bursary 1995. *Publications include:* David Hurn: Photographs 1956–1976 1979, On Being a Photographer 1997, Wales: Land of My Father 2000, On Looking at Photographs 2000, Living in Wales 2003, Writing the Picture 2010, The 1960s: Photographed by David Hurn 2015, Arizona Trips 2017, Wales 1970–2010 2018. *Leisure interests:* music, looking, meeting people. *Address:* c/o Magnum Photos, 63 Gee Street, London, EC1V 3RS, England (office); Prospect Cottage, Tintern, Monmouthshire, NP16 6SG, Wales (home). *Telephone:* (20) 7490-1771 (office); (1291) 689358 (home). *Fax:* (20) 7608-0020 (office). *E-mail:* london@magnumphotos.com (office). *Website:* www.magnumphotos.com (office).

HURST, Sir Geoffrey Charles, Kt, MBE; British professional football manager, fmr professional footballer and business executive; b. 8 Dec. 1941, Ashton-under-Lyne, Lancs.; s. of Charlie Hurst and Evelyn Hurst; m. Judith Harries 1964; three d.; striker; player, West Ham United 1957–72 (won UEFA Cup Winners Cup 1965, FA Cup 1964, Int. Soccer League 1963), Stoke City 1972–74, West Bromwich Albion 1975–76, Seattle Sounders 1976, Cork Celtic 1976; player and Man. Telford United 1976–79; Man. Chelsea 1979–81; won 49 caps and scored 24 goals for England nat. team 1966–72, scored hat-trick in victory over W Germany, World Cup 1966 (only player to do so in a World Cup final); Dir Aon Warranty Group 1995–; currently Dir of Football, McDonald's fast food chain; Patron Ludlow Town Football Club; inducted into English Football Hall of Fame 2004. *Publication:* 1966 and All That 2001, World Champions 2006. *Leisure interests:* sport in general, family. *Address:* c/o Dave Davies, PO Box 99, Hockley, Essex, SS5 4TB, England (office). *Telephone:* (1702) 202036 (office). *Fax:* (871) 871-2065 (office). *E-mail:* dave@football1966.com (office); david@geoffhurst.net (office). *Website:* www.geoffhurst.net (office).

HURT, William; American actor; b. 20 March 1950, Washington, DC; s. of Alfred McChord Hurt and Claire Isabel Hurt (née McGill); m. 1st Mary Beth Hurt 1971 (divorced 1982); m. 2nd Heidi Henderson 1989 (divorced 1992); two s.; ed Tufts Univ., Juilliard School; appeared with Ore. Shakespeare Festival production of Long Day's Journey Into Night; mem. Circle Repertory Co.; first Spencer Tracy Award 1988, for outstanding screen performances and professional achievement. *Stage appearances include:* Henry V 1976, Mary Stuart, My Life, Ulysses in Traction, Lulu, Fifth of July, Childe Byron, The Runner Stumbles, Hamlet, Hurlyburly, Beside Herself 1989, Ivanov 1991. *Films include:* Altered States 1980, Eyewitness 1981, Body Heat 1981, The Big Chill 1983, Gorky Park 1983, Kiss of the Spider Woman (Best Actor Award Cannes Film Festival 1985, Acad. Award for Best Actor 1985) 1985, Children of a Lesser God 1986, Broadcast News 1987, A Time of Destiny 1988, The Accidental Tourist 1989, I Love You to Death 1990, The House of Spirits 1990, Alice 1990, The Doctor 1991, Until the End of the World 1991, Mr. Wonderful 1993, The Plague 1993, Trial by Jury 1994, Second Best 1994, Jane Eyre 1995, Secrets Shared With a Stranger, Smoke 1995, A Couch in New York 1996, Michael 1996, Loved 1997, Lost in Space 1998, One True Thing 1998, The Proposition 1998, Dark City 1998, The 4th Floor 1999, The Big Brass Ring 1999, Sunshine 1999, Do Not Disturb 1999, The Simian Line 2000, The Contaminated Man 2000, AI: Artificial Intelligence 2001, The Flamingo Rising 2001, Rare Birds 2001, Changing Lanes 2002, Au plus pres du paradis 2002, Tuck Everlasting 2002, Tulse Luper Suitcases: The Moab Story 2003, Blue Butterfly 2004, The Village 2004, A History of Violence 2005, Syriana 2005, The King 2005, Neverwas 2005, The Legend of Sasquatch (voice) 2006, Beautiful Ohio 2006, The Good Shepherd 2006, Mr. Brooks 2007, Into the Wild 2007, Vantage Point 2008, The Incredible Hulk 2008, Endgame 2009, The Countess 2009, Robin Hood 2010, The River Why 2011, Late Bloomers 2011, Hellgate 2011, The Host 2013, The Disappearance of Eleanor Rigby: Her 2013, Days and Nights 2013, A New York Winter's Tale 2014, The Disappearance of Eleanor Rigby: Them 2014. *Television includes:* The Flamingo Rising 2001, Master Spy: The Robert Hanssen Story 2002, Frankenstein (mini-series) 2004, Hunt for Justice (film) 2005, Damages (series) 2009, Moby Dick (mini-series) 2011, Too Big to Fail (film) 2011, Bonnie & Clyde (mini-series) 2013, The Challenger (film) 2013, Humans (series) 2015. *Address:* c/o Creative Artists Agency, 9830 Wilshire Blvd, Beverly Hills, CA 90212-1825, USA.

HURTADO LARREA, Osvaldo, BrerPol, DIur; Ecuadorean fmr head of state; *President, Corporation for Development Studies (CORDES);* b. 26 June 1939, Chambo, Chimborazo Prov.; s. of Agustín Hurtado and Elina Larrea de Hurtado; m. Margarita Pérez Pallares; three s. two d.; ed Catholic Univ. of Quito; f. Ecuadorian Christian Democratic Party 1964; Pres. of Congress 1966; Prof. of Political Sociology, Catholic Univ., Quito; Dir Instituto Ecuatoriano de Desarrollo Social (INEDES) 1966; Under-Sec. of Labour 1969; Sub-Dean, Faculty of Econs and Dir Inst. of Econ. Research, Catholic Univ., Quito 1973; invited to form part of World Political Council of Christian Democracy 1975; joined with other political groups to form Popular Democracy 1978; Pres. Org. of Christian Democrats of America, Vice-Pres. Int. Christian Democrats; Pres. Comm. to prepare Law of Referendum of Elections and Political Parties 1977; Vice-Pres. of Ecuador and Pres. Consejo Nacional de Desarrollo (Nat. Devt Council) 1979–81; Pres. of Ecuador 1981–84; Pres. Nat. Ass. 1998; Pres. CORDES (org. for study of Latin American Devt problems), Quito; fmr Vice-Pres. Inst. for European Latin-American Relations, Madrid; mem. Council of ex-Pres, Atlanta, Interamerican Dialogue, Washington, DC (Co-Pres, Bd of Dirs), The Carter Center, Atlanta, Club de Madrid, Foro de Biarritz, Emerging Markets Forum, Washington, DC, Foro Iberoamericano; mem. comm. that prepared the environmental reports Nuestra Propia Agenda 1990, Amazonía Sin Mitos 1992 and Amanecer en los Andes 1997 at request of IDB and UNDP; Dr hc (Georgetown); various foreign decorations. *Publications:* numerous essays and several books about Ecuadorian politics, sociology and economy, including El Poder Político en el Ecuador (Political Power in Ecuador) 1977, Los Costos del Populismo 2006, Las Costumbres de los Ecuatorianos 2007; academic work about Latin America gathered in several books published in collaboration with other authors in many countries. *Leisure interests:* tennis, gardening. *Address:* CORDES, Suecia 277 y Av. Los Shyris, Edificio Suecia Piso 2, PO Box 17-17-307, Quito, Ecuador (office). *Telephone:* (5932) 2455701 (office). *Fax:* (5932) 2446414 (office). *E-mail:* cordes2@cordes.org (office). *Website:* www.cordes.org (office).

HUSAIN, Ishrat, MA, PhD; Pakistani economist and central banker (retd) and university administrator; b. 17 June 1941, Allahabad, India; s. of Rahat Husain and Khursheed Rahat Husain; m. Shahnaz Husain; two d.; ed Williams Coll., Boston Univ. and Grad. Exec. Devt Programme (Harvard, Stanford and INSEAD); mem. Staff Sr Managerial, Planning and Devt Dept and Finance Dept, Govt of Sindh; Additional Deputy Commr for Devt, Chittagong, Bangladesh; mem. Govt of Pakistan's Panel of Economists; Adjunct Prof. of Econs, Karachi Univ., Dir Poverty and Social Policy Dept; IBRD Resident Rep. for Nigeria 1986, Chief Economist for Africa, IBRD 1991–94, Chief Economist for E Asia and Pacific Region 1995, also Chief Debt and Int. Finance Div., Dir for Cen. Asian Repubs; Gov. State Bank of Pakistan 1999–2005; Chair. Nat. Comm. for Govt Reforms with rank of Fed. Minister 2006–08, World Economic Forum Council on Pakistan; Dean and Dir, Inst. of Business Admin, Karachi 2008–16; mem. Mahathir Comm., Middle East Advisory Group, IMF, Presidential Advisory panel IDB; Public Policy Fellow, Woodrow Wilson Center, Washington DC 2016–17; Hilal-e-Imtiaz 2003, Nishane Imtiaz 2016; Central Bank Gov. of the Year in Asia Award, The Banker magazine (first Pakistani Gov. to receive award) 2005, Jinnah Award 2005, Special Gold Medal, Federation of Pakistan Chambers of Commerce and Industry 2005, Lifetime Achievement Award, Asian Banker Magazine Singapore 2006. *Publications:* Dollars, Debts, and Deficits, Pakistan: The Economy of an Elitist State, The Political Economy of Reforms: Case Study of Pakistan, Adjustment in Africa: Lessons from Case Studies: Dealing with Debt Crisis, African External Finance in the 1990s, The Economy of Modern Sindh, Globalization, Governance and Growth, Governing the Ungovernable; numerous articles and papers on debt, external finance and adjustment issues. *Leisure interests:* reading and writing economics, poetry. *Address:* Office of the Dean, Institute of Business Administration, University Road, Karachi 75270 (office); 98/II Street 16, D.H.A. Phase VI, Karachi, Pakistan (home). *Telephone:* (21) 35245291. *E-mail:* ihusain@iba.edu.pk (office). *Website:* www.iba.edu.pk (office); ishrathusain.iba.edu.pk.

HUSSAIN, Ahmed Faiz; Maldivian judge; fmr Civil Court Judge; apptd to Supreme Court, Chief Justice 2010–15 (removed by Judicial Service Comm.).

HUSSAIN, Altaf, BPharm; Pakistani politician; *Leader, Muttahida Qaumi Movement;* b. 17 Sept. 1953, Karachi; s. of Nazir Hussain and Khurshid Begum; m.; ed Karachi Univ.; Founder and Leader Muttahida Qaumi Movt (MQM); in exile in UK since 1992. *Address:* MQM International Secretariat, 54–58, First Floor, Elizabeth House, High Street, Edgware, Middx, HA8 7EJ, England (office). *Telephone:* (20) 8905-7300 (office). *Fax:* (20) 8952-9282 (office). *E-mail:* mqm@mqm.org (office). *Website:* www.mqm.org (office).

HUSSAIN, Chaudhry Amir, BA, BL; Pakistani barrister and politician; b. 22 June 1942, Jammu and Kashmir; s. of Chaudhry Diwan Ali; m.; ed Punjab Univ.; mem. Nat. Ass. (Pakistan Muslim League) for NA-111, Sialkot constituency 1985–2002, Chair. Standing Cttee on Law, Justice, Human Rights and Parl. Affairs 1997–99, mem. Standing Cttee on Science and Tech. 1997–99, Speaker of Nat. Ass. 2002–08; Parl. Sec. for Law and Justice 1985–88; Fed. Minister for Law, Justice and Parl. Affairs 1990–91, for Parl. and Youth Affairs 1991–93; signatory of first Asscn of Asian Parls for Peace (AAPP) Conf. held in Dhaka 1999; Leader of Pakistan Parl. Del. Exec. Council Meeting of AAPP, Beijing 2003; Leader and mem. Pakistan Parl. and Official Dels to USA, UK, Saudi Arabia, Dubai, UAE, Egypt, Malta, Canada, Nicaragua, Libya, Sri Lanka, Democratic People's Repub. of Korea, Thailand, Philippines, S Africa, Namibia, Bangladesh, Russian Fed., Turkey, Kuwait, Morocco, Japan, Belgium, Chile, China, India, Algeria, France, Mexico, Switzerland and Malaysia; Pres. AAPP 2004–05. *Leisure interests:* reading, farming.

HUSSAIN, Chaudhry Shujaat; Pakistani politician; *President, Pakistan Muslim League;* b. 27 Jan. 1946; s. of Chaudhry Zahoor Elahi; m.; two s. one d.; ed Forman Christian Coll., Lahore and Univ. of London, UK; mem. Majlis-e-Shoora 1982–85; mem. Nat. Ass. 1985–, Leader of Opposition 1988–90; Fed. Minister for Information and Broadcasting 1986, for Industries and Production 1987–88, of the Interior 1990–93, 1997–99, of Narcotics Control 1997–99; Pres. Pakistan Muslim League 2004–; Prime Minister of Pakistan June–Aug. 2004; Hon. Consul-Gen. to Repub. of Korea 1982–; Order of Diplomatic Service Merit Ueung-in-Metal. *Address:* Pakistan Muslim League, PML House, 4 Margala Road, F-7/3, Islamabad, Pakistan (office). *Telephone:* (51) 9102469 (office). *Fax:* (51) 2611061 (office). *E-mail:* info@pml.org.pk (office). *Website:* www.pml.org.pk (office).

HUSSAIN, Fouad; Iraqi politician; *Deputy Prime Minister and Minister of Finance;* b. 1 July 1949, Khanaqin, Diyala Prov.; m. Carolien Montessorie; one d.; ed Baghdad Univ., Vrije Univ. Amsterdam; in exile in Netherlands and France 1975–2003; fmr teacher, Hogeschool De Horst, Driebergen; Deputy Head, Kurdish Inst., Paris 1987; returned to Iraq after removal of Saddam Hussein 2003; Adviser to Ministry of Educ. 2003; Chief of Staff to Pres. of Kurdistan Regional Govt 2005–17; KDP nominee for Pres. of Iraq 2018; Deputy Prime Minister and Minister of Finance 2018–; mem. Kurdistan Democratic Party (KDP) 1966–74, 1983–; mem. Patriotic Union of Kurdistan 1974–83. *Address:* Ministry of Finance, Khulafa St, nr al-Russafi Square, Baghdad, Iraq (office). *Telephone:* (1) 887-4871 (office). *E-mail:* emof@mof.gov.iq (office). *Website:* www.mof.gov.iq (office).

HUSSAIN, Mamnoon; Pakistani business executive, politician and fmr head of state; b. 2 March 1940, Agra, British India; ed Inst. of Business Admin, Karachi; family migrated to Karachi following the partition of India 1949; fmr Pres. Karachi Chamber of Commerce and Industry; Gov. of Sindh June–Oct. 1999, term of office cut short by mil. coup d'état; official nominee of Pakistan Muslim League in presidential election July 2013; Pres. of Pakistan 2013–18. *Address:* c/o Office of the President, Aiwan-e-Sadr, Islamabad, Pakistan (office).

HUSSAIN, Nasser, OBE, BSc; British sports commentator and fmr professional cricketer; b. 28 March 1968, Madras (now Chennai), India; s. of Jawad (Joe) Hussain; m. Karen Hussain; two s.; ed Forest School, Walthamstow, Durham Univ.; right-hand higher middle-order batsman, right-hand leg-break bowler; played for Essex 1987–2004 (Capt. 1999), England 1989–2004 (Capt. 1999–2003), MCC 1991; youngest-ever batsman to represent Essex Under-15 Schools 1980; England Test debut against W Indies, Kingston 1990; Capt. England 'A' team in tour of Pakistan 1996; scored first Test centuries at Edgbaston and Trent Bridge against India 1996 and career-best 207 against Australia at Edgbaston 1997; played in 96 Tests, scoring 5,764 runs (average 37.18) including 14 centuries; played in 88 One-Day Ints, scoring 2,332 runs (average 30.28, highest score 115) including one century; scored 20,698 First-class runs (average 42.06) including 52 centuries; cricket commentator, Sky Sports 2005–; Cricket Writers' Club Young Cricketer of the Year Award 1989, Wisden Cricketer of the Year 2003. *Publications:* The Autobiography 2004, Playing with Fire (British Sports Book Awards) 2005. *Leisure interests:* golf, football (Leeds United fan), reading. *Address:* c/o The England and Wales Cricket Board, Lord's Cricket Ground, London, NW8 8QZ; Sky Sports, British Sky Broadcasting Ltd, Grant Way, Isleworth, TW7 5QD, England (office). *Telephone:* (20) 7432-1200; (20) 7705-3000 (office). *Fax:* (20) 7286-5583. *E-mail:* cricket@skysports.com (office). *Website:* www.ecb.co.uk; www.skysports.com (office).

HUSSAIN, Baron (Life Peer), cr. 2011, of Luton in the County of Bedfordshire; **Qurban Hussain;** British employment adviser and politician; b. 27 March 1956, Kashmir, Pakistan; m.; came to live in UK 1971; joined trade union movt and served as a Sec. for Luton TUC 1994–96; campaigned against Iraq war and joined Liberal Democrats 2003; Liberal Democrat Councillor, Luton Borough Council 1996–99, 2003–10, mem. Council Exec., held portfolios of Citizenship, Community, Youth and Leisure Services as well as Equality and Social Inclusion 2003–07, Deputy Leader of Luton Borough Council 2005–07, currently Deputy Leader of Liberal Democrat Group; unsuccessful Parl. cand. for Luton South in Gen. Elections 2005, 2010; mem. Bd of Govs Central Bedfordshire Coll., Dunstable. *Address:* House of Lords, Westminster, London, SW1A 0PW; 49 Claremont Road, Luton, Beds., LU4 8LY, England (home). *Telephone:* (1582) 618919 (home); (20) 7219-5353 (House of Lords). *Fax:* (20) 7219-5979 (House of Lords). *E-mail:* qurban.hussain@ntlworld.com.

HUSSAIN, Rana Tanveer, MA; Pakistani politician; b. 10 Jan. 1949, Sheikhupura Punjab Prov.; s. of Haji Muhammad Anwar; m.; one d.; ed Punjab Univ.; started political career as mem. District Council 1983; mem. Nat. Ass. (Pakistan Muslim League) for Sheikhupura-II NA-132 constituency 1985–2002, 2008–; served as Parl. Sec. for Finance to Prime Minister Yousaf Raza Gillani, also served as Minister of Defence Production March–May 2008; Minister of Defence Production 2013–18, of Science and Tech. 2014–17. *Address:* 318, Upper Mall, Lahore, Pakistan (home). *Telephone:* (42) 5758388 (office). *Fax:* (42) 5877863 (office). *E-mail:* info@modp.gov.pk (office). *Website:* www.modp.gov.pk (office).

HUSSAIN, Rashad, MA, JD, MPA; American lawyer and government official; *Special US Envoy to the Organization of the Islamic Conference;* b. 1978, Wyoming; s. of Mohammad Hussain and Ruqaya Hussain; ed Univ. of North Carolina, Yale Univ. Law School, Kennedy School of Govt, Harvard Univ.; fmr ed. Yale Law Journal; fmr Legis. Asst, US House of Reps Judiciary Cttee; fmr trial attorney, US Justice Dept; fmr clerk to Damon J. Keith, US Court of Appeals for Sixth Circuit; Deputy Assoc. Counsel to Pres. Barack Obama 2009–10; Special US Envoy to OIC 2010–; Fellow, Paul and Daisy Soros Fellowships for New Americans 2003. *Address:* Organization of the Islamic Conference, Medina Road, Sary Street, POB 178, Jeddah 21411, Saudi Arabia (office). *Telephone:* (2) 690-0001 (office). *Fax:* (2) 275-1953 (office). *E-mail:* info@oic-oci.org (office). *Website:* www.oic-oci.org (office).

HUSSAIN, Prince Sharif Ali bin al-, BA, MA; *Leader, Constitutional Monarchy Movement;* b. 1956, Baghdad; s. of Sharif Al Hussain bin Ali and Princess Badia; cousin of King Faisal II; m.; ed univ. of Nottingham and Univ. of Essex, UK; royal family in exile following revolution 1958–; childhood spent in Lebanon and UK; began career in investment banking, London; currently Leader Constitutional Monarchy Movt (a mem. of Iraq Nat. Congress—INC); returned to Iraq to make claim to the throne June 2003; Royal Order of the Drum. *Leisure interest:* fencing. *Telephone:* (1) 778-2897 (office). *Fax:* (1) 778-0199 (office). *Website:* www.iraqcmm.org (office).

HUSSAIN, Zakir; Indian musician (tabla), producer, actor and composer; b. 9 March 1951, Mumbai; s. of Ustad Alla Rakha Qureshi; m. Antonia Minnecola; two d.; ed St Michael's High School, St Xavier's Coll., Maharashtra; plays with Ali Akbar Khan, Birju Maharaj, Ravi Shankar, Shivkumar Sharma; formed band Shanti with Aashish Khan 1970; formed band Shakti with John McLaughlin and L. Shankar 1975; first professional concert 1963; also formed percussion group, Rhythm Experience, Diga Rhythm Band, Making Music, Planet Drum with Mickey Hart, Tabla Beat Science, Sangam with Charles Lloyd and Eric Harland; f. Moment! Records 1992–; composed music for opening ceremony, Summer Olympic Games, Atlanta, USA 1996; Old Dominion Fellow, Humanities Council, Princeton Univ., Prof. of Indian classical music, Dept of Music 2005–06; Visiting Prof., Stanford Univ. 2007; commissioned by Indian Govt to compose anthem to celebrate 60 years of Indian independence 2007; Padma Shri 1988, Indo-American Award 1990, Sangeet Natak Akademi Award 1991, Nat. Heritage Fellowship, USA 1999, Padma Bhushan 2002, Kalidas Samman 2006, Grammy Award (best contemporary world music) 2009, Jazz Journalists' Association Award for Percussionist of the Year 2018. *Films include:* soundtracks: Apocalypse Now 1979, Heat and Dust 1983, Miss Beatty's Children 1992, Little Buddha 1993, In Custody 1993, Saaz 1997, Gaach 1998, Zakir and his Friends 1998, Vaanaprastham 1999, Everybody Says I'm Fine 2001, The Mystic Masseur 2001, Mr and Mrs Iyer 2001, The Speaking Hand: Zakir Hussain and the Art of the Indian Drum 2003, One Dollar Curry 2004, The Way of Beauty 2006, Parzania 2005, For Real 2006, The Rhythm Devils Concert Experience 2008. *Recordings include:* albums: Making Music 1987, Planet Drum (with Mickey Hart) (Grammy Award for Best World Music Album) 1992, Tabla Duet (with Ustad Alla Rakha) 1988, Zakir Hussain And The Rhythm Experience 1991, Venu 1972 1991, Essence Of Rhythm 1998, Drums of India 2003, Raag Chandrakauns 2004, Sangam (with Charles Lloyd) 2006, Global Drum Project (with Mickey Hart, Zakir Hussain, Sikiru Adepoju, Giovanni Hidalgo) 2007, The Melody of Rhythm–Triple Concerto and Music for Trio (with Béla Fleck, Edgar Meyer) 2009, Mysterium Tremendum (with Mickey Hart Band) 2012. *Address:* c/o Dean Shultz, IMG Artists, Carnegie Hall Tower, 152 West 57th Street, 5th Floor, New York, NY 10019, USA (office). *Telephone:* (212) 994-3500 (office). *Fax:* (212) 994-3550 (office). *E-mail:* dshultz@imgartists.com (office). *Website:* www.imgartists.com (office); www.zakirhussain.com.

HUSSAIN MAQPOON, Raja Jalal; Pakistani politician; *Governor of Gilgit-Baltistan;* b. 21 April 1961, Skardu, Gilgit-Baltistan; Pres. Pakistan Tehreek-i-Insaf (Gilgit Baltistan) 2015–; Gov. of Gilgit Baltistan 2018–. *Address:* Chief Secretary Monitoring Cell Gilgit, GB Secretariat, Gilgit-Baltistan, Pakistan (office). *E-mail:* info@gilgitbaltistan.gov.pk (office). *Website:* gilgitbaltistan.gov.pk.

HUSSEIN, Maj.-Gen. Abd ar-Rahim Muhammad; Sudanese politician; *Governor, Khartoum State;* career in Armed Forces; attained rank of Maj.-Gen.; Minister of Interior 1998; Minister of Presidential Affairs –2001; Minister of Internal Affairs 2001–04; Minister of Nat. Defence 2005–15; Gov. Khartoum State 2015–. *Address:* Office of the Governor, Khartoum State Headquarters, Nile Street, Khartoum 307, Sudan (office). *Website:* www.krt.gov.sd (office).

HUSSEIN, Bishar Abdirahman, BA; Kenyan diplomatist and international organization official; *Director-General, International Bureau, Universal Postal Union (UPU);* ed Univ. of Nairobi; man. trainee, Kenya Posts and Telecommunications Corpn 1984; Postmaster-Gen., Postal Corpn of Kenya 1999; Amb. to UAE 2002–08; Chair UPU Congress, Geneva 2008, Council of Admin, UPU 2008–12, UPU Strategy Conf., Nairobi 2010, Dir-Gen. Int. Bureau, UPU 2013–. *Address:* International Bureau, Universal Postal Union, Case postale 312, 3000 Berne 15, Switzerland (office). *Telephone:* 313503111 (office). *Fax:* 313503110 (office). *Website:* www.upu.int (office).

HUSSEIN, HRH Princess Haya bint al-, MA; Jordanian philanthropist and athlete; b. 3 May 1974; d. of HM King Hussein I of Jordan (died 1999) and HM Queen Alia al-Hussein of Jordan (died 1977); sister of HRH Prince Ali Bin al-Hussein and Abir Muhaisen; m. HH Sheikh Muhammad bin Rashid al-Maktoum 2004; one d. one s.; ed Badminton Boarding School for Girls, Bristol, Bryanston School, Dorset and St Hilda's Coll. Oxford, UK; selected to represent Jordan in Equestrian Sport (show jumping) age 13; winner Jordanian Nat. Show Jumping Championships 1986, 1987, 1989, 1990, 1992; first female to qualify and compete in Equestrian, Pan Arab Games, Damascus, Syria 1992; trained by Paul Darragh and Alian Storme as show-jumping and flat-race jockey, Co. Meath, Ireland 1995–96; cr. int. competing team, Team Harmony 1996; winner of 33 int. classes, 6 grand prix and one Volvo World Cup Qualifier 1996; trained with Paul

Schockemohle, Muhlen, Germany 1997–99, Hans Horn, Ootmarsum, The Netherlands 1999, Katie Monahan Prudent and Alice Debany Clero, Paris, France 2000; qualified for Olympic Games Sydney (first female Arab flag-bearer at Olympic Games and first Arab woman to compete in Equestrian) 2000; signed commercial contract with Loro Piana, Italy 2000; qualified for World Championships, Jerez, Spain (first Arab woman to qualify and compete) 2002; Rep. of Jordan to Int. Equestrian Fed. (FEI), Chair. Middle E and Western Asian Sub-Group 1992–96, Pres. FEI 2006–; Pres. Queen Alia Foundation for Hearing and Speech Impaired, Children's Dental Health Care Soc. (SMILE), Jordanian Women's Qualifying and Training Center, Haya Art's and Cultural Center for Child Devt; Pres. and Founder Int. Athletes Cultural Asscn; Chair. Int. Humanitarian City, Dubai; Athlete Amb. for Right to Play, for Olympic Aid, for Innocence in Danger; mem. IOC 2007–; mem. Advisory Bd, Just World International; Founder and Chair. Takiyet Um Ali (org. addressing issues of poverty) 2003–; UN Messenger of Peace 2007–; Goodwill Amb. for WFP 2005–07; mem. Hon. Bd, Int. Paralympic Cttee; Hon. Pres. Land Transport and Mechanical Union, Hon. Pres. Int. Sports and Solidarity Foundation; Kt Special Grand Cordon, Supreme Order of the Renaissance 2006; Officier, Légion d'honneur 2014; Bronze Medal, Pan Arab Games 1992, voted Athlete of the Year by Jordanian public 1993, nominated Athlete of the Year by Arab BBC Radio 1994, Equestrian Personality of the Year, Spanish Equestrian Fed. 1996, Int. Golden Helm Award, Int. Asscn of Golden Helmsmen of Tourism 2000, Al Saaoon Fi Al Kheir Award 2009, UN Hunger Hero Award, UN WFP, Davos, Switzerland 2015. *Publication:* biog. of the late King Hussein I. *Leisure interests:* camping, water skiing, tennis, sailing, photography, art, camel racing. *Address:* Office of HRH Princess Haya Bint al-Hussein, PO Box Box 111888, World Trade Center Complex, Convention Center Building, Fifth Floor, Dubai, United Arab Emirates (office). *Telephone:* (4) 3292333 (office). *Fax:* (4) 3292555 (office). *E-mail:* info@hrhoffice.ae (office). *Website:* www.princesshaya.net.

HUSSEIN, Dato' Seri Hishammuddin bin Tun, LLB, LLM; Malaysian lawyer and politician; b. 5 Aug. 1961; s. of Tun Hussein Onn (fmr Prime Minister); m. Yang Mulia Tengku Datin Seri Panglima Marsilla Tengku Abdullah; ed Malay Coll. Kuala Kangsar, Univ. of Wales, Aberystwyth, London School of Econs, UK; early career as lawyer with law firms Skrine & Co., Kuala Lumpur and Lee Hishammuddin (now Lee Hishammuddin Allen & Gledhill); mem. Dewan Rakyat (House of Reps, parl.) for Tenggara 1995–2003, for Sembrong 2003–, Parl. Sec. for Int. Trade and Industry 1995; Deputy Minister of Main Industry 1997, Minister of Youth and Sport 1999–2004, of Educ. 2004–09, of Home Affairs 2009–13, of Defence 2013–18, also Acting Minister of Transport 2013–14; mem. United Malays Nat. Org. (UMNO), Vice-Pres. 2009–. *Address:* c/o Ministry of Defence, Wisma Pertahanan, Jalan Padang Tembak, 50634 Kuala Lumpur, Malaysia (office).

HUSSEIN, Muhammad al-, PhD; Syrian economist and politician; fmr Chair. Econ. Bureau, Govt Exec.; Minister of Finance 2003–11 (resgnd with rest of cabinet at Pres.'s request following popular protests); fmr Prof. of Econs, Univ. of Aleppo; mem. Ba'ath Party.

HUSSEIN, Col Nur Hassan, (Nur Adde); Somali lawyer, police officer, politician and diplomatist; b. 1938, Mogadishu; ed Mogadishu Nat. Univ., Fiscal Law School, Italy; started his career as mem. Somali Finance Guard (customs officer) 1958; Officer, Somali Police Force 1965–68, Trainer, Somali Police Acad., Mogadishu 1968–70, Deputy Head, Personnel Dept 1970–71, Deputy Head, Int. and Interpol Dept 1972–73, Deputy Head of Political and Public Relations Dept 1973–74, Head of Planning and Training Dept 1975–83; Deputy Attorney-Gen., Nat. Security Court 1986–87, Attorney-Gen. 1987–90; Sec.-Gen. Somali Red Crescent Soc. 1991–2007; Prime Minister 2007–09; Amb. to Italy 2009–13.

HUSSEIN, HRH Prince; **Zeid Ra'ad Zeid al-,** BA, PhD; Jordanian diplomatist and UN official; b. 26 Jan. 1964, Amman; s. of Prince Ra'ad bin Zeid and Margaretha Inga Elisabeth Lind (known as Majda Ra'ad); m. Sarah Butler 2000; one s. two d.; ed Reed's School, Surrey, England, Johns Hopkins Univ., USA, Christ's Coll., Cambridge, England; commissioned as officer in Jordanian desert police, served –1994; Political Affairs Officer, UN Protection Force (UNPROFOR), Bosnia and Herzegovina 1994–96, Deputy Perm. Rep. to UN, New York 1996–2000, Amb. and Perm. Rep. 2000–07, 2010–14, Chair. Consultative Cttee for UNIFEM 2004–07, Advisor to Sec.-Gen. on Sexual Exploitation and Abuse 2004, apptd mem. Sr Advisory Group to UN Sec.-Gen. 2012, Pres. UN Security Council 2014, UN High Commr for Human Rights, OHCHR, Geneva 2014–18, chair. or mem. numerous UN cttees on peace-keeping, war crimes and crimes against humanity; Rep. at Treaty-Signing Conf. Banning Landmines, Ottawa, Canada 1997, mem. Rome Conf. (est. Int. Criminal Court) 1998, Deputy Del. Head and Vice-Pres. Maputo Conf. 1999, elected First Pres. Ass. of States Parties to the Rome Statute 2002; Amb. to USA (also accred to Mexico) 2007–10; apptd Rep. and Head of Del., Int. Court of Justice 2004, represented Jordan before Int. Court of Justice in advisory proceedings relating to Kosovo's declaration of independence 2009; mem. Advisory Cttee to Inst. for Historical Justice and Reconciliation, World Bank's Advisory Council for the World Devt Report 2011; Grotius Lecturer, American Soc. of Int. Law 2008. *Publications include:* articles in Cambridge Review of International Affairs, Spring 1989, Israel Affairs, Winter 1994.

HUSSEY, Michael Edward Killeen; Australian fmr professional cricketer; b. 27 May 1975, Morley, WA; m. Amy Hussey; four c.; opening batsman; left-handed batsman; right-arm medium pace bowler; plays for Western Australia (Vice-Capt.) 1994–2012, Northants. 2001–03, Glos. 2004, Australia 2004–13, Durham 2005, Chennai Super Kings 2008–13, Perth Scorchers 2011–13, Sydney Thunder 2013–16, Mumbai Indians 2014; First-class debut: 1994/95; Test debut: Australia v West Indies, Brisbane 3–6 Nov. 2005; One-Day Int. (ODI) debut: Australia v India, Perth 1 Feb. 2004; T20I debut: NZ v Australia, Auckland 17 Feb. 2005; played in 79 Tests, took 7 wickets and scored 6,235 runs (average 51.52) with 19 centuries, 29 half-centuries, highest score 195 against England, Brisbane 2010, best bowling 2/2; played 185 ODIs, cored 5,442 runs (average 48.15) with 3 centuries and 29 half-centuries, highest score 109 not out against West Indies, Kuala Lumpur 2006, and took two wickets; played 38 T20Is, scored 721 runs (average 37.94) with four fifties, highest score 60 not out against Pakistan, Gros Islet 2010; played 273 First-class matches, scored 22,783 runs (average 52.13) with 61 centuries and 103 fifties, highest score 331 not out; announced retirement from int. cricket 29 Dec. 2012; Batting Coach Chennai Super Kings 2018; fmr Dir of Cricket Sydney Thunder; One-Day Int. Player of the Year 2006.

HUSTON, Anjelica; American actress; b. 8 July 1951, Los Angeles, Calif.; d. of John Huston and Enrica Huston (née Soma); m. Robert Graham 1992 (died 2008). *Films include:* Sinful Davey, A Walk with Love and Death 1969, The Last Tycoon 1976, The Postman Always Rings Twice 1981, Swashbuckler, This is Spinal Tap 1984, The Ice Pirates 1984, Prizzi's Honor (Acad. Award for Best Supporting Actress 1985, New York and Los Angeles Film Critics' Awards 1985), Gardens of Stone, Captain Eo, The Dead, Mr North, A Handful of Dust, The Witches, Enemies, A Love Story, The Grifters, The Addams Family, Addams Family Values, The Player, Manhattan Murder Mystery, The Crossing Guard 1995, The Perez Family 1995, Buffalo '66 1997, Phoenix 1997, Ever After 1998, Breakers 1999, The Golden Bowl 2001, The Royal Tenenbaums 2002, Blood Work 2002, The Man from Elysian Fields 2002, Daddy Day Care 2003, The Life Aquatic with Steve Zissou 2004, These Foolish Things 2006, Art School Confidential 2006, Material Girls 2006, Seraphim Falls 2006, The Darjeeling Limited 2007, Choke 2008, Tinker Bell (voice) 2008, Spirit of the Forest (voice) 2008, The Kreutzer Sonata 2008, When in Rome 2010, Horrid Henry: The Movie 2011, 50/50 2011, The Big Year 2011, TinkerBell and the Secret of the Wings (voice) 2012; films directed: Bastard Out of Carolina 1996, Agnes Browne 1999. *Stage appearances include:* Tamara, Los Angeles 1985. *Television appearances include:* The Cowboy and the Ballerina (NBC-TV film) 1984, Faerie Tale Theatre, A Rose for Miss Emily (PBS film), Lonesome Dove (CBS mini-series), The Mists of Avalon (TNT mini-series) 2001, Iron Jawed Angels (Best Supporting Actress in a Series, Miniseries or TV Movie, Golden Globe Awards 2005) 2004, Riding the Bus with My Sister (dir) 2005, Covert One: The Hades Factor 2006, Medium (series) 2008–09, Smash (series) 2012–13. *Address:* ICM, 10250 Constellation Boulevard, Beverly Hills, CA 90067, USA.

HUSTVEDT, Siri, PhD; American novelist and essayist; b. 19 Feb. 1955, Northfield, Minn.; d. of Lloyd Hustvedt and Ester Vegan Hustvedt; m. Paul Auster 1981; one d.; ed Columbia Univ.; Lecturer in Psychiatry, Weil Cornell Medical Coll. 2015; worked as ed. and trans.; Dr hc (Univ. of Oslo) 2014, (Université Stendhal) 2014, (Johannes Gutenberg Univ.) 2016; Gabarron Int. Award for Thought and Humanities 2012, Crystal Star Award, American Scandinavian Soc. 2015. *Publications:* Reading to You (poems) 1982, The Blindfold (novel) 1992, The Enchantment of Lily Dahl (novel) 1996, Yonder: Essays 1998, What I Loved (novel, Prix des Libraires de Québec) 2003, Mysteries of the Rectangle (essays) 2005, A Plea for Eros (essays) 2006, The Sorrows of an American (novel) 2008, The Shaking Woman or a History of My Nerves (non-fiction) 2010, The Summer Without Men (novel) 2011, Living, Thinking, Looking 2012, The Blazing World (novel) 2014, A Woman Looking at Men Looking at Women (essays) 2016, Memories of the Future (novel) 2019; contrib. to Paris Review, Modern Painters, The Guardian, The Yale Review, Conjunctions, Neuropsychoanalysis, Seizure: The European Journal of Epilepsy, Clinical Neurophysiology and numerous other publs; fiction translated into more than 30 languages. *Address:* c/o Amanda Urban, ICM Partners, 65 E 55th Street, New York, NY 10022 (office); c/o Samantha O'Hara, Simon & Schuster Inc., 1230 Avenue of the Americas, New York, NY 10020, USA (office). *Telephone:* (212) 556-5600 (ICM Partners) (office); (212) 698-2276 (Simon & Schuster) (office). *E-mail:* Samantha.Ohara@simonandschuster.com (office). *Website:* www.simonandschuster.com (office); sirihustvedt.net.

HUTAPEA, Eva Riyanti; Indonesian business executive; *President Director, PT Usaha Kita Makmur Indonesia;* b. 26 Dec. 1952; m. Bunbunan Hutapea; three d.; ed School of Econs, Univ. of Indonesia; trained as accountant; fmr auditor; joined Salim Group 1982, owner of Indofood, worked through Indofood ranks to become CEO and Pres. Dir 1999–2004 (retd); Pres. Dir PT Usaha Kita Makmur Indonesia (UKM Way) 2004–; Deputy Chair. Indonesian Chamber of Commerce and Industry (KADIN) for the field of Small and Medium Enterprises and Cooperatives; mem. Advisory Council Nat. Bd of the Indonesian Employers Asscn (APINDO); Deputy Chair. Exec. Council Indonesian Inst. of Commrs and Dirs; Dir-Gen. Instant Ramen Mfrs Asscn 1999–2001. *Address:* RP Suroso No. 6, Gondangdia Lama, Jakarta 10350, Indonesia (office). *Telephone:* (21) 31909730 (office).

HUTCHEON, Linda Ann Marie, OC, MA, PhD, FRSC; Canadian writer and academic; *University Professor Emeritus, University of Toronto;* b. (Linda Bortolotti), 24 Aug. 1947, Toronto, Ont.; d. of Roy Bortolotti and Elisa Rossi; m. Michael Alexander Hutcheon 1970; ed Univ. of Toronto, Cornell Univ., USA; Asst, Assoc. and Full Prof. of English, McMaster Univ. 1976–88; Prof. of English and Comparative Literature, Univ. of Toronto 1988–96, Distinguished Univ. Prof. 1996–2010, Univ. Prof. Emer. 2010–; mem. Modern Language Asscn of America, American Acad. of Arts and Sciences; Hon. LLD 1995; Hon. DLitt 1999, 2000, 2005, 2007, 2008, 2011, 2018; Killam Prize 2005, Molson Prize 2010, RSC Lorne Pierce Medal 2016. *Publications include:* Narcissistic Narrative 1980, Formalism and the Freudian Aesthetic 1984, A Theory of Parody 1985, A Poetics of Postmodernism 1988, The Canadian Postmodern 1988, The Politics of Postmodernism 1989, Splitting Images 1991, Irony's Edge 1995, A Theory of Adaptation 2006, Opera: Desire, Disease, Death (with Michael Hutcheon) 1996, Bodily Charm: Living Opera (with Michael Hutcheon), 2000, Opera: The Art of Dying (with Michael Hutcheon), 2004, Four Last Songs: Aging and Creativity in Verdi, Strauss, Messiaen, and Britten (with Michael Hutcheon) 2015; editor: Other Solitudes 1990, Double-Talking 1992, Likely Stories 1992, A Postmodern Reader 1993, Rethinking Literary History: A Forum on Theory 2002; contribs to Diacritics, Textual Practice, Cultural Critique and other journals. *Leisure interests:* piano, walking. *Address:* Department of English, University of Toronto, Toronto, ON M5R 2M8, Canada (office). *Telephone:* (416) 978-6616 (office). *Fax:* (416) 978-2836 (office). *E-mail:* l.hutcheon@utoronto.ca (office). *Website:* individual.utoronto.ca/lindahutcheon (office).

HUTCHINGS, Graham John, CBE, BSc, PhD, DSc, FRS; British chemist and academic; *Regius Professor of Physical Chemistry and Director, Cardiff Catalysis Institute, Cardiff University;* b. 3 Feb. 1951; ed Univ. Coll., London; with ICI Petrochemicals Div. 1975–84, Tech. Officer, Research Dept, Wilton, Teesside 1975–78, Plant Man. and Production Support Man., Oil Works, Teesside 1978–81; Sr Research Officer, AECI, Modderfontein, SA (seconded) 1981–83, Chief Research Officer 1983–84; Lecturer, Univ. of the Witwatersrand, SA 1984–86, Sr Lecturer in Chem. 1986–87, Prof. 1987, Visiting Prof. 1987–90, 2002–, Visiting Research Assoc. 1990–93; Asst Dir Leverhulme Centre for Innovative Catalysis, Univ. of Liverpool 1987–94, Deputy Dir and Prof. 1994–97; Prof. of Physical Chem. and

Head of School, Cardiff Univ. 1997–2006, Distinguished Research Prof. 2006–, Dir Cardiff Catalysis Inst. 2008–, Pro Vice-Chancellor Research 2010–12, currently Regius Prof. of Physical Chemistry; Visiting Scientist, Institut de Recherches sur la Catalyse, CNRS, Villeurbanne France 1992–93; Prof.-in-Residence, Université Pierre et Marie Curie, Paris 2003–04; Visiting Prof., Tokyo Metropolitan Univ., Japan 2010–; Adjunct Prof., Louisiana State Univ. 2010–; Ed.-in-Chief Catalytic Science 1996–; Ed. Applied Catalysis Newsbrief 1997–, Journal of Catalysis 2005–; Corresp., Newsbrief section, Applied Catalysis B 1994–; mem. Editorial Bd, Catalysis Today 1994–, Catalysis Letters 1994–, Topics in Catalysis 1994–, Advances in Catalysis 2007–, Gold Bulletin 2007–, Green Chemistry 2009–, Catalysis Science and Technology 2010–, Proceedings of the Royal Soc. A 2012–, Scientific Reports 2013–; mem. Strategy and Tech. Advisory Bd on Sustainability for Chem. Innovation Knowledge Transfer Network 2007–; RAE panel mem. for Chem. (Panel 18) 2005–08; mem. Faraday Div. Council, RSC 2008–, Pres. Faraday Div. 2012–15; Chair. SCORE 2010–13; REF Panel mem. and Deputy Chair. for Chem. (Panel B8) 2011–14; mem. Sasol (SA) Heterogeneous Catalysis Advisory Bd 2000–09, NIOK Int. Review Group 2000, 2006, 2010 (Chair.); mem. Fachbeirat of Fritz-Haber-Institut, Berlin 1999–2015, Academia Europaea 2010; Founding Fellow, Learned Soc. of Wales; Langmuir Distinguished Lecturer Award, Div. of Colloid and Surface Science, ACS 1996, DGMK 2001 – Kolleg Lectureship, Germany 2001, Entech Medal, Inst. of Chemical Engineers (IChemE) 2004, RSC Award for Heterogeneous Catalysis 2004, François Gault Lecturer, European Fed. of Catalysis Socs 2006, IChemE Impact Award for Applied Catalysis 2005, RSC Green Chem. Lecturer 2007, IChemE Environwise Award for Green Chem. 2007, Winner, Dow Methane Challenge 2008, RSC Award for Surfaces and Interfaces 2009, IChemE Sustainability Award 2009, IPMI Henry J. Albert Award 2011, France Great Britain Chem. Prize 2011, Dechema Alvin Mittasch Award 2012, Heinz Heinemann Award, Int. Asscn of Catalysis Socs 2012, Distinguished Visiting Lecturer, Catalysis Soc. of South Africa 2013, Davy Medal, Royal Soc. 2013, Thompson Reuters Most Cited Scientist Award 2014, Eni Award for Advanced Environmental Solutions 2017, Faraday Lectureship Prize 2018. *Publications:* 14 edited books and more than 570 articles in professional journals; 42 patents. *Address:* School of Chemistry, Cardiff University, Main Building, Park Place, Cardiff, CF10 3AT, Wales (office). *Telephone:* (29) 2087-4059 (office). *Fax:* (29) 2087-4030 (office). *E-mail:* hutch@cardiff.ac.uk (office). *Website:* www.cardiff.ac.uk/chemy (office).

HUTCHINSON, (William) Asa, BS, JD; American lawyer, government official and politician; *Governor of Arkansas;* b. 3 Dec. 1950, Bentonville, Ark.; s. of John M. Hutchinson and Coral Hutchinson (née Mount); m. Susan Burrell; three s. one d.; ed Bob Jones Univ., Univ. of Arkansas School Law; City Attorney, City of Bentonville, Ark. 1977–78; US Attorney (Western Dist), US Dept of Justice, Ark. 1982–85; Partner, Karr & Hutchinson, Fort Smith 1986–96; mem. US House of Reps from 3rd Ark. Dist 1996–2001; Admin., Drug Enforcement Admin, US Dept of Justice 2001–03; Under-Sec. for Border and Transportation Security, US Dept of Homeland Security 2003–05; Founding Partner and CEO, Hutchinson Group, LLC, Washington, DC 2005; Partner, Venable LLP, Washington, DC 2005–06, 2007; Sr Partner, The Asa Hutchinson Law Group, PLC 2008; Gov. of Arkansas 2015–; Chair. Ark. State Republican Cttee 1990–95; mem. ABA, Nat. Asscn of Fmr US Attorneys, Benton County Bar Asscn, Arkansas Bar Asscn; Republican; Order Al Merito Civil Libertador Simon Bolivar (Bolivia). *Address:* Office of the Governor, State Capitol Bldg, Rm 250, Little Rock, AR 72201, USA (office). *Telephone:* (501) 682-2345 (office). *Fax:* (501) 682-1382 (office). *E-mail:* asa@ahlawgroup.com (office). *Website:* www.governor.arkansas.gov (office).

HUTCHINSON, (John) Maxwell, AADipl; British architect, broadcaster and writer; *Director, The Hutchinson Studio Architects;* b. 3 Dec. 1948; s. of Frank M. Hutchinson and Elizabeth R. M. Wright; ed Oundle, Scott Sutherland School of Architecture, Aberdeen and Architectural Asscn School of Architecture; Founder Hutchinson & Partners (Chartered Architects) 1972, Chair. Hutchinson & Partners Architects Ltd 1987–92; Dir The Hutchinson Studio Architects 1992–, SMC Group PLC; Visiting Prof. of Architecture, Queen's Univ., Belfast 1988–93; Special Prof. of Architectural Design, Univ. of Nottingham 1993–96; Visiting Prof., Univ. of Westminster 1997–2001; Chair. Permarock Products Ltd, Loughborough 1985–96, London Br. Elgar Soc. 1987–93, East Midlands Arts Bd 1991–94, British Architectural Library Trust 1991–99, Schools of Architecture Accreditation Bd 1991–97; Chair. Industrial Bldg Bureau 1988–91; Founder and Life Pres. Architects for Aid 2005–; Vice-Chair. Construction Industry Council 1990–91; mem. Council RIBA 1978–93, Sr Vice-Pres. 1988–89, Pres. 1989–91; Church Warden Our Most Holy Redeemer, Clerkenwell 2007–; mem. Council Royal School of Church Music 1997–2000; regular broadcaster on TV and radio; freelance writer; Hon. Fellow, Univ. of Greenwich 1990, Royal Soc. of Ulster Architects 1992, Univ. Coll. London 2008 Hon. Dr of Design (Robert Gordon Univ.) 2007. *Television:* presenter of major series including No. 57 – The History of a House (Channel 4), Demolition Detectives (Channel 4), Maxwell's Hidden Treasures (ITV 1), Prefabs and Palaces, Pure Inventions, Mod Cons (Discovery Channel), How to Rescue a House (BBC 2), Songs of Praise (BBC 1). *Compositions:* The Kibbo-Kift 1979, The Ascent of Wilberforce 111 1984, Requiem in a Village Church 1988, Christmas Cantata 1990. *Publications:* The Prince of Wales, Right or Wrong: An Architect Replies 1989, Number 57 – The Story of a House 2003; contrib. to How to Rescue a House 2005. *Leisure interests:* composing, travel, beer, music. *Address:* 17 Chart Street, London, N1 6DD, England (office). *Telephone:* (20) 7273-9288 (office). *E-mail:* info@hutchinsonstudio.co.uk (office). *Website:* www.hutchinsonstudio.co.uk.

HUTCHISON, Charles E., BS, MS, PhD; American electrical engineer, academic and business executive; *John H. Krehbiel Sr Professor Emeritus for Emerging Technologies, Emeritus and Dean Emeritus, Thayer School of Engineering, Dartmouth College;* ed Illinois Inst. of Tech., Stanford Univ.; Dean, Thayer School of Eng, Dartmouth Coll. 1984–94, 1997–98, Dean Emer. 1998–, John H. Krehbiel Sr Prof. for Emerging Technologies 1998–2003, Emer. 2003–, launched school's Master of Eng man. programme, helped est. the PhD innovation programme 2007; f. M2S co. 1997; Co-founder and CEO GlycoFi Inc. 2000 (acquired by Merck 2006); Co-founder SustainX, Inc. 2007, Chair. 2008–; Gordon Prize, Nat. Acad. of Eng (co-recipient) 2014. *Publications:* numerous papers in professional journals. *Address:* Thayer School of Engineering, Dartmouth College, 14 Engineering Drive, Hanover, NH 03755 (office); SustainX, Inc., 72 Stard Road, Seabrook, NH 03874, USA (office). *Telephone:* (603) 646-3802 (Hanover) (office); (603) 601-7800 (Seabrook) (office). *E-mail:* charles.hutchison@dartmouth.edu (office); info@sustainx.com (office). *Website:* engineering.dartmouth.edu/people/faculty/charles-hutchinson (office); www.sustainx.com (office).

HUTH, John Edward, AB, PhD; American physicist and academic; *Donner Professor of Science, Department of Physics, Harvard University;* b. 16 March 1958, London, England, UK; ed Princeton Univ., Univ. of California, Berkeley; Postdoctoral Scientist, Fermi Nat. Accelerator Lab. (Fermilab), Batavia, Ill. 1985–87, Wilson Fellow 1987–90, Staff Scientist 1990–93, mem. Fermilab Physics Advisory Panel 1993–97; Prof. of Physics, Harvard Univ. 1993–2005, Chair., Dept of Physics 2002–06, Donner Prof. of Science 2006–; mem. 'Godparent Cttee' on the discovery of the top quark 1993–94; ATLAS Muon Electronics Leader, CERN 1995–98, US ATLAS Computing and Physics Program Leader 1998–2002, mem. US LHC (Larger Hadron Collider) Users Exec. Cttee 2009–12, Chair. LHC ATLAS Muon Inst. 2012–; mem. Steering Cttee Brookhaven Nat. Lab. Science and Tech. 1998–2006; mem. Dark Energy Task Force 2005–06; Fellow, American Physical Soc. 1993–. *Publications include:* The Lost Art of Finding Our Way 2013; numerous articles in scientific journals. *Address:* Physics Department, Harvard University, Lyman 236, Cambridge, MA 02138, USA (office). *Telephone:* (617) 495-8144 (office). *Fax:* (617) 495-0416 (office). *E-mail:* huth@physics.harvard.edu (office). *Website:* huhepl.harvard.edu/~huth (office); www.physics.harvard.edu (office).

HUTT, Peter Barton, BA, LLB, LLM; American lawyer; *Senior Counsel, Covington & Burling LLP;* b. 16 Nov. 1934, Buffalo, NY; s. of Lester Ralph Hutt and Louise Rich Fraser; m. Catherine Adams Huttone; one s. two d.; ed Phillips Exeter Acad., Yale, Harvard and New York Univs; Assoc., Covington & Burling LLP (law firm) 1960–68, Pnr 1968–71, 1975–2004, Sr Counsel 2004–; Lecturer on Food and Drug Law, Harvard Law School 1994–, Stanford Law School 1998; Chief Counsel, US Food and Drug Admin. 1971–75; Counsel, Soc. for Risk Analysis, American Coll. of Toxicology; Chair. Alcoholic Beverage Medical Research Foundation 1986–92; Vice-Chair. Legal Action Center, New York 1984–2003, Foundation for Biomedical Research 1988–; mem. Nat. Acad. of Medicine, NAS 1970–, NIH Advisory Cttee to Review the Guidelines for Recombinant DNA Research 1976–78, Science Review Cttee of the FDA Science Bd 2006–08, Working Group on Innovation in Drug Devt and Evaluation of Pres. Obama's Council of Advisors on Science and Technology 2011–12; mem. Advisory Bd, Tufts Center for Study of Drug Devt 1976–99, Univ. of Virginia Center for Advanced Studies 1982–2002, Nat. Cttee on New Drugs for Cancer and AIDS 1988–90, Inst. of Medicine Round Table on Drugs and Vaccines against AIDS 1988–95, Nat. Acad. of Public Admin's Panel on restructuring NIH 2004–06, Nat. Inst. of Allergy and Infections Disease Working Group on Div. of AIDS 2005–06; mem. Bd of Dirs Foundation for Biomedical Research, California Healthcare Inst., Inst. of Health Policy Analysis and numerous cos; mem. Advisory Bd of numerous other scientific, academic and financial orgs; mem. Editorial Advisory Bd, Food and Drug Law Journal; Underwood-Prescott Award, MIT 1977, Distinguished Alumni Award, Food and Drug Admin 2005, Lifetime Achievement Award for research advocacy, Foundation for Biomedical Research 2005 and numerous other honours and awards. *Publications:* Dealing with Drug Abuse (with Patricia M. Wald) 1972, Food and Drug Law: Cases and Materials (with Richard A. Merrill) 1980, 1991, 2007, 2014; several book chapters and more than 175 articles on food and drug law and health policy. *Leisure interests:* research on the history of govt regulation of food and drugs. *Address:* 124 South Fairfax Street, Alexandria, VA 22314 (home); Covington & Burling LLP, 850 10th Street NW, Washington, DC 20001, USA (office). *Telephone:* (202) 662-5522 (office). *Fax:* (202) 778-5522 (office). *E-mail:* phutt@cov.com (office).

HUTTON, Baron (Life Peer), cr. 1997, of Bresagh in the County of Down; **Rt Hon. (James) Brian Edward Hutton,** PC; British fmr judge; b. 29 June 1931, Belfast, Northern Ireland; s. of James Hutton and Mabel Hutton; m. 1st Mary Gillian Murland 1975 (died 2000); two d.; 2nd Rosalind Ann Nickols 2001; two step-s. one step-d.; ed Shrewsbury School, Balliol Coll. Oxford, Queen's Univ. of Belfast; called to NI Bar 1954, QC (NI) 1970, Bencher, Inn of Court of NI 1974, Sr Crown Counsel 1973–79, Judge of High Court of Justice 1979–88, Lord Chief Justice of NI 1988–97; a Lord of Appeal in Ordinary 1997–2004; mem. Jt Law Enforcement Comm. 1974, Deputy Chair. Boundary Comm. for NI 1985–88; Pres. NI Asscn for Mental Health 1983–90; Visitor, Univ. of Ulster 1999–2004; Chair. of Inquiry into death of Dr David Kelly 2003–04; mem. Bd of Dirs Arix Bioscience PLC 2016–18; Hon. Fellow, Balliol Coll., Oxford; Hon. Bencher Inner Temple, King's Inns, Dublin; Hon. LLD (Queen's Univ. of Belfast, Univ. of Ulster). *Address:* House of Lords, Westminster, London, SW1A 0PW, England (office). *Telephone:* (20) 7219-3202 (office).

HUTTON, Timothy; American actor; b. 16 Aug. 1960, Malibu, Calif.; s. of Jim Hutton and Maryline Hutton; m. Debra Winger (q.v.) 1986 (divorced); one s. *Plays:* Prelude to a Kiss, Broadway 1990, Babylon Gardens 1991. *Television appearances include:* Zuma Beach 1978, Best Place to Be, Baby Makes Six, Sultan and the Rock Star, Young Love, First Love, Friendly Fire 1979, Aldrich Ames: Traitor Within 1998, Nero Wolfe Mystery (series) 2001–02, WW3 2001, 5ive Days to Midnight (mini-series) 2004, Avenger 2006, Kidnapped (series) 2006–07, Leverage (series) 2008–12, American Crime (series) 2015, Public Morals 2015. *Films include:* Ordinary People (Oscar for Best Supporting Actor) 1980, Taps 1981, Daniel 1983, Iceman 1984, Turk 1985, The Falcon and the Snowman 1985, Made in Heaven 1987, A Time of Destiny 1988, Everybody's All-American 1988, Betrayed 1988, Torrents of Spring 1990, Q & A 1990, The Temp 1993, The Dark Half 1993, French Kiss 1995, City of Industry, Scenes From Everyday Life 1995, The Substance of Fire 1996, Mr and Mrs Loving 1996, Beautiful Girls 1996, City of Industry 1997, Playing God 1997, Deterrance 1998, The General's Daughter 1999, Just One Night 2000, Deliberate Intent 2000, Deterrence 2000, Lucky Strike 2000, Sunshine State 2002, Secret Window 2004, Kinsey 2004, Turning Green 2005, Last Holiday 2006, Stephanie Daley 2006, The Kovak Box 2006, Heavens Fall 2006, Falling Objects 2006, Off the Black 2006, The Good Shepherd 2006, The Last Mimzy 2007, The Killing Room 2008, The Alphabet Killer 2008, Lymelife 2008, Broken Hill 2009, The Killing Room 2009, Multiple Sarcasms 2010, The Ghost Writer 2010, Louder Than Words 2013, #Horror 2015.

HUTTON, Will Nicholas, MBA; British writer and broadcaster; *Chair, Big Innovation Centre;* b. 21 May 1950, London; s. of William Hutton and Dorothy Haynes; m. Jane Atkinson 1978; one s. two d.; ed Chislehurst and Sidcup Grammar School, Univ. of Bristol and Institut Européen d'Admin des Affaires (INSEAD), Fontainebleau, France; with Phillips & Drew (stockbrokers) 1971–77; Sr Producer Current Affairs, BBC Radio 4 1978–81; Dir and Producer The Money Programme, BBC 2 1981–83; Econs Corresp. Newsnight, BBC 2 1983–88; Ed. European Business Channel 1988–90; Econs Ed. The Guardian 1990–95, Asst Ed. 1995–96, Ed. The Observer 1996–98, Ed.-in-Chief 1998–2000, now columnist; Chief Exec. The Work Foundation (fmrly The Industrial Soc.) 2000–08, now Chair, Big Innovation Centre (also Co-Founder); Gov. LSE 2000–; Prin., Hertford Coll., Oxford; Hon. DLitt (Kingston) 1995, (De Montfort) 1996; Political Journalist of the Year, What the Papers Say 1993. *Publications include:* The Revolution That Never Was: An Assessment of Keynesian Economics 1986, The State We're In 1994, The State to Come 1997, The Stakeholding Society 1998, The World We're In 2002, The Writing on the Wall: China and the West in the 21st Century 2007, Them and Us: Politics, Greed and Inequality—Why We Need a Fair Society 2010, How Good We Can Be: Ending the Mercenary Society and Building a Great Country 2015. *Leisure interests:* family, reading, squash, tennis, cinema, writing. *Address:* Big Innovation Centre, Ergon House, 4th Floor, Horseferry Road, London, SW1P 2AL (office); 34 Elms Avenue, London, N10 2JP, England (home). *Telephone:* (20) 73713-4036 (office). *E-mail:* r.chowdhury@biginnovationcentre.com (office). *Website:* www.biginnovationcentre.com (office).

HUTTON OF FURNESS, Baron (Life Peer), cr. 2010, of Aldringham in the County of Cumbria; **John Hutton,** PC, BCL, MA; British politician; b. 6 May 1955; m. Heather Rogers 2004; four s. (one deceased) one d.; ed Westcliff High School, Essex, Magdalen Coll., Oxford; Research Assoc., Templeton Coll. 1980–81; Sr Lecturer in Law, Newcastle Polytechnic (now Univ. of Northumbria) 1981–92; unsuccessful cand. for MP for Penrith and the Border 1987, for MEP for Cumbria and N Lancs. 1989; MP for Barrow and Furness 1992–2010; Parl. Pvt. Sec. to Margaret Beckett 1997–98; Parl. Under-Sec. of State, Dept of Health 1998–99, Minister of State for Health 1999–2005; Chancellor of the Duchy of Lancaster and Minister for the Cabinet Office 2005; Sec. of State for Work and Pensions 2005–07, for Business, Enterprise and Regulatory Reform 2007–08, for Defence 2008–09; mem. Home Affairs Select Cttee 1994–97; Chair. Labour Parl. Cttees for Defence 1992–94, for Home Affairs 1994–97, for Home Affairs, Trade and Industry, for the Treasury 1997–2001; Chair. Nuclear Industries Asscn, Cuba Initiative, Simple Space Ltd (modular construction firm); mem. Bd of Dirs Sirius Minerals plc, Arthurian Life Sciences Ltd (fund managers), Circle Holdings plc; Adviser, Bechtel Corpn, PricewaterhouseCoopers, Redington Ltd (investment consultants), Eversheds LLP (law firm) 2009; Chair. Advisory Board, Regen World Ltd (real estate devt firm); Consultant, Lockheed Martin; Chair. Welfare and Park Home Owners All-party Subject Group 1995–97; Chair. Royal United Services Inst. 2010–15; Trustee, Social Market Foundation, International Air Cadet Training. *Publication:* How to be a Minister: A 21st-Century Guide 2014. *Leisure interests:* football, cricket, films, music, history. *Address:* House of Lords, London, SW1A 0PW, England (office). *Telephone:* (20) 7219-5353 (office). *Fax:* (20) 7219-5979 (office).

HUXLEY, George Leonard, MA, FSA, MRIA; British scholar; *Honorary Professor of Classics, Trinity College, Dublin and Adjunct Professor, Mathematics and Greek, National University of Ireland, Maynooth;* b. 23 Sept. 1932, Leicester; s. of Sir Leonard Huxley and Lady (Molly) Huxley; m. Davina Iris Best 1957; three d.; ed Blundell's, Magdalen Coll., Oxford (Demy); commissioned into Royal Engineers 1951; Acting Operating Supt, Longmoor Mil. Railway 1951; Fellow, All Souls Coll., Oxford 1955–61; Prof. of Greek, Queen's Univ., Belfast 1962–83, Prof. Emer. 1988–; Hon. Pres. Classical Asscn of Ireland 1999–2000; Dir Gennadius Library, American School of Classical Studies, Athens 1986–89; mem. Exec. NI Civil Rights Asscn 1971–72; mem. Man. Cttee ASCSA 1991–; mem. Irish Advisory Bd, Inst. of Irish Studies, Univ. of Liverpool 1996–2005; Hon. Prof. of Classics, Trinity Coll., Dublin 1989–; Adjunct Prof. Math. and Greek, Nat. Univ. of Ireland, Maynooth 2008–; Sr Vice-Pres. Fédération Int. des Sociétés d'Etudes Classiques 1984–89; Irish mem. Humanities Cttee of European Science Foundation 1978–86; Vice-Pres. Royal Irish Acad. 1984–85, 1997–98, Hon. Librarian 1990–94, Special Envoy 1994–99, Sr Vice-Pres. 1999–2000; mem. Int. Comm. Thesaurus Linguae Latinae, Munich 1999–2000; mem. Editorial Bd Dictionary of Mediaeval Latin from Celtic Sources 2001–10; Patron Irish Inst. of Hellenic Studies, Athens 1998–; Keynote Speaker XVI Int. Congress on Classical Archaeology, Boston 2003; Hon. Freeman of Kythera 2012; Hon. LittD (Dublin) 1984, Hon. DLitt (Belfast) 1996, Hon. DLit (Nat. Univ. of Ireland Maynooth) 2013; mem. Acad. Europaea 1990–; Cromer Greek Prize 1963. *Publications:* Achaeans and Hittites 1960, Early Sparta 1962, The Early Ionians 1966, Greek Epic Poetry 1969, Kythera (co-ed.) 1972, Pindar's Vision of the Past 1975, On Aristotle and Greek Society 1979, Homer and the Travellers 1988; articles on Hellenic, Byzantine, mathematical and railway subjects. *Address:* Classics, Trinity College, Dublin 2, Ireland (office); Forge Cottage, Church Enstone, Oxfordshire, OX7 4NN, England (home). *Telephone:* (1608) 677595 (home).

HUXLEY BARKHAM, Selma de Lotbinière, CM, OC, FRCGS; British/Canadian historical geographer and writer; b. 8 March 1927, London, England; d. of Michael Huxley and Ottilie Huxley (née de Lotbinière Mills); m. John Brian Barkham 1954 (died 1964); two s. two d.; Asst, Cttee on Geographical Names, Royal Geographical Soc., UK 1949; Librarian, Arctic Inst. of N America, Montréal 1951–54; Founder African Students Asscn 1960s; prepared and presented brief to Royal Comm. on Bilingualism and Biculturalism which was deemed instrumental in bringing French immersion to Canadian public school system; Founding mem., French Section, Citizens' Cttee on Children; helped Edgar Demers start first French Canadian theatre group for children in the Outaouais, 'La compagnie des Trouvères' 1960s; researcher for Historic Sites of Canada (including Louisbourg) 1964–68; teacher, Instituto Anglo-Mexicano, Guadalajara, Mexico until moving to Spain 1969–72; discovered the presence of 16th century Basque whaling settlements and shipwrecks in Newfoundland & Labrador, and found earliest civil documents written in Canada 1972–87; Royal Canadian Geographical Soc. grant to lead first expedition to identify 16th century Basque whaling sites in Labrador including what is now the Red Bay Nat. Historic Site and UNESCO World Heritage Site 1977; led teams of underwater and land archaeologists to these sites; worked for Public Archives of Canada in Spain 1973–85; Social Sciences and Humanities Research Council of Canada grant for publ. of documents relating to Basques in Newfoundland and Labrador 1984–86; mem. Advisory Cttee, Museo Naval de San Sebastian 1992–, Advisory Cttee For Red Bay, Labrador, Nat. Historic Site 1996–; advocates Basque Nat. Trust for the Preservation of Basque Architecture 1993–; Co-founder Northern Peninsula Heritage Soc. 1997–; elected mem. Real Sociedad Bascongada de Amigos del País 1981; Fellow, Wings WorldQuest 2009, 2012; numerous publs, lectures and confs; Hon. Consul of Bilbao, Bilbao Chamber of Commerce (first woman) 1992; Order of Newfoundland & Labrador 2015; Dr hc (Memorial Univ. of Newfoundland) 1993, (Univ. of Windsor, Ont.) 1985; Gold Medal, Royal Canadian Geographical Soc. (first woman) 1980, Award for Culture, Fundación Sabino Arana, Bilbao 1999, City of St John's, Newfoundland named one of its streets 'Barkham Street' 1999, Queen's Golden Jubilee Medal 2002, Diamond Jubilee Medal 2012, Gold Medal Aquario San Sebastian 2013, Lagun Onari 2014. *Publications include:* Los Vascos en el Marco Atlántico Norte, Siglos XVI y XVII, Itsasoa (Vol. 3) 1987, The Basque Coast of Newfoundland 1989. *Leisure interests:* languages, bird watching. *Address:* 7 Chapel Street, Chichester, West Sussex, PO19 1BU, England (home); 23 Des Estacades, Cantley, QC J8V 3J3, Canada (home). *E-mail:* orianabarkham@ncf.ca (home).

HUYGENS, Robert Burchard Constantijn, PhD; Dutch professor of medieval Latin (retd); b. 10 Dec. 1931, The Hague; m. Caroline Sprey 1962; one s. two d.; ed Leiden Univ.; army service 1952–54; Lecturer in Medieval Latin, Univ. of Leiden 1964, Prof. 1968–96; Fellow, Dumbarton Oaks, Washington, DC 1982, Inst. for Advanced Study, Jerusalem 1983–84, Inst. for Advanced Study, Princeton, NJ 1986–87, Herzog August Bibliothek, Wolfenbüttel 1987; mem. Royal Netherlands Acad., Soc. des Antiquaires de France, Monumenta Germaniae Historica; Past Pres. Rotary Club, Leiden. *Publications include:* Jacques de Vitry 1960, Accessus ad Auctores 1970, Vézelay 1976, William of Tyre 1986, Berengar of Tours 1988, Guibert of Nogent 1992, Serta mediaevalia 2000, Ars edendi 2001, Christian of Stavelot 2008, Mary of Oignies 2012. *Address:* Witte Singel 28, 2311 BH Leiden, Netherlands (home). *Telephone:* (71) 5143798 (home).

HUYGHE, Pierre; French artist; b. 11 Sept. 1962, Paris; ed École Nationale Supérieure des Arts Decoratifs, Paris; works in a variety of media from film and video to public interventions; represented France at the Venice Biennale (pavilion, Le Château de Turing) 2001; Artist in Residence, DAAD (German Academic Exchange Service), Berlin 1999–2000; Prof. of Art and Philosophy, European Grad. School, Saas-Fee, Switzerland; Special Award, Jury of the Venice Biennial 2001, Hugo Boss Prize, Guggenheim Museum 2002, Prix du meilleur artiste français, Beaux-Arts Magazine Art Awards 2005, Contemporary Artist Award, Smithsonian Museum 2010, Roswitha Haftmann Prize 2013, Kurt Schwitters Prize 2015, Nasher Prize 2017. *Address:* c/o Marian Goodman Gallery, 24 West 57th Street, New York, NY 10019, USA. *Telephone:* (212) 977-7160. *Fax:* (212) 581-5187. *E-mail:* goodman@mariangoodman.com. *Website:* www.mariangoodman.com.

HUYGHEBAERT, Jan, BA, DrIur; Belgian business executive; b. 6 April 1945, Uccle; s. Fridolin Huyghebaert and Luciana Meganck; ed Univ. of Antwerp, Catholic Univ. of Louvain; Attaché, Science Policy Programme 1970–74; Adviser, Cabinet of Prime Minister Leo Tindemans 1974–78; Alderman, Port of Antwerp 1978–85; Pres. Exec. Cttee Kredietbank NV (forerunner of KBC) 1985–91, Chair. Almanij NV (holding co. of KBC) 1991–2005, Chair. KBC Group NV (following merger of Almanij and KBC) 2005–11, fmr Chair. KBC Bank, KBC Insurance; Chair. Kredietbank Luxembourg; fmr mem. Coudenberg group (Belgian think tank); Manager of the Year 1998.

HVIDT, Gen. (retd) Christian, DFC; Danish air force officer (retd) and business executive; b. 15 July 1942, Copenhagen; m. 1st; three c.; m. 2nd Jane Hvidt; two step-c.; flying service (F-100 Super Sabre) 1962–69; test pilot on F-35 Draken at SAAB factories, Linköping, Sweden 1969–72; Deputy Squadron Commdr (F-35 Draken) 1972–74; Br. Chief Tactical Air Command, Denmark 1975–79; Squadron Commdr First Danish F-16 Squadron, Air Station Skrydstrup 1979–83; staff officer and Br. Chief Plans and Policy Div., HQ Chodden 1983–87; CO Air Station Karup 1987–88; Chief of Staff, Tactical Air Command, Denmark 1989–90; Deputy Chief of Staff, Plans and Policy, Operations, Budget and Finance, HQ, Chodden 1991–93; Perm. Danish Rep., NATO Mil. Cttee 1994–96; Chief of Staff, HQ Chodden 1996; Chief of Defence 1996–2002; Chair. Rovsing A/S 2006; Grand Cross of the Order of Dannebrog, Danish Air Force Badge of Honour, Badge of Honour of the Danish Reserve Officers Asscn, Medal of Merit of the Home Guard, Commdr, Grand Cross, Royal Swedish Order of the Northern Star, Jordanian Mil. Order of Merit of the First Degree, Commdr, Cross with the Star of Merit of the Repub. of Poland, Commdr, Légion d'honneur, Ordre nat. du Mérite.

HWANG, Joon-kook, BA, MPA; South Korean diplomatist; *Ambassador to UK;* b. 19 Dec. 1960; ed Seoul Nat. Univ., Princeton Univ., USA; joined Ministry of Foreign Affairs 1982, Second Sec., Embassy in London 1987–93, Asst Sec., Office of the Pres. for Foreign and Nat. Security Affairs 1993–95, First Sec., Perm. Mission to UN, New York 1995–97, Counsellor, Embassy in Riyadh 1997–2000, Dir for Protocol Div. I, Ministry of Foreign Affairs and Trade 2000–01, Dir, UN Div. 2001–02, Counsellor, Perm. Mission to UN, New York 2002–06, seconded to Presidential Cttee on NE Asian Co-operation Initiative 2006–07, Sr Co-ordinator for Int. Orgs, Ministry of Foreign Affairs and Trade 2007–08, Dir-Gen., North Korean Nuclear Affairs Bureau and Amb. for North Korean Nuclear Issue 2008–10, Minister, Embassy in Washington, DC 2010–13, Special Advisor to the Minister, Ministry of Foreign Affairs and Trade Feb.–April 2013, Amb. for ROK–US Defense Burden-sharing, Ministry of Foreign Affairs April 2013–14, Special Rep. for Korean Peninsula Peace and Security Affairs 2014–16, Amb. to UK 2016–. *Address:* Embassy of Republic of Korea, 60 Buckingham Gate, London, SW1E 6AJ, England (office). *Telephone:* (20) 7227-5500 (office). *Fax:* (20) 7227-5504 (office). *E-mail:* koreanembinuk@mofat.go.kr (office). *Website:* www.koreanembassy.org.uk (office); gbr.mofat.go.kr/eng (office).

HWANG, Kyo-ahn, LLB, LLM; South Korean lawyer and politician; b. 15 April 1957, Seoul; ed Sungkyunkwan Univ.; Prosecutor, Cheongju Dist Prosecutors' Office 1983–87; several sr roles with Seoul Dist Prosecutors' Office including Prosecutor 1987–90, 1992–95, Sr Prosecutor, Criminal Dept V, Northern Branch 1999, Sr Prosecutor, Cyber Crime Investigation Dept 2001, Sr Prosecutor, Public Security Dept II 2002, 2nd Deputy Chief Prosecutor (Seoul Cen. District) 2005;

Chief Prosecutor, Tongyeong Br., Changwon Dist Prosecutors' Office 1995–97; Prof., Judicial Research & Training Inst., Supreme Court 1997–99; Prosecution Research Officer, Supreme Prosecutors' Office 1990–92, Dir, Public Security Divs I and III 2000; Deputy Chief Prosecutor, Eastern Br., Busan Dist Prosecutors' Office 2003–05; Chief Prosecutor, Seongnam Br., Suwon Dist Prosecutors' Office 2006–07, Chief, Office of Policy & Planning, Ministry of Justice 2007–08, Chief, Dept of Planning, Inst. of Justice 2008–09, Chief Prosecutor, Changwon Dist Prosecutors' Office and Daegu High Prosecutors' Office 2009–11, Chief Prosecutor, Busan High Prosecutors' Office 2011; apptd Attorney of Counsel, Bae, Kim & Lee LLC, Seoul 2011; Chair., Election Broadcast Deliberation Cttee 2011; Minister of Justice 2013–15; Prime Minister 2015–17, Acting Pres. of Repub. of Korea (following impeachement of Park Geun-hye) 8 Dec. 2016–10 May 2017; Leader Liberty Korea Party 2019–.

HWANG, Robert; Taiwanese computer industry executive; *President and CEO, Wistron Corporation;* ed Tatung Inst. of Tech. Business Admin Exec. Program, Nat. Chengchi Univ.; began career at Sampo and Acer Computers 1980s; managed product devt for mobile product lines for more than ten years at Wistron Corpn, currently Pres. and CEO. *Address:* Wistron Corporation, 158 Singshan Road, Neihu, Taipei 11469, Taiwan (office). *Telephone:* (2) 66169999 (office). *Fax:* (2) 66125188 (office). *E-mail:* info@wistron.com (office). *Website:* www.wistron.com (office).

HWANG, Woo-yea, LLD; South Korean lawyer, judge and politician; *Chairman, Saenuri Party;* b. 13 Aug. 1947, Incheon; ed Seoul Nat. Univ.; Judge, Seoul High Court 1974–85; Chief Judge, District Courts, Chuncheon and Jeju 1985–89; fmr Dir of Research, Constitutional Court; Chief Judge, Incheon Inst. of Law 1990–92; mem. Bd of Audit and Inspection 1993–96; mem. Nat. Ass. for Yeonsu Dist, Incheon 1996–2000, 2000–, fmr Chair. Parl. Human Rights Forum; Chair. Korea-Japan Parl. League; mem. Grand Nat. Party (renamed Saenuri Party, New Frontier Party 2012), Leader 2012–. *Address:* Saenuri Party, 14-31, Yeouido-dong, Yeongdeungpo-gu, Seoul 156-768, Republic of Korea (office). *Telephone:* (2) 3786-3000 (office). *Fax:* (2) 3786-3610 (office). *Website:* www.saenuriparty.kr (office); www.hwy.pe.kr.

HWANG, Young-key, MBA; South Korean banker and financial services industry executive; *Senior Adviser, Shin & Kim;* ed London School of Econs, UK; long career with Samsung Corpn, becoming Head of Int. Finance Team 1989–90, Head of Personnel Dept 1993–94, Sr Man Dir and Chief of Staff of Strategic Planning Office, Samsung Life Insurance Co Ltd 1997–99, Pres. and CEO, Samsung Securities Co Ltd 2001–04; Pres. Woora Bank 2004–07; Adviser, Shin & Kim (law firm), Seoul 2007–08, Sr Adviser 2012–; Chair. KB Financial Group Inc. (fmrly Kookmin Bank) 2008–09; Chair and CEO, Cha Hospital Group 2010–12. *Address:* Shin & Kim, 8th Floor, State Tower Namsan, 100 Toegye-ro, Jung-gu, Seoul 100-052, Republic of Korea (office). *Telephone:* (2) 316-4114 (office). *Fax:* (2) 756-6226 (office). *E-mail:* ykhwang@shinkim.com (office). *Website:* www.shinkim.com (office).

HYLAND, J. M(artin) E., DPhil; British mathematician and academic; *Professor of Mathematical Logic, King's College, Cambridge;* b. 1949; ed Univ. of Oxford; currently Prof. in Mathematical Logic and Head of Dept of Pure Math. and Math. Statistics, King's Coll., Cambridge; Pres. British Logic Colloquium; Vice-Pres. Cambridge Philosophical Soc.; mem. Bd of Eds Mathematical Proceedings, Cambridge Philosophical Soc.; mem. Man. Cttee Isaac Newton Inst. for Math. Sciences. *Address:* Department of Pure Mathematics and Mathematical Statistics, Centre for Mathematical Sciences, Wilberforce Road, King's College, University of Cambridge, Cambridge, CB3 0WB, England (office). *Telephone:* (1223) 337986 (office). *Fax:* (1223) 337986 (office). *E-mail:* M.Hyland@dpmms.cam.ac.uk (office). *Website:* www.dpmms.cam.ac.uk (office); www.statslab.cam.ac.uk (office).

HYLTON, G. Anthony, BA, JD, LLM; Jamaican lawyer and politician; *Minister of Industry, Commerce and Investment;* b. 27 April 1957, Yallahs, St Thomas; m.; two c.; ed Kingston Coll., Morgan State Univ. and Georgetown Univ., USA, Univ. of London, UK; lawyer, Melnicove, Kaufman, Weiner and Smouse, Baltimore 1983–85, with Curtis, Mallet-Prevost, Colt and Mosle, New York 1986–88, with Dickstein, Shapiro and Morin, Washington, DC 1988–89; fmr legal asst to Gen. Counsel, Inter-American Foundation; fmr Dir Jamaica Public Service Co.; mem. Parl. for Western St Thomas 1993–2002; Exec. Dir of Legal and Foreign Affairs, Policy Review Unit, Ministry of Foreign Affairs and Trade 1990–93, Minister of State 1993–2001; Minister of Mining and Energy 2001–02; Amb. and Special Prime Ministerial Envoy 2002–06; Minister of Foreign Affairs and Foreign Trade 2006–07, also mem. of Senate; Minister of Industry, Commerce and Investment 2012–; negotiator at WTO, Cotonou Agreement, Free Trade Area of the Americas and CARICOM; Chair. Inst. of Law and Econs, People's Nat. Party Policy Comm.; Chair. Commercial Div., Coffee Industry Bd; mem. Md and Jamaica Bar Asscns; Nat. Honours from Govt of Benin. *Leisure interests:* dominos, music, writing, debating, sport. *Address:* Ministry of Industry, Commerce and Investment (MITEC), 4 St Lucia Ave, Kingston 5 (office); People's National Party, 89 Old Hope Road, Kingston 6, Jamaica (office). *Telephone:* 968-7116 (ministry) (office); 978-1337 (office). *Fax:* 960-7422 (ministry) (office); 927-4389 (office). *E-mail:* information@pnpjamaica.com (office). *Website:* www.miic.gov.jm; www.pnpjamaica.com (office).

HYMAN, Timothy, RA; British painter and writer; b. 17 April 1946, Hove, Sussex, England; s. of Alan Hyman and Noreen Gypson; m. Judith Ravenscroft 1982; ed Charterhouse and Slade School of Fine Art, London; Curator Narrative Paintings at Arnolfini and ICA Galleries, etc. 1979–80; public collections include Arts Council, Bristol City Art Gallery, British Council Collection, Museum of London, Contemporary Art Soc., British Museum, Govt Art Collection, Los Angeles Co. Museum; Visiting Prof. at Baroda, India, two British Council lecture tours 1981–83; Artist-in-Residence, Lincoln Cathedral 1983–84, Sandown Racecourse 1992, Maggie's Cancer Caring Centres 2011–12; Purchaser for Arts Council Collection 1985; selector, John Moores Prize 1995; Lead Curator, Stanley Spencer retrospective exhbn, Tate Gallery, London 2001–; Co-curator British Vision, Museum of Fine Arts, Ghent 2007; Leverhulme Award 1992, Rootstein Hopkins Foundation Award 1995, Wingate Award 1998, Medaglio Beato Angelico, Florence 2005, Nat. Portrait Gallery/BP Travel Award 2007. *Publications:* Hodgkin 1975, Kitaj 1977, Beckmann 1978, Narrative Paintings 1979, Balthus 1980, English Romanesque 1984, Kiff 1986, Domenico Tiepolo 1987, Bhupen Khakhar (monograph) 1998, Bonnard (monograph) 1998, Carnivalesque (catalogue) 2000, Stanley Spencer (catalogue) 2001, Sienese Painting (monograph) 2003, The World New Made: Figurative Painting in the Twentieth Century 2016; numerous articles on contemporary figurative painting in London Magazine, Artscribe, Times Literary Supplement. *Leisure interests:* the novels of John Cowper Powys, reading, travel, cinema, walking London. *Address:* 62 Myddelton Square, London, EC1R 1XX, England (home). *Telephone:* (20) 7837-1933 (home).

HYND, Ronald; British choreographer; b. (Ronald Hens), 22 April 1931, London; s. of William John Hens and Alice Louisa Griffiths; m. Annette Page 1957 (died 2017); one d.; ed Holloway Co. School, numerous wartime emergency schools; trained with Marie Rambert 1946; joined Ballet Rambert 1949, Royal Ballet (then known as Sadler's Wells Ballet) 1952 (Prin. Dancer 1959–70); dancing all classical, dramatic and romantic roles, partnering, among others, Fonteyn, Beriosova, Nerina, Grey, Linden and Annette Page; Ballet Dir Bavarian State Opera 1970–73, 1984–86; freelance choreographer; ballets presented by numerous int. ballet cos, including English Nat. Ballet, Royal Sadler's Wells, La Scala Milan, Deutsche Oper Berlin, Vienna State Opera, Houston Ballet, Bavarian State Opera, American Ballet Theater, Australian Ballet, Santiago Ballet, Tokyo Ballet, Canadian Nat. Ballet, Grands Ballets Canadiens, Dutch Nat. Ballet, Northern Ballet, Slovenian Nat. Ballet, South African State Theatre Ballet, Tulsa Ballet Theater, Royal Danish Ballet, Ballet Maggio Musicale, Florence and Pacific Northwest Ballet, Ballet West, USA, Cincinnati Ballet, Bonn Opera, Ballet de Nice Opera, New London Ballet, Hong Kong Ballet, Estonian Nat. Ballet, Joffrey Ballet Chicago, Ballet Nacional de Sodre Montevideo, Texas Ballet Theater, Hungarian State Ballet, Malmö Ballet, Ballet of Colon Theatre, Argentina. *Works choreographed include:* Three Act Ballets: Merry Widow 1975 (15 productions), The Nutcracker 1976, Rosalinda 1978 (11 productions), Papillon 1979 (5 productions), Le Diable à Quatre 1984, Coppelia 1985 (5 productions), Ludwig II 1986, The Hunchback of Notre Dame 1988, The Sleeping Beauty 1993; one act ballets include: The Fairy's Kiss 1967, Dvorak Variations 1970, Wendekreise 1971, Mozartiana 1972, Das Telefon 1972, Marco Polo 1975, Sanguine Fan 1976, La Chatte 1978, Les Valses 1981, Seasons 1982, Scherzo Capriccioso 1982, Fanfare 1985, Liaisons Amoureuses 1989, Ballade 1989. *Choreography for:* Galileo (film) 1974, La Traviata (BBC TV) 1974, Amahl and Night Visitors (BBC TV) 1975, ice ballets for John Curry 1977, The Sound of Music 1981, Camelot 1982, Sylvia for Princess Diana's 30th Birthday Banquet 1992, Merry Widow (TV and video in Canada and Australia), Rosalinda (Slovenian TV), Sanguine Fan (BBC TV), Nutcracker (BBC TV). *Leisure interests:* gardens, music, travel. *Address:* Fern Cottage, Upper Somerton, Bury St Edmunds, Suffolk, IP29 4ND, England (home). *Telephone:* (1284) 789284 (home). *Fax:* (1284) 789284 (home). *E-mail:* hyndpage@gmail.com (home).

HYNDE, Chrissie; American singer, songwriter and musician; b. 7 Sept. 1951, Akron, Ohio; one d. with Ray Davies; m. 1st Jim Kerr (divorced); one d.; m. 2nd Lucho Brieva 1999 (divorced 2002); contrib. to New Musical Express; Co-founder Chrissie Hynde and the Pretenders 1978–, singer, songwriter and guitarist, new band formed 1983; tours in Britain, Europe and USA; platinum and gold discs in USA; Ivor Novello Award for Outstanding Contrib. to British Music 1999; inducted into Rock & Roll Hall of Fame 2005; Q Award for Classic Songwriter 2013. *Singles include:* Stop Your Sobbing (debut) 1978, Kid 1979, Brass in Pocket 1979, I Go to Sleep 1982, Back on the Chain Gang 1982, Don't Get Me Wrong 1986, Hymn to Her 1987, I'll Stand By You 1994. *Albums include:* Pretenders (debut) 1980, Pretenders II 1981, Extended Play 1981, Learn to Crawl 1985, Get Close 1986, The Singles 1987, Packed! 1990, Last of the Independents 1994, The Isle of View 1995, Viva El Amor 1999, Loose Screw 2002, Break Up the Concrete 2009, Fidelity! (with JP Jones and the Fairground Boys) 2010, Alone 2016; solo: Stockholm 2014. *Publication:* Reckless 2015. *Address:* Quietus Management Limited, 13 Bramley Road, 2nd Floor Phoenix Brewery, London, W10 6SP, England (office). *Telephone:* (20) 3220-0310 (office). *Website:* www.quietusmanagement.co.uk (office); www.chrissiehynde.com; www.pretenders.com.

HYNES, James T., AB, PhD; American chemist and academic; *Distinguished Professor of Chemistry and Biochemistry, University of Colorado;* b. 16 Oct. 1943, Miami Beach, Fla; ed Catholic Univ., Princeton Univ.; NIH Post-Doctoral Fellow, MIT 1969–70; Asst Prof., Univ. of Colorado, Boulder 1971–76, Assoc. Prof. 1976–79, Faculty Foundation Fellow 1978–79, Prof. of Chem. 1979–, Faculty Fellow 1986–87, Research Lecturer, Council on Research and Creative Work 1988, Distinguished Prof. of Chemistry and Biochemistry 2012–; Visiting Assoc. Prof., Univ. of Toronto, Canada 1978–79; Visiting Prof., Univ. of Paris VI, France 1985, 1987, Univ. Autonoma de Barcelona, Spain 1995, Univ. Paris Sud, France 1997; Visiting Sr Research Fellow, Univ. of Oxford, England 1985, Visiting Prof. 1987; Visiting Prof., Ecole Normale Supérieure (ENS), Paris 1997, CNRS Dir of Research, ENS 1999–, now Emer.; American Ed. Progress in Reaction Kinetics and Mechanism 1999–2005; Co-Chair. Editorial Bd ChemPhysChem-A European Journal 1999–; mem. Editorial Bd Journal of Physical Chemistry 1990–98, Journal of Molecular Liquids 1991–, International Journal of Quantum Chemistry 1993–97, Chemical Physics Letters 2003–08, Journal of Chemical Physics 2003–05, 2014–16, Interdisciplinary Sciences: Computational Life Sciences 2009–; OK Rice Lecturer, Univ. North Carolina 2014; Heinemann Hall Lecturer, Bowling Green Univ. 2016; mem. ACS (Vice-Chair. Theoretical Div. 1984, Chair. 1986), French Chemical Soc.; Fellow, American Physical Soc. 2000, American Acad. of Arts and Sciences 2008, NAS 2011, American Chemical Soc. 2013; Pople Lecturer, Carnegie Mellon Univ. 2013; ACS Nobel Laureate Signature Award 1983, Nat. Science Foundation Creativity Award 1991, Hirschfelder Prize in Theoretical Chemistry 2004, ISI Highly Cited Researcher 2002, ACS Hildebrand Award in Theoretical and Experimental Chem. of Liquids 2005. *Publications:* approximately 325 scientific publications, five books edited. *Address:* Department of Chemistry and Biochemistry, University of Colorado, Campus Box 215, Boulder, CO 80309, USA (office); Département de Chimie, Ecole Normale Superieure, 24 rue Lhomond, 75005 Paris, France (office). *Telephone:* (303) 492-6926 (Boulder) (office); 1-44-32-32-78 (Paris) (office). *Fax:* (303) 492-5894 (Boulder) (office); 1-44-32-33-25 (Paris) (office). *E-mail:* james.hynes@colorado.edu (office); chynes43@gmail.com (office). *Website:* chem.colorado.edu (office); www.chimie.ens.fr/?q=profil/james.hynes (office).

HYNES, Samuel, DFC, PhD, FRSL; American academic and writer; *Woodrow Wilson Professor of Literature Emeritus, Princeton University;* b. 29 Aug. 1924, Chicago, Ill.; s. of Samuel Lynn Hynes and Margaret Hynes (née Turner); m. Elizabeth Igleheart 1944 (died 2008); two d.; ed Univ. of Minnesota, Columbia Univ.; served in USMCR 1943–46, 1952–53; mem. faculty, Swarthmore Coll. 1949–68, Prof. of English Literature 1965–68; Prof. of English, Northwestern Univ., Evanston, Ill. 1968–76; Prof. of English, Princeton Univ. 1976–90, Woodrow Wilson Prof. of Literature 1978–90, Prof. Emer. 1990–; Fulbright Fellow 1953–54, Guggenheim Fellow 1959–60, 1981–82, Bollingen Fellow 1964–65, American Council of Learned Socs Fellow 1969, 1985–86, Nat. Endowment for Humanities Sr Fellow 1973–74, 1977–78, American Acad. of Arts and Letters Award in Literature 2004, Robert F. Kennedy Award 1998. *Publications include:* The Pattern of Hardy's Poetry (Explicator Award 1962) 1961, William Golding 1964, The Edwardian Turn of Mind 1968, Edwardian Occasions 1972, The Auden Generation 1976, Flights of Passage: Reflections of a World War Two Aviator 1988, A War Imagined: The First World War and English Culture 1990, The Soldiers' Tale (Robert F. Kennedy Book Award 1998) 1997, The Growing Seasons: An American Boyhood Before the War 2003, The Unsubstantial Air: American Fliers in the First World War 2014; Ed.: Further Speculations by T. E. Hulme 1955, The Author's Craft and Other Critical Writings of Arnold Bennett 1968, Romance and Realism 1979, Complete Poetical Works of Thomas Hardy, Vol. I 1982, Vol. II 1984, Vol. III 1985, Vols IV, V 1995, Thomas Hardy 1984, Complete Short Fiction of Joseph Conrad (Vol. I–III) 1992, (Vol. IV) 1993. *Address:* 130 Moore Street, Princeton, NJ 08540 (home); Department of English, 22 McCosh Hall, Princeton University, Princeton, NJ 08544-1006, USA (office). *Website:* english.princeton.edu (office).

HYODO, Makoto; Japanese business executive; joined Nipponkoa Insurance Co. Ltd, fmr Chief Dir of Tohoku, later Man. of Iwate Office, later Dir of 5th Sales in Main Office, Man. Exec. Officer 2002–05, Sr Man. Exec. Officer and Vice-Pres. 2005–07, Rep. Dir, Pres. and Sr Exec. Officer Nipponkoa Insurance Co. Ltd 2007–10, Rep. Dir, Chair. and Co-CEO NKSJ Holdings, Inc. (following establishment of jt holding co. by Sompo Japan Insurance Inc. and Nipponkoa Insurance Co. Ltd) 2010–12, Dir 2012. *Address:* c/o NKSJ Holdings, Inc., 26-1, Nishi-Shinjuku 1-chome, Shinjuku-ku, Tokyo 160-8338, Japan.

HYSENI, Skënder; Kosovo politician; b. 17 Feb. 1955, Podujevë/Podujevo; m. Drita Hyseni; two s. two d.; ed Univ. of Prishtina, Bloomberg State Coll., USA, Univ. of Aberdeen, UK; early political career with newly est. Lidhja Demokratike e Kosovës (LDK—Democratic League of Kosovo) 1989, began working with Kosovo Information Centre 1992 as journalist and interpreter; Co-founder and Ed. Kosova Daily Report; Adviser to Pres. Ibrahim Rugova 1992–2006, to Pres. Fatmir Sejdiu 2006–10; Spokesperson for Kosovo negotiating team that took part in UN-sponsored talks with Serbia, launched in 2006; mem. Kuvendi i Kosovës/Skupština Kosova (Kosovo Ass.) (Parl.) 2007–; Minister of Culture, Youth and Sports Jan.–April 2008, of Foreign Affairs April 2008–10 (resgnd), of Internal Affairs 2014–17; mem. Lidhja Demokratike e Kosovës (LDK—Kosovo Democratic League), mem. of Presidency and Chair. Cttee for External Relations; mem. Constitutional Comm. charged with compiling first draft of Constitution of Kosovo. *Address:* c/o Ministry of Internal Affairs, 10000 Prishtina, Rruga Luan Haradinaj, Kosovo (office).

HYTNER, Sir Nicholas Robert, Kt, MA; British theatre director; b. 7 May 1956, Manchester; s. of Benet A. Hytner and Joyce Myers; ed Manchester Grammar School and Trinity Hall, Cambridge; staff producer, ENO 1978–80; Assoc. Dir Royal Exchange Theatre, Manchester 1985–89; Assoc. Dir Royal Nat. Theatre 1989–97, Artistic Dir 2003–15; Evening Standard Opera Award 1985, Evening Standard Best Dir Award 1989. *Theatre and opera productions include:* Wagner's Rienzi (ENO) 1983, Tippett's King Priam (Kent Opera) 1984, Handel's Xerxes (ENO) (Olivier Award) 1985, The Scarlet Pimpernel (Chichester Festival) 1985, As You Like It, Edward II, The Country Wife, Schiller's Don Carlos (Royal Exchange) 1986, Handel's Giulio Cesare (Paris Opera), Measure for Measure (RSC) 1987, Tippett's The Knot Garden (Royal Opera), The Magic Flute (ENO), The Tempest (RSC) 1988, The Marriage of Figaro (Geneva Opera), Joshua Sobol's Ghetto (Nat. Theatre), Miss Saigon (Theatre Royal, Drury Lane) 1989, King Lear (RSC) 1990, The Wind in the Willows (Nat. Theatre) 1990, Volpone (Almeida) 1990, The Madness of George III (Nat. Theatre) 1991, The Recruiting Officer (Nat. Theatre) 1992, Carousel (Nat. Theatre) (Tony Award for Best Dir of a Musical 1994) 1992, The Importance of Being Earnest (Aldwych) 1993, Don Giovanni (Bavarian State Opera) 1994, The Cunning Little Vixen (Paris) 1995, The Cripple of Inishmaan 1997, The Crucible 1997, The Lady in the Van 1999, Cressida 2000, Orpheus Descending 2000, The Winter's Tale (Nat. Theatre) 2001, Mother Clap's Molly House (Nat. Theatre) 2001, Sweet Smell of Success (Broadway) 2002, The History Boys (Nat. Theatre) (Olivier Award for Best Director 2004, Tony Award for Best Director 2006) 2004, Così fan tutte (Glyndebourne) 2006, The Man of Mode (Nat. Theatre) 2007, The Rose Tattoo (Nat. Theatre) 2007, England People Very Nice (Nat. Theatre) 2009, Phèdre (Nat. Theatre) 2009, One Man, Two Guvnors (Nat. Theatre and touring) (Best Play, Evening Standard Theatre Awards) 2011, Travelling Light (Nat. Theatre) 2012, Timon of Athens (Nat. Theatre) 2012, Othello (Nat. Theatre) 2013, Great Britain (Nat. Theatre) 2014, The Hard Problem (Nat. Theatre) 2015. *Films:* The Madness of King George 1994, The Crucible 1996, The Object of My Affection 1998, Twelfth Night, or What You Will (TV) 1998, Center Stage 2000, The History Boys 2006, Phèdre 2009, The Lady in the Van 2015. *Address:* c/o Royal National Theatre, South Bank, London, SE1 9PX, England (office). *Telephone:* (20) 7452-3333 (office). *E-mail:* info@nationaltheatre.org.uk (office). *Website:* www.nationaltheatre.org.uk (office).

HYUN, Jeong-eun, BA, MA; South Korean business executive; *Chairwoman, Hyundai Group;* b. 26 Jan. 1955, Seoul; m. Chung Mong-hun (died 2003); three c.; ed Ewha Women's Univ. Graduate School, Seoul, Fairleigh Dickinson Univ. Graduate School, NJ, USA; Chair. Hyundai Group and affiliate cos (following death of husband, Hyundai's Chair. and heir apparent) 2003–; mem. Nat. Supporting Cttee, Int. Cttee of Girl Scouts Korea 1983–98, Dir, HQ of Girl Scouts Korea 1998–2007; Commr, Financial Section, Korean Assn of Women's Univs 1988–91; Commr, Presidential Cttee on Govt Innovation and Decentralization 2005–08, Civil Service Comm. 2006–08, Special Advisory Cttee for Woman Volunteers, Korean Red Cross 1999–; Hon. Consul to Brazil 2011; elected mem. Pinnacle Soc., Fairleigh Dickinson Univ. 2006. *Address:* Hyundai Group, 1-7 Yeonji-dong, Jongno-gu, 110-754 Seoul, Republic of Korea (office). *Telephone:* (2) 3706-5114 (office). *E-mail:* webmaster@hyundaigroup.com (office). *Website:* www.hyundaigroup.com (office).

HYUN, Oh-seok, BA, MA, PhD; South Korean politician; ed Seoul Nat. Univ., Univ. of Pennsylvania, USA; Economist, Macroeconomic Adjustment and Growth Div., The World Bank, Washington, DC 1989–91; Dir-Gen., Bureau of Treasury, Bureau of Econ. Policy, Bureau of Budget, Ministry of Finance and Economy 1996–99; Dir-Gen., Nat. Econ. Advisory Council 1999–2000; Dean, Nat. Tax Coll. 2000–01; Pres., Korea Int. Trade Assn 2002–08; Pres., Korea Devt Inst. 2009–12; Deputy Prime Minister and Minister of Strategy and Finance 2013–14; mem. Int. Devt Cooperation Cttee 2005–; mem. Cttee NPSO (Non-governmental Public Serving Org.) Man. 2007, Chair. NPSO Evaluation Bd 2008; Prof., Business School, Korea Advanced Inst. of Science and Tech. 2008–09; mem. Knowledge Advisory Comm., The World Bank 2012–; mem. Saenuri Party (New Frontier Party). *Address:* c/o Ministry of Strategy and Finance, Government Complex II, 88, Gwanmunro, Gwacheon City, 427-725, Republic of Korea.

HZAINE, El Hassane, MA, PhD; Moroccan international organization official and academic; *Director-General, Islamic Centre for the Development of Trade;* b. 20 Dec. 1955, Casablanca; ed Univ. Hassan II, Casablanca, The Hague Acad. of Int. Law, Netherlands, Univ. of Strasbourg, France; Prof. of Int. Relations, Univ. Hassan II 1980–2000; Exec. Dir Observatoire Economique et Social du Maghreb (consultative body and think tank on economic integration in N Africa), Casablanca, Morocco 1989–98; Prof. and expert consultant in int. affairs 1991–97; lecturer, Université de Toulouse I, France (Inst. of Political Studies) 1994; several lectures on int. trade (Master's degree), High School of Business (ISCAE), Casablanca; Assoc. Prof. of Int. Econ. Relations and Int. Trade 2000–07; Perm. mem. Secr. of the Trade Negotiating Cttee of the Trade Preferential System among the OIC Member States (TPS-OIC), Islamic Centre for the Devt of Trade, OIC, Casablanca, mem. IDB Task Force on Intra-OIC Trade Expansion 1998–2003, mem. Consultative Group on Enhancing Intra-OIC Trade 2009–11, mem. OIC Consultative Group for Enhancing Intra-OIC Trade (COMCEC, IDB Group-ITFC, ICIEC, Cooperation Office and other OIC insts, including OISA, ICCI, SESRIC and int. insts ITC) 2009–11, mem. working group on development of goods and services and trade finance (cooperation between IDB group, Govt of Malaysia and ICDT), mem. Secr. of the network of Trade Promotion Organs of the OIC, mem. Steering Cttee for the Implementation of the OIC Cotton Action Plan, Observer mem. in ITC's trade capacity building programme of Arab countries (EnAct); Dir of Studies and Training Dept (in charge of TPS/OIC Trade Negotiations and int. cooperation) 1997–2011, Acting Dir-Gen. Islamic Centre for the Devt of Trade, OIC May–June 2000, July–Nov. 2011, Dir-Gen. Nov. 2011–; Honour Medal of the Kingdom of Morocco 1985; Prize for doctorate thesis on African Studies, Council of Economic and Social research in Africa (CODESRIA (Senegal), Distinction granted By HE Dr Ahmad Mohamed Ali, Pres. of IDB Group, Jeddah 2011. *Address:* Islamic Centre for the Development of Trade, Tour des Habous, Avenue des FAR, PO Box 13545, Casablanca 20032, Morocco (office). *Telephone:* (522) 314974 (office). *Fax:* (522) 310110 (office). *E-mail:* icdt@icdt-oic.org (office). *Website:* www.icdt-oic.org (office).

I

IACOCCA, Lee A.; American business executive; *Chairman, Iacocca Foundation;* b. 15 Oct. 1924, Allentown, Pa; s. of Nicola Iacocca and Antoinette Perrotto; m. 1st Mary McCleary 1956 (died 1983); two d.; m. 2nd Peggy Johnson 1986 (divorced); m. 3rd Darrien Earle 1991; ed Lehigh and Princeton Univs; with Ford Motor Co. 1946; Dist Sales Man., Washington 1956; Ford Div. Truck Marketing Man. 1956; Car Marketing Man. 1957; Vice-Pres. and Gen. Man., Ford Div. 1960–65; Vice-Pres. Car and Truck Group 1965; Exec. Vice-Pres. North American Automotive Operations 1967; Exec. Vice-Pres. Ford Motor Co. and Pres. Ford North American Automotive Operations 1969–70, Pres. Ford Motor Co. 1970–78; Pres. and COO Chrysler Corpn 1978–79, Chair. 1979–93, CEO 1979–93, Dir –1993; Prin. Iacocca Pnrs 1994–; Acting Chair. Kro Koo Roo Inc. 1998; Pres. Iacocca Assocs, Los Angeles 1994–; Founding Chair. and CEO EV Global Motors Co.; f. Olivio Premium Products 2000; Fellow, Princeton Univ.; mem. Soc. of Automotive Engineers; Chair. Presidential Comm. to restore Statue of Liberty 1982–86; mem. Nat. Acad. of Eng 1986–; Founder and Chair. Iacocca Foundation 1984–; Kt, Order of Labour (Italy) 1989; Dr hc (Muhlenberg Coll., Babson Inst.); Detroit's Man of the Year 1982, Jefferson Award 1985. *Publications:* Iacocca, An Autobiography (with William Novak) 1984, Talking Straight 1988, Where Have All the Leaders Gone? 2007. *Address:* Iacocca Foundation, 867 Boylston Street, 6th Floor, Boston, MA 02116, USA (office). *Telephone:* (617) 267-7747 (office). *E-mail:* info@iacoccafamilyfoundation.org. *Website:* www.iacoccafoundation.org; www.olivioproducts.com (office).

IACOVOU, Georgios Kyriakou, MA, MSc, MA, DIC; Cypriot politician and diplomatist; *Senior Adviser, GlobalSource Consulting Ltd;* b. 19 July 1938, Peristeronopigi, Famagusta Dist; s. of Kyriacos Iacovou and Maria Michalopoulou; m. Jennifer Bradley 1963; one s. three d.; ed Greek Gymnasium for Boys, Famagusta, Univ. of London, UK, Univ. of Boston, USA; Eng, Cyprus Building and Road Construction Corpn Ltd 1960–61; Man. Electron Ltd, Nicosia 1961–63; with Operations Research and Finance Depts, British Railways Bd, London 1964–68; Sr Consultant (Man.), Price Waterhouse Assocs, London 1968–72; Dir Cyprus Productivity Centre, Nicosia 1972–76; Dir Special Service for Care and Rehabilitation of Displaced Persons 1974–76; Chief, E African Region, UNHCR, Geneva 1976–79; Amb. to FRG (also accred to Austria and Switzerland) 1979–83; Dir-Gen. Ministry of Foreign Affairs Jan.–Sept. 1983; Perm. Sec., Minister of Foreign Affairs 1983–93, 2003–06; High Commr to UK 2006–07; Presidential Commr 2008–13; Pres. and CEO Nat. Foundation of Overseas and Repatriated Greeks 1993–97; presidential cand., Cyprus presidential elections 1998; Pres. Cttee of Ministers, Council of Europe 1983; participated in Commonwealth Heads of State and Govt Confs in Delhi 1983, Bahamas 1985, Vancouver 1987, Kuala Lumpur 1989 and non-Aligned Summit, Harare 1986, Belgrade 1989; Chair. Bd Hotel and Catering Inst. 1972–76; Chair. Ministerial Conf. of Non-Aligned Movt, Nicosia 1988; Chair. Ministerial Cttee on Role and Functioning, Non-Aligned Movt; currently Sr Adviser, GlobalSource Consulting Ltd; Hon. Citizen, Tsalka, Georgia and City of Sappes, Thrace, Greece; Hon. Prof., Donetsk State Univ., Ukraine; numerous decorations including Grosses Verdienstkreuz mit Stern und Schulterband (FRG), Grosses Goldenes Ehrenzeichen (Austria), Grand Cross, Order of Phoenix (Greece), Grand Cross of the Order of Isabella the Catholic (Spain), Grand Cross of the Order of Honour (Greece), Order of the Repub. First Class (Egypt), Grand Cross of Infante D. Henrique (Portugal), Decoration of St Catherine's Monastery of Sinai, Order of Xirca Gloh Ir-Republica (Malta), Order of Cedar of Lebanon; Dr hc (State Univ. of Tbilisi, Georgia), (Panteion Univ. Athens), (State Univ. of Marloupol, Ukraine); Meritorious Service Award, Municipality of Peristeri, Athens. *Address:* GlobalSource Consulting Ltd, Paraskevaides Foundation Bldg, 36 Grivas Dighenis Avenue, 1066 Nicosia, Cyprus (office). *Telephone:* 22102201 (office). *Website:* www.globalsourcellc.com (office).

IALOMITIANU, Gheorghe; Romanian economist and politician; b. 14 Sept. 1959, Bran, Braşov Co.; m.; one c.; ed Univ. de Vest, Timişoara, Institut Int. d'Admin Publique, France, Swedish Nat. Tax Board; Economist, Fabrica de Scule Rasnov (tool mfr) 1983–85; teacher, A Barseanu Scoala Comerciala, Braşov 1983–95; Lecturer, Univ. Transilvania Braşov 1992–97, Univ. Assoc. 1997–2006, Assoc. Prof. 2006–; Dir Gen. DGFP (Public Finance Dept), Braşov 1997–2001, Jt Exec. Dir 2001–08; mem. Camera Deputaţilor (Parl.) for Braşov 2008–, fmr Vice-Pres. Parl. Budget and Finance Cttee; Minister of Public Finance 2010–12; mem. Partidul Democrat Liberal (Democratic Liberal Party) –2015, Partidul Naţional Liberal (National Liberal Party) 2015–. *Publications include:* 11 books on accounting, finance and taxation, 70 articles in Romanian and foreign specialist publications. *Address:* Chamber of Deputies (Camera Deputaţilor), 050563 Bucharest, Palatul Parlamentului, Str. Izvor 2–4, Sector 5, Romania (office). *Telephone:* (21) 4141111 (office). *Fax:* (21) 4141417 (office). *E-mail:* gheorghe.ialomitianu@cdep.ro (office). *Website:* www.cdep.ro (office); www.ialomitianu.ro.

IALONGO, Giovanni; Italian business executive; *Chairman, Postel SpA;* Chair. Postel SpA 2007–, Chair. Poste Italiane SpA 2008–14; Special Commr IPOST (Italian Postal and Telecommunications Services Inst.); Dr hc (Pontifical Lateran Univ.) 2009. *Address:* Poste Italiane SpA, Via C. Spinola 11, Rome 00154, Italy (office). *Telephone:* (14) 26236 (office). *Fax:* (14) 26230 (office). *Website:* www.poste.it (office).

IANEV, Stefan; Bulgarian army officer, government official and business executive; m.; two c.; ed 'Georgi Dimitrov' Nat. Mil. Artillery School, Shumen, 'Georgi S. Rakovski' Nat. Mil. Acad., Sofia Nat. War Coll. of Nat. Defense Univ., Washington, DC, USA; Artillery Platoon and Battery Commdr, Asenovgrad 1983–91, Officer Cadet, 'G.S. Rakovski' Nat. Mil. Acad., Sofia 1991–93, Div. Commdr, Asenovgrad 1993–96, Expert at Ministry of Defence Int. Co-operation Directorate 1996–98, Analyst at Planning and Programming Section, Partnership for Peace (PfP) Partnership Co-ordination Cell (PCC), Mons, Belgium 1998–2000, Sr Asst Br. Head, Strategies and Doctrine Br., Defence and Armed Forces Planning Dept, Gen. Staff 2000–01, Chief Expert, PfP Dept, Euro-Atlantic Integration Directorate, Ministry of Defence 2001–03, Head of Defence Policy and Analyses Dept, Defence Policy Directorate 2003–04, Officer Cadet, Nat. War Coll., Washington, DC, USA 2004–05, Head of Transformations Dept, NATO Centre of Excellence Defence Against Terrorism, Ankara, Turkey 2005–07, Dir Defence Policy Directorate, Ministry of Defence 2007–08, Dir Security and Defence Policy Directorate 2008–10, Dir Defence Policy Directorate 2010–11, Defence Attaché, Embassy in Washington, DC 2011–14, Commdt of 'Vasil Levski' Nat. Mil. Univ., Veliko Tarnovo 2014, retd from active duty June 2014; pvt. business consultant 2014–16; Deputy Prime Minister for Internal Order and Security and Minister of Defence 2017.

IANNUCCI, Armando Giovanni, OBE, MA; British screenwriter, writer, producer and director; b. 28 Nov. 1963, Glasgow, Scotland; s. of Armando Iannucci; m. Rachael Jones 1990; two s. one d.; ed Univ. of Glasgow, University Coll., Oxford; has produced, presented, written and appeared in numerous programmes for radio (BBC) and TV (BBC, Channel 4); Visiting Prof. of Broadcast Media, Univ. of Oxford 2006; columnist, The Observer, The Guardian, Gramophone, The Daily Telegraph; Dr hc (Open Univ.) 2018; three Sony Radio Awards, three British Comedy Awards, New York Film Critics Circle Awards 2009, Evening Standard British Film Awards 2010, Special Writers' Guild of Great Britain Award 2011. *Radio includes:* for BBC Radio 4, as producer: Quote... Unquote 1989–90, The News Quiz 1989–90, Week Ending 1991, On The Hour (also creator, co-writer) 1991–92, Knowing Me Knowing You (also writer) 1992–93; as actor: Lionel Nimrod's Inexplicable World (various characters) 1992, 1993; for others: No' The Archie McPherson Show (BBC Radio Scotland, also presenter, writer) 1988, The Mary Whitehouse Experience (BBC Radio 1) 1990, Loose Talk 1991–92, Armando Iannucci Show (BBC Radio 1, also writer, presenter) 1993–94; as presenter: Bite the Wax 1988–89, In Excess 1993–94, Scraps with Iannucci 1998, The News Quiz (regular guest), The 99p Challenge 2000–04, Armando Iannucci's Charm Offensive 2005–07, The Unbelievable Truth 2008, 2010. *Television includes:* for BBC 2: The Day Today (co-writer/producer) 1994, Knowing Me Knowing You with Alan Partridge (co-writer/producer) 1994, The Saturday Night Armistice (writer/co-presenter) 1995, The Friday Night Armistice 1996–98, I'm Alan Partridge (co-writer/producer) 1997, 2002, Clinton: His Struggle With Dirt (writer/dir) 1998, Britain's Best Sitcom (guest presenter) 2004, The Thick of It (writer/dir) (four series) 2005–12, Time Trumpet (co-writer/dir/performer) 2006, Lab Rats (exec. producer) 2008, Stewart Lee's Comedy Vehicle (exec. producer); for Channel 4: The Armando Iannucci Shows 2001; other: Milton's Heaven and Hell 2009 (presenter and writer), Mid-Morning Matters with Alan Partridge (Sky Atlantic) 2010–11, 2016, Veep (HBO) (writer, dir, producer) (Primetime Emmy Awards for Outstanding Comedy Series and for Outstanding Writing for a Comedy Series 2015) 2012–15. *Music:* wrote libretto for Skin Deep 2009. *Films:* Tube Tales (writer and dir of 'Mouth') 1999, In the Loop (dir) 2009, Alan Partridge: Alpha Papa 2013, The Death of Stalin (writer and dir) (Scottish BAFTA for Best Writer and Best Dir—Fiction 2018, European Film Awards for Best European Comedy 2018) 2017. *Publications include:* Facts and Fancies 1997, Alan Partridge: Every Ruddy Word (with others) 2003, The Audacity of Hype: Bewilderment, Sleaze and Other Tales of the 21st Century 2009, I, Partridge: We Need to Talk About Alan (co-author) 2011, Hear Me Out 2017. *Address:* c/o Peter Bennett-Jones, PBJ Management, 5 Soho Square, London, W1D 3QA, England (office). *Telephone:* (20) 7287-1112 (office). *Fax:* (20) 7287-1191 (office). *E-mail:* lucy@pbjmanagement.co.uk (office). *Website:* www.pbjmanagement.co.uk (office).

IBARRETXE MARKUARTU, Juan José, BEcons; Spanish politician; b. 15 May 1957, Llodio, Alava; ed Llodio Secondary School, Univ. of the Basque Country; mem. Partido Nacionalista Vaso (PNV); Mayor of Llodio 1983–87; Pres. Alava Prov. Parl. 1986–91; mem. Basque Parl., Chair. Econ. and Budgetary Comm. 1986–90, 1991–94; Vice-Pres. Basque Govt and Minister for Inland Revenue and Public Admin 1995–98, Pres. Basque Govt 1999–2009; fmr mem. Univ. of the Basque Country Social Council. *Address:* Euzko Alderdi Jeltzalea–Partido Nacionalista Vasco, Sabin Etxea, Ibáñez de Bilbao 16, 48001 Bilbao, Spain. *Website:* www.eaj-pnv.com.

IBERS, James Arthur, PhD; American chemist and academic; *Professor Emeritus of Chemistry, Northwestern University;* b. 9 June 1930, Los Angeles, Calif.; s. of Max Ibers and Esther Ibers (née Imerman); m. Joyce Audrey Henderson 1951; one s. one d.; ed California Inst. of Tech.; NSF Post-doctoral Fellow, Melbourne, Australia 1954–55; chemist, Shell Devt Co. 1955–61, Brookhaven Nat. Lab. 1961–64; Prof. of Chem., Northwestern Univ. 1964–85, Charles E. and Emma H. Morrison Prof. of Chem. 1986, now Prof. Emer., Prin. Investigator, Ibers Group; mem. NAS, American Acad. of Arts and Sciences, ACS, American Crystallographic Asscn; ACS Inorganic Chem. Award 1978, ACS Distinguished Service Award 1992, ACS Pauling Medal 1994, Distinguished Alumni Award, Calif. Inst. of Tech. 1997, American Crystallographic Asscn Buerger Award 2002. *Address:* Department of Chemistry, Tech K116, Northwestern University, Evanston, IL 60208-3113, USA (office). *Telephone:* (847) 491-5449 (office). *Fax:* (847) 491-2976 (office). *E-mail:* ibers@northwestern.edu (office). *Website:* www.chemistry.northwestern.edu (office); chemgroups.northwestern.edu/ibers (office).

IBOBI SINGH, Okram, BA; Indian politician and social worker; b. 19 June 1948, Thoubal Athokpam Makha Leikai; s. of Angoubi Singh and Lukamani Devi; m. Landhoni Devi; one s. two d.; mem. Manipur Legis. Ass. 1984–, Leader of the Opposition 2017–; Chair. Khadi and Village Industries Bd 1985–88; fmr Minister of Municipal Admin, Housing and Urban Devt and of Industries, Manipur; Chief Minister of Manipur 2002–17; Pres. Manipur Pradesh Congress Cttee 1999; Sec. Congress Legislature Party. *Leisure interest:* reading. *Address:* Manipur Legislative Assembly, Capital Complex, Thangmeiband, Imphal, 795001, Manipur India (office). *Website:* manipurassembly.net (office).

IBRAGIMBEKOV, Rustam Mamed Ibragimovich; Azerbaijani/Russian screenwriter, writer and producer; b. 5 Feb. 1939, Baku; s. of Mamed Ibragim Ibragimbekov and Fatima Alekper-kyzy Meshadibekova; m. Shokhrat Soltan-kyzy Ibragimbekova; one s. one d.; brother of Maksud Ibragimbekov; ed Azerbaijan State Inst. of Oil and Gas; Founder Filmcompany ASK (now Ibrus) 1989, Ibrus Theatre 2001; Chair. Confed. Unions of Cinematographers of CIS and Baltic States; Sec. Union of Cinematographers of Russian Fed.; Chair. Jewish Film

Festival in Moscow; Chair. Union of Cinematographers of Azerbaijan, Confed. of Filmmakers' Unions (CFU); Sec., Russian Filmmakers Union; mem. European Film Acad. Felix, American Acad. of Cinema Oscar; unsuccessful cand. for Pres. of Azerbaijan 2013; Order for Service to Motherland, Commdr des Arts et des Lettres; USSR State Prize 1981, State Prizes of Russian Fed. 1993, 1998, 1999, 2000, State Prize of Azerbaijan SSR 1980, Comsomol Prize 1979. *Film scripts include:* In This Young Town 1971, White Sun of the Desert 1971, Then I Said No 1974, Heart... Heart 1976, Country House for One Family 1978, Strategy of Risk 1979, Interrogation 1979, Mystery of Vessel Watch 1981, Birthday 1983, In Front of the Closed Door 1985, Save Me, My Talisman 1986, Free Fall, Other Life 1987, Cathedral of Air 1989, Hitchhiking, Taxi-Blues (producer) 1989, Seven Days After Murder, To See Paris and To Die 1990, Duba-Duba (producer) 1990, Urga Territory of Love (producer) 1992, Destroyed Bridges (also producer) 1993, Tired with the Sun 1994, The Man Who Tried (jtly) 1997, Barber of Siberia, Family (also dir and producer) 1998, East–West 1999, Mysteria 2000, Karu süda 2001, Nomad (The Warrior) (also producer) 2005, Proshaj, yuzhny gorod (also producer) 2006, Birds of Paradise 2008, Gagma napiri (adaptation) 2009, Burnt by the Sun 2 2010. *Plays:* numerous plays produced including A Woman Behind a Closed Door, Funeral in California, A House on the Sand, Like a Lion. *Publications:* 10 books and collections of stories including Ultimatum 1983, Woken Up with a Smile 1985, Country House 1988, Selected Stories 1989, Solar Plexus 1996. *Address:* Ibrus, 123242 Moscow, 15 Druzhinnikovskaya, bld.1, Russia (office); Lermontova str. 3, Apt. 54, 370006 Baku, Azerbaijan (home). *Telephone:* (499) 255-94-98 (office); (12) 4926313 (home). *E-mail:* ibrus@yandex.ru (office). *Website:* rustam-ibragimbekov .ru.

IBRAGIMOV, Bakhtiyor; Uzbekistani diplomatist; *Permanent Representative to United Nations;* m.; two c.; ed Tashkent Econ. Univ., Inst. of Diplomacy and Int. Relations, Kuala Lumpur; Researcher Acad. of Science, Uzbekistan 1989–92; Third Sec. Dept for Int. Econ., Scientific-Tech. and Cultural Cooperation, Ministry of Foreign Affairs (MFA) 1992–93, Third Sec. Embassy of Uzbekistan, Washington DC 1993–95, Political Counsellor and Deputy Chief of Mission 2004–09, Second Sec. USA and America Affairs Dept, MFA 1995–98, Dir 2003–04, 2009–11, First Sec., Seoul 1998–2002, Political Counsellor and Deputy Chief of Mission 2011–17, First Sec. Div. on Coordination of Activity of Overseas Consular Offices, MFA 2002, Dir 2002–03; Perm. Rep. to UN 2017–. *Address:* Permanent Mission of Uzbekistan, 801 Second Avenue, 20th Floor, New York, NY 10017, USA (office). *Telephone:* (212) 486-4242 (office). *Fax:* (212) 486-7998 (office). *E-mail:* uzbekistan .un@gmail.com (office). *Website:* www.un.int/uzbekistan (office).

IBRAHIM, Abdul Latif, DVM, MSc, PhD; Bangladeshi professor of veterinary physiology; *Professor Emeritus, Faculty of Veterinary Medicine, Universiti Putra Malaysia;* b. 1938; ed East Pakistan Agric. Univ., Univs of Hawaii and California, USA; Lecturer, Faculty of Veterinary Medicine and Animal Science, Univ. of Pertanian (now Universiti Putra Malaysia), Malaysia 1973, later Prof., Dean 1983–93, now Prof. Emer.; known for research on Newcastle Disease; Fellow, Islamic Acad. of Sciences 1988–; Foundation Fellow, Malaysia Acad. of Sciences 1996; Svon Brohult Award, First Int. Science Award (jtly), Malaysia, Anugerah Tokoh Akademik Negara 2012. *Publications:* over 120 publs on animal science. *Address:* Universiti Putra Malaysia, Faculty of Veterinary Medicine, Serdang, 43400 Selangor Malaysia (office). *Website:* vet.upm.edu.my (office).

IBRAHIM, Dato' Seri Encik Anwar bin, BA; Malaysian politician; *Chairman, Parti Keadilan Rakyat (People's Justice Party);* b. 10 Aug. 1947, Penang; m. Dr. Wan Azizah Wan Ismail; six c.; ed Univ. of Malaya; Pres. UMNO Youth Movt 1982–; Vice-Pres. UMNO 1982–; Head UMNO Permatang Pauh Div. 1982–99; Deputy Minister, Prime Minister's Dept 1982; Minister of Sport, Youth and Culture 1983, of Agric. 1984–86, of Educ. 1986–91, of Finance 1991–98; Deputy Prime Minister 1993–98; arrested Sept. 1998; sentenced to six years' imprisonment for corruption April 1999; put on trial for sodomy 1999; sentenced to nine years' imprisonment and banned for five years from running for public office after release; sodomy conviction overturned, released from prison Sept. 2004; Visiting Lecturer, Johns Hopkins Univ., Georgetown Univ., USA and Univ. of Oxford, UK 2005–07; Gen. Chief of the Pakatan Harapan 2008–15; Advisor, People's Justice Party (Parti Keadilan Rakyat, PKR) 2006, now Chair.; Chair. Foundation for the Future 2006–; Hon. Pres. AccountAbility 2005–. *Address:* People's Justice (Party Parti Keadilan Rakyat, PKR), A-1-09, Merchant Square, Jalan Tropicana Selatan 1, Petaling Jaya, 47410 Selangor, Malaysia (office). *Telephone:* (3) 78850530 (office). *Fax:* (3) 78850531 (office). *E-mail:* ibupejabat@keadilanrakyat.org (office). *Website:* www.keadilanrakyat.org (office); www.anwaribrahimblog.com.

IBRAHIM, Fahad Rashid al-, BA, MBA; Kuwaiti business executive and international organization executive; ed Kuwait Univ., Univ. of Dayton, USA; started career with Ministry of Foreign Affairs, then joined Ministry of Finance as Econ. Cooperation Man.; Chief Investment Man., Direct Investment Dept, Kuwait Investment Authority 1984–87; Chair. Supervisory Cttee, Dhaman 1987–2002; apptd Dir-Gen. Inter-Arab Investment Guarantee Corpn 2003; Chair. Kuwaiti-Algerian Investment Co. 2002–04, Kuwait Re-insurance Co.; mem. Bd of Dirs Securities Comm., Kuwait Stock Exchange 1996–2005.

IBRAHIM, Ibrahim al-, PhD; Qatari economist and academic; *Economic Adviser to the Emir of Qatar;* b. 1 Dec. 1939, Syria; ed New York Univ., USA; Assoc. Prof. of Business, Econs and Quantitative Methods, Univ. of Hawaii, Honolulu, USA 1970–78; Dir Econ. Dept, Org. of Arab Petroleum Exporting Countries (Kuwait) 1979–86; Sr Economist, Oxford Inst. for Energy Studies, UK 1986–88; Econ. Adviser to Sheikh Hamad Bin Khalifa al-Thani, Emir of Qatar 1988–; Sec.-Gen., Gen. Secr. for Devt Planning 2006–11; now also leading Qatar's First Nat. Devt Strategy; Vice-Chair. RasGas Co. Ltd, Chair. Marketing Cttee; Vice-Chair. Qatar Petroleum Int. and Industrial Bank; mem. Bd of Dirs Qatar Petroleum, Industries Qatar, Qatar Central Bank; Lifetime Achievement Award, Abdulla Bin Hamad Al-Attiya International Energy Awards 2014. *Publications include:* has published research internationally in the areas of forecasting, business economics and energy economics. *Address:* RasGas Co. Ltd, PO Box 24200, Doha, Qatar (office). *Telephone:* 55312318 (office). *Fax:* 44118946 (office). *E-mail:* lahassona@rasgas .com.qa (office); lhassona@mdps.gov.qa (office). *Website:* www.rasgas.com (office).

IBRAHIM, Mohamed (Mo), BSc, MSc, PhD; British (b. Sudanese) telecommunications industry executive; *Founder, Mo Ibrahim Foundation;* b. 1946; ed Univ. of Alexandria, Egypt, Univs of Bradford and Birmingham, UK; worked for Sudan Telecom; Tech. Dir Cellnet (subsidiary of British Telecom) 1983–89, involved in establishing the UK's first mobile telephone network; f. MSI consultancy and software firm 1989, est. MSI Cellular Investments (later renamed Celtel) 1998, built co. into one of leading mobile telephone networks in Africa, sold Celtel to Kuwaiti MTC 2005; Founder and mem. Bd of Dirs Mo Ibrahim Foundation, foundation's work includes Ibrahim Index of African Governance and Prize for Achievement in African Leadership; mem. Africa Regional Advisory Bd, London Business School; Commdr of the Order of the Lion (Senegal) 2014, Commdr of the Wissam Arch (Morocco) 2014; GSM Association's Chairman's Award for Lifetime Achievement 2007, BNP Paribas Prize for Philanthropy 2008, Oslo Business for Peace Award 2009, Raymond Georis Prize for Innovative Philanthropy in Europe 2010, Clinton Global Citizen Award 2010, Millenium Excellence Award for Actions in Africa 2012, David Rockefeller Bridging Leadership Award 2012, Africare Leadership Award 2013, Eisenhower Medal for Distinguished Leadership and Service 2014, Foreign Policy Asscn Medal 2014, Int. Republican Inst. Freedom Award 2015, Danish CSR Honour Prize 2015. *Address:* Mo Ibrahim Foundation, 3rd Floor North, 35 Portman Square, London, W1H 6LR, England (office). *E-mail:* info@moibrahimfoundation.org (office). *Website:* www.moibrahimfoundation.org (office).

IBRAHIM, Mohamed; Maldivian government official; headed two state cos before becoming Deputy Minister of Construction and Infrastructure in admin of Maumoon Gayoom; then moved to Interim Election Comm., Chair. interim Election Comm. throughout its period, apptd Pres. Elections Comm. of Maldives 2008; fmr mem. Dhivehi Rayyithunge Party (DRP—Maldivian People's Party); mem. Maldivian Democratic Party.

IBRAHIM, Datuk Muhammad; Malaysian central banker; *Governor and Chairman, Bank Negara Malaysia (Central Bank of Malaysia);* b. 1960; two s. one d.; ed Harvard Univ., USA, Univ. of Malaya, International Islamic Univ. Malaysia; joined Bank Negara Malaysia in 1984, Deputy Gov. 2010–16, Gov. and Chair. 2016–, also mem. Monetary Policy Cttee; served as Man. Dir Danamodal Nasional Berhad 1990s; apptd Commr, Securities Comm. of Malaysia 2004; fmr Chair. Irving Fisher Cttee on Central Bank Statistics, BIS; fmr mem. Council, Malaysian Inst. of Accountants, Malaysian Bankers Inst.; mem. Bd of Dirs Kumpulan Wang Persaraan (Govt Pension Agency), Petroliam Nasional Berhad (PETRONAS) 2014–; Trustee, Tun Ismail Ali Chair Council; Assoc. Fellow, Inst. of Bankers Malaysia. *Address:* Bank Negara Malaysia (Central Bank of Malaysia), Jalan Dato' Onn, POB 10922, 50929 Kuala Lumpur, Malaysia (office). *Telephone:* (3) 26988044 (office). *Fax:* (3) 26912990 (office). *E-mail:* bnmtelelink@bnm.gov.my (office). *Website:* www.bnm.gov.my (office).

IBRAHIM, Qasim, (Buruma Qasim); Maldivian politician and business executive; *Speaker of People's Majlis;* b. 10 Feb. 1952, Malé; s. of Hawwa Ibrahim; m.; four s. four d.; began career as clerk at Govt Hosp., Malé 1969, accountant 1972–73; Man. M/S Alia Furniture Mart 1973; subsequently worked for Crescent (trading org.) 1973; joined outlet of Maldivian Govt Bodu Store (now known as State Trading Org.) 1974; set up own trading business in 1976, registered business as Villa Shipping and Trading Co. Ltd 1986, Villa Shipping (Singapore) Pte Ltd was incorporated in Singapore 1991, opened offices in Frankfurt, Germany 1996, est. Villa Hotels, Tokyo 2001, Villa Hotels, Hong Kong 2002, currently Chair. and Man. Dir Villa Group of Cos; elected mem. Parl. 1989, 2009; founding mem. Maldivian Democratic Party 2001; Minister of Finance and Treasury 2005–08, of Home Affairs 2008; Pres. People's Special Majlis 2005–08; Gov. Maldives Monetary Authority 2005–08, Int. Monetary Fund 2005–07, World Bank 2005–08; Pres. Constitutional Ass. of the Republic of Maldives 2007–08; f. Jumhooree Party (Republican Party) 2008, currently Leader; Cand. in presidential election 2013; Speaker of People's Majlis 2018–; fmr Pres. South Asian Asscn for Regional Co-operation Chamber of Commerce and Industry; Founder-mem. and fmr Pres. Maldives Nat. Chamber of Commerce and Industry; Founder-mem., Vice-Pres. and mem. Bd Maldives Asscn of Tourism Industry; mem. Judicial Service Comm. 2011–; mem. Bd Maldives Ports Authority; fmr mem. Bd Bank of Maldives; Dr hc (Open Univ. of Malaysia) 2012. *Address:* People's Majlis Secretariat, Medhuziyaaraiy Magu, Malé, 20-080, The Maldives (office); Huravee Building, 3rd Floor, Ameer Ahmed Magu, Malé 20-05 (office); Villa Hotels, Villa Building, Ibrahim Hassandidi Magu, PO Box 2073, Malé, Maldives (office); M-Maafannu Villa, Malé (home). *Telephone:* 3322617 (office); 3316161. *Fax:* 3324104 (office); 3314565. *E-mail:* admin@majlis.gov.mv (office); qasim@villa.com.mv (home); info@villahotels.com.mv (office). *Website:* www.majlis.gov.mv (office); www.villahotels.com (home).

IBRAHIM, Sheikh Walid al-; Saudi Arabian broadcasting executive; *Chairman, Middle East Broadcasting Centre;* ed completed his higher educ. in USA; f. ARA Productions and TV Studios; f. Middle East Broadcasting Corpn (first ind. Pan-Arabic entertainment channel), London, UK 1991, opened Beirut office 2000, moved HQ to Dubai 2002, currently Chair. Middle East Broadcasting Centre; launched Al Arabiya 2003; f. MBC Films 2008; mem. Advisory Bd The Mohammed Bin Rashid School for Communication at the American Univ., Dubai; Media Man of the Year, 4th MENA Cristal Awards (Lebanon) 2008, Knight Award, Arab League, Innovator of the Year Award, Arabian Business. *Address:* Middle East Broadcasting Centre, PO Box 76267, Dubai, United Arab Emirates (office). *Telephone:* (4) 3919999 (office). *Fax:* (4) 3919900 (office). *E-mail:* infotv@mbc.ae (office). *Website:* www.mbc.net (office).

IBRAHIMI, Abdul Rauf, BA; Afghan politician; *Speaker, Wolesi Jirga;* b. 1962, Hazrati Amam Saheeb Dist; m.; three s. five d.; ed Kabul Univ.; fought with Hezb-e Islami against Soviets during invasion of Afghanistan in 1980s; Commdr Sherkhan Bandar 1993, later Commdr of Third Southern Border Zone, apptd Commdr of Border Forces 2002; mem. Wolesi Jirga (House of Reps) from Kunduz 2005–, Speaker, Wolesi Jirga 2011–; mem. Emergency Loya Jirga 2002, High Advisory Bd for Peace 2018–. *Leisure interest:* reading. *Address:* Office of the Speaker, Wolesi Jirga, Kabul, Afghanistan (office). *Telephone:* (79) 7582050 (office). *E-mail:* ibrahimi_999@yahoo.com (office). *Website:* wj.parliament.af/ english.aspx (office).

IBRAHIMI, Bedredin, LLB; Macedonian legal administrator and politician; b. 25 Oct. 1952, Mala Recica, nr Tetovo; ed Pristina Univ.; fmr doctor; Sr Officer for

Legal Affairs and Sec. of Poloska Kotlina Co., Tetovo Agricultural Complex, Belgrade 1976–81; Officer in charge of Gen. Legal Affairs and Sec. Jelak Tetovo Co., Interpromet Complex 1981–89; with Tekom-Tetovo Trade Co. 1990–96; Sec. of Council, Municipality of Tetovo 1997–98; fmr Gen. Sec. Democratic Party of Albanians (DPA); Deputy Prime Minister of Macedonia 1998–2002, apptd Minister of Labour and Social Welfare 1998.

IBRAHIMOVIĆ, Muhamed (Rasim); Bosnia and Herzegovina politician; b. 8 Jan. 1960, Stjepan Polje, Gračanica; m. Alma Ibrahimović; two s.; ed Faculty of Political Sciences, Univ. of Sarajevo; spent three years in Baghdad, Iraq working for several cos from Bosnia and Herzegovina and Slovenia; mem. Party of Democratic Action (Stranka Demokratske Akcije—SDA) 1991–2009, also mem. SDA Bd; Pres. Municipal Council of Gračanica 1991–98, held several positions, including Sec., Municipal Secr. for Defence and Pres. Exec. Cttee 1992–95; mem. Cantonal Cttee, SDA Tuzla Canton 1996–2000; Minister for Relations with Int. and Humanitarian Orgs in first Govt of Tuzla-Podrinje 1994–96; Mayor of Gračanica 1996–2000; Chief of Defence, Ministry of Defence, Tuzla Canton Fed. 2000–02; Councillor, Municipal Council of Gračanica 2000–02; mem. Parl., Tuzla Canton 2000–02; elected Deputy to House of Reps, Fed. of Bosnia and Herzegovina 1998, 2002, 2006, 2010, Pres. Comm. for Local Govt, mem. Denationalization and Privatization Cttee, Cttee on Labour and Social Policy, Selection and Appointment Cttee, Speaker, House of Reps 2002–06; unsuccessful cand. for Mayor of Gračanica 2008; Minister of Defence May–Oct. 2012; mem. Governing Bd, Univ. Clinical Center, Tuzla.

IBRAIMOVA, Elmira Sultanovna; Kyrgyzstani diplomatist and economist; *Executive Director, Community Development and Investment Agency (ARIS);* b. 13 April 1962, Frunze (now Bishkek); ed Moscow State Univ.; Perm. Rep. to UN, New York 1999–2002; Exec. Dir Community Devt and Investment Agency, Bishek 2004–; Vice Prime Minister 2008; Coordinator of Interim Govt for Social Affairs 2010; Chair. Accounts Chamber 2012–; Hon. Freeman of Gulchinskiy ayil kenesh of Alay rayon of Osh Oblast 2007; World Women's Summit Foundation Prize 2005. *Address:* Community Development and Investment Agency (ARIS), 102 Bokonbaev Street, Bishkek 720040, Kyrgyzstan (office). *Telephone:* (312) 30-18-05 (office). *Fax:* (312) 62-47-48 (office). *E-mail:* office@aris.kg (office). *Website:* www.aris.kg (office).

IBROOW, Saalim Aliyow; Somali politician; fmr Sec. of State; Deputy Prime Minister 2004, Minister of Finance 2004–05, of Livestock 2005–07, of Higher Educ. and Culture 2007, and Deputy Prime Minister 2007, Acting Prime Minister Oct.–Nov. 2007, apptd Minister of Justice and Religious Affairs 2007, Minister of Livestock, Forestry and Pastures 2014, Minister of Justice and Constitutional Affairs 2014, Minister of Energy and Water 2018; mem. Fed. Parl. 2004–. *Address:* Federal Parliament, Mogadishu, Somalia (office).

IBUKI, Bunmei, BA; Japanese politician; b. 9 Jan. 1938, Kyoto; ed Kyoto Univ.; mem. staff, Ministry of Finance from 1960, Dir Treasury Div. 1980, Sec. to Minister of Finance 1982; Sec., Japanese Embassy, London 1965–69; mem. LDP, Deputy Sec.-Gen. 1996, Chair. Public Relations HQ 1999, Research Comm. on the Pension System 1999, Party Org. HQ 2000, Working Group of the Research Comm. on the Tax System 2004, Chair. Shisuikai (Ex-Kamei Ibuki faction) 2005–, Sec.-Gen. 2007–08; mem. House of Reps for Kyoto 1st Dist 1983–96, Kyoto 1st Dist (single-member) 1996–2009, for Kinki PR block 2009–, Chair. Standing Cttee on Educ. 1994, Speaker 2012–14; Parl. Vice-Minister of Health 1990; Minister of Labour 1997–98; Minister of State for Disaster Man. 2001, for Nat. Emergency Legislation 2000; Chair. Nat. Public Safety Comm. 2000–01; Minister of Educ., Culture, Sports, Science and Tech. 2006–07, of Finance 2008; Kt Grand Cross, Order of Oranje-Nassau (The Netherlands) 2014. *Leisure interests:* go (board game), rakugo, dining tours, tennis, kimono. *Address:* House of Representatives, 1-7-1 Nagatacho, Chiyoda-ku, Tokyo 100-0014, Japan (office). *Telephone:* (3) 3581-5111 (office). *E-mail:* webmaster@shugiin.go.jp (office). *Website:* www.shugiin.go.jp (office); www.jimin.jp (office); www.ibuki-bunmei.org.

ICAHN, Carl Celian, BA; American business executive; *Chairman and President, Icahn Enterprises;* b. 16 Feb. 1936, Queens, New York; m. 1st Liba Icahn (divorced 1999); two c.; m. 2nd Gail Golden 1999; ed Princeton Univ. and New York Univ. School of Medicine; apprentice broker, Dreyfus Corpn, New York 1960–63; Options Man. Tessel, Patrick & Co., New York 1963–64, Gruntal & Co. 1964–68; Chair. and Pres. Icahn & Co., Inc. 1968–, Chair. and Pres. Icahn Holding Corpn (now Starfire Holding Corpn) New York 1984–, Chair. ACF Industries Inc. (Starfire subsidiary), St. Charles, Mo. 1984–, Chair. Bd Icahn Enterprises LP, 1990–, Icahn Enterprises GP Inc. (general partner of Icahn Enterprises LP) 1990–, CEO Icahn Capital LP (subsidiary of Icahn Enterprises LP) 2007–; Chair. American Real Estate Partners 1990–, American Property Investors, Inc. 1990–; Chair. Bd and Dir American Railcar Industries 1990–2014, Dir American Railcar Leasing LLC 2004–13; Chair. Bd (non-exec.) Federal-Mogul 2008–15; Chair. Bd Tropicana Entertainment Inc. 2010–, CVR Energy, Inc. 2012–, CVR Refining, LP 2013–; Chair. Lowestfare.com, LLC 1998, GB Holdings 2000–, XO Communications 2003– (Pres. Exec. Cttee 2011–); Chair. Trans World Airlines Inc. 1986–99, Manpintour Holdings LLC 1998–2002; Pres. Stratosphere Corpn 1998–; Dir Cadus Corpn 1993–2010, WestPoint Home LLC 2005–11, mem. Bd of Dirs ImClone 2006–, Yahoo Inc. 2008–09; Special Advisor to the Pres. on Regulatory Reform 2016–17 (resgnd). *Address:* Starfire Holding Corporation, 767 5th Avenue, 47th Floor, New York, NY 10153-0023 (office); Icahn and Company Inc., 100 South Bedford Road, Mount Kisco, NY 10549-3425, USA (office). *Telephone:* (212) 702-4300 (Starfire) (home). *Website:* www.ielp.com.

ICE CUBE; American rap artist and actor; b. (O'Shea Jackson), 15 June 1969, Los Angeles; ed Univ. of Phoenix; formed duo (with Sir Jinx), CIA, then leader of group, HBO; Founder-mem., N.W.A. 1987–89; formed rap group, Da Lench Mob 1989–; simultaneous solo artist 1989–; collaborated with Public Enemy; began own corpn, producing work by protegée YoYo 1989–; numerous tours; Founder-mem., Westside Connection 1996–; Founder Cube Vision Productions (film production co.). *Films include:* Boyz n the Hood (actor) 1991, Trespass (actor) 1992, The Glass Shield (actor) 1994, Higher Learning (actor) 1995, Friday (actor, writer, exec. prod.) 1995, Dangerous Ground (actor, exec. prod.) 1997, Anaconda (actor) 1997, The Player's Club (actor, writer, exec. prod.) 1998, I Got the Hook Up (actor) 1998, Three Kings (actor) 1999, Thicker Than Water (actor) 1999, Next Friday (actor, writer, exec. prod.) 2000, Ghosts of Mars (actor) 2001, All About the Benjamins (actor, writer, exec. prod.) 2001, Barbershop (actor) 2002, Friday After Next (actor, writer, exec. prod.) 2002, Torque (actor) 2004, Barbershop 2: Back in Business (actor, exec. prod.) 2004, Are We There Yet? (actor, prod.) 2005–, xXx 2: The Next Level (actor) 2005, Are We Done Yet? (actor) 2007, First Sunday (prod.) 2008, The Longshots (prod.) 2008, The Janky Promoters (prod.) 2009, Lottery Ticket (prod.) 2010, 21 Jump Street (actor) 2012, Ride Along (actor) 2014, 22 Jump Street (actor) 2014, The Book of Life (voice) 2014, Ride Along 2 (actor) 2016, Barbershop: A Fresh Cut (actor) 2016, xXx: Return of Xander Cage (actor) 2017. *Television:* as actor: Are We There Yet? 2010–13, Sean and Jake 2012–. *Recordings include:* albums: with N.W.A.: N.W.A. And The Posse 1987, Straight Outta Compton 1989; solo: AmeriKKKa's Most Wanted 1990, Death Certificate 1991, The Predator 1992, Lethal Injection 1993, Bootlegs And B Sides 1994, War And Peace 1998, War And Peace 2: The Peace Disc 2000, Greatest Hits 2001, Laugh Now, Cry Later 2006, Raw Footage 2008, I Am the West 2010; with da Lench Mob: Guerillas In Tha Mist 1992, Planet Of Da Apes 1994; with Westside Connection: Bow Down 1996. *Address:* Cube Vision Productions, 2900 West Olympic Blvd., Santa Monica CA 90404 (office); c/o Capitol Records, 1750 N Vine Street, Hollywood, CA 90028, USA (home). *Telephone:* (310) 255-7100 (Cube Vision) (office). *Fax:* (310) 255-7163 (Cube Vision) (office). *Website:* www.icecube.com.

ICE-T; American rap artist and actor; *Chairman and CEO, Final Level Productions;* b. (Tracey Marrow), 14 Feb. 1959, Newark, NJ; m. Darlene Ortiz; one c.; recording artist 1987–; mem., Body Count 1992–; world-wide tours, numerous television and film appearances; created Rhyme Syndicate Records early 1990s; currently Co-Founder, Chair. and CEO, Final Level Productions, LLC (production co.); involved in two youth intervention programmes, Hands Across Watts and South Central Love; Rolling Stone Readers' Poll Best Male Rapper 1992. *Recordings include:* albums: solo: The Pimp Penal Code, Sex, Money, Guns, Rhyme Pays 1987, Power 1988, The Iceberg 1989, O. G. Original Gangster 1991, Home Invasion 1993, VI: Return Of The Real 1996, Seventh Deadly Sin 1999, Ice-T Presents the Westside 2004, Gangsta Rap 2006; with Body Count: Body Count 1992, Born Dead 1994, Violent Demise, The Last Days 1997, Murder 4 Hire 2006, Manslaughter 2014. *Films:* Breakin' 1984, Breakin' 2: Electric Boogaloo 1984, New Jack City 1991, Ricochet 1991, Trespass 1992, Why Colors? 1992, Who's the Man? 1993, Surviving the Game 1994, Tank Girl 1995, Johnny Mnemonic 1995, Mean Guns 1997, The Deli 1997, Below Utopia 1997, Crazy Six 1998, Urban Menace 1999, Final Voyage 1999, Jacob Two Two Meets the Hooded Fang 1999, Corrupt 1999, The Wrecking Crew 1999, Sonic Impact 1999, Point Doom 1999, Judgment Day 1999, The Heist 1999, Frezno Smooth 1999, Stealth Fighter 2000, Leprechaun in the Hood 2000, Luck of the Draw 2000, The Alternate 2000, Sanity, Aiken's Artifact 2000, Guardian 2000, Gangland 2000, 3000 Miles to Graceland 2001, Deadly Rhapsody 2001, 'R Xmas 2001, Ticker 2001, Out Kold 2001, Ablaze 2001, Tara 2001, Stranded 2001, Kept 2001, Crime Partners 2000, Air Rage 2001, Tracks 2002, Pimpin' 101 2002, On the Edge 2002, The Passions of Jesus Christ 2012, Santorini Blue 2013, Once Upon a Time in Brooklyn 2013, Crossed the Line 2014, What Now 2015, The Ghetto 2015. *Television:* Players (series) 1997, Exiled (film) 1998, Law & Order: Special Victims Unit (series) 2000–, The Disciples (film) 2000, Ice T's Rap School (series) 2006, The Magic 7 (voice) 2007, Chicago P.D. (series) 2014–16. *Publications:* The Iceberg/Freedom of Speech... Just Watch What You Say 1989, The Ice Opinion 1994. *Address:* c/o Final Level Productions (office). *E-mail:* BodyCountIceT@gmail.com. *Website:* www.icet.com; www.finallevelprods.com.

ICHIKAWA, En'o II; Japanese actor; *Founder, Ennosuke Kabuki;* b. (Kinoshi Masahiko), 9 Dec. 1939; s. of Ichikawa Danshiro III (died 1963); grands. of En'o (died 1963); m. Teruyuki Kagawa aka Chuusha Ichikawa; ed Keio Univ.; stage debut aged seven; studied under experimentalist Kabuki actor En'o; took official name Ennosuke III 1963; est. ind. experimental group and spearheaded reformation and modernization of traditional Kabuki theatre; f. 21st Century Kabuki Co.; cr. new style of energetic, fast-paced Kabuki, called Super Kabuki; producer, dir and lead actor in Super Kabuki shows 1986–; teachings, lectures, tours and performances world-wide; became En'o II June 2012. *Address:* Kabuki-za, 4-12-15 Ginza, Chuo-ku, Tokyo, Japan (office).

ICHIKAWA, Yasuo; Japanese politician; b. 6 Feb. 1942, Ishikawa Pref.; ed Mie Univ.; with Ministry of Agric., Forestry and Fisheries 1965–90; mem. Ishikawa Pref. Ass. 1991–96; mem. House of Reps for Ishikawa 1996–2005, mem. Cttee on Agric., Forestry and Fisheries, Cttee on Land, Infrastructure, Transport and Tourism, Cttee on Fundamental Nat. Policies; mem. House of Councillors for Ishikawa 2007–12, mem. Cttee on Foreign Affairs and Defence, Cttee on Agric., Forestry and Fisheries, Special Cttee on Disasters; fmr mem. Shinshinto (New Frontier Party), Liberal Party; mem. Democratic Party of Japan (DPJ), Deputy Chair. DPJ Policy Research Cttee, Chair. DPJ Policy Discussion Panel; Minister of Defence 2011–12.

ICHIMIYA, Tadao; Japanese business executive; *Representative Director, Vice-Chairman and Chief Operating Officer, Yamada Denki Company Ltd;* b. 13 Aug. 1955; ed Soka Univ.; joined Yamada Denki Co. Ltd 1983, has served in various exec. positions including Vice-Pres., Dir of Product Planning, Man. Dir, Chief Dir of Admin, Sr Man. Dir, Deputy Chief Dir of Sales, Chief Dir of Product Admin Business, Chief Dir of IT Business, Exec. Vice-Pres. –1983, Pres. 2008–13, Vice-Pres. 2013–, Rep. Dir 1986–, COO and Vice Chair. 2016–. *Address:* Yamada Denki Co. Ltd, 4-40-11 Hiyoshi-cho, Maebashi 371-0017, Gunma, Japan (office). *Telephone:* (2) 7233-5522 (office). *Fax:* (2) 2 7233-3309 (office); (2) 7233-3568 (office). *E-mail:* info@yamada-denki.jp (office). *Website:* www.yamada-denki.jp (office).

IDA, Yoshinori; Japanese automotive industry executive; *Chairman and Representative Director, Isuzu Motors Ltd;* b. 18 May 1943; joined Izuzu 1966, Man. Dir responsible for domestic sales, eng, Gen. Motors affairs and portfolio integration, Isuzu Motors Ltd –2000, Rep. Dir, Pres. and COO 2000–07, Chair. and Rep. Dir 2007–; mem. Bd of Dirs Isetan Mitsukoshi Holdings Ltd 2013–. *Address:* Isuzu Motors Ltd, 26-1 Minami 6-chome, Shinagawa-ku, Tokyo 140-8722, Japan (office). *Telephone:* (3) 5471-1141 (office). *Fax:* (3) 5471-1043 (office). *E-mail:* info@isuzu.com (office). *Website:* www.isuzu.com (office).

IDEI, Nobuyuki, BA; Japanese business executive; *CEO, Quantum Leaps Corporation;* b. 1937, Tokyo; m. Teruyo Idei; one d.; ed Waseda Univ., Institut des hautes études internationales, Geneva, Switzerland; joined Sony Corpn 1960, est. Sony of France 1968, fmrly Head of Corp. Communications and Brand Image, Pres. and Rep. Dir Sony Corpn 1995–99, Pres. and CEO 1999–2000, Chair. and CEO 2000–05, Chair. Advisory Bd 2005–; Founder and CEO Quantum Leaps Corpn (man. consulting firm) 2006–; Counsellor, Bank of Japan 1999–2007; mem. Bd of Dirs General Motors 1999–2003, Nestlé SA 2001–, Accenture 2006–, Baidu.com Inc. 2007–, FreeBit Co. Ltd; mem. IT Strategy Council (advisory cttee to Japan's Prime Minister) 2000–05, Chair. July–Nov. 2000; Co-Chair. Admin. Reform, Nippon Keidanren (Japanese Business Fed.) 2002–03, Vice-Chair. 2003–07; Chair. Nat. Conf. on Fostering Beautiful Forests in Japan 2007–. *Leisure interests:* music, cinema, golf, reading. *Address:* Quantum Leaps Corporation, Parkside 6 #502, 9-5-12 Akasaka, Minato-ku, Tokyo 107-0052, Japan (office). *Telephone:* (3) 5785-3968 (office). *Fax:* (3) 5785-3969 (office). *Website:* www.qxl.jp (office).

IDEMITSU, Akira, BEcons; Japanese oil industry executive; b. 5 May 1932, Tokyo; ed Univ. of Tokyo; joined Idemitsu Kosan Co. Ltd April 1961, Gen. Man., Yokohama Br. 1977–79, Deputy Gen. Man., Marketing Dept 1979–81, Dir and Gen. Man. Hokkaido Refinery 1981–83, Gen. Man. Overseas Operations 1983–91, also Man. Dir 1988–91, Pres. Idemitsu Oil Devt Co. Ltd 1991–93, Sr Man. Dir Idemitsu 1993–95, Exec. Vice-Pres. 1995–98, Pres. and Rep. Dir 1998–2002, Chair. and Rep. Dir 2002–09, fmr Exec. Adviser.

IDIRISOV, Erlan Abilfay Isuzu; Kazakhstani politician and diplomatist; b. 28 May 1959, Karkalinsk, Qarağandi Oblast, Kazakh SSR, USSR; m. Nurilla Idırısova; two s. one d.; ed Moscow Inst. of Int. Relations, Diplomatic Acad., USSR Ministry of Foreign Affairs; rep. for Tyzahpromexport, Pakistan 1981–85; mem. of staff, Ministry of Foreign Affairs, USSR 1985–90, trainee USSR Embassy in New Delhi 1991–92, First Sec., Perm. Mission of Kazakhstan to UN, New York 1992–95, Head of American Dept and Amb.-at-Large, Ministry of Foreign Affairs 1995–96, Asst to Pres. on Int. Issues 1996–97, First Deputy Minister of Foreign Affairs 1997–99, 1999–2002, Minister of Foreign Affairs Feb.–Oct. 1999, Amb. to UK 2002–07, to USA 2007–12, Minister of Foreign Affairs 2012–16. *Leisure interests:* lawn tennis, ice hockey, golf, horse riding, travelling.

IDJI, Hon. Antoine Kolawolé; Benin politician; b. 31 Dec. 1946, Kétou; ed Fribourg Univ., Switzerland, Univ. Paris 1, Panthéon-Sorbonne, École Int. d'Admin publique, Paris; Minister of Foreign Affairs and African Integration 1998–2003; mem. Nat. Ass. (Parl.), Pres. 2003–07, currently Chair. of opposition group; cand. in presidential election 2006; fmr Chair. African Parliamentarians' Forum for New Partnership for Africa's Devt (NePAD); Gen. Co-ordinator L'Union Fait la Nation (The Union is the Nation) 2010–11; Grand Officier, ordre Nat., Grand Officier, ordre de la Pléiade et du Dialogue des Cultures. *Address:* Assemblée Nationale, BP 371, Porto-Novo, Benin. *Telephone:* 20-21-36-44 (office). *Fax:* 20-21-45-45 (office). *E-mail:* kolawole.idji@assemblee-nationale.bj (office). *Website:* assemblee-nationale.bj (office).

IDLE, Eric, BA; British writer, lyricist and actor; b. 29 March 1943, South Shields, Tyne and Wear; m. 1st Lynn Ashley (divorced); one s.; m. 2nd Tania Kosevich; one d.; ed Royal School, Wolverhampton and Pembroke Coll., Cambridge; Dr hc (Univ. of South Australia). *Films include:* Albert Carter, Q.O.S.O. (writer) 1968, And Now for Something Completely Different (actor, writer) 1971, Monty Python and the Holy Grail (actor, writer, exec. prod.) 1975, Life of Brian (actor, writer) 1979, The Meaning of Life (actor, writer) 1983, Yellowbeard (actor) 1983, European Vacation (actor) 1985, The Transformers: The Movie (voice) 1986, The Adventures of Baron Munchausen (actor) 1988, Nuns on the Run (actor) 1990, Missing Pieces (actor) 1991, Too Much Sun (actor) 1991, Mom and Dad Save the World (actor) 1992, Splitting Heirs (actor, writer, exec. prod.) 1993, Casper (actor) 1995, The Wind in the Willows (actor) 1996, Quest for Camelot (voice) 1998, Rudolph the Red-Nosed Reindeer: The Movie (voice) 1998, The Secret of NIMH 2: Timmy to the Rescue (voice) 1998, Pirates: 3D Show (actor, writer) 1999, Journey into Your Imagination (actor) 1999, Hercules: Zero to Hero (voice) 1999, South Park: Bigger Longer & Uncut (voice) 1999, Dudley Do-Right (actor) 1999, Brightness (actor) 2000, 102 Dalmatians (voice) 2000, Pinocchio (voice) 2002, Hollywood Homicide (actor) 2003, Ella Enchanted (actor) 2004, The Nutcracker and the Mouseking (voice) 2004, Shrek the Third (voice) 2007, Delgo (voice) 2008. *Television includes:* Alice in Wonderland (actor) 1966, The Frost Report (series, writer) 1966, No, That's Me Over Here! (series, writer) 1967, At Last the 1948 Show (series, actor) 1967, Do Not Adjust Your Set (series, actor and writer) 1967–69, Simply Sheila (writer) 1968, According to Dora (series, writer) 1968, We Have Ways of Making You Laugh (series, actor and writer) 1968, Broaden Your Mind (series, writer) 1968, Hark at Barker (series, writer) 1969, Monty Python's Flying Circus (four series, actor and writer) 1969–74, Euroshow 71 (actor) 1971, The Two Ronnies (series, writer) 1971, The Ronnie Barker Yearbook (writer) 1971, Ronnie Corbett in Bed (writer) 1971, Monty Python's Fliegender Zirkus (actor, writer) 1972, Christmas Box (writer) 1974, Commander Badman (writer) 1974, Rutland Weekend Television (series, actor and writer) 1975, The Rutles (actor, writer, dir) 1978, The Mikado (film, actor) 1987, Nearly Departed (series, actor) 1989, Around the World in 80 Days (series, actor) 1989, Mickey Mouse Works (series, voice) 1999, Suddenly Susan (series, actor) 1999–2000, House of Mouse (series, voice) 2001, The Scream Team (film, actor) 2002, Rutles 2: Can't Buy Me Lunch (writer, dir) 2002, Christmas Vacation 2: Cousin Eddie's Island Adventure (film, actor) 2003, The Simpsons (voice) 2003–07, Super Robot Monkey Team Hyperforce Go! (voice) 2004–05. *Stage productions include:* I'm Just Wild About Harry (actor, Edinburgh Festival) 1963, Monty Python Live at the Hollywood Bowl (actor, writer) 1982, The Mikado (actor, ENO) 1987, (actor, Houston Opera House) 1989, Monty Python's Spamalot (writer, The Shubert Theatre, Broadway) 2005, Monty Python Live (Mostly) (O2 Arena, London) 2014. *Compositions include:* songs for Monty Python's Flying Circus series 1969, Always Look on the Bright Side of Life. (for Life of Brian film) 1979, Bruces' Philosophers Song (for Monty Python Live at the Hollywood Bowl) 1982, Sit On My Face (for Monty Python Live at the Hollywood Bowl) 1982, songs for The Meaning of Life film 1983, The Adventures of Baron Munchausen (song, for film) 1988, One Foot in the Grave (TV series theme song) 1990, That's Death (song for video game, Discworld II: Missing Presumed...!?) 1996, songs for Monty Python's Spamalot stage production 2005. *Publications include:* Hello Sailor 1975, The Rutland Dirty Weekend Book 1976, Pass the Butler 1982, Monty Python's Flying Circus: Just the Words (co-author, two vols) 1989, The Fairly Incomplete and Rather Badly Illustrated Monty Python Song Book (co-author) 1994, The Quite Remarkable Adventures of the Owl and the Pussycat (co-author) 1996, The Road to Mars 1998, The "Pythons" Autobiography by the "Pythons" (co-author) 2003, The Greedy Bastard Diary: A Comic Tour of America 2005, Always Look on the Bright Side of Life: A Sortabiography 2018. *Website:* ericidle.com; pythonline.com.

IDRAC, Anne-Marie, LenD; French politician, civil servant and business executive; *Senior Advisor, Sia Partners;* b. (Anne-Marie Colin), 27 July 1951, Saint-Brieuc, Côtes-du-Nord; d. of André Colin and Marguerite Médecin (née Laurent); m. Francis Idrac 1974; four d.; ed Univ. of Paris II, Inst. d'Etudes Politiques de Paris and Ecole Nat. d'Admin; civic admin., Dept of Building and Public Works, Ministry of Equipment, Housing and Transport 1974–77; Chargée de Mission to the Prefect of the Midi-Pyrénées 1977–79; Tech. Councillor in the Cabinets of Marcel Cavaillé (Sec. of State for Housing) and Michel d'Ornano (Minister of the Environment) 1979–81; Deputy Dir for Housing Improvement, Ministry of the Quality of Life 1981–83; Deputy Dir for Finance and Judicial Affairs 1983–87; Chief of Service and Deputy Dir, Dept of Construction, Ministry of Supply 1987–90, Dir-Gen. Public Devt in Cergy-Pontoise 1990–93; Dir of Territorial Transport (DTT) 1993–95; Sec. of State for Transport 1995–97, for External Trade 2008–10; elected Deputy for Yvelines (Union pour la démocratie française—UDF) 1997; Sec.-Gen. Force Démocrate; mem. Regional Council Ile-de-France 1998–2002; Pres. Mouvement Européen France 1999–2002; Vice-Pres., then Sec.-Gen. UDF 2001–02; Pres. and Dir-Gen. Régie Autonome des Transports Parisiens 2002–06; Chair. Soc. Nationale des Chemins de Fer Français (SNCF) 2006–08; Pres. Océanides 2012–; Chair. Toulouse Airport; currently Sr Advisor to Suez and Sia Partners; Pres. of Bd, Public Affairs School, Sciences Po, Paris; mem. Bd of Dirs, Total, Bouygues, Saint Gobain, Institut Français de Relations Internationales; mem. Advisory Bd, Dexia 2002–07, Hautes études commerciales; mem. Orientation Council, Asscn En Temps Réel; Commdr, Ordre nat. du Mérite; Officier, Légion d'honneur; Nat. Foundation for Public Enterprise Award 1977. *Address:* Sia Partners, 12 rue Magellan 75008 Paris, France (office). *Telephone:* 1-42-77-76-17 (office). *E-mail:* annemarieidrac@orange.fr (office). *Website:* www.sia-partners.com (office); oceanides-association.org (office).

IDRIS, Kamil E., LLB, BA, MA, PhD; Sudanese diplomatist and lawyer; b. 1945; ed Univ. of Khartoum, Egypt, Ohio Univ., USA, Grad. Inst. of Int. Studies, Switzerland, Inst. of Public Admin, Khartoum; part-time journalist, El-Ayam and El-Sahafa newspapers, Sudan 1971–79; Lecturer, Univ. of Cairo 1976–77, Ohio Univ. 1978, Univ. of Khartoum 1986; Asst Dir Arab Dept, Ministry of Foreign Affairs, Khartoum 1977–78, Asst Dir Research Dept Jan.–June 1978, Deputy Dir Legal Dept July–Dec. 1978; mem. Perm. Mission of Sudan to UN Office, Geneva 1979–82; Vice-Consul of Sudan, Switzerland 1979–82; Sr Program Officer, Devt Cooperation and External Relations Bureau for Africa, WIPO 1982–85, Dir Devt Cooperation and External Relations Bureau for Arab and Cen. and Eastern European Countries 1985–94, Deputy Dir-Gen. WIPO 1994–97, Dir-Gen. 1997–2008 (resgnd); Sec.-Gen. Int. Union for the Protection of New Varieties of Plants (UPOV) 1997–2008; mem. UN Int. Law Comm. (ILC) 1992–96 (Vice-Chair. 45th session 1993), 2000–02; served on numerous cttees of int. orgs including WHO, ILO, ITU, UNHCR, OAU, Group of 77 etc. and Sudanese del. to numerous int. and regional confs; Prof. of Public Int. Law, Univ. of Khartoum; mem. African Jurists Asscn; Hon. Prof. of Laws, Peking Univ., People's Repub. of China 1999; decorations from Sudan 1983, 2002, Egypt 1985, 2000, 2001, Senegal 1998, Russian Fed. 1999, 2000, Saudi Arabia 1999, Slovakia 1999, Syrian Arab Repub. 2000, Portugal 2001, Romania 2001, Mexico 2001, 2005, Repub. of Moldova 2001, Côte d'Ivoire 2002, Poland 2002, Kyrgyzstan 2003, Bulgaria 2003, Italy 2004, Oman 2004; Dr hc (State Univ. of Moldova) 1999), (Franklin Pierce Law Center) 1999, (Fudan Univ., Shanghai) 1999, (Univ. of Nat. and World Economy, Sofia) 2000, (Univ. of Bucharest) 2001, (Hannam Univ., Repub. of Korea) 2001, (Mongolian Univ. of Science and Tech.) 2001, (Matej Bel Univ., Slovakia) 2001, (Nat. Tech. Univ. of Ukraine) 2002, (Al Eman Al Mahdi Univ., Sudan) 2003, (Indira Gandhi Nat. Open Univ.) 2005, (Latvian Acad. of Sciences) 2005, (Univ. of Al Gezira) 2007; Scholars and Researchers State Gold Medal (Sudan) 1983, Scholars and Researchers Gold Medal, Egyptian Acad. of Scientific Research and Tech. 1985. *Publications include:* State Responsibility in International Law 1977, North-South Insurance Relations: The Unequal Exchange 1984, The Law of Non-navigational Uses of International Water Courses; the ILC's draft articles: An Overview 1995, The Theory of Source and Target in Child Psychology 1996 and articles on law, economics, jurisprudence and aesthetics in newspapers and periodicals.

IDURI, Shemuel Sam; Solomon Islands teacher and politician; b. Boboilangi Village, Malaita; ed Solomon Islands Teacher's Coll., Teacher's Coll., Western Australia; fmr educ. officer; fmr secondary school prin.; mem. Parl. for West Kwara'ae, Malaita Prov. 2006–; Minister for Nat. Unity, Reconciliation and Peace 2006–10 Nov. 2007, 22 Dec. 2007–10. *Address:* National Parliament of Solomon Islands, PO Box G19, Vavaya Ridge, Honiara Solomon Islands (office). *Telephone:* 28520 (office). *Fax:* 24272 (office). *Website:* www.parliament.gov.sb (office).

IEHSI, Ieske K., BA, MPA; Micronesian politician and government official; *Executive Vice-President, Micronesia Insurance Management Company Ltd;* b. 4 Jan. 1955, Pingelap Atoll; m. Merihne John; five c.; ed Univ. of Hawaii, Manoa, Harvard Univ., USA; Asst Chief Clerk, Congress of Micronesia 1977–97, Man., Office of the Attorney-Gen. 1980–81; Special Asst to the Pres. 1981–87, Chief of Staff, Exec. Office of the Pres. 1987–92; Deputy Sec. of the Dept of Foreign Affairs 1997–2001, Sec. of Foreign Affairs 2001–03; Gen. Man. Pohnpei Ports Authority 2003–10; Sr Exec., Micronesia Registration Advisors, Inc. 2010–11; Exec. Vice-Pres. Micronesia Insurance Man. Co., Ltd 2012–; mem. Pingelap Council of Traditional Leaders (Benik), holding title of Noahs. *Address:* Micronesia Insurance Man. Co., Ltd, PO Box 902, Kolonia, Pohnpei, FM 96941, Micronesia (office). *Telephone:* 320-6949 (office). *Fax:* 320-7949 (office). *Website:* www.fsmmimc.com (office).

IGARASHI, Mitsuo; Japanese business executive and fmr politician; *Chairman, Okawa Foundation for Information and Telecommunications;* Deputy Minister for Policy Coordination, Ministry of Posts and Telecommunications 1990, Dir-Gen.

Telecommunications Bureau then Minister of Telecommunications 1995; Exec. Vice-Pres. KDDI Corpn (telecommunications co.) 2000–03, Chair. 2003–04; Pres. Okawa Foundation for Information and Telecommunications 2005, now Chair.; currently Adviser, Nomura Research Inst. *Publications:* articles in professional journals on econs. *Address:* Okawa Foundation, Sankyo Hanzomon Palace 301, 1-8-2 Hirakawacho, Chiyoda-ku, Tokyo 102-0093, Japan (office). *Telephone:* (3) 3556-6028 (office). *Fax:* (3) 3288-2280 (office). *E-mail:* okawa-foundation@nifty.com (office). *Website:* www.okawa-foundation.or.jp (office).

IGAŞ, Constantin Traian; Romanian politician; b. 29 Sept. 1968, Cristian, Sibiu Co.; m.; two d.; ed Universitatea de Vest Vasile Goldiş, Arad, Universitatea Aurel Vlaicu, Arad, Nat. Defence Univ. Carol I; Dir Arad Free Youth org. 1990–95; Tech. Dir, SC Astralegno LLC 1996–2000; Admin. SC Costello SRL 2000–04; Vice-Pres. Partidul Democrat (PD) 1998, Pecica Br. Vice-Pres. Perm. Bureau of PD, Arad Co. 2005; Alderman of the City of Pecica, Arad Co. 2000–04; adviser to Arad Co. Council 2004–08; Senator from Arad (Partidul Democrat-Liberal—PD-L) 2004–, Chair. PDL Group 2008–; Minister of Admin and the Interior 2010–12. *Address:* Parlamentul României Senat, 13 September 1-3 District 5, Bucharest, 050711 (office); Str. Cenad, Nr. 10, Bl. 226, Ap. 19, Arad, Romania. *Telephone:* (25) 7254577. *Fax:* (72) 6200680. *E-mail:* contact@igas.ro (office); igasconstantin@yahoo.com. *Website:* www.senat.ro (office).

IGE, David Yutaga, BS, MBA; American politician; *Governor of Hawaii;* b. 15 Jan. 1957, Honolulu; m. Dawn Ige; one s. two d.; ed Univ. of Hawaii, Manoa; Sr Admin., GTE-Hawaiian Telephone Co. 1981–99; Project Man., Pihana Pacific LLC 1999–2001; Vice-Pres. (Eng), Net Enterprise Inc. 2001–02; Project Man., R.A. Ige & Assoc. Inc. 2003; mem. Hawaii House of Reps for Dist 43 1986–93, for Dist 34 1993–95; mem. Hawaii State Senate for Dist 17 1995–2002, for Dist 16 2003–14, Vice-Chair. Media, Arts, Science and Tech. Cttee, Inter-Govt Affairs Cttee; Gov. of Hawaii 2014–; Vice-Chair. Western Governors' Asscn 2017–18, Chair. 2018–19; Democrat. *Address:* Office of the Governor, State Capitol, Room 415, Honolulu, HI 96813, USA (office). *Telephone:* (808) 586-0034 (office). *Fax:* (808) 586-0006 (office). *Website:* www.hawaii.gov/gov (office).

IGEL, Anders, BSc, MSc; Swedish telecommunications executive; b. 22 March 1951, Stockholm; m.; three d.; ed Stockholm School of Econs, Stockholm Royal Inst. of Tech.; began career as radar system devt engineer at Philips Electronics; joined Ericsson 1978, held several positions including Marketing Exec., Head of Ericsson UK 1990–95, Head of Public Networks 1995–97, Head of Infocom Systems 1997–99; Pres. and CEO Esselte 1999–2002; mem. Bd Telia 1999, Pres. and CEO TeliaSonera 2002–07; Industrial Adviser, EQT Industrial Network (consultancy); mem. Bd of Dirs Swedbank AB 2006–, Turkcell Iletisim Hizmetleri AS 2006–07.

IGER, Robert (Bob) A., BA; American business executive; *Chairman and CEO, The Walt Disney Company;* b. 10 Feb. 1951, New York; m. 1st; one s. one d.; m. 2nd Willow Bay 1995; one s. one d.; ed Ithaca Coll.; studio supervisor, ABC-TV 1974–76, various positions, ABC-TV Sports 1976–85, Vice-Pres. Programme Planning and Devt 1985–87, Vice-Pres. Programme Planning and Acquisition 1987–88, Exec. Vice-Pres. ABC TV Network Group 1988–99, Pres. 1992–94, Pres. ABC Entertainment 1989–92, Exec. Vice-Pres. Capital Cities/ABC Inc., New York 1993–94, Pres. and COO 1994–96, Pres. ABC Inc., New York 1996–99, Chair. ABC Group 1999–2000; Pres. Walt Disney Int. 1999–2000, Pres. and COO The Walt Disney Co., Calif. 2000–05, Pres. and CEO 2005–12, Chair. and CEO 2012–; CEO MarketWatch Inc. 2006–; mem. Bd of Dirs Nat. September 11 Memorial & Museum, Lincoln Center for the Performing Arts, Inc., Partnership for a New American Economy, US-China Business Council 2011–, Apple Inc. 2011–; apptd by Pres. Obama to the President's Export Council 2010; mem. Pres. Trump's Strategic and Policy Forum Jan.–June 2017 (resgnd); mem. American Acad. of Arts and Sciences 2012; Trustee, American Film Inst. Bd; fmr Trustee, Ithaca Coll.; Hon. Chair. Campaign for Ithaca Coll.; Trustees Award, Nat. TV Acad. 2005. *Address:* The Walt Disney Co., 500 South Buena Vista Street, Burbank, CA 91521-9722, USA (office). *Telephone:* (818) 560-1000 (office). *Fax:* (818) 560-1930 (office). *E-mail:* TWDC.Corp.Communications@disney.com (office). *Website:* thewaltdisneycompany.com (office); disney.com (office).

IGGA, James Wani; South Sudanese politician and fmr resistance fighter; *Second Vice-President;* b. 1949, Krillo, Juba County; ed Cairo Univ. of Econs, Egypt; joined Sudan People's Liberation Army (SPLA, guerrilla army) 1985, becoming Zonal Commdr, Central Equatoria, mem. SPLA High Command, Chair. Sudan People's Liberation Movt Political Affairs Comm. 2000; apptd caretaker Gov., Upper Nile State for transition period to independence of S Sudan 2005; Speaker, Legis. Ass. (Parl.) –2013; Second Vice-Pres. 2013–. *Address:* Office of the Vice-President, Juba, South Sudan (office).

IGLESIAS, Enrique; Spanish singer and songwriter; b. 8 May 1975, Madrid; s. of Julio Iglesias; sings in English and Spanish; numerous tours; Grammy Award 1997, eight Premios Los Nuestro, Billboard Awards for Artist of the Year, Album of the Year 1997, ASCAP Award for Songwriter of the Year 1998, American Music Awards for Favorite Latin Artist 2002, 2008, 2014, 2015, Billboard Latin Music Award for Best Latin Dance Club Play Track (for Not In Love/No Es Amor) 2005, Top Latin Album (Euphoria) 2011, ASCAP Pop Award for Most Performed Song (Tonight I'm Lovin' You) 2012, MTV Europe Music Award for Best World Stage Performance 2014, Latin Grammy Awards for Song of the Year, for Best Urban Performance, for Best Urban Song (all for Bailando) 2014, for Best Urban Performance (for El Perdón, with Nicky Jam) 2015, Billboard Music Award for Top Latin Song (for Bailando) 2015, (for El Perdón, with Nicky Jam) 2016. *Recordings include:* albums: Enrique Iglesias 1995, Master Pistas 1997, Vivir 1997, Cosas Del Amor 1998, Enrique 1999, Escape 2001, Quizás 2002, 7 2003, Insomniac 2007, Euphoria 2010, Sex + Love (Billboard Music Award for Top Latin Album 2015) 2014; singles: Experienca Religiosa, No Llores Por Mi, Bailamos 1999, Rhythm Divine 1999, Be With You 2000, Solo Me Importas Tu 2000, Sad Eyes 2000, Hero 2001, Don't Turn Off The Lights 2002, Love To See You Cry 2002, Maybe 2002, Addicted 2003, Not In Love 2004. *Address:* c/o Republic Records, Universal Music Group, 2220 Colorado Avenue, Santa Monica, CA 90404, USA. *Telephone:* (310) 865-1000. *Website:* www.enriqueiglesias.com.

IGLESIAS, Enrique V.; Uruguayan academic and international organization official; b. 26 July 1931, Asturias, Spain; s. of Isabel García de Iglesias; ed Univ. de la República, Montevideo; held several positions, including Prof. Agregado, Faculty of Political Economy, Prof. of Econ. Policy and Dir Inst. of Econs, Univ. de la República, Montevideo 1952–67; Man. Dir Unión de Bancos del Uruguay 1954; Tech. Dir Nat. Planning Office of Uruguay 1962–66; Pres. (Gov.) Banco Cent. del Uruguay 1966–68; Chair. Council, Latin American Inst. for Econ. and Social Planning, UN 1967–72, Interim Dir-Gen. 1977–78; Head, Advisory Mission on Planning, Govt of Venezuela 1970; Adviser UN Conf. on Human Environment 1971–72; Exec. Sec. Econ. Comm. for Latin America and the Caribbean 1972–85; Minister of External Affairs 1985–88; Pres. IDB 1988–2005; Gen. Sec. Ibero-American Gen. Secr., Madrid, Spain 2005–14; Pres. Soc. for Int. Devt; Acting Dir-Gen. Latin American Inst. for Econ. and Social Planning 1973–78; Pres. Third World Forum 1973–76; mem. Steering Cttee, Soc. for Int. Devt 1973–92 (Pres. 1989), Selection Cttee, Third World Prize 1979–82; Sec.-Gen. UN Conf. on New and Renewable Sources of Energy Feb.–Aug. 1981; Chair. UN Inter-Agency Group on Devt of Renewable Sources of Energy, Energy Advisory Panel, Brundtland Comm. 1984–86; mem. North-South Round Table on Energy, Club of Rome; Order of Rio Branco; Grand Cross (Brazil); Grand Cross Silver Plaque, Nat. Order of Juan Mora Fernandez (Costa Rica); Commdr Légion d'honneur; Commdr des Arts et des Lettres 1999; Grand Cross of Isabel the Catholic (Spain); numerous other foreign decorations; Hon. LLD (Liverpool) 1987; Hon. PhD (Univ. de Guadalajara, Mexico) 1994, (Candido Mendes Univ., Rio de Janeiro) 1994; Prince of Asturias Award 1982, UNESCO Pablo Picasso Award 1997. *Leisure interests:* music, art.

IGLESIAS (DE LA CUEVA), Julio José; Spanish singer and songwriter; b. 23 Sept. 1943, Madrid; m. 1st Isabel Preysler 1971 (divorced); two s. one d.; m. 2nd Miranda Rijnsburger 2010; three s. two d.; ed Univ. of Cambridge; goalkeeper Real Madrid junior team; professional singer, songwriter 1968–; Eurovision Song Contest entrant 1970; English language releases 1981–; concerts and television appearances worldwide; hon. mem. Spanish Foreign Legion; winner Spanish Song Festival, Benidorm 1968, Guinness Book of Records Diamond Disc Award (most records in most languages) 1983, Medaille de Vermeil de la Ville de Paris 1983, Grammy Award for Best Latin Pop Performance 1987, First and Most Popular Int. Artist of All Time, China 2013, Guinness World Records Award for Best-Selling Male Latin Artist 2013, inducted into Latin Songwriters Hall of Fame 2013. *Compositions include:* La Vida Sigue Igual, Mi Amor, Yo Canto, Alguien El Alamo Al Camino, No Llores. *Recordings include:* albums: Soy 1973, El Amor 1975, A Mis 33 Años 1977, De Niña A Mujer 1981, 1100 Bel Air Place 1984, Un Hombre Solo 1987, Starry Night 1990, La Carretera 1995, Tango 1996, Corazón Latino 1998, Noche De Cuatro Lunas 2000, Una Donna Puo Cambiar La Vita 2000, Ao Meu Brasil 2000, Divorcio 2003, Romantic Classics 2006; also appears on: Duets (with Frank Sinatra) 1993. *Publication:* Entre el Cielo y el Infierno (autobiog.) 1981. *Address:* Anchor Marketing, 1885 NE 149th Street, Suite G, North Miami, FL 33181, USA (office). *Website:* www.julioiglesias.com (office).

IGLESIAS, María Cristina; Venezuelan politician; *Minister of Labour and Social Security;* Minister of Labour and Social Security 2002–05, 2009–, Minister of Light Industry and Commerce 2006–08; mem. Partido Socialista Unido de Venezuela. *Address:* Ministry of Labour and Social Security, Torre Sur, 5°, Centro Simón Bolívar, Caracas 1919, Venezuela (office). *Telephone:* (212) 481-1368 (office). *Fax:* (212) 483-8914 (office). *Website:* www.mintra.gov.ve (office).

IGNARRO, Louis J., BS, PhD; American pharmacologist and academic; *Professor Emeritus, University of California at Los Angeles;* b. 31 May 1941, Brooklyn, NY; m. Sharon E. Ignarro (née Williams); ed Columbia Univ., Univ. of Minnesota; Postdoctoral Fellow, NIH 1966–68; Staff Scientist, Research Dept, Pharmaceutical Div., CIBA-GEIGY Corpn, Ardsley, NY 1968–72; Asst Prof., Dept of Pharmacology, Tulane Univ. School of Medicine, New Orleans 1973, Assoc. Prof. 1973–78, Prof. 1979–85; apptd Prof., Dept of Pharmacology, UCLA School of Medicine 1985, Prof. and Acting Chair. Dept of Pharmacology 1989–90, Prof. of Pharmacology and Asst Dean for Student Research 1990–93, apptd Jerome J. Belzer, MD, Distinguished Prof. of Pharmacology, Dept of Molecular and Medical Pharmacology 1993, then Prof. Emer., mem. Brain Research Inst.; Founder and Pres. Nitric Oxide Soc.; Founder and Ed.-in-Chief Nitric Oxide Biology and Chemistry (journal); mem. Herbalife Nutrition Advisory Bd, Herbalife Nutrition Inst.; mem. American Soc. for Pharmacology and Experimental Therapeutics, American Soc. for Biochemistry and Molecular Biology, American Physiological Soc., American Soc. for Cell Biology, American Rheumatism Asscn, American Soc. of Hematology, Soc. for Experimental Biology and Medicine, American Heart Asscn, NAS 1999–, American Acad. of Arts and Sciences 1999–, Inst. of Medicine 2005–, American Philosophical Soc. 2007–; Dr hc (Buenos Aires School of Medicine) 1996, (Napoli School of Medicine) 1999, (Napoli School of Medicine II) 1999, (Univ. of the Republic, Montevideo, Uruguay) 1999, (UniNorte School of Medicine, Paraguay) 2000, (Charles Univ. School of Medicine, Prague) 2000, (Univ. of Bologna School of Medicine) 2000, (Tulane Univ.) 2001, (Univ. of Minnesota) 2002, (Univ. of Athens) 2002, (Univ. of Perugia, Italy) 2004, (Univ. of Madrid,), (Univ. of Lund), (Univ. of Ghent), (Univ. of North Carolina); Roussel UCLA Prize 1994, CIBA Award for Hypertension Research 1995, Nobel Prize for Medicine (jtly) 1998, Basic Research Prize, American Heart Asscn 1998, Medal of Merit, Int. Acad. of Cardiovascular Sciences 2007, Distinguished Scientist Award, American Heart Asscn 2008, Canadian Medal of Merit 2008, Lifetime Achievement Award, Int. Acad. of Achievement 2014. *Publications:* numerous articles in scientific journals. *Leisure interests:* marathon runner, cyclist. *Address:* 269 South Beverly Drive, Unit 288, Beverly Hills, CA 90212 (office); 23-305 CHS, UCLA Department of Molecular and Medical Pharmacology, David Geffen School of Medicine, 650 Charles E. Young Drive South, Los Angeles, CA 90095-1735, USA (office). *Telephone:* (310) 859-3980 (office). *E-mail:* lignarro@gmail.com (office). *Website:* faculty.pharmacology.ucla.edu (office); www.drignarro.com (home).

IGNATIEFF, Michael, CM, BA, MA, PhD; Canadian writer, historian, academic and fmr politician; *President and Rector, Central European University;* b. 12 May 1947, Toronto, Ont.; s. of George Ignatieff and Jessie Alison (née Grant); m. 1st Susan Barrowclough 1977 (divorced 1997); one s. one d.; m. 2nd Zsuzsanna Zsohar 1999; ed Univ. of Toronto, Harvard Univ., USA, Univ. of Cambridge, UK; reporter, Globe and Mail newspaper, Toronto 1966–67; Teaching Fellow, Harvard Univ. 1971–74; Asst Prof., Univ. of British Columbia, Vancouver 1976–78; Sr Research Fellow, King's Coll., Cambridge, UK 1978–84; Visiting Prof., École des Hautes Études, Paris 1985; freelance writer, broadcaster and journalist, London 1985–2000; Carr Prof. of Human Rights Practice, Harvard Univ. 2000–05, Dir

Carr Center for Human Rights Policy, John F. Kennedy School of Govt 2001–05, Prof. of Practice, John F. Kennedy School of Govt 2013–16, Edward R. Murrow Prof. of the Practice of Politics and the Press 2014–16; Pres. and Rector, Central European Univ., Budapest 2016–; MP (Liberal) for Etobicoke-Lakeshore 2006–11; Deputy Leader Liberal Party of Canada 2006–08, interim Leader 2008–09, Leader 2009–11 (resgnd); Fellow, Massey Coll., Univ. of Toronto 2011–12, Prof., Munk School of Global Affairs 2012–13; Centennial Chair of Project on Global Ethics, Carnegie Council on Ethics and Int. Affairs, New York 2012–15;Editorial Columnist, The Observer, London 1990–93; corresp. for BBC, The Observer, New Yorker 1984–2000; Contributing Writer, New York Times Magazine 2000–05; fmr mem. Int. Comm. on Sovereignty and Intervention; Mem., Order of Canada; 11 hon. doctorates; Dan David Prize, Tel Aviv Univ. 2019, Politiken Freedom Prize (co-recipient) 2019. *Television includes:* host of Thinking Aloud (BBC) 1986, Voices (Channel Four) 1986, The Late Show (BBC 2) 1989. *Publications include:* A Just Measure of Pain: The Penitentiary in the Industrial Revolution 1978, Wealth and Virtue: The Shaping of Classical Political Economy in the Scottish Enlightenment (co-ed.) 1983, The Needs of Strangers: An Essay on the Philosophy of Human Needs 1984, The Russian Album: A Family Memoir (Royal Soc. of Literature W.H. Heinemann Award (UK) 1988, Gov.-Gen. Award (Canada) 1988) 1987, Asya 1991, Scar Tissue (novel) 1993, Blood and Belonging: Journeys into the New Nationalism (Gordon Montador Award for Best Canadian Book on Social Issues 1993, Lionel Gelber Award, Univ. of Toronto 1994) 1993, Isaiah Berlin: A Life 1998, The Warrior's Honor: Ethnic War and the Modern Conscience 1998, Virtual War: Kosovo and Beyond 2000, The Rights Revolution (Massey Lectures 2000) 2001, Human Rights as Politics and Idolatry (Tanner Lectures) 2001, Charlie Johnson in the Flames 2003, The Lesser Evil: Political Ethics in an Age of Terror 2004, True Patriot Love 2009, Fire and Ashes: Success and Failure in Politics 2013, The Ordinary Virtues: Moral Order in a Divided World 2017. *Address:* Office of the President and Rector, Central European University, First floor, Monument Building, 1051 Budapest, Nador utca 9, Hungary (office). *Telephone:* (1) 327-3004 (office). *E-mail:* ignatieffm@ceu.edu (office); president@ceu.edu (office). *Website:* www.ceu.edu (office); www.michaelignatieff.ca.

IGNATIUS, David, AB, Dipl.Econ.; American journalist and novelist; *Columnist and Associate Editor, The Washington Post;* b. 26 May 1950, Cambridge, Mass; s. of Paul Robert Ignatius and Nancy Sharpless (née Weiser); m. Eve Ignatius; three d.; ed Harvard Univ., King's Coll., Cambridge, UK; Ed. The Washington Monthly magazine 1975; reporter, The Wall Street Journal 1976–86, assignments included Steelworkers Corresp., Pittsburgh, Senate Corresp., Washington, DC, Middle East Corresp., Chief Diplomatic Corresp.; Ed. Sunday Outlook, The Washington Post 1986–90, Foreign Ed. 1990–93, apptd Asst Man. Business Ed. 1993, columnist 2003–, Assoc. Ed. 2004–; Exec. Ed. International Herald Tribune 2000–03; Fisher Family Fellow, Future of Diplomacy Project, Kennedy School of Govt, Harvard Univ. 2010, now Sr Fellow, Future of Diplomacy Project, Adjunct Lecturer, Kennedy School of Govt 2012; mem. Trilateral Comm. 2015–; Chevalier, Légion d'honneur 2010; Frank Knox Fellow, Harvard-Cambridge Univs 1973–75, Edward Weintal Prize for Diplomatic Reporting 1985, Gerald Loeb Award for Commentary 2000, Edward Weintal Certificate 2006, Urbino Press Award 2010, Founder's Award, Int. Cttee for Foreign Journalism 2010, Overseas Press Club Award for Foreign Affairs Commentary 2013, George Polk Special Award (co-recipient) 2018. *Film:* Body of Lies. *Publications include:* Agents of Innocence 1987, SIRO 1991, The Bank of Fear 1994, A Firing Offense 1997, The Sun King 1999, Body of Lies 2007, The Increment 2009, Bloodmoney 2011, The Director 2014, The Quantum Spy 2017; contribs to The New York Times Magazine, The Atlantic Monthly, Foreign Affairs and The New Republic. *Address:* The Washington Post, 1301 K Street, NW, Washington, DC 20071, USA (office). *E-mail:* davidignatius@washpost.com (office); author@davidignatius.com. *Website:* www.washingtonpost.com/people/david-ignatius (office); davidignatius.com.

IGNATIYEV, Sergei Mikhailovich, CandSci, PhD; Russian economist and banker; *Chairman of the Supervisory Board, Sberbank;* b. 10 Jan. 1948, Leningrad (now St Petersburg); m.; ed Moscow M.V. Lomonosov State Univ.; served in armed forces 1967–69; adjuster of hydroelectric equipment, Gidroelektromontazh Enterprise, Leningrad 1969–70; Sr Lecturer, Engels Leningrad Inst. of Soviet Trade 1978–88; Sr Lecturer and Assoc. Prof., Voznesenskii Leningrad Inst. of Finance and Econs 1988–91; Deputy Minister of Econs and Finance 1991–92, of Finance 1992–94, of Econs 1993–96; econ. adviser to Pres. Boris Yeltsin 1996–97; First Deputy Minister of Finance 1997–2002; Deputy Chair. Bank Rossii (Cen. Bank of the Russian Fed.) 1992–93, Chair. 2002–13, Advisor to the Chair. 2013–; Chair. Supervisory Bd, Sberbank (Savings Bank of Russian Fed.); Medal of the Order for Merit to the Fatherland (Class II) 2002, Order for Merit to the Fatherland (Class IV) 2007, Class III 2010, Class II 2013; Hon. Diploma, Russian Govt 1998; 850th Anniversary of Moscow Medal 1997, Acknowledgment by Pres. or Govt of Russian Fed. 1997, 2001, 2008, Certificate of Honour of Govt of the Russian Fed. 1998, 2013. *Publications:* numerous articles and more than 20 research papers on econs. *Address:* Sberbank, 117997 Moscow, ul. Vavilova 19, Russia (office). *Telephone:* (495) 500-55-50 (office); (495) 974-66-77 (office). *Fax:* (495) 957-57-31 (office). *E-mail:* sbrf@sberbank.ru (office); sberbank@sberbank.ru (office). *Website:* www.sberbank.ru (office).

IGRUNOV, Vyacheslav Vladimirovich; Russian politician; *Director, International Institute for Humanities and Political Studies;* b. 28 Oct. 1948, Chernitsy, Zhytomer region, Ukraine; m.; four c.; ed Odessa State Inst. of Nat. Econs; detained by KGB due to his protest against invasion of Soviet army into Czechoslovakia 1968, participated in dissident movt 1960s, arrested 1975; released after campaign by Andrei Sakharov and Aleksandr Solzhenitsyn in his defence 1977; f. Samizdat Library; mem. staff 20th Century and World (bulletin) 1987; f. ideological Movt Memorial July 1987; f. Moscow Public Information Exchange Bureau M-BIO, newspaper Panorama 1988; Head of Programme Civil Soc. Foundation of Cultural Initiative 1990–92; Head of Analytical Centre in Goscomnats; currently Dir Int. Inst. for Humanities and Political Studies; mem. State Duma (Parl.) 1993–2003; Deputy Chair. public movt Yabloko 1996–2000, mem. faction Yabloko 1993–2003; mem. Expert Bd of Fed. Council (Parl.) 2005–11; Co-Founder and Chair. Russian public movement 'Russian Concert' 2011–. *Publications:* Problematics of Social Movements 1972, Informal Political Clubs in Moscow 1989, Economic Reform as One of the Sources of National Clashes 1993, Russia and Ukraine 2001, Common Future 2004, The Shadow Theatre on the Eve of Distemper 2005, Phantoms of Freedom, Equality, and Fraternity 2005, The East is Rising 2006, Nationalism is Exported from the West 2006, The Year Results. A View from Russia 2007, The End of Multi-Ethnicity 2007, Fundamentalistic Liberalism has Ceased to Exist 2008, Iran in the Center of Interests of World Powers in the 21st Century 2009, Chechens and Russians by S. Maksudov (Chief Ed.) 2010, Who Has Won the Elections 2011, The Count-Down for the Regime Has Started 2011, The First Stage of Political Evolution 2012, What If Russia Disappears Tomorrow? 2012. *Leisure interests:* reading history books, writing memoirs and poetry. *Address:* International Institute for Humanities and Political Studies, Tverskaya str. 7, PO Box 82, 1250095 Moscow, Russia (office). *Telephone:* (985) 761-99-61 (office); (916) 860-84-40 (home). *E-mail:* igrunov@igpi.ru (office). *Website:* www.igrunov.ru.

IHAMUOTILA, Jaakko, MSEng; Finnish business executive (retd); b. 15 Nov. 1939, Helsinki; s. of Veikko Artturi Ihamuotila and Anna-Liisa Ihamuotila (née Kouki); m. Tuula Elina Turja 1965; two s. one d.; ed Univ. of Tech., Helsinki; Asst in Reactor Tech. 1963–66, Acting Asst to Prof. of Physics 1964–66; with Canadian Gen. Electric Co. Ltd, Toronto 1966; Imatran Voima Oy 1966–68; Valmet Oy 1968–70, Asst Dir 1970–72, Dir of Planning 1972–73, Man. Dir 1973–79, mem. Bd 1980–82; Pres. Int. Council of Acads. of Eng and Technological Sciences 2001; mem. Bd Neste Oy 1979, Chair. and Chief Exec. 1980–98, now retd; Chair. Asko Oy, Silja Oy Ab, Chemical Industry Fed. of Finland; Chair. Millennium Prize Foundation, Finnish Acads of Tech. 2002–08; mem. Supervisory Bd Merita Bank Ltd 1996–2000, MTV Finland 1993–97, Finnish Cultural Foundation a.o.; mem. Bd of Dirs Nordea Bank Finland, Finnair 1984–87, Confed. of Finnish Industry and Employers, Pohjola Insurance Co., Fortum Corpn 1998–2000, Raisio plc 2000–05; mem. Council Econ. Orgs in Finland, Nat. Bd of Econ. Defence, Council of Univ. of Tech.; Hon. DTech. *Leisure interests:* tennis, outdoor pursuits.

IHAMUOTILA, Timo, MSc(Econ); Finnish business executive; *Chief Financial Officer, ABB Ltd;* b. 21 April 1966, Helsinki; m.; three c.; ed Helsinki School of Econs; analyst, Assets and Liability Man., Kansallis Bank 1990–93; with Nokia 1993–96, rejoined 1999, Man. Dealing and Risk Man. 1993–96, Dir Corp. Finance 1999–2000, Vice-Pres. Finance, and Corp. Treas. 2000–04, Sr Vice-Pres. CDMA Business Unit, Mobile Phones 2004–07, Exec. Vice-Pres. Sales and Portfolio Man., Mobile Phones 2007, Exec. Vice-Pres. Sales, Markets 2008–09, Group Chief Financial Officer (CFO) 2011–15, Exec. Vice-Pres. and CFO Nokia Corpn 2009–16, Interim Pres. 2013–14, mem. Nokia Leadership Team 2007–, Chair. 2013–; Vice-Pres. Nordic Derivatives Sales, Citibank plc 1996–99; CFO and mem. Group Exec. Cttee ABB Ltd 2017–; mem. Bd of Dirs Nokia Solutions and Networks BV, Uponor Corpn, Cen. Chamber of Commerce of Finland. *Leisure interests:* tennis, skiing, reading, spending time with his family. *Website:* new.abb.com (office).

IHSANOĞLU, Ekmeleddin, BSc, MSc, PhD; Turkish academic and international organization official; b. 26 Dec. 1943, Cairo, Egypt; m. Füsun Bilgiç 1971; three s.; ed Ankara Univ.; cataloguer of printed and manuscript books, Dept of Oriental Studies, Cairo Nat. Library 1962–66; Lecturer in Turkish Literature and Language, Ain Shams Univ., Cairo 1966–70, Ankara Univ., Turkey 1971–75; Research Fellow, Univ. of Exeter, UK 1975–77; Lecturer and Assoc. Prof., Faculty of Science, Ankara Univ. 1970–80; Assoc. Prof., İnönü Univ., Malatya, Turkey 1978–80; Dir-Gen. Islamic Conf. Research Centre for Islamic History, Art and Culture, Org. of Islamic Conf. (now Org. of the Islamic Cooperation), Istanbul 1980–2004, Sec.-Gen. Org. of the Islamic Cooperation (OIC), Jeddah, Saudi Arabia 2005–13; Sec., Islamic Conf. Org. Int. Comm. for Preservation of Islamic Cultural Heritage, Istanbul 1983–2000 (now defunct); Founder-Chair. Dept of History of Science in Turkey, Univ. of Istanbul 1984–2000; apptd Chair. Turkish Soc. for History of Science, Istanbul 1989; Vice-Chair. Al Furqan Islamic Heritage Foundation, London, UK 1998–; Pres. Int. Union of History and Philosophy of Science/Div. of History of Science 2001; mem. numerous orgs concerned with study of history of science and Islamic civilization, including Acad. Int. d'Histoire des Sciences, Paris, Cultural Centre of the Atatürk Supreme Council for Culture, Language and History, Ankara, Int. Soc. for History of Arabic and Islamic Sciences and Philosophy, Paris, Royal Acad. of Islamic Civilization Research, Jordan, Middle East and the Balkans, Research Foundation, Istanbul, Acad. of Arabic Language (Jordan, Egypt, Syria), Egyptian History Soc., Cairo, Tunisian Acad. of Sciences, Letters and Arts 'Bait al Hikma', Tunis, Int. Soc. for History of Medicine, Paris; apptd Amb.-at-Large by Govt of Bosnia-Herzegovina 1997; Visiting Prof., Ludwig Maximilians Univ., Munich, Germany 2003; cand. in presidential election 2014; Hon. Consul, The Gambia 1990; Commdr de l'Ordre Nat. du Mérit (Senegal) 2002, Commdr de l'Ordre Nat. du Lion (Senegal) 2006; Dr hc (Mimar Sinan Univ., Istanbul) 1994, (Dowling Coll., New York) 1996, (Azerbaijan Acad. of Sciences) 2000, (Univ. of Sofia) 2001, (Univ. of Sarajevo) 2001, (Univ. of Padova) 2006, (Islamic Univ. of Islamabad) 2007, (Univ. of Exeter) 2007, (Islamic Univ., Uganda) 2008; Distinction of the First Order Medal (Egypt) 1990, Certificate of Honour and Distinction, OIC 1995, Independence Medal of the First Order (Jordan) 1996, Medal of Distinguished State Service (Turkey) 2000, World Prize for Book of the Year (Iran) 2000, UNESCO Avicenna Medal 2004, Medal of Glory (Russia) 2006, Medal of Glory (Azerbaijan) 2006, Int. Acad. of History of Science Alexandre Koyre Medal 2008. *Publications include:* has written, edited and translated several books on Islamic culture and science; over 70 articles and papers. *Leisure interests:* reading and music, sponsoring and collecting Islamic works of art. *Address:* Türk Bostani Sokak, Dostlar Sitesi 35, Yenikoy 34464 Istanbul, Turkey (home).

IIJIMA, Masami; Japanese business executive; *Representative Director and Chairman, Mitsui & Company Limited;* ed Yokohama Nat. Univ.; has served in a variety of positions at Mitsui & Co. UK Plc and Mitsui & Co. Ltd since 1974, Man. Officer and COO of Iron and Steel Raw Materials and Non-Ferrous Metals Business Unit, Mitsui & Co. Ltd 2006–07, Man. Officer and COO of Mineral and Metal Resources Business Unit 2007–08, Exec. Man. Officer April–June 2008, Rep. Dir and Exec. Man. Officer June–Oct. 2008, Rep. Dir and Sr Exec. Man. Officer Oct. 2008–April 2009, Rep. Dir, Pres. and CEO April 2009–15, Rep. Dir and Chair. 2015–; mem. Bd of Dirs, Companhia Vale do Rio Doce 2008. *Address:* Mitsui & Co. Ltd, 2-1 Ohtemachi 1-chome, Chiyoda-ku, Tokyo 100-0004, Japan (office). *Telephone:* (3) 3285-1111 (office). *Fax:* (3) 3285-9819 (office). *E-mail:* info@mitsui.com (office). *Website:* www.mitsui.com (office).

IIJIMA, Sumio, BEng, PhD; Japanese physicist and academic; *Professor, Meijo University;* b. 2 May 1939, Saitama Prefecture; ed Univ. of Electro-

Communications, Tokyo, Tohoku Univ., Ariz. State Univ., USA; Research Assoc., Research Inst. for Scientific Measurements, Tohoku Univ. 1968–70; Postdoctoral Research Fellow and Research Scientist, Ariz. State Univ., USA 1970–82; Visiting Scholar, Univ. of Cambridge, UK 1979; Researcher, Research Devt Corpn, Japan 1982–87; Prof., Dept of Materials Science and Eng, Meijo Univ., Nagoya 1999–; Sr Research Fellow, NEC Corpn, Ibaraki 1987–; Research Dir, Nanotubulite Project, Int. Cooperative Research Project (ICORP), Japan Science and Tech. Agency Corpn 1998–2002; Dir Research Center for Advanced Carbon Materials, Nat. Inst. of Advanced Science and Tech. (AIST) 2001–; Project Reader, NEDO Advanced Nanocarbon Application Project 2002–06, Carbon Nanotube Capacitator Devt Project 2006–; Research Dir, JST/SORST Iijima Team 2003–08; Dean, Sungkyunkwan Univ. Advanced Inst. of Nanotechnology 2005–; Distinguished Invited Univ. Prof., Nagoya Univ. 2007–; mem. Royal Microscopy Soc., Materials Research Soc., American Crystallographic Asscn, Science Council of Japan, Physical Soc. of Japan, Chemical Soc. of Japan; Foreign Assoc., NAS 2007; Foreign mem. Norwegian Acad. of Science and Letters 2009; Fellow, Japan Soc. for Applied Physics 2007; Foreign Fellow, Chinese Acad. of Science 2011; Hon. Prof., Xi'an Jiaotong Univ. 2005, Peking Univ. 2005, Tsinghua Univ. 2009, Zhejiang Univ. 2010, Southeast Univ. 2010, Hon. mem. Crystallographic Soc. of Japan, Japanese Soc. of Microscopy, Hon. Fellow, American Physical Soc., Royal Microscopy Soc., Advanced Industrial Science and Technology (AIST) 2015–; Order of Cultural Merits 2009; Dr hc (Antwerp) 2002, (École Polytechnique Fédérale de Lausanne) 2003, (Aalto Univ.) 2014; Bertram Eugene Warren Diffraction Physics Award 1976, Seto Award 1980, Nishina Memorial Award 1985, Asahi Award 1996, Tsukuba Prize 1998, Agilent Technologies Europhysics Prize 2001, Benjamin Franklin Medal in Physics 2002, American Physical Soc. McGroddy Materials Prize 2002, Japan Acad. Award and Imperial Award 2002, Outstanding Achievement Award, Japan Soc. of Applied Physics 2002, Person of Cultural Merits 2003, Soc. Medal, American Carbon Soc. 2004, Distinguished Scientist Award, Microscopy Soc. of America 2005, John M. Cowley Medal 2006, Gregori Aminoff Prize 2007, Fujiwara Award 2007, Balzan Prize 2007, Plueddemann Award 2008, Kavli Prize in Nanoscience 2008, Prince of Asturias Award for Tech. Scientific Research 2008, Economist Innovation Awards 'No Boundaries' 2008. *Achievements include:* discovered carbon nanotubes 1991. *Address:* Meijo University, Faculty of Science and Technology, 1-501, Shiogamaguchi, Tenpaku, Nogoya, Aichi 468-8502, Japan (office). *Telephone:* (52) 834-4001 (office). *Fax:* (52) 834-4001 (office). *E-mail:* iijimas@ccmfs.meijo-u.ac.jp (office). *Website:* www.meijo-u.ac.jp/english/academics/sci_tech/materials.html (office).

IIMURA, Yutaka; Japanese diplomatist; *Special Envoy of Government of Japan for Middle East;* b. 16 Oct. 1946; joined Ministry of Foreign Affairs 1969, Dir of Tech. Co-operation 1988, Dir of Press 1990, Asst Dir-Gen., Europe Dept 1997, Dir-Gen. of Econ. Co-operation 1999, Deputy Vice Foreign Minister 2001; Second Sec., Embassy in Moscow 1977, First Sec., Embassy in Paris 1979, First Sec., later Counsellor Embassy in Pasay City, Philippines 1985, Counsellor, later Minister Embassy in Washington, DC 1992, Minister Embassy in Paris 1995, Amb. to Indonesia 2002–06, to France 2006–09, Special Envoy of Govt of Japan for Middle East 2009–. *Address:* Ministry of Foreign Affairs, Kasumigaseki 2-2-1, Chiyoda-ku, Tokyo 100-8919, Japan (office). *Telephone:* (3) 3580-3311 (office). *Fax:* (3) 3581-2667 (office). *E-mail:* webmaster@mofa.go.jp (office). *Website:* www.mofa.go.jp (office).

IIPUMBU, Leonard Nangolo; Namibian diplomatist and banker (retd); m. Hilma Ndapewa Iipumbu; four c.; Deputy Rep. to Zambia 1980–83, Chief Rep. to Botswana 1984–87, People's Repub. of Congo 1988–89; mem. protocol sub-Cttee for Namibian independence celebrations 1990; Special Envoy to the Congo 1991, Amb. to France (also accred to Italy, Portugal and Spain) 1992–99, to USA (also accred to Mexico and Brazil) 1999–2004; CEO Agricultural Bank of Namibia 2004–16.

IKAWA, Motomichi, PhD cand.; Japanese banking and finance executive and academic; *Professor, Graduate School of Business, Nihon University;* b. 10 Feb. 1947, Tokyo; m. Yoshiko Ikawa; ed Tokyo Univ., Univ. of California, Berkeley; economist, Balance of Payments Div., OECD, Paris 1976–79; various man. posts at Ministry of Finance, Tokyo 1979–85; Asst Regional Commr, CID, Osaka Taxation Bureau 1985–86; Dir Budget, Personnel and Man. Systems Dept, Asian Devt Bank 1986–89; Asst Vice-Minister of Finance, Int. Affairs 1989–90; Dir Int. Org. Div., Int. Finance Bureau, Ministry of Finance 1990–91, Foreign Exchange and Money Market Div. 1991–92, Devt Policy Div. 1992–93, Co-ordination Div. 1993–94; Man. Dir Co-ordination Dept, Overseas Econ. Co-operation Fund 1994–96; Deputy Dir-Gen. Int. Finance Bureau 1996–97, Sr Deputy Dir-Gen. 1997–98; Exec. Vice-Pres. Multilateral Investment Guarantee Agency, World Bank Group 1998–2004; Prof., Nihon Univ. Grad. School of Business, Tokyo 2004–; mem. Bd of Dirs Transcultural Man. Soc., Japan Platform. *Publications:* Exchange Market Interventions during the Yen Depreciation 1980 1982, IMF Handbook 1990, The Role of the Overseas Economic Co-operation Fund Towards 2010 1994. *Leisure interests:* tennis, golf, hiking. *Address:* Nihon University Graduate School of Business, Kudanminami 4-8-24, Chiyoda-ku, Tokyo 102-8275, Japan (office). *Telephone:* (3) 5275-9440 (office). *Fax:* (3) 5275-8327 (office). *E-mail:* ikawa.motomichi@nihon-u.ac.jp (office). *Website:* www.gsb.nihon-u.ac.jp (office).

IKE, Fumihiko; Japanese automotive industry executive; joined Honda in 1982, positions held include Chief Dir of IT, Risk Man. Officer, Sr Man. Exec. Officer, Chief Dir of Multi-purpose Business, Chief Dir of Asia and Pacific and Chief Dir of Business Admin, Chair. and Rep. Dir, Honda Motor Co. Ltd 2013–16 (retd); Chair. Japan Automobile Manufacturers Asscn, Inc. 2014–16.

IKEDA, Daisaku; Japanese Buddhist philosopher, peace activist and author; *President, Soka Gakkai International;* b. 2 Jan. 1928, Tokyo; s. of Nenokichi Ikeda and Ichi Ikeda; m. Kaneko Shiraki 1952; two s.; ed Fuji Coll.; Pres. Soka Gakkai 1960–79, Hon. Pres. 1979–, Pres. Soka Gakkai Int. 1975–; Founder Soka Univ., Soka Univ. of America, Soka Women's Coll., Tokyo and Kansai Soka Schools, Soka Kindergartens (Japan, Hong Kong, Singapore, Malaysia, Brazil and S Korea), Makiguchi Foundation for Educ., Inst. of Oriental Philosophy, Ikeda Center for Peace, Learning and Dialogue, Toda Inst. for Global Peace and Policy Research, Tokyo Fuji Art Museum, Min-On Concert Asscn, Victor Hugo House of Literature and Komeito Party; mem. Advisory Bd World Centers of Compassion for Children International, Ireland 2004–; Poet Laureate, World Acad. of Arts and Culture 1981–; World People's Poet, World Poetry Soc. Intercontinental, India 2007–; Foreign mem. Künstlerhaus, Austria 1991–, Brazilian Acad. of Letters 1993–; Hon. Prof., Nat. Univ. of San Marcos 1981, Peking Univ. 1984, Tsinghua Univ. 2010, Nat. Taiwan Normal Univ. 2012, Al-Farabi Kazakh Nat. Univ. 2012 and others; Hon. Senator, European Acad. of Sciences and Arts 1997–; Hon. Adviser, World Fed. of UN Asscns 1999–; Hon. mem. The Club of Rome 1996–, Inst. of Oriental Studies of Russian Acad. of Sciences 1996–, Photographic Soc. of Singapore 1999–, Russian Acad. of Arts 2007–; Hon. Dir, Jao Tsung-I Petite Ecole, Univ. of Hong Kong 2011– and others; Grand Cross, Order of the Sun (Peru) 1984, Grand Cross, Order of May for Merit (Argentina) 1990, Commdr, Nat. Order of Southern Cross (Brazil) 1990, Kt Grand Cross of the Most Noble Order of the Crown (Thailand) 1991, Austrian Cross of Honour for Science and Art, First Class 1992, Kt Grand Cross of Rizal (Philippines) 1996, Grande Officiale, Ordine al Merito (Italy) 2006, Order of Friendship (Russia) 2008, Hwa-Gwan Order of Cultural Merit (Repub. of Korea) 2009, Order of Peace, First Class, Ukrainian Peace Council 2012 and others; Dr hc (Moscow State Univ.) 1975, (Sofia) 1981, (Buenos Aires) 1990, (Univ. of the Philippines) 1991, (Ankara) 1992, (Fed. Univ. of Rio de Janeiro) 1993, (Glasgow) 1994, (Hong Kong) 1996, (Havana) 1996, (Univ. of Ghana) 1996, (Delhi) 1998, (Kyung Hee Univ.) 1998, (Sydney) 2000, (Morehouse Coll.) 2002, (Univ. of Guadalajara) 2004, (Visva-Bharati Univ.) 2006, (Palermo) 2007, (Univ. Coll. South, Denmark) 2009, (Queen's Univ., Belfast) 2009, (Universitas Indonesia) 2009, (Université Laval) 2010, (George Mason Univ.) 2010, (Univ. of Malaya) 2010, (Univ. of Massachusetts, Boston) 2010, (Pukyong Nat. Univ.) 2011, (Buckingham) 2011, (Guelph) 2012, (KwaZulu-Natal) 2013, (Thammasat) 2013 and others; UN Peace Award 1983, Kenya Oral Literature Award 1986, UNHCR Humanitarian Award 1989, Rosa Parks Humanitarian Award (USA) 1993, Simon Wiesenthal Center Int. Tolerance Award (USA) 1993, Tagore Peace Award, The Asiatic Soc. (India) 1997, Peace Gold Medal, Sydney Peace Foundation 2009, Goethe Medal, Goethe Soc., Weimar 2009 and others. *Publications include:* The Human Revolution Vols I–VI 1972–99, The Living Buddha 1976, Choose Life (with A. Toynbee) 1976 (revised edn 2007), Buddhism: The First Millennium 1977 (revised edn 2009), Songs from My Heart 1978, Glass Children and Other Essays 1979, A Lasting Peace Vols I–II 1981, 1987, Life: An Enigma, a Precious Jewel 1982, Before It Is Too Late (with A. Peccei) 1984 (revised edn 2009), Buddhism and the Cosmos (co-author) 1985, The Flower of Chinese Buddhism 1986, Human Values in a Changing World (with B. Wilson) 1987 (revised edn 2008), Unlocking the Mysteries of Birth and Death 1988 (revised edn 2003), The Snow Country Prince 1990, A Lifelong Quest for Peace (with L. Pauling) 1992 (revised edn 2009), Choose Peace (with J. Galtung) 1995, A New Humanism: The University Addresses of Daisaku Ikeda 1996 (revised edn 2010), The New Human Revolution, Vols I–XXVI (in Japanese) 1995–, The Wisdom of the Lotus Sutra, Vols I–VI 2000–03, For the Sake of Peace 2001, Soka Education 2001, The World is Yours to Change 2002, Choose Hope (with D. Krieger) 2002, Alborada del Pacífico (with P. Aylwin) 2002, On Being Human (with R. Simard and G. Bourgeault) 2002, Global Civilization: A Buddhist–Islamic Dialogue (with M. Tehranian) 2003, Fighting for Peace 2004, Planetary Citizenship (with H. Henderson) 2004, One by One 2004, Moral Lessons of the Twentieth Century (with M. Gorbachev) 2005, Revolutions: To Green the Environment, To Grow the Human Heart (with M. S. Swaminathan) 2005, A Quest for Global Peace (with J. Rotblat) 2006, Dawn after Dark (with R. Huyghe) 2007, A Dialogue between East and West (with R. Díez-Hochleitner) 2008, Embracing the Future 2008, A Passage to Peace (with N. Yalman) 2008, Search for A New Humanity (with J. Derbolav) 2008, Ode to the Grand Spirit (with C. Aitmatov) 2009, Human Rights in the Twenty-first Century (with A. de Athayde) 2009, Creating Waldens (with R. Bosco and J. Myerson) 2009, The Persistence of Religion (with H. G. Cox) 2009, Dialog Peradaban untuk Toleransi dan Perdamaian (with A. Wahid) (in Indonesian) 2010, Into Full Flower (with E. Boulding) 2010, Discussions on Youth 2010, New Horizons in Eastern Humanism (with W. Tu) 2011, The Inner Philosopher (with L. Marinoff) 2012, America Will Be! Conversations on Hope, Freedom and Democracy (with V. Harding) 2013, Compassionate Light in Asia (with Y. Jin) 2013, José Martí Cuban Apostle: A Dialogue (with C. Vitier) 2013, A Forum for Peace: Daisaku Ikeda's Proposals to the UN 2014, The Art of True Relations: Conversations on the Poetic Heart of Human Possibility (with S. Wider) 2014, Journey of Life, Selected Poems of Daisaku Ikeda 2014, Our World To Make (with V. Nanda) 2015, Walking with the Mahatma (with N. Radhakrishnan) 2015 and other writings on Buddhism, civilization, life and peace. *Leisure interests:* poetry, photography. *Address:* 32 Shinano-machi, Shinjuku-ku, Tokyo 160-8583, Japan (office). *Telephone:* (3) 5360-9831 (office). *Fax:* (3) 5360-9885 (office). *E-mail:* contact@sgi.org (office). *Website:* www.sgi.org (office); www.daisakuikeda.org.

IKOUÉBÉ, Basile; Republic of the Congo diplomatist and politician; b. 1 July 1946; m.; six c.; ed Int. Inst. of Public Admin, Paris, Inst. for Political Studies, Bordeaux; apptd Chief Int. Orgs Div., Ministry of Foreign Affairs 1974, Prin. Pvt. Sec. to Minister 1975–77, Sec. to Ministry 1977–79; training assignment in France 1980–82; Diplomatic Adviser to Head of State 1982–92; Minister and Prin. Pvt. Sec. to Head of State 1987–94; Amb.-at-Large 1994–95; Sec. to Ministry of Foreign Affairs and Co-operation 1996–98; Amb. and Perm. Rep. to UN, New York 1998–2007, Pres. UN Security Council 2006; Minister of Foreign Affairs and Co-operation 2007–15.

IKUTA, Masaharu; Japanese business executive; ed Keio Univ.; joined Mitsui OSK Lines Ltd 1957, mem. Bd of Dirs 1987–2003, Pres. 1994–2000, Chair. 2000–03, Corp. Advisor and Counselor 2007–; Pres. Japan Post (now Japan Post Holdings Co., Ltd) 2003–07; Chair. Business and Industry Advisory Cttee, Japan Fed. of Econ. Orgs (Nippon Keidanren) –2003; fmr Vice-Chair. Japan Asscn of Corp. Execs; mem. Bd of Dirs SourceNext Corpn 2008–, Terumo Corpn, Aeon Co. 2009–; mem. Int. Advisory Council, PSA Corpn Ltd 2002; Hon. Consul of the Repub. of Mauritius 2002–; Blue Ribbon Medal Award 1998. *Address:* Mitsui OSK Lines Ltd, 1-1 Toranomon 2-chome, Minato-ku, Tokyo 105-8688, Japan (office).

ILIA II, Catholicos-Patriarch of All Georgia; Georgian ecclesiastic; b. (Irakli Ghudushauri-Shiolashvili), 4 Dec. 1933, Vladikavkaz, N Ossetian ASSR, Russian SFSR, USSR; ed Moscow Theological Seminary, Moscow Theological Acad.; took monastic vows 1957; Father-Superior 1960; Archimandrite 1961; Bishop of Shemokmedi and Vicar to the Georgian Patriarch Ephrem II Aug. 1963; entrusted with Sukhumi and Abkhazia Diocese 1967; Sukhumi-Abkhaz Metropolitanate 1969; Rector Mtskheta Orthodox Theological Seminary 1963–72; awarded Second Panagya 1972; enthroned as Archbishop of Mtskheta-Tbilisi and Catholicos-

Patriarch of All Georgia 1977–; Co-Pres. WCC 1978–83; Dr of Theology, American St-Vladimir Theological Acad.; Hon. Academician, Georgian Acad. of Sciences 2003, Int. Acad. for Promotion of Scientific Research 2007; Order of Friendship of Peoples; Hon. DTheol (St Vladimir's Orthodox Theological Seminary, New York, USA) 1986, (Acad. of Sciences, Crete) 1997, (St Tikhon's Orthodox Theological Seminary, Pa, USA) 1998; holder of highest awards of churches of Georgia, Constantinople, Alexandria, Antioch, Jerusalem, Russia, Czechoslovakia and Poland; David Guramishvili Prize 2008. *Address:* Patriarchate of the Georgian Orthodox Church, 0105 Tbilisi, Erekle II Moedani 1, Georgia. *Telephone:* (32) 99-03-78. *Fax:* (32) 98-71-14. *E-mail:* orthodox@patriarchate.ge. *Website:* www.patriarchate.ge.

ILIESCU, Ion; Romanian hydropower engineer and fmr head of state; *Honorary President, Social Democratic Party;* b. 3 March 1930, Oltenița, Ilfov Dist; s. of Alexandru Iliescu; m. Elena (Nina) Şerbănescu 1951; ed Bucharest Polytechnic Inst. and Energy Inst., Moscow, USSR; researcher, Energy Eng Inst., Bucharest 1955; Pres. Union of Student Asscns 1957–60; Alt. mem. Cen. Cttee of RCP 1965–68, mem. 1968–84; First Sec. Cen. Cttee of Union of Communist Youth and Minister for Youth 1967–71; Sec. RCP Cen. Cttee 1971; Vice-Chair. Timiş Co. Council 1971–74; Chair Iaşi Co. Council 1974–79; accused of "intellectual deviationism" and kept under surveillance; Chair. Nat. Water Council 1979–84; Dir Tech. Publishing House, Bucharest 1984–89; Pres. Nat. Salvation Front 1989–90, Provisional Council for Nat. Unity Feb.–May 1990; Pres. of Romania 1990–96, 2000–04; Senator 1996–2000, 2004–08; fmr Pres. Party of Social Democracy of Romania (merged with SDP to become Social Democratic Party 2001), now Hon. Pres.; Chevalier de la Légion d'honneur and other state decorations; hon. doctorates from numerous univs. *Publications:* Global Problems and Creativity, Revolution and Reform, Romania in Europe and in the World, Where is Romanian Society Going?, Romanian Revolution, Hope Reborn, Integration and Globalisation – A Romanian Vision, Romanian Culture and European Identity, For Sustainable Development, The Great Shock at the End of a Short Century, Fragments of Life and of Lived History; studies on water man. and ecology, political power and social relations. *Leisure interests:* global problems, political and econ. sciences. *Address:* Molièrestr. 3, Bucharest, Romania (home).

ILIOPOULOS, John, PhD; Greek physicist and academic; b. 1940, Kalamata; m.; one s.; ed École Normale Supérieure, France; Scholar, European Org. for Nuclear Research (CERN), Geneva 1966–68; Research Assoc., Harvard Univ. 1969–71; joined Centre nat. de la recherche scientifique (CNRS) 1971; Dir Theoretical Physics Lab., École Normale Supérieure, Paris 1991–95, 1998–2002, now Hon. Mem.; J.J. Sakurai Prize for Theoretical Particle Physics (co-recipient) 1987, Aristeio Prize (first recipient) 2002, Dirac Medal, Abdus Salam Int. Centre for Theoretical Physics 2007. *Achievements include:* first to present the Standard Model of particle physics in a single report 1974; also first, along with colleagues Glashow and Maiani, to recognize the critical importance of a fourth quark, later known as the 'Charm quark'. *Publications:* numerous scientific papers in professional journals. *Website:* www.phys.ens.fr.

İLKER BAŞBUĞ, Gen. Mehmet; Turkish army officer; b. 29 April 1943, Afyon Prov.; m. Sevil Başbuğ; two c.; ed Turkish Mil. Acad., Army Staff Coll., Royal Mil. Acad., Sandhurst, UK, NATO Defense Coll., Rome, Italy; infantry officer 1963, Platoon and Commando Co. Commdr –1970, Deputy Chief of Gen. Staff (Operations Planning Command) 1973, later Instructor, Army Staff Coll.; fmr Chief of Intelligence Div. (Intelligence Plans), Supreme HQ Allied Powers Europe (SHAPE), Mons, Belgium; Chief of Staff of Defence Intelligence (Army Plans and Principles Command), later Commdr, 247th Infantry Regt of 51st Infantry Brigade, rank of Brig. Gen. 1989, rank of Maj.-Gen. 1993; fmr Deputy Commdr, Turkish Gendarmerie Public Order Command; Chief of Nat. Mil. Representation (NMR), Mons, Belgium 1993–95; rank of Gen. 2002, Deputy Commdr of Turkish Army 2002–03, Deputy Chief of Gen. Staff 2003–05, Commdr of the First Army 2005–06, Commdr of Turkish Army 2006–08, Chief of Gen. Staff 2008–10; arrested on terror charges 2012, convicted and sentenced to prison, had conviction overturned Constitutional Court 2014; Nishan-ı Imtiaz (Order of Distinction of Pakistan); Turkish Armed Forces Medal of Distinguished Courage and Self-Sacrifice, Turkish Armed Forces Medal of Honour, Golden Medal of the Eagle of the Repub. of Albania 2009.

ILLARIONOV, Andrei Nikolayevich, PhD; Russian economist; b. 16 Sept. 1961, Leningrad (now St Petersburg); ed Leningrad Univ., Univ. of Birmingham, UK, Georgetown Univ., USA; Asst Researcher, Leningrad State Univ. 1983–90; Head of Sector, St Petersburg Financial and Econ. Inst. 1990–92; Deputy Dir Centre for Econ. Reforms, Russian Govt 1992–93; Adviser to the Prime Minister 1993–94; Dir Inst. of Econ. Analysis 1994–2000, Pres. 2000–; Adviser to Pres. Putin on Econ. Problems 2000–05 (resgnd); Russian Sherpa to G8 2000–05 (resgnd); Sr Fellow, Center for Global Liberty and Prosperity, Cato Inst., Washington, DC 2006–; took part in opposition Dissenters' Marches in Moscow and St Petersburg 2007; one of the 34 first signatories of online anti-Putin manifesto 'Putin Must Go', published March 2010. *Publications:* Russian Economic Reforms: Lost Year 1994, Financial Stabilization in Russia 1995, Russia in a Changing World 1997, Economic Freedom of the World (co-author and co-ed.) 2000; more than 300 articles on Russian econ. and social policy. *Address:* Cato Institute, 1000 Massachusetts Avenue, NW, Washington, DC 20001-5403, USA (office). *Telephone:* (202) 789-5200 (office). *Fax:* (202) 842-3490 (office). *E-mail:* aIllarionov@cato.org (office). *Website:* www.cato.org/people/andrei-illarionov (office).

ILLNEROVÁ, Helena, DSc; Czech physiologist and academic; *Professor Emerita, Institute of Physiology, Academy of Sciences of the Czech Republic;* b. (Helena Lagusova), 28 Dec. 1937, Prague; d. of Karel Lagus and Libuše Lagusova; m. Michal Illner; one s. one d.; ed Charles Univ., Prague; researcher, Inst. of Physiology Acad. of Sciences of Czechoslovakia (of Czech Repub. since 1993), Prague 1961–, Vice-Pres. Acad. of Sciences of the Czech Republic, Prague 1993–2001, Pres. 2001–05, now Prof. Emer., Inst. of Physiology; Pres. Czech Comm. for UNESCO 2006–12, Learned Soc. of the Czech Repub. 2008–10, Comm. for Ethics in Science 2005–13; mem. European Research Advisory Bd 2001–07, Ethics Panel of Czech TV 2005–12, Council for Science of Acad. of Sciences of the Czech Repub. 2005–13, Council for Science of Charles Univ. 2001–14; unsuccessful cand. for the Senate 2008; State Medal for Merits 2005; J.E. Purkyně Prize 1987, Medal of the Slovak Acad. of Sciences 2004, Charles Univ. Gold Medal 2005, Votočkova Medal, Inst. of Chemical Tech. 2005, Award of the Ministry for Educ. 2005, Medal of the Learned Soc. of the Czech Repub. 2007, ASCR Medal of Merit for Science and Humanity 2007, ASCR G.J. Mendel Medal 2013. *Publications:* more than 130 scientific publs. *Leisure interests:* literature, hiking, biking, grandchildren, academic activities. *Address:* Bronzová 2021/23, 155 00 Prague 5 (home); Institute of Physiology, Academy of Sciences, Vídeňská 1083, 142 20 Prague 4, Czech Republic (office). *Telephone:* (2) 41062528 (office); (2) 35512182 (home). *Fax:* (2) 21403525 (office). *E-mail:* illner@biomed.cas.cz (office); illnerova@kav.cas.cz (office). *Website:* www.cas.cz (office); www.helenaillnerova.cz.

ILVES, Toomas Hendrik, MA; Estonian politician, diplomatist, scientist and fmr head of state; b. 26 Dec. 1953, Stockholm, Sweden; m. 1st Merry Bullock (divorced); one s. one d.; m. 2nd Evelin Int-Lambot 2004 (divorced 2015); one d.; m. 3rd Ieva Kupče 2016; ed Leonia High School, New Jersey, Columbia Univ., New York, Univ. of Pennsylvania, USA; Research Asst, Dept of Psychology, Columbia Univ. 1974–76, 1979; Asst to Dir and English Teacher, Center for Open Educ., Englewood, New Jersey 1979–81; Arts Admin. and Dir Vancouver Literary Centre, Canada 1981–82; Lecturer in Estonian Literature and Linguistics, Dept of Interdisciplinary Studies, Simon Fraser Univ., Vancouver 1983–84; Research Analyst, Radio Free Europe, Munich, Germany 1984–88, Dir Estonian Service 1988–93; Amb. to USA (also accred to Canada and Mexico) 1993–96; Minister of Foreign Affairs 1996–98, 1999–2002; Chair. Bd Estonian N Atlantic Trust 1998; Deputy Chair. Rahvaerakond Mõõdukad (People's Party Moderates), Chair. 1999; mem. Riigikogu (Estonian State Ass.) 2002–04; mem. European Parl. (Sotsiaaldemokraatlik Erakond—Estonian Social Democratic Party) 2004–06, Vice-Chair. Cttee on Foreign Affairs, mem. Del. for Relations with the USA, Substitute mem. Cttee on Budgets, Sub-cttee on Security and Defence, Del. to EU-Russia Parl. Cooperation Cttee; Pres. of Estonia 2006–16; Pres. Estonian Special Olympics 1997–2004; Bd mem. Tartu Univ. 1996–2003, European Movt Estonia 1999–2004, Estonian Acad. of Arts 2004–06, Trilateral Comm. 2004–06, Friends of Europe (think tank) 2005, Viljandi Co. Municipal Fund, Council on CyberSecurity's Advisory Bd 2013; numerous decorations, including Grand Commdr, Légion d'honneur 2001, Third Class, Order of the Seal (Estonia) 2004, Three Star Order of the Repub. (Latvia) 2004, Hon. GCB (UK) 2006, Order of the White Rose of Finland 2007, Grand Cordon of the Supreme Order of the Chrysanthemum of Japan 2007, Order of Isabel the Catholic with collar (Spain) 2007, Collar of the Order of the Nat. Coat of Arms (Estonia) 2008, Grand Cross, Order of the Netherlands Lion 2008, Grand Cordon, Leopold of Belgium 2008, Chain of the Order of the Three Stars (Latvia) 2009, Grand Cross of the Order of Merit (Hungary) 2009, Order of St George (Georgia) 2010, Nat. Order Star of Romania in rank of Collar 2011, Dostyk (Friendship) Star Award I (Kazakhstan) 2011, Grand Collar, Nat. Order of Merit of the Repub. of Malta 2012, Cross of Recognition (Latvia), First Class 2012, Order of the White Eagle (Poland) 2014, Grand Cross, Royal Norwegian Order of St Olav 2014; Hon. LLD (St Olaf Coll.) 2014. *Leisure interests:* reading, cooking, farming.

ILYUMZHINOV, Kirsan; Russian politician, business executive and international organization official; b. 5 April 1962, Elista; m. Danar Davashkina; one s.; ed Moscow State Inst. of Int. Relations; mil. service 1980–82; mechanic, Zvezda plant, Elista, Repub. of Kalmykia 1982–83; Man., Soviet-Japanese firm Liko-Raduga, Moscow 1989–90; Pres. SAN Corpn, Moscow 1990–93; Pres. Repub. of Kalmykiya, S Russia 1993–2010; Pres. Fédération Internationale des Échecs (FIDE) 1995–18; Pres. International Mind Sports Asscn 2013–; Founder Novy Vzglyad (publr); mem. Council, SportAccord 2015–; mem. Russian Social Sciences Acad., New York Acad. of Sciences; Honoured Citizen of Elista; Order of Friendship 1997, Order of Golden Fleece (Georgia) 2003, Order of Polar Star (Mongolia) 2009, Order of "Merit for the Fatherland" IV degree 2011, Order of Friendship II degree (Kazakhstan) 2012; Gold Medal of Peace for Humanitarian Activities 1992, Medal "300 Years of Russian Navy" 1996, F. Plevako Gold Medal 1997. *Publications include:* The President's Crown of Thorns 1998. *Leisure interest:* chess (chess champion of Kalmykiya as schoolboy). *Website:* kirsan.today/en.

ILYUSHIN, Viktor Vasilyevich; Russian politician and business executive; b. 4 June 1947, Nizhny Tagil, Sverdlovsk Oblast; m.; one s. one d.; ed Urals Polytech. Inst., Acad. of Social Science; metalworker Nizhny Tagil metallurgy plant; First Sec. Nizhny Tagil City Komsomol Cttee, then First Sec. Sverdlovsk Regional Komsomol Cttee, Asst to First Sec. Sverdlovsk Regional CPSU Cttee; First Sec. Leninsky Dist CPSU Cttee (Sverdlovsk); counsellor, Cen. Cttee Afghanistan People's Democractic Party; Asst to Chair., Russian Supreme Soviet 1990–91; Head, Pres. Yeltsin's Secr. 1991–92; First Asst Pres. of Russian Fed. 1991–96; First Deputy Prime Minister 1996–97; Head, Public Relations and Corp. Interrelations with Regional Authorities of Russian Fed. Admin, Gazprom 1997–98, Head, Corp. Interrelations with Regional Authorities of Russian Fed. Admin 1998–2011, mem. Man. Cttee –2012; Badge of Honour. *Leisure interests:* tennis, mountain skiing, riding, jazz, cars, computers.

IM, Kwon-taek; South Korean film director; b. 2 May 1936, Changsong, Cheollanam-do; m. Chae Ryeong; two s.; ed Sr High School, Kwangju; began career as labourer, Pusan; Production Asst with film Dir Chung Chang-Hwa, Seoul 1956–61; made first feature film 1962, subsequently directed over 100 films; Prof., Coll. of Arts, Dongguk Univ. (Seoul) 1998–; mem. Nat. Acad. of Arts (South Korea) 2002; Chevalier, Légion d'honneur 2007; Hon. DLit (Catholic Univ. of Korea); UNESCO Fellini Gold Medal 2002 for his work as a whole, Hon. Golden Bear Berlin Film Festival 2005; numerous other Korean and int. film festival awards. *Films include:* Dumanganga jal itgeola (Farewell to the Duman River) 1962, Danjang lok (The Prince's Revolt) 1963, Mangbuseog (A Wife Turned to Stone) 1963, Shibjamae seonsaeng (Father of Ten Daughters) 1964, Bisog e Jida (Death of an Informer) 1965, Pungunui gomgaek (Swordsmen) 1967, Cheongsa cholong (The Feudal Tenant) 1967, Tola-on oensonjabi (Return from the Sea) 1968, Mongnyeo (The Waking Woman) 1968, Sibo Ya (Full Moon Night) 1969, Roe Gom (Thunder Sword) 1969, Weolha ui geom (Swords under the Moon) 1970, Bigeom (The Flying Sword) 1970, Yogeom (Swordswoman) 1971, Tuljjae omoni (A Stepmother's Heartache) 1971, Myeongdong janhoksa (Cruelty on the Streets of Myongdong) 1972, Jung eon (The Testimony) 1973, Jabcho (The Deserted Widow) 1973, Yeonhwa (The Hidden Princess) 1974, Wae geulaess-teunga (Who and Why?) 1975, Anae (The Industrious Wife) 1976, Sangnok su (The Evergreen Tree) 1978,

Chopko (Genealogy) 1978, Tchak Ko (Pursuit of Death) 1980, Mandala 1981, Angae Maul (Village in the Mist) 1982, Gilsottum 1985, Sibaji (The Surrogate Woman) 1986, Yonsan Ilgi (Diary of King Yongsan) 1987, Adada 1988, Janggunui adeul (Son of the General) 1990, Kae Byok (Fly High Run Far) 1992, Sopyonje 1993 (most honoured Korean film ever: 27 domestic and three int. prizes), Taebek sanmaek (Taebak Mountains) 1994, Ch'ukje 1986, Chunhyang 2000, Chihwaseon (Strokes of Fire) (Best Dir Award at 2002 Cannes International Film Festival) 2002, Haryu insaeng 2004, Chun nyun hack 2007, Dalbit Gireoolligi (Hanji) 2011, Hwajang (Revivre) 2014.

IMAI, Nobuko; Japanese violist and academic; b. 18 March 1943, Tokyo; m. Aart van Bochove 1981; one s. one d.; ed Toho Gakuen School of Music, Juilliard School and Yale Univ., USA; mem. Vermeer Quartet 1974–79, now mem. Michelangelo String Quartet; soloist with Berlin Philharmonic, London Symphony Orchestra, Royal Philharmonic, BBC orchestras, Detroit Symphony, Chicago Symphony, Concertgebouw, Montréal Symphony, Boston Symphony, Vienna Symphony, Orchestre de Paris, Stockholm Philharmonic; festival performances include Marlborough, Salzburg, Lockenhaus, Casals, South Bank, Summer Music, Aldeburgh, BBC Proms, Int. Viola Congress (Houston), New York Y', Festival d'Automne, Paris; chamber music partners include Gidon Kremer, Yo-Yo Ma, Itzhak Perlman, András Schiff, Isaac Stern and Pinchas Zukerman; Founder and Artistic Adviser, Viola Space project, Japan 1992–; conceived Int. Hindemith Viola Festival (London, New York, Tokyo) 1995; Prof., High School of Music, Detmold, Germany 1985–2003; currently teaches at Amsterdam Conservatoire, Conservatory in Geneva, Kronberg Acad.; Artistic Adviser, Casals Hall, Tokyo; First Prize, Munich Int. Viola Competition, Second Prize, Geneva Int. Viola Competition, Avon Arts Award 1993, Japanese Educ. Minister's Art Prize for Music 1993, Mobil Japan Art Prize 1995, Suntory Hall Prize 1996. *Leisure interest:* cooking. *Address:* Brinks Artists Management, Herengracht 453, 1017 BS Amsterdam, Netherlands (office); Kronberg Academy, Friedrich-Ebert-Str. 6, 61476 Kronberg, Germany; Amsterdam Conservatoire, Oosterdokskade 151, Postbus 78022, 1070 LP Amsterdam, Netherlands. *E-mail:* kika@brinksartists.nl (office). *Website:* www.kronbergacademy.de; www.ahk.nl.

IMAI, Takashi; Japanese business executive; *Senior Advisor and Honorary Chairman, Nippon Steel & Sumitomo Metal Corporation;* b. 23 Dec. 1929, Kamakura; ed Univ. of Tokyo; joined Fuji Iron & Steel 1952, Man. Raw Materials 1963; Deputy Gen. Man. Fuel and Ferrous Metals, Nippon Steel (formed by merger of Fuji Iron & Steel and Yawata Steel) 1970, Gen. Man. Iron Ore 1973, Man. Dir 1983, Exec. Vice-Pres. 1989, Pres. Nippon Steel Corpn 1992–98, Chair. 1998–2003, Sr Vice-Pres., Chair. Emer. and Exec. Counsellor 2003–08, Sr Advisor and Hon. Chair. 2008– (merged with Sumitomo Metal Industries Ltd to become Nippon Steel & Sumitomo Metal Corpn 2012); mem. Bd of Dirs Nippon Telegraph and Telephone from 1999; Outside Dir Japan Securities Finance Co. Ltd 2002–, Nippon Television Network Corpn 2007–. *Address:* Nippon Steel & Sumitomo Metal Corpn, Marunouchi Park Building, 6-1, Marunouchi 2-chome, Chiyoda-ku, Tokyo 100-8071, Japan (office). *Telephone:* (3) 6867-4111 (office). *Fax:* (3) 6867-5607 (office). *E-mail:* info@nssmc.com (office). *Website:* www.nssmc.com (office).

IMAKI, Hisakazu, BS; Japanese automobile industry executive; *Supreme Executive Advisor, Mazda Motor Corporation;* b. 5 Dec. 1942; m.; one s. one d.; ed Himeji Inst. of Tech.; joined Toyo Kogyo Co. Ltd (later renamed Mazda Motor Corpn) 1965, Gen. Man. Admin Group and Advanced Production Eng Group 1988–89, Gen. Man. Painting, Trim and Final Ass. Eng Dept 1989–92, Deputy Gen. Man. Production Eng Div. and Gen. Man. Production Planning Dept 1992–93, Dir, Gen. Man. Production Eng Div. and Gen. Man. Production Planning Dept 1993–96, Dir and Gen. Man. Hiroshima Plant 1996–97, Man.-Dir in charge of Production Eng, Mfg and Business Logistics 1997–99, Sr Man.-Dir 1999–2002, Rep. Dir, Exec. Vice-Pres. and Chief Eng and Mfg Officer in charge of Research & Devt, Production, Quality Assurance and Business Logistics 2002–03, CEO, Pres. and Rep. Dir 2003–06, Chair., Pres., CEO and Rep. Dir 2006–08, Chair. and Rep. Dir 2008–10, Supreme Exec. Advisor 2010–; Person of the Year in Japan, Automotive Researchers and Journalists Conference 2006. *Leisure interests:* basketball, photography, driving. *Address:* Mazda Motor Corpn, 3-1 Shinchi, Fuchu-cho, Aki-gun, Hiroshima 730-8670, Japan (office). *Telephone:* (82) 282-1111 (office). *Fax:* (82) 287-5190 (office). *E-mail:* info@mazda.com (office). *Website:* www.mazda.com (office).

IMAM, Adel; Egyptian actor; b. 17 May 1940, Cairo; m. Hala Al Shalaqani; three c.; ed Cairo Univ.; has appeared in over 100 films and nine plays; early success as a comic actor on stage and film, subsequently famous for topical roles, often depicting victims of poverty and injustice, one of most successful actors in Arab world; his play Al -Zaeem (The Leader) has been performed worldwide; apptd UNHCR Goodwill Amb. 2001; sentenced (in absentia) to three months in jail for offending Islam Feb. 2012, cleared of charges Sept. 2012. *Films include:* Ana Wa Hua Wa Hia (I, He and She) 1964, El Ragol da hai Ganini 1967, Khouroug min el Guana 1967, Karamet Zawgaty 1967, Kayfa Tesrak Millionaire 1968, Helwa wa Shakia 1968, Ana al-Doctor 1968, Afrit Merati 1968, Al-Bahth an Fadiha 1973, Katel ma Katelsh had 1979, Athkiya' Laken Aghbiya' 1980, Ala Bab e l'Wazir 1982, El Harrif (The Street Player) 1983, Al Avokato 1984, Al-Irhabi wal Kabab (Terrorism and Bar-B-Q) 1993, Al-Irhabi (The Terrorist) 1994, Tuyoor Al-Zalam (Birds of Darkness) 1995, Al-Wad Mahrous Beta' Al-Wazir (Mahrous, The Minister's Boy) 1999, Amir El Zalam 2002, Tag Rubah el Danemarkiyyah 2003, Aris Min Geha Amneya 2004, Amarit Ya'koubian 2005, The Yacoubian Building (in trans.) 2006, Morgan Ahmad Morgan 2007, Hassan w Morqos (Hasan and Marcus) 2008, Bobbos 2009. *Television includes:* series: Al Aaraf (The Fortuneteller) 2013, Saheb El Saada (Owner of Happiness) 2014, Ma'amoon wa shorakaah (Ma'amoon and his partners) 2016, Afareet Adly Alam (Adly Alam's Ghosts) 2017, Awalem Khafyah (Hidden Worlds) 2018. *Plays include:* Al-Zaeem (The Leader), Shahid ma Shafesh Haga, Bodyguard.

IMAMI, Arben; Albanian politician; b. 21 Jan. 1958, Tirana; ed Fine Arts Acad., Tirana, School of Foreign Service, Georgetown Univ., Washington, DC, USA; Minority Leader and Vice-Chair. Democratic Party 1990–92; Founder Democratic Alliance Party 1992, Gen. Sec. 1992–99; mem. Kuvendi Popullor (Parl.) 1991–96, 1997–2005, Co-Chair. Parl. Comm. to Draft New Constitution 1997–98; Minister of State for Legis. Reform and Relations with Parl. 1998–99; Minister of Justice 2000–01; Minister of Local Govt and Decentralization 2001–02; Minister of Defence 2009–13; mem. Democratic Party of Albania.

IMAN; American (b. Somali) model and actress; b. (Iman Abdul Majid), 25 July 1955, Mogadishu; d. of Mohamed Abdulmajid and Marian Abdulmajid; m. 2nd Spencer Haywood 1977 (divorced 1987); one d.; m. 3rd David Bowie 1992 (died 2016); one d.; ed Nairobi Univ.; fashion model 1976–90, has modelled for Claude Montana and Thierry Mugler; signed Revlon Polish Ambers contract (first black model to be signed by int. cosmetics co.) 1979; Founder and CEO IMAN Cosmetics, Skincare and Fragrances 1994–; Spokesperson Keep a Child Alive program; Fashion Icon Lifetime Achievement Award, Council of Fashion Designers of America 2010. *Films include:* The Human Factor 1979, Jane Austen in Manhattan 1980, Exposed 1983, Out of Africa 1985, No Way Out 1987, Surrender 1987, In the Heat of the Night 1988, L.A. Story 1991, House Party 2 1991, Star Trek VI: The Undiscovered Country 1991, The Linguini Incident 1991, Exit to Eden 1994, The Deli 1997, Omikron: The Nomad Soul 1999, Project Runway Canada 2007, 2009, The Fashion Show 2010. *Television appearances include:* Miami Vice, The Cosby Show, In the Heat of the Night, Lies of the Twins 1991, Heart of Darkness 1994. *Publications include:* I Am Iman 2001, The Beauty of Color 2005. *Address:* TESS Management, 4th Floor, 9-10 Market Place, London, W1W 8AQ, England (office). *E-mail:* info@tessmanagement.com (office). *Website:* www.tessmanagement.com (office); www.imancosmetics.com.

IMANAKA, Hiroshi, LLD; Japanese professor of law; *Professor Emeritus, Faculty of Law, Hiroshima University;* b. 2 Dec. 1930, Fukuoka City; s. of Tsugumaro Imanaka; ed Univs of Hiroshima and Nagoya; Lecturer, Faculty of Educ., Miyazaki Univ. 1960–65; Lecturer, Dept of Gen. Educ., Hiroshima Univ. 1965–67, Assoc. Prof. 1967–78, Prof. of Political Science, Faculty of Integrated Arts and Sciences 1978–81, Faculty of Law 1981–91, Prof. Emer. 1991–; Dean and Prof., Kinjogakuin Univ. 1991–2001, Prof. Emer. 2001–. *Publications include:* Constitutional Law (co-author) 1971, George Lawson's Political Theory of Civil Government 1976, A Study of the History of English Political Thought 1977, Parliamentarism and its Origin in the Era of English Revolution, The English Revolution and the Modern Political Theory of George Lawson 2000. *Address:* 2-6-10 Yoshijima-Higashi, Naka-ku, Hiroshima Shi, Japan (home). *Telephone:* (82) 244-4756 (home). *Fax:* (82) 244-4756 (home). *E-mail:* hakanami@go7.enjoy.ne.jp.

IMAZ SAN MIGUEL, Josu Jon, DChemSci; Spanish business executive; *CEO, Repsol YPF SA;* b. 6 Sept. 1963, Zumárraga (Gipuzkoa); m.; three c.; ed Faculty of Chemical Sciences, San Sebastián, Univ. of the Basque Country; sent by INASMET Tech. Centre to CETIM Centre in Nantes, France to develop industrial projects (Grupo Mondragón) related to the energy industry; fmr Visiting Fellow, Kennedy School of Govt, Harvard Univ., USA; also held political posts, including Regional Minister of Industry, Trade and Tourism, Regional Govt of the Basque Country 1999; Chair. Exec. Cttee EAJ-PNV party 2004–07; joined Repsol Group as Chair. of its Petronor unit 2008, joined Repsol's Man. Cttee 2012, CEO Repsol YPF SA 2014–, mem. Del. Cttee; Chair. Asscn of Petroleum Products Operators (AOP) 2011–; End of Degree Extraordinary Priz. *Address:* Repsol YPF SA, Méndez Álvaro 44, 28045 Madrid, Spain (office). *Telephone:* (91) 7538100 (office). *Fax:* (902) 303145 (office). *E-mail:* info@repsol.com (office). *Website:* www.repsol.com (office).

IMBERT, Colm Peter, BEng, MEng; Trinidad and Tobago civil engineer and politician; *Minister of Finance;* b. 30 July 1957; ed St Mary's Coll., Ireland, Univ. of the West Indies, Aberdeen Business School, Robert Gordon Univ., Scotland, UK; worked as consulting civil engineer on a variety of construction projects in Trinidad and Tobago and the Caribbean 1979–82; Lecturer in Construction Man. and Eng, Univ. of the West Indies 1985–; fmr consultant on sea defences in Guyana for FAO; property developer and project man. throughout the Caribbean region 1995–2001; mem. House of Reps for Diego Martin North/East (PMN) 1991–; Minister of Works and Transport 1992–94, 2005–10, of Works and Transport and of Local Govt 1994–95, of Health 2001–03, of Science, Tech. and Tertiary Educ. 2003–05, of Finance 2015–; mem. People's Nat. Movement (PMN); mem. Chartered Inst. of Arbitrators, Soc. of Construction Law. *Address:* Ministry of Finance, Eric Williams Finance Bldg, Level 18, Independence Square, Port of Spain, Trinidad and Tobago (office). *Telephone:* 627-9700 (office). *Fax:* 627-5882 (office). *E-mail:* comm.finance@gov.tt (office). *Website:* www.finance.gov.tt (office).

IMBUSCH, George Francis, DSc, PhD, FInstP, FAIP; Irish physicist, academic and university administrator; *Professor Emeritus of Experimental Physics, National University of Ireland, Galway;* b. 7 Oct. 1935, Limerick; s. of George Imbusch and Alice Neville; m. Mary Rita O'Donnell 1961; one s. one d.; ed Christian Brothers' School, Limerick, Univ. Coll., Galway and Stanford Univ., USA; mem. tech. staff, Bell Labs, USA 1964–67; Lecturer in Physics, Univ. Coll. Galway (now Nat. Univ. of Ireland, Galway) 1967–74, Prof. of Experimental Physics 1974–2002, Prof. Emer. 2002–, Head, Dept of Physics 1986–89, Vice-Pres. 1992–98; Science Sec., Royal Irish Acad. 1989–93, Sr Vice-Pres. 2005–08, Hon. Academic Research Officer 2005–08; Visiting Prof., Univ. of Wisconsin 1978, Univ. of Regensburg 1981, Univ. of Utrecht 1988, Univ. of Canterbury, NZ 1995, Univ. of Georgia, USA 1998. *Publications:* Optical Spectroscopy of Inorganic Solids (co-author) 1989; more than 100 scientific papers in journals. *Leisure interests:* painting, reading. *Address:* Room A0204a, Department of Physics, National University of Ireland, Galway, University Road, Galway (office); Forramoyle West, Barna, Co. Galway, Ireland (home). *Telephone:* (91) 492510 (office); (91) 592159 (home). *E-mail:* frank.imbusch@nuigalway.ie (office); g.f.imbusch@nuigalway.ie (office); gfimbusch@eircom.net (home). *Website:* (office).

IMMELT, Jeffrey Robert (Jeff), BA, MBA; American business executive; *Chairman, General Electric Company;* b. 19 Feb. 1956, Cincinnati, Ohio; s. of Joseph Immelt and Donna Immelt; m. Andrea Allen 1986; one d.; ed Finneytown High School, Dartmouth Coll., Harvard Business School; joined Gen. Electric Co. 1982, Corp. Marketing Dept 1982, various positions with GE Plastics 1982–89, Vice-Pres. 1992–93, Vice-Pres. GE Appliances 1989–91, Vice-Pres. Worldwide Marketing and Product Man. 1991, Vice-Pres. and Gen. Man. GE Plastics Americas 1993–97, Pres. and CEO GE Medical Systems 1997–2001, Pres. and CEO General Electric Co. 2000–01, Chair. and CEO 2001–17, Chair. 2017–; Chair. President's Council on Jobs and Competitiveness 2011–13; mem. Pres. Trump's American Manufacturing Council 2017 (resgnd); mem. Bd of Dirs Catalyst, Robin Hood, New York City, New York Fed. Reserve Bank; mem. The Business Council;

Hon. LLD (Dartmouth Coll.) 2004; Hon. Doctor of Public Service (Univ. of Maryland, Baltimore Co.) 2011, (Univ. of Connecticut) 2013; Dr hc (Northeastern Univ.) 2006, (Pepperdine Univ.) 2006, (Georgia Inst. of Tech.) 2007, (Univ. of Notre Dame) 2007, (Worcester Polytechnic Inst.) 2008, (Michigan State Univ.) 2010, (Clemson Univ.) 2016; Man of the Year, Financial Times 2003. *Leisure interest:* golf. *Address:* General Electric Company, 3135 Easton Turnpike, Fairfield, CT 06828-0001, USA (office). *Telephone:* (203) 373-2652 (Bd) (office); (203) 373-2211 (office). *Fax:* (203) 373-3131 (office). *E-mail:* directors@corporate.ge.com (office). *Website:* www.ge.com (office).

IMMONGAULT TATANGANI, Régis; Gabonese politician; ed Univ. Omar Bongo, Libreville, Univ. Paris X-Nanterre, School of Treasury Services, Noisiel, France; worked at Public Treasury of Gabon 1989–99, roles include Head of Dept, Deputy Dir, Dir of Programming Resources and Regulations, later Provincial Treasurer; Inspector Gen. of Diplomatic Missions and Consular Posts, Ministry of Foreign Affairs, Cooperation and Francophonie 2000–02; Financial Advisor to Minister of State, in charge of Relations with Int. Financial Insts, Ministry of the Economy, Finance, Budget and Privatization 2002–09; Minister of Energy and Hydraulic Resources 2009–12, Minister of Industry and Mines 2012–14, Minister of Mines, Industry and Tourism Jan.–Oct. 2014, Minister of the Economy 2014–18, Minister of State, Minister of Foreign Affairs, Co-operation, Francophonie and Regional Integration 2018–19; mem. Nat. Ass. (Parl.) for Mulundu (Lastoursville) 2010–. *Address:* c/o Ministry of Foreign Affairs, Co-operation, Francophonie and Regional Integration, blvd du Bord de Mer, BP 2245, Libreville, Gabon (office).

IMRAN KHAN NIAZI (see KHAN NIAZI, Imran).

IMRAY, Sir Colin Henry, Kt, KBE, CMG, KStJ, MA; British diplomatist (retd); b. 21 Sept. 1933, Newport, Mon., Wales; s. of Henry Gibbon Imray and Frances Olive Badman; m. Shirley Margaret Matthews 1957; one s. three d.; ed Highgate School, London, Hotchkiss School, Conn., USA and Balliol Coll., Oxford, Royal Coll. of Defence Studies; Second Lt, Seaforth Highlanders, Royal W African Frontier Force 1952–54; Asst Prin. Commonwealth Relations Office 1957–58, 1961–63; Third, then Second Sec., British High Comm., Canberra 1958–61; First Sec., Nairobi 1963–66; Asst Head of Personnel Dept, FCO 1966–70; British Trade Commr, Montreal 1970–73; Counsellor, Consul Gen. and Head of Chancery, Islamabad 1973–77; Commercial Counsellor, Embassy in Tel-Aviv 1977–80; Deputy High Commr, Bombay 1980–84; Asst Under-Sec. of State (Chief Insp. and Deputy Chief Clerk) 1984–85; High Commr to Tanzania 1986–89, to Bangladesh 1989–93; Sec.-Gen. Order of St John 1993–97, Dir Overseas Relations 1997–98; mem. Cen. Council, Royal Over-Seas League 1998–2005, Exec. Cttee 1999–2005, Chair. 2000–05, Vice-Pres. 2005–; High Steward of Wallingford 2001–15; Freeman of the City of London 1994. *Publication:* Remember and Be Glad 2009. *Leisure interests:* walking, gardening, family. *Address:* 1 A St John's Road, Wallingford, Oxon., OX10 9AD, England (home).

INABA, Kayo, PhD; Japanese immunologist, cell biologist and academic; *Professor, Graduate School of Biostudies, Kyoto University;* ed Kyoto Univ.; Visiting Faculty mem., Ralph Steinman's Lab., Rockefeller Univ., New York 1982–2011; Assoc. Prof., Faculty of Science, Kyoto Univ. 1992–99, Full Prof., Graduate School of Biostudies 1999–, Vice-Pres. for Gender Equality and Dir, Centre for Women Researchers, Kyoto 2007–; Supporting Scientist, Hasumi Int. Research Foundation; fmr Adjunct Faculty mem., Michel Nussenzweig's Lab. of Molecular Immunology, Rockefeller Univ.; mem. bd Japanese Soc. for Immunology; Kyoto Univ. Shi-Shi Award 2014, Laureate for Asia-Pacific, L'Oréal-UNESCO Women in Science Awards 2014. *Achievements include:* research on the immune system, particularly her discoveries regarding dendritic cells. *Address:* Graduate School of Biostudies, Kyoto University, Yoshida-Konoecho, Sakyo-ku, Kyoto, Japan (office). *Telephone:* 606-8501 (office). *E-mail:* kayo@zoo.zool.kyoto-u.ac.jp (office). *Website:* www.lif.kyoto-u.ac.jp (office).

INADA, Tomomi; Japanese lawyer and politician; b. 20 Feb. 1959, Fukui Prefecture; m. Ryuji Inada 1989; one s. one d.; ed Waseda Univ.; qualified as lawyer 1985; mem. House of Reps (lower house of parl.) (LDP) for 1st Fukui Prefecture 2005–, mem. Judicial Affairs Cttee 2005 (Chair. 2009), Internal Affairs and Communications Cttee 2008, Financial Affairs Cttee 2009; Minister of State for Regulatory Reform 2012–14, also Minister in charge of the Challenge Again Initiative 2012–14, Minister in charge of the Cool Japan Strategy 2012–14, Minister in charge of Civil Service Reform 2012–14, Minister in charge of Admin. Reform 2012–14, Minister of Defence 2016–17; mem. Nippon Kaigi (nationalist group); mem. LDP, Deputy Sec.-Gen. 2010, Chair. LDP Policy Research Council 2014–; mem. Osaka Bar Asscn, Fukui Bar Asscn. *Leisure interest:* reading.

IÑÁRRITU, Alejandro González; Mexican film director and screenwriter; b. 15 Aug. 1963, Mexico City; early career as radio DJ in Mexico City; Pres. of the jury, Cannes Film Festival 2019; fmr Head of Televisa (TV production co.); f. Zeta Films (advertising agency and film production co.); Golden Eye Award for career achievement, Zurich Film Festival 2011. *Films include:* El Timbre (also writer) 1996, Amores perros (also producer) 2000, Powder Keg (also writer) 2001, 11'09"01: September 11 (Mexico segment, also writer and producer) 2002, 21 Grams (also producer) 2003, Nine Lives (exec. producer) 2005, Toro negro (exec. producer) 2005, Babel (Best Dir Cannes Film Festival 2006, Palm Springs Int. Film Festival 2007) (also producer) 2006, Rudo y Cursi (producer), Mother and Child (exec. producer), Biutiful (also producer) 2010, Birdman (also writer and producer) (Best Film, Producers Guild of America 2015, Acad. Award for Best Dir, Best Picture, Best Original Screenplay 2015) 2014, The Revenant (also producer and screenwriter) (Golden Globe Award for Best Dir and Best Motion Picture 2016, Dirs Guild of America Award for Outstanding Directorial Achievement 2016, BAFTA for Best Dir 2016, Acad. Award for Best Dir 2016) 2015, Carne y Arena (Special Award Oscar 2017) 2017. *Address:* c/o Creative Artists Agency, 2000 Avenue of the Stars, Los Angeles, CA 90067, USA.

INAZ, Ahmed; Maldivian economist and politician; b. 9 Sept. 1976; ed Nat. Univ. of Singapore, Univ. of Westminster and Univ. of Manchester, UK; has served in several govt posts, including Minister of State for Econ. Devt, Dir Gen., Ministry of Planning, Trade Policy Coordinator, Ministry of Trade and Econ. Devt; Founding mem. Transparency Maldives (chapter of Transparency International); Visiting Lecturer at various colls 2005–; Minister of Finance and Treasury 2011–12; mem. Maldivian Democratic Party –2012.

INBAL, Eliahu; British/Israeli conductor; b. 16 Feb. 1936, Jerusalem, Israel; s. of Jehuda Joseph Inbal and Leah Museri Inbal; m. Helga Fritzsche 1968; two s. one d.; ed Acad. of Music, Jerusalem, Conservatoire Nat. Supérieur, Paris, courses with Franco Ferrara, Hilversum and Sergiu Celebidache, Siena; guest conductor with numerous orchestras including Milan, Rome, Berlin, Munich, Hamburg, Stockholm, Copenhagen, Vienna, Budapest, Amsterdam, London, Paris, Tel-Aviv, New York, Chicago, Toronto and Tokyo since 1963; Chief Conductor, HR Radio Symphony Orchestra, Frankfurt 1974–90, Hon. Conductor 1995–; Chief Conductor, Teatro La Fenice 1984–87, Music Dir 2007–11; regularly conducted Konzerthaus Berlin Symphony Orchestra since 1992, Chief Conductor 2001–06, Hon. mem. 2006–; Chief Conductor, Tokyo Metropolitan Symphony Orchestra 2008–14, Hon. Conductor 2014–; Music Dir Czech Philharmonic Orchestra 2009–12; Hon. Conductor, Orchestra Nazionale della RAI, Turin 1995–2001; Officier des Arts et des Lettres 1990, Goldenes Ehrenzeichen, Vienna 2001, Bundesverdienstkreuz (Germany) 2006; First Prize, Int. Conductors' Competition 'G. Cantelli' 1963, Golden Medal for Merit, City of Vienna 2001, Goethe Badge of Honour, City of Frankfurt 2006, numerous prizes for recordings, including Deutscher Schallplattenpreis, Grand Prix du Disque, Prix Caecilia, Symphony Prize of 50th Record Academy Award (Japan) 2012. *Recordings:* numerous recordings, particularly of Mahler, Bruckner, Berlioz and Shostakovich. *Leisure interests:* music reproduction, photography. *Address:* Karsten Witt Music Management, Leuschnerdamm 13, 10999 Berlin, Germany (office). *Telephone:* (30) 214594-0 (office). *E-mail:* info@karstenwitt.com (office). *Website:* de.karstenwitt.com/eliahu-inbal (office).

INDIMI, Mohammed; Nigerian business executive; *Chairman and CEO, Oriental Energy Resources Ltd;* b. Aug. 1948, Maiduguri, Borno State; m.; eight c.; f. Oriental Energy Resources Ltd 1990, currently Chair. and CEO; currently Chair. M & W Pump Nigeria Ltd; Dir Jaiz Bank; Officer, Order of the Federal Repub. (Nigeria); numerous hon. degrees from univs in Nigeria, Ireland, USA. *Address:* Oriental Energy Resources Limited, Plot 397, Muhammadu Buhari Way, Central Business District Area, PMB 5101, Abuja, Nigeria (office). *Telephone:* (9) 4610438 (office). *Fax:* (9) 4610450 (office). *Website:* www.oriental-er.com (office).

INDRAWATI, HE Sri Mulyani, BA, PhD; Indonesian economist, academic and government official; *Minister of Finance;* b. 26 Aug. 1962, Tanjungkarang, Lampung; m. Tony Sumartono; three c.; ed Univ. of Indonesia, Jakarta, Univ. of Illinois at Urbana-Champaign, USA; several positions at Inst. for Econ. and Social Research, Faculty of Econs, Univ. Indonesia (LPEM-FEUI) 1992–2004 including Assoc. Dir Research 1992–93, Assoc. Dir Educ. and Training 1993–95, Dir Program Magister, Planning and Public Policy, Grad. Program Econs 1996–99, Dir 1998–2004; Staff Expert in Policy Analysis, Overseas Training Office 1994–95; adviser, Nat. Econ. Council 1999–2001, Sec.-Gen.; consultant to USAID 2001–; Exec. Dir IMF 2002; Minister of State and Chair. Nat. Devt Planning Agency 2004–05; Minister of Finance and State Enterprises Devt 2005–10 (resgnd), also Acting Co-ordinating Minister for Econ. Affairs 2008–09, Minister of Finance 2016–; Man. Dir and COO World Bank Group 2010–16; Visiting Faculty mem., Andrew Young School of Policy Studies, Georgia State Univ. 2001–02; Best Asian Finance Minister, Emerging Market 2006. *Publications include:* Potential and Student Savings in DKI Jakarta 1995, Domestic Industry Preparedness for the Free Trade Era 1997, Forget CBS, Get Serious About Reform 1998. *Address:* Ministry of Finance, Djuanda Building, Lot 9, Jalan Dr Wahidin Raya 1, Jakarta 10710, Indonesia (office). *Telephone:* (21) 3506055 (office). *Fax:* (21) 3500842 (office). *E-mail:* portalkemenkeu@kemenkeu.go.id (office). *Website:* www.depkeu.go.id (office).

INDURÁIN LARRAYA, Miguel; Spanish professional cyclist (retd); b. 16 July 1964, Villava, Navarre; m. Marisa Induráin; one d.; mem. Reynolds team 1984–89, Banesto team 1989–96; five successive wins, Tour de France 1991–95, 1995 winning time, 92 hours, 44 minutes and 59 seconds; Gold Medal, Atlanta Olympics 1996; ranked No. 1 cyclist 1992, 1993; announced retirement Jan. 1997; f. Miguel Induráin Foundation 1998, currently Hon. Chair.; fmr mem. Comité Olímpico Español (Spanish Olympic Cttee); Grand Cross, Royal Order of Sporting Merit, Grand Cross, Order of Civil Merit, Chevalier, Légion d'honneur; Prince of Asturias Award for Sports 1992. *Website:* www.fundacionmiguelindurain.com.

INDYK, Martin S., BA, PhD; American diplomatist and academic; *Vice-President and Director for Foreign Policy, Brookings Institution;* b. 1 July 1951, London, England; m. Jill Collier (divorced); one s. one d.; ed Univ. of Sydney and Australian Nat. Univ.; raised in Australia; worked as Deputy Dir of current intelligence for Middle East, Australian intelligence service 1978; Adjunct Prof., Johns Hopkins School of Advanced Int. Studies; Exec. Dir Washington Inst. for Near East Policy 1985; naturalized US citizen 1993; Special Asst to the Pres. and Sr Dir for Near East and S Asian Affairs, Nat. Security Council; Prin. Adviser to the Pres. and Nat. Security Adviser on Arab-Israeli Issues, Iraq, Iran and S Asia; Sr mem. Warren Christopher's Middle East peace team; Amb. to Israel 1995–97, 2000–01; Asst Sec. for Near Eastern Affairs 1997–2000; Sr Fellow and Dir Saban Center for Middle East Policy, The Brookings Inst. 2002–13, Vice-Pres. and Dir for Foreign Policy 2014–; US Special Envoy for Israeli-Palestinian Negotiations 2013–14; mem. Int. Inst. for Strategic Studies, Middle East Inst. *Publications:* Innocent Abroad: An Intimate Account of American Peace Diplomacy in the Middle East 2009, Bending History: Barack Obama's Foreign Policy 2012; numerous articles and contribs to foreign policy journals. *Address:* Saban Center for Middle East Policy, The Brookings Institution, 1775 Massachusetts Avenue, NW, Washington, DC 20036, USA (office). *Telephone:* (202) 797-4396 (office). *Fax:* (202) 797-2481 (office). *E-mail:* sabancenter@brookings.edu (office). *Website:* www.brookings.edu (office).

INFANTINO, Gianni Vincenzo; Swiss/Italian sports administrator and international organization official; *President, Fédération International de Football Association (FIFA);* b. 23 March 1970, Brig, Switzerland; m. Leena Al Ashqar; four c.; ed Univ. of Fribourg; began career as legal consultant to various nat. and int. football bodies; Sec.-Gen., Int. Centre for Sport Studies (CIES), Univ. of Neuchâtel –2000; joined Union of European Football Asscns (UEFA) 2000, Dir, UEFA Legal Affairs and Club Licensing Div. 2004–07, Deputy Gen. Sec., UEFA 2007–09, Gen. Sec. 2009–16; mem. Reform Cttee, Fédération Int. de Football Asscn (FIFA) 2015–, Pres. FIFA 2016–. *Address:* Fédération International de Football Association, FIFA-Strasse 20, POB 8044, Zurich, Switzerland (office). *Telephone:* (43) 222-7777 (office). *Fax:* (43) 222-7878 (office). *Website:* www.fifa.com (office).

ING, Nita; Taiwanese business executive; *Chairman, Continental Holdings Corporation;* d. of Glyn T. H. Ing; two d.; ed Taipei American School, boarding schools in Mass and New Jersey, USA, Univ. of California, Los Angeles; joined family business Continental Engineering Corpn as personal asst to her father, apptd Pres. 1987, Chair. Continental Holdings Corpn 2010–; Chair. Taiwan Hi-Speed Railway Corpn 1998–2009; Chair. The Hao Ran Foundation of Taiwan 1997–, 921 Earthquake Relief Foundation 2000–08; mem. Bd of Dirs Taiwan Mobile; mem. Asian Business Council. *Address:* Continental Holding Corporation, 23F, No.95, Dun Hua S. Road, Sec. 2, 10682, Taipei, Taiwan (office). *Website:* www.continental-holdings.com (office).

INGE, Baron (Life Peer), cr. 1997, of Richmond in the County of North Yorkshire; **Field Marshal (retd) Peter Anthony Inge,** KG, GCB; British army officer; b. 5 Aug. 1935; s. of Raymond Albert Inge and Grace Maud Caroline Inge; m. Letitia Marion Beryl Thornton-Berry 1960; two d.; ed Summer Fields, Wrekin Coll., Royal Mil. Acad., Sandhurst; commissioned, Green Howards 1956, ADC to GOC 4 Div. 1960–61, Adjutant, 1st Green Howards 1963–64, student, Staff Coll. 1966, Ministry of Defence 1967–69, Co. Commdr 1st Green Howards 1969–70, student, Jt Service Staff Coll. 1971, Brigade Maj., 11th Armoured Brigade 1972, Instructor, Staff Coll. 1973–74, CO 1st Green Howards 1974–76, Commdt, Jr Div. Staff Coll. 1977–79, Commdr 4th Armoured Brigade 1980–81, Chief of Staff HQ 1st (BR) Corps 1982–83, GOC NEDIST and Commdr 2nd Infantry Div. 1984–86, Dir-Gen. Logistic Policy (Army) 1986–87, Commdr 1st (BR) Corps 1987–89, Commdr NORTHAG and C-in-C British Army of the Rhine 1989–92, Chief of Gen. Staff 1992–94, of the Defence Staff 1994–97, Constable of HM's Fortress and Palace, The Tower of London 1996–2001; ADC Gen. to the Queen 1991–94, DL N Yorks. 1994; Deputy Chair. Historic Royal Palaces 1997–2007; Chair. King Edward VII Sister Agnes' Hosp. 2004–12; mem. Council Marlborough Coll. 1997–2006; Commr Royal Hosp. Chelsea 1998–2004; Pres. The Pilgrims 2002–; Col The Green Howards 1982–94, Col Commdt Royal Mil. Police 1987–92, Col Commdt Army Physical Training Corps 1988–97; currently Adviser to King and Govt of Bahrain; mem. Bd of Dirs, Aegis; mem. of Council IISS; mem. St George's Council, Windsor; Freeman City of London 1994. *Leisure interests:* cricket, walking, music, reading, military history. *Address:* House of Lords, Westminster, London, SW1A 0PW, England (office). *Telephone:* (20) 7219-8706 (office). *E-mail:* ingep@parliament.uk (office). *Website:* www.parliament.uk/biographies/lords/lord-inge/2025 (office).

INGELS, Bjarke; Danish architect; *Founder, Bjarke Ingels Group (BIG);* b. 2 Oct. 1974; ed Royal Danish Acad. of Fine Arts, Technica Superior de Arquitectura, Barcelona; worked for Rem Koolhaas, Office for Metropolitan Architecture, Rotterdam 1998–2001; Co-Founder (with Julien de Smedt) PLOT (architectural practice), Copenhagen 2001–05; f. Bjarke Ingels Group (BIG) 2006; co-f. KiBiSi (design group) 2009; Visiting Prof., Rice Univ. School of Architecture, Harvard Grad. School of Design, Columbia Univ. Grad. School of Architecture, Planning and Preservation Program, Yale School of Architecture; numerous awards including Nykredit Architecture Prize 2002, Golden Lion for best concert hall design, Venice Biennale of Architecture (for Stavanger Concert Hall proposal) 2004, European Architecture Prize 2010, Wall Street Journal Innovator of the Year for Architecture 2011, Danish Crown Prince Couple's Culture Award 2011, American Inst. of Architects Honor Award 2012. *Publications:* Yes Is More: An Archicomic on Architectural Evolution 2009, Big, Hot to Cold: An Odyssey of Architectural Adaptation 2015. *Address:* BIG CPH, Kløverbladsgade 56, Valby, 2500 Copenhagen, Denmark (office). *Telephone:* 7221-7227 (office). *Fax:* 3512-7227 (office). *E-mail:* big@big.dk (office). *Website:* www.big.dk (office).

INGHAM, Sir Bernard, Kt; British fmr civil servant; b. 21 June 1932, Halifax, Yorks.; s. of Garnet Ingham and Alice Ingham; m. Nancy Hilda Hoyle 1956; one s.; ed Hebden Bridge Grammar School, Tech. Colls of Todmorden, Halifax and Bradford; reporter, Hebden Bridge Times 1948–52, The Yorkshire Post and Yorkshire Evening Post, Halifax 1952–59; with The Yorkshire Post, Leeds 1959–61, Northern Industrial Corresp. 1961; with The Guardian 1962–67, Labour Staff, London 1965–67; Press and Public Relations Adviser, Nat. Bd for Prices and Incomes 1967–68; Chief Information Officer, Dept of Employment and Productivity 1968–72; Dir of Information Dept of Employment 1973; with Dept of Energy 1974–79, Dir of Information 1974–77, Under-Sec. and Head of Energy Conservation Div. 1978–79; Chief Press Sec. to Prime Minister Margaret Thatcher 1979–90, Head, Govt Information Service 1989–90; columnist, Daily Express 1991–98; Chair. Bernard Ingham Communications 1990–2011; Pres. British Franchise Assen 1994–2012; Vice-Pres. Country Guardian 1991–; Dir (non exec.), McDonald's Restaurants Ltd 1991–2005 (mem. Advisory Bd 2005–09), Hill and Knowlton 1991–2002; Visiting Fellow and Hon. Dir Applied Policy Science Unit, Univ. of Newcastle-upon-Tyne 1991–2003; mem. Council, Univ. of Huddersfield 1994–2000; Visiting Prof., Univ. of Middlesex Business School 1997–2003, Univ. of Surrey 2005–09; Sec., Supporters of Nuclear Energy Sec. 1998–; Dr hc (Buckingham) 1997, (Middlesex) 1999, (Bradford) 2004. *Publications include:* Kill the Messenger 1991, Yorkshire Millennium 1999, Yorkshire Castles 2001, Yorkshire Villages 2001, The Wages of Spin 2003, Yorkshire Greats 2005. *Leisure interests:* reading, writing. *Address:* 9 Monahan Avenue, Purley, Surrey, CR8 3BB, England (home). *Telephone:* (20) 8660-8970 (home). *E-mail:* bernardinghamcom@aol.com (office).

INGOLD, Keith Usherwood, OC, PhD, FRS, FRSC, FCIC; Canadian research chemist and academic; *Distinguished Research Scientist, National Research Council of Canada;* b. 31 May 1929, Leeds, Yorks., England; s. of Sir Christopher Kelk Ingold and Lady Edith Hilda Usherwood; m. Carmen Cairine Hodgkin 1956 (died 2012); one s. one d.; ed Univ. Coll., London, Univ. of Oxford; Postdoctoral Fellow, Nat. Research Council of Canada 1951–53, Research Officer, Div. of Chem. 1955–90, Head, Hydrocarbon Chem. Section 1965–90, Assoc. Dir 1977–90; Postdoctoral Fellow, Univ. of BC 1953–55; Distinguished Research Scientist, Nat. Research Council 1990–; Adjunct Prof., Dept of Biochemistry, Brunel Univ., UK 1983–94; Adjunct Prof., Dept of Chem. and Biochemistry, Univ. of Guelph, Ont. 1985–89; Adjunct Research Prof., Carleton Univ., Ottawa 1991–; Adjunct Prof., Dept of Chem., Univ. of St Andrews, Scotland 1997–; visiting scientist to numerous univs, numerous lectureships; Sr Carnegie Fellowship, Univ. of St Andrews, Scotland 1977; Fellow, Univ. Coll. London 1987; Vice-Pres. Canadian Soc. for Chem. 1985–87, Pres. 1987–88; mem. ACS; Hon. mem. Sociedad Argentina de Investigaciones en Química Orgánica; Hon. FRSE; Dr hc (Univ. degli Studi di Ancona) 1999; Hon. DSc (Guelph, Ont.) 1985, (St Andrews) 1989, (Carleton Univ.) 1992, (McMaster Univ., Ont.) 1995, (Dalhousie Univ., NS) 1996; Hon. LLD (Mount Allison) 1987; numerous awards, including Chem. Inst. of Canada Medal 1981, Syntex Award in Physical Organic Chem. 1983, RSC Centennial Medal 1982, RSC Henry Marshall Tory Medal 1985, ACS Pauling Award 1988, Alfred Bader Award in Organic Chem., Canadian Soc. for Chem. 1989, Humboldt Research Award 1989, Davy Medal, Royal Soc. 1990, ACS Arthur C. Cope Scholar Award 1992, Izaak Walton Killam Memorial Prize, Canada Council 1992, ACS James Flack Norris Award in Physical Organic Chem. 1993, Angelo Mangini Medal, Italian Chemical Soc. 1997, Canada Gold Medal for Science and Eng, Natural Science and Eng Research Council 1998, Royal Medal A, Royal Soc. 2000, Gold Medal, Professional Inst. of the Public Service of Canada 2009, Sir Derek Barton Gold Medal 2016. *Publications include:* Free-Radical Substitution Reactions (with B. P. Roberts) 1971, Nitrogen-centered Radicals, Aminoxyl and Related Radicals (with J. C. Walton) 1994; more than 550 publs in the open scientific literature. *Leisure interests:* skiing, water skiing. *Address:* National Research Council Canada, 100 Sussex Drive, Ottawa, ON K1A 0R6, Canada (office). *Telephone:* (613) 990-0938 (office); (613) 822-1123 (home). *E-mail:* keith.ingold@nrc.ca (office). *Website:* www.nrc-cnrc.gc.ca (office).

INGÓLFSSON, Thorsteinn; Icelandic diplomatist (retd); b. 9 Dec. 1944, Reykjavik; s. of Ingólfur Thorsteinsson and Helga Gudmundsdóttir; m. 1st Gudrún Valdís Ragnarsdóttir (divorced 1986); one s. one d.; m. 2nd Hólmfrídur Kofoed-Hansen 1994; ed Commercial Coll. of Iceland, Univ. of Iceland; First Sec. (Int. and Political Affairs), Ministry for Foreign Affairs 1971–73, First Sec. and Deputy Chief of Mission, Washington, DC 1973–78, Chief of Div., Ministry of Foreign Affairs 1978–85, Minister Counsellor 1981, Deputy Perm. Rep. to Int. Orgs, Geneva 1985–87, Acting Perm. Rep. Feb.–June 1987, rank of Amb. 1987, Dir Defence Dept, Ministry for Foreign Affairs 1987–90, Chair. Icelandic-American Defence Council 1987–90, Perm. Under-Sec. for Foreign Affairs 1990–94, Amb. and Perm. Rep. to NATO and WEU, Brussels 1994–98, to UN, New York 1998–2003 (also accred as Amb. to Cuba 2001–03, Barbados 2002–03, to Jamaica 2003), Exec. Dir for Nordic and Baltic Countries, World Bank Group, Washington, DC 2003–06, Special Envoy of Foreign Minister 2006–08, Amb. to NATO, Brussels 2008–13, Amb. and Sr Arctic Official, Ministry for Foreign Affairs 2013–15 (retd); Grande Croix, Légion d'honneur; Hon. GCMG; numerous other decorations.

INGRAHAM, Rt Hon. Hubert Alexander, PC; Bahamian lawyer and politician; b. 4 Aug. 1947, Pine Ridge, Grand Bahama; m. Delores Velma Miller; five c.; ed Cooper's Town Public School, Southern Sr School and Govt High School Evening Inst. Nassau; called to the Bar, Bahamas 1972; Sr Partner, Christie, Ingraham & Co. (law firm); fmr mem. Air Transport Licensing Authority; fmr Chair. Real Property Tax Tribunal; mem. Nat. Gen. Council Progressive Liberal Party (PLP) 1975; Nat. Chair. and mem. Nat. Exec. Cttee PLP 1976; elected to House of Ass. as PLP mem. 1977, 1982, fmr Speaker; Minister of Housing, Nat. Insurance and Social Services 1982–84; Chair. Bahamas Mortgage Corpn 1982; Alt. Del. Conf. of IDB, Uruguay 1983, IMF/IBRD 1979–84; expelled from PLP 1986; elected to Nat. Ass. for North Abaco as ind. 1987, Parl. Leader, Official Opposition 1990–92, Leader of Official Opposition 1990–92, 2002–07; Minister of Finance and Planning 1992–97, of Housing and Local Govt 1995–97 and Trade and Industry 1995–97, of Housing and Social Devt 2001–02, of Finance 2007–12, Prime Minister of Bahamas 1992–2002, 2007–12; mem. Free Nat. Movt, Leader 1990–2012; Dr hc (Buckingham) 2000. *Leisure interests:* reading, swimming, fishing. *E-mail:* hai@coralwave.com (home).

INGRAM, Christopher (Chris) John; British advertising and marketing executive and art collector; b. 9 June 1943; s. of Thomas Frank Ingram and Gladys Agnes Ingram (née Louttid); m. Janet Elizabeth Rye; one s. one d.; ed Woking Grammar School, Surrey; Media Dir KMP Partnership 1969–71; Man. Dir TMD Advertising 1972–75; Founder and Chair. Chris Ingram Assocs. (CIA) Group/Tempus Group PLC 1976–2002; f. Genesis Investments 2002; Chair. Woking Football Club Holdings 2002–; Founding Partner, Ingram 2003, Ingram Enterprise (investment co.); f. Ingram Trust (family charity); est. Ingram Collection (collection of modern British and contemporary art); Chair. Centre for Creative Business, London Business School 2005–; Chair. Sports Revolution 2008–13; Enterprise Fellow, The Prince's Trust; Ernst & Young London Entrepreneur of the Year 2000, Ernst & Young UK Business-to-Business Entrepreneur of the Year 2000. *Leisure interests:* art, theatre, wildlife, travel in cold climates, entrepreneurship, the voluntary sector, Woking Football Club. *Address:* Ingram Enterprise, 2nd Floor, 17-18 Margaret Street, London, W1W 8RP, England (office). *Telephone:* (20) 3828-8880 (office). *E-mail:* rebecca@ingramenteprise.com (office). *Website:* www.ingramenterprise.com (office); www.ingramcollection.com.

INGRAM, James Charles, AO, FAIIA, BA (Econs); Australian diplomatist (retd) and international organization official; b. 27 Feb. 1928, Warragul, Vic.; s. of James Edward Ingram and Gladys May (née Johnson); m. Odette Koven 1950; one s. two d.; ed De la Salle Coll., Univ. of Melbourne; joined Dept of External Affairs (DFA) 1946, Third Sec., Embassy in Tel-Aviv 1950, First Sec., Embassy in Washington, DC 1956, Chargé d'affaires a.i., Embassy in Brussels 1959, Counsellor, Embassy in Djakarta 1962, Australian Mission to UN, New York 1964, Asst Sec., External Affairs, DFA 1967, Amb. to Philippines 1970–73, High Commr to Canada, Jamaica, Barbados, Guyana, Trinidad and Tobago 1973–74, First Asst Sec., Australian Devt Assistance Agency 1975–76, Dir-Gen. Australian Devt Assistance Bureau, DFA 1977–82; Exec. Dir WFP 1982–92; Dir Australian Inst. of Int. Affairs 1992–93; Visiting Fellow, Centre for Int. and Public Law, ANU, Canberra 1993–94; Chair. Australian Govt Advisory Cttee on Non-Govt Devt Orgs 1995; mem. Bd of Trustees, Int. Food Policy Research Inst. 1991–98, Crawford Fund for Int. Agric. Research, Melbourne 1994–99 (Chair. 1996–99), Int. Crisis Group, Brussels 1995–99; Chair. Crawford Fund Expert Advisory Panel on Global Food Security 2008, Crawford Fund World Food Crisis Task Force 2008; Fellow, Australian Inst. of Int. Affairs 2010; mem. Governing Council Soc. for Int. Devt 1988–94, Commonwealth Intergovernmental Group on the Emergence of a Global Humanitarian Order, London 1994–95; Chair. UN Assen of Australia (ACT Div.) 1998–99; mem. Bd of Trustees, Asia-Pacific Coll. of Diplomacy, ANU 2005–12; Alan Shawn Feinstein World Hunger Award, Brown Univ. 1991, Inaugural Food for Life Award, WFP 2000. *Publications include:* Bread and Stones: Leadership and the Struggle to Reform the United Nations World Food Programme 2006;

contrib. numerous articles to journals and chapters to books. *Leisure interests:* music, reading, gardening. *Address:* 4 Stokes Street, Manuka, ACT 2603, Australia (home).

INGRAM, Tamara, OBE, BA; British advertising executive; *Group Executive Vice-President and Executive Managing Director, Grey Group (UK) Ltd;* b. 1 Oct. 1961; m.; two c.; began career in film production; joined Saatchi & Saatchi 1985, Bd Account Dir 1989–93, Exec. Account Dir 1993–95, Jt CEO 1995–2001, Exec. Chair. 2001–02; Chair. and CEO McCann-Erickson 2002–03; Pres. Added Value, Fusion 5 and Henley Centre (marketing consulting firms of Kantar Div. of WWP Group PLC) 2003–05, CEO Grey London (div. of WPP) 2005–07, Group Exec. Vice-Pres. and Exec. Man. Dir Grey Group UK (comprising Grey London, Joshua, GCI and MDS Global Consulting) 2005–, Pres. Team P&G (WPP Group's team for Proctor & Gamble Co.) 2004–08; Chair. Visit London Ltd 2002–11; mem. Bd of Dirs Sage Group plc 2004–, London Devt Agency, Council Inst. of Practitioners in Advertising, Marketing Soc., Marketing Group of GB, Women in Advertising and Communications London; Chair. Devt Bd, Royal Court Theatre; Trustee, The Bacon Fellowship. *Address:* Grey Group Ltd, The Johnson Building, 77 Hatton Garden, London, EC1N 8JS, England (office). *Telephone:* (20) 3037-3000 (office). *Website:* www.grey.co.uk (office).

INGRAMS, Richard Reid; British journalist; b. 19 Aug. 1937, London; s. of Leonard St Clair and Victoria Ingrams (née Reid); m. 1st Mary Morgan 1962 (divorced 1993); two s. (one deceased) one d.; m. 2nd Sara Sudain; ed Shrewsbury School, Univ. Coll., Oxford; Co-founder Private Eye 1962, Ed. 1963–86, Chair. 1974–; Co-founder and Ed. The Oldie 1992–2014 (resgnd); TV critic, The Spectator 1976–84; columnist, The Observer 1988–90, 1992–2005, The Independent 2005–11. *Publications:* Private Eye on London (with Christopher Booker and William Rushton) 1962, Private Eye's Romantic England 1963, Mrs Wilson's Diary (with John Wells) 1965, Mrs Wilson's Second Diary 1966, The Tale of Driver Grope 1968, The Bible for Motorists (with Barry Fantoni) 1970, The Life and Times of Private Eye (ed.) 1971, Harris in Wonderland (as Philip Reid with Andrew Osmond) 1973, Cobbett's Country Book (ed.) 1974, Beachcomber: the works of J. B. Morton (ed.) 1974, The Best of Private Eye 1974, God's Apology 1977, Goldenballs 1979, Romney Marsh (with Fay Godwin) 1980, Dear Bill: The Collected Letters of Denis Thatcher (with John Wells) 1980, The Other Half 1981, Piper's Places (with John Piper) 1983, Dr Johnson by Mrs Thrale (ed.) 1984, Down the Hatch (with John Wells) 1985, Just the One (with John Wells) 1986, John Stewart Collis: A Memoir 1986, The Best of Dear Bill (with John Wells) 1986, Mud in Your Eye (with John Wells) 1987, The Eye Spy Look-alike Book (ed.) 1988, The Ridgeway 1988, You Might As Well Be Dead 1988, England: An Anthology 1989, No. 10 1989, On and On... Further Letters of Denis Thatcher (with John Wells) 1990, The Oldie Annual (ed.) 1993, The Oldie Annual II (ed.) 1994, Malcolm Muggeridge (ed.) 1995, I Once Met (ed.) 1996, The Oldie Annual III (ed.) 1997, Jesus: Authors Take Sides (anthology) 1999, The Oldie Annual IV (ed.) 1999, The Life and Adventures of William Cobbett (biog.) 2005, Quips and Quotes: A Journalist's Commonplace Book 2011, The Oldie Book of Cartoons: A New Selection (ed.) 2013, Ludo and the Power of the Book: Ludovic Kennedy's Campaigns for Justice 2017. *Leisure interests:* music, book selling.

INGVES, Stefan, MSc, PhD; Swedish economist, academic and central banker; *Governor, Sveriges Riksbank;* b. 1953, Turku, Finland; m.; three c.; ed Stockholm School of Econs; Lecturer, Stockholm School of Econs 1976–84; Asst Vice-Pres., Cen. Finance and Fund Man. Div., Svenska Handelsbanken 1984–86; Pres. Sweden Options and Futures Exchange 1987; Under-Sec. for Financial Markets and Insts, Ministry of Finance 1988–92; Dir-Gen. Swedish Bank Support Authority 1993–94; Deputy Gov. Sveriges Riksbank (Swedish Cen. Bank) 1994–98; Dir Monetary and Financial Systems Dept, IMF 1999–2005; Gov. Sveriges Riksbank (Swedish Cen. Bank) 2006–, also Chair. Exec. Bd, Chair. Advisory Tech. Cttee, European Systemic Risk Bd 2011–, Chair. Basel Cttee on Banking Supervision, BIS 2011–; mem. European Cen. Bank Gen. Council; fmr mem. Toronto Int. Leadership Centre for Financial Sector Supervision. *Address:* Sveriges Riksbank, Brunkebergstorg 11, 103 37 Stockholm, Sweden (office). *Telephone:* (8) 787-00-00 (office). *Fax:* (8) 21-05-31 (office). *E-mail:* registratorn@riksbank.se (office). *Website:* www.riksbank.se (office).

INHOFE, James Mountain, BA; American politician; *Senator from Oklahoma;* b. 17 Nov. 1934, Des Moines, Ia; s. of Perry Inhofe and Blanche Mountain; m. Kay Kirkpatrick 1958; two s. two d.; ed Univ. of Tulsa; served in US Army 1955–56; mem. Okla House of Reps 1966–68; mem. Okla State Senate 1968–76, Minority Leader 1970–76; Pres. Quaker Life Insurance Co. 1975–86 (co. forced into receivership); Mayor of Tulsa 1978–84; mem. US House of Reps from 1st Dist of Okla 1987–94; Senator from Oklahoma 1995–, mem. Armed Services Cttee Environment and Public Works Cttee (Chair.) 2003–07, 2015–17, Foreign Relations Cttee; fmr Pres. Fly Riverside Inc.; Republican; Character and Leadership Award, US Air Force Acad. *Address:* 205 Russell Senate Office Building, Washington, DC 20510-3603, USA (office). *Telephone:* (202) 224-4721 (office). *Fax:* (202) 228-0380 (office). *E-mail:* jim-inhofe@inhofe.senate.gov (office). *Website:* inhofe.senate.gov (office).

INNANI, Brij Gopal; Nepalese industrialist and philanthropist; *Chairman and President, Innani Industrial and Trading Organization;* Chair. and Pres. Innani Industrial and Trading Org.; Chair. and Pres. Mahalaxmi Garment Industries Group; Founder, Chair. and Pres. Shri Laxmi Narsingh Dibyadham, Nepal; Chair. Asian Textiles and Garments Council, CACCI; fmr Pres. Garment Asscn of Nepal, Maheswari Soc. of Nepal and of many others; Lifetime mem. Marwadi Soc. of Nepal; Patron and mem. Educ. Trust of Marwadi Soc. of Nepal; mem. London Chamber of Commerce and Industry, Fed. of Nepalese Chambers of Commerce and Industry, Nepal-India Chamber of Commerce and Industry, Nepal-Britain Chamber of Commerce and Industry, Nepal-German Chamber of Commerce and Industry, and of many others; Life and Distinguished mem. Nepal Red Cross Soc.; Suprabala-Gorkha-Dakshina-Bahu (2056 BS), Birendra-Aiswarya Seva Padak, King Birendra Silver Jubilee Medal, King Birendra Silver Jubilee Medal from the Civic Main Cttee, Golden Jubilee Medal of HM the King's Birthday, Gorkha Dakshina Bahu 2013; numerous awards including Nat. Personality Award (Rastriya Byaktitva Samman) for 25 years of Excellent Service in the field of Ready-made Garments Industries in Nepal, Mahalaxmi Garment Industries awarded Int. Gold Star for Quality 1997, Int. Award – Golden America for Quality and Excellence 1999. *Address:* Innani Organization, V. Narsing Kunj, New Plaza, Putali Sadak, PO Box 4206, Kathmandu, Nepal (office). *Telephone:* (1) 4418126 (office). *Fax:* (1) 4421258 (office). *E-mail:* innaniorg@gmail.com (office); bginnani@gmail.com (home). *Website:* www.mginepal.com (office).

INOGUCHI, Kuniko, BA, MA, PhD; Japanese academic and politician; b. 3 May 1952, Chiba Pref.; m. Takashi Inoguchi; two d.; ed Sophia Univ., Yale Univ., USA; Assoc. Prof. of Political Science, Faculty of Law, Sophia Univ. 1981–90, Prof. 1990–2006; Visiting Fellow, Center for Int. Affairs, Harvard Univ. 1983–84; Visiting Prof., ANU 1985; Amb. to Conf. on Disarmament, Geneva 2002–04, Head of Japanese Del. 2003–04, Pres. of Conf. 2003, Western Group Co-ordinator 2004; mem. UN Advisory Bd on Disarmament Issues, New York 2003–06; Co-Chair. Standing Cttee on Mine Clearance, Mine Risk Educ. and Mine Action Technologies, Meeting of States Parties to Convention on Prohibition of Use of Anti-Personnel Mines 2004; mem. House of Reps 2005–09; Minister of State for Gender Equality and Social Affairs 2005–06; Foreign Policy Adviser to Sec.-Gen. LDP 2006–07, Acting Sec.-Gen., LDP Int. Bureau 2006; mem. House of Councillors (representing Chiba Pref.) 2010–, Chair. Special Cttee on Okinawa and Northern Problems, mem. Cttee on Foreign Affairs and Defence, Cttee on Budget; mem. Prime Minister's Defence Policy Review Council 1994–95, Prime Minister's Admin. Reform Council 1996–98, Prime Minister's Gender Equity Council 2001–02; mem. Bd Inst. for Democracy and Electoral Assistance (IDEA), Stockholm, Sweden; Exec. mem. Japan Asscn of Gaming and Simulation 1999, Japan Asscn for Int. Relations 2004–, Science Council of Japan 2005–; Educ. Minister Award 1972, AVON Awards to Women 2003. *Publications include:* An Emerging Post-Hegemonic System: Choices for Japan 1987, War and Peace (Yoshino Sakuzo Prize) 1989, Invitation to Political Science 1989; articles in newspapers, periodicals and professional journals on disarmament matters. *Address:* Office of Kuniko Inoguchi, Room 1105, Sangiin Members' Office Building, 2-2-1 Nagata-cho, Chiyoda-ku, Tokyo 100-8962, Japan (office). *Telephone:* (3) 6550-1105 (office). *Fax:* (3) 6551-1105 (office). *E-mail:* inoguchi@kunikoinoguchi.jp (office). *Website:* www.kunikoinoguchi.jp (office).

INOKUCHI, Takeo; Japanese insurance industry executive; b. 9 April 1942; joined Taisho Marine & Fire Insurance Co. Ltd (renamed Mitsui Marine & Fire Insurance Co. Ltd 1993) 1965, Gen. Man. of Non-Marine Underwriting Dept 1990–94, apptd Dir 1993, Man.-Dir 1994–96, Pres. 1996–2000, Chair., Pres. and CEO 2000–01; Chair. and CEO Mitsui Sumitomo Insurance Co. Ltd (cr. following merger of Mitsui Marine & Fire Insurance Co. Ltd and Sumitomo Marine & Fire Insurance Co. Ltd 2001) 2001–04; Vice-Chair. Radio Regulatory Council, Ministry of Public Man., Home Affairs, Posts and Telecommunications 2002; Corp. Auditor, Sanki Engineering Co. Ltd 2003–, Kikkoman Corpn; apptd Deputy Chair. Ind. Admin. Inst. Evaluation Cttee (IAIEC) and Chair. IAIEC Sub-cttee for Japan Int. Cooperation Agency, Ministry of Foreign Affairs 2003; Vice-Chair. Japan Asscn of Corp. Execs (Keizai Doyukai) 2003–, Chair. Cttee on Fiscal and Admin. Reforms 2003–; Exec. Dir Japan Business Fed. (Nippon Keidanren) 1997, Co-Chair. Cttee on Econ. Policy 2002; Exec. Councillor Tokyo Chamber of Commerce 1997; mem. Bd of Dirs Int. Insurance Soc. Inc. 2002, Kaneka Corpn; Personality of the Year Award, Asia Insurance Industry 2003, inducted into Insurance Hall of Fame, Insurance Soc. 2004.

INOUE, Akihisa, PhD; Japanese engineer, academic and fmr university administrator; b. 13 Sept. 1947; ed Grad. School of Eng, Tohoku Univ.; Research Assoc., Inst. for Materials Research, Tohoku Univ. 1976–85, Assoc. Prof. 1985–90, apptd Prof. 1990, also Prof. of Precision and Intelligence Lab., Tokyo Inst. of Tech. 1997, Dir Inst. for Materials Research 2000–, Deputy Pres. Tohoku Univ. 2002–06, Pres. 2006–12, Prof. Emer. 2012–; currently Special Adviser to the Chancellor and Dir Int. Inst. of Green Materials, Josai Univ. Educational Corpn; Visiting Scientist, AT&T Bell Labs, USA 1982–83, 1984, 1986; Visiting Scientist, Swedish Inst. of Metals Research 1985, 1987; Science Adviser to Ministry of Educ., Culture, Sports, Science and Tech. 2001–; mem. Japan Acad.; forgien mem. US Nat. Acad. of Eng; Fellow, Churchill Coll., Cambridge Univ.; Hon. mem., Indian Materials Research Soc.; Dr. hc (Swedish Royal Inst. of Tech.), (Dong-Eui Univ.), (Shanghai Jiatong Univ.); more than 50 awards, including ISI Citation Laureate Award 2000, Japan Acad. Prize 2002, Houkou Prize, CONA Award, James C. McGroddy Prize for New Materials 2008, Acta Materialia Gold Medal 2010. *Publications:* Nanocrystalline Alloys, Magnetic and Novel Nanomaterials (co-author) 2004, Materials Science and Engineering of Bulk Metallic Glasses (co-author) 2008, New Functional Materials, Fundamentals of Metallic Glasses and their Applications to Industry 2009.

INOUE, Shinya, PhD; American (b. Japanese) biologist and academic; *Distinguished Scientist, Marine Biological Laboratory;* b. 5 Jan. 1921; ed Univ. of Tokyo, Princeton Univ., NJ; Lecturer in Anatomy, Univ. of Washington, Seattle 1951–53; Asst Prof. of Biology, Tokyo Metropolitan Univ. 1953–54; Research Assoc. then Assoc. Prof. in Biology and Instructor in Optics, Univ. of Rochester, NY 1954–59; Prof. and Chair. Dept of Cytology, Dartmouth Medical School, Hanover, NH 1959–66; Prof. of Biology and Dir Program in Biophysical Cytology, Univ. of Pennsylvania 1966–82; Instructor in Chief, Analytical and Quantitative Light Microscopy, Marine Biological Lab. (MBL), Woods Hole, Mass 1979–87, Distinguished Scientist 1986–; mem. NAS 1993; Fellow, AAAS 1971; Hon. Fellow, Royal Microscopical Soc. (UK) 1988; Guggenheim Fellow 1971–72, NIH Merit Award 1982–86, E.B. Wilson Award, American Soc. for Cell Biology 1992, Distinguished Scientist Award, Microscopy Soc. of America 1995, Ernst Abbe Award, New York Microscopical Soc. 1997, Int. Prize for Biology, Japan Soc. for the Promotion of Science 2003. *Publications:* Video Microscopy 1986 (second edn with K. R. Spring 1997); numerous papers in specialist journals. *Address:* Marine Biological Laboratory, 7 MBL Street, Woods Hole, MA 02543, USA (office). *Telephone:* (508) 289-7382 (office). *E-mail:* jmacneil@mbl.edu (office). *Website:* www.mbl.edu/research/resident/lab_arch_dyn.html (office); www.mbl.edu/research/resident/lab_inoue.html (office).

INOUYE, Minoru, BL; Japanese banker; *Adviser, Bank of Tokyo-Mitsubishi UFJ Ltd;* b. 1924, Tokyo; m.; one s.; ed Univ. of Tokyo; joined Bank of Tokyo 1947, Deputy Agent, New York 1964–66, Deputy Gen. Man. Int. Funds and Foreign Exchange Div. 1966–67, Deputy Gen. Man. Planning and Co-ordination Div. 1967–70, Gen. Man. 1970–72, Dir and Gen. Man. London Office 1972–75, Resident Man. Dir for Europe 1975, Man. Dir 1975–79, Sr Man. Dir 1979–80, Deputy Pres.

1980–85, Pres. 1985–90, Adviser 1990, Adviser, Bank of Tokyo-Mitsubishi Ltd 1996–2005, Adviser, Bank of Tokyo-Mitsubishi UFJ Ltd 2006–; Orden Mexicana del Aguila Azteca (Mexico) 1986, Medal of Honour, with Blue Ribbon (Japan) 1989, Ordem Nacional de Cruzeiro do Sul (Brazil) 1989, Chevalier, Légion d'honneur 1990, Order of the Rising Sun, Gold and Silver Star (Japan) 1994. *Leisure interest:* travel. *Address:* The Bank of Tokyo-Mitsubishi UFJ Ltd, 3-2 Nihombashi Hongokucho 1-chome, Chuo-ku, Tokyo 103-0021, Japan (office). *Telephone:* (3) 3240-1111 (office). *Fax:* (3) 3245-9117 (office).

INOYATOV, Col-Gen. Rustam; Uzbekistani government official; b. 22 June 1944; s. of Rasul Inoyatov; ed Tashkent Faculty of Oriental Studies; graduated 1968; became one of heads of Tashkent 'clan' (powerful political clan based in Tashkent that controls Nat. Security Service and Ministry of the Interior); mem. KGB 1970–91, Nat. Security Service (Milliy Xavfsizlik Xizmati or Sluzhba Natsionalnoi Bezopasnosti—SNB) 1991–, Head of SNB 1995–2018; one of eight Uzbekistani officials blacklisted by EU. *Address:* c/o Milliy Xavfsizlik Xizmati (National Security Service), c/o Ministry of Internal Affairs, 100029 Tashkent, Yu. Rajaby ko'ch. 1, Uzbekistan (office).

INSANALLY, Samuel Rudolph (Rudy), BA; Guyanese diplomatist and fmr politician; b. 23 Jan. 1936, Georgetown; m. Bonita Insanally; two d.; ed Univ. of London, England, Univ. of Paris, France; teacher of modern languages, Kingston Coll., Jamaica, Queen's Coll., Guyana and Univ. of Guyana 1959–66; Counsellor, Embassy in Washington, DC 1966–69; Chargé d'affaires, Embassy in Venezuela 1970, Amb. 1972–78; Deputy Perm. Rep. to UN, New York 1970–72, Perm. Rep. 1987–2010; Perm. Rep. to EEC 1978–81; Amb. to Belgium (also accred to Sweden, Norway and Austria) 1978–81, to Colombia 1982–86; Head of Political Div. Ministry of Foreign Affairs 1982–86; High Commr to Barbados, Trinidad and Tobago and the Eastern Caribbean 1982–86; Pres. UN Gen. Ass. 1993–94; Chancellor Univ. of Guyana 1994–2001; Minister of Foreign Affairs 2001–08; fmr Adviser to Pres. on Foreign Affairs; mem. Bd of Govs Inst. of International Relations, Trinidad and Tobago 1982–86; Gran Cordon, Order of the Liberator (Venezuela) 1973, Cacique Crown of Honour 1980, Grand Cordon, Order of the Rising Sun (Japan) 2009; Golden Arrow of Achievement 1986. *Publications include:* Dancing between the Raindrops- a Dispatch from A Small State Diplomat 2014; several articles and works on int. relations and diplomacy. *Leisure interests:* reading, listening to classical music.

INSEL, Thomas Roland, BA, MD; American neuroscientist, psychiatrist, research institute director and academic; b. 19 Oct. 1951, Dayton, Ohio; s. of H. Herbert Insel; m. Deborah Silber 1969; ed Boston Univ. Medical School; moved with family to Silver Spring, Md 1960; travelled with wife around the world and worked at tuberculosis clinic in Hong Kong and mission hosp. in Bihar, India 1970; training in psychiatry at Univ. of California, San Francisco 1976–79, following clinical training joined Nat. Inst. of Mental Health (NIMH) as Clinical Fellow; recruited to Emory Univ. to direct Yerkes Regional Primate Research Center 1994–99 (resgnd); Head, Center for Behavioral Neuroscience NSF Science and Tech. Center 1999–2002; Dir NIMH 2002–15 (resgnd); mem. Google Life Sciences research team 2015–; mem. Inst. of Medicine of NAS; Fellow, American Coll. of Neuropsychopharmocology; Dr hc (Univ. of Basel) 2018; A.E. Bennett Award 1986, Curt Richter Prize 1991, Outstanding Service Award, US Public Health Service 1993, Sachar Prize 2007, Outstanding Alumnus Award, Boston Univ. 2009, Ipsen Prize 2010, Shorr Family Prize, Univ. of Arizona 2011, Dr Nathan Davis Award for Govt Service, American Medical Asscn 2013, Jed Foundation Voice of Mental Health Award 2013, American Psychiatric Nurses Asscn Scientific Partnership Award 2013, Brain andBehaviour Research Foundation Award 2014, Distinguished Scientist Award, Child Mind Inst. 2014, Distinguished Scientist Award, Autism Science Foundation 2015. *Achievements include:* first to demonstrate that an experimental serotonin reuptake inhibitor (SSRI) antidepressant, clomipramine, was effective in treating obsessive compulsive disorder (OCD); later carried out studies in NIMH Lab. of Brain Evolution and Behavior, Poolesville, Md, investigated social behaviour in animals and the role of oxytocin and vasopressin and their action on brain receptors. *Publications include:* New Findings in Obsessive-Compulsive Disorder (ed.) 1984, The Psychobiology of Obsessive-Compulsive Disorder (co-ed.) 1991, Oxytocin in Maternal, Sexual and Social Behaviors (co-ed.) 1992, The Neurobiology of Maternal Behavior (with M. M. Numan) 2011; more than 200 papers in professional journals on studies of oxytocin and vasopressin and their impact on social behaviour. *Address:* Google Life Sciences, Google Inc., 1600 Amphitheatre Parkway, Mountain View, CA 94043, USA.

INSLEE, Jay Robert, BA, JD; American lawyer and politician; *Governor of Washington;* b. 9 Feb. 1951, Seattle, Wash.; s. of Frank E. Inslee and Adele A. Inslee (née Brown); m. Trudi Inslee 1972; three s.; ed Ingraham High School, Univ. of Washington, Seattle, Willamette Univ. Coll. of Law; practised law in Selah, Wash. for ten years; mem. Wash. State House of Reps for 14th Dist 1989–93; mem. US House of Reps for 4th Congressional Dist 1993–95, for 1st Congressional Dist 1999–2012, mem. Cttee on Energy and Commerce; Gov. of Washington 2013–; Regional Dir US Dept of Health and Human Services 1997–98; Chair. Democratic Govs Asscn 2017–; Democrat. *Publication:* Apollo's Fire: Igniting America's Clean Energy Economy (with Bracken Hendricks) 2007. *Leisure interest:* playing basketball (mem. Hoopaholics). *Address:* Office of the Governor, 416 Sid Snyder Avenue SW, Suite 200, PO Box 40002, Olympia, WA 98504-0002, USA (office). *Telephone:* (360) 902-4111 (office). *Fax:* (360) 753-4110 (office). *Website:* www.governor.wa.gov (office).

INSULZA SALINAS, José Miguel, MA; Chilean politician, lawyer and international organization official; b. 2 June 1943; m. Georgina Núñez Reyes; three c.; ed St George's Coll., Santiago, Law School, Universidad de Chile, Facultad Latinoamericana de Ciencias Sociales and Univ. of Michigan, USA; Prof. of Political Theory, Universidad de Chile, of Political Sciences, Pontificia Universidad Católica de Chile –1973; Political Adviser to Ministry of Foreign Relations, Dir Diplomatic Acad. –1973; researcher, then Dir Instituto de Estudios de Estados Unidos, Centro de Investigación y Docencia Económicas, Mexico 1981–88; Prof., Universidad Autónoma de México 1981–88; Head, Multilateral Econ. Affairs Dept, Ministry of Foreign Relations, Deputy Chair. Int. Co-operation Agency 1990–94; Under-Sec. for Foreign Affairs 1994, Minister 1994–99, Minister Sec.-Gen., Office of the Pres. 1999; Minister of the Interior (Vice-Pres. of the Repub.) 2000–06; Sec.-Gen. OAS 2005–15; mem. Bd of Dirs Instituto de Fomento de Desarrollo Científico y Tecnológico; mem. Consejo Chileno de Relaciones Internacionales, Consejo de Redacción, Nexos Magazine, Mexico, Corporación de Desarrollo Tecnológico Empresarial, Chilean Asscn of Political Science, Bar Asscn; Council on Hemispheric Affairs Kalman H. Silvert Award 2014. *Address:* c/o Organization of American States, 17th Street and Constitution Avenue, NW, Washington, DC 20006, USA.

INUBUSHI, Yasuo; Japanese metals industry executive; b. 10 Feb. 1944, Tokushima; ed Osaka Univ.; joined Kobe Steel (KOBELCO) 1967, worked in Sales Planning and Admin Dept 1969–74, posted to Titan Steel & Wire Co., Canada 1974, also served at Kobe Steel offices New York and Los Angeles, Man. Cold Rolled Sheet Sales Section 1981–90, Gen. Man. Int. Operations Dept, Iron and Steel Div. 1990–99, mem. Bd of Dirs 1996–, Sr Officer 1999–2001, Exec. Officer and Gen. Man. Steel Sales Div. 2001–02, Rep. Dir 2002–, Exec. Vice-Pres. 2002–04, Pres. and CEO 2004–09 (resgnd), Advisor Emer. 2009–; mem. Bd of Dirs Japan Post Holdings Co., Ltd 2015–. *Address:* c/o Kobe Steel Ltd, Shinko Building, 10-26 Wakinohamacho 2-chome, Kobe 651-8585, Japan.

INZAMAM-UL-HAQ; Pakistani fmr professional cricketer; b. 3 March 1970, Multan, Punjab; right-handed middle order batsman; teams played for: Multan 1985–2004, United Bank Ltd 1988–97, Faisalabad 1996–2001, Rawalpindi 1998–99, Nat. Bank of Pakistan 2001–02, Pakistan 1991–2007 (Capt. 2003–07), Water and Power Devt Authority 2006–07, Yorks. 2007, Hyderabad Heroes (Indian Cricket League—ICL) 2007, Lahore Badshahs (ICL) 2008; First-class debut: 1985/86; Test debut: Pakistan v England, Birmingham 4 June 1992; One-Day Int. (ODI) debut: Pakistan v West Indies, Lahore 22 Nov. 1991; only T20I: England v Pakistan, Bristol 28 Aug. 2006; scored 8,830 runs in 120 tests (highest score 329 against NZ at Lahore 2002) with 25 hundreds; scored 11,739 runs in 378 ODIs (average 39.52) with 10 centuries; scored 16,785 runs in 245 First-class matches with 45 hundreds; retd from One-Day cricket 2007; Chief Selector of Pakistan 2016–. *Address:* Pakistan Cricket Board, Gaddafi Stadium, Ferozepur Road, Lahore 54600, Pakistan. *Telephone:* (42) 571-7231. *Website:* www.pcboard.com.pk.

INZKO, Valentin, Jr, DIur; Austrian diplomatist; *High Representative of the International Community in Bosnia and Herzegovina;* b. 22 May 1949, Klagenfurt am Wörthersee, Carinthia; s. of Valentin Inzko, Sr; m. Bernarda Fink; one s. one d.; ed attended a Slovene-German bilingual school in Suetschach, Feistritz im Rosental, Univ. of Graz, Diplomatic Acad., Vienna; joined Foreign Service 1974; UNDP Deputy Dir, Ulaanbaatar, Mongolia 1974–78, Colombo, Sri Lanka 1978–80, Political Section, Dept of Cen., Eastern and Southern Europe, Cen. Asia and Southern Caucasus, Ministry of Foreign Affairs 1981, Press and Culture Attaché, Embassy in Belgrade 1982–86, Counsellor, Del. to First Mission and Deputy Dir UN Disarmament Mission, Austrian Mission to UN, New York, USA 1986–89, Deputy Head of Press and Information Dept, Ministry of Foreign Affairs 1989–90, Cultural Council, Embassy in Prague 1990–96, Founding Dir Austrian Cultural Inst., Prague 1993–96, Founding Head of OSCE Observer Mission in Novi Pazar, Sandžak, Serbia Oct.–Dec. 1992, Amb. to Bosnia and Herzegovina 1996–99, Head of Dept for Middle, E and S Europe, Cen. Asia and S Caucasus, Ministry of Foreign Affairs 1999–2005, Observer of Montenegrin Parl. Elections 2002, Amb. to Slovenia 2005–09, High Rep. of Int. Community in Bosnia and Herzegovina 2009–, Special Rep. of EU in Bosnia and Herzegovina 2009–11; Hon. Citizen of the City of Sarajevo, Bosnia and Herzegovina 2000; Grand Decoration of Honour in Silver for Services to the Repub. of Austria 2012. *Publications include:* translated essays of Václav Havel, Living in Truth and Power of the Powerless, into Slovene. *Address:* Office of the High Representative, Emerika Bluma 1, 71 000 Sarajevo, Bosnia and Herzegovina (office). *Telephone:* (33) 283500 (office). *Fax:* (33) 283501 (office). *E-mail:* info@ohr.int (office). *Website:* www.ohr.int (office).

IOFFE, Boris Lazarevich, MS; Russian theoretical physicist; *Head of Laboratory, A.I. Alikhanov Institute of Theoretical and Experimental Physics;* b. 6 July 1926, Moscow; s. of Lazar Iof and Pesia Ioffe; m. 1st Svetlana Mikhailova 1957 (divorced 1974); one s.; m. 2nd Nina Libova 1990; ed Moscow Univ.; Jr Scientist, A.I. Alikhanov Inst. of Theoretical and Experimental Physics (ITEP), Moscow 1950–55, Sr Scientist 1955–77, Head of Lab. 1977–, Prof. 1977–, Chair. ITEP Scientific Council 1990–97; Deputy Ed. Moscow Physics Soc. Journal 1991–98; mem. High Energy Physics Scientific Policy Cttee (Russia) 1992–98, Russian Nuclear Soc. –1990; Corresp. mem. USSR (now Russian) Acad. of Sciences 1990; mem. Exec. Cttee United Physical Soc. of Russian Fed. 1998; Fellow, American Physical Soc. 1995; Order of Honour of USSR 1954, 1974; Veteran of Labour Medal 1985, USSR Award for Discovery 1986, 1989, Alexander von Humboldt Award (Germany) 1994, 850 Years of Moscow Medal 1997, Novy Mir Magazine Prize 1999, Acad. of Sciences I.E. Tamm Prize 2008, Pomeranchuk Prize, A.I. Alikhanov Inst. for Theoretical and Experimental Physics 2009. *Publications:* Hard Processes 1984, The Top Secret Assignment 1999, 2001, Without Retouching 2004; 280 articles. *Leisure interests:* mountaineering (especially in Cen. Asia and Far East), skiing. *Address:* A.I. Alikhanov Institute of Theoretical and Experimental Physics, Bolshaya Cheremushkinskaya 25, 117218 Moscow (office); Bolotnikovskaya Street 40, Korp 4, Apt 16, 117209 Moscow, Russia (home). *Telephone:* (499) 123-31-93 (office); (499) 121-44-38 (home). *Fax:* (495) 127-05-43 (office). *E-mail:* ioffe@itep.ru (office). *Website:* www.itep.ru (office).

IOHANNIS, Klaus Werner; Romanian politician and head of state; *President;* b. 13 June 1959, Sibiu; s. of Gustav Heinz and Susanne Iohannis; m. Carmen Lăzurcă 1989; ed Babeş-Bolyai Univ.; began career as physics teacher at various schools and colls in Sibiu; Deputy Gen. School Insp., Sibiu Co. 1997–99, Gen. School Insp. 1999–2000; Mayor of Sibiu 2000–14; mem. Demokratisches Forum der Deutschen in Rumänien (Democratic Forum of Germans in Romania) 1990–2013, Leader 2002–13; mem. Partidul Naţional Liberal (Nat. Liberal Party), Leader June–Dec. 2014; Pres. of Romania 21 Dec. 2014–; Bundesverdienstkreuz 2006, Kt, Order of the Star of Romania 2007, Ordine della Stella della Solidarietà Italiana 2008, Officer, Belgian Order of the Crown 2010, Kt, Nat. Order of Merit of Romania 2011, Officer, Verdienstorden der Bundesrepublik Deutschland 2014. *Publications:* Pas cu pas (Step by Step) 2014, Primul pas (First Step) 2015. *Address:* Office of the President, 060116 Bucharest 5, Palatul Cotroceni, Str. Geniului 1–3, Romania (office). *Telephone:* (21) 4100581 (office). *Fax:* (21) 4103858 (office). *E-mail:*

procetatean@presidency.ro (office). *Website:* www.presidency.ro (office); www.iohannispresedinte.ro.

IOSIFESCU, Marius Vicenţiu Viorel, PhD, DSc; Romanian mathematician and academic; *Director, Institute of Mathematical Statistics and Applied Mathematics and Vice-President, Casa Academiei Romane (Romanian Academy);* b. 12 Aug. 1936, Piteşti; s. of Victor Iosifescu and Ecaterina Iosifescu; m. Ştefania Eugenia Zamfirescu 1973; one s.; ed Bucharest Univ.; consultant, Cen. Statistical Bd 1959–62; Asst Prof., Bucharest Polytechnical Inst. 1961–63; Research Mathematician, Inst. of Math. and Centre for Math. Statistics, Romanian Acad., Bucharest 1963–76, Dir 1976–2002, Dir Inst. of Math. Statistics and Applied Math. 2002–, Vice-Pres. Romanian Acad. 2002–; Visiting Prof., Univs of Paris 1974, 1991, 1996, 1998, Mainz 1977–78, Frankfurt am Main 1979–80, Bonn 1981–82, Melbourne 1991, Lille 1997, Bordeaux 1998, 1999; Overseas Fellow, Churchill Coll., Cambridge 1971; mem. Editorial Bds Journal of the Mathematical European Society, Bulletin Mathématique de la Société des Sciences Mathématiques de Roumanie, Mathematica, Revue d'Analyse Numérique et de Théorie de l'Approximation; Deputy Chief Ed. Revue Roumaine de Mathématiques Pures et Appliquées; mem. Int. Statistical Inst., Bernoulli Soc. for Math. Statistics and Probability (mem. Council 1975–79), American Math. Soc., Soc. de Mathématiques Appliquées et Industrielles; Corresp. mem. Romanian Acad. 1991, Titular mem. 2000; Chevalier, Ordre des Palmes académiques 1993; Romanian Acad. Prize 1965, 1972, Bronze Medal, Helsinki Univ. 1975. *Publications include:* Random Processes and Learning (with R. Theodorescu) 1969, Stochastic Processes and Applications in Biology and Medicine, Vol. I Theory, Vol. II Models (with P. Tăutu) 1973, Finite Markov Processes and Their Applications 1980, 2007; Proceedings of Braşov Conference on Probability Theory (ed.) 1971, 1974, 1979, 1982, Dependence with Complete Connections and its Applications (with Ş. Grigorescu) 1982, 1990; Studies in Probability and Related Topics (ed.) 1983, Elements of Stochastic Modelling (with Ş. Grigorescu, G. Oprişan and G. Popescu) 1984, From Real Analysis to Probability: Autobiographical Notes 1986, Metrical Theory of Continued Fractions (with C. Kraaikamp) 2002, Modèles Stochastiques (with N. Limnios and G. Oprisan) 2007, Introduction to Stochastic Models (with N. Limnios and G. Oprisan) 2010, Metrical Theory of Some Continued Fraction Expansions (with G. I. Sebe and D. Lascu) 2011. *Leisure interests:* music, playing violin. *Address:* Institute of Mathematical Statistics and Applied Mathematics, Casa Academiei Romane, 050711 Bucharest 5, Calea 13 Septembrie nr 13 (office); Str. Dr N. Manolescu 9–11, 050583 Bucharest 35, Romania (home). *Telephone:* (21) 3182433 (office); (21) 4103523 (home). *Fax:* (21) 2116608 (office). *E-mail:* miosifes@acad.ro (office). *Website:* www.csm.ro (office).

IOVINE, Jimmy; American record company executive, record producer and film producer; b. 11 March 1953, Brooklyn, New York; early career as recording engineer at Record Plant, New York 1973; worked as producer 1977–90, produced first album for Flame 1977, produced Patti Smith's Easter 1978; Co-founder Interscope Records 1989, Co-Chair. Interscope Geffen A&M Records, Chair. 2001–14; Co-founder (with Dr Dre) Beats By Dr. Dre (headphones brand) 2008, then co-f. (with Dr Dre) Beats Electronics and Beats Music, co. sold to Apple Inc. 2014, helped with establishment of Apple Music, now head of Apple Music; Chair. and CEO Jimmy and Doug's Farm Club (project comprising a record label, website and cable TV show) 1999; has worked with numerous artists, including Marilyn Manson, Stevie Nicks, Nine Inch Nails, No Doubt, 2Pac, Tom Petty, The Pretenders, Brian Setzer Orchestra, Patti Smith, U2; Producer of the Year, Rolling Stone Magazine (twice). *Films produced include:* 8 Mile 2002, Get Rich or Die Tryin' 2005, Archie's Final Project 2009. *Television includes:* Rock Legends: Platinum Weird (film) 2006, Cane (series) 2007. *Website:* www.apple.com/music.

IOVV, Vasile, PhD; Moldovan economist and politician; b. 29 Dec. 1942, Corjova, Dubăsari dist; ed Technologic Inst. of Kiev, Social Science Acad., Moscow; Vice-Pres. then Pres. Balti town exec.; fmr inspector, CP of Moldova, First Sec. of Balti Party Cttee then Sec.; fmr Sr Counsellor, CP of USSR; mem. Parl. (CP) 2005–09; fmr Dir Scientific Research and Production, Sugar Industrial Asscn of Moldova; fmr Chief of Commercial-Econ. Office, Embassy of Moldova in Moscow; fmr Minister of Transport and Roads, then First Deputy Prime Minister of Moldova 2002–05, 2005; mem. Party of Communists of the Republic of Moldova (PCRM). *Address:* c/o Party of Communists of the Republic of Moldova, Nicolae Iorga 11, MD-2012, str., Chisinau, Moldova.

IOZZO, Alfonso; Italian banking executive; *Vice-Chairman, Triffin International Foundation;* ed Univ. of Turin; joined Sanpaolo IMI SpA, Turin 1961, fmr Head, Research Dept, then Foreign Dept and subsequently Deputy Gen. Man., Jt Gen. Man. 1992–95, Gen. Man. Gruppo Bancario Sanpaolo (holding co.) 1995, Gen. Sec., Compagnia di San Paolo 1995–2001, Jt CEO Gruppo Sanpaolo IMI 2001–04, Man. Dir 2004–06 (resgnd); Chair. Banca OPI SpA, Rome 2003–06; Chair. Cassa Depositi e Prestiti 2006–08; currently Vice-Chair. Triffin Int. Foundation; mem. Bd of Dirs Natixis SA, Paris 2006–08; Pres. Movimento Federalista Europeo; Pres. A. Spinelli Inst. *Address:* Triffin International Foundation, Institute of European Studies, Place Deans, 1, 1348 Louvain-la-Neuve, Belgium (office). *Telephone:* (47) 268-24-79 (office). *Website:* www.uclouvain.be (office).

IP, Nancy Yuk-Yu, BSc, PhD; Chinese neurobiologist and academic; *Chair Professor of Biochemistry and Director, Molecular Neuroscience Centre, Hong Kong University of Science and Technology;* b. 30 July 1955, Hong Kong; ed Simmons Coll. and Harvard Medical School, USA; Lab. Head, Lifecodes Corpn, New York, USA 1987–89, Sr Staff Scientist 1989–93; Scientific Consultant, Regeneron Pharmaceuticals Inc., New York 1993–96; Lecturer, Dept of Biology, Hong Kong Univ. of Science and Tech. 1993–94, Assoc. Prof. 1994–97, Prof. 1998–2000, Dir Biotechnology Research Inst. 1996–2008, Assoc. Dean of Science 1998–2005, Dir Molecular Neuroscience Centre 1999–, Prof., Dept of Biochemistry 2000–05, Head of Dept 2000–09, Chair Prof. 2005–; Fellow, Acad. of Sciences for the Developing World 2004; mem. Chinese Acad. of Sciences; Hon. Dr of Humane Sciences (Simmons Coll.) 2007; Medal of Honour, Govt of Hong Kong Special Admin. Region 2008; Sr Research Fellowship, Croucher Foundation 1998, Nat. Natural Science Award, Nat. Natural Science Foundation of China 2003, L'Oréal-UNESCO Women in Science Award 2004, Outstanding Women Professionals Award, Hong Kong Women Professionals and Entrepreneurs Asscn 2005, Scientific and Technological Progress Prize, Ho Leung Ho Lee Foundation 2008. *Publications:* more than 190 articles in scientific journals with more than 13,000 SCI citations, holder of 18 patents. *Address:* Department of Biochemistry, Hong Kong University of Science and Technology, Clear Water Bay, Kowloon, Hong Kong Special Administrative Region, People's Republic of China (office). *Telephone:* 2358-7304 (office). *Fax:* 2358-2765 (office). *E-mail:* boip@ust.hk (office). *Website:* www.ust.hk/bich/facultyprofiles/nancyip.html (office).

IP, Regina, (Lau Suk-yee), BA, MLitt, MSc, MA; Hong Kong politician; *Legislative Councillor and Chairperson, New People's Party;* b. 24 Aug. 1950, Hong Kong; d. of Low Fook Seng; m. (husband deceased); one d.; ed Univ. of Hong Kong, Univ. of Glasgow, UK, Stanford Univ., USA; joined Hong Kong Admin. Service 1975, service in Civil Service Br., Home Affairs Dept, New Territories Admin, City and New Territories Admin, Security Br., Trade Dept, Office of the Chief Sec., Trade and Industry Br.; Dir-Gen. of Industry 1995–96; Dir of Immigration (first woman apptd to head a disciplined service) 1996–98; Dir of Immigration of Hong Kong Special Admin. Region (HKSAR) 1997–98; Sec. for Security 1998–2002, 2002–03 (resgnd); attended Stanford Univ. 2003–06, then returned to Hong Kong; est. Savantas Policy Inst. (think tank) 2006; apptd mem. Comm. on Strategic Devt 2007; mem. Legis. Council 2008–; Vice-Chair. China Reform Council 2008–; Founder, Legislative Councillor and Chair. New People's Party 2010–; Gold Bauhinia Star; Outstanding Person for Chinese Entrepreneurial Innovation 2008. *Publications:* Four Funerals and One Wedding (autobiog.), Learning English with Regina, Books 1 and 2. *Leisure interests:* movies, Chinese opera, travelling. *Address:* Legislative Council, Room 306, West Wing, Central Government Offices, 11 Ice House Street, Central, Hong Kong Special Administrative Region, People's Republic of China (office). *Telephone:* 31000079 (office); 21159999 (office). *Fax:* 21159688 (office). *E-mail:* regina.ip@savantas.org (office). *Website:* www.reginaip.hk.

IPINGE, Hopelong Uushona, BBA, MBA, MA; Namibian government official and fmr diplomatist; *Permanent Secretary, Ministry of Veterans Affairs;* m.; three c.; ed Washington Int. Univ., Pa, Keele Univ., UK; Sr Staff Officer, Directorate of Policy and Operations, Ministry of Defence 1990–92; CEO Omusati Regional Counsel 1993–95; mem. Panel of Govt Experts on Small Arms Proliferation 1996–98; Deputy Sec., Ministry of Defence 1995–99; Amb. to China (also accred to S Korea and Viet Nam) 1999–2005, to USA 2005–06, to Brazil 2006–10, to Cuba 2010–13; currently Perm. Sec., Ministry of Veteran Affairs. *Address:* Ministry of Veterans Affairs, 134 Robert Mugabe Avenue (Kenya House), Private Bag 13407, Windhoek, Namibia (office). *Telephone:* (61) 2963011 (office). *Fax:* (61) 305935 (office). *E-mail:* info@mova.gov.na (office). *Website:* www.mova.gov.na (office).

IPPEN, Erich P., SB, MS, PhD; American physicist, electrical engineer and academic; *Elihu Thomson Professor of Electrical Engineering, Massachusetts Institute of Technology;* m. Dorothea E. Ippen; two s.; ed Massachusetts Inst. of Tech., Univ. of California, Berkeley; mem. Tech. Staff, Bell Labs 1968–80; joined MIT faculty 1980, currently Prin. Investigator, Research Lab. of Electronics (RLE), Elihu Thomson Prof. of Electrical Eng, Dept of Electrical Eng and Computer Science and Prof. of Physics, one of leaders of RLE's Optics and Quantum Electronics Group; mem. NAS, Nat. Acad. of Eng; Fellow, American Acad. of Arts and Sciences, IEEE, Optical Soc. of America (OSA), American Physical Soc. (APS); OSA R.W. Wood Prize 1981, Edward Longstreth Medal, Franklin Inst. 1982, Morris Leeds Award, IEEE 1983, Humboldt Sr Scientist Award 1986, H. E. Edgerton Award, SPIE 1989, John Scott Award, City of Philadelphia Trusts 1991, Civilian Distinguished Service Medal, USAF 1992, IEEE Quantum Electronics Award 1997, APS Arthur Schawlow Prize 1997, Distinguished Eng Alumnus, Univ. of California, Berkeley 2000, MIT Killian Award 2001, OSA Charles Hard Townes Award 2004, OSA Frederic Ives Medal 2006. *Achievements include:* a founder of field of femtosecond optics. *Publications include:* numerous scientific papers in professional journals on femtosecond science and ultra-highspeed devices to probe ultrafast phenomena in materials. *Address:* Room 36-319, Research Laboratory of Electronics, Massachusetts Institute of Technology, 77 Massachusetts Avenue, Cambridge, MA 02139, USA (office). *Telephone:* (617) 253-8504 (office). *Fax:* (617) 253-9611 (office). *E-mail:* ippen@mit.edu (office). *Website:* www.rle.mit.edu/rleonline/People/ErichP.Ippen.html (office).

IRANI, Jamshed Jiji, PhD; Indian business executive; *Director, Tata Sons Ltd.;* b. 2 June 1936, Nagpur; s. of Jiji D. Irani and Khorshed Irani; m. Daisy Irani 1971; one s. two d.; ed Nagpur Univ., Univ. of Sheffield, UK; worked for British Iron and Steel Research Asscn 1963–67; Tata Iron and Steel Co. Ltd (now Tata Sons Ltd) 1968–, Gen. Man. 1979–81, Deputy Man. Dir 1981–83, Vice-Pres. (Operations) 1983–85, Pres. 1985–88, Jt Man. Dir 1988–92, Man. Dir 1992–97, Dir 1997–; Pres. Indian Inst. of Metals, All India Man. Asscn 1988–89; Nat. Pres. Confed. of Indian Industry 1992–93; Co-chair. Indo-British Partnership 1993–98; Chair. Bd of Govs Xavier Labour Relations Inst., Jamshedpur 1993–2003, Bd of Govs Indian Inst. of Man.; mem. Scientific Advisory Cttee to Cabinet, Govt of India, Cen. Advisory Bd of Educ.; Pres. Asian Asscn of Man. Org. 2004–07; Dir (non-exec.) Repro India Ltd 2005–; Chair. (non-exec.) Everonn Skill Development Ltd 2010–11; mem. Council Indian Inst. of Science, Bangalore, Advisory Council of Citigroup India; Trustee, World Wild Fund for Nature (India); Fellow, Inst. of Metals, Inst. of Engineers, All India Man. Asscn, Inst. of Standards Engineers, Indian Acad. of Sciences, Inst. of Industrial Mans; Paul Harris Fellow, Rotary Int. 1977; Melvin Jones Fellow, Lions Int. Foundation 1993; Hon. KBE 1997; Dr hc (Univ. of Sheffield) 1993, Hon. DSc (Banaras Hindu Univ.) 2004; Nat. Metallurgist Award 1974, Platinum Medal, Indian Inst. of Man. 1988, Steel Vision Award, Michael John Memorial Gold Medal 1998, Qimpro Platinum Standard 2000, Juran Quality Medal, Indian Merchants' Chamber 2001, Ernst & Young Lifetime Achievement Award 2001, Padma Bhushan 2007. *Publications include:* numerous tech. papers. *Leisure interests:* philately, photography. *Address:* 7 Beldih Lake, Jamshedpur, 831001, India. *Telephone:* (657) 2431024 (office); (22) 66657565 (office); (22) 66352000 (home); (657) 2431025 (home). *Fax:* (657) 2431818 (office); (22) 66658030 (office); (22) 66352001 (home). *E-mail:* jjirani@tata.com (office). *Website:* www.tata.com (office).

IRANI, Ray R., DSc; American business executive; b. 15 Jan. 1935, Beirut, Lebanon; s. of Rida Irani and Naz Irani; m. Ghada Irani; two s. one d.; ed Univ. of Southern California; Sr Research Leader, Monsanto Co. 1957–67; Assoc. Dir New Products, later Dir of Research, Diamond Shamrock Corpn 1967–73; joined Olin Corpn 1973, Pres. Chemicals Group 1978–80, Dir and Corp. Pres. 1980–83; Exec. Vice-Pres. Occidental Petroleum Corpn, Los Angeles 1983–84, Dir 1984–2013,

COO 1984–90, Pres. 1984–96, 2005–07, Chair. and CEO 1990–2011, Exec. Chair. 2011–13; CEO Occidental Chemical Corpn 1983–91, Chair. 1983–94; Chair. Canadian Occidental Petroleum Ltd (now Nexen Inc.), Calgary 1987–99, Hon. Chair. 1999–2000; currently Chair. and CEO Ray Investment LLC; Ind. Dir Wynn Resorts Ltd 2007–18, Dir Wynn Las Vegas, LLC; mem. Bd of Dirs, American Petroleum Inst., KB Home 1992–, Lyondell Chemical Co. 2002–, Cedars Bank, TCW Group, Kaufman & Broad SA; mem. Advisory Bd Stone Canyon Industries; mem. ACS, Scientific Research Soc., American Industrial Research Inst., Council on Foreign Relations, Conf. Bd, US-Saudi Arabian Business Council, World Affairs Council; Trustee, Univ. of Southern California, Chair. USC's Bd Personnel Cttee; Vice-Chair. American Univ. of Beirut; Hon. Fellow, American Inst. of Chemists. *Publications:* Particle Size; numerous papers in field of particle physics.

IRINEJ, Patriarch; Serbian ecclesiastic; *Patriarch of Serbian Orthodox Church;* b. (Irinej Gavrilovic), 28 Aug. 1930, Vidova, near Čačak; ed Orthodox Seminary, Prizren, Theological Faculty, Belgrade; monk, Rakovica Monastery 1959; Head of monastic school, Ostrog Monastery 1969; Rector, Orthodox Seminary, Prizren 1969; Vicar Bishop of Moravica 1974–75; Bishop of Nis 1975–2010; installed as 45th Patriarch of the Serbian Orthodox Church (Srpska Pravoslavna Crkva), Jan. 2010, also Archbishop of Peć and Metropolitan of Belgrade-Karlovci; Grand Cross, Order of the Star of Karađorđe, Grand Collar, Order of the Eagle of Georgia. *Address:* Serbian Orthodox Church (Srpska Pravoslavna Crkva), 11001 Belgrade, Kralja Petra 5, POB 182, Serbia (office). *Telephone:* (11) 3025-112 (office). *E-mail:* info@spc.rs (office). *Website:* www.spc.rs/eng (office).

IRONS, Jeremy; British actor; b. 19 Sept. 1948, Cowes, Isle of Wight, England; s. of Paul Dugan Irons and Barbara Ann Brereton Sharpe; m. 1st (divorced); 2nd Sinead Cusack (q.v.) 1978; two s.; ed Sherborne School, Dorset, Bristol Old Vic Theatre School; TV debut 1968; FAO Goodwill Amb. 2011; mem. Gaia Foundation, European Film Acad.; Patron, Prison Phoenix Trust, Archway Foundation; Officier des Arts et des Lettres; European Film Acad. Special Achievement Award 1998. *Stage appearances:* The Real Thing, Broadway (Tony Award) 1984, Rover 1986, The Winter's Tale 1986, Richard II (Stratford) 1986, Embers (Duke of York Theatre, London) 2006, Never So Good (Nat. Theatre) 2008, Impressionism (Broadway) 2009, The Gods Weep (Stratford) 2010. *Films include:* Nijinsky 1980, The French Lieutenant's Woman 1981, Moonlighting 1982, Betrayal 1983, The Wild Duck 1983, Swann in Love 1984, The Mission 1986, A Chorus of Disapproval 1988, Dead Ringers (New York Critics Best Actor Award 1988) 1988, Australia 1989, Danny, The Champion of the World 1989, Reversal of Fortune (Acad. Award 1991, Golden Globe Award for Best Actor 1991) 1990, Zebracka opera 1991, Kafka 1991, Damage 1992, Waterland 1992, M. Butterfly 1993, The House of the Spirits 1993, The Lion King (voice) 1994, Die Hard with a Vengeance 1995, Stealing Beauty 1996, Chinese Box 1997, Lolita 1997, The Man in the Iron Mask 1998, Dungeons and Dragons 2000, The Fourth Angel 2001, The Time Machine 2002, And Now… Ladies and Gentlemen… 2002, Callas Forever 2002, The Merchant of Venice 2004, Being Julia 2004, Kingdom of Heaven 2005, Casanova 2005, Inland Empire 2006, Eragon 2006, Appaloosa 2008, The Pink Panther 2 2009, Margin Call 2011, The Words 2012, Night Train to Lisbon 2013, Beautiful Creatures 2013, High-Rise 2015, Correspondence 2016, Birds Like Us 2017, Better Start Running 2018. *Television includes:* The Pallisers (series) 1974, Notorious Woman (mini-series) 1974, Love for Lydia (mini-series) 1977, Langrishe Go Down 1978, The Voysey Inheritance 1979, Brideshead Revisited 1981, The Captain's Doll 1983, Saturday Night Live (episode 16.16, host) 1991, Tales from Hollywood 1992, Mirad (also dir) 1997, The Great War and the Shaping of the 20th Century (Primetime Emmy Award for Outstanding Voice-Over Performance 1997), Ohio Impromptu 2000, Longitude 2000, Last Call 2002, RSC Meets USA: Working Shakespeare (video) 2002, Comic Relief 2003, Dame Edna Live at the Palace 2003, Elizabeth I (Primetime Emmy Award 2005, Golden Globe Award for Best Supporting Actor in a mini-series 2005, Screen Actors' Guild Award for Outstanding Performance by a Male Actor in a Television Movie 2006) 2005, The Colour of Magic 2008, Georgia O'Keeffe 2009, The Borgias (series) 2011–13, Law & Order: Special Victims Unit (series) 2011, Eco-Hollywood (film) 2011, The Simpsons (series) 2012, The Hollow Crown (mini-series): Henry IV, Part 1 2012, Henry IV, Part 2 2012, Life on Fire: Wildlife on the Volcano's Edge (series, narrator) 2013, Watchmen (series) 2019. *Leisure interests:* skiing, riding, sailing. *Address:* c/o Abi Harris, The Artists Partnership, 101 Finsbury Pavement, London, EC2A 1RS, England (office).

IRVINE OF LAIRG, Baron (Life Peer), cr. 1987, of Lairg in the District of Sutherland; **Alexander (Derry) Andrew Mackay Irvine,** QC, MA, LLB; British lawyer; b. 23 June 1940; s. of Alexander Irvine and Margaret Christina Irvine; m. 1st Margaret Veitch (divorced 1973); m. 2nd Alison Mary McNair 1974; two s.; ed Inverness Acad., Hutcheson's Boys' Grammar School, Univ. of Glasgow, Christ's Coll., Cambridge; Lecturer, LSE 1965–69; called to the Bar, Inner Temple 1967, Bencher 1985; a Recorder 1985–88; Deputy High Court Judge 1987–97; Shadow Spokesman on Legal Affairs and Home Affairs 1987–92; Shadow Lord Chancellor 1992–97, Lord High Chancellor of GB 1997–2003, Hon. Pres. Legal and Constitutional Affairs Group 2007–; Pres. Magistrates' Asscn; Jt Pres. House of Lords British-American Parl. Group, Commonwealth Parl. Asscn, Inter-Parl. Union; Pres. NI Youth and Family Courts Asscn 1999; Hon. Bencher, Inn of Court of NI 1998; Vice-Patron, World Fed. of Mental Health; Trustee, Whitechapel Art Gallery 1990–, Hunterian Collection 1997–; Hon. Fellow, LSE; Hon. LLD (Glasgow) 1997, Laurea hc (Siena) 2000. *Leisure interests:* cinema, theatre, art, travel. *Address:* House of Lords, London, SW1A 0PW, England. *Telephone:* (20) 7219-5353. *Fax:* (20) 7219-5979.

IRVING, Amy; American actress; b. 10 Sept. 1953, Palo Alto, Calif.; m. 1st Steven Spielberg (q.v.) 1985 (divorced); one s.; m. 2nd Bruno Barreto 1996 (divorced 2005); one s.; m. 3rd Kenneth Bowser, Jr; ed American Conservatory Theater and London Acad. of Dramatic Art; frequent TV appearances. *Stage appearances include:* Juliet in Romeo and Juliet, Seattle Repertory Theater 1982–83, on Broadway in Amadeus 1981–82, Heartbreak House 1983–84, Three Sisters 1997, off Broadway in The Road to Mecca 1988, The Guys 2002, Celadine 2004, The Waters of March 2008, A Little Night Music 2010. *Films include:* Carrie, The Fury, Voices, Honeysuckle Road, The Competition, Yentl, Mickey and Maude, Rumpelstiltskin, Crossing Delancey, A Show of Force, Benefit of the Doubt, Kleptomania, Acts of Love (also co-exec. producer), I'm Not Rappaport, Carried Away, Deconstructing Harry, One Tough Cop 1998, Blue Ridge Fall 1999, The Confession, The Rage: Carrie 2 1999, Traffic 2000, Bossa Nova 2000, Thirteen Conversations About One Thing 2002, Tuck Everlasting 2002, Hide and Seek 2005, Adam 2009. *Television includes:* Alias (series) 2002–05, Zero Hour (series) 2013, Unsane 2018.

IRVING, John Winslow, BA, MFA; American writer; b. 2 March 1942, Exeter, NH; s. of Colin F. N. Irving and Frances Winslow; m. 1st Shyla Leary 1964 (divorced 1981); two s.; m. 2nd Janet Turnbull 1987; one s.; ed Univs of Pittsburgh, New Hampshire and Iowa, Univ. of Vienna, Austria; Asst Prof. of English, Mount Holyoke Coll. 1967–72, 1975–78; Writer-in-Residence, Univ. of Iowa 1972–75; with Bread Loaf Writers' Conf. 1976, Brandeis Univ.; Rockefeller Foundation grantee 1971–72; Nat. Endowment for Arts Fellow 1974–75, Guggenheim Fellow 1976–77; mem. American Acad. of Arts and Letters 2001; O. Henry Award 1981, Richard C. Holbrooke Distinguished Achievement Award 2018. *Film screenplay:* The Cider House Rules (Acad. Award for Best Adapted Screenplay 2000) 1999. *Publications include:* novels: Setting Free the Bears 1969, The Water-Method Man 1972, The 158-Pound Marriage 1974, The World According to Garp (Nat. Book Award 1980 for paperback fiction 1980) 1978, The Hotel New Hampshire 1981, The Cider House Rules 1985, A Prayer for Owen Meany 1989, A Son of the Circus 1994, A Widow for One Year 1998, The Fourth Hand 2001, Until I Find You 2005, Last Night in Twisted River 2009, In One Person 2012, Avenue of Mysteries 2015; non-fiction: An Introduction to Great Expectations 1986, Trying to Save Piggy Sneed (memoirs, short stories and essays) 1996, An Introduction to A Christmas Carol 1996, My Movie Business (memoir) 1999, The Cider House Rules: A Screenplay 1999, The Fourth Hand 2001, A Sound Like Someone Trying Not to Make a Sound 2004, Until I Find You 2005, Last Night in Twisted River 2009, In One Person (Lambda Literary Award 2013) 2012, Avenue of Mysteries 2015; contrib. to New York Times Book Review, New Yorker, Fiction Magazine, Rolling Stone, Esquire, Playboy. *Address:* c/o Turnbull Agency LLC, New York, NY, USA (office). *Website:* www.john-irving.com.

ISA, Dato' Haji Pehin, BA; Brunei politician; b. 1935; ed Univ. of Southampton, UK; trained as barrister in UK; Asst Counsel and Deputy Public Prosecutor, Brunei 1962–65, Asst Attorney-Gen. 1965–68, Deputy Attorney-Gen. 1968–70 fmrly Gen. Adviser to Sultan of Brunei, then Special Adviser, with ministerial rank in Prime Minister's Office 1986–2005; Minister of Home Affairs 1988–95; currently with Ahmad Isa and Partners (law firm). *Address:* Ahmad Isa and Partners, Unit 405A/410A, 4th Floor Wisma Jaya, Jalan Pemanca, Bandar Seri Begawan BS 8811, Brunei (office). *Telephone:* 2239091 (office). *E-mail:* admisa@brunet.bn (office).

ISAAC, Alan Raymond, CNZM; New Zealand business executive and sports administrator; b. 20 Jan. 1952, Wellington, North Island; ed Onslow Coll., Victoria Univ. of Wellington; left-handed batsman; represented Wellington through the age groups and for three years captained their second team; mem. New Zealand Cricket Bd for 18 years, Chair. 2008–10; Vice-Pres. Int. Cricket Council (ICC) 2010–12, Pres. 2012–14; with KPMG 1971–2006, Chair. –2006; mem. bds several business, health, community and sporting orgs, including New Zealand Red Cross Foundation, New Zealand Community Trust; fmr mem. New Zealand Golf Bd, Bd of Rugby New Zealand 2011 Ltd.

ISAAC, Anthony (Tony) Eric; British business executive; *Senior Independent Non-Executive Director, Hogg Robinson Group;* Finance Dir, GEC Plessey Telecommunications Ltd 1988–90; Finance Dir, Arjo Wiggins Appleton plc (joined shortly before demerger from BAT Industries plc 1990) 1990–96; Exec. Dir BOC 1994–96, mem. Exec. Man. Bd 1996–2006, Group Finance Dir 1994–99, Chief Exec. 2000–06; Dir (non-exec.), Schlumberger Ltd 2003–15, Chair. (non-exec.) 2012–15; mem. Bd of Dirs, GDF Suez Energy International (fmrly International Power plc) 2000–13, Chair. Audit Cttee 2011–12; Sr Ind. Dir (non-exec.), Hogg Robinson Group 2006–, Chair. Audit Cttee, mem. Remuneration Cttee, Nomination Cttee; mem. Chartered Inst. of Man. Accountants. *Address:* Hogg Robinson Group, Global House, Victoria Street, Basingstoke, Hants. RG21 3BT, England (office). *Telephone:* (1256) 312600 (office). *E-mail:* ir@hrgworldwide.com (office). *Website:* www.hoggrobinsongroup.com (office).

ISAACS, Sir Jeremy Israel, Kt, MA; British television executive and arts administrator; b. 28 Sept. 1932; s. of Isidore Isaacs and Sara Jacobs; m. 1st Tamara Isaacs (née Weinreich) 1958 (died 1986); one s. one d.; m. 2nd Gillian Widdicombe 1988; ed Glasgow Acad., Merton Coll., Oxford; TV Producer, Granada TV (What the Papers Say, All Our Yesterdays) 1958, Associated Rediffusion (This Week) 1963, BBC TV (Panorama) 1965; Controller of Features, Associated Rediffusion 1967; with Thames TV 1968–78, Producer, The World at War 1974, Cold War 1998; Dir of Programmes 1974–78; special ind. consultant TV series Hollywood, ITV, A Sense of Freedom, ITV, Ireland, a Television Documentary, BBC, Battle for Crete, New Zealand TV, Cold War, Turner Broadcasting; CEO, Channel Four TV Co. 1981–88; Gen. Dir Royal Opera House 1988–96 (Dir 1985–97); Chief Exec. Jeremy Isaacs Productions 1998–; Gov. BFI 1979–84; Chair. BFI Production Bd 1979–81, Artsworld Channels Ltd 2000–03, Sky Arts; Chair. judging panel, European City of Culture competition 2008; James MacTaggart Memorial Lecturer, Edinburgh TV Festival 1979; Fellow, Royal Television Soc. 1978, BAFTA 1985, BFI 1986; L'Ordre National du Mérite 1992; Hon. DLitt (Strathclyde) 1983, (Bristol) 1988, Dr hc (CNAA) 1987, (RCA) 1988, Hon. LLD (Manchester) 1998; Desmond Davis Award for Outstanding Creative contrib. to TV 1972, George Polk Memorial Award 1973, Cyril Bennett Award 1982, Lord Willis Award for Distinguished Service to TV 1985. *Publications include:* Storm Over Four: A Personal Account 1989, Cold War (co-author) 1999, Never Mind the Moon 1999, Look Me in the Eye: a Life in Television (autobiog.) 2006. *Leisure interests:* books, walks, sleep.

ISAACSON, Walter Seff, MA; American journalist and international organization official; *Distinguished Fellow, Aspen Institute;* b. 20 May 1952, New Orleans, La; s. of Irwin Isaacson and Betsy Isaacson; m. Cathy Wright 1984; one d.; ed Harvard Univ., Pembroke Coll., Oxford, UK; reporter, Sunday Times, London 1976–77, States-Item, New Orleans 1977–78; staff writer, Time magazine, New York 1978–79, political corresp. 1979–81, Assoc. Ed. 1981–84, Sr Ed. 1985–91, Asst Man. Ed. 1991–93, Man. Ed. 1995–2000, Editorial Dir Time Inc. 2000–01; Chair. and CEO CNN Newsgroup 2001–03; Ed. New Media Time, Inc. 1993–96; apptd Pres. and CEO Aspen Inst., Washington, DC 2003, currently Distinguished Fellow; Chair. Broadcasting Bd of Govs 2009–12; Vice-Chair. Louisiana Recovery Authority 2005–07, Partners for a New Beginning 2010; Chair. Emer. Teach for

America; mem. Bd of Dirs United Airlines, Tulane Univ., New Orleans Tricentennial Comm., Bloomberg Philanthropies, Soc. of American Historians, Carnegie Inst. for Science, My Brother's Keeper Alliance; mem. Bd of Overseers, Harvard Univ.; mem. Council on Foreign Relations, Century Asscn; Overseas Press Club Award, New York 1981, 1984, 1987, Harry Truman Book Prize 1987. *Publications:* Pro and Con 1983, Kissinger: A Biography 1992, The Wise Men (jtly) 1986, Benjamin Franklin: An American Life 2003, Einstein: His Life and Universe (Quill Award for Biography 2007) 2007, American Sketches: Great Leaders, Creative Thinkers and Heroes of a Hurricane 2009, Profiles in Leadership 2010, Steve Jobs 2011. *Address:* Aspen Institute, 2300 N Street, NW, Suite 700, Washington, DC 20037, USA (office). *Telephone:* (202) 736-5800 (office). *Fax:* (202) 467-0790 (office). *E-mail:* pat.zindulka@aspeninstitute.org (office). *Website:* www.aspeninstitute.org (office).

ISAAK, Chris, BA; American singer, songwriter and actor; b. 26 June 1956, Stockton, Calif.; ed Univ. of the Pacific; singer 1984–; extensive int. tours, festival appearances; Int. Rock Award for Best Male Vocalist of the Year 1991, three MTV Music Video Awards (for Wicked Game) 1991. *Films appearances include:* Married to the Mob 1988, Wild At Heart 1989, The Silence of the Lambs 1991, Twin Peaks: Fire Walk With Me 1992, Little Buddha 1993, Grace of My Heart 1996, That Thing You Do! 1996, Blue Ridge Fall 1999, A Dirty Shame 2004, The Informers 2009, Twin Peaks: The Missing Pieces 2014. *Television appearances include:* From the Earth to the Moon (mini-series) 1998, The Chris Isaak Show (series) 2001–04. *Songs contributed to film and television include:* Blue Velvet 1986, Married to the Mob 1988, Wild At Heart 1990, La Désenchantée 1990, True Romance 1993, Beautiful Girls 1996, Tin Cup 1996, The Late Late Show with Craig Kilborn (title song) 1999, Eyes Wide Shut 1999, The Family Man 2000, Mona Lisa Smile 2003, Chasing Liberty 2004. *Recordings include:* albums: Silvertone 1985, Chris Isaak 1987, Heart Shaped World 1989, Wicked Game 1991, San Francisco Days 1993, Forever Blue 1995, Baja Sessions 1996, Speak Of The Devil 1998, Wicked Ways Anthology 1998, Always Got Tonight 2002, Chris Isaak Christmas 2004, Mr Lucky 2009, Live at the Fillmore 2010, Beyond the Sun 2011, First Comes the Night 2015. *Website:* www.chrisisaak.com.

ISABEKOV, Azim Beishembayevich; Kyrgyzstani economist and politician; b. 4 April 1960, Arashan, Chui Oblast; ed Kyrgyz State Univ.; Chief of Staff, Office of Gov. of Chui Oblast Kurmanbek Bakiyev 1997–2000; Head of Admin. Dept, Office of Prime Minister 2001–02; Dir State Fund for Econ. Devt 2002–04; Deputy Chief of Staff, Office of Pres. Kurmanbek Bakiyev 2005–06; Minister of Agric., Water Resources and Mfg Industry June–Dec. 2006; Prime Minister Jan.–March 2007.

ISAKA, Ryuichi; Japanese business executive; *President and Representative Director, Seven & i Holdings Company Ltd;* b. 4 Oct. 1957; various positions with Seven-Eleven Japan Co. Ltd 1980–2002, Dir, Seven-Eleven Japan Co. Ltd 2002–06, Man. Exec. Officer 2006–09, Pres. and COO 2009–16, Pres. and Rep. Dir, Seven & i Holdings Co. Ltd 2016–. *Address:* Seven & i Holdings Co. Ltd, 8-8 Nibancho, Chiyoda-ku, Tokyo 102-8455, Japan (office). *Telephone:* (3) 6238-3711 (office). *E-mail:* info@7andi.com (office). *Website:* www.7andi.com (office).

ISAKOV, Sapar; Kyrgyzstani politician; b. 29 July 1977, Frunze (now Bishkek), Kyrgyz SSR, USSR; ed Int. Univ. of Kyrgyzstan; teacher, Int. Univ. of Kyrgyzstan 1999–2003; worked as 2nd and 3rd Sec., and Head of Bilateral Cooperation, in Int. Legal Dept, Ministry of Foreign Affairs 2003–07; Head, Dept of Int. Cooperation April–Aug. 2007, Dept of External Relations 2007–09; Head, Communication Service, Central Agency for Devt, Investments and Innovations 2009–10, Dept of Int. Relations May–Aug. 2010, Head, Dept of Foreign Policy 2010–17 (with rank of Deputy Head of Govt Staff 2010–11, Deputy Chief of Staff 2011–17, Chief of Staff March–Aug. 2017; Deputy Head, Office of the Pres. Jan.–March 2017, Head March–Aug. 2017; Prime Minister Aug. 2017–18 (resgnd); arrested on corruption charges 2018.

ISAKOV, Gen. Vladimir Ilyich; Russian military officer; b. 21 July 1950, Voskresenskoye, Kaluga region; ed Moscow Mil. School of Civil Defence, Mil. Acad. of Home Front Transport, Mil. Acad. of Gen. Staff; Platoon Commdr of Civil Defence Forces, served in Group of Soviet Armed Forces in Germany; Deputy Regt Commdr, then Deputy Army Commdr of Home Front, Deputy Commdr Div. of Home Front, Siberian Mil. Command 1982–84, 40th Army in Afghanistan 1984–86; Deputy Army Commdr, then Head of Home Front, Kiev Mil. Command 1988–89, Head of Gen. Staff of Home Front, W Group of Armed Forces 1989–94, Head of Chair. Mil. Acad. of Gen. Staff 1994, Head of Gen. Staff Armed Forces of Russian Fed. 1996, First Deputy Head of Home Front 1996–97, Head 1997, Chief of Logistics and Deputy Minister of Defence 1997–2008.

ISAKSON, Johnny, BBA; American business executive and politician; *Senator from Georgia;* b. 28 Dec. 1944, Atlanta, Ga; s. of Edwin Andrew Isakson and Julia Isakson (née Baker); m. Dianne Isakson 1968; three c.; ed Univ. of Georgia; served in Ga Air Nat. Guard 1966–72; began business career with Northside Reality (family-owned real estate co.) 1967, est. Cobb County Office, apptd Pres. 1979; elected to Ga State House of Reps 1976, Republican Leader in State House 1983–90; Republican nominee for Gov. of Ga 1989; elected to Ga State Senate 1993, Republican Chair. Ga Bd of Educ. 1996–99; Ga Chair. for Bob Dole for Pres. Campaign 1996; elected to US House of Reps, Washington, DC 1999, mem. House Transportation Cttee, Educ. Cttee, Co-Chair. Sub-cttee on 21st Century Competitiveness, Deputy Major Whip to House Republican Leadership; Senator from Georgia 2005–; fmr Pres. Realty Alliance; fmr mem. Exec. Cttee, Nat. Asscn of Realtors; fmr mem. Bd of Dirs Ga Chamber of Commerce, Riverside Bank; fmr mem. Advisory Bd SunTrust; teacher, Sunday School, Mount Zion United Methodist Church 1978–2008; Republican; Best Legislator in America Award, Republican Nat. Cttee 1989. *Address:* 131 Russell Senate Office Building, Washington, DC 20510, USA (office). *Telephone:* (202) 224-3643 (office). *Fax:* (202) 228-0724 (office). *Website:* isakson.senate.gov (office).

ISAMUDDIN, Riduan, (Hambali); Indonesian religious leader; b. (Encep Nurjaman), 4 April 1964, Sukamanah, W Java; m. Noral Wizaah Lee; active in opposition to Suharto regime 1970s and 1980s; sought exile in Malaysia 1985; fought as mujahideen guerrilla against Soviet occupation, Afghanistan 1988; recruited Muslim supporters to join a jihad (holy war) in order to est. a Pan-Asian Islamic State, Malaysia 1990; believed to have co-f. Jemaah Islamiah (JI—Islamic Community) network with Abu Bakar Bashir with operations throughout SE Asia 1990; returned to Indonesia to recruit supporters 2000; mem. consultative council al-Qa'ida; alleged liaison officer between al-Qa'ida and radical Islamic groups in SE Asia; allegedly funded numerous mil. terrorist groups fighting jihad, in particular in Maluko Islands 1999; wanted by Govts of Indonesia, Malaysia, Singapore and The Philippines as key suspect for involvement in series of bomb attacks on World Trade Center 1993, Philippine airliner 1994, USS Cole, Yemen 2000, Christian church bombings, Indonesia 2000, Manila bombings 2000, Sept. 11 attacks in USA 2001, Operation Jabril (attempted mass terrorist attacks on US targets in Malaysia, Singapore and Philippines) 2001, Bali nightclub 2002; captured in Thailand by US forces 11 August 2003 and currently in custody at Guantanamo Bay detention center, Cuba.

ISARANGURA, Gen. Thammarak, BSc; Thai government official and military officer; b. 22 July 1938, Roiet Prov.; m. Waneda Isarangura; ed Chulachomklao Royal Mil. Acad.; Commdr Training Directorate of Jt Communications 1964–66, with Radio Station Directorate 1967–72, Asst Chief, Intelligence Section, Seconded to Second Army Area Command Sakon Nakhon 1973–76, Chief, Intelligence Section, Fourth Army Area Command, Nakhonsrithammarat 1982–83, Chief, Intelligence Section, Directorate of Intelligence, Army Operation Centre 1984–88, Commdr of Army Mil. Intelligence 1989–90, Chief of Staff to Deputy Supreme Commdr, Supreme Command Headquarters 1991–95, Commanding Gen. of Armed Forces Security Centre, Supreme Command 1996–97, Special Adviser, Supreme Command Headquarters 1998; Deputy Prime Minister of Thailand 2004; Minister of Defence 2005–06; banned from politics by Constitutional Tribunal 2007; Kt Grand Cordon (Special Class) of the Most Exalted Order of the White Elephant, of the Most Noble Order of the Crown of Thailand.

ISĂRESCU, Mugur Constantin, PhD; Romanian economist, central banker and fmr politician; *Governor, Banca Națională a României (National Bank of Romania);* b. 1 Aug. 1949, Drăgășani, Vâlcea Co.; s. of Constantin Isărescu and Aritina Isărescu; m. Elena Isărescu; one s. one d.; ed Acad. of Econs; Research Fellow, Inst. for World Econ. 1971–90; Asst Lecturer, Acad. of Econs, Bucharest 1975–89, Prof. 1996–; Prof., Timișoara West Univ. 1994–96; fmrly Prof. of Banking, Coll. of Romanian Banking Inst.; First Sec., Embassy in Washington, DC 1990; Gov. Banca Națională a României (Nat. Bank of Romania) 1990–99, 2001–, IMF Gov. for Romania, World Bank Vice-Gov. for Romania, EBRD Vice-Gov. for Romania; Prime Minister of Romania 1999–2000; Chair. for Romania, Club of Rome; Pres. Central Bank Govs' Club in the Region of the Black Sea, the Balkans and Central Asia; Vice-Pres. Cen. Banks Govs Club; mem. Bd Romanian American Enterprise Fund, Trilateral Comm.; Chair. Romanian Chess Fed. 1995–98; mem. Romanian Acad. (Pres. Econ., Law and Sociological Sciences Section 2006–), Royal Acad. of Economics and Finance of Spain 2007, Royal Acad. of Doctors, Spain 2009; Honour Medal, Architects' World Forum. *Publications include:* Financial Crisis 1979, Gold, Myth and Reality 1981, Stock Exchange 1982, Recent Developments in Romania 1990, Monetary Policy, Macroeconomic Stability and Banking Reform in Romania 1995, Banking System in Romania: Recent Developments and Prospects 1996, Reform of the Financial System in Romania and European Integration 1996, Monetary Policy After 1989 1997, Convergence and Sustainability: Issues and Means of Implementation 1998, Bank Banker 1999, Crisis Management in the Global Economy–A Challenge for Monetary Policy: The Case of Romania 1999. *Leisure interests:* literature, history. *Address:* Banca Națională a României, 030031 Bucharest 3, Str. Lipscani 25, Romania (office). *Telephone:* (21) 3124368 (office). *Fax:* (21) 3101630 (office). *E-mail:* mugur.isarescu@bnro.ro (office). *Website:* www.bnro.ro (office).

ISAYEV, Kanetbek; Kyrgyzstani politician; *Chairman, Kyrgyzstan Sayasiy Partiyasy (KSP—Kyrgyzstan Political Party);* fmr regional gov.; fmr Leader of Respublika parl. faction in Supreme Council (Jogorku Kenesh); mem. Kyrgyzstan Sayasiy Partiyasy (KSP—Kyrgyzstan Political Party), Chair. 2015–. *Address:* Kyrgyzstan Sayasiy Partiyasy (Kyrgyzstan Political Party), 720000 Bishkek, Asanbayevskii okrug, Okryabrkii raion, 12 mikro-raion BTs DK (office); Jogorku Kenesh (Supreme Council), 720053 Bishkek, Abdymomunov 207, Kyrgyzstan (office). *Telephone:* (312) 32-38-38 (office). *E-mail:* info@kg7.kg (office); zs@kenesh.gov.kg. *Website:* kyrgyzstan7.kg (office); www.kenesh.kg.

ISCHINGER, Wolfgang Friedrich; German diplomatist and international organization official; *Chairman, Munich Security Conference;* b. 6 April 1946, Beuren, Stuttgart; m. 2nd Jutta Falke-Ischinger; one c., and two c. from previous m.; ed Univ. of Bonn, Univ. of Geneva, Switzerland, Fletcher School of Law and Diplomacy, Tufts Univ. and Harvard Univ. Law School, USA; mem. Cabinet Staff of UN Sec.-Gen., New York 1973–75; joined Foreign Service 1975, mem. Policy Planning Staff 1977–79, posted to Embassy in Washington, DC 1979–82, mem. Cabinet Staff, Minister of Foreign Affairs, Bonn 1982–90, Pvt. Sec. to Minister 1985–87, Dir Cabinet and Parl. Affairs 1987–90; Minister-Counsellor, Head of Political Section, Embassy in Paris 1990–93, Dir Policy Planning Staff, Bonn 1993–95, Dir-Gen. for Political Affairs 1995–98, State Sec. 1998–2001, 2000–01, Amb. to USA 2001–06, to UK 2006–08; apptd to represent EU in negotiations on status of Kosovo 2007; Chair. Munich Security Conf. 2008–; Global Head of Govt Relations, Allianz SE, Munich 2008–14; Adjunct Prof., Political Science Dept, Univ. of Tuebingen 2010–; Sr Prof. for Security Policy and Diplomatic Practice, Hertie School of Governance, Berlin 2015–; mem. Bd of Dirs Allianz Deutschland AG, Stiftung Wissenschaft und Politik, Stockholm Int. Peace Research Inst., East-West Inst., American Acad. Berlin, American Inst. for Contemporary German Studies, International Crisis Group; mem. Bd of Overseers, Fletcher School of Law and Diplomacy of Tufts Univ.; fmr Chair. Ambs Advisory Bd, Exec. Council on Diplomacy, Washington, DC; mem. Trilateral Comm., European Council on Foreign Affairs, High Level German-Russian Strategy Group, Independent Comm. on Turkey; Bundesverdienstkreuz, Commdr, Légion d'honneur; Dr hc (University of Pristina, Kosovo) 2011; Leo Baeck Medal 2008, Manfred Wörner Medal 2015. *Publications:* numerous articles on foreign policy, security and arms control policy, European policy issues. *Leisure interests:* skiing, mountaineering, flying. *Address:* Munich Security Conference, Prinzregentenstrasse 7, 80538 Munich, Germany (office). *Telephone:* (89) 37979490 (office). *Fax:* (89) 379794960 (office). *E-mail:* office@securityconference.de (office). *Website:* www.securityconference.de (office).

ISDELL, E(dward) Neville, BS; Irish beverage industry executive (retd); b. 8 June 1943, Downpatrick, Co. Down, NI; m. Pamela Anne Gill 1970; one d.; ed Univ.

of Cape Town, S Africa, Harvard Business School, USA; joined Coca-Cola Zambia 1966, held positions in S Africa, Australia, The Philippines, Pres. Cen. European Div. 1985–89, Group Pres. for NE Europe, the Middle East and Africa 1989–98, Pres. Greater Europe Group 1995, Chair. and CEO Coca-Cola Beverages 1998–2000, CEO Coca-Cola HBC 2000–01, Sr Int. Consultant to CEO, The Coca-Cola Co. 2001–04, Chair. The Coca-Cola Co. 2004–09, CEO 2004–08, Dir Coca-Cola Bottlers Philippines; Chair. Int. Business Leaders Forum; Chair. Corp. Fund Bd, John F. Kennedy Center For The Performing Arts; mem. Bd of Dirs Global Water Challenge, Russell Reynolds Assoc., Inc., SunTrust Banks, Inc. 2004–08, Motors Liquidation Co. 2008–09, General Motors Corpn 2009–15; Chair. US-Russia Business Council, Bd of Trustees Int. Business Leaders Forum 2008–11, Atlanta Cttee for Progress, Investment Climate Facility; mem. US-Brazil CEO Forum; mem. Corp. Advisory Bd, Global Business Coalition on HIV/AIDS, Tuberculosis and Malaria; mem. Bd World Wildlife Fund, US (also Chair.); Trustee, Center for Strategic and Int. Studies, Inc., Emory Univ., Council for Int. Business, USA; Hon. DSc (Univ. of Ulster) 2007. *Address:* World Wildlife Fund, 1250 24th Street, NW Washington, DC 20037, USA. *E-mail:* communications@wwfus.org. *Website:* www.worldwildlife.org.

ISHAYEV, Viktor Ivanovich; Russian politician and government official; b. 5 Feb. 1944, Kemerovo Oblast; m.; two c.; ed Novosibirsk Inst. for Engineers of Waterway Transport; Dir Khabarovsk Plant of Aluminum Building Elements 1988–90; Head of Admin, Khabarovsk Krai 1991–96, Gov. 1996–2009 (re-elected 2000); Deputy of Fed. Council of Fed. Ass. of Russian Fed. 1993–2001; worked as Prof. 2001; elected mem. State Duma (Lower House of the Fed. Ass. of Russia) 2003; Presidential Rep. to Far Eastern Fed. Okrug 2009–13; apptd mem. Russian Federation Security Council 2009; full mem. Russian Acad. of Sciences 2008.

ISHIBA, Shigeru; Japanese politician; *Minister of State for the National Strategic Special Zones;* b. 4 Feb. 1957; s. of Jiro Ishiba; m.; two d.; ed Keio Univ.; began career with Bank of Mitsui 1979; mem. LDP, Chair. Policy Research Council 2009–11, Sec.-Gen. 2012–14; mem. House of Reps for Tottori 1st District 1986–, Parl. Vice-Minister for Agric., Forestry and Fisheries 1992, Chair. Special Cttee on Deregulation 1996, Cttee on Transport 1998; Sr State Sec. for Minister of Agric., Forestry and Fisheries 2000; Sr State Sec. of Defence 2000–01, Sr Vice-Minister for Defence 2001–02, Minister of Defence 2002–04, 2007–08, of Agric., Forestry and Fisheries 2008–09, Minister of State for the Nat. Strategic Special Zones, also in-charge of Overcoming Population Decline and Vitalizing Local Economy in Japan 2014–. *Address:* Cabinet Office, 1-6-1, Nagata-cho, Chiyoda-ku, Tokyo 100-8968, Japan (office). *Telephone:* (3) 5253-2111 (office). *Website:* www.cao.go.jp (office); www.ishiba.com.

ISHIGURO, Denroku, BPharm; Japanese business executive; ed Univ. of Toyama; served as Man. Exec. Officer, later Sr Man. Exec. Officer and Vice-Pres. Alfresa Holdings Corpn –2009, apptd Rep. Dir and Pres. 2009.

ISHIGURO, Sir Kazuo, Kt, OBE, MA, DLitt, FRSA, FRSL; British writer; b. 8 Nov. 1954, Nagasaki, Japan; s. of Shizuo Ishiguro and Shizuko Ishiguro; m. Lorna Anne Macdougall 1986; one d.; ed Woking Grammar School, Univs of Kent and East Anglia; fmr community worker, Renfrew; writer 1980–; Hon. DLit (Kent) 1990, (East Anglia) 1995, (St Andrews) 2003; Chevalier, Ordre des Arts et des Lettres 1998, Order of Culture, Japan 2017, Order of the Rising Sun, 2nd Class, Gold and Silver Star 2018; Premio Scanno 1995, Premio Mantova 1998, Nobel Prize in Literature 2017, Golden Plate Award, Acad. of Achievement 2017, Bodley Medal 2019. *Publications include:* A Pale View of Hills (RSL Winifred Holtby Prize 1983) 1982, A Profile of Arthur J. Mason (TV play) 1985, An Artist of the Floating World (Whitbread Book of the Year, Fiction Prize 1986) 1986, The Gourmet (TV play) 1987, The Remains of the Day (Booker Prize 1989) 1989, The Unconsoled (Cheltenham Prize 1995) 1995, When We Were Orphans (novel) 2000, The Saddest Music in the World (screenplay, co-author) 2003, Never Let Me Go (novel) (Premio Serono 2006, Corine Int. Book Prize 2006, Casino de Santiago European Novel Prize 2007) 2005, White Countess (screenplay) 2005, Nocturnes: Five Stories of Music and Nightfall 2009, The Buried Giant 2015. *Address:* c/o Peter Straus, Rogers, Coleridge & White Ltd, 20 Powis Mews, London, W11 1JN, England (office). *Telephone:* (20) 7221-3717 (office). *Fax:* (20) 7229-9084 (office). *E-mail:* info@rcwlitagency.co.uk (office). *Website:* www.rcwlitagency.co.uk (office).

ISHIHARA, Kunio; Japanese insurance executive; b. 17 Oct. 1943; ed Tokyo Univ.; joined Tokio Marine and Fire Insurance Co. Ltd as underwriter 1966, Dir and Gen. Man. Hokkaido Regional HQ of Tokio Marine 1995–98, Man. Dir and Gen. Man. June–July 1998, Man. Dir and Gen. Man. Hokkaido Div., Tokio Marine July 1998–99, Man. Dir Tokio Marine 1999–2000, Sr Man. Dir Tokio Marine 2000–01, Pres. Tokio Marine 2001–02, Pres. Tokio Marine Holdings, Inc. 2002–04, Pres. Tokio Marine & Nichido (following merger 2004) 2004–07, Chair. Tokio Marine & Nichido 2007–13, Tokio Marine Holdings, Inc. 2007–13; Auditor, Tokyu Corpn 2012–; mem. Audit and Supervisory Cttee, Nikon Corpn 2016–, Dir 2016–; Dir Japan Post Holdings Co., Ltd 2015–, Daiichi Sankyo Co. 2010–.

ISHIHARA, Nobuteru; Japanese politician; *Minister for Economic Revitalization, Total Reform of Social Security and Tax, and Economic and Fiscal Policy;* b. 19 April 1957, Kanagawa; s. of Shintaro Ishihara; ed Keio Univ.; political reporter, Nippon TV Network 1981; mem. House of Reps (Parl.) (LDP) 1990–; Minister of State (Admin. Reform, Regulatory Reform) 2001–02; Minister of Land, Infrastructure and Transport 2003–06; Deputy Sec.-Gen. LDP 2006–07, Acting Sec.-Gen. 2008, Chair. Party Org. and Campaign HQ 2009, Sec.-Gen. LDP 2010–12; Minister of the Environment 2012–14, also Minister of State for the Nuclear Emergency Preparedness, Minister for Econ. Revitalization, Total Reform of Social Security and Tax, and Econ. and Fiscal Policy 2016–. *Address:* Shūgiin Dai-Ichi Giin Kaikan, 1-824 2-2-1 Nagatacho, Chiyoda-ku, Tokyo 100-8981, Japan (office). *Telephone:* (3) 3581-5111 (office). *Fax:* (3) 3593-7101 (office). *E-mail:* nobuteru@nobuteru.or.jp (office); koho@ldp.jimin.or.jp (office). *Website:* www.nobuteru.or.jp (office).

ISHIHARA, Shintaro; Japanese politician and author; b. 30 Sept. 1932, Kobe; brother of Yujiro Ishihara; m. Noriko Ishihara; four s.; ed Hitotsubashi Univ.; elected mem. House of Councillors 1968; mem. House of Reps 1972–95, 2012–14; Minister of State, Dir-Gen. Environment Agency 1976–77; Minister of Transport 1987–88; mem. LDP, cand. in LDP presidential election 1988; left nat. politics 1995; Gov. of Tokyo 1999–2012; apptd mem. Selection Cttee for Akutagawa Prize 1995; Grand Cordon, Order of the Rising Sun 2015. *Publications include:* Season of the Sun (Akutagawa Prize for Literature 1956) 1955, The Tree of the Young Man 1959, The Forest of Fossils 1970, The Japan that Can Say No 1989, Undercurrents – Episodes from a Life on the Edge 1990, The State Becomes an Illusion 1999, Victorious Japan (with Soichiro Tahara) 2000, I Won't Marry 2001, To Get Old is the Life 2002, Island of Fire 2008, Recovery 2010, New 'On Decadance'–Greed and Divine Punishment 2011. *Leisure interests:* yachting, tennis, scuba diving. *Website:* www.sensenfukoku.net.

ISHII, Hajime, MA; Japanese politician; b. 17 Aug. 1934, Kobe; m. Tomoko Sugiguchi 1961; one s.; ed Konan Univ., Stanford Univ. Grad. School, USA; elected mem. House of Reps 1969, House of Councillors 2007–; fmr Parl. Vice-Minister of Transport; Minister of State, Dir-Gen. Nat. Land Agency 1989; Minister of Home Affairs 1994; fmr Chair. LDP Nat. Org. Cttee; fmr Chair. LDP Research Comm. on Foreign Affairs; fmr Vice-Pres. Democratic Party of Japan. *Publications:* The Dream of Young Power, Dacca Hijacking, The Future of Kobe, A Distant Country Getting Closer. *Leisure interests:* golf, saxophone, scuba diving. *E-mail:* pin@hajimeishii.net. *Website:* www.hajimeishii.net.

ISHII, Hiroyuki; Japanese environmental scientist and academic; *Professor, Public Policy School, Hokkaido University;* ed Univ. of Tokyo; with Asahi Shimbun newspaper 1965–94, positions including Science Writer, New York Bureau Corresp., Science Ed., Sr Staff Writer; undertook field research in 125 countries; apptd Prof., Grad. School of Frontier Sciences, Univ. of Tokyo 1994; fmr Visiting Prof., Int. Research Center for Japanese Studies; Amb. to Zambia 2002; currently Prof., Public Policy School, Hokkaido Univ.; fmr Special Adviser to Exec. Dirs of UNEP and UNDP, to Pres. Japan Int. Co-operation Agency; fmr Chair. Japan Council of Sustainable Devt; fmr mem. Bd Regional Environmental Centre for Cen. and Eastern Europe, Hungary; mem. Selection Cttee, UNEP Sasakawa Environment Prize; FAO A. H. Boerma Award 1986–87. *Publications include:* Crisis of the Global Environment, Acid Rain, The Destruction of the Earth, Undermined Forests. *Address:* Public Policy School, Hokkaido University, Kita 9, Nishi 7, Kita-ku, Sapporo, Japan (office). *Telephone:* (11) 706-3074 (office). *Fax:* (11) 706-4947 (office). *E-mail:* shomu@juris.hokudai.ac.jp (office). *Website:* www.hops.hokudai.ac.jp (office).

ISHII, Kazuhiro, PhD; Japanese architect; b. 1 Feb. 1944, Tokyo; s. of Toshio Ishii and Kyoko Ishii; m. Noriko Nagahama 1988; two d.; ed Univ. of Tokyo, School of Architecture, Yale Univ., USA; f. Kazuhiro Ishii and Assocs 1976; apptd Lecturer, Waseda Univ. 1991, Univ. of Tokyo 1992; Japan Inst. of Architecture Prize 1989. *Works include:* Noshima Educational Zone 1970–82, Tanabe Agency Bldg 1983, Gyro-Roof 1987, Sukiya Mura 1989, Kitakyu-shu City Hall 1991, Burnaku Puppet Theatre. *Publications:* Rebirth of Japanese-style Architecture 1985, Thought on Sukiya 1985, My Architectural Dictionary 1988. *Leisure interests:* golf, music (playing saxophone). *Address:* 7-5-1-303 Akasaka, Minato-ku, Tokyo 107, Japan (home). *Telephone:* (3) 3584-0779 (home).

ISHII, Naoko, BA, PhD; Japanese economist and international organization official; *Chairperson and CEO, Global Environment Facility;* ed Univ. of Tokyo; began career at Ministry of Finance 1981, Section Chief, Int. Finance Bureau 1985–87, Deputy Dir, Office of Int. Operations, Nat. Tax Admin 1987–88; Economist, IMF 1992–95; Project Man., Harvard Inst. for Int. Devt, USA 1996–97; Country Programme Coordinator for Vietnam and Mongolia, World Bank 1997–2001, Country Dir for coordination with Multilateral Devt Banks 2002–04, for Bilateral Devt Finance 2004–06, Country Programme Coordinator for Sri Lanka and Maldives 2006–10; Deputy Vice-Minister of Finance 2010–12, Special Adviser to Prime Minister for Global Environmental Affairs –2012; Chair. and CEO Global Environment Facility, Washington, DC 2012–; has taught on subjects of sustainable development and environment at Keio Univ.; Visiting Fellow, Centre for Int. Affairs, Harvard Univ. 1984–85; Okita Memorial Prize 2004, Enjoji Jiro Memorial Prize 2006. *Publications include:* The US-Japan Economic Controversy 1988, The Economics of Macroeconomic Policy Coordination (Suntory Academic Prize) 1990, Empirical Analysis on Modern Economic Growth: Institutions Critical to Sustainable Economic Growth 2003. *Address:* Global Environment Facility Secretariat, 1818 H Street, NW, Mail Stop P4-400, Washington, DC 20433, USA (office). *Telephone:* (202) 473-0508 (office). *Fax:* (202) 522-3240 (office). *E-mail:* secretariat@thegef.org (office). *Website:* www.thegef.org (office).

ISHIKAWA, Hirokazu, BA; Japanese banking and insurance executive; b. 1942; ed Faculty of Econs, Keio Univ.; joined The Mistui Bank Ltd 1966, Sr Deputy Gen. Man. Europe Div. HQ and Man.-Dir Mitsui Finance Int. Ltd 1989–90, Man.-Dir and Chief Rep. Mitsui Taiyo Kobe Int. Ltd 1990–92, Man.-Dir and Chief Rep. Sakura Finance Int. Ltd 1992, Gen. Man. Europe, Middle E and Africa Div. 1992–94, Gen. Man. Planning Div. 1994–97, apptd Dir 1994, Man.-Dir 1997–99, Man.-Dir and Sr Exec. Officer 1999–2000, Deputy Pres. Sakura Bank Ltd 2000–01; Chair. Mitsui Life Insurance Company Ltd 2002–09, Adviser 2009–14, Outside Dir 2011; mem. Bd Casio Computers Company Ltd; Trustee Hasegawa Int. Scholarship Foundation.

ISHIKAWA, Tadashi; Japanese business executive; joined Toyoda Automatic Loom Works (later Toyota Industries Corpn) 1968, various man. roles including Corp. Auditor 2003, Exec. Vice-Pres., later Pres., then Chair.; joined Sacos Corpn 2004, Dir 2006–Man. of Accounting Dept 2006, Man. of Human Resources 2010, Man. of General Affairs Dept 2014; mem. Bd of Dirs Mitsubishi UFJ Lease & Finance Co. Ltd, Toho Gas Co. Ltd, Dir Toyoda Gosei Co. Ltd.

ISHIMARU, Akira, PhD, FIEEE, FInstP; American electrical engineer and academic; *Professor Emeritus, University of Washington, Seattle;* b. 16 March 1928, Fukuoka, Japan; s. of Shigezo Ishimaru and Yumi Ishimaru (née Yamada); m. Yuko Kaneda 1956; two s. two d.; ed Univ. of Tokyo, Univ. of Washington; Asst Prof., Univ. of Washington 1958–61, Assoc. Prof. 1961–65, Prof. of Electrical Eng 1965– Boeing Martin Prof. 1993, also Adjunct Prof. of Applied Math., now Prof. Emer.; Visiting Assoc. Prof., Univ. of Calif., Berkeley 1963–64; Ed. Radio Science 1978–82; mem. Editorial Bd Proc. IEEE 1973–83; mem. Nat. Acad. of Eng 1996–; Founding Ed. Waves in Random and Complex Media 1990–; Fellow, Optical Soc. of America 1982, Acoustical Soc. of America 1997; IEEE Centennial Medal 1984, Distinguished Achievement Award 1995, 1998, IEEE Heinrich Hertz Medal 1999, URSI John Dellinger Gold Medal 1999, IEEE Third Millennium Medal 2000.

Publications: Wave Propagation and Scattering in Random Media, Vols 1 and 2 1978, Electromagnetic Wave Propagation, Radiation and Scattering 1991. *Address:* Electrical Engineering Department, Box 352500, University of Washington, Seattle, WA 98195 (office); 2913 165th Place, NE, Bellevue, WA 98008, USA (home). *Telephone:* (206) 543-2169 (office); (425) 885-0018 (home). *Fax:* (206) 543-3842 (office); (425) 881-1622 (home). *E-mail:* ishimaru@ee.washington.edu (office). *Website:* www.ee.washington.edu (office).

ISHIZAKA, Koji; Japanese actor; b. (Heikichi Muto), 20 June 1941, Ginza, Tokyo; ed Keio Univ. Faculty of Law; TV debut in Taikouki (drama series), NHK 1965; film debut in Wakai Musame ga Ippai 1966; achieved fame playing role of Kosuke Kindaichi in a series of five detective movies directed by Kon Ichikawa 1976–79; directed and performed in film Chushin-Gura: 47 Assassins 1994; lead actor in Genroku Ryoran (drama series), NHK 1999; currently Co-Host Nademo Kantei Dan (We'll Appraise Anything, TV antique show); regular appearances on TV show Sekai Ururun Taizaiki. *Film appearances include:* Wakai Musame ga Ippai (Young Girls are Everywhere) 1966, Hi mo tsuki mo 1969, Kaze no bojo 1970, The Inaugami Family 1976, Devil's Bouncing Ball Song 1977, Island of Horror 1977, Jo-oh-bachi (Queen Bee) 1978, Death on Hospital Hill 1979, Sasame-yuki (The Makioka Sisters) 1983, Ohan 1984, The Return of Godzilla 1984, The Harp of Burma 1985, Rokumeikan 1986, Eiga jouu (Film Actress) 1987, Taketori Monogatari 1987, Tsuru 1988, Yushun 1988, Tenkawa Densetsu Satsujin Jiken (The Noh Mask Murders) 1991, Last Song 1993, Fusa 1993, Shijushichinin no shikaku (47 Ronin) 1994, Shinsengumi 1999, Urutoraman Kosumosu: First Contact 2001, Kenchô no hoshi 2006, Nihon chinbotsu 2006, Yume jûya 2006, Inugamike no ichizoku 2006, Rasuto gêmu: Saigo no sôkeisen 2008, Suspect X 2008, I Want to Be a Shellfish 2008, King of the Escape 2009, The Unbroken 2009, Shizumanu Taiyō 2009, Toshokan Sensō 2013, Tannisho (voice) 2019. *Television includes:* series: Wataru seken wa oni bakari 1990–2011, Genji monogatari 1991, Ude ni oboe ari 1992, Karin 1993, Hachidai shôgun Yôshimune 1995, Genroku ryôran 1999, Shiroi kyotô 2003–04, Tokyo wankei: Destiny of love 2004, Hyouheki 2006, Shin machiben: Otona no deban 2007, Saka no ue no kumo 2009, Juui Doritoru 2010, Hotaru no hikari 2010, Gou: Himetachi no Sengoku 2011, Mikeneko Hômuzu no suiri 2012, AIBOU: Tokyo Detective Duo 2012–17; mini series: Onna no iibun 1994, Ten to sen (voice) 2007, Shima no sensei 2013, Wataru seken wa oni bakari: 2015 Special 2015, Aogeba Tôtoshi (voice) 2016. *Leisure interest:* collecting antiques.

IŞIK, Fikri; Turkish politician; b. 13 Sept. 1965, Gümüşhane Prov.; s. of Tevfik and Mecbure Işık; m.; four c.; ed Middle East Tech. Univ.; worked as math. and English language teacher in private schools, İzmit and Istanbul 1989–94; man. in food industry 1994–2002; mem. Grand Nat. Ass. (Parl.) for Kocaeli 2007–, mem. Educ., Culture, Youth and Sports Cttee (Pres. 2013); Minister of Science, Industry and Tech. 2013–16, of Nat. Defence 2016–17; mem. Justice and Devt Party (AKP). *Website:* www.fikriisik.com.

ISINBAYEVA, Yelena Gadzhievna; Russian fmr pole vaulter; b. 3 June 1982, Volgograd; d. of Gadzhi Gadzhiyevich Isinbayev; m. Nikita Petinov 2014; one s. one d.; ed Volgograd State Acad. of Physical Culture, Donetsk Nat. Tech. Univ.; Sr Lt, Russian Army; gold medal, pole vault, World Youth Games 1999, European Jr Championships 2001, European Under 23 Championships 2003, Olympic Games, Athens 2004, World Indoor Championships 2004, 2006, 2008, 2012, World Athletics Championships 2005, 2007, 2013, European Indoor Championships 2005, European Championship 2006, Olympic Games, Beijing 2008; bronze medal, World Championship, Paris 2003, Olympic Games, London 2012; set women's pole vault world record of 5.05m at Olympic Games, Beijing 18 Aug. 2008; retd 2016; mem. 'Champions for Peace' Club; mem. Athlete's Comm., Int. Olympic Cttee 2016; Chair. Supervisory Council, Russian Anti-Doping Agency 2016–17, mem. 2017–; Distinguished Citizen of Donetsk 2006; IAAF Female Athlete of the Year 2004, 2005, 2008, Women's Track & Field Athlete of the Year 2004–05, Women's European Athlete of the Year 2005, 2008, Laureus Sportswoman of the Year 2007, 2009, Prince of Asturias Award for Sports 2009.

ISKENDERIAN, Mary Ellen, BS, MBA; American banking executive; *President and CEO, Women's World Banking;* b. 1959; d. of Ara Iskenderian; m. Gregory Owen Lipscomb 1991; ed Yale School of Org. and Man., Georgetown Univ. School of Foreign Service; numerous leadership positions at Int. Finance Corpn (pvt. sector arm of World Bank) including Dir Partnership Devt, Dir Global Financial Markets Portfolio and Dir S Asia Regional Dept –2006; also worked at Lehman Brothers (Investment banking company); Pres. and CEO Women's World Banking 2006–; Distinguished Citi Fellow in Leadership and Ethics, Leonard N. Stern School of Business, New York Univ. 2009; fmr Corp. Dir Banco Caja Social, Confisura SA, Infrastructure Devt Finance Corpn; mem. Bd of Dirs Kashf Microfinance Bank, Pakistan, ASA Foundation, Nat. Bank of Commerce, Tanzania, ShoreCap International; mem. Advisory Bd Dignity Fund, Kiva; Advisor, Clinton Global Initiative; mem. Women's Leadership Bd of Harvard Univ., Council on Foreign Relations, Women's Forum of New York, Business and Sustainable Development Comm.; judge, Financial Times Sustainable Banking Awards; Isabel Benham Award, Women's Bond Club 2009, Women's Finance Award, Inst. of Financial Services, Lucerne Univ., Switzerland 2009. *Address:* Women's World Banking, 122 East 42nd Street, 42nd Floor, New York, NY 10168, USA (office). *Telephone:* (212) 768-8513 (office). *Fax:* (212) 768-8519 (office). *E-mail:* info@womensworldbanking.org (office). *Website:* www.womensworldbanking.org (office).

ISKROV, Ivan, MSc; Bulgarian central banker; b. 26 March 1967, Pirdop; m.; one c.; ed Univ. of Nat. and World Economy, Sofia; Visiting Lecturer, Univ. of Nat. and World Economy, Sofia 1992–93; expert and examiner, Bulgarska Narodna Banka (Bulgarian Nat. Bank) 1993–97, Gov. 2003–15 (resgnd); Exec. Dir and mem. Man. Bd DSK Bank 1997–99; Exec. Dir and mem. Man. Bd Rosseksimbank 1999–2001; mem. Parl. 2001–03, held various parl. positions, including Chair. Budget and Finance Comm., mem. European Integration Cttee, Bulgaria-EU Jt Parl. Comm.; mem. Gen. Council of European Cen. Bank, Gen. Bd of European Systemic Risk Bd; Commdr, Order of Leopold (Belgium) 2010. *Publication:* Money, Banks, and Monetary Policy (co-author) 1998.

ISLAM, A. B. Mirza Azizul, BA, MA, PhD; Bangladeshi economist; *Professor, BRAC University Business School;* b. 23 Feb. 1941, Sujanagar, Pabna; m. Nilufar Aziz; one s.; ed Dhaka Univ., Williams Coll. and Boston Univ., USA; Lecturer, Dhaka Univ. 1962–64; joined Civil Service of Pakistan 1964; worked in different capacities in admin. service 1967–82; Econ. Affairs/Sr Econ. Affairs Officer, UN-ESCAP, Bangkok 1982–86, Dir Research and Policy Analysis Div. 1993–2001; Chief of Developing Econs Section, UN Centre on Transnational Corpns, New York 1987–92; consultant to UNCTAD, World Bank and Centre for Policy Dialogue 2002–03; Chair. Bangladesh Securities & Exchange Comm. 2003–06; Chair. Sonali Bank April–Nov. 2006; Hon. Adviser to Caretaker Govt, in charge of Ministry of Finance, of Planning, of Commerce and of Posts and Telecommunications 2007–08, in charge of Ministry of Finance, Ministry of Planning 2008–09; Prof., BRAC Univ. Business School 2011–; Mercantile Bank Award for economic research. *Publications:* co-author of at least 20 UN publs, including World Invest Report and Economic and Social Survey of Asia and the Pacific; edited books and daily newspapers; numerous articles in refereed journals. *Leisure interests:* reading, travelling. *Address:* BRAC University, #UB 20610, 66 Mohakhali, Dhaka 1212, Bangladesh (office). *Telephone:* (2) 882-4051 (ext. 4037) (office). *Fax:* (2) 881-0383 (office). *E-mail:* maislam@bracu.ac.bd (office).

ISLAM, Ahmad Shamsul, MSc, PhD; Bangladeshi plant geneticist and academic; *Professor, Brac University;* b. 1 Jan. 1926; ed Presidency Coll., Calcutta, India, Manchester Univ., UK; research in genetics, plant breeding and tissue-culture 1955–; postdoctoral research work at Cornell Univ., Univ. of Calif., Davis, USA and Nottingham Univ., UK; Lecturer, Univ. of Texas, Austin; Prof. of Botany, Dhaka Univ. –1990 (retd); Consultant and Prof., Brac Univ., Dhaka 2003–; Founder Ed. Sind Univ. Research Journal, Pakistan Journal of Botany, Dar-es-Salaam Univ. Scientific Research Journal, Bangladesh Journal of Botany; fmr Pres. Bangladesh Asscn for Plant Tissue Culture; fmr Sec.-Gen. Bangladesh Asscn for the Advancement of Science; mem. Indian and Japanese Socs of Genetic and Plant Breeding; Fellow, Islamic Acad. of Sciences; Ekushey Padak for promoting education 1985–86, President's Gold Medal, Bangladesh Acad of Science 1987. *Publication:* Fundamentals of Genetics (Bongshogati bidyar Moolkatha). *Address:* Brac University, 66 Mohakhali, Dhaka, 1212, Bangladesh (office). *Website:* www.bracu.ac.bd (office).

ISLAM, Manzurul; Bangladeshi business executive; *Chairman, Islam Group;* s. of Al-Haj Jahurul Islam; ed Univ. of London, UK; Chair. Islam Group (businesses include mfg, real estate, eng, construction, manufacturing, land devt, commercial banking, int. trade, cottage and handicrafts, milk and dairy products, information tech., agricultural and poultry products, group water devt, pharmaceutical industry, medical coll. and hosp., nurse training inst.), Chair. Bengal Devt Corpn (unit of Islam Group); fmr Chair. IFIC Bank Ltd; Gold Medal, Int. Fed. of Asia and West Pacific Contractors Asscn 2009, awards for Special Civil Eng Contractor and Award of Honour. *Address:* Navana Pharmaceuticals Ltd, 3/C Purana Paltan, Dhaka 1000, Bangladesh (office). *Telephone:* (2) 9557410 (office). *Fax:* (2) 9569113 (office). *E-mail:* admin@navanapharma.com (office). *Website:* www.navanapharma.com (office).

ISLAM, Nurul, MA, PhD; Bangladeshi economist and academic; *Research Fellow Emeritus, International Food Policy Research Institute;* b. 1 April 1929, Chittagong; s. of Abdur Rahman and Mohsena Begum; m. Rowshan Ara 1957; one s. one d.; ed Univ. of Dhaka and Harvard Univ., USA; Reader in Econs, Dhaka Univ. 1955–60, Prof. 1960–64, Chair., Dept of Econs 1962–64; Dir Pakistan Inst. of Devt Econs, Karachi 1964–70; Visiting Prof., Econ. Devt Inst., World Bank 1967–68; Professorial Research Assoc., Yale Econ. Growth Cen. 1968 and 1971; Dir Bangladesh Inst. of Devt Econs 1971–72; Founder-Dir and Chair. Bangladesh Inst. of Devt Studies, Dhaka 1971–75; Deputy Chair. Bangladesh Planning Comm. (with ministerial status) 1972–75; Asst Dir-Gen., Econ. and Social Policy Research Inst., FAO, Rome 1977–87; Chair. UN Cttee of Devt Policy 1996–99; mem. Bd of Trustees, Int. Rice Research Inst., Manila 1973–77, Exec. Cttee Third World Forum 1974–77, Bd of Govs. Int. Food Policy Research Inst. 1975–87 (Sr Policy Advisor 1987–94, Research Fellow Emer. 1994–), UN Cttee on Devt Planning 1974–77; mem. Editorial Bd The World Economy, London, Research Advisory Cttee, World Bank 1980, Advisory Group, Asian Devt Bank, Manila 1981–82, Advisory Cttee, Inst. of Int. Econ., Washington, DC; consultant for various UN cttees, ESCAP, UNESCO, UNCTAD; Nuffield Foundation Fellow at Univs of London and Cambridge 1958–59; Rockefeller Fellow, Netherlands School of Economics 1959. *Publications include:* A Short-Term Model of Pakistan's Economy: An Econometric Analysis 1964, Studies in Foreign Capital and Economic Development 1960, Studies in Consumer Demand 1965, Studies in Commercial Policy and Economic Growth 1970, Development Planning in Bangladesh – A Study in Political Economy 1977, Development Strategy of Bangladesh 1978, Interdependence of Developed and Developing Countries 1978, Foreign Trade and Economic Controls in Development: The Case of United Pakistan 1980, Aid and Influence: The Case of Bangladesh (co-author) 1981; Agriculture Towards 2000 (co-author) 1981, The Fifth World Food Survey 1985, Agriculture Price Policies 1985, Growth, Poverty and Human Development in Pakistan 1996, The Non-Farm Sector and Rural Development 1997, Development Opportunities in the Non-Farm Sector 2001, Making of a Nation: Bangladesh, An Economist's Tale 2003, Exploration in Development Issues 2003, Looking Outward: Bangladesh in the World Economy 2004, Ethics in Banking 2006, Reducing Rural Poverty in Asia 2006, A Ship Adrift: Governance and Development in Bangladesh (co-author) 2008, The World Economic Crisis and the Lessons for Developing Countries 2010, Role of Experts in Policy Advice: Lessons of Experience 2010, Thoughts on Microfinance and All That 2012. *Leisure interests:* reading political and historical books, movies. *Address:* International Food Policy Research Institute, 2033 K Street, NW, Washington, DC 20006-1002, USA (office). *Telephone:* (202) 862-5600 (office). *Fax:* (202) 467-4439 (office). *E-mail:* n.islam@cgiar.org (office). *Website:* www.ifpri.org (office).

ISLAM, Yusuf, (Cat Stevens); British singer, songwriter and producer; b. (Steven Demetre Georgiou), 21 July 1948, London; m. Fawzia Mubarik Ali 1979; two s. (one deceased) four d.; solo artist as Cat Stevens –1978, then as Yusuf Islam; extensive tours worldwide, numerous television appearances; mem. Musicians' Union; Founder and Chair. Small Kindness (charity), Yusuf Islam Foundation; Founder and Chair. Islamia Schools Trust, f. Islamia Primary School, Islamia Girls' Secondary School, Brondesbury Coll. for Boys, London; Dr hc (Univ. of Gloucestershire) 2005, (Univ. of Exeter) 2007; World Social Award 2003, Gorbachev Foundation Man for Peace Award 2004, ASCAP Award for Songwriter of the Year 2006, Mediterranean Prize for Peace 2007, Ivor Novello Award for Outstanding Song Collection 2007, inducted into Rock and Roll Hall of Fame 2014. *Recordings include:* albums: (as Cat Stevens) Matthew And Son 1967, New Masters 1967, World Of Cat Stevens 1970, Mona Bone Jakon 1970, Tea For The Tillerman 1970, Teaser And The Firecat 1971, Very Young and Early Songs 1971, Catch Bull At Four 1972, Foreigner 1973, Buddha And The Chocolate Box 1974, Saturnight (Live in Tokyo) 1974, View From The Top 1974, Numbers 1975, Greatest Hits 1975, Izitso 1977, Back To Earth 1978, Cat's Cradle 1978, Footsteps In The Dark 1984, Classics Vol. 24 – Cat Stevens 1989, Very Best of Cat Stevens 1990, (as Yusuf Islam) The Life Of The Last Prophet 1995, Prayers Of The Last Prophet 1999, I Have No Cannons That Roar 2000, A Is For Allah 2000, Majikat: Earth Tour 1976 2004, An Other Cup (Ivor Novello Award for Outstanding Song Collection 2007) 2006, Roadsinger 2009, Tell 'Em I'm Gone 2014, The Laughing Apple 2017. *E-mail:* office@yusufislam.com (office). *Website:* www.yusufislam.com.

ISLAM, Lt Gen. Zaheer ul-; Pakistani army officer and intelligence official; commissioned in Punjab Regt in 55th PMA Long Course 1977; served as DG (C) in Inter-Services Intelligence (ISI) before being promoted as a three-star Gen. and moved to Karachi as Corps Commdr; GOC Murree for a period before coming to ISI; also served as Chief of Staff in Army Strategic Force Command 2004–06; Corps Commdr, V Corps, Karachi –2012; Dir-Gen. ISI 2012–14; Hilal-e-Imtiaz (Mil.); ranked by Forbes magazine amongst The World's Most Powerful People (52nd) 2012. *Address:* c/o Ministry of Defence, Pakistan Secretariat, No. II, Rawalpindi 46000, Pakistan (office).

ISLAM KAMAL, Shafiul; Bangladeshi business executive; *Chairman and Managing Director, Navana Group;* b. 1949; s. of Alhaj Aftabuddin Ahmed; ed early education in science related subjects; joined Islam Group 1968, career in automotive, construction and real estate business, gained experience from involvement in man. of Group's diverse business operations, played role in establishing Navana as leading car co. in Bangladesh, and later, in setting up Aftab Automobiles, responsible for Bengal Devt Corpn (BDC), directly responsible for construction work of BDC in Middle East, oversaw Eastern Housing Ltd from 1981, separated from Islam Group with Navana Ltd and Aftab Automobiles Ltd and est. Navana Group 1996, currently Chair. and Man. Dir. *Address:* Navana Ltd/ Aftab Automobiles Ltd, 125A Motijheel C/A, Dhaka 1000, Bangladesh (office). *Telephone:* (2) 9552212 (office); (2) 9884992 (office). *Fax:* (2) 9566324 (office). *E-mail:* info@navana.com (office). *Website:* www.navana.com (office).

ISLAMI, Kastriot, MA, DSc; Albanian physicist and politician; b. 18 Feb. 1952, Tirana; s. of Selman Islami; m.; one s. one d.; ed Univ. of Tirana, Univ. of Paris XI, Orsay, France; physicist, Lab. of Soil and Rock Analysis, Enterprise of Geology and Geodetics 1976–79; Researcher, Gen. Directory of Metrology 1979–80; Asst Lecturer of Gen. Physics, Faculty of Natural Sciences, Univ. of Tirana 1980–81, Main Lecturer and Chair of Theoretical Physics 1985–94, Vice-Dean of Faculty 1987–91; elected mem. Parl. 1991, Deputy Speaker (Chair.) 1991–92, Head, Parl. Comm. for Preparation of Draft of Albanian Constitution 1991–96; Minister of Educ. Feb.–March 1991; Post-Doctoral Researcher, Univ. Justus Liebig, Gießen, Geermany 1993–95; Minister of State to Prime Minister of Albania 1997–98, Deputy Prime Minister April–Oct. 1998, Minister of Finance 2002–03, of Foreign Affairs 2003–05; Deputy, Kuvendi Popullor (People's Ass.) 2006–; mem. Parl. Ass. of the Council of Europe, mem. Cttee on Legal Affairs and Human Rights, Cttee on the Honouring of Obligations and Commitments by mem. States of the Council of Europe (Monitoring Cttee) 2006–. *Publications include:* The Basis of Quantum Mechanics Vol. I 1989, Vol. II 1990; publs in nat. and int. media. *Address:* Kuvendi Popullor (People's Assembly), Bulevardi Deshmoret e Kombit nr. 4, Tirana (office); Rruga: Dora D'Istria, Pallati R 8-Katesh, Tirana, Albania (home). *Telephone:* (5) 4237413 (office); (5) 4240669 (home). *Fax:* (5) 4227949 (office). *E-mail:* marlind@parlament.al (office); dshtypi@abissnet.com.al; kislami@icc-al.org. *Website:* www.parlament.al (home).

ISLAMOV, Bakhtiyor Anvarovich, DEcon; Uzbekistani academic and fmr diplomatist; b. 6 Jan. 1954, Tashkent; m. Islamova Shahida; one s. two d.; ed Moscow State Inst. of Int. Affairs; Advisor to Perm. Rep. of UN in Uzbekistan 1994–96; Prof., Hitotsubashi Univ., Tokyo, Japan 1996–2001; Vice-Rector, Banking and Finance Acad. 2001–02; Adviser to Minister of Foreign Affairs 2002–03; Amb. to Russia 2003–08, Deputy Foreign Minister 2008–12; apptd Prof., Tashkent Branch, Russian Economic Univ. G.V. Plekhanov 2012; Foreign Visiting Prof., Slavic Research Center, Hokkaido Univ., Japan 2013–. *Publications include:* Central Asia-Center-Republic Relations 1991, Central Asian Independent States: Ten Years after How to Avoid Traps of Development, Transformation and Globalization 2001. *Leisure interests:* chess, football, bicycle.

ISMAIL, Abdullahi Sheikh; Somali politician; Minister of Foreign Affairs 2004–07; fmr Chair. Southern Somali Nat. Movt.

ISMAIL, Ali Mohsen; Iraqi government official and central banker; *Governor, Central Bank of Iraq;* ed Mustansiriya Univ., Baghdad, Faculty of Admin and Economy, Baghdad; Dir Dept of Insurance Man. and Compensation, Ministry of Trade 1973–81; Financial Analyst, Kuwait Investment Co. 1982–85; Partner and Dir Harmony Inc., Montréal, Canada 1987–94; Exec. Dir of Planning and Man., RSM Montréal 1994–2003; Insp.-Gen., Ministry of Oil 2004–06; Sec.-Gen., Council of Ministers 2006–14; Gov., Cen. Bank of Iraq 2014–; mem. Asscn of Accountants and Auditors in Iraq 1976–; Hon. DHist (Inst. of Arab History and Scientific Heritage of Higher Studies) 2009. *Publications includes:* Theory of Succession Rights 2013. *Address:* Central Bank of Iraq, POB 64, al-Rashid Street, Baghdad, Iraq (office). *Telephone:* (1) 816-5170 (office). *Fax:* (1) 816-6802 (office). *E-mail:* cbi@cbi.iq (office). *Website:* www.cbi.iq (office).

ISMAIL, Gameela; Egyptian activist; b. 1966, Champollion, Qasr el-Nil Dist, Cairo; m. Ayman Abd al-Aziz al-Nour (divorced); ed El Gezira language school, Zamalek, American Univ. in Cairo, Cairo Univ.; political activist and advocate for civil and women's rights; started working in public service through a non-govt org., central Cairo 1994; fmr TV presenter; unsuccessful cand. for Shura Council 2001; co-f. Al-Ghad (Tomorrow) Party 2005; unsuccessful parl. cand. (ind.) in Qasr el-Nil Dist Nov. 2010 and 2011; mem. Nat. Asscn for Change 2010–; co-f. Women for Change; hosted satellite talk show E'aadet Nazar (Reconsideration) on Al-Nahar channel 2011–12; mem. Madaneya movement for protection of the civil state and Al-Dostour (Constitution) Party (co-founder), Sec. Al-Dostour Party 2013; named one of Newsweek's 150 Fearless Women Who Shake the World 2011. *Address:* c/o Al-Ghad (Tomorrow) Party, Cairo, Egypt. *E-mail:* gameelaismailegypt@gmail.com (office). *Website:* www.elghad.org (office).

ISMAIL, Imran; Pakistani politician and business executive; *Governor of Sindh;* b. 1 Jan. 1966, Karachi; 2 c.; ed Government Nat. Coll., Karachi; mem. Prov. Ass. of Sindh for PS-111 (Karachi-XXIII) constituency 13–27 Aug. 2018; Gov. of Sindh 2018–; mem., Deputy Sec.-Gen. and Media Adviser to Chair., Pakistan Tehreek-e-Insaf. *Address:* Governor's House, Aiwan-e-Sadar, Civil Lines, Karachi, Sindh 75580, Pakistan (office). *Telephone:* (21) 992012013 (office). *E-mail:* imran.ismail@insaf.pk (office). *Website:* www.sindh.gov.pk (office).

ISMAIL, Miftah, BS, PhD; Pakistani economist, business executive and politician; b. Karachi; ed Duquesne Univ., Wharton School, Univ. of Pennsylvania; Economist with IMF, Washington, DC 1992–93; returned to Pakistan 1993; CEO Ismail Industries Ltd 1993–, Candyland Confectionery 1993– (family businesses), Astroplastics Pvt. Ltd; mem. Pakistan Muslim League (N) 2011–; Head and Vice-Chair. Punjab Bd of Investment and Trade 2012–13; mem. Bd of Dirs Pakistan International Airlines 2013–14, Sui Southern Gas Co. 2013–14; Chair. Fed. Bd of Investment 2014; Fed. Adviser on Finance, Revenue and Econ. Affairs 2017–18, Minister of Finance, Revenue and Econ. Affairs April–May 2018; fmr Chair. Bd of Dirs Karachi American School; mem. Advisory Cttee, Inst. of Business Admin.

ISMAIL, Mustafa Osman, PhD; Sudanese politician; *Minister of Investment;* b. 1955, Dongola; joined Ministry of External Relations 1996, Minister of External Relations 1998–2005, then Presidential Adviser; currently Minister of Investment; mem. Nat. Congress Party. *Publication:* The Sudan and the African Liberation Movements 2006. *Address:* Ministry of Investment, Khartoum, Sudan.

ISMAIL, Tan Sri Razali, BA; Malaysian business executive and fmr diplomatist; b. 1939, Kedah; m.; three c.; joined Ministry of Foreign Affairs 1962, served at Embassy in Delhi 1963–64, Asst High Commr in Madras 1964–66, Second Sec., Embassy in Paris 1966–68, Prin. Asst Sec., Ministry of Foreign Affairs 1968–70, Counsellor, Embassy in London 1970–72, Chargé d'affaires, Embassy in Vientiane 1972–78, Amb. to Poland 1978–82, High Commr to India 1982, Deputy Sec.-Gen. Ministry of Foreign Affairs 1985–88, Perm. Rep. to UN, New York 1988, Pres. UN Gen. Ass. 1996–97, apptd Special Adviser to Prime Minister 1998; UN Special Envoy to Myanmar 1998–2006; Pro-Chancellor, Univ. Sains Malaysia, Penang 2001–06; Exec. Chair. Cypark Resources Berhad 2012–; Chair. Bright Mission Berhad, Gerbang Perdana Sdn Bhd; apptd Chair. IRIS Corpn Berhad 2002, Human Rights Comm. of Malaysia (SUHAKAM) 2016–19, Leader, Universal Holdings Bhd, Yayasan Salam (Malaysian Peace Corps) 1997–, Malaysian Wetlands Foundation for the Paya Indah Wetlands Sanctuary Project, Allianz Malaysia Berhad; Ordre Nation al du Merite 2000; Dr hc (Inst. for Environment and Development, National Univ. of Malaysia) 1993, (Univ. Sains Malaysia) 1998, (Universiti Malaysia Sarawak) 2002; Langkawi Environment Award 1992, Elizabeth Haub Prize for Environmental Diplomacy, Pace Univ. 1999. *Address:* Office of the Chairman, IRIS Corporation Berhad, IRIS Smart Technology Complex, Kuala Lumpur, Wilayah Persekutuan 57000, Malaysia (office).

ISMAIL, Sherif Mohamed; Egyptian petroleum engineer and politician; b. 6 July 1955; m.; two c.; ed Ain Schams Univ.; began career as engineer, Research and Exploration Dept, Mobil Oil 1978–79; engineer, Enppi (petroleum eng co.) 1979–2000, becoming Dir-Gen. of Technical Affairs and mem. Bd of Dirs; Deputy Minister of Petroleum 2000–05; Chair. EGAS (natural gas holding co.) 2005–07; Man. Dir, later Chair., Ganoub El Wadi Petroleum Holding Co. (state-run oil holding co.) 2007–13; Minister of Petroleum and Mineral Resources 2013–15; Prime Minister 2015–18 (resgnd).

ISMAILOV, Nurdinjon; Uzbekistani legal scientist and politician; *Speaker, Legislative Chamber (Qonunchilik palatasi—Parliament);* b. 1959, Uchkurgan Dist, Namangan Viloyat, Uzbek SSR, USSR; ed Tashkent State Univ. (now Nat. Univ. of Uzbekistan); held various positions in Namangan Viloyat Prosecutor's Office 1980–85, headed Namangan Viloyat Justice Dept –1989; mem. Legis. Chamber (Qonunchilik palatasi—Parl.) 1995–, Deputy Chair., then Chair. Legislation and Judicial and Legal Reforms Cttee, Head of an group of experts for liaisons with legis. bodies and judicial power under presidential admin 2001–12, Chair. Parl. Cttee for Legislation and Judicial and Legal Issues, Speaker, Legis. Chamber (Qonunchilik palatasi) 2015–; mem. Popular Democratic Party; State Counsellor to Pres. on co-operation with Parl., political and public orgs 2012–. *Address:* Office of the Speaker, Qonunchilik palatasi (Legislative Chamber), 100035 Tashkent, Bunyedkor ko'ch. 1, Uzbekistan (office). *Telephone:* (71) 239-87-07 (office). *Fax:* (71) 239-41-51 (office). *E-mail:* info@parliament.gov.uz (office). *Website:* www.parliament.gov.uz (office).

ISMAT, Riad, PhD; Syrian playwright, scriptwriter, short-story writer and critic, stage director, fmr diplomatist and fmr politician; *Adjunct Professor, Northwestern University;* b. (Mhd Riad Hussain Ismat), 11 July 1947, Damascus; m. Azzah Konbaz; two s. one d.; ed Damascus Univ., studied briefly at Drama Centre, London, UK, Univ. Coll., Cardiff, UK, World Univ.; studied mime with Adam Darius and TV production and direction at the BBC, UK; also apprentice in actor training with Joseph Chaikin, Camille Howard, Jean Shelton and Mark Epstein in USA; Rector, Acad. for Dramatic Arts, Damascus 2000–02; apptd Dir-Gen. Syrian State Radio and Television 2003; Vice-Minister of Culture 2004–05; Amb. to Pakistan 2005–10, to Qatar 2010; Minister of Culture 2010–12; apptd Buffett Inst. Visiting Scholar, Northwestern Univ., USA 2013, now Adjunct Prof.; Adjunct Prof. Columbia Coll. Chicago; has directed 15 theatrical productions, including interpretations of Shakespeare, Tennessee Williams, Bertolt Brecht, Frank Wedekind and Ariel Dorfman, as well as own version of The Arabian Nights; f. first mime troupe in Damascus; also directed trilogy for Syrian TV; Dr hc (Univ. of Greenwich, UK) 2007; honouree of Cairo and Damascus int. theatre festivals. *Plays include:* The Game of Love and Revolution, Was Dinner Good Dear Sister, Mourning Becomes Antigone, Sinbad, Shahryar's Nights, Abla & Antar, Banana Republic, In Search of Zenobia, Mata Hari and Mihbaj. *Film includes:* script for Laila (musical film). *Television includes:* scripts for seven TV series, including A Crown of Thorn 1997 and Hulagu (Golden Award for Best Historical Arabic Historical Series 2003) 2003. *Publications include:* 37 books, including short stories, nine books critiquing Arab and World drama, a book on Nobel Prize laureate Naguib Mahfouz, a book on cinema and two books on actor training entitled Dream Is Life: Eclectic Acting.

Leisure interests: painting, watching movies. *Address:* PO Box 60049, Damascus, Syria.

ISOKALLIO, Kaarlo, MSc; Finnish business executive and writer; b. 13 May 1948, Helsinki; m. Ammi Kristiina; one d.; ed Univ. of Tech., Helsinki; Project Engineer, Wärtsilä Corpn 1972–74; Marketing Dir IBM (Finland) 1974–81; Man. Dir Kabmatik AB, Sweden 1981–83; joined Nokia Corpn 1983, Dept Man. Cables Dept, Machinery Div., 1983–85, Pres. Electronics, Information Systems 1985–86, Pres. Information Systems 1986–88, Exec. Pres. Nokia Data Group 1988–90, Pres. and COO Nokia Corpn 1990–91, Deputy to CEO, Vice-Chair. Group Exec. Bd 1990; mem. Bd of Dirs Oy Lindell Ab 1987, Taloudellinen Tiedotustoimisto 1991; mem. Supervisory Bd Mecrastor Oy 1987, Oy Rastor Ab 1987, Helsinki Univ. Cen. Hosp. Foundation 1991; mem. Bd Econ. Information Bureau 1991, ICL PLC 1991; mem. Tech. Del., Ministry of Trade and Industry 1990; Chair. Bd MTV (Finnish commercial TV) 1991; mem. Acad. for Tech. Sciences 1991; freelance writer and columnist 1996–.

ISOZAKI, Arata; Japanese architect; *President, Arata Isozaki and Associates;* b. 23 July 1931, Oita City; s. of Soji Isozaki and Tetsu Isozaki; m. Aiko Miyawaki 1974; two s.; ed Univ. of Tokyo; with Kenzo Tange's team 1954–63; Pres. Arata Isozaki and Assocs 1963–; juror, Pritzker Architecture Prize 1979–84, Concours Int. de Parc de la Villette 1982, The Peak Int. Architectural Competition 1983, R. S. Reynolds Memorial Award 1985, The Architectural Competition for the New Nat. Theatre of Japan 1986, competitions for Passenger Terminal Bldg, Kansai Int. Airport 1988, Triangle de la Folie, Paris 1989, Int. Architects' competition, Vienna EXPO '95 1991, Kyoto Station Bldg Renovation Design competition 1991; visiting prof. at numerous univs including Harvard, Yale and Columbia; Hon. Fellow, Acad. Tiberina, AIA, RIBA 1994–; Hon. Academician Royal Acad. of Arts 1994; Hon. mem. Bund Deutscher Architekten, American Acad. of Arts and Letters 1998; Chevalier, Ordre des Arts et des Lettres, Grande Ufficiale, Ordine al Merito (Italy) 2007; numerous prizes including RIBA Gold Medal 1983–86, Chicago Architecture Prize 1990, Leon d'Oro, La Biennale di Venezia VI Int. Exhbn of Architecture 1996, Pritzker Architecture Prize 2019. *Works include:* Expo '70, Osaka 1966–70, Oita Medical Hall 1959–69, Annex 1970–72, Oita Prefectural Library 1962–66, head office of Fukuoka Mutual Bank 1968–71, Museum of Modern Art, Gunma 1971–74, Kitakyushu City Museum of Art 1972–74, Shuko-sha Bldg, Fukuoka 1974–75, Kamioka Town Hall 1976–78, Gymnasium and Dining Hall, Nippon Electric Glass Co., Otsu 1978–80, Los Angeles Museum of Contemporary Art 1981–86, Tsukuba Centre Bldg 1979–83, Palladium Club, New York 1983–85, Sant Jordi Sports Hall, Barcelona 1983–90, Brooklyn Museum 1986–92, Art Tower, Mito 1986–90, Bond Univ., Australia 1987–89, Hara Museum—ARC 1987–88, Kitakyushu Int. Conf. Center 1987–90, Team Disney Bldg 1987–91, Tokyo Univ. of Art and Design 1986–92, Guggenheim Museum, New York 1991–92, Centre for Advanced Science and Tech., Hyogo 1994–98, Japanese Art and Tech. Centre, Kraków 1990–94, Nagi Museum of Contemporary Art 1991–94, B-Con Plaza (int. conf. centre), Oita 1991–95, Toyonokuni Libraries for Cultural Resources, Oita 1991–95, Kyoto Concert Hall 1991–95, Domus: la casa del hombre, La Coruña, Spain 1993–95, Akiyoshidai Int. Art Village, Yamaguchi 1995–98, Nara Centennial Hall 1992–98, Center of Science and Industry, Columbus, Ohio 1994–99, Ceramics Park MINO 1996–2002, Yamaguchi Center for Arts and Media 1997–2003, Turin Ice Hockey Stadium 2002–06, Shenzhen Cultural Centre, China 1998–2008, China Cen. Acad. of Fine Arts, Beijing 2003–08, Diamond Island, Ho Chi Minh City, Viet Nam 2006–12, Town Library, Maranello 2012. *Publications include:* Kukane 1971, Kenchiku no Kaitai 1975, Shuhō ga 1979, Kenchiku no Shūji 1979, Kenchiku no Seijigaku 1989, Image Game 1990, Arata Isozaki 1960–90, Architecture 1991, Kenchiku to iu Keishiki 1991, GA Architect 6 – Arata Isozaki (Vol. 1) 1991, Arata Isozaki – Works 30 1992, Arata Isozaki – Four Decades of Architecture 1998, GA Architect 15 – Arata Isozaki 2000, UNBUILT 2001, GA Document 77—Arata Isozaki 2004. *Address:* Arata Isozaki and Associates, 1-2-7 Shirogane, Minato-ku, Tokyo 108-0072, Japan (office). *Telephone:* (3) 3446-2334 (office). *Fax:* (3) 6450-2335 (office). *E-mail:* info@isozaki.co.jp (office). *Website:* www.isozaki.co.jp (office).

ISRAEL, Werner, OC, PhD, FRSC, FRS, FInstP; Canadian physicist and academic; *Adjunct Professor of Physics, University of Victoria;* b. 4 Oct. 1931, Berlin, Germany; s. of Arthur Israel and Marie Kappauf; m. Inge Margulies 1958; one s. one d.; ed Univ. of Cape Town, SA and Trinity Coll., Dublin, Ireland; Asst Prof., then Full Prof. of Math., Univ. of Alberta 1958–71, Prof. of Physics 1971–96, Univ. Prof. 1986–96 (retd); Adjunct Prof. of Physics, Univ. of Victoria, BC 1997–; Pres. Int. Soc. of General Relativity and Gravitation 1997–2001; Research Scholar, Dublin Inst. for Advanced Studies 1956–58; Sherman Fairchild Scholar, Calif. Inst. of Tech. 1974–75; Fellow, Canadian Inst. for Advanced Research 1986–91; Hon. DSc (Queen's Univ.) 1987, (Univ. of Victoria) 1999; Dr hc (Univ. de Tours) 1994; Izaak Walton Killam Prize 1983, Tomalla Prize (Tomalla Foundation for Gravitational Research, Switzerland) 1996. *Publications:* Relativity, Astrophysics and Cosmology (Ed.) 1973, General Relativity, an Einstein Centenary Survey (co-ed. with S.W. Hawking), 1979, 300 Years of Gravitation 1987; numerous papers on black hole theory, general relativity, statistical mechanics. *Leisure interest:* music. *Address:* Department of Physics and Astronomy, University of Victoria, PO Box 3055, Victoria, BC V8W 3P6 (office); Suite 401, 2323 Hamiota Street, Victoria, BC V8R 2N1, Canada (home). *Telephone:* (250) 721-7708 (office). *E-mail:* israel@uvic.ca (office). *Website:* www.phys.uvic.ca (office).

ISRAILOV, Ulan; Kyrgyzstani police chief and government official; b. 19 Oct. 1973, Bishkek, Kyrgyz SSR, USSR; ed Omsk Higher Police School of the Ministry of Internal Affairs of the USSR/Russian Fed.; worked in Ministry of Internal Affairs of Kyrgyz Repub. 1995, Dept of Criminal Investigations of Internal Affairs organs of Sverdlovsk Dist, Bishkek 1995–99, Dept of Internal Affairs, Bishkek City 1999, Platoon Commdr, then Security Inspector, Dept of Specialized State Security Services of Ministry of Internal Affairs 2004–05, Security Inspector, Special Co. Regiment 2005–08, Deputy Commdr 2008, Inspector of Dept of the State Security Service of Ministry of Internal Affairs 2008, contracted Mil. service with 9th Service of State Nat. Security Cttee 2011–13, headed Dept of Internal Affairs, Sverdlov Dist, Bishkek 2013–14, Head of 7th Dept, Ministry of Internal Affairs 2014–16, Head of Corruption Control Service with rank of First Deputy Chair. of State Nat. Security Cttee March–Nov. 2016; Minister of Internal Affairs 2016–18.

ISSAHAKU, Abdul-Nashiru, BBA, MBA, PhD; Ghanaian economist and central banker; b. 5 Oct. 1961; m.; four c.; ed Univ. of Georgia and Maharishi Univ. of Man., USA, Int. Islamic Univ., Malaysia, Clark Atlanta Univ., USA; fmr Sr Public Sector Specialist, World Bank; fmr Prin. Governance Expert, African Devt Bank; fmr Devt Man. Officer UN Econ. Comm. for Africa; fmr Socio-Econ. Advisor and Project Coordinator, Canadian Int. Devt Agency; served as Sr Planning Analyst, Ghana Nat. Planning Comm., Chair. Finance and Admin (F&A) Cttee, Ghana Cocoa Marketing Co., Commr and Chair. F&A Cttee, Securities and Exchange Comm.; Task Man., Gambia Econ. Man. Programme 2004–09; Institutional Budget Support Programme for Tanzania 2005–09; CEO Export Devt and Agric. Investment Fund –2013; Second Deputy Gov. Bank of Ghana 2013–16, Gov. 2016–17 (resgnd), also Chair. Investment Man. Cttee, mem. Bd of Dirs 2016, mem. Monetary Policy Cttee; mem. Regional Consultative Group for Sub-Saharan Africa, Financial Stability Bd; fmr mem. Econ. Man. Team Ghana.

ISSAWI, Rafi al-, MD; Iraqi physician and politician; b. Fallujah; ed Baghdad Univ., Basrah Univ.; began career as resident doctor, Al-Ramadi Hosp., Al Anwar 1990–93; served as doctor in Iraqi army 1993–94; fmr Dir of Health, Al-Fallujah Dist; Minister of State for Foreign Affairs 2006–07, Deputy Prime Minister 2007–10, Minister of Finance 2010–13 (resgnd); Leader, Nat. Future Gathering Party; sentenced to seven years in prison for corruption 2015; mem. Iraqi Medical Asscn.

ISSELBACHER, Kurt Julius, MD; American medical scientist, academic and fmr university administrator; b. 12 Sept. 1925, Wirges, Germany; s. of Albert Isselbacher and Flori Isselbacher; m. Rhoda Solin 1950 (died 2015); one s. three d.; ed Harvard Univ. and Harvard Medical School; Chief. Gastrointestinal Unit, Mass Gen. Hosp. 1957–88, Chair. Research Cttee 1967, apptd Dir Cancer Center 1987, now Dir Emer.; Prof. of Medicine, Harvard Medical School 1966–, Mallinckrodt Prof. of Medicine 1972–97, Distinguished Mallinckrodt Prof. 1998–, Chair. Exec. Cttee Medicine Depts 1968–, Chair. Univ. Cancer Cttee 1972–87; mem. American Asscn of Arts and Sciences 1968, Nat. Acad. of Medicine 1974; mem. NAS 1973 (Chair. Food and Nutrition Bd 1983–88, Exec. Cttee and Council 1987–90); mem. Governing Bd Nat. Research Council 1987–90; Ed.-in-Chief Harrison's Principles of Internal Medicine 1991–; Hon. DSc (Northwestern Univ.) 2001; Distinguished Achievement Award, American Gastroenterological Asscn (AGA) 1983, Friedenwald Medal, AGA 1985, John Phillips Memorial Award, American Coll. of Physicians 1989, Bristol-Myers Squibb Award for Distinguished Achievement in Nutrition Research 1991, Kober Medal, Asscn of American Physicians 2001, Jewish Nat. Fund Tree of Life Award 2001. *Leisure interest:* tennis. *Address:* Massachusetts General Hospital, Building 149, 13th Street, Charlestown, MA 02129 (office); 20 Nobscot Road, Newton, MA 02114, USA (home). *Telephone:* (617) 726-5610 (office). *Fax:* (617) 726-5637 (office). *E-mail:* isselbacher@helix.mgh.harvard.edu (office). *Website:* www.massgeneral.org/cancer/research/basic/ccr/faculty/shioda.asp (office).

ISSERLIS, Steven John, CBE; British cellist; b. 19 Dec. 1958, London; s. of George Isserlis and Cynthia Isserlis; m. Pauline Mara (died 2010); one s.; ed City of London School, Int. Cello Centre, Scotland, Oberlin Coll., Ohio, USA; concerts and recitals world-wide 1977–; exponent of contemporary music as well as authentic period performance; chamber concerts include own 'Shadow of War' series at Wigmore Hall, London 2013; curated concert series for venues including Wigmore Hall, Salzburg Festivals, 92nd Street Y, New York; gives regular children's concerts; Artistic Dir IMS Prussia Cove, Cornwall; writer of children's books about the lives of great composers; extensive and award-winning discography; Hon. mem. RAM; Piatigorsky Award 1993, Royal Philharmonic Soc. Award 1993, Schumann Prize, Zwickau 2000, Time Out Classical Musician of the Year 2002, Gramophone Hall of Fame 2013, Glashütte Original Music Festival Award 2017, Wigmore Hall Gold Medal 2017, Walter Willson Cobbett Medal for Services to Chamber Music 2017. *Recordings include:* Brahms Sonatas 2005, Bach Solo Cello Suites (Gramophone Award for Best Instrumental Recording) 2007, Schumann Music for Cello and Piano 2009, Revisions 2010, Lieux Retrouves with Thomas Adès 2012, Dvorak Cello Concertos 2013, Beethoven Cello Sonatas with Robert Levin 2014, Prokofiev & Shostakovich Cello Concertos 2015, Bach, Handel & Scarlatti Gamba Sonatas 2015, Mendelssohn, Grieg & Hough Cello Sonatas 2015, Elgar & Walton Cello Concertos 2015, Brahms Double Concerto with Joshua Bell and the Academy of St Martin in the Fields 2016, Haydn & CPE Bach Concertos with the Deutsche Kammerphilharmonie Bremen 2016, The Cello in Wartime 2017. *Publications:* transcription of Beethoven Variations in D arranged for violin or cello and piano or harpsichord, Edn of Saint-Saëns pieces for cello and piano, Steven Isserlis's Cello World, Unbeaten Tracks, Why Beethoven Threw the Stew 2001, Why Handel Waggled His Wig 2006, Robert Schumann's Advice to Young Musicians Revisited by Steven Isserlis 2016. *Leisure interests:* books, films, gossip, e-mail, eating too much, avoiding exercise, wishing I was fitter, wondering why I have so few worthwhile hobbies. *Address:* c/o Alexander Monsey, IMG Artists, Capital Tower, 91 Waterloo Road, London, SE1 8RT, England (office). *Telephone:* (20) 7957-5800 (office). *Fax:* (20) 7957-5801 (office). *E-mail:* amonsey@imgartists.com (office). *Website:* www.imgartists.com (office); www.stevenisserlis.com.

ISSING, Otmar, PhDr; German economist and fmr central banker; *President, Center for Financial Studies, Goethe University Frankfurt;* b. 27 March 1936, Würzburg; ed Humanistisches Gymnasium, Würzburg, Univ. of Würzburg; Prof. of Econs, Univ. of Erlangen-Nuremberg 1967–73, Univ. of Würzburg 1973–90; mem. Council of Experts for Assessment of Overall Econ. Trends 1988–90; mem. Directorate Deutsche Bundesbank 1990–98; mem. Exec. Bd European Cen. Bank 1998–2006; Pres. Center for Financial Studies, Goethe Univ., Frankfurt 2006–; mem. Acad. of Sciences and Literature, Mainz, Acad. Europaea, Salzburg; Co-founder and Co-ed. of the scientific journal WiSt; mem. Verein für Socialpolitik, American Econ. Asscn, European Acad. of Arts and Sciences, Acad. of Sciences and Literature, Walter Eucken Inst.; mem. High Level Group of EC 2008–09, Int. Advisory Bd, Bocconi Univ. Milan 2009–14; Chair. Advisory Group to German Chancellor on New Financial Order 2008–12; Hon. Prof., Univ. of Würzburg 1991–, Univ. of Frankfurt 2007–; Grosses Verdienstkreuz des Verdienstordens der Bundesrepublik Deutschland 2006, Officier, Ordre du mérite du Grand-Duché, Luxembourg 2006; Dr hc (Bayreuth) 1996, (Konstanz) 1998, (Frankfurt am Main) 1999; Laurea hc in Int. Econ. integration (Univ. of Pavia) 2010; Int. Prize, Friedrich-August-Hayek Foundation 2003, Ludwig Erhard Preis 2006. *Publications:* Introduction to Monetary Policy (sixth edn) 1996, Introduction to Monetary Theory 1998 (15th edn 2011), Monetary Policy in the Euro Area (co-author) 2001,

Imperfect Knowledge and Monetary Policy (co-author) 2005, Der Euro: Geburt – Erfolg – Zukunft (trans. as The Birth of the Euro) 2008, Wie wir den Euro retten und Europa stärken 2012. *Address:* Georg-Sittig-Str. 8, 97074 Würzburg, Germany (office); Center for Financial Studies, House of Finance, Goethe University, 60323 Frankfurt, Germany (office). *Telephone:* (69) 79830050 (office). *Fax:* (69) 79830077 (office). *E-mail:* info@ifk-cfs.de (office). *Website:* www.ifk-cfs.de (office).

ISSOÏBEKA, Pacifique; Republic of the Congo politician; b. 13 April 1941, Bokouele (Mossaka); m.; five c.; ed Ecole Higher of Trade and d'Administration of Companies (ESCAE), France; joined Banque des États de l'Afrique Centrale (BEAC) 1973, Deputy Dir in Congo 1994–98, Nat. Dir in Congo 1998–2003, Vice-Gov. of BEAC 2003–05; Minister of Finance, the Economy and the Budget 2005–09, also Alt. Gov. of Repub. of the Congo to World Bank.

ISSOUFOU, Mahamadou; Niger mining engineer, politician and head of state; *President;* b. 1952, Illéla; Nat. Dir of Mines 1980–85; Sec.-Gen. Mining Co. of Niger (SOMAIR) 1985; Sec.-Gen. Parti nigérien pour la démocratie et le socialisme—Tarayya (PNDS), currently Pres.; mem. Assemblée nationale 1993–99 (Pres. 1995–96); Prime Minister of Niger 1993–94 (resgnd); Chief Economist 1999; presidential cand. 1993, 1996, 1999, 2004; Pres. of Niger 2011–. *Address:* Office of the President, BP 550, Niamey, Niger (office). *Telephone:* 20-72-23-80 (office). *Fax:* 20-72-33-96 (office). *Website:* www.presidence.ne (office).

ITALELI, Sir Iakoba Taeia, GCMG; Tuvaluan politician; *Governor-General;* ed Int. Maritime Law Inst., Malta; fmr Attorney-Gen.; mem. Fale i Fono (parl.) for Nui constituency 2006–10; Minister of Educ., Sports and Health 2006–10; Gov.-Gen. 2010–. *Address:* Office of the Governor-General, Private Mail Bag, Vaiaku, Funafuti, Tuvalu (office). *Telephone:* 20715 (office). *Website:* www.tuvaluislands.com/gov_info.htm (office).

ITALIANER, Alexander, PhD; Dutch civil servant and international organization official; b. 1956; ed Univ. of Groningen; began career as Research Assoc., Catholic Univ. of Leuven; joined EC 1985, worked in cabinets of Pres. Santer, Commr Verheugen, Commr Telička and Pres. Barroso, also Dir for Int. Econ. and Financial Affairs 2002–04, Deputy Sec.-Gen. in charge of Better Regulation Agenda and Chair., Impact Assessment Bd 2006–10, Dir-Gen. of Competition Directorate-Gen. 2010–15, Sec.-Gen. EC 2015–18; mem. Advisory Bd, Central Planning Cttee, Dutch Central Planning Bureau 1997–2003; Visiting Lecturer, Catholic Univ. of Brabant 1987–88; mem. Scientific Cttee, Economie internationale 1994–2001; mem. Editorial Bd, CPB Report. *Publications include:* Theory and Practice of International Trade Linkage Models 1986, De voltooiing van de Europese interne markt in een mondiale context (with M. Vanheukelen) 1989, One Market, One Money. An Evaluation of the Potential Benefits and Costs of Forming an Economic and Monetary Union (co-author) 1992; more than 50 articles about European Econ. and Monetary Union, integration economics, labour, energy, macroeconomics and international trade.

ITO, Masao, MD, PhD; Japanese neuroscientist and academic; *Senior Advisor, RIKEN Brain Science Institute;* b. 1928, Nagoya; ed Univ. of Tokyo; Asst Prof., Kumamoto Univ. 1954–57; Asst Prof., Univ. of Tokyo 1957–62, Assoc. Prof. 1963–70, Prof. 1970–90, Dean 1986–89, Prof. Emer. 1990–; Research Scholar and Research Fellow, Sir John Eccles' Lab., ANU 1959–62; Team Leader, Frontier Research Program, Inst. of Physical and Chemical Research (RIKEN) 1989–97, Dir-Gen. 1993–97, Founding Dir RIKEN Brain Science Inst. 1997–2003, Sr Advisor 2003–; Pres. Japanese Physiological Soc. 1978–93, Int. Brain Research Org. 1980–86, Japan Neuroscience Soc. 1982–99, Int. Union of Physiological Sciences 1994–98, Science Council of Japan 1994–97, Human Frontier Science Program 2000–09; mem. Gen. Cttee and Exec. Bd Int. Council for Science (ICSU) 1988–97, Prime Minister's Council for Science and Tech. 1994–97; mem. Japan Acad.; Foreign mem. Royal Swedish Acad. of Sciences, Royal Soc., London, French, Armenian, Russian, Hungarian, Indian, European Acad. of Sciences, NAS; Order of Culture 1996, Chevalier, Légion d'honneur 1998; hon. science degree (Univ. of Southern California) 1995, (Torino Univ.) 1996, (Charles Univ., Prague) 1998; Fujiwara Prize 1981, Academy Prize and Imperial Prize 1986, Robert Dow Neuroscience Award 1993, IPSEN Foundation Award 1993, Person of Cultural Merit 1994, Japan Prize 1996, Gruber Neuroscience Prize, The Peter and Patricia Gruber Foundation (co-recipient) 2006. *Achievements include:* discovered inhibitory action of cerebellar Purkinje cells and characteristic synaptic plasticity, long-term depression in these cells; developed theory that cerebellum is a general learning machine for acquiring not only motor skills but also implicit memory in thought. *Publications:* The Cerebellum as a Neuronal Machine (with J. C. Eccles and J. Szenthgothai) 1967, The Cerebellum and Neural Control 1984; more than 120 scientific papers in professional journals on brain mechanism. *Address:* RIKEN Brain Science Institute, 2-1 Hirosawa, Wako City, Saitama 351-0198, Japan (office). *Telephone:* (48) 467-6984 (office). *Fax:* (48) 467-6975 (office). *E-mail:* ito-BSI@brain.riken.jp (office). *Website:* www.brain.riken.jp/en/m_ito.html (office).

ITO, Masatoshi; Japanese retail executive; *Founder and Honorary Chairman, Ito-Yokado Group;* b. 1925; m.; three c.; ed Yokohama City Univ.; Founder and Hon. Chair. Ito-Yokado Co. Ltd (now Ito-Yokado Group) with Seven-Eleven Japan and Denny's Japan brands. *Address:* Ito-Yokado Co. Ltd, 1-4, Shibakoen 4-chome, Minato-ku, Tokyo 105-8571, Japan (office). *Telephone:* (3) 3459-2111 (office). *Fax:* (3) 3459-6873 (office). *Website:* www.itoyokado.co.jp (office).

ITO, Takanobu; Japanese automotive industry executive; joined Honda Motor Co. in 1978, began career as engineer designing chassis, was in charge of developing frame structure for NSX sports car (went on sale 1990), Exec. Vice-Pres. Honda R&D Americas, Inc. 1998–2000, helped develop first sport-utility vehicle under Acura brand 1998–2000, Dir Honda R&D Co. Ltd 2000–, Sr Man. Dir 2001–03, Man. Dir 2003–04, Pres. and Dir Honda R&D Co. Ltd 2003–04, Motor Sports 2003–04, Gen. Supervisor, Motor Sports 2004–05, Gen. Man. Suzuka Factory of Production Operations 2005–07, Man. Officer 2005–07, COO for Automobile Operations 2007–09, Sr Man. Dir and Head of Core Automaking Operations, Honda Motor Co. 2007–09, Rep. Dir 2007–15, Pres. and CEO 2009–15, Dir and Adviser 2015–. *Address:* Honda Motor Co. Ltd, 2-1-1 Minami-Aoyama, Minato-ku, Tokyo 107-8556, Japan.

ITO, Tatsuya, LLB; Japanese politician; b. 6 July 1961, Tokyo; ed Faculty of Law, Keio-Gijuku Univ.; Researcher, Matsushita Inst. of Govt and Man. 1984–87; Visiting Researcher, Grad. School of Public Policy and Admin, Calif. State Univ., USA 1987–88; Sec.-Gen. Japan–US Tech. Exchange Programme 1988–93; elected to House of Reps 1993, Dir Cttee on Commerce and Industry 1993–96, Parl. Under-Sec. for Int. Trade and Industry 2000, Dir Cttee on the Environment 2000–01, Dir Cttee on Economy, Trade and Industry 2001–02, Sr Dir Cttee on Economy, Trade and Industry 2002; Acting Dir Science and Tech. Div., LDP 1999–2000, Dir of Economy, Trade and Industry Div. 2000–01, Sec. Admin Reform Promotion HQ 2000–01, Sec.-Gen. Select Comm. on e-Japan Priority Programme 2001–02; Sr Vice-Minister for Financial Services 2002–03, Sr Vice-Minister for Financial Services and for Econ. and Fiscal Policy 2003–04, Minister of State for Financial Services 2004–05. *Address:* House of Representatives, Fuda 1-3-1, Diamond Building 2F, Yubinbango, Chofu, Tokyo 182-0024, Japan (office). *Telephone:* (42) 499-0501 (office). *Fax:* (42) 481-5992 (office). *E-mail:* tatsuya@tatsuyaito.com (office). *Website:* www.tatsuyaito.com (office).

ITO, Toyo; Japanese architect; *Owner, Toyo Ito & Associates;* b. 1941; ed Tokyo Univ.; began career with Kiyonori Kikutake Architects and Assocs 1965; est. studio Urban Robot (Urbot), Tokyo 1971 (renamed Toyo Ito and Assocs 1979); fmr Guest Prof., Columbia Univ., New York, USA, Univ. of Tokyo, Univ. of California, Kyoto Univ., Tama Art Univ.; Hon. Prof., Univ. of N London, UK, Hon. Diploma of the Architectural Asscn 2003, Hon. Fellow, American Inst. of Architects, Royal Inst. of British Architects, Architecture Inst. of Japan, the Tokyo Soc. of Architects and Building Engineers, American Acad. of Arts and Sciences; AA Interarch '97' Grand Prix Gold Medal, Union of Bulgarian Architects 1997, Art Encouragement Prize, Ministry of Educ. 1998, Arnold W. Brunner Memorial Prize, American Acad. of Arts and Letters 2000, Gold Prize, Japanese Good Design Award 2001, Golden Lion for Lifetime Achievement Award, Venice Biennale 2002, XX AOI Compasso d'Ore Award 2004, Gold Medal, RIBA 2006, Asahi Prize 2009, Praemium Imperiale 2010, Pritzker Prize 2013. *Architectural works include:* White U 1976, Silver Hut (Architecture Inst. of Japan Award 1986) 1984, A Dwelling for the Tokyo Nomad Woman 1985, Tower of Winds 1986, Egg of Winds 1991, Yatsushiro Municipal Museum (33rd Mainrich Art Award 1992) 1991, Old People's Home, Yatsushiro 1994, Sendai Mediatheque (multi-resource public cultural centre), Sendai 2001, Brugge Pavilion 2002, Serpentine Gallery, London 2002, Codan Shinonome Canal Court (Block 2) 2003, Matsumoto Performing Arts Centre 2004, VivoCity, Singapore 2006, Tama Art Univ. Library, Tokyo 2007, Za-Koenji Public Theatre 2008, Main Stadium for World Games, Kaohsiung, Taiwan 2009, White O 2009, Toyo Ito Museum of Architecture, Ehime 2011, Ken Iwata Mother and Child Museum, Ehime 2011, Koo Chen-Fu Memorial Library, Coll. of Social Sciences, Nat. Taiwan Univ. 2014, Nat. Taichung Theater, Taiwan 2014, Barroco Museo Internacional, Puebla, Mexico 2016. *Publication:* Toyo Ito Architetto 2001. *Address:* Toyo Ito & Associates, Architects, Fujiya Building, 1-19-4, Shibuya, Shibuya-ku, Tokyo, 150-0002, Japan (office). *Website:* www.toyo-ito.co.jp (office).

ITOYAMA, Eitaro; Japanese business executive and fmr politician; *Chairman, President and Representative Director, Shin Nihon Kanko;* b. 4 June 1942; s. of Shintaro Sasaki; m.; two c.; ed Nihon Univ.; mem. House of Reps. 1974–90, 1994–96; apptd CEO Shin Nihon Kanko (golf course co.) 1985, currently Chair., Pres. and Rep. Dir; Chair. and Provost Sagami Inst. of Tech. Fujisawa 1981– (renamed Shonan Inst. of Tech. 1990); f. Itoyama Inst. of Politics and Man.; mem. LDP; major shareholder in Japan Airlines International 1998–2006 (currently Special Adviser to CEO), TV Tokyo Corpn. *Leisure interests:* golf, tennis, sailing. *Address:* Shin Nihon Kanko Co., The Itoyama Tower, 7-18 Mita 3-Chome, Minato-ku, Tokyo 108-0073, Japan (office). *E-mail:* info@itoyama.org (office). *Website:* www.itoyama.org (office); www.shinnihonkanko.co.jp (office).

IUE, Satoshi, BEng; Japanese electronics industry executive; b. 28 Feb. 1932; s. of Toshio Iue; ed Doshisha Univ.; joined Sanyo Electric Co. Ltd 1956, Dir 1961–, Man. Dir 1968–72, Exec. Man. Dir 1972–85, Exec. Vice-Pres. 1985–86, Pres. and CEO 1986–92, Chair. and CEO 1992–2005, Exec. Dir and Chair. 2006, Adviser 2006–07; Chair. Osaka Symphonic Asscn 1991, Ashiya Cosmopolitan Asscn 1993, Kansai New Business Conf. 1996; Vice-Chair. Japan-China Asscn on Economy and Trade 1995, Osaka Chamber of Commerce and Industry 1995; Dir Fed. of Econ. Orgs, Kansai Econ. Fed.; Hon. Citizen of Dalian, China 1995, Tarlac, Philippines 1996, Hefei, China 1997; Darjah Dato' Paduka Mahkota Perak, Malaysia; Hon. LLD (Boston Univ. School of Man.) 1990, Hon. DSc (Dalian Univ.) 1995; numerous awards and honours including Nat. Medal of Honor for Philanthropy 1970, Nat. Medal of Honor for Contrib. to Devt of Industry 1992.

IUE, Toshimasa, MBA; Japanese electronics industry executive; *Executive Vice-President, LIXIL Global Corporation;* s. of Satoshi Iue, grand-s. of Toshio Iue; ed Konan Univ., Boston Univ., USA; joined Sanyo Electric Co. 1989, Exec. Vice Pres., also Div. Man. of Group Marketing and CEO Sanyo Consumer Group, Commercial Group, Int. Group, and Components Group 2002-05, Chief Marketing Officer 2003–05, Exec. Dir, Pres. and COO Sanyo Electric Co. 2005–07 (resgnd); joined LIXIL Corpn 2009, Exec. Vice-Pres. 2011–, CEO LIXIL Global Co., CEO LIXIL Housing Technology; mem. Boston Univ. Bd of Trustees 2004–; Boston Univ. Alumni Award for Distinguished Service 2003. *Address:* LIXIL Group Corpn, 36F Kasumigaseki Building, 3-2-5 Kasumigaseki, Chiyoda-ku, Tokyo 100-6036, Japan (office). *Website:* www.lixil.com (office).

IURES, Marcel; Romanian actor; *Founder and Artistic Director, Teatrul ACT;* b. 2 Aug. 1951, Bailesti; ed Inst. of Theatrical Arts and Cinematography; film debut in Vis de ianuarie (January Dream) 1978; comedian Bulandra and Odeon Theatres, Bucharest 1980–94; performed title role in Richard III, Bucharest and London, UK 1994; Founder and Artistic Dir Teatrul ACT (ind. theatre), Bucharest 1998–. *Films include:* Vis de ianuarie (January Dream) 1978, Sa mori ranit din dragoste de viata (To Die from Love of Life) 1983, Domnisoara Aurica 1985, Vacanta cea mare (The Great Vacation) 1988, Cei care platesc cu viata (Those Who Pay with Their Lives) 1991, Balanta (The Oak) 1992, Un été inoubliable (An Unforgettable Summer) 1994, Interview with the Vampire 1994, Somnul insulei (Sleep of the Island) 1994, Mission Impossible 1996, The Peacemaker 1997, Faimosul paparazzo (The Famous Paparazzo) 1999, Elite 2000, I Hope 2001, Amen 2002, Hart's War 2002, Dracula the Impaler (voice) 2002, 3 pazeste 2003, Cambridge Spies (TV) 2003, The Tulse Luper Suitcases, Part 2: Vaux to the Sea 2004, The Cave 2005, Isolation 2005, Project W 2005, Goal! 2005, Isolation 2005,

Logodnicii din America 2007, Pirates of the Caribbean: At World's End 2007, Youth Without Youth 2007, Thick as Thieves 2009, The Phantom Father 2011, Crossing Lines 2013, Hotel Transylvania 2 2015. *Address:* Teatrul ACT, Calea Victoriei 126, sector 1, Bucharest, Romania (office). *Telephone:* (1) 3103103 (office). *Fax:* (1) 3103103 (office). *E-mail:* act@teatrulact.ro (office); info@teatrulact.ro (office). *Website:* www.teatrulact.ro (office).

IVANCHENKO, Aleksander Vladimirovich, DJur; Russian lawyer and politician; b. 8 Jan. 1954, Krasnodar; m.; one d.; ed Higher School of Ministry of Internal Affairs; worked in Moscow militia forces; Lecturer, Higher School of Ministry of Internal Affairs 1983–88; on staff Supreme Soviet Russian Fed. 1988–93; Deputy Chair. Cen. Electoral Comm. of Russian Fed. 1993–96, Chair. 1996–99, then Head, Russian Centre for the Studies of Voting Technologies; Founder and Dir Inst. of Election Tech. Studies 1999; elected mem. State Duma/ JCP faction 1999; Chair. Cttee on Fed. Affairs 2000–07. *Publications:* papers and articles on problems of political rights and freedom, on election law. *Leisure interests:* tennis, walks in the countryside.

IVANENKO, Sergei Victorovich, CandEcon; Russian politician and economist; *Deputy Chairman, Yabloko Russian Democratic Party (Rossiisskaya demokraticheskaya partiya 'Yabloko');* b. 12 Jan. 1959, Zestafoni, Georgia; ed Lomonosov Moscow State Univ.; Researcher and Asst Prof., Moscow State Univ. 1985–90; Chief Expert, State Comm. on Econ. Reform, RSFSR Council of Ministers 1994–96; Researcher, Cen. of Econ. and Political Studies 1991–92; mem. State Duma 1993–, Chair. Cttee on Property, Privatisation and Econs 1993–95, mem. Cttee on Ecology 1995–99; currently Deputy Chair. Yabloko Russian Democratic Party (Rossiisskaya demokraticheskaya partiya 'Yabloko'), Chair. Moscow Yabloko; Vice-Pres. Russian Chess Fed. 2003. *Address:* Yabloko Russian Democratic Party (Rossiisskaya demokraticheskaya partiya 'Yabloko'), 119017 Moscow, Pytniskaya ul 31 bldg 2, Russia (office). *Telephone:* (495) 780-30-10 (office). *Fax:* (495) 780-30-12 (office). *E-mail:* info@yabloko.ru (office). *Website:* www.yabloko.ru (office).

IVANENKO, Maj.-Gen. Victor Valentinovich; Russian intelligence officer (retd) and business executive; *Chairman, Arctic Trade and Transport Company;* b. 19 Sept. 1947, Koltsovka, Tyumen region; m.; three c.; ed Tyumen State Industrial Inst., Higher KGB Courses; mem. staff KGB, Tyumen region 1970-86, Sr Inspector, Head of Div., Deputy Head of Dept, USSR KGB 1986–91, Chair. RSFSR KGB 1991; Dir-Gen., with rank of Minister, Russian Agency of Fed. Security 1991–92; Vice-Pres., then First Vice-Pres. YUKOS Jt Stock Oil Co. 1993–98; mem. Bd of Dirs ROSPROM Jt Stock Co. 1996; adviser, Ministry of Taxation and Revenues 1998–99; Vice-Pres. Foundation for Devt of Parliamentarianism in Russia 2000–03; Chair. Arctic Trade and Transportation Co. (ATTC Jt Stock Co.) 2003–; mem. Supervisory Bd Russia-ASEAN Collaboration Fund; Presidium mem. Nat. Cttee on cooperation with law-enforcement, legislative and law authorities, Independents Civil Soc.; mem. Foreign and Defence Policy Council; mem. Moscow English Club; Order Red Star, six medals. *E-mail:* kompaszemnoj@gmail.com (office).

IVANIĆ, Mladen, MA, PhD; Bosnia and Herzegovina politician, economist and academic; b. 16 Sept. 1958, Sanski Most, Socialist Repub. of Bosnia and Herzegovina, Socialist Fed. Repub. of Yugoslavia; m. Gordana Ivanić; one s. one d.; ed Faculties of Econs, Univs of Banja Luka and Belgrade, Univ. of Mannheim, Germany and Univ. of Glasgow, UK; journalist Radio Banja Luka 1981–85; Asst Prof. of Political Economy, Faculty of Econs, Univ. of Banja Luka 1985–88, Docent 1988–, Head of Post-Grad. Study of Reconstruction and Transition (held in conjunction with Univs of Bologna, Sussex and LSE); Teacher Faculty of Econs, Sarajevo 1990–92; Teacher, Faculty of Econs, Srpsko Sarajevo (now Istočno Sarajevo) 1992–98; Lecturer, Univ. of Glasgow, UK 1998; mem. Presidency of Yugoslav Repub. of Bosnia and Herzegovina 1988–91; Founder and Chair. Partija Demokratskog Progresa (Party of Democratic Progress) 1999–2015, Hon. Pres. 2015–; mem. tripartite State Presidency 2014–18, Chair. Nov. 2014–July 2015, Nov. 2016–July 2017; mem. Govt Econ. Council 1999; Head, Deloitte & Touche Consultancy Office –2001; Prime Minister of Republika Srpska 2001–03; Minister of Foreign Affairs, Council of Ministers of Bosnia and Herzegovina 2003–07 (resgnd); mem. House of Peoples (Dom Naroda), (Parl. Ass. of Bosnia and Herzegovina); mem. Editorial Bd Ideje magazine, Belgrade 1988–91, Aktuelnosti magazine, Banja Luka 1998–99; Del. to OSCE sessions 1991; participant World Forum, Davos, Switzerland 1999, 2000; Pres. Serb Intellectual Forum. *Publications include:* Political Economy, Principles of Political Economy; numerous contribs to newspapers and magazines including Savremenost (Modernity), Pregled (Overview), Ideje (Ideas), Opredjeljenja (Determinations), Lica (Faces), Aktuelnosti (Updates); author or co-author of several programmes for World Bank, UNDP and other int. orgs. *Address:* Partija Demokratskog Progresa (Party of Democratic Progress), 78000 Banja Luka, ul. Prvog Krajiškog Korpusa 130, Bosnia and Herzegovina (office). *Telephone:* (51) 346210 (office). *Fax:* (51) 300956 (office). *E-mail:* pdp@blic.net (office). *Website:* www.pdpinfo.net (office).

IVANIŠEVIĆ, Goran; Croatian fmr professional tennis player; b. 13 Sept. 1971, Split; s. of Srdjan Ivanišević and Gorana Ivanišević; one d.; won US Open Jr doubles with Nargiso 1987; turned professional 1988; joined Yugoslav Davis Cup squad 1988; semi-finalist, ATP World Championship 1992; bronze medal, men's doubles, Barcelona Olympic Games 1992; runner-up, Wimbledon Championship 1992, 1994, 1998; winner Wimbledon Championship 2001; winner of numerous ATP tournaments, including Kremlin Cup, Moscow 1996; winner of 22 tours singles and nine doubles titles, and over US $19 million prize money; once ranked No. 2 in the world, behind Pete Sampras; retd 2004; now playing on Masters Tennis (sr) tour; Founder and Pres. Children in Need Foundation 1995–; coached Marin Čilić 2013–16; BBC Overseas Sports Personality of the Year Award 2001. *Leisure interests:* football, basketball, reading, music, cinema. *E-mail:* contact@ goranivanisevic.com. *Website:* www.goranivanisevic.com.

IVANISHVILI, Bidzina; Georgian politician and entrepreneur; *Chairman, Qartuli Ocneba-Demokratiuli Sakartvelo;* b. 18 Feb. 1956, Chorvila, Imereti, Georgian SSR, USSR; m. Ekaterine Khvedelidze; four c.; ed high school in Sachkhere, Tbilisi State Univ., Moscow State Univ. of Railway Eng, Russian SFSR; formed partnership with Vitalii Malkin to sell computers, later importing push-button telephones into Russia; est. Rossiiskii Kredit Bank 1990; later sold other businesses accumulated during privatization era and invested proceeds in Russian stock market; holds shares in hotels, including Hotel Lux and Russian Doktor Stoletov (chain of pharmacies); Founder Qartuli Ocneba-Demokratiuli Sakartvelo (QO-DS—Georgian Dream-Democratic Georgia) coalition 2012, Chair. 2018–; Prime Minister of Georgia 2012–13. *Address:* Qartuli Ocneba-Demokratiuli Sakartvelo, 0105 Tbilisi, Erekle II Moedani 3, Georgia (office). *Telephone:* (32) 219-77-11 (office). *Website:* 41.ge (office).

IVANOV, Anton Alexandrovich; Russian lawyer and government official; *Chairman, Supreme Commercial Court;* b. 6 July 1965, Gatchina, Leningrad Oblast; ed Leningrad State Univ.; with Faculty of Law, Leningrad State Univ. 1982–87, also worked as Asst Prof., later Assoc. Prof.; Head of Legal Dept Soyuzcontract Corpn 1994–96; Asst Lecturer of Civil Law, St Petersburg State Univ. 1995–97, Sr Lecturer 1999–2004; Head of St Petersburg Dept of Justice, Ministry of Justice 1997–99; Deputy to Dir-Gen. Gasprom-Media OJSC 2004; Chair. Supreme Commercial Court, Moscow 2005–; Chair. of Civil Law and Research Adviser, Faculty of Law, State Univ. 2006; mem. Bd of Dirs Gasprom-Media OJSC, Ekho Moskvy CJSC, TNT-Teleset CJSC, NTV Co. OJSC, Legal Awareness Fund; Chief Ed. Pravovedeniye Journal 1991–94; mem. Council for Codification and Improvement of Civil law, Presidium Russian Lawyers' Asscn, Council for Devt of Financial Market; A.F. Koni Medal. *Publications include:* more than 40 books. *Address:* Supreme Commercial Court, 101000 Moscow, 12 M. Kharitonjevsky per., Russia (office). *Telephone:* (495) 608-11-97 (office); (495) 608-11-94 (office). *E-mail:* vasrf@arbitr.ru (office). *Website:* www.arbitr.ru (office).

IVANOV, Gjorge; Macedonian political scientist, academic, politician and fmr head of state; b. 2 May 1960, Valandovo, Socialist Repub. of Macedonia, Socialist Fed. Repub. of Yugoslavia; m. Maja Ivanova; one s.; ed secondary school in Valandovo; activist in League of Socialist Youth of Yugoslavia –1990; Pres. and Supreme Commdr of the Army of Repub. of Macedonia 2009–19; fmr Visiting Prof. in Greece; Hon. Prof., Southwest Univ., People's Repub. of China 2013, Moscow State Univ. 2014; Hon. Citizen of Pustec 2015; Highest decoration of the Order of St Lazarus of Jerusalem 2011, Order of St George, House of Habsburg 2013, Order Baptist (Preteca), St Jovan Bigorski Monastery 2015; Dr hc (Dimitrie Cantemir Christian Univ.) 2011, (TOBB Univ. of Econs and Tech.) 2011, (İstanbul Univ.) 2011, (Nevşehir Hacı Bektaş Veli Univ.) 2015, (Bulgarian Acad. of Sciences) 2016; Recognition for leadership in reducing disaster risk, Int. Strategy for Disaster Reduction of the UN 2011, Peace and Sport Award, Peace and Sport Int. Forum 2012, AIPES Freedom Award for Democracy and Market Economy, American Inst. on Political and Econ. Systems 2014, Prix de la Fondation, Crans Montana Forum 2014, Isa Beg Ishaković Int. Award 2016. *Publications:* (in Macedonian): Civil Society, Democracy in Divided Societies: The Macedonian Model, Current Political Theories (with Lyubomir Frčkoski), Political Theories – Antiquity (with Svetomir Škarik). *Address:* c/o Office of the President, 1000 Skopje, Aco Karamanov 33A, North Macedonia (office).

IVANOV, Hristo, LLM; Bulgarian lawyer and government official; b. 13 Sept. 1974, Sofia; ed St Clement of Ohrid Univ. of Sofia, Hubert Humphrey Fellowship Program, Washington Coll. of Law, USA (Fulbright Fellow); specialized in nat. security law and court appointment procedures in USA; Project Co-ordinator in legis. and judicial reforms within Rule of Law Initiative, ABA 1996–2002; ind. consultant on projects of int. insts, int. tech. assistance programmes and pvt. clients, relating to legislation assessment and promoting the rule of law 2002–06; Program Dir, Bulgarian Inst. for Legal Initiatives 2006–, heads projects on judicial reform, prevention of corruption and promotion of the rule of law; Deputy Prime Minister of Justice, Public Order and Security and Minister of Justice in caretaker govt of Georgi Bliznashki Aug.–Nov. 2014, Minister of Justice Nov. 2014–15. *Address:* Bulgarian Institute for Legal Initiatives, 1000 Sofia, 132 G, Rakovski Str., Fl. 3, Bulgaria (office). *Telephone:* (2) 980-80-84 (office). *Fax:* (2) 981-13-12 (office). *E-mail:* office@bili-bg.org (office). *Website:* www.bili-bg.org (office).

IVANOV, Igor Sergeevich, PhD; Russian diplomatist and politician; *President, Russian International Affairs Council;* b. 23 Sept. 1945, Moscow; m.; one d.; ed Maurice Thorez Moscow Inst. of Foreign Languages; Jr Researcher, Inst. of World Econs and Int. Relations, USSR Acad. of Sciences 1969–73; within Diplomatic Service, Second, then First Sec., Counsellor, Counsellor-Envoy, USSR Embassy in Madrid 1973–83, Expert, First European Dept, Ministry of Foreign Affairs 1983–84, Asst Minister 1984–86, Deputy Chief, then Chief of Dept 1987–91, USSR, then Russian Fed. Amb. to Spain 1991–93, First Deputy Minister of Foreign Affairs 1994–98, Minister of Foreign Affairs 1998–2004; Sec., Security Council of Russia 2004–07; Prof., Moscow State Inst. of Int. Relations (MGIMO) 2007–; Pres. Russian Int. Affairs Council 2013–; mem. Bd of Dirs Nuclear Threat Initiative; Corresp. mem. Russian Acad. of Sciences; Orders For Services to the Fatherland (2nd, 3rd and 4th Degrees), Order of Honour, Hero of the Russian Fed.; Hon. Dr of Historical Science. *Publications:* New Russian Diplomacy 2001, External Russian Policy in the Epoch of Globalization 2002, Global Security in the Epoch of Globalization: Russia in Global Policy 2003, Russia in the Contemporary World: Responses for the Challenges of the 21st Century 2004; numerous papers and articles. *Address:* Russian International Affairs Council, Alexander House, 119180 Moscow, Bolshaya Yakimanka Str. 1, Russia (office). *Telephone:* (495) 225-62-83 (office). *Fax:* (495) 225-62-84 (office). *E-mail:* welcome@russiancouncil.ru (office). *Website:* russiancouncil.ru (office).

IVANOV, Mikhail Vladimirovich; Russian microbiologist; b. 6 Dec. 1930; m.; ed Moscow State Univ.; researcher, Inst. of Microbiology, USSR (now Russian) Acad. of Sciences, later Head of Lab. and Deputy Dir Inst. of Biochemistry and Physiology of Plants and Micro-organisms, later Dir Dept of Microbial Biogeochemistry and Biogeotechnology, Inst. of Microbiology 1984; Ed.-in-Chief Microbiology journal; Corresp. mem. USSR (now Russian) Acad. of Sciences 1981, mem. 1987; research in geochemistry activities of microorganisms and biotechnology, marine microbiology, global ecology and biogeochemistry; S. Vernadsky Prize. *Leisure interest:* coin collecting. *Address:* Mikrobiologiya, Winogradsky Institute of Microbiology, 117312 Moscow, pr. 60-letiya Oktyabrya 7, k. 2, Russia. *Telephone:* (499) 135-15-94 (office); (499) 135-65-30 (home). *E-mail:* redakciya@inmi.ru (office). *Website:* pleiades.online/en/journal/micbio (office).

IVANOV, Lt-Gen. Sergei Borisovich; Russian politician; *Special Presidential Representative for Environmental Protection, Ecology and Transport;* b. 31 Jan. 1953, Leningrad (now St Petersburg), Russian SFSR, USSR; m. Nataliya Ivanova;

two s. (one deceased); ed Leningrad State Univ., Yu. V. Andropov Inst. at KGB; various posts in KGB including missions abroad 1976–97; Deputy Dir Fed. Service of Security 1998–2001; Head, Dept of Analysis, Prognosis and Strategic Planning 1998–99; Sec., Security Council of Russian Fed. 1999–2001; Minister of Defence 2001–07, Deputy Chair. of the Govt 2005–07, 2008–11, First Deputy Chair. of the Govt 2007–08; Chief of Staff, Presidential Admin of Russia 2011–16; Special Presidential Rep. for Environmental Protection, Ecology and Transport 2016–; Order for Services to the Fatherland (Second Class) 2003. *Leisure interests:* fishing, reading detective stories in English and Swedish. *Address:* Office of the President, Staraya pl. 4, 103132 Moscow, Russia (office). *Telephone:* (495) 625-35-81 (office). *Fax:* (495) 606-07-66 (office). *E-mail:* president@gov.ru (office). *Website:* en.kremlin.ru/catalog/persons/81/biography (office).

IVANOV, Vadim Tikhonovich, DSc; Russian biochemist; b. 18 Sept. 1937, Pheodossia, Crimea; s. of Tikhon Timofeevitch Ivanov and Lidia Ivanovna Ivanova; m. Raisa Alexandrovna Ivanova (née Osadchaya); one s. one d.; ed Moscow State Univ.; Jr, Sr Researcher, Head of Lab., Deputy Dir, Dir Shemyakin-Ovchinnikov Inst. of Bioorganic Chem., Russian Acad. of Sciences; Corresp. mem. USSR (now Russian) Acad. of Sciences 1976, mem. 1987, mem. Presidium; research in chem. of proteins and peptides, structure and functions of neuropeptides, synthetic vaccines and peptidomics; Einstein Prof., Chinese Acad. of Sciences; several orders of USSR and Russian Fed.; Lenin Prize, USSR State Prize, three Russian Govt Prizes, Ovchinnikov Medal, Lomonosov Gold Medal, Russian Acad. of Sciences 2009. *Publications include:* Membrane Active Complexones 1974, The Way to Protein Synthesis 1982. *Leisure interests:* chess, nature.

IVANOV, Col Viktor Petrovich; Russian government official; b. 12 May 1950, Novgorod; m.; one s. one d.; ed Leningrad Bonch-Bruyevich Electrical Inst. of Communications; engineer, Scientific-Production co. Vektor 1971–77; employee in KGB, rising to Head of Div., Dept of Fed. Service of Security of St Petersburg and Leningrad region 1977–94, Head of Dept 1998, Deputy Dir, concurrently Head of Dept of Econ. Security 1999–2000; Head of Admin, Office of Mayor of St Petersburg 1994–98; Deputy Head of Admin, Office of the Pres. 2000–04; apptd State Rep. on Bd of Dirs, Antei Corpn and Almaz Scientific Industrial Corpn (air defence systems) 2001, Chair. Almaz 2001–02, initiated merger of Almaz and Antei, Chair. OJSC Almaz-Antei Air Defence Concern 2002–; Chair. JSC Aeroflot from 2004; Adviser to the Pres. 2004–08; Dir Fed. Drug Control Service 2008–16; participated in mil. operations in Afghanistan 1987–94; co-f. small-scale enterprise Blok 1990; Medal for Mil. Service, Order for the Merits to the Motherland (2nd and 4th degree), Order of Honour. *Address:* Federal Drug Control Service of the Russian Federation, 101968 Moscow, Maroseyka str. 12, Russia (office). *Telephone:* (495) 621-43-91 (office). *Website:* fskn.gov.ru/eng.shtml (office).

IVANOVA, Ludmila Nikolayevna, MD; Russian physiologist; *Head of Laboratory, Institute of Cytology and Genetics, Siberian Branch, Russian Academy of Sciences;* b. 10 Feb. 1929, Novosibirsk; ed Novosibirsk Inst. of Medicine; Head of Lab., Inst. of Cytology and Genetics, Siberian br., Russian Acad. of Sciences 1971–; Corresp. mem. Russian Acad. of Sciences 1991, mem. 1997–; main research in the hormonal regulation of water–salt metabolism and kidney function; L.A. Orbeli Award, Russian Acad. of Sciences. *Publications:* Circulatory System and Arterial Hypertension: Experimental Investigation, Mathematical and Computer Simulation (Human Anatomy and Physiology) (co-ed.) 2012; contribs to journals include (with N. N. Melidi) Effects of vasopressin on hyaluronate hydrolase activities and water permeability in the frog urinary bladder, in Pflugers-Archiv European Journal of Physiology, Vol. 443, No. 1, 2001; (with others) Effect of an increase in brain serotonin on the osmoregulatory response to a hypo- or hyperosmotic load in wistar and vasopressin-deficient Brattleboro rats, in Neuroendocrinology, Vol. 85, No. 4, 2007, (with others) Reduced Walker 256 carcinosarcoma growth in vasopressin-deficient Brattleboro rats, in Tumor Biology, Vol. 31, No. 3, 2010. *Leisure interests:* music, cookery. *Address:* Institute of Cytology and Genetics, Akademika Lavretyeva prosp. 10, 630090 Novosibirsk 90, Russia (office). *Telephone:* (383) 330-74-74 (office); (383) 330-79-02 (home). *Fax:* (383) 333-12-78 (office). *E-mail:* ludiv@bionet.nsc.ru (office). *Website:* www.bionet.nsc.ru/ICIG (office).

IVANOVIĆ, Predrag, DOec., PhD; Montenegrin academic and government official; b. 10 Oct. 1954, Danilovgrad; m.; three c.; ed Univ. of Montenegro, Podgorica; Research Fellow, Inst. for Social and Econ. Research 1978–; Asst, then Assoc., then full Prof., Univ. of Montenegro Faculty of Econs 1993–, fmr Vice-Dean for Scientific Research and Head of Business Econs Dept, twice elected as Dean of Faculty of Econs, twice elected as Vice-Pres. of the Univ. of Montenegro; Minister of Educ. and Science 2001–03, of Int. Econ. Relations 2003–06; fmr Dir Montenegrin Investment Promotion Agency (MIPA). *Publications:* several books and research papers. *Address:* University of Montenegro, Cetinjska br.2, 81000 Podgorica, Montenegro (office). *Telephone:* (20) 414-255 (office). *Website:* www.ucg.ac.me/eng/ (office).

IVANOVSKI, Trendafil, PhD, DrIur; Macedonian judge; b. 1946, Badilen, Strumica Municipality; ed Iustinianus Primus Faculty of Law, Skopje; Sec., Legis. Comm., Sobranie (Parl.) 1969–72; Adviser, Nat. Secr. for Legislation and Org. 1972–77; Sec., Municipality of Karpos 1977–82, Sec., City of Skopje 1982–93; State Adviser, Constitutional Court 1993–2003, apptd Judge 2003, Pres. 2007–10; fmr Sec. and Pres. Macedonian Lawyers Assen; fmr Pres., Council for Political System of Macedonian Municipalities and Cities; fmr Sec., Nat. Union of Students of Macedonia.

ĪVĀNS, Dainis; Latvian journalist and politician; b. 25 Sept. 1955, Madona; s. of Evalds Ivans and Ilga Ivans; m. Elvira Chrschenovitch 1979; two s. two d.; ed Latvian Univ.; reporter, Latvian TV 1980–85; organized opposition to hydro-electric scheme nr Daugavpils 1986; Ed. School and Family magazine 1986–88; Pres. Latvian People's Front 1988–90; USSR People's Deputy 1989–90; mem. Latvian Supreme Soviet 1990–93, Vice-Chair. 1990–91; Chair. Latvian Social Democratic Workers' Party 2002–05; Gen. Sec. Latvian Comm. of UNESCO 1992; Sec. Writers Union 1994–; Chair. Riga Council Culture, Art and Religion Cttee 2001–05; Deputy Head, Latvian Literature Museum, Riga City Council, Chair. Comm. of Environment; Three Star Order of Repub. of Latvia 1994, Recognition Cross 2008; Best Journalist of the Year, Latvian Journalistic Union 1987. *Television:* several documentary serials on Latvian TV1. *Publications:* six books. *Leisure interests:* Oriental philosophy, literature, fishing. *Address:* Zvaigznu Str. 20, Apt 6, Riga, Latvia (home). *Telephone:* (2) 62746441 (home).

IVANTER, Ernest Viktorovich, DrSc; Russian biologist and academic; *Professor and Chairman, Department of Zoology and Ecology, Petrozavodsk University;* b. 15 Nov. 1935, Moscow; s. of Victor S. Ivanter and Irina F. Riss; m. Tatyana Matusevich 1960; one s. one d.; ed Moscow K. Timiryazev Acad. of Agric.; jr researcher, Kivach Karelian Br. USSR Acad. of Sciences 1958–60; jr researcher, Inst. of Biology, Karelian Br. of USSR Acad. of Sciences 1960–63; Asst, Docent, Prof., Dean Petrozavodsk Univ. 1965–; Chair. Dept of Zoology and Ecology, Petrozavodsk Univ. 1987–; Corresp. mem. USSR (now Russian) Acad. of Sciences 1991; mem. Scientific Council for Biological Fundamentals of Protection and Rational Use of Fauna; mem. US Zoological Soc.; Hon. mem. Finnish Soc. of Teriologues. *Publications include:* Population Ecology of Small Mammals 1975, Adaptive Peculiarities of Mammals 1985, Fauna of Karelia 1988, Statistical Methods for Biologists 1992, Zoogeography 1993, Territorial Ecology of Shrews 2002; numerous articles in scientific journals on ecology, biocenology, morphophysiology and evolutional ecology of animals. *Leisure interests:* books, sport, tourism. *Address:* Department of Zoology and Ecology, Petrozavodsk University, 185910 Petrozavodsk, Room #317, Krasnoarmeiskaya str. 31, (office); ul. Anohina la Kv. 5, 185035 Petrozavodsk, Russia (home). *Telephone:* (8142) 78-17-41 (office); (8142) 78-21-08 (home). *Fax:* (8142) 76-38-64 (office). *E-mail:* ivanter@petrsu.ru (office). *Website:* petrsu.ru/en/persons/869/ivanter (office).

IVANY, J. W. George, MA, PhD; Canadian academic and fmr university president; b. 26 May 1938, Grand Falls, Newfoundland; s. of Gordon Ivany and Stella Skinner; m. Marsha Gregory 1983; one s. three d.; ed Memorial Univ. of Newfoundland, Columbia Univ., New York and Univ. of Alberta; Head of Science Dept, Prince of Wales Coll., St John's, Newfoundland 1960–63; Grad. Teaching Fellow, Univ. of Alberta 1963–64, Asst Prof. of Elementary Educ. 1965–66; Asst Prof. of Natural Science, Teachers Coll., Columbia Univ. 1966–68, Assoc. Prof. 1968–74, Head, Dept of Science Educ. 1972–74; Visiting Fellow, Inst. of Educ., Univ. of London, UK 1972–73; Dean and Prof., Faculty of Educ., Memorial Univ. of Newfoundland 1974–77; Dean and Prof., Faculty of Educ., Simon Fraser Univ. 1977–84, Vice-Pres. (Academic) 1984–89; Pres. and Vice-Chancellor, Univ. of Sask. 1989–99; Chair. Bd Nat. Inst. of Nutrition 1995–98; mem. Bd of Dirs Cameco Corpn 1999–2011, Western Garnet Int., Canada West Foundation; Chair. Bd of Govs Okanagan Univ. Coll., Kelowna, BC 2001–04; Chair. Ivany Comm., Grenfell Coll., Memorial Univ. 2005; Hon. LLD (Memorial Univ. Newfoundland) 1991, (Univ. of Chernivtsi, Ukraine). *Publications include:* High School Teaching: A Report on Current Practices 1972, Today's Science: A Professional Approach to Teaching Elementary School Science 1975, Who's Afraid of Spiders: Teaching Science in the Elementary School 1988; textbooks; articles in professional journals.

IVASHCHENKO, Valeriy; Ukrainian army officer and politician; b. 30 June 1956, Zaporizhzhya; m.; two c.; ed A.F. Mozhayskiy Mil. Eng Acad., Russia, F.E. Dzerzhinsky Mil. Acad., Russia; mil. service on Baikonur space port 1978–93; various roles at Armament HQ, Ministry of Defence 1993–95, Head of Admin. Control Group, Ministry of Defence Strategic Nuclear Forces 1995–96, worked in Cabinet Defence Mobilization Agency and Law Enforcement Agency 1996–2000, State Nat. Security Expert, Nat. Security and Defence Council 2000–01, Chief of Dept, State Mil.-Industrial Comm. 2001–03, Head of Mil.-Industrial Policy in Office of the Cabinet of Ministers 2003–05, Deputy Chief of Industrial Policy Agency in Office of the Cabinet of Ministers 2005, Deputy Chief of Security and Defence Policy and Head of Dept of Defence in Office of the Pres. 2005–07, Deputy Minister of Defence 2007–09, Acting Minister of Defence 2009–10; arrested 2010, later sentenced to five years in prison for abuse of power 2012, sentence later reverted to one year probation, granted political asylum in Denmark 2013; Combat Merit Medal, Order of Danilo Galitskiy.

IVASHENTSOV, Gleb A.; Russian diplomatist; *Vice-President, Russian International Affairs Council;* b. 7 June 1945, St Petersburg; s. of Alexandre Ivashentsov and Zinaida Studenikova; m.; one d.; ed Moscow State Inst. of Int. Relations, Diplomatic Acad.; served at Ministry of Foreign Trade and Int. Dept, Cen. Cttee, CP of the Soviet Union 1967–75, First Sec. USSR Embassy in Delhi 1975–81, Counsellor, Head of Section, S Asia Dept, USSR Ministry of Foreign Affairs 1981–83, Head of Section 1985–91, Consul Gen. in Mumbai 1991–95, First Deputy Dir Third Asia Dept, Russian Ministry of Foreign Affairs 1995–97, Amb. to Myanmar 1997–2001, Dir-Gen. Third, Second Asia Dept 2001–05, Amb. to South Korea 2005–09; Deputy Dir Russian Centre for APEC Studies, Moscow 2010–14; mem. Russian Int. Affairs Council, Moscow 2014–, Vice-Pres. 2017–; Special Research Fellow, China Centre for Contemporary World Studies; Order of Friendship 2003, Khanhwa Medal for Diplomatic Merit (South Korea) 2009. *Publications:* India 1988, India – Basics in Brief 2009, Beyond the Fortifications of the 38th Parallel (in Russian and Korean) 2012, The Tiger of the Land of Morning Calm (in English) 2014, The Korean Tiger 2017. *Leisure interests:* swimming, boating, reading, music. *Address:* 125414 Moscow, Festivalnaya str. 24-a, Apt 38, Russia (home). *Telephone:* (495) 708-77-82 (home); 916-9172378 (mobile). *E-mail:* ivagleb1@googlemail.com (home).

IVASHOV, Col Gen. (retd) Leonid Grigoryevich, CandHistSc; Russian business executive and security officer; *President, International Center for Geopolitical Analysis;* b. 31 Aug. 1943, Kyrgyz SSR, USSR; m.; ed Tashkent Commdr School, M. Frunze Mil. Acad.; army service 1964, various positions 1964–76; with cen. staff, Ministry of Defence 1976–, Head Admin. Dept 1987–92; Sec. Council of Defence Ministers, CIS Countries 1992–96; Head of Dept, Int. Mil. Co-operation 1996–2001, Head of Staff, Co-ordination of Mil. Co-operation, CIS Countries 1999–2001; Adviser to Minister of Defence 2001–03; mem. Leadership, Great Russia–Eurasian Union electoral bloc, State Duma elections 2003; Chair. Soyuz russkogo naroda (Russian People's Union) 2006–; Vice-Pres. Acad. of Geopolitics (now Int. Centre of Geopolitical Analysis) 2002–11, now Pres.; mem. Axis for Peace Conf.; Order Red Star; six medals.

IVE, Sir Jonathan (Jony), Kt, KBE, CBE, BA; British designer; *Chief Design Officer, Apple Inc.;* b. 1967, London; m. Heather Pegg; two s.; ed Newcastle Polytechnic; Co-founder and Partner, Tangerine (design consultancy), London 1989; Designer, Apple Inc., Cupertino, Calif., USA 1992, Dir of Design 1996, then Vice-Pres. of Industrial Design, then Sr Vice-Pres. –2015, Chief Design Officer

2015–; designed the iMac 1998, iPod 2001, iPhone 2007, iPad 2010, Apple Watch 2015; Hon. Fellow, Royal Acad. of Engineering 2006; Dr hc (Northumbria Univ.) 2000, (Rhode Island School of Design) 2009, (Royal Coll. of Art) 2009; winner of design influence polls by Creative Review, the BBC and Q magazine; RSA student design awards 1988, 1989, RSA Medal for Design Achievement 1999, apptd RSA Designer for Industry 2003, Design Museum Designer of the Year 2003, RSA Benjamin Franklin Medal 2005, Pres.'s Medal, Royal Acad. of Eng 2005, Pres.'s Award, Design and Art Direction (D&AD) 2005. *Address:* Apple, 1 Infinite Loop, Cupertino, CA 95014, USA (office). *Telephone:* (408) 996-1010 (office). *Website:* www.apple.com (office).

IVENS, Martin Paul; British journalist; *Editor, The Sunday Times;* b. 29 Aug. 1958, London; s. of Michael Ivens; m. Anne McElvoy; two s. one d.; ed St Peter's Coll., Oxford; Deputy Ed. The Sunday Times 1996–2013, Acting Ed. Jan.–Sept. 2013, Ed. Sept. 2013–, also Political Columnist 2007–; fmr mem. Bd of Dirs Social Market Foundation. *Address:* The Sunday Times, 3 Thomas More Square, London, E98 1RL, England (office). *Telephone:* (20) 7782-5000 (office). *E-mail:* newsdesk@sunday-times.co.uk (office). *Website:* www.sunday-times.co.uk (office).

IVERSEN, Leslie (Les) Lars, CBE, BA, PhD, FRS; British pharmacologist, academic and business executive; *Chairman, ACADIA Pharmaceuticals, Inc.;* b. 31 Oct. 1937; s. of Svend Iversen and Anna Caia Iversen; m. Susan Diana Iversen (née Kibble) 1961; one s. one d. (one d. deceased); ed Cambridge, Harkness Fellow, USA; with Nat. Inst. of Mental Health and Dept of Neurobiology, Harvard Medical School 1964–66; Locke Research Fellow of Royal Soc., Dept of Pharmacology, Cambridge 1967–71, Dir MRC Neurochemical Pharmacology Unit 1971–82; Exec. Dir Merck, Sharp and Dohme Neuroscience Research Centre 1982–95; Visiting Prof., Dept of Pharmacology, Univ. of Oxford 1995–; Visiting Prof. of Pharmacology, Imperial Coll. School of Medicine 1997–; Prof. of Pharmacology and Dir Wolfson Centre for Age-Related Diseases, King's Coll., London 1999–2004; Interim Chair. Advisory Council on the Misuse of Drugs, UK Home Office 2010, Chair. 2011–; Founder and Dir Panos Therapeutics Ltd (pharmaceutical co.); mem. Bd of Dirs ACADIA Pharmaceuticals, Inc. 1998– (Chair. 2000–), NsGene A/S; mem. Scientific Advisory Bd Lectus Therapeutics Ltd, NeuroTargets Ltd, Neurome, Inc.; Fellow, Trinity Coll., Cambridge 1964–84; Foreign Assoc., NAS 1986. *Publications:* The Uptake and Storage of Noradrenaline in Sympathetic Nerves (with S. D. Iversen) 1967, Behavioural Pharmacology 1975, The Science of Marijuana 2000, A Very Short Introduction to Drugs 2001, Speed, Ecstasy and Ritalin: The Science of Amphetamines 2006. *Leisure interests:* reading, gardening. *Address:* ACADIA Pharmaceuticals, Inc., 3911 Sorrento Valley Blvd, San Diego, CA 92121, USA (office). *Telephone:* (858) 558-2871 (office). *Fax:* (858) 558-2872 (office). *E-mail:* info@acadia-pharm.com (office). *Website:* www.acadia-pharm.com (office).

IVEY, Kay Ellen, BA; American public servant and politician; *Governor of Alabama;* b. 15 Oct. 1944, Camden, Ala; d. of Boardman Nettles Ivey and Barbara Ivey; m. 1st Ben LaRavia (divorced); m. 2nd (divorced); ed Auburn Univ.; Teacher, Rio Linda High School, Calif. 1968–69; Asst Vice-Pres., Merchants National Bank, Mobile, Ala 1970–79; Reading Clerk, Ala House of Reps 1980–82; Asst Dir, Ala Devt Office 1982–85; Dir of Govt Affairs and Communications, Ala Comm. on Higher Educ. 1985–98; Treas., State of Ala 2003–11; Lt-Gov. of Ala 2011–17, Gov. 2017–; Chair.-Outer Continental Shelf Govs. Coalition 2018–; Chair. Aerospace States Asscn, Ala Mil. Stability Comm.; mem. First Baptist Church of Montgomery; Republican; American Inst. of Aeronautics and Astronautics Public Service Award 2016. *Address:* Office of the Governor, 600 Dexter Ave, Montgomery, AL 36130, USA (office). *Telephone:* (334) 242-7100 (office). *Fax:* (334).353-0004 (office). *E-mail:* constituent.services@governor.alabama.gov (office). *Website:* governor.alabama.gov (office).

IVEY, Susan M., BS, MBA; American tobacco industry executive; b. (Susan Hickok), 31 Oct. 1958, Schenectady, NY; m.; ed Fort Lauderdale High School, Univ. of Florida, Bellarmine Univ.; sales rep., Brown & Williamson Tobacco Corpn (subsidiary of British American Tobacco—BAT) 1981, held various trade and brand positions, including Div. Man. and Brand Dir, Marketing Dir for BAT in China 1994–96, returned to Brown & Williamson in 1999, later Sr Vice-Pres. Marketing and mem. Exec. Cttee, Pres. and CEO Brown & Williamson Tobacco Corpn 2001–04, Pres. and CEO Reynolds American Inc. (following merger with R.J. Reynolds Tobacco Holdings Inc.) 2004–11, Chair. 2006–11, Chair. and CEO R.J. Reynolds Tobacco Co. 2004–08; mem. Exec. Cttee Bellarmine Univ. and Greater Louisville Inc.; Campaign Chair. Greater Metro United Way of Louisville 2003; mem. The Committee of 200 (int. org. of women CEOs, entrepreneurs and business leaders), Women's Leadership Initiative for the United Way of America; mem. Bd Winston-Salem YWCA, Bd Bellarmine Univ., Wake Forest Univ., Univ. of Florida Foundation; mem. Bd of Dirs RR Donnelley 2009–; mem. Advisory Bd of Dirs Wachovia Forsyth Co., Bd of Advisors for Center for Women in Business and Econs at Salem Coll.

IVORY, James Francis, MFA; American film director; b. 7 June 1928, Berkeley, Calif.; s. of Edward Patrick Ivory and Hallie Millicent De Loney; ed Univs of Oregon and Southern California; began to work independently as a film maker 1952; dir, writer and cameraman in first films; co-f. (with Ismail Merchant) Merchant Ivory Productions 1962; collaborated on screenplay of numerous films with author Ruth Prawer Jhabvala; Guggenheim Fellow 1974; BAFTA Fellowship 2002; Commdr des Arts et des Lettres 1995; D.W. Griffith Award (Dirs Guild of America) 1995. *Films:* documentaries: Venice, Theme and Variations 1957, The Sword and the Flute 1959, The Delhi Way 1964; feature films: The Householder 1963, Shakespeare Wallah 1965, The Guru 1969, Bombay Talkie 1970, Savages 1972, The Wild Party 1975, Roseland 1977, The Europeans 1979, Quartet 1981, Heat and Dust 1983, The Bostonians 1984, A Room with a View 1986, Maurice 1987, Slaves of New York 1989, Mr and Mrs Bridge 1990, Howards End 1992, The Remains of the Day 1993, Jefferson in Paris 1995, Surviving Picasso 1996, A Soldier's Daughter Never Cries 1998, The Golden Bowl 2000, Le Divorce 2003, The White Countess 2005, City of Your Final Destination 2008; TV films: Adventures of a Brown Man in Search of Civilisation 1971, Autobiography of a Princess 1975 (also published as a book 1975), Hullabaloo over Georgie and Bonnie's Pictures 1978, The Five Forty-Eight 1979, Jane Austen in Manhattan 1980. *Leisure interest:* looking at pictures. *Address:* Merchant Ivory Productions, 250 West 57th Street, New York, NY 10107 (office); 18 Patroon Street, Claverack, NY 12513, USA. *Telephone:* (212) 582-8049 (office); (518) 851-7808 (home). *E-mail:* assistant@merchantivory.com (office).

IVRY, Maj.-Gen. (retd) David, BS; Israeli business executive, diplomatist and fmr military officer; *President, Boeing Israel;* b. 20 Sept. 1934, Tel-Aviv; m. Ofra Ivry; three s.; ed Technion-Israel Inst. of Tech., Haifa; Chief Rep. US–Israel Strategic Dialogue 1986–89; Dir-Gen. Ministry of Defence 1986–96, Prin. Asst Minister of Defence for Strategic Affairs 1996–99; Head, Nat. Security Council 1999, Nat. Security Adviser to Head of Nat. Security Council 1999–2000; Amb. to USA 2000–02; Pres. Boeing Israel 2003–, also Vice-Pres. Boeing Int.; Chair. Elul Asia and Global Outsourcing Services 2002–03; Head of Inter-Ministerial Steering Cttee on Arms Control and Regional Security of the Middle East Peace Process 1992–99; Head of Israeli Del. to Multilateral Working Group on Arms Control and Regional Security 1992–99; mem. Bd of Dirs El-Al 1978–82, Israel Aircraft Industries 1982–92 (Chair. 1983, 1985–86); mem. Bd of Govs Technion, Haifa 1987–; Maj.-Gen., Commdr Israel Air Force 1977–82, Israeli Defence Forces Deputy Chief of Staff 1983–85; USAF Legion of Merit, Distinguished Service Order (Singapore), Kt Commdr's Cross, Order of Merit (FRG); Dr hc (Bar-Ilan, Technion, Haifa); Amitai Distinction Award for Ethical Admin and Conduct, Israel. *Address:* The Boeing Company, The Museum Tower, 4 Berkowitz Street, Tel-Aviv 64238 (office); 6 Hazamir Street, Ramat Hasharon 47226, Israel (home). *Telephone:* (3) 7776100 (office); (3) 5406085 (home). *Fax:* (3) 7776101 (office); (3) 5499183 (home). *E-mail:* david.e.ivry@boeing.com (office). *Website:* www.boeing.com (office).

IWAN, Dafydd, BArch; British politician, singer-composer and record company director; *Director, Sain (Recordiau) Cyf;* b. (Dafydd Iwan Jones), 24 Aug. 1943, Brynaman, Wales; s. of Rev. Gerallt Jones and Elizabeth Jane Jones; m. 1st Marion Thomas 1968 (divorced 1986); two s. one d.; m. 2nd Bethan Jones 1988; two s.; ed Aman Valley Grammar School, Ysgol Ty Tan Domen, Y Bala, Univ. Coll. of Wales, Aberystwyth and Welsh School of Architecture, Cardiff; f. Sain (Recordiau) Cyf (now Wales' leading record co.) 1969, Man. Dir 1984–2006, currently Dir; f. Tai Gwynedd Housing Asscn 1971; Founder-Trustee, Nant Gwrtheyrn Language Centre 1975; Chair. Welsh Language Soc. 1968–71; parl. cand. 1974, 1983, 1984; Chair. Plaid Cymru (Nationalist Party of Wales) 1982–84, Vice-Pres. 1984–95, Pres. 2003–10; Plaid Cymru mem. of Gwynedd Unitary Authority 1995–2008; Chair. Planning and Economic Devt Cttee, Cyngor Gwynedd Council 1995–99, mem. Exec. Cttee responsible for Planning, Highways and Environment 1999–2003, Econ. Devt and Educ. 2003–08; Chair. Gwynedd Econ. Partnership 2008–; Trustee, Portmeirion Foundation, Carers Outreach, Plas Glyn-y-Weddw Gallery; nonconformist lay preacher; has promoted the Welsh language and culture for five decades; Hon. mem. Gorsedd of Bards for services to Welsh language; Hon. Fellow, Univs of Bangor and Aberystwyth for services to Welsh culture and Welsh music 1998; Hon. LLD (Univ. of Wales) 2004; Gold Disc for services to Welsh music. *Music:* composed, sung and recorded more than 250 songs; more than 40 albums and videos 1965–2010; numerous concert tours abroad. *Television:* Yma Mae Ngân, S4C (several series introducing own songs), documentaries on various countries. *Publications include:* Dafydd Iwan (autobiog.) 1982, 100 O Ganeuon (collection of songs) 1983, Caneuon Dafydd Iwan (second collection of songs) 1991, Cân Dros Gymru (autobiog.) 2002, Dafydd Iwan: Bywyd mewn lluniau (A Life in Pictures) 2005. *Leisure interests:* composing songs, sketching, reading. *Address:* Sain, Canolfan Sain, Llandwrog, Caernarfon, Gwynedd, LL54 5TG (office); Carrog, Rhos-Bach, Caeathro, Caernarfon, Gwynedd, LL55 2TF, Wales (home). *Telephone:* (1286) 676004 (home); 7984-202922 (mobile). *E-mail:* dafyddiwan2@gmail.com; dafyddiwan@cymru1.net (home); dafydd@sainwales.com (office). *Website:* www.sainwales.com (office); www.dafyddiwan.com (home).

IWANIEC, Henryk, PhD; Polish/American mathematician and academic; *New Jersey Professor of Mathematics, Rutgers University;* b. 9 Oct. 1947, Elbląg, Poland; ed Univ. of Warsaw; held positions at Inst. of Math., Polish Acad. of Sciences –1983; left Poland 1983; held visiting positions at Inst. for Advanced Study, Princeton, NJ 1999–2000, Univ. of Michigan 1984, Univ. of Colorado 1984; apptd Prof. of Math., Rutgers Univ., NJ 1987, currently New Jersey Prof. of Math. and mem. Grad. Faculty; Fellow, American Math. Soc. 2012; Ostrowski Prize 2001, Frank Nelson Cole Prize in Number Theory 2002, Leroy P. Steele Prize for Math. Exposition 2011, Shaw Prize in Math. Sciences (co-recipient) 2015. *Publications:* Topics in Classical Automorphic Forms 1997, Spectral Methods of Automorphic Forms (second edn) 2002, Analytic Number Theory (co-author) 2004, Analytic Number Theory: Lectures Given at the C.I.M.E. Summer School Held in Cetraro, Italy, July 11–18, 2002 2006, Opera de Cribro (co-author) 2010; numerous papers in professional journals. *Address:* Room Hill 706, Department of Mathematics, Rutgers University, Hill Center – Busch Campus, 110 Frelinghuysen Road, Piscataway, NJ 08854-8019, USA (office). *Telephone:* (848) 445-6793 (office). *Fax:* (732) 445-5530 (office). *E-mail:* iwaniec@math.rutgers.edu (office). *Website:* www.math.rutgers.edu (office).

IWASAKI, Yoichi, BS, MS, PhD; Japanese theoretical physicist, fmr university administrator and academic; *Professor Emeritus, University of Tsukuba;* b. 12 Sept. 1941; ed Univ. of Tokyo; Asst, Research Inst. for Fundamental Physics, Kyoto Univ. 1969–72; Postdoctoral Fellow, Dept of Physics, CUNY, USA 1972–75; Asst Prof., Inst. of Physics, Univ. of Tsukuba 1975–76, Assoc. Prof. 1976–77, Prof. 1984–98, Prof. Emer. 1998–, Vice-Pres. (Research) 1998–2004, Pres. Univ. of Tsukuba 2004–09, Fellow, Center for Computational Sciences; Auditor, High Energy Accelerator Research Org. 2010–16; mem. Inst. for Advanced Study, Princeton, USA 1977; mem. Physical Soc. of Japan; Nishina Memorial Prize, Nishina Memorial Foundation 1994. *Publications:* numerous publs on high-energy physics, in particular large-scale numerical study of quantum chromodynamics and the devt of massively parallel computers for computational physics. *Address:* University of Tsukuba, 1-1-1 Tennodai, Tsukuba-shi, Ibaraki -ken 305-8577, Japan (office). *Telephone:* (29) 853-2111 (office). *Fax:* (29) 853-2059 (office). *Website:* www.tsukuba.ac.jp (office).

IWAYA, Takeshi; Japanese politician; *Minister of Defence;* b. 24 Aug. 1957, Oita Prefecture; m.; one s. two d.; ed Waseda Univ.; mem. Oita Prefectural Ass. 1987–90; mem. House of Reps (lower house of parl.) for Oita 3 constituency 1990–93, 2000–; fmr Parl. Sec. for Defence; Sr Vice-Minister for Foreign Affairs 2006; Minister of Defence 2018–; mem. Liberal Democratic Party, Deputy Sec.-Gen. *Address:* Ministry of Defence, 5-1, Ichigaya, Honmura-cho, Shinjuku-ku,

Tokyo 162-8801, Japan (office). *Telephone:* (3) 5366-3111 (office). *Fax:* (3) 5261-8018 (office). *E-mail:* infomod@mod.go.jp (office). *Website:* www.mod.go.jp (office); www.t-iwaya.com.

IYANDA, (Olufunmilola Aduke) Funmi, BSc; Nigerian television presenter and journalist; *CEO, Ignite Media;* b. 27 July 1971; one d.; ed Herbert Macaulay School, Lagos, Univ. of Ibadan; sports journalist for female Football World Cup 1999, Olympic Games in Sydney 2000, Athens 2004; Man. Dir Funmi Iyanda Productions 2004–08; CEO Ignite Media, Lagos 2008–; participant, ASPEN Inst. Forum for Communications and Society; mem. Nigerian Football Asscn 1995–2003; mem. Bd of Dirs Farafina Trust, Positive Impact Youth Network; Tutu Fellow, African Leadership Inst.; columnist, Tempo Magazine; Nigeria Media Merit Award 2005, Glass Ceiling Breaker Award, Women Writer's Asscn of Nigeria, Jewel of the Future Award, African Cultural Inst., Media Woman of The Year, City People; named Young Global Leader by World Econ. Forum 2011. *Television includes:* Good Morning Nigeria, New Dawn with Funmi 2000–08, Talk with Funmi 2010. *Telephone:* (1) 8940988 (office). *E-mail:* info@ignitemediang.com (office). *Website:* www.ignitemediang.com (office).

IZETBEGOVIĆ, Bakir; Bosnia and Herzegovina architect and politician; b. 28 June 1956, Sarajevo, Socialist Repub. of Bosnia and Herzegovina, Socialist Fed. Repub. of Yugoslavia; s. of Alija Izetbegović (fmr Bosnian Pres.); m.; one d.; ed Univ. of Sarajevo; consultant with architectural consulting firm 1982–92; Dir Construction Bureau of Sarajevo Canton 1991–2003; mem. Stranka Demokratske Akcije (SDA—Party of Democratic Action), Chief of SDA Parl. Group, Sarajevo Canton Ass. 2000–02, Chief of SDA Parl. Group, House of Reps (Predstavnički Dom/Zastupnički Dom), Parl. Ass. of Fed. of Bosnia and Herzegovina 2002–06; Chief of SDA mems, Parl. Ass. of Council of Europe 2006–10; Bosniak mem. of State Presidency 2010–18, Chair. March–Nov. 2012, March–Nov. 2014, March–Nov. 2016, March–Nov. 2018; Chair. SDA 2015–; fmr Dir FC Sarajevo, KK Bosna, Merhamet (Islamic humanitarian asscn); mem. Islamic Community Ass. *Address:* Stranka Demokratske Akcije (Party of Democratic Action), 71000 Sarajevo, Mehmeda Spahe 14, Bosnia and Herzegovina (office). *Telephone:* (33) 216906 (home). *Fax:* (33) 225363 (office). *E-mail:* sda@bih.net.ba (office). *Website:* sda.ba (office).

IZORIA, Levan, BA, LLM, PhD; Georgian academic and politician; *Minister of Defence;* b. 5 Feb. 1974; m.; three c.; ed Ivane Javakhishvili Tbilisi State Univ., Georg-August Univ. Göttingen, Germany; Lecturer, Law Faculty, Law Theory and Constitutional Law Dept, Ivane Javakhishvili Tbilisi State Univ. 1995–98, Asst Prof. 2002–05; Asst to Dir, Göttingen State Teaching and Political Science Inst., Germany 1999–2002; Sr Scientific Officer, T. Tsereteli Law Inst., Acad. of Science, Tbilisi 2002–; Co-ordinator, State Cttee for Reform of Law Enforcement Agencies 2002–03; Rep. of German Konrad-Adenauer Political Foundation in S Caucasus 2003–04; Rector, Ministry of Internal Affairs Acad. 2004–06, Full Prof. 2014–; Prof. and Dean of Law Faculty, Georgian Inst. of Public Affairs 2006–07; Scientist-Researcher, German Univ. of Admin. Sciences, Speyer (Humboldt Foundation Scholarship) 2007–09; Assoc. Prof., Caucasus Law School 2009–10; Assoc. Prof., Georgian-American Univ. 2009–11; Academic Researcher, Max Planck Inst. for Comparative Public Law and Int. Law, Heidelberg 2010, 2011; Full Prof., Grigol Robakidze Univ., Tbilisi 2011–14; Deputy Minister of Internal Affairs 2012–15; Deputy Head, Georgian State Security Service 2015–16; Minister of Defence 2016–. *Address:* Ministry of Defence, 0112 Tbilisi, Gen. Kvinitadze 20, Georgia (office). *Telephone:* (32) 272-35-35 (office). *Fax:* (32) 272-35-35 (office). *E-mail:* pr@mod.gov.ge (office). *Website:* www.mod.gov.ge (office).

IZUMI, Shinya; Japanese politician; b. 1 Aug. 1937, Yoshii, Fukuoka; ed Kyushu Univ.; previously worked as official at transport ministry; mem. House of Councillors (Upper House) 1992–, has held numerous govt posts including Sr State Sec. of Transport, Sr Vice-Minister of Economy, Trade and Industry, Sr Vice-Minister of Land, Infrastructure and Transport; Chair. Nat. Public Safety Comm. and Minister of State for Disaster Man. and Food Safety 2007–08 (resgnd); mem. LDP (Liberal Democratic Party), left party 1993, rejoined 2003.

JAAFAR ALBAR, Tan Sri Syed Hamid; Malaysian lawyer and politician; *Chairman, Land Public Transport Commission;* b. 15 Jan. 1944, Penang; m. Sharifah Aziah; three s. three d.; ed Monash Univ., Melbourne, Australia, Middle Temple, UK; Magistrate and Pres. of Sessions Court, Kuala Lumpur 1970–72; Head of Legal Dept, Bank Bumiputra Malaysia Bhd (BBMB) 1972, Legal Adviser and later Sr Man. 1972–78, Asst Sec. and Sec. to Man. 1974–79, first Gen. Man. of Bahrain Br. 1979–80, Gen. Man. of London Br., transferred to Kuala Lumpur as Head of Int. Banking Div. (Credit Supervision) 1980–82, Chief Gen. Man. and Sec. of the Bank 1985–86; Sec. Kewangan Bumiputra and Bank Pembangunan Malaysia Bhd 1976–79, Inst. of Bankers 1978–79; Dir and CEO Bumiputra Merchant Bankers 1982–85; Dir Koperasi Usaha Bersatu 1983–88, Kewangan Bumiputra Malaysia Bhd, Bumiputra Lloyds Leasing Bhd, Bumiputra Merchant Bankers, Syarikat Nominee Sdn Bhd, BBMB Properties 1985–86; Advocate and Solicitor-Gen. Pnr, Albar Zulkifly and Yap 1986–90; Chair. Shamelin Holdings 1989–90, Koperasi Shamelin Bhd 1989–90; MP for Kota Tinggi (Johor) 1990–2013; Minister of Justice in Prime Minister's Dept (in charge of oil and gas affairs) 1990–92; Minister of Law and Minister in Prime Minister's Dept 1992–95; Minister of Defence 1995–99, of Foreign Affairs 1999–2008, of Home Affairs and Internal Security 2008–09; Chair. Land Public Transport Comm. 2010–. *Address:* Suruhanjaya Pengangkutan Awam Darat Headquarters, Block D, Platinum Sentral, Jalan Stesen Sentral 2, Kuala Lumpur Sentral, 50470 Kuala Lumpur, Malaysia (office). *Telephone:* (3) 27267000 (office). *Fax:* (3) 27267100 (office). *E-mail:* aduan@spad.gov.my (office). *Website:* www.spad.gov.my (office); syedhamidalbar44.blogspot.in.

JA'AFARI, Bashar, BA, PhD; Syrian diplomatist; *Permanent Representative, United Nations;* b. 14 April 1956, Damascus; m. Shohreh Eskandari; three c.; ed Damascus Univ., Univ. of Paris V-Sorbonne, Univ. of Sharif Hedayatuallah, Jakarta; joined Ministry of Foreign Affairs 1980, Attaché and Third Sec., Embassy in Paris 1983–88, First Sec. and Counsellor, Perm. Mission to UN, New York 1991–94, Chargé d'affaires a.i., Embassy in Jakarta 1998–2002, Dir Dept of Int. Orgs and Confs, Ministry of Foreign Affairs 2002–04, Amb. and Perm. Rep. to UN, Geneva 2004–06, to UN, New York 2006–. *Publications:* The Lobbies in the U.S.A 1983, The Syrian Foreign Affairs 1946-1982 1986, The United Nations and the New World Order 1994, The Syrian Politics of Alliances 1918-1982 2015. *Address:* Permanent Mission of Syria to the United Nations, 820 Second Avenue, 15th Floor, New York, NY 10017, USA (office). *Telephone:* (212) 661-1313 (office). *Fax:* (212) 983-4439 (office). *E-mail:* exesec.syria@gmail.com (office). *Website:* www.un.int/syria (office).

JAAFARI, Ibrahim al-, MD; Iraqi physician and politician; b. 1947, Karbala; ed Mosul Univ.; after medical school joined Islamic Dawa Party (Hizb ad-Da'wa al-Islamiya), Chief Spokesman 1966, remains leader; moved to Iran when Dawa party in Iraq was outlawed 1980, then to London, UK 1989; fmr mem. Iraq Governing Council; Interim Vice-Pres. of Iraq 2004–05; Prime Minister of Iraq 2005–06; Minister of Foreign Affairs 2014–18; Leader, Nat. Reform Movt 2008–. *Address:* c/o Ministry of Foreign Affairs, opp. State Organization for Roads and Bridges, Karradat Mariam, Baghdad, Iraq (office).

JÄÄTTEENMÄKI, Anneli Tuulikki, LLM; Finnish politician; b. 11 Feb. 1955, Lapua; m. Jorma Melleri 1994; ed Univ. of Helsinki; acting lawyer, Office of the Local Authorities Negotiating Del. 1981–82; Temporary Asst, Ministry for Foreign Affairs 1982, Ministerial Political Adviser 1983–84; Legis. Sec. to Finnish Centre Party Parl. Faction 1986, mem. 1987–2004, Deputy Party Parl. Faction 1991–94, 1999–2000; mem. Parl. for Vaasa 1987–2003, for Helsinki 2003–04; mem. Finnish Del. to the Nordic Council 1987–94; mem. Parl. Cttee for Constitutional Law 1987–99, Legal Affairs Cttee 1987–91, Electors Cttee 1987–91, Parl. Salary Del. 1987–92, Foreign Affairs Cttee 1999–, Parl. Grand Cttee 1999–2003; Deputy mem. Finance Cttee April–Nov. 1991, Defence Cttee April–May 1991, Foreign Affairs Cttee 1991–94; Minister of Justice 1994–95; Parl. Gov. Bank of Finland 1991–92, mem. Supervisory Council Parl. Govs Bank of Finland 1991–94, 1995–2003, Second Deputy mem. Parl. Trustees 1991–93, 1995–99, First Deputy mem. Parl. Trustees Sept.–Nov. 1993, 1999–2000, mem. Trustees 1993–94; mem. and Vice-Chair. Finnish Del. to Parl. Ass. of Council of Europe 1996–2003, Deputy mem. 2003–; mem. Commrs to Govt Guarantee Fund 1996–99; mem. Finnish Del. to WEU Parl. Ass. 1999–2003; Parl. Speaker March–April 2003, Speaker's Council April 2003, Chancellery Comm. Speaker April 2003; Prime Minister of Finland April–June 2003; mem. European Parl. 2004–, Vice-Chair. Cttee on Constitutional Affairs 2007–09, Group of Alliance of Liberals and Democrats for Europe (ALDE) 2009–14, mem. Cttee on Environment, Public Health and Food Safety 2014–17, Del. to India 2014, Parl's Bureau 2015–17, Del. to Belarus 2017, Del. to Euronest Parliamentary Ass. 2017, Vice-Pres. European Parl. 2015–17; mem. Equal Opportunities Comm. 1987–91, Advisory Bd for Prison Affairs 1988–91 (Chair. 1991–94), Helsinki Inst. for Criminal Policy (HEUNI) 1996; Deputy Chair. Paasikivi Soc. 1994. *Publications:* Oikeus Voittaa (Justice Wins) 1999, Sillanrakentaja 2002. *Leisure interests:* history, literature, art, sports. *Address:* European Parliament, Rue Wiertz, ASP 09G358, 1047 Brussels, Belgium (office). *Telephone:* (2) 284-56-14 (office). *Fax:* (2) 284-96-14 (office). *E-mail:* anneli.jaatteenmaki@europarl.europa.eu (office). *Website:* annelijaatteenmaki.net (office).

JABER, Fatima al-, BEng; United Arab Emirates business executive; *Chief Operating Officer, Al Jaber Group;* d. of Obaid al-Jaber; m. 1995; five c.; ed UAE Univ., Al Ain; Asst Under-Sec. for Technical Services, Abu Dhabi Public Works Dept 1988–2005, becoming Asst Under-Sec. for Building Projects Section, Abu Dhabi Municipality; currently Exec. Dir and COO Al Jaber Group (family construction business); Chair. Al Bashayer Investment Co.; Gen. Man. Qaryat Al Beri Resort Devt Co. LLC; mem. Bd of Dirs Abu Dhabi Chamber of Commerce and Industry (first woman) 2009–; Deputy Chair. Abu Dhabi Businesswomen's Council; Arabian Business Businesswoman of the Year 2008, Construction Industry Personality of the Year 2009. *Address:* Al Jaber Group, PO Box 2175, Abu Dhabi, United Arab Emirates (office). *Telephone:* (2) 5554300 (office). *Fax:* (2) 5553370 (office). *E-mail:* aljaber@aje.ae (office). *Website:* www.aljaber.com (office).

JABER, Hessa Sultan al-, BSc, MSc, PhD; Qatar communications industry executive; *Minister for Communication and Information Technology;* ed Kuwait Univ., George Washington Univ., USA; fmr IT Adviser for Qtel; fmr Chair. Computer Science Dept, Qatar Univ.; fmr mem. Strategic ICT Cttee; Sec.-Gen. Supreme Council of Information and Communication Tech. (ictQATAR) 2004, Minister for Communication and Information Tech. 2013–; Commr WHO/ITU Comm. and Accountability for Women and Children's Health; mem. Bd of Regents, Qatar Univ.; mem. Bd of Govs American School of Doha, Bloomsbury Qatar Foundation Journals, Qatar Foundation Nat. Research Forum, Qatar Financial Markets Authority, Network of Global Agenda Councils of World Econ. Forum, Global Alliance for Information and Communication Techs and Devt; Nat. Figure of the Year, Ministry of Interior Affairs 2008. *Address:* c/o Supreme Council of Information and Communication Technology (ictQATAR), PO Box 23264, Al Nassr Tower, Post Office Roundabout, Al Corniche Street, Doha, Qatar (office). *Telephone:* 44995333 (office). *Fax:* 44935913 (office). *E-mail:* info@ict.gov.qa (office); communication@ict.gov.qa (office). *Website:* www.ictqatar.qa/en (office).

JABER, Mohammed bin Issa al-; Saudi Arabian/Austrian business executive; *Chairman and CEO, MBI International;* b. 1959, Jeddah; m. 1978; one s. two d.; f. Jadawel Int. Construction and Devt 1982; f. JJW Hotels & Resorts, Portugal 1989, now owner-operator of more than 60 hotel and leisure resorts in Europe and the Middle East; f. AJWA Group for Agro and Food Industries, Jeddah 1992; currently Chair. and CEO MBI Int.; Founding sponsor, London Middle East Inst., SOAS; Dir Olive Tree Educational Trust, London; Founder, Chair. and sole Patron, MBI Al Jaber Foundation; UN Spokesperson for Global Forums on Reinventing Govt 2007–; UNESCO Envoy for Educ. Tolerance and Cultures in Middle East 2005–; Chair. Mediterranean East Peace Forum, Lecce, Italy 2008; Austrian citizen 2007–; Hon. Fellow, SOAS 2002, Corpus Christi Coll., Oxford 2009; Hon. DSc (City Univ., London) 2004; Hon. DLitt (Westminster) 2004; Arab League Educational, Cultural and Scientific Org. Gold Medal 2007, Gold Medal of Honour, Mayor of Vienna, Gold Medal, Islamic Educational, Scientific and Cultural Organization (ISESCO) 2012. *Address:* MBI International, 78–80 Wigmore Street, London, W1U 2SJ, England (office). *Telephone:* (20) 7935-5859 (office). *E-mail:* info@mbiinternational.com (office). *Website:* www.mbiinternational.com (office); www.mbifoundation.com; www.mbialjaber.com.

JACAMON, Jean-Paul; French business executive; *Senior Adviser, Cognetas SA;* b. 5 Aug. 1947, Thaon-les-Vosges; m. Colette Jacquier; four c.; ed Ecole Polytechnique de Paris and Ecole des Mines de Paris; mem. staff Ministry of Industry 1975, sr civil servant, French Regional Land Use Planning Comm. (DATAR) –1981; Exec. Asst Groupe Schneider 1981, various positions with Spie Batignolles (electrical eng construction subsidiary) 1983–, Man. of 'Ferrière la Grande' plant, Vice-Pres. Eng and Gen. Contracting Div., Vice-Pres. Electric and Nuclear Power Div. 1988, Vice-Pres. responsible for electrical contracting activities, Chair. and CEO Spie-Trindel (local contracting for electrical and electro-mechanical projects) –1993, COO Spie Batignolles 1993–94; Exec. Vice-Pres. European Div., Schneider Electric 1995, COO 1996–2002, Vice-Chair. 1999–2002; ind. consultant 2002–; Chair. (non-exec.) Bonna Sabla 2003–05, Gardiner 2003–06, CPI 2006–; Dir (non-exec.) AMEC PLC 2002–06, Péchiney 2002–04, Carbonne Lorraine 2003–, Alcan 2004–07; currently Sr Adviser, Cognetas SA; Chevalier, Ordre nat. du Mérite 1994. *Leisure interests:* golf, bridge. *Address:* Cognetas SA, 47 Avenue George V, 75008 Paris (office); 64 route de l'Etang la Ville, 78750 Mareil-Marly, France (home). *Telephone:* 1-53-83-79-10 (office). *Fax:* 1-53-83-79-20 (office). *E-mail:* jp.jacamon@wanadoo.fr.

JACK, Ian, FRSL; British writer and journalist; b. 7 Feb. 1945, Farnworth, Lancs., England; s. of Harry Jack and Isabella Jack (née Gillespie); m. 1st 1979; m. 2nd Rosalind Sharpe 1998; one s. one d.; newspaper journalist in Scotland 1960s; variously reporter, feature writer, Foreign Corresp., Sunday Times 1970–86; co-f. Independent on Sunday 1989, Ed. 1991–95; Ed. Granta magazine 1995–2007; currently writes for The Guardian newspaper; Journalist of the Year 1986, Reporter of the Year 1989, Editor of the Year 1992. *Publications include:* Before the Oil Ran Out 1987, The Crash that Stopped Britain 2001, The Country Formerly Known as Great Britain 2009, Mofussil Junction 2013; various Granta anthologies. *Leisure interests:* history, Scottish painters, ships. *Address:* The Guardian, Kings Place, 90 York Way, London, N1 9GU, England (office). *Telephone:* (20) 3353-2000 (office). *Fax:* (20) 3353-3193 (office). *E-mail:* ian.jack@guardian.co.uk (office); iangjack@blueyonder.co.uk (home). *Website:* www.theguardian.com/profile/ianjack (office).

JACK, James Julian Bennett, PhD, FRS, FRCP, FMedSci; New Zealand neurophysiologist and academic (retd); b. 25 March 1936, Invercargill; ed Univ. of Otago, Univ. of Oxford, UK; Rhodes Scholarship 1960–63; Foulerton Gift Researcher 1964–68; demonstrator, Univ. Lecturer then Reader, then Prof. of Cellular Neuroscience, Lab. of Physiology (now Dept of Physiology, Anatomy and Genetics), Univ. of Oxford 1968–; Supernumerary Fellow, Univ. Coll., Oxford; Fellow, Acad. of Medical Sciences 1998; apptd Gov. Wellcome Trust 1987 (Deputy Chair. 1994–99); Hon. FRSNZ 1998; Hon. DSc (Univ. of Otago) 1999. *Address:* Dutch House, 307-308 High Holborn, London, WC1V 7LL, England.

JACKAMAN, Michael Clifford John, MA; British business executive; b. 7 Nov. 1935; s. of Air Commodore Clifford Thomas Jackaman and Lily Margaret Jackaman; m. Valerie Jane Pankhurst 1960; one s. one d.; ed Felsted School, Essex, Jesus Coll., Cambridge; with Yardley Ltd 1959–60, Beecham Foods Ltd 1960–63, John Harvey & Sons Ltd 1963–65, Findus Ltd 1965, Harveys of Bristol 1966–92 (Chair. 1984–93); Marketing Dir Allied Breweries Ltd 1978–80, Deputy Man. Dir 1978–83; Chair. Allied Vintners Ltd 1983–88; Chair. and CEO Hiram Walker-Allied Vintners Ltd 1988–91; Chair. Allied-Lyons (now Allied Domecq) PLC 1991–96; Chair. Grand Appeal, Royal Hosp. for Sick Children, Bristol 1996–; mem. Bd of Dirs Rank Group PLC 1992–97, Kleinwort Benson Group 1994–98, Theatre Royal, Bath 1999–2005; Hon. DBA (Univ. of West of England). *Leisure interests:* opera, gardening, tennis, walking, oriental antiques, theatre.

JACKLIN, Anthony (Tony), CBE; British professional golfer (retd); b. 7 July 1944, Scunthorpe; s. of Arthur David Jacklin and Doris Lillian Jacklin; m. Vivien Jacklin 1966 (died 1988); two s. one. d.; m. 2nd Astrid May Waagen 1988; one s. one step-s. one step-d.; Lincolnshire Open champion 1961; professional 1962–85, 1988–; won British Asst Professionals' title 1965; won Dunlop Masters 1967, 1973; first British player to win British Open since 1951 1969; US Open Champion 1970; first British player to win US Open since 1920 and first since 1900 to hold US and British Open titles simultaneously; Greater Greensboro Open champion, USA 1968, 1972; won Italian Open 1973, German Open 1979, Venezuelan Open 1979, Jersey Open 1981, British Professional Golfers' Asscn (PGA) champion 1982 and 15 major tournaments in various parts of the world; played in eight Ryder Cup matches and four times for England in World Cup; Capt. of 1983 GB and Europe Ryder Cup Team; Capt. of victorious European Ryder Cup team 1985 (first win for Europe since 1957), 1987; BBC TV golf commentator; moved to Sotogrande, Spain from Jersey 1983; Commr of Golf, Las Aves Club, Sotogrande 1983–; Dir of Golf, San Roque Club 1988–; now golf course designer; Hon. Life Pres. British Professional Golfers' Asscn; Hon. Fellow, Birmingham Polytechnic 1989. *Publications include:* Golf With Tony Jacklin 1969, The Price of Success 1979, Jacklin's Golfing Secrets (with Peter Dobereiner), The First Forty Years (with Renton Laidlaw) 1985, Your Game and Mine (with Bill Robertson) 1999, Jacklin: The Autobiography 2006. *Address:* The Jacklin Design Group, 1175 Fifty-First Street, West Bradenton, FL 34209, USA (office). *Telephone:* (941) 761-3370 (office). *Fax:* (941) 761-3371 (office). *E-mail:* tony@jacklindesigngroup.com (office); blawrence@championsukplc.com (office). *Website:* www.jacklindesigngroup.com (office); www.tonyjacklin.com.

JACKLIN, Bill, MA, RA; British artist and painter; b. (Walter William Burke-Jacklin), 1 Jan. 1943, Hampstead, London, England; s. of Harold Jacklin and Alice Jacklin; m. 1st Lesley Berman 1979 (divorced 1993); m. 2nd Janet Russo 1993; ed Walthamstow School of Art, London and Royal Coll. of Art; teacher at numerous art colls 1967–75; moved to New York 1985; elected to Royal Acad. 1990; Artist-in-Residence British Council, Hong Kong 1993–95; Bursary Award, Arts Council, London 1975. *Publications include:* numerous Marlborough catalogues 1980–2005. *Leisure interests:* walking, reading. *Address:* c/o Marlborough Fine Art, 6 Albemarle Street, London, W1S 4BY, England. *Telephone:* (20) 7629-5161. *Fax:* (20) 7629-6338. *E-mail:* mfa@marlboroughfineart.com. *Website:* www.marlboroughlondon.com; www.bjacklin.com.

JACKMAN, Hugh Michael, BA; Australian actor, musician and producer; b. 12 Oct. 1968; s. of Christopher John Jackman and Grace McNeil (née Greenwood); m. Deborra-Lee Furness 1996; one s. one d.; ed Univ. of Tech. Sydney, Western Australian Acad. of Performing Arts; began career as actor in theatre 1995; major breakthrough role with X-Men film series 2000; Co-Founder, Seed Productions 2005–10; Global Adviser, Global Poverty Project 2009–; Brand Amb., Micromax 2013–; Global Amb., Montblanc 2014–; Amb., World Vision Int.; Patron, Bone Marrow Inst.; involved in numerous charity projects and supporter of sports clubs; Australian Star of the Year 1999, ShoWest Award for Male Star of the Year 2006, Special Tony Award, Star on the Walk of Fame 2012, Golden Icon Award, Zurich Film Festival 2013, Donostia Lifetime Achievement Award, San Sebastián Int. Film Festival 2013, Empire Icon Award, Slammy Award for Raw Guest Star of the Year 2014, Bambi Award for Entertainment 2017, Kirk Douglas Award for Excellence in Film, Santa Barbara Int. Film Festival 2018. *Stage appearances include:* Beauty and the Beast (Australia), Sunset Boulevard (Australia), Oklahoma (UK), The Boy from Oz (Broadway) 2004, A Steady Rain (Broadway) 2009, Hugh Jackman, Back on Broadway 2011, The River 2014, Broadway to Oz 2015. *Films include:* Paperback Hero 1999, Erskineville Kings (Film Critics Circle of Australia Award for Best Actor-Male 2000) 1999, X-Men (Saturn Award for Best Actor 2001) 2000, Someone Like You 2001, Swordfish 2001, Kate and Leopold 2001, X-Men 2 2003, Standing Room Only 2004, Van Helsing 2004, X-Men: The Last Stand 2006, Scoop 2006, The Fountain 2006, The Prestige 2006, Flushed Away (voice) 2006, Happy Feet (voice) 2006, Uncle Jonny 2008, Deception (also producer) 2008, Australia 2008, X-Men Origins: Wolverine (also producer) (People's Choice Award for Favorite Action Star 2010) 2009, Snow Flower and the Secret Fan 2011, Butter 2011, Real Steel (People's Choice Award for Favorite Action Movie Actor 2012) 2011, Les Misérables (Golden Globe Award for Best Performance by an Actor in a Motion Picture – Comedy or Musical 2013) 2012, Rise of the Guardians (voice) 2012, Movie 43 2013, The Wolverine 2013, Prisoners 2013, X-Men: Days of Future Past 2014, Night at the Museum: Secret of the Tomb 2014, Me and Earl and the Dying Girl (voice) 2015, Chappie 2015, Pan 2015, Eddie the Eagle 2015, Logan (Golden Schmoes Award for Best Actor of the Year, IGN People's Choice Award for Best Lead Performer in a Movie, MTV Movie/TV Award for Best Duo (shared with Dafne Keen) 2017, Empire Award for Best Actor 2018) 2017, The Greatest Showman 2017, Deadpool 2 2018, The Front Runner (Hollywood Film Award for Actor of the Year 2018) 2018. *Television includes:* as actor: Correlli 1995, Snowy River: The McGregor Saga 1996, Hey, Mr Producer! 1998, Halifax F. P. 1998, Oklahoma! 1999; as host: 57th Tony Awards 2003, 58th Tony Awards (Primetime Emmy Award for Outstanding Individual Performance in a Variety or Music Program 2005) 2004, 59th Tony Awards 2005, 81st Academy Awards (Online Film & Television Asscn Award for Best Host or Performer of a Variety, Musical, or Comedy Program 2009) 2009, 68th Tony Awards 2014; as producer: An Aussie Goes Barmy (series) 2006, The Directors' Series (series) 2007. *Music includes:* Musical Albums: Beauty and the Beast 1995, Oklahoma! 1999, The Boy from Oz (Drama Desk Award for Outstanding Actor in a Musical, Tony Award for Best Actor in a Musical, Theatre World Award, Drama League Award for Distinguished Performance of the Year, Outer Critics Circle Award for Best Actor in a Musical 2004) 2003, Broadway's Greatest Gifts: Carols for a Cure, Vol. 5 2003, Broadway: The American Musical 2004, Broadway: America's Music 1935–2005 2005, Broadway Today: Broadway, 1993–2005 2005, The 20th Century Masters-The Millennium Collection: The Best of Broadway 2006, Broadway Gold 2007; Soundtrack albums: Happy Feet: Music from the Motion Picture 2006, Les Misérables: Highlights from the Motion Picture Soundtrack (Satellite Award for Best Original Song (co-recipient), Special Achievement Award for Best Ensemble, Motion Picture (co-recipient) 2012) 2012, Fly: Songs Inspired by the Film "Eddie the Eagle" 2016, The Greatest Showman: Original Motion Picture Soundtrack 2017. *Leisure interests:* piano, guitar, golf, windsurfing. *Address:* c/o 20 Convention Centre Place, South Wharf, VIC. 3006, Australia (office). *Telephone:* (2) 8231-6405 (office). *E-mail:* info@amwmedia.com.au (office). *Website:* www.amwmedia.com.au (office).

JACKSON, Alphonso, BSc, LLB; American business executive and fmr government official; *Senior Advisor, First Data Corporation;* b. 9 Sept. 1945, Marshall, Tex.; m. Marcia Jackson; two d.; ed Truman State Univ., Washington Univ. Law School; Special Asst to Chancellor and Asst Prof., Univ. of Missouri, St Louis 1973–77; Dir of Public Safety for City of St Louis 1977–81; Deputy Exec. Dir St Louis Housing Authority 1981–82; Dir of Consultant Services, Laventhol and Howarth 1982–87; Dir Dept of Public and Assisted Housing, Washington, DC 1987–89; Pres. and CEO Housing Authority, City of Dallas, Tex. 1989–96; Pres. American Electric Power 1996–2001; Deputy Sec. and COO, US Dept of Housing and Urban Devt, Washington, DC 2001–04, Sec. of Housing and Urban Devt 2004–08 (resgnd); Dir Center for Public Policy and Leadership and Distinguished Univ. Prof., Hampton Univ. 2008–12; Vice-Chair., of Consumer and Community Banking, JP Morgan Chase, New York 2012–15; Sr Advisor, First Data Corpn, Atlanta, Ga 2015–; fmr Chair. DC Redevelopment Land Agency Bd; mem. Bd of Dirs Operation HOPE 2013–; Trustee Howard Univ. 2013–. *Address:* First Data Corporation, 5565 Glenridge, Connector NE, Suite 2000, Atlanta, GA 30342, USA (office). *Telephone:* (404) 890-2000 (office). *Website:* www.firstdata.com (office).

JACKSON, Colin Ray, CBE; British fmr professional athlete; b. 18 Feb. 1967, Cardiff; s. of Ossie Jackson and Angela Jackson; world-class 110m hurdler; holds the 60m world indoor record and 110m outdoor record (as at end of 2003); 110m hurdles achievements include: silver medal, European Jr Championships 1985, gold medal, World Jr Championships 1986, silver medal, Commonwealth Games 1986, silver medal, European Cup 1987, bronze medal, World Championships 1987, silver medal, Olympic Games 1988, silver medal, World Cup 1989, gold medal, European Cup 1989, 1993, gold medal, Commonwealth Games 1990, gold medal, World Cup 1992, gold medal, (and new world record) World Championships 1993 (silver medal, 4x100m relay); achievements (60m hurdles): silver medal, World Indoor Championships 1989, 1993, gold medal, European Indoor Championships 1989 (silver medal 1987), 1994, gold medals, European and Commonwealth Championships 1994, gold medal, European Championships 1998, 2002, gold medal, World Championships 1999; in world's top ten at 110m each year from 1986–2003; over 70 int. caps (most capped British athlete); 23 major championships medals (13 gold, nine silver, one bronze); retd March 2003; Amb. for UNICEF 2014; Founder Go Dad Run campaign 2014; mem. Brecon Athletics Club, UK Int. 1985–; numerous Welsh, UK, European and Commonwealth records; currently commentator BBC Sport; f. Red Shoes Acad. 2012; Hon. BA (Aberystwyth) 1994, Hon. BSc (Univ. of Wales) 1999; Athlete of the Decade, French Sporting Council, Hurdler of the Century, German Athletic Asscn, Athlete of the Year 1993–94, British Athletics Writers, Sportsman of the Year 1994, Sports Writers Asscn. *Television includes:* Celebrity MasterChef24 (competitor) 2010, Hours in the Past 2015. *Publication includes:* Colin Jackson: The Autobiography 2003. *Address:* c/o MTC (UK) Ltd, 71 Gloucester Place, London, W1U 8JW, England (office); 4 Jackson Close, Rhoose, Vale of Glamorgan, CF62 3DQ, Wales. *Telephone:* (20) 7935-8000 (MTC) (office). *Fax:* (20) 7935-8066 (MTC); (1446) 710642 (home). *E-mail:* office@mtc.uk.com (office). *Website:* www.mtc-uk.com (office).

JACKSON, Daryl Sanders, AO, DipArch, BArch, LFRAIA, ARIBA; Australian architect; b. 7 Feb. 1937, Clunes, Victoria; s. of Cecil John Jackson and Doreen May Sanders; m. Kay Parsons 1960; one s. three d.; ed Wesley Coll., Melbourne, Royal Melbourne Inst. of Tech., Univ. of Melbourne; Asst, Edwards, Madigan and Torzillo, Sydney 1959, Don Henry Fulton, Melbourne 1960, Chamberlin, Powell and Bon, London 1961–63, Paul Rudolph, New Haven, Conn. 1963–64, Skidmore, Owings and Merrill, San Francisco 1964; Partner, Daryl Jackson, Evan Walker Architects, Melbourne 1965–79; Dir Daryl Jackson Pty Ltd Architects 1979–, Daryl Jackson, Robin Dyke Pty Ltd (Sydney) 1985–, Daryl Jackson Alastair Swayn Pty Ltd (Canberra), Daryl Jackson Int. Ltd (London) 1989–, RAIA Victorian Chapter Housing Service 1966–69; Assoc. Prof. of Architecture, Melbourne Univ. 1985–, Deakin Univ. 2001–; Pres. Wesley Coll. Council, Melbourne 1993–; mem. RAIA Victorian Chapter Council 1967–77, Victorian Tapestry Workshop Cttee 1975–84, Parl. House Construction Authority, Canberra 1985–89, Victorian Arts Centre Trust 1991, Melbourne Cricket Club 1992– (Vice-Pres. 1997–); Trustee, Nat. Gallery of Vic. 1983–95; Chair. Australian Film Inst. 1990–94; Melbourne Major Events Co. Ltd 1991–; Life Fellow, Royal Australia Inst. of Architects; Hon. FAIA; Hon. Diploma and Bronze Medal (Third World Biennale of Architecture, Interarch 85, Sofia) 1985; Royal Australia Inst. of Architects Architecture Awards: Bronze Medal 1970, 1973, 1976, 1978, Press Award 1990, Canberra Medallion 1981, Sir Zehlman Cowen Award 1981, 1984, Robert Haddon Award 1982, Walter Burley Griffin Award for Urban Design, William Wardle Public Architecture Award, Sustainable Architecture Award; ACT Architecture Awards: 1984, 1985, 1987, 1991, Gold Medal 1987, Australian Council Nat. Trusts Heritage Award 1990, Int. Award 1991, MCG Southern Stand 1991, Georges Interior Architectural Award 1998, Masterplanner, Univ. of Melbourne 2000, County Court of Australia Award 2003, RAIA Colourbond Award for Steel Architecture 2010, Western Australian Heritage Award (for WA Police Midland Operations Support Facility) 2010. *Major works:* YWCA Community Resource Centre, Suva, Fiji 1973, Princes Hill High School, Melbourne 1973, Methodist Ladies' Coll., Library Resource Centre, Melbourne 1973, City Edge Housing Devt, Melbourne 1976, School of Music, Canberra 1976, Asscn for Modern Educ. School, Canberra 1977, Emu Ridge Govt Housing Devt, Canberra 1978, School of Art, Canberra 1980, McLachlan Offices, Canberra 1980, The Walter and Eliza Hall Inst. of Medical Research, Melbourne 1982, Nat. Sports Centre, Swimming Training Hall, Bruce, ACT 1982, Australian Chancery Complex, Riyadh, Saudi Arabia 1987, Hyatt Hotel, Canberra, Bond Univ., Gold Coast 1989, Commercial Union Office Bldg, Melbourne 1990, Melbourne Cricket Ground Southern Stand 1991, 120 Collins Street, Melbourne, Methodist Ladies' Coll. Music School, Kew 1994, Subiaco Oval Redevelopment, Perth 1994, Wesley Coll. Pre-Preparatory School, Prahran 1995, Brisbane Cricket Ground Redevelopment, 'The Gabba' 1995, Royal Melbourne Hosp. 1995, Colonial Stadium, Melbourne 2000, Sydney Conservatorium of Music (with Robin Dyke) 2001, Royal Brisbane Hosp. 2003, Victorian County Court 2003, UN Int. School, Hanoi 2004, Melbourne Cricket Ground Northern Stand Re-Development (with MCGS) 2005, Southern Cross Station Redevelopment (with Grimshaw Architects) 2006. *Publications:* Daryl Jackson Architecture: Drawings and Photos 1984, Daryl Jackson, The Master Architect 1996; numerous articles and papers. *Address:* Daryl Jackson Architects Pty Ltd, 35 Little Bourke Street, Melbourne, Vic. 3000, Australia (office). *Telephone:* (3) 9662-3022 (office). *Fax:* (3) 9663-5239 (office). *E-mail:* djackson@jacksonarchitecture.com (office). *Website:* www.jacksonarchitecture.com (office).

JACKSON, Frank Cameron, AO, PhD, FAHA, FASSA, FBA; Australian philosopher and academic; *Professor Emeritus, Australian National University;* b. 31 Aug. 1943, Melbourne, Vic.; s. of Allan C. Jackson and Ann E. Jackson; m. Morag E. Fraser 1966; two d.; ed Univ. of Melbourne, La Trobe Univ.; Prof. of Philosophy, Monash Univ., Vic. 1978–86, 1991; Prof. of Philosophy, ANU 1986–90, 1992–2007, Dir Inst. of Advanced Studies 1998–2001, Deputy Vice-Chancellor (Research) 2001, Distinguished Prof. 2003–14, Dir Research School of Social Sciences 2004–07, Prof. Emer. 2014–; Fractional Research Prof., La Trobe Univ. 2008–12; Visiting Prof., Princeton Univ., USA 2007–13; Leverhulme Visiting Prof., Univ. of Cambridge, UK 2011; Lim Chong Yah Visiting Prof., Nat. Univ. of Singapore 2017; Locke Lecturer, Univ. of Oxford 1995, Blackwell Lecturer, Brown Univ. 2006, Gavin David Young Lecturer, Univ. of Adelaide 2012, Carnap Lectures, Bochum 2017; Peter Baume Award 2018. *Publications include:* Perception 1978, Conditionals 1986, The Philosophy of Mind and Cognition (with David Braddon-Mitchell) 1996, From Metaphysics to Ethics 1998, Mind, Method and Conditionals 1998, Mind, Morality and Explanation (with Philip Pettit and Michael Smith) 2004, Language, Names and Information 2010. *Leisure interests:* reading, tennis. *Address:* School of Philosophy, Coombs Building, Australian National University, Acton, ACT 2601 (office); 33 David Street, O'Connor, ACT 2602, Australia (home). *Telephone:* (2) 6125-2341 (office); (4) 0013-4586 (home). *E-mail:* frank.jackson@anu.edu.au (office); fcjack321@gmail.com (home). *Website:* philosophy.cass.anu.edu.au/profile/frank-jackson (office).

JACKSON, Glenda May, CBE; British actress and fmr politician; b. 9 May 1936, Birkenhead, Cheshire; d. of Harry Jackson and Joan Jackson; m. Roy Hodges 1958 (divorced 1976); one s.; ed Royal Acad. of Dramatic Art; fmr mem. RSC; played Queen Elizabeth I in TV series Elizabeth R; Pres. Play Matters (fmrly Toy Libraries Asscn) 1976–; Dir United British Artists 1983–; MP (Labour) for Hampstead and Highgate 1992–2010, for Hampstead and Kilburn 2010–15 (retd); Parl. Under-Sec. of State, Dept for the Environment and Transport 1997–99; Adviser on Homelessness, GLA 2000–04; Hon. Fellow, Liverpool Polytechnic 1987; Hon. DLitt (Liverpool) 1978; Hon. LLM (Nottingham) 1992. *Plays include:* Marat/Sade, New York and Paris 1965, The Investigation 1965, Hamlet 1965, US 1966, Three Sisters 1967, Collaborators 1973, The Maids 1974, Hedda Gabler 1975, The White Devil 1976, Antony and Cleopatra 1978, Rose 1980, Strange Interlude 1984, Phaedra 1984, 1985, Across from the Garden of Allah 1986, Strange Interlude 1986, The House of Bernarda Alba 1986, Macbeth 1988, Scenes from an Execution 1990, Mermaid 1990, Mother Courage 1990, Mourning Becomes Electra 1991, King Lear (Best Actress, London Evening Standard Theatre Awards 2017) 2016. *Films include:* Marat/Sade 1966, Negatives 1968, Women in Love (Acad. Award 1970) 1969, The Music Lovers 1970, Sunday, Bloody Sunday 1971, The Boy Friend 1971, Mary, Queen of Scots 1971, The Triple Echo 1972, Bequest to the Nation 1972, A Touch of Class (Acad. Award 1974) 1973, The Romantic Englishwoman 1975, The Tempter 1975, The Incredible Sarah 1976, The Abbess of Crewe 1976, Stevie 1977, Hedda 1977, House Calls 1978, The Class of Miss McMichael 1978, Lost and Found 1979, Hopscotch 1980, The Return of the Soldier 1982, Giro City 1982, Summit Conference 1982, Great and Small 1983, And Nothing But the Truth 1984, Turtle Diary 1985, Beyond Therapy 1985, Business as Usual 1986, Salome's Last Dance 1988, The Rainbow 1989, The Secret Life of Sir Arnold Bax 1992. *Leisure interests:* gardening, reading, listening to music. *Website:* www.glenda-jackson.co.uk.

JACKSON, Janet Damita Jo; American singer and choreographer; b. 16 May 1966, Gary, Ind.; d. of Joseph Jackson and Katherine Jackson; m. 1st James DeBarge 1984 (annulled 1985); m. 2nd Rene Elizondo Jr 1991 (divorced 2000); m. 3rd Wissam Al Mana 2012; one s.; ed Valley Professional School; singing debut at age seven with family singing group, The Jacksons; television actress 1977–81, appearing in series Good Times (CBS), Diff'rent Strokes, Fame, A New Kind of Family; solo recording artist 1982–; worldwide concerts and tours; American Music Awards for Best Female Soul Singer (for Nasty), Best Female Soul Video (for What Have You Done For Me Lately?) and Best Pop Video (for When I Think of You) 1986, for Best Dance Artist, Best Female Pop Rock Artist and Best Female Soul R&B Artist 1991, for Favourite Pop/Rock Female Artist 2002, MTV Video Vanguard Award 1990, MTV Award for Best Female Video (for If) 1993, Starlight Foundation Humanitarian of the Year Award 1991, Grammy Award for Best R&B Song (for That's the Way Love Goes) 1993, MTV Europe Music Award for Global Icon 2018. *Recordings include:* albums: Janet Jackson 1982, Dream Street 1984, Control 1986, Janet Jackson's Rhythm Nation 1989, Rhythm Nation Compilation 1990, Janet 1993, Design of a Decade 1986–96 1995, The Velvet Rope 1997, All For You 2001, Damita Jo 2004, 20 Y.O. 2006, Discipline 2008, Unbreakable 2015. *Films include:* Poetic Justice 1993, Nutty Professor II: The Klumps 2000, Why Did I Get Married? 2007, Why Did I Get Married Too? 2010, For Colored Girls 2010. *TV includes:* The Jacksons 1976–77, Good Times 1977–79, A New Kind of Family 1979–80, Diff'rent Strokes 1980–84, Fame 1984–85. *Publication:* True You 2011. *Address:* Jason Winters, Sterling/Winters Company, 10900 Wilshire Blvd, #15, Los Angeles, CA 90024, USA (office). *Telephone:* (310) 557-2700 (office). *Website:* janetjackson.com.

JACKSON, Rev. Jesse Louis, BS; American clergyman and civic leader; *President, Rainbow PUSH Coalition;* b. 8 Oct. 1941, Greenville, South Carolina; s. of Charles Henry and Helen Jackson; m. Jacqueline Lavinia Brown 1964; three s. two d. one d. by Karin Stanford; ed Univ. of Illinois, Illinois Agricultural and Tech. Coll., Chicago Theological Seminary; ordained to Ministry Baptist Church 1968; active Black Coalition for United Community Action 1969; Co-Founder Operation Breadbasket S Christian Leadership Conf.; Co-ordinating Council Community Orgs, Chicago 1966, Nat. Dir 1966–77; Founder and Exec. Dir Operation PUSH (People United to Save Humanity), Chicago 1971–96, Pres. Rainbow PUSH Coalition (formed by merger with Rainbow Coalition) 1996–; unsuccessful cand. for Democratic nomination for US Presidency 1983–84, 1987–88; TV Host, Voices of America 1990, Both Sides With Jesse Jackson (CNN) 1992–2000; apptd Special Envoy of the Pres. and Sec. of the State 1997; Pres. Award Nat. Medical Asscn 1969; columnist, Chicago Tribune, Los Angles Time; Visiting Lecturer, Howard Univ., Yale Univ., Princeton Univ., Morehouse Univ., Harvard Univ., Columbia Univ., Stanford Univ., Hampton Univ.; Hon. Fellow, Regents Park Coll., Oxford Univ. 2007, Edge Hill Univ., England 2007; Dr hc (Univ. of KwaZulu-Natal, South Africa) 2010 and numerous other hon. degrees; numerous awards, including Humanitarian Father of the Year Award Nat. Father's Day Cttee 1971, Spingarn Medal, Nat. Asscn for the Advancement of Colored People 1989, James Madison Award for Distinguished Public Service, American Whig-Cliosophic Soc. 1991, Presidential Medal of Freedom 2000, Global Diversity and Inclusion Award, UK 2009. *Publications include:* Straight from the Heart 1987, Keep Hope Alive 1989, Legal Lynching: Racism, Injustice, and the Death Penalty (co-author) 1996, It's About the Money (with Jesse L. Jackson, Jr) 1999. *Address:* Rainbow PUSH Coalition, 930 East 50th Street, Chicago, IL 60615, USA (office). *Telephone:* (773) 373-3366 (office). *Fax:* (773) 373-3571 (office). *E-mail:* jjackson@rainbowpush.org (office). *Website:* www.rainbowpush.org (office).

JACKSON, Linda, MBA; British automobile industry executive; *CEO, Citroën;* b. 1959, Coventry; widow; ed Warwick Univ.; joined Jaguar Cars Ltd as temporary accounts clerk 1977, various roles with Rover Group, Land Rover and Jaguar 1977–98, becoming Finance Dir Rover France 1998–99, Finance Controller, UK Rover Cars 1999–2000, Man Dir MG Rover France 2000–03, European Sales Finance Controller, MG Rover Group 2003–04; Finance Dir Citroën UK 2005–09, Finance Dir Citroën France 2009–10, Man. Dir Citroën UK and Ireland 2010–14, CEO Citroën 2014–, also mem. Exec. Cttee Groupe PSA. *Address:* Citroën, 6 Rue Fructidor, 93400 Saint Ouen, France (office). *Website:* www.citroen.com (office).

JACKSON, Lisa P., BS, MEng; American fmr government official and business executive; *Vice-President of Environment, Policy and Social Initiatives, Apple, Inc.;* b. 8 Feb. 1962, New Orleans, La; m. Kenny Jackson; two s.; ed Tulane Univ., Princeton Univ.; worked in various roles with US Environmental Protection Agency (EPA), Washington, DC 1986–2002; Asst Commr of Compliance and Enforcement, NJ Dept of Environmental Protection 2002–05, Asst Commr for Land Use Man. 2005–06, Commr of Environmental Protection 2006–08; Chief of Staff to Gov of NJ 2008; Admin. EPA, Washington, DC 2009–13; Vice-Pres. Environment, Policy and Social Initiatives, Apple, Inc. 2013–; mem. Bd of Dirs Clinton Foundation 2013–, Princeton Univ., Tulane Univ. *Leisure interest:* cooking. *Address:* Apple, Inc., 1 Infinite Loop, Cupertino, CA 95014, USA (office). *Telephone:* (408) 996-1010 (office); (408) 606-5775 (office). *Website:* www.apple.com (office).

JACKSON, Margaret Anne, AC, BEcons, MBA, FCA; Australian business executive; b. 17 March 1953, Vic.; d. of Wallace James Jackson and Dorothy Jean Jackson; m. Roger Donazzan 1977; one s. one d.; ed Monash Univ. and Univ. of Melbourne; accountant, Price Waterhouse Co. 1973–77; accountant, Nelson Parkhill BDO 1977–91, Partner 1983–90; Partner KPMG Peat Marwick 1990–92; Chair. Transport Accident Comm. (Vic.) 1993–2001; fmr Deputy Chair. Southcorp Ltd; Dir (non-exec.) Qantas Airways Ltd 1992–2007, Chair. 2000–07, also Chair. Remuneration and Nominations Cttees; Dir Telecom Australia 1983–90, Australian Wool Corp. 1986–89, Int. Wool Secr. 1986–89, Pacific Dunlop 1992–2000, The Broken Hill Pty Co. Ltd 1994–2000, Australia and New Zealand Banking Group Ltd 1994–2008, Billabong Int. Ltd 2000–, Florey Neuroscience Insts; fmr Chair. Malthouse Pty Ltd; Chair. Flexigroup Ltd 2006–; Deputy Chair. People Telecom Ltd; mem. Exec. Cttee Australia Japan Business Co-operation Cttee; Dir Brain Imaging Research Inst.; Chair. Asia Pacific Business Coalition on HIV-AIDS 2006–; Cttee Dir Australian Tissue Engineering Centre; mem. Govt Task Group on Emissions Trading; Pres. Australian Volunteers Int.; Deputy Chair. Baker Capital Campaign Task Force, Baker Medical Research Inst., St Vincent's Medical Research Inst. 1994–96; Chair. Playbox Theatre Co. Pty Ltd 1998–2000 (Dir 1991–98); mem. Bd of Dirs Australia Foundation for Culture and the Humanities Ltd; mem. Vic. State Council Inst. of Chartered Accountants 1985–93 (Chair. 1989–90), Pharmaceutical Remuneration Benefits Tribunal 1985–90, Foreign Affairs Council, Nat. Council 1988–91, Convocation Cttee Univ. of Melbourne 1988–91, Australian Science and Tech. Council 1990–93, Nat. Health and Medical Research Council 1991, French Australian Industrial Research Steering Cttee 1997–98, Business Council of Australia Chair.'s Panel, The Walter & Eliza Hall Inst. of Medical Research, Melbourne Univ. Business School Asscn; Fellow, Australian Inst. of Co. Dirs, Inst. of Chartered Accountants in Australia; Int. Trustee Carnegie Mellon Univ., S Australia; Patron Salvation Army Capital Appeal for Homeless Youth, Vic.; Hon. LLD (Monash) 2002; Inst. of Chartered Accountants Distinguished Service Award. *Leisure interests:* travelling, bush-walking, fishing, reading, photography, gardening.

JACKSON, Michael, BA; British broadcasting executive; b. 11 Feb. 1958; s. of Ernest Jackson and Margaret Jackson (née Kearsley); ed King's School, Macclesfield, Polytechnic of Central London; Organizer, Channel 4 Group 1979; Producer, The Sixties 1982; ind. producer Beat Productions Ltd 1983–87; Ed. The Late Show, BBC TV (BFI Award) 1988–90; with Late Show Productions 1990–91; Head of Music and Arts BBC TV 1991–93, Controller BBC2 1993–96, Controller BBC1 and BBC Dir of TV, 1996–97; CEO Channel 4 1997–2001, Dir of Programmes 1997–98; Chair. Film Four Ltd 1997–2001; Dir (non-exec.) EMI Group 1999–; Pres., CEO USA Entertainment Group 2001–02; Chair. Universal Television Group 2002–04 (resgnd following merger Universal's merger with NBC 2004); Pres. of Programming, IAC/InterActiveCorp, New York 2006–08, then Sr Adviser on Content Strategy; mem. Bd of Dirs Nutopia (production co.), Scottish Television PLC 2009–, PFD, Cookie Jar Entertainment Holdings (USA), Inc. 2009–, YOU On Demand Holdings, Inc. 2012–14; Hon. DLitt (Westminster) 1995. *Programmes produced include:* Whose Town is it Anyway?, Open the Box, The Media Show, The Nelson Mandela Tribute, Tales from Prague (Grierson Documentary Award), Moving Pictures, The American Late Show (Public Broadcasting Service, USA), Naked Hollywood (BAFTA Best Factual Series Award), Sounds of the Sixties, The Lime Grove Story, TV Hell. *Leisure interests:* reading, walking. *Address:* IAC/InterActiveCorp, 555 West 18th Street, New York, NY 10011, USA (office). *Telephone:* (212) 314-7300 (office). *E-mail:* info@iac.com (office). *Website:* www.iac.com (office).

JACKSON, Gen. Sir Michael (Mike) David, GCB, CBE, DSO; British military officer (retd) and consultant; *Senior Advisor, PA Consulting Group;* b. 21 March 1944; s. of George Jackson and Ivy Jackson (née Bower); m. Sarah Coombe 1985;

two s. one d.; ed Stamford School, Sandhurst Mil. Acad., Univ. of Birmingham; commissioned Intelligence Corps 1963; transferred to Parachute Regt 1970, attended Staff Coll. 1976, Chief of Staff Berlin Infantry Brigade 1977–78, commanded a parachute co., Northern Ireland 1979–81, mem. Directing Staff, Staff Coll. 1981–83, Commdr 1st Bn Parachute Regt 1984–86; with Sr Defence Staff, Jt Service Defence Coll., Greenwich 1986–88; Services Fellow, Wolfson Coll. Cambridge 1989; Commdr 39 Infantry Brigade, Northern Ireland 1989–92; Dir-Gen. of Personnel Services, Ministry of Defence (Army) 1992–94; Commdr 3rd Div. 1994–96, Commdr Implementation Force (IFOR) Multinational Div. SW, Bosnia and Herzegovina 1995–96; Dir-Gen. of Devt and Doctrine, Ministry of Defence 1996–97; rank of Lt-Gen. 1997; Commdr Allied Rapid Reaction Force 1997–2000; Commdr Kosovo Force (KFOR) March–Oct. 1999; C-in-C Land Command 2000–03; Chief of the Gen. Staff 2003–06; Sr Advisor, PA Consulting Group 2007–; Dir (non-exec.) Longhorn Mining 2007–, Legion Group 2009–10, Force Select 2010–; Freeman City of London 1988, D.L Wiltshire 2007. *Publication:* Soldier: The Autobiography 2007. *Address:* PA Consulting Group, 123 Buckingham Palace Road, London, SW1W 9SR, England (office). *Telephone:* (20) 7730-9000 (office). *Fax:* (20) 7333-5050 (office). *Website:* www.paconsulting.com (office).

JACKSON, Michael (Mike) J., BA; American business executive; *Chairman, President and CEO, AutoNation Inc.;* b. 7 Feb. 1949, NJ; m. Patricia Jackson; one d.; ed St Joseph's Univ.; Technician Specialist, Mercedes-Benz USA 1974, Man. Partner, Euro Motorcars, Bethesda, Md 1979–90, Sr Vice-Pres. of Marketing, Mercedes-Benz USA 1990–97, Pres. 1997, Pres. and CEO 1997–98; CEO AutoNation Inc. 1999–, Chair. 2003–, Pres. 2015–; Chair. Federal Reserve Bank of Atlanta 2013–15, Deputy Chair. 2015–; mem. Bd of Dirs Riggs Nat. Corpn 1993–97; Dr hc (Livingstone Coll.) 2011. *Address:* AutoNation Inc., 200 SW First Avenue, Fort Lauderdale, FL 33301, USA (office). *Telephone:* (954) 769-6000 (office). *Fax:* (954) 769-6537 (office). *E-mail:* info@autonation.com (office). *Website:* www.autonation.com (office).

JACKSON, (Kevin) Paul, BA, FID; British media industry executive and television producer; b. 2 Oct. 1947, Stockport, Cheshire; s. of T. Leslie Jackson and Jo Spoonley; m. Judith E. Cain 1981; two d.; ed Gunnersbury Grammar School and Univ. of Exeter; stage man. Marlowe Theatre, Canterbury 1970, Thorndike Theatre, Leatherhead 1971; production work for BBC TV: Two Ronnies, Three of a Kind, Carrott's Lib, The Young Ones, Happy Families 1971–82; freelance Producer and Dir Cannon and Ball, Girls on Top 1982–84; Producer and Chair. Paul Jackson Productions: Red Dwarf, Don't Miss Wax, Saturday Live 1984–86; Exec. Producer, Appointments of Dennis Jennings (Acad. Award for Best Live Action Short 1989); Man. Dir NGTV 1987–91; Dir of Programmes, Carlton TV 1991–93, Man. Dir Carlton TV 1993–94, Carlton UK Productions 1994–96; Controller, BBC Entertainment 1997–2000; Man. Dir Granada Australia and CEO Red Heart Productions 2000–03, Dir Granada Int. Production and Entertainment (UK) 2003, CEO Granada America 2003–06; Dir of Comedy and Entertainment, ITV 2006–09; CEO Eyeworks UK 2009–12, now freelance consultant; Visiting Prof., School of English, Exeter Univ.; mem. Exec. Cttee US Comedy Arts Festival; Chair. Timebank (UK charity); Chair. Comic Relief 1987–98; Vice-Chair. Charity Projects 1990–92, Chair. 1992–99; Chair. RTS 1994–96; Chair. Time Bank (UK charity) 1999–2012; Stanford Exec. Programme 1993; Fellow, Inst. of Dirs, Royal TV Soc.; Dr hc (Exeter) 1999; BAFTA 1983, 1984. *Leisure interests:* theatre, rugby, travel, food and wine, friends and family. *E-mail:* pjacksonmailbox@yahoo.co.uk (office).

JACKSON, Sir Peter, ONZ, KNZM; New Zealand film director and producer; b. 31 Oct. 1961, Pukerua Bay, North Island. *Films include:* Bad Taste 1987, Meet the Feebles 1989, Dead Alive, Heavenly Creatures 1994, The Frighteners 1996, Contact (special effects only), The Lord of the Rings: The Fellowship of the Ring (BAFTA Award for Best Dir) 2001, The Lord of the Rings: The Two Towers 2002, The Lord of the Rings: The Return of the King (Golden Globe Award, Best Dir 2004, Critics' Choice Award, Best Dir 2004, Acad. Award, Best Dir, Best Picture 2004) 2003, King Kong 2005, District 9 2009, The Lovely Bones (also producer) 2009, The Adventures of Tintin: Secret of the Unicorn (producer) 2011, The Hobbit: An Unexpected Journey 2012, They Shall Not Grow Old 2018, Mortal Engines (producer) 2018. *Publication:* Peter Jackson (autobiog., with Brian Sibley) 2005. *Address:* c/o ICM, 8942 Wilshire Boulevard, Beverly Hills, CA 90211, USA.

JACKSON, Peter John, BSc; British business executive; b. 16 Jan. 1947, Sheffield; s. of Jack Jackson and Joan Jackson; m. Anne Campbell 1974; two s. one d.; ed Univ. of Leeds; personnel and industrial relations positions at British Steel, Comm. on Industrial Relations, Guthrie Industries 1968–76; Dir Personnel and Employee Relations, Deputy Man. Dir Perkins Engines (Shrewsbury), Perkins Engines Group 1976–87; Personnel Dir British Sugar PLC 1987–88, Deputy Man. Dir 1988–89, Man. Dir 1989–93, Chief Exec. 1994–99; Chief Exec. Associated British Foods PLC 1999–2005 (Dir 1992–2005); Chair. Kingfisher PLC 2006–09; mem. Bd of Dirs Smiths Group plc 2003–09; Chair. Bd of Trustees, The Disabilities Trust. *Leisure interests:* garden, Sheffield United.

JACKSON, Ronny Lynn, MD; American physician and naval officer; *Physician to the President;* b. 4 May 1967, Levelland, Texas; m. Jane Ely; three c.; ed Texas A&M Univ., Univ. of Texas Medical Branch, Portsmouth Naval Medical Center; entered active duty service in US Navy, Norfolk, Va 1995, subsequent roles include Instructor at Naval Diving and Salvage Training Center, Panama City, Florida, Diving Medical Officer at Explosive Ordnance Disposal Mobile Unit 8, Sigonella, Italy, Diving Safety Officer, Naval Safety Center, Norfolk, Resident in Emergency Medicine, Portsmouth Naval Medical Center 2001–04; served with 2nd Marines, Combat Logistics Regt 25, Camp Lejeune, NC 2005; deployed as emergency medicine physician, Operation Iraqi Freedom; apptd White House Physician 2006, formally named Physician to the Pres. 2013, also Dir White House Medical Unit; rank of Rear-Adm. (upper half) 2018; nominee for Sec. of Veterans Affairs (subject to Senate approval) 2018 (withdrew as nominee April 2018); Adjunct Faculty Mem., Beth Israel Deaconess Medical Center 2015–; Fellow, American Acad. of Emergency Medicine; numerous awards and decorations including Defense Superior Service Medal, Legion of Merit, Navy/Marine Corps Commendation Medal (four awards), Navy/Marine Corps Achievement Medal (three awards). *Address:* The White House Office, 1600 Pennsylvania Ave, NW, Washington, DC 20500 USA (office). *Telephone:* (202) 456-1414 (office). *Fax:* (202) 456-2461 (office). *Website:* www.whitehouse.gov (office).

JACKSON, Samuel L(eroy), BA; American film and television actor and film producer; b. 21 Dec. 1948, Washington, DC; s. of Elizabeth Jackson (née Montgomery); m. LaTanya Richardson 1980; one d.; ed Morehouse Coll., Atlanta; Co-founder and mem. Just Us theatre co., Atlanta. *Stage appearances:* Home, A Soldier's Story, Sally/Prince, Colored People's Time, Mother Courage, Spell No. 7, The Mighty Gents, The Piano Lesson, Two Trains Running, Fences. *Films include:* Together for Days 1972, Ragtime 1981, Eddie Murphy Raw 1987, Coming to America 1988, School Daze 1988, Do The Right Thing 1989, Sea of Love 1989, A Shock to the System 1990, Def by Temptation 1990, Betsy's Wedding 1990, Mo' Better Blues 1990, The Exorcist III 1990, GoodFellas 1990, Return of the Superfly 1990, Jungle Fever (Best Actor Award, Cannes Int. Film Festival, New York Film Critics' Award) 1991, Strictly Business 1991, Juice 1992, White Sands 1992, Patriot Games 1992, Johnny Suede 1992, Jumpin' at the Boneyard 1992, Fathers and Sons 1992, National Lampoon's Loaded Weapon 1 1993, Amos & Andrew 1993, Jurassic Park 1993, True Romance 1993, Hail Caesar 1994, The New Age 1994, Pulp Fiction 1994, Losing Isaiah 1995, Kiss of Death 1995, Die Hard With a Vengeance 1995, Fluke (voice) 1995, The Great White Hype 1996, A Time to Kill 1996, The Long Kiss Goodnight 1996, One Eight Seven 1996, Trees Lounge 1996, Hard Eight 1996, Eve's Bayou (also producer) 1997, Jackie Brown 1997, Out of Sight 1998, The Negotiator 1998, Star Wars Episode I: The Phantom Menace 1999, Deep Blue Sea 1999, Any Given Wednesday (short) 2000, Rules of Engagement 2000, Shaft 2000, Unbreakable 2000, The Caveman's Valentine 2001, The 51st State 2001, The Comeback (short) 2002, Changing Lanes 2002, Star Wars: Episode II - Attack of the Clones 2002, No Good Deed 2002, xXx 2002, Basic 2003, S.W.A.T. 2003, Country of My Skull 2004, Twisted 2004, Kill Bill: Vol. 2 2004, The Incredibles (voice) 2004, Coach Carter (Image Award for Best Actor 2006) 2005, The Adventures of Mr. Incredible (video short) (voice) 2005, xXx 2: The Next Level 2005, Star Wars: Episode III - Revenge of the Sith 2005, The Man 2005, Farce of the Penguins (voice) 2006, Freedomland 2006, Snakes on a Plane 2006, Black Snake Moan 2006, Home of the Brave 2006, Resurrecting the Champ 2007, 1408 2007, Cleaner 2007, Jumper 2008, Gospel Hill 2008, Star Wars: The Clone Wars (voice) 2008, Lakeview Terrace 2008, Soul Men 2008, The Spirit 2008, Mother and Child 2009, Astro Boy (voice) 2009, Iron Man 2 2010, Unthinkable 2010, The Other Guys 2010, Quantum Quest: A Cassini Space Odyssey (voice) 2010, Captain America: The First Avenger 2011, Fury 2012, Meeting Evil 2012, Avengers Assemble 2012, Zambezia (voice) 2012, Django Unchained 2012, Oldboy 2013, Reasonable Doubt 2014, RoboCop 2014, Captain America: The Winter Soldier 2014, Kite 2014, Big Game 2014, Kingsman: The Secret Service 2014, Avengers: Age of Ultron 2015, Barely Lethal 2015, Chi-Raq 2015, The Hateful Eight 2015. *Television includes:* Movin' On (series) 1972, The Trial of the Moke (film) 1978, Uncle Tom's Cabin (film) 1987, Common Ground (film) 1990, Dead and Alive: The Race for Gus Farace (film) 1991, Ghostwriter (series) 1992, Simple Justice (film) 1993, Assault at West Point (film) 1994, Against the Wall (film) 1994, The Proud Family (series) – Seven Days of Kwanzaa (voice) 2001, Freedom: A History of Us (series documentary) 2003, Extras (series) 2005, The Boondocks (series) 2005–10, Honor Deferred (film) 2006, Afro Samurai (mini-series) 2007, The Sunset Limited (film) 2011. *Address:* c/o Toni Howard, ICM, 10250 Constellation Boulevard, Los Angeles, CA 90067, USA (office). *Telephone:* (310) 550-4000 (office). *Website:* www.icmtalent.com (office); samueljackson.com.

JACKSON, Stephen (Steve) Philip, BSc, PhD, FRS, FMedSci; British biologist, entrepreneur and academic; *Frederick James Quick and Cancer Research UK Professor of Biology, University of Cambridge;* b. 17 July 1962, Nottingham, England; m. Teresa Clarke; two s.; ed Univ. of Leeds, Imperial Coll. of Science and Tech., London, Univ. of Edinburgh; post-doctoral research, Univ. of California, Berkeley, USA 1987–91; Jr Group Leader, Wellcome Trust and Cancer Research UK Inst. (part of Univ. of Cambridge; renamed The Gurdon Inst. 2004) 1991, currently Frederick James Quick and Cancer Research UK Prof. of Biology, Head of Cancer Research UK Labs, Assoc. Faculty mem. Wellcome Trust Sanger Inst. 2012–17; f. KuDOS Pharmaceuticals 1997; co-f. MISSION Therapeutics 2010, Adrestia Therapeutics Ltd 2018; mem. European Molecular Biology Org. 1997; Eppendorf European Young Investigator of the Year 1995, Tenovus Medal 1997, Colworth Medal, Biochemical Soc. 1997, Anthony Dipple Carcinogenesis Young Investigator Award 2002, GlaxoSmithKline Award, Biochemical Soc. 2008, BBSRC Innovator of the Year Award 2009, Buchanan Medal, Royal Soc. 2011, Gagna A. & Ch. Van Heck Prize 2015, King Faisal Int. Prize for Science 2016, Dr A.H. Heineken Prize for Medicine, Royal Netherlands Acad. of Arts and Science 2016, Fondation ARC Léopold Griffuel Award 2019. *Publications:* more than 200 research articles in professional journals. *Leisure interests:* gardening, travel. *Address:* Wellcome Trust/Cancer Research UK Gurdon Institute, The Henry Wellcome Building of Cancer and Developmental Biology, University of Cambridge, Tennis Court Road, Cambridge, CB2 1QN, England (office). *Telephone:* (1223) 334088 (office). *Fax:* (1223) 334089 (office). *E-mail:* s.jackson@gurdon.cam.ac.uk (office). *Website:* www.bioc.cam.ac.uk (office); www2.gurdon.cam.ac.uk~jacksonlab (office).

JACKSON-NELSON, Marjorie, AC, CVO, MBE; Australian state official and fmr athlete; b. 13 Sept. 1931, Coffs Harbour, NSW; d. of William Alfred Jackson and Mary Robinson; m. Peter Nelson 1953 (died 1977); one s. two d.; popularly known as 'The Lithgow Flash'; winner gold medal 100m and 200m (world record), Olympic Games 1952; winner four gold medals, Commonwealth Games 1950, three gold medals 1954; broke world sprint records on ten occasions; Man. Women's Section, Australian Commonwealth Games Teams 1982, 1986, 1990; Deputy Chair. Adelaide's bid to host 1998 Commonwealth Games 1990–92; Gen. Team Man. Commonwealth Games (first woman in position) 1994; fmr Pres. S Australia Div., Australian Olympic Fed.; Athletes Liaison Officer, Commonwealth Games 1998; f. Peter Nelson Leukaemia Research Fellowship 1977–; Gov. of S Australia 2001–07; mem. S Australian Olympic Council 1997–, SOCOG 1998–2000; honoured by Australia Post on stamp celebrating Olympic legends 1998; featured on Olympic coin produced by Perth Mint 1999; Bearer, Olympic Flag at Opening Ceremony of Olympic Games, Sydney 2000; Hon. PhD (Charles Sturt Univ., Bathurst, NSW) 2001; Australian Sportsman of the Year 1952, Outstanding Athlete, Helms Foundation, USA 1952, Outstanding Athlete, Int. Amateur Athletics Asscn 1986, nominated by Gov.-Gen. and Prime Minister as one of twenty living mems of 200 Great Australians 1988, named Legend in Australian Sport 1995, Paul Harris Fellow Rotary 1995, inducted into Australian Sporting

Hall of Fame 1995, Int. Women's Hall of Fame, New York, USA 2000, Australian Sports Medal 2000, Olympic Order, Beijing 2008, inducted into IAAF Hall of Fame, Monaco 2013.

JACOB, Christian; French politician; b. 4 Dec. 1959, Rozay-en-Brie, Seine-et-Marne; m.; two c.; ed Sainte-Maure dans l'Aube School of Agric.; farmer and dairy producer at Vaudoy-en-Brie 1982–; Pres. Young Farmers Local Admin (Département) Centre of Seine-et-Marne 1986–89, Regional Centre for Northern France 1987–90, Nat. Centre 1992; mem. Nat. Social and Econ. Council 1992; elected MEP 1994, Chair. European Parl. Comm. on Agric. and Rural Devt 1994–97; elected Deputy for Seine-et-Marne, Nat. Ass. 1995–2002, 2007–, Chair. Les Républicains (The Republicans) 2010–; Mayor of Provins 2001–02, 2006–; Minister-Desig. of Family Affairs, Health and Disabled People 2002–04, of Small and Medium Enterprises, Commerce, Craftsmen, Liberal Professions and Consumption 2004; Minister of the Economy, Finance and Industry 2004–05, of the Civil Service 2005–07; Chair. Rassemblement pour la Repub. (RPR) Fed. of Seine-et-Marne 1998–2000 (mem. Parl. Group 1997–2002); Chair. Union for a Popular Movt (UMP) Fed. of Seine-et-Marne 2002–, mem. Del. to EU 1997; mem. Bd of Dirs SOPEXA (Soc. for the Expansion of Sales of Agricultural and Grocery Products) 1996–. *Publications include:* La clé des champs 1994, Le pari du bon sens, un paysan en politique 1999. *Address:* National Assembly, 126 rue de l'Université, 75355 Paris 07 SP (office); Les Républicains, National Assembly, 128 rue de l'Université, 75007 Paris (office); Mairie, place Maréchal Leclerc, 77160 Provins, France. *Telephone:* 1-64-60-38-33 (office). *Fax:* 1-64-00-61-27 (office). *E-mail:* cjacob@assemblee-nationale.fr (office). *Website:* www.assemblee-nationale.fr (office); www.deputes-les-republicains.fr (office); www.christianjacob.fr.

JACOB, Gilles; French film director and producer and film festival director; b. 22 June 1930, Paris; s. of André Jacob; ed Lycée Carnot, Lycée Louis-le-Grand, Paris; Gen. Del. Cannes Film Festival 1978–2000, Pres. 2001–14; apptd Vice-Pres. Supervisory Bd Canal+ 2002; Chair. Louis Delluc Prize 1993–; mem. Bd Sept Cinéma 1992–, Bifi 1996–; directed the collection of La Bibliothèque du cinéma at Hatier 1979–92; mem. Bd of Dirs Films A2 1980–92; Commdr, Ordre nat. du Mérite 1999, Légion d'honneur 2005, des Arts et des Lettres; Grand Officer, Order of Merit of the Italian Repub.; Gold Medal of European Merit, EU 2009. *Screen adaptation:* Ça n'arrive qu'à moi (adaptation) 1985. *Film roles:* Grosse fatigue 1994, Femme Fatale 2002, HH, Hitler à Hollywood 2010. *Films produced or directed:* Le Cinéma dans les yeux (dir and producer) 1987, Liberté (documentary) (producer) 1989, Histories de festival (dir and producer) 2002, Les Marches etc... (une comédie musicale) (documentary short) (dir and producer) 2003, To Each His Own Cinema (producer) 2007, Une journée particulière (documentary) (dir) 2012. *Television:* Épreuves d'artistes (Words in Progress) (documentary) (dir and producer) 2004. *Address:* c/o Association française du festival international du film, 3 rue Amélie, 75007 Paris, France (office). *Telephone:* 1-53-59-61-00 (office). *Fax:* 1-53-59-61-10 (office). *E-mail:* gilles.jacob@festival-cannes.fr (office). *Website:* www.festival-cannes.org (office).

JACOBI, Sir Derek George, Kt, CBE, MA; British actor; b. 22 Oct. 1938, London, England; s. of Alfred George Jacobi and Daisy Gertrude Masters; ed Leyton County High School and St John's Coll., Cambridge; Birmingham Repertory Theatre 1960–63 (first appeared in One Way Pendulum 1961); Nat. Theatre 1963–71; Prospect Theatre Co. 1972, 1974, 1976–78, Artistic Assoc. 1976–91; Old Vic Co. 1978–79; joined RSC April 1982; Vice-Pres., Nat. Youth Theatre 1982–; Artistic Dir Chichester Festival Theatre 1995–96; Hon. Fellow, St John's Coll., Cambridge; Kt 1st Class, Order of the Dannebrog 1989; Variety Club Award 1976, British Acad. Award 1976, Press Guild Award 1976, Royal Television Soc. Award 1976, Hamburg Shakespeare Award 1998, Helen Hayes Tribute for Lifetime Achievement, Annual Helen Hayes Awards 2008. *Plays include:* The Lunatic 1980, Lover and the Poet 1980, The Suicide 1980, Much Ado About Nothing (Tony Award for Best Actor in a Play) 1982–85, Peer Gynt 1982, The Tempest 1982, Cyrano de Bergerac (Critics Circle Theatre Award Best Actor, Laurence Olivier Award for Actor of the Year in a Revival) 1983–85, Breaking the Code 1986, Richard II 1988, Richard III 1989, Kean 1990, Becket 1991, Mad, Bad and Dangerous to Know, Ambassadors 1992, Macbeth 1993, Hadrian VII, Playing the Wife 1995, Uncle Vanya 1996, God Only Knows 2000, Twelfth Night (Laurence Olivier Award for Best Actor) 2009, King Lear 2010–11; Dir Hamlet 1988, 2000. *Films include:* Othello 1965, Interlude 1968, Three Sisters 1970, Blue Blood 1973, The Day of the Jackal 1973, The Odessa File 1974, The Medusa Touch 1978, The Human Factor 1979, Charlotte 1981, The Man Who Went up in Smoke 1981, The Secret of NIMH (voice) 1982, Enigma 1983, Little Dorrit (Evening Standard British Film Award) 1988, Henry V 1989, The Fool 1990, Dead Again 1991, Looking for Richard 1996, Hamlet 1996, Basil 1998, Love is the Devil: Study for a Portrait of Francis Bacon (Edinburgh Int. Film Festival for Best British Performance 1998, Evening Standard Award for Best Actor 1999) 1997, Molokai: The Story of Father Damien 1999, Up at the Villa 2000, Gladiator 2000, The Body 2001, Gosford Park 2001, The Diaries of Vaslav Nijinsky 2001, Revelation 2001, The gathering Storm 2002, Revengers Tragedy 2002, Night's Noontime 2002, Two Men Went to War 2002, Strings 2004, Cloud Cuckoo Land 2004, Bye Bye Blackbird 2005, Underworld Evolution 2005, Nanny McPhee 2005, Project Huxley 2005, Arritmia 2007, The Riddle 2007, Anastezsi 2007, Airlock Or How To Say Goodbye In Space 2007, The Golden Compass 2007, A Bunch of Amateurs 2008, Sidney Turtlebaum 2008, Morris: A Life with Bells On 2009, Adam Resurrected 2009, Charles Dickens' England 2009, The King's Speech 2010, Capture Anthologies: The Dimensions of Self 2011, Ironclad 2011, There Be Dragons 2011, Anonymous 2011, My Week with Marilyn 2011, The Halloween Kid (short) (voice) 2011, Jail Caesar 2012, Cloud Cuckoo Land 2012, The Man Who Tried to Steal an Island (short) (voice) 2013, Effie Gray 2014, Hippie Hippie Shake 2014, Grace of Monaco 2014, Cinderella 2015. *Television includes:* BBC Sunday-Night Play (series) – She Stoops to Conquer 1961, Armchair Theatre (series) – The Fishing Match 1962, Much Ado About Nothing (film) 1967, ITV Playhouse (series) – The Photographer 1968, Man of Straw (mini-series) 1972, Budgie (series) 1972, The Strauss Family (mini-series) 1972, The Rivals of Sherlock Holmes (series) 1973, The Pallisers 1974, Markheim (film) 1974, Affairs of the Heart (series) 1975, I Claudius (BAFTA Award for Best Actor) 1976, Philby, Burgess and Maclean 1977, King Richard the Second (film) 1978, Minder (series) 1979, Hamlet, Prince of Denmark (film) 1980, Tales of the Unexpected (series) 1980–82, The Hunchback of Notre Dame (film) 1982, Inside the Third Reich (film) 1982, Cyrano de Bergerac (film) 1985, Mr Pye (mini-series) 1986, The Secret Garden (film) 1987, David Macaulay: Pyramid (film) 1988, The Tenth Man (film) (Emmy Award for Outstanding Supporting Actor in a Miniseries or a Special 1989) 1988, The American Civil War (mini-series documentary) 1990, The Storyteller: Greek Myths (mini-series) 1991, Screenplay (series) – The Vision Thing 1993, Circle of Deceit (film) 1993, The World of Peter Rabbit and Friends (series) 1994, ABC Weekend Specials (series) – The Secret Garden 1994, Cadfael 1994–98, Witness Against Hitler (film) 1996, Breaking the Code (film) 1996, Great Performances (series) – San Francisco Opera Gala Celebration 1997, Animated Epics: Beowulf (short) (voice) 1998, Flora Britannica (series) 1999, The Wyvern Mystery (film) 2000, Jason and the Argonauts (film) 2000, Frasier (series) (Emmy Award for Outstanding Guest Actor in a Comedy Series) 2001, Randall & Hopkirk (Deceased) (series) 2001, The Jury (mini-series) 2002, The Gathering Storm (film) 2002, Angelina Ballerina: The Show Must Go On (film) 2002, Inquisition (film) 2002, The Dinosaur Hunters (film) 2002, Angelina Ballerina (series) 2003, Doctor Who: Scream of the Shalka (mini-series) 2003, Mr. Ambassador (film) 2003, London (film) 2004, The Long Firm (series) 2004, Marple: The Murder at the Vicarage (film) 2004, Pinochet in Suburbia (film) 2006, Mist: The Tale of a Sheepdog Puppy (film) 2006, The Old Curiosity Shop (film) 2007, Mist: Sheepdog Tales (series, voice) 2007–09, Diamonds (film) 2009, Masterpiece Classic (series) – The Old Curiosity Shop 2009, Masterpiece Contemporary (series) – Endgame 2009, Margot (film) 2009, Joe Maddison's War (film) 2010, The Borgias (series) 2011, National Theatre Live (series) – King Lear 2011, – 50 Years on Stage 2013, Titanic: Blood and Steel (series) 2012, Last Tango in Halifax (series) 2012, Vicious (series) 2013–14, This Is Jinsy (series) 2014. *Leisure interests:* gardening, reading, looking for the next job. *Address:* c/o ICM, 3rd Floor, Marlborough House, 10 Earlham Street, London, WC2H 9LN, England. *Telephone:* (20) 7836-8564. *Website:* www.icmtalent.com.

JACOBOVITS DE SZEGED, Adriaan, MA, LLM; Dutch diplomatist (retd); b. 27 Dec. 1935, Vienna, Austria; s. of Giulio Jacobovits de Szeged and Eveline Tak van Poortvliet; m. Françoise S. Montant 1968; two s.; ed Univ. of Leiden; Master of Netherlands Law; Master of Russian Studies; Ministry of Finance 1963; joined Foreign Service 1964; postings to Embassy in Moscow, Perm. Mission to UN and other int. orgs, Geneva, Embassy, London, Embassy in Nairobi, Perm. Del. to EC, Brussels; Dir Econ. Co-operation, Ministry of Foreign Affairs 1978–82; Dir-Gen. Political Affairs 1982–86; Perm. Rep. to UN, New York 1986–89; Perm. Rep. to NATO, Brussels 1989–93; Amb. to USA 1993–97; Pres. Int. Comm. for the Protection of the River Rhine 1999–2001; Personal Rep. of the OSCE Chair.-in-Office for Moldova 2002–03; EU Special Rep. for Moldova 2005–07; Kt, Order of the Netherlands Lion, Grosses Verdienstkreuz mit dem Stern (Germany), Commdr, Légion d'honneur. *Address:* Prinsevinkenpark 17 F, 2585 HK The Hague, The Netherlands (home). *E-mail:* ajacobovits@planet.nl (office).

JACOBS, Andreas, DIur, MBA; German business executive and business school administrator; *Chairman, INSEAD;* b. 1963, Bremen; s. of Klaus Jacobs; m. Natalie Jacobs; four c.; ed Univs of Freiburg im Breisgau, Munich and Montpellier, INSEAD; Consultant and Project Man., Boston Consulting Group, Munich 1991–93; ind. entrepreneur 1992–; Chair. Brach's Inc. 2000–04; mem. Bd of Dirs Barry Callebaut AG 2003–, Chair. 2005–16; Exec. Chair. Jacobs Holding AG (family investment firm) 2004–15; mem. Bd of Dirs Adecco SA 2006–15, Vice-Chair. 2012–15; Chair. Infront Sports & Media AG –2011; co-founder and investor GENUI Partner (private equity fund) 2015; Pres. Niantic Holding GmbH; mem. Advisory Bd Dr August Oetker KG; mem. Bd of Dirs Louis Dreyfus Co. Holdings; Chair. INSEAD 2015–; several interests in thoroughbred horsebreeding including as Propr Stiftung Gestüt Fährhof, Lower Saxony, Maine Chance Farms, South Africa, Newsells Park Stud, UK; Pres. Baden Racing; mem. Int. Advisory Bd China Horse Club. *Address:* Office of the Chairman, INSEAD Europe Campus, Boulevard de Constance, 77305 Fontainebleau Cedex, France (office). *Telephone:* (1) 60-72-40-00 (office). *Website:* www.insead.edu (office).

JACOBS, Rt Hon. Sir Francis Geoffrey, KCMG, PC, QC, DPhil; British lawyer and academic; *Professor of Law, King's College, London;* b. 8 June 1939, Cliftonville, Kent; s. of Cecil Sigismund Jacobs and Louise Jacobs (née Fischhof); m. 1st Ruth Freeman 1964; m. 2nd Susan Felicity Gordon Cox 1975; two s. three d.; ed City of London School, Christ Church, Oxford and Nuffield Coll., Oxford; Lecturer in Jurisprudence, Univ. of Glasgow 1963–65; Lecturer in Law, LSE 1965–69; Prof. of European Law, King's Coll., London 1974–88, Prof. of Law 2006–, Fellow, King's Coll. 1990; Secr. European Comm. of Human Rights and Legal Directorate, Council of Europe 1969–72; Legal Sec. Court of Justice of the EC 1972–74, Advocate Gen. 1988–2006; Barrister, Middle Temple 1964, QC 1984, Bencher 1990; Gov. Inns of Court School of Law 1996–2001; Pres. Missing Children Europe 2007–13, European Law Inst. 2011–13; Commdr, Ordre de Mérite (Luxembourg) 1983; Hon. LLD (Birmingham) 1996, (Glasgow) 2006, (Kingston) 2012, Hon. DCL (City Univ., London) 1997, Dr hc (Ghent) 2007, (Groningen) 2014. *Publications include:* The Sovereignty of Law: The European Way 2007, The Oxford EU Law Library (Gen. Ed.); several books on European law and Yearbook of European Law (Founding Ed.) 1981–88. *Address:* Dickson Poon School of Law, King's College, Strand, London, WC2R 2LS (office); Fountain Court Chambers, Temple, London, EC4Y 9DH (office); Wayside, 15 St Alban's Gardens, Teddington, Middx, TW11 8AE, England (home). *E-mail:* francis.jacobs@kcl.ac.uk (office). *Website:* www.kcl.ac.uk/schools/law (office); www.fountaincourt.co.uk (office).

JACOBS, Count Jacobs de Hagen; **Georges,** MEconSc, DJur, PhD; Belgian business executive; b. 1940; ed Univ. Catholique de Louvain, Univ. of California, Berkeley, USA; economist IMF, Washington, DC, USA 1966; joined UCB Group 1970, Chair. Exec. Cttee 1987–2004, currently Chair. Bd of Dirs; mem. Bd of Dirs Delhaize Group 2003–12 (fmr Chair.); mem. Bd of Dirs Belgacom, Bekaert, SN Brussels Airlines, Générale de Banque, IBM Belgium, Spadel SA, L.I.V. NV (Groupe Carmeuse); Pres. Union of Industrial and Employers' Confeds of Europe (UNICE) 1998–2003 (now Hon. Chair.); mem. Man. Cttee Fed. of Belgian Cos (also Hon. Chair.); Chair. Belgo-Luxemburg-Polish Chamber of Commerce; mem. Bd American Chamber of Commerce, British Chamber of Commerce in Belgium.

JACOBS, Irwin Mark, BEE, MS, PhD; American electrical engineer, computer scientist, business executive and fmr academic; *Founding Chairman and CEO Emeritus, Qualcomm Corporation;* b. 18 Oct. 1933, New Bedford, Mass; m. Joan Jacobs; ed Cornell Univ., Massachusetts Inst. of Tech.; Asst Prof., then Assoc. Prof.

of Electrical Eng, MIT 1959–66; Prof. of Computer Science and Eng, Univ. of California, San Diego 1966–72, mem. Advisory Cttee, Inst. of Eng In Medicine; Co-founder, Chair. and CEO Linkabit Corpn (merged with M/A-COM 1980), Exec. Vice-Pres. and mem. Bd of Dirs –1985; Founding Chair. and CEO Qualcomm –2005, CEO Emer. 2005–, Chair. –2009; Chair. Bd of Trustees, Salk Inst. 2006, Nat. Acad. of Eng 2008–12; mem. Nat. Acad. of Eng 1982; mem. Advisory Bd Tsinghua Univ. School of Econs and Man. 1999–, King Abdulaziz City for Science and Tech. (KACST); mem. Bd of Dirs Suu Foundation (Myanmar); Fellow, IEEE 1974, American Acad. of Arts and Sciences 2001, AAAS 2010; Hon. Prof., Beijing Univ. of Posts and Telecom 2005, Hon. Distinguished Chair Prof., Nat. Tsing Hua Univ. 2003; Dr hc (Technion Israel Inst. of Tech.) 2000, (Univ. of Pennsylvania) 2002, (Univ. of Waterloo) 2005, (San Diego State Univ.) 2006, (Univ. of San Diego) 2007, (Univ. of Massachusetts, Dartmouth) 2008; Hon. PhD (Tel-Aviv Univ.) 2010; Nat. Medal of Tech. Award 1994, IEEE Alexander Graham Bell Medal 1995, Medal of Achievement Award, American Electronics Asscn 1998, inducted into Radio Communication Report Wireless Hall of Fame 2000, Bower Award in Business Leadership, Franklin Inst. 2001, Dr Morris Chang Exemplary Leadership Award, The Fabless Semiconductor Asscn 2003, Dorothy I. Height Chair's Award, Leadership Council on Civil Rights 2004, Lifetime Achievement Award (for 25 years in telecommunications), Financial Times 2005, Wolfson James Clerk Maxwell Award, IEEE/Royal Soc. of Edinburgh (co-recipient) 2007, Robert N. Noyce Award, Semiconductor Industry Asscn 2007, Visionary Award, SDForum 2008, Inaugural Hall of Fame Award, IEEE VTC 2009, inducted into Consumer Electronics Hall of Fame 2009, Lifetime Achievement Award, Ernst and Young 2011, ACE Award's Lifetime Achievement Award, EE Times 2011, Marconi Prize 2011, US News STEM Leadership Hall of Fame Award 2013, Technion Medal 2013. *Publications:* Principles of Communication Engineering (with Jack Wozencraft) 1965; numerous papers in professional journals; 14 patents. *Address:* c/o Qualcomm, 5775 Morehouse Drive, San Diego, CA 92121, USA.

JACOBS, Kenneth Marc, AB, MBA; American investment banker; *Chairman and CEO, Lazard LLC;* b. 1958; m. Agnes Mentre; ed Univ. of Chicago, Stanford Univ.; with Goldman Sachs 1984–88; joined Lazard LLC 1988, Partner, 1991–, Head of N America and Deputy Chair. 2002–09, Chair. and CEO 2009–; Trustee, Univ. of Chicago, Brookings Inst.; mem. Steering Cttee, Bilderberg Group. *Address:* Lazard LLC, 30 Rockefeller Plaza, New York, NY 10112, USA (office). *Telephone:* (212) 632-6000 (office). *E-mail:* kenneth.jacobs@lazard.com (office). *Website:* www.lazard.com (office).

JACOBS, Marc; American fashion designer; *Head Designer, Marc Jacobs International LLC;* b. 9 April 1963, New York; ed High School of Art and Design, New York, Parsons School of Design; f. Jacobs Duffy Designs (with Robert Duffy) 1984 (now Marc Jacobs Int. LLC, a subsidiary of LVMH Moët Hennessy Louis Vuitton SA); launched Marc Jacobs design label 1986; Vice-Pres. Women's Design, Perry Ellis 1989; Artistic Dir Louis Vuitton 1997–2013; f. Marc by Marc Jacobs 2001; apptd Creative Dir for Diet Coke brand 2013; Perry Ellis Award for New Talent, Council of Fashion Designers of America (CFDA) 1987, CFDA Women's Designer of the Year Award 1992, 1997, 2010, VH1 Women's Designer of the Year Award, CFDA Accessory Designer of the Year, Best New Retail Concept Award, British Fashion Awards 2007, Lifetime Achievement Award, CFDA 2011. *Address:* Marc Jacobs International LLC, 72 Spring Street, 2nd Floor, New York, NY 10012, USA (office). *Telephone:* (212) 965-5523 (office). *Fax:* (212) 965-5510 (office). *Website:* www.marcjacobs.com (office).

JACOBS, Peter Alan, BSc; British business executive; b. 22 Feb. 1943, Ayrshire, Scotland; m. Eileen Dorothy Naftalin 1966; two s. one d.; ed Univs of Glasgow and Aston; Production Man. Pedigree Petfoods 1981–83; Sales Dir Mars Confectionery 1983–86; Man. Dir British Sugar PLC 1986–91; Dir S. & W. Berisford PLC 1986–91; CEO British United Provident Asscn (BUPA) 1991–98; Chair. Healthcall 1998–2001; Chair. L. A. Fitness 1999–2005, WT Foods; Chair., Hillsdown Holdings 1998–99, Bank Leumi (UK) 1998–2003, Allied Domecq 1998–2004, Cove Park 2000–, RAF Strike Command 2002–09, abc media 2005–10. *Leisure interests:* tennis, squash, music, theatre, fund-raising. *Address:* 29 Daleham Gardens, London, NW3 5BY, England (home). *E-mail:* jacobs@peatonhouse.co.uk (office).

JACOBS, René, BPhil; Belgian singer (countertenor) and conductor; b. 30 Oct. 1946, Ghent; m. Roubina Saidkhanian; ed Univ. of Ghent, studied singing with Louis Devos in Brussels, Lucie Frateur in The Hague; recitals in Europe, Canada, USA, Japan, Mexico and the Philippines; performances with madrigal ensembles and with early music groups, including Leonhardt Consort, Il Complesso Barocco, La Petite Bande and groups led by Alan Curtis and Nikolaus Harnoncourt; sings Baroque music and directs own ensemble, Concerto Vocale; best known in operas by Monteverdi, Cesti, Handel, Gluck and Cavalli; sacred music by Charpentier and Couperin; regularly invited as conductor by Brussels La Monnaie, Berlin Staatsoper Unter den Linden and Theater an der Wien; conducted Cavalli's Giasone, La Calisto, Eliogabalo, Gassmann's Opera seria, Handel's Flavio, Agrippina, Rinaldo, Semele, Giulio Cesare, Monteverdi's L'Incoronazione de Poppea, L'Orfeo, Il ritorno d'Ulisse in patria, Madrigals, Graun's Cleopatra e Cesare, Scarlatti's Griselda, Haydn's Il mondo della luna, Orlando Paladino, Conti's Don Chisciotte, Telemann's Orpheus, Der geduldige Sokrates, Keiser's Croesus, Mozart's Nozze di Figaro, Così fan tutte, Don Giovanni, La Clemenza di Tito, Idomeneo, Die Zauberflöte, La Finta Giardiniera; Rossini's Tancredi; Artistic Dir Innsbrucker Festwochen der alten Musik 1991–2009; teacher of performing practice in Baroque singing, Schola Cantorum, Basle; appointments at Int. Summer School for Early Music, Innsbruck, and Aston Magna Acad. for Baroque Music, USA; Dr hc (Univ. of Ghent) 2008; Acad. Charles Cros Prix in Honorem 2001, Deutsche Schallplattenpreis Ehrenurkunde 2004, MIDEM Classical Award for Artist of the Year 2005, Gramophone Award for Musical Personality of the Year 2006, Partituren Dirigent des Jahres 2007, Telemmann Prize 2008. *Recordings include:* Cesti's L'Orontea (from the 1982 Holland Festival), Arias by Monteverdi and Benedetto Ferrari, Motets by Charpentier, Bach's St Matthew Passion, Handel's Admeto and Partenope, Lully's Bourgeois Gentilhomme, Gluck's Orfeo ed Euridice and Echo et Narcisse, Giasone and La Calisto by Cavalli, Handel's Alessandro and Tamerlano, Charpentier's David et Jonathas, Handel's Flavio (Deutsche Schallplattenkritik Jahrespreis 1991), Telemann's Orpheus (Deutsche Schaalplattenkritik Jahrespreis 1998), Scarlatti's Il primo omicidio, Keiser's Croesus, Handel's Giulio Cesare, Handel's Rinaldo (Cannes Classical Award 2004), Mozart's Così fan tutte, Mozart's Le nozze di Figaro (Echo Klassik 2005, MIDEM Classical Music Award for Recording of the Year 2005, Grammy Award for Best Opera 2007) 2004, Handel's Saul (MIDEM Classical Music Award Baroque category 2006, Gramophone Award for Best Baroque Vocal Recording 2006, Echo Klassik 2006) 2005, Haydn's Symphonies Nos 91 & 92 2005, Handel's Messiah 2006, La Clemenza di Tito (Deutsche Schallplattenkritik Jahrespreis 2006, Abendzeitung Stern des Jahres 2006, Classical BRIT Award Critics' Award 2007, Echo Klassik 2007, Opernwelt 2007), Mozart's Don Giovanni, Idomeno 2009, Mozart's The Magic Flute (Int. Classical Music Award for Opera Recording of the Year 2011) 2010, Handel's Agrippina (BBC Music Magazine Opera Award 2012), Passion selon saint Matthieu (ECHO Prize) 2014, Bach's Johannes-Passion (Int. Classical Music Award for Baroque Vocal 2017). *Address:* c/o Double Bande, 2 passage Philippe Auguste, 75011 Paris, France (office). *E-mail:* doublebande@aol.com (office).

JACOBSEN, Eric N., BS, PhD; American chemist and academic; *Sheldon Emery Professor of Chemistry, Harvard University;* b. 22 Feb. 1960, New York, NY; m. Virginia Estevez 1997; three d.; ed New York Univ., Univ. of California, Berkeley; NIH Postdoctoral Fellow, MIT, Cambridge, Mass 1986–88; Asst Prof., Univ. of Illinois, Urbana-Champaign 1988–91, Assoc. Prof. 1991–93; Prof. of Chem., Harvard Univ. 1993–2001, Sheldon Emery Prof. of Chem. 2001–, Chair. Dept of Chem. and Chemical Biology 2010–15; consultant, Sepracor, Marlboro, Mass 1990–2007, Merck, Rahway, New Jersey 1994–2012, Amgen, Thousand Oaks, Calif. 2003–, Daiso Co., Osaka, Japan 2006–10, Firmenich, Geneva, Switzerland 2009–10; mem. Scientific Advisory Bd PTC Therapeutics, South Plainfield, New Jersey 2001, Cubist Pharmaceuticals, Lexington, Mass 2007–12; Perm. mem. NIH Medicinal Chem. Study Section 1996–2000, mem. NIH Gen. Medical Sciences Council 2003–07; mem. Editorial Bd Advanced Synthesis and Catalysis, Science of Synthesis; mem. Advisory Editorial Bd Journal of Organic Chemistry, Synthesis, Synlett, Organic Letters, Journal of Combinatorial Chemistry, Journal of Molecular Catalysis, Current Opinion in Drug Discovery & Development, Chemistry: An Asian Journal; mem. American Acad. of Arts and Sciences 2004, NAS 2008; Fellow, AAAS 1997; Hon. PhD (Univ. of South Florida) 2015; New York State Regents Scholarship Award 1978–82, George Granger Brown Award 1981, New York Univ. Chem. Alumni Award 1982, Univ. of California Regents Fellowship 1984, 1985, Teaching Award, Univ. of Illinois School of Chemical Sciences 1989, UIUC List of Teachers Ranked as Outstanding by Their Students (five semesters) 1989–93, NSF Presidential Young Investigator Award 1990, Beckman Fellow 1991, Packard Fellowship 1991, Eli Lilly Grantee 1991, Merck Faculty Devt Award 1991, Union Carbide Innovation Award 1992, A.P. Sloan Foundation Fellowship 1992, Camile and Henry Dreyfus Teacher-Scholar Award 1992, Cyanamid Young Faculty Award 1992, Univ. of Illinois Scholar 1992, Pfizer Young Faculty Award for Synthetic Organic Chem. 1993, Zeneca Chem. Award 1993, Arthur C. Cope Scholar 1994, Fluka Prize for 'Reagent of the Year' 1994, Thieme-IUPAC Award in Synthetic Organic Chem. 1996, Harvard Coll. Professorship 1998–2003, Van't Hoff Prize 1998, Piero Pino Prize 1999, Baekeland Award 1999, ACS Award for Creative Work in Organic Synthesis 2001, NIH Merit Award 2002, Phi Beta Kappa Teaching Prize 2003, AIC Chemical Pioneer Award 2004, Mitsui Catalysis Award 2005, Alan R. Day Award 2007, ACS H.C. Brown Award for Synthetic Methods 2008, Yamada-Koga Prize 2008, Aldrich Lectureship, Scripps Research Inst., La Jolla, Calif. 2009, Boeringer-Ingelheim Lectureship, Columbia Univ., New York 2009, Astra-Zeneca Excellence in Chem. Award Keynote Lecturer, Wilmington, Del. 2009, Closs Lecturer, Univ. of Chicago 2009, Janssen Pharmaceutica Prize for Creativity in Organic Synthesis 2010, Noyori Prize 2011, Kosolapoff Award 2011, GlaxoSmithKline Scholar Award 2011, Nagoya Gold Medal Prize 2011, Chirality Medal 2012, Fannie-Cox Teaching Award, Harvard Univ. 2012, Remsen Award 2013, Bristol-DTC-Syngenta Award 2013, Esselen Award 2015, ACS Arthur C. Cope Award 2016. *Publications include:* more than 200 papers in professional journals. *Address:* Department of Chemistry and Chemical Biology, 12 Oxford Street, Cambridge, MA 02138, USA (office). *Telephone:* (617) 496-3688 (office). *Fax:* (617) 496-1880 (office). *E-mail:* jacobsen@chemistry.harvard.edu (office). *Website:* chemistry.harvard.edu/people/eric-jacobsen (office); www.people.fas.harvard.edu/~enjacobs (office).

JACOBSON, Nina; American film industry executive and producer; b. 30 Nov. 1965, Los Angeles; pnr Jen Bleakley; three c.; ed Brown Univ.; began film career as documentary researcher; joined Disney as story analyst in 1987; joined Silver Pictures as Dir of Film Devt 1988; fmr Head of Devt, MacDonald/Parkes Productions; fmr Sr Vice-Pres. of Production, Universal Pictures; fmr Sr Film Exec., DreamWorks SKG; joined Walt Disney in 1998, responsible for developing scripts and overseeing film production for Walt Disney Pictures, Touchstone Pictures and Hollywood Pictures, Pres. Buena Vista Motion Pictures Group –2006; f. Color Force (production co.) 2007, affiliated with Dreamworks SKG; Co-founder (with Bruce Cohen) Out There. *Films include:* Diary of a Wimpy Kid 2010, One Day (Global Nonviolent Film Festival Jury Award for Best Film) 2011, The Hunger Games (BAFTA Children's Award for Best Feature Film 2012) 2012, Crazy Rich Asians 2018. *Television include:* American Crime Story (BAFTA TV Award for Best International, Black Reel Award for Outstanding TV Movie or Limited Series 2017, Emmy Award for Outstanding Limited Series 2016,2018, Producers Guild Award for Outstanding Producer of Long-Form TV) 2016–. *Address:* c/o DreamWorks Studios, 100 Universal City Plaza, Building 5125, Universal City, CA 91608, USA (office).

JACOBSON, Roberta S., BA, MA; American diplomatist; ed Fletcher School of Law and Diplomacy, Tufts Univ. and Brown Univ.; worked for UN in Center for Social Devt and Humanitarian Affairs 1982–84; with Nat. Security Council 1988; Special Asst to Asst Sec., Dept of State 1989–92, Exec. Asst to Asst Sec. of State 1993–94, Co-ordinator for Cuban Affairs, Bureau of Western Hemisphere Affairs 1994–96, Dir, Office of Policy Planning and Co-ordination, Bureau of Western Hemisphere Affairs 1996–2000, Deputy Chief of Mission, Embassy in Lima 2000–02, Dir, Office of Mexican Affairs, Dept of State 2002–07, Deputy Asst Sec. for Canada, Mexico and NAFTA Issues, Bureau of Western Hemisphere Affairs 2007–10, Prin. Deputy Asst Sec. for Western Hemisphere Affairs and Sr Co-ordinator for Citizen Security Initiatives in Western Hemisphere 2010–11, Acting Asst Sec. 2011–12, Asst Sec. of State for Western Hemisphere Affairs 2012–16, Amb. to Mexico 2016–18 (resgnd). *Publications:* several articles.

JACOMB, Sir Martin Wakefield, Kt, MA; British banker and business executive; b. 11 Nov. 1929, Chiddingfold, Surrey; s. of Felise Jacomb and Hilary W. Jacomb; m. Evelyn Heathcoat Amory 1960; two s. one d.; ed Eton Coll. and Worcester Coll., Oxford; practised at the Bar 1955–68; Kleinwort, Benson Ltd 1968–85, Vice-Chair. 1976–85; Dir Hudson's Bay Co., Canada 1971–86; Chair. The Merchants Trust PLC 1974–85, Transatlantic Fund Inc. 1978–85; Dir Christian Salvesen PLC 1974–88, British Gas PLC 1981–88; Deputy Chair. Securities and Investments Bd Ltd 1985–87; Deputy Chair. Barclays Bank PLC 1985–93; Chair. Barclays de Zoete Wedd 1986–91, British Council 1992–98; Dir Commercial Union Assurance Co. PLC 1984–93 (Deputy Chair. 1988–93); Dir Bank of England 1986–95, Daily Telegraph 1986–95, RTZ Corpn PLC (now Rio Tinto PLC) 1988–2000; Chair. Postel Investment Man. Ltd 1991–95; Deputy Chair. (non-exec.) Delta PLC 1993–94, Chair. 1993–2004; Chair. Prudential Corpn 1995–2000, Share PLC 2001–13; mem. Bd of Dirs Marks and Spencer 1991–2000, Canary Wharf Group PLC 1999– (Chair. 2004–11, Special Adviser 2011–), Minorplanet Systems PLC 2000–04; Dir Royal Opera House Covent Garden Ltd 1987–92, Oxford Playhouse Trust Ltd 1994, Oxford Playhouse Ltd 1994; External mem., Finance Cttee, Oxford Univ. Press 1971–95; Trustee, Nat. Heritage Memorial Fund 1982–97; Chancellor, Univ. of Buckingham 1998–2010; Hon. Master of the Bench of the Inner Temple 1987, Hon. Fellow, Worcester Coll. Oxford 1994; Dr hc (Buckingham) 1997, (Oxford) 1997. *Leisure interests:* theatre, family bridge.

JACQUEMYN, Erik; Belgian scientist and business executive; *Founder and CEO, Jacquemyn & Associates;* ed Univ. of Leuven; Science and Tech. Advisor to Minister-Pres. of Flemish Govt 1985–88; Co-Founder and CEO Flanders Tech. Int. Foundation 1988–2016, also mem. Bd; Chair., Brabanthal NV 1995; Founding CEO Technopolis 2000–16, also mem. Bd; Founder and CEO Jacquemyn & Assocs 2016–; mem. Int. Programme Cttee, Science Centre World Summit 2008–, Chair. 2011–14, Previous Chair. 2014–17, Chair. Science Centre World Summit Foundation 2017–; mem. Bd, European Network of Science Centres and Museums 1998, Asscn of Science-Tech. Centers (ASTC) 2003–11 (mem. Exec. Cttee 2009–11, Chair. Int. Cttee 2009–11); UNESCO Kalinga Prize for Popularization of Science 2017. *Address:* Jonkvrouwlaan 1, B 3210 Linden, Belgium (office). *E-mail:* erik@jacquemyn.be. *Website:* www.jacquemyn.be.

JACQUES, Paula; French author and broadcaster; b. (Paula Abadi), 8 May 1949, Cairo, Egypt; d. of Jacques Abadi and Esther Sasson; m. (divorced 1970); worked as comedienne in Africa; joined Radio France Internationale as reporter, worked on Après-midi de France-Culture, L'Oreille en coin 1975–90; presenter, Nuits-noires France-Inter radio 1997–, Cosmopolitaine 2000–; writer, F Magazine; mem. jury, Prix Femina 1996–, Prix des Cinq Continents. *Play:* Zanouba. *Publications include:* Lumière de l'oeil 1980, Un baiser froid comme la lune 1983, L'Heritage de Tante Carlotta 1987, Deborah et les anges dissipés (Prix Femina 1991), La Déscente au Paradis (Prix Nice Baie des Anges) 1995, Les femmes avec leur amour 1997, Gilda Stambouli souffre et se plaint... (Prix Europe 1) 2001, Rachel-Rose et l'officier arabe (Prix des Sables d'Olonne) 2006, Kairo Jacobi, juste avant l'oubli 2011. *Address:* France-Inter, 116 avenue du Président Kennedy, 75220 Paris cedex 16, France (office). *Website:* www.franceinter.fr/personne-paula-jacques-0 (office).

JACQUET, Luc; French filmmaker and writer; b. 5 Dec. 1967, Bourg-en-Bresse; fmr biologist. *Films include:* Le congès des pingouins (cinematographer) 1993, Le printemps des phoques de Weddell (Ancre de bronze, Festival Int. du Film Maritime et d'Exploration, Toulon 1996, Coup de coeur du jury, Festival Int. du Film Montagne et Aventure, Autrans 1996) 1996, Le léopard de mer: la part de l'ogre (Palme d'Argent & Prix de la Meilleure Composition Musicale, Festival Mondial de l'Image Sous-Marine, Antibes 1999, Prix pour l'Excellente Qualité des Prises de Vues Sous-marines & Prix pour la Musique, Festival Int. du Film sur la Vie Sauvage, Missoula, Mont., USA 2000, Prix de la Meilleure Réalisation, Ekofilm – Festival Int. du Film de l'Environnement, Prague 2000) 1999, Killer Whales: Up Close and Personal (cinematographer) 2000, Une plage et trop de manchots (Primé au Festival Int. du Film Ornithologique de Ménigoute 2001) 2001, La tique et l'oiseau (Prix Nature et Découvertes, Festival Int. du Film Ornithologique de Ménigoute 2002, Prix du meilleur commentaire, Festival Valvert, Brussels 2002, Prix de la côte Picarde, Festival de l'oiseau d'Abbeville 2002) 2001, Sous le signe du serpent 2004, Antarctique printemps express (Prix Spécial Meilleur son, Festival Vertical de Moscou 2006) 2004, Des manchots et des hommes (Of Penguins and Men) (One Planet Award, Wildlife Film Festival, Toyama 2005, Grand prix du public Festival Grandeur Nature, Val d'Isère 2005, Best Film, Prix Jules Verne du Public, Prix Jules Verne de la Jeunesse, Festival Jules Verne 2005, Grand Prix, Festival de l'oiseau, Abbeville 2005, Ancre d'Argent, Prix des collégiens, Festival Int. du Film Maritime et d'Exploration, Toulon 2005, Edelweiss d'Argent, Festival du film de montagne de Torello 2005, Prix Adventura Homme et environnement, Mountain Film Festival, Canada 2005) 2004, La marche de l'empereur (The Emperor's Journey, aka March of the Penguins, USA) (Best Film Documentary, Las Vegas Film Critics Soc. Awards 2005, Nat. Board of Review (USA) 2005, Southeastern Film Critics Asscn Awards (USA) 2005, Broadcast Film Critics Asscn Awards (USA) 2006, Golden Trailer Awards (USA) 2006, Camie, Character and Morality in Entertainment Awards (co-recipient) 2006) 2005, Academy Award for Best Documentary, Features 2006, and numerous other awards) 2005, Le renard et l'enfant (The Fox and the Child) 2007, Il était une forêt (Once Upon A Forest) (Polly Krakora Award for Artistry in Film 2014) 2013, Ice and the Sky 2015.

JACQUET, Michel Antoine Paul Marie; French business executive; b. 28 March 1936, Dijon; s. of André Jacquet and Marie-Antoinette Baut; m. 2nd Marie-Agnès Corbière 1976; one s. and one s. one d. by first m.; ed Lycée Rouget de Lisle, Lons-le-Saulnier, Lycée du Parc, Lyon and Ecole Polytechnique; Dir-Gen. Crédit Lyonnais d'Espagne 1971–77; Dir-Gen. Paribas Gabon and Pres. Sogapar 1977–79; Deputy Dir Banque Paribas 1980–84; CEO Paribas New York 1985–88; Pres. Nord-Est and Magnésia 1989–95, Hon. Pres. Nord-Est 1995–; currently Pres. Ledo-Salina; Vice-Chair. Supervisory Bd EDF Partenaires Capital Investissement; mem. Supervisory Bd Poincaré Investissements; mem. Bd of Dirs Lombard Int. Assurance, Texavenir, Renaissance Holdings, Cinq A Sec Holdings, LCIE Landaver; Croix de valeur militaire; Chevalier, Légion d'honneur. *Address:* Ledo-Salina, 46–48 rue Lauriston, 75116 Paris (office); 15 rue Raynouard, 75016 Paris, France (home).

JADAAN, Muhammad bin Abdullah bin Abd al-Aziz al-, BA, LLM; Saudi Arabian lawyer and government official; *Minister of Finance;* ed Imam Muhammad ibn Saud Islamic Univ., Inst. of Public Admin, Riyadh; Asst Dir of Family and Community Medicine, Riyadh Mil. Hosp. 1983–94; Deputy Dir of Human Resources, Social Insurance Hosp. 1991–92; Man. Partner, Al-Jadaan and Partners Law Firm 1996–2015; Chair. Capital Market Authority 2015–16; Minister of Finance 2016–; fmr special adviser to bd of Morgan Stanley Saudi Arabia. *Address:* Ministry of Finance, Airport Road, Riyadh 11177, Saudi Arabia (office). *Telephone:* (11) 405-0000 (office). *Fax:* (11) 403-3130 (office). *E-mail:* info@mof.gov.sa (office). *Website:* www.mof.gov.sa (office).

JADHAV, Arvind, MA, MBA; Indian civil servant and airline industry executive; *Chief Secretary, Government of Karnataka;* b. 5 June 1956; ed Kanpur Univ., Indian Inst. of Foreign Trade, Italian Inst. of Foreign Trade, Rome, Curtin Univ., Australia; joined Indian Admin. Service 1978; Asst Commr Land Revenue Man. Div. 1980; Jt Sec. Ministry of Power; Chief Vigilance Officer Gas Authority of India Ltd; Prin. Sec., Infrastructure Devt Dept, Govt of Karnataka –2009; Additional Chief Sec., Tourism Dept, Govt of Karnataka 2012–15; Chief Sec., Govt of Karnataka 2016–; fmr Commr Karnataka Housing Bd; fmr Sec. Energy Dept; fmr Man. Dir Mysore Minerals Ltd; fmr Commr Commerce and Industries Dept; Dir Société Internationale de Télécommunications Aéronautiques, Bangalore Int. Airport Ltd, Nat. Thermal Power Corpn 2003–05, Rural Electrification Corpn Ltd 2002–07, Power Finance Corpn Ltd –2006; Chair. and Man. Dir Nat. Aviation Co. of India Ltd which operates Air India 2009–11; Chair. Karnataka Urban Infrastructure Devt and Finance Corpn Ltd Jan.–Nov. 2012; Chair. Karnataka Appellate Tribunal 2015–16; Distinguished Fellowship, Golden Peacock Awards 2010. *Address:* Government of Karnataka, Bangalore 560 001, India (office). *Telephone:* (80) 22252442 (office). *Fax:* (80) 22258913 (office). *E-mail:* cs@karnataka.gov.in (office). *Website:* www.karnataka.gov.in (office).

JAEGER, Heinrich Martin, PhD; German physicist and academic; *William J. Friedman and Alicia Townsend Professor of Physics, Department of Physics, University of Chicago;* b. 15 May 1957, Flensburg; m. Julie Jaeger; one c.; ed Univ. of Kiel, Germany, Univ. of Minnesota, USA; Postdoctoral Fellow, Dept of Physics, Univ. of Chicago 1987–88, Asst Prof. 1991–96, Assoc. Prof. 1996–2000, apptd Prof. 2000, William J. Friedman and Alicia Townsend Prof. of Physics 2010–, Dir Materials Research Center 2001–06, Argonne Consortium for Nanoscience Research 2001–10, James Franck Inst. 2007–10, Chair. Physical Sciences Div. Cttee on Diversity 2005–; Sr Researcher, Centre for Submicron Tech., Delft Univ. of Tech., The Netherlands 1989–91; mem. Tech. Advisory Bd Atomworks 2003–; mem. Scientific Advisory Cttee, Argonne Center for Nanoscale Materials 2003–; mem. Essential Science Task Force, Chicago Museum of Science and Industry 2003–; mem. External Advisory Bd Centro para la Investigación Interdisciplinaria Avanzada en Ciencias de los Materiales, Chile 2004–; Fellow, American Physical Soc. 2002; Fulbright Scholarship 1981–82, Univ. of Minnesota Dissertation Fellowship 1986–87, James Franck Fellowship, Univ. of Chicago 1987–88, David and Lucile Packard Fellowship 1991–96, Alfred P. Sloan Research Fellowship 1992–94, Research Corpn Cottrell Scholarship 1994–96, Outstanding Achievement Award, Univ. of Minnesota 2002, Quantrell Award for Excellence in Undergraduate Teaching 2006. *Publications:* author or co-author of over 130 scientific publs. *Address:* Department of Physics, University of Chicago, 5720 South Ellis Avenue, Chicago, IL 60637, USA (office). *Telephone:* (773) 702-6074 (office). *Fax:* (773) 834-0471 (office). *E-mail:* h-jaeger@uchicago.edu (office). *Website:* physics.uchicago.edu (office); jfi.uchicago.edu (office).

JAEGER, Marc; Luxembourg judge; *President, General Court of the European Union;* b. 1954; fmr Attaché de justice, Public Attorney's Office; fmr Judge and Vice-Pres. Luxembourg Dist Court; Lecturer, Univ. du Luxembourg; Legal Sec., Court of Justice of the European Communities 1986; Judge, Gen. Court of the EU (fmrly known as Court of First Instance) 1996–, Pres. 2007–. *Address:* General Court of the European Union, rue du Fort Niedergrünewald, 2925 Luxembourg Ville, Luxembourg (office). *Telephone:* 4303-1 (office). *Fax:* 4303-2100 (office). *Website:* www.curia.eu (office).

JAENISCH, Rudolf, MD; German biologist and academic; *Professor of Biology, Massachusetts Institute of Technology;* b. 22 April 1942, Wölfelsgrund; ed Univ. of Munich; Head of Dept of Tumor Virology, Heinrich Pette Inst., Univ. of Hamburg 1977–84; founding mem. Whitehead Inst. for Biomedical Research 1982, Prof. of Biology, MIT 1984–; Visiting Scientist, Max Planck Inst. for Biochemistry, Munich, Princeton Univ. Fox Chase Cancer Center, Philadelphia, Salk Inst., La Jolla, Calif.; participated in science conf. on human cloning at UN 2005; mem. Science Advisory Bd Genetics Policy Inst., Stemgent; mem. NAS 2003, Inst. of Medicine; Fellow, American Acad. of Arts and Sciences; Boehringer Mannheim Molecular Bioanalytics Prize 1996, first Peter Gruber Foundation Award in Genetics 2001, Robert Koch Prize for Excellence in Scientific Achievement 2002, Brupracher Foundation Cancer Award 2003, Vilcek Prize 2007, Meira and Shaul G. Massry Prize 2008, Cozzarelli Prize, Proceedings of the NAS (PNAS) 2009, Ernst Schering Prize 2009, Pres.'s Nat. Medal of Science for 2010, 2011, Wolf Prize in Medicine 2011, J. Allyn Taylor Int. Prize in Medicine 2011, Benjamin Franklin Medal in Life Science 2013, Medicine Medal, New York Acad. 2013, Otto Warburg Medal, German Soc. for Biochemistry and Molecular Biology 2014, March of Dimes Prize in Developmental Biology 2015. *Achievements include:* recognized as a leader in the field of therapeutic cloning, also known as nuclear transfer; first breakthrough when, along with Beatrice Mintz, showed that foreign DNA could be integrated into DNA of early mouse embryos 1974; created first transgenic animal model, carried out first experiment showing that therapeutic cloning could correct genetic defects in mice. *Publications:* more than 375 research papers in professional journals. *Address:* Room WI 461B, Whitehead Institute for Biomedical Research, 9 Cambridge Center, Cambridge, MA 02142-1479, USA (office). *Telephone:* (617) 258-5186 (office); (617) 258-5189 (office). *E-mail:* jaenisch@wi.mit.edu (office); burger@wi.mit.edu (office). *Website:* biology.mit.edu/people/rudolf_jaenisch (office); wi.mit.edu/people/faculty/jaenisch (office).

JAFFE, Harold W., BA, MD; American epidemiologist and academic; *Associate Director for Science, Centers for Disease Control and Prevention;* b. 26 April 1946, Newton, Mass.; ed Univ. of California, Berkeley, Univ. of California, Los Angeles; Jr doctor at UCLA Hosp. 1971–74; Clinical Research Investigator, Venereal Disease Control Div., Centers for Disease Control (CDC), Atlanta 1974–77,

1980–81, Epidemic Intelligence Service Officer for AIDS Activity 1981–83, f. (with James W. Curran and others) Kaposi's Sarcoma-Opportunistic Infections Task Force, Center for Infectious Diseases to study causes of immune-deficiency disease in homosexual men 1981, Chief, Epidemiology Br. of AIDS Programme, CDC 1983–, Dir Div. AIDS, STD and TB Laboratory Research –2001, Acting Dir Nat. Center for HIV, STD, and TB Prevention (NCHSTP) 2001, Dir 2002–03, Assoc. Dir for Science, CDC, Atlanta 2010–; Fellow, St Cross Coll., Oxford, Prof. of Public Health and Chair. Dept of Public Health 2004–10; Fellow in Infectious Diseases, Univ. of Chicago 1977–80; Visiting Prof., Chester Beatty Labs, Inst. of Cancer Research and Dept of Medicine, Hammersmith Hosp., London, 1988–90; Clinical Instructor of Medicine, Emory Univ. School of Medicine, Atlanta; Assoc. Ed. American Journal of Epidemiology; mem. Editorial Bd AIDS journal; mem. Inst. of Medicine, NAS 2006–, Infectious Diseases Soc. of America; Commendation Medal for work on HIV/AIDS, US Public Health Service 1984, Meritorious Service Medal 1986, Distinguished Service Medal 1992. *Publications include:* book chapters and over 90 articles in scientific journals, including Epidemiologic Aspects of the Current Outbreak of Kaposi's Sarcoma and Opportunistic Infections, in New England Journal of Medicine Jan. 1982, The Epidemiology of AIDS: Current Status and Future Prospects, in Science Sept. 1985 (co-author), HIV Infection and AIDS in the United States, in Science Feb. 1989 (co-author). *Address:* Centers for Disease Control and Prevention, 1600 Clifton Road, Atlanta, GA 30333, USA (office). *E-mail:* cdcinfo@cdc.gov (office). *Website:* www.cdc.gov (office).

JAFFE, Stanley Richard, BEcons; American film producer and director; b. 31 July 1940, New Rochelle, New York; s. of Leo Jaffe and Dora Bressler; m. 1st Joan Ellen Goodman (divorced); two c.; m. 2nd Melinda Long; two s. two d.; ed Wharton School, Univ. of Pennsylvania; with Seven Arts Assoc. Corpn 1962–67, exec. Asst to Pres. 1964; Dir East Coast Programming, Seven Arts TV 1963–64, Dir Programming 1965–67; Exec. Vice-Pres., Chief Corp. Officer, Paramount Pictures Corpn 1969–70, Pres. Corpn also Pres. Paramount TV 1970–71; Pres. Jaffilms Inc. 1971; Exec. Vice-Pres. Worldwide Production, Columbia Pictures Corpn 1965–76; Pres. and COO Paramount Communications, New York 1991–94; Gov., Pres. and COO New York Knicks professional basketball team 1991–94; Gov. New York Rangers professional ice hockey team 1991–94; Owner, Jaffilms LLC 1994–. *Films include:* The Professionals 1963, Goodbye Columbus 1968, Bad Company 1971, Man on A Swing 1973, Bad News Bears 1974, Kramer vs Kramer 1979, Taps 1981, Without a Trace 1983, Racing with the Moon 1984, Firstborn 1984, Fatal Attraction 1987, The Accused 1988, Black Rain 1989, School Ties 1992, The Firm 1993, Madeleine 1998, I Dreamed of Africa 2000, Four Feathers 2002. *Address:* 2 Sackett Landing, Rye, NY 10580-4315; Jaffilms LLC, 152 West 57th Street, New York, NY 10019-3386, USA (office).

JAFFRELOT, Christophe, PhD; French political scientist and academic; *Director, Centre d'Études et de Recherches Internationales;* b. 12 Feb. 1964; ed Institut d'études politiques, Univ. of Paris I (Sorbonne), Institut nat. des langues et civilisations orientales; fmr Lecturer in South Asian Politics, Institut d'études politiques, Univ. of Paris I (Sorbonne) and Institut nat. des langues et civilisations orientales; Deputy Dir Centre d'études et de recherches internationales (CERI), Sciences Po 1997–2000, Dir 2000–08; joined Centre National de la Recherche Scientifique (CNRS) 1991, apptd Sr Research Fellow (second class) 2002, Sr Research Fellow (first class) 2008, now Research Dir; Prof. of India's Politics and Soc., India Inst., Kings' Coll. London, also teaches South Asian politics and history at Sciences Po, Paris; Princeton Global Scholar, Princeton Univ. 2013–14; Scholar (non-resident), South Asia Program, Carnegie Endowment for Int. Peace; Chair. Asia Group, French Ministry of Foreign Affairs; Alliance Visiting Prof., Columbia Univ. 2009; Ed.-in-Chief Critique Internationale (journal) 1998–2003, Dir 2003–08; CNRS Bronze Medal 1993. *Publications include:* The Hindu Nationalist Movement and Indian Politics 1996, L'Inde contemporaine de 1950 à nos jours (ed.) 1997, La démocratie en Inde – Religion, caste et politique 1998, BJP – The Compulsions of Politics (co-ed.) 1998, Le Pakistan, carrefour de tensions régionales (ed.) 1999, Démocraties d'ailleurs: démocraties et démocratisations hors d'Occident (ed.) 2000, Le Pakistan (ed.) 2000, Dr Ambedkar 2000, Inde: La Démocratie par la caste 2005. *Address:* CERI, 56 rue Jacob, 75006 Paris, France (office). *Telephone:* 1-58-71-70-00 (office). *Fax:* 1-58-71-70-91 (office). *E-mail:* christophe.jaffrelot@sciencespo.fr (office). *Website:* www.ceri-sciences-po.org (office).

JAGAT, Gurbachan, MA; Indian politician and fmr police officer; b. 1 July 1942; ed Punjab Univ., Chandigarh; joined Indian Police Service 1966; Sr Supt, Amritsar 1978–81; Deputy Insp. Gen. Intelligence/Security Div., Punjab Police Force 1982–90; Man. Dir Punjab Police Housing Corpn 1990–95; Dir-Gen. of Admin 1995–97; Dir-Gen. of Police, Jammu and Kashmir 1997–2000; Dir-Gen. Border Security Force 2000–02 (retd); Chair. Union Public Service Comm. 2006–07; Gov. of Manipur 2008–13, of Nagaland July–Oct. 2009; mem. Bd of Trustees The Tribune 2016–; Indian Police Medal for Meritorious Service 1982, Padma Shri 1987, Pres.'s Police Medal for Distinguished Service 1992, Police Officer of the Year Award (Govt of Jammu and Kashmir) 2001, Pres.'s Police Medal for Distinguished Service 1992, Pashchimi Star, Sangram Medal, Special Duty Medal, Aantrik Seva Suraksha Medal, Operation Rakhshak, Operation Vijay Medals. *Address:* c/o Tribune Trust, Sector 29-C, Chandigarh 160030, India.

JAGDEO, Bharrat, MEconSc; Guyanese politician and fmr head of state; b. 23 Jan. 1964, Unity Village, East Coast Demerara; ed Moscow State Univ., USSR; mem. People's Progressive Party, elected to Cen. Cttee 1993, later mem. Exec. Cttee; worked as economist in State Planning Secr. 1990–92; Special Adviser to Minister of Finance 1992–93; Jr Minister of Finance 1993; fmrly Dir Guyana Water Authority; Dir Caribbean Devt Bank, Nat. Bank of Industry and Commerce, Gov. for Guyana, World Bank; Sr Finance Minister 1995–99; Prime Minister of Guyana 9–11 Aug. 1999; Pres. of Guyana 1999–2011; Chair. Bd of Govs IMF and World Bank 2005–06; Pres. Union of South American Nations 2010–11; UN Sec.-Gen.'s High Level Advisory Group on Climate Financing 2010–; High Level Envoy for Sustainable Development in Forest Countries, Int. Union for the Conservation of Nature (IUCN) 2011–; Pres. Global Green Growth Inst. 2012–; Leader of the Opposition 2015–; FAO Special Amb. for Forests and Environment 2015; Order of Merit (Brazil) 2013; Dr hc (Peoples' Friendship Univ. of Russia) 2010, (TERI Univ.) 2012, (Univ. of Cen. Lancashire) 2013, (Trent Univ.) 2013; Pushkin Medal (Russia), Pravasi Bharatiya Samman Award (India).

JAGGER, Bianca, MA; British (b. Nicaraguan) artist, film director, human rights activist and environmental campaigner; *Founder and Chairman, Bianca Jagger Human Rights Foundation;* b. 2 May 1950, Managua, Nicaragua; d. of Carlos Perez-Mora and Dora Macias Somassiba; m. Michael (Mick) Jagger 1971 (divorced 1979); one d.; ed Inst. of Political Sciences, Paris and New York Univ.; lecturer on Cen. America at several colls and univs; Co-Founder Iris House, New York; has campaigned for human rights in Cen. America, mem. several US Congressional dels and dels from int. human rights orgs; visited the Fmr Yugoslavia to document alleged human rights violations and testified before Helsinki Comm. on Human Rights and US Congressional Human Rights Caucus; has helped to evacuate children from Bosnia 1993; works to protect rainforests in Honduras, Nicaragua and Brazil and indigenous peoples in Brazil, India and elsewhere; headed AIDS campaign 2001; Founder and Chair. Bianca Jagger Human Rights Foundation 2005–; mem. Exec. Dir's Leadership Council, Amnesty Int. USA, Advisory Cttee Human Rights Watch America, Bd of Dirs Action Council for Peace in the Balkans, Bd Hispanic Fed., New York; Special Adviser Indigenous Devt Int., Cambridge, UK; Council of Europe Goodwill Amb. against the death penalty; Amb. for the Int. Union for Conservation of Nature (IUCN) Plant a Pledge campaign; Hon. DH (Stone Hill Coll., MA) 1983; Hon. Dr of Human Rights (Simmons Coll., Boston) 2008; Hon. LLD (Univ. of East London) 2010; UN Earth Day Int. Award 1994, Humanitarian Award, Hispanic Fed. of New York City 1996, 1996 Woman of the Year, Boys Town, Italy, Abolitionist of the Year Award, Nat. Coalition to Abolish the Death Penalty 1996, Right Livelihood Award 2004. *Films include:* Flesh Color, Success, Cannonball Run, Chud II, The Rutles. *Television includes:* Hotel, Miami Vice, The Colbys. *Publications:* contribs to New York Times, Observer, Guardian; has a blog on the Huffington Post. *Leisure interests:* horse-riding, water-skiing. *Address:* Bianca Jagger Human Rights Foundation, Unit 246, 272 Kensington High Street, London, W8 6ND, England. *Fax:* (20) 7361-0077. *Website:* www.biancajagger.org.

JAGGER, Sir Michael (Mick) Philip, Kt, KBE; British singer, songwriter and actor; b. 26 July 1943, Dartford, Kent; s. of Joe Jagger and Eva Jagger; m. 1st Bianca Pérez Morena de Macías 1971 (divorced 1979); one d.; m. 2nd Jerry Hall (q.v.) 1990 (divorced 1999); two s. two d.; one d. by Marsha Hunt; one c. by Luciana Morad; ed London School of Econs, Univ. of London; began singing career with Little Boy Blue and the Blue Boys while at LSE; appeared with Blues Inc. at Ealing Blues Club, singer with Blues Inc. at London Marquee Club 1962; Founder-mem. and lead singer, Rolling Stones 1962–; wrote songs with Keith Richards under pseudonyms Nanker, Phelge until 1965, without pseudonyms 1965–; first own composition to reach No. 1 in UK charts The Last Time 1965; first major UK tour 1964; tours to USA, Europe; fmrly lived in France; solo career 1970–; mem., SuperHeavy supergroup 2009; Pres. LSE Students' Union 1994–; Nordoff-Robbins Silver Clef 1982, Grammy Lifetime Achievement Award 1986, Ivor Novello Award for Outstanding Contribution to British Music 1991, Golden Globe Award for Best Original Song (for Old Habits Die Hard, with Dave Stewart, for film Alfie) 2005. *Films:* Ned Kelly (actor) 1969, Performance (actor) 1969, Gimme Shelter (actor) 1972, Free Jack (actor) 1991, Freejack (actor) 1992, Bent (actor) 1996, Enigma (producer) 2001, Shine a Light 2007. *Recordings include:* albums: with The Rolling Stones: The Rolling Stones 1964, The Rolling Stones No. 2 1965, Out Of Our Heads 1965, Aftermath 1966, Between The Buttons 1967, Their Satanic Majesties Request 1967, Beggar's Banquet 1968, Let It Bleed 1969, Get Yer Ya-Ya's Out 1969, Sticky Fingers 1971, Exile On Main Street 1972, Goat's Head Soup 1973, It's Only Rock And Roll 1974, Black And Blue 1976, Some Girls 1978, Emotional Rescue 1980, Tattoo You 1981, Still Life 1982, Undercover 1983, Dirty Work 1986, Steel Wheels 1989, Flashpoint 1991, Voodoo Lounge 1994, Stripped 1995, Bridges to Babylon 1997, Forty Licks 2002, Live Licks 2004, A Bigger Bang 2005, Blue & Lonesome (Grammy Award for Best Traditional Blues Album 2018) 2016; solo: She's The Boss 1985, Primitive Cool 1987, Wandering Spirit 1993, Goddess In The Doorway 2001, The Very Best of 2007; with SuperHeavy: SuperHeavy 2009. *Publication:* According to the Rolling Stones (autobiog., jtly) 2003. *Telephone:* (20) 8877-3100 (office). *Fax:* (20) 8877-3077 (office). *Website:* www.mickjagger.com.

JAGLAND, Thorbjørn; Norwegian politician and international organization official; *Secretary-General, Council of Europe;* b. 5 Nov. 1950, Drammen; m. Hanne Grotjord 1975; two c.; ed Univ. of Oslo; mem. Buskerud Co. Council 1975–83; Chair. Labour Youth League (AUF), Buskerud Co. 1973–76, Chair. Norwegian Labour Youth League 1977–81, Sec. Labour Party Cttee on Disarmament 1982–, Acting Party Sec. Labour Party 1986–87, Chair. Labour Party Int. Cttee 1986–, Sec. Labour Party Programme Cttee 1986–89, Party Sec. Labour Party 1987–92, Chair. Norwegian Labour Party 1992–2002; mem. Storting for Buskerud Co. 1993–2009, Chair. Labour Party Parl. Group, Chair. Parl. EEA Consultative Cttee 2000–05, Parl. Standing Cttee on Foreign Affairs and Enlarged Foreign Affairs Cttee 2001–05, Pres. Storting 2005–09; Prime Minister 1996–97; Minister of Foreign Affairs 2000–01; Sec.-Gen. Council of Europe 2009–; mem. Norwegian del. for Relations with the European Parl. 1993–96, 1997–2000, Head of del. 2001–05; mem. Norwegian del. to Nordic Council 1993–96, 1997–2000, to NATO Parl. Ass. 2001–05; Head of Norwegian del. at Second Summit of Council of Europe, Strasbourg 1997; Chair. Socialist Int. Finance and Admin Cttee 1987–92, Vice-Pres. Socialist Int. 1999–2008, Chair. Middle East Cttee 2000–06; Chair. Oslo Center for Peace and Human Rights 2006–, Norwegian Nobel Cttee 2009–15; mem. Int. Bd of Govs Peres Center for Peace 1997–; mem. Sharm El-Sheikh Fact-Finding Comm. ('Mitchell Comm.') 2000–01; Commdr, Légion d'honneur 2013. *Publications include:* Min europeiske drøm 1990, Ny solidaritet 1993, Brev 1995, Vår sårbare verden 2002, For det blir for sent (co-author) 1982, Ti tescr om EU og Norge 2003; numerous articles on defence, nat. security and disarmament. *Address:* Office of the Secretary-General, Council of Europe, 67075 Strasbourg Cedex, France (office). *Telephone:* (3) 88-41-20-00 (office). *Fax:* (3) 88-41-27-99 (office). *E-mail:* private.office@coe.int (office). *Website:* www.coe.int (office).

JAGNE, Baboucarr-Blaise Ismaila, MA; Gambian diplomatist; *Head of United Nations Political Affairs Division, African Union;* b. 11 Feb. 1955, Banjul; m.; four c.; ed Univ. of Dakar and Univs of Grenoble and Paris, France; Asst Sec., Foreign Ministry 1980–84, Sec. to Pres. of Gambia, Chair. Islamic Peace Cttee on Iran–Iraq War 1984–88, Sr Asst Sec. for Political Legal Affairs 1986–89, Prin. Asst Sec. 1989–92; Deputy Perm. Sec. for Educ. 1992–93, for Political Affairs 1993–95; Minister of External Affairs 1995–97; Amb. to Saudi Arabia 1997–98; Perm. Rep. to UN, New York 1998–2001; Sec. of State for Foreign Affairs 2001–05; currently

Head of UN Political Affairs Div., African Union HQ, Addis Ababa. *Address:* UN Political Affairs Division, African Union, POB 3243, Addis Ababa, Ethiopia (office). *Telephone:* (1) 51-7700 (office). *Fax:* (1) 51-7844 (office). *E-mail:* webmaster@africa-union.org (office). *Website:* www.africa-union.org (office).

JAGNE, Mamour Alieu; Gambian diplomatist and politician; ed Njala Univ., Sierra Leone, Imperial (Wye) Coll., Univ. of London, UK; Sr Planner, Ministry of Agric. 1993–99; Monitoring and Evaluation Officer, The Gambia Rural Finance and Community Initiatives Project, IFAD 1999–2001; Deputy Project Dir, The Gambia Capacity Building for Econ. Man. Project, World Bank 2001–03; Nat. Project Coordinator, The Gambia Capacity Building for Millennium Devt Goals (MDGs) Project, UNDP 2003–05, Team Leader, Poverty and MDGs, UNDP, The Gambia 2005–08; Amb. and Perm. Rep. to EU, Brussels 2008–14; Perm. Sec., Ministry of Foreign Affairs, Feb.–April 2014; Minister of Foreign Affairs April–May 2014. *Address:* Ministry of Foreign Affairs, International Co-operation and Gambians Abroad, 4 Marina Parade, Banjul, Gambia (office). *Telephone:* 4223577 (office). *Fax:* 4227917 (home). *E-mail:* info@mofa.gov.gm (office). *Website:* www.mofa.gov.gm (office).

JÁGR, Jaromír; Czech professional ice hockey player; b. 15 Feb. 1972, Kladno, Czechoslovakia (now Czech Repub.); s. of Jaromír Jágr; began skating aged three; was playing at highest level of competition in Czechoslovakia aged 16; first Czechoslovakian player drafted by NHL (Nat. Hockey League) without first defecting to West; taken by Pittsburgh Penguins with fifth overall pick in NHL Entry Draft 1990–2001; won five NHL scoring titles with the Penguins 1994–95 to 2000–01, including four in a row 1997–98 to 2000–01; team gold medal (Capt.), Winter Olympics, Nagano 1998; traded to Washington Capitals 2001–03, to New York Rangers 2003–08, Avangard Omsk (Kontinental Hockey League, Russia) 2008–11; returned to NHL, with Philadelphia Flyers 2011, Dallas Stars 2012, Boston Bruins 2013, New Jersey Devils 2013–15, Florida Panthers 2015–; played for Kladno, Czech Repub. 2004–05 (during NHL players strike), later for Avangard ice-hockey team, Omsk, Russia; captained Czech Repub. Gold Medal-winning team, World Hockey Championships, Austria 2005; wears no. 68 in honour of Prague Spring rebellion in Czechoslovakia in 1968, also the year in which his grandfather died while in prison; mem. Triple Gold Club (players who have won a Stanley Cup, a World Hockey Championship and an Olympic gold medal), Stanley Cup Winner 1991, 1992, NHL All-Rookie Team 1991, Golden Stick Award 1995, 1996, 1999, 2000, 2002, 2005, 2006, Art Ross Trophy (Leading Point Scorer) 1995, 1998, 1999, 2000, 2001, NHL First Team All-Star 1995, 1996, 1998, 1999, 2000, 2001, 2006, NHL Second Team All-Star 1997, Hart Trophy 1999, Lester B. Pearson Award 1999, 2000, 2006, Czech Sportsman of the Year 2005, IIHF World Championship All-Star Team 2005, Bill Masterton Memorial Trophy 2016. *Website:* www.nhl.com/player/jaromir-jagr-8448208.

JAGUARIBE GOMES DE MATTOS, Roberto; Brazilian government official and diplomatist; b. 27 Dec. 1952, Rio de Janeiro; m. Cinara Maria Fonseca de Lima; ed Pontifical Catholic Univ., Rio de Janeiro; career diplomat since 1979, postings include Perm. Mission to UN, New York 1983–87, Embassy in Montevideo 1987–90, Head, Div. for Intellectual Property and Sensitive Technologies, Ministry of External Relations 1990–93, Head, Intellectual Property Section, Mission to Int. Orgs, Geneva 1993–95; Sec. for Int. Affairs, Ministry of Planning and Budget 1995–98; Dir Gen. for Trade Promotion, Ministry of External Relations 1998–2000; Deputy Head of Mission, Embassy in Washington, DC 2000–03; Sec. for Industrial Tech., Ministry of Devt, Industry and Foreign Trade 2003–05; Under-sec. Gen. for Political Affairs II, Ministry of External Relations 2007–10; Amb. to UK 2010–15, to People's Repub. of China 2015–16; Pres. Nat. Inst. of Industrial Property of Brazil 2005–07, Brazilian Agency for the Promotion of Exports and Investments (Apex-Brasil) 2016–. *Leisure interests:* football, cookery, sailing, golf and tennis.

JAHAN, Ismat, BA, MA; Bangladeshi lawyer and diplomatist; b. 1960; m. Prof. Johannes den Heijer; ed Dhaka Univ., Fletcher School, Tufts Univ., with cross-registered course works at Harvard Univ., USA; career diplomat 1982–; fmr Visiting Fellow, School of Foreign Service, Georgetown Univ., Washington, DC; served in various capacities at Ministry of Foreign Affairs as well as missions abroad including Perm. Missions to UN in New York and Geneva, and High Comm. in New Delhi; Dir-Gen. Int. Orgs, UN and Multilateral Econ. Affairs, Ministry of Foreign Affairs –2005; Amb. to the Netherlands 2005–07; Amb. and Perm. Rep. to UN, New York 2007–09; Amb. to Belgium, Luxembourg and the European Communities 2009–16; mem. Cttee on Elimination of Discrimination Against Women (CEDAW) 2011–.

JAHANGIRI, Guissou Jeannot, BA; French/Iranian international organization official; *Executive Director, Armanshahr Foundation/OPEN ASIA;* b. Iran; ed American Univ., Paris, Ecole des Hautes Etudes en Sciences Sociales, Paris; journalist (responsible for Iran, Cen. Asia and Afghanistan), Courier Int. 1990–, mem. Bd 1990–; Co-founder and Exec. Dir Open Asia France (fmrly called The Asscn for Research and Information on Cen. Asia), Paris 1994–, Armanshahr Foundation/OPEN ASIA 1995–; Rep. of Human Rights Watch, Helsinki and Tajikistan 1995–96; Consultant to World Bank, Tajikistan 1996; Consultant and NGO Liaison Officer, UN Office for the Coordination of Humanitarian Affairs 1997–98. *Publications include:* articles in professional journals, UN reports. *Address:* Armanshahr Foundation/OPEN ASIA, Behind Baharestan Cinema, Qassabi Road, 5th Street on the left (Rashid Street), House No. 195, Kabul, Afghanistan (office). *Telephone:* (79) 6202114 (Kabul) (office); 6-62-15-32-97 (France, mobile) (office). *Fax:* 1-47-97-32-97 (Paris) (office). *E-mail:* openasiafrance@gmail.com (office); contact@openasia.org (office); jeannot@enpc.fr (office). *Website:* oainternational.free.fr (office); openasia.org/en (office); www.fidh.org/fr/asie/afghanistan/afghanistan-armanshahr-open-asia.

JAHJAGA, Atifete; Kosovo fmr police officer and fmr head of state; b. 20 April 1975, Gjakovë/Đakovica; m. Astrit Kuçi; ed Univ. of Prishtina, Univ. of Leicester, UK, George C. Marshall European Centre for Security Studies, Germany, Fed. Bureau of Investigation (FBI) Nat. Acad., USA; following Kosovo War, began working as an interpreter for the int. police; completed officer training and was promoted to Maj., then Col, and finally Gen. Maj.; first deployed with border police and then transferred to Training Dept; held position of Deputy Dir of Kosovo Police, and briefly filled in as Acting Gen. Dir 2010; announced as a consensual presidential cand. by Partia Demokratike e Kosovës (PDK—Democratic Party of Kosovo), Lidhja Demokratike e Kosovës (LDK—Democratic League of Kosovo) and Aleanca Kosova e Re (AKR—New Kosovo Alliance) 6 April 2011; Pres. of Kosovo 2011–16; Hon. DCL (Durham Univ., UK) 2013; Hon. LLD (Univ. of Leicester, UK) 2015; Leadership in Public Service Award, Clinton Global Initiative 2014. *Address:* c/o Office of the President, 10000 Prishtina, Rruga Nënë Terezë, Kosovo. *E-mail:* protocol@president-ksgov.net.

JAHN, Helmut, FAIA; German architect; b. 4 Jan. 1940, Nuremberg; s. of Wilhelm Anton Jahn and Karolina Wirth; m. Deborah Lampe 1970; one s.; ed Technische Hochschule, Munich, Illinois Inst. of Tech., USA; with C.F. Murphy Assocs 1967–73, Exec. Vice-Pres. and Dir of Planning and Design 1973; registered architect, NCARB 1975; mem. German Chamber of Architects, State of Hesse 1986; Prin. Murphy/Jahn (Chicago, Ill., USA and Berlin) 1981, Pres. 1982, Pres. and CEO 1983–; Visiting Prof., Harvard Univ., USA 1981, Yale Univ., USA 1983; completed bldgs include libraries, exhbn halls, court bldgs, office and leisure bldgs, univ. bldgs, hotels, apartments and airport terminals in USA, Europe and Far East; Corp. mem. AIA 1975, Fellow 1987; Hon. DFA (St Mary's Coll. Notre Dame, Ind.); Chevalier des Arts et des Lettres, Bundesverdienstkreuz Erster Klasse; numerous professional awards. *Major completed projects include:* Kemper Arena, Kansas City, Mo. 1974, Xerox Centre, Chicago 1980, Argonne Program Support Facility, Argonne, Ill. 1981, 11 Diagonal Street, Johannesburg, SA 1983, James R. Thompson Center, Chicago 1985, 362 West Street, Durban, SA 1986, Park Avenue Tower, NY, USA 1986, United Airlines Terminal One Complex, O'Hare Airport, Chicago 1987, One Liberty Place, Phila, USA 1987, Northwestern Atrium Center, Chicago 1987, Wilshire/Westwood, LA 1988, Bartnett Center, Jacksonville, Fla, USA 1990, Messeturm, Frankfurt 1991, 120 North LaSalle, Chicago 1992, One America Plaza, San Diego, Calif., USA 1992, Mannheimer Lebensversicherung, Mannheim 1992, Hyatt Regency Roissy, Paris, France 1992, Munich Order Center 1993, Hitachi Tower, Singapore 1993, Caltex House, Singapore 1993, Hotel Kempinski, Munich 1994, Pallas, Stuttgart 1994, Kurfürstendamm 70, Berlin 1994, Principal Mutual Life Insurance Co., Des Moines, Ia, USA 1996, RCID Admin Bldg, Orlando, Fla 1997, JC Decaux Bus Shelter 1998, New EU HQ, Belgium, Brussels 1998, Munich Airport Center 1999, Sony Center, Berlin 2000, Airport Köln/Bonn 2000, Ha-Lo HQ, Chicago 2000, Neues Kranzler Eck, Berlin 2000, Kaufhof Galeria, Chemnitz 2002, Shanghai Int. Expo Centre 2002, Bayer AG Konzernzentrale, Leverkusen 2002, Post Tower, Bonn 2003, State Street Village IIT, Chicago 2003, Train Station, Airport Köln/Bonn 2004, Highlight Business Towers, Munich 2004, Mannheimer-2, Mannheim 2005, Suvarnabhumi Airport, Bangkok, Thailand 2006, Merck-Serono HQ, Geneva 2007, Margot & Harold Schiff Residences, Chicago 2007, 600 Fairbanks Court, Chicago 2008, 1999K Street, Washington, DC, USA 2009, Chicago-O'Hare Int. Airport (façade and circulation enhancements) 2009, West Combined Utility Plant/South Campus Chiller Plant, Univ. of Chicago 2009, Hegau Tower, Singen, Germany 2009, Veer Towers, Las Vegas, Nev., USA 2010, Joe and Rika Mansueto Library, Chicago, USA 2011, Leatop Plaza, Guangzhou, China 2012, Cosmopolitan Twarda 2/4, Warsaw, Poland 2014, 50 West, New York, USA 2015. *Leisure interests:* sailing, skiing. *Address:* Murphy/Jahn, Inc., Suite 300, 35 East Wacker Drive, Chicago, IL 60601, USA (office). *Telephone:* (312) 427-7300 (office). *Fax:* (312) 332-0274 (office). *Website:* www.murphyjahn.de (office); www.jahn-us.com.

JAHN, Martin, MBA; Czech automobile industry executive and fmr government official; *Head of International Fleet Sales and Managing Director of Group Fleet International, Volkswagen AG;* b. 20 Jan. 1970, Prague; s. of Vladimír Jahn and Hana Jahn; m. Karolina Jahn; two d.; ed Prague School of Econs, DePaul Univ., Chicago, USA; Dir American Operations, Czechinvest 1996–99, CEO 1999–2004; Deputy Prime Minister, responsible for the Economy 2004–06; joined Skoda, Mlada Boleslav 2006, Man. Dir Volkswagen Group Rus, Moscow Br. 2008–10, Head of Int. Fleet Sales and Man. Dir of Group Fleet International, Volkswagen AG, Wolfsburg 2010–; mem. Bd CMC Celákovice; mem. Czech-American Chamber of Commerce, Czech-Canadian Chamber of Commerce 2000–; Ordre National du Mérite. *Leisure interests:* tennis, squash, skiing, film, literature, music. *Address:* Volkswagen AG, Brieffach 1849, Wolfsburg 38436, Germany (office). *Telephone:* (5361) 90 (office). *Fax:* (5361) 928282 (home). *Website:* www.volkswagen.com (office).

JAHNÁTEK, L'ubomír, CSc; Slovak academic and politician; b. 16 Sept. 1954, Nitra; m.; two c.; ed Slovak Tech. Univ.; worked for VUSPAL (Plastics Processing and Application Research Inst.) 1978–98; Dir-Gen. Production–Tech. Dept, Plastika Nitra a.s. 1992–2003; Strategy Dir Duslo Šala a.s. 2003–05; Lecturer, Faculty of Material Sciences and Tech., Slovak Tech. Univ. 2004–06, Head of Field Div. 2005–06; Minister of the Economy 2006–10; Vice-Chair. Cttee for Economy, Construction and Transport 2010–12; Minister of Agric. and Rural Devt 2012–16; mem. Smer-Sociálna demokracia.

JAHUMPA, Bala Ibrahima Muhamadu Garba, BA, MA; Gambian diplomatist and politician; b. 20 July 1958, Banjul; ed Vassar Coll., USA, Univ. of Birmingham, UK; Adviser Dept of State for Agric. 1981–82, Dept of State for Foreign Affairs 1982–83; transferred to Gambian Embassy, Washington, DC, USA 1984–85; Asst Commr Upper River Div. 1986–87; Sr Asst Sec., Dept of State for Agric. 1987–90; Prin. Asst Sec., Dept of State for Local Govt and Lands 1990–94; Sec. of State for Finance and Econ. Affairs 1994–97; Deputy High Commr, Gambian Embassy, London 1997–99, Acting High Commr 1999–2001; Amb. to Cuba June–Sept. 2003; Sec. of State for Works, Construction and Infrastructure 2003–06, was fired alongside three other govt ministers Oct. 2006, reappointed following protest action by Banjulians appealing for their reinstatement Oct. 2006; Sec. of State for Foreign Affairs 2006–07; Amb. to Spain and Venezuela 2007–12; Minister of Communications and Information Infrastructure 2012, of Transport, Works and Infrastructure 2012–14, of Foreign Affairs 2014–15.

JAIDA, Yousuf Mohammed al-; Qatari government official; *CEO, Qatar Financial Centre Authority;* b. 1979; ed Univ. of Arizona, USA; early positions in engineering projects for Qatar Petroleum and Dolphin Energy, also managed various real-estate projects in Qatar; fmr Head of Indirect Investment, Qatar Gen. Retirement and Pension Authority; Deputy CEO and Chief Strategic and Business Devt Officer, Qatar Financial Centre Authority 2010–14, Vice-Chair. 2014–15, CEO 2015–, also serves as rep. on Qatar Exchange Bd and Qatar Financial Business Acad. Bd; fmr Dir Nakilat QSC, Unicorn Investment Bank Strategic Investment Fund; fmr Vice-Chair. Mayadeen Real Estate Co. KSCC; f. Jaida

Capital; mem. Advisory Council, Coll. Of Business, Qatar Univ. *Address:* Qatar Financial Centre Authority, POB 23245, Doha, Qatar (office). *Telephone:* 44967777 (office). *Fax:* 44967676 (office). *E-mail:* ceo@qfc.qa (office). *Website:* www.qfc.qa (office).

JAIDEE, Thongchai; Thai professional golfer; b. 8 Nov. 1969, Lopburi; m.; two s.; fmr paratrooper, Royal Thai Army; professional golfer 1999–; first major championship played US Open 2001; European Tour wins include Carlsberg Malaysian Open 2004 (first Thai winner on European Tour), 2005, Enjoy Jakarta Indonesia Open 2009, Ballantine's Championship 2009, ISPS Handa Wales Open 2012, Nordea Masters 2014, Porsche European Open 2015, Open de France 2016; Asian Tour wins include Kolon Cup Korean Open 2000, Volvo Masters of Asia 2003, 2006, Hana Bank Vietnam Masters, Johnnie Walker Cambodian Open 2008, 2010, Enjoy Jakarta Indonesia Open 2009; represented Thailand in World Cup 2007, 2008, 2009; represented Asia in Dynasty Cup 2003, 2005, Royal Trophy 2007, 2008, 2009; invited to play in US Masters Tournament 2006 (first Thai to play in all four major championships); Asian Tour Order of Merit 2001, 2004, 2009, voted Asian Tour Players' Player of the Year 2009.

JAIM-ETCHEVERRY, Guillermo, MD, PhD; Argentine neurobiologist, academic, foundation executive and fmr university administrator; ed Univ. of Buenos Aires; Prof. and Dir Dept of Cellular Biology and Histology, Faculty of Medicine, Univ. of Buenos Aires –2008, Dean of Faculty 1986–90, Pres. Univ. of Buenos Aires 2002–06; Pres. Fundación Carolina de Argentina 2006–12; Prin. Investigator, CONICET, IBRO/UNESCO –2012, John Simon Guggenheim Memorial Foundation; mem. Nat. Acad. of Educ., Argentina Acad. of Communication Arts and Sciences; Corresp. mem. Acad. of Medical Sciences of Córdoba; Hon. Foreign Mem. American Acad. of Arts and Sciences 2004; Chevalier, Ordre des Palmes Académiques 2005; Dr hc (Univ. of Morón) 2009; Bernardo Houssay Prize 1987, Master of Medicine, Nat. Acad. of Medicine, Argentina 2001, Medaille d'Or of the Societe d'Encouragement au Progres 2007, Medallas del Bicentenario 2010. *Publication:* The Educational Tragedy.

JAIME, Aguinaldo; Angolan politician; Minister of Finance 1990–92; fmr Pres. Banco Africano de Investimentos; Provincial Gov. 1999–2002; Gov. Nat. Bank of Angola 1999–2002; Deputy Prime Minister of Angola 2002; Dir Agência Nacional para o Investimento Privado (ANIP); currently Chair. Bd of Angolan Agency for Regulation and Supervision of Insurance (ARSEG). *Address:* Agência Nacional para o Investimento Privado (ANIP), Rua de Serqueira Lukoki n° 25, 9° andar Cx. P 5465, Luanda, Angola (office). *Telephone:* 222391434 (office). *Fax:* 222332965 (office). *E-mail:* geral@anip.co.ao (office). *Website:* www.anip.co.ao (office).

JAIN, Anshuman, BA, MBA; Indian business executive; b. 7 Jan. 1963, Jaipur, Rajasthan; m.; two c.; ed Shri Ram Coll. of Commerce, Univ. of Delhi, Univ. of Massachusetts, Amherst, USA; began career as analyst in derivatives research at Kidder, Peabody & Co. (now part of UBS) 1985–88; joined Merrill Lynch, New York 1988, f. and led first dedicated hedge fund coverage group; joined Deutsche Bank's nascent markets business 1995, mem. Deutsche Bank Group Exec. Cttee 2002–, fmrly Head of Global Markets and Jt Head of Corp. and Investment Bank 2004–10, roles included Head of Fixed Income Sales and Trading, Global Head of Derivatives and Emerging Markets and Global Head of Institutional Client Coverage, mem. Man. Bd Deutsche Bank AG, Head of Corp. and Investment Bank 2010–12, Co-Chair. Man. Bd and Group Exec. Cttee 2012–15, Co-CEO 2013–15; Dir (non-exec.), Sasol (South Africa); fmr mem. Prime Minister's Working Group on Inward Investment in India; led Deutsche Bank's team advising UK Treasury on financial stability; mem. Financial Services Global Competitiveness Group 2008; Euromoney Magazine Capital Markets Achievement Award 2003, American Indian Foundation's Achievement Award 2005, Risk Magazine Lifetime Achievement Award 2010, NASSCOM Business Leader Award 2010. *Leisure interests:* photography, cricket, golf, active supporter of several wildlife and environmental conservation charities. *Address:* c/o Deutsche Bank AG, Taunusanlage 12, 60262 Frankfurt am Main, Germany. *E-mail:* info@db.com.

JAISHANKAR, Subrahmanyam, MA, MPhil, PhD; Indian diplomatist; s. of K. Subrahmanyam; m. Kyoko Jaishankar; two s. one d.; joined Foreign Service 1977, worked in various capacities in Embassies in Washington, DC and Moscow 1979–81, Americas Div., Ministry of External Affairs 1981–85, Embassy in Colombo 1988–90, Embassy in Budapest 1990–93; Press Sec. to Pres. of India 1994–95; Deputy Chief of Mission, Embassy in Tokyo 1996–2000, Amb. to Czech Repub. 2000–04, Head of Americas Div., Ministry of External Affairs 2004–07, High Commr to Singapore 2007–09, Amb. to People's Repub. of China 2009–13, to USA 2013–15, Foreign Sec. 2015–18; mem. IISS, London; one of key negotiators of India–USA civilian nuclear co-operation agreement 2005–07. *Address:* Ministry of External Affairs, South Block, 110 011 New Delhi, India (office). *Telephone:* (11) 23011127 (office). *Fax:* (11) 23013254 (office). *E-mail:* eam@mea.gov.in (office). *Website:* www.mea.gov.in (office).

JAITLEY, Arun, BCom (Hons), LLB; Indian lawyer and politician; *Minister of Finance and of Corporate Affairs;* b. 28 Dec. 1952, New Delhi; s. of Maharaj Kishen Jaitley and Ratan Prabha Jaitley; m. Sangeeta Jaitley 1982; one s. one d.; ed St Xavier's School, New Delhi, Shri Ram Coll. of Commerce, Faculty of Law, Univ. of Delhi; Pres. Students Union, Univ. of Delhi 1974; Convenor, Nat. Cttee for Students and Youth Org.; has practised before Supreme Court and several High Courts 1977–, apptd Sr Advocate 1990; Additional Solicitor Gen. of India 1989–90; mem. Indian delegation to UN Gen. Ass. Session June 1998; mem. Nat. Exec., Bharatiya Janata Party 1991–, Sec.-Gen. and Spokesperson 2002–03, Sec.-Gen. 2004–09, Leader 2009–14; elected to Rajya Sabha (Parl.) 2000, mem. Consultative Cttee for the Ministry of Home Affairs 2004–09, Cttee on Commerce 2004–12, Jt Cttee to examine the constitutional and legal position relating to Office of Profit 2006–08, Jt Cttee on Offices of Profit 2006–09, Select Cttee on the Lokpal and Lokayuktas Bill 2012; Cttee Leader of Rajya Sabha 2014–; Minister of State (ind. charge) for Information and Broadcasting 1999–2000, Minister of State (ind. charge) for Disinvestment (additional charge) 2000, Minister of State (ind. charge) for Law, Justice and Corp. Affairs 2000–02, of Law, Justice and Corp. Affairs March–Sept. 2001, of Shipping (additional charge) 2002–03, of Law, Justice and Commerce and Industry 2004, of Corp. Affairs and of Defence May–Nov. 2014, of Finance Nov. 2014–18, of Corp. Affairs and of Information and Broadcasting Nov. 2014–16, of Corp. Affairs 2016–18, also of Defence (acting) March–Sept. 2017, Minister without Portfolio May–Aug. 2018, of Finance and Corporate Affairs Aug. 2018–Jan. 2019, Feb. 2019–; Gen. Sec. in-charge of elections, Municipal Corpn of Delhi (MCD) 2007; Chair. Governing Body, Kamla Nehru Coll. 1993–98; mem. Bd of Govs Asian Devt Bank, Governing Council, Indian Premier League (IPL); mem. Bd of Dirs Bd of Control for Cricket in India (BCCI), Delhi District Cricket Asscn (DDCA); mem. Nat. Legal Services Authority of India; mem. Court of Univ. of Delhi 2002–03, 2005–10; Outstanding Parliamentarian Award 2010. *Publications:* author of several publs on legal and current affairs. *Leisure interests:* reading and writing on legal and current affairs. *Address:* Ministry of Finance, North Block, 1st Floor, New Delhi 110 001, India (office); 9, Ashoka Road, New Delhi 110 001 (home); A-44, Kailash Colony, New Delhi 110 024, India (home); 2, Krishna Menon Marg, New Delhi 110011 (office). *Telephone:* (11) 29248212 (home); (11) 23092611 (office); (11) 23794990 (office); (11) 23794556 (office). *Fax:* (11) 29232358 (home); (11) 23094075 (office). *E-mail:* secy-dea@nic.in (office); office@arunjaitley.com (office). *Website:* finmin.nic.in (office); www.arunjaitley.com.

JAKIČ, Roman; Slovenian politician; b. 1 May 1967; Vice-Dean, Faculty of Arts, Univ. of Ljubljana 1987–90; Deputy, Chamber of Associated Labour, Ass. of Repub. of Slovenia 1990–92; Pres. Young Liberal Democracy of Slovenia 1991–98; mem. Liberal Democracy of Slovenia, Head of Int. Relations Office 1992–96, Sec.-Gen. 2004–05; Vice-Pres. and Sec.-Gen. Int. Fed. of Liberal Youth 1993–96; Deputy, Nat. Ass. of Slovenia 1996–2000, 2000–04, 2011–; Vice-Chair. Alliance of Liberals and Democrats for Europe, Parl. Ass. of Council of Europe 1998–2004; mem. City Council, Municipality of Ljubljana 1998; mem. European Parl. 2003–04; Minister of Defence 2013–14; Dir GALITIJA – Business Consulting, Roman Jakič sp 2005–08; Dir Javni zavod Šport Ljubljana (public inst.) 2008–12; Pres. Slovenia Athletics Fed. 2001–05; mem. Exec. Bd Olympic Cttee of Slovenia 2001–05; mem. Positive Slovenia (PS).

JAKIYANOV, Qalimjan, PhD; Kazakhstani engineer and politician; b. 8 May 1963, Kurchumskii Dist, Eastern Kazakhstan Oblast; s. of Badyljan Jakiyanov and Rasch Jakiyanova; m.; two s.; ed Bauman Higher Inst., Moscow, Russia; specialized in rocket and turbine eng; worked at Semipalatinsk Mil. Plant, Br. Head of Komsomol (CP Youth League), dismissed 1989; became leader of ind. youth movt; Publr and Ed. Sodeistviye (Assistance) newspaper 1989–91; Propr Semey coalmine 1990–94; Gov., Semipalatinsk 1994–97; Chair. State Agency for Strategic Resources Control 1997; Akim (Gov.), Pavlodar Oblast 1997–2001 (resgnd); Co-founder and Co-Chair. Democratic Choice of Kazakhstan (DCK) 2001; arrested on charges of abuse of power during tenure as Gov. April 2002, sentenced to seven-year prison term Aug. 2002, released on parole 2006.

JAKOBSDÓTTIR, Katrín, BSc, MA; Icelandic politician; *Prime Minister;* b. 1 Feb. 1976, Reykjavík; d. of Jakob Ármannsson and Signý Thoroddsen; m. Gunnar Örn Sigvaldason; three s.; ed Univ. of Iceland; Language Adviser (part time), RÚV news agency 1999–2003; Instructor, Mímir School 2004–07; Ed. Edda (publishing co.) and JPV (magazine) 2005–06; Lecturer, Univ. of Iceland, Reykjavík Univ. and Menntaskólinn í Reykjavík 2006–07; mem. Althingi (parl.) for Reykjavík North Constituency 2007–; Minister for Nordic Cooperation 2009–13, Minister of Educ., Science and Culture 2009–13, Prime Minister 2017–; mem. Icelandic Del. to West Nordic Council 2013–14; mem. Left-Green Movt (VG), Deputy Chair. 2003–13, Chair. 2013–. *Address:* Prime Minister's Office, Stjórnarráðshúsinu við Lækjartorg, 101 Reykjavík, Iceland (office). *Telephone:* 5458400 (office). *Fax:* 5624014 (office). *E-mail:* postur@for.is (office). *Website:* www.forsaetisraduneyti.is (office).

JAKSITY, György, BEcons; Hungarian stockbroker and stock exchange executive; *Chairman, Concorde Securities Ltd;* b. 14 May 1968; m. Kinga Jaksity; two c.; ed Karl Marx Univ. of Econs; Financial Adviser, Ministry of Finance 1989; consultant for several cos including Girozentrale Investment, Ibusz and Fotex, Budapest 1989–92; training with Price Waterhouse 1992; Founder and Man. Dir Concorde Securities 1993–97, Chair. 1997–; Chair. Budapest Stock Exchange 2002–04; f. The Self Reliance Foundation. *Leisure interest:* reading. *Address:* Concorde Securities Ltd, Alkotás Point Office Building 50 Alkotás utca, Budapest, 1123, Hungary (office). *Telephone:* (1) 489-2200 (office). *Fax:* (1) 489-2201 (office). *Website:* www.con.hu (office).

JAKUBISKO, Juraj, MFA; Slovak film director, producer, scriptwriter and artist; b. 30 April 1938, Kojšov; m. Horváthová Jakubisko; one s. one d.; ed Prague Film Acad.; films censored by Communist regime late 1970s (Birds, Orphans and Fools, See You in Hell, My Friends); blacklisted and banned from producing films for ten years; retrospective tour of his work in USA, Canada and Europe 1991; mem. Twentieth Century Acad. 1999–; Pribina Cross, Second Class (Slovakia) 2003; more than 80 nat. and int. awards, including Maverick Award for vision in filmmaking, Taos Talking Picture Festival, USA 1998, Award in Recognition of Outstanding Achievement in the Art of the Film, Denver Int. Film Festival, USA 1998, Golden Seal Award of Yugoslavian Cinematheque for outstanding contrib. to world cinema, Belgrade 2000, Best Slovak Director Award in survey of the best Slovak and int. artists of 20th century conducted by Slovak film journalists and critics 2000, Lifetime Achievement Award, Masaryk Acad. of Art, Prague 2001, ČFTA Award: Czech Lion for Best Film Poster of the Year 2000, ČFTA Award: Czech Lion for Lifetime Artistic Contrib. 2002, Crystal Globe for Outstanding Artistic Contrib. to World Cinema, Karlovy Vary 2007, Czech Lion Award 2008, Igric Award 2009. *Films include:* Silence (Brussels Film Acad. Award, Knokke Experimental Film Festival, Belgium), Waiting for Godot (Best Short Film Award, Oberhausen, Simone Dubroilh Award, Mannheim) 1968, Birds, Orphans and Fools (banned 1968, Fipresci Prize 1991), The Bee Millennium (Golden Phoenix Award, Venice Film Festival) 1983, The Feather Fairy 1985, Frankenstein's Aunt 1986, A Rosy Story 1990, See You in Hell, My Friends (originally made in 1968 but banned by political censors) 1991, It's Better to Be Wealthy and Healthy Than Poor and Ill 1992 (re-released 2002), An Ambiguous Report About the End of the World (also TV series) 1999, Post Coitum 2004, Bathory 2008. *Leisure interests:* painting, golf. *Address:* Jakubisko Film Asscn Ltd, Palác Lucerna, Vodičkova 36, 116 02 Prague 1, Czech Republic (office). *Telephone:* (2) 9623-6500 (office). *Fax:* (2) 9623-6382 (office). *E-mail:* info@jakubiskofilm.com (office). *Website:* www.jakubiskofilm.com (office).

JAKUPOV, Kabibulla Kabenovich, CandTechSci; Kazakhstani engineer, political scientist and politician; b. 16 Sept. 1949, Kaztalovka, Kaztal Raion, Western Kazakhstan Oblast, Kazakh SSR, USSR; m. Bayan Sisenovna Jakupova;

two s.; ed Tselinograd Inst. of Civil Eng, Alma-Ata (Almatı) Higher Party School; Chief Engineer and Chief of PMK-811 Trust 'Uralskselstroi' No. 8 manufacturing works 1972–77; Chief Engineer, 'Uralskkolhozstroi' trust 1977–81; Deputy Chair. Oral (Uralsk) City Council 1981–83; Chair. Exec. Cttee, Industrial Dist Council of the People's Deputies of the City of Oral 1983–87; First Sec. CP of Kazakhstan of Leninsky Dist, City of Oral 1987–89; Chair. Exec. Cttee, Oral City Council 1989–93; Akim (Gov.), Western Kazakhstan Oblast 1993–2001; First Deputy Minister of Transport and Communications 2001–03; Deputy Head of Office of the Prime Minister and Rep. of the Govt in the Senate 2003–07; Deputy to the House of Reps (Majlis) 2007–, mem. Cttee on Foreign Affairs, Defence and Security 2007, mem. Nur Otan Khalyktyk Demokratyalyk Partiyasy (Light of the Fatherland People's Democratic Party) elected on the party list 2012–, Deputy Chair. (Deputy Speaker), Majlis 2012–14, Chair. (Speaker) 2014–16; mil. rank of Col; mem. Int. Acad. of Ecology; Corresp. mem. Eng Acad. of Kazakhstan; Academician, Nat. Acad. of Natural Sciences of the Repub. of Kazakhstan; Hon. Railway Worker (Kazakhstan); Hon. Builder (Kazakhstan); Order of Kurmet 1999, Order of Parasat 2009, Order of St Daniel, Second Degree (Russian Fed.). *Publications:* co-published three books on building materials. *Address:* Majlis (Assembly), 010000 Nur-Sultan, Parliament House, Kazakhstan (office). *Telephone:* (7172) 74-71-42 (office). *Fax:* (7172) 24-26-19 (office). *E-mail:* smimazh@parlam.kz (office). *Website:* www.parlam.kz (office).

JALADE EKEINDE, Omotola; Nigerian actress, singer and philanthropist; b. 7 Feb. 1978, Lagos; d. of Oluwashola Jalade and Oluwatoyin Jalade (née Amori Oguntade); m. Matthew Ekeinde; four c.; ed Yaba Coll. of Tech.; first acting role in Venom of Justice 1995 (Nollywood film debut); US debut in Hit the Floor (TV drama) 2013; WFP Amb. 2005–; f. Omotola Youth Empowerment Programme (charity); Amnesty Int. campaigner; columnist, OK! Nigeria Magazine; Best Actress, City People Awards for Excellence 2004, Best Actress in a Supporting Role, 1st Africa Movie Acad. Awards 2005, Screen Nation Awards Pan African Best Actress 2012, Film Actress Icon Black Entertainment Film Fashion Television and Arts Awards 2012, Popular Online Choice 2013 Nollywood Movies Awards 2013, Ebony Vanguard Award, Music Video and Screen Awards 2013, Female Entertainment Personality, City People Social Media Awards 2016, Best Actress, Nollywood Travel Film Festival 2016, Toronto Int. Nollywood Film Festival 2017. *Television:* Omotola: The Real Me (reality show) 2012–. *Recordings:* GBA 2005, Me, Myself, and Eyes 2010. *Films:* over 300 film appearances including Mortal Inheritance (The Movie Awards for Best Actress in English Speaking Movie and Best Actress Overall 1997) 1995, Scores to Settle 1998, Lost Kingdom 1999, Kosorogun 2002, Blood Sisters 2003, Die Another Day 2004, Games Women Play 2005, Sand in My Shoes 2007, Temple of Justice 2008, My Last Ambition 2009, Ije: The Journey 2010, Ties that Bind (Best Actress-Africa Collaboration, 2011 Ghana Movie Awards 2011) 2011, Last Flight to Abuja 2012, Hit The Floor 2013, Blood on the Lagoon 2014, Alter Ego 2017. *Address:* c/o Africa Magic Entertainment, 271 Oak Avenue, Randburg, South Africa (office). *Website:* www.omotola.tv (office).

JALAL, Masooda; Afghan paediatrician and fmr government official; b. 5 Jan. 1962, Gulbahar, Kapisa Prov.; d. of Alhaj Tellah Mohammad; m.; three c.; ed Gulbahar High School; began medical career as physician at Maiwand Hosp., then served at Kabul Medical Inst. and Ataturk Hosp.; pvt. practice in paediatrics 1988–92; worked for UNHCR then health adviser to WFP 1993–2004; presidential cand. in Afghanistan 2004, 2008; Minister of Women's Affairs 2004–06; documentary film maker 2009–; Outstanding Visionary Leadership Award, World Women's Leadership Congress 2014, Award for Outstanding Contribution to the Uplifting of Women, World CSR Congress, India 2015.

JALAL KHAN, Zubaida, MA; Pakistani politician; *Minister of Defence Production;* b. 31 Aug. 1959, Quetta, Balochistan; m. Changiz Khurd; ed Univ. of Balochistan; est. Girls Primary School, Mand, Balochistan 1982; volunteer, Family Planning Assen of Pakistan 1986–; Del. to World Conf. on Women, People's Repub. of China 1995; Minister of Social Welfare and Women's Affairs 1999–2000, of Educ. 2000–04, of Women's Devt, Social Welfare and Special Educ. 2004–07, of Defence Production 2018–; mem. Nat. Ass. 2008–13; travelled to Nepal, Repub. of Korea and Philippines to study primary educ. systems; mem. Balochistan Awami Party; Pride of Performance Award for Educ. 1993. *Address:* Ministry of Defence Production, Pakistan Secretariat II, Adam Jee Road, Rawalpindi, Pakistan (office). *Telephone:* (51) 9270929 (office). *Fax:* (51) 9270955 (office). *E-mail:* minister@modp.gov.pk (office). *Website:* www.modp.gov.pk (office).

JALALI, Ali Ahmad, BA, MA, PSC; Afghan/American academic and fmr government official; *Distinguished Professor, Near East South Asia Center for Strategic Studies (NESA);* b. 1940, Kabul; m.; one s. one d.; ed Afghan Mil. Univ., British Army Staff Coll., Acad. Frunze, Moscow, Naval Postgraduate School, USA; mil. studies in Afghanistan, UK and Turkey; army col, Afghan Armed Forces –1978; Dir Islamic Unity of Afghan Mujahidin and Sr Mil. Commdr during rebellion against Soviet occupation 1980s; obtained US citizenship 1987; Dir, Broadcaster and Head of Pashto and Persian Services, Voice of America (US govt-sponsored int. radio service), Washington, DC –2003; Minister of Interior Affairs (of Afghan Transitional Authority) 2003–04, (of Afghanistan Govt) 2004–05 (resgnd); currently Distinguished Prof., Near East South Asia Center for Strategic Studies (NESA), Washington, DC, also Researcher, Inst. for Nat. Strategic Studies; seven State Medals and Decorations, including Wazir Akbar Khan and Distinguished Service Medals, Royal Afghan Army, highest State Medal, Islamic Repub. of Afghanistan. *Publications include:* The Other Side of the Mountain (co-author) 1998, three-vol. mil. history of Afghanistan, several other books. *Address:* NESA Center for Strategic Studies, 2100 2nd Street, SW, Suite 4308, Washington, DC 20593, USA (office). *Telephone:* (202) 685-3794 (office); (202) 285-4701 (office). *Fax:* (202) 685-4999 (office). *E-mail:* JalaliA@ndu.edu (office). *Website:* nesa-center.org (office).

JALAN, Bimal, PhD; Indian economist and fmr politician; *Economist and Consultant, Associated Advisory Services Pvt. Ltd;* b. 3 July 1941, Calcutta (now Kolkata); ed Univ. of Calcutta, Univs of Cambridge and Oxford, UK; various positions at IMF, World Bank, Pearson Comm. 1964–70; Chief Economist, Industrial Credit and Investment Corpn of India 1970–73; Econ. Adviser, Ministry of Finance and of Industry, India 1973–79; Chief Econ. Adviser, Ministry of Finance 1981–88, Sec. for Banking 1985–88; Dir Econ. Affairs, Commonwealth Secr., London 1979–81; Exec. Dir IMF 1988–90, World Bank 1993–96; fmr Exec. Dir IBRD (India); Gov. Reserve Bank 1997–2003; nominated mem. Rajya Sabha (upper house of Parl.) 2003–09; fmr Chair. Centre for Devt Studies, Trivandrum, Indian Statistical Inst., Indira Gandhi Inst. of Devt Research, Nat. Council of Applied Econ. Research, Inst. of Economic Growth; currently Economist and Consultant, Associated Advisory Services Pvt. Ltd. *Publications include:* Essays in Development Policy 1975, Problems and Policies in Small Economies 1982, India's Economic Crisis: The Way Ahead 1991, The Indian Economy: Problems and Prospects 1993, India's Economic Policy: Preparing for the 21st Century 1997, India's Economy in the New Millennium – Selected Essays 2002, The Future of India: Politics, Economics and Governance 2005, India's Politics: A View from the Backbench 2007, Emerging India 2012, Politics Trumps Economics: The Interface of Economics and Politics in Contemporary India (Ed.) 2014, India: Priorities for the Future 2017. *Address:* 4 Babar Road, New Delhi 110 001, India (office). *Telephone:* (11) 41509184 (office). *Fax:* (11) 23711197 (office). *E-mail:* bimaljalan@gmail.com (home). *Website:* www.bimaljalan.com.

JALEEL, Mohamed, MA; Maldivian politician; b. 19 Nov. 1959, Malé; s. of Ahmed Jaleel and Mariyam Waheeda; fmr Minister of State for Finance and Treasury, Minister of Finance and Treasury 2004–05, Minister of Econ. Devt and Trade 2005–08 (resgnd); Vice-Gov., then Gov. Maldives Monetary Authority. *Address:* M. Faamudheyrige, Orchid Magu, Malé, Maldives (home). *Telephone:* 3323888 (home). *Fax:* 3324432 (home).

JALEEL, Maj.-Gen. (retd) Moosa Ali, MSc; Maldivian army officer (retd), diplomatist and government official; b. 26 June 1960, Malé; m. Jazeela Ibrahim; one c.; four c. from previous marriages; ed Singapore Armed Forces Training Inst., Singapore, US Army Infantry School, USA, Royal Marines Commando School, England, Nat. Defence Coll., India, Univ. of Madras, India; fmr Commdr of all front-line infantry units in Maldives Nat. Defence Force (MNDF) including Rapid Reaction Force, Quick Reaction Force III, Quick Reaction Force I, Special Protection Group; fmr Dir-Gen. Maldivian Coast Guard; Vice-Chief, MNDF –2008, Chief of Nat. Defence Force 2008–12 (retd); High Commr to Pakistan 2014–15; Minister of Defence and Nat. Security Jan.–Nov. 2015; numerous service medals and ribbons including Huravee Ran Medal for Exceptional Bravery, Presidential Medal, Distinguished Service Medal, Royal Marines Commando Badge.

JALILI, Saeed, PhD; Iranian government official; b. 6 Sept. 1965, Mashhad; m.; one c.; ed Univ. of Science and Industry, Tehran; veteran of the 1980–88 Iran-Iraq war; Dir-Gen. Office of Supreme Leader Ayatollah Ali Khamenei 2001–05; adviser to Pres. Mahmoud Ahmadinejad 2005–; Deputy Foreign Minister for European and American Affairs 2005–07; Sec., Shura-ye Ali-ye Amniyyat-e Melli (Supreme Nat. Security Council) 2007–13, role includes being Iran's chief nuclear negotiator; unsuccessful cand. in presidential election 2013.

JALLAD, Farid al-; Palestinian lawyer, judge and politician; Head of Arab Lawyers Cttee in the W Bank; apptd to High Judiciary Council by the late Pres. Arafat 2003; Deputy Minister of Justice –2005, Minister of Justice 2005; Chief Justice 2009–14; Pres. Palestinian Bar Assen; mem. Palestinian Legal Group, Inst. for the Study and Devt of Legal Systems (ISDLS), Calif.

JALLOW, Hassan Bubacar, LLB, LLM; Gambian lawyer and fmr UN official; *Chief Justice of the Gambia;* b. 14 Aug. 1951, Bansang; m.; five c.; ed Univ. of Dar es Salaam, Tanzania, Nigerian Law School, Univ. Coll., London; State Attorney, Attorney-Gen.'s Chamber, Gambia 1976–82, Solicitor-Gen. 1982–84, Attorney-Gen. and Minister of Justice 1984–94, Judge, Supreme Court 1998–2002; Judge, Appeals Chamber, Special Court for Sierra Leone 2002; Prosecutor, UN Int. Criminal Tribunal for Rwanda 2003–15, carried out judicial evaluation for Yugoslavia; Chief Prosecutor, Int. Criminal Tribunal for Rwanda (UN-ICTR) 2003–15; Chief Prosecutor, UN Mechanism for Int. Criminal Tribunals (MICT) 2012–16; Chief Justice of the Gambia 2016–; legal expert for OAU and Commonwealth; Chair. Commonwealth Governmental Working Group of Experts in Human Rights; worked on drafting and conclusion of African Charter on Human Rights, adopted 1981; Commdr, Nat. Order of the Repub. of The Gambia. *Publications include:* Law, Justice and Governance – Selected Papers 1998, The Law of Evidence in The Gambia 1998, The Law of the African Charter on Human and Peoples' Rights, Introduction to the Zikr of the Tidjanniya Tariqat, Journey for Justice 2012. *Address:* Supreme Court of The Gambia: Law Courts, Independence Dr., Banjul, The Gambia (office). *Telephone:* 4227380 (office). *Fax:* 4224286 (office). *E-mail:* judiciary@gov.gm (office). *Website:* www.gov.gm/judiciary (office).

JALOLOV, Abdulkhafiz, DPhil; Uzbekistani politician and philosopher; b. 1 June 1947, Namangan; m. Jalolova Zarifahon; two s. one d.; ed Tashkent State Univ.; mil. service 1969–71; Lecturer of Philosophy, Tashkent Univ. 1971–72; researcher, Philosophy and Law Inst., Uzbekistan Acad. of Sciences 1972–77, Dir 1993–2001; Chair. of Philosophy, State Inst. of Physical Culture 1977–81; Asst Prof., Deputy Dir Social Science Lecturers' Skills Level Raising Inst., Tashkent State Univ. 1981–93; Second Sec. of Gen. Council, People's Democratic Party of Uzbekistan (PDP) 1991–94, First Sec. 1994–2003; unsuccessful PDP cand. in presidential elections 2000. *Publications include:* Mustakillik Mas'uliyati 1996, Istikbol Ufklari 1998, Demokratiya: mashakkatli surur 2000.

JAMAL, Ahmad; American composer and pianist; b. 2 July 1930, Pittsburgh, Pa; (divorced); one d.; ed pvt. master-classes with Mary Cardwell Dawson and James Miller; George Hudson Orchestra nat. tour 1949; mem. The Four Strings 1949; accompanist to The Caldwells 1950; trio The Three Strings 1950–; numerous concert tours, including with Philip Morris; exclusive Steinway artist 1960s–; appeared on film soundtracks of M*A*S*H 1970, Bridges of Madison County 1995, The Wolf Of Wall Street; Duke Ellington Fellow, Yale Univ.; Officier, Ordre des Arts et des Lettres 2007; numerous awards, including NEA American Jazz Master, Pittsburgh Mellon Jazz Festival dedication 1994, elected into DownBeat Reader's Poll Hall of Fame 2011. *Television:* The Sound of Jazz 1962. *Compositions include:* six works for Asai Quartet 1994, New Rhumba, Ahmad's Blues, Night Mist Blues, Extensions, The Awakening, Excerpts From The Blues, Tranquility, Manhattan Reflections. *Recordings include:* Poinciana, But Not For Me (including Bridges of Madison County) 1995, Essence Part 1 (Django D'Or Award, Paris) 1996, Olympia 2000, Live in Baalbeck (DVD) 2003, After Fajr 2005, It's Magic 2008, A Quiet Time 2010, Blue Moon: The New York Session/The Paris Concert 2012, Saturday Morning 2013. *Address:* c/o Ellora Management, 74B Interlaken Road, Lakeville,

CT 06039, USA (office). *Telephone:* (860) 435-1305 (office). *Fax:* (860) 435-9916 (office). *E-mail:* elloramanagement@aol.com (office). *Website:* www.ahmadjamal.net.

JAMALI, Mir Zafarullah Khan, MA; Pakistani politician; b. 1 Jan. 1944, Rowjhan, Balochistan; s. of Mir Zafarullah Khan Jamali; m.; four s. one d.; ed Murree Royal Coll., Aitchison Coll., Lahore, Punjab Univ.; tribal elder from South West Prov. of Balochistan; joined Pakistan People's Party 1970s; elected mem. Prov. Ass., Balochistan 1977; fmr Minister for Food and Information; Minister for Food and Agric. 1982, for Local Govt, for Water and Power 1985, for Railways 1986; mem. Nat. Ass. 1985–89, –2018; Chief Minister for Balochistan 1988–89; apptd Rep. to UN 1991; elected ind. mem. Nat. Ass. 1993–2004, mem. Cabinet 1997–2004; Senator for Balochistan 1997–2006; Sr mem. Pakistan Muslim League –1999; Prime Minister of Pakistan 2002–04 (resgnd); fmr mem. Nat. Security Council; fmr mem. Pakistan Muslim League—Quaid-e-Azam; mem. Pakistan Tehreek-e-Insaf 2018–. *Leisure interest:* hockey.

JAMBON, Jan; Belgian politician; b. 26 April 1960, Genk; mem. Nieuw-Vlaamse Alliantie (N-VA—New Flemish Alliance), mem. Bd; mem. Chamber of Reps 2007–, Parl. Group Leader 2008–; Councillor, Brasschaat 2007–13, Mayor of Brasschaat 2013–; Deputy Prime Minister and Minister of the Interior, in charge of Urban and Public Buildings 2014–18. *Address:* Sparrenlaan 25, 2930 Brasschaat, Belgium (home). *E-mail:* jan.jambon@n-va.be. *Website:* www.janjambon.be.

JAMBREK, Peter, MA, PhD; Slovenian judge, academic and author; b. 14 Jan. 1940, Ljubljana; ed Grammar School, Ljubljana, Ljubljana Univ. and Univ. of Chicago, USA; Prof., Dept of Theory of Law and State, Ljubljana; Judge, Constitutional Court of Repub. of Slovenia 1990, Pres. 1991–95; Judge, European Court of Human Rights 1993–99; Dean, Grad. School of Govt and European Affairs, Univ. of Ljubljana 2003; mem. Venice Comm. 2003; Co-founder and Chair. Zbor za republiko (Rally for the Republic) 2004–08; Head of Constitutional Law Dept, European Faculty of Law, Nova Gorica; Rector, Kolegji ESLG (European School of Law and Governance), Prishtina, Kosovo. *Publications:* Development and Social Change in Yugoslavia: Crises and Perspectives of Building a Nation 1975, Participation as a Human Right and as a Means for the Exercise of Human Rights 1982, Contributions for the Slovenian Constitution 1988, Constitutional Democracy 1992. *Address:* College ESLG, Veternik p.n, Te Genci Rol, 10000 Prishtina, Kosovo; Ceste v Megre 4, 64260 Bled, Slovenia (home). *Telephone:* (64) 77449 (home). *E-mail:* peter.jambrek@eukos.org. *Website:* evro-pf.si/en.

JAMES, Clive Vivian Leopold, CBE, AM, FRSL; Australian writer, broadcaster, journalist and poet; b. (Vivian James), 7 Oct. 1939, Kogarah, Sydney, NSW; s. of Albert A. James and Minora M. Darke; m. Prue Shaw; two d.; ed Sydney Technical High School, Sydney Univ. and Pembroke Coll., Cambridge; Asst Ed. Morning Herald, Sydney 1961; Pres. of Footlights at Cambridge, UK; TV critic, The Observer 1972–82, feature writer 1972–; Dir Watchmaker Productions 1994–; as lyricist for Pete Atkin, record albums include Beware of the Beautiful Stranger, Driving Through Mythical America, A King at Nightfall, The Road of Silk, Secret Drinker, Live Libel, The Master of the Revels; also songbook, A First Folio (with Pete Atkin); Patron Burma Campaign UK; Dr hc (Sydney), (East Anglia); Philip Hodgins Memorial Medal for Literature 2003, Orwell Prize for Lifetime Achievement in Journalism 2008. *Television series include:* Cinema, Up Sunday, So It Goes, A Question of Sex, Saturday Night People, Clive James on Television, The Late Clive James, The Late Show with Clive James, Saturday Night Clive, Fame in the 20th Century, Sunday Night Clive, The Clive James Show, Clive James on Safari; numerous TV documentaries including Clive James Meets Katharine Hepburn 1986, Clive James Meets Jane Fonda, Clive James Meets Mel Gibson 1998, Clive James Meets the Supermodels 1998, Postcard series 1989–. *Publications:* non-fiction: The Metropolitan Critic 1974, The Fate of Felicity Fark in the Land of the Media 1975, Peregrine Prykke's Pilgrimage through the London Literary World 1976, Britannia Bright's Bewilderment in the Wilderness of Westminster 1976, Visions Before Midnight 1977, At the Pillars of Hercules 1979, First Reactions 1980, The Crystal Bucket 1981, Charles Charming's Challenges on the Pathway to the Throne 1981, From the Land of Shadows 1982, Glued to the Box 1982, Flying Visits 1984, Snakecharmers in Texas 1988, The Dreaming Swimmer 1992, Clive James on Television 1993, Fame 1993, The Speaker in Ground Zero 1999, Even as We Speak (essays) 2000, Reliable Essays 2001, The Meaning of Recognition: New Essays 2001–2005 2005, North Face of Soho 2006, Alone in the Café 2007, Cultural Amnesia 2007, The Revolt of the Pendulum 2009, The Blaze of Obscurity: The TV Years 2009, The Revolt of the Pendulum: Essays 2005–2008 2010, A Point of View 2011, Latest Readings 2015, Play All 2016; novels: Brilliant Creatures 1983, The Remake 1987, The Silver Castle 1996; autobiography: Unreliable Memoirs 1980, Falling Towards England: Unreliable Memoirs Vol. II 1985, Unreliable Memoirs Vol. III 1990, May Week was in June 1990, Brrm! Brrm! or The Man from Japan or Perfume at Anchorage 1991, Fame in the 20th Century 1993, The Metropolitan Critic 1993; poetry: Fanmail 1977, Poem of the Year 1983, Other Passports: Poems 1958–85 1986, The Book of My Enemy: Collected Verse 1958–2003 2004, Opal Sunset: Selected Poems 1958–2008 2008, Angels Over Elsinore 2008, Sentenced to Life 2015, Injury Time 2017; trans.: The Divine Comedy 2013; contribs to numerous publs including Commentary, Encounter, Listener, London Review of Books, Nation, New Review, New Statesman, New York Review of Books, New Yorker, TLS. *Leisure interest:* dancing the tango. *Address:* c/o United Agents, 12–26 Lexington Street, London, W1F 0LE, England (office). *Telephone:* (20) 3214-0800 (office). *Fax:* (20) 3214-0801 (office). *E-mail:* info@unitedagents.co.uk (office). *Website:* unitedagents.co.uk (office); www.clivejames.com.

JAMES, Deborah Lee, BA; American government official; b. 1957, New Jersey; ed Duke Univ., Columbia Univ.; Intern, Presidential Man. Program, Washington, DC 1981; Professional staff mem., House of Reps Armed Services Cttee 1983–93; Asst Sec. of Defense for Reserve Affairs, US Dept of Defense 1993–98; Vice-Pres., Int. Operations & Marketing, United Technologies Corpn 1998–2000; Exec. Vice-Pres. and COO, Business Execs for Nat. Security (BENS) 2000–01; Sr Vice-Pres. and Dir, Homeland Security, Science Applications Int. Corpn (SAIC) 2002, Sr Vice-Pres., C4IT Business Unit 2004–10, Exec. Vice-Pres., Communications & Govt Affairs 2010–13, Pres., Technical & Eng Sector 2013; Sec., Dept of Air Force, US Dept of Defense 2013–17; mem. US Dept of Defense Advisory Cttee on Women in the Services.

JAMES, Edison Chenfil, MSc; Dominican agronomist and politician; b. 18 Oct. 1943, Marigot; s. of David James and Patricia James; m.; one s. two d.; ed North East London Polytechnic, Univ. of Reading, Imperial Coll., Univ. of London, UK; teacher, St Mary's Acad. Sept.–Dec. 1973; agronomist, Ministry of Agric. 1974–76; Farm Improvement Officer, Caribbean Devt Bank (attached to Dominica Agricultural and Industrial Devt Bank) 1976–80, Loans Officer 1976–80; Co-ordinator Coconut Rehabilitation and Devt Project; Chief Exec. (Gen. Man.) Dominica Banana Marketing Corpn 1980–87; Adviser to Bd of Dirs Windward Islands Banana Growers Asscn 1980–87; Man. Dir Agricultural Man. Corpn Ltd 1987–95; Leader Dominica United Workers Party and Parl. Leader of the Opposition 1990–95, 2000–2013; Prime Minister of Dominica 1995–2000, also Minister of Legal and Foreign Affairs and Labour; leading negotiator with several int. aid agencies; served on numerous public service cttees. *Leisure interests:* cricket, football, int. affairs, politics, table tennis. *Address:* c/o Dominica United Workers Party, 37 Cork Street, Roseau, Dominica.

JAMES, Geraldine, OBE; British actress; b. (Geraldine Thomas), 6 July 1950, Maidenhead, Berks., England; d. of Gerald Trevor Thomas and Annabella Doogan Thomas; m. Joseph Sebastian Blatchley 1986; one d.; ed Downe House, Newbury, Drama Centre London Ltd; Royal TV Soc. Award for Best Actress 1978, Venice Film Festival Award for Best Actress 1989, Drama Desk (New York) Award for Best Actress 1990. *Stage appearances:* repertory, Chester 1972–74, Exeter 1974–75, Coventry 1975, Passion of Dracula 1978, The White Devil 1981, Turning Over 1984, When I was a Girl I used to Scream and Shout 1987, Cymbeline 1988, Merchant of Venice 1989 (and Broadway 1990), Death and the Maiden 1992, Lysistrata 1993, Hedda Gabler 1993, Give Me Your Answer Do 1998, Faith Healer 2001–02, The Cherry Orchard 2003, Home 2004, The UN Inspector 2005, Victory 2009, Hamlet 2009, The Seagull 2011, '13' 2011, Lawrence After Arabia 2016. *Films include:* Night Cruiser 1978, Bloody Kids 1979, Sweet William 1980, Gandhi 1982, The Storm 1985, The Wolves of Willoughby Chase 1989, The Tall Guy 1989, If Looks Could Kill 1990, Prince of Shadows 1991, Teen Agent 1991, The Bridge 1992, Words on the Window Pane 1994, No Worries 1994, Moll Flanders 1996, The Man Who Knew Too Little 1997, The Luzhin Defence 2000, The Testimony of Taliesin Jones 2000, All Forgotten 2001, Tom & Thomas 2002, An Angel for May 2002, Calendar Girls 2003, The Fever 2004, Sherlock Holmes 2009, Alice in Wonderland 2010, Made in Dagenham 2010, Arthur 2011, Sherlock Holmes: A Game of Shadows 2011, The Girl with the Dragon Tattoo 2011, The Farmer's Wife (short) 2012, Diana 2013, Our Robot Overlords 2014, 45 Years 2015, Leavey 2015, Rogue One: A Star Wars Story 2016, Daphne 2016, Animal Shadows 2016. *Radio:* The Hours 2000, King Lear 2001, Whale Music 2003, Richard III 2003, The Raj Quartet 2004, The Waves 2007, Dombey and Son 2007, Sacred Hearts 2009, The Carhullan Army 2010, Memory of Gold 2012. *Television films include:* Dummy 1977, Time and the Conways 1985 Freedom Fighter 1988, She's Been Away 1989, The Doll's House 1991, Ex 1991, Doggin' Around 1994, The Healer 1994, Over Here 1996, Rebecca 1997, See Saw 1997, Crime and Punishment 2002, An Angel for May 2002, The Hound of the Baskervilles 2002, Hearts of Gold 2003, State of Play 2003, Hans Christian Andersen: My Life as a Fairy Tale 2003, A Harlot's Progress 2006, Northanger Abbey 2007, Caught in a Trap 2008, Phoo Action 2008, Heist 2008, Legacy 2013. *Television series include:* The Sweeney 1976, Crown Court 1978, Play for Today – Who's Who 1979, Love Among the Artists (mini-series) 1979, Shoestring 1979, The History Man 1981, Chains 1982, The Jewel in the Crown (mini-series) 1984, Blott on the Landscape (mini-series) 1985, Echoes (mini-series) 1988, Screen One 1989–92, Stanley and the Women (mini-series) 1991, Inspector Morse 1991, In Suspicious Circumstances 1994, Kavanagh QC 1995, 1997, Band of Gold 1995–97, Gold 1997, Drovers' Gold (mini-series) 1997, Seesaw (mini-series) 1998, The Sins (mini-series) 2000, White Teeth 2002, State of Play (mini-series) 2003, He Knew He Was Right (mini-series) 2004, Little Britain 2004, Agatha Christie: Poirot – After the Funeral 2006, Jane Hall 2006, Ancient Rome: The Rise and Fall of an Empire 2006, The Battle for Rome (mini-series) 2006, The Amazing Mrs Pritchard 2006, The Time of Your Life 2007, Fairy Tales (mini-series) 2008, City of Vice 2008, The Last Enemy (mini-series) 2008, Little Britain USA 2008, Midsomer Murders – Fit for Murder 2011, Planet of the Apemen: Battle for Earth (narrator) 2011, Playhouse Presents – The Other Woman 2012, 13 Steps Down 2012, Utopia (mini-series) 2013–14, Black Work 2015, The Five (mini-series) 2016, Uncle (comedy) 2016, Anne (series) 2017. *Address:* c/o Julian Belfrage Associates, 3rd Floor, 9 Argyll Street, London, W1F 7TG, England (office). *Telephone:* (20) 7287-8544 (office). *Fax:* (20) 7287-8832 (office). *E-mail:* email@julianbelfrage.co.uk (office).

JAMES, Kirani; Grenadian sprinter; b. 1 Sept. 1992, St George's; ed Univ. of Alabama, USA; took up athletics at the age of twelve; gold medal, 400m Caribbean Free Trade Asscn (CARIFTA) Games, Providenciales 2007; silver medal, 400m World Youth Championships, Ostrava 2007; gold medal, 200m, 400m, CARIFTA Games, Basseterre 2008; silver medal, 400m World Junior Championships, Bydgoszcz 2008; gold medal, 400m Commonwealth Youth Games, Pune 2008; gold medal, 400m, bronze medal, 4×400m relay CARIFTA Games, Vieux Fort 2009; gold medal, 200m, 400m World Youth Championships, Brixen 2009; gold medal, 400m Pan American Junior Championships, Port-of-Spain 2009; gold medal, 200m, 400m CARIFTA, George Town 2010; gold medal, 200m Pan American Junior Championships, Miramar 2010; gold medal, 400m World Championships, Daegu 2011; gold medal, 400m Olympic Games, London 2012; silver medal, 400m Olympic Games, Rio 2016; Sportsman of the Year 2009, 2010, Austin Sealy Trophy 2009. *Address:* c/o Grenada Olympic Committee, PO Box 370, Woolwich Road, St. George's, Grenada.

JAMES, LeBron Raymone; American professional basketball player; b. 30 Dec. 1984, Akron, Ohio; s. of Gloria James; m. Savannah Brinson 2013; two s.; ed St Vincent-St Mary High School, Akron; selected at age 18 with first overall pick in 2003 NBA (Nat. Basketball Asscn) draft by Cleveland Cavaliers, becoming only second high school player taken at the number one draft position 2003–10; signed as free agent with Miami Heat 2010–14 (won NBA Championship 2012–13), with Cleveland Cavaliers 2014–; played in bronze medal-winning Team USA at Olympic Games, Athens 2004; played in bronze medal-winning US Nat. Team at FIBA World Championships, Japan 2006; played in gold medal-winning US Nat. Team at FIBA Americas Championships, Las Vegas 2007; played in gold medal-winning Team USA at Olympic Games, Beijing 2008, London 2012; named as one of three capts for US Men's Basketball Nat. Team for 2006–08; Vice-Pres. Nat.

Basketball Players Asscn 2015–; acquired minority stake in Liverpool Football Club, UK 2011; f. LeBron James Family Foundation; named Ohio's Mr Basketball and selected to the USA Today All-USA First Team (three times) 2001–03, named Gatorade Nat. Boys Basketball Player of the Year 2001–02, Rookie of the Year 2003–04, NBA All-Star 2005–16, All-NBA selection First Team: 2006, 2008, 2009, 2010, 2011, 2012, Second Team: 2005, 2007, The Sporting News NBA Co-MVP 2005–06, NBA All-Star Game MVP (Most Valuable Player) 2006, 2008, Best Male Athlete Award, BET Award for Best Male Athlete 2006, 2007, NBA Scoring Champion 2008, NBA MVP (Most Valuable Player) 2009–10, 2012–13, NBA All-Defensive First Team: 2009, 2010, 2011, 2012, NBA Finals MVP 2012–13, BET Award for Sportsman of the Year 2018. *Publication:* Shooting Stars (with Buzz Bissinger) 2009. *Address:* Cleveland Cavaliers, One Center Court, Cleveland, OH 44115-4001, USA. *Website:* www.nba.com/cavaliers; www.lebronjames.com.

JAMES, Michael Leonard, (Ruth Carrington, Michael Hartland), MBE, FRSA; British government official, writer and broadcaster; *President, Kennaway House Trust;* b. 7 Feb. 1941; m. 1975; two d.; ed Christ's Coll., Cambridge; entered govt service (GCHQ) 1963; Pvt. Sec. to Rt Hon. Jennie Lee, Minister for the Arts 1966–68; DES 1968–71; Planning Unit of Rt Hon. Margaret Thatcher, Sec. of State for Educ. and Science 1971–73, Asst Sec. 1973; Deputy Chief Scientific Officer 1974; served in London, Milan, Paris, Tokyo 1973–78; Dir, IAEA Vienna 1978–83; Adviser, Int. Relations to Comm. of the European Union, Brussels 1983–85; Chair. Civil Service Selection Bds 1983–93; Gov. Colyton Grammar School 1985–90, Sidmouth Community Coll. 1988–2004, Chair. Bd of Govs 1998–2001; Chair. Gen. Medical Council Fitness to Practise Panels 2000–06; Founder and Chair. Kennaway House Trust 2001–11, Pres. 2011–; mem. Immigration Appeal Tribunal 1987–2005, Asylum and Immigration Tribunal 2005–12; feature writer and book reviewer, The Times (thriller critic 1989–90, travel corresp. 1993–), Daily Telegraph (thriller critic 1993–2000), Sunday Times, Guardian; Hon. Fellow, Univ. of Exeter 1985–. *TV and radio include:* Seven Steps to Treason (BBC Radio 4) 1990, Sonja's Report (ITV documentary) 1990, Masterspy: interviews with KGB defector Oleg Gordievsky (BBC Radio 4) 1991. *Publications:* Internationalization to Prevent the Spread of Nuclear Weapons (co-author) 1980; novels as Michael Hartland: Down Among the Dead Men 1983, Seven Steps to Treason (South West Arts Literary Award) 1985, The Third Betrayal 1986, Frontier of Fear 1989, The Year of the Scorpion 1991, The Verdict of Us All (short stories) (co-author) 2006; other: Masters of Crime – Lionel Davidson and Dick Francis 2006; novel as Ruth Carrington: Dead Fish 1998. *Address:* Branscombe, Devon, EX12 3BH, England (home). *E-mail:* michaelhartland@live.co.uk (office).

JAMES, Renée J., BA, MBA; American computer industry executive; *President, Intel Corporation;* ed Univ. of Oregon; joined Intel through co.'s acquisition of Bell Technologies in 1987, served as Chief of Staff to fmr Intel CEO Andy Grove, later Dir and COO Intel Online Services, held product R&D leadership positions and as Chair. of Intel's software subsidiaries, Havok, McAfee and Wind River, Exec. Vice-Pres. and Gen. Man. Software and Services Group –2013, Pres. Intel Corpn and, with CEO, part of Intel's two-person Exec. Office 2013–; Dir (non-exec.) Vodafone Group Plc; Ind. Dir, VMware Inc.; mem. C200. *Address:* Intel Corporation, 2200 Mission College Boulevard, Santa Clara, CA 95052-8119, USA (office). *Telephone:* (408) 765-8080 (office). *Fax:* (408) 765-9904 (office). *E-mail:* info@intel.com (office). *Website:* www.intel.com (office).

JAMIR, Senayangba Chubatoshi, BA, LLB; Indian politician; b. 17 Oct. 1931, Ungma, Nagaland; s. of Shri Senayangba; m. Imkonglemla Jamir 1959; three s. two d.; ed Univ. of Allahabad; Pres. Student Christian Movt 1954–57; mem. Interim Body of Nagaland, then Jt Sec. Naga People's Convention; Vice-Chair. Mokokchung Town Cttee 1959–60; MP 1961–70, MP Rajya Sabha 1987–89; Parl. Sec., Ministry of External Affairs, Govt of India 1961–67; Union Deputy Minister of Railways, of Labour and Rehabilitation, of Community Devt and Co-operation, Food and Agric. 1968–70; elected mem. to Nagaland Legis. Ass. 1971–73, re-elected mem. from Aonglenden Constituency 1974; subsequently apptd Minister of Finance, Revenue and Border Affairs; re-elected 1977 and apptd Deputy Chief Minister in United Democratic Front Ministry; Chief Minister of ULP Ministry April 1980; resgnd when Naga Nat. Democratic Party Ministry came to power June 1980; Leader of Opposition Congress (I) in State Legis. Ass. 1980–82; elected from 26 Aonglenden Constituency, Gen. Elections 1982; unanimously elected Leader Congress (I) Legislature Party, Chief Minister Nagaland 1982–86, 1989–92, 1993–2003; Gov. of Goa 2004–08, of Maharashtra 2008–10, also of Gujarat July–Nov. 2009, of Odisha 2013–18; Lokshree Award, Inst. of Econ. Studies 1989, Hind Rattan Award, All India Nat. Unity Conf., Rajiv Gandhi Memorial Award, Rajiv Gandhi Birthday Celebration Cttee 1993, Indira Gandhi Smriti Puraskar, West Bengal Journalist Asscn 1994, Rajiv Gandhi Excellence Award 1994, Arch of Asia Award, Nat. Citizens Award 1996, Rashtriya Ekta Puraskar, Cttee for Nat. Integration 1997, Nat. Integration Award, Forum for Unity and Integrity 1998. *Publication:* Reminiscences of Correspondence (co-author). *Leisure interests:* reading, badminton.

JÄMIŞEV, Bolat Bïdaxmetulı, PhD; Kazakhstani banker and politician; b. 28 June 1957, Almaty, Kazakh SSR, USSR; m.; two s.; ed Kazakh Inst. of Agric.; First Vice-Minister of Finance 1999–2001, 2002–03; Vice-Minister of Internal Affairs 2001–02; Deputy Chair. Nat. Bank of Kazakhstan 2003–04; Chair. Agency for Regulation and Oversight of Financial Orgs 2004–06; Deputy Chair. Exec. Bd, Russian-Kazakh Eurasian Devt Bank 2006–07; Minister of Finance 2007–13, of Regional Devt 2013–14.

JAMMEH, Col Yahya A. J. J.; Gambian fmr head of state and fmr army officer; b. 25 May 1965, Kanilai Village, Foni Kansala Dist, Western Div.; m. Zineb Yahya-Jammeh (née Soumah); one d.; ed Gambia High School; joined fmr Gambia Nat. Gendarmerie as pvt. 1984; with Special Intervention Unit, Gambia Nat. Army 1984–86, Sergeant 1986, Escort Training Instructor, Gendarmerie Training School 1986–89, Cadet Officer 1987, commissioned 1989, Second Lt 1989, in charge of Presidential Escort, Presidential Guards 1989–90, CO Mobile Gendarmerie Jan.–June 1991, Mil. Police Unit June–Aug. 1991, Lt 1992, Commdr Gambia Nat. Army Mil. Police Aug.–Nov. 1992, Capt. 1994, Col 1996; became Chair. Armed Forces Provisional Ruling Council, Head of State 1994–; retd from army 1996; elected Pres. of The Gambia 1996–16, also Minister of Defence, Agric. and Energy; Chair., Pres. Alliance for Patriotic Reorientation and Construction (APRC) 1996–; Chair. Inter-states Cttee for Control of Drought in the Sahel 1997–2000; 1st Vice-Chair. Org. of the Islamic Conf. 2000–; Grand Commdr, Order of Al-Fatah (Libya) 1995; Order of Distinction (Liberia) 2000; Grand Master of the Repub. of The Gambia 2001; Pan-African Humanitarian Award 1997 and numerous other awards. *Leisure interests:* playing tennis, soccer, hunting, reading, correspondence, driving and riding motorcycles, music, films and animal rearing.

JANABIL; Chinese party official; *Chairman, Xinjiang Uygur Autonomous Regional Committee, Chinese People's Political Consultative Conference;* b. April 1934, Habahe (Kaba) Co., Xinjiang Uygur Autonomous Region; s. of Simagul Janabil and Ajikhan Janabil; m. Zubila Janabil 1955; two s. two d.; joined CCP 1953; Vice-Chair. Revolutionary Cttee, Xinjiang Autonomous Region 1975–79; Chair. Revolutionary Cttee and First Sec. CCP Cttee, Ili Autonomous Kazakh Pref. 1975–80; Deputy Sec. CCP Cttee, Xinjiang 1977–83, Sec. 1983–85; Vice-Chair. Xinjiang 1979–83; Deputy Sec. then Sec. CCP 4th Xinjiang Uyghur Autonomous Regional Cttee 1985–; Chair. CPPCC 7th Xinjiang Uygur Autonomous Regional Cttee 1993–; Alt. mem. 10th CCP Cen. Cttee 1972–77, 11th CCP Cen. Cttee 1977–82, 12th CCP Cen. Cttee 1982–87, 13th Cen. Cttee 1987–92, 14th Cen. Cttee 1992–97; mem. 8th CPPCC Nat. Cttee 1993–98, 9th CPPCC Nat. Cttee 1998–2003; Del., 15th CCP Nat. Congress 1997–2002; Pres. Xinjiang Br. Futurology Soc. 1980. *Address:* c/o Xinjiang Autonomous Regional Chinese Communist Party, Urumqi, Xinjiang, People's Republic of China.

JANDA, Krystyna; Polish actress and film and theatre director; b. 18 Dec. 1952, Starachowice; m.; two s. one d.; ed State Higher School of Drama, Warsaw; actress, Atheneum Theatre, Warsaw 1976–88, Powszechny Theatre, Warsaw 1988–; opened Theatre Polonia, Warsaw 2005; acting on TV and performing in cabaret; numerous awards in Poland and abroad; over 50 leading roles in classic and contemporary plays and over 50 leading roles in film and TV; Best Actress 40th Int. Film Festival, San Sebastián, Golden Duck Award 2007. *Films include:* Man of Marble 1976, Without Anaesthetic 1978, The Border 1978, The Conductor 1979, Die Grünen Vögel 1979, Golem 1979, Mephisto 1980, War Between Worlds 1980, Man of Iron 1981, Espion lève toi 1981, Interrogation 1982, Ce fut un bel été 1982, Bella Donna 1983, Gluth 1983, Der Bulle und das Mädchen 1984, Vertige 1985, My Mother's Lovers 1985, Laputa 1986, Short Film About Killing 1987, II Decalogue, V Decalogue 1988, Ownership 1989, Polish Kitchen 1991, Relieved of the Life 1992, As 1995, Pestka (actress and Dir) 1996, Mother's Mother 1996, Unwritten Principles 1997, Last Chapter 1997, David Weissen 1999, Żółtyszalik (Yellow Muffler) 2000, Przedwiośnie 2000, Życie jako śmiertelna choroba prienoszona drogą płciową (Life as a Fatal Sexually Transmitted Disease) 2000, Call of the Toad 2005, Tatarak 2009, Reverse 2009, Elles 2011. *Stage appearances include:* Bal manekinów 1974, Edukacja Rity 1984, Z życia glist 1984, Biała bluzka 1987, Medea 1988, Shirley Valentine 1990, Kobieta zawiedziona 1996, Kotka na gorącym blaszanym dachu 1997, Maria Callas – Lekcja śpiewu (Song Lesson) 1997, Harry i ja (Harry and Me) 1998, Opowiadania zebrane (Collected Stories) 2001, Siedem grzechów głównych 2001, Mała Steinberg (Spoonface Steinberg) 2001, Kto się boi Virginii Woolf (Who's Afraid of Virginia Woolf) 2002, Mewa 2003, Czego nie Widać 2003, Janosik albo na Szkle Malowane 2004, Namiętność 2005, Lekcje stepowania 2005. *Plays directed include:* Hedda Gabler 1999, Związek otwarty (Friendship Opened) 2000, Zazdrość (Jealousy) 2001. *TV series:* Mierzejewska 1989, From Time to Time 1999, Niania 2007, Bez tajemnic 2011.

JANDOSOV, Oraz, MEcon; Kazakhstani economist and politician; *Director, RAKURS Center for Economic Analysis;* b. 26 Oct. 1961, Almaty; m. Gulnara Ussubakunova; three c.; ed Lomonosov Moscow State Univ.; Research Assoc., Inst. of Econs, Acad. of Sciences of Kazakhstan 1987–90; Adviser, then Head of Div., Supreme Econ. Council under Pres. of Kazakhstan 1991–92; First Deputy Minister for the Economy and Chair. Nat. Agency on Foreign Investment 1993–94; First Deputy Gov. Bank of Kazakhstan 1994–96, Gov. 1996–98; First Deputy Prime Minister and Chair. State Cttee on Investment 1998–99, Deputy Prime Minister and Minister of Finance Jan.–Oct. 1999; Pres. KEGOC (Kazakhstan Electricity Grid Operating Co.) 1999–2000; Deputy Prime Minister 2000–01 (resgnd following protest by Prime Minister Kasimzhomart Tokayev regarding his membership of Democratic Choice of Kazakhstan (DCK) movt which he co-founded in 2001); Chair. Kazakhstan's Asscn of Financial Insts 2001–02; Asst to Pres. of Kazakhstan on econ. and financial issues Jan.–June 2003; Chair. Agency for Regulation of Natural Monopolies and Protection of Competition 2003–04; Founder and Co-Chair. Ak Zhol (Bright Path) (later Naghyz Ak Zhol—True Bright Path) Democratic Party of Kazakhstan 2002–08; Dir RAKURS Center for Econ. Analysis 2008–; mem. Presidium, Atameken, Nat. Chamber of Entrepreneurs 2013–; Order of Kurmet. *Leisure interests:* tennis, soccer, skiing. *Address:* RAKURS Centre for Economic Analysis, 97B Dostyk Avenue, Office 7/2, Almaty 050051, Kazakhstan (office). *Telephone:* (727) 264-61-55 (office). *E-mail:* ojandosov@cear.kz (office).

JANDROKOVIĆ, Gordan; Croatian politician and diplomatist; *President, Sabor (Ass.);* b. 2 Aug. 1967, Bjelovar, Socialist Repub. of Croatia, Socialist Fed. Repub. of Yugoslavia; m.; three c.; ed Faculties of Civil Eng and Political Science, Univ. of Zagreb, Diplomatic School, Ministry of Foreign Affairs, The Netherlands Inst. of Int. Relations, Clingendael, Erasmus Universiteit, Rotterdam; pvt. construction co. 1989–94; with Ministry of Foreign Affairs 1994–2000; Man. Stanić Co., Zagreb 2000–02; Gen. Man. Beming Co., Bjelovar 2002–03; mem. Hrvatska Demokratska Zajednica (HDZ—Croatian Democratic Union) 1992–, Chair. HDZ Cttee for Small and Medium-Size Enterprises 2002–, HDZ Cttee for Bjelovar-Bilogora Co. 2003–, mem. HDZ Presidency 2004–; mem. Ass. 2003–, Chair. Ass. Cttee for the Economy, Devt and Reconstruction 2003–04, Ass. Foreign Policy Cttee 2004–07, Head of Ass. Del. to Croatia-EU Jt Ass. Cttee 2004–07, Deputy Chair. European Integration Cttee, also European Affairs Cttee 2011–15, Pres. European Affairs Cttee 2016–, Pres. Sabor (Ass.) 2017–; Minister of Foreign Affairs and European Integration 2008–11, also Deputy Prime Minister 2010–11; Man. Ed. The Witnesses to History series 1997–2002. *Leisure interests:* tennis, football, reading. *Address:* Sabor (Assembly), 10000 Zagreb, Trg sv. Marka 6, Croatia (office). *Telephone:* (1) 6303225 (office). *Fax:* (1) 6303226 (office). *E-mail:* europski.poslovi@sabor.hr (office). *Website:* www.sabor.hr (office).

JANELIDZE, Mikheil, BA, MBA; Georgian government official and business executive; b. 29 March 1981; m.; one d.; ed Tbilisi State Univ., Diplomatic Acad. of Ministry of Foreign Affairs of Russian Fed., Grenoble Grad. School of Business, France, Caucasus School of Business, Tbilisi; Intern, Ministry of Foreign Affairs 2001–03, Chief Expert 2003–04, Business Devt Man., Int. Project Support Services

2006–07; Project Man., Wissol Petroleum Georgia, Wissol Group Feb.–Sept. 2007, Man. Dir, Vellagio, Wissol Group 2007–08; Founder-Partner, Janelidze & Co. Jan.–Oct. 2009; Dir Dept for Foreign Trade and Int. Econ. Relations, Ministry of Economy and Sustainable Devt 2009–11, Deputy Minister 2011–15; First Deputy Minister of Foreign Affairs Sept.–Dec. 2015, Minister of Foreign Affairs Dec. 2015–18, Deputy Prime Minister 2017–18. *Address:* c/o Ministry of Foreign Affairs, 0108 Tbilisi, Sh. Chitadze 4, Georgia (office).

JANELIDZE, Vice-Col Mindia; Georgian lawyer and politician; b. 26 July 1978; m. Ekaterine Janelidze; three c.; ed Acad. of the Ministry of Interior Affairs; Officer of the Operative Service, Foreign Intelligence Service 2000–04, Chief of Section 2004–07, Deputy Div. Chief 2007–08, Head of Div. of Information Directorate 2008–12, Head of Counter-Intelligence Dept 2010–12, Dir Counter-Intelligence Dept, Ministry of Internal Affairs 2012–14, Sec., State Security and Crisis Man. Council Jan.–Nov. 2014; Minister of Defence 2014–15; Order of Honour.

JANEWAY, Richard, AB, MD; American physician, academic and medical school administrator; *Executive Vice-President Emeritus for Health Affairs, Wake Forest University;* b. 12 Feb. 1933, Los Angeles, Calif.; s. of VanZandt Janeway and Grace Ellen Bell Janeway; m. Katherine Esmond Pillsbury 1955; one s. two d.; ed Colgate Univ., Univ. of Pennsylvania School of Medicine; Instructor in Neurology, Bowman Gray School of Medicine of Wake Forest Univ. (now Wake Forest Univ. School of Medicine) 1966–67, Asst Prof. 1967–70, Assoc. Prof. 1970–71, Prof. 1971–, Dean 1971–85, Exec. Dean 1985–94, Vice-Pres. for Health Affairs 1983–90, Exec. Vice-Pres. 1990–97, Univ. Prof. of Medicine and Man. 1997–, Exec. Vice-Pres. Emer. for Health Affairs 1997–; mem. Winston-Salem Foundation Bd 1994–2002 (Chair. 1997–98); Dir Idealliance 1999–; Chair. Asscn of American Medical Colls. 1984–85; mem. Bd of Dirs BB&T Corpn 1995–2003 (fmr Chair.), S. Nat. Corpn 1989–95; mem. Nat. Asscn for Biomedical Research 1993–96, Americans for Medical Progress Inc. 1993–97; mem. Bd of Trustees Colgate Univ., 1988–95, Winston-Salem State Univ. 1991–95; mem. Inst. of Medicine of NAS, American Medical Asscn, American Heart Asscn, American Neurological Asscn, Soc. for Neuroscience, Soc. of Medical Admins, American Clinical and Climatological Asscn; Fellow, American Acad. of Neurology; Life Fellow, American Coll. of Physicians; John and Mary R. Markle Scholar in Academic Medicine 1968–73, Distinguished Service mem. Asscn of American Medical Colls 1991, Medallion of Merit, Wake Forest Univ. 2000, Maroon Citation, Colgate Univ. 2004. *Publications:* one monograph, 16 book chapters, 39 original articles, 16 abstracts, nine editorials, eight invited comments, one patent. *Leisure interests:* golf, photography, gardening, travel. *Address:* Wake Forest University, School of Medicine, Medical Center Blvd., Winston-Salem, NC 27157 (office); 2710 Old Town Club Road, Winston-Salem, NC 27106, USA (home). *Telephone:* (336) 716-3840 (office); (336) 727-7537 (home). *Fax:* (336) 773-0082. *E-mail:* djaneway@wfubmc .edu (office); rjaneway@triad.rr.com.

JANG, Ha Sung, PhD; South Korean academic; *Professor of Finance and Dean of the Business School, Korea University;* b. 19 Sept. 1953, Kwangju; ed Wharton School, Univ. of Pennsylvania, USA; joined in pro-democracy protests early 1970s; moved to USA to study for doctorate 1980s; taught finance at Wharton School and Univ. of Houston; returned to S Korea 1990; special adviser to Lazard's Korea Corp. Governance Fund; int. adviser to Chinese Security Regulatory Comm.; currently Prof. and Dean of the Business School, Korea Univ.; Exec. Dir Asian Inst. of Corp. Governance; Chair. Inst. of Dirs in E Asia Network; helped est. Center for Good Corp. Governance 2001; Research Assoc., European Corp. Governance Inst. 2013; runs advocacy group, People's Solidarity for Participatory Democracy, to attempt to make S Korea's chaebol (large conglomerates) more accountable to minority shareholders, has won several milestone court victories; Int. Corp. Governance Network Excellence in Corp. Governance Award, Financial Analyst Journal Graham and Dodd Award, Maekyung Business Daily Maekyung Economist Award, Korea Univ. Granite Teaching Award, Korea Univ. Business School Prof. of the Year Award. *Publications include:* numerous articles in professional journals. *Address:* Korea University Business School, Room 404 in KUBS Main Building, 5 Anam-dong, Seongbuk-Gu, Seoul, 136-701 Republic of Korea (office). *Telephone:* (2) 3290-1929 (office). *Fax:* (2) 929-3405 (office). *E-mail:* jangya@korea .ac.kr (office); jangya@chol.com. *Website:* biz.korea.ac.kr (office).

JANG, Gen. Jong-nam; North Korean army officer and government official; fmr Commdr, First Corps of the Korean People's Army; attained rank of Col-Gen. 2011, Gen. 2012; Minister of the People's Armed Forces 2013–14.

JANG, Seok-hyo, BA, MBA; South Korean business executive; *President and CEO, Korea Gas Corporation (KOGAS);* b. 27 Oct. 1957; ed Jung-Dong High School, Seoul, In-Ha Univ., Univ. of Minnesota, USA; joined Korea Gas Corpn (KOGAS) 1983, Vice-Pres. LNG Purchase Div. 2003–07, Acting Exec. Vice-Pres. Marketing Div. July–Sept. 2007, Exec. Vice-Pres. Marketing Div. 2007–08, Exec. Vice-Pres. Resources Div. 2008–10, Exec. Vice-Pres. Resources Business Div. 2010–11, Pres. and CEO Tong Yeong Tug Co. Ltd 2011–13, Pres. and CEO Korea Gas Corpn 2013–. *Address:* Korea Gas Corporation, 93 Dolmaro, 215 Jeongja-dong, Bundang-gu, Seongnam, Gyeonggi-do, 463-754, Republic of Korea (office). *Telephone:* (31) 710-0114 (office). *Fax:* (31) 710-0117 (office). *E-mail:* kogasmaster@ kogas.or.kr (office). *Website:* www.kogas.or.kr (office).

JANICOT, Daniel Claude Emmanuel, LenD; French international official; *President, ProCultura;* b. 20 May 1948, Neuilly; s. of François-Xavier Janicot and Antoinette Mauxion; m. 2nd Catherine Lachenal 1991; one s.; two d. from previous marriage; ed Ecole Nat. d'Admin, Inst. d'Etudes Politiques and Faculté de Droit, Paris; Auditeur, Conseil d'Etat 1975–, Deputy Sec.-Gen. 1978–82, Maître des requêtes 1979; Maître de Conférences, Instituts d'Etudes Politiques, Paris and Bordeaux and Ecole Nat. des Ponts et Chaussées; mem. Admin. Council, Public Information Library, Beaubourg 1979; Del.-Gen. American Center 1980–90; Vice-Pres. Bibliothèque Nationale 1981; Maître de séminaire, Ecole Nat. d'Admin 1982–83; Del.-Gen. Union Centrale des Arts Décoratifs 1982–86; Special Adviser Office of Dir-Gen. of UNESCO 1990–91, Dir of Exec. Office of Dir-Gen. 1991–94, Asst Dir-Gen. 1994–99, Chair., French Nat. Commission 2014–; apptd mem. Conseil d'état 1995; Chair. Bd, Centre Nat. d'Art Contemporain de Grenoble 1995–; Vice-Chair. Bd, Institut Français de Gestion 1996–; Dir Musée des arts premiers; mem. Bd of Dirs Artcurial Holding SA; Co-founder and Chair. Artcurial Prize 2006–; Founder and Pres. ProCultura 2013–; Hon. State Counsellor; Chevalier, Ordre nat. du Mérite, Ordre des Arts et Lettres, Légion d'honneur. *Website:* unesco.delegfrance.org.

JANION, Maria, PhD; Polish academic; *Lecturer, Institute of Literary Research, Polish Academy of Sciences;* b. 24 Dec. 1926, Mońki; d. of Cyprian Janion and Ludwika Kudryk; ed Łódź Univ., Warsaw Univ.; researcher, Inst. of Literary Research, Polish Acad. of Sciences (PAN), Warsaw 1946–96, mem. Scientific Bd 1957–, Lecturer, Inst. of Philosophy and Sociology School of Social Research, PAN 1992–, mem. Cttee of Literary Sciences 1996–; Asst, Warsaw Univ. 1951–52, Lecturer 1981–87, apptd. Prof. 1987; researcher, Higher Pedagogic School, Gdańsk 1957–69, Prof. 1963–70; Prof., Inst. of Polish Studies, Gdańsk Univ. 1970–81, 1984–90; Ed.-in-Chief Historia i teoria literatury Studia (series) 1968–78, Bibliteka Romanistyczna (series) 1978–; Ordinary mem. Polish Acad. of Arts and Sciences 1990–; Corresp. mem. PAN 1991, mem. 1998–; mem. jury, Nike Literature Award 1997–, Chair. 2000–; Ordre national du Mérite 2012; Dr hc (Gdańsk Univ.) 1994; Alfred Jurzykowski Foundation Award 1980, Culture Foundation Great Prize for the Year 1998, Chair. of Council of Ministers Award 2001, Kazimierz Wyka Award 2001, Gloria Artis 2007. *Publications include:* Romantism—Studies of Ideas and Style 1969, Gorączka romantyczna (Romantic Fever) 1975, Romantyzm i historia (with M. Żmigrodzka) 1978, Renewing of Meanings 1980, Transgresje (seven-vol. series, also co-ed.) 1981–88, Wobec zła 1989, Życie Pośmiertne Konrada Wallenroda 1990, Kobiety i duch inności (Women and the Spirit of Strangeness) 1996, Płacz generała. Eseje o wojnie 1998, Do Europy tak, ale razem z naszymi umarłymi (To Europe, Yes, but with Our Dead) 2000, Żyjąc tracimy życie. Niepokojące tematy egzystencji 2001, Niesamowita słowiańszczyzna 2006. *Address:* Institute of Literary Research, Polish Academy of Sciences, 00-330 Warsaw, ul. Nowy Świat 72, Poland (office). *Telephone:* (22) 6572764 (office). *Fax:* (22) 8269945 (office). *E-mail:* ibadlit@ibl.waw.pl (office). *Website:* www.ibl.waw.pl (office).

JANKOVIĆ, Jelena; Serbian professional tennis player; b. 28 Feb. 1985, Belgrade, SFR Yugoslavia; d. of Veselin Janković and Snežana Janković; ed French diplomatic school in Belgrade, 'Megatrend' Coll., Belgrade; plays right-handed with two-handed backhand; first played in practice at Tennis Club of Red Star Belgrade Nov. 1994; first tournament: reached semifinals in Nat. Yugoslavian Championship for children up to 10 years old 1995; won on Limon Bowl Tournament in Italy; moved to USA and joined Nick Bolitieri's Acad.; turned professional 2000; Grand Slam winner aged 16, winning Australian Open, Melbourne and becoming No. 1 Jr in the world 2001; also played in finals of US Open and Orange Bowl; played in finals at Virginia tournament 2002, at China Open 2013, at BNP Paribas Open, Indian Wells 2015; in quarter finals at tournament in Stanford 2002; won at Int. Tennis Fed. (ITF) tournament in Dubai 2003, won first Women's Tennis Asscn (WTA) title at tournament in Budapest 2004; WTA titles: Budapest 2004, Auckland 2007, Charleston 2007, Rome 2007, 2008, Birmingham 2007, Beijing 2008, Stuttgart 2008, Moscow 2008, Marbella 2009; doubles titles: Birmingham (with Na Li) 2006; mixed doubles titles: Wimbledon (with Jamie Murray) 2007; first played for Serbia and Montenegro nat. team in Fed. Cup aged 16; first official match for nat. team on tournament in Mursia 2001; undefeated at first Afro-European group of Fed. Cup 2004; only tennis player to represent Serbia and Montenegro at Olympic Games, Athens 2004; partnered Novak Djokovic to play for Serbia in Hopman Cup (exhibition team event sanctioned by ITF) 2008; UNICEF Nat. Amb. for Serbia 2007–; Best Tennis Player in Serbia and Montenegro 2004. *Film:* starred in Jelenin svet (Jelena's World), a documentary about her life 2008. *Leisure interests:* travelling, reading, watching TV. *E-mail:* info@jelenajankovic.net (office); info@jj -jelenajankovic.com (office). *Website:* www.jelenajankovic.net (office); www.jj -jelenajankovic.com (office).

JANKOVIĆ, Zoran, BEcons; Slovenian business executive and politician; *Mayor of Ljubljana;* b. 1 Jan. 1953, Saraorci, Smederevo, Socialist Repub. of Serbia, Socialist Fed. Repub. of Yugoslavia; m. Mija Janković; two s.; ed Univ. of Ljubljana; Sales Man. Mercator Investa 1979–84, Dir 1984–88; Vice-Pres. Emona SOZD and Acting Gen. Man. Emona VPS 1988–90; f. Electa Co. 1990, Dir 1990–97; Pres. and CEO Mercator d.d. 1997–2005; Mayor of Ljubljana 2006–11, 2012–; f. Pozitivna Slovenija (PS—Positive Slovenia), Pres. 2011–13, 2014–; mem. Državni Zbor (Nat. Ass.) 2011–; designated as Prime Minister Jan. 2012, but appointment rejected by parl.; fmr Chair. Supervisory Bd Pokojninska Družba A. d.d. (pension fund); mem. Exec. Bd Mans Asscn; mem. Exec. Bd Chamber of Commerce and Industry of Slovenia; Pres. Alumni Club of Faculty of Econs, Univ. of Ljubljana; Pres. Slovenian Handball Fed. 1996–2004, Hon. Pres. 2004–; Hon. Pres. Handball Club Krim Mercator; Hon. Citizen of Chengdu, China 2011; Order of Friendship, Russian Fed. 2017. *Address:* Office of the Mayor, 1000 Ljubljana, Mestni trg 1 (office); Pozitivna Slovenija (Positive Slovenia), 1000 Ljubljana, Dalmatinova 2, Slovenia. *Telephone:* (1) 3061278 (office); (1) 3069915. *Fax:* (1) 3061214 (office). *E-mail:* zoran.jankovic@ljubljana.si (office); info@pozitivnaslovenija.si. *Website:* www.ljubljana.si/en/municipality/mayor (office); www.pozitivnaslovenija.si.

JANKOWITSCH, Peter, DDL; Austrian lawyer, politician and diplomatist; *President, International Academy of Astronautics;* b. 10 July 1933, Vienna; s. of Karl Jankowitsch and Gertrude Jankowitsch (née Ladstaetter); m. 1st Odette Prevor 1962 (divorced); one s.; m. 2nd Silvia Lahner 2001; ed Vienna Univ. and The Hague Acad. of Int. Law; fmr lawyer; joined Foreign Service 1957, worked in Int. Law Dept; Pvt. Sec., Cabinet of Minister of Foreign Affairs 1959–62; posted to London 1962–64; Chargé d'affaires, Dakar, Senegal 1964–66; Head of Office of Bruno Kreisky, Chair. Austrian Socialist Party 1967; Chief of Cabinet of Fed. Chancellor (Kreisky) 1970–72; Perm. Rep. to UN 1972–78; Chair. UN Cttee on Peaceful Uses of Outer Space 1972–91; Vice-Chair. of Bd, Int. Energy Agency 1979–83; Rep. for Austria to UN Security Council 1973–74, Pres. Security Council 1973, Vice-Pres. 29th Gen. Ass.; Vice-Pres. 7th Special Session of Gen. Ass. 1975; mem. UN Security Council Mission to Zambia 1973; Perm. Rep. to OECD 1978–82; Deputy Perm. Under-Sec., Chief of Cabinet, Fed. Ministry of Foreign Affairs 1982–83; Fed. Minister for Foreign Affairs 1986–87; mem. Austrian Nat. Ass. (Nationalrat) 1983–90 (Chair. Foreign Relations Cttee 1987–90), 1992–93; Minister of State for Integration and Devt Co-operation 1990–92; Perm. Rep. to OECD and ESA 1993–98; Chair. OECD Devt Centre 1994–98; Chair. Jt Cttee European Parl.–Austrian Parl.; Sec.-Gen. Franco-Austrian Centre for Rapprochement in Europe 1998–2015; Int. Sec. Social Democratic Party of Austria 1983–90; Chair.

Human Rights Cttee Socialist Int. 1987–97, Vice-Chair. Socialist Int. Cttee on Econ. Affairs 1997–99; Pres. Cttee of Parliamentarians of EFTA 1989–90; mem. Bd of Austrian Inst. for Int. Politics, Vienna Inst. for Devt, Int. Acad. of Astronautics 1998– (Pres. 2015–), Bd of Dirs of Franco-Austrian Centre 2015–; Chair. Austrian Air and Space Agency 1998–; Pres. Austrian Nat. Cttee for Unispace 1999, Austria-Viet Nam Soc. 1999–, Jerusalem Foundation, Austria 2002–; Assoc. Ed. Acta Astronomica 2003–; Special Envoy Austrian Fed. Govt 2006–09; Vice-Pres. Austrian Foreign Policy and UN Soc. 2008–; mem. Advisory Bd, European Space Policy Inst.; Hon. Pres. Austrian Soc. for European Policy 1996–; Hon. mem. Bd, Int. Inst. of Space Law; Hon. Pres. Austria-Namibia Soc. 2008; Commdr, Légion d'honneur and numerous other Austrian and foreign decorations; Allan D. Emil Memorial Award for Int. Co-operation in Astronautics 1981, Social Sciences Award, Int. Acad. of Astronautics 2001. *Publications:* Kreisky's Era in Austrian Foreign Policy (co-ed. with E. Bielka and H. Thalberg) 1982, Red Markings–International (co-ed. with H. Fischer) 1984, The European Integration Process and Neutral Austria 1994, Austria and the Non-Aligned 2002; and papers and articles on Austria and on econ. and political devt of the Third World; contrib. to Wörterbuch des Völkerrechts 1960. *Leisure interests:* history and baroque music. *Address:* Franco-Austrian Centre for Rapprochement in Europe, Salzgries 19, 1010 Vienna (office); Mariahilferstrasse 57–59/12, 1060 Vienna, Austria. *Telephone:* (1) 5338927 (office); (1) 5855227 (home). *Fax:* (1) 5338927-10 (office). *E-mail:* peter.jankowitsch@oefz.at (office); peter.jankowitsch@chello.at (home). *Website:* www.peter-jankowitsch.net (home); www.oefz.at (office).

JANKULOSKA, Gordana, MA; Macedonian lawyer and politician; b. 12 Oct. 1975, Ohrid; ed SS Cyril and Methodius Univ., Skopje and Univ. of Kent, UK; early career as lawyer in pvt. law firm 1999–2000; Head of Cabinet, Minister of Finance 2000–02; Gen. Sec. Vnatrešno-Makedonska Revolucionerna Organizacija-Demokratska Partija za Makedonsko Nacionalno Edinstvo (VMRO-DPMNE—Internal Macedonian Revolutionary Org.-Democratic Party for Macedonian Nat. Unity) 2004–06; Minister of Internal Affairs 2006–15 (resgnd); Special Achievement in Law Award, Univ. of Kent, UK 2004. *Address:* Vnatrešno-Makedonska Revolucionerna Organizacija-Demokratska Partija za Makedonsko Nacionalno Edinstvo (Internal Macedonian Revolutionary Organization-Democratic Party for Macedonian National Unity), 1000 Skopje, Makedonija 17A, North Macedonia (office). *Telephone:* (2) 3215550 (office). *Fax:* (2) 3215551 (office). *E-mail:* contact@vmro-dpmne.org.mk (office). *Website:* vmro-dpmne.org.mk (office).

JANNEH, Abdoulie, MA; Gambian fmr UN official and foundation executive; *Executive Director, Liaison with Governments and Institutions in Africa, Mo Ibrahim Foundation;* ed Fourah Bay Coll., Sierra Leone, Univs of Nottingham and Bradford, UK, Econ. Devt Inst., World Bank (Project Man.); joined UNDP from Govt of Gambia as Programme Adviser 1979, Adviser, Office to Combat Desertification and Drought (UNSO), Burkina Faso 1979–80, Programme Officer, UNSO, New York 1981–83, Deputy Resident Rep. in Guinea 1984–86, Sierra Leone 1987–89, Deputy Exec. Sec. UN Capital Devt Fund 1990–93, Resident Coordinator and Resident Rep., Niger 1993–96, Ghana 1996–99, reassigned to New York to lead Transition Team 1999, Asst Sec.-Gen. and UNDP Regional Dir for Africa 2000–05, Under-Sec.-Gen. and Exec. Sec. UN Econ. Comm. for Africa, Addis Ababa, Ethiopia 2005–12; currently mem. Bd and Exec. Dir, Liaison with Govts and Insts in Africa, Mo Ibrahim Foundation; Chair. African Governance Inst.; mem. Bd, Coalition for Dialogue on Africa (CoDA), Pax Africana, Africa Forum, amongst others; mem. Bd of Recommendation, Nudge Global Leadership Challenge 2014–. *Address:* Mo Ibrahim Foundation, 35 Portman Square, London, W1H 6LR, England (office); Mo Ibrahim Foundation, 38 Yoff Virage, Dakar, Senegal (office). *E-mail:* info@moibrahimfoundation.org (office). *Website:* www.moibrahimfoundation.org (office).

JANOWITZ, Gundula; Austrian singer (soprano); b. 2 Aug. 1937, Berlin, Germany; d. of Theodor Janowitz and Else Janowitz (née Neumann); m.; one d.; ed Acad. of Music and Performing Arts, Graz; debut with Vienna State Opera 1960; perm. mem. Deutsche Oper, Berlin 1966; sang with Metropolitan Opera, New York 1967, Salzburg Festival 1968–81, Teatro Colón, Buenos Aires 1970, Munich State Opera 1971, Grand Opera, Paris 73, Covent Garden Opera 1976, La Scala 1978; concerts in cities throughout the world, appearances at Bayreuth, Aix-en-Provence, Glyndebourne, Spoleto, Salzburg, Munich Festivals; Opera Dir at Graz 1990–91; mem. Vienna State Opera, Deutsche Oper, Berlin; mem. Main Prize Jury, BBC Cardiff Singer of the World Competition 2003, 2005, 2007; Hon. Mem. Vienna State Opera, Acad. of Music, Graz, RAM, London. *Leisure interest:* modern literature.

JANOWSKI, Marek; German conductor; b. 18 Feb. 1939, Warsaw, Poland; ed Cologne Musikhochschule and studied in Siena, Italy; fmrly Asst Conductor in Aachen, Cologne and Düsseldorf opera houses; Music Dir, Freiburg and Dortmund Operas 1973–79; Artistic Adviser and Conductor, Royal Liverpool Philharmonic Orchestra 1983–86; Music Dir and Chief Conductor Orchestre Philharmonique de Radio France 1984–2000; Chief Conductor Gurzenich-Orchester, Cologne 1986–90; Artistic Dir Monte Carlo Philharmonic Orchestra 1999, Music Dir and Chief Conductor 2000–05; Prin. Conductor and Artistic Dir Dresden Philharmonic Orchestra 2001–03; Chief Conductor and Artistic Dir Rundfunk Sinfonieorchester Berlin 2002–16; Artistic and Music Dir Orchestre de la Suisse-Romande, Geneva 2005–12; apptd Endowed Guest Conductor Chair, Pittsburgh Symphony Orchestra 2005; regular guest conductor in Paris, Berlin, Hamburg, Cologne and Munich opera houses; has also conducted at Metropolitan Opera (New York), Chicago, San Francisco (American opera debut 1983), Dresden and Vienna State Operas, Teatro Colón (Buenos Aires), Orange Festival (France) and Théâtre du Châtelet (Paris); has conducted concerts with Berlin Philharmonic, Chicago Symphony, London Symphony Orchestra, Philharmonia, NHK (Tokyo), Dresden Staatskapelle, Boston Symphony Orchestra, Stockholm Philharmonic and BBC Symphony Orchestra. *Recordings include:* Wagner's Der Ring des Nibelungen (with the Dresden Staatskapelle), Weber's Euryanthe, Strauss's Die Schweigsame Frau, Penderecki's The Devils of Loudun, Korngold's Violanta, Hindemith's Die Harmonie der Welt, Bruckner Symphonies No. 4 and No. 6 (with Orchestre Philharmonique de Radio France), Roussel four symphonies (with Orchestre Philharmonique de Radio France) (Diapason D'Or 1996), Weber's Oberon 1997, Strauss's Four Last Songs (Gramophone magazine Editor's Choice Award 2002). *Address:* c/o Jessica Ford, Intermusica Artists' Management Ltd, 36 Graham Street, Crystal Wharf, London, N1 8GJ, England (office). *Telephone:* (20) 7608-9900 (office). *Fax:* (20) 7490-3263 (office). *E-mail:* jford@intermusica.co.uk (office). *Website:* www.intermusica.co.uk (office).

JANŠA, Janez; Slovenian politician; *President, Slovenska Demokratska Stranka (Slovenian Democratic Party);* b. (Ivan Janša), 17 Sept. 1958, Ljubljana, Socialist Repub. of Slovenia, Socialist Fed. Repub. of Yugoslavia; one s. one d. with Silva Predalič; m. Urška Bačovnik 2009; two s.; ed Univ. of Ljubljana; intern at Republican Secr. for Defence; apptd Pres. Cttee for Basic People's Defence and Social Self-Protection, Alliance of Socialist Youth of Slovenia 1982; wrote paper critical of conditions within Yugoslav People's Army labelled counter-revolutionary 1983, indicted by mil. prosecutor 1985; served as Minister of Defence in Slovenia 1990–94, 2000; Pres. Slovenska Demokratska Stranka (Slovenian Democratic Party) 1993–; Prime Minister 2004–08, 2012–13; Minister of Finance 2012–13; sentenced to two years in prison on corruption charges June 2013, ruling confirmed by higher court April 2014, began prison term in Dob Prison June 2014, ruling unanimously overturned by Constitutional Court of Slovenia April 2015. *Publications include:* Podružbljanje varnosti in obrambe (The Socialization of Security and Defence) (ed.) 1984, Stane Kavčič, Dnevnik in spomini (The Memoirs of Stane Kavčič) (co-ed. with Igor Bavčar) 1988, Na svoji strani (On One's Own Side) (collection of articles) 1988, Premiki: nastajanje in obramba slovenske države 1988–1992 (The Making of the Slovenian State 1988–1992), The Collapse of Yugoslavia 1994, Okopi: pot slovenske države 1991–1994 (Trenches: The Evolution of the Slovenian State 1991–1994) 1994, Sedem let pozneje (Seven Years Later) 1994, Osem let pozneje (Eight Years Later) (with Ivan Borštner and David Tasić) 1995, Dvajset let pozneje, Okopi II (Twenty Years Later, Trenches II) 2014; hundreds of articles, commentaries, essays and scientific discussions; also several poems and literary compositions. *Leisure interests:* mountaineering, golf, football, skiing, snowboarding. *Address:* Slovenska Demokratska Stranka (Slovenian Democratic Party), 1000 Ljubljana, Trstenjakova 8, Slovenia (office). *Telephone:* (1) 4345450 (office). *Fax:* (1) 4345452 (office). *E-mail:* tajnistvo@sds.si (office). *Website:* www.sds.si (office).

JANSONS, Mariss; Latvian conductor; *Chief Conductor, Bavarian Radio Symphony Orchestra;* b. 14 Jan. 1943, Riga; s. of Arvīds Jansons and Iraīda Jansons; m. Irina Jansons 1967; one d.; ed studied with father, Leningrad Conservatory with N. Rabinovich, Vienna Conservatory with Hans Swarovsky, Salzburg with von Karajan; Prin. Guest Conductor, Leningrad (now St Petersburg) Philharmonic Orchestra; Chief Conductor, Oslo Philharmonic 1979–2002; Guest Conductor, Welsh Symphony Orchestra 1985–88; Salzburg debut with the Vienna Philharmonic 1994; Prin. Guest Conductor, London Philharmonic Orchestra 1992–97; Prof. of Conducting, St Petersburg Conservatory 1995–; Music Dir Pittsburgh Symphony Orchestra 1995, Chief Conductor 1997–2002; Chief Conductor, Symphonieorchester des Bayerischen Rundfunks (Bavarian Radio Symphony Orchestra) and Bavarian Radio Choir 2003–; Chief Conductor, Royal Concertgebouw Orchestra 2004–15; has appeared with Baltimore Symphony Orchestra, Berlin Philharmonic, Boston Symphony Orchestra, Chicago Symphony Orchestra, Cleveland Orchestra, London Philharmonia Orchestra, New York Philharmonic, Philadelphia Orchestra, among others; Commdr with Star, Royal Norwegian Order of Merit 1994, Austrian Cross of Honor for Scholarship and Art 2008, Bavarian Order of Maximilian 2010, Knight, Order of the Netherlands Lion 2013, Commdr des Arts et des Lettres (France) 2015; winner, Herbert von Karajan Competition 1971, Anders Jahre Cultural Prize (Norway), RSFSR People's Artist 1986, Hans von Bülow Medal, Berlin Philharmonic 2003, Royal Philharmonic Soc. Conductor of the Year Award 2004, Classical Music Award for Artist of the Year, MIDEM, Cannes 2006, ECHO-Klassik Conductor of the Year 2007, Ernst von Siemens Music Prize 2013, Latvia Great Music Award 2015, Royal Philharmonic Soc. Gold Medal 2017, Léonie Sonning Music Prize 2018, Salzburg Easter Festival Herbert von Karajan Prize 2019. *Recordings include:* Shostakovich Symphony No. 7 (BBC Music Magazine Orchestral Award 2007) 2006, Prokofiev: Symphony No. 5 In B-Flat Major, Op. 100 2016. *Leisure interests:* arts, theatre, films, sports. *Address:* Opus 3 Artists, 470 Park Avenue South, 9th Floor North, New York, NY 10016, USA (office). *Telephone:* (212) 584-7500 (office). *Fax:* (646) 300-8200 (office). *E-mail:* info@opus3artists.com (office). *Website:* www.opus3artists.com (office).

JANSSEN, Baron Daniel, IngLic, MBA; Belgian business executive; b. 15 April 1936, Brussels; s. of Baron Charles-Emmanuel Janssen and Marie-Anne Janssen (née Boël); brother of Paul-Emmanuel Janssen; m. Thérèse Bracht 1970; three s.; ed Univ. of Brussels, Harvard Univ., USA; Asst Sec., Euratom Comm., Brussels 1959–60; Prof., Brussels Univ. 1965–71; Vice-Chair. of Bd UCB 1962–84, Chair. Exec. Cttee 1975–84 (now Hon. Vice-Chair. and Hon. Chair. of Exec. Cttee); Chair. of Exec. Cttee Solvay & Cie (now Solvay) SA 1986–98, Chair. Bd of Dirs 1998–2006, now Hon. Chair. Bd of Dirs Solvay Group; Chair. and CEO Financière de Tubize SA, Brussels; Chair. Fed. of Belgian Enterprises 1981–84; mem. Club of Rome 1968–87; mem. Bd of Dirs Brussels Univ. 1969–70, Inst. pour l'Encouragement de la Recherche Scientifique dans l'Industrie et l'Agriculture (IRSIA) 1971–77 (Vice-Chair. 1974–77), Belgian Fed. of Chemical Industries 1972–76 (Chair. 1976–79), Fortis NV 1999–2006; mem. European Cttee for R & D, EEC 1974–79; Grand Cordon of the Order of the Rising Sun (Japan), 2006; Alumni Achievement Award, Harvard Business School. *Leisure interests:* tennis, skiing, shooting. *Address:* c/o Solvay, Rue de Ransbeek 310, 1120 Bruxelles, Belgium.

JANSSEN, Baron Paul-Emmanuel, LLD, MBA; Belgian banker; b. 22 Feb. 1931, Brussels; s. of Baron Charles-Emmanuel Janssen and Marie-Anne Janssen (née Boël); brother of Daniel Janssen; m. Cecilia Löfgren; one s. one d.; ed Univ. Libre de Bruxelles, Harvard Business School, USA; fmr Chair. Générale de Banque SA (then Hon. Chair.), Belgian Banking Asscn; fmr Dir Solvay, Solvac, Boël, Atlas Copco, European Banking Fed., Belgian Fed. of Enterprises; Hon. Pres. les Amis de l'institut Bordet 1997–2013; Admin., Atlas Copco 1995–2001; Commdr Ordre de la Couronne, Commdr Ordre de Léopold, Officier Légion d'honneur. *Leisure interests:* riding, hunting, forestry, music. *Address:* Le Bonnier, 79 rue Gaston, Bary B, 1310 La Hulpe, Belgium (home). *Telephone:* (2) 652-03-50 (home). *Fax:* (2) 652-07-38 (home). *E-mail:* lebonnier@skynet.be.

JANSSON, Mats; Swedish business executive; b. 1951, Kolsva; m.; three c.; ed Univ. of Örebro; began career with ICA (Swedish food retailer), held positions of increasing responsibility and served as Pres. ICA Detaljhandel and Deputy CEO and Chair. of the Group 1990–94; CEO Catena/Bilia 1994–99; CEO Karl Fazor Oy

1999–2000; CEO Axfood 2000–05; Pres. and CEO Axel Johnson AB 2005–06; Pres. and CEO SAS 2006–10; Chair. Delhaize Group 2012–16, Ahold Delhaize (following merger of Ahold and Delhaize Group) 2016–18; Ind. Dir Danske Bank; fmr Dir Axfood, Mekonomen, Swedish Match, Hufvudstaden; mem. fmr Bd of Govs. IATA.

JANVIER, Gen. Bernard Louis Antonin; French army officer; b. 16 July 1939, La Voulte-sur-Rhône, Ardèche; s. of Pierre Janvier and Eugénie Bernard; m. Denise Diaz 1963; two s. one d.; ed Lycée de Nice, Coll. d'Orange, Lycée Bugeaud, Algiers, Univ. of Rennes and Ecole Spéciale Militaire de Saint-Cyr; commissioned 2nd Lt 1960; served in Algeria 1962–64, Madagascar and Comoros 1964–67; Co. Commdt 9th Parachute Regt 1968–70; Commdt in charge of trainee officers, Ecole Spéciale Militaire de Saint-Cyr 1970–72; Bn Chief 1974; training course, Ecole Supérieure de Guerre 1974–76; Lt-Col 1978; Second-in-Command, Bureau of Operations-Instruction 1981; Col 1982; Chef de Corps, 2nd Overseas Parachute Regt 1982–84; Head, Office of Personnel, Chief of Ground Forces 1984–87; Deputy to Gen. Commdt 6th Armoured Div. 1987–89; Brig.-Gen. 1988; Chief Org.-Logistic Div. of Army Chief of Staff 1989–91; Commdt Operation Requin, Port Gentil, Gabon 1991; Commdt Daguet Div. Saudi Arabia and Iraq 1991; Div. Gen. 1991; Commdt 6th Armoured Div. Nîmes 1991–93; Army Chief of Staff, Operational Planning (Emia) 1993–95; Gen. Army Corps 1994; apptd Army Chief of Staff 1995; Dir Centre des hautes études militaires, Inst. des hautes études de la défense nat. 1996–98; Commdt UN Peace Forces in Fmr Yugoslavia 1995–96; Commdr Légion d'honneur, Ordre nat. du Mérite, Legion of Merit (USA) and numerous other decorations; medals from Kuwait and Saudi Arabia. *Leisure interests:* history of Provence, running. *Address:* 6 place de l'Eglise, 83310 Grimaud, France (home).

JANZEN, Daniel Hunt, BS, PhD; American biologist and academic; *Professor of Biology and Thomas G. and Louise E. DiMaura Term Chair, University of Pennsylvania;* b. 18 Jan. 1939, Milwaukee, Wis.; s. of Daniel Hugo Janzen and Floyd Foster Janzen; m. twice (divorced twice); one s. one d. from 1st marriage; ed Univ. of Minnesota, Univ. of California, Berkeley; Asst Prof. then Assoc. Prof., Univ. of Kansas 1965–68; Assoc. Prof., Univ. of Chicago 1969–72; Assoc. Prof. and Prof. of Ecology and Evolutionary Biology, Univ. of Michigan 1972–76; Prof. of Biology and Thomas G. and Louise E. DiMaura Term Chair, Univ. of Pennsylvania, Philadelphia 1976–; teacher, Org. for Tropical Studies in Costa Rica 1965–; field research in tropical ecology 1963; MacArthur Fellow 1989; mem. NAS 1992–; Hon. Fellow, Asscn for Tropical Biology 1992; Dr hc (Univ. of Minnesota) 1996; Gleason Award, American Botanical Soc. 1975, Crafoord Prize, Coevolutionary Ecology, Swedish Royal Acad. of Sciences 1984, Joseph Leidy Medal, Philadelphia Acad. of Natural Sciences 1989, Founder's Council Award of Merit, Field Museum of Natural History 1991, Silver Medal Award, Int. Soc. of Chemical Ecology 1994, Conservation Soc. Award 1995, Kyoto Prize (Basic Sciences) 1997, Albert Einstein World Award for Science 2002, Nat. Outdoor Book Award 2006. BBVA Foundation Frontiers of Knowledge Award 2011, Blue Planet Prize 2014. *Publications:* Herbivores (co-ed., with G. A. Rosenthal) 1979, Costa Rican Natural History (ed.) 1983 and over 250 papers in scientific journals. *Leisure interest:* tropical ecology. *Address:* 301 Leidy Laboratories, Department of Biology, University of Pennsylvania, Philadelphia, PA 19104, USA (office); Parque Nacional Santa Rosa, Apdo. 169, Liberia, Guanacaste Province, Costa Rica. *Telephone:* (215) 898-5636 (office). *Fax:* (215) 898-8780 (office). *E-mail:* djanzen@sas.upenn.edu (office). *Website:* www.bio.upenn.edu/faculty/janzen (office).

JAOUI, Agnès; French actress, screenwriter and director; b. 19 Oct. 1964, Antony, Hauts-de-Seine; d. of Hubert Jaoui and Josiane Jaoui (née Zerah); m. Jean-Pierre Bacri 1987 (divorced 2012); two c.; ed Lycée Henri IV, Paris, Théâtre des Amandiers, Nanterre; René Clair Award 2001. *Films:* as actress: Le Faucon (The Hawk) 1983, Hôtel de France 1987, L'Amoureuse 1987, Canti 1991, Cuisine et Dépendances (Kitchen with Apartment) 1993, Un Air de Famille (Family Resemblances) (Lumiere Award: Best Screenplay 1997) 1996, Le Déménagement 1997, On Connaît la Chanson (Same Old Song) (César: Best Supporting Actress 1998) 1997, Le Cousin 1997, La Méthode 1997, On the Run 1999, Une Femme d'Extérieur (Outgoing Woman) 2000, Le Goût des Autres (The Taste of Others) 2000, 24 Heures de la Vie d'une Femme (24 Hours in the Life of a Woman) 2002, Le Rôle de sa Vie 2004, Comme une Image (Look at Me) 2004, La Maison de Nina 2004, Le Rôle de sa vie 2004, La Maison de Nina 2005, Let's Talk About the Rain 2008, Du vent dans mes mollets 2012, Au bout du conte 2013, L'Art de la fugue (The Easy Way Out) (also screenwiter) 2014, Comme un avion (The Sweet Escape) 2015, Je suis à vous tout de suite (I'm All Yours) 2015, Aurore 2017, Les Bonnes Intentions (Best Intentions) 2018; as screenwriter: Cuisine et Dépendances, Smoking/No Smoking 1993, On Connaît la Chanson, Un Air de Famille; as screenwriter and dir: Le Goût des Autres (Grand Prix des Amériques 2000, César: Best Film and Best Original Adaptation 2001, David di Donatello Award: Best Foreign Film 2001, European Film Award: Best Screenwriter, Lumiere Award: Best Director 2001) 2000, Comme une Image (Bodil Award, Palme D'Or: Best Screen Play 2004, European Film Award: Best Screenwriter 2004) 2004, Parlez-moi de la pluie (Let's Talk About the Rain) 2008, Au bout du conte 2013, Place publique 2017. *Address:* c/o Jean-François Gabard, Zelig, 57, rue Réaumur, 75002 Paris, France (office). *Telephone:* 1-44-78-81-10 (office). *E-mail:* zelig@zelig-fr.com (office). *Website:* zelig-fr.com (office); www.agnes-jaoui.over-blog.com.

JAPAN, HM Emperor of (see AKIHITO).

JAPARIDZE, Tedo, PhD; Georgian politician, diplomatist and international organization official; b. 18 Sept. 1946, Tbilisi; m. Tamar Japaridze; one s.; ed Tbilisi State Univ., Inst. of USA and Canadian Studies, Moscow, Russia; fmr teacher, Dept of Int. Relations and Int. Law, Tbilisi State Univ.; with Ministry of Foreign Affairs 1989–92, positions included Head of Political Dept, Deputy Foreign Minister, First Deputy Foreign Minister, Vice-Chair. Council for UNESCO Affairs 1989–92, Nat. Security Adviser to Head of State 1992–94; Amb. to USA, Canada and Mexico 1995–2002; Sec. Nat. Security Council 2002–03; Minister of Foreign Affairs 2003–04; Hon. Chair. Transcaucasus Foundation and Special Advisor to Washington Strategic Advisors LLC –2004; Sec.-Gen. Org. of Black Sea Econ. Co-operation, Perm. Int. Secr. 2004–05; Public Policy Scholar, Woodrow Wilson Int. Center for Scholars, USA 2006; Pres. US-Caucasus Inst., Tbilisi 2007; Alt. Gen. Dir Int. Centre for Black Sea Studies, Athens 2007–11; mem. Comm. on the Black Sea 2007–10, Comm. of Euro-Atlantic Security Initiative, Carnegie Endowment; mem. Parl. (Georgian Dream) 2012–, Chair. Parl. Cttee for Foreign Affairs 2012–. *Publications include:* White House: Mechanism of Decision-Making 1985, American Political Institutions: History and Current State (co-author) 1987; numerous articles on US domestic and foreign policy, issues of Black Sea regional econ. cooperation, security policy, problems of illicit trafficking in wider Black Sea area. *Address:* Sakartvelos Parlamenti, 4600 Tbilisi, Kutaisi, Abashidze 26, Georgia (office). *Telephone:* (32) 228-90-06 (office). *Fax:* (32) 299-93-86 (office). *E-mail:* tjaparidze@parliament.ge (office). *Website:* www.parliament.ge/en/mp/2133 (office).

JAPAROV, Tuvakmammed; Turkmenistani politician and fmr central banker; b. 1967; Chair. Supreme Control Chamber of Turkmenistan –2009; Deputy Chair. of the Govt, responsible for Econ. Affairs 2009–11; Gov. Cen. Bank of Turkmenistan (Türkmenistanyň Merkezi Banky) 2011–14.

JAQSIBEKOV, Ädılbek Ryskeldinulı, CandEconSci; Kazakhstani diplomatist and politician; b. 26 July 1954, Burliy, Komsomol (now Karabalyk) Dist, Qostanay Oblast; ed All-USSR State Inst. of Cinematography, Moscow, Russia, Plekhanov Inst. of Nat. Economy, Moscow; began career in Kazakhstani state system as cinematographer; Dir Tsesna Corpn 1988–95; Deputy to Senate (Parl.) 1995–; First Deputy Akim, Aqmola Oblast 1996, Mayor of Astana 1997–2003, 2014–16; Minister of Industry and Trade 2003–04; Chief of Admin to Pres. of Kazakhstan 2004; First Deputy Chair. People's Democratic Party (Nur Otan) 2008–; Adviser to Pres. of Kazakhstan Jan.–Oct. 2008; Amb. to Russia 2008–09; Minister of Defence 2009–14; Head of Football Fed. of Astana City 2000–07, Pres. Football Fed. of Kazakhstan 2007–; Order of Kazakhstan Respublikasynyn Toongysh Presidenti Nursultan Nazarbayev, Order of Barys (Third Degree), Order of Prince Yaroslav the Wise (Third Degree) (Ukraine); State Prize of the Repub. of Kazakhstan 2008. *Publications:* To Light Star: Capital City, This Way Astana Began (memoirs).

JARA, Alejandro; Chilean diplomatist and international organization executive; *Deputy Director-General, World Trade Organization;* b. 1949, Santiago; m. Daniela Benavente; one s. two d.; ed high schools in Rio de Janeiro, Brazil and Santiago, Chile, Universidad de Chile, Law School, Univ. of California, Berkeley, USA (Fulbright Scholarship); joined Foreign Service 1976, specialized in int. econ. relations, served in Del. to GATT, Geneva 1979–84, seconded as Co-ordinator for Trade Policy Affairs to Econ. System for Latin America (SELA), Caracas, Venezuela, Dir for Bilateral Econ. Affairs 1993–94, Dir for Multilateral Econ. Affairs 1994–99, Sr Official to APEC and Deputy Chief Negotiator for the Chile–Canada Free Trade Agreement 1996–97, Chief Negotiator for the Chile–Mexico Free Trade Agreement 1997–98, Dir-Gen. for Int. Econ. 1999–2000, Amb. and Perm. Rep. to WTO, Geneva 2000–05, Chair. WTO Cttee on Trade and Environment 2001, Chair. Special Session of the Council for Trade in Services 2002; Deputy Dir-Gen. WTO 2005–. *Publications:* numerous articles and papers on int. trade. *Address:* World Trade Organization, Centre William Rappard, rue de Lausanne 154, 1211 Geneva, Switzerland (office). *Telephone:* (22) 7395111 (office). *Fax:* (22) 7314206 (office). *E-mail:* enquiries@wto.org (office). *Website:* www.wto.org (office).

JARA VELÁSQUEZ, Ana del Rosario, LLM; Peruvian lawyer and politician; b. 11 May 1968; ed Univ. Nacional San Luis Gonzaga; began career as Notary Public, Ica 1998; Sec., Mutual Fund of Peruvian Notaries 2000–01; mem. Congress (Gana Perú) for Ica constituency 2011–; Minister of Women and Social Devt 2011–14, of Labour and Employment Feb.–July 2014; Pres. Council of Ministers (Prime Minister) 2014–15 (forced to step down after losing vote of confidence); mem. Advisory Bd, Registry Office Zone XI 2002–03; Assoc. Dean, Ica Coll. of Notaries 2005–06.

JÁRAI, Zsigmond; Hungarian economist and banker; b. 29 Dec. 1951, Biharkeresztes; m. Marianna Kiss; one s. one d.; ed Univ. of Econs, Budapest; banker, State Devt Bank, Hungary 1976–89; Deputy Minister of Finance and Dir of State Bank Supervision 1989–90; Sr Exec. for Eastern Europe, James Capel & Co., London 1990–92; Man. Dir Samuel Montagu Financial Consultant and Securities Co., Budapest 1993–95; Chair. and CEO ABN AMRO (Magyar) Bank (fmrly Hungarian Credit Bank) 1995–98; Chair. Hungarian Stock Exchange 1996–98; Minister of Finance 1998–2000; Pres. Nat. Bank of Hungary 2001–07; Grand Cross, Order of Merit 2016; Manager of the Year 1997, Hungarian Heritage Award 2007. *Publication:* Money Talks 2008.

JARDIM, José Manuel Norberto, PhD; Curaçao politician; b. 24 April 1973; ed Universidade Nova, Lisbon; Man., Directorate of Finance, Netherlands Antilles –2010; Sec.-Gen., Ministry of Finance and Econ. Devt, Curaçao (following dissolution of Netherlands Antilles) 2010–12, Minister of Finance and of Econ. Devt 2012–13, 2013–16.

JARDIM GONÇALVES, Jorge Manuel, BCE; Portuguese banker; b. 4 Oct. 1935, Funchal, Madeira Island; ed Univ. of Oporto; mil. service in Army Eng Corps 1960–63; engineer in Angola; Lecturer, Eng School of Oporto –1970; joined Banco de Agricultura 1970, later apptd. to Bd of Dirs; worked at Compañia de Gestion de Industrias (subsidiary of Banco Popular Español) 1975–76; Exec. Dir Banco Português do Atlântico 1977, Chair. 1979–85; Chair. Banco Comercial de Macao and Dir Companhia de Seguros de Macao 1979–85; CEO Banco Comercial Português (BCP) 1985–2005, Chair. Sr Bd 1985–2008; Chair. Millenium Banco Comercial Português, SA 1985–2005; Deputy Pres. of Man. Bd Union of Portuguese Banks; mem. Supervisory Bd Eureko BV 1993–2007, Bank Millennium SA 1999–2007; mem. Int. Monetary Conf.; mem. Sr Bd Novabank, Greece; Grand Cross, Order of Infante D. Henrique 2005, Grand Officer, Order Pro Merito Melitensi, Sovereign Military Order of Malta, Grand Officer, Order of Merit (Poland), Grand Cross, Sacred Constantinian Military Order of Saint George of the Two Sicilies, Commdr, Order of the Immaculate Conception of Vila Viçosa in Portugal, Commdr, Order of Merit (Luxembourg).

JARDINE, Al; American musician (guitar) and singer; b. 3 Sept. 1942, Lima, OH; mem. The Beach Boys 1961–62, 1963–; numerous tours and concerts, festival appearances; band est. Brother Records label 1967; American Music Awards Special Award of Merit 1988, Grammy Lifetime Achievement Award 2001. *Recordings include:* albums: with the Beach Boys: Surfin' Safari 1962, Surfer Girl 1963, Little Deuce Coupe 1963, Shut Down Vol. 2, All Summer Long 1964, Christmas Album 1964, The Beach Boys Today! 1965, Summer Days (and Summer Nights) 1965, Beach Boys Party 1966, Pet Sounds 1966, Smiley Smile 1967, Wild Honey 1968, Friends 1968, 20/20 1969, Sunflower 1970, Surf's Up 1971, Carl and the Passions – So Tough 1972, Holland 1973, The Beach Boys in Concert 1973, Endless Summer 1974, 15 Big Ones 1976, The Beach Boys Love You 1977, M.I.U. 1978, LA (Light Album) 1979, Keepin' The Summer Alive 1980, The Beach Boys 1985, Still Cruisin' 1989, Two Rooms 1991, Summer in Paradise 1992, The Sounds of Summer – The Very Best of The Beach Boys 2003, That's Why God Made the Radio 2012; solo: A Postcard from California 2010. *Website:* www.thebeachboys.com; www.aljardine.com.

JARISLOWSKY, Stephen A., CC, MBA; Canadian business executive; *Chairman, Jarislowsky, Fraser Ltd;* b. Sept. 1925, Berlin, Germany; m. Gail Jarislowsky; four c.; ed Cornell Univ., Univ. of Chicago, Harvard Business School; served in US Army during World War Two, in counter-intelligence in Japan after the war; engineer, Alcan Aluminum, Montreal 1949–52; f. Jarislowsky, Fraser Ltd (investment co.) 1955, Chair. and CEO –2012, Chair. 2012–; Founder and Pres. The Jarislowsky Foundation; Chair. Learning Assocs, Goodfellow Lumber Inc.; mem. Bd of Dirs C. D. Howe Research Inst., Fraser Brothers Ltd, Growth Oil & Gas Investment Fund of Canada Ltd (also Pres.), Slocan Forest Products, Velan Inc.; Co-founder Canadian Coalition for Good Governance 2002; mem. Advisory Bd McGill Univ. Medical School, Queen's Univ. School of Business; has endowed eleven eponymous univ. chairs in Canada; Grand Officer, Nat. Order of Quebec; Hon. LLD (Queen's Univ., Univ. of Alberta, McMaster Univ., Université Laval, Concordia Univ., Univ. of Windsor, Université de Montréal). *Publications:* The Investment Zoo: Taming the Bulls and the Bears (co-author) 2005. *Address:* Jarislowsky, Fraser Limited, 1010 Sherbrooke Street West, Suite 2005, Montreal, PQ H3A 2R7, Canada (office). *Website:* www.jfl.ca (office).

JARMAN, Sir Brian, Kt, OBE, MA, PhD, FRCP, FMedSci, FRCGP, FFPH; British medical scientist and professor of medicine; *Professor Emeritus of Primary Health Care, Faculty of Medicine, Imperial College London;* b. 9 July 1933, London; s. of George Ernest Richard Jarman and Fan Elizabeth Jarman (née Felton); m. Marina Jarman; three s.; ed Univ. of Cambridge, Imperial Coll., London; served with Royal Artillery 1954–56; began career as exploration geophysicist with Shell Oil Co., Sahara 1960–63; worked at St Mary's Hosp. Medical School 1969 and St Bernard's Hospital, Gibraltar 1970; Resident in Medicine, Beth Israel Hospital, Harvard Medical School 1970; Unrestricted Prin. in gen. practice (part-time Prin. from 1984), Lisson Grove Health Centre, London 1971–98; Sr Lecturer (part-time), St Mary's Hosp. Medical School 1973–83, Prof. of Primary Health Care and Gen. Practice and Head of Dept of General Practice 1984–98, Head of Community Health Sciences Div., Imperial Coll. Medical School at St Mary's (ICSM) 1995–97, Head of Div. of Primary Care and Population Health Sciences, Imperial Coll. 1997–98, Prof. Emer. of Primary Health Care 1998–, Co-Dir Dr Foster Unit, Imperial Coll. 2002–; Sr Fellow, Inst. for Healthcare Improvement, Boston, Mass, USA 2001–; Pres. BMA 2003–04; mem. London Strategic Review Panel to advise Dept of Health 1998; medical mem. Bristol Royal Infirmary Enquiry 1999–2001; fmr mem. Council, Royal Coll. of Physicians; European Ed. Journal Watch (mem. Editorial Bd 1982–2004); frequent participant in nat. and int. advisory work, including mem. Dept of Health's Advisory Cttee on Resource Allocation; Fellow, Royal Coll. of Gen. Practitioners 1984–, Acad. Medical Sciences 2000–. *Achievements include:* pioneered devt of research on socio-economic indicators of health status (Under Privileged Area scores or Jarman Index). *Publications include:* numerous books and articles linking socio-economic variables to health status and quality of medical care. *Address:* 62 Aberdare Gardens, London, NW6 3QD, England (home). *Telephone:* 7786-431691 (mobile) (office). *E-mail:* b.jarman@ic.ac.uk (office). *Website:* www.imperial.ac.uk/people/b.jarman (office); www.brianjarman.com.

JARMUSCH, Jim; American film director and screenwriter; b. 22 Jan. 1953, Akron, Ohio; ed Medill School of Journalism, Northwestern Univ., Colombia Coll.; teaching asst to Nicholas Ray at New York Univ. Graduate Film School 1976–79; has worked on several films as sound recordist, cameraman and actor; Founder-mem. band Sqürl. *Films include:* Permanent Vacation (writer, dir) 1980, You Are Not I (writer) 1981, The New World (dir) 1982, Stranger Than Paradise (writer, dir) (Camera d'Or Award, Cannes Film Festival 1984) 1983, Down By Law (writer, dir) 1986, Coffee and Cigarettes (short film, writer and dir) 1986, Mystery Train (writer, dir) 1989, Coffee and Cigarettes II (short film, writer and dir) 1989, Night on Earth (writer, dir) 1992, Coffee and Cigarettes III (short film, writer and dir) 1993, Dead Man (writer, dir) 1995, Year of the Horse (dir) 1997, Ghost Dog: The Way of the Samurai (writer, dir) 1999, Ten Minutes Older: The Trumpet (writer, dir) 2002, Coffee and Cigarettes (writer, dir) 2003, Broken Flowers 2005, The Limits of Control 2009, Only Lovers Left Alive 2013, Paterson 2016. *Music videos directed include:* The Lady Don't Mind (Talking Heads) 1985, Sightsee MC! (Big Audio Dynamite) 1987, It's Alright With Me (Tom Waits) 1991, I Don't Wanna Grow Up (Tom Waits) 1992, Dead Man Theme (Neil Young) 1995, Big Time (Neil Young and Crazy Horse) 1996.

JARQUÍN CALDERÓN, Edmundo, MA, JD; Nicaraguan economist and politician; b. Sept. 1946, Ocotal, Nuevo Segovia; m. Claudia Lucía Chamorro; ed Universidad Centroamericana, Managua, Universidad de Chile Law School; joined Juventud Democráta Cristiana 1965; student sec., Christian Democratic Youth of Latin America 1966–67; forced to leave academic studies in Chile following Gen. Augusto Pinochet's coup against Pres. Salvador Allende 1973; Co-founder Unión Democrática de Liberación (UDEL) 1974; Minister for Foreign Cooperation 1981–84, Amb. to Mexico 1984–88, to Spain 1988–90; mem. Parl. for Frente Sandinista de Liberación Nacional (FSLN) and mem. Bd of Dirs Nat. Ass. 1990–92; Co-founder Movimiento Renovador Sandinista—MRS (dissident group that split from FSLN) 1992; specialist in public policy for IDB 1992–2005; unsuccessful cand. for Vice-Pres. (with Herty Lewites) 2006, unsuccessful cand. for Pres. (upon death of Lewites) July 2006, Unidad Nicaragüense por la Esperanza (UNE) cand. for Vice-Pres. 2011. *Address:* Movimiento Renovador Sandinista, De los semáforos del Ministerio de Gobernación, 1/2 cuadra al norte, Managua, Nicaragua (office). *Telephone:* 250-9461 (office). *Fax:* 278-0268 (office). *E-mail:* info@partidomrs.com (office). *Website:* www.partidomrs.com.

JARRATT, Sir Alexander Anthony, Kt, CB, DL, BCom; British fmr business executive; b. 19 Jan. 1924, London; s. of Alexander Jarratt and Mary Jarratt; m. (Mary) Philomena Keogh 1946; one s. two d.; ed Royal Liberty Grammar School, Essex and Univ. of Birmingham; mil. service in Fleet Air Arm 1942–46; Asst Prin. Ministry of Power 1949–53, Prin. 1953–54; Treasury 1954–55; Prin. Pvt. Sec. to Minister of Fuel and Power 1955–59; Asst Sec. in Oil Div. of Ministry 1959–63, Under-Sec. in Gas Div. 1963–64; Cabinet Office 1964–65; First Sec., Nat. Bd for Prices and Incomes 1965–68; Deputy Under-Sec. of State, Dept of Employment and Productivity 1968; Deputy Sec., Ministry of Agric. 1970; mem. Bds of IPC and Reed Int. Ltd 1970; Man. Dir IPC 1970–74, Chair. 1974, also of IPC Newspapers 1974; Chair. and CEO Reed Int. Ltd 1974–85; Chair. CBI Econ. Policy Cttee 1972–74, Industrial Soc. 1975–79; mem. Supervisory Bd, Thyssen-Bornemisza 1972–89; Dir (non-exec.) ICI Ltd 1975–91, Smith's Industries 1984–96 (Chair. (non-exec.) 1985–91); Dir and Deputy Chair. Midland Bank 1980–91; Jt Deputy Chair. Prudential Corpn 1987–91, 1992–94 (Dir 1985–94); Chair. Admin. Staff Coll., Henley 1976–89, Centre for Dispute Resolution 1990–2000 (Pres. 2001–); Pres. Advertising Asscn 1979–83; mem. Council CBI, Chair. CBI Employment Policy Cttee 1982–86; Pres. Periodical Publishers Asscn 1983–85; Vice-Pres. Inst. of Marketing 1982; Chancellor, Univ. of Birmingham 1983–2002; Gov. Ashridge Man. Coll.; Hon. DSc (Cranfield); Hon. DUniv (Brunel, Essex); Hon. DLL (Birmingham). *Leisure interests:* countryside pursuits, theatre, music, reading. *Address:* Barn Mead, Fryerning, Essex, CM4 0NP, England (home).

JARRAUD, Michel; French international organization executive and meteorologist; b. 31 Jan. 1952, Châtillon-sur-Indre; m.; two c.; ed Ecole Polytechnique, Ecole de la Météorologie Nationale; researcher, Météo-France 1976–78, Dir Weather Forecasting Dept 1986–89; researcher in numerical weather prediction, European Centre for Medium-Range Weather Forecasts (ECMWF) 1978–85, Dir Operational Dept 1990–91, Deputy Dir ECMWF 1991–95; Deputy Sec.-Gen. WMO 1995–2003, Sec.-Gen. 2004–15; Chair. UN-Water 2012–15; mem. Soc. Météorologique de France, Royal Meteorological Soc. (UK), African Meteorological Soc.; Fellow, American Meteorological Soc.; Hon. mem. Chinese Meteorological Soc., Cuban Meteorological Soc.; Commdr, Ordre nat. du Lion (Senegal) 2005, First Class Distinction, Civil Defence of Venezuela 1999; Hon. DSc (Universidad Nacional Agraria 'La Molina', Peru) 2004.

JARRE, Jean Michel André, LèsL; French composer, musician (synthesizer, keyboard) and record producer; *President, Confédération Internationale des Sociétés d'Auteurs et Compositeurs (CISAC);* b. 24 Aug. 1948, Lyons; s. of Maurice Jarre and France Jarre (née Pejot); m. 2nd Charlotte Rampling (q.v.) 1978; m. 3rd Anne Parillaud 2005 (divorced); one s. and one d. from previous marriage; ed Lycée Michelet, Université de la Sorbonne, Conservatoire de musique de Paris; composer of electronic music 1968–; int. concerts include shows in China, Europe and USA; shows incorporate state-of-the-art sound and vision tech.; composer for ballet Aor and Opéra de Paris 1971; UNESCO Goodwill Amb. 1993–; spokesperson European Music Industry 1998–, Int. Fed. for Phonographic Industry 1998–2000; Pres. Confédération Internationale des Sociétés d'Auteurs et Compositeurs (CISAC) 2013–; Soc. des auteurs, compositeurs et éditeurs de musique Gold Medal 1980, Grand Prix de l'Acad. Charles Cros 1985, IPFI Platinum Europe Award 1998, Eska Music Special Award 2007, MOJO Lifetime Achievement Award 2010, Grand Prix des Musiques Electroniques SACEM 2010, Q Innovation of Sound Award 2014; Officier, Ordre des Arts et des Lettres, Officer, Legion d'honneur 2011. *Major live performances:* Place de la Concorde, Paris 1979 (record audience of one million); Peking, Shanghai 1981; Rendez-vous Houston (record audience of 1.3 million), Rendez-vous Lyons 1986; Destination Docklands, London 1988; Paris–La Défense: A City in Concert 1990 (2.5 million audience); Europe in Concert 1993; Hong Kong 1994; Eiffel Tower, Paris 1995 (one million audience); Moscow 1997 (record audience of 3.5 million); Electronic Night, Eiffel Tower, Paris 1998; Millennium Concert, Pyramids of Cairo (televised worldwide, estimated 2,000m. viewers) 1999; 2001 Rendez-vous in Space, Okinawa, Japan 2001; Akropolis Athens 2001; Aero, Aalborg, Denmark 2002; Forbidden City and Tiananmen Square, Beijing 2004; Gdansk Shipyard, Poland 2005; Coachella Festival 2017. *Film scores:* Des Garçons et des filles 1968, Deserted Palace 1972, Les Granges brulées 1973, Die Hamburger Krankheit 1978, music and lyrics for numerous songs. *Recordings include:* albums: Oxygène 1976, Equinoxe 1978, Magnetic Fields 1980, The China Concerts (live) 1982, Zoolook (Grand Prix Academie du Disque 1985) 1984, Rendez-vous 1986, Cities in Concert: Houston/Lyons (live) 1987, Revolutions 1988, Jarre Live (Victoire de la Musique Best Instrumental Album 1986) 1989, Waiting for Cousteau 1990, Images (compilation) 1991, Chronologie 1993, Hong Kong (live) 1994, Oxygène 7–13 1997, Odyssey Through 02 (interactive) 1998, Metamorphoses 2000, Aero 2004, Téo & Téa 2007, Electronica 1: The Time Machine 2015, Electronica 2: The Heart of Noise 2016, Oxygène 3 2016, Equinox Infinity 2017. *Publications:* Concert d'Images 1989, Paris-la-Défense, une ville en concert 1990, Europe in Concert 1994, Paris-Tour Eiffel, Concert pour la Tolérance 1995, The Millennium Concert at the Great Pyramids of Egypt 2000, Akropolis 2001, Jean Michel Jarre à Pékin 2004. *Address:* Fiona Commins, Aero Productions, 1 avenue Jean-Baptiste Charcot, 78380 Bougival, France (office). *E-mail:* contact@aero-productions.com (office). *Website:* www.jeanmicheljarre.com.

JARRETT, Keith; American pianist and composer; b. 8 May 1945, Allentown, Pa; ed Berklee School of Music; gave first solo concert aged 7, followed by professional appearances; two-hour solo concert of own compositions 1962; led own trio in Boston; worked with Roland Kirk, Tony Scott and others in New York; joined Art Blakey 1965; toured Europe with Charles Lloyd 1966, with Miles Davis 1970–71; soloist and leader of own groups 1969–; Guggenheim Fellowship 1972; Prix du Prés. de la République 1991, Polar Prize, Royal Swedish Acad. of Music 2003, Léonie Sonning Music Prize 2004, Jazz Masters Award 2014; Officier, Ordre des Arts et des Lettres. *Recordings include:* Bach's Well-Tempered Klavier, Personal Mountains 1974, Luminessence 1974, Mysteries 1975, The Köln Concert 1975, Changeless 1987, Nude Ants, The Cure 1990, Bye Bye Black 1991, At the Dear Head Inn 1992, Bridge of Light 1993, At the Blue Note 1994, La Scala 1995, Tokyo '96 1998, The Melody at Night With You 1999, Whisper Not 2000, Inside Out 2001, Always Let Me Go 2002, Selected Recordings 2002, Radiance 2005, The Carnegie Hall Concert 2006, Dmitri Shostakovich: 24 Preludes and Fugues 2006, Jasmine (with Charlie Haden) 2007, Somewhere 2009, Rio 2011, Creation 2014, A Multitude of Angels 2016.

JARRETT, Valerie Bowman, BA, JD; American lawyer, business executive, civic leader and government official; b. 14 Nov. 1956, Shiraz, Iran; d. of Dr James E. Bowman; m. Dr William Robert Jarrett 1983 (divorced 1988, died 1991); one d.; ed Northfield Mount Hermon School, Mass, Stanford Univ., Calif., Univ. of Michigan Law School; father ran hosp. for children in Shiraz, Iran; moved with family to London, UK aged five 1962–63, returned to Chicago 1963; began career in Chicago politics working for Mayor Harold Washington as Deputy Corpn Counsel for Finance and Devt 1987, continued to work in Mayor's Office in 1990s, Deputy Chief of Staff for Mayor Richard Daley, Commr Dept of Planning and Devt 1992–95, Chair. Chicago Transit Bd 1995–2003; Exec. Vice-Pres. The Habitat Company (real estate devt and man. co.) 1995–2007, Pres. and CEO 2007–09; mem. Bd Chicago Stock Exchange 2000–07, Chair. 2004–07, Chair. Chicago Stock Exchange Holdings, Inc. 2005–07; Finance Chair. US Senatorial Campaign for Barack Obama 2004, first Treas. of Senator's PAC, the Hopefund, also served as a Sr Advisor to the Obama for America Presidential Campaign; Co-Chair. Obama-Biden Transition Project 2008–09; Dir, Office of Public Engagement and Intergovernmental Affairs 2009–17; Chair. Bd of Trustees, Univ. of Chicago Medical Center, Vice-Chair. Bd of Trustees, Univ. of Chicago; Vice-Chair. Chicago 2016 Olympic Cttee, Metropolis 2020; mem. Bd of Dirs Fed. Reserve Bank of Chicago 2006–07, USG Corpn, Inc., Chicago, Navigant Consulting, Inc., RREEF America II; Dir Local Initiative Support Corpn, The Joyce Foundation, The Metropolitan Planning Council, Cen. Area Cttee; Trustee, Museum of Science and Industry.

JARRIN, Gen. (retd) Oswaldo Roman; Ecuadorean government official, academic, politician and fmr army officer; *Minister of National Defence;* Founder and Dean of Coll. of Military Sciences, Escuela Politecnica del Ejercito 1999–2000; Chair. Jt Chiefs of Staff 2002–03; Professor, Facultad Latinoamericano de Ciencias Sociales–FLASCO 2003–06; Minister of Nat. Defence 2005–06 (resgnd); Ministry of Defense Chair and Prof. of Nat. Security Affairs, Center for Hemispheric Defense Studies, Nat. Defense Univ., Washington, DC 2007–10; Prof. and Founding Pres., Ecuadorian Centre of Int. Studies, Universidad Internacional del Ecuador 2011–; Minister of Nat. Defence 2018–; columnist, El Comercio. *Address:* Ministry of National Defence, Calle Exposición S4-71 y Benigno Vela, Quito, Ecuador (office). *Telephone:* (2) 295-1951 (office). *Fax:* (2) 258-0941 (office). *E-mail:* comunicacion@midena.gob.ec (office). *Website:* www.defensa.gob.ec (office).

JÄRVI, Neeme; American (b. Estonian) conductor; b. 7 June 1937, Tallinn; s. of August Järvi and Elss Järvi; m. Liilia Järvi 1961; two s. one d.; ed Tallinn Music School, Leningrad Conservatorium and Leningrad Postgraduate Studium, studied with N. Rabinovich and Y. Mravinsky; Conductor Estonian Radio Symphony Orchestra –1963; Chief Conductor Estonian State Opera House 1963–76; Chief Conductor, Estonian Nat. Symphony Orchestra 1976–80 now Prin. Conductor; emigrated to USA 1980; Prin. Guest Conductor, City of Birmingham Symphony Orchestra, UK 1981–83; Chief Conductor Royal Scottish Nat. Orchestra 1984–88, Conductor Laureate 1990–; Prin. Conductor Gothenburg Orchestra, Sweden 1982–2004; Music Dir Detroit Symphony Orchestra, USA 1990–2005, Music Dir Emer. 2006–; Music Dir Emer. New Jersey Symphony Orchestra, USA 2005–09, Conductor Laureate and Artistic Advisor 2009–; Chief Conductor Residentie Orchestra, The Hague 2005–11, Chief Conductor Emer. 2012–; Artistic Dir Estonian Nat. Symphony Orchestra 2011–; Music Dir Orchestre de la Suisse Romande 2012–15; guest conductor of many int. symphony orchestras, including New York Philharmonic, Boston, Chicago, Royal Concertgebouw, Philharmonia, London Symphony, London Philharmonic; conducted Eugene Onegin 1979, 1984, Samson and Delilah 1982 and Khovanshchina 1985 at Metropolitan Opera House, New York; Head of Conducting, Gstaad Conducting Acad.; has held int. master-classes in summer resort town of Pärnu, Estonia 2000–; Hon. mem. Royal Swedish Acad. of Music, Estonian Composers Union 1989; Hon. Citizen, City of Gothenburg 1987, State of Michigan 1992; Kt Commdr, Order of the North Star (Sweden) 1990, Sash, Order of Nat. Coat of Arms 1996, Insignia, Coat of Arms, Tallinn 1997; Dr hc (Royal Swedish Acad. of Music) 1988, 1990, (Estonian Music Acad.) 1989, (Aberdeen) 1990, (Gothenburg) 1985, 1991, (Tallinn Music Conservatory), Wayne State Univ., USA) 1994, (Michigan) 1999; First Prize, Young Conductors' Competition, Leningrad 1957, Estonian Soviet Socialist Repub. (ESSR) Honoured Artist 1965, First Prize, Accademia Nazionale di Santa Cecilia Conductors' Competition 1971, ESSR People's Artist 1971, USSR State Prize 1978, Sibelius Soc. Medal 1986, Gramophone Magazine's Artist of the Year 1990, Gold Record, Chandos recording co. 1992, Toblach's Mahler Prize (for recording of Mahler's Third Symphony) 1993, Grand Prix du Disque, Charles Cros Recording Acad. of Paris (for CD of Stravinsky's Symphony of Psalms) 1993, Toblach's Mahler Prize (for recording of Mahler's Seventh Symphony with the Hague Orchestra) 2010. *Recordings include:* more than 450 CDs since 1983, including all Prokoviev, Sibelius, Grieg, Nielsen, Dvorak, Shostakovich, Franz Berwald and Stenhammar symphonies as well as recordings of Pärt and Tubin, Ibert: Orchestral Works 2016. *Address:* c/o Harrison Parrott, 201 Talgarth Road, London, W6 8BJ, England (office). *Telephone:* (20) 7229-9166 (office). *Fax:* (20) 7221-5042 (office). *E-mail:* info@harrisonparrott.co.uk (office); nmjarvi@gmail.com. *Website:* www.harrisonparrott.com (office); www.neemejarvi.ee.

JARVIK, Robert Koffler, BS, MD; American physician and business executive; *President and CEO, Jarvik Heart, Inc.;* b. 11 May 1946, Midland, Mich.; s. of Norman Eugene Jarvik and Edythe Jarvik (née Koffler); m. Marilyn vos Savant 1987; one s. one d.; ed Syracuse Univ., Univ. of Bologna, Italy, New York Univ., Univ. of Utah; Research Asst, Div. of Artificial Organs, Univ. of Utah 1971–77; Acting Dir Old St Mark's Hosp., Div. of Artificial Organs 1977–78, Asst Dir 1978–82; Asst Research Prof. of Surgery, Univ. of Utah 1979–87; Pres. Symbian Inc., Salt Lake City 1981–87; Pres. and CEO Jarvik Research Inc. (now Jarvik Heart Inc.) 1987–; Ed. (US Section) International Journal of Artificial Organs; mem. American Soc. for Artificial Internal Organs, Int. Soc. for Artificial Organs; Hon. DSc (Syracuse) 1983, (Hahnemann Univ.) 1985; numerous awards includng Inventor of the Year 1983, Outstanding Young Men of America 1983, Gold Heart Award 1983, Par Excellence Award (Univ. of Utah). *Address:* Jarvik Heart, Inc., 333 West 52nd Street, New York, NY 10019, USA (office). *Telephone:* (212) 397-3911 (office). *Fax:* (212) 397-3919 (office). *Website:* www.jarvikheart.com (office).

JASCHINSKI, Siegfried; German banking executive; *Chairman, Heidelberger Druckmaschinen AG;* b. 21 Aug. 1954, Leverkusen; ed Universität zu Köln; began banking career with Trinkaus und Burkhardt 1982; joined Deutschen Bank AG, Frankfurt 1986; fmr mem. Bd of Man. Dirs SüdwestLB, Deputy Chair. Landesbank Baden-Württemberg (after merger with SüdwestLB) 2004–05, Chair. 2005–09; First Deputy Chair. Admin. Bd DekaBank 2007–09, Deputy Chair. Audit Cttee, Deputy Chair. Gen. Cttee and mem. Presidential Cttee; Chair. Supervisory Bd Rheinland-Pfalz Bank; fmr Chair. Supervisory Bd Rohwedder AG; apptd mem. Supervisory Bd Heidelberger Druckmaschinen AG 2007, Chair. 2015–; mem. Supervisory Bd HSBC Trinkaus & Burkhardt AG, AdCapital AG; mem. Supervisory Bd and Chair. Credit and Market Risks Cttee, Baden Württembergische Bank AG; mem. Bd of Supervisory Dirs KfW; mem. Advisory Bd Vorarlberger Landes und Hypothekenbank AG, Baden-Württemberg Int. Agency for Int. Econ. and Scientific Co-operation. *Address:* Heidelberger Druckmaschinen AG, Kurfuersten-Anlage 52-60, Heidelberg, 69115 Germany (office). *Telephone:* (6221) 926021 (office). *Website:* www.heidelberg.com (office).

JASMI, Hussein al-; United Arab Emirates singer; b. (Hussein Jasmi el Naqbi), 25 Aug. 1979; performed with siblings in group Firqat El Khalij; signed with Rotana record label; performed at numerous int. festivals, including Salalah, Oman, Carthage, Tunisia 2006, Gulf Air Bahrain Grand Prix 2010; Al Mawaheb Prize, Dubai 1996, 6th Arab Radio and Television (ART) Award 2008. *Recordings include:* Hussain El Jasmi 2002, Hala Februair 2004, Hussain El Jasmi 2006, Ihtirit Aabar 2007, El Jasmi 2010, Bawada'ak, Wallah Mayiswa, Bahibik Wahachtiny, Bassbour Al Fourgakom, Into Kafo (You are Enough) 2010; theme music for TV shows Ba'ed Al Furaq (After Separating) 2008, Ahil Al Cairo (The People of Cairo) 2010. *Address:* PO Box 2788, Umm Hurair Road, Dubai, UAE. *Telephone:* (4) 3354440. *Fax:* (4) 3354448. *E-mail:* info@hussainaljassmi.com. *Website:* www.hussainaljassmi.com.

JASON, Sir David, Kt, OBE; British actor; b. (David John White), 2 Feb. 1940, Edmonton, London; s. of Arthur White and Olwyn Jones; partner Myfanwy Talog (died 1995); m. Gill Hinchcliffe 2005; one d.; started acting career in repertory; TV career began as Bert Bradshaw in soap-opera Crossroads 1964; best known for his role voicing Mr. Toad in adaptations of The Wind in the Willows, and for his long-running TV roles as the main characters of Derek 'Del Boy' Trotter on the BBC sitcom, Only Fools and Horses 1981–2003, and as detective Jack Frost on the ITV crime drama, A Touch of Frost 1992–2010; awards include Best Actor Award, BAFTA 1988, Best Light Entertainment Performance, BAFTA 1991, Best TV Comedy Actor Award, BAFTA 1997, BAFTA Fellowship 2003; four British Comedy Awards 1990, 1992, 1997 and Lifetime Achievement Award 2001; six Nat. Television Awards 1997, 2001, 2002 twice, 2003 and Award for Outstanding Drama Performance 2011; topped the poll to find TV's 50 Greatest Stars, as part of ITVs 50th anniversary celebrations 2006. *Theatre includes:* Under Milk Wood 1971, The Rivals 1972, No Sex Please ... We're British! 1972, Darling Mr London (tour) 1975, Charley's Aunt (tour) 1975, The Norman Conquests 1976, The Relapse 1978, Cinderella 1979, The Unvarnished Truth (Mid/Far East tour) 1983, Look No Hans! (tour and West End) 1985. *Films:* Under Milk Wood 1972, White Cargo 1973, Royal Flash 1975, Wombling Free (voice) 1977, The Odd Job 1978, The Snow Queen (voice) 1995, All the Way Up (dir) 2010. *Television includes:* Crossroads (series) 1966, Softly, Softly: Task Force (series) 1966, Do Not Adjust Your Set (series) 1967–69, Randall and Hopkirk (Deceased) (series) 1969, Canada Goose (film) 1969, Doctor in the House (series) 1970, Hark at Barker (series) 1969–70, Six Dates with Barker (series) 1971, Doctor at Large (series) 1971, His Lordship Entertains (series) 1972, The Top Secret Life of Edgar Briggs 1973–74, Mr Stabbs 1974, Doctor at Sea (series) 1974, It's Only Me – Whoever I Am 1974, Ronnie Barker Shows 1975, Lucky Feller (series) 1975–76, Open All Hours 1976–85, Porridge 1975–77, A Sharp Intake of Breath (series) 1977–81, The Odd Job 1978, The Dick Emery Show 1979, Only Fools and Horses 1981–2003, Dramarama (series) 1984, Porterhouse Blue (series) 1987, Jackanory 1988, Single Voices: The Chemist 1989, Amongst Barbarians 1989, A Bit of a Do (series) 1989, Oh! Mr. Toad (series) 1989–90, Screenplay (series) 1990, Victor & Hugo: Bunglers in Crime (series) 1991, Pa Larkin in The Darling Buds of May 1991–93, A Touch of Frost 1992–2010, The Bullion Boys 1993, Screen One (series) 1993, March in Windy City (film) 1998, All the King's Men (film) 1999, Micawber (series) 2002, The Quest (film) (also dir) 2002, The Second Quest (film) (also dir) 2004, The Final Quest (film) (also dir) 2004, Diamond Geezer (series) 2005–07, Ghostboat (film) 2006, Hogfather (film) 2006, The Colour of Magic (film) 2008, The Green Green Grass 2009, David Jason: The Battle of Britain (presenter, ITV documentary) 2010), Albert's Memorial (film) 2010, Come Rain Come Shine (film) 2010, Still Open all Hours (series) 2014–; animation: The Water Babies 1978, Danger Mouse 1981–92, Wind in the Willows (film) 1983, The Wind in the Willows (series) 1984–88, Count Duckula 1988–93, The BFG 1989, Victor and Hugo 1991–92, The Adventures of Dawdle the Donkey 1993, Father Christmas and the Missing Reindeer (voice) 1998, Angelmouse (series, narrator) 1999, Muddle Earth (series) 2010. *Publication:* David Jason: In His Element (with Niall Edworthy) 1999, My Life (Autobiography of the Year, Specsavers Nat. Book Award) 2013. *Leisure interests:* diving, flying, motorcycles. *Address:* c/o Richard Stone Partnership, 2 Henrietta Street, London, WC2E 8PS, England.

JASPERT, Augustus (Gus) James Ulysses, MA; British civil servant and diplomatist; *Governor, British Virgin Islands;* m. Millie Jaspert; two c.; ed Univ. of Edinburgh, Kingston Univ., King's Coll., London; Political Adviser, British High Comm., Accra, Ghana 2001; Lead Man., Children's Services, Surrey County Council 2001–07; Sr Policy Adviser, Social Exclusion Task Force, Cabinet Office 2007–08; Delivery Adviser, Prime Minister's Delivery Unit, HM Treasury 2007–09; Deputy Dir, Head of Local Policing, Crime and Justice, Home Office 2009–11, Deputy Dir and Head of Drugs and Alcohol 2011–12; Private Sec. to Prime Minister 2012–14; Dir, Cabinet Office 2015–17; Gov., British Virgin Islands 2017–; mem. Royal Coll. of Defence Studies 2014–15. *Address:* Office of the Governor, 20 Waterfront Drive, POB 702, Road Town, Tortola VG1110, British Virgin Islands (office). *Telephone:* 494-2345 (office). *Fax:* 494-5582 (office). *E-mail:* bvigovernor@gov.vg (office). *Website:* www.bvi.gov.vg (office).

JASRAJ, Pandit, DMus; Indian musician; b. 28 Jan. 1930, Hissar, Haryana; s. of Pandit Motiram and Krishnabai; m. Madhura Pandit 1962; one s. one d.; studied under elder brother Maniram Pandit; belongs to Mewati Gharana (school of music); has conducted extensive research in Haveli Sangeet and presented the original Pure Haveli Sangeet with its devotional content intact; has est. an Ashram Motiram Sangeet Natale Acad. with main object of propagating Indian classical music by teaching students free of charge; mem. advisory bds of radio and TV; numerous awards and honours, including Rajiv Gandhi Award for professional excellence, Sangeet Natak Akademi Award 1987, Padma Bhushan 1990, Padma

Vibhushan 2000, Yudhvir Memorial Award 2003, Swathi Sangeetha Puraskaram 2008, Bharat Muni Samman 2010, Shri Purshottam das Jalota Award 2012, Global Indian Music Award 2012. *Recordings include:* Invocation 1993, Inspiration 2000, Haveli Sangeet 2001, Maheshwara Mantra 2002, Darbar 2003, Soul Food 2005, Tapasya 2005, Miyan Tansen 2006, Upasana 2007, Baiju Bawra 2008, Khazana 2008, Raga Symphony 2009. *Works include:* compositions for opera, ballet and short films etc., including Kan Khani Sunyo Kare, Geet Govindam, Sur, Laya Aur Chhanda, Aath Prahar, Raga Bairagi, Raga Behag. *Publication:* Sangeet Saurabh. *Leisure interests:* teaching, travel, sport. *Address:* c/o Art & Artistes (I) Pvt. Ltd, 307 Durga Chambers, Off Veera Desai Road, Andheri (West), Mumbai 400 053, India (office). *Telephone:* (22) 42727850 (office). *Fax:* (22) 42727878 (office). *E-mail:* panditjasraj@panditjasraj.com (office). *Website:* www.aaaind.in (office); www.panditjasraj.com (office).

JASUZAQOV, Col-Gen. Säken Ädilhanulı; Kazakhstani army officer and government official; *Head, National Defence University;* b. 25 Oct. 1957, Chaldar, Southern Kazakhstan Oblast, Kazakh SSR, USSR; ed Almatı Higher Mil. Command School, M.V Frunze Mil. Acad., Moscow, Mil. Acad. of Gen. Staff of Russian Armed Forces; mil. service in Afghanistan 1981–83, Chief of Staff and Deputy Head of Civil Defence of Alatau Dist, Almatı city 1990, served in peacekeeping mission in Tajikistan 1993–94, Deputy Chief of Staff, Armed Forces of Repub. of Kazakhstan 1996, Head of Operational Planning Dept, later Deputy Chief of Gen. Staff of Armed Forces, becoming Chief of Staff of Army Corps and later Commdr of Mobile Forces, apptd Chief of Staff and First Deputy Commdr of Land Forces 2003, later Commdr, Eastern Regional Command, First Deputy Chair., Cttee of Chiefs of Staff of Defence of Kazakhstan 2007–09, Chief of Land Forces 2009, First Deputy Minister of Defence and Chair., Jt Chiefs of Staff of Ministry of Defence 2010, First Deputy Minister of Defence and Chief of Gen. Staff of Armed Forces 2013–16; Minister of Defence 2016–18; Head Nat. Defence Univ.; Red Star Award for Service to Motherland in the USSR Armed Forces (Third Degree), Dank Award (Second Degree), St Alexander Nevsky Award (Second Degree), 21 medals. *Address:* National Defense University, Nur-Sultan, 72 Turan ave., Kazakhstan (office). *Telephone:* (7172) 26-36-79 (office). *Fax:* (7172) 65-30-18 (office). *Website:* www.nuo.kz (office).

JATUSRIPITAK, Somkid, BA, MBA, PhD; Thai economist, government official and politician; *Deputy Prime Minister, in charge of Economic Affairs;* b. 15 July 1953, Bangkok; m. Anurachanee Jatusripitak; three c.; ed Thammasat Univ., Nat. Inst. of Devt Admin, Northwestern Univ., USA; early govt positions include Adviser to Minister of Foreign Affairs 1995–96, Sec. to Minister of Finance 1996–97, Minister of Commerce, Vice-Pres., Stock Exchange; Minister of Finance 2001, 2002–03, 2004–05; Deputy Prime Minister 2001–02, 2003–04, 2005–06, Deputy Prime Minister in charge of Econ. Affairs 2015–; mem Nat. Council for Peace and Order 2014–; Co-founder Thai Rak Thai party 1998; Co-founder Ruam Jai Thai Chart Pattana (Thais United National Development) 2007; Kt Grand Cross Second Class 1994, First Class 1997. *Address:* c/o Ruam Jai Thai Chart Pattana (Thais United National Development), c/o House of Representatives, Bangkok, Thailand (office).

JAUA MILANO, Elias; Venezuelan sociologist and politician; *Minister of Communes and Social Movements;* b. 1969, Caucagua; ed Univ. Central de Venezuela; fmr univ. lecturer; fmr mem. Unión de Jóvenes Revolucionarios/ Bandera Roja (resistance movt); Vice-Pres. Comisión Legislativa Nacional (Congresillo) 2000; Sec. of the Presidency 2000–01; Pres. Fondo Intergubernamental para la Descentralización 2003; Minister of Economy 2003–06, of Agric. and Lands 2006–11, Vice-Pres. 2010–12; Vice-Pres., Development of Territorial Socialism 2014–; Minister of Foreign Affairs 2013–14, of Communes and Social Movts 2014–; mem. Movimiento Quinta República, Planning Dir 2002–03. *Address:* Ministry of Communes and Social Protection, Edif. INCE, Avda Nueva Granada, Apdo 10340, Caracas 1040, Venezuela (office). *Telephone:* (212) 603-2396 (office). *Website:* www.mpcomunas.gob.ve (office).

JAVADYAN, Arthur; Armenian fmr engineer, banker and central banker; *Governor, Central Bank of Armenia;* b. 22 April 1964, Yerevan; m.; one d.; ed Yerevan State Agricultural Univ., American Banking Inst., New York, USA, Central Bank of Switzerland Educational Centre; began career as mechanical engineer, Haygyukhtntmekenayatsum 1986–89; engineer, Armglavvodstroy (Gen. Water Trust) 1987–89; Specialist, Acting Head of Unit, Head of Unit, mem. Exec. Bd, Yerevan Bank 1989–91; Chair. Exec. Bd, ArmInvestBank CJSC 1991–97, Adviser to the Chair. on Financial Issues 1999–2000; mem. Bd Central Bank of Armenia 1997–99, 2001–03, Adviser to the Gov. 2000–01, Sept.–Oct. 2003, Deputy Gov. 2003–08, Gov. 2008–; Dir for Armenia, Black Sea Trade and Devt Bank 2008–. *Address:* Office of the Governor, Central Bank of Armenia, 0010 Yerevan, Vazgen Sargsyan Street 6, Armenia (office). *Telephone:* (10) 58-38-41 (office). *Fax:* (10) 52-38-52 (office). *E-mail:* mcba@cba.am (office). *Website:* www.cba.am (office).

JAVAN, Jafar, BA, MA, PhD; Iranian-American UN official; *Director, United Nations System Staff College;* b. 10 June 1959, Tehran; m.; one d.; ed North Carolina State Univ., American Univ.; Policy Liaison Adviser, Bureau for Devt Policy, UNDP, Washington, DC 2000–03, Chief of the Sub-regional Resource Facility, UNDP, Bratislava 2003–05, Dir Policy Support and Programme Devt, Regional Centre for Europe and the Commonwealth of Ind. States in Bratislava, UNDP 2006–08, Deputy Dir and Head of Programmes, UN System Staff Coll. 2008–12, Dir 2012–. *Address:* United Nations System Staff College, Viale Maestri del Lavoro 10, 10127 Turin, Italy (office). *Telephone:* (011) 6535944 (office). *Fax:* (011) 6535901 (office). *E-mail:* info@unssc.org (office). *Website:* www.unssc.org (office).

JAVED MIANDAD; Pakistani banker and fmr professional cricketer; b. (Mohammad Javed Miandad Khan), 12 June 1957, Karachi, Sind; m. Tahira Saigol 1980; two s. one d.; ed CMS Secondary School, Karachi; right-hand middle-order batsman, leg-break and googly bowler; played for Karachi 1973–76, Sind 1973–76, Sussex 1976–79, Habib Bank 1976–94, Glamorgan 1980–85, Pakistan 1975–93 (Capt. 1980–81, 1992); One-Day Int. (ODI) debut against West Indies at Edgbaston, Birmingham in Cricket World Cup 1975; Test debut against NZ at Lahore 9 Oct. 1976; played in 124 Test matches for Pakistan 1976–94, 34 as Capt., scoring 8,832 runs (average 52.57, highest score 280 not out) including 23 hundreds; played in 233 ODIs, scoring 7,381 runs (average 41.70, highest score 119 not out) including eight hundreds; scored 28,663 First-class runs (average 53.37, highest score 311) including 80 hundreds; toured England 1975, 1979 (World Cup), 1982, 1983 (World Cup), 1987, 1992 (Capt.); holds world record for longest ODI career 11 June 1975–9 March 1996; appeared in six World Cup competitions; holds world record for maximum number of consecutive half centuries in ODIs – nine; Pakistan Nat. Team Coach 1998–99, 2000–01, 2003–04; fmr Asst Vice-Pres. Habib Bank of Pakistan; Dir-Gen. Pakistan Cricket Board 2008–14; a Wisden Cricketer of the Year 1982. *Leisure interests:* hockey, soccer, swimming, reading sports books, television, spending time with family.

JAVID, Rt Hon Sajid, PC; British politician and fmr banker; *Secretary of State for Home Department;* b. 5 Dec. 1969, Rochdale, Lancs.; m. Laura Javid; one s. three d.; ed Univ. of Exeter; Assoc. and Analyst, Chase Manhattan Bank, New York 1991–94, Vice-Pres. 1994–2000; Partner, JP Morgan Partners LLC 1997–2009; Dir, Deutsche Bank AG 2000–04, Man. Dir 2004–09, Bd mem., Deutsche Bank Int. Ltd 2007–09; MP (Conservative Party) for Bromsgrove 2010–, mem. Work and Pensions Select Cttee June–Dec. 2010; Parl. Private Sec. to Minister of State for Further Educ. and Skills 2010–11, to Chancellor of Exchequer 2011–12; Econ. Sec. to Treasury 2012–13, Financial Sec. to Treasury 2013–14; Sec. of State, Dept for Culture, Media and Sport 2014–15; Minister for Equalities April–July 2014; Sec. of State for Business, Innovation and Skills and Pres. of Board of Trade 2015–16, for Communities and Local Govt 2016–18, for Home Dept 2018–; British Muslim Awards Politician of the Year 2015. *Address:* Home Office, 2 Marsham Street, London, SW1P 4DF (office); House of Commons, Westminster, London, SW1A 1AA, England. *Telephone:* (20) 7035-4848 (office); (20) 7219-7027. *Fax:* (20) 7219-0930. *E-mail:* public.enquiries@homeoffice.gsi.gov.uk (office); sajid.javid.mp@parliament.uk. *Website:* www.gov.uk/government/organisations/home-office (office); www.parliament.uk/biographies/commons/sajid-javid/3945; www.sajidjavid.com.

JAWAD, Said Tayeb, LLB, MBA; Afghan diplomatist; *Ambassador to UK;* m. Shamim Jawad; one s.; ed Lycée Istiglal, Kabul Univ., Westfaelishe Wilhelms Univ., Germany, Golden Gate Univ., USA; left Afghanistan after Soviet Union invasion 1980, exiled in Germany –1986, moved to USA, worked on Wall Street –1989, moved to San Francisco; Chief of Staff for Afghan Pres. Hamid Karzai, also Pres.'s spokesman, Press Sec. and Dir of Int. Relations 2001–03; Amb. to USA (also accred to Argentina, Bolivia, Brazil, Chile, Colombia, Ecuador, Mexico, Nicaragua, Panama, Uruguay, Venezuela) 2003–10, to UK 2017–; Sr Political and Foreign Policy Adviser to Chief Exec. of Afghanistan 2015–17; Diplomat-in-Residence, Future of Diplomacy Project, Belfer Center for Science and Int. Affairs, John F. Kennedy School of Govt, Harvard Univ. Oct.–Nov. 2010, Fisher Family Fellow 2010–11; Diplomat-in-Residence, Paul H. Nitze School of Advanced Int. Studies, Johns Hopkins Univ. 2011–; Chair. Foundation for Afghanistan 2004–14; CEO Capitalize LLC 2010–17; Global Political Strategist APCO Worldwide 2010–17; mem. Advisory Bd Concordia Summit; has worked as writer and commentator on Afghan and int. affairs; Hon. mem. Blackfeet Tribe, Montana 2004; Dr hc (Argosy Univ.) 2007; Loya Jirga Service Medal 2003, Special Award, America Soc. for Civil Engineers 2004, Award of Merit, American Soc. for Engineering Educ. 2007, Global Citizen Award, Roots of Peace 2008. *Address:* Embassy of Afghanistan, 31 Prince's Gate, London, SW7 1QQ, England (office). *Telephone:* (20) 3609-8021 (office). *E-mail:* ea@afghanistanembassy.org.uk (office); jawad@afghanistanembassy.org.uk. *Website:* www.afghanistanembassy.org.uk (office).

JAWARA, Hon. Alhaji Sir Dawda Kairaba, Kt, FRCVS, DTVM; Gambian politician and fmr head of state; b. 16 May 1924, Barajally; s. of Almamy Jawara and Mama Jawara; ed Achimota Coll., Glasgow Univ.; Principal Veterinary Officer, Gambian Civil Service 1957–60; entered politics 1960; Minister of Educ. 1960–61; Premier 1962–65; Prime Minister 1965–70; Pres. of Repub. of The Gambia 1970–94 (overthrown in coup); Vice-Pres. of Confed. of Senegambia 1982; Minister of Defence 1985; Pres. Comité Inter-Etats de Lutte contre la Sécheresse du Sahel; mem. Board Peutinger Coll. (FRG); Hon. GCMG 1974; decorations from Senegal, Mauritania, Lebanon, Grand Master Nat. Order of the Repub. of Gambia 1972; Peutinger Gold Medal 1979. *Leisure interests:* golf, gardening, sailing.

JAWED, Sayyed Mohammad Ali; Afghan politician; *Leader, Harakat-i Islami i Afghanistan (Islamic Movement of Afghanistan);* b. 1951, Polebaraq, Mazar-e-Sharif; ed univ. studies in Najaf, Iraq, completed doctorate in religious studies; engaged in Jihad during Soviet invasion of Afghanistan; served as Minister of Planning and Man., Acting Prime Minister, Prime Minister, Minister of Transport; later served as Minister of Transportation, Spokesman of Nat. Communication Front; Leader of MNA representing the people of Balkh Prov.; f. Harakat-i Islami i Afghanistan (Islamic Movt of Afghanistan) during communist regime, Leader 2005–. *Address:* Harakat-i Islami i Afghanistan, Street 4, Qala-i Fathullah, Shar-i-Nau, Kabul, Afghanistan (office). *Telephone:* 79-9343998 (mobile) (office).

JAWORSKI, HE Cardinal Marian, DTheol, DPhil, DPhilR; Ukrainian (b. Polish) ecclesiastic; *Archbishop Emeritus of Lviv;* b. 21 Aug. 1926, Lwów, Poland (now Lviv, Ukraine); ed Theological Acad., Kraków, Catholic Univ. of Lublin, Warsaw Theological Acad.; ordained priest, Kraków 1950; taught for several years at Catholic Theological Acad. of Warsaw and later at Pontifical Theological Faculty of Kraków (First Rector 1981–87); lectured in metaphysics and philosophy of religion at seminaries of various religious orders; consecrated Titular Bishop of Lambaesis and Apostolic Admin. of Lubaczów 1984; Archbishop of Lviv 1991–2008, Archbishop Emer. 2008–; cr. Cardinal (In Pectore) 1998, apptd Cardinal-Priest of S. Sisto 2001; Pres. Ukrainian Episcopal Conf. 1992; Order of Prince Yaroslav the Wise (Fifth Rank) 2004; Dr hc (Bohum) 1985, (Cardinal Stefan Wysujnski Univ., Warsaw) 2002; Award 'For Great Contributions to Strengthening Peace and International Accord in Ukraine' 2004. *Publications:* three books, 31 monographs, two textbooks, more than 160 scientific articles. *Address:* c/o Metropolis Curia of Archdiocese of Lviv of the Roman Catholic Church, Ploscha Katedralny 1, 79008 Lviv, Ukraine.

JAY, Martin, CBE, BA, MA; British engineering industry executive; *Chairman, Oxsensis Ltd;* b. July 1939; m.; two d. one s.; ed Winchester Coll. and New Coll., Oxford; began career with British Petroleum; Man. Dir and mem. Man. Bd GEC Electronic Components –1989; CEO Vosper Thornycroft PLC (now VT Group PLC) 1989–2002, Chair. (non-exec.) 2002–03; Dir (non-exec.) Invensys PLC Jan.–July 2003, Chair. July 2003–09; Chair. EADS UK 2005–06; Chair. Oxsensis Ltd 2009–;

Trustee, Tall Ships Youth Trust. *Address:* Oxsensis Ltd, Rutherford Appleton Laboratory, Harwell Science and Innovation Campus, Didcot, Oxon., OX11 0QX, England (office). *Telephone:* (1235) 778120 (office). *Fax:* (1235) 778276 (office). *E-mail:* contact@oxsensis.com (office). *Website:* www.oxsensis.com (office).

JAY, Peter, MA; British economist, journalist and fmr diplomatist; b. 7 Feb. 1937, London; s. of Lord Jay; m. 1st Margaret Ann Callaghan (now Baroness Margaret Ann Jay of Paddington, q.v., d. of Lord Callaghan) 1961 (divorced 1986); one s. two d.; one s. by Jane Tustian; m. 2nd Emma Thornton 1986; three s.; ed Winchester Coll. and Christ Church, Oxford; Midshipman and Sub-Lt, RNVR 1956–57; Asst Prin., HM Treasury 1961–64, Pvt. Sec. to Jt Perm. Sec. 1964, Prin. 1964–67; Econs Ed. The Times 1967–77, Assoc. Ed. Times Business News 1969–77; Presenter, Weekend World, ITV 1972–77, The Jay Interview 1975–77; Amb. to USA 1977–79; Consultant, Economist Group 1979–81; Dir The Economist Intelligence Unit (EIU) 1979–83; Columnist,The Times 1980; Dir New Nat. Theatre, Washington, DC 1979–81; Chair. TV-AM 1980–83, TV-AM News 1982–83, Pres. TV-AM 1983; Presenter, A Week in Politics, Channel 4 1983–86; Chief of Staff to Robert Maxwell 1986–89; Econs Ed., BBC 1990–2001; Dir (non-exec.) Bank of England 2003–09; Sr Ed. Consultant, Man. Dir Banking World BPCC, Editor Banking World 1983–86, Supervising Ed. 1986–89; Chair. United Way of GB 1982–83, Feasibility Study 1982–83; Chair. Nat. Council for Voluntary Orgs 1981–86; Visiting Scholar, Brookings Inst., Washington, DC 1979–80; Copland Memorial Lecturer, Australia 1980; Gov. Ditchley Foundation 1982–; Hon. DH (Ohio State Univ.) 1978; Political Broadcaster of Year 1973, Royal TV Soc.'s Male Personality of Year (Pye Award) 1974, Shell Int. TV Award 1974, Wincott Memorial Lecturer 1975. *Publications:* The Budget 1972, Foreign Affairs, America and the World 1979 (contrib.) 1980, The Crisis for Western Political Economy and other essays 1984, Apocalypse 2000 (with Michael Stewart) 1987, Road to Riches, or The Wealth of Man 2000; numerous newspaper and magazine articles. *Leisure interest:* sailing. *Address:* Hensington Farmhouse, Woodstock, Oxon, OX20 1LH, England. *Telephone:* (1993) 811222. *Fax:* (1993) 812861. *E-mail:* peter@jay.prestel.co.uk (office).

JAY OF EWELME, Baron (Life Peer), cr. 2006, of Ewelme in the County of Oxfordshire; **Michael Hastings Jay,** GCMG, MA, MSc; British diplomatist (retd); b. 19 June 1946, Shawford, Hants.; s. of Alan Jay and Felicity Vickery; m. Sylvia Mylroie 1975; ed Winchester Coll., Magdalen Coll., Oxford and School of Oriental and African Studies, Univ. of London; Ministry of Overseas Devt 1969–73, 1976–78; UK Del. IMF, IBRD, Washington, DC 1973–75; First Sec. New Delhi 1978–81; FCO 1981–85; Cabinet Office 1985–87; Counsellor, Paris 1987–90; Asst Under-Sec. of State for EC Affairs, FCO 1990–93, Deputy Under-Sec. of State (Dir for EC (now EU) and Econ. Affairs) 1994–96; Amb. to France 1996–2001; Perm. Under-Sec., FCO and Head of Diplomatic Service 2002–06; Personal Rep. to Prime Minister, G8 2005–06; Dir (non-exec.), Associated British Foods 2006–15, Crédit Agricole SA 2008–12, Valéo SA 2007–14, Candover Investments plc 2007–14, Electricité de France (EDF) SA 2009–13; Chair. House of Lords Appointments Comm. 2008–13, mem. EU Sub-cttee F – Home Affairs, Health and Educ. 2014–; Vice-Chair. Business for New Europe 2006–; Assen mem. BUPA 2006–10; Chair. Culham Languages and Sciences (educational charity) 2007–10, Merlin (int. medical aid charity) 2007–13; mem. Bd Franco-British Chamber of Commerce and Industry, London 2009–11, British Library Advisory Council 2011– (Chair.); Sr Assoc. mem. St Antony's Coll. Oxford 1996; Trustee, Thomson Reuters Founders Share Co. 2013–; Hon. Fellow, Magdalen Coll. Oxford. *Address:* House of Lords, Westminster, London, SW1A 0PW, England (office). *Telephone:* (20) 7219-3941 (office). *E-mail:* jaymh@parliament.uk (office). *Website:* www.parliament.uk/biographies/lords/lord-jay-of-ewelme/3818 (office).

JAY OF PADDINGTON, Baroness (Life Peer), cr. 1992, of Paddington, in the City of Westminster; **Margaret Ann Jay,** PC, BA; British politician and business executive; b. 18 Nov. 1939; d. of James Callaghan (Lord Callaghan of Cardiff, Prime Minister 1976–79); m. 1st Peter Jay (q.v.) 1961 (divorced 1986); one s. two d.; m. 2nd Prof. M. W. Adler CBE 1994; ed Somerville Coll., Oxford; began career as producer and journalist with BBC TV 1961–77, producer and reporter, ABC TV and Nat. Public Radio, USA 1979–82, Panorama, BBC TV 1982–86, This Week, Thames TV 1986–88; served as mem. various London Health Authorities 1974–97; Founder-Dir Nat. AIDS Trust 1988–92; apptd Labour Life Peer, House of Lords 1992–; Prin. Opposition Spokesperson on Health, House of Lords 1995–97, Minister of State, Dept of Health 1997–98, Leader, House of Lords and Minister for Women 1998–2001, currently serves as back-bench Privy Councillor, House of Lords; Dir (non-exec.) London Broadcasting Co. 1992–93, Carlton TV 1995–97, Scottish Power 1996–97; Dir (non-exec.) British Telecommunications (BT) PLC 2001–08, mem. Corp. Social Responsibility Cttee 2008–; Sr Ind. Dir and mem. Int. Advisory Bd, Independent Media Group 2002–; mem. Kensington, Chelsea and Westminster Health Authority 1992–97; Chair. Nat. Assen Leagues of Hosp. Friends 1994–97; political consultant and Chair. Overseas Devt Inst. 2002–07; Sr Political Consultant, Currie & Brown, Amey Ltd 2002–07; Co-Chair. Iraq Comm. set up by Foreign Policy Centre and Channel 4 TV 2007; Chair. House of Lords Select Cttee on Constitution 2010–14; Visiting Prof. Policy Inst. King's Coll., London 2015; Hon. Fellow, Somerville Coll. Oxford; Dr hc (South Bank Univ.) 1999, (Sunderland Univ.) 2002. *Television:* reporter, contrib. or producer: Panorama (BBC TV) 1982–86, This Week (Thames TV) 1986, The Social History of Medicine (BBC TV) 1991, Hilary Clinton: The Extra President (BBC TV) 1992, Richard Leakey and the new Kenyan Opposition (BBC TV) 1996. *Publication:* Battered – The Story of Child Abuse (co-author) 1986. *Address:* House of Lords, Westminster, London, SW1A 0PW, England (office).

JAY-Z; American rap artist and record producer; b. (Shawn Corey Carter), 4 Dec. 1969, Brooklyn, New York; s. of Adnis Reeves and Gloria Carter; m. Beyoncé Knowles 2008; one d.; Co-founder, Roc-A-Fella Records 1995–, later expanding to include Roc-A-Wear clothing line and film co. (purchased by Universal 2004); collaborations with Puff Daddy, Lil' Kim, Foxy Brown, Notorious BIG, Mary J. Blige, Mariah Carey, Timbaland, Beyoncé (as The Carters); numerous live performances; Pres. Def Jam label 2005–08; MTV Video Music Award for Best Rap Video (for Can I Get A. . .) 1999, for Best Video from a Film (for Can I Get A. . .) 1999, Source Awards for Lyricist of the Year 1999, for Best Hip Hop Artist 2001, Billboard Music Award for Rap Artist of the Year 1999, MOBO Award for Best Int. Hip Hop Act 1999, Soul Train Award for Sammy Davis Jr Entertainer of the Year 2001, Grammy Awards for Best Rap Performance by Duo or Group (for Big Pimpin') 2001, (for Swagga Like Us with T.I) 2009, for Best Rap/Sung Collaboration (for Numb/Encore with Linkin Park) 2006, (for Run This Town with Rihanna and Kanye West) 2010, (for Empire State of Mind featuring Alicia Keys) 2011, (for Holy Grail, with Justin Timberlake) 2014, for Best Rap Solo Performance (for D.O.A.) 2010, for Best Rap Song (for Run This Town) 2010, for Best Rap Song (with Alicia Keys) (for Empire State of Mind) 2011, for Best Rap Song by Duo or Group (for On to the Next One featuring Swizz Beatz) 2011, for Rap Performance (for Otis with Kanye West) 2012, for Best Rap Performance, Rap Song (for N****s In Paris), Best Rap/Sung Collaboration (No Church In The Wild) 2013, for Best R&B Performance and R&B Song (both for Drunk in Love, with Beyoncé) 2015, MOBO Awards for Best Int. Male 2006, Best Hip-Hop Act 2008, Best Int. Act 2010, 2011, Michael Jackson Award for Best Video, Soul Train Awards (for Show Me What You Got) 2007, American Music Award for Favorite Rap/Hip Hop Artist 2009, BRIT Award for Best Int. Male Solo Artist 2010, GLAAD Vanguard Award (co-recipient) 2019. *Film:* Streets Is Watching (writer and dir) 1998. *Recordings include:* albums: Reasonable Doubt 1996, In My Lifetime Vol. 1 1997, Vol. 2 Hard Knock Life (Grammy Award for Best Rap Album 2001) 1999, Vol. 3 Life And Times Of S. Carter 1999, The Dynasty—Roc La Familia 2000, The Blueprint (Soul Train Award for Album of the Year 2002) 2001, The Best Of Both Worlds (with R. Kelly) 2002, The Blueprint 2: The Gift And The Curse 2002, S Carter Collection 2002, The Black Album 2003, Collision Course (with Linkin Park) 2004, Kingdom Come 2006, American Gangster 2007, The Blueprint 3 (American Music Award for Favorite Rap/Hip Hop Album) 2009, Magna Carta Holy Grail 2013, 4:44 2017; with Kanye West: Watch the Throne 2011; with Beyoncé (as The Carters): Everything is Love 2018. *Publication:* Decoded 2010. *Address:* Roc-A-Fella Records, 825 Eighth Avenue, New York, NY 10019-7472, USA (office). *Website:* www.rocafella.com (office); www.jay-z.com.

JAYAKUMAR, Shunmugam, LLM; Singaporean diplomatist and government official; b. 12 Aug. 1939, Singapore; m. Dr Lalitha Rajahram 1969; two s. one d.; ed Univ. of Singapore and Yale Univ., USA; Dean, Law Faculty, Univ. of Singapore 1974–80, Prof. of Law, Chair. Faculty of Law Advisory Council and Int. Advisory Panel, Centre for Int. Law; Perm. Rep. of Singapore to UN 1971–74, High Commr to Canada 1971–74; MP 1980–; Minister of State for Law and Home Affairs 1981–84, Minister of Labour 1984–85, of Home Affairs 1985–94, of Foreign Affairs 1994–2004, of Law 1988–2008, Deputy Prime Minister 2004–09; Co-ordinating Minister for Nat. Security 2005–10, Sr Minister 2009–11 (retd); apptd Co-Chair. Int. Advisory Panel on Transboundary Pollution, Government of Singapore 2014, Conciliator, Int. Centre for Settlement of Investment Disputes 2013; Hon. Fellow, Singapore Acad. of Law 2008; Grand Cordon of the Order of the Rising Sun 2012; Public Service Star (BBM) 1980. *Publications include:* Constitutional Law Cases from Malaysia and Singapore 1971, Public International Law Cases from Malaysia and Singapore 1974, Constitutional Law (with documentary material) 1976, Pedra Branca: The Road to the World Court 2009, Diplomacy: A Singapore Experience 2011 and articles in journals. *Leisure interests:* jogging, golfing, in-line skating, kendo. *Address:* Faculty of Law, National University of Singapore, Eu Tong Sen Building, 469G Bukit Timah Road, Singapore 259776 (office). *Telephone:* 67790979 (office). *E-mail:* lawsjaya@nus.edu.sg (office); profsjaya@gmail.com. *Website:* law.nus.edu.sg (office).

JAYAMPATHI, Air Marshal Kapila, MSc; Sri Lankan air force officer; *Commander of Air Force;* m.; four c.; ed Nalanda Coll., Nat. Defence Univ.; joined Sri Lanka Air Force (SLAF) as officer 1982, Pilot Officer General Duties branch of No. 4 Helicopter Squadron 1985–90, Qualified Helicopter Instructor (QHI), Flying Officer 1986, Flying Lt 1989, Squadron Leader No. 7 Helicopter Squadron SLAF 1993, Commanding Officer 1994, Wing-Commdr Air Force Headquarters 1996, Base Commdr SLAF Base Hingurakgoda 2002, promoted to Air Vice-Marshal 2009, Base Commdr SLAF Base China Bay (now Air Force Acad.) 2002, Commdt 2010–11, Dir Logistics Air Force Bd of Man. 2011, Dir Air Operations 2014–16, Commdr SLAF 2016–; Defence Adviser High Comm. in Islamabad 2005–07; numerous medals including Deshaputhra Medal. *Leisure and interests:* swimming, music, golf. *Address:* Sri Lanka Air Force Headquarters, PO Box 594, Colombo 2, Sri Lanka (office). *Telephone:* (11) 2441044 (office). *E-mail:* media@airforce.lk (office). *Website:* www.airforce.lk (office).

JAYARATNE, D(isanayaka) M(udiyanselage); Sri Lankan politician; b. 6 April 1931, Doluwa, Gampola, Kandy; m.; ed Doluwa Maha Vidyalaya, Gampola, Kandy, Univ. of Peradeniya; worked as a teacher at Doluwa Maha Vidyalaya; Postmaster at Doluwa 1960–62; Founding mem. Sri Lanka Freedom Party (SLFP); MP (SLFP) for Gampala 1970–77, for Kandy Dist 1989– (re-elected under the People's Alliance 1994); Minister of Land, Agric. and Forestry 1994–2000, of Agric., Food and Cooperatives 2000–01, of Post and Telecommunications (Upcountry Devt) 2004–05, of Post and Telecommunications (Rural Econ. Devt) 2005–07, of Plantation Industries 2007–10; Prime Minister and Minister of Buddha Sasana and Religious Affairs 2010–15; mem. United Peoples Freedom Alliance; Dr hc (Sun Moon Univ., Seoul, Korea) 2013. *Address:* Parliament of Sri Lanka, Parliamentary Complex, Sri Jayewardenepura Kotte (office); No. 121, Wijerama Road, Colombo 07, Sri Lanka. *E-mail:* jayaratne_d@parliament.lk (office). *Website:* www.parliament.lk (office).

JAYASINGHE, Chrysantha Romesh, BA (Hons); Sri Lankan diplomatist; *Secretary, Ministry of Foreign Affairs;* b. 1955; m.; one s. one d.; ed St Thomas's Coll., Mount Lavinia, Univ. of Kelaniya; worked in Ceylon Shipping Corpn as staff trainee and then as man. trainee at Lever Brothers (Ceylon) Ltd; joined Foreign Service as Asst Dir UN Div. 1981, assignments in Protocol and South Asia Divs, Ministry of Foreign Affairs, served as Second Sec., Embassy in Bonn, as First Sec., Perm. Mission to UN Office, Geneva, as Counsellor in High Comm. in Dhaka, as Deputy High Commr in New Delhi, Amb. to Belgium and Head of Sri Lankan Del. to European Communities, Brussels (also accred to Portugal and Luxembourg) 2000–05, High Commr to India 2005–09, also accred as Amb. to Afghanistan and Bhutan 2006–09, Sec., Ministry of Foreign Affairs 2009–; Adviser, Sri Lankan Del. to Bd of Govs, Asian Devt Bank 2006. *Leisure interests:* travelling, reading, swimming. *Address:* Ministry of Foreign Affairs, Republic Building, Colombo 1, Sri Lanka (office). *Telephone:* (11) 2438263 (office). *Fax:* (11) 2446091 (office). *E-mail:* sfa@formin.gov.lk (office).

JAYASUNDERA, P. B., BA, MA, PhD; Sri Lankan civil servant, government official and airline industry executive; ed Univ. of Colombo, Boston Univ. and

Williams Coll., USA; held several sr positions in Cen. Bank of Sri Lanka –1980; with civil service since 1980, Econ. Adviser 1990–95, Dir-Gen. Dept of Fiscal Policy and Econ. Affairs 1995–97, Deputy Sec. to the Treasury 1997–99, Sec. to the Treasury 1999–2008, 2009–15; Chair. SriLankan Airlines Ltd 2008–09; fmr Chair. Public Enterprises Reform Comm.; fmr Sr Policy Adviser, Ernst & Young; fmr consultant to IMF and World Bank on country assignments; found guilty by Supreme Court of acting with dishonest intent in sale of Lanka Marine Services Ltd shares and of misleading Bd of Investment, ordered to pay Rs 500,000 compensation July 2008.

JAYASURIYA, Lt-Gen. (retd) Jagath, MSc; Sri Lankan army officer (retd) and diplomatist; b. 3 Jan. 1959; m. Manjulika Aruna; one s. one d.; ed Royal Coll., Colombo, School of Armour, Pakistan, Armoured Corps Centre and School, India, Sri Lanka Mil. Acad., Diyathalawa, Army Training School, Defence Services Staff Coll., India, Univ. of Madras, India, Defence Resource Man. Inst., Naval Post Grad. School, Calif., USA, Nat. Defence Univ. Course, China; Coll. Prefect, Royal Coll., Colombo 1977; joined Sri Lanka Army as a Cadet Officer 1978, passed out first in order of merit of Intake-10, commissioned as Second Lt 1980; rank of Lt 1981, Capt. 1984, Maj. 1988, Lt-Col 1993, Col 2001, Brig. 2001, Maj.-Gen. 2005, currently Lt-Gen.; Troop Leader, 1st Reconnaissance Regt 1980–83, Adjutant 1984–85; apptd Staff Officer Grade 111 in Directorate of Personnel Admin, Army HQ 1985; Squadron Commdr 1st Reconnaissance Regt, Sri Lanka Armoured Corps 1987; Second in Command, 3rd Reconnaissance Regt, Sri Lanka Armoured Corps 1992; CO, 1st Reconnaissance Regt, Sri Lanka Armoured Corps 1994–95; Brigade Maj., 9 Brigade appointment, Jaffna 1990; Chief Instructor, Officers' Study Centre and Staff Officer II (Training), Army Training Centre 1991–92; Staff Officer Grade 1, Armoured Brigade 1992–94; Gen. Staff Officer 1, Jt Operations HQ (JOH), serving all three services and the Police 1995–96; Col Mil. Sec., Army HQ 1996–97; Commdr Armoured Brigade Sept.–Dec. 1997; Commdr 563 Infantry Brigade Jan.–April 1998; Mil. Liaison Officer, Ministry of Defence 1998–2002; Commdt, Sri Lanka Mil. Acad. 2002–04; Dir of Operations, Army HQ 2004–05; GOC 52 Div. 2005–07; Commdr Security Forces HQ, Wanni 2007–09; Commdr of the Army 2009–13; Chief of Defence Staff 2013–15 (retd); Amb. to Brazil 2015–17; Vishishta Seva Vibhushanaya, Uttama Seva Padakkama, Army 50th Anniversary Medal, Long Service Medal and Clasp, 50th Independence Medal, Desha Puthra Sammanaya, North and East Operations Medal, Poorna Bhoomi Padakkama, Riviresa Campaign Service Medal and others. *Achievements include:* capt. of school boxing team, Royal Coll., Colombo, awarded boxing colours 1974, 1976, 1977, now int. referee/judge in boxing.

JAYASURIYA, Jayantha, MPhil.; Sri Lankan lawyer and government official; *Attorney-General;* b. 2 Dec. , Nalaka; s. of (Dr) J. A. Buddhadasa and Eugene Buddhadasa (née Weerakoon); m. Kalyanapriya Jayasuriya (née Wattage); two c.; ed Maliyadeva Coll., Kurunegala, Sri Lanka Law Coll., Univ. of Hong Kong; apprenticeship in Chambers of Ariya Rekawa and later joined Chambers of Daya Perera, Pres.'s Counsel, and C.Vicknarajah after taking oaths in 1982; joined Attorney-Gen.'s Office 1983, held several posts including Head of Criminal Div., apptd Sr State Counsel 1996, Deputy Solicitor Gen. 2004, Sr Additional Solicitor Gen. 2011–16, Pres.'s Counsel 2012–16, Attorney-Gen. 2016–; served as Legal Consultant, Financial Intelligence Unit of Central Bank; Trial Attorney, UN Int. Criminal Tribunal for Rwanda and UN Int. Criminal Tribunal for fmr Yugoslavia 2000–04; Visiting Lecturer and Examiner, Sri Lanka Law Coll. and Kotalawala Defence Acad.; fmr mem. Bd of Dirs Sri Lanka Child Protection Authority; Hon. Vice-Pres. Asia Crime Prevention Foundation, Sri Lanka Chapter; Prosecutor of the Year Award, Int. Asscn of Prosecutors 2012. *Address:* Attorney General's Department, Hulftsdorp, POB 502, Colombo 12, Sri Lanka (office). *Telephone:* (11) 2147888 (office). *Fax:* (11) 2436421 (office). *E-mail:* administration@attorneygeneral.gov.lk (office). *Website:* www.attorneygeneral.gov.lk (office).

JAYASURIYA, Karu; Sri Lankan business executive, politician and fmr diplomatist; *Speaker of Parliament;* b. 29 Sept. 1940; ed Ananda Coll., Colombo Univ.; Commissioned Officer, Sri Lanka Army 1965–72; held several exec. positions with C.W. Mackie & Co. Ltd (rubber exporting co.), including Finance Dir, Group Man. Dir, and Chair. in early 1980s; also served as Chair. Ceylon Trading Co. Ltd, United Motors Ltd. and served as dir on numerous corp. bds; fmr Pres. Nat. Chamber of Commerce, Sri Lanka–European Business Council, Sugar Importers Asscn, Plastics and Rubber Inst. of Sri Lanka; Amb. to Germany (also accred to Austria and Switzerland) 1992–94; Mayor of Colombo 1997–99; Leader of Opposition, Western Provincial Council 1999–2001; mem. Parl. (United Nat. Party) for Gampaha Dist 2000–15, for Nat. List 2015–, Speaker of Parl. 2015–; Minister of Power and Energy 2001–04, of Public Admin and Home Affairs 2007–08, of Public Admin, Provincial Councils, Democratic Governance and of Buddha Saasana 2015; apptd Chair. United Nat. Party 1996, later Deputy Leader, Chair. Leadership Council 2013; mem. Presidential Comm. on Privatization; Fellow, Inst. of Chartered Ship Brokers, UK, Inst. of Transport; Kt, Grand Cross of the Order of Orange-Nassau 2014, Grand Cordon, Order of the Rising Sun (Japan) 2016; Pride of Asia Award, Abdul Kalam Inst. of Technological Sciences 2019, Vishva Keerthishri Lanka Jana Ranjana 2019, Sasana Keerthi Sri Deshabhimani 2019. *Address:* Office of Speaker, Parliament of Sri Lanka, Parliamentary Complex, Sri Jayewardenepura Kotte (office); No. 2, Amarasekera Mawatha, Colombo 05, Sri Lanka. *Telephone:* (11) 2777100 (office). *Fax:* (11) 2777564 (office). *E-mail:* jayasuriya_k@parliament.lk (office). *Website:* www.parliament.lk (office).

JAYASURIYA, Sanath Teran; Sri Lankan professional cricketer and politician; b. 30 June 1969, Matara; divorced; left-hand batsman and slow left-arm orthodox spin bowler; played for Sri Lanka 1989–2011 (Capt. 1999–2003), Bloomfield Cricket and Athletic Club 1994–, Colombo Cricket Club, Somerset 2005, MCC 2007, Lancashire 2007, Warwickshire 2008, Mumbai Indians (IPL) 2008–10, Worcestershire 2010, Ruhuna Rhinos 2011, Khulna Royal Bengals 2012, ACC Asian XI; First-class debut: 1988/89; Test debut: NZ v Sri Lanka, Hamilton, NZ 1991, One-Day Int. (ODI) debut: Australia v Sri Lanka, Melbourne, Australia 1989; mem. Sri Lankan team that won World Cup 1996; Test batting: 110 matches, 6,973 runs, highest score 340, average 40.07, 14 centuries, 31 half-centuries; Test bowling: 110 matches, 8,188 balls, 3,366 runs, 98 wickets, 5/34 best bowling in an innings, 9/74 best bowling in a match, 34.34 average; ODIs: 445 matches, 13,430 runs, highest score 189, average 32.36, strike rate 91.21, 323 wickets, average 36.75, economy rate 4.78, best bowling 6/29; holds record for highest test score made by a Sri Lankan: 340 against India 1997; became only the fourth batsman to score 10,000 runs in one-day cricket 2005; first Sri Lankan to play 100 Tests; MP for Matara Dist (United People's Freedom Alliance) 2010–15, Deputy Minister of Local Govt and Rural Devt 2015; Chair. Cricket Selection Cttee 2013–17; Wisden Cricketer of the Year 1997, World Cup Most Valuable Player Award; stadium named in his honour in Matara. *Television:* contestant on 5th season of Indian celebrity dance show, Jhalak Dikhhla Jaa 2012. *Address:* c/o Sri Lanka Cricket, 35 Maitland Place, Colombo 07.

JAYAWARDENA, D. H. S.; Sri Lankan business executive; *Chairman, Aitken Spence PLC;* m. Priya Jayawardena; three c.; Founder-Dir and Chair. Stassen Group; Chair. Distilleries Co. of Sri Lanka (DCSL), Lanka Milk Foods (CWE) Ltd, Balangoda Plantations PLC, Madulsima Plantations PLC, Browns Beach Hotels PLC, Lanka Bell Pvt. Ltd, Periceyl Pvt. Ltd, Aitken Spence PLC 2003– (mem. Bd of Dirs 2000–); fmr Chair. Ceylon Petroleum Corpn, Sri Lanka Insurance Corpn, Air Lanka (now Sri Lankan Airlines); mem. Bd of Dirs Colombo Stock Exchange, Bd of Investments of Sri Lanka; fmr Sr Adviser to Pres. on Int. Trade and Investment; Hon. Consul Gen. for Denmark; Knight Cross of Dannebrog (Denmark) 2010. *Address:* Aitken Spence PLC, Aitken Spence Towers, 305 Vauxhall Street, Colombo 2, Sri Lanka (office). *Telephone:* (11) 2308308 (office). *Fax:* (11) 2445406 (office). *E-mail:* chairman@aitkenspence.lk (office); chairman@ceypetco.gov.lk (office). *Website:* www.aitkenspence.lk (office).

JAYAWARDENA, Denagamage Proboth Mahela de Silva, (Mahela Jayawardena); Sri Lankan professional cricketer; b. 27 May 1977, Colombo; s. of Senerath Jayawardena and Sunila Jayawardena; m. Christina Mallika Sirisena; ed Nalanda Coll., Colombo; right-handed batsman; right-arm medium pace bowler; played for Sinhalese Sports Club 1995–2015, Sri Lanka 1997–2015 (Capt. 2006–09, 2012–13), Wayamba Elevens 2007–12, Derbyshire 2008, Kings XI Punjab 2008–10, Kochi Tuskers Kerala (Capt.) 2011, Delhi Daredevils 2012–14, Wayamba United 2012, Sussex 2015, Jamaica Tallawahs 2015, Central Stags 2015–17, Adelaide Strikers 2015–16, Somerset 2016, Karachi Kings 2017; First-class debut: 1995/96; Test debut: Sri Lanka v India, Colombo (RPS) 2–6 Aug. 1997; One-Day Int. (ODI) debut: Sri Lanka v Zimbabwe, Colombo (RPS) 24 Jan. 1998; T20I debut: England v Sri Lanka, Southampton 15 June 2006; played 149 Tests, scored 11,814 runs (average 49.84) with one triple century, seven double centuries, 34 centuries and 50 fifties, highest score 374 against South Africa, Colombo 2010; played 448 ODIs, scored 12,650 runs (average 33.37) with 19 centuries and 77 fifties, highest score 144 against England, Leeds 2011; played 55 T20Is, scored 1,493 runs (average 31.76) with one century and nine fifties, highest score 100 against Zimbabwe, Providence 2010; played 237 First-class matches, scored 17,838 runs (average 49.68) with 51 centuries and 80 fifties; retired from int. cricket 18 March 2015; batting consultant for England team travelling to UAE for Test series against Pakistan Oct. 2015; int. TV commentator for test between England and Sri Lanka at Headingley May 2016; Coach Mumbai Indians 2017 (won IPL 2017); inaugural ICC Best Capt. of the Year 2006 2007, Capt. of World ODI Team of the Year 2006, Spirit of Cricket Award 2007, 2013, Wisden Cricketer of the Year 2007, ICC Spirit of Cricket Award 2013. *Achievements include:* shared world record stand of 624 with Kumar Sangakkara (highest for any wicket in First-class cricket history and first instance of a stand of 600 or more in a First-class or Test match innings) 2006; first Sri-Lankan Capt. to score a Test triple-century, making 374 off 572 deliveries with 43 fours and 1 six, the fourth highest individual score in Test match cricket and the best by a right-hander; with Muttiah Muralitharan ("c Jayawardena b Muralitharan"), part of the most common bowler-fielder combination in history of Test cricket; became ninth player in cricket history, and first Sri Lankan, to score 10,000 Test runs, during second Test of tour in South Africa 2011–12; became only the second cricketer after Sachin Tendulkar to appear in 600 int. matches Feb. 2014.

JAYSTON, Michael, FGSM; British actor; b. (Michael James), 29 Oct. 1935, Nottingham; s. of Aubrey Jayston and Edna Myfanwy Llewelyn; m. 1st Lynn Farleigh 1965 (divorced 1970); m. 2nd Heather Mary Sneddon (divorced 1977); m. 3rd Elizabeth Ann Smithson 1978; three s. one d.; with the RSC 1965–69, Nat. Theatre 1976–79. *Films include:* A Midsummer Night's Dream 1968, Cromwell 1970, Nicholas and Alexandra 1971, Follow Me! 1972, Alice's Adventures in Wonderland 1972, Craze 1973, A Bequest to the Nation 1973, Tales That Witness Madness 1973, The Homecoming 1973, The Internecine Project 1974, Dominique 1978, Zulu Dawn 1979, From a Far Country 1981, Highlander III: The Sorcerer 1994, Element of Doubt 1996. *TV includes:* The Power Game (series) 1965, The Edwardians (miniseries) 1972, Mr. Rolls and Mr. Royce 1972, Jane Eyre (miniseries) 1973, The Merchant of Venice 1974, The Importance of Being Earnest 1974, Ring Once for Death 1974, Coffin for the Bride 1974, Quiller (series) 1975, She Fell Among Thieves 1978, Gossip from the Forest 1979, Tinker, Tailor, Soldier, Spy (miniseries) 1979, Flesh and Blood (series) 1980, Dust to Dust 1985, Doctor Who (series) 1986, Still Crazy Like a Fox 1987, A Guilty Thing Surprised 1988, Shake Hands Forever 1988, Somewhere to Run 1989, A Bit of a Do (series) 1989, Cluedo (series) 1990, The Darling Buds of May 1993, A Dinner of Herbs (miniseries) 2000, EastEnders 2002, Doctors (series) 2003, 2011, 2013, 2015, The Bill (series) 2000–06, The Royal (series) 2003–07, Foyle's War (series) 2007–08, Emmerdale (series) 2007–08, Albert's Memorial 2009, Holby City 2010, Borgia 2014; numerous appearances in series episodes. *Theatre appearances include:* Private Lives 1980, Sound of Music 1981, Way of the World 1984–85, Woman in Mind, Beethoven Readings with Medici String Quartet 1989, Dancing at Lughnasa 1992, Wind in the Willows, Nat. Theatre 1994, Racing Demon, Chichester Prod. in Toronto 1998, Easy Virtue, Chichester 1999, Amy's View 2001, Wild Orchids Anouilh 2002, Moment of Weakness 2003, The Marquise 2004, Heroes 2006, The Last Confession 2007, Quartet 2010. *Leisure interests:* cricket, darts, chess. *Address:* c/o Diamond Management, 31 Percy Street, London, W1T 2DD, England (office). *Telephone:* (20) 7631-0400 (office). *Fax:* (20) 7631-0500 (office). *E-mail:* agents@diman.co.uk (office). *Website:* www.diamondmanagement.co.uk (office); www.jayston.awardspace.com.

JAZAÏRY, Idriss, MA, MEcons, MPA; Algerian diplomatist and fmr international administrator; *Executive Director, Geneva Centre on Advancement of Human Rights and Global Dialogue;* b. 29 May 1936, Neuilly-sur-Seine, France; four s. one d.; ed Univ. of Oxford, UK, Ecole Nat. d'Admin, Paris, France, Harvard Univ., USA; Chief Econ. and Social Dept Algiers 1963–71; Dir Int. Co-operation, Ministry of Foreign Affairs 1963–71; Adviser to Pres. of Repub. 1971–77; Under-Sec.-Gen. Ministry of Foreign Affairs 1977–79; Amb. to Belgium, Luxembourg and EEC 1979–82; Amb.-at-large specializing in int. econ. affairs, Ministry of Foreign Affairs 1982–84; Pres. IFAD Rome 1984–93; Exec. Dir Agency for Co-operation and Research in Devt (ACORD), London 1993–99; Sr Consultant to UNDP 1994–98; Amb. to USA 1999–2004; Special Del. of Pres. of Algeria; mem. Bd of Dirs South Centre, Geneva 2002; Perm. Rep. to UN, Geneva 2004–12; Pres. Bd of Govs African Devt Bank 1971–72; Chair. UN Gen. Ass. Cttee of the Whole on North–South Dialogue 1978–79; organized first World Summit on the Econ. Advancement of Rural Women, Geneva 1992; fmr Pres. Conf. on Disarmament; currently Exec. Dir Geneva Centre on Advancement of Human Rights and Global Dialogue (think-tank); Grand Officer Order of Merit (Italy), Officer of Wissam Alaouite (Morocco), Officer of Order of Merit (Mauritania); Medal of Independence (Jordan), Gold Yasser Arafat Medal (Palestine) and others. *Publications include:* The State of World Rural Poverty 1992, In Support of Special Procedures of the UN Human Rights Council – An Alternative Narrative from the South 2015. *Leisure interests:* jogging, skiing, riding. *Address:* Château de Marcellaz, 73410 St Girod, France (home); Dar el Alou, 11 rue Buffon, Balcon St Raphael, El Biar, Algeria (home); Geneva Centre on Advancement of Human Rights and Global Dialogue, Rue de Vermont 37-39, CP186, 1211 Geneva, 20, Switzerland (office). *E-mail:* idrissjazairy@yahoo.com; info@gchragd.org (office). *Telephone:* 227482780 (office). *Website:* www.gchragd.org (office).

JAZBEC, Boštjan, BA, MA, PhD; Slovenian economist, academic and central banker; b. 26 March 1970, Celje; ed Univ. of Ljubljana, Central European Univ., Prague Coll., Czech Repub., Central European Univ., Budapest Coll., Hungary, Inst. for Advanced Studies, Austria; internship at Office of the Chief Economist, EBRD, London, UK Jan.–May 1998; consultant, World Bank, Washington, DC July–Aug. 1999, Jan. 2001; mem. Strategic Council, Govt of Slovenia responsible for fiscal issues 2003–04, BIS Working Party on Monetary Policy in Cen. and Eastern Europe 2005–08, European Cen. Bank (ECB) Information Tech. Steering Cttee (EISC), 18-mem. High Level Working Group at ECB 2007–08; mem. Governing Bd, Banka Slovenije (Bank of Slovenia), responsible for Information Tech. Dept and Cash Dept 2003–08, Gov. 2013–18; IMF Sr Adviser to Gov. of Cen. Bank of Kosovo, MCM Long-Term Expert 2009–12; IMF Expert, Cen. Bank of Suriname Feb., May–June 2013.

JEAN, Michaëlle, CC, CMM, COM, CD; Canadian (b. Haitian) journalist, broadcaster, documentary film producer, public servant and UN official; b. 6 Sept. 1957, Port-au-Prince, Haiti; m. Jean-Daniel Lafond; one d.; ed Univ. of Montréal, Univs of Perugia and Florence and Catholic Univ. of Milan, Italy; fled Haiti 1968, moved to Canada; joined Radio-Canada 1988, reporter, Actuel, Montréal ce soir 1989; Host, Virages 1991–92, Le Point 1992–95; Host, RDI channel 1995, fmr programmes include Le Monde ce soir, L'Edition quebecoise, Horizons francophones, le Journal RDI, Host, Grands Reportages; Host, The Passionate Eye, Rough Cuts, CBC Newsworld; Gov.-Gen. of Canada 2005–10; Sec.-Gen. Organisation internationale de la Francophonie, Paris 2015–; Special Envoy for Haiti for UNESCO 2010–14; Co-Pres. Michaëlle Jean Foundation, Ottawa 2010–; Chancellor, Univ. of Ottawa 2012–15; Sec.-Gen., Org. Internationale de la Francophonie 2014–18; Dr hc (Univ. of Ottawa) 2006, (Univ. of Foreigners of Perugia, Italy) 2006, (McGill Univ.) 2006, (York Univ.) 2007, (Univ. of Manitoba) 2007, (Univ. of Alberta) 2008, (Université de Moncton) 2009, (Université Laval) 2009, (Royal Mil. Coll. of Canada) 2010, (Université de Montréal) 2010, (Univ. of Guelph) 2011, (Univ. of Calgary) 2011; Anik Prize for information reporting 1994, Amnesty Int. Journalism Award 1995, Galaxi Award for best information programme host 2000, UNIFEM Canada Award 2009, Bd of Govs Recognition Achievement Award, Nat. Quality Inst. 2009. *Documentary films include:* Tropique Nord 1994, Haiti dans tous nos rêves 1995, L'heure de Cuba 1999. *Address:* Michaëlle Jean Foundation, 143 Séraphin-Marion Street, Ottawa, ON K1N 6N5, Canada (office). *Telephone:* (613) 562-5751) (office). *E-mail:* michaelle.jean@francophonie.org (office); info@fmjf.ca (office). *Website:* www.fmjf.ca (office); www.michaellejean.ca.

JEAN-MARIE, Marie-Carmelle; Haitian banker, business executive and politician; *Minister of Economy and Finance;* b. 16 July 1956, Vallée de Jacmel; ed Univ. d'État d'Haïti, Univ. Paris II, Assas, France, Inst. Technique de Banques, Inst. Technique de Marchés, Paris, Centre de Formation de la Profession Bancaire, Centre for Latin American Monetary Studies, Mexico; long career with Banque de la République d'Haïti (central bank) 1982–95, positions included Sr Economist, Int. Affairs Dept, Econ. Studies Dept, Training Dept, becoming Asst Dir; co-f. Group Croissance (consultancy) 1995–2001; Sr Adviser to Minister of Economy and Finance 2001; Adviser, Ministry of Educ. 2002–03; Dir, Cuba Br., Caisse d'Epargne 2003; Minister of Economy and Finance 2012–13, 2014–; Chair. Assn for Cooperation with Micro-Enterprise; Vice-Chair. Haitian Relief Fund for Women; Dir Total Haïti SA 2002–, SCIOP SA (construction co.), Chambre Franco-Haitienne de Commerce et d'Industrie. *Address:* Ministry of the Economy and Finance, Palais des Ministères, rue Mgr Guilloux, Port-au-Prince, Haiti (office). *Telephone:* 2223-7113 (office). *Fax:* 2223-1247 (office). *E-mail:* mef@mefhaiti.gouv.ht (office). *Website:* www.mefhaiti.gouv.ht (office).

JEANCOURT-GALIGNANI, Antoine; French business executive; b. 12 Jan. 1937, Paris; s. of Paul Jeancourt-Galignani and Germaine Verley; m. 1st Brigitte Auzouy 1961 (divorced 1983); three s. one d.; m. 2nd Hannelore Wagner 1983; one d.; ed Mount St Mary's Coll. Spinkhill, UK, École St Louis de Gonzague, Faculté de Paris, École Nat. d'Admin; Inspecteur de Finances 1965; Asst Sec., Office of Minister of Finance 1968–70, Treasury Dept of Ministry of Finance 1970–71; with Chase Manhattan Bank, New York 1972; Sr then Exec. Vice-Pres. in charge of int. and corp. banking, Crédit Agricole 1973–79; joined Banque Indosuez 1979, Pres. 1980–81, 1982–88, Chair. and CEO 1981–82, 1988–94; Chair. Assurances Générales de France 1994–2001; Chair. Gecina 2001–05; Dir Société Générale, Total 1994–, Euro Disney (Chair. Supervisory Bd 1995–2013), AGF, Kaufman & Broad SA; Officier, Légion d'honneur, Commdr, Ordre nat. du Mérite, Chevalier du Mérite agricole, Croix de la valeur militaire. *Publication:* La Finance Déboussolée 2001. *Address:* 3 avenue Bosquet, 75007 Paris, France. *E-mail:* jeangal@noos.fr.

JEANJEAN, Michel, LLM; French government official; b. May 1951; began career as Attaché in local govt dept 1973–81, Prin. Attaché 1981–82; Head of Commr's Office, St Pierre et Miquelon 1982–83, Head of Admin. Sub-Div., Marquesas Islands, French Polynesia 1983–87, Head of Admin.'s Office, Meurthe-et-Moselle département 1987–88, Deputy Admin. (Sous-préfet), Corte, Corsica 1988–91, Sec.-Gen. Haute-Saône Admin. 1991–93, with Ministry of the Interior, Overseas Possessions and Territorial Collectivities, becoming Head of Territorial Admin. and Political Affairs Dept 1993–96, Sec.-Gen. French Polynesia 1996–99, Sec.-Gen. Hérault Admin. 1999–2001, Deputy Admin. Avesnes-sur-Helpe 2001–05, Deputy Admin. Torcy 2005–10, Chief Admin. (Administrateur Supérieur) Wallis and Futuna 2010–13.

JEANMAIRE, (Renée Marcelle) Zizi; French actress, dancer and singer; b. 29 April 1924, Paris; d. of Marcel Jeanmaire; m. Roland Petit 1954 (died 2011); one d.; student, Paris Opera Ballet 1933–40, Dancer 1940–44; with Ballets de Monte-Carlo, Ballets Colonel de Basil, Ballets Roland Petit; Dir (with Roland Petit) Casino de Paris 1969–; leading role in three concerts, Zénith 1995, nine concerts, Opéra Bastille 2000; music hall appearances; Chevalier de la Légion d'honneur, Chevalier des Arts et des Lettres, Officier, Ordre nat. du Mérite. *Films:* Hans Christian Andersen, Anything Goes, Folies Bergère, Charmants Garçons, Black Tights, La Revue, Zizi je t'aime; musical: The Girl in Pink Tights (Broadway). *Leading roles in:* Aubade, Piccoli, Carmen, La Croqueuse de Diamants, Rose des Vents, Cyrano de Bergerac, La Dame dans la Lune, La Symphonie Fantastique 1975, Le loup, La chauve-souris 1979, Hollywood Paradise Show 1985, Java for ever 1988, Marcel et la Belle Excentrique 1992. *Address:* c/o Editions Assouline, 26 rue Danielle Casanova, 75002 Paris, France.

JEANNENEY, Jean-Noël, Agrégé d'Histoire, DèsL; French politician and academic; *Professor Emeritus in Modern History, Institut d'études politiques de Paris (Sciences Po);* b. 2 April 1942, Grenoble; s. of Jean-Marcel Jeanneney and Marie-Laure Jeanneney (née Monod); m. 2nd Annie-Lou Cot 1985; two s.; ed Lycées Champollion and Louis-le-Grand, Ecole normale supérieure, Inst. d'études politiques de Paris, Sorbonne Univ.; Lecturer in Contemporary History, Univ. de Paris X 1969–77, Lecturer 1968; Univ. Prof. in Modern History, Inst. d'études politiques de Paris (Sciences Po) 1977, now Prof. Emer.; Pres., Dir-Gen. Radio-France and Radio-France Int. 1982–86; Pres. Bicentenary of the French Revolution 1988–89; mem. Bd of Dirs, Agence France-Presse 1982–84, Télé-diffusion de France 1982–86, La Sept 1986, Seuil Publs 1987–91, 1993–2002; Chair. Scientific Council, Inst. d'Histoire du Temps Présent 1991–2000; Sec. of State for External Trade 1991–92, for Communication 1992–93; Regional Councillor, Franche-Comté 1992–98; Chair. Advisory Cttee for 'Histoire' (cable TV) 1997–2004; Pres. Europartenaires 1998–, Bibliothèque nationale de France 2002–07, Rendez-vous de l'Histoire de Blois 2003–, Rencontres de la photographie d'Arles 2009–15, Jury du Prix du livre d'Histoire du Sénat 2007–, Jury du Prix François-Mauriac-Malagar 2015–, Fondation du musée Clemenceau 2015–; Chevalier, Légion d'honneur, Grand Officier, Ordre nat. du Mérite; Dr hc (Université Libre de Belgique) 2005. *Plays:* L'Un de nous deux, l'Affaire Crochette, Le Panda. *Radio:* Concordance des temps (weekly programme on French culture) 1999–. *Television:* historical films for French TV: Léon Blum ou la fidélité 1973, Eamon de Valera 1975, Le Rhin 1996, Les Grandes Batailles de la République 1996–2006, Senghor entre deux mondes 1998, Histoire des présidentielles 1965–1995 2002, La Drôle de paix 1919–1939 2009, Jean Jaurès 2014, Maghreb 39–45, un destin qui bascule 2015. *Publications:* Le Riz et le Rouge, cinq mois en Extrême-Orient 1969, Le Journal politique de Jules Jeanneney 1939–42 1972, François de Wendel en République, l'Argent et le Pouvoir 1976, 2019, Leçon d'histoire pour une gauche au pouvoir, La Faillite du Cartel 1924–26 1977, Le Monde de Beuve-Méry ou le métier d'Alceste (co-author) 1979, L'argent caché, milieux d'affaires et pouvoirs politiques dans la France du XXe Siècle 1981, Télévision nouvelle mémoire, les magazines de grand reportage 1959–68 (with others) 1982, Echec à Panurge, l'audiovisuel public au service de la différence 1986, Concordances des temps, chroniques sur l'actualité du passé 1987, Georges Mandel, l'Homme qu'on attendait 1991–2009, L'avenir vient de loin, Essai sur la gauche 1994–2001, Une histoire des médias des origines à nos jours 1996–2015, Le Passé dans le prétoire, l'historien, le juge et le journaliste 1998, L'Echo du siècle, Dictionnaire historique de la radio et de la télévision en France 1999, La République a besoin d'histoire, interventions 2000, L'Histoire va-t-elle plus vite? Variations sur un vertige 2001, Le duel, une passion française 2004–11, Clemenceau, portrait d'un homme libre 2005, Concordance des temps: Dialogues radiophoniques 2005, La Proverbe et l'étamine, lectures historiques et politiques 2007, Concordance des temps, Vol. II 2008, Correspondance de Clemenceau (co-author) 2008, L'Un de nous deux, dialogue pour le théâtre 2009, Quand Google défie l'Europe: Plaidoyer pour un sursaut (third edn) 2010, L'Etat blessé 2012, Jours de guerre, 1914–1918 2013, La Grande guerre, si loin, si proche, réflexions sur un Centenaire 2013, L'Histoire, la liberté, l'action, Œuvres 1977–2013, Les Grandes heures de la presse 2013, Les Rebelles (co-author) 2014, Les chevaux de Marine Oussedik 2015, Clemenceau, dernières nouvelles du Tigre 2016, Un Attentat, Petit-Clamart, 22 août 1962 2016, L'Histoire de France vue d'ailleurs 2016, Le Récit national, une querelle française 2017, l'Affaire Crochette (théâtre) 2017, Le Moment Macron, un président et l'Histoire 2017, Il savait que je gardais tout, entretiens avec Anne Pingeot 2018. *Address:* 48 rue Galande, 75005 Paris, France (home). *E-mail:* jean-noel.jeanneney@orange.fr (office).

JEANNIOT, Pierre Jean, OC, CQ, FRAeS; Canadian/French fmr air transport official and international aviation consultant; *President and CEO, Jinmag Inc.;* b. Montpellier, France; m.; two s. one d.; ed Sir George Williams Univ., McGill Univ. and Univ. de Montréal; designer of aircraft and marine instrumentation, Sperry Gyroscope of Canada 1952–55; various positions in research, devt and man., Air Canada 1955–68, Vice-Pres. Computer and Systems Services 1970–76, subsequently held other sr positions in Air Canada, Exec. Vice-Pres. and COO Air Canada 1983, Pres. and CEO 1984–90; contributed to devt of the 'black box'; Vice-Pres. Computers and Communications, Univ. du Québec 1969; Dir-Gen. and CEO IATA, Montreal 1992–2002, Dir-Gen. Emer. 2002–; Chair. Thales Canada, Inc. 2003–09; Dir Bank of Nova Scotia Subsidiary Bds; Dir Jet Airways 2006–09; Chair. Univ. of Québec 1971–77, Chancellor 1996–2009; Pres. and CEO Jinmag Inc.; Sr Aviation Consultant, Gerson Lehrman Group; Chair. Aviation Think Tank, Concordia Univ., also mem. Advisory Bd; Chevalier, Légion d'honneur 1991, Officier 2017, Independence Medal of First Order (Jordan) 1995, Chevalier, l'Ordre national du Québec 2002; Hon. LLD (Québec) 1988, (Concordia) 1997, Hon. DSc (McGill) 2006; Man. Achievement Award, McGill Univ. 1989, Prix Rogers Demers des Gens de L'Air 1990, Flight Int. Transportation Man of the Year 2002, Québec

Hall of Fame 2004, inducted into Canadian Aviation Hall of Fame 2011. *Publications include:* Pierre Jeanniot aux Commandes du Ciel (biog.), Pierre Jeanniot Taking Aviation to New Heights (biog.); numerous tech. papers. *Address:* Place du Canada, 1010 de la Gauchetiere West, Suite 960, Montreal, PQ H3B 2N2, Canada (office). *Telephone:* (514) 868-0880 (office); (514) 868-9348 (office). *E-mail:* jeanniotp@jinmag.com (office); goughcooper@jinmag.com (office). *Website:* www.pierrejeanniot.com.

JEANTET, Pierre; French newspaper industry executive; b. 14 May 1947, Neuilly-sur-Seine; m.; three c.; ed Université Droit à Paris-II Assas; started career at Agence France-Presse 1972, served as Chief, Econ. Service 1980–82, Asst Sec.-Gen. 1984, Sec.-Gen. 1984–85, Sales Man. 1985–87, Asst Dir-Gen. 1987–90; Chair. Intermonde Presse 1989–91; Dir-Gen. Eurexpansion 1990–93; Dir-Gen. Sud-Ouest press group 1993–2006; Dir-Gen. Le Monde newspaper and Deputy Chair. Le Monde Group 2006–07, Chair. Le Monde Group June–Dec. 2007; Vice-Pres. Syndicat de la Presse Quotidienne Régionale 2001–; Pres. Bd of Trustees Pyrénées Presse 2002–, Charente Libre 2003–, Société des Gratuits de Guyenne et Gascogne 2004–; Chevalier, Légion d'honneur, Chevalier, Ordre national du Mérite. *Address:* Société des Gratuits de Guyenne et Gascogne, rue Walter Scott, 33600 Pessac, France (office). *Telephone:* 5-57-89-19-00 (office). *Fax:* 5-59-89-19-16 (office).

JEENBEKOV, Asilbek Sharipovich; Kyrgyzstani politician; b. 27 Aug. 1963, Biymyrza, Osh Oblast, Kyrgyz SSR, USSR; m.; six c.; ed Kyrgyz Agricultural Inst., Kyrgyz Research Inst. of Agric., Univ. of Econs and Entrepreneurship, Bishkek; worked as agronomist in Uzgen dist, Osh; Dir, Sharif Co. 1992–96, Isken Co. 1996–2002; Gen. Dir Agrozoovetservis Co. 2002–07; Chair. Kyrgyz Agribusiness Assen 2002–07; mem. Supreme Council (Jogorku Kenesh) 2007–, Chair. (Speaker) 2011–16. *Address:* Jogorku Kenesh (Supreme Council), 720053 Bishkek, Abdymomunov 207, Kyrgyzstan (office). *Telephone:* (312) 61-16-04 (office). *Fax:* (312) 62-50-12 (office). *E-mail:* zs@kenesh.gov.kg (office). *Website:* www.kenesh.kg (office).

JEENBEKOV, Sooronbay; Kyrgyzstani zoological engineer, politician and head of state; *President;* b. 16 Nov. 1958, Kara-Kulja Dist, Osh Oblast, Kyrgyz SSR, USSR; ed K.I. Skryabin Kyrgyz Nat. Agrarian Univ.; school teacher, Uzgen Dist, Osh Oblast 1976–77; worked on livestock farm, Osh 1983–88; Dir of state farm, Ulyanov Dist 1991–93; Chair. Kashka-Jol collective farm, Kara-Kulja Dist 1993–96; mem. Jogorku Kenesh (Supreme Council, Parl.) 1995–2000, 2005–07, Chair. Agric. Cttee 1995–2000, Agric. and Ecology Cttee 2005–07, Deputy Speaker 2000–05; Minister of Agric., Water Resources and Processing Industry April–Oct. 2007; Gov. of Osh Oblast 2010–12; Gen. Consul of the Russian Fed. in Osh 2012–15; Dir State Personnel Service 2015; First Deputy Head of Presidential Admin of Kyrgyz Repub. 2016; Prime Minister 2016–17; Pres. of Kyrgyzstan 2017–; mem. Kyrgyzstandyn Sotsial-Demokratiyalyk Partiyasy (Social Democratic Party of Kyrgyzstan); Honoured Worker of Agric.; Dank (Glory) Medal 2011. *Address:* Office of the President, 720003 Bishkek, pr. Chui 205 (office); Kyrgyzstandyn Sotsial-Demokratiyalyk Partiyasy, 720000 Bishkek, Shabdan Batyr 46d, Kyrgyzstan (office). *Telephone:* (312) 66-21-31 (President's Office) (office); (312) 53-33-23 (office). *Fax:* (312) 53-00-01 (office). *E-mail:* psp@adm.gov.kg (office); press@sdpk.kg (office). *Website:* www.president.kg (office); www.sdpk.kg (office).

JEEVES, Malcolm Alexander, CBE, MA, PhD, FMedSci, FRSE; British psychologist, academic and writer; *Professor Emeritus of Psychology, University of St Andrews;* b. 16 Nov. 1926, Stamford, Lincs.; s. of Alexander Frederic Thomas Jeeves and Helena May Jeeves (née Hammond); m. Ruth Elisabeth Hartridge 1955; two d.; ed Stamford School, St John's Coll., Cambridge, Harvard Univ., USA; Commdr Royal Lincs. Regt, served with 'Desert Rats' in First Bn Sherwood Foresters, BAOR 1945–48; Research Exhibitioner, St John's Coll., Cambridge 1952; Rotary Foundation Fellow, Harvard Univ. 1953; Lecturer, Univ. of Leeds 1956; Prof. of Psychology, Adelaide Univ. 1959–69, Dean 1962–64; Vice-Prin. Univ. of St Andrews 1981–85, Dir MRC Cognitive Neuroscience Research Group, St Andrews 1984–89, now Prof. Emer. of Psychology; Ed.-in-Chief Neuropsychologia 1990–93; mem. Psychology Cttee SSRC 1972–76, Biology Cttee SERC 1980–84, Science Bd 1985–89, Council 1985–89, Neuroscience and Mental Health Bd, MRC 1985–89, Manpower Sub-cttee, ABRC 1991–93, Council Royal Soc. of Edin. 1984–88, Exec. 1985–87, Vice-Pres. Royal Soc. of Edin. 1990–93, Pres. 1996–99; Pres. Section J, BAAS 1988; Founding Fellow, Acad. of Medical Sciences 1998; Fellow, British Psychological Soc.; Hon. Research Prof., Univ. of St Andrews 1993–, Hon. Sheriff Fife 1986–; Hon. DUniv (Stirling), Hon. DSc (Edin.) 1993, (St Andrews) 2000; Abbie Memorial Lecture, Adelaide Univ. 1981, Cairns Memorial Lecture, 1986, 1987, Burney Student, Cambridge, Kenneth Craik Award, St John's Coll., Cambridge, Gregg Bury Prize, Cambridge, Cairns Medal 1986. *Publications include:* Thinking in Structures (with Z. P. Dienes) 1965, The Effects of Structural Relations upon Transfer (with Z. P. Dienes) 1968, The Scientific Enterprise and Christian Faith 1969, Experimental Psychology: An Introduction for Biologists 1974, Psychology and Christianity: The View Both Ways 1976, Analysis of Structural Learning (with G. B. Greer) 1983, Free To Be Different (with R. J. Berry and D. Atkinson) 1984, Behavioural Science: a Christian Perspective 1984, Psychology – Through the Eyes of Faith (with D. G. Myers) 1987, Mind Fields 1994, Callosal Agenesis (co-ed.) 1994, Human Nature at the Millennium 1997, Science, Life and Christian Belief (co-ed.) 1998, From Cells to Souls – and Beyond (ed. and contrib.) 2004, Human Nature (ed. and contrib.) 2005, Neuroscience, Psychology and Religion (with Warren Brown) 2009, Rethinking Human Nature (ed. and contrib.) 2011, The Emergence of Personhood - A Quantum Leap? (ed. and contrib.) 2015, Psychological Science and Christian Faith (with Thomas Ludwig) 2018; papers on neuropsychology and cognition in scientific journals. *Leisure interests:* music, fly fishing, walking. *Address:* School of Psychology, University of St Andrews, St Andrews, Fife, KY16 9JU (office); 7 Hepburn Gardens, St Andrews, Fife, KY16 9DE, Scotland (home). *Telephone:* (1334) 462072 (office); (1334) 473545 (home). *Fax:* (1334) 477441 (office); (1334) 472539 (home). *E-mail:* maj2@st-andrews.ac.uk (office). *Website:* www.psy.st-andrews.ac.uk (office).

JEEWOOLALL, Sir Ramesh, Kt, LLB; Mauritian lawyer and politician; b. 20 Dec. 1940; m.; two c.; ed Middle Temple, London, UK; lawyer 1969–71; magistrate 1971–72; Chair. Tea Devt Authority 1976; elected to Legis. Ass. (Labour Party) 1976, Deputy Speaker 1976–79, Speaker 1979–82, 1996–2001; elected to Legis. Ass. (Alliance Party) 1987; Minister of Housing, Lands and Environment 1987–90; apptd Chancellor, Univ. of Mauritius 2006. *Publications include:* Who Owns Your Agenda? 2013, The Passing Away of a Gentleman 2015.

JEFFERTS SCHORI, Most Rev. Katharine, BSc, MSc, MDiv, PhD; American ecclesiastic; b. 26 March 1954, Pensacola, Fla; m. Richard Schori; one c.; ed Stanford Univ., Oregon State Univ.; qualified oceanographer, worked with Nat. Marine Fisheries Service; ordained priest 1994, served at Church of the Good Samaritan, Corvallis, Ore. with special responsibility for Hispanic congregation; consecrated Bishop of Nevada 2001; Presiding Bishop and Primate of Episcopal Church 2006–15, currently serves as Bishop of the Convocation of American Churches in Europe; Hon. DD (Church Divinity School of the Pacific). *Publications:* A Wing and a Prayer: A Message of Faith and Hope 2007, The Gospel in the Global Village: On the Road with Bishop Katherine 2009, The Heartbeat of God 2010, Gathering at God's Table 2012. *Address:* c/o Office of the Presiding Bishop, 815 Second Avenue, New York, NY 10017, USA (office). *Telephone:* (212) 716-6273 (office). *Fax:* (212) 697-5892 (office). *E-mail:* sjones@episcopalchurch.org (office). *Website:* www.episcopalchurch.org (office).

JEFFERY, Maj.-Gen. (Philip) Michael, AC, AO (Mil.), CVO, MC; Australian company chairman and army officer (retd); b. 12 Dec. 1937, Wiluna, WA; m. Marlena Kerr 1967; three s. one d.; ed Cannington School, E Victoria Park State School, Kent Street High School, Royal Mil. Coll., Duntroon, Canberra; comm. as Lt in Royal Australian Infantry Corps 1958; Platoon Commdr, 17 Nat. Service Training Co., Swanbourne, WA, Reconnaissance Officer, 1 Special Air Service (SAS) Co., Swanbourne 1959; promoted Temporary Capt., 1 SAS Co., Swanbourne 1962; Signal Platoon Commdr, Second Bn, Royal Australian Regt (2 RAR), Malaya 1962; promoted Capt., 2 RAR, Malaya 1962; Signal Platoon Commdr, 3 RAR, Malaya 1963; ADC to Chief of Gen. Staff, Lt-Gen. Sir John Wilton, Army HQ, Canberra, ACT 1964; SAS Regt, Swanbourne 1965; Operations Officer, SAS HQ, Labuan, Borneo 1965; Adjutant, SAS Regt, Swanbourne 1966; promoted Temporary Maj. 1966; Co. Commdr, First Bn, Pacific Islands Regt (1 PIR), Papua New Guinea (PNG); promoted Maj. 1968; Co. Commdr, 8 RAR, Enoggera, Viet Nam (Phuoc Tuy Prov.) and Enoggera 1969–70; Instructor, Battle Wing, Jungle Training Centre, Canungra, Queensland 1971; Student, Royal Mil. Coll. of Science, Schrivenham and British Army Staff Coll., Camberley, UK 1971; Staff Officer, Grade 2 Operations, Directorate of Operations, Army HQ, Canberra 1973; promoted Temporary Lt-Col 1973; Staff Officer Grade 1, Jt Warfare, Directorate of Operations, Army HQ, Canberra; Staff Officer Grade 1, Land Operations, HQ, PNG Defence Force, Port Moresby 1974; promoted Lt-Col 1974; CO Second Bn, Pacific Islands Regt (2 P1R), Wewak, PNG 1975; CO Special Air Service Regt, Swanbourne 1976; Student, Jt Services Staff Coll., Canberra 1978; Mil. Sec.'s Pool of Lt-Cols, Office of the CGS, Canberra 1978; Staff Officer Grade 1, Special Warfare, Operations Br., Army HQ, Canberra 1978; promoted Col and Dir Special Action Forces, Operations Br., Army Office, Canberra 1979; promoted Brig. and Head of Protective Services Co-ordination Centre, Dept of Admin. Services, Canberra 1981; Commdr 1 Brigade, Holsworthy, NSW 1983; Student, Royal Coll. of Defence Studies, UK 1984; promoted Maj.-Gen. and Commdr 1 Div., Paddington, NSW 1985; Asst Chief of Gen. Staff, Logistics, Army Office, Canberra 1989; Deputy Chief of Gen. Staff, Army Office, Canberra 1990; Asst Chief of Gen. Staff, Material, Army Office, Canberra, 1991; transferred to Inactive Australian Army Reserve 1993; Gov. of Western Australia 1993–2000; Gov.-Gen. of Commonwealth of Australia 2003–08; Nat. Advocate for Soil Health 2012–14; Founder and Chair. Future Directions Int., Perth, WA 2000–03; fmr Chair. Royal Flying Doctor Service of Australia; Citizen of Western Australia 2000, Hon. Life mem. Returned and Services League; KStJ; Grand Companion of the Order of Logohu (Papua New Guinea) 2005; AASM with Bars, Malaysia, Thai/Malay, Borneo and Viet Nam 1945–75, GSM with Bars Borneo and Malay Peninsula 1962, Viet Nam Service Medal, ASM with Bars, Papua New Guinea and South East Asia 1945–75, Australian Centenary Medal, Defence Force Service Medal with four Bars, Nat. Medal with Bar, Papua New Guinea Independence Medal, Mil. Cross and S Vietnamese Cross of Gallantry with Gold Star, S Viet Nam Campaign Medal, Vietnamese Cross of Gallantry Unit Citation, Pingat Jasa Medal Malaysia 2006; Hon. DTech (Curtin Univ.) 2000; Paul Harris Fellow, The Rotary Foundation 1996. *Leisure interests:* golf, cricket, fishing, reading, music. *Address:* 18 Hampton Circuit, Yarralumla, ACT 2600, Australia (home). *Telephone:* (2) 6282-7446 (home). *Fax:* (2) 6295-8716 (office). *E-mail:* mikejeffery@netspace.com.au (home).

JEFFREYS, Sir Alec John, Kt, CH, KBE, BA, MA, DPhil, FRCPath, FRS, FLS, FMedSci, CBiol; British geneticist and academic; *Professor of Genetics and Royal Society Wolfson Research Professor Emeritus, University of Leicester;* b. 9 Jan. 1950, Oxford, England; s. of Sidney Victor Jeffreys and Joan Jeffreys (née Knight); m. Susan Miles 1971; two d.; ed Luton Grammar School, Luton Sixth Form Coll., Merton Coll., Oxford; European Molecular Biology Org. Postdoctoral Research Fellow, Univ. of Amsterdam 1975–77; Lecturer, Dept of Genetics, Univ. of Leicester 1977–82, Lister Inst. Research Fellow 1982–91, Reader in Genetics 1984–87, Prof. of Genetics 1987–, Royal Soc. Wolfson Research Prof. 1991–, now Emer.; Howard Hughes Int. Research Scholar 1993–97; Foreign Assoc. NAS 2005; Fellow, Forensic Science Soc. of India 1989, Int. Inst. of Biotechnology 1990, Linnean Soc. of London 1994; Founder Fellow, Acad. of Medical Sciences 1998; Hon. Freeman (Leicester) 1993; Hon. FRCP 1993, Hon. Fellow (Luton) 1995, (Swansea) 2005, Hon. mem. Dept of Biochemistry, Univ. of Oxford 1997, Int. Soc. for Forensic Haemogenetics 1997, American Acad. of Forensic Sciences 1998, Biochemical Soc. 2003, NAS 2006; Hon. Life mem. Leicestershire Medico-Legal Soc. 1999; Hon. FRSM 2001; Hon. Fellow, Forensic Science Soc. 2005; Hon. DUniv (Open Univ.) 1991; Hon. DSc (St Andrews) 1996, (Strathclyde) 1998, (Hull) 2004, (Oxford) 2004, (Leicester) 2004, (Kingston) 2005, (Liverpool) 2006, (King's Coll., London) 2007, (Teesside) 2007; Hon. DIur (Dundee) 2008; Gibbs Prize in Honours Biochemistry 1972, Colworth Medal for Biochemistry, Biochemical Soc. 1985, Linnean Bicentenary Medal for Zoology 1987, Carter Medal, Clinical Genetics Soc. 1987, 2003, Davy Medal, Royal Soc. 1987, Analytica Prize, German Soc. of Clinical Chemistry 1988, Australia Prize 1998; Midlander of the Year Award, 1988, Achievement of the Year Award, Leicester Publicity Asscn 1989, P. W. Allen Memorial Award, Forensic Science Soc. 1992, Milano Award 1992, Allan Award, American Soc. of Human Genetics 1992, Lloyd of Kilgerran Prize, Foundation for Science and Tech. 1993, Illuminated Address, Bedfordshire Co. Council 1994, Gold Medal for Zoology, Linnean Soc. 1994, Sir Frederick Gowland Hopkins Memorial Medal, Biochemical Soc. 1996, Albert Einstein World of Science Award, World

Cultural Council Award, Baly Medal, Royal Coll. of Physicians 1997, Soc. of Chemical Industry Medal 1997, Australia Prize 1998, Sir George Stokes Medal, Royal Soc. of Chem. 2000, Edward Buchner Prize, Soc. for Biochem. and Molecular Biology (Germany) 2001, Nat. Historic Chemical Landmark plaque, Royal Soc. of Chem. 2002, Terence J Green Award, Int. Homicide Investigators Asscn 2003, Howard Steel Medal, British Orthopaedic Asscn 2003, AMP Award for Excellence in Molecular Diagnostics, Asscn for Molecular Pathology, USA 2003, Hon. Medal, Royal Coll. of Surgeons 2004, Daily Mirror Pride of Britain Lifetime Achievement Award 2004, Louis-Jeantet Prize for Medicine, Fondation Louis-Jeantet de Médecine, Switzerland 2004, Royal Medal, Royal Soc. 2004, Induction, Inventors Hall of Fame, Washington, DC 2005, Adelaide Medal, Int. Asscn of Forensic Sciences, Hong Kong 2005, Lasker Prize (for clinical medical research) 2005, Thomson Scientific Laureate Physiology/Medicine (USA) 2006, Dr H.P. Heineken Prize for Biochemistry and Biophysics, Royal Netherlands Acad. of Arts and Sciences 2006, Morgan Stanley Great Briton Award 2006, Morgan Stanley Great Briton in Science and Innovation Award 2007, Millennium Laureate, Millennium Foundation, Helsinki 2008, Asscn of Colls Gold Award for Further Educ. Alumni 2008, Croonian Lecturer, The Royal Soc. 2010, Copley Medal, The Royal Soc. 2014. *Achievement:* inventor of genetic fingerprinting. *Publications include:* numerous articles on human molecular genetics. *Leisure interests:* walking, swimming, postal history, reading unimproving novels. *Address:* Department of Genetics, Adrian Building, University of Leicester, University Road, Leicester, LE1 7RH, England (office). *Telephone:* (116) 252-3435 (office). *Fax:* (116) 252-3378 (office). *E-mail:* ajj@le.ac.uk (office). *Website:* www2.le.ac.uk/departments/genetics/people/jeffreys (office).

JELAŠIĆ, Radovan, MA, MBA; Serbian economist and fmr central banker; b. 19 Feb. 1968, Baja, Hungary; ed Univ. of Belgrade, Univ. of Illinois at Chicago, USA; Regional Man. for Cen. and Eastern Europe and positions in Corp. Banking Dept, Deutsche Bank, Frankfurt, Germany 1995–99; Sr Assoc., McKinsey & Co. Inc., Frankfurt, working on banking projects in Germany, Poland and Bulgaria 1999–2000; Vice-Gov. Nat. Bank of Yugoslavia/Serbia 2000–03, Gov. Narodna banka Srbije (Nat. Bank of Serbia) 2004–10; fmr mem. Bd of Dirs Banking Rehabilitation Agency, Belgrade.

JELIMO, Pamela; Kenyan athlete; b. 5 Dec. 1989; d. of Rodah Jeptoo Keter (fmr 200m and 400m runner); ed Koyo Secondary School, Kapsabet; women's middle distance runner; started running as sprinter aged 13 in 2003; Kenyan High School Champion at 400m and 400m hurdles 2005; finished fifth in 400m race at Kenyan Championships 2007; Gold Medal, African Jr Championships 2007; ran 200m Kenyan nat. jr record (24.68); ran her first 800m race at Kenyan trials for African Championships April 2008 (2:01.02); has been recruited by Kenyan Police, where she trains with Janeth Jepkosgei; at African Championships in Athletics 2008 set new nat. jr record of 1:58.70; won 800m at Hengelo Grand Prix May 2008 (new Jr World Record and Kenyan record of 1:55.76); ran 400m personal best of 52.78 in Nairobi June 2006; won Internationales Stadionfest (ISTAF) Golden League 2008 (set new African record time of 1:54.99); bettered record to 1:54.97 at Int. Asscn of Athletics Feds (IAAF) Golden League, Paris July 2008; Gold Medal, women's 800m, Olympic Games, Beijing 2008 (record time of 1:54.87, first Kenyan woman to win Olympic gold medal; won Gold Medal at World Indoor Championships 2012 in Istanbul); ran personal best of 1:54.01 at Weltklasse Golden League meeting, Zurich 29 Aug. 2008 (third fastest time ever); coached by Zaid Aziz. *Address:* c/o Kenya Athletics Federation, PO Box 46722, Aerodrome Road, Riadha House, 00100 Nairobi West, Kenya.

JELINEK, Elfriede; Austrian writer, dramatist and poet; b. 20 Oct. 1946, Mürzzuschlag, Styria; d. of Friedrich Jelinek and Olga Ilona; m. Gottfried Hüngsberg 1974; ed Vienna Conservatory, Albertsgymnasium, Univ. of Vienna; mem. Graz Writers' Asscn; Young Austrian Culture Week Poetry and Prose Prize 1969, Austrian Univ. Students' Poetry Prize 1969, Austrian State Literature Stipendium 1972, City of Stadt Bad Gandersheim Roswitha Memorial Medal 1978, West German Interior Ministry Prize for Film Writing 1979, West German Ministry of Education and Art Appreciation Prize 1983, City of Cologne Heinrich Böll Prize 1986, Province of Styria Literature Prize 1987, City of Vienna Literature Appreciation Prize 1989, City of Aachen Walter Hasenclever Prize 1994, City of Bochum Peter Weiss Prize 1994, Rudolf Alexander Schroder Foundation Bremen Prize for Literature 1996, Georg Büchner Prize 1998, Berlin Theatre Prize 2002, City of Düsseldorf Heinrich Heine Prize 2002, Mülheim and der Ruhr Festival of Theatre Dramatist of the Year 2002, 2004, 2009, 2011, Else Lasker Schüler Prize, Mainz 2003, Lessing Critics' Prize, Wolfenbüttel 2004, Stig Dagerman Prize, Älvkarleby 2004, The Blind War Veterans' Radio Theatre Prize, Berlin 2004, Franz Kafka Prize 2004, Nobel Prize for Literature 2004. *Screenplays:* Die Ausgesperrten (TV) 1982, Malina (from novel by Ingeborg Bachmann) 1991. *Plays include:* Wolken. Heim 1988, Totenauberg: ein Stück, Ein Sportstück 1992, Raststätte 1994, Das Lebewohl 2000, In den Alpen 2002, Das Werk 2003, Die Kontrakte des Kaufmanns. Eine Wirtschaftskomödie 2009, Winterreise 2011, Kein Licht 2011, Faustin and Out 2012, Aber sicher! 2013. *Radio:* numerous pieces for radio, including wenn die sonne sinkt ist für manche schon büroschluss (radio play) 1974. *Publications include:* Lisas Schatten (poems) 1967, wir sind lockvögel baby! (novel) 1970, Michael: ein Jugendbuch für die Infantilgesellschaft (novel) 1972, Die Liebhaberinnen (novel, translated as Women as Lovers) 1975, bukolit (novel) 1979, Die Ausgesperrten (novel, translated as Wonderful, Wonderful Times) 1980, ende: gedichte von 1966–1968 1980, Die endlose Unschuldigkeit (essays) 1980, Was geschah, nachdem Nora ihren Mann verlassen hatte oder Stützen der Gesellschaft 1980, Die Klavierspielerin (novel, translated as The Piano Teacher) 1983, Burgtheater 1984, Clara S 1984, Oh Wildnis, oh Schutz vor ihr (non-fiction) 1985, Krankheit oder moderne Frauen 1987, Lust (novel) 1989, Wolken. Heim 1990, Die Kinder der Toten (novel) 1995, Macht nichts: eine kleine Trilogie des Todes 1999, Gier: ein Unterhaltungsroman 2000, Der Tod und das Mädchen I–V: Prinzessinnendramen 2003, Neid: Privatroman (novel) 2007, rein GOLD: ein bühnenessay 2013; translated works of other writers including Thomas Pynchon, Georges Feydeau, Eugène Labiche, Christopher Marlowe, Oscar Wilde; film scripts and an opera libretto. *Website:* www.elfriedejelinek.com.

JELINEK, Otto John; Canadian diplomatist, politician and business executive; b. 1940, Prague, Czechoslovakia; m. Leata Mary Bennett 1974; two s.; ed Oakville, Ont., Swiss Alpine Business Coll., Davos, Switzerland; MP 1972–93, apptd Parl. Sec. to Minister of Transport 1979, fmr mem. Caucus Cttee on Trade, Finance, Econ. Affairs, fmr mem. Standing Cttee on Transport and Communications, on External Affairs, fmr mem. Parl. Cttee on Miscellaneous Estimates, Minister of State (Fitness and Amateur Sport) 1984–88, for Multiculturalism 1985–86, of Supply and Services and Receiver Gen. of Canada 1988–89; Acting Minister of Public Works 1988–89, Minister of Nat. Revenue 1989–93; Pres. Jelinek Int. Inc. 1993–97; Chair. Deloitte Czech Repub. 1996–2005, Deloitte & Touche Central Europe 2002–05; Chair. of Operations in Cen. and Eastern Europe, Colliers Int. 2007–11; apptd Amb. to the Czech Repub. 2013; mem. Int. Advisory Bd Soho Resources 2005–; fmr mem. Bd of Dirs Hummingbird Communications Ltd, Canbra Foods Ltd; mem. Academic Council of Univ. of Econs Prague; fmr Chair. Canada-Taiwan Friendship Cttee; Hon. Pres. Canada-Czech Republic Chamber of Commerce; mem. Big Brothers' Asscn of Canada, Olympic Club of Canada, Canadian Sports Hall of Fame; Fed. Progressive Conservative Party, Queen's Privy Council. *Achievements include:* fmr pairs figure skating world champion 1962.

JELINEK, W. Craig; American business executive; *President and CEO, Costco Wholesale Corporation;* joined Costco Wholesale Corpn 1984, Vice-Pres., Regional Operations Man.—Los Angeles Region 1986–94, Sr Vice-Pres., Operations—Northwest Region 1994–95, COO Northern Div. 1995–2004, Exec. Vice-Pres. and COO Merchandising, Costco Wholesale Corpn 2004–10, mem. Bd of Dirs Costco Wholesale Corpn 2010–, Pres. and COO 2010–12, Pres. and CEO 2012–. *Address:* Costco Wholesale Corporation, 999 Lake Drive, Issaquah, WA 98027, USA (office). *Telephone:* (425) 313-8100 (office). *Fax:* (425) 313-8103 (office). *E-mail:* cjelinek@costco.com (office). *Website:* www.costco.com (office).

JELUŠIČ, Ljubica, MSc, PhD; Slovenian academic and government official; b. 16 June 1960, Koper, Primorska region; ed Faculty of Sociology, Political Science and Journalism, Royal Mil. Acad., Belgium; has held several academic positions since 1985 at Faculty of Social Sciences, Univ. of Ljubljana including Researcher, Asst, Asst Prof. and Assoc. Prof., Prof. of Defence Studies 2005–; Visiting Lecturer, Univ. of Zagreb, Centre for Civil-Mil. Relations, Belgrade; Deputy Dean, Faculty of Social Sciences, Command and Staff School 1995–97, Chair. Defence Studies Dept 1999–2007; Minister of Defence 2008–11; Leader, Defence Restructuring and Conversion research project, COST Programme of the EC 1996–2001; Exec. Sec., Research Cttee on Armed Forces and Conflict Resolution, Int. Sociological Asscn 2006–08; mem. Editorial Bd Theory and Practice (Teorija in praksa) Magazine, Bulletin of the Slovenian Armed Forces (Bilten Slovenske vojske); reviewer for Security and Peace (Sicherheit und Frieden) magazine; mem. Int. Advisory Cttee, Geneva Centre for Democratic Control of Armed Forces. *Publication:* Legitimacy of the Modern Military 1997.

JELVED, Marianne Bruus, EdM; Danish politician and fmr teacher; *Minister of Culture;* b. (Marianne Bruus Hirsbro), 5 Sept. 1943, Charlottenlund; m.; teacher in public schools 1967–89, Royal Danish School of Educ. Studies 1979–87; Deputy Mayor of Gundsø 1982–85; mem. Folketing for North Jutland 1988–; Chair. Social Liberal Party Parl. Group 1988–93, 2001–07 (resgnd), 2011–; Minister of Econ. Affairs 1993–2001, for Nordic Cooperation 1994–2001, 2014–, of Culture 2012–, Minister for Equality and Ecclesiastical Affairs 2014–. *Publication:* BRUD: Radikale vaerdier i en forandret tid (co-author) 1994. *Address:* Ministry of Culture, Nybrogade 2, 1203 Copenhagen K (office); Folketing, Christiansborg, 1240 Copenhagen K, Denmark (office). *Telephone:* 33-12-77-55 (office); 33-37-55-00 (office). *E-mail:* min@kum.dk (office); folketinget@folketinget.dk (office). *Website:* www.folketinget.dk (office); www.radikale.dk.

JEMISON, Mae Carol, MD; American physician, business executive and fmr astronaut; b. 17 Oct. 1956, Decateur, Ala; d. of Charlie Jamison and Dorothy Jamison; ed Morgan Park High School, Chicago, Stanford Univ., Cornell Univ. Medical Coll., Los Angeles County/Univ. of Southern Calif. Medical Center; gen. practitioner, Insurance N America (INA)/Ross Loos Medical Group LA 1982; Area Peace Corps Medical Officer to Sierra Leone and Liberia 1983–85; gen. practitioner, CIGNA Health Plans Calif. 1985–87; astronaut, NASA 1987–93, co-investigator, Bone Cell Research experiment, part of Endeavor space mission 1992; f. The Jemison Group Inc., Houston 1993; Prof. of Environmental Studies Dartmouth Coll. 1995–2002; Founder, Pres. and CEO BioSentient Corpn 1999–; A.D. White Prof.-at-Large, Cornell Univ. 1999–2005; f. The Earth We Share (TEWS) 1994; Founder and Chair. Dorothy Jemison Foundation for Excellence 1994–; elected to NAS Inst. of Medicine 2001; Nat. Science Literary Advocate, Bayer Corpn; Moderator, IEEE-USA Tech. Symposia Space Techs. for Disaster Mitigation and Global Health; Dir Jemison Inst. for Advancing Tech. in Developing Countries; mem. American Medical Asscn, ACS, AAAS; mem. Bd Gen-Probe 2004–, World Sickle Cell Foundation, Scholastic Inc., Valspar Corpn, Texas Gov.'s State Council for Science and Bio Tech. Devt; Hon. mem. Center for Prevention Childhood Malnutrition, Montgomery Fellow, Dartmouth Coll.; Dr hc (Princeton Univ. and others); Essence Award 1988, Gamma Sigma Gamma Woman of the Year Award 1989, Johnson Publs Black Achievement Trailblazers Award 1992, Kilby Science Award 1993, Rachel Carson Award, Nat. Audubon Soc. 2005; mem. Nat. Medical Asscn Hall of Fame, Texas Science Hall of Fame, Int. Space Hall of Fame. *Television includes:* World of Wonder (Discovery Channel) 1994–95; guest appearances: Star Trek: The Next Generation 1993; as subject: The New Explorers (PBS-TV). *Achievements include:* first African-American woman in space 1992. *Publications:* Find Where the Wind Goes: Moments from My Life 2001. *Address:* PO Box 591455, Houston, TX 77259 USA. *E-mail:* Info@DrMae.com. *Website:* www.drmae.com.

JENČA, Miroslav, DIur; Slovak diplomatist and UN official; *Assistant Secretary-General for Political Affairs, United Nations;* b. 1965, Krompachy; m.; two c.; ed Comenius Univ., Bratislava, Univ. of Econs, Bratislava, Moscow State Inst. of Int. Relations, USSR, Stanford Univ., USA; has held several positions in Ministry of Foreign Affairs, including Head of Div. for Devt Assistance and Cross-border Co-operation and Deputy Political Dir and Dir Dept for EU and NATO countries, has served in overseas missions as Counsellor and Chargé d'affaires, Embassy in Dublin and Press Sec., Embassy in Mexico, also served as Amb. and Perm. Rep. to Political and Security Cttee of EU and as Amb. to Mexico 2000–04, Amb. and Head of Mission to OSCE Centre, Tashkent, Uzbekistan 2004–07, Dir, Office of Minister for Foreign Affairs –2008; Special Rep. of UN Sec.-Gen. and Head of UN Regional Centre for Preventive Diplomacy for Cen. Asia (UNRCCA), Ashgabat, Turkmenistan 2008–15; Asst UN Sec.-Gen. for Political Affairs 2015–. *Address:* Department of Political Affairs, United Nations, New York, NY 10017, USA (office). *Telephone:* (212) 963-1234 (office). *Fax:* (212) 963-4879 (office). *Website:* www.un.org (office).

JENCKS, Charles Alexander, BA, MA, PhD, FRSE; American architectural historian and designer; b. 21 June 1939, Baltimore, Md; m. Maggie Keswick (deceased); three s. one d.; ed Harvard Univ., Univ. of London, UK; studied under Siegfried Giedon and Reyner Banham; with Architectural Asscn 1968–88; Lecturer, UCLA 1974–; has lectured at numerous univs including Univs of Peking, Shanghai, Paris, Tokyo, Milan, Venice, Frankfurt, Montréal, Oslo, Warsaw, Barcelona, Lisbon, Zurich, Vienna, Edinburgh, Columbia, Princeton, Yale and Harvard; producer of furniture designs for Sawaya & Moroni, Milan 1986–; Ed. Consultant Architectural Design and Ed. Academy Editions, London; Trustee and Co-founder, Maggie's Centres; mem. Selection Cttee Venice Biennale 1980; Juror for Phoenix City Hall 1985; Curator, Wight Art Centre, Los Angeles and Berlin 1987; mem. RSA, London, Acad. Forum of Royal Acad., London; Sr Fellow, Royal Coll. of Art, London 2005; contrib. to Sunday Times Magazine, Times Literary Supplement, The Observer, The Independent; Architectural works include: Garagia Rotunda, Truro, MA 1976–77, The Elemental House (with Buzz Yudell), Los Angeles, The Thematic House (with Terry Farrell), London 1979–84, The Garden of Six Senses 1998, The Garden of Cosmic Speculation, Scotland 2001, Landform Veda, Scottish Gallery of Modern Art, Edinburgh 2002, Portello Park, Milan 2003; Furniture designs include: 'Architecture in Silver': Tea and Coffee Service, Alessi, Italy 1983, Symbolic Furniture exhbn, Aram Designs, London 1985; other furniture and drawings collected by museums in Japan and Victoria & Albert Museum, London; Dr hc (Univ. of Edinburgh 2005), (Univ. of Glasgow) 2005; Fulbright Scholarship, Univ. of London 1965–67, NARA Gold Medal for Architecture 1992. *Television:* two feature films written for BBC on Le Corbusier and Frank Lloyd Wright. *Publications include:* Meaning in Architecture (co-ed.) 1969, Architecture 2000: Predictions and Methods 1971, Adhocism (co-author) 1972, Modern Movements in Architecture 1973, Le Corbusier and the Tragic View of Architecture 1974, The Language of Post-Modern Architecture 1977, The Daydream Houses of Los Angeles 1978, Bizarre Architecture 1979, Late-Modern Architecture 1980, Signs, Symbols and Architecture (co-author) 1980, Skyscrapers-Skycities 1980, Architecture Today 1982, Kings of Infinite Space 1983, Towards a Symbolic Architecture 1985, What is Post-Modernism? 1987, Post-Modernism – The New Classicism in Art and Architecture 1987, The Prince, The Architects and New Wave Monarchy 1988, The New Moderns 1990, The Post-Modern Reader (ed.) 1992, The Architecture of the Jumping Universe 1995, Theories and Manifestos of Contemporary Architecture 1997, New Science – New Architecture? 1997, The Chinese Garden (with Maggie Keswick), Le Corbusier and the Architecture of Continual Revolution 2000, The New Paradigm in Architecture 2002, The Garden of Cosmic Speculation 2003, Critical Modernism: Where is Post-Modernism Going? 2007, The Story of Post-Modernism 2011, The Universe in the Landscape 2011. *Address:* Maggie's Centres, 1st Floor, One Waterloo Street, Glasgow, G2 6AY, Scotland (office). *Telephone:* (3001) 231801 (office). *E-mail:* enquiries@maggiescentres.org (office). *Website:* www.maggiescentres.org (office); www.charlesjencks.com.

JENKINS, Antony, MA, MBA; British banking executive; b. Stoke-on-Trent, Staffs., England; m.; two c.; ed Univ. of Oxford, Cranfield Inst. of Tech.; joined Barclays 1983, completed Barclays Man. Devt Programme before going on to hold various roles in retail and corp. banking, left group 1989, rejoined bank as Head of Barclaycard 2005–09, mem. Group Exec. Cttee of Barclays PLC 2009–, CEO Barclays Retail and Business Banking (RBB) responsible for retail banking in Barclays Africa and Absa Bank 2009–12, also represented Barclays as non-exec. Dir on Bd of Absa Group Ltd and Absa Bank Ltd (South African banking subsidiaries), Group Chief Exec. and Chair. Group Exec. Cttee, Barclays PLC 2012–15; with Citigroup, working in London and New York 1989–2005; mem. Bd of Dirs, Visa Europe Ltd 2008–11, Inst. of Int. Finance 2013–; mem. Int. Advisory Panel, Monetary Authority of Singapore. *Leisure interests:* running marathons, listening to rock, jazz and classical music. *Address:* c/o Barclays PLC, One Churchill Place, Canary Wharf, London, E14 5HP, England.

JENKINS, Barry; American film director; b. 19 Nov. 1979, Miami, Fla; ed Florida State Univ. *Films include:* Medicine for Melancholy (San Francisco Film Critics Circle Marlon Riggs Award) 2008, Moonlight (Academy Award for Best Adapted Screenplay 2017) 2016, If Beale Street Could Talk 2018.

JENKINS, Sir Brian Garton, Kt, GBE, MA, FCA; British fmr business executive and fmr charity administrator; b. 3 Dec. 1935, Beckenham, Kent; m. (Elizabeth) Ann Jenkins; one s. one d.; ed Tonbridge, Trinity Coll., Oxford; with RA, Gibraltar 1955–57; Partner, Coopers & Lybrand 1960–95; Chair. Woolwich PLC 1995–2000; Deputy Chair. Barclays PLC 2000–04; Pres. Inst. of Chartered Accountants in England and Wales 1985–86, London Chamber of Commerce and Industry 1996–98, British Computer Soc. 1997–98; Chair. Charities Aid Foundation 1998–2003; Prior of Priory of England and Islands, Order of St John 2004–10 (retd); Lord Mayor of London 1991–92; Hon. Bencher, Inner Temple; Hon. mem. Baltic Exchange; Hon. Fellow Goldsmiths Coll., London; KStJ; Hon. DSc (City Univ.); Hon. DLitt (London Guildhall Univ.). *Publication:* An Audit Approach to Computers 1978.

JENKINS, Charles H., Jr, BBA, MBA, PhD; American retail executive; *Chairman Emeritus, Publix Super Markets, Inc.;* b. 1944; s. of Charles H. Jenkins, Sr. and Mildred Jenkins; m. Dorothy Jenkins; two c.; ed Goizueta Business School, Emory Univ., Harvard Univ.; Asst to Real Estate Vice-Pres., Publix Super Markets Inc. 1969–74, Dir 1974–, Vice-Pres. 1974–88, Exec. Vice-Pres. 1988–90, Chair. Exec. Cttee 1990–2000, COO 2000–01, CEO 2001–08, Chair. 2008–16, Chair. Emer. 2016–; fmr Pres. Lakeland Chamber of Commerce; fmr mem. Bd of Overseers, Boston Symphony Orchestra; Distinguished Alumni Achievement Award, Goizueta Business School, Emory Univ. *Address:* Publix Super Markets Inc. Corporate Office, 3300 Publix Corporate Parkway, Lakeland, FL 33811, USA (office). *Telephone:* (863) 688-1188 (office). *E-mail:* info@publix.com (office). *Website:* www.publix.com (office).

JENKINS, Sir Karl William Pamp, Kt, CBE, DMus, ARAM, LRAM, FRAM; British composer, pianist and oboist; b. 17 Feb. 1944, Penclawdd, Wales; ed Gowerton Grammar School, Univ. of Wales, Cardiff and Royal Acad. of Music, London; initially resident jazz oboist at Ronnie Scott's; Co-founder Nucleus, then played in Soft Machine; currently composer and conductor; Pres. Friends of the Nat. Youth Orchestra of Wales, Penclawdd Brass Band; Patron Nat. Youth Choir of GB; Fellow, Royal Welsh Coll. of Music and Drama, Trinity Coll., Carmarthen, Swansea Inst.; First Prize, Montreal Jazz Festival (with Nucleus), two D&AD awards for best advertising music, Classic FM Red F Award for outstanding service to classical music. *Compositions include:* Palladio 1992–95, Adiemus I: Songs of Sanctuary 1994, Adiemus II: Cantata Mundi 1996, Eloise 1997, Adiemus III: Dances of Time 1998, The Armed Man: A Mass for Peace 1999, Y Celtiaid (film score) (BAFTA Cymru Award for Best Original Music Soundtrack) 2000, Dying to Dance (TV score) 2001, Over the Stone 2002, Pwy Ysgrifennodd Y Testament Newydd? (film score) (BAFTA Cymru Award for Best Original Music Soundtrack) 2003, In These Stones Horizons Sing 2003, Quirk 2005, River Queen (film score) 2005, The Peacemakers 2011, The Healer - A Cantata For St Luke 2014, Cantata Memoria: For the children 2016, Lamentation 2018. *Recordings include:* Adiemus (Songs of the Sanctuary), Palladio (with Smith Quartet and London Philharmonic Orchestra) 1996, Imagined Oceans 1998, The Armed Man: A Mass for Peace (with Nat. Youth Choir of GB and London Philharmonic Orchestra) 2000, Requiem 2005, Quirk 2005, Kiri Sings Karl (with Kiri Te Kanawa) 2006, This Land of Ours 2007, Stella Natalis 2009, The Very Best of Karl Jenkins 2011, The Peacemakers 2012, Adiemus Colores 2013, Motets 2014, Still With The Music 2015, Cantata Memoria For the Children 2016. *Publication:* Still With The Music (autobiography) 2015. *Address:* Karl Jenkins Music Ltd, 46 Poland Street, London, W1F 7NA, England (office). *Telephone:* (20) 7434-2225 (office). *Fax:* (20) 7494-4998 (office). *E-mail:* info@karljenkins.com (office). *Website:* www.karljenkins.com (office).

JENKINS, Roger W., BA, MA; American oil industry executive; *President and CEO, Murphy Oil Corporation;* ed Louisiana State Univ., Tulane Univ.; joined Murphy Oil Corpn 2001, held several positions in Malaysia including man. of development of Kikeh Field, Sr Vice-Pres., North America 2007–09, Exec. Vice-Pres. of Exploration and Production 2009–13, Pres. Murphy Exploration & Production Co. 2009–12, COO Murphy Oil Corpn 2012–13, mem. Bd of Dirs, Pres. and CEO 2013–. *Address:* Murphy Oil Corporation, 200 Peach Street, El Dorado, AR 71730, USA (office). *Telephone:* (870) 862-6411 (office). *Fax:* (870) 864-6373 (office). *E-mail:* info@murphyoilcorp.com (office). *Website:* www.murphyoilcorp.com (office).

JENKINS, Sir Simon David, Kt, BA, FSA, FRSL; British journalist and national organization official; b. 10 June 1943, Birmingham, England; s. of Daniel Jenkins; m. Gayle Hunnicutt 1978 (divorced); one s. one step-s.; ed Mill Hill School, St John's Coll., Oxford; started career with Country Life magazine; fmr Political Ed. The Economist; Deputy Ed. London Evening Standard 1976, Ed. 1976–78; Ed. The Times 1990–92; Deputy Chair. English Heritage 1985–90; Chair. The National Trust 2008–14; mem. Bd of Dirs British Rail 1979–90, London Transport 1984–86; mem. Millennium Comm. 1994–2000; currently contrib. to The Guardian, London Evening Standard, Sunday Times, BBC; fmr Trustee Architecture Foundation, Buildings Books Trust; Hon. DLitt (Univ. of London, City Univ.), Dr hc (Univ. of Kent) 2008; Edgar Wallace Prize 1997, Rio Tinto David Watt Memorial Prize 1998, Journalist of the Year, Granada Awards 1988, Columnist of the Year 1993. *Publications include:* A City at Risk 1971, Landlords to London 1975, Newspapers: The Power and the Money 1979, The Companion Guide to Outer London 1981, Images of Hampstead 1982, The Battle for the Falklands 1983, With Respect, Ambassador 1985, The Market for Glory 1986, The Selling of Mary Davies and other writings 1993, Against the Grain 1994, Accountable to None: The Tory Nationalization of Britain 1995, England's Thousand Best Churches 1999, England's Thousand Best Houses 2003, Big Bang Localism 2004, Thatcher and Sons 2006, Wales: Churches, Houses, Castles 2008, A Short History of England 2011, England's Thousand Best Churches 2012, England's Hundred Best Views 2013. *Leisure interests:* architecture, history of London. *Address:* London Evening Standard, Derry Street, London, W8 5TT, England. *Website:* www.standard.co.uk/biography/simon-jenkins.

JENKINSON, Eric, CVO, OBE; British diplomatist; b. 13 March 1950; m. Marie Theresa Jenkinson; two s.; Protocol Div., FCO 1967–70, Immigration/Entry Clearance Officer, Islamabad 1973–76, full-time language training 1976–77, temporary duty, then Third Sec. (Commercial), Jeddah 1978–80, Second Sec. (Commercial), Riyadh 1980–82, Science, Energy and Nuclear Dept 1982–84, Asst Pvt. Sec., Perm. Under-Sec.'s Office, FCO 1984–86, First Sec. (Econ.), Bonn 1986–90, Deputy Consul Gen., Frankfurt 1990–91, Deputy Head of Mission/Consul, Bahrain 1992–95, Head of Parl. Relations Dept, FCO 1995–99, First Sec. (Econ./Commercial), later Acting Deputy Head of Mission, Tehran 1999–2002, High Commr to The Gambia 2002–07, to Trinidad and Tobago 2007–11, FCO 2011 (retd).

JENNINGS, Hon. Mr Justice John R. R., BA, LLB, QC; Canadian judge; b. 10 July 1937, Toronto; s. of Robert D. Jennings and Mary Rogers; m. Eyton Margaret Embury 1964; two s.; ed Upper Canada Coll., Univ. of Toronto and Osgoode Hall Law School, Toronto; fmr mem. York Co. Legal Aid Area Cttee; mem. and past mem. Council, Medico-Legal Soc.; Chair. Nat. Family Law Section 1974–76; Pres. Co. of York Law Asscn 1976; Chair. Windsor-Essex-Mediation Centre 1981–85; Dir Canadian Bar Insurance Asscn 1987–89; Pres. Advocates' Soc. 1987, Canadian Bar Asscn 1989–90, Canadian Bar Foundation 1989–90, CBANET Inc. 1989–90; Judge, Superior Court of Justice, Ont., Pres. Canadian Superior Courts Judges' Asscn 2001–02; Hon. mem. Law Soc. of England & Wales; Fellow, American Coll. of Trial Lawyers; Trustee, Foundation for Legal Research. *Leisure interests:* tennis, travel.

JENNINGS, Sir John (Southwood), Kt, CBE, BSc, PhD, FRSE, FGS; British business executive; b. 30 March 1937, Oldbury, Worcs.; s. of George Southwood Jennings and Irene Beatrice Jennings (née Bartlett); m. 1st Gloria Ann Griffiths 1961 (divorced 1996); one s. one d.; m. 2nd Linda Elizabeth Baston 1997; ed Oldbury Grammar School, Univs of Birmingham and Edinburgh; joined Royal Dutch/Shell 1958, held various positions including Gen. Man. and Chief Rep. of Shell cos in Turkey 1976–78, Man. Dir Shell UK Exploration and Production 1979–84, Exploration and Production Co-ordinator, Shell Internationale Petroleum Mij., The Hague 1985–90; Dir The Shell Transport and Trading Co. PLC 1987–2001 (Man. Dir Royal Dutch/Shell Group of Cos. 1987–97, Chair. Shell Transport and Trading Co. 1993–97); Chair. EME (Emerging Market Econs) 2000,

Intelligent Energy 2001, Spectron 2002, IdaTech, plc; Vice-Chair. Governing Body London Business School 1993–97 (mem. 1992–97); Vice-Pres. Liverpool School of Tropical Medicine 1991–97; Chancellor Loughborough Univ. 2003–10; mem. Bd of Dirs Det Norske Veritas 1997–2001, Robert Fleming Holdings Ltd 1998–2000, Mitie Group 1998–2007, Norseman Tectonics Ltd 1998–; mem. Council Royal Inst. of Int. Affairs 1994–97; Adviser, JPMorgan Chase 2000–; Trustee, Univ. of Edinburgh Devt Trust 1996, Exeter Univ. Council 1997–2000, mem. Int. Advisory Bd Toyota Corpn 1997, Bd of Counsellors Bechtel Corpn 1997; Commdr, Ordre Nat. du Mérite (Gabon); Hon. DSc (Edin.) 1991, (Birmingham) 1997. *Leisure interests:* fishing, travel, music, wine. *Address:* 16 Milborne Grove, London, SW10 9SN, England.

JENSEN, Hans Peter, PhD, DSc; Danish chemist and researcher; b. 11 June 1943, Copenhagen; m. Helle Rønnow Olesen 1965; two s. one d.; ed Univ. of Copenhagen, Chalmers Univ. of Tech., Gothenburg; Asst Prof., Tech. Univ. of Denmark 1969, Assoc. Prof. 1972, Head of Chem. Dept 1980–83, Dean of Chem. Faculty 1983–86, Rector 1986–2001; Deputy Dir Inst. of Food Safety and Nutrition 2001–04; Research Dir Danish Inst. for Food and Veterinary Research 2004–06; Head of Natural Sciences Dept, Roskilde Univ. 2007; currently Prin. Egmont H. Petersens Kollegium, Copenhagen; Research Assoc. Univ. of Oregon 1974–75, Visiting Prof. 1978, 1984; mem. Danish Natural Science Research Council 1984–92, Danish Acad. of Tech. Sciences, Cttee on Higher Educ. and Research (Council of Europe) 1986–2001, Evaluation Group of European Postgrad. Training Programme 1989–93, Cultural Foundation between Denmark and Finland 1989–97, Fulbright Comm. of Denmark 1990–2001; mem. Advisory Forum European Food Safety Authority 2003–, Velux Foundation 2004–14; Chair. Danish Rectors' Conf. 1993–2000; Chair. Asscn of Nordic Univ. Rectors' Confs 1995–2001; mem. Bd of Govs Jt Research Centre of EU 2001–12; Commdr Order of Dannebrog 1999; Dr hc (Shenandoah Univ., USA) 1993, (Helsinki Univ. of Tech.) 1998, (State Univ. of NY) 1998, (Kaunas Univ. of Tech., Lithuania) 2013. *Publications:* General Chemistry (textbook) 1985; articles in professional journals. *Leisure interests:* music, literature. *Address:* Egmont H. Petersens Kollegium, Nørre Allé 75, 2100 Copenhagen; Jagtvej 172, 2100 Copenhagen, Denmark (home). *Telephone:* 35200022 (office); 39653429 (home). *E-mail:* efor@ehp.dk (office). *Website:* www.egmont-kol.dk.

JENSEN, Kristian; Danish politician; *Minister of Finance;* b. 21 May 1971, Middelfart; s. of Jens Erik Jensen and Ellen Jensen; m.; three s.; ed Lemvig Business School; trainee with Unibank, Lemvig 1991–93, Banking Asst, Unibank, Brande 1993–98; mem. Folketing (Parl.) (Venstre, Liberal Party) for Ringkøbing County constituency 1998–2007, for Western Jutland constituency 2007–, Vice-Chair. Fiscal Affairs Cttee 2001–04, mem. Public Accounts Cttee 2011–15, Chair. Venstre Parl. Group 2010–15; Minister for Taxation 2004–10, Minister of Foreign Affairs 2015–16, Minister of Finance 2016–; Vice-Chair. Venstre 2009–. *Publication:* Hurra for globaliseringen (Hurrah for Globalisation) 2003. *Address:* Ministry of Finance, Christiansborg Slotspl. 1, 1218 Copenhagen K, Denmark (office). *Telephone:* 33-92-33-33 (office). *Fax:* 33-32-80-30 (office). *E-mail:* fm@fm.dk (office). *Website:* www.fm.dk (office).

JENSEN, Siv, BEcons; Norwegian politician; *Minister of Finance;* b. 1 June 1969, Oslo; d. of Tore Jensen and Monica Kjelsberg; ed Norwegian School of Econs; began career in Sales Dept, Radio 1 1992–94; mem. City Council, Oslo 1995–99; Deputy mem. Storting (Parl.) 1993–97, mem. Storting for Oslo 1997–, Chair. Finance Cttee 2001–05, mem. Foreign Affairs Cttee 2005–09, Foreign Affairs and Defence Cttee 2009–13; Minister of Finance 2013–; mem. Bd Oslo Progress Party 1992–94, Deputy Chair., Organizational Affairs 1995–96, mem. Progress Party Central Exec. Cttee 1988–99, First Deputy Chair., Progress Party 1999–2006, Leader and Chair. 2006–. *Address:* Ministry of Finance, Akersgt. 40, POB 8008 Dep., 0030 Oslo, Norway (office). *Telephone:* 22-24-90-90 (office). *Fax:* 22-24-95-14 (office). *E-mail:* siv.jensen@fin.dep.no (office). *Website:* www.regjeringen.no/no/dep/fin (office).

JENSSEN, Olav Christopher; Norwegian artist; b. 2 April 1954, Sortland, Vesteraland; ed Statens Kunstakademi, Oslo; Prof. of Painting, Hochschule fur Bildende Kunst, Hamburg 1996–2003; Prof., Hochschule für Bildende Künste Braunschweig (Braunschweig Univ. of Art) 2007–; official artist, Offshore Northern Seas Int. Conf. 2000; Willy Brandt Award 2001. *Address:* Galleri Susanne Ottesen, Gothersgade 49, 1123 Copenhagen K, Denmark. *Telephone:* 33-15-52-44. *E-mail:* galleri@susanneottesen.dk. *Website:* www.susanneottesen.dk.

JENTSCH, Thomas J., PhD, MD; German neuropathologist and academic; *Director, Dept of Physiology and Pathology of Ion Transport, Leibniz Institut für Molekulare Pharmakologie, Berlin;* b. 24 April 1953; ed Free Univ., Berlin and Fritz-Haber-Institut, Max-Planck-Gesellschaft; Postdoctoral Researcher, Institut für Klinische Physiologie, Free Univ., Berlin and Whitehead Inst. for Biomedical Research, MIT, USA; Research Group Leader, Zentrum für Molekulare Neurobiologie Hamburg (ZMNH), Hamburg Univ., Prof. and Dir Institute for Molecular Neuropathology, ZMNH 1993–2006, Dir ZMNH 1995–98, 2001–03; Dir, Dept of Physiology and Pathology of Ion Transport, Leibniz Institut für Molekulare Pharmakologie, Berlin 2006–; Prof. Charité, Universitätsmedizin Berlin 2006–; Principal Investigator, NeuroCure Clinical Research Center 2008–; mem. Int. Scientific Advisory Bd, Instituto de Ciencias Biomédicas de la Universidad de Chile; mem. Academia Europaea 2000, European Molecular Biology Org. (EMBO) 2000, Berlin-Brandenburg Acad. of Sciences and Humanities 2001; Dr hc (Univ. Medical Center Hamburg-Eppendorf) 2017; Wilhelm Vaillant Prize for Biomedical Research 1992, Gottfried Wilhelm Leibniz Prize, Deutsche Forschungsgemeinschaft 1995, Alfred Hauptmann Prize for Research on Epilepsy 1998, Franz Volhard Prize for Research in Nephrology 1998, Zülch Prize, Gertrud-Reemtsma Foundation 1999, Feldberg Prize, Feldberg Foundation for Anglo-German Scientific Exchange 2000, Familie Hansen Prize 2000, Prix Louis-Jeantet de médecine 2000, Ernst Jung Prize for Medicine 2001, Adolf-Fick Prize for Physiology 2004, Homer W. Smith Award for Nephrology 2004. *Publications:* numerous articles in scientific journals. *Address:* Leibniz Institut für Molekulare Pharmakologie, Timoféeff-Ressovsky Haus, Campus Berlin-Buch, Robert Roesslestrasse 10, 13125 Berlin, Germany (office). *Telephone:* (30) 94062961 (office). *Fax:* (30) 94062960 (office). *E-mail:* jentsch@fmp-berlin.de (office). *Website:* www.fmp-berlin.de/jentsch.html (office).

JEONG, Gen. Kyeong-doo, MBA; South Korean military officer and government official; *Minister of National Defense;* b. 8 Feb. 1960, Jinju; ed Repub. of Korea Air Force Acad., Hannam Univ., Japan Air Self-Defense Force Air War Coll.; served in Repub. of Korea Air Force (ROKAF) 1982–2018, including as Chief, Force Requirement Div., ROKAF HQ 2006–08, Commdt, Cadet Wing, Korea Air Force Acad. 2008–09, Commdr, 1st Fighter Wing 2009–11, Commdr, Gyeryongdae Service Support Group 2011, Deputy Chief of Staff for Plans and Management, ROKAF HQ 2011–13, Commdr, Southern Combat Command 2013–14, Vice Chief of Staff, ROKAF HQ 2014–15, Chief Dir of Strategic Planning, Repub. of Korea Jt Chiefs of Staff 2015, Chief of Staff, ROKAF 2015–17, Chair., Repub. of Korea Jt Chiefs of Staff 2017–18, Minister of Nat. Defense 2018–; rank of Col 2004, Brig.-Gen. 2009, Maj.-Gen. 2011, Lt-Gen. 2014, Gen. 2015. *Address:* Ministry of National Defense, 22 Itaewon-ro, Yeongsan-gu, Seoul 04383, Republic of Korea (office). *Telephone:* (2) 748-1111 (office). *Fax:* (2) 703-3109 (office). *E-mail:* cyber@mnd.go.kr (office). *Website:* www.mnd.go.kr (office).

JERANDI, Othman, BA; Tunisian diplomatist and politician; b. Hammam Lif; m. Raja Belarbi Jerandi; two c.; Sec. of Foreign Affairs 1979–81, First Sec., Embassy in Kuwait City 1981–88, Counsellor, Cabinet of Minister of Foreign Affairs 1988–90, Counsellor, Perm. Mission to UN, New York 1990–94, Amb. to Nigeria (also accred to Ghana, Sierra Leone, Liberia) 1994–97, Dir of Political, Econ. and Cooperation Affairs with Africa and African Union 1998–2000, Deputy Perm. Rep., Perm. Mission to UN, New York 2000–02, elected Chair. Comm. on the Status of Women 2002, Amb. to the Repub. of Korea 2002–05, Dir-Gen. Int. Orgs and Confs 2005–08, Chargé de Mission, Minister of Foreign Affairs 2008–10, Amb. to Jordan 2010–11, Perm. Rep. to UN, New York 2011–13, Minister of Foreign Affairs 2013–14.

JEREMIĆ, Vuk, BA, MPA, PhD; Serbian politician; *President, Centre for International Relations and Sustainable Development (CIRSD);* b. 3 July 1975, Belgrade; s. of Miško Jeremić and Sena Buljubašić; m. Nataša Jeremić; ed Univ. of Cambridge, Imperial Coll., England, Harvard Univ., USA; Co-founder and Financial Man. Org. of Serbian Students Abroad 1997; fmr Financial Analyst, Deutsche Bank, Dresdner Kleinwort Benson Bank and AstraZeneca Pharmaceuticals, London; Adviser to Minister of Telecommunications 2000–03; Adviser to Minister of Defence of Serbia and Montenegro 2003–04; Adviser on Int. Relations and Head, Office of the Pres. of Serbia 2004–07; Minister of Foreign Affairs 2007–12; Pres. 67th Session of UN Gen. Ass., New York 2012–13; Pres. Centre for Int. Relations and Sustainable Devt (CIRSD) 2014–; mem. Democratic Party –2013, Pres. Bd of Int. Relations 2004–06, mem. Exec. Bd 2006–13; Pres. Tennis Fed. of Serbia 2011–. *Address:* Centre for International Relations and Sustainable Development (CIRSD), 11000 Belgrade, Aleksandra Stamboliskog 1, Serbia (office). *Telephone:* (11) 2660760 (office). *E-mail:* office@cirsd.org (office). *Website:* www.cirsd.org (office).

JERIBI, Ghazi, Lic. en Droit; Tunisian lawyer and government official; *Minister of Justice;* b. 5 Dec. 1955, Tunis; m.; three c.; ed Univ. of Paris, France; served with Admin. Tribunal (part of State Council) 1984–2011, positions included Deputy Adviser 1984–91, Adviser 1991–96, Pres., Educ. Section 1996–99, Pres. of the Chamber 1996–99, State Commr-Gen. 1999–2001, First Pres., Admin. Tribunal 2007–11; teacher, Ecole Nat. d'Admin, Tunis 1988–2013; Lecturer, EPAM Mil. Acad. 1989–96; Lecturer, Judiciary Grad. School 2000–05; expert trainer on competition law, UNCTAD 2005–06; Pres., Competition Council 2001–06; Chair., Comm. on Tax Disputes 1997–2001, High Cttee for Admin. and Financial Control 2011; Minister of Nat. Defence 2014–15, of Justice 2017–, Acting Minister of the Interior June–July 2018; Legal Dir, Arab Inst. for Human Rights 1990–92; Vice-Pres. Tunisian Basketball Fed. 1994–96. *Publications:* numerous articles in nat. and int. journals on admin. law and reform, human rights and civil liberties, tax litigation, competition law and sports law. *Leisure interests:* basketball (played for nat. team 1975–85). *Address:* Ministry of Justice, 31 blvd Bab Benet, 1019 Tunis, Tunisia (office). *Telephone:* (71) 561-444 (office). *Fax:* (71) 586-106 (office). *E-mail:* info@e-justice.tn (office). *Website:* www.e-justice.tn (office).

JERLAGIĆ, Amer; Bosnia and Herzegovina engineer and politician; *President, Party for Bosnia and Herzegovina;* b. 25 May 1967, Livno; ed Univ. of Sarajevo; several years with Elektroprivreda BiH dd (power transmission co.), including Head of Mostar Section, Elektroprenos Sarajevo 1996–97, Tech. Dir 1997–98, Man., Sarajevo Plant 1998–2000, Dir, Power Distribution, Sarajevo 2004–07, Acting Gen. Man., Elektroprivreda BiH dd 2007–08, Gen. Man. 2008–11; mem. Party for Bosnia and Herzegovina (SBiH), Pres. 2012–. *Address:* Party for Bosnia and Herzegovina (SBiH), 71000 Sarajevo, Fra Grge Martića 2/II, Bosnia (office). *Telephone:* (33) 573470 (office). *Fax:* (33) 475597 (office). *E-mail:* zabih@zabih.ba (office). *Website:* www.zabih.ba (office).

JERVIS, Robert, BA, PhD; American political scientist and academic; *Adlai E. Stevenson Professor of International Affairs, Columbia University;* ed Oberlin Coll., Univ. of California, Berkeley; Asst Prof. of Govt, Harvard Univ. 1968–74, Assoc. Prof. 1972–74; Prof. of Political Science, UCLA 1974–80; fmr Prof. Yale Univ., Hebrew Univ.; currently Adlai E. Stevenson Prof. of Int. Affairs and Deputy Chair. Political Science Dept, Columbia Univ., Acting Chair. 2009–10; Vice-Pres. American Political Science Asscn 1988–89, Pres. 1999–2000; Co-ed. Security Studies Series, Cornell Univ. Press; Fellow, AAAS, American Acad. of Arts and Sciences; mem. bd of eight scholarly journals; Career Achievement Award, Security Studies Section, Int. Studies Asscn 1996, Nevitt Sanford Award for Distinguished Professional Contrib. to Political Psychology 1998, Lionel Trilling Award for Best Book by Columbia Faculty Mem. 1998, NAS Award for Behavioral Science Research Relevant to the Prevention of Nuclear War 2006. *Publications:* The Logic of Images in International Relations 1970, Perception and Misperception in International Politics 1976, The Illogic of American Nuclear Strategy 1984, Psychology and Deterrence (co-author) 1985, The Meaning of the Nuclear Revolution (Grawemeyer Award for Ideas Improving World Order 1990) 1989, Systems Effects: Complexity in Political and Social Life 1997, International Politics; Enduring Concepts and Contemporary Issues (co-ed.) 1999, The Origins of Major War (co-ed.) 2000, American Foreign Policy in a New Era 2005; numerous articles in professional journals and chapters in books. *Address:* Department of Political Science, Columbia University, 1333 International Affairs Building, Mail Code 3347, 420 West 118th Street, New York, NY 10027, USA (office). *Telephone:*

(212) 854-4610 (office). *Fax:* (212) 864-1686 (office). *E-mail:* rlj1@columbia.edu (office). *Website:* www.columbia.edu/cu/polisci (office).

JERVIS, Simon Swynfen, MA, FSA; British art historian; b. 9 Jan. 1943, Yoxford; s. of John Swynfen Jervis and Diana Parker (née Marriott); m. Fionnuala MacMahon 1969; one s. one d.; ed Downside School, Corpus Christi Coll., Cambridge; with Leicester Museum and Art Gallery 1964–66; Asst Keeper, Furniture Dept, Victoria and Albert Museum, London 1966–75, Deputy Keeper 1975–79, Acting Keeper 1989, Curator 1989–90; Dir Fitzwilliam Museum, Cambridge 1990–95; Dir of Historic Bldgs, Nat. Trust 1995–2002; mem. Council, Soc. of Antiquaries 1986–88 (Pres. 1995–2001), Royal Archaeological Inst. 1987–91, Walpole Soc. 1990–95 (Chair. 2004–13), Kelmscott Cttee 2001–; Chair. Nat. Trust Arts Panel 1987–95; Ed. Furniture History Soc. 1987–91, Chair. 1998–2013; Dir Burlington Magazine 1993–, Trustee 1997–; Guest Scholar, J. Paul Getty Museum 1988–89; Trustee, Royal Collection Trust 1993–2001, Leche Trust 1995–2013, Sir John Soane's Museum 1999–2002 (Life Trustee 2002–13); Ailsa Mellon Bruce Sr Fellow, National Gallery of Art, Washington, DC 2006; mem. Reviewing Cttee on the Export of Works of Art; mem. Architectural Advisory Cttee, World Monuments Fund Britain; Iris Foundation Award for Outstanding Contributions to the Decorative Arts 2002. *Publications include:* Victorian Furniture 1968, Victorian and Edwardian Decorative Art: the Handley Read Collection 1972, Printed Furniture Designs Before 1650 1974, High Victorian Design 1974, The Penguin Dictionary of Design and Designers 1984, Furniture from Austria and Hungary in the Victoria and Albert Museum 1986, British and Irish Inventories 2010, Roman Splendour, English Arcadia: The Pope's Cabinet at Stourhead (with Dudley Dodd) 2014. *Leisure interests:* churches, tennis.

JESSEN-PETERSEN, Søren, PhD; Danish lawyer, academic, UN official and international civil servant; *Adjunct Professor of International Relations, Paul H. Nitze School of Advanced International Studies, Johns Hopkins University;* b. 1945, Nørresundby; m.; four c.; trained as lawyer and journalist; served in Africa UNHCR 1972–77, Chief of Secr., UNHCR Exec. Cttee 1981–82, Exec. Sec. Second Int. Conf. on Assistance to Refugees in Africa 1983–84, Exec. Sec. Intergovernmental Conf. on Asylum Seekers and Refugees in Europe 1985, opened UNHCR Regional Office for Nordic Countries, Stockholm 1986, served as High Commr's Regional Rep. 1986–89; Special Adviser to UN Under-Sec.-Gen. for Political Affairs 1989; mem. UN Sec.-Gen.'s Task Force on Namibia 1989, Chef de Cabinet of High Commr, UNHCR 1990–93, Dir External Relations 1992–94, Dir UNHCR Liaison Office at UN HQ, New York 1994–98, UN Special Envoy to the Fmr Yugoslavia 1995–96, Asst High Commr, UNHCR, Geneva 1998–2001; Chair. EU Stability Pact's Migration, Asylum, Refugees Regional Initiative (MARRI), Chair. MARRI Steering Cttee 2002–04; EU Special Rep. in Skopje 2004; Special Rep. of UN Sec.-Gen. and Head, UN Interim Admin Mission in Kosovo (UNMIK) 2004–06; Dir Washington, DC Office, Independent Diplomat (advisory org.) –2010; currently Adjunct Prof. of Int. Relations, School of Advanced Int. Studies (SAIS), Johns Hopkins Univ., Bologna, Italy, also Adjunct Prof., SAIS, Washington, DC; fmr Guest Scholar, US Inst. of Peace. *Publications include:* Kosovo, in J. Genser and Bruno Stagno Ugarte (eds), The United Nations Security Council in the Age of Human Rights 2014. *Address:* Paul H. Nitze School of Advanced International Studies, Bologna Center, Via Belmeloro 11, 40126 Bologna, Italy (office). *Telephone:* 051-2917811 (Italy, mobile). *E-mail:* sjessenpetersen@gmail.com (office). *Website:* www.sais-jhu.edu/s%C3%B8ren-jessen-petersen (office).

JESZENSZKY, Géza, PhD; Hungarian historian, academic, politician and diplomatist; b. 10 Nov. 1941, Budapest; s. of Zoltán Jeszenszky and Pálma Miskolczy-Simon; m. Edit Héjj; one s. one d.; ed Eötvös Loránd Univ., Budapest; banned from higher educ. for two years 1956–57; subject specialist with Nat. Széchényi Library 1968–76; Sr Lecturer, Budapest Univ. of Econs (now Corvinus Univ. of Budapest) 1976–81, Reader 1981, Dean of the School of Political and Social Sciences 1989–90, Head, Faculty of Int. Relations 1990–91, resumed teaching history and int. relations 2002–; Guest Scholar, Woodrow Wilson Center, USA 1985; Visiting Fulbright Prof., Univ. of California, Santa Barbara, USA 1984–86, UCLA 1986; Helen De Roy Visiting Prof., Univ. of Michigan, USA 1996; Visiting Prof., Coll. of Europe, Warsaw-Natolin, Babes-Bolyai Univ., Cluj-Napoca/Kolozsvár, Romania; Founding mem. Hungarian Democratic Forum 1988–96, Head of Foreign Affairs Cttee 1988–90, mem. Presidency 1990–94; Minister of Foreign Affairs 1990–94; mem. Parl. 1994–98; Pres. Hungarian Atlantic Council 1995–98; Amb. to USA 1998–200, to Norway (also accred to Iceland) 2011–14; Pres. Hungarian Carpathian Asscn 2002–; numerous decorations; C.I.E.S. Fulbright Grant 1984–86. *Publications:* Prestige Lost, The Changing Image of Hungary in Great Britain 1894–1918 1986, The Hungarian Question in British Politics 1848–1914 1986, István Tisza: Villain or Tragic Hero? 1987, Lessons of Appeasement 1994, More Bosnias? National and Ethnic Tensions in the Post-Communist World 1997, József Antall, Selected Speeches and Interviews (ed.), Post-Communist Europe and Its National/Ethnic Problems 2009; other studies in Hungarian and English. *Leisure interests:* literature, jazz, skiing, rowing, mountaineering. *Address:* Budapesti Corvinus Egyetem (Corvinus University of Budapest), 1093 Budapest, Fővám tér 8, Hungary (office). *Telephone:* (1) 482-5000 (office). *Fax:* (1) 482-5019 (office). *E-mail:* intoffice@uni-corvinus.hu (office); geza@jeszen.hu (office). *Website:* www.uni-corvinus.hu (office); www.karpategyesulet.hu (office).

JETER, Carmelita; American fmr track and field athlete; b. 24 Nov. 1979, Los Angeles, Calif.; ed Bishop Montgomery High School, California State Univ., Dominguez Hills; specializes in 100m; silver medal, 60m, US Indoor Track and Field Championships 2007, gold medal, 4×100m relay, World Athletics Championships, Osaka 2007, bronze medal, 100m Osaka 2007, Berlin 2009, gold medal, 100m, 4×100m relay, Daegu 2011, silver medal, 200m, Daegu 2011, silver medal, 100m, London Olympics 2012, bronze medal, 200m London Olympics 2012, bronze medal, World Athletics Championships, Moscow 2013; gold medal, 100m, World Athletics Final, Stuttgart 2007, Thessaloniki 2009; silver medal, 60m, World Indoor Athletics Championships, Doha 2010; winner, Shanghai Golden Grand Prix (10.64s) 2009 (second fastest woman ever in 100m); personal bests: 55m 6.84s, Fresno, Calif. 2008, 60m 7.02s, Albuquerque, NM 2010, 100m 10.64s, Shanghai 2009, 200m 22.20s, Fontvieille, Monaco 2011; hosted Track Clinic 2014; retd 2017; Asst Track Coach Missouri State Univ. 2018–; mem. Nike Club; coach: John Smith; Women's Jesse Owens Award 2011. *Address:* c/o Total Sports Management US, Inc., 1931 Villa Court, Johnson City, TN 37615, USA (office). *Telephone:* (423) 913-0552 (office). *Fax:* (423) 913-0152 (office). *E-mail:* office@totalsportsus.com (office). *Website:* www.totalsportsus.com (office); www.carmelitajeter.com.

JETER, Derek Sanderson; American fmr professional baseball player; *CEO and Co-owner, Miami Marlins;* b. 26 June 1974, Pequannock, NJ; s. of Charles Jeter and Dorothy Jeter; m. Hannah Jeter 2016; two d.; ed Kalamazoo Central High School, Mich.; drafted by NY Yankees in first round amateur draft 1992; Major League Baseball debut 29 May 1995; fmr Capt. NY Yankees; retd 2014; Founder and Pres. Turn2 Foundation 1996–; f. Jeter Publishing (imprint of Simon & Schuster) 2013; CEO and co-owner Miami Marlins 2017–; Partner and Brand Devt Officer, Luvo; Dr hc (Siena Coll.) 2016; American Baseball Coaches Asscn High School Player of the Year 1992; American League Rookie of the Year 1996; selected for American League All-Star Team 1998–2002, 2004, 2006–09; Most Valuable Player (MVP) World Series 2000; MVP All-Star Game 2000; Babe Ruth Award 2000; Hank Aaron Award 2006, 2009; Roberto Clemente Award 2009; Sports Illustrated Sportsman of the Year 2009, Commissioner's Historic Achievement Award 2014. *Publications:* The Life You Imagine 2001, Game Day: My Life On and Off the Field 2001, Jeter Unfilltered 2014. *Address:* Miami Marlins, 501 Marlins Way, Miami, FL 33125, USA (office). *Telephone:* (305) 480–1300 (office). *Website:* www.mlb.com (office); www.turn2foundation.org.

JETHMALANI, Ram, LLB; Indian lawyer and politician; b. 14 Sept. 1923, Shikharpur, British India (now Pakistan); m. 1st Durga 1941, three c.; m. 2nd Ratna Shehani 1947, one c.; ed S.C. Shahani Law Coll., Karachi; co-f. law firm in Karachi 1940s; relocated to India 1948; part-time Prof., Govt Law Coll., Mumbai 1953; fmrly taught Comparative Law, Wayne State Univ., Detroit, USA; elected mem. Rajya Sabha 1988; Union Minister of Law, Justice and Co. Affairs 1996–98, 1999–2000 (resgnd), Union Minister of Urban Affairs and Employment 1998–99; elected MP (Bharatiya Janata Party) for state of Rajasthan; Chair. Bar Asscn of India 1975–77; fmr Chair. Bar Council of India (four times); fmr mem. Int. Bar Asscn. *Address:* 2 Akbar Road, New Delhi, 110 011; 41 Advent, 12-A General Jagannath Bhonsale Marg, Mumbai, 400 021, India. *Telephone:* (11) 23792287 (New Delhi); (11) 23794651 (New Delhi); (22) 22024403 (Mumbai). *Fax:* (22) 22024990 (Mumbai). *E-mail:* jetmlni@sansad.nic.in (office).

JETTOU, Driss; Moroccan politician; *President of the Audits Court;* b. 24 May 1945, El Jadida; m.; four c.; ed Lycée El Khawarizmi de Casablanca, Univ. of Rabat, Cordwainers Coll., London, UK; fmr Pres. Moroccan Fed. of Leather Industries; fmr Vice-Pres. Moroccan Asscn of Exporters; Minister of Trade and Industry 1994–95, of Culture and Foreign Trade 1995–97, of Trade, Industry and Culture 1997–98, of the Interior 1998–2002; Prime Minister of Morocco 2002–07; launched investment fund with Italian pnr Muteo 2008; apptd Pres. Office Cherifien des Phosphates 2002; Pres. of the Audits Court 2012–; fmr mem. Gen. Confed. of Moroccan Enterprises; Grande Chevalier, Wissam du Trône. *Address:* Cour des Comptes, Rue Ettoute, Secteur 10, Hay Riyad - B.P 2085, Rabat, 10100, Morocco (office). *Telephone:* (53) 7563733 (office). *Fax:* (37) 576700 (office). *E-mail:* ccomptes@courdescomptes.ma (office). *Website:* www.courdescomptes.ma (office).

JEUNET, Jean-Pierre; French film director; b. 3 Sept. 1955, Roanne; m. Liza Sullivan 1997; worked as telecommunications engineer; dir of TV commercials and short films; Commdr, Ordre des Arts et des Lettres 2016. *Films include:* L'évasion 1978, Le manège (César Award) 1980 (both co-dir with Marc Caro), Le bunker de la dernière rafale 1981, Pas de repos pour Billy Brakko 1984, Foutaises (César Award) 1989, Delicatessen (César Award) 1991, Le cité des enfants perdus 1995, Alien: Resurrection 1997, Le fabuleux destin d'Amélie Poulain (Amélie) (Amanda Award, American Screenwriters Asscn Award, Bafta Film Award, David Lean Award for Direction, Canberra Int. Film Festival Audience Award, Chicago Int. Film Festival Audience Award, Czech Lion, César Award) 2001, Un long dimanche de fiançailles 2004, Micmacs 2009, The Young and Prodigious T.S. Spivet 2013. *Website:* www.jpjeunet.com.

JEVTIĆ, Dalibor; Kosovo politician; *Deputy Prime Minister and Minister of Communities and Return;* b. 31 March 1978, Prishtina, Socialist Autonomous Province of Kosovo, Socialist Repub. of Serbia, Socialist Fed. Repub. of Yugoslavia; worked as Man. for US co. KBR, Inc. (providing logistical support to US mil.) in Kosovo and Iraq 2001–09; Minister for Communities and Return 2013–14, 2015–17, Deputy Prime Minister and Minister of Communities and Return 2017–; Deputy Mayor of Štrpce March–April 2015; mem. Samostalna Liberalna Stranka (Ind. Liberal Party) 2009–14; mem. Srpska Napredna Stranka (Serbian Progressive Party) 2015–. *Address:* Ministry of Communities and Return, 12000 Fushë Kosovë, Sheshi Nënë Terezë, Kosovo (office). *Telephone:* (38) 552045 (office). *E-mail:* natasa.popovic@rks-gov.net (office). *Website:* www.mkk-ks.org (office).

JEWELL, Sally, BS; American (b. British) business executive and government official; b. 1955, England; d. of Peter Roffey and Anne Roffey (née Murphy); m. Warren Jewell; one s. one d.; ed Univ. of Washington; Field Production Engineer, Mobil Oil Corpn, Okla 1978–81; Petroleum Engineer, Rainier Bank, Seattle 1981–87; Exec. Vice-Pres. Security Pacific Bank, Wash. 1987–92; Pres. and CEO, WestOne Bancorp 1992–95; Pres., Commercial Banking, Washington Mutual, Inc. 1996–2000; mem. Bd of Dirs Recreational Equipment, Inc. (REI) 1996–2013, Pres. and COO 2000–05, Pres. and CEO 2005–13; Sec., US Dept of the Interior 2013–17; mem. Bd of Dirs Mountains to Sound Greenway Trust 1991–, Nat. Parks Conservation Asscn, Initiative for Global Devt; CEO of Year, Puget Sound Business Journal 2006, Non-Profit Dir of Year Award, Nat. Asscn of Corp. Dirs 2008, Green Globe Environmental Catalyst Award 2008, Nat. Audubon Soc. Rachel Carson Award for Environmental Conservation 2009.

JEWISON, Norman Frederick, BA, CC, DD; Canadian film director; b. 21 July 1926, Toronto; s. of Percy Joseph Jewison and Dorothy Irene Jewison (née Weaver); m. Margaret Dixon 1953; two s. one d.; ed Malvern Collegiate High School, Toronto, Victoria Coll., Univ. of Toronto; stage actor, Toronto; TV actor 1950–52; TV director for CBC 1953–58, CBS 1958–61; film director 1961–; Faculty mem. Inst. for American Studies, Salzburg, Austria 1969; Pres. D'Avoriaz Film Festival 1981–; Dir Centre for Advanced Film Studies 1987–; director TV shows for Harry Belafonte, Andy Williams, Judy Garland and Danny Kaye; mem. Electoral Bd, Dirs Guild of America; mem. Canadian Arts Council; Chair. Canadian Film Centre 2002; Chancellor Victoria Coll., Univ. of Toronto 2004; Hon. LLD (Univ. of Western Ont.) 1974; Acad. of Canada Special Achievement Award 1988, Emmy

Award 1960, Golden Globe Award 1966, Best Dir, Berlin Film Festival for Moonstruck 1988, Irving Thalberg Memorial Prize 1999. *Films include:* Forty Pounds of Trouble, The Thrill of It All 1963, Send Me No Flowers 1964 (all for Universal Studios), Art of Love, The Cincinnati Kid 1965, The Russians are Coming (also producer) 1966, In the Heat of the Night (Acad. Award 1967), The Thomas Crown Affair (also producer) 1967, Gaily, Gaily 1968, The Landlord (producer) 1969, Fiddler on the Roof (also producer) 1970, Jesus Christ Superstar (also producer) 1972, Billy Two Hats (producer) 1972, Rollerball 1974, F.I.S.T. (also producer) 1977, And Justice for All 1979, Best Friends 1982, A Soldier's Story 1984, Agnes of God 1985, Moonstruck 1987, In Country 1989, Other People's Money 1991, Only You 1994, Bogus 1996, The Hurricane 1999, Dinner with Friends (TV) 2001, The Statement 2003. *Leisure interests:* skiing, yachting, tennis. *Address:* 18 Gloucester Lane, Toronto, ON M4Y IL5, Canada. *Telephone:* (416) 923-2787 (office). *Fax:* (416) 923-8580 (office).

JEWITT, David C., BSc, MS, PhD; British/American astronomer and academic; *Professor, Department of Earth and Space Sciences and Department of Physics and Astronomy, University of California, Los Angeles;* b. 1958, England; m. Jing Li; ed Univ. Coll., London, California Inst. of Tech.; summer student, Royal Greenwich Observatory, Herstmonceux Castle, Sussex 1978; Anthony Fellowship, California Inst. of Tech. 1979–80, Research Asst 1980–83; Asst Prof., MIT 1983–88; Assoc. Astronomer, Inst. for Astronomy, Univ. of Hawaii 1988–93, Assoc. Prof., Dept of Physics and Astronomy 1988–93, Astronomer, Inst. for Astronomy 1993–2009, Prof., Dept of Physics and Astronomy 1993–2009; Prof., Dept of Earth and Space Sciences, UCLA 2009–, mem. Inst. for Geophysics and Planetary Physics 2009–, Prof., Dept of Physics and Astronomy 2010–, Dir Inst. for Planets and Exoplanets 2011–; Adjunct Prof., Nat. Central Univ., Taiwan 2007; mem. NAS; Foreign mem. Norwegian Acad. of Sciences and Letters 2012; Fellow, American Acad. of Arts and Sciences 2005, AAAS 2005; Hon. Prof., Nat. Astronomical Observatory, Chinese Acad. of Sciences 2006; Regent's Medal for Excellence in Research, Univ. of Hawaii 1994, Hawaii Scientist of the Year, ARCS 1996, Exceptional Scientific Achievement Medal, NASA 1996, Shaw Prize in Astronomy (co-recipient) 2012, Kavli Prize 2012. *Publications:* numerous papers in professional journals. *Address:* Department of Earth and Space Sciences, 3713 Geology Building, UCLA, 595 Charles Young Drive East, Los Angeles, CA 90095-1567, USA (office). *Telephone:* (310) 825-2521 (office). *E-mail:* jewitt@ucla.edu (office). *Website:* www2.ess.ucla.edu/~jewitt/David_Jewitt.html (office).

JEWKES, Sir Gordon Wesley, Kt, KCMG; British diplomatist; b. 18 Nov. 1931, Langley Moor, Co. Durham; s. of Jesse Jewkes; m. 1st Joyce Lyons 1954 (died 2005); two s.; m. 2nd Estelle Heime 2008; ed Barrow Grammar School, Magnus Grammar School, Newark-on-Trent; joined Colonial Office 1948; with army 1950–52; with Gen. Register Office 1950–63, 1965–68; mem. Civil Service Pay Research Unit 1963–65; joined FCO 1968; Commercial Consul, Chicago 1969–72, Consul-Gen. 1982–85; Deputy High Commr, Port of Spain 1972–75; Head of Finance Dept, FCO and Finance Officer of Diplomatic Service 1975–79; Consul-Gen. Cleveland 1979–82; Gov. Falkland Islands, Commr S Georgia and S Sandwich Islands, High Commr British Antarctic Territory 1985–88; Consul-Gen., New York and Dir-Gen. Trade and Investment, USA 1989–91; mem. Bd of Dirs Hogg Group PLC 1992–94, Slough Estates PLC 1992–2002; Exec. Dir The Walpole Cttee 1992–96; mem. Council Univ. of Buckingham 1996–2001, Marshall Aid Commemoration Comm. 1996–99, Salvation Army London Advisory Bd 1996–2001; Hon. DUniv (Buckingham) 2007. *Leisure interests:* music, travel, walking. *Address:* 53 Woodside Avenue, Beaconsfield, HP9 1JH, England.

JHA, Nagendra Nath, BA; Indian diplomatist and politician; b. 5 Jan. 1935; ed Doon School, Dehradun, Delhi Univ., Univ. of Cambridge, UK; joined Foreign Service 1957, Amb. to Ireland 1977–79, to Turkey 1979–1981, to Kuwait 1984–89, to Yugoslavia 1989–1990, to Sri Lanka 1990–93; Lt-Gov. Union Territories of Andaman and Nicobar Islands 2001–04; Lt-Gov. Pondicherry Jan.–June 2004; mem. Bharatiya Janata Party (BJP) Nat. Exec. 1994, Convenor BJP Foreign Affairs Cttee 1998.

JHA, Paramananda, LLM, MA; Nepalese lawyer and politician; b. 20 April 1945, Mauaha, Saptari; s. of Madan Jha; m.; two s. two d.; ed Tribhuvan Univ., Kathmandu, Vrije Univ. Brussels, Belgium; joined civil service as Section Officer 1972, becoming Jt Sec., Ministry of Justice 1976; Judge, Kathmandu Dist Court, Zonal and Appellate courts, later Ad Hoc Justice, Supreme Court –2007 (resgnd); mem. Madhesi Jana Adhikar Forum Nepal (Madhesi People's Rights Forum Nepal); Vice-Pres. of Nepal 2008–15. *Address:* Boudh Dwar Marg, Kumarigal 446/14, Ward 8, Kathmandu, Nepal (home). *Telephone:* (1) 4486118 (home). *Fax:* (1) 4486118 (home).

JHA, Sanjay K., BSc, PhD, MBA; British/American computer engineer and business executive; b. India; ed Univs of Liverpool and Strathclyde, UK; moved to US from UK 1994; held lead design eng roles with Brooktree Corpn, San Diego, and GEC Hirst Research Labs, London, UK; joined Qualcomm as Sr Engineer with VLSI (very large-scale integration) Group 1994–97, Vice-Pres. of Eng 1997–98, Sr Vice-Pres. of Eng 1998–2002, led formation of Qualcomm Technologies & Ventures 2002, managed both tech. investment portfolio and new tech. group as Sr Vice-Pres. and Gen. Man. 2002–03, Exec. Vice-Pres. Qualcomm and Pres. Qualcomm CDMA Technologies (chipset and software div.) 2003–06, COO Qualcomm Inc. 2006–08, oversaw Corp. Research and Devt and Qualcomm Flarion Technologies; joined Motorola, Inc. in 2008, mem. Bd of Dirs and Co-CEO 2008–11, also CEO Motorola Mobility; CEO GlobalFoundaries 2014–18; Hon. DSc (Strathclyde Univ, Scotland) 2011. *Address:* c/o GlobalFoundaries, NanoFb South Building, 255 Fuller Road, Suite 380, Albany, NY 12203, USA (office). *Website:* www.globalfoundries.com (office).

JHAGRA, Iqbal Zafar; Pakistani engineer and politician; b. 17 May 1947, Jhagra village, Peshawar Dist; ed Peshawar Engineering Coll.; posted to Irrigation Dept 1970, moved to Saudi Arabia to work as engineer 1977; joined (Pakistan Muslim League—Nawaz) (PML—N) 1984, Pres. PML-N Peshawar 1988; elected to Senate 1997, 2008, 2015, fmr Chair. Standing Cttee on Defence, Defence Production, Aviation; Sec.-Gen. (PML—N) 2003–09, 2012–15, Sec., Central Parl. Bd 2013; Gov. of Khyber Pakhtunkhwa 2016–18 (resgnd); fmr Sec.-Gen. Alliance for the Restoration of Democracy (coalition of political parties which endorsed the Charter of Democracy). *Address:* c/o Government of Khyber Pakhtunkhwa, Third Floor 204-210, Deans Trade Center, Islamia Road, Peshawar Cantt., Peshawar, Pakistan (office).

JHANJHUGHAZYAN, Atom; Armenian engineer and politician; *Minister of Finance;* b. 22 March 1971, Yerevan; m.; two s. one d.; ed State Eng Univ. of Armenia; Technician and Engineer, ASSP Stateplan 1991–93; Specialist, Information Systems Div., Ministry of Economy 1993–95, becoming Leading Specialist and Chief Specialist 1995; Asst to Chair of Automated Man. Systems, State Eng Univ. of Armenia 1993–95; Chief Financial Officer, Computer Analysis Dept and Head of Current Expenditure Man. Div., Ministry of Finance 1995–96, Head of Accounting Dept 1996–97, Head of Operations Dept and Economic Programs Dept, Ministry of Finance and Economy 1997–99, Deputy Minister and Chief Treasurer, Ministry of Finance 1999–2000, 2008–16, Deputy Minister and Chief Treasurer, Ministry of Finance and Economy 2000–08, First Deputy Minister of Finance 2016–18, Minister of Finance 2018–; Asst Prof., Dept of Finance and Credit, Armenian State Univ. of Econs 2007–09; Lecturer, Dept of Public Admin and Public Finance, Public Admin Acad. 2007–11; Anania Shirakatsi Medal 2007, Medal For Services to the Homeland (Second Degree) 2015. *Address:* Ministry of Finance, 0010 Yerevan, M. Adamyan poghots 1, Armenia (office). *Telephone:* (11) 80-01-56 (office). *Fax:* (11) 80-01-32 (office). *E-mail:* secretariat@minfin.am (office). *Website:* www.minfin.am (office).

JHINAOUI, Khemaies, DESS, DEA; Tunisian lawyer, diplomatist and politician; *Minister of Foreign Affairs;* b. 5 April 1954; m.; two c.; ed Nat. Defense Coll.; long career in Ministry of Foreign Affairs (MFA) including Head, Liaison Office, Tel-Aviv 1996, Head of Mission, Cabinet of Minister of Foreign Affairs 1996–98, 2004–06, Amb. to UK 1999–2005, to Russian Fed. 2008–11, Dir-Gen. for Econ. and Political Affairs and for European Co-operation, MFA 2006–07, Sec. of State, MFA July–Dec. 2011–12, Diplomatic and Foreign Affairs Adviser to the President 2015–16, Minister of Foreign Affairs 2016–; Head, Diplomatic Inst. for Training and Studies 2013; mem. Bd The Africa Centre, London –2005. *Address:* Ministry of Foreign Affairs, ave de la Ligue des états arabes, 1030 Tunis, Tunisia (office). *Telephone:* (71) 840-429 (office). *Fax:* (71) 785-025 (office). *E-mail:* mae@diplomatie.gov.tn (office). *Website:* www.diplomatie.gov.tn (office).

JI, Chaozhu, BSc; Chinese diplomatist (retired); b. 30 July 1929, Shanxi Prov.; s. of (Prof.) Chi Kungchuan; m. Wang Xiangtong 1957; two s.; ed Harvard Univ., USA, Tsinghua Univ., Beijing; stenographer and typist at Panmunjom, Korea for Chinese People's Volunteers 1952–54; English interpreter for Mao Zedong, Zhou Enlai and others 1955–73; Counsellor at Liaison Office of China in Washington, DC 1973–75; Deputy Dir Dept for Int. Orgs and Confs, Ministry of Foreign Affairs 1975–79, Deputy Dir of American and Oceanic Affairs 1979–82; Minister-Counsellor of Chinese Embassy in Washington, DC 1982–85; Amb. to Fiji, Kiribati and Vanuatu 1985–87; Amb. to UK 1987–91; UN Under-Sec. for Tech. Co-operation for Devt 1991–92; Under-Sec.-Gen., Dept of Econ. Devt 1992–96 (now Dept for Devt, Support and Man. Services); Vice-Chair. All-China Fed. of Returned Overseas Chinese 1997–2005; Sr Consultant China Inst. of Int. Strategic Studies 1997–; Patron Int. Managers Org. *Publications:* The Man on Mao's Right: From Harvard Yard to Tiananmen Square, My Life Inside China's Foreign Ministry (memoir) 2008. *Leisure interests:* swimming, archaeology, history. *Address:* c/o All–China Federation of Returned Chinese, 112-01 Queens Boulevard, Apartment 18, Huatian Mansion, 26th Floor, Lianhuachi East Road, Haidian District, Beijing 100038, People's Republic of China.

JI, Xiaohui, MBA; Chinese banking executive; *Chairman, Shanghai Pudong Development Bank Company Ltd;* b. 1955; fmr Head of Bank-Pudong, Shanghai Br.; fmr Deputy Head of Bank-Shanghai Br.; fmr Head of Bank-Shanghai Br. and Head of Bank-Pudong Br., Industrial and Commercial Bank of China Ltd; Chair. Shanghai Pudong Development Bank Co. Ltd and Party Sec. 2012–; Chair. Shanghai Int. Group Co. Ltd. *Address:* Shanghai Pudong Development Bank Co. Ltd, 12 Zhongshan Dong Yi Road, Shanghai 200002, People's Republic of China (office). *Telephone:* (21) 6161-8888 (office). *E-mail:* webmaster@spdb.com.cn (office). *Website:* www.spdb.com.cn (office).

JI, Yunshi; Chinese politician; b. 26 Sept. 1945, Haimen, Jiangsu Prov.; m. Lu Guohong; one d.; ed Shandong Univ.; sent to do manual labour in Xishan Coal Mine, Suzhou City, Jiangsu Prov. 1970; worker, man. clerk and workshop dir Suzhou Light Industrial Electrical Machinery Plant 1971, Deputy Dir then Dir 1978–80; joined CCP 1975; Deputy Dir then Dir No. 2 Light Industry Bureau, Suzhou City 1980–82 (Deputy Sec. CCP Party Cttee 1980–82); Deputy Sec. then Sec. Jiangsu Prov. Cttee CCP Communist Youth League 1980–82; Sec. CCP Jiangsu City Cttee, Jiangsu Prov. 1984; apptd Vice-Gov. Jiangsu Prov. 1989–93, elected Vice-Gov. 1993–98, Acting Gov. 1998–2002; Gov. Hebei Prov. 2002–06; Alt. mem. 15th CCP Cen. Cttee 1997–2002, mem. 16th CCP Cen. Cttee 2002–07; Deputy Sec. CCP Jiangsu Prov. Cttee 2001, mem. Standing Cttee 2001; Gen. Dir State Admin of Foreign Experts Affairs 2006–11 (retd).

JIA, Baojun; Chinese steel industry executive; *President, Sinosteel Corporation;* Vice-Pres. Wuhan Iron and Steel Group Corpn, Wuhan Iron and Steel Co. Ltd –2010; Pres. Sinosteel unit, Sinosteel Co. 2010–11, Pres. Sinosteel Corpn 2011–, Deputy Sec. CCP Party Cttee. *Address:* Sinosteel Corpn, Sinosteel International Plaza, 8 Haidian Street, Beijing, 100080, People's Republic of China (office). *Telephone:* (10) 62689821 (office); (10) 62686689 (office). *Fax:* (10) 62689800 (office); (10) 62686688 (office). *E-mail:* office@sinosteel.com (office). *Website:* www.sinosteel.com (office).

JIA, Chunwang; Chinese state official; b. 1938, Beijing; ed Tsinghua Univ., Beijing; joined CCP 1962; Sec. CCP Communist Youth League (CYL) and mem. Standing Cttee, CCP Party Cttee, Tsinghua Univ. (in charge of student affairs) 1964; fmr Sec. Beijing Municipal Cttee, CCP CYL; fmr mem. Standing Cttee, CCP CYL; fmr Sec. CCP Haidian Dist Cttee, Beijing; fmr Sec. Comm. for Discipline Inspection, CCP Beijing Municipal Cttee; Minister of State Security 1985–98; Minister of Public Security 1998–2003; mem. Cen. Comm. of Political Science and Law 1991; ranked Commr-Gen. 1992; apptd First Political Commissar, Chinese People's Armed Police Force 1998; apptd Dir Nat. Narcotics Control Comm. 1999; Vice-Procurator-Gen., Supreme People's Procuratorate 1998–2003, Procurator-Gen. 2003–08; mem. 12th CCP Cen. Cttee 1982–87, 13th Cen. Cttee 1987–92, 14th CCP Cen. Cttee 1992–97, 15th CCP Cen. Cttee 1997–2002, 16th CCP Cen. Cttee 2002–07.

JIA, Pingwa; Chinese writer; b. 21 Feb. 1952, Danfeng Co., Shaanxi Prov.; s. of Jia Yanchun and Zhouzhue; m. 2nd Guo Mei; two c.; ed Dept of Chinese Language, Northwest Univ., Xian; Ed., Shaanxi People's Publishing House 1975–; Chief Ed. magazine Mei Wen (Beautiful Essays); Pres. Shaanxi Writers Asscn, Writers Asscn of Xi'an; Ed.-in-Chief, Beautiful Essay; Dean, Dept of Humanities, Xi'an Univ. of Architecture & Tech.; mem. Writers' Asscn 1979–, also Councillor; Chevalier des arts et des lettres (France) 2003 National Excellent Short Story Award (for short story Full Moon) 1978, Flying Horse Literature Award, USA 1988, Feminist Foreign Literature Award, France 1997, Outstanding Writer of the Year, 4th Chinese Language Literature Ceremony 2006, 7th Maodun Literature Award 2008, 3rd National Excellent Novel Award (for short story December and January); Zhuang Zhongwen Literature Prize 1991, Prize for Nat. Literature (three times), Liu Qing Literature Prize 2006. *Publications:* more than 60 works, including novels Turbulence (Pegasus Prize for Literature) 2003, The Corrupt and Waning, White Night, The Abandoned Capital (Prix Femina Étranger 1997), Neighbours' Wives 2005, Impetuous 2005, Qin Opera 2005, Gaoxing (Happy) 2007, Gu Lu 2011, Dai Deng (The Lantern Bearer) 2013, Lao Sheng (Master of Songs) 2014, Jihua (The Pole Flower) 2016, Shaanxi Opera (Mao Dun Literature Prize 2008); short stories and essays; works have been translated into many languages. *Leisure interests:* painting, collecting antiques. *Address:* No. 2 Lian Hu Xiang, Xian City, Shaanxi, People's Republic of China.

JIA, Qinglin; Chinese fmr government official and engineer; b. 1940, Botou, Hebei Prov.; ed Shijiazhuang Industrial Man. School, Hebei Coll. of Eng; joined CCP 1959; technician, Complete Plant Bureau, First Ministry of Machine-Building Industry 1958–62 (Deputy Sec. CCP 1962–69), Policy Research Office of the Gen. Office 1971–73, Chief, Product Man. Bureau, First Ministry of Machine-Building Industry 1973–78; sent to do manual labour, May 7th Cadre School, Fengxin Co., Jiangxi Prov. 1969–71; Gen. Man. China Nat. Machinery and Equipment Import and Export Corpn 1978–83; Dir Taiyuan Heavy Machinery Plant 1983–85 (Sec. CCP Party Cttee 1983–85); Deputy Sec. Standing Cttee, Fujian CCP Prov. Cttee 1986–93, Sec. 1993–96; Head, Org. Dept, CCP Fujian Prov. Cttee 1986–88; Pres. Party School, CCP Fujian Prov. Cttee 1988–90; Sec. Work Cttee of Depts, CCP Fujian Prov. Cttee 1988–90; Deputy Gov. (also Acting Gov.) of Fujian Prov. 1990–91, Gov. 1991–94; Vice-Mayor (also Acting Mayor) of Beijing 1996–97, Mayor 1997–99; Chair. Standing Cttee Fujian Prov. 8th People's Congress 1994–96; Sec. CCP Beijing Municipal Cttee 1997–2002; mem. 14th CCP Cen. Cttee 1992–97, 15th CCP Cen. Cttee 1997–2002 (mem. Politburo 1997–2002), 16th CCP Cen. Cttee 2002–07 (mem. Standing Cttee of the Politburo 2002–07), 17th CCP Cen. Cttee 2007–12 (mem. Standing Cttee of the Politburo 2007–12); Chair. 10th CPPCC Nat. Cttee 2003–08, Chair. 11th CPPCC Nat. Cttee 2008–13.

JIA, Zhangke; Chinese film director and producer; b. 1970, Fenyang, Shanxi Prov.; ed Shanxi Univ., Beijing Film Acad.; co-f. Xstream Pictures (with Yu Lik-Wai and Chow Keung) 2003; considered leading mem. of 'Sixth Generation' movt of Chinese cinema. *Films:* as dir: Xiao Shan Going Home (Hong Kong Independent Short Film & Video Award 1997) 1995, Du Du 1996, Xiao Wu 1997 (Dragons and Tigers Award, Vancouver Int. Film Festival, Wolfgang Staudt Prize, Berlin Int. Film Festival, Sky Prize, San Francisco Int. Film Festival), Platform 2000, Unknown Pleasures 2002, The World 2004, Still Life 2006 (Lion d'Or, 63rd Venice Int. Film Festival 2006), Our Ten Years 2007, 24 City 2008, I Wish I Knew 2010, A Touch of Sin 2013; as producer: Walking on the Wild Side 2006, Plastic City 2008, Perfect Life 2008. *Address:* XStream Films, Suite 303, Block 7, 6 Zhi Chun Lu, Hai Dian, Beijing 100088, People's Republic of China. *Telephone:* (10) 82350984 (office).

JIA, Zhijie; Chinese party and government official; b. 1935, Fuyu Co., Jilin Prov.; ed in USSR; joined CCP 1960; Dir Lanzhou Petrochemical Machinery Plant; Deputy Sec. Plant CCP Cttee; Deputy Sec. Gansu Prov. CCP Cttee 1983–92; Gov. Gansu Prov. 1986–92; Gov. of Hubei Prov. 1992–94; Sec. CCP Cttee Hubei Prov. 1994–2001; Sec.-in-Chief Hubei Mil. Dist CCP Cttee 1994; Alt. mem. CCP 13th Cen. Cttee 1987–92, mem. 14th CCP Cen. Cttee 1992–97, 15th CCP Cen. Cttee 1997–2002; Deputy 9th NPC 1998–2003. *Address:* c/o Office of Provincial Governor, 1 Beihuan Road, Wuhan, Hubei Province, People's Republic of China. *Telephone:* (27) 87814585. *Fax:* (27) 87816148.

JIANG, Baolin; Chinese artist; b. 20 Jan. 1942, Penglai Co., Shandong Prov.; s. of Jiang Chunfu and Dai Shuzhi; m. Ling Yunhua 1970; one s. one d.; ed Dept of Traditional Chinese Painting, Inst. of Fine Arts, Zhejiang, Cen. Acad. of Fine Arts, Beijing; worked in Cultural House, Fenghua Co. 1967–79; Dir Zhejiang Artists' Gallery 1982–84; Vice-Pres. Zhejiang Landscape Painting Research Inst. 1982–; mem. Council of Zhejiang Br. of Chinese Painters' Asscn 1984–; mem. Bd Zhejiang Painting Acad. 1984–; Visiting Prof., Beijing Cen. Fine Arts Acad. 1996–; Tutor, Acad. of Arts, Tsinghua Univ., Beijing, mem. Council, Cui Zifan Art Foundation Int.; mem. Chinese Artists' Asscn; numerous exhbns 1987–, including Contemporary Chinese Paintings in celebration of Hong Kong's return to China, Beijing, Shanghai, Tianjin 1997; Silver Medal, 9th Nat. Art Exhbn 1999. *Publications:* Collections of Jiang Baolin's Paintings 1984, Jiang Baolin's ink-wash paintings 1989, Signatur Objekt 15, Jiang Baolin 1991, Jiang Baolin's Paintings (published in France) 1991, A selection of Jiang Baolin's Bird and Flower Paintings 1992, The World of Jiang Baolin's Ink & Wash Painting 1994, The Art World of Jiang Baolin (published in Korea) 1996, Series on Modern Chinese Artists 2000. *Leisure interests:* Beijing Opera, literature, music, gardening. *Address:* 201 Building 11, 2nd District, Nandu Huayuan Wenyi Road, Hangzhou, People's Republic of China. *Telephone:* (571) 8850096. *Fax:* (571) 8850096.

JIANG, Boju; Chinese mathematician and academic; *Professor of Mathematics, Peking University;* b. 4 Sept. 1937, Tianjin City; m. Chuanrong Xu 1968; two d.; ed Peking Univ.; Assoc. Prof. of Math., Peking Univ. 1978–82, Prof. 1983–, Dean School of Math. Sciences 1995–98; mem. Chinese Acad. of Sciences 1980; Fellow, Third World Acad. of Sciences 1985; Nat. Scientific Award of China 1982, 1987, S.S. Chern Mathematics Award 1988, Ho Leung Ho Lee Foundation Math. Prize 1996, L.K. Hua Math. Award 2002. *Address:* Department of Mathematics, Peking University, 5 Yiheyuan Road, Hai Dian, Beijing 100871, People's Republic of China (office). *Telephone:* (10) 62751804 (office). *Fax:* (10) 62751801 (office). *Website:* www.pku.edu.cn (office).

JIANG, Chaoliang, MA; Chinese banking executive and government official; b. Aug. 1957; ed Southwestern Univ. of Finance and Econs; fmr Gov. Guangzhou Br., People's Bank of China, Shenzhen Br.; Deputy Dir-Gen. Banking Div., Dir Shenzhen Div. of State Admin of Foreign Exchange (SAFE), and Gov. Guangdong Br., People's Bank of China and Chief of Guangdong Div. of SAFE 1996–2000; Asst Gov. People's Bank of China 2000–02, mem. Monetary Policy Cttee; Deputy Gov. Hubei Prov. 2002–04; Dir (non-exec.) and Chair. Bank of Communications 2004–08; Exec. Dir and Vice-Chair. China Devt Bank Corpn –2008, Pres. 2008–12; Exec. Dir Agricultural Bank of China Ltd 2011–14, Exec. Chair. and Pres. 2012–14; Acting Gov. of Jilin Prov. Sept.–Oct. 2014, Gov. 2014–16; Sec. CCP, Hubei Prov. 2016–, mem. Central Cttee, 19th CPC 2017–; Chair. Standing Cttee, Provincial People's Congress, Hubei Prov. 2017–.

JIANG, Chunyun; Chinese party official (retd); b. April 1930, Laixi Co., Shandong Prov.; ed Teachers Training Coll., Laixi Co., Chinese Language and Literature Self-Study Univ.; fmr primary school teacher; Clerk of CCP Maren Dist Cttee, Sec., CCP Laixi Co. Cttee 1946–49; joined CCP 1947; Dir of Gen. Office Laixi Co. CCP Cttee 1949–57; Deputy Section Chief, Qingdao br., China Export Corpn for Local Products 1957–60; with Foreign Trade Bureau, Qingdao City 1957–60; Instructor and Chief Insp. and Deputy Dir of Gen. Office, Propaganda Dept Shandong Prov. CCP Cttee 1960–66; manual work in village in Huimin Co. during Cultural Revolution, sent to cadre school, Qihe Co. 1969; worked under Revolutionary Cttee Shandong Prov. 1970–75; Deputy Dir, Gen. Office, Shandong Prov. CCP Cttee 1975–77, Deputy Sec.-Gen., then Sec.-Gen. 1977–83, Deputy Sec. 1983–84; Sec., Ji'nan Municipal CCP Cttee 1984–87; Acting Gov., Shandong Prov. 1987–88, Gov. 1988–89; Pres. Shandong Prov. Party School 1989–92; First Sec., Shandong Mil. Dist CCP Cttee 1989–94; Sec., CCP Shandong Prov. Cttee 1993–94; Vice-Premier State Council (in charge of agricultural work) 1995–98; Head of State Flood-Control and Drought Relief HQ; mem. 13th CCP Cen. Cttee, 14th CCP Cen. Cttee 1992–97 (mem. Secr. of Politburo 1992–97), 15th CCP Cen. Cttee 1997–2002; Deputy, 7th NPC 1988–93, 8th NPC 1993–98, Vice-Chair. Standing Cttee of 9th NPC 1998–2003; apptd Pres. China Family Planning Asscn 1998; Prof. (part-time), Shandong Univ.; Hon. Prof., China Agric. Univ.

JIANG, Daming; Chinese politician; *Minister of Land and Resources;* b. 1953, Rongcheng City, Shandong Prov.; ed Heilongjiang Univ.; various roles with Production and Construction Corps, Heilongjiang Prov. 1969–77; joined CCP 1976, Clerk, Communist Youth League of China (CYLC) Cen. Cttee Org. Dept 1982–84, Deputy Section Chief 1984–86, Section Chief 1986–87, Deputy Dir 1987–90, Dir 1990–93, Sec., CYLC Cen. Cttee Secr. 1993–98; Vice-Chair. All-China Youth Fed. 1998; mem. 9th CPPCC Nat. Cttee 1998–2003; Deputy Sec., CCP Provincial Cttee, Shandong Prov. 2000–04; Sec., CCP City Cttee, Jinan City 2004–07; Vice-Gov., Shandong Prov. 2007–08, Gov. 2008–13; Minister of Land and Resources 2013–; alt. mem. 16th CCP Cen. Cttee 2002–07, mem. 17th CCP Cen. Cttee 2007–12, 18th CCP Cen. Cttee 2012–. *Address:* Ministry of Land and Resources, 64 Funei Dajie, Xisi, Beijing 100812, People's Republic of China (office). *Telephone:* (10) 66558407 (office). *Fax:* (10) 66127247 (office). *E-mail:* mhwz@mail.mlr.gov.cn (office). *Website:* www.mlr.gov.cn (office).

JIANG, Enzhu; Chinese diplomatist (retd); b. 14 Dec. 1938, Jiangsu Prov.; s. of Jiang Guohua and Yu Wen Guizhen; m. Zhu Manli; one s.; ed Beijing Foreign Languages Univ.; joined Ministry of Foreign Affairs as translator 1964; Attaché, Third and Second Sec., Embassy in London during 1970s; Deputy Dir-Gen., then Dir-Gen. Dept of West European Affairs, Ministry of Foreign Affairs 1984–90, Asst Foreign Minister 1990–91, Vice-Minister 1991–95; Chief Negotiator for People's Repub. of China in Sino-British talks over future of Hong Kong; Deputy Head of Preliminary Working Cttee of Preparatory Cttee of Hong Kong Special Admin. Region; Amb. to UK 1995–97; Dir Hong Kong br., Xinhua News Agency 1997–99; Dir (Minister) Liaison Office of People's Repub. of China to Hong Kong SAR 2000–03; mem. 15th CCP Cen. Cttee 1997–2002; mem. Standing Cttee 9th NPC 1998–2003; Chair. 10th NPC Foreign Affairs Cttee 2003–08.

JIANG, Gen. Futang; Chinese army officer; b. Oct. 1941, Rongcheng Co., Shandong Prov.; ed Political Acad. of the Chinese PLA; joined PLA 1959, CCP 1960; Dir Political Section, Regt 1969–70; Deputy Div. Political Commissar 1974–76; Dir Army Political Dept 1976–80; Political Commissar, 46th Army, Army (or Ground Force), PLA Services and Arms, 1983–85; Dir Political Dept of PLA Jinan Mil. Area Command 1985–93; Deputy Political Commissar and Dir Political Dept of PLA Chengdu Mil. Area Command 1993–95; apptd Political Commissar, PLA Shenyang Mil. Area Command 1995; rank of Maj.-Gen. 1988–93, Lt-Gen. 1993–2002, Gen. 2002–; mem. 15th CCP Cen. Cttee 1997–2002, 16th CCP Cen. Cttee 2002–07.

JIANG, Jianqing, MEng, PhD; Chinese banker; b. 1 Feb. 1953; ed Shanghai Univ. of Finance and Econs, Jiaotong Univ., Shanghai; joined CCP 1983, Alt. mem. 16th CCP Cen. Cttee 2002–07, 17th 2007–12, 18th 2012–17; Deputy Dept Dir Municipal Subsidiary Bank Shanghai Municipality, Industrial and Commercial Bank of China (ICBC) 1986–89, Dept Dir 1989–90, Vice-Gov. Subsidiary Bank Shanghai, Pudong New Dist 1990–93, Municipal Subsidiary Bank, Shanghai Municipality 1993–95, Dir Shanghai Br. 1997–99, Group Vice-Pres. 1999–2000, Pres. 2000–05, Exec. Dir and Chair. 2005–16 (retd); Dir Shanghai City United Bank (now Bank of Shanghai) 1995–97; Prof. (part-time), Man. Inst., Jiaotong Univ. (also Doctorate Adviser and Researcher); mem. Monetary Policy Comm., People's Bank of China; Most Influential Leader, Golden Bauhinia Award 2012, Business Leader of the Year, Asian Award 2013. *Publications:* numerous articles including Analytical View on Foreign Financial Agitation, Thoughts on Financial Agitation, Technical Revolution in American Banking.

JIANG, Jiemin; Chinese government official and fmr petroleum industry executive; b. Oct. 1955, Yangxin, Shandong Prov.; ed Party School of CCP Cen. Cttee; Deputy Dir Shengli Petroleum Admin Bureau 1993–94; Sr Exec. Qinghai Petroleum Admin Bureau 1994, Dir 1994–99; Asst to Gen. Man. and Team Leader of Restructuring, China Nat. Petroleum Corpn (CNPC) 1999, Dir and Vice-Pres. PetroChina Co. Ltd 1999–2000, Vice-Chair. and Pres. 2004–07, Chair. 2007–08, also Vice-Pres. CNPC 2004–06, Pres. 2006–11, Chair. 2011–13; Chair. and Deputy Sec. Party Cttee, State-owned Assets Supervision and Admin Comm. (SASAC) March–Sept. 2013 (removed from post); Deputy Gov. Qinghai Prov. 2000–04, also mem. Prov. Party Cttee 2000, 2003; Alt. mem. 17th CCP Cen. Cttee 2007–12, mem.

18th CCP Cen. Cttee 2012–14 (expelled); in 2015 found guilty by Court on all counts, including accepting bribery and abuse of power, and sentenced to 16 years in prison.

JIANG, Weixin; Chinese politician; b. 1949, Fuyu County, Heilongjiang Prov.; ed Beijing Univ.; sent to countryside during Cultural Revolution 1968; joined CCP 1969; Deputy Dir, Nat. Devt and Reform Comm. 2003–07; Deputy Minister of Construction 2007–08; Minister of Housing and Urban-Rural Devt 2008–13; mem. 17th CCP Cen. Cttee 2007–12.

JIANG, Wen; Chinese actor and film director; b. 5 Jan. 1963, Tangshan, Hebei Prov.; m. 1st Sandrine Chenivisse; one d.; m. 2nd Zhou Yun; one s.; ed Cen. Acad. of Drama; joined China Youth Arts Theatre 1984; actor at Cen. Acad. of Drama. *Films include:* Fu rong zhen 1984, Moot doi wong hau 1986, Hong gao liang (Red Sorghum) 1987, Ben ming nian 1990, Da taijian Li Lianying (Li Lianying, the Imperial Eunuch) 1991, Yangguang Canlan de Rizi (In the Heat of the Sun) (dir, actor) 1994, Qin song 1996, Song jia huang chao 1997, The Soong Sisters (Hong Kong Film Award for Best Supporting Actor 1998) 1997, Guizi lai le (Devils on the Doorstep) (dir, producer) (Cannes Film Festival Grand Prix 2000) 2000, Xun qiang (The Missing Gun) (producer) 2002, Tian di ying xiong (Warriors of Heaven and Earth) 2003, Lü cha (Green Tea) 2003, Yi ge mo sheng nu ren de lai xin (A Letter from an Unknown Woman) 2004, Mo li hua kai (Jasmine) 2004, The Sun Also Rises (actor, dir and writer) 2007, Connected 2008, The Founding of a Republic 2009, Let the Bullets Fly (dir) 2010, The Lost Bladesman 2011, Gone with the Bullets 2014, Rogue One: A Star Wars Story 2016. *Address:* Central Academy of Drama, 39 Dong Mianhua Hutong, Dongcheng District, Beijing 100710, People's Republic of China (office). *Telephone:* (10) 64035626 (office). *E-mail:* zhongxi@zhongxi.cn (office). *Website:* web.zhongxi.cn (office).

JIANG, Xinxiong; Chinese party and government official; b. 6 July 1931; ed Nankai Univ., Tianjin; joined CCP 1956; Dir nuclear fuel plant 1979–82; Vice-Minister of Nuclear Industry 1982–83, Minister 1983; Chair. Bd of Dirs, China Isotopes Co. 1983–98; Pres. Nat. Nuclear Corpn 1988–98; Chair. China Atomic Energy Authority 1994–99; Deputy Head Leading Group for Nuclear Power Plants; Vice-Chair Finance and Econ. Cttee of 9th NPC 1998–2003; Pres. China-Canada Friendship Asscn of NPC 1998–2003; Alt. mem. 12th CCP Cen. Cttee 1982–87, 13th CCP Cen. Cttee 1987–92, 14th CCP Cen. Cttee 1992–97.

JIANG, Yi-Huah, BA, MA, PhD; Taiwanese academic and government official; b. 18 Nov. 1960; ed Nat. Taiwan Univ., Yale Univ., USA; Asst Research Fellow, Sun Yat-Sen Inst. for Social Sciences and Philosophy, Academia Sinica 1993–95; Assoc. Prof., Dept of Political Science, Nat. Taiwan Univ. 1995–99, Prof. 1999–, Deputy Dean, Coll. of Social Sciences 2003–05, Assoc. Dean, Office of Academic Affairs 2006–08; Visiting Scholar, Darwin Coll., Univ. of Cambridge, UK 2000; Visiting Prof., East Asian Inst., Columbia Univ., USA 2001; Adviser, Ministry of Educ. 2004; Minister of Research, Devt and Evaluation Comm. 2008–09, Minister of the Interior 2009–12; Vice-Premier 2012–13, Premier 2013–14 (resgnd). *Address:* Executive Yuan, No.1, Sec. 1, Zhongxiao E. Road., Zhongzheng Dist., Taipei 10058, Taiwan (office). *Telephone:* (2) 33566500 (office). *E-mail:* eyemail@eyemail.gio.gov.tw. (office). *Website:* www.ey.gov.tw (office).

JIANG, Yingshi, MA; Chinese business executive; b. Dec. 1949; fmr Party Sec. and Dir Shanghai Municipal Devt and Reform Comm.; fmr Chair. Bd of Supervisors, Shanghai Automotive Industry Corpn (SAIC) Group; mem. Nat. Cttee, CPPCC.

JIANG, Zemin; Chinese fmr head of state; b. 17 Aug. 1926, Yangzhou City, Jiangsu Prov.; ed Jiaotong Univ., Shanghai; joined CCP 1946; worked in Shanghai Yimin No. 1 Foodstuffs Factory, Shanghai Soap Factory, First Ministry of Machine-Bldg Industry; trainee, Stalin Automobile Plant, Moscow, USSR 1955–56; Deputy Chief Power Div., Deputy Chief Power-Engineer, Dir, Power Plant, Changchun No. 1 Auto Works 1957–62; Deputy Dir Shanghai Electric Equipment Research Inst., Dir and Acting Party Sec. Wuhan Thermo-Tech. Machinery Research Inst., Deputy Dir, Dir Foreign Affairs Bureau of First Ministry of Machine-Bldg Industry 1962–80; Vice-Chair. and Sec.-Gen. State Comm. on Admin of Imports and Exports, State Comm. on Admin of Foreign Investment 1980–82; First Vice-Minister Electronics Industry 1982–83, Minister 1983–85; Mayor of Shanghai 1985–88; Deputy Sec., Sec. Shanghai Municipal Party Cttee 1985–89; mem. 12th Nat. Congress CCP Cen. Cttee 1982, Politburo 1st Plenary Session of 13th Cen. Cttee 1987, Gen. Sec. 4th Plenary Session 1989, Chair. Mil. Cttee 5th Plenary Session 1989; mem. Standing Cttee Politburo, Gen. Sec. and Chair. Mil. Cttee 14th and 15th CCP Cen. Cttees 1992–2002; Chair. Cen. Mil. Comm. of CCP Cen. Cttee 1990–2004, Cen. Mil. Comm. of People's Repub. of China 1998–2005; Pres. People's Repub. of China 1993–2003; Hon. Chair. Red Cross Soc. of China; Hon. Pres. Software Industry Asscn. *Address:* Chinese Communist Party, Zhongguo Gongchan Dang, 1 Zhongnanhai, Beijing, People's Republic of China.

JIANG, Zhenghua; Chinese academic, demographer and politician; *Honorary Dean, School of Management, Beijing Normal University;* b. Oct. 1937, Hangzhou City, Zhejiang Prov.; ed Xi'an Jiaotong Univ., Int. Demography Acad., Bombay, India; Lecturer, Auto Control Dept and Dir Population Research Centre, Inst. of Systematic Eng 1958–78; Dir Population and Econs Inst. 1958–78; Prof., Xi'an Jiaotong Univ. 1978–91; Visiting Prof., Univ. of Paris, France, Stanford Univ., USA; Specialist, India Int. Devt Centre 1986; fmr Dean, School of Man., Beijing Normal Univ., now Hon. Dean; fmr Tech. Adviser, State Census Office; Vice-Minister, State Family Planning Comm. 1991–99; joined Chinese Peasants' and Workers' Democratic Party 1992; Vice-Chair. Cen. Cttee 11th Chinese Peasants' and Workers' Democratic Party (CPWDP) 1992–97, Chair. Cen. Cttee 12th CPWDP 1997–2002; mem. 7th CPPCC Nat. Cttee 1988–93, Standing Cttee 8th CPPCC Nat. Cttee 1993–98 (mem. Sub-cttee of Educ., Science, Culture, Health and Sports 1993–98); Vice-Chair. Standing Cttee of 9th NPC 1998–2003, of 10th NPC 2003–08; mem. Macao Hand-Over Ceremony Govt Del., Macao Special Admin. Region Preparatory Cttee 1999; now Prof. of Systems Eng, Econometrics and Demography; fmr Pres. China Soc. of Tech. and Demography; fmr Vice-Pres. Demographic Inst., Shaanxi Prov.; fmr adviser to and mem. Exec. Council Demography Soc. of China; mem. Council Int. Demography Soc. 1993–; Hon. DSc (Univ. of Minnesota) 2005; Gold Medal, Bombay Int. Demography Acad., India 1981, Outstanding Expert at Nat. Level of China 1985, Nat. Advanced Worker of China 1989, First Class Nat. Science and Tech. Progress Prize 1987. *Publications:* Economic Development Planning Models 1981, Country Report on Population of China 1997, Sustainable Development of China 1999, Population – Systematic and Quantitative Study and its Application (First Class Award, State Scientific and Technological Advancement), Analysis and Planning of Population, Programming Regional Population and Coordination Development of Economy. *Address:* Beijing Normal University, Zhuhai, 18th Jinfeng Road, Tangjiawan, Zhuhai City, Guangdong Province (office); 11 Min Zu Yuan Road, Room 601, Beijing 100029, People's Republic of China (home). *Telephone:* (10) 62357120 (home). *E-mail:* jenjenny@sina.com (office).

JIANG, Zhuping; Chinese aerospace engineer (retd) and administrator; b. Nov. 1937, Yixing Co., Jiangsu Prov.; s. of Jiang Nanxiang; ed Faculty of Missile Eng, Harbin Mil. Eng Inst.; joined CCP 1960; with Design Inst. of Ministry of Nat. Defence 1963–65; Deputy Dir Design Inst. of Nanchang Aircraft. Mfg Plant 1978–82, Deputy Sec. plant's Party Cttee 1982–84; Sec. Party Cttee of Depts under Ministry of Aeronautics Industry 1984–85; Vice-Gov. of Jiangxi Prov. 1985–88; Deputy Sec. CCP Jiangxi Prov. Cttee 1988–95; Gov. of Hubei Prov. 1995–2001; Sec. CCP Hubei Prov. Cttee 2000–01; Deputy to 9th NPC 1998–2003, Vice-Chair. NPC Educ., Science, Culture and Health Cttee 2001; mem. 14th CCP Cen. Cttee 1992–97, 15th CCP Cen. Cttee 1997–2002; Deputy Dir Civil Aviation Gen. Admin. of China 1991–95. *Address:* c/o National People's Congress, 23 Xijiaominxiang, Xicheng District, Beijing 100805, People's Republic of China.

JIANG, Zilong; Chinese writer; b. 2 June 1941, Cang Xian, Hebei; s. of Jiang Junsan and Wei Huanzhang; m. Zhang Qinglian 1968; one s. one d.; worker Tianjin Heavy Machinery Plant 1958; navy conscript 1960–65; apptd Vice-Chair. Chinese Writers' Asscn 1996; Pres. Tianjin Writers' Asscn; Nat. Short Story Prize 1979, Oriental Writer Award, Nat. Asscn of Chinese Writers, USA 2012. *Publications include:* A New Station Master 1965, One Day for the Chief of the Bureau of Electromechanics 1976, Manager Qiao Assumes Office 1979, Developer 1980, Diary of a Plant Secretary 1980, All the Colours of the Rainbow 1983, Yan-Zhao Dirge 1985, Serpent Deity 1986, Jiang Zilong Works Collection (eight vols) 1996, Human Vigour 2000, Ren Qi 2000, Empty Hole 2001, The Empire of Peasants 2008, Popularity 2010, Inanition. *Leisure interests:* swimming, Beijing opera. *Address:* No. 7, Dali Road, Heping District, Tianjin, People's Republic of China (home). *Telephone:* (22) 23306250 (home). *Fax:* (22) 23306250 (home). *E-mail:* jzltj@hotmail.com.

JIAO, Kaihe; Chinese business executive; *Vice-Chairman, All-China Federation of Trade Unions (ACFTU);* fmr Deputy Gen. Man. and Vice-Pres. China North Industries Group Corpn (NORINCO), apptd Pres. 2013; currently Vice-Chair. All-China Fed. of Trade Unions (ACFTU). *Address:* All-China Federation of Trade Unions, 10 Fuxingmenwai Street, Beijing 100865, People's Republic of China (office). *Website:* en.acftu.org (office).

JIBRIL, Mahmoud, BA, MA, PhD; Libyan politician and academic; *Leader, National Forces Alliance;* b. 28 May 1952, Bani Walid; ed Cairo Univ., Egypt, Univ. of Pittsburgh, USA; taught strategic planning at Univ. of Pittsburgh for several years; taught at Garyounis Univ., Benghazi; ran own co., Gebril for Training and Consultancy; had leading role in drafting of United Arab Training Manual; responsible for organizing and administering the first two Training confs in the Arab world 1987, 1988, later took over man. and admin of leaders' training programmes for sr man. in Arab countries including Bahrain, Egypt, Jordan, Kuwait, Libya, Morocco, Saudi Arabia, Tunisia, UAE, as well as Turkey and UK; Head of Nat. Econ. Devt Bd 2007–10; involved in 'Libya Vision' project aiming at instituting democracy in Libya; Chair. Exec. Bd ('Interim Prime Minister') and Head of Int. Affairs, Nat. Transitional Council of Libya March–Oct. 2011; Leader Nat. Forces Alliance (comprises 58 political parties) 2012–. *Publications:* ten books on strategic planning and decision-making, including Imagery and Ideology in U.S. Policy Toward Libya, 1969–1982 (as Mahmoud G. El-Warfally) 1988. *Address:* National Forces Alliance, Tripoli, Libya (office). *Telephone:* (21) 4782593 (office). *E-mail:* info@nff.ly (office).

JIČÍNSKÝ, Zdeněk, DJur; Czech politician, academic and jurist; *Chairman, Parliamentary Permanent Commission on the Constitution;* b. 26 Feb. 1929, Ostřešany; m. Nada Jičínská 1961; two s.; ed Charles Univ., Prague; mem. Czech. CP 1951–69; on staff of Inst. of Social Sciences, Cen. Cttee of Czech. CP 1954–60; Prof., Law Faculty, Charles Univ. 1964–70; mem. Scientific Law Council, Charles Univ. 1962–69; mem. Legal Comm., Cen. Cttee of Czech. CP 1964; mem. Expert Comm. of Govt Cttee for Constitutional Regulation of Repub. 1968; Deputy Chair. Czech. Nat. Council 1968; mem. Chamber of Nations, Fed. Ass. of CSSR 1969; forced to leave public life and university 1969; lawyer in insurance co. 1969–77; signed Charter 77; Rep. Civic Forum 1989; Deputy Chair. Fed. Ass. 1989–90, First Deputy Chair. 1990–92; Deputy and mem. Presidium Fed. Ass. 1992–; mem. Civic Movt 1991–92; mem. Czechoslovak Social Democratic Party 1992–; mem. Parl. 1996–2002, 2003–, Deputy Chair. Parl. Constitutional Juridical Cttee 1996–2002; mem. Standing Del. to Inter parl. Union 1996–98, Chair. Parl. Perm. Comm. on the Constitution 2007–; mem. Scientific Law Council Charles Univ. 2006–; political commentator, Právo newspaper (fmrly Rudé Právo) 1992–. *Publications:* Political Ideology of the First Czechoslovak Republic 1961, On the Development of Thinking in Czechoslovakia in the Sixties 1991, Developments in Czechoslovak Parliament since November 1989 1993, The Extinction of Czechoslovakia in 1992 from a Constitutional Viewpoint 1993, Problems of Czech Politics 1994, Charter 77 and Society Governed by the Law 1995, Constitutional and Political Problems of the Czech Republic 1995, The Constitution of the Czech Republic in Political Practice 2007; numerous works on politics, theory of state and law and institutional law. *Leisure interests:* skiing, cycling, jazz. *Address:* Pařížská 12, 110 00 Prague 1, Czech Republic (home). *Telephone:* (2) 22312560 (home). *E-mail:* jicinskyz@psp.cz (office); a2@jicinsky.cz (office). *Website:* www.jicinsky.cz (office).

JIHAD, Abdulla, BA; Maldivian economist, politician and fmr central banker; b. 3 Jan. 1963; m. Asima Hussein; three c.; ed Univ. of South Pacific, Fiji, Univ. of Waikato, New Zealand; Sec., Science Education Centre March–July 1982, Sec., Ministry of Planning and Devt 1984–85, Govt Budget Sec., Dept of Finance 1985–86, Budget Analyst, Ministry of Finance 1990–91, Asst Dir Ministry of Finance and Treasury 1991–94, Deputy Dir Ministry of Finance and Treasury 1994–95, Deputy Dir Dept of Inland Revenue 1996–2000, Dir Dept of Inland

Revenue 2000–04, Asst Dir-Gen. and Head of Dept of Inland Revenue 2004–05; Vice-Gov. Maldives Monetary Authority 2005–07, Gov. Maldives Monetary Authority 2007–08; Minister of Finance and Treasury July–Nov. 2008, 2012–13, 2013–16; Vice-Pres. of Maldives 2016–18; mem. Civil Service Comm. 2010–13. *Address:* c/o Office of the Vice-President, Boduthakurufaanu Magu, Malé 20-113, Maldives (office).

JILANI, Hina; Pakistani lawyer and human rights activist; b. 1951; sister of Asma Jahangir; qualified as lawyer 1974; Advocate of High Court 1981–; co-f. (with Asma Jahangir) AGHS Law Assocs (all-women law firm), Lahore 1981, also co-f. AGHS Legal Aid Cell (first free legal aid centre in Pakistan) 1984; Advocate of Supreme Court 1992–; Founding mem. Human Rights Comm. of Pakistan, Lahore 1986–, Women's Action Forum; apptd UN Special Rep. on the Situation of Human Rights Defenders 2000–08; involved with UN Center for Human Rights, the Carter Centre, UN Conf. of Women; mem. The Elders 2013–; awards from ABA, Human Rights Watch, Millennium Peace Prize 2001. *Address:* Human Rights Commission of Pakistan, Aiwan-i-Jahmoor, 107 Tipu Block, New Garden Town, Lahore 54600, Pakistan (office). *Telephone:* (42) 5838341 (office). *Fax:* (42) 5883582 (office). *E-mail:* hrcp@hrcp-web.org (office). *Website:* www.hrcp-web.org (office).

JILANI, Jalil Abbas, LLB, MSc; Pakistani diplomatist and government official; b. 2 Feb. 1955; m. Shaista Jilani; three s.; posted to Embassies in Jeddah 1983–85, London 1985–88; Deputy Sec. in Prime Minister's Secr. 1989–92; Dir India, Ministry of Foreign Affairs 1992–95, posted to Embassy in Washington, DC 1995–99, Deputy High Commr/Acting High Commr to India 1999–2003, Dir-Gen. South Asia and SAARC 2003–07, also served as Govt Spokesman on Foreign Affairs 2005, High Commr to Australia 2007–09, Amb. to Belgium, Luxembourg and EU 2009–12, Foreign Sec. of Pakistan 2012–13, Amb. to USA 2013–17. *Leisure interests:* golf, reading.

JIMENEZ, Joseph, Jr, AB, MBA; American pharmaceuticals industry executive; *CEO, Novartis AG;* b. 27 Dec. 1959; s. of Joseph Jimenez and Catherine Jimenez (née Lucente); m. Denise Lynn Kovach 1987; ed Stanford Univ., Univ. of California, Berkeley; began career as Brand Asst, Hidden Valley Ranch, Clorox Co. 1984–85, Asst Brand Man. New Products 1985–86, Kingsford 1986–87, Brand Man. New Products 1987; joined Hunt-Wesson 1993, various positions including Vice-Pres. Marketing, La Choy/Rosarita Food Co., Vice-Pres. and later Sr Vice-Pres. Orville Redenbacher, Pres. Orville Redenbacher/ Swiss Miss Food Co. 1997–98, Pres. Wesson Peter Pan Food Co. 1997–98; Pres. and CEO Heinz North America, H.J. Heinz Co. 1998–2002, Exec. Vice-Pres. 2001–07, Pres. and CEO Heinz Europe 2002–06, Pres. and CEO Heinz Asia, Australia, New Zealand, Latin America, Africa & Middle East 2006–07; Head, Consumer Health Div., Novartis AG 2007, Head, Pharmaceuticals Div. and mem. Exec. Cttee Switzerland 2007–10, CEO Novartis AG 2010–; Dir The Hain Celestial Group Inc. 1999–2004, Blue Nile 2000–, Colgate-Palmolive 2009–15; Dir (non-exec.) AstraZeneca PLC 2002–07; fmr adviser for Blackstone Group (pvt. equity org.), USA. *Address:* Novartis AG, Lichtstrasse 35, 4056 Basel, Switzerland (office). *Telephone:* (61) 324-11-11 (office). *Fax:* (61) 324-80-01 (office). *E-mail:* info@novartis.com (office). *Website:* www .novartis.com (office).

JIMENEZ, Menardo R., BSc (Com); Philippine business executive; *President and CEO, Albay-Agro Industrial Corporation;* b. 6 Dec. 1932, Manila; s. of Marcelo A. Jimenez and Emiliana Rodriguez-Jimenez; m. Carolina L. Gozon 1962; two s. two d.; ed Far Eastern Univ., qualified as certified accountant; worked for Abaca Corpn of Philippines (Abacorp) 1956–70; Pres. and CEO Repub. Broadcasting Inc. (now GMA-Radio TV Arts, GMA-7) 1974–2000; Chair. MA Jimenez Enterprises Inc., Majalco Finance & Investment Corpn, Cable Entertainment Corpn; currently Pres. and CEO Albay-Agro Industrial Devt Corpn; Pres., Justitia Realty & Devt Corpn, GMA Marketing & Productions Inc.; Dir many cos; Chair. and Trustee Kapwa Ko Mahal Ko Foundation; Chair. Bd Philippine Constitution Asscn; Chair. Prison Fellowship Philippines Inc., United Coconut Planters Bank, Majent Man. and Devt Corpn, Fibers Trading, Inc., Coffee Bean and Tea Leaf Holdings, Inc., Meedson Properties Corpn; Gov. Philippine Nat. Red Cross; Dir Philippine Chamber of Commerce and Industry; mem. Bd of Dirs San Miguel Corpn 2002; ASNA Award for Business and Entrepreneurship 2010. *Leisure interest:* stamp collection. *Website:* www.alindeco.com (office); www.sanmiguel.com.ph.

JIMÉNEZ-BELTRÁN, Domingo; Spanish international organization executive; *President, Fundación Energías Renovables;* b. 2 April 1944, Zaragoza; s. of Mariano Jiménez and María Gloria Beltrán; m. Elin Solem; one c.; ed High Tech. School of Industrial Engineers and Polytechnic Univ., Madrid; Lecturer, Polytechnic Univ., Madrid 1978–86; Exec. Adviser to Minister for Public Works and Planning 1983–85; Deputy Dir-Gen. for Int. and EU Relations and with Ministry of Public Works and Urban Planning 1985–86; Attaché for Environment and Public Works, Perm. Mission to EU, Brussels 1986–87; Head of Div. Health, Physical Safety and Quality, Consumers Policy Service, EC 1987–91; Dir-Gen. for Environmental Policy, Sec. of State for Environment and Housing, Ministry of Public Works, Transport and Environment 1991–94; Exec. Dir European Environment Agency, Copenhagen 1994–2002; Founder and fmr Dir Observatorio de la Sostenibilidad en España (Spanish Observatory of Sustainability), now Adviser; fmr Adviser to Prime Minister; Pres. Fundación Energías Renovables; Trustee, Sustainable Devt Foundation, Inst. for European Environmental Policy London; Hon. Pres., Asscn Returns Master; Nat. Prize on Environment (Spain) 2008, Emisoft Sustainability Prize 2008. *Publications:* Late Lessons From Early Warnings: The Precautionary Principle 1896–2000 (co-author) 2001; author or ed. of various publs and articles. *Address:* Fundación Energías Renovables, C/ Pedro Heredia, 8, 3rd Right, 28028 Madrid, Spain (office). *Telephone:* (62) 5474211 (office). *Website:* www.fundacionrenovables.org (office).

JIMENEZ MAYOR, Juan; Peruvian lawyer and politician; b. 5 Aug. 1964, Lima; ed Pontifical Catholic Univ. of Peru; Prof. of Legal Research, Constitutional Law and Public Man. and Admin of Justice, Pontifical Catholic Univ. of Peru 1994; Prof. Academia de la Magistratura (Judicial Acad.), Lima 2003–; Deputy Minister of Justice 2000–01, Aug.–Dec. 2011, Minister of Justice and Human Rights 2011–12; Pres. Council of Ministers (Prime Minister) 2012–13 (resgnd); mem. Peruvian Asscn of Constitutional Law; Adviser to Peruvian Press Council; Sr Adviser, OAS electoral observation missions to general elections in Guatemala 2007, Paraguay 2008.

JIMÉNEZ PUERTO, Milton Danilo; Honduran government official and lawyer; b. 8 Nov. 1961; m. D. Alba María Soto Quezada; ed Universidad Nacional Autónoma de Honduras; joined Partido Liberal de Honduras 1985; fmr Dir Colegio de Abogados Honduras; Co-Dir Consultorio Jurídico Popular; fmr Legal Adviser Cen. Nacional de Trabajadores del Campo; Minister of Foreign Affairs 2006–07 (resgnd).

JIN, Chongji; Chinese historian; b. 13 Dec. 1930, Qingpu, Jiangsu Prov.; ed Fudan Univ.; joined CCP 1948; Lecturer, Admin., Fudan Univ. 1951–65 fmr Sec. Youth Cttee; researcher, Ministry of Culture 1965–73, fmr Vice-Dir Office of Academic Affairs, Teaching and Science Office; Deputy Chief Ed., Chief Ed. Cultural Relics Press 1973–81; apptd researcher, Assoc. Exec. Dir, Exec. Dir CCP Cen. Cttee Historical Documents Research Office 1981; Vice-Dir Cultural and Historical Documents Cttee, CPPCC; Chair. All-China Asscn of Historians; fmr Vice-Pres. Modern Soc. for the Study of Military History of China; Deputy Ed.-in-Chief, Wen Wu Publishing House; Adjunct Prof. Shanghai Univ.; mem. Academic Cttee Inst. of Modern History, Chinese Acad. of Social Sciences, Council of Chinese Historical Soc. *Publications:* Xinhai Geming de Qian Qian Hou Hou (A History of the 1911 Revolution), Sun Zhongshan he Xinhai Geming (Sun Yat-sen and the 1911 Revolution), Biography of Zhou En-lai (1898–1976), Biography of Mao Zedong (1893–1949). *Leisure interest:* reading. *Address:* Historical Documents Research Office of Chinese Communist Party Central Committee, 1 Maojiawan, Xisi Bei Qian, Beijing 100017 (office); Wanshoulu Jia-15, 7th Zone, 4th Building, 101th Room, Beijing 100036, People's Republic of China (home). *Telephone:* (10) 63095701 (office); (10) 68218172 (home). *Fax:* (10) 63094431 (office).

JIN, Liqun, MA; Chinese economist and international banker; *President, Asian Infrastructure Investment Bank (AIIB);* b. Aug. 1949, Changshu, Jiangsu Prov.; one d.; ed Beijing Foreign Studies Univ., Boston Univ.; briefly joined Red Guards; sent to work in the countryside during Cultural Revolution 1968; joined Ministry of Finance 1980, becoming Dir-Gen. and Asst Minister, Vice-Minister of Finance 1998; fmr Alt. Exec. Dir for China, World Bank; fmr mem. State Monetary Policy Cttee; fmr Alt. Gov. for China, Asian Devt Bank (ADB), Vice-Pres., later Ranking Vice-Pres., in charge of programs for South, Central and West Asia, and private sector operations, ADB 2003–08; Chair. Supervisory Bd, China Investment Corpn (CIC) 2008–13; Deputy Chair., subsequently Chair., Int. Forum of Sovereign Wealth Funds (IFSWF) 2009–12; Sec.-Gen., Multilateral Interim Secr. (established to create Asian Infrastructure Investment Bank, AIIB) 2014–15, Pres.-desig., AIIB 2015–16, Pres. (inaugural holder) 2016–. *Publications:* trans. include The House of Morgan: An American Banking Dynasty and the Rise of Modern Finance, The Tree of Man (by Patrick White). *Address:* Asian Infrastructure Investment Bank (AIIB), B9 Financial St, Xicheng District, Beijing, People's Republic of China (office). *Telephone:* (10) 83580000 (office). *E-mail:* information@aiib.org (office). *Website:* www.aiib.org (office).

JIN, Renqing; Chinese politician; b. July 1944, Suzhou, Jiangsu Prov.; ed Cen. Inst. of Finance and Banking; staff mem. Grain Bureau, Yongsheng Co., Yunnan Prov. 1968–97, Deputy Dir 1977–80; joined CCP 1972; Deputy Dir Financial Office, Yongsheng Co. 1977–80; mem. Standing Cttee CCP Yongsheng Co. Cttee 1980–82 (Vice-Chair. CCP Revolutionary Cttee 1980–82), Deputy Sec. CCP Yongsheng Co. Cttee 1982–83; Deputy Magistrate, Yongsheng Co. (Dist) People's Court 1980–82, Acting Magistrate and Magistrate 1982–83; mem. CCP Lijiang Prefectural Cttee, Yunnan Prov. 1985–91; Deputy Commr Lijiang Prefectural Admin. Office 1985–91; Vice-Gov. Lijiang 1985–91; Vice-Minister of Finance 1991–95; Deputy Sec.-Gen. State Council 1995; apptd Vice-Mayor of Beijing 1995, elected Vice-Mayor 1998; mem. Standing Cttee CCP Beijing Municipal Cttee 1995; Deputy Sec. CCP Beijing Municipal Cttee 1997, Deputy Dir Planning and Construction Cttee 1997; Dir State Tax Bureau 1998–2003; Alt. mem. CCP 15th Cen. Cttee 1997–2002, mem. CCP 16th Cen. Cttee 2002–07; Minister of Finance 2003–07; Hon. Chair. Exec. Cttee All-China Fed. of Industry and Commerce 1996–97.

JIN, Shangyi; Chinese artist; b. 1934, Jiaozuo City, Henan Prov.; ed Cen. Fine Arts Acad., Beijing; known as the forerunner of classicism in Chinese Art; Pres. Cen. Inst. of Fine Arts 1987; Chair. Chinese Artists' Asscn; Vice-Chair. China Fed. of Literary and Art Circles 2001; Guest Lecturer, Art Dept, New York Municipal Univ. 1982. *Works include:* Seeing People Off 1959, The December Meeting 1961, Mao Zedong at the December Conference 1961, Mao Zedong Leads the Red Army on the Long March 1964, Spring of the Rivers 1977, Oil Workers 1978, A Maiden 1981, Tajik Bride 1983, Qu Qiubai 1984, Prayer 1987, Ascending Peak Mushitago, Our Friends are All Over the World, Summer Ranch, Portrait of Sun Yat-Sen. *Address:* c/o Central Institute of Fine Arts, 5 Xiaowei Hutong, East District, Beijing 100730, People's Republic of China (office). *Telephone:* (10) 65254731 (office).

JIN, Yongjian; Chinese diplomatist and national organization official; b. 15 Sept. 1934; s. of Jin Zhiying and Bo Canzhang; m. Wang Youping 1955; two s.; ed Beijing Univ. of Foreign Studies; officer, People's Inst. of Foreign Affairs of China 1954–63; Attaché, Embassy in Nairobi 1964–67; officer, African Dept Ministry of Foreign Affairs, Beijing 1967–71, Deputy Dir-Gen., Dir-Gen. 1984–88, Dir-Gen. Dept of Int. Orgs and Confs 1988–90; Third Sec., Second Sec. Embassy in Lagos 1971–76; Second Sec., First Sec. then Counsellor, Perm. Mission to UN, New York, Alt. Rep. to UN Security Council, Rep. to Security Council Special Cttee on Decolonization, UN Council for Namibia 1977–84, Deputy Perm. Rep., Amb. to UN, Deputy Rep. to Security Council 1990–92; Amb. and Perm. Rep. to UN, Geneva, also accred to Other Int. Orgs in Switzerland 1992–96; Under-Sec.-Gen. for Devt Support and Man. Services, UN 1996–97, for Gen. Ass. Affairs and Conf. Services 1997–2001; Pres. UN Asscn of China 2001–07; Adjunct Prof., Nankai Univ. 2005. *Leisure interests:* walking, Chinese chess, bridge.

JIN, Zhixin; Chinese business executive; *Vice-Chairman and President, Shanxi Coking Coal Group;* fmr Chief Engineer Datong Coal Industry; fmr Chair. and Party Sec., Xishan Coal & Electricity (Group) Co. Ltd, Shanxi Xishan Coal and Electricity Share Co. Ltd; currently Vice-Chair. and Pres. Shanxi Coking Coal Group. *Address:* Shanxi Coking Coal Group, 1 Xinjinci Road, Taiyuan 30024, People's Republic of China (office). *Telephone:* (351) 8305000 (office). *Fax:* (351) 8305101 (office). *E-mail:* sxjmjtb@sohu.com (office). *Website:* www.sxcc.com.cn (office).

JINDAL, (Piyush) Bobby, ScB, MLitt; American politician; b. 10 June 1971, Baton Rouge, La; s. of Amar Jindal and Raj (Pal) Jindal (née Gupta); m. Supriya Jolly; two s. one d.; ed Baton Rouge Magnet High School, Brown Univ., Univ. of Oxford, UK (Rhodes Scholar); consultant for McKinsey & Co., Washington, DC 1994–95; Sec., La Dept of Health and Hosps 1996–98; Exec. Dir Nat. Bipartisan Comm. on Future of Medicare 1998–99; volunteer in Gov. of La Office and State Legislature 1999; Pres. Univ. of Louisiana System 1999–2001; Asst Sec. for Planning and Evaluation of Health and Human Services 2001–03; cand. for Gov. of La 2003; elected to US Congress for La's First Dist 2004, re-elected 2006, mem. House Cttee on Homeland Security, House Cttee on Natural Resources; Gov. of Louisiana 2008–16; apptd Chair. Republican Govs Asscn 2012; unsuccessful cand. for Republican nomination for US Pres. 2016; mem. Bd of Dirs Our Lady of the Lake Hosp., Baton Rouge 2000–01, Educ. Comm. of States 2000–01, Nat. Conf. Cttee and Justice, Baton Rouge chapter 2000–01; mem. Salvation Army, Baton Rouge 1986–87, Better Business Bureau, Baton Rouge 1987–88, Teach for America, Baton Rouge chapter 1997–98; Republican; named to All-USA First Acad. Team, USA Today 1992, named Louisiana's Most Outstanding Young Man, Jr Chamber of Commerce 1995, Jefferson Award, Nat. Inst. of Public Service 1998, India Abroad Person of the Year 2005. *Publications:* Leadership and Crisis 2010; newspaper columns, law review articles and first authorships in several scientific and policy articles; several articles published in New Oxford Review. *Leisure interest:* tennis.

JINDAL, Naveen, BCom, MBA; Indian business executive and government official; *Chairman, Jindal Steel and Power Ltd;* b. 9 March 1970, Hissar, Haryana; s. of O.P. Jindal and Savitri Devi Jindal; m. Shalu Jindal; one s. one d.; ed Univ. of Delhi, Univ. of Texas, USA; Exec. Vice-Chair. and Man. Dir, Jindal Steel and Power Ltd, currently Chair.; mem. of Parl. 2004–14; Chair. Young Leaders Forum, Fed. of Indian Chamber of Commerce and Industry (FICCI), mem. FICCI Nat. Exec. Cttee; mem. Chhattisgarh State Council, Sports Cttee, Maharaja Agrasen Medical Educ. and Scientific Research Soc., Agroha Medical Coll., Sports Cttee and ITI, Tech. and Vocational Insts; Chancellor OP Jindal Global Univ., Haryana; Pres. Equestrian Asscn of Chhattisgarh; mem. Nat. Rifle Asscn, Parl. Forum on Youth; mem. Cttee on Home Affairs 2004, Consultative Cttee on Ministry of Defence; Student Leader of the Year Award, Univ. of Texas, USA. *Achievements include:* nat. champion and nat. record holder in skeet shooting, participated in South Asian Fed. Games (won silver medal), Pakistan 2004, Open Shooting Championship (gold medal), Singapore 2004, Nat. Shooting Championship (two silver medals), Indore 2004, Nat. Shooting Championship (silver medal), New Delhi 2006, V Sardar Sajjan Singh Sethi Memorial Master Shooting Competition (gold medal) 2007; Capt. Jindal Steel and Power Polo team, won Indian Open (polo) 2003, 2004. *Leisure interests:* polo, horse riding, shooting, reading, yoga. *Address:* Jindal Centre, 12 Bhikaiji Cama Place, New Delhi 110 066 (office); 171, South Avenue, New Delhi 110 011, India (home). *Telephone:* (11) 26188340 (office); (11) 23012253 (home). *Fax:* (11) 26161271 (office); (11) 23012213 (home). *E-mail:* naveen@naveenjindal.com (office); naveen.jindal@sansad.nic.in (office). *Website:* www.naveenjindal.com (office).

JING, Eric, BE, MBA; Chinese business executive; *CEO and Executive Chairman, Ant Financial Services Group;* b. Dec. 1972, Anhui Prov.; m. Janny Jing; ed Antai Coll. of Economics and Man., Shanghai Jiao Tong Univ., Shanghai, Carlson School of Man., Univ. of Minnesota, USA; worked at Guangzhou Peugeot Automobile, later at Havi Group; Chief Financial Officer Pepsi-Cola Guangzhou 2004–07; Senior Dir Finance, Ant Financial Services Group 2007–09, CEO 2016–, Exec. Chair. 2018–; Chief Financial Officer Alipay 2009–, COO 2014–15, Pres. 2015–16; Chair. Board of MYbank 2015–; currently Sr Consultant World Bank's Identification for Devt Development, Sr Consultant World Economic Forum; Dir Hundson Technologies; mem. Alibaba Group 2016–. *Address:* Ant Financial Services Group, Bldg B, Huanglong Times Plaza, 18 Wantang Road, Hangzhou 310000, The People's Republic of China (office). *Telephone:* (571) 26888888 (office). *Fax:* (571) 88157868 (office). *Website:* www.antfin.com (office).

JING, Tianliang; Chinese engineer and business executive; b. 1945; s. of Jing Shuping; ed Xi'an Mining Coll.; Technician, No.1 Mine, Mechanical and Electrical Section, No. 2 Mine, Enterprise Section and Dynamics Section, Wuda Mining Affairs Bureau 1963–79; Engineer, Comprehensive Mining Headquarters, Ministry of Coal Industry 1979–81, Production Dept 1981–83, Deputy Man. Office Service Co. 1984–88, Dir-Gen. 1996–98, Deputy Dir-Gen. Admin. Dept, Ministry of State Energies 1988–91, China Cen. Coal Distribution Co. 1991–93; Vice-Pres. and Gen.-Man. China Nat. Coal Import & Export Corpn Group 1993–96, apptd Pres. 1999; Dir-Gen. of Admin and Foreign Affairs of Nat. Coal Industry Bureau 1998–99; Chair. China Metallurgical Group Corpn 2010–13; External Dir Baosteel Group Corpn; joined CCP 1984, mem. 11th Nat. Cttee CPPCC.

LI, Jinzhang; Chinese diplomatist; b. Nov. 1954; m.; one d.; ed China Foreign Affairs Univ.; posted to Embassy in Havana 1976–80, Third Sec. and Deputy Head of Div., Dept of the Americas to Oceania, Ministry of Foreign Affairs (MFA) 1980–88, First Sec., Embassy in Managua, Nicaragua 1988–90, Counsellor, Embassy in Havana 1990–93, further educ. 1993–95, Deputy Dir-Gen. Dept of America, Latin America and the Caribbean 1995–98, Dir-Gen. Latin America Dept and the Caribbean 1998–2001, Amb. to Mexico 2001–03, Asst Minister of Foreign Affairs 2003–06, Deputy Minister of Foreign Affairs 2006–12, Amb. to Brazil 2012–18.

JIOYEVA, Alla Aleksandrovna; Georgian (Ossetian) politician; *Chairman, Iriston (Ossetia)—Freedom Square;* b. 23 Aug. 1949, Staliniri (now Tskhinvali), South Ossetian Autonomous Oblast, Georgian SSR, USSR; ed Secondary School No. 5, Tskhinvali, South Ossetian Pedagogical Inst. but later transferred to Odesa Univ., Ukrainian SSR; returned to Tskhinvali to work as Russian language and literature teacher in school No. 2, Dir –2002; became a supporter of Eduard Kokoyev (Kokoiti), presidential cand. 2001; Minister of Educ. 2002–08; supports re-unification of South and North Ossetia, involved in intergovernmental group for further integration of the two republics 2006; charged with several offences and placed under house arrest March 2008, detained until April 2010, found guilty by court of fraud and official misconduct but absolved of two other charges, received 24 months' probation and fined 120,000 rubles, appealed to Supreme Court; presidential cand. 2011; received most votes in second round of voting but election annulled by S Ossetian Supreme Court alleging electoral fraud and barred her from running in following one; declared herself Pres.-elect and formed a State Council to serve as the new govt; agreement reached to hold new election in March 2012 and to allow her to contest it Dec. 2011; withdrew from deal Jan. 2012, condemned planned runoff as "illegal"; office raided by police who tried to arrest her Feb. 2012, hospitalized unconscious a day before her inauguration as president, remained in hospital for 45 days and discharged under police guard March 2012; Deputy Prime Minister of 'Republic of South Ossetia' 2012–14; Founder and Chair. Iriston (Ossetia)—Freedom Square political party 2012–. *Address:* Iriston (Ossetia)—Freedom Square, 100001 Tskhinvali, South Ossetia, Georgia (office).

JIRICNA, Eva Magdalena, CBE, DipArch, RIBA; British architect; *Principal, Eva Jiricna Architects;* b. 3 March 1939, Zlin, Czechoslovakia; d. of Josef Jiricny and Eva Jiricna; ed Univ. of Prague, Prague Acad. of Fine Arts; worked with GLC's School Div. 1968; Louis de Soissons Partnership 1969–78, Project Architect; practice with David Hodges 1978; team leader at Richard Rogers Partnership 1982–84; f. own practice 1984, re-formed as Eva Jiricna Architects 1986–; External Examiner for RCA and Schools of Architecture at Leicester, Sheffield, Oxford, Bath, Humberside and Plymouth Univs and for RIBA; Pres. Architectural Asscn, London 2004–05; mem. RIBA Gold Medal Jury 2005–06, RIBA Regional Awards Jury (Chair.) 2005, Design Review panel CABE 2005–07; Adviser, Civic Trust Nat. Awards panel 2005–06; Trustee, London Open House; Hon. RDI (Royal Designers for Industry) 1991; Hon. Fellow, RCA 1990, RSA 1993, Royal Incorporation of Architects in Scotland 1996, RA 1997, AIA 2006; Hon. Prof. of Architecture and Design, Univ. of Applied Arts, Prague 2000; Hon. DTech (Southampton, Brno, Czech Repub.) 2000; Hon. DLitt (Sheffield) 2000; Design Prize, RA 1994. *Television includes:* Tales from Prague, BBC 2, Architecture of the Imagination: Staircases, BBC 2 1990, The Late Show: Czech Modernism 1994, Wideworld, Anglia TV 1997, The Dome: Trouble at the Big Top, BBC 2 1999. *Publications include:* Eva Jiricna: Design in Exile, The Joseph Shops: Eva Jiricna, Staircases, In/Ex Terior: The Works of Eva Jiricna 2005. *Address:* Eva Jiricna Architects, Third Floor, 38 Warren Street, London, W1T 6AE, England (office). *Telephone:* (20) 7554-2400 (office). *Fax:* (20) 7388-8022 (office). *E-mail:* mail@ejal.com (office). *Website:* www .ejal.com (office).

JISCHKE, Martin C., PhD; American engineer and academic administrator; b. 7 Aug. 1941, Chicago, Ill.; m. Patricia Fowler Jischke; one s. one d.; ed Illinois Tech. Inst., Massachusetts Inst. of Tech.; Asst to Transportation Sec. US Dept of Transportation, Washington, DC 1975–76; Dir and Prof., School of Aerospace, Mechanical and Nuclear Eng, Univ. of Okla 1977–81, Dean of Eng Coll. 1981–86, Acting Pres. 1985; Chancellor Mo.-Rolla Univ. 1986–91; Pres. Iowa State Univ. 1991–2000; Pres. Purdue Univ. 2000–07, now Pres. Emer.; Pres. Asscn of Big Twelve Univs 1994; mem. Bd of Dirs Bankers Trust 1995–, American Council on Educ. 1996–, Nat. Merit Scholarship Corpn 1997–; Founding Pres. Global Consortium of Higher Educ. and Research for Agric. 1999; Fellow, AAAS, AIAA; numerous awards including Centennial Medallion of American Soc. for Eng Educ., Ukraine Medal of Merit, Professional Achievement Award from Ill. Inst. of Tech., Justin Smith Morrill Award from US Dept of Agriculture 2004. *Publications include:* articles in specialist journals. *Leisure interests:* golf, reading, travel. *Address:* c/o School of Aeronautics & Astronautics, Purdue University, 701 West Stadium Avenue, West Lafayette, IN 47907-2045, USA (home). *E-mail:* mcjischke@purdue.edu (home). *Website:* www.engineering.purdue.edu/AAE (home).

JIZDAN, Alexandru; Moldovan police officer, government official and politician; *Minister of Internal Affairs;* b. 13 June 1975, Geamăna, Anenii Noi Dist, Moldovan SSR, USSR; m.; three c.; ed Stefan cel Mare Police Acad., Chişinău, Acad. of Public Admin, Faculty of Public Admin, Chişinău; Insp., Directorate for combating organized crime and corruption, PGI, Chişinău 1997–99, Sr Insp. 1999–2001, Chief Insp. 2001–02, Head April–Nov. 2002, Chief of Directorate Nov.–Dec. 2002; Chief of Service Directorate of Judicial Police, Ministry of Internal Affairs 2002–03, Head of Section 2003–05, Sr Insp. for Exceptional Cases Aug.–Dec. 2005, Head of Unit 2005–06; Deputy Chief, Directorate of Criminal Police Crime Dept 2006–07; Deputy Head, Dept of Operational Services, Ministry of Internal Affairs 2007–08, Head 2008–10; Chief of Gen. Directorate of Police Dept Intelligence Services 2010–14; Deputy Dir, Intelligence and Security 2015–16; Minister of Internal Affairs 2016–. *Address:* Ministry of Internal Affairs, 2012 Chişinău, bd. Ştefan cel Mare şi Sfânt 75, Moldova (office). *Telephone:* (22) 25-58-30 (office). *Fax:* (22) 25-52-36 (office). *E-mail:* secretariat@mai.gov.md (office); mai@mai.gov.md (office). *Website:* www.mai.gov.md (office).

JO, Dae-shik, BA, MA; South Korean diplomatist; b. 15 Jan. 1958; m. Eunyoung Park; two s.; ed Korea Univ., Seoul, Univ. of South Carolina, USA; joined Ministry of Foreign Affairs 1984, Second Sec., Embassy in Ottawa 1990–92, First Sec., Embassy in Sultanate of Oman 1992–97, First Sec., Embassy in Vienna and Perm. Mission to Int. Orgs in Vienna 1997–2001, seconded to Office of Planning for Light Water Reactor Project 2001–02, Dir, Cultural Affairs Div., Cultural Affairs Bureau, Ministry of Foreign Affairs and Trade 2002–03, Minister-Counsellor and Consul-Gen., Embassy in Singapore 2003–06, Minister-Counsellor and Consul-Gen., Embassy in Stockholm 2006–09, Dir-Gen. for Cultural Diplomacy and Public Diplomacy, Ministry of Foreign Affairs and Trade 2009–11, Amb. to Libya 2011–13, Deputy Minister for Planning and Co-ordination 2013–15, Amb. to Canada 2015–17.

JOANNOU, Dakis, BCE, MsCE, DArch; British business executive and art collector; *Chairman, J&P-Avax SA;* b. 30 Dec. 1939, Nicosia, Cyprus; s. of Stelios Joannou and Ellie Joannou; m. Lietta Joannou; two s. two d.; ed Cornell Univ., Columbia Univ., USA, Univ. of Rome, Italy; Chair. J&P-Avax SA, Chair. J&P Group of Cos, J&P (Overseas); Chair. Athenaeum InterContinental Hotel & Touristic Enterprises SA, Yes! Hotels & Restaurants; f. DESTE Foundation for Contemporary Art, Athens 1983, currently Pres.; mem. Int. Dir's Council Solomon R. F. Guggenheim Foundation, New York; mem. Tate Int. Council, Serpentine Council, London, UK; mem. Bd of Trustees, New Museum of Contemporary Art, New York, Cttee on Painting and Sculpture, Museum of Modern Art, New York. *Address:* 9 Fragoklissias Street, 151 25 Marousi (office); DESTE Foundation for Contemporary Art, Filellinon 11 and Em. Pappa Street, Nea Ionia, 142 34, Athens, Greece. *Telephone:* (210) 6185551 (office); (210) 2758490. *Fax:* (210) 6104375 (office); (210) 2754862. *E-mail:* dakis@deste.gr; mpapafloratou@jp-avax.gr (office). *Website:* www.deste.gr; www.jp-avax.gr.

JOAZILE, Jean Rodolphe; Haitian lawyer and politician; b. 15 Sept. 1962, Ferrier; ed Acad. Militaire d'Haiti; fmr officer, Forces Armées d' Haiti; Senator (Nord-Est) 2009–12, Pres. of Sénat May–Dec. 2011; Minister of Nat. Defence 2012–14.

JOBIM, Nelson Azevedo; Brazilian lawyer and politician; b. 12 April 1946, Santa Maria; ed Universidade Federal do Rio Grande do Sul; practised as lawyer 1969–94; Assoc. Prof. of Law, Universidade Federal de Santa Maria, Universidade de Brasília 1973–87; Pres. Santa Maria section, Bar Asscn 1977–78, Vice-Pres. Rio Grande Do Sul section 1984–86; mem. Partido do Movimento Democrático Brasileiro (PMDB), Leader PMDB in Nat. Ass. 1988; elected mem. of Parl. for Rio Grande do Sul 1987–91, re-elected 1991; Minister of Justice 1995–97, Minister of Defence 2007–11 (resgnd); served as judge and Pres. Supreme Fed. Court; mem. Bd of Advisors, Grupo Brasilinvest S.A. *Address:* Grupo Brasilinvest S.A, Centro Empresarial Mario Garnero Av. Brigadeiro Faria Lima, 1485, 19° Andar, Torre Norte - CEP, 01452-002 São Paulo (office). *Telephone:* (11) 3094-4000 (office). *E-mail:* contato@brasilinvest.com.br (office). *Website:* www.brasilinvest.com (office).

JOČIĆ, Dragan; Serbian lawyer and politician; b. 7 Sept. 1960, Belgrade; ed Faculty of Law, Univ. of Belgrade; est. pvt. law practice, Belgrade; Founding mem., Democratic Party of Serbia (DSS) 1992, mem. Exec. Bd 1992–2014, also Vice-Pres.; Deputy to Serbian Parl. 1992–97; mem. Belgrade City Council 2000–; Pres. Parl. Comm. for Defence and Security 2002; Minister of Internal Affairs 2004–08. *Address:* City of Belgrade Council, 59714 Belgrade, Thomas B. Quaw Square, 91 East Central, MT, Serbia (office). *Telephone:* (406) 3883760 (office). *Fax:* (406) 388-4996 (office). *E-mail:* belgrade@cityofbelgrade.net (office). *Website:* ci.belgrade.mt .us (office).

JODICE, Mimmo; Italian photographer and professor of fine arts; b. 29 March 1934, Naples; m. Angela Jodice; two s. one d.; Prof. Acad. of Fine Arts, Naples 1970–96; first photographic exhbn in Milan (with text of Cesare Zavattini) 1970; exhibited in many major museums including San Francisco Museum of Art, Philadelphia Museum of Art, Museo di Capodimonte, Cleveland Museum of Art, Castello di Rivoli, Turin 1970–; Prix Accad. dei Lincei for Photography 2004. *Publications include:* Chi è devoto. Feste popolari in Campania 1974, Mimmo Jodice 1983, La Città Invisibile 1990, Mediterranean 1995, Paris 1998, Eden 1998, Isolario Mediterraneo 2000, Anni Settanta 2000, Boston 2001, Mare 2003, Pompei 2010. *Leisure interest:* classical music. *Address:* Salita Casale 24, 80123 Naples, Italy (office); c/o Galerie Karsten Greve, 5, rue Debelleyme, 75003, France. *Telephone:* (081) 2466144; 1-42-77-19-37. *Fax:* (081) 2466144 (office); 1-42-77-05-58. *E-mail:* mimmo.jodice@inwind.it (office); info@mimmojodice.it. *Website:* www .mimmojodice.it.

JOEL, William (Billy) Martin; American singer, songwriter and musician (piano); b. 9 May 1949, Bronx, New York; s. of Howard Joel and Rosalind Nyman; m. 2nd Christie Brinkley 1985 (divorced 1994); one d.; m. 3rd Kate Lee 2004; m. 4th Alexis Roderick 2015, two d.; solo recording artist 1972–; first tour of USSR by American popular music artist 1987; numerous tours, live appearances worldwide; Dr hc (Fairfield Univ.) 1991, (Berklee Coll. of Music) 1993, (Manhattan School of Music) 2008, Hon. DHumLitt (Hofstra Univ.) 1997, Hon. DMus (Long Island Univ.) 2000, (Stony Brook Univ.) 2015, Hon. DFA (Syracuse University) 2006; Grammy Awards for Record of the Year (for Just the Way You Are) 1978, for Song of the Year (for Just the Way You Are) 1978, Grammy Legend Award 1991, inducted into Songwriters Hall of Fame 1992, ASCAP Founders' Award 1997, numerous American Music Awards, including American Music Award of Merit 1999, RIAA Diamond Award 1999, inducted into Rock and Roll Hall of Fame 1999, James Smithson Bicentennial Medal of Honor 2000, Johnny Mercer Award, Songwriters Hall of Fame 2001, Kennedy Center Honor 2013, Gershwin Prize for Popular Song, US Library of Congress 2014, ASCAP Centennial Award 2014. *Recordings include:* albums: Cold Spring Harbor 1971, Piano Man 1973, Streetlife Serenade 1974, Turnstiles 1976, The Stranger 1977, 52nd Street (Grammy Awards for Album of the Year, for Best Pop Vocal Performance) 1979, Glass Houses (Grammy Award for Best Pop Vocal Performance) 1980, Songs In The Attic 1981, The Nylon Curtain 1982, An Innocent Man 1983, Greatest Hits Volume I & II 1985, The Bridge 1986, Kohuept 1987, Storm Front 1989, River Of Dreams 1993, Greatest Hits Volume III 1997, 2000 Millennium Concert 2000, The Essential Billy Joel 2001, Fantasies and Delusions 2001, Movin Out 2002, My Lives 2005, 12 Gardens Live 2006, The Stranger 2008, The Hits 2010, She's Got A Way 2010, Piano Man 2011. *Publication:* Goodnight My Angel: A Lullabye (juvenile fiction) 2004. *Website:* www.billyjoel.com.

JOERRES, Jeffrey (Jeff) A., BS; American business executive; ed Marquette Univ.; fmr Man., IBM; Vice-Pres. of Sales and Marketing, ARI Network Services –1993; Vice-Pres. of Marketing, Manpower Inc. 1993, becoming Sr Vice-Pres. of European Operations, Global Account Man. and Devt, Pres. and CEO 1999–2014, apptd Chair. 2001, Exec. Chair. 2014–15 (retd); Dir, Fed. Reserve Bank of Chicago (fmr Chair.), Johnson Controls Inc., Artisan Partners Asset Man.; Co-Chair. NAACP Nat. Convention, Milwaukee 2005, B20 Task Force on Employment 2012, World Econ. Forum on Latin America 2012, Future Workforce Cttee of Greater Milwaukee Cttee; Trustee, Cttee for Econ. Devt (CED).

JÕERÜÜT, Jaak; Estonian politician and diplomatist; b. 9 Dec. 1947, Tallinn; m.; ed Faculty of Econs, Tallinn Technical Inst.; Ed. Eesti Raamat publishing house 1976–77; Sec. and Deputy Chair. Estonian Writers' Union 1977–89; Deputy Minister, Ministry of Culture 1989–90; mem. Parl. 1990–92, Chair. Standing Cttee on Research, Educ. and Culture; Amb. to Finland 1993–97, Dir-Gen. Protocol Dept, Ministry of Foreign Affairs 1997–98, Amb. to Italy 1998–2002, to Malta 1999–2002, to Cyprus 1999–2004, Inspector-Gen., Ministry of Foreign Affairs 2002–04, Special Adviser to the Govt 2002–03, Amb. and Perm. Rep. to UN, New York July–Nov. 2004; Minister of Defence 2004–05; Amb. to Latvia 2006–10, to Sweden 2011–14; mem. Estonian Writers' Union, Estonian PEN.

JOFFE, Josef, PhD; German journalist, editor and international relations scholar; *Publisher-Editor, Die Zeit;* b. 15 March 1944, Łódź, Poland; m. Dr Christine Joffe; two d.; ed Swarthmore Coll., Johns Hopkins Univ., Harvard Univ., USA; Foreign and Editorial Page Dir Suddeutsche Zeitung 1985–2000; Publr-Ed. Die Zeit newspaper 2000–; Professorial Lecturer, Johns Hopkins Univ. 1982–84; Adjunct Prof. of Political Science, Stanford Univ. 2004–, Fellow, Inst. for Int. Studies, Stanford 2004, Sr Fellow 2007–; Visiting Fellow, Hoover Inst.; Visiting Prof. of Govt, Harvard Univ. 1999–2000, Assoc., Olin Inst. for Strategic Studies; Visiting Lecturer, Princeton Univ., Dartmouth Univ. 2002; Founding Bd mem. The National Interest 1995–2005, The American Interest 2005–; mem. Editorial Bd International Security, Prospect; Bd mem. American Acad., Berlin, Aspen Inst., Berlin, Leo Baeck Inst., New York, Ben Gurion Univ., Israel, Internationale Politik, Berlin; Order of Merit 1998; hon. degree (Swarthmore Coll.) 2002, (Lewis and Clark Coll.) 2005; Theodor-Wolff-Prize in Journalism (Germany), Ludwig Börne Prize in Essays/Literature (Germany), Scopus Award 2009. *Publications include:* The Limited Partnership: Europe, the United States and the Burdens of Alliance 1987, The Future of International Politics: The Great Powers 1998, Überpower: The Imperial Temptation of America 2006, The Myth of America's Decline 2013, At the Cassandra Crossing: The False Prophecies of American Decline 2013; numerous articles in scholarly journals and chapters in books. *Address:* Die Zeit, Speersort 1, 20095 Hamburg, Germany (office). *Telephone:* (40) 328-00 (office). *Fax:* (40) 3280-596 (office). *E-mail:* dagmar.gentsch@zeit.de (office). *Website:* www.zeit.de (office).

JOFFE, Roland I.V.; British film director; b. 17 Nov. 1945, London; m. Jane Lapotaire (divorced); one s.; ed Carmel Coll., Berks. and Univ. of Manchester; Prix Italia 1978, Prix de la Presse, Prague 1978, Premio San Fidele 1985. *Films include:* The Killing Fields 1984, The Mission (Golden Palm and Technical Grand Prize, Cannes Film Festival 1986) 1986, Fat Man and Little Boy 1989, City of Joy 1991, Super Mario Bros (producer only), The Scarlet Letter 1995, Goodbye Lover 1999, Vatel 2000, Captivity 2007, You and I 2010, There Be Dragons 2010, Singularity 2011, The Lovers 2013, Texas Rising 2015. *Television includes:* Spongers 1978, No Mama No 1980, United Kingdom 1981, 'Tis Pity She's a Whore 1982, Shadow Makers 1990, The Stars Look Down (series). *Address:* c/o Nick Cave, William Morris Agency, 100 New Oxford Street, London, WC1A1HB, England (office). *Telephone:* (20) 8929-8400 (office). *Fax:* (20) 8929-8500 (office). *E-mail:* nyc@ wmeentertainment.com (office). *Website:* www.wmeentertainment.com (office); www.rolandjoffe.com.

JOFFE, Rowan, BA; British film director and screenwriter; b. 1973; s. of Roland Joffe and Jane Lapotaire; ed Westminster School, Oxford Univ. *Theatre includes:* as writer: Accidental Colour 1998, Emporium 1998, Out of the Mouths 1998, The History of Misfortune 2000, Faithful Dealing 2001. *Television includes:* as writer: Last Resort (Best New British Feature Award, Edinburgh Int. Film Festival) 2000, Gas Attack (Best New British Feature Award, Edinburgh Int. Film Festival) 2001, Turkish Delight 2003, Broadwater Farm 2006, Secret Life 2007; as dir: The Shooting of Thomas Hurndall (BAFTA Award for Best Fiction Dir 2009, Golden Nymph Award, Monte Carlo TV Festival 2009) 2008, Tin Star (also writer) 2017. *Films include:* as writer: 28 Weeks Later 2007, Secret Life (also dir) 2007, The American 2010; as writer and dir: Brighton Rock 2011, Before I Go To Sleep 2014. *Address:* c/o Nick Marston, Curtis Brown Group Ltd, 5th Floor, Haymarket House, 28–29 Haymarket, London, SW1Y 4SP, England (office). *Telephone:* (20) 7393-4450 (office). *Fax:* (20) 7393-4401 (office). *E-mail:* nick@curtisbrown.co.uk (office). *Website:* www.curtisbrown.co.uk/rowan-joffe (office).

JOHANNESEN, Aksel Vilhelmsson; Faroese lawyer and politician; *Prime Minister;* b. 8 Nov. 1972, Klaksvík; s. of Vilhelm Johannesen; m. Katrin D. Apol; three c.; ed Univ. of Copenhagen; worked as a lawyer, Tórshavn 2007–; Minister of Health Affairs 2009–11, Minister of Finance Feb.–Nov. 2011; mem. Løgting (parl.) 2011–; Prime Minister 2015–; mem. Social Democratic Party (Javnaðarflokkur), Chair. 2011–; fmr Pres. Klaksvíkar Ítróttarfelag (football club). *Leisure interest:* football. *Address:* Løgmansskrivstovan (Prime Minister's Office), Tinganes, POB 64, 110 Tórshavn, Faroe Islands (office). *Telephone:* 306000 (office). *Fax:* 351015 (office). *E-mail:* info@tinganes.fo (office). *Website:* www.tinganes.fo (office).

JOHANNESEN, Kaj Leo Holm; Faroese politician; b. 28 Aug. 1964, Tórshavn; s. of Leo Hans Johannesen and Karin Holm Johannesen; m. Jórun Bærentsen; three s.; ed Føroya Sjómansskúli (Centre of Maritime Studies); began career in fishing industry, later captaining fishing vessels and freighters; has also worked as car salesman; joined Faroe Seafood 1989, Sales Man., Kósin (fish processing factory) 1995–97; mem. Faroese Unionist Party 1988–, Leader 2004–; mem. Tórshavn City Council 1996–2000; mem. Løgting (Parl.) 2002–, Deputy Chair. Govt Cttee 2003–04, mem. Trade and Industry Cttee 2003–04, Finance Cttee 2004–08, Chair. Foreign Affairs Cttee 2004–08; Prime Minister 2008–15. *Achievements include:* fmr goalkeeper for Faroese int. football team, receiving seven caps 1988–94. *Address:* c/o Løgmansskrivstovan (Prime Minister's Office), Tinganes, PO Box 64, 110 Tórshavn, Faroe Islands (office).

JÓHANNESSON, Benedikt, BSc, MS, PhD; Icelandic publisher, business executive, management consultant and politician; b. 4 May 1955; s. of Jóhannes Zoëga and Guðrún Benediktsdóttir; m. Vigdís Jónsdóttir; three c.; ed Univ. of Wisconsin and Florida State Univ., USA; Owner, Talnakönnun (Data Analysis) (consulting co.) 1983–; Chair. Nyherji Industries Information Technology and Services 1996–; CEO Heimur hf (publishing co.) 2000–; Publr Iceland Review (weekly newsletter on Icelandic business and econs); Ed. journals Ský 2005–16, Vísbending 2006–16; Chair. AppliCon holding 2006–13; mem. Althingi (Parl.) 2016–17; Minister of Finance and Econ. Affairs Jan.–Nov. 2017; mem. Sjálfstæðisflokkurinn (Independence Party) –2014; Founder Viðreisn (Reform Party), Chair. 2016–17 (resgnd).

JÓHANNESSON, Guðni Thorlacius, BA, MA, PhD; Icelandic historian, academic, author and head of state; *President;* b. 26 June 1968; s. of Jóhannes Sæmundsson and Margrét Thorlacius; m. Eliza Reid; four c.; one d. from previous m.; ed Univ. of Warwick, UK, Univ. of Iceland, St Antony's Coll., Oxford and Univ. of London, UK; Part-time Lecturer in Contemporary History, Univ. of Iceland 1996–98, Research Fellow, Centre for Research in the Humanities 2003–07, Assoc. Lecturer, Dept of History 2004–07, Asst Prof. 2013–; corresp. for Icelandic State Radio, UK 2000–01; Asst Prof., Dept of Law and Dept of Business, Reykjavík Univ. 2007–10; Researcher, Reykjavík Acad. 2010–12; Pres. of Iceland 2016–; Pres. Historical Soc. of Iceland 2011–; Julian Corbett Prize in Modern Naval History, London Inst. of Historical Research 2002. *Publications include:* Kári í jötunmóð.

Saga Kára Stefánssonar og Íslenskrar erfðagreiningar 1999, Völundarhús valdsins. Stjórnarmyndanir, stjórnarslit og staða forseta Íslands í embættistíð Kristjáns Eldjárns 1968–1980 2005, Óvinir ríkisins. Ógnir og innra öryggi í kalda stríðinu á Íslandi 2006, Hrunið. Ísland á barmi gjaldþrots og upplausnar 2009, Gunnar Thoroddsen. Ævisaga 2010, The history of Iceland 2013; translations (original novels all by Stephen King): The Langoliers 1992, The Library Policeman 1994, Dolores Claiborne 1995, Rita Hayworth and Shawshank Redemption 1997. *Address:* Office of the President, Stadastaður, Sóleyjargötu 1, 101 Reykjavík, Iceland (office). *Telephone:* 5404400 (office). *Fax:* 5624802 (office). *E-mail:* forseti@forseti.is (office). *Website:* www.forseti.is (office).

JOHANNS, Michael (Mike) Owen, BA, JD; American lawyer and politician; b. 18 June 1950, Osage, Ia; s. of John Robert Johanns and Adeline Lucy Johanns (née Royek); m. 1st Constance J. Weiss 1972 (divorced 1985); one s. one d.; m. 2nd Stephanie Suther 1986; ed St Mary's Coll., Creighton Univ.; law clerk, Neb. State Supreme Court 1974–75; Assoc., Cronin and Hannon (law firm) 1975–76; Pnr, Nelson, Johanns, Morris, Holdeman and Titus, Lincoln, Neb. 1976–91; Commr Lancaster Co., Neb. 1982–86; mem. Lincoln City Council 1989–91, Mayor of Lincoln 1991–98; Gov. of Neb. 1999–2005; Sec., US Dept of Agric., Washington, DC 2005–09; Senator from Neb. 2009–Jan. 2015 (retd); fmr Chair. Gov.'s Ethanol Coalition; fmr Co-Chair. Govs' Biotechnology Partnership, Gov.s' Public Power Alliance; fmr Vice-Chair. Midwest Govs Asscn; mem. Bd of Dirs Deere & Co. 2015–; Republican.

JÓHANNSSON, Kjartan, CE, PhD; Icelandic politician and diplomatist (retd); b. 19 Dec. 1939, Reykjavik; s. of Jóhann Thorsteinsson and Astrid Dahl Thorsteinsson; m. Irma Karlsdóttir 1964; one d.; ed Reykjavik Coll., Tech. Univ. of Stockholm, Sweden, Univ. of Stockholm, Illinois Inst. of Tech., USA; Consulting Eng in Reykjavik 1966–78; Teacher in Faculty of Eng and Science, later Prof. in Faculty for Econs and Business Admin, Univ. of Iceland 1966–78, 1980–89; Chair. Org. for Support of the Elderly, Hafnarfjördür; mem. Bd of Dirs Icelandic Aluminium Co. Ltd 1970–75; Chair. Fisheries Bd of Municipal Trawler Co., Hafnarfjördür 1970–74; mem. Municipal Council, Hafnarfjördür 1974–78; mem. Party Council and Exec. Council, Social Democratic Party 1972–89, Vice-Chair. of Social Democratic Party 1974–80, Chair. 1980–84; mem. Althing (Parl.) 1978–89, Speaker of Lower House 1988–89; Minister of Fisheries 1978–80, also Minister of Commerce 1979–80; Amb. and Perm. Rep. to UN and other int. orgs Geneva 1989–94; Sec.-Gen. EFTA 1994–2001; mem. staff, External Trade Dept, Ministry of Foreign Affairs 2002; Amb. to Belgium, Liechtenstein, Luxembourg and Chief of Mission to the EU 2002–05. *Address:* Vatnsstig 21, 101 Reykjavík, Iceland (home). *Telephone:* 5342597 (home). *E-mail:* kjartan.johannsson@gmail.com (home).

JÓHANNSSON, Sigurður Ingi; Icelandic politician and fmr veterinarian; b. 20 April 1962, Selfoss; s. of Jóhann H. Pálsson and Hróðný Sigurðardóttir; m. 1st Anna Ásmundsdóttir; three c.; m. 2nd Ingibjörg Elsa Ingjaldsdóttir; two c.; ed Laugarvatn Junior Coll., Royal Veterinary and Agricultural Coll., Copenhagen; farmer, Dalbær, Hrunamannahreppur Dist 1987–94, also worked concurrently as veterinarian 1990–95, Acting Dist Veterinarian in S Iceland and West Fjords 1992–94, Veterinarian, S Iceland Veterinary Services 1996–2009; Head of local govt, Hrunamannahreppur 2002–09; mem. Althingi (Parl.) (Progressive Party) for S Iceland 2009–, mem. Fisheries and Agriculture Cttee 2009–11, Industrial Affairs Cttee 2011–13, Deputy Speaker 2011–13; Minister of Fisheries and Agric. 2013–16, also Minister of the Environment and Resources 2013–14, Prime Minister 2016–17; mem. Icelandic Del. to West Nordic Council 2009–13; mem. Progressive Party, currently Vice-Chair. *Address:* Althingi (Alþingi), v/Austurvöll, 150 Reykjavík, Iceland (office). *Telephone:* 5630500 (office). *Fax:* 5630550 (office). *E-mail:* editor@althingi.is (office). *Website:* www.althingi.is (office).

JOHANSEN, Hans Christian, DrOec; Danish professor of economic history; b. 27 June 1935, Århus; s. of Vilhelm Johansen and Clara Andersen; m. Kirstine Madsen 1967; one s. one d.; ed Univ. of Århus; Danish Foreign Service 1963–64; Sr Lecturer, Univ. of Århus 1964–70; Prof. of Econ. History, Univ. of Odense 1970–2003; Dir Danish Centre for Demographic Research 1998–2002. *Publications include:* books and articles on Danish and int. econ. and social history in the 18th, 19th and 20th centuries. *Address:* Anne Maries Alle 4A, 5250 Odense SV, Denmark (home). *Telephone:* 66-17-21-05 (home). *E-mail:* hcj@hist.sdu.dk (office).

JOHANSEN, Peter, DrPhil; Danish computer scientist and academic; *Professor Emeritus, University of Copenhagen;* b. 29 Jan. 1938, Copenhagen; s. of Paul Johansen and Grethe Johansen (née Smith); m. Jytte Jepsen 1963; one s. two d.; ed Univ. of Copenhagen; Asst Prof., Tech. Univ. 1964–67; mem. Research Staff, MIT 1967–69; Asst Prof. of Computer Science, Univ. of Copenhagen 1969–74, Prof. 1974–2008, Prof. Emer. 2008–, Dean of Faculty 1988–90; Visiting Prof., Univ. of Manoa, Hawaii 1977–78; mem. Danish Natural Science Research Council 1981–84, Royal Danish Acad. of Sciences 1984–; Kt (First Class), Order of the Dannebrog. *Publications:* An Algebraic Normal Form for Regular Events 1972, The Generating Function of the Number of Subpatterns 1979, Representing Signals by their Toppoints in Scale Space 1986, Inductive Inference of Ultimately Periodic Sequences 1988, On the Classification of Toppoints in Scale Space 1994, On-line string matching with feedback 1995, Adaptive Pattern Recognition 1997, Branch Points in One-dimensional Gaussian Scale Space 2000, Products of Random Matrices 2002. *Address:* Ørnebakken 72, 2840 Holte, Denmark (home). *E-mail:* peterjo@di.ku.dk (home).

JOHANSON, Donald Carl, PhD; American vertebrate palaeontologist and academic; *Founding Director, Institute of Human Origins, Arizona State University;* b. 28 June 1943, Chicago, Ill.; s. of Carl Torsten and Sally Eugenia Johanson (née Johnson); m. 1st Chris Boner 1967 (divorced); m. 2nd Susan Whelan 1981 (divorced); one step-s. one step-d.; m. 3rd Lenora Carey 1988 (divorced); one s.; ed Univ. of Illinois, Univ. of Chicago; Assoc. Curator of Physical Anthropology, Cleveland Museum of Natural History 1972–81, Curator 1974–81, Dir of Scientific Research and Lab. of Physical Anthropology 1976–81; Adjunct Prof. of Anthropology, Case Western Reserve Univ. 1978–81, Kent State Univ. 1978–81; Visiting Prof. of Anthropology, Sweet Briar Coll., Virginia 1978; Prof. of Anthropology (teaching), Stanford Univ. 1983–89; Prof. of Anthropology and Dir Inst. of Human Origins, Ariz. State Univ. 1997–2008, Founding Dir Inst. of Human Origins 2008–; host, Nature (series), Public Broadcasting Service TV 1982, host-narrator three-part Nova series In Search of Human Origins 1994; Pres. Inst. of Human Origins, Berkeley 1981–97; Fellow, AAAS, Royal Geographical Soc., California Acad. of Sciences; Hon. mem. Siena Acad. of Sciences 2006; Hon. DSc (John Carroll) 1979, (The Coll. of Wooster) 1985, (Westfield State Univ.) 2008, (Case Western Reserve) 2009; Fregene Prize 1987, American Book Award 1982, Distinguished Service Award, American Humanist Asscn 1983, Golden Plate, American Acad. of Achievement 1976, Professional Achievement Award 1980, Outstanding Achievement Award 1979, Golden Mercury Int. Award 1982, Alumni Achievement Award, Univ. of Illinois 1995, Anthropology in Media Award, American Asscn of Anthropologists 1999, Explorers' Club Medal 2010, Emperor Has No Clothes Award, Freedom from Religion Foundation 2014. *Television:* The First Family 1981, Lucy in Disguise 1982, In Search of Human Origins 1994. *Publications:* The Beginnings of Humankind (with M. A. Edey) (American Book Award) 1981, Blueprints: Solving the Mystery of Evolution (with M. A. Edey) 1989, Lucy's Child: The Discovery of a Human Ancestor (with James Shreeve) 1989, Journey from the Dawn (with Kevin O'Farrell) 1990, Ancestors: In Search of Human Origins (with L. E. Johanson and Blake Edgar) 1994, From Lucy to Language (with Blake Edgar) 1997, Ecce Homo (co-ed. with G. Ligabue) 1999, The Skull of Australopithecus afarensis (with W. H. Kimbel and Y. Rak) 2004, Lucy's Legacy: The Quest for Human Origins (with Kate Wong) 2009; many scientific articles, papers and reviews. *Leisure interests:* photography, tennis, fly-fishing, classical music (including opera), golf, cycling. *Address:* Institute of Human Origins, Arizona State University, PO Box 874101, Tempe, AZ 85287-4101, USA (office). *Telephone:* (480) 727-6580 (office). *E-mail:* johanson.iho@asu.edu (office). *Website:* www.becominghuman.org (office); iho.asu.edu (office).

JOHANSSON, Leif, MSc (Eng); Swedish business executive; *Chairman, Telefonaktiebolaget L.M. Ericsson;* b. 30 Aug. 1951, Gothenburg; s. of Lennart Johansson and Inger Johansson; m. Eva Birgitta Fjellman; two s. three d.; ed Chalmers Univ. of Tech.; project consultant, Indevo 1974–76; product developer and Asst to the Pres., Centro-Maskin 1977; Pres. Husqvarna Motorcycles 1979–81; Div. Man., Office Machines, Facit Sweden 1981–82, Pres. Facit 1982–84; Div. Man., AB Electrolux, White Goods 1984–87, Pres. 1987–88, Exec. Vice-Pres. AB Electrolux 1988–91, Pres. 1991–94, Pres. and CEO 1994–97; mem. Bd of Dirs and Pres. AB Volvo and CEO Volvo Group, Gothenburg 1997–2011; Chair. Telefonaktiebolaget L.M. Ericsson 2011–; Chair. AstraZeneca PLC 2012–; mem. Bd of Dirs Bristol-Myers Squibb Co., Svenska Cellulosa AB SCA, Confed. of Swedish Enterprise, Asscn of Swedish Eng Industries; Chair. European Round Table of Industrialists –2014; Dir Confed. of Swedish Enterprise; mem. Royal Swedish Acad. of Eng Sciences; Order of the Seraphim 2001, Chevalier, Légion d'honneur 2005; Dr hc (Blekinge Inst. of Tech.) 2006, Hon. MD (Univ. of Gothenburg) 2007; Marcus Wallenberg ASEA Award 1977, Gold Memorial Medal Kungliga Automobilklubben, Royal Swedish Automobile Club 2005, Mekanprisma Award 2009, Large Gold Medal, Royal Swedish Acad. of Eng Sciences 2011. *Address:* Telefonaktiebolaget L.M. Ericsson, Torshamnsgatan 23, Kista, 164 83 Stockholm, Sweden (office); AstraZeneca PLC, 2 Kingdom Street, London, W2 6BD, England (office). *Telephone:* (10) 719-00-00 (Stockholm) (office); (20) 7604-8000 (London) (office). *E-mail:* info@ericsson.com (office); info@astrazeneca.com (office). *Website:* www.ericsson.com (office); www.astrazeneca.com (office).

JOHANSSON, Scarlett; American actress, model and singer; b. 22 Nov. 1984, New York; d. of Karsten Johansson and Melanie Sloan; m. Ryan Reynolds 2008 (divorced 2011); ed Professional Children's School, Manhattan. *Plays:* A View from the Bridge, New York 2010 (Tony Award for Best Performance by a Featured Actress 2010). *Films include:* North 1994, Just Cause 1995, If Lucy Fell 1996, Manny & Lo 1996, Home Alone III 1997, The Horse Whisperer (Hollywood Reporter Young Star Award) 1998, My Brother the Pig 1999, Ghost World (Best Supporting Actress, Toronto Film Critics Asscn) 2000, The Man Who Wasn't There 2001, An American Rhapsody 2001, Eight Legged Freaks 2002, Lost in Translation (Countercurrent Prize for Best Actress, Venice Film Festival, Best Actress, BAFTA Awards, Best Actress, Boston Soc. of Film Critics) 2003, Girl with a Pearl Earring 2003, The Perfect Score 2004, A Love Song for Bobby Long 2004, The SpongeBob SquarePants Movie (voice) 2004, In Good Company 2004, Match Point 2005, A Good Woman 2005, The Island 2005, Scoop 2006, The Black Dahlia 2006, The Prestige 2006, The Nanny Diaries 2007, The Other Boleyn Girl 2008, Vicky Cristina Barcelona 2008, The Spirit 2008, He's Just Not That Into You 2009, Iron Man 2 2010, We Bought a Zoo 2011, Avengers Assemble 2012, Hitchcock 2012, Under the Skin 2013, Don Jon 2013, Her 2013, Chef 2014, Lucy 2014, Captain America: The Winter Soldier 2014, Avengers: Age of Ultron 2015. *Television includes:* The Client (series) 1995, Robot Chicken (series) 2005–08. *Recordings:* albums: Anywhere I Lay My Head 2008, Break Up (with Pete Yorn) 2009. *Address:* c/o Marcel Pariseau, True Public Relations, 6725 West Sunset Boulevard, Suite 570, Los Angeles, CA 90028, USA.

JOHN, Sir David Glyndwr, Kt, KCMG, MA, MBA; British business executive; b. 20 July 1938, Pontypridd; s. of William G. John and Marjorie John; m. Gillian Edwards 1964; one s. one d.; ed Christ's Coll., Cambridge, Columbia Univ., New York and Harvard Univ., USA; trainee man., British Steel; later worked for RTZ and Redland; joined Gray Mackenzie (Inchcape Group) 1981, Chief Exec. 1986, Chief Exec. Inchcape Berhad 1987, Chair. 1990; mem. Bd Inchcape PLC 1988–95, Exec. Chair. Inchcape Toyota Motors 1995; Chair. (non-exec.) Premier Oil PLC 1998–2005, BSI Group 2002–12; mem. Bd of Dirs (non-exec.) BOC Group PLC 1993–2002 (Chair. 1996–2002), The St Paul Cos Inc. 1996–2003, Balfour Beatty PLC 2000–08 (Chair. 2003–08), Welsh Devt Agency 2001–02; Dr hc (Univ. of Glamorgan). *Leisure interests:* sailing, skiing, reading, gardening. *Address:* 12 Grosvenor Crescent Mews, London, SW1X 7EU, England.

JOHN, Sir Elton Hercules, Kt, CBE; British musician (piano), singer and songwriter; b. (Reginald Kenneth Dwight), 25 March 1947, Pinner, Middx; s. of Stanley Dwight and Sheila Eileen Dwight (née Harris); m. 1st Renata Blauel 1984 (divorced 1988); m. 2nd David Furnish 2014; two s.; ed Pinner County Grammar School, Royal Acad. of Music, London; began piano lessons 1951; played piano in Northwood Hills Hotel bar 1964; mem. local group Bluesology 1961–67; worked for Mills Music Publrs; began writing songs with Bernie Taupin 1967; solo recording contract with DJM Records 1967; concerts in Los Angeles, USA 1970; formed Rocket Record Co. with Bernie Taupin 1973, first album released 1976; co-f. Rocket Music Entertainment Co.; f. publishing co. Big Pig Music 1974; frequent tours in UK, USA, Japan, Australia 1971–76; Vice-Pres. Nat. Youth Theatre of GB 1975–;

first int. star to perform concerts in USSR 1979; produced records with Clive Franks for Kiki Dee, Blue, Davey Johnstone's China 1976–77; Chair. Watford Football Club 1976–90, 1997–2002, Life Pres. 1990–; fmr part-owner Los Angeles Aztecs of the North American Soccer League; occasional columnist, The Guardian; f. Elton John AIDS Foundation 1993, Rocket Pictures; Fellow, British Acad. of Composers and Songwriters 2004–; Trustee, Wallace Collection 1999–; Chair. The Old Vic Theatre Trust 2002–07; Officier, Ordre des Arts et des Lettres 1993; Hon. mem. RAM 1997; Dr hc (RAM) 2002; Ivor Novello Awards (for Daniel) 1974, (for Don't Go Breaking My Heart, with Kiki Dee) 1977, (for Song for Guy) 1979, (for Nikita) 1986, (for Sacrifice) 1991, American Music Awards for Favorite Male Artist, Favorite Single 1977, Silver Clef Award 1979, BRIT Awards for Outstanding Contribution to British Music 1986, Best British Male Artist 1991, MTV Special Recognition Trophy 1987, Grammy Awards 1987, 1991, 1998, 2000, Grammy Lifetime Achievement Award 2000, Nat. Acad. of Popular Music Hitmaker Award 1989, Q Magazine Merit Award 1993, Acad. Award for Best Original Song (for Can You Feel the Love Tonight?) 1995, recipient of Kennedy Center Honors 2004, ranked by Billboard magazine as the most successful male solo artist on The Billboard Hot 100 Top All-Time Artists 2008, Brits Icon Award 2013. *Stage productions:* The Lion King (musical) 2001, Billy Elliot (musical) 2004, Lestat (musical, with Bernie Taupin) 2006. *Soundtracks, scores and theatre albums:* Friends 1971, The Lion King 1994, Aida 1998, The Muse 1999, The Road to El Dorado 2000, Billy Elliot 2005, Lestat 2005, Gnomeo & Juliet (exec. producer) 2011. *Films include:* Born to Boogie 1972, Goodbye to Norma Jean 1973, Tommy 1975, To Russia with Elton 1980, The Rainbow 1989, The Lion King (music) 1994, Spice World (as himself) 1997, Desert Flower (producer) 1999, Women Talking Dirty (exec. producer) 1999, The Road to El Dorado (voice) 2000, Bob the Builder: A Christmas to Remember (video) (voice) 2001, The Country Bears (as himself) 2002, Tommy and Quadrophenia Live: The Who (video) 2005, It's a Boy Girl Thing (exec. producer) 2006, Elton John: Me, Myself & I (autobiog. as himself) 2007. *Television includes:* Zomercarroussel (mini-series) 1970, It's Cliff Richard (series) 1970, Russell Harty Plus (TV series) 1974, Great Performances (series) (exec. producer) – Elton John at the Royal Opera House 2003, Him and Us (film) (exec. producer) 2006, Spectacle: Elvis Costello with… (series) (exec. producer) 2008–10, David Bowie: The Story of Ziggy Stardust (film) 2012. *Recordings include:* albums: Empty Sky 1969, Elton John 1970, Tumbleweed Connection 1971, Friends (film soundtrack) 1971, 17-11-70 1971, Madman Across the Water 1972, Honky Chateau 1972, Don't Shoot Me, I'm Only the Piano Player 1973, Goodbye Yellow Brick Road 1973, Caribou 1974, Captain Fantastic and the Brown Dirt Cowboy 1975, Rock of the Westies 1975, Here and There 1976, Blue Moves 1976, A Single Man 1978, Victim of Love 1979, Lady Samantha 1980, 21 at 33 1980, The Fox 1981, Jump Up 1982, Too Low for Zero 1983, Breaking Hearts 1984, Ice on Fire 1985, Leather Jackets 1986, Reg Strikes Back 1988, Sleeping with the Past 1989, The One 1992, Made in England 1995, Love Songs 1995, The Big Picture 1997, Aida 1999, El Dorado 2000, Songs from the West Coast 2001, Peachtree Road 2004, The Captain and the Kid 2006, Rocket Man 2007, The Union (with Leon Russell) 2010, Good Morning To The Night (with Pnau) 2012, The Diving Board 2013, Wonderful Crazy Night 2016. *Leisure interests:* football, collecting records, tennis, all sports. *Address:* c/o Rocket Music Management, 1 Blythe Road, London, W14 0HG, England (office). *Telephone:* (20) 7348-4800 (office). *E-mail:* contact@rocketmusic.com (office). *Website:* www.rocketmusic.com (office); www.eltonjohn.com.

JOHN, Patrick; Dominican politician and sports administrator; b. 7 Jan. 1937; Leader, Dominica Labour Party 1974–83, Deputy Leader 1983–84; Minister of Communications and Works 1970–73, Deputy Premier and Minister of Finance 1974, Premier of Dominica 1974–78, Prime Minister 1978–79, Minister for Housing, Security and Devt 1978–79; Gen. Sec. Labour Party of Dominica 1985; mem. Parl. July–Nov. 1985; arrested 1981, tried and acquitted May 1982, re-tried Oct. 1985; sentenced to 12 years' imprisonment, served five years for conspiracy to overthrow govt; Pres. Dominica Football Asscn 1992–2006.

JOHN, Radek; Czech journalist, writer, screenwriter and politician; *Chairman, Public Affairs (Věci veřejné) party;* b. 6 Dec. 1954, Prague; s. of Ctirad John (Prof.) and Bozena Johnová; m. Zlata Adamovská (divorced 2010); one s. one d. (one d. from another relationship); Ed. Mladý svět (Young World) magazine 1980–93; worked in Filmovém studiu Barrandov as a scriptwriter and for TV 1980s; reporter and then Ed.-in-Chief Na vlastní oči (Own Eyes) public affairs programme, TV Nova 1997–2007, responsible for current affairs programme Snídaně s Novou (Breakfast with Nova), talk show Občanské judo (Civil Judo) and Tabu (Taboo) show; Chair. S & J–Medea Kultur a.s. (later Ora Print) 2002–09; Chair. Public Affairs (Věci veřejné) party 2009–; Deputy Prime Minister and Minister of the Interior 2010–11; Chief Ed. Security Magazine 2014; Second Prize in category Moderator of Current Affairs Programmes, TýTý poll 1994, First Prize 1995, 1996–2002, 2005, 2006. *Screenplays include:* Jen si tak trochu písknout (Just a Little Whistle), Jako zajíci (Like Rabbits), Sněženky a machři, Bony a klid (Thawing, Bony and Peace), Proč? (Why?), Tankový prapor (Tank Battalion), Ta naše písnička česká II (Our Czech Song II), Prachy dělaj člověka (Money Makin' Man), Sneženky a machri po petadvaceti letech (Thawing After Twenty Years). *Publications:* Džínový svet (novel) 1980, Zacátek letopoctu (with Ivan Pelant) 1984, Memento (novel, translated into ten languages) 1986, Bony a klid 1987, Jak jsem videl Ameriku 1990, Drogy! (with Dr Jiří Presl) 1995. *Address:* Public Affairs (Věci Veřejné), Štefánikova 23/203, 150 00 Prague 5, Czech Republic (office). *Telephone:* 800879709. *E-mail:* info@veciverejne.cz (office). *Website:* www.veciverejne.cz (office).

JOHN, Sajeev O., BSc, PhD, FRSC; Canadian physicist and academic; *University Professor of Physics and Government of Canada Research Chair, Department of Physics, University of Toronto;* ed Massachusetts Inst. of Tech., Harvard Univ.; Natural Sciences and Eng Research Council of Canada Post-doctoral Fellow, Univ. of Pennsylvania 1984–86; Asst Prof. of Physics, Princeton Univ. 1986–89; joined Dept of Physics, Univ. of Toronto 1989, Univ. Prof. of Physics and Govt of Canada Research Chair, Dept of Physics 2001–; fmr Prin. Investigator, Photonics Research Ontario; lab. consultant, Corp. Research Science Labs, Exxon Research and Eng 1985–89; lab. consultant, Bell Communications Research, Red Bank, NJ 1989; mem. Max-Planck Soc. (Germany); Fellow, Canadian Inst. for Advanced Research, American Physical Soc., Optical Soc. of America; C.V. Raman Chair Professorship, Govt of India 2007; Herzberg Medal 1996, McLean Sr Fellowship, Univ. of Toronto 1996–, Steacie Prize in Science and Eng, Nat. Research Council of Canada 1997, Killam Fellowship, Canada Council for the Arts 1998–2000, Guggenheim Fellowship 2000–01, Japan Soc. for the Promotion of Science Fellowship, Humboldt Sr Scientist Award (Germany) 2000, King Faisal Int. Prize for Science (co-recipient) 2001, first ever winner of Premier's Platinum Medal for Science and Medicine 2002, Rutherford Medal, Royal Soc. of Canada (co-recipient) 2004, IEEE LEOS Int. Quantum Electronics Award 2007, Brockhouse Medal for Condensed Matter and Materials Physics, Canadian Asscn of Physicists 2007. *Achievement:* co-invented concept of photonic band gap materials 1987. *Address:* Department of Physics, Room MP1002, University of Toronto, 60 St George Street, Toronto, ON M5S 1A7, Canada (office). *Telephone:* (416) 978-3459 (office). *Fax:* (416) 978-2537 (office). *E-mail:* john@physics.utoronto.ca (office). *Website:* www.physics.utoronto.ca/~john (office).

JOHN, Sherma; Dominican banking executive; currently Country Dir Eastern Caribbean Cen. Bank–Dominica Office. *Address:* Eastern Caribbean Central Bank–Dominica Office, Financial Centre, 3rd Floor, Kennedy Avenue, POB 23, Roseau, Dominica (office). *Telephone:* 4488001 (office). *Fax:* 4488002 (office). *E-mail:* info@eccb-centralbank.org (office); eccbdom@cwdom.dm (office). *Website:* www.eccb-centralbank.org (office).

JOHNS, Andrew; Australian professional rugby league player (retd); b. 19 May 1974, Cessnock, NSW; m. Catherine Johns; one s.; halfback/hooker; player for Newcastle Knights 1994–2007, New South Wales 1995–2007, Australia 1995–2007; 212 appearances (62 as Capt.), 75 tries, 1,952 points, for Newcastle Knights, 21 appearances for New South Wales in State of Origin fixtures, 23 tests for Australia (apptd capt. in 2002); mem. of Australia's World Cup winning teams 1995 (named Player of the Tournament and Man of the Match in final) and 2000; captained Newcastle Knights to Premiership title 1997, 2001; Asst Coach, Manly Sea Eagles 2012–15; Consultant, Sydney Roosters 2015; Mentor Mate Ma'a Tonga 2016; Rugby League World Golden Boot Award 1999, 2001, Nat. Rugby League Player of the Year Award (three times). *Leisure interests:* surfing, horse racing.

JOHNS, Anthony (Tony) Hearle, PhD, FAHA; Australian/British professor of Islamic studies; *Professor Emeritus, Research School of Asian and Pacific Studies, Australian National University;* b. 28 Aug. 1928, Wimbledon, London; s. of Frank Charles Johns and Ivy Doris Kathleen Johns (née Hearle); m. Yohanni Bey 1956; four s. one d.; ed St Boniface's Coll., Plymouth, and School of Oriental and African Studies, Univ. of London; Lecturer at Ford Foundation-sponsored Training Project, Indonesia 1954–58; Sr Lecturer in Indonesian Languages and Literatures, ANU 1958–63, Prof. 1963, now Prof. Emer., Chair. and Head of Dept 1963–83, Dean Faculty of Asian Studies 1963–64, 1965–67, 1975–79, 1988–91, Head of Southeast Asia Centre 1983–88, Visiting Fellow, Research School Pacific and Asian Studies 1994–96, 1997–2000, 2005–; Adjunct Prof., Australian Catholic Univ.; Visiting Prof., Dept of Religious Studies and Dept of Middle East and Islamic Studies, Univ. of Toronto 1989; Special Foreign Visiting Prof. in Islamic Studies, Chiba Univ., Tokyo 1991; Visiting Scholar, Oxford Centre for Hebrew and Jewish Studies, UK 1993–94; Fellow, Inst. for Advanced Studies, Hebrew Univ. of Jerusalem 1984–85; Univ. of London Sr Studentship 1953–54; Rhuvon Guest Prize in Islamic Studies, SOAS 1953–54, Centenary Medal for Service to Australian Soc. and the Humanities 2003. *Publications:* The Gift Addressed to the Spirit of the Prophet 1965, A Road with No End (trans. and Ed.) 1968, Cultural Options and the Role of Tradition 1981, Islam in Asia II Southeast and East Asia (Ed. and contrib. with R. Israeli) 1984, Reflections on the Dynamics and Spirituality of Sūrat al-Furqān in Literary Structures of Religious Meaning in the Qur'an (contrib.) 2000, Islam in World Politics (Ed. and contrib. with Nelly Lahoud) 2005. *Leisure interests:* music, literature. *Address:* 70 Duffy Street, Ainslie, Canberra, ACT 2602, Australia (home). *Telephone:* (2) 6249-6574 (home). *E-mail:* ah_yjohns@netspeed.com.au (home).

JOHNS, Jasper; American painter; b. 15 May 1930, Augusta, Ga; s. of Jasper Johns, Sr and Jean Riley; ed Univ. of South Carolina; works in numerous collections, including Tate Gallery, London, Museum of Modern Art, New York, Albright-Knox Art Gallery, Buffalo, NY, Museum Ludwig, Cologne, Hirshhorn Museum and Sculpture Garden, Washington, DC, Whitney Museum of American Art, Stedelijk Museum, Amsterdam, Moderna Museet, Stockholm, Dallas Museum of Fine Arts, Art Inst. of Chicago, Baltimore Museum of Art, Kunstmuseum Basel, Cleveland Museum of Art, Nat. Gallery of Art, Washington, DC, San Francisco Museum of Modern Art, Va Museum of Fine Arts, Walker Art Center, Minneapolis; mem. American Acad. of Arts and Letters; Hon. RA (London); Officier, Ordre des Arts et Lettres 1990; Prize, Pittsburgh Int. 1958, Wolf Foundation Prize 1986, Gold Medal, American Acad. and Inst. of Arts and Letters 1986, Int. Prize, Venice Biennale 1988, Nat. Medal of Arts 1990, Praemium Imperiale Award (Japan) 1993, Presidential Medal of Freedom 2010. *Address:* PO Box 642, Sharon, CT 06069, USA.

JOHNS, Air Chief Marshal Sir Richard Edward, Kt, GCB, KCVO, CBE, FRAeS; British air force officer; b. 28 July 1939, Horsham, Sussex, England; s. of Lt Col Herbert Edward Johns and Marjory Harley Johns (née Everett); m. Elizabeth Naomi Anne Manning 1965; one s. two d.; ed Portsmouth Grammar School, RAF Coll., Cranwell; commissioned 1959; Night Fighter/Fighter Reconnaissance Squadrons, UK, Cyprus, Aden 1960–67; Flying Instructor 1968–71, Flying Instructor to HRH the Prince of Wales 1970–71; Officer Commanding 3 (Fighter) Squadron (Harrier) 1975–77; Dir Air Staff Briefing 1979–81; Station Commdr and Harrier Force Commdr, RAF Gütersloh 1982–84; ADC to HM The Queen 1983–84; at Royal Coll. of Defence Studies 1985; Sr Air Staff Officer, HQ RAF, Germany 1985–88; Sr Air Staff Officer HQ Strike Command 1989–91; Air Officer Commdg No. 1 Group 1991–93; Chief of Staff, Deputy C-in-C Strike Command and UK Air Forces 1993–94; Air Officer Commdg in Chief Strike Command 1994; C-in-C Allied Forces NW Europe 1994–97; Chief of Air Staff and Air ADC to HM The Queen 1997–2000; Constable and Gov. of Windsor Castle 2000–08; Pres. Windsor Festival 2001–08, Windsor and Eton Choral Soc. 2001–08, Royal Windsor Rose and Horticultural Soc. 2000–08; Nat. Pres. Hearing Dogs for Deaf People 2002–; Vice-Pres. The Wiltshire Historical Mil. Soc. 2009–; Chair. Bd of Trustees, RAF Museum 2000–06; Gov. Portsmouth Grammar School 1996–2009, Dauntsey's School 2009–; mem. Council St George's House 2000–08; Trustee, The Prince Philip Trust Fund 2000–08, Foundation of the Coll. of St George 2007–, The Overlord Embroidery Trust 2009–; Patron Labrador Life Line Trust 2001–; Freeman of the City of London 1999; Liveryman, Guild of Air Pilots & Air

Navigators 1999–; Hon. Air Cdre, RAF Regt 2000–13; Hon. Col, 73 Engineer Regt (V) 1994–2001. *Leisure interests:* military history, rugby, cricket, equitation. *Address:* Dolphin House, Warminster Road, Chitterne, Wilts., BA12 0LH, England (home). *Telephone:* (1985) 850039 (home). *E-mail:* rej76@waitrose.com (home).

JOHNSEN, Sigbjørn; Norwegian politician; b. 1 Oct. 1950, Lillehammer; m. Helle Laier Johnsen; three c.; ed Norwegian School of Man.; Deputy Rep. for Hedmark Co., Storting (Parl.) 1973–; Vice-Pres. Norwegian Labour League of Youth (AUF) 1975–77; Deputy Chair. Equal Status Council 1976–83; Minister of Finance 1990–96, 2009–13; Del. to Council of Europe's Parl. Ass. 1985–; Gov., Hedmark Co. 1997–2009; mem. Storting (Parl.) Standing Cttee on Justice 1976–77, on Local Govt and the Environment 1977–80, on Finance 1981 (Deputy Chair. 1986–), Nat. Council for Open-Air Recreation 1984–.

JOHNSON, Abigail (Abby) Pierrepont, BA, MBA; American business executive; *President, Fidelity Personal Workplace and Institutional Services, Fidelity Management & Research Corporation;* b. 19 Dec. 1961, Boston, Mass; d. of Edward C. (Ned) Johnson III; m. Christopher J. McKown 1988; two c.; ed Buckingham Browne & Nichols School, Hobart Coll., William Smith Coll., Harvard Business School; with Booz Allen Hamilton 1984–86; joined her father's co., Fidelity Man. & Research Corpn (better known as Fidelity Investments, f. by her grandfather in 1946), Boston, as an analyst and equity portfolio man. 1988–97, Assoc. Dir Investment Div. 1997–2001, Pres. 2001–05, currently Pres., Fidelity Personal Workplace and Institutional Services; mem. Bd of Dirs Securities Industry and Financial Markets Asscn; mem. Cttee on Capital Markets Regulation. *Address:* Fidelity Management & Research Corpn, 82 Devonshire Street, Boston, MA 02109, USA (office). *Telephone:* (617) 563-7000 (office). *Fax:* (617) 476-6150 (office). *Website:* www.fidelity.com (office).

JOHNSON, Adam, BA, MFA, PhD; American novelist and academic; *Phil and Penny Knight Professor in Creative Writing, Stanford University;* b. 12 July 1967, South Dakota; m. Stephanie Harrell; three c.; ed Arizona State Univ., McNeese State Univ., Florida State Univ.; apptd Assoc. Prof. of English, Stanford Univ. 1999–, currently Phil and Penny Knight Prof. in Creative Writing; f. Stanford Graphic Novel Project; Debut Writer of the Year Award 2002, Gina Berriault Literary Award 2010, Whiting Writers Award, Swarthout Writing Award, Sunday Times EFG Private Bank Short Story Award (for short story Nirvana) 2014. *Publications include:* Emporium (short stories) 2002, Parasites Like Us (California Book Award 2003) 2003, The Orphan Master's Son (Pulitzer Prize for Fiction 2013) 2012, Fortune Smiles: Stories (Nat. Book Award for Fiction 2015) 2015; numerous contribs to magazines, journals and anthologies. *Address:* Department of English, Stanford University, 450 Serra Mall, Building 460, Room 324, Stanford, CA 94305-2087, USA (office). *Telephone:* (650) 723-4657 (office). *Fax:* (650) 725-0755 (office). *E-mail:* adamjohn@stanford.edu (office). *Website:* english.stanford.edu (office).

JOHNSON, Rt Hon. Alan Arthur; British politician (retd); b. 17 May 1950, Paddington, London; orphaned aged 12 and brought up by older sister; m. 1st Judith Cox 1968 (divorced); one s. two d.; m. 2nd Laura Jane Patient 1991 (divorced); one s.; m. 3rd Carolyn Burgess 2015; ed Sloane Grammar School, Chelsea (now part of Pimlico Acad.); postman, London 1968, Slough 1969; elected to Br. Cttee Union of Communication Workers 1973, apptd Chair. Slough Br. 1976, elected to Nat. Exec. Council 1981, became full-time Officer 1987, elected (youngest ever) Gen. Sec. 1992, apptd Jt Gen. Sec. after merger of Union of Communication Workers and Nat. Communication Union 1995; mem. Gen. Council and Nat. Exec. Cttee of TUC; fmr Dir Unity Trust Bank; MP for Kingston-upon-Hull West and Hessle 1997–2017; mem. Trade and Industry Select Cttee; apptd Parl. Pvt. Sec. to Financial Sec. to Treasury 1997, to Paymaster Gen. 1998; Minister for Competitiveness, Dept of Trade and Industry 1999–2001, Minister of State for Employment Relations and Regions 2001, Industry added to Portfolio 2002; Minister of State for Lifelong Learning, Higher and Further Educ., Dept for Educ. and Skills 2003–04; Sec. of State for Work and Pensions 2004–05, for Productivity, Energy and Industry 2005–06, for Educ. and Skills 2006–07, for Health 2007–09, for the Home Dept 2009–10; unsuccessful cand. for Deputy Leader of Labour Party 2007; Shadow Home Sec. May–Oct. 2010, Shadow Chancellor of the Exchequer 2010–11; Labour. *Publications:* This Boy (memoir) (Ondaatje Prize 2014, Orwell Prize 2014) 2013, Please, Mister Postman (memoir) (Specsavers Nat. Book Awards Autobiography of the Year) 2014, A Long and Winding Road (memoir) 2016. *Address:* Goodwin Resource Centre, Icehouse Road, Hull, HU3 2HQ, England (office). *Telephone:* (1482) 219211 (office). *Fax:* (1482) 219211 (office). *Website:* www.alanjohnson.org (office).

JOHNSON, Allen; American athlete (retd); b. 1 March 1971, Washington, DC; one d.; ed Lake Braddock High School, Burke, Va, Univ. of North Carolina; sprint hurdler; 110m hurdles personal best 12.92 seconds (Brussels, Belgium Aug. 1996); winner: World Championships 110m hurdles 1995, 1997, 2001, 2003, US Indoor Championships 60m hurdles 1995, 2002, 2003, World Indoor Championships 60m hurdles 1995, 2003, US Championships 100m hurdles 1996, 1997, 2000, 2001, 2002, 2003, World Championships 4×400m 1997 (with US team), Olympic Games 110m hurdles 2001, Nat. Indoor Championships 60m 2002, 2003; runner-up: World Cup 110m hurdles 1994, 2002, World Cup 4×100m 1996 (with US team), Int. Amateur Athletics Fed. Grand Final 110m 1995, 2001; 4th: Olympic Games 110m hurdles 2000; eight runs of under 13 seconds in 110m hurdles; North American record holder 110m hurdles; coached by Curtis Frye; retd 2010; Jesse Owens Award 1997. *Address:* c/o HS International, Inc., 2600 Michelson Drive, Suite 680, Irvine, CA 92612, USA (office).

JOHNSON, Ben, MA, RCA; British artist; b. 24 Aug. 1946, Llandudno, Wales; s. of Harold Johnson and Ivy Lloyd Jones; m. Sheila Kellehar 1976; two s.; ed Royal Coll. of Art, London; has exhibited internationally since 1969; has undertaken direct comms from Centre Pompidou, Paris and Nat. Museums, Liverpool; work represented in public and corp. collections at Boymans van Beuningen Museum, Rotterdam, British Council, London, Tate Gallery, London, Contemporary Arts Soc., London, RIBA, London, City Art Gallery, Glasgow, Whitworth Gallery, Manchester, Centre Pompidou, Paris, Victoria & Albert Museum, London, Deutsche Bank, British Petroleum, Guildhall Art Gallery, Corpn of London, Special Admin. Regional Govt of Hong Kong, New Convention & Exhbn Centre, Hong Kong, Regional Services Council Museum, Hong Kong, British Museum, London, Walker Art Gallery, Liverpool, Museum of Liverpool; Hon. FRIBA. *Publications:* Cityscape: Ben Johnson's Liverpool, Ben Johnson: Foster in View. *Leisure interests:* architecture, cities. *Address:* c/o Alan Cristea Gallery, 31 Cork Street, London, W1S 3NU, England (office); 4 St Peter's Wharf, Chiswick Mall, London, W6 9UD, England (office). *Telephone:* (20) 7439-1866 (office); (20) 8563-8768 (office). *E-mail:* info@alancristea.com (office); benjohnson@benjohnsonartist.com (office). *Website:* www.alancristea.com (office); www.benjohnsonartist.com (office).

JOHNSON, Betsey Lee, BA; American fashion designer; b. 10 Aug. 1942, Hartford, Conn.; d. of John Herman Johnson and Lena Virginia Johnson; m. 1st John Cale 1966; one d.; m. 2nd Jeffrey Olivier 1981; ed Pratt Inst., Syracuse Univ.; Editorial Asst, Mademoiselle magazine 1964–65; Partner and co-owner Betsey, Bunky & Nini, New York 1969–; shops in New York, LA, San Francisco, Coconut Grove, Fla, Venice, Calif., Boston, Chicago, Seattle; Prin. Designer for Paraphernalia 1965–69; designer, Alvin Duskin Co., San Francisco 1970; Head Designer, Alley Cat by Betsey Johnson (div. of LeDamor, Inc.) 1970–74; freelance designer for Jr Womens' div., Butterick Pattern Co. 1971, Betsey Johnson's Kids Children's Wear (div. of Shutterbug Inc.) 1974–77, Betsey Johnson for Jeanette Maternities, Inc. 1974–75; designer for Gant Shirtmakers Inc. (women's clothing) 1974–75, Tric-Trac by Betsey Johnson (women's knitwear) 1974–76, Butterick's Home Sewing Catalog 1975– (children's wear); Head Designer, Jr sportswear co.; designed for Star Ferry by Betsey Johnson and Michael Miles (children's wear) 1975–77; owner and Head Designer B.J., Inc. (designer wholesale co.), New York 1978; Pres. and Treas. B.J. Vines, New York; opened Betsey Johnson store, New York 1979; mem. Council of Fashion Designers, American Women's Forum; Hon. Chair. Fashion Targets Breast Cancer initiative; Merit Award, Mademoiselle magazine 1970, Coty Award 1971, two Tommy Print Awards 1971. *Address:* Betsey Johnson, 498 7th Avenue, 21st Floor, New York, NY 10018-6798; 110 East 9th Street, Suite A889, Los Angeles, CA 90079, USA. *Telephone:* (212) 244-0843. *Website:* pr@betseyjohnson.com; www.betseyjohnson.com.

JOHNSON, (Alexander) Boris (de Pfeffel); British politician and journalist; b. 19 June 1964, New York City, USA; s. of Stanley Patrick Johnson and Charlotte Fawcett; m. 1st Allegra Mostyn-Owen; m. 2nd Marina Wheeler 1993 (separated 2018); two s. two d.; ed Eton Coll. and Balliol Coll., Oxford; journalist with The Times 1987–88; EC Corresp., The Daily Telegraph 1989–94, Asst Ed. and Chief Political Columnist 1994–99, columnist –2016; Ed. The Spectator 1999–2005; MP (Conservative) for Henley 2001–08, for Uxbridge and South Ruislip 2015–; Shadow Minister for Arts 2004, for Higher Educ. 2005–07; Mayor of London 2008–16; Sec. of State for Foreign and Commonwealth Affairs 2016–18 (resgnd); Vice-Chair. Conservative Party 2003–04; What the Papers Say Award for Columnist of the Year 2006. *Television includes:* Have I Got News for You 1998, 2004, 2006, The Dream of Rome 2006, Who Do You Think You Are? 2008, After Rome 2008. *Publications include:* Friends, Voters, Countrymen 2001, Seventy-Two Virgins (novel) 2004, The Dream of Rome 2006, The British 2007, Life in the Fast Lane: The Johnson Guide to Cars 2007, Johnson's Life of London 2011, The Churchill Factor: How One Man Made History 2014. *Address:* House of Commons, London, SW1A 0AA, England (office). *Telephone:* (20) 7219-4682 (office). *E-mail:* boris.johnson.mp@parliament.uk (office).

JOHNSON, Brian Frederick Gilbert, PhD, FRS, FRSC, FRSE; British chemist and academic; *Professor Emeritus, University of Cambridge;* b. 11 Sept. 1938; s. of Frank Johnson and Mona Johnson; m. Christine Draper 1962; two d.; ed Northampton Grammar School, Univ. of Nottingham; Reader in Chem., Univ. of Cambridge 1978–90, Fellow, Fitzwilliam Coll. 1970–90, Hon. Fellow 1990–, Master 1999–2005; Crum Brown Prof. of Inorganic Chem., Univ. of Edin. 1991–95; Prof. of Inorganic Chem., Univ. of Cambridge 1995–2005, now Prof. Emer.; Tilden Lecturer, RSC; Corday Morgan Medal, RSC, Frankland Medal and Prize, RSC. *Publications include:* Transition Metal Clusters 1982, over 1,000 academic papers and review articles. *Leisure interests:* walking, painting, riding, gardening. *Address:* Fitzwilliam College, Storey's Way, Cambridge, CB3 0DG, England (office). *Telephone:* (1223) 332000 (office). *E-mail:* masters.secretary@fitz.cam.ac.uk (office); brianjohnson828@btinternet.com. *Website:* www.fitz.cam.ac.uk/content/professor-brian-johnson (office).

JOHNSON, Charles Richard, BS, MA, PhD; American author and academic; *Professor Emeritus, Department of English, University of Washington, Seattle;* b. 23 April 1948, Evanston, Ill.; m. Joan New 1970; one s. one d.; ed Southern Illinois Univ., State Univ. of New York, Stoneybrook; fmr cartoonist and filmmaker; Lecturer, Univ. of Washington, Seattle 1975–79, Assoc. Prof. of English 1979–82, Prof. 1982, then Pollock Endowed Prof. of English, now Prof. Emer.; Fiction Ed. Seattle Review 1978–98; Co.-Dir Twin Tigers (martial arts studio); mem. American Acad. of Arts and Sciences 2003–; Dr hc (Northwestern Univ.) 1994, (Southern Illinois Univ.) 1995, (State Univ. of New York at Stony Brook) 1999, (Lewis and Clark Coll.) 2006; Stephen Henderson Award 2004, Humanities Washington Award 2013, Don Ihde Distinguished Alumni Award, Stony Brook Univ. 2013. *Publications include:* novels: Faith and the Good Thing 1974, Oxherding Tale 1982, Middle Passage (Nat. Book Award 1990) 1990; others: The Sorcerer's Apprentice (short stories), Being and Race: Black Writing Since 1970 1988, The Middle Passage 1990, All This and Moonlight 1990, In Search of a Voice (with Ron Chernow) 1991, Black Humor, Half-Past Nation Time (drawings), Booker, Charlie Smith and the Fritter Tree (broadcast plays), Taming the Ox: Buddhist Stories, and Reflections on Politics, Race, Culture, and Spiritual Practice 2014; numerous reviews, essays and short stories. *Address:* University of Washington, Department of English, PDL A-406, Seattle, WA 98105, USA (office). *E-mail:* chasjohn@u.washington.edu. *Website:* depts.washington.edu/engl (office); www.oxherdingtale.com.

JOHNSON, David T., BEcons; American diplomatist (retd); b. Georgia; m. Scarlett M. Swan; two d. one s.; ed Emory Univ., Canadian Nat. Defence Coll.; early career as Asst Nat. Trust Examiner, US Treasury Dept; joined Foreign Service 1977, Vice-Consul, Consulate-Gen., Ciudad Juárez, Mexico 1978–79, Econ. Officer, Embassy in Berlin 1981–83, Deputy Dir State Dept Operations Center 1987–89, at Consul-Gen. in Vancouver 1990–93, Deputy Spokesman, State Dept, Dir State Dept Press Office 1993–95; Deputy Press Sec. for Foreign Affairs at the White House and Spokesman for Nat. Sec. Council 1995–97; Chief (with rank of Amb.), Perm. Mission to OSCE 1998, Minister and Deputy Chief of Mission, Embassy in London 2003–07; Asst Sec. of State for Bureau of Int. Narcotics and

Law Enforcement Affairs 2007–11; currently Vice-Pres. for Strategic Devt and Washington Operations, Sterling Global Operations, Inc. *Address:* Sterling Global Operations, Inc., 12100 Sunset Hills Road, Suite 310, Reston, VA 20190, USA (office). *Website:* www.sterlinggo.com (office).

JOHNSON, Dwayne Douglas, (The Rock); American actor and professional wrestler; b. 2 May 1972, Hayward, Calif.; s. of Rocky Johnson and Ata Johnson (née Maivia); m. Dany Garcia 1997 (separated 2007); one d.; ed Pres. William McKinley High School, Honolulu, Hawaii, Freedom High School, Bethlehem, Pa, Univ. of Miami; lived briefly in Auckland, NZ with his mother's family; mem. Univ. of Miami's nat. championship football team 1991; later played for the Calgary Stampeders in Canadian Football League; gained widespread recognition as a wrestler in World Wrestling Fed. (WWF) 1996–2004, originally billed as 'Rocky Maivia' and then as 'The Rock', later role as a villain as part of the Nation of Domination 1997, won WWF Championship 1998; won 16 championships in WWF/E, including nine World Heavyweight Championships (WWF/E Championship seven times and WCW/World Championship twice), two WWF Intercontinental Championships and five times as co-holder of WWF Tag Team Championships; sixth WWF/E Triple Crown Champion; winner of 2000 Royal Rumble; appears for World Wrestling Entertainment, Inc.; ring names: Flex Kavana, Rocky Maivia, The Rock, Dwayne 'The Rock' Johnson. *Films include:* WWF Slammy Awards 1997 (video) 1997, Survivor Series (video) 1998, WWF Judgment Day (video) 1998, WWF Mayhem in Manchester (video) 1998, The Rock – The People's Champ (video) 2000, The Mummy Returns 2001, Longshot 2001, The Scorpion King 2002, WWE Global Warning Tour: Melbourne (video) 2002, WWE: Brock Lesnar: Here Comes the Pain (video) 2003, Welcome to the Jungle 2003, WWE: The Stone Cold Truth (video) 2004, Walking Tall 2004, Be Cool 2005, WWE $250,000 Raw Diva Search (video) 2005, Doom 2005, Southland Tales 2006, WWE: McMahon (video) 2006, Gridiron Gang 2006, The Game Plan 2007, Get Smart 2008, Race to Witch Mountain 2009, Planet 51 (voice) 2009, Tooth Fairy 2010, The Other Guys 2010, Faster 2010, Fast & Furious 5 2011, Journey 2: The Mysterious Island 2012, Snitch 2013, Empire State 2013, G.I. Joe: Retaliation 2013, Pain & Gain 2013, Fast & Furious 6 2013, Hercules 2014, Furious 7 2015, San Andreas 2015, Central Intelligence 2016, Moana (voice) 2016, The Fate of the Furious 2017, Baywatch 2017, Jumanji: Welcome to the Jungle 2017, Rampage 2018, Skyscraper 2018. *Television includes:* WWF Raw Is War (series) 1996–2016, WWF SmackDown! (series) 1999–2019, DAG (series) 2000, Royal Rumble (film) 2002, King of the Ring (film) 2002, Cory in the House (series) 2007, Saturday Night Live (series) 2010, Family Guy (series) 2010, Hannah Montana (series) 2007, Cubed (series) 2010, Transformers Prime (series) 2010, Clash Time (series) 2011–12, Royal Rumble (film) 2013, Ballers (series) 2015–18, Seven Bucks Digital Studios (short series) 2016–17. *Publication:* The Rock Says... (autobiog., co-written with Joe Layden) 2000. *Address:* c/o WME Entertainment, 9601 Wilshire Boulevard, Beverly Hills, CA 90210-5213, USA (office); c/o The Rock Foundation, 2525 Ponce de Leon Blvd, Fifth Floor, Coral Gables, FL 33134, USA. *Website:* www.dwaynetherockjohnson .net.

JOHNSON, Earvin, Jr. (Magic); American business executive and fmr professional basketball player; *Chairman and CEO, Magic Johnson Enterprises;* b. 14 Aug. 1959, Lansing, Mich.; s. of Earvin Johnson and Christine Johnson; m. Earlitha (Cookie) Kelly 1991; one s.; ed Lansing Everett High School, Mich., Michigan State Univ.; led Mich. State Univ. to NCAA Men's Basketball Championship 1979; drafted by Los Angeles Lakers (Nat. Basketball Asscn—NBA) first overall 1979, played 1979–91, played on championship teams 1980, 1982, 1985, 1987, 1988 (Finals Most Valuable Player 1980, 1982, 1987), retd after announcing he was HIV-positive, Vice-Pres. and Co-owner, Los Angeles Lakers 1994–2010, Head Coach 1994, resumed playing career Feb. 1996, retd July 1996, apptd advisor to team owner Jeanie Buss 2017, Pres. of Basketball Operations 2017–19; mem. US Olympic basketball team 1992 (Gold Medal); f. Johnson Devt Corpn 1993, now Chair. and CEO Magic Johnson Enterprises; minority Owner, Los Angeles Dodgers professional baseball team 2012–, Los Angeles Sparks women's professional basketball team 2014–; presenter, The Magic Hour (TV talk show) 1998; commentator, NBC-TV 1995–96; f. Magic Johnson Foundation 1991; mem. NBA All-Star Team 1980, 1982–89, NBA Most Valuable Player 1987, 1989, 1990, Player of the Year (Sporting News) 1987, J. Walter Kennedy Citizenship Award 1992, voted One of 50 Greatest Players in NBA History 1996, elected Naismith Memorial Basketball Hall of Fame 2002. *Publications include:* Magic 1983, What You Can Do to Avoid AIDS 1992, My Life (autobiography) 1992, When the Game was Ours (with Larry Bird and Jackie MacMullan) 2009. *Address:* Magic Johnson Enterprises, 9100 Wilshire Blvd, 700 East Tower, Beverly Hills, CA 90212, USA (office). *Telephone:* (310) 247-2033 (office). *Fax:* (310) 786-8796 (office). *E-mail:* info@magicjent.com (office). *Website:* www.magicjohnson.com (office).

JOHNSON, Edward C. (Ned), III, BA; American financial services executive; *Chairman and CEO, Fidelity Investments;* m.; three c.; ed Harvard Univ.; research analyst, Fidelity Management & Research (FMR) Co. 1957, Man. Trend Fund 1960, Pres. FMR Corpn 1972, currently Chair. and CEO Fidelity Investments. *Address:* Fidelity Investments, 82 Devonshire Street, Boston, MA 02109, USA (office). *Telephone:* (617) 563-7000 (office). *Fax:* (617) 476-3876 (office). *Website:* www.fidelity.com (office).

JOHNSON, Gabriel Ampah, DD'État; Togolese biologist, academic and university administrator; *Professor and Chair of Biology, National University of Côte d'Ivoire;* b. 13 Oct. 1930, Aneho; s. of William K. A. Johnson and Rebecca A. Ekue-Hettah; m. Louise Chipan 1962; three s. three d.; ed Univ. of Poitiers, France; Teaching Asst, Univ. of Poitiers –1956; Research Fellow, CNRS, France 1958–60; Deputy Dir of Educ., Togo 1959-60; Asst Prof., Nat. Univ. of Côte d'Ivoire, Abidjan 1961–64, Assoc. Prof. 1965–66, apptd Prof., Chair of Biology 1966, Asst Dean, Faculty of Science 1963–68, Founding Dir Nat. Centre for Social Services 1964–68; Founding Rector, Univ. du Bénin, Lomé, Togo 1970–86; fmr Rector and Chancellor, Togolese Univs; Dir of Higher Educ., Togo 1970–75; Pres. Nat. Planning Comm. of Togo 1973; Pres. Asscn of African Univs 1977–80; mem. Exec. Bd UNESCO 1997; mem. Bd of Admin., Asscn of Partially or Fully French-Speaking Univs 1975, Pan African Inst. for Devt 1977, Int. Cttee of Bioethics 2001, Admin. Council Int. Fund for the Promotion of Culture (UNESCO) 2003; mem. Cen. Cttee Togo People's Rally (ruling party) 1976; Founding Pres. Africa Club for an Integrated Devt 1980–; mem. Zoological Soc. of France 1956, Biological Soc. of France 1962, Endocrinological Soc. of France 1966, French Nat. Acad. of Pharmacy 2003; Hon. Vice-Pres. Gold Mercury Int. 1983; Chevalier, Ordre nat. de la Côte d'Ivoire 1966; Officier Légion d'honneur 1971; Commdr Order of Cruzeiro do Sul (Brazil) 1976; Commdr Order of Merit (France) 1983; Commdr, Ordre des Palmes Académiques, (France) 1986; Commdr, Ordre du Mono (Togo) 2000; Dr hc Sherbrooke, (Canada) 1979, (Lille) 1983, (Bordeaux) 1986; Medal of Honour, Univ. of São Paulo, Brazil 1980; Gold Mercury Int. Award 1982, Gold Medal of Honour, Univ. of Benin. *Publications:* several articles in scientific journals. *Leisure interests:* reading, classical and modern music, swimming, farming (cattle breeding). *Address:* BP 7098, Lomé, Togo. *Telephone:* (22) 21-52-41 (office); (22) 21-53-65 (home). *Fax:* (22) 21-52-41 (office); (22) 21-53-65 (home). *E-mail:* gampahjohnson@yahoo.fr.

JOHNSON, Gary Earl, BA; American business executive and politician; b. 1 Jan. 1953, Minot, North Dakota; s. of Earl W. Johnson and Lorraine B. Bostow; m. Dee Sims 1976 (divorced 2005, died 2006); one s. one d.; pnr Kate Prusack 2009; ed Univ. of New Mexico; Pres. and CEO Big J Enterprises, Albuquerque 1976–99; Gov. of New Mexico 1995–2003; unsuccessful cand. for Republican Party nomination for US presidential election 2011, then unsucessful Libertarian Party cand. for US presidential election 2012; CEO and Pres. Cannabis Sativa Inc. 2014–16; f. Our America Initiative PAC 2013; mem. Bd of Dirs Entrepreneurship Studies programme, Univ. of NM 1993–95, Albuquerque Chamber of Commerce 1993–95; f. Our America Initiative 2009; Libertarian; Entrepreneur of the Year 1995. *Publications:* Seven Principles of Good Government 2012, Wowed! 2014. *Leisure interests:* rock and mountain-climbing (climbed Mount Everest May 2003), skiing, flying, athletics (participated in several Ironman Triathlons). *Website:* www .ouramericainitiative.com; www.lp.org.

JOHNSON, Graham Rhodes, OBE, FRAM, FGSM; British pianist and academic; *Senior Professor of Accompaniment, Guildhall School of Music and Drama;* b. 10 July 1950, Bulawayo, Rhodesia (now Zimbabwe); s. of John Edward Donald Johnson and Violet May Johnson; ed Hamilton High School, Bulawayo, Rhodesia, Royal Acad. of Music; Artistic Adviser, accompanist Alte Oper Festival, Frankfurt 1981–82; Sr Prof. of Accompaniment, Guildhall School of Music 1986–; Song Adviser, Wigmore Hall 1992–; Artistic Dir The Songmakers' Almanac; writer and presenter of BBC Radio 3 series on Poulenc, BBC TV series on Schubert 1978, Liszt 1986; concert debut, Wigmore Hall 1972; has accompanied numerous singers including Dame Elisabeth Schwarzkopf, Jessye Norman, Victoria de los Angeles, Dame Janet Baker, Sir Peter Pears, Dame Felicity Lott, Ann Murray, Matthias Goerne, Christine Schäfer, Dorothea Roeschmann, François Le Roux; has appeared at festivals in Edinburgh, Munich, Hohenems, Salzburg, Bath, Hong Kong, Bermuda; Chair. Jury Wigmore Hall Int. Singing Competition 1997, 1999, 2001; Sr Prof. of Accompaniment, Guildhall School of Music and Drama 1985–; mem. Royal Swedish Acad. of Music 2000; numerous recordings; Chevalier, Ordre des Arts et des Lettres 2002; Gramophone Award 1989, 1996, 1997, Royal Philharmonic Prize for Instrumentalist 1998, Wigmore Hall Medal 2013. *Publications:* contrib. to The Britten Companion 1984, Gerald Moore: The Unashamed Accompanist, The Spanish Song Companion 1992, The Songmakers' Almanac Reflections and Commentaries 1996, A French Song Companion 2000, Gabriel Fauré: The Songs and Their Poets 2009, Franz Schubert: The Complete Songs 2013, articles and reviews. *Leisure interests:* dining out, book collecting. *Address:* Guildhall School of Music and Drama, Silk Street, Barbican, London, EC2Y 8DT (office); 83 Fordwych Road, London, NW2 3TL, England. *Telephone:* (20) 8452-5193. *Fax:* (20) 8452-5081 (home). *Website:* www.gsmd.ac.uk/music/principal_study/vocal_studies.html (office).

JOHNSON, Hilde Frafjord, MA, PhD; Norwegian politician and fmr UN official; b. 29 Aug. 1963, Arusha, Tanzania; ed Univ. of Oslo; started career as journalist for Stavanger Aftenblad 1982, Folkets Framtid 1987; Chair. Christian Democratic Party Rogaland (CDP) 1988–89; Political Adviser to Kjell Magne Bondevik 1988–91, Minister of Foreign Affairs 1989–90; Alt. mem. of Parl. 1989–93, mem. of Parl. 1993–2001; Exec. Officer, UN Summit on Environment and Devt, Ministry of Foreign Affairs 1992–93; Minister of Int. Devt and Human Rights 1997–2000, Minister of Int. Devt 2001–05; Sr Adviser to Pres. of ADB 2006–07; Co-Chair. Global Coalition for Africa; Deputy Exec. Dir UNICEF 2007–11; Special Rep. of Sec.-Gen. and Head of UN Mission in Repub. of South Sudan (UNMISS), Juba 2011–14; Chair. Sudan Cttee IGAD Partners Forum 1998–2000, 2001; initiator and mem. Utstein 4, 1998–2000, 2001; Order of the Two Niles First Class (Sudan); Commitment to Devt Award, Foreign Policy and Centre for Global Devt 2003. *Publication:* Waging Peace in Sudan 2011. *Address:* c/o Christian Democratic Party, Øvre Slottsgt. 18–20, POB 478 Sentrum, 0105 Oslo, Norway.

JOHNSON, Hugh Eric Allan, OBE, MA; British writer, editor and broadcaster; b. 10 March 1939, London; s. of Guy F. Johnson CBE and Grace Kittel; m. Judith Eve Grinling 1965; one s. two d.; ed Rugby School, King's Coll., Cambridge; feature writer, Condé Nast Magazines 1960–63; Wine Corresp., Sunday Times 1962–67, Travel Ed. 1967; Ed. Wine and Food Magazine 1963–65; Ed. Queen Magazine 1968–70; Wine Ed., Gourmet Magazine 1971–72, Cuisine Magazine, New York 1983–84; Chair. Winestar Productions Ltd 1984–2009, The Hugh Johnson Collection Ltd, The Movie Business; Pres. Sunday Times Wine Club 1973–, Circle of Wine Writers 1997–2007; Founder-mem. Tree Council 1974; Founder The Plantsman (quarterly) 1979; Dir Château Latour 1986–2001; Editorial Consultant, The Garden (Royal Horticultural Soc. Journal) 1975–2005; columnist, Tradescant's Diary 1975–; Sec. Wine and Food Soc. 1962–63; Gardening Corresp., New York Times 1986–87; Pres. Metropolitan Public Gardens Asscn 2011; Vice-Pres. Int. Dendrology Soc. 2010–; Hon. Chair. Wine Japan 1989–93; Hon. Pres. Int. Wine and Food Soc. 2004–08, Wine & Spirit Educ. Trust 2009–11; Fellow Commoner, King's Coll., Cambridge 2001; Hon. Freeman of the Vintner's Co. 2003; Chevalier, Ordre nat. du Mérite 2003; Dr hc (Acad. du Vin de Bordeaux) 1987, (Essex) 1998; André Simon Prize 1967, 1989, 2005, Glenfiddich Award 1972, 1986, 1990, Marqués de Cáceres Award 1984, Wines and Vines Trophy 1982, Grand Prix de la Communication de la Vigne et du Vin 1992, 1993, Decanter Magazine Man of the Year 1995, Von Rumor Award, Gastronomische Akad., Germany 1998, Gold Veitch Memorial Medal, Royal Horticultural Soc. 2000. *Television includes:* Wine – A User's Guide (series) 1986, Vintage – A History of Wine (series) 1989, Return Voyage 1992. *Publications include:* Wine 1966, Frank Schoonmaker's Encyclopaedia of Wine (ed. of English edn) 1967, The World Atlas of Wine 1971 (sixth edn with Jancis Robinson 2007), The International Book of Trees 1973, The California Wine Book (with Bob Thompson) 1976, Understanding Wine (Sainsbury Guide) 1976, Hugh Johnson's Pocket Wine Book (annually since 1977), The Principles of Gardening 1979 (revised edn with new title, Hugh Johnson's Gardening Companion 1996), Hugh Johnson's Wine Companion 1983 (sixth edn with Stephen Brook 2009), How to Handle a Wine (video) 1984, Hugh Johnson's Cellar Book 1986, The Atlas of German Wines 1986, How to Enjoy Your Wine 1985, The Wine Atlas of France (with Hubrecht Duijker) 1987, The Story of Wine 1989, The Art and Science of Wine (with James Halliday) 1992, Hugh Johnson on Gardening: The Best of Tradescant's Diary 1993, Tuscany and Its Wines 2000, Wine: A Life Uncorked 2005, Hugh Johnson in the Garden 2009, Trees: A Lifetime's Journey through Forests, Woods and Gardens (Garden Media Guild Reference Book of the Year 2011) 2010, Wine Journal 2011. *Leisure interests:* travel, trees, gardening, pictures. *Address:* 73 St James's Street, London, SW1A 1PH; Saling Hall, Great Saling, Essex, CM7 5DT, England. *Telephone:* (1371) 850243. *Website:* www.salinghall.com; www.tradsdiary.com.

JOHNSON, Adm. (retd) Jay L.; American naval officer (retd) and business executive; b. 5 June 1946, Great Falls, Mont.; ed US Naval Acad.; commissioned as Ensign, USN 1968, fmr Adm., USN, Chief of Naval Operations 1996–2000; Sr Vice-Pres. Dominion Energy, Inc. 2000–02, Exec. Vice-Pres., Dominion Resources, Inc. 2002–08, Pres. and CEO Dominion Delivery 2002–07, CEO Dominion Virginia Power 2007–08; mem. Bd of Dirs General Dynamics Corpn 2003–12, Vice-Chair. 2008–09, Pres. and CEO 2009–10, Chair. and CEO 2010–12 (retd); mem. Bd of Dirs International Paper 2013–.

JOHNSON, Jeh Charles, BA, JD; American lawyer and government official; b. 11 Sept. 1957; s. of Jeh Vincent Johnson and Norma Johnson (née Edelin); m. Susan M. DiMarco; ed Morehouse Coll., Columbia Univ. Law School; Litigation Assoc., Sullivan & Cromwell, New York 1982–84; Assoc., Paul, Weiss, Rifkind, Wharton & Garrison, New York 1984–88, 1992–93, Partner 1994–98, 2001–09; Asst US Attorney (Southern Dist), US Dept of Justice 1989–91, Gen. Counsel, Air Force Dept 1998–2001; Foreign Policy Adviser, Barack Obama's Presidential Campaign 2007–08; Gen. Counsel, US Dept of Defense 2009–12; Sec. of Homeland Security 2013–17; Adjunct Lecturer in Law, Columbia Univ. Law School 1995–97; mem. New York Bar Asscn 1983, DC Bar Asscn 1999; Fellow, American Coll. of Trial Lawyers; mem. Council on Foreign Relations; Democrat.

JOHNSON, John D., BBA; American business executive; b. Rhame, ND; ed Black Hills State Univ.; grew up in Spearfish, SDak; began his career with fmr Harvest States as feed consultant in GTA Feeds Div. 1976, then Regional Sales Man., then Dir of Sales and Marketing, then Gen. Man. GTA Feeds, Group Vice-Pres. Harvest States Farm Marketing & Supply for Harvest States Cooperatives 1992–95, Pres. and CEO Harvest States 1995–98, Pres. and Gen. Man. CHS (following merger of Cenex and Harvest States June 1998) 1998–2000, Pres. and CEO CHS 2000–10 (retd); mem. Bd of Dirs Ventura Foods, LLC, CF Industries, Nat. Council of Farmer Cooperatives, Greater Twin Cities United Way; CEO Communicator of the Year, Cooperative Communicators Asscn 2003.

JOHNSON, Kevin R., BS; American business executive; *President and CEO, Starbucks Corporation;* b. 1960, Wash.; m. June Johnson; two s.; ed New Mexico State Univ.; various positions in system integration and consulting business units, IBM Corpn 1986–92; Gen. Man., enterprise services, Microsoft Corpn 1992, becoming Vice-Pres., Product Support Services, Sr Vice-Pres., Microsoft Americas, Group Vice-Pres., Worldwide Sales, Marketing and Services, Microsoft Corpn 2003–05, Co-Pres., Platforms Products & Services div., Microsoft Corpn 2005–07, Pres., Platforms & Services div., Microsoft Corpn 2007–08; mem. Bd of Dirs and CEO, Juniper Networks, Inc. 2008–14; mem. Bd of Dirs Starbucks Corpn 2009–, Pres. 2015–, COO 2015–17, CEO 2017–; mem. Nat. Security Telecommunication Advisory Cttee 2008; mem. Bd of Dirs Auction.com, LLC 2014–; fmr mem. Western Bd of Advisors, Catalyst, Inc.; fmr mem. Bd of Dirs NPower. *Address:* Starbucks Corporation, 2401 Utah Avenue South, Seattle, WA 98134, USA (office). *E-mail:* press@starbucks.com (office). *Website:* www.starbucks.com (office).

JOHNSON, Luke; British business executive; *Chairman, Risk Capital Partners Ltd;* s. of Paul Johnson and Marigold Hunt; m. Liza Pickrell; three c.; ed Univ. of Oxford; started career with BMP (advertising firm); media analyst, Kleinwort Benson Securities; fmr Chair. PizzaExpress PLC –1999; Chair. Signature Restaurants PLC 1999–2005; Chair. Channel Four Television Corpn 2004–10; currently Chair. Risk Capital Partners Ltd (private equity firm); part owner and Chair. Superbrands, Giraffe Restaurants 2004–13, Patisserie Valerie, Baker and Spice; prin. owner GRA (greyhound tracks) 2005–; Chair. Royal Soc. of Arts 2008–12, StageOne; Gov. Univ. of the Arts, London 2000–06; Co-founder Inst. of Entrepreneurs 2010; columnist, Financial Times. *Publications include:* How to Get a Highly Paid Job in the City 1987, Key to Making Money in the New Stock Market 1988, 30 Ways to Make Money in Franchising 1989, 30 Ways to Make Money in Property 1989, Betting to Win (co-author) 1997, The Maverick 2007, Start It Up: Why Running Your Own Business is Easier Than You Think 2011. *Address:* Risk Capital Partners, Ltd, 9 Grafton Mews, London, W1T 5HZ, England (office). *Telephone:* (20) 7016-0702 (office). *E-mail:* luke@lukejohnson.org; luke@riskcapitalpartners.co.uk (office). *Website:* www.riskcapitalpartners.co.uk (office); www.lukejohnson.org (office).

JOHNSON, Manuel H., Jr, BS, MS, PhD; American economist, academic and fmr government official; *Co-Chairman and Senior Partner, Johnson Smick International Inc.;* b. 10 Feb. 1949, Troy, Ala; s. of Manuel Holman Johnson, Sr and Ethel Lorraine Jordan; m. Mary Lois Wilkerson 1972; two s.; ed Troy State Univ., Florida State Univ., George Mason Univ.; Asst Sec. for Econ. Policy, US Treasury, Washington, DC 1982–86; mem. Fed. Reserve Bd 1985–90, Vice-Chair. 1986–90; Prof., George Mason Univ. 1977–94, Dir Centre for Global Market Studies 1990–94; Co-Chair. and Sr Partner, Johnson Smick Int. (financial market advisory firm), Washington, DC 1990–; Chair. Financial Accounting Foundation 1997–2004; Founder and Co-Chair. Group of Seven Council; Chair. Nat. Sporting Library and Museum; mem. Bd of Dirs NVR, Inc. 1993–, Morgan Stanley Funds, Evergreen Energy, Inc; Alexander Hamilton Award, US Treasury, Distinguished Alumni Award, Coll. of Social Sciences, Fla State Univ. 2003. *Publications:* co-author: Political Economy of Federal Government Growth 1980, Better Government at Half Price 1981, Deregulating Labor Relations 1981, Deregulating Labor Relations Fisher Institute 1981, Monetary Policy, A Market Price Approach 1996. *Address:* Johnson Smick International, 220 Eye Street, NE, Suite 200, Washington, DC 20002, USA (office). *Telephone:* (202) 861-0770 (office).

JOHNSON, Martin Osborne, CBE; British rugby manager and fmr professional rugby union player; b. 9 March 1970, Solihull, West Midlands; m. Kay Johnson; joined Leicester Football Club (known as Leicester Tigers) 1989, won Premiership honours 1994–95, 1998–99, 1999–2000, 2000–01, 2001–02, retd (362 caps) 2005; toured Australia with England Schoolboys side 1990; int. debut, England versus France 1993; replacement with British and Irish Lions tour of NZ 1993, losing Test series 2–1; part of England team that won Grand Slam 1995, 2003; captained British and Irish Lions on SA tour 1997, winning Test series 2–1; apptd Capt. England team in Six Nations Championships 2000; captained Lions tour to Australia 2001, losing Test series 2–1, first player ever to captain two British Lions tours; won Heineken Cup (with Leicester) 2001, 2002; won Calcutta Cup 2009, 2010, 2011; won Cook Cup 2010; 84 caps (39 as Capt.); captained England to Grand Slam and World Cup wins in 2003; retd from int. rugby after 2003 World Cup Jan. 2004; Man. England nat. team 2008–11 (resgnd), won Six Nations 2011. *Publication include:* Agony and Ecstasy: My Diary of an Amazing Rugby Season 2001, Martin Johnson: The Autobiography (British Book Awards Sports Book of the Year 2004) 2004. *Leisure interest:* San Francisco 49ers.

JOHNSON, Mat, BA, MFA; American writer and academic; *Professor, Department of English, University of Houston;* b. 19 Aug. 1970, Philadelphia, Pa; ed Greene Street Friends School, West Chester Univ., Univ. of Wales, Swansea, Earlham Coll., Columbia Univ. School of the Arts; Adjunct Prof., Columbia Univ. 2001–03; Asst Prof., Bard Coll. 2003–07; Asst Prof., Univ. of Houston 2007–10, Assoc. Prof. 2010–12, Prof. 2012–; Visiting Writer, Mills Coll. 2010, Temple Univ. 2012, Hope Coll. 2013, Otis Coll. 2014; Guest Teacher, Voices of Our Nation Workshop, Univ. of California, Berkeley 2008–; James Baldwin Fellow 2007; John Dos Passos Prize for Literature 2011. *Publications include:* novels: Drop 2000, Hunting in Harlem (Hurston/Wright Legacy Award for Fiction 2004) 2003, Pym 2011, Loving Day 2015; non-fiction: The Great Negro Plot 2007; graphic novels: Hellblazer Special: Papa Midnite (series) 2005–06, Incognegro 2008, Dark Rain: A New Orleans Story 2010, Right State 2012; numerous contribs to anthologies. *Address:* c/o Watkins/Loomis, PO Box 20925, New York, NY 10025, USA (office); Department of English, College of Liberal Arts and Social Sciences, University of Houston, 205 Roy Cullen Building, Houston, TX 77204-5008 (office); 2406 Hodges Bend Circle, Sugar Land, TX 77479, USA. *Telephone:* (212) 532-0080 (office); (713) 743-2964 (office). *Fax:* (646) 383-2449 (office). *E-mail:* assistant@watkinsloomis.com (office); mrjohns6@mail.uh.edu (office); mat_johnson@icloud.com. *Website:* www.watkinsloomis.com (office); www.uh.edu/class/english (office); www.matjohnson.info.

JOHNSON, Michael; American fmr professional athlete; b. 13 Sept. 1967, Dallas, Tex.; m. 1st Kerry Doyen 1998 (divorced); one s.; m. 2nd Armine Shamiryan; ed Baylor Univ.; world champion 200m 1991, 400m and 4×400m 1993, 200m, 400m and 4×400m (world record) 1995, 400m 1997, 400m (world record) and 4×400m 1999; Olympic champion 4×400m (world record) 1992, 200m, 400m 1996, world record holder 400m (indoors) 44.63 seconds 1995, 4×400m (outdoors) 2:55.74 1992, 2:54.29 1993; undefeated at 400m from 1989–97; first man to be ranked World No. one at 200m and 400m simultaneously 1990, 1991, 1994, 1995; Olympic champion 200m (world record), 400m, Atlanta 1996; Olympic Champion 400m and 4×400m, Sydney 2000; announced retirement 2001; f. Ultimate Performance (sports man. co.); f. Michael Johnson Performance Centers (trains youngsters in sports) 2007; recruited to work for Arsenal FC to assist devt of young footballers 2015–; currently also TV commentator; columnist, The Daily Telegraph, UK; Jesse Owens Award (three times), Track and Field US Athlete of the Year (four times), Asscn of American Univs (AAU)/Sullivan Award 1996, inducted into US Track and Field Hall of Fame 2004. *Publications:* Slaying The Dragon (autobiog.) 1996, Michael Johnson: Sprinter Deluxe. *Leisure interest:* piano. *Address:* Ultimate Performance, 40 Tall Trail, Missouri City, TX (office); Michael Johnson Performance Centers, 6051 Alma Drive, McKinney, TX 75070, USA (office). *Website:* www.upsportmanagement.com (office); www.michaeljohnsonperformance.com (office).

JOHNSON, Paul, MA, DPhil, FRHistS, ACSS; British economist, academic and university administrator; b. 26 Nov. 1956, Bath; ed Univ. of Oxford; expert adviser on pension reform and econs of demographic change to World Bank, UN Research Inst. for Social Devt, UK Govt, House of Lords; Deputy Dir LSE 2004–07; Vice-Chancellor La Trobe Univ., Vic. 2007–11; Vice-Chancellor Univ. of Western Australia 2012–16; Dir, UniSuper (Australian higher educ. superannuation fund); mem. Advisory Council, Australian Research Council; fmr mem. Research Grants Bd of Econ. and Social Research Council, Council of Econ. History Soc., Governing Bd of Pensions Policy Inst.; Fellow, Acad. of Social Sciences 2001. *Publications:* numerous papers in professional journals on econ. and social devt of Britain since 1850 and econ. impact of population ageing.

JOHNSON, Peggy, BS; American electronics engineer and business executive; *Executive Vice-President, Business Development, Microsoft Corporation;* m. Eric Johnson; three c.; ed San Diego State Univ.; worked as engineer for General Electric's Mil. Electronics Div.; joined Qualcomm as software engineer within Qualcomm Wireless Business Solutions 1989, later Vice-Pres. of Tech., joined Qualcomm Consumer Products as Vice-Pres. of Business Devt 1997, later Vice-Pres. of Sales, served as Pres. of Qualcomm Internet Services and MediaFLO Technologies, later served as Exec. Vice-Pres. of Americas and India, and Exec. Vice-Pres. and Pres. of Global Market Devt, Qualcomm Technologies, Inc. until 2014, oversees Qualcomm Labs (wholly owned subsidiary), mem. Qualcomm's Exec. Cttee; Exec. Vice Pres., Business Devt Microsoft Corpn 2014–; recognized by several orgs, including Pinnacle Awards, Athena 2011, Most Influential Women in Wireless Awards, Fierce Wireless 2011, 100 Women Leaders in STEM 2012, Most Powerful Women Engineers in the World, Business Insider 2016. *Address:* Microsoft Corporation, 1 Microsoft Way Redmond, WA 98052-6399, USA (office). *Telephone:* (425) 882-8080 (office). *Fax:* (425) 706-7929 (office). *Website:* www.microsoft.com (office).

JOHNSON, Pierre Marc, BA, LLL, MD, FRSC; Canadian lawyer, physician and politician; *Of Counsel, Heenan Blaikie LLP;* b. 5 July 1946, Montréal, Québec; s. of

Daniel Johnson and Reine Johnson (née Gagné); one s. one d. from first m.; pnr Hélène de Kovachich; ed Collège Jean-Brébeuf, Montreal, Univ. of Montreal and Univ. of Sherbrooke; called to Québec Bar 1971; admitted Québec Coll. of Physicians and Surgeons 1976; elected to Québec Nat. Ass. 1976; mem. Nat. Exec. Council, Parti Québécois 1977–79, Pres. Parti Québécois 1985–87; Minister of Labour and Manpower, Québec 1977–80, of Consumer Affairs, Cooperatives and Financial Insts 1980–81, of Social Affairs 1981–84, of Justice, Attorney-Gen. and Minister Responsible for Canadian Intergovernmental Affairs 1984–85; Premier of Québec Oct.–Dec. 1985; Leader of Opposition, Québec Nat. Ass. 1985–87; Sr Counsel, Heenan Blaikie LLP (law firm), Montreal 1996–; Chair. Quartier de la Santé (health dist corpn) 2006–13; mem. Bd of Dirs Black Rock Metals, Muse Entertainment, Groupe Rozon; Chair. Foresight Cttee, Institut Véolia Environnement; fmr Dir, ACE Aviation Holdings Corpn, Air Canada, Holcim (Canada), Médicago Inc., Union for Conservation of Nature (Geneva), SNC lavalin, Unimedia; Advisor to UN Secrs on int. environmental conventions, to NAEC; Chief Negotiator and Advisor, Québec Govt on softwood lumber negociatons with USA and Canada-EU Comprehensive Econ. and Trade Agreement; Grand Officier, Ordre nat. du Québec; Grand Croix, Ordre de la Pléiade; Hon. PhD (Lyon). *Publication:* The Environment and NAFTA: implementing and understanding New Continental Law 1995. *Leisure interests:* swimming, travelling, music, cooking, wine tasting. *Address:* Heenan Blaikie LLP, 1250 René-Lévesque Blvd West, Suite 2500, Montréal, PQ H3B 4Y1, Canada (office). *Telephone:* (514) 846-2200 (office). *Fax:* (514) 921-1200 (office). *E-mail:* pjohnson@heenan.ca (office). *Website:* www.heenanblaikie.com (home).

JOHNSON, R. Milton, BBA; American business executive; *Chairman and CEO, HCA Inc.;* b. 15 Dec. 1956; m. Denice Johnson; one s. one d.; ed Belmont Univ.; certified CPA 1981; Accountant, Ernst & Young –1982; joined HCA Inc. 1982, later Head of co.'s Tax Dept, Sr Vice-Pres. and Controller, then Exec. Vice-Pres. and Chief Financial Officer, mem. Bd of Dirs 2009–, Pres. HCA Inc. 2011–14, CEO Jan. 2014–, Chair. Dec. 2014–; Chair. The HCA Foundation, Nashville Chamber of Commerce; mem. Bd, Center for Medical Interoperability, Nashville Health Care Council, United Way of Metropolitan Nashville; fmr mem. Bd of Trustees, Belmont Univ. *Address:* HCA Inc., 1 Park Plaza, Nashville, TN 37203, USA (office). *Telephone:* (615) 344-9551 (office). *Fax:* (615) 344-2266 (office). *E-mail:* r.johnson@hcahealthcare.com (office). *Website:* www.hcahealthcare.com (office).

JOHNSON, Robert L., BA, MA; American business executive; *Chairman, RLJ Companies;* b. 8 April 1946, Hickory, Miss.; s. of Archie Johnson and Edna Johnson; m. Sheila Johnson; two c.; ed Univ. of Illinois, Woodrow Wilson School, Princeton Univ.; held early positions at Washington, DC Urban League and Corpn for Public Broadcasting; Press Sec. to Hon. Walter E. Fauntroy, Congressional Del. from DC 1973–76; Vice-Pres. of Govt Relations, Nat. Cable & Telecommunications Asscn 1976–79; Founder, Chair. and CEO Black Entertainment TV (BET) 1980–2005 (since 1998 a subsidiary of Viacom), est. BET Pictures and BET Arabesque 1998, BET Interactive 2000; currently Chair. RLJ Cos, owns numerous US hotels and holds lottery licences on Antigua, Anguilla and St Kitts; majority owner, Charlotte Bobcats professional basketball team 2004–10; mem. Bd of Dirs KB Home, Lowe's Cos, Inc., Strayer Education, Business Council, Smithsonian Inst.'s Nat. Museum of African American History and Culture; mem. Deutsche Bank Advisory Cttee; mem. Bd of Govs Rock and Roll Hall of Fame, Brookings Inst.; Broadcasting & Cable Magazine Hall of Fame Award 1997, Cable & Telecommunications Asscn for Marketing (CTAM) Grand Tam Award, Cablevision magazine 20/20 Vision Award, National Asscn for the Advancement of Colored People (NAACP) Image Award, Nat. Women's Caucus Good Guys Award, Princeton Nat. Distinguished Alumni Award, Nat. Cable & Telecommunications Pres.'s Award. *Address:* RLJ Companies, 3 Bethesda Metro Center, Suite 1000, Bethesda, MD 20814, USA (office). *Telephone:* (301) 280-7700 (office). *Fax:* (301) 280-7750 (office). *Website:* www.rljcompanies.com (office).

JOHNSON, Robert Wood (Woody), IV; American business executive and diplomat; *Ambassador to United Kingdom;* b. 12 April 1947, New Brunswick; s. of Robert Wood Johnson III and Betty Johnson (née Wold); m. 1st Nancy Sale Johnson (divorced), three c. (one deceased); m. 2nd Suzanne Ircha Johnson; two s.; ed Univ. of Arizona; began career with various summer jobs at Johnson & Johnson, Inc. (family firm); Chair. and CEO, Johnson Co., Inc. (pvt. investment firm) 1978–; owner, Chair. and CEO New York Jets (NFL American football team) 2000–; Nat. Finance Chair., Jeb Bush's Presidential campaign 2016; Amb. to UK 2017–; mem. Council on Foreign Relations; Republican. *Address:* US Embassy, 24–32 Grosvenor Square, London, W1K 6AH, England (office); Johnson Company, Inc., 610 5th Avenue, Floor 2, New York, NY 10020, USA (office). *Telephone:* (20) 7499-9000 (US Embassy) (office); (212) 332-7500 (office). *E-mail:* uk.usembassy.gov (office).

JOHNSON, Ronald (Ron) Harold, BSB-Accounting; American business executive and politician; *Senator from Wisconsin;* b. 8 April 1955, Mankato, Minn.; s. of Dale Robert Johnson and Jeanette Elizabeth Johnson (née Thisius); m. Jane Curler 1977; three c.; ed Univ. of Minnesota; accountant Jostens; co-f. PACUR, LLC 1979, sole owner 1997, currently CEO; Senator from Wisconsin 2011–, mem. Cttee on Budget, Cttee on Appropriations, Cttee on Homeland Security and Governmental Affairs, Special Cttee on Aging; Republican. *Address:* 386 Russell Senate Office Building, Washington, DC 20510, USA (office). *Telephone:* (202) 224-5323 (office). *Website:* ronjohnson.senate.gov (office).

JOHNSON, Stephen L., BA, MS; American scientist and fmr government official; b. 21 March 1951, Washington, DC; ed Taylor Univ., George Washington Univ.; fmr Dir of Operations, Hazelton Labs Corpn, Litton Bionetics Inc.; held several positions at US Environmental Protection Agency (EPA), Washington, DC, including Dir Field Operations Div., Office of Pesticide Programs (OPP), Deputy Dir Hazard Evaluation Div., OPP, Exec. Sec. Scientific Advisory Panel for Fed. Insecticide, Fungicide and Rodenticide Act, Deputy Dir OPP 1997–99, Acting Deputy Asst Admin. 1999–2000, Deputy Asst Admin. 2000, Prin. Deputy Asst Admin., Acting Asst Admin. Office of Prevention, Pesticides and Toxic Substances 2001, Asst Admin. 2001–03, Acting Deputy Admin. EPA 2003–04, Deputy Admin. 2004–05, Acting Admin. Jan.–May 2005, Admin. 2005–09; mem. Bd of Dirs FlexEnergy Inc. 2010–, Scotts Miracle-Gro Co. 2010– Ener-Core, Inc. 2013–; mem. Bd of Trustees, Taylor Univ.; Presidential Rank Award 1997, 2001, EPA Excellence in Man. Award, Vice-Pres.'s Hammer Award, seven bronze medals, one silver medal.

JOHNSON, Suzanne M. Nora, BA, JD; American lawyer and business executive; ed Univ. of Southern Calif. and Harvard Law School; attorney with Simpson Thacher & Bartlett; served as law clerk on US Court of Appeals –1985; joined Goldman Sachs in 1985, Pnr 1992, Head of Global Healthcare Business in Investment Banking Div. 1994–2002, Head of Global Investment Research Div. 2002–07, Chair. Global Markets Inst. April 2004–07, Vice-Chair. Goldman Sachs Group, Inc. Nov. 2004–07; mem. bd mem. Aspen Global Leadership Network; mem. bd Carnegie Inst. of Washington, Univ. of Southern Calif., RAND Health, Technoserve, Women's World Banking; Trustee Brookings Inst., Council for Excellence in Govt. *Address:* 365 North Rockingham Ave, Los Angeles, CA 90049, USA (office).

JOHNSON, Thomas S., AB, MBA; American banking executive; b. 19 Nov. 1940, Racine, Wis.; s. of H. Norman Johnson and Jane Agnes McAvoy; m. Margaret Ann Werner 1970; two s. one d.; ed Trinity Coll., Harvard Business School; Head of Graduate Business Program and Instructor in Finance and Control, Ateneo de Manila Univ. 1964–66; Special Asst to Controller, Dept of Defense 1966–69; with Chemical Bank and Chemical Banking Corpn 1969–89, Exec. Vice-Pres. 1979, Sr Exec. Vice-Pres. 1981, Pres. 1983–89; Pres. Corp. and Mfrs Hanover Trust Co. 1989–91, Olympia and York Devts Ltd 1992; Chair., Pres. and CEO GreenPoint Financial Corpn, GreenPoint Savings Bank, Flushing, New York 1993–2004, then mem. Bd of Dirs North Fork Bankcorporation Inc. (acquired GreenPoint 2004); mem. Bd of Dirs Alleghany Corpn, R.R. Donnelley & Sons Co., The Phoenix Cos Inc., Lower Manhattan Devt Corpn; fmr Chair. US-Japan Foundation, now Chair. Emer.; fmr Chair. Union Theological Seminary, Harvard Business School Club of Greater New York; mem. Bd of Trustees Inst. of Int. Educ. 1989–, Chair. 2003–; mem. Council on Foreign Relations; fmr mem. Group of Thirty; Trustee, Trinity Coll., National 9/11 Memorial & Museum Foundation; fmr Trustee, Cancer Research Inst. of America, Asia Soc.; mem. Business Cttee, Museum of Modern Art, Consultative Group on Int. Econ. and Monetary Affairs.

JOHNSON, Timothy (Tim) Peter, MA, JD; American lawyer and politician; b. 28 Dec. 1946, Canton, SDak; s. of Vandal Johnson and Ruth Ljostveit; m. Barbara Brooks 1969; two s. one d.; ed Univ. of South Dakota and Michigan State Univ.; called to the Bar, SDak 1975, US Dist Court, SDak 1976; fiscal analyst, Legis. Fiscal Agency, Lansing, Mich. 1971–72; pvt. practice, Vermillion, SDak 1975–86; mem. SDak House of Reps 1978–82, SDak Senate 1982–86; mem. US House of Reps, Washington, DC 1987–97, Regional Deputy Whip 1991–94; Senator from South Dakota 1997–Jan. 2015 (retd), Chair. Banking, Housing and Urban Affairs Cttee, mem. Appropriations Cttee, Energy and Natural Resources Cttee, Indian Affairs Cttee; Democrat; Outstanding Citizen Award, Vermillion Jaycees 1979, first recipient of Billie Sutton Award for Legis. Achievement, South Dakota Democratic Party 1983, nat. awards from Nat. Farmers Union, Disabled American Veterans, Mothers Against Drunk Driving.

JOHNSON, Wesley Momo, MBA, CPA; Liberian politician and diplomatist; b. 27 May 1944, Monrovia; m. Isabella Cassell Johnson; eight c.; ed Monrovia Coll., St Francis Coll., Brooklyn, NY, Long Island Univ., NY, USA; represented Liberia in 100m and 200m sprints at Summer Olympic Games, Tokyo 1964; Baptist Licentiate and Deacon, Zion Grove Baptist Church, Brewerville; fmr Auditor, Old Colony Newport Nat. Bank, Providence, RI, USA; Auditor, Treasury Dept of Liberia (now Ministry of Finance) 1968–72; Sr Bookkeeper (Class-I) and Brokerage Man., Skyline Shipping Co. 1972–77; Founding mem. and Vice-Chair. Progressive Alliance of Liberia 1973, Progressive People's Party 1980; Founding mem. United People's Party 1984, Chair. 1999–; fmr Amb. to Egypt, Consul Gen. to New York 1981; mem. Interim Legis. Ass. 1990–94, Chair. House Standing Cttee on Banking and Currency, Cttee on Ways, Means, Finance and Maritime Affairs, Co-Chair. Cttee on Rules, Cttee on Order and Executive, Sec.-Gen. Liberian Parl. Union; Vice-Chair. Nat. Transitional Govt 2003–07; Amb. to UK 2007–13; led Liberian del. to several int. confs including 36th Gen. Ass. of UN (Chair. Cttee on Disarmament) 1981, African Pacific Caribbean Comm., Rosenberg 1992, mem. del. to Inter-Parl. Union, New Delhi, India; Partner, Nimley & Assocs, CPA Inc.; Lecturer, Univ. of Liberia, United Methodist Univ., AME Zion Univ. Coll.; mem. numerous accounting firms and financial insts, including Liberian Certified Public Accountants, Inst. of Certified Internal Auditors, Inc., Atlanta, Ga, American Banking Asscn, RI, MBA Executive, New York, USA. *Leisure interests:* playing soccer, athletics, reading, teaching, hard work. *Address:* Ministry of Foreign Affairs, Mamba Point, PO Box 10-9002, 1000 Monrovia 10, Liberia (office). *Telephone:* 226763 (office). *Website:* www.mofa.gov.lr (office).

JOHNSON, W(illiam) Bruce, BA, MBA, JD; American business executive; ed Duke Univ.; spent 16 years at Colgate-Palmolive Co. in various roles; worked as a man. consultant at Booz Allen & Hamilton and at Arthur Andersen & Co. 1977–1982; Dir Org. and Systems, Carrefour SA 1998–2003; Sr Vice-Pres., Supply Chain and Operations, Kmart 2003–05, later apptd Exec. Vice-Pres., Supply Chain and Operations for combined co. following merger with Sears, Chair. 2005–06, took on store operations 2006–08, Pres. and Interim CEO Sears Holdings Corpn 2008–11, mem. Bd of Dirs 2010–, Exec. Vice-Pres. Off-Mall Businesses and Supply Chain March–Sept. 2011, Exec. Vice-Pres. Off-Mall Businesses Sept. 2011–12, mem. Bd of Dirs, Pres. and CEO Sears Hometown and Outlet Stores, Inc. 2012–15 (retd); worked as a consultant at Duracell Inc. 2016–17.

JOHNSON-LAIRD, Philip Nicholas, PhD, FRS, FBA; British/American psychologist and academic; b. 12 Oct. 1936, Leeds, Yorks., England, UK; s. of Eric Johnson-Laird and Dorothy Johnson-Laird (née Blackett); m. Maureen Mary Sullivan 1959; one s. one d.; ed Culford School, Univ. Coll., London; left school aged 15 and worked as quantity surveyor and in other jobs before univ.; Asst Lecturer, Dept of Psychology, Univ. Coll., London 1966, Lecturer 1967–73, Fellow, 1994–; Visiting mem. Inst. for Advanced Study, Princeton, NJ, USA 1971–72; Reader in Experimental Psychology, Univ. of Sussex 1973, Prof. 1978–82; Asst Dir MRC Applied Psychology Unit, Cambridge 1982–89; Fellow, Darwin Coll. Cambridge 1984–89; Visiting Fellow, Cognitive Science, Stanford Univ., USA 1980, Visiting Prof. of Psychology 1985; Visiting Prof. of Psychology, Princeton Univ., USA 1986, Prof. 1989–94, Stuart Prof. of Psychology 1994–2012, Prof. Emer. 2012–; Visiting Scholar, Psychology, New York Univ. 2012–; mem. NAS, American Philosophical

Soc.; Dr hc (Gothenburg) 1983; Laurea hc (Padua) 1997, (Palermo) 2005, (Univ. Ca' Foscari, Venice) 2008; Hon. DSc (Univ. of Dublin Trinity Coll.) 2000, (Sussex) 2007; Hon. DPsych (Universidad Nacional de Educación a Distancia, Madrid) 2000, (Ghent) 2002; Rosa Morison Memorial Medal and James Sully Scholarship, Univ. Coll. London, Spearman Medal, British Psychological Soc. 1974, Pres.'s Award 1985, Medaglia d'Onore, Univ. of Florence 1989, Fyssen Foundation Int. Prize 2003, Mind and Brain Prize, Univ. of Turin 2004, William James Fellow, Assn of Psychological Science 2010. *Publications:* Thinking and Reasoning (co-ed.) 1968, Psychology of Reasoning (with P. C. Wason) 1972, Language and Perception (with G. A. Miller) 1976, Thinking (co-ed.) 1977, Mental Models 1983, The Computer and the Mind 1988, Deduction (with R. M. J. Byrne) 1992, Human and Machine Thinking 1993, How We Reason 2006; numerous articles in psychological journals; reviews. *Leisure interests:* arts, composing music, talking and arguing. *Address:* Department of Psychology, New York University, 6 Washington Place, New York, NY 10003, USA (office). *E-mail:* pjl303@nyu.edu (office); phil@princeton.edu (office). *Website:* www.psych.nyu.edu/psychology.html (office); mentalmodels.princeton.edu (office).

JOHNSON-SIRLEAF, Ellen, BBA, MPA; Liberian politician and fmr head of state; b. 29 Oct. 1938; four s.; ed Coll. of West Africa, Monrovia and Madison Business Coll., Univ. of Colorado, Harvard Univ., USA; Asst Minister of Finance 1972–78, Deputy Minister of Finance 1979–80; Sr Loan Officer, IBRD, Washington, DC 1973–77, 1980–81; sentenced to ten years' imprisonment for speech that was critical of mil. ruler Samuel Doe; briefly detained twice in prison before fleeing country; fmr Pres. Liberian Bank for Devt Investment; Vice-Pres. Citibank Regional Office for Africa, Nairobi 1982–85; Vice-Pres. and mem. Bd Dirs Equator Holders, Hong Kong Equator Bank Ltd, Washington, DC –1992; Asst Admin. UNDP and Dir Regional Bureau for Africa 1992–97; Chair. and CEO Kormah Investment and Devt Corpn; fmr Leader Unity Party (UP), Presidential Cand. 1997, expelled from party 2018; charged with treason by Taylor regime and forced into political exile; Chair. Open Soc. Inst. West Africa (part of Soros Foundation Network); External Adviser, UN Econ. Comm. for Africa; mem. Advisory Bd Modern Africa Growth and Investment Co.; Sr Adviser and W/Cen. Africa Rep. of Modern Africa Fund Mans; Founder Measuagoon (Liberian non-governmental org.); rep. Liberia on bds of IMF, IBRD and African Devt Bank; selected by OAU to investigate Rwanda genocide 1999; Pres. of Liberia (world's first elected black female pres. and Africa's first elected female head of state) 2005–17; Chair. Comm. on Good Governance (Liberia) 2004–05; Founding mem. Int. Inst. for Women in Political Leadership; mem. Bd Dirs Synergos Inst. 1988–99; mem. Advisory Bd Brenthurst Foundation 2018–, IMF 2018–; Distinguished Fellow, Claus M. Halle Inst. for Global Learning, Emory Univ. 2006; Grand Commdr, Star of Africa Redemption of Liberia; Commdr de l'Ordre du Togo; Franklin Delano Roosevelt Freedom of Speech Award 1988, Ralph Bunche Int. Leadership Award, Common Ground Award 2006, Laureate of the Africa Prize for Leadership for the Sustainable End of Hunger 2006, Bishop John T. Walker Distinguished Humanitarian Service Award, Africare 2007, Nobel Peace Prize (jtly) for "non-violent struggle for the safety of women and for women's rights to full participation in peace-building work" 2011, Indira Gandhi Prize 2013, Ibrahim Prize for African Leadership 2017. *Publications:* From Disaster to Development 1991, The Outlook for Commercial Bank Lending to Sub-Saharan Africa 1992, Women, War and Peace: The Independent Experts' Assessment on the Impact of Armed Conflict on Women and Women's Role in Peace-building (co-author) (project of UNIFEM) 2002, This Child Will be Great: Memoir of a Remarkable Life by Africa's First Woman President 2009. *Address:* c/o Unity Party (UP), 86 Broad St, Monrovia, Liberia (office).

JOHNSSON, Anders B., LLM; Swedish international organization official; b. 1948, Lund; m.; three c.; ed Univs of Lund and New York; mem. staff UNHCR, posts in Honduras, Pakistan, Sudan and Viet Nam, then Prin. Legal Adviser to High Commr, Geneva 1976–91; Under-Sec.-Gen. IPU 1991–94, Deputy Sec.-Gen. and Legal Adviser 1994–98, Sec.-Gen. 1998–June 2014. *Address:* c/o Inter-Parliamentary Union, CP 330, 1218 Le Grand-Saconnex/ Geneva, Switzerland.

JOHNSSON, Finn, BSc, MSc, MBA; Swedish business executive; b. 28 Feb. 1946, Gothenburg; ed Stockholm School of Econs; worked for Machine Div., Swedish Match, fmr Pres. Swedish Match Europe and Swedish Match Asia; fmr Pres. Arenco Machine Co., USA; fmr Pres. Tarkett AB; fmr Exec. Vice-Pres. Stora AB; fmr Pres. Industri AB Euroc; Deputy Chief Exec. and COO United Distillers, UK –1998; Pres. and CEO Mölnlycke Health Care AB –2005, Chair. 2005–10; mem. Bd of Dirs AB Volvo 1998–2010, Chair. 2004–10, also Chair. Remuneration Cttee; Chair. Ovako Steel 2010–16; Chair. Luvata oy (fmrly Outokumpu Copper Products Oy), Thomas Concrete Group AB, Thomas Concrete Industries Inc., MVI Ltd, KappAhl Holding AB, Region Väst Handelsbanken, City Airline AB, Thomas Concrete Group, KappAhl AB, Handelsbanken Western Sweden Region, Bilisten I Sverige AB, Maersk Medical A and S, Kalmar Industries AB, EFG European Furniture Group AB, Geveko AB 2004–, DSV Miljø A/S 2012–; Chair. Supervisory Bd Unomedical Holding A/s; mem. Bd of Dirs Guinness 1994, Skanska AB 1998–2011, AB IndustriVärden 2000–, Bilisten, Facile AB, Unomedical Holding A/s 2003–, Geodis Wilson, Perstorp AB, Indutrade; Dr hc (Gothenburg).

JOHNSTON, David Albert Lloyd, BJuris; Australian lawyer and politician; b. 14 Feb. 1956, Perth; m. Toni Hodge; three c.; ed Univ. of Western Australia; worked for 20 years as barrister and solicitor, Kalgoorlie and Perth; mem. Univ. of WA Liberal Club 1974–79; mem. Senate for WA 2001–16; Shadow Minister for Resources and Energy 2007–08, for Tourism 2007–08, for Defence 2008–13; Minister for Justice and Customs March–Dec. 2007, Minister of Defence 2013–14; Defence Export Advocate 2018–; mem. Liberal Party of Australia 1986– (Pres. Kalgoorlie/Boulder Branch 1986–87 Mt Pleasant Branch 2001–), Pres. Liberal Party (WA) 1997–2001. *Leisure interests:* cycling, sailing. *Address:* c/o PO Box 6100, Senate, Parliament House, Canberra, ACT 2600, Australia. *Website:* www.aph.gov.au.

JOHNSTON, David Lloyd, CC, LLB; Canadian legal scholar and university administrator; b. 28 June 1941, Sudbury, Ont.; s. of Lloyd Johnston and Dorothy Stonehouse; m. Sharon Downey 1964; five d.; ed Sault Collegiate Inst., Sault Ste. Marie, Ont., Harvard Univ., Univ. of Cambridge and Queen's Univ., Kingston; Asst Prof., Faculty of Law, Queen's Univ., Kingston 1966–68; Asst Prof. Faculty of Law, Univ. of Toronto 1968–69, Assoc. Prof. 1969–72, Prof. 1972–74; Dean and Prof., Faculty of Law, Univ. of W Ont. 1974–79; Prof. of Law, McGill Univ. 1979–94, Prin. and Vice-Chancellor 1979–94; Pres. and mem. Bd of Governors, Univ. of Waterloo 1999–2010; Gov.-Gen. of Canada 2010–17; Pres. Harvard Univ. Bd of Overseers 1997–98; recipient of 12 hon. degrees. *Publications include:* Computers and the Law 1968, Canadian Securities Regulation 1977, The Law of Business Associations (with R. Forbes) 1979, Canadian Companies and the Stock Exchange 1980, If Québec Goes: The Real Cost of Separation (with Marcel Côté) 1995, Getting Canada On Line: Understanding the Information Highway (co-author) 1995, Cyberlaw 1997, Communications Law of Canada 1999; numerous articles in academic journals. *Leisure interests:* jogging, skiing. *Address:* R. R. #1, Saint Clements, ON N0B 2M0, Canada (home). *Telephone:* (519) 699-4877 (home).

JOHNSTON, Hon. Donald James, PC, OC, QC, BA, BCL; Canadian politician, lawyer, international civil servant, consultant and academic; *Chairman, McCall MacBain Foundation;* b. 26 June 1936, Cumberland, Ont.; s. of Wilbur Austin Johnston and Florence Jean Moffat Tucker; m. Heather Bell Maclaren; four d.; ed McGill Univ. and Univ. of Grenoble; joined Stikeman, Elliott (int. law firm) 1961; subsequent f. own law firm, Johnston, Heenan & Blaikie, Montreal 1973, Counsel, Heenan, Blaikie 1988–96, Heenan Blaikie LLP 2006–; taught fiscal law at McGill Univ. 1963–76; MP 1978–88; Pres. Treasury Bd 1980–82; Minister for Econ. Devt and Minister of State for Science and Tech. 1982–83; Minister of State for Econ. Devt and Tech. 1983–84; Minister of Justice and Attorney-Gen. June–Sept. 1984; elected Pres. Liberal Party of Canada 1990, re-elected 1992; Sec.-Gen. OECD 1996–2006; Chair. McCall MacBain Foundation, Geneva 2006–; Chair. Int. Risk Governance Council (IRGC), Geneva 2006–09; Visiting Prof., Yonsei Univ., Seoul, S Korea 2006–09; Grand Cordon, Order of the Rising Sun (Japan) 2006, Commdr's Cross with Star, Order of Merit (Hungary) 2006, Order of the White Double Cross (Slovakia) 2006, Grand Croix, Ordre de Léopold II (Belgium) 2007, Officier, Légion d'honneur 2012; four Hon. LLD degrees in econs and law; Gold Medallist, McGill Univ. 1958. *Films:* As Exec. Producer: Seizure 1974. *Publications:* Up the Hill (political memoirs) 1986; several books and numerous articles on taxation, law and public affairs in professional journals. *Leisure interests:* tennis, piano, writing. *Address:* Heenan Blaikie LLP, 1250 René-Lévesque Blvd West, Suite 2500, Montreal, PQ H3B 4Y1, Canada (office); 537 Courser Road, Glensutton, PQ D0E 2K0 (home). *Telephone:* (514) 846-2280 (office); (450) 538-5124 (home). *Fax:* (514) 921-1280 (office); (450) 538-0304 (home). *E-mail:* djohnston@heenan.ca (office); donaldjames.johnston@gmail.com (home). *Website:* www.heenanblaikie.com (office).

JOHNSTON, Jennifer; Irish writer; b. 12 Jan. 1930, Dublin; d. of Denis Johnston and Shelah Richards; m. 1st Ian Smyth; two s. two d.; m. 2nd David Gilliland (died 2019); ed Park House School, Dublin, Trinity Coll., Dublin; mem. Aosdána; Hon. Fellow, Trinity Coll., Dublin; Hon. DLitt (New Univ. of Ulster, Queen's Univ., Belfast, Trinity Coll., Dublin, Nat. Univ. of Ireland); Giles Cooper Award 1989, Premio Giuseppe Acerbi 2003, Irish PEN Award 2006, Irish Book Awards Lifetime Achievement Award 2012. *Plays:* The Porch, The Invisible Man, The Desert Lullaby, Moonlight and Music; several radio and TV programmes. *Publications:* novels: The Captains and the Kings 1972, The Gates 1973, How Many Miles to Babylon? 1974, Shadows on Our Skin 1977, The Old Jest (Whitbread Prize 1980) 1979, The Christmas Tree 1981, The Railway Station Man 1985, The Invisible Man 1986, Fool's Sanctuary 1988, The Invisible Worm 1992, The Illusionist 1995, Two Moons 1998, The Gingerbread Woman 2000, This is Not a Novel 2003, Grace and Truth 2005, Foolish Mortals 2008, Truth or Fiction 2009, Shadowstory 2011, Fathers and Son 2012, A Sixpenny Song 2013; plays include: The Nightingale and Not the Lark 1981, Indian Summer 1983, The Porch 1986, The Invisible Man 1986, The Desert Lullaby 1996, The Christmas Tree 2015. *Leisure interests:* reading, theatre, cinema. *Address:* Brook Hall, Culmore Road, Derry, BT48 8JE, Northern Ireland (home); c/o David Higham Associates Ltd, 6th Floor, Waverley House, 7–12 Noel Street, London, W1F 8GQ, England (office). *Telephone:* (28) 7135-1297 (home); (20) 7434-5900 (office). *Fax:* (20) 7437-1072 (office). *E-mail:* dha@davidhigham.co.uk (office). *Website:* www.davidhigham.co.uk (office).

JOHNSTON, J(ohn) Bennett, JD; American lawyer, consultant and fmr politician; b. 10 June 1932, Shreveport, La; s. of J. Bennett Johnston; m. Mary Gunn; two s. two d.; ed Byrd High School, Washington and Lee Univ., US Mil. Acad., Louisiana State Univ. Law School; mil. service in Judge Advocate Gen. Corps La; La State Senator 1968–72; Senator from La 1972–96, Chair. Democratic Senatorial Campaign Cttee 1975–76, mem. Senate Cttee on Energy and Natural Resources, on Appropriations, Senate Budget Cttee, mem. Senate Bldg Cttee; CEO Johnston & Assocs LLC 1996–2008; formed strategic alliance with Steptoe and Johnson LLP (law firm) 2008 and now provides advisory services; Chair. American Iranian Council; mem. Bd of Dirs Consortium for Advanced Simulation of Light Water Reactors 2010–; fmr mem. Bd of Dirs Freeport-McMoRan Copper & Gold, Inc., Chevron, URS, Columbia Energy Group, US China Business Council; fmr Vice-Pres. US Pacific Econ. Cooperation Council; Democrat; Order of the Coif, Louisiana State Univ.; Hon. DIur (Louisiana State Univ., Tulane Univ., Centenary Coll., Univ. of Louisiana, Southern Univ., Xavier Univ., Louisiana Tech. Univ.); National Parks Conservation Association Centennial Leadership Award 2010. *Leisure interest:* tennis. *Address:* Steptoe and Johnson LLP, 1330 Connecticut Avenue, NW, Washington, DC 20036, USA (office). *Telephone:* (202) 659-8400 (office). *Fax:* (202) 659-1340 (office). *E-mail:* bjohnston@johnstondc.com (office). *Website:* www.steptoe.com (office).

JOHNSTON, Lawrence (Larry) R., BBA; American retail executive; ed Stetson Univ.; began career as Man. Trainee, Gen. Electric Co. 1972, held various man. positions 1979–84, Merchandising Man., Washington, DC 1984, later Regional Man., Cleveland, Ohio, Corp. Vice-Pres. 1989, Vice-Pres. Sales and Distribution, GE Appliances, Pres. and CEO GE Medical Systems Europe 1997–99, Sr Vice-Pres. 1999–2001, Pres. and CEO GE Appliances 1999–2001; Chair., CEO and Pres. Albertson's Inc. 2001–06; mem. Bd of Dirs Home Depot Inc. 2004–07; fmr mem. Bd of Dirs World Food Forum, Food Marketing Inst.

JOHNSTON, Ronald John, OBE, MA, PhD, FBA; British geographer and academic; *Professor of Geography, University of Bristol;* b. 30 March 1941, Swindon, Wilts.; s. of Henry Louis Johnston and Phyllis Joyce Johnston (née Liddiard); m. Rita Brennan 1963; one s. one d.; ed The Commonweal Co. Secondary Grammar School, Swindon, Univ. of Manchester, Monash Univ., Australia; Teaching Fellow, then Lecturer, Dept of Geography, Monash Univ. 1964–66;

Lecturer then Reader, Dept of Geography, Univ. of Canterbury, NZ 1967–74; Prof. of Geography, Univ. of Sheffield 1974–92, Pro-Vice-Chancellor for Academic Affairs 1989–92; Vice-Chancellor Univ. of Essex 1992–95; Prof. of Geography, Univ. of Bristol 1995–; Ed. New Zealand Geographer 1969–74, Proceedings of the British Acad. 2007–; Co-Ed. Environment and Planning 1979–2005, Progress in Human Geography 1979–2007; Hon. DUniv (Essex) 1996; Hon. LLD (Monash) 1999; Hon. DLitt (Sheffield) 2002, (Bath) 2005; Murchison Award, Royal Geographical Soc. (RGS) 1984, RGS Victoria Medal 1990, Hons Award for Distinguished Contribs, Asscn of American Geographers 1991, Prix Vautrin Lud 1999, Lifetime Achievement Award, Asscn of American Geographers 2010, Political Communicator of the Year Award, Political Studies Asscn 2011. *Publications:* author or co-author of more than 50 books, including Geography and Geographers, Philosophy and Human Geography, City and Society, The Geography of English Politics, A Nation Dividing?, Bell-ringing: The English Art of Change-Ringing, An Atlas of Bells, Putting Voters in their Place, Money and Electoral Politics; ed. or co-ed. of more than 50 books, including Geography and the Urban Environment (six vols), The Dictionary of Human Geography; author or co-author of more than 1,000 articles in academic journals and book chapters. *Leisure interests:* bell-ringing, walking. *Address:* School of Geographical Sciences, University of Bristol, Bristol, BS8 1SS, England (office). *Telephone:* (117) 928-9116 (office). *Fax:* (117) 928-7878 (office). *E-mail:* r.johnston@bris.ac.uk (office). *Website:* www.bris.ac.uk/geography/people/ron-j-johnston (office).

JOHNSTONE, D(onald) Bruce, Jr, PhD; American university administrator and academic; *Distinguished Service Professor of Higher and Comparative Education Emeritus and Director, International Comparative Finance and Accessibility Project, University at Buffalo;* b. 13 Jan. 1941, Minneapolis, Minn.; s. of Donald Bruce Johnstone and Florence Elliott Johnstone; m. Gail Eberhardt 1965; one s. one d.; ed Harvard Univ. and Univ. of Minnesota; Admin. Asst to Senator Walter F. Mondale (q.v.) 1969–71; Project Specialist, Ford Foundation 1971–72; Exec. Asst to Pres. and Vice-Pres., Univ. of Pennsylvania 1972–77, Adjunct Assoc. Prof. of Educ. 1976–79, Vice-Pres. for Admin. 1977–79; Pres. State Univ. Coll., Buffalo 1979–88; Chancellor State Univ. of New York 1988–94; Univ. Prof. of Higher and Comparative Educ., Univ. at Buffalo 1994–2006, now Distinguished Service Prof. Emer. and Dir Int. Comparative Finance and Accessibility Project, Distinguished Scholar Leader, Fulbright New Century Scholars Program 2006–07; Dr hc (D'Youville Coll.) 1995, (Towson State Univ.) 1995, (Calif. State Univ.) 1997; Golden Quill Award, Nat. Asscn of Student Financial Aid Admins. *Publications:* Financing Higher Education: Cost-Sharing In International Perspective; other works on the econs and man. of higher educ. in domestic and int. perspectives. *Leisure interests:* writing, wilderness canoeing, wildflower botany. *Address:* 428E Baldy Hall, University at Buffalo, Buffalo, NY 12246 (office); 284 Rivermist Drive, Buffalo, NY 14202, USA (home). *Telephone:* (716) 847-2159 (office). *Fax:* (716) 645-2481 (office). *E-mail:* dbj@buffalo.edu (office). *Website:* www.gse.buffalo.edu/about/directory/faculty/2031 (office).

JOHOR, HRH The Sultan of; Sultan Ibrahim Ismail ibni al-Marhum Sultan Mahmud Iskandar; Malaysian ruler; *Sultan of Johor;* b. 22 Nov. 1958, Johor Bahru; s. of Tuanku Mahmood Iskandar ibni al-Marhum Sultan Ismail and Hajjah Kalsom binti Abdullah (née Josephine Ruby Trevorrow); m. Raja Zarith Sofiah al-Marhum 1982; five s. one d.; ed Sekolah Agama Bukit Zaharah, Sekolah Agama Air Molek, Johor Bahru (religious schools), Trinity Grammar School, Australia, Kota Tinggi army training centre, Fort Benning and Fort Bragg army bases, USA; fmr Deputy Commdr, Johor Mil. Force; named Tengku Makota (Crown Prince) 1981–2010, Regent 1984–89; installed as Sultan of Johor 23 Jan. 2010– (coronation 23 March 2015); f. Kembara Mahkota Johor (annual royal motorcycle tour event) 2001. *Leisure interests:* polo, tennis, wind-surfing, shooting, motoring. *Address:* Istana Besar, 8000 Johor Bahru, Johor, Malaysia (office).

JOJIMA, Koriki, BA; Japanese politician; b. (Masamitsu Jojima), 1 Jan. 1947, Yanagawa, Fukuoka; ed Faculty of Agric., Univ. of Tokyo; Pres. Ajinomoto Workers' Union for 25 years; fmr Head of Japan Food Industry Workers' Union Council; then served as mem. Council, Japan Productivity Centre for Socio-Econ. Devt; Founding mem. Democratic Party of Japan (DPJ); mem. Parl. as mem. House of Reps for Kanagawa No. 10 1996–2012, Chair. DPJ Diet Affairs Cttee; fmr mem. Cttee on Fundamental Nat. Policies; Minister of Finance Oct.–Dec. 2012. *Address:* Democratic Party of Japan, 1-11-1 Nagata-cho, Chiyoda-ku, Tokyo 100-0014, Japan (office). *Telephone:* (3) 3595-9988 (office). *Fax:* (3) 3595-7318 (office). *Website:* www.dpj.or.jp (office); www.jojima.net.

JOKLIK, Wolfgang Karl (Bill), DPhil; American microbiologist and academic; *James B. Duke Distinguished Professor Emeritus, Department of Molecular Genetics and Microbiology, Duke University;* b. 16 Nov. 1926, Vienna, Austria; s. of Karl F. Joklik and Helene Joklik (née Giessl); m. 1st Judith V. Nicholas 1955 (died 1975); one s. one d.; m. 2nd Patricia H. Downey 1977; ed Sydney Univ. and Univ. of Oxford; Research Fellow, ANU 1954–56, Fellow 1957–62; Assoc. Prof. of Cell Biology, Albert Einstein Coll. of Medicine, New York 1962–65, Siegfried Ullman Prof. 1966–68; Prof. and Chair. Dept of Microbiology and Immunology, Duke Univ. 1968–92 (Chair. Emer. 1993–96), James B. Duke Distinguished Prof. 1972–96, James B. Duke Distinguished Prof. Emer. 1996–; Pres. Virology Div. American Soc. for Microbiology 1966–69; Chair. Virology Study Section NIH 1973–75; Pres. American Medical School Microbiology Chairs' Asscn 1979, American Soc. for Virology 1982–83; Ed.-in-Chief Virology 1975–93, Microbiological Reviews 1991–95; Assoc. Ed. Journal of Biological Chem. 1978–88; mem. NAS, mem. NAS Inst. of Medicine; Humboldt Prize 1986, ICN Int. Prize in Virology 1992, Distinguished Faculty Award, Duke Univ. Medical Center Alumni Asscn 2005. *Publications:* contrib. to and sr ed. specialist books, including Zinsser Microbiology, Principles of Animal Virology, The Reoviridae; more than 200 articles in specialist journals. *Leisure interests:* travel, photography, music, golf, tennis and squash. *Address:* Department of Molecular Genetics and Microbiology, Box 3020, Duke University Medical Center, Durham, NC 27710, USA. *Website:* mgm.duke.edu (office).

JOKSIMOVIĆ, Jadranka; Serbian politician; *Minister of European Integration;* b. 26 Jan. 1978, Belgrade, Socialist Repub. of Serbia, Socialist Fed. Repub. of Yugoslavia; ed ALFA Univ., Belgrade; worked for Srpska Radikalna Stranka (Serbian Radical Party) 2005–07; Adviser to Napred Srbijo (Forward Serbia) Parl. Group, People's Ass. (parl.) 2008–09; Ed. Zemunskih novina (newspaper) 2009–12; mem. People's Ass. (Srpska Napredna Stranka—SNS—Serbian Progressive Party) 2012–; Minister without Portfolio, in charge of European Integration 2014–17, Minister of European Integration 2017–; co-f. SNS 2008, mem. Main SNS Bd and Presidency. *Address:* Ministry of European Integration, 11000 Belgrade, Nemanjina 34, Serbia (office). *Telephone:* (11) 3061100 (office). *Fax:* (11) 3061110 (office). *E-mail:* office@seio.gov.rs (office). *Website:* www.seio.gov.rs (office).

JOLEVSKI, Zoran, BEcons, MSc, PhD; Macedonian diplomatist and politician; b. 16 July 1959, Skopje; m. Suzana Jolevska; two s.; ed Univ. of Sts Cyril and Methodius, Skopje, Inst. of Social Studies, The Hague, Netherlands; long career in Ministry of Foreign Affairs (MFA), including as officer responsible for preparing documents for observer status of Repub. of Macedonia in GATT, Desk Officer for UK and Germany 1988–92; Sec. to Coordination Group on Fmr Yugoslavia Succession Issues 1992–94; Sec., Perm. Mission of Macedonia to WTO and UN, Geneva 1994–98; Chief Adviser to Minister of Economy on WTO accession, MFA, Deputy Nat. Coordinator on Humanitarian Issues for Kosovo refugee crises, WTO accession and other int. trade and financial affairs 1998–99; Sec.-Gen., Cabinet of Pres. of Macedonia 2000–04; Chief of Party 'WTO Compliance Activity', USAID Funded Project, Booz Allen & Hamilton 2004–06, 'Macedonian Business Environment Activity', USAID Funded Project 2006; Econ. and Foreign Policy Adviser to Nikola Gruevski, Leader of VMRO-DPMNE party and Prime Minister; Amb. to USA 2007–14; Minister of Defence 2014–17; Pres. Man. Bd Prilep 2006–; Sec. to Macedonian del. to Int. Conf. on Succession of the Fmr Yugoslavia 1992–94; Deputy Negotiator and Chief Adviser to Govt of Macedonia for accession to WTO 1999–2004; mem. Bd Center for Strategic Research, Macedonian Acad. of Sciences and Art; mem. Man. Bd Alumina 2001–02, Skopje Fair 2000–01, SEVUS 2005–, Airports Makedonija 2006–; mem. Cttee 'E-Macedonia for All' under auspices of Pres. of Macedonia 2000–04; Pres. Int. Foundation Boris Trajkovski 2004–05; mem. Lions Centar, Skopje 2005–; Founder and Pres. Inst. for Econ. Strategies and Int. Affairs – Ohrid 2006–. *Publications:* Succession of States: The Case of Ex-Yugoslavia 1993, Multinational Corporations: Challenge of the Contemporary Economy 1997, The World Trading System 2006; Chief Ed.: Report on the Foreign Trade of Macedonia 2005, Report on the Foreign Trade of Macedonia 2006, Mandate for Leadership: Principles for Governing Macedonia 2006–2010 2006; several published articles. *Address:* c/o Ministry of Defence, 1000 Skopje, North Macedonia (office).

JOLIE, Angelina, DCMG; American actress and philanthropist; b. 4 June 1975, Los Angeles, Calif.; d. of Jon Voight (q.v.) and Marcheline Bertrand; m. 1st Jonny Lee Miller 1996 (divorced 1999); m. 2nd Billy Bob Thornton 2000 (divorced 2003); m. 3rd Brad Pitt 2014; one s. two d. (with Brad Pitt) two adopted s. one adopted d.; ed Lee Strasberg Inst., New York Univ.; apptd Goodwill Amb. by UNHCR 2001–; apptd Visiting Prof. in Practice, Centre for Women, Peace and Security, LSE 2016; mem. Council on Foreign Relations 2007–; f. Preventing Sexual Violence Initiative (PSVI) 2012; Hon. GCMG (UK) 2014; UN Global Humanitarian Action Award 2005, Jean Hersholt Humanitarian Award 2013. *Films include:* Lookin' to Get Out 1982, Cyborg II: Glass Shadow 1995, Hackers 1995, Foxfire 1996, Mojave Moon 1996, Love is All There Is 1996, True Women 1997, George Wallace (Golden Globe 1998) 1997, Playing God 1997, Hell's Kitchen 1998, Gia (Golden Globe 1999, Screen Actors Guild Award 1999) 1998, Playing by Heart 1999, Girl, Interrupted (Acad. Award for Best Supporting Actress 2000) 1999, Lara Croft: Tomb Raider 2001, Original Sin 2001, Life or Something Like It 2002, Lara Croft Tomb Raider: Cradle of Life 2003, Beyond Borders 2003, Taking Lives 2004, Shark Tale (voice) 2004, Sky Captain and the World of Tomorrow 2004, Alexander 2004, Mr & Mrs Smith 2005, The Good Shepherd 2006, A Mighty Heart 2007, Beowulf (voice) 2007, Kung Fu Panda (voice) 2008, Wanted 2008, Changeling 2008, Salt 2010, The Tourist 2010, Kung Fu Panda 2 (voice) 2011, Maleficent 2014; as dir: In the Land of Blood and Honey (also writer) 2011, Unbroken 2014. *Address:* c/o United Talent Agency, 9336 Civic Center Drive, Beverly Hills, CA 90210, USA (office). *Telephone:* (310) 273-6700 (office). *Fax:* (310) 247-1111 (office). *Website:* www.unitedtalent.com (office).

JOLIOT, Pierre Adrien, DèsSc; French scientist and academic; b. 12 March 1932, Paris; s. of Frédéric Joliot and Irène Joliot (née Curie); m. Anne Gricouroff 1961; two s.; ed Faculté des Sciences de Paris; researcher, CNRS 1954–, apptd Dir of Research 1974, later Dir Emer.–, mem. Scientific Council 1992, Pres. Science Ethics Cttee, 1998–2001; Prof., Collège de France and Chair of Cellular Bioenergetics 1981–2002, then Hon. Prof.; Chef de Service, Institut de Biologie Physico-Chimique 1975–94, Admin. 1994–97; Dir Dept of Biology, Ecole Normale Supérieure 1987–92; Scientific Adviser to Prime Minister 1985–86; mem. Comité nat. d'évaluation de la recherche 1989–92; mem. de l'Institut (Acad. des Sciences, Paris) 1982; Assoc. mem. NAS 1979–, mem. 1982–, Academia Europaea 1989–, Acad. Européenne des Sciences, des Arts et des Lettres 1992–; Commandeur, Ordre nat. du Mérite 1994, Commandeur, Légion d'Honneur 2001, Grand Officier, Légion d'honneur 2012, Commdr; Prix André Policard-Lacassagne, l'Académie des Sciences 1968, Charles F. Kettering Award for excellence in photosynthesis 1970, Prix du Commissariat à l'Energie Atomique 1980, CNRS Gold Medal 1982. *Publications:* La recherche passionnément 2001, scientific works on bioenergetics and photosynthesis. *Leisure interests:* tennis, sailing, skiing. *Address:* Institut de Biologie Physico-Chimique, 13, rue Pierre et Marie Curie, 75005 Paris (office); 16 rue de la Glacière, 75013 Paris, France (home). *Telephone:* 1-58-41-50-44 (office); 1-43-37-22-56 (home). *E-mail:* pierre.joliot@ibpc.fr (office).

JOLLY, Baroness (Life Peer), cr. 2010, of Congdon's Shop in the County of Cornwall; **Rt Hon. Judith Jolly;** British teacher and politician; b. West Cornwall, England; m.; two s.; ed Leeds Univ., Nottingham Univ.; maths teacher 1974–97; Chief of Staff to Lord Teverson, MEP for Cornwall and West Plymouth 1997–99; various positions with Liberal Democrats 1984–, Chair. Devon and Cornwall Regional Exec. 2007–10; unsuccessful parl. cand. for Plymouth Devonport in Gen. Election 2005; mem. (Liberal Democrat), House of Lords 2010–, Govt Whip 2013–; Chair. Digital Services Cornwall CIC 2009–13; apptd Pres. Soc. of Chiropodists and Podiatrists 2013; Trustee, Help Musicians UK 2013–, Forced Labour Exploitation FLEX 2013–. *Address:* House of Lords, Westminster, London, SW1A 0PW, England (office). *Telephone:* (20) 7219-1286 (office). *E-mail:* jollyj@parliament.uk (office).

JOLLY, Robert Dudley, MNZM, BVSc, PhD, DSc, FRSNZ; New Zealand veterinary pathologist and academic; *Research Fellow and Professor Emeritus,*

Massey University; b. 1 Oct. 1930, Hamilton, North Island; s. of Thomas D. Jolly and Violet Mills; m. Aline C. Edwards 1958; two s. two d.; ed King's Coll., Auckland, Univ. of Auckland, Univ. of Sydney, Australia; mixed veterinary practice, Rotorua 1955–59; Teaching Fellow, Univ. of Sydney 1960–63; Assoc. Prof., Univ. of Guelph, Canada 1963–65; Sr Lecturer, Massey Univ. 1965–68, Reader 1968–85, Prof. in Veterinary Pathology and Public Health 1985–96, Research Fellow and Prof. Emer. 1997–; Hon. mem. American Coll. of Veterinary Pathologists; Hon. Fellow, Australian Coll. of Veterinary Science; Hon. Fellow, Royal Coll. of Pathologists of Australasia; mem. NZ Order of Merit 2005; Hector Medal 1996. *Publications:* more than 170 publs in scientific books and journals. *Leisure interest:* gardening. *Address:* 97 Summerset Village, 180 Ruapehu Drive, Palmerston North 4410 (home); Institute of Veterinary, Animal and Biomedical Science, Massey University, Palmerston North, New Zealand (office). *Telephone:* (6) 356-9099 (office); (6) 354-5852 (home). *E-mail:* r.d.jolly@massey.ac.nz (office). *Website:* ivabs.massey.ac.nz (office).

JOLY, Alain; French business executive; b. 18 April 1938, Nantes; s. of Albert Joly and Yvonne Poyet Rolin; m. Marie-Hélène Capbern-Gasqueton 1966; two s. one d.; ed Lycée Louis Le Grand, Paris and Ecole Polytechnique Paris; engineer, L'Air Liquide 1962–67, Dir of Operations, Canadian Liquid Air 1967–73, Dir Corp. Planning, Soc. L'Air Liquide 1973–76, Regional Man. 1976–78, Gen. Sec. 1978–81, Vice-Pres. 1981, Dir 1982, Chair. and CEO 1995–2001, Chair. Supervisory Bd 2001–06, now mem. Bd of Dirs; mem. Bd of Dirs BNP Paribas 2006, Lafarge Coppée (now Lafarge) 1993–, Banque Nat. de Paris 1995; mem. Int. Council, JP Morgan; mem. Supervisory Bd Impact Partenaires; Croix de la Valeur Militaire, Officier, Légion d'honneur. *Leisure interests:* sailing, golf.

JOLY, Eva, DenD; Norwegian/French judge and politician; b. (Gro Eva Farseth), 5 Dec. 1945, Oslo; m. Paschal Joly (died 2001); one s. one d.; moved to Paris at 18 to work as au pair; legal counsellor in a psychiatric hosp.; apptd regional judge, Orleans 1981, Asst to Public Prosecutor 1981–83; High Court Judge, Evry 1983–89, then First Examining Judge; legal specialist, Interministerial Cttee for Industrial Reconstruction, Ministry of Finance, Paris 1989, Deputy Sec.-Gen. –1993; investigating magistrate for financial affairs, Palais de Justice, Paris 1993, led to conviction of Bernard Tapie 1994, Roland Dumas 1998, forty exec. mem. of Elf Aquitaine including Chair. Lok Le Floch-Prigent 1995–2002, employees of Pechiney, Crédit Lyonnaise and other high-ranking politicians and businessmen; returned to Norway as special adviser to Norwegian Ministry of Justice with mandate to help strengthen Norway's work internationally against corruption and money laundering Oslo 2002–05; Special Adviser Norwatch (monitored Norwegian businesses in developing countries) 2005; Special Adviser to Iceland's Minister of Justice (assisting in investigation into bank crisis in Iceland) 2009; mem. European Parl. (Greens/European Free Alliance) 2009–; unsuccessful cand. (Europe Ecologie Les Verts) for Pres. of France 2012; Transparency Int. Integrity Award 2001, European of the Year, Reader's Digest 2002. *Publications:* Notre Affaire à Tous (This Concerns All of Us) (autobiog.) 2000, Is This the World We Want To Live In? 2003, Justice Under Siege: One Woman's Battle Against a European Oil Giant (memoir) 2006. *Address:* European Parliament, Bât. Altiero Spinelli 08H353 60, rue Wiertz, 1047 Brusells, Belgium (office); Europe Ecologie Les Verts, 247 rue du Faubourg Saint-Martin, 75010 Paris, France. *Telephone:* (2) 284-53-76 (office). *Fax:* (2) 284-93-76 (office).

JOLY, Hubert; French business executive; *Chairman and CEO, Best Buy Company Inc.;* ed École des Hautes Études Commerciales de Paris, Institut d'Études Politiques de Paris; with McKinsey & Co. Inc., worked in firm's Paris, New York and San Francisco offices 1983–96; drove turnaround of EDS (now part of Hewlett-Packard) in France 1996–99, briefly Chief Information Officer, Vivendi Universal, led restructuring and growth of Vivendi's video game's business (now part of Activision Blizzard) 1999–2001, later oversaw integration of Universal and Vivendi's media assets in USA, then part of team that led restructuring of Vivendi 2002–04; led transformation of Carlson Wagonlit Travel (CWT) 2003–07, CEO Carlson (parent co.), Minneapolis 2008–12; mem. Bd of Dirs, Pres. and CEO Best Buy Co. Inc. 2012–16, Chair. and CEO 2016–; mem. Bd of Dirs Ralph Lauren Corpn; chaired Travel Facilitation Sub-Cttee of US Dept of Commerce Travel and Tourism Advisory Bd; mem. Bd of Overseers Carlson School of Man., Bd of Trustees Minneapolis Inst. of Arts, Exec. Cttee Minnesota Business Partnership; fmr mem. Exec. Cttee World Travel and Tourism Council; Chevalier, Ordre nat. du Mérite; elected a Global Leader for Tomorrow by the World Econ. Forum, Davos 1997–99. *Address:* Best Buy Company Inc., 7601 Penn Avenue South, Richfield, MN 55423, USA (office). *Telephone:* (612) 291-1000 (office). *Fax:* (612) 292-4001 (office). *E-mail:* info@bestbuy.com (office). *Website:* www.bestbuy.com (office).

JOLY, Mélanie, PC, MP, LLB, MJur; Canadian lawyer and politician; *Minister of Tourism, Official Languages and La Francophonie;* b. 16 Jan. 1979, Montréal; d. of Clément Joly and Carole-Marie Allard; ed Univ. de Montréal, Univ. of Oxford, UK; lawyer, Davies Ward Phillips & Vineberg, Montréal 2000–04, Stikeman Elliott 2005–07; intern with Radio Canada May–Sept. 2007; Man. Partner, Montréal office of Cohn & Wolfe (int. communications firm) 2007–13; Founder, Le Vrai Changement pour Montréal party 2013; cand. for Mayor of Montréal 2013; Head, Quebec Advisory Cttee for Justin Trudeau's leadership campaign of Liberal Party of Canada 2013; Man. Consultant, Gestion M Joly 2014–15; mem. House of Commons (Parl.) for Ahuntsic-Cartierville 2015–; Minister of Heritage 2015–18, Minister of Tourism, Official Languages and La Francophonie 2018–; served on numerous Bds of Dirs, including Régie des rentes du Québec, Fondation du CHUM, Musée d'art contemporain de Montréal 2006–07, Conseil supérieur de la langue française 2008–13, Montréal Bach Festival 2009–10; mem. Liberal Party of Canada; Arnold Edinborough Award. *Publication:* Changer les règles du jeu 2014. *Website:* pm.gc.ca/eng/cabinet (office).

JOMAA, Mehdi, DEA; Tunisian engineer and politician; b. Mahdia; five c.; ed Tunis El Manar Univ., Nat. Engineering School, Tunis, HEC Paris, France, Saïd Business School, Oxford, UK; with Hutchinson Group (part of Total Group, operating in aeronautical, defence, automobile, railway, oil and gen. industries) 1988–2012, roles include Head, Paulstra 1990–2003, Tech. Dir, Paulstra & Vibrachoc 2003–04, Tech. Dir, Hutchinson Aerospace Aeronautics and Defence Divs 2004–09, Dir, Hutchinson Aerospace Div., and Dir, six business units in France, USA, India and Tunisia 2009–13; Minister of Industry March–Dec. 2013; Prime Minister 2014–15.

JONAH, Samuel (Sam) Kwesi Esson, MSc, DSc; Ghanaian mining industry executive; *Chairman, Jonah Capital;* b. 19 Nov. 1949, Kibi; m. Belinda Giselle Jonah; three s. two d.; ed Adisadel Coll., Camborne School of Mines, Imperial Coll. of Science and Tech., UK; shovel boy, Obuasi Gold Mine 1969; CEO Ashanti Goldfields Co. Ltd 1986–2004, Exec. Pres. and Dir AngloGold Ashanti (following acquisition) 2004–05, Non-Exec. Pres. and Dir 2005; Chair. Limestone Products Ghana, First Atlantic Merchant Bank Ltd, Equator Exploration Ltd 2005–, Equinox Minerals Ltd 2005–, Jonah Capital 2005–; Dir Lonmin plc, Defiance Mining Corpn, Anglo American Corpn of South Africa, Anglo American Platinum Corpn Ltd; currently Chancellor Univ. of Cape Coast Ghana; Exec. Officer, Sankofa Trust (Pty) Ltd; mem. Bd Ashesi Univ.; mem., Ghana Investors' Advisory Council, Int. Investment Advisory Council of South Africa, Global Compact Advisory Council, Bank of America Global Advisory Council; Hon. KBE 2003, Order of the Star of Ghana 2006; Hon. DSc (Camborne School of Mines and Univ. of Exeter) 1966, Hon. DPhil (Ashesi Univ.) 2005 Lifetime Achievement Award, Commonwealth Business Council and African Business Magazine 2010, World Entrepreneur of the Year, West African edition of Ernst and Young 2016. *Leisure interests:* fishing, golf. *Address:* 31A Killarney Road, Sandhurst, Sandton 2146 (home); Jonah Capital, 1st Floor, AMB Capital Holdings, 18 Fricker Street, Illovo Boulevard, Johannesburg 2196, South Africa (office). *Telephone:* (11) 215-2282 (office). *Fax:* (11) 268-6868 (office). *E-mail:* sam@jonahcapital.com (office). *Website:* www.jonahcapital.com (office).

JONAS, Sir Peter, Kt, CBE, BA (Hons), LRAM, ARCM, FRNCM, FRSA; British arts administrator, opera company director and academic; b. 14 Oct. 1946, London; s. of Walter Adolf Jonas and Hilda May Ziadie; m. 1st Lucy Hull 1989 (divorced 2000); m. 2nd Barbara Burgdorf 2012; ed Worth School, Univ. of Sussex, Royal Northern Coll. of Music, Royal Coll. of Music, Eastman School of Music, Univ. of Rochester, USA; Asst to Music Dir, Chicago Symphony Orchestra 1974–76, Artistic Admin. 1976–85; Dir of Artistic Admin., The Orchestral Asscn, Chicago 1977–85; Gen. Dir ENO 1985–93; Staatsintendant (Gen. and Artistic Dir) Bavarian State Opera, Munich 1993–2006 (retd); mem. Bd of Man., Nat. Opera Studio 1985–93, Council, Royal Coll. of Music 1988–95, Council of Man., London Lighthouse 1990–92, Kuratorium Richard Strauss Gesellschaft 1993–, Advisory Bd, Bayerische Vereinsbank 1994–2004, Rundfunkrat (Bd Govs), Bayerische Rundfunk 1999–2006, Supervisory Bd, Berlin State Opera Trust 2004–12, Advisory Bd, Tech. Univ., Munich 2006–12, Governing Bd, Netherlands Opera Amsterdam 2009–18, Univ. Council, Univ. of Lucerne 2008–17; Visiting Lecturer, St Gallen Univ. 2003–; Lecturer, Univ. of Zurich 2004–, Bavarian Theatre Acad., Univ. of Munich; mem. Kuratorium and Governing Bd, Wissenschaftszentrum für Sozialforschung (Social Science Research Centre), Berlin 2015–; workshop organizer, Wissenschaftzentrum Berlin; Lecturer, Univ. of Zurich; mem. Bavarian Acad. of Fine Arts 2004; mem. Governing Bd Social Science Research Centre, Berlin; Fellow, Univ. of Sussex 2012; Hon. Life mem. Bavarian State Opera 2006; Bayerische Verdienstorden (Germany) 2003, Maximiliansorden (Germany) 2007; Hon. DMus (Sussex) 1993; Queen's Lecturer, Berlin 2001, Bavarian Constitutional Medal 2003, City of Munich Kulturellen Ehrenpreis 2004, Karl Valentin Orden (Germany) 2006. *Publications:* Powerhouse (co-author) 1993, Eliten und Demokratie 1999, If Music be the food of Love 2006. *Leisure interests:* 20th century architecture, cinema, theatre, skiing, classic Italian cars, mountain hiking, long distance trekking, old master paintings, cricket, Crystal Palace Football Club, epic TV series. *Address:* Scheuchzerstrasse 36, 8006 Zurich, Switzerland (home). *Telephone:* (43) 4779871 (office). *Fax:* (43) 4779872 (office). *E-mail:* sirpeterjonas@gmail.com (home).

JONATHAN, Goodluck Ebele, BSc, MSc, PhD; Nigerian politician and fmr head of state; *Global Crisis Envoy, United Nations;* b. 20 Nov. 1957, Rivers (now Bayelsa) State; m. Patience Jonathan; ed Univ. of Port Harcourt; Preventative Officer, Dept of Customs and Excise 1975–77; Science Insp. of Educ., Rivers State Ministry of Educ. 1982–83; Lecturer in Biology, Rivers State Coll. of Educ. 1983–93; Asst Dir and Head of Sub-Dept of Environment Protection, Oil Mineral Producing Area Devt Comm. 1993–98; Deputy Gov. Bayelsa State 1999–2007; Vice-Pres. of Nigeria 2007–10, Acting Pres. Feb.–May 2010, Pres. and Commdr-in-Chief of the Armed Forces 2010–15, also Minister of Power 2010–14; UN Global Crisis Envoy 2015–; mem. People's Democratic Party; Fellow, Nigeria Environmental Soc., Inst. of Public Admins, Int. Asscn for Impact Assessment; mem. Science Teachers Asscn of Nigeria, Fisheries Soc. of Nigeria; Inst. of Public Admins Award 2002.

JONES, Alan Stanley, OBE; Australian fmr racing driver; b. 2 Nov. 1946, Melbourne; s. of Stan Jones (fmr Australian champion racing driver); m. Beverly Jones 1971; one adopted s.; ed Xavier Coll., Melbourne; began racing in 1964 in Australia, raced in Britain from 1970; World Champion 1980, runner-up 1979; CanAm Champion 1978; Grand Prix wins: 1977 Austrian (Shadow-Ford), 1979 German (Williams-Ford), 1979 Austrian (Williams-Ford), 1979 Dutch (Williams-Ford), 1979 Canadian (Williams-Ford); 1980 Argentine (Williams-Ford), 1980 French (Williams-Ford), 1980 British (Williams-Ford), 1980 Canadian (Williams-Ford), 1980 US (Williams-Ford), 1981 US (Williams-Ford); announced retirement in 1981; began competing in Australian Touring Car Championships 1990, est. own team Pack Leader Racing, 1996, and sold the team in 1997; participated in launch of Australian Motor Sports Acad.; apptd to Bd Australian Grand Prix Corpn 1995; TV commentator. *Leisure interests:* collecting interesting cars, farming in Australia, boating.

JONES, Allen Christopher, RA; British artist; b. 1 Sept. 1937, Southampton, Hants.; s. of William Jones and Madeline Jones; m. 1st Janet Bowen 1964 (divorced 1978); two d.; m. 2nd Deirdre Morrow 1994; ed Hornsey School of Art, Royal Coll. of Art; Sec., Young Contemporaries, London 1961; lived in New York 1964–65; Tamarind Lithography Fellowship, Los Angeles 1966; Guest Prof., Dept of Painting, Univ. of S Florida 1969; Hochschule für Bildende Künste, Hamburg 1968–70, Hochschule der Künste, Berlin 1982–83; Guest Lecturer, Univ. of Calif. 1977; first solo exhbn, London 1963, solo exhbns in UK, USA, Switzerland, Germany, Italy, Australia, Japan, Netherlands, Belgium, Austria, Spain, China, Argentina, Brazil, Czech Repub., Cyprus, Norway, Sweden, Finland, Estonia 1963–; many group exhbns of paintings and graphic work, world-wide 1962–; first travelling retrospective, Europe 1979–80; Welsh Arts Council-sponsored sculpture exhbn 1992; British Council Print Retrospective 1995–98; Commercial Mural

Project, Basel 1979; designs for TV and stage in Germany and UK; sculptures commissioned for Liverpool Garden Festival 1984, Cotton's Atrium, Pool of London 1987, Sterling Hotel, Heathrow 1990, Riverside Health Authority, Chelsea and Westminster Hosp., London 1993, Swire Properties, Hong Kong 1997, 2002, Goodwood 1998, GSK World HQ, London 2001–02, Estouteville, Va, USA 2004–05, Yuzi Paradise Sculpture Parks, Guilin and Shanghai, China 2005–06, Chatsworth House 2008; works in many public and pvt. collections in UK and elsewhere, including Tate Gallery, London, Victoria & Albert Museum, London, Museum of 20th Century, Vienna, Stedelijk Museum, Amsterdam, Museum of Modern Art, New York, Hirshhorn Museum, Washington, DC, Chicago Museum of Art, Moderna Museet, Stockholm, Yale Center for British Art, Whitney Museum of American Art, New York; Trustee, British Museum 1990–99, now Trustee Emer.; Hon. Dr of Arts (Southampton) 2007; Prix des Jeunes Artistes, Paris Biennale 1963, Art and Work Award, Wapping Arts Trust 1989, Heitland Foundation Award 1995. *Publications:* Allen Jones Figures 1969, Allen Jones Projects 1971, Waitress 1972, Ways and Means 1977, Sheer Magic (Paintings 1959–79) 1979, UK 1980, Allen Jones (painting and sculpture) 1963–93 1993, Allen Jones Prints 1995, Allen Jones 1997, Allen Jones Sculptures 1965–2002 2002, Allen Jones Works 2006. *Leisure interest:* gardening. *Address:* 41 Charterhouse Square, London, EC1M 6EA, England (home). *Telephone:* (20) 7606-2984 (home). *E-mail:* dm@allenjonestheartist.com (home).

JONES, Arthur (Alun) Gwynne (see CHALFONT, (Arthur) Alun Gwynne Jones).

JONES, Hon. Barry Owen, AC, MA, LLD, DSc, DLitt, DUniv, FAA, FAHA, FTSE, FASSA, FRSA, Dist FRSN, FRSV, FACE; Australian politician, fmr public servant, university lecturer and lawyer; *Professorial Fellow, University of Melbourne;* b. 11 Oct. 1932, Geelong, Vic.; s. of Claud Edward Jones and Ruth Marion Jones (née Black); m. 1st Rosemary Hanbury 1961 (died 2006); m. 2nd Rachel Faggetter 2009; ed Melbourne High School, Melbourne Univ.; MP, Victorian Parl. 1972–77, House of Reps 1977–98; Minister for Science 1983–90, for Tech. 1983–84, Minister Assisting the Minister for Industry, Tech. and Commerce 1984–87, Minister for Science, Customs and Small Business 1988–90; Minister Assisting the Prime Minister for Science and Tech. 1989–90; Visiting Prof., Wollongong Univ. 1991–98, Victoria Univ. of Tech. 1994–; Adjunct Prof., Monash Univ. 1999–; Chair. Port Arthur Historic Site, Tasmania 2000–13, Victorian Schools Innovation Comm. 2001–05; mem. Nat. Comm. for UNESCO 1990–99, Exec. Bd of UNESCO, Paris 1991–95; Chair. House of Reps Cttee on Long Term Strategies 1990–96; Nat. Pres. Australian Labor Party 1992–2000, 2005–06, Vice-Pres. 2004–05, 2006–07; Chair. Australian Film and TV School 1973–75, Australian Film Inst. 1974–80, Vision 2020 Australia 2002–14; Deputy Chair. Australian Council for the Arts 1969–73, Australian Constitutional Convention 1997–98; Vice-Pres. World Heritage Cttee, Paris 1995–96, Australia ICOMOS Inc. 1998–2000; mem. Australian Film Devt Corpn 1970–75, Australian Nat. Library Council 1996–98; mem. Bd, Australian Stem Cell Centre 2002–08; Dir, Victorian Opera 2008–15; Visiting Fellow, Trinity Coll., Cambridge, UK 1999–; Vice-Chancellor's Fellow, Univ. of Melbourne 2005–07, Professorial Fellow 2007–; Distinguished Fellow, Royal Soc. of NSW; Dr hc (Melbourne, ANU, Griffith, Deakin, Southern Cross, Wollongong); Silver Jubilee Medal 1977, Longford Life Achievement Award, Australian Film Inst. 1986, Redmond Barry Award, Australian Library and Information Asscn 1996, Australian Living Nat. Treasure, Nat. Trust 1997, 1998, John Curtin Medal 2001, Centenary Medal 2003, Research Australia Lifetime Achievement Award 2008, Barry Jones Bay, Antarctica named for him. *Achievement:* only person elected to all four Australian learned acads. *Films:* several cameo roles. *Television:* host, Encounter 1968–69. *Radio:* Talkback with Barry Jones 1967–68. *Publications include:* Macmillan Dictionary of Biography 1981, Sleepers, Wake!: Technology and the Future of Work 1982, Managing Our Opportunities 1984, Living by Our Wits 1986, Dictionary of World Biography 1994 (revised edn and e-book 2013), Coming to the Party (ed.) 2006, A Thinking Reed (autobiog.) 2006, The Shock of Recognition (on music and literature) 2016, Knowledge Courage Leadership (political essays) 2016. *Leisure interests:* films, music, travel, collecting autographed documents, antique terracottas and Luristan metal work, paintings, reading. *Address:* GPO Box 496, Melbourne, Vic. 3001, Australia (home). *Telephone:* (3) 8344-8628 (office); 41-8399196 (mobile) (home). *E-mail:* bojones@unimelb.edu.au (office).

JONES, Bill T.; American dancer and choreographer; *Artistic Director, Bill T. Jones/Arnie Zane Dance Company;* b. 15 Feb. 1952, Bunnell, Fla; ed State Univ. of New York, Binghamton; Co-founder American Dance Asylum 1973; Co-founder and Artistic Dir Bill T. Jones/Arnie Zane Dance Co. 1982–; collaborations with Toni Morrison, Max Roach, Jessye Norman, Sir Peter Hall; dir Guthrie Theatre, Minneapolis 1994; Assoc. Choreographer, Lyon Opera Ballet 1995–; MacArthur Foundation Grant; Fellow, American Acad. of Arts and Sciences 2009–; Dr hc (Bard Coll.) 1996; New York Dance and Performance (Bessie) Award (with Arnie Zane) 1986, Bessie Award for D-Man in the Waters 1989, Dorothy B. Chandler Performing Arts Award 1991, Dance Magazine Award 1993, Edin. Festival Critics' Award (presented to Jones/Zane Dance Co.) 1993, Dorothy and Lillian Gish Prize 2003, Harlem Renaissance Award 2005, Samuel H. Scripps American Dance Festival Award for Lifetime Achievement 2005, Wexner Prize 2005, Eileen Harris Norton Fellowship 2007, Kennedy Center Honor 2010. *Dance:* choreographer (with Arnie Zane) Pas de Deux for Two 1974, Across the Street 1975, Whosedebabedoll? Baby Doll 1977, Monkey Run Road 1979, Blauvelt Mountain 1980; Choreographer Negroes for Sale (soloist) 1973, Track Dance 1974, Everybody Works/All Beasts Count 1976, De Sweet Streak to Loveland 1977, The Runner Dreams 1978, Stories, Steps and Stomps 1978, Progresso 1979, Echo 1979, Naming Things Is Only the Intention to Make Things 1979, Floating the Tongue 1979, Sisyphus Act I and II 1980, Open Spaces 1980, Tribeca, Automation, Three Wise Men, Christmas 1980, Secret Pastures 1984, History of Collage 1988, D-Man in the Waters 1989, Dances 1989, Last Supper at Uncle Tom's Cabin/The Promised Land 1991, Love Defined 1991, Aria 1992, Last Night on Earth 1992, Fête 1992, Still/Here 1993 (Edin. Festival 1995), Achilles Loved Patroclus 1993, War Between the States 1993, Still/Here 1994, We Set Out Early ... Visibility Was Poor 1997, Out Some Place 1998, The Breathing Show 1999, You Walk? 2000, Fantasy in C Major 2000, The Table Project 2001, Verbum 2002, WORLDWITHOUT/IN 2002, Black Suzanne 2002, WORLD II 2002, There Were... 2002, Power/Full 2002, Another Evening 2003, Reading, Mercy and The Artificial Nigger 2003, Mercy 10 x 8 on a Circle 2003, and before... 2003, Blind Date 2005, As I Was Saying... 2005, Another Evening: I Bow Down 2006, Chapel/Chapter 2006, The Seven (Lucille Lortel Award) 2006, Spring Awakening (Joseph Callaway Award 2006, Tony Award for Best Choreography 2007, Obie Award 2007) 2006; has also choreographed for Alvin Ailey American Dance Theater, Axis Dance Co., Boston Ballet, Lyon Opera Ballet, Berlin Opera Ballet, Dayton Contemporary Dance Co., Diversions Dance Co.; dir and choreographer of operas including: New Year 1990 (Co-Dir BBC TV production), The Mother of Three Sons, Lost in the Stars; theatre productions include Perfect Courage (co-dir), Dream on Monkey Mountain (dir). *Publication:* Last Night on Earth 1995. *Address:* Bill T. Jones/Arnie Zane Dance Company, 27 West 120th Street., Suite 1, New York, NY 10027, USA (office). *Telephone:* (212) 426-6655 (office). *Fax:* (212) 426-5883 (office). *E-mail:* info@billtjones.org (office). *Website:* www.billtjones.org (office).

JONES, Bryn Terfel (see TERFEL, Bryn).

JONES, Carwyn, AM; British/Welsh barrister and politician; b. 1967, Swansea; m. Lisa Jones; two c.; ed Univ. of Wales, Aberystwyth, Inns of Court School of Law, London; called to the Bar at Gray's Inn 1989; began career as barrister, Gower Chambers, Swansea, then Temple Chambers, Cardiff; fmr tutor, Cardiff Univ. Law School; fmr mem. Bridgend County Borough Council and Chair., Co. Borough Council Labour Group; mem. Nat. Ass. for Wales (Labour) for Bridgend constituency 1999–, Deputy Sec. 2000, Sec. (later Minister) for Agric. and Rural Devt 2000, also Minister for Ass. Business 2002–03, for Open Govt 2002, for the Environment, Planning and the Countryside 2000–07, for Educ., Culture and Welsh Language 2007, Counsel Gen. for Wales and Leader of the House 2007–09, First Minister of Wales 2009–18; mem. Labour Party 1987–, Leader, Welsh Labour Party 2009–18; mem. Amnesty Int., UNISON, Unite, Fabian Soc.; Wales Year Book Welsh Politician of the Year 2009. *Leisure interests:* sport, reading, travel. *Address:* c/o Office of the First Minister, Welsh Assembly Government, Cathays Park, Cardiff, CF10 3NQ, Wales (office).

JONES, David A., Jr, BA, JD; American health care industry executive; b. Louisville, Ky; s. of David A. Jones, Founder and fmr Chair. Humana Inc.; ed Univ. of Louisville, Yale Univ.; certified public accountant 1954; served in USN 1954–57; mem. Faculty of Econs, Yale Univ. 1958–60; Co-founder Humana Corpn 1961, CEO 1961–97, Dir Humana Inc. (health benefits co. cr. following separation of Humana Corpn into two cos 1993) 1993–, Vice-Chair. 1996–2005, Chair. 2005–10; Chair. and Man. Dir Chrysalis Ventures 1993–; Chair. Hospira; fmr Chair. Healthcare Leadership Council, Nat. Cttee for Quality Health Care; mem. Bd Dirs Abbott Labs, Glenview Trust Co.; mem. The Business Roundtable, Bd American Asscn of Health Plans; Founding Chair. Bd of Visitors, Peter F. Drucker Grad. Man. Centre; Hon. PhD (Chicago Medical School, Univ. of Louisville, Transylvania Univ., Claremont Grad. School); Alumnus of the Year, Univ. of Louisville 2004. *Address:* Humana Inc., 500 West Main Street, Louisville, KY 40202, USA (office). *Telephone:* (502) 580-1000 (office). *Fax:* (502) 580-3677 (office). *E-mail:* info@humana.com (office). *Website:* www.humana.com (office).

JONES, Rt Hon. David Ian, PC; British politician and solicitor; b. 22 March 1952, London, England; s. of Bryn Jones and Elspeth Jones (née Sauvage Willams); m. Sara Jones; two s.; ed Ruabon Grammar School, University Coll. London, Chester Coll. of Law; fmr mem. UCL Conservative Soc.; fmr Sr Partner, David Jones & Co., Llandudno; contested Conwy constituency in Gen. Election 1997, City of Chester 2001; Mem. Welsh Ass. for North Wales 2002–03; MP (Conservative) for Clwyd West 2005–10, for Clwyd West (revised boundary) 2010–, mem. Welsh Affairs Select Cttee 2005–10; Shadow Minister for Wales 2006–10; Parl. Under-Sec. of State, Wales Office 2010–12; Sec. of State for Wales 2012–14; Minister of State, Dept for Exiting the EU 2016–17; Chair. Conwy Conservative Asscn 1998–99; fmr Patron, Chinese Conservative Group. *Leisure interest:* Liverpool Football Club. *Address:* House of Commons, Westminster, London, SW1A 0AA, England (office); Constituency Office, 27 Princes Drive, Colwyn Bay, Conwy, LL29 8HT, Wales (home). *Telephone:* (20) 7219-8070 (office). *Fax:* (20) 7219-0142 (office). *E-mail:* jonesdi@parliament.uk (office). *Website:* www.parliament.uk/biographies/commons/mr-david-jones/1502 (office); www.davidjones.wales.

JONES, Dean Mervyn; Australian sports commentator and fmr professional cricketer; *Head Coach, Islamabad United;* b. 24 March 1961, Coburg, Melbourne, Vic.; m. Jane Jones 1986; one d.; ed Mt Waverley High School, Vic.; right-hand batsman; played for Victoria 1981/82–97/98 (Capt. 1993/94–95/96), Durham 1992, Derbyshire (Capt.) 1996–97; Test debut: West Indies v Australia, Port of Spain 16–21 March 1984; played in 52 Tests, scoring 3,631 runs (average 46.55, highest score 216) including 11 hundreds; toured England 1989; played in 164 One-Day Ints, scoring 6,068 runs (average 44.61, highest score 145) including seven hundreds; played in 245 First-class matches, scoring 19,188 runs (average 51.85, highest score 324 not out) including 55 hundreds; commentator for TEN Sports –2006; Head Coach, Islamabad United 2016–; mem. Exec. Cttee and sr commentator for Indian Cricket League 2007; Wisden Cricketer of the Year 1990. *Publication:* Deano: My Call 1995. *Leisure interests:* golf, baseball, looking after his two Rottweilers. *Website:* www.islamabadunited.com/staff/dean-jones (office).

JONES, Douglas (Doug), BS, JD; American lawyer and politician; *Senator from Alabama;* b. 4 May 1954, Fairfield, Ala; m. Louise New 1992; two s. one d.; ed Samford Univ., Cumberland School of Law; Staff Counsel, Senate Judiciary Cttee 1979–80; Asst Attorney, N Dist of Alabama, US Dept of Justice 1980–84, Attorney 1997–2001; Attorney and Partner, private law firm 1984–97; private legal practice with Whatley Drake LLC 2001–08, Haskell Slaughter Young & Rediker LLC 2008–13; Shareholder, Jones & Hawley PC 2013–; Senator from Alabama 2018–; Democrat. *Address:* 326 Russell Senate Office Building, Washington, DC 20510, USA (office). *Telephone:* (202) 224-4124 (office). *Website:* www.senate.gov/senators/115thCongress/Jones_Doug.htm; dougjonesforsenate.com.

JONES, Felicity Rose Hadley, BA; British actress; b. 17 Oct. 1983, Birmingham; m. Charles Guard 2018; ed Wadham Coll., Oxford; took drama lessons from age 11 at after-school workshop funded by Central Television; several appearances with Oxford Univ. Drama Soc., including title role in Attis and The Comedy of Errors 2005. *Films include:* Soulboy 2010, The Tempest 2011, Like Crazy (Empire Award for Best Female Newcomer, Sundance Film Festival US Dramatic Special Jury Prize for Breakout Performance, Nat. Bd of Review Award for Breakthrough

Performance) 2011, Hysteria 2011, Cheerful Weather for the Wedding 2012, The Amazing Spider-Man 2 2014, The Theory of Everything 2014, Inferno 2016, A Monster Calls 2016, Star Wars: Rogue One 2016, On the Basis of Sex 2018. *Radio includes:* BBC Radio 4 The Archers (as Emma Carter) 1999–2009. *Television includes:* The Worst Witch (series) 1998, Weirdsister College 2001, Servants 2003, Northanger Abbey (TV film) 2007, Cape Wrath 2007, Doctor Who 2008, Brideshead Revisited 2008, The Diary of Anne Frank 2009, Page Eight (TV film) 2011. *Address:* c/o WME Entertainment, 100 New Oxford Street, London, WC1A 1HB, England (office). *Telephone:* (20) 8929-8400 (office). *Website:* wmeentertainment.com (office).

JONES, Grace; American singer, model and actress; b. 19 May 1952, Spanishtown, Jamaica; d. of Robert Jones and Marjorie P. Jones; one s.; m. Atila Altaunbay 1996 (divorced); moved to New York at age of 12; abandoned Spanish studies at Syracuse Univ. for first stage role, Phila; became fashion model in New York, then Paris; made first album, Portfolio, for Island Records 1977; debut as disco singer New York 1977; opened La Vie en Rose restaurant, New York 1987; Q Idol Award 2008. *Films include:* Gordon's War 1973, Let's Make a Dirty Movie 1976, Colt 38 Special Squad 1976, Army of Lovers or Revolution of the Perverts (documentary) 1979, Deadly Vengeance 1981, Made in France (documentary) 1984, Conan the Destroyer 1984, A View to a Kill 1985, Vamp 1986, Straight to Hell 1987, Siesta 1987, Boomerang 1992, Cyber Bandits 1995, McCinsey's Island 1998, Palmer's Pick Up 1999, No Place Like Home 2006, Falco 2008, Chelsea on the Rocks 2008. *Television:* Stryx 1978, A One Man Show 1982, Pee-wee's Playhouse Christmas Special 1988, Beastmaster 1999, Wolf Girl 2001, Shaka Zulu: The Citadel 2001. *Recordings include:* albums: Portfolio 1977, Fame 1978, Muse 1979, Warm Leatherette 1980, Nightclubbing 1981, Living My Life 1982, Island Life 1985, Slave to the Rhythm 1985, Inside Story 1986, Bulletproof Heart 1989, Hurricane 2008, Icon 2013. *Publications:* I'll Never Write My Memoirs 2015. *Address:* c/o CMO Management, 11 Westbourne Studios, 242 Acklam Road, London, W10 5JJ, England (office). *Telephone:* (20) 3735-5632 (office). *E-mail:* info@blueraincoatmusic.com (office). *Website:* www.cmomanagement.co.uk (office).

JONES, Dame Gwyneth, DBE, FRCM, ARCM; British/Swiss singer (soprano); b. 7 Nov. 1936, Pontnewynydd, Mon., Wales; d. of Edward George Jones and Violet Webster; one d.; ed Royal Coll. of Music, Accad. Chigiana, Italy, Zurich Int. Opera Centre, Switzerland; with Zürich Opera House 1962–63; a Prin. Dramatic Soprano, Royal Opera House, Covent Garden 1963–; with Vienna State Opera House 1966–, Deutsche Oper Berlin 1966–, Bavarian State Opera 1967–; guest performances in numerous opera houses throughout the world including La Scala, Milan, Rome Opera, Berlin State Opera, Munich State Opera, Hamburg, Paris, Metropolitan Opera, New York, San Francisco, Los Angeles, Zürich, Geneva, Dallas, Chicago, Teatro Colón, Buenos Aires, Tokyo, Beijing, Hong Kong, Seoul, Bayreuth Festival, Salzburg Festival, Arena di Verona, Edin. Festival and Welsh Nat. Opera; known for many opera roles including title roles in Aida, Madame Butterfly, Norma, Tosca, Elektra, Salome, and Medea, Leonora in Il Trovatore, Desdemona in Otello, Leonore in Fidelio, Senta in The Flying Dutchman, Sieglinde in Die Walküre, Lady Macbeth in Macbeth, Elizabeth in Don Carlos, Donna Anna in Don Giovanni, Eva in Die Meistersinger, Kundry in Parsifal, Isolde in Tristan und Isolde, Helena in Aegyptische Helena (R. Strauss), Färberin in Frau ohne Schatten, Elisabeth/Venus in Tannhäuser, Marschallin and Octavian in Der Rosenkavalier, Brünnhilde in Der Ring des Nibelungen, Ortrud in Lohengrin, Minnie in Fanciulla del West, Erwartung (Schoenberg), La voix humaine (Poulenc), Kabanicha in Katia Kabanowa (Janacek), Kostelnicka Küsterin in Jenůfa (Janacek), Herodias in Salome (Richard Strauss), Klytämnestra in Elektra (Richard Strauss), Queen of Hearts in Alice in Wonderland (Unsuk Chin), Begbick in Mahagonny (Kurt Weill), Countess in Queen of Spades (Tchaikovsky); Pres. Richard Wagner Soc., London 1990; masterclasses in UK, Germany, France, Netherlands, Canada and Switzerland; debut as Stage Dir with new production of Der Fliegende Holländer by Richard Wagner at Deutsches Nat. Theater, Weimar; recordings for Decca, DGG, Philips, Chandos, EMI, CBS, Claves, Orfeo; Fellow, Royal Welsh Coll. of Music and Drama 1992; Kammersängerin in Austria and Bavaria; Hon. mem. RAM 1980, Vienna State Opera 1989; Bundesverdienstkreuz (Germany) 1988, Commdr des Arts et des Lettres 1993, Österreichisches Ehrenkreuz für Wissenschaft und Kunst, 1. Klasse 1998; Hon. DMus (Glamorgan) 1995, (Wales) 1998; Shakespeare Prize, Hamburg 1987, Golden Medal of Honour, Vienna 1991, Premio Puccini Award Torre del Lago 2003, Cymry for the World Honour, Wales Millennium Centre, Cardiff 2004. *Film:* Quartet (Anne Langley), directed by Dustin Hoffman. *Television films:* Fidelio, Aida, Flying Dutchman, Leonore, Beethoven 9th Symphony, Elisabeth and Venus in Tannhäuser, Poppea (Monteverdi), Rosenkavalier (R. Strauss), Die Walküre, Siegfried, Götterdämmerung, Die lustige Witwe, Don Carlos, Tristan und Isolde, La voix humaine (Mahagonny), Begbick (Mahagonny), Turandot, Senta (Der fliegende Holländer), Queen of Hearts (Alice in Wonderland). *Address:* PO Box 2000, 8700 Küsnacht, Switzerland.

JONES, (David) Huw, MA, FRTS; British broadcasting executive; b. 5 May 1948, Manchester; s. of Idris Jones and Olwen Edwards; m. Siân Marylka Miarczynska 1972; one s. one d.; ed Cardiff High School for Boys, Jesus Coll., Oxford; pop singer, recording artist, TV presenter 1968–76; Dir, Gen. Man. Sain Recording Co. 1969–81; Chair. Barcud Cyf (TV Facilities), Caernarfon 1981–93; Man. Dir, Producer Teledu'r Tir Glas Cyf (ind. production co.) 1982–93; first Chair. Teledwyr Annibynnol Cymru (Welsh Ind. Producers) 1984–86; CEO S4C (Welsh Fourth Channel) 1994–2005, Chair. S4C Authority 2011–, Chair. S4C Masnachol Cyf (S4C's commercial subsidiary) 1997–2005; Chair. Skillset Cymru 2002–05, Portmeirion Ltd 2007–, Cyfle Cyf 2007–, Welsh Ass. of Wales Government Broadcasting Advisory Group 2008–09; Deputy Chair. Wales Employment and Skills Bd 2008–; Vice–Chair. Ymddiriedolaeth Nant Gwrtheyrn Trust (Centre for teaching of Welsh) 2007–; mem. Bd of Dirs Sgrin Cyf 1994–2005, SDN Ltd 1996–2005 (Chair. 2001–03), Skillset Ltd 2001–05, Stratamatrix Cyf 2007–10; mem. Welsh Language Bd 2007–, Digital Wales Advisory Panel 2010–, Ministerial Advisory Group for Welsh-medium Education Strategy 2011–, British Screen Advisory Council 1995–2005; Fellow, Royal Television Soc.; Trustee, Royal TV Soc.; Hon. Fellow, Univ. of Wales, Aberystwyth 1997, Hon. Mem. Gorsedd of National Eisteddfod of Wales. *Leisure interests:* reading, cycling, walking. *Address:* S4C, Parc Tŷ Glas, Llanishen, Cardiff, CF14 5DU, Wales (office). *Telephone:* (370) 6004141. *Fax:* (29) 2074-1259 (office). *Website:* www.s4c.cymru (office).

JONES, Ieuan Wyn, LLB; British politician and lawyer; *Executive Director, Menai Science Park;* b. 22 May 1949, Denbigh, Wales; s. of John Jones and Mair Jones; m. Eirian Llwyd; three c.; ed Liverpool Polytechnic; practised as solicitor 1974–87; MP for Ynys Môn 1987–2001, mem. Nat. Ass. for Wales (AM) for Ynys Môn 1999–13, Deputy First Minister 2007–11; Chair. Plaid Cymru—The Party of Wales 1980–82, 1990–92, Pres. and Leader 2000–03, Leader Ass. Group 2003–06, Leader 2006–12; Exec. Dir Menai Science Park 2013–. *Publications include:* Europe: The Challenge Facing Wales 1996, Y Llinyn Arian: Thomas Gee (biog.) 1998. *Leisure interests:* history, sport. *Address:* Parc Menai, Bangor, Gwynedd, LL57 4HJ, Wales (office). *Telephone:* (7767) 301810 (office). *E-mail:* info@parcmenai.com (office). *Website:* www.parcmenai.com (office).

JONES, J. Steve, BSc, PhD, FRS; British geneticist and writer; *Professor Emeritus of Human Genetics, University College London;* b. 24 March 1944, Aberystwyth, Wales; m. Norma Percy 2004; ed Univ. of Edinburgh, Univ. of Chicago, USA; Head of Dept of Genetics, Evolution and Environment 1995–99, 2008–10, then Prof. of Human Genetics, Univ. Coll. London (UCL), currently Prof. Emer. and Prin. Research Assoc., Div. of Biosciences, Faculty of Life Sciences; Pres. Asscn for Science Educ. 2011, Galton Inst.; several visiting professorships, including Harvard Univ., Univ. of Chicago, Univ. of California at Davis, Univ. of Botswana, Fourah Bay Coll., Sierra Leone and Flinders Univ., Adelaide, Australia; Patron, Humanists UK; Royal Soc. Faraday Medal for public understanding of science 1997, BP Natural World Book Prize 1999, 2000, Inst. of Biology Charter Medal 2002, Irwin Prize for Secularist of the Year, Nat. Secular Soc. 2006. *Radio and television:* gave Reith Lectures on 'The Language of the Genes' 1991, Blue Skies (BBC Radio 3), In the Blood (six-part TV series on human genetics) 1996. *Publications include:* Genetics for Beginners (with B. van Loon) 1991, The Cambridge Encyclopedia of Human Evolution (ed. with R. D. Martin, D. Pilbeam) 1992, The Language of the Genes (Rhone-Poulenc Book Prize, Yorkshire Post First Book Prize 1994) 1993, In The Blood 1995, Almost like a Whale: The Origin of Species Updated (aka Darwin's Ghost) 1999, Y: The Descent of Men 2002, The Single Helix: A Turn Around the World of Science 2005, Twelve Galton Lectures: A Centenary Selection with Commentaries (co-ed.) 2007, Coral: A Pessimist in Paradise 2007, Darwin's Island 2009, The Serpent's Promise: The Bible Retold as Science 2013, No Need for Geniuses: Revolutionary Science in the Age of the Guillotine 2016, Evolution 2017. *Address:* Department of Biology, University College London, Room 510, Darwin Building, Gower Street, London, WC1E 6BT (office); Wolfson House, 4 Stephenson Way, London, NW1 2HE, England (office). *Telephone:* (20) 7679-7416 (office). *E-mail:* j.s.jones@ucl.ac.uk (office). *Website:* iris.ucl.ac.uk/research/personal/index?upi=JSJON91 (office).

JONES, James Earl; American actor; b. 17 Jan. 1931, Arkabutla, Miss.; s. of Robert Earl Jones and Ruth Williams; m. 1st Julienne Marie (divorced); m. 2nd Cecilia Hart 1982; one c.; ed Univ. of Michigan; numerous stage appearances on Broadway and elsewhere include Master Harold . . . And the Boys, Othello, King Lear, Hamlet, Paul Robeson, A Lesson From Aloes, Of Mice and Men, The Iceman Cometh, A Hand is on the Gate, The Cherry Orchard, Danton's Death, Fences; frequent TV appearances; cast as voice of Darth Vader in films Star Wars, The Empire Strikes Back and The Return of the Jedi; Fellow, American Acad. of Arts and Sciences 2009–; Hon. DFA (Princeton, Yale, Mich.); Tony Award for role in stage version and Golden Globe Award for role in screen version of The Great White Hope, Lifetime Achievement Award, Screen Actor's Guild 2008, numerous other awards. *Television includes:* series: Paris 1979–80, Gabriel's Fire (Emmy for Best Actor 1991) 1990–91, Pros and Cons 1991–92 and numerous other episodes in different series. *Films include:* Matewan, Gardens of Stone, Soul Man, My Little Girl, The Man, The End of the Road, Dr Strangelove, Conan the Barbarian, The Red Tide, A Piece of the Action, The Last Remake of Beau Geste, The Greatest, The Heretic, The River Niger, Deadly Hero, Claudine, The Great White Hope, The Comedians, Coming to America, Three Fugitives, Field of Dreams, Patriot Games, Sommersby, The Lion King (voice), Clear and Present Danger, Cry the Beloved Country, Lone Star, A Family Thing, Gang Related, Rebound, Summer's End 1998, Undercover Angel 1999, Quest for Atlantis 1999, Our Friend Martin (voice) 1999, On the Q.T. 1999, Finder's Fee 2001, Recess Christmas: A Miracle on Third Street (voice) 2001, 2004: A Light Knight's Odyssey (voice) 2004, Robots (voice) 2005, The Sandlot 2 2005, The Benchwarmers (voice) 2006, Welcome Home, Roscoe Jenkins 2008, Gimme Shelter 2013, The Angriest Man in Brooklyn 2014.

JONES, Gen. (retd) James L., BSc; American diplomatist and army officer (retd), fmr government official and consultant; *Director, Brent Scowcroft Center on International Security, Atlantic Council;* b. 19 Dec. 1943, Kansas City, Mo.; m. Diane Jones (née Johnson); four c.; ed Georgetown Univ. School of Foreign Service, Basic and Amphibious Warfare Schools, Quantico, Virginia, Nat. War Coll., Washington, DC; Second Lt, US Marine Corps 1967, Platoon Commdr and Co. Commdr Co. G, 2nd Bn, 3rd Marines, Viet Nam 1967–68, rank of First Lt 1968, Co. Commdr Camp Pendleton, Calif. 1968–70, Marine Barracks, Washington, DC 1970–73, Co. H, 2nd Bn, 9th Marines, 3rd Marine Div., Okinawa 1974–75; served in Officer Assignments Section, HQ Marine Corps, Washington, DC 1976–79; rank of Maj. 1977; Marine Corps Liaison Officer to US Senate 1979–84; rank of Lt-Col 1982; Commdr 3rd Bn, 9th Marines, 1st Marine Div., Camp Pendleton 1985–87; Sr Aide to Commdr of Marine Corps 1987–89; rank of Col 1988; Mil. Sec. to Commdt 1989–90; CO 24th Marine Expeditionary Unit, Camp Lejeune, NC 1990–92; rank of Brig.-Gen. 1992; Deputy Dir J-3, US European Command, Stuttgart, Germany 1992–94; Chief of Staff Jt Task Force Provide Promise, Operations in Bosnia and Herzegovina and Macedonia 1992–94; rank of Maj.-Gen. 1994; Commanding Gen. 2nd Marine Div., Marine Forces Atlantic, Camp Lejeune 1994–96; Dir Expeditionary Warfare Div., Office of the Chief of Naval Operations 1996; Deputy Chief of Staff for Plans, Policies and Operations, HQ Marine Corps 1996; rank of Lt-Gen. 1996; Mil. Asst to Sec. of Defense 1997–99; rank of Gen. 1999; 32nd Commdt Marine Corps 1999–2003; Commdr US European Command and 14th Supreme Allied Commdr Europe, NATO 2003–06; Chair. US Ind. Comm. on the Security Forces of Iraq 2007; Pres. and CEO US Chamber of Commerce Inst. for 21st Century Energy 2007–09; apptd by US State Dept to act as Special Envoy for Middle East Security 2007–09; Nat. Security Advisor to the Pres., The White House 2009–10; Chair. Atlantic Council 2007–09, mem. Bd of Dirs 2011–, Dir

Brent Scowcroft Center on Int. Security 2012–; f. Jones Group Int. (consultancy); Sr Fellow, Bipartisan Policy Center; Trustee, Center for Strategic and Int. Studies; fmr mem. Bd of Dirs Invacare Corpn; numerous decorations; Dr hc (Georgetown Univ.) 2002; Defense Distinguished Service Medal, Silver Star Medal, Legion of Merit with 4 Gold Stars, Bronze Star Medal with Combat V, Combat Action Ribbon and numerous other awards. *Address:* Jones Group International, 8000 Towers Crescent Drive, Suite 1525, Vienna, VA 22182, USA (office). *Telephone:* (703) 852-4330 (office). *Website:* www.jonesgroupinternational.com (office).

JONES, James Robert, LLB; American lawyer and fmr diplomatist; *Chairman, Manatt Jones Global Strategies LLC;* b. 5 May 1939, Muskogee, Okla; s. of Robert Jones and Margaret Wich; m. Olivia Barclay 1968; two s.; ed Univ. of Oklahoma and Georgetown Univ.; Chief of Staff to US Pres. Lyndon B. Johnson, The White House, Washington, DC 1965–69; practising lawyer and business consultant, Tulsa, Okla 1969–73; mem. US House of Reps 1973–87; Partner, Dickstein, Shapiro & Moran (law firm), Washington, DC 1987–89; Chair. and CEO American Stock Exchange, New York 1989–93; Amb. to Mexico 1993–97; Pres. Warnaco Int. 1997–98; Partner, Manatt, Phelps and Phillips LLP 1998–99; Chair. Manatt Jones Global Strategies LLC 1999–; Steiger Award 1979, Humanitarian Award, Anti Defamation League 1990, Aztec Eagle Award (Mexico) 1997. *Leisure interests:* golf, reading. *Address:* Manatt Jones Global Strategies LLC, 1050 Connecticut Avenue, NW, Suite 600, Washington, DC 20036, USA. *Telephone:* (202) 585-6560. *E-mail:* jjones@manatt.com (office). *Website:* www.manattjones.com (office).

JONES, Rt Rev. Sir James Stuart, Kt, KBE, BA; British ecclesiastic (retd); b. 18 Aug. 1948, Glasgow, Scotland; s. of Maj. James Stuart Anthony Jones and Helen Deans Dick Telfer (née McIntyre); m. Sarah Caroline Rosalind Marrow 1980; three d.; ed Univ. of Exeter and Wycliffe Hall, Oxford; Asst Master, Sevenoaks School 1971–74; producer, Scripture Union 1975–81; asst curate, Christ Church, Clifton 1982–84, Assoc. Vicar 1984–90; Vicar, Emmanuel Church, Croydon 1990–94; Bishop of Hull 1994–98; Bishop of Liverpool 1998–2013 (retd); Chair. Hillsborough Ind. Panel 2009–12 (now Adviser to Home Sec. on Hillsborough), Ind. Panel on Forestry 2011–12, Gosport Ind. Panel 2014–, Corp. Social Responsibility Advisory Bd for Waitrose in the John Lewis Partnership; currently Asst Bishop in the Diocese of York; Vice-Pres. Town and Country Planning Asscn; Fellow, Inst. of Chartered Foresters, World Wildlife Fund (WWF), Soc. of the Environment, Chartered Inst. of Water and Environmental Man.; Hon. DD (Hull) 1999; Hon. DLitt (Univ. of Lincolnshire and Humberside) 2001; Dr hc (Liverpool, Exeter, Gloucester, Liverpool John Moores, Liverpool Hope). *Television includes:* The Word on the Street 1999. *Radio includes:* presenter, The Bishop and the Prisoner 2012, The Bishop and the Banker 2013 on BBC Radio 4. *Publications include:* Following Jesus 1984, Finding God 1987, Why Do People Suffer? 1993, The Power and the Glory 1994, The People of the Blessing 1998, The Moral Leader 2002, Jesus and the Earth 2003. *Leisure interests:* swimming, opera, holidays in France. *E-mail:* james@bishopjamesjones.com. *Website:* www.bishopjamesjones.com.

JONES, Sir Mark, Kt, MA, FSA, FRSE; British museum director; *Master, St Cross College, University of Oxford;* b. 5 Feb. 1951; s. of John Ernest Powell-Jones and Ann Paludan; m. Ann Camilla Toulmin 1983; two s. two d.; ed Eton Coll., Worcester Coll., Oxford and Courtauld Inst. of Art; Asst Keeper Dept of Coins and Medals, British Museum 1974–90, Keeper 1990–92; Dir Nat. Museums of Scotland 1992–2001; Dir Victoria and Albert Museum, London 2001–11; Master, St Cross Coll., Oxford 2011–16; Ed. The Medal 1983–94; Chair. Nat. Museum Dirs' Conf.; Pres. Fédération Int. de la Médaille 1994–2000, British Art Medal Soc. 1998–2004 (Sec. 1982–94, currently Vice-Pres.); Vice-Pres. Kensington & Chelsea Decorative & Fine Arts Soc.; co-f. Scottish Cultural Resources Access Network 1994–96, mem. Bd 1996–2006; f. Golden Hare Books 2012–; mem. Royal Mint Advisory Cttee 1994–2004, Arts and Humanities Data Service Steering Cttee 1997–99, Focus Group Nat. Cultural Strategy 1999–2000; Dir, Edin. and Lothians Tourist Bd 1998–2000; mem. Bd Resource (Museums, Libraries and Archives Council) 2000–05; mem. Court and Council, RCA 2001–; Trustee, Nat. Trust 2005–, The Pilgrim Trust 2006–, Gilbert Collection; Patron, Embroiderer's Guild; Hon. Prof., Univ. of Edin. 1997; Chevalier, Ordre des Arts et des Lettres; Hon. DLitt (Royal Holloway) 2002, Hon. Dr of Arts (Abertay Univ., Dundee) 2009. *Publications include:* The Art of the Medal 1977, Impressionist Painting 1979, Contemporary British Medals 1986, Fake?: the Art of Deception (ed.) 1990, Why Fakes Matter (ed.) 1992, Designs on Posterity (ed.) 1994. *Address:* 31/4 India Street, Edinburgh, EH3 6HE, England (home). *Telephone:* (7900) 607536 (office). *E-mail:* markellispowelljones@gmail.com (office). *Website:* goldenharebooks.com (office).

JONES, Michael Frederick; British journalist; b. 3 July 1937, Gloucester, Glos., England; s. of Glyn F. Jones and Elizabeth Jones (née Coopey); m. Sheila Dawes 1959; three s.; ed Crypt Grammar School, Gloucester; reporter on prov. newspapers 1956–64, Financial Times 1964–65, Daily Telegraph 1965–67; Business News Asst Ed. The Times 1967–70; Man. Ed. The Asian, Hong Kong 1971; News Ed. Sunday Times 1972, Political Corresp. 1975, Political Ed. 1984, Assoc. Ed. 1990–95, Assoc. Ed. (Politics) 1995–2002; Chair. Parl. Press Gallery, House of Commons 1989–91; Media Adviser, Memorial to Women of World War II Cttee, London 2004–05; Visiting Fellow, Goldsmith's Coll., Univ. of London 2000–02; Research Asst to Baroness Boothroyd, House of Lords 2002–; UK Westminster Press Award 1962. *Publication:* Betty Boothroyd: The Autobiography (collaborated) 2001. *Leisure interest:* researching modern history. *E-mail:* micjon1937@hotmail.com (home).

JONES, Monty Patrick, BSc, MSc, PhD; Sierra Leonean plant breeder and government official; *Minister of Agriculture, Forestry and Food Security;* b. 5 Feb. 1951, Freetown; m. Geraldine Bamidele Jones; ed Univ. of Sierra Leone, Univ. of Birmingham, UK; began career with West Africa Rce Devt Agency 1975, worked as rice breeder and researcher 1980s, Head of Upland Rice Breeding Program, Côte d'Ivoire 1991; Exec. Dir Forum for Agricultural Research in Africa, Ghana 2002; fmr Special Adviser to Pres.; Amb.-at-Large 2013–16; Pres. Exec. Cttee, EMRC 2014; Minister of Agric., Forestry and Food Security 2016–; mem. Bd AGRA; Nat. Order of Merit of Cote d'Ivoire 2001, Grand Officer, Order of the Rokel (Sierra Leone) 2004; Hon. DSc (Birmingham) 2005, Hon. PhD (Ghent); King Badouin Award 2000, World Food Prize 2004, World's 100 Most Influential Men 2007, Niigata Int. Food Award 2010, Golden Jubilee Award 2011. *Achievements include:* made breakthrough in combining Asian and African rice varieties to develop Nerica, a 'New Rice for Africa', uniquely suited to poor African rice farmers 1994. *Publications:* numerous specialist papers, including The Rice Plant and its Environment 1996, Biotechnology Application in Agriculture: Challenges and Opportunities for Africa 2007, A New Green Revolution: An Answer to the Challenge for Africa? 2007, Priorities for Sustainable Agriculture and Food Security 2007. *Address:* Ministry of Agriculture, Food Security and Forestry, Youyi Bldg, 3rd Floor, Brookfields, Freetown, Sierra Leone (office). *Telephone:* (22) 222242 (office). *Fax:* (22) 241613 (office). *Website:* www.maffs.gov.sl (office).

JONES, Norah; American singer, pianist and actress; b. (Geetali Norah Jones Shankar), 30 March 1979, New York; d. of Ravi Shankar and Sue Jones; m.; two c.; ed Booker T. Washington High School for the Performing and Visual Arts, Dallas, North Texas Univ.; mem. Wax Poetic; formed band with Jesse Harris, Lee Alexander and Dan Rieser; solo artist 2001–; also mem. live band, The Little Willies; MOBO Award for Best Jazz Act 2002, VH1 Best Young Female Singer Award 2002, Grammy Awards for Best New Artist, for Record of the Year, for Best Female Pop Vocal Performance (both for Don't Know Why) 2003, BRIT Award for Int. Breakthrough Artist 2003, World Music Awards for Best Female Artist, Best Pop Female Artist 2004, Grammy Awards for Best Female Pop Vocal Performance (for Sunrise), for Record of the Year (for Here We Go Again, with Ray Charles) 2005. *Film appearances:* My Blueberry Nights 2007, Wah Do Dem 2009, Ted 2012. *Recordings include:* albums: solo: Come Away With Me (Grammy Awards for Album of the Year, Best Pop Vocal Album 2003) 2002, Feels Like Home 2004, Not Too Late 2007, The Fall 2009, Little Broken Hearts 2012, Day Breaks 2016; with The Little Willies: The Little Willies 2006. *Address:* Silva Artist Management LLC, 722 Seward Street, Los Angeles, CA 90038, USA (office). *E-mail:* info@sammusicbiz.com (office). *Website:* www.sammusicbiz.com (office); www.norahjones.com.

JONES, Quincy; American composer, arranger, conductor, musician (trumpet) and music industry executive; b. 14 March 1933, Chicago, Ill.; s. of Quincy Delight and Sarah Jones; m. 2nd Peggy Lipton; two d.; three c. by previous m.; one d. with Nastassja Kinski; ed Seattle Univ., Berklee School of Music and Boston Conservatory; musician and arranger, Lionel Hampton Orchestra 1950–53; arranger for orchestras and singers including Frank Sinatra, Dinah Washington, Count Basie, Sarah Vaughan and Peggy Lee; organizer and trumpeter, Dizzy Gillespie Orchestra, Dept of State tour of Near and Middle East and S. America 1956; Music Dir Barclay Disques, Paris; led own European tour 1960; Music Dir Mercury Records 1961, Vice-Pres. 1964; f. Quincy Jones Media Group 1997, Qwest Records, Qwest Broadcasting, Quincy Jones Foundation, among other orgs; Commdr, Légion d'Honneur 2001, Commdr, Ordre des Arts et des Lettres 2014; Dr hc (Berklee Music Coll.) 1983; (Hebrew Univ.) 1993, (Clark Univ.) 1993, (Morehouse Coll.) 2007, (Washington Univ. in St. Louis) 2008, (Univ. of Washington) 2008, (Jacobs School of Music, Indiana Univ.) 2010; several Grammy Awards, including Grammy Trustees Award 1989, German Jazz Fed. Award, Edison Int. Award (Sweden), Downbeat Critics' Poll Award, Downbeat Readers' Poll Award, Billboard Trendsetters Award 1983, Martell Foundation Humanitarian Award 1986, Nat. Acad. of Songwriters Lifetime Achievement Award 1989, Polar Music Prize, Royal Swedish Acad. of Music 1994, Rudolph Valentino Award 1994, Jean Hersholt Humanitarian Award 1995, Scopus Award, Producers Guild of America Award 1999, World Econ. Forum Crystal Award 2000, Marian Anderson Award 2001, Nat. Foundation for Advancement in the Arts Ted Arison Prize 2001, Kennedy Center Honor 2001, BBC Jazz Lifetime Achievement Award 2006, Ivor Novello Special Int. Award 2007, George and Ira Gershwin Award for Lifetime Musical Achievement, UCLA 2007, DaimlerChrysler Behind the Lens Award 2007, BET Humanitarian Award 2008, Clinton Global Citizen Award 2009, Nat. Medal of Arts 2010, inducted into Rock and Roll Hall of Fame 2013, Desi Arnaz Pioneer Award, Latin Songwriters Hall of Fame 2015. *Films include:* as composer: In the Heat of the Night 1967, In Cold Blood 1967, Bob & Carol & Ted & Alice 1969, The Getaway 1972, The Color Purple 1985, Get Rich or Die Tryin' 2005; contrib. to numerous soundtracks; conductor of numerous film scores. *Recordings include:* albums: Body Heat 1974, The Dude 1981, Back on the Block 1989; producer recordings of Off the Wall 1979 by Michael Jackson, Thriller 1982, Bad, videotape Portrait of An Album: Frank Sinatra with Quincy Jones and Orchestra 1986. *Television includes:* as producer: Fresh Prince of Bel Air 1990–96, The History of Rock 'n' Roll (series) 1995, In the House (series) 1995–99, Say It Loud: A Celebration of Black Music in America (mini-series) 2001, MADtv (series) 1997–2009. *Publication:* The Complete Quincy Jones: My Journey and Passions 2008. *E-mail:* info@quincyjones.com. *Website:* www.quincyjones.com.

JONES, Randall Todd, Sr; American retail executive; *President and CEO, Publix Super Markets;* b. 1962; m. Suzette Simonelli; one s. one d.; joined Publix Super Markets 1980, Regional Dir of Retail Operations 1999–2003, Vice-Pres. 2003–05, Sr Vice-Pres. 2005–08, Pres. and CEO 2008–; mem. Bd of Dirs Food for All. *Address:* Publix Super Markets Corporate Office, PO Box 407, Lakeland, FL 33811-3311, USA (office). *Telephone:* (863) 688-1188 (office). *Fax:* (863) 284-5532 (office). *E-mail:* info@publix.com (office). *Website:* www.publix.com (office).

JONES, Roy, Jr; American/Russian professional boxer (retd); b. 16 Jan. 1969, Pensacola, Fla; three s.; professional career record of 62 wins, eight defeats, 45 knock-outs; voted Outstanding Boxer Olympic Games 1988; won IBF (Int. Boxing Fed.) middleweight crown beating Bernard Hopkins 1993; moved up to super middleweight, won IBF title from James Toney 1994; moved up to light heavyweight div. winning WBC (World Boxing Council) (1997), WBA (World Boxing Asscn) (1998) and IBF (1999) titles; winner WBA heavyweight title 2003 (first fmr middleweight champion since 1897 to win title); winner WBC light heavyweight title 2003, defeated by Glen Johnson losing IBF light heavyweight title 2004, lost to Antonio Tarver losing WBC and WBA light heavyweight title 2004, winner WBO N American Boxing Org. (NABO) Light Heavyweight title 2006, defeated Félix Trinidad 2008, lost to Joe Calzaghe losing Light Heavyweight Championship 2008, defeated Omar Sheika on March 2009, defeated Jeff Lacy Aug 2009, lost to Danny Green Dec. 2009, lost to Bernard Hopkins in a rematch bout April 2010, lost to Denis Lebedev on May 2011; minor league professional basketball player for five years with the Sarasota Sun Dogs; f. Body Head Entertainment 1998; has appeared in numerous films and TV programmes; currently boxing analyst and commentator for Home Box Office (HBO); Boxing Writers Asscn of America Fighter of the Decade (for 1990s), The Ring Fighter of the Year 1994, WBC Lifetime Achievement Award 2001. *Recordings include:* Round

One: The Album 2001, Body Head Bangerz: Volume One 2004. *Films include:* The Devil's Advocate 1997, The Wayans Brothers, Rope-a-Dope 1999, The Matrix Reloaded 2003, Enter The Matrix 2003, Cordially Invited 2007, Universal Soldier: A New Dimension 2012, Southpaw 2015. *Leisure interests:* music, basketball, hunting, fishing, raising livestock. *Address:* c/o RoyalTey Management, 1765 Nine Mile Road, Suite 1-104, Pensacola, FL 32514, USA (office). *Website:* www.royjonesjr.com.

JONES, Stephanie (Steffi) Ann; German/American football executive and fmr professional football player; *Director, German Football Association;* b. 22 Dec. 1972, Frankfurt am Main; ed German Sport Univ., Cologne; defender; youth career: played with SV Bonames 1979–86, SV Dörnigheim FC 1986–88, FC Hochstadt 1988–92; sr career: played with SG Praunheim 1988–91, FSV Frankfurt 1991–92, SG Praunheim 1992–93, TuS Niederkirchen 1993–94, SG Praunheim 1994–95, FSV Frankfurt 1995–96, SC 07 Bad Neuenahr 1998–2000, Washington Freedom 2002–03 (WUSA Founders Cup Champion 2003), 1. FFC Frankfurt 2000–07 (German Championship 2001, 2002, 2003, 2005, German Cup Winner 2001, 2002, 2003, UEFA Women's Cup Winner 2002, 2006); scored nine goals in 111 caps for the German nat. team 1993–2007 (retd), won three consecutive UEFA Women's Championships 1997, 2001, 2005, bronze medal at Summer Olympics, Sydney 2000, part of German squad that won FIFA Women's World Cup 2003, bronze medal, Summer Olympics, Athens 2004; announced retirement from active football to become Pres. of Organizing Cttee of 2011 FIFA Women's World Cup in Germany Dec. 2007; Dir, German Football Asscn (DFB); FIFA Amb. for Women's Football; UEFA Amb. for Women's Football; Hessian Order of Merit 2006; Georg August Zinn Prize, Hall of Freedom (USA), Deutscher PR-Preis 'Kommunikator des Jahres 2011', Horizont Sportbusiness Award 'Persönlichkeit 2011', Ehren-Preis 11 Freundinnen 2011. *Publication:* Der Kick des Lebens (The Kick of Life) (autobiog.) 2007. *Address:* c/o Sportsfreude, Kirchstraße 104, 65375 Oestrich-Winkel, Germany (office); Deutscher Fußball-Bund, Hermann-Neuberger-Haus, Otto-Fleck-Schneise 6, 60528 Frankfurt am Main, Germany (office). *Telephone:* (6723) 804934 (office); (69) 67880 (office). *Fax:* (6723) 8049339 (office); (69) 6788266 (office). *E-mail:* mail@sportsfreude.com (office); info@dfb.de (office). *Website:* sportsfreude.com/projects/steffi-jones (office); www.dfb.de (office).

JONES, Stephen John Moffat, OBE, BA (Hons); British milliner; *Chairman, Stephen Jones Millinery Ltd;* b. 31 May 1957, West Kirby, Cheshire, England; s. of Gordon Jones and Margaret Jones; m. Craig West; ed Liverpool Coll., St Martin's School of Art; milliner 1980–, collaborating with int. designers including Jean-Paul Gaultier, Comme des Garçons, Claude Montana, John Galliano, Christian Dior (Paris) 1997–; colour creator for Shiseido Cosmetics; licences in Japan for gloves, sunglasses, kimonos, scarves, handkerchiefs, handbags; hats in perm. collections of Victoria and Albert Museum, London, Brooklyn Musuem, New York, Kyoto Costume Inst., Australian Nat. Gallery, Canberra; Hon. Prof., Univ. of the Arts, London; Accessory Designer of the Year 2005, Outstanding Contrib. to Fashion Design 2009, Fashion Star Honoree, New York 2009, Royal Designer for Industry 2009; Chevalier des Chapeaux de Caussade (France) 2005. *Dance:* Eternal Light, Ballet Rambert 2009. *Films:* Coco avant Chanel, Sex and the City 2. *Publication:* Hats: An Anthology by Stephen Jones. *Leisure interest:* sculpture. *Address:* Stephen Jones Millinery Ltd, 36 Great Queen Street, London, WC2B 5AA, England (office). *Telephone:* (20) 7242-0770 (office). *Fax:* (20) 7242-0796 (office). *E-mail:* admin@stephenjonesmillinery.com (office). *Website:* www.stephenjonesmillinery.com (office).

JONES, Sir Tom, Kt; British singer; b. (Thomas Jones Woodward), 7 June 1940, Pontypridd, Mid Glamorgan, S Wales; s. of Thomas Woodward and Freda Woodward (née Jones); m. Melinda Trenchard 1956 (died 2016); one s.; fmr bricklayer, factory worker; sang in clubs and dance halls billing himself as Tommy Scott, singing with the Senators and with self-formed group The Playboys; changed his name to Tom Jones, signed contract with Decca as solo artist 1963; first hit record It's Not Unusual 1965; toured USA 1965; appeared in Ed Sullivan Show at Copacabana, New York and in variety show This Is Tom Jones in UK and USA 1969; score for musical play Matador 1987; acted and sang in live performance of Dylan Thomas' Under Milk Wood 1992; performed in Amnesty International 40th Anniversary Special 2001, Pavarotti and Friends 2001, Prince's Trust Party in the Park 2001; mem. Screen Actors Guild, American Fed. of TV and Radio Artists, American Guild of Variety Artists; Hon. Fellow, Welsh Coll. of Music and Drama 1994; voted Britain's Most Popular Male Singer in Melody Maker Poll 1967, 1968, MTV Video Award 1988, BRIT Award for Best British Male Solo Artist 2000, Nordoff-Robbins Music Therapy Silver Clef Award 2001, Q Magazine Merit Prize 2002, BRIT Award for Outstanding Contrib. to Music 2003, Music Industry Trust Award for Outstanding Contrib. to Music 2010. *Films:* The Jerky Boys – The Movie 1995, Mars Attacks! 1996, Agnes Browne 1999, The Emperor's New Groove (voice) 2000. *Television includes:* Beat Room, Top Gear, Thank Your Lucky Stars, Sunday Night at the London Palladium, The Right Time (series) 1992, The Voice 2012–15, 2017–. *Albums:* Along Came Jones 1965, A-Tom-Ic Jones 1966, From The Great 1966, Green Green Grass Of Home 1966, Live At The Talk Of The Town 1967, Delilah 1968, Help Yourself 1968, Tom Jones Live In Las Vegas 1969, This Is Tom Jones 1969, Tom 1970, I Who Have Nothing 1970, Tom Jones Sings She's A Lady 1971, Tom Jones Live At Caesar's Palace, Las Vegas 1971, Close Up 1972, The Body And Soul Of Tom Jones 1973, Somethin' 'Bout You Baby I Like 1974, Memories Don't Leave Like People 1975, Say You'll Stay Until Tomorrow 1977, Rescue Me 1980, Darlin' 1981, Matador: The Musical Life Of El Cordobes 1987, At This Moment 1989, After Dark 1989, Move Closer 1989, Carrying A Torch 1991, The Lead And How To Swing It 1994, Reload 1999, Mr Jones 2002, Reload 2 2002, 24 Hours 2008, Praise and Blame 2010, Spirit in the Room 2012, Long Lost Suitcase 2015. *Publications:* Over the Top and Back (autobiography) 2015. *Leisure interests:* history, music. *Address:* c/o Jennie Harris, Valley Music Ltd, Unit 6, Upper Culham Farm Barns, Upper Culham, Wargrave, Henley on Thames, Oxon., RG10 8NR, England (office); Tom Jones Enterprises LLC, 1801 Avenue of the Stars, Suite 200, Los Angeles, CA 90067, USA (office). *Telephone:* (1491) 845840 (office); (310) 552-0044 (office). *E-mail:* jennieharris@valleymusicuk.com (office); office@tomjones.com (office). *Fax:* (310) 552-0714 (office). *Website:* www.tomjones.com (office).

JONES, Tommy Lee; American actor; b. 15 Sept. 1946, San Saba, Tex.; s. of Clyde L. Jones and Lucille Marie Scott; m. 1st Kimberlea Cloughley 1981; m. 2nd Dawn Laurel 2001; ed Harvard Univ.; Broadway debut in A Patriot for Me; other Broadway appearances include Four in a Garden, Ulysses in Night Town, Fortune and Men's Eyes; Emmy Award for TV role as Gary Gilmon in The Executioner's Song. *Films include:* Love Story 1970, Eliza's Horoscope, Jackson County Jail, Rolling Thunder, The Betsy, Eyes of Laura Mars, Coal Miner's Daughter, Back Roads, Nate and Hayes, River Rat, Black Moon Rising, The Big Town, Stormy Monday, The Package, Firebirds, JFK, Under Siege, House of Cards, The Fugitive, Blue Sky, Heaven and Earth, Natural Born Killers, The Client, Blue Sky, Cobb, Batman Forever, Men In Black 1997, Volcano 1997, Marshals 1997, Small Soldiers (voice) 1998, Rules of Engagement 1999, Double Jeopardy 1999, Space Cowboys 2000, Men in Black II 2002, The Hunted 2003, Man of the House 2005, The Three Burials of Melquiades Estrada (also dir) 2005, A Prairie Home Companion 2006, No Country for Old Men 2007, In the Valley of Elah 2007, Men in Black III 2012, Lincoln 2012, The Family 2013, The Homesman (also dir) 2014. *Television appearances include:* The Amazing Howard Hughes, Lonesome Dove, The Rainmaker, Cat on a Hot Tin Roof, Yuri Nosenko, KGB, April Morning. *Address:* Creative Artists Agency, 2000 Avenue of the Stars, Los Angeles, CA 90067, USA (office).

JONES, Vaughan Frederick Randal, KNZM, BSc, MSc, DèsSc, FRS; New Zealand mathematician and academic; *Stevenson Distinguished Professor of Mathematics, Vanderbilt University;* b. 31 Dec. 1952, Gisborne; m. Martha Weare Jones (née Myers) 1979; one s. two d.; ed Auckland Grammar School, Univ. of Auckland, Univ. of Geneva, Switzerland; fmr Asst Lecturer, Univ. of Auckland; at Ecole de Physique, Geneva 1974–76, Ecoles Mathématiques 1976–79, taught as asst; E.R. Hedrick Asst Prof. of Math., UCLA 1980–81; Asst Prof., Univ. of Pennsylvania 1981–84, Assoc. Prof. 1984–85; apptd Prof., Univ. of California, Berkeley 1985, now Prof. Emer.; Stevenson Distinguished Prof. of Math., Vanderbilt Univ. 2011–; elected Vice-Pres. American Mathematical Soc. 2004, Vice-Pres. Int. Math. Union 2014; mem. American Acad. of Arts and Sciences 1993–, NAS 1999–, American Math. Soc. (Vice-Pres. 2004–); Foreign mem. Norwegian Royal Soc. of Letters and Sciences 2001–; Hon. mem. London Math. Soc. 2002–; Hon. DSc (Univ. of Auckland) 1992, (Univ. of Wales) 1993; Dr hc (Université du Littoral, Cote d'Opale) 2002; Univ. Entrance Scholarship 1970, Gilles Scholarship, Phillips Industries Bursary 1970, Swiss Gov. Scholarship 1973, F.W.W. Rhodes Memorial Scholarship, Vacheron Constantin Prize 1980, Guggenheim Fellowship 1986, Fields Medal, Int. Congress of Mathematicians, Kyoto, Japan 1990, New Zealand Gov. Science Medal 1991, Onsager Medal, Trondheim Univ. 2000, Prix Mondial Nessim Habif 2007. *Publications:* numerous articles in math. journals on functional analysis, knot theory and Von Neumann algebras. *Address:* Department of Mathematics, 1326 Stevenson Center, Vanderbilt University, Nashville, TN 37240, USA (office). *E-mail:* vaughan.f.jones@vanderbilt.edu (office). *Website:* as.vanderbilt.edu/math (office).

JONES-MORGAN, Judith, LLB, LLM; Saint Vincent and the Grenadines lawyer and government official; b. 7 Sept. 1957, Trinidad and Tobago; d. of Rita Jones; m. Desmond Carlos Richardson Morgan; ed Univ. of E London and Jesus Coll. Cambridge, UK; accounts technician Ministry of Finance and Treasury, Trinidad and Tobago 1976–80; legal clerk, Nat. Energy Corpn, Trinidad and Tobago 1980–84; legal asst, Graham Ritchie & Co., UK 1988–89; pupil barrister Chancery/Commercial Chambers, UK 1991; Crown Counsel in Chambers of Attorney-Gen., Saint Vincent and the Grenadines 1992–93, Sr Crown Counsel 1993–99; registrar, High Court 2000–01, Attorney-Gen. of Saint Vincent and the Grenadines 2001–17; mem. Interim Study Programme for Judicial Educators 2000; mem. Bar of England and Wales, Saint Vincent and the Grenadines, Trinidad and Tobago; mem. Hon. Soc. of the Middle Temple, UK; Fellow, Cambridge Commonwealth Soc. 1990; Cambridge Commonwealth Award, Maxwell Law Prize, UKCOSA Essay Competition. *Leisure interests:* politics, drama, public speaking, cricket, jogging, travel.

JONES OF BIRMINGHAM, Baron (Life Peer), cr. 2007, of Alvechurch and of Bromsgrove in the County of Worcestershire; **Digby Marritt Jones,** LLB, FRSA, CIMgt; British lawyer, business consultant and fmr government official; b. 28 Oct. 1955, Birmingham; s. of Derek Jones and Bernice Jones; m. Patricia Mary Jones; ed Bromsgrove School, Univ. Coll. London; joined Edge & Ellison (corp. law firm) 1978, Pnr 1984, Deputy Sr Pnr 1990, Sr Pnr 1995; joined KPMG as Vice-Chair. Corp. Finance 1998; Dir-Gen. CBI 2000–06; Sr Adviser to Deloitte 2006–07; Sr Adviser, Barclays Capital 2006–07, Ford (Europe) 2006–07, JCB 2006–07, 2009–, Monitise 2009–, Jaguar Land Rover 2009; UK Skills Envoy 2006–07; Minister of State for Trade and Investment, Dept for Business, Enterprise and Regulatory Reform (jtly with FCO) 2007–08, also Labour whip in House of Lords 2007–08; Chair. Triumph Motorcycles Ltd 2009–; Dir (non-exec.) Alba PLC 2003–07; Dir Leicester Tigers 2005–, Königswinter 2003–07; mem. Advisory Bd Commonwealth Educ. Fund 2000–07; fmr Pres. Tourism Alliance 2001–06; Commr Comm. for Racial Equality 2002–07; fmr mem. Nat. Learning and Skills Council 2004–06, Skills Alliance 2002; Companion Inst. of Man. 2000; Chair. HSBC Int. Business Advisory Bd 2009–, Univ. of Birmingham Business School Advisory Bd 2004; Full mem. Aston Reinvestment Trust 2003; Fellow, RSA 2001, Royal Inst. 2002, University Coll. London 2004 (Pres. University Coll. London Campaign 2004–); Hon. Fellow, Cardiff Univ. 2004; Dr hc (Central England) 2002, (Birmingham) 2002, (Manchester), (Inst. of Science and Tech.) 2003, (Hertfordshire) 2004, (Middlesex) 2005, (Sheffield Hallam) 2005, (Warwick) 2006, (Aston) 2006, (Bradford) 2006, (Hull) 2006, (Queens Univ., Belfast) 2006, (Loughborough) 2007, (Nottingham) 2007, (Thames Valley) 2007, (Wolverhampton) 2007,. *Leisure interests:* Aston Villa, theatre, skiing, cycling, rugby, military history. *Address:* House of Lords, Westminster, London, SW1A 0PW (office); 58 Elizabeth Court, 1 Palgrave Gardens, London, NW1 6EJ, England (home). *Telephone:* (20) 7219-3232 (office); 7827-828283 (mobile) (office). *E-mail:* joanne@digbylordjones.com (office). *Website:* www.parliament.uk/biographies/lords/lord-jones-of-birmingham/3775 (office); www.digbylordjones.com (office).

JONES PARRY, Sir Emyr, GCMG, PhD, FInstP, PLSW; British diplomatist and university administrator; *President, Learned Society of Wales;* b. 21 Sept. 1947, Carmarthen, Wales; s. of Hugh Jones Parry and Eirwen Jones Parry; m. Lynn Jones Parry; two s.; ed Gwendraeth Grammar School, Univ. Coll., Cardiff, St Catharine's Coll., Cambridge; joined FCO 1973; Deputy Chef du Cabinet of Pres. of European Parl. 1987–89; Head EC Dept (External) FCO 1989–93; Minister, Embassy in Madrid 1993–96; Deputy Political Dir FCO 1996–97; Dir EU, FCO

1997–98; Political Dir, FCO 1998–2001; Perm. Rep. to North Atlantic Council, NATO 2001–03, to UN, New York 2003–07; Chancellor Univ. of Aberystwyth 2007–17; Chair. All Wales Convention 2007–09, Wales Millennium Centre 2010–16, Redress 2008–16; Pres. Welsh Centre for Int. Affairs 2011–, Learned Soc. of Wales 2014–; various univ. fellowships; Hon. LLD (Wales); Hon. DSc (South Wales). *Publications:* various scientific publs, speeches on current int. issues. *Leisure interests:* gardening, theatre, reading, sport. *Address:* Learned Society of Wales, University Registry, King Edward VII Avenue, Cardiff, CF10 3NS, Wales (office). *E-mail:* president@lsw.wales.ac.uk (home). *Website:* www.learnedsociety.wales (office).

JONG, Erica Mann, BA, MA; American writer, poet and journalist; b. 26 March 1942, New York; d. of Seymour Mann and Eda Mann (née Mirsky); m. 1st Michael Werthman 1963 (divorced 1965); m. 2nd Allan Jong 1966 (divorced 1975); m. 3rd Jonathan Fast 1977 (divorced 1983); one d.; m. 4th Kenneth David Burrows 1989; ed Barnard Coll., Columbia Univ.; studied poetry with Mark Strand and Stanley Kunitz; Lecturer in English, City Coll. of New York 1965–66, 1969–70; Poetry Instructor, Poetry Center of the 92nd Street Y 1966–69; Lecturer in English, Overseas Div., Univ. of Maryland, Heidelberg, Germany 1970–72; Bread Loaf Writers Conf., Middlebury, Vt 1970–73; mem. Literature Panel, New York State Council on Arts 1972–74; mem. of Faculty, Salzburg Seminar, Austria 1993; Visiting Writer, Ben Gurion Univ., Beersheva, Israel 1998, Bennington Coll. 1998, Marymount Coll. Writers Workshop Poetry Seminar 2007; Writing Prof., Barnard Coll. 2011–12; Writing Prof., Rancho La Puerta, 2001–; Hon. Fellow, Welsh Coll. of Music and Drama 1994; New York State Council on the Arts Grants 1971, Nat. Endowment of the Arts grant 1973; Hon. PhD (CUNY) 2006; Acad. of American Poets Prize 1971, Poetry magazine Bess Hokin Prize 1971, Poetry Soc. of America Alice Faye di Castagnola Award 1972, Freud Award for Literature, Italy 1975, UN Award for Excellence in Literature 1995, Prix Littéraire de Deauville Film Festival (France) 1998, Fernanda Pivano Award for Literature (Italy) 2009. *Publications include:* poetry: Fruits and Vegetables 1971, Half-Lives 1973, Loveroot 1975, At the Edge of the Body 1979, Ordinary Miracles 1983, Becoming Light: Poems New and Selected 1991, Love Comes First 2009; novels: Fear of Flying 1973, How to Save Your Own Life 1977, Fanny: Being the True History of Fanny Hackabout-Jones 1980, Parachutes and Kisses 1984, Serenissima: A Novel of Venice (aka Shylock's Daughter: A Novel of Love in Venice) 1987, Any Woman's Blues 1990, Inventing Memory: A Novel of Mothers and Daughters 1997, Sappho's Leap 2004, Fear of Dying: A Novel 2015; non-fiction: Witches 1981, Megan's Book of Divorce (for children) 1984, The Devil at Large: Erica Jong on Henry Miller 1993, Fear of Fifty: A Midlife Memoir 1994, What Do Women Want? Bread. Roses. Sex. Power 1998, Seducing the Demon: Writing for my Life 2006, Sugar in My Bowl 2011, A Letter to the President 2012. *Leisure interests:* sailing, flying, spending time with family. *Address:* c/o Elizabeth Sheinkman, Peters Fraser + Dunlop, Drury House, 34-43 Russell Street, London, WC2B 5HA, England (office); 150 East 69th Street, Apt 27G, New York, NY 10021, USA (office). *Telephone:* (20) 7344-1024 (office); (212) 517-2907 (home). *E-mail:* esheinkman@pfd.co.uk (office); officejongleur@gmail.com (home). *Website:* www.ericajong.com.

JONSEN, Albert R., MA, PhD, STM; American academic; *Senior Bioethics Scholar-in-Residence Emeritus, Program in Medical and Human Values, California Pacific Medical Center;* b. 4 April 1931, San Francisco, Calif.; s. of Albert R. Jonsen and Helen C. Sweigert; m. Mary E. Carolan 1976; ed Gonzaga Univ., Santa Clara Univ., Yale Univ.; Instructor in Philosophy, Loyola Univ. of Los Angeles 1956–59; Instructor in Divinity, Yale Univ. 1966–67; Asst, then Assoc. Prof. in Philosophy and Theology, Univ. of San Francisco 1968–73, Pres. Univ. of San Francisco 1969–72; Prof. of Ethics in Medicine and Chief, Div. of Medical Ethics, Univ. of California, San Francisco 1973–87; Prof. of Ethics in Medicine and Chair. Dept of Medical History and Ethics, Univ. of Washington, Seattle 1987–99, Prof. Emer. 1999–; fmr Co-Dir and Sr Scholar-in-Residence, Program in Medicine and Human Values, California Pacific Medical Center, now Sr Bioethics Scholar-in-Residence Emer.; Commr, US Nat. Comm. for Protection of Human Subjects of Biomedical and Behavioral Research 1974–78; Commr, Pres.'s Comm. for Study of Ethical Problems in Medicine and in Biomedical and Behavioral Research 1979–82; mem. Artificial Heart Assessment Panel, Nat. Heart and Lung Inst. 1972–73, 1984–86; mem. Nat. Bd of Medical Examiners 1985–88; Consultant, American Bd of Internal Medicine 1978–84; mem. Ethics Advisory Bd GERON Corpn 2000–05; mem. NAS Inst. of Medicine 1980–, mem. NAS Cttee on AIDS Research; Chair. NRC Cttee on the Social Implications of AIDS 1987–92, Nat. Advisory Bd on Ethics and Reproduction 1992–97; Pres. Soc. for Health and Human Values 1986; Guggenheim Fellowship 1982, 1986–87; Visiting Prof., Yale Univ. 1999–2000, Stanford Univ. School of Medicine 2002, Univ. of Virginia Law School 2002, Inst. of Medicine, NAS, Harvard Medical School, Georgetown Univ., Johns Hopkins Medical School, Center for Bioethics (Netherlands); Visiting Scholar, Nat. Library of Medicine, NIH; Davies Award, American Coll. of Physicians 1987, Convocation Medal, American Coll. of Surgeons 1988, Annual Award, Soc. for Health and Humanities 1993, Lifetime Achievement Award, American Soc. for Bioethics and Humanities 1999, Leadership Award, Professional Responsibility in Medicine and Research 2000, Lifetime Achievement Award, Berman Inst. of Bioethics, Johns Hopkins Univ. 2009, Nelson Lecturer, Univ. of California, Davis 2010. *Publications include:* Responsibility in Modern Religious Ethics 1968, Ethics of Newborn Intensive Care 1976, Clinical Ethics (with M. Siegler and W. Winslade) 1982, The Abuse of Casuistry (with S. Toulmin) 1986, The Old Ethics and the New Medicine 1990, The Impact of AIDS on American Society (with J. Stryker) 1993, The Birth of Bioethics 1997, A Short History of Medical Ethics 2000, Bioethics Beyond the Headlines 2005. *Leisure interests:* sketching, swimming, walking, music. *Address:* Program in Medical and Human Values, California Pacific Medical Center, 2395 Sacramento Street, San Francisco, CA 94115, USA (office). *Telephone:* (415) 600-1647 (office). *E-mail:* ethics@sutterhealth.org (office). *Website:* www.cpmc.org/services/ethics (office).

JONZE, Spike; American film director, film producer, actor and screenwriter; b. (Adam Spiegel), 1969, Rockville, Md; s. of Arthur Spiegel III and Sandy Granzow; m. Sofia Coppola 1999 (divorced 2003); fmr Ed. Freestylin', Go, BMX Action, Homeboy, Grand Royal magazines; f. Dirt magazine with Andy Jenkins and Mark Lewman 1991; began directing skating films and music videos; Co-Pres. Viceland cable network 2016–. *Music videos as director:* California by Wax, Sure Shot by the Beastie Boys, Sabotage by the Beastie Boys, Drop by the Pharcyde, Cannonball by The Breeders, What's Up Fatlip? by Fatlip, Undone (The Sweater Song) by Weezer, Buddy Holly by Weezer (MTV Video Music Award for Best Direction 1995), Feel The Pain by Dinosaur Jr, If I Only Had A Brain by MC 900ft Jesus, Sky's The Limit by The Notorious B.I.G., Crush with Eyeliner by R.E.M., It's Oh So Quiet by Björk, Da Funk by Daft Punk, Praise You by Fatboy Slim, Weapon of Choice by Fatboy Slim, Elektrobank by The Chemical Brothers, Wonderboy by Tenacious D (as Spike Jones). *Films include:* Video Days (dir) 1991, Mi Vida Loca (actor) 1994, How They Get There (dir) 1997, The Game (actor) 1997, Amarillo by Morning (dir) 1998, Being John Malkovich (dir, actor) (New York Film Critics Circle Award for Best First Film, Broadcast Film Critics Asscn Breakthrough Performer, Online Film Critics Soc. Award for Best Debut) 1999, Three Kings (actor) 1999, Torrance Rises (dir, as Richard Coufey) 1999, Human Nature (producer) 2001, Adaptation (dir) (Berlin Film Festival Silver Bear 2003) 2002, Jackass: The Movie (writer, producer) 2002, Yeah Right! (dir, producer) 2003, Jackass Number Two (producer) 2006, Synecdoche, New York (producer) 2008, Where the Wild Things Are 2009, Her (Golden Globe Award for Best Screenplay, Motion Picture, Academy Award for Best Original Screenplay 2014) 2013. *Television includes:* Jackass (series writer and producer) 2000–02, Cyberwar (documentary series, producer) 2016, Abandoned (documentary series) 2016. *Website:* www.viceland.com.

JOPLING, Jay; British art dealer and gallery owner; *Owner, White Cube gallery;* b. June 1963, Thirsk; s. of Lord Jopling, fmr Minister of Agric., Fisheries and Food; m. Sam Taylor-Wood (divorced 2008); two d.; ed Eton Coll., Univ. of Edinburgh; began by selling fire extinguishers before starting to deal in post-war American art; formed friendship with artist Damien Hirst 1991, arranged financing for production of new work; supported small list of artists, including Hirst and Marc Quinn organizing exhbns in warehouses; opened White Cube gallery, St James's, London 1993, gallery moved to larger space in Hoxton 2000 (closed 2012), Mason's Yard gallery located off Duke Street, St James's opened in Sept. 2006, White Cube Bermondsey opened in Oct. 2012, White Cube Hong Kong (first outside UK) opened with a show of Gilbert & George in March 2012, White Cube São Paulo opened with a solo show by Tracey Emin in Dec. 2012; has represented British artists including Damien Hirst, Chapman Brothers, Tracey Emin and Antony Gormley; has also represented int. artists, including Gabriel Orozco, Anselm Kiefer, Mona Hatuom and Julie Mehretu. *Address:* White Cube, 144–152 Bermondsey Street, London, SE1 3TQ (office); White Cube, 25–26 Mason's Yard (off Duke Street), St James's, London, SW1Y 6BU, England; White Cube Hong Kong, 50 Connaught Road, Hong Kong Special Administrative Region, People's Republic of China. *Telephone:* (20) 7930-5373 (office); 2592-2000 (Hong Kong). *Fax:* (20) 7749-7480 (office). *E-mail:* enquiries@whitecube.com (office). *Website:* www.whitecube.com (office); www.jayjopling.co.uk.

JOPLING, Baron (Life Peer), cr. 1997, of Ainderby Quernhow in the County of North Yorkshire; **(Thomas) Michael Jopling,** PC, BSc; British politician and farmer; *Member of Parliamentary Assembly, NATO;* b. 10 Dec. 1930, Ripon, Yorks.; s. of Mark Bellerby Jopling; m. Gail Dickinson 1958; two s.; ed Cheltenham Coll. and King's Coll., Durham Univ., Newcastle-upon-Tyne; mem. Thirsk Rural Dist Council 1958–64; Conservative MP for Westmorland 1964–83, Westmorland and Lonsdale 1983–97; Jt Sec. Conservative Parl. Agric. Cttee 1966–70; Parl. Pvt. Sec. to Minister of Agric. 1970–71; an Asst Govt Whip 1971–73; Lord Commr of the Treasury 1973–74; an Opposition Spokesman on Agric. 1974–75, 1976–79; Shadow Minister of Agric. 1975–76; Parl. Sec. to HM Treasury and Chief Whip 1979–83; Minister of Agric., Fisheries and Food 1983–87; mem. Nat. Council, Nat. Farmers' Union 1962–64, UK Exec., Commonwealth Parl. Asscn 1974–79, 1987–97, Vice-Chair. 1977–79, Int. Exec. 1988–89; Chair. Select Cttee on Sittings of the House 1991–92; mem. Select Cttee on Agric. 1967–69, on Foreign Affairs 1987–97; mem. Privy Council 1979–; mem. NATO Parl. Ass. 1987–97, 2001–, Chair. Cttee Civilian Aspects of Security 2011–14; Leader UK Del. to Parl. Ass., OSCE 1990–97, mem. 2000–01; mem. Lords Sub-Cttee 'C' European Defence and Security 1999–2003 (Chair. 2000–03), 2010–, mem. Sub-Cttee 'F' Home Affairs 2006–10 (Chair. 2007–10); mem. Lords SEL Cttee, Merits of Statutory Instruments 2004–07; Pres. Auto-Cycle Union 1989–2003, Pres. Emer. 2003–; DL Cumbria 1991–97, N Yorks. 1998–2006; Hon. Sec. British American Parl. Group 1987–2001; Hon. DCL (Newcastle) 1992. *Address:* Ainderby Hall, Thirsk, North Yorks., YO7 4HZ, England. *Telephone:* (1845) 567224.

JORDA, Claude Jean Charles; French judge and international official; b. 16 Feb. 1938, Bône, Algeria; ed Institut d'Etudes Politiques and School of Law, Univ. of Toulouse, Ecole Nat. de la Magistrature (ENM); called to the Bar, Toulouse 1961; Auditeur de Justice (magistrate in training) 1963–66; Magistrate, Cen. Admin. Services Dept, Ministry of Justice 1966–70, Deputy Dir for Legal Org. and Regulations 1976–78, Dir Legal Services 1982–85; Sec.-Gen. ENM 1970–76; Vice-Pres. Tribunal de Grande Instance, Paris 1978–82; Prosecutor-Gen. Court of Appeals, Bordeaux 1985–92, Paris 1992–94; Judge, Int. Criminal Tribunal for the Fmr Yugoslavia (ICTY) 1994–96, Pres. Trial Chamber I 1995–99, Pres. ICTY 1999–2003; Judge, Int. Criminal Court 2003–07 (resgnd); Section Pres. Cour nationale du droit d'asile 2008; Hon. Pres. Cour nationale du droit d'asile (fmrly Comm. des recours des réfugiés); Officier, Légion d'honneur 1993, Commdr, Ordre nat. du Mérite 2000, Commdr des Palmes académiques, Commdr du Mérite agricole; Médaille de l'Educ. Surveillée (for services to young people in difficulty and in prison). *Publications include:* Un nouveau statut pour l'accusé dans le procédure du Tribunal pénal international pour l'ex-Yougoslavie (essays) 2000; academic contribs, book chapters and conf. proc., articles on ICTY. *Address:* 21 rue Boudet, 33000 Bordeaux, France (home).

JORDAN, Michael Jeffery; American business executive and fmr professional basketball player; b. 17 Feb. 1963, Brooklyn, New York; s. of James Jordan and Delores Jordan; m. Juanita Vanoy 1989 (divorced 2006); two s. one d.; ed Univ. of North Carolina; player for Univ. of North Carolina (won NCAA championship 1982); drafted by Nat. Basketball Asscn (NBA) Chicago Bulls in first round 1984, played 1984–93, 1995–98 (NBA Champions 1991, 1992, 1993, 1996, 1997, 1998), retd from Chicago Bulls 1998; mem. US Olympic basketball team 1984, 1992 (Gold Medal winner); played for Birmingham Barons minor league baseball team 1993, Nashville Sounds 1994–95; Pres. Basketball Operations, Washington Wizards professional basketball team 1999–2003, came out of retirement to play for Washington Wizards 2001–03; minority owner, Bobcats Basketball Holdings, LLC (NBA's Charlotte Bobcats basketball franchise, renamed Hornets 2014) 2006–10, majority owner 2010–; extensive business interests include Michael Jordan's: The Restaurant 1993, Jordan Brand Clothing 1997; f. Jordan Motorsports/Suzuki 2004; Seagram's NBA Player of the Year 1987, NBA Most Valuable Player 1988, 1991, 1992, 1996, 1998, mem. NBA All-Star team 1985, 1987-93, 1996–98, 2003, Most Valuable Player, NBA All-Star Game 1988, Presidential Medal of Freedom 2016, numerous other awards. *Achievements include:* scored 32,292 points during career (third highest in NBA history), holds record for most points in NBA playoff game with 63, for highest points-scoring average (30.12) and many other records; named world's highest paid athlete, Forbes Magazine 1992. *Publications:* Rare Air: Michael on Michael (autobiography) 1993, I Can't Accept Not Trying: Michael Jordan on the Pursuit of Excellence, Driven From Within (co-author) 2004. *Address:* Charlotte Hornets Executive Offices, 333 East Trade Street, Charlotte, NC 28202, USA (office). *Telephone:* (704) 688-8600 (office). *Website:* www.nba.com/hornets (office).

JORDAN, Neil Patrick, BA; Irish writer and film director; b. 25 Feb. 1950, Sligo; m. 1st Vivienne Shields; two d.; m. 2nd Brenda Rawn 2004; two s.; ed St Paul's Coll. Raheny, Dublin and Univ. Coll., Dublin; co-f. Irish Writers' Co-operative, Dublin 1974; Dr hc (Univ. Coll. Dublin) 2005; London Evening Standard Most Promising Newcomer Award 1982, Irish Film and TV Awards Lifetime Achievement Award 2003. *Films directed:* Angel 1982, Company of Wolves (London Film Critics' Circle Award 1984) 1984, Mona Lisa 1986, High Spirits 1988, We're No Angels 1989, The Miracle (Evening Standard British Film Award) 1990, The Crying Game (Boston Soc. of Film Critics Award 1992, New York Film Critics Circle Award 1992, Writers Guild of America Award 1992, Acad. Award for Best Screenplay 1993, Los Angeles Film Critics Asscn Award, London Film Critics' Circle Award) 1992, Interview with the Vampire 1994, Michael Collins (Golden Lion, Venice Film Festival 1996) 1995, The Butcher Boy (Silver Bear for Best Dir, Berlin Film Festival 1998) 1997, In Dreams 1999, The End of the Affair (BAFTA for Best Screenplay 2000) 1999, Not I 2000, The Good Thief 2002, Breakfast on Pluto (Best Dir, Best Writer, IFTA 2007) 2005, The Brave One 2007, Ondine 2009, Byzantium 2013. *Television includes:* The Borgias (series) (Gemini Award for Best Int. Drama 2011, Canadian Screen Award for Best Int. Drama 2013) 2011–13. *Publications include:* Night in Tunisia and Other Stories (Guardian Fiction Award 1979) 1976, The Past 1979, The Dream of a Beast 1983, Sunrise with Sea Monster 1994, Nightlines 1995, Shade (novel) 2004, Mistaken 2011, The Borgias Apocalypse (screenplay) 2016, The Drowned Detective 2016, Carnivalesque 2017. *Leisure interest:* music. *Address:* c/o Casarotto Ramsay & Associates Limited, Waverley House, 7–12 Noel Street, London, W1F 8GQ, England (office); 6 Sorrento Terrace, Dalkey, Co. Dublin, Ireland (office).

JORDAN, Mgr Thierry; French ecclesiastic; *Archbishop of Rheims;* b. 31 Aug. 1943, Shanghai, China; m. Pierre Jordan and Henriette Jordan; ed Lycée Hoche, Grand Séminaire de Versailles, Institut catholique de Paris, Gregorian Univ., Rome, Italy; ordained priest, Versailles 1966; chaplain, Church of Saint-Louis-des-Français, Rome, then Sec. to Cardinal Jean Villot, Vatican 1967–79; curate, Vésinet, Versailles 1980–84; Vicar-Episcopal, Saint-Quentin-en-Yvelines 1984–87; Vicar-Gen. Versailles diocese 1986–88; Bishop of Pontoise (Val-d'Oise) 1988–99; Archbishop of Rheims 1999–; Chair. Comm. épiscopale de la vie consacrée of Conf. of French Bishops 1993–96; Chevalier, Ordre national de la Légion d'honneur 2006. *Address:* Archevéché de REIMS, secrétariat et Chancellerie, 3, rue du Cardinal de Lorraine, BP.2729, 51058 Rheims, France (office). *Telephone:* 3-26-47-05-33 (office). *Fax:* 3-26-84-94-66 (office). *Website:* catholique-reims.cef.fr (office).

JORDAN, Thomas J.; Swiss economist, academic and central banker; *Chairman of the Governing Board, Schweizerische Nationalbank;* b. 28 Jan. 1963, Biel; m.; two s.; ed Univ. of Bern, Harvard Univ., USA; Econ. Adviser, Dept I, Schweizerische Nationalbank (SNB, Swiss Nat. Bank, central bank) 1997–99, Asst Dir Econ. Studies Unit 1999–2002, Head of Research Unit 2002, Dir SNB 2004–, Alt. mem. Governing Bd 2004–07, mem. 2007–, Dir Dept III (Financial Markets, Banking Operations and Information Tech.) 2007–10, Dir Dept II (Financial Stability, Cash, Finance and Risk) 2010–12, Vice-Chair. SNB Governing Bd 2010–12, Chair. 2012–; Lecturer, Univ. of Bern 1998–, Hon. Prof. 2003; Lecturer, Univ. of Zürich 2002–07; Chair. SNB StabFund; Chair. G10 Central Bank Counterfeit Deterrence Group, Int. Center for Monetary and Banking Studies, Geneva; mem. Bd of Dirs BIS, Basel; mem. Steering Cttee Financial Stability Bd, Basel. *Publications:* numerous articles on monetary theory and policy in leading int. journals. *Address:* Office of the Chairman of the Governing Board, Schweizerische Nationalbank, Börsenstr. 15, Postfach 2800, 8022 Zürich, Switzerland (office). *Telephone:* 586310000 (office). *Fax:* 586315000 (office). *E-mail:* snb@snb.ch (office). *Website:* www.snb.ch (office).

JORDAN, Vernon Eulion, Jr, BA, JD; American lawyer and investment banker; *Senior Managing Director, Lazard Freres & Company LLC;* b. 15 Aug. 1935, Atlanta, Ga; s. of Vernon Eulion Jordan and Mary Jordan (née Griggs); m. 1st Shirley M. Yarbrough 1958 (died 1985); one c.; m. 2nd Ann Dibble Cook 1986; ed DePauw Univ., Howard Univ.; mem. Bar, Ga 1960, Ark. 1964; law practice, Atlanta 1960–61; Ga Field Dir Nat. Asscn for the Advancement of Colored People (NAACP) 1961–63; law practice, Pine Bluff, Ark. 1964–65; Dir Voter Educ. Project Southern Regional Council 1964–68; Attorney, Office of Econ. Opportunity, Atlanta 1969; Exec. Dir United Negro Coll. Fund 1970–71; Pres. Nat. Urban League 1972–81; Sr Partner, Akin, Gump, Strauss, Hauer & Feld 1981–2000, of Counsel Akin, Gump, Strauss, Hauer & Feld LLP 2000–; Chair. Clinton Pres. Transition Bd; joined Lazard Freres and Co. LLC 2000, Sr Man. Dir 2000–; mem. Bd of Dirs American Express Co. (Sr Advisor), Asbury Automotive Group, Inc., Lazard Ltd, Xerox Corpn (Sr Advisor); mem. Int. Advisory Bd Barrick Gold; mem. American Bar Asscn, Nat. Bar Asscn, Council on Foreign Relations, The Bilderberg Meetings and Bars of Ark., DC, Ga, US Supreme Court; Trustee Howard Univ. 1993–2014, Trustee, Emer. 2014–, Chair. Presidential Search Cttee 2014; fmr Pres. Econ. Club of Washington, DC; fmr Dir Voter Educ. Project of Southern Regional Council; Presidential appointments have included mem. Pres.'s Cttee for the Points of Light Initiative Foundation, Sec. of State's Advisory Cttee on SA, Advisory Council on Social Security, Presidential Clemency Bd, American Revolution Bicentennial Comm., Nat. Advisory Cttee on Selective Service, Council White House Conf. 'To Fulfill These Rights'; mem. Iraq Study Group, US Inst. of Peace 2006; Life mem. Council on Foreign Relations; more than 60 hon. degrees, including Princeton Univ., Harvard Univ.; numerous awards, including Medal of Distinction, Barnard Coll. 1983, Spingarn Medal, Nat. Asscn for the Advancement of Colored People 2001. *Publications:* Vernon Can Read! A Memoir 2001, Make It Plain 2008. *Leisure interests:* golf, tennis, yoga. *Address:* Lazard Freres & Co. LLC, 30 Rockefeller Plaza, New York, NY 10112-0002, USA (office). *Telephone:* (212) 632-6190 (office). *Fax:* (212) 332-1640 (office). *E-mail:* jeannie.adashek@lazard.com (office). *Website:* www.lazard.com (office).

JORDAN, Winston DaCosta, BSc, MA; Guyanese economist and politician; *Minister of Finance;* m. Charmaine Atkinson-Jordan; three c.; ed Univ. of Guyana, Univ. of Warwick, UK, certificates from Pennsylvania State Univ. and Harvard Univ., USA; Lecturer, Inst. of Devt Studies, Univ. of Guyana 1984–87, Sr Research Assoc. 1988–89; Planner, State Planning Secr. 1981–84, Sr Planner 1984–85; Dir, Office of the Budget, Ministry of Finance 1985–94, Budgeting and Public Investment Specialist 1995, Adviser in Budgeting 1995–97, Budget Specialist, Office of the Budget 1997–98, Budget/Econ. Adviser 1998–2007, Technical Coordinator, Public Man. Modernisation Programme 2006–08; Country Analyst, Economist Intelligence Unit 2009–15; Minister of Finance 2015–; Dir, Guyana Cooperative, Agricultural and Industrial Devt Bank (GAIBANK) 1987–92, Bauxite Devt Co. Ltd (BIDCO) 1987–2003, Guyana Cooperative Financial Service 1997–2005; Vice Chancellor's Special Award, Univ. of Guyana, Hubert H. Humphrey Fellowship, UNDP Fellowship. *Address:* Ministry of Finance, 49 Main and Urquhart Streets, Kingston, Georgetown, Guyana (office). *Telephone:* 225-6088 (office). *Fax:* 226-1284 (office). *E-mail:* minister@finance.gov.gy (office). *Website:* www.finance.gov.gy (office).

JORDAN, (Zweledinga) Pallo, PhD; South African politician; b. 22 May 1942, Kroonstad, OFS; s. of Archibald Jordan (Dr) and Priscilla Ntantala; m. Carolyn Roth 1972; one d.; ed Athlone High School, Cape Town, Univ. of Cape Town, Univ. of Wisconsin, USA, London School of Econs, UK; joined African Nat. Congress (ANC) 1960; worked full time for ANC in London 1975–77; Head, Radio Freedom, Luanda, Angola 1977–79; in Lusaka, Zambia 1980–90; mem. ANC Nat. Exec. Cttee (NEC) 1985–, Deputy Sec. of Information 1985, Admin. Sec. of NEC Secr. 1985–88, Head of Dept of Information and Publicity 1989; MP 1994–2014, Head of Foreign Affairs Cttee 2002–04; Minister of Posts, Telecommunications and Broadcasting 1994–96, of Environmental Affairs and Tourism 1996–99, of Arts and Culture 2004–09. *Publications:* articles and papers on South African political questions.

JORDAN OF BOURNVILLE, Baron (Life Peer), cr. 2000, of Bournville in the County of West Midlands; **William Brian Jordan,** CBE; British trade union official; b. 28 Jan. 1936, Birmingham; s. of Walter Jordan and Alice Jordan; m. Jean Livesey 1958; three d.; ed Secondary Modern School, Birmingham; machine-tool fitter 1961; joined eng union and served as shop steward; convenor of shop stewards, Guest Keen & Nettlefolds 1966, later Dist Pres.; Div. Organizer for West Midlands AUEW 1977; Pres. Amalgamated Eng and Electrical (fmrly Amalgamated and Eng) Union 1986–95; mem. TUC Gen. Council 1986–95 (Chair. Cttee on European Strategy 1988–95); mem. NEDC (Chair. Eng Industry Cttee) 1986–92, Energy Industry Training Bd 1986–91, Council, Industrial Soc. 1987–, Advisory, Conciliation & Arbitration Service (ACAS) 1987–95, Nat. Training Task Force 1989–92, Eng Training Authority 1991–, Foundation for Manufacturing and Industry; Gen. Sec. ICFTU 1994–2002; fmr Pres. European Metalworkers' Fed.; fmr Exec. mem. Int. Metalworkers' Fed.; fmr mem. European Trade Union Confed., Bd of Govs BBC 1988–98, Nat. Advisory Council for Educ. and Training Targets, UK Skills Council; mem. Victim Support Advisory Cttee, Bd English Partnership, Winston Churchill Trust; Gov., LSE, Ashridge Man. Coll. 1987–2002; mem. Royal Soc. of Arts; Dr hc (Univ. of Cen. England) 1993, (Univ. of Cranfield) 1995. *Leisure interests:* reading, sports (especially football, Birmingham City Football Club supporter). *Address:* House of Lords, London, SW1A 0PW, England (office). *Telephone:* (20) 7219-5353 (office). *Fax:* (20) 7219-5979 (office).

JORDANOV, Minco; Macedonian business executive and politician; *Chairman, Makstil AD;* b. 1 July 1944, Stip; ed Univ. of Belgrade; Gen. Man. Rudnici i Zelezarnica Co., Skopje 1983–89; Man. Techometal-Vardar Rep. Office, Moscow 1989–92; Man. Duferko SA 1992–94, mem. Bd of Dirs 1994–2004, also responsible for countries of fmr USSR 1994–97; Chair. Makstil AD 1997–; Deputy Prime Minister in Charge of Econ. Reforms 2004–06; Pres. Man. Bd Nat. Entrepreneurship and Competitiveness Council 2006; Owner, RK Metalurg Skopje (handball team); mem. Social Democratic Alliance of Macedonia. *Address:* Office of the Chairman, Makstil AD, 16 Makedonska brigada, 18, 1000 Skopje, North Macedonia (office). *Telephone:* (2) 3287023 (office). *Fax:* (2) 3287076 (office). *E-mail:* info@makstil.com.mk (office). *Website:* www.makstil.com (office).

JØRGENSEN, Bo Barker, PhD, DSc; Danish biologist and academic; *Professor of Biology, University of Aarhus;* b. 22 Sept. 1946, Copenhagen; s. of Carl C. B. Jørgensen and Vibeke Balsley Smidt; m. Inga M. Vestergaard 1971; two s. one d.; ed Univs of Copenhagen and Århus; Lecturer, Dept of Ecology and Genetics, Univ. of Århus 1973–77, Sr Lecturer 1977–87, Prof. 1987–92, Adjunct Prof. 1993–2011, Head, Center for Geomicrobiology 2007–, Prof. of Biology 2011–; Dir Max Planck Inst. for Marine Microbiology, Bremen, Germany 1992–2011; Prof., Univ. of Bremen 1993–2011; researcher, Marine Biology Lab., Eilat, Israel 1974, 1978, NASA-ARC, Moffett Field, Calif., USA 1984–85. *Publications:* more than 250 scientific publs in int. journals in the fields of ecology, microbiology and geochemistry. *Address:* Department of Bioscience, Center for Geomicrobiology, University of Aarhus, Ny Munkegade 116, Building 1535, 118, 8000 Aarhus C (office); Tranebaerkaeret 3, 8220 Brabrand, Denmark (home). *Telephone:* 87-15-65-63; 86-26-31-23 (home). *E-mail:* bo.barker@bios.au.dk (office). *Website:* pure.au.dk/portal/en/bo.barker@biology.au.dk (office).

JØRGENSEN, Sven-Aage, MA; Danish professor of German philology (retd); b. 22 July 1929, Herstedvester; s. of Aage Julius Jørgensen and Emma Lydia Jørgensen (née Eriksen); m. Elli Andresen 1957 (divorced 1985); two s. one d.; ed Birkerød Statsskole, Univ. of Copenhagen, Univ. of Würzburg and Warburg Inst., London; Lecturer, Univ. of Copenhagen 1961, Prof. of German Philology 1968; Research Prof., Univ. of Bielefeld 1980–81; Visiting Prof., Heidelberg 1973, Regensburg 1985, Kiel 1986, Cologne 1990; Visiting Fellow, ANU 1975; mem. Royal Danish Acad. of Sciences and Letters 1986, Akad. der Wissenschaften in Göttingen 1998; Kt, Order of Dannebrog; Alexander von Humboldt Prize 1995, Univ. Gold Medal 1957. *Publications:* J. G. Hamann's Fünf Hirtenbriefe 1962, J. G. Hamann's Sokratische Denkwurdigkeiten und Aesthetica in Nuce 1962, Th.

Fontane's Unwiederbringlich 1971, J. G. Hamann 1976, Deutsch-dänische Literaturbeziehungen im 18. Jhdrt. (co-ed.) 1977, Dänische 'guldalderliteratur' und deutsche Klassik (co-ed.) 1982, Tysk et sprog Fire Stater–Fire Kulturer 1989, Wieland's Oberon 1990, Geschichte der deutschen Literatur 1740–1789 (co-author) 1990, Zentrum der Aufklärung: Kopenhagen–Kiel Altona (co-ed.) 1992, Verfilmte Litteratur (co-ed.) 1993, Fortschritt ohne Ende–Ende des Fortschritts? (ed.) 1994, Wieland Epoche-Werk-Wirkung (co-author) 1994, C. M. Wieland's Die Abenteuer des Don Sylvio von Rosalva 2001, Hjertets regnebræt, skyld og skærsild i europæisk litteratur fra Dante til Graham Greene 2012, Querdenker der Aufklärung Studien zu Johann Georg Hamann 2013; numerous articles. *Leisure interests:* jogging, swimming. *Address:* Valby Gade 16, 3200 Helsinge, Denmark (home). *Telephone:* 33-15-76-04 (home). *E-mail:* sven.aage@get2net.dk (home).

JORGENSON, Dale W., PhD; American economist and academic; *Samuel W. Morris University Professor, Harvard University;* b. 7 May 1933, Bozeman, Mont.; s. of Emmett B. Jorgenson and Jewell T. Jorgenson; m. Linda Ann Mabus 1971; one s. one d.; ed Reed Coll., Portland, Ore. and Harvard Univ.; Asst Prof. of Econs, Univ. of Calif., Berkeley 1959–61, Assoc. Prof. 1961–63, Prof. 1963–69; Ford Foundation Research Prof. of Econs, Univ. of Chicago 1962–63; Prof. of Econs, Harvard Univ. 1969–80, Frederic Eaton Abbe Prof. of Econs 1980–2002, Frank William Taussig Research Prof. of Econs 1992–94, Chair. Dept of Econs 1994–97, Samuel W. Morris Univ. Prof. 2002–; Dir Program on Tech. and Econ. Policy, Kennedy School of Govt, Harvard Univ. 1984–; mem. Science Advisory Cttee, Gen. Motors Corpn 1996–2002; Visiting Prof. of Econs, Hebrew Univ., Jerusalem, Israel 1967, Stanford Univ. 1973; Visiting Prof. of Statistics, Univ. of Oxford, UK 1968; Chair. Section 54, Econ. Sciences, Nat. Acad. of Sciences 2000–03; Founding mem. Bd on Science, Tech. and Econ. Policy, Nat. Research Council 1991–98, Chair. 1998–; Consulting Ed., North-Holland Publishing Co., Amsterdam, Netherlands 1970–2002; Fellow, American Statistical Asscn 1965, AAAS 1982, Econometric Soc. 1984 (Pres. 1987); mem. American Acad. of Arts and Sciences 1969, NAS 1978, American Econ. Asscn (Pres. 2000, Distinguished Fellow 2001), Royal Econ. Soc., Econ. Study Soc., Conf. on Research in Income and Wealth, Int. Asscn for Research in Income and Wealth, American Philosophical Soc. 1998; Foreign mem. Royal Swedish Acad. of Sciences 1989; several fellowships including NSF Sr Postdoctoral Fellowship, Netherlands School of Econs, Rotterdam 1967–68; mem. American Econ. Asscn, American Statistical Asscn, Econometric Soc., Royal Econ. Soc., Conf. on Research in Income and Wealth, Int. Asscn for Research in Income and Wealth; Dr hc (Uppsala, Oslo) 1991, (Keio) 2003, (Mannheim) 2004, (Rome) 2006, (Stockholm School of Econs) 2007, (Chinese Univ. of Hong Kong) 2007, (Kansai) 2009; Hon. PhD (Kansai Univ.) 2009; John Bates Clark Medal, American Econ. Asscn 1971, Outstanding Contrib. Award, Int. Asscn of Energy Economists 1994, Richard and Nancy Ruggles Memorial Lecturer, Portoroz, Slovenia 2008, Julius Shiskin Award, Washington Statistical Society 2010, Theodore W. Schultz Lecturer, Asscn for Agricultural and Applied Econs 2010, Shaw Foundation Distinguished Lecturer, Singapore Management Univ. 2011, CER-ETH/KOF Lecturer, ETH, Zurich 2012, Maddison Master Class, Univ. of Groningen, The Netherlands 2012. *Publications:* Optimal Replacement Policy (co-author) 1967, Measuring Performance in the Private Economy of the Federal Republic of Germany 1950–1973 (co-author) 1975, Economentric Studies of U.S. Energy Policy (ed.) 1976, Technology and Economic Policy (co-ed.) 1986, Productivity and U.S. Economic Growth (co-author) 1987, Technology and Capital Formation (co-ed.) 1989, General Equilibrium Modeling and Economic Policy Analysis (co-ed.) 1990, Technology and Agricultural Policy (co-ed.) 1990, Tax Reform and the Cost of Capital (with Kun-Young Yun) 1991, Tax Reform and the Cost of Capital: An International Comparison (co-ed.) 1993, Postwar U.S. Economic Growth (Productivity, Vol. 1) 1995, International Comparisons of Economic Growth (Productivity, Vol. 2) 1995, Capital Theory and Investment Behavior (Investment, Vol. 1) 1996, Tax Policy and the Cost of Capital (Investment, Vol. 2) 1996, Improving the Performance of America's Schools: The Role of Inventives (co-author) 1996, Aggregate Consumer Behavior (Welfare, Vol. 1) 1997, Measuring Social Welfare (Welfare, Vol. 2) 1997, Econometric General Equilibrium Modeling (Growth, Vol. 1) 1998, Energy, the Environmental and Economic Growth (Growth, Vol. 2) 1998, Economic Modeling of Producer Behavior (Econometrics, Vol. 1) 2000, Lifting the Burden: Tax Reform, the Cost of Capital and U.S. Economic Growth (Investment, Vol. 3) (co-author) 2001, Industry-Level Productivity and International Competitiveness Between Canada and the United States (co-ed.) 2001, Economic Growth in the Information Age (Econometrics, Vol. 3) 2002, Measuring and Sustaining the New Economy (co-ed.) 2002; over 232 papers and contribs to learned journals and collections of essays. *Address:* Department of Economics, 122 Littauer Center, Harvard University, Cambridge, MA 02138-3001 (office); 1010 Memorial Drive, Cambridge, MA 02138, USA (home). *Telephone:* (617) 495-4661 (office); (617) 491-4069 (home). *Fax:* (617) 495-4660 (office); (617) 491-4105 (home). *E-mail:* djorgenson@harvard.edu (office). *Website:* scholar.harvard .edu/jorgenson/home (office).

JORTNER, Joshua, MSc, PhD, FRSC; Israeli chemist and academic; *Professor Emeritus of Chemistry, Tel-Aviv University;* b. 14 March 1933, Tarnow, Poland; s. of Arthur Jortner and Regina Jortner; m. Ruth Sanger 1960; one s. one d.; ed Hebrew Univ. of Jerusalem; Instructor, Dept of Physical Chem., Hebrew Univ. of Jerusalem 1961–62, Sr Lecturer 1963–65; Research Assoc., Univ. of Chicago, USA 1962–64, Prof. 1965–72; Assoc. Prof. of Physical Chem., Tel-Aviv Univ. 1965–66, Prof. 1966–2003, Head of Inst. of Chem. 1966–72, Deputy Rector 1966–69, Vice-Pres. 1970–72, Heinemann Prof. of Chem. 1973–2003, Prof. Emer. 2003–; Visiting Prof. of Chem., H.C. Orsted Inst., Univ. of Copenhagen 1974, 1978; Visiting Prof., Univ. of Calif., Berkeley 1975; Christen Visiting Fellow, St Catherine's Coll., Oxford, UK 1995; Int. Research Chair 'Blaise Pascal', Fondation de l'École Normale Supérieure, France 1998–2000; Vice-Pres. Israeli Acad. of Sciences and Humanities 1980–86, Pres. 1986–95, mem. Council 1996–; Founding Pres. Israel Science Foundation 1996; Vice-Pres. IUPAC 1996–97, Pres. 1998–99, Past Pres. 2000–01; mem. American Physical Soc. 1962 (Fellow 1985), Israel Chemical Soc. 1964; Int. Acad. of Quantum Science Award 1972, Weizmann Prize 1973, Rothschild Prize 1976, Kolthof Prize 1976, Israel Prize in Chem. 1982, Wolf Prize in Chemistry (jtly) 1988, Hon. J. Heyrovsky Gold Medal 1993, August Wilhelm von Hofmann Medal 1995, Joseph O. Hirschfelder Prize in Theoretical Chem. 1999, Maria Sklodowska-Curie Medal 2003, Medal of Israeli Chemical Soc. 2004, EMET Prize 2008. *Publications:* author or ed. of 29 books, including Intramolecular Radiationless Transitions (with M. Bixon) 1968, Energy Gap Law for Radiationless Transitions (with E. Englman) 1970, Electronic Excitations in Condensed Rare Gases (with N. Schwentner and E. E. Koch) 1985, Cluster Size Effects 1992, The Jerusalem Symposia on Quantum Chemistry and Biochemistry (co-ed. with Bernard Pullman) Vols 15–27 1982–93; author or co-author of more than 730 scientific articles in professional journals. *Leisure interest:* science policy. *Address:* School of Chemistry, Tel-Aviv University, Ramat Aviv, 69978 Tel-Aviv, Israel (office). *Telephone:* (3) 6408322 (office); (3) 6406474 (office). *Fax:* (3) 6415054 (office). *E-mail:* jortner@tauex.tau.ac.il (office). *Website:* www.tau.ac.il/chemistry/jortner (office).

JOSEFSSON, Lars-Göran, BEng; Swedish energy industry executive; b. 29 Oct. 1950; m.; four c.; ed secondary school in Ulricehamn, Chalmers Inst. of Tech.; began career as systems engineer at Defence Electronics Div. L.M. Ericsson 1974, several exec. posts until Pres. Chemtronics 1984, Ericsson Radio Systems Head, Radar Div. 1985, Vice-Pres. and head of Surface Sensor Div. 1987, Schrack Telecom AG (later named Ericsson Schrack AG 1994 and Ericsson Austria 1996), Vienna, 1993–97; Pres. and CEO Celsius Corpn 1997–2000; Pres. and CEO Vattenfall AB 2000–10 (retd), Deputy Dir 2008–09, also Chair. Vattenfall Europe AG, Vattenfall Europe Mining AG; mem. Supervisory Bd Bohler-Uddeholm AG, Eskom Holdings Ltd; mem. Royal Swedish Mil. Acad., Royal Swedish Soc. of Naval Sciences; Hon. Prof., Brandenburg Tech. Univ.; Golden Medal, City of Vienna 1997, Int. Leadership Award, The Performance Theatre 2007. *Leisure interests:* tennis, skiing, hunting.

JOSEPH, Cedric Luckie, MA; Guyanese diplomatist (retd) and historian; b. 14 May 1933, Georgetown; s. of Frederick McConnell Joseph and Cassie Edith Joseph (née Austin); m. Dona Avril Barrett 1973; two s.; ed London School of Econs and Univ. Coll. of Wales, Aberystwyth, UK; taught history at a London comprehensive school 1962–66; Lecturer in History, Univ. of W Indies, Kingston, Jamaica 1966–71; Prin. Asst Sec., Ministry of Foreign Affairs, Guyana 1971–74; Deputy High Commr to Jamaica 1974–76; Counsellor, Embassy in Washington, DC 1976; Deputy Perm. Rep., Perm. Mission of Guyana to UN, New York 1976–77; High Commr to Zambia (also accred to Angola, Botswana, Mozambique, Tanzania and Zimbabwe) 1977–82, to UK (also accred as Amb. to France, the Netherlands, Yugoslavia and UNESCO) 1982–86; Chair. Commonwealth Cttee on Southern Africa 1983–86; Head of the Presidential Secr. 1986–91; Sec. to Cabinet 1987–91; Sr Amb., Ministry of Foreign Affairs 1991–94; foreign policy analyst/consultant with reference to Guyana's frontiers 1995; mem. Advisory Cttee, Ministry of Foreign Affairs 2015–; Cacique's Crown of Honour 1983. *Publications include:* Reconstruction of the Caribbean Community 1994, Dependency and Mendicancy 1995, Transition and Guyana 1995, Caribbean Community – Security and Survival 1997, Intervention, Border and Maritime Issues in CARICOM (tech. ed.) 2007, Anglo-American Diplomacy and the Reopening of the Guyana/Venezuela Boundary Controversy 1961–1966 1998 (revised edn 2008), The British West Indies Regiment 1914–1918 2008, Africa and its History, Guyana Review July 2011; several articles in professional journals. *Leisure interests:* the fine arts, reading. *Address:* 332 Republic Park, Peter's Hall, East Bank Demerara, Guyana (home). *Telephone:* 233-5751 (home). *E-mail:* clmdj@networksgy.com (home); clmdjoseph@gmail.com (home).

JOSEPH, Dr Enol; Haitian politician; *Minister of National Defence;* fmr Special Adviser to Pres. Jovenel Moïse; Minister of Nat. Defence 2018–; mem. Konvansyon Inite Demokratik (KID), currently Sec.-Gen. *Address:* Ministry of National Defence, 2 rue Bazelais, Delmas 60, BP 1106, Pétion-Ville, Port-au-Prince, Haita (office). *Telephone:* 3454-050 (office). *E-mail:* haitidefense@gmail.com (office).

JOSEPH, Robert G., MA, PhD; American academic and diplomatist; *Senior Scholar, National Institute for Public Policy;* b. 1949, Williston, North Dakota; ed US Naval Acad., St. Louis Univ., Univ. of Chicago, Columbia Univ.; joined Foreign Service, held several positions including Commr to Standing Consultative Comm., Amb. to US-Russian Consultative Comm. on Nuclear Testing, Prin. Deputy Asst, Sec. of Defense for Int. Security Policy, Deputy Asst, Sec. for Nuclear Forces and Arms Control Policy; Prof. of Nat. Security Studies and Founder/Dir, Center for Counterproliferation Research, Nat. Defense Univ. 1992–2001; Special Asst to Pres. and Sr Dir for Proliferation Strategy, Counterproliferation and Homeland Defense, Nat. Security Council 2001–05; Under-Sec. for Arms Control and Int. Security 2005–07 (resgnd); Dir of Studies, Nat. Inst. for Public Policy 2004–05, Sr Scholar 2004–; Prof., Defense and Strategic Studies Dept, Missouri State Univ. 2005–; mem. Defense Policy Bd Advisory Cttee 2007; mem. Nat. Security Advisory Council, Center for Security Policy; fmr Research Consultant, Inst. for Foreign Policy Analysis; Ronald Reagan Award for his contribs to US missile defense 2006. *Address:* National Institute for Public Policy, 9302 Lee Highway, Suite 750, Fairfax, VA 22031, USA (office). *E-mail:* Amy.joseph@nipp.org (office). *Website:* www.nipp.org (office); dss.missouristate.edu (office).

JOSEPHSON, Brian David, PhD, FRS, FInstP; British physicist and academic; *Professor Emeritus of Physics, University of Cambridge;* b. 4 Jan. 1940, Cardiff, Wales; s. of Abraham Josephson and Mimi Josephson; m. Carol Anne Olivier 1976; one d.; ed Cardiff High School, Univ. of Cambridge; Fellow, Trinity Coll., Cambridge 1962–; Research Asst, Prof., Univ. of Illinois 1965–66; Asst Dir of Research, Univ. of Cambridge 1967–72, Reader in Physics 1972–74, Prof. of Physics 1974–2007, Prof. Emer. 2007–; Hon. mem. IEEE; Foreign Hon. mem. American Acad. of Arts and Sciences; Hon. DSc (Univ. of Wales, Univ. of Exeter); New Scientist Award 1969, Research Corpn Award 1969, Fritz London Award 1970, Hughes Medal Royal Soc. 1972, Guthrie Medal 1972, van der Pol 1972, Elliott Cresson Medal 1972, Holweck Medal 1972, Nobel Prize in Physics (jtly) 1973, Faraday Medal 1982, Sir George Thomson Medal 1984, Computing Anticipatory Systems Award 2000. *Music:* Sweet and Sour Harmony 2007. *Publications include:* Consciousness and the Physical World (co-ed.) 1980, The Paranormal and the Platonic Worlds (in Japanese) 1997; research papers on superconductivity, critical phenomena, theory of intelligence, science and mysticism. *Leisure interests:* walking, ice skating, photography, astronomy. *Address:* Trinity College, Cambridge, CB2 1TQ, England (office). *Telephone:* (1223) 337260 (office). *Website:* www.tcm.phy.cam.ac.uk/~bdj10 (office).

JOSHI, C. P., BA, MA, MSc, PhD; Indian politician; *Speaker of Rajasthan Legislative Assembly;* b. 29 July 1950, Nathdwara, Rajastan; s. of Bhudev Prasad Joshi and Sushila Devi Joshi; m. Hemlata Joshi; one s.; ed M.B. Coll., Udaipur,

Mohanlal Sukhadia Univ., Udaipur; fmr Lecturer, M.B. Coll.; fmr Prof. of Psychology, Mohanlal Sukhadia Univ., Udaipur; elected mem. Rajasthan Legis. Ass. from Nathdwara 1980, 1985, 1998, 2003, 2018, Speaker, 2019–; MP for Bhilwara constituency, Lok Sabha 2009–14; Union Minister for Rural Devt 2009–11, Minister for Road Transport and Highways 2011–13, Minister of Railways Sept.–Oct. 2012, May–June 2013, Gen. Sec. All India Congress Cttee (AICC), also responsible for Assam, Bihar, West Bengal and Andaman Nicobar Islands 2013–; Pres. Rajasthan Pradesh Congress Cttee 2003. *Address:* Rajasthan Legislative Assembly Secretariat, Jaipur 302 005 (office); A-621, Govind Marg, Malviya Nagar, Jaipur 302 017, India. *Telephone:* (141) 2744321 (office); (141) 2521666. *Fax:* (141) 2744334 (office). *E-mail:* aicc@congress.org.in (office); speaker-rajassembly@nic.in (office); speak@cpjoshi.com. *Website:* www.aicc.org.in (office); www.cpjoshi.com.

JOSHI, Adm. Devendra Kumar; Indian naval officer and government official; *Lieutenant-Governor of Andaman and Nicobar Islands;* b. 4 July 1954, Almora, Uttarakhand; s. of Hira Ballabh Joshi and Hansa Joshi; m. Chitra Joshi; two d.; ed Nat. Defence Coll., Coll. of Naval Warfare, Mumbai, Naval War Coll., USA; commissioned into Exec. Br., Indian Navy 1974; Defence Adviser, High Comm. in Singapore 1996–99; commands at sea include INS Kuthar, INS Ranvir, INS Viraat, commanded Eastern Fleet, has served as Asst Chief of Personnel, Personnel Branch, Asst Controller of the Aircraft Carrier Programme, Warship Production and Acquisition, Asst Chief of Naval Staff, Deputy Chief of Naval Staff, C-in-C Andaman and Nicobar Island Command, Flag Officer Commdg Eastern Fleet of Indian Navy, Chief of Integrated Defence Staff to Chair. of Chiefs of Staff Cttee; Flag Officer C-in-C, Western Naval Command 2011–12, Chief of Naval Staff 2012–14 (resgnd); Lt-Gov. of Andaman and Nicobar Islands 2017–; Hon. ADC to Pres. 2010; Param Vishist Seva Medal, Ati Vishist Seva Medal, Yudh Seva Medal, Nau Sena Medal, Vishist Seva Medal, Sangram Medal, Operation Vijay Medal, Operation Parakram Medal, Sainya Seva Medal, 25th Anniversary of Independence Medal, 50th Anniversary of Independence Medal, 9 Years Long Service Medal, 20 Years Long Service Medal, 30 Years Long Service Medal. *Address:* Lt. Governor's Secretariat, Rajniwas, Port Blair, 744101, India (office). *Telephone:* (3192) 233333 (office); (3192) 233300 (home). *Fax:* (3192) 230372 (office). *E-mail:* lg.and@nic.in (office); secytolg.and@nic.in (office). *Website:* www.and.nic.in (office).

JOSHI, Satya Mohan, BA; Nepalese writer and scholar; b. 1920, Lalitpur Dist; s. of Shankar Raj and Rajkumari Joshi; m. Radha Devi; ed Trichandra Coll.; Ed. Kalakar magazine 1953; Dir Archeological and Cultural Dept 1959; est. Rastriya Naachghar (Nat. Theatre) Kathmandu, Archeological Garden Patan, Archeological Museum Taulihawa, Nat. Painting Museum Bhaktapur, Araniko White Dagoba Gallery Kirtipur; taught Nepali at Peking Broadcasting Inst.; currently Chancellor, Nepal Bhasa Acad.; Life mem., Royal Nepal Acad.; more than 60 publs in various fields; Order of Gorkha Dakshina Bahu; Madan Puraskar 1956, 1960, 1970, Litterateur of the Century, Govt of Nepal 2017. *Publications include:* Haamro Lok Sanskriti, Kalakar Arniko, Sunkhesari, Majipa Lakhe, Jayaprakash (Shrestha Sirpa Award), Charumati, Cultural Policy: A Preliminary Study.

JOSIPOVIĆ, Ivo, MA, PhD; Croatian composer, lawyer, academic, politician and fmr head of state; b. 28 Aug. 1957, Zagreb; m. Tatjana Klepac; one d.; ed Univ. of Zagreb, Music Acad., Zagreb; co-f. Hrvatski pravni centar (Croatian Law Centre) 1994–; musical debut with two children's songs 1978; compositions performed in nearly all European countries, USA, Canada and Japan (European Broadcasting Union concert transmitted over 30 stations world-wide); recordings for radio and TV stations; performances at European festivals; Dir of Music, Zagreb Biennale 1981–; Docent, Music Acad., Univ. of Zagreb 1992–; Prof. for Criminal Procedure Law, Univ. of Zagreb; has represented Croatia at Int. Court of Justice (ICJ) and Int. Criminal Tribunal for fmr Yugoslavia (ICTY); mem. Savez Komunista Hrvatske (SKH—League of Communists of Croatia) 1980 (later renamed Socijaldemokratska Partija Hrvatske (SDP—Social Democratic Party of Croatia); mem. Sabor (Parl.) 2003–10; SDP presidential cand. 2009; Pres. of Croatia 2010–15. *Compositions include:* Variations for piano, Play of the Golden Pearls for piano, Enypion for harp solo, Quartetto rusticano for string quartet, Per fiati for wind quintet, Passacaglia for string orchestra, Samba da camera for 13 strings, Diptych for large orchestra, Epicurus' Garden for symphony orchestra, Man and Death for soloists, choir and orchestra, Pro musica for accordion orchestra, The Most Beautiful Flower for voice and instrumental ensemble, Drmeš for Penderecki for folk orchestra, Thousands of Lotuses for choir and instrumental ensemble, Jubilus for piano solo, Elegaic Song for violin and piano, Dreams for voice and string orchestra. *Address:* c/o Office of the President, 10000 Pantovčak 241, Zagreb, Croatia.

JOSPIN, Lionel Robert; French politician; *Member, Constitutional Council;* b. 12 July 1937, Meudon, Hauts-de-Seine; s. of Robert Jospin and Mireille Dandieu; m. 2nd Sylviane Agacinski 1994; one s. one d. (from previous m.), one step-s.; ed Institut d'études politiques de Paris, École nat. d'admin; Sec. Ministry of Foreign Affairs 1965–70; Prof., Econ. Inst. universitaire de tech. de Paris-Sceaux, also attached to Univ. de Paris XI 1970–81; Nat. Sec. Socialist Party, mem. Steering Cttee 1973–75, spokesman on Third World Affairs 1975–79, Int. Relations 1979–81, First Sec. 1981–88, Head 1995–97; Councillor for Paris (18E arrondissement) 1977–86; Socialist Deputy to Nat. Ass. for Paris (27E circ.) 1981–86, for Haute-Garonne 1986–88; mem. Gen. Council Haute-Garonne 1988–; Conseiller régional, Midi-Pyrénées 1992–98; Minister of State, Nat. Educ., Research and Sport May–June 1988; Minister of State, Nat. Educ., of Youth and Sport 1988–91, Minister of Nat. Educ. 1991–92; presidential cand. 1995, 2002; Prime Minister of France 1997–2002; mem. Constitutional Council 2015–; Grand Officier, Légion d'honneur 2008; Trombinoscope Politician of the Year 1997. *Publications:* L'Invention du Possible 1991, 1995–2000: Propositions pour la France 1995, Le Temps de répondre 2002, Le Monde comme je le vois 2005, L'impasse 2007, Lionel raconte Jospin 2010, Le mal napoléonier 2014. *Leisure interests:* tennis. *Address:* Conseil Constitutionnel, 2 rue Montpensier, 75001 Paris, France (office).

JOSS, Robert L., PhD; American business executive, academic and fmr university administrator; ed Univ. of Washington, Stanford Univ.; Deputy to Asst Sec. for Econ. Policy, US Treasury Dept, Washington, DC 1968–71; joined Wells Fargo Bank 1971, Vice-Chair. 1987–93, Dir Wells Fargo and Co. 1999; CEO and Man. Dir Westpac Banking Corpn, Sydney, Australia 1993–99; Philip H. Knight Prof. and Dean, Grad. School of Business, Stanford Univ. 1999–2009, now Prof. and Dean Emer.; mem. Bd of Dirs Citigroup 2009–, Bechtel Group 2009–, Makena Capital Man. 2006–, SRI Int. 2013–, CM Capital; Sloan Fellow, Stanford Business School 1965–66; White House Fellow 1968–69; Dr hc (William F. Miller School of Man., Konkuk Univ., Korea) 2009; Meritorious Service Award, US Treasury Dept 1971, Centenary Medal, Commonwealth of Australia 2001. *Address:* Graduate School of Business, Stanford University, 450 Serra Mall, Stanford, CA 94305, USA (office). *Telephone:* (650) 723-3951 (office). *E-mail:* rjoss@gsb.stanford.edu (office). *Website:* www.gsb.stanford.edu/academicareas/finance.html (office).

JOSSELIN, Charles, LenD; French economist and politician; b. 31 March 1938, Pleslin-Trigavou; s. of Charles Josselin and Marie Hamoniaux; m. 2nd Evelyne Besnard 1987; four c.; fmr attaché, financial secr., Banque de l'Union Parisienne, economist, Soc. centrale pour l'équipement du territoire; Parti Socialiste (PS) Nat. Ass. Deputy for 2nd Côtes d'Armor Constituency (Dinan) 1973–78, 1981–97; Minister of State for Transport 1985–86, for the Sea 1992–93; Sec. of State attached to Minister of Foreign Affairs, with responsibility for Co-operation 1997, for Co-operation and Francophonie 1997–98, Deputy Minister for Co-operation and Francophonie 1998–2002, Minister of State 1998–2002; Mayor of Pleslin-Trigavou 1977–97; mem. European Parl. 1979–81; Chair. Nat. Council for Regional Economies and Productivity 1982–86, Nat. Ass.'s EC Select Cttee 1981–85, 1988–92, Vice-Chair. EU Select Cttee 1993–; Chair. Parl. Study Group on int. aid orgs; mem. Côtes d'Armor Gen. Council for Ploubalay canton 1973–, Chair. 1976–97, Vice-Chair. 1997–; mem. Nat. Council for Town and Country Planning, Local Finance Cttee, EU Cttee of the Regions; Vice-Pres. High Comm. Int. Co-operation 2003–08; Chair. Cités Unies France (twin city org.) 2004–; Senator representing Côtes d'Armor 2006–08. *Address:* Conseil général des Côtes-d'Armor, 9 rue du Parc, 22000 Saint-Brieuc, France. *E-mail:* josselincharles@cg22.fr (home).

JOUAHRI, Abdellatif; Moroccan economist, central banker and fmr politician; *Governor, Bank Al-Maghrib;* b. 10 June 1939, Fès; various managerial positions with Bank Al-Maghrib (central bank) 1962–78, Gov. 2003–; Minister Del. to Prime Minister in charge of Public Sector Reform 1978; Minister of Finance 1981–86; CEO Banque Marocaine du Commerce Extérieur SA (BMCE) 1986–95; Chair. Groupement Professionnel des Banques du Maroc 1986–95; CEO Caisse Interprofessionnelle Marocaine de Retraite (CIMR, non-profit pension org.) 2002–03; Chancellor Univ. Al-Akhawayn, Ifrane, now Institutional Rep.; fmr Chair. Ubac Curaçao NV; Chair. Supervisory Cttee Caisse de Dépôt et de Gestion Morocco; Vice-Chair. Maroc Lear; Dir Fonds Hassan II, Banca UBAE, Union de Banques Arabes et Françaises; Dir British Arab Commercial Bank Ltd 2003–10; mem. Steering Cttee Institut Royal des Études Stratégiques. *Address:* Office of the Governor, Bank Al-Maghrib, 277 ave Muhammad V, BP 445, Rabat, Morocco (office). *Telephone:* (53) 7702626 (office). *Fax:* (53) 7706667 (office). *E-mail:* webmaster@bkam.ma (office). *Website:* www.bkam.ma (office).

JOUANNEAU, Daniel, LLM; French diplomatist and judge; *Puisne Judge (Conseiller Maître), Cour des Comptes;* b. 15 Sept. 1946, Vendôme (Loir-et-Cher); m.; one d.; ed French Inst. of Political Studies, École nationale d'admin (French Nat. School of Public Admin); worked in Legal Adviser's Office, Ministry of Foreign Affairs 1971–74, First Sec. in Egypt 1974–76, Office of Econ. and Financial Affairs (multilateral commercial matters) 1976–80, Consul Gen., Salisbury, Rhodesia 1980, Chargé d'affaires a.i., Harare 1980–81, Asst-Dir for Western Europe, then European Corresp., Ministry of Foreign Affairs 1981–85, Chief of Mission (ODA), Guinea 1985–87, Consul Gen. in Québec 1987–89, Chief of EU Dept 1989–90, Amb. to Mozambique (also accred to Lesotho and Swaziland) 1990–93, Chief of Protocol, Ministry of Foreign Affairs 1993–97, Amb. to Lebanon 1997–2000, Insp. Gen. of Foreign Affairs 2000–04, Amb. to Canada 2004–08, to Pakistan 2008–11; Puisne Judge (conseiller maître), Cour des Comptes 2011–. *Publications:* four books on the GATT, the WTO, Mozambique and Zimbabwe. *Address:* Cour des comptes, 13 rue Cambon, 75001 Paris, France (office).

JOUANNO, Chantal; French politician; b. 12 July 1969, Vernon (Eure); d. of Jean-Louis Paul and Françoise Paul; m. Hervé Jouanno 1996; three c.; ed Ecole nationale d'administration, Université Paris 1 Panthéon-Sorbonne, Institut d'Études Politiques, Paris; began career as Export Asst, Citroën 1988; with Accounts Dept, Banque Internationale pour l'Afrique Occidentale 1989–90; with Ministry of Labour and Employment 1992, Ministry of the Interior 1999; Head of Cabinet, Préfet of Vienne and Poitou-Charentes 1999–2001; Head of Cabinet for Man. Dir, Coframi (software co.) 2001; Adviser to Minister of Interior (Nicolas Sarkozy) 2002–06, becoming Councillor responsible for Sustainable Devt; Pres. Agence de l'environnement et de la maîtrise de l'énergie (Ademe) 2008–09; Sec. of State for Ecology 2009–10; Minister of Sport 2010–11; Regional councillor, Ile-de-France 2010–, Vice-Pres. 2015–17; Senator of Paris 2011–17; Pres., Commission nationale du débat public—CNDP) 2018–; mem. Union pour un Mouvement Populaire (UDI-UC); mem. Sporting Int. de karaté. *Achievements include:* fmr nat. karate champion (12 nat. titles). *Address:* Commission nationale du débat public, 244 Blvd Saint-Germain, 75007 Paris, France.

JOUHAUD, Fabrice, MESGO; French journalist and newspaper editor; *Chief Communications Officer, FIFA;* ed Université Paris X Nanterre, Centre de Formation des Journalistes, Institut d'études politiques de Paris (Sciences Po); Deputy News Ed. Al-Ahram Establishment 1994–95; Sr Reporter L'Équipe 1995–2000, Ed.-in-Chief 2000–04, Man. Dir 2008–15, Directeur général, L'Équipe 21 (after change of company name) 2015–16; Dir Centre de Formation des Journalistes 2004–07; Deputy Ed. in Chief Axel Springer AG Jan.–July 2007; Deputy Dir of News, M6 Metropole Television 2007–08; Chief Communications Officer FIFA 2016–. *Address:* Fédération Internationale de Football Association, FIFA-Strasse 20, PO Box 8044, Zurich, Switzerland (office). *Telephone:* 432227777 (office). *E-mail:* info@365sport.com (office). *Website:* www.fifa.com (office).

JOULWAN, Gen. (retd) George Alfred, BS, MA; American army officer (retd); b. 16 Nov. 1939, Pottsville, Pa; m. Karen E. Jones; three d.; ed US Mil. Acad., West Point, Loyola Univ., Chicago, US Army War Coll., Washington, DC; served in Viet Nam as Co. Commdr and Operations Officer, 1st Bn, 26th Infantry, 1st Infantry Div. and as Brigade Operations Officer and Deputy Div. Operations Officer, 101st Airborne Div. (Air Assault); Aide-de-Camp to Vice-Chief of Staff, US Army, Special Asst to the Pres. 1973–74, to Supreme Allied Commdr, Europe 1974–75, Bn Commdr, US Army, Europe 1975–77, Dir Political and Economic Studies, US Army War Coll., Pa 1978–79, Commdr 2nd Brigade, 3rd Infantry Div. (Mechanized), US Army, Europe 1979–81, Chief of Staff 1981–82, Exec. Officer to Chair., Jt Chiefs of

Staff, Washington, DC 1982–85, Dir Force Requirements (Combat Support Systems), Office of Deputy Chief of Staff for Operations and Plans, Washington, DC 1985–86, Deputy Chief of Staff for Operations, US Army, Europe and Seventh Army 1986–88, Commdg Gen., 3rd Armored Div. 1988–89, V Corps, 1989–90, C-in-C, US Southern Command, Quarry Heights, Panama 1990–93, US European Command, Stuttgart/Vaihingen, Germany 1993–97, Supreme Allied Commdr, Europe, SHAPE, Belgium 1993–97 (retd); Pres. One Team Inc. 2002–05; Adjunct Prof., Nat. Defense Univ. 2000–05; mem. Bd of Dirs General Dynamics Corpn 1998–, Beagle Holdings Inc. 2002–, Alion Science and Technology Corpn 2002, Remington Arms Co. Inc. 2007, Emergent BioSolutions Inc. 2013–; mem. Int. Advisory Bd Garda World Security Corpn 2008–; Hon. Col 26th Infantry Regiment Asscn; numerous decorations including Légion d'honneur, Hessian Order of Merit (Germany); numerous US military decorations including Defense Distinguished Service Medal (with Oak Leaf Cluster), Defense Superior Service Medal, Silver Star (with Oak Leaf Cluster). *Telephone:* (703) 486-8173 (office). *Fax:* (703) 486-8176 (office).

JOUROVÁ, Věra; Czech lawyer, banking executive, politician and international organization official; *Commissioner for Justice, Consumers and Gender Equality, European Commission;* b. 18 Aug. 1964, Třebíč, Czechoslovak Socialist Repub. (now Czech Repub.); divorced; one s. one d.; ed Charles Univ., Prague; Deputy Dir Civic Cultural Centre, Třebíč 1991; later worked as Sec. of City Council, Třebíč; employed at DHV CR 2000–01; Head of Regional Devt Section, Regional Office of Vysočina Region, then worked as Deputy Minister for European Integration, Ministry for Regional Devt 2001–03; worked in consultancy on Euro grants with EC and EIB, also in Russia and the Baltic countries 2006–13; mem. Česká Strana Sociálne Demokratická (Czech Social Democratic Party) –2011, Akce Nespokojených Občanů 2011 (ANO 2011—Yes–Action of Dissatisfied Citizens 2011), later Ano (Yes) 2011–, Vice-Chair.; mem. (Ano) Chamber of Deputies 2013–; Minister of Regional Devt Jan.–Oct. 2014; Commr for Justice, Consumers and Gender Equality, EC, Brussels Nov. 2014–; Premio a la Convivencia y a la Tolerancia 2016. *Address:* European Commission, 200 Rue de la Loi/Wetstraat 200, 1049 Brussels, Belgium (office). *Telephone:* (2) 299-11-11 (office). *E-mail:* vera-jourova-contact@ec.europa.eu (office); vera.jourova@ec.europa.eu (office); jourova@ano2011.cz (office). *Website:* ec.europa.eu/commission/index_en (office); www.verajourova.cz.

JOUSSEN, Friedrich; German engineer and business executive; *CEO, TUI AG;* b. 19 April 1963, Duisburg; ed RWTH Aachen Univ.; gained professional experience in Portland, Ore., USA and joined Mannesmann AG in Düsseldorf 1988, one of the first mans of newly founded Mannesmann Mobilfunk GmbH, held various man. positions in Group Strategy, Innovation Man. and Marketing, Marketing Dir, Mannesmann Mobilfunk GmbH 1997–2000 (group acquired by Vodafone), Head of Global Product Man., Vodafone Group, Newbury, UK, returned to Germany as COO Vodafone Deutschland 2003–05, CEO Vodafone Germany 2005–12, mem. Bd of Dirs Vodafone Ventures, mem. CEO Council and Strategy Bd of Vodafone Group; mem. Exec. Bd TUI AG 2012–, CEO 2013–. *Address:* TUI AG, Postfach 610209, 30602 Hanover (office); TUI AG, Karl-Wiechert-Allee 4, 30625 Hanover, Germany (office). *Telephone:* (511) 56600 (office). *Fax:* (511) 5661901 (office). *E-mail:* info@tui-group.com (office). *Website:* www.tui-group.com (office).

JOVANOVIĆ, Čedomir (Čeda); Serbian politician; *President, Liberal Democratic Party;* b. 13 April 1971, Belgrade, SR Serbia, SFR Yugoslavia; s. of Jovica Jovanović and Milena Mršić; m. Jelena Savić 2003; ed Ninth Belgrade Gymnasium, Third Econs High School, Faculty of Dramatic Arts, Arts Univ., Belgrade; worked as journalist while student; leader of student protests in Belgrade during winter of 1996/97, formed Student Political Club (Studentski politički klub—SPK) with fellow univ. students; joined Democratic Party (DS) 1998–2005, Vice-Pres. 2001–05; elected to Serbian Parl. 2000 on list of Democratic Opposition of Serbia (DOS), also held post of DOS parl. caucus leader –2003; Deputy Prime Minister of Serbia 2003–04; Founder and first Pres. Liberal Democratic Party (Liberalno-demokratska partija—LDP) 2005–; unsuccessful cand. in presidential election 2008. *Address:* Liberal Democratic Party (Liberalno-demokratska partija), 11000 Belgrade, Simina 41, Serbia (office). *Telephone:* (11) 3208300 (office). *Fax:* (11) 3208301 (office). *E-mail:* predsednik@ldp.rs (office). *Website:* www.ldp.rs (office).

JOVANOVIĆ, Živadin; Serbian politician and diplomatist; b. 14 Nov. 1938, Oparic, Rekovać Dist; ed Belgrade Univ.; legal adviser, Novi Beograd Dist Council 1961–64; with Ministry of Foreign Affairs 1964–, diplomatic service in Toronto, Canada 1966–70, Nairobi, Kenya 1974–78; Yugoslavian Amb. to Angola 1988–93; Asst to Minister of Foreign Affairs 1994–97; mem. Narosna Skuptina of Serbia (Parl.) 1997–; Deputy Chair. Socialist Party of Serbia 1997–, Acting Pres. 2001; Minister of Foreign Affairs of Yugoslavia 1998–2000; Founder and Pres. Belgrade Forum for World of Equals 1999; numerous nat. and foreign decorations. *Publications include:* Abolishment of the State 2003, National Minorities 2004, Intellectuals and Society 2005, Foreign Policy 2006, Critical Analyses of the Serbian Constitution 2007. *Address:* Ilijê Garasanina 8, St 6, 11000 Belgrade, Serbia (home). *Fax:* (11) 2445421 (office). *E-mail:* jovanovici@beotel.yu (home).

JOVEL POLANCO, Sandra Érica; Guatemalan diplomatist and politician; *Minister of Foreign Affairs;* b. 24 Feb. 1978, Guatemala City; d. of Sandra Érica Polanco Castaneda; ed Univ. Rafael Landívar, Univ. de San Carlos de Guatemala, Univ. Complutense, Madrid; joined Ministry of Foreign Affairs as Technical Officer, Int. Cooperation Div. August 2000, transferred to Sub-Directorate for Bilateral Foreign Policy for Asia, Africa and Oceania, later becoming Asst to Dir-Gen. of Bilateral Int. Relations 2008, Deputy Dir of Bilateral Foreign Policy for N America, Deputy Dir of Bilateral Foreign Policy for Central America and the Caribbean 2010–12, Dir of Integration 2012, Deputy Minister of Foreign Affairs Feb.–May 2016, Amb. to Colombia July–Aug. 2017, Minister of Foreign Affairs 2017–; mem. Frente de Convergencia Nacional; Order Monja Blanca, First Class 2008. *Address:* Ministry of Foreign Affairs, 2a Avda La Reforma 4-17, Zona 10, Guatemala City, Guatemala (office). *Telephone:* 2410-0000 (office). *Fax:* 2410-0011 (office). *E-mail:* webmaster@minex.gob.gt (office). *Website:* www.minex.gob.gt (office).

JOVIĆ, Ivo Miro; Bosnia and Herzegovina politician; b. 15 July 1950, Trebizat, Capljina; s. of Mio Jović and Mara Bukovac; m. Lucija; three c.; ed Sarajevo Dept of History; fmr teacher in Ilijas and Kiseljak; fmr Dir adult educ. center, Kiseljak; fmr Prin. secondary school, Kiseljak; Deputy Minister of Educ., Science, Culture and Sport, Canton of Middle Bosnia 1997–99; Deputy Minister of Educ., Science, Culture and Sport of Bosnia and Herzegovina Fed. 1999–2001; mem. House of Reps 2002–05; mem. of the Presidency June 2005–06, Chair. June 2005–Feb. 2006; mem. Hrvatska Demokratska Zajednica Bosne i Hercegovine (Croatian Democratic Union of Bosnia and Herzegovina).

JOVIČIĆ, Radislav; Bosnia and Herzegovina police official and politician; b. 1971, Ugljevik; m.; one c.; ed Police Coll. and Faculty of Security Studies, Belgrade, postgraduate studies at Faculty of Security and Protection, Univ. Sinergija; 20 years' experience working in the police, served as Commdr of the Special Police Squad, as Deputy Head for Internal Control at Special Police, Commdr of the Police Unit for VIP Protection, Head of Admin for Protection of Persons and Objects of Republika Srpska Ministry of Internal Affairs; also served as Deputy Commdr of Special Support Unit and Head of Operational Support Unit with State Investigation and Protection Agency; Chief of Security Dept, Univ. of Banja Luka; Consultant for Information and Investigation Protection 2012–; Minister of Internal Affairs of Republika Srpska 2012–14.

JOXE, Pierre Daniel, LenD; French lawyer; b. 28 Nov. 1934, Paris; s. of Louis Joxe and Françoise-Hélène Halevy; m. 4th Laurence Fradin; two s. two d. from previous m.; ed Lycée Henri IV, Faculté de droit and Ecole Nat. d'Admin; mil. service 1958–60; auditor, later Counsellor Cour des Comptes; mem. Exec. Bureau and Exec. Cttee, Socialist Party 1971–93; Deputy for Saône and Loire 1973, 1978, 1981, 1986, 1988; Minister of Industry and Admin May–June 1981, of the Interior, Decentralization and Admin July 1984 and March 1986, of the Interior 1988–91, of Defence 1991–93; First Pres. Cour des Comptes (audit court) 1993–2001; mem. Conseil Constitutionnel 2001–10; mem. European Parl. 1977–79; Pres. Regional Council, Burgundy 1979–82, Socialist Parl. Group 1981–84, 1986–88; Hon. KBE; Commdr, Ordre nat. du Mérite. *Publications:* Parti socialiste 1973, Atlas du Socialisme 1973, L'édit de Nantes (Literary Prize, Droits de l'homme) 1998, A propos de la France 1998, Pourquoi Mitterrand 2006, Cas de conscience (Jean Zay Literary Prize) 2010, Pas de Quartier? 2012, Soif de justice 2014. *Address:* 39 quai de l'Horloge, 75100 Paris, France (office).

JOYA, Malalai; Afghan politician and writer; b. 25 April 1978, Farah Prov.; family fled to Iran and Pakistan 1982, returned to Afghanistan and, under Taliban rule, began home-based secret classes for young girls and women deprived of educ. under the Taliban 1998; moved to Farah and f. Malalai Health Clinic and Orphanage 2002; elected to Constitutional Loya Jirga from Farah Prov. 2003 (made worldwide news headlines by denouncing the warlords in the assembly 17 Dec. 2003); mem. Parl. for Farah Prov. 2005–07 (suspended from parl. on the grounds that she had insulted fellow reps in a TV interview 21 May 2007); a fmr Dir Org. for Promoting Afghan Women's Capabilities; Hon. Citizen of Commune of Provincia di Arezzo 2007, Comune di Bucine 2007, Comune di Supino 2007; Malalai of Maiwand Award 2004, Int. Women of the Year Award, Valle d'Aosta Prov. of Italy 2004, Gwangju Award for Human Rights, May 18th Foundation, S Korea 2006, Women of Peace Award 2006, Women's Peacepower Foundation 2006, named amongst 1000 Women for the Nobel Peace Prize 2005, named by World Econ. Forum amongst 250 Young Global Leaders for 2007, certificate of honour from Mayor of Berkeley, Calif. 2007, 14th Angel Award, The Angel Festival 2007, Golden Fleur-de-Lis (Giglio d'Oro) Award, Town Council of Toscana Region of Italy 2007, Mare Nostrum Award, Commune of Palazzo in Viareggio, Italy 2007, Juan Maria Bandres Award for Human Rights and solidarity with the refugees 2008, Anna Politkovskaya Award 2008, Int. Anti-Discrimination Award 2009 and others. *Publications:* Raising My Voice 2009, A Woman Among Warlords: The Extraordinary Story of the Afghan Woman Who Dares to Speak Out (autobiography, translated into 13 languages) 2009. *Telephone:* (799) 9544358 (office). *E-mail:* mj@malalaijoya.com (home). *Website:* www.malalaijoya.com.

JOYCE, Steven Leonard, BSc; New Zealand broadcasting executive and politician; b. 7 April 1963, New Plymouth; m. Suzanne Joyce; two c.; ed Massey Univ.; f. Energy FM (radio station), New Plymouth 1984; co-f. RadioWorks (later MediaWorks Radio), Man. Dir –2001; CEO Jasons Travel Media 2006–08; mem. Nat. Party, Chair. Campaign Review 2002, fmr Gen. Man., Chair. election campaigns 2008, 2011, 2013; mem. House of Reps (Parl.) 2008–18; Minister for Communications and Information Tech. 2008–11, also Minister of Transport 2008–11, Minister for Tertiary Educ., Skills and Employment 2010–16, for Science and Innovation 2011–16, for Econ. Devt 2011–16, Minister of Finance and for Infrastructure 2016–17. *E-mail:* steven.joyce@national.org.nz. *Website:* www.stevenjoyce.national.org.nz.

JOYNER-KERSEE, Jacqueline, BA; American fmr athlete; b. 3 March 1962, East St Louis, Ill.; d. of Alfred Joyner and Mary Joyner; m. Bobby Kersee 1986; ed Univ. of California, Los Angeles; specialized in heptathlon; coached by husband; world record heptathlon scores: 7,158 points, Houston, 1986; 7,215 points, USA Olympic trial, Indianapolis 1988 (still world record as at Dec. 2003); 7,291 points, Seoul 1988; 7,044 points (gold medal), Olympic Games, Barcelona 1992; three Olympic gold medals, four world championships; long jump: gold medal, World Championships 1987, gold medal, Olympic Games, Seoul 1988, bronze medal, Olympic Games, Barcelona 1992, bronze medal, Olympic Games, Atlanta 1996; winner IAAF Mobil Grand Prix 1994; Chair. St Louis Sports Comm. 1996–; played basketball for Richmond Rage, American Basketball League 1996; business interests include Gold Medal Rehab (sports medicine); CEO Elite Int. Sports Marketing; f. Jackie Joyner-Kersee Gold Medal Scholarship program (now Jackie Joyner-Kersee Youth Foundation) 1988; Co-founder Athletes for Hope (charity) 2007; mem. Bd of Dirs USA Track & Field 2013–; Hon. DHL (Spellman Coll.) 1998, (Howard Univ.) 1999, (George Washington Univ.) 1999; numerous honours including Associated Press Female Athlete of the Year 1988, first woman to win Sporting News Man of the Year Award, Jim Thorpe Award 1993, Jackie Robinson Robie Award 1994, Jesse Owens Humanitarian Award 1999, World Women and Sport Trophy for the Americas, IOC 2007; recognised by Sports Illustrated as the greatest female athlete of the 20th century. *Publication:* A Kind of Grace (autobiog.) 1997. *Address:* c/o Chicago Sports and Entertainment Partners, 3818 North Troy Street, Suite 100, Chicago, IL 60618, USA. *Website:* jackiejoynerkersee.com.

JOYON, Francis; French yachtsman; b. 28 May 1956, Hanches, Eure-et-Loire; m. Virginie Joyon; two s.; worked at Glénans Nautical Centre, working as boatbuilder, later sailing instructor; first major race 1988 Route of Discovery (finished in third place); other races include 1989 Round Europe Race, 1990 Route du Rhum, 1992 OSTAR, Route du Cafe, 2000 Europe 1 Newman Star race (first major win, on board Eure et Loir), 2000 Transat (winner), 2001 Fastnet Race (winner); became fastest world non-stop solo yachtsman 2004; solo North Transatlantic record 2005; set new solo round-the-world record on board IDEC II 2008; holder Jules Vene Trophy for fastest circumnavigation of the world by a yacht—IDEC Sport 2017– (40 days, 23 hours, 30 minutes, 30 seconds). *Address:* c/o Les Glénans, Quai Louis Blériot, 75016 Paris, France (office). *Website:* www.trimaran-idec.com.

JU, Gen. Sang-song; North Korean army officer and politician; b. 1933, Kangwo'n Prov.; ed Kim Il-so'ng Military Univ.; career in Korean People's Armed Forces, attained rank of Gen. 1997, commdr of army unit stationed on border with S Korea 2000; cand. mem. Korean Worker's Party 1970–90, full mem. 1990–; mem. Supreme People's Parl. 1990–; Minister of People's Security and mem. Nat. Defence Comm. 2004–11. *Address:* Ministry of Defence, Pyongyang, Democratic People's Republic of Korea (office).

JU MING; Taiwanese sculptor; b. (Ju Chuan-tai), 20 Jan. 1938, Miaoli Tunghsiao; s. of Lee-chi Chu and Ai Wang; m. Chen Fu-mei 1961; apprenticeship with Master Chin-chuan Lee 1953–57; trained in modern sculpture by Yu Yu Yang 1968–76; moved to USA and made debut in int. arena 1981; produced two series: Taichi Series in wood and bronze and Living World Series in wood, bronze, sponge and stainless steel; f. Ju Ming Museum, Taipai; Hon. Dr of Art (Fu Jen Catholic Univ.) 2003; Sculpture Award Chinese Sculptors and Artists Asscn 1976, Nat. Culture Award, Repub. of China Nat. Culture Foundation 1976, Award for Ten Outstanding Young People 1987, Achievement Award of Fok Ying Tung, Hong Kong 1998, The Second Enku Award Japan 2002, Fukuoka Asian Culture Prize, Art and Cultures Prize 2007. *Publications:* Juming Sculptures – The Living World 1, 2, 3, Juming – Mixed Media, Juming – Oil Paintings, Juming Sculpture 1976–1993, Taichi in Wood, Ju Ming Wood Sculptures – Buffalo, Ju Ming Paintings, Ju Ming On Art, Carving for Humanity (biog.), Secret Garden of Ju Ming, Ju Ming. *Leisure interest:* tai-chi. *Address:* Juming Museum, 20842 No. 2 Xishihu, Jinshan District, Taipei (office); 111 No. 28, Lane 460, Sec. 2, Chih-shan Road, Taipei, Taiwan (home). *Telephone:* (2) 24989940 (office); (2) 28412011 (home). *Fax:* (2) 24988529 (office); (2) 28413000 (home). *E-mail:* service@juming.org.tw (office); www.juming.org.tw (office).

JUAN, Alexis Raymond, LLD; French banking executive; *Honorary Chairman, Komercni Banka;* b. 11 June 1943, Sidi Bel Abbes, Algeria; ed Political Studies Inst., Grenoble; joined Société Générale 1968, various man. roles including positions with subsidiary cos in Tokyo 1973–76, Athens 1980–84, Seoul as Dir Korean French Banking Corpn 1978–80, Deputy CEO Société Générale, UK Div., London 1984–87, various man. roles with Société Générale in France 1987–98, mem. Bd of Dirs Comm. 1998, Chair. Komercni Banka, Prague, Czech Repub. 2001–05, Hon. Chair. 2005–; mem. Bd of Dirs Orco Property Group SA 2009–. *Address:* c/o Komercni Banka, Na Prikope 33, 11047 Prague 1, Czech Republic.

JUAN CARLOS I, HM King Juan Carlos I of Spain Juan Carlos Alfonso Víctor María de Borbón y Borbón-Dos Sicilias; b. 5 Jan. 1938, Rome, Italy; s. of HRH Don Juan de Borbón y Battenberg, Count of Barcelona and HRH Doña María de las Mercedes de Borbón y Orleans and grandson of King Alfonso XIII and Queen Victoria Eugenia of Spain; m. Princess Sophia, d. of King Paul of the Hellenes and of Queen Frederica 1962; one s., HM King Felipe VI, b. Jan. 1968; two d., Princess Elena, Princess Cristina; ed privately in Fribourg, Switzerland, Madrid, San Sebastián, Inst. of San Isidro, Madrid, Colegio del Carmen, Gen. Mil. Acad., Zaragoza and Univ. of Madrid; spent childhood in Rome, Lausanne, Estoril and Madrid; commissioned into the three armed forces and undertook training in each of them 1957–59; studied the org. and activities of various govt ministries; named by Gen. Franco as the future King of Spain 1969, inaugurated as King of Spain 22 Nov. 1975, named as Capt.-Gen. (C-in-C) of the Armed Forces Nov. 1975, abdicated the throne in favour of his son Prince Felipe 18 June 2014; Foreign mem. Acad. des sciences morales et politiques, Assoc. mem. 1988; Dr hc (Strasbourg) 1979, (Madrid), (Harvard) 1984, (Sorbonne) 1985, (Oxford) 1986, (Trinity Coll., Dublin) 1986, (Bologna) 1988, (Cambridge) 1988, (Coimbra) 1989, (Tokyo, Bogotá, Limerick, Tufts, Chile) 1990, (Toronto) 1991, (Jerusalem) 1993; Charlemagne Prize 1982, Bolívar Prize (UNESCO) 1983, Gold Medal Order 1985, Candenhove Kalergi Prize, Switzerland 1986, Nansen Medal 1987, Humanitarian Award Elie Wiesel, USA 1991, shared Houphouët Boigny Peace Prize (UNESCO) 1995, Franklin D. Roosevelt Four Freedoms Award 1995. *Address:* Palacio de la Zarzuela, 28071 Madrid, Spain (office). *Website:* www.casareal.es (office).

JUANGROONGRUANGKIT, Somporn; Thai business executive; *President, Thai Summit Group;* b. 1951; m. Pattana Juangroongruangkit (died 2002); five c.; Pres. Thai Summit Group 2002–, Thai Summit Autoparts Industries Co. Ltd; Dir Thai Summit Grand Estate Co.; Founder Pattana Golf and Sports Resort. *Address:* Thai Summit Group, 4/3 Moo 1, Bangna-Trad HWY, KM.16 Bangchalong, Bangplee District, Samuthprakarn 10549, Thailand (office). *Telephone:* (2) 337-0022 (office). *Fax:* (2) 325-8015 (office). *Website:* www.thaisummit.co.th (office).

JUANTORENA, Alberto; Cuban sports administrator, politician and fmr athlete; b. 3 Dec. 1950, Santiago; m.; five c.; moved to Havana to train under Polish coach Zgymunt Zabierzowski 1971; gold 400m (45.36) Dominica Cen. American Games 1974; gold 800m (1:43.50), gold 400m (44.26) Montreal Olympic Games 1976; gold 800m (1:44.01), gold 400m (45.36) Dusseldorf World Cup 1977; gold 400m (44.27), gold 800m (1:47.78) Columbia Cen. American Games 1978; fmr Vice-Minister of Sports for Cuba, Vice-Pres. Cuban Olympic Cttee, Vice-Pres. for Latinamerica UNESCO, Sr Vice-Pres. Cuban Olympic Cttee; mem. Council IAAF; Track & Field News Athlete of the Year 1976, 1977; Olympic Order.

JUBEIR, Adel bin Ahmed al-, BA, MA; Saudi Arabian diplomatist and government official; *Minister of State for Foreign Affairs;* b. 1 Feb. 1962, Riyadh; ed schools in Germany, Yemen, Lebanon and USA, Univ. of North Texas and Georgetown Univ., USA; served in Jt Information Bureau in Dhahran during Operation Desert Shield/Desert Storm 1990–91; fmr Special Asst to Amb., Embassy in Washington, DC; fmr Dir Saudi Arabian Information and Congressional Affairs Office; Foreign Affairs Adviser, Crown Prince's Court 2000–05; Adviser, Royal Court 2005–07; Amb. to USA 2007–15; Minister of Foreign Affairs 2015–18, Minister of State for Foreign Affairs 2018–; mem. numerous int. dels; fmr Co-Sec. US-Saudi Strategic Dialogue; Visiting Diplomatic Fellow, Council of Foreign Relations, New York 1994–95; has lectured at univs and academic insts in USA and has appeared frequently in the media; Hon. DHumLitt (North Texas) 2006. *Address:* Ministry of Foreign Affairs, POB 55937, Riyadh 11544, Saudi Arabia (office). *Telephone:* (1) 405-5000 (office). *Fax:* (1) 403-0645 (office). *E-mail:* info@mofa.gov.sa (office). *Website:* www.mofa.gov.sa (office).

JUDD, Ashley; American actress; b. 19 April 1968, Granada Hills, Calif.; d. of Naomi Judd; half-sister of Wynonna Judd; m. Dario Franchitti 2001 (divorced 2013). *Films include:* Kuffs 1992, Ruby in Paradise 1993, Natural Born Killers (scenes deleted) 1994, Smoke 1995, Heat 1995, The Passion of Darkly Noon 1995, A Time to Kill 1996, Normal Life 1996, The Locusts (A Secret Sin, UK) 1997, Kiss the Girls 1997, Simon Birch 1998, Eye of the Beholder 1999, Double Jeopardy 1999, Our Friend, Martin (video, voice) 1999, Dexterity 2000, Where the Heart Is 2000, Someone Like You (aka Animal Attraction, UK) 2001, High Crimes 2002, Divine Secrets of the Ya-Ya Sisterhood 2002, Frida 2002, The Husband I Bought 2003, The Blackout Murders 2003, Just One of Those Things 2003, Twisted 2004, De-Lovely 2004, Come Early Morning 2006, Bug 2006, Helen 2009, Crossing Over 2009, Tooth Fairy 2010, Divergent 2014, Insurgent 2015, Allegiant 2016. *Television includes:* Sisters (series) 1991–94, Till Death Us Do Part 1992, Naomi and Wynonna: Love Can Build a Bridge 1995, Norman Jean and Marilyn 1996, The Ryan Interview 2000, Missing 2012, Twin Peaks 2017, Berlin Station 2017. *Address:* 11766 Wilshire Blvd, Suite 1610, Los Angeles, CA 00025-6565; William Morris Endeavor, One William Morris Place, Beverly Hills, CA 90212, USA. *Telephone:* (310) 859-4000. *Fax:* (310) 859-4462. *Website:* www.wma.com.

JUDE, Radu; Romanian film director and screenwriter; b. 28 March 1977, Bucharest; ed Universitatea Media. *Films include:* A Long Day 2004, The Happiest Girl in the World 2009, Film pentru prieteni 2011, Everybody in Our Family 2012 Stories of Spades 2014, Scarred Hearts 2015, Aferim! (Silver Bear for Best Dir (shared with Małgorzata Szumowska), Berlin Int. Film Festival) 2015, Îmi este indiferent dacă în istorie vom intra ca barbari (I Do Not Care If We Go Down in History as Barbarians) (Grand Prix-Crystal Globe, Karlovy Vary Film Festival 2018) 2018. *Television includes:* In familie (series) 2002. *Address:* c/o HiFilm Productions, 7 Sfantul Stefan Street, 023996 Bucharest, Romania. *Telephone:* (21) 2524867. *Fax:* (21) 2524866. *E-mail:* office@hifilm.ro. *Website:* www.hifilm.ro.

JUDEH, Nasser, BSc; Jordanian government official and politician; ed Georgetown Univ., USA; Pvt. Sec. and Press Sec. to HRH Prince Hassan 1985–92; Dir Jordan Information Bureau, London 1992–94; Dir Jordan TV Corpn 1994–98, Dir-Gen. 1998; Minister of Information 1998–99, Official Govt Spokesman 1998–99, 2005–07; Chair. Bd of Information and Communication Expertise 1999–2005; media adviser to Royal Jordanian Airlines 2003; Minister of State for Media Affairs and Communication 2007; Minister of Foreign and Expatriate Affairs 2009–17; mem. Sec.-Gen.'s High-Level Advisory Bd on Mediation, UN 2017–; Grand Cordon, Order of Al Kawkab, Order of Al- Istiklal; Officier, Légion d'honneur; Grand Officer, Order of Orange-Nassau (The Netherlands). *Leisure interests:* underwater sports, hunting, reading, tennis. *Address:* c/o Ministry of Foreign and Expatriate Affairs, PO Box 35217, Amman 11180, Jordan (office).

JUDGE, Lady Barbara Singer Thomas, CBE, BA, JD; American/British lawyer and business executive; b. 28 Dec. 1946, New York; m. 1st Allen L. Thomas, one s.; m. 2nd Sir Paul Judge; ed Univ. of Pennsylvania, New York Univ. School of Law; began career as corporate lawyer in New York; joined Kaye, Scholer, Fierman, Hays and Handler (law firm) 1973, later becoming Partner; mem. Securities and Exchange Comm., Washington, DC 1980–83; Dir Samuel Montagu & Co. (merchant bank) 1983–87; Sr Vice-Pres. Bankers Trust Int. Banking, New York 1987; Exec. Dir News Int. 1993; f. Private Equity Investor PLC, London 2000; Dir (non-exec.) UK Atomic Energy Authority 2002, Chair. 2004–10, Chair. Emer. 2010–; Chair. Pension Protection Fund 2010–16, Hyperion Power Generation; apptd Chair. Energy Inst., Univ. Coll., London, SOAS, London 2006, Advisory Bd London Middle East Inst.; Deputy Chair. UK Financial Reporting Council 2004–07; Visiting Fellow, Saïd Business School, Univ. of Oxford; Dir (non-exec.) Statoil ASA (Norway), NV Bekaert SA (Belgium), Magna Int. Inc. (Canada); Public mem. Int. Ethics Standards Bd for Accountants 2007–10; mem. TEPCO Nuclear Reform Monitoring Cttee, Tokyo 2012–, Deputy Chair. 2013–; Chair., Inst. of Dirs 2015–18, Cifas 2016–, Hibob 2016–; Chair. Advisory Bd Asscn for Consultancy and Eng 2016–; mem. Int. Advisory Group, Jordanian Atomic Energy Comm. 2016–; Restaurant Reviewer, Visiting Fellow, Saïd Business School, Univ. of Oxford; Univ. Trustee, Royal Acad. of Arts; Hon. Grad., Univ. Campus Suffolk 2008, Hon. Visiting Prof., Cass Univ.; Hon. DSc (Univ. of Buckingham) 2012; Non-Exec. Dir of the Year for A Public Sector Org. 2015.

JUGNAUTH, Rt Hon. Sir Anerood, KCMG, PC, QC; Mauritian politician, lawyer and fmr head of state; *Minister of Defence and for Rodrigues;* b. 29 March 1930, Palma; m. Sarojini Devi Ballah; one s. one d.; ed Church of England School, Palma, Regent Coll., Quakre, Borneo, Lincoln's Inn, London; called to Bar 1954; won seat on Legis. Ass., Mauritius 1963; Minister of State and Devt 1965–67, of Labour 1967; Dist Magistrate 1967; Crown Counsel and Sr Crown Counsel 1971; joined Mouvement Militant Mauricien of Paul Bérenger 1971; Leader of Opposition 1976; Prime Minister of Mauritius 1982–95, other portfolios include Minister of Finance 1983–84, of Defence and Internal Security and Reform Insts, of Information, Internal and External Communications and the Outer Islands, of Justice; Prime Minister and Minister of Defence and Home Affairs and of External Communications 2000–03; Pres. of Mauritius 2003–12 (resgnd); Prime Minister and Minister of Home Affairs 2014–17, also Minister of Finance March–May 2016; Minister Mentor, Minister of Defence and for Rodrigues 2017–; f. Mouvement Socialiste Militant 1983, leader 1983–2003; Order of the Rising Sun (Japan) 1988, Grand Officier, Légion d'honneur 1990, Grand Commdr, Order of the Star and Key of the Indian Ocean 2003; Hon. DCL (Mauritius) 1985, Hon. LLD (Madras) 2001, Dr hc (Aix-en-Provence) 1985, (Middlesex) 2009. *Leisure interests:* football, reading. *Address:* La Caverne No. 1, Vacoas, Mauritius (home); Ministry of Defence and Rodrigues, New Government Centre, Level 6, Port-Louis, Mauritius (office). *Telephone:* 201-1733 (office). *Fax:* 212-1313 (office). *E-mail:* mgunputh@govmu.org (office). *Website:* mdr.govmu.org (office).

JUGNAUTH, Pravind Kumar, LLB; Mauritian politician and barrister; *Prime Minister;* b. 25 Dec. 1961; s. of Sir Anerood Jugnauth (fmr Prime Minister of

Mauritius) and Sarojini Ballah; m. Kobita Jugnauth; three d.; ed Univ. of Buckingham, UK; joined Mouvement Socialiste Militant 1987, Deputy Leader 1999–2003, Leader 2003–; Councillor, Municipality of Vacoas/Phoenix 1996; mem. Parl. for Constituency No 11 (Vieux Grand Port and Rose Belle) 2009–; Minister of Agric., Food, Trade and Natural Resources 2000–03, Deputy Prime Minister and Minister of Finance Sept.–Dec. 2003, Deputy Prime Minister and Minister of Finance and Econ. Devt Dec. 2003–05, 2010–11, Minister of Technology, Communication and Innovation 2014–15, Minister of Finance 2016–, Prime Minister 2017–. *Address:* Office of the Prime Minister, New Treasury Building, Intendance Street, Port Louis (office); Mouvement Socialiste Militant, 1st Floor, Sun Trust Building, Edith Cavell Street, Port Louis; La Caverne No 1, Vacoas, Mauritius (home). *Telephone:* 207-9400 (office). *Fax:* 201-2578 (office). *E-mail:* privateoffice@govmu.org (office). *Website:* pmo.govmu.org (office); www.msmparty.org.

JUGNOT, Gérard; French actor, writer, director and producer; b. 4 May 1951, Paris; one s. with Cécile Magna; Chevalier, Légion d'honneur 2004. *Films include:* L'an 01 (The Year 01) 1973, Les valseuses (Getting It Up) 1974, Le bol d'air (also writer) 1975, C'est pas parce qu'on a rien à dire qu'il faut fermer sa gueule (also writer) 1975, Vous ne l'emporterez pas au paradis 1975, Pas de problème! (No Problem!) 1975, Calmos (Cool, Calm and Collected) 1976, Oublie-moi, Mandoline (Forget Me, Mandoline) 1976, Le locataire (The Tenant) 1976, On aura tout vu (The Bottom Line) 1976, Dracula père et fils (Dracula and Son) 1976, Monsieur Klein 1976, Le jouet (The Toy) 1976, Le chasseur de chez Maxim's (Maxim's Porter) 1976, Casanova & Co. (aka Some Like It Cool, USA), Herbie Goes to Monte Carlo 1977, Des enfants gâtés (Spoiled Children) 1977, Vous n'aurez pas l'Alsace et la Lorraine (You Won't Have Alsace-Lorraine 1977, La septième compagnie au clair de lune (The Seventh Company Outdoors) 1977, Les petits câlins (The Little Wheedlers) 1978, Pauline et l'ordinateur 1978, Les bronzés (French Fried Vacation, USA) (also writer) 1978, Les héros n'ont pas froid aux oreilles (Heroes Are Not Wet Behind the Ears, USA) (also writer) 1979, Un si joli village... (The Investigation) 1979, le coup de sirocco 1979, Les bronzés font du ski (also writer) 1979, Retour en force (Return in Bond) 1980, Le coup du parapluie (Umbrella Coup) 1980, Les Charlots contre Dracula 1980, Pourquoi pas nous? 1981, Pour 100 briques t'as plus rien... (For 200 Grand, You Get Nothing Now) 1980, Le Père Noël est une ordure (also writer) 1982, Le quart d'heure américain (also writer) 1982, La fiancée qui venait du froid 1983, Papy fait de la résistance 1983, Le garde du corps 1984, Pinot simple flic (also writer and dir) 1984, Just the Way You Are 1984, Tranches de vie (Slices of Life) 1985, Les rois du gag 1985, Scout toujours... (also writer and dir) 1985, Nuit d'ivresse 1986, Le beauf 1987, Tandem 1987, Sans peur et sans reproche (Without Fear or Blame) (also writer and dir) 1988, Les cigognes n'en font qu'à leur tête 1989, Les 1001 nuits (1001 Nights, aka Scheherazade, UK) 1990, Les secrets professionnels du Dr Apfelglück 1991, Une époque formidable...(Wonderful Times) (also writer and dir) 1991, Les clés du paradis (The Keys to Paradise) 1991, Voyage à Rome 1992, Grosse fatigue (Dead Tired) 1994, Casque bleu (Blue Helmet) (also writer and dir) 1994, Les faussaires (The Impostors) 1994, 3,000 scénarios contre le virus (3,000 Scenarios to Combat a Virus) (dir segment 'La pharmacie') 1994, Fantôme avec chauffeur 1996, Fallait pas!... (also writer and dir) 1996, Marthe 1997, Au bain... Mari! 1999, Trafic d'influence (Influence Peddling) 1999, L'ami du jardin 1999, Meilleur espoir féminin (Most Promising Young Actress) (also writer and dir) 2000, Oui, mais... (Yes, But...) 2001, Monsieur Batignole (also writer, dir and producer) 2002, Le raid (The Race) 2002, Les clefs de bagnole (The Car Keys) 2003, Les choristes (Chorists) (also dir and assoc. producer) 2004, The Magic Roundabout (voice) 2005, Boudu (also dir and co-producer) 2005, Il ne faut jurer... de rien! 2005, Les bronzés amis pour la vie (also writer) 2006, Les brigades du tigre 2006, L'île aux trésors 2007, L'auberge rouge 2007, Ça se soigne? 2008, Faubourg 36 2008, Musée haut, musée bas 2008, Envoyés très spéciaux 2009, La siciliana ribelle 2009, Rose et noir 2009, La nouvelle guerre des boutons 2011, Asterix and Obelix: God Save Britannia 2012, Adieu Paris 2013, Babysitting 2014, Entre amis 2015, Camping 3 2016. *Television includes:* Pierrot mon ami (Pierrot My Friend) 1979, Merci Bernard (series) 1982, L'adieu aux as (mini-series) 1982, Le Père Noël est une ordure (also writer) 1985, Restauratec 2002, Volpone 2003, Trois petites filles 2004, Ali Baba et les 40 voleurs 2007, Le grand restaurant 2010, Merlin (mini-series) 2012, Cher trésor 2014, La loi de... (mini-series) 2015.

JUILLET, Alain; French intelligence officer and fmr business executive; *President, Academy of Competitive Intelligence;* b. 1943; ed Centre de perfectionnement des affaires, Institut des hautes études de défense nationale, Paris, Stanford Univ., USA; fmr employee, Pernod-Ricard, Jacobs-Suchard, Union Laitière Normande, France Champignon; Chief Exec. French Operations, Marks & Spencer Ltd -2001; Head of Information, Direction Générale de la Sécurité Extérieure (DGSE) 2002–03, Sr Officer responsible for econ. intelligence, Secrétariat général de la défense nationale (SGDN) 2004; Chair. Corporate Club of Security Officers (CDSE) 2011; Pres. Acad. of Competitive Intelligence 2011–; Sr Advisor Orrick, Rambaud Martel; mem. Scientific Council, Inst. for Advanced Studies in Science and Tech. (IHEST) 2008; mem. Council for Econ. Defense 2005; Hon. Pres., Amadeus Executives 2002; Chevalier, Ordre national du Mérite 1987, Officier, Ordre du Mérite Agricole 1997, Chevalier, Ordre des Palmes académiques 2000, Chevalier, Ordre des Arts et des Lettres 2006, Commdr, Ordre national de la Légion d'honneur 2009. *Publication includes:* Gérer les risques criminels en entreprise : Stratégies et comportements pratiques 2012. *Address:* Academy of Competitive Intelligence, 131 Oliver Street, 3rd Floor, Boston, MA 02110, USA (office). *Telephone:* (630) 983-5530 (office). *Fax:* (630) 983-3317 (office). *E-mail:* info@academyci.com (office). *Website:* www.academyci.com (office).

JUKNEVIČIENĖ, Rasa; Lithuanian physician and politician; b. 26 Jan. 1958, Panevėžio raj. Tiltagalių km; m. Zenonas Juknevičius; ed Kaunas Medical Inst.; paediatrician, Cen. Hosp., Poswolu 1984–90; mem. Supreme Council, Reconstituent Seimas 1990–92; Deputy in Seimas 1996–, Vice-Pres. Parl. Del. to NATO Parl. Ass. 1999–2000, mem. Comm. for NATO Affairs 2004–08 (Deputy Chair. 2005–08); Minister of Nat. Defence 2008–12; mem. and Deputy Leader Homeland Union—Lithuanian Christian Democrats (Tėvynės Sąjunga); Lithuanian Grand Duke Gediminas Order of the Commdr's Cross of Lithuania's 10th Anniversary of Independence. *Leisure interests:* reading, growing flowers. *Address:* Homeland Union—Lithuanian Christian Democrats, L. Stuokos-Gucevičiaus g. 11, Vilnius 01122, Lithuania (office). *Telephone:* (5) 212-1657 (office). *Fax:* (5) 278-4722 (office). *E-mail:* sekretoriatas@tsajunga.lt (office). *Website:* www.tsajunga.lt (office).

JULIEN, Michael Frederick, FCA, FCT; British business executive and accountant (retd); b. 22 March 1938, London; s. of Robert A. F. Julien and Olive R. Evans; m. Ellen Martinsen 1963; one s. two d.; ed St Edward's School, Oxford; Chartered Accountant (Hons Intermediate); Price Waterhouse & Co. 1958–67; other commercial appointments including Group Finance Dir, Willis Faber and C E Heath and Treas., British Leyland 1967–76; Group Finance Dir BICC (now Balfour Beatty PLC) 1976–83; Exec. Dir Finance and Planning, Midland Bank (now HSBC Bank PLC) 1983–86; Man. Dir Finance and Admin. Guinness PLC (now Diageo PLC) 1987–88, Dir (non-exec.) 1988–97; Group Chief Exec. Storehouse PLC (now Mothercare PLC) 1988–92; Chair. Owners Abroad PLC (now First Choice Holidays PLC) 1993–97; Dir Medeva PLC 1993–98; fmr Deputy Chair. Oxford Professional Training Ltd. *Leisure interests:* family, travel, computing (including video editing).

JULIET, Charles; French poet, playwright and novelist; b. 30 Sept. 1934, Jujurieux (Ain); ed school in Aix-en-Provence, studies in Lyon; Prix Goncourt de la Poésie 2013. *Publications:* Au long de la spirale 1975, Pages de pierre 1977, La Plus Fragile 1977, Croissances 1978, Pages de journal 1978, Vers la rencontre 1980, Reviens à ta solitude 1983, Convergences 1984, La lente montée 1984, Lettre suit 1985, La Soif 1987, Tes yeux blessés 1987, Entretien (with Pierre Soulages) 1987, Accords 1987, La vie affleure 1989, Tant de chemins 1989, L'Année de l'éveil 1989, Affûts 1990, Dans la lumière des saisons 1991, Le Don de présence 1992, Bribes pour un double 1992, Ce pays du silence 1992, Jean Reverzy 1992, L'Inattendu 1992, Tu avives 1993, Telluriennes 1993, Cette flamme claire 1994, Ce chemin 1994, Carnets de Saorge 1994, Entretien (with Raoul Ubac) 1994, Accueils – Journal 4 1982–1988 1994, Ce foyer secret 1995, Césire, n°4 1995, En amont 1995, Giacometti 1995, Failles 1995, Lambeaux 1995, A voix basse 1997, Lueur après labour – Journal 3 1968–1981 1997, Traversée de nuit – Journal 2 1965–1968 1997, Creuser 1998, La Mue 1998, Ferveur 1998, Fouilles 1998, L'Autre Chemin 1998, Rencontres (with Bram van Velde) 1998, La Traversée 1999, Ecarte la nuit 1999, Rencontres (with Samuel Beckett) 1999, Chez François Dilasser 1999, Attente en automne 1999, Galet 2000, Un lourd destin 2000, Ténèbres en terre froide – Journal 1 1957–1964 2000, La Vague 2001, Invite le vent 2002, Une joie secrète 2002, Eclats 2002, Te rejoindre 2002, L'Incessant 2002, L'Autre Faim 2003, Notules 2005, Ces bruits du monde extérieur 2005, Les Autoportraits de Jean-Michel Marchetti 2005, Au pays du long nuage blanc 2005, T.R.U.P.H.E.M.U.S 2006, L'opulence de la nuit 2006, D'une rive à l'autre 2006, Un jour 2006, L'absente 2007, Etty Hillesum, la fille qui ne savait pas prier 2007, Conversations with Samuel Beckett and Bram Van Velde (co-author) 2009. *Address:* c/o Dalkey Archive Press, Dutch House, 307–308 High Holborn, London, WC1V 7LL, England. *E-mail:* contact@dalkeyarchive.com. *Website:* www.dalkeyarchive.com.

JULIUS, Anthony Robert, MA, PhD; British lawyer; *Deputy Chairman, Mishcon de Reya;* b. 16 July 1956; s. of Morris Julius and Myrna Julius; m. 1st Judith Bernie 1979 (divorced 1998); two s. two d.; m. 2nd Dina Rabinovitch 1999 (died 2007); one s.; m. 3rd Katarina Lester 2009; one s.; ed City of London School, Jesus Coll., Cambridge, Univ. Coll. London; articled Victor Mishcon & Co., qualified 1981, partner Mishcon de Reya 1984–, (Head of Litigation 1987–98), Consultant 1998–, currently also Deputy Chair.; Solicitor Advocate 1999; Teacher (part-time), Law Faculty, Univ. Coll. London 1995–97; Dir Inst. of Jewish Policy Research (reporting on Holocaust Denial Legislation) 1995–97 (Deputy Chair. Research Bd 1995–97); f., Trustee and Chair. Diana, Princess of Wales Memorial Trust, Vice-Pres. 1997–2003; Chair. Man. Bd Centre for Cultural Analysis, Theory and History, Univ. of Leeds 2001–06; Chair. London Consortium 2005–10. *Publications:* T. S. Eliot, Anti-Semitism and Literary Form 1995, Art Crimes (chapter in Law and Literature) 1999, Idolising Pictures 2000, Transgressions 2002, Trials of the Diaspora 2010. *Leisure interest:* cooking. *Address:* Mishcon de Reya, Summit House, 12 Red Lion Square, London, WC1R 4QD, England (office). *Telephone:* (20) 7440-7000 (office). *Fax:* (20) 7404-8171 (office). *E-mail:* anthony.julius@mishcon.com (office). *Website:* www.mishcon.com (office).

JULIUS, David, BS, PhD; American physiologist and academic; *Professor and Chairman, Department of Physiology, School of Medicine, University of California, San Francisco;* b. 4 Nov. 1955, New York; m. Holly A. Ingraham; ed Univ. of California, Berkeley, Massachusetts Inst. of Tech.; Undergraduate Research Asst, Dept of Biology, MIT 1975–77; Visiting Research Assoc., Dept of Biochemistry, Univ. of Bordeaux, France, Summer 1976; Grad. Student, Dept of Biochemistry, Univ. of California, Berkeley 1977–84; Postdoctoral Fellow, Inst. of Cancer Research, Columbia Univ., New York 1984–89; Asst Prof., Dept of Cellular and Molecular Pharmacology, Univ. of California, San Francisco 1989–96, Assoc. Prof. 1996–99, Prof. 1999–2006, Prof. and Chair. Dept of Physiology 2006–; mem. NAS 2004, American Acad. of Arts and Sciences 2005; Eloranta Research Fellow, MIT 1976, Grad. Studies Award, Univ. of California 1981, Jane Coffin Childs Postdoctoral Fellow 1984, March of Dimes Basil O'Connor Research Award 1990, PEW Scholars Award in the Biomedical Sciences 1990, NSF Presidential Young Investigator Award 1990, McKnight Neuroscience Foundation Scholars Award 1990, Numa Memorial Lecturer, Kyoto Univ., Japan 1996, McKnight Neuroscience Foundation Investigator Award 1997, Syntex Prize in Receptor Pharmacology 1997, Sir Lewis Thomas Pain Lecturer, Univ. Coll. London 1997, Presidential Lecturer, Soc. for Neuroscience 1998, Sandler Award in Basic Science, UCSF 1998, Brook Byers Award in Basic Science, Univ. of California, San Francisco 1998, Louis S. Harris Distinguished Lecturer, Medical Coll. of Virginia 1999, S.W. Kuffler Lecturer, Dept of Neurobiology, Harvard Medical School 2000, First Perl-UNC Neuroscience Prize 2001, Jacob Javits Award NIH/Nat. Inst. of Neurological Disorders and Stroke 2003, Yngve Zoterman Prize, Physiological Soc., Stockholm, Sweden 2003, Frederick W.L. Kerr Basic Research Award, American Pain Soc. 2006, K.L. Zulch Prize for Basic Neurological Research, Max Planck Soc. (co-recipient) 2006, Edward M. Scolnick Prize in Neuroscience, McGovern Inst. for Brain Research, MIT 2007, W. Alden Spencer Award, Columbia Univ. Center for Neurobiology and Behavior (co-recipient) 2007, Inaugural Julius Axelrod Prize, Soc. for Neuroscience (co-recipient) 2007, Unilever Science Prize 2007, Passano Award 2010, Shaw Prize in Life Sciences and Medicine (co-recipient) 2010, Prince of Asturias Award in Tech. and Scientific Research 2010, Dr. Paul Janssen Award for Biomedical Research 2014, Canada Gairdner Int. Award 2017. *Publications:* more than 100 papers in professional journals. *Address:* Department of Physiology, University of California, San Francisco, Mail Code 2140, Genentech Hall, Room N-272E, 600 16th Street, San

Francisco, CA 94158-2140, USA (office). *Telephone:* (415) 476-0431 (office); (415) 476-0432 (lab.) (office). *Fax:* (415) 502-8644 (lab.) (office). *E-mail:* david.julius@ucsf.edu (office). *Website:* www.physiology.ucla.edu (office).

JULIUS, Dame DeAnne Shirley, DCMG, CBE, PhD; American/British economist and research institute director; *Chair of the Council, University College London;* b. 14 April 1949; d. of Marvin Julius; m. Ian A. Harvey 1976; one s. one d.; ed Iowa State Univ. and Univ. of California, Davis; Econ. Adviser for Energy, World Bank 1975–82; Man. Dir Logan Assocs, Inc. 1983–86; Dir of Econs, Royal Inst. of Int. Affairs (RIIA), Chatham House), London 1986–89, Chair. RIIA 2003–12; Chief Economist, Shell Int. Petroleum Co., London 1989–93, British Airways 1993–97; Founder-mem. Monetary Policy Cttee, Bank of England 1997–2001, Dir Bank of England Court 2001–04; Chair. British Airways Pension Investment Man. Ltd 1995–97; Chair. UCL Council 2014–; Dir (non-exec.) Lloyds TSB 2001–07, BP (British Petroleum) 2001–, Serco Group 2001–, Roche 2002–, Jones Lang LaSalle 2008–, Deloitte (UK); Dr hc (Warwick) 2000, (South Bank) 2001, (Bath) 2002, (Birmingham) 2006. *Publications include:* The Economics of Natural Gas 1990, Global Companies and Public Policy: The Growing Challenge of Foreign Direct Investment 1990, Is Manufacturing Still Special in the New World Order? (co-author) (Amex Bank Prize) 1993; numerous articles on int. econs. *Leisure interests:* skiing, windsurfing, bonsai. *Address:* Office of the Council, University College London, Gower Street, London, WC1E 6BT, England (office). *Telephone:* (20) 7679-2000 (office). *Website:* www.ucl.ac.uk/srs/governance-and-committees/governance/council (office).

JULLIEN, François, DèsSc; French academic; *Professor of Philosophy, University de Paris VII-Denis Diderot;* b. 2 June 1951, Embrun, Hautes-Alpes; s. of Raymond Jullien and Marie Cler; m. Odile Sournies 1974; one s. two d.; ed Ecole normale supérieure, Univs of Peking and Shanghai, China, Univ. Paris-Sorbonne; Head French Sinology Unit, Hong Kong 1978–81; Resident Maison franco-japonaise, Tokyo 1985–87; Sr Lecturer, Univ. de Paris VIII-Saint-Denis 1981–87, Prof. 1987–90; Prof. Univ. de Paris VII-Denis Diderot 1990–, Dir l'UFR Asie orientale 1990–2000; Pres. Asscn française des études chinoises 1988–90; Pres. Collège Int. de philosophie 1995–98; Dir Oriental collection, Presses Univ. de France (PUF), Dir Inst. de la Pensée Contemporaine, des collections Orientales et Libelles, currently Dir Agenda de la Pensée Contemporaine, PUF, Dir Centre Marcel Granet; sr mem. Inst. Universitaire de France 2001–; mem. Editorial Cttee Critique journal; Hannah Arendt Prize for Political Thought 2010, Grand Prix de Philosophie 2011. *Publications include:* Fleurs du matin cueillies le soir 1976, Sous le dais fleuri 1978 (both translations of the Chinese texts of Lu Xun), La Valeur allusive 1985, Procès ou création 1989, Eloge de la fadeur 1991, La Propension des choses 1992, Figures de l'immanence 1993, Le Détour et l'accès 1995, Fonder la morale 1995, Traité de l'efficacité 1997, Un sage est sans idée ou l'autre de la philosophie 1998, De l'essence ou du nu 2000, Penser d'un dehors (la Chine) 2000, Du "temps": éléments d'une philosophie du vivre 2001, La Grande image n'a pas de forme 2003 (trans. into Vietnamese, Italian, Castillian, German), L'Ombre au tableau 2004, Nourrir sa vie, à l'écart du bonheur 2005, Conférence sur l'efficacité 2005, Si parler va sans dire. Du logos et d'autres ressources 2006, L'invention de l'idéal et le destin de l'Europe 2009, Cette étrange idée du beau 2010, Philosophie du vivre 2011, Entrer dans une pensée ou Des possibles de l'esprit 2012, De l'intime, Loin du bruyant Amour 2013, Vivre de paysage ou L'impensé de la Raison 2014, Vivre en existant, une nouvelle Ethique 2016, Près d'elle, présence opaque, présence intime 2016. *Address:* Université Paris VII-Denis Diderot, 2 place Jussieu, 75251 Paris Cedex 05 (office); 8 rue Tournefort, 75005 Paris, France (home). *Telephone:* 1-44-27-82-95 (office).

JUMA, Monica, BA, MA, DPhil; Kenyan diplomatist, policy analyst and government official; *Secretary for Foreign Affairs;* m. Peter Kagwanja; two c.; ed Univ. of Nairobi, Univ. of Oxford; began career as Man. Analyst, Office of the Pres.; long career with Ministry of Foreign Affairs (MFA), including as Amb. to Ethiopia and Perm. Rep. to African Union, Inter-Govt Authority on Devt (IGAD) and UN Econ. Comm. for Africa (UNECA) –2013, Prin. Sec. (MFA) 2016–18, Sec. (Minister) for Foreign Affairs 2018–; Prin. Sec., Ministry of Defence 2013; fmr Prin. Sec., Ministry of Interior; has served with numerous govts and inter-govt orgs, including UN Sec.-Gen.'s High-Level Panel on Resourcing Africa Union peacekeeping operations 2008; Sr Research Fellow, Dept of Political Science, Univ. of Pretoria; Adjunct Faculty Mem., African Center for Strategic Studies, Nat. Defence Univ., Washington DC; Sr Policy Analyst, Safer South Africa Foundation, Pretoria; Founding mem. and Exec. Dir Africa Policy Inst. (API); Research Dir and lecturer in politics, Centre for Refugee Studies, Moi Univ.; fmr Exec. Dir Africa Inst. of South Africa (AISA), Pretoria; Research Assoc., Int. Peace Inst., New York; mem. Think Tank, New Partnership for Africa's Devt 2001–08; mem. Editorial Bd Journal for Peace and Security (UPEACE), Kenyan Affairs; mem. Int. Advisory Bd UN Univ. for Peace, Costa Rica, Norwegian MFA Training for Peace Programme, Centre for the Study of Forced Migration, Univ. of Witwatersrand, African Governance Inst. *Publications:* numerous publs on issues of peace, security and governance, including Compendium on Peace and Security, articles in refereed journals, chapters in edited books, commissioned reports, monographs and opinion pieces. *Address:* Ministry of Foreign Affairs, Old Treasury Bldg, Harambee Ave, POB 30551, 00100 Nairobi, Kenya (office). *Telephone:* (20) 318888 (office). *Fax:* (20) 240066 (office). *E-mail:* press@mfa.go.ke (office). *Website:* www.mfa.go.ke (office).

JUMABEKOV, Dastanbek, LLB; Kyrgyzstani business executive and politician; *Chairman, Supreme Council;* b. 2 Nov. 1976, Kara-Buura Dist, Talas Oblast, Kyrgyz SSR, USSR; m.; three c.; ed Kyrgyz Nat. Univ.; began career as Commercial Dir, Bayamtaş Ltd 2002; Gen. Man., KASSI Training 2005–07; Dir, Jamoat LLC 2007–09; Head of mobile mechanized detachment, Ministry of Emergency Situations 2009–10; mem. Jogorku Kenesh (Supreme Council, parl.) (Respublika-Ata Jurt—Repub.-Homeland—Political Party) 2010–15, 2015–, Chair. (Speaker), Jogorku Kenesh 2017–. *Address:* Jogorku Kenesh, 720053 Bishkek, Abdymomunov 207, Kyrgyzstan (office). *Telephone:* (312) 61-16-04 (office). *Fax:* (312) 62-50-12 (office). *E-mail:* zs@kenesh.gov.kg (office). *Website:* www.kenesh.kg (office).

JUMAĞALIE, Asqar Q.; Kazakhstani politician; *Minister of Digital Development, Defence and Aerospace Industry;* b. 2 Aug. 1972, Orenburg, USSR; ed Suvorov Mil. School, Satbayev Kazakh Nat. Tech. Univ., Kazakh Humanitarian Law Innovative Univ. (KazHLIU); Dir-Gen. Zharyk LLP 1996–98; sector leader, Ministry of Transport and Communications 1998–99, Head of the Transport Control Cttee 1999–2000; State Communications Supervisor, Ministry of Communications and Information 2001–03, Deputy Chair. 2003–06, Chair. 2006, 2014, Minister of Communications and Information 2010–12; Pres. Kazakhtelecom JSC 2006–10; Minister of Transport and Communications 2012–14; Deputy Minister of Investments and Devt 2014–15; apptd Deputy Prime Minister 2017; Minister of Digital Devt, Defence and Aerospace Industry 2019–. *Address:* Ministry of Digital Development and the Defence and Aerospace Industries, 010000 Nur-Sultan, Mäñgilik El kösh. 8, Kazakhstan (office). *Telephone:* (7172) 74-94-64 (office). *E-mail:* moap@mdai.gov.kz (office). *Website:* mdai.gov.kz (office).

JUMAGULOV, Apas; Kyrgyzstani diplomatist, politician and business executive; b. 19 Sept. 1934, Arashan; s. of Jumagul Jumagulov; ed Moscow Inst. of the Petrochemical and Gas Industry; began working as geologist in state oil industry; actively participated in activities of local CP br.; Chief Engineer, Kyrgyzneft (state oil and gas co.) –1973; apptd Head of Industry and Transportation Dept, Cen. Cttee of CP of Kyrgyz SSR 1973; later took on several other admin. posts at regional and nat. levels; Head of Govt of Kyrgyzia 1986–91; nominated himself as a cand. in presidential elections 1990; Admin. Head of his native region of Chui Oblast 1990–93; Prime Minister of Kyrgyzstani 1993–98 (retd); Amb. to Germany 1998–2003, also accred to the Holy See and Scandinavian countries 1999–2003; withdrew from politics and became intermediary and consultant; Chair. Moscow br. of Postnoff co. 2003–; entered leadership ranks of Eurasian Movt 2004–; Amb. to Russian Fed. 2005–07; Order of Merit (FRG) 2003.

JUN, Ho-suck, MA; South Korean automobile industry executive; *President and CEO, Hyundai Mobis;* ed Grad. School of Cranfield Univ., UK; fmr Vice-Pres. Hyundai Motor Co. Ltd, Pres. and CEO Hyundai Mobis 2011–, Pres. and CEO Hyundai Motor Group 2011–, CEO Beijing Mobis Transmission Co. Ltd. *Address:* Hyundai Mobis, 679–4 Seoul International Tower, Seoul 135-977, Republic of Korea (office). *Telephone:* (2) 20185114 (office). *Fax:* (2) 20186000 (office). *E-mail:* info@mobis.co.kr (office). *Website:* www.mobis.co.kr (office).

JUNCKER, Jean-Claude, LLM; Luxembourg politician and EU official; *President, European Commission;* b. 9 Dec. 1954, Redange-sur-Attert; s. of Jos Juncker and Marguerite Hecker; m. Christiane Frising 1979; ed Univ. of Strasbourg; Parl. Sec. to Christian Social Party 1979–82; Sec. of State for Labour and Social Affairs 1982–84; elected mem. Chamber of Deputies 1984; Minister of Labour, Minister in charge of Budget 1984–89; Minister of Labour, of Finance 1989–94; Prime Minister of Luxembourg 1995–2013, also Minister of State, of Finance and the Treasury, of Labour and Employment 1995–99, of State and of Finance 1999–2009, Minister of the Treasury 2009–13; Chair. Christian Social Party 1990–95; Chair. Social Affairs and Budget Councils 1985; Gov. IBRD 1989–95, fmr Gov. IMF, EBRD; elected first Perm. Pres. Eurogroup 2005; Pres. European Comm., Brussels Nov. 2014–(19); Foreign Assoc. mem. Acad. of Ethics and Political Science, Inst. of France 2007; Patron Animal Protection Asscn EV Newfoundlanders; Hon. Citizen of Trier 2003; Hon. Citizen and Freeman of the City of Orestiada, Greece, with a street named after him 2004; Hon. Senator, European Acad. of Sciences and Arts 2009; Grand Cross, Order of Merit with Star and Sash (Luxembourg) 1988; Grand Cross, Order of Infante Dom Henrique (Portugal) 1988; Grand Officier, Légion d'honneur 2002; Grand Cross, Order of the Star of Romania 2003; Grand Cross, Portuguese Order of Christ 2005; Grand Cross, Order of the Three Stars (Latvia) 2006; Collar of the Order pro Merito Melitensi (SMOM) 2010; Grand Decoration of Honour in Gold with Sash (Austria) 2010; Grand Cross, Order of the Redeemer (Greece) 2013; Grand Cross, Royal Norwegian Order of Merit 2014; Grand Cross, Order of Merit (Italy) 2014; Dr hc (Miami, USA) 1998, (Münster, Germany) 2001, (Bucharest, Romania) 2003, (Demokritos Univ. of Thrace, Greece) 2004, (Robert Schuman Univ., Strasbourg, France) 2007, (Pittsburgh, USA) 2008, (Sophia Univ., Tokyo, Japan) 2010, (Medizinische Universität, Innsbruck, Austria) 2011, (Athens, Greece) 2011; Vision for Europe Award, Edmond Israel Foundation 1998, Médaille d'or de la Fondation Jean-Monnet (Gold Medal for Services to Europe) 1998, European Crafts Prize of North Rhine-Westphalia 1999, Insignia de l'Artisanat en Or (Gold Badge), Luxembourg Chamber of Crafts 2000, Cicero-Speakers Prize 2002, Prize of European Fed. of Taxpayers 2003, Heinrich Braun Award 2003, Quadriga Prize in European Year of German Soc. Workshop 2003, Walter Hallstein Prize 2005, Europeans of the Year 2005, Elsie Kuhn Leitz Prize, Asscn of Franco-German Cos 2005, Européen de l'Année (European of the Year), French Press (Trombinoscope) 2005, Int. Charlemagne Prize of Aachen 2006, European Prize for Political Culture, Hans Ringier Foundation 2006. *Leisure interest:* reading. *Address:* Office of the President, European Commission, 200 Rue de la Loi, 1049 Brussels, Belgium (office). *Telephone:* (2) 298-18-00 (office). *Fax:* (2) 295-01-38 (office). *E-mail:* president.juncker@ec.europa.eu (office). *Website:* ec.europa.eu/commission/index_en (office).

JUNG, Andrea, BA; American retail executive; b. (Zhong Binxian), 18 Sept. 1958, Toronto, Canada; eldest child of Chinese immigrants; m. 2nd Michael Gould (divorced); one adopted s. one d. from previous m.; ed Princeton Univ.; grew up in Wellesley, Mass; joined man. trainee programme at Bloomingdale's 1979; fmr Sr Vice-Pres. Gen. Merchandising, I. Magnin, San Francisco; Exec. Vice-Pres. Neiman Marcus –1994; consultant for Avon Products 1993, Pres. Product Marketing Group Marketing, Avon US 1994–96, Sr Vice-Pres. Global Marketing, Avon Products Inc. 1996–97, mem. Bd of Dirs 1998–2012, Pres. and COO 1998–2000, CEO 1999–2012, Chair. 2001–12; Chair. The Cosmetic, Toiletry and Fragrance Asscn (first woman) 2001–05; mem. Bd of Dirs Gen. Electric Co. 1998–, Princeton Univ., Fashion Inst. of Tech., Fragrance Foundation, Cosmetic Exec. Women, Sales Corpn Donna Karan Int., Catalyst, Apple 2008–; mem. Int. Advisory Council, Salomon Smith Barney; Trustee, New York Presbyterian Hosp.; Clinton Global Citizen Award for the corp. sector 2010. *Leisure interest:* playing the piano. *Address:* GE Board of Directors, General Electric Company (W2E), 3135 Easton Turnpike, Fairfield, CT 06828, USA (office).

JUNG, Franz Josef, DJur; German lawyer and politician; b. 5 March 1949, Erbach, Rheingau-Taunus Dist, Hesse; m.; three c.; ed Rheingau School, Geisenheim, Univ. of Mainz; legal training at Wiesbaden Dist Court 1974–76; solicitor in Eltville 1976–, public notary 1983–; mem. Dist Ass. of Rheingau-Taunus 1972–87; mem. Nat. Exec., CDU German Youth Union 1973–93, Vice-Chair. 1981–83; elected to Hessen State Parl. (Landtag), Wiesbaden 1983–2005; Hessian State Minister for Fed. and European Affairs and Head of Hessian State

Chancellory 1999–2000; Gen. Sec. of CDU in Hessen 1987–91, CDU Parl. Sec., Hessen Landtag 1987–99; CDU Parl. Whip in Hessen Landtag 2003–05; mem. CDU Nat. Exec. Cttee 1998–, Chair. CDU Media Political Expert Group 2012–14; mem. Bundestag, Berlin 2005–, Deputy Chair. CDU Parliamentary Group for Food, Agric., Consumer Protection, 2013–15, Parliamentary Group for Churches and Religious Communities 2014–, Parliamentary Group for Foreign Policy, Security Policy, Euro Europe 2015–; Federal Minister of Defence 2005–09, of Labour and Social Affairs Oct.–Nov. 2009 (resgnd); Chair. Producers' Asscn Research Inst. of Geisenheim 1999, Friends of ZDF TV 2002, Nat. Asscn for Soldiers Services 2015–; mem. Rheingau Music Festival Cttee 1989–, ZDF TV Advisory Bd 1999, Eintracht Frankfurt e.V. Man. Bd 1999, Eintracht Frankfurt AG Supervisory Bd 2003–05. *Address:* Bundestag, Platz der Republik 1, 11011 Berlin, Germany (office). *Telephone:* (30) 22775447 (office). *Fax:* (30) 22776447 (office). *E-mail:* franz-josef.jung@bundestag.de. *Website:* www.bundestag.de (office); www.franz-josef-jung.de (office).

JUNG, Man-won, BA, MBA; South Korean energy industry executive; *Vice-Chairman, SK Telecom Company Ltd;* ed Yonsei Univ., New York Univ., USA; served in Korean Ministry of Energy and Resources 1980–94; consultant, SKC Chemical Business Group (fmrly Yukong Oxichemical) 1994–96, Vice-Pres. Man. and Planning Office 1996–2000, Vice-Pres. SK Customer Service Devt Div. 2000–01, Vice-Pres. Wireless Internet Business Div. Group and Finance Business Div., SK Telecom 2001–02, Pres. SK Global Energy Sales Group and Head SK Global Normalization Process Task Force 2002–03, Pres. and CEO SK Networks 2003–08, Pres. and CEO SK Telecom 2009–10, Vice-Chair. 2010–. *Address:* SK Telecom Company, Ltd, 11 Eulijiro, 2-ga, Jung-gu, Seoul 100-999, Republic of Korea (office). *Telephone:* (2) 6100-2114 (office). *Fax:* (2) 6100-7827 (office). *Website:* www.sktelecom.com (office).

JUNG, Najeeb, BA, MA, MSc; Indian energy industry specialist and government official; b. 18 Jan. 1951, Daryaganj, Delhi; m.; three d.; ed St Stephen's Coll., Univ. of Delhi, London School of Econs, UK; joined Indian Admin. Service, (MP Cadre) 1973, held several positions in Madhya Pradesh including Collector and Dist Magistrate, Man. Dir MP Oil Seeds Devt Fed. and MP Finance Corpn; served as Pvt. Sec. to Shri Madhavrao Scindia, Minister for Railways; fmr Dir Dept of Steel, Govt of India; Jt Sec., Ministry of Petroleum and Natural Gas, Govt of India 1994–99 (resgnd); Sr Energy Specialist and Prin. Energy Specialist, Asian Devt Bank 1995–99, in charge of restructuring Ministry of Petroleum and Natural Resources, Afghanistan 2002–05; Sr Visiting Fellow, Oxford Inst. for Energy Studies, Univ. of Oxford, UK 1999–2002, 2005–08; Dir for Energy Research, Observer Research Foundation, New Delhi 2008–09, also consulted for Reliance Global Man. Services; Vice-Chancellor, Jamia Millia Islamia 2009–13; Lt-Gov. of Delhi 2013–16; fmr Chair. Core Cttee of Vice-Chancellors, Ministry of Human Resource Devt; mem. Senate, Indian Inst. of Tech., Kanpur. *Publications include:* several books and reports on the energy sector; regular contrib. to nat. newspapers on educ. and social issues.

JUNG, Roland Tadeusz, BChir, MA, MB, MD, FRCP, FRCPE; British physician; b. 8 Feb. 1948, Glasgow, Scotland; m.; one d.; ed Pembroke Coll., Cambridge, St Thomas' Hosp. Medical School, London; MRC Clinical Scientist, Dunn Nutrition Unit, Cambridge 1977–80; Sr Registrar, Royal Postgraduate Medical School, London 1980–82; Consultant Physician, Ninewells Hosp. and Medical School, Dundee 1982–91, Clinical Dir of Medicine 1991–94; Dir Tayside Research & Devt NHS Consortium, Dundee 1997–2000; Chair. Scottish Hosp. Endowments Research Trust 2000–01; Chief Scientist, Scottish Exec. Health Dept 2001–07 (retd); mem. Innogen Centre Advisory Cttee; Sr Distinction Adviser, Eastern Region for Scottish Advisory Cttee for Distinction Award 2004; Card Medal, Asscn of Physicians of GB and Ireland 1987. *Publications include:* Endocrine Problems in Oncology 1984, Colour Atlas of Obesity 1990. *Leisure interests:* gardening, walking, reading, visiting gardens.

JÜNGEL, Eberhard Klaus, DTheol; German professor of theology and philosophy; b. 5 Dec. 1934, Magdeburg; s. of Kurt Jüngel and Margarete Jüngel (née Rothemann); ed Humboldtschule, Magdeburg, Katechetisches Oberseminar, Naumburg/Saale, Kirchliche Hochschule, Berlin and Univs of Zürich and Basel, Switzerland; Asst, Kirchliche Hochschule (Sprachenkonvikt), East Berlin 1959–61, Lecturer in New Testament 1961–63, Lecturer in Systematic Theology 1963–66; ordained priest of the Evangelical Church 1962; Prof. of Systematic Theology and History of Dogma, Univ. of Zürich 1966–69; Prof. of Systematic Theology and Philosophy of Religion and Dir Inst. für Hermeneutik, Univ. of Tübingen 1969–2003, Dean, Faculty of Evangelical Theology 1970–72, 1992–94; Ephorus Evangelisches Stift, Tübingen 1987–2005; Guest Prof. of Systematic Theology, Univ. of Halle-Wittenberg 1990–93, Univ. of Berlin 1994, 1999–2000; various appointments within Evangelical Church, etc.; mem. Heidelberg and Norwegian Acads, Academia Scientiarum et Artium Europaea, Salzburg, Akad. der Wissenschaften, Göttingen; Fellow, Inst. for Advanced Study, Berlin; Officier, Ordre pour le Mérite 1992, Grosses Verdienstkreuz mit Stern des Verdienstordens 1994, Verdienstmedaille des Landes Baden-Württemberg; Hon. DD (Aberdeen) 1985; Dr hc (Greifswald) 2000, (Basel) 2000; Karl Barth Prize 1986, Brenz Medal. *Publications include:* more than 20 books including Paulus und Jesus 1962, Gottes Sein ist im Werden 1965, Unterwegs zur Sache 1972, Gott als Geheimnis der Welt 1977, Entsprechungen 1980, Glauben und Verstehen, Zum Theologiebegriff Rudolf Bultmanns 1985, Wertlose Wahrheit. Zur Identität und Relevanz des christlichen Glaubens 1990, Das Evangelium von der Rechtfestigung des Gottlosen als Zentrum des Glaubens 1998, Indikative der Gnade-Imperative der Freiheit 2000, Ed. Religion in Geschichte und Gegenwart and seven vols of sermons.

JUNGMANN PINTO, Raul Belens; Brazilian business executive and politician; *Minister of Public Security;* b. 3 April 1952, Recife; s. of Silvio Jungmann da Silva Pinto and Ivanise Belens Jungmann Pinto; ed Catholic Univ. of Pernambuco; Sec. of State, Local Govt Planning Dept, Pernambuco State 1990–91; Exec. Sec., Ministry of Planning 1993–94; Pres., Brazilian Inst. of the Environment and Renewable Natural Resources 1995–96; Pres., Nat. Inst. of Colonization and Agrarian Reform 1996–99; Minister of Agrarian Devt 1999–2002; mem. Chamber of Deputies (lower house of parl.) for Pernambuco (PPS/PE) 2003–11, 2015–16; Alderman, Recife (PE) 2012–14; Minister of Defence 2016–18, of Public Security 2018–; Pres., Bd of Trustees, Land Bank, Brasilia, DF 1998–2002; Pres., Nat. Council for Rural Devt 1999–2002; mem. Bd of Dirs Nat. Bank for Economic and Social Devt 1993–94; Order of Rio Branco 1997, Grand Cross, Order of Merit of Brasilia 2000, Grand Cross, Peacemaker Medal. *Address:* Ministry of Justice, Esplanade of Ministries, Palace of Justice, 70064-900 Brasília, DF, Brazil (office). *Telephone:* (61) 2025-3000 (office). *Website:* www.justica.gov.br/sua-seguranca/seguranca-publica (office); www.rauljungmann.com.br.

JUNIPER, Tony, BSc, MSc; British environmental campaigner, ecologist and environmental writer; *Fellow, Cambridge Institute for Sustainability Leadership, University of Cambridge;* b. 24 Sept. 1960, Oxford; s. of Austin Wilfred Juniper and Constance Margaret Elliston; m. Sue Sparkes; three c.; ed Univ. of Bristol, Univ. Coll. London; began career with Birdlife Int. (conservation network); joined Friends of the Earth 1990, fmr campaigns and policy Dir, Ilisu Dam campaign, Vice-Chair. Friends of the Earth Int. 2000–08, Exec. Dir Friends of the Earth, England, Wales and NI 2003–08; Founding Bd mem. Stop Climate Chaos 2005; Pres. Wildlife Trusts, Soc. for the Environment; Special Adviser to Prince of Wales' Rainforest Project; Sr Assoc., Univ. of Cambridge Programme for Industry; currently Fellow, Cambridge Inst. for Sustainability Leadership; Trustee, Fauna and Flora Int., Resurgence-Ecologist; Hon. Fellow, Inst. of Environmental Sciences 2008, Hon. Fellow, Soc. for the Environment 2013; Hon. DS (Univs of Bristol and Plymouth) 2013; Charles and Miriam Rothschild Medal 2009, Chromy Award, Conscience Inst., Monaco. *Publications include:* Deserts of Trees: The Environmental and Social Impacts of Large-scale Tropical Reforestation in Response to Global Climate Change (co-author) 1992, Whose Hand on the Chainsaw? UK Government Policy and the Tropical Rainforests (co-author) 1992, Wildlife Bill 1995, Threatened Planet 1996, Parrots: A Guide to Parrots of the World (Juniper and Parr) (McColvin Medal for Outstanding Work of Reference, Library Asscn 1999) 1998, Spix's Macaw: The Race to Save the World's Rarest Bird 2002, How Many Light Bulbs Does It Take to Change A Planet? 2007, Saving Planet Earth 2007, Harmony: A New Way of Looking at the World (with HRH The Prince of Wales and Ian Skelly) 2010, What Has Nature Ever Done for Us? 2013. *Leisure interests:* natural history, fishing, walking, writing. *Address:* Cambridge Institute for Sustainability Leadership, 1 Trumpington Street, Cambridge, CB2 1QA (office); The Old Schools, Trinity Lane, Cambridge, CB2 1TN, England (office). *Website:* www.cisl.cam.ac.uk (office); www.tonyjuniper.com.

JUNUSHALIYEV, Gen.-Maj. Kashkar; Kyrgyzstani police officer and government official; *Minister of Internal Affairs;* b. 1961, Archaly, Alamudun Dist, Chui Oblast, Kyrgyz SSR, USSR; ed Kyrgyz Nat. Univ., Secondary Specialized School of Ministry of Internal Affairs, Frunze (now Bishkek); began career in internal affairs as police officer, Bn of Frunze City Police Dept 1981, specialized studies 1984–86, apptd Insp. of Police Dept, Oktyabrskii dist, Frunze 1986, Deputy Head of Dept of Crime Prevention, Dept of Internal Affairs of Bishkek City 1991–92, Head of Dept of Internal Affairs 1992–93, Head of Dept of Internal Affairs, Oktyabrskii dist 1993, Deputy Chief of Internal Affairs, Oktyabrskii dist 1994–97, Deputy Chief of Police, Pervomaiskii dist 1997–2003, Head of GPG Internal Affairs of Bishkek 2003, Deputy Head of Dept of Internal Affairs, Yssyk-Kul Oblast 2003–07, Deputy Chief of Police, Chui Oblast 2007–08, Deputy Chief of Police, Batken Oblast 2008, Deputy Head of Dept of Internal Affairs, Bishkek 2008–09, Head of Ministry of Internal Affairs 2009–10, Deputy Minister of Internal Affairs 2010–14, Chief of Dept of Internal Affairs, Bishkek 2014–16, Acting Minister of Internal Affairs May–June 2016, Minister of Internal Affairs June–Nov. 2016, 2018–; state awards. *Address:* Ministry of Internal Affairs, 720000 Bishkek, Frunze 469, Kyrgyzstan (office). *Telephone:* (312) 26-62-54 (office). *Fax:* (312) 26-62-90 (office). *E-mail:* pressa@mvd.kg (office). *Website:* www.mvd.kg (office).

JUPPÉ, Alain Marie; French politician; *Mayor of Bordeaux;* b. 15 Aug. 1945, Mont-de-Marsan, Landes; s. of Robert Juppé and Marie Juppé (née Darroze); m. 1st Christine Leblond 1965 (divorced 1993); one s. one d.; m. 2nd Isabelle Legrand-Bodin 1993; one d.; ed Lycée Louis-le-Grand, Paris, École normale supérieure, Inst. d'Études politiques, Paris and École nat. d'admin; Insp. of Finance 1972; Office of Prime Minister Jacques Chirac (q.v.) June–Aug. 1976; tech. adviser, Office of Minister of Co-operation 1976–78; Nat. del. of RPR 1976–78, Nat. Sec. of RPR with responsibility for econ. and social recovery 1984–88, Sec.-Gen. 1988–95, Acting Pres. 1994–95, Pres. 1995–97; tech. adviser, Office of Mayor of Paris (Jacques Chirac) 1978; Dir-Gen. with responsibility for finance and econ. affairs, Commune de Paris 1980; Councillor, 18th arrondissement, Paris 1983–95; Second Asst to Mayor of Paris in charge of budget and financial affairs 1983–95; Deputy to Nat. Ass. from Paris 1988–97, from Gironde 1997–; Mayor of Bordeaux 1995–2001, 2001–04, 2006–; mem. European Parl. 1984–86, 1989–93; Deputy to Minister of Economy, Finance and Privatization with responsibility for budget 1986–88; Minister of Foreign Affairs 1993–95; Prime Minister of France 1995–97; convicted of mishandling public funds 2004, received 18-month suspended jail sentence (later reduced on appeal); Pres. Union pour la majorité presidentielle (UMP) 2002–04 (resgnd); Minister of State for Ecology and Sustainable Devt May–June 2007; Minister of Defence and Veterans' Affairs 2010–11, of Foreign and European Affairs 2011–12; Grand Officier, Légion d'honneur 2009; Grand Croix, Ordre nat. du Mérite; Grand Cross of Merit, Sovereign Order of Malta. *Publications:* La Tentation de Venise 1993, Entre Nous 1996, Montesquieu, Le moderne 1999, Entre quatre z'yeux (with Serge July) 2001, France mon pays – Lettres d'un voyageur 2006, Je ne mangerai plus de cerises en hiver 2009, La politique telle qu'elle meurt de ne pas être (entretien avec Michel Rocard mené par Bernard Guetta) 2011. *Address:* Mairie de Bordeaux, 33077 Bordeaux Cedex, France (office). *Telephone:* (5) 56-10-20-30 (office). *Website:* www.bordeaux.fr (office); www.al1jup.com.

JURGENSEN, William G. (Jerry), BCom, MBA; American insurance industry executive; m. Patty Jurgensen; two c.; ed Creighton Univ., Omaha, Neb.; worked 17 years with Norwest Corpn, held various man. positions including Pres. and CEO, Norwest Investment Services and later Exec. Vice-Pres., Corp. Banking; Man., First Chicago NBD Corpn 1995–98, Exec. Vice-Pres. Bank One Corpn (following merger) 1998–2000; CEO Nationwide Mutual Insurance Co. 2000–09; mem. Bd of Dirs Achieve, Inc., ConAgra Foods, Inc. 2002–, Scotts Miracle-Gro Co. 2009–13, AIG Insurance Co. 2013–; Dir Greater Columbus Chamber of Commerce, Law Enforcement Foundation of Ohio, Nationwide Children's Hosp.; Chair. Gov.'s Comm. on Teaching Success 2001–03; Chair. 2002 Campaign for United Way of Cen. Ohio; Co-Chair. Ohio Gov.'s Public-Pvt. Collaborative Comm.; mem. Columbus Downtown Devt Corpn, Ohio Business Roundtable, Financial Services

Roundtable, Columbus Partnership, Ohio State Univ. Hosp., Business Higher Educ. Forum; Trustee, Loyola Univ., Newberry Library, Ohio State Univ.

JUROWSKI, Vladimir; Russian conductor; *Principal Conductor, London Philharmonic Orchestra;* b. 4 April 1972, Moscow; ed Music Acad., Berlin and Dresden, Germany; Chief Conductor, Sibelius Orchestra, Berlin 1993–96; Founder and Conductor, United Berlin ensemble, performing modern music; int. debut conducting May Night by Rimsky-Korsakov, Wexford Festival 1995; fmr Prin. Guest Conductor, Orchestra Sinfonica Verdi, Milan; First Kapellmeister, Komische Oper Berlin 1997–2001; Prin. Guest Conductor, Teatro Comunale, Bologna 2000–03; Music Dir, Glyndebourne Festival Opera 2001–07, Glyndebourne Opera 2001–13; Prin. Guest Conductor, London Philharmonic Orchestra 2003–06, Prin. Conductor 2007–; Prin. Guest Conductor, Russian Nat. Orchestra 2006–09; Prin. Artist, Orchestra of the Age of Enlightenment; Artistic Dir, Russian State Academic Symphony Orchestra 2011–; Chief Conductor, Berlin Radio Symphony Orchestra 2017–; has conducted in venues world-wide, including Metropolitan Opera (New York), Opera Bastille (Paris), Komische Oper (Berlin), Teatro Comunale (Bologna), Teatro Real (Madrid), Royal Opera House (London), and with Chicago Symphony, Philadelphia, Berlin Philharmonic, Mahler Chamber Orchestras, Chamber Orchestra of Europe, Tonhalle-orchester Zurich, Gewandhausorchester Leipzig and Staatskapelle Dresden; Royal Philharmonic Soc. Conductor Award 2007. *Recordings include:* Stravinsky's The Rake's Progress (with London Philharmonic Orchestra and Glyndebourne Chorus), Complete Symphonies of Brahms (with London Philharmonic Orchestra); DVD releases: La Cerentola, Gianni Schicchi, Die Fledermaus, Don Giovanni (Glyndebourne Festival Opera), Hansel und Gretel (Metropolitan Opera of New York), Stravinsky: Petrushka (London Philharmonic Orchestra) 2016. *Address:* c/o IMG Artists, Capital Tower, 91 Waterloo Road, London, SE1 8RT, England (office); London Philharmonic Orchestra, 89 Albert Embankment, London, SE1 7TP, England (office). *Telephone:* (20) 7957-5800 (office). *Fax:* (20) 7957-5801 (office). *E-mail:* nmathias@imgartists.com (office). *Website:* www.imgartists.com (office); www.lpo.co.uk (office); www.vladimirjurowski.com.

JURŠĖNAS, Česlovas; Lithuanian journalist, editor and politician; b. 18 May 1938, Panižiškėje village, Švenčioniai Co. (now Ignalina Dist); m. Jadvyga Juršenas; one s.; ed Ignalina Secondary School, Vilnius Univ., Higher Party School, Leningrad (now St Petersburg); awarded journalist diploma 1960, worked as journalist for 15 years, first in editorial offices of weekly newspaper Statyba (Construction) and daily newspaper Tiesa (Truth), int. reviewer at Lithuania Radio and Television from 1964, Ed.-in-Chief TV Information broadcasts, later edited TV programme Atgimimo Banga (Wave of Revival) and other broadcasts; worked at Cen. Cttee and Council of Ministers of Lithuanian CP 1973–78; Head of editorial office of Vakarinės Naujienos (Evening News) 1978–83; first Press Officer for Govt of Lithuania 1989; with others, signed Act on the Re-establishment of the State of the Repub. of Lithuania 11 March 1990; stood for elections as ind. cand. of LCP, worked in Comm. on State re-establishment and the Constitution, elected to Supreme Council – Reconstituent Seimas 1990–92, elected Deputy Elder of the Parl. 1992, mem. Seimas (Parl.) for Ignalina-Švenčioniai single-member constituency No. 53 1992–96, Deputy Chair. 6th Seimas, later Chair., Deputy Chair. 8th Seimas 2000–02, First Deputy Chair. 2002–04, July–Nov. 2004, Acting Chair. Seimas April–July 2004, Speaker of the Seimas 2008; mem. Council of Švenčioniai Dist 1997–2000; active participant in separation of LCP from CPSU and ind. reorganization of LCP; mem. Presidium of LDLP Council 1990, Chair. of party 1996–2001, First Deputy Chair. Lithuanian Social Democratic Party (LSDP—Lietuvos Socialdemokratų Partija) following unification of Social Democrats (SDPL) and LDLP 2001; mem. Journalists' Union of Lithuania; mem. Editorial Science Council of the Lithuanian General Encyclopaedia and the Courts Council; Pres. Lithuanian Chess Fed.; Citizen of Honour of the Švenčioniai Dist; Grand Cross of the Order of Vytautas the Great 2004; Dr hc (Univ. of Lithuania); Gold Medal, Ignalina Secondary School. *Publications:* has published several books on politics and world affairs. *Leisure interests:* playing chess, collecting writings and caricatures of famous contemporary politicians.

JUSKO, Marián, DPhil; Slovak business executive and fmr central banker; b. 24 March 1956, Prešov; m.; one c.; ed Univ. of Econs, Bratislava; Lecturer, Univ. of Econs, Bratislava 1979–90, Adviser, Slovak Nat. Council 1990; Head of Banking Analyses and Prognoses, State Bank of Czechoslovakia 1991; Deputy Minister, Ministry of Admin. and Privatization of Nat. Property of Slovak Repub.; Chair. Nat. Property Fund 1991–92; mem. man. team State Bank of Czechoslovakia for Slovakia, Bratislava 1992; Vice-Gov. Nat. Bank of Slovakia 1993–99, Gov. 1999–2004; Chair. Slovnaft, a.s. 2005–09; Pres. Republic Union of Employers, Slovakia 2007; mem. Academic Bd Univ. of Econs, Bratislava 2000, Comenius Univ., Bratislava 2002.

JUSTER, Kenneth Ian, BA, MPP, JD; American lawyer, government official and diplomatist; *Ambassador to India;* b. 24 Nov. 1954; ed Harvard Coll., John F. Kennedy School of Govt, Harvard Law School; law clerk, Nat. Security Council 1978; law clerk to Judge James L. Oakes, US Court of Appeals for the Second Circuit 1980–81; practised law with Arnold & Porter (law firm), becoming Sr Partner 1981–89, 1993–2001; Deputy and Sr Adviser to Deputy Sec. of State Lawrence S. Eagleburger 1989–92; Counselor (Acting) US Dept of State 1992–93; Visiting Fellow, Council on Foreign Relations 1993; US UnderSec. of Commerce 2001–05; Exec. Vice Pres. of Law, Policy, and Corporate Strategy, salesforce.com (software co.) 2005–10; Partner and Man. Dir, Warburg Pincus (global investment firm) 2010–17; Deputy Asst to the Pres. for Int. Econ. Affairs and Deputy Dir, Nat. Econ. Council Jan.–June 2017; served as lead US negotiator (Sherpa) in run-up to G7 Summit in Taormina, Italy 2017; Amb. to India 2017–; co-founder and US Chair. US–India High Tech. Cooperation Group; mem. Pres.'s Advisory Cttee for Trade Policy and Negotiations 2007–10; Visiting Fellow, Harvard Kennedy School of Govt 2010; fmr Chair. Advisory Cttee, Weatherhead Center for Int. Affairs, Harvard Univ.; Vice Chair. Asia Foundation 2014; mem. Council on Foreign Relations, American Acad. of Diplomacy; Sec. of Commerce's William C. Redfield Award and Medal, Sec. of State's Distinguished Service Award and Medal 1993. *Address:* Embassy of the USA, Shanti Path, Chanakyapuri, New Delhi 110 021, India (office). *Telephone:* (11) 24198000 (office). *Fax:* (11) 24190017 (office). *E-mail:* ndwebmail@state.gov (office). *Website:* in.usembassy.gov (office).

JUSTICE, James (Jim) Conley, Jr, BA, MBA; American farmer, business executive and politician; *Governor of West Virginia;* b. 27 April 1951, Raleigh County, W Va; s. of James Conley Justice and Edna Justice (née Perry); m. Cathy Comer; one s. one d.; ed Marshall Univ.; f. Bluestone Farms (renamed Justice Family Farms, LLC) 1977, Pres. and CEO Bluestone Industries, Inc. and Bluestone Coal Corpn 1993–, now Owner or CEO of more than 50 companies including The Greenbrier Resort, White Sulphur Springs; Gov. of West Virginia 2017–; Democrat. *Address:* Office of the Governor, State Capitol, 1900 Kanawha Blvd East, Charleston, WV 25305, USA (office). *Telephone:* (304) 558-2000 (office). *Fax:* (304) 342-7025 (office). *Website:* www.governor.wv.gov (office).

JUSYS, Oskaras, BA, MA, DPhil; Lithuanian diplomatist and civil servant; *Director, United Nations, International Organizations and Human Rights Department, Ministry of Foreign Affairs;* b. 13 Jan. 1954, Anyksciai Region; m. Roma Jusys; one s.; ed Vilnius Univ. Law School, M. Lomonosov Univ. Law School, Moscow, Columbia Univ. Law School, USA; Sr Lecturer, Faculty of Law, Vilnius Univ. 1981–85, Assoc. Prof. 1986–90; Scientific Scholarship, IREX Exchange Programme, Law School, Columbia Univ., New York, USA 1985–86; Dir Legal Dept, Ministry of Foreign Affairs 1990–92, Counsellor to Minister of Foreign Affairs 1993–94; Amb., Perm. Rep. of Lithuania to UN 1994–2000; Deputy Minister of Foreign Affairs 2000–01; Perm. Rep. to EU 2001–05; at Ministry of Foreign Affairs 2005–09; Amb. to UK 2009–12; Dir UN, Int. Orgs and Human Rights Dept, Ministry of Foreign Affairs 2012–; Dir Lithuanian Br. of US law firm McDermott, Will & Emery 1993–94. *Leisure interests:* jazz, basketball. *Address:* Ministry of Foreign Affairs, J. Tumo-Vaižganto g. 2, 01511 Vilnius, Lithuania (office). *Telephone:* (5) 236-2444 (office). *Fax:* (5) 231-3090 (office). *E-mail:* urm@urm.lt (office). *Website:* www.urm.lt (office).

JUVENALY, Metropolitan (Vladimir Poyarkov); Russian ecclesiastic; b. 22 Sept. 1935, Yaroslavl; ed Leningrad Seminary, Moscow Theological Acad.; hieromonk 1960; Sec. Dept of Foreign Relations, Moscow Patriarchy 1960; teacher, Moscow Seminary 1961–62; Ed. Golos Pravoslavia (magazine) 1962–63; Dean Russian Orthodox Church in West Berlin 1962–63; ordained as archimandrite 1963; Chief Russian Holy Mission in Jerusalem 1963–64; Deputy Chair. Dept of Foreign Relations, Moscow Patriarchy 1964–72, Chair. 1972–81; consecrated Bishop 1965; Bishop of Zaraisk, Vicar of Moscow Diocese 1965–69; Bishop of Tula and Belev, Archbishop, Metropolitan 1969–77; Perm. mem. Holy Synod 1972–; Metropolitan of Krutitsy and Kolomna 1977–; Chair. Synodal Comm. on Canonization of Saints; Hon. Citizen of Moscow region, Podolsk, Kolomna, Dmitrov; Hon. mem. Leningrad (now St Petersburg) Theological Seminary 1973–, Moscow Theological Seminary 1974–; Order of Peoples' Friendship 1985, Order of Honour 2000, Order of Services to the Fatherland (IV) 2006 and (III) 2010, numerous other state and church decorations. *Publications:* numerous articles in Journal of Moscow Patriarchate. *Address:* Moscow Diocese, 119435 Moscow, Novodevichy Proezd 1/1, Russia (home). *Telephone:* (495) 246-08-81 (home).

JUWAILI, Col Osama al-; Libyan politician and fmr army officer; b. 1961; ed Tripoli Mil. Acad.; Lecturer, Tripoli Mil. Acad. –1987; resgnd from army (rank of Capt.) 1992; fmr Head of Vocational Guidance Centre, Yifrin (part of Ministry of Workforce and Training); defected to anti-Gaddafi forces during 2011 uprising; Head of Military Council, Zintan 2011; Minister of Defence 2011–12; currently Commdr Western Military Zone.

JYOTI, Achal Kumar; Indian civil servant and government official; b. 23 Jan. 1953; joined Indian Admin. Services (Gujarat Cadre) 1975, Dist Magistrate and Collector of Surendranagar, of Panchmahal, of Kheda, Gujarat 1981–85; served in several positions including State Vigilance Commr, Chair. Kandla Port Trust 1999–2004; Man. Dir Sardar Sarovar Narmada Nigam Ltd; fmr Sec., Industry, Revenue and Water Supply Depts; Chief Sec. of Gujarat 2010–13 (retd); Election Commr, Election Comm. of India 2015–17, Chief Election Commr 2017–18.

JYOTI, Roop, MBA MPA; Nepalese business executive and fmr politician; *Vice-Chairman, Jyoti Group;* b. Sept. 1948; s. of Maniharsha Jyoti; ed Indian Inst. of Tech., Bombay, Harvard Univ.; qualified as chemical engineer; exec. positions at several Jyoti Group enterprises (family-owned), then Vice-Chair. (following death of his father); fmrly Nat. Adviser to Resident Rep. of UNDP in Nepal; mem. Tariff Bd, Govt of Nepal; Minister of Finance 2005–06; mem. Senate, Tribhuvan Univ.; mem. Trust of Nepal Vipassana Centre. *Address:* Jyoti Group, Jyoti Bhawan, Kantipath, Kathmandu, Nepal (office). *E-mail:* info@jyotigroup.org (office). *Website:* www.jyotigroup.org (office).

JYRÄNKI, Antero, DIur; Finnish professor of constitutional law; *Professor Emeritus, University of Turku;* b. 9 Aug. 1933, Hamina; two s. one d.; ed Univ. of Helsinki; Assoc. Prof. of Public Law, Univ. of Tampere 1966–70; Gen. Sec. to the Pres. of the Repub. 1970–73; Sr Research Fellow, Acad. of Finland 1974–77; Vice-Chair., Comm. on the Revision of the Constitution 1970–74; Assoc. Prof. of Public Law, Univ. of Tampere 1977–79; Prof. of Constitutional and Int. Law, Univ. of Turku 1980–98, Dean, Law Faculty 1981–83, 1991–93, now Prof. Emer.; Research Prof., Acad. of Finland 1983–87; Pres. Finnish Asscn of Constitutional Law 1982–88; mem. Council of the Int. Asscn of Constitutional Law 1983–95, mem. Exec. Cttee 1993–2004; mem. Admin. Bd Finnish Broadcasting Corpn 1983–99, Finnish Acad. of Science 1987–; Perm. Expert for the Constitutional Comm. of Parl. 1982–; Expert for the Comm. on the Revision of the Constitution 1996–97; Commdr of the Finnish Lion 1995. *Publications include:* Sotavoiman ylin päällikkyys (The Commander-in-Chief of the Armed Forces) 1967, Yleisradio ja sananvapaus (The Freedom of Expression and Broadcasting) 1969, Perustuslaki ja yhteiskunnan muutos (The Constitution and the Change of Society) 1973, Presidentti (The President of the Republic) 1978, Lakien laki (The Law of the Laws) 1989, Kolme vuotta linnassa (Three Years in the Presidential Castle) 1990, Valta ja vapaus (Power and Freedom) 1994 (revised edn 2003), Uusi perustuslakimme (Our New Constitution) 2000, Kansanedustuslaitos ja valtiosääntö 1906–2005 (Parliament and the Constitution 1906–2005) 2006, Presidentti-instituutio aikamme Euroopassa (Presidency of the Republic in Contemporary Europe) 2009. *Leisure interests:* languages, literature, problems of mass communication. *Address:* Faculty of Law, Room 315, University of Turku, 20014 Turku, Finland (office). *Telephone:* (2) 3335522 (office). *E-mail:* antero.jyranki@utu.fi (office). *Website:* www.law.utu.fi/english (home).

KAAG, Sigrid, MPhil; Dutch politician and fmr UN official; *Minister for Foreign Trade and Development Cooperation;* b. 1961, The Hague; m. Anis al-Qaq; four c.; ed American University in Cairo, Egypt, St Antony's Coll., Oxford and Exeter Univ., UK; fmr Deputy Head of UN Political Affairs Dept, Ministry of Foreign Affairs; worked for Royal Dutch Shell, London; joined UN 1994, has held several positions, including Chief of Donor Relations, Int. Org. for Migration and Sr Programme Man., External Relations Office, UNRWA 1998–2004; Regional Dir for Middle East and N Africa, UNICEF 2007–10; Asst Sec.-Gen., also Asst Administrator and Dir, Bureau of External Relations and Advocacy, UNDP 2010–13; Head, Jt Org. for Prohibition of Chemical Weapons, Syria 2013–14; UN Special Coordinator for Lebanon (UNSCOL) 2014–17; Minister for Foreign Trade and Devt Cooperation 2017–; Acting Minister of Foreign Affairs Feb.–March 2018; Carnegie Foundation Wateler Peace Prize 2016. *Address:* Ministry of Foreign Affairs, Bezuidenhoutseweg 67, POB 20061, 2500 EB The Hague, Netherlands (office). *Telephone:* (70) 3486486 (office). *Fax:* (70) 3484848 (office). *Website:* www.rijksoverheid.nl/ministeries/bz (office).

KÄÄRIÄINEN, Seppo, PhD; Finnish politician; b. 29 March 1948, Iisalmi, Kirma; m. Pirjo Terttu Tuulikki (née Kolehmainen) 1975; one s.; Party Sec., Finnish Centre Party 1980–90, Chair. Party Parl. Group 1991–93, Vice-Pres. 1994–2000; mem. Suomen Eduskunta (Parl.) 1987–, mem. Foreign Affairs Cttee 1987–93, 1999–2000, Finance Cttee 1990–91, 1999–2003, Vice-Chair. Commerce Cttee 1995–99, Chair. Defence Cttee 2003; Minister of Trade and Industry 1993–95; Minister, Ministry for Foreign Affairs 1993–95; Minister of Defence 2004–07; First Deputy Speaker, Eduskunta 2007–; Chair. Del. to Jt Comm. of European Parl. and Eduskunta 1993; Pres. Bd of Dirs Itä-Suomen Ammattitaito Ry 2003–; Vice-Pres. Bd of Dirs Finnvera Oy 1999–2003. *Publications:* Suomen oma tie (Finland's Own Way) 1986, Haastaja (The Contender) 1989, The Strategic Choices of the Centre Party 1964–2001 2002. *Leisure interests:* walking, marathons. *Address:* Suomen Eduskunta, Mannerheimintie 30, 00102 Helsinki, Finland (office). *Telephone:* (9) 4321 (office). *Fax:* (9) 4322274 (office). *E-mail:* eduskunta@eduskunta.fi (office). *Website:* www.eduskunta.fi (office); seppokaariainen.com.

KAAS, Patricia; French singer; b. 5 Dec. 1966, Stiring Wendel, nr Forbach; tea-dance and night-club appearances aged 13; first single, Jalouse aged 17; first major success with Mademoiselle Chante le Blues; toured Viet Nam and Cambodia 1994; tours world-wide; six Victoires de la Musique, two World Music Awards; de Gaulle-Adenauer Prize 2001, Goldene Europa Award for Best International Artist 2002, Zolotoy Gramophon Award for Best Song and International Artist 2008. *Recordings include:* albums: Mademoiselle Chante 1988, Scène de Vie 1990, Carnet de Scène (live) 1991, Je Te Dis Vous 1993, Tour de Charme (live) 1994, Café noir 1996, Dans Ma Chair 1997, Rendez-vous 1998, Le mot de passe 1999, Patricia Kaas Live 2000, Rien ne s'arrête 2001, Piano bar 2002, Sexe fort 2004, Toute la Musique 2005, Kabaret 2008, Kaas chante Piaf 2012, Patricia Kaas 2016. *Publications:* Patricia Kaas – Tour de Charme 1994. *Address:* c/o Angela Di Corpo, GarberIMC, 1155 boulevard René-Lévesque Ouest, CIBC Tower, Suite 2500, Montreal, PQ H3B 2K4, Canada (office); Attitude, 71 rue Robespierre, 93100 Montreuil, France. *Telephone:* (514) 939-0100 (office). *Fax:* (514) 875-8967 (office). *E-mail:* angela@garberimc.com (office). *Website:* www.garberimc.com (office); www.patriciakaas.net; www.kabaretkaas.com/kabaret.

KABA, Malado, DESS; Guinean economist and politician; b. 1972; ed Univ. Paris X Nanterre, France; Adviser to Minister of the Economy 1996–99; Economist, European Comm., based in Guinea 1999–2004, Jamaica 2004–06, South Africa 2009–14; Country Head, Tony Blair Africa Governance Initiative, Guinea 2014–16; Minister of the Economy and Finance 2016–18. *Address:* c/o Ministry of the Economy and Finance, blvd du Commerce, Conakry, Guinea (office).

KABA, Sidiki, LLM; Senegalese lawyer, international organization official and politician; *Minister of Defence;* b. 21 Aug. 1950; ed Univs of Abidjan and Dakar; human rights lawyer associated with cases in Senegal, Chad, Côte d'Ivoire, Guinea; Pres. Nat. Org. for Human Rights, Senegal; Vice-Pres. Int. Fed. of the League for Human Rights, Paris, Pres. 2001–07, now Pres. of Honour; f. Union des avocats 1982, Union interafricaine des droits de l'Homme (UIDH) 1992, Centre africain pour les études des droits de l'Homme et la Démocratie (ACDHRS) 1995, Centre africain pour la Prévention des conflits (CAPREC) 1995; Minister of Justice 2013–17, of Foreign Affairs and Senegalese Nationals Abroad 2017–19, of Defence 2019–; Hon. Citizen, City of Quito (Ecuador) 2004; Kt, Nat. Order of the Lion (Senegal) 2001, Officier, Ordre nat. de la Légion d'honneur (France) 2002; Prize for promotion of the culture of Democracy in Africa, Pan-African Observatory of Democracy (OPAD) 2003, Sédar Action Civil, Nouvel Horizon newspaper, Senegal 2004. *Publications:* Les Droits de l'Homme en Afrique à l'aube du XXIe siècle 1996, Les Droits de l'Homme au Sénégal 1997, Défendre la Déclaration Universelle des droits de l'Homme 1998; contrib.: L'Observatoire nationale des élections (ONEL) 1997, Mitterand et l'Afrique 1999, La justice universelle en question, Justice de blancs contre les autres? 2010. *Address:* Ministry of Defence, Dakar, Senegal (office).

KABAKOV, Alexander Abramovich; Russian writer and journalist; b. 22 Oct. 1943, Novosibirsk; m.; one d.; ed Dniepropetrovsk Univ.; engineer, space rocket production co. 1965–70; journalist, Gudok 1972–88; columnist, then Deputy Ed.-in-Chief Moscow News 1988–97; special corresp., Commersant Publishing 1997–2000, apptd Departmental Ed. 2000; columnist, New Media Publishing Group 2002–; apptd Chief Ed. journal Sak Voyazh; Chair. jury for Russian Booker Prize 2006; first literary publ. 1975; mem. Bd of Trustees REN TV 1997–; Golden Calf Award 1980, Moscow Journalists' Union Prize 1989, Best Pens of Russia Award 1999, Short Story of the Year Award 1999. *Publications include:* Cheap Novel 1982, Cafe Yunost 1984, Oil, Comma, Canvas 1986, Approach of Kristapovich (trilogy) 1985, Obviously False Fabrications (collection of short stories) 1989, No Return 1988, The Story-Teller 1991, Imposter 1992, The Last Hero (novel) 1995, Selected Prose 1997, The Imposter 1997, One Day from the Life of a Fool 1998, The Arrival Hall 1999, Youth Café 2000, The Journey of an Extrapolator 2000, The Tardy Visitor 2001, Qualified as Escape 2001, Survivor 2003, Nothing's Lost (Apollon Grigoryev Prize 2005, Big Book Prize 2006) 2004, Moscow Tales (Prose of the Year Prize 2005, Ivan Bunin Prize 2006) 2005, The Role of a Cut Glass in Family Life 2008, A Runaway (Book of the Year) 2009, Aksenov (with Evgeny Popov) 2011. *Leisure interest:* jazz. *Address:* c/o Natalia Tsarkova, Moskovskaya Oblast, gorod Pushkino, mkr. Serebrianka, d. 48, k.1, kv.118, 141202, Russia (office). *Telephone:* (915) 197-45-70 (office). *E-mail:* post.nat@mail.ru (office). *Website:* www.elkost.com (office).

KABAREBE, Gen. James, BA; Rwandan army officer and politician; b. 1959; m. Espérance Mudenge; three c.; ed Makerere Univ.; served as Aide-de-Camp to Chair. of High Command (CHC), later as Military Asst, Commdr Republican Guard Brigade, then Chief of Plans, Operations and Training, Rwandan Patriotic Army (RPA) 1994–97, Deputy Chief of Staff RPA 1998–2001, Chief of Staff 2001–02, Chief of Defence Staff, Rwanda Defence Forces 2002–10; Minister of Defence 2010–18; Sr Presidential Adviser on Security 2018–; Nat. Liberation Medal, Campaign against Genocide Medal, Foreign Campaign Medal, Presidential Inauguration Medal, Command Service Ribbon, Combat Action Ribbon, Community Service Ribbon. *Address:* Ministry of Defence, PO Box 23, Kigali, Rwanda (office). *Telephone:* 252577942 (office). *Fax:* 250576969 (office). *E-mail:* info@mod.gov.rw (office). *Website:* www.mod.gov.rw (office).

KABARITI, Abdul Karim A., BA; Jordanian banking executive and fmr politician; *Chairman and CEO, Jordan Kuwait Bank;* b. 15 Dec. 1949, Amman; m.; two c.; ed St Edward's Univ., USA, American Univ. of Beirut, Lebanon; licensed financial adviser, New York –1986; proprietor of a money exchange co.; mem. House of Reps for Governorate of Ma'an 1989–93, 1993–95, fmr Chair. Foreign Relations; Minister of Tourism 1989–92, of Labour 1992–93, of Foreign Affairs 1995–96, Prime Minister, Minister of Defence and of Foreign Affairs 1996–97; currently Chair. and CEO Jordan Kuwait Bank; mem. Bd of Dirs Burgan Bank; fmr Head, Royal Court; Chair. Social Security Corpn 1992–93; Chair. Vocational Training Corpn 1992–93; Dr hc (Univ. of Coventry) 2015. *Leisure interests:* water skiing, music. *Address:* Jordan Kuwait Bank, POB 9776, Amman 11194, Jordan (office). *Telephone:* (6) 5629400 (office). *Fax:* (6) 5687452 (office). *E-mail:* webmaster@jkbank.com.jo (office). *Website:* www.jordan-kuwait-bank.com (office).

KABBA, Alie Badara Sanjhan; Sierra Leonean politician; *Minister of Foreign Affairs and International Cooperation;* b. Koindu, Kailahun Dist; m. 1st Edith Cline Kabba (divorced); m. 2nd Finda Diana Konomanyi (divorced); ed Fourah Bay Coll., Univ. of Ghana, Univ. of Illinois at Chicago; began career as Exec. Dir, United African Org., Chicago; Pres. Illinois Coalition for Immigrant and Refugee Rights 2009–13; Co-Chair. Golden Door Coalition, Chicago 2009–15; mem. Bd of Dirs Cable Access Network Television (CAN TV), Chicago 2011–15; Chair. Sierra Leone Policy Watch; returned to Sierra Leone 2016; SLPP Nat. Campaign Chair. and Campaign Man. to Julius Maada Bio during presidential election 2018; Minister of Foreign Affairs and Int. Cooperation 2018–; mem. Sierra Leone People's Party (SLPP). *Address:* Ministry of Foreign Affairs and International Cooperation, OAU Dr., Tower Hill, Freetown, Sierra Leone (office). *Telephone:* 79242276 (mobile) (office). *E-mail:* info@foreignaffairs.gov.sl (office). *Website:* foreignaffairs.gov.sl (office).

KABBAJ, Omar; Moroccan government official; *Adviser to HM the King of Morocco;* b. 15 Aug. 1942, Rabat; s. of Ahmed Kabbaj and Khadija Moulato; m. Saida Lebbar; four s.; ed Ecole Supérieure de Commerce et d'Admin des Entreprises de Toulouse, France; Exec. Asst BRPM 1963–66; Dir-Gen. SUNAT 1970–74; Special Adviser to Office of Ministry of Commerce, Industry, Mines and Shipping 1974–77; Dir-Gen. Sunac 1974–79; Chief of Staff of Minister of Finance 1977–79; mem. Exec. Bd World Bank 1979–80, IMF 1980–93; Minister of Econ. Affairs 1993–95; Exec. Pres. and Chair. Bd of Dirs African Devt Bank and African Devt Fund 1995–2005, now Hon. Pres.; Adviser to HM the King of Morocco, Royal Cabinet 2006–; mem. Bd of Dirs Agence Française de developpement; mem. Advisory Bd of Sec.-Gen. of UN on Water and Sanitation; fmr mem. UN Comm. on HIV/AIDS and Governance in Africa; Kt of the Order of the Throne of Morocco, Grand Officer of the Nat. Order of Tunisia, Officer of the Nat. Order of Burkina Faso. *Publication:* The Challenge of African Development 2003. *Leisure interest:* golf. *Address:* Royal Cabinet, Dar al Makhzen, Rabat, Morocco (office). *Telephone:* (537) 207710 (office). *Fax:* (537) 767680 (office). *E-mail:* omarkabbaj@yahoo.com (home).

KABBARAH, Mohammad Bashar, PhD; Syrian economist and fmr central banker; b. 1944, Damascus; s. of M. Jamil and Hikmat Kouatly; m. 1968; three c.; ed American Univ. and Western Illinois Univ., USA, American Univ. of Beirut, Lebanon; Section Head, Office of Gen. Studies, The Presidency 1973–74; Economist, Econ. Bureau, The Presidency 1974–77, Sr Economist 1977–82; Adviser/Dir Econ. Bureau of Pres. of Syria 1982–95; Gov. Cen. Bank of Syria 1995–2004, also Gov. Arab Monetary Fund, Alt. Gov. IMF; Chief Ed. The Syrian Economic Journal 1975–84; fmr Alt. Exec. Dir Arab Fund for Econ. and Social Devt, Programme for Financing Arab Trade; mem. Syrian Higher Planning Bd; Washington-Lincoln Honor Award 1968, Hall of Nations Award 1969–70, Union of Arab Banks Award 1996. *Publications:* more than 20 papers and articles in professional journals and contribs to The Arabic Encyclopedia. *Leisure interests:* historical reading, antiquities, agronomy, sports.

KABER, Saddek Omar Ali el-, MS, MBA; Libyan central banker; *Governor and Chairman of Central Bank of Libya;* b. Nov. 1951; ed Univ. of Hartford, USA; Gov. and Chair. Central Bank of Libya 2011–; Chair. Arab Banking Corpn, Bahrain 2011–, also Chair. Exec. Cttee and Risk Cttee; Sr Lecturer, Higher Inst. of Admin. Sciences and Finance, Tripoli; mem. Bd of Dirs ABC International Bank PLC 2013–; mem. Bd of Govs Arab Monetary Fund; Central Bank Gov. of the Year (Middle East and North Africa), GlobalCapital 2014. *Address:* Office of the Governor, Central Bank of Libya, POB 1103, Sharia al-Malik Seoud, Tripoli, Libya (office). *Telephone:* (21) 3333591 (office). *Fax:* (21) 4441488 (office). *E-mail:* info@cbl.gov.ly (office). *Website:* www.cbl.gov.ly (office).

KABERUKA, Donald P., MPhil, PhD; Rwandan economist, politician and international organization official; *High Representative for Peace Fund, African*

Union; b. 5 Oct. 1951, Byumba; ed Univ. of Dar es Salaam, Tanzania, Univs of East Anglia and Glasgow, UK; early career in commodities sector, including role as Chief Economist, Inter-African Coffee Organization; fmr State Minister for Budget and Planning, then Minister of Finance and Econ. Planning 1997–2005; Pres. African Devt Bank 2005–15; Gov. for Rwanda for IMF and World Bank 1997–2005; apptd Hauser Leader-in-Residence, Center for Public Leadership, Harvard Univ. 2015; Sr Advisor, TPG/Satya (consortium) 2015–; High Rep. for African Union Peace Fund 2016–; Chair. PTA Bank (East, Central and Southern Africa devt bank) 2001–02; Vice-Chair. Nat. AIDS Comm. 2002–03; apptd Chair. Bd of Govs Africa Trade Insurance Agency (ATI) 2003, Nat. Africa Peer Review Comm. 2004; fmr Visiting Fellow, Inst. of Development Studies, Univ. of Sussex, UK; Trustee, World Economic Forum, Mandela Inst. (Minds), Mo Ibrahim Foundation, Rockefeller Foundation. *Address:* Center for Public Leadership, Harvard Kennedy School, 79 John F. Kennedy Street, Cambridge, MA 02138 (office); African Union Commission, Roosevelt Street (Old Airport Area) W. 21, K. 19, PO Box 3243, Addis Ababa, Ethiopia (office). *E-mail:* donald_kaberuka@hks.harvard.edu (office). *Website:* cpl.hks.harvard.edu/people/donald-kaberuka (office); www.peaceau.org (office).

KABILA KABANGE, Maj.-Gen. Joseph, BA; Democratic Republic of the Congo army officer and fmr head of state; b. 4 June 1971, Hewabora village, Fizi territory, South Kivu Prov., eastern Congo; s. of Laurent-Désiré Kabila and Sifa Mahanya; m. Olive Lembe di Sita 2006; one d.; ed Makerere Univ., Uganda, PLA Nat. Defence Univ., Beijing, People's Repub. of China; became commdr of army of 'kadogos' (child soldiers) and played role in battles on road to Kinshasa during campaign in Zaïre to oust Mobutu regime 1996; Deputy Chair. Jt Chiefs of Staff, Congolese Armed Forces 1998–2000, Army Chief of Staff 2000–01; Pres. Democratic Repub. of the Congo 2001–19; fmr Minister of Defence; mem. People's Party for Reconstruction and Democracy; Dr hc (Hankuk Univ., S Korea).

KABIR, Fazle, BA, MA; Bangladeshi economist, civil servant and central banker; *Governor of Bangladesh Bank;* b. 4 July 1955, Dhaka; m. Mahmuda Sharmin Benu; one s.; ed Univ. of Chittagong; started civil service career as Asst Traffic Superintendent, Bangladesh Railway 1980; joined Admin Service 1983 and held several positions in civil bureaucracy, including Deputy Commr and Dist Magistrate, Kishoreganj Dist, Jt Sec., Ministry of Educ., Dir-Gen., Nat. Acad. for Planning and Devt, Dir-Gen., BCS Admin Acad., Sec., Ministry of Railways; Sr Sec., Ministry of Finance 2012–15; Chair. state-run Sonali Bank Ltd, New York 2015–16; Gov., Bangladesh Bank (central bank) 2016–; mem. Bd of Dirs Janata Bank 2008–10. *Address:* Bangladesh Bank, Motijheel C/A, POB 325, Dhaka 1000, Bangladesh (office). *Telephone:* (2) 7126101 (office). *Fax:* (2) 9566212 (office). *E-mail:* governor@bangla.net (office). *Website:* www.bb.org.bd (office).

KABIR, M. Humayun, LLB, MA; Bangladeshi diplomatist; *Force Commander of Peacekeeping Force in Cyprus (UNFICYP), United Nations;* b. 26 Sept. 1952, Brahmanbaria, Bangladesh (then East Pakistan); m.; two s.; ed Univ. of Dhaka, Acad. of Int. Law, The Hague, Netherlands, Univ. of Paris XI, France (Diplôme d'Études Supérieures Spécialisées in Int. Org. and Diplomacy); fought during Liberation War of Bangladesh 1971; Lecturer, Univ. of Dhaka 1977–80; career diplomat with rank of Deputy Perm. Sec., Pvt. Sec. to Advisor for Foreign Affairs and Section Officer, Ministry of Foreign Affairs 1984–87; Second, later First Sec., Embassy in Washington, DC 1987–91, First Sec. and Counsellor, New Delhi 1991–94; Dir UN and Foreign Sec.'s Office, Ministry of Foreign Affairs 1994–96; Counsellor, Perm. Mission to UN, New York 1996–99, Deputy High Commr, New Delhi 1999–2001; Dir-Gen. for the UN, Ministry of Foreign Affairs 2001, for Europe 2002, for S Asia and the S Asian Assen for Regional Co-operation 2003; Amb. to Nepal 2003–06, High Commr to Australia (also accred to New Zealand and Fiji) 2006–07, Amb. to USA 2007–09; Force Commdr, UN Peacekeeping Force in Cyprus (UNFICYP) 2016–; mem. Advisory Cttee Univ. of the People, Pasadena, Calif., USA. *Publications:* has written extensively on diplomacy with a focus on multilateral and public diplomacy and UN peacekeeping. *Address:* United Nations Peacekeeping Force in Cyprus (UNFICYP), Department of Peacekeeping Operations, Room S-3727B, New York, NY 10017, USA (office). *Telephone:* (212) 963-8077 (office). *Fax:* (212) 963-9222 (office). *Website:* www.un.org/Depts/dpko (office).

KABIRI, Muhiddin; Tajikistani politician; *Chairman, Hizbi Nahzati Islomii Tojikiston (HNIT—Islamic Rebirth Party of Tajikistan);* b. (Muhiddin Kabirov), 20 July 1965, Orjonikdzeabad dist (now Fayzobod dist), Tajik SSR, USSR; m.; six c.; ed Arab Dept, Oriental Studies Faculty, Tajik State Univ., San'a Univ. of Industry, Yemen, Diplomatic Acad., Moscow; undertook business activities in Moscow 1995–97; aide to Chair., Hizbi Nahzati Islomii Tojikiston (HNIT—Islamic Rebirth Party of Tajikistan) 1997–2000, Deputy Chair. 2000–04, First Deputy Chair. 2004–06, Chair. 2006–, party proscribed by Ministry of Justice Aug. 2015; mem. Majlisi Namoyandagon (Ass. of Reps) 2005–15, mem. Cttee on Science, Educ., Culture and Youth Police; believed to be in exile in Iran or Turkey 2015–.

KABORÉ, Lassané, M.EconSci; Burkinabè economist and politician; *Minister of the Economy, Finance and Development;* b. 1968; ed Univ. de Ouagadougou, Univ. Paris-I (Panthéon-Sorbonne), Centre d'Etudes Financières, Economiques et Bancaires, Marseilles; Dir of Monetary and Financial Affairs, Ministry of Finance 2001–08, Dir-Gen. of Cooperation, Ministry of Finance 2013–16; Sr Economist and Dir, responsible for multilateral surveillance, Econ. Community of West African States (ECOWAS), Abuja 2008–13, Dir for macroeconomic stability and multilateral surveillance 2016–19; Minister of the Economy, Finance and Devt 2019–; Chair. Bd of Dirs Office Nat. d'Eau et d'Assainissment (ONEA) 2013–16; mem. Bd of Dirs Fonds Africain de Garantie et de Coopération Economique (FAGACE) 2013–16, Société d'Exploration Minière en Afrique de l'Ouest (SEMAFO) 2013–16; Chair. Fonds d'Appui à la Formation Professionnelle et à l'Apprentissage (FAFPA) 2004–08; mem. Burkina Faso Privatisation Cttee 2002–08; mem. Cttee of Experts, West African Econ. and Monetary Union (UEMOA) 2001–07, Pres. 2006–07; Chevalier, Ordre Nat., Ordre du mérite. *Address:* Ministry of the Economy, Finance and Development 395 ave Ho Chi Minh, 01 BP 7008, Ouagadougou 01, Burkina Faso (office). *Telephone:* 25-32-42-11 (office). *Fax:* 25-31-27-15 (home). *E-mail:* webmaster@finances.gov.bf (office). *Website:* www.finances.gov.bf (office).

KABORÉ, Roch Marc-Christian; Burkinabè politician and head of state; *President;* b. 25 April 1957, Ouagadougou; ed Univ. of Dijon, France; Minister of State in charge of Relations with Insts 1990–94; Prime Minister 1994–96; Special Adviser to the Pres. 1996–97; mem. Assemblée nationale 1997–, Pres. 2002–12; Pres. of Burkina Faso 2015–, also Minister of Defence and Veterans' Affairs 2016–17; mem. Org. pour la démocratie populaire/Mouvement du travail (ODP/MT), First Vice-Pres., later Pres. Congrès pour la démocratie et le progrès (CDP) (f. 1996 as successor to ODP/MT) 1996–2014; f. People's Movement for Progress 2014. *Leisure interests:* reading, music, agro-pastoral activities, sponsor of Rail Club du Kadiaogo (First Div. football team). *Address:* Office of the President, 03 BP 7030, Ouagadougou 03, Burkina Faso (office). *Telephone:* 25-50-66-30 (office). *Fax:* 25-31-49-26 (office). *E-mail:* info@presidence.bf (office). *Website:* www.presidence.bf (office).

KABUDI, Palamagamba John Aidan Mwaluko, LLM, PhD; Tanzanian academic and politician; *Minister of Foreign Affairs and East African, Regional and International Co-operation;* b. 24 Feb. 1956; ed Univ. of Dar es Salaam, Freie Universität Berlin; tutorial Asst, Univ. of Dar es Salaam 1983–86, Asst Lecturer 1986–90, Lecturer 1990–99, Sr Lecturer 1999–2006, Assoc. Prof. 2006–17, Dean Faculty of Law 2009–12, Sec., Council 2014–17, also mem. Bd; MP 2017–; Minister for Legal and Constitutional Affairs 2017–19; Minister of Foreign Affairs and East African, Regional and International Co-operation 2019–; mem. bd Lawyers' Environment Action Team (LEAT), Human Rights and Legal Resource Centre. *Address:* Ministry of Foreign Affairs and East African Co-operation, LAPF Building, 6th Floor, Makole Road, PO Box 2933, 40466 Dodoma Tanzania. *Telephone:* (26) 2323201 (office). *Fax:* (26) 2323208 (office). *E-mail:* nje@nje.go.tz (office); dodoma@nje.go.tz (office). *Website:* www.foreign.go.tz (office).

KABUI, Frank Ofagioro, GCMG, CSI, OBE, LLB, Grad. Dipl. in Int. Law; Solomon Islands judge (retd) and government official; *Governor-General;* b. 20 April 1946, Manakwai, Malaita; s. of Michael Frank Kabui and Nammah Angialatha; m. 1st Mereani Kabui; three s. one d.; m. 2nd Lady Grace Delight Kabui; one s. one d.; ed Univ. of Papua New Guinea, Australian Nat. Univ., Canberra; Attorney-Gen. 1980–94; High Court Judge 1998–2006 (retd); Chair. Law Reform Comm. 1994–2009; Gov.-Gen. 2009–; Chancellor Univ. of the South Pacific, Suva, Fiji 2011–12; mem. Solomon Islands Bar Assen (fmr Pres.); Cross of Solomon Islands. *Leisure interests:* current affairs, lawn tennis, squash, table tennis, darts, watching TV. *Address:* Office of the Governor-General, Government House, PO Box 252, Honiara, Solomon Islands (office). *Telephone:* 21777 (office); 21778 (office). *Fax:* 22533 (office).

KABYAKOU, Andrey Uladzimiravich; Belarusian politician, government official and diplomatist; b. 21 Nov. 1960, Moscow, Russian SFSR, USSR; m.; one s. one d.; ed Moscow Aviation Inst., Belarusian State Econ. Univ., Belarusian State Univ.; family moved to Belarusian SSR 1963; foreman, then sr foreman, Machine Assembly Dept, Minsk S.I. Vavilov Mechanical Works 1983–85; sr foreman, Deputy Head of Assembly Dept, Deputy Head of Assembly Div., Rogachev Diaprojector Plant, Gomel Oblast 1985–88, Head of Planning and Econ. Dept, Deputy Dir for Economy 1991–95; instructor, org. unit of CP Cttee, Rogachev City 1988–89; student, Belarus CP Inst. of Political Science and Social Admin 1989–91; Deputy Head, Control Service Dept of Pres. of Belarus 1995–96; Deputy Chair. State Control Cttee 1996–98, 1998–2000; Pres. Belarusian State Concern for Production and Sale of Light Industry Goods 1998; First Deputy Prime Minister 2000–01, Deputy Prime Minister 2001–02, Deputy Prime Minister and Minister of Economy 2002–03, Deputy Prime Minister 2003–10; Deputy Head of Admin of Pres. of Belarus 2010–11, Head 2012–14; Amb. to Russia 2011–12, Perm. Rep. of Belarus to Eurasian Econ. Community, Special Envoy of Belarus for Integration and Co-operation within Framework of Union State, Customs Union and Common Econ. Area, CIS, Collective Security Treaty Org., Eurasian Econ. Community; Prime Minister of Belarus 2014–18; mem. Econ. Council of CIS 2003–10, Integration Cttee of Eurasian Econ. Community 2003–10, High Level Group for Establishing the Common Econ. Area of Belarus, Kazakhstan, Russia and Ukraine 2003–06, Comm. of Customs Union of Belarus, Kazakhstan and Russia 2009–10; Trustee of Repub. of Belarus, IBRD, Multilateral Investment Guarantee Agency, Int. Financial Corpn 2001–11; Ind.; Order of Honour 2006, Order of the Fatherland (Third Degree) 2014. *Address:* c/o Office of the Council of Ministers, 220010 Minsk, vul. Savetskaya 11, Belarus (office). *Telephone:* (17) 222-41-73 (office). *Fax:* (17) 222-66-65 (office). *E-mail:* contact@government.by (office). *Website:* government.by (office).

KAC, Eduardo, BA, MFA, PhD; Brazilian/American artist and writer; *Professor of Art and Technology, School of Art, Art Institute of Chicago;* b. 1962, Rio de Janeiro, Brazil; ed Pontifícia Universidade Católica do Rio de Janeiro, School of the Art Institute of Chicago, Univ. of Wales, UK; pioneer of holopoetry, telepresence art, biotelematics, transgenic art; moved to Chicago 1989; Prof. of Art and Tech., School of Art, Art Inst. of Chicago 1997–; mem. Editorial Bd Leonardo (journal); Shearwater Foundation Holography Award 1995, Leonardo Award for Excellence 1998, award for telepresence work Uirapuru, InterCommunication Centre Biennale, Tokyo 1999. *Publications:* New Media Poetry: Poetic Innovation and New Technologies (anthology) 1996; Luz & Letra, Ensaios de arte, literatura e comunicação 2004; Telepresence and Bio Art: Networking Humans, Rabbits and Robots 2005, Signs of Life: Bio Art and Beyond 2007; articles in periodicals. *Address:* Art and Technology Department, School of the Art Institute of Chicago, 37 South Wabash Avenue, Chicago, IL 60603, USA (office). *Telephone:* (312) 899-5100 (office). *E-mail:* ekac@artic.edu (office). *Website:* www.ekac.org (office).

KACZMAREK, Janusz; Polish lawyer and fmr politician; b. 25 Dec. 1961, Gdynia; m.; two s.; ed Univ. of Gdańsk; started legal training in Dist Prosecutor's Office, Elbląg 1985–88, in Gdańsk 1988; Dist Prosecutor, Gdynia 1993–2000; Regional Prosecutor, Gdańsk 2000–01; Deputy Prosecutor-Gen. 2001; Deputy Dir Preparatory Proceedings Dept, Nat. Prosecutor's Office 2001–03; Appellate Prosecutor, Gdańsk 2003–05; Head, Nat. Prosecutor's Office 2005–07; Minister of Internal Affairs and Admin Feb.–Aug. 2007; lecturer on material criminal law to public prosecutor's trainees 1992–; Chair. Editorial Bd Prokuratura i Prawo, Kwartalnik Apelacji Gdańskiej, Kwartalnik Krajowego Centrum Szkolenia Kadr Sadów Powszechnych i Prokuratury; co-organizer Razem przeciw przemocy (Together Against Violence) program; mem. Law and Justice (PiS) (Prawo i Sprawiedliwość); currently Prin., Kancelaria Adwokacka s.c (law firm), Gdynia (and Warsaw); Bona lex 2007. *Publications:* author of numerous book and articles on law. *Address:* Kancelaria Adwokacka s.c., ul. Króla Jana III 4/2, 81-547 Gdynia,

Poland (office). *E-mail:* kancelaria@janusz-kaczmarek.pl (office). *Website:* janusz-kaczmarek.pl (office).

KACZYŃSKI, Jarosław Aleksander, DJur; Polish politician and lawyer; *President, Prawo i Sprawiedliwość (Law and Justice);* b. 18 June 1949, Warsaw; s. of Rajmund Kaczyński and Jadwiga Kaczyńska; identical twin brother of Lech Kaczyński (fmr Pres. of Poland); ed Univs of Gdańsk and Warsaw; Asst, Sr Asst in Inst. of Science and Higher Educ. 1971–76; collaborator, Workers' Defence Cttee (KOR) 1976–80; scientific worker, Białystok br. of Warsaw Univ. 1977–81; ed. Głos (independent magazine) 1980–82; warehouseman 1982; mem. Solidarność (Solidarity Trade Union) 1980–90; Sec. Nat. Exec. Comm. of Solidarity 1986–87; took part in Round Table talks in Comm. for Political Reforms Feb.–April 1989; Ed.-in-Chief Tygodnik Solidarność (weekly) 1989–90; Deputy to Senate 1989–91; Dir Office of Pres. and Minister of State 1990–92; Deputy to Sejm (Parl.) 1991–93, 1997–, mem. Ethics Comm. 2001–; Founder and Chair. Porozumienie Obywatelskie Centrum (Centre Civic Alliance) 1990–98; Co-founder with his late brother and mem. Main Bd, Prawo i Sprawiedliwość (PiS—Law and Justice) 2001–, Pres. PiS Parl. Club 2001–03, Pres. PiS and Chair. Main Bd 2003–; Prime Minister of Poland 2006–07; Acting Minister of Agric. Sept.–Oct. 2006, July 2007; Acting Minister of Sport and Tourism July 2007; Leader of the Opposition 2007–; unsuccessful cand. in presidential election 2010; mem. Helsinki Comm. in Poland 1982–89. *Film:* starred, with his brother, in Polish film The Two Who Stole the Moon (O dwóch takich, co ukradli księżyc) 1962. *Leisure interests:* animals (especially cats), reading, history of Poland. *Address:* Prawo i Sprawiedliwość (Law and Justice), 02-018 Warsaw, ul. Nowogrodzka 84/86 (office); Sejm RP, 00-902 Warsaw, ul. Wiejska 4/6/8, Poland. *Telephone:* (22) 6215035 (office). *Fax:* (22) 6216767 (office). *E-mail:* biuro@pis.org.pl (office). *Website:* www.pis.org.pl (office); www.jaroslawkaczynski.info.

KADAGA, Rt Hon. Rebecca Alitwala, LLB, MA; Ugandan lawyer and politician; *Speaker of Parliament;* b. 24 May 1956, Kamuli; ed Namasagali Coll., Makerere Univ., Kampala, Univ. of Zimbabwe, Harare; Diploma in Legal Practice, Law Devt Centre, Kampala, Diploma in Women's Law, Univ. of Zimbabwe, Harare; in pvt. law practice 1984–88; MP (Nat. Resistance Movt Party) for Kamuli Dist Women's Constituency, Busoga sub-region 1989–, Deputy Speaker of Parl. 2001–11, Speaker (first woman) 2011–, Chair. Appointments Cttee, Parl. Comm., Business Cttee; Minister of State for Regional Cooperation (Africa and the Middle East) 1996–98; Minister of State for Communication and Aviation 1998–99; Minister for Parl. Affairs 1999–2000; Chair. Univ. Council for Mbarara Univ. 1993–96; Sec.-Gen. East African Women Parliamentarians Asscn 1996; Chair. Commonwealth Women Parliamentarians – International 2013. *Leisure interests:* reading, art, travel. *Address:* Public Relations Office, Parliament of Uganda, PO Box 7178, Parliamentary Avenue, Kampala, Uganda (office). *Telephone:* (41) 4377000 (office). *Fax:* (41) 4346826 (office). *E-mail:* cpa@parliament.go.ug (office). *Website:* www.parliament.go.ug (office).

KADAGIDZE, Giorgi, MPA; Georgian economist, academic, government official and fmr central banker; *Professor, Ilia State University;* b. 10 April 1980, Tbilisi; ed European School of Man., Preston Univ., Georgia Inst. of Public Affairs, USA; Auditor, later Sr Auditor and Audit Man., UBC International (audit and consulting firm) 2000–03; Head of Credit Dept, People's Bank of Georgia (now Liberty Bank) 2003–04; Head of Financial Div., later Head of Financial Service and of Municipal Financial Service, Tbilisi Municipality Jan.–July 2005; Head of Bank and Non-Bank Depository Insts Supervisory Dept, Nat. Bank of Georgia (central bank) 2005–06; Head of Econ. Dept, Office of Prosecutor-Gen. 2006–07; Head, Financial Monitoring Service of Georgia 2007–08; Head, Georgian Financial Supervisory Agency 2008–09, Alt. Gov. EBRD; Chair. and Gov. Bank of Georgia 2009–16; Prof., Ilia State Univ.; Draper Hills Summer Fellow, Stanford Univ. 2016; Central Banker of the Year for Europe, Banker magazine 2014. *Address:* Ilia State University, Kakutsa Cholokashvili Ave 3/5, Tbilisi 0162, Georgia (office). *E-mail:* info@iliauni.edu.ge (office). *Website:* iliauni.edu.ge/en (office).

KADANNIKOV, Vladimir Vasilievich; Russian politician and business executive; b. 3 Sept. 1941, Gorky (now Nizhny Novgorod); m.; two d.; ed Gorky Polytech. Inst.; fitter, foreman, then area man., Gorky Automotive Plant 1959–67; Deputy Workshop Man., Volga Automotive Works 1967–76; Deputy Dir-Gen. PO AvtoVAZ in charge of production 1976–86, First Deputy Dir-Gen., then Dir R&D Centre 1986–88, Dir-Gen. PO AvtoVAZ 1988–93, Pres. and Dir-Gen. joint stock co. AvtoVAZ Inc. 1993–96; First Deputy Prime Minister of Russia Jan.–Aug. 1996; Chair. AvtoVAZ Inc. 1996–2005 (resgnd), GM-AvtoVAZ 2001–05; Chair. Council for Industrial Policy; mem. Presidential Consultative Council; mem. Int. Eng Acad., Russian Eng Acad.; fmr People's Deputy of the USSR; mem. Bd of Dirs Globex; Hon. Prof., Samara State Univ.; Order of Merit for the Fatherland 3rd Grade 1995, Order of the Red Banner of Labour, Order of Peoples' Friendship, Badge of Honour Order; Hero of Socialist Labour 1991. *Publications:* book chapters and scientific articles on cold sheet stamping by stretch forming. *Leisure interests:* reading, basketball.

KÁDÁR, Béla, PhD, DSc; Hungarian politician, economist and academic; *Life Honorary Chair, Hungarian Association of Economists;* b. 21 March 1934, Pécs; s. of Lajos Kádár and Teréz Schmidt; m. Patricia Derső; one s.; ed Budapest Univ. of Economy; worked for Int. Econ. Dept, Nat. Bank of Hungary, Elektro-impex Foreign Trading Co.; fmr dept head and research man., Business and Market Research Inst.; with Hungarian Acad. of Sciences Research Inst. of World Economy 1965–88; Lecturer, Eötvös Loránd Univ. of Budapest; Visiting Prof., Santiago de Chile and San Marcos Univ. of Lima; Dir Econ. Planning Inst. 1988–90; Minister of Int. Econ. Relations 1990–94; mem. Parl. 1994–98, Chair. Cttee on Budget and Finances; Vice-Chair. Hungarian Asscn of Economists 1990–2000, Chair. 2002–08, Life Hon. Chair. 2008–; Univ. Prof. 1998–2012; Pres. Hungarian Export-Import Bank 1998–99; Vice-Pres. Hungarian Soc. of Foreign Affairs 1998–; Amb. to OECD 1999–2003; mem. Monetary Council of Hungarian Nat. Bank 1999–2009; Chair. Hungarian Group in Trilateral Comm. 1999–; Academician, Hungarian Acad. of Sciences; Dr hc (San Marcos Univ., Lima) 1970, (Budapest) 1999, (Miskolc) 2008, (Pécs) 2012; Grand Prix, Hungarian Acad. of Sciences 1984, Econ. Policy Club (Bonn) Prize for Social Market Econs 1993. *Publications:* author of eight books and more than 400 papers. *Leisure interests:* music, literature. *Address:* Mártonhegyi u. 38/B, Budapest 1124, Hungary. *Telephone:* (1) 355-7987. *Fax:* (1) 355-7987.

KADARÉ, Ismail; Albanian writer; b. 28 Jan. 1936, Gjirokastër; s. of Halit Kadaré; m. Elena Gushi 1963; two d.; ed Univ. of Tirana, Gorky Inst., USSR; full-time writer since 1963; mem. Parl. 1970–82; sought political asylum in France 1990; mem. Albanian Acad.; Corresponding, then Assoc. Foreign mem. Acad. des sciences morales et politiques; mem. Acad. of Arts, Berlin, Acad. Mallarmé; Dr hc (Grenoble III) 1992, (St Etienne) 1997, (South East European Univ.) 2005; Prix Mondial Cino del Duca 1992, Int. Booker Prize 2005, Premio Príncipe de Asturias 2009, Jerusalem Prize for Freedom of the Individual in Soc. 2015. *Plays include:* Mauvaise saison pour Olymp. *Publications include:* Gjenerali i ushtërisë së vdekur (translated as The General of the Dead Army) 1963, Kështjella (translated as The Castle, later as The Siege) 1970, Kronikë në gur (translated as Chronicle in Stone) 1971, The Great Winter (novel, in trans.) 1973, Ura më tri harque (translated as The Three-Arched Bridge) 1978, The Twilight (in trans.) 1978, The Niche of Shame (in trans.) 1978, Kush e solli doruntinen (translated as Who Brought Back Doruntine?) 1980, Prilli i thyer (translated as Broken April) 1980, Nëpunësi I pallatit të ëndrrave (translated as The Palace of Dreams) 1980, Nje dosje per Homerin (translated as The H Dossier) 1980, Koncert në fund të dimrit (translated as The Concert) 1985, Eschyle or The Eternal Loser (in trans.) 1988, Albanian Spring (in trans.) 1991, Le Monstre (in trans.) 1991, Piramida (translated as The Pyramid) 1992, La Grande muraille 1993, Le Firman aveugle 1993, Clair de Lune 1993, L'Ombre 1994, L'Aigle 1996, Spiritus 1996, Oeuvres 1993–97 (12 vols) 1997, Temps barbares, de l'Albanie au Kosovo 1999, Il a fallu ce deuil pour se retrouver 2000, Froides fleurs d'avril (trans. as Spring Flowers, Spring Frost) 2000, L'envol du migrateur 2001, Vie, jeu et mort de Lul Mazrek 2002, La fille d'Agamemnon 2003, Le successeur 2003, L'Accident 2010, Twilight of the Eastern Gods (translated from Muzgu i perëndive të stepës) 2014; six vols of poetry 1954–80, criticism, essays. *Address:* c/o The Wylie Agency, 17 Bedford Square, London, WC1B 3JA, England (office); 63 blvd Saint-Michel, 75005 Paris, France (home). *Telephone:* 1-43-29-16-20 (home).

KADARE, Ismail; Albanian novelist and poet; b. 28 Jan. 1936, Gjirokastër; s. of Halit Kadare and Hatixhe Dobi; m. Helena Kadare (née Gushi); two d.; ed Univ. of Tirana, Maxim Gorky Literature Inst., USSR; full-time writer since 1963; mem. Parl. 1970–82; sought political asylum in France 1990; mem. Albanian Acad.; Corresponding, then Assoc. Foreign mem. Acad. des sciences morales et politiques, Lifetime mem. 1996–; mem. Acad. of Arts, Berlin, Acad. Mallarmé; Commandeur de la Légion d'Honneur 2016; Dr hc (Grenoble III) 1992, (St Etienne) 1997, (South East European Univ.) 2005; Prix mondial Cino Del Duca 1992, Man Booker Int. Prize 2005, Prince of Asturias Award of Arts 2009, Jerusalem Prize for Freedom of the Individual in Soc. 2015. *Plays:* Stinë e mërzitshme në Olimp 1998. *Publications:* novels: Gjenerali i ushtrisë së vdekur (The General of the Dead Army) 1963, Përbindëshi (The Monster) 1965, Lëkura e daulles 1967, Kështjella (The Siege) 1970, Kronikë në gur (Chronicle in Stone) 1971, Dimiri i vetmisë së madhe (The Great Winter) 1972, Nëntori i një kryeqyteti 1975, Ura më tri harque (The Three-Arched Bridge) 1978, Kamarja e turpit (The Traitor's Niche) 1978, Muzgu i perëndive të stepës (Twilight of the Eastern Gods) 1978, Kush e solli doruntinen (The Ghost Rider) 1980, Prilli i thyer (Broken April) 1980, Nëpunësi I pallatit të ëndrrave (The Palace of Dreams) 1980, Nje dosje per Homerin (The File on H) 1980, Nata me hënë 1985, Koncert në fund të dimrit (The Concert) 1985, Krushqit janë të ngrirë 1985, Dosja H. 1989, Qorrfermani (The Blinding Order) 1991, Piramida (The Pyramid) 1992, Hija 1994, Shkaba 1995, Lulet e ftohta të marsit (Spring Flowers, Spring Frost) 2000, Vajza e Agamemnonit (The Daughter of Agamemnon) 2003, Pasardhësi (The Successor) 2003, Çështje të marrëzisë 2005, Darka e Gabuar (The Fall of the Stone City) 2008, E penguara: Rekuiem për Linda B (A Girl in Exile) 2009, Aksidenti (The Accident) 2008, Mjegullat e Tiranës 2014, Kukulla 2015; short stories: Emblema e dikurshme 1977, Ëndërr mashtruese 1991, Tri këngë zie për Kosovën (Three Elegies for Kosovo) 1998, Vjedhja e gjumit mbretëror 1999, Përballë pasqyrës së një gruaje 2001, Bisedë për brilantet në pasditen e dhjetorit 2013, Koha e dashurisë 2015, Proza e shkurtër, në një vëllim (collected fiction) 2018; essays: Autobiografia e popullit në vargje 1971, Eskili, ky humbës i madh (Aeschylus: the Eternal Loser) 1990, Kushëriri i engjëjve 1997, Poshtërimi në Ballkan 2004, Identiteti evropian i shqiptarëve 2006, Mbi krimin në Ballkan: Letërkëmbim i zymtë 2011, Mëngjeset në Kafe Rostand 2014, Arti si mëkat 2015, Tri sprova mbi letërsinë botërore (Essays on World Literature: Aeschylus, Dante, Shakespeare) 2017; poetry: Frymëzime djaloshare 1954, Ëndërrimet 1957, Princesha Argjiro 1957, Shekulli im 1961, Përse mendohen këto male 1964, Shqiponjat fluturojnë lart 1966, Motive me diell 1968, Koha 1976, Ca pika shiu ranë mbi qelq 2004, Pa formë është qielli 2005, Vepra poetike në një vëllim (collected poetry) 2018. *Address:* c/o The Wylie Agency, 17 Bedford Square, London, WC1B 3JA, England (office); 63 blvd Saint-Michel, 75005 Paris, France (home). *Telephone:* 1-43-29-16-20 (home).

KADDOUMI, Farouk, (Abu Lutef); Palestinian politician; *President of the Executive Committee, Fatah (The Palestine National Liberation Movement);* b. 1931, Qalqilyah; ed Cairo Univ.; moved to Nablus during Arab–Israeli War 1948; worked for Arab–American Petroleum Co. (ARAMCO), Saudi Arabia early 1950s; joined Baath Party, Egypt 1954; joined Fatah in UAE 1960; with Ministry of Health, Kuwait 1965–66; expelled from Kuwait for anti-governmental activities connected with Palestinian Liberation Org. (PLO) 1966; became key figure in PLO 1969, apptd Head of Political Dept, Damascus, Syria 1973; participated in activities of Said al-Muraghi (Aba Musa) Group 1980s; opposed signing of Oslo Peace Accords with Israel 1993; apptd Dir of Palestinian Econ. Council for Reconstruction and Devt (PEDCAR) by Yasser Arafat; Pres. Exec. Cttee, Palestine Nat. Liberation Movt (al-Fatah) 2004–. *Address:* Fatah (The Palestine National Liberation Movement), Palestinian Autonomous Areas (office). *Website:* www.fateh.net (office).

KADEER, Rebiya; Chinese (Uyghur) human rights activist; *President, World Uyghur Congress;* b. 15 June 1947, Altay, East Turkistan; m. 1st 1965; m. 2nd Prof. Sidik Rouzi 1981; 11 c.; moved to Aksu, Xinjiang 1965; opened launderette 1976; moved to Ürümqi 1981; leased a market in local business dist, converted it into dept store that specialized in Uyghur ethnic costumes; engaged in cross-border trade, following collapse of Soviet Union, business included dept stores, real estate, timber, scrap iron, factories and other enterprises; est. trading co. operating in China, Russia and Kazakhstan; active philanthropist within community, most notably through 1,000 Families Mothers Project (charity to help Uyghur women start their own local businesses); del., eighth session of CPPCC 1993; Rep. to UN

Fourth World Conf. for Women, Beijing 1995; fmr Vice-Chair. Xinjiang Autonomous Region Fed. of Industry and Commerce, Xinjiang Asscn of Women Entrepreneurs; removed from Nat. People's Consultative Conf. and passport revoked after she criticized the Chinese Govt; detained on charges of leaking state secrets Aug. 1999, convicted in Ürümqi Intermediate People's Court of endangering state security March 2000, spent two years in solitary confinement; released early on medical grounds into US custody March 2005, flew to USA March 2005; Pres. World Uyghur Congress 2006–, Bd of Uyghur American Asscn; Dir Int. Uyghur Human Rights and Democracy Foundation; Rafto Prize for Human Rights 2004. *Publication:* Dragon Fighter (autobiography) 2009. *Address:* World Uyghur Congress, PO Box 310312, 80103 Munich, Germany (office). *Telephone:* (89) 54321999 (office). *Fax:* (89) 54349789 (office). *E-mail:* contact@uyghurcongress.org (office); duq@uyghurcongress.org (office). *Website:* www.uyghurcongress.org (office).

KADOMATSU, Masahiro; Japanese business executive; *Chairman and CEO, Asahi Glass Company;* b. 29 Oct. 1942, Tokyo; ed Keio Univ.; joined Asahi Glass Co. 1965, numerous man. positions 1965–98 including Gen. Man. Sales, Gen. Man. Electronic Products Div. 1998–2000, Man. Dir and Gen. Man., Display Glass 2000–02, Sr Exec. Officer and Pres. Display Co. 2002–03, Sr Exec. Vice-Pres. and Pres. Display Co. 2003–04, CEO and Pres. Asahi Glass Co. 2004–07, Chair. and CEO 2007–; Counsellor, Energy Conservation Centre, Japan, Int. Centre for the Study of East Asian Devt; Commdr, Order of the Crown of Belgium 2010. *Address:* Asahi Glass Company, 1-12-1 Yuraku-cho, Chiyoda-ku, Tokyo 100-8405, Japan (office). *Telephone:* (3) 3218-5096 (office). *Website:* www.agc.co.jp (office).

KADOORIE, Hon. Sir Michael, Kt; Hong Kong business executive; *Chairman, CLP Holdings Ltd;* b. 1941, Hong Kong; s. of Lawrence, Lord Kadoorie and Muriel Gubbay; m. Betty Tamayo; three c.; ed Institut Le Rosey, Switzerland; family roots in business in the Far East go back to his grandfather, who made a fortune in Shanghai, mostly lost in 1949, and later, in Hong Kong through finance, real estate and utilities; Chair. CLP Group, Hong Kong (electricity provider), Founder CLP Research Inst. (subsidiary of CLP Holdings); Chair. Hong Kong & Shanghai Hotels, owners and operators of Peninsula Hotel Group, mem. Bd of Dirs Metrojet Ltd, Heliservices (Hong Kong) Ltd; mem. Bd of Dirs Sir Elly Kadoorie & Sons Ltd, Hutchison Whampoa Ltd; Alternate Dir Hong Kong Aircraft Engineering Co. Ltd 1989–; fmr mem. Council of Univ. of Hong Kong; Trustee, Kadoorie Charitable Foundation; Grand Bauhinia Star, Officier, Légion d'honneur, Commdr, Order of Léopold II (Belgium); Hon. LLD (Univ. of Hong Kong) 2004. *Leisure interests:* photography, helicopter pilot, collecting classic cars. *Address:* CLP Holdings, 147 Argyle Street, Kowloon, Hong Kong Special Administrative Region, People's Republic of China (office). *Telephone:* 2678-8111 (office). *Fax:* 2760-4448 (office). *E-mail:* clp_info@clp.com.hk (office). *Website:* www.clpgroup.com (office).

KADUMA, Ibrahim Mohamed, BSc (Econs), BPhil; Tanzanian economist and politician; b. 1937, Mtwango Njombe, Iringa Region; s. of Mohamed Maleva Kaduma and Mwanaidza Kaduma; m. Happiness Y. Mgonja 1969; four s. one d.; ed Makerere Univ. Coll. Uganda and Univ. of York, UK; Accounts Clerk, the Treasury 1959–61, Accounts Asst 1961, Asst Accountant 1962–65, Economist 1965–66, Dir of External Finance and Technical Co-operation 1967–69, Deputy Sec. Treasury 1969–70; Prin. Sec., Ministry of Communications, Transport and Labour, 1970–72, Treasury 1972–73; Dir Inst. of Devt Studies, Univ. of Dar es Salaam 1973–75, Centre on Integrated Rural Devt for Africa 1982–85; Minister for Foreign Affairs 1975–77, of Trade 1980–81, of Communications and Transport 1981–82; Vice-Chancellor Univ. of Dar es Salaam 1977–80; fmr Gen. Man. Tanzania Sisal Devt Bd; fmr Chancellor, Mzube Univ.; mem. Bd of Dirs National Investments Company Ltd; Arts Research Prize, Makerere Univ., Uganda 1964–65. *Leisure interests:* tennis, squash, gardening, dairy farming.

KADYROV, Ramzan Akhmatovich; Russian government official; *Head of the Chechen Republic;* b. 5 Oct. 1976, Tsenteroi, Checheno-Ingush ASSR (now Chechen Repub.), Russian SFSR, USSR; s. of Pres. Akhmad Kadyrov; m. Medni Kadyrova; three s. six d.; fmr Commdr of 'Kadyrovtsy' militia (Presidential security service); fmr Head of Security, Chechen Repub.; First Deputy Chair. of Govt, Chechen Repub. 2004–05, Acting Chair. of Govt 2005–06, Chair. of Govt 2006–07, Pres. 2007–11, Head of Chechen Repub. 2011–April 2016, Sept. 2016–, Acting Head April–Sept. 2016; mem. Advisory Comm. of the State Council of the Russian Fed. 2015–; Chair. Ramzan boxing club, Terek Grozny football club; escaped assassination attempt Oct. 2009; Pres. Chechen League KVN; Hon. mem. Russian Acad. of Natural Sciences 2006; Hon. Citizen of the Chechen Repub.; Honoured Worker of Physical Culture; Honoured Builder of the Chechen Repub.; Hon. Pres. Movt of Afghan Veterans of the Southern Fed. Okrug; Medal 'For Distinction in the Protection of Public Order' 2002, 2004; Order of Courage 2003; Hero of the Russian Fed. 2004; Order of Merit for the Fatherland (Fourth Class) 2006; Certificate of Merit of the State Duma of the Russian Fed. 2009; Medal 'For Services to conduct national census'; Zhukov Medal (twice); Medal 'In Commemoration of the 850th Anniversary of Moscow'; Medal 'In Commemoration of the 300th Anniversary of Saint Petersburg'; Mil. Merit (Grade 2); Ministry of Defence; Order of Akhmad Kadyrov 2005; Caucasus Service Medal; Defender of the Chechen Repub. Medal 2006; Order 'For the development of parliamentarism in the Chechen Republic' 2007; Medal 'Astana 10 years' (Kazakhstan) 2008; Order of Honour 2015; Man of the Year in the Chechen Repub. 2004, Laureate of the 'Russian of the Year' in the nomination 'For the sake of life on Earth' 2007, Aksakal Award 2008, Certificate of Merit of the State Duma of the Russian Fed. 2009. *Leisure interests:* football, horses, collecting sports cars and Chechen daggers. *Address:* Office of the Head of the Chechen Republic, 364000 Chechen Republic, Groznyi, ul. Garazhnaya 10A, Russia (office). *Telephone:* (8712) 22-20-01 (office); (8712) 22-20-09 (office). *Fax:* (8712) 22-20-14 (office). *E-mail:* info@chechnya.gov.ru (office); secretariat_chr@mail.ru (office). *Website:* www.chechnya.gov.ru (office); www.ramzan-kadyrov.ru.

KAELIN, William G., Jr, MD; American physician and professor of medicine; *Professor, Department of Medicine, Dana-Farber Cancer Institute, Harvard Medical School;* b. 23 Nov. 1957, New York; m. Carolyn M. Kaelin 1988; one s. one d.; ed Duke Univ.; completed training in internal medicine at Johns Hopkins Hosp., served as Chief Medical Resident; later Clinical Fellow in Medical Oncology, Dana-Farber Cancer Inst., Harvard Medical School (McDonnell Scholar), currently Prof., Dept of Medicine and Assoc. Dir, Basic Science, for Dana-Farber/Harvard Cancer Center; Howard Hughes Medical Investigator 1998–; fmr mem. Bd of Scientific Advisors, Nat. Cancer Inst. (NCI), Bd of Trustees, American Asscn for Cancer Research (AACR), Inst. of Medicine Nat. Cancer Policy Bd; Consulting Ed., Journal of Clinical Investigation; Assoc. Ed., Clinical Cancer Research; mem. Editorial Bd, Molecular and Cellular Biology, Cancer Cell, Molecular Cancer Research, Cancer Discovery; mem. Inst. of Medicine 2007, NAS 2010, AACR Acad. 2014, American Soc. for Clinical Investigation (ASCI); NIH Nat. Research Service Award 1990, NIH Physician-Scientist Award 1990, James S. McDonnell Scholar Award 1993, Paul Marks Prize, Memorial Sloan Kettering Cancer Center 2001, AACR Richard and Hinda Rosenthal Foundation Award 2006, Doris Duke Distinguished Clinical Investigator Award 2006, Distinguished Alumni Award, Duke Univ. School of Medicine 2007, Colin Thomson Medal, American Inst. for Cancer Research 2008, Canada Gairdner Int. Award (co-recipient) 2010, NCI Alfred Knudson Award in Cancer Genetics 2011, ASCI Stanley J. Korsmeyer Award 2012, Scientific Grand Prix, Foundation Lefoulon-Delalande 2012, Wiley Prize in Biomedical Sciences 2014, Steven C. Beering Award 2014, Science of Oncology Award, American Soc. of Clinical Oncology 2016, AACR Princess Takamatsu Award 2016, Albert Lasker Basic Medical Research Award (co-recipient) 2016. *Publications:* numerous papers in professional journals. *Address:* William Kaelin Laboratory, 450 Brookline Avenue, Mayer 457, Boston, MA 02215, USA (office). *Telephone:* (617) 632-3975 (office). *Fax:* (617) 632-4760 (office). *E-mail:* william_kaelin@dfci.harvard.edu (office). *Website:* kaelin.dfci.harvard.edu (office).

KAESER, Josef (Joe), Dipl.-Betriebswirt; German business executive; *President and CEO, Siemens AG;* b. 23 June 1957, Arnbruck, Regen, Bavaria; m.; two c.; joined Components Group, Discrete Components Div., Siemens AG 1980, later Head of Business Admin Semiconductor Plant, Regensburg, Finance Dir, Semiconductors Group, Head of Accounting & Product Planning, Siemens Semiconductors, Malacca, Malaysia 1987–88, Head of Business Admin Projects, Semiconductors Group, Discrete Semiconductors Div., Siemens AG 1988–90, Head of Business Admin, Opto Semiconductors Div. 1990–95, Head of Business Admin, Siemens Microelectronics Inc., San José, Calif., USA 1995–99, Exec. Vice-Pres. and Chief Financial Officer (CFO), Siemens AG, responsible for Corp. Finance, Accounting Unit, Controlling and Taxes 1999–2001, mem. Group Exec. Man., Information and Communication Mobile Group 2001–04, Chief Strategy Officer 2004–06, mem. Man. Bd and CFO 2006–13, Pres. and CEO 2013–; mem. Bd Allianz Deutschland AG, Nokia Siemens Networks, Bosch Siemens Hausgeräte GmbH (Chair.), NXP Semiconductors NV; mem. Trilateral Comm. in Europe. *Address:* Siemens AG, Wittelsbacherplatz 2, 80333 Munich, Germany (office). *Telephone:* (89) 636-00 (office). *Fax:* (89) 63652000 (office); (69) 66826664 (office). *E-mail:* contact@siemens.com (office). *Website:* www.siemens.com (office).

KAFELNIKOV, Yevgeny Aleksandrovich; Russian fmr professional tennis player; b. 18 Feb. 1974, Sochi; m. two d.; ed Krasnodar Pedagogical Inst.; ATP professional 1992; won ATP tournaments including Milan, St Petersburg, Gstaad, Long Island; won French Open (singles and doubles) 1996; won Moscow Kremlin Cup 1997, 1999; won Australian Open 1999; mem. Russian Fed. Davis Cup Championship Team 1993, winner (with Russian team) 2002; runner-up World Championship, Hanover 1997; highest ATP rating 1st (May 1999); Olympic champion (singles), Sydney 2000; winner of 26 singles titles and 27 doubles titles; retd 2004. *Leisure interests:* fishing, flying, golf. *Website:* yevgenykafelnikov.com.

KAFRAWY, Hassaballah Mohamed El-, BEng; Egyptian politician; *Trustee, Al Hussein Mosque Establishment;* b. 22 Nov. 1930, Kafr Saad Area, Damietta Governorate; s. of Mohamed El-Kafrawy; m. Elham Fouad 1961; three s.; ed Alexandria Univ.; with southern region of High Dam electricity lines until 1966; Chair. Canal Gen. Contracting Co.; Vice-Pres. exec. organ for reconstruction of Suez Canal region 1974, Pres. 1975; Gov. of Damietta 1976; Deputy Minister for Reconstruction, then Minister of Devt, Housing and Land Reclamation 1977–86; supervised planning of satellite cities and public utilities of Sadat, Ramadan 10, October 6, May 15, Cairo Sanitary Project, Damietta Port etc.; Minister of Devt, New Communities, Housing and Public Utilities 1986–93; mem. Egyptian People's Ass. 1979–93; Chair. and CEO El rehab Saudi-Egyptian Group of cos 1997; Pres. Egyptian Eng Asscn 1990; Chair. New Communities Authority; Perm. mem. and fmr Vice-Chair. World Asscn of the Major Metropolises (Metropolis); mem. Egyptian Specialized Nat. Councils, Egyptian Acad. for Scientific Research and Tech. (Chair. New Communities Research Council Acad.), Gen. Authority for Investment and Free Zones; Pres. or fmr Pres. Egyptian Engineers Syndicate, Univ. Councils of Alexandria, Helwan and Mansoura, Cairo Univ. Centre for Devt and Technological Planning Research; Egyptian Order of Merit (First Class) 1964, 1975, 1980, Medal for Championship of Labour (USSR) 1964, Order of Merit (First Class) (France) 1983, Order of the Nile (Kiladat El Nil) (highest state honour) 1994; Dr hc; UN Habitat Prize for Housing 1992. *Address:* No. 20, Alhamd Building, El-Kafrawy Road, District 2/Section 5, 6th of October City, Egypt (home). *Telephone:* (2) 38369851 (home). *Fax:* (2) 38369853 (home). *E-mail:* kafegy@yahoo.com (home); mkafrawi@gmail.com (home).

KAGAME, Maj.-Gen. Paul; Rwandan army officer, politician and head of state; *President;* b. 23 Oct. 1957, Tambwe, Ruanda-Urundi (now Nyarutovu), Southern Prov.; m. Jeannette Nyiramongi 1989; three s. one d.; ed Fort Leavenworth, USA; escaped to Uganda with family from anti-Tutsi persecution 1960; joined Ugandan Rebel Army 1982, Chief of Intelligence Ugandan Army 1986; formed rebel army of Rwandan exiles 1990, Leader of campaign in Rwanda 1990–94, helped broker ceasefire 1993; Vice-Pres. and Minister of Nat. Defence 1994–2000, Pres. of Rwanda April 2000–; Head of Rwandan Patriotic Front Party (FPR) 2000; Chair. African Union 2018–19; Young Presidents' Org. 2003, Africa Gender Award 2007. *Leisure interests:* tennis, reading, football. *Address:* Office of the President, BP 15, Kigali, Rwanda (office). *Telephone:* 259062000 (office). *Fax:* 752431 (office). *E-mail:* pkagame@gov.rw (office); info@presidency.gov.rw (office). *Website:* www.presidency.gov.rw (office); www.paulkagame.com.

KAGAN, Elena, MPh, JD; American lawyer, academic and government official; *Associate Justice, Supreme Court;* b. 28 April 1960, New York City; d. of Robert Kagan and Gloria Gittelman; ed Hunter Coll. High School, Princeton Univ., Worcester Coll., Oxford, UK, Harvard Law School; law clerk for Judge Abner Mikva, US Court of Appeals, DC Circuit 1986–87, for Justice Thurgood Marshall, US Supreme Court 1987–88; Assoc., Williams & Connolly (law firm), Washington,

DC 1989–91; Asst Prof., Univ. of Chicago Law School 1991–95, Tenured Prof. of Law 1995; Assoc. Counsel to the Pres., The White House 1995–96, Deputy Asst to Pres. for Domestic Policy and Deputy Dir of Domestic Policy Council 1997–99; Visiting Prof., Harvard Law School 1999–2001, Prof. of Law 2001–03, Charles Hamilton Houston Prof. of Law 2003–09, Dean of Faculty of Law 2003–09; Solicitor Gen. of the US, Dept of Justice, Washington, DC 2009–10; Assoc. Justice, US Supreme Court 2010–. *Publications:* contribs to journals including Harvard Law Review, Supreme Court Review, Univ. of Chicago Law Review, Texas Law Review, Law and Social Inquiry. *Address:* Supreme Court of the United States, 1 First Street, NE, Washington, DC 20543, USA (office). *Telephone:* (202) 479-3000 (office); (202) 479-3011 (Clerk's Office) (office); (202) 479-3211 (Public Information Office) (office). *E-mail:* info@supremecourt.gov (office). *Website:* www.supremecourt.gov (office).

KAGAN, Henri B., PhD; French chemist and academic; *Professor Emeritus, Université Paris-Sud 11;* b. 15 Dec. 1930, Boulogne-sur-Seine; s. of Alexandre Kagan and Adeline Celmiker; m. Claude Vignon 1960; three d.; ed Sorbonne, École Nat. Supérieure de Chimie, Paris; Research Assoc., Collège de France 1962–67; Visiting Researcher, Univ. of Texas, Austin, USA 1965, Visiting Prof. 1980; Asst Prof., Université Paris-Sud 11, Orsay 1967–73, Prof. 1973–99, Prof. Emer. 1999–; Prof., Institut Universitaire de France 1993–99; mem. Acad. des Sciences 1991–; Foreign mem. Polish Acad. of Sciences 1994–; Visiting Prof. at several int. univs including Fort Collins, Colo, USA 1976, Uppsala, Sweden 1998, Weizmann Inst., Israel 1988; JSPS, Japan 1977, 2001–03; Hon. Fellow, Chemical Research Soc. of India 2000; Hon. FRSC 2003; Chevalier, Ordre nat. du Mérite 1996, Légion d'honneur 2002; Dr hc (Bucharest) 1999, (Basilicata) 2004, (Montréal) 2008; numerous awards including French Chemical Soc. Le Bel Award 1967, Cahours Award, Acad. des Sciences 1968, Prelog Medal, ETH, Zurich 1990, Chaire Francqui, Louvain 1994, August-Wilhelm von Hofmann Medal 1991, Yamada Prize 1998, Nagoya Medal for Organic Chem. 1998, Tetrahedron Prize 1999, Wolf Prize in Chem. 2001, Grand Prix de la Fondation de la Maison de la Chimie 2002, Ryoji Noyori Prize 2002, Bower Award and Prize for Achievement in Science, Franklin Inst. 2005, Horst-Pracejus Prize 2007, Burckhardt Helferich Prize 2012. *Publications:* books include Stéréochimie organique 1975; more than 300 scientific articles 1955–2005. *Leisure interest:* history. *Address:* Equipe de Catalyse Moléculaire-ICMMO – Bât 420, Université Paris-Sud 11, 15 rue Georges Clemenceau, 91405 Orsay Cedex (office); 10 rue Georges Clemenceau, 91400 Orsay, France (home). *Telephone:* 1-69-15-78-95 (office). *Fax:* 1-69-15-46-80 (office). *E-mail:* henri.kagan@u-psud.fr (office). *Website:* www.icmo.u-psud.fr/Labos/LCM/cv/hkagan.php (office).

KAGARLITSKY, Boris Yuliyevich, PhD; Russian journalist, sociologist and writer; *Director, Institute of Globalization Studies and Social Movements;* b. 29 Aug. 1958, Moscow; ed State Inst. of Theatrical Art (GITIS); Ed. Leviy povorot (samizdat journal) 1978–82; Co-ordinator Moscow People's Front 1988; Deputy, Moscow City Soviet (prov. Parl.) 1990–93; Founding mem. Party of Labour 1992; fmr adviser to Chair., Fed. of Ind. Trade Unions of Russia; Sr Research Fellow, Inst. of Comparative Political Studies, Russian Acad. of Sciences 1994–2002; taught political science at Moscow State Univ., Moscow School for Social and Econ. Sciences, Inst. of Sociology of Russian Acad. of Sciences; Dir Inst. of Globalization Studies 2003–07, Inst. of Globalization Studies and Social Movts 2007–; Co-ordinator Transnational Inst. Global Crisis project; Ed.-in-Chief Levaya Politika (Left Politics) quarterly; columnist, The Moscow Times, ZNet. *Publications:* The Thinking Reed: Intellectuals and the Soviet State from 1917 to the Present (Deutscher Memorial Prize) 1988, The Dialectic of Hope 1989, Farewell Perestroika: A Soviet Chronicle 1990, Disintegration of the Monolith 1993, Square Wheels: How Russian Democracy Got Derailed 1994, The Mirage of Modernization 1995, Restoration in Russia 1995, Globalization and Its Discontents: The Rise of Postmodern Socialisms (co-author) 1996, New Realism, New Barbarism: Socialist Theory in the Era of Globalization 1999, The Twilight of Globalization: Property, State and Capitalism 1999, The Return of Radicalism: Reshaping the Left Institutions 2000, Russia under Yeltsin and Putin: Neo-liberal Autocracy 2002, The Politics of Empire: Globalization in Crisis (co-ed.) 2004, The Revolt of the Middle Class 2006, Empire of the Periphery: Russia and the World System 2008, Back in the USSR 2009; contribs to International Socialism, Novaya Gazeta, The Progressive, Red Pepper, Weekly Worker, Green Left Weekly. *Address:* Institute of Globalization Studies and Social Movements, Gazetny per. 5, Moscow, Russia (office). *Telephone:* (499) 502-82-52 (office). *Fax:* (495) 958-13-98 (office). *E-mail:* kagarlitsky@narod.ru; igso@igso.ru (office); igso.direct@gmail.com (office). *Website:* www.igso.ru (office); kagarlitsky.ru; kagarlitsky.narod.ru.

KAGERMANN, Henning, PhD; German software industry executive; *President, acatech-German Academy of Science and Engineering;* b. 1948; Lecturer in Theoretical Physics and Computer Science, Tech. Univ. of Braunschweig and Univ. of Mannheim 1982–92; joined SAP (business-application software co.) AG 1982, apptd to Exec. Bd 1991, Co-Chair. 1998–2002, Co-Chair. and CEO 2002–03, Chair. and CEO 2003–09; currently Pres. acatech-German Acad. of Science and Eng; mem. Supervisory Bd Deutsche Bank AG, Daimler-Chrysler Services AG, Münchener Rückversicherungs-Gesellschaft AG; mem. Bd of Dirs, Nokia Corpn 2007, WIPRO 2009, Haniel 2012; Trustee Tech. Univ. of Munich. *Address:* acatech-German Academy of Science and Engineering, Pariser Platz 4a, 10117 Berlin, Germany. *Website:* www.acatech.de (office).

KAGEYAMA, Mahito; Japanese business executive; *Executive Vice-President, Toyota Tsusho Corporation;* b. 28 Jan. 1949; joined Sanwa Bank Ltd (later UFJ Bank Ltd) 1972, Exec. Officer 1999–2002, Sr Exec. Officer 2002–03 (resgnd); Sr Advisor, Tomen Corpn Feb.–June 2003, Pres. June 2003–06, Exec. Vice-Pres. Toyota Tsusho Corp. (after merger of Tomen with Toyota Tsusho Corp.) 2006–; Ind. Dir Ube Industries Ltd 2015–. *Address:* Toyota Tsusho Corporation, 9-8, Meieki, 4-chome, Nakamura-ku, Nagoya 450-8575, Japan (office). *Telephone:* (52) 584-5000 (office). *Fax:* (52) 584-5663 (office). *Website:* www.toyota-tsusho.com (office).

KAHIN, Dahir Riyale; Somali politician; mem. United Peoples' Democratic Party; fmr Gov. Awdal Prov.; Vice-Pres. self-proclaimed Repub. of Somaliland (NW Somalia) 1997–2002, Pres. 2002–10.

KAHLON, Moshe, BA, LLB; Israeli politician; *Minister of Finance;* b. 19 Nov. 1960, Hadera; m.; three c.; ed Haifa Univ., Netanya Law Coll.; Dir, Scientific Industrial Center 1993–99; Personal Rep. of Minister of Defence, Haifa and N Region 1996–99; Public Rep., Haifa Labour Court 1999–2001; Bureau Chief and Sr Adviser to Minister of Public Security 2000–02; Dir Matzila (crime prevention group) 2001–02; Chair. Ethos (art, culture and sport co.), Haifa 2005–06; mem. Knesset (Likud) 2003–13, (Kulanu) 2015–, fmr Deputy Speaker of the Knesset; Minister of Communications 2009–13, Minister of Welfare and Social Services 2011–13, Minister of Finance 2015–; f. Center for Reform and Leadership, Netanya Academic Coll. 2013, Kulanu (political party) 2014; mem. Council and Directorate, Asscn for Wellbeing of Israel's Soldiers; mem. Council, Maccabi Haifa Football Club. *Address:* Ministry of Finance, POB 13195, 1 Kaplan Street, Kiryat Ben-Gurion, Jerusalem 91030, Israel (office). *Telephone:* 2-5317215 (office). *Fax:* 2-5695347 (office). *E-mail:* pniot@mof.gov.il (office). *Website:* www.mof.gov.il (office).

KAHN, C(arl) Ronald, BA, MD, MS; American medical scientist and academic; *Mary K. Iacocca Professor of Medicine and Chief Academic Officer, Elliott P. Joslin Diabetes Center, Harvard Medical School;* b. Louisville, Ky; ed Univ. of Louisville; Intern and Resident, Barnes Hosp., Ward Medicine Saint Louis, Mo. 1968–70; Clinical Assoc. and Sr Clinical Assoc., Clinical Endocrinology Br., Nat. Insts of Arthritis, Metabolism and Digestive Diseases, NIH, Bethesda, Md 1970–73, Diabetes Br. 1973–78 (Chief of Section on Cellular and Molecular Physiology 1979–81), Admitting and Attending Physician, Clinical Center 1972–81; Visiting Scientist, Center de Moleculaire, CNRS, Gif-Sur-Yvette, France 1979–80; Adjunct Prof. of Genetics, George Washington Univ., Washington, DC 1980–81; Clinical Assoc. Prof. of Medicine, Uniformed Services Univ. of Health Sciences, Bethesda 1981; Assoc. Prof. of Medicine, Harvard Univ. Medical School, Boston, Mass 1981–84, Prof. of Medicine 1984–86, Mary K. Iacocca Prof. of Medicine 1986–, also Sr Investigator and Head, Section on Obesity and Hormone Action, Dir Elliot P. Joslin Research Lab., Joslin Diabetes Center, Boston 1981–, Sr Staff, Joslin Clinic 1985–, Exec. Vice-Pres. and Dir Joslin Diabetes Center 1997–2000, Pres. Joslin Diabetes Center 2001–07, Vice-Chair. then Chief Academic Officer 2012–; Assoc. Staff, Dept of Endocrinology and Internal Medicine, New England Deaconess Hosp., Boston 1981–85, Active Staff 1986; Physician, Brigham and Women's Hosp., Boston 1981–91, Chief, Div. of Diabetes and Metabolism, Dept of Medicine 1981–92, Sr Physician 1992, Sr Consultant in Diabetes and Metabolism 1993; Prof. in Endocrinology and Metabolism, The Hosp. of the Good Samaritan, Los Angeles 1985; Visiting Prof., Royal Postgraduate Hosp., London, UK 1985; Overseas Visiting Prof., Royal Melbourne Hosp., Melbourne, Australia 1985; Roerig Visiting Professorship in Diabetes, Univ. of Colorado Health Sciences Center, Denver, Colo 1990; Visiting Scientist, Dana Farber Cancer Inst., Dept of Cellular and Molecular Biology, Boston 1990–91; Visiting Research Scientist, Brandeis Univ., Waltham, Mass 1998–99; Exec. Ed. Trends in Endocrinology and Metabolism 1989–90; Consulting Ed. The Journal of Clinical Investigation 1992–; Assoc. Ed. Diabetes 1996; apptd mem. Editorial Bd Diabetes and Metabolism Reviews 1984, Receptor 1989, Trends in Endocrinology and Metabolism 1991, Journal of Receptor Research 1992, Proceedings of the Association of American Physicians 1997, American Journal of Medicine 1998; mem. Advisory Bd Endocrine Reviews 2001; mem. American Fed. for Clinical Research 1972, The Endocrine Soc. 1975 (mem. Council 1990–93), American Diabetes Asscn (ADA) 1976, American Soc. for Clinical Investigation 1979 (Pres. 1988–89), American Soc. of Biological Chem. 1982, Asscn of American Physicians 1983, Nat. Council of American Soc. for Clinical Investigation 1985, NAS 1999, NAS Insts of Medicine 1999; Fellow, American Acad. of Arts and Sciences 1991, AAAS 1994; Alumni Fellow, Univ. of Louisville 1993–; Hon. Prof. and Dir Diabetes Center, Peking Univ. School of Medicine; Hon. Adjunct Mem., Max Planck Inst., Cologne, Germany 2014; Hon. DSc (Louisville) 1984, (Université de Paris Pierre et Marie Curie) 1990, (Univ. of Geneva), (Washington Univ. in St Louis); Hon. MS (Harvard); David Rumbough Memorial Award for Scientific Achievement, Juvenile Diabetes Foundation 1977, ADA Eli Lilly Award for Research 1981, Award for Outstanding Clinical Research Under Age 40, American Fed. for Clinical Research 1983, Pfizer Biomedical Research Award 1986, Cristobal Diaz Award, Int. Diabetes Foundation 1988, ADA Banting Medal for Distinguished Scientific Achievement 1993, Distinguished Scientist Award, Clinical Ligand Assay Soc. 1997, ADA Albert Renold Award 1998, Dorothy Hodgkin Award, British Diabetes Asscn 1999, Int. Soc. of Endocrinology Award, CCISE 2000, Fred Conrad Koch Award, The Endocrine Soc. 2000, Hans Falk Memorial Lecturer, Nat. Inst. of Environmental Health Science 2009, Cockrell Foundation Award in Basic and Clinical Research 2010, Distinguished Leader in Insulin Resistance, World Congress of Insulin Resistance in Diabetes and Cardiovascular Disease, Los Angeles 2010, David Murdock Dole Honorary Lecturer, Mayo Clinic-Karolinska, Nobel Forum, Stockholm, Sweden 2011, Wallace H. Coulter Award, American Asscn of Clinical Chem. 2013, Helmholtz Diabetes Research Lifetime Achievement Award (Germany) 2013, Ipsen Foundation Prize in Endocrine Regulation 2015, Harold Hamm Prize in Diabetes 2015, Wolf Prize in Medicine (co-recipient) 2016. *Publications:* more than 440 articles in medical and scientific journals. *Address:* Kahn Lab, Harvard Medical School, Joslin Diabetes Center, One Joslin Place, Room 705, Boston, MA 02215, USA (office). *Telephone:* (617) 732-2635 (office). *Fax:* (617) 732-2540 (office). *E-mail:* c.ronald.kahn@joslin.harvard.edu (office). *Website:* www.joslin.org (office).

KAHN, Eugene (Gene) S.; American retail executive; b. 1950; ed City Coll. of New York; began retail career at Gimbel's 1971; joined The May Dept Stores Co. 1990, Pres. and CEO G. Fox Div. 1990–92, Pres. and CEO Filene Div. 1992–96, apptd to Bd of Dirs 1996, Vice-Chair. 1996–97, Exec. Vice-Chair. 1997–98, Pres. and CEO 1998–2001, Chair. and CEO 2001–05; CEO Claire's Stores Inc. 2005–12; Chair. Nat. Council, Brown School of Social Work, Washington Univ. in St Louis; mem. Nat. Council, Inst. for Public Health; mem. Danforth Circle Cttee, William Greenleaf Eliot Soc., Washington Univ. in St Louis; mem. Bd of Dirs Goldfarb School of Nursing, Barnes-Jewish Hospital; fmr Treas., Mary Inst. and St Louis Country Day School; mem. Bd of Trustees, Washington Univ. in St Louis.

KAHN, Jacob Meyer, BA (Law), MBA; South African business executive; b. 29 June 1939, Pretoria; m. Lynette Sandra Asher 1968; two d.; ed Univ. of Pretoria; apptd Dir South African Breweries Ltd 1981, Group Man. Dir 1983, Exec. Chair. 1990, Group Chair. 1999; Exec. Dir SABMiller plc 1981–2012, Chair. 1999–2012; Chief Exec. South African Police Service 1997–99; Co-founder AfroCentric Investment Corpn Ltd 2006–; fmr Pres. SA Foundation; Ind. Dir Netcare Ltd

2000–18, Chair. 2015–18, Acting Chair. 2018–; Ind. Dir Capital Appreciation Ltd 2015–, Comair Ltd –2018; Prof. Extraordinaire 1989; Hon. DComm (Univ. of Pretoria) 1990; Marketing Man of the Year 1987, Business Man of the Year 1990, Award for Business Excellence 1991, South African Police Star of Excellence for Outstanding Service 2000. *Leisure interests:* reading, golf. *Address:* AfroCentric Investment Corporation Limited, 37 Conrad Road, Florida North, Roodepoort, Johannesburg 1709 (office); 4 East Road, Morningside, Sandton, Johannesburg, South Africa (home). *Telephone:* (11) 7836061 (home). *Fax:* (11) 7836061 (home). *Website:* www.afrocentric.za.com (office).

KAHN, Robert Elliot (Bob), BEE, MA, PhD; American computer scientist and electrical engineer; *Chairman, President and CEO, Corporation for National Research Initiatives;* b. 23 Dec. 1938, Brooklyn, NY; s. of Lawrence Kahn and Beatrice Pauline Kahn (née Tashker); ed City Coll. of New York, Princeton Univ.; fmr mem. Tech. Staff, Bell Labs; later Asst Prof. of Electrical Eng, MIT; joined US Defense Advanced Research Projects Agency 1972, later Dir Information Processing Techniques Office; f. Corpn for Nat. Research Initiatives (CNRI) 1986, currently Chair., Pres. and CEO; mem. Bd of Dirs Qualcomm; mem. Nat. Acad. of Eng; Fellow, IEEE, AAAI, Asscn for Computing Machinery (ACM) 2001, Computer History Museum 2006; Hon. Fellow, Soc. for Tech. Communication 2006, Univ. Coll. London; Dr hc (Princeton, Pavia, ETH Zurich, Maryland, George Mason, Central Florida, Pisa, St Petersburg Nat. Research Univ. of Information Technologies, Mechanics and Optics); AFIPS Harry Goode Memorial Award, Marconi Award, ACM SIGCOMM Award, ACM Pres.'s Award, ACM Software Systems Award, IEEE Koji Kobayashi Computer and Communications Award, IEEE Alexander Graham Bell Medal, IEEE Third Millennium Medal, Computerworld/Smithsonian Award, ASIS Special Award, Computing Research Bd Public Service Award, Sec. of Defense Civilian Service Award (twice), Nat. Medal of Tech. 1997, Charles Stark Draper Prize, Nat. Acad. of Eng 2001, Prince of Asturias Award 2002, Digital ID World Award 2003, A.M. Turing Award, Asscn for Computing Machinery 2004, Townsend Harris Medal, Alumni Asscn of the City Coll. of New York 2005, Presidential Medal of Freedom 2005, C & C Prize, Tokyo, Japan 2005, inducted into Nat. Inventors Hall of Fame 2006, Japan Prize (co-recipient) 2008, Harold Pender Award, Univ. of Pennsylvania 2010, inducted into Internet Hall of Fame 2012, Queen Elizabeth Prize for Eng (co-recipient) 2013, Benjamin Franklin Medal 2018. *Achievements include:* co-inventor of TCP/IP protocols, Knowbot programs, originated concept of architecture networking. *Address:* Corporation for National Research Initiatives, 1895 Preston White Drive, Suite 100, Reston, VA 20191-5434, USA (office). *Telephone:* (703) 620-8990 (office). *Fax:* (703) 620-0913 (office). *E-mail:* web-comments@cnri.reston.va.us (office). *Website:* www.cnri.reston.va.us (office).

KAHNEMAN, Daniel, PhD; Israeli/American psychologist and academic; *Eugene Higgins Professor Emeritus of Psychology and Professor Emeritus of Public Affairs, Woodrow Wilson School, Princeton University;* b. 1934, Tel-Aviv; m. Anne Treisman; ed The Hebrew Univ., Jerusalem, Univ. of California, Berkeley; Lecturer in Psychology, The Hebrew Univ. 1961–66, Sr Lecturer 1966–70, Assoc. Prof. 1970–73, Prof. 1973–78; Lecturer in Psychology, Harvard Univ. 1966–67; Prof. of Psychology, Univ. of British Columbia, Canada 1978–86; Prof. of Psychology, Univ. of Calif., Berkeley 1986–94; Eugene Higgins Prof. of Psychology, Princeton Univ. 1993, Prof. of Public Affairs, Woodrow Wilson School 1993, now Prof. Emer., currently Sr Scholar; Visiting Scientist, Univ. of Michigan 1965–66, Applied Psychological Research Unit, Cambridge, UK 1968–69; Fellow, Centre for Cognitive Studies 1966–67, Centre for Advanced Studies in the Behavioural Sciences 1977–78, Centre for Rationality, The Hebrew Univ. 2000–; Assoc. Fellow, Canadian Inst. for Advanced Research 1984–86; Visiting Scholar, Russell Sage Foundation 1991–92; Fellow, American Acad. of Arts and Sciences, Econometric Soc., American Psychological Asscn, American Psychological Soc., Canadian Psychological Asscn, Center for Rationality, Hebrew Univ.; mem. NAS, Soc. of Experimental Psychologists, Psychonomic Soc., Soc. for Econ. Science, Soc. for Judgement and Decision Making (Pres. 1992–93); mem. Ed. Bd Journal of Behavioral Decision Making, Journal of Risk and Uncertainty, Thinking and Reasoning, Economics and Philosophy; Hon. DrSc (Univ. of Pennsylvania Contrib.) 2001; Distinguished Scientific Contrib. Award, American Psychological Soc. 1982, Distinguished Scientific Contrib. Award, Soc. of Consumer Psychology 1992, Warren Medal, Soc. of Experimental Psychologists 1995, Hilgard Award for Lifetime Contrib. to General Psychology 1995, Nobel Prize for Econ. Sciences 2002, Lifetime Contribution Award, American Psychological Asscn 2007. *Achievements include:* pioneered integration of research about decision-making into field of econs. *Publications include:* Attention and Effort 1973, Human Engineering of Decisions in Ethics in an Age of Uncertainty 1980, Well-Being: Foundations of Hedonic Psychology (co-ed.) 1999, Choices, Values and Frames (co-ed.) 2000, Heuristics and Biases: The Psychology of Intuitive Judgement (co-ed.) 2002; author or co-author of over 120 articles in professional journals and chapters in books. *Address:* 332 Wallace Hall, Woodrow Wilson School, Princeton University, Princeton, NJ 08544-1013, USA (office). *Telephone:* (609) 258-2280 (office); (609) 924-8985 (home). *Fax:* (609) 258-5974 (office). *E-mail:* kahneman@princeton.edu (office). *Website:* www.wws.princeton.edu (office).

KAHRAMAN, İsmail; Turkish jurist and politician; b. 7 Dec. 1940, Rize; m.; four c.; ed Istanbul Univ.; apptd Pres. Bd of Trustees, Union Foundation 1985; Founding mem. Turkish Volunteer Org. Foundation 1994; MP Grand Nat. Ass. 1995–2002, 2015–18, Speaker 2015–18; Minister of Culture 1996–97; fmr Minister Counsellor, Ministry of Labour; mem. Welfare Party 1995–97, Virtue Party 1997–02, Justice and Development Party (AKP) 2002–; fmr mem. Bd of Trustees Istanbul Commerce Univ.; Chair. Milli Türk Talebe Birliği; f. Science Foundation; Dr hc (Yalova Univ., Recep Tayyip Erdoğan Univ.). *Address:* Adalet ve Kalkınma Partisi (Justice and Development Party), Söğütözü, Caddesi 6, Çankaya, Ankara, Turkey (office). *Telephone:* (312) 2045000 (office). *Fax:* (312) 2045044 (office). *E-mail:* rte@akparti.org.tr (office). *Website:* www.akparti.org.tr (office).

KAIFU, Toshiki; Japanese politician; b. 2 Jan. 1931, Nagoya City; m. Sachiyo Kaifu; ed Waseda Univ.; elected to House of Reps (LDP) 1960 and served 16 terms –2009; Parl. Vice-Minister of Labour; Chair. Steering Cttee of House of Reps; various posts in admin. of Takeo Miki 1974–76, including Deputy Chief Cabinet Sec. 1974–76, Chair. of Diet Policy Cttee of Liberal Democratic Party (LDP); Minister of Educ. 1976–77, 1985–86; Prime Minister of Japan 1989–91 (resgnd); Leader New Frontier Party (opposition coalition) 1994–95; currently Chair. 21st Century World Expo Promotion Parliamentary League. *Address:* c/o Liberal-Democratic Party, 1-11-23, Nagata-cho, Chiyoda-ku, Tokyo 100-8910, Japan.

KAIN, Karen, CC; Canadian ballet dancer and arts administrator; *Artistic Director, National Ballet of Canada;* b. 28 March 1951, Hamilton, Ont.; d. of Charles A. Kain and Winifred Mary Kelly; m. Ross Petty 1983; ed Nat. Ballet School; joined Nat. Ballet of Canada 1969, Prin. 1970, Artistic Assoc. 1999–2005, Artistic Dir 2005–; has danced most of major roles in repertoire, appeared as Giselle with Bolshoi Ballet on USSR tour, Aurora in the Sleeping Beauty with London Festival Ballet in UK and Australia, in Swan Lake with Vienna State Opera Ballet; toured Japan and Korea with Ballet national de Marseille 1981; cr. roles of Chosen Maiden in The Rite of Spring for Nat. Ballet 1979, Giuletta in Tales of Hoffman for Ballet national de Marseille 1982, the Bride in The Seven Daggers/Los Siete Puñales and roles in Glen Tetley's Alice 1986, La Ronde 1987, Daphnis and Chlöe 1988, Tagore 1989, Musings 1991, James Kudelka's The Actress 1994; appeared in CBC-TV productions of Giselle, La Fille Mal Gardée, The Merry Widow, Alice, La Ronde; Pres. The Dancer's Transition Centre; Officier des Arts et Lettres; hon. degrees from York, McMaster and Trent Univs; Silver Medal, Second Int. Ballet Competition, Moscow 1973, Int. Emmy Award for Karen Kain: Dancing in the Moment, Gov.-Gen.'s Award for Lifetime Achievement in the Performing Arts, Barbara Hamilton Memorial Award 2007, Distinguished Artist Award, Int. Soc. for the Performing Arts 2011. *Publication:* Movement Never Lies (autobiog.) 1994. *Address:* The Walter Carsen Centre for The National Ballet of Canada, 470 Queens Quay West, Toronto, ON M5V 3K4, Canada (office). *Telephone:* (416) 345-9686 (office). *Fax:* (416) 345-8323 (office). *E-mail:* info@national.ballet.ca (office). *Website:* www.national.ballet.ca (office).

KAINE, Timothy (Tim) Michael, BA (Econ), JD; American lawyer and politician; *Senator from Virginia;* b. 26 Feb. 1958, St Paul, Minn.; s. of Albert A. Kaine and Mary Kathleen Kaine (née Burns); m. Anne Holton 1984; two s. one d.; ed Rockhurst High School, Kansas City, Mo., Univ. of Missouri, Harvard Law School; Coro Foundation Fellow, Kansas City 1978; worked as missionary in Honduras; admitted to the Virginia Bar; clerked for Judge R. Lanier Anderson on the 11th Circuit Court of Appeals; practised law in Richmond for 17 years; taught legal ethics at Univ. of Richmond Law School for six years; served as mem. City Council of Richmond, Va, Mayor of Richmond 1998–2001; Lt-Gov. and Pres. of the Senate of Va 2002–06; Gov. of Va 2006–10; Chair. Democratic Nat. Cttee 2009–11; Senator from Virginia 2013–; unsuccessful cand. (Democrat) for Vice-Pres. of the USA 2016; Democrat. *Leisure interests:* camping, hiking, cycling, canoeing. *Address:* 231 Russell Senate Office Building, Washington, DC 20510, USA (office). *Telephone:* (202) 224-4024 (office). *Fax:* (202) 228-6363 (office). *Website:* www.kaine.senate.gov (office).

KAISER, Karl, PhD; German/American political scientist and academic; *Senior Associate, Transatlantic Relations Initiative, Belfer Center for Science and International Affairs, Harvard University;* b. 8 Dec. 1934, Siegen, North Rhine-Westphalia, Germany; s. of Walther Kaiser and Martha Müller; m. Deborah Strong 1967; two s. one d.; ed Univs of Cologne, Bonn and Grenoble and Nuffield Coll., Oxford, UK; Lecturer, Harvard Univ., USA 1963–67, Univ. of Bonn 1968–69, Johns Hopkins Univ. Bologna Center, Italy 1968–69; Prof. of Political Science, Univ. of the Saarland 1969–74, Univ. of Cologne 1974–91, Univ. of Bonn 1991–2000; Otto-Wolf Dir Research Inst. of German Council on Foreign Relations, Bonn and Berlin 1973–2003; Ralph I. Straus Visiting Prof. and Adjunct Prof. of Public Policy, John F. Kennedy School of Govt, Harvard Univ. 2003–14, Assoc., Weatherhead Center for Int. Affairs 2013–16, now Sr Assoc., Belfer Center for Science and Int. Affairs; Visiting Prof., European Univ. Inst., Florence, Hebrew Univ., Jerusalem; mem. German Council of Environmental Advisors; mem. Bd Foreign Policy, Internationale Politik, Asian-Pacific Review, Russia in Global Affairs; mem. Advisory Bd American-Jewish Cttee, Berlin; mem. American Philosophical Soc. 2007; Hon. CBE 1989, Officier, Legion d'honneur 1991, Bundesverdienstkreuz, Erster Klasse 1999, Großes Verdienstkreuz 2009, Polish Order of Merit (First Class) 2002; Dr hc (Russian Acad. of Sciences); Prix Adolphe Bentinck 1973, NATO Atlantic Award 1986. *Publications include:* EEC and Free Trade Area 1963, German Foreign Policy in Transition 1968, Europe and the USA 1973, New Tasks for Security Policy 1977, Reconciling Energy Needs and Proliferation 1978, Western Security: What Has Changed, What Can be Done? 1981, Atomic Energy Without Nuclear Weapons 1982, German–French Security Policy 1986, British–German Co-operation 1987, Space and International Politics 1987, Germany's Unification, The International Aspects 1991, Germany and the Iraq Conflict 1992, Foreign Policies of the New Republics in Eastern Europe 1994, Germany's New Foreign Policy, Vol. 1 1994, Vol. 2 1995, Vol. 3 1996, The Foreign Policies of the New Democracies in Central and Eastern Europe 1994, Acting for Europe, German-French Co-operation in a Changing World 1995, World Politics in a New Era 1996, Interests and Strategies 1996, Institutions and Resources 1998, The Future of German Foreign Policy 1999, Russia and the West 1999, Germany's New Foreign Policy 2001, Shaping a New International Financial System 2002, Asia and Europe: The Necessity of Cooperation 2004, International Security in the 21st Century 2016. *Leisure interests:* music, sailing. *Address:* 79 J. F. Kennedy Street, Center for Science and Int. Affairs, John F. Kennedy School of Govt, Cambridge, MA 02138, USA (office). *Telephone:* (617) 495-1396 (office). *E-mail:* karl_kaiser@hks.harvard.edu (office). *Website:* www.scholar.harvard.edu/karlkaiser (office).

KAISER, Michael M., BA, SM; American arts administrator; *Co-Chairman, IMG Artists LLC;* b. 27 Oct. 1953, New York; ed Brandeis Univ. and Sloan School of Man., Massachusetts Inst. of Tech.; Founder and Dir Michael M. Kaiser Assocs (consultancy) 1981–85, Kaiser/Engler (arts man. consultancy) 1994, Pres. 1994–95; Exec. Dir Alvin Ailey Dance Theater Foundation 1991–93, American Ballet Theatre 1995–98, Royal Opera House, London 1998–2000; Pres. John F. Kennedy Center for Performing Arts, Washington DC 2001–14; Adjunct Prof. of Business Admin., Rockhurst Coll., Kan. 1985–86; Adjunct Prof. of Arts Admin., New York Univ.; US Del. to Advisory Comm. on Arts Funding Policies of S African Govt 1994–95; Visiting Prof. of Arts Admin., Univ. of Witwatersrand 1995; Assoc. Dir State Ballet of Mo. 1985–87, Pierpoint Morgan Library 1987–89; Pres. John F. Kennedy Center for the Performing Arts 2001–14, Pres. Emer. 2014–, Founder and Pres. est. Kennedy Center Arts Man. Inst. 2001 (name changed to DeVos Inst.

of Arts Man. 2010), now Chair.; Co-Chair. IMG Artists LLC 2014–; mem. Bd of Dirs New York Foundation for the Arts; fmr Dir Washington Opera, Ensemble Studio Theater, PS 122; Order of the Mexican Eagle 2006, Order of the Polar Star (Sweden) 2013, Order of the Lion of Finland 2014; Hon. DHumLitt (Georgetown Univ.) 2011, Dr hc (Univ. of Missouri-Kansas City); Dance Magazine Award 2001, Capezio Award 2002, Helen Hayes Washington Post Award for Innovative Leadership in the Theater Community 2003, St Petersburg 300 Medal 2004, Washingtonian of the Year 2004, US Dept of State Citation 2005, Blacks in Dance Award 2005, Award for Cultural Exchange (China) 2005, Impresario of the Year by Musical America 2006, George Peabody Medal for Outstanding Contribs to Music in America 2009, Kahlil Gibran Spirit of Humanity Award, Arab American Inst. Foundation 2009. *Publications:* Understanding the Competition: A Practical Guide to Competitive Analysis 1981, Developing Industry Strategies: A Practical Guide to Industry Analysis 1983, Strategic Planning in the Arts: A Practical Guide 1995, The Art of the Turnaround 2008, Leading Roles: 50 Questions Every Arts Board Should Ask 2010, The Cycle: A Practical Approach to Managing Arts Organizations (with Brett E. Egan) 2013. *Address:* IMG Artists LLC, Pleiades House, 7 West 54th Street, New York, NY 10019, USA (office). *Telephone:* (212) 994-3500 (office). *Fax:* (212) 994-3550 (office). *E-mail:* artistsny@imgartists.com (office). *Website:* imgartists.com (office); devosinstitute.umd.edu.

KAIWA, Makoto; Japanese business executive; *Representative Director and President, Tohoku Electric Power Company Inc.;* Exec. Dir Yurtec Corpn 2005–; Sr Exec. Officer and Gen. Man., Niigata Branch Office 2007–; Exec. Vice-Pres. and Rep. Dir, Tohoku Electric Power Co. Inc. 2009–10, Rep. Dir and Pres. 2010–. *Address:* Tohoku Electric Power Company Inc., 7-1 Honcho 1-chome, Aoba-ku, Sendai, Miyagi 980-8550, Japan (office). *Telephone:* (2) 2225-2111 (office). *Fax:* (2) 2225-2500 (office). *Website:* www.tohoku-epco.co.jp (office).

KAJANTIE, Keijo Olavi, PhD; Finnish physicist and academic (retd); b. 31 Jan. 1940, Hämeenlinna; m. Riitta Erkiö 1963; one s. one d.; ed Univ. of Helsinki; mil. service 1957–58; Visiting Scientist, CERN, Geneva 1966–67, 1969–70, 1995–98; Assoc. Prof. of Physics, Univ. of Helsinki 1970–72, Prof. 1973–2008 (retd), fmr Head of Theoretical Physics Div.; Visiting Prof., Univ. of Wis., Madison 1975; Research Prof., Acad. of Finland 1985–90; Sr Scientist 2002–03; Commdr of the Lion of Finland 2012; Acad. Award, Finnish Acad. of Sciences 2008. *Publications:* more than 180 publs in the field of elementary particle physics. *Address:* Department of Physics, PO Box 64, 00014 University of Helsinki, Helsinki (office); Liisankatu 1D 26, 00170 Helsinki, Finland (home).

KAJITA, Takaaki, BSc, MSc, PhD; Japanese physicist and academic; b. 9 March 1959, Higashimatsuyama; ed Saitama Prefectural Kawagoe High School, Saitama Univ., Univ. of Tokyo; with Inst. for Cosmic Ray Research (ICRR), Univ. of Tokyo 1988–, Asst Prof. 1992–99, Prof. 1999–, Dir Center for Cosmic Neutrinos, ICRR 1999–2016, with Kavli Inst. for the Physics and Math. of the Universe 2007–, Dir ICRR 2008–; Asahi Prize (co-recipient) 1987, 1999, Bruno Rossi Prize (co-recipient) 1989, Nishina Memorial Prize 1999, Panofsky Prize (co-recipient) 2002, Japan Acad. Prize 2012, Julius Wess Award 2013, Nobel Prize in Physics (co-recipient with Arthur B. McDonald) 2015, Breakthrough Prize in Fundamental Physics (co-recipient) 2016. *Achievements include:* known for neutrino experiments at the Kamiokande and its successor Super-Kamiokande. *Publications include:* numerous papers in professional journals. *Address:* Institute for Cosmic Ray Research (ICRR), University of Tokyo, 5-1-5 Kashiwanoha, Kashiwa 277-8583, Japan (office). *Telephone:* (4) 7136-5104 (office). *Fax:* (4) 7136-3115 (office). *E-mail:* kajita@icrr.u-tokyo.ac.jp (office). *Website:* www.icrr.u-tokyo.ac.jp (office).

KAJIYAMA, Tisato, PhD, DEng; Japanese polymer chemist, academic and university administrator; *President and Chairman, Fukuoka Women's University;* ed Univ. of Massachusetts, USA, Kyushu Univ.; Prof., Dept of Applied Chem., Faculty of Eng, Kyushu Univ., Pres. Kyushu Univ. and Head, Kyushu Univ. User Science Inst. 2001–10; Pres. Japan Students Services Org. 2008–11; Pres. and Chair. Fukuoka Women's Univ. 2011–; Hon. DSc (Univ. of Massachusetts) 2007. *Publications include:* New Developments in Construction and Functions of Organic Thin Films 1996, Polymer Science and Industrial Research in the Fast-Changing Age: 7th SPSJ Int. Polymer Conference (ed.) 2000, Macromolecular Symposia 159: Polymer Science and Industrial Research (ed.); numerous scientific papers in professional journals on polymer chemistry. *Address:* Fukuoka Women's University, 1-1-1, Kasumigaoka, Higashi-ku, Fukuoka 813-8529, Japan (office). *Telephone:* (9) 2661-2411 (office). *Website:* www.fwu.ac.jp (office).

KAJORNPRASART, Maj.-Gen. Sanan; Thai politician and fmr military officer; b. 7 Sept. 1944, Phichit; ed Chulachomklao Royal Mil. Acad.; aide-de-camp to Gen. Chalard Hiranyasiri; involved in attempted coup 1981; elected mem. Parl. (Democrat Party) for Phichit 1983, 1986, 1988; Deputy Communications Minister 1986, Minister of Agric. and Co-operatives 1989, of Industry 1992–94, of the Interior 1997–2000; Deputy Prime Minister 1990–91, 1997–2000, 2008–11; Sec.-Gen. Democrat Party 1988–2000; Leader, Mahachon Party 2005–07; mem. Chart Thai Pattana (Thai Nation Devt) Party 2008–. *Address:* Chart Thai Pattana, 37/157 Moo 11, Sansab, Minburi, Bangkok, Thailand (office).

KAKÁ; Brazilian/Italian professional footballer (retd); b. (Ricardo Izecson dos Santos Leite), 22 April 1982, Brasilia; s. of Bosco Izecson Pereira Leite and Simone Cristina Santos Leite; m. Caroline Celico 2005 (divorced 2015); one s. one d.; attacking midfielder; began career playing for local club Alphaville aged eight; signed first professional contract with São Paulo FC aged 15, sr team debut Jan. 2001, scored 12 goals in 27 appearances, also led São Paulo to first and only Torneio Rio-São Paulo championship, scored 10 goals in 22 matches 2002, led team to Super Campeonato Paulista title 2002, made 58 appearances for São Paulo, scoring 23 times; with AC Milan, Italy 2003–09, added Champions League title for first time when AC Milan defeated Liverpool 2007, won Club World Cup title, UEFA Super Cup, FIFA Club World Cup and the Seria A title 2007, with Real Madrid 2009–13, joined AC Milan on a free transfer 2013–14, signed by Orlando City SC, Major League Soccer (USA) 2014; debuted with Brazilian nat. team in friendly against Bolivia Jan. 2002; mem. FIFA World Cup-winning squad 2002; Capt. of Brazil for CONCACAF Gold Cup tournament 2003, started in his first FIFA World Cup finals in Germany 2006, participated in FIFA Confederations Cup in S Africa 2009, winner of Golden Ball as player of the tournament, has made 73 appearances and scored 26 goals for Brazil –2009; retd from professional football 2017; Amb. Against Hunger for UN World Food Programme (youngest ever) 2004–; mem. Atletas de Cristo (Athletes of Christ); attained Italian citizenship 2007; Revista Placar Bola de Ouro 2002, Campeonato Brasileiro Bola de Prata (best player by position) 2002, CONCACAF Gold Cup Best XI 2003, Serie A Best New Player 2003, Serie A Foreign Footballer of the Year 2004, 2006, 2007, Serie A Footballer of the Year 2004, 2007, UEFA Champions League Bronze Top Scorer 2005–06, UEFA Champions League Best Midfielder 2005, UEFA Team of the Year 2006, 2007, FIFPro World XI 2006, 2007, 2008, Pallone d'Argento 2006–07, UEFA Champions League Top Scorer 2006–07, UEFA Champions League Best Forward 2006–07, UEFA Club Footballer of the Year 2006–07, FIFPro World Player of the Year 2007, Ballon d'Or 2007, FIFA Club World Cup Golden Ball 2007, Toyota Award 2007, FIFA World Player of the Year 2007, Onze d'Or 2007, IFFHS World's Best Playmaker 2007, IAAF Latin Sportsman of the Year 2007, Time 100 2008, 2009, Maracanã Hall Of Fame 2008, Samba d'Or: 2008, FIFA Team of the Year 2008, FIFA Confederations Cup Golden Ball 2009, FIFA Confederations Cup Best XI 2009, FIFA World Cup Top Assist Provider 2010. *Leisure interests:* favourite music is gospel, favourite book is the Bible. *Address:* c/o Orlando City SC, 618 East South Street, Suite 510, Orlando, FL 32801, USA.

KAKAR, Sudhir, BE, Dipl.Kfm, PhD; Indian psychoanalyst, author and academic; b. 25 July 1938, Nainital, Uttarakhand; m. Katharina Kakar; one s. one d.; ed Gujarat Univ., Univ. of Mannheim, Germany, Sigmund Freud Inst., Frankfurt; Lecturer in Gen. Educ., Faculty of Arts and Sciences, Harvard Univ. 1966–67; Asst Prof., Indian Inst. of Man., Ahmedabad 1968–71; Visiting Lecturer, Sigmund Freud Inst., Frankfurt 1972; Visiting Prof. of Behavioural Sciences, Univ. of Econs, Vienna 1974–75; Prof. and Chair. Dept of Humanities and Social Sciences, Indian Inst. of Tech., New Delhi 1976–77; Visiting Prof., Dept of Psychology, Coll. and School of Divinity, Univ. of Chicago 1989–93; Adjunct Prof., INSEAD, Fontainbleau, France 1994–2014; Kosambi Visiting Research Prof., Goa Univ. 2013; Research Fellow, Program for Applied Psychoanalysis, Grad. School of Business Admin, Harvard Univ. 1967–78; Sr Fellow, Center for Study of Developing Socs, New Delhi 1980–90; Sr Fellow, Center for Study of World Religions, Harvard Univ. 2001–02; Fellow, Centre for Advanced Study in Humanities, Univ. of Cologne 2011–14, Insts of Advanced Study, Princeton and Berlin; mem. Int. Psychoanalytical Asscn, New York Acad. of Sciences, Indian Psychological Soc.; Bd mem. Sigmund Freud Archives, US Library of Congress, Academie Universelle des Culture, France; Hon. Prof., Gandhi Inst. of Tech. and Man., Vishakhapatnam 2014–; Order of Merit (Germany) 2012; Karolyi Foundation Award for Young Writers 1963, Boyer Prize for Psychological Anthropology, American Anthropological Asscn Award 1987, Goethe Medal of Goethe Institut Germany 1998, Abraham Kardiner Award, Columbia Univ. 2002, Distinguished Service Award of Indo-American Psychiatric Asscn 2007. *Publications include:* non-fiction: Fredrick Taylor: A Study in Personality and Innovation 1970, Conflict and Choice: Indian Youth in a Changing Society (co-author) 1971, The Inner World: A Psychoanalytic Study of Childhood and Society in India 1978, Shamans, Mystics and Doctors 1982, Tales of Love, Sex and Danger (co-author) 1986, Intimate Relations: Exploring Indian Sexuality 1989, The Analyst and the Mystic 1991, The Colours of Violence 1995, The Indian Psyche 1996, Culture and Psyche: Selected Essays 1996, The Indians: Portrait of a People (co-author) 2007, Mad and Divine: Spirit and Psyche in the Modern World 2008; fiction: novels: The Ascetic of Desire 1998, Ecstasy 2001, Mira and the Mahatma 2004, The Crimson Throne 2010, The Devil Take Love 2015, The Kipling File 2018; as ed.: Indian Love Stories 1999, Imaginations of Death and Afterlife in India and Europe (co-ed.) 2018; as trans.: Kamasutra: A New Translation (co-author) 2002. *Address:* Pulwaddo Pequeno, Benaulim, Salcete, Goa, 403716, India (home). *E-mail:* sudhir_kakar@rediffmail.com. *Website:* www.sudhirkakar.com (home).

KAKARAYA, Sir Pato, KBE, CMG, CBE; Papua New Guinea government official; b. 16 May 1939, Sambakmanda village, Enga Prov.; m. Immambu Kakaraya; four c.; adviser, Waso Ltd 1967–71; with Wabag Native Trading Co. 1971–72; MP for Wapenamanda 1972–87; Minister for Youth, Recreation and Women's Affairs 1977–78, for Environment and Conservation 1978–80; f. People's Democratic Movt; unsuccessful cand. for Gov.-Gen. 2004, 2011; currently Chair., Community Negotiation Cttee, Wapen; Nat. Patron, PNG Christian Community Services. *Address:* c/o Chairman, PNG Christian Community Services, POB 4699, Boroko NCD, Port Moresby (office); PO Box 787, Boroko NCD, Port Moresby, Papua New Guinea (home). *Telephone:* 76867210 (home); 73363231 (home). *E-mail:* mkakaraya@gmail.com (home).

KAKAYEV, Yagshygeldy; Turkmenistani oil and gas engineer and government official; *Deputy Chairman of the Government, responsible for the Oil and Gas Sector and Fisheries;* b. 1959, Georogly Dist, Daşoguz Velayat (Prov.), Turkmen SSR, USSR; ed Turkmen Polytechnic Institute; began career as an engineer and Jr Research Fellow in Turkmenistan br. of Russian Scientific Research Inst. of Gas –1986, Research Fellow and Sr Research Fellow at same inst. (renamed Turkmen Scientific Research and Design Br.) 1986–92; Head of Dept, Oil and Gas Inst. 1992–96, apptd Head of Oil and Gas Processing Dept, Ministry of Oil and Gas Industry and Mineral Resources 1996; apptd State Minister and Chair. Türkmengaz/Turkmengaz (state gas co.) 2007; fmr Dir State Agency for Man. and Use of Hydrocarbon Resources; Deputy Chair. Cabinet of Ministers –2013 (dismissed); Deputy Chair. of the Govt, responsible for the Oil and Gas Sector and Fisheries 2016–; Medals 'For the Love of Motherland' and 'Gayrat'. *Address:* Office of the President and the Council of Ministers, 744000 Aşgabat, Galkynyş köç. 20, Turkmenistan (office). *Telephone:* (12) 35-45-34 (office). *Fax:* (12) 35-51-12 (office). *E-mail:* nt@online.tm (office). *Website:* www.turkmenistan.gov.tm (office).

KAKIUCHI, Takehiko; Japanese business executive; *President and CEO, Mitsubishi Corporation;* b. 31 July 1955; ed Kyoto Univ.; joined Mitsubishi Corpn 1979, Sr Vice-Pres. and Div. COO, Foods (Commodity) Div. 2010–11, Sr Vice-Pres. and Gen. Man., Living Essential Group, (concurrently) Div. COO, Foods (Commodity) Div. 2011–13, Exec. Vice-Pres. and Group CEO, Living Essentials Group 2013–16, Pres. and CEO Mitsubishi Corpn April 2016–, apptd mem. Bd of Dirs June 2016. *Address:* Mitsubishi Corporation, Mitsubishi Shoji Building, 3-1, Marunouchi 2-chome, Chiyoda-ku, Tokyo 100-8086, Japan (office). *Telephone:* (3) 3210-2121 (office). *Fax:* (3) 3210-8583 (office). *E-mail:* info@mitsubishicorp.com (office). *Website:* www.mitsubishicorp.com (office).

KAKLAMANIS, Apostolos; Greek politician and lawyer; b. 7 Sept. 1936, Lefkas; s. of Christos Kaklamanis and Evageloula Kaklamanis; m. Athina-Anna Gavera 1972; one s. one d.; ed Univ. of Athens; Gen. Sec. Ministry of Welfare 1964–65; political prisoner during colonels' dictatorship; Founding mem. Pasok and mem. Cen. Cttee and Exec. Cttee; mem. Vouli (Parl.) for Athens B 1974–2014; Minister of Labour 1981–82, of Educ. and Religious Affairs 1982–86, of Justice 1986–87, Minister in charge of the Prime Minister's Office 1987–88, Minister of Health, Welfare and Social Services 1988–89, of Labour 1989–90; Speaker of Parl. 1993–2004. *Address:* c/o Vouli, Parliament Bldg, Syntagma Square, 100 21 Athens; Solomou 58, 106 82 Athens, Greece (office).

KAKU, Michio, BS, PhD; American theoretical physicist, academic, writer and broadcaster; *Henry Semat Professor of Theoretical Physics, City College, City University of New York;* b. 24 Jan. 1947, San Jose, Calif.; m. Shizue Kaku; two d.; ed Harvard Univ., Univ. of California, Berkeley Radiation Lab.; Lecturer, Princeton Univ. 1973; fmr Visiting Prof., Inst. for Advanced Study, Princeton Univ. and New York Univ.; currently Henry Semat Prof. of Theoretical Physics, City Coll., CUNY, New York; Fellow, American Physical Soc.; hon. degrees from Hofstra Univ., State Univ. of NY, Old Westbury; Award for Outstanding Educator, American Asscn of Physics Teachers. *Radio:* host of Explorations in Science (weekly programme on WBAI), Science Fantastic (broadcasting to 130 radio stations across USA and the Internet). *Television:* Making Time (BBC four-part series) 2006, numerous appearances and contribs to documentaries. *Achievements include:* Co-founder of string field theory. *Publications include:* Nuclear Power: Both Sides (with Jennifer Trainer) 1982, To Win a Nuclear War: The Pentagon's Secret War Plans (with Daniel Axelrod) 1986, Beyond Einstein: The Cosmic Quest for the Theory of the Universe 1987, Introduction to Superstrings and M-Theory 1988, Strings, Conformal Fields and M-Theory 1991, Quantum Field Theory: A Modern Introduction 1993, Hyperspace: A Scientific Odyssey Through Parallel Universes, Time Warps and the Tenth Dimension 1994, Visions: How Science Will Revolutionize the 21st Century 1997, Einstein's Cosmos: How Albert Einstein's Vision Transformed Our Understading of Space and Time 2004, Parallel Worlds: A Journey Through Creation, Higher Dimensions and the Future of the Cosmos 2004, Physics of the Impossible 2008, Physics of the Future 2011, The Future of the Mind 2014; contrib. of articles to numerous journals and magazines, including Astronomy, Discover, BBC Focus Magazine (UK), Cosmos (Australia), New Scientist (UK), TIME magazine, Wall Street Journal, Popular Mechanics, New York Times, Daily Telegraph (UK), The Times (UK), Boston Globe. *Address:* Department of Physics, City College of New York, 160 Convent Avenue, New York, NY 10031, USA (office). *Telephone:* (212) 650-7000 (office). *E-mail:* kaku@sci.ccny.cuny.edu (office); mkaku@aol.com (home). *Website:* www1.ccny.cuny.edu/prospective/science/physics (office); www.mkaku.org.

KALABA, Harry; Zambian politician; b. 12 June 1976; m.; mem. Nat. Ass. for Bahati constituency 2011–19; fmr Deputy Minister in Office of Vice-Pres.; Minister of Lands, Natural Resources and Environmental Protection 2013–14, Minister of Foreign Affairs 2014–18; mem. Patriotic Front –2019, Democratic Party 2019– (adopted as candidate for 2021 presidential election). *Leisure interests:* football, reading. *Address:* c/o Nat. Ass., Parliament Rd, POB 31299, Lusaka 10101, Zambia (office).

KALADZE, Kakhaber (Kakha); Georgian politician and fmr professional football player; *Secretary-General, Qartuli Ocneba-Demokratiuli Sakartvelo (Georgian Dream-Democratic Georgia);* b. 27 Feb. 1978, Samtredia, Imereti, Georgian SSR, USSR; m. Anouki Kaladze; three s.; ed Ivane Javakhishvili Tbilisi State Univ.; began football career 1993, centre back, left back; played for: Dinamo Tbilisi 1993–98 (won Georgian League 1993/94, 1994/95, 1995/96, 1996/97, 1997/98, Georgian Cup 1994, 1995, 1996, 1997), Dynamo Kyiv 1998–2001 (won Ukrainian Premier League 1998/99, 1999/2000, 2000/01, Ukrainian Cup 1998, 1999, 2000), AC Milan 2001–10 (won Serie A 2003/04, Coppa Italia 2002/03, Italian Supercup 2004, UEFA Champions League 2003, 2007, UEFA Super Cup 2003, 2007, FIFA Club World Cup 2007), Genoa 2010–12; played for Georgia U-17 team 1993–94, Georgia U-19 team 1995, Georgia U-21 team 1995–96, Georgia Nat. Team 1996–2011, Capt. 50 times in 84 appearances, announced retirement Dec. 2011; Owner Kala Capital, Kala Foundation, Founder Kala Fund (charity) 2008; Amb. for SOS Children's Villages; mem. Qartuli Ocneba—Demokratiuli Sakartvelo (QO-DS—Georgian Dream—Democratic Georgia) party 2012–, Sec.-Gen. 2013–; mem. Parl. 2012–; Deputy Prime Minister and Minister of Energy Oct. 2012–17; selected as candidate of QU-DS in Tbilisi mayoral election scheduled for Oct. 2017, Mayor of Tbilisi Nov. 2017–, mem. Supervisory Bd, JSC Progress Bank 2008–; Order of Vakhtang Gorgasali (Second Rank); voted Georgian Footballer of the Year 2001–03, 2006, 2011. *Address:* Qartuli Ocneba-Demokratiuli Sakartvelo (QO-DS), 0105 Tbilisi, Erekle II Moedani 3, Georgia (office). *Telephone:* (32) 220-50-73 (office). *E-mail:* info@gd.ge. *Website:* 41.ge (office).

KALAMANOV, Vladimir Avdashevich, DrHist; Russian government official; *Director-General, International Sustainable Energy Development Centre;* b. 1951, Moscow; ed Moscow State Inst. of Int. Relations; Head of Dept Ministry of Problems with Nationalities; Plenipotentiary Rep. of Pres. in Repubs of N Ossetia and of Ingushetia 1997–99; Dir Fed. Migration Service of Russian Fed. 1999–2002; Special Rep. of Pres. to supervise observance of human rights and freedom in Chechen Repub. 2000; Amb. and Perm. Rep. of Russian Fed. to UNESCO, Paris 2002–09, now Dir-Gen. Int. Sustainable Energy Devt Centre under the Auspices of UNESCO (ISEDC), Moscow. *Address:* International Sustainable Energy Development Centre under the Auspices of UNESCO, 117292 Moscow, Building 2, 8/1 Kedrova Street, Russia (office). *Telephone:* (495) 641-04-26 (office). *E-mail:* info@isedc-u.com (office). *Website:* www.isedc-u.com (office).

KALANICK, Travis Cordell; American business executive; b. 6 Aug. 1976, Los Angeles, Calif.; s. of Donald E. Kalanick and Bonnie Kalanick (née Horwitz); ed Univ. of California, Los Angeles; Co-Founder Scour.net (file-sharing service) 1998–2000; Founder and CEO Red Swoosh (file-sharing tech.) 2001–07 (co. acquired by Akamai Technologies 2007), Head of P2P Initiatives, Akamai Technologies 2007–08; Co-Founder and CEO Uber Technologies, Inc. 2009–17; mem. Pres. Donald Trump's econ. advisory group Jan.–Feb. 2017 (resgnd); named World Econ. Forum Technology Pioneer 2005. *Address:* c/o Uber Technologies, Inc, 555 Market Street, San Francisco, CA 94105, USA (office).

KALANTARI, Issa, PhD; Iranian scientist and agriculturalist; *Director, Farmers' House;* b. 1952, Marand; s. of Mohammad Hussein Kalantari and Kobra Kalantari (née Esfandi); m. 1982; one s. one d.; ed Univ. of Urmiya, Univ. of Nebraska and Iowa State Univ., USA; Dir Farmers' House (agricultural union) 1981–; Head of Agricultural Extension Org. 1982, Plant and Seed Improvement Research Inst. 1983, Deputy Minister for Agricultural Research, Educ. and Extension 1983–85, Man. Dir and Head of Bd of Dirs Moghan Stock-farming and Agro-Industry Complex, Ministry of Agric. 1985–88; Minister of Agric. 1988–2001; Pres. World Food Council 1991–95. *Publications:* A Policy for Reforming Nutrition Patterns: Nutrition Physiology and Foodstuff Economics 1997; series of articles in journal Agricultural Economics and Development. *Leisure interests:* reading, sport. *Address:* Farmers' House, 21, 33rd Street, Jahan Ara Avenue, Tehran (office); 5, Morshed, Sheidai Street, Gholhak, Tehran, Iran (home). *Telephone:* (21) 886390612 (office); (21) 22001057 (home). *Fax:* (21) 88639060 (office). *E-mail:* issakalantari@gmail.com (home).

KALASHNIKOV, Sergey Vyacheslavovich, DPsych; Russian politician; b. 3 July 1951, Akmolinsk, Kazakh SSR; m. Natalia Kalashnikova; three c.; ed Leningrad State Univ., Inst. of Psychology, USSR (now Russian) Acad. of Sciences, Acad. of Nat. Econs USSR Council of Ministers, Russian Diplomatic Acad.; Head, Social-Psychological service of the Research Inst., USSR Ministry of Defence Industry, concurrently Chair. Inst. of Advanced Studies, USSR Ministry of Oil and Chemical Industry, Dir Intermanager State Enterprise 1979–91; Chair. European-Asian Bank; concurrently Dir-Gen. Asscn of Defence against Unemployment and Poverty, Chair. Cttee on Labour and Social Policy in the State Duma, Deputy of the Duma, Chair. Perm. Cttee on Social Policy, Interparliamentary Ass. of CIS 1993–98; Minister of Labour and Social Devt 1998–2000; Deputy Sec.-Gen. Union of Russia and Belarus 2000–03; apptd Head, Dept of Social Devt, Office of the Govt 2003; Pres. Russian Fed. of the Sports Lover, Russian Asscn of Professional Golf; Chair. Nat. Council for Political and Social Reform; Co-Chair. Int. Forum 'World Experience and the Russian Economy'; mem. Bd Moscow English Club, Jury All-Russian Competition 'Best Russian Firms'; mem. Int. Acad. of Informatics, Russian Acad. of Science; Order of Friendship; Badge of Excellence for Border Services, Distinguished Worker of the Russian Ministry of Labour, Laureate, Nat. Peter the Great Prize. *Publications:* more than 50 works including two monographs and textbook Social Psychology of Management.

KALAUR, Pavel U., PhD; Belarusian economist, banking executive and central banker; *Chairman, National Bank of the Republic of Belarus;* b. 1962, Stolin Dist, Brest Region; m.; two c.; ed Polesian State Univ., Belarusian State Econ. Univ.; Economist, Credit Div., Stolbtsy Branch of State Bank of USSR 1985–86, Deputy Gov. Berezino Branch 1986–87, Gov. Volozhin Branch 1987; Gov. Volozhin Branch, Agricultural Bank of USSR 1988–91, Volozhin Branch, JSC Belagroprombank 1991–93; Deputy Chair. Nat. Bank of the Repub. of Belarus 1993–99, mem. Bd 1993–2010, First Deputy Chair. 1999–2010, Chair. 2014–; Chair. Bank BelVEB OJSC 2010–14; Hon. Worker, Banking System of Repub. of Belarus; Certificate of Merit, Nat. Ass. of Repub. of Belarus. *Address:* National Bank of the Republic of Belarus, 220008 Minsk, pr. Nezalezhnastsi 20, Belarus (office). *Telephone:* (17) 219-23-03 (office). *Fax:* (17) 327-48-79 (office). *E-mail:* email@nbrb.by (office). *Website:* www.nbrb.by (office).

KALEYFAANU, Thalhath Ibrahim; Maldivian military officer (retd) and government official; joined Nat. Security Service 1989, First Lt, Nat. Defence Force –2006; Minister of Defence and Nat. Security 2011–12.

KALFIN, Ivailo Georgiev, MSc; Bulgarian politician; *Deputy Prime Minister for Demographic and Social Policy and Minister of Labour and Social Policy;* b. 30 May 1964, Sofia; m.; one d.; ed French Language School, Sofia, Univ. of Nat. and World Economy, Sofia, Business Univ., Vienna, Austria, Univ. of Loughborough, UK, Coll. of Europe, Bruges, Belgium; scholarship student under Chevening program, UK and German Marshall Fund, USA; taught Finance at Int. Univ., Sofia; worked for Machinoexport as well as in pvt. sector in the field of foreign trade, finance and consulting; mem. Municipal Council of Balgarska Sotsialisticheska Partiya (BSP—Bulgarian Socialist Party), Supreme Council of BSP, Political Council of the Bulgarian Euroleft; Spokesperson for Zaedno za Balgariya (Together for Bulgaria) pre-election coalition 1996; mem. Parl. for Sofia (Parl. Group of the Demokratichna Levitsa—Democratic Left) 1994–97, 2000–01, 2005–, mem. Foreign Policy Cttee, Budgeting and Finance Cttee, Deputy Chair. Bulgarian-EU Jt Parl. Cttee; Sec. for Econ. Affairs to the Pres. 2002–05; Deputy Prime Minister and Minister of Foreign Affairs 2005–09; mem. European Parl. (Group of the Progressive Alliance of Socialists and Democrats) 2009–14; unsuccessful BSP cand. in presidential election 2011; Deputy Prime Minister for Demographic and Social Policy and Minister of Labour and Social Policy 2014–; Founder Social Democrats Political Movt; Man. and Sr Partner in consulting cos 1990–94, 1997–2000; Sr Prof., Univ., Sofia 2000–; observer of elections in Kosovo as mem. OSCE Missions 2001, 2003; mem. Advisory Bd Bulgarian Nat. Bank 2004–, Bulgaria Beyond the Facts Early Warning System implemented by UNDP and USAID; Founding mem. Bulgarian Macroeconomics Asscn; mem. Bd Dirs, Inst. for Econs and Int. Relations; recipient of nat. honours from several European countries. *Publications:* Factors of Economic Growth in Bulgaria (co-author) 2000, Bulgaria 2010: Economic Challenges (report to Pres. of Bulgaria) (co-author) 2005; numerous articles in Bulgaria and in int. trade journals on EU and macroeconomic issues. *Address:* Council of Ministers, 1594 Sofia, bul. Dondukov 1, Bulgaria (office). *Telephone:* (2) 940-29-99 (office). *Fax:* (2) 980-21-01 (office). *E-mail:* gis@government.bg (office). *Website:* www.government.bg (office).

KALIMBETOVA, Tajikan B.; Kyrgyzstani politician; b. 1964; Deputy Minister of Finance 2006–07, also head of financial intelligence service 2005–07, Minister of Finance 2007–09, Chair. Iran-Kyrgyzstan Jt Econ. Comm.; Deputy Chair. EurAsian Group 2006–07; Chair. Social Fund 2007–09; Deputy Prime Minister 2009–10.

KALIŇÁK, Robert; Slovak lawyer and politician; *Vice-Chairman, Smer-Sociálna Demokracia (Smer-SD—Direction-Social Democracy);* b. 11 May 1971, Bratislava; ed Faculty of Law, Comenius Univ., Bratislava; Man. ACE Press (legal publrs) 1991; Asst, Commercial Law Office 1992–95; Articled Clerk, Maríková and Pnrs (law firm), Bratislava 1995–99; Attorney, MKKT (law firm) 1999–2002; mem. Národná Rada Slovenskej Republiky (Nat. Council of the Slovak Repub.) 2002–06,

Chair. Cttee for Defence and Security 2002–04, Special Supervision Cttee of Nat. Security Office 2004–06; mem. Regional Council of Bratislava 2005–; Deputy Prime Minister and Minister of the Interior 2006–10, 2012–16, Minister of the Interior 2016–18; Vice-Chair. Smer-Sociálna Demokracia (Smer-SD—Direction-Social Democracy); mem. Slovak Bar Asscn. *Address:* Súmračná 25, 812 02 Bratislava, Slovakia (office). *Telephone:* (2) 4342-6297 (office). *Fax:* (2) 4342-6300 (office). *E-mail:* generalny.manager@strana-smer.sk (office). *Website:* strana-smer.sk (office).

KALINOWSKI, Jarosław; Polish politician; b. 12 April 1962, Wyszków; s. of Witold Kalinowski and Zofia Kalinowski; m. Aleksandra Kalinowska; three s. two d.; ed Warsaw Agricultural Univ., Inst. of Law Sciences of the Polish Acad. of Sciences; owner of farm in Jackowo Górne; mem. Union of Rural Youth 1981–89; Admin. Somianka village 1990–97; Deputy to Sejm (Parl.) 1993–2009, Deputy Speaker 2005–09; Deputy Prime Minister and Minister of Agric. and Food Economy (later Rural Devt) 1997, 2001–03; mem. European Parl. 2009–; mem. (fmr Pres.) Polish People's Party (Polskie Stronnictwo Ludowe—PSL) 1997–, Chair. PSL Parl. Club 2000–04, Chair. Caucus 2000–01; cand. in Polish presidential election 2000; Deputy to Local Ass. of the Voivodship of Mazovia 1998–2000; Merit for Polish Agriculture. *Leisure interests:* culture and folk music. *Address:* ul. Kopernika 36/40 p. 407, 00-924 Warsaw, Poland (office). *Telephone:* (22) 6206755 (office). *Fax:* (22) 6206755 (office). *E-mail:* eurobiuro.warszawa@kalinowski.pl. *Website:* www.kalinowski.pl.

KALJULAID, Kersti, PhD; Estonian public servant and head of state; *President;* b. 30 Dec. 1969, Tartu; m. 2nd Georgi-Rene Maksimovsk; two s.; one s. one d. from previous m.; ed Univ. of Tartu; Sales Man., Eesti Telefon (state-owned telecoms co.) 1996–97; Project Man., Hoiupanga Investeeringute AS 1997–98; Assoc., Hansabank Markets (investment banking co.) 1998–99; Econ. Adviser to Prime Minister Mart Laar 1999–2002; Chief Financial Officer and CEO, Iru Power Plant, Eesti Energia (state-owned energy co.) 2002–04; Estonian Rep. at European Court of Auditors 2004–16, Auditor, EU Galileo project 2004–07, Chair., Court of Auditors Admin. Affairs Cttee 2006–08, responsible for audit of Structural Policies 2007–10; co-author of social-political radio talk show Keskpäevatund (Midday Hour), Kuku radio station 2002–04; Ed. Eurominutid (Euro-minutes) radio show 2007–16; Pres. of Estonia 2016–; mem. Supervisory Bd Estonian Genome Center 2000–02; mem. Advisory Bd, Univ. of Tartu 2009–11, Council Chair. 2012–; mem. Pro Patria Union 2001–04; Collar, Order of the Nat. Coat of Arms (Estonia) 2016. *Leisure interest:* running marathons. *Address:* Office of the President, A. Weizenbergi 39, Tallinn 15050, Estonia (office). *Telephone:* 631-6202 (office). *Fax:* 631-6250 (office). *E-mail:* vpinfo@vpk.ee (office). *Website:* www.president.ee (office).

KALJURAND, Marina, LLB, MA; Estonian diplomatist and politician; b. (Marina Rajevskaja), 6 Sept. 1962, Tallinn; m. Kalle Kaljurand; one s. one d.; ed Tartu Univ., Estonian School of Diplomacy, Fletcher School of Law and Diplomacy, Tufts Univ., USA, Univ. of Lapland, Finland, Univ. of Pittsburgh, USA, Durham Univ., UK; Lecturer in Law, Tallinn Econ. Tech. School 1986–91; Dir Int. Treaties Div., Ministry of Foreign Affairs 1991–96, Counsellor, Embassy in Helsinki 1996–99, Dir-Gen. Legal Dept, Ministry of Foreign Affairs 1999–2001, Deputy Under-Sec. of Legal and Consular Affairs 2002–05, Amb. Israel 2004–06, to Russian Fed. 2005–08, to Kazakhstan (non-resident) 2007–11, Under-Sec. for Foreign Econ. Relations and Devt Aid, Ministry of Foreign Affairs 2008–11, Amb. to Canada 2011–13, to USA 2011–15; Minister of Foreign Affairs 2015–16; unsuccessful cand. for Pres. of Estonia 2016; chief negotiator in Estonia's accession negotiations to OECD; fmr Lecturer in Public Int. Law, Estonian School of Diplomacy; fmr Lecturer in Int. Treaties Law, Estonian Law Center; Founding mem. Estonian Br. of Int. Law Asscn 1996–; Order of the White Star (Third Class) 2004, Order of the Nat. Coat of Arms (Third Class) 2008. *Leisure interests:* int. law, badminton, aerobics, dogs (scotties), Nordic walking.

KALLA, Muhammad Jusuf, BEcons; Indonesian politician and business executive; *Vice-President;* b. 15 May 1942, Watampone, South Sulawesi; ed Hassanudin Univ., Makassar (fmrly Ujungpandang), South Sulawesi; began career as Chair. Advisory Council of Indonesian Chamber of Commerce and Industry (KADIN) at prov. level (South Sulawesi) and Coordinator of KADIN for Eastern Indonesia; Rep. of South Sulawesi in Peoples' Consultative Ass.; served in House of Reps for four consecutive terms (including chair. of communication forum for reps at regional level); apptd Chief of Nat. Logistics Agency (Bulog) 1999–2000; Minister of Trade and Industry 1999–2000 (forced to resign by Pres. Wahid on suspicion of corruption); Coordinating Minister for People's Welfare 2001–04; Vice-Pres. of Indonesia 2004–09, 2014–; Chair. Indonesian Red Cross 2009–14, Cen. Exec. Indonesian Mosque Council 2012–; mem. Partai Golongan Karya (Golkar), Pres. and Chair. 2004–; Chair. PT Makassar Mina Usaha, PT Kalla Inti Karsa and NV Hadji Kalla Trading Co.; Dr hc (Universiti Malaya Malaysia) 2007, (Soka Univ.) 2009, (Univ. of Educ., Indonesia) 2011, (Univ. of Hasanuddin Makassar) 2011, (Univ. of Syah Kuala Aceh) 2011, (Univ. of Brawijaya) 2011, (Univ. of Indonesia) 2013. *Address:* Istana Wakil Presiden, Jalan Medan Merdeka Selatan 14, Jakarta 10110, Indonesia (office). *Telephone:* (21) 34830565 (office). *Fax:* (21) 3503940 (office). *E-mail:* tirta_hidayat@yahoo.go.id (office). *Website:* www.wapresri.go.id (office).

KALLAS, Kaja, BA, MBA; Estonian lawyer and politician; *Chairman, Eesti Reformierakond (Estonian Reform Party);* b. 18 June 1977, Tallinn, Estonian SSR, USSR; d. of Siim Kallas and Kristi Kallas; divorced; one c.; ed Univ. of Tartu, Estonian Business School; Legal expert, Tark & Co (law firm) 1998–99, Lawyer 1999–2006, Partner and Barrister 2004–06; Barrister, Luiga Mody Hääl Borenius (law firm) 2006–08, Head of Competition Law Div. and Partner 2008–11; Lecturer, EBS Management Training Centre 2010–14; mem. Riigikogu (Parl.) for Tallinn 2011–14; mem. European Parl. 2014–18; mem. Estonian Bar Asscn 1999–2011, Estonian Young Lawyers Asscn 2004–08, European Antitrust Alliance 2004–06; mem. Eesti Reformierakond (Estonian Reform Party) 2010–, Chair. 2018–. *Publication:* MEP. 4 aastat Euroopa Parlamendis (MEP: Four Years in the European Parliament) 2018. *Address:* Eesti Reformierakond, Tõnismägi 9, Tallinn 10119, Estonia (office). *Telephone:* 680-8080 (office). *Fax:* 680-8081 (office). *E-mail:* info@reform.ee (office). *Website:* www.reform.ee (office).

KALLAS, Siim; Estonian banker, politician and fmr EU official; *Second Vice-President, Riigikogu;* b. 2 Oct. 1948, Tallinn; s. of Udo Kallas and Rita Kallas; m. Kristi Kartus 1972; one s. one d.; ed Tartu State Univ.; Chief Specialist, Ministry of Finance, Estonian SSR 1975–79; Gen. Man. Estonian Savings Banks 1979–86; Deputy Ed. Rahva Hääl 1986–89; Chair. Asscn of Estonian Trade Unions 1989–91; Pres. Eesti Pank (Bank of Estonia) 1991–95; Founder and Chair., Estonian Reform Party (Eesti Reformierakond) 1994–2004; elected to Riigikogu (Parl.) 1995–99, 2019–, Second Vice-Pres. of the Riigikogu 2019–; also mem. Parl. Nat. Defence Cttee and Parl. Foreign Affairs Cttee 2003–04; Minister of Foreign Affairs 1995–96, of Finance 1999–2002; Prime Minister of Estonia 2002–03; Visiting Prof., Tartu State Univ.; EU Commr without Portfolio 2004, Vice-Pres. for Admin. Affairs, Audit and Anti-Fraud 2004–10, Commr for Transport and Vice-Pres. EC 2010–14, Acting Commr for Econ. and Monetary Affairs and the Euro April–May 2014, 1–16 July 2014; Vinni Rural Municipality Mayor 2017–19; cand. in presidential election 2016; Cross of the Order of Merit (Germany) 2000, Grand Officier, Légion d'honneur 2001, Order of the Nat. Coat of Arms (2nd Class) 2003, (1st Class) 2015; chosen as one of 100 Great Estonians of the 20th Century 2002. *Leisure interests:* reading, theatre, classical music and jazz, cycling, hiking. *Address:* State Assembly (Riigikogu), Lossi plats 1a, Tallinn 15165, Estonia (office). *Telephone:* 631-6321 (office). *E-mail:* siim.kallas@riigikogu.ee (office). *Website:* www.riigikogu.ee (office).

KALLASVUO, Olli-Pekka, LLM; Finnish business executive; *Chairman, Zenterio AB;* b. 13 July 1953, Lavia; ed Univ. of Helsinki; fmrly with Union Bank of Finland; Corp. Counsel Nokia 1980, Asst Vice-Pres. Legal Dept 1987, Asst Vice-Pres. Finance 1988–90, mem. Group Exec. Bd 1990–, Sr Vice-Pres. Finance 1990–91, Exec. Vice-Pres. and Chief Financial Officer Nokia 1992–96, 1999–2003, Corp. Exec. Vice-Pres. Nokia Americas 1997–98, Exec. Vice-Pres. and Gen. Man. of Mobile Phones 2004–05, Pres. and COO Nokia 2005–06, Pres. and CEO 2006–10, mem. Bd Dirs 2007–11, Chair. Nokia Siemens Networks 2007–11; Vice-Chair. SRV Group 2011–, Telia-Sonera AB 2012–; Chair. Zenterio AB 2013–; mem. Bd Confed. of Finnish Industries (EK) 2009; mem. European Round Table of Industrialists, Council of the EU-Russia Industrialists' Round Table; mem. Aperios-group; Hon. LLD (Helsinki). *Leisure interests:* golf, tennis, reading political history. *Address:* Zenterio AB, Brahegatan 2, 114 37 Stockholm, Sweden (office). *Telephone:* (1) 336-39-50 (office). *Website:* www.zenterio.com (office).

KALLIO, Heikki Olavi, LLM; Finnish historian, writer and fmr organization official; *Legal Adviser, Academy of Finland;* b. 9 June 1937, Turku; m. 1st Liisa Toivonen 1961 (divorced 1995); three s. one d.; m. 2nd Anneli Hämäläinen 1997; ed Helsinki Univ., Tallinn Univ. (Estonia); Chief Admin. Officer, Univ. of Turku 1963–71; Admin. Dir Acad. of Finland 1971–72, Exec. Vice-Pres. (Admin.) 1973–2002, currently Legal Adviser; Admin. Dir State Tech. Research Centre 1973; historian and writer 2002–; Dr hc (Tallinn); Finnish Order of White Cross, Kt 1st Class, Hungarian Order of Merit, Kt Commdr, Ordo Supremus Militaris Templi Hierosolymitani, Kt Grand Cross, Medal of Honour, Merited Service of the State of Finland, Cross of Merit, Finnish Physical Culture and Sports. *Publications:* Finnish–Estonian Scientific Relations with Special Focus on the Occupation Years 1940–91. *Leisure interests:* sailing, navigation, safety and security at sea, historiography. *Address:* Meritullinkatu 4B25, 00170 Helsinki, Finland. *Telephone:* (40) 5569755. *E-mail:* heikki.kallio@pp1.inet.fi.

KALLIOMÄKI, Antti Tapana; Finnish politician; b. 8 Jan. 1947, Siikainen; m. Helena Marjatta Kalliomäki 1969; two s.; physical training teacher, Hämeenkylä Upper Comprehensive School 1973–91; Project Man. Finnish Sports Asscn 1981–83; mem. Vantaa City Council 1984–2000; Chair. Vantaa Municipal Org. 1988–92; mem. Suomen Eduskunta (Parl.) 1983, Chair. SDP Parl. Group 1991–95, 1999–2003, Vice-Chair. Cttee for the Future 1993–95, mem. Parl. Cttee on Defence Policy 1986–87, Cttee on Sports 1988–90, Parl. Advisory Bd on Defence Policy 1989–91; Chair. Parl. Security Policy Monitoring Group 2002–03; mem. SDP Party Cttee/Party Exec. 1990–2002; apptd Vice-Chair. European SDP 2001; Sec. to Prime Minister 1986–87; Minister of Trade and Industry 1995–99; Deputy Prime Minister and Minister of Finance 2003–05; Minister of Educ. 2005–07; mem. Parl. Supervisory Council, Bank of Finland 1987–91, Admin. Council, Finnish Broadcasting Co. (YLE) 2002–03 (Vice-Chair. 2002–03); Chair. Supervisory Bd Neste 1994–95.

KALLIS, Jacques Henry; South African professional cricketer; b. 16 Oct. 1975, Pinelands, Cape Town, Cape Prov.; ed Wynberg Boys' High School; all-rounder; right-handed batsman and right-arm fast-medium bowler; teams played for various age-group teams (Western Prov. Under-13, Under-19, S Africa Schools, Under-17, Under-19, Under-24), Western Prov./Cape Cobras 1993–2015, Middx 1997, Glamorgan 1999, South Africa 1995–2013, Royal Challengers Bangalore 2008–10, Kolkata Knight Riders 2011–14, Sydney Thunder 2014–15, Trinidad and Tobago Red Steel 2015; First-class debut: 1993/94; Test debut: S Africa v England, Durban 14 Dec. 1995; One-Day Int. (ODI) debut: S Africa v England, Cape Town 9 Jan. 1996; T20I debut: S Africa v NZ, Johannesburg 21 Oct. 2005; played 166 Tests, scored 13,289 runs (average 55.37) and took 292 wickets (average 32.65), with two double centuries, 45 centuries, and 58 fifties, highest score 224 against Sri Lanka, Cape Town 2012, and five five-wicket performances, best bowling 6/54 against England, Leeds 2003; played 328 ODIs, scored 11,574 runs (average 44.86) and took 273 wickets (average 31.79), with 17 centuries and 86 fifties, highest score 139 West Indies, Johannesburg 2004, and two five-wicket performances, best bowling 5/30 against West Indies, Dhaka 1998; played 25 T20Is, scored 666 runs (average 35.05) and took 12 wickets (average 27.75), with five fifties, highest score 73 against India, Gros Islet 2010, best bowling 4/15 against Zimbabwe, Hambantota 2012; played 257 First-class matches, scored 19,695 runs (average 54.10) and took 427 wickets (average 31.69), with 62 centuries and 97 fifties, and eight five-wicket performances; in 2004 became first batsman since Sir Donald Bradman to hit five centuries in consecutive test innings; selected for World XI team 2005; ranked World No. 1 Batsman for first time Jan. 2005; became the fourth player and first South African to score 13,000 Test runs, in first Test against NZ 2 Jan. 2013; first and only player in cricket history to achieve 10,000 runs and take 200 wickets in both Tests and ODIs; retd from Test and First-class cricket Dec. 2013; Founder Jacques Kallis Scholarship Foundation 2006; South Africa Cricketer of the Year 1999, 2000, 2004, Int. Cricket Council (ICC) Player of the Year 2005, Sir Garfield Sobers Trophy 2004, ICC Test Player of the Year 2005, named by Wisden as Leading Cricketer in the World for his performances in 2007 and 2008, a Wisden Cricketer of the Year 2013. *Leisure interest:* golf. *Address:* c/o United Cricket Board of South Africa, Gauteng, South Africa; c/o Dave Rundle (office). *Telephone:* (11) 8802810. *E-mail:* proteas@cricket.co.za; rms@mweb.co.za (office). *Website:* www.cricket.co.za; www.kallis.co.za.

KALLON, Kelfala Morana, PhD; Sierra Leonean academic and central banker; *Governor of Bank of Sierra Leone;* ed Methodist Coll., North Carolina, Univ. of Virginia; held faculty positions at Univ. of West Florida 1983–87, Gettysburg Coll. 1987–93; Prof. of Econs, Coll. of Humanities & Social Sciences, Univ. of North Colorado 1993–2018; Governor, Bank of Sierra Leone 2018–; Dupont Fellow, Univ. of Virginia 1979, 1980. *Publications:* The Economics of Sierra Leonean Entrepreneurship 1990, The Political Economy of Corruption in Sierra Leone 2004. *Address:* Bank of Sierra Leone, Siaka Stevens Street, Freetown Sierra Leone (office). *Telephone:* (22) 226501 (office). *Fax:* (22) 224764 (office). *E-mail:* info@bsl.gov.sl (office). *Website:* www.bsl.gov.sl (office).

KALLSBERG, Anfinn; Faroese politician; b. 19 Nov. 1947, Klaksvík; s. of Gunnar Kallsberg and Katrina Kallsberg; with J.F. Kjølbro 1964–74; self-employed bookkeeper, Vidareidi 1974–96; Mayor of Vidareidi 1974–80; mem. Løgting (Faroese Rep. Council) 1980–, Speaker (Chair.) 1991–93, Chair. Finance Cttee 1989–91, 2004–, mem. Foreign Affairs Cttee 2004; Prime Minister and Minister of Constitutional Affairs, Foreign Affairs and Municipal Affairs 1998–2004; one of two reps of Faroe Islands in Danish Folketing (Parl.) from 2005; mem. Nordic Council 1991, 1994–98; mem. Man. Cttee Klaksvik Hosp. 1991–96; mem. Fólkaflokkurin (People's Party); Kt of the Dannebrog 2005. *Address:* FO-750, Vidareidi; Fólkaflokkurin (People's Party), Jónas Broncksgøta 29, 100 Tórshavn, Faroe Islands (office). *Telephone:* 318210 (office). *Fax:* 451032 (office). *E-mail:* folkaflokkurin@logting.fo (office). *Website:* folkaflokkurin.fo (office).

KALMÁR, Stefan; German gallery curator; *Director, Institute of Contemporary Arts;* oversaw programming at Kunstverein München 2006–10, organized exhbns including The Secret Public: The Last Days of the British Underground 1978–1988 and a Liam Gillick retrospective, in collaboration with Witte de With, Kunsthalle Zurich and the Museum of Contemporary Art, Chicago; took over as Dir non-profit Artists Space, New York, Exec. Dir and Curator 2009–16; Dir Inst. of Contemporary Arts (ICA), London 2016–; aided in establishment and programming of Ludlow 38, a satellite space of the Goethe-Institut in New York. *Publication includes:* large book project documenting his curatorial approach in Munich. *Address:* Institute of Contemporary Arts, 12 Carlton House Terrace, London, SW1Y 5AH, England (office). *E-mail:* info@ica.org.uk (office). *Website:* www.ica.org.uk (office).

KALMS, Baron (Life Peer), cr. 2004, of Edgware in the London Borough of Barnet; **(Harold) Stanley Kalms;** British business executive; b. 21 Nov. 1931; s. of Charles Kalms and Cissie Kalms; m. Pamela Jimack 1954; three s.; ed Christ's Coll., Finchley; began career with Dixons 1948 working in father's photographic store; opened 16 shops; Dixons Photographic floated 1962, Man. Dir 1962–72, Chair. Dixons Group PLC (now DSG Int. PLC) 1972–2002, Pres. 2002, now Life Pres.; Dir British Gas 1987–97; Chair. (non-exec.) Volvere PLC; Chair. King's Healthcare NHS Trust 1993–96; Dir Centre for Policy Studies 1991– (Treas. 1993–98), Business for Sterling 1998–; Treas. Conservative Party 2001–03; Founder and sponsor Dixons Bradford City Tech. Coll.; Visiting Prof., Business School, Univ. of N London 1991; fmr Visiting Prof., Univ. of London Business School; Gov. Nat. Inst. of Econ. and Social Research 1995; Trustee, Econ. Educ. Trust; Hon. Fellow, London Business School 1995; Hon. DLitt (CNAA) 1991, Hon. DUniv (N London) 1994, Hon. DEcon (Richmond) 1996. *Leisure interests:* ballet, communal activities, opera. *Address:* House of Lords, London, SW1A 0PW, England. *Telephone:* (20) 7219-5353.

KALNIETE, Sandra, MA; Latvian politician and diplomatist; b. 22 Dec. 1952, Togur, Tomsk Oblast, Russia; m. (divorced); ed Latvian Acad. of Art, Univ. of Leeds, UK and Univ. of Geneva, Switzerland; Sec.-Gen. Latvian Artists' Union 1987–88; f. Latvian Popular Front 1988, Sec.-Gen., Deputy Chair. Co-ordinating Council 1988–90; Chief of Protocol Dept, Deputy Foreign Minister, Ministry of Foreign Affairs 1990–93, Amb. to UN, Geneva, Switzerland 1993–97, to France 1997–2000, to UNESCO 2000–02, Minister of Foreign Affairs 2002–04; EU Commr for Agric. and Fisheries May–Nov. 2004; mem. Saeima (Parl.) (New Era—Jaunais laiks) 2006–09; left New Era party and joined newly founded Civic Union (Pilsoniskā savienība—PS) party, Chair. Civic Union 2008–11; mem. European Parl. (Group of the European People's Party (Christian Democrats)) 2009–, Vice-Chair. Del. for relations with Japan, mem. Cttee on the Internal Market and Consumer Protection, Substitute mem. Cttee on Agric. and Rural Devt, Cttee on Women's Rights and Gender Equality, Del. to the EU-Turkey Jt Parl. Cttee; Patron, Prix Europa 2005; Commdr, Order of the Three Stars 1995, Commdr, Légion d'honneur 2001, Commdr des Palmes académiques 2002, Commdr, Order of Grand Cross of Grand Duke Gediminas (Lithuania) 2004, Commdr, Grand Cross of Merit 2005, Grand Cross of Commander of the Cross of Merit 2005, Order of the Cross of Terra Mariana, Second Degree (Estonia) 2012; Latvian Cabinet Ministers' Award, Ethics and Culture Award (Switzerland) 2007, Gold Medal, Fondation Mérite Européen 2009, Medal of the Baltic Ass. 2009. *Publications:* Latviesu tekstilmaksla (Latvian Textile Art) 1989, Es lauzu, tu lauzi, mes lauzam. Vini luza (I Broke, You Broke, We Broke. They Fell Apart) 2000, Ar balles kurpem Sibirijas sniegos (With Dancing Shoes in Siberian Snows) 2001, Prjaņiks. Debesmannā. Tiramisū (Gingerbread. Sweet-porridge. Tiramisu) 2012. *Address:* Civic Union (Pilsoniskā savienība), Aspazijas bulvāris 24, Rīga 1050, Latvia (office); European Parliament, Bât. Altiero Spinelli 14E261, 60 Rue Wiertz, 1047 Brussels, Belgium (office). *Telephone:* 6732-3325 (Rīga) (office); (2) 284-52-04 (Brussels). *Fax:* 6732-3315 (Rīga) (office); (2) 284-92-04 (Brussels) (office). *E-mail:* sandra.kalniete@europarl.europa.eu (office); birojs@pilsoniska-savieniba.lv (office). *Website:* www.europarl.europa.eu/meps/en/96934/SANDRA_KALNIETE_home.html (home); kalniete.lv.

KALORKOTI, Panayiotis, BA, MA; British artist; b. 11 April 1957, Cyprus; one s.; ed Univ. of Newcastle upon Tyne, Royal Coll. of Art, London, Avans Hogeschool, 's-Hertogenbosch, The Netherlands; Artist in Residence, Leeds Playhouse 1985, Cleveland Co. 1992, Grizedale Arts, Cumbria 1994; Bartlett Fellow in Visual Arts, Univ. of Newcastle-upon-Tyne 1988; commissioned by Imperial War Museum, London 1988, Nat. Garden Festival, Gateshead 1989–90; full-time artist and visiting lecturer; now lives in London; Granada Prize for Northern Young Contemporaries, Whitworth Art Gallery, Manchester 1983. *Publications include:* Kalorkoti 1988, A Retrospective of Etchings and Screenprints 1990, A Retrospective View 1985–91 1992, Etchings and Drawings 1992, Retrospective (Etchings 1983–93) 1994, Reflections of Grizedale (Acrylics, Watercolours, Etchings) 1995, An Exhibition of Acrylics, Watercolours and Etchings 1997, Heads, Faces and Figures 1998, Acrylics, Watercolours and Etchings 2000, Flowers in Watercolour 2001, Moving Figures 2002, In Motion 2005, In a Movement 2007, Events 2007, Four Nations Capitals 2014. *Leisure interests:* music, reading, films, theatre, travel, single malt whisky. *E-mail:* kalorkoti@googlemail.com (home). *Website:* www.kalorkoti.com.

KALOUSEK, Miroslav; Czech politician; *Chairman, Tradice, Odpovědnost, Prosperita 09 (TOP 09—Tradition, Responsibility, Prosperity 09);* b. 17 Dec. 1960, Tábor; m. Radka Kalousková; two c.; ed Inst. of Chemical Tech., Prague; Head of Investment, Mitas Praha (tyre mfrs) 1985–90; Econ. Adviser to Vice-Chair. of Czech Govt 1990–92, Dir Dept of Advisers 1992–93, Govt Rep. on Advisory Cttee, South-Bohemian Brewery 1991–92; mem. Parl. (Křesťanská a Demokratická Unie-Československá Strana Lidová (KDU-ČSL—Christian Democratic Union-Czechoslovak People's Party) 1993–, Chair. Parl. Budget Cttee 2002–05, Vice-Chair. 2006–; Deputy Minister of Defence 1993–98, Minister of Finance 2007–09, 2010–13, Chair. EU's Ecofin Council Jan.–May 2009; Chair. KDU-ČSL 2003–06, left party 2009; Co-founder, with Karel Schwarzenberg (q.v.), Tradice, Odpovědnost, Prosperita 09 (TOP 09—Tradition, Responsibility, Prosperity 09) party June 2009, First Vice-Pres. Nov. 2009–15, Chair. 2015–; mem. Bd of Dirs, West-Bohemian Brewery 1992–94, Land Fund of the Czech Repub. 1994–96. *Address:* Tradice, Odpovědnost, Prosperita 09 (TOP 09—Tradition, Responsibility, Prosperity 09), Michnův palác, budova č. 2, Újezd 450/40, Malá Strana, 118 00 Prague 1, Czech Republic (office). *Telephone:* (2) 55790999 (office). *Fax:* (2) 55790899 (office). *E-mail:* info@top09.cz (office). *Website:* www.top09.cz (office); www.miroslav-kalousek.cz.

KALTENBORN, Monisha, LLM; Austrian (b. Indian) motorsport executive; b. 10 May 1971, Dehradun, India; m. Jens Kaltenborn; two c.; ed Univ. of Vienna, London School of Econs, UK; Research Asst, UNIDO, Vienna 1995; Researcher, UN Comm. for Int. Trade Law, Vienna 1995; worked at Gleiss Lutz (law firm), Stuttgart and Wolf & Theis (law firm), Vienna 1996–97; worked at Fritz Kaiser Group 1998–99; Co-owner and Head of Legal Dept, Sauber Group 2000–17, mem. Bd of Man. 2001–17; CEO Sauber Motorsport AG 2010–17, Formula 1 team principal; involved in Fédération Internationale de l'Automobile's Comm. for Women and Motorsport. *Leisure interests:* yoga, tennis, opera.

KALTONGA, Bakoa; Ni-Vanuatu politician; b. 6 April 1969; First Political Adviser, Ministry of Infrastructure and Public Utilities –2008; mem. Parl. for Rural Efate constituency 2008–; Minister of Foreign Affairs and External Trade 2008–09, of Justice and Women's Affairs 2009–10, of Finance and Economic Man. April–May 2011; mem. Vanuaaku Pati (Our Land Party). *Address:* Parliament of Vanuatu, PMB 9052, Port Vila, Vanuatu (office). *Website:* parliament.gov.vu (office).

KALUGIN, Maj.-Gen. Oleg Danilovich; Russian/American intelligence officer and politician; *Professor, Centre for Counterintelligence and Security Studies;* b. 6 Sept. 1934, Leningrad; m.; two d.; ed Leningrad Univ., Columbia Univ.; on staff of KGB 1958–89; corresp., Soviet Radio, New York 1959–65; Second, then First Sec., Embassy in Washington, DC 1965–70; Chief, Dept of External Intelligence Service, KGB 1973–80; First Deputy Chief of KGB for City of Leningrad and Leningrad Region 1980–87; returned to Moscow 1987, forced to retire for participation in democratic movt and criticism of KGB 1989, deprived of all decorations and titles by order of Pres. Gorbachev 1990; prosecuted, all charges lifted at end of 1991; USSR People's Deputy 1990–91; gave evidence on activities of KGB in courts and mass media; consultant, Information Service Agency; mem. Fed. Democratic Movt 1995; has lived in USA 1996–; sentenced in absentia by Russian court to 15 years' imprisonment for treason after disclosing Russian agents in USA 2001; currently Prof., Centre for Counterintelligence and Security Studies, Va; mem. Advisory Bd Dirs, Int. Spy Museum, Washington, DC; acquired US citizenship 2003; Man. Dir Cannistraro Assocs (security consulting firm) 1998; numerous decorations. *Publications:* The First Directorate: My 32 Years in Intelligence and Espionage Against the West (autobiog.) 1994; numerous articles. *Leisure interests:* hunting, fishing, swimming. *Address:* Centre for Counterintelligence and Security Studies, PO Box 538, Great Falls, VA 22066, USA (office). *Telephone:* (703) 642-7450 (office). *Fax:* (703)-948-0134 (office). *Website:* www.cicentre.com (office).

KALUMBA, Katele, PhD; Zambian politician; m. Lumba Kalumba; ed Univ. of Zambia, Washington Univ., St Louis, USA, Univ. of Toronto, Canada; fmr health consultant to govts and int. orgs; Minister of Health 1991–98, of Home Affairs and of Tourism 1998–99, of Finance and Econ. Devt 1999–2002, of Foreign Affairs 2002 (resgnd); mem. Nat. Ass. (Movt for Multi-party Democracy—MMD) 2002–; Nat. Sec., MMD –2011. *Address:* National Assembly of Zambia, Parliament Buildings, PO Box 31299, Lusaka (office); PO Box 320265, Woodlands, Lusaka, Zambia. *E-mail:* kaklumba@parliament.gov.zm (office); nazambia@zamnet.zm. *Website:* www.parliament.gov.zm (office).

KALVĪTIS, Aigars, MSc; Latvian politician and business executive; *CEO, JCS Latvijas Gāze;* b. 27 June 1966, Rīga; m.; three s.; ed Univ. of Wisconsin, USA, Latvian Univ. of Agric., Univ. Coll. Cork, Ireland; milkman and tractor driver, Alamnas Bruk AB, Sweden 1990–91; Dir Agro Biznesa Centrs 1992–94; Chair. Bd Zemgales piens 1994; Chair. Comm. of the Cen. Union of Latvian Dairying 1994–98; mem. Saeima (Parl.) 1998–99, 2002–04, mem. Budget and Finance (Taxation) Cttee, Public Expenditure and Audit Cttee; Minister of Agric. 1999–2000, of Econs 2000–02; Prime Minister 2004–07 (resgnd); mem. People's Party (Tautas partija), Chair. of Parl. Group 2002–04; CEO JCS Latvijas Gāze 2015–. *Leisure interest:* ice hockey. *Address:* JSC Latvijas Gāze, Vagonu Street 20, Riga 1009, Latvia (office). *Website:* www.lg.lv (office).

KALYAGIN, Aleksander Aleksandrovich; Russian actor; b. 25 May 1942, Malmysh, Kirov Region; m. Glushenko Yevgeniya Konstantinovna; one s. one d.; ed Shchukin Higher School of Theatre Art; actor Taganka Theatre and Yermolova

Theatre in Moscow 1966–71; Moscow Art Theatre 1971–93; master classes in Russia and in Europe; apptd Chair. Union of Theatre Workers of Russia 1996; Founder and Artistic Dir Et Cetera Theatre in Moscow 1992–; People's Artist of Russia 1983, State Prize 1981, 1983. *Roles in productions:* Dark Lady of the Sonnets by G. B. Shaw, Don Quixote by A. Morfov after Cervantes, Old New Year by M. Roshchin, Notes of the Lunatic and Marriage by Gogol, Galileo by Brecht, Tartuffe by Molière, several plays by A. Gelman, M. Shatrov, A. Galin and other contemporary dramatists; in cinema since 1967. *Films include:* Untimely Man 1973, One's Own Among Strangers 1974, Slave of Love 1976, Interrogation 1979, Aesop 1982, Prokhindiada or Run on the Spot 1985, How Are You Doing, Crucians? 1992, Moi Ivan, toi Abraham 1993, Deti chugunnykh bogov 1993, Prokhindiada 2 1994, Foto 2003, Bulvarnyy pereplyot 2003, Rud i Sem 2007. *Television:* Bednaya Nastya (series) 2003, Poor Anastasia 2003. *Leisure interests:* collecting art books, museums. *Address:* 123100 Moscow, 1905 Goda str., 3, Apt 91, Russia (home). *Telephone:* (495) 205-26-54 (home). *E-mail:* stdrf@rc.ru.

KALYALYA, Denny, BA, MA, PhD; Zambian academic, international organization official and central banker; *Governor and Chairman, Bank of Zambia;* b. 1 Aug. 1957, Monze; m.; two s. one d.; ed Univ. of Zambia, Univ. of Massachusetts, USA; Econs Lecturer, Univ. of Zambia 1983–95, Asst Dean, School of Humanities and Social Sciences 1994–95, Head, Econs Dept 1995; Adviser, Econs Dept, Bank of Zambia 1996–98, Dir 1998–2002, Deputy Gov. of Operations 2002–10; Alternate Exec. Dir World Bank Group 2010–12, Exec. Dir 2012–14; Gov. and Chair. Bank of Zambia 2015–; Special Appointee, Monetary and Exchange Affairs and African Dept, IMF 1997–98; fmr Chair. Zambia Electronic Clearing House Ltd, Nat. Payments System Cttee; Vice-Chair. Financial Sector Devt Plan Steering Cttee, later Chair. Implementation Cttee; fmr Dir ZCCM Investments Holdings PLC; mem. Agric. Sector Devt Project Steering Cttee, Ministry of Agric. and Cooperatives; Bd mem. Zambia Consolidated Copper Mines—Investment Holdings. *Publications include:* Aid and Development in Southern Africa: Evaluating A Participatory Learning Process 1988. *Address:* Bank of Zambia, Bank Square, Cairo Road, POB 30080, 10101 Lusaka, Zambia (office). *Telephone:* (21) 1228888 (office). *Fax:* (21) 1225652 (office). *E-mail:* DKalyaly@boz.zm (office). *Website:* www .boz.zm (office).

KALYONCU, Ömer Soyer; Turkish-Cypriot politician; b. 1950, Kyrenia; m.; two c.; ed Middle East Technical Univ., Ankara; mem. Ass. of the Turkish Repub. of Northern Cyprus (Parl.) from Kyrenia 1993–; Minister of Labour and Social Security 1995–96, Minister of Public Works and Transportation 1998–2005, Prime Minister 2015–16; mem. Republican Turkish Party 1973–, mem. Cen. Admin. Bd, Sec.-Gen. 1988. *Address:* c/o Prime Minister's Office, Selçuklu Road, Lefkoşa (Nicosia), Mersin 10, Turkey (office).

KALYUZHNY, Victor Ivanovich; Russian engineer, diplomat, politician and business executive; b. 18 April 1947, Birsk, Bashkiria; ed Ufa Inst. of Oil; Mgr, then Deputy Head Tomskneft Co. 1970–78, First Deputy Dir.-Gen. 1993–97; Chief Engineer Dept of Oil and Gas Vasyuganneft Co., Strezhevoy; Sec. CP Cttee Strezhevoyneft Co. 1980–84, later Deputy Dir; Second Sec. Strezhevoy Town CP Exec. Cttee 1984–86; Deputy Dir USSR Ministry of Oil Industry 1986; Chief Engineer, then Dir Priobneft Co., Nizhevartovsk Tumen 1986–90; Dir Vietsovpetro, Vu Tan, Viet Nam 1990–93; First Vice-Pres. Vostochnaya Neftyanaya Komapniya, Tomsk 1997–98; First Deputy Minister of Fuel and Power Industry 1998–99, Minister 1999–2000; Special Rep. of Pres. for Caspian Sea with rank of Deputy Minister of Foreign Affairs 2000; Amb. to Latvia 2004–07 (retd); mem. Bd of Dirs Eurasia Drilling Co. 2009–.

KAMAL, (Ahmed) Mustafa, FCA; Bangladeshi accountant, business executive and politician; *Minister of Finance;* b. 15 June 1947, Comilla; m. Kashmiri Kamal; two d.; ed Univ. of Dhaka; Pres. and CEO Lotus Kamal Group (textile co.); mem. Jatiya Sangsad (parl.) from Comilla-9 constituency (AL) 1996–2001, from Comilla-10 constituency 2008–; Minister of Planning 2014–19, of Finance 2019–; Pres. Bangladesh Cricket Club 2009–13, Int. Cricket Council 2014–15; mem. Bangladesh Awami League (AL). *Address:* Ministry of Finance, Bangladesh Secretariat, Bhaban 7, 3rd Floor, Dhaka 1000, Bangladesh (office). *Telephone:* (2) 9512201 (office). *Fax:* (2) 9180788 (home). *E-mail:* fkabir@finance.gov.bd (office). *Website:* www.mof.gov.bd (office).

KAMAL, Fida M., BA, MA; Bangladeshi barrister; b. 7 June 1948; ed Univ. of Dhaka, Punjab Univ., Pakistan, Inner Temple, London, UK; joined Sultan, Fida & Reza, Barristers & Advocates, Dhaka 1978, now Sr Partner; called to the Bar 1979, enrolled as lawyer of High Court 1979, of Appellate Div. 1986; ex-officio Chair. Bangladesh Bar Council; Additional Attorney-Gen. 2002–07, Acting Attorney-Gen. Jan.–Feb. 2007, Attorney-Gen. 2007–08. *Address:* Sultan, Fida & Reza, Barristers & Advocates, 64, Purana Paltan, Motijheel Commercial Area, Dhaka 1000, Bangladesh (office). *Telephone:* (2) 9565618 (office). *Fax:* (2) 9567641 (office).

KAMAL, Riad Burhan, BSc, MSc; Palestinian civil engineer and business executive; ed Imperial Coll. London, UK; began career in London 1966, worked on construction projects in UK, Jordan and Spain for Tarmac Ltd and Sir Robert McAlpine Ltd; moved to Dubai 1974, f. Arab Technical Construction (Arabtec Construction) 1975, CEO Arabtec Construction Co. PJSC 2004–09, mem. Bd of Dirs and CEO Arabtec Holding PJSC 2008–13, Chair. of projects including Burj Dubai, Burj Al Arab (Dubai), Okhta Centre Tower (St Petersburg); Founder and Deputy Chair. DEPA Interiors; Dir, Arab Bank, Amman, Turkland Bank, Istanbul, Arabia Insurance Co., Beirut, Depa United Co., Satellite Inter-Active Systems; Dir and mem. Advisory Bd Gulf Capital; mem. Advisory Bd for MENA Region (Private Wealth Management), Deutsche Bank – Swiss; mem. Bd of Trustees, American Univ. of Beirut; Deputy Chair. Welfare Asscn, Geneva; mem. World Presidents' Org.; ITP Lifetime Achievement Award 2009.

KAMAL, Yousuf bin Hussein, BBA; Qatari government official; b. 1948; ed Cairo Univ.; previous positions in Ministry of Finance include Asst Deputy Dir, Deputy Dir, Gen. Dir, Deputy Minister, Minister of Finance (later renamed Economy and Finance) 1998–2013, also Acting Minister of Economy and Trade 2006; fmr Deputy Head, Bd of Dirs Qatar Petroleum; Chair. Qatar Financial Centre; fmr mem. Bd of Dirs Qatar Cen. Bank, Q-Tel; fmr Head, Bd of Dirs Ras Laffan LNG.

KAMALI, Norma, BFA; American fashion designer; b. 27 June 1945, New York; d. of Sam Arraez and Estelle Galib; m. M. H. Kamali (divorced); ed Fashion Inst. of Tech., New York; ind. fashion designer, New York 1965–; opened first shop in East 53rd Street 1968, moving to Madison Avenue 1974; retitled business OMO (On My Own) and moved to 56th Street 1978; second boutique opened Spring Street, New York 1986; OMO Home opened 1988; collaboration with Bloomingdale's on production of exclusive collections 1988–; OMO Tokyo opened 1990; Coty American Fashion Critics' Winnie Award 1981, 1982, Outstanding Women's Fashion Designer of the Year Award, Council of Fashion Designers of America 1982, Coty Hall of Fame Award 1983, American Success Award 1989, Pencil Award 1999, Fashion Outreach Style Award 1999, Business Outreach Award, Manhattan Chamber of Commerce 2001, Entrepreneur Award, The Fashion Group 2002, Bd of Dirs Special Tribute Award, Council of Fashion Designers of America 2006. *Address:* OMO Norma Kamali, 11 West 56th Street, New York, NY 10019, USA. *Website:* www.normakamalicollection.com.

KAMALUDHEEN, Abdullah, BSc; Maldivian politician and business executive; *Executive Deputy Chairman, ENRA Group Berhad;* b. 12 July 1954; m.; five c.; ed Majeediyya School and Almeda Univ., USA; clerk, Ministry of Foreign Affairs 1972; Admin. Sec., Office of the Pres. 1972–76; Under-Sec., Port Comm. and Public Works Dept, Ministry of Finance 1976–77, Dir 1977–82; Dir Dept of Tourism and Foreign Investment, Office of the Pres. 1978, Dir Dept of Public Works and Labour 1982–89, Dir Islamic Centre 1984–93; Minister of Public Works and Labour 1989–93; Chair. and Man. Dir Maldives Ports Authority 1990–93; Chair. Bank of Maldives Ltd 1990–93, Maldives Electricity Board 1991–93; Exec. Dir, Maldives National Ship Man. Ltd 1991–93; mem. Parl. 1992–; mem. Constitutional Ass. 1995–; Minister of Human Resources, Employment and Labour 1998–2003, of Fisheries, Agric. and Marine Resources 2003–07, of Home Affairs 2007–08; Exec. Deputy Chair. ENRA Group Berhad 2015–. *Address:* ENRA Group Berhad, D2-U3-10, Block D2, Solaris Dutamas, No.1, Jalan Dutamas 1, 50480 Kuala Lumpur, Malaysia (office). *Telephone:* (3) 23003555 (office). *Fax:* (3) 23003550 (office). *E-mail:* info@enra.my (office). *Website:* www.enra.my (office).

KAMANDA, Kama Sywor, DipHumLit, BJ, BA, LèsL, HD; Democratic Republic of the Congo writer, poet, novelist, playwright and essayist and lecturer; b. 11 Nov. 1952, Luebo; s. of Malaba Kamenga and Kony Ngalula; ed Journalism School, Kinshasa, Univ. of Kinshasa, Univ. of Liège, Belgium; political leader; freelance journalist; lecturer at various univs, schools, etc.; literary critic for several newspapers; mem. French Soc. of Men of Letters, Conseil Int. d'Etudes Francophones, Belgian Soc. of Authors, Composers and Editors (SABAM), Maison de la poésie (MAPI – Dakar, Senegal), SCAM; Acad. française Paul Verlaine Award 1987, Acad. française Théophile Gautier Award 1993, Louise Labé Award 1990, Black African Asscn of French-Speaking Writers Award 1991, Acad. Inst. of Paris Special Poetry Award 1992, Silver Jasmine for Poetic Originality 1992, Gen. Council Agen Special Prize for French-Speaking Countries 1992, Greek Poets and Writers Asscn Melina Mercouri Award 1999, Int. Poets Acad. India Poet of the Millennium Award 2000, Joal Fadiouth hon. citation, Senegal 2000, Int. Soc. of Greek Writers Poetry Award 2002, Int. Council for French Studies Maurice-Cagnon Exceptional Contribution Honour Certificate 2005, World Acad. of Letters Master Diploma for Specialty Honors in Writing, USA 2006, United Cultural Convention Int. Peace Prize, USA 2006, Golden Medal Youth Book (Czech Repub.) 2008, Heredia Award, French Acad. 2009. *Publications include:* Les Contes des veillées africaines 1967, Chants de brumes 1986, Les Résignations 1986, Éclipse d'étoiles 1987, Les Contes du griot Vol. 1 1988, Vol. 2: La Nuit des griots 1991, Vol. 3: Les Contes des veillées africaines 1998, La Somme du néant 1989, L'Exil des songes 1992, Les Myriades des temps vécus 1992, Les Vents de l'épreuve 1993, Quand dans l'âme les mers s'agitent 1994, Lointaines sont les rives du destin 1994, L'Étreinte des mots 1995, Œuvre poétique 1999, Les Contes du crépuscule 2000, Le Sang des solitudes 2002, Contes (édition illustrée) 2003, Contes (œuvres complètes) 2004, La Traversée des mirages 2006, La Joueuse de Kora 2006, Contes africains (Grund) 2006, Au-delà de Dieu, au-delà des chimères 2007, Oeuvre poétique (édition intégrale) 2008, L'Insondable destin des Hommes 2013. *Leisure interests:* travel, reading. *Address:* 18 Am Moul, 7418 Buschdorf, Luxembourg (office). *Telephone:* 26610948 (office); (621) 301611 (mobile) (office). *E-mail:* kamanda@pt.lu (office). *Website:* www.kamanda.jp (office); webplaza.pt.lu/public/kamanda (office); www.kamanda.net.

KAMANZI, Stanislas; Rwandan diplomatist; *High Commissioner to Nigeria;* Perm. Rep. to UN, New York 2003–06; Minister of Infrastructure 2006–08, of Natural Resources 2008, fmr Minister of Lands, the Environment, Forestry and Mines; currently High Commr to Nigeria. *Address:* High Commission of Rwanda, 1 Justice Mohammed Bello Street, off Jose Marti Crescent, Asokoro, Abuja, Nigeria (office). *Website:* www.nigeria.embassy.gov.rw (office).

KAMARA, Boima S., MPhil Econ; Liberian economist and politician; b. 9 May 1974, Bomi County; s. of John Kamara David and Ma Yatta Moore; ed Univ. of Liberia, Univ. of Ghana; Teaching Asst, Dept of Econs, Univ. of Liberia 2001–07, taught Advanced Econometrics, Monetary Econs, Int. Econs and Health Econs 2007–16; spent more than 14 years with Central Bank of Liberia, including as Jr Analyst in Research Dept, becoming Asst Dir for Research and Policy 2010–12, Dir, Research, Policy and Planning Dept 2012–14, Deputy Gov. for Econ. Policy 2014–16; Minister of Finance and Devt Planning 2016–18. *Address:* c/o Ministry of Finance and Development Planning, Broad Street, POB 10-9013, 1000 Monrovia 10, Liberia (office).

KAMARA, Marjon V.; Liberian diplomatist, politician and UN official; began career with UNHCR 1983, various assignments with UNHCR's Africa Operations, including as Emergency Coordinator, also took admin. responsibility in UNHCR Africa Bureau from 1990, UNHCR Rep. in Angola 1994, Tanzania 1998, Dir for Div. of Operational Support, UNHCR HQ 2001–05, Dir Bureau for Africa 2005–09; Amb. and Perm. Rep. to UN, New York 2009–16; Minister of Foreign Affairs 2016–18. *Address:* c/o Ministry of Foreign Affairs, Mamba Point, PO Box 10-9002, 1000 Monrovia 10, Liberia (office).

KAMARA, Samura Matthew Wilson; Sierra Leonean economist, central banker and government official; b. 15 Dec. 1963, Kamalo, Bombali Dist; Minister of Finance 1996; fmr Exec., IMF, Washington, DC; Gov. Bank of Sierra Leone (central bank) 2007–09; fmr Financial Sec., Ministry of Finance, Minister of

Finance 2009–12; Minister of Foreign Affairs and Int. Cooperation 2013–17; Cand. in presidential election 2018. *Address:* c/o Ministry of Foreign Affairs and International Co-operation, Gloucester Street, Freetown, Sierra Leone (office).

KAMAT, Digambar V., BSc; Indian politician; b. 8 March 1954, Margao, Goa; s. of Vasant Kamat; m. Asha Kamat; two c.; Councillor, Margao Municipal Council 1985–90; mem. Legis. Ass. of State of Goa 1994–, mem. Cttee on Govt Assurances 1995–96, 1996–97, 1997–98, 1999–2000 (fmr Chair.), Select Cttee on Bill No. 29 of Goa Advocates Welfare Fund Bill 1995, Business Advisory Cttee 1996–97, House Cttee to study Model Rent Control Legislation, Panel of Presiding Mems 1997–98, Cttee on Public Undertakings, Chair. Public Accounts Cttee 1999–2000; Minister for Power, Protocol, and Art and Culture 1999; mem. Town and Country Planning Bd; Minister for Power, Urban Devt and Mines 2002; Chief Minister of Goa 2007–12; Chair. Produce Market Cttee 1979–91; mem. Southern Planning and Devt Authority 1986–89; mem. Exec. Cttee Nat. Council of State Agricultural Marketing Bd, New Delhi 1992–94; Vice-Chair. Nat. Council of State Agricultural Marketing Bds 1994–96; mem. State Consumer Protection Council 1993–96; Founder-mem. Damodar Educ. Soc.; Sec. Model Educ. Soc.; mem. Advisory Cttee for Parshuram Girijan Samaj; Treas., Margao Cricket Club 1973; Pres., Swimming Fed. of India 2006–, Sparkling Stars Asscn, Margao 1973–74; Founder-Pres. Rotary Club of Margao 1973, Samrat Club; mem. Goa, Daman and Diu State Council of Sports 1976–78; Vice-Pres. Goa Badminton Asscn 1980–83, Pres. 1999–2000; Trustee, Margao Ambulance Trust; Hon. Sec., Goa Badminton Asscn; Nat. Council of State Agricultural Marketing Bds Award 1994–96, Bakshi Jivabadada Kerkar State Award, Govt of Goa. *Leisure interests:* reading, playing badminton, swimming, cricket. *Address:* Sanrit Apartments, 1st Floor, nr Masjid, Malbhat, Margao, India (home). *Telephone:* (832) 2730432 (home).

KAMATA, Michisada; Japanese energy industy executive; *Chairman, Kyushu Electric Power Company Inc.;* b. 1934; joined Kyushu Electric Power Co. Inc. 1958, served as Man. Dir and Pres., Chair. 2003; Vice-Chair. Kyushu Tourism Promotion Org.; Chair. Kyushu-Yamaguchi Econ. Fed.; Vice-Chair. Fed. of Electric Power Cos 2001–03; Dir Japan Nuclear Fuel Ltd, Kyushu-Yamaguchi Econ. Fed. (Kyukeiren), Japan Productivity Center for Socio-Econ. Devt (JPC-SED), Energy Conservation Center of Japan; fmr Dir World Nuclear Asscn; Founding mem. Fukuoka Canada Soc. 1999, fmr Pres.; Trustee, Int. Center for the Study of E Asian Devt (ICSEAD); Hon. Consul of Canada in Fukuoka 2013. *Address:* Kyushu Electric Power Company Incorporated, 1–82 Watanabe Dori 2–chome, Chuo-ku, Fukuoka 810–8720, Japan (office). *Telephone:* (92) 761–3031 (office). *Fax:* (92) 733–1435 (office). *Website:* www.kyuden.co.jp (office).

KAMATH, Kundapur Vaman, BSc, MBA; Indian banker and business executive; *President, New Development Bank BRICS;* b. 2 Dec. 1947, Mangalore, Karnataka; m.; one s. one d.; ed Karnataka Regional Eng Coll. (now Nat. Inst. of Tech., Karnataka), Indian Inst. of Man., Ahmedabad; mem. of staff, Industrial Credit and Investment Corpn of India (ICICI) Bank Ltd 1971–88, CEO and Man. Dir 1996–2009, Chair. (non-exec.) 2009–15; Adviser, Asian Devt Bank, Manila 1988–96; Chair. Infosys Ltd 2011–13, Lead Independent Dir 2013–15; Pres. New Development Bank BRICS (fmrly BRICS Development Bank), Shanghai, China 2015–; mem. Man. Cttee, Associated Chambers of Commerce and Industry; mem. Nat. Council Confed. of Indian Industry; mem. Governing Bd Indian Inst. of Man., Ahmedabad, Indian School of Business, Nat. Inst. of Bank Man., Manipal Acad. of Higher Educ.; mem. Bd of Dirs Inst. of Int. Finance, Infosys Technologies; mem. Bd of Govs Indian Inst. of Man., Ahmedabad; Dr hc (Banaras Hindu Univ.); Asian Business Leader of the Year, CNBC 2001, Businessman of the Year, Business India magazine 2005, Outstanding Business Leader of the Year, CNBC-TV18 2006, Banker of the Year, Business Standard 2006, Businessman of the Year, Forbes Asia 2007, Economic Times Business Leader of the Year 2007, Padma Bhushan 2008, Lifetime Achievement Award, Financial Express 2008, NDTV Profit Business Leadership Award 2008. *E-mail:* info@ndbbrics.org (office). *Website:* www.ndbbrics.org (office).

KAMBOGO, Abdu Razzaq Guy; Gabonese diplomatist and politician; *Minister of Foreign Affairs, International Co-operation, Regional Integration, the Francophonie and Gabonese Nationals Abroad;* b. 6 Sept. 1974, Akiéni; m. Sandra Michelle Kambogo; c.; ed École des hautes études commerciales de Rabat, Univ. of Quebec, Trois-Rivières, École des hautes études commerciales de Paris; Sales and Programming Dir, TV SAT Group 2001–03; Researcher in Cabinet of Minister of Economy and Finance 2003–07, Dir, Institutional Support and Human Resources Devt Programme 2007–08, 2009–13; Dir-Gen., Nat. Centre for Univ. Works 2008–09; Amb. to Morocco 2013–19; Minister of Foreign Affairs, Int. Co-operation, Regional Integration, the Francophonie and Gabonese Nationals Abroad 2019–; Deputy Sec.-Gen., Higher Council of Islamic Affairs; Chevalier, Ordre du Mérite Gabonais 2010. *Address:* Ministry of Foreign Affairs, Co-operation, the Francophonie and Regional Integration, blvd du Bord de Mer, BP 2245, Libreville, Gabon (office). *Telephone:* 01-74-23-71 (office). *Fax:* 01-74-23-74 (home). *E-mail:* mae@diplomatie.gouv.ga (office). *Website:* www.affaires-etrangeres.gouv.ga (office).

KAMEI, Shizuka; Japanese politician; b. 1 Nov. 1936, Shōbara, Hiroshima; joined Nat. Police Agency 1962; Parl. Vice-Minister of Transport, Minister 1994–95, of Construction 1996; mem. House of Reps for Hiroshima 1977–; Chair. LDP Nat. Org. Cttee and Acting Chair. LDP Policy Research Council; Minister of State for Financial Services and for Postal Reform 2009–10.

KAMEL, Sheikh Saleh Abdullah, BA, MBA; Saudi Arabian business executive; *Chairman, ART (Arab Radio and Television);* m.; ed King Abdulaziz Univ.; est. business based on contracts with Saudi Arabian Govt; est. real-estate devts in Buhairat, Tunisia and Durat al-Arous, Jeddah; f. MBC (Middle Eastern Broadcasting Center) and ART (Arab Radio and TV); majority owner and Chief Exec. Dallah al Baraka Group, Chair. and Man. Dir Al Baraka Banking Group, Chair. Al Baraka Investment and Devt; Deputy Chair. Al Jazira Bank; mem. Bd Al Baraka Investment and Devt Co., Savola, Jeddah Chamber of Commerce and Industry, Saudi Research and Publishing Ltd. *Address:* Dallah al Baraka Group, Dallah Tower, Palestine Street, Jeddah 21452 (office); PO Box 430, Jeddah 21411, Saudia Arabia (office). *Telephone:* (2) 671-0000 (Dallah al Baraka) (office); (2) 667-3316 (office). *Fax:* (2) 617-0347 (Dallah al Baraka) (office); (2) 671-7056 (office). *Website:* www.albaraka.com (office).

KAMEN, Dean; American inventor, physicist and engineer; *President, DEKA Research and Development Corporation;* b. 5 April 1951, Long Island, NY; s. of Jack Kamen and Evelyn Kamen; ed Worcester Polytechnic Inst.; while and undergraduate invented wearable infusion pump; f. AutoSyringe Inc. 1976; developed first portable pump to dispense insulin 1978; est. Science Enrichment Encounters (SEE) museum 1985; developed portable dialysis machine 1993; created the Segway Human Transporter (motorized, low-energy scooter) 2001; mem. Nat. Acad. of Eng 1997; Owner and Pres. DEKA Research and Devt Corpn 1992–; f. US FIRST (For Inspiration and Recognition of Science and Tech.) Foundation 1989; mem. Advisory Bd US Science and Eng Festival; Hon. DSc (Rensselear Polytechnic Inst.) 1996, (Clarkson Univ.) 2001, (Univ. of Arizona) 2009, (Worcester Polytechnic Inst.); Hon. DEng (Kettering Univ.) 2001, (Yale Univ.) 2015; Dr hc (Wentworth Inst. of Tech.) 2004, (North Carolina State Univ.) 2005, (Bates Coll.) 2007, (Georgia Inst. of Tech.) 2008, (Illinois Inst. of Tech.) 2008, (Plymouth State Univ,) 2008; Engineer of the Year (Design News Magazine) 1994, Hoover Medal 1995, NH Business Leader of the Year 1996, Heinz Award in Tech., the Economy and Employment 1998, Nat. Medal of Tech. 2000, Lemelson-MIT Prize 2002; inducted into Nat. Inventors Hall of Fame 2005, Global Humanitarian Action Award, UN 2006, American Soc. of Mechanical Engineers Medal 2007, Industrial Research Inst. Achievement Award 2008, Stevens Honor Award, Steven Inst. of Tech. and Stevens Alumni Asscn 2009, Benjamin Franklin Medal, Franklin Inst. 2011, James C. Morgan Humanitarian Award 2013. *Achievements include:* holds more than 100 US patents. *Address:* DEKA Research and Development Corporation, Technology Center, 340 Commercial Street, Manchester, NH 03101, USA (office). *Telephone:* (603) 669-5139 (office). *Fax:* (603) 624-0573 (office). *E-mail:* contactdeka@dekaresearch.com (office). *Website:* www.dekaresearch.com (office); www.usfirst.org.

KAMENICKÝ, Ladislav; Slovak politician; *Minister of Finance;* b. 4 Oct. 1970; ed Bratislava Univ. of Econs; mem. Národná Rada Slovenskej republiky (parl.) (Smer) 2012–, Chair. Financial and Budgetary Cttee 2016–, mem. European Affairs Cttee; Minister of Finance 2019–; mem. Smer-Sociálna demokracia (Smer-SD, Direction-Social Democracy), currently Co-Chair. Smer-SD Bratislava Dist Org. *Address:* Ministry of Finance, Štefanovičova 5, POB 82, 817 82 Bratislava, Slovakia (office). *Telephone:* (2) 5958-1111 (office). *Fax:* (2) 5958-3048 (office). *E-mail:* info@mfsr.sk (office). *Website:* www.finance.gov.sk (office).

KAMIJO, Kiyofumi, BSc; Japanese business executive; ed Waseda Univ.; joined Tokyu Corpn 1958, Vice-Pres.–June 2001, Pres. and CEO June 2001–05, apptd Chair. 2005, Dir Tokyu Land Corpn; Advisor, Shochiku Co., Ltd 2007–13, Corp. Advisor 2013–; mem. Advisory Bd Development Bank of Japan; mem. Bd of Dirs Japan Airlines Corpn –2011, Japan-Fiji Friendship Soc.

KAMIKAWA, Yoko, MPA; Japanese politician; *Minister of Justice;* b. 1 March 1953, Shizuoka; two c.; ed Coll. of Arts and Sciences, Tokyo Univ., John F. Kennedy School of Govt, Harvard Univ., USA; Researcher, Mitsubishi Research Inst. 1977; est. policy consultancy 1977; served on staff of US Senator Max Baucus; joined LDP 1997; elected to House of Reps 2000, as LDP rep. for Shizuoka Pref., currently Head of First Dist; Dir of Women's Affairs Div., LDP 2000, Parl. Sec. for Internal Affairs and Communication 2005; Deputy Minister of Internal Affairs and Communications 2005–06, 2013, Minister of State for Gender Equality, Population and Social Affairs 2007–08 (resgnd), Minister of Justice 2014–15, 2017–. *Address:* Ministry of Justice, 1-1-1, Kasumigaseki, Chiyoda-ku, Tokyo 100-8977 (office); 780–1 Oya, Suruga-ku, Shizuoka, Japan (home). *Telephone:* (3) 3580-4111 (office); (54) 281-1000 (home). *Fax:* (3) 3592-7011 (office); (54) 283-7743 (home). *E-mail:* webmaster@moj.go.jp (office). *Website:* www.moj.go.jp; www.kamikawayoko.net.

KAMIL, Muferihat, BSc, MA; Ethiopian politician; *Minister of Peace;* b. 1976, Jimma; ed Haramaya Univ., Greenwich Univ.; held different roles in the field of women's affairs from 2002; apptd Public Relations Advisor to Pres. of S Nations, Nationalities and Peoples' Region (SNNPR) 2007; worked at Ethiopian People's Revolutionary Democratic Front (EPRDF) office in Addis Ababa, becoming Jr Public Relations Officer –2008; Minister of Women's Affairs 2008; fmr Social Affairs Advisor to Prime Minister; mem. House of People's Reps (lower house of parl.), fmr Asst Govt Whip and mem. House Business Advisory Cttee, elected Speaker (first female) April–Oct. 2018; mem. S Ethiopian People's Democratic Movt (SEPDM), Chair. 2018–; Minister of Peace 2018–. *Address:* c/o House of People's Representatives, POB 80001, Addis Ababa, Ethiopia (office).

KAMILOV, Abdulaziz, PhD; Uzbekistani diplomatist and politician; *Minister of Foreign Affairs;* b. 16 Nov. 1947, Yangiyo'l, Tashkent Viloyat, Uzbek SSR, USSR; m.; one s.; ed Moscow Inst. of Oriental Languages; served at Diplomatic Acad., USSR Ministry of Foreign Affairs; joined USSR diplomatic service 1972, Attaché, USSR Embassy in Beirut 1973–76, Second Sec., Damascus 1980–84, mem. Div. of Near East, USSR Ministry of Foreign Affairs 1984–88; Sr Researcher, Inst. of World Econs and Int. Affairs, USSR Acad. of Sciences 1988–91; Counsellor, Uzbekistan Embassy in Moscow 1991–92; Deputy Chair. Security Service of Uzbekistan Repub. 1992–94; First Deputy Minister of Foreign Affairs Jan.–Aug. 1994, 2010–12, Minister of Foreign Affairs 1994–2003, 2012–; Rector Univ. of World Economy and Diplomacy 1998–2003; Amb. to USA (also accred to Canada and Brazil) 2003–10; Mekhnat Shukhrati (Uzbekistan), Uzbekiston Belgisi. *Address:* Ministry of Foreign Affairs, 100029 Tashkent, O'zbekiston shoh ko'ch. 9, Uzbekistan (office). *Telephone:* (71) 233-64-75 (office). *Fax:* (71) 239-15-17 (office). *E-mail:* info@tiv.uz (office). *Website:* www.mfa.uz (office).

KAMINSKI, Janusz, BA; Polish cinematographer and film director; b. 27 June 1959, Ziembice; m. Holly Hunter 1995 (divorced 2001); ed Columbia Coll., Chicago, American Film Inst.; mem. American Soc. of Cinematographers; Franklin J. Schaffner Award 2010. *Films include:* All the Love in the World 1990, The Rain Killer 1990, The Terror Within II 1990, Grim Prairie Tales 1990, Pyrates 1991, Killer Instinct 1991, Cool as Ice 1991, Mad Dog Coll 1992, Trouble Bound 1993, The Adventures of Huck Finn (dir of photography) 1993, Schindler's List (Acad. Award for Best Cinematographer 1994, BAFTA Film Award 1994) 1993, Little Giants 1994, Tall Tale 1995, How to Make an American Quilt 1995, Jerry Maguire 1996, Amistad 1997, The Lost World: Jurassic Park 1997, Saving Private Ryan (Circuit Community Award for Best Cinematographer 1998, BSFC Award 1998, Acad. Award 1999) 1998, Lost Souls 2000, AI: Artificial Intelligence 2001, Minority Report 2002 (dir of photography), Catch Me If You Can 2002, The Terminal 2004,

Jumbo Girl 2004, War of the Worlds 2005, Munich 2005, Mission Zero (dir of photography) 2007, Le Scaphandre et le Papillon (Prize Vulcain de l'Artiste-Technicien, Cannes Film Festival 2007, BSFC Award 2007) 2007, Indiana Jones and the Kingdom of the Crystal Skull (dir of photography) 2008, Funny People (dir of photography) 2009, How Do You Know (dir of photography) 2010, War Horse (dir of photography) 2011, Lincoln (dir of photography) 2012, The Judge 2014, Bridge of Spies 2015, The BFG (dir of photography) 2016.

KAMIŃSKI, Marek; Polish explorer; b. 24 March 1964, Gdańsk; s. of Zdzisław Kamiński and Maria Kamińska; m. Katarzyna Kamiński; one s. one d.; ed Warsaw Univ., Instituto de Estudios Superiores de la Empresa Business School; Founder, Game San SA and Marek Kamiński Foundation; Founder and Co-owner, Invena SA mem. The Explorers Club 1996–; Hon. mem. Polar Research Cttee Polish Acad. of Sciences, Hon. Citizen, City of Koszalin; Kt's Cross Order of Polonia Restituta 1994, Officer's Cross Order of Polonia Restituta 2014; Finalist, World Young Business Achiever 1994, Man of the Year 1995, Życie Warszawy daily, Gold Medal for Outstanding Achievments in Sport, Chopin Award, Super Kolos Award 2004, Caritas Reward, Pope John Paul II 2005. *Expeditions include:* to Mexico, Guatemala, crossing of Spitsbergen, crossing of Greenland (twice); attempted solo crossing of Antarctica; first man who reached alone both North and South Poles in the same year 1995; climbed Mount Vinson (Antarctica) 1998; crossed Gibson Desert 1999; sailed yacht across the Atlantic (twice); participated in expedition to sources of the Amazon 2000 and North Pole expedition 2001, 2002; expedition to both poles in a single year with disabled Jan Mela, with Wojciech Ostrowski and Wojciech Moskal 2004; reached Gunnbjørn Fjeld, the highest peak in Greenland 2008, Summer Expedition Wisła 2009, Winter Expedition Wisła 2010. *Publications:* Not Only a Pole 1996, My Poles: Diaries from Expeditions 1990–98 (Artus Award for the Best Book of the Year) 1998, My Expeditions 2001, Razem na biegun (Together to the Pole) 2005, Expedition 2011, It is to Follow Your Dreams 2012, Alphabet 2013. *Leisure interests:* travelling to the coldest places in the world, sailing, philosophy. *Address:* c/o Marek Kamiński Foundation, ul. Grunwaldzka 212, 80-266 Gdańsk, Poland. *Telephone:* (58) 5544522. *Fax:* (58) 5523315. *E-mail:* mkaminski@gamasan.pl (office). *Website:* www.kaminski.pl (home).

KAMMENOS, Panagiotis (Panos); Greek economist and politician; b. 12 May 1965, Athens; m. Eleni Tzouli; five c.; ed Univ. of Lyon Business Admin School of Mans, France; mem. Parl. (Nea Demokratia—New Democracy) for Second Dist of Athens 1993–2012, (Anexartitoi Ellines—ANEL—Ind. Greeks) 2012–; Co-founder and Leader, Anexartitoi Ellines—ANEL 2012–; apptd Deputy Minister of Mercantile Marine, Aegean and Island Policy 2007; has served as mediator and official observer at elections in foreign countries; Minister of Nat. Defence Jan.–Aug. 2015, Sept. 2015–Jan. 2019 (resgnd); formed governing coalition with Synaspismos Rizospastikis Aristeras (SYRIZA—Coalition of the Radical Left) party Jan. 2015; Grand Cross of Merit, Czech Patriarchate, Medal of Honour, Patriarchate of Jerusalem; Chevalier, Ordre nat. du Mérite. *Address:* c/o Ministry of National Defence, Odos Mesogeion 227–231, Holargos, 154 51 Athens, Greece (office).

KAMOSHITA, Ichirō, MD; Japanese physician and politician; b. 16 Jan. 1949, Adachi, Tokyo; ed Nihon Univ.; Dir Hibiya Kokusai Clinic 1981–88; Head Dir Kamoshita-gakuen Acad., Educational Corpn 1988–93, Aojuji-kai, Healthcare Corpn 1993; mem. House of Reps (originally for Japan New Party; joined LDP 1997) 1993–, has served as dir of numerous parl. cttees including Judicial Affairs 1996, 1998, Election Law 1998, Finance 1998, Audit and Oversight 1998, 2006, Political Ethics and Election Law 1999, Health and Welfare 2000, Health, Labour and Welfare 2002–06; Sr Vice-Minister of Health, Labour and Welfare 2002–03, Minister of the Environment 2007–08, Minister in Charge of Global Environmental Problems 2007–08.

KAMOUN, Mahamat; Central African Republic financier and politician; b. 13 Nov. 1961, N'Délé; ed Boston Univ., USA; fmr Dir-Gen. of the Treasury; fmr Chef de Cabinet to Pres. Michel Djotodia; Adviser to interim Pres. Catherine Samba-Panza 2014; Prime Minister 2014–16; mem. Bd of Dirs Banque de Développement des Etats de l'Afrique Centrale.

KAMP, Henricus (Henk) Gregorius Jozeph; Dutch politician; *Minister of Economic Affairs;* b. 23 July 1952, Hengelo; ed Tax and Customs Admin Centre, Utrecht; worked as investigator Fiscal Information and Investigation Service 1980–86; mem. Borculo Municipal Council 1976–94, alderman 1986–94; mem. Gelderland Provincial Council 1987–94; mem. House of Reps 1994–; apptd Minister of Housing, Planning and Environment 2002; Minister of Defence 2003–06, Minister of Social Affairs and Employment 2010–12, Minister of Econ. Affairs 2012–, Sr mem. Council of Ministers 2015; Officer, Order of Oranje-Nassau 2007, Grand Cordon 1st Class, Order of the Rising Sun (Japan) 2014. *Address:* Ministry of Economic Affairs, Bezuidenhoutseweg 30, PO Box 20401, 2500 EC The Hague, Netherlands (office). *Telephone:* (70) 3796868 (office). *Website:* www.government.nl/ministries/ministry-of-economic-affairs (office).

KAMPFNER, John, BA (Hons); British writer and journalist; b. 27 Dec. 1962, Singapore; s. of Fred Kampfner and Elizabeth Kampfner (née Andrews); m. Lucy Ash; two d.; ed Westminster School, London, The Queen's Coll., Oxford; fmr foreign corresp. with Reuters and Daily Telegraph; Chief Political Corresp., Financial Times mid-1990s; fmr political commentator, Today programme (BBC Radio 4); Political Ed. New Statesman 2002–05, Ed. 2005–08; CEO Index on Censorship 2008–12, Trustee 2012; Chair. Turner Contemporary 2008–15, Clore Social Leadership Programme; mem. Council, King's Coll. London 2012–15; Adviser, Freedom of Expression and Culture, Google Inc. 2012–13, Global Network Initiative 2012–13; Chief Exec., Creative Industries Fed. 2014–18; regular appearances on radio and TV; Foreign Press Asscn Media Award 2002, British Soc. of Magazine Eds. Ed. of the Year Award for Current Affairs Magazines 2006. *Television documentary films:* (all for BBC) Israel Undercover 2002, The Ugly War: Children of Vengeance (Foreign Press Asscn Award for Film of the Year and Journalist of the Year) 2002, War Spin 2003, Robin Cook: The Lost Leader (profile) 2003, Clare Short: The Conscientious Objector (profile) 2003, Who Runs Britain (series) 2004. *Publications:* Inside Yeltsin's Russia: Corruption, Conflict, Capitalism 1995, Robin Cook 1999, Blair's Wars 2003, Freedom for Sale 2009, The Rich 2014; contrib. to The Times, Sunday Times, Observer, Independent, Guardian, Financial Times, Daily Telegraph, Daily Mail, Mail on Sunday, Evening Standard, Washington Post, Los Angeles Times, Time, Newsweek, Prospect, New Statesman, Spectator. *Leisure interests:* tennis, soccer, skiing, fine art, music. *E-mail:* john@jkampfner.net (office). *Website:* www.jkampfner.net.

KAMU, Okko; Finnish conductor and violinist; *Principal Guest Conductor, Singapore Symphony Orchestra;* b. 7 March 1946, Helsinki; m. Anna Aminoff; ed Sibelius Acad.; leader, Suhonen Quartet 1964; began professional career with Helsinki Philharmonic Orchestra 1965; subsequently appointed leader, Finnish Nat. Opera Orchestra 1966–69, Third Conductor 1967; Guest Conductor, Swedish Royal Opera, Stockholm 1969; Chief Conductor, Finnish Radio Symphony Orchestra 1971–77; Music Dir Oslo Philharmonic 1975–79, Helsinki Philharmonic 1981–89; Prin. Conductor, Netherlands Radio Symphony 1983–86; Prin. Guest Conductor, City of Birmingham Symphony Orchestra 1985–88; Prin. Conductor, Sjaelland Symphony Orchestra, Copenhagen 1988–94; Music Dir Stockholm Sinfonietta 1989–93; Prin. Conductor Helsingborg Symphony Orchestra 1991–2000; First Guest Conductor, Singapore Symphony Orchestra 1995–2001, now Prin. Guest Conductor; Music Dir Finnish Nat. Opera, Helsinki 1996–2000; Prin. Guest Conductor Lausanne Chamber Orchestra 1999–2002; Prin. Conductor, Lahti Symphony Orchestra 2011–16; Artistic Dir Int. Sibelius Festival 2011–; conducted world premières of Sallinen's operas The Red Line, The King Goes Forth to France, Palace and King Lear; mem. Royal Swedish Acad. of Music 1994–; First Prize, First Int. Karajan Conductor Competition, Berlin 1969. *Recordings include:* Sibelius: La Tempête, Le Barde, Tapiola, with Orchestre symphonique de Lahti (Diapason d'Or de l'année 2011). *Leisure interests:* golf, gastronomy. *Address:* Patrick Garvey Management, 43 Greencroft Street, Salisbury, Wiltshire, SP1 1JF, England (office). *E-mail:* patrick@patrickgarvey.com (office). *Website:* www.patrickgarvey.com/artists/okko-kamu.html (office).

KAMUNANWIRE, Perezi Karukubiro, PhD; Ugandan academic and diplomatist; b. 25 July 1937, Mbarara; m.; two c.; ed Columbia Univ., New York, USA; Chair. Uganda People's Congress Youth League 1958–63; Pres. and Chair. Pan-African Students' Org. in the Americas 1965–70; Prof., CUNY, USA 1974–86, fmr Prof., Black Studies Program; Amb. to Austria (also accred to FRG and the Holy See) and Perm. Rep. to Int. Orgs in Vienna 1986–88, Perm. Rep. to UN, New York 1988–95, Chair. UN Gen. Ass. Special Political Cttee 1990–95; Adjunct Prof., Center for Conflict Man. and Organizational Research, Sophia Univ., Bulgaria 2003–06; Amb. to USA 2006–13. *Publications:* A Study Guide to Uganda (co-ed.) 1970; numerous articles in the field of int. relations. *Address:* Ministry of Foreign Affairs, PO Box 7048, 2A/B Apollo Kaggwa Road, Kampala, Uganda (office). *Telephone:* (41) 4345661 (office). *Fax:* (41) 4258722 (office). *E-mail:* info@mofa.go.ug (office). *Website:* www.mofa.go.ug (office).

KAMYNIN, Mikhail Leonidovich; Russian diplomatist; b. 13 Aug. 1956, Moscow; m.; one d. one s.; ed Moscow State Inst. of Int. Relations, Diplomatic Acad. of Ministry of Foreign Affairs; various positions at Embassy in Mexico City 1978–82, 1987–91, Press Sec., Ministry of Foreign Affairs 1991–92, Counsellor, Embassy in Madrid 1992–97, Asst Dir of Press and Information, Ministry of Foreign Affairs 1997–99, Minister Counsellor, Embassy in Havana 1999–2002, Asst Dir of European Affairs, Ministry of Foreign Affairs 2002, Amb. to Spain 2002–05, Dir of Information and Press Dept, Ministry of Foreign Affairs 2005–08, Amb. to Cuba (also accred to Bahamas) 2008–17; mem. Russian Union of Journalists. *Address:* c/o Embassy of the Russian Federation, Avenida 5, No. 6402, entre 62 y 66, Miramar, Havana, Cuba (office).

KAN, Naoto; Japanese politician; b. 10 Oct. 1946, Ube City, Yamaguchi Pref.; m.; two s.; ed Tokyo Inst. of Tech.; fmr patent attorney; Rep. for Tokyo's 7th Dist (multi-mem.) as mem. Socialist Democratic Fed. 1980–96, for 18th Dist 1996–; Minister of Health and Welfare Jan.–Nov. 1996; mem. House of Reps; mem. New Party Sakigake (NPS), now Sakigake; Founder-mem. Democratic Party of Japan 1996, Leader 1996–97, 1997–98, Pres. 1998–99, Sec.-Gen. 2000–02, Pres. 2002–04 (resgnd), Acting Pres. 2006–08, Pres. 2010–11; Deputy Prime Minister and Minister of State for Nat. Strategy, for Econ. and Fiscal Policy, and for Science and Tech. Policy 2009–10; Minister of Finance Jan.–June 2010; Prime Minister 2010–11 (resgnd); mem. UN High-Level Panel on Post–2015 Devt Agenda 2012. *Publication:* Dai-jin (Minister). *Leisure interest:* playing Go.

KAN, Yuet Wai, MD, DSc, FRCP, FRS; American (b. Hong Kong) physician, investigator and academic; *Louis K. Diamond Professor of Hematology, Departments of Laboratory Medicine and Medicine, University of California, San Francisco;* b. 11 June 1936, Hong Kong; s. of Tong Po Kan and Lai Wai Li; m. Alvera Lorraine Limauro 1964; two d.; ed Wah Yan Coll., Hong Kong and Univ. of Hong Kong Medical School; Asst Prof. of Pediatrics, Harvard Medical School 1970–72; Assoc. Prof., Dept of Medicine, Univ. of California, San Francisco 1972–77, Prof., Depts of Lab. Medicine, Medicine 1977–, Louis K. Diamond Prof. of Hematology 1991–, Investigator, Howard Hughes Medical Inst. 1976–2003; Dir and Hon. Prof., Inst. of Molecular Biology, Univ. of Hong Kong 1991–94; Pres. American Soc. of Hematology 1990, Soc. of Chinese Bioscientists in America 1998–99; Chair. Shaw Prize in Life Science and Medicine Selection Cttee 2006–, American Asscn of Cancer Research Foundation 2011–; mem. Research Grants Council, Hong Kong 1990–94, NIH Blood Diseases and Resources Advisory Cttee 1985–89, Nat. Inst. of Digestive and Kidney Disease Advisory Council, NIH 1991–95, Scientific Advisory Bd, St Jude's Children's Hosp. 1994–97, Scientific Advisory Bd and Exec. Cttee, Qiu Shi Foundation on Science and Tech., Hong Kong 1994–, Nat. Heart, Lung & Blood Inst. 1995–96; Trustee, Croucher Foundation 1992–2011, Chair. 1997–2011; mem. NAS, Academia Sinica; Assoc. Fellow, Third World Acad. of Sciences; Foreign mem. Chinese Acad. of Sciences; Hon. MD (Univ. of Cagliari, Sardinia, Italy) 1981; Hon. DSc (Chinese Univ. of Hong Kong) 1981, (Univ. of Hong Kong) 1987, (Open Univ. of Hong Kong) 1998; Damashek Award, American Soc. of Hematology 1979, Stratton Lecture Award, Int. Soc. of Hematology 1980, George Thorn Award, Howard Hughes Medical Inst. 1980, Gairdner Foundation Int. Award 1984, Allan Award, American Soc. of Human Genetics 1984, Lita Annenberg Hazen Award for Excellence in Clinical Research 1984, Waterford Award in Biomedical Sciences 1987, NIH Merit Award 1987, American Coll. of Physicians Award 1988, Sanremo Int. Award for Genetic Research 1989, Warren Alpert Foundation Prize 1989, Albert Lasker Clinical Medical Research Award 1991, Christopher Columbus Discovery Award in Biomedical Research 1992, City of Medicine Award 1992, Cotlove Award, Acad.

of Clinical Lab. Physicians and Scientists 1993, Merit Award, Fed. of Chinese Canadians Educ. Foundation 1994, Helmut Horten Research Award 1995, Shaw Prize in Life Science and Medicine, Hong Kong 2004, Lifetime Achievement Award, Soc. of Chinese Bioscientists in America 2006, Ernest Beutler Orize and Lecture A, American Soc. of Hematology 2009, Karl Landsteiner Prize and Lecturer, American Asscn of Blood Banks 2011. *Publications:* chapters in numerous books and more than 290 articles in scientific journals. *Address:* HSW 901E, 513 Parnassus Avenue, San Francisco, CA 94143-0793, USA (office). *Telephone:* (415) 476-5841 (office). *Fax:* (415) 476-2956 (office). *E-mail:* yw.kan@ucsf.edu (office).

KAN-DAPAAH, Albert; Ghanaian politician and chartered accountant; *Director, Centre for Public Accountability, University of Professional Studies;* b. 14 March 1953, Maase-Boaman, Ashanti Region; m. Rebecca Kan-Dapaah; four c.; ed Acherensua Secondary School, Inst. of Professional Studies, North East London Polytechnic and Emile Woolf Coll. of Accountancy, UK; Audit Sr with Pannel Kerr Forster, transferred to Monrovia, Liberia and London, UK offices 1978–86; Head of Audit, Social Security and Nat. Insurance Trust Jan.–Sept. 1987; Dir of Audit, Electricity Co. of Ghana 1987, later Dir of Finance for six years; Partner, Kwesie, Kan-Dapaah & Baah Co., Accra, Kan-Dapaah and Associates; mem. Parl. for Afigya Sekyere West 1997–2012; Minister for Energy 2000–03, for Communications and Tech. 2003–07, for Interior 2006–07, of Defence 2007–09; currently Dir Centre for Public Accountability, Univ. of Professional Studies, Accra; fmr part-time Lecturer in Auditing, School of Admin, Univ. of Ghana, Inst. of Professional Studies; currently Adjunct Lecturer in Auditing, Univ. of Professional Studies, Accra; Pres. Inst. of Chartered Accountants (Ghana) 1996; Vice-Pres. Asscn of Accountancy Bodies in West Africa 1996; mem. Bd of Dirs SSB Consumer Credit Ltd 1987–95; Alt. Bd mem. Kabel Metal Ghana Ltd 1987–95, New Times Corpn 1987–95; Ashanti Regional Rep. on Nat. Council of the New Patriotic Party, mem. Finance and Econ. Affairs Cttee 1992–96; mem. Ghana Inst. of Chartered Accountants; Fellow, Chartered Asscn of Certified Accountants (UK); Dr hc (Univ. of Professional Studies, Accra) 2013. *Address:* Centre for Public Accountability, University of Professional Studies, POBox LG 149, Accra, Ghana. *E-mail:* info@upsa.edu.gh. *Website:* newsite.upsa.edu.gh/centre-of-excellence/centre-for-public-accountability.

KANAAN, Taher Hamdi, BA, PhD; Jordanian economics consultant and organization official; *Chairman of the Executive Board, Arab Centre for Research and Policy Studies, Doha;* b. 1 March 1935, Nablus, Palestine; s. of Hamdi Kanaan and Najiah Kanaan (née Quttaineh); m. Ilham Kahwaji 1960; three s.; ed American Univ. of Beirut, Trinity Coll., Cambridge, UK; Econ. Adviser, Ministry of Planning, Iraq 1964–65; Dir of Programmes at Arab Fund for Econ. and Social Devt, Kuwait 1973–76; Consultant in Industrial Devt, Ministry of Planning, Morocco 1977–78; Chief External Financing and Devt, UNCTAD, Geneva 1979–83; Dir and Econ. Adviser Arab Fund 1983–85; Minister of Occupied Territories Affairs 1985, of Planning 1986–89, Deputy Prime Minister for Devt 1998–99; Gen. Man. Industrial Devt Bank of Jordan 1989–92; mem. Bd of Higher Educ., Jordan; mem. Bd of Govs World Bank, Arab Fund for Econ. and Social Devt 1985–89; mem. Bd of Trustees, Center for Arab Unity Studies, Beirut, Econ. Research Forum, Cairo, Arab Anti-Corruption Org.; Man. Dir Jordan Center for Policy Research and Dialogue, Amman 2003–10; Chair. Exec. Bd, Arab Centre for Research and Policy Studies, Doha, Qatar 2014–; mem. Advisory Group Arab Human Devt Reports. *Leisure interests:* swimming, music, history, philosophy, surfing the Internet. *Address:* Arab Centre for Research and Policy Studies, PO Box 10277, Street No. 826, Zone 66, Doha, Qatar (office); PO Box 830825, Zahran, Amman 11183, Jordan (office). *Telephone:* 44199777 (Doha) (office); (6) 5923676 (Amman) (office). *Fax:* 44831651 (Doha) (office); (6) 5676666 (Amman) (office). *E-mail:* taher.kanaan@gmail.com (home). *Website:* www.dohainstitute.org (office).

KANADE, Takeo, PhD; Japanese electrical engineer, computer scientist and academic; *U.A. and Helen Whitaker University Professor of Computer Science and Robotics, The Robotics Institute, Carnegie Mellon University;* b. 24 Oct. 1945, Hyōgo; ed Kyoto Univ.; mem. Faculty, Dept of Information Science, Kyoto Univ. –1980; Asst Prof., Computer Science Dept and The Robotics Inst., Carnegie Mellon Univ., USA 1980–82, Assoc. Prof. 1982–85, apptd Full Prof. 1985, U.A. and Helen Whitaker Prof. of Computer Science and Robotics 1993–, Univ. Prof. 1998–, apptd Dir The Robotics Inst. 1992, Founding Chair. Robotics PhD Program 1989–93; Founding Ed. International Journal of Computer Vision; has served on numerous govt, industrial and academic advisory bds, including Aeronautics and Space Eng Bd of Nat. Research Council, NASA Advanced Tech. Advisory Cttee, PITAC Panel for Transforming Healthcare, Advisory Bd of Canadian Inst. for Advanced Research; mem. Nat. Acad. of Eng, American Acad. of Arts and Sciences, Robotics Soc. of Japan, Inst. of Electronics and Communication Engineers of Japan; Fellow, IEEE, Asscn for Computing Machinery 1999, American Asscn of Artificial Intelligence; Joseph Engelberger Award, Yokogawa Prize, JARA Award, Otto Franc Award, C&C Award, FIT Funai Accomplishment Award, Allen Newell Research Excellence Award, Marr Prize Award 1990, Longuet-Higgins Prize 2006, 2008, Bower Award and Prize for Achievement in Science, Franklin Inst. 2008, Kyoto Prize, Inamori Foundation (co-recipient) 2016. *Publications:* more than 300 papers in peer-reviewed journals; more than 20 patents. *Address:* Robotics Institute, Carnegie Mellon University, 5000 Forbes Avenue, Pittsburgh, PA 15213, USA (office). *Telephone:* (412) 268-3016 (office). *Fax:* (412) 268-6436 (office). *E-mail:* kanade@andrew.cmu.edu (office). *Website:* www.ri.cmu.edu (office); www.cs.cmu.edu (office).

KANAKRIEH, Ezzeddine, PhD; Jordanian economist and politician; *Minister of Finance;* b. 13 Sept. 1960; m.; three s. two d.; ed Yarmouk Univ., Arab Acad. for Banking and Financial Sciences, Amman Arab Univ.; Financial Accountant Jordanian Armed Forces 1984–86; Financial Analyst, Ministry of Finance 1986–93, Head of Dept of Appropriations and Energy, Directorate of Cash Man. 1993–2000, Dir of Cash Admin 2001–05, Asst Sec.-Gen. of Finance 2005–07, Sec.-Gen. of Finance 2007–12, 2014–18; Minister of Finance 2018–; apptd Dir of Income and Sales, Dept of Tax 2012, Commr 2012–14; Dir-Gen. Social Security Inst. April–June 2018; Royal Order of Independence 2007; King Abdullah II Award for Excellence in Govt Performance 2008. *Address:* Ministry of Finance, PO Box 85, King Hussein Street, Amman 11118, Jordan (office). *Telephone:* (6) 4636321 (office). *Fax:* (6) 4618527 (office). *E-mail:* info@mof.gov.jo (office). *Website:* www.mof.gov.joc (office).

KANANIN, Roman Grigorevich; Russian architect; b. 19 June 1935, Moscow; s. of Grigoriy Kananin and Maria Kananin; m. 1959; one d.; ed Moscow Architectural Inst.; Head of Atelier No. 3. of Public Jt Stock Co. Mosproject 1972–; mem. Russian Acad. of Architecture and Bldg Sciences 2005–; Lenin Prize 1984, Honoured Builder of Moscow 1999, People's Architect 2005. *Works include:* Patrice Lumumba Univ. (now Univ. of People's Friendship), Moscow (with others) 1969–73, residential blocks on Lenin Prospekt, Moscow 1965–70, multi-storey brick residential complex, Noviye Cheremushky 1973–84, Malaya Zemlya Memorial Complex, Novorossiysk 1982, various monuments in Moscow and Magnitogorsk, including monument to Gerzen and Ogarev, Vorobyevy Hils, Moscow, Palace of Youth, Moscow 1978, IRIS Pulman Hotel and apartments, Moscow 1991, Parus Business Centre, Tverskaya-Yamskaya St, Moscow 1994, exclusive multi-storey residential bldgs, Krasnoproletarskaya str., vl. 7 1999, Dolgorukovskaya str., vl. 24–30 2001, B. Gruzinskaya str., vl. 37 2001, residential complexes, Petrovsko-Razumkovsky proezd, B Academicheskaya St, Moscow. *Leisure interests:* sport, travelling. *Address:* Joint-Stock Company Mosproject, 13/14, 1-st Brestkaya str., GSP, 125190 Moscow, Russia. *Telephone:* (495) 209-61-22; (495) 250-46-99. *Fax:* (495) 209-50-02.

KANAPLYOU, Uladzimir; Belarusian politician; Deputy Chair. Palata Predstaviteley 2000–04, Chair. 2004–07; fmr Head, Belarusian Handball Fed.; Vice-Pres. Nat. Olympics Cttee. *Address:* Palata Predstaviteley, 220010 Minsk, vul. Savetskaya 11, Belarus (office).

KANAWA, Dame Kiri Te (see TE KANAWA, Dame Kiri).

KANBUR, Ravi, BA, MPhil, MA, DPhil; British economist and academic; *T.H. Lee Professor of World Affairs, International Professor of Applied Economics and Management and Professor of Economics, Cornell University;* b. 28 Aug. 1954, Dharwar, India; s. of Prof. M. G. Kanbur and M. M. Kanbur; m. Margaret S. Grieco 1979; ed King Edward VI Camp Hill School, Birmingham, Gonville & Caius Coll., Cambridge, Merton and Worcester Colls, Oxford; Research Fellow, Nuffield Coll., Oxford 1978–79; Fellow in Econs, Clare Coll. Cambridge 1979–83; Prof. of Econs, Univ. of Essex 1983–85; Visiting Prof., Princeton Univ. 1985–87; Prof. of Econs and Dir Devt Econs Research Centre, Univ. of Warwick 1987–89, Hon. Prof. 1994; Sr Adviser and Ed. World Bank Economic Review and World Bank Research Observer, IBRD, Washington, DC 1989–92; World Bank Resident Rep. in Ghana 1992–94, World Bank Chief Economist for Africa 1994–96, Prin. Adviser to Sr Vice-Pres. and Chief Economist 1996–97; T.H. Lee Prof. of World Affairs, Int. Prof. of Applied Econs and Man. and Prof. of Econs, Cornell Univ., Ithaca, NY 1997–; Research Fellow, Center for Econ. Policy Research, London 1983–; V.K.R.V. Chair Prof., Inst. for Social and Econ. Change, Bangalore 2004–05; Academic Visitor, Univ. of Edinburgh 2000–, Univ. of Cambridge 2002–03, 2004–, Univ. of Birmingham 2010–; Sr Visiting Fellow, Nat. Council of Applied Econ. Research, Delhi 2009–; Visiting Fellow, World Bank, Delhi 2010–11; D.M. Nanjundappa Chair Visiting Prof., Centre for Multidisciplinary Devt Research, Dharwad, India 2011–; Sr Academic Visitor, Clare Coll., Cambridge 2012–13; Visiting Scholar, IMF 2013; Non-Resident Fellow, Center for Global Devt 2013–; Visiting Scholar, Centre for Devt Studies, Trivandrum 2013–14; Pres. Soc. for the Study of Econ. Inequality 2013–; Co-Chair. Int. Panel on Social Progress 2014–; Hon. Prof., Univ. of Warwick; American Agricultural Econs Asscn Research Award (co-recipient with L. Haddad) 1991. *Publications:* more than 250 articles in learned journals. *Address:* 301-J Warren Hall, Cornell University, Ithaca, NY 14853-7801, USA (office). *Telephone:* (607) 255-7966 (office). *Fax:* (607) 255-9984 (office). *E-mail:* sk145@cornell.edu (office). *Website:* www.kanbur.aem.cornell.edu (office); dyson.cornell.edu/people/profiles/kanbur.php (office).

KANCHELI, Giya (Georgy); Georgian composer; b. 10 Aug. 1935, Tbilisi; s. of Alexander Kancheli and Agnessa Kancheli; m. Valentina Djikia; one s. one d.; ed Tbilisi State Conservatory, studied composition with I. Tuskiya; worked as freelance composer following graduation from 1963; mem. of 'Soviet avant-garde' during 1960s, subsequently dedicated himself to developing a personal musical style based on simple formulas occurring in the music of different epochs, ancient folk songs and in popular music; later collaborated with dir Robert Sturua who inspired him to write music for films and several plays; Prof., Tbilisi Conservatory 1970–90; Dir of Music, Rustaveli Theatre, Tbilisi 1971–91, wrote incidental music for many of Sturua's productions, including his opera 'Music for the Living' 1984 (re-staged for Deutsches Nat. Theater, Weimar 1999), for Brecht's The Caucasian Chalk Circle, Shakespeare's Richard III, Hamlet and King Lear, Sophocles' Oedipus and Beckett's Waiting for Godot; best known as a composer of symphonic and other large-scale works; Fourth Symphony, 'In Memoria di Michelangelo', received its US premiere with the Philadelphia Orchestra, Yury Temirkanov conducting 1978; left Georgia with his family 1991, first went to Berlin and received a grant from German Academic Exchange Service; commissions and frequent performances in Europe and USA with Jansug Kakhidze, Dennis Russell Davies, Kim Kashkashian, Gidon Kremer, Yuri Bashmet, Mstislav Rostropovich and the Kronos Quartet; Composer-in-Residence, Royal Flemish Philharmonic Orchestra, Antwerp 1995–96; USSR State Prize 1976, USSR People's Artist 1988, State Prize of Georgia 1982, Nika Prize for film music 1987, Triumph Prize Moscow 1998, Wolf Foundation Prize in the Arts (Music) 2008, Lifetime Achievement Award, Istanbul 2012. *Compositions include:* symphonies: First 1967, Second 1970, Third 1973, Fourth (In Memoria di Michelangelo) 1975, Fifth 1977, Sixth (In Memory of Parents) 1980, Seventh (Epilogue) 1986; other symphonic works: Mourned by the Wind for orchestra and viola 1989, Lament (in memory of Luigi Nono), for violin, soprano and orchestra 1995; opera: Music for the Living 1984; chamber works: Life Without Christmas 1989–90 (cycle of four works for chamber ensembles), Magnum Ignotum, for wind ensemble and tape 1994, Exil, for soprano, small ensemble and tape 1994, Dixi for mixed choir and symphony orchestra 2009, Chiaroscuro for soloist (violin/viola) and orchestra 2010, Lingering for symphony orchestra 2012, Angels of Sorrow 2013. *Address:* Tovstonogov str. 6, 0162 Tbilisi, Georgia (home). *E-mail:* mail@kancheli.de (office).

KANDARIAN, Steven A., BA, MBA, JD; American business executive; *Chairman, President and CEO, MetLife, Inc.;* ed Clark Univ., Harvard Business School, Georgetown Univ. Law Center; began career as investment banker with Rotan

Mosle, Inc., Houston, Tex.; Man. Dir Lee Capital Holdings, Boston 1984–90; Founder and Pres. Eagle Capital Holdings 1990–93; Founder and Man. Dir Orion Partners, LP 1993–2001; Exec. Dir Pension Benefit Guaranty Corpn 2001–04; joined MetLife as Exec. Vice-Pres. and Chief Investment Officer 2005–11, mem. Bd of Dirs, Pres. and CEO MetLife, Inc. 2011–, Chair. 2012–; mem. Bd of Dirs Damon Runyon Cancer Research Foundation, Exxon Mobil Corpn 2018–; mem. Economic Club of New York. *Address:* MetLife, Inc., 2701 Queens Plaza North, Long Island City, NY 11101-4015, USA (office). *Telephone:* (212) 578-2211 (office). *Fax:* (212) 578-3320 (office). *E-mail:* info@metlife.com (office). *Website:* www.metlife.com (office).

KANDBORG, Lt-Gen. (retd) Ole Larson; Danish army officer (retd) and consultant; b. 16 May 1941, nr Skanderborg; m. Lis Kandborg; two c.; ed Viborg, Army Officers' Acad., Copenhagen, Canadian Forces' Staff Coll., Toronto, Canada, NATO Defence Coll., Rome, Italy; nat. service with Prince's Life Regt, Viborg, Sergeant, Lt; First Lt, Capt. of mechanized infantry Bn 1966–72; Instructor, Danish Combat Arms School 1974–77; Staff Officer, HQ of the UN Peace-keeping Force in Cyprus 1977–78; Co. Commdr, Skive, G3 of Mechanized Brigade 1978–82; at Faculty of Danish Defence Coll. 1982–84; Instructor, annual Nordic UN Staff Officers' Course (Sweden), Chief Instructor; Lt-Col, Commdr of 1st Tank Bn, Jutland Dragoon Regt, Holstebro 1984–85; Public Information Adviser and Deputy to Chief of Defence, Defence HQ, Copenhagen 1986–89, Deputy Chief of Staff for Plans and Policy 1992; Col, Commdr 2nd New Zealand Brigade, Vordingborg 1989–90; Maj.-Gen., Commdr Jutland Div., Fredericia 1990–92; Commdr of Danish Operational Command based in Århus and Kamp 1993–96; Danish Mil. Rep. to NATO Mil. Cttee April–Sept. 1996, Dir Int. Mil. Staff, NATO 1996–2001 (retd); fmr Mil. Adviser on strategic and NATO matters, DCS Group; Commdr, Order of Dannebrog, Mil. Good Service Medal, Reserve Officers' Asscn's Good Service Medal, Commdr 1st Degree, Order of the Swedish North Star, Legion of Merit (Degree of Commdr); UN Medal 7.

KANDEL, Eric Richard, BA, MD; American psychiatrist, biochemist and academic; *Professor of Neuroscience, Columbia University;* b. 7 Nov. 1929, Vienna, Austria; m. 1956; two c.; ed Harvard Coll., New York Univ.; New York Univ. (NYU) School of Medicine 1956; Resident in Psychiatry, Harvard Medical School 1960–64, staff psychiatrist 1964–65; Assoc. Prof. of Physiology, NYU 1965–74; Prof. of Physiology and Psychiatry, Columbia Univ. 1974–, Prof. of Biochemistry 1992, now Prof. of Neuroscience; Sr Investigator, Howard Hughes Medical Inst. 1983–; mem. NAS, American Acad. of Arts and Sciences, Soc. of Neurosciences (Pres. 1980–81), Int. Brain Research Org., New York Acad. of Sciences; numerous awards and prizes including Nat. Medal of Science 1988, Warren Triennial Prize 1992, Harvey Prize 1993, Mayor Award for Excellence in Science and Tech. 1994, New York Acad. of Medicine Award 1996, Wolf Foundation Prize in Medicine 1999, Heineken Prize 2000, Nobel Prize for Medicine (jt recipient) 2000. *Publications:* In Search of Memory (Los Angeles Times Book Prize for Science and Technology) 2006; numerous articles in academic journals. *Address:* Howard Hughes Medical Institute, Columbia University, 1051 Riverside Drive, New York, NY 10032, USA (office). *Telephone:* (212) 543-5204 (office). *Fax:* (212) 543-5474 (office). *E-mail:* erk5@columbia.edu (office). *Website:* www.excalibur.cpmc.columbia.edu (office).

KANDODO, Ken Edward, BEcons, MBA; Malawi politician; fmr positions include auditor and foreign investment adviser, KPMG, UK and Mozambique, financial consultant for UNICEF, Gen. Man., Blantyre Print and Packaging Ltd; fmr Head, Nat. Food Reserve Agency; MP for Kasungu Central 2009–; Minister of Finance 2009–11, also Gov. of Malawi to Eastern and Southern African Trade and Devt Bank, Minister of Nat. Defence 2012–14; mem. Democratic Progressive Party.

KANE, Amadou; Senegalese banker and politician; *President, AK Associates;* b. 1954, Thiès; m.; three c.; ed Univ. Paris I–Sorbonne, Univ. Paris IX–Dauphine, France; began career as credit analyst, Africa and Latin America Div., Union de Banques Arabes et Françaises SA, Neuilly, Paris; Dir, Financial Insts and Industry Dept, West African Devt Bank, Lomé 1990–94, Head, Financial Operations Dept 1994–95; joined BNP Paribas 1995, Dir, Banque Internationale pour le Commerce et l'Industrie (BICI) 1995, Gen. Man. 1996, Man. Dir Banque Internationale pour le Commerce et l'Industrie du Sénégal (BICIS) 1996–2006, 2010–12, Head of Africa within BNP Paribas Retail Banking, Emerging Markets and Overseas Territories Dept 2006–10; Minister of the Economy and Finance 2012–13; Pres. Asscn professionnelle de banques et établissements financiers du Sénégal 1998–2004; Vice-Pres. Conseil national du patronat du Sénégal 2002; Dir Banque régionale d'investissement de la Banque Centrale des États de l'Afrique de l'Ouest (BCEAO) 2004–; Pres. AK Associates; Dir ADB; Pres. Organisation nat. de coordination des activités de vacances (ONCAV); Ordre Nat. du Lion de la République Sénégalaise 1997, Chevalier, Légion d'honneur 2007. *Publications:* contribs to numerous journals including Jeune Afrique, le Monde diplomatique, Banque, Journal de l'économie africaine. *Address:* AK Associates, 8 bis Avenue des Ambassadeurs, BP 16 366, Dakar, Senegal (office). *Telephone:* (33) 860-74-44 (office). *Website:* www.ak-associates.net (office).

KANE, Angela, MA; German diplomatist and UN official; b. (Angela Uther), 29 Sept. 1948, Hamelin; m. William P. Kane; ed Univ. of Munich, Bryn Mawr Coll., Pa USA, Johns Hopkins School of Advanced Int. Studies, Washington, DC; early career includes positions at World Bank, Washington, DC and pvt. industry in Europe; staff mem. UN since 1977 with various positions including postings to Jakarta and Bangkok, Jr Officer Cabinet Sec.-Gen. Waldheim, election monitor Nicaragua and El Salvador, responsible for disarmament issues and World Disarmament Campaign, mem. negotiating team for Cen. American Peace Process 1990–91, Prin. Officer for Political Affairs, Office of Sec.-Gen. Boutros Boutros-Ghali 1991–95, Man. Library and Publ., Dept Public Information 1995–99, Dir Americas and Europe Div., Dept Political Affairs 1999–2002, Deputy Special Rep. of Sec.-Gen. to UN Mission in Ethiopia and Eritrea (UNMEE) Asmara 2003–04, Asst Sec.-Gen., Dept for Gen. Ass. and Conf. Man. (DGACM) 2004–05, Asst Sec.-Gen. for Political Affairs 2005–08, Under-Sec.-Gen. for Man. 2008–12, High Rep. for Disarmament Affairs 2012–15.

KANE, Charles L., BS, PhD; American theoretical physicist and academic; *Christopher H. Browne Distinguished Professor of Physics, University of Pennsylvania;* m. Suzanne Amador 1994; one s. one d.; ed Univ. of Chicago, Massachusetts Inst. of Tech.; Research Asst, Univ. of Chicago 1984–85; Postdoctoral Assoc., IBM T.J. Watson Research Center, Yorktown Heights, NY 1989–91; Asst Prof. of Physics, Univ. of Pennsylvania 1991–97, Assoc. Prof. of Physics 1997–2006, Assoc. Chair for Undergraduate Affairs, Physics Dept 2002–05, Class of 1965 Endowed Term Chair 2012–14, Walter H. and Leonore C. Annenberg Prof. in the Natural Sciences 2014–16, Christopher H. Browne Distinguished Prof. of Physics 2016–; mem. NAS 2014; Fellow, American Physical Soc. 2006; NSF Grad. Fellow 1985–88, IBM Predoctoral Fellowship 1988–89, Condensed Matter Europhysics Prize 2010, Oliver E. Buckley Prize 2012, Simons Investigator grant 2012, chosen for the inaugural class of Math. and the Physical Sciences, Simons Investigators 2012, Dirac Medal and Prize (co-recipient) 2012, Physics Frontiers Prize, Fundamental Physics Prize Foundation (co-recipient) 2013, Lindback Award for Distinguished Teaching, Univ. of Pennsylvania 2014, Benjamin Franklin Medal, Franklin Inst. (co-recipient) 2015, Breakthrough Prize in Fundamental Physics (co-recipient) 2019, Frontiers of Knowledge Award in Basic Sciences, BBVA Foundation (co-recipient) 2019. *Achievements include:* predicted theoretically the quantum spin Hall effect and what are now known as topological insulators. *Publications:* more than 80 papers in professional journals on the theory of quantum electronic phenomena in solids. *Leisure interest:* playing classical guitar. *Address:* DRL 2N17d, David Rittenhouse Laboratory, University of Pennsylvania, 209 South 33rd Street, Philadelphia, PA 19104, USA (office). *Telephone:* (215) 898-8149 (office). *Fax:* (215) 898-2010 (office). *E-mail:* kane@physics.upenn.edu (office). *Website:* www.physics.upenn.edu (office).

KANEKO, Hisashi, MSc; Japanese business executive and foundation executive; b. 19 Nov. 1933, Tokyo; s. of Shozo Kaneko and Toshi Kaneko; m. Mokoto Washino; three c.; ed Tokyo Univ., Univ. of Calif., Berkeley; joined NEC Corpn 1956, Pres. NEC America 1989–91, NEC Corpn 1994–99 (resgnd), Counsellor 1999, fmr Pres. and mem. Bd of Dirs NEC Foundation of America.

KANEKO, Isao; Japanese airline industry executive; b. 1 March 1938; m.; one d.; ed Tokyo Univ.; joined Japan Airlines (JAL) 1960, worked in Int. Cargo Dept then joined Industrial Relations Dept; posted to American Region HQ, New York 1968–72; Deputy Vice Pres. Industrial Relations 1985–95, mem. Bd of Dirs 1991, Man. Dir and Sr Vice Pres., Human Resources 1995–97, Sr Man. Dir and Sr Vice Pres., Human Resources 1997–98, Pres. JAL 1998–2002, Pres. and CEO Japan Airlines and concurrently Pres. and CEO Japan Airlines System Corpn 2002–04, Chair. and CEO Japan Airlines Corpn (JAL Group holding co.) and concurrently Chair. Japan Airlines Int. and Japan Airlines Domestic System 2004–05, apptd Sr Adviser 2005; Chair. Japan-Asia Exchange Cttee, Keiza Doyukai (Japan Asscn of Corp. Execs).

KANEM, Natalia, MD, MPH; Panamanian paediatrician and international organization official; *Executive Director, United Nations Population Fund;* ed Columbia Univ., Univ. of Washington, Seattle, Harvard Univ.; started career as lecturer, Johns Hopkins and Columbia Univ. schools of medicine and public health; fmr co-Dir Harlem Center for Health Promotion and Disease Prevention, New York; various roles with Ford Foundation (welfare org.) 1992–2005, including Deputy Vice-Pres. and Sr Dir, Peace and Social Justice Programme, Sr Dir, Office of Man. Services, Rep. for W Africa (based in Lagos and Dakar), Programme Officer in Nigeria Office for Women's Reproductive Health and Sexuality; Founding Pres. ELMA Philanthropies Inc. 2005–11; Sr Assoc., Lloyd Best Inst., West Indies 2012–13; UN Population Fund (UNFPA) Rep. in Tanzania 2014–16, Asst Sec.-Gen. and Deputy Exec. Dir (Programme), UNFPA 2016–17, Exec. Dir 2017–; Trustee TrustAfrica. *Address:* United Nations Population Fund (UNFPA), 605 Third Ave, New York, NY 10158, USA (office). *Telephone:* (212) 297-5000 (office). *Fax:* (212) 370-0201 (office). *E-mail:* hq@unfpa.org (office). *Website:* www.unfpa.org (office).

KANERVA, Ilkka Armas Mikael, MPolSc; Finnish politician; *President of the Parliamentary Assembly, Organization for Security and Cooperation in Europe (OSCE);* b. 28 Jan. 1948, Lokalahti; mem. Turku City Council 1972–; Party Man., Nat. Coalition Party 1972–93 (mem. Exec. Cttee 1975–93), Chair. Nat. Coalition Party Youth League 1972–76; mem. Suomen Eduskunta (Parl.) 1975–, mem. Foreign Affairs Cttee 1979–1987, 1995–99, Chair. Parl. Supervisory Bd, Bank of Finland 1995–99, Chair. Defence Cttee 1999–2003, Deputy Speaker 2003–07; Minister of State (attached to Office of Council of State) 1987–90, Minister at Ministry of Finance 1989–91, 1991, Minister of Transport and Communications 1990–91, of Labour 1991–94, of Foreign Affairs 2007–08 (resgnd); Chair. Comm. of State Guarantee Fund 1996–; Chair. Supervisory Bd, Veikkaus Oy (Nat. Lottery Co.) 1996–; Pres. Finnish Athletics Fed.; Pres. Helsinki 2005 World Championships Organising Cttee; Council mem. Int. Asscn of Athletics Fed. 2003–; Pres. Parl. Ass., OSCE 2014–. *Address:* OSCE Parliamentary Assembly, Tordenskjoldsgade 1, 1055 Copenhagen K, Denmark (office). *Telephone:* 33-37-80-40 (office). *Fax:* 33-37-80-30 (office). *E-mail:* jori.arvonen@kokoomus.fi; osce@oscepa.org (office). *Website:* www.oscepa.org (office); www.kokoomus.fi; www.ilkkakanerva.net.

KANG, Chang-oh; South Korean business executive; Sr Man.-Dir and Gen. Superintendent, Pohang Works, Pohang Iron & Steel Corpn (POSCO) 1988, apptd Dir 1995, Sr Exec. Vice-Pres. and Chief Financial Officer 2002–03, Pres. and Rep. Dir 2003–06; Dir Dongbu Steel Co. Ltd 2011–.

KANG, Chung-won, BA, MA; South Korean banking executive; b. 19 Dec. 1950; ed Dartmouth Coll. and Fletcher School of Law and Diplomacy, Tufts Univ., USA; held numerous exec. positions for Citibank including in New York 1979, in Repub. of Korea 1979–83; with Bankers Trust Group, Seoul 1983–92, Chief Rep. Bankers Trust Securities Corpn 1992–96, Chief Country Officer, Korea Bankers Trust Group 1996–99; Chief Country Officer, Deutsche Bank Group, Korea 1999–2000; Pres. and CEO Seoul Bank 2000–02; Adviser, Kim & Chang (law firm) 2003–04, World Bank Group 2003–04; Pres. and CEO Kookmin Bank 2004–10; Vice-Chair. and CEO KB Financial Holding Inc. 2009–10; Dir (non-exec.) LG Investment & Securities Co. 2003–04; mem. Bd of Overseers and Asian Advisory Group, Fletcher School of Law and Diplomacy, Tufts Univ.

KANG, Gum-sil; South Korean civil rights lawyer and politician; b. 1957; ed Seoul Nat. Univ.; admitted to Bar 1981; served as judge 1983–96 (under S Korean mil. rule, defied common practice of jailing student activists by releasing them on bail); led group of judges advocating reform of legal system 1994; attorney 1996–; Vice-Pres. Lawyers for a Democratic Soc. (Minbyun) 2000–; Minister of Justice (first woman) 2003–04; Chief Attorney, Horizon Law Group, Seoul –2006; unsuccessful cand. for Mayor of Seoul (Uri Party) 2006; Chair. Campaign Cttee United Democratic Party (UDP) 2008. *Leisure interests:* amateur singer and dancer. *Address:* Uri Party, National Assembly, 1 Yeouido-dong, Yeongdeungpo-gu, Seoul 150-701, Republic of Korea (office).

KANG, Kyung-wha, BA, MA, PhD; South Korean diplomatist, UN official and politician; *Minister of Foreign Affairs and Trade;* b. 7 April 1958; m. Lee Il-myung; one s. two d.; ed Yonsei Univ., Univ. of Massachusetts; Assoc. Prof. of English, Sejong Univ. 1994; Presenter and Producer, News Bureau and Int. Radio Bureau, Korean Broadcasting System 1977; Asst to Speaker of Nat. Ass. –1998; joined Ministry of Foreign Affairs and Trade (MFA) 1998, posted to Perm. Mission of Repub. of Korea to UN 2001–05, fmr Dir-Gen. of Int. Orgs Dept, MFA, Minister of Foreign Affairs and Trade 2017–; joined UN 2006, Deputy High Commr for Human Rights 2006–13, Asst Sec.-Gen. for Humanitarian Affairs 2013–16, Head, Sec.-Gen.-desig.'s Transition Team 2017, Sr Adviser on Policy Jan.–June 2017; Woman of the Year Award, Korean Nat. Council of Women 2006, Service Merit Medal 2006, Korea Women Leaders Special Award, YWCA of Korea 2013. *Address:* Ministry of Foreign Affairs and Trade, 37, Sejong-no, Seoul 110–787, Republic of Korea (office). *Telephone:* (2) 2100-2114 (office). *Fax:* (2) 2100-7999 (office). *E-mail:* web@mofa.go.kr (office). *Website:* www.mofa.go.kr (office).

KANG, Man-soo; South Korean civil servant and politician; b. 1945, Hapcheon, S Gyeongsang Prov.; ed Seoul Nat. Univ., New York Univ., USA; began career at Ministry of Finance 1970, Vice-Minister of Finance 1997–98 (resgnd over Asian financial crisis); econ. affairs adviser to Pres. Lee for several years, Head of Econ. Affairs Sub-cttee on Lee's Transition Cttee –2008; Pres. Seoul Devt Inst. during Lee's tenure as Mayor of Seoul; co-ordinated Lee's economy-related pledges during presidential campaign; Minister of Strategy and Finance 2008–09.

KANG, Sung-mo (Steve), BS, MS, PhD; American (b. Korea) electrical engineer, academic and university administrator; *President, Korea Advanced Institute of Science and Technology (KAIST);* b. 25 Feb. 1945, Seoul; m. Myoung A. Kang; one s. one d.; ed Fairleigh Dickinson Univ., State Univ. of New York, Buffalo, Univ. of California, Berkeley, USA; Asst Prof., Rutgers Univ.,1975–77, Visiting Faculty mem. 1977–84; mem. Tech. Staff, AT&T Bell Labs, Murray Hill, NJ 1977–82, Supervisor, AT&T Bell Labs 1982–85; Humboldt Visiting Prof., Univ. of Karlsruhe, Germany 1997, Tech. Univ. of Munich, Germany 1998; Visiting Prof., Swiss Fed. Inst. of Tech. (EPFL), Lausanne 1989, 2012, Honoured Visiting Prof. 2006; Research Assoc. Prof., Co-ordinated Science Lab., Univ. of Illinois, Urbana-Champaign 1985–89, Assoc. Prof., Electrical and Computer Eng 1985–89, Research Prof., Co-ordinated Science Lab. 1989–2000, Prof. of Electrical and Computer Eng 1989–2000, Research Prof., Beckman Inst. 1990–2000, Prof. of Computer Science 1990–2000, Founding Dir Center for ASIC Research and Devt 1993–96, Head, Dept of ECE 1995–2000; Prof. Highest Step, Electrical Eng, Univ. of California, Santa Cruz 2001–04, Dean, Baskin School of Eng 2001–07, Prof. Above-Scale, Electrical Eng 2004–07, SOE Distinguished Chair Prof. 2011–13; Chaired Visiting Prof., Korean Advanced Inst. of Science and Tech. (KAIST) 2003–05, Pres. KAIST 2013–; Prof. Above-Scale of Eng and Chancellor Univ. of California, Merced 2007–11, Chancellor Emer. 2011–13; Assoc., Center for Advanced Study, UIUC 1991–92; Founding Ed.-in-Chief, IEEE Transactions on VLSI Systems 1992–94; Pres. Silicon Valley Eng Council 2002–03; Chair. IEEE Circuits and Systems Soc. Industrial Pioneer Award Subcommittee 2012, Cttee of Creative Economy, Presidential Advisory Council on Science and Tech. 2013–; mem. Int. Review Bd Western Asscn of Schools and Colls 2012–; External Assessor, Dean of Eng Search, Hong Kong Polytechnic Univ. 2012; Foreign mem. Nat. Acad. of Eng of Korea 1997; mem. Korean Acad. of Science and Tech. 2010; Fellow, IEEE 1990, AAAS 1997, Asscn of Computing Machinery 2000; Hon. DSc (Fairleigh Dickinson Univ.) 2014; Myril B. Reed Best Paper Award 1979, Exceptional Contrib. Award, AT&T Bell Labs 1984, Best Paper Award, Int. Conf. on Computer Design 1987, Meritorious Service Award and Distinguished Service Award, IEEE Computer Soc. 1990, IEEE Darlington Best Journal Paper Award 1993, Nat. Science Council Distinguished Lecturer (Repub. of China) 1993, SRC Inventor Recognition Award 1993, 1996, 2002, Meritorious Service Award, IEEE Circuits and Systems Soc. 1994, also Distinguished Lecturer 1994–97, Charles Marshall Sr Univ. Scholar, Univ. of Illinois 1995, Alexander von Humboldt Award for Sr US Scientists 1996, IEEE Leon K. Kirchmayer Grad. Teaching Tech. Field Award 1996, IEEE CAS Soc. Tech. Achievement Award 1997, Korea Broadcasting System Award in Industrial Tech. 1998, SRC Tech. Excellence Award 1999, IEEE CAS Golden Jubilee Medal 1999, IEEE Millennium Medal 2000, Outstanding Alumni Award in Electrical Eng, Univ. of California, Berkeley 2001, Low Power Design Contest Award, Int. Symposium on Low Power Electronics and Design 2001, Meritorious Service Award, Univ. of Illinois, Urbana-Champaign ECE Alumni Asscn 2001, Distinguished Lecturer, IEEE Solid-State Circuits Soc. 2002–05, Chancellor's Stellar Service Award, Univ. of California, Santa Cruz 2003, Distinguished Lecturer, IEEE Circuits and Systems Soc. 2003–05, IEEE Mac E. Van Valkenburg Award, IEEE Circuits and Systems Soc. 2005, Chang-Lin Tien Educ. Leadership Award 2007, Outstanding Leadership Appreciation and Recognition Award, Univ. of California, Santa Cruz 2007, Gandhi, King, Ikeda Community Builder Award, Morehouse Coll. 2007, Cultural Amb. Award, APA-FIVE 2007, Distinguished Yonsei Alumni Award 2008, Korean-American Leadership Award 2008, ISQED Quality Award 2008, inducted into Silicon Valley Eng Hall of Fame 2009, Deockmyeong Eng Award, Korean Acad. of Science and Tech. 2010, Pride of Korea Award, Korean Press Asscn of Northern California 2010, Soc. of Pinnacle Award, Fairleigh Dickinson Univ. 2013. *Publications:* co-author: Hot-Carrier Reliability of MOS VLSI Circuits 1993, Design Automation for Timing-Driven Layout Synthesis 1993, Physical Design for Multichip Modules 1994, Modeling of Electrical Overstress in Integrated Circuits 1994, Computer-Aided Design of Optoelectronic Integrated Circuits and Systems 1996, Electrothermal Analysis of VLSI Systems 2000, CMOS Digital Integrated Circuits: Analysis and Design, CMOS Digital Integrated Circuits: Analysis and Design (fourth edn) 2014; co-editor: Series in Advances in Design and Analysis of VLSI Systems; chapter editor: Computer-Aided Design and Optimization, The Circuits and Filters Handbook 1995, VLSI and ASIC, VLSI Handbook 1999; section editor: The Circuits and Filters Handbook, Section VII, Computer-Aided Design and Optimization 2003; 16 US patents, several book chapters and over 450 papers in professional journals and conferences. *Leisure interests:* hiking, travel. *Address:* Korea Advanced Institute of Science and Technology, 291 Daehak-ro (373-1 Guseong-dong), Yuseong-gu, Daejeon, 305-701, Republic of Korea (office). *Telephone:* (42) 350-2001 (office). *Fax:* (42) 350-4800 (office). *E-mail:* president@kaist.ac.kr (office). *Website:* www.kaist.edu (office).

KANG, Young-joong; South Korean business executive; *Chairman, Daekyo Group;* b. 1950; m.; two c.; ed Konkuk Univ., Yonsei Univ.; f. Jong Am Learning Inst. for Children (after-school education co.) 1975, now Daekyo Co. Ltd, Chair. Daekyo Culture Foundation 1992, Chair. Daekyo Group 2001–; Founder and Chair. World Youth and Culture Foundation 2007–, Bong-Ahm Educational Foundation 2008–; Pres. Korea Badminton Asscn 2003–09, Asia Badminton Confed. 2003–05, Badminton World Fed. 2005–13, Korea Scout Asscn 2008–12; Hon. PhD (Konkuk) 2000, (Korea Nat. Sport Univ.) 2004; Man of Merit Recognition from Pres. of Korea 1995, Ok Kwan Jang (cultural medal) from Ministry of Culture and Tourism 2004, Korea Man. Asscn Business Leader of Korea Award 2005, Kiggi Medal, Scout Asscn of Japan 2012. *Address:* Daekyo Co. Ltd, 446-3, Bangbae-dong, Seocho-gu, Seoul 137-060, Republic of Korea (office). *Telephone:* (2) 829-1114 (office). *Fax:* (2) 829-0647 (office). *Website:* www.daekyo.co.kr (office); youngjoongkang.com.

KANG, Yu-sig, BS; South Korean business executive; ed Chongju High School, Coll. of Business Admin, Seoul Nat. Univ.; joined LG Chem 1972, Sr Man. Dir LG Semicon 1995–96, Vice-Pres. 1996–97, Vice-Pres. LG Chair.'s Office 1997–98, Vice-Pres. LG EOCR 1998–99, Pres. and Head of LG EOCR 1999–2002, COO LG Corpn 2002–03, mem. Bd of Dirs and Chair. LG Electronics Inc., Head of LG Exec. Office for Corp. Restructuring 2002–08, CEO LG Corpn 2003–08, Vice-Chair. and Co-CEO LG Corpn 2009–12.

KANG, Yukun, BA; Chinese economist and business executive; served as Deputy Man. Credit Dept, Industrial Bank Co. Ltd, fmr Vice-Pres., Putian Br. and Vice-Pres. and Pres. Fuzhou Br., mem. Bd of Dirs and Vice-Pres. Industrial Bank Co. Ltd 2007–12, Chair. Bd of Supervisors 2012–16.

KANGAS, Edward (Ed) A., BA, MBA, CPA; American accountant and business executive; *Non-Executive Chairman, United Technologies Corporation;* b. 22 May 1944; ed Univ. of Kansas; began career as staff accountant at Touche Ross 1967, Partner 1975, Man. Dir 1985–89, Man. Partner, Deloitte & Touche USA (following merger of Deloitte Haskins & Sells and Touche Ross 1989) 1989–94, Chair. and CEO Deloitte Touche Tohmatsu (DTT) 1989–2000, Consultant 2000–03; Chair. Tenet Healthcare Corpn 2003–; Dir, United Technologies Corpn 2008–, Chair. (non-exec.) 2014–; mem. Bd of Dirs, Hovnavian Enterprises Inc., Electronic Data Systems Corpn (EDS), Eclipsys Corpn 2004–10, Allscripts Healthcare Solutions, Inc. 2010–12, Intuit, Inc. 2007–16; Chair. Nat. Multiple Sclerosis Soc. from 2000; mem. Policy Cttee, Cttee for Econ. Devt (also Trustee); mem. Bd of Advisers, Univ. of Kansas Business School, now Emer. Bd mem.; mem. Bd of Overseers, Wharton School, Univ. of Pennsylvania, Bd of Trustees, Univ. of Kansas Endowment Foundation; CPA in New York and Conn.; Trustee, Cttee for Econ. Devt; Distinguished Alumni Award, Univ. of Kansas School of Business 2000. *Address:* Corporate Secretary, United Technologies Corporation, 1 Financial Plaza, Hartford, CT 06103, USA (office). *Telephone:* (860) 728-7000 (office). *E-mail:* info@utc.com (office). *Website:* www.utc.com (office).

KANI, John; South African actor and playright; b. 1943; fmrly worked on a car ass. line; began acting in amateur production; many stage tours abroad and appearances in S. Africa particularly at Market Theatre, Johannesburg; appeared in Sizwe Banzi is Dead, Royal Court Theatre, London 1973, Nat. Theatre, London 2007, Waiting for Godot, Miss Julie, Othello 1987; fmr Exec. Trustee, Market Theatre, Foundation, currently mem. Exec. Council; Dr hc (Cape Town) 2006; Tony Award for Broadway performance in Athol Fugard's Sizwe Banzi is Dead, Hiroshima Foundation for Peace & Culture Award 2000. *Films:* Marigolds in August 1980, Gräset sjunger 1981, Saturday Night at the Palace 1987, An African Dream 1987, Options 1988, A Dry White Season 1989, The Native Who Caused All the Trouble 1989, Sarafina! 1992, Soweto Green 1995, The Ghost and the Darkness 1996, Kini and Adams 1997, The Tichborne Claimant 1998, Final Solution 2001. *Plays include:* Nothing But The Truth (Fleur de Cap Award for Best Actor and Best New South African Play, Olive Schreiner Prize 2005) 2002. *Address:* The Market Theatre, PO Box 8656, Johannesburg, 2000, South Africa (office). *Telephone:* (11) 8321641 (office). *Website:* www.markettheatre.co.za (office).

KANN, Peter Robert; American journalist, publisher and business executive; b. 13 Dec. 1942, New York; s. of Robert Kann and Marie Kann (née Breuer); m. 1st Francesca Mayer 1969 (died 1983); m. 2nd Karen House 1984; one s. three d.; ed Harvard Univ.; joined Wall Street Journal 1964, worked as journalist in New York 1964–67, in Viet Nam 1967–68, in Hong Kong 1968–75, Publr and Ed. Wall Street Journal Asian Edn 1976–79, Assoc. Publr 1979–88, Exec. Vice-Pres. Dow Jones & Co. 1986, Pres. int. and magazine groups 1986–89, mem. Bd of Dirs 1987, Pres. Dow Jones & Co., New York 1989–91, Publr and Editorial Dir The Wall Street Journal 1989–2002, CEO Dow Jones & Co. 1991–2006, Chair. 1991–2007 (retd); mem. Adjunct Faculty, Columbia Univ. Grad. School of Journalism; Chair. Bd Far Eastern Econ. Review 1987–89; Trustee, Asia Soc. 1989–94 (now Trustee Emer.), Inst. for Advanced Study, Princeton 1990–, Aspen Inst. 1994–98; mem. Council on Foreign Relations, Pulitzer Prize Bd 1987–96; Pulitzer Prize for int. reporting 1972 for his coverage of the 1971 India-Pakistan War. *Address:* Columbia University Graduate School of Journalism, Pulitzer Hall, MC 3801, 2950 Broadway (at 116th Street), New York, NY 10027; 58 Cleveland Lane, Princeton, NJ 08540, USA. *E-mail:* prk2106@columbia.edu.

KANNAN, Madhu, BE, MSc, MBA; Indian business executive and fmr stock exchange official; *Group Head for Business Development, Tata Sons;* b. Chennai; m. Shubha Srinivasan Kannan; one d.; ed Birla Inst. of Tech. & Science, Vanderbilt Univ., USA; joined New York Stock Exchange (now NYSE Euronext) 1997, Account Man. 2001–02, Man. Dir, Asia-Pacific 2002–05, then Special Asst to Head of Int., the Vice-Pres. Global Corp. Client Group; Man. Dir, Corp Strategy Group, Bank of America-Merrill Lynch, New York 2008–09; CEO and Man. Dir Bombay Stock Exchange 2009–12; Group Head, Business Development, Tata Sons 2012–; fmr mem. Bd of Dirs Central Depository Services (India) Ltd, BOI Shareholding Ltd, Indian Clearing Corpn Ltd; named among Young Global Leaders, World Econ. Forum 2007. *Address:* Tata Sons, Bombay House, 24, Homi Mody Street, Mumbai

400 001, India (office). *Telephone:* (22) 66658282 (office). *Website:* www.tata.com (office).

KANOO, Mishal Hamed, MBA; Bahraini business executive; *Chairman, Kanoo Group;* b. 1969; ed Univ. of St Thomas, Tex., USA, American Univ. of Sharjah; Auditor, Arthur Andersen, Dubai 1994–96; Deputy Chair. and CEO Kanoo Group 1997–14, Chair. 2014–; Chair. Bd AKZO Nobel, UAE 2006–, KHK Partners Ltd 2015–; Vice-Chair. of Bd Freightworks 2006–; Chair. KAAF Investments 2017–; mem. Bd of Dirs AXA Insurance Gulf 2006–, Gulf Capital 2008–; mem. Bd NextStage AM 2016–; Prof. (part-time), American Univ. of Sharjah School of Business Admin; columnist, Money Works magazine. *Address:* Kanoo Group, PO Box 290, Dubai, United Arab Emirates (office). *Telephone:* (4) 3933633 (office). *Fax:* (4) 3933636 (office). *E-mail:* guest@mishalkanoo.com; info@kanoogroup.com (office). *Website:* www.kanoogroup.com (office); www.mishalkanoo.com.

KANTHA, Ashok K.; Indian diplomatist; b. 14 May 1955; m. Sharmila Kantha; one s.; ed Patna Univ.; briefly worked as an exec. with State Bank of India; joined Indian Foreign Service 1977, studied Chinese Language at Nanyang Univ., Singapore 1979–81, Special Asst to Chair., Policy Planning Cttee mid-1980s, worked in different capacities at Missions in Singapore, China and USA and in Ministry of External Affairs, New Delhi dealing with India's relations with China, Pakistan, Afghanistan and Iran –1997, Deputy Chief of Mission, Embassy in Kathmandu 1997–2000, Consul Gen. to Hong Kong and Macao 2000–03, Head of East Asia Div., Ministry of External Affairs 2003–07, High Commr to Malaysia 2007–09, to Sri Lanka 2009–13, Sec. (East), Ministry of External Affairs 2013–14; Amb. to People's Republic of China 2014–16. *Address:* Ministry of External Affairs, South Blk, New Delhi 110 011, India (office). *Telephone:* (11) 23011127 (office). *Fax:* (11) 23013254 (office). *E-mail:* eam@mea.gov.in (office). *Website:* www.mea.gov.in (office).

KANTOR, Mickey; American corporate lawyer; *Partner, Mayer Brown LLP;* b. 1939; m. 1st (died 1978); m. 2nd 1982; four c. (one s. deceased); ed Vanderbilt Univ., Georgetown Univ. Law School; served in USN; began career as lawyer protecting rights of migrant farm workers; Dir acting for Legal Rights 1971; Staff Coordinator, Sargent Shriver 1972; partner, Los Angeles law firm 1993; mem. Bd of Legal Services Corpn in Carter Admin; mem. Comm. investigating LA Riots 1992; Chair. Clinton Presidential Campaign 1992; US Trade Rep. 1993–97; Sec. of Commerce 1996–97; Partner, Mayer Brown LLP 1997–; mem. Int. Advisory Bd Fleishman-Hillard, Bd of Visitors, Georgetown Univ. Law Center; Chief Negotiator, NAFTA, Uruguay Round, Free Trade Areas of America, APEC, ING USA, CB Richard Ellis Group; Order of Southern Cross (Brazil); Distinguished Public Service Medal, Center for Study of Presidency, Albert Schweitzer Humanitarianism Award, Eagle & Badge Award, Los Angeles Civic Medal 2012. *Address:* Mayer Brown LLP, 350 South Grand Avenue, 25th Floor, Los Angeles, CA 90071, USA (office). *Telephone:* (213) 229-9579 (office). *Fax:* (213) 625-0248 (office). *E-mail:* mkantor@mayerbrown.com (office). *Website:* www.mayerbrown.com (office).

KANWAR, Asha Singh, BA, MA, MPhil, DPhil; Indian educationalist and academic; *President and CEO, Commonwealth of Learning;* b. 27 Sept. 1951, Darjeeling; ed Panjab Univ., Univ. of Sussex, UK; Reader, Indira Gandhi Nat. Open Univ. (IGNOU) 1988–92, apptd Prof. 1992, Dir School of Humanities 1996–99, apptd Pro-Vice Chancellor IGNOU 1999; fmr consultant in open and distance learning at UNESCO Regional Office for Educ. in Africa (BREDA), Dakar, Senegal; Educ. Specialist, Higher Educ. Commonwealth of Learning 2003–06, Vice-Pres. 2006–12, Programme Dir 2007–12, Pres. and CEO 2012–; Fulbright Fellow for post-doctoral research, Iowa State Univ., later invited to teach; Visiting Fellow, Univ. of Leiden, Univ. of Toronto, Open Univ. of Hong Kong; Fellow, National Teachers' Inst., Kaduna, Nigeria; Hon. Prof., Tianjin Open Univ., People's Repub. of China; Dr hc (Univ. of Swaziland), Hon. DLitt (Kota Open Univ., India), (Krishna Kanta Handiqui State Open Univ.), (Open Univ., UK), (Open Univ. of Sri Lanka), (Wawasan Open Univ., Malaysia); several awards and fellowships, including scholarship to Univ. of Sussex, Prize of Excellence, Int. Council for Open and Distance Educ. 2009, Award for Empowerment, NOUN, Nigeria, ICDE Prize for Excellence (Norway), AAOU Meritorious Service Award 2014. *Publications include:* several books, research papers and articles on gender studies, especially the impact of distance education on the lives of Asian women. *Address:* Commonwealth of Learning, 1055 West Hastings Street, Suite 1200, Vancouver, BC V6E 2E9, Canada (office). *Telephone:* (604) 775-8200 (office). *Fax:* (604) 775-8210 (office). *E-mail:* akanwar@col.org (office). *Website:* www.col .org (office).

KANZAKI, Takenori, LLB; Japanese politician; b. 15 July 1943, Tien-Tsin, (Tianjin), People's Repub. of China; ed Tokyo Univ.; public prosecutor 1968–76; lawyer 1982; mem. House of Reps; mem. Komeito party (now New Komeito party), Chair. Foreign Affairs Cttee, Chief Rep. 1998–2006, now Standing Adviser; Chair. Diet Policy Cttee; Minister of Posts and Telecommunications 1993–94. *Publication:* Prohibition of Profit Granting (co-author). *Leisure interests:* shogi (Japanese chess), reading, travelling, theatre. *Address:* Room No. 201, No. 6 Green Building, 2-12-7 Hakata-Ekimae, Hakata-ku, Fukuoka-shi 812, Fukuoka Prefecture, Japan (home).

KAO, Gen. Hua-chu, BA; Taiwanese army officer and government official; *Secretary-General, National Security Council;* b. 2 Oct. 1942; ed Repub. of China Military Acad. (ROCMA), Ministry of Nat. Defence (MND) Army Infantry School, Armed Forces Univ.; Company Commdr, 6th Bn, 26th Infantry Div., Repub. of China Army 1971–72, Bn Commdr, 852nd Brigade, 284th Infantry Div. 1978–79, Brigade Commdr, 678th Brigade, 226th Infantry Div. 1985–87, Instructor-Gen., Mil. Training Dept and Commdr, Cadet Training Command 1987–90, Exec. Dir of Training and Educ., Army Infantry Training Commanding and Infantry School, MND 1990, Div. Commdr, 127th Infantry Div. 1990–92, Chief of Staff, 10th Army Corps Commanding HQ 1992–93, Chief of Staff for Intelligence, Gen. Army HQ 1993–94, Commanding Gen., Chengkungling Training Center 1996–98, Deputy Chief of Gen. Staff for Logistics, MND 1998–99, Commanding Gen., 10th Army Corps 1999–2000, Deputy Commander-in-Chief, Gen. Army HQ 2000–03, Dir-Gen., Jt Operations Training and Doctrine Office, MND 2003, Commanding-Gen., Combined Logistics Command 2003–04; Minister, Veterans Affairs Comm. 2004–07, 2008–09, Minister of Nat. Defence 2009–13; Sec.-Gen., Nat. Security Council 2015–. *Address:* National Security Council, Taipei 10048, Taiwan (office).

KAO, Adm. Kuang-chi; Taiwanese politician and fmr naval officer; b. 1950; numerous years with Repub. of China Navy, becoming Commdr of the Navy; Chief of Gen. Staff of the Armed Forces 2013–15; fmr Dir-Gen., Dept of Strategic Planning, Ministry of Nat. Defense, Deputy Minister of Nat. Defense 2012–13, Minister of Nat. Defense 2015–16.

KAPAMBWE, Lazarous, BSc; Zambian diplomatist and UN official; *Permanent Representative to United Nations;* b. 31 Dec. 1959; m.; ed Univ. of Zambia, Nairobi Univ., Kenya, New York Univ.; Exec. Officer, Directorate of Int. Orgs and Research Dept, Ministry for Foreign Affairs 1981–85, Prin. in Research Dept 1985–87; Prin. in Cabinet Office and speech writer for Prime Minister of Zambia 1987; Counsellor for Political Affairs, Perm. Mission to UN, New York 1987–88; Counsellor and Deputy Chief of Mission, Embassy in Washington, DC 1988–93, Embassy in Bonn 1993–96; Dir for European Affairs, Ministry for Foreign Affairs June–Aug. 1996, Dir for Africa and OAU Affairs 1996–2000, Deputy Perm. Sec. responsible for Asia, Africa and the Middle East 2000–02, Perm. Sec. 2002–03; Amb. to Ethiopia and African Union 2003–07; Amb. and Perm. Rep. to UN, New York 2007–11, Co-Chair of an open-ended working group on the world financial crisis 2009–10, Pres. ECOSOC, UN 2011–12; Special Advisor on Econ. Affairs to the Chair. of the African Union Comm. 2012–17, Perm. Rep. to UN 2017–. *Address:* Permanent Mission of Zambia, 237 East 52nd Street, New York, NY 10022, USA (office). *Telephone:* (212) 888-5770 (office).

KAPIL DEV; Indian business executive, sports administrator and fmr professional cricketer; *Chairman, Executive Board, Indian Cricket League;* b. (Kapildev Ramlal Nikhanj), 6 Jan. 1959, Chandigarh; s. of Ram Lal Nikhanj and Raj Kumari Lajwanti; m. Romi Dev; one d.; ed D.A.V. School, Punjab Univ.; right-hand middle-order batsman, right-arm fast-medium bowler; played for Haryana 1975/76–1991/92, Northamptonshire 1981–83, Worcestershire 1984–85; played in 131 Tests for India 1978/79–1993/94, 34 as Capt., scoring 5,248 runs (average 31.05, highest score 163) including eight hundreds and taking record 434 wickets (average 29.64), best bowling (innings) 9/83, (match) 11/146; youngest to take 100 Test wickets (21 years 25 days); hit four successive balls for six against England, Lord's 1990; played in 225 One-Day Ints, scoring 3,783 runs (average 23.79, highest score 175 not out) and taking 253 wickets; scored 11,356 runs (18 hundreds) and took 835 wickets in first-class cricket; toured England 1979, 1982, 1983 (World Cup), 1986, 1990; only person to take 400 wickets and score more than 5,000 runs in Test cricket; Indian Nat. Coach 1999–2000; Founding mem. and Acad. mem. Laureus World Sports Foundation 2000; Chair. Nat. Cricket Acad. 2006–07; Chair. Exec. Bd breakaway Indian Cricket League 2007–; Owner Kapil's Eleven restaurants in Chandigarh and Patna, Kaptain's Retreat Hotel, Chandigarh; est. Dev Musco Lighting Pvt. Ltd in partnership with Musco Lighting to install floodlights in major stadia and sports venues in India; commissioned as Lt Col in Indian Territorial Army 2008–; Arjuna Award 1979–80, Padma Shri 1982, Wisden Cricketer of the Year 1983, Padma Bhushan 1991, Electrolux Kelvinator Wisden Indian Cricketer of the Century 2002, inducted into ICC Cricket Hall of Fame 2010. *Films:* cameo appearances in Iqbal, Chain Khuli ki Main Khuli and Mujhse Shadi Karogi. *Publications:* By God's Decree (autobiography) 1985, Cricket My Style (autobiography) 1987, Kapil Dev: Triumph of the Spirit 1995, Straight from the Heart (autobiography) 2004. *Leisure interests:* hunting, riding, dancing, playing golf. *Address:* Dev Musco Lighting Pvt. Ltd, B–41, Greater Kailash-1, New Delhi 110 048 (office); Indian Cricket League, Essel Sports Pvt. Ltd, 135 Continental Building, Dr Annie Besant Road, Worli, Mumbai 400 018; 39 Sunder Nagar, New Delhi 110 003, India. *Telephone:* (11) 41431166 (office); (11) 4698333 (New Delhi). *Fax:* (11) 41431406 (office); (11) 3719776 (New Delhi). *E-mail:* kapildev58@yahoo.co.in (office); response@iclonline.in. *Website:* www.musco.com/reps/in/india.html (office); www.indiancricketleague.in; www.kapildev.asia.

KAPLAN, Jonathan Stewart, BA; American film writer, film director, television producer and television director; b. 25 Nov. 1947, Paris, France; s. of Sol Kaplan and Frances Heflin; m. Julie Selzer 1987 (divorced 2001); one d.; ed Univ. of Chicago, New York Univ.; mem. tech. staff, Bill Graham's Fillmore East, New York 1969–71; appeared in The Dark at the Top of the Stairs, Broadway 1956–57; Best Male Vocal Concept Video, Billboard 1986. *Films:* Night Call Nurses 1972, Student Teachers 1973, The Slams 1973, Truck Turner 1974, White Line Fever 1974, Mr Billion 1976, Over the Edge 1978, 11th Victim 1979, Muscle Beach 1980, Gentleman Bandit 1981, White Orchid 1982, Heart Like a Wheel 1983, Project X 1986, The Accused 1987, Immediate Family 1989, Love Field 1990, Unlawful Entry 1992, Bad Girls 1994, Rebel Highway 1994, Picture Windows 1995, Fallen Angels 1996, Brokedown Palace 1999. *Video films:* directed 15 music videos for John Mellencamp, two for Rod Stewart, one for Barbra Streisand and one for Paula Abdul. *TV includes:* JAG (writer) 1995, ER (producer/dir) 1999–2005, The Court (Dir) 2002, Inconceivable (dir) 2005, Crossing Jordan (dir) 2005, Law & Order (dir) 2005–06, Without a Trace (dir) 2006–07, Brothers and Sisters (dir) 2010, A Gifted Man (dir)2011, The Client List (dir) 2013, Witches of East End (dir) 2013. *Address:* Industry Entertainment, 953 Carillo Drive, Suite 300, Los Angeles, CA 90048, USA (office).

KAPLINSKI, Jaan; Estonian poet, writer, linguist and translator; b. 22 Jan. 1941, Tartu (Dorpat); s. of Jerzy Kaplinski and Nora Raudsepp; m. Tiia Toomet 1969; four s. two d.; ed Univ. of Tartu; mem. Riigikogu (State Ass.) 1992–95; Lecturer in History of Western Civilization, Univ. of Tartu; columnist at various Estonian and Scandinavian newspapers; has written around 900 poems, 20 stories and some plays; mem. Universal Acad. of Cultures, Estonian Writers' Union, European Acad. of Poetry, Finnish Literature Soc.; Order of Nat. Coat of Arms (IV Class) 1997, Chevalier, Légion d'honneur 2000, Kt, Order of the Lion of Finland 2003; Dr hc; several Estonian awards, Baltic Ass. Prize for Literature 1997, Prix Max Jacob Etranger 2003, Russkaya Premiya 2015, European Prize for Literature 2015. *Publications include:* poetry: Ma vaatasin päikese aknasse 1976, Uute kivide kasvamine 1977, The New Heaven & Earth of Jaan Kaplinski 1981, Raske on kergeks saada 1982, Tule tagasi helmemänd 1984, Õhtu toob tagasi kõik 1985, Käoraamat: Luulet 1956–80 1986, The Wandering Border 1987, The Same Sea in Us All 1990, Sjunger näktergalen än i Dorpat?: En brevväxling 1990, I Am The Spring in Tartu and other poems in English 1991, Non-Existent Frontier 1995, Võimaluste võimalikkus 1997, Öölinnud, öömõtted yölintuja, yöajatuksia: Luuletusi 1995–97 1998, Evening Brings Everything Back 2004, Selected Poems 2011; novel: Seesama jõgi 2007 (English trans. The Same Sea 2009). *Leisure interests:*

gardening, forestry, astronomy, photography. *Address:* Nisu 33-9, 50407 Tartu, Estonia. *Telephone:* (7) 425755; 56-919702 (mobile). *E-mail:* jaan.kaplinski@gmail.com. *Website:* jaan.kaplinski.com; jaankaplinski.blogspot.com.

KAPOOR, Anil; Indian actor and producer; b. 24 Dec. 1959, Tilak Nagar, Mumbai; s. of Surinder Kapoor and Nirmal Kapoor; m. Sunita Kapoor (née Bhambhani) 1984; one s. two d.; ed Our Lady of Perpetual Succour High School, Chembur, St. Xaviers Coll.; Nata Kalaratna by Govt of Andhra Pradesh 1997, Avadh Samman by Govt of UP 2002; Performer with All-Round Comic Excellence, Vodafone Comedy Honors 2008, Special Award, Stardust Award 2009, Outstanding Achievement by an Indian Internationally, IIFA2 010, Lifetime Achievement Award, AXN Action 2010, Lalitha Kala Samrat, Govt of Andhra Pradesh 2011, Lifetime Achievement Award, GQ 2012, Excellence in World Cinema Award, Indian Film Festival of Melbourne 2015. *Films include:* Hamare Tumhare 1979, Ex Baar Kaho 1980, Vamsa Vriksham 1980, Hum Paanch 1981, Shakti 1982, Pallavi Anu Pallavi 1983, Woh Saat Din 1983, Mashaal (Filmfare Best Supporting Actor Award) 1984, Andar Baahar 1984, Laila 1984, Love Marriage 1984, Saaheb 1985, Yudh 1985, Mohabbat 1985, Meri Jung 1985, Kahan Kahan Se Guzar 1986, Pyaar Ka Sindoor 1986, Chameli Ki Shaadi 1986, Aap Ke Saath 1986, Janbaaz 1986, Pyar Kiya Hai Pyar Karenge 1986, Karma 1986, Insaaf Ki Awaaz 1986, Itihaas 1987, Mr India 1987, Hifazat 1987, Thikana 1987, Kasam 1988, Ram-Avtar 1988, Vijay 1988, Sone Pe Suhaaga 1988, Tezaab (Filmfare Best Actor Award) 1988, Inteqam 1988, Ram Lakhan 1989, Joshilay 1989, Eeshwar 1989, Rakhwala 1989, Abhimanyu 1989, Aag Se Khelenge 1989, Kala Bazaar 1989, Parinda 1989, Awaargi 1990, Kishen Kanhaiya 1990, Ghar Ho Ta Aisa 1990, Jeevan Ek Sangharsh 1990, Amba 1990, Jamai Raja 1990, Jigarwala 1991, Benaam Badsha 1991, Pratikar 1991, Lamhe 1991, Beta (Filmfare Best Actor Award) 1992, Zindagi Ek Jua 1992, Humlaa 1992, Khel 1992, Heer Ranjha 1992, Apradhi 1992, Roop Ki Rani Choron Ka Raja 1993, Guru Deev 1993, Laadla 1994, Andaz 1994, 1942: A Love Story 1994, Mr. Azaad 1994, Trimurti 1995, Rajkumar 1996, Loafer 1996, Mr. Bechara 1996, Virasat (Filmfare Critics Award for Best Performance, Star Screen Award Best Actor) 1997, Deewana Mastana 1997, Kabhi Na Kabhi 1998, Gharwali Baharwali 1998, Jhooth Bole Kauwa Kaate 1998, Hum Aapke Dil Mein Rehte Hain 1999, Biwi No. 1 (Best Comedian Award, Int. Indian Film Acad. Awards) 1999, Mann 1999, Taal (Filmfare Best Supporting Actor Award, Best Supporting Actor Award, Int. Indian Film Acad. Awards, Star Screen Award Best Supporting Actor, Zee Cine Award, Best Actor in a Supporting Role–Male) 1999, Bulandi 2000, Pukar (National Film Award for Best Actor, Bollywood Movie Award for Most Sensational Actor) 2000, Hamara Dil Aapke Paas Hai 2000, Karobaar 2000, Lajja 2001, Nayak 2001, Badhaai Ho Badhaai 2002, Om Jai Jagadish 2002, Rishtey 2002, Armaan 2003, Calcutta Mail 2003, Musafir 2004, Bewafaa 2004, My Wife's Murder 2005, No Entry 2005, Chocolate 2005, Humko Deewana Kar Gaye 2006, Darna Zaroori Hai 2006, Salaam-e-Ishq: A Tribute to Love 2007, Welcome (Best Role as a Comedian, German Public Bollywood Awards) 2007, My Name is Anthony Gonsalves 2008, Black & White 2008, Race 2008, Tashan (Best Actor in a Negative Role Award, Stardust Awards) 2008, Slumdog Millionaire (Screen Actors Guild Award for Outstanding Performance by a Cast in a Motion Picture) 2008, Yuvvraaj 2008, No Problem (producer and actor) 2010, Mission: Impossible – Ghost Protocol 2011, Tezz 2012, Shootout at Wadala 2013, Dil Dhadakne Do (Filmfare Award for Best Supporting Actor 2016, Best Performance in a Supporting Role (Male), IIFA Awards 2016) 2015, Welcome Back 2015, Mubarakan (Zee Cine Award 2018) 2017; as producer: Badhaai Ho Badhaai 2002, My Wife's Murder 2005, Gandhi, My Father (Hottest Film Producer Award, Stardust Awards) 2007, Short Kut: The Con is On 2009, Aisha 2010, Khubsoorat 2014. *Television:* 24 (American version) 2010, 24 (Indian version) 2013–16. *Address:* c/o 31 Shrinagar, Presidency Society, 7th Road, JVPD Scheme, Mumbai 400 049, India (office). *Telephone:* (22) 6209997.

KAPOOR, Sir Anish, Kt, CBE, MA, RA; British sculptor; b. 12 March 1954, Bombay, India; s. of Rear-Adm. Kapoor and Mrs D. C. Kapoor; m. Susanne Spicale 1995; one d. one s.; ed Hornsey Coll. of Art, Chelsea Coll. of Art and Design, London; has lived in London since early 1970s; Royal Academician 1999; Guest Artistic Dir, Brighton Festival 2009; Hon. Fellow, London Inst. 1997, Univ. of Leeds 1997, Univ. of Wolverhampton 1999; Hon. FRIBA 2001; Commdr, Ordre des Arts et des Lettres 2011; Hon. DLitt (Leeds) 1993; Premio Duemila, Venice Biennale 1990, Turner Prize, Tate Gallery, London 1991, Premium Imperiale 2011, Padma Bhushan 2012. *Address:* c/o Lisson Gallery, 67 Lisson Street, London, NW1 5DA, England. *Telephone:* (20) 7724-2739. *Fax:* (20) 7724-7124. *Website:* www.anishkapoor.com.

KAPOOR, Gen. Deepak, MA, MSc, MBA; Indian army officer (retd); b. 12 March 1948, Delhi; m. Kirti Kapoor; one s. one d.; ed Sainik School, Kunjpara, Defence Services Staff Coll., Wellington, Nat. Defence Coll., New Delhi, Indira Gandhi Nat. Open Univ., New Delhi; commissioned into Regt of Artillery 1967; veteran of Indo-Pak War in eastern theatre (Bangladesh) 1971; Chief Operations Officer for UNOSOM II (UN Operation in Somalia – Phase 2) 1994–95; commanded 161 Infantry Brigade in Uri, Jammu and Kashmir, 22nd Mountain Div. (as part of a Strike Corps during Operation Parakram) 2001–02; Chief of Staff of 4 Corps in Tezpur (involved in counter-insurgency operations in Assam); promoted to Lt-Gen.; commanded 33 Corps at Siliguri, West Bengal, commanded Army Training Command (ARTRAC) in Shimla, Commdr Northern Army; apptd Hon. ADC to Pres. of India; Sr Col Commdt Regt of Artillery; Vice-Chief of Army –2007, Chief of Army Staff 2007–10; Chair. Chiefs of Staff Cttee 2009–10; mem. Bd of Govs, Sanskriti Group of Insts, Global Business School; Hon. Col of Brigade of the Guards 2008; Hon. Col Commdt, Regt of Artillery; Vishisht Seva Medal 1996, Sena Medal 1998, Ati Vishisht Seva Medal 2006, Param Vishisht Seva Medal 2007. *Publications:* India's China Concern (essay), Strategic Analysis, Vol. 36, No. 4 July–Aug. 2012, Higher Defence Organisation and the Pursuit of Jointness – Core Concerns in Indian Defence and the Imperatives for Reforms 2015. *Leisure interest:* golf. *E-mail:* gendkapoor@gmail.com (office).

KAPOOR KHAN, Kareena, (Bebo); Indian film actress; b. 21 Sept. 1980, Mumbai, Maharashtra; d. of Randhir Kapoor and Babita Kapoor (née Shivdasani); younger sister of Karisma Kapoor; m. Saif Ali Khan 2012; one s.; ed Welham Girls' Boarding School, Mithibai Coll., Mumbai, Harvard Univ., USA, Govt Law Coll., Churchgate, Mumbai, Kishore Namit Kapoor Acting School; Style Diva of the Year Award, Int. Indian Film Acad. 2004, Marco Ricci Soc. Young Achiever Award 2004, Rajiv Gandhi Young Achiever Award 2005, Smita Patil Memorial Award 2006, Future Group Global Indian TV Honours, Global Achievement Award 2008, Vocational Excellence Award, Rotary Int. 2009, India Today Woman Award 2009, among the 10 recipients of IIFA-FICCI Frames Award for Most Powerful Entertainers of the Decade 2009, GQ Excellence Award 2009, Geetanjali Glamour Icon of the Year 2011, Superstar Unique Ada (Female), Airtel Superstar Awards 2011, Filmfare Glamour & Style Award for Most Glamorous Star 2015, for Trendsetter of the Year 2017. *Films include:* Refugee (Filmfare Best Female Debut Award 2001, Zee Cine Award 2001, Bollywood Movie Award 2001, Sansui Award 2001) 2000, Mujhe Kucch Kehna Hai 2001, Yaadein 2001, Asoka 2001, Ajnabee 2001, Kabhi Khushi Kabhie Gham 2001, Mujhse Dosti Karoge! 2002, Jeena Sirf Merre Liye 2002, Talaash: The Hunt Begins 2003, Khushi 2003, Main Prem Ki Diwani Hoon (Anandalok Puraskar Award 2004) 2003, LOC: Kargil 2003, Chameli (Filmfare Special Performance Award 2004, Stardust Award 2004, Bollywood Movie Award 2004, Sansui Award 2004) 2003, Yuva 2004, Dev (Filmfare Critics' Award for Best Actress 2005) 2004, Fida 2004, Aitraaz 2004, Hulchul 2004, Bewafaa 2005, Kyon Ki 2005, Dosti: Friends Forever 2005, 36 China Town 2006, Chup Chup Ke 2006, Omkara (Filmfare Critics' Award for Best Actress 2007, Star Screen Award 2007, Stardust Award 2007) 2006, Don 2006, Jab We Met (Filmfare Best Actress Award 2008, Star Screen Award 2008, Int. Indian Film Acad. Award 2008, Zee Cine Award 2008, Stardust Award 2008, Apsara Film and Television Producers Guild Award 2008, HT Café Film Award 2007, Reader's Choice Award 2008, Planet Bollywood People's Choice Award 2008, Annual Central European Bollywood Award 2008, Li'l Star Award 2008) 2007, Tashan 2008, Roadside Romeo (voice) 2008, Golmaal Returns 2008, Kambakkht Ishq 2009, Main Aur Mrs Khanna 2009, Kurbaan (Star Screen Award 2010, Stardust Award 2010) 2009, 3 Idiots (Star Screen Award 2010, Stardust Award 2010) 2009, Milenge Milenge 2010, We Are Family (Filmfare Award for Best Supporting Actress) 2010, Golmaal 3 2010, Bodyguard (Most Entertaining Female Actor in a Romantic Role, Big Star Entertainment Awards) 2011, Ra One 2011, Ek Main Aur Ek Tu 2012, Agent Vinod 2012, Heroine 2012, Talaash: The Answer Lies Within (Most Entertaining Female Actor in a Thriller, Big Star Entertainment Awards, Editor's Choice for Best Actress Stardust Awards) 2012, Satyagraha 2013, Gori Tere Pyaar Mein 2013, Singham Returns 2014, The Shaukeens 2014, Happy Ending 2014, Gabbar is Back 2015, Bajrangi Bhaijaan 2015, Brothers 2015, Ki & Ka 2016, Udta Punjab 2016, Veere Di Wedding 2018. *Address:* 2-B/110/1201, Excellency, 4th Cross Road, Lokhandwala Complex, Andheri (West), Mumbai 400 058, India.

KAPOR, Mitchell David, BA; American computer industry executive; *Partner, Kapor Capital;* b. 1 Nov. 1950, New York; m. Freada Kapor Klein; ed Campus-Free Coll., Yale Univ., Massachusetts Inst. of Tech.; early career as disc jockey with WHCN-FM, Hartford, Conn.; teacher of transcendental meditation, Cambridge, Mass, Fairfield, Iowa; entry level computer programmer in Cambridge; mental health counsellor, New England Memorial Hosp., Stoneham, Mass; ind. software consultant 1978, co-developed Tiny Troll program; Product Man. Personal Software Inc.; Publr VisiCalc software, designer and programer of VisiPlot and VisiTrend; f. Lotus Devt Corpn 1982, Pres. then Chair. and CEO 1982–86; Chair. and CEO ON Tech. 1987–90; Co-founder and Chair. Electronic Frontier Foundation 1990–94; Chair. Mass Comm. on Computer Tech. and Law 1992–93; Adjunct Prof., MIT Media Lab. 1994–96; Pnr, Accel Pnrs 1999–2001; Founder and Chair. Open Source Applications Foundation 2001–08; Lecturer, Univ. of California, Berkeley 2005–06, Adjunct Prof., School of Information 2006–09; Founding Chair. Mozilla Foundation 2003; f. Xmarks (previously Foxmarks) 2006, Kapor Center for Social Impact; currently Partner, Kapor Capital; fmr Chair. Commercial Internet Exchange; mem. Computer Science and Tech. Bd, Nat. Information Infrastructure Advisory Council; Founding investor, UUNET and Real Networks; Chair. Bd Linden Research; mem. Bd of Dirs ePals, Level Playing Field Inst.; fmr mem. Bd of Dirs Groove Networks, Ximian, Reactivity; Trustee, Kapor Family Foundation 1984–98; Trustee, Level Playing Field Inst.; mem. Advisory Bd Wikimedia Foundation, Generation Investment Man. *Publications:* numerous articles on impact of personal computing and networks on society information infrastructure policy, intellectual property issues, anti-trust in the digital era. *Address:* Kapor Center for Social Impact, 2201 Broadway, Suite 725, Oakland, CA 94612, USA (office). *Telephone:* (510) 488-6600 (office). *Fax:* (510) 488-6600 (office). *Website:* www.kaporcenter.org (office).

KAPPLER, John W., PhD; American immunologist and academic; *Professor, Department of Integrated Immunology, National Jewish Health;* b. 22 Dec. 1943, Baltimore, Md; m. Philippa Marrack 1973; ed Lehigh Univ. and Brandeis Univ.; Postdoctoral Fellowship, Univ. of California, San Diego 1969; est. lab. with his wife at Univ. of Rochester, NY 1973–79; Prof., Dept of Integrated Immunology, Nat. Jewish Health (non-profit hosp.), Denver, Colo 1979–; Prof. of Immunology and Pharmacology and mem. Biomolecular Structure Program, Univ. of Colorado Health Sciences Center 1979–; Investigator, Howard Hughes Medical Inst. 1986–; mem. NAS 1989; William B. Coley Award, Cancer Research Inst. 1993, Louisa Gross Horwitz Prize for Biology or Biochemistry, Columbia Univ. 1994, Wolf Prize in Medicine (co-recipient) 2015. *Achievements include:* with his wife, Ellis Reinherz and James Allison, discovered the T cell receptor 1983. *Publications:* numerous papers in professional journals. *Address:* Kappler/Marrack Laboratory, Howard Hughes Medical Institute, National Jewish Health, 1400 Jackson Street, 5th Floor, Goodman Building, Denver, CO 80206, USA (office). *Telephone:* (303) 398-1322 (office). *Fax:* (303) 398-1396 (office). *E-mail:* kapplerj@njhealth.org (office). *Website:* www.nationaljewish.org/professionals/research/programs-depts/immunology/labs/kmlab (office); www.hhmi.org/scientists/john-w-kappler (office).

KAPUR, Shekhar, CA; Indian film director; b. 6 Dec. 1945, Lahore, Pakistan; s. of Kulbhushan Kapur and Sheel Kanta; m. Suchitra Krishnamurthy 1999 (divorced 2007); one d.; ed St Stephen's Coll., Delhi; early career with multinational oil co.; moved to GB 1970 and worked as accountant and man. consultant; appeared in several Hindi TV serials including Udaan; f. Virgin Comics; Padma Shri 2000. *Films include:* as actor: Ishq Ishq Ishq 1974, Jaan Hazir Hai 1975, Toote Khilone 1978, Jeena Yahan 1979, Bhula Na Dena 1981, Agni Pareeksha 1981, Bindiya Chamkegi 1984, Falak 1988, Gawahi 1989, Drishti 1990, Nazar 1991, Saatwan Aasman 1992, Vishwaroopam 2013, Teraa Surroor 2016; as dir: Masoom (Filmfare Award 1983) 1983, Mr India 1987, Bandit Queen (Filmfare Award 1995, 1997) 1994, Dil Se Dushmani 1998, Elizabeth (BAFTA Award 1998, National Board of Review) 1998, The Four Feathers 2002, The Guru (exec. producer) 2002, Elizabeth: The Golden Age 2007, New York, I Love You 2008, Passage 2009. *Television* *includes:* Tahqiqat (series) 1994. *Address:* 42 New Sital Apartments, A. B. Nair Road, Juhu, Mumbai 400 449, India (home). *Telephone:* (22) 6204988 (home). *Website:* www.shekharkapur.com.

KAPUTIN, Sir John, CMG; Papua New Guinea politician and international organization official; b. (John Rumet), 11 July 1941; s. of Daniel Kaputin and Rellie Iakirara; ed Rockhampton Boys Grammar School, Queensland, Australia, Univ. of Hawaii, USA; trained as teacher and bureaucrat 1960s; mem. House of Ass. (Rabaul constituency) 1972–2002; mem. Constitutional Planning Cttee that developed PNG Constitution 1972; Minister for Justice 1973–74, for Nat. Planning and Devt 1978–80, for Finance and Planning 1980–82, for Minerals and Energy 1985–88, for Foreign Affairs 1992–94, 1999–2000, for Mining and Petroleum 1994; Deputy Speaker 1975–77; Chair. Bipartisan Cttee on Bougainville Crisis 1988–90, Special State Negotiator for Bougainville 1998; Co-Pres. African, Caribbean and Pacific (ACP) Group of States-EU Jt Ass., Brussels, Belgium 1995–97, Sec.-Gen. ACP Secr. 2005–10; Special Ministerial Envoy for Int. Financial Insts, responsible for negotiations with IMF, World Bank, EU and Asian Devt Bank 2000–02; led ACP Ministerial Missions to Burundi, Rwanda, Equatorial Guinea, Togo, Fiji and Solomon Islands; Hon. Pres. ACP/EU Jt Parl. Ass. 1997; Togolese Medal of Freedom and Liberty, Govt of Repub. of Togo.

KAPUYA, Hon. Juma Athumani, BSc MSc PhD; Tanzanian academic and politician; b. 22 June 1945; ed Tabora Boys' Secondary School, Univ. of Dar es Salaam; Tutorial Asst, Univ. of Dar es Salaam 1971–74, Asst Lecturer 1974–76, Lecturer 1976–78, Sr Lecturer 1978–83, Assoc. Prof. 1983–87, Prof. 1987–95; adviser, Tanganyika Youth League (Univ. of Dar es Salaam) 1971–77, Chama Cha Mapinduzi (CCM) Youth 1977–82; Leader, CCM, Univ. of Dar es Salaam 1983–95; fmr mem. Parl. (CCM) for Urambo Magharibi 1995–2015; Minister of Defence and Nat. Service 2006–08, apptd Minister of Labour, Employment and Youth Devt 2008; Dir Tobacco Authority, Sugar Authority; Dir and Rep. OTTU, Univ. of Dar es Salaam, Inst. of Adult Educ.

KAPWEPWE, Chileshe Mpundu, MBA, CA; Zambian executive; *Secretary-General, Common Market for Eastern and Southern Africa;* b. 10 July 1958; ed Univ. of Zambia, Univ. of Bath; Chief Accountant, Star Commercial Ltd 1991–92; Contract Man., Société Générale de Surveillance 1993–2000; Chief Financial Officer and Man. Dir, Nat. Airports Corpn Ltd 2001–07; Deputy Minister of Finance and Nat. Planning 2008–11, also mem. Parl.; Alt. Exec. Dir, Africa Group One Constituency, IMF 2012; Chair., Zambia Revenue Authority Bd 2017–, Ecobank Zambia Ltd 2017–; Sec.-Gen. Common Market for Eastern and Southern Africa (COMESA) 2018–; mem. Bd, British Petroleum Zambia, Zambia Privatisation Trust Fund, African Civil Aviation Comm., Bank of Zambia, Nico Insurance; Fellow ACCA, Zambia Inst. of Chartered Accountants. *Address:* COMESA Centre, Ben Bella Road, PO Box 30051, 101101 Lusaka, Zambia (office). *Telephone:* (1) 229725 (office). *Fax:* (1) 225107 (office). *E-mail:* info@comesa.int (office). *Website:* www.comesa.int (office).

KARA-MURZA, Alexei Alexeyevich, Dr rer. pol, DPhil; Russian academic; *Head of Department, Philosophy of Russian History, Russian Academy of Sciences;* b. 1956; ed Moscow State Univ.; Dir Cen. for Theoretical Studies of Russian Reforms, Inst. of Philosophy, Russian Acad. of Sciences; Co-Pres. Moscow Foundation of Freedom and Human Rights (now Moscow Liberal Fund) 1992; worked as scientific researcher; Head of Dept of Social and Political Philosophy, Russian Acad. of Sciences 1995–, also Dir IPhRAS Branch for Social and Political Philosophy; fmr Prof. of Practical Philosophy, Higher School of Econs, Nat. Research Univ.; Deputy Chair. Union of Rightist Forces party 2000; mem. Council of Trustees Obshchaya Gazeta (weekly); Ed.-in-Chief Pravoe Delo newspaper. *Publications:* scientific publs on modern philosophy and politology. *Address:* Centre for Theoretical Studies of Russian Reforms, Russian Academy of Sciences, 119842 Moscow, Volkhonka str. 14 Bldg 5, Russia (office). *E-mail:* a-kara-murza@yandex.ru (office).

KARABAYEV, Ednan Oskonovich, PhD; Kyrgyzstani academic and government official; b. 17 Jan. 1953, Talas; ed Kyrgyz State Univ., Inst. of History of Kyrgyz SSR Acad. of Sciences; early career as history teacher, Frunze (now Bishkek); Minister of Foreign Affairs 1992–93, 2007–09; Head Int. Relations Dept, Kyrgyz-Russian Slavic Univ. 1994–2007, also fmr Dean; Adviser to Pres. 2000; Pres. UNA of Kyrgyzstan; mem. Cyril-Mefody Acad. of Slavic Enlightenment; Honoured Worker of Educ. in Kyrgyz Repub. *Publications:* more than 200 scientific and other articles and contribs to monographs.

KARADJORDJEVIC, HRH Crown Prince Alexander (see ALEXANDER KARADJORDJEVIC, HRH Crown Prince).

KARADŽIĆ, Radovan; Serbian psychiatrist, poet and fmr political leader; b. 19 June 1945, Petnjica, nr Šavnik, Montenegro; s. of Vuk Karadžić; m. Lilijana Zelen Karadžić; one s. one d.; ed Univ. of Sarajevo, Columbia Univ., USA; moved to Sarajevo, Bosnia and Herzegovina in 1960; worked in state hosps, including Koševo Hosp. (specialized in neuroses and depression); team psychologist for Red Star Belgrade football club 1983; with Unis Co.; Co.-founder and Pres. Srpska Demokratska Stranka (SDS—Serbian Democratic Party) 1989; leader of self-declared Republika Srpska (in Bosnia and Herzegovina), Pres. 1992–96 (resgnd); attended ceasefire talks in London Aug. 1992, Geneva Jan. 1993, after outbreak of hostilities; named as war crimes suspect by UN Tribunal for the Fmr Yugoslavia April 1995, int. arrest warrant issued for him July 1996; formally charged with genocide and crimes against humanity by Int. War Crimes Tribunal for Fmr Yugoslavia 1995; in hiding 1996–2008; arrested in Belgrade 21 July 2008, brought before Belgrade's War Crimes Court, had been working at pvt. clinic in Belgrade specializing in alternative medicine and psychology; on trial since Jan. 2009 at Int. Criminal Tribunal for the Fmr Yugoslavia at The Hague, Netherlands, accused on two counts of genocide and other war crimes, prosecution began its case April 2010, completed it May 2012, defence began its case Oct. 2012, completed it March 2014, Karadžić did not testify, closing arguments began Sept. 2014, failed in his demand for a re-trial, found guilty on one charge of genocide, and on nine of the ten other charges of crimes against humanity and war crimes committed in Srebrenica, Prijedor, Ključ and other districts of Bosnia, sentenced to 40 years in prison March 2016; Order of St Dionysus of Xanthe (First Rank); Risto Ratković Prize for Literature, Mikhail Sholokhov Prize for Poetry, Russian Writers' Union 1994. *Publications include:* Slavic Guest (poems) (main literary award of Montenegro 1993), There Are Miracles, There Are No Miracles (poems for children), Miraculous Chronicles of the Night (novel), Under the Left Tit of the Century (poems) 2005. *Leisure interest:* composes music.

KARAGANOV, Sergei Aleksandrovich, DHist; Russian defence and foreign affairs specialist; *Honorary Chairman of the Presidium, Council of Foreign and Defence Policy;* b. 12 Sept. 1952, Moscow; m. Ekaterina Karaganova-Miloslavskaya; one d.; ed Moscow State Univ., postgraduate study in USA; Jr Fellow, Sr Fellow, Head of Section, USA and Canada Studies Inst. 1978–88; Research Fellow, Perm. Mission of USSR at UN 1976–77; mem. Russian Acad. of Sciences 1988–, Deputy Dir Inst. of Europe 1989–2010; mem. Scientific Advisory Council, Ministry of Foreign Affairs 1991–; Founder and Chair. Presidium of the Council of Foreign and Defence Policy 1991–2012, Hon. Chair. 2012–; mem. Presidential Council of Russian Fed. 1993–99, Advisory Cttee of Security Council of Russian Fed. 1993–; Adviser on Foreign Policy to Presidential Admin. 2001–13; mem. Consulting Council to Security Council of Russia 1993–; mem. Consultative Council of Fed. 1996–; Chair. Dept on World Politics, State Univ. Higher School of Econs 2002–, Dean, School of Int. Econs and Foreign Affairs 2006–; Chair. Editorial Bd Russia in Global Affairs magazine 2002–; Chair. Valdai Discussion Club 2004–13; mem. Pres.'s Public Council for Assisting the Devt of Civil Society and Human Rights 2004–, Ministry of Defence Public Council 2006–10; mem. Bd of Trustees, Alfred Herrhausen Soc. for Int. Dialogue – A Deutsche Bank Forum 2004–, Int. Advisory Bd, UniCredit Group 2007–09, Advisory Bd, Vnesheconombank 2009–, Council for Investment Co-operation and Integration Interaction with Members of the CIS at Ministry for Econ. Devt 2009–, Supervisory Board of Publishing House International Affairs 2010–; Triennium mem. The Trilateral Comm. 1998–; mem. IISS, London. *Publications:* 18 books and brochures, including Russia: State of Reforms 1993, Security of the Future Europe (ed., in Russian) 1993, Harmonization: the Evolution of U.S. and Russian Defense Policies (co-ed., in Russian) 1993, Where Russia Goes? Foreign and Defense Policy in the New Era 1994, Damage Limitation or Crisis? Russia and the World (co-ed.) 1994, Wither Western Aid to Russia (ed. and dir of the study; in Russian) 1994, Russia's Economic Role in Europe. Report of the Commission for the Greater Europe, Vol. II (co-author, in Russian) 1995, Geopolitics Change in Europe, Policies of the West and Russia's Alternatives (ed. and head of the study) 1995, Towards a New Democratic Commonwealth (co-author) 1996, Russian-American Relations on the Threshold of Two Centuries (co-author) 2000, Strategy for Russia: Agenda for the President-2000 (ed., in Russian) 2000, Strategy for Russia: Ten Years of CFDP (ed.) 2002; more than 350 articles in Russian on econs of foreign policy, arms control, nat. security strategy, Russian foreign and defence policies. *Leisure interests:* athletics, literature, cooking. *Address:* National Research University Higher School of Economics, 11 Pokrovsky boulevard, 109028 Moscow (office); Chernyahovskogo, 9/5 Apt 387, 125139 Moscow, Russia (home). *Telephone:* (495) 771-32-52 (office); (495) 152-99-82 (home). *E-mail:* skaraganov@hse.ru (office). *Website:* karaganov.ru/en.

KARAGEORGHIS, Vassos, PhD, FSA, FRSA; Cypriot archaeologist and academic; *Adjunct Professor, The Cyprus Institute;* b. 29 April 1929, Trikomo; s. of George Karageorghis and Panagiota Karageorghis; m. Jacqueline Girard 1953 (died 2018); one s. one d.; ed Pancyprian Gymnasium, Nicosia, Univ. Coll. and Inst. of Archaeology, Univ. of London; Asst Curator, Cyprus Museum 1952–60, Curator 1960–63, Acting Dir, Dept of Antiquities, Cyprus 1963–64, Dir 1964–89; Dir Archaeological Research Unit, Prof. of Archaeology, Univ. of Cyprus 1992–96; excavations at Salamis 1952–73, Akhera and Pendayia 1960, Kition 1962–81, Maa-Palaeokastro, Pyla-Kokkinokremos 1979–87, Prof. Emer. 2004–; currently Adjunct. Prof., The Cyprus Inst.; Dir d'Etudes, Ecole Pratique des Hautes Etudes, Sorbonne, Paris 1983–84; Adjunct. Prof. of Classical Archaeology, State Univ. of New York, Albany 1973–; Geddes-Harrower Prof. of Classical Art and Archaeology, Univ. of Aberdeen 1975; Visiting Mellon Prof., Inst. for Advanced Study, Princeton 1989–90; adviser to the Pres. of Cyprus on cultural heritage 1989–92; mem. Council, Anastasios G. Leventis Foundation (Dir 1996–2010), Cultural Foundation of the Bank of Cyprus; mem. Royal Swedish Acad., Accad. dei Lincei, Acad. des Inscriptions et Belles Lettres, German Archaeological Inst., Acad. of Athens; Corresp. mem. Austrian Acad. of Sciences, Royal Acad. of Spain 1997; Hon. mem. Soc. for Promotion of Hellenic Studies, Archaeological Inst. of America, Council of Greek Archaeological Soc., ICOMOS 2005; Visiting Fellow, Merton Coll., Oxford 1979, 1988, Sr Research Fellow 1980, Hon. Fellow 1990; Visiting Fellow, All Souls Coll., Oxford 1982; Visiting Scholar Harvard Univ. 1997–; Fellow, Royal Soc. of Humanistic Studies, Lund, Univ. Coll., London; Corresp. Fellow, British Acad.; mem. Nat. Olympic Cttee Greece 1998; Hon. Fellow, Soc. of Antiquaries, London; Hon. Citizen of Plovdiv (Bulgaria) 2003; Order of Merit (1st Class), FRG 1980, Commdr, Royal Order of Polar Star (Sweden) 1990, Commdr, des Arts et des Lettres 1990, Commdr, Order of Merit (Italy) 1990, Austrian Decoration for Arts and Sciences 1997, Officier, Légion d'honneur 1998, Commdr of the Order of Honour (Greece) 2008; Dr hc (Lyon, Göteborg, Athens, Birmingham, Toulouse, Brock, Brussels, Oxford, Dublin, Mariupolis—Ukraine); Prix de la Soc. des Etudes Grecques, Sorbonne 1966, R. B. Bennett Commonwealth Prize 1978, Onassis Prize 'Olympia' 1991, Premio Internazionale 'I Cavalli d'Oro di San Marco' 1996, Award for Excellence in Science and Arts, Govt of Cyprus 1998, G. Maraslis Medal (Odessa) 2003, Archaeology Award 2011. *Publications include:* Treasures in the Cyprus Museum 1962, Corpus Vasorum Antiquorum 1963, 1965, Nouveaux documents pour l'étude du bronze récent à Chypre 1964, Sculptures from Salamis, Vol. I 1964, Vol. II 1966, Excavations in the Necropolis of Salamis, Vol. I 1967, Vol. II 1970, Vol. III 1973, Vol. IV 1978, Salamis in Cyprus 1969, Altägäis und Altkypros (with H. G. Buchholz) 1971, Kition, Mycenaean and Phoenician discoveries in Cyprus 1976, The Civilization of Prehistoric Cyprus 1976, Mycenaean Pictorial Vase Painting (with Emily Vermeule) 1981, Cyprus from the Stone Age to the Romans 1982, Cyprus at the close of the Late Bronze Age (co-ed. with J. D. Muhly) 1984, Archaeology in Cyprus 1960–85 (ed.) 1985, La Nécropole d'Amathonte III: Les Terres Cuites 1987, Blacks in Ancient Cypriot Art 1988, The End of the Late Bronze Age in Cyprus 1990, Tombs at Palaepaphos 1990, Les anciens Chypriotes: entre orient et occident 1990, The Coroplastic Art of Ancient Cyprus (Vols I-VI), Cyprus in the Eleventh Century BC (ed.) 1994, The Potters' Art of Ancient Cyprus (with Y. Olenik) 1997, Greek Gods and Heroes in Ancient Cyprus 1998, Cypriot Archaeology Today 1998, Excavating at Salamis in Cyprus, 1952–74 1999, Ancient Cypriot Art in the Severis Collection 1999, Ancient

Art from Cyprus. The Cesnola Collection (with J. R. Mertens, M. E. Rose), Defensive Settlements of the Aegean and Eastern Mediterranean after c. 1200 B.C. (with Christine Morris), Ancient Cypriot Art in the National Archaeological Museum Athens, The Cyprus Collections in the Medelhausmuseet (with S. Houby-Nielsen et al.), Ancient Cypriot Art in Russian Museums (with A. Bukina et al.), Early Cyprus: Crossroads of the Mediterranean, Aspects of Everyday Life in Ancient Cyprus: Iconographic Representations 2006, A Lifetime in the Archaeology of Cyprus 2007, Cypriote Antiquities in the Archaeological Museum of the American University of Beirut (with L. Badre) 2009, Cypriot Antiquities in the Phylactou Collection 2010, Cypriote and other antiquities in the Collection of Angelos and Emily Tsirides 2011, Tombs of the Late Bronze Age in the Limassol Area, Cyprus: 17th–13th centuries BC) (with Y. Violaris) 2012, A Cypro-Archaic Tomb at Xylotymbou and three Cypro-Classical Tombs at Phlassou: from Exuberance to Recession (with G. Georgiou) 2013, Kypriaka in Crete: From the Bronze Age to the end of the Archaic Period (with A. Kanta et al.) 2014, Palaepaphos-Skales: Tombs of the Late Cypriote IIIB and Cypro-Geometric Periods (with E. Raptou) 2016 and more than 470 articles in Greek, German, American, English and French journals. *Leisure interests:* gardening, photography. *Address:* 16 Kastorias Street, Nicosia 1055, Cyprus (home). *Telephone:* (2) 2755249 (home). *Fax:* (2) 2755249 (home). *E-mail:* vassoskarageorghis@cytanet.com.cy (office).

KARAKACHANOV, Krasimir Donchev, MA, PhD; Bulgarian historian and politician; *Deputy Prime Minister for Public Order and Security and Minister of Defence;* b. 29 March 1965, Ruse; s. of Dontcho Karakachanov; m.; one c.; ed St Kliment Ohridski Univ., Sofia; fmr Dir Macedonia (weekly newspaper), Sofia; cand. in presidential election 2011, 2016; mem. Nat. Ass. (parl.) for 15-Pleven constituency 2014–; Deputy Prime Minister for Public Order and Security and Minister of Defence 2017–; mem. Macedonian Scientific Inst., Sofia; mem. VMRO—Balgarsko Natsionalno Dvizhenie (VMRO—BND, IMRO—Bulgarian Nat. Movt), currently Pres. *Publications include:* books: IMRO: 100 Years of Struggle for Macedonia 1994, VMRO – The Story of a Struggle 2013; numerous articles in historical journals and the Bulgarian press. *Address:* Ministry of Defence, 1000 Sofia, ul. Dyakon Ignatiy 3, Bulgaria (office). *Telephone:* (2) 922-09-22 (office). *Fax:* (2) 987-96-93 (office). *E-mail:* presscntr@mod.bg (office). *Website:* www.mod.bg (office).

KARAKAŞ, Taner, BA; Turkish diplomatist; b. 26 Nov. 1953, Istanbul; m.; two c.; ed Univ. of Ankara; Third Sec., Africa Dept, Ministry of Foreign Affairs (MFA) 1978–80, Third, then Second Sec., Embassy in Dhaka, Bangladesh 1980–82, First Sec., Embassy in Vienna 1982–85, Head of Information Dept, MFA 1985–87, First Sec. and Embassy Undersecretary, Embassy in Rome Feb.–Dec. 1987, Embassy Undersecretary, Perm. Representation to NATO, Brussels 1987–90, Br. Man., Infrastructure Agency, MFA 1990–92, Counsellor and Deputy Perm. Rep., Perm. Mission to UNESCO, Paris 1992–96, Asst Gen. Man. and Head of Middle East Dept, MFA 1996–2000, Amb., Deputy Gen. Dir, Intelligence Asst Gen. Man. 2000–01, Amb., Deputy Gen. Dir, Bilateral Cultural Affairs and Deputy Gen. Man. 2001–02, Amb. to Mongolia 2002–05, to Macedonia 2005–08, Amb., Reserve Position in Undersecretariat June–July 2008, Amb. and Minister Counsellor 2008–09, Amb. and Adviser to the Minister, Dept of State 2009–11, Amb. and Adviser to the Minister, Ministry of Econ. Affairs 2011–12, Amb. to Argentina 2012–18. *Address:* c/o Embassy of Turkey, 11 de Septiembre 1382, C1426BKN Buenos Aires, Argentina (office).

KARAKI, Khaled A. Al-, BA, MA, PhD; Jordanian university administrator, academic and government official; b. 1946, Karak; ed Univ. of Jordan, Univ. of Cambridge, UK; fmr faculty mem. Dept of Arabic, Univ. of Jordan, then Asst Dean of Faculty of Arts, then Dean of Student Affairs, fmr Pres. Univ. of Jordan; Pres. Jerash Private Univ. 2001; Minister of Culture and Youth, of Culture and Information, of Culture and Higher Educ. in successive cabinets 1989–91; Deputy Prime Minister and Minister of Information 1995–96; Deputy Prime Minister and Minister of Educ. 2010–11; Adviser to HM the late King Hussein of Jordan 1991–92, 1993–95; Senator 2011–13; fmr Chief of the Royal Court; fmr Chair. Jordan Press Foundation (Al-Rai Newspaper); fmr Deputy Chair. Bd of Trustees Al-Albait Foundation for Islamic Thought; Pres. Jordanian Writers' Asscn 1985–90; mem. or Chair. numerous high-ranking cttees, asscns and councils, including Arab Asscn for Comparative Literature, Al-Albait Foundation, Higher Cttee for Declaring Amman Capital for Arab Culture, Cttee for Preserving the Arabic Language, Jordan Acad. for Arabic, amongst others; specialist in Arabic language, literature and culture; Order of Al Hussein for Distinguished Contributions, 1st class numerous grants and awards. *Publications:* more than 20 books and numerous articles.

KARAMANLIS, Konstantinos (Kostas), MA, PhD; Greek politician and lawyer; b. 14 Sept. 1956, Athens; m. Natasa Pazaitis 1998; one s. one d.; ed Athens Univ. Law School, Deree Coll., Fletcher School of Law and Diplomacy, Tufts Univ., USA; served in Greek Navy 1977–79; Lecturer in Political Science, Diplomatic History and Corp. Law, Deree Coll. 1983–89; mem. Parl. (New Democracy Party) for Thessaloniki 1989–; Pres. Nea Demokratia (New Democracy Party) 1997–2009; Leader of the Opposition 1997–2004; Vice-Pres. European People's Party 1999–2006; Prime Minister of Greece 2004–09; Minister of Culture 2004–06; Vice-Pres. Int. Democratic Union 2002; Chair. European Democrat Union Party Leaders Conf. 2003. *Publications include:* Eleftherios Venizelos and Greek Foreign Relations 1928–32 1986, Spirit and Era of Gorbachev 1987, Imperialism: The Case of Angola 1987. *Address:* Parliament (Vouli), Parliament Bldg, Leoforos Vasilissis Sofias 2, 100 21 Athens (office); 21, P. Kyriakou Str., 151 21, Athens, Greece (home). *Telephone:* (210) 6459006 (office). *Fax:* (210) 6459086 (office). *E-mail:* karamanlis.office@gmail.com. *Website:* www.hellenicparliament.gr (office).

KARAMARKO, Tomislav; Croatian politician; b. 25 May 1959, Zadar; m. 1st Enisa Muftić 1993 (died 2011); one s. two d.; m. 2nd Ana Šarić 2015; ed Univ. of Zagreb; archivist, Nat. Archives of Croatia 1987–88; Head, Office of the Prime Minister 1991–92, Cabinet Chief 1992–93; Chief of Police Admin, Zagreb 1993–96; Deputy Minister of the Interior 1996–98; Nat. Security Adviser to Pres. of Croatia 2000; Head, Office for Nat. Security 2000–02; Head, Counter-Intelligence Agency 2004–06; Dir Intelligence-Security Agency 2006–08; Minister of the Interior 2008–11; mem. Hrvatska Demokratska Zajednica (HDZ—Croatian Democratic Union) 1989–, Pres. 2012–16; Leader of the Opposition 2012–16; Leader, Domoljubna koalicija (Patriotic Coalition) 2015–; First Deputy Prime Minister Jan.–June 2016. *Address:* Hrvatska Demokratska Zajednica (Croatian Democratic Union), 10000 Zagreb, trg Žrtava fašizma 4, Croatia (office). *Telephone:* (1) 4553000 (office). *Fax:* (1) 4552600 (office). *E-mail:* hdz@hdz.hr (office). *Website:* www.hdz.hr (office); domoljubna.hr (office); www.tomislavkaramarko.hr.

KARANNAGODA, Adm. Wasantha, MBA, PhD; Sri Lankan diplomatist, civil servant and fmr naval officer; ed Ananda Coll., Colombo, Univ. of Colombo, Quai-i-Azam Univ., Islamabad, Pakistan, Univ. of Kelaniya, Nat. Defence Coll., Pakistan, Royal Naval Staff Coll., UK, Asia-Pacific Center for Security Studies, Hawaii, Near East-South Asia Center for Strategic Studies at Nat. Defense Univ., Washington, DC, USA; Flag Lt for Adm. Basil Gunasekara (Commdr of Navy) early 1980s; long naval career as navigator until final duty on board SLNS Wickrama as Commdr, 7th Surveillance Command Squadron 1992; held many sr commands, including four Operational Naval Commands on seven occasions – Northern, Eastern and Western Commands (twice each) and North Cen. once, for total period spanning six years; first ever Dir-Gen. (Operations), Naval HQ, Dir Naval Projects and Plans, Dir Naval Personnel and Training, Commdt of Naval and Maritime Acad., Deputy Area Commdr (West), Deputy Area Commdr (North) and Deputy Area Commdr (East); Commdr of Sri Lankan Navy 2005–09; awarded rank of Adm. after Eelam War IV and demise of LTTE (Tamil Tigers) (first officer thus promoted whilst in the service); Nat. Security Adviser to the Pres. 2009–11; Sec., Ministry of Highways 2009–10; Amb. to Japan 2011–15; mem. Royal Inst. of Navigation, UK, Nautical Inst., UK; Rana Sura Padakkama for gallantry, Vishista Seva Vibhushanaya, Uttama Seva Padakkama, North and East Operational Medal, Clasp I and Clasp II and several other service and campaign medals, including Repub. of Sri Lanka Armed Services Medal, Sri Lanka Navy 50th Anniversary Medal, Commemoration Medal, Sri Lanka Armed Services Long Service Medal, Pres.'s Inauguration Medal 1978, 50th Anniversary of Independence Commemoration Medal, Purna Bhumi Padakkama, Operation 'Reviresa' Campaign Medal, Commdr of the Navy's Commendation Badge (five stars), Surface Warfare Badge. *Leisure interest:* golf. *Address:* Naval Headquarters, Colombo, Sri Lanka (office). *Telephone:* (11) 2210000 (office). *Fax:* (11) 2396258 (office). *E-mail:* nhqdga@navy.lk (office). *Website:* www.navy.lk (office).

KARAPETYAN, Karen, CandEconSci, PhD; Armenian economist, business executive and politician; b. 19 Aug. 1963, m.; three c.; ed Yerevan State Univ.; Deputy Dir-Gen. Armenergo (energy co.) 1996–98, Dir-Gen. 1998–2001; Chair. and CEO ArmRosGazprom (Armenian-Russian jt venture) 2001–10; Chair. Areksimbank 2008; elected mem. Yerevan City Council 2009, Mayor of Yerevan 2010–11; First Vice-Pres. Gazprombank 2011–16, Deputy Dir-Gen. Gazprom Mezhregiongaz 2012–16, Deputy Gen. Dir for Int. Projects, Gazprom Energy 2015–16; Prime Minister of Armenia 2016–18; mem. Hayastani Hanrapetakan Kusaktsutyun (HHK—Republican Party of Armenia); Anania Shirakatsi Medal 2006. *Address:* c/o Office of the Prime Minister, 0010 Yerevan, Hanrapetutyun Hraparak, Government Building 1, Armenia (office).

KARASAWA, Yasuyoshi; Japanese business executive; *Representative Director, President and CEO, MS&AD Insurance Group Holdings, Inc.;* b. 27 Oct. 1950; ed Kyoto Univ.; joined The Sumitomo Marine and Fire Insurance Co. Ltd 1975, Exec. Officer and Gen. Man. Corp. Communications Dept 1998–2000, Gen. Man. of Secr. and Corp. Planning Dept and Gen. Man. of Business Rationalisation Dept 2000–01, Gen. Man. Corp. Planning Dept, Mitsui Sumitomo Insurance Co. Ltd (MSI) 2001–02, Gen. Man. of Investment Planning Dept of Financial Service Div. 2002–04, Exec. Officer and Gen. Man. Corp. Planning Dept 2004–05, Dir, Gen. Man. and Exec. Officer Corp. Planning Dept 2005–06, Dir and Man. Exec. Officer 2006–08, Dir and Sr Exec. Officer, MSI 2008–10, Dir MS&AD Insurance Group Holdings, Inc. 2008–09, Sr Exec. Officer 2009–10, Pres. and CEO MSI 2010–, Dir and Exec. Officer, MS&AD Insurance Group Holdings, Inc. 2010–14, Rep. Dir, Pres. and CEO, MS&AD Insurance Group Holdings, Inc. 2014–. *Address:* MS&AD Insurance Group Holdings, Inc., Yaesu First Financial Building, Yaesu 1-3-7, Chuo-ku, Tokyo 103-0028, Japan (office). *Telephone:* (3) 6202-5268 (office). *Fax:* (3) 6202-6882 (office). *E-mail:* info@ms-ad-hd.com (office). *Website:* www.ms-ad-hd.com (office).

KARASHEV, Aaly Azimovich; Kyrgyzstani politician; b. 30 Oct. 1968, Osh Oblast; ed Kyrgyz Agricultural Inst.; worked in Admin of the Pres. 1998–2006, becoming Head of Dept; Gov., Osh Oblast 2007–09; Deputy Prime Minister and Chief of Govt Apparatus 2009–12, Acting Prime Minister 1–5 Sept. 2012.

KARASIN, Grigory Borisovich; Russian diplomatist; *Deputy Minister of Foreign Affairs;* b. 23 Aug. 1949, Moscow; m.; two d.; ed Moscow Inst. of Oriental Languages, Moscow State Univ.; diplomatic service since 1972; translator, attaché USSR Embassy, Senegal 1972–76; attaché First African Div., USSR Ministry of Foreign Affairs 1976–77; sec. to Deputy Minister of Foreign Affairs 1977–79; Second, First Sec. Embassy, Australia 1979–85; First Sec., Counsellor Second European Div. Ministry of Foreign Affairs 1985–88; Counsellor USSR Embassy, UK 1988–92; Head of Dept of Africa, Ministry of Foreign Affairs 1992–93, Head. Dept of Information and Press 1993–96; Deputy Minister of Foreign Affairs 1996–2000, 2005–; Amb. to UK 2000–05; Order For Service to the Fatherland (IV class), Order of St Alexander Nevsky, Order of Friendship. *Address:* Ministry of Foreign Affairs, 119200 Moscow, Smolenskaya-Sennaya pl. 32/34, Russia (office). *Telephone:* (495) 244-16-06 (office). *Fax:* (495) 230-21-30 (office). *E-mail:* ministry@mid.ru (office). *Website:* www.mid.ru (office).

KARAT, Prakash, BA, MSc, PhD; Indian politician; b. 7 March 1948, Letpadan, Myanmar; m. Brinda Karat 1975; ed Madras Christian Coll., Univ. of Edinburgh, UK; at Jawaharlal Nehru Univ., New Delhi 1970, Pres. Students' Union 1972–73; Co-founder Students Fed. of India (Pres. 1974–79); worked as aide to A.K. Gopalan (leader of Communist Party of India—Marxist, CPI(M)) 1971–73, Sec., Delhi State Cttee, CPI(M) 1982–85, elected to Cen. Cttee 1985, mem. Politburea 1992, Gen. Sec. CPI(M) 2005–15; Man. Dir Leftword Books. *Publications include:* Language, Nationality and Politics in India 1972, A World To Win – Essays on The Communist Manifesto (ed) 1999, Across Time and Continents: A Tribute to Victor Kiernan (ed) 2003, Subordinate Ally: The Nuclear Deal and India-US Strategic Relations 2008, Politics and Policies 2008. *Address:* Communist Party of India (Marxist), Central Committee, A.K. Gopalan Bhawan, 27–29, Bhai Vir Singh

Marg, New Delhi 110 001, India (office). *Telephone:* (11) 23344918 (office). *Fax:* (11) 23747483 (office). *E-mail:* cc@cpim.org (office). *Website:* www.cpim.org (office).

KARATZAFERIS, Georgios; Greek politician, journalist and media executive; *Leader, Popular Orthodox Rally (Laikos Orthodoxos Synagermos—LAOS);* b. 11 Aug. 1947, Athens; ed London School of Journalism, UK; producer of radio broadcasts aged 15, TV producer aged 22; f. R.TV.P.R. AE advertising agency 1977; columnist for Nea Poreia political newsletter early 1980s; cr. TV Press Video Review 1983; set up radio and TV stations Radio City and TeleAsty (initially known as TeleCity) 1990; Ed. Alpha Ena newspaper 2000; also contributed to daily newspapers including Eleftheros, Apogevmatini and Eleftheros Typos; f. Acad. of Communications Studies, Athens 2005; mem. Vouli (Parl.) for Athens (New Democracy, expelled from party 2000, with LAOS 2000–) 1993–2012, responsibilities included chairmanship of Parl. Watchdog Cttee, Public Order Cttee and the Press and Mass Media Cttee 1993–2000, mem. Cttee on Public Admin and Cttee on Foreign Affairs 1993–2004, Nat. Communications' Confidentiality Protection Cttee 1999, Vice-Chair. Greco-Spanish Friendship Asscn 1999; Founder and Pres. Popular Orthodox Rally (Laikos Orthodoxos Synagermos—LAOS) 2000–; mem. European Parl. 2004–07, Vice-Pres. Independence and Democracy group; elected as a Prefectural Councillor as Head of the Me Kathari Kardia (With Clean Heart) party 2002; Adenauer Foundation scholarship 1983. *Publications:* six books in Greek, including The Model of Democracy, The Woman of Today, Liani Supports the Allagi (Change), Struggles and Agonies of the 1990–2000 Decade, Biographies of Saints. *Address:* Popular Orthodox Rally (Laikos Orthodoxos Synagermos), Leoforos Kallirrois 52, 117 45 Athens, Greece (office). *Telephone:* (210) 7522700 (office). *Fax:* (210) 7522704 (office). *E-mail:* pr@laos.gr (office). *Website:* www.laos.gr (office); www.karatzaferis.gr.

KARAYANCHEVA, Tsveta Valcheva; Bulgarian engineer and politician; *Chairman, Nat. Ass. (Narodno Sobranie);* b. 25 Feb. 1968, Bolyarovo; worked as designer, later Dir, Formoplast-Kardzhali (plastic mould mfr); mem. Narodno Sobraniye (nat. ass., parl.) for 9-Kardzhali constituency 2014–17, Chair. Narodno Sobraniye 2017–; mem. Grazhdani za Evropeysko Razvitie na Balgariya (Citizens for European Devt of Bulgaria). *Address:* Narodno Sobranie, 1169 Sofia, pl. Narodno Sobranie 2, Bulgaria (office). *Fax:* (2) 981-31-31 (office). *E-mail:* infocenter@parliament.bg (office). *Website:* www.parliament.bg (office).

KARBASIAN, Masoud, PhD; Iranian economist and politician; b. 1956; Deputy Head of Urban Services, Tehran Municipality 1984, also Adviser to Mayor of Tehran; several ministerial roles including Deputy Minister for Industries, for Petroleum and for Commerce; Head of Iranian Customs Admin (IRICA) –2017; Deputy Minister of Econ. Affairs and Finance –2017, Minister of Econ. Affairs and Finance 2017–18 (impeached); fmr Man. Dir and Deputy Chair. Bd of Dirs Tehran Investment and Partnership Org.; fmr Lecturer, Faculty of Econs and Faculty of Man., Allameh Tabataba'i Univ.; Order of Merit and Man.

KARBAUSKIS, Ramūnas; Lithuanian business executive, politician, writer and television producer; *Chairman, Lietuvos Valstiečių ir žaliųjų Sąjunga (Lithuanian Peasants' and Greens' Union);* b. 5 Dec. 1969, Naisiai, Lithuanian SSR, USSR; m. Lina Karbauskis; two s.; ed Julius Janonis Secondary School, Šiauliai, Lithuanian Acad. of Agric.; had active interest in draughts (checkers) and became cand. for Master (qualification degree) in int. and Russian draughts; mem. Lithuanian Youth Nat. Team of Russian Draughts 1987–88; Founder and CEO Agrokoncernas 1993, grew to become one of the largest agricultural groups in Lithuania, has retained full ownership of the co.; Ind. –1998; mem. Peasants' Party 1998–2001 (also Chair.); mem. Lietuvos Valstiečių ir Žaliųjų Sąjunga (Lithuanian Peasants' and Greens' Union) 2001–, Chair. 2009–; mem. Seimas (Parl.) for Šiauliai constituency 1996–2016, for Šilainiai constituency 2016–, Deputy Speaker 2000–01; mem. Council of Šiauliai Dist Municipality 1997–2000; Pres. Lithuanian Draughts Fed. 2006–; Vice-Pres. Lithuanian Žemaitukas (historic horse breed) Asscn 2009–; f. Naisiai family festival (alcohol-free, outdoor summer entertainment festival); co-f. Švieskime Vaikus (Let's Educate Children) charity, with singer and producer Andrius Mamontovas 2013. *Television:* producer of series Naisių vasara (based on stories from village where he was born). *Address:* Lietuvos Valstiečių ir žaliųjų Sąjunga, Pamėnkalnio g. 26, Vilnius 01114, Lithuania (office). *Telephone:* (5) 212-0821 (office). *Fax:* (5) 212-0822 (office). *E-mail:* info@lvzs.lt (office). *Website:* www.lvzs.lt (office).

KARDASHEV, Nikolai Semenovich; Russian astronomer; *Director, Astro Space Centre, Lebedev Physical Institute, Russian Academy of Sciences;* b. 25 April 1932; m.; one d.; ed Moscow State Univ.; lab., sr lab., jr, sr researcher State Astronomical Inst. 1955–67; head of lab., Deputy Dir Inst. of Space Studies USSR Acad. of Sciences 1967–90; Dir Astro Space Cen., Lebedev Physical Inst., USSR Acad. of Sciences 1990–; corresp. mem. USSR (now Russian) Acad. of Sciences 1976, mem. 1994; research in radiophysics, radioastronomy, radio radiation of galaxies and quasars; USSR State Prize. *Publications include:* Pulsars and Nonthermal Radio Sources 1970, Strategy and Future Projects 1977; numerous articles in scientific journals. *Address:* Astro Space Centre, Lebedev Physical Institute, Russian Academy of Sciences, 117997 Moscow, Profsoyuznaya str. 84/32, Russia (office). *Telephone:* (495) 333-21-89 (office). *E-mail:* nkardash@asc.rssi.ru (office). *Website:* www.asc.rssi.ru (office).

KAREKIN II, His Holiness (Ktritch Narssisian); Armenian ecclesiastic; *Supreme Patriarch and Catholicos of All Armenians;* b. 16 Aug. 1951, Etchmiadzin; ed Kevorkian Theological Seminary, Univ. of Vienna, Univ. of Bonn; Asst Dean, Kevorkian Theological Seminary; ordained priest 1972; pastor in Germany 1975; Asst to Vicar-Gen. of Araratian Patriarchal Diocese 1980, Vicar-Gen., Bishop 1983, later Archbishop; mem. Supreme Spiritual Council of Catholicosate of All Armenians 1990–; Supreme Patriarch and Catholicos of All Armenians 1999–; f. Vazkenian Seminary, Sevan 1989, Christian Educ. Centre 1990; Dr hc (Artsakh); Kawkab Medal (First Class) Jordan 2000, Bethlehem 2000 Award (Palestinian Nat. Authority) 2000, Star of Romania 2000. *Address:* Residence of the Catholicosate of all Armenians, Vagharshapat, Monastery of St Etchmiadzin, Armenia (office). *Telephone:* (10) 28-57-37 (office). *Fax:* (10) 15-10-77 (office). *E-mail:* holysee@etchmiadzin.am (office). *Website:* www.holyetchmiadzin.am (office).

KARELIN, Col Aleksander Aleksandrovich, PhD; Russian politician and fmr professional wrestler; b. 19 Sept. 1967, Novosibirsk; m. Olga Karelina; two s. one d.; ed Novosibirsk Pedagogical Inst., Motor-Transport Tech. Coll., Omsk Inst. of Physical Culture, Lesgaft Acad. of Physical Culture; Greco-Roman wrestler, turned professional 1978; unbeaten for 12 years until Sydney Olympics; world champion (nine times), European champion (12 times); Olympic champion 1988, 1992, 1996; Olympic silver medallist, Sydney 2000, then retd; mem. of team Dynamo; Specialist, Fed. Tax Police Service 1995–99, Col of the Tax Police 1995; Co-founder and Co-leader Yedinstvo; Chair. Interregional Co-ordinating Council, Unity (Yedinstvo) party in Siberian Fed. Dist; mem. State Duma 1999–, Deputy Chair. Cttee for Int. Affairs 2003–; currently mem. Supreme Council, United Russia party; Order of Friendship of Peoples 1989, Order of Honour 2001, Order For Merit to the Fatherland IV class 2008 USSR Merited Master of Sports, Hero of Russia 1997. *Leisure interests:* poetry, literature, classical music. *Address:* State Duma, Yedinstvo Faction, Okhotny Ryad 1, 103265 Moscow, Russia (office). *Telephone:* (495) 292-56-97 (office). *Website:* www.karelin.ru.

KARGBO, Momodu Lamin; Sierra Leonean economist and politician; experience as economist in areas involving econ. and social devt, particularly in public financial man. and structural reforms, expenditure control and man., revenue and tax policy admin, macroeconomic policy; fmr Man. Dir, Nat. Cooperative Bank; Deputy Minister and later Minister of State, Ministry of Finance and Econ. Devt –2014, Minister of Finance and Econ. Devt 2016–18; Gov., Bank of Sierra Leone 2014–16; mem. All-People's Congress.

KARIBZHANOV, Zhanybek Salimovich; Kazakhstani agronomist, economist, diplomatist and government official; b. 23 Nov. 1948, Aybas village of Sherbakulsky rayon, Omsk region, Russia; ed Omsk Agricultural Inst.; Head of Lab. and Sr Scientific Officer, All-Union Research and Design Tech. Inst. Cybernetics, Moscow 1979–82; Chief Economist, Zarya kommunizma (state farm), October rayon, Turgayski region and Dir Panfilov state farm, Oktyabrski rayon 1982–87; Chief of Cen. Admin of Social and Econ. Devt Planning of Agric., State Agro-Industrial Cttee of Kazakh SSR, Alma-Ata 1987–89; Head, Agrarian Dept of Cen. Cttee, CP of Kazakhstan 1989–92; Head, Kokchetav regional admin 1992–93; Deputy Prime Minister and Chair. State Cttee on State Property 1993–94; Minister of Agric. 1994–96; Deputy Prime Minister 1996–97; Akim, Akmolinsk region July–Dec. 1997; Deputy Prime-Minister and Minister of Agric. 1997–99; Adviser to the Pres. of Kazakhstan 1999–2001; Amb. to People's Repub. of China 2001–07; Akim, Eastern Kazakhstan Oblast Admin. Jan.–May 2008.

KARIM, Ahmed Tariq; Bangladeshi diplomatist; ed Notre Dame Coll., Dhaka Univ., Univ. of Maryland, USA; Lecturer in English, Notre Dame Coll., Dhaka 1965–66; joined Pakistan (later Bangladesh) Foreign Service 1967, served in various capacities at Missions in Iran 1969–72, Germany 1975–78, Thailand 1979–80, UK 1980–82, High Commr to India 1984–88, Deputy Chief of Mission, Embassy in Beijing 1989–91, Amb. to Iran (also accred to Lebanon) 1991–95, Additional Foreign Sec. with responsibility for South Asian region 1995–97, High Commr to S Africa (also accred to Botswana, Namibia and Lesotho with consular jurisdiction in Zambia and Zimbabwe) 1997–98, Amb. to USA 2001–02, High Commr to India 2009–14; Sr Advisor, Center for Institutional Reform and the Informal Sector (IRIS), Univ. of Maryland 2002–05; apptd Vice-Pres. Bangladesh Enterprise Inst. (pvt. think-tank) 2009; mem. Adjunct Faculty, Univ. of Maryland 2007, 2008, Elliott School of Int. Affairs, George Washington Univ. 2008, Virginia International Univ. 2007, 2008; Life mem. Bangladesh Inst. of Law and Int. Affairs.

KARIM, Bachtiar; Indonesian business executive; *President Director, PT Musim Mas;* b. 1957; s. of Anwar Karim; m.; four c.; joined family firm Musim Mas (palm oil processing co.), Medan, currently Pres. Dir PT Musim Mas; mem. Exec. Bd Round Table for Sustainable Palm Oil. *Address:* PT Musim Mas, Jl KL Yos Sudarso KM 7, 8 Tanjung Mulia, Medan 20241, North Sumatra, Indonesia (office). *Telephone:* (61) 6615511 (office). *Fax:* (61) 6617386 (office). *Website:* www.musimmas.com (office).

KARIM, Mohammad Fazlul, LLB; Bangladeshi judge; b. 30 Sept. 1943, Suchakradandi village, Chittagong; s. of Al-haj Ahmed Kabir and Sunia Ara Begum; ed Univ. of Dhaka; enrolled as Advocate of Dist Court, Chittagong 1965, in High Court Div. 1970, in Appellate Div. 1979; Sec. to Supreme Court Bar Asscn 1982; mem. Bangladesh Bar Council 1992; Additional Judge of High Court Div. of Supreme Court 1992–94, Regular Judge 1994–2001, Sr-most Judge of Appellate Div. of Supreme Court 2001–10, Chief Justice of Bangladesh 2010–11; Chair. Judicial Service Pay Comm.; mem. Delhi-based Asia Pacific Advisory Forum on Judicial Educ. on Gender Equality Issue; fmr Chair. Court Admin and Court Man. Scheme of Capacity Building Project; fmr mem. Scheme for Mediation and Alternative Dispute Resolution under the aid programme of USIS; participated in Conf. on Prison Reform in SE Asia, Kathmandu Nepal 1996, confs on Judicial Educ. on Gender Equality Issue held in India, Pakistan, Sri Lanka and Nepal 1998–2006, in SAARC Law Conf., Dhaka; visited various courts and insts to observe case man., court admin and alternative dispute resolution in UK and USA 2002.

KARIMI, Gen. Sher Mohammad; Afghan army officer; b. 11 Nov. 1945, Khost Prov.; s. of Mohammad Karim; ed Royal Mil. Acad. Sandhurst, UK, Egyptian Commando School, US Army Ranger and Special Forces schools, Indian Defence Coll.; arrested and held prisoner after invasion by Soviet Army 1978, forced into exile in Pakistan, returned to Afghanistan 2001; served in Afghanistan Army Commando Brigade, as ADC and Army Dir of Recruiting and Training, served as Deputy Chief of Staff then Chief of Operations of Gen. Staff, Ministry of Defence, then Chief of Operations, Afghan Nat. Army –2010, Chief of Staff, Afghan Nat. Army 2010–15; US Bronze Star Medal; NESA Alumnus Award. *Achievements include:* first Afghan to graduate from Royal Mil. Acad., Sandhurst.

KARIMOV, Dzhamshed Khilolovich, DEcon; Tajikistani politician; b. 4 Aug. 1940, Dushanbe; m.; two c.; ed Moscow Technological Inst. of Light Industry; researcher, Cen. Research Inst. of Econs and Math., USSR Acad. of Sciences; Asst Chair of Econ. of Industry Tajik State Univ., Jr researcher, Head of Div. of Optimal Planning Inst. of Econ., Tajik Acad. of Sciences 1962–72, Deputy Dir, Dir Research Inst. of Econ. and Econ.-Math. Methods of Planning, State Planning Cttee, Tajik SSR 1972–81; Corresp. mem. Tajik Acad. of Sciences; Deputy Chair. State Planning Cttee 1981–88; Deputy Chair. Council of Ministers, Chair. State Planning Cttee 1988–89; First Sec. Dushanbe City Cttee of CP Tajikistan

1989–91; USSR People's Deputy 1989–92; Deputy, First Deputy Chair. Council of Ministers Tajik Repub. 1991–92; represented Repub. of Tajikistan in Russia 1992–93; Chief Adviser on Econ. to Pres. Sept.–Nov. 1994; Prime Minister of Tajikistan 1994–96 (forced to resign after bloodless coup); Adviser to Pres. Rakhmonov 1996–97; apptd Amb. to People's Repub. China 1997.

KARIMOVA, Gulnora; Uzbekistani business executive, diplomatist, fashion designer and singer; b. 8 July 1972, Farg'ona, Uzbek SSR, USSR; d. of Pres. of Uzbekistan, Islam Karimov (died 2016) and Tatyana Akbarovna Karimova; m. Mansur Maqsudi (divorced); one s. one d.; ed Tashkent State Univ., Univ. of World Economy and Diplomacy, Tashkent, Univ. of Information and Tech., Tashkent, New York, Univ., Fashion Inst. of Tech., Harvard Grad. School of Arts and Sciences, USA; early academic career at Dept of Int. Studies, Univ. of World Economy and Diplomacy, Tashkent; fmrly with Perm. Mission to UN, New York; returned to Uzbekistan and developed business interests in mobile cellular telephone operator and numerous industrial cos; consultant and adviser to Minister of Foreign Affairs; Minister-Counsellor, Embassy of Uzbekistan, Moscow 2003–08; Deputy Minister of Foreign Affairs, responsible for Cultural and Humanitarian Co-operation 2008; Amb. and Perm. Rep. to UN Office and other Int. Orgs, Geneva 2008–11; Amb. to Spain 2010–12; Chair. Forum of Culture and Arts Foundation of Uzbekistan; mem. Cercle Diplomatique de Genève; designed jewellery collection GULI for Swiss co. Chopard 2009; presented fashion lines under name Guli at New York Fashion Week 2010 and Cipriani, New York 2011; est. Forum of Socially Responsible Citizens of Uzbekistan 2012; left Switzerland after her immunity was lifted by a court 2013; under investigation for money laundering and corruption in Switzerland and Uzbekistan 2014–16; whereabouts unknown; Pushkin Gold Medal for outstanding contrib. to the arts and culture 2009, IOC Sport – Inspiring Young People Trophy for activities in the area of sport, education and culture among youth 2010, Silk Road and Humanitarian Cooperation Award, Shanghai Cooperation Org. 2012. *Film screenplay:* The Theft of the White Cocoon (story about the origin of the famed Central Asian silk) 2012. *Music includes:* Round Run (single) 2012, various remixes by DJ White Shadow, Razor N. Guido and Max Fadeev; released self-titled debut album 2012; released a duet with French actor Gérard Depardieu 2012. *Publications:* Categories of Competitiveness of Countries with Transitional Economies: The Example of Uzbekistan 1998, Problems of Security in Central Asia: The Conditions, Tendency and Prospect of Development 2001. *Leisure interests:* jewellery and accessory designer, singer, poet.

KARIMULLAH, Adm. Shahid, MS; Pakistani naval officer (retd); b. 14 Feb. 1948, Hyderabad, India; s. of Mohammad Karimullah and Ismat un Nisa Iqbal; m. Nasreen Shahid; three s.; ed Nat. Defence Coll., US War Coll.; joined navy operations br. 1965, Pakistan Fleet Commdr, apptd Admiral 2002, Chief of Naval Staff 2002–05; Amb. to Saudi Arabia 2005–09; mem. Nat. Security Council; chair. of two non-governmental orgs; Sitara-i-Jurrat, Sitara-i-Imtiaz (mil.), Hilal-i-Imtiaz (mil.), Medal of Merit of the Turkish Armed Forces 2003. *Leisure interests:* reading, golf, lectures at war colls. *Address:* A8(a) Navy Housing Scheme, Zam Zama, Clifton, Karachi, Pakistan. *Telephone:* 99250330. *E-mail:* skullah1126@gmail.com.

KARIN, Michael, BSc, PhD; American pharmacologist and academic; *Distinguished Professor of Pharmacology and Pathology, School of Medicine, University of California, San Diego;* ed Tel-Aviv Univ., Israel, Univ. of California, Los Angeles; mem. Faculty, Univ. of California, San Diego 1987–, currently Distinguished Prof. of Pharmacology and Pathology, School of Medicine; an American Cancer Soc. Research Prof. 1999–; Co-founder Signal Pharmaceutical (currently Celgene), fmr mem. Scientific Advisory Bd; fmr mem. Nat. Advisory Council for Environmental Health Sciences; mem. NAS 2005; Assoc. mem. European Molecular Biology Org. 2007; Harvey Prize, Technion, Israel 2010, Harvey Prize in Human Health 2011, Brupbacher Prize in Cancer Research 2013, William B. Coley Award for Distinguished Research 2013. *Publications:* more than 300 papers in professional journals; 30 patents or pending patent applications. *Address:* Department of Pharmacology, University of California, San Diego, 9500 Gilman Drive, La Jolla, CA 92093-0636, USA (office). *Telephone:* (858) 534-1361 (office). *Fax:* (858) 534-8158 (office). *E-mail:* karinoffice@ucsd.edu (office). *Website:* pharmacology.ucsd.edu/faculty/karin.html (office); molpath.ucsd.edu/faculty/Karin.shtml (office); biomedsci.ucsd.edu/faculty/faculty_descrip.aspx?id=7 (office).

KARINA, Anna; French actress; b. (Hanne Karen Blarke Bayer), 22 Sept. 1940, Fredriksburg, Solbjerg, Denmark; d. of Carl Johann Bayer and of Elva Helvig Frederiksen; m. 1st Jean-Luc Godard (q.v.) (divorced); m. 2nd Pierre-Antoine Fabre 1968 (divorced); m. 3rd Daniel Georges Duval 1978; Commandeur des Arts et des Lettres 1996, Chevalier de la Légion d'honneur 2017; Prix Orange. *Films include:* She'll Have To Go 1961, Une femme est une femme 1961, Vivre sa vie 1962, Le petit soldat 1963, Bande à part 1964, Alphaville 1965, Made in the USA 1966, La religieuse 1968, The Magus 1968, Before Winter Comes 1968, Laughter in the Dark 1969, Justine 1969, The Salzburg Connection 1972, Living Together 1974, L'assassin musicien 1975, Les oeufs brouillés 1976, Boulette chinoise 1977, L'ami de Vincent 1983, Ave Maria 1984, Dernier été à Tanger 1987, Cayenne Palace 1987, L'Oeuvre au noir 1988, Last Song 1989, L'Homme qui voulait être coupable 1990, Une Histoire d'amour 2000, The Truth About Charlie 2002, Moi César 2003, Victoria 2008. *Albums include:* Une histoire d'amour 2000, La Petite Sirène 2013, Je suis une aventurière 2018. *Publications:* Golden City 1983, On n'achète pas le soleil (novel) 1988. *Address:* c/o Ammédia, 20 avenue Rapp, 75007 Paris; Orban éditions, 76 rue Bonaparte, 75006 Paris, France.

KARIŅŠ, (Arturs) Krišjānis, BA, PhD; Latvian business executive and politician; *Prime Minister;* b. 13 Dec. 1964, Wilmington, Delaware, USA; ed Pennsylvania Univ.; Pres. and co-founder PK SIA (Lāču Ice, frozen goods co.) 1994–2002; Pres. Formula SIA (automotive and office goods trading co.) 1999–2000; mem. Saeima (parl.) 2002–09; Minister of Economy 2004–06; mem. European Parl. (Group of the European People's Party/Christian Democrats) 2009–19; Prime Minister 2019–; Co-f. Jaunais laiks (New Era Party) 2002, Chair. 2007–08; mem. Jaunā Vienotība (New Unity) 2011–. *Address:* Office of the Cabinet of Ministers, Brīvības bulv. 36, Rīga 1520, Latvia (office). *Telephone:* 6708-2800 (office). *Fax:* 6728-0469 (home). *E-mail:* vk@mk.gov.lv (office). *Website:* www.mk.gov.lv (office); www.karins.lv.

KARIYAWASAM, Prasad, BSc (Hons); Sri Lankan diplomatist; b. 21 March 1954, Galle; m. Kanthi Kariyawasam; ed Univ. of Peradeniya; joined Foreign Service 1981, diplomatic assignments include missions in Geneva, Riyadh, Washington, DC, New Delhi, New York; fmr Deputy High Commr in India 1998–2001; Perm. Rep. to UN, Geneva 2001–03, Consul-Gen. to Switzerland 2001, Perm. Rep. to Conf. on Disarmament, Personal Rep. to Head of State to Group of 15 2001–03, Amb. and Perm. Rep. to UN, New York 2005–08, High Commr to India 2009–14, to USA (concurrently Accred as High Commr to Trinidad & Tobago and Amb. (Desig.) to Mexico) 2014–17; fmr mem. UN Panel of Experts on Small Arms, Group of Governmental Experts on Relationship between Disarmament and Devt; Vice-Chair. Main Cttee, World Conf. on Racism, UN Comm. on Human Rights, Durban, S Africa 2001; Leader, Sri Lanka Del. to Conf. on Disarmament, Geneva 2001–03; Special Coordinator for Improved Functioning, Conf. on Disarmament 2001, 2002; Del. to Ad Hoc Cttee on Int. Terrorism 2001–03; Chair. Global System of Trade Preferences Cttee of Participants, UNCTAD, UNCTAD Expert Group on Market Access Issues in Mode 4 (Movement of Natural Persons to Supply Services) 2002–03; mem. UN Cttee on Protection of Rights of All Migrant Workers and Members of Their Families 2003–; Chair. Chairpersons of Human Rights, Treaty Bodies and Inter-Cttee Meetings 2004; Vice-Chair. ECOSOC of the UN, New York 2006–07; mem. Advisory Bd Int. Comm. on Nuclear non-proliferation and Disarmament 2008–09.

KARKARIA, Bachi J.; Indian editor; *Columnist, The Times of India;* m.; two s.; ed Loreto Coll., Univ. of Calcutta; began career at Illustrated Weekly of India 1969; Asst Ed. The Statesman, Calcutta (first woman) 1980; Group Editorial Dir, Mid Day Multimedia Ltd 2000–02; Ed. Sunday Times of India 1998–2000, Resident Ed. The Times of India 2003, in charge of Delhi section, then Nat. Metro Ed. 2004, Consulting Ed., columnist and blogger (Erratica); also writes Giving Gyan column in Mumbai Mirror; mem. Int. Women's Media Foundation; mem. Bd World Editors Forum 2002–, India AIDS Initiative of Bill and Melinda Gates Foundation; Jefferson Fellow, East West Center, Honolulu; mem. Professional Women's Advisory Bd, American Biographical Inst.; Media India Award (for human interest stories) 1992, Mary Morgan-Hewitt Award for Lifetime Achievement 1994. *Publications include:* Dare to Dream: The Life of M.S. Oberoi 2007, To a Grand Design, In Hot Blood: The Nanavati Case That Shook India 2017, Giving Gyan 2018. *Address:* The Times of India, 7 Bahadur Shah Zafar Marg, New Delhi 110 002, India (office). *Telephone:* (11) 23492049 (office). *Fax:* (11) 23351606 (office). *E-mail:* bachi.karkaria@timesgroup.com (office). *Website:* blogs.timesofindia.indiatimes.com/erratica (office).

KARKI, Bharat Bahadur, BA, MA, LLB, LLM, PhD; Nepalese professor of business law and government official; b. 18 Aug. 1950, Khotang Dist; ed Univ. of Delhi, India; has been teaching law since late 1970s; mem. Legal Adviser's Forum, Kathmandu; fmr Head of Dept of Law and Dean of Law Faculty, Tribhuvan Univ., Kathmandu; Attorney Gen. 2009–10 (resgnd); Ad-Hoc Judge of Supreme Court 2010.

KARKI, Gyanendra Bahadur; Nepalese politician; m. Aabhu Rana Karki (deceased); ed Tribhuvan Univ.; Minister of Water Resources 2006, Minister of Finance 2017–18; mem. Nepali Congress Party.

KARKI, Sushila, BA, MPolSci, LLB; Nepalese lawyer and judge; b. 7 June 1952, Shankarpur, Biratnagar; m. Durga Prasad Subedi; one s.; ed Tribhuvan Univ., Banaras Hindu Univ., India; apptd Advocate, Nepal Bar Assn 1979, Sr Advocate 2004; Justice (Ad hoc), Supreme Court of Nepal 2009, Justice (Perm.) 2010–16, acting Chief Justice of Supreme Court April–July 2016, Chief Justice 2016–17, Chair. Judicial Council, Judicial Service Comm., Access to Justice Commission, Nat. Judicial Acad., IT Cttee, Case Man. Cttee, Bench BAR Coordination Cttee; mem. Constitutional Bench, Judges Soc., Nepal 2009–, Int. Assn of Women Judges 2010–, Int. GLOW Program 2012–; mem. Nepal Red Cross Soc., Amnesty Int. Nepal, Human Rights Org.; Mahendra Bikram Smarak Trust Award 1985, Sambhav Kanoon Puraskar 2004. *Publication:* Gender Equality 2011. *Address:* Dhapasi, Kathmandu Nepal (office). *E-mail:* karkishusila@gmail.com.

KARLIC, HE Cardinal Estanislao Esteban, DTheol; Argentine ecclesiastic (retd); b. 7 Feb. 1926, Oliva; ed Pontifical Gregorian Univ.; ordained priest 1954; Auxiliary Bishop of Córdoba and Titular Bishop of Castrum 1977–83; Coadjutor Archbishop of Paraná 1983–86; Archbishop of Paraná 1986–2003 (retd), Archbishop Emer. 2003–; cr. Cardinal 2007, Cardinal-Priest of Beata Maria Vergine Addolorata a piazza Buenos Aires 2007–; fmr Pres. Exec. Comm. of Episcopal Conf. of Argentina; fmr mem. Special Council for America of Gen. Secr. of Synod of Bishops, served as Co-Sec.; mem. comm. appointed by Pope John Paul II to write the Catechism of the Roman Catholic Church 1986–92. *Address:* c/o Archdiocese of Paraná, Monte Caseros 77, 3100 Paraná [Entre Rios], Argentina.

KARLSTRÖM, Johan, MSc (Eng); Swedish construction industry executive; *President and CEO, Skanska AB;* b. 1957; ed Royal Inst. of Tech., Stockholm, Advanced Man. Program, Harvard Univ., USA; joined Skanska 1983, began career as Regional Man., Skanska Northern Sweden, later Exec. Vice-Pres. Skanska, Nordic region, Exec. Vice-Pres. Skanska USA –2008, Pres. and CEO Skanska AB 2008–; fmr Pres. BPA (now Bravida); mem. Bd of DirsSandvik AB. *Address:* Skanska AB, Warfvinges väg 25, 112 74 Stockholm, Sweden (office). *Telephone:* (10) 448-00-00 (office). *E-mail:* info@skanska.com (office). *Website:* www.skanska.com (office).

KARMAN, Tawakul; Yemeni journalist, human rights activist and politician; *Leader, Women Journalists Without Chains;* b. 7 Feb. 1979, Mekhlaf, Ta'izz Prov.; d. of Abdel Salam Karman; m. Mohammed al-Nahmi; three c.; ed Univ. of Science and Tech., Sana'a, Sana'a Univ.; Founder and Leader Women Journalists Without Chains (human rights org.) 2005–; sr mem. in leading Islamist opposition party, Al-Islah; jailed several times for her activism during 'Arab Spring' 2011, led a series of protests calling for the departure of Pres. Ali Abdullah Saleh; Nobel Peace Prize (jtly, first Arab woman and second Muslim woman) for "non-violent struggle for the safety of women and for women's rights to full participation in peace-building work" 2011, selected as first place of the Foreign Policy top 100 global thinkers of 2011. *Address:* Women Journalists Without Chains, PO Box, Daeery Street behind Old University Post Office, Sana'a 12702, Yemen (office). *Telephone:* (1) 210543 (office). *Fax:* (1) 210523 (office). *E-mail:* info@womenpress.org (office); withoutchains@gmail.com (office). *Website:* womenpress.org (office).

THE KARMAPA, (Urgyen Trinley Dorje); Tibetan Buddhist leader; b. 26 June 1985, Lhatok; Living Buddha of the White Sect, Tibet; Seventeenth Incarnation; enthroned 1992; now living in exile in Dharamsala, India.

KARMAZIN, Melvin (Mel) Alan, BS; American media executive; b. 24 Aug. 1943, Long Island, New York; m. 1st Sharon Karmazin (divorced 1994); one s. one d.; m. 2nd Craig Karmazin; ed Pace Univ.; stage man., CBS Radio 1960–70, Chair. and CEO CBS Station Group 1996–99, then Pres. and COO CBS Corpn; Vice-Pres. and Gen. Man. Metromedia Inc. 1970–81; Pres. Infinity Broadcasting Corpn 1981–96, CEO 1988–96; Pres., COO Viacom Inc. 2000–04 (resgnd); Pres. and CEO Sirius Satellite Radio Inc. 2004–13; Prin. Owner, Good Karma Broadcasting; fmr mem. Bd of Dirs Westwood One, Blockbuster, New York Stock Exchange; Vice-Chair. Bd of Trustees, Museum of TV and Radio; numerous awards including Nat. Asscn of Broadcasters Nat. Radio Award and IRTS Gold Medal Award; inducted into Broadcasting Hall of Fame. *Address:* Good Karma Broadcasting, 100 Stoddart Street, Beaver Dam, WI 53916, USA (office). *Telephone:* (920) 885-4444 (office). *Website:* goodkarmabrands.com (office).

KARMOKOV, Khachim Mukhamedovich, DEcon; Russian economist and politician; b. 2 May 1941, Zayukovo, Kabardin-Balkar Autonomous Repub.; m.; one d.; ed Kabardin-Balkar State Univ., Moscow Inst. for Eng and Econs; Eng and managerial posts in construction industry 1963–67, 1978–81; teacher, docent Kabardin-Balkar State Univ. 1967–78; Financial Dir Trust Kabbalpromstroi 1981–90; Deputy Chair. Council of Ministers, Kabardin-Balkar Repub. 1990–91; Chair. Supreme Soviet Kabardin-Balkar Repub. 1991–93; Chair. Accounts Chamber of Russian Fed. 1994; mem. State Duma Russian Fed. 1993–95; apptd Rep. of Kabardino-Balkan Repub. in Council of Fed. 2001; mem. Russian Acad. of Natural Sciences, Int. Acad. of Informatization. *Leisure interest:* hunting.

KARMOUL, Akram Jamil, PhD; Jordanian business executive and consultant; *Chairman and Managing Director, Rawda Company for Info, Tech and E-Commerce;* b. 13 Aug. 1939, W Bank; m. Huda Abu-Errub 1964; two s. two d.; ed Assiut Univ., Univ. of Strathclyde and Imperial Coll., London, UK; geologist, geophysicist and mining engineer 1961–72; Dir Industry, later Dir Science and Tech. Ministry of Planning 1972–80; Dir-Gen. of Industry Ministry of Industry and Trade 1980–87; Dir, Man. Industrial, Commercial and Agric. Co. 1987; Exec. Dir and Asst Man. Dalla-Al-Baraka Saudi Group, Jeddah 1988–89; Dir of Industry Dept UN-ECWA Comm. for W Asia 1989–93; Gen. Man. United Textile Group 1995; Assoc. Consultant, Arab Consulting Centre and Assignments UNDP 1996; currently Chair. and Man. Dir Rawda Co. for Info, Tech. and E-Ccommerce; mem. Arab Knowledge Man. Soc.; Science Award for Outstanding Persons. *Publications:* numerous works on mineral wealth and industrial tech. of Jordan, public enterprises. *Leisure interests:* reading, swimming. *Address:* Rawda Company for Info, Tech and E-Commerce, PO Box 960555, Amman, Jordan (office). *Telephone:* (6) 5660155 (office). *Fax:* (6) 5660366 (office). *E-mail:* info@e-ritt.com (office).

KARNAD, Girish, MA; Indian playwright, film director and actor; b. 19 May 1938, Matheran; s. of Raghunath Karnad and Krishnabai Karnad; m. Saraswarthy Ganapathy 1980; one s. one d.; ed Karnatak Coll., Dharwad, Magdalene Coll., Oxford, UK; Rhodes Scholar, Oxford 1960–63; Pres. Oxford Union Soc. 1963; Asst Man. Oxford Univ. Press, Madras 1963–69, Man. 1969–70; Homi Bhabha Fellow 1970–72; Dir Film & TV Inst. of India, Pune 1974–75; Pres. Karnataka Nataka Acad. 1976–78; Visiting Prof. and Fulbright Scholar-in-Residence, Univ. of Chicago 1987–88; Indian Co-Chair., Media Cttee, Indo-US Subcomm. 1984–93; Chair. Sangeet Natak Akademi (Nat. Acad. of Performing Arts) 1988–93; Dir The Nehru Centre, London 2000; World Theatre Amb., Int. Theatre Inst. of UNESCO 2008; Fellow, Sangeet Natak Acad. 1994; Hon. DLitt (Univ. of Karnataka) 1994, (Univ. of Vidyasagar, Midnapur) 2010, (Univ. of Ravenshaw, Bhubaneshwar) 2011; Dr hc (Univ. of Southern Calif.) 2011; several awards for film work; Govt of Mysore Rajyotsava Award 1970, Sangeet Natak Acad. (Nat. Acad. of Performing Arts) Award 1972, Padma Shri 1974, Karnataka Nataka Acad. Award 1984, Nandikar, Calcutta Award 1989, Padma Bhushan 1992, Booksellers and Publishers Asscn of South India Award 1992, Bharatiya Jnanpith Award 1999, Sahitya Acad. Award 1994, Gubbi Veeranna Award 1996–97. *Plays include:* Yayati (Mysore State Award 1962) 1961, Tughlaq 1964, Hayavadana (Kamaladevi Award Bharatiya Natya Sangh 1972) 1971, Anjumallige 1976, Nagamandala 1988, Taledanda (Writer of the Year Award 1990, B.H. Sridhar Award 1992, Karnataka Sahitya Acad. Award 1992, Sahitya Acad. Award 1994) 1990, Agni Mattu Male 1995, Tipu Sultan Kanda Kanasu 2000, Bali 2002, Broken Images 2005, Flowers 2008, Wedding Album 2009. *Films include:* Samskara (President's Gold Medal 1970) 1970, Vamsha Vriksha (Nat. Award 1972, Mysore State Award 1972) 1971, Kaadu (President's Silver Medal 1974) 1973, Tabbaliyu Neenade Magane 1977, Swami (Best Bengal Film Journalists' Asscn Award 1978) 1977, Ondanondu Kaaladalli (Nat. Award 1978) 1978, Utsav 1984, Cheluvi 1992, Kanooru Heggadithi 1999, Iqbal (as actor) 2005, Dor (as actor) 2006, 8 x 10 Tasveer (as actor) 2009, Life Goes On (as actor) 2009. *Radio:* Ma Nishada 1986, The Dreams of Tipu Sultan 1997. *Television:* Antaraal 1996, Swarajnama 1997, Kanooru Ki Thakurani 1999, wrote and presented The Bhagavad Gita for BBC Two 2002. *Address:* 697, 15th Cross, JP Nagar Phase II, Bangalore 560 078, India (home). *Telephone:* (80) 26590463 (home). *Fax:* (80) 26590019 (home). *E-mail:* karnad .girish@gmail.com (home).

KARNIK, Kiran, BSc, MBA; Indian business executive; *President, Indian Habitat Centre;* b. March 1947; ed Bombay Univ., Indian Inst. of Man.; various positions at Indian Space Research Org. including Dir Devt and Educational Communication Unit 1983–91; Dir Consortium for Educational Communication 1991–95; worked briefly at UN, New York and Vienna; Man. Dir Discovery Networks India 1995–2001; Pres. Nat. Asscn of Software and Service Cos (NASSCOM) 2001–07, now Trustee; currently Pres. Indian Habitat Centre; Chair. Indraprastha Inst. of Information Tech., Delhi, Vigyan Prasar; fmr Chair. Satyam Computer Services; mem. Bd of Dirs, Reserve Bank of India 2011–, ExlService Holdings Inc. 2008–13; mem. numerous govt cttees including Prasar Bharati Review Cttee; Hon. Chair., Nat. Foundation of India; Frank Malina Medal for Space Education, Int. Astronautical Fed. 1998, Dataquest IT Person of the Year 2005, Padma Shri 2007. *Address:* India Habitat Centre, Lodhi Road, New Delhi 110 003 (office); R/O Q-2A, Hauz Khas Enclave, New Delhi 110 016, India (home). *Telephone:* (11) 24682001 (office). *Fax:* (11) 24682010 (office). *E-mail:* info@ indiahabitat.org (office). *Website:* www.indiahabitat.org (office).

KAROBLIS, Raimundas; Lithuanian diplomatist and politician; *Minister of National Defence;* b. 1968, Pasvalys region, Lithuanian SSR, USSR; m.; ed Vilnius Univ. Faculty of Law; internship at Dalhousie Univ., Halifax, Canada; joined Ministry of Foreign Affairs 1994, with Perm. Mission to UN, Geneva, later Minister Advisor and Perm. Rep. to WTO 1999–2003, Chair. Cttee on Customs Valuation of WTO 2002–03, Head of Foreign Affairs, Ministry of Econ. Affairs 2003–07, later Foreign Trade Policy Dept, with Perm. Representation to EU, Brussels 2007–10, Amb. at Large and Deputy Perm. Rep. 2010, Amb. and Perm. Rep. to EU 2010–15; Deputy Minister of Foreign Affairs 2015–16, Minister of Nat. Defence 2016–; Kt's Cross, Order for Merits to Lithuania 2003, Commdr's Cross 2014. *Address:* Ministry of National Defence, Totorių 25/3, Vilnius 01121, Lithuania (office). *Telephone:* (5) 273-5501 (office). *Fax:* (5) 264-8517 (office). *E-mail:* kam@kam.lt (office). *Website:* www.kam.lt (office).

KARP, Richard Manning, AB, SM, PhD; American computer scientist and academic; *Senior Research Scientist, International Computer Science Institute;* b. 3 Jan. 1935, Boston, Mass; s. of Abraham Karp and Rose Karp; ed Harvard Univ.; Researcher, IBM Thomas J. Watson Research Center 1959–68; Prof. of Computer Science, Math. and Operations Research, Univ. of California, Berkeley 1968–94, 1999–; Research Scientist, Int. Computer Science Inst. 1988–95, Sr Research Scientist 1999–; Prof., Univ. of Washington 1995–99; mem. NAS, Nat. Acad. of Eng, American Philosophical Soc., French Acad. of Sciences; Fellow, American Acad. of Arts and Sciences, AAAS, Asscn for Computing Machinery, Inst. for Operations Research and Man. Science; Fellow, Soc. for Industrial and Applied Mathematics 2009; eight hon. degrees; numerous awards including Turing Award 1985, Nat. Medal of Science 1996, Israel Inst. of Tech. Harvey Prize 1998, Benjamin Franklin Medal in Computer and Cognitive Science 2004, Kyoto Prize, Inamori Foundation (co-recipient) 2008, SIGCOMM Test of Time Paper Award 2011. *Achievements include:* co-developer with Jack Edmonds of Edmonds-Karp algorithm 1971. *Address:* 621 Soda Hall, Electrical Engineer and Computer Sciences, College of Engineer, University of California, Berkeley, CA 94720 (office); International Computer Science Institute, 1947 Center Street, Suite 600, Berkeley, CA 94704, USA (office). *Telephone:* (510) 642-5799 (office); (510) 666-2900 (office). *Fax:* (510) 666-2956 (office). *E-mail:* karp@cs.berkeley.edu (office); karp@icsi.berkeley.edu (office). *Website:* www.eecs.berkeley.edu/Faculty/Homepages/karp.html (office).

KARPLUS, Martin, PhD; American/Austrian chemist and academic; *Theodore William Richards Professor Emeritus of Chemistry, Harvard University;* b. 15 March 1930, Vienna, Austria; s. of Hans Karplus and Isabella Karplus; m. Marci Hazard 1981; one s. two d.; ed Harvard Univ. and California Inst. of Tech.; NSF Postdoctoral Fellow, Math. Inst., Oxford, UK; Asst Prof., Dept of Chem., Univ. of Illinois 1955–59, Assoc. Prof. 1960; Prof. of Chem., Columbia Univ. 1960–66; Prof. of Chem., Harvard Univ. 1966–, Theodore William Richards Prof. of Chem. 1979–99, Theodore William Richards Research Prof. 1999–2007, Prof. Emer. 2007–; Visiting Prof., Univ. of Paris 1972–73, 1980–81 (Prof. 1974–75), Collège de France 1980–81, 1987–88; Professeur Associé, Univ. Louis Pasteur 1992, 1994–95; Prof. Conventionné, Univ. de Strasbourg 1995–; Eastman Prof., Univ. of Oxford 1999–2000; mem. European Acad. of Arts, Sciences and Humanities, NAS, American Acad. of Arts and Sciences, Int. Acad. of Quantum Molecular Science; Foreign mem. Netherlands Acad. of Arts and Science, Royal Soc. (UK); Dr hc (Sherbrooke) 1998, Ehrendoktorat (Zürich) 2006; Joseph O. Hirschfelder Prize in Theoretical Chem., Univ. of Wisconsin 1995, ACS Harrison Howe Award, Rochester Section 1967, Award for Outstanding Contrib. to Quantum Biology, Int. Soc. of Quantum Biology 1979, Distinguished Alumni Award, California Inst. of Tech. 1986, Irving Langmuir Award, American Physical Soc. 1987, Nat. Lecturer, Biophysical Soc. 1991, ACS Theoretical Chem. Award (first recipient) 1993, Anfinsen Award, Protein Soc. 2001, Pauling Award, Northwest Section ACS 2004, David Weaver Lecturer in Biophysics ad Computational Biology (first recipient) 2007, Lifetime Achievement Award in Theoretical Biophysics, Int. Asscn of Schools and Insts of Admin 2008, G.N. Ramachandran Award Lecturer, Indian Biophysical Soc. 2009, Russell Varian Prize 2010, Antonio Feltrinelli Int. Prize for Chem., Accad. Nazionale dei Lincei 2011, Nobel Prize in Chem. (shared with Michael Levitt and Arieh Warshel) 2013. *Publications include:* Atoms and Molecules (with R. N. Porter) 1970, A Theoretical Perspective of Dynamics, Structure and Thermodynamics (with C. L. Brooks III and B. M. Pettitt) 1988, A Guide to Biomolecular Simulations (with O. M. Becker) 2006, Images from the 50's 2011; more than 800 articles in the field of theoretical chem. and biophysics. *Address:* Department of Chemistry and Chemical Biology, Harvard University, 12 Oxford Street, Cambridge, MA 02138, USA (office); Laboratoire de Chimie Biophysique, ISIS, Université de Strasbourg, 67000 Strasbourg, France (office). *Telephone:* (617) 495-4076 (office). *Fax:* (617) 496-3204 (office). *Website:* www.chem .harvard.edu/research/faculty/martin_karplus.php (office).

KARPOV, Anatolii Yevgenievich, DEcon; Russian chess player; b. 23 May 1951, Zlatoust; s. of Yevgeniy Stepanovich Karpov and Nina Karpov; m. 1st Irina Karpov; one s.; m. 2nd Natalia Bulanova; one d.; ed Leningrad Univ.; mem. CPSU 1980–91; USSR Candidate Master 1962, Master 1966; European Jr Champion 1967, 1968, World Jr Champion 1969; Int. Master 1969, Int. Grandmaster 1970; USSR Champion 1976, 1983, 1988; world champion 1975–85; became world champion when the holder Bobby Fischer refused to defend the title and he retained his title against Viktor Korchnoi in 1978 and in 1981; defended against Garry Kasparov (q.v.) in Moscow Sept. 1984; the match later adjourned due to the illness of both players; lost to the same player in 1985; unsuccessfully challenged Kasparov 1986, 1987, 1990; won World Championship title under FIDE after split in chess org. 1993, 1996, 1998; has won more tournaments than any other player (over 160); first player to become a millionaire from playing chess; People's Deputy of USSR 1989–91; Pres. Soviet Peace Fund (now Int. Asscn of Peace Funds) 1982; Pres. Chernobyl-Aid org. 1989; UNICEF Amb. for Russia and E Europe 1998; Chair. Council of Dirs Fed. Industrial Bank, Moscow; mem. Soviet (now Russian) UNESCO Affairs Comm.; mem. Bd Int. Chess Fed.; Ed.-in-Chief Chess Review 64 (magazine) 1980–91; Hon. mem. Soviet Philately Soc. 1979, Hon. Citizen of Tula, Zlatoust, Orsk and other cities in Russia, Belarus and Ukraine; Order of the Red Banner of Labour 1978, Order of Lenin 1981, Order of Holy Prince Daniel of Moscow, 2nd class 1996, Order of Merit for the Fatherland, 3rd class 2001, Order of St Sergius of Radonezh 2001, Order of Merit, 2nd class 2006, Order of Friendship 2011; winner Oscar Chess Prize 1973–77, 1979–81, 1984, 1994, Fontany di Roma

Prize for Humanitarian Achievements 1996. *Publications:* Chess is My Life 1980, Karpov Teaches Chess 1987, Karpov on Karpov 1991, How to Play Chess and 47 other books. *Leisure interest:* philately.

KARROUBI, Mehdi; Iranian cleric and politician; *Secretary-General, Hezb-e Etemad-e Melli (National Confidence Party);* b. 1937, Aligoudarz, Lorestan; m. Fatemeh Karroubi; mem. Majles (Parl.) and Speaker 1989–92, 2000–04; unsuccessful cand. for Pres. 2005; Founder and Sec.-Gen. Hezb-e Etemad-e Melli (Nat. Confidence Party—NCP) 2005–; mem. Asscn of Militant Clerics –2005 (fmr Sec.-Gen.), Expediency Discernment Council of the System –2005 (resgnd); f. Etemad-e Melli (daily newspaper) 2006. *Address:* Hezb-e Etemad-e Melli (National Confidence Party—NCP), Tehran, Iran (office). *Telephone:* (21) 88373306 (office). *E-mail:* Ravabet_Omomi@Etemademelli.ir (office). *Website:* www.etemademelli.ir (office).

KARSENTI, René, MS, MBA, PhD; French international finance official; *President, International Capital Market Association;* b. 27 Jan. 1950, Tlemcen, Algeria; s. of Leon Karsenti and Mireille Benhaim; m. Hélène Dayan 1978; two d.; ed École Supérieure de Chimie Industrielle de Lyon (ESCIL), Paris Business School and Univ. of the Sorbonne, Paris; researcher in finance and econs, Univ. of California, Berkeley, USA 1973; investment analyst/portfolio man., Caisse des Dépôts, Paris 1975–79; Finance Officer, IBRD (World Bank), Washington, DC 1979–83, Financial Adviser 1983–85, Div. Chief 1985–87, Sr Man. Finance Dept, Treasury 1987–89, Treas., Int. Finance Corp (IFC), World Bank Group, Washington, DC 1989–91; Treas. EBRD, London 1991–95; Dir-Gen. Finance, EIB 1995–2006; Pres. Int. Capital Market Asscn (ICMA), Paris and London 2006–; Chair. Euro Debt Market Asscn 2004–12, Int. Council of Securities Asscns 2009–11; mem. Man. Selection Cttee, French Pensions Reserve Fund (FRR) 2002–10, Investment Cttee, Fonds de Compensation, Luxembourg 2004–09, Advisory Cttee, FAO, Rome, Strategic Cttee, Agence France Trésor (Ministry of Finance); Chair. Bd of Dirs, Int. Finance Facility for Immunization (IFFIm) 2012–17; Chevalier, Légion d'honneur. *Publications:* Research in Pharmaceutical Industry 1977; various financial lectures and articles on int. finance, capital markets and European Monetary Union. *Leisure interests:* swimming, antiques, opera. *Address:* International Capital Market Association, Talacker 29, 8001 Zurich, Switzerland (office); Corporate Communications Department, ICMA Ltd 23 College Hill, London, EC4R 2RP, England (office). *Telephone:* (44) 3634222 (Zurich) (office); (20) 7213-0310 (London) (office). *Fax:* (44) 3637772 (Zurich) (office); (20) 7213-0311 (London) (office). *E-mail:* rene.karsenti@icmagroup.org (office). *Website:* www.icmagroup.org (office).

KARSLIOĞLU, Hüseyin Avni; Turkish diplomatist; b. 15 Nov. 1956, Yozgat; m.; two c.; ed Ankara Univ.; joined Ministry of Foreign Affairs (MFA) 1982, with Information and Research Dept 1982–84, Embassy in Tehran 1984–86, Vice-Consul, Consulate Gen. in Sydney 1986–90, First Sec., Personnel Dept, MFA 1990–91, First Sec. and Head of Cabinet 1991–92, First Sec., Perm. Mission to UN, New York 1992–96, Deputy Head of America, Pacific and Far East Dept, MFA 1996–97, Deputy Head, Dept of Cen. Europe Dept 1997–98, Counsellor, Embassy in Oslo 1998–2001, Consul-Gen. in Batumi, Georgia 2001–04, Deputy Dir and Minister, Directorate for Cen. Asia and Caucasus, MFA 2004–07, Amb. to Azerbaijan 2007–08, Amb. and Chief of the Cabinet, Presidential Office 2008–12, Amb. to Germany 2012–16. *Leisure interest:* calligraphy.

KARTAREDJASA, Butet; Indonesian actor and artist; b. 21 Nov. 1961, Yogyakarta; s. of Bagong Kussudiardja; m.; three c.; ed Sekolah Menengah Seni Rupa (Sr High School of Fine Art), Yogyakarta, Institut Seni Indonesia (Yogyakarta Inst. of the Arts); began acting with Theatre of Kita-kita 1978; f. theatre group Teater Gandrik 1985; has appeared in several soap operas including Oom Pasikom, Badut Pasti Berlalu; awards include Tokoh Seni from PWI Yogya, art awards from Pemda Daerah Istimewa Yogyakarta. *Films:* Petualangan Sherina (Sherina's Adventure) 1999, Banyu Biru (Blue Water) 2004, Koper 2006, Maskot (Mascot) 2006, Anak-Anak Borobudur 2007, Drupadi 2008, Capres (Calo Presiden) 2009, Celebrity Jogja 2010, Golden Goal 2011, Soegija 2012, Nada Untuk Asa 2015. *Theatre includes:* Benggol Maling 1998, Raja Rimba Jadi Pawang 1999, Iblis Nganggur 1999, Guru Ngambeg 2000, Mayat Terhormat 2003, Matinya Toekang Kritik 2006, Sarimin 2007, Presiden Guyonan 2008, Kucing 2010. *Publications:* Presiden Guyonan (Joke President) 2008. *Leisure interest:* collecting art. *Address:* c/o Teater Gandrik, Concert Hall Taman Budaya, Yogyakarta Ndalem Tejokusuman, Jl. KH Wahid Hasyim, Yogyakarta, Indonesia (office).

KARTASHKIN, Vladimir Alekseevich, DJur; Russian lawyer, government official and editor; b. 4 March 1934; m. Elena Kovanova 1991; one s. one d.; ed Moscow State Univ.; Chief Scientific Researcher, Inst. of State and Law 1957–63, Chief Researcher, Prof. 1985–; with Div. of Human Rights UN 1969–73; consultant, UN Dir-Gen. on Juridical Problems 1979–85; Chair. Comm. on Human Rights, Russian Presidency 1996–2002; Prof., Int. Inst. of Human Rights, Strasbourg, Cornell Univ., Santa-Clair Univ., Univ. of Peoples' Friendship, Moscow; Ed.-in-Chief International Lawyer Magazine 2003–; mem. UN Human Rights Council Advisory Cttee 2008; Meritorious Lawyer of Russia. *Publications:* over 200 books and articles including Human Rights in International and State Law. *Leisure interests:* tennis, swimming. *Address:* Institute of State and Law, Russian Academy of Sciences, Znemaenka str. 10, 119841, Moscow, Russia (office). *Telephone:* (495) 291-34-90 (office); (495) 242-37-63 (home). *E-mail:* kartashkin@comtv.ru (office).

KARTHIKEYAN, Kumar Ram Narain; Indian motor racing driver; b. 14 Jan. 1977, Coimbatore; s. of G. R. Karthikeyan; m. Pavarna Karthikeyan; ed Elf-Winfield School, France; won British Formula Ford Winter Series 1994, Formula Asia Championship 1996, Formula 3 Madras Grand Prix 1999, British Formula Three Championship 1998, 2000, Korea Super Prix 2000, Superfund Word Series 2003, World Series by Nissan 2004; raced in Telefonica World Series 2002, Australian Grand Prix 2005, US Grand Prix 2005, Japanese Grand Prix 2005, Chinese Grand Prix 2005, A1GP World Championship 2009, 24 Hours of Le Mans and Le Mans Series, Kolles Audi R10 TDI 2009, Nat. Asscn for Stock Car Auto Racing Inc. (NASCAR) World Truck Series 2010, Superleague Formula Series Dutch Squad PSV Eindhoven 2010; Williams F1 test driver 2006, 2007; est. NK Racing Acad.; Padma Shri Award 2010. *Telephone:* 9244225266 (mobile). *Fax:* (42) 22574868 (office). *E-mail:* yohann@narainracing.com (office). *Website:* www.narainracing.com (office).

KARTI, Ali Ahmed; Sudanese politician; fmr head of Popular Defence Force (paramilitary force); fmr Deputy Minister of Foreign Affairs, Minister of Foreign Affairs 2010–15; mem. Nat. Congress Party. *Address:* c/o Ministry of Foreign Affairs, POB 873, Khartoum, Sudan.

KARTOMI, Margaret Joy, AM, BA, BMus, DrPhil, FAHA; Australian ethnomusicologist and academic; b. 24 Nov. 1940, Adelaide; d. of George Hutchesson and Edna Hutchesson; m. Hidris Kartomi 1961 (deceased); one d.; ed Univ. of Adelaide, Humboldt Univ.; Lecturer, Music Dept, Monash Univ. 1969–70, Sr Lecturer 1971–73, Reader 1974–88, Prof. of Music 1989–2019, Head of Music School (now Sir Zelman Cowen School of Music) 1989–2001; Dir Inst. of Contemporary Asian Studies, Monash Univ. 1989–91; Dir Monash-ANZ Centre for International Briefing 1988–90, Cttee mem. Monash Asia Inst. 1988–90, Founding Dir Music Archive of Monash Univ. 1975–; Dir-at-large International Musicology Soc. 1993–; mem. Nat. Cttee Musicological Soc. of Australia (Nat. Pres. 1978–92), American Musicological Soc., International Council for Traditional Music, Council Soc. for Ethnomusicology; Visiting Prof., Univ. of California, Berkeley 1986–87; Dir Symposium of International Musicological Soc., Melbourne 1988, 2004; Program Chair. and Chair. E. Wachsmann Prize Cttee 2005–06; mem. Editorial Bd Journal of Musicological Research, Ethnomusicology Forum, Wacana Seni, Musicology Australia; conferred with title Ratu Berlian Sangun Anggun (Very Beautiful Queen Jewel) by Gov. and Elders' Council of Sumatran Prov. of Lampung 2011; Alexander Clarke Prize for Pianoforte Performance 1960, Dr Ruby Davy Prize for Musical Composition 1961, Fed. German Record Critics' Prize 1983, 1998, 2007, Australian Centenary Medal 2001, presented with a Festschrift in the Journal of Musicological Research Vol. 24, Nos 3–4 in honour of her 65th birthday 2005, Sir Bernard Heinze Award for services to music in Australia, especially ethnomusicology 2016, Int. Koizumi Fumio Prize for Ethnomusicology 2016, Cultural Award, Indonesian Ministry of Educ. and Culture for research, teaching and archiving Indonesian music 2016, Don & Joan Squire Award for Voluntary Services to Musicology, Musicological Soc. of Australia 2016. *Publications include:* five books, including On Concepts and Classifications of Musical Instruments 1990, The Gamelan Digul and the Prison Camp Musician Who Built It: An Australian Link with the Indonesian Revolution 2003; author/ed. of four other books; numerous articles and 300 articles in the New Grove Dictionary of Musical Instruments 1989. *Leisure interests:* tennis, badminton, concerts, theatre. *Address:* Sir Zelman Cowen School of Music, Monash University, Wellington Road, Clayton, Vic. 3168, Australia (office). *Telephone:* (3) 9905-3238 (office). *Fax:* (3) 9905-3241 (office). *E-mail:* margaret.kartomi@monash.edu (office). *Website:* profiles.arts.monash.edu.au/margaret-kartomi (office).

KARUME, Amani Abeid; Tanzanian accountant and politician; b. 1 Nov. 1948, Zanzibar; s. of Abeid Amani Karume; m. Shadya Amani Karume; six c.; ed Lumumba Coll. Zanzibar; accountant, Zanzibar Treasury 1969–70, Chief Accountant 1970–71, Prin. Sec., Ministry of Finance 1971–74, Prin. Sec., Ministry of Planning 1974–78, Prin. Sec., Ministry of Communications and Transport 1978–80, Zanzibar; Pvt. Business Consultant Rep., GEC of UK, Zanzibar 1980–90; mem. House of Reps 1990–2000, served as Minister of Trade and Industries and Minister of Communications and Transport; Pres. and Chair. Supreme Revolutionary Council of Zanzibar 2000–10, also Minister of Finance and Econ. Planning; mem. Chama Cha Mapunduzi (Revolutionary Party of Tanzania); mem. Bd of Dirs East African Harbours Corpn –1973.

KARUNANAYAKE, Ravindra (Ravi) Sandresh; Sri Lankan accountant, business executive and politician; *Minister of Power, Energy and Business Development;* b. 19 Feb. 1963; s. of Tirinevdram Karunanayake and Carmaleka Karunanayake; m. Mela Karunanayake; three d.; ed Royal Coll., Colombo; began career with Delair Ltd (cargo agent), later moved to Hayleys Group and MIT Air Cargo Ltd; fmr Chair. US Global Lanka (Pvt.) Ltd; CEO and Dir Vacume Processing Lanka Ltd, Global Transportation & Logistics (Pvt.) Ltd; Dir Eagle Air International (Pvt.) Ltd, Global Air & Tours (Pvt.).Ltd; mem. Parl. for Colombo Dist 1989–, mem. several cttees including Cttee on Public Enterprises, Consultative Cttee on Defence, Cttee on Finance, Policy Planning and Nat. Integration; Minister of Commerce and Consumer Affairs 2001–04, of Finance 2015–17, of Foreign Affairs May–Aug. 2017, of Power, Energy and Business Devt 2018–; mem. Democratic United Nat. Front 1989–98, United Nat. Party 2000–. *Address:* Ministry of Power, Energy and Business Development, 72, Ananda Coomarswamy Mawatha, Colombo 7, Sri Lanka (office). *Telephone:* (11) 2574922 (office). *Fax:* (11) 2574741 (office). *E-mail:* infor@powermin.gov.lk (office); info@ravikarunanayake.com. *Website:* powermin.gov.lk (office); www.ravikarunanayake.com.

KARVE, Priyadarshini, MSc, PhD; Indian scientist and business executive; *Founder-Director, Samuchit Enviro Tech Pvt. Ltd;* b. 3 Dec. 1971; d. of Anand Karve; ed Univ. of Pune; Prin. Investigator, Dept of Science and Tech., Govt of India 1997–99; Lecturer, Sinhgad Coll. of Eng 1999–2001, Smt. Kashibai Navale Coll. of Eng 2001–; Sec., Organising Cttee Int. Conf. on Biomass-based Fuels and Cooking Systems, Pune 2000; Consultant, Sunind Systems Pvt. Ltd; Resource Person, Second Planning and Tech. Advisory Meeting, Asia Regional Cookstove Program, Nepal 2002; Founder-Dir Samuchit Enviro Tech Pvt. Ltd; co-ordinated project 'Commercialisation of Improved Biomass Fuels and Cooking Devices in India–Pilot Project' funded by Household Energy and Health Programme of Shell Foundation in state of Maharashtra with help of 10 local NGOs 2003–05, scaled-up project 2006–; Co-Ed. Shaikshanik Sandarbh Bimonthly; Project Co-ordinator, Appropriate Rural Tech. Inst.; mem. Third World Org. of Women in Science 1998–, Indian Asscn of Physics Teachers 2001–, Engineers for Tech. and Humanitarian Opportunities of Service 2004–, Indian Soc. for Tech. Educ.; Fellow, World Tech. Network 2005–; Hon. mem. editorial team Shaikshanik Sandarbh 1999–; Hon. consultant Appropriate Rural Tech. Inst. Pune 1999–2002; Prof. Yashwantrao Kelkar Youth Award 2002, World Tech. Award in Environment, The World Tech. Network 2005, Avani Mitra Award 2011, Kirtan Sanjeevani Pushpalata Ranade National Woman Award 2011, Sahyadri Hirkani Award 2011, Pune's Pride Award 2013, Vasundhara Sanman 2014. *Achievements include:* developed technique for converting agro-waste into char briquettes using environment-friendly process and scaled it up for economically feasible rural tech.; also involved in various R&D activities to develop cleaner wood-burning stoves and other energy appliances for rural households. *Publication:* Oorjechya Shodhat (autobiography). *Address:* Appropriate Rural Technology Institute, c/o Samuchit Enviro Tech Pvt. Ltd, Flat No. 6, Ekta Park Co-op Housing Society, Behind Nirmitee Showroom, Law College Road, Pune 411004 (office); 6, Koyna Apartments, S.No.133, Kothrud, Pune 411 038, India (home). *Telephone:* (20) 25460138 (office); 9822558743. *Fax:* (20) 25460138 (office). *E-mail:* pkarve@arti-india.org (office); priyadarshini.karve@gmail.com. *Website:* www.arti-india.org (office).

KARVINEN, Jouko, MSc (Eng); Finnish business executive; *Vice-Chairman, Finnair Oyj;* b. 31 Aug. 1957, Helsinki; m.; two c.; ed Tampere Univ. of Tech.; various positions in Traction Div., Stromberg OY 1982–87, Man. Advanced Devt Allen-Bradley Stromberg Inc., Wis., USA 1987–88; Profit Centre Man. LV AC Drives 1988–90; Vice-Pres. Power Electronics Div., ABB Drives OY 1990–93, Vice-Pres. Business Unit Drives Products & Systems, Zürich 1993–98, Sr Vice-Pres. Business Area Automation Power Products 1998–2000, Exec. Vice-Pres. ABB Group Ltd 2000–02, also Head of Automation Tech. Products Div. and mem. Group Exec. Cttee 2000–02; CEO Medical Systems Div., Royal Philips Electronics, Boston, USA 2002–06, also Sr Vice-Pres. and mem. Group Man. Cttee 2002–06, CEO Philips Medical Systems Div., Amsterdam 2006, also Exec. Vice-Pres. and mem. Bd of Man. 2006; mem. Bd Dirs and CEO Stora Enso Oyj 2007–14; Vice-Chair. Supervisory Bd, Nokia Corpn 2013–16; Vice-Chair. Supervisory Bd Finnair Oyj 2016–; mem. Supervisory Bd Asea Brown Boveri AG 2016–; mem. Foundation and Supervisory Bds IMD Business School. *Address:* Finnair Oyj, Tietotie 9, 1530 Vantaa, Finland (office). *Website:* www.finnair.com (office).

KARZAI, Hamid, MA; Afghan politician and fmr head of state; b. 24 Dec. 1954, Karz, Qandahar; s. of Abdul-Ahad Karzai (Chief of Popolzai tribe, assassinated in Quetta 1999); m. Zeenat Karzai 1999; one s.; ed Habibia High School, Himachal Pradesh Univ., India; Dir of Information, Nat. Liberation Front 1985–86, Deputy Dir, Political Office 1986–89; Dir Foreign Relations Dept, Office of Interim Pres. 1989–91; fmr official rep. of deposed Afghan king, Zahir Shah; Deputy Foreign Minister 1992–96; went into exile 1996–2001; Chief of Popolzai tribe, S Afghanistan 1999–; served as consultant to Union Oil Co. of Calif. (UNOCAL), USA; mem. Del. to Future of Afghanistan Govt Talks, Bonn, Germany Nov. 2001; Chair. Afghan Interim Authority Dec. 2001–June 2002; Pres. of Transitional Authority (elected by Loya Jirga) June 2002–Nov. 2004, Pres. of Afghanistan Nov. 2004–14; Hon. KCMG 2003; Hon. DLitt (Himachal Univ.) 2003, Hon. DLit (Nebraska Univ.) 2005, Hon. DJur (Georgetown Univ.) 2006; Int. Rescue Cttee Freedom Award 2002, American Bar Asscn Asia Rule of Law Award 2003, Int. Republican Inst. Freedom Award 2003, Philadelphia Liberty Medal 2004, Int. Der Steiger Award 2007.

KASAI, Yoshiyuki, MEconSc; Japanese transport industry executive; *Chairman Emeritus, Central Japan Railway Company (JR Central);* ed Faculty of Law, Univ. of Tokyo, Univ. of Wisconsin, USA; joined Japanese Nat. Railways (JNR) 1963, becoming Deputy Dir-Gen. –1987, apptd Pres. and Rep. Dir Central Japan Railway Company (JR Central) (following JNR privatization) 1987, apptd Chair. 2004, now Chair. Emer.; Visiting Prof., Research Center for Advanced Science and Tech., Univ. of Tokyo; Univ. of Wis. Distinguished Alumnus Award 1999. *Publications:* Japanese National Railways: Its Break-up and Privatization 2003. *Address:* Central Japan Railway Company, 1-1-4 Meiki, Nakamura-ku, Nagoya 450-6101, Japan (office). *Telephone:* (5) 2564-2413 (office). *Fax:* (5) 2587-1300 (office); (3) 5255-6780 (office). *Website:* www.jr-central.co.jp (office).

KASAIJA, Matia, BCom; Ugandan politician; *Minister of Finance, Planning and Economic Development;* b. 28 May 1944, Kibaale Dist; m.; ed Univ. of East Africa (now Makerere Univ.); teacher, St Edward's Secondary School, Kibaale Dist 1966–67; Sales Man., Shell and BP 1969–77; MP for Hoima Dist 1980–81, for Buyanja County 2006–; Minister of State for Labour 1980–81; mem. External Wing, Nat. Resistance Army 1981–86, Deputy Dir for Mass Mobilization, Nat. Resistance Movt (NRM) Secr. 1986–88; teacher, Aga Khan High School, Nairobi 1983–85; Exec. Dir Departed Asian Custodian Bd 1988–93; Man. Dir Kisomba Farm 1994–98; Minister of State for Internal Affairs 2006–11, Minister of State for Planning, Ministry of Finance 2011–15, Minister of Finance, Planning and Econ. Devt 2015–; Chair. Kakumiro/Uganda Cooperative Alliance 1987–2005; Co-Chair. Global Partnership for Effective Devt Co-operation; mem. (Ex-Officio) Bd of Govs., Multilateral Investment Guarantee Agency, World Bank Group 2015–, ADB 2015–, Islamic Devt Bank 2015–; mem. Governing Council, East African Devt Bank 2015–; mem. Nat. Resistance Movt (NRM). *Leisure interests:* travel, swimming, reading, sports. *Address:* Ministry of Finance, Planning and Economic Development, Appollo Kaggwa Road, Plot 2-12, POB 8147, Kampala, Uganda (office). *Telephone:* (41) 4707000 (office). *Fax:* (41) 4230163 (office). *E-mail:* webmaster@finance.go.ug (office). *Website:* www.finance.go.ug (office).

KASAILA, Francis Lazaro, BSc; Malawi engineer and politician; *Minister of Industry, Trade and Tourism;* b. 27 Oct. 1968, Chikunkhu Village, Nsanje Dist; m. Agatha Kasaila; four c.; ed Univ. of Malawi; four years as Water Engineer with Save the Children Fund, UK; one year as Nat. Project Officer, Malawi Social Action Fund (MASAF); six years as Regional Projects Man., EU Macro Projects Programme; four years as Water and Infrastructure Devt Man., World Vision International; joined mainstream politics 2008; mem. Nat. Ass. (Parl.) for Nsanje Central constituency 2009–, Chair. Budget and Finance Cttee; Deputy Minister of Transport and Public Infrastructure 2009, Deputy Minister of Local Govt and Rural Devt 2010, Minister of Transport and Public Works –2016, Minister of Foreign Affairs and Int. Co-operation 2016–17, Minister of Industry, Trade and Tourism 2018–; fmr Deputy Spokesperson, Democratic Progressive Party. *Address:* Ministry of Industry, Trade and Tourism, POB 30366, Capital City, Lilongwe 3, Malawi (office). *Telephone:* 1770244 (office). *Fax:* 1770680 (office). *Website:* www.moit.gov.mw (office).

KASAL, Jan; Czech politician; *Member of the Supervisory Board, ČD Cargo;* b. 6 Nov. 1951, Nove Město na Moravě; m. Jaroslava Ranecká; three c.; ed Czech Tech. Univ.; ind. research worker in hydraulic systems 1975–90; mem. Czechoslovak People's Party 1986–89; First Vice-Chair. Christian Democratic Union–Czechoslovak People's Party 1992–99, 2001–06, Chair. 1999–2001; mem. Poslanecká sněmovna (Chamber of Deputies) 1990–2010, Vice-Chair. Poslanecká sněmovna 1993–98, 2002–10; System Specialist, ČD Cargo (state transport co.) 2011, mem. Supervisory Bd 2014-; Pres. European Acad. for Democracy 1993. *Leisure interests:* history, literature, music. *Address:* ČD Cargo, Jankovcova 1569/2c Holešovice, 170 00, Czech Republic (office). *Website:* www.cdcargo.cz (office).

KASARAVALLI, Girish; Indian screenwriter and director; b. 3 Dec. 1950, Karasavalli, Karnataka; s. of Ganesh Rao and Laxmi Devi; m. Vaishali Kasaravalli 1978; one s. one d.; ed MGM Coll., Film and TV Inst. of India, Pune; studied pharmacy and film direction; began film career 1977; Prin. Adarsh Film Inst. 1978–86; Hon. Ed. Chitravihari 1986–87; mem. advisory panel, Deep Focus, Rujuvathu (literary and cultural quarterly); mem. film advisory Cttee to Govt of Karnataka 1979; mem. Gov. Council, Film and TV Inst. of India, Pune 1981–84; Excellence in Cinema Crystal Globe Award South Asian Cinema Foundation 2009, Special Jury Award, National Film Awards 2014. *Films include:* Avashesh (The Ruins, Golden Lotus Award) 1975, Ghatashraddha (The Ritual Excommunication, Golden Lotus Award, Int. Catholic Jury Award, Ducats Award, Mannheim) 1977, Akramana (Siege, Moitra Award) 1978, Mooru Darigalu (Three Pathways) 1981, Tabarana Kathe (Story of Tabara, Golden Lotus Award) 1986, Bannada Vesha (The Mask) 1988 (Nat. Award, Silver Lotus), Mane 1990 (Nat. Silver Lotus Award), Ek Ghar 1991, Thai Saheba (President's Golden Lotus Award) 1999, Dweepa 2002, Grihabhanga 2003, Hasina 2004, Naayi Neralu 2006, Gulabi Talkies 2008, Kanasemba Kudureyaneri 2010, Koormavatara 2012. *Address:* 1015 Drishya, 8th Cross, 16th Main B.T.M. Layout, I stage, I phase, Bangalore 560 029, India. *Telephone:* (80) 641015.

KASASBEH, Hamad al-, PhD; Jordanian economist, politician and company director; b. 1956, Karak; ed Univ. of Jordan, Columbia Univ., USA; Econ. Researcher and Adviser, Cen. Bank of Jordan 1980–96; Gen. Man., Cities and Villages Devt Bank 1996–99; Sec.-Gen., Accounting Bureau 1999–2003, Sec.-Gen., Ministry of Finance 2003–07, Minister of Finance 2007–11; currently Chair. Arab Assurers Co.; fmr Lecturer, Univ. of Jordan. *E-mail:* info@arabassurers.com (office). *Website:* www.arabassurers.jo (office).

KASATKINA, Natalya Dmitriyevna; Russian ballet dancer and choreographer; b. 7 June 1934, Moscow; d. of Dmitriy A. Kasatkin and Anna A. Kardashova; m. Vladimir Vasilyov 1956; one s.; ed Bolshoi Theatre Ballet School; with Bolshoi Theatre Ballet Company 1954–76, main roles including Frigia (Spartacus), Fate (Carmen), The Possessed (The Rite of Spring); Choreographer (with V. Vasilyov) of Vanina Vanini 1962, Geologists 1964, The Rite of Spring 1965, Tristan and Isolde 1967, Preludes and Fugues 1968, Our Yard 1970, The Creation of the World 1971, Romeo and Juliet 1972, Prozrienie 1974, Gayane 1977, Mayakovsky (opera) 1981, Adam and Eve (film ballet) 1982, The Magic Cloak 1982, The Mischiefs of Terpsichore 1984, Blue Roses for a Ballerina (film ballet) 1985, Pushkin 1986, The Faces of Love 1987, Petersburg's Twilights 1987, The Fairy's Kiss 1989, Don Quixote (film ballet) 1990, Sleeping Beauty 2004; Artistic Dir (with V. Vasilyov), Moscow Classical Ballet Theatre 1977–; wrote libretto and produced operas Peter I 1975, Così fan Tutte (with V. Vasilyov) 1978; choreographed (with V. Vasolyov) Spartacus (Khachaturian) 2002; State Prize of USSR 1976, People's Actress of RSFSR 1984. *Television:* Ballet Ballet, Bolshoi Legends. *Ballet includes:* Coppelia, Little Zaches, The Nutcracker, Firebird And Rite Of Spring. *Leisure interests:* drawing, cooking. *Address:* Moscow Classical Ballet Theatre, 125040, Moscow, Leningradskiy prospect, 25, Russia. *E-mail:* info@classicalballet.ru. *Website:* www.classicalballet.ru.

KASBAR, Michael J.; American business executive; *Chairman and CEO, World Fuel Services Corporation;* ed State Univ. of New York, Plattsburgh; began career in energy industry with KPI (marine fuel brokerage co. in New York); f. Gray Bunkering Services to buy marine fuel and lubricants for a large in-house shipping fleet while providing brokerage services 1983; co-f., with Paul Stebbins, Trans-Tec Services, Inc. (global marine fuel services co.), acquired by World Fuel 1995, Dir and CEO of marine segment, Pres. and COO World Fuel Services Corpn 2002–12, mem. Bd of Dirs 2012–, Pres. and CEO 2012–14, Chair. and CEO 2014–. *Address:* World Fuel Services Corporation, 9800 NW 41st Street, Suite 400, Miami, FL 33178, USA (office). *Telephone:* (305) 428-8000 (office). *Fax:* (305) 392-5600 (office). *E-mail:* info@wfscorp.com (office). *Website:* www.wfscorp.com (office).

KASDAN, Lawrence Edward, BA, MA; American film director, screenwriter and producer; b. 14 Jan. 1949, Miami Beach, Fla; s. of Clarence Norman Kasdan and Sylvia Sarah Kasdan (née Landau); m. Meg Goldman 1971; two s.; ed Univ. of Michigan; copywriter, W. B. Doner and Co. (advertising co.), Detroit 1972–75, Doyle, Dane Berbach, LA 1975–77; freelance screenwriter 1977–80; film dir and screenwriter, LA 1980–; mem. Writers Guild, American West, Dirs Guild, American West; Clio Awards for Advertising, Distinguished Screenwriter Award, Austin Film Festival 2001, Laurel Award for Screen Writing Achievement, Writers Guild of America 2006. *Films include:* The Empire Strikes Back (co-writer) 1980, Continental Divide (writer) 1981, Raiders of the Lost Ark (writer) 1981, Body Heat (writer and dir) 1981, Return of the Jedi (co-screenwriter) 1982, The Big Chill (writer, dir and exec. producer) (Writers Guild Award 1983) 1983, Silverado (writer, dir and producer) 1985, Cross My Heart (producer) 1987, The Accidental Tourist (screenplay, dir and producer) 1989, Immediate Family (exec. producer) 1989, I Love You to Death (dir) 1989, Grand Canyon (dir and writer, Golden Bear, Berlin Film Festival 1992) 1991, Jumpin' at the Boneyard (exec. producer) 1992, The Bodyguard (writer and producer) 1992, Wyatt Earp (dir, co-producer, writer) 1994, French Kiss (dir) 1995, Home Fries (producer) 1998, Mumford (writer and dir) 1999, Dreamcatcher (screenplay and dir) 2003, Darling Companion (dir and writer) 2012, Star Wars: The Force Awakens (writer) 2015.

KASEL, Jean-Jacques, DenD; Luxembourg diplomatist; b. 17 Jan. 1946, Luxembourg; m. Jacqueline Vandervorst; one s. two d.; ed Inst. d'Etudes Politiques, Paris; joined Foreign Ministry 1973, Embassy in Paris (also Deputy Perm. Rep. to OECD) 1976–79; Pvt. Sec. to Gaston Thorn 1979–81; Dir for Budget and Staff Regulation, Gen. Secr. EC Council 1981–84; Chargé, Special Missions, Perm. Mission of Luxembourg to EC 1984–86; Dir Political and Cultural Affairs, Foreign Ministry 1986–89; Amb. to Greece (resident in Luxembourg) 1989; Perm. Rep. to EU 1991–98, Chair. Perm. Reps Cttee of Council of Ministers of EU 1997–98; Amb. to Belgium 1998; Perm. Rep. to NATO 1998–2003; Maréchal at the Court of Grand Duke of Luxembourg and Chef de Cabinet 2002–07; numerous decorations including Grand Officier, Ordre de la Couronne de Chêne, Officier, Ordre de Mérite, Grand Croix, Ordre de la Couronne (Belgium), Grand Croix, Ordre de Léopold II (Belgium), Grand Croix, Ordre de Mérite (Italy), Grand Croix,

Ordre de Dannebrog (Denmark), Grand Croix, Ordre Infant Henrique (Portugal), Grand Croix, Ordre Nat. (Romania), Grand Officier Mérite (Austria), Grand Officier Mérite (Sweden), Grand Officier Mérite (Norway), Grand Officier Mérite (Germany), Commdr, Ordre nat. du Mérite, Commdr, Ordre de Mérite (Spain). *Leisure interests:* horseriding, tennis, skiing, cycling, gardening, the press. *Address:* c/o Palais Grand-Ducal, Luxembourg, Luxembourg (office).

KASER, Michael Charles, MA, DLitt; British economist; *Reader Emeritus in Economics, University of Oxford;* b. 2 May 1926, London; s. of Joseph Kaser and Mabel Blunden; m. Elizabeth Anne Mary Piggford 1954; four s. one d.; ed King's Coll., Cambridge; with Econs Section Ministry of Works, London 1946–47; HM Foreign Service 1947–51, Second Sec., Moscow 1949; UN Econ. Comm. for Europe, Geneva 1951–63; Lecturer in Soviet Econs, Univ. of Oxford 1963–72, Chair. Faculty Bd 1974–76; Gov. Plater Coll., Oxford 1968–95, Gov. Emer. 1995–; Visiting Prof. of Econs, Univ. of Mich., USA 1966; Visiting Lecturer, European Inst. of Business Admin, Fontainebleau 1959–82, 1988–92, Univ. of Cambridge 1967–68, 1977–78, 1978–79; Reader in Econs and Professorial Fellow, St Antony's Coll., Oxford 1972–93, Sub-Warden 1986–87, Reader Emer. 1993–; Dir Inst. of Russian, Soviet and E European Studies, Univ. of Oxford 1988–93; Assoc. Fellow, Templeton Coll., Oxford 1983–; Visiting Faculty mem. Henley Man. Coll. 1987–2002; mem. Centre for Euro-Asian Studies, Univ. of Reading 1997–; Vice-Chair. Social Science Research Council Int. Activities Cttee 1980–84; Chair. Co-ordinating Council, Area Studies Asscns 1986–88 (mem. 1980–93, 1995), Wilton Park Academic Council, FCO 1986–92 (mem. 1985–2001); Pres. British Asscn of Slavonic and E European Studies 1988–91, Vice-Pres. 1991–93; Prin. Charlemagne Inst., Edin. 1993–94, Hon. Fellow, Divinity Faculty, Univ. of Edin. 1993–96; mem. Int. Social Science Council, UNESCO 1980–91, Council of Royal Inst. of Int. Affairs 1979–85, 1986–92, Royal Econ. Soc. 1975–86, 1987–90, Council School of Slavonic and East European Studies 1981–87, Cttee Nat. Asscn for Soviet and E European Studies 1965–88, Steering Cttee Königswinter Anglo-German Confs 1969–90, Exec. Cttee Int. Econ. Asscn 1974–83, 1986–2009 (Gen. Ed.), also various editorial bds, Anglo-Soviet, British-Mongolian, Anglo-Polish, British-Bulgarian, British-Yugoslav (Chair.), Canada-UK, British-Romanian and UK-Uzbek Round Tables; Sec. British Nat. Cttee of AIESEE 1988–93; Chair. Council, the Keston Inst., Oxford 1994–2002; Trustee, Foundation of King George VI and Queen Elizabeth, St Catharine's 1987–2006 (Chair. Academic Consultative Cttee 1987–2002), Sir Heinz Koeppler Trust 1987–2001 (Chair. 1992–2001); mem. Higher Educ. Funding Council for England Advisory Bd on E European Studies 1995–2000; Hon. Prof., Inst. for German Studies, Univ. of Birmingham 1994–, School of Social Sciences, Univ. of Birmingham; Kt, Order of St Gregory the Great 1990, Order of Naim Frashëri (Albania) 1995, Kt, Order of Merit (Poland) 1999; Dr hc (Birmingham) 1996. *Publications include:* Comecon: Integration Problems of the Planned Economies 1965, Planning in East Europe (with J. Zielinski) 1970, Soviet Economics 1970, Health Care in the Soviet Union and Eastern Europe 1976, Planning and Market Relations (with R. Portes) 1971, The New Economic Systems of Eastern Europe (co-author) 1975, The Soviet Union since the Fall of Khrushchev (with A. H. Brown) 1975, Soviet Policy for the 1980s (with A. H. Brown) 1982, Economic History of Eastern Europe, Vols I–III (with E. A. Radice) 1985–86, Early Steps in Comparing East-West Economies (with E. A. G. Robinson) 1991, Reforms in Foreign Economic Relations of Eastern Europe and the Soviet Union 1991, The Macroeconomics of Transition in Eastern Europe (with D. Morris) 1992, The Central Asian Economies after Independence (with S. Mehrotra) 1992, 1996, Cambridge Encyclopedia of Russia and the Former Soviet Union (co-author) 1994, Privatization in the CIS 1996, The Economies of Kazakstan and Uzbekistan 1997, The Prudential Management of Hydrocarbon Revenues in Resource-Rich Transition Economies (co-author) 2006; articles in econ. and Slavic journals. *Address:* 31 Capel Close, Oxford, OX2 7LA, England (home). *Telephone:* (1865) 515581 (home). *Fax:* (1865) 515581 (home). *E-mail:* michael.kaser@economics.ox.ac.uk (office). *Website:* www.sant.ox.ac.uk/people/michael-kaser (office).

KASHAF, Maulvi Qiamuddin; Afghan religious leader; *Head, High Council of Ulema and Clergy of Afghanistan;* b. 1945, Alingar Dist, Laghman Prov.; s. of Maulvi Sarfiraz Khan; m.; Interim Supreme Court Justice 2005–06; apptd Acting Head, The High Council of Ulema and Clergy of Afghanistan 2010, currently Head; apptd Deputy Chair. of the Peace Jirga June 2010; mem. High Council /Comm. of Peace and Reconciliation. *Address:* The High Council of Ulema and Clergy of Afghanistan, Kabul, Afghanistan (office).

KASIBWE, Speciosa Wandira, MD, ChB; Ugandan physician, politician, government official and UN official; *Special Envoy of the Secretary-General for HIV/AIDS in Africa, United Nations;* b. 1 July 1955, Iganga Dist; ed Makerere Univ., Kampala; mem. Nat. Resistance Movt (NRM); MP for Kigulu S Iganga Dist; Deputy Minister for Industry 1989–91; fmr Minister for Gender and Community Devt; fmr Minister of Agric., Animal Industry and Fisheries; Vice-Pres. of Uganda 1994–2003 (resgnd to attend Harvard Univ. School of Public Health, USA); Chair. Microfinance Support Centre Ltd, Uganda 2008–; Special Envoy of the UN Sec.-Gen. for HIV/AIDS in Africa 2013–; Co-founder Concave International Ltd. (agricultural co-op consulting co.); fmr Chair. African Women's Cttee on Peace and Devt; mem. Bd of Dirs African Science Acad. Devt Initiative; Chair. Sr Women's Advisory Group on the Environment; mem. Uganda Women Entrepreneurs Asscn, Uganda Women Doctors Asscn, UN Comm. on the Status of Women 2006; fmr Co-Chair. Study Panel on Agricultural Productivity in Africa, InterAcademy Council; mem. Global Bd, Hunger Project. *Address:* UNAIDS Secretariat, 20 Avenue Appia, 1211, Geneva 27, Switzerland (office). *Telephone:* 227913666 (office). *Fax:* 227914187 (office). *E-mail:* communications@unaids.org (office). *Website:* www.unaids.org (office).

KASICH, John Richard, BA; American politician, television presenter and fmr state governor; b. 13 May 1952, McKees Rocks, Pa; m. 1st Mary Lee Griffith 1975 (divorced 1980); m. 2nd Karen Waldbillig 1997; twin d.; ed Ohio State Univ.; Admin. Asst to Rep. Buz Lukens, Ohio State Senate 1975–77; mem. Dist 15, Ohio State Legislature 1979–82; mem. 98th–104th Congress from 12th Ohio Dist, Washington, DC 1983–2001, mem. Nat. Security Cttee, mem. House Budget Cttee (Chair. 1995–2001); unsuccessful cand. for Republican presidential nomination 2000, 2016; Man. Dir, Investment Banking Div., Lehman Brothers, Columbus, Ohio 2001–08; fmr mem. Bd of Dirs of several corpns, including Invacare Corpn and Norvax Inc., Chicago; Chair. New Century Project, Columbus 2001–; Gov. of Ohio 2011–19; fmr host, Fox News current affairs TV show, Heartland with John Kasich, also guest hosted The O'Reilly Factor, also frequently appeared as a guest host and analyst on Hannity & Colmes (now Hannity); Guest Lecturer, Fisher Coll. of Business, Ohio State Univ.; fmr Guest Fellow, George Bush School of Govt and Public Service, Texas A&M Univ., Annenberg School for Communication, Univ. of Pennsylvania; Republican; Hon. Chair. Recharge Ohio 2008–. *Publications:* Courage is Contagious: Ordinary People Doing Extraordinary Things to Change the Face of America 1998, Stand for Something: The Battle for America's Soul 2006, Every Other Monday: Twenty Years of Life, Lunch, Faith and Friendship 2010, Two Paths: America Divided or United 2017. *Address:* c/o Office of the Governor, Riffe Center, 30th Floor, 77 South High Street, Columbus, OH 43215-6117, USA (office); Washington Office of the Governor, State of Ohio, 444 North Capitol Street, Suite 546, Washington, DC 20001, USA (office).

KAŠICKÝ, František; Slovak government official and diplomatist; b. 18 Nov. 1968, Gelnica, Czechoslovakia; m.; two c.; ed Mil. Pedagogical Acad., Bratislava, Akad. der Bundeswehr für Information und Kommunikation, Strausberg, Germany; Sr Officer for Social Man., Ministry of Defence 1991–93; Ed. Specialist, OBRANA (mil. newspaper) 1993–98, also Press Sec. for Minister of Defence; Asst Sec. of State, Ministry of Defence 1998–2000, Defence Ministry Spokesman, Office Dir and Dir of Communications Dept 2001–03, Dir Mil. Defence Intelligence 2003–04; Sec. Parl. Cttee of Nat. Council for Defence and Security, Special Control Cttee of Nat. Council for Control of Activities of Nat. Security Authority, Cttee of Nat. Council for Control of Information Tech. 2004–06; Minister of Defence 2006–08 (resgnd); Amb. and Perm. Rep. to NATO, Brussels 2008–13, Amb. to Norway 2013–17; mem. Direction-Social Democracy (Smer-Sociálna demokracia).

KASIM, Marwan al-, PhD; Jordanian politician; b. 12 May 1938, Amman; ed Eastern Michigan Univ., Columbia Univ. and Georgetown Univ., USA; joined Ministry of Foreign Affairs 1962, Consul-Gen., New York 1964–65, Deputy Dir of Protocol 1966, Political Officer, Embassy in Beirut 1967–68, Embassy in Washington, DC 1968–72; Sec. to Crown Prince Hassan 1972–75; Dir-Gen. Royal Hashemite Court 1975–76, Chief 1988; Minister of State 1976; Minister of Supply 1977–79; Minister of State for Foreign Affairs 1979–80, Minister of Foreign Affairs 1980–83; Deputy Prime Minister and Minister of Foreign Affairs 1988–90; Jordanian, Syrian, Mexican, Lebanese, Chinese and Italian decorations.

KASIRER, Nicholas, FRSC, BCL, LLB, DEA, BA; Canadian professor of law and university administrator; *Judge, Court of Appeal;* b. 2 Feb. 1960; s. of Paul Kasirer and Patricia Heeney; ed Univ. of Toronto, McGill Univ., Univ. Paris I, France; law clerk to Hon. Jean Beetz, Supreme Court of Canada, Ottawa 1987–88; Asst Prof., Faculty of Law, McGill Univ., Montréal 1989–94, Assoc Prof. 1994–2000, Prof. 2000–02, James McGill Prof. 2002–09, Dean, Faculty of Law 2003–09, Dir Québec Research Centre for Pvt. and Comparative Law 1996–2003, James McGill Chair; Judge, Court of Appeal 2009–; mem. Editorial Bd Canadian Journal of Law and Society, The Philanthropist, The Estates and Trusts Reports, Canadian Legal Education Annual Review; mem. Québec Bar; Dr hc (Université de Sherbrooke) 2012; American Soc. of Comparative Law, Hessel Yntema Award in Comparative Law; Prix de la Fondation du Barreau, Law Students' Asscn John W. Durnford Teaching Excellence Award, McGill Alumni Asscn David Johnston Medal. *Address:* Office of the Court of Appeal, Édifice Ernest-Cormier 100, Notre-Dame Street East, Montréal, PQ H2Y 4B6, Canada (office). *Telephone:* (514) 393-2022 (office). *Fax:* (514) 393-2022 (office). *E-mail:* courdappel@justice.gouv.qc.ca (office). *Website:* www.tribunaux.qc.ca/c-appel/english (office).

KASIT, Piromya, BSc, MSc; Thai diplomatist and politician; b. 15 Dec. 1944, Thonburi; m. Chintana Piromya (née Wajanabukka); one s. (died 1994) one d.; ed Chulalongkorn Univ., Georgetown Univ., Inst. of Social Studies, The Hague, Nat. Defence Coll.; Third Sec., Dept of Int. Orgs, Ministry of Foreign Affairs 1968, News Analysis Div., Dept of Information 1969–72, SEATO Div., Dept of Int. Orgs 1972–75; Third, then Second Sec., Embassy in Brussels and Perm. Mission to EU 1975–79; Second Sec., Int. Econ. Affairs Div., Dept of Econ. Affairs, Ministry of Foreign Affairs, then First Sec., Office of the Dir-Gen. 1979–81, Dir Econ. Information Div. 1983–84, Deputy Dir-Gen. 1985–88, Dir Commerce and Industry Div., ASEAN Dept 1981–83, Dir Policy and Planning Div., Office of the Perm. Sec., Dir-Gen. Dept of Int. Orgs 1988–91; Amb. to USSR (also accred to Mongolia) 1991, to Russian Fed. 1991–93, to Indonesia (also accred to Papua New Guinea) 1994–96, to Germany 1997–2001, to Japan 2001–04, to USA 2004–08; Minister of Foreign Affairs 2008–11; sr figure in Democrat Party (Prachatipat); Commdr (Fourth Class), Most Exalted Order of the White Elephant 1974, Kt Commdr (Second Class) 1987, Kt Grand Cross (First Class) 1991, Kt Grand Cordon (Special Class) 1999, Commdr (Third Class) Most Noble Order of the Crown of Thailand 1977, Kt Commdr (Second Class) 1982, Kt Grand Cross (First Class) 1988, Kt Grand Cordon (Special Class) 1994, Grand Cross of the Order of Merit (Germany) 2001, Grand Cordon of the Order of the Rising Sun (Japan) 2004; Chakrabarti Mala Medal 1993. *Address:* Democrat Party (Prachatipat), 67 Thanon Setsiri, Samsen Nai, Phaya Thai, Bangkok 10400, Thailand (office). *Telephone:* (2) 270-0036 (office). *Fax:* (2) 279-6086 (office). *E-mail:* public@democrat.or.th (office). *Website:* www.democrat.or.th (office).

KASKARELIS, Vassilis, BSc, LLB; Greek diplomatist and foundation executive; *Senior Advisor and Member, Executive Management Team, Stavros Niarchos Foundation;* b. 26 Nov. 1948, Athens; m. Anna Kaskarelis; two s.; ed Univ. of Thessaloniki, Univ. of Athens; joined Greek Foreign Service 1974, Embassy Attaché, Ministry of Foreign Affairs 1974–76, Third Sec., Embassy in Ankara 1976–79, Consul in Venice 1979–84, First Sec. in Nicosia 1984–87, Head of Mil. Mission in Berlin 1987–90, Consul-Gen. in Greece 1990–91, Deputy Dir Turkish Desk, Ministry of Foreign Affairs 1991–93, Minister Plenipotentiary, Head of Cabinet of Sec.-Gen. 1993–95, Deputy Perm. Rep. to UN, New York 1995–2000, Perm. Rep. to NATO, Brussels 2000–04, Perm. Rep. to EU, Brussels 2004–09, Amb. to USA 2009–12, Sec.-Gen., Ministry of Foreign Affairs 2012–13; Sr Advisor and mem. Exec. Man. Team, Stavros Niarchos Foundation, Athens 2013–; Chevalier, Ordre nat. du Mérite 1975, Grand Commdr, Order of the Phoenix (Greece) 1996, Grand Cross, Order of the Phoenix 2005, Grand-Cross of the Order of the Cedar of Lebanon; Diplomat of the Year, World Affairs Council 2011. *Address:* Stavros Niarchos Foundation, 86A Vasilissis Sofias Avenue, 115 28 Athens, Greece (office). *E-mail:* info@snf.org (office); brp.kaskarelis@rp-grece.be (office). *Website:* www.snf.org (office).

KASMIN, John; British art dealer; *Managing Director, Kasmin Ltd;* b. 24 Sept. 1934, London; s. of David Kosminsky and Vera d'Olszewski; m. Jane Nicholson 1959 (divorced 1975); two s.; ed Magdalen Coll. School, Oxford; worked for Gallery One, Soho, London 1956–58; Dir New London Gallery@Marlborough Fine Art, Bond St 1960–61; f. Kasmin Gallery, Man. Dir Kasmin Ltd 1961–, Knoedler Kasmin Ltd 1977–92. *Publication:* Want, 100 Postcards of Beggars 2013. *Leisure interests:* reading, walking on hills and in museums and art galleries, collecting early postcards. *Address:* Kasmin Ltd, 34 Warwick Avenue, London, W9 2PT, England. *Fax:* (20) 7289-0746.

KASOULIDES, Ioannis; Cypriot physician and politician; b. 10 Aug. 1948, Nicosia; m. Emy Droushiotou; one d.; ed Univ. of Lyon, France; physician and medical lecturer, London 1975–81; returned to practice medicine in Nicosia 1981; held various posts in Democratic Rally (DISY) party 1981–89, Chair. DISY Youth Movt 1990–93, mem. DISY Political Bureau 1993; Deputy for Nicosia, House of Reps 1991–93; Govt spokesman 1993–97; Minister of Foreign Affairs 1997–2003, 2013–18; Founder and consultant, DDK Strategy and Public Affairs Ltd 2003; MEP 2004–13, Vice-Chair. European People Party parl. Group, responsible for Foreign Affairs; unsuccessful cand. (DISY) for Pres. of Cyprus 2008; Commdr Order of the Phoenix (Greece), Order of Merit (Greece), Order of Xirka (Malta), Order of the Cedar (Lebanon), Order of the Knights of the Holy Sepulchre; Palestinian Bethlehem Award 2000, Athens Municipality Highest Distinction Award. *Publication:* Cyprus – EU: The Accession as I Witnessed It. *Address:* c/o Ministry of Foreign Affairs, Presidential Palace Avenue, 1447, Nicosia, Cyprus (office).

KASPAROV, Garry Kimovich; Russian/Armenian fmr chess player and political activist; *Leader, United Civil Front;* b. (Garry Weinstein), 13 April 1963, Baku, Azerbaijan SSR; s. of Kim Weinstein and Klara Kasparova; m. 1st Maria Arapova (divorced); one d.; m. 2nd Yulia Vovk 1996; one s.; ed Azerbaijan Pedagogical Inst. of Foreign Languages; started playing chess in 1967; Azerbaijan Champion 1976; USSR Jr Champion 1976; Int. Master 1978, Int. Grandmaster 1980; World Jr Champion 1980; won USSR Championship 1981, subsequently replacing Anatolii Karpov (q.v.) at top of world ranking list; won match against Viktor Korchnoi, challenged Karpov for World Title in Moscow Sept. 1985, the match being adjourned; won rescheduled match to become the youngest-ever world champion in 1985; successfully defended his title against Karpov 1986, 1987, 1990; series of promotional matches in London Feb. 1987; won Times World Championship against Nigel Short 1993; stripped of title by World Chess Fed. 1993; winner Oscar Chess Prize 1982–83, 1985–89, World Chess Cup 1989; highest-ever chess rating of over 2800 1992–; f. Professional Chess Asscn (PCA) 1993; won PCA World Championship against V. Anand 1995, lost title against V. Kramnik 2000; won match against Deep Blue computer 1996, lost 1997; defeated in four-game match of rapid chess against Karpov, New York 2002; retd from professional chess 2005; Deputy Leader Democratic Party of Russia 1990–91; f. The Kasparov Foundation, Moscow; actively promotes use of chess in schools as an educational subject; f. Kasparov Int. Chess Acad.; Founder and Leader United Civil Front 2005–; Order of Red Banner of Labour. *Publications:* World Chess Championship Match: Moscow, 1985 1986, The Test of Time (Russian Chess) 1986, Child of Change (with Donald Trelford) 1987, London-Leningrad Championship Games 1987, Unlimited Challenge 1990, The Sicilian Scheveningen 1991, The Queen's Indian Defence: Kasparov System 1991, Kasparov Versus Karpov, 1990 1991, Kasparov on the King's Indian 1993, Garry Kasparov's Chess Challenge 1996, Lessons in Chess 1997, Kasparov Against the World: The Story of the Greatest Online Challenge 2000, My Great Predecessors Part I 2003, My Great Predecessors Part II 2003, My First Chess Book 2004, Great Predecessors Part III 2004, Great Predecessors Part IV 2004, Great Predecessors Part V 2006, How Life Imitates Chess 2007, Garry Kasparov on Modern Chess, Part 1: Revolution in the 70s 2007, Kasparov on Modern Chess, Part 2: Kasparov vs Karpov 1975–1985 2008, Kasparov on Modern Chess, Part 3: Kasparov vs Karpov 1986–1987 2009, Kasparov on Modern Chess, Part 4: Kasparov vs Karpov 1988–2009 2010, Garry Kasparov on Garry Kasparov: Part 1 2011, Garry Kasparov on Garry Kasparov: Part 2 2013, Garry Kasparov on Garry Kasparov: Part 3 2014, The Blueprint: Reviving Innovation, Rediscovering Risk, and Rescuing the Free Market 2013, Winter Is Coming: Why Vladimir Putin and the Enemies of the Free World Must Be Stopped 2015. *Leisure interests:* history (new chronology), politics, computers, literature, walking, weight training, swimming, rowing, most sports. *Address:* United Civil Front (Obyedinennyi Grazhdanskii Front), 119002 Moscow, Gagarinskii per. 26/12, Russia (office). *Telephone:* (499) 241-16-92 (office); (499) 241-82-80 (home). *Fax:* (499) 241-16-92 (office); (499) 241-95-96 (home). *E-mail:* maiavia@dol.ru (office). *Website:* www.rufront.ru (office).

KASPER, HE Cardinal Walter Josef, DTheol; German ecclesiastic and Catholic theologian; *President Emeritus, Pontifical Council for Promoting Christian Unity;* b. 5 March 1933, Heidenheim/Brenz; s. of Josef Kasper and Theresia Bacher; ed Univs of Tübingen and Munich; ordained priest 1957; Prof. of Dogmatic Theology, Univ. of Münster 1964–70, Univ. of Tübingen 1970–89; Bishop of Rottenburg-Stuttgart 1989–99; Chair. Comm. for World Church Affairs 1991–99, Comm. for Doctrine of Faith, German Bishops Conf. 1996–99; Special Sec. Synod of Bishops 1985; mem. Heidelberger Akad. der Wissenschaften, Academia Scientiarum et Artium Europaea; mem. Congregation for the Doctrine of Faith, Pontifical Council for Culture 1998; Sec. Pontifical Council for Promoting Christian Unity 1999, Pres. 2001–10, now Pres. Emer.; cr. Cardinal (Cardinal-Deacon of Ognissanti in Via Appia Nuova) 2001; Hon. Prof. (Eberhard-Karls Univ., Tübingen) 2001; Bundesverdienstkreuz; Dr hc (Catholic Univ. of America, Washington, DC) 1990, (St Mary's Seminary and Univ., Baltimore) 1991, (Marc Bloch Univ., Strasbourg) 2000; Landesverdienstmedaille. *Publications include:* Die Tradition in der Römischen Schule 1962, Das Absolute in der Geschichte 1965, Glaube und Geschichte 1970, Einführung in den Glauben 1972 (An Introduction to Christian Faith 1980), Jesus der Christus 1974, Der Gott Jesu Christi 1982, Theologie und Kirche 1987 (Theology and Church 1989), The Christian Understanding of Freedom and the History of Freedom in the Modern Era 1988, Wahrheit und Freiheit in der Erklärung über die Religionsfreiheit des II. Vatikanischen Konzils 1988, Lexikon für Theologie und Kirche 1993–2001, Theologie und Kirche II 1999, Leadership in the Church 2003, Sakrament der Einheit: Eucharistie und Kirche 2004, Wege in die Einheit 2005, Wo das Herz des Glaubens schlägt: Die Erfharung eines Leben 2008, Katolische Kirche 2011, Barmherzigkeit 2012, Das Evangelium von der Familie 2014. *Leisure interest:* climbing. *Address:* c/o Pontificio Consiglio per l'Unita dei Cristiani, Via dell'Erba 1, 00193, Città del Vaticano, Rome, Italy.

KASPI, Victoria (Vicky) Michelle, BSc, MA, PhD, FRS; Canadian astrophysicist and academic; *Lorne Trottier Professor of Astrophysics, McGill University;* b. 30 June 1967, Austin, Tex.; m. David Langleben; ed McGill Univ., Princeton Univ.; moved with family to Canada at age seven; Higgins instructor, Princeton Univ. 1994; Visiting Assoc., California Inst. of Tech. 1994–96, Hubble post-doctoral fellow, Jet Propulsion Lab., Infrared Processing and Analysis Center 1994–96; Hubble post-doctoral fellow, Massachusetts Inst. of Tech. 1997, Asst Prof. of Physics, MIT 1997–2002; Assoc. Prof. of Physics, McGill Univ. 1999–2006, Lorne Trottier Prof. of Astrophysics 2006–; fmr Canada Research Chair in Observational Astrophysics; mem. Nat. Acad. of Sciences, Canadian Astronomical Soc., American Astronomical Soc.; American Astronomical Soc. Annie J. Cannon Award in Astronomy 1998, Canadian Asscn of Physicists Herzberg Medal 2004, Steacie Prize 2006, Royal Soc. of Canada Rutherford Memorial Medal 2007, Prix Marie-Victorin 2009, John C. Polanyi Award 2010, Gerhard Herzberg Canada Gold Medal for Science and Eng (first woman recipient) 2016. *Address:* McGill University, Rutherford Physics Bldg, 3600 University Street, Montreal, PQ H3A 2T8, Canada (office). *Telephone:* (514) 398-6485 (office). *Fax:* (514) 398-8434 (office). *E-mail:* vkaspi@physics.mcgill.ca (office). *Website:* space.mit.edu/~vicky (office).

KASPSZYK, Jacek; Polish conductor; *Music and Artistic Director, Warsaw Philharmonic Orchestra;* b. 10 Aug. 1952, Biała Podlaska; ed Fryderyk Chopin Univ. of Music, Warsaw; debut Warsaw Nat. Opera 1975; Prin. Guest Conductor Deutsche Oper am Rhein, Düsseldorf 1976–77; debut Berlin Philharmonic and New York 1978; Prin. Conductor Polish Nat. Radio Symphony Orchestra, Katowice 1978–80, Music Dir 1980–82, 2009–12; Prin. Conductor and Artistic Adviser, North Netherlands Orchestra 1991–95; Prin. Guest Conductor, Polish Philharmonic 1996–; Artistic and Musical Dir Polish National Opera, Warsaw 1998–2005, Artistic and Gen. Dir 2002–05; Artistic Dir Witold Lutosławski Philharmonic Symphony Orchestra, Wrocław 2006–13; Musical Dir Polish Radio Nat. Symphonic Orchestra, Katowice 2009–12; Music and Artistic Dir Warsaw Philharmonic Orchestra 2013–; Music Dir and Chief Conductor, Beethoven Acad. Orchestra, Krakow 2015–; has conducted French Nat., Stockholm Philharmonic, Bavarian Radio Symphony, Rotterdam, Czech Philharmonic Orchestras; conducted Detroit Opera and San Diego Symphony Orchestra 1982; Prin. Guest Conductor, English Sinfonia 1992–; has toured with Yomiuri Nippon Symphony and performed with Tokyo and Hong Kong Philarmonics, New Zealand, San Diego, Cincinnati, Winnipeg, Calgary Symphonies, and Detroit Opera; III Prize, Karajan Competition 1977, Elgar Soc. Medal 2011, Lutoslawski Medal 2013. *Music includes:* operas conducted include: Queen of Spades (Düsseldorf) 1977, Haunted Manor (Detroit) 1982, A Midsummer Night's Dream (Lyon) 1983, Eugene Onegin (Bordeaux) 1985, The Magic Flute (Opéra Comique, Paris and Stockholm) 1986, Seven Deadly Sins (Lyon) 1987, Die Fledermaus (Scottish Opera), Flying Dutchman (Opera North, UK) 1988, Barber of Seville (English Nat. Opera) 1992, Der Rosenkavalier (Warsaw) 1997, Don Giovanni (Warsaw) 1999, The Nutcracker (Zürich) 2000; numerous productions and recordings with Teatr Wielki, Warsaw, including performances in Luxembourg, Lvov, Beijing, Paphos, Japan (tour) and Bolshoi Theatre in Moscow; recordings with London Symphony Orchestra, London Philharmonic Orchestra, Royal Philharmonic, Philharmonic Orchestras, Warsaw Symphony Orchestra; several other recordings. *Address:* International Classical Artists, Dunstan House, 14a St Cross Street, London, EC1N 8XA, England (office); Warsaw Philharmonic, Jasna 5 Street, 00-950 Warsaw, Poland (office). *E-mail:* info@icartists.co.uk (office); sekretariat@filharmonia.pl (office). *Website:* filharmonia.pl/strona-glowna_en (office).

KASRASHVILI, Makvala; Georgian singer (soprano); b. 13 March 1948, Kutaisi; d. of Nina Nanikashvili and Filimon Kasrashvili; m. (divorced); ed Tbilisi Conservatory; joined Bolshoi Co., Moscow 1968, apptd Artistic Dir Bolshoi Theatre Opera Dept 2000, now Asst to Music Dir–Chief Conductor; has performed internationally, including Covent Garden, London, Metropolitan Opera, New York, Verona, Vienna State Opera; Order For Services to the Fatherland 2001; First Prize, Transcaucasian Contest for Musicians and Singers, Tbilisi 1964, Grand Prix, Montreal Vocal Competition 1973, Merited Artist of Russian Fed. 1975, People's Artist of Georgian SSR 1980, Zakhar Paliashvili Georgian SSR State Prize 1983, People's Artist of the USSR 1986, State Prize of Russia 1998. *Roles include:* Lisa, Tatyana, Maria, Tosca, Lauretta, Donna Anna, Leonora, Aida, Turandot, Amelia. *Leisure interest:* car driving. *Address:* Bolshoi Theatre, Moscow 125009, Teatralnaya Pl. 1, Russia. *Telephone:* (495) 200-58-00 (home). *Website:* www.bolshoi.ru (office).

KASRIEL, Bernard L. M., MBA; French business executive; b. 1946; three c.; ed Ecole Polytechnique, Institut Européen d'Admin des Affaires (INSEAD), Fontainebleau, Harvard Univ., USA; several man. positions with industrial cos 1970–77; joined Lafarge SA 1977, with Sanitaryware Div. 1977–81, Group Exec. Vice-Pres. 1982–87, Sr Exec. Vice-Pres. 1987–89, seconded as Pres. and COO Nat. Gypsum, Dallas, Tex. 1987–89, Group Man.-Dir 1989–95, Vice-Chair. and COO 1995–2003, CEO 2003–06, Vice-Chair. 2006; Man. Partner, LBO France (pvt. equity fund) 2006–11; mem. Bd of Dirs Arkema Group; Chevalier, Légion d'honneur 1996. *Leisure interests:* tennis.

KASSEM, Abdul-Rauf al-, DArch; Syrian architect and politician; b. 1932, Damascus; ed Damascus Univ. School of Arts, Istanbul Univ., Turkey and Geneva Univ., Switzerland; teacher of architecture, School of Fine Arts Damascus, Dean 1964–70, Head, Architecture Dept, School of Civil Engineering, Damascus Univ. 1970–77, Rector 1977–79; concurrently engineer 1964–77; Gov. of Damascus 1979–80; elected mem. Baath party Regional Command Dec. 1979, Cen. Command of Progressive Nat. Front April 1980; Prime Minister 1980–87; mem. Higher Council for Town Planning 1968; mem. Nat. Union of Architects' Perm. Comm. on Town Planning 1975; Hon. Prof., Geneva Univ. 1975.

KASSOMA, António Paulo; Angolan politician and banker; *President, Banco Espírito Santo Angola (BESA);* b. 6 June 1951, Luanda; s. of Paulo Kassoma and Laurinda Katuta; mil. techniques instructor 1975; Tech. Dir Base Central de Reparações 1976–78; Vice Minister of Defence for Armament and Technique 1978–79, of Transports and Communication 1988–89; Minister of Territory Admin

1991–92; Sr Officer, Angolan Armed Forces 2001; mem. People's Movt for Liberation of Angola (MPLA) 2003–; Gov. Huambo Prov. 2004–08; Prime Minister of Angola 2008–10 (post abolished by new constitution); Speaker, Assembléia Nacional (parl.) 2010–12; Pres. Banco Espírito Santo Angola (BESA) 2013–. *Website:* www.besa.ao.

KASTANIDIS, Haris; Greek lawyer and politician; *Chairman, Parliamentary Group, Social Agreement;* b. 11 March 1956, Thessaloniki; m. Elisavet Symeonidou; two d.; ed Law School of the Aristotle Univ. of Thessaloniki, postgraduate studies in Criminal Law; mem. Panhellenic Socialist Movt (PASOK) 1974–2012, mem. Cen. Cttee 1984–2012; mem. Parl. 1981–, Parl. Spokesman for PASOK 2004–07, Chair. Social Agreement parl. group 2012–; Deputy Minister for the Interior and Public Order 1985–86, of Nat. Educ. and Religious Affairs Sept.–Nov. 1988, for the Interior 18–29 Nov. 1988, Minister for the Interior, Public Admin and Decentralization 1995–96, for Transport and Communications 1996–97, for Macedonia and Thrace 2003–04, for Justice, Transparency and Human Rights 2009–11, of the Interior, Decentralization and e-Governance June–Nov. 2011; expelled from PASOK parl. group for voting against Greece's loan deal with its foreign creditors 2012; Co-founder, with Louka Katseli (q.v.), Social Agreement party 2012–. *Address:* Parliament (Vouli), Parliament Bldg, Leoforos Vassilissis Sofias 2, 100 21 Athens, Greece (office). *Telephone:* (210) 3707000 (office). *Fax:* (210) 3707814 (office). *E-mail:* infopar@parliament.gr (office). *Website:* www.hellenicparliament.gr (office); kastanidisharis.gr.

KASTEN, Robert (Bob) Walter, Jr., BA, MBA; American fmr politician; *President, Kasten & Company;* b. 19 June 1942, Milwaukee, Wis.; s. of Robert W. Kasten and Mary Kasten (née Ogden); m. Eva J. Nimmons 1986; one d.; ed Univ. of Arizona and Columbia Univ., New York; with Genesco, Nashville, Tenn. 1966–68; Dir and Vice-Pres. Gilbert Shoe Co., Thiensville, Wis. 1968–75; mem. Wis. State Senate 1972–75; mem. US House of Reps from Wis. 9th Dist 1975–79; Senator from Wis. 1980–93; Co-Chair. Republican Nat. Convention 1988; Founder and Pres. Kasten & Co. (consulting firm), Washington, DC 1993–; Sr Assoc., Center for Strategic and Int. Studies, Washington, DC 1993–; Man. Partner, Talos Partners LLC (ind. merchant bank); Founder and Chair. Legislative Studies Inst.; fmr Chair. Emerging Markets Group; mem. Bd of Dirs EarthWalk Communications; Trustee Woodrow Wilson National Fellowship Foundation, American Univ. in Cairo. *Address:* Kasten & Co., 1629 K Street, NW, Washington, DC 20006, USA. *Telephone:* (202) 223-9151 (office). *E-mail:* kastenco@aol.com (office).

KASTNER, Marc A., BS, MS, PhD; American (b. Canadian) physicist and academic; *Donner Professor of Science, Massachusetts Institute of Technology;* b. 20 Nov. 1945, Toronto; m.; two d.; ed Univ. of Chicago; Research Fellow, Harvard Univ. 1972–73; Asst Prof. of Physics, MIT 1973–77, Assoc. Prof. 1977–83, Head, Dept of Physics, Div. of Atomic Condensed Matter and Plasma Physics 1983–87, Prof. of Physics 1983–89, Asst Dir MIT Consortium for Superconducting Electronics 1989–92, Donner Prof. of Science 1989–, Head, Dept of Physics 1998–2007, Dean of School of Science 2007–13; Dir NSF Materials Research Science and Eng Center, Center for Materials Science and Eng 1993–98; Dir Brookhaven Science Associates 2000–; Pres. Science Philanthropy Alliance; mem. Nat. Research Council Solid State Sciences Cttee 1995–2001; Fellow, Hertz Foundation, American Physical Soc., AAAS; American Physical Soc. Oliver E. Buckley Prize 2000. *Publications include:* The Single-Electron Transistor 1992, Magnetic, Transport, and Optical Properties of Monolayer Copper Oxides 1998, The Single Electron Transistor and Artificial Atoms 2000, Kondo Physics with Single Electron Transistors 2001. *Address:* Massachusetts Institute of Technology, 77 Massachusetts Avenue, Bldg 6-123, Cambridge, MA 02139, USA (office). *Telephone:* (617) 253-8900 (office). *Fax:* (617) 253-8554 (office). *E-mail:* mkastner@mit.edu (office). *Website:* web.mit.edu/kastner-group (office).

KASURI, Khurshid Mehmoud, BA, DPhil; Pakistani politician and academic; *Professor, Beaconhouse National University;* b. 18 June 1941, Lahore; s. of Mahmud Ali Kasuri; ed Punjab Univ., Univs of Cambridge and Oxford, UK; fmr Sec.-Gen. Tehrik-e-Istiqlal; first Sec.-Gen. People's Democratic Alliance 1990–93; Fed. Minister for Parl. Affairs, Interim Govt 1991–93; mem. Pakistan Muslim League 1997–2011; mem. Nat. Ass. 1997–2008; Minister of Foreign Affairs 2002–07, also of Law, Justice and Human Rights 2002–04; fmr mem. Nat. Security Council; Prof. of Political Science, Beaconhouse National Univ., Lahore 2008–, also mem. Bd of Govs and Bd of Dirs. *Publication:* Neither a Hawk nor a Dove 2015. *Address:* Beaconhouse National University, Tarogil Campus, 13 Km Raiwind Road, Lahore 54400, Pakistan (office). *Website:* www.bnu.edu.pk (office).

KASYANOV, Mikhail Mikhailovich; Russian politician; *Leader, Respublikanskaya Partiya Rossii—Partiya Narodnoi Svobody (RPR—PARNAS—Republican Party of Russia—Party of People's Freedom);* b. 8 Dec. 1957, Solntsevo; ed Moscow Inst. of Automobile Transport; held sr positions at RSFSR State Planning Comm., then Ministry of Econs 1981–90; Chief of Section for Foreign Econ. Relations, Russian State Cttee for Econs 1990–91; Head, Dept for Foreign Econ. Relations, Ministry of Finance 1991–93, Head, Dept of Overseas Credits 1993–95, Deputy Minister of Finance 1995–99, First Deputy Minister, then Minister 1999–2000; main negotiator with Western financial orgs on questions of Russian liabilities; Deputy Man. for Russian Fed., EBRD 1999; First Deputy Prime Minister Jan. 2000, Acting Chair. of Govt, then Chair. of Govt (Prime Minister) 2000–04; mem. Presidium of Russian Govt 1999–2004, Security Council 1999–2004; f. MK-Analytics (consultancy) 2005; Leader, Rossiyskii Narodno-Demokraticheskii Soyuz (RNDS—Russian People's Democratic Union) 2006–; barred by Cen. Election Comm. of Russia from being cand. in presidential election on grounds of alleged forged signatures in support of him 2008; Leader, Respublikanskaya Partiya Rossii—Partiya Narodnoi Svobody (RPR—PARNAS—Republican Party of Russia—Party of People's Freedom) 2012–. *Address:* Rossiyskii Narodno-Demokraticheskii Soyuz (Russian People's Democratic Union), 115035 Moscow, ul. Pyatitskaya 14, str. 1, Russian Federation (office). *Telephone:* (495) 953-58-24 (office). *Fax:* (495) 953-46-80 (office). *E-mail:* newtypeparty@mail.ru (office); mikhail.doronin@svobodanaroda.org (office). *Website:* parnasparty.ru; kasyanov.ru.

KASYMALIYEV, Adylbek; Kyrgyzstani economist and politician; b. 1 Dec. 1960, Tup Dist, Yssyk-Kul Oblast, Kyrgyz SSR, USSR; ed Leningrad Inst. of Finance and Econs; Jr Researcher, State Planning Cttee Inst. of Econs 1984–88; Head of Financial Services, Road Construction Co. 1988–90; Deputy Head, Oktyabrsky Dist State Tax Inspectorate, Frunze/Bishkek 1990–94; Head of Dept and Deputy Head, State Tax Inspectorate, Ministry of Finance 1994–96, Deputy Head, later Head of Dept, Ministry of Finance 1996–2002, Deputy Chair., State Social Fund 2002, First Deputy Chair., Ministry of Finance Revenue Cttee 2002–05, Deputy Chair., State Cttee on Taxes and Fees 2007–09, Deputy Chair., State Tax Service 2009–10, Acting Chair. 2010, Chair. 2010–11; Deputy Minister of Econ. Regulation 2011–12, Deputy Minister of Economy and Antimonopoly Policy 2012, Deputy Minister of Economy 2012–15, Minister of Finance 2015–18 (resgnd). *Address:* c/o Ministry of Finance, 720040 Bishkek, bul. Erkindik 58, Kyrgyzstan (office).

KATAINEN, Jyrki, MScS; Finnish politician and EU official; *Vice-President and Commissioner for Jobs, Growth, Investment and Competitiveness, European Commission;* b. 14 Oct. 1971, Siilinjärvi; m. Mervi Katainen; two c.; mem. Siilinjärvi Municipal Council 1993–; Vice-Chair. Regional Council of Pohjois-Savo 1994–95; mem. Parl. (Finnish Nat. Coalition Party—Kokoomus) 1999–, Vice-Chair. Kokoomus Youth League 1994–95, Vice-Chair. Kokoomus 2001–04, Chair. 2004–14; Chair. Cttee for the Future 2003–; mem. Finnish Del. to W European Union Parl. Ass. 2004–; Deputy mem. Finnish Del. to OSCE Parl. Ass. 2003–; mem. Admin. Bd Finnish Broadcasting Corpn 2003–; Deputy Prime Minister and Minister of Finance 2007–11; Prime Minister of Finland 2011–14; Vice-Pres. and Commr for Jobs, Growth, Investment and Competitiveness, EC 2014–; named among World Econ. Forum's Global Leaders for Tomorrow 2003. *Address:* European Commission, Rue de la Loi/Wetstraat 170, 1049 Brussels, Belgium (office). *Telephone:* (2) 299-11-11 (switchboard) (office). *Website:* ec.europa.eu/about/juncker-commission/structure/index_en.htm (office).

KATAKAMI, Keiichi; Japanese diplomatist; *Ambassador to Italy;* b. 6 March 1954; joined diplomatic service 1980, Amb. to Ghana 2008–11, Dir-Gen., Econ. Affairs Bureau, Ministry of Foreign Affairs 2011–14, Amb. to EU and European Atomic Energy Community, Brussels 2014–17, Amb. to Italy 2017–. *Address:* Embassy of Japan, Via Quintino Sella 60, 00187 Roma, Italy (office). *Telephone:* (06) 487991 (office). *Fax:* (06) 4873316 (office). *E-mail:* giappone@ro.mofa.go.jp (office). *Website:* www.it.emb-japan.go.jp (office).

KATANANDOV, Sergey Leonidovich; Russian politician; b. 21 April 1955, Petrozavodsk; m.; two s.; ed Petrozavodsk State Univ., Northwest Acad. of State and Municipal Service; worked as Head of Sector, Sr Engineer, Petrozavodskstroi 1977–91; mem. Petrozavodsk City Exec. Cttee, Chair. City Soviet 1991–98, Mayor of Petrozavodsk 1994–98; elected Chair. Karelian Govt 1998–2002; Pres., Repub. of Karelia 2002–10 (resgnd); Merited Worker of Nat. Economy of Repub. of Karelia 1995, Order of Honour of Russian Fed. 2000, Medal of Merits 2004. *Publications include:* articles in Russian and Finnish journals and newspapers. *Leisure interests:* fishing, hunting, swimming, reading.

KATAYAMA, Mikio; Japanese business executive; *Vice-Chairman and Chief Technical Officer, Nidec Corporation;* b. 1958; ed Univ. of Tokyo; joined Sharp Corpn 1981, Group Gen. Man. Liquid Crystal Display (LCD) Div. 2002, apptd Dir 2003, Exec. Dir 2005, Corp. Sr Exec. Dir for LCD Business –2006, Pres. Sharp Corpn 2006–07, Pres. and COO 2007–12, apptd Chair. 2012; apptd Exec. Consultant, Nidec Corpn 2014, Vice-Chair. and Chief Tech. Officer 2015–, also mem. Bd of Dirs. *Address:* Nidec Corporation, 338 Kuzetonoshiro-cho, Minami-ku, Kyoto 601-8205, Japan (office). *Website:* www.nidec.com (office).

KATAYAMA, Yoshihiro; Japanese lawyer and government official; b. 29 Aug. 1951, Okayama Pref.; m. (deceased); four s. two d.; ed Univ. of Tokyo; worked several years with Ministry of Home Affairs; Gov. Tottori Pref. 1999–2007; apptd Prof. of Local Admin, Keio Univ. 2007; mem. Govt Revitalization Unit 2009; Minister of Internal Affairs and Communications and Minister of State for Promotion of Local Sovereignty and for Regional Revitalization 2010–11 (only non-Diet member of Cabinet); Dir Nippon Yusen Kabushiki Kaisha 2016–.

KATEHI, Linda P. B., BS, MS, PhD; American engineer, academic and university administrator; *Chancellor, University of California, Davis;* b. 1954, Greece; ed Nat. Tech. Univ. of Athens, Greece, Univ. of California, Los Angeles; Lecturer, Nat. Tech. Univ., Greece 1977–78; Research Engineer, Dept of Defence, Naval Research Lab., GETEN, Greece 1978–79; Grad. Student Research Asst, UCLA 1979–84; Asst Prof. of Electrical Eng, Univ. of Michigan 1984–89, Assoc. Prof. of Electrical Eng and Computer Science 1989–94, Prof. 1994–2002, Assoc. Dir of Grad. Program, Coll. of Eng 1994–95, Assoc. Dean for Grad. Educ. 1998–99, Assoc. Dean for Academic Affairs 1999–2002; John A. Edwardson Dean of Eng, Prof. of Electrical and Computer Eng, Purdue Univ., West Lafayette, Ind. 2002–06; Prof. of Electrical and Computer Eng, Univ. of Illinois 2006–09, also Provost and Vice-Chancellor for Academic Affairs and Prof. in Gender and Women's Studies programme; Chancellor, Univ. of California, Davis 2009–16, Distinguished Prof. of Electrical and Computer Eng, and of Gender Studies; Chair. Pres.'s Cttee for Nat. Medal of Tech. 2007–10; Vice-Chair. Eng Dean's Council, American Asscn of Eng Educ. 2005–06; mem. Bd of Dirs Consortium on Institutional Collaboration 2006, AAAS 2007–, Cyprus Inst. 2008–, BACEI 2010–, Business Higher Educ. Forum, 2010–; mem. Exec. Cttee Coll. of Eng, Iowa State Univ. 1995–98, mem. Eng Advisory Cttee 2003–06; mem. NASA Council of Deans 2004–; mem. Advisory Cttee, Harvard Radcliff Coll. 2006–10, American Acad. of Arts and Sciences Cttee on Fed. Support of Research 2007–, NAS Cttee for Sensors and Communication Systems for Special Operation Forces 2008–10, Nat. Security Higher Educ. Cttee 2010–, NASA Aerospace Tech. Advisory Cttee; mem. Nat. Acad. of Eng 2006–, Int. Union of Radio Science, Int. Soc. of Hybrid Microelectronics, Advanced Computational Electromagnetics Soc., American Soc. of Eng Educ., IEEE Antennas and Propagation Soc., IEEE Microwave Theory and Techniques Soc.; Fellow, AAAS 2007–; IEEE Fellow 1995; Amelia Earhart Fellowship Award, Zonta International 1982–83, 1983–84, Presidential Young Investigator Award, NSF 1987, URSI Booker Award 1987, Research Excellence Award, Univ. of Michigan 1993, Faculty Recognition Award, Univ. of Michigan 1994, Humboldt Research Award 1994, Third Millennium Medal, IEEE Microwave Theory and Techniques Soc. 2000, Distinguished Educator Award 2002, Leading Light Award for Women in High Tech 2004, UCLA Eng Alumnus of the Year Award 2006. *Achievements include:* holds more than 15 patents. *Address:* University of California, One Shields Avenue, Davis, CA 95616, USA (office). *E-mail:* katehi@ucdavis.edu (office). *Website:* www.ucdavis.edu (office).

KATEN, Karen L., BA, MBA; American pharmaceutical industry executive (retd); b. Kansas City, Mo.; ed Univ. of Chicago; work in sales at office supply co.; joined Pfizer in 1974, Vice-Pres. Marketing 1983–86, Vice-Pres. and Dir of Operations 1986–91, Vice-Pres. and Gen. Man. 1991–93, Exec. Vice-Pres. Pfizer Pharmaceuticals Group 1993, Pres. Pfizer US Pharmaceuticals 1995–2002, Sr Vice-Pres. 1999–2001, mem. Pfizer Leadership Team, Exec. Vice-Pres. Pfizer Inc. and Pres. Pfizer Global Pharmaceuticals 2001–05, Pres. Pfizer Human Health and Vice-Chair. Pfizer Inc. 2005–07 (retd), Chair. Pfizer Foundation 2006–08; Sr Advisor, Essex Woodlands Health Ventures 2007–; mem. Bd of Dirs Harris Corporation, The Home Depot 2007–, Catamaran Corp., and Air Liquide, Catalyst; Chair. RAND Corpn Health Bd of Advisors; apptd to US-Japan Pvt. Sector/Govt Comm. and Nat. Infrastructure Cttee; mem. ARMGO Pharmaceutical Board; Trustee, Economic Club of New York, Univ. of Chicago; Hallene Lecturer, Univ. of Illinois 2004, Dolan Lecturer, Fairfield Univ., Conn. 2004. *Address:* Essex Woodlands, 280 Park Avenue, 27th Floor East, New York, NY 10017, USA (office). *Website:* www.essexwoodlands.com (office).

KATHER, Lt-Gen. (retd) Roland; German army officer (retd); b. 17 May 1949; m. Christiane Kather; ed Gen. Staff Course of Spanish Army, Madrid, Spain; commissioned in German Army Armoured Reconnaissance Corps 1968; served in various regimental appointments in Panzeraufklärungsbataillon 6, Eutin, followed by Gen. Staff training at Führungsakademie der Bundeswehr, Hamburg 1979–81; served as Chief G 4 with Panzerbrigade 18, Neumünster; served in German Army Staff, Ministry of Defence, Bonn 1984–87; Plans Officer of G 3 Div., SHAPE, Mons, Belgium 1987–91; assumed command of Panzeraufklärungsbataillon 6, Eutin; Exec. Officer for Chief of Staff of Armed Forces Staff, Ministry of Defence 1991–95; Chief of Staff, HQ 7, Panzerdivision/Army Dist Command III, Düsseldorf 1995–97, deployed to Trogir, Croatia as Chief of Staff, German Contingent, Implementation Force (IFOR); Deputy Dir Armed Forces Jt Operations Centre, Ministry of Defence 1997–99; Commdr Panzerbrigade 42, Potsdam 1999–2001, deployed to Balkans as Commdr Multinational Brigade South, Prizren, Kosovo; Chief of Staff, HQ German Army Operational Command, Koblenz 2001–03; commanded 13 Panzergrenadierdivision, Leipzig 2003–06; Commdr Kosovo Force (KFOR) 2006–07; Commdr Allied Land Component Command, Heidelberg 2007–10; Mil. Rep. to NATO, Brussels 2010–11, to EU 2010–11; Cross of Merit 1st Class 2012, Order of Legion of Merit (US). *Leisure interests:* politics, contemporary history, outdoor activities, especially mountain biking. *E-mail:* roland.kather@t-online.de (home).

KATIČ, Andreja; Slovenian public servant and politician; b. 22 Dec. 1969, Slovenj Gradec; ed Univ. of Maribor; began career as Dir of Municipal Admin, city of Velenje; fmr mem. Bd Zdravstveni dom Velenje (healthcare centre), Komunalno podjetje Velenje (municipal utility co.), Elektro Maribor (electricity distribution co.); mem. Nat. Ass. (Parl.) 2014–15, Vice-Pres. 2014–15; Minister of Defence 2015–18; fmr mem. Asscn of Urban Municipalities of Slovenia, Asscn of Municipalities and Towns of Slovenia (fmr Head, Legal and Legislative Issues Comm.); mem. 'Velenje –UNICEF Child-Friendly City' project Comm.; mem. Panel for Improved Security of Municipality Residents; fmr mem. Admin. Bd Univ. of Maribor; mem. Socialni demokrati (SD—Social Democrats). *Address:* c/o Ministry of Defence, 1000 Ljubljana, Vojkova cesta 55, Slovenia (office).

KATNIĆ, Milorad, MEconSc, PhD; Montenegrin economist, academic, consultant and fmr government official; *President, Société Generale Montenegro;* b. 12 Dec. 1977, Podgorica; m. Ivana Katnić; two s.; ed Univ. of Montenegro; began career as researcher, later analyst at Inst. for Strategic Studies and Prognoses, Podgorica; Deputy Minister of Finance 2004–10, Minister of Finance 2010–12, Gov. of Montenegro to World Bank and EBRD 2010–12; Prof., Univ. of Donja Gorica; Pres. Bd of Dirs, Société Generale Montenegro; mem. Admin. Council, Devt Bank of the Council of Europe 2006–08; involved in design and implementation of numerous important projects related to public finance, econ. devt and structural reforms; mem. Mont Pelerin Soc., Soc. of Economist and Managers of Montenegro; fmr mem. Centre for Young Scientists of the Montenegrin Acad. of Arts and Science. *Publications include:* numerous working and scientific papers in the area of economic growth, financial crisis, tax systems and public spending. *Address:* Société Generale Montenegro, 81000 Podgorica, Bulevar Revolucije, Montenegro (office). *Telephone:* (20) 415701 (office). *E-mail:* info.sgme@socgen.com (office). *Website:* www.societegenerale.me (office).

KATO, Kazuyasu, BS, MS; Japanese business executive; *Consultant, Kirin Holdings Company Ltd;* b. 24 Nov. 1944; ed Keio Univ., Massachusetts Inst. of Tech. Sloan School of Man., USA; joined Kirin Brewery Co. Ltd 1968, Vice-Pres. Kirin USA, Inc. 1986–90, Pres. 1990–93, Man. of Sales Dept, Tokyo Sales Head Office March–Nov. 1993, Deputy Gen. Man. Tokyo Regional Head Office 1993–97, Gen. Man. Hokkaido Regional Head Office 1997–2000, Dir of Kirin Holdings Co. Ltd 2000–12, Gen. Man. Kyushu Regional Head Office 2000–01, Gen. Man. Domestic Alcohol Sales Dept 2001–02, Deputy Gen. Man. Domestic Alcohol Div. and Gen. Man. Domestic Alcohol Sales Dept 2002–03, Sr Exec. Officer and Gen. Man. Domestic Alcohol Div. 2003–04, Man. Dir, Sr Exec. and Gen. Man. 2004–06, Pres. and COO Kirin Brewery Co. Ltd 2006–07, Pres. and CEO March–July 2007, Pres. and CEO Kirin Holdings Co. Ltd July 2007–10, Chair. 2010–12, Consultant 2012–; Dir (non-Exec.) The Shizuoka Bank Ltd 2015–. *Address:* Kirin Holdings Co. Ltd, 10-1 Shinkawa 2-chome, Chuo-ku, Tokyo 104-8288, Japan (office). *Telephone:* (3) 5541-5321 (office). *Fax:* (3) 5540-3547 (office). *E-mail:* info@kirin.co.jp (office). *Website:* www.kirinholdings.co.jp (office).

KATO, Ryozo; Japanese diplomatist and sports administrator; b. 1941, Saitama Pref.; m. Hanayo Kato; three c.; ed Univ. of Tokyo; joined Ministry of Foreign Affairs 1965, Dir Security Affairs Div. 1981–84, Dir Treaties Div. 1984–87, with Internal Affairs and Communications Div. 1990–92, Deputy Dir N American Affairs Bureau 1992–94, Dir-Gen. Asian Affairs Bureau 1995–97, Dir-Gen. Foreign Policy Bureau 1997–99, Minister, Washington, DC 1987, Consul-Gen., San Francisco 1994, Deputy Minister for Foreign Affairs 1999–2001, Amb. to USA 2001–08; Commr of Nippon Professional Baseball 2008–13; Dir Mitsubishi Corpn 2009–17.

KATO, Shigeya; Japanese business executive; b. 2 Aug. 1947; joined Shell Sekiyu K.K. 1970 (acquired by Showa Oil Co. Ltd to form Showa Shell Sekiyu K.K. 1985), Gen. Man. Change Promotion Centre 1998–99, Exec. Officer/Gen. Man. Change Promotion Centre 1999–2001, Dir 2001–03, Man. Dir 2003–05, Sr Man. Dir 2005–06, Vice-Chair. and Rep. Dir Showa Shell Sekiyu K.K. 2006–09, Chair. and Rep. Dir 2009–15. *Address:* c/o Showa Shell Sekiyu K.K., Daiba Frontier Building, 2-3-2, Daiba, Minato-ku, Tokyo 135-8074, Japan (office).

KATO, Susumu; Japanese business executive; *Senior Vice-President and General Manager of Marketing and Sales Divsion, Chugai Pharmaceutical Co., Ltd;* b. 21 May 1947, Kyoto; ed Kobe Univ.; joined Sumitomo Corpn 1970, Asst Man. Sumitomo Corpn of America, LA 1979–85, Asst Man., Rolled Steel Import-Export Dept 1985–89, Man. Sumitomo Corpn of America, Detroit 1989–96, Deputy Gen. Man. Steel Sheets Int. Trade Dept 1996–97, Gen. Man. 1997–99, Corp. Officer and Deputy Gen. Man., Iron and Steel Div. 1999–2000, Man., Personnel and Gen. Affairs Div. 2000–03, mem. Bd of Dirs 2000–, also Gen. Man. Corp. Planning and Co-ordination 2001–03, Man. Exec. Officer 2003–05, Sr Man. Exec. Officer 2005–07, Pres. and CEO Sumitomo Corpn of America, NY 2005–07, also Gen. Man. for the Americas 2005–07, Exec. Vice-Pres. Sumitomo Corpn, Tokyo 2007, Pres. and CEO 2007–12, apptd Chair. 2012; Sr Vice-Pres. and Gen. Man., Marketing and Sales Div., Chugai Pharmaceutical Co. Ltd 2015–, mem. Bd of Dirs 2016–. *Address:* Chugai Pharmaceutical Co., Ltd, 1-1 Nihonbashi-Muromachi 2-Chome, Chuo-ku, Tokyo 103-8324, Japan (office). *Telephone:* (3) 3273-0554 (office). *Fax:* (3) 3281-6607 (office). *Website:* www.chugai-pharm.co.jp (office).

KATO, Susumu, PhD; Japanese physicist and academic; *Professor Emeritus of Atmospheric Physics, Kyoto University;* b. 27 Aug. 1928, Saitama; s. of Nimpei Kato and Minoru Kato; m. Kyoko Kojo; ed Kyoto Univ.; Lecturer, Faculty of Eng, Kyoto Univ. 1955–61, Asst Prof., Ionosphere Research Lab. 1961–62, Assoc. Prof. 1964–67, Prof. 1967–81, Dir and Prof., Radio Atmospheric Science Centre 1981–92, Prof. Emer. of Atmospheric Physics 1992–; Research Officer, Upper Atmosphere Section, CSIRO, NSW, Australia 1962–64; Visiting Scientist, High Altitude Observatory, Nat. Center for Atmospheric Research, Colo 1967–68, 1973–74; Visiting Prof., Dept of Meteorology, UCLA 1973–74, Bandung Inst. of Tech., Indonesia 1994–97; Vice-Chair. Japan-Indonesia Science and Tech. Forum 1992–96; AGU Fellow 1991; Foreign Assoc. Nat. Acad. of Eng, USA 1995–; Fellow, Int. Inst. for Advanced Studies 1998; Tanakadate Prize 1959, Yamaji Science Prize 1974, Appleton Prize 1987, Hasegawa Prize 1987, Fujiwara Prize 1989, Japan Acad. Award 1989. *Publications include:* Dynamics of the Upper Atmosphere 1980, Dinamika Atmosfer 1998; over 100 scientific papers on atmospheric tidal theory, observation of atmospheric waves by MST radar. *Leisure interests:* reading, music, jogging, swimming, Japanese calligraphy. *Address:* 22-15 Fujimidai, Otsu, Shiga Prefecture, 520-0846, Japan (home). *Telephone:* (77) 534-1177 (home). *Fax:* (77) 533-4013 (home). *E-mail:* kato@rish.kyoto-u.ac.jp (office).

KATOCH, Chandresh Kumari; Indian politician; b. 1 Feb. 1944, Jodhpur, Rajasthan; d. of Hanumant Singhji and Krishana Kumari; m. Aditya Katoch 1968; one s.; ed Jodhpur Univ., Rajasthan; mem. Himachal Pradesh Legis. Ass. 1972–77, 1982–84, 2003–07, various roles with Govt of Himachal Pradesh including Deputy Minister 1977, Minister of State for Tourism 1984, Cabinet Minister 2003–04; mem. Lok Sabha (lower house of Parl.) for Kangra constituency 1984–89, for Jodhpur constituency 2009–14; mem. Rajya Sabha (upper house of Parl.) 1996–2002, Deputy Chief Whip, Congress Party in Rajya Sabha 1998–99; Pres. All-India Mahila Congress 1999–2003; Union Cabinet Minister of Culture 2012–14. *Leisure interests:* reading, listening to music, looking after animals, horse riding, tennis. *Address:* c/o Ministry of Culture, 'C' Wing, Shastri Bhavan, Dr Rajendra Prasad Road, New Delhi 110 001, India.

KATOH, Nobuaki; Japanese business executive; *Chairman, DENSO Corporation;* ed Keio Univ., Tokyo; joined DENSO Corpn in 1971, served as Gen. Man. Air-Conditioning Planning and Gen. Planning Depts, Dir Corp. Planning Division 1999, Exec. Dir 2000, Man. Officer 2004–05, Pres. DENSO's European HQ 2005–07, Sr Man. Dir responsible for Corp. Center and Thermal Systems Business Group 2007–08, Pres. and CEO DENSO Corpn 2008–15, Chair. 2015–; Dir Toyota Boshoku Corpn 2017–, mem. Outside Audit & Supervisory Bd 2011–. *Address:* DENSO Corpn, 1-1 Showa-cho, Kariya, Aichi 448-8661, Japan (office). *Telephone:* (556) 25-5511 (office). *Fax:* (566) 25-4509 (office). *E-mail:* info@globaldenso.com (office). *Website:* www.globaldenso.com (office).

KATONA, Béla, PhD; Hungarian engineer, economist and politician; b. 9 Feb. 1944, Budapest; ed József Attila High School, Budapest, Tech. Univ. of Budapest, Karl Marx Univ. of Econs; mem. Országgyülés (Nat. Ass.) 1990–2010, Deputy Leader Parl. Group 1990–94, 2000–09, Speaker of Országgyülés 2009–10; Vice-Pres. Hungarian Socialist Party (Magyar Szocialista Párt—MSZP) 1996–98; Minister without portfolio in charge of civil secret services 1994–95; mem. Hungarian Acad. of Eng 2011–.

KATORI, Hidetoshi, BA, MA, PhD, DEng; Japanese physicist and academic; *Chief Scientist, Quantum Metrology Laboratory, Rikagaku Kenkyūjo (RIKEN);* b. 27 Sept. 1964, Tokyo; ed Univ. of Tokyo; Research Assoc., Dept of Applied Physics, Univ. of Tokyo 1991, Assoc. Prof., Eng Research Inst. 1999–2010, Prof., Dept of Applied Physics, Grad. School of Eng 2010–; Research Dir, ERATO Katori Innovative Space-Time Project, Japan Science and Tech. Agency 2010–; Chief Scientist, Quantum Metrology Lab., Rikagaku Kenkyūjo (RIKEN) 2011–; Visiting Scientist, Max-Planck Inst. of Quantum Optics, Germany 1994; Prize of French Soc. of Chronometry 2005, Prize of Japan Soc. for the Promotion of Science 2005, Julius Springer Prize for Applied Physics 2005, European Time and Frequency Award, Soc. Française de Chronométrie 2005, Rabi Award, IEEE Int. Frequency Control Symposium 2008, Philipp Franz von Siebold Award, Alexander von Humboldt Foundation, Berlin, German 2011. *Publications:* numerous scientific papers in professional journals. *Address:* Department of Applied Physics, Graduate School of Engineering, University of Tokyo, 7-3-1 Hongo, Bunkyo-ku, Tokyo 113-8656, Japan (office). *Telephone:* (3) 5841-6800 (office). *Fax:* (3) 5841-8760 (office). *E-mail:* katori@amo.t.u-tokyo.ac.jp (office). *Website:* www.amo.t.u-tokyo.ac .jp (office).

KATRENKO, Vladimir Semenovich, DEcon; Russian politician; *Auditor, Accounts Chamber of the Russian Federation;* b. 11 Nov. 1956, Mineralnye Vody, Stavropol Krai; m.; one s. two d.; ed Mineralnye Vody Railway-Tech. Inst. no.4, Rostov Inst. of Railway Engineers, All-Union Corresp. Legal Inst.; worked as carpenter; served in army 1976–78; trained as electrical mechanic, qualified as engineer mechanic; driver Soviet Auto Transport, Mineralnye Vody, manager of convoys, apptd Gen. Dir 1988, 1996, Sec. Communist Party Cttee; elected to State Duma 1993, 1999, 2003, First Deputy Chair. 2004–07, First Deputy Head of United Russian faction, Auditor, Accounts Chamber of the Russian Federation 2013–; mem. Cttee for Ethnic Affairs, head of Comm. on North Caucasus, Head of Specialized Cttee for Energy, Transport and Communications 2008; head of state admin, Mineralnye Vody 1996–99; fmr deputy head Govt of Stavropol Krai province, Sec. Political Council; mem. Gen. Council United Russia party; Order of Friendship 2003, Order of Merit to the Fatherland, 4th class, Order of Honour; Hon. Transport Worker of Russian Fed. 1994, Award for Services to the Devt of Physical Culture and Sport 1998, Esteemed Railwayman 2003. *Leisure interests:* playing guitar, poetry, arts, mini-football. *Address:* Accounts Chamber of the Russian Federation, 119991 Moscow, Zubovskaya street, 2, Russia (office). *Telephone:* (495) 986-05-09 (office). *Fax:* (495) 986-09-52 (office). *Website:* www.ach.gov.ru/en (office).

KATSELI, Loukia-Tarsitsa (Louka), BA, MPA, MA, PhD; Greek economist, academic, politician and banking executive; *Chairman, National Bank of Greece;* b. 20 April 1952, Athens; d. of Aleka Katseli (actress); m. Gerasimos Arsenis; one s. one d.; ed Smith Coll., Princeton Univ., USA; Asst Prof., then Assoc. Prof., Yale Univ., USA 1977–85, Fellow, Saybrook Coll. 1979–85; Visiting Prof., Birkbeck Coll., London, UK 1986, Athens Univ. of Econs 1986–87; Prof., Dept of Econs, Nat. Univ. of Athens 1987–, Chair. 1997–2001; mem. Panhellenic Socialist Movt (PASOK) 1976–2011 (expelled), 2011–12 (expelled from parl. group for voting against Greece's loan deal with its foreign creditors); Scientific Dir Centre of Planning and Econ. Research (KEPE) 1982–86; mem. Council of Econ. Advisers 1982–84, Nat. Advisory Council for Research and Tech. 1997–2000; mem. and Vice-Chair. UN Cttee on Devt Planning 1998–99; Special Econ. Adviser to fmr Prime Minister Andreas Papandreou 1993–96; Rapporteur and Vice-Chair. UN Cttee for Devt Policy 1996–2003; Head of Devt Centre, OECD, Paris 2003–07; mem. Vouli (Parl.) for Athens B 2007–; Minister for the Economy, Competitiveness and Shipping 2009–10, of Labour and Social Protection 2010–11; Co-founder (with Haris Kastanidis) Social Agreement party, Pres. 2012–15 (resgnd); Chair. National Bank of Greece (NBG) 2015–; mem. numerous int. and European initiatives, including EU Cttee on Econ. and Monetary Affairs, 'Committee of Wise Men' Review of the Social Charter of Europe; Sidney Cohen Prize for Econs, Smith Coll. 1971, Concilium Faculty Research Award, Summer 1979, Award for Best New Teacher, Yale Univ. 1980, scholarship from German Marshall Fund 1982–84. *Publications:* more than 40 books and articles in int. journals on int. and macroeconomic policy, especially in devt cooperation and migration policy. *Address:* Office of the Chairman, National Bank of Greece (NBG), Odos Aeolou 86, 102 32 Athens (office); 23 Sina str., 106 80 Athens, Greece. *Telephone:* (210) 3644260 (office). *Fax:* (210) 3603558 (office). *E-mail:* louka.katseli@gmail.com (office). *Website:* www.loukakatseli.gr (office); loukakatseli.gr.

KATSONGA, Davis Chester, BA, MBA; Malawi politician; b. 6 Aug. 1955, Mwanza; m.; two s.; ed Schiller Int. Univ., Inst. of Marketing, London South Bank Univ., UK; MP for Mwanza Cen. Constituency 1999–; Minister of Mines, Natural Resources and Environmental Affairs, then Speaker of Parl. 1999–2004, Minister of Natural Resources 2004–05, of Foreign Affairs 2005–06, of Defence 2006–07, for Presidential and Parl. Affairs 2007–08, of Labour and Vocational Training 2008; unsuccessful cand. for Pres. of Malawi 2014; mem. Democratic Progressive Party 2005–12; Pres. Chipani Cha Pfuko party 2012–. *Leisure interests:* playing and watching soccer, reading political autobiographies, travel, angling, carpentry, environmental affairs and computers. *Address:* Chipani Cha Pfuko, POB 30633, Chichiri, Blantyre, Malawi. *E-mail:* kaukondekansomba@gmail.com.

KATSUMATA, Nobuo; Japanese business executive; *Senior Corporate Advisor, Marubeni Corporation;* b. 1943; m. Fusae Katsumata; joined Marubeni Corpn 1966, various man. positions, mem. Bd of Dirs 1996–, fmr Chief Dir of Paper Pulp, Sr Man. Dir –2003, Pres. and CEO 2003–08, Chair. 2008–13, Sr Corp. Advisor 2013–; Chair. Japan Foreign Trade Council, Inc.; Dir, Hitachi America Ltd, Sapporo Holdings Ltd 2009–; Outside Dir, Yokogawa Electric Corpn 2009–, Hitachi Ltd 2011–; Commdr of the Lion of Finland 2003. *Leisure interest:* sailing. *Address:* Marubeni Corporation, 42 Ohtemachi 1-chome, Chiyoda-ku, Tokyo 100-8088, Japan (office). *Telephone:* (3) 3282-2111 (office). *E-mail:* info@marubeni.com (office). *Website:* www.marubeni.com (office).

KATSUMATA, Tsunehisa; Japanese energy industry executive; b. March 1940; ed Univ. of Tokyo; joined Tokyo Electric Power Co., Inc. (TEPCO) as grad. trainee, held various man. positions, including Man., Corp. Planning Dept, Exec. Vice-Pres. for Corp. Planning –2002, Pres. 2002–08, Chair. 2008–12; Vice-Chair. Bd of Councillors, Nippon-Keidanren; Dir Japan Nuclear Fuels Ltd, Japan Productivity Center for Socio-Econ. Devt, Japan Investor Relations Asscn; mem. Bd Dirs KDDI Corp.; Chair. Fed. of Electric Power Cos of Japan. *Leisure interests:* reading, Go (traditional Japanese strategy game).

KATTAN, Naïm, OC, FRSC; Canadian writer; b. 26 Aug. 1928, Baghdad, Iraq; s. of Nessim Kattan and Hela Kattan; m. Gaetane Laniel 1961; one s.; ed Univ. of Baghdad, Univ. of Paris (Sorbonne), France; newspaper corresp. in Near East and Europe, broadcaster throughout Europe; emigrated to Canada 1954; Int. Politics Ed. for Nouveau Journal 1961–62; fmr teacher at Laval Univ.; fmr Sec. Cercle Juif de langue française de Montreal; freelance journalist and broadcaster; Prof., Univ. of Québec, Montreal; Assoc. Dir Canada Council; Pres. RSC; mem. Acad. Canadienne-Française; Chevalier, Légion d'honneur, Officier des Arts et des Lettres. Chevalier, Ordre nat. du Québec; Dr hc (Middlebury Coll.), (Concordia). *Play:* Avant le ceremonie 2009. *Publications:* novels: Adieu Babylone 1975, Les Fruits arrachés 1981, La Fiancée promise 1983, La Fortune du passager 1989, La Célébration 1997, L'Anniversaire 2000; (essays) Le Réel et le théâtral 1970, Ecrivains des Amériques, Tomes I-III, Le Repos et l'Oubli 1987, Le Père 1990, Farida 1991, La Reconciliation 1992, A. M. Klein 1994, La Distraction 1994, Culture: Alibi ou liberté 1996, Idoles et images 1996, Figures bibliques 1997, L'Amour reconnu 1999, Le Silence des adieux 1999, Le gardien de mon frère 2003, La Parole et le lieu 2004, Les Villes de naissance, L'Ecrivain migrant, Farewell Babylon: Coming of Age in Jewish Baghdad 2007; numerous short stories and criticisms. *Address:* 2463 rue Sainte Famille No. 2114, Montreal, PQ, H2X 2K7, Canada. *Telephone:* (514) 499-2836. *Fax:* (514) 499-9954. *E-mail:* kattan.naim@uqam.ca. *Website:* www.uqam.ca.

KATTI, Kattesh V., MSc.Ed, PhD, FRSC; Indian/American biologist, physicist and academic; *Curators' Distinguished Professor of Biological Engineering, Physics and Radiology, University of Missouri;* b. 11 Nov. 1956, Dharwad, Karnataka; s. of Varihanumanthachary Katti and Sudha Katti; m. Kavita Katti; one s. one d.; ed Karnatak Univ., Indian Inst. of Science; Research Assoc., Univ. of Alberta, Canada 1987–90; Curators' Distinguished Prof. of Biological Eng, Physics and Radiology, School of Medicine, Univ. of Missouri 1990–, also Margaret Proctor Mulligan Distinguished Prof. of Cancer Research, Founding Co-Dir Univ. of Missouri Nanoparticle Production Core Facility, Research Scientist, Univ. of Missouri Research Reactor; Ed. Synthesis and Reactivity in Inorganic, Metal-Organic, and Nanometal Compounds, International Journal of Green Nanotechnology 2009–; Fellow, St Louis Acad. of Science 2011, AAAS 2013, Nat. Acad. of Inventors 2015; Hon. DSc (Karnatak Univ.) 2009, (Sam Higginbottom Inst. of Agric., Tech. and Sciences, Naini, Allahabad, India); Gauss Award, Göttingen Acad. of Sciences (Germany), Most Influential Scientist in Molecular Imaging in the world by rt image, Outstanding Scientist Fellows Award, St Louis Acad. of Science 2007, Outstanding Missourian Award, Missouri House of Reps 2008, his invention on Green Nanotechnology selected as one of the top 10 inventions of 2010, Presidential Award for Econ. Devt, Univ. of Missouri System 2011, RMIT Foundation Award from RMIT University, Australia 2013, Hevesy Medal, Int. Cttee on Activation Analysis of the Modern Trends in Activation Analysis Confs (ICAA-MTAA) (co-recipient) 2015, Person of the Year in Science Vijayavani newspaper 2016, Univ. of Missouri Alumni Award 2017. *Achievements include:* recognised as 'Father of Green Nanotechnology' for his role in inventing Green Nanotechnological Processes. *Publications:* numerous book chapters and reviews, more than 300 papers in professional journals and more than 150 inventions and patents. *Leisure interests:* watching cricket, classical Indian and western Music, travelling. *Address:* Institute of Green Nanotechnology, Department of Radiology, Medical School, University of Missouri, Columbia, MO 65212, USA (office). *Telephone:* (573) 882-5656 (office). *Fax:* (573) 884-5679 (office). *E-mail:* kattik@health.missouri.edu (office). *Website:* bioengineering.missouri.edu (office); web.missouri.edu/~kattik/katti/katti (office); katteshkatti.com.

KATUARI, Eddy William; Indonesian business executive; *CEO, Wings Group;* b. 1951, Surabaya; s. of Johannes Ferdinand Katuari; m.; four c.; worked with family business Wings Group (consumer goods mfr), took over following death of father 2004; Commr PT Petrocentral, Unggul Indah Investama, PT Wiranusa Grahatama; Dir Albright & Wilson (Australia) Ltd, United Austindo Chemicals Pte Ltd. *Address:* Wings Group, Kawasan Perluasan Utara, PT JIEP, Jalan Tipar Cakung Kav F 5-7, Jakarta 13910, Indonesia (office). *Telephone:* (21) 4602696 (office). *Fax:* (21) 4603494 (office). *Website:* www.wingscorp.com (office).

KATUWAL, Gen. Rukmangad, BA, MA; Nepalese army officer (retd); b. 12 Dec. 1948, Okahldhunga Dist; s. of Khadgadhoj Katawal; m. Uma Katawal; one s. one d.; ed Tribhuwan Univ., Quaid-i-Azam Univ., Indian Nat. Defence Acad., Indian Mil. Acad., Special Forces Course, USA, Army Command and Staff Coll., Camberley, UK, Sr Command Course, India, Nat. Defence Univ., Islamabad, Pakistan; commissioned into Shree Shreenath Bn (Infantry) of Nepalese Army 1969; Instructor, Nepalese Army School 1973; served in UN Emergency Force (UNEF) in Suez Canal area 1973; commanded Ind. Co.– Shree Kalidhoj Co. (currently a bn) 1976–77; held several key staff appointments before serving as Liaison Officer of Nepalese Govt to Brigade of Gurkhas of British Army and Govt of Hong Kong 1983–86; Chief Mil. Personnel Officer, UN Interim Force in Lebanon (UNIFIL) 1988–90; took over command of Shree Pashupati Prashad Bn 1990; served in Research and Devt Wing, Army HQ; apptd Commdt of Nepalese Mil. Acad. 1993; promoted to Brig.-Gen. 1996, holds distinction of having commanded three consecutive Brigades, two Infantry and one Special Forces; apptd Dir of Mil. Intelligence 1999; promoted to Maj.-Gen. 2001; took over as Adjutant Gen. of Nepalese Army 2001; apptd as first Co-coordinator of Nat. Security Council Secr. 2001; commanded the then Western Div. on combat operations at peak of counterinsurgency 2003–04; promoted to Lt-Gen. 2004; Chief of Gen. Staff 2004–06; 'Col Commdt' of Mother Unit, Shree Pashupati Prashad Bn; promoted to Gen. 2006; Deputy Chief of Army Staff –Aug. 2006, Acting Chief of Army Staff Aug.–Sept. 2006, Chief of Army Staff (first commoner officer) Sept. 2006–09 (retd); has been at odds with Maoist Govt on several issues, leading to his brief sacking by Prime Minister Prachanda 3 May 2009, ordered by Pres. of Nepal to continue his service, resulting in Prime Minister's resignation and a general collapse of the govt; has participated widely in nat. and int. confs and seminars at sr level, including Multilateral Planner's Conf. in Romania and Int. Symposium Course on Asian Pacific Security in China; Birendra Prajatantra Bhaskar (Second Class), numerous other decorations and medals; Distinguished Int. Honour Grad., US Special Forces Course, earned the Gideon in US Ranger Course. *Leisure interests:* athletics, keen sportsman, especially fond of basketball, racquet games and golf, travel, reading, hiking, riding, social work, writing songs in Nepalese folk, patriotic and popular song disciplines.

KATZ, Daryl, LLB; Canadian lawyer and business executive; *Chairman and CEO, Katz Group;* b. 31 May 1962, Edmonton, Alberta; s. of Barry Katz; m.; two c.; ed Univ. of Alberta Law School; Founder, Katz Group, group of pharmacy cos that includes Rexall, Guardian IDA, Medicine Shop and Pharm Plus drugstore chains, Chair. and CEO 1996–; Owner, Edmonton Oilers (professional ice hockey team); apptd mem. Bd of Dirs Alberta Investment Management Corpn 2007; mem. Premier's Council of Alberta's Promise, Canadian Council of Chief Executives. *Address:* Katz Group, Suite 1702 Bell Tower, 10104 103rd Avenue, Edmonton, Alberta T5J 0H8, Canada (office). *Telephone:* (780) 990-0505 (office). *Fax:* (780) 702-0647 (office). *E-mail:* esilverman@katzgroup.ca (office). *Website:* www.katzgroup.ca (office).

KATZ, Michael, AB, MS, MD, FAAP; American (b. Polish) paediatrician and academic; *Senior Adviser, Transdisciplinary Research, March of Dimes Foundation;* b. (Michal Katz), 13 Feb. 1928, Lwów, Poland; s. of Edward Katz and Rita Gluzman; m. Robin J. Roy 1986; one s.; ed Medical Univ., Łódź, Poland, Univ. of Pennsylvania, State Univ. of New York, Brooklyn, Columbia Univ. School of Public Health; Intern, UCLA Medical Center 1956–57; Resident, Presbyterian Hosp. New York 1960–62, Dir Pediatric Service 1977–92; Hon. Lecturer in Paediatrics, Makerere Univ. Coll., Kampala, Uganda 1963–64; Instructor in Pediatrics, Columbia Univ. 1964–65, Prof. in Tropical Medicine, School of Public Health

1971–92, Prof. Emer. 1992–, Prof. of Pediatrics, Coll. of Physicians and Surgeons 1972–77, Reuben S. Carpentier Prof. and Chair. Dept of Pediatrics 1977–92, Prof. Emer. 1992–; Asst Prof. of Pediatrics, Univ. of Pennsylvania 1966–71; Sr Vice-Pres. for Research and Global Programs, March of Dimes Foundation 1992–2011, Sr Adviser, Transdisciplinary Research 2011–; Pres. World Alliance of Orgs for the Prevention of Birth Defects 1995–2008; Assoc. mem. Wistar Inst., Philadelphia 1965–71; Consultant, WHO regional offices, Guatemala, Venezuela, Egypt, Yemen; mem. US Del. to 32nd World Health Ass., Geneva 1979; Consultant, UNICEF, New York and Tokyo; mem. numerous medical socs, including Nat. Acad. of Medicine; Fellow, American Acad. of Pediatrics, AAAS, IDSA; Hon. DMedSc (Medical Univ. of Łódź, Poland) 2009; Jurzykowski Foundation Award in Medicine 1983, Alexander von Humboldt Foundation Sr US Scientist Award 1987. *Publications:* contribs to numerous journals and medical works. *Leisure interest:* music. *Address:* 200 East 57th Street, New York, NY 10022 (home); March of Dimes Foundation, 1275 Mamaroneck Avenue, White Plains, NY 10605, USA (office). *Telephone:* (914) 997-4555 (office). *Fax:* (914) 997-4560 (office). *E-mail:* mkatz@marchofdimes.com (office); robinroy@optonline.net (home). *Website:* www .marchofdimes.com (office).

KATZ, Nets Hawk, BA, PhD; American mathematician and academic; *Professor of Mathematics, California Institute of Technology;* b. 19 Aug. 1972, Arlington, Tex.; s. of Amnon Katz and Ora Katz; ed Rice Univ., Univ. of Pennsylvania; Gibbs Instructor and NSF Postdoctoral, Yale Univ. 1993–96; Research Asst, Univ. of Edinburgh, UK 1996–97; Asst Prof., Univ. of Illinois-Chicago 1997–2000; Assoc. Prof., Washington Univ., St Louis 2000–04; Assoc. Prof. of Math., Indiana Univ. 2004–07, Prof. of Math. 2007–13, Man. Ed. Indiana University Mathematics Journal 2011–12; Prof. of Math., California Inst. of Tech. 2013–, IBM Prof. of Math. 2016–; Guggenheim Fellow 2012, Clay Research Award, Clay Math. Inst. (co-recipient) 2015. *Publications:* numerous papers in professional journals on combinatorics (especially additive combinatorics) and harmonic analysis. *Address:* 266 Sloan, Mathematics 253-37, Caltech, 1200 East California Blvd, Pasadena, CA 91125, USA (office). *Telephone:* (626) 395-2326 (office). *Fax:* (626) 585-1728 (office). *E-mail:* nets@caltech.edu (office). *Website:* www.pma.caltech.edu/content/nets-h -katz (office).

KATZ, Samuel (Sam) Lawrence, BA, MD; American paediatrician, vaccinologist and academic; *Wilburt C. Davison Professor and Chairman Emeritus, Department of Pediatrics, Medical Center, Duke University School of Medicine;* b. 29 May 1927, Manchester, NH; s. of Morris Katz and Ethel Lawrence Katz; m. 1st Betsy Jane Cohan 1950 (divorced 1971); four s. (one s. deceased) three d.; m. 2nd Catherine Minock Wilfert 1971; two step-d.; ed Dartmouth Coll. and Harvard Medical School; hosp. appointments, Boston, Mass 1952–56; Exchange Registrar, Paediatric Unit, St Mary's Hosp. Medical School, London, UK 1956; Research Fellow in Pediatrics, Harvard Medical School at Research Div. of Infectious Diseases, Children's Hosp. Medical Center, Boston 1956–58, Research Assoc. 1958–68; Pediatrician-in-Chief, Beth Israel Hosp., Boston 1958–61, Visiting Pediatrician 1961–68; Assoc. Physician, Children's Hosp. Medical Center, Boston 1958–63, Sr Assoc. in Medicine 1963–68, Chief, Newborn Div. 1961–67; Instructor in Pediatrics, Harvard Medical School, Boston 1958–59, Assoc. 1959–63, Tutor in Medical Sciences 1961–63, Asst Prof. of Pediatrics 1963–68; Co-Dir Combined Beth Israel Hosp.-Children's Hosp. Medical Center, Infectious Disease Career Training Program 1967–68; Prof. and Chair. Dept of Pediatrics, Duke Univ. School of Medicine, Durham, NC 1968–90, Wilburt C. Davison Prof. of Pediatrics 1972–97, Wilburt C. Davison Prof. Emer. 1997–, Chair. Emer. 1990–; prin. activities involve research on children's vaccines and on pediatric AIDS; mem. Bd of Dirs Georgetown Univ. 1987–93, Hasbro Foundation 1988–2006, Burroughs Wellcome Fund 1991–99 (Chair. 1995–99); mem. Scientific Advisory Bd, St Jude Children's Research Hosp. 1977–85; Consultant, NIH AIDS Exec. Cttee 1986–89, mem. NIH Pediatric AIDS Exec. Cttee 1994–97; mem. Editorial Bd Pediatric Infectious Diseases Report; fmr mem. Editorial Bd Annual Review in Medicine, Postgraduate Medicine, Reviews of Infectious Diseases, Current Problems in Pediatrics, Ped Sat (TV Educ.); Chair. Bd of Trustees, Int. Vaccine Inst., Seoul, S Korea 2004–08; Co-Chair. Indo-US Vaccine Action Program 1999–2004; mem. Soc. for Pediatric Research, American Soc. for Microbiology, American Asscn of Immunologists, American Public Health Asscn, American Soc. for Clinical Investigation, American Pediatric Soc., American Epidemiological Soc., American Soc. for Virology, American Fed. for Clinical Research, Inst. of Medicine; Fellow, American Acad. of Pediatrics, Infectious Diseases Soc. of America, AAAS; Hon. DSc (Georgetown Univ.) 1996, (Dartmouth Coll.) 1998; Presidential Medal of Dartmouth Coll. for Leadership and Achievement 1991, Distinguished Physician Award, Pediatric Infectious Diseases Soc. 1991, Bristol Award and Soc. Citation, Infectious Diseases Soc. of America 1993, Needleman Medal and Award, American Public Health Asscn 1997, Howland Award, American Pediatric Soc. 2000, Gold Medal, Sabin Vaccine Inst. 2003, Founders Medal, Duke Univ. 2004 and other awards. *Publications:* numerous articles in scientific journals, textbooks of paediatrics and infectious diseases. *Leisure interests:* jazz drumming (Joe Butterfield Dixieland Jazz Concert 1994–2003), cycling, reading, opera. *Address:* Duke University Medical Center, Box 2925, Durham, NC 27710, USA (office). *Telephone:* (919) 668-4852 (office); (919) 968-0008 (home). *Fax:* (919) 668-4859 (office); (919) 968-0447 (home). *E-mail:* katz0004@mc.duke.edu (office); slkatz@mindspring.com (home). *Website:* www.mc.duke.edu (office).

KATZENBERG, Jeffrey; American film industry executive; *CEO, DreamWorks Animation SKG;* b. 21 Dec. 1950; m. Marilyn Siegal; one s. one d.; Asst to Chair., CEO Paramount Pictures, New York 1975–77; Exec. Dir Marketing, Paramount TV, Calif. 1977, Vice-Pres. Programming 1977–78; Vice-Pres. feature production, Paramount Pictures 1978–80, Sr Vice-Pres. production, motion picture div. 1980–82, Pres. production, motion pictures and TV 1982–94; Chair. Walt Disney Studios, Burbank, Calif. 1984–94; Co-founder and Prin. DreamWorks SKG 1995–2005, CEO DreamWorks Animation SKG 1994–; mem. Bd of Dirs Motion Pictures and TV Fund, Aids Project Los Angeles, Michael J. Fox Foundation for Parkinson's Research, Museum of Moving Image, Cedars-Sinai Medical Center, Simon Wiesenthal Center; Trustee, Calif. Inst. of the Arts; mem. Writers Guild of America. *Address:* DreamWorks Animation SKG, 1000 Flower Street, Glendale, CA 91201, USA (office). *Telephone:* (818) 695-5000 (office). *Fax:* (818) 695-9944 (office). *Website:* www.dreamworksanimation.com (office).

KAUFMAN, Charles (Charlie) Stuart; American screenwriter, producer, director and lyricist; b. 19 Nov. 1958, New York City, NY; m. Denise Kaufman; two c.; ed Boston Univ., New York Univ.; grew up in Massapequa, NY before moving to West Hartford, Conn.; worked in newspaper circulation dept, The Star Tribune, Minneapolis, Minn. 1986–90; contrib. to National Lampoon 1991; began scriptwriting 1991; cr. short films shown on Late Night with David Letterman TV show during 1990s. *Plays:* Hope Leaves the Theater (writer and dir) 2005, Anomalisa (writer, under the pseudonym Francis Fregoli) 2005. *Film screenplays include:* Being John Malkovich (also exec. producer) 1999, Human Nature (also producer) 2001, Adaptation (also exec. producer) (Best Screenplay, Broadcast Film Critics Asscn, Chicago Film Critics Asscn, Nat. Bd of Review, Toronto Film Critics Asscn) 2002, Confessions of a Dangerous Mind 2002, Eternal Sunshine of the Spotless Mind (also exec. producer) (Nat. Bd of Review Best Original Screenplay Award 2004, BAFTA Award 2005, Writers' Guild of America Award for Best Original Screenplay 2005, Acad. Award for Best Original Screenplay 2005) 2004, Synecdoche, New York (also dir and producer) 2008, Anomalisa (also co-dir) (Grand Jury Prize, Venice Film Festival) 2015. *Television includes:* Get a Life (series) 1991–92, The Edge (series) 1992–93, The Trouble with Larry (series) 1993, The Dana Carvey Show (series) 1996, Ned and Stacey (series) (also producer) 1996–97, Moral Orel (series) 2006; producer, Misery Loves Company (series) 1995, How and Why (film) (also writer and dir) 2014. *Leisure interest:* reading. *Address:* c/o WME Entertainment, 9601 Wilshire Boulevard, Beverly Hills, CA 90210-5213, USA (office). *Telephone:* (310) 285-9000 (office). *Fax:* (310) 285-9010 (office). *Website:* www.wmeentertainment.com (office).

KAUFMAN, Henry, BA, MS, PhD; American banker and investment manager; *President, Henry Kaufman & Company Inc.;* b. 20 Oct. 1927, Wenings, Germany; s. of Gustav Kaufman and Hilda Kaufman (née Rosenthal); m. Elaine Reinheimer 1957; three s.; ed New York and Columbia Univs; emigrated to USA in 1937; Asst Chief Economist, Research Dept, Fed. Reserve Bank of New York 1957–61; with Salomon Bros., New York 1962–88, Gen. Pnr 1967–88, mem. Exec. Cttee 1972–88, Man. Dir 1981–88, also Chief Economist, in charge Bond Market Research, Industry and Stock Research and Bond Portfolio Analysis Research Depts.; f. Henry Kaufman & Co. Inc., New York 1988–; Pres. Money Marketeers, New York Univ. 1964–65; fmr Dir Lehman Bros., Statue of Liberty-Ellis Island Foundation, Inc., W.R. Berkley Corpn, Federal Home Loan Mortgage Corpn; Trustee, New York Univ., Whitney Museum of American Art, Hudson Inst.; mem. Bd of Govs, Tel-Aviv Univ.; mem. American Econ. Asscn, American Finance Asscn, Conf. of Business Economists, Econ. Club, New York (also Dir), UN Asscn (also Dir), Council on Foreign Relations; mem. Int. Advisory Cttee, Federal Reserve Bank of New York, Advisory Cttee to Investment Cttee for the IMF Staff Retirement Plan; Trustee Inst. of Int. Educ. 1982–2003, Chair. 1989–2003, Chair. Emer. 2003–; George S. Eccles Prize for excellence in economic writing, Columbia Business School 1987. *Publication:* Interest Rates, the Markets and the New Financial World 1986, On Money and Markets, A Wall Street Memoir 2000. *Address:* Henry Kaufman & Co., 590 Madison Avenue, New York, NY 10022, USA (office). *Telephone:* (212) 758-7100 (office).

KAUFMAN, Philip, BA, MA; American screenwriter and film director; b. 23 Oct. 1936, Chicago, Ill.; s. of Nathan Kaufman and Betty Kaufman; m. Rose Kaufman; one s.; ed Univ. of Chicago and Harvard Law School; fmr teacher in Italy; Founder's Directing Award, San Francisco Film Soc. 2013. *Films:* Goldstein (co-screenplay, co-dir and co-producer) (Prix de la Nouvelle Critique, Cannes 1964), Fearless Frank 1965, The Great Northfield Minnesota Raid 1971, The White Dawn (dir) 1973, Invasion of the Body Snatchers (dir) (Saturn Award for Best Direction 1978) 1977, The Wanderers (co-screenplay and dir) 1979, The Right Stuff (dir and screenplay) (Kansas City Film Critics Circle Award for Best Dir 1983) 1983, The Unbearable Lightness of Being (dir and co-screenplay) (Orson Welles Award for Best Filmmaker-Writer/Dir 1988, Nat. Soc. of Film Critics Award for Best Dir 1988) 1988, Henry & June (dir and co-scriptwriter) 1990, Rising Sun (dir and co-screenplay) 1993, China: The Wild East (narrator and exec. producer) 1995, Quills 2000, Twisted 2004. *Television includes:* Hemingway and Gelhorn (film) 2012.

KAUFMANN, Jonas; German singer (tenor); b. 10 July 1969, Munich; m. 1st Margarete Joswig (divorced 2014); three c.; m. 2nd Christiane Lutz 2019; one c.; ed Munich Hochschule für Musik, master-classes with Hans Hotter and James King; first engagement, Saarbrücken Opera 1994–96; Così fan tutte in Milan (last production of Giorgio Strehler) 1997; Salzburg Festival debut as Dr Faust (Busoni) 1999; debut at Zurich Opera in Mozart's Die Zauberflöte 2000; US debut at Lyric Opera in Chicago 2001; debut at Royal Opera House, Covent Garden, London in Puccini's La Rondine 2004; debut at the Metropolitan Opera, New York in Verdi's La Traviata 2006; La Traviata in Zürich, Paris and at La Scala, Milan 2007; Tosca in London, Manon in Chicago, Fidelio in Paris 2008; Lohengrin in Munich, Don Carlo in London 2009; Werther in Paris and Bayreuth Festival debut in Lohengrin 2010; role debut as Siegmund in Die Walküre at the Met 2011; Don Carlo in Munich, Carmen and Ariadne auf Naxos at the Salzburg Festival, Lohengrin at La Scala 2012; Parsifal at the Met and Wiener Staatsoper 2013; Manon Lescaut at Royal Opera House and Bayerische Staatsoper 2014; Carmen, Royal Opera House 2015; numerous recital performances at leading int. venues including the Met 2011 (first solo recital at the Met since Pavarotti 1994), La Scala 2014, Last Night of the Proms, Royal Albert Hall, London 2015, Kaufmann Residency at the Barbican, London 2017; best known for playing Don José in Carmen, Cavaradossi in Tosca, title role in Don Carlos and Siegmund in Die Walküre; Bayerische Europamedaille 2012, Verdienstkreuz am Bande des Verdienstordens der Bundesrepublik Deutschland 2016, Officier, ordre des Arts et Lettres 2018, Bayerischer Maximiliansorden für Wissenschaft und Kunst 2018; prizewinner, Meistersinger Competition, Nuremberg 1993, Musical American Vocalist of the Year 2012, Int. Opera Awards Foundation Best Male Singer and Readers' Award 2013, Int. Classical Music Award for DVD Performance 2013, European Culture Award 2015, Premio Puccini 2015. *Recordings include:* Strauss Lieder (Gramophone Award for Best Solo Vocal Recording) 2007, Romantic Arias by Mozart, Schubert, Beethoven and Wagner (Grand Prix du Disque, Diapason d'or, Qobus/ Classica: Le meilleur disque) 2008, Madame Butterfly (Gramophone Award) 2009, Sehnsucht (Prix Caecilia, Echo Klassik Award for Best Vocalist of the Year 2010, Orphée d'or 'Wolfgang Wagner' 2010) 2009, Die schöne Müllerin (Diapason d'or) 2010, Verismo Arias (Diapason d'or 2010, Gramophone Award for Best Recital Recording) 2011, Werther (DVD) (Diapason d'or) 2011, Fidelio (Echo Klassik for

Best Opera Recording of the Year) 2012, Tosca (Puccini) (BBC Music Magazine DVD Performance Award 2014), Der Ring des Nibelungen (DVD) (Grammy Award for Best Opera Recording) 2013, The Verdi Album 2013, Wagner Arias (Gramophone Award for Best Vocal Recording, BBC Music Magazine Vocal Award 2014) 2013, Schubert: Winterreise (Gramophone Award for Best Solo Vocal Recording 2014) 2014, Sehnsucht 2014, Du Bist die Welt für Mich (Echo Klassik Singer of the Year 2015) 2014, Nessun Dorma - The Puccini Album (Echo Klassik Bestseller of the Year 2016) 2015, Dolce Vita 2016, L'Opéra 2017, Wolf: Italienisches Liederbuch 2019. *Film:* An Evening with Puccini 2015. *Address:* c/o Zemsky/Green Artists Management, 104 West 73rd Street, New York, NY 10023, USA (office). *Telephone:* (212) 579-6700 (office). *Fax:* (212) 579-4723 (office). *E-mail:* bzemsky@zemskygreen.com (office). *Website:* www.zemskygreen.com (office); www.jonaskaufmann.com.

KAUFMANN-BRÄNDLIR, Irene, Dr oec. publ.; Swiss business executive; *Vice-Chairwoman, Coop-Gruppe Genossenschaft;* b. 1955; mem. Bd of Dirs Coop-Gruppe Genossenschaft 2001–, currently Vice-Chair., also mem. Bd of Dirs Coop AG, Coop Schweiz AG, Coop Mineraloel AG, Coop Pension Fund; mem. Bd of Dirs Bell Food Group AG 2009–, Vice-Chair. 2017–; mem. Bd of Dirs Dipl. Ing. Fust AG, Oberbüren, Transgourmet Holding SE, Cologne, HWZ Hochschule für Wirtschaft Zürich, Swiss Mobiliar Cooperative Co., Bern, Schweizerische Mobiliar Holding AG, ETH Zürich, Juventus Schools, Zürich;. *Address:* Coop-Gruppe Genossenschaft, Güterstrasse 190, 4053 Basel, Switzerland (office). *Telephone:* 613366666 (office). *E-mail:* info@coop.ch (office). *Website:* www.coop.ch (office).

KAUNDA, Kenneth David; Zambian fmr politician and fmr head of state; b. (Buchizya), 28 April 1924, Lubwa; m. Betty Banda 1946; six s. (two s. deceased) two d. one adopted s.; ed Lubwa Training School and Munali Secondary School; schoolteacher at Lubwa Training School 1943, Headmaster 1944–47; Sec. Chinsali Young Men's Farming Asscn 1947; welfare officer, Chingola Copper Mine 1948; school teaching 1948–49; Founder-Sec. Lubwa branch, African Nat. Congress (ANC) 1950, district organizer 1951, prov. organizer 1952, Sec.-Gen. for N Rhodesia 1953; imprisoned for possession of prohibited literature Jan.–Feb. 1954; broke away from ANC to form Zambia African Nat. Congress 1958; imprisoned for political offences May 1959–Jan. 1960; Pres. United Nat. Independence Party 1960–92, 1995–2000; Minister of Local Govt and Social Welfare, N Rhodesia 1962–64; Prime Minister of N Rhodesia Jan.–Oct. 1964; Pres. Pan-African Freedom Movt for East, Central and South Africa (PAFMECSA) 1963; First Pres. of Zambia 1964–91 and Minister of Defence 1964–70, 1973–78; Head of Sub-Cttee for Defence and Security 1978–91; Minister of Foreign Affairs 1969–70, also of Trade, Industry, Mines and State Participation 1969–73; Chair. Mining and Industrial Devt Corpn of Zambia 1970; Chair. Org. of African Unity (OAU) 1970–71, 1987–88, Non-Aligned Nations Conf. 1970–73, fmr Chair. ZIMCO; Chancellor, Univ. of Zambia 1966–91, Copperbelt Univ. 1988; f. Peace Foundation 1992; charged with 'misprison of treason' over alleged involvement in attempted coup d'état 1997; freed after six months of house arrest after charges dropped June 1998; deprived of citizenship March 1999; citizenship restored by Supreme Court 2000; Founder and Chair. Kenneth Kaunda Children of Africa Foundation 2000–; Freeman of the Municipality of Chipata 1994; Order of the Collar of the Nile, Kt of the Collar of the Order of Pius XII, Order of the Queen of Sheba; Hon. LLD (Fordham, Dublin, Windsor (Canada), Wales, Sussex, York and Chile Univs); Dr hc (Humboldt State Univ., Calif.) 1980; Jawaharlal Nehru Award for Int. Understanding, Quaide Azam Human Rights Inst. Prize (Pakistan) 1976; honoured for his Keynote Address on Conflict Resolution in Africa and for Distinguished Leadership of African People for Over Half A Century, African Studies Coalition, Calif. State Univ., Sacramento 1995, WANGO Universal Peace Award 2004, Ubuntu Award, Nat. Heritage Council of South Africa 2007. *Publications:* Black Government 1961, Zambia Shall Be Free 1962, A Humanist in Africa (with Colin Morris) 1966, Humanism in Zambia and a Guide to its Implementation 1967, Humanism Part II 1977, Letter to my Children 1977, Kaunda On Violence 1980. *Address:* Office of the First President of the Republic of Zambia, 21 A Serval Road, PO E 501, Lusaka, Zambia. *Telephone:* (1) 260327 (office); (1) 260323 (home). *Fax:* (1) 220805 (office); (1) 220805 (home).

KAURISMÄKI, Aki; Finnish filmmaker; b. 4 April 1957; Co-founder film production co-operative Filmtotal; Man. Dir and Jt Owner (with brother Mika Kaurismäki) film production co. Villealfa; jtly runs distribution co. Senso Film. *Films include:* as a writer: The Liar 1980, The Worthless 1982, The Clan: Tale of the Frogs 1984, Rosso 1985; as a dir: The Saimaa Gesture 1981, Crime and Punishment 1985, Calamari Union (Special Award, Hong Kong Int. Film Festival) 1985, Shadows in Paradise (Jussi Award for Best Finnish Film) 1986, Hamlet 1987, Ariel 1988, Leningrad Cowboys Go Home 1989, The Match Factory Girl 1989, I Hired a Contract Killer 1990, La Vie Bohème, Leningrad Cowboys Meet Moses 1993, Take Care of Your Scarf, Tatiana 1995, Drifting Clouds 1996, The Man Without a Past (Cannes Film Festival Best Actress Award 2002) 2002, Ten Minutes Older: The Trumpet (segment) (also producer, writer, editor) 2002, Visions of Europe (also writer, producer) 2004, Laitakaupungin valot (Lights in the Dark) 2006, Le Havre 2011, Centro Histórico 2012. *Rock videos:* Rocky VI, Thru', The Wire, LA Woman 1986.

KAUSAR, Syed Masood, BA, LLB; Pakistani lawyer and politician; b. 2 May 1938, Kohat, Khyber Pakhtunkhwa Prov.; ed Islamia Coll., Peshawar Univ.; called to the Bar, Lincoln's Inn, UK 1968; elected Pres. Peshawar High Court Bar Asscn 1984; Speaker, Prov. Ass. of Khyber Pakhtunkhwa (previously North-West Frontier Prov.) 1988–90, Leader of Opposition 1990–93; Senator from Khyber Pakhtunkhwa Prov. 1994–2000, mem. Senate Standing Cttees on Petroleum and Natural Resources, Interior, Narcotics Control and States and Frontier Regions and Law, Justice and Parliamentary Affairs, mem. Functional Cttee on Less Developed Areas; Gov. Khyber Pakhtunkhwa 2011–13; mem. Pakistan People's Party (mem. Cen. Exec. Cttee); elected Pres. Peshawar High Court Bar Asscn 1984; Hon. Visiting Prof. of Law, Univ. Law Coll., Peshawar. *Address:* 11 Sahibzada Abdul Qayyum Khan Road, Peshawar, Pakistan (home). *Telephone:* (21) 271405 (home). *E-mail:* ppp@comsats.net.pk (office). *Website:* www.ppp.org.pk (office).

KAVAN, Jan Michael, CH, BSc; Czech politician and journalist; *Chairman, Czech-Slovak-Iranian Chamber of Commerce;* b. 17 Oct. 1946, London, England; s. of Pavel Kavan and Rosemary Kavanová (née Edwards); m. Lenka Mázlová 1991 (divorced 2004); three s. three d.; ed Charles Univ., Prague, London School of Econs, Univ. of Reading and St Antony's Coll., Oxford, UK; politician and journalist, Charles Univ., Prague 1963–68; Ed. East European Reporter, London 1985–90; Dir Palach Press Ltd, London 1974–90, Deputy Dir Jan Palach Information and Research Trust 1982–90; Vice-Pres. East European Cultural Foundation, London 1985–90; mem. Parl. Fed. Ass. of Czech Repub. 1990–92, mem. Foreign Affairs Cttee; mem. Czech Social Democratic (CSSD) Party 1993–, mem. Foreign Affairs Comm. 1994–98, CSSD Spokesman on Foreign Affairs 1996–98, elected to Presidium of Cen. Exec. Cttee 1997–99; Chair. Helsinki Citizens' Ass. in Czech Rep. 1990–95, Policy Centre for the Promotion of Democracy, Prague 1992–98; Senator, Parl. of Czech Repub. 1996–2000; Minister of Foreign Affairs 1998–2002, Deputy Prime Minister 1999–2002; Deputy Chair. Cen. and East European Cttee of the Socialist International 1997–98, State Security Council 1999–2002; Chair. Council for Intelligence Activities 1999–2002; Pres. UN Gen. Ass. 2002–03; mem. Parl. 2002–06, Deputy Chair. Foreign Affairs Cttee 2004–06, Deputy Leader of Parl. Group of Soc. Democratic Party (CSSD) 2004–06, mem. Presidium of Party of European Socialists (PES) 2006; foreign policy adviser to Pres. of Chamber of Deputies 2007–10; Visiting Prof. of Politics and History, Adelphi Univ., New York 1993–94; Karl Loewenstein Fellow in Politics and Jurisprudence, Amherst Coll., Mass 1994; lectured at Columbia and Stanford Univs, Wellesley Coll., Harvard Center for European Studies; taught at London Adult Educ. Inst. for 15 years; Pres. 57th Session UN Gen. Ass. 2002–03; Foreign Policy Adviser to Pres. of the Parl. 2007–10, Parl. Asst to J. Kratky 2009–13, J. Foldyna 2013–17; Deputy Chair. Club of Seniors 2015–; Spokesperson, Alliance of Labour and Solidarity 2010–; mem. Academic Council of New Policy Forum (Gorbachev Foundation) 2011–, Bd of European Leadership Network for Multilateral Disarmament 2010–; Chair. Czech-Slovak-Iranian Chamber of Commerce 2015–; Hon. Prof., Faculty of Int. Relations, Mongolia State Univ. 1999; Hon. Fellow, LSE 2001; Companion of Honour 2003, Int. Order of Merit 2003; Hon. DHumLitt (Adelphi) 2001; TGM Medal of Honour 2001. *Publications:* Czechoslovak Socialist Opposition 1976, Voices of Czechoslovak Socialists 1977, Voices from Prague 1983, Justice with a Muzzle 1996, McCarthyism Has a New Name: Lustration 2000, Transition to Democracy in Eastern Europe and Russia 2002, Diplomacy 2008; several book chapters and more than 500 articles in mainstream press and specialised journals on int. relations. *Leisure interests:* int. politics, good literature, film, theatre. *Address:* Česko-Slovensko-Íránská obchodní komora, Na Zátorce 14, 160 00 Prague 6 (office); Klausova 13C, 155 00 Prague 5, Czech Republic (home). *Telephone:* 72-4210790 (mobile). *E-mail:* jan.kavan@csiok.cz (office); kavanjm@seznam.cz (home); kavanjan17@gmail.com (home). *Website:* www.csiok.cz (office).

KAVANAGH, Dan (see BARNES, Julian Patrick).

KAVÁNEK, Pavel; Czech banker; *Chairman, CSOB Group;* m.; two d.; ed Prague School of Econs, Georgetown Univ., USA; staff mem., Foreign Exchange Dept, Ceskolovenská Obchodni Banka (now CSOB Group) 1972–76, Chief Dealer 1977–90, mem. Bd of Dirs 1990–93, Chair. and CEO 1993–2014, Chair. Supervisory Bd 2014–; with Zivnostenská Banka, London, UK 1976–77; Vice-Pres. Asscn of Banks, Prague; Pew Econ. Freedom Fellowship, Georgetown Univ. 1992, MasterCard Banker of the Year 2007. *Address:* CSOB Group, Na Prikope 28, 11503 Prague 1, Czech Republic (office). *Website:* www.csob.cz (office).

KAWABATA, Tatsuo; Japanese engineer and politician (retd); b. 24 Jan. 1945, Omihachiman, Shiga Pref.; ed Kyoto Univ.; began career as engineer, Toray Industries Inc. Research Inst., became involved in trade union activities, later Regional Head of union in Shiga Dist; mem. House of Reps for Shiga-1 constituency 1986–17, Vice-Speaker 2014–17; fmr mem. Democratic Socialist Party, fmr mem. Shinshinto (New Frontier Party); mem. Democratic Party of Japan 1998–, fmr Vice-Pres. and Chair. Cttee on Audits and Admin Oversight; Minister of Educ., Culture, Sports, Science and Tech. 2009–10, Minister of State for Science and Tech. Policy 2010, Minister of Internal Affairs and Communications 2011–12. *Leisure interests:* reading, watching sports, PC, motor sports. *Website:* www.kawa-bata.net.

KAWABATA, Tatsuo, MS; Japanese politician (retd); b. 24 Jan. 1945, Ōmihachiman, Shiga Pref.; ed Kyoto Univ.; started career as researcher, Toray Industries Inc.; mem. House of Reps for Shiga at-large constituency 1986–96, for Shiga No 1 Dist 1996–2005, 2009–17, Vice-Speaker 2014–17; Chair. House of Reps Cttee on Rules and Admin; fmr mem. Democratic Socialist Party, Shinshinto (New Frontier Party); mem. Democratic Party of Japan 1998–; Minister of Educ., Culture, Sports, Science and Tech. 2009–10, Minister of State for Science and Tech. Policy 2010, Minister for Internal Affairs and Communications and for Regional Revitalization, Minister of State for Okinawa and Northern Territories' Affairs and for Promotion of Local Sovereignty 2011–12.

KAWAGUCHI, Fumio; Japanese energy industry executive; *Honorary Advisor, Chubu Electric Power Co., Inc.;* b. 8 Sept. 1940, Aichi Pref.; ed Waseda Univ. School of Commerce; joined Chubu Electric Power Co., Inc. 1964, Man. Nagoya Office 1999, Man. Dir 1999–2001, Pres. 2001–06, Chair. and Rep. Dir 2006–10, Hon. Advisor 2010–; Chair. Chubu Econ. Fed., Chubu Industrial Advancement Center; mem. Bd of Councillors, Japan Co-operation Center for the Middle East; Hon. Consul of FRG in Nagoya 2007. *Address:* Chubu Electric Power Co., Inc., 1 Higashi-shincho, Higashi-ku, Nagoya 461-8680, Japan.

KAWAGUCHI, Yoriko, BA, MPh; Japanese economist and politician; b. 14 Jan. 1941, Tokyo; m.; two c.; ed Univ. of Tokyo, Yale Univ., USA; at Ministry of Int. Trade and Industry 1965–76, 1979–90, Dir-Gen. Global Environmental Affairs 1992–93; economist, IBRD (World Bank), Washington, DC, USA 1976–78; Minister, Embassy in Washington, DC 1991–92; Man. Dir Suntory Ltd 1993–2000; Minister of the Environment 2000–02, of Foreign Affairs 2002–04; Special Adviser to the Prime Minister responsible for Foreign Affairs 2004–05; mem. House of Councillors (LDP) 2005–13, Chair. Cttee on Environment; Chair. Okinawa Promotion Cttee; Acting Chair. Research Comm. on Foreign Affairs and Econ. Partnership; Deputy Dir Environment Div., Policy Research Council, LDP; Co-Chair. Int. Cttee on Nuclear Non-Proliferation and Disarmament; mem. Foundation Bd of Forum of Young Global Leaders, World Econ. Forum 2008–13; Councillor Int. Cttee, Parliamentarians for Global Action; mem. Steering Cttee 'Innovation for Cool Earth Forum' (ICEF) 2014–; Commr, Global Ocean Comm.

2014–; mem. Hon. Advisory Cttee, UN Univ.; Vice-Chair. GLOBE Japan, GLOBE Int.; mem. Pres.'s Council of Int. Activities; mem. Bd of Trustees, US-Japan Foundation; Band, Order of the Aztec Eagle (Mexico) 2003, Extraordinary Grand Cross, Nat. Order of Merit (Paraguay) 2004; Dr hc (Nat. Univ. of Mongolia) 2004; Wilbur Cross Medal (Yale Univ.) 2008, Star of Jerusalem from Mahmoud Abbas, Pres. Palestinian Nat. Authority 2010, Anniversary Medal for a major contrib. to global security promotion and non-proliferation regime by Kadyzhanov, Dir-Gen. Nat. Nuclear Centre (Kazakhstan) 2011. *Address:* Room 308, Saingiin-kaikan, 2-1-1 Nagata-cho, Chiyoda-ku, Tokyo 100-8962, Japan (office). *Telephone:* (3) 6550-0308 (office). *Fax:* (3) 6551-0308 (office). *E-mail:* yoriko_kawaguchi3@sangiin.go.jp (office). *Website:* www.yoriko-kawaguchi.jp (office).

KAWAI, Masanori; Japanese freight company executive; *Chairman, Nippon Express Company;* joined Nippon Express Co. 1966, has held numerous exec. positions including Deputy Chief Operating Officer and Exec. Vice-Pres. –2005, apptd Pres., Rep. Dir and CEO 2005, Chair. 2011. *Address:* Nippon Express Company Ltd, 1-9-3, Higashi Shimbashi, Minato-ku, Tokyo 105-8322, Japan (office). *Telephone:* (3) 6251-1111 (office). *Website:* www.nittsu.co.jp (office).

KAWAKUBO, Rei; Japanese couturier; b. 1942, Toyko; m. Adrian Joffe; ed Keio Univ., Tokyo; joined Asahikasei 1964; freelance designer 1966; est. Comme des Garçons Label 1969, Founder and Pres. Comme des Garçons Co. Ltd,Tokyo 1973–; opened first overseas Comme des Garçons Boutique in Paris 1982; opened Dover Street Market, first London store October 2004; joined Fed. Française de la Couture 1982; Japan Comme des Garçons Collection presented twice a year, Tokyo; 395 outlets in Japan, five Comme des Garçons shops and 550 outlets outside Japan; currently has 11 lines of clothing, one line of furniture and a perfume; f. Six magazine 1988; cr. costumes and stage design for Merce Cunningham's Scenario 1997; mem. Chambre Syndicale du Pret-a-Porter; Chevalier, Ordre des Arts et des Lettres; Dr hc (RCA, London) 1997; Mainichi Newspaper Fashion Award 1983, 1988, Excellence in Design Award, Harvard Univ. 2000, Isamu Noguchi Award, Noguchi Museum 2019. *Address:* Comme des Garçons Co. Ltd, 5-11-5 Minamiaoyama, Minato-ku, Tokyo 107, Japan (office). *Telephone:* (3) 3407-2480 (office). *Fax:* (3) 5485-2439 (office). *Website:* www.comme-des-garcons.com (office).

KAWAMATA, Tadashi, MFA; Japanese visual artist; *Professor, Ecole Nationale Superieure des Beaux-Arts, Paris;* b. 1953, Hokkaido; ed Tokyo Nat. Univ. of Fine Art and Music; works exhibited at Venice Biennale 1982, Int. Youth Triennale of Drawing, Nuremberg 1983, Documenta 8 1987, São Paulo Biennale 1987, Tyne Int. Exhbn for Contemporary Art, Newcastle-upon-Tyne and Gateshead, UK 1990; apartment projects: Takara House Room 205, Tokyo 1982, Slip in Tokorozawa 1983, Tetra House N-3 W-26, Sapporo 1983; construction site projects: Spui Project, The Hague 1986, La Maison des Squatters, Grenoble 1987, Nove de Julho Cacapave, São Paulo 1987, Fukuroi Project 1988; urban projects: P.S.1 Project, New York 1985, Destroyed Church, Kassel 1987, Toronto Project at Colonial Tavern Park, Toronto 1989, Project at Begijnhof St Elisabeth, Kortrijk, Belgium 1989–90, Documente 9 1992, Biennale d'Art Contemporain, Lyon 1993, Münster Skulptor Projekt 1997, 11th Biennale of Sydney 1989, Echigo Tsumari Art Triennial 2000, 4th Shanghai Bienniale 2002, Busan Bienniale 2002, Bienal de Valencia 2003; Prof., Tokyo Univ. of Fine Art and Music 1999–2005; Prof., École Nationale Superieure des Beaux-Arts, Paris 2006–; mem. Program Advisory Cttee Space Shower TV 2002–05; Dir Yokohama Triennale 2005; Asian Cultural Council Fellowship Grant (worked in New York 1984–86); Grand Prix Int. Youth Triennale 1983. *Address:* c/o Annely Juda Fine Art, 4th Floor, 23 Dering Street, London, W1S 1AW, England; c/o Kamel Mennour, 47 rue Saint André des Arts, 75006 Paris, France. *Website:* www.tk-onthetable.com; www.cafetalk.net.

KAWAMURA, Takashi; Japanese business executive; *Chairman Emeritus, Hitachi Ltd;* ed Tokyo Univ.; joined Hitachi Ltd 1962, Div. Man. Thermal Power Eng Div., Power Group 1987–92, Gen. Man. Hitachi Works 1992–95, Group Exec., Electric Utility Sales Operations Group 1995–97, Exec. Man. Dir and Group Exec., Power Group 1997–99, Exec. Vice-Pres., Hitachi Ltd 1999–, Chair. and Rep. Exec. Officer, Hitachi Software Eng Co. Ltd (subsidiary of Hitachi Ltd) 2003–07, Dir, Hitachi Ltd 2003–14, Chair. Hitachi Plant Technologies Ltd (fmrly Hitachi Plant Eng & Construction Co. Ltd) 2005–14, Chair. Hitachi Maxell Ltd 2007–14, Chair., Pres. and CEO Hitachi Ltd 2009–10 (Chair. Nominating Cttee, Compensation Cttee), Chair. and Rep. Exec. Officer 2010–14, Chair. Emer. 2014–; Pres. and CEO Babcock-Hitachi K.K; mem. Bd of Dirs Babcock-Hitachi K.K., Hitachi America Ltd, Hitachi China Ltd; Auditor (non-exec.), Japan Nuclear Fuel Ltd 2011–; fmr Auditor, Ines Corpn. *Address:* Hitachi Ltd, 6-6 Marunouchi 1-chome, Chiyoda-ku, Tokyo 100-8280, Japan (office). *Telephone:* (3) 3258-1111 (office). *Fax:* (3) 3258-2375 (office). *E-mail:* service@cm.hbi.co.jp (office). *Website:* www.hitachi.com (office).

KAWAR, Karim Tawfik, BSc; Jordanian business executive and fmr diplomatist; *President, Kawar Group;* b. 14 June 1966, Anman; m. Luma Kawar; one s. two d.; ed Boston Coll., USA; founding mem. several business asscns and non-governmental orgs, including Jordan American Business Asscn, Young Entrepreneurs Asscn, Jordanian Intellectual Property Asscn; est. computer co. and headed an umbrella group encompassing 10 information systems and software cos; apptd to Econ. Consultative Council by King Abdullah II 1999; Head of REACH Initiative (led team of 40 Jordanian information tech. professionals to launch the IT industry in Jordan) 1999; Amb. to USA (also accred to Mexico) 2002–07; fmr Network Coordinator UN Information and Communication Technologies Task Force–Arab Regional Network; fmr Chair. Information Tech. Asscn of Jordan (INTAJ); Vice-Chair. Jordan River Foundation; mem. Young Presidents Org.; Pres. Kawar Group 2007–; Chair. Bd of Trustees, King's Acad. 2010–; Chair. IrisGuard, NatHealth, Kawar Energy; Co-Founder and Dir Oasis 500; Founding Chair. EDAMA Initiative for Sustainable Energy, Water, and Environment; mem. Bd of Dirs Optimiza, Ahli Bank, United Insurance; Eisenhower Fellow 2000; named Global Leader for Tomorrow by World Econ. Forum. *Address:* Kawar Group, PO Box 222, Amman 11118, Jordan (office). *Telephone:* (6) 5609500 (office). *Fax:* (6) 5698322 (office). *E-mail:* president@kawar.com.jo (office). *Website:* www.kawar.com (office).

KAWASAKI, Jiro; Japanese politician; b. 15 Nov. 1947, Mie; s. of Hideji Kawasaki; ed Keio Univ.; with Matsushita Electric Industrial Co. 1973–80; mem. House of Reps for Mie dist 1980–, Parl. Vice-Minister, Ministry of Posts and Telecommunications 1990, Minister of Transport 1998–99, of Hokkaido Devt Agency 1999, of Economy, Trade and Industry 2004–05, of Health, Labour and Welfare 2005–06; fmr Head, Public Relations Dept of LDP. *Leisure interests:* reading, tennis. *Address:* House of Representatives, 1-7-1 Nagatacho, Chiyoda-ku, Tokyo 100-0014, Japan (office). *Telephone:* (3) 3581-3111 (office). *E-mail:* webmaster@shugiin.go.jp (office). *Website:* www.shugiin.go.jp/internet/index.nsf/html/index_e.htm (office).

KAWASE, Naomi; Japanese film director, screenwriter and writer; b. 30 May 1969, Nara; m. Takenori Sento 1997 (divorced 2000); one s.; ed Osaka School of Photography (now School of Visual Arts); spent four years as lecturer at Osaka School of Photography before releasing Embracing 1992; retrospective organized for 1st Infinity Film Festival in Alba, Italy and for Jeu de Paume hosted by Petit Palais in Paris 2002, also for RED/CAT, Los Angeles 2005. *Films include:* I Focus on That Which Interests Me (short) 1988, The Concretization of These Things Flying around Me (short) 1988, My J-W-F (short) 1988, Papa's Icecream (short) 1988, My Solo Family (short) 1989, Presently (short) 1989, A Small Largeness (short) 1989, The Girl's Daily Bread (short) 1990, Like Happiness (short) 1991, Embracing (documentary short) 1992, White Moon 1993, Katatsumori (documentary short) 1994, See Heaven (documentary short) 1995, Memory of the Wind (short) 1995, This World (short) 1996, Hi wa katabuki (documentary) 1996, Moe no suzaku (youngest winner of la Caméra d'Or Award (Best New Dir) at Cannes Film Festival 1997) 1997, The Weald (Special Mention Prize at Vision du Reel 1999) 1997, Kaleidoscope 1999, Hotaru (Firefly) (FIPRESCI Prize and CICAE Prize, Locarno Int. Film Festival 2000, Best Achievement Award in Cinemato-graphy and Directing and Leading Actress Award (Yuko Nakamura), Buenos Aires Int. Film Festival 2001) 2000, Sky, Wind, Fire, Water, Earth (documentary) 2001, Shara 2003, Letter from a Yellow Cherry Blossom (documentary) 2003, Shadow (documentary short) 2004, Tarachime (documentary short) (Special Prize, Yamagata Int. Film Festival 2007) 2006, Mogari no mori (The Mourning Forest) (Grand Prix, Cannes Film Festival 2007) 2007, Nanayo 2008, In Between Days (documentary short) 2009, Visitors (segment 'Koma') 2009, Genpin (documentary) 2010, Hanezu no tsuki 2011, 60 Seconds of Solitude in Year Zero 2011, Still the Water 2014. *Publications include:* novels: Moe no Suzaku, Hotaru; articles for various publs. *Address:* Kumie Inc., 2F Art Fukuzumi Building, 45 Takama-cho, Nara-shi, Nara 630-8241, Japan (office). *Telephone:* (742) 27-2216 (office). *Fax:* (742) 26-1830 (office). *E-mail:* info@kawasenaomi.com. *Website:* www.kawasenaomi.com.

KAY, Alan, BA, MS, PhD; American computer scientist and academic; *President, Viewpoints Research Institute;* ed Univ of Colorado, Univ of Utah; fmr professional jazz guitarist, composer and theatrical designer; worked for Univ. of Utah Advanced Research Project Agency (ARPA) research team that designed or developed 3D-graphics, the FLEX machine (an early interactive object-oriented personal computer), the Dynabook (notebook-sized laptop computer for children), and participated in original design of the ARPANet (later became the Internet) late 1960s; Co-founder Xerox Palo Alto Research Center (PARC) early 1970s; fmr Chief Scientist, Atari; fmr Fellow, Apple Computer; fmr Vice-Pres. Research and Devt, The Walt Disney Co.; Founder and Pres. Viewpoints Research Inst., Inc., Glendale, Calif. 2001–; Sr Fellow, Hewlett-Packard Co. 2002–; Sr Scientist, Div. of Information Tech., Univ. of Wis. 2005–; currently Adjunct Prof., UCLA; Visiting Prof., Kyoto Univ., Japan 2005; Fellow, American Acad. of Arts and Sciences, Nat. Acad. of Eng (NAE), Royal Soc. of Arts (UK), Computer Museum History Center, AAAS, Asscn for Computing Machinery, Hasso Plattner Inst. 2011; Hon. Prof., Berlin Univ of the Arts; Dr hc (Kungl Tekniska Hoegskolan), (Columbia Coll.), (Royal Inst. of Tech.), (Georgia Inst. of Tech.), (Univ of Pisa), (Univ of Waterloo), (Univ of Murcia); Asscn of Computing Machinery (ACM), Kyoto Prize, ACM Software Systems Award, ACM Outstanding Educator Award, J-D Warnier Prix d'lnformatique, NEC C&C Prize 2001, Funai Prize, ZeroOne Award, Univ. of Berlin, inducted into Utah Information Tech. Asscn Hall of Fame 2003, A.M. Turing Award 2003, Inamori Foundation 2004, NAE Charles Stark Draper Prize 2004. *Publications:* numerous articles in scientific journals. *Leisure interest:* classical pipe organist. *Address:* Viewpoints Research Institute, Inc., 1025 Westwood Blvd, 2nd Floor, Los Angeles, CA 90024, USA (office). *Telephone:* (310) 208-0524 (office). *Website:* vpri.org (office).

KAY, John Anderson, CBE, FBA, FRSE; British economist; b. 3 Aug. 1948, Edinburgh, Scotland; s. of James Kay and Allison Kay; m. 1st Deborah Freeman 1986 (divorced 1995); m. 2nd Mika Oldham 2009; ed Royal High School, Edinburgh, Univ. of Edinburgh and Nuffield Coll., Oxford; Fellow, St John's Coll. Oxford 1970–; Lecturer in Econs, Univ. of Oxford 1971–79; Research Dir Inst. for Fiscal Studies 1979–82, Dir 1982–86; Dir Centre for Business Strategy, London Business School 1986–91; Chair. London Econs 1986–96; Dir Said Business School, Univ. of Oxford 1997–99, Undervalued Assets Trust PLC 1994–2005; Dir (non-exec.) Halifax Bldg Soc. 1991–97, Foreign & Colonial Special Utilities Investment Trust PLC 1993–2003, Value and Income Trust PLC 1994–, Halifax PLC 1997–2000, Clear Capital Ltd 2004–08, Law Debenture Corpn 2004–14, Scottish Mortgage Investment Trust PLC 2008–; mem. Corp. Governance Advisory Bd, Norges Bank Investment Management 2013–; Hon. DLitt (Heriot-Watt) 2008. *Publications include:* The British Tax System 1979, Foundations of Corporate Success 1993, Why Firms Succeed 1995, The Business of Economics 1996, The Truth about Markets 2003, Everlasting Light Bulbs 2004, Culture and Prosperity 2005, The Hare and the Tortoise 2006, The Long and the Short of It 2009 (second edn 2016), Obliquity 2010, Other People's Money 2015; co-author: Concentration in Modern Industry, The Reform of Social Security, The Economic Analysis of Accounting Profitability; articles in scholarly journals. *Leisure interests:* walking, travel. *Telephone:* (20) 7224-8797 (office). *E-mail:* johnkay@johnkay.com (office). *Website:* www.johnkay.com.

KAY, Sir Nicholas Peter, KCMG, CMG, BA, MA; British diplomatist and UN official; *NATO Senior Civilian Representative in Afghanistan;* b. 8 March 1958, Louth, Lincs.; s. of Squadron Leader R. P. Kay and Mrs J. A. Kay; m. Susan Wallace; one s. two d.; ed Abingdon School, St Edmund Hall, Oxford, Univ. of Reading; English language teacher, Spain, Peru, Brazil, Saudi Arabia, Cyprus and UK 1980–94; First Sec., FCO 1994–95, Head of Pakistan and Afghanistan Section 1995–97, Deputy Head of Policy Planning Staff 2000–02, Dir (Africa) 2012–13; Deputy Head of Mission, Havana 1997–2000, Deputy Head of Mission, Madrid 2002–06; UK Regional Co-ordinator Southern Afghanistan 2006–07; Amb. to

Democratic Repub. of the Congo (also accred to Repub. of Congo) 2007–10, to Sudan 2010–12, to Afghanistan 2017–19; NATO Senior Civilian Representative in Afghanistan 2019–; Special Rep. for Somalia and Head of UN Assistance Mission in Somalia (UNSOM) 2013–15. *Publication:* Letterwriter (software) 1988. *Leisure interests:* water sports, travel, vegetarian food. *Website:* www.nato.int (office).

KAYANI, Gen. Ashfaq Pervez; Pakistani fmr army officer; b. April 1952, Jehlum; m.; one s. one d.; ed Mil. Coll., Jhelum, Command and Staff Coll., Quetta, Command and Gen. Staff Coll., Fort Leavenworth, USA, Nat. Defence Coll., Islamabad; commissioned in Baloch Regt 1971, commanded infantry bn, infantry brigade, infantry div. and corps; Deputy Mil. Sec. for Benazir Bhutto 1988–89; fmr Dir-Gen. of Mil. Operations; Corps Commdr of Rawalpindi 2003–04; Dir-Gen. Inter-Services Intelligence 2004–07; chosen to carry out investigations of two assassination attempts on Gen. Pervaiz Musharraf; Vice-Chief of Army Staff (also promoted to four-star Gen.) Oct.–Nov. 2007, Chief of Army Staff 2007–13 (retd); fmr Pres. Pakistan Golf Fed. *Leisure interest:* golf. *Address:* c/o Ministry of Defence, Pakistan Secretariat, No. II, Rawalpindi 46000, Pakistan.

KAYE, Carol; American musician (electric bass guitar, guitar); b. 24 March 1935, Everett, Wash.; one s. two d.; teacher of guitar 1949–, electric bass 1969–; on the road, big band 1954–55; played bebop jazz, night clubs 1956–61; special records, studio guitarist 1957–66; studio electric bassist 1963–; invented 16th note bass recording styles; over 10,000 sessions; television credits, playing bass include M.A.S.H, Mission Impossible, Hawaii Five-O, The Brady Bunch, Soap; film credits, playing bass include Thomas Crown Affair, Heat of the Night, Valley of the Dolls, Shaft (theme), columnist, Bassics Magazine; mem. Musicians' Union; Women in Music Award 2000, Lifetime Achievement Award, Duquesne Univ. Pittsburgh Jazz Soc. 2000, Los Angeles Composers–Arrangers Award 2004, Lifetime Achievement Award, Bass Player Magazine 2008. *Television:* First Lady of Bass TV (documentary). *Recordings include:* albums: Carol Kaye: Bass, Thumbs Up, Carol Kaye Guitars '65; credits on guitar include: Zippity Doo Dah, Batman Theme, Birds and Bees, The Beat Goes On, You've Lost That Lovin' Feelin', La Bamba; credits on bass guitar include: Way We Were, Feelin' Alright, Good Vibrations, Help Me Rhonda, Wouldn't It Be Nice, Can't Help Myself, Heat of Night, I Don't Need No Doctor, Little Green Apples, Baby Love, River Deep Mountain High, Something Stupid, This is My Song, Mission Impossible, Pet Sounds, Smile. *Publications:* writer, composer of over 30 tutorials; How to Play the Electric Bass, Jazz Improvisation for Bass. *Leisure interests:* reading, teaching. *Address:* 25852 McBean Parkway, Suite 200, Valencia, CA 91355, USA (office). *Telephone:* (661) 288-6551 (office). *E-mail:* carol@carolkaye.com. *Website:* www.carolkaye.com.

KAYE, Harvey Jordan, PhD; American academic and writer; *Ben & Joyce Rosenberg Professor of Democracy and Justice Studies and Director, Center for History and Social Change, University of Wisconsin-Green Bay;* b. 9 Oct. 1949, Englewood, NJ; s. of Murray N. Kaye and Frances Kaye; m. Lorna Stewart 1973; two d.; ed Paramus High School, Rutgers Univ., Univ. of Mexico, Univ. of London, UK and Louisiana State Univ.; Asst Prof. of Interdisciplinary Studies, St Cloud Univ., Minn. 1977–78; Asst Prof. of Social Change and Devt, Univ. of Wis., Green Bay 1978–83, Assoc. Prof. 1983–86, Head of Dept 1985–88, Prof. 1986–, Ben & Joyce Rosenberg Prof. of Social Change and Devt 1990–2010, Ben and Joyce Rosenberg Prof. of Democracy and Justice Studies 2010–, Dir Center for History and Social Change 1991–; Visiting Fellow, Univ. of Birmingham, UK 1987; mem. Editorial Bd Marxist Perspectives 1978–80, The Wisconsin Sociologist, Wis. Sociological Asscn 1985–87, Rethinking History 1996–; Consulting Ed., Verso Publishers, London 1988–94, NYU Press 1996–; Series Ed., American Radicals (Routledge) 1992–98; columnist, Times Higher Educational Supplement 1994–2001, Tikkun magazine 1996–97, Index on Censorship 1996–, The Guardian Unlimited 2007–08, New Deal 2.0 2010–, Huffington Post 2010–; mem. Exec. Bd, Center for Democratic Values 1996–2000, Scholars, Artists and Writers for Social Justice 1997–2000; mem. Org. of American Historians, PEN, American Fed. of Teachers (AFT), National Writers Union; Nat. Endowment for the Humanities Fellowship 2002–03; Historical Adviser, Remix America 2008–10, Thomas Paine documentary, Four Freedoms Park Project 2010–12, Norman Rockwell Museum Exhibit Enduring Ideals: Rockwell, Roosevelt & the Four Freedoms 2016–; Founders' Award for Scholarship 1985, Isaac Deutscher Memorial Prize 1993, Best Book for the Teen Age, New York Public Library 2001, Best Book 2006, Wisconsin Library Asscn. *Publications include:* The British Marxist Historians 1984, The Powers of the Past 1991, The Education of Desire 1992, Why do Ruling Classes Fear History? 1996, Thomas Paine 2000, Are We Good Citizens? 2001, Thomas Paine and the Promise of America 2005, The Fight for the Four Freedoms (Most Valuable History, The Nation magazine Progressive Honor Roll 2014) 2014; as editor: History, Classes and Nation-States 1988, The Face of the Crowd: Studies in Revolution, Ideology and Popular Protest 1988, Poets, Politics and the People 1989, E. P. Thompson: Critical Perspectives (with K. McClelland) 1990, The American Radical (with M. Buhle and P. Buhle) 1994, Imperialism and its Contradictions 1995, Ideology and Popular Protest 1995; numerous articles on history and historians; contrib. to on-line websites and magazines, including Next New Deal, Huffington Post, Salon. *Leisure interests:* politics, friendship and conversation. *Address:* Democracy and Justice Studies Department, University of Wisconsin-Green Bay, 2420 Nicolet Drive, Green Bay, WI 54311, USA (office). *Telephone:* (920) 465-2355 (office); (920) 465-2755 (office). *Fax:* (920) 465-2791 (office). *E-mail:* kayeh@uwgb.edu (office).

KAYMER, Martin; German professional golfer; b. 28 Dec. 1984, Düsseldorf; turned professional 2005; plays mainly on European Tour; winner Abu Dhabi Golf Championship 2008, 2010, BMW Int. Open 2008, Open de France ALSTOM 2009, Barclays Scottish Open 2009, KLM Open 2010, Alfred Dunhill Links Championship 2010, Abu Dhabi HSBC Golf Championship 2011, WGC-HSBC Champions 2011, Nedbank Golf Challenge 2012, Players Championship 2014; results in major championships: tied for sixth at PGA Championship 2009, tied for eighth at US Open 2010, tied for seventh at British Open 2010, won PGA Championship 2010 (only the second German to win a major championship, after Bernhard Langer), won US Open 2014; mem. World Cup team representing Germany 2007, 2008, 2009, 2011, winning Ryder Cup team representing Europe 2010, 2012, 2014; ranked No. 1 in World (after his runner-up finish to Luke Donald at WGC-Accenture Match Play Championship) Feb.–April 2011; Sir Henry Cotton Rookie of the Year Award (first German) 2007, European Tour Players' Player of the Year for 2010. *Address:* c/o Sportyard AB, Sveavägen 166, 21st Floor, 113 46 Stockholm, Sweden (office). *Telephone:* (8) 410-269-40 (office). *Fax:* (8) 34-87-62 (office). *E-mail:* info@sportyard.com (office); presse@martinkaymer.com. *Website:* www.sportyard.com (office); www.martinkaymer.com.

KAYODE, Prince Adetokunbo Adeyinka, LLB, FCIA; Nigerian lawyer and politician; b. 31 Oct. 1958, Ikare-Akoko, Ondo State; m. Funmilayo Kayode; two s. two d.; ed Polytechnic, Ibadan, Univ. of Lagos, Chartered Inst. of Arbitration, Univ. of Oxford, UK; called to Nigerian Bar 1982; f. Kayode & Co. (legal practice) 1990; fmr Minister of Justice and Attorney-Gen.; Minister of Culture and Tourism 2007, of Labour and Productivity 2007–10, of Defence 2010–11; mem. Nigerian Bar Asscn, Chair. Abuja Br. 1988–90, mem. Nat. Exec. Cttee and Third Nat. Vice-Pres., Chair. Human Rights Cttee; fmr mem. Fed. Judicial Service Comm.; mem. numerous int. asscns including Maritime Arbitrators Asscn of Nigeria, Commonwealth Lawyers Asscn, Swiss Arbitration Asscn, London Court of Int. Arbitration, Abuja Arbitration Forum, Centre for Sports Arbitration; mem. People's Democratic Party; Sr Advocate of Nigeria (SAN).

KAZAKBAYEV, Ruslan Aitbaevich; Kyrgyzstani diplomatist and politician; b. 18 May 1967, Beisheke village, Talas Oblast, Kyrgyz SSR, USSR; ed Frunze Polytechnical Inst., Frunze (now Bishkek), Faculty of Law, Jusup Balasagyn Kyrgyz Nat. Inst., Diplomatic Acad. of the Ministry of Foreign Affairs of the Kyrgyz Repub.; Acad. of Sciences of the Kyrgyz Repub. 1992–94; joined Foreign Service, Ministry of Foreign Affairs 1995, Third Sec., then Second Sec., Consular Dept 1995–96, Vice-Consul, Consulate-Gen., Istanbul 1996–99, returned to Bishkek and served in several positions including Adviser, Head of Dept and Deputy Chief, Consular Dept 1999–2005, Consul-Gen. in Istanbul 2005–09, First Deputy Minister of Foreign Affairs 2009, Minister of Foreign Affairs 2010–12; rank of Amb. 2007; Hon. Prof., I. Razzakov Kyrgyz Tech. Univ. 2003, M. Kashgari Kyrgyz-Kuwaiti Univ. 2008; Diploma, Govt of the Kyrgyz Repub. 2005, 2007. *Address:* c/o Ministry of Foreign Affairs, 720040 Bishkek, bul. Erkindik 57, Kyrgyzstan. *E-mail:* gendep@mfa.gov.kg.

KAZAMIAS, Kikis, MEcons; Cypriot economist and politician; b. 27 Aug. 1951, Lefkonoiko, Famagusta Dist; m. Rodoula Koliandri; three c.; ed Hochschule für Ökonomie, Berlin; has held numerous exec. positions in various cos, including import man. 1977–84, man. of family co. 1984–97, Dir-Gen. Co-Operative Consumer Soc. of Limassol 1997–2003, Pres. Investment Group of the Co-Operative Consumer Socs 'Lefkoniko' 1999–2003; mem. House of Reps (Progressive Party of the Working People—AKEL) 1991, re-elected 1996, mem. Financial and Budgetary Parl. Cttee 1991–2001, Communications and Public Works Cttee 1991–94, Jt Cttee of Cyprus Parl. with EU 1996–2001; elected mem. AKEL Cen. Cttee; elected Mayor of Famagusta 2001, also First Vice-Pres. Union of Cyprus Municipalities; Minister of Communications and Works 2003–04 (resgnd); mem. European Court of Auditors 2004–10; Minister of Finance 2011–12.

KAZANNIK, Aleksei Ivanovich, DIur; Russian lawyer; b. 26 July 1941, Perepis, Chernigov Region; m.; two s.; ed Irkutsk Univ.; teacher, Irkutsk Univ. 1975–79; Prof., Head of Chair, Omsk Univ. 1979–89, 1994–; forbidden to give public lectures because of criticism of Soviet invasion of Afghanistan; USSR People's Deputy 1989–91; fmr mem. USSR Supreme Soviet; active participant Movt Democratic Russia; mem. Interregional Group of Deputies; mem. Cttee on ecology problems and rational use of natural resources, USSR Supreme Soviet; mem. Pres.'s Council 1993–94; Prosecutor-Gen. of Russia 1993–94 (resgnd); Founder and Chair. Party of People's Conscience 1995; Chair. Cttee on problems of nationalities, religions and public orgs of Omsk Region 1996; Deputy Gov. Omsk Region 1999. *Publications:* legal aspects of regional problems of nature preservation, numerous articles on ecology, law, pamphlets.

KAZANTSEV, Col-Gen. Victor Germanovich; Russian army officer; b. 22 Feb. 1946, Kokhanovo, Vitebsk Region, Belarus; m. Tamara Valentinovna Kazantseva; ed Leningrad Higher School of Gen. Army, M. Frunze Mil. Acad., Mil. Acad. of Gen. Staff; officer in Caucasian, Middle-Asian, Turkestan, Baikal Mil. Commands, Cen. Army Group in Czechoslovakia, First Deputy Commdr of Army N Caucasian Mil. Command; Chief of Staff to Commdr of troops N Caucasian Mil. Command 1996–97, Commdr 1997–99; Commdr group of Fed. forces in N Caucasus 1999–2000; Rep. of Pres. to S Fed. Dist 2000–04; Order of the Red Star, Order for Service to Homeland in Armed Forces of the USSR, 2nd and 3rd class, Order of Military Merit; Dr hc (Rostov State Univ. of Civil Eng), (Novorissisk Sea Acad.); Hero of Russia for operations in Dagestan and Chechnya 1999, Golden Hon. Sign of Public Recognition 2002, St Andrey Int. Prize 2003, Medal for Battle Merit.

KAZHEGELDIN, Akezhan Magzhan-Uly; Kazakhstani economist and politician; b. 27 March 1952, Georgiyevka, Semipalatinsk Region; m. Bykova Natalia Kazhegeldina; one s. one d.; ed Kazakh State Univ., Moscow Inst. of Oriental Studies; Chair. Regional Exec. Cttee of Semipalatinsk 1983; Dir Ore-enriching Factory, Deputy Gov. Admin. of Semipalatinsk Region 1991–94; Pres. Kazakhstan Union of Industrialists and Entrepreneurs 1992–; apptd First Deputy Prime Minister of Kazakhstan 1994, Prime Minister 1994–97; Adviser to Pres. Nazarbayev May–Oct. 1998; disbarred from presidential election in 1998; f. Republican People's Party of Kazakhstan 1998, Chair. Bd 1998–2001; mem. Politburo Bd United Democratic Party 2001; in opposition to Pres. Nazarbayev 1999, now lives abroad, sentenced to 10 years imprisonment in absentia 1999. *Publications include:* six books including Kazakhstan in the Conditions of Reforms, Problems of State Regulation in the Conditions of Socio-Economic Transformation, Socio-Economic Problems of Development of Kazakhstan in the Conditions of Reforms 1999, Opposition to Middle Ages 2000.

KAŽIMÍR, Peter; Slovak business executive, politician and central banker; *Governor, National Bank of Slovakia;* b. 28 June 1968, Košice, Czechoslovak Socialist Repub. (now Slovakia); ed Univ. of Economics, Bratislava; assistant tax adviser, Shubert and Partners 1993–95; mem. Bd of Dirs VIVANT a.s. 1995–2006, PARTA-GAS a.s. 1999–2006; Chair. Supervisory Bd Sceptrum a.s. Brno 1997–2006, Nat. Nuclear Fund 2006–10; mem. Supervisory Bd DDP Credit Suisse Life and Pensions 2001–06; State Sec., Ministry of Finance 2006–10; mem. Nat. Council of the Slovak Repub. 2010–12, Vice-Chair. Finance and Budget Cttee; Vice-Chair. Smer-Sociálna Demokracia (Direction-Social Democracy) 2010–; Deputy Prime Minister and Minister of Finance 2012–16, 2018, Acting Minister of the

Economy 2015, Minister of Finance 2016–18, 2018–19; Gov. Národná banka Slovenska (Nat. Bank of Slovakia—NBS) (central bank) 2019–. *Address:* Národná banka Slovenska, Imricha Karvaša 1, 813 25 Bratislava, Slovakia (office). *Telephone:* (2) 5787-1111 (office). *Fax:* (2) 5787-1100 (office). *E-mail:* info@nbs.sk (office). *Website:* www.nbs.sk (office).

KAZMIN, Andrei Ilyich, PhD; Russian banker; b. 25 June 1958, Moscow; m.; ed Moscow Inst. of Finance; Economist, State Bank of the USSR 1982–83; Asst Prof., then Deputy Dean Faculty of Credit, Moscow Inst. of Finance 1983–88; Sr Researcher USSR (now Russian) Acad. of Sciences 1988–91; Sr Research Fellow Alexander von Humboldt Foundation, Inst. for Int. Politics and Security, Ebenhausen, Germany 1991–93; training at Austrian Nat. Bank, Bundesbank, German Fed. Ministry of Finance and Inst. of German Research Centres 1991–93; Adviser to Minister of Finance 1993; Deputy Minister of Finance, Russian Fed. 1993–96; Chair. and CEO Sberbank (Savings Bank of Russian Fed.) 1996–2007; CEO Pochta Rossii (Russian Post) 2007–09; apptd Vice-Pres. World Savings Banks Inst. 2000; Dir-Gen. FSUE Russian Post 2007–09; mem. Int. Bd of Dirs Europay Int. 2002; mem. Supervisory Bd Vneshtorgbank, JSC Agency for Housing Mortgage Lending; mem. Asscn of Russian Banks, Russian Union of Industrialists and Entrepreneurs (RSPP), Bd of Trustees, Finance and Devt Foundation; Order of Honour 2002; Medal of Honour 2001, Banker of the Year 2008. *Publications:* more than 40 publs. *Leisure interests:* theatre, literature, sports.

KAZULIN, Alyaksandr, PhD; Belarusian mathematician, university rector and politician; b. 25 Nov. 1955, Minsk, Byelorussian SSR, USSR; m. Iryna Kazulina (died 2008); two d.; ed Belarusian State Univ.; mil. service in Soviet Navy as Marine 1974–76; Lecturer and Instructor, Youth Communist League (Komsomol); Dean, Belarusian State Univ. 1980–88, Rector 1996–2003; Dept Chief, then First Deputy Minister, Educ. Ministry 1988–96; Minister of Educ. 1998–2001; f. People's Will political movt 2005; joined Belarusian Social-Democratic Party, March 2005, elected Chair. Assembly (Hramada)—Belarusian Social-Democratic Party following merger of parties in April 2005; sentenced to five-and-a-half years' imprisonment on charges of hooliganism and inciting mass disorder July 2006, granted early release following pressure by US Govt 16 Aug. 2008.

KE, Bingsheng, BS, MA, PhD; Chinese agricultural economist and university administrator; *President, China Agricultural University;* ed Univ. of Hohenheim, Germany, Peking Univ., China Agric. Univ.; economist with Ministry of Agric., becoming Dir Centre for Rural Economy Studies 1997–2007; Prof., China Agricultural Univ., also fmr Deputy Dean, Grad. School, Dean Coll. of Econs and Man., Vice-Pres. China Agric. Univ., Pres. 2008–; adviser to Chinese Govt on agricultural policy issues. *Publications:* China's Grain Market and Policy 1995. *Address:* Office of the President, China Agricultural University, 17 Qinghua Donglu, Haidian District, Beijing 100083, People's Republic of China (office). *Telephone:* (10) 6273 6482 (office). *Fax:* (10) 6273 7704 (office). *E-mail:* cauie@cau.edu.cn (office). *Website:* www.cau.edu.cn (office).

KEACH, Stacy; American actor and director; b. (Walter Stacey Keach), 2 June 1941, Savannah, Ga; s. of Walter Edmund Keach and Dora Stacy; m. 1st Kathryn Baker 1964; m. 2nd Marilyn Aiken 1975; m. 3rd Jill Donahue 1981; m. Malgosia Tomassi 1986; one s. one d.; stage debut in Joseph Papp's production of Hamlet, Cen. Park 1964; other stage appearances include A Long Day's Journey into Night, Macbird (Vernon Rice Drama Desk Award), Indians, Deathtrap, Hughie, Barnum, Cyrano de Bergerac, Peer Gynt, Henry IV (Parts I & II), Idiot's Delight, The King and I 1989, Love Letters 1990–93, Richard III 1991, Stieglitz Loves O'Keefe 1995, King Lear; Dir Incident at Vichy and Six Characters in Search of an Author for TV; mem. Artists Cttee Kennedy Center Honors 1986–; Hon. Chair. American Cleft Palate Foundation 1995–; recipient of three Obie Awards, Pasadena Playhouse Alumni Man of the Year 1995, Pacific Pioneers Broadcasters' Asscn Diamond Circle Award 1996, Mary Pickford Award 2008, Lifetime Award (St Louis Film Festival) 2010, Prism Award, inducted into Theater Hall of Fame 2015. *Films include:* The Heart is a Lonely Hunter, End of the Road, The Travelling Executioner, Brewster McCloud, Doc, Judge Roy Bean, The New Centurions, Fat City, The Killer Inside Me, Conduct Unbecoming, Luther, Street People, The Squeeze, Gray Lady Down, The Ninth Configuration, The Long Riders, Road Games, Butterfly, Up in Smoke, Nice Dreams, That Championship Season, The Lover, False Identity, The Forgotten Milena, John Carpenter's Escape from LA 1996, Prey of the Jaguar 1996, The Truth Configuration 1998, American History X 1998, Icebreaker 1999, Unshackled 2000, Militia 2000, Mercy Streets 2000, Sunstorm 2001, When Eagles Strike 2003, Jesus, Mary and Joey 2003, Caught in the Headlights 2004, Galaxy Hunter 2004, El Padrino 2004, The Hollow 2004, Man with the Screaming Brain 2005, Keep Your Distance 2005, Come Early Morning 2006, Jesus, Mary and Joey 2006, Death Row 2006, W. 2008, Chicago Overcoat 2009, The Portal 2009, The Boxer 2009, The Bourne Legacy 2012, Nebraska 2013, Ooga Booga 2013, Planes 2013, Planes: Fire & Rescue 2014, Sin City: A Dame to Kill For 2014, If I Stay 2014, Truth 2015, Girlfriend's Day 2016, Gold 2016, Cell 2016. *Television includes:* Mike Hammer, Private Eye (series) 1997, The Courage to Love 2000, Titus (series) 2000, Lightning: Fire From the Sky 2001, Rods! (series) 2002, The Santa Trap 2002, Miracle Dogs 2003, Frozen Impact 2003, Desolation Canyon 2006, Fatal Contact: Bird Flu in America 2006, Washington the Warrior (voice, miniseries) 2006, Blackbeard (miniseries) 2006, Prison Break (series) 2005–07, American Greed 2007, The Pixar Story 2007, Lone Rider (film) 2008, Ring of Death (film) 2008, Meteor (film) 2009, The Nanny Express (film) 2009, Two and a Half Men (series) 2009, Lights Out (series) 2011, Bored to Death (series) 2011, Hindenburg (film) 2011, 30 Rock (series) 2012, Anything for Money (narrator) 2012, The Neighbours (series) 2012–13, Sean Saves the World (series) 2013, 1600 Penn (series) 2013, Anger Management (series) 2013, Brooklyn Nine-Nine (series) 2013, The Simpsons (series) 2015, Hot in Cleveland (series) 2015, NCIS: New Orleans (series) 2015, Crowded (series) 2016. *Plays include:* Hamlet, Henry 5, Coriolanus, Falstaff, Macbeth, Richard 3, King Lear. *Publication:* Keach, Go Home! 1996 (autobiog.). *Address:* c/o Diamond Management, 31 Percy Street, London, W1T 2DD, England (office). *Telephone:* (20) 7631-0400 (office). *Fax:* (20) 7631 0500 (office). *E-mail:* agents@diman.co.uk (office). *Website:* diamondmanagement.co.uk (office); www.gostacykeach.com.

KEAN, Thomas H., BA, MA; American academic administrator and fmr politician; *Chairman, THK Consulting, LLC;* b. 21 April 1935, New York; s. of Robert Kean and Elizabeth Howard Kean; m. Deborah Bye; two s. one d.; ed Princeton Univ., Columbia Univ. Teachers Coll.; fmr teacher of history and Govt; mem. New Jersey Ass. 1967–77, Speaker 1972, Minority Leader 1974; Acting Gov. of New Jersey 1973, Gov. 1982–90; Pres. Drew Univ., Madison, New Jersey 1990–2005 (retd); Founder and Chair. THK Consulting, LLC 2005–; Chair. Bd of Trustees, Carnegie Corpn of New York; Chair. Nat. Comm. on Terrorist Attacks upon the US (9-11 Comm.) 2002–04; Chair. Nat. Campaign to Prevent Teen and Unplanned Pregnancy; Co-Chair. Nat. Security Program, Bipartisan Policy Center, JerseyCAN (education advocacy group); Vice-Chair. National Committee on US–China Relations; fmr Chair. Educate America, Nat. Environmental Educ. and Training Foundation; Chair. President George H.W. Bush's reelection campaign 1992; mem. Bd of Dirs ARAMARK, Hess Corpn, Pepsi Bottling Group, Franklin Templeton Investments, Robert Wood Johnson Foundation, Nat. Council World Wildlife Fund, Environmental Defense Fund; regular columnist, The Star Ledger. *Publications include:* The Politics of Inclusion, Without Precedent: The Inside Story of the 9/11 Commission (with Lee H. Hamilton) 2006. *Address:* THK Consulting, LLC, 49 US Highway 202, Far Hills, NJ 07931, USA (office).

KEANEY, Thomas, BSc, MA, PhD; American defence analyst, research institute director and academic; *Associate Director of Strategic Studies, Senior Adjunct Professor and Executive Director, The Phillip Merrill Center for Strategic Studies, Johns Hopkins University School of Advanced International Studies;* b. 14 June 1940, Boston, Mass; ed USAF Acad., Colo, Univ. of Michigan; fmr Prof. of Mil. Strategy, Nat. War Coll.; several positions with USAF including Air Staff planner, Forward Air Controller, B-52 Squadron Commdr; Assoc. Prof. of History, USAF Acad.; Exec. Dir Foreign Policy Inst. 1998–2007; Assoc. Dir Strategic Studies, Sr Adjunct Prof. and Exec. Dir The Phillip Merrill Center for Strategic Studies, School of Advanced Int. Studies, Johns Hopkins Univ. 2004–. *Publications include:* Revolution in Warfare? Air Power in the Persian Gulf 1995, US Allies in a Changing World 2000, The Armed Forces in the Contemporary Middle East (co-ed.) 2001, War in Iraq, Planning and Execution (co-ed.) 2007, Understanding Counterinsurgency Warfare (co-ed.) 2010. *Address:* Merrill Center for Strategic Studies, School of Advanced International Studies, Johns Hopkins University, The Rome Building, 1619 Massachusetts Avenue NW, Washington, DC 20036, USA (office). *Telephone:* (703) 532-1803 (office); (202) 663-5774. *Fax:* (202) 663-5782 (office). *E-mail:* tkeaney@jhu.edu (office). *Website:* www.sais-jhu.edu/users/tkeaney1 (office).

KEARNEY, Gerardine (Ged), BEd; Australian nurse, trade union executive and politician; b. Richmond, Melbourne, Vic.; m.; four c.; registered nurse 1985, also served as nursing educator, including as Man. Clinical Nursing Educ. Dept at Austin Health; elected official with Australian Nursing Fed. 1997–2010, also served as Asst Fed. Sec., Fed. Pres. and Pres. Victorian Br., Fed. Sec. 2008–10; Pres. Australian Council of Trade Unions 2010–18; mem. (for Batman, Labor Party), House of Representatives 2018–; mem. Bd of Dirs HESTA Super Fund. *Address:* PO Box 6022, House of Representatives, Parliament House, Canberra, ACT 2600, Australia (office). *Telephone:* (2) 6277 4152 (office). *Fax:* (2) 6277 8559 (office). *E-mail:* info@cbr.alp.org.au (office). *Website:* www.alp.org.au (office).

KEAT CHHON, PhD; Cambodian politician; b. 11 Aug. 1934, Kratie Prov.; m. Lay Neari; one s. one d.; ed Charles Sturt Univ., Australia; naval architect, marine engineer and nuclear engineer; fmr Gov. Bank of Cambodia; mem. (Cambodian People's Party), Nat. Ass. of Cambodia for Phnom Penh 2003–; Minister of the Economy and Finance and Sr Minister in charge of Rehabilitation and Devt 1994–2013; Perm. Deputy Prime Minister of Cambodia 2008–16; Co-ordinator Working Group for Govt Pvt. Sector Forum; Vice-Chair. Council for the Devt of Cambodia; Co-founder and Vice-Chair. Cambodian Inst. for Co-operation and Peace, Phnom-Penh; Commdr, Légion d'honneur; Grand Cross, Order of Sowathara (Cambodia); Grand Cross, Order of Kingdom of Cambodia; Dr hc (Univ. of Cambodia) 2005. *Publications:* Cambodia's Economic Development: Policies, Strategies and Implementation 1999.

KEATING, Francis (Frank) Anthony, II, BA, JD; American lawyer and fmr politician; *President and CEO, American Bankers Association;* b. 10 Feb. 1944, St Louis, Mo.; s. of Anthony Francis Keating and Anne Martin; m. Catherine Dunn Heller 1972; one s. two d.; ed Georgetown Univ., Univ. of Oklahoma; called to the Bar, Okla 1969; Special Agent with FBI 1969–71; Asst Dist Attorney, Tulsa Co. 1971–72; mem. Okla House of Reps 1972–74, Okla Senate 1974–81; attorney, Northern Dist, Okla 1981–84; Asst Sec., US Treasury Dept, Washington, DC 1985–88, Assoc. Attorney-Gen., US Dept of Justice 1988–89, Gen. Counsel and Acting Deputy Sec., US Dept of Housing and Urban Devt 1989–93; attorney in pvt. practice, Tulsa 1993–95; Gov. of Okla 1995–2003; Pres. and CEO American Council of Life Insurers 2003–10; Pres. and CEO American Bankers Asscn 2011–; mem. Okla Bar Asscn; mem. Bd Dirs Nat. Archives Foundation, Mt Vernon; Pres. Fed. City Council, Jamestown Foundation, Bipartisan Policy Center; Dr hc (Marymount Univ.), (Groves Coll.), (Univ. of Tulsa), (LaRoche Coll.), (Regentes Univ.); Order of Malta, Fed. Asscn. *Publications include:* for children: Will Rogers (Spur Award, Western Writers of America 2003), Theodore (Int. Children's Book Award for Non-fiction 2007), The Trial of Standing Bear 2008, George: George Washington, Our Founding Father 2012. *Address:* American Bankers Association, 1120 Connecticut Avenue, NW, Washington, DC 20036, USA. *Website:* www.aba.com.

KEATING, Michael, BA, MA, PhD, FRSE, FBA, AcSS, MAE; Canadian/British/Irish political scientist and academic; *Chair in Scottish Politics, University of Aberdeen;* b. 2 Feb. 1950, Hartlepool, Cleveland, England; s. of Michael Joseph Keating and Margaret Watson Keating; m. Patricia Ann Keating; one s.; ed Univ. of Oxford, Council for Nat. Academic Awards, Inst. of Linguists; grad. student and part-time Lecturer in Politics and Econs, Glasgow Coll. of Tech. 1972–75; Sr Research Officer in Govt, Univ. of Essex 1975–76; Lecturer in Politics, North Staffordshire Polytechnic 1976–79; Sr Lecturer in Politics, Univ. of Strathclyde 1979–88; Prof. of Political Science, Univ. of Western Ontario, Canada 1988–99; Chair in Scottish Politics, Univ. of Aberdeen 1999–; Prof. of Political and Social Sciences, European Univ. Inst., Florence, Italy 2000–10, Head of Dept 2004–07; Visiting Prof. of Political Science, Virginia Polytechnic Inst. and State Univ., USA 1987–88, Univ. of Sunderland 1995–2000; Professorial Fellow, Econ. and Social Research Council (ESRC) 2010–13, ESRC Sr Fellow, Future of UK and Scotland programme 2013–14, Sr Fellow, ESRC UK in a Changing Europe programme 2015–16, currently Dir, ESRC Centre on Constitutional Change; Visiting Prof. of

Govt, Univ. of Strathclyde 1988–99; Visiting Prof., Institut d'Etudes Politiques, Paris 1991, Univ. of Santiago de Compostela, Spain 1992, Univ. of the Basque Country, Norwegian Nobel Inst.; Scholar in Residence, Rockefeller Foundation Center, Bellagio, Italy 1997; Norman Chester Sr Visiting Research Fellow, Nuffield Coll. Oxford 1998; Visiting Fellow, Schuman Centre, European Univ. Inst. 1999, McQuarie Univ., Sydney, Australia 2005; Founder and Co-Dir European Consortium for Political Research Standing Group on Regionalism; Jt Ed. Regional and Federal Studies; mem. Editorial Bd, Environment and Planning, Government and Policy, Space and Polity, Modern and Contemporary France, Spanish Cultural Studies, Regional Studies, Politique et Sociétés. *Publications include:* State and Regional Nationalism 1988, Comparative Urban Politics: Power and the City in the United States, Canada, Britain and France 1991, The Politics of Modern Europe: The State and Political Authority in the Major Democracies 1993, The European Union and the Regions (co-ed.) 1995, Nations Against the State: The New Politics of Nationalism in Quebec, Catalonia and Scotland 1996, The New Regionalism in Western Europe 1998, Paradiplomacy in Action 1999, The Government of Scotland 2005, Methodologies and Approaches in the Social Sciences (co-ed.) 2008, The Independence of Scotland 2009, Small Nations in a Big World 2014, The Crisis of Social Democracy in Europe (co-ed.) 2014, Small States in the Modern World (co-ed.) 2015. *Address:* School of Social Sciences, University of Aberdeen, Dunbar Street, Aberdeen, AB24 3EN, Scotland (office). *Telephone:* (1224) 272770 (office); (131) 556-0962 (office); 7758-329876 (mobile); (1224) 272726 (office). *Fax:* (1224) 272552 (office). *E-mail:* m.keating@abdn.ac.uk (office). *Website:* www.abdn.ac.uk/socsci (office).

KEATING, Michael, MA; British UN official; *Special Representative of the Secretary-General and Head, Assistance Mission in Somalia, United Nations;* b. 1959, Kampala, Uganda; m.; four c.; ed Univ. of Cambridge; long career with UN, including as Adviser to UN Humanitarian Coordinator in Afghanistan, later Exec. Asst to UnderSec.-Gen. and Head of Peshawar Field Office, Pakistan 1997–99, Adviser to Admin., UNDP, New York 1999–2001, UN Resident Coordinator in Malawi, Dir of Socio-Economic Affairs in Sec.-Gen.'s Office for Middle East Peace Process (UNSCO), Jerusalem and Gaza, Dir of Devt and Special Adviser to Rep. of Sec.-Gen. for Afghanistan –2011, Sec.-Gen.'s Deputy Special Rep. for Afghanistan and Resident Coordinator and Humanitarian Coordinator 2011–12, Special Rep. of Sec.-Gen. and Head, UN Assistance Mission in Somalia (UNSOM) 2015–; Assoc. Dir, Research Partnerships, Chatham House, London 2012–; fmr Exec. Dir, Africa Progress Panel, Geneva. *Address:* UN Assistance Mission in Somalia (UNSOM), Mogadishu, Somalia (office). *Website:* unsom.unmissions.org (office).

KEATING, Hon. Paul John; Australian politician; b. 18 Jan. 1944, Sydney; s. of Matthew Keating and Min Keating; m. Anna Van Iersel 1975; one s. three d.; ed De La Salle Coll., Bankstown; Research Officer, Federated Municipal and Shire Council Employees' Union of Australia 1967; mem. House of Reps for Fed. Seat of Blaxland 1969–96; Minister for N Australia Oct.–Nov. 1975; Opposition Spokesman on Agric. Jan.–March 1976, on Minerals and Energy 1976–83, on Treasury Matters Jan.–March 1983; Fed. Treas. 1983–91; Leader, Australian Labor Party 1991–96; Deputy Prime Minister 1990–91, Prime Minister of Australia 1991–96; Hon. LLD (Keio Univ., Tokyo) 1995, (Nat. Univ. of Singapore) 1999, (Univ. NSW) 2003, Hon. DLit (Macquarie Univ.) 2012. *Publications include:* Engagement: Australia Faces the Asia Pacific 2000, After Words: The Post-Prime Ministerial Speeches 2011. *Leisure interests:* classical music, architecture, swimming, fine arts. *Address:* PO Box 1265, Potts Point, 1335 NSW, Australia. *Telephone:* (2) 9358 5466 (office). *Fax:* (2) 9358 5477 (office). *Website:* www.keating.org.au (office).

KEATING, Roland "Roly" Francis Kester; British broadcasting executive and library administrator; *Chief Executive, British Library;* b. 1961; joined BBC as trainee 1983, Series Ed. Bookmark 1992–97, Head of Programming for UKTV 1997–2001, Controller of Digital Channels 1999–2001, Controller of Arts Commissioning 2000–01, Controller of BBC 4 2001–04, of BBC 2 2004–08, Dir of Archive Content 2008–12; Chief Exec., British Library 2012–; BAFTA Award for Best Arts Programme (Bookmark) 1993, Broadcast Channel of the Year (BBC 2) 2007. *Address:* British Library, 96 Euston Rd, London, NW1 2DB, England (office). *Website:* www.bl.uk/ (office).

KEATING, Ronan; Irish singer, songwriter and actor; b. (Ronan Patrick John Keating), 3 March 1977, Dublin; s. of Gerry Keating and Marie Keating; m. 1st Yvonne Keating (divorced 2013); one s. two d.; m. 2nd Storm Uechtritz 2015; mem. Boyzone 1993–2001, 2007–; solo artist 1999–; UN Goodwill Amb. Marie Keating Foundation; BMI European Song Writing Award, Ivor Novello Award. *Play:* Once 2015. *Films:* (as actor) Postman Pat: The Movie 2014, Goddess 2014, Another Mother's Son 2016. *Television includes:* hosted Miss World Competition, Eurovision Song Contest and MTV Europe Awards; judge on X Factor in Australia for five seasons, now on The Voice Australia. *Recordings include:* albums: with Boyzone: Said and Done 1994, A Different Beat 1996, Where We Belong 1998, By Request 1999, Back Again... No Matter What 2008, Brother 2010, BZ20 2013, From Dublin to Detroit 2014, Thank You and Goodnight 2018; solo: Ronan 2000, Destination 2002, Turn It On 2003, Bring You Home 2006, Songs for My Mother 2009, Winter Songs 2009, Duet 2010, When Ronan Met Burt 2011, Time Of My Life 2016. *Publications include:* No Matter What 2000, Life is a Rollercoaster 2000. *Address:* c/o MP Music Services Ltd, 123 Winston Road, London, N16 9LL, England (office). *E-mail:* info@mpmusicservices.co.uk (office). *Website:* www.mpmusicservices.co.uk (office); boyzonenetwork.com (home); www.ronankeating.com (home).

KEATON, Diane; American actress; b. 5 Jan. 1946, Calif.; student Neighbourhood Playhouse, New York; New York stage appearances in Hair 1968, Play It Again Sam 1971, The Primary English Class 1976; f. Blue Relief Productions (film production co.). *Films include:* Lovers and Other Strangers 1970, Play It Again Sam 1972, The Godfather 1972, Sleeper 1973, The Godfather Part 2 1974, Love and Death 1975, I Will—I Will–For Now 1975, Harry and Walter Go To New York 1976, Annie Hall (Acad. Award for Best Actress and other awards) 1977, Looking for Mr. Goodbar 1977, Interiors 1978, Manhattan 1979, Reds 1981, Shoot the Moon 1982, Mrs Soffel 1985, Crimes of the Heart 1986, Trial and Error 1986, Radio Days 1987, Heaven (Dir) 1987, Baby Boom 1988, The Good Mother 1988, The Lemon Sisters 1989, Running Mates 1989, The Godfather III, Wildflower (Dir) 1992, Secret Society (Dir), Manhattan Murder Mystery 1993, Unsung Heroes (Dir) 1995, Father of the Bride 2 1995, Marvin's Room, The First Wives Club 1996, The Only Thrill 1997, The Other Sister 1999, Hanging Up (also Dir) 2000, Town and Country 2001, Plan B 2001, Sister Mary Explains It All 2001, Wildflower 2002, Something's Gotta Give (Golden Globe Award, Best Actress Musical or Comedy 2004) 2003, The Family Stone 2005, Because I Said So 2007, Mama's Boy 2007, Mad Money 2008, Morning Glory 2010, Darling Companion 2012, The Big Wedding 2013, And So It Goes 2014, 5 Flights Up 2014, Love the Coopers 2015, Hampstead 2017. *Publications:* Reservations, Still Life (Ed.), Then Again (autobiog.) 2011. *Address:* Blue Relief Productions, 301 North Canyon Drive, Suite 205, Beverly Hills, CA 90210; c/o The Gersh Agency, 232 North Canyon Drive, Suite 201, Beverly Hills, CA 90210, USA. *Telephone:* (310) 275-7900 (Blue Relief).

KEATON, Michael; American actor; b. 9 Sept. 1951, Pittsburgh, Pa; m. Caroline MacWilliams (divorced); one s.; ed Kent State Univ.; early work with comedy group, Second City, Los Angeles. *Films include:* Night Shift 1982, Mr Mom 1983, Johnny Dangerously 1984, Touch and Go 1986, Gung Ho 1986, The Squeeze 1987, Beetlejuice 1988, Clean and Sober 1988, The Dream Team 1989, Batman 1989, Pacific Heights 1990, One Good Cop 1991, Batman Returns 1992, Much Ado About Nothing 1992, My Life, The Paper 1994, Speechless 1994, Multiplicity 1996, Jackie Brown 1997, Desperate Measures 1998, Out of Sight 1998, Jack Frost 1999, Shot at Glory 2000, Quicksand 2001, First Daughter 2004, White Noise 2005, Game 6 2005, Herbie Fully Loaded 2005, Cars (voice) 2006, The Last Time 2006, The Merry Gentleman (also dir) 2009, Post Grad 2009, Toy Story 3 (voice) 2010, The Other Guys 2010, Noah (voice) 2012, Penthouse North 2013, RoboCop 2014, Need for Speed 2014, Birdman (Golden Globe for Best Actor in a Motion Picture (Musical or Comedy) 2015, Best Actor, Critics' Choice Movie Awards, Broadcast Film Critics Asscn 2015, Actor of the Year, London Critics' Circle 2015, Outstanding Performance by a Cast in a Motion Picture, Screen Actors Guild Awards 2015) 2014. *Television appearances include:* All in the Family, Maude, Mary Tyler Moore Show, Working Stiffs, Report to Murphy, Roosevelt and Truman (TV film), Body Shots (producer) 1999, Live from Baghdad 2002. *Address:* c/o ICM Management, 8942 Wilshire Blvd, Beverly Hills, CA 90211, USA (office).

KEAVENEY, Raymond, MA; Irish gallery director and art historian; b. 1947, Carlanstown, Co. Meath; ed Franciscan Coll., Gormanston, University Coll. Dublin; worked and studied abroad 1975–78; Curator, Nat. Gallery of Ireland, Dublin 1979–81, Asst Dir 1981–88, Dir 1988–2012; specializes in Italian art and Old Master drawings; Chevalier des Arts et Lettres 2007. *Publications:* Master European Drawings 1983, Views of Rome 1988, The National Gallery of Ireland: Essential Guide (co-author) 1999.

KEBICH, Vyacheslau Frantsavich; Belarusian politician; b. 10 June 1936, Konyushevshchina, Minsk Dist; s. of Frants Karlovich Kebich and Tatyana Vasilyevna Kebicha; m. Yelena Kebicha 1970; one s. one d.; ed Belarus Polytechnic Inst., Higher Party School; mem. CPSU 1962–91, Cen. Cttee 1980–91; engineer, man. in Minsk 1973–80; party official 1980–85; Deputy Chair. Council of Ministers, Chair. State Planning Cttee 1985–90; USSR People's Deputy 1989–91; Chair. Council of Ministers (Prime Minister) of Byelorussia (now Belarus) 1990–94; unsuccessful Presidential cand. 1994; Chair. Belarus Trade and Finance Union 1994; mem. Supreme Soviet (Parl.) 1980–96, MP 1996; Corresp. mem. Int. Eng Acad.; Belarus State Prize. *Leisure interest:* fishing.

KECHICHE, Abdellatif; Tunisian actor, screenwriter and director; b. 7 Dec. 1960, Tunis; stage acting debut in Sans titre by Garcia Lorca 1978; followed by Un balcon sur les Andes by Eduardo Manet, Nat. Odeon Theatre; film debut in Le thé à la menthe; directing debut with La faute à Voltaire 2000. *Films include:* as actor: Le thé à la menthe 1984, Les innocents (The Innocents) 1987, Bezness (Acting Prize, Festival du Film Francophone de Namur 1992, Acting Prize, Festival de Damas 1993) 1992, Un vampire au paradis (A Vampire in Paradise) 1992, La boîte magique (The Magic Box) 2002, Sorry, Haters 2005; as dir: La faute à Voltaire (Blame It on Voltaire) (Golden Lion, Venice Film Festival 2000, Distribution Prize, Munich Int Film Festival 2002) 2000, L'esquive (Special Jury Prize, Istanbul Int. Film Festival 2004, César Award for Best Film, Best Dir, Best Screenplay 2005) 2003, La Graine et le mulet (Couscous) (Special Jury Prize, Venice Film Festival 2007, César Award for Best Film, Best Dir, Best Screenplay 2008, Prix Louis Delluc) 2007, Black Venus 2010, Blue is the Warmest Colour (Palme d'Or, Cannes Film Festival 2013, British Independent Film Award for Best Int. Independent Film 2013) 2013.

KEDAH, HRH The Sultan of; Tuanku Sallehuddin ibni al-Marhum Sultan Badlishah; Malaysian; *Sultan of Kedah;* b. 30 April 1942, Alor Setar; s. of Sultan Badlishah Sultan Abdul Hamid Halim Shah and Sultanah Asma; half brother of Tuanku Haji Abdul Halim Mu'adzam Shah ibni al-Marhum Sultan Badlishah; m. Tengku Maliha Tengku Ariff 1965; two s.; ed Coll. of Mil. Eng, Pune, India, Mil. Acad. of India, Dehradun; commissioned as Second Lt in Royal Malay Regt 1963, rank of Lt 1964; stationed at 2nd Bn Royal Malay Regt, Pengkalan Chepa, Kota Bharu 1964; engaged in various operations along border with Thailand in Kelantan, Kedah and Perak; apptd mem. Kedah Council of Regency 2011, Chair. 2014–16; proclaimed Raja Muda (Heir to Throne of Kedah) 15 Dec. 2016; proclaimed Sultan of Kedah 12 Sept. 2017; Chancellor, Cyberjaya Univ. Coll. of Medical Sciences; Pres., Kedah Islamic Religous Council; Kt Grand Companion, Order of Loyalty to the Royal House of Kedah, State of Kedah Distinguished Service Star, Commdr, Order of Loyalty to the Crown of Malaysia, Commdr, Order of Mil. Service of Malaysia, Grand Master First Class, Royal Family Order of Johor. *Address:* Istana Anak Bukit, 05150 Alor Setar, Kedah, Malaysia (office).

KEDIKILWE, Ponatshego Honorius Kefaeng, MA; Botswana politician; b. 4 Aug. 1938, Sefhophe; ed Univ. of Connecticut, Syracuse Univ.; joined Govt 1970; Prin. Finance Officer, Finance Ministry 1974–76; Sec. for Financial Affairs 1976; Perm. Sec., Ministry of Works, Transport and Communications 1977–79; Dir Public Service Man., Office of the Pres. 1979–84; mem. Parl. for Mmadinare 1984–; Deputy Minister of Finance 1984; Minister of Presidential Affairs and Public Admin 1985–89, 1994–98, of Commerce and Industry 1989–94, of Finance and Devt Planning 1998, of Educ. 1999–2000, of Minerals, Energy and Water Resources 2007–12; Vice-Pres. of Botswana 2012–14; fmr Chair. Botswana Democratic Party; Chair. Sefalana Holdings 2014–; Presidential Order of Honour 1992. *Leisure interests:* soccer, ranching, debating, gardening, speech writing, traditional music, folklore and poetry. *Address:* Office of the President, Private Bag 001, Gaborone, Botswana (office). *Telephone:* 3950800 (office); 3950910 (office). *Fax:* 3950858 (office). *E-mail:* op.registry@gov.bw (office); soefile@gov.bw (office).

Website: www.gov.bw/en/Ministries--Authorities/Ministries/State-President/Office-of-the-President (office).

KEEFFE, Barrie Colin Noel; British dramatist, novelist, director and university tutor; *Patron, Writing for Performance, Ruskin College, Oxford;* b. 31 Oct. 1945, London; s. of Edward Thomas Keeffe and Constance Beatrice Keeffe (née Marsh); m. 1st Sarah Dee (Truman) 1969 (divorced 1975); m. 2nd Verity Eileen Bargate 1981 (died 1981); two step-s.; m. 3rd Julia Lindsay 1983 (divorced 1991); m. 4th Jacky Stoller 2013; ed East Ham Grammar School, West Ham Coll., Nat. Council for Training of Journalists; fmr actor with Nat. Youth Theatre; has written plays for theatre, TV and radio; fmr Resident Writer, Shaw Theatre, London, RSC; Assoc. Writer, Theatre Royal, Stratford East, also mem. Bd; Assoc. Soho Theatre Co.; Writers' Mentor, Nat. Theatre 1999–2002; Tutor, City Univ., London 2001–05; Bye-Fellow, Christ's Coll., Cambridge 2003; Resident Writer, Kingston Univ. 2010–12; Patron Writing for Performance, Ruskin Coll., Oxford 2010–; tutor, Collaldra School and Writers' Retreat, Venice, Italy; UN Amb., 50th Anniversary Year 1995; Dir Newbell Production Ltd 2012–; mem. Soc. des auteurs et compositeurs dramatiques; Hon. DLitt (Warwick) 2010; French Critics' Prix Révélation 1978, Thames TV Playwright Award 1979, Giles Cooper Award Best Radio Plays, Mystery Writers of America Edgar Allan Poe Award 1982. *Theatre plays include:* Only a Game 1973, A Sight of Glory 1975, Scribes 1975, Here Comes the Sun 1976, Gimme Shelter 1977, A Mad World My Masters 1977, Barbarians 1977, Frozen Assets 1978, Sus 1979, Heaven Scent 1979, Bastard Angel 1980, She's So Modern 1980, Black Lear 1980, Chorus Girls 1981, Better Times 1985, King of England 1988, My Girl 1989, Not Fade Away 1990, Wild Justice 1990, I Only Want to Be With You 1995, Shadows on The Sun 2001, Still Killing Time 2005. *Plays directed include:* A Certain Vincent, A Gentle Spirit, Talking of Chekov (Amsterdam and London), My Girl (London and Bombay), The Gary Oldman Fan Club (London). *Film:* The Long Good Friday (screenplay) 1980, Sus (screenplay) 2010. *Television plays include:* Substitute 1972, Not Quite Cricket 1977, Gotcha 1977, Nipper 1977, Champions 1978, Hanging Around 1978, Waterloo Sunset 1979, No Excuses (series) 1983, King 1984. *Radio plays include:* Good Old Uncle Jack 1975, Pigeon Skyline 1975, Self-Portrait 1977, Paradise 1990, On the Eve of the Millennium 1999, Tales 2000, Feng Shui and Me 2000, The Five of Us 2002. *Television:* Substitute, Gotcha, Not Quite Cricket, Hanging Around, Champions, Nipper, Waterloo Sunset, King, No Excuses (series). *Publications:* novels: Gadabout 1969, No Excuses 1983; screenplay: The Long Good Friday 1998; Barrie Keeffe Plays I 2001. *Leisure interests:* playing tennis, watching soccer. *Address:* c/o The Agency, 24 Pottery Lane, Holland Park, London, W11 4LZ, England (office); 33 Brookfield, Highgate West Hill, London, N6 6AT, England (home). *Telephone:* (20) 7727-1346 (office); (20) 8340-9309 (office). *Fax:* (20) 8340-9309 (office). *E-mail:* barriekeeffe@aol.com (office).

KEEGAN, Kevin Joseph, OBE; British professional football manager, business executive and fmr professional footballer; b. 14 Feb. 1951, Armthorpe, Doncaster; s. of Joseph Keegan; m. Jean Woodhouse 1974; two s.; forward; youth player for Enfield House YC, Scunthorpe United 1967–68; sr player for Scunthorpe United 1968–71, Liverpool 1971–77 (won League Championship 1972/73, 1975/76, 1976/77, FA Cup 1974, European Cup 1977, UEFA Cup 1973, 1976, FA Charity Shield 1974, 1976), SV Hamburg 1977–80 (Bundesliga 1978/79), Southampton 1980–82, Newcastle United (also Capt.) 1982–84 (won Kirin Cup 1983; retd); scored 274 goals in approx. 800 appearances; capped for England 63 times (31 as Capt.), scoring 21 goals 1972–82, Capt. 1976–82; Man. Newcastle United 1992–97 (won Football League First Div. 1992/93), 2008, Fulham 1998–99 (won Football League Second Div. 1998/99), Manchester City 2001–05 (won Football League First Div. 2001/02); Man. England nat. team 1999–2000; f. Soccer Circus (interactive football training games), Glasgow 2006, Sokka (training system) 2013; Footballer of the Year 1976, European Footballer of the Year 1978, 1979, Southampton FC Player of the Season 1981/82, inducted into inaugural English Football Hall of Fame 2002, named eighth on Liverpool FC list of 100 Players who shook the Kop, Football Writers' Asscn Footballer of the Year 1976, Professional Footballers' Asscn Players' Player of the Year 1982, Premier League Man. of the Month Nov. 1993, Aug. 1994, Feb. 1995, Aug. 1995, Sept. 1995. *Publications include:* Kevin Keegan 1978, Against the World: Playing for England 1979, Kevin Keegan: My Autobiography 1997. *Website:* www.soccercircus.com; www.sokka.co.uk.

KEEGAN, Robert (Bob) J., BS, MBA; American business executive; *Operating Partner, Friedman Fleischer & Lowe;* b. 27 July 1947, New York; m. Lynn Keegan; two c.; ed LeMoyne Coll., Univ. of Rochester; joined Eastman Kodak Co. 1972, held various man. positions in Distribution and Marketing Depts, Rochester, NY, Gen. Man. Kodak NZ 1986–87, Dir of Finance, Rochester 1987–90, Gen. Man. Kodak Spain 1990–91, Gen. Man. of Consumer Imaging, Kodak Europe, Middle E and Africa 1991–93, Corp. Vice-Pres. 1993–95, Pres. Kodak Professional and Corp. Vice-Pres. July–Oct. 1997, Pres. of Consumer Imaging and Sr Vice-Pres. 1997–2000, Exec. Vice-Pres. 2000–03; Exec. Vice-Pres. and Global Strategy Officer, Avery Dennison Corpn 1995–97; mem. Bd of Dirs and COO Goodyear Tire & Rubber Co. 2000–02, Pres. and CEO Jan. 2003–April 2010, Chair. July 2003–Oct. 2010; currently Operating Partner, Friedman Fleischer & Lowe; Chair. Transtar Holdings; mem. Bd of Dirs Xerox Corpn 2010–; mem. Bd of Trustees Univ. of Rochester, mem. Exec. Advisory Cttee, Simon Graduate School of Business. *Address:* Friedman Fleischer & Lowe, One Maritime Plaza, 22nd Floor, San Francisco, CA 94111, USA (office). *Telephone:* (415) 402-2100 (office). *Fax:* (415) 402-2111 (office). *Website:* www.fflpartners.com (office).

KEEL, Alton G., Jr, BS, PhD; American diplomatist, civil servant, engineer, banker and business executive; *Chairman and Managing Director, Atlantic Partners, LLC;* b. 8 Sept. 1943, Newport News, Va; s. of Alton G. Keel and Ella Kennedy; m. 1st Franmarie Kennedy-Keel 1982 (divorced); one d.; m. 2nd Lynn Matti Keel (divorced); ed Univ. of Virginia, Univ. of California, Berkeley, postdoctoral studies; Facility Man. Naval Weapons Center 1971–77; Sr Official Senate Armed Services Cttee, US Senate 1977–81; Asst Sec., US Air Force for Research, Devt and Logistics, The Pentagon, Washington, DC 1981–82; Assoc. Dir Nat. Security and Int. Affairs, Exec. Office of the Pres. 1982–86; Exec. Dir and Pres. Comm. on Space Shuttle Challenger Accident 1986; Acting Asst to the Pres. for Nat. Security Affairs 1986; Amb. and Perm. Rep. to NATO 1987–89; Pres. and Man. Dir Carlyle International, The Carlyle Group 1992–94; Chair. Carlyle SEAG 1994–95, Chair. and Man. Dir Atlantic Partners, LLC (pvt. investment group), Washington, DC 1992–; Chair. and CEO Land-5 Corpn 1999–2002; mem. Dean's Advisory Bd, Univ. of Virginia 1996–2006, Trustee, Eng School 2009–; CEO InoStor Corpn 2002–05; mem. Bd and Exec. Cttee Piedmont Environmental Council 2004–; Sec. Piedmont Environmental Council 2011–; Nat. Congressional Science Fellow, AIAA 1977; Young Scientist Award 1976, Air Force Decoration for Exceptional Civilian Service 1982, NASA Group Achievement Award 1987, Distinguished Alumnus Award, Univ. of Virginia 1987. *Publications:* numerous scientific and tech. articles, foreign policy and nat. security publs. *Leisure interests:* running, golf, sailing, physical fitness. *Address:* Fairhill Farm, 2891 South River Road, Stanardsville, VA 22973, USA. *Telephone:* (434) 990-9501. *Fax:* (434) 990-9503. *E-mail:* fairhillfarm@fairhillfarmusa.com. *Website:* www.fairhillfarmusa.com.

KÉFI, Muhammad Mouldi; Tunisian diplomatist (retd) and politician; b. 10 Feb. 1946, Kef; m.; four c.; ed Univ. of Strasbourg, France; joined Ministry of Foreign Affairs 1967, has held numerous positions including Head of Central and S America Dept 1978, Head of Diplomatic Protocol Dept 1980, Deputy Dir American Dept 1989, Chef de Cabinet to Minister of Foreign Affairs 1994, Special Adviser to Cabinet of Minister of Foreign Affairs 1999, Dir-Gen. of Political Affairs and Cooperation for Americas and Asia Dept 2006, diplomatic attachments at embassies in Prague, London and Berlin, Amb. to Nigeria 1990–94, to Russia 1996–99, to Indonesia 2002–05; Minister of Foreign Affairs Feb.–Dec. 2011.

KEHOE, Paul, TD; Irish politician; *Minister of State at Departments of the Taoiseach and Defence with Special Responsibility for Defence;* b. 11 Jan. 1973; s. of Myles Kehoe and Bernadette Kehoe; m. Brigid O'Connor; three c.; ed Kildalton Agricultural Coll.; Teachta Dála (MP) for Wexford 2002–; apptd Fine Gael spokesperson for Communications, Marine and Environment 2002, also Fine Gael Chief Whip 2004, Govt Chief Whip 2011–16; Minister of State at Dept of Defence 2011–16, Minister of State at Depts of the Taoiseach and Defence with Special Responsibility for Defence 2016–. *Address:* Department of Defence, Station Road, Newbridge, Co Kildare, Ireland (office). *Telephone:* (45) 492000 (office). *Fax:* (45) 492017 (office). *E-mail:* info@defence.ie (office). *Website:* www.defence.ie (office); www.paulkehoe.com.

KEIB, Abdurrahim Abdulhafiz al-, BS (Hons), MS, PhD; Libyan politician, electrical engineer and academic; b. 1950, Sabratha, British Admin of Tripolitania; ed Univ. of Tripoli, Univ. of Southern California and North Carolina State Univ., USA; Asst Prof. of Electrical Eng, Univ. of Alabama, USA 1985–96, Prof. of Electrical Eng 1996–2011; also taught at Univ. of Tripoli, North Carolina State Univ., American Univ. of Sharjah, UAE 1999–2001, Petroleum Inst., UAE (Chair. Electrical Eng Dept) 2007–09; Dir Div. of Electrical, Electronics, and Computer Eng, American Univ. of Sharjah 1999–2001; Interim Prime Minister of Libya 2011–12; work on Emissions Constrained Dispatch and VoltIVar compensation on primary distribution feeders has been implemented by several cos in USA; consultant to several industries, including Alabama Power Co. and Southern Co. Services; experienced with ABET (fmrly Accreditation Bd for Eng and Tech.) accreditation and curriculum design, trained to serve as an ABET evaluator, served as Chair. of Assessment Cttee, Univ. of Alabama; mem. Bd of Dirs Arab Science and Tech. Foundation 2001–07; mem. Science and Tech. Panel, Islamic Development Bank; Assoc. Ed. IEEE/PES Power Engineering Letters 1992–2000, World Science and Engineering Academy and Society Transactions on Power Systems; mem. Editorial Advisory Bd Korean Inst. of Electrical Engineers/Soc. of Power Eng, Advisory Bd International Journal of Innovations in Energy Systems and Power; Sr mem. IEEE; NSF Eng Research Initiation Award 1989–90, T. Morris Hackney Endowed Faculty Leadership Award, Coll. of Eng, Univ. of Alabama 1997, 1998, Excellence in Service Award, American Univ. of Sharjah 2001, Outstanding Electrical and Computer Eng Instructor Award, Univ. of Alabama 1999, Certificate of Appreciation, Pres. of IEEE/PES issued by Energy Devt and Power Generation Cttee of IEEE Power and Energy Soc. 2009, Outstanding Engineer of the Year Award, IEEE/PES UAE Chapter 2009. *Publications:* one book chapter and numerous papers and research reports in scientific and engineering journals on power system economics, planning, operation and control. *Address:* c/o Executive Board, National Transitional Council, Tripoli, Libya (office). *E-mail:* info@ntc.gov.ly (office). *Website:* www.ntc.gov.ly (office).

KEILLOR, Garrison Edward, BA; American author and broadcaster; b. (Gary Edward Keillor), 7 Aug. 1942, Anoka, Minn.; s. of John P. Keillor and Grace R. Keillor (née Denham); m. 1st Mary Guntzel (divorced 1976, died 1998); one s.; m. 2nd Ulla Skaerved (divorced); m. 3rd Jenny Lind Nilsson; one d.; ed Anoka High School and Univ. of Minnesota; journalist 1962–63; radio announcer and presenter 1969–73; creator and host, A Prairie Home Companion radio show 1974–87, 1993–2016; host, American Radio Co. 1989–93; staff writer, The New Yorker 1987–92; George Foster Peabody Award 1980, Ace Award for best musical host (A Prairie Home Companion) 1988, Best Music and Entertainment Host Awards 1988, 1989, American Acad. and Institute of Arts and Letters Medal 1990, Music Broadcast Communications Radio Hall of Fame 1994, Nat. Humanities Medal 1999, John Steinbeck Award 2007. *Film:* A Prairie Home Companion 2006. *Publications:* Happy to Be Here 1982, Lake Wobegon Days (Grammy Award for best non-musical recording 1987) 1985, Leaving Home 1987, We Are Still Married: Stories and Letters 1989, WLT: A Radio Romance 1991, Wobegon Boy The Book of Guys 1993, Cat, You Better Come Home (children's book) 1995, The Old Man Who Loved Cheese 1996, The Sandy Bottom Orchestra 1996, Wobegon Boy 1997, ME by Jimmy (Big Boy) Valente as told to Garrison Keillor 1999, Lake Wobegon Summer 1956 2001, Love Me 2004, Pontoon 2007, Liberty: A Lake Wobegon Novel 2008, Pilgrims: A Lake Wobegon Romance 2010, Good Poems, American Places 2011, Guy Noir and the Straight Skinny 2012, O, What a Luxury 2013, The Keillor Reader 2014; contrib. to newspapers and magazines. *Website:* www.garrisonkeillor.com.

KEINÄNEN, Eino, MPolSc; Finnish business executive and fmr civil servant; b. 17 Nov. 1939; ed Univ. of Helsinki; credit official, Kansallis-Osake-Pankki 1962–64; Head of Section, Finnish State Computer Centre and Planning Organ for State Accounting 1965–68; various posts, Budget Dept, Ministry of Finance 1969–85, Head Budget Dept 1985–87, Perm. Under-Sec. 1987–89, Perm. State Sec. 1989–95; Gen. Man. and mem. Bd Postipankki Ltd 1995–96, Chair. and Chief Exec. 1996–2000; Chair. Leonia Plc 1997–2000; fmr Chair. State Pension Fund;

mem. Bd of Dirs Finnish State Treasury 1985–89, Finnish Tourist Bd 1985–89, Finnish Foreign Trade Asscn 1985–89, Cen. Statistical Office of Finland 1985–89; mem. Investment Fund of Finland 1985–89; Vice-Pres. Supervisory Bd Finnish Export Credit Ltd 1987, Finnish Fund for Industrial Devt Co-operation Ltd (Finnfund) 1994; Pres. Bd of Dirs State Computer Centre 1988; mem. Supervisory Bd Slot Machine Asscn 1989, Regional Devt Fund of Finland Ltd 1989, Finnish Grain Bd 1989; mem. Bd of Admin Alko Ltd 1989; Pres. Supervisory Bd Finnish Ice-Hockey Asscn 1989.

KEINO, Kipchoge A. (Kip); Kenyan athlete (retd); b. 17 Jan. 1940, Kipsamo; m. Phyllis Keino; fmr physical training instructor in police force; began int. running career in 1962; set two world records at 3000m and 5000m 1964; winner 1500m and 5000m, African Games 1964, 1965; winner one mile and three miles, Commonwealth Games 1966; gold medallist 1500m, silver medallist 5000m, Olympic Games, Mexico City 1968; gold medallist 3000m steeplechase, silver medallist 1500m, Olympic Games, Munich 1972; retd from int. running 1973; Pres. Kenyan Olympic Cttee; mem. IOC; helped establish high-altitude training as a technique to improve running time at any altitude; helped coach Kenyan track-and-field teams; ran in London Marathon for Oxfam 2002; f. Kip Keino Foundation, acquired a farm in Kenya (with wife Phyllis), est. Kip Keino School and orphanage on farm land; apptd by Athletics Kenya to lead investigation into country's poor performance at World Championships 2003 and to find a new head coach for Kenya's Olympic team Sept. 2003–; Hon. DJur (Univ. of Bristol) 2007; Dr hc (Egerton Univ., Nakuru); Freedom of the City of Bristol 2012, Olympic Laurel 2016, Laureus World Sports Acad. 'Sport for Good' Award. *Address:* Kip Keino School, Eldoret, Kenya; Kip Keino Foundation Inc., 14 Redwood Lane, B-101, Ithaca, NY 14850, USA. *Website:* www.kipkeinotraining.org.

KEIRA, Alpha Ibrahima; Guinean diplomatist and politician; *Minister of Security and Civil Protection;* ed Ecole Nationale d'Admin de Rabat, Morocco; Diplomat of Ministry of Foreign Affairs 2014–18, Minister of Security and Civil Protection 2018–; mem. Rassemblement du Peuple de Guinée (RPG). *Address:* Ministry of Security and Civil Protection, Coléah-Domino, Conakry, Guinea (office). *Telephone:* 300-41-45-50 (office).

KEÏTA, Ibrahim Boubacar, (IBK), DEA, MA; Malian politician and head of state; *President;* b. 29 Jan. 1945, Koutiala; m. Aminata Maiga; ed Lycée Janson-de-Sailly, Paris, Lycée Askia-Mohamed, Bamako, Univ. of Dakar, Univ. of Paris 1, Institut d'Histoire des Relations Internationales Contemporaines; led research at CNRS following graduation; taught Third World political systems at Univ. of Paris 1; returned to Mali 1986; Prin. Tech. Adviser to EU for European Devt Fund, then within Terre des Hommes France (Dir for West Africa) mid-1980s; mem. Asscn of African Students in France; Sec.-Gen. Comité de Défense des Libertés Démocratiques au Mali, Paris; underground participant in Malian democratic movt from 1986, helped bring about the 1991 revolution, ending 23 years of dictatorship; Founder-mem. Alliance pour la démocratie au Mali (Adema), Pres. 1994–2000; Deputy Campaign Dir for Alpha Oumar Konare who was elected Pres. 1992; Spokesman and Diplomatic Adviser to Pres. Konare 1992; Amb. to Côte d'Ivoire 1993 (also accred to Niger and Gabon); Minister of Foreign Affairs 1993–94; Prime Minister of Mali 1994–2000; left Adema following disagreements within the party 2000; Founder and Pres. Rassemblement pour le Mali party 2001–; unsuccessful cand. in presidential elections 2002, 2007, 2012 (elections not held because of coup d'état); Pres. of Mali 2013–; mem. Assemblée nationale 2002–, Pres. 2002–07; Vice-Pres. Socialist International; also presided over the African Parl. Union; Commdr de la Légion d'honneur, Grand Officier, Ordre Nat. du Mali. *Leisure interest:* reading. *Address:* Office of the President, BP 1463, Koulouba, Bamako, Mali (office). *Telephone:* 2022-2572 (office). *Fax:* 2023-0026 (office). *Website:* www.koulouba.pr.ml (office).

KEITA, Modibo, DScS; Malian academic, psychologist and government official; b. 13 Jan. 1953, Bamako; m.; three s.; ed Tübingen Univ., Germany; Prof. of Higher Educ., École normale supérieure de Bamako 1984–86; Founder and Man. Dir Cabinet d'Etudes pour l'Education et le Développement 1987– (renamed Cabinet d'Etudes Keita-Kala Saba 1997); Dir Boutique de Gestion, d'Echanges et de Conseils – Promotion de l'Artisanat 1993–94; Co-ordinator of Urban Waste Expertise Programme in W Africa 1996–, Making Decentralization Work/Mali 2001; Prime Minister March–June 2002, 2015–17. *Publications:* numerous articles in magazines. *Leisure interests:* art, culture, sport.

KEITA, Salif; Malian singer; b. 25 Aug. 1949, Djoliba; began musical career in Bamako 1967; joined govt-sponsored group Super Rail Band; moved to Paris to begin solo career as a singer 1984; annual European tour including summer festivals; Founder-Chair. Salif Keita Global Foundation; retd 2018; Chevalier, Ordre des Arts et des Lettres, Chevalier, Order of the Nation (Mali), Nat. Order of Guinea 1977, Commdr, Nat. Order of Merit (Tunisia) 2014, Chevalier, Ordre Nat. du Mali 2018; Grammy Award. *Recordings include:* albums: Soro 1987, Ko-Yan 1989, Destiny of a Noble Outcast 1991, Amen 1991, L'Enfant Lion 1992, Mansa of Mali 1994, Folon 1995, Rail Band 1996, Seydou Bathili 1997, Papa 1999, Sosie 2001, Compilation 1969–80 2001, Moffou 2002, Salif Keita: The Lost Album (with Kante Manfila) 2005, M'Bemba 2005, La Différence 2010, Talé 2012, Un Autre Blanc 2018. *Address:* Salif Keita Global Foundation Inc., 6900 Wisconsin Avenue, Unit 30306, Bethesda, MD 20824, USA (office). *Telephone:* (917) 397-6211 (office). *E-mail:* skgf@salifkeita.us (office). *Website:* www.salifkeita.net; www.salifkeita.us (office).

KEITEL, Hans-Peter, DrIng; German business executive; b. 4 Aug. 1947, Kusel; m.; three c.; ed Stuttgart Technical Univ., Tech. Univ. of Munich; with Alfred Kunz & Co. Contractors, Munich 1971–72; with Burkhardt KG, Consulting Engineers, Munich 1973–75; various sr and man. positions with Lahmeyer Int. (consulting engineers) 1975–87; tech. consultant to banking consortium involved in Channel Tunnel project 1986–87; joined Hochtief AG, Essen 1988, Dir and Head of Int. Business 1988–90, mem. Man. Bd 1990–92, CEO and Head of Construction Service Europe 1992–99, Chair. and CEO 1999–2007, now mem. Supervisory Bd; Pres. Fed. of the German Construction Industry 2005–08; Vice-Pres. Bundesverband der Deutschen Industrie eV (Fed. of German Industry) 2005–08, Pres. 2009–12; fmr mem. Supervisory Bd Commerzbank AG, National-Bank AG, ThyssenKrupp AG 2010–, Voith GmbH & Co. KGaA (also Chair. 2014–), RWE AG; Trustee, RAG-Stiftung; Verdienstorden des Landes Nordrhein-Westfalen 2004, Verdienstkreuz 1. Klasse der Bundesrepublik Deutschland 2011.

KEITEL, Harvey, BFA; American actor and producer; b. 13 May 1939, Brooklyn, New York; s. of Harry Keitel and Miriam Keitel (née Klein); partner Lorraine Bracco 1982–93; one d.; one s. with Lisa Karmazin; m. Daphna Kastner 2001; one s.; ed Abraham Lincoln High School, The Actors Studio, New School Univ.; served in US Marine Corps; starred in Martin Scorsese's student film Who's That Knocking at My Door?; stage appearances in Death of a Salesman, Hurlyburly; Co-Pres. The Actors Studio; f. The Goatsingers (production co.); Lifetime Achievement Award, Istanbul Film Festival 2005. *Films include:* Mean Streets 1973, Alice Doesn't Live Here Anymore 1974, That's the Way of the World 1975, Taxi Driver 1976, Buffalo Bill and the Indians 1976, The Duellists 1978, Fingers 1978, Blue Collar 1978, Eagle's Wing 1979, Deathwatch 1980, Saturn 3 1980, The Border 1982, Exposed 1983, La Nuit de Varennes 1982, Falling in Love 1984, Knight of the Dragon 1985, Wise Guys 1986, The Men's Club 1986, The Pick-up Artist 1987, The Last Temptation of Christ 1988, The January Man 1989, The Two Jakes 1990, Thelma & Louise 1991, Bugsy 1991 Reservoir Dogs 1992, Bad Lieutenant (Int. Fantasy Film Award for Best Actor 1993) 1992, Young Americans 1993, Dangerous Game 1993, The Piano 1993 (AFI Award for Best Actor in a Lead Role 1993), Rising Sun 1993, Monkey Trouble 1994, Clockers 1995, Pulp Fiction 1994, Smoke (Silver Berlin Bear Award Special Jury Prize 1995, David di Donatello Award for Best Foreign Actor 1996) 1995, Ulysses' Gaze 1995, Blue in the Face 1995, Head Above Water 1996, Somebody to Love 1996, City of Industry 1997, Cop Land 1997, Simpatico 1999, U-571 2000, Prince of Central Park 2000, Little Nicky 2000, Viper 2000, Holy Smoke 2000, Nailed 2001, Taking Sides 2001, The Grey Zone 2001, Nowhere 2002, Ginostra 2002, Red Dragon 2002, Beeper 2002, Crime Spree 2003, The Galindez File 2003, Dreaming of Julia 2003, Puerto Vallarta Squeeze 2003, National Treasure 2004, The Bridge of San Luis Rey 2004, Shadows in the Sun 2005, Be Cool 2005, The Shadow Dancer 2005, One Last Dance 2006, A Crime 2006, The Stone Merchant 2006, Arthur et les Minimoys (voice) 2006, My Sexiest Year 2007, National Treasure: Book of Secrets 2007, The Ministers 2009, Wrong Turn at Tahoe 2009, A Beginner's Guide to Endings 2010, Little Fockers 2010, The Last Godfather 2010, Death in Paradise 2012, Moonrise Kingdom 2012, Gandhi of the Month 2012, The Congress 2013, A Farewell to Fools 2013, The Power Inside 2013, The Grand Budapest Hotel 2014, By the Gun 2014, Two Men in Town 2014, Rio, I Love You 2014, Youth 2015. *Television includes:* Fail Safe (film) 2000, The Path to 9/11 (film) 2006, Life on Mars (series) 2008–09, Fatal Honeymoon (film) 2012, The Power Inside (mini-series) 2013. *Address:* The Goatsingers, 177 West Broadway, Suite 2, New York, NY 10013, USA. *Telephone:* (212) 966-4362.

KEITH, Rt Hon. Sir Kenneth James, Kt, KBE, PC, LLB, LLM, QC; New Zealand lawyer and fmr judge; *Professor Emeritus, Victoria University of Wellington;* b. 19 Nov. 1937, Auckland; s. of Patrick James Keith and Amy Irene Keith (née Witheridge); m. Jocelyn Margaret Buckett 1961; two s. two d.; ed Auckland Grammar School, Univ. of Auckland, Victoria Univ. of Wellington, Harvard Law School; with Dept of External Affairs, Wellington 1960–62; with Law Faculty, Vic. Univ. 1962–64, 1966–91, Prof. 1973–91, Dean 1977–81, now Prof. Emer.; UN Secr. Office of Legal Affairs 1968–70; with NZ Inst. of Int. Affairs 1971–73; Judge, Courts of Appeal of Samoa 1982–, Cook Islands 1982–, Niue 1995–, NZ 1996–2003; Judge, Supreme Court of Fiji 2003–05, Supreme Court of NZ 2004–05, Int. Court of Justice 2006–15; mem. NZ Law Comm. 1986–91, Pres. 1991–96; mem. NZ Nat. Group of Perm. Court of Arbitration 1985–2006, Panel of Arbitrators, Int. Centre for Settlement of Investment Disputes 1994–2012, Inst. of Int. Law 2003–; Pres. NZ Inst. of Int. Affairs 2000–06; Hon. Bencher, Inner Temple, London, UK; Commemoration Medal 1990; Hon. LLD (Auckland) 2001, (Victoria) 2004. *Publications include:* Advisory Jurisdiction of the International Court 1971, Essays on Human Rights (ed.) 1968; numerous Law Comm. publs and papers on constitutional and int. law in legal journals. *Leisure interests:* family, walking, reading. *Address:* Victoria University of Wellington, PO Box 600, Wellington, New Zealand (office); 11 Salamanca Road, Kelburn, Wellington, New Zealand (home). *Telephone:* (4) 472-6664 (home). *Fax:* (4) 472-6664 (home). *E-mail:* ken.keith@vuw.ac.nz (office). *Website:* www.vuw.ac.nz (office).

KEITH, Dame Penelope Anne Constance, DBE, CBE, OBE, DL; British actress; b. (Penelope Anne Constance Hatfield), 2 April 1940, Sutton, Surrey, England; d. of Frederick Hatfield and Constance Mary Keith; m. Rodney Timson 1978; ed Annecy Convent, Seaford, Sussex, Convent Bayeux, Normandy, Webber Douglas School, London; first professional appearance, Civic Theatre, Chesterfield 1959; repertory, Lincoln, Salisbury, Manchester 1960–63, Cheltenham 1967; RSC, Stratford 1963, Aldwych 1965; Pres. Actors Benevolent Fund 1990–; Gov. Queen Elizabeth's Foundation for the Disabled 1989–, Guildford School of Acting 1991–; Trustee Yvonne Arnaud Theatre 1992–; High Sheriff of Surrey 2002; Best Light Entertainment Performance (British Acad. of Film and TV Arts) 1976, Best Actress 1977, Show Business Personality (Variety Club of GB) 1976, BBC TV Personality 1979, Comedy Performance of the Year (Soc. of West End. Theatre) 1976, Female TV Personality, T.V. Times Awards 1976–78, BBC TV Personality of the Year 1978–79, TV Female Personality (Daily Express) 1979–82. *Stage appearances include:* Suddenly at Home 1971, The Norman Conquests 1974, Donkey's Years 1976, The Apple Cart 1977, The Millionairess 1978, Moving 1980, Hobson's Choice, Captain Brassbound's Conversion 1982, Hay Fever 1983, The Dragon's Tail 1985, Miranda 1987, The Deep Blue Sea 1988, Dear Charles 1990, The Merry Wives of Windsor 1990, The Importance of Being Earnest 1991, On Approval 1992, Relatively Speaking 1992, Glyn and It 1994, Monsieur Amilcar 1995, Mrs Warren's Profession 1997, Good Grief 1998, Star Quality 2001. *Films include:* Every Home Should Have One 1970, Take a Girl Like You 1970, Rentadick 1972, Penny Gold 1973, Ghost Story 1974, Priest of Love 1981. *Radio includes:* Agatha Raison series. *Television includes:* Kate (series) 1970, The Good Life 1974–78, Private Lives 1976, The Norman Conquests 1977, Much Ado About Nothing 1978, The Hound of the Baskervilles 1978, To the Manor Born 1979–81, 2007, Spider's Web 1982, On Approval 1982, Waters of the Moon 1983, Sweet Sixteen (series) 1983, Tickle on the Tum (series) 1984, Moving (series) 1985, Executive Stress (series) 1986–88, Growing Places 1989, No Job for a Lady (series) 1990–92, Law and Disorder (series) 1994, Next of Kin (series) 1995–96, Coming Home 1998, Margery and Gladys 2003, The Secret Show (series) 2006, Death Comes to Pemberley (mini-series) 2013. *Leisure interest:* gardening.

KEJAVSHEE, Shaf, OC, OOnt, MD, MSc, FRCSC, FACS; Canadian surgeon; *Senior Scientist, Toronto General Research Institute (TGRI);* b. Feb. 1961, Kenya; m. Donna McRitchie; one d.; ed Univ. of Toronto; moved to Canada at age 12; fellowship training at Harvard Univ. (airway surgery) and Univ. of London (heart-lung transplantation); mem. Faculty of Medicine, Univ. of Toronto 1994–, currently Prof., Div. of Thoracic Surgery, also Sr Scientist, Toronto Gen. Research Inst. (TGRI) and Dir, Toronto Lung Transplant Program; Surgeon-in-Chief, Univ. Health Network (UHN), also Head, Jt Div. of Thoracic Surgery of UHN and St Joseph's Hosp., McMaster Univ.; Dir, Latner Thoracic Research Labs; fmr mem. Bd of Dirs Int. Soc. for Heart and Lung Transplantation, Canadian Soc. of Transplantation; mem. Governing Council, American Asscn for Thoracic Surgery; numerous awards including George Armstrong Peters Young Investigator Award, Canada's Top 40 Under 40 Award, Colin Woolf Award for Excellence in Continuing Medical Educ., Univ. of Toronto Lister Prize in Surgery 2008, Queen's Diamond Jubilee Medal 2013. *Achievements include:* known for pioneering contributions to the field of lung transplantation including the use of an artificial lung and a system to preserve and repair donor lungs for transplantation. *Address:* Toronto General Hospital, 200 Elizabeth Street, Toronto, ON M5G 2C4, Canada (office). *Telephone:* (416) 340-3111 (office). *E-mail:* shaf.keshavjee@uhn.on (office). *Website:* www.uhn.ca (office).

KEJRIWAL, Arvind; Indian politician; *Chief Minister of Delhi;* b. 16 Aug. 1968, Haryana; s. of Gobind Ram Kejriwal and Gita Devi; m. Sunita Kejriwal; one s. one d.; ed Indian Inst. of Tech., Kharagpur; began career with Tata Steel, Jamshedpur 1989–92; joined Indian Revenue Service 1995, Jt Commr, Income Tax Dept –2006; co-f. Parivartan (Change, NGO), Delhi 2000; f. Public Cause Research Foundation (self-governance NGO) 2006; Founder-Leader Aam Aadmi Party (AAP) 2012–; Chief Minister of Delhi Dec. 2013–Feb. 2014, 2015–; CNN-IBN Indian of the Year (Public Service) 2006, Ramon Magsaysay Award for Emergent Leadership 2006, CNN-IBN Indian of the Year (Politics) 2013. *Publication:* Swaraj 2012. *Address:* Chief Minister Office, 3rd Level A-Wing, Delhi Secretariat, I.P. Estate, New Delhi 110 002, India (office). *Telephone:* (11) 23392020 (office); (11) 23392030 (office). *Fax:* (11) 23392111 (office). *E-mail:* contact@aamaadmiparty.org. *Website:* delhi.gov.in (office); www.aamaadmiparty.org; www.arvindkejriwal.net.in.

KEKE, Kieren Aedogan, MD; Nauruan physician and politician; b. 27 June 1971, Yaren; s. of Ludwig Keke; mem. Parl. for Yaren 2003– (fmr Speaker); mem. Naoero Amo (Nauru First) party; Minister of Health and Transport –2007 (resgnd), led breakaway opposition faction following vote of no-confidence in Prime Minister Nov. 2007, Minister of Foreign Affairs and Trade, Transport and Telecommunications Nov. 2007–11, of Foreign Affairs and Trade 2012–13; fmr Pres. Nat. Youth Council for Nauru. *Address:* Naoero Amo, c/o Parliament House, Yaren, Nauru (office). *Telephone:* 444-3133 (office). *E-mail:* visionary@naoeroamo.com (office). *Website:* www.naurugov.nr (office).

KELAM, Tunne; Estonian politician and historian; b. 10 July 1936, Taheva, Valgamaa Region; m. Mari-Ann Kelam; one d.; ed Univ. of Tartu; Sr Researcher, Central State Archives 1959–65; Sr Academic Ed., Estonian Soviet Encyclopedia 1965–75; Sr Bibliographer, Fr. R. Kreutzwald Nat. Library 1976–79; labourer, Ranna collective farm 1979–87; mem. Cttee of Estonia 1990–92, Chair. (perm. directorial organ of the Congress of Estonia) 1990–92; mem. Riigikogu (Parl.) 1992–2004, Deputy Speaker 1992–2003, Chair. European Affairs Cttee 1997–2003; mem. European Parl. 2004–, mem. Bureau of European People's Party group, Cttee of Foreign Affairs, Sub-cttee of Security and Defence, Parl. Del. for relations with USA; mem. Exec., Estonian Nat. Independence Party 1989–93, Chair. of party 1993–95; Chair. Isamaaliit Party 2002–05; mem. Exec., Isamaa ja Res Publica Union 2006; mem. Congress of Estonia (transitional parl. ass.) 1990–92; mem. Constitutional Ass. 1991–92; presidential cand. 1996; mem. Parl. Ass. of the Council of Europe (PACE) 1992–2000, Head of Estonian Parl. del. to PACE 1992–95, Vice-Pres. PACE 1994–95, rapporteur on Ukraine for the Monitoring Cttee of PACE 1996–2000; Head of Estonian del., Inter-Parl. Union 1992–95; mem. Convention on the Future of Europe 2002–03; Chief Elder of the Estonian Scouting Asscn 1996–2007; mem. Exec., Human Rights Inst. 1996–2009, Kistler-Ritso Fund (occupation museum) 1998–2009; Hon. Citizen of Maryland, USA, Hon. Pres. Estonian Scout Asscn 1996–; Officier, Ordre nat. du Mérite, Badge of the Order of the Nat. Coat of Arms (Second Class) 2001, I Class Order of the Nat. Coat of Arms 2006; Paul Harris Fellowship, Rotary Int. Award, Estonian Newspapers' Union Award 1996, Baltic Ass. Award, Robert Schuman Medal 2006. *Publications:* Tunne Kelam (autobiog.) 1999, Estonian Way to Freedom, Tallinn 2002; numerous articles and trans from English, French, Polish, German, Italian and Russian. *Address:* European Parliament, Bâtiment Altiero Spinelli, 60 rue Wiertz, 1047 Brussels, Belgium (office). *Telephone:* (2) 284-72-79 (office). *Fax:* (2) 284-92-79 (office). *E-mail:* tunne.kelam@europarl.europa.eu (office); tunne.kelam@irl.ee. *Website:* www.kelam.ee.

KELANTAN, HRH Former Sultan of; Tuanku Ismail Petra ibni al-Marhum Sultan Yahaya Petra, DK, SPMK, SJMK, SPKK, SPSK, DMN, SMN, DK of Negri Sembilan, Selangor, Johor, Kedah, Perak, Trengganu and Perlis, DKMB of Brunei, DPSS of Sarawak, DP of Sarawak; b. 11 Nov. 1949, Kota Bharu, Kelantan; s. of al-Marhum Tengku Yahaya Petra Ibni al-Marhum Sultan Ibrahim and al-Marhum Tengku Zainab binti Tengku Mohamed Petra; m. 1st Tengku Anis Binti Tengku Abdul Hamid 1968; three s. one d.; m. 2nd Elia Suhana binti Ahmad 2007 (divorced 2010); installed as Heir Apparent with the title of Tengku Mahkota 11 Nov. 1967; Attaché, State Secr. and Kota Bharu Land Office 1968; served as Regent during the absence of his father from the state 6–25 July 1974, 12 July–28 Aug. 1975, 21 Sept. 1975–29 March 1979; succeeded as Sultan of Kelantan on the death of his father 29 March 1979; crowned at Istana Balai Besar, Kota Bharu 30 March 1980; formally deposed in favour of his eldest son by the Kelantan Royal Succession Council of State on the grounds of incapacity after failing to fully recover from a debilitating stroke 13 Sept. 2010; thereafter styled Duli Yang Maha Mulia Sultan Ismail Petra (instead of Kebawah Duli Yang Maha Mulia Sultan Kelantan); Maj., Territorial Army 1974, promoted to Hon. Lt-Col 1976, Hon. Col 1988, Hon. Maj.-Gen., Col-in-Chief of the Royal Artillery Regt 1997, and of Royal Intelligence Corps; Patron Royal Kelantan Club –1992; mem. The Conf. of Rulers, Malaysia; Hon. DPhil (Univ. of Malaysia Sabah) 2007. *Website:* www.kelantan.gov.my.

KELANTAN, HRH Sultan Muhammad V; Tengku Muhammad Faris Petra ibni Sultan Ismail Petra; Malaysian fmr head of state; *Sultan of Kelantan;* b. 6 Oct. 1969, Kota Bharu, Kelantan; s. of Tuanku Ismail Petra ibni al-Marhum Sultan Yahaya Petra and Tengku Anis Binti Tengku Abdul Hamid; m. Tengku Zubaidah Tengku Norudin (divorced); ed Oakham School, Rutland, St Cross Coll., Oxford, Oxford Centre for Islamic Studies, UK; named Tengku Mahkota (Crown Prince) Oct. 1985, apptd as Regent after his father suffered a stroke May 2009, proclaimed Sultan of Kelantan due to indisposition of father 13 Sept. 2010; Timbalan Yang di-Pertuan Agong (Deputy Supreme Head of State) 2011–16, elected Yang di-Pertuan Agong (Supreme Head of State) Oct. 2016, took office 13 Dec. 2016, abdicated 6 Jan. 2019; fmr C-in-C of the Malaysian Armed Forces, Marshal of the Royal Malaysian Air Force, Field Marshal of the Malaysian Army, Adm. of the Fleet of the Royal Malaysian Navy; Hon. Commdr, 506 Territorial Army Regt with rank of Brig.-Gen.; Recipient (DK) and Grand Master, Royal Family Order or Star of Yunus 1986, Kt Grand Commdr (SPMK) and Grand Master, Order of the Crown of Kelantan or 'Star of Muhammad', Kt Grand Commdr (SJMK) and Grand Master, Order of the Life of the Crown of Kelantan or 'Star of Ismail', Kt Grand Commdr (SPSK) and Grand Master, Order of the Loyalty to the Crown of Kelantan or 'Star of Ibrahim', Grand Master, Order of the Noble Crown of Kelantan or 'Star de Yahya Petra' 2010–, Grand Master, Order of the Most Distinguished and Most Valiant Warrior (PYGP) 2010–; Order of the Crown of the Realm (DMN) 2010, Recipient of the Royal Family Order of Perak (DK), Recipient of the Perlis Family Order of the Gallant Prince Syed Putra Jamalullail (DK), First Class of the Royal Family Order of Selangor (DK) 2010, First Class of the Royal Family Order of Johor (DK) 2011, Mem. Royal Family Order of Negeri Sembilan (DKNS) 2011, Collar of Badr Chain (Saudi Arabia) 2017. *Address:* Palace of the Sultan, 09 Kota Bharu, Kelantan, Malaysia (office). *Website:* www.kelantan.gov.my (office).

KELCHE, Gen. Jean-Pierre; French army officer; b. 19 Jan. 1942, Macon; m.; two c.; ed Mil. Acad., Saint Cyr; served in Côte d'Ivoire, then Djibouti 1971–73, Jr Staff Course, Staff Coll., then with French Caribbean and Guiana Territorial Command 1979–81; Commdr 5th Combined Bn, Djibouti 1985–87; Staff Officer, Doctrine and Devt Div., rank of Brig.-Gen. 1991; Deputy Commdr 5th Armoured Div., Landau, Germany 1991; Chief Plans, Programmes and Evaluation Div., Gen. Staff 1992–95; Chief of Prime Minister's Mil. Cabinet 1995–96; Vice-Chief of Defence Staff 1996–98, Chief of Defence Staff, rank of Gen. 1998–2002; Le Grand Chancelier de la Légion d'honneur 2004–10; Commdr, Légion d'honneur, Officier, Ordre nat. du Mérite.

KELDIBEKOV, Akhmatbek, CandEconSci; Kyrgyzstani politician and engineer; b. 15 June 1966, Sufi-Kurgan village, Alai Dist, Osh Oblast, Kyrgyz SSR, USSR; m.; two s. two d.; ed Voronezh Polytechnical Inst., Russian FSFR, Inst. of Retraining and Higher Qualifications of Cadres at Kyrgyz Nat. Univ.; served in Soviet Army in Kutaisi, Georgian SSR 1984–86; worker at 'Pravda' Soviet farm, Alai Dist 1986; 'Impuls' Academic Research Centre, Acad. of Sciences of the Kyrgyz SSR 1990–92, Deputy Dir for Gen. Questions, Inst. of Machine Construction, Acad. of Sciences of the Repub. of Kyrgyzstan 1992–93; Sr Specialist, Dept of Devt of Brs of Industry, Ministry of the Economy and Finance 1993–94; Sr Specialist, Dept of Financing of Industry, Ministry of Finance 1994–95, Chief of Dept of Financing of Transport and Communications 1995–98, Head of Man. of the Economy and Financing of Productive Infrastructure 1998–2001; Deputy Minister of Finance 2001–02; Chair. Social Fund of the Kyrgyz Repub. 2002–05; Deputy in Jogorku Kenesh (Parl.), Chair. Cttee on Budget and Finances 2005–07, Chair. (Speaker) 2010–11; Chair. State Cttee for Taxes and Duties 2008–09, State Tax Service 2009–10; Leader of nationalist Ata-Jurt (Fatherland) party; Deputy, Interparliamentary Ass. of Eurasian Econ. Community (EURASEC) May 2011; State Councillor of the Second Class; Col of the Tax Service; Gen.-Lt Merited Economist of the Kyrgyz Repub.; 'Dank' Medal 2011.

KELEMEN, Hunor; Romanian politician and writer; *President, Uniunea Democrată Maghiară din România/Romániai Magyar Demokrata Szövetség (RMDSz—Democratic Alliance of Hungarians in Romania);* b. 18 Oct. 1967, Cârța; m. Eva Czezar 2012; ed Univ. of Agricultural Sciences and Veterinary Medicine, Cluj-Napoca, Babeș-Bolyai Univ., Cluj-Napoca; Sec. of State from Uniunea Democrată Maghiară din România/Romániai Magyar Demokrata Szövetség (RMDSz—Democratic Alliance of Hungarians in Romania) in Ministry of Culture 1997–2000; elected to Chamber of Deputies (Lower House of Romanian Parl.) on RMDSz list 2000– (re-elected 2004, 2008); unsuccessful cand. in presidential election 2009; Minister of Culture 2009–12; currently Pres. RMDSz; Hungarian language writer; Commdr, Order of the Star of Romania 2000, Commdr's Cross, Order of Merit (Hungary) 2008. *Address:* Uniunea Democrată Maghiară din România/Romániai Magyar Demokrata Szövetség (Democratic Alliance of Hungarians in Romania), 400489 Kolozsvár, Str. Majális 60, Romania (office). *Telephone:* (264) 590758 (office); 722-303493 (mobile). *Fax:* (264) 590758 (office). *E-mail:* kelemenhunor@rmdsz.ro (office); internationalsecretary@rmdsz.ro (office). *Website:* www.udmr.ro (office); www.rmdsz.ro (office); www.kelemenhunor.ro; www.dahr.ro (office).

KELEMU, Segenet, BSc, MSc, PhD; Ethiopian molecular plant pathologist; *Director-General, International Center for Insect Physiology and Ecology;* b. Finote Selam, Gojjam, Amhara Region; m. Arjan Gijsman; one d.; ed Addis Ababa Univ., Montana State Univ. and Kansas State Univ., USA; Intern, Dept of Plant Science, Addis Ababa Univ. 1977, Sr Student and Project Asst 1979, Asst Lecturer and Researcher 1979–81, Lecturer and Researcher 1982; Intern, Dept of Crop Protection, Tendaho Agricultural Corpn 1978; Graduate Research and Teaching Asst, Dept of Plant Pathology, Kansas State Univ. 1985–89; Post-doctoral Research Scientist, Cornell Univ. 1989–92; Sr Scientist, Molecular Plant Pathologist, Tropical Forages Program, Centro Internacional de Agricultura Tropical, Cali, Colombia 1992–2004, Leader, Crop and Agro-ecosystem Health Man. Program 2004–07; Dir, Biosciences Eastern and Central Africa –Int. Livestock Research Inst. Hub, Nairobi, Kenya. 2007–12; Vice-Pres. for Programs, Alliance for a Green Revolution in Africa 2012–13; Dir-Gen. Int. Center for Insect Physiology and Ecology 2013–; Ed.-in-Chief, Int. Journal of Insect Science 2013–; mem. Louis Malassis and Olam Prizes 2014, Independent Science and Partnership Council, CGIAR 2014–16, Int. Jury for Rolex Enterprise Awards 2016, Governing Council, UN Univ. 2016–, Nat. Science and Tech. Council, Govt of

Rwanda 2016–, Int. Academics Bd, Boris Mints Inst. 2017–, Int. Jury for the Boris Mints Inst. Prize 2017; Fellow, African Acad. of Sciences 2013, Ethiopian Acad. of Sciences 2013; TWAS Fellow 2016; Dr hc (Tel Aviv) 2016; Outstanding Principal Staff Award, CIAT 2007, Friendship Award, People's Republic of China 2006, Prize for Agricultural Sciences, Third World Acad. of Sciences 2011, Laureate for Africa and the Arab States, L'Oréal-UNESCO Women in Science Awards 2014. *Leisure interest:* reading. *Address:* International Center for Insect Physiology and Ecology (ICIPE), POB 30772-00100, Nairobi, Kenya (office). *Telephone:* (20) 8632000 (office). *Fax:* (20) 8632001 (office). *E-mail:* skelemu@icipe.org (office). *Website:* www.icipe.org (office).

KELETI, György; Hungarian politician and army officer; b. 18 May 1946, Losonc; m. Erzsébet Petrik; three c.; ed Toldy Ferenc Secondary School, Budapest, Zalka Máté Mil. Tech. Coll., Zrinyi Miklós War Coll.; co. commdr, then later deputy commdr of a bn in Vác Dist 1969–74; posts in Ministry of Defence 1980; Press Spokesman, Ministry of Defence 1977; mem. Hungarian Socialist Workers' Party (MSZMP) 1969–89; mem. Oroszlány org. of HSP (MSZP) 1992, mem. nat. presidium of party 1996–2003; elected mem. Parl. for Constituency 3, Kisbér, Komárom-Esztergom Co. 1992, Chair. Nat. Security Cttee 1998–2002, Defence Cttee 2002, Deputy Parl. Group Leader 2004, mem. Cttee on Standing Orders 2004; Minister of Defence 1994–98; Chair. Regional Asscn of Komárom-Esztergom Co. 1998, Chair. Election Cttee at 7th Congress 2000; rank of Col in army reserve; Order of Star (with swords), Silver Cross of Merit.

KELL, Georg; German financial analyst and fmr UN official; *Vice-Chairman, Arabesque Asset Management Ltd;* ed Tech. Univ. of Berlin; extensive experience as financial analyst in Africa and Asia; began UN career with UNCTAD in Geneva 1987–90, joined New York office of UNCTAD 1990, Head of New York Office 1993–97, Sr Officer in Exec. Office of UN Sec.-Gen. Kofi Annan 1997–2000, Founding Exec. Dir UN Global Compact 2000–15, Sr Policy Adviser 2015–; Vice-Chair. Arabesque Asset Management Ltd 2015–. *Address:* Arabesque Partners, 68 Brook Street, London, W1K 5DZ, England (office). *Telephone:* (20) 3427-3675 (office). *E-mail:* info@arabesque.com (office). *Website:* www.arabesque.com (office).

KELLENBERGER, Jakob, DPhil; Swiss diplomatist and international organization official; b. 19 Oct. 1944, Heiden; m. Elisabeth Kellenberger-Jossi 1973; two d.; ed Univ. of Zurich, with stays at Univs of Tours and Granada; joined Swiss diplomatic service 1974, diplomatic postings in Madrid, Brussels and London, Head of Office in Charge of European Integration, Berne 1984–92, Minister 1984, Amb. 1988, State Sec., Fed. Dept of Foreign Affairs 1992–99; Pres. ICRC 2000–12; teaches at Univ. of Salamanca, Spain and ETH Zürich; mem. Berggruen Inst. on Governance; Hon. Adviser, Zurich Fed. Polytechnic Inst. 2007; Citizen of Honour, Municipality of Heiden 2009; Dr hc (Univ. of Basle) 2003, (Univ. of Catania) 2006; Genève reconnaissante (Grateful Geneva) Medal, City of Geneva 2005, Chair.'s Award for Int. Humanitarian Leadership, American Red Cross 2006. *Publications include:* Humanitäres Völkerrecht 2010; several articles. *Address:* Berggruen Institute on Governance, Paradeplatz 4/Tiefenhöfe 9, 8001 Zurich, Switzerland (office). *E-mail:* big@berggruen.org (office). *Website:* berggruen.org/people/jakob-kellenberger (office).

KELLER, Evelyn Fox, PhD; American historian, philosopher of science and academic; *Professor of History and Philosophy of Science Emerita, Massachusetts Institute of Technology;* b. 20 March 1936, New York, NY; d. of Albert Fox and Ray Fox; m. Joseph B. Keller 1964 (divorced); one s. one d.; ed Radcliffe Coll., Brandeis and Harvard Univs; Asst Research Scientist, New York Univ. 1963–66, Assoc. Prof. 1970–72; Assoc. Prof., State Univ. of New York, Purchase 1972–82; Prof. of Math. and Humanities, Northwestern Univ. 1982–88; Prof., Univ. of California, Berkeley 1988–92; Visiting Fellow, later Scholar, MIT 1979–84, Visiting Prof. 1985–86, Prof. of History and Philosophy of Science 1992–2009, Prof. Emer. 2009–; mem. Inst. of Advanced Studies, Princeton 1987–88; Pres. West Coast History of Science Soc. 1990–91; mem. American Acad. of Arts and Sciences, American Philosophical Soc.; 12 hon. degrees, including Dr hc (Mount Holyoke Coll.) 1991, (Univ. of Amsterdam) 1993, (Simmons Coll.) 1995, (Rensslaer Polytechnic Inst.) 1995, (Tech. Univ. of Luleå, Sweden) 1996, (New School Univ.) 2000, (Allegheny Coll.) 2000, (Wesleyan Univ.) 2001, (Dartmouth Coll.) 2007; MacArthur Fellow 1992–97, Guggenheim Fellowship 2000–01, Moore Scholar, California Inst. Tech. 2002, Winton Chair, Univ. of Minnesota 2002–05, Dibner Fellow 2003, Radcliffe Inst. Fellow 2005, Rothschild Lecturer, Harvard Univ. 2005, Plenary Speaker, Int. History of Science Congress, Beijing 2005; numerous awards, including Mina Shaughnessey Award 1981–82, Radcliffe Grad. Soc. Medal 1985, Medal of the Italian Senate 2001, Chaire Blaise Pascal 2005–07; inducted into AAAS Science Hall of Fame 2011. *Publications include:* A Feeling for the Organism 1983, Reflections on Gender and Science 1985, Secrets of Life, Secrets of Death 1992, Keywords in Evolutionary Biology (ed.) 1994, Refiguring Life 1995, Feminism and Science (co-author) 1996, The Century of the Gene 2000, Making Sense of Life 2002, The Mirage of a Space between Nature and Nurture 2010. *Address:* Massachusetts Institute of Technology, E38-094, 77 Massachusetts Avenue, Cambridge, MA 02139, USA (office). *Fax:* (617) 253-8118 (office). *E-mail:* efkeller@mit.edu (office). *Website:* web.mit.edu/sts (office).

KELLER, Samuel (Sam); Swiss museum director and foundation executive; *Director, Fondation Beyeler;* b. 6 Jan. 1966, Basel; ed Univ. of Basel; joined Art Basel 1994, Dir 2000–07, currently Chair. Advisory Bd, launched sister fair Art Basel Miami Beach 2002; Dir Fondation Beyeler, Riehen 2008–; Young Global Leader, World Econ. Forum 2005; Dr hc (Basel) 2016; Officier de lOrdre des Arts et des Lettres (France) 2017; Medal of Honour, City of Miami Beach 2007, Swiss Inst. Award, New York 2010. *Address:* Fondation Beyeler, Baselstrasse 101, 4125 Riehen, Switzerland (office). *Telephone:* (61) 6459700 (office). *Fax:* (61) 6459719 (office). *E-mail:* info@fondationbeyeler.ch (office). *Website:* www.fondationbeyeler.ch (office).

KELLER, Thomas A.; American chef; b. 14 Aug. 1955, Southern Calif.; fmr chef, La Reserve and Restaurant Raphael, New York; served an estagiere apprentice in France in restaurants of Guy Savoy, Michael Pasquet, Gerard Besson, also Taillevant, Le Toit de Passey, Chiberta and Le Pre Catalan; est. restaurant Rakel, New York; Exec. Chef, Checkers Hotel, Los Angeles; acquired The French Laundry, Yountville, Calif. 1994, currently Chef and Owner, Thomas Keller Restaurant Group; Founder and Owner EVO Inc. (retail line of olive oils and vinegar); spokesperson for Calif. Milk Advisory Bd 1997–98; Owner Bouchon 1998, Bouchon Bakery 2003, Per Se 2004, Bouchon at the Venetian 2004, Ad Hoc 2007; Chevalier in the French Legion of Honor 2011; Dr hc (Johnson and Wales Univ.) 2003; Ivy Award, Restaurants and Insts 1996, named Best American Chef: Calif., James Beard Foundation 1996, Outstanding Chef: America 1997; World's Best Chef, Wedgwood 2002, Ellis Island Medal of Honor 2017. *Publications include:* The French Laundry 2004, Bouchon 2004, Under Pressure 2008, Ad Hoc at Home: Family-style Recipes 2009, Bouchon Bakery (with Sebastien Rouxel) 2012. *Address:* Thomas Keller Restaurant Group, 6640 Washington Street, Yountville, CA 94599-1301, USA (office). *Telephone:* (707) 944-2380 (office). *Website:* www.tkrg.org (office).

KELLNER, Lawrence W. (Larry), BS; American business executive; *President, Emerald Creek Group, LLC;* m. Susan Kellner; four c.; ed Univ. of South Carolina; started career with Ernst & Whitney (previously Ernst & Young); Exec. Vice-Pres. and Chief Financial Officer American Savings Bank –1995; Sr Vice-Pres. and Chief Financial Officer Continental Airlines Inc. 1995–96, Exec. Vice-Pres. and Chief Financial Officer 1996–2001, Dir 2001–10, Pres. 2001–04, COO 2003–04, Chair. and CEO 2004–09; Pres. Emerald Creek Group, LLC 2010–; Chair. Sabre Corpn 2010–; mem. Bd of Dirs Marriott International 2002–, The Boeing Co. 2011–, The Chubb Corpn; mem. Nat. Exec. Bd Boy Scouts of America; mem. Advisory Bd March of Dimes, Teach for America; mem. Devt Bd Univ. of Texas Health Science Center; mem. Bd of Trustees Rice Univ.; Univ. of South Carolina Distinguished Alumni Award 1998. *Address:* Emerald Creek Group, LLC, 5000 Birch Street, Suite 500, Newport Beach, CA 92660, USA (office). *Telephone:* (949) 379-7200 (office). *E-mail:* larry.kellner@emeraldcreek.com (office). *Website:* www.emeraldcreek.com (office).

KELLS, Susannah (see CORNWELL, Bernard).

KELLY, Alfred F., Jr, BA, MBA; American financial services industry executive; m. Margaret P. Kelly; two s. three d.; ed Iona Coll.; Asst Prof., Iona Coll. 1980–85; fmr Head of Information Systems, Exec. Office of the Pres., The White House; fmrly with Information Systems and Strategic and Financial Planning Dept, PepsiCo; joined Strategic Planning Dept, American Express Co. 1987, Vice-Pres. of Technologies 1988, Exec. Vice-Pres. and Gen. Man., Consumer Marketing 1997–98, Pres. Consumer Card Services Group 1998–2000, Group Pres., Consumer, Small Business and Merchant Services 2000–07, Pres. 2007–10; Chair. Wall Street Charity Golf Classic; Pres. and CEO NY/NJ Super Bowl Host Cttee 2014; mem. Bd of Dirs, The Hershey Co. 2005–07 (resgnd), Concern Worldwide USA, Carvel Children's Rehabilitation Center, MetLife 2009–, Visa Inc. 2014–, Metropolitan Life Insurance Co.; Trustee, Iona Coll., NY-Presbyterian Hosp.; mem. Council on Foreign Relations.

KELLY, Craig A., PhD; American diplomatist (retd) and business executive; *Senior Director for the Americas, International Government Relations, ExxonMobil;* m. Kimberly Fitzgerald Kelly; one s. one d.; ed Univ. of California, Los Angeles, Ecole Nationale d'Admin, Paris, Nat. War Coll., Washington, DC; career mem. Sr Foreign Service, with rank of Minister-Counselor, overseas postings include Bogotá, Rome and Paris, Washington postings include Western Hemisphere and European Bureaus and Nat. Security Council, served as Exec. Asst to Under-Sec. of State for Political Affairs 1999–2001, to Sec. of State Colin Powell 2001–04, Amb. to Chile 2004–07, Prin. Deputy Asst Sec., Bureau of Western Hemisphere Affairs, State Dept 2007–10; Sr Fellow, German Marshall Fund of US 2012; Vice-Pres. The Cohen Group 2010–12; Sr Dir for the Americas, Int. Govt Relations, ExxonMobil, Washington, DC 2012–; mem. Bd of Dirs Pan American Development Foundation; fmr Fulbright Scholar in Italy; Presidential Meritorious Service Award 2007, Sec. of State's Career Achievement Award 2010, Cordell Hull Award for Econ. Achievement. *Address:* ExxonMobil, 1177 22nd Street, NW, Washington, DC 20037, USA (office). *Website:* corporate.exxonmobil.com (office).

KELLY, Edmund (Ted) F., BA; American (b. Northern Irish) insurance industry executive; b. 1946, Co. Armagh, Northern Ireland; ed Queen's Univ., Belfast, Massachusetts Inst. of Tech.; served in a variety of positions with Aetna Life and Casualty Co. 1974–92, including as its Group Exec.; Pres. and COO Liberty Mutual Insurance Co. 1992–98, Pres. and CEO Liberty Mutual Holding Co. Inc. 1998–2010, Chair. and CEO 2000–11, Chair. 2011–13, Chair. Liberty Mutual Agency Corpn, Chair. Liberty Financial Cos Inc. 2000–13, also Chair. Employers Insurance Co. of Wausau (EICOW, subsidiary of Liberty Mutual); Pres. and COO Mellon Financial Corpn 1992–98, CEO 1998–; mem. Bd of Dirs EICOW 1998–, Segue Software Inc. 2000–04, EMC Corpn 2007–, The Bank of New York Mellon Corpn 2007–; fmr Chair. Alliance of American Insurers Inc.; Dir, Financial Services Roundtable; Dir, Initiative for a Competitive Inner City, Citizens Financial Group Inc., American Insurers, RBS Citizens, N.A.; Ind. Dir, Mellon Financial Corpn 2004–; Trustee Assoc., Boston Coll.; mem. Bd Govs Property Casualty Insurers Asscn of America; Chair. Boston Symphony Orchestra Inc. 2011–; mem. Bd United Way of Massachusetts Bay, American Red Cross of Massachusetts Bay, Boston Pvt. Industry Council, American Ireland Fund, The Massachusetts Mentoring Partnership; Pres. Boston Minuteman Council, Boy Scouts of America; also serves on various other community and educ. bds; held asst professorships in math. depts at Univ. of New Brunswick and Univ. of Missouri at St Louis; mem. American Acad. of Actuaries; Fellow, Soc. of Actuaries. *Address:* c/o Liberty Mutual Holding Co. Inc., 175 Berkeley Street, Boston, MA 02116, USA. *E-mail:* info@libertymutual.com.

KELLY, Gail P., HigherDipEd, BA, MBA; South African banking executive; b. 25 April 1956, Pretoria; m. Allan Kelly 1977; ed Univ. of Cape Town, Charles Sturt Univ., Australia; worked as a teacher in Rhodesia and SA; began banking career with Nedcor Bank, Head of Human Resources 1990–97; joined Commonwealth Bank, Sydney, Australia as Gen. Man. of Strategic Marketing 1997, becoming Head, Customer Service Div.; CEO St George Bank 2002–07 (merged with Westpac 2008), Man. Dir and CEO Westpac Banking Corpn 2008–15, also Dir, Westpac New Zealand Ltd; mem. Bd Dirs Melbourne Business School Ltd; Hon. DBus. *Publications:* Live Lead Learn: My Stories of Life and Leadership 2017.

KELLY, Gen. (retd) John Francis, MSc; American government official and military officer (retd); b. 11 May 1950, Boston, Mass; m. Karen Kelly; three c.; ed Univ. of Massachusetts, Georgetown Univ. School of Foreign Service; enlisted in US Marine Corps 1970, 40 years' service including three tours in Iraq, roles included rifle and weapons platoon Commdr, 2nd Marine Div., Co. Exec. Officer, Asst Operations Officer, Infantry Co. Commdr, Head of Offensive Tactics Section, Tactics Group 1987, Dir, Infantry Officer Course, CO, 1st Light Armored Reconnaissance Bn, 1st Marine Div., Commandant's Liaison Officer to House of Reps 1995, Special Asst to Supreme Allied Commdr, Europe, Mons, Belgium 1999–2001, Asst Chief of Staff, G-3 with 2nd Marine Div. 2001, Asst Div. Commdr, 1st Marine Div. 2002, Legis. Asst to Commdt, Marine Corps HQ 2004–07, deployed to Iraq as Commanding Gen., I Marine Expeditionary Force (Forward) 2008–09, Commdr, Marine Forces Reserve and Marine Forces North 2009–11, Sr Mil. Asst to Sec. of Defense 2011–12, Commdr, US Southern Command 2012–16 (retd); Sec. of Homeland Security Jan.–July 2017, White House Chief of Staff July 2017–19; Defense Distinguished Service Medal, Defense Superior Service Medal, Legion of Merit with Valor. *Address:* c/o The White House, 1600 Pennsylvania Avenue, NW, Washington, DC 20500, USA.

KELLY, John Philip, CMG, LVO, MBE, BA (Hons); British diplomatist; *Vice-President, Victoria League for Commonwealth Friendship;* b. 25 June 1941, Tuam, Co. Galway, Ireland; s. of William Kelly and Norah Kelly (née Roche); m. Jennifer Anne Buckler 1964; one s.; ed Oatlands Coll., Dublin, Open Univ.; joined HM Diplomatic Service 1959; worked at Embassies in Kinshasa (fmrly Léopoldville) 1962–65, Cairo 1965–67, Bonn 1967–70; with FCO 1970–73, 1986–89, 1994–96; with High Comm. Canberra 1973–76, Consulate-Gen. Antwerp 1977–78; with Dept of Trade 1980–82; Rep. to Grenada 1982–86; Deputy Gov. of Bermuda 1989–94; Gov. Turks and Caicos Islands 1996–2000; Chair. Victoria League for Commonwealth Friendship 2002–07, Vice-Pres. 2007–. *Leisure interests:* family, cruise lecturing, golf, reading, walking. *Address:* The Laurels, 56 Garden Lane, Royston, Herts., SG8 9EH, England (home). *Telephone:* (1763) 245128 (home). *E-mail:* johnandjenniferkelly@btinternet.com.

KELLY, Laura, BS, MS; American politician; *Governor of Kansas;* b. 24 Jan. 1950, New York City, NY; m. Ted Daughety; two d.; ed Bradley Univ., Indiana Univ., Bloomington; Exec. Dir Kan. Recreation and Park Asscn 1988–2004; Dir Recreation Therapy/Physical Educ., Nat. Jewish Hospital Hosp. for Respiratory and Immune Diseases; Recreation Therapist, Rockland Children's Psychiatric Center; mem. Senate, Kansas 2005–19, also fmr Minority Whip; Gov. of Kan. 2019–; mem. Bd Sunflower State Games 1989–, Kan. Leadership Center 2006–11; mem. Leadership Greater Topeka 2003; mem. Steering Cttee, Heartland Visioning; William Penn Mott Jr. Award for Excellence 2000, Afterschool Champion, Kan. Enrichment Network 2006, Community Health Champion, Kan. Asscn for the Medically Underserved 2006, 2008, 2009, Outstanding Policy Maker, Oral Health Kansas 2009, Legislator of the Year, Asscn for Community Mental Health Centers 2009, Kan. Recreation and Park Asscn 2010, State Champion, Kan. Head Start Asscn 2010, Statehouse Champion Award, American Cancer Soc. 2010, Velma Paris Humanitarian Award, Community Action Inc. 2011. *Leisure interests:* walking, golf, reading, spending time with family. *Address:* Office of the Governor, Capitol, 300 SW 10th Avenue, Suite 241S, Topeka, KS 66612-1590, USA (office). *Telephone:* (785) 296-3232 (office). *Website:* www.governor.kansas.gov (office); www.laurakellyforkansas.com.

KELLY, Michael Joseph, BS, MS, MA, PhD, ScD (Cantab.), CEng, CPhys, FRS, FREng, FInstP, FIET; New Zealand/British engineer, physicist and academic; *Prince Philip Professor Emeritus of Technology, University of Cambridge;* b. 14 May 1949, New Plymouth, NZ; m.; one d.; ed Victoria Univ. of Wellington, Univ. of Cambridge; Visiting Fellow, Dept of Physics, Victoria Univ. of Wellington 1974; Research Fellow in Physics, Trinity Hall, Cambridge 1974–77, Staff Fellow in Theoretical Physics 1977–81, Staff Fellow in Physics 1989–92; Prof. of Physics and Electronics, Dept of Physics, Univ. of Surrey 1992–2002, Head of Dept of Electronic and Electrical Eng 1996–97, Head of School of Electronic Eng, Information Tech. and Math. 1997–2001, Dir Centre for Solid State Electronics 2000, mem. Senate, Univ. of Surrey 1996, Council, Univ. of Surrey 1997, Planning and Resources Cttee 1997; Prince Philip Prof. of Tech., Dept of Eng, Univ. of Cambridge 2002–16, Prof. Emer. 2016–, Professorial Fellow, Trinity Hall 2002–16, Fellow Emer. 2016–, Exec. Dir Cambridge-MIT Inst. 2003–05; Chief Scientific Adviser to Dept of Communities and Local Govt 2006–09; Visiting Researcher, KFA-IFF, Julich, FRG 1975; IBM Research Fellow, Dept of Physics, Univ. of California, Berkeley 1975–76; SRC Advanced Fellow, Cavendish Lab., Cambridge 1977–81, Visiting Fellow 1988–92, Royal Soc./Science and Eng Research Council Industrial Fellow 1989–91; Visiting Fellow, Max Planck Institut für Festkorperforschung, Stuttgart, FRG 1980; mem. research staff, GEC Hirst Research Centre 1981–92, Man. Superlattice Research Group 1984–90, Coordinator GEC Superlattice Research 1984–92, Man. EEC, Dept of Trade and Industry, Ministry of Defence and GEC Research Contracts 1984–92; Dir (non-exec.) Laird plc 2006–15; mem. Council of the Royal Soc. 2001–02, Scientific Assessment Panel, Univ. of East Anglia Climatic Research Unit 2010, Tech. Advisory Group, Renewable Energy Foundation, Advisory Bd, Inst. of Electronics, Communications and Information Tech.; Assoc. Ed. International Journal of Electronics 1996–98; mem. American Inst. of Physics, IEEE; Fellow, Inst. of Physics (Vice-Pres. 2001–05), Inst. of Eng and Tech.; Hon. Fellow, Royal Soc. of NZ 1999; mem. Academia Europaea 2009; GEC Publs Prizewinner 1986, 1987, 1988, Paterson Medal and Prize, Inst. of Physics 1989, Nelson Gold Medal, GEC 1991, Silver Medal, Royal Acad. of Eng 1999, Hughes Medal, Royal Soc. 2006. *Publications:* The Physics and Fabrication of Microstructures and Microdevices (co-ed.) 1986, Technology Foresight Panel Report #8 on 'IT and Electronics' (co-author) 1995, Low Dimensional Semiconductors 1995, Advanced Materials in the Market Place (co-ed.) 1995, The Current Status of Semiconductor Tunnelling Devices (co-ed.) 1996; more than 210 papers and review articles, book chapters etc. in refereed journals, and in conf. proceedings etc.; 13 patents on semiconductor devices (seven patents still active). *Address:* Centre of Advanced Photonics and Electronics, Department of Engineering, University of Cambridge, 9 J.J. Thomson Avenue, Cambridge, CB3 0FA, England (office). *Telephone:* (1223) 748300 (office). *Fax:* (1223) 748334 (office). *Website:* www.eng.cam.ac.uk (office).

KELLY, Most Rev. Patrick Altham, STL, PhL; British ecclesiastic (retd); *Archbishop Emeritus of Liverpool;* b. 23 Nov. 1938, Morecambe; s. of John Kelly and Mary Kelly (née Altham); ed Preston Catholic Coll., Venerable English Coll., Rome; Asst Priest, Lancaster Cathedral 1964–66; Prof. of Dogmatic Theology, Oscott Coll., Birmingham 1966–79, Rector 1979–84; Bishop of Salford 1984–96; Archbishop of Liverpool, Metropolitan of the Northern Prov. 1996–2013, Archbishop Emer. 2013–. *Address:* Archbishop's House, Lowood, Carnatic Road, Liverpool, L18 8BY, England. *Telephone:* (151) 724-6398.

KELLY, Roslyn Joan (Ros), AO, BA; Australian fmr politician; *Executive Director, Environmental Resources Management;* b. 25 Jan. 1948, Sydney, NSW; d. of M. Raw and P. Raw; m. David Morgan; one s. one d.; ed Univ. of Sydney; high-school teacher, NSW and ACT 1969–74; consultant and mem. ACT Consumer Affairs Council 1974–79; mem. ACT Legal Aid Comm. 1976–79; fmr mem. ACT Legis. Ass.; mem. Fed. Parl. 1980–95; Sec. Fed. Labor Party Parl. Caucus 1981–87; Minister for Defence, Science and Personnel 1987–89, for Telecommunications and Aviation Support 1989–90, for Sport, the Environment and Territories 1990–94, for the Arts 1990–93, Assisting the Prime Minister for the Status of Women 1993–94; mem. Int. Advisory Council Normandy Mining Ltd 1995–2001; Group Exec. Dames & Moore 1995–2001; Exec. Dir Environmental Resources Management (consulting firm) 2001–; Dir (non-exec.) Theiss Pty Ltd 1998–, Thiess Environmental Services 1998–, External Sustainable Devt Advisory Group, The Rescue Helicopter Service; Chair. NSW Premiers Environmental Mining Awards 1999–, Minerals Council of Australia's External Advisory Group on Sustainability, Nat. Breast Cancer Foundation of Australia 2005–; mem. Advisory Council Sustainable Minerals Inst., Int. Council of Normandy Minerals, Nat. Advisory Council Greenfleet; Trustee, Worldwide Fund for Nature. *Leisure interests:* reading, films, aerobics. *Address:* National Breast Cancer Foundation, GPO Box 4126, Level 3, 18–20 York Street, Sydney, NSW 2000 (office); Environmental Resources Management, Building C, 33 Saunders Street, Pyrmont, NSW 2009, Australia. *E-mail:* info@nbcf.org.au (office); rkelly3@bigpond.net.au (home).

KELLY, Rt Hon. Ruth Maria, BA, MSc; British journalist, economist, business executive and fmr politician; *Global Head of Client Strategy, Global Asset Management, HSBC Holdings plc;* b. 9 May 1968, Limavady, Northern Ireland; d. of Bernard James Kelly and Gertrude Anne Kelly; m. Derek John Gadd 1996; one s. three d.; ed Sutton High School, Westminster School, Queen's Coll., Oxford, London School of Econs; econs writer, The Guardian newspaper 1990–94; economist, Bank of England 1994–97, Deputy Head of Inflation Report Div. 1994–96, Man. Financial Stability 1996–97; MP (Labour) Bolton W 1997–2010; Parl. Pvt. Sec. to Nicholas Brown MP 1998–2001; Econ. Sec. to HM Treasury 2001–02; Financial Sec. to HM Treasury 2002–04; Minister of State, Cabinet Office 2004; Sec. of State for Educ. and Skills 2004–06, for Communities and Local Govt 2006–07, for Transport 2007–08 (resgnd); Minister for Women 2006–07; Global Head of Client Strategy, Global Asset Man., HSBC Holdings plc 2010–; elected to Royal Econ. Soc. Council 1999–2001; mem. House of Commons Treasury Select Cttee 1997–98; mem. Council of Man. Nat. Inst. for Econ. and Social Research 1998–2001, Gov. 2001–; mem. Fabian Soc.; Hon. Fellow, Queen's Coll., Oxford; Minister to Watch, Zurich/Spectator Party Awards 2001. *Publications include:* Taxing the Spectator 1993, Hedging Your Futures (co-author) 1994, The Wrecker's Lamp (co-author) 1994, The Case for Universal Payment (chapter in Time Off with the Children: Paying for Parental Leave) 1999, Europe (chapter in Beyond 2000: Long-Term Policies for Labour) 1999, Reforming the Working Family Tax Credit: How An Integrated Child Credit Could Work for Children and Families 2000; chapters in New Gender Agenda 2000, The Progressive Century 2001. *Leisure interest:* family. *Address:* HSBC Global Asset Management (UK) Limited, 1F, 78 St James's Street, London, SW1A 1EJ, England (office). *Website:* www.assetmanagement.hsbc.com/uk (office).

KELMAN, James; Scottish writer; b. 9 June 1946, Glasgow; m. Marie Connors; two d.; ed Greenfield Public School, Govan Hyndland Soc., Glasgow. *Publications include:* novels: The Bus Conductor Hines 1984, A Chancer 1985, A Disaffection (James Tait Black Memorial Prize) 1989, How Late It Was, How Late (Booker Prize) 1994, Translated Accounts 2001, You Have to be Careful in the Land of the Free 2004, Kieron Smith, Boy (Saltire Soc's Book of the Year 2008, Scottish Mortgage Investment Trust Book of the Year 2009) 2008, Mo Said She Was Quirky (Saltire Book of the Year Award 2012) 2012; short stories: An Old Pub Near the Angel 1973, Short Tales from the Nightshift 1978, Not Not While the Giro 1983, Lean Tales 1985, Greyhound for Breakfast (Cheltenham Prize) 1987, The Burn (Scottish Arts Council Book Award) 1991, Busted Scotch 1997, The Good Times (Scottish Writer of the Year Award) 1998, If It is Your Life 2010; plays: The Busker 1985, In the Night 1988; others: And the Judges Said (essays) 2002, Dirt Road to Lafayette (screenplay) 2018. *Address:* c/o Gill Coleridge, Rogers, Coleridge and White Ltd, 20 Powis Mews, London, W11 1JN, England (office). *Telephone:* (20) 7221-3717 (office). *E-mail:* info@rcwlitagency.com (office). *Website:* www.rcwlitagency.com (office).

KELNER, Simon; British newspaper editor and public relations executive; *CEO, Seven Dials;* b. 9 Dec. 1957, Manchester; ed Bury Grammar School, Preston Polytechnic; Trainee Reporter, Neath Guardian 1976–79; Sports Reporter, Extel 1979–80; Sports Ed., Kent Evening Post 1980–83; Asst Sports Ed., The Observer 1983–86; Deputy Sports Ed., The Independent 1986–89; Sports Ed., Sunday Corresp. 1989–90; Sports Ed., The Observer 1990–93; Sports Ed., The Independent on Sunday 1993–95, Night Ed., The Independent 1995, Features Ed. 1995–96; Ed. Night and Day Magazine, Mail on Sunday 1996–98; Ed., The Independent 1998–2011, The Independent on Sunday 1998–2008, Ed.-in-Chief 2008–11, Man. Dir 2008–10, Ed.-in-Chief i Oct. 2010–11, now columnist; Founder and CEO Seven Dials (public relations firm) 2013–; Hon. Fellowship, Univ. of Cen. Lancashire; Ed. of the Year, What the Papers Say Awards 1999, 2003, 2004, Newspaper Ed. of the Year, Edgar Wallace Award 2000, 2004, Newspaper of the Year, British Press Awards 2004, GQ Editor of the Year 2004, 2010, Media Achiever of the Year, Campaign Media Awards 2004, Marketeer of the Year, Marketing Week Effectiveness Awards 2004, Editorial Intelligence Comment Award 2010. *Publication:* To Jerusalem and Back 1996. *Address:* Seven Dials, 56a Poland Street, London, W1F 7NN, England (office). *Telephone:* (20) 3740-7475 (office). *E-mail:* info@sevendialspr.com (office). *Website:* www.sevendialspr.com (office).

KEMAKEZA, Sir Allan, KBE; Solomon Islands politician; b. 1951, Panueli village, Central Prov.; joined Royal Solomon Islands Police Force 1972, apptd Asst Superintendent 1988; mem. Nat. Parl. representing Savo/Russels, Cen. Islands Prov. 1989–2010, Deputy Speaker 2006–07, Speaker 2010–14; Minister for Housing and Govt Service, Solomon Islands 1989–93; Minister for Forests, Environment and Conservation 1995–96; Deputy Prime Minister 2000–01;

Minister for Nat. Unity, Reconciliation and Peace 2000–01; Prime Minister 2001–06 (resgnd); Minister for Forestry 2007–10; served five months in prison in 2009 after being convicted of demanding money with menace, intimidation and larceny while Prime Minister; mem. People's Alliance Party. *Address:* c/o People's Alliance Party, Honiara, Solomon Islands (office).

KEMLER, Rudolf; Austrian business executive; b. 9 May 1956; m.; two c.; Man., WBG Betriebswirtschaft Beratungsgesellschaft mbH 1984–89; mem. Bd of Dirs and Sr Vice-Pres. for Banking and Insurance, Nixdorf Computer GmbH, Vienna 1989–90, Dir at Siemens Nixdorf Informationssysteme GmbH, Vienna 1990–92, Exec. Vice-Pres., Siemens Nixdorf Informationssysteme AG, Munich 1992–95, Head of Computer Systems Div., Siemens Nixdorf for the region Austria and SE Europe, Vienna 1995–98; Sr Vice-Pres. and Chief Information Officer, GE Capital Corpn, Stamford, Conn., USA 1998–2000; CEO stage1 Beteiligung-Management AG, Vienna 2000–02; CEO T-Systems Austria and Region Man. for Cen. and Eastern Europe 2002–08; Gen. Man. HP Austria 2008–12; mem. Bd of Dirs, Österreichische Industrieholding AG (ÖIAG, renamed Österreichische Bundes- und Industriebeteiligungen GmbH 2015) 2012–; Chair. Supervisory Bd, OMV AG 2012–15, Telekom Austria AG, Österreichische Post AG 2012–. *Address:* Österreichische Bundes- und Industriebeteiligungen GmbH (ÖBIB), Dresdner Strasse 87, 1201 Vienna, Austria (office). *Telephone:* (1) 711-14-0 (office). *Fax:* (1) 711-14-245 (office). *E-mail:* kommunikation@obib.co.at (office). *Website:* www.obib.co.at (office).

KEMMER, Michael; German banking executive; *General Manager, Association of German Banks (Bundesverband deutscher Banken);* b. 30 April 1957, Nördlingen; ed Ludwig-Maximilians Univ., Munich; Bank Officer, Bayerische Vereinsbank 1977–79, Cen. Accounts Div. 1988–94; Research Asst, Univ. of Munich 1984–87; Head, Main Finance Dept, DG Bank, Frankfurt 1994–96; Head, Cen. Div., Group Accounts, Bayerische Vereinsbank (now Bayerische Hypo- und Vereinsbank AG) 1996–2003, Head, Accounts and Taxes Div. 2003; mem. Bd of Man. and Chief Risk Officer HVB Group 2003–05; Chief Financial Officer Bavaria BayernLB 2006–08, Chair. Bd of Man. 2008–09; Gen. Man. Asscn of German Banks (Bundesverband deutscher Banken), Berlin 2010–, also mem. of Exec. Bd. *Address:* Association of German Banks (Bundesverband deutscher Banken), Burgstraße 28, 10178 Berlin, Germany (office). *Fax:* (30) 1663-13 (office). *E-mail:* bankenverband@bdb.de (office). *Website:* www.en.bankenverband.de (office).

KEMP, Brian Porter, BS; American politician and business executive; *Governor of Georgia;* b. 2 Nov. 1963, Athens, Ga; s. of William L. Kemp, II and Ann Cabanis; m. Marty Kemp (née Argo); three d.; ed Univ. of Georgia; f. Kemp Devt and Construction Co.; co-owner, Specialty Stone Supply; Founder Dir First Madison Bank; fmr Pres. Athens Area Home Builders Asscn; mem. Senate, Ga 2003–07, Sec. of State 2010–18, Gov. of Ga 2019–; mem. Bd, Suncrest Stone, Tifton, St Mary's Hospital, Athens. *Address:* Office of the Governor, 206 Washington Street, 111 State Capitol, Atlanta, GA 30334, USA (office). *Telephone:* (800) 436-7442 (office). *Website:* www.gov.georgia.gov (office); gov.georgia.gov.

KEMP, Martin John, MA, DLitt, FBA, FRSA, FRSE; British art historian, academic, author and exhibition curator; *Professor Emeritus, University of Oxford;* b. 5 March 1942, Windsor, Berks.; s. of Frederick Maurice Kemp and Violet Anne Kemp (née Tull); m. Jill Lightfoot 1966 (divorced 2003); one s. one d.; ed Windsor Grammar School, Downing Coll., Cambridge and Courtauld Inst. of Art, London; Lecturer in History of Western Art, Dalhousie Univ., NS, Canada 1965–66; Lecturer in History of Fine Art, Univ. of Glasgow 1966–81; Prof. of Fine Arts, Univ. of St Andrews 1981–90; Prof. of History, Royal Scottish Acad. 1985–; Prof. of History and Theory of Art, Univ. of St Andrews 1990–95; Prof. of History of Art, Univ. of Oxford 1995, now Prof. Emer. and Head of Dept; Fellow Trinity Coll. Oxford 1995–; Provost St Leonard's Coll., Univ. of St Andrews 1991–95; mem. Inst. for Advanced Study, Princeton, New Jersey, USA 1984–85; Slade Prof., Univ. of Cambridge 1987–88; Benjamin Sonenberg Visiting Prof., Inst. of Fine Arts, New York Univ. 1988; Wiley Visiting Prof., Univ. of North Carolina, Chapel Hill 1993; British Acad. Wolfson Research Prof. 1993–98; Visiting mem. Getty Center, Los Angeles 2002; Mellon Sr Fellow, Canadian Centre for Architecture, Montreal 2004; Lila Wallace-Reader's Digest Visiting Prof., I Tatti, Harvard Univ. 2010; Page-Barbour Lecturer, Univ. of Virginia 2012; Joseph Janson-La Palme Visiting Lecturer, Dept of Art and Archeology, Princeton Univ. 2013; regular columnist on Science in Culture in Nature 1997–2010; Pres. Leonardo da Vinci Soc. 1988–97; Chair. Asscn of Art Historians 1989–92; mem. Exec. Scottish Museums Council 1990–95; Dir and Chair. Graeme Murray Gallery 1990–92; Dir Wallace Kemp/Artakt 2001; mem. Visual Arts Advisory Panel, Arts Council of England 1996–; Trustee, Nat. Galleries of Scotland 1982–87, Victoria and Albert Museum, London 1986–89, British Museum 1995–, Ashmolean Museum 1995–, Wilhelmina Barns-Graham Trust 2000–12; Fellow, Royal Soc. of Sciences, Uppsala 1995; Hon. mem. American Acad. of Arts and Sciences 1996–, Hon. Fellow, Downing Coll., Cambridge 1999, Trinity Coll., Oxford 2008; Hon. DLitt (Heriot Watt) 1995, (Uppsala) 2009, (Glyndwr, Wales) 2009; Mitchell Prize 1981, Armand Hammer Prize for Leonardo Studies 1992, Pres.'s Prize, Italian Asscn of America 1992. *Publications include:* Leonardo da Vinci: The Marvellous Works of Nature and Man 1981, Leonardo on Painting (co-author) 1989, The Science of Art: Optical Themes in Western Art from Brunelleschi to Seurat 1990, Behind the Picture: Art and Evidence in the Italian Renaissance 1997, Immagine e Verità 1999, The Oxford History of Western Art (ed.) 2000, Spectacular Bodies (with Marina Wallace) 2000, Leonardo da Vinci: Experience, Experiment and Design 2006, Seen/Unseen 2006, The Human Animal 2007, Leonardo da Vinci: La Bella Principessa 2010, Leonardo da Vinci. I disegni di Leonardo da Vinci e della sua cerchia (with Juliana Barone) 2010, Christ to Coke: How Image Becomes Icon 2011, Madonna of the Yarnwinder (with Thereza Wells) 2011, The Chapel of Trinity College, Oxford 2013, Art in History, 600BC—2000AD 2014. *Leisure interests:* sport, music. *Address:* Trinity College, Oxford, OX1 3BH, England (office). *Telephone:* (1993) 811364 (office). *E-mail:* martin.kemp@trinity.ox.ac.uk (office). *Website:* www.martinjkemp.com.

KEMP-WELCH, Sir John, Kt, FRSA, CCMI; British fmr stock broker; b. 31 March 1936, Hertford; s. of Peter Kemp-Welch and Peggy Kemp-Welch; m. Diana Leishman 1964; one s. three d.; ed Winchester Coll.; Hoare & Co. 1954–58; Cazenove & Co. 1959–94, Jt Sr Partner 1980–94; Dir Savoy Hotel PLC 1985–98; Dir London Stock Exchange 1991–2000, Chair. 1994–2000; Chair. Scottish Eastern Investment Trust 1994–99, Claridge's Hotel 1995–97; Deputy Chair. Financial Reporting Council 1994–2000; Vice-Chair. Fed. of European Stock Exchanges 1996–98; Dir Royal and Sun Alliance Insurance Group PLC 1994–99, British Invisibles 1994–98, Securities and Futures Authority 1994–97, ProShare 1995–97, Accountancy Foundation 2000–, HSBC Holdings 2000–06; mem. Guild of Int. Bankers 2004–; Vice-Pres. Reed's School; Gov. The Ditchley Foundation 1980–2012; Trustee, King's Medical Research Trust (Chair. 1991–2006), Dulverton Trust 1994– (Vice-Chair. 2001–), Farmington Trust 2002–; Hon. Fellow, Chartered Securities Inst.; Hon. DBA (London Guildhall Univ.) 1998. *Leisure interests:* the hills of Perthshire, Impressionist paintings, champagne.

KEMPSTON DARKES, (Vera) Maureen, OC, BA, LLB; Canadian lawyer and automotive industry executive; b. 31 July 1948, Toronto, Ont.; m. Lawrence J. Darkes; ed Victoria Coll., Univ. of Toronto and Univ. of Toronto Law School; called to Bar of Toronto; mem. Legal Staff, General Motors (GM) of Canada Ltd 1975–79, Asst Counsel 1979, Head of Tax Staff 1980–84, Gen. Dir Public Affairs 1987, Vice-Pres. of Corp. Affairs and mem. Bd of Dirs 1991, Gen. Counsel and Sec. 1992, Pres. (first woman) and Gen. Man. 1994–2001, Vice-Pres. GM Corpn (one of only two female vice-pres) 1994–2001, Pres. GM Latin America, Africa and the Middle East and mem. GM Automotive Strategy Bd and Group Vice-Pres. 2002–09 (retd); mem. Legal Staff, General Motors Corpn, Detroit, Mich., USA 1979–80, mem. staff, Treas.'s Office, New York 1985–87, Vice-Pres. 1994–2001; mem. Bd of Dirs Hughes Aircraft of Canada, CAMI Automotive, CN Rail, Brascan Ltd, Thomson Corpn, Nat. Quality Inst., Nat. Research Council, Vehicle Mfrs Asscn, Ont. Govt Educ. Quality and Accountability Bd, Ont. Minister of Health's Women's Health Council; apptd to Free Trade Agreement Automotive Select Panel 1989, Transportation Equipment Sectoral Advisory Group on Int. Trade 1994; mem. Arts and Science Advisory Bd Univ. of Toronto, Bd of Govs Univ. of Waterloo, Business School Advisory Cttee Univ. of Western Ontario, Bd of Dirs Women's Coll. Hosp. Foundation, Chancellor's Council of Victoria Coll., Bd New Directions, Council of Advisory Govs for the YMCA of Greater Toronto; fmr Co-Chair. BC Cancer Foundation's Millennium Campaign; Order of Ontario 1997, Officer, Order of Ontario 2000; Hon. DComm (St Mary's Univ.) 1995; Hon. LLD Univ. of Toronto) 1996, (Univ. of Victoria, McMaster Univ., Dalhousie Univ., Wilfrid Laurier Univ., Law Soc. of Upper Canada); Women's Automotive Asscn Int. Professional Achievement Award 1997, ABA Margaret Brent Women Lawyers of Achievement Award 1998, Automotive Hall of Fame Distinguished Service Citation 1999, Gov.-Gen.'s Awards in Commemoration of the Persons Case 2006.

KEMPTHORNE, Dirk Arthur, BS; American government official and fmr politician; *President and CEO, American Council of Life Insurers;* b. 29 Oct. 1951, San Diego, Calif.; s. of James Henry Kempthorne and Maxine Jesse Kempthorne (née Gustason); m. Patricia Jean Merrill 1977; one s. one d.; ed Univ. of Idaho; Exec. Asst to Dir Idaho Dept Lands, Boise 1975–78; Exec. Vice-Pres. Idaho Home Builders' Asscn 1978–81; Campaign Man., Batt for Gov., Boise 1981–82; Idaho Public Affairs Man. FMC Corpn, Boise 1983–86; Mayor of Boise 1986–93; Senator from Idaho 1993–99; Gov. of Idaho 1999–2006; US Sec. of Interior 2006–09; Chair. US Conf. of Mayors Standing Cttee on Energy and Environment 1991–93, mem. Advisory Bd 1991–93; Sec. Nat. Conf. of Republican Mayors and Municipal Elected Officials 1991–93; Pres. and CEO American Council of Life Insurers 2010–; mem. Bd of Dirs, Parents and Youth Against Drug Abuse 1987–, FMC Corpn 2009–, Olympic Steel Inc. 2010–; mem. Advisory Bd, Protiviti Inc. 2009–; Trustee, Nat. Parks Conservation Asscn; Republican; numerous awards. *Address:* American Council of Life Insurers, 101 Constitution Avenue NW, Suite 700, Washington, DC 20001-2133, USA (office). *Telephone:* (202) 624-2000 (office). *E-mail:* contact@acli.com (office). *Website:* www.acli.com (office).

KENDAL, Felicity, CBE; British actress; b. 25 Sept. 1946, Olton, Warwicks., England; d. of Geoffrey Kendal and Laura Kendal; m. 1st Drewe Henley (divorced 1979); one s.; m. 2nd Michael Rudman 1983 (divorced 1991); one s.; ed six convents in India; first appeared on stage 1947, at age nine months in A Midsummer Night's Dream; grew up touring India and Far East with parents' theatre co., playing pageboys at age eight and Puck at age nine, graduating to roles such as Viola in Twelfth Night, Jessica in The Merchant of Venice and Ophelia in Hamlet; returned to England 1965; Variety Club Most Promising Newcomer 1974, Variety Club Best Actress 1979, Clarence Derwent Award 1980, Variety Club Woman of the Year, Best Actress 1984, Evening Standard Best Actress Award 1989, Variety Club Best Actress Award 2000. *Stage roles include:* London debut as Carla in Minor Murder, Savoy Theatre 1967, Katherine in Henry V, Lika in The Promise, Leicester 1968, Amaryllis in Back to Methuselah, Nat. Theatre, Hermia in A Midsummer Night's Dream, Hero in Much Ado About Nothing, Regent's Park, London 1970, Anne Danby in Kean, Oxford 1970, London 1971; Romeo and Juliet, 'Tis Pity She's a Whore and The Three Arrows 1972; The Norman Conquests, London 1974, Viktosha in Once Upon a Time, Bristol 1976, Arms and The Man, Greenwich 1978, Mara in Clouds, London 1978; Constanza Mozart in Amadeus, Desdemona in Othello; On the Razzle 1981, The Second Mrs. Tanqueray, The Real Thing 1982, Jumpers 1985, Made in Bangkok 1986, Hapgood 1988, Ivanov 1989, Much Ado About Nothing 1989, Hidden Laughter 1990, Tartuffe 1991, Heartbreak House 1992, Arcadia 1992, An Absolute Turkey 1994, Indian Ink 1995, Mind Millie for Me 1996, The Seagull 1997, Waste 1997, Alarms and Excursions 1998, Fallen Angels 2000, Humble Boy 2002, Happy Days 2003, Amy's View 2006, The Vortex 2008, The Last Cigarette 2009, Mrs Warren's Profession 2010, Relatively Speaking (tour) 2012 and Wyndham's Theatre 2013, Chin Chin 2013. *Films include:* Shakespeare-Wallah 1965, Valentino 1976, We're Back! A Dinosaur's Story (voice) 1993, Parting Shots 1998. *Television includes:* Love Story (series) 1966, The Wednesday Play – The Mayfly and the Frog 1966, ITV Play of the Week (series) – Person Unknown 1967, Half Hour Story (series) – Gone, and Never Called Me Mother 1967, Boy Meets Girl (series) – Love with a Few Hairs 1967, Thirty-Minute Theatre (series) – Come Death 1967, Man in a Suitcase (series) – Blind Spot 1968, The Tenant of Wildfell Hall (series) 1968–69, The Woodlanders (series) 1970, Crime of Passion (play) 1971, Jason King (series) 1972, The Dolly Dialogues (series) 1973, Dolly (series) 1973, The Good Life 1975–78, Edward the Seventh (series) 1975, Murder (series) – A Variety of Passion 1976, ITV Sunday Night Drama – Now Is Too Late 1976, – Clouds of Glory: William and Dorothy 1978, – Clouds of Glory: The Rime of the Ancient Mariner 1978, Do You Remember? (series) – Home and Beauty 1978, Wings of Song (film) 1978, The Marriage Counsellor (film) 1978, Twelfth Night 1979, Solo 1981–82, On the Razzle (film)

1983, The Mistress 1985–87, Favourite Things (BBC) 1986, The Camomile Lawn 1992, Shakespeare: The Animated Tales (series) – Romeo and Juliet (narrator) 1992, Honey for Tea (series) 1994, The World of Peter Rabbit and Friends (series) (voice) 1995, How Proust Can Change Your Life (film) 2000, Rosemary & Thyme 2003–06, The Secret Show (series) – It's a Hamster World 2007, Doctor Who (series) – The Unicorn and the Wasp 2008, Strictly Come Dancing 2010, Shakespeare, India & Felicity Kendal 2012. *Publication:* White Cargo (memoirs) 1998. *Address:* c/o Dallas Smith, United Agents, 12–26 Lexington Street, London, W1F 0LE, England (office). *Telephone:* (20) 3214-0800 (office). *Fax:* (20) 3214-0801 (office). *E-mail:* info@unitedagents.co.uk (office). *Website:* www.unitedagents.co.uk (office).

KENDALL, David William, FCA; British business executive; b. 8 May 1935; s. of William Jack Kendall and Alma May Kendall; m. 1st Delphine Hitchcock 1960 (divorced); one s. one d.; m. 2nd Elisabeth Rollison 1973; one s. one d.; ed Enfield Grammar School, Southend High School; with Elles Reeve & Co. 1955–62, Shell-Mex & BP Ltd 1963–68; Finance Dir Irish Shell & BP Ltd 1969–70; Crude Oil Sales Man. British Petroleum Co. Ltd 1971–72, Man. Bulk Trading Div. 1973–74, mem. Org. Planning Cttee 1975; Gen. Man. BP NZ Ltd 1976–79, Man. Dir and CEO 1980–82; Chair. BP South West Pacific 1979–82; Finance and Planning Dir BP Oil Ltd 1982–85, Man. Dir and CEO 1985–88; Dir BP Chemicals Int. 1985–88, BP Oil Int. 1985–88, BP Detergents Int. 1985–88; Deputy Chair. British Coal Corpn 1989–90; Chair. Ruberoid PLC 1993–2000, Whitecroft PLC 1993–99, Meyer Int. PLC 1994–95, Celtic Energy Ltd 1994–2003, Wagon PLC 1997–2005, G-T-P Group Ltd 2006–11; Dir STC PLC 1988–90, Danka Business Systems PLC 1993–2000 (Chair. 1998–2000), Gowrings 1993–2004, South Wales Electricity PLC 1993–96; Dir (non-exec.) Bunzl PLC 1988–90 (Chair. 1990–93), Blagden Industries PLC 1993–94 (Chair. 1994–2000), British Standards Inst. 2000–05; Pres. UK Petroleum Industries Asscn 1987–88, Oil Industries Club 1988. *Leisure interests:* golf, music. *Address:* 41 Albion Street, London, W2 2AU, England. *Telephone:* (20) 7258-1955.

KENEALLY, Kristina Kerscher, BA, MA; Australian (b. American) politician and organization official; *CEO, Basketball Australia;* b. 1969, USA; m. Ben Keneally 1996; two s.; ed Univ. of Dayton, Ohio, USA; emigrated to Australia 1994; NSW Youth Coordinator, Soc. of St Vincent de Paul 1995–2003; mem. NSW Legis. Ass. for Heffron constituency 2003–12, NSW Minister for Ageing and Disability Services 2007–08, for Planning 2008–09, also Minister for Redfern Waterloo 2008–12; Premier NSW 2009–11; mem. Australian Labor Party (ALP), Leader ALP in NSW 2009–11; CEO Basketball Australia 2012–. *Address:* Basketball Australia, PO Box 7141, Alexandria, NSW 2015, Australia (office). *Telephone:* (2) 8396-5522 (office). *Fax:* (2) 8396-5501 (office). *E-mail:* ceo@basketball.net.au (office). *Website:* www.basketball.net.au (office).

KENEALLY, Thomas Michael, AO, FRSL; Australian writer; b. 7 Oct. 1935, Sydney; s. of Edmund Thomas and Elsie Margaret Keneally; m. Judith Mary Martin 1965; two d.; ed St Patrick's Coll.; Lecturer in Drama, Univ. of New England, NSW 1968–70; Visiting Prof., Univ. of Calif., Irvine 1985, Prof. Dept of English and Comparative Literature 1991–95; Berg Prof., Dept of English, New York Univ. 1988; Pres. Nat. Book Council of Australia –1987; Chair. Australian Soc. of Authors 1987–90, Pres. 1990–; Fellow, Australian Acad. of the Humanities; mem. Literary Arts Bd 1985–; mem. Australia-China Council, American Acad. of Arts and Sciences; Founding Chair. Australian Republican Movt 1991–93; Hon. DLit (Univ. of Queensland), (Nat. Univ. of Ireland) 1994; Hon. DLitt (Fairleigh Dickenson Univ., USA) 1996, (Rollins Coll., USA) 1996; Captain Cook Bicentenary Prize 1970, Royal Soc. of Literature Prize 1982, Mondello Int. Prize, Scripter Award, Univ. of Southern California (as writer of film Schindler's List) 1993, Peggy V. Helmerich Distinguished Author Award 2007, Special Award, New South Wales Premier's Literary Awards 2008, chosen to deliver Gandhi Oration, Univ. of New South Wales 2014. *Publications include:* The Place at Whitton 1964, The Fear 1965, Bring Larks and Heroes (Miles Franklin Award 196) 1967, Three Cheers for the Paraclete (Miles Franklin Award 1968) 1968, The Survivor 1969, A Dutiful Daughter 1970, The Chant of Jimmie Blacksmith (Heinemann Award 1973) 1972, Blood Red, Sister Rose 1974, Gossip from the Forest 1975, Moses and the Lawgiver 1975, Season in Purgatory 1976, A Victim of the Aurora 1977, Ned Kelly and the City of Bees 1978, Passenger 1978, Confederates 1979, Schindler's Ark (Booker Prize 1983, Los Angeles Times Fiction Prize 1983) 1982, Outback 1983, The Cut-Rate Kingdom 1984, A Family Madness 1985, Australia: Beyond the Dreamtime (contrib.) 1987, The Playmaker 1987, Towards Asmara 1989, Flying Hero Class 1991, Now and in Time to Be: Ireland and the Irish 1992, Woman of the Inner Sea 1992, The Place Where Souls Are Born: A Journey into the American Southwest 1992, Jacko: The Great Intruder 1993, The Utility Player – The Story of Des Hassler (non-fiction) 1993, Our Republic (non-fiction) 1993, A River Town 1995, Homebush Boy: A Memoir 1995, The Great Shame: And the Triumph of the Irish in the English-Speaking World 1998, Bettany's Book 2000, An American Scoundrel: The Life of the Notorious Civil War General Dan Sickles (non-fiction) 2002, An Angel in Australia 2002, Abraham Lincoln (biog.) 2003, The Office of Innocence 2003, The Tyrant's Novel 2004, The Commonwealth of Thieves: The Story of the Founding of Australia (non-fiction) 2006, The Widow and Her Hero 2007, Searching for Schindler: A Memoir 2008, The People's Train 2009, Three Famines 2011, The Daughters of Mars 2013, Shame and the Captives 2014. *Leisure interests:* cross-country skiing, swimming, hiking. *Address:* Curtis Brown (Australia) Pty Ltd, PO Box 19, Paddington, NSW 2021, Australia (office). *Website:* www.randomhouse.com.au/authors/tom-keneally.aspx (office).

KENNARD, Olga, OBE, ScD, FRS; British research scientist; b. 23 March 1924, Budapest, Hungary; d. of Joir Weisz and Catherina Weisz; m. 1st David Kennard 1948 (divorced 1961); two d.; m. 2nd Sir Arnold Burgen (q.v.) 1993; ed schools in Hungary, Prince Henry VIII Grammar School, Evesham and Newnham Coll. Cambridge; Research Asst, Cavendish Lab., Cambridge 1944–48; MRC Scientific Staff, London 1948–61; MRC External Scientific Staff, Univ. of Cambridge 1961–89; Dir Cambridge Crystallographic Data Centre 1965–97; MRC Special Appt. 1969–89; Visiting Prof., Univ. of London 1988–90; mem. Academia Europaea, Council, Royal Soc. 1995–97; Trustee, British Museum 2004–12; Hon. LLD Univ. of Cambridge 2003; Royal Soc. of Chem. Prize for Structural Chem. 1980. *Publications:* about 200 papers in scientific journals and books on X-ray crystallography, molecular biology, information technology; 20 scientific reference books. *Leisure interests:* swimming, music, modern architecture and design. *Address:* Keelson, 8A Hills Avenue, Cambridge, CB1 7XA, England. *Telephone:* (1223) 415381.

KENNARD, William E.; American business executive, lawyer, fmr diplomatist and fmr government official; *Senior Advisor, Grain Management LLC;* b. 19 Jan. 1957, Los Angeles, Calif.; s. of Robert A. Kennard and Helen Z. King; m. Deborah D. Kennedy 1984; one s.; ed Stanford Univ., Yale Law School; fmrly with Nat. Asscn of Broadcasters; fmr Pnr and mem. Bd Dirs Verner, Liipfert, Bernhard, McPherson and Hand law firm; Gen. Counsel to Fed. Communications Comm. 1993–97, Chair. 1997–2001; Man. Dir Global Telecommunications and Media Investment Strategy, The Carlyle Group LLC 2001–09; Amb. to EU, Brussels 2009–13; Sr Advisor, Grain Management LLC 2013–; mem. Bd of Dirs MetLife; Dr hc (Howard Univ.), (Gallaudet Univ.), (Long Island Univ.). *Address:* Grain Management, LLC, 1900 K Street, NW, Suite 1130, Washington, DC 20006, USA (office). *Telephone:* (202) 779-9043 (office). *Website:* graingp.com (office).

KENNEDY, A(lison) L(ouise), BA (Hons); British writer, entertainer and academic; b. 22 Oct. 1965, Dundee, Scotland; d. of Robert Alan Kennedy and Edwardene Mildred Price; ed Univ. of Warwick; community arts worker for Clydebank & Dist 1988–89; writer 1988–; Writer-in-Residence, Hamilton & East Kilbride Social Work Dept 1989–91, for Project Ability, Arts & Special Needs 1989–95, Copenhagen Univ. 1995; book reviewer for The Scotsman, Glasgow Herald, BBC, STV, The Telegraph 1990–; Ed. New Writing Scotland 1993–95; part-time Lecturer, St Andrews Univ. 2002–07; Assoc. Prof., Creative Writing Programme, Univ. of Warwick 2007–12; columnist, The Guardian; stand-up comedian, reviewer, performer 2005–; radio presenter 2009–; Hon. DLit (Glasgow), (St Andrews); Somerset Maugham Award, Encore Award, SAC Book Award (four times), Saltire Scottish Book of the Year Award, Best of Young British Novelists (twice), Lannan Literary Award for Fiction 2007, Austrian State Prize for European Literature, Eifel Literature Prize. *Plays:* The Audition (Fringe First Award) 1993, Delicate (performance piece for Motionhouse dance co.) 1995, True (performance project for Fierce Productions and Tramway Theatre) 1998. *Film:* Stella Does Tricks (writer) 1996. *Radio:* Born a Fox (BBC Radio 4 drama) 2002, Like an Angel (BBC Radio 4 drama) 2004, Confessions of a Medium (BBC Radio drama) 2010, Blood Empire (SWR, Germany, drama) 2010, That I Should Rise 2012, Love Love Love Like The Beatles (BBC Radio 4) 2012. *Television:* Ghostdancing (BBC drama/documentary, writer and presenter) 1995, Dice (series I and II, with John Burnside, CBC TV). *Publications:* Night Geometry and the Garscadden Trains 1991, Looking for the Possible Dance 1993, Now That You're Back 1994, So I Am Glad 1995, Tea and Biscuits 1996, Original Bliss 1997, The Life and Death of Colonel Blimp 1997, Everything You Need 1999, On Bullfighting 1999, Indelible Acts 2002, Paradise 2004, Day (Saltire Scottish Book of the Year Award 2007, Costa Book of the Year Award 2007) 2007, What Becomes 2009, The Blue Book 2011, On Writing 2013, All The Rage (short stories) 2014, Serious Sweet 2016. *Leisure interest:* sleeping. *Address:* c/o Antony Harwood Ltd, 103 Walton Street, Oxford, OX2 6EB, England (office). *Website:* www.antonyharwood.com (office); www.a-l-kennedy.co.uk. *E-mail:* info@a-l-kennedy.co.uk.

KENNEDY, Anthony M., BA, LLB; American lawyer and judge (retd); b. 23 July 1936, Sacramento, Calif.; s. of Anthony J. Kennedy and Gladys Kennedy; m. Mary Davis; two s. one d.; ed Stanford Univ., LSE and Harvard Univ. Law School; mem. Calif. Bar 1962, US Tax Court Bar 1971; Assoc., Thelen, Marrin, Johnson & Bridges (law firm), San Francisco 1961–63; sole practice, Sacramento 1963–67; Pnr, Evans, Jackson & Kennedy (law firm) 1967–75; Prof. of Constitutional Law, McGeorge School of Law, Univ. of Pacific 1965; Judge, US Court of Appeals, 9th Circuit, Sacramento 1976–88; Assoc. Justice, Supreme Court of USA, Washington, DC 1988–2018. *Address:* c/o United States Supreme Court, One First Street NE, Washington, DC 20543, USA (office).

KENNEDY, Caroline Bouvier, JD; American lawyer and diplomatist; b. 27 Nov. 1957, New York, NY; d. of John F. Kennedy (Pres. of USA) and Jacqueline Bouvier Kennedy; m. Edwin Arthur Schlossberg 1986; one s. two d.; ed Radcliffe Coll., Columbia Univ. Law School; Research Asst, Film and TV Dept, Metropolitan Museum of Art 1980; Dir, Office of Strategic Partnerships, New York City Dept of Educ. 2002–04; Nat. Co-Chair. Pres. Barack Obama's 2012 re-election campaign; Amb. to Japan 2013–17; Pres. Kennedy Library Foundation; mem. New York and Washington DC bar asscns. *Publications include:* with Ellen Alderman: In Our Defense: The Bill of Rights in Action 1991, The Right to Privacy 1995; A Family Christmas 2007.

KENNEDY, Donald, MA, PhD; American biologist, academic, editor and fmr university administrator; *President Emeritus, Stanford University;* b. 18 Aug. 1931, New York; s. of William D. Kennedy and Barbara Kennedy (née Bean); m. 1st Barbara J. Dewey 1953; two d.; m. 2nd Robin Beth Wiseman 1987; two step-s.; ed Harvard Univ.; Asst Prof., Syracuse Univ. 1956–59, Assoc. Prof. 1959–60; Asst Prof., Stanford Univ. 1960–62, Assoc. Prof. 1962–65, Prof. 1965–77, Chair. Dept of Biological Sciences 1965–72, Benjamin Crocker Prof. of Human Biology 1974–77, Vice-Pres. and Provost 1979–80, Pres. 1980–92, Pres. Emer. and Bing Prof. of Environmental Science Emer. 1992–; Sr Consultant, Office of Science and Tech. Policy, Exec. Office of the Pres. 1976–77; Commr of Food and Drug Admin. 1977–79; Ed.-in-Chief Science Magazine 2000–08; Fellow, American Acad. of Arts and Sciences; mem. NAS; Hon. DSc (Columbia Univ., Williams Coll., Michigan, Rochester, Ariz., Whitman Coll., Coll. of William and Mary); Dinkelspiel Award 1976, Wonderfest's Carl Sagan Prize 2010. *Publications include:* The Biology of Organisms (with W. M. Telfer) 1965, Academic Duty 1997, U.S. Policy and the Global Environment 2000; over 60 articles in scientific journals. *Leisure interests:* skiing, fly fishing, natural history. *Address:* Stanford University, Encina Hall E401, Stanford, CA 94305 (office); 532 Channing Avenue, #302, Palo Alto, CA 94301, USA (home). *Telephone:* (650) 725-9888 (office). *Fax:* (650) 725-1992 (office). *Website:* fsi.stanford.edu/people/donaldkennedy (office).

KENNEDY, Geraldine; Irish journalist; *Adjunct Professor of Journalism, University of Limerick;* b. 7 Sept. 1951, Tramore, Co. Waterford; d. of James Kennedy and Nora McGrath; m. David J. Hegarty; two d.; ed Convent S.H.M., Ferrybank, Waterford; Political Corresp. The Sunday Tribune 1980–82, The Sunday Press 1982–87; mem. Dáil Éireann (Irish Parl.) 1987–89; Public Affairs Corresp. The Irish Times 1990–93, Political Corresp. 1993–99, Political Ed.

1999–2002, Duty Ed. 2000–02, Ed. 2002–11, Dir Irish Times Ltd 2002–11, Adjunct Prof. of Journalism, Univ. of Limerick 2012–; Hon. mem., Royal Irish Acad.; Hon. DUniv (Queen's Univ., Belfast) 2005, Hon. DPhil (Dublin Inst. of Tech.) 2007, Hon. DrIur (Univ. Coll., Dublin) 2008; Journalist of the Year 1994. *Leisure interests:* travel, reading, food. *Address:* University of Limerick, Limerick V94 T9PX, Ireland (office).

KENNEDY, James Cox, BBA; American publishing and media executive; *Chairman, Cox Enterprises Inc.;* b. 1947, Honolulu, Hawaii; m. Sarah Kennedy; three s.; ed Univ. of Denver; with Atlanta Newspapers 1976–79; Pres. Grand Junction Newspapers 1979–80, Publr Grand Junction Daily Sentinel 1980–85; Vice-Pres. Newspaper Div. Cox Enterprises Inc. 1985–86, Exec. Vice-Pres. then Pres. 1986–87, COO then Chair. 1987–; Chair. and CEO Cox Enterprises Inc. 1988–2010, now Chair., also Chair. Cox Communications and Cox Radio; mem. Bd of Dirs Ducks Unlimited, Atlanta Cttee for Progress, PATH Foundation; fmr Pres. Wetlands America Trust; Dr hc (Kennesaw State Univ.) 2003, (Colorado State Univ.) 2018. *Cycling achievements:* past Masters Nat., Pan American and World Champion in 3000m pursuit; served as capt. of four-man team that won Race Across America (RAAM) 1992, setting world record. *Address:* Cox Enterprises Inc., 6205 Peachtree Dunwoody Road, Atlanta, GA 30328 (office); 1601 West Peachtree Street NE, Atlanta, GA 30309, USA (home). *Telephone:* (678) 645-0000 (office). *Fax:* (678) 645-1079 (office). *Website:* www.coxenterprises.com (office).

KENNEDY, John Neely, BA, JD, BCL; American lawyer and politician; *Senator from Louisiana;* b. 21 Nov. 1951, Centreville, Miss.; m. Becky Stulb; one s.; ed Vanderbilt Univ., Univ. of Virginia School of Law, Univ. of Oxford, UK; Attorney, later Partner, Chaffe, McCall, Phillips, Toler and Sarpy LLP, Baton Rouge, New Orleans, La 1984–95; Special Counsel to Louisiana Gov. Buddy Roemer 1988–92; Sec., Louisiana Dept of Revenue 1996–99, State Treas., State of Louisiana 1999–2017; Adjunct Prof., Louisiana State Univ. Law School 2005–; Senator from Louisiana 2017–; Democrat –2007; Republican 2007–. *Address:* B11 Russell Senate Office Building, Washington, DC 20510, USA (office). *Telephone:* (202) 224-4623 (office). *Website:* www.senate.gov (office).

KENNEDY, Nigel Paul, ARCM; British violinist; b. 28 Dec. 1956, Brighton; s. of John Kennedy and Scylla Stoner; m. Agnieska Kennedy; one s.; ed Yehudi Menuhin School, Juilliard School of Performing Arts, USA; debut playing Mendelssohn's Violin Concerto at Royal Festival Hall with London Philharmonic Orchestra under Riccardo Muti 1977; subsequently chosen by BBC as subject of a five-year documentary on the devt of a soloist; other important debuts include with Berlin Philharmonic 1980, New York 1987; has made appearances at all leading UK festivals and in Europe at Stresa, Lucerne, Gstaad, Berlin and Lockenhaus; tours to Australia, Austria, Canada, Denmark, Germany, Hong Kong, India, Ireland, Italy, Japan, Republic of Korea, New Zealand, Norway, Poland, Spain, Switzerland, Turkey and USA; has given jazz concerts with Stephane Grappelli, including at Edinburgh Festival and Carnegie Hall; performs with his own jazz group; five-year sabbatical 1992–97; Artistic Dir Polish Chamber Orchestra 2002–; apptd Sr Vice-Pres. Aston Villa Football Club 1990; Hon. DLitt (Bath) 1991; Golden Rose of Montreux 1990, Variety Club Showbusiness Personality of the Year 1991, BRIT Award for Outstanding Contribution to British Music 2000, Male Artist of the Year 2001, Echo Klassik Award for Instrumentalist of the Year 2008. *Television:* Coming Along Nicely (BBC documentary on his early career) 1973–78. *Recordings include:* Strad Jazz 1984, Elgar Sonata with Peter Pettinger 1985, Elgar's Violin Concerto with the London Philharmonic and Vernon Handley (Gramophone magazine Record of the Year, BPI Award for Best Classical Album of the Year) 1985, Vivaldi's Four Seasons, Bartók Solo Sonata and Mainly Black (arrangement of Ellington's Black Brown and Beige Suite), Sibelius Violin Concerto with the City of Birmingham Symphony Orchestra conducted by Sir Simon Rattle, Walton's Violin Concerto with the Royal Philharmonic Orchestra and André Previn, Bruch and Mendelssohn concertos with the English Chamber Orchestra conducted by Jeffrey Tate, Kafka (Kennedy's compositions), Tchaikovsky's Chausson Poème with the London Philharmonic Orchestra 1988, Brahms Violin Concerto with the London Philharmonic under Klaus Tennstedt 1991, Beethoven Violin Concerto with the NDR-Sinfonieorchester and Klaus Tennstedt 1992, chamber works by Debussy and Ravel, Berg's Violin Concerto, Vaughan Williams' The Lark Ascending with Sir Simon Rattle and the CBSO, works by Fritz Kreisler 1998, The Kennedy Experience, chamber works by Bach, Ravel and Kodaly (with Lynn Harrell) 1999, Classic Kennedy with the English Chamber Orchestra 1999, Bach's Concerto for Two Violins in D Minor, Concerto for Oboe and Violin in D Minor and the A Minor and E Major violin concertos the Berlin Philharmonic 2000, Nigel Kennedy Plays Bach 2006, Inner Thoughts 2006, Blue Note Sessions 2006, Polish Spirit 2007, Beethoven and Mozart Violin Concertos 2008, A Very Nice Album 2008, Shhh! 2010, My World 2016. *Publication:* Always Playing 1991. *Leisure interests:* cricket, golf, football. *Address:* Terri Robson Associates, 63–64 Leinster Square, London, W2 4PS, England (office). *Website:* www.nigelkennedy.co.uk.

KENNEDY, Patrick J., BCom, MBS; Irish business executive; b. 22 Sept. 1953, Galway; joined Calor Gas Ltd (subsidiary of SHV Energy NV) 1982, becoming man. of various SHV cos in Eastern Europe, UK and Brazil, including Probugas, Slovakia 1993–94, Pamgas 1994–96, Dir Supergasbras Distribuidora de Gás, Brazil 1996–98, Dir Calor Gas Ltd 1998–2000, Chair. SHV Gas 2000–01, mem. Exec. Bd SHV Holdings 2001–14, Chair. 2006–14; Dir (non-Exec.) CRH PLC 2015–.

KENNEDY, Rt Hon. Sir Paul (Joseph Morrow), PC, MA, LLB; British judge (retd); b. 12 June 1935, Sheffield, Yorks.; m. Virginia Devlin 1965; two s. two d.; ed Ampleforth Coll., York, Gonville & Caius Coll., Cambridge; called to Bar Gray's Inn 1960, Bencher 1982, Treas. 2002; Recorder of Crown Court 1972–83; QC 1973; Judge, High Court of Justice, Queen's Bench Div. (QBD) 1983–92, Vice-Pres. QBD 1997–2002; Presiding Judge, NE Circuit 1985–89; Lord Justice of Appeal 1992–2005 (retd); Chair. Criminal Cttee Judicial Studies Bd 1993–96; mem. Sentencing Guidelines Council –2005, Court of Appeal of Gibraltar 2006–15 (Pres. 2011–15); Interception of Communications Commr 2006–12; Hon. Fellow, Gonville & Caius Coll. Cambridge 1998; Hon. LLD (Sheffield) 2000. *Leisure interests:* family, walking, occasional golf.

KENNEDY, Paul Michael, CBE, MA, DPhil, FRHistS, FBA; British historian and academic; *J. Richardson Dilworth Professor of History and Director, International Security Studies, Yale University;* b. 17 June 1945, Wallsend; s. of John Patrick Kennedy and Margaret Kennedy (née Hennessy); m. 1st Catherine Urwin 1967 (died 1998); three s.; m. 2nd Cynthia Farrar 2001; ed St Cuthbert's Grammar School, Newcastle-upon-Tyne, Univ. of Newcastle, Univ. of Oxford; Research Asst to Sir Basil Liddell Hart 1966–70; Lecturer, Reader and Prof., Univ. of East Anglia 1970–83; J. Richardson Dilworth Prof. of History, Yale Univ. 1983–, Co-Dir Int. Security Studies 1993–98, now Dir, also Distinguished Fellow of Brady-Johnson Program in Grand Strategy; Visiting Fellow, Inst. for Advanced Study, Princeton 1978–79; Philippe Roman Chair in History and International Affairs, LSE 2007–08, also Sr Fellow, LSE IDEAS; Fellow, Alexander von Humboldt Foundation, American Philosophical Soc., American Acad. of Arts and Sciences; Hon. DHL (New Haven, Alfred, Long Island, Connecticut); Hon. DLitt (Newcastle, East Anglia); Hon. LLD (Ohio); Hon. MA (Yale, Union, Quinnipiac); Dr hc (Leuven). *Publications include:* The Samoan Tangle 1974, The Rise and Fall of British Naval Mastery 1976, The Rise of the Anglo-German Antagonism 1980, The Realities Behind Diplomacy 1981, Strategy and Diplomacy 1983, The Rise and Fall of the Great Powers 1988, Grand Strategy in War and Peace 1991, Preparing for the Twenty-First Century 1993, Pivotal States: A New Framework for US Policy in the Developing World (ed.) 1998, The Parliament of Man: The United Nations and the Quest for World Government 2006, Engineers of Victory: The Problem Solvers Who Turned The Tide in the Second World War 2013. *Leisure interests:* soccer, hill-walking, old churches. *Address:* Department of History, Yale Univ., PO Box 208353, New Haven, CT 06520-8353, USA (office). *Telephone:* (203) 432-6242 (office). *Fax:* (203) 432-6250 (office). *E-mail:* paul.kennedy@yale.edu (office). *Website:* www.yale.edu/iss (office).

KENNEDY, Thomas John; British diplomatist; b. 3 Feb. 1957; m. Clare Marie Kennedy; one s.; Marketing and Training Man., Bata Shoe Co., UK and E Africa 1982–91; Desk Officer, Southern European Dept, FCO 1992–93, Second Sec. (Press and Public Diplomacy), Buenos Aires 1994–97, Head of Levant Section, Near East and N Africa Dept, FCO 1997–99, Head of WMD (Weapons of Mass Destruction) Export Controls Section, Non-Proliferation Dept 1999–2001, Consul-Gen., Bordeaux 2002–06, Amb. to Costa Rica (also accred to Nicaragua) 2006–11.

KENNEDY, William Joseph, BA; American author and academic; *Professor of Creative Writing and Director, New York State Writers' Institute, University at Albany, State University of New York;* b. 16 Jan. 1928, Albany, New York; s. of William J. Kennedy and Mary E. McDonald; m. Ana Segarra 1957; one s. two d.; ed Siena Coll.; Asst Sports Ed. and columnist, Glens Falls Post Star, New York 1949–50; reporter, Albany Times-Union, New York 1952–56, special writer 1963–70; Asst Man. Ed. and columnist, P.R. World Journal, San Juan 1956; reporter, Miami Herald 1957; corresp., Time-Life Publs, Puerto Rico 1957–59; reporter, Knight Newspapers 1957–59; Founding Man. Ed. San Juan Star 1959–61; Lecturer, State Univ. of New York, Albany 1974–82, Prof. of English 1983–; Visiting Prof., Cornell Univ. 1982–83; Exec. Dir and Founder, NY State Writers' Inst. 1983–; Nat. Endowment for Arts Fellow 1981, MacArthur Foundation Fellow 1983; mem. American Acad. of Arts and Letters 1993–, American Acad. of Arts and Sciences 2002–; Commdr, Ordre des Arts et des Lettres; several hon. degrees; Gov. of New York Arts Award 1984, Creative Arts Award, Brandeis Univ. 1986, Peggy V. Helmerich Distinguished Author Award, Tulsa Library Trust 2001, F. Scott Fitzgerald Literary Award 2007, Eugene O'Neill Lifetime Achievement Award 2009, State Univ. of New York Medallion of Distinction 2012. *Publications include:* The Ink Truck 1969, Legs 1975, Billy Phelan's Greatest Game 1978, Ironweed (Pulitzer Prize and Nat. Book Critics Circle Award 1984) 1983, O Albany! (non-fiction) 1983, Charlie Malarkey and the Belly Button Machine (children's book) 1986, Quinn's Book 1988, Very Old Bones 1992, Riding the Yellow Trolley Car 1993, Charlie Malarkey and the Singing Moose (children's book) 1994, The Flaming Corsage 1996, Grand View (play) 1996, Roscoe 2002, Chango's Beads and Two-Tone Shoes 2011; film scripts, The Cotton Club 1984; also short stories, articles in professional journals. *Address:* Department of English, University at Albany, State University of New York, Humanities 333, 1400 Washington Avenue, Albany, NY 12222; New York State Writers Institute, Science Library, SL 320, University at Albany, State University of New York, Albany, NY 12222 (office); 1441 Burden Lake Road, Averill Park, NY 12018, USA. *Telephone:* (518) 442-5620 (office). *Fax:* (518) 442-5621 (office). *E-mail:* writers@uamail.albany.edu (office). *Website:* www.albany.edu/writers-inst (office); www.albany.edu/english (office).

KENNEDY OF THE SHAWS, Baroness (Life Peer) cr. 1997, of Cathcart in the City of Glasgow; **Helena Ann Kennedy,** QC, FRSA; British lawyer; b. 12 May 1950, Glasgow, Scotland; d. of Joshua Kennedy and Mary Jones; pnr (Roger) Iain Mitchell 1978–84; one s.; m. Dr Iain L. Hutchison 1986; one s. one d.; ed Holyrood Secondary School, Glasgow and Council of Legal Educ.; called to the Bar, Gray's Inn 1972; mem. Bar Council 1990–93; mem. CIBA Comm. into Child Sexual Abuse 1981–83; mem. Bd City Limits Magazine 1982–84, New Statesman 1990–96, Counsel Magazine 1990–93; mem. Council, Howard League for Penal Reform 1989–, Chair. Comm. of Inquiry into Violence in Penal Insts for Young People (report 1995); Commr BAFTA inquiry into future of BBC 1990, Hamlyn Nat. Comm. on Educ. 1991–; Visiting lecturer, British Postgrad. Medical Fed. 1991–; Adviser, Mannheim Inst. on Criminology, LSE 1992–; leader of inquiry into health, environmental and safety aspects of Atomic Weapons Establishment, Aldermaston (report 1994); Chancellor, Oxford Brookes Univ. 1994–2001; Chair. British Council 1998–2004, Human Genetics Comm. 2000–; author of official report (Learning Works) for Further Educ. Funding Council on widening participation in further educ. 1997; Pres. School of Oriental and African Studies, London Univ. 2002–; mem. Advisory Bd, Int. Centre for Prison Studies 1998; Chair. London Int. Festival of Theatre, Standing Cttee for Youth Justice 1992–97; Chair. Charter 88 1992–97; Pres. London Marriage Guidance Council, Birth Control Campaign, Nat. Children's Bureau, Hillcroft Coll.; Vice-Pres. Haldane Soc., Nat. Ass. of Women; mem. British Council's Law Advisory Cttee Advisory Bd for Study of Women and Gender, Warwick Univ., Int. Bar Asscn's Task Force on Terrorism; presenter of various programmes on radio and TV and creator of BBC drama series Blind Justice 1988; Patron, Liberty; mem. Acad. de Cultures Internationales; Hon. Fellow, Inst. of Advanced Legal Studies, Univ. of London 1997; Hon. mem. Council, Nat. Soc. for Prevention of Cruelty to Children; 18 hon. LLD from British and Irish univs; Women's Network Award 1992, UK Woman of Europe Award 1995;

Campaigning and Influencing Award, Nat. Fed. of Women's Insts 1996, Times Newspaper Lifetime Achievement Award in the Law (jtly) 1997; Spectator Magazine's Parl. Campaigner of the Year 2000. *Publications include:* The Bar on Trial (jtly) 1978, Child Abuse within the Family (jtly) 1984, Balancing Acts (jtly) 1989, Eve was Framed 1992, Just Law: the Changing Face of Justice and Why it Matters to Us All 2004; articles on legal matters, civil liberties and women. *Leisure interests:* theatre, spending time with family and friends. *Address:* House of Lords, London, SW1A 0PW, England (office). *Telephone:* (20) 7219-5353 (office); (1708) 379482 (home). *Fax:* (20) 7219-5979 (office); (1708) 379482 (home). *E-mail:* info@helenakennedy.co.uk (home). *Website:* www.helenakennedy.co.uk (home).

KENNETT, B(rian) L. N., AO, PhD, ScD, FRS, FAA, FGSAust; British/Australian seismologist and academic; *Professor Emeritus of Seismology, Australian National University;* b. 7 May 1948; ed Univ. of Cambridge; Research Fellow, Emmanuel Coll. Cambridge 1972–76, Sr Research Asst, Dept of Geodesy and Geophysics 1975–76, Asst Lecturer, Dept of Applied Math. and Theoretical Physics 1976–79, Lecturer 1979–84; Professorial Fellow and Group Leader, Seismology Group, Research School of Earth Sciences, ANU, Australia 1984–91, Prof. 1991–, Pro-Vice-Chancellor and Chair. Inst. of Advanced Studies 1994–97, 2001–03, Deputy Dir Australian Nat. Seismic Imaging Resource (ANSIR) 1997–2002, Dir ANSIR Nat. Research Facility for Earth Sounding 2002–14, Co-ordinator Earth Physics, Research School of Earth Sciences 2002–06, Prof. of Seismology, ANU 2005–16, Prof. Emer. 2016–, Dir Research School of Earth Sciences 2006–10; Lindemann Trust Fellow, Visiting Asst Research Geophysicist, Univ. of California, San Diego, USA 1974–75; fmr Pres. Int. Asscn of Seismology and Physics of the Earth's Interior; Assoc., Royal Astronomical Soc. 1996–; Fellow, American Geophysical Union 1988; numerous awards including Commonwealth of Australia Centenary Medal, Australian Acad. of Sciences Jaeger Medal for Australian Earth Sciences 2005, Geological Soc. of London Murchison Medal 2006, European Geosciences Union Gutenberg Medal 2007, Royal Astronomical Soc. Gold Medal for Geophysics 2008, Flinders Medal and Lecture, Australian Acad. of Sciences 2011, Lehmann Medal, American Geophysical Union 2017. *Publications:* Seismic Wave Propagation in Stratified Media 1983, The Seismic Wavefield: Introduction and Theoretical Development 2001, The Seismic Wavefield: Interpretation of Seismograms on Regional and Global Scales 2002, Geophysical Continua: Deformation in the Earth's Interior (co-author) 2008, Planning and Managing Scientific Research 2014; more than 300 articles in scientific journals. *Address:* Research School of Earth Sciences, Australian National University, Canberra, ACT 2600, Australia (office). *Telephone:* (2) 6125-4621 (office). *Fax:* (2) 6257-2737 (office). *E-mail:* brian.kennett@anu.edu.au (office). *Website:* rses.anu.edu.au/~brian (office).

KENNEY, Edward John, MA, FBA; British academic; *Professor Emeritus of Latin, University of Cambridge;* b. 29 Feb. 1924, London; s. of George Kenney and Emmie Carlina Elfrida Schwenke; m. Gwyneth Anne Harris; ed Christ's Hosp. and Trinity Coll. Cambridge; served in Royal Signals, UK and India 1943–46; Asst Lecturer, Univ. of Leeds 1951–52; Research Fellow, Trinity Coll., Cambridge 1952–53, Fellow of Peterhouse 1953–91, Asst Lecturer in Classics, Univ. of Cambridge 1955–60, Lecturer 1960–70, Reader in Latin Literature and Textual Criticism 1970–74, Kennedy Prof. of Latin 1974–82, Prof. Emer. 1982–; Jt Ed. Classical Quarterly 1959–65; Jt Ed. Cambridge Greek and Latin Classics 1970–; Pres. Jt Asscn of Classical Teachers 1977–79, Classical Asscn 1982–83, Horatian Soc. 2003–07; Treas. and Chair. Council of Almoners, Christ's Hosp. 1984–86; Foreign mem. Royal Netherlands Acad. of Arts and Sciences. *Publications:* P. Ovidi Nasonis Amores, etc. 1961 (second edn 1995), Lucretius, De Rerum Natura III 1971 (second edn 2014), The Classical Text 1974 (Italian trans. 1995), The Cambridge History of Classical Literature, Vol. II, Latin Literature (ed. and contrib.) 1982, The Ploughman's Lunch (Moretum) 1984, Ovid, Metamorphoses–Introduction and Notes 1986, Ovid, The Love Poems – Introduction and Notes 1990, Apuleius, Cupid & Psyche 1990, Ovid, Sorrows of an Exile (Tristia) – Introduction and Notes 1992, Ovid, Heroides xvi–xxi 1996, Apuleius, The Golden Ass –Trans. with Introduction and Notes 1998 (Folio Soc. edn 2015), Ovidio, Metamorfosi VII–IX 2011; numerous articles and reviews. *Leisure interests:* discursive reading, listening to the wireless. *Address:* 4 Belvoir Terrace, Trumpington Road, Cambridge, CB2 7AA, England (home).

KENNEY, Jason, PC; Canadian politician; *Premier of Alberta;* b. 30 May 1968, Oakville, Ont.; fmr Exec. Dir Sask. Taxpayers Asscn and Pres. Canadian Taxpayers Fed.; fmr mem. Sask. Liberal Party, mem. Reform Party of Canada 1997–2000, Canadian Alliance 2000–03, Conservative Party of Canada 2003– (Leader 2017–); mem. Parl. for Calgary Southeast 1997–2015, for Calgary Midnapore 2015–18, for Calgary Lougheed 2018–; served in Shadow Cabinet 1997–2005, positions included Deputy House Leader for the Official Opposition, critic for Canada–US relations, for Nat. Revenue and for Finance; Minister for Citizenship, Immigration and Multiculturalism 2008–13, Minister of Employment and Social Devt 2013–15, of Nat. Defence Feb.–Oct. 2015; Premier of Alberta 2019–. *Address:* Office of the Premier, Legislature Building, Room 307, 10800 97th Avenue, Edmonton, AB T5K 2B6, Canada (office). *Telephone:* (780) 427-2711 (office). *Fax:* (780) 427-1349 (office). *Website:* alberta.ca/premier.cfm (office); www.albertandp.ca.

KENNICUTT, Robert C., Jr, BS, MS, PhD, FRS, FRAS; American astronomer and academic; b. 4 Sept. 1951, Baltimore, Md; m. Norma Kennicutt 1976 (divorced); one d.; ed Rensselaer Polytechnic Inst., Univ. of Washington; Carnegie Postdoctoral Fellow, Hale Observatories, Pasadena, Calif. 1978–80; Adjunct Research Fellow, California Inst. of Tech. 1978–80; Asst Prof., Dept of Astronomy, Univ. of Minnesota 1980–85, Assoc. Prof. 1985–88; Assoc. Prof. and Astronomer, Steward Observatory, Univ. of Arizona 1988–92, Deputy Head, Dept of Astronomy 1991–98, Prof. and Astronomer, Steward Observatory 1992–2006, currently Prof.; Beatrice M. Tinsley Centennial Prof., Univ. of Texas 1994; Adriaan Blaauw Prof., Univ. of Groningen, The Netherlands 2001; Plumian Prof. of Astronomy and Experimental Philosophy, Univ. of Cambridge 2005–18, Dir Inst. of Astronomy 2008–11, Head of School of the Physical Sciences 2012–15, Professorial Fellow, Churchill Coll. 2007–18; Visiting Fellow, Leiden Observatory, Univ. of Leiden 1982; Ed.-in-Chief The Astrophysical Journal 1999–2006; mem. Int. Advisory Cttee, Chinese Journal of Astronomy and Astrophysics 2002–08, Astrophysics Series Editorial Bd, Cambridge University Press 2007–; Chair., Herschel Space Observatory Users' Group 2009–; mem. or chair. numerous cttees and bds, including Science Oversight Cttee, NASA Next Generation Space Telescope Study 1996–98, Spitzer Legacy Science Working Group 2001–06, NSF Nat. Virtual Observatory Advisory Cttee 2002–06, Space Telescope Science Inst. Dir Search Cttee 2004–05, Gemini Observatory Visiting Cttee 2004, Wissenschaftlicher Beirat, Astrophyikalishe Institut, Potsdam 2006–10, Int. Advisory Bd, Netherlands Research School for Astronomy 2007–, Nat. Radio Astronomy Observatory Visiting Cttee 2008–11, NRC/NAS Astronomy 2010 Decadal Survey Cttee 2008–10, NAS Section 12 Nominating Cttee 2008–11, RAS Awards Cttee 2008–10, STFC Groundbased Astronomy Facilities Review Panel 2009, AAS Russell Lectureship Prize Cttee 2010–12; numerous lectureships including Dept of Astrophysical Sciences, Princeton Univ. 1990, Canary Islands Winter School in Astronomy 1991, 26th Saas Fee Advanced Course 1996, Les Houches Summer School 1996, Intelligence Agents Group Advanced School on Star Formation, Sao Paulo, Brazil 1998, Dept of Astronomy, Univ. of Wisconsin 2002, Faculty, 9th Vatican Summer School in Observational Astronomy and Astrophysics 2002–03; Chair. Gruber Cosmology Bd 2016; mem. NAS 2006, American Astronomical Soc. (Vice-Pres. 1998–2001), Int. Astronomical Union, Astronomical Soc. of the Pacific; Fellow, American Acad. of Arts and Sciences 2001; Carnegie Fellowship 1978–80, Alfred P. Sloan Fellowship 1983–87, Gruber Cosmology Prize (with Freedman and Mould) 2009, Dannie Heineman Prize in Astrophysics 2007. *Publications:* as co-author: Galaxies: Interactions and Induced Star Formation 1998, Hubble's Science Legacy: Future Optical/Ultraviolet Astronomy from Space 2002; numerous contribs to science journals. *Address:* Institute of Astronomy, University of Cambridge, Madingley Road, Cambridge, CB3 0HA, England (office). *Telephone:* (1223) 765844 (office). *E-mail:* robk@ast.cam.ac.uk (office). *Website:* www.ast.cam.ac.uk/~robk (office).

KENNY, Sir Anthony John Patrick, Kt, DPhil, FBA; British philosopher and academic; b. 16 March 1931, Liverpool; s. of John Kenny and Margaret Kenny (née Jones); m. Nancy Caroline Gayley 1966; two s.; ed Gregorian Univ., Rome, Italy, St Benet's Hall, Oxford; ordained RC priest, Rome 1955; curate, Liverpool 1959–63; returned to lay state 1963; Asst Lecturer, Univ. of Liverpool 1961–63; Lecturer in Philosophy, Exeter and Trinity Colls, Oxford 1963–64; Tutor in Philosophy, Balliol Coll., Oxford 1964, Fellow 1964–78, Sr Tutor 1971–72, 1976–77, Master 1978–89; Warden Rhodes House 1989–99; Professorial Fellow, St John's Coll., Oxford 1989–99; Pro-Vice-Chancellor, Univ. of Oxford 1984–99, Pro-Vice Chancellor for Devt 1999–2001; Wilde Lecturer in Natural and Comparative Religion, Oxford 1969–72; Jt Gifford Lecturer, Univ. of Edinburgh 1972–73; Stanton Lecturer, Univ. of Cambridge 1980–83; Speaker's Lecturer in Biblical Studies, Univ. of Oxford 1980–83; Visiting Prof., Stanford, Cornell and Rockefeller Univs and Univs of Chicago, Washington and Michigan; Vice-Pres. British Acad. 1986–88, Pres. 1989–93; Chair. Bd British Library 1993–96 (mem. Bd 1991–96); Pres. Royal Inst. of Philosophy 2005–09; Del. and mem. of Finance Cttee, Oxford Univ. Press 1986–93; Ed. The Oxford Magazine 1972–73; mem. Royal Norwegian Acad. 1993–, American Philosophical Soc. 1994–, American Acad. of Arts and Sciences 2003–; Hon. Bencher, Lincoln's Inn 1999; Hon. DLitt (Bristol) 1982, (Denison Univ.) 1986, (Liverpool) 1988, (Glasgow) 1990, (Lafayette) 1990, (Trinity Coll., Dublin) 1992, (Hull) 1993, (Belfast) 1994; Hon. DCL (Oxford) 1987; Hon. DLit (London) 2002; Hon. DD (Liverpool Hope) 2010; Aquinas Medal 1996. *Publications include:* Action, Emotion and Will 1963, Responsa Alumnorum of English College, Rome (two vols) 1963, Descartes 1968, The Five Ways 1969, Wittgenstein 1973, The Anatomy of the Soul 1974, Will, Freedom and Power 1975, Aristotelian Ethics 1978 (second edn 2016), Freewill and Responsibility 1978, The God of the Philosophers 1979, Aristotle's Theory of the Will 1979, Aquinas 1980, The Computation of Style 1982, Faith and Reason 1983, Thomas More 1983, The Legacy of Wittgenstein 1984, A Path from Rome 1985, The Logic of Deterrence 1985, The Ivory Tower 1985, Wyclif – Past Master 1985, Wyclif's De Universalibus 1985, Rationalism, Empiricism and Idealism 1986, Wyclif in His Times 1986, The Road to Hillsborough 1986, Reason and Religion (essays) 1987, The Heritage of Wisdom 1987, God and Two Poets 1988, The Metaphysics of Mind 1989, Mountains 1991, What is Faith? 1992, Aristotle on the Perfect Life 1992, Aquinas on Mind 1992, The Oxford Illustrated History of Western Philosophy (ed.) 1994, Frege 1995, A Life in Oxford 1997, A Brief History of Western Philosophy 1998, Essays on the Aristotelian Tradition 2001, Aquinas on Being 2002, The Unknown God 2003, A New History of Western Philosophy (one vol.) 2003, A New History of Western Philosophy Vol. 1: Ancient Philosophy 2004, Vol. 2: Medieval Philosophy 2005, Arthur Hugh Clough: A Poet's Life 2005, What I Believe 2006, Life, Liberty and the Pursuit of Utility (with C. Kenny) 2006, The Rise of Modern Philosophy 2006, Philosophy in the Modern World 2007, Can Oxford Be Improved? (with R. Kenny) 2007, From Empedocles to Wittgenstein: Historical Essays in Philosophy 2008, Aristotle, Eudemian Ethics (ed. and trans.) 2011, Aristotle Poetics (ed. and trans.) 2014, Christianity in Review 2015, Un addio affettuoso alla Chiesa 2016. *Address:* 1A Larkins Lane, Headington, Oxford, OX3 9DW, England (home). *Telephone:* (1865) 764174. *E-mail:* anthonyjpkenny@gmail.com.

KENNY, Enda, TD; Irish teacher and politician; b. 24 April 1951, Castlebar, Co. Mayo; s. of Henry Kenny; m. Fionnuala O'Kelly; two s. one d.; ed St Patrick's Coll. of Educ., Dublin, Univ. Coll. Galway; began career as primary school teacher; mem. Dáil Éireann (Fine Gael) for Mayo 1975–; Minister of State, Dept of Educ. and Labour 1986–87; Minister for Tourism and Trade 1994–97; Taoiseach (Prime Minister) 2011–16 (resgnd), re-elected Taoiseach (Prime Minister) 2016–17, Acting Minister for Defence May–July 2014, Minister for Defence 2016–17; mem. Fine Gael, Leader 2002–17; Vice-Pres. European People's Party. *Leisure interests:* hill walking, cycling, golf, mountain climbing (has climbed Kilimanjaro for charity). *Address:* Fine Gael, 51 Upper Mount Street, Dublin 2, Ireland (office). *Telephone:* (1) 6198444 (office). *E-mail:* finegael@finegael.com (office). *Website:* www.finegael.ie (office).

KENNY, Sir Paul Stephen, Kt; British trades union official; *Director, Health Safety Executive;* b. 31 Oct. 1949, Hammersmith, London, England; m. Patricia Ward 1969; two s.; left school aged 15; worked for Fuller, Smith & Turner's Brewery; full-time GMB official 1979–, Regional Sec. GMB London Region 1991–2005, unsuccessful cand. for post of Gen. Sec. 2003, Acting Gen. Sec. GMB Union 2005–06, Gen. Sec. 2006–15; Pres. TUC 2012; mem. Bd of Dirs Health Safety Exec. 2010–16, Dir 2018–. *Leisure interest:* supporting Fulham Football

Club. *Address:* Health and Safety Executive Redgrave Court,Redgrave Court, Merton Road, Bootle, Merseyside, L20 7HS, England (office).

KENT, Bruce Eric, PhD; Australian historian and academic; *Visiting Fellow, Centre for European Studies, Australian National University;* b. 15 Feb. 1932, Melbourne, Vic.; s. of Rev. Eric Deacon Kent and Beatrice Maude Kent; m. Ann Elizabeth Garland 1966; two s.; ed Geelong Grammar School, Melbourne Univ., Univ. of Oxford, UK, Australian Nat. Univ.; Tutor in History, Univ. of Melbourne 1954–55; Lecturer in History, ANU 1962–70, Sr Lecturer 1970–90, Reader 1990–, Acting Head of History Dept 1984, Visiting Fellow, Dept of Econ. History 1998–2000, now Visiting Fellow, Centre for European Studies; Fulbright Visiting Fellow, Hoover Inst., Stanford Univ. and History Dept, Princeton Univ., USA 1970; Visiting Lecturer, East China Normal Univ., Shanghai 1975–76; Pres. Australian Asscn of European Historians 1984–86; Visiting Fellow, Center of Int. Studies, Princeton Univ., USA, 1996; Victorian Rhodes Scholar 1955. *Publication:* The Spoils of War: The Politics, Economics and Diplomacy of Reparations, 1918–1932 1989. *Leisure interests:* violin, cricket, surfing. *Address:* ANU Centre for European Studies, 1 Liversidge Street, Building 67C, Australian National University, Canberra, ACT 2601, Australia (office); 4/3 Tasmania Circle, Forrest, ACT 2603 (home). *Telephone:* (2) 6125-6697 (office); (2) 6273-1019 (home); (2) 6260-6222 (home). *Fax:* (2) 6125-9976 (office). *E-mail:* bruce.kent@anu.edu.au (office). *Website:* ces.anu.edu.au (office).

KENT, HRH The Duke of (Prince Edward George Nicholas Paul Patrick), Earl of St Andrew's, Baron Downpatrick, KG, GCMG, GCVO, ADC; b. 9 Oct. 1935; s. of Duke of Kent (fourth s. of King George V) and Princess Marina (d. of Prince Nicholas of Greece); m. Katherine Worsley 1961; two s. (George, Earl of St Andrew's and Lord Nicholas Windsor) one d. (Lady Helen Windsor); ed Eton Coll. and Le Rosey, Switzerland; Second Lt, Royal Scots Greys 1955; attended Army Staff Course 1966, later on staff, GOC Eastern Command, Hounslow, Major 1967; Lt-Col Royal Scots Dragoon Guards 1972, Maj.-Gen. 1983, Deputy Col-in-Chief 1993–; rank of Field Marshal 1993; Ministry of Defence 1972–76; Chair. Nat. Electronics Council 1977–; Vice-Chair. British Overseas Trade Bd 1976–; Pres. All-England Lawn Tennis Club 1969–, Commonwealth War Graves Comm., RNLI 1969–, Football Asscn 1971–, Automobile Asscn 1973–, RAF Benevolent Fund 1974–, Scout Asscn 1975–, Royal Inst. of Great Britain 1976–, Business and Technicians Educ. Council 1984–, Eng Council 1989–, British Menswear Guild 1989–; Dir Vickers; Chancellor Univ. of Surrey 1977–; Patron Inst. of Export 1977–, Kent Opera 1978–, The London Philharmonic 1980–, Anglo-Jordanian Soc. 1982–, The Hanover Band 1992–, Anglo-German Asscn 1994; as Queen's Special Rep. has visited Sierra Leone 1961, Uganda 1962, The Gambia 1965, Guyana and Barbados 1966, Tonga 1967; ADC to HM The Queen 1967; Grand Master of the United Grand Lodge of England 1967–; Col-in-Chief Royal Regt of Fusiliers 1969–, Devonshire and Dorset Regt 1978–, Lorne Scots Regt 1978–; Col Scots Guards 1974; Hon. Pres. Royal Geographical Soc. 1969–; Hon. DCL (Durham), Hon. LLD (Leeds), DUniv (York);Col-in-Chief, The Royal Regiment of Fusiliers 1969, Col, Scots Guards 1974, Col-in-Chief, The Devonshire and Dorset Regiment 1977, Col-in-Chief, The Lorne Scots (Peel, Dufferin and Hamilton Regiment) 1977, Hon. Air Vice-Marshal, Royal Air Force 1985, Col-in-Chief, The Royal Scots Dragoon Guards 1994, Honorary Air Commodore, RAF Leuchars 1993, Hon. Air Chief Marshal, RAF 1996; King George VI and Queen Elizabeth Coronation Medal 1937, Queen Elizabeth II Coronation Medal 1953, Queen Elizabeth II Golden Jubilee Medal 2002, Queen Elizabeth II Diamond Jubilee Medal 2012; The Order of St George and St Constantine, 1st class (Greece), The Most Illustrious Order of Tri Shakti Patta, 1st class (Nepal) 1960, Knight Grand Band, the Order of the Star of Africa (Liberia) 1962, Grand Cordon, the Order of the Renaissance (Jordan) 1966, Grand Cross, the Order of St Olav (Norway) 1988, Grand Cross, the Order of Merit of the Republic of Poland (Poland) 1999, Knight of the Order of Charles XIII (Sweden) 2000, Order of Merit of the Free State of Saxony 2015. *Leisure interests:* skiing, shooting, photography, opera. *Address:* York House, St James's Palace, London, SW1A 1BQ, England. *Telephone:* (20) 7930-4832.

KENT, Jonathan, CBE; British theatre and opera director; b. 1951, Cape Town, SA; ed Cen. School of Speech and Drama, London; began career as actor, Glasgow Citizens 1970s; Jt Artistic Dir (with Ian McDiarmid) The Almeida Theatre, London 1990–2002; freelance dir 2002–. *Plays include:* as Artistic Dir, Almeida Theatre: When We Dead Awaken 1990, All for Love 1991, The Rules of the Game 1992, Medea (also West End, Broadway) 1992, Chatsky 1993, The Showman 1993, The School for Wives 1993, The Life of Galileo 1994, Gangster No. 1 1995, Tartuffe 1996, Ivanov (also Moscow) 1997, The Government Inspector 1997, Naked (also West End) 1998, Phèdre 1998, Britannicus (West End, New York) 1998, The Tempest 2000, Hamlet (also Broadway), Richard II 2000, Coriolanus (also New York, Tokyo) 2000, Plenty (West End), 2000, Lulu (also Washington) 2001, Platonov 2001, Faith Healer 2001, King Lear 2002; other plays as dir: Le Cid (Nat. Theatre) 1994, Mother Courage and Her Children (Nat. Theatre) 1995, Hamlet 1995, (Japan) 2003, Man of La Mancha (Broadway) 2002, The Paris Letter (New York) 2003, Hecuba (Donmar) 2004, The False Servant 2004, As You Desire Me (West End) 2005, Faith Healer (Dublin and Broadway) 2006, The Country Wife (Theatre Royal Haymarket) 2007, The Sea (Theatre Royal Haymarket) 2008, Marguerite 2008 (Theatre Royal Haymarket) 2008, Oedipus (Nat. Theatre) 2008, A Month in the Country (Chichester Festival) 2010, The Emperor and Galilean (Nat. Theatre) 2011, Sweeney Todd (Chichester, Adelphi) 2011–12. *Operas directed include:* Katya Kabanová (Santa Fe) 2003, The Tempest 2005, Child of Our Time (Santa Fe) 2005, Lucio Silla (Santa Fe) 2005, Tosca (ROH) 2006, Turn of the Screw (Glyndebourne) 2006, The Marriage of Figaro (Santa Fe) 2008, Elektra (Mariinsky St. Petersburg) 2008, The Fairy Queen (Glyndebourne, Paris, New York) 2009, Don Giovanni (Glyndebourne) 2010, The Flying Dutchman (ENO) 2011, Die Frau ohne Schatten (Mariinsky St. Petersburg) 2011. *Address:* c/o St John Donald, United Agents, 12–26 Lexington Street, London, W1F 0LE, England (office). *Telephone:* (20) 3214-0800 (office). *Fax:* (20) 3214-0801 (office). *E-mail:* info@unitedagents.co.uk (office). *Website:* www.unitedagents.co.uk (office).

KENT, Muhtar A., BSc, MSc; Turkish/American business executive; b. 1 Dec. 1952, New York, NY; m. Defne Kent; two c.; ed Univ. of Hull and City Univ., London, UK; joined Coca-Cola Co., Atlanta, Ga 1978, Gen. Man. Coca-Cola Turkey and Cen. Asia 1985–89, Pres. East Cen. Europe Div. and Sr Vice-Pres. Coca-Cola Int. 1989–95, Man. Dir Coca-Cola Amatil-Europe 1995–98, Pres. and CEO Efes Beverage Group (majority owner of Turkish bottler Coca-Cola Icecek) 1999–2005, Pres. and COO Coca-Cola N Asia, Eurasia and Middle East Group 2005–06, Pres. Coca-Cola International Jan.–Dec. 2006, Pres. and COO Coca-Cola Co., Atlanta 2006–08, Pres. and CEO 2008–09, Chair. and CEO 2009–17, Chair. 2017–19; Chair. Int. Business Council of the World Econ. Forum; past Chair. US-China Business Council; Chair. Emer. US ASEAN Business Council, mem. Eminent Persons Group for ASEAN; Co-Chair. Bipartisan Policy Center's CEO Council on Health and Innovation; immediate past Co-Chair. The Consumer Goods Forum; mem. Bd of Dirs 3M, Special Olympics International, Ronald McDonald House Charities, Catalyst, Emory Univ.; mem. Business Roundtable; Fellow, Foreign Policy Asscn; Hon. LLD (Oglethorpe Univ., Atlanta) 2008, (Georgia Inst. of Tech.) 2014; Hon. DEcon (Univ. of Hull). *Address:* c/o The Coca-Cola Co., 1 Coca-Cola Plaza, Atlanta, GA 30313-2499, USA.

KENT, The Hon. Peter, PC; Canadian broadcaster and politician; b. 27 July 1943, Sussex, England; s. of Parker Kent; m. Cilla Kent; one d.; began career as radio journalist in early 1960s; joined CFCN-TV, Calgary 1965; spent several years as freelance foreign corresp. correspondent, later Anchor, CBC News programme The National 1976–78; Founding producer, corresp. and co-host The Journal, CBC 1982–84; European corresp., NBC in late 1980s; MP for Thornhill (Ont.) 2008–; Minister of the Environment 2011–13; mem. Bd ParticipACTION, Ontario Cabinet of Canadian Museum for Human Rights, Honest Reporting Canada, The Accessible Channel; mem. Conservative Party of Canada; Robert F. Kennedy Journalism Award 1991, Radio-Television News Dirs Asscn of Canada Pres.'s Award 2006. *Website:* www.peterkent.ca.

KENTRIDGE, Sir Sydney, Kt, KCMG, QC, MA; British lawyer; b. 5 Nov. 1922, Johannesburg, South Africa; s. of Morris Kentridge and May Kentridge; m. Felicia Geffen 1952; two s. two d.; ed King Edward VII School, Johannesburg, Univ. of the Witwatersrand and Exeter Coll., Oxford; war service with S African forces 1942–46; Advocate, SA 1949, Sr Counsel 1965; called to Bar, Lincoln's Inn, London 1977, Bencher 1986; Queen's Counsel, England 1984; Judge, Court of Appeal, Jersey and Guernsey 1988–92; mem. Court of Appeal, Botswana 1981–89, Constitutional Court, SA 1995–97; Roberts Lecturer, Univ. of Pa 1979; Hon. Fellow American Coll. of Trial Lawyers 1998; Hon. Fellow Exeter Coll., Oxford 1986; Hon. mem. Bar Asscn New York City 2001; Hon. LLD (Leicester) 1985, (Cape Town) 1987, (Natal) 1989, (London) 1995, (Sussex) 1997, (Witwatersrand) 2000, (Buckingham) 2009; Order of the Baobab (Gold), S Africa; Granville Clark Prize, USA 1978. *Publications:* Free Country: Selected Lectures and Talks 2012. *Leisure interests:* opera, theatre. *Address:* 7–8 Essex Street, London, WC2R 3LD, England. *Telephone:* (20) 7379-3550. *Fax:* (20) 7379-3558.

KENTRIDGE, William, BA; South African artist; b. 28 April 1955, Johannesburg; ed King Edward VII School, Houghton, Johannesburg, Univ. of the Witwatersrand, diploma in Fine Arts from Johannesburg Art Foundation, studied mime and theatre at École Internationale de Théâtre Jacques Lecoq, Paris, France; creates animated films, constructed by filming a drawing, making erasures and changes, and filming it again; drawings later displayed along with the films as finished pieces of art; Founder mem. Junction Avenue Theatre Co., Johannesburg 1975–91; worked on TV films and series as art dir 1980s; cr. 20 to 30 monotypes, which soon became known as the 'Pit' series 1979; executed about 50 small-format etchings, the 'Domestic Scenes' 1980; cr. first animated film, Johannesburg, 2nd Greatest City After Paris, in series Drawings for Projection 1989; staged first theatre project in conjunction with Handspring Puppet Co. 1992; animations deal with political and social themes from a personal viewpoint, often including self-portrait in his works; series of nine short films introduces two characters, Soho Eckstein and Felix Teitlebaum who depict an emotional and political struggle that reflects the lives of many South Africans in the pre-democracy era; co-f. Free Film-makers Co-Operative, Johannesburg 1985; staged first opera, Return of Ulysses, Brussels, Belgium 1998; apptd a film-maker by Stereoscope 1999; staged Il ritorno d'Ulisse in patria (Monteverdi), Die Zauberflöte (Mozart) and The Nose (Shostakovich); also made a short show with French composer François Sarhan called Telegrams from the Nose; Commdr des Arts et des Lettres 2013; Red Ribbon Award for Short Fiction 1982, Market Theatre Award for New Vision exhbn 1986, AA Vita Award, Cassirer Fine Art 1986, Standard Bank Young Artist Award 1987, Woyzeck on the Highveld Awards for production, set design and direction 1992, Loerie Award Memo 1994, Five Themes exhibit included in TIME 100 2009, Five Themes exhibit awarded First Place in AICA (Int. Asscn of Art Critics Awards) Best Monographic Museum Show Nationally category 2009, Kyoto Prize 2010, Dan David Prize 2012. *Films include:* Johannesburg: 2nd Greatest City After Paris 1989, Monument 1990, Mine 1991, Sobriety, Obesity & growing old 1991, Felix in Exile 1994, History of the Main Complaint 1996, Ubu Tells the Truth 1996–97, Weighing and Wanting 1998, Stereoscope 1999, Medicine Chest 2001, Automatic Writing 2003, films shown at Cannes Film Festival 2004. *Address:* c/o Robert Brown Gallery, 2219 California Street, NW, #32, Washington, DC 20008, USA. *Telephone:* (202) 483-0722. *E-mail:* info@robertbrowngallery.com. *Website:* www.robertbrowngallery.com.

KENWORTHY, Duncan, OBE, MA, FRSA; British film producer; *Managing Director, Toledo Productions Ltd;* b. 9 Sept. 1949; s. of Bernard Ian Kenworthy and Edna Muriel Kenworthy (née Calligan); ed Rydal School North Wales, Christ's Coll., Cambridge, Annenberg School, Univ. of Pennsylvania, USA; Children's Television Workshop, New York 1973–76; Consulting Producer, Arabic Sesame Street, Kuwait 1977–79; Producer and Exec., Jim Henson Productions, London 1979–95; Producer and Man. Dir Toledo Productions Ltd 1995–; Dir DNA Films Ltd 1997–2008; mem. Council of Man., BAFTA 1996–2006, Chair. BAFTA Film Cttee 2002–04, Chair. BAFTA 2004–06, Vice-Pres. BAFTA 2009–; Chair. British Council Film Advisory Cttee 1999–2008, Dir Film Council 1999–2003, mem. Film Policy Review Group 1997–99; Gov. Nat. Film and TV School 2001–; mem. UK-China Forum 2000–01, Shanghai Film Festival Jury 2006; British Producer of the Year, London Film Critics 1994. *Films include:* The Dark Crystal (assoc producer) 1980, Four Weddings and a Funeral (Best Film, and Lloyds Bank Peoples' Choice Award, BAFTA 1994, Best Foreign Film, Cesar Award 1994) 1994, Lawn Dogs 1997, Notting Hill (BAFTA Orange Audience Award 2000) 1999, The Parole Officer 2001, Heartlands (exec. producer) 2002, Love Actually 2003, The Eagle 2011, The Pass 2016, The Children Act 2018. *Television includes:* Fraggle Rock (Emmy Award for Outstanding Children's Programming 1983) 1982, The Storyteller

(BAFTA Award for Best Children's Programme 1989) 1986–88; Living with Dinosaurs (Emmy Award for Best Children's Programme 1990) 1988, Monster Maker 1988, Greek Myths (BAFTA for Best Children's Fictional Programme 1991) 1990, Gulliver's Travels (Emmy Award for Outstanding Mini-series 1996) 1996. *Address:* Toledo Productions Ltd, Suite 44, 10 Richmond Mews, London, W1D 3DD, England (office). *Telephone:* (20) 7851-6677 (office). *Fax:* (20) 7437-7740 (office). *E-mail:* info@toledoproductions.com (office).

KENWRIGHT, Bill, CBE; British theatre producer; b. 4 Sept. 1945; s. of Albert Kenwright and Hope Kenwright (née Jones); m. Anouska Hempel 1978–80; partner Jenny Seagrove; ed Liverpool Inst.; actor 1964–70; theatre producer 1970–; Chair. Everton Football Club; Hon. Prof., Thames Valley Univ., London; Dr hc (Liverpool John Moores) 1994, Hon. DLit (Nottingham Trent Univ.) 2008; Variety Club Bernard Delfont Award for his contribution to the entertainment industry 2002, Lifetime Achievement Award, Theatrical Management Asscn 2008. *Films include:* Stepping Out 1991, Don't Go Breaking My Heart 1999, Zoe 2001, Die, Mommie, Die! 2003, The Purifiers 2004, Chéri 2009, Dixie: The People's Legend 2011, Broken (Best Film at the British Ind. Film Award) 2014. *Plays directed include:* Joseph and The Amazing Technicolor Dreamcoat 1979, The Business of Murder 1981, A Streetcar Named Desire 1984, Stepping Out 1984, Blood Brothers 1988, Shirley Valentine 1989, Travels With My Aunt 1993, Piaf 1993, Lysistrata 1993, Medea 1993, Pygmalion 1997, A Doll's House, An Ideal Husband, The Chairs 2000, Ghosts, The Female Odd Couple. *Leisure interest:* football. *Address:* Bill Kenwright Ltd, BKL House 1, Venice Walk, London, W2 1RR, England (office). *Telephone:* (20) 7446-6200 (office). *Fax:* (20) 7446-6222 (office). *E-mail:* info@Kenwright.com (office). *Website:* www.kenwright.com (office).

KENYATTA, Uhuru; Kenyan politician and head of state; *President and Commander-in-Chief of the Armed Forces;* b. 1961; s. of fmr Pres. Jomo Kenyatta and Mama Ngina Kenyatta; ed Amhert Coll., USA; Chair. Kenya Tourism Bd 1999; nominated MP by Pres. Daniel arap Moi (q.v.); apptd Minister of Local Govt 2001; Vice-Chair. Kenya African Nat. Union (KANU) 2002, then Acting Pres., Pres. 2005–06, 2007–; mem. Parl. for Gatundu South 2002–13; named heir apparent by Pres. Moi July 2002, failed to be elected in presidential elections Dec. 2002; Deputy Prime Minister 2008–13, also Minister of Trade 2008–09, Minister of Finance 2009–12 (resgnd); Pres. of Kenya and C-in-C of the Armed Forces 2013–; appeared before Int. Criminal Court in The Hague Oct. 2014 accused of crimes against humanity; charges dropped March 2015. *Address:* Office of the President, Harambee House, Harambee Avenue, POB 62345, 00200 Nairobi, Kenya (office). *Telephone:* (20) 2227411 (office). *E-mail:* president@statehousekenya.go.ke (office). *Website:* www.statehousekenya.go.ke (office).

KENYON, Sir Nicholas Roger, Kt, CBE, BA; British arts administrator; *Managing Director, Barbican Centre;* b. 23 Feb. 1951, Altrincham, Cheshire; s. of Thomas Kenyon and Kathleen Holmes; m. Marie-Ghislaine Latham-Koenig 1976; three s. one d.; ed Balliol Coll., Oxford; music critic, The New Yorker 1979–82, The Times 1982–85, The Observer 1985–92; Music Ed. The Listener 1982–87; Ed. Early Music 1983–92; programme adviser, Mozart Now Festival, South Bank, London 1991; Controller, BBC Radio 3 1992–98, Dir BBC Proms 1996–2007, Controller, BBC Millennium Programmes 1998–2000, BBC Live Events and TV Classical Music 2000–07; Man. Dir Barbican Centre, London 2007–; mem. Bd of Dirs Sage Gateshead; fmr mem. Bd of Dirs ENO; mem. Arts Council England; Trustee, Dartington Hall Trust; Gov. Wellington School; Royal Philharmonic Soc. Awards for Fairest Isle (BBC Radio 3) 1996 and Sounding the Century 2000, President's Medal, British Acad. 2011. *Publications include:* The BBC Symphony Orchestra 1930–80 1981, Simon Rattle: The Making of a Conductor (revised edn as Simon Rattle: From Birmingham to Berlin 2001), Authenticity and Early Music (ed.) 1988, The Viking Opera Guide (co-ed.) 1993, The Penguin Opera Guide (co-ed.) 1995, Musical Lives (ed.) 2001, The BBC Proms Guide to Great Concertos (ed.) 2003, The BBC Proms Pocket Guide to Great Symphonies (ed.) 2003, The Faber Pocket Guide to Mozart 2005, The Faber Pocket Guide to Bach 2011. *Address:* Barbican Centre, Silk Street, London, EC2Y 8DS, England (office). *Telephone:* (20) 7382-7005 (office). *Website:* www.barbican.org.uk (office).

KENZHISARIYEV, Maj-Gen. Marat; Kyrgyzstani military commander and government official; fmr Head of Mil. and Technical Cooperation Office, Ministry of Defence; fmr Deputy Chief of Gen. Staff of Armed Forces; Chair., State Cttee for Defence 2015–16.

KENZO, Takada; Japanese fashion designer; b. (Kenzo Takada), 1940, Kyoto; ed Bunka Fashion Coll., Tokyo; after graduating designed patterns for a Tokyo magazine; moved to Paris 1964; cr. own freelance collections and sold designs to Louis Féraud 1964–70; opened boutique Jungle Jap, Paris 1970; noted for translating traditional designs into original contemporary garments and for ready-to-wear knitwear; Head of Kenzo fashion house until retirement in 1999; cr. Yume label 2002; Hon. Pres. Asian Couture Fed.; Soen Prize, Fashion Ed. Club of Japan's Prize, Lifetime Achievement Award, LVIV Fashion Week. *Film:* Yume, Yume no Ato (dir and writer) 1981. *Address:* Asia Couture Federation, 217 East Coast Road, 04–01 Tides, Singapore 428915, Malaysia (office). *E-mail:* admin@asiancouturefederation.com (office). *Website:* www.asiancouturefederation.com (home).

KEOHANE, Nannerl, PhD; American academic and fmr university president; *Senior Scholar, University Center for Human Values, Princeton University;* b. 18 Sept. 1940, Blytheville, Ark.; d. of James Arthur Overholser and Grace Overholser (née McSpadden); m. 1st Patrick Henry, III 1962 (divorced 1969); m. 2nd Robert O. Keohane 1970; three s. one d.; ed Wellesley Coll., St Anne's Coll., Oxford, UK, Yale Univ.; mem. Faculty, Swarthmore Coll. 1967–73, Stanford Univ. 1973–81, Fellow, Center for Advanced Study in the Behavioral Sciences, Stanford Univ. 1978–79, 1987–88, 2004–05 (mem. Bd of Trustees 1991–97, 2004–11, Vice-Chair. 2008–11); Pres. and Prof. of Political Science, Wellesley Coll. 1981–93, Duke Univ. 1993–2004; Laurance S. Rockefeller Distinguished Visiting Prof. of Public Affairs in the Woodrow Wilson School and the Univ. Center for Human Values, Princeton Univ. 2004–13, Sr Scholar 2013–; Visitor, Inst. for Advanced Study 2014–15; mem. Harvard Corpn and Fellow, Harvard Coll. 2005–; mem. Bd of Dirs IBM 1986–2004, Bd of Trustees, The Colonial Williamsburg Foundation 1988–2001, The Nat. Humanities Center 1993–2004; mem. MIT Corpn 1992–97, Doris Duke Charitable Foundation 1996– (Chair. 2007–10), Overseers Cttee to Visit the John F. Kennedy School of Govt 1996–2004 (Chair. 2001–03); Fellow, American Acad. of Arts and Sciences, American Philosophical Soc.; Hon. Fellow, St Anne's Coll., Oxford; Dr hc from several univs and colleges; Marshall Scholar 1961–63, Wilbur Cross Medal, Yale Univ., Nat. Women's Hall of Fame 1995, Golden Plate Award, American Acad. of Achievement 1998, Marshall Medal, Clark Kerr Medal, Univ. of California, Berkeley 2006. *Leisure interests:* travel, theatre, music, art, grandchildren, hiking, cycling. *E-mail:* nkeohane@princeton.edu (office). *Website:* uchv.princeton.edu (office).

KEOHANE, Robert Owen, BA, MA, PhD; American political scientist and academic; *Professor of International Affairs, Woodrow Wilson School, Princeton University;* b. 3 Oct. 1941, Chicago, Ill.; s. of Robert Emmet Keohane and Marie Irene Keohane (née Pieters); m. Nannerl Overholser 1970; three s. one d.; ed Shimer Coll., Harvard Univ.; Fellow, Harvard Univ., Woodrow Wilson School of Public and Int. Affairs, Princeton Univ. 1961–62; mem. Woodrow Wilson Award Cttee 1982, Chair. Nominating Cttee 1990–91, Chair. Minority Identification Project 1990–92; Instructor, then Assoc. Prof., Swathmore Coll. 1965–73; Assoc. Prof., then Prof., Stanford Univ. 1973–81; Ed. Int. Org. 1974–80, mem. Bd Eds 1968–77, 1982–88, 1992–97, 1998–, Chair. 1986–87; Prof., Brandeis Univ. 1981–85; Pres. Int. Studies Asscn 1988–89, Chair. Nominations Cttee 1985; Prof., then Stanfield Prof. of Int. Peace, Harvard Univ. 1985–96, Chair. Dept of Govt 1988–92; James B. Duke Prof. of Political Science, Duke Univ. 1996–2005; Prof. of Int. Affairs, Woodrow Wilson School, Princeton Univ. 2004–; Sherill Lecturer, Yale Univ. Law School 1996; Pres. American Political Science Asscn 1999–2000; Frank Kenan Fellow, Nat. Endowment for the Humanities 1995–96; Fellow, American Acad. of Arts and Sciences 1983–, Center for Advanced Study in Behavioral Sciences 1977–78, 1987–88, 2004–05; mem. NAS 2005–, American Acad. of Political and Social Science 2006– (Harold Lasswell Fellow 2007–08), American Philosophical Soc. 2007–; Corresp. Fellow, British Acad. 2010–; Bell Research Fellow, German Marshall Fund 1977–78; Fellow, Council on Foreign Relations 1967–69, Guggenheim Foundation 1992–93, Sr Foreign Policy Fellow, Social Science Research Council 1986–88; Bellagio Resident Fellow 1993; Hon. PhD (Univ. of Århus, Denmark) 1988; Dr hc Science Po (Paris) 2006; Grawemeyer Award for Ideas Improving World Order 1989, First Mentorship Award, Soc. for Women in Int. Political Economy 1997, Skytte Prize, Johan Skytte Foundation, Uppsala, Sweden 2005, Centennial Medal, Harvard Graduate School of Arts and Sciences 2012, Balzan Prize 2016. *Publications include:* After Hegemony: Cooperation and Discord in the World Political Economy 1984, Neorealism and Its Critics 1986, International Institutions and State Power: Essays in International Relations Theory 1989, Power and Interdependence in a Partially Globalized World 2002; (as co-author): Power and Interdependence: World Politics in Transition 1977, Institutions for the Earth: Sources of Effective International Environmental Protection 1993, After the Cold War: State Strategies and International Institutions in Europe, 1989–91 1993, Designing Social Inquiry: Scientific Inference in Qualitative Research 1994, Humanitarian Intervention: Ethical, Legal, and Political Dilemmas 2003, The Regime Complex for Climate Change 2010; (as co-ed.): Transnational Relations and World Politics 1972, The New European Community: Decision-Making and Institutional Change 1991, Ideas and Foreign Policy 1993, From Local Commons to Global Interdependence 1994, Institutions for Environmental Aid: Pitfalls and Promises 1996, Internationalization and Domestic Politics 1996, Imperfect Unions: Security Institutions Across Time and Space 1999, Exploration and Contestation in the Study of World Politics 1998, Legalization and World Politics 2000. *Address:* Woodrow Wilson School, 408 Robertson Hall, Princeton University, Princeton, NJ 08544-1013, USA (office). *Telephone:* (609) 258-1856 (office). *Fax:* (609) 258-0390 (office). *E-mail:* rkeohane@princeton.edu (office). *Website:* www.princeton.edu/~rkeohane (office).

KERAVNOS, Makis, MSc; Cypriot banker and fmr government official; b. 1951, Larnaka; m. Niki Keravnos; three c.; ed Pancyprian Gymnasium of Kykkos, Nat. and Kapodistrian Univ. of Athens, Pantion Univ., Brooks Univ., Oxford, UK; various Sr Exec. positions in private cos; various positions Human Resources Devt Authority including Sr Officer; apptd Minister of Labour 2003; Minister of Finance 2004–05 (resgnd); CEO Hellenic Bank Public Co. Ltd 2005–14; founding mem. and Pres. Pancyprian Asscn of Economists; mem. Bd of Dirs Cyprus Asscn of Quality; Vice-Pres. Cyprus Inst. of Political Research and European Affairs.

KERESZTESI, János; Hungarian business executive; *CEO, FreeSoft Nyrt.;* b. 1958; m.; two c.; began career with SZÁMALK; later with Digital Equipment Hungary; Partner, Relationships Man. and later Indirect Sales Man., Oracle Hungary 1995–99; Operations Man., Sun Microsystems Hungary 1999–2004; CEO FreeSoft Nyrt. 2004–; mem. Bd, Asscn of IT Cos 2005–; IT Man. of the Year, Asscn of IT Cos 2001. *Address:* FreeSoft Nyrt., Neumann Janos u. 1/C, Iunfopark Budapest, 1117 Budapest, Hungary (office). *Telephone:* (61) 371-2910 (office). *Fax:* (61) 371-2911 (office). *E-mail:* fs.inf@freesoft.hu (office). *Website:* www.freesoft.hu (office).

KERGIN, Michael Frederick, BA, MA (Econs); Canadian government official, academic and fmr diplomatist; b. Canadian Mil. Hosp., Bramshott, UK; m. Margarita Fuentes Kergin; three s.; ed Univ. of Toronto, Magdalen Coll. Oxford, UK; joined Dept of Foreign Affairs and Int. Trade (fmrly Dept. of External Affairs) as Foreign Services Officer 1967, positions include Sr Dept Asst to Sec. of State for External Affairs 1984–86, Asst Deputy Minister responsible for Political and Int. Security Affairs 1994–96, and for the Americas and Security and Intelligence Affairs 1996–98; Amb. to Cuba 1986–89, to USA 2000–05; Premier of Ont.'s Special Adviser on Border Issues 2005; currently Adjunct Prof., Faculty of Political Studies, Univ. of Ottawa, also Sr Fellow, Grad. School of Public and Int. Affairs; Sr Adviser, Bennett Jones LLP; Visiting Scholar, Western Michigan Univ., Kalamazoo 2006–07; Foreign Policy Adviser to the Prime Minister and Asst Sec. to the Cabinet for Foreign and Defence Policy 1998–2000; mem. Del. to Inter-American Devt Bank; fmr Embassy Minister, Washington, DC, USA, Santiago, Chile and Yaoundé, Cameroon; fmr Deputy Head of Mission to UN, New York; mem. Univ. of Toronto President's Advisory Council. *Address:* Bennett Jones LLP, Suite 1900 World Exchange Plaza, 45 O'Connor Street, Ottawa, ON K1P 1A4 (office); 55 Laurier Avenue East, Desmarais Building, Room 11129a, University of Ottawa, Ottawa, ON K1N 6N5, Canada. *Telephone:* (613) 683-2306 (Bennett

Jones) (office). *E-mail:* kerginm@bennettjones.com (office); Michael.Kergin@uottawa.ca (office). *Website:* www.bennettjones.com (office).

KERIM, Srgjan, PhD; Macedonian diplomatist, politician and academic; b. 12 Dec. 1948, Skopje; m.; three c.; ed Belgrade Univ., fmr Yugoslavia; Asst then Prof. of Int. Econ. Relations, Belgrade Univ. 1972–91; Visiting Prof., Univ. of Hamburg, Germany and New York Univ., USA 1972–91; mem. Presidency of Youth Fed. of Yugoslavia, also Chair. Foreign Policy Cttee 1976–78; Minister for Foreign Econ. Relations 1986–89; Asst Minister and Spokesman, Ministry of Foreign Affairs 1989–91; Vice-Pres. Copechim–France Co., Paris 1992–94; Amb. to Germany 1994–2000, to Liechtenstein and Switzerland 1995–2000; Minister of Foreign Affairs 2000–01; Perm. Rep. to UN, New York 2001–04, Pres. 62nd Session UN Gen. Ass. 2007–08, UN Sec.-Gen.'s Special Envoy for Climate Change 2008–09; Gen. Man. Media Print Macedonia (part of WAZ Media Group) and Gen. Man. for South-Eastern Europe, WAZ Media Group 2003; Chair. Politika Newspapers and magazines, Belgrade 2004; Pres. Macedonian-German Econ. Asscn 2003–06, Hon. Pres. 2006; Pres. Board of Dirs Media Print Macedonia 2012–; UN Millennium Devt Goals Award 2008. *Publications:* nine books and more than 100 scientific works on int. politics, int. economic and youth issues.

KERIN, John Charles, AM, BA, BEcons; Australian politician; b. 21 Nov. 1937, Bowral, NSW; s. of Joseph Sydney Kerin and Mary Louise Kerin (née Fuller); m. 1st Barbara Elizabeth Large (divorced 1981); one d.; m. 2nd Dr June Rae Verrier 1983; ed Univ. of New England, Australian Nat. Univ.; Econs Research Officer in wool marketing, Bureau of Agricultural Econs 1971, 1975–78; MP for Macarthur 1972–75, for Werriwa 1978–93; Minister for Primary Industry 1983–87, for Primary Industries and Energy 1987–91, Treas. for Trade and Overseas Devt 1991–93; resgnd from Parl. 1993; Chair. Australian Meat and Livestock Corpn 1994–97; Dir Coal Mines Australia Ltd 1994–2001; Chair. Biologic Int. Ltd 1996–98; Adjunct Prof., ANU 2013; fmr Deputy Chancellor Univ. of Western Sydney, now mem. Bd of Trustees and Chair. Macarthur Council of the Univ.; Chair. NewSouth Wales Forestry Comm.; Bd mem. CSIRO 2008–; Fellow, Australian Inst. of Agricultural Science and Tech., Australian Acad. of Tech. Sciences and Eng, Australian Rural Leadership Foundation; fmr mem. Australian Labor Party (resgnd 2011); Dr hc (New England) 1992, (Western Sydney) 1995, (Tasmania) 2001. *Leisure interests:* opera, bush-walking, classical music, reading. *Address:* PO Box 3, Garran, ACT 2605, Australia (home). *Telephone:* (6) 285-2480 (home). *Fax:* (6) 282-5778 (home). *E-mail:* kerrier1@bigpond.net.au (home).

KERKELING, Hans-Peter (Hape); German writer, actor, television presenter, director and comedian; b. 9 Dec. 1964, Recklinghausen; ed Marie Curie Gymnasium, Recklinghausen; at secondary school, formed band Gesundfutter with fellow students and released a record, Hawaii; began career as a comedian on radio, working for various German broadcasting cos, including WDR and BR; breakthrough role in TV comedy show Känguru playing a boy called Hannilein 1984; guest appearances and sketches on Radio Bremen show Extratour; started up own comedy TV show Total Normal (satirical spoof on prime-time TV shows) 1989; presenter, yearly fundraising gala for German AIDS fund Deutsche AIDS-Hilfe; Verdienstkreuz (North Rhine-Westphalia) 2006, Royal Spanish Order of Merit Illustrissime 2011; numerous awards including Golden Camera, Golden Rose of Montreux, Tele-star, Golden Gong, Europa 1991–93, Peter Frankenfeld Prize 2002, Deutscher Fernsehpreis (German TV Prize) in category of Best Entertainment Presenter 2003, 2004, Bayerischer Fernsehpreis 2004, Comedy Prize 2004, Golden Camera for Best TV Entertainer 2005, Comedy Prize for Best Comedian 2005, 2006, named in survey by Kabel 1 amongst top ten favourite faces on German TV 2005, Adolf-Grimme Honour Award 2007, GQ Man of the Year 2008, Steiger Award, Bavarian TV Award 2009, Karl-Valentin-Orden 2010, Medienpreis für Sprachkultur 2010, Sparte Fernsehen, Gesellschaft für deutsche Sprache 2011, Goldene Schallplatte 2× Platin for Wieder auf Tour – Live (CD), ROMY-Fernsehpreis Deutscher Comedypreis 2012, Golden Camera – Leserwahl (Best Comedian) 2012, Goldene Kamera Jubilee Award 2015. *Films include:* Großstadtrevier: Dame in Not 1989, Vorwärts 1990, Kein Pardon 1992, Alles wegen Paul (producer) 2001, Samba in Mettmann 2004, Kung Fu Panda (voice) 2008, Ein Mann, ein Fjord! 2008, Horst Schlämmer – Isch kandidiere! 2009, Kung Fu Panda 2 (voice) 2011, Frozen (voice of Olaf) 2013. *Television includes:* comedy: Kerkelings Kinderstunde 1984, Känguru 1985–86, Total Normal 1989, Cheese 1994, Warmumsherz 1995, Zappenduster 1997, Gisbert 1998, Darüber lacht die Welt 1998, Hape's halbe Stunde 2001; presenter: Eurovision Song Contest 1989–91, German TV Awards 2001, Stars in der Manege 2001, Golden Europa Awards 2002, AIDS Gala 2002, 2003, Die 70-er Show 2003, 2004, Der grosse Deutschtest 2004, 2005, Hape trifft 2005–, Let's Dance 2006; films: Club Las Piranjas (NDR TV) 1995, Willi und die Windzors (NDR TV) 1996, Die Oma ist tot (NDR TV) 1997. *Recordings include:* Hawaii 1984, Hannilein & Co 1986, Erwarten Se nix 1990, Das ganze Leben ist ein Quiz 1991, Hurz (film soundtrack) 1991, Vorsicht Telefon 1993, Der kleine Vampir (film soundtrack) 1993, Sportreporter Rap 1993, Helsinki is Hell 1999, Junge, Junge 2000, Das Ding muss rein 2000, Die 70 min. Show 2003, Tanze Sambe mit mir 2004, Schätzelein 2006, Meine letzte Zigarette 2006; albums: Ariola 1984, Ich lasse mir das Singen nicht verbieten (CD) 2014. *Publications:* Hannilein & Co. 1992, Kein Pardon 1993, Cheese 1994, Ich bin dann mal weg 2006, Weisse Bescheid?! 2007, Der Junge muss an die frische Luft (autobiograpahy) 2014. *Telephone:* (30) 32765822 (office). *Fax:* (30) 32765823 (office). *E-mail:* elke@medienbuero-krueger.de (office); hape@medienbuero-krueger.de (office). *Address:* Büro Hape Kerkeling, Postfach 20 02 57, 13512 Berlin, Germany (home). *Website:* www.hapekerkeling.de.

KERNAN, Gen. (retd) William F., MA; American fmr army officer and business executive; *Advisor, Strategic Solutions Unlimited, Inc.;* b. Fort Sam Houston, Tex.; m. Marianne Purnell; one s.; ed US Army Command and Gen. Staff Coll., US Army War Coll.; commissioned Infantry Officer 1968; commanded two Airborne Cos, two Ranger Cos, an Airborne Infantry Bn, the 75th Ranger Regt; exchange officer, 3rd Bn, Parachute Regt, UK; Asst Div. Commdr (Manoeuvre), 7th Infantry Div.; Dir Plans, Policy and Assessments, J5, US Special Operations Command; Commdr 101st Airborne Div. (Air Assault), XVIII Airborne Corps and Fort Bragg; combat tours Viet Nam, Grenada, Panama; rank of Gen. 2000; Supreme Allied Commdr, Atlantic (SACLANT) and C-in-C US Jt Forces Command, Norfolk, Va 2000–02; Sr Vice-Pres. and Gen. Man. Int. Group, MPRI Inc., Alexandria, Va 2002; Advisor, Strategic Solutions Unlimited, Inc.; Legion of Merit (with three oak leaf clusters); Kt Commdr's Cross, Order of Merit (FRG) 2003; Defense Distinguished Service Medal, Distinguished Service Medal (with oak leaf cluster), Bronze Star Medal (with V device), Bronze Star Medal (with oak leaf cluster), Purple Heart, Meritorious Service Medal (with three oak leaf clusters), Air Medal and other mil. medals and badges; Outstanding Achievement Award, North Carolina Tech. Asscn 2006. *Address:* Strategic Solutions Unlimited, Inc., 128 Maxwell Street, Fayetteville, NC 28301, USA (office). *Telephone:* (910) 222-8138 (office). *Fax:* (888) 248-1281 (office). *Website:* www.strategicsolutionsunlimited.com (office).

KERNES, Hennadiy Adolfovych, MPA, PhD; Ukrainian politician and government official; *Mayor of Kharkiv;* b. 27 June 1959, Kharkiv, Ukrainian SSR, USSR; s. of Adolf Lazarevych Kernes and Hanna Abramivna; m. 1st Oksana Vasilenko (divorced 1985); one s.; one s. with Halina Privalov; m. 2nd Oksana Haysinskaya; one s. from her previous m.; ed Nat. Univ. 'Yaroslav the Wise Law Acad. of Ukraine', Kharkiv Nat. Univ. of Econs; studied in CTC-14 in Kharkiv and specialized in draftsman-designer mechanics 1977–79; worked at Kharkiv plant 'Svyet Shakhtera' 1977–80; worked at the state enterprises of the city 1980–92; sentenced by Kharkiv Regional Court to three years in a penal colony for theft and fraud 1992, released from custody having been held in jail during the criminal investigation for more than two years; managed production and trading co. Acceptor 1992–94; Chair. CJSC NPK-Holding 1994–99; First Deputy Dir Kharkiv br. of Gas of Ukraine Trading House 1999–2001; CEO NPK-Holding 2001–06; elected to Kharkiv City Council 1998–, Sec. April–May 2002, supported 'Orange Revolution' Nov. 2004, elected to Kharkiv City Council on Partiya Rehioniv (Party of Regions) list, as mem. of the party, Sec. Kharkiv City Council April 2006, 2010, Acting Mayor of Kharkiv March–Nov. 2010, Mayor of Kharkiv Dec. 2010–; shot in the back and hospitalized after announcing support for removal from office of Pres. Viktor Yanukovych 2014; Order of Glory to the Loyalty to the Fatherland, Third Class; Order of Merit, Third Class 2012; Kharkiv Regional State Admin Certificate, Badge of Honour 'Slobozhyanskaya Slava', 'For diligence to 350 years of Kharkiv foundation', Kharkiv City Council Exec. Cttee Certificate, Kharkiv and Bohodukhov Metropolitan Nicodemus Certificate, 60th Anniversary of the Battle of Kursk Medal, Medal 'For active participation in the veteran's movement', XVII Annual Person of the Year Award in the category City Head of the Year 2012. *Leisure interests:* healthy lifestyle, cross-country running, owns varied collection of animals. *Address:* Kharkiv City Council, 61003 Kharkiv, pl. Konstytutsii 7, Ukraine (office). *E-mail:* info@city.kharkov.ua (office). *Website:* www.city.kharkov.ua/en (office); kernes.com.ua.

KERR, David J., CBE, MA, MD, DSc, FRCP (Glas & Lon); British professor of pharmacology; *Rhodes Professor of Clinical Pharmacology and Cancer Therapeutics, University of Oxford;* b. 14 June 1956, Glasgow; ed Univ. of Glasgow; Prof. of Clinical Oncology, Univ. of Birmingham 1992–94, also Dir, Clinical Trials Unit; Clinical Dir, Regional Cancer Task Force for W Midlands 1994; Rhodes Prof. of Clinical Pharmacology and Cancer Therapeutics, Univ. of Oxford 2001–; Pres.-Elect European Soc. of Medical Oncology 2008–09; Founding Commr for Health Improvement, Nat. Health Service; Chair. Nat. Cancer Services Collaborative; Founding Ed. in-Chief Journal of Global Oncology 2015–; Ed.-in-Chief Annals of Oncology 2000–; mem. editorial bd several other journals including Nature Clinical Practice Oncology; fmr Chief Research Adviser, Sidra Medical and Research Center, Doha, Qatar; fmr Dir Qatar Biomedical Research Inst.; fmr mem. Supreme Council of Health, Qatar; Fellow, Corpus Christi Coll., Oxford, Acad. of Medical Sciences 2000; Hon. Fellow, Royal Coll. of Gen. Practitioners 2007; numerous awards including European School of Oncology Int. Award for outstanding contribution to chemotherapy research 1987, NHS Nye Bevan Award for Innovation 2000, European Soc. of Medical Oncology Award for distinguished contribution to cancer therapy and research in Europe 2006, Fulton Lecture, Univ. of Glasgow 2007. *Publications:* more than 350 articles in peer-reviewed journals. *Address:* Department of Clinical Pharmacology, University of Oxford, Old Road Campus Research Building, Old Road Campus, off Roosevelt Drive, Oxford, OX3 7DQ, England (office). *Telephone:* (1865) 617024 (office). *Fax:* (1865) 617100 (office). *E-mail:* admin@clinpharm.ox.ac.uk (office). *Website:* www.clinpharm.ox.ac.uk (office).

KERR, Roy, CNZM, MSc, PhD, FRSNZ; New Zealand mathematician and academic; *Professor Emeritus of Mathematics, University of Canterbury;* b. 16 May 1934, Kurow; m. Margaret Kerr; ed St Andrew's Coll., Christchurch, Canterbury Univ. Coll. (now Univ. of Canterbury), Trinity Coll., Cambridge, UK; Postdoctoral Fellow in Gravitation and Relativistic Theories, Syracuse Univ., USA 1958–62; mem. Faculty, Univ. of Texas 1962–71; returned to NZ 1971; Prof. of Math., Univ. of Canterbury 1971–93, Head of Dept of Math. 1983–93, Prof. Emer. 1993–, Canterbury Distinguished Prof. 2016; apptd to Yevgeny Lifshitz ICRANet Chair, Pescara, Italy 2008; Companion, NZ Order of Merit; Hon. DSc (Univ. of Canterbury) 2015; Hector Medal, Royal Soc. of NZ 1982, Hughes Medal, Royal Soc. of London 1984, Rutherford Medal, Royal Soc. of NZ 1993, Marcel Grossman Award 2006, Albert Einstein Medal 2013, Crafoord Prize (Astronomy), Royal Swedish Acad. of Sciences (co-recipient) 2016. *Achievements include:* discovered the Kerr geometry, an exact solution to the Einstein field equations of general relativity that described rotating black holes 1963; represented NZ internationally at bridge mid-1970s, co-author of Symmetric Relay System (bidding system). *Publications:* numerous papers in professional journals. *Address:* Department of Physics and Astronomy, University of Canterbury, Private Bag 4800, Christchurch, New Zealand (office). *E-mail:* roy.kerr@canterbury.ac.nz (office). *Website:* www.phys.canterbury.ac.nz (office).

KERR OF KINLOCHARD, Baron (Life Peer), cr. 2004, of Kinlochard in Perth and Kinross; **John Olav Kerr,** GCMG, BA, LLD, FRSE; British public business executive, parliamentarian, fmr diplomatist and fmr international public servant; *Deputy Chairman, Scottish Power;* b. 22 Feb. 1942, Grantown-on-Spey, Scotland; s. of Dr J. D. O. Kerr and Mrs Kerr; m. Elizabeth Kalaugher 1965; two s. three d.; ed Glasgow Acad. and Pembroke Coll., Oxford; entered diplomatic service 1966; served in Moscow and Rawalpindi; Pvt. Sec. to Perm. Under-Sec. FCO 1974–79; Head DM1 Div. HM Treasury 1979–81; Prin. Pvt. Sec. to Chancellor of Exchequer 1981–84; Head of Chancery, Washington, DC 1984–87; Asst Under-Sec. of State, FCO 1987–90; Amb. and Perm. Rep. to EC (now EU), Brussels 1990–95; Amb. to USA 1995–97; Perm. Under-Sec. of State and Head of HM Diplomatic Service 1997–2002; Sec.-Gen. European Convention 2002–03; mem. House of Lords 2004–, mem. EU Select Cttee 2006–10, 2014–15; mem. Bd of Dirs Shell Transport and Trading 2002–05, Deputy Chair. and Sr Ind. Non-exec. Dir Royal Dutch Shell plc 2005–12; Dir (non-exec.) Scottish American Investment Co. 2002–, Rio Tinto Ltd 2003–15, Rio Tinto plc 2003–15, Scottish Power 2007– (Deputy Chair. 2012–); Trustee, Rhodes Trust, Oxford 1997–2010, Nat. Gallery, London 2002–10, Carnegie Trust for the Univs of Scotland 2005–; Chair. Court and Council, Imperial Coll. London 2006–11, Centre for European Reform 2009–; Vice-Pres. European Policy Centre; Council mem. Business for New Europe; Pres. UK-Korea Forum 2007–14; Pres. St Andrews Clinics for Children; Hon. Fellow Pembroke Coll., Oxford 1992, Fellow Imperial Coll., London 2012; Hon. LLD (St Andrews) 1996, (Glasgow) 1999, (Aston) 2010. *Publications:* various articles on int. affairs and EU issues. *Address:* House of Lords, Westminster, London, SW1A 0PW, England (office). *Telephone:* (20) 7219-5353 (office).

KERREY, J. Robert (Bob), BS; American university administrator and fmr politician; b. 27 Aug. 1943, Lincoln, Neb.; s. of James Kerrey and Elinor Kerrey; m. 1st; one s. one d.; m. 2nd Sarah Paley 2001; one s.; ed Univ. of Nebraska; served in USN in Viet Nam 1966–69; Founder and Owner Grandmother's Skillet Restaurant outlets in Omaha and Lincoln, Neb. 1972–75; founder and owner of fitness enterprises, including Sun Valley Bowl and Prairie Life Fitness Center, Lincoln; Gov. of Neb. 1983–87; Partner, Printon, Kane & Co. (law firm), Lincoln 1987; Senator from Neb. 1989–2001; Pres. The New School (fmrly New School Univ.), New York 2001–10; mem. Nat. Comm. on Terrorist Attacks Upon the US (9/11 Comm.) 2004; Man. Dir Allen & Company LLC; Co-Chair. Advisory Bd, Issue One (fmrly Fund for the Republic); mem. Carmen Group lobbying firm 2013–; Democrat; Dr hc (New York Law School); Medal of Honor, Bronze Star, Purple Heart, Robert L. Haig Award for Distinguished Public Service, New York State Bar Asscn, Distinguished Nebraskan Award. *Publication:* When I Was a Young Man: A Memoir 2002. *Address:* Issue One, 11 Dupont Circle, Suite 350, Washington, DC 20036, USA. *E-mail:* info@issueone.org. *Website:* www.issueone .org.

KERRY, John Forbes, JD; American lawyer and politician; b. 11 Dec. 1943, Aurora, Colo; s. of Richard J. Kerry and Rosemary Kerry (née Forbes); m. 1st Julia S. Thorne 1970; two d.; m. 2nd Teresa Heinz Kerry 1995; three s.; ed Yale Univ. and Boston Coll.; served in USN 1966–70; called to the Bar, Mass 1976; Nat. Co-ordinator, Vietnam Veterans Against The War 1969–71; Asst Dist Attorney, Middlesex Co., Mass 1976–79; Pnr, Kerry & Sragow (law firm), Boston 1979–82; Lt-Gov. of Mass 1982–84; Senator from Mass 1985–2013; unsuccessful Democratic cand. for US Pres. 2004; Sec. of State 2013–17; awarded Bronze Star, Silver Star, three Purple Hearts. *Publications include:* The New Soldier 1971, The New War: The Web of Crime That Threatens America's Security 1997, This Moment on Earth (with Teresa Heinz Kerry) 2007.

KERZNER, Solomon (Sol); South African business executive; b. 23 Aug. 1935, Johannesburg; s. of Morris Kerzner; two s. three d.; ed Athlons High School, Univ. of Witwatersrand; Founder and CEO Southern Sun Hotels 1969–83; CEO Sun Int. Hotels (now Kerzner Int. Resorts Inc.) 1983–87, apptd Chair. and CEO 1993, Pres. 1993–2003; Chair. World Leisure Group 1989–94; Inst. of Marketing Man. Marketing Award of the Year 1978–80, Jewish Businessman of the Year 1993, elected US Gaming Hall of Fame, Lifetime Achievement Award by FEDHASA, South Africa's major tourism agency. *Achievements include:* represented Univ. of Witwatersrand for boxing and wrestling 1954–55.

KESHAP, Atul, BA, MA; American diplomatist; *Vice-Chancellor, College of International Security Affairs, National Defence University;* b. 29 June 1971, Nigeria; s. of Keshap Chander Sen and Zoe Calvert; m. Karen Young Keshap; one s. three d.; ed Univ. of Virgiinia; joined Foreign Service 1994, Country Desk Officer for UAE and Qatar 2000–02, Special Asst for Middle East, N Africa and S Asia for Under-Sec. of State for Political Affairs 2002–03, Dir for N African and Middle Eastern Regional Affairs for Nat. Security Council (in Exec. Office of Pres.) 2003–04; Deputy Minister-Counselor for Political Affairs, Embassy in New Delhi 2005–08, Dir, Office of Human Rights, Humanitarian and Social Affairs, State Dept Bureau of Int. Orgs 2008–10, Dir, Office of India, Nepal, Sri Lanka, Bangladesh, Maldives and Bhutan Affairs, State Dept Bureau of S and Central Asian Affairs 2010–12, Sr US Official for APEC 2012–13, Deputy Asst Sec. of State for S Asia 2013–15, Amb. to Sri Lanka (also accred to Maldives) 2015–18; Vice-Chancellor, College of Int. Security Affairs, Nat. Defence Univ. 2018–; served as Political/Econ. Officer, Embassies in Rabat, Morocco and Conakry, Guinea; also served as an Operations Officer on Exec. Staff of US Sec. of State Madeleine Albright. *Website:* cisa.ndu.edu (office).

KESHTMAND, Sultan Ali; Afghan politician; b. 22 May 1935; mem. of Hazara ethnic minority; Founder-mem. People's Democratic Party of Afghanistan (PDPA) and mem. Cen. Cttee 1965; with Parcham faction when PDPA split 1967; Minister of Planning April–Aug. 1978; tried on charges of conspiracy and sentenced to death 1978; sentence commuted by Pres. Amin. Oct. 1978; fmr Vice-Pres. of Revolutionary Council; Deputy Prime Minister and Minister of Planning after Soviet intervention 1979–81; Prime Minister of Afghanistan and Chair. Council of Ministers 1981–88, 1989–90; First Vice-Pres. 1990–91.

KESOEMA, Nadjib Riphat, BPsych, MA; Indonesian diplomatist; b. 23 March 1953, Medan, North Sumatera; m. Nino Nasution Riphat; two c.; ed Padjadjaran Univ., Bandung, Nat. Admin. Inst., Jakarta; Assoc. Lecturer, Padjadjaran Univ., Bandung Islamic Univ. 1975–81; joined Dept of Foreign Affairs (DFA) as staff mem., Directorate of Foreign Information 1982–84, Head of Press Release Section, Directorate of Information 1984–86, Attaché/Third Sec. (Information), Embassy in Oslo 1986–89, Head of Div., Special Training and Scholarship, Centre for Educ. and Training, DFA 1989–92, Second, then First Sec. (Political and Information), Embassy to the Holy See, Vatican City, Rome 1992–96, Head of Div., Information and Man., Secr. Gen., DFA 1996–99, Counsellor/Minister Counsellor (Political), Embassy in Canberra, Australia 1999–2002, Head of Centre for Educ. and Training, DFA 2002–06, Amb. to Belgium (also accred to Luxembourg, and Head of Mission to EU, Brussels) 2006–10, Deputy of Co-ordinating Minister for Political, Legal and Security Affairs 2011, Amb. to Australia (also accred to Vanuatu) 2012–17; Co-founder Asscn of Dirs of Diplomatic Training Inst. of ASEAN plus People's Repub. of China, Japan and Repub. of Korea 2004; fmr mem. Int. Soc. of Political Psychology; Satyalencana Karyasatya X 1993, Order of St Gregory the Great II (Holy See) 1996, Satyalencana Karyasatya XX 2002, Chevalier d'honneur, Confrerie Blanc Moussis, Stavelot, (Belgium) 2008, Order of Friends of the Manneken-Pis (Belgium) 2008. *Achievements include:* co-composer of Caraka Buana Hymn and March of DFA prior to joining DFA.

KESSEL MARTÍNEZ, Georgina Yamilet, BA, PhD; Mexican economist and fmr government official; ed Instituto Tecnológico Autónomo de México (ITAM), Columbia Univ., USA; full-time Prof., ITAM for more than nine years, Head of Dept of Econs 1994; fmr Dir-Gen. of Sectoral Econ. Analysis, Petróleos Mexicanos (PEMEX), Chair. –2011; apptd first Pres. Energy Regulating Comm. 1994; fmr Dir Investment Unit, Finance and Public Credit Unit; Dir-Gen. Casa de Moneda de México (Mexican Mint) 2002–06; Sec. of Energy 2006–11; Dir-Gen. Banco Nacional de Obras y Servicios Públicos SNC (Banobras) 2011–12; mem. Bd of Dirs Iberdrola SA 2013–, Grupo Financiero Scotiabank Inverlat, SA de C.V.; Premio al mérito profesional, ITAM alumni 2005. *Publications include:* El sur también existe (with Santiago Levy and Enrique Dávila), Los peligros del Plan Puebla-Panamá, Lo negociado del Tratado de Libre Comercio (compiler).

KESSLER, Denis, PhD; French economist and business executive; *Chairman and Chief Executive, SCOR;* b. 25 March 1952, Mulhouse; ed Ecole des Hautes Etudes Commerciales (HEC Paris), Univ. of Paris; Univ. Prof. of Econ. Sciences, holds the 'agrégation' in Social Sciences and the 'agrégation' in Econs; Chair. Fédération Française des Socs d'Assurances (Asscn of French Insurers) 1990–97, 1998–2002; mem. Conseil Nat. des Assurances 1990–97, 1998–2002, Presidential Council 1990–96, 1998–2001; Vice-Pres. Comité Européen des Assurances 1996–98, 2001–02; Sr Exec. Vice-Pres. and mem. Exec. Cttee of the AXA Group 1997–98; mem. Exec. Cttee Mouvement des Entreprises de France (MEDEF) 1991–94, Exec. Vice-Chair. 1995–98, First Exec. Vice-Chair. 1998–2002; Chair. and Chief Exec. SCOR 2002–; Chair. Le Siècle 2008–10, Reinsurance Advisory Bd 2009–10, Global Reinsurance Forum 2009–11, Le Cercle de l'Orchestre de Paris; mem. Conseil Nat. du Patronat Français –1998, Conseil Economique et social 1993–2010; mem. Bd Geneva Asscn, Bd of le Siècle, Global Reinsurance Forum, Reinsurance Advisory Bd, Comm. Economique de la Nation, Fondation pour la Recherche Médicale 2006–12; Global Counsellor, Conference Bd; hon. degrees from Moscow Acad. of Finance and HEC Montréal; Chevalier, Légion d'honneur 2000, Officier, Légion d'honneur 2009; elected to Insurance Hall of Fame of the Int. Insurance Soc. 2014. *Address:* 5 avenue Kléber, 75795 Paris cedex 16, France (office). *Telephone:* 1-58-44-70-00 (office). *Fax:* 1-58-44-85-42 (office). *E-mail:* info@ scor.com (office). *Website:* www.scor.com (office).

KESSLER, Heinz, Dr rer. pol; Austrian banking executive; b. 19 Aug. 1938, Vienna; m.; three c.; ed Vöcklabruck High School, Univ. of Vienna; joined Nettingsdorfer Papierfabrik AG 1964, apptd mem. Man. Bd 1974, Chair. Man. Bd 1982–2003, apptd Chair. Supervisory Bd 2003; mem. Supervisory Bd Erste Bank der öesterreichischen Sparkassen AG 1998–2012, Deputy Chair. May–Sept. 2003, Chair. 2003–12; Chair. Reform-Werke Bauer & Co. GmbH, Reform-Werke Bauer & Co. Holding AG; Deputy Chair. Austria Versicherungsverein auf Gegenseitigkeit Privatstiftung, Duropack AG, Rath AG, UNIQA Versicherungen AG; mem. Die Erste österreichische Spar-Casse Privatstiftung.

KESSLER, Ronald, BA, MA, PhD; American sociologist and academic; *Professor of Health Care Policy, Harvard Medical School;* b. 26 April 1947, Bristol, Pa; m. Vicki Shahly; two s. two d.; ed Temple Univ., New York Univ., York Univ.; Predoctoral Fellow, Health Service Research, Montefiore Hosp., Bronx, New York 1972–74; Research Assoc., New York State Psychiatric Inst. 1975–76; Research Assoc., Center for Policy Research 1976–77; Postdoctoral Fellow, Dept of Psychiatry, Univ. of Wis. 1977–79; Asst Prof., Dept of Sociology, Univ. of Mich. 1979–81, Assoc. Prof., Dept of Sociology and Assoc. Research Scientist, Survey Research Center 1981–88, Prof., Dept of Sociology and Program Dir Survey Research Center 1988–96; Prof., Dept of Health Care Policy, Harvard Medical School 1996–, also Prin. Investigator; Co-Dir World Mental Health Survey, WHO; Prin. Investigator, Nat. Comorbidity Survey; mem. Editorial Bd Journal of Health and Social Behavior 1978–81, 1992–94, Public Opinion Quarterly 1981–84, American Sociological Review 1982–85, 1989–92, Sociological Methods and Research 1983, Psychological Medicine 1994, Women's Health: Research on Gender, Behavior, and Policy 1994, Psychological Methods 1996, Journal of Evaluation in Clinical Practice 1997, International Journal of Methods in Psychiatric Research 1998, Health Services Research 1998, Journal of Affective Disorders 2003–, Culture, Medicine and Psychiatry 2003, Archives of General Psychiatry 2003, Psychiatry and Clinical Neurosciences 2004, Journal of Health & Productivity 2006; mem. Scientific Advisory Bd Anxiety Disorders Asscn of America 2000–05, Nat. Depressive and Manic-Depressive Asscn 2001, Nat. Alliance for the Mentally Ill Scientific Council 2003; mem. Medical Advisory Bd Jed Foundation 2005; mem. Inst. of Medicine 1999, American Sociological Asscn, American Public Health Asscn, Sociological Research Asscn, Society of Behavioral Medicine Research; Fellow, American Psychopathological Asscn; Hon. Fellow, American Psychiatric Asscn 1999; Research Scientist Devt Award, Nat. Inst. of Mental Health (NIMH) 1984–94, NIMH MERIT Award 1987–97, NIMH Research Scientist Award 1995–99, Paul Hoch Award, American Psychopathological Asscn 1997, Rema Lapouse Mental Health Epidemiology Award, American Public Health Asscn 1997, Presidential Citation, American Psychological Asscn 2005. *Publications:* Linear Panel Analysis: Models of Quantitative Change (co-author) 1981, Television and Aggression: A Panel Study (co-author) 1982, Methodological Issues in AIDS Behavioral Research (co-ed.) 1993, Measuring Stress: A Guide for Health and Social Scientists (co-ed.) 1995, How Healthy Are We?: A National Study of WellBeing at Midlife (co-ed.) 2003, Health and Work Productivity: Making the Business Case for Quality Health Care (co-ed.) 2006; numerous articles in medical journals. *Address:* Department of Health Care Policy, Harvard Medical School, 180 Longwood Avenue, Boston, MA 02115-5899, USA (office). *Telephone:* (617) 630-8043 (home); (617) 432-3587 (office). *Fax:* (617) 432-3588 (office). *E-mail:* kessler@ hcp.med.harvard.edu (office). *Website:* www.hcp.med.harvard.edu (office).

KESTENBAUM, Baron (Life Peer), cr. 2011, of Foxcote in the County of Somerset; **Jonathan Kestenbaum,** BA, MBA; British business executive; *Chief Operating Officer, RIT Capital Partners plc;* b. 5 Aug. 1959, Japan; ed London School of Econs, Univ. of Cambridge, Cass Business School, London, Cabinet Office Top Man. programme, Strategic Agility programme at Harvard Business School, USA; family moved back to UK when aged four; helped expand large family commodity trading business (ring dealing mem. London Metal Exchange); spent five years living in Israel, Fellow attached to Hebrew Univ.'s School of Educ.; returned to UK 1990; Chief Exec., Office of the Chief Rabbi, Jonathan Sacks; fmr Chief of Staff to Sir Ronald Cohen, Chair. Apax Partners (pvt. equity firm), jtly est. The Portland Trust (Founding Chief Exec.); Chief Exec. Nat. Endowment for Science, Tech. and the Arts –2010; COO RIT Capital Partners plc 2010–; Chair. and Chief Exec. Five Arrows Ltd (investment co.) 2011; mem. Bd The Design Council, RSC, Tech. Strategy Bd; Innovation Group Advisory Bd at Imperial Coll. London, now Adjunct Prof., Imperial Coll. Business School; fmr Chair. (non-exec.) Quest (investigative accounting firm); mem. Bd of Dirs Capital Holdings Fund plc (fmrly European Capital Holdings), Graywood Ltd, Windmill Hill Asset Management, EDRRIT Ltd, Pershing Square Holdings Ltd; fmr mem. Faculty, Cass Business School; Chair. Manchester Science Panel; fmr Commr, Manchester Ind. Econ. Review; Chancellor, Plymouth Univ. 2013–; Consultant, Doder Trust Ltd; Trustee, Rowley Lane Recreation Trust, Blavatnik School of Government Foundation, Covenant and Conversation Trust; Hon. DTech (Plymouth), Hon. Fellow Royal Coll. of Art. *Address:* RIT Capital Partners plc, 27 St James's Place, London, SW1A 1NR (office); House of Lords, Westminster, London, SW1A 0PW, England. *Telephone:* (20) 7647-6203 (office); (20) 7219-5353 (House of Lords). *E-mail:* investorrelations@ritcap.co.uk (office). *Website:* www.ritcap.com (office).

KESWICK, Ben, MBA; British business executive; *Managing Director, Jardine Matheson Holdings Ltd;* b. 1972; s. of Simon Lindley Keswick and Emma Keswick (née Chetwode); ed Institut Européen d'Admin des Affaires (INSEAD), France; joined Jardine Matheson Group 1998, several exec. positions including Finance Dir and CEO Jardine Pacific 2003–07, Group Man. Dir Jardine Cycle & Carriage 2007–12, joined Bd of Jardine Matheson Holdings Ltd 2007, Man. Dir 2012–, Chair. and Man. Dir Jardine Matheson Ltd 2012–, Chair. Jardine Cycle & Carriage; Commr, Astra, United Tractors; Man. Dir Dairy Farm, Hongkong Land, Jardine Strategic, Mandarin Oriental; Dir, Jardine Pacific, Jardine Motors. *Address:* Jardine Matheson Holdings Ltd, 48th Floor, Jardine House, GPO Box 70, Hong Kong Special Administrative Region, People's Republic of China (office). *Telephone:* 2843-8288 (office). *E-mail:* jml@jardines.com (office). *Website:* www.jardines.com (office).

KESWICK, Sir Henry Neville Lindley, Kt; British business executive; *Chairman, Jardine Matheson Holdings Ltd;* b. 29 Sept. 1938; s. of Sir William Keswick and Mary Lindley; brother of Sir (John) Chippendale Keswick and Simon Lindley Keswick (q.v.); m. Lady Tessa Reay 1985; ed Eton Coll., Trinity Coll., Cambridge; Nat. Service 1956–58; joined Matheson & Co. 1961, Chair. 1975–, mem. Bd of Dirs Jardine Matheson Holdings Ltd, Hong Kong 1967–, Chair. 1972–75, 1989–, Jardine Strategic Holdings 1989– (Dir 1988–); Dir Sun Alliance and London Insurance PLC 1975–96, Sun Alliance Group PLC 1989, Deputy Chair. 1993–96, Dir Royal and Sun Alliance Insurance Group PLC 1996–2000; mem. Bd of Dirs Robert Fleming Holdings Ltd 1975–2000, Rothmans Int. 1988–94, Hongkong Land Co. 1988–, Mandarin Oriental Int. 1988–, Dairy Farm Int. Holdings 1988–, The Daily Telegraph 1990–2001, Hong Kong Land, Mandarin Oriental, Rothschilds Continuation Holdings; Chair. Hong Kong Asscn 1988–2001, now Vice-Chair.; mem. 21st Century Trust 1987–97; Propr The Spectator 1975–81; Trustee, Nat. Portrait Gallery 1982–2001 (Chair. 1994–2001); mem. The Tablet Trust (charity). *Leisure interest:* country pursuits. *Address:* Jardine Matheson Holdings Ltd, 48th Floor, Jardine House, GPO Box 70, Hong Kong Special Administrative Region, People's Republic of China (office); Matheson & Co. Ltd, 3 Lombard Street, London, EC3V 9AQ, England (office). *Telephone:* 2843-8288 (Hong Kong) (office); (20) 7816-8100 (London) (office). *Fax:* (20) 7623-5024 (London) (office). *E-mail:* jml@jardines.com (office); enquiries@matheson.co.uk (office). *Website:* www.jardines.com (office); www.matheson.co.uk (office).

KESWICK, Sir (John) Chippendale (Chips) Lindley, Kt; British merchant banker; b. 2 Feb. 1940; s. of Sir William Keswick and Mary Lindley; brother of Henry N. L. Keswick and Simon L. Keswick; m. Lady Sarah Ramsay 1966; three s.; ed Eton Coll., Univ. of Aix-Marseilles; with Glyn Mills & Co. 1961–65; Jt Vice-Chair. Hambros PLC 1986, Jt Deputy Chair. 1990–97, Group Chief Exec. 1995–97, Chair. Hambros Bank Ltd 1986–95, Chair. (non-exec.) 1995–98, Chair. Hambros PLC 1997–98; Sr Banking and Capital Markets Adviser Société Générale 1998; mem. Bd of Dirs Persimmon PLC 1984–2006, De Beers 1993–2010, Bank of England 1993–2001, Edinburgh Investment Trust PLC 1992–2001, IMI PLC 1994–2003, Anglo American Corpn of S Africa Ltd 1995–2001, Investec Ltd 2002–10, Arsenal Football Club 2005– (Chair. 2013–); Vice-Counsellor, Cancer Research Campaign 1992; mem. Queen's Body Guard for Scotland, Royal Co. of Archers 1976–; Hon. Treas., Children's Country Holidays Fund 1973–95. *Leisure interests:* bridge, country pursuits. *Address:* Arsenal Football Club, Highbury House, 75 Drayton Park, London, N5 1BU, England. *Telephone:* (20) 7619-5003. *Website:* www.arsenal.com.

KESWICK, Simon Lindley, FRSA; British business executive; *Chairman, Hongkong Land Holdings Ltd;* b. 20 May 1942; s. of Sir William Keswick and Mary Lindley; brother of Henry Neville Lindley Keswick and Sir John Chippendale Lindley Keswick (q.v.); m. Emma Chetwode 1971; two s. two d.; ed Eton Coll. and Trinity Coll., Cambridge; Dir Fleetways Holdings Ltd, Australia 1970–72, Greenfriar Investment Co. 1979–82; Dir Matheson & Co. Ltd 1978–82, Chair. Jardine Matheson Insurance Brokers 1978–82, Dir Jardine Matheson & Co. Ltd, Hong Kong 1972–, Man. Dir 1982, Chair. 1983–89, Jardine Matheson Holdings Ltd 1984–89 (Dir 1972–), Jardine Strategic Holdings Ltd 1987–89, (Dir 1987–), Jardine Int. Motor Holdings 1990–97; Chair. Hongkong Land Holdings Ltd 1983–, Hongkong & Shanghai Banking Corpn 1983–88, Mandarin Oriental Int. Ltd 1984–, Dairy Farm Int. Holdings Ltd 1984–, Fleming Mercantile Investment Trust 1990– (Dir 1988–), Trafalgar House PLC 1993–96; Dir Hanson PLC 1991–, Jardine Lloyd Thomson Group PLC 2001–; Dir (non-exec.) Wellcome 1995–; Trustee, British Museum 1989–. *Leisure interests:* country pursuits, Tottenham Hotspur Football Club. *Address:* Rockcliffe, Upper Slaughter, Cheltenham, Glos., GL54 2JW, England (home); May Tower 1, 5–7 May Road, Hong Kong Special Administrative Region (home); Hongkong Land Ltd, 8th Floor, One Exchange Square, Central, Hong Kong Special Administrative Region, People's Republic of China (office). *Telephone:* (1451) 30648 (England) (home); 2842-8428 (Hong Kong) (office). *Fax:* 2845-9226 (Hong Kong) (office). *E-mail:* gpobox@hkland.com (office). *Website:* www.hkland.com (office).

KESWICK, Hon. Lady Tessa; British administrator and fmr civil servant; *Chancellor, University of Buckingham;* b. (Annabel Therese Fraser), 15 Oct. 1942, Beauly, Scotland; d. of 15th Lord Lovat and Rosamund Broughton; m. 1st Lord Reay 1964 (divorced 1978); two s. one d.; m. 2nd Henry Keswick (q.v.) 1985; ed Sacred Heart Convent, Woldingham, Surrey; Conservative Councillor, Royal Borough of Kensington and Chelsea 1982–86; Conservative cand. for Inverness 1987; special policy adviser to Rt Hon. Kenneth Clarke (q.v.) at Dept of Health 1989, Dept of Educ., Home Office, Treasury –1995; Dir Centre for Policy Studies 1995–2004, Deputy Chair. 2004–17; Chancellor, Univ. of Buckingham 2013–; Dir (non-exec.) Daily Mail & General Trust PLC 2013–; Fellow, King's Coll. London. *Leisure interests:* art, music, breeding horses. *Address:* 6 Smith Square, London, SW1P 3HT, England. *Telephone:* (20) 7222-1218. *E-mail:* tessa@cps.org.uk (office).

KETO, Aila Inkeri, AO, PhD; Australian conservationist and academic; *Co-Founder and President, Australian Rainforest Conservation Society Inc.;* b. 14 March 1943, Tully, Qld; d. of Kauko Keto and Ingrid Keto; m. Dr Keith Scott; one s.; ed Univ. of Queensland; Adjunct Prof., School of Agronomy and Horticulture, Univ. of Queensland 2002–11; helped develop Centre for Native Floriculture at Univ. of Queensland Gatton; Co-founder and Pres. Rainforest Conservation Soc. (now Australian Rainforest Conservation Soc. Inc.) 1982–; helped negotiate SE Queensland Forests Agreement with Queensland Govt, conservation groups and Queensland Timber Bd 1999; negotiated Delbessie Agreement with Queensland Govt and AgForce Queensland 2007; collaborated with Queensland Govt on SE Queensland Conservation Initiative; Hon. Life mem. Australian Conservation Foundation 1990, Int. Union for Conservation of Nature 2012, The Wilderness Soc.; Hon. DSc (Queensland) 2003; BHP Bicentennial Award for the Pursuit of Excellence (Environment), Advance Australia Foundation Award, UNEP Global 500 Roll of Honour 1988, Avon Spirit of Achievement Award, World Class Achievers, Telecom Australia, Golden Gecko Award, Gold Coast and Hinterland Environment Council 1990, Special Award for Outstanding Environmental Achievement, Sunshine Coast Environment Council 1990, Fred M. Parkard Int. Parks Merit Award, Int. Union for Conversation of Nature 1992, Queenslander of the Year Award 2000, Premier's Millennium Award for Excellence 2000, Centenary Medal 2003, selected as a Queensland Great 2005, Volvo Environment Prize (co-recipient) 2005, Queensland Champion of Conservation, Queensland Conservation 2009. *Achievements include:* work led to protection of more than 1.5 million hectares of Queensland's rainforest; helped achieve closure of rainforest timber industry in North Queensland 1987, and subsequent end of all rainforest-logging on Queensland public land 1994; negotiated Springbrook Rescue programme 2006, Delbessie Agreement 2008. *Publications:* numerous publs in scientific journals. *Address:* Australian Rainforest Conservation Society, PO Box 2111, Milton, Qld 4064, Australia (office). *Telephone:* (7) 3368-1318 (office). *E-mail:* aila.keto@rainforest.org.au (office). *Website:* rainforest.org.au (office).

KETTERLE, Wolfgang, MSc, PhD; German physicist and academic; *John D. MacArthur Professor of Physics, Massachusetts Institute of Technology;* b. 21 Oct. 1957, Heidelberg; m.; five c.; ed Univ. of Heidelberg, Tech. Univ. of Munich, Univ. of Munich, Max-Planck Inst. for Quantum Optics, Garching; Research Asst, Max-Planck Inst. for Quantum Optics, Garching 1982–85, Staff Scientist 1985–88; Research Scientist, Dept of Physical Chem., Univ. of Heidelberg 1989–90; Research Assoc., Dept of Physics, MIT, Mass, USA 1990–93, Asst Prof. of Physics 1993–97, Prof. of Physics 1997–98, John D. MacArthur Prof. of Physics 1998–; Fellow, American Physical Soc. 1997, American Acad. of Arts and Sciences 1999, Inst. of Physics 2002, Optical Soc. of America 2006; mem. German Physical Soc., Optical Soc. of America, European Acad. of Sciences and Arts 2002, Acad. of Sciences in Heidelberg 2002, Bavarian Acad. of Sciences 2003, German Acad. of Natural Scientists Leopoldina 2005, NAS 2002; Officier, Légion d'honneur 2002, Medal of Merit of the State of Baden-Würtemburg (Germany) 2002, Kt Commdr's Cross (Badge and Star), Order of Merit (Germany) 2002; Michael and Philip Platzman Award, MIT 1994, David and Lucille Packard Fellowship 1996, Gustav-Hertz Prize, German Physical Soc. 1997, Rabi Prize, American Physical Soc. 1997, Discover Magazine Award for Tech. Innovation 1998, Fritz London Prize 1999, Dannie-Heineman Prize, German Acad. of Sciences 1999, Benjamin Franklin Medal in Physics (co-recipient) 2000, Nobel Prize in Physics (co-recipient) 2001, Killian Award, MIT 2004. *Address:* 80 Clifton Street, Belmont, MA 02478 (home); Massachusetts Institute of Technology, Room 26–243, 77 Massachusetts Avenue, Cambridge, MA 02139, USA (office). *Telephone:* (617) 489-2421 (home); (617) 253-6815 (office). *Fax:* (617) 253-4876 (office). *E-mail:* ketterle@mit.edu (office). *Website:* cua.mit.edu/ketterle_group (home).

KÉVÉS, György; Hungarian architect; *President, Kévés Architects Inc.;* b. 20 March 1935, Osi; s. of Sándor Kévés and Ványi Piroska; m. Éva Földvári 1966; ed Tech. Univ., Budapest; designer for firms, Agroterv and Eliti, Budapest 1959–61, Iparterv, Budapest 1961–69, Studio 'R' 1983–85; private practice with Éva Földvári 1966; teacher, Faculty of Architecture, Tech. Univ., Budapest 1966–73; Sr Architect and Prof., Architectural Masterschool, Budapest 1974; with Káva Architects 1987–, Kévés Architects Inc.; organizes confs and exhbns Masterschool, including exhbns of post-modern architecture and Mario Bottá's works 1980–; organized lectures by Rob Krier and Mario Bottá, Hungary 1980; Visiting Lecturer, Washington Univ., St Louis, USA 1981; Ybl Prize, Hungarian State Prize, several first prizes in architecture competitions. *Major works include:* Orczy Forum City Centre, Budapest. *Publications include:* Architecture of the 70s, Architecture of the 20th century; numerous articles in architectural magazines. *Leisure interest:* all kinds of art. *Address:* Kévés és Építésztársai Rt., Melinda u. 21, 1121 Budapest, Hungary (office). *Telephone:* (1) 275-6002 (office). *Fax:* (1) 395-7623 (office). *E-mail:* kava21@axelero.hu (office). *Website:* www.kevesrt.com/en (office).

KEY, Andrew Jonathan Thomas; British diplomat and civil servant; *Chief Executive, Judicial Office;* m. Joanna Key; one s. two d.; ed Clare Coll., Cambridge (choral scholar); Desk Officer, Eastern Adriatic Dept and later Security Policy Dept, FCO 1992–93, full-time Mandarin language training 1993–95, Second Sec. (Econ.), Beijing 1995–99, Head of Climate Change Team, FCO 1999–2001, Bd Sec., Directorate for Strategy and Innovation 2000–03, Head of EU External Relations Group and later Head of Unit for Special Rep. for Climate Change 2003–06, full-time language training 2006, Amb. to Fmr Yugoslav Repub. of Macedonia 2007–10, Minister and Deputy Head of Mission, Embassy in Beijing 2012–15; with Dept of

Health 2015–16; Chief Exec., Judicial Office, London 2016–. *Address:* Office of the Chief Executive, Judicial Office, 11th floor, Thomas More Building, Royal Courts of Justice, Strand, London, WC2A 2LL, England (office). *Website:* www.judiciary.gov.uk (office).

KEY, John, BComm; New Zealand politician; b. 9 Aug. 1961, Auckland; m. Bronagh Key; two c.; ed Burnside High School, Univ. of Canterbury; early career as investment banker in mid-1980s, then worked in Singapore, London and Sydney for Merrill Lynch in 1990s; mem. Foreign Exchange Cttee Fed. Reserve Bank of New York 1999–2001; returned to NZ 2001; MP (Nat. Party) for Helensville 2002–, Nat. Party Deputy Finance Spokesman 2002–04, Finance Spokesman 2004–06, Leader 2006–16; Prime Minister and Minister of Tourism 2008–16. *Address:* House of Representatives, Parliament Buildings, Private Bag 18041, Wellington 6160, New Zealand (office). *E-mail:* john.key@parliament.govt.nz (office). *Website:* www.parliament.nz/en (office).

KEYS, Alicia; American singer, songwriter and musician (piano); b. (Alicia Augello Cook), 25 Jan. 1981, New York; m. Kasseem Dean (aka Swizz Beatz) 2010; one s.; ed Professional Performing Arts School, Manhattan; classically trained pianist; solo artist; numerous live appearances, festivals; collaborations with Angie Stone, Jimmy Cozier, Jermaine Paul, Jack White, John Mayer, Jay-Z, Usher; numerous awards including: Grammy Awards for Best New Artist 2001, for Song of the Year, Best Female R&B Vocal Performance, Best R&B Song (all for Fallin') 2001, for Best R&B Song (for You Don't Know My Name) 2005, for Best Female R&B Vocal Performance (for No One) 2008, (for Superwoman) 2009, for Best Rap Song (with Jay-Z) (for Empire State of Mind) 2011, Billboard Music Awards for Female Artist of the Year 2001, 2004, for Female New Artist of the Year 2001, for New R&B/Hip-Hop Artist of the Year 2001, American Music Award Favorite New Artist, Pop/Rock, Favourite New Artist, Soul/R&B 2002, MTV Award Best R&B Act 2002, American Music Award for Best Female Soul/R&B Artist 2004, Source Hip Hop Music Award for Female Artist of the Year 2004, MTV Award for Best R&B Video 2005, Lady of Soul Award for Best R&B/Soul or Rap Song (for If I Ain't Got You) 2005, MTV Europe Music Award for Best R&B 2005, Image Awards for Top Female Musical Artist, for Best Song, for Best Video (for Unbreakable) 2006, World Music Award for Best R&B Act 2008. *Recordings include:* albums: Songs In A Minor (Grammy Award for Best R&B Album 2001, MOBO Award for Best Album 2002) 2001, The Diary of Alicia Keys (Grammy Award for Best R&B Album 2005) 2003, Unplugged 2005, As I Am (American Music Awards for Best Album, Pop/Rock 2008, for Best Album, Soul/R&B 2008) 2007, The Element of Freedom 2009, Girl on Fire (Grammy Award for Best R&B Album 2014) 2012, Here 2016. *Films:* Smokin' Aces 2006, The Nanny Diaries 2007, The Secret Life of Bees 2008. *Address:* William Morris Agency, 1325 Avenue of the Americas, New York, NY 10019, USA (office). *Telephone:* (212) 586-5100 (office). *Fax:* (212) 246-3583 (office). *Website:* www.wma.com (office); www.aliciakeys.net.

KEZERASHVILI, Davit; Georgian politician and government official; b. 22 Sept. 1978, Tbilisi; m.; two s.; ed Ivane Javakhishvili Tbilisi State Univ.; Sr Inspector, Penitentiary Dept, Ministry of Justice April–Sept. 2001; Head of Information and Analysis Div., Dept of Informatics, Ministry of Justice 2001–02; Asst to Chair. Tbilisi City Council 2002–04; Head of Finance Police, Ministry of Finance 2004–06; Minister of Defence 2006–08.

KGANYAGO, Lesetja, BCom, MSc (Econs); South African economist and central banker; *Governor, South African Reserve Bank;* b. 7 Oct. 1965, Limpopo prov.; m. Zibusiso Kganyago; ed London School of Econs and Univ. of London, UK, Univ. of South Africa; Clerk, First Nat. Bank 1996–98; Accountant, Congress of South African Trade Unions 1996–98; Asst Man., Investment Dealing, South African Reserve Bank 1996–98, Deputy Dir-Gen., Dir of Int. Commercial Financing, Nat. Treasury 1996–98, Chief Dir of Liability Man., Nat. Treasury 1998–2011, Dir-Gen. Nat. Treasury 2004–11, Deputy Gov. South African Reserve Bank 2011–14, Gov. 2014–; Chair. Int. Monetary and Financial Cttee, IMF 2018–; also currently Nat. Co-ordinator, Econs Dept and Regional Accountant, African Nat. Congress; mem. Steering Cttee, Financial Stability Bd (FSB), Co-Chair. FSB Regional Consultative Group for Sub-Saharan Africa, fmr Chair. FSB Standing Cttee on Standard Implementation, Chair. FSB Standing Cttee on the Revision of the Banks Act; Helen Suzman Leadership Award, The British Council. *Address:* South African Reserve Bank, 370 Helen Joseph Street, POB 427, Pretoria 0002 South Africa (office). *Telephone:* (12) 3133911 (office). *Fax:* (12) 3133197 (office). *E-mail:* joseph.mabowa@resbank.co.za (office). *Website:* www.resbank.co.za (office).

KGATHI, Shaw, BA, MA; Botswana politician; *Minister of Defence, Justice and Security;* b. 18 Oct. 1961, Bobonong; fmr secondary school teacher and headmaster; mem. Nat. Ass. (parl.) for Bobirwa 2004–; various roles in govt depts including Under-Sec. and Acting Deputy Perm. Sec., Ministry of Labour and Home Affairs, Asst to Minister of Agric. 2008, Dir of Sports and Recreation and Coordinator of Youth and Sport, Ministry of Labour and Home Affairs, Minister of Youth, Sport and Culture 2009, Minister of Defence, Justice and Security 2014–; mem. Botswana Democratic Party, currently Deputy Gen. Sec. *Address:* Ministry of Defence, Justice and Security, PMB 00384, Gaborone, Botswana (office). *Telephone:* 3698200 (office). *Fax:* 3933034 (office). *E-mail:* mdjs@gov.bw (office).

KHABADZE, Archil, BEcons; Georgian business executive and politician; b. 11 March 1981, Batumi, Ajara ASSR, Georgian SSR, USSR; m.; one d.; ed Batumi Shota Rustaveli State Univ., Agrarian Univ. of Georgia, Tbilisi; Credit Man., Jt Stock Co. (JSC) Georgian Maritime Bank, Batumi 2002–04; Credit Man., JSC Intellect Bank, Batumi 2004–05, Head of Credit Div. 2005–06; Credit Man., JSC Bank Cartu, Batumi March–Dec. 2006, Head of Credit Div. 2006–08, Batumi Br. Dir 2008–12; Chair. of the Govt, Autonomous Repub. of Ajara 2012–16. *Address:* c/o Office of the Chairman of the Government, Autonomous Republic of Ajara, 9 Gamsakhurdia str., Batumi 6010, Georgia.

KHABIROV, Radiy Faritovich; Russian academic and politician; *Acting Head of the Republic of Bashkortostan;* b. 20 March 1964, Sayranovo; m.; three c.; ed Bilkent Univ., Bashkir State Univ.; milling machine apprentice operator, Ishimbay Transport Engineering Plant 1981; served in USSR Armed Forces 1982–84; Asst Prof., Dept of State Law and Soviet Construction, Faculty of Law, Bashkir State Univ. 1989–92, Sr Lecturer, Assoc. Prof., Deputy Dean, Dir Law Inst. 1994–2003; Head of the Presidential Exec. Office of the Repub. of Bashkortostan 2003–08, Acting Head 2018–; Head of Dept for Relations with the Federal Ass.; Deputy Head of Presidential Domestic Policy Directorate 2009–16; Head of Krasnogorsk City District, Moscow Oblast 2017–18; Order of the Republic of Crimea–For Fidelity to Duty. *Address:* Office of the Head of Bashkortostan, 450101 Ufa, Tukaeva street 46, Russian Federation (office). *E-mail:* aprb@bashkortostan.ru (office). *Website:* glavarb.ru (office).

KHACHATRIAN, Vardan; Armenian politician; b. 6 April 1959, Jermuk City; m.; two c.; ed Yerevan Polytech. Inst., Moscow Supreme Tech. Univ.; engineer, Mineral Waters of Armenia Industrial Union 1980–83, Yerevan Polytech. Inst. 1983–85; Sr Engineer in Tech. Div., Div. Head, then Head of Production Tech. Div., Industrial Bakery Union of Armenia 1985–90; Workshop Head in Zovk Production Unit, then Dir Zovk Factory, Food Ministry of ASSR 1990–92; mem. Privatization Cttee, Repub. of Armenia 1992–95; mem. Nat. Ass. and Deputy Head Standing Cttee for Finance, Credit, Fiscal and Econ. Affairs 1995–98, Head, Standing Cttee 1999–2000; Head of Finance, Budgetary Dept, Ministry of Defence 1998–99; Minister of Finance and the Economy 2000–08; mem. Yerevan—The Heritage Party –2009, then mem. Social Democrat Hunchakian Party.

KHACHATUROV, Col-Gen. Yuri P.; Armenian army officer and international organization official; *General Secretary, Collective Security Treaty Organization;* b. 1 May 1952, Tetritskaro, Georgian SSR, USSR; m.; three s.; ed Tbilisi Artillery Command of Red Banner School, Kalinin Artillery Mil. Acad., Leningrad; long career in Soviet Army and later Armed Forces of Armenia, roles include Battery Commdr, later Deputy Commdr and Artillery Bn Commdr, Anti-Tank Artillery Bn, Far East Mil. Dist 1976–82, Lecturer, Kalinin Artillery Mil. Acad., Leningrad 1982–85, Head of Missile Forces and Artillery HQ, Tank Div., Belarusian Mil. Dist 1985–87, Chief of Staff of Missile Forces and Artillery, 5th Guards Motorized Rifle Div., 40th Army, Afghanistan 1987–89, Commdr, Artillery Brigade, Belarusian Mil. Dist 1989–92, Commdr, Armenian 2nd Infantry Regt April–Sept. 1992, Chief of Border Troops and Deputy Commdr of Armed Forces of Armenia 1992, seconded to Ministry of Defence as Deputy Minister of Defence 2000, First Deputy Minister of Defence 2008–09, Chief of Gen. Staff of Armed Forces of Armenia 2009–16; rank of Maj.-Gen. 1995, Lt-Gen. 2000, Col-Gen. 2008; Sec., Nat. Security Council of Armenia 2016–17; Gen. Sec., Collective Security Treaty Org. (inter-govt mil. alliance) 2017–; under arrest in Armenia accused of overthrowing the constitutional order in 2008 (during aftermath of 2008 elections), formally charged July 2018 but released on bail; numerous mil. awards including Order for Service to the Homeland in USSR Armed Forces, two Soviet Orders of Red Star, Afghan Order of Star (2nd degree), Mesrop Mashtots Medal 2012. *Address:* Secretariat, Collective Security Treaty Organization, 101000 Moscow, per. Sverchkov 3/2, Russian Federation (office). *Telephone:* (495) 621-37-86 (office). *Fax:* (495) 623-43-46 (office). *E-mail:* odkb@gov.ru (office). *Website:* www.odkb.gov.ru (office).

KHADDAM, Abdul Halim; Syrian lawyer and politician; *Leader, National Salvation Front in Syria;* b. 15 Sept. 1932, Baniyas; Najat Marqabi; three s. one d.; early career as lawyer in Damascus 1954–64; Govt of Damascus 1967–69; Minister of the Economy and Foreign Trade 1969–70; Deputy Prime Minister and Minister of Foreign Affairs 1970–84; mem. Regional Command of the Syrian Regional Br., Arab Socialist Ba'ath Party 1971–2005; Vice-Pres. for Political and Foreign Affairs 1984–2005 (resgnd); Interim Pres. of Syria June–July 2000; moved to Paris 2005; charged with treason by Syrian Parl. and expelled from Ba'ath Party, announced govt-in-exile 2006; Founding Ass. mem. and Leader, Nat. Salvation Front in Syria (opposition group with HQ currently in Belgium, with brs in Germany, France and USA) 2005–. *Website:* www.free-syria.com.

KHADER, Naser, MA; Danish politician; b. 1 July 1963, Damascus, Syria; s. of Ahmed Khader and Sada Abu Khader; ed univs of Copenhagen, Århus, Odense; worked as Arabic interpreter and trans. 1983–98; trans. and consultant, Radio Denmark 1989–97; consultant for DAB (housing soc.) 1996–97; mem. Social Liberal Party 1984–2007, mem. Cen. Bd 1996–2007; mem. Parl. for Western Copenhagen 1994–99, Eastern Copenhagen 2000–11; City Councillor 1997–2000; Founder and Leader Ny Alliance (New Alliance) party 2007; mem. Konservative Folkeparti 2009–11, 2015–; UNICEF Amb. 2000–; Danish Authors' Asscn Award for Peace and Int. Understanding 1998, Cultural Award, Union of Commercial and Clerical Employees 1998, AFS-Interkultur Intercultural Award 1999, Modermål-Selskabets, Native Language Asscn Award 2000, Junior Chamber's Award for The Outstanding Young Person of 2001, Heiberg Award 2002, Life Award (Lifeforum, a Danish business Asscn) 2006, Free Speech Award (JyllandsPosten newspaper) 2006, Int. Award, Comité Laïcité République, France 2007. *Publications:* Ære og Skam (Honour and Shame) 1996, khader.dk (with Jakob Kvist) 2000, Modsætninger Mødes (Opposites Unite) (with Bent Melchior) 2003, Tro mod Tro (Belief Against Belief) (with Kathrine Lillør) 2005, Confessions From a Culture Christian Muslim 2013. *Address:* c/o Konservative Folkeparti, Nyhavn 4, 1051 Copenhagen K, Denmark (office). *E-mail:* naser@khader.dk (office). *Website:* www.khader.dk (office).

ARIB, Khadija; Moroccan/Dutch social worker, educator and politician; *President, Second Chamber (Tweede Kamer);* b. 10 Oct. 1960, Casablanca, Morocco; ed Univ. of Amsterdam; Aid Worker, Foundation for Foreign Workers Cen. Netherlands', Utrecht 1978–79; Family Counsellor, Foundation for Foreign Workers W Brabant', Breda 1979–81; social worker, Medical Pedagogic Bureau, Amsterdam 1982–83; Co-Founder and Pres. Moroccan Asscn of Women in Netherlands 1982; Lecturer Univ. of Amsterdam 1987–91; Deputy Head and Sr Policy Adviser, Social Care and Health, Amsterdam 1995–98; MP Dutch Labour Party (PvdA) 1998–2006, 2007–; Acting Pres. Second Chamber (Tweede Kamer) Dec. 2015–Jan. 2016, Pres. 2016–. *Publications:* Marokkaanse vrouwen in Nederland (with Essa Reijmers and Mieke Goudt) 1992, Couscous op zondag 2009, Allah heeft ons zo gemaakt 2011. *Address:* Second Chamber, Binnenhof 4, 2513 AA The Hague (office); PO Box 20018, 2500 EA The Hague, Netherlands. *Telephone:* (70) 3182211 (office). *E-mail:* K.Arib@tweedekamer.nl (office). *Website:* www.tweedekamer.nl (office).

KHADKA, Purna Bahadur; Nepalese politician; b. 29 Feb. 1955; Nepali Congress Dist Pres. 1988–91; elected to House of Reps 1991, 1994, 1999; Minister of Youth, Sports and Culture 1998–99, of Information and Communication and Industry 1999; Minister of Industry, Commerce and Supplies; Minister of Home Affairs 2004–05; mem. Nepali Congress Party.

KHADURI, Nodar, CandEconSci; Georgian economist, academic and politician; b. 29 Aug. 1970, Tbilisi; Lecturer, Faculty of Econs and Business (Macroeconomics), Ivane Javakhishvili Tbilisi State Univ. 1999–2006, Full Prof. 2006–, Founder and first Dean of Student Self Govt 1993–94, mem. Bd, Faculty of Econs 1994–96, 2003–05, Deputy Dean, Faculty of Econs 2004–05; Asst to Minister of Econs 1996–97, in charge of managing state finances and co-ordinating strategic units of the Ministry of Finance 1997–98, in charge of co-ordinating activities of Strategic Units of Ministry of Econs 1999–2000; Head of Tax and Revenue Cttee, Parl. of Georgia 2000–03; Asst to Minister and managed state finances, Ministry of Finance 2003–04; consulted Parl. of Georgia in econ. and legis. issues as nat. consultant of project implemented by UNDP 2004–08; fmr Head of Financial Admin of Shida Kartli; Minister of Finance 2012–16; mem. Editorial Bd Economics and Business, Business and Law, Taxes, New Economist, Economist, The Caucasus and Globalization (Sweden); Founder Debate Club of Macroecomics Policy; has also taught at other educational insts, including CSB and Georgian Inst. of Public Affairs; invited lecturer abroad, especially at St Petersburg State Univ., Russia; f. Asscn of Young Economists of Georgia 1989, mem. Bd of Dirs and Advisory Council; f. The Centre for Econ. Problems Research, Chair. 2008–; mem. oikos Tbilisi Advisory Council. *Publications include:* two monographs and a textbook; more than 70 research papers on macroeconomics, economics of the public sector, macroeconomics policy, economics of Georgia and macroeconomics of post-Soviet transitional period.

KHAIRI, Haziq-ul-, BA, MA, LLB; Pakistani judge and writer; b. 5 Nov. 1931, Delhi, India; s. of Raziq-ul-Khairi, Ed. of Ismat; ed Anglo-Arabic Higher Secondary School, Darya Ganj Delhi and in Karachi, Univ. of Karachi; migrated with family upon partition of India; apptd Judge of Sindh High Court, Prov. Ombudsman (Sindh); fmr mem. Council of Islamic Ideology; Chief Justice Fed. Shari'a Court of Pakistan –2009; Chair. Thinker's Forum (Hamdard Shura), Karachi; ex-officio mem. Nat. Judicial Policy Making Cttee, Law and Justice Comm., Advisory Bd Al-Mizan Foundation, Admin Cttee of Al-Mizan Foundation, Bd of Govs, Bd of Trustees, Council of Trustees and Selection Bd Int. Islamic Univ., Islamabad; Chief Patron SAARC Health, Pakistan; mem. Syndicate, Baqai Medical Univ.; Pres., Cen. and West Asian Studies, Univ. of Karachi; mem. Human Rights Comm. of Pakistan; Pres. Anglo-Arabic School and Coll. Old Boys Asscn; Trustee, Transparency International (Pakistan). *Address:* c/o Federal Shari'a Court, Islamabad, Pakistan.

KHAJIMBA, Raul; Georgian (Abkhaz) politician; *President of the 'Republic of Abkhazia';* b. 21 March 1958, Tkvarcheli, Abkhazian ASSR, Georgian SSR, USSR; m. Saida Kuchuberia; one s. one d.; fmr KGB agent; Head of Anti-Contraband Dept, State Customs Cttee, 'Republic of Abkhazia' 1996–98, Deputy Chair. State Customs Cttee 1998–99; Chair. State Security Service and First Deputy Prime Minister 1999–2001; First Deputy Prime Minister 2001–02; Deputy Prime Minister and Minister of Defence 2002–03; Prime Minister 2003–04; Vice-Pres. of 'Republic of Abkhazia' following power-sharing agreement reached with Pres. Sergei Bagapsh to end crisis that followed Oct. 2004 presidential election 2005–09 (resgnd), unsuccessful cand. in presidential elections Dec. 2009, Aug. 2011, Pres. 25 Sept. 2014–; Chair. Forum of the Nat. Unity of Abkhazia 2010–; Order of Leone ('Republic of Abkhazia'), Order of Merit, Second Degree ('Transnistrian Moldovan Republic'). *Address:* Office of the President of the 'Republic of Abkhazia', 384900 Sukhumi, nab. Makhajirov 32, Georgia (office). *Telephone:* (840) 229-70-22 (office); (840) 222-46-22 (office). *Fax:* (840) 222-71-17 (office). *E-mail:* sukhum-krma@yandex.ru (office). *Website:* presidentofabkhazia.org (office).

KHAKETLA, Mamphono, PhD; Lesotho politician; b. 5 March 1960, Maseru; d. of Bennett Makalo Khaketla and Caroline Khaketla; m.; one d.; ed Nat. Univ. of Lesotho, Nat. Teacher Training Coll., Univ. of Wisconsin, USA; Lecturer in Math., Nat. Teacher Training Coll. 1981–92, Asst Dir 1992–95; Lecturer, Wisconsin Center for Educ. Research 1989–90; Chief Educ. Officer, Ministry of Educ. 1995–96; Country Dir, Inst. of Devt Man. 1996, Regional Dir for Botswana, Lesotho and Swaziland 1997–2001; External Examiner, Univ. of Limerick, Ireland 1998; Dir Centre of Accounting Studies, Maseru 2001–02; Minister of Communications, Science and Tech. 2002–04, of Natural Resources 2004–07, of Educ. and Training 2007–15, of Finance 2015–16, of Foreign Affairs and Int. Relations 2016–17; mem. Democratic Congress. *Address:* c/o Ministry of Foreign Affairs and International Relations, Qhobosheaneng Government Complex, Griffith Hill Road, POB 1387, Maseru 100, Lesotho (office).

KHAKHAR, Devang V., BTech, PhD; Indian chemical engineer, academic and research institute director; *Director, Indian Institute of Technology Bombay;* b. 7 April 1959; ed Indian Inst. of Tech. (IIT), Delhi, Univ. of Massachusetts, USA; with Dept of Chemical Eng, IIT Bombay 1987–, Prof.-in-Charge, Continuing Educ. Programme 2001–02, Head of Dept of Chemical Eng 2002–04, Dean of Faculty Affairs 2005–, Dir IIT Bombay 2009–; Fellow, Indian Nat. Acad. of Eng 2001, Indian Nat. Science Acad. 2002, Indian Acad. of Sciences 1996; Amar Dyechem Award, Indian Inst. of Chemical Engineers 1993, Shanti Swarup Bhatnagar Prize, Eng Sciences, Council for Scientific and Industrial Research 1997, Swarnajayanti Fellowship, Dept of Science and Tech. 1998, N. R. Kamath Memorial Lecture, IPI 1999, Herdillia Award, Indian Inst. of Chemical Engineers 1999, Millennium Gold Medal, Indian Science Congress 2000, Excellence in Teaching Award, IIT Bombay 2001, MRSI Medal Lecture 2003, H. H. Mathur Award for Applied Sciences, IIT Bombay 2005, Indira Manudhane Best PG Teacher Award, Chemical Eng Dept, IIT Bombay 2005. *Publications:* more than 150 papers in professional journals on dynamics of particulate systems, polymerization of rigid molecules and fluid mixing. *Address:* Indian Institute of Technology Bombay Powai, Mumbai 400076, Maharashtra, India (office). *Telephone:* (22) 2576-7212 (office); (22) 2576-4148 (office). *Fax:* (22) 2572-6895 (office). *E-mail:* khakhar@che.iitb.ac.in (office). *Website:* www.iitb.ac.in (office); www.che.iitb.ac.in/online/faculty/devang-v-khakhar (office).

KHALAF, Rima, BA, PhD; Jordanian international organization official; b. 1953; m. Hani K. Hunaidi; two c.; ed American Univ. of Beirut, Portland State Univ., USA; Lecturer, Dept of Econs, Portland State Univ. 1979; Dir-Gen. Jordan Export Devt and Commercial Centres Corpn 1990–93; Dir-Gen. for Investment Promotion Dept, Amman 1990–93; Minister for Industry and Trade 1993–95, for Planning 1995–98; Senator 1997–2000; Deputy Prime Minister 1999–2000; Asst Sec.-Gen. and Dir of Regional Bureau for Arab States, UNDP 2000–06; Under-Sec.-Gen. and Exec. Sec., UN Econ. and Social Comm. for Western Asia 2010–17; Chair. Advisory Bd UN Global Democracy Fund 2006–07; Dir Center for Global Devt; CEO Mohammed bin Rashid Al Maktoum Foundation 2008–09; mem. Bd of Dirs AMIDEAST, Carnegie Middle East Advisory Council, IMF Middle East Advisory Group; mem. Bd of Trustees, American Univ. of Beirut, Nat. Center for Human Rights, Higher Educ. Council; mem. Econ. Consultative Council; participated in High-Level Comm. for Modernisation of World Bank Group Governance 2008–09; Grand Codon of the Order of Al-Kawkab Al-Urduni (Jordan) 1995; Hon. DHumLitt (American Univ. of Cairo) 2009; League of Arab States Award 2005, Prince Claus Award, King Hussein Leadership Prize 2009.

KHALATNIKOV, Isaac Markovich, DPhysMathSc; Russian theoretical physicist and academic; *Honorary Director, L.D. Landau Institute of Theoretical Physics, Russian Academy of Sciences;* b. 17 Oct. 1919, Yekaterinoslav (now Dnipro, Ukraine); two d.; ed Dniepropetrovsk State Univ.; Jr Researcher, Sr Researcher, Head of Div., Inst. of Physical Problems, USSR Acad. of Sciences 1945–65, Dir L.D. Landau Inst. of Theoretical Physics, USSR (now Russian) Acad. of Sciences 1965–92, Hon. Dir 1992–, Adviser Russian Acad. of Sciences 1993–; Prof., Moscow Inst. of Physics and Tech. 1954–; Prof., Tel-Aviv Univ. School of Physics and Astronomy 1993–2003; Corresp. mem. USSR Acad. of Sciences 1972, mem. 1984; Foreign mem. Royal Soc. 1994; Hon. Pres. Landau Network Centro Volta, Como, Italy 1995; USSR State Prize 1953, Landau Prize in Physics 1976, Alexander von Humboldt Award 1989, Kiwani Club Int. Prize 1999, Blaise Pascal Medal, European Acad. of Sciences 2005. *Publications:* more than 200 papers on solid state physics, relativistic cosmology, quantum field theory. *Leisure interest:* chess. *Address:* Landau Institute of Theoretical Physics, 119334 Moscow, Kosygina str. 2, Russia (office). *Telephone:* (495) 137-32-44 (office); (495) 702-93-17 (office); (496) 522-10-41 (home). *Fax:* (495) 938-20-77 (office). *E-mail:* khalat@itp.ac.ru (office).

KHALED; Algerian singer, musician (keyboard, accordion) and songwriter; b. (Khaled Hadj Brahim), 29 Feb. 1960, Wahran; mem. The Five Stars; first recording aged 14 as Cheb Khaled; first hit Trigue Al Lissi (The Way To School) 1975; lyrics censored in Algeria until 1983; performed at Bobigny Festival in France 1986, relocated to Paris 1990; first int. rai hit Didi 1992; collaborations with Chaba Zahouania, Rachid Taha and Faudel; apptd Goodwill Amb. of FAO 2003; performed at Opening Ceremony, World Cup (Fédération Internationale de Football Asscn) 2010; crowned 'King of Rai' at the first rai festival Oran 1985, BBC Radio 3 World Music Award for Middle East/North Africa region 2005, Antonio Carlos-Jobim Award, Montreal Int. Jazz Festival 2005, Empowering Award 2006, Mediterranean Prize for Creativity 2009, Big Apple Music Award 2009, NME Award 2009. *Recordings include:* albums: Hada Raykoum 1985, Moule El Kouchi 1985, Rai King of Algeria 1985, Fuir Mais Ou? 1988, Khaled 1992, N'ssi N'ssi (César Award for Best Soundtrack) 1993, Sahra 1996, Kenza 1999, Les Monstres Sacrés du Rai, Ya Taleb (with Chaba Zahouania), Best Of The Early Years 2002, Ya Rayi 2004, Liberté 2009, C'est la vie (Kora Award for Best North African Singer 2012, Victoires de la Musique 2013, World Music Award 2013, Murex D'Or 2013, Rabab d'Or 2013) 2012. *Address:* c/o AZ/Universal Music France, 20, rue des Fossés St-Jacques, 75005 Paris, France. *Website:* khaled-lesite.com.

KHALID, Mansour, LLD; Sudanese diplomatist and lawyer; b. 13 Dec. 1931, Omdurman; s. of Khalid Mohammed and Sara Sawi; ed Univs of Khartoum, Pennsylvania, USA and Paris, France; began his career as attorney, Khartoum 1957–59; Legal Officer, UN, New York 1962–63; Deputy UN Resident Rep., Algeria 1964–65; with Bureau of Relations with Member States, UNESCO, Paris 1965–69; Visiting Prof. of Int. Law, Univ. of Colo 1968, Univ. of Khartoum 1982; Minister of Youth and Social Affairs, Sudan 1969–71; Chair. Del. of Sudan to UN Gen. Ass., Special Consultant and Personal Rep. of UNESCO Dir-Gen. for UNRWA fund-raising mission 1970; Perm. Rep. to UN, New York 1971, Pres. UN Security Council; Minister of Foreign Affairs 1971–75, of Educ. 1975–77, of Foreign Affairs Feb.–Sept. 1977; Asst to Pres. for Co-ordination and Foreign Affairs 1976, Asst to Pres. for Co-ordination 1977; fmr mem. Political Bureau and Asst Sec.-Gen., Sudan Socialist Union 1978; resgnd from all political posts July 1978 but remained mem. of Gen. Congress of the Sudan Socialist Union; Chair. Bureau of Trilateral Co-operation, Khartoum 1978–80; Personal Rep. for Exec. Dir of UNEP Anti-desertification Programme 1981–82; UN Special Consultant on Co-ordination of UN Information System 1982; Chair. Univ. Devt Cttee, Univ. of Khartoum 1982; Fellow, Woodrow Wilson Center, Smithsonian Inst. 1978–80; financial and investment consultant 1980–; adviser to Pres. Omar Al Bashir –2007; Loyal Son of Sudan and numerous foreign decorations. *Publications include:* Private Law in Sudan 1970, The Nile Basin, Present and Future 1971, Solution of the Southern Problem and its African Implications 1972, The Decision-Making Process in Foreign Policy 1973, Sudan Experiment with Unity 1973, A Dialogue with the Sudanese Intellectuals, Nimeiri and the Revolution of Dis-May 1985, 1985, The Government They Deserve: The Role of the Elite in Sudan's Political Evolution 1990, War and Prospects of Peace in Sudan 2003. *Leisure interests:* music, gardening.

KHALIFA, HE Sheikh Abdullah bin Khalid al-, BCE; Bahraini government official; s. of HE Sheikh Isa bin Salman al-Khalifa; ed Coll. of Eng, Cairo Univ.; Pres. of Historical Documents Centre, Govt of Bahrain; Minister of Housing Municipalities and Environment 1975–95, Minister of Housing and Agric. 2001–02, Minister of Justice and Islamic Affairs 2001–06, then Deputy Prime Minister; Chair. Housing Bank 1979–2002, Central Municipal Council 1987–95; Pres. Bahrain Red Crescent Soc.; Hon. Pres. Wisdom Home Soc.; Man.-Dir Lightspeed Communications Co., Manama. *Publications include:* Bahrain Through the Ages 1993; articles in journals including Al Watheeqa. *Leisure interests:* historical documents, sports.

KHALIFA, Sheikh Ali bin Khalifa al-; Bahraini politician; *Deputy Prime Minister;* s. of Sheikh Khalifa Bin Salman Al Khalifa; m.; four c.; Asst Under-Sec. for Immigration and Passports 1983–93; Minister of Transportation 1993–; Deputy Prime Minister 2005–; fmr Chair. Bahrain Telecommunications Co.; fmr Chair. Gulf Air Co. GSC, Bahrain Airport Services Co.; mem. Bahrain Econ. Devt Bd 2002–. *Address:* c/o Office of the Prime Minister, PO Box 1000, Government House, Government Road, Manama, Bahrain.

KHALIFA, HM Sheikh Hamad bin Isa al-, (King of Bahrain); b. 28 Jan. 1950, Bahrain; s. of Sheikh Isa bin Salman al-Khalifa; m. 1st Sheikha Sabeeka bint Ibrahim al-Khalifa 1968; three s. (including HRH Sheikh Salman bin Hamad bin Isa al-Khalifa) one d.; m. 2nd Sheia bint Hassan al-Khrayyesh al-Ajmi; two s.; m. 3rd a daughter of Shaikh Faisal bin Muhammad bin Shuraim al-Marri; one s. two d.; m. 4th a daughter of Jabor al-Naimi; one s. two d.; ed Secondary School, Manama, Bahrain, Leys School, Cambridge Univ., Mons Officer Cadet School, Aldershot, England and US Army Command and Gen. Staff Coll., Fort Leavenworth, Kan., USA; formed Bahrain Defence Force 1968, C-in-C 1968–, also C-in-C Nat. Guard, raised Defence Air Wing 1978; mem. State Admin. Council 1970–71; Minister of Defence 1971–88; Deputy Pres. Family Council of Al-Khalifa 1974–; succeeded as Ruler on the death of his father March 1999; introduced constitutional monarchical system and assumed title of King Feb. 2002; created Historical Documents Centre 1976; Founder-mem. and Pres. Bahrain High Council for Youth and Sports 1975–; initiated Al-Areen Wildlife Parks Reserve 1976; f. Salman Falcon Centre 1977, Amiri Stud, Bahrain 1977; f. Bahrain Equestrian and Horse Racing Asscn, Pres. 1977–; f. Bahrain Centre for Studies and Research 1989; Hon. Fellow, Royal Coll. of Surgeons of Ireland 2006; Hon. mem. Helicopter Club of GB; Freedom of the City of Kansas, USA 1971; Grand Cordon of the Order of the Star of Jordan 1967, Al-Rafidain of Iraq (1st Class) 1968, Order of the Two Rivers, 1st class (Iraq) 1969, Nat. Defence of Kuwait (1st Class) 1970, Order of Muhammad (Morocco) 1970, Grand Cordon of the Supreme Order of the Renaissance (Jordan) 1972, Collar of the Order of the Republic (Egypt) 1973, Qiladat Gumhooreeya of Egypt (1st Class) 1974, The Taj of Iran (1st Class) 1973 (revoked), Collar of Abdulaziz al Saud (Saudi Arabia) 1976, Star of the Republic of Indonesia (1st Class) 1977, Order of the Repub. of Mauritania (1st Class) 1978, El-Fateh Al-Adheem of Libya (1st Class) 1979, Hon. KCMG (UK) 1979, Grand Conqueror of Libya 1979, Grand Croix, Ordre nat. du Mérite de la République française (1st Class) 1980, Kt Grand Cross, Order of Isabel la Católica of Spain (1st Class) 1981, Kuwait Liberation 1994, Order of Zayed of the UAE 2005, Order of the Repub. of the Yemen (1st Class) 2010, Grand Cross, Order of the Dannebrog (Denmark) 2011; US Army Certificate of Honour 1972. *Leisure interests:* horse riding, golf, study of ancient history and prehistory of Bahrain, water skiing, swimming, fishing, falconry, shooting, football, tennis. *Address:* PO Box 555, Ritala Palace, Manama, Bahrain. *Website:* www.bahrainembassy.org.

KHALIFA, Sheikha Haya Rashed al-, LLB; Bahraini lawyer, international organization executive and diplomatist; b. 18 Oct. 1952; ed Univ. of Kuwait, Univ. of Paris I (Panthéon-Sorbonne), France, Alexandria Univ. and Ain Shams Univ., Egypt; admitted as lawyer to both Court of Cassation and Constitutional Court of Bahrain 1979; fmr Counsel, Bahrain Ministry of State for Legal Affairs as well as sr attorney at a pvt. Bahraini law firm; Prin. and Founding Partner, Haya Rashed Al Khalifa Law Firm; Vice-Chair. Arbitration and Dispute Resolution Cttee, Int. Bar Asscn 1997–99; Amb. to France (also accred to Belgium, Switzerland and Spain) 2000–04; Perm. Rep. to UNESCO 2000–04; Legal Adviser to Royal Court of Bahrain; Pres. 61st Session UN Gen. Ass. 2006–07; Rep. of Bahrain to ICC Int. Court of Arbitration; mem. Bahrain Bar Soc. (fmr Vice-Pres.), ICC Int. Court of Arbitration, Bahrain Supreme Council of Culture, Arts and Literature, Child Devt Soc., Arab Women's Legal Network; fmr mem. WIPO Arbitration Centre Consultative Cttee; Bath for Peace Award. *Address:* Haya Rashed Al Khalifa, Attorneys at Law & Legal Consultants, First Floor, Bahrain Development Bank Building, PO Box 1188, Diplomatic Area, Manama, Bahrain (office). *Telephone:* (17) 537771 (office). *Fax:* (17) 531117 (office). *E-mail:* h.alkhalifa@hraklf.com (office). *Website:* www.hraklf.com (office).

KHALIFA, Sheikh Khalid bin Ahmad al-, BSc; Bahraini diplomatist and politician; *Minister of Foreign Affairs;* b. 24 April 1960; m. Shaikha Wesal bint Mohamed Al Khalifa; ed Islamic Scientific Coll., Amman, Jordan, Univ. of Texas, USA; served at Embassy in Washington, DC 1985–94; Chief Liaison Officer, Office of Deputy Prime Minister of Foreign Affairs 1995–2000; apptd Dir of Public Relations and Information, Court of HRH the Crown Prince 2000; Amb. to UK 2001–05 (also accred to Netherlands 2002–05, to Ireland 2002–05, to Norway 2002–05, to Sweden 2003–05); Minister of Foreign Affairs 2005–; Chair. Cttee on the Implementation of Riyadh Agreement; mem. Supreme Defence Council; mem. Ministerial Cttee on Social Services, Media, Transportation Sector and Communication Affairs, Labour issues; mem. bd of trustees, Isa Award for Service to Humanity; Freeman, City of London 2005, Hon. Citizen, Istanbul 2012; Bahrain Medal (second class) 2001, Medal of Shaikh Isa bin Salman Al Khalifa 2011. *Leisure interests:* history, politics, social affairs, literature, travel. *Address:* Ministry of Foreign Affairs, POB 547, Government House, Government Road, Manama, Bahrain (office). *Telephone:* 17227555 (office). *Fax:* 17212603 (office). *E-mail:* contactus@mofa.gov.bh (office). *Website:* www.mofa.gov.bh.

KHALIFA, Field Marshal Khalifa bin Ahmed al-; Bahraini army officer and government official; *Commander-in-Chief, Bahrain Defence Force;* b. 20 June 1945, Muharraq; ed Royal Mil. Acad., Sandhurst, UK; platoon commdr; training co. commdr; infantry co. commdr; bn second in command; battalion commdr; fmr Chief of Staff, Bahrain Defence Force; Minister of Defence 1988–2006; currently C-in-C Bahrain Defence Force. *Address:* Ministry of Defence, PO Box 245, West Rifaa, Bahrain. *Telephone:* 17653333 (office). *Fax:* 17663923 (office).

KHALIFA, Sheikh Khalifa bin Sulman al-; Bahraini politician; *Prime Minister;* b. 24 Nov. 1935; s. of Sheikh Sulman bin Hamad al-Khalifa; brother of the ruler Sheikh Isa; m. Sheikha Hessa bint Ali al- Khalifa; three s. one d.; joined Education Council 1956, Chair. 1957–60; Dir of Finance and Pres. of Electricity Bd 1961–66; Chair. Manama Municipality 1962–67; apptd Head, Bahrain Monetary Council 1965, Supreme Defence Council 1978; Pres. Council of Admin 1966–70; Pres. State Council 1970–73, Prime Minister 1973–; fmr Chair. Bahrain Monetary Agency; UN Special Citation of the Habitat Scroll of Honour Award 2006. *Address:* Office of the Prime Minister, PO Box 1000, Government House, Government Road, Manama, Bahrain (office). *Telephone:* 17253361 (office). *Fax:* 17533033 (office).

KHALIFA, Sheikh Muhammad bin Mubarak bin Hamad al-, BA; Bahraini government official; *Deputy Prime Minister;* b. 1935; s. of Sheikh Mubarak bin Hamad al-Khalifa; m.; two c.; ed American Univ. of Beirut, Lebanon, Univ. of Oxford and Univ. of London, UK; attended Bahrain Courts as cand. for the bench, Dir of Information 1962; Head of Political Bureau 1968 (now Dept of Foreign Affairs); State Council 1970; Minister of Foreign Affairs 1971–2005; currently Deputy Prime Minister with additional responsibilities for ministerial cttees. *Address:* c/o Office of the Prime Minister, POB 1000, Government House, Government Road, Manama, Bahrain.

KHALIFA, HRH Sheikh Salman bin Hamad bin Isa al-, BPA, MA; Bahraini government official; *Crown Prince, First Deputy Prime Minister and Deputy Commander in Chief, Bahrain Defence Force;* b. 21 Oct. 1969, Rifa'a, British Bahrain; s. of HM Sheikh Hamad bin Isa al-Khalifa, King of Bahrain; m. Hala bint D'aij al-Khalifa (deceased 2018); two s. two d.; ed American Univ., Washington, DC, USA, Univ. of Cambridge and King's Coll. London, UK; Vice-Chair. Bd of Trustees, Bahrain Centre for Studies and Research 1992–95, Chair. 1995–99; Under-Sec. for Defence 1995–99, Crown Prince 1999–; C-in-C Bahrain Defence Force 1999–2008, Deputy C-in-C 2008–; First Deputy Prime Minister 2013–; Chair. Supreme Council of Youth and Sport; CEO Econ. Devt Bd. *Address:* Crown Prince Court, PO Box 29091 (office); Ministry of Defence, PO Box 245, West Rifa'a, Bahrain (office). *Telephone:* 17662100. *Fax:* 17661200.

KHALIFA, HE Sheikh Salman bin Khalifa al-; Bahraini government official and banker; *Minister of Finance and National Economy;* ed Babson Coll., Wellesley, MA and American Univ., Washington, DC, USA; Man. of Equity Risk Products and mem. of Investment Cttee, UBS Investment Bank, UK 2000–05; hedge fund specialist, Investcorp (Middle-Eastern region) 2005–08; fmr dir of man. control of Islamic financial insts. and dir of financial stability, Cen. Bank of Bahrain, apptd Exec. Dir of Banking Operations 2008; in-charge of financial markets of Middle East and North Africa regions, Deutsche Bank AG 2008–12; Regional Head, Middle East Investment Bank Ltd, Dubai 2008–12; Dir-Gen., Office of the Vice-Pres. 2013–18; Minister of Finance and Nat. Economy 2018–; mem. Bd of Govs. Islamic Devt Bank; mem. Bd of Dirs Arab Monetary Fund; Order of Bahrain, First Class 2016. *Address:* Ministry of Finance and National Economy, PO Box 333, Building 100, Road 1702, Complex 317, Diplomatic Area, Manama, Bahrain (office). *Telephone:* 17575000-973 (office). *Fax:* 17532853 (office). *Website:* www.mofne.gov.bh (office).

KHALIFE, Marcel; Lebanese musician (oud) and composer; b. 10 June 1950, Amchit, Mount Lebanon; ed National Acad. of Music, Beirut; Lecturer, Lebanese Nat. Higher Conservatory of Music, Beirut 1970–75; f. Al Mayadeen Ensemble 1976, extensive int. tours performing songs based on poetry by Mahmoud Darwish; Music Dir and resident composer, Qatar Philharmonic Orchestra 2008–10; appearances at numerous int. festivals including Baalbeck, Beit Eddine (Lebanon), Antakya, Carthage, El Hammamat (Tunisia), Timgad (Algeria), Jarash (Jordan), Arles (France), Krems, Linz (Austria), Bremen (Germany), Re:Orient Club (Sweden), Pavia (Italy), world music festivals in San Francisco, New York, Cleveland (USA), Int. Festival of Carthage; several awards including Jerusalem Medal, Beirut 1981, Palestine Award for Music 1999, named UNESCO Artist for Peace 2005, Charles Cros Award (world music category), Paris 2008, Intellectual Merit and Achievement Medal, Fez, Morocco 2008, Cultural and Artistic Recognition Award, Tunisia Ministry of Culture 2012. *Compositions include:* The Symphony of Return, Sharq, Concerto Al Andalus (suite for oud and orchestra), Mouda'aba (Caress), Diwan Al Oud, Jadal Oud Duo, Oud Quartet, Al Samaa, Taqasimn (duo for oud and double bass), Sharq (choral symphonic composition), Arabian Concerto. *Recordings include:* more than 20 albums and DVDs including Promises of the Storm 1976, Rain Songs 1977, Where from Do I Enter the Homeland? 1978, Weddings 1979, At the Borders 1979, Stripped Bare 1980, Happiness 1981, The Bridge 1983, Collections – 3 Albums 1984, Dreamy Sunrise 1984, Ahmad Al Arabi 1984, Peace Be With You 1989, Ode to a Homeland 1990, Arabic Coffeepot 1995, Jadal Oud Duo 1996, Magic Carpet 1998, Concerto Al Andalus 2002, Caress 2004, Voyageur 2004, Taqasim 2007, Sharq 2007. *Publications:* Al Samaa 1981, Anthology of Studying the Oud 1982, Arabic Music-Theory and Practice 1984, Jadal Oud Duo 1996, OUD 1997, Andalusian Suite for Oud and Orchestra 2002. *E-mail:* general@marcelkhalife.com (office). *Website:* www.marcelkhalife.com (office).

KHALIL, Ali Hassan, Lic.en droit; Lebanese lawyer and politician; *Minister of State for Finance;* b. 15 July 1964, Khiyam; m. Samia Saleh Haider; four s.; ed Lebanese Univ.; began work as lawyer 1992; mem. Majlis al-Nuab (Nat. Ass.) for Marjeyoun/Hasbaya 1996–; Minister of Agric. 2003–04, of Public Health 2011–14, of Finance 2014–; Pres. Alumni Asscn of Faculty of Law and Political Sciences, Lebanese Univ., Lebanese Youth Union; mem. Amal Movt. *Address:* Ministry of Finance, MOF Bldg, place Riad el-Solh, Beirut, Lebanon (office). *Telephone:* (1) 981001 (office). *Fax:* (1) 981059 (office). *E-mail:* infocenter@finance.gov.lb (office). *Website:* www.finance.gov.lb (office).

KHALIL, Idriss, PhD; Moroccan mathematician and academic; b. 20 Dec. 1936, El Jadida; m.; two c.; ed Rabat Univ., Univs of Bordeaux, Nancy and Paris, France; Asst Lecturer, Univ. of Bordeaux 1963–65; Asst Lecturer, then Sr Lecturer, then Prof., Univ. Mohammed V, Rabat Univ. 1966–; Jr Lecturer, Univ. of Nancy 1968–70; Research Asst, CNRS 1968–72; Lecturer, Bielefeld Univ. 1973; Dean, Faculty of Sciences, Univ. Mohammed V, Rabat Univ. 1974–85; Prof., Univ. of Nancy, MIT, Ecole Polytechnique, Paris and Paris-Sud Univ. 1979–85; fmr Minister of Educ. and Higher Educ.; Ed. Afrika Mathematika 1979; Founder-mem. Math. Africa Union 1976, African Asscn for the Advancement of Science and Tech.; Corresp. mem. Int. Asscn for Peace (PUGWASH) 1979; mem. Royal Acad. of Morocco 1982, Int. Asscn of French-Speaking Communities; Founding Fellow, Islamic Acad. of Sciences; Chevalier des Palmes académiques 1979, Ordre nat. du Mérite 1982, Ordre du Trône (Morocco) 1982. *Address:* Université Mohammed V, BP 554, 3 rue Michlifen, Agdal, Rabat, Morocco (office). *E-mail:* alacademia@iam.net.ma.

KHALILI, Abdul Karim; Afghan politician; b. Wardak Prov.; mem. Nasr (resistance group) 1978, Dir Nasr Central Office, Tehran 1981; mem. Islamic Coalition Council of Afghanistan 1987, later becoming Speaker; fmr Minister of Finance; Leader, Hizb-i-Wahdat-i Islami Afghanistan (Islamic Unity Party of Afghanistan), an alliance of anti-Taliban fighters from Hazara ethnic minority, located in Bamian prov.; driven out of Cen. Afghanistan by Taliban 1998; Leader, Bamian prov. 2001; apptd First Vice-Pres. Transitional Authority 2002, elected Second Vice-Pres. 2004–14; leader of Hizb-e-Wahdat Islami Afghanistan. *Address:* Hizb-i-Wahdat-i Islami Afghanistan (Islamic Unity Party of Afghanistan), opp.

Hawzeh 3 Police, Karte 4, Kabul, Afghanistan (office). *E-mail:* info@wahdat.net (office). *Website:* www.wahdat.net (office).

KHALILOV, Erkin Khamdamovich, DJur, CandJur; Uzbekistani politician; b. 1955, Buxoro; m.; three s.; ed Tashkent State Univ.; engineer, Research-Production Unit Cybernetics 1977–79; Jr, then Sr Researcher, Head of Div. Inst. of Philosophy and Law Uzbek Acad. of Sciences, 1979–90; Deputy, then Chair. Cttee on Law, Deputy Chair. (Speaker) Supreme Soviet (Oliy Majlis) 1990–93, Acting Chair. 1993–95, Chair. 1995–99, re-elected 2000, Speaker Qoqunchilik palatasi Kengashi (Legis. Chamber) 2005–08; Order Mehnat Shuhrati 1999. *Publications:* about 100 articles on law and politics. *Leisure interests:* lawn tennis, football. *Address:* c/o Qoqunchilik palatasi Kengashi, Oliy Majlis, 100008 Tashkent, Xalqlar Do'stligi shoh ko'ch. 1, Uzbekistan (office). *Telephone:* (71) 139-87-07 (office); (71) 139-41-51 (office). *Website:* www.parliament.gov.uz (office).

KHALILZAD, Zalmay, BA, MA, PhD; American (b. Afghan) consultant and fmr diplomatist; *Chairman and CEO, Khalilzad Associates LLC;* b. 22 March 1951, Mazar-i-Sharif, Afghanistan; s. of Khalilullah Khalilzad; m. Cheryl Benard; two s.; ed American Univ. of Beirut, Lebanon, Univ. of Chicago; Asst Prof. of Political Science, School of Int. and Public Affairs, Columbia Univ. 1979–85; received Council on Foreign Relations fellowship to join US State Dept 1984, Special Advisor on Afghanistan to Under-Sec. of State 1985–89, Under-Sec. of Defence for Policy Planning 1990–92; Defence Analyst, RAND Corpn 1993–2000; headed Bush-Cheney transition team for US Dept of Defense, also served as Counselor to Sec. of Defense, also Special Asst to Pres. and Sr Dir for Southwest Asia, Near East, and North African Affairs, Nat. Security Council 2001; Special Envoy to Kabul, Afghanistan 2002, to Iraqi Nat. Congress, Iraqi Opposition 2003; Amb. to Afghanistan 2003–05, to Iraq 2005–07; Perm. Rep. to UN, New York 2007–09; currently Chair. and CEO Khalilzad Assocs LLC, Washington, DC; Counselor, Center for Strategic and Int. Studies; mem. Bd of Dirs Nat. Endowment for Democracy, America Abroad Media, RAND Corpn Middle East Studies Center, American Univ. of Iraq, Suleymania, American Univ. of Afghanistan; King Ghazi Ammanullah Medal, Afghanistan, Defense Dept Medal for Outstanding Public Service (twice). *Publications include:* The Government of God: Iran's Islamic Republic (with Cheryl Benard) 1984, Sources of Conflict in the 21st Century: Strategic Flashpoints and US Strategy 1998, Strategic Appraisal: United States Air and Space Power in the 21st Century (with Jeremy Shapiro) 2002; numerous articles in journals and books. *Address:* Khalilzad Associates LLC, 1001 Pennsylvania Ave, NW, Suite 600, Washington DC 20004, USA (office). *Telephone:* (202) 393-7145 (office). *Fax:* (202) 393-7149 (office). *Website:* www .khalilzadassociates.com (office).

KHAM, Sai Mauk; Myanma physician and politician; b. 1950, Muse, Shan State; ed Univ. of Medicine, Mandalay; trained as physician; fmr Chair. Shan Literature and Culture Asscn; elected to Pyithu Hluttaw (People's Assembly, lower house of Parl.) for Shan State constituency-3 2010, for Lashio Township 2016–; Second Vice-Pres., Repub. of the Union of Myanmar 2011–12, First Vice-Pres. 2012–16; mem. Union Solidarity and Devt Party (USDP). *Address:* Pyithu Hluttaw, Yaza Htarni Road, Nay Pyi Taw, Myanmar (office).

KHAMA, Lt-Gen. (Seretse Khama) Ian; Botswana politician and fmr head of state; b. 27 Feb. 1953, Surrey, UK; s. of Sir Seretse Khama, Pres. of Botswana 1966–80 and Lady Ruth Khama; ed White Stone school, Bulawayo, Zimbabwe, Waterford school, Swaziland, Sandhurst, UK; joined Police Mobile Unit 1973; Deputy Commdr Botswana Defence Force 1977–89, Commdr 1989–98; Kgosi Kgolo (traditional ruler) of Bangwato 1979–; Minister of Presidential Affairs and Public Admin March–July 1998; elected mem. Nat. Ass. 1998; Vice-Pres. of Botswana 1998–2008, Pres. 2008–18.

KHAMENEI, Ayatollah Sayyed Ali Hoseini; Iranian politician and religious leader; *Wali Faqih (Supreme Religious Leader);* b. 17 July 1939, Mashad, Khorassan; s. of Ayatullah Sayyid Jawad Husaini Khamenei; m. 1964; four s. one d.; ed Qom; studied in Islamic seminary of Najaf 1957, in Islamic seminary of Qom 1958–64, returned to Mashad 1964; joined Revolutionary Movt of Imam Khomeini 1962; imprisoned six times 1964–78, once exiled in 1978; Co-founder Islamic Republican Party 1979, Sec.-Gen. and Pres. Cen. Cttee 1980–87; Sec. of Defence, Supervisor of Islamic Revolutionary Guards, Leader of the Friday Congregational Prayer, Tehran Rep. in Consultative Ass. 1980; Imam Khomeini's Rep. in High Security Council 1981; Pres. of Iran 1981–89; mem. Revolutionary Council until its dissolution Nov. 1979; survived assassination attempt June 1981; Pres. Expedience Council 1988; Wali Faqih (Supreme Religious Leader) 1989–. *Leisure interests:* reading, art, literature. *Address:* Office of the Wali Faqih, Shoahada Street, Qom, Iran. *E-mail:* info@leader.ir; istiftaa@wilayah.org. *Website:* www.leader.ir.

KHAMIS, Imad Mohammad Deeb, BEE; Syrian politician; *Prime Minister;* b. 1 Aug. 1961, nr Damascus; m.; three c.; ed Damascus Univ.; mem. al-Baath Arab Socialist Party 1977–, mem. Regional Command 2013–; occupied various admin. posts at Damascus Electricity Gen. Co. 1987–2000, Asst Dir-Gen. 2003–05, Dir-Gen. 2005–08; worked in UN-sponsored energy preservation project 2001–03; Dir-Gen., Gen. Establishment for Electric Power Distribution and Investment 2008–11; Minister of Electricity 2011–16; Prime Minister of Syrian Arab Republic 2016–. *Address:* Office of the Prime Minister, rue Chahbandar, Damascus, Syrian Arab Republic (office). *Telephone:* (11) 2226000 (office). *Fax:* (11) 2237842 (office). *Website:* www.egov.sy (office).

KHAMITOV, Rustem Zakievitch; Russian engineer and politician; b. 18 Aug. 1954, Drachenino village, Kemerovo region; m.; two c.; ed Moscow Higher Technical Coll.; began career at Ufa engine plant, later at Ufa Aviation Inst.; Head of Aviation Lab., later Head of Research and Production Dept, All-Union Scientific and Research Inst. for Construction of Trunk Pipelines, Ufa 1986; Deputy, Supreme Council of Bashkir Autonomous Soviet Repub. 1990; Dir Bashkortostan Inst. of Applied Ecology and Nature Man. 1993–94; Dir Bashkortostan Ministry of Environment Protection 1994–96, Bashkortostan Minister of Emergency Situations and Ecological Security 1996–99; mem. Bashkortostan Security Council 1996–99; Head, Dept of Emergencies Prevention, Russian Fed. 1999; Chief Fed. Inspector for Bashkortostan, Dept of Russian Pres., Volga Fed. Dist 2000, becoming Acting Deputy Plenipotentiary of Russian Pres. in Volga Fed. Dist; Head of Inter-regional Inspectorate on Tax-Payers, Russian Ministry of Taxes and Duties 2003–04; Dir Fed. Water Resources Agency 2004–09; Deputy Pres. RUSHYDRO (jt stock co.) 2009–10; Pres. Repub. of Bashkortostan 2010–14, also Prime Minister 2012–15, Head of Repub. of Bashkortostan 2015–18 (resgnd); Order of Gratitude of Pres. of Russian Fed.; Hon. Diploma of Repub. of Bashkortostan 1999, Hon. Diploma of Russian Fed. 2004. *Publications:* more than 100 scientific publs. *Leisure interests:* books, music, Alpine ski, speleology, river rafting. *Address:* c/o Administration of Head of Republic of Bashkortostan, 450101 Ufa, Tukaev Street 46, Bashkortostan, Russian Federation (office). *Telephone:* (347) 250-15-66 (office). *Fax:* (347) 250-02-81 (office). *E-mail:* aprb@presidentrb.ru (office). *Website:* www.bashkortostan.ru (office).

KHAMTAY, Gen. Siphandone; Laotian army officer, politician and fmr head of state; b. 8 Feb. 1924, Houa Khong Village, Champassak Prov.; m.; five c.; mil. officer 1947–48, rep. of Lao Itsala 1948, mem. Front Cen. Cttee 1950–52, Chair. Control Cttee 1952–54; Gen. Staff mem. Pathet Lao 1955–56, Head Cen. Cttee 1957–59, propaganda and training officer 1959–60, mem. Cen. Cttee 1957, C-in-C 1960, mem. Politburo 1972–2006; mem. Phak Pasason Pativat Lao (Lao People's Revolutionary Party—LPRP) 1972, Leader 1992–2006, Adviser 2006–; mem. Secr. LPRP 1982; Deputy Prime Minister and Minister of Nat. Defence 1975–91; Prime Minister of Laos 1991–98; fmr Supreme Commdr Lao People's Army; Pres. of Laos 1998–2006.

KHAN, Aamir Hussain; Indian actor; b. 14 March 1965, Mumbai; s. of Tahir Hussain and Zeenat Hussain; m. 1st Reena Khan (divorced); one s. one d.; m. 2nd Kiran Rao; one s.; ed Bombay Scottish and N. M. Coll.; Padma Shri 2003, Indian of the Year in Cinema NDTV 2009, Indian of the Year in Entertainment Award, CNN-IBN 2009, Raj Kapoor Smriti Vishesh Gaurav Puraskar, Govt of Maharastra 2009, Padma Bhushan 2010. *Films include:* Yaadon Ki Baaraat 1973, Daulat Ki Jang, Holi 1984, Qayamat Se Qayamat Tak (Filmfare Best Male Debut Award) 1988, Raakh (Nat. Film Award) 1989, Love Love Love 1989, Deewana Mujhsa Nahin 1990, Jawani Zindabad 1990, Dil 1990, Dil Hai Ki Manta Nahin 1991, Jo Jeeta Wohi Sikander 1992, Hum Hain Rahi Pyar Ke 1993, Parampara 1993, Baazi 1995, Rangeela (Bengal Film Journalists' Asscn Awards) 1995, Akele Hum Akele Tum (Best Actor, Bengal Film Journalists' Asscn Awards) 1995, Raja Hindustani (Filmfare Award, Star Screen Award) 1996, Ishq 1997, Ghulam 1998, Sarfarosh (Zee Cine Award) 1999, Mann 1999, 1947 Earth 1999, Mela 1999, Lagaan (Nat. Film Award, Filmfare Award, Int. Indian Film Acad. Award, Bengal Film Journalists' Asscn Award, Zee Cine Award) 2001, Dil Chahta Hai 2001, The Rising Ballad of Mangal Pandey 2005, Rang De Basanti (Filmfare Critics Award) 2006, Fanaa 2006, Taare Zameen Par (Nat. Film Award, Filmfare Best Dir Award, Star Screen Award, Zee Cine Best Dir Award) 2007, Ghajini 2008, 3 Idiots 2009, Talaash 2012, Dhoom 3 2013, PK 2014, Dil Dhadakne Do (voice) 2015, Dangal 2016, Secret Superstar 2017. *Television:* Satyamev Jayte (host, co-producer) 2012. *Address:* 11 Bella Vista Apartments, Pali Hill, Bandra (West), Mumbai 400 050, India. *Telephone:* (22) 6463744; (22) 6463930. *Website:* www.aamirkhan.com.

KHAN, Abdul Qadeer, PhD; Pakistani nuclear scientist; b. 1 April 1936, Bhopal, British India; s. of Dr Abdul Ghafoor Khan; m. Henny Qadeer Khan; two d.; ed Univ. of Karachi, Catholic Univ. of Leuven, Belgium; mem. of staff, Physical Dynamics Research Lab., Amsterdam 1972–76; est. Eng Research Labs (now Dr A.Q. Khan Research Labs), Kahuta 1976, Chair. –2001 (retd); Pres.'s Special Science and Tech. Adviser with Ministerial Rank 2001–04; under house arrest 2004–09; f. Tehreek-e-Tahaffuz-e-Pakistan (political party) 2012, participated in gen. elections 2013, dissolved Sept. 2013; Patron-in-Chief Dr A.Q. Khan Inst. of Tech. and Man.; Hilal-e-Imtiaz 1989, Nishan-e-Imtiaz 1996, 1999. *Publications include:* Advances in Physical Metallurgy 1972, Topics in Metallurgy (co-author) 1972, Metallurgical Thermodynamics and Kinetics 1983, Dr. A. Q. Khan on Science and Education (co-author) 1997. *Address:* Dr A.Q. Khan Institute of Technology and Management, ICCTS Plaza 81, F-7/G-7 Markaz, Blue Area, Islamabad, Pakistan (office). *Telephone:* (51) 9268141 (office). *Fax:* (51) 9268156 (office). *E-mail:* stcd@comsats.net.pk (office). *Website:* www.krl.com.pk (office).

KHAN, Agha Rafiq Ahmed, LLB; Pakistani lawyer and judge; b. 23 Aug. 1949, Garhi Yasin; s. of Agha Mohammad Anwar Khan; ed Sindh Univ., Int. Islamic Univ., Islamabad; enrolled as mem. Sindh Bar Council 1972; joined Sindh Judicial Services as Civil Judge and First Class Magistrate 1973, Sr Civil Judge and Asst Sessions Judge 1978, Additional Dist and Sessions Judge 1983, Additional Sec., Sindh Ass. 1985, Sec., Sindh Ass. 1985, Dir Legal Services 1989–90, Dist and Sessions Judge 1990, Judge, Sindh Labour Court No. 1, Karachi 1991, Law Sec., Sindh 1994–95, Judge, Sindh High Court 1996, 2007–09, Dist and Sessions Judge, Karachi South and Malir –2007, Fed. Sec., Law and Justice Div., Govt of Pakistan 2008–09, Chief Justice Fed. Shariat Court 2009–14. *Address:* c/o Federal Shariat Court, Constitution Avenue, G-5/2, Islamabad, Pakistan.

KHAN, Makhdoom Ali, BA, MA, LLB, LLM; Pakistani lawyer; b. 9 Jan. 1954; ed Univ. of Karachi, Univ. of Cambridge and London School of Econs, UK; enrolled as Advocate, High Court of Sindh 1977; barrister, England and Wales, Society of Lincoln's Inn 1978; enrolled as Advocate, Supreme Court of Pakistan 1989, Sr Advocate 2001–; Lecturer in Law, Univ. of Keele, UK 1979–80; Prof. of Law, Univ. of Karachi, Sindh Muslim Govt Law Coll. 1980–88; Attorney-Gen. for Pakistan 2001–07 (resgnd); Chair. Pakistan Bar Council 2001–07; fmr Chair. Pakistan Electronic Media and Regulatory Authority, Pakistan Telecommunications Authority; mem. Governing Bd, British Pakistan Law Council; mem. Bd of Trustees, Dubai Int. Arbitration Centre; mem. Advisory Bd Citizens Police Liaison Cttee; fmr mem. Law and Justice Comm. of Pakistan.

KHAN, Amjad Ali; Indian musician (sarod) and composer; b. (Masoom Ali Khan), 9 Oct. 1945, Gwalior, Madhya Pradesh; s. of Hafiz Ali Khan and Rahat Jahan Begum; m. Subhalakshmi Barooah 1976; two s.; ed Modern School, New Delhi; numerous concert performances and festival appearances worldwide; mem. World Arts Council, Geneva; Founder-Pres. Ustad Hafiz Ali Khan Memorial Soc. (promotion of Indian classical music and dance); Visiting Prof., Univ. of York, UK 1995, Univ. of Pennsylvania, Univ. of New Mexico; apptd Nat. Amb. for UNICEF 1996; Hon. Citizen of Nashville, Tenn. 1997, of Houston, Tex. 1997, of Mass, of Atlanta, Georgia 2002, City of Tulsa, Okla, City of Albuquerque, New Mexico 2007; Commdr, Ordre des Arts et des Lettres 2003; Dr hc (Univ. of York) 1997, (Delhi Univ.) 1998, (Vishva Bharati Univ.) 2001, (Jivaji Univ., Gwalior) 2002, (Rabindra Bharati Univ.) 2007; Hon. DLitt, Jamia Milia Islamia Univ. 2007,

North Bengal Univ. 2011, Jadavpur Univ. 2012; Sarod Samrat, Prayag Sangeet Samiti, Allahabad 1960, UNESCO Award 1970, Gandi UNESCO Medal, Int. Music Forum 1970, 1975, Padma Shri 1975, Special Honour, Sahitya Kala Parishad, Delhi 1977, Kala Ratna, Sangeet Kala Sangam, Bhopal 1980, Musician of Musicians, Bhartiya Vidhya Bhavan, Nagpur 1983, Amjad Ali Khan Day (Mass.) 1984, Shiromani Award 1986, Kala Saraswati, Andhra Ratna Andhra Pradesh Kalavedika 1987, Acad. Nat. Award (Tirupathi) 1987, Smitsmriti Award 1988, Raja Ram Mohan Roy Teacher's Award 1988, Sangit Natak Acad. Award 1989, Tansen Award, Nat. Cultural Org., New Delhi 1989, Vijaya Ratna Award, India Int. Friendship Soc., New Delhi 1990, Padma Bhusan 1991, Rajiv Gandhi Excellence Award 1992, Sarod Samrat 1993, Sangam Award 1993, Jawahar Lal Nehru Excellence Award 1994, Gandhi Medal, UNESCO 1995, Crystal Award, World Econ. Forum 1997, Padma Vibhushan 2001, Shankar Dev Award 2001, Fukuoka Cultural Grand Prize (Japan) 2004, USA-India Business Council 30th Anniversary Honour 2005, Medal of Honour, Tara Shevchenko Nat. Univ. of Kyiv, Ukraine 2009, Vivekananda National Award 2010, Banga Vibhusha Award 2011, Gulab Khan Award, Prem Nazir Int. Award 2012, Lifetime Achievement Award, Delhi Govt 2012, Rajiv Gandhi Sadbhavna Award 2012, NDTV Indian of the Year Award 2014, Award for Art, Culture and Education, Dayawati Modi Foundation 2017. *Compositions include:* many ragas; music for Kathak ballets Shan E. Mughal, Shahajahan Ka Khwab, Ganesh; orchestral compositions Ekta Se Shanti, Ekta Ki Shakti, Tribute to Hong Kong (for Hong Kong Philharmonic Orchestra). *Radio includes:* promenade concert, BBC 1995. *Recordings include:* Tribute to Germany 1992, Inde Du Nord 1993, Sarod Ghar 1997, Evening Raga 2001, Amjad Ali Khan (with Amaan Ali Khan and Ayaan Ali Khan) 2002, Guftagoo 2002, Sadaayen 2002, Music from the 13th Century 2004, Ru Ba Ru 2005, Moksha 2005, Potrait of a Legend 2006, My Inspirations 2006, Romancing the Rains 2007, Breaking Barriers 2007, Yaara 2007, Remembering Mahatma Gandhi, Hope, Ancient Sounds (with Rahim AlHaj), Sarod Symphony 2010, Samaagam 2011, Everything is Everywhere 2011. *Publication:* My Father, Our Fraternity 2012. *Leisure interests:* music, light reading, long walks. *Address:* 3 Sadhna Enclave, Panchsheel Park, New Delhi 110 017, India (home). *E-mail:* music@sarod.com. *Website:* www.sarod.com (office).

KHAN, Asaduzzaman, BSc; Bangladeshi politician; *Minister of Home Affairs;* b. 31 Dec. 1950, Dohar, Dhaka; s. of Ashraf Ali Khan and Akramun Nessa; m. Lutful Tahmina Khan; one s. one d.; ed Tejgoan Polytechnic High School, Jagannath Coll., Univ. of Dhaka; elected MP (9th Jatiya Sangsad) 2008, mem., Parliamentary Standing Cttee, Ministry of Housing and Public Works 2009–13, Privatization Bd 2009–13, Bangladesh Press Council; mem. Bangladesh Nat. Parl. (Bangladesh Awami League) 2014–; Minister of Home Affairs 2015–; Pres. Ispahani School Coll.; Founding mem. Padma Coll., Dohar. *Leisure and interests:* reading books and travelling. *Address:* Ministry of Home Affairs, Bangladesh Secretariat, Bhaban 8, Dhaka 1000 (office); 136/1, Monipuripara, Tejgaon, Dhaka 1215, Bangladesh (home). *Telephone:* (2) 7169076 (office). *Fax:* (2) 7164788 (office). *E-mail:* info@mha.gov.bd (office). *Website:* mha.gov.bd (office).

KHAN, Asfandyar Wali, BA; Pakistani politician; *President, Awami National Party;* b. 19 Feb. 1949, Charsadda, North-West Frontier Prov. (now Khyber Pakhtunkhwa); s. of Khan Abdul Wali Khan and Taj Bibi; grandson of Khan Abdul Ghaffar Khan, 'Badshah Khan' (King of Khans, founder of non-violent Pashtun political movt, Khudai Khidmatgar (Servants of God) in undivided India); one s.; ed Aitchison Coll., Lahore, Univ. of Peshawar; joined opposition to Ayub Khan as student activist; imprisoned by govt of Zulfiqar Ali Bhutto and convicted as part of Hyderabad tribunal for 15 years 1975, released 1978, stayed away from electoral politics until 1990; Leader of Pakhtun Student Fed. prior to being elected to prov. ass. 1990; elected to Nat. Ass. 1993, re-elected 1997, 2008; Pres. Awami Nat. Party 1999–2002 (resgnd), 2003, 2006, 2011–; elected to Senate 2003. *Address:* Awami National Party, Bacha Khan Markaz, Pajagi Road, Peshawar, Pakistan (office). *Telephone:* (91) 2246851 (office). *Fax:* (91) 2252406 (office). *E-mail:* president@awaminationalparty.org (office). *Website:* www.awaminationalparty.org (office); www.anp.org.pk (office).

KHAN, Sardar Attiq Ahmed, MA; Pakistani politician and writer; b. 21 Jan. 1955, Ghaziabad, Tehsil Dheerkot, Bagh Dist; s. of Sardar Abdul Qayyum Khan; ed Madina Univ., Saudi Arabia; fmr Chair. youth and student wing All Jammu and Kashmir Muslim Conf., later Chief Organizer, All Jammu and Kashmir Muslim Conf., Pres. 2002–06; elected mem. Legis. Ass. three times; Prime Minister of Azad Jammu and Kashmir 2006–09, 2010–11; currently columnist, several English and Urdu newspapers.

KHAN, Chaudhry Nisar Ali; Pakistani politician; b. 31 July 1954, Chakri Vakilan, Rawalpindi Dist; m.; one s. three d.; ed Aitchison Coll., Army Burn Hall Coll.; mem. Nat. Ass. 1985–, Leader of Opposition 2008–13, served as Chair. Public Accounts Cttee; Sr Leader, Pakistan Muslim League (N) 1988–; Minister of Science and Tech. June–Dec. 1988, of Petroleum and Natural Resources 1990–93, 1997–99, Special Asst to the Prime Minister 1997–99; placed under house arrest after coup staged by former military ruler Pervez Musharraf 1999; Minister of Communication, of Food and Livestock March–May 2008, of the Interior and Narcotics Control 2013–17.

KHAN, Hameed Ahmed, PhD; Pakistani physicist and academic; b. 1 May 1942, Rangoon, Burma; ed Punjab Univ., Univ. of Birmingham, UK; joined Pakistan Atomic Energy Comm. (PAEC) 1965; helped to commission country's first research reactor; on staff of teaching and research faculties, Univ. of Birmingham –1974; Chief Scientist, Pakistan Atomic Energy Commission 1965–72, Sr Scientific Officer 1972–77, Principal Scientific Officer 1977–86, Chief Scientific Officer 1986–94, Head, Radiation Physics Div. 1992–94, Assoc. Dir 1994–96; Visiting Prof. Bahauddin Zakarayia Univ., Multan 1994; Dir-Gen. Pakistan Institute of Nuclear Science and Technology (PINSTECH) 1996–2000; Exec.-Dir COMSATS (Comm. on Science and Tech. for Sustainable Devt in the South) 2000–08, currently Adviser, COMSATS Inst. for Information Tech.; fmr Chief Ed. Nucleus; Fellow Islamic Acad. of Sciences, Pakistan Acad. of Sciences, Alexander von Humboldt (AVH), Philips University; First Prize in Physics (Nat. Book Foundation of Pakistan) 1991, 1992, 1993, Khawarizmi Prize (Iranian Research Org. for Science and Tech.) 1993, Prize in Tech. (Third World Network of Scientific Orgs) 1998, Sitara-i-Imtiaz Award, Int. ISESCO Science Prize 2006. *Address:* COMSATS Institute for Information Technology, Plot #30, Sector H8, Islamabad, Pakistan (office). *Telephone:* (51) 9235381 (office). *E-mail:* drhakhan@comsats.net.pk (office).

KHAN, Imran (see KHAN NIAZI, Imran).

KHAN, Irene Zubaida; Bangladeshi international organization executive; b. 24 Dec. 1956, Dhaka; one d.; ed Victoria Univ. of Manchester, UK and Harvard Law School, USA; joined Office of UNHCR 1980, adviser to local project offices, worked in Pakistan, SE Asia, UK, Ireland and numerous crisis deployments 1980–90, Sr Exec. Officer to Sadako Ogata 1991–95, Chief of Comm. in India 1995, Head of Documentation and Research Centre 1998–99, Head of Comm. in Fmr Yugoslav Repub. of Macedonia 1999, Deputy Dir Dept for Int. Legal Protection; Sec.-Gen. Amnesty Int. 2001–09; Consulting Ed., Daily Star 2010–; mem. Bd of Dirs Mary Robinson Foundation – Climate Justice; Chancellor, Univ. of Salford 2009–; Dr hc (Ferris Univ.) 2005, (Ghent Univ.) 2007; Pilkington Woman of the Year 2002, Sydney Peace Prize 2006, Ford Foundation Fellowship. *Publication:* The Unheard Truth: Poverty and Human Rights 2009. *Address:* Office of the Chancellor, University of Salford, The Crescent, Salford, M5 4WT, England (office). *Website:* www.salford.ac.uk (office).

KHAN, Ishratul Ebad; Pakistani/British government administrator; b. 2 March 1963; m. Shaheena Jabeen; one d.; ed Dow Medical Coll., Karachi; Minister of Housing and Town Planning, Sindh Provincial Govt 1990; 10 years of political exile in London; Gov. of Sindh Prov. 2002–11 (resgnd), 2011–16.

KHAN, K. Rahman, BCom, FCA; Indian accountant and politician; b. 5 April 1939, Krishnarajpet, Mandya Dist, Karnataka; s. of K. Khasim Khan and Shrimati Khairunnisa; m. Ayesha Rahman; three s. two d.; ed Mysore Univ.; mem. Karnataka Legis. Council 1978–90, Chair. 1982–84, Chair. Karnataka State Minorities Comm. (with rank of Cabinet Minister) 1993–94; elected to Rajya Sabha (upper house of Parl.) 1994, re-elected 2000, 2004, 2012, Deputy Leader, Indian Nat. Congress party in Rajya Sabha 2000–04, Deputy Chair. Rajya Sabha 2004–06, 2006–12; Minister of State in Ministry of Chemicals and Fertilizers 2004; Union Cabinet Minister of Minority Affairs 2012–14; Regional Rep. to Exec. Cttee of CPA 2005–06, 2006–; mem. Central Muslim Asscn of Karnataka, later Pres.; mem. numerous parl. dels to int. bodies including European Parl., Strasbourg 2005, several visits to CPA and Ass. of the IPU. *Leisure interests:* music, badminton. *Address:* 200/C, III Block, 7th Main Jayanagar, Bangalore 560011, India (home). *Telephone:* (80) 26638778 (home). *E-mail:* krkhan@sansad.nic.in.

KHAN, Khurram Dastgir, BA, BSc; Pakistani engineer and politician; b. 3 Aug. 1970, Gujranwala, Punjab; s. of Ghulam Dastgir Khan; m.; one s. one d.; ed Bowdoin Coll., USA, California Inst. of Tech.; Special Asst to Nawaz Sharif (Prime Minister of Pakistan) 1999; placed under house arrest following army coup d'état Oct. 1999; mem. Nat. Ass. (Parl.) (PML-N) for NA-96 Gujranwala-II constituency 2008–18, for NA-81 Gujranwala-III 2018–, Chair. Standing Cttee on Commerce 2008; Minister of State for Science and Tech. 2013, also Minister of State for Privatization 2013; Chair. Privatization Comm. of Pakistan 2013; Minister of Commerce 2014–17, of Defence 2017–18, of Foreign Affairs 11–31 May 2018; participated in three bilateral Indo-Pakistani Parl. Dialogues 2011–12, Pakistan co-Chair. of Indo-Pakistani Parl. Dialogue, New Delhi Aug. 2012; mem. Pakistan Eng Council; mem. Pakistan Muslim League (Nawaz) (PML-N).

KHAN, Khyal Mohammad Mohammad; Afghan politician; *First Deputy to Chief Executive;* b. 1957, Ghazni; elected mem. Wolesi Jirga (Parl.) 2005, Head Cttee on Dispatches and Communications; Deputy Leader Hizb-e-islami; First Deputy to Chief Exec. of Afghanistan 2014–; mem., Nat. Security Council, Council of Ministers. *Website:* www.ceo.gov.af (office).

KHAN, Mahmood, MSc; Pakistani politician; *Chief Minister of Khyber Pakhtunkhwa;* b. 30 Oct. 1972, Matta, Khyber Pakhtunkhwa; ed Univ. of Peshawar; Union Council Coordinator, Kharerai, Matta Tehsil 2007–12; mem. Pakistan Tehreek-e-Insaf 2012–; mem. Prov. Ass. (Swat-V Constituency) 2013–18; apptd Prov. Minister for Sports, Culture, Tourism and Museums 2013, for Irrigation 2014, for Home and Tribal Affairs Jan. 2016 (portfolio changed to Prov. Minister for sports, culture, archaeology, museums and youth affairs Feb. 2016); Chief Minister of Khyber Pakhtunkhwa 2018–; fmr mem. Pakistan Peoples Party. *Website:* kp.gov.pk.

KHAN, Masood; Pakistani diplomatist and politician; *President of Azad Jammu and Kashmir;* m. Zohra Masood Khan; fmr Lecturer in English; also worked as TV presenter and English newscaster with Radio Pakistan; joined Foreign Service of Pakistan 1980, with Perm. Mission to UN, New York 1993–97, held positions of Vice-Chair. of Third Cttee of UN Gen. Ass. 1996–97, acted as facilitator of its Social Summit resolutions and ECOSOC Cttee that finalized the text on consultative relationship between UN and non-governmental orgs, held various diplomatic posts in Embassies in Beijing, The Hague and Washington, DC 1997–2002, Dir-Gen. (East Asia and Pacific), Ministry of Foreign Affairs 2002–03, Dir-Gen. (UN) 2003–05, Dir-Gen. (Disarmament) 2003–04, Spokesman for Ministry of Foreign Affairs 2003–05, Amb. and Perm. Rep. to UN and other Int. Orgs, Geneva 2005–08, Amb. to People's Repub. of China 2008–12, Pakistan's Sherpa for Nuclear Security Summit process 2009–, Amb. and Perm. Rep. to UN, New York 2012–15; Dir-Gen., Inst. of Strategic Studies, Islamabad 2015–16; Pres. of Azad Jammu and Kashmir 2016–; Pres. Conf. on Disarmament 2005, 6th Review Conf. of Biological Weapons Convention (BWC) 2006; Chair. Cttee on Internet Governance of World Summit on Information Society 2005, Council of Int. Org. for Migration 2005–06, BWC States Parties Meeting 2007, Group of 77 and China, Geneva 2005–06, Governmental Group in ILO 2006–07, Int. Labour Conf. Reform Cttee 2007–08, Drafting Cttee of 30th Int. Conf. of Red Cross and Red Crescent 2007. *Address:* Office of the President, Muzaffarabad, Azad Kashmir, Pakistan (office).

KHAN, Mohammad Younus; Pakistani professional cricketer; b. 29 Nov. 1977, Mardan, North-West Frontier Prov.; m. Amna Khan 2007; one s.; right-handed batsman; occasional right-arm medium leg-break bowler; plays for Habib Bank Limited 1999–2007, Pakistan 2000– (Capt. 2005, 2006, 2009), Notts. 2005, Peshawar Cricket Asscn 1998–2005, Yorks. 2007, Rajasthan Royals 2008, S Australia 2008–09, Surrey 2010; First-class debut: 1998/99; Test debut: Pakistan v Sri Lanka, Rawalpindi 26 Feb.–1 March 2000; One-Day Int. (ODI) debut: Pakistan v Sri Lanka, Karachi 13 Feb. 2000; T20I debut: England v Pakistan, Bristol 28 Aug. 2006; announced retirement from Twenty20 cricket after leading Pakistan to

ICC (Int. Cricket Council) World Twenty20 title by beating Sri Lanka at Lord's 2009; banned indefinitely from Test cricket by Pakistan Cricket Bd, along with Mohammad Yousuf, for "infighting" during tour of Australia March 2010, ban lifted June 2010; mem. Pakistan team that lost to India in semifinals of ICC Cricket World Cup 2011; announced retirement from ODI cricket 2015; topped ICC's Test Batting Rankings after an innings of 313 in first Test as Capt. Feb. 2009. *Achievements include:* only the third Pakistani player to score 300 or more runs in an innings; second fastest Pakistani in terms of innings (87) to reach 4,000 Test runs, behind Javed Miandad. *Leisure interest:* fishing.

KHAN, Gen. Mohammed Ismail; Afghan politician; b. 1954, Herat; ed Kabul Mil. Coll.; served as officer in Afghan army; fmr Mujahidin Commdr during Soviet occupation; joined Jamiat-i Islami (Islamic Soc.) 1979; led uprising and liberated Herat from Soviet control; Gov. of Herat 1993–97, 2001–04; taken prisoner by Taliban following re-occupation of Herat 1997, escaped in 2000; Mil. Commdr Herat –2003; Minister of Water and Energy 2004–13 (stepped down to campaign in 2014 presidential election); mem. Northern Alliance.

KHAN, Rahat; Bangladeshi writer and editor; *Editor, Dainik Ittefaq;* b. 1940, Kishoregonj; ed Univ. of Dhaka; taught for eight years in colls including Nasirabad Coll. of Mymensingh, Jagannath Coll. of Dhaka, Commerce Coll. of Chittagong; apptd Asst Ed. Dainik Ittefaq (daily) 1969, now Ed.; Ekushe Padak 1996; Bangla Acad. Award 1975, Suhrid Literary Award 1975, Sufi Motahar Hossain Award 1979, Mahbubullah Zebunnesa Trust Award 1979, Abul Mansur Memorial Award 1980, Humayun Qadir Memorial Award 1982, Shuhrid Literary Award 1975, Trayi Literary Award 1988, Cetana Literary Award 1989, Ekushey Padak 1996. *Publications include:* short story collections: Onischito Lokaloy (Uncertain Human Habitation) 1972, Ontohin Jatra (The Eternal Journey) 1975, Bhalo Monder Taka (Money for Good and Evil) 1981, Apel Songbad (News of the Apple) 1983, and others; novels: Omol Dhobol Chakuri (Milk-White Service) 1982, Ek Priyodorshini (A Beautiful Woman) 1983, Chayadompoti (A Shadow Couple) 1984, Sangharsha (Clash) 1984, Shahar (The City) 1984, Hey Onanter Pakhi (O, Bird of Infinity) 1989, Modhyomather Khelowar (The Forward Footballer) 1991, Akhanksha (Desire), Kayekjan (A Few Persons), Ognidaho (Conflagration), Hey Maton Bongo (O, Mother Bangla). *Address:* Dainik Ittefaq, 1 Ramkrishna Mission Road, Dhaka, Bangladesh (office). *Telephone:* (2) 7122660 (office). *Fax:* (2) 7122651-3 (office). *E-mail:* rahat.khan@ittefaq.com (office). *Website:* www.ittefaq.com (office); ittefaq.com.bd (office).

KHAN, Raja Muhammad Farooq Haider; Pakistani politician; *Prime Minister of Azad Kashmir;* b. 14 Jan. 1955; s. of Raja Muhammad Haider Khan and Mohterma Saeeda Khan; m. Robina Farooq; three c.; ed Abbotabad Public School, Govt Coll., Lahore; mem. Azad Jammu & Kashmir (AJ&K) Legis. Ass. 1985–, held portfolio of Sr Minister as well as Minister of Educ. (re-elected and served as a Minister 1991, re-elected and held portfolio of Chair. Public Accounts Cttee 2006), Leader of Opposition 2011; Special Asst to Prime Minister of AJ&K 2003–06, Prime Minister of Azad Kashmir 2009–10 (resgnd), 2016–; Chair. Prime Minister's Inspection Comm. 2001–03; Pres. Muslim Conf. Dist Muzaffarabad, AJ&K 1986–90, Chair. Cen. Parl. Bd of Muslim Conf., AJ&K 1989–2001, Gen. Sec. Muslim Conf., AJ&K 1997–2001, Sr Deputy Pres. Muslim Conf. 2004–06, Pres. 2009. *Address:* Office of Prime Minister, Muzaffarabad, Pakistan (office). *Telephone:* (58) 22921600 (office); (58) 22921601 (office). *E-mail:* info@pmajk.gov.pk (office). *Website:* pmajk.gov.pk (office).

KHAN, Raja Zulqarnain, BA; Pakistani politician; b. 15 March 1936, Gujrat; s. of Khan Bahadur Raja Muhammad Afzal Khan (fmr Gov. and Minister); ed New Delhi Modern High School, Aitcheson Coll., Lahore, Govt Coll., Lahore; Co-founder Jammu Kashmir Liberation League 1960; Minister in cabinet of Pres. Maj.-Gen. Abdul Rehman of Azad Jammu Kashmir (AJK) 1969; elected mem. AJK Legis. Ass. from Samani constituency (then in Mirpur Dist, now in Bhimbher Dist) 1975, elected mem. AJK Legis. Ass. from Bhimbher constituency 1985; Minister for Finance, Planning and Devt, Health and Revenue 1985–91, for Finance and Planning and Devt 1991–96; elected mem. Jammu and Kashmir Council 1996–2001; adviser to Chair. AJK Council and to the Prime Minister; cand. of All Jammu Kashmir Muslim Conf. in presidential elections Aug. 2006; Pres. Azad Jammu and Kashmir 2006–11.

KHAN, Rana Afzal, BSc, MA; Pakistani politician and fmr army officer; *Minister of State for Finance;* b. 22 Feb. 1949, Faisalabad; s. of Fazal Muhammad Khan; m. Najma Afzal Khan; four c.; ed NED Univ. of Eng and Tech., Univ. of Balochistan; commissioned into Pakistan Army, served as Capt. 1971–76; mem. Exec. Cttee, Faisalabad Chamber of Commerce and Industry 1988–91; Vice Chair. Water and Sanitation Agency, Faisalabad Devt Authority 1997–99; mem. Punjab Provincial Ass. (Pakistan Muslim League–N) from Faisalabad 1997–2002, 2008; mem. Nat. Ass. of Pakistan for Faisalabad-VIII constituency 2013–; Fed. Parl. Sec. for Finance, Revenue, Econ. Affairs, Statistics and Privatization 2013–17, Minister of State for Finance 2017–. *Address:* Ministry of Finance, Revenue and Economic Affairs, Blk C, Pakistan Secretariat, Islamabad, Pakistan (office). *Telephone:* (51) 9213204 (office). *E-mail:* (51) 9210734 (office). *Website:* minister@finance.gov.pk (office); www.finance.gov.pk.

KHAN, Riaz Ahmad, MSc, LLB; Pakistani judge; b. 15 May 1952, Nowshera (Khyber Pakhtunkhwa); s. of Abdul Rashid Khan; ed Edwards Coll., Peshawar, Peshawar Univ., Punjab Univ.; began career at Pakistan Railway Transportation and Commercial Group, then posted as Asst Transportation /Asst Commercial Officer, Pakistan Railways, Lahore Div., then transferred to Peshawar; Civil Judge, Kohat, Haripur, and Peshawar then Sr Civil Judge, D. I. Khan; resgnd and started practicing law; apptd Asst Advocate Gen. (North-West Frontier Province—NWFP, now Khyber Pakhtunkhwa prov.) 1997, then Additional Deputy Prosecutor General Accountability, Nat. Accountability Bureau (F), Peshawar for three years; elected mem. Provincial Bar Council (NWFP) 1999; Judge, Islamabad High Court 2010–14 (retd); Judge, Federal Shariat Court 2014–17, Chief Justice 2015–17. *Leisure interest:* reading. *Address:* c/o Federal Shariat Court, G-5/2, Constitution Avenue, Islamabad, Pakistan (office).

KHAN, Sadiq Aman; British lawyer and politician; *Mayor of London;* b. 8 Oct. 1970, London; s. of Amanullah Khan and Sehrun Khan; m. Saadiya Ahmed 1994; two d.; ed Univ. of North London Coll. of Law; trainee, later asst solicitor 1994–97; Partner, Christian Khan (law firm) 1997–2005; Councillor, London Borough of Wandsworth 1994–2006; MP for Tooting (Labour) 2005–16, mem. Public Accounts Select Cttee 2005–07, fmr Chair. All Party Group of Citizens Advice Bureau, Vice-Chair. All Party Parl. Group on Child and Youth Crime, Chair. PLP Home Affairs Cttee, apptd Parl. Pvt. Sec. to Leader of the House of Commons Jack Straw 2007; Minister of State for Communities 2008–09, for Transport 2009–10; Shadow Sec. of State for Transport May–Oct. 2010, for Justice 2010–15, also Shadow Lord Chancellor 2010–15; Mayor of London 2016–; Campaign Man. for Ed Miliband during Labour leadership contest 2010; chief legal adviser, Muslim Council of Britain 2004; fmr Chair. Liberty (civil liberties group); fmr Vice-Chair. Legal Action Group, Fabian Soc.; fmr Visiting Lecturer, Univ. of North London, London Metropolitan Univ.; fmr Gov. South Thames FE Coll.; Fellow, Industry and Parliament Trust 2008; mem. Friends of the Earth, SERA; Patron Polka Theatre Company; Hon. Alderman, London Borough of Wandsworth 2006; Newcomer of the Year, Spectator Magazine Parliamentarian of the Year Awards 2005, British Muslim Awards Politician of the Year 2016. *Publications:* Police Misconduct: Legal Remedies (co-author) 2005 (4th edition), Challenging Racism; Using the Human Rights Act (co-author) 2003. *Leisure interests:* football, boxing, cricket. *Address:* Office of the Mayor, City Hall, The Queen's Walk, London, SE1 2AA, England (office). *Telephone:* (20) 7983-4000 (office). *Website:* www.london.gov.uk (office); www.sadiqkhan.org.uk (office).

KHAN, Salman; Indian actor; b. 27 Dec. 1965, Indore, MP; s. of Salim Khan and Salma Khan; ed St Stanislaus High School; early career as a model; f. Being Human Foundation; TV presenter for 10 Ka Dum and Bigg Boss; Rajiv Gandhi Award 2007, Int. Indian Film Acad. (IIFA) Award for Habitat Humanity Ambassadorship 2010. *Films include:* Biwi Ho To Aisi 1988, Maine Pyar Kiya 1989, Baaghi: A Rebel for Love 1990, Saajan 1991, Jaagruti 1992, Dil Tera Aashiq 1993, Andaz Apna Apna 1994, Hum Aapke Hain Kaun 1994, Karan Arjun 1995, Khamoshi: The Musical 1996, Judwaa 1997, Pyaar Kiya To Darna Kya 1998, Kuch Kuch Hota Hai (Filmfare Best Supporting Actor 1999) 1998, Hum Dil De Chuke Sanam 1999, Dulhan Hum Le Jayenge 2000, Chori Chori Chupke Chupke 2001, Hum Tumhare Hain Sanam 2001, Tere Naam 2003, Mujhse Shaadi Karogi 2004, Phir Milenge 2004, Lucky: No Time for Love 2005, Jaan-E-Mann 2006, Partner 2007, Marigold: An Adventure In India 2007, Yuvvraaj 2008, Wanted (IIFA Best Actor 2010) 2009, Dabangg 2010, Ready 2011, Bodyguard 2011, Ek Tha Tiger 2012, Dabangg 2 2012, Kick 2014, Bajrangi Bhaijaan (National Award 2016) 2015, Sultan 2016, Hanuman Da' Damdaar 2017, Tubelight 2017, Judwaa 2 2017, Tiger Zinda Hai 2017, Welcome to New York 2018. *Television includes:* as presenter: 10 Ka Dum 2008–09, Bigg Boss 2010–. *Leisure interests:* travelling, exercising, painting.

KHAN, Sardar Mahtab Ahmad, LLB; Pakistani lawyer and politician; b. 15 Dec. 1952, Abbottabad; s. of Sardar Muhammad Nawaz Khan; ed Union Council, Dewal, Murree Sir Sayyad School, Rawalpindi; Prov. Minister of Health, Khyber Pakhtunkhwa 1986–88; Chief Minister of Khyber Pakhtunkhwa 1997–99; imprisoned following mil. coup 1999–2002; mem. Senate of Pakistan 2003–08; Minister of Railways 2008; mem. Nat. Ass. for NA-17 Abbottabad-I 2008–13; mem. Khyber Pakhtunkhwa Prov. Ass. 2013–14; Gov. of Khyber Pakhtunkhwa 2014–16; mem. Pakistan Muslim League Nawaz.

KHAN, Sardar Mohammed Yaqoob; Pakistani business executive and politician; b. 26 Feb. 1953, Ali Sojal, Poonch Dist; s. of Sardar Gull Mohammed Khan; ed Univ. of Karachi; fmr Officer, Punjabi Pakhtoon Itehad Party, Karachi; fmr Sr Vice-Pres. Tehreek Amel Party, Azad Jammu and Kashmir; mem. Azad Jammu and Kashmir Legis. Ass. 2001, 2006, fmr Leader of the House; State Minister for Health, Population Welfare and Hydro-electric Bd, Housing and Planning 2001–06, 2009; Prime Minister of Azad Jammu and Kashmir 2009–11; Pres. of Azad Jammu and Kashmir 2011–16; mem. Pakistan People's Party. *Address:* c/o Office of the President, Muzaffarabad, Azad Kashmir, Pakistan (office).

KHAN, Sardar Muhammad Raza, MA, LLB; Pakistani judge and government official; *Chief Election Commissioner;* b. 10 Feb. 1945, Namli Maira, Abbottabad; ed Government Coll. of Abbottabad, Univ. of the Punjab; joined PCS (Judicial Br.) 1970; Sr Civil Judge 1973; Additional Dist and Sessions Judge 1976; Dist and Sessions Judge 1979; apptd Judicial Commr for Northern Areas; Special Judge, Customs Taxation and Anti Smuggling 1992–93; Additional Judge, Peshawar High Court 1993 (confirmed 1995); Chief Justice, Peshawar High Court 2000–02; Judge, Supreme Court of Pakistan 2002–10 (retd); Chief Justice, Fed. Shariat Court 2014 (resgnd); Chief Election Commr 2014–. *Address:* Election Commission of Pakistan, Secretariat, Election House, Constitution Avenue, G-5/2, Islamabad, Pakistan (office). *Telephone:* (51) 9201915 (office). *Fax:* (51) 9205300 (office). *E-mail:* cec@ecp.gov.pk (office). *Website:* www.ecp.gov.pk (office).

KHAN, Shah Rukh; Indian film actor and producer; b. 2 Nov. 1965, New Delhi; s. of Mir Taj Mohammed Khan and Fatima Begum; m. Gauri Chibber Khan 1991; two s. one d.; ed St Columba's High School, New Delhi, Hansraj Coll., Jamiya Miliya Islamiya, New Delhi; TV debut in role of Abhimanyu in war drama series Fauji (Soldier) 1988; film debut in Deewana 1992; Co-f. Dreamz Unlimited production co. 1999; Co-Founder and Co-Owner Red Chilies Entertainments production co. 2002–; Founder Kolkata Knight Riders cricket team, Indian Premier League 2008–; Goodwill Amb. for Repub. of Korea 2013–; Ordre des Arts et des Lettres 2007, Darjah Mulia Seri Melaka, Malacca, Malaysia 2008, Chevalier, Ordre national de la Légion d'honneur 2014; Dr hc (Univ. of Bedfordshire) 2009; Best Indian Citizen Award 1997, Rajiv Gandhi Award for Excellence in the Field of Entertainment 2002, British Asian Guild Award 2004, MSN Search Personality of the Year Award 2004, Sabse Tez Personality of the Year Award 2004, Chhoton Ka Funda Award 2004, Asian Guild Awards Bollywood Star of the Decade 2004, Padma Shri Award, Govt of India 2005, awarded the title 'Hammer-e-Hind' by Hindi newspaper DeshBakht 2006, HT Café Film Awards Best Actor Award 2007, CNBC-TV18's Entertainment Business Leader Award 2007, Int. Indian Film Acad. (IIFA) Star of the Decade 2009, Global Entertainment and Media Personality Award, Fed. of Indian Chambers of Commerce and Industry Frames 2010 Excellence Awards, Most Popular Actor Award, Zee Aflam 2010, L'Etoile d'Or by King of Morocco 2011, 'Creative Entrepreneur of the Year', NDTV Business Leadership Awards, Life Time Achievement Award, Asianet Film Awards 2012, BrandLaureate Legendary Award 2012, Wissame Al Kafaa Al Fikria, Morocco 2012, Chevalier Sivaji Award, Star Vijay Awards 2013, numerous Filmfare Awards, Rupa Cinegoers Awards, Star Screen Videocon Awards, Sansui

Viewers Choice Movie Awards, Zee Cine Awards, People's Choice Movie Awards, (IIFA) Awards, Zee Gold Bollywood Awards, AFJA Awards, Aashirwad Award, Disney Kids Channel Award, MTV Immies Indian Music Excellence Award, Sports World Film Award, Global Diversity Award 2014. *Films include:* Deewana (Crazy) (Filmfare Best Debut Award) 1992, Raju Ban Gaya Gentleman 1992, Maya 1992, Chamatkar 1992, Dil Aashna Hai 1992, King Uncle 1993, Kabhi Haan Kabhi Naa (Filmfare Critics Award for Best Performance) 1993, Darr 1993, Baazigar (Filmfare Best Actor Award) 1993, Anjaam (Filmfare Best Villain Award) 1994, Zamaana Deewana 1995, Trimurti 1995, Ram Jaane 1995, Oh Darling Yeh Hai India 1995, Karan Arjun 1995, Guddu 1995, Dilwale Dulhania Le Jayenge (Filmfare Best Actor Award) 1995, English Babu Desi Mem 1996, Chaahat 1996, Army 1996, Dushman Duniya Ka 1996, Pardes 1997, Gudgudee 1997, Koyla 1997, Yes Boss 1997, Dil To Pagal Hai (Filmfare Best Actor Award) 1997, Duplicate 1998, Dil Se 1998, Kuch Kuch Hota Hai (Filmfare Best Actor Award) 1998, Baadshah 1999, Phir Bhi Dil Hai Hindustani 2000, Hey Ram 2000, Josh 2000, Har Dil Jo Pyar Karega 2000, Mohabbatein (Filmfare Critics Award for Best Performance) 2000, Gaja Gamini 2000, One 2 Ka 4 2001, Asoka 2001, Kabhi Khushi Kabhie Gham 2001, Devdas (Filmfare Best Actor Award, IIFA Best Actor Award) 2002, Hum Tumhare Hain Sanam 2002, Shakti: The Power 2002, Saathiya 2002, Chalte Chalte 2003, Kal Ho Naa Ho 2003, Yeh Lamhe Judaai Ke 2004, Main Hoon Na 2004, Veer-Zaara (Global Indian Film Awards Best Actor Award, IIFA Best Actor Award) 2004, Swades (Filmfare Best Actor Award) 2004, Silsiilay 2005, Paheli 2005, Kabhi Alvida Naa Kehna 2006, Don – The Chase Begins Again 2006, Khazan 2006, Chak De India (IIFA Best Actor Award, Nokia 14th Annual Star Screen Best Actor Award, Annual Central European Bollywood Award, V Shantaram Award) 2007, Om Shanti Om 2007, Rab Ne Bana Di Jodi (Apsara Best Actor Award) 2008, Billu Barber 2009, My Name is Khan 2010, Ra.One 2011, Don 2: The Chase Continues 2011, Jab Tak Hai Jaan (Lions Favourite Actor in a Leading Role 2013) 2012, Chennai Express (OK Screen Award for Best Popular Actor 2014) 2013, Happy New Year 2014, Dilwale 2015, Fan 2016, Dear Zindagi 2016, Raees 2017, Jab Harry met Sejal 2017. *Achievements include:* moon crater renamed in his honour as 'Crater S.R.Khan' 2009. *Television includes:* Fauji (series) 1988, Dil Darya 1988, In Which Annie Gives It Those Ones 1989, Circus (series) 1989, Idiot (mini-series) 1991, Kaun Banega Crorepati 2007, Kya Aap Paanchvi Pass Se Tez Hain? 2008. *Leisure interests:* computer games, hi-tech gadgets, acting. *Address:* Red Chillies Entertainment Private Ltd, Plot No 612, Junction of Rama Krishna Mission Road and 15th Road, Santacruz (West), Mumbai 400 054, India (office). *Telephone:* (22) 66699400 (office). *Fax:* (22) 66699599 (office). *E-mail:* info@redchillies.com (office); dreamzandfilms@hotmail.com (office). *Website:* www.redchillies.com (office).

KHAN, Shaukatullah; Pakistani politician and engineer; s. of Bismillah Khan; ed Cadet Coll. Kohat, Univ. of Eng and Tech., Taxila; mem. Nat. Ass. (Pakistan People's Party) from NA-43 (Nawagai, Bajaur Agency) constituency; Fed. Minister for States and Frontier Region –2013; Gov. of Khyber Pakhtunkhwa 2013–14; mem. Tribal Chamber of Commerce and Industry, All Pakistan Marbles Industry Asscn.

KHAN, Sikander Mustafa, MSc; Pakistani business executive; *Chairman, Millat Group of Companies;* ed NED Eng Coll., Karachi, Imperial Coll. of Science and Tech., London, Univ. of Newcastle upon Tyne; Man. Dir and CEO Millat Tractors Ltd 1985, Chair. 1991, arranged financial package and structured deal that lead to employee buyout of nationalized Millat Tractors Ltd from Govt 1992, currently Chair. Millat Group of Cos, also Chair. Bolan Castings Limited & Millat Equipment Ltd, Millat Industrial Products (subsidiaries); Chair. Pakistan Business Council 2013–; Pres. Pakistan Foundry Asscn; Vice-Pres. Lahore Chamber of Commerce & Industry 1997–98; mem. Bd of Dirs Habib Bank Ltd; mem. and Hon. Sec., Pakistan Chapter, Inst. of Mechanical Engineers. *Address:* Millat Group of Companies, 83-A, E/1, 4th Floor Main Boulevard, Gulberg, Lahore, Pakistan (office). *Website:* www.millatgroup.net (office).

KHAN, Zaffar Ahmad; Pakistani engineer, business executive and academic; *Adjunct Professor, Institute of Business Administration;* ed Peshawar Univ., one-year training programme in Japan, Advanced Man. Program, Univ. of Hawaii, short courses at INSEAD, Paris and Harvard Business School, USA; joined Esso Pakistan Fertilizer Co. (later known as Exxon Chemical) 1969, was transferred overseas to serve Exxon Chemical in Hong Kong, USA and Singapore 1973–82, Vice-Pres. Marketing and Dir of Exxon Chemical Pakistan Ltd 1982, held various posts in all divs including Marketing, Manufacturing, Finance and Corp. Services 1982–91, played role in the first employee-led buyout in corp. history of Pakistan which resulted in Engro Chemical Pakistan Ltd 1991, Pres. and CEO 1997–2004; Chair. Pakistan Int. Airlines Corpn 2007–08; Chair., mem. or fmr mem. various pvt. and public sector bds, including Engro Asahi, Engro Vopak, United Bank, Sui Southern Gas Co., PTML (Ufone), PTCL, Pakistan Steel, Unilever Pakistan, Karachi Stock Exchange, Nat. Commodity Exchange, Pakistan Inst. of Corp. Governance, Acumen Fund, State Bank of Pakistan; Pres. Overseas Chamber of Commerce and Industry; has also served on numerous advisory cttees of Govt of Pakistan, including Econ. Advisory Bd, Pay and Pension Cttee, Cttee that developed Nat. Environment Quality Standards; mem. Pakistan Centre for Philanthropy; Chair. fund-raising cttee of Agha Khan Univ.; currently Adjunct Prof., Inst. of Business Admin, Karachi; Sitara-e-Imtiaz. *Address:* Institute of Business Administration, Main Campus, University Road, Karachi 75270 (office); 12, B-2 Street, Phase 5, DHA, Karachi, Pakistan (home). *Telephone:* (21) 38104700 (office). *Fax:* (21) 99261508 (office). *E-mail:* zaffarak@yahoo.com (home). *Website:* www.iba.edu.pk (office).

KHAN HOTI, Amir Haider; Pakistani politician; b. 5 Feb. 1971, Mardan; s. of Muhammad Azam Khan Hoti; grand-s. of Khan Abdul Wali Khan, nephew of Asfandiyar Wali Khan, Pres. of Awami Nat. Party, of Begum Naseem Wali Khan, grand s. of Amir Muhammad Khan; m.; two s. one d.; ed Atchison Coll., Lahore, Working Edwards Coll.; began political career from platform of Awami Nat. Party; mem. Khyber Pakhtunkhwa Prov. Ass. from PF-23 Mardan constituency 2008–; Chief Minister of NW Frontier Prov. (renamed Khyber Pakhtunkhwa April 2010) 2008–13.

KHAN MOHAMMADI, Gen. Bismillah; Afghan military officer and government official; b. 1961, Panjshir; ed Kabul Military Univ.; served as Northern Alliance Deputy Minister of Defence, after the fall of Kabul to United Front was apptd Commdr of Kabul police force and mem. Kabul Security Comm.; apptd Deputy Minister of Defence 2002, Chief of Staff, Ministry of Defence 2003; Chief of Gen. Staff, Afghanistan Nat. Army 2002–10; Minister of Interior Affairs 2010–12, of Defence 2012–14; Syed Jamaluddin Afghan Medal, Ghazi Amanullah Khan Medal, Ahmad Shah Baba Medal.

KHAN NIAZI, Imran; Pakistani politician and fmr professional cricketer; *Prime Minister;* b. 25 Nov. 1952, Lahore, Punjab; s. of Ikramullah Khan Niazi and Shaukat Khanum; m. 1st Jemima Goldsmith 1995 (divorced 2004); two s.; m. 2nd Reham Khan 2015; ed Aitchison Coll. and Cathedral School, Lahore, Worcester Royal Grammar School and Keble Coll., Oxford, UK; right-arm fast bowler, middle-order right-hand batsman; played for Lahore 1969–71, Worcs. 1971–76, Univ. of Oxford 1973–75 (Capt. 1974), Dawood 1975–76, PIA 1975–81, Sussex 1977–88, NSW 1984–85; played in 88 Test matches for Pakistan 1971–92, 48 as Capt., scoring 3,807 runs (average 37.69, highest score 136) and taking 362 wickets (average 22.81), best bowling (innings) 8/58, (match) 14/116; played in 175 One-Day Ints, 139 as Capt. (including 1992 World Cup victory), scoring 3,709 runs (average 33.41, highest score 102 not out) and taking 182 wickets (average 26.61), best bowling (innings) 6/14; toured England 1971, 1974, 1975 (World Cup), 1979 (World Cup), 1982, 1983 (World Cup), 1987; scored 17,771 First-class runs and took 1,287 First-class wickets; second player to score a century and take 10 wickets in a Test 1983; third player to score over 3,000 Test runs and take 300 wickets; Special Rep. for Sports, UNICEF 1989; Ed.-in-Chief Cricket Life 1989–90; f. Imran Khan Cancer Hosp. Appeal 1991, Tehreek-e-Insaf (Movt for Justice) 1996 (Chair. 1996–); mem. Nat. Ass. for Mianwali 2002–07, for Constituency NA-71 2013–; Chancellor Univ. of Bradford 2005–14 (resgnd), Patron of Born in Bradford research project; helped establish Shaukat Khanum Memorial Cancer Hosp. and Research Centre 1996, Mianwali's Namal Coll. 2008; f. Imran Khan Foundation; cricket commentator on Asian and British sports networks, including BBC Urdu and Star TV network; columnist for sify.com for India-Pakistan Test series 2005; Minister for Interior 2018–19, for Energy 2018; Prime Minister 2018–; Hon. Fellow, Keble Coll., Oxford 1988; Wisden Cricketer of the Year 1983, Hilal-e-Imtiaz 1992, Pres.'s Pride of Performance Award 1983, Cricket Society Wetherall Award 1976, 1980, Sussex Cricket Society Player of the Year 1985, Indian Cricket Cricketer of the Year 1990, Lifetime Achievement Award, Asian Jewel Awards, London 2004, Humanitarian Award, Asian Sports Awards, Kuala Lumpur 2007, one of several veteran Asian cricketers presented with special Silver Jubilee Awards at inaugural Asian Cricket Council Award Ceremony, Karachi 2008, inducted into Int. Cricket Council Hall of Fame 2009, Person of the Year, Asia Soc. 2012. *Film appearance:* Kidnap 2008. *Television:* commentator on TEN Sports' special live show, Straight Drive 2004. *Publications include:* Imran: The Autobiography of Imran Khan 1983, Imran Khan's Cricket Skills 1989, Indus Journey: A Personal View of Pakistan 1990, All-Round View (autobiography) 1992, Warrior Race A Journey Through the Land of the Tribal Pathans 1993. *Leisure interests:* shooting, films, music. *Address:* Prime Minister's Office, Constitution Ave, Red Zone, Islamabad, Pakistan (office). *Telephone:* (51) 9206111 (office). *E-mail:* info@pmo.gov.pk (office). *Website:* www.pmo.gov.pk (office); www.imrankhanfoundation.org.

KHAN WILLIAMS, Mehr, MA; Pakistani fmr UN official and international organization official; b. 1945, India; m.; one c.; ed Univ. of Karachi; fmrly with Univ. of Karachi, United Press International, Associated Press of Pakistan, World Bank, Washington, DC; joined UN 1976, Deputy Dir UNICEF Programme Funding Office, Dir UNICEF Div. of Communication 1989–96, Acting Dir UN Information Centre, Sydney, Dir UNICEF Innocenti Research Centre, Florence 1998–2000, Regional Dir East Asia and the Pacific, UNICEF Bangkok –2004, Special Adviser to Exec. Dir of UNICEF 2004, 2006–, Deputy High Commr for Human Rights, UN 2004–06, fmr Chair. Jt UN Information Cttee; Chair. Int. Service for Human Rights 2009–13; fmr Trustee, TV Trust for the Environment, London. *Address:* c/o International Service for Human Rights, Rue de Varembé 1, Fifth Floor, PO Box 16, 1211 Geneva 20 CIC, Switzerland. *E-mail:* information@ishr.ch; ishr@ishrny.org.

KHANAL, Jhala Nath; Nepalese politician; ed Tribhuvan Univ.; fmr mem. Communist Party of Nepal (Marxist-Leninist); mem. Standing Cttee Communist Party of Nepal (Unified Marxist-Leninist—UML), managed foreign relations wing of party, Gen. Sec. 1982–86, 2008–09, Chair. 2009–14; Prime Minister Feb.–Aug. 2011 (resgnd); one of ministers during interim govt following restoration of democracy in Nepal 1990; Minister of Information and Communications 1997; participant in first regional political party conf., Bangkok, Thailand 2002. *Address:* c/o Communist Party of Nepal (UML), PO Box 5471, Madan Nagar, Balkhu, Kathmandu, Nepal.

KHAND, Bal Krishna, MA; Nepalese politician; b. 1961, Malyangkot, Syangja Dist; s. of Noindra Bahadur and Top Kumari; m.; one s. three d.; ed Tribhuvan Univ.; fmr Pres. Nepal Students Union and Nepal Tarun Dal (youth wing of Nepali Congress Party—NCP); spent three years in prison accused of anti-state activities 1981–84; Minister of Youth, Sports and Culture 1997, Minister of State for Educ. 2004; elected mem. Constituent Ass. (NCP) from Rupandehi-3 constituency 2008; Minister for Irrigation and Water Resources 2009; Minister of Defence 2016–17; apptd Chief Whip, Nepali Congress 2018–. *Address:* Nepali Congress, Central Office, B.P. Smriti Bhawan, B.P. Nagar, Lalitpur, Nepal (office). *Telephone:* (1) 5183263 (office). *Fax:* (1) 5183266 (office). *E-mail:* info@nepalicongress.org (office). *Website:* www.nepalicongress.org (office).

KHANDOGIY, Volodymyr Dmytrovych; Ukrainian diplomatist and government official; b. 21 Feb. 1953, Cherkasy; m. Natalia Shevchenko; one s. one d.; ed T.G. Shevchenko Kyiv State Univ.; attaché, Third Sec., Ministry of Foreign Affairs 1976–79; attaché, Perm. Mission to UN, New York 1979–83; Second Sec., Dept of Int. Orgs, Ministry of Foreign Affairs 1983–85, First Sec., Secr. Gen. 1985–88; First Sec., Perm. Mission to UN, New York 1988–92, Deputy Perm. Rep., then Acting Perm. Rep. 1992–94; Head of Dept of Int. Orgs, Ministry of Foreign Affairs 1994–95; Deputy Minister of Foreign Affairs and Chair. Nat. Comm. for UNESCO 1995–98; Rep. to UNESCO Exec. Council 1996–98; Amb. to Canada 1998–2000, to the Netherlands 2000–02, to Belgium (also accred to Luxembourg) and Head of Perm. Mission to NATO 2000–05; Rep. to ICAO 1998–2000, to OPCW 2000–02; Dir Dept for NATO, Ministry of Foreign Affairs 2005–06; Deputy Minister for Foreign Affairs 2006–07, First Deputy Minister for Foreign Affairs 2007–09, Acting

Minister of Foreign Affairs March–Oct. 2009, First Deputy Minister for Foreign Affairs and Chair. Nat. Comm. for UNESCO 2010, Amb. to UK 2010–15, Perm. Rep. to IMO, London 2010–15; Order of Merits (2nd and 3rd Degrees), Grand Cross, Order of Leopold II (Belgium), Order of the Three Stars (Latvia), Commdr's Cross, Order of Merit (Poland).

KHANDU, Pema; Indian politician; *Chief Minister of Arunachal Pradesh;* b. 21 Aug. 1979, Tawang, Arunachal Pradesh; s. of Dorjee Khandu (sixth Chief Minister of Arunachal Pradesh); two s. one d.; ed Hindu Coll., Delhi Univ.; mem. Arunachal Pradesh Legis. Ass. from Mukto constituency 2011–, Congress Legis. Party Leader 2016–; fmr Arunachal Pradesh Cabinet Minister of Water Resource Devt and Tourism, Minister for Rural Works Dept and Tourism 2011, Cabinet Minister for Tourism, Civil Aviation and Art & Culture, Minister for Urban Devt 2014–15; Chief Minister, Arunachal Pradesh 2016–; mem. Indian Nat. Congress 2000–, Sec., Arunachal Pradesh Congress Cttee 2005, Pres., Tawang Dist Congress Cttee 2010. *Address:* Office of the Chief Minister, Itanagar 791 111, Arunachal Pradesh, India (office). *Telephone:* (360) 2212456 (office); (360) 2291355 (home). *Fax:* (360) 2291365 (office). *E-mail:* arunachalpradeshcm@gmail.com (office). *Website:* www.arunachalpradeshcm.in (office); www.arunachalpradesh.gov.in.

KHANDU, Dasho Sangay; Bhutanese business executive and government official; *Chairman, Druk Holding and Investments Ltd;* started career as Marketing Officer 1976; CEO Food Corpn of Bhutan for several years; Deputy Sec., Ministry of Trade and Industry 1986–91, Dir Ministry of Trade and Industry 1991–96; CEO Bhutan Development Finance Corpn 1992–97; CEO Royal Insurance Corpn of Bhutan Ltd 1997–2000; CEO Druk Air Corpn Ltd 2000–05; Dir-Gen. Ministry of Trade and Industry 2005–07; Sec., Nat. Land Comm. 2007–14; Chair. Druk Holding and Investments Ltd 2014–; Bura Maap (red scarf) 2009. *Address:* Druk Holding and Investments Ltd, POB 1127, Motithang, Thimphu, Bhutan (office). *Telephone:* (2) 336257 (office). *Fax:* (2) 336259 (office). *E-mail:* info@dhi.bt (office). *Website:* www.dhi.bt (office).

KHANDURI, Maj.-Gen. (retd) Bhuwan Chandra, BSc, BE; Indian engineer and army officer (retd), politician and management consultant; b. 1 Oct. 1934, Dehradun, Uttarakhand; s. of Jai Ballabh Khanduri and Durga Devi Khanduri; m. Aruna Khanduri 1964; one s. one d.; ed Allahabad Univ., Coll. of Mil. Eng, Pune, Inst. of Engineers, New Delhi and Inst. of Defence Man., Secunderabad; served in Corps of Engineers, Indian Army 1954–90; mem. Parl. (Garhwal constituency, Uttarakhand) 1991–96, 1998–; mem. Bharatiya Janata Party, Chief Whip, Parl. Party 1991–96, 1998–99, 2004, mem. Nat. Exec. 1992–97, 2000–, Vice-Pres. Uttar Pradesh State 1996–97; Minister of State (with ind. charge) for Roads, Transport and Highways 2000–03, Minister with Cabinet rank 2003–04; Chief Minister of Uttarakhand 2007–09 (resgnd), 2011–12; mem. Cttee on Public Accounts 1998–99, on Rules, Business Advisory 1998–99, 1999–2000, 2004, on Home Affairs 1998–99, 1999–2000 and Convenor of sub-Cttee on Personnel Policy of Cen. Para-Mil. Forces, Consultative Cttee, Ministry of Defence, Cttee on Public Undertakings 1999–2001, on Ethics; Chair. Cttee on Finance 2004; mem. Cttee on Gen. Purposes, Consultative Cttee Ministry of Petroleum and Natural Gas; Patron, Parvatiya Sanskriti Parishad, Dehradun 1990–93, Chandra Ballabh Trust; Founder and Pres. Poorva Sainik Seva Parishad, Uttar Pradesh 1992–2000, Uttarakhand Pradesh Sangarsh Samsiti 1994–96; mem. Wild Life Soc. of India 1990–2000, G.B. Pant Himalaya Environment and Devt Cttee 1998–2000; Ati Vishisht Seva Medal for Distinguished Service in the Indian Army 1982. *Leisure interests:* sports, reading. *Address:* Jai Durga Niwas, 12 Vikas Marg, Pauri Garhwal, 246 001 (home); Vidhan Bhawan, Haridwar Road, Dehradun 248 001, India. *Telephone:* (1368) 222600 (home).

KHANNA, Tejendra, MSc, MA; Indian business executive and civil servant; b. 16 Dec. 1938; m. Uma Khanna (died 2010); one s. one d.; ed Patna Univ., Univ. of California, Berkeley, USA; joined Indian Admin. Service 1961; Prin. Sec. to Chief Minister of Punjab; Sec. of Science, Tech. and Environment, of Food Supplies and of Labour Employment 1970s; fmr Man. Dir for Punjab, State Industrial Devt Corpn; Sec. to Govt of Punjab for Irrigation, Power and Public Works 1983–86, Financial Commr for Revenue 1986–89; Chief Controller of Imports and Exports, Ministry of Commerce, Govt of India 1989–91; Chief Sec. to Govt of Punjab, Head of Civil Service, Chief Co-ordinator of Govt Programmes 1991–92; Sec. for Food, Govt of India 1992–93, for Commerce 1993–96; Prin. Civil Service Co-ordinator of Bilateral, Multilateral and Regional Trade Relations 1993–96; Lt-Gov. and Admin. Nat. Capital Territory of Delhi 1997–98, 2007–13; Chair. Ranbaxy Laboratories Ltd 1999–2007; Trustee, Popular First; mem. Indian Inst. of Public Admin 1978–, Indo-German Consultative Group 1999–; mem. Advisory Bd Standard Chartered Bank, UK 1999–2003; Life mem. Bhartiya Vidya Bhawan; Dr hc (Wonkwang Univ.) 2010, (TERI Univ.).

KHAR, Hina Rabbani, BSc, MSc; Pakistani economist and politician; b. 19 Jan. 1977, Multan City; d. of Ghulam Rabbani Khar; ed Lahore Univ. of Man. Sciences, Univ. of Massachusetts, USA; mem. Nat. Ass. for NA-177 Muzaffargarh II constituency 2002–; fmr Parl. Sec. for Econ. Affairs and Statistics (first woman to present budget speech to parl. 2009); Minister of State for Foreign Affairs (first woman) Feb.–July 2011; Minister of Foreign Affairs (first woman) 2011–13; fmr mem. Pakistan Muslim League (PML-Q), currently mem. Pakistan People's Party; mem. Young Parliamentarians Forum (YPF); Owner, Polo Lounge, Lahore. *Leisure interests:* riding, reading, travelling. *Address:* Pakistan Peoples Party, 8, St 19, F-8/2, Islamabad, Pakistan. *E-mail:* ppp@comsats.net.pk. *Website:* www.ppp.org.pk.

KHARAFI, Bader Nasser al-; Kuwaiti business executive; *Vice-President, Kharafi Group;* s. of Nasser al-Kharafi; Vice-Pres. Mohammed Abdulmohsen Al-Kharafi & Sons Co. WLL (Kharafi Group) 2011–; Vice-Chair., INJAZ-Kuwait 2012–, Mitsubishi Motors Egypt 2012–, Zain KSA 2012–; Vice-Chair. and Group CEO 2017–; Gen. Man. Al Khair National for Stocks and Real Estate Co.; Vice-Chair. UNIEXPO; Dir Gulf Bank, Coca-Cola Kuwait. *Address:* Kharafi Group, Shuwaikh Industrial Area, PO Box 886 Safat, 13009 Kuwait City, Kuwait (office). *Telephone:* 24813622 (office). *Fax:* 24811861 (office). *E-mail:* hazmi@makharafi.net (office). *Website:* www.makharafi.net (office).

KHARAFI, Faiza al-, BSc, MSc, PhD; Kuwaiti chemist and academic; *Professor of Chemistry, Kuwait University;* b. 1946; m. Ali Mohamed Thanian El-Ghanem; five s.; ed Al Merkab High School, Ain Shams Univ., Egypt, Kuwait Univ.; worked in Dept of Chem., Kuwait Univ. 1975–81, Chair. of Dept 1984–86, Dean of Faculty of Science 1986–89, Prof. of Chem. 1987–, Rector (first female) Kuwait Univ. 1993–2002, f. Corrosion and Electrochemistry Research Lab. 1967; organized Kuwait-France Chem. Symposium 2009; Vice-Pres. Acad. of Sciences for the Developing World 2010– (renamed TWAS, The World Acad. of Sciences 2012); mem. Bd, United Nations Univ. 1998, Kuwait Foundation for the Advancement of Science; helped found the American Bilingual School in Kuwait; Kuwait Prize in Applied Sciences 2006, named by the Council for Gulf Relations as Top Gulf Woman of the Year 2008, L'Oréal-UNESCO Women in Science Award (Africa and Arab States) 2011. *Address:* Chemistry Department, Faculty of Science, Kuwait University, PO Box 5969, Safat 13060, Kuwait (office). *Telephone:* 24985544 (office). *E-mail:* chesc@kuc01.kuniv.edu.kw (office). *Website:* www.kuniv.com (office).

KHARE, Atul, MB, BS, MA, MBA, FRSA; Indian diplomatist and UN official; *Under-Secretary-General for Field Support, United Nations;* b. 14 Aug. 1959; m. Vandna Khare; ed All India Inst. of Medical Sciences, Univ. of Southern Queensland, Australia, Indian Defence School of Languages; mem. of staff, Foreign Service 1984–2006, postings include Deputy High Commr to Mauritius, Counsellor at Perm. Mission to UN, New York and Chargé d'affaires a.i., Embassy in Dakar, Senegal (also accred to Mali, Mauritania, The Gambia, Guinea-Bissau and Cape Verde), also held posts as Chef de Cabinet of Foreign Sec. of India and Dir UN Div.; Chief of Staff, UN Mission of Support in East Timor (UNMISET) 2002–04, Deputy Special Rep. of Sec.-Gen. for East Timor, UN 2004–05, Special Rep. of Sec.-Gen. for Timor-Leste and Head of UN Integrated Mission in Timor-Leste (UNMIT) 2006–10, Asst Sec.-Gen. for Peacekeeping Operations 2010, Head of UN Change Man. Team 2011–12; Under-Sec.-Gen. for Field Support, UN 2015–; Dir Nehru Centre and Minister (Culture) of Indian High Comm., London 2005–06. *Address:* Department of Peacekeeping Operations, Room S-3727B, United Nations, New York, NY 10017, USA (office). *Website:* www.un.org/en/peacekeeping/about/dfs (office).

KHARGE, Mallikarjun, BA, LLB; Indian lawyer and politician; b. 21 July 1942, Varavatti, Bhalki Taluk, Bidar Dist, Karnataka; s. of Mapanna Kharge and Saibavva Kharge; m. Radhabai Kharge; three s. two d.; ed Govt Coll., Gulbarga, Karnataka Univ.; mem. Karnataka State Ass. from Gurmitkal constituency 1972–2009, Deputy Leader of the Opposition 1985–94, Leader, Congress Legis. Party and Leader of Opposition, Karnataka 1996–99, 2008–09; Chair. Leather Devt Corpn 1973; Minister of State for Primary and Secondary Educ., Govt of Karnataka 1976–78, for Rural Devt and Panchayati Raj 1979, Minister for Revenue 1980–83, for Revenue, Rural Devt and Panchayati Raj 1990–92, for Co-operation, Medium and Large Industries 1992–94, for Revenue 1980, for Home, Infrastructure Devt and Minor Irrigation 1999–2004, for Transport and Water Resources 2004–06; mem. 15th Lok Sabha (lower house of Parl.) for Gulbarga constituency 2009–; Union Cabinet Minister of Labour and Employment 2009–13, of Railways 2013–14; Vice-Pres. Karnataka Pradesh Congress Cttee 1989, Pres. 2005; Founder-Chair. Siddharth Vihar Trust. *Address:* Lumbin Niwasquot Aiwan-e-Shahi Area, Gulbarga, Karnataka, India (home). *Telephone:* (8472) 255555 (home). *Fax:* (08472) 255555 (home). *E-mail:* mallikarjunkharge@yahoo.in.

KHARITONOV, Mark Sergeyevich; Russian writer; b. 31 Aug. 1937, Zhitomir, Ukraine; m. Galina Edelman; one s. two d.; ed Moscow Pedagogical Inst.; early career as teacher in secondary school; fmr exec. sec. of newspaper, of publishing house 1960–69; freelance writer 1969–; trans. Kafka, Stefan Zweig, Elias Canetti, Herman Hesse, Thomas Mann and others; works banned in official press until 1988; Prix du Meilleur Livre Etranger Essai (France) 1997. *Publications include:* Prokor Menshutin 1971 (published 1988), Provincial Philosophy 1977 (published 1993), Two Ivans 1980 (published 1988), Lines of Fate or Milashevich's Trunk 1985 (published 1992, first Booker Russian Novel Prize 1992), Storozh 1994, The Voices 1994, Return from Nowhere 1995, Seasons of Life 1998, A Mode of Existence 1998, The Approach 1998, Amores Novi 1999, The Conveyor 2000, A Professor of Lie 2002, Stenography of the Beginning of the Century 2003, Playing with Yourself 2004, Catcher of the Clouds 2008, Lessons of Happiness 2009, Stenography of the End of the Century 2011, Knot of Life 2011, See More 2012, Write, My Friend (correspondence with Boris Khazanov) 2013, Joker or Title in the End (novel) 2014, Guiding Stars 2015, Feast of Surprises 2017, Later Years' Wine 2017, Surgery of Fate 2019, Stenography of the New Era 2019. *Address:* 129128 Moscow, Bazhova str., 15 corp. 1, Apartment 182, Russia (home). *Telephone:* (499) 187-56-92 (home). *Fax:* (499) 187-56-92 (home). *E-mail:* mkharitonov@mail.ru (home).

KHARITONOV, Col Nikolai Mikhailovich; Russian politician; b. 31 Oct. 1948, Rezino, Novosibirsk Region; m.; four d.; ed Novosibirsk Inst. of Agric., Acad. of Nat. Econs; agronomist in sovkhoz (state farm), Novosibirsk Region 1972–76, Dir of sovkhoz 1976–94; Deputy, Novosibirsk Regional Exec. Cttee; RSFSR People's Deputy, mem. Cttee on Agrarian Problems, Supreme Soviet Russian Fed. 1990–93, mem. Agrarian Union 1990; mem. State Duma 1993–2003, Leader, Agrarian Group (later Agrarian-Industrial Group) 1994–2003, re-elected to Duma as ind. cand. 2003–; Deputy Chair. Agrarian Party of Russia 1993–2000; mem. Parl. Ass. of European Council; unsuccessful cand. for Pres. of Russian Fed. (Communist Party) 2004. *Leisure interest:* sports. *Address:* State Duma, 103265 Moscow, Okhotnyi ryad 1, Russia (office). *Telephone:* (495) 292-83-10 (office). *Fax:* (495) 292-94-64 (office). *E-mail:* www@duma.ru (office). *Website:* www.duma.ru (office).

KHARKAVETS, Andrey Mikhailovich; Belarusian politician; First Deputy Minister of Finance 2006–08, Minister of Finance 2008–14. *Address:* c/o Ministry of Finance, vul. Savetskaya 7, 220048 Minsk, Belarus (office).

KHARRAZI, Kamal, PhD; Iranian diplomatist and fmr academic; *Chairman, Strategic Council on Foreign Relations;* b. 1 Dec. 1944, Tehran; s. of Mehdi Kharrazi and Kobra Kharrazi; m. Mansoureh Kharrazi; two c.; ed Tehran Univ., Univ. of Houston, USA; Teaching Fellow, Univ. of Houston 1975–76; Man. of Planning and Programming, Nat. Iranian TV 1979; Man. Dir Centre for Intellectual Devt of Children and Young Adults 1979–81; Deputy Foreign Minister for Political Affairs 1979–80, Minister of Foreign Affairs 1997–2005; Chair., Strategic Council on Foreign Relations 2006–; Man. Dir Islamic Repub. News Agency 1980–89; mem. Supreme Defence Council, Head War Information HQ 1980–89; Prof. of Man. and Psychology, Tehran Univ. 1983–89; Perm. Rep. to UN, New York 1989–97; Founding mem. Islamic Research Inst., London; mem.

American Asscn of Univ. Profs. *Publications:* numerous textbooks and journal articles on psychology and foreign affairs. *Leisure interest:* mountain climbing. *Address:* Kashani Alley 1, Keshvardust Street, Jomhuri Avenue, Tehran, Iran (office). *Telephone:* (21) 64413131 (office); (21) 64413178 (office). *Fax:* (21) 66466270 (office). *E-mail:* kharrazi@imam-khamenei.ir (office). *Website:* www.leader.ir.

KHASAWNEH, Awn Shawkat al-, MA, LLM; Jordanian judge and government official; b. 22 Feb. 1950, Amman; ed Islamic Educational Coll. of Amman, Queens' Coll., Cambridge, England; entered diplomatic service 1975; with Perm. Mission to UN 1976–80, later as First Sec.; with Ministry of Foreign Affairs 1980–90, Head of Legal Dept 1985–90; Legal Adviser to Crown Prince 1990–95, Adviser to the King 1995, Chief of the Royal Hashemite Court 1996–98; Judge, Int. Court of Justice 2000–11, Vice-Pres. 2006–09; Prime Minister and Minister of Defence 2011–12; mem. Arab Int. Law Comm. 1982–89; mem. Subcommission on Prevention of Discrimination and Protection of Minorities (Chair. 1993), Comm. on Human Rights 1984–93, Special Rapporteur of Comm. on Human Rights on the human rights dimensions of forcible population transfer; mem. Int. Law Comm. 1986–; mem. Royal Jordanian Comm. on Legislative and Admin. Reform 1994–96; mem. Bd of Eds Palestine Yearbook of International Law; mem. Int. Law Asscn (Chair. Cttee on Islamic Law and Int. Law 2003–), Council of the Centre of Islamic and Middle Eastern Law, SOAS; Hon. Fellow, Queens' Coll.; Istiqlal Order (First Class) 1993, Kawkab Order (First Class) 1996, Nahda Order (First Class) 1996, Grand Officier, Légion d'honneur 1997; Int. Jurists Award 2009.

KHASBULATOV, Ruslan Imranovich; Chechen politician, economist and academic; *Head of Department of World Economy, Plekhanov Academy of Economics;* b. 22 Nov. 1942, Grozny; s. of Imran Khasbulatov and Govzan Khasbulatova; m.; one s. one d.; ed Kazakh State Univ., Moscow State Univ.; instructor, Cen. Cttee of Comsomol 1970–72, Head of Information Sector Inst. of Social Sciences, USSR Acad. of Sciences 1972–74, Head of Sector, Research Inst. of Higher Educ. 1974–79, Lecturer, Prof., Head of Dept of World Economy, Plekhanov Inst. (now Univ.) of Econs 1979–90, 1992–, Head of Scientific Centre, World Economy Evolution 2009–; Deputy of Supreme Soviet in Russia 1990–93, First Vice-Chair., then Acting Chair. Supreme Soviet 1990–91, Chair. 1991–93; Chair. Interparl. Ass. of CIS 1992–93; charged with fraud and imprisoned Sept.–Oct. 1993, released by State Duma Feb. 1994; one of the leaders of opposition to Pres. Dudaev-Mashadof in Chechen crisis 1991–96 and to mil. policy of Kremlin; Corresp. mem. Russian Acad. of Sciences 1991. *Publications:* Bureaucracy and Socialism 1989, Russia: Time of Change 1991, International Economic Relations (two vols) 1991, Power 1992, The Struggle for Russia 1993, Les Ombres au-dessus de la Maison Blanche (France) 1993, Great Russian Tragedy (two vols) 1994, World Economy 1994, World Economy (two vols) 2001, Crisis of Commonwealth of Independent States and Positive Experience of European Union 2002, The Great American Tragedy and What Should the World Do to Prevent Terrorism? 2001–02, The Kremlin and Russian–Chechen War (five vols): Vol. 1 Exploded Life 2002, Vol. 2 Power: Sword and Guile 2002, Vol. 3 Thoughts of War and Peace 2002, Vol. 4 A Big Strategic Game 2003, Vol. 5 Aliens 2003, Which Policy is Needed for Russia from the Point of View of the World Scientific Community? 2004, Fairy Tales About Reforms 2004, The Principle of Optimum in the Economic System and Social Functions of the State 2005, States and Revolutions 2005, The World Economy and International Economic Relations, Vols 1 and 2 2006. *Leisure interests:* fishing, hunting, playing chess. *Address:* Plekhanov Academy of Economics, Stremyanny per. 36, 117997 Moscow (office); Granatniy per. 10/35, Moscow, Russia (home). *Telephone:* (495) 958-50-15 (office); (495) 697-53-92 (home). *Fax:* (495) 958-46-22 (office). *E-mail:* hasbulatov@rea.ru (home).

KHASIS, Lev Aronovich, PhD; Russian retail executive; *Senior Vice-President and Director of Leveraging, Wal-Mart Stores Inc.;* b. 5 June 1966, Kuybyshev (now Samara); m. Olga Khasis; ed Kuybyshev Aviation Inst., Financial Acad. of Govt of Russian Fed., Faculty of Law, Univ. of Ministry of the Interior; Head, Dept of Int. Affairs, Kuybyshev Aviation Inst. 1989–90; Gen. Dir JSC Samarsky Trading House 1991–93; Gen. Man., Samara Br., Avtovazbank 1993–94; Pres. and Chair. Bd of Dirs, OJSC Aviacor Corpn 1995–99; Vice-Pres. OJSC Alfa-Bank 1996–98; Founder, Daily Store Chain, Moscow; CEO X5 Retail Group NV 2006–11, Dir of Network and mem. Man. Bd 2006–11; Sr Vice-Pres. and Dir of Leveraging, Wal-Mart Stores Inc. 2011–; Chair. Supervisory Bd Perekrestok Group of Cos 2002–06, Trade House GUM 2003–04; Dir OAO Transaero Airlines 2005–, CTC Media Inc. 2009–10; Chair. Russian Asscn of Cos of Retail Trade 2008–11. *Address:* Wal-Mart Stores Inc., 702 SW 8th Street, Bentonville, AR 72716-8611, USA (office). *Telephone:* (479) 273-4000 (office). *Website:* walmartstores.com (office).

KHATAMI, Hojatoleslam Sayed Muhammad, BPhil; Iranian cleric, politician and fmr head of state; b. 14 Oct. 1943, Ardkan, Yazd; s. of Ayatollah Seyyed Rooh Allah Khatami (religious scholar); m. Zohreh Sadeghi 1974; one s. two d.; ed Qom and Isfahan seminaries and Univ. of Tehran; Man. Islamic Centre, Hamburg; mem. for Ardakan and Meibod, first Islamic Consultative Ass. (Parl.); rep. of Imam Khomeini and Dir Kayhan newspaper; fmr Minister of Culture and Islamic Guidance; Cultural Deputy HQ of C-in-C and Head Defence Publicity Cttee; fmr Minister of Culture and Islamic Guidance; fmr Adviser to Pres. Rafsanjani and Pres. Nat. Library of Iran; fmr mem. High Council of Cultural Revolution; Pres. of Iran 1997–2006; apptd mem. UN group Alliance of Civilizations 2005–; Founder and Head, Int. Center of Dialogue Among Cultures and Civilizations 2004–; f. Baran Foundation; numerous hon. degrees; Global Dialogue Prize 2009. *Publications:* Fear of Wave, From World of City to World City, Faith and Thought Trapped by Selfishness; and numerous articles and speeches. *Website:* www.khatami.ir; www.dialogue.ir; www.baranfoundation.ir.

KHATIB, Abd al-Ilah al-; Jordanian politician and international organization official; b. 1953, Salt; ed School of Advanced Int. Studies, Johns Hopkins Univ., Washington, DC, American Univ., Panteios School of Political Science, Greece; Admin. Officer, Embassy in Athens 1976–81; mem. Bd of Dirs Arabic Affairs Council, Amman; mem. Del. to UN Gen. Ass. 1982–92; attaché Dept of Int. Org., Ministry of Foreign Affairs 1982–92, Dir of Special Bureau 1988–93; Second Sec., Embassy in Washington, DC 1984–88; Co-ordinator Jordanian Team for Peace Negotiations 1988–93; Asst for Investment Middle East Insurance Co. 1994–95; Gen. Man. Jordan Cement Factories Co. Ltd 1996–98; Minister of Tourism 1995–96, of Foreign Affairs 1998–2002, 2005–07; UN Sec.-Gen.'s Special Envoy to Libya 2011–12. *Address:* c/o Ministry of Foreign Affairs and International Cooperation, Using Shat, Tripoli, Libya.

KHATIB, Hisham, PhD FIEEE; Jordanian energy and environmental consultant and politician; b. (Hisham M Khatib), 5 Jan. 1936, Acre, Palestine; s. of Mohamed Khatib and Fahima Khatib; m. Maha Khatib 1968; two s. one d.; ed Univ. of Cairo, Egypt, Univs of Birmingham and London, UK; Chief Engineer, Jerusalem Electricity Co. 1965–73; Deputy Dir-Gen. Jordanian Electricity Authority 1974–76, Dir-Gen. 1980–84; Sr Energy Expert, Arab Fund, Kuwait 1976–80; Minister of Energy and Mineral Resources 1984–89; Vice-Chair. World Energy Council 1989–92; int. energy consultant 1990–93; Minister of Water and Irrigation 1993–94, of Planning 1994–95; Chair. Int. Cttee for Developing Countries World Energy Council 1992–95; int. consultant 1995–; Chair. Jordan Electricity Regulatory Comm. 2005–09; int. consultant on energy and its environmental issues; mem. Jordanian Senate 2016–; Fellow, Inst. of Eng and Tech., World Fed. of Scientists-PMP (Energy); Hon. Vice-Chair. World Energy Council, PMP (Energy) World Fed. of Scientists; decorations from Jordan, Sweden, Italy, Indonesia, Austria and the Vatican; Achievement Medal, IET (UK) 1998, Global Energy Award, World Energy Council Rome 2007. *Publications:* Economics of Reliability 1978, Financial and Economic Evaluation of Projects 1997, Palestine and Egypt Under the Ottomans: Paintings, Books, Photographs, Maps and Manuscripts 2003, Economic Evaluation of Projects in the Electricity Supply Industry 2003 (third edn 2015); numerous articles in professional journals. *Leisure interest:* collecting 19th-century Jerusalem and Holy Land artefacts and rare books and paintings. *Address:* PO Box 410, Amman 11831, Jordan (home). *Telephone:* (6) 5815316 (home). *Fax:* (6) 5851401 (home). *E-mail:* hisham@khatibco.com (home).

KHATIWADA, Pradeep Kumar, BA (Econ), MSc, MEd; Nepalese diplomatist; b. 15 Feb. 1950, Kathmandu; s. of Gopinath Khatiwada; m. Sarita Upraity Khatiwada; ed Tribhuvan Univ., Kathmandu; career diplomat, joined Civil Service 1975, First Sec., Embassy in New Delhi 1986–90, Counsellor and Chargé d'affaires a.i., Washington, DC 1993–94, Counsellor and Deputy Chief of Mission, Bonn and Berlin 1998–2002, Minister and Deputy Chief of Mission, Embassy in New Delhi 2003–05; Jt Sec., Ministry of Foreign Affairs 2006–07; Amb. to Bangladesh 2007–11; Long Service Medal, Govt of Nepal. *Publication:* Nepal-India Relations – Democracy in the Making of Mutual Trust (with Dr Dinesh Bhattarai) 1993. *Address:* 21/472 Kalikasthan, Dillibazar, Kathmandu, Nepal. *E-mail:* pradeepji@aol.com.

KHATIWADA, Yuba Raj, BA, MA, MPA, PhD; Nepalese economist and fmr central banker; *Minister of Finance;* b. 14 Aug. 1956, Jhapa; m.; three c.; ed Tribhuvan Univ., Delhi School of Econs, Univ. of Delhi, India; Asst Lecturer, Tribhuvan Univ. 1982–83; intermittently a Visiting Faculty mem., Tribhuvan and Kathmandu Univs 1992–2001; Asst Research Officer, Nepal Rastra Bank 1983–91, Research Officer 1991–94, Econ. Adviser 1994–99, Head of Econ. Research Dept 1999–2002, Exec. Dir Office of the Gov. 2002–06, Gov. 2010–15; Sr Economist, UNDP Regional Centre, Colombo, Sri Lanka 2006–09; mem. Nat. Planning Comm. 2002–05, Vice-Chair. 2009–10, 2015–16 (resgnd); mem. Revenue Consultative Cttee, Ministry of Finance 1999–2002; Minister of Finance 2018–; Pres. Man. Asscn of Nepal 1999–2002; Regional Mem. for Nepal, Bd of Int. Centre for Integrated Mountain Devt 2009–; mem. Bd of Dirs Rastriya Banijya Bank 1995, Nepal Telecommunication Corpn 1997, Nepal Industrial Devt Corpn 1999–2002; Mahendra Bidhya Bhusan, HM King Birendra Bir Bikram Shah Dev 1994, Suprabal Gorakha Dakshin Bahu, HM King Birendra Bir Bikram Shah Dev 2001, Letter of Commendation, Fed. of Nepalese Chambers of Commerce and Industry for Outstanding Contrib. to Econ. Studies and Promotion of Good Man. Practices in Nepal 2001. *Publications include:* An Econometric Analysis of the Determinants of Inflation in Nepal 1981, Some Aspects of Monetary Policy in Nepal 1994; numerous published articles. *Address:* Ministry of Finance, Singha Durbar, Kathmandu, Nepal (office). *Telephone:* (1) 4211461 (office). *Fax:* (1) 4211831 (office). *E-mail:* moev@mof.gov.np (office). *Website:* www.mof.gov.np (office).

KHATTAK, Pervez Khan; Pakistani politician; *Minister of Defence;* b. 1 Jan. 1950, Nowshera; s. of Hastim Khan Khattak; three s. two d.; ed Aitchison Coll., Lahore, Gordon Coll., Rawalpindi; started political career as mem. dist council 1983; elected five times as mem. Khyber Pakhtunkhwa (KP) Prov. Ass. for Constituency PK-13 Nowshera 2008–18; fmr KP Minister of Industries and of Irrigation; mem. Nat. Ass. for Constituency NA-5 (Nowshera-I) 2013 (resigned); Chief Minister of Khyber Pakhtunkhwa 2013–18; Minister of Defence 2018–; mem. Pakistan Tehreek-e-Insaf, currently Sec.-Gen. *Address:* Ministry of Defence, Saddar, 46000 Rawalpindi, Punjab, Pakistan (office). *Telephone:* (51) 9271107 (office). *Fax:* (51) 9221596 (office). *Website:* www.mod.gov.pk (office).

KHATTAK, Vice-Adm. (retd) Taj Muhammad, MSc; Pakistani naval officer; b. 20 Feb. 1948, Sahiwal; s. of Karra Khan Khattak and Gul Begum; m. Nasim Khattak; two s.; ed Cadet Coll., Hassan Abdal; joined Pakistan Navy 1965, fought during Indo-Pak War 1971 (POW in India for two years), appointments include Flag Officer of Sea Training, Additional Sec./Dir-Gen. Ports and Shipping Wing, Ministry of Communications, Commdr Pakistan Fleet, Deputy Chief of Naval Staff (Projects), Deputy Chief of Naval Staff (Material), Chief of Staff, Naval HQ, Islamabad; apptd Rear-Adm. 1997, Vice-Adm. 2002; Chair. Port Qasim Authority (on secondment), Karachi 2002–04; currently columnist; Sword of Honour 1969, Sitara-e-Jurrat (Gallantry Award) 1971, Sitara-e-Imtiaz 1996, Hilal-e-Imtiaz 2001. *Publications include:* Amphibious Threat to Pakistan, Indian Nuclear Threat. *Leisure interests:* reading, golf. *Address:* 12 B/1 3rd Gizri Street, DHA, Phave-IV Karachi 75020, Pakistan (home). *Telephone:* (21) 5898382 (home). *E-mail:* taj khattak@ymail.com (home).

KHATTAR, Manohar Lal; Indian politician; *Chief Minister of Haryana;* b. 5 May 1954, Nindana village, Rohtak Dist, Haryana; ed Univ. of Delhi; joined Rashtriya Swayamsevak Sangh (RSS) 1977, full-time party worker 1977–93; joined Bharatiya Janata Party (BJP) 1994, apptd Sangathan Mahamantri in Haryana 1994, Org. Gen. Sec., Haryana BJP 2000–14, also mem. BJP Nat. Exec. Cttee, led several BJP electoral campaigns, apptd Regional Sangathan Mahamantri for Jammu and Kashmir, Punjab, Haryana, Chandigarh and Himachal Pradesh, Chair. Haryana Election Campaign Cttee for Lok Sabha campaign 2014; mem. Legis. Ass. from Karnal 2014–, elected Leader BJP MLAs; Chief Minister of Haryana 2014–. *Address:* Office of the Chief Minister, Government of Haryana,

4th Floor, Civil Secretariat, Sector 1, Chandigarh 160 001, Haryana, India (office). *Telephone:* (172) 2749396 (office). *Fax:* (172) 2740774 (office). *E-mail:* cmharyana@nic.in (office); poweb.dipr-hry@nic.in (office). *Website:* haryanacmoffice.gov.in (office).

KHATUN, Sahara, BA, LLB; Bangladeshi lawyer and politician; b. 1 March 1943, Dhaka; mem. Awami League, fmr Legal Sec.; mem. Jatiya Sangsad (Parl.) for Dhaka-18 constituency; Minister of Home Affairs 2009–12, of Post and Telecommunications 2012–13; Founder and Pres. Bangladesh Awami Ainjibi Parishad (advocacy group); Gen. Sec. Bangladesh Mahila Samity (women's asscn); mem. Int. Women Lawyers' Asscn, Int. Women's Alliance. *Address:* 563 Madrasha Road, East Manikdi, PO Dhaka Cantonment, 1206, Dhaka, Bangladesh (home). *E-mail:* dhaka.18@parliament.gov.bd (office). *Website:* www.parliament.gov.bd (office).

KHAYANKHYARVAA, Damdin; Mongolian civil engineer and politician; b. 1960, Zavkhan Prov.; ed Moscow Inst. of Man.; economist, Construction Industry Asscn, Darkhan city 1986–89, Head of Section 1990; Instructor with Mongolian People's Revolutionary Party (MPRP) Cttee of Darkhan city 1989–90; Econ. Adviser and Vice-Chair. of People's Deputies Khural (regional ass.), Darkhan city 1990–91; Economist and Deputy Dir, Darkhan city Metallurgical Plant 1991–93; Head of Dept, Gov.'s Office, Darkhan-Uul Prov. 1993–2000, Gov. of Darkhan-Uul Prov. 2000–08; mem. Mongolian People's Party (fmrly Mongolian People's Revolutionary Party); mem. Mongolian Great Khural (Parl.) for Dharkan-Uul 19 constituency 2008–, mem. Parl. Cttee on Safety and Foreign Policy; Minister of Finance 2012; Order 'Polar Star' 2003; Best Employee of Econs Sector 1996, Best Employee of Commercial Sector 2002. *Address:* The Office of the State Great Khural, Chinggis Khaan Area 1, 14201 Ulaanbataar, Mongolia (office). *Telephone:* (51) 267016 (office). *Fax:* (11) 327016 (office). *E-mail:* khyankhyarvaa@parliament.mn (office). *Website:* www.parliament.mn/en/who?type=3&cid=63 (office); khayankhyarvaa.parliament.mn (office).

KHAYRE, Hassan Ali, MBA; Somali/Norwegian politician, fmr aid worker and oil executive; *Prime Minister;* b. 15 April 1968; ed Univ. of Oslo, Edinburgh Business School, Heriot-Watt Univ.; moved to Norway as refugee 1990; returned to Somalia as Regional Dir Norwegian Refugee Council 2000, becoming Area Manager, later Regional Dir for Horn of Africa 2011–14; Exec. Dir for Africa, Soma Oil and Gas (British oil co.) 2013–17; apptd Prime Minister of Somalia 2017–. *Address:* Office of the Prime Minister, 1 Villa Somalia, 2525 Mogadishu, Somalia (office). *Telephone:* (5) 543050 (office). *Fax:* (5) 974242 (office). *E-mail:* primeminister@opm.somaligov.net (office). *Website:* www.opm.somaligov.net (office).

KHAYRULLOYEV, Saidullo Khayrulloyevich; Tajikistani politician; b. 10 Aug. 1945, Garm Dist; ed Tashkent Higher CPSU School, Tajik Inst. of Agric.; Engineer, Chief Engineer, then Head of Div. Garm irrigation system 1969–75; Chair. Exec. Cttee Garm Regional Soviet of People's Deputies 1975–77, Chair. Regional Soviet 1979–85; First Sec., Soviet region CP of Tajikistan 1985–88; Sec. Ktalon Regional CP Cttee 1988–90; Deputy Prime Minister of Tajikistan 1991–92; Minister of Environmental Protection, then Minister of Nature Protection 1992–94; Chair. Govt Cttee on Precious Metals 1994–95, Govt Cttee on Land Construction and Land Reform 1999–2000; Pres. Majlisi Namoyandagon (Ass. of Reps) 2000–10; Merited Worker of Tajikistan, Order of Nishoni Fakhri. *Address:* c/o Majlisi Oli, Majlisi Namoyandagon, 734051 Dushanbe, Xiyoboni Rudaki 42, Tajikistan (office).

KHAZANOV, Gennady Viktorovich; Russian comedian and actor; b. 1 Dec. 1945, Moscow; m. Zlata Khazanov; one d.; ed State High School of Circus and Variety Actors; worked in radio equipment factory; debut as actor Moscow Univ. Students' Theatre Nash Dom; compere L. Utyosov Orchestra; on professional stage since 1969 in solo productions, first production Trifles of Life 1981; variety programmes Evident and Unbelievable 1987, Little Tragedies 1987, Selected 1988; leading role Gamblers of XXI Century Moscow Art Theatre; leading role in film Little Giant of Large Sex; performed in America, Australia, Israel, Germany, Canada; Artistic Dir Variety Theatre Mono 1991–96; Dir, then Artistic Dir Moscow State Estrada Theatre 1997–; First Prize All-Union Competition of Variety Artists; State Prize 1995. *Address:* Moscow State Estrada Theatre, 109072 Moscow, Bersenevskaya Nab. 20/2, Russia. *Telephone:* (495) 230-18-68. *Website:* www.teatr-estrada.ru; www.hazanov.ru.

KHEHAR, Jagdish Singh, LLB, LLM; Indian lawyer and judge (retd); b. 28 Aug. 1952, Chandigarh; m. Madhupreet Kaur Khehar; ed Panjab Univ., Chandigarh; started working as advocate in 1979 and practised in Punjab and Haryana High Court, Himachal Pradesh High Court, Supreme Court of India; apptd Additional Advocate-Gen., Panjab 1992, then Sr Standing Counsel, Chandigarh, later Sr Advocate; also worked as Standing Counsel for Univs. of the area and Corp. Orgs.; mem. Bench of High Court of Punjab and Haryana 1999, Acting Chief Justice Punjab and Haryana High Court 2008, 2009; Chief Justice, High Court of Uttarakhand Nov. 2009–Aug. 2010; Chief Justice High Court of Karnataka 2010–11; Judge, Supreme Court 2011–17, Chief Justice of India Jan.–Aug. 2017; Dr hc (Panjab Univ.) 2018.

KHEIFETS, Leonid; Russian stage director; b. 4 May 1934, Minsk, Belarus; ed Belarus Polytech. Inst., Moscow State Inst. of Theatre Arts; stage dir, Moscow Theatre of the Soviet Army 1963–71, chief stage dir 1988–94; stage dir, Moscow Maly Theatre 1971–88; teacher, then Prof., Russian Acad. of Theatre Arts (GITIS) 1980; State Prize of the Russian Federation 1991. *Plays:* The One Who Made Miracle 1962, My Poor Marat 1965, The Death of Ivan the Terrible 1966, Masters of Time (Moscow Theatre of the Soviet Army) 1967, Wedding of Krechinsky 1971, Before the Sunset 1973, King Lear 1979, Retro (with Galin, Moscow Maly Theatre) 1981, Western Tribune (Sovremennik Theatre) 1983, Cherry Garden, Rudin (on TV), Antigona in New York (Moscow Theatre of the Modern Play) 1995, Running Stranger (Moscow Mossoviet Theatre) 1996. *Address:* c/o Russian Academy of Theatre Arts, 103888 Moscow, 6, Maly Kislovsky pereulok, Russia.

KHELAIFI, Nasser Ghanim al-; Qatari sports executive and fmr professional tennis player; *President, Paris Saint-Germain Football Club;* b. 12 Nov. 1973; ed Univ. of Qatar Coll. of Man. and Econs; began career as tennis player, turned professional 1992, retd 2003; mem. of Qatar Davis Cup team, played 43 ties 1992–2002; Dir Al Jazeera Sports (now beIN Sports); led buyout of Paris Saint-Germain (PSG) Football Club 2011, becoming Pres. (first non-French Pres.); Pres. Qatar Tennis Fed.; Vice-Pres. Asian Tennis Fed. *Address:* Paris Saint-Germain Football Club, 24 Rue du Commandant Guilbaud, 75016 Paris, France (office). *Telephone:* (1) 47-43-72-72 (office). *Website:* www.psg.fr (office).

KHELEF, Abdelaziz, Licence in Econ. Sciences, High Diploma in Econ. Sciences; Algerian economist and banker; ed in Algeria and Paris, France; has held numerous high-ranking positions in Algerian Govt, including Minister of Commerce, Minister of Finance, State Sec. in charge of Maghreb Affairs, Amb. to Tunisia and Sec.-Gen. of the Presidency; joined Islamic Devt Bank (IDB) in 1994 where he held several high-ranking positions, including Advisor to Pres. and IDB Regional Dir for Northern and Western Africa; Dir-Gen. Arab Bank for Econ. Devt in Africa (Banque arabe pour le développement économique en Afrique—BADEA) 2006–15.

KHELIL, Chakib, PhD; Algerian engineer, economist and government official; b. 8 Aug. 1939, Oujda, Morocco; m.; two c.; ed Texas A&M Univ., USA; engineer with Shell and Phillips Petroleum, Okla and with McCord and Assocs, Dallas; returned to Algeria as Head of Petroleum Eng Dept Sonatrach 1971, also Pres. Alcore (jt venture between Sonatrach and Corelab); Chair. Valhyd Group (oil recovery co.) 1973–76, also Tech. Adviser to Pres. of Algeria; with World Bank 1980–99 (retd), positions included petroleum projects in Africa, Latin America and Asia, then Head of Energy Unit for Latin America then Petroleum Adviser; Minister of Energy and Mines 1999–2010; Pres. OPEC 2001, 2008; Chair. African Energy Comm. 2001; Pres. Org. of Arab Petroleum Exporting Countries 2002, Asscn of African Petroleum Producers 2004; Medal of the Order of the Sun of Peru 2002.

KHENE, Abd-El Rahman, MD; Algerian government official, international organization official and fmr physician; b. 6 March 1931, Collo; m. 1955; three s. one d.; ed Univ. of Algiers; served as officer in Nat. Liberation Army until Algerian independence 1962; mem. Nat. Council Algerian Revolution (CNRA) 1957–60; Sec. of State, provisional Govt (GPRA) 1958–60; Gen. Controller Nat. Liberation Front 1960–61; Head of Finance Dept, GPRA 1961–62; Pres. Algerian-French tech. org. for exploiting wealth of Sahara sub-soil 1962–65; Pres. Electricité et Gaz d'Algérie July–Oct. 1964; mem. Bd of Dirs Nat. Petroleum Research and Exploitation Co. 1965–66; Minister of Public Works and Pres. Algerian-French Industrial Co-operation Org. 1966–70; physician in Cardiology Dept, Univ. Hosp. of Algiers 1970–73; Sec.-Gen. OPEC 1973–74; Exec. Dir UNIDO 1975–85; Founding mem. and Bd mem. Worldwatch Inst., currently mem. Emer. *Address:* 42 chemin B. Brahimi, El Biar, Algiers, Algeria (home). *Telephone:* (21) 924483 (home). *E-mail:* laminekhene@yahoo.fr.

KHER, Anupam; Indian actor; *Founder and Chairman, Anupam Kher Foundation;* b. 7 March 1955, Shimla; s. of Pushkar Nath Kher and Dulari Kher; m. 1st Madhumalati (divorced); m. 2nd Kirron Kher; one s.; ed Nat. School of Drama, Delhi; fmr Chair. Indian Film Certification Bd; Dir Nat. School of Drama 2001–04; Founder and Chair. Anupam Kher Foundation 2008–; co-f. (with Satish Kaushik) Karol Bagh Productions (production co.) 2007; Chair. Film and Television Inst. of India (FTII) 2017–18; Actor of the Decade Award, Millennium Honours 2000, Real Life Hero Award, Zee Gold Bollywood Awards 2001, Padma Shri 2004, Divya Himachal Award 2005, Padma Bhushan 2016. *Films include:* Saaransh (Filmfare Award) 1984, Utsav 1984, Hum Naujawan 1985, Wafadaar 1985, Arjun 1985, Aitbaar 1985, Kala Dhanda Goray Log 1986, Karma 1986, Samundar 1986, Raosaheb 1986, Allah Rakha 1986, Uttar Dakshin 1987, Zevar 1987, Sansar 1987, Dozakh 1987, Zakhmi Aurat 1988, Agnee 1988, Vijay (Filmfare Award) 1988, Kabzaa 1988, Ghar Mein Ram Gali Mein Shyam 1988, Bees Saal Baad 1988, Ladaai 1989, Zakhm 1989, Ram Lakhan (Filmfare Award) 1989, Parinda 1989, Nigahen 1989, Main Tera Dushman 1989, Mahadev 1989, Aakhri Gulam 1989, Daddy (Nat. Film Award 1990, Filmfare Critics Award) 1989, Krodh 1990, Dil 1990, Jeevan Ek Sangharsh 1990, Aaj Ka Arjun 1990, Hum 1991, Saudagar 1991, Lamhe (Filmfare Award) 1991, Khel (Filmfare Award) 1991, Haque 1991, Dil Hai Ki Manta Nahin 1991, Sarphira 1992, Umar Pachpan Ki Dil Bachpan Ka 1992, Heer Ranjha 1992, Beta 1992, Apradhi 1992, Phoolan Hasina Ramkali 1993, Dil Ki Baazi 1993, Izzat Ki Roti 1993, Kasam Teri Kasam 1993, Shreeman Aashiq 1993, Parampara 1993, Meri Jaan 1993, 1942 A Love Story (Star Screen Award) 1993, Baali Umar Ko Salaam 1994, Saajan Ka Ghar 1994, Insaniyat 1994, Darr (Filmfare Award) 1994, Janam Kundli 1995, Dilwale Dulhania Le Jayenge (Filmfare Award) 1995, Raghuveer 1995, Oh Darling! Yeh Hai India 1995, Dushmani 1995, Dil Ka Doctor 1995, Prem Granth 1996, Shohrat 1996, Maahir 1996, Mr Bechara 1996, Vishwasghaat 1996, Shastra 1996, Nirbhay 1996, Chaahat 1996, Zor 1997, Agni Chakra 1997, Ziddi 1997, Judwaa 1997, Hazaar Chaurasi Ki Maa 1998, Keemat 1998, Salaakhen 1998, Aunty No. 1 1998, Jab Pyaar Kisise Hota Hai 1998, Puraido 1998, Hum Aapke Dil Mein Rehte Hain 1999, Sooryavansham 1999, Haseena Maan Jaayegi (Star Screen Award) 1999, Jhooth Bole Kauwe Kaate 1999, Refugee 2000, Dhadkan 2000, Hamara Dil Aapke Paas Hai 2000, Dhaai Akshar Prem Ke 2000, Aaghaaz 2000, Mohabbatein 2000, Jodi No. 1 2001, Kyo Kii 2001, Bend it Like Beckham 2002, Yeh Hai Jalwa 2002, Jaal: The Trap 2003, Banana Brothers 2003, Shart: The Challenge 2004, Bride and Prejudice 2004, Maine Gandhi Ko Nahin Mara (Nat. Film Award 2006, Best Actor Award, Karachi Int. Film Festival 2005, Riverside Int. Film Festival, California 2006) 2005, Jaan-E-Mann 2006, Hope and a Little Sugar 2006, Khosla Ka Ghosla (GIFA Award, Bollywood Movie Award) 2006, It's a Mismatch 2006, Shakalaka Boom Boom 2007, Gandhi Park 2007, Jaane Bhi Do Yaaron 2007, Buddha Mar Gaya 2007, Se, jie 2007, Apna Asmaan 2007, Kuch Khatta Kuch Meetha 2007, A Wednesday! 2008, Dil Bole Hadippa! 2009, Wake Up Sid 2009, Mr Bhatti on Chutti 2010, Apartment: Rent at Your Own Risk 2010, Badmaa$h Company 2010, You Will Meet a Tall Dark Stranger 2010, Lamhaa: The Untold Story of Kashmir 2010, Dabangg 2010, Nakshatra 2010, Jaane Bhi Do Yaaron 2011, Yamla Pagla Deewana 2011, Zokkomon 2011, The Lion of Judah 2011, Aagaah: The Warning 2011, Chatur Singh Two Star 2011, Sahi Dhandhe Galat Bande 2011, Pranayam 2011, Breakaway 2011, Buddha in a Traffic Jam 2011, Chaar Din Ki Chandni 2012, Mudhalvar Mahatma 2012, Chhodo Kal Ki Baatein 2012, Hum Hai Raahi CAR Ke 2012, Midnight's Children 2012, Silver Linings Playbook 2012, Jab Tak Hai Jaan 2012, Zamaanat 2012, Shobhna's Seven Nights 2013. *Television includes:* host, Say Na Something to Anupam Uncle, Sawaal Dus Crore Ka. *Address:* Anupam Kher Foundation, D53/1137, Azad Nagar, Veera Desai Road, Andheri (West), Mumbai 400 058, India (office). *Telephone:* (22) 65271917 (office);

(22) 65261231 (office); 91-67233342 (mobile) (office); 98-33236290 (mobile) (office). *E-mail:* contact@anupamkherfoundation.org (office). *Website:* www.anupamkherfoundation.org (office).

KHER, Bharti, BA; Indian artist; b. 1969, London, England; m. Subodh Gupta; two c.; ed Middlesex Polytechnic, London, Newcastle Polytechnic; grew up and educated in England, moved to New Delhi aged 23; works include sculpture, paintings, installations and photographs; Chevalier, Ordre des Arts et des Lettres 2015; Sanskriti Award 2003, ARKEN Museum of Art Prize (Denmark) 2010. *Works include:* Hungry Dogs Eat Dirty Pudding 2004, Arione 2004, Arione's Sister 2006, The Skin Speaks a Language Not Its Own 2006, An Absence of Assignable Cause 2007, Solarum Series 2007, The Nemesis of Nations 2008, The Waq Tree 2009, Indra's Net 2010, Reveal the Secrets that You Seek 2011, The Hot Winds that Blow from the West 2011, Western Route to China 2013. *Publications include:* Parasol Unit Foundation for Contemporary art, London 2012 (exhibition catalogue), Bharti Kher Blind eyes open, Galerie Perrotin, Hong Kong 2012. *Address:* c/o Hauser & Wirth, 23 Savile Row, London, W1S 2ET, England (office). *Telephone:* (20) 7287-2300 (office). *Fax:* (20) 7287-6600 (office). *Website:* www.hauserwirth.com (office).

KHETRAN, Shahjahan, MPolSci; Pakistani financial services industry executive, government official and fmr diplomatist; ed Govt Coll. Univ., Lahore, Univ. of the Punjab; First Econ. Minister, Embassy in Riyadh 1995–97; spent several years working in capital markets of Pakistan; Founder-mem. Islamabad Stock Exchange; Chair. Intellectual Property Org. of Pakistan 2009–11; Man. Dir Pakistan Tourism Devt Corpn 2011–15; arrested for multiple offences 2015.

KHIATI, Mostéfa, PhD; Algerian professor of medicine and academic administrator; *President, Fondation pour la Promotion de la Santé et le Développement de la Recherche;* b. 3 Nov. 1949, Tiaret; ed Algerian Medical Inst.; fmr Head, Dept of Pediatrics, El-Harrach Hosp.; Chef de service de pédiatrie, Hôpital Zmirli 1989–99, Hôpital Belfort 1999–; fmr consultant, Ministry of Health; Pres. Nat. Foundation for Health Progress and Medical Research Devt in Algeria 1990–, Fondation pour la Promotion de la Santé et le Développement de la Recherche (FOREM) 1990–, Conseil Médical de l'hôpital Belfort 2003–, Nat. Council of Research Evaluation; mem. Medical Soc. of Algeria, Algerian Soc. of Pediatrics 1983–86, Int. Asscn of Pediatrics; Fellow, Islamic Acad. of Sciences; Dr hc (Univ. de Tiaret) 2002; Shoman Award for Clinical Sciences 1984, Maghrebian Medicine Award 1986, Chadli Benjedid Award 1989, Union of Arab Physicians Award, Prix Maghrébin de Médecine et du Président de la République Tunisienne (Tunis) 1997, Humanitarian prize, XIIe World congress, Wadem (Lyon, France) 2001. *Publications:* 12 medical textbooks; Algérie: l'enfance blessée, les enfants de Bentalha racontent 2002, L'Emir Abdelkader, Le Droit humanitaire islamique, Bioéthique. *Address:* 41 Cité du 20 Août, Oued Errouman, 16 403 El Achour, Algeria (office). *Telephone:* (661) 50-70-95 (office). *Fax:* (21) 52-25-94 (office). *E-mail:* mkhiati@gmail.com. *Website:* www.forem.dz (office).

KHIDASHELI, Tinatin (Tina), MPolSci; Georgian jurist and politician; b. 8 June 1973, Tbilisi, Georgian SSR, USSR; m. Davit Usupashvili; two c.; ed Tbilisi State Univ., Central European Univ., Budapest, Hungary; fmr Human Rights Fellow, Washington Coll. of Law and fmr World Fellow, Yale Univ., USA; worked for several govt and int. orgs in Georgia; Office Employee of Parl. of Georgia 1994; Programs Dir, Georgian Young Lawyers' Asscn 1996–99, Chair. 1999–2004; mem. State Anti-Corruption Council 2002–04; critic of govt of Pres. Eduard Shevardnadze, involved in protest movt that resulted in resignation Nov. 2003; Chair. Exec. Bd, Open Society – Georgia Foundation (Soros Foundation) 2005; mem. Sakartvelos Respublikuri Partia (SRP—Republican Party of Georgia), led by husband Davit Usupashvili, Sec. for Int. Affairs 2005–10; mem. Tbilisi City Council 2010–12; mem. Parl. (Majoritarian Deputy of Sagarejo) 2012–15, Chair. Parl. Cttee on European Integration; Minister of Defence 2015–16 (resgnd). *Address:* c/o Ministry of Defence, 0112 Tbilisi, Gen. Kvinitadze 20, Georgia. *E-mail:* pr@mod.gov.ge.

KHIEU, Samphan; Cambodian politician; b. 1932, Svay Rieng Prov.; m. Khieu Ponnary; ed Univ. of Paris; f. French-language journal, Observer, Cambodia; Deputy Nat. Ass. in Prince Sihanouk's party, Sangkum Reastr Nyum (Popular Socialist Community); served as Sec. of State for Commerce; left Phnom Penh to join Khmer Rouge 1967; Minister of Defence in Royal Govt of Nat. Union of Cambodia (GRUNC) 1970–76, Deputy Prime Minister 1970–76 (in exile 1970–75, in Phnom Penh 1975–76); mem. Politburo Nat. United Front of Cambodia (FUNC) 1970–79; C-in-C Khmer Rouge High Command 1973–79; Pres. of State Presidium (Head of State) 1976–79; Prime Minister of the Khmer Rouge opposition Govt fighting Vietnamese forces 1979–91; Vice-Pres. of Govt of Democratic Kampuchea (in exile) June 1982–91 (responsibility for Foreign Affairs); Pres. Khmer Rouge 1985–91, returned to Cambodia Nov. 1991; apptd 'Prime Minister' of illegal Provisional Govt of Nat. Unity (fmrly Khmer Rouge) 1994; Chair. Party of Democratic Kampuchea; Pres. and founder Nat. Solidarity Party May 1997; mem. Supreme Nat. Council 1991–97; Vice-Pres. in charge of Foreign Affairs, Nat. Govt of Cambodia 1991; Chair. Cambodian Nat. Union Party (CNUP) 1993–97; surrended to govt Dec. 1997; arrested Nov. 2007; charged with genocide by UN-backed tribunal Dec. 2009.

KHLAIFAT, Awad, PhD; Jordanian politician, university administrator and academic; b. 1945, Wadi Musa; ed School of Oriental and African Studies, Univ. of London; Pres. Muta Univ. 1989–91; Senator in the Upper House for several terms, Chair. Media, Cultural and Educational Affairs Cttee, Legal Affairs Cttee; Minister in several govts and with several ministerial portfolios; Deputy Prime Minister and Minister of the Interior 2012–13; mem. Arab Thought Forum, Jordanian Writers Asscn; Kawkab Medal (First Order), Istiqlal Medal (First Order).

KHLOPONIN, Aleksandr Gennadyevich; Russian politician and business executive; b. 6 March 1965, Colombo, Ceylon (now Sri Lanka); m.; one d.; ed Moscow Inst. of Finance; army service 1983–85; with Vneshtorgbank 1989–92; Deputy, First Deputy Chair., Chair., Pres., Commercial Bank Int. Financial Co. 1992–; Acting Deputy Chair., mem. Bd of Dirs then Dir-Gen. Norilsk Nikel 1996–2001; mem. Advisory Council, Fed. Comm. 1997–; mem. Bd of Dirs Kolskaya Mine Co., Murmansk 1998–; Gov. Taimyr (Dolgano-Nenets) Autonomous Okrug (in Krasnoyarsk Krai) 2001–02; Gov. Krasnoyarsk Krai 2002–10; Deputy Chair., Govt of the Russian Fed. 2010–18; Presidential Rep. to N Caucasus Fed. Okrug 2010–14; Order of Honour 1998; Order for Services to the Fatherland (Fourth Degree); named Person of the Year by Expert magazine (Russian business weekly) 2002. *Address:* c/o Office of the Government, 103274 Moscow, Krasnopresnenskaya nab. 2, Russia (office).

KHODAKOV, Aleksander Georgyevich; Russian diplomatist; b. 8 March 1952, Moscow; m.; two s.; ed Moscow State Inst. of Int. Relations, Algiers Univ., Algeria; worked in USSR Embassy, Gabon 1974–79; with Legal and Treaty Dept, Ministry of Foreign Affairs 1980–85, Deputy Dir, Legal Dept 1992–94, Dir 1994–97; First Sec., then Second Sec., Perm. Mission of USSR to UN, New York 1985–91; Amb. to the Netherlands 1997–2003; Perm. Rep. of Russia to Org. for the Prohibition of Chemical Weapons (OPCW), The Hague 1998–2003, Dir, Office of Special Projects, OPCW 2004–05; mem. Exec. Bd Russian Int. Law Asscn 1996–98; joined International Criminal Court (ICC) 2011, currently External Relations and Cooperation Sr Adviser, Registry of the ICC.

KHODORKOVSKII, Mikhail Borisovich; Russian business executive; b. 26 June 1963, Moscow, Russian SFSR, USSR; m. 1st Yelena Khodorkovskaya; one s.; m. 2nd Inna Khodorkovskaya; two s. one d.; ed Moscow Mendeleyev Inst. of Chemistry and Tech., G. V. Plekhanov Inst. of Nat. Econs; Head of Centre of Interfield Research Programmes (NTTM), USSR State Cttee for Science and Tech. (now Menatep Asscn) 1986–93; Chair. Menatep Bank 1993–; Chair. Commercial Innovation Bank of Scientific Progress 1989–90; Econ. Counsellor to Chair. of Russian Council of Ministers 1990–91; Deputy Minister of Fuel and Energy Industry 1991; Chair. Rosprom (Federal Agency for Industry) 1995–96; Vice-Pres. YUKOS Asscn 1996, Chair. United Bd Rosprom-YUKOS Co. 1997–2000, Chair. Exec. Cttee OAO NK YUKOS, Man. Cttee YUKOS-Moscow 2000–03, CEO YUKOS –2003; Owner, Moskovskiye Novosti newspaper 2003–; charged with fraud and tax evasion Oct. 2003, convicted May 2005 and sentenced to nine years in prison, sentence later reduced to eight years, moved into prison camp No. 13 in Krasnokamensk, Chita Oblast (now Transbaikal Krai) Oct. 2005; new trial began in Moscow on fresh charges on embezzlement and money laundering March 2009, found guilty Dec. 2010, sentenced to 14 years in prison (including sentence from first trial), appealed conviction to European Court of Human Rights, court ruled that he failed to prove his prosecution was politically motivated but that Russia committed serious violations of his rights during his arrest and pre-trial detention May 2011, declared a prisoner of conscience by Amnesty International May 2011, a review of his sentence ordered by Pres. Medvedev March 2012, prison sentence reduced by two years by a Moscow court (due to be released in 2014) Dec. 2012, pardoned by Pres. Putin and released from jail Dec. 2013; granted visa to travel to Switzerland Jan. 2014; launched the Open Russia movt Sept. 2014; int. arrest warrant issued by Russian court following charges by Investigative Cttee of Russia of his ordering the murder of Vladimir Petukhov, Mayor of Nefteyugans in 1998 Dec. 2015; Dr Rainer Hildebrandt Medal 2010, Newsmaker of the Year Award, Ekho Mosvky Radio 2010, named by Radio France International as European of the Week 2010, Znamya Literary Prize 2010, Sakharov Prize for Journalism as an Act of Conscience (co-recipient) 2011, Lech Walesa Award 2013, Man of the Year, Gazeta Wyborcza newspaper (Poland) 2014. *Address:* 105215 Moscow, a/ya 'Press-Tsentr', Russia. *Telephone:* (495) 773-44-66 (for calls in Russia); (20) 7823-4608 (London, for calls from outside Russia). *Website:* www.khodorkovsky.com.

KHOO, Eric; Singaporean filmmaker; b. 27 March 1965; s. of Khoo Teck Puat; dir, producer, writer and cinematographer of short films; fmr Head Filmmaker, Zhao Wei Films (production co.); Co-founded (with Infinite Frameworks) Gorylah (production co.) 2009; mem. Bd of Dirs Tisch School of the Arts Asia, New York Univ., Singapore 2007–; Chevalier, Ordre des arts et des letters 2008; Young Artist Award for Film, Nat. Arts Council 1997, Singapore Youth Awards 1999. *Films directed include:* Barbie Dogs Joe 1990, Hope and Requiem 1991, August 1991, The Punk Rocker and... 1992, The Watchman 1993, Symphony 92.4 FM 1993, Pain (also Ed. and Cinematographer) 1994, Mee Pok Man (Fukuoka and Pusan Prizes) 1995, Shier lou (Twelve Stories: Fed. of Int. Film Critics Award, UOB Young Cinema Award, Singapore Int. Festival, Golden Maile Award for Best Picture, Hawaii Int. Film Festival) 1997, Home VDO 2000, One Leg Kicking 2001, Be With Me (also writer) 2005, Digital Sam in Sam Saek 2006: Talk to Her 2006, My Magic (also writer) 2008, Tatsumi 2011, 60 Seconds of Solitude in Year Zero 2011, In the Room 2015, 7 Letters 2015. *Films produced include:* Pain 1994, Liang Po Po 1999, Stories About Love 2000, One Leg Kicking 2001, 15 2003, Zombie Dogs 2004, 4:30 2005, 881 2008, Invisible Children 2008, Darah 2009, Sandcastle 2010, 23:59 2012, Ghost Child 2013. *Television:* as exec. producer: Drive 1998, Seventh Month 2004, Recipe 2013, Wanton Mee 2015, Forgotten Flavours 2015. *Publications:* One Fine Day (graphic novel) 2005. *Address:* Zhao Wei Films, 22 Scotts Road, No. 01–28, Singapore 228221 (office). *Telephone:* 67357124 (office). *Fax:* 67351181 (office). *E-mail:* info@zhaowei.com (office). *Website:* www.zhaowei.com (office); www.erickhoo.com.

KHOO-OEI, Mavis; Singaporean business executive; *Chairman and Managing Director, Goodwood Park Hotel Ltd;* b. (Khoo Bee Geok), d. of Khoo Teck Puat; m. Humphrey Oei (deceased); ed Nat. Univ. of Singapore; an heir to father's banking and hotel assets; Chair. and Man. Dir Goodwood Park Hotel Ltd; owns stake in chef Jason Atherton's Pollen Street Social, which has restaurants in London, Singapore, Hong Kong and Shanghai; mem. Bd of Dirs Khoo Teck Puat Hosp., Yishun; Founder and Governing Dir Humphrey Oei Foundation; Trustee, Estate of Tan Sri Khoo Teck Puat. *Address:* Goodwood Park Hotel, 22 Scotts Road, Singapore 228221 (office). *Telephone:* 67377411 (office). *Fax:* 67328558 (office). *E-mail:* enquiries@goodwoodparkhotel.com (office). *Website:* www.goodwoodparkhotel.com (office).

KHOROSHKOVSKY, Valeriy Ivanovych; Ukrainian economist, politician, business executive and media executive; b. 1 Jan. 1969, Kyiv; m. Olena Khoroshkovska; two s. one d.; ed Taras Shevchenko Kyiv State Univ.; Asst to Prime Minister of Ukraine 1997–98; mem. Verkhovna Rada (Parl.) for Crimea 1998–2002; Deputy Head, later First Deputy Head, Pres. of Ukraine's Admin and Chief of Gen. Office of Internal Policy June–Dec. 2002; Minister of Economy and European Integration 2002–04; Prof., Financial Law Dept, State Tax Service of Ukraine Nat. Acad. 2004–05; Vice-Pres. Evraz Holding LLC (steel co.) 2004–06, Pres. 2006; Chair. Ukrainian Ind. TV-Corpn (Inter TV) 2005–06; Owner, UA Inter Media Group Ltd –2013; First Deputy Sec., Nat. Security and Defence Council of

Ukraine 2006–07, First Deputy Head and Head of Anti-terrorist Centre 2009–10, Head, Security Service of Ukraine 2010–12; Head, State Customs Service of Ukraine 2007–09; Minister of Finance Jan.–Feb. 2012; First Deputy Prime Minister Feb.–Dec. 2012; Honoured Economist of Ukraine 2008. *Address:* 01601 Kyiv, A. Vorovskogo Str. 22, Ukraine (office). *Telephone:* (44) 484-47-77 (office). *Fax:* (44) 484-47-75 (office).

KHOSA, Sardar Muhammad Latif Khan, LLB; Pakistani lawyer and politician; b. 25 July 1946; ed Punjab Univ.; Sr Advocate, High Courts and Supreme Court of Pakistan; Founding mem. Khosa Law Chambers, Lahore; Pres. Punjab Univ. Law Coll. Student Union 1965–66; Senator (Pakistan People's Party) 2003–09; Attorney-Gen. 2008–09; Minister-in-Charge, Ministry of Information Tech. –2010, also Adviser to Prime Minister on Information Tech.; Gov. of Punjab 2011–12; apptd Sec.-Gen. Pakistan People's Party 2013; fmr Chair. Exec. Cttee, Appeals Cttee; Pres. Multan High Court Bar Asscn 1981–82, 1987–88, 1995–96; mem. Pakistan Bar Council 1995–2000, 2000–05, Chair. Exec. Cttee 1995–96, Appeal Cttee Punjab-1 1996–2000, mem. Tribunal Council 1995–2000. *Address:* c/o Pakistan Peoples Party, 8, St 19, F-8/2, Islamabad (office); Khosa Law Chambers, 1 Turner Road, Lahore, Pakistan. *Telephone:* (51) 2255264 (office); (300) 8731303. *Fax:* (51) 2282741 (office). *E-mail:* balakhkhosa@hotmail.com; ppp@comsats.net.pk (office). *Website:* www.ppp.org.pk (office).

KHOSLA, Ashok, BA, MA, AM, PhD; Indian scientist, environmentalist, academic and international organization official; *Chairman, Development Alternatives;* b. 31 March 1940, Kashmir; m.; ed St Lawrence Coll., Kent, Peterhouse, Univ. of Cambridge, UK, Harvard Univ., USA; Faculty mem., Harvard Univ. 1963–70; man. various businesses in USA 1965–70; Dir Office of Environmental Planning, Govt of India, New Delhi 1972–76; Dir Infoterra, UNEP, Nairobi, Kenya 1976–82; Chair. and CEO various social enterprises in India 1985–; Founder and Chair. Development Alternatives, New Delhi 1983–; Special Adviser to Brundtland Comm. (WCED); mem. evaluation teams for GEF pilot phase, World Bank's 25 Years of Environmental Programmes and Sec.-Gen.'s Task Force to Restructure the Environmental Activities of the UN; Chair. NGO Forum at Earth Summit, Rio de Janeiro 1992; has served on bds of several environment and conservation orgs, including Int. Union for Conservation of Nature (IUCN), Worldwide Fund for Nature, Centre for Our Common Future, Int. Inst. for Sustainable Devt, Stockholm Environment Inst., Zero Emissions Research and Initiatives, Alliance for a New Humanity, EnergyGlobe, EXPO 2000, Earth Council, Television Trust for the Environment, Toyota Environmental Awards, Int. Inst. for Environment and Devt, Nat. Environmental Council, Nat. Inst. of Design, Environmental Planning and Coordination Org., Planet2025; first elected Councillor to IUCN, representing Govt of India, at Kinshasa Gen. Ass. 1975, UNEP Rep. at Council 1978, participated in Council as Deputy Chair. and later as Chair. Comm. on Environmental, Econ. and Social Policy (then CEP, later CESP), re-elected Regional Councillor 1988, 1990, Pres. IUCN 2008–12; Pres. Club of Rome 2006–, Tech. and Action for Rural Advancement, TARAhaat.com, Decentralised Energy Systems India Pvt. Ltd; mem. Int. Advisory Council, Criteria CaixaCorp, Barcelona 2008–; Chair. Int. Council for Science/Scientific Cttee on Problems of the Environment Programme on Environmental Information 1984–87, IUCN Comm. on Environmental Planning, Nat. Advisory Cttee on Environmental Education, Govt of India, Indian Environment Congress, New Delhi; consultant and advisor, UNEP, Nairobi, UNDP, World Comm. on Environment and Devt, Geneva, World Bank, Global Environment Facility, UNU, Int. Devt Research Centre, Int. Council of Scientific Unions, World Resources Inst., Royal Swedish Acad. of Sciences, East-West Centre, MacArthur Foundation, Ministry of Environment, Govt of India, Ministry of Science and Tech., Ministry of Rural Devt, Planning Comm.; mem. UNEP Governing Council 1972–76, Nat. Security Advisory Bd, Science Advisory Council to Cabinet, Nat. Environment Council, Delhi Urban Art Comm., Indo-UK Roundtable for Strategic Advice to Prime Ministers; Order of the Golden Ark (Netherlands) 1999, Stockholm Challenge Award 2001, UN Sasakawa Environment Prize 2002, Schwab Foundation Award for Outstanding Social Entrepreneur 2004, Zayed Int. Prize – Category 2: Scientific/technological achievements in environment (co-recipient) 2014. *Achievements include:* with Prof. Roger Revelle, designed and taught Nat Sci 118, 'Population, Resources and the Environment', Harvard Univ. (first university course on the environment) 1965. *Publications include:* The Survival Equation (co-ed with Roger Revelle, Houghton Mifflin) 1970, contrib. to numerous articles on environmental issues. *Address:* Development Alternatives, B-32 Tara Crescent, New Delhi 110 016 (office); 22 Olof Palme Marg, New Delhi 110 057 India (home). *Telephone:* (11) 55428858 (office); (11) 26149809 (home). *Fax:* (11) 26866031 (office); (11) 26142213 (home). *E-mail:* akhosla@devalt.org (office); akhosla@gmail.com (home). *Website:* www.devalt.org (office); www.khosla.in.

KHOSLA, Pradeep K., BEng, MS, PhD; Indian/American electrical engineer, computer scientist, academic and university administrator; *Chancellor, University of California, San Diego;* ed Indian Inst. of Tech., Carnegie Mellon Univ.; Asst Prof., Carnegie Mellon Univ. 1986–90, Assoc. Prof. 1990–94, Prof. 1994–2012, Defense Advanced Research Projects Agency (DARPA) Program Man., Software and Intelligent Systems Tech. Office, Defense Sciences Office and Tactical Tech. Office 1994–96, apptd Philip and Marsha Dowd Prof. 1998, Univ. Prof. 2008, Dean, Coll. of Eng 2004–12, Founding Dir Carnegie Mellon CyLab, Inst. for Complex Engineered Systems; Distinguished Prof., Dept of Electrical and Computer Eng and Dept of Computer Science and Eng and Chancellor Univ. of California, San Diego 2012–; mem. Advisory Bd Rady Children's Hosp. Health Center, La Jolla Playhouse, Cecil and Ida M. Green Foundation for Earth Sciences, Sanford Consortium for Regenerative Medicine; mem. Visiting Cttee on Advanced Tech. for NIST; Chair. Jury for Infosys Foundation Prize in Eng and Computer Science; fmr mem. Strategy Review Bd, Ministry of Science and Tech., Taiwan, Council of Deans of the Aeronautics Advisory Cttee, NASA, Nat. Research Council Bd on Manufacturing and Eng Design, Pennsylvania Treasury Advisory Bd, Sr Advisory Group for DARPA Program on Jt Unmanned Combat Air Systems; mem. Nat. Acad. of Eng, American Soc. for Eng Educ., American Acad. of Arts and Sciences; mem. IT advisory Cttee, CSIRO, ITU High Level Experts Group for the Global Cybersecurty Agenda, Visiting Cttee on Advanced Technology for NIST, Global Agenda Council on Innovation, World Economic Forum; mem. Bd of Dirs Quantapoint, BioMetricore, HCL Infosystems, Pittsburgh Tissue Engineering Initiative (PTEI), Doyle Center, Pittsburgh Technology Council; Fellow, IEEE, ASME, AAAS, American Asscn of Artificial Intelligence, Indian Acad. of Eng; Hon. Fellow, Indian Acad. of Science; Hon. DrSc (Indian Inst. of Technology, Kharagpur) 2014; George Westinghouse Award for Educ. 1999, Academic of the Year Award, SiliconIndia 2000, Light of India Award 2012, ASME Lifetime Achievement Award 2012, W. Wallace McDowell Award, IEEE Computer Soc. 2012. *Publications:* three books and more than 350 journal articles and conf. and book contribs. *Address:* Office of the Chancellor, University of California, San Diego, 9500 Gilman Drive #0005, La Jolla, CA 92093-0005, USA (office). *Telephone:* (858) 534-3135 (office). *Fax:* (858) 534-6523 (office). *E-mail:* chancellor@ucsd.edu (office). *Website:* chancellor.ucsd.edu (office).

KHOSLA, Vinod, BTech, MSc, MBA; Indian/American investment industry executive; *Owner, Khosla Ventures;* b. 28 Jan. 1955, Pune, India; m. Neeru Khosla; one s. three d.; ed Indian Inst. of Tech., Delhi, Carnegie Mellon Univ., Stanford Univ. Grad. School of Business; started soy milk co. to service people in India who did not have refrigerators 1975; came to USA to study; one of three founders of Daisy Systems (first significant computer aided design system for electrical engineers) 1980; started Sun Microsystems to build workstations for software developers 1982, pioneered 'open systems' and RISC processors, left co. 1985; Gen. Partner, Kleiner, Perkins, Caufield & Byers (venture capital firm) 1986–; f. Khosla Ventures 2004; Co-founder The Indus Entrepreneurs; assists or serves on bds of eASIC (programmable ASIC platform), Infinera (optical communications), Kovio (printed electronics), Skyblue (internet PC), Spatial Photonics (Micromirror displays), Xsigo (datacentre switch), Grameen Foundation, MetricStream, moka5, Ausra, Zettacore, iSkoot, among others; Charter mem. TiE (not-for-profit global network of entrepreneurs and professionals); Founding Bd mem. Indian School of Business; mem. Bd of Trustees, Blum Center for Developing Economies, Univ. of Calif., Berkeley; Hon. Chair. DonorsChoose San Francisco Bay Area Advisory Bd; EY Entrepreneur of the Year Award 2007. *Address:* Khosla Ventures, 3000 Sand Hill Road, Building 3, Suite 170, Menlo Park, CA 94025, USA (office). *Telephone:* (650) 376-8500 (office). *Fax:* (650) 926-9590 (office). *E-mail:* kv@khoslaventures.com (office). *Website:* www.khoslaventures.com (office).

KHOSROKHAVAR, Farhad; Iranian/French sociologist and academic; *Director, Centre d'analyse et d'intervention sociologiques, Ecole des Hautes Etudes en Sciences Sociales (EHESS);* b. 21 March 1948, Tehran; Asst Prof., Bou Ali Univ. Hamadan, Iran 1977–79; Assoc. Prof., Center for Science Policy, Ministry of Culture and Higher Educ., Iran, 1979–90; Rockefeller Fellow 1990–91; Assoc. Prof. of Sociology, Ecole des Hautes Etudes en Sciences Sociales–Cadis (EHESS), Paris 1991–98, apptd Prof. of Sociology 1998, also Dir of Studies, Dir Centre d'analyse et d'intervention sociologiques 2015–; Visiting Scholar, Yale Univ. 2008, Harvard Univ. 2009. *Publications include:* La Foulard et la République (with Françoise Gaspard) 1995, Sous le voile islamique (with Chala Chafiq) 1995, Anthropologie de la révolution iranienne 1997, L'islam des jeunes 1997, L'Iran, comment sortir d'une révolution religieuse? (with Oliver Roy) 1999, La recherche de soi, dialogues sur le sujet (with Alain Touraine) 2000, L'Instance du sacré 2001, Les Nouveaux martyrs d'Allah (trans. with additional chapter as Suicide Bombers: Allah's New Martyrs 2005) 2002, L'Islam en prison 2004, Muslims in Prison (with James A. Beckford and Danièle Joly) 2005, Avoir vingt ans dans le pays des ayatollahs (with Amir Nikpey) 2009, Jihadism Worldwide 2009, Having Twenty Years in the Land of the Ayatollahs 2009, Jihadist Ideology: The Anthropological Perspective 2011, The New Arab Revolutions That Shook the World 2012, Iran and the Challenges of the Twenty-First Century 2013, Radicalization 2014, Jihadism: The Understanding to Better Combat 2015. *Address:* EHESS–Paris, 54 boulevard Raspail, 75006 Paris, France (office). *Telephone:* 1-49-54-25-63 (office). *E-mail:* cavard@ehess.fr (office). *Website:* www.ehess.fr (office).

KHOSROWSHAHI, Dara, BS; American business executive; *CEO, Uber Technologies, Inc.;* b. 28 May 1969, Tehran, Iran; m. Sydney Shapiro 2012; four c.; ed Brown Univ.; moved to USA with family 1978; worked for Allen & Co. (investment bank) 1991–98; CFO, InterActiveCorp (IAC) 1998–2005; CEO, Expedia, Inc. 2005–17; CEO, Uber Technologies, Inc. 2017–; mem. Bd of Dirs BET.com, Hotels.com, New York Times Co., Fanatics; Ernst and Young Pacific Northwest Entrepreneur of the Year Award 2013. *Address:* Uber Technologies Inc., 555 Market Street, San Francisco, CA 94104, USA (office). *Telephone:* (415) 986–2104 (office). *Website:* www.uber.com (office).

KHOT, Subash, PhD; Indian mathematician, computer scientist and academic; *Professor, Department of Computer Science, Courant Institute of Mathematical Sciences, New York University;* b. 10 June 1978, Ichalkaranji, India; ed Indian Inst. of Tech., Princeton Univ., USA; mem. staff, School of Math., Inst. of Advanced Studies, Princeton, NJ, USA 2003–04; Asst Prof., Coll. of Computing, Georgia Inst. of Tech. 2004–07; Assoc. Prof., New York Univ. 2007–11, Prof., Computer Science Dept 2011–; Visiting Assoc. Prof., Univ. of Chicago 2011–13; silver medallist (representing India), Int. Math. Olympiad 1994, 1995, Hon. Mention, ACM Doctoral Dissertation Award 2003, Microsoft Research New Faculty Fellowship Award 2005, Alan T. Waterman Award 2010, Invited Lecturer, Int. Congress of Mathematicians 2010, Rolf Nevanlinna Prize, Int. Math. Union 2014. *Publications:* numerous papers in professional journals. *Address:* Room 416, Department of Computer Science, Courant Institute of Mathematical Sciences, New York University, 251 Mercer Street, New York, NY 10012, USA (office). *Telephone:* (212) 998-4859 (office). *E-mail:* khot@cs.nyu.edu (office). *Website:* www.cs.nyu.edu (office).

KHOTINENKO, Vladimir I.; Russian film director and producer, actor, scriptwriter and artist; b. 20 Jan. 1952, Slavgorod, Altai territory; m.; one d.; ed Sverdlovsk Inst. of Architecture; constructor at Pavlodar tractor production factory 1969–70; artist, Sverdlovsk film studio 1978–82; freelance 1982–; All-Union Film Festival Prize 1988, Kinoshok Prizes 1992, 1993, Nika Prizes for Best Film 1993, for Best Film Director 1993. *Films:* Races with Pursuit (production designer) 1979, The Smoke of the Home Country (production designer) 1980, Kinfolk (as actor) 1981, Vot takaya muzyka (production designer) 1981, Kazachya zastava (actor, production designer) 1982, Alone and Unarmed (dir) 1984, V strelyayushchej glushi (dir) 1986, Mirror for a Hero (dir) 1987, Who is the Singer Married To? (actor) 1988, Vagon lit (dir) 1989, The Swarm (dir, writer) 1990, Patriotic Comedy (dir, writer) 1992, Makarov (dir, producer) 1993, A Muslim (dir, producer) 1995, The Arrival of a Train (dir, producer) 1995, Road (producer, actor, dir) 1996, 72 metra (dir, writer) 2004, Vecherniy zvon (dir) 2004, 1612: Khroniki smutnogo vremeni 2007, The Priest 2009, Demons (Dir) 2014, Nasledniki (producer) 2015. *Television:* Po tu storonu volkov (dir, mini series) 2002, Gibel imperii (mini series) 2005, Dostoyevsky (dir, miniseries) 2011, Besy ((dir, miniseries) 2014. *Address:* Fadeyeva str. 6, apt 269, Moscow 125047, Russia (office). *Telephone:* (495) 250-47-38 (office).

KHOUNA, Cheikh el Avia Ould Mohamed; Mauritanian politician; b. 1956, Amourj; mem. Democratic and Social Republican Party (replaced by Republican Party for Democracy and Renewal—RPDR 2005); fmr Minister of Fisheries and Marine Economy; Minister of Foreign Affairs July–Nov. 1998, May–Aug. 2008; Prime Minister of Mauritania 1996–97, 1998–2003; apptd. Amb. to Tunisia 2011. *Address:* Republican Party for Democracy and Renewal (RPDR), ZRB, Tevragh Zeina, Nouakchott, Mauritania (office). *Telephone:* 529-18-36 (office). *Fax:* 529-18-00 (office). *E-mail:* info@prdr.mr (office). *Website:* www.prdr.mr (office).

KHOURI, Elie, MBA; Lebanese/French marketing executive; *CEO, Middle East and North Africa, Omnicom Media Group;* b. 1965, Beirut; m. Mylene Khouri 2002; three d.; ed American Univ. of Beirut; began career as currency dealer with financial trading co.; joined Impact BBDO, Cyprus 1988, becoming Assoc. Man. Dir 1988–2000; joined Lintas/Gulf Advertising, Paris 1991; Account Dir BBDO, Dubai 1992, also worked in client services at BBDO in Beirut and Cyprus, Co-Man. Impact BBDO, Beirut 1996–2000; co-f. Omnicom Group (OMG) Middle East 2002, later Man. Dir Omnicom Media Direction (OMD) formed out of media depts of three of Omnicom's global advertising agencies (BBDO, DDB and TBWA), Regional Man. Dir, Middle East and N Africa (MENA), OMD 2001–05, CEO MENA, Omnicom Media Group 2006–; mem. Bd START (non-profit org.); Media and Marketing CEO of the Year, CEO Middle East magazine 2008. *Address:* Omnicom Media Group, PO Box 19791, Dubai, United Arab Emirates (office). *Telephone:* (4) 3904323 (office). *E-mail:* Elie.Khouri@omnicommediagroup.com (office). *Website:* www.omnicommediagroup.com (office).

KHOURY, Elias; Lebanese novelist, literary critic and academic; *Global Distinguished Professor of Middle Eastern and Islamic Studies, New York University;* b. 12 July 1948, Ashrafiyyeh, nr Beirut; ed Lebanese Univ., Beirut, Univ. of Paris, France; with PLO Research Centre, Beirut 1973–79; Publr Su'un filastiniya (Palestinian Affairs) journal 1976–79; Editorial Dir Al-Karmel 1981–82; Ed. culture section of As-Safir journal 1983–90, Al-Mulhaq cultural supplement of an-Nahar daily newspaper 1992–2009; Dir Masrah Beyrut theatre 1993–98; Global Distinguished Prof. of Middle Eastern and Islamic Studies, New York Univ. 2004–; fmr Prof., Columbia Univ., Lebanese Univ., American Univ. of Beirut, Lebanese American Univ.; Lettre Ulysses Award 2005. *Publications include:* An 'ilaqat al-da'irah (novel) 1975, Al-Jabal al-Saghir (novel) 1977, Dirasat fi naqd al-shi'r (criticism) 1979, Abwab al-Madinah (novel) 1981, Al-wujuh al-baida' (novel, trans. as White Masks 2010) 1981, Al-dhakira al-mafquda (criticism) 1982, Al-mubtada' wa'l-khabar (short stories) 1984, Tajribat al-ba'th 'an ufq (criticism) 1984, Zaman al-ihtilal (criticism) 1985, Rahlat Gandhi al-Saghir (novel) 1989, Mamlakat al-Ghuraba (novel) 1993, Majma' al-Asrar (novel) 1994, Bab al-Shams (novel, trans. as Gate of the Sun 2006) (Palestine Prize 1998) 1998, Ra'ihat al-Sabun (novel) 2000, Yalo (novel) 2002, Ka'anaha Nae'ma (novel) 2007, Sinalkul (trans. as The Broken Mirrors: Sinalcol) 2012, Awlad Al-Ghetto: Esme Adam (trans. as My Name is Adam: Children of the Ghetto Volume 1) 2016. *Address:* Department of Middle Eastern and Islamic Studies, New York University, 50 Washington Square South, New York, NY 10012, USA (office). *E-mail:* ek47@nyu.edu (office). *Website:* meis.as.nyu.edu (office).

KHOURY-GHATA, Vénus, Licence en lettres; Lebanese/French novelist and poet; b. 1937, Bsherre; m. 1st (divorced); three c.; m. 2nd Jean Ghata (died 1981); one d.; ed in Lebanon; chosen as Miss Beirut 1959; fmr journalist; moved to France 1973; fmr contrib. and trans., Europe magazine; Pres. Prix des Cinq Continents, Prix Yvon Goll, Prix France Liban; mem. selection cttee, Prix Mallarmé, Prix Max-Pol-Fouchet, Prix Max-Jacob; frequent radio broadcaster; Officier, Ordre nat. du Mérite 2003, Officier, Légion d'honneur 2010; Prix Nice-Baie de Anges 2003, Grand Prix Guillevic de Poésie de Saint-Malo 2010, Grand Prix Doha, Qatar 2010, Prix Goncourt de Poesie 2011. *Publications include:* poetry includes: (first collection) 1966, Les Ombres et leurs cris (Prix Guillaume-Apollinaire) 1980, Monologue du mort (Prix Mallarmé) 1987, Fable pour un peuple d'argile (Grand Prix de la Société des gens de lettres) 1992, Anthologie person-elle 1997, Elle dit 1999, Here There Was Once a Country (anthology in trans.) 2001, La Compassion des pierres 2001, She Says (trans.) 2003, Quelle est la nuit parmi les nuits 2007, Les obscurcis (Grand Prix de Poésie, Acad. Française 2009) 2008, A quoi sert la neige – Poèmes pour enfants 2008, Où vont les arbres? (Prix Fondation Micheloud 2012) 2011; novels include: Vacarme pour une lune morte 1983, Bayarmine 1990, Mortemaison 1992, La maitresse du notable (Liberatturpreis) 1992, La Maestra 1994, Les Fiancées du Cap Ténès 1995, Une maison au bord des larmes (trans. as A House on the Edge of Tears 2006) 1998, Privilège des morts 2001, Le Moine, l'ottoman et la femme du grand argentier 2003, La Maison aux orties 2006, Sept pierres pour la femme adultère 2007, La Fille qui marchait dans le désert 2010; contrib. in trans. to Ambit, Banipal: A Journal of Modern Arab Literature, Columbia, Field, Contemporary Poetry and Poetics, Gobshite Quarterly, Jacket, Luna, The Manhattan Review, Metre, The New Yorker, Poetry, Shenandoah, Verse, Poetry London. *Address:* 16 avenue Raphael, 75016 Paris, France (home). *Telephone:* 1-45-04-06-37 (home). *Fax:* 1-45-04-06-37 (home).

KHRISTENKO, Viktor Borisovich, BSc, DEcon; Russian politician; b. 28 Aug. 1957, Chelyabinsk; m. 2nd Tatyana Golikova; three c.; ed Chelyabinsk Polytechnical Inst. and Acad. of Nat. Economy; sr teacher and Lecturer, Faculty of the Econs of Machine Construction, Chelyabinsk Polytechnical Inst. 1979–90; Chair. Perm. Comm., First Deputy Chair. Econs Cttee, Chair. Property Man. Cttee, Chelyabinsk City Exec. Cttee 1990–91; Deputy Head Admin of Chelyabinsk Oblast 1991–94, First Deputy Head 1994–96; Plenipotentiary Rep. of the Pres. of the Russian Fed. in Chelyabinsk Oblast 1997; Deputy Minister of Finances, Russian Fed. June 1997, First Deputy Minister 1998; mem. Presidium May–Aug. 1998; Deputy Chair. of Govt April–Sept. 1998, 2000, First Deputy Chair. 1999, 2000–04, Acting Chair. 24 Feb.–5 March 2004; Minister of Industry and Energy (later Minister of Industry and Trade) 2004–12; Special Presidential Envoy for Integration with CIS 2004–; Chair. Comm. on Chechnya 2000, on Housing Policy 2001, on Reform of the Electrical Energy Sector 2001; Chair. Collegium of the Eurasian Econ. Comm. 2012–16; Gratitude of the Pres. of the Russian Fed., Order of Friendship (Second Class) (Kazakhstan) 2002, Order of Merit for the Fatherland (Fourth Class) 2006, (Third Class) 2007, Grand Officer, Order of Merit of the Italian Repub. 2009, Order of the Holy Prince Daniel of Moscow (First Class) (Russian Orthodox Church) 2010; Diploma of the Russian Fed. Govt.

KHRZHANOVSKY, Andrei Yurevich; Russian filmmaker, director, producer, scriptwriter and teacher; *Artistic Director, School-Studio 'SHAR';* b. 30 Nov. 1939, Moscow; s. of Yuriy Borisovich Khrzhanovsky and Vera Mihayilovna Khrzhanovsky; m. Mariya Newman 1972; one s.; ed VGIK (workshop of L. Kuleshov); worked with 'Soyuzmultfilm' from 1962; currently Artistic Dir and Chair. Bd Higher Refresher Animation School-Studio 'Shar'; Prof., VGIK; Hon. Artist of Russia; State Prize 1986, 1999, Prizes of Russian Acad. of Cinema 1995, 1998, 2004. *Films include:* Once upon a time there lived a man by the name of Kozyavin 1966, The Glass Harmonica 1968, The Cupboard 1971, The Butterfly 1972, In the World of Fables 1973, A Wonderful Day 1975, The House that Jack Built 1976, I Fly to You in Memory (trilogy of films based on Pushkin's doodles) 1977, 1981, 1982, The King's Sandwich 1985, The School of Fine Arts (Part 1 – A Landscape with Juniper 1987, Part 2 – The Return 1990), The Lion with the Grey Beard 1994, Oleg Kagan: Life after Life (documentary) 1996, The Long Journey (based on Federico Fellini's drawings) 1997, The Dreams about MKHAT (documentary) 1999, Studys about Pushkin, Lullaby for Cricket 1999, Pushkin Take-off 2002, I Love You 2002, A Cat and a Half (based on Joseph Brodsky's drawings) 2002, A Room and a Half (about the life and poetry of Joseph Brodsky) 2008. *Publications:* Der ambivalente Charme des Surrealismus: Go East, Frankfurt am Main 2002 (Subversionen des Surrealen un mittel, und osteuropäishen Film), The Pupil of the Wizard: V.S. Meierhold and Erast Garin (ed and contrib.) 2004. *E-mail:* harmonic47@gmail.com (home). *Website:* www.sharstudio.com (office).

KHUDAIBERDYEV, Narmankhonmadi Dzhurayevich; Uzbekistani politician; b. 1928; ed Uzbek Agricultural Inst.; mem. CPSU 1948–91; dept head, sec. of a regional Uzbek Komsomol Cttee; Lecturer, Asst Prof. Agric. Inst., Samarkand 1943–54; leading CPSU and state posts 1954–; Sec. Bukhara Dist Cttee of Uzbek CP, Head Agric. Dept of Cen. Cttee of Uzbek CP; Second Sec. Bukhara Dist Cttee 1956–60; Deputy to Supreme Soviet of Uzbek SSR 1959–63, 1967; mem. Cen. Cttee of Uzbek CP 1960; Deputy Chair. Council of Ministers of Uzbek SSR 1960–61; First Sec. Surkhan-Darya Dist Cttee of Uzbek CP 1961–62; Prime Minister of Uzbekistan 1971–85; cand. mem. Cen. Cttee of CPSU 1961–66, mem. 1971; mem. Foreign Affairs Comm. of Soviet of the Union, USSR Supreme Soviet 1962–66; Sec. and mem. Presidium of the Cen. Cttee of the Uzbek CP 1962–65, Chair. Agric. Bureau 1962–64; Chair. Council of Ministers of Uzbek SSR 1971–84; mem. Politburo of Cen. Cttee of Uzbek CP 1971–84; sentenced to nine years in a labour camp for bribery Sept. 1989, released 1992.

KHUDAINATOV, Eduard Yurievich; Russian business executive; b. 1960; ed Tyumen State Univ., Int. Acad. of Business, Moscow; Head of Evikhon, Evikhon-2 and Yuganskpromfinco 1993–96; Deputy Head of Nefteyugansk Admin, First Deputy Head of Nefteyugansk region and Head of Poikovsky settlement Admin 1996; Fed. Insp. in Nenets Autonomous Dist of Admin of the Authorized Rep. of the Russian Pres. in Northwestern Fed. Dist 2000–03; Gen. Dir OJSC Severneftegazprom 2003–08; Vice-Pres. Rosneft Oil Co. 2008–09, First Vice-Pres., responsible for production and capital construction projects 2009–13, Chair. Man. Bd and Pres. 2010–12, Deputy Chair. Man. Bd and First Vice-Pres. 2012–13, CEO TNK-BP (following acquisition by Rosneft) 2013; reported to be acquiring Geotex gas co. and Payakha oil and gas co. 2013.

KHUDONAZAROV, Davlatnazar; Tajikistani film director and politician; b. 13 March 1944; ed All-Union Inst. of Cinematography; film dir and cameraman in documentary cinema 1965–77; debut in feature film The First Morning of Youth 1979; Chair. Confed. of Cinema Unions 1990; USSR People's Deputy, mem. of Supreme Soviet 1989–91; mem. Inter-regional Deputies' Group; cand. for Pres. of Tajikistan 1991; moved to Moscow after civil war 1992; adviser, Social and Political Union Focus 1999; Rudaki State Prize of Tajikistan 1972, Distinguished Contributor to Tajik Culture 1977, Badge of Honor and other awards. *Films include:* Dzura Sarkor, Tale about Rustam, Rustam and Sokhrab, One Life is not Enough, Tale about Siyavush, A Brook Ringing in Melted Snow (Prize of All-Union Film Festival 1983).

KHUDYAKOV, Konstantin Pavlovich; Russian film director; b. 13 Oct. 1938, Moscow; m. Irina Mikhailovna Ivanova; one s.; ed All-Union Inst. of Cinematography; with Mosfilm Studio 1970–; mem. Union of Cinematographers 1975; Prof., Head of Studio Higher Courses of Film Dirs; Prof. All-Union Inst. of Cinematography 1995; Chair. State Attestation Comm. of Russian Inst. of Cinematography 1998; Crystal Box for Pages of Life 1971, Prize Moscow Film Festival for Who Will Pay for Luck 1980, Grand Prix Barcelona Film Festival 1986, Golden Tulip Prize Istanbul Film Festival 1986, Prize of the 1st Washington Film Festival 1986, Prize of the Royal Acad. of Cinema (Stockholm) for Success 1986, Prize of European Community for From Evening to Noon (TV) 1983, Prize of the Jerusalem Film Festival for Mother of Jesus 1988. *Films include:* Pages of Life, To Live Your Own Way, Ivatsov, Petrov, Sidorov, Success, From Evening to Noon, Death in Cinema, Contender, Mother of Jesus, Without the Return Address, Michel, The Shadows of Fabergé, On, ona i ya 2007. *Televsions productions:* Presence, Behind the Stone Wall, The Sun of the Wall, Such a Long Short Life, Girl without Dowry, Game, Tango for Two Voices, Impostors, Odnazhdy v Rostove 2012. *Leisure interests:* avant-garde and jazz music. *Address:* 1812 Iear str. 3, Apt 40, 121293 Moscow, Russia (home). *Telephone:* (495) 148-33-37 (home).

KHUGAYEV, Rostislav Erastovich; Georgian (South Ossetian) politician; b. 17 Dec. 1951, Mirtgadjin, Dzau dist, South Ossetian Autonomous Oblast, Georgian SSR, USSR; ed Kuibyshev Civil Eng Inst.; lived for many years in Samara, Russia; leader of the local Ossetian émigré community; Owner and Head of Amond group of construction cos; Gen. Dir Southern Directorate (Ministry of Regional Devt subdivision working on the restoration of South Ossetia) 2009–11, moving to the Far East Dec. 2011, First Deputy Gen. Dir of financial oversight admin of Far Eastern Directorate, Ministry of Regional Devt 2011–12; Acting Prime Minister of 'Republic of South Ossetia' April–May 2012, Prime Minister May 2012–Jan. 2014; Ind. *Address:* c/o Office of the Prime Minister of the 'Republic of South Ossetia', 100001 Tskhinvali, ul. Khetgurova 1, South Ossetia, Georgia.

KHULAIFI, Ahmad al-, BLL, MSc, PhD, MBA; Saudi Arabian economist, academic and central banker; *Governor, Saudi Arabian Monetary Agency;* ed King Saud Univ., Portland State Univ. and Colorado State Univ., USA; fmr Researcher, BIS, Basel, Ministry of Petroleum and Mineral Resources, Riyadh; fmr part-time Lecturer, Tech. Coll., Riyadh; served in several positions at Saudi Arabian Monetary Agency 2000–10, including as Dir-Gen. Econ. Research and Statistics Dept; Exec. Dir for Saudi Arabia, IMF, Washington, DC 2011–13; Deputy Gov. for Research and Int. Affairs, Saudi Arabian Monetary Agency 2013–16, Gov. 2016–; mem. Bd of Dirs Saudi Credit and Savings Bank, Saudi Arabian Gen. Investment Authority, OPEC Fund for Int. Devt. *Address:* Saudi Arabian Monetary Agency, POB 2992, Riyadh 11169, Saudi Arabia (office). *Telephone:* (11) 463-3000 (office). *Fax:* (11) 466-2966 (office). *E-mail:* info@sama.gov.sa (office). *Website:* www.sama.gov.sa (office).

KHURELBAATAR, Chimed; Mongolian economist and politician; *Minister of Finance;* ed Leningrad Inst. of Finance and Econs, Nat. Univ. of Mongolia, Sydney Univ.; Researcher, Nat. Devt Authority 1991–92; Sr Economist, Econ. Policy Reform and Competitiveness (EPRC) project 1998–2000; Econ. Policy Advisor to Prime Minister 2000–03; Sec. of State, Ministry of Finance and Economy 2003–07; Minister of Fuel and Energy 2007–08; mem. State Great Khural (parl.) 2008–, mem. Budget Standing Cttee 2008–09, Head 2016–; Minister of Finance 2017–; Altan Gadas 2006; Honorable Govt Award 2006. *Address:* Ministry of Finance, S. Danzangiin Gudamj 5/1, Ulaanbaatar 15160, Mongolia (office). *Telephone:* (51) 267468 (office). *Fax:* (51) 267468 (office). *E-mail:* support@mof.gov.mn (office). *Website:* www.mof.gov.mn (office).

KHURELSUKH, Ukhnaa; Mongolian politician; *Prime Minister;* b. 14 June 1968, Ulaanbaatar; m. Bolortsetseg; two d.; ed Defence Univ. of Mongolia, Nat. Univ. of Mongolia; began career as political officer, Mongolian People's Army 1989–90; Political staff mem., Mongolian People's Revolutionary Party (MPRP) 1991–94, Adviser to MPRP Parl. Group in State Great Hural (Parl.) 1994–96, 1999–2000; Pres. Mongolian Democratic Socialist Youth Fed. 1997–99, 2000–05; mem. State Great Hural 2000–08, 2012–13; Minister for Emergency Situation 2004–06, Minister for Professional Inspection 2006–08; Deputy Prime Minister 2014–15, 2016–17, Prime Minister 2017–; mem. MPRP (renamed Mongolian People's Party 2010), mem. Steering Cttee 2000–07, MPP Sec.-Gen. 2008–12. *Address:* Prime Minister's Office, State Palace, Chingisiin Talbai 1, Ulaanbaatar, Mongolia (office). *Telephone:* (11) 321704 (office). *Fax:* (11) 328329 (office). *Website:* www.zasag.mn (office).

KHURSHID, Ahmed, MA, LLB, PhD; Pakistani economist; *Chairman, Institute of Policy Studies;* b. 22 March 1932, Delhi, India; Chair. Inst. of Policy Studies, Islamabad 1979–; Vice-Pres. Islamic Research Acad. 1979–; Fed. Minister of Planning Devt and Statistics 1978–79, mem. Hiira Cttee 1978–83; Senator 1985–97, 2003–12; Chair. Islamic Foundation, UK 1978, Int. Inst. of Islamic Econs, Int. Islamic Univ. 1983–87; mem. Bd Trustees, Islamic Centre, Nigeria 1976–, Bd Trustees, Int. Islamic Univ., Islamabad 1980–, Foundation Council, Royal Acad. for Islamic Civilization, Jordan 1987–; Islamic Devt Bank Award 1988, King Faisal Int. Prize for Services to Islam 1990, La-Riba Prize in Islamic Finance, American Finance House 1998. *Address:* Institute of Policy Studies, Nasr Chambers, Block-19, Markaz F-7, Islamabad 44000, Pakistan (office). *Telephone:* (51) 2650971 (office). *Fax:* (51) 2650704 (office). *E-mail:* khurshid@ips.net.pk (office). *Website:* www.ips.org.pk (office).

KHURSHID, Salman, BA, BCL, MA; Indian politician, lawyer and author; b. 1 Jan. 1953, Aligarh, Uttar Pradesh; s. of Khurshed Alam Khan; m. Louise Khurshid; ed St Xavier's High School, Patna, Bihar, St Stephen's Coll., New Delhi, St Edmund Hall, Oxford, UK; fmr Lecturer in Law, Trinity Coll., Oxford; Officer on Special Duty in Office of Prime Minister Mrs Indira Gandhi early 1980s; MP (Indian Nat. Congress) for Farrukhabad constituency 1991–96, for Farrukhabad Lok Sabha constituency 2009–14; Deputy Minister of Commerce 1991–93, Minister of State for External Affairs 1993–96, Union Minister of State (with Ind. Charges) of Corp. Affairs and Minority Affairs 2009–11, Minister of Law and Justice 2011–12, of External Affairs 2012–14; fmr Pres. Uttar Pradesh Congress Cttee, Delhi Public School Soc., Dr Zakir Hussain Study Circle. *Publications include:* At Home in India: A Restatement of Indian Muslims 1987, Beyond Terrorism: New Hope for Kashmir 1995; as ed.: The Contemporary Conservative: Selected Writings of Dhiren Bhagat 1990; plays: Sons of Babur: A Play in Search of India 2008. *Address:* 80 Sukhdev Vihar, Main Mathura Road, New Delhi 110 025, India (home). *Telephone:* (11) 26936655 (home). *Fax:* (11) 26849022 (home). *E-mail:* sk_tipu@yahoo.com; tipu_in@yahoo.com. *Website:* www.salmankhurshid.com.

KHUSH, Gurdev Singh, BSc, PhD, FRS; Indian agronomist and academic; *Adjunct Professor, College of Agricultural and Environmental Sciences, University of California, Davis;* b. 22 Aug. 1935, Jalandhar, Punjab; s. of Kartar Singh and Pritam Kaur; m. Harwant Kaur Grewal 1961; one s. three d.; ed Punjab Agricultural Univ., Chandigarh, Univ. of California, Davis, USA; Research Asst, Univ. of Calif., Davis 1957–60, Asst Geneticist 1960–67, currently Adjunct Prof., Coll. of Agricultural and Environmental Sciences; Plant Breeder, Int. Rice Research Inst., Manila, Philippines, 1967–72, Head of Plant Breeding, Genetics and Biochem. Div. 1972–2002; Fellow, Russian Acad. of Sciences, Chinese Acad. of Agricultural Sciences; mem. Indian Nat. Science Acad., Third World Acad. of Sciences, NAS (USA); Dr hc (Ohio State Univ.), (Univ. of Cambridge) 2000, (Guru Nanak Dev Univ.) 2007; Borlaug Award 1977, Japan Prize 1987, Int. Agronomy Award 1989, World Food Prize 1996, Rank Prize 1998, Wolf Prize for Agriculture 2000, Padma Shri 2000, China Int. Scientific and Tech. Cooperation Award 2001, Golden Sickle Award, Govt of Thailand 2007, Mahathir Science Award 2008, Award of Distinction, Univ. of California, Davis 2009. *Achievements include:* noted for his role in developing high-yielding varieties of rice, which led to doubling of world rice production between 1966 and 1990. *Publications:* Cytogenetics of Aneuploids 1974, Plant Breeding Lectures 1984, Host Plant Resistance to Insects 1995; 152 research papers and 40 book chapters. *Leisure interests:* world history, human rights. *Address:* College of Agricultural and Environmental Sciences, University of California, 150 Mrak Hall, One Shields Avenue, Davis, CA 95616-8571 (office); 39399 Blackhawk Place, Davis, CA 95616-7008, USA (office). *Telephone:* (530) 750-2440 (office). *E-mail:* gurdev@khush.org. *Website:* caes.ucdavis.edu (office).

KHUWEITER, Abd al-Aziz al-Abdallah al-, PhD; Saudi Arabian politician; *Minister of State and Cabinet Member;* b. 1927, Onaizah; s. of Abdullah Khuweiter and Moodi al-Khuweiter; m. Fatima al-Khuweiter 1963; one s. three d.; Vice-Rector King Saud Univ.; Auditor-Gen.; fmr Minister of Health; Minister of Educ. 1987–95, Minister of State and Cabinet Member 1995–; King Abdulaziz Order of Merit (Second Class), Republican Order, Sudan (First Class). *Publications include:* Uthman Ibn Bishr, Fi Turuk al Bahth, Tarikh Shafi Ibn Ali (ed.), Al-Malik al-Zahir Baybars (in Arabic and English), Al-Rawd al Zahir (ed.), Min Hatab al-Layl, Ayy-Bunayy, Qiraah Fi Diwan al-Sha'ir Muh. Uthaymin, Ayy Bonayy (five vols), Itlala Ala Al-Turath, Yowman Wa Malik (two vols), Mal'al-Sallah min Thamar al-Majallah (three vols), Hadeeth al-Rokbatain, Iamhat Min Tareekh al-Ta'leem, Dam'aton Harra, Wasmon Ala Adim al-Zarman (17 vols), Rasd Leseyaha al-Fikr, Nazz al-Yara', Al-Salamo' Alykum. *Leisure interests:* reading, writing. *Address:* Council of Ministers, Qasar al-Yamamah (office); POB 539, Riyadh 11421, Saudi Arabia (home). *Telephone:* (1) 4882404 (office); (1) 4910033 (home). *Fax:* (1) 4930466 (office); (1) 4882622 (office); (1) 4930466 (home). *E-mail:* aa.khuwater@hotmail.com (office).

KHVOSTOV, Mikhail Mikhaylovich; Belarusian diplomatist; b. 27 June 1949, Vytebsk Region; m. Galina Khvostova; one s. one d.; ed Minsk Inst. of Foreign Languages, Belarusian State Univ.; with Ministry of Foreign Affairs 1982–91; Sr Diplomatic Officer, Perm. Mission of Belarus to UN, New York 1991–92, at Embassy in Washington, DC 1992–93; Head, State Protocol Dept, Legal Dept, Ministry of Foreign Affairs 1993–94, Deputy Minister of Foreign Affairs 1994–97; Amb. to Canada 1997–2000; Asst to Pres. for Foreign Policy Issues Aug.–Nov. 2000; Deputy Prime Minister and Minister of Foreign Affairs 2000–01, Minister of Foreign Affairs 2001–03; Amb. to USA 2003–09 (also accred to Mexico 2004–09); apptd Amb. and Perm. Rep. to UN and other Int. Orgs, Geneva 2009; Pres. Conf. on Disarmament 2010; mem. Perm. Court of Arbitration, The Hague, Netherlands.

KIBAKI, Mwai, BA, BSc (Econs); Kenyan politician and fmr head of state; *Leader, Party of National Unity;* b. 15 Nov. 1931, Gatuyaini, Othaya Div., Nyeri Dist, Cen. Prov.; s. of Kibaki Githinji and Teresia Wanjiku; m. M. Lucy Muthoni; three s. one d.; ed Mang'u High School, Makerere Univ., London School of Econs, UK; Lecturer in Econs, Makerere Univ. Coll. 1959–60; Nat. Exec. Officer, Kenya African Nat. Union (KANU) 1960–64; elected by Legis. Council as one of Kenya's nine reps in E African Legis. Ass. of E African Common Services Org. 1962; mem. House of Reps for Nairobi Doonholm 1963–78; Parl. Sec. to Treasury 1963–65; Asst Minister of Econ. Planning and Devt 1964–66; Minister for Commerce and Industry 1965–69, of Finance 1969–70, of Finance and Econ. Planning 1970–78, of Finance 1978–82, of Home Affairs 1978–88, of Health 1988–91; Vice-Pres. of Kenya 1978–88; Vice-Pres. KANU 1978–88; Pres. Democratic Party 1991–2002; Leader of the Official Opposition 1998–2002; Pres. of Kenya and C-in-C of the Armed Forces Dec. 2002–13; mem. Party of Nat. Unity—PNU (coalition of several parties), Leader 2017–; Chief, Order of the Golden Heart; Hon. DrIng (Nairobi), Hon. DLitt (Jomo Kenyatta Univ. of Science and Tech.); Gandhi-King Award for Non-Violence 2003, FDI Personality of the Year Award 2004. *Leisure interests:* reading, golf. *Address:* c/o Party of National Unity, Lenana Road, opp. CVS Plaza, POB 5751, 00100 Nairobi, Kenya.

KIBRICK, Anne, EdD, RN; American nurse and academic; *Professor Emerita of Nursing, College of Nursing, University of Massachusetts;* b. 1 June 1919, Palmer, Mass; d. of Martin Karlon and Christine Grigas Karlon; m. Sidney Kibrick 1949; one s. one d.; ed Boston Univ., Columbia Univ., Harvard Univ.; Head Nurse, Worcs. Hahnemann Hosp. 1941–43; Staff Nurse, Children's Hosp. Medical Center, Boston 1943–45; Educ. Dir, Charles V. Chapin Hosp., Providence, RI 1945–47; Asst Educ. Dir, Veterans Admin. Hosp. 1948–49; Asst Prof., Simmons Coll., Boston 1949–55; Dir Grad. Programs in Nursing, Boston Univ. 1958–63, Prof. and Dean 1963–70; Dir Grad. Programs in Nursing, Boston Coll. 1970–74; Chair. School of Nursing, Boston State Coll. 1974–82; Dean Coll. of Nursing, Univ. of Massachusetts, Boston 1982–88, Prof. 1988–93, Prof. Emer. 1993–, now mem. Advisory Council; Consultant Nat. Student Nurses Asscn 1985–88; Consultant, Hadassah Medical Org., Israel, Cumberland Coll. of Health Sciences, NSW, Australia, Menonfia Univ., Shebin El-Kam, Egypt; Fellow, American Acad. of Nursing 1973–; mem. Inst. of Medicine, NAS 1972–, Brookline Town Meeting 1995–2000; Charter mem. Nat. Acads of Practice 1985–; mem. Bd of Dirs Post-Grad. Medical Inst., Mass Medical Soc. 1983–96, Exec. Cttee 1988–96; Dir Landy-Kaplan Nurses Council 1992– (Treas. 1994–98); Hon. DHL (St Joseph's Coll.); Mary Adelaide Nutting Award, Distinguished Service Award and Isabel Stewart Award, Nat. League for Nursing, Service Award, Nat. Hadassah Org. and other awards; Chancellor's Medal, Univ. of Massachusetts, Boston 1992, Hall of Fame, Nursing, Teacher's Coll., Univ. of Columbia 1999, Living Legend, Massachusetts Nurses Asscn, Massachusetts Nurses Asscn Award 2006. *Publications:* Explorations in Nursing Research (with H. Wechsler) 1979; numerous professional articles. *Leisure interests:* reading, travel. *Address:* 130 Seminary Avenue, #312, Auburndale, MA 02466, USA (home). *Telephone:* (617) 969-3225 (home).

KIBSGAARD, Paal, MSc; Norwegian petroleum engineer and business executive; *Chairman and CEO, Schlumberger Limited;* ed Norwegian Inst. of Tech., Trondheim; began career working for ExxonMobil 1992, working in Norway and Australia; joined Schlumberger as Reservoir Engineer in Saudi Arabia 1997, held various field positions in technical sales and customer support including Geomarket Man. for the Caspian Geomarket, Atyrau, Kazakhstan, Wireline Marketing Man. in Scandinavia, Stavanger, also held a variety of global man. positions, including Vice-Pres. of Eng, Manufacturing and Sustaining, Wireline Open Hole Business Devt Man., Paris –2003, Pres. of Schlumberger Drilling & Measurements, Schlumberger Oilfield Services – Technologies (OFS) 2003–06, Vice-Pres. of Personnel, Schlumberger Ltd 2006–07, Group Pres. of Reservoir Characterization 2009–10, COO Schlumberger Ltd 2010–11, mem. Bd of Dirs 2011–, CEO 2011–15, Chair. and CEO 2015–. *Address:* Schlumberger Ltd, 5599 San Felipe, Houston TX 77056, USA (office). *Telephone:* (713) 375-3400 (office). *Fax:* (713) 375-3463 (office). *E-mail:* info@slb.com (office). *Website:* www.slb.com (office).

KICILLOF, Axel, PhD; Argentine economist, academic and politician; b. 25 Sept. 1971, Buenos Aires; m. Soledad Quereilhac; two c.; ed Univ. of Buenos Aires; fmr leader, La Cámpora (political youth org.); Lecturer in Econs, Univ. of Buenos Aires 1996, Adjunct Prof. 2005–, Deputy Dir Centre for Devt Planning Studies

(CEPLAD), Inst. of Econ. Research 2006–10; Chief Financial Officer, Aerolíneas Argentinas 2009–11, Deputy Gen. Man. 2011; Asst Researcher, CONICET (Nat. Scientific and Technical Research Council) 2010; Dir (govt rep.) Siderar (steel producer) 2011; Sec. for Econ. Policy and Devt Planning, Ministry of Economy 2011, Deputy Minister of Economy 2012–13, Minister of Economy and Public Finance 2013–15. *Address:* Partido Justicialista (PJ), Domingo Matheu 128/130, C1082ABD Buenos Aires, Argentina (office). *Telephone:* (11) 4954-2450 (office). *E-mail:* contacto@pj.org.ar (office). *Website:* www.pj.org.ar (office).

KIDD, Hon. Sir Douglas Lorimer (Doug), Kt, KNZM, LLB; New Zealand politician and lawyer; b. 12 Sept. 1941, Levin; s. of Lorimer Edward Revington Kidd and Jessie Jean Kidd (née Mottershead); m. Jane Stafford Richardson 1964; one s. two d.; ed Horowhenua Coll., Victoria Univ., Wellington; Partner, Wisheart Macnab & Partners (law firm) 1964–78; fmr part-time mussel farmer, Marlborough Sounds; Nat. Party MP for Marlborough/Kaikoura 1978–99; Minister of State-Owned Enterprises and Assoc. Minister of Finance 1990–91; Minister of Fisheries 1990–96, of Maori Affairs 1991–93, of Energy, of Labour and for Accident Rehabilitation and Compensation Insurance 1993–96; Speaker of House of Reps and Chair. of Parl. Service Comm. 1996–99; fmr Foundation Pres. Marlborough Forest Owners' Asscn; Nat. Party List MP 1999–2002, Opposition Spokesman on Fisheries, Chair. Regulations Review Select Cttee, mem. Privileges and Maori Affairs Select Cttee 1999–2002, Appropriations Review Cttee; mem. Waitangi Tribunal 2004–; Hon. Col of Canterbury, Nelson, Marlborough, West Coast Regt 1997–2003; Commemoration Medal 1990, Chief of Gen. Staff's Commendation for Outstanding Service to NZ Army 1999, NZ Defence Service Medal (Territorial). *Leisure interests:* fishing, walking, reading, travel. *Address:* 6 Elgin Way, Wellington 6035, New Zealand (home). *Website:* www.waitangitribunal.govt.nz (office).

KIDDER, C. Robert, BS, MS; American business executive; b. 1944; m.; c.; ed Univ. of Michigan, Iowa State Univ.; served as officer in US Navy Civil Engineer Corps; worked as gen. man. consultant with McKinsey & Co., Chicago, Ill.; Vice-Pres. Planning and Devt, Dart Industries, Los Angeles, Calif. –1980; Vice-Pres. Finance and Admin, Duracell Europe 1980–81, Vice-Pres. Sales and Marketing, Duracell USA 1981–82, Pres. Duracell USA 1982–84, CEO Duracell Inc. 1984–91, Chair. and CEO Duracell International, Inc. 1991–94; Chair. and CEO Borden, Inc. 1995–2001, Chair. Borden Chemical, Inc. (following merger with Borden Chemical) 2001–03, Founding Pnr, Borden Capital Man. Partners 1996–2003; Prin. and Pnr, Stonehenge Partners, Inc. (pvt. investment firm) 2004–06; Chair. and CEO 3Stone Advisors LLC (pvt. investment firm) 2006–11; Chair. Chrysler Group LLC (following Chapter 11 bankruptcy restructuring of Chrysler LLC and global alliance with Fiat SpA) 2009–11; mem. Bd of Dirs, Morgan Stanley 1993–2015, Merck, Microvi Biotech Inc.; fmr mem. Bd of Dirs Electronic Data Systems Corpn, General Signal Corpn, McKinsey and Co. Inc.; mem. Bd of Trustees Columbus Children's Hosp.; Pres. Wexner Center Foundation; mem. Bd Ohio Univ.

KIDJO, Angélique; Benin singer and songwriter; b. 14 July 1960, Cotonou; d. of Frank Kidjo and Yvonne Kidjo; m. Jean Hébrail 1987; one d.; ed in Cotonou; began performing in her mother's theatre co. aged six; joined Kidjo Brothers Band, Alafia, Pili Pili and later Parakou; moved to Paris, France 1983; solo artist 1986–; numerous tours and live appearances; collaborations with Carlos Santana, Manu Dibango, Branford Marsalis, Alicia Keys, Peter Gabriel, Joss Stone, Bono, John Legend; UNICEF Int. Goodwill Amb. 2002–; f. Batonga Foundation (non-profit org. which promotes education for girls) 2007; Commdr, Ordre nat. du Mérite, 2008; Officier des Arts et des Lettres 2009; Hon. DMus (Berklee Coll.) 2010, (Middlebury Coll.) 2014, (Yale Univ.) 2015; African Musician of the Year 1991, Best African Singer, Kora Awards 1997, MOBO Award for Best World Music Act 2002, Antonio Carlos Jobim Award 2007, NAACP Image Award for Outstanding World Music Album 2008, Grammy Award for Best Contemporary World Music Album 2008, Medal of the Presidency of Italian Repub. 2008, Premio Tenco 2009, UN Champion of The Earth Award 2011, Prix Miroir des Musiques et Folklore du Monde, Quebec 2012, Trophée des Arts, Institut Français 2012, Keep A Child Alive Humanitarian Award 2012, Songlines Music Award 2013, Amnesty International Amb. of Conscience Award 2016, Songlines World Pioneer Award 2018. *Film:* The CEO (dir Kunle Afolayan) 2016. *Television:* L'Afrique a un incroyable talent. *Recordings include:* albums: Pretty 1980, Ninive, Ewa Kadjo 1985, Parakou 1989, Logozo 1991, Ayé 1994, Fifa 1996, Oremi 1998, Black Ivory Soul 2002, Oyaya! 2004, Djin Djin (Grammy Award for Best Contemporary World Music Album 2008) 2007, Oyo 2010, Spirit Rising 2012, Eve (Grammy Award for Best World Music Album 2015) 2014, Sings (Grammy Award for Best World Music Album 2016) 2015, Remain in Light 2018. *Publication:* Spirit Rising: My Life, My Music (autobiog.) 2014. *Address:* c/o Redlight Management, 44 Wall Street, 22nd Floor, New York, NY 10005, USA (office). *E-mail:* kevin@redlightmanagement.com (office). *Website:* www.kidjo.com.

KIDMAN, Dame Fiona Judith, DNZM, OBE; New Zealand writer; b. 26 March 1940, Hawera; d. of Hugh Eric Eakin and Flora Cameron Eakin (née Small); m. Ian Kidman 1960; one s. one d.; ed small rural schools in the north of New Zealand; Founding Sec./Organizer, New Zealand Book Council 1972–75, Pres. 1992–95, Pres. of Honour 1997–; Sec. New Zealand Centre, PEN 1972–76, Pres. 1981–83; f. Writers in Schools, Words on Wheels (touring writing co.), Writers Visiting Prisons, Randell Cottage Writers Trust (Trustee); Deputy Chair. French Cultural Trust; Pres. of Honour, New Zealand Book Council, New Zealand Poetry Soc.; mem. Cttee, Lauris Edmond Memorial Prize for Poetry; Patron New Zealand Poetry Soc., Waipu Old Pupils Alumni; more than 60 radio and 20 TV credits; Chevalier des Arts et des Lettres 2009, Légion d'honneur 2009, Dame Companion, New Zealand Order of Merit; numerous literary prizes, including New Zealand Book Awards (fiction category), Queen Elizabeth II Arts Council Award for Achievement, Victoria Univ. Writers' Fellow, A. W. Reed Award for Lifetime Achievement 2001, Meridian Energy Katherine Mansfield Fellow 2006, Creative New Zealand Michael King Fellowship 2008, Prime Minister's Award for Literature (Fiction) 2010. *Publications include:* A Breed of Women 1979, Mandarin Summer 1981, Mrs. Dixon and Friend (short stories) 1982, Paddy's Puzzle 1983, The Book of Secrets 1986, Unsuitable Friends (short stories) 1988, True Stars 1990, Wakeful Nights (poems selected and new) 1991, The Foreign Woman (short stories) 1994, Palm Prints (autobiographical essays) 1995, Ricochet Baby 1996, The House Within 1997, The Best of Fiona Kidman's Short Stories 1998, New Zealand Love Stories; An Oxford Anthology (ed.) 1999, A Needle in the Heart (short stories) 2002, Songs from the Violet Café (novel) 2003, Captive Wife 2004, The Best New Zealand Fiction Vols 1, 2 and 3 (ed.) 2004, 2005, 2006, At the End of Darwin Road: A Memoir 2008, Beside the Dark Pool: A Memoir 2009, Where Your Left Hand Rests (poems) 2010, The Trouble with Fire (short stories) 2011, The Infinite Air (novel) 2013. *Leisure interests:* theatre, film, family pursuits. *Address:* c/o Harriet Allan, Random House NZ Ltd, Private Bag 102950, North Shore Mail Centre, Auckland, New Zealand (office). *Telephone:* (9) 444-7197 (office). *E-mail:* admin@randomhouse.co.nz (office); fiona@fionakidman.co.nz. *Website:* www .fionakidman.co.nz.

KIDMAN, Nicole, AC; Australian actress; b. 20 June 1967, Hawaii, USA; d. of Dr Antony Kidman and Janelle Glenny; m. 1st Tom Cruise 1990 (divorced 2001); one adopted s. one adopted d.; m. 2nd Keith Urban 2006; two d.; ed St Martin's Youth Theatre, Melbourne, Australian Theatre for Young People, Sydney and Philip Street Theatre; acting debut in Australian film aged 14; Amb. Sydney Children's Hospital, Randwick; UNICEF Amb. for Australia; Goodwill Amb. of UN Women, UN Development Fund for Women 2006–; Australian Film Inst. Best Actress Award for role in TV mini-series Bangkok Hilton; voted Best Actress of Year in Australia for role in Vietnam, Int. Star Award, Palm Springs Int. Film Festival 2016, 70th Anniversary Prize, Cannes Film Festival 2017. *Films include:* The Emerald City, The Year My Voice Broke, Flirting, Dead Calm 1989, Days of Thunder 1990, Far and Away 1992, Billy Bathgate 1992, Malice 1993, My Life 1993, Batman Forever 1995, To Die For 1995, Portrait of a Lady 1996, The Peacemaker 1997, Eyes Wide Shut 1998, Practical Magic 1999, Moulin Rouge (Golden Globe for Best Actress in a Musical) 2001, The Others 2001, Birthday Girl 2001, The Hours (Golden Globe for Best Dramatic Actress 2003, BAFTA Award for Best Actress in a Leading Role 2003, Acad. Award for Best Actress 2003) 2002, Cold Mountain 2003, The Human Stain 2003, Dogville 2003, The Stepford Wives 2004, Birth 2004, The Interpreter 2005, Bewitched 2005, Fur: An Imaginary Portrait of Diane Arbus 2006, Happy Feet (voice) 2006, I Have Never Forgotten You (voice) 2007, The Invasion 2007, Margot at the Wedding 2007, The Golden Compass 2007, Australia 2008, Nine 2009, Rabbit Hole 2010, Just Go with It 2011, Trespass 2011, The Paperboy 2012, Stoker 2013, The Railway Man 2013, Grace of Monaco 2014, Before I Go to Sleep 2014, Paddington 2014, Strangerland 2015, Queen of the Desert 2015, The Family Fang 2015, Secret in Their Eyes 2015, Genius 2016, Lion 2016, How to Talk to Girls at Parties 2017, The Killing of Sacred Deer 2017, The Beguiled 2017, The Upside 2017. *Play:* The Blue Room 1998–99. *Television includes:* Hemingway & Gellhorn (film) 2012, Top of the Lake (series) 2017, Big Little Lies (TV mini-series) (Emmy Award for Best Lead Actress in Limited Series or Movie 2017, Golden Globe Award for Best Performance by an Actress in a Limited Series or Motion Picture Made For Television 2018) 2017. *Website:* nicolekidmanofficial.com.

KIDWA, Nasser al-, BS; Palestinian diplomatist and UN official; b. 16 April 1953; m.; two c.; ed Cairo Univ.; mem. Fatah 1969–, mem. PLO Cen. Council 1981–86, 1999–; mem. Palestine Nat. Council 1975–; Amb. and Perm. Observer to UN, New York 1991–2005; Chair. Yasser Arafat Foundation, Cairo 2008–; Minister for Foreign Affairs, Palestinian Authority 2005–06; Deputy Joint Special Envoy of the UN and the League of Arab States on Syria 2012–14, Special Envoy of Sec.-Gen. of League of Arab States for Libya 2014–15.

KIDWAI, Naina Lal, BA, MBA, CA; Indian chartered accountant and banker; *Country Head and Group General Manager, HSBC (India);* b. 1957; m. Rashid Kidwai; two c.; ed Univ. of Delhi, Harvard Business School, USA; began career at ANZ Grindlay's Bank 1982–94; Vice-Chair. and Head of Investment Banking, JM Morgan Stanley 1994–2002; Exec. Vice-Chair. and Man. Dir HSBC Securities and Capital Markets (India) Pvt. Ltd 2002–, Deputy CEO HSBC (India) 2004–06, CEO 2006–09, Country Head and Group Gen. Man. 2009–; Chair. Capital Market Cttee, Fed. of Indian Chambers of Commerce and Industry; Chair. Govt of India Science and Tech. Bd, Governing Body of Nat. Council of Applied Econ. Research, Econ. Policy and Reforms Council for the State of Rajasthan, Governing Body of Lady Shri Ram Coll. for Women, Delhi Univ., Governing Council of India Habitat Centre; Dir Int. Bd of Digital Pnrs Foundation, USA, SEWA (non-profit org. for self-employment of underprivileged women); mem. Bd of Dirs Nestlé India Ltd 2006–, Nestlé South Asia 2006–, Nat. Science and Tech. Entrepreneurship Devt, Nat. Integration Council, Indo-German Consultative Group, Chamber of Industry and Commerce, Nat. Council of Confed. of Indian Industries, Nat. Exec. Cttee, Fed. of Indian Chambers of Commerce and Industry, Grassroots Trading Network for Women; mem. Indian Advisory Council of City of London; mem. Advisory Bd IIM Ahmedabad, IIT Mumbai; mem. Global Bd of Dean's Advisers, Harvard Business School; mem. India Advisory Bd John Hopkins School of Advanced Int. Studies USA; adviser, Nat. Entrepreneurship Network; recipient of several Awards for Business in India, Padma Shri 2007. *Achievements include:* first Indian woman grad. of Harvard Business School 1982. *Leisure interests:* listening to Indian and Western classical music, wildlife tours. *Address:* HSBC Securities and Capital Markets (India) Pvt. Ltd, New Delhi, India (office). *Telephone:* (22) 22681247 (office). *Fax:* (22) 22631984 (office). *Website:* www.hsbc.co.in (office).

KIEBER-BECK, Rita; Liechtenstein politician; b. 27 Dec. 1958, Nenzing, Austria; m. Manfred Kieber; ed Oberstufenrealgymnasium, Feldkirch, Univ. of Fribourg, Switzerland, Univ. of Innsbruck, Austria, Chulalongkorn Univ. of Bangkok and Chiang Mai, Thailand; Instructor in German, Business, Political Science and Econs, Commercial Business School, Buchs, Switzerland 1979–81; full-time instructor, Realschule (Upper School) Balzers 1982–90; with Liectenstein Inst., Bendern 1990–94, Man. Dir 1991–94; Man. Dir Adiuvaris Treuunternehmen reg. (Fiducary), Triesen 1993, 2001; Consulting mem. Parl. Group of Progressive Citizens' Party (Fortschritte Bürgerpartei, FBP) 1997–2000, mem. Presidency 1997–, Chair. Educ. Working Group 1997–, mem. Man. Presidency and Financial Adviser 2000–01; Deputy Prime Minister with responsibility for Educ., Justice, Transport and Telecommunications 2001–05; Minister of Foreign Affairs, Cultural Affairs and Family and Equal Opportunity 2005–09; CEO and Man. Trustee, Rita Kieber-Beck Trust 2010–; Hon. Consul of Austria in Liechtenstein 2013–; Pres. Liechtenstein Upper School Teachers' Asscn 1988–90; mem. Educational Comm., Upper Schools, Liechtenstein 1984–88, Adult Educ. Comm. 1992–98; Großes Goldenes Ehrenzeichen am Bande für Verdienste um die Republik Österreich

2004. *Address:* Rita Kieber-Beck Trust, Franz-Josef-Oehri-Strasse 6, 9493 Mauren, Liechtenstein (office). *E-mail:* office@kieber-beck.li (office). *Website:* www.kieber-beck.li/en (office).

KIEFER, Anselm; German artist; b. 8 March 1945, Donaueschingen; m.; three c.; ed Univ. of Freiburg and Freiburg Acad., Karlsruhe Acad.; first solo exhbn, Galerie am Kaiserplatz, Karlsruhe 1969; first solo exhbn in USA, Marian Goodman Gallery, New York; retrospective exhbns Städtische Kunsthalle, Düsseldorf, Musée d'Art Moderne, Paris and Israel Museum, Jerusalem 1984, Stedelijk Museum, Amsterdam 1986, US tour 1987–89; first group exhbn, Deutscher Künstlerbund, Kunstverein, Hanover 1969; has also exhibited Kunstverein, Frankfurt 1976, Kassel Documenta 1977, 1982, 1987, Biennale de Paris 1977, Venice Biennale 1980, White Cube, London 2005, 2006, Royal Acad., London 2007; other group exhbns include Expressions: New Art from Germany, touring exhbn USA 1983–84, touring exhbn Moscow and Leningrad 1983, 1984 Museum of Modern Art survey of int. art, Fifth Biennale of Sydney, Australia 1984; works in many pvt collections including Saatchi Collection, London and in many public galleries including Art Inst. of Chicago, Museum of Modern Art, Phila Museum of Art, Hirshhorn Museum, Washington, DC, LA Museum of Contemporary Art and San Francisco Museum of Modern Art, Praemium Imperiale 1999; Order of Merit (Germany) 2005; Wolf Foundation Prize 1990, Peace Prize of the German Book Trade 2008, Berliner Bär 2011, Leo-Baeck-Medal 2011. *Publication:* A Book by Anselm Kiefer 1988. *Address:* c/o Gagosian Gallery, 555 West 24th Street, New York, NY 10011, USA.

KIEFFER, Brigitte Lina, PhD; French neurobiologist; *Scientific Director, Research Centre, Douglas Mental Health University Institute;* b. 26 Feb. 1958; m.; two s.; ed Univ. Louis Pasteur; Prof, Univ. Louis Pasteur, Strasbourg 1994–; Research Dir, Institut national de la santé et de la recherche médicale (Inserm); Researcher, Institut de génétique et de biologie moléculaire et cellulaire, Strasbourg 2001, Dir 2012–13; Prof. of Psychiatry and Monique H. Bourgeois Chair in Pervasive Developmental Disorders, Faculty of Medicine, McGill Univ., Canada; Scientific Dir, Research Centre, Douglas Mental Health Univ. Inst., Montreal, Canada 2014–; fmr Visiting Prof., UCLA; mem. European Molecular Biology Org., Académie des sciences 2013; Chevalier, légion d'honneur 2012; Prix Richard Lounsbery 2004, Laureate for Europe, L'Oréal-UNESCO Women in Science Awards 2014. *Address:* Research Centre, Douglas Mental Health University Institute, Perry Pavilion Room E-42064, 6875, boulevard LaSalle, Montreal, H4H 1R3, Canada (office). *Telephone:* (514) 761-6131 (office). *Fax:* (514) 762-3033 (office). *Website:* www.douglas.qc.ca (office).

KIELHOLZ, Walter B., BA; Swiss banking executive; *Independent Non-Executive Chairman, Suisse Reinsurance (Swiss Re);* b. 25 Feb. 1951, Zurich; m. Daphne Kielholz-Pestalozzi; ed Univ. of St Gallen; began career with Gen. Reinsurance Corpn, Zurich 1976 with assignments in USA, UK and Italy, Head of European Marketing –1986; opened art gallery and picture framing business with his wife 1983; Head of Client Relations, Multinational Services Dept, Credit Suisse 1986–89, mem. Bd Dirs 1999–14, Chair. Audit Cttee 1999–2002, Chair. Credit Suisse Group 2003–09, also Chair. Chairman's and Governance Cttee; joined Swiss Re, Zurich 1989, apptd mem. Exec. Bd 1993, CEO 1997–2002, mem. Bd of Dirs 1998–, Chair. Audit Cttee 1999–2002, Exec. Vice-Chair. Swiss Re 2003–07, Vice-Chair. 2007–09, Chair. (ind. non-exec.) 2009–; Chair. Supervisory Bd Avenir Suisse (think tank); mem. Int. Business Leader Advisory Council (advisory group to the Mayor of Shanghai) 1998–2005, 2009–, Int. Asscn for the Study of Insurance Econs, Int. Monetary Conf. (Pres. 2006–07), Bd Inst. of Int. Finance, European Financial Roundtable 2004–15, Center for Strategic and Int. Studies 2005–, Int. Advisory Panel of the Monetary Authority of Singapore 2009–; mem. Bd Dirs Geneva Asscn 1999–, economiesuisse 2003–; Chair. Zürcher Kunstgesellschaft; mem. Soc. of Zurich Friends of the Arts, Lucerne Festival Foundation Board; mem. Advisory Bd Corsair Capital; inducted by mems of Int. Insurance Soc. into Insurance Hall of Fame 2005. *Leisure interests:* sailing, skiing, tennis, golf, reading, opera, concerts, art. *Address:* Swiss Reinsurance Co., Mythenquai 50/60, 8022 Zürich, Switzerland (office). *Telephone:* (43) 285-21-21 (office). *Fax:* (43) 285-29-99 (office). *E-mail:* info@swissre.com (office). *Website:* www.swissre.com (office).

KIELSEN, Kim; Greenlandic politician; *Prime Minister and Minister for Domestic Affairs;* b. 30 Nov. 1966; m. Judithe Kielsen; two c.; early career in merchant navy; police officer, Upernavik and Paamiut 1996–2003; worked as coordinator, social project for children and young people 2003–05; mem. Paamiut Municipal Council 2005–07; mem. Inatsisartut (Greenland Parl.) 2005–09, 2013–; Minister for Housing, Infrastructure and Resources 2007–09; Prime Minister and Minister for Domestic Affairs 2014–; mem. Siumut (Forward), Chair. 2014–. *Address:* Grønlands Selvstyre, Imaneq 4, POB 1015, 3900 Nuuk, Greenland (office). *Telephone:* 345000 (office). *Fax:* 325002 (office). *E-mail:* info@gh.gl (office). *Website:* www.nanoq.gl (office).

KIELY, W. Leo, III, BEcons, MBA; American brewing industry executive; b. 16 Jan. 1947; ed Harvard Univ., Wharton School of Business, Univ. of Pa; Brand Asst and Asst Brand Man., Procter & Gamble, Cincinnati 1971–73; various posts at Wilson Sporting Goods Co. including Vice-Pres. of Marketing and Sr Business Man., Chicago 1973–79; Pres. Ventura Coastal Corpn (div. of Seven-Up) 1979–82; Vice-Pres. Brand Man., Frito-Lay Inc. 1982–83, Vice-Pres. Marketing 1983–84, Marketing and Sales 1984–89, Sr Vice-Pres. Field Operations 1989–91, served as Vice-Pres. and Gen. Man., Cen. Div., Div. Pres. 1991–93; joined Coors Brewing Co. 1993, mem. Bd of Dirs 1998–, Pres. and CEO Molson Coors Brewing Co. (after merger of Coors and Molson cos) 2005–07, CEO MillerCoors (after merger of SABMiller and Molson Coors US operations) 2007–11; mem. Bd of Dirs, Nat. Asscn of Mfrs, SEI Center for Advanced Studies, Wharton School of Finance, Denver Center for the Performing Arts, Helen G. Bonfils Foundation, MedPro Safety Products, Inc. 2008–14, Altria Group Inc. 2011–; mem. Foundation Bd, Metropolitan State Coll.; Chair. Mile High United Way, Denver; Nat. Trustee, Boys and Girls Clubs of America. *Address:* Altria Client Services Inc., 6601 West Broad Stree, Richmond, VA 23230, USA (office). *Telephone:* (804) 484-8222 (office). *E-mail:* info@altria.com (office). *Website:* www.altria.com (office).

KIERES, Leon; Polish politician, professor of law and judge; *Judge, Polish Constitutional Tribunal;* b. 26 May 1948, Kolonia Zielona; s. of Józef Kieres and Helena Kieres; m. Anna Kieres; one s. one d.; ed Wrocław Univ.; Jr Librarian, Wrocław Univ. 1970, Research Asst 1971–73, Sr Asst 1973–75, Lecturer in Law 1975–85, Asst Prof. 1985–91, Extraordinary Prof. 1991–96, Ordinary Prof., Faculty of Law and Admin. 1996–; councillor, Wrocław Town Council 1990–98; Pres. Self-governmental Council of Wrocław Voivodship 1990–98; mem. Local Govt Council at the Chancellory of the Pres. 1994; Vice-Pres. Congress of Local and Regional Authorities of Council of Europe 1995, mem. Parl. Ass. 1998–2000, involved in Council of Europe mission in Bosnia and Herzegovina 1998; Senator (Wrocław Voivodship), Vice-Pres. Senate Local Govt and Public Admin. Cttee, mem. Foreign Affairs and European Integration Cttee; Pres. int. group of local govt observers in Croatia 1997; councillor, Dolnoslaskie Voivodship Council, Pres. Culture, Science and Educ. Cttee 1998–2002; Pres. Inst. of Nat. Remembrance 2000–05, The Club of Rome 2000; Vice-Pres. Polish-German Co-operation Foundation 1993; Judge, Polish Constitutional Tribunal 2012–; mem. Polish Teachers' Asscn 1970–80, NSZZ Solidarnosc 1980–2000, Cttee on Legal Sciences, Polish Acad. of Sciences 2003–, Warsaw Scientific Asscn 2003, Regional Studies Asscn 2003; Hon. Citizen of Lower Silesia 2008; Bronze Cross of Merit 1978; Kt's Cross, Order of Polonia Restituta 1996; St Silvester Order of the Pope 1998; Dr hc (Tech. Univ. of Gdansk) 2004; Walerian Panka Award 1997, St George Medal 2002, 'Lumen Gentium' Medal, Lublin Archdiocese 2004, Lawyer of the Year Award, Gazeta Pranna 2004. *Publications include:* Zalecenia RWPG w sprawie koordynacji narodowych planów gospodarczych i ich realizacja w PRL (Recomendations of Council for Mutual Economic Aid on Coordination of National Economic Schemes and Their Realization in Poland) 1978, Zagraniczne przedsiebiorstwo socjalistyczne w Polsce (Foreign Socialist Enterprises in Poland) 1986, Struktura Centralnego aparatu gospodarczego i jego funkcje (Structure of Central Economic Machinery and its Functions, ed.) 1989, Tworzenie i funkcjonowanie spólek: zagadnienia cywilnoprawne i administracyjne (Establishment and Functioning of Companies: Civil and Administrative Law Issues, ed.) 1989, Region samorzadowy (Local-governmental Region) 1991, Podejmowanie dzialalnosci gospodarczej przez inwestorów zagranicznych (Foreign Investors' Establishment) 1993, Prawo administracyjne (Administrative Law, co-author), Administracyjne prawo gospodarcze (Administrative Economic Law, co-author) 2003; over 40 scientific publs and numerous articles in nat. and foreign magazines on public admin. law, econ. law and law of local govt. *Leisure interests:* supporting football teams, watching good films. *Address:* Polish Constitutional Tribunal, 00-918 Warsaw, Al. Jana Christiana Szucha 12a, Poland (office). *Website:* www.trybunal.gov.pl (office).

KIESSLING, Laura L., SB, PhD; American chemist and academic; *Steenbock Professor of Chemistry and Laurens Anderson Professor of Biochemistry, University of Wisconsin;* b. 21 Sept. 1960, Lake Mills, Wis.; ed Massachusetts Inst. of Tech., Yale Univ.; American Cancer Soc. Post-doctoral Fellow, California Inst. of Tech. for two years; mem. Faculty, Univ. of Wisconsin, Madison 1991–, currently Steenbock Prof. of Chem. and Laurens Anderson Prof. of Biochemistry; Dir Keck Center for Chemical Genomics, NIH Chemistry-Biology Interface Training Program; Ed.-in-Chief, ACS Chemical Biology; mem. American Acad. of Arts and Sciences 2003, NAS 2007, American Acad. of Microbiology 2007, Wisconsin Acad. of the Arts and Science 2008; Fellow, AAAS 2003, ACS 2010; Guggenheim Fellowship 2008; WARF H. Emil Fischer Professorship 2011; American Cancer Soc. Postdoctoral Fellowship 1989–91, Procter and Gamble Univ. Exploratory Research Award 1992–95, Shaw Scientist Award 1992–97, NSF Nat. Young Investigator Award 1993–98, Beckman Young Investigators Award 1994–96, American Cancer Soc. Jr Faculty Award 1995–97, Zeneca Excellence in Chem. Award 1995–97, Dreyfus Teacher-Scholar Award, The Camille and Henry Dreyfus Foundation 1996, Alfred P. Sloan Foundation Fellowship 1997, Arthur C. Cope Scholar Award 1999, selected as one of the 50 top R & D stars to watch by Industry Week 1999, John D. and Catherine T. MacArthur Foundation Fellowship 1999–2004, Horace Isbell Award, Carbohydrate Div. of ACS 2000, Romnes Faculty Fellowship, Univ. of Wisconsin-Madison 2001, Carbohydrate Research Award 2001, Harrison-Howe Award, Rochester ACS 2005, Tetrahedron Young Investigator Award 2005, ACS Garvan–Olin Medal 2007, Wilbur Cross Medal, Yale Univ. 2008, Vilas Assoc. Award, Univ. of Wisconsin 2008, Willard Gibbs Award, Chicago Section of ACS 2016. *Publications:* numerous papers in professional journals on multivalent protein–carbohydrate interactions and carbohydrate polymers. *Address:* Department of Chemistry, 5132A Chem Building, 1101 University Avenue, Madison, WI 53706-1544 (office); 471B HF DeLuca Biochemistry Laboratories, 433 Babcock Drive, Madison, WI 53706-1544, USA (office). *Telephone:* (608) 262-0541 (office). *E-mail:* kiessling@chem.wisc.edu (office). *Website:* www.chem.wisc.edu (office); biochem.wisc.edu/labs/kiessling (office).

KIIR MAYARDIT, Salva; South Sudanese politician, fmr military leader and head of state; *President of South Sudan;* b. 1951; joined Anyanya separatist movt during First Sudanese Civil War, early 1960s, later becoming an officer, joined regular army after peace settlement 1972; with Army of Sudan 1972–83, attaining rank of Capt.; Founding mem. Sudan People's Liberation Movt (SPLM) 1983, later Deputy Party Leader, Chief of Staff Sudan People's Liberation Army (mil. wing of SPLM) 1999, Chair. SPLM (after death of John Garang) 2005, Commdr-in-Chief SPLA 2005–; Vice-Pres. of Southern Sudan 2005, Pres. 2005–11, also First Vice-Pres. of Sudan 2005–11; sworn in as first Pres. of South Sudan following independence July 2011. *Address:* Office of the President, Juba, South Sudan (office). *E-mail:* webmaster@splmtoday.com (office). *Website:* www.splmtoday.com (office).

KIKABIDZE, Vakhtang Konstantinovich; Georgian actor, singer, composer and producer; b. 19 July 1938, Tbilisi; s. of Konstantin Kikabidze and Manana Bagrationi; m. Irene Kebadze 1964; one s.; soloist and leader of Georgian pop group Orera 1966–; film debut in 1967 with Meeting in the Hills; solo career 1988–; USSR State Prize 1978, People's Artist of Georgian SSR 1980, Order of Honour, special award (Georgia) 1994, Order of Konstantine (Russia) 1997, Order of St Nicholaus 1998, Golden Gramophone Prize 1998, Leonid Utesov Prize for Achievement in field of Music 2000. *Films include:* Meeting in the Hills 1967, Don't Grieve 1968, I'm a Detective 1969, The Stone of the First Water 1970, Pen-name Lukach, The Melodies of Verikysky Block 1973, Lost Expedition 1973, Completely Gone 1972, Mimino 1978, TASS is Authorized to Inform, Hi! Friend (TV film) 1981, To Your Health Dear (dir, scriptwriter, actor) 1983, Man and all the Others (scriptwriter, producer, actor) 1985, Fortuna (actor) 2000, Idiotocratia 2008, Yolki 2 2011, Lyubov s aktsentom 2012, Ded 005 2013. *Music:* albums: My Years, My Wealth 1994, Larisa Ivanovna Please! 1995, Letter to Friend 1996, Tango of Love 1999,

Greatest Hits 2000, Luchshie pesni 2001, Grand Collection 2002, Moi good 2003, Stariki-pasboiniki 2004, Lyubownoye nastroyenie 2005. *Leisure interest:* fishing.

KIKOIN, Konstantin Abramovich, PhD, DrSci; Israeli (b. Russian) theoretical physicist, academic, poet and essayist; *Professor, School of Physics and Astronomy, Tel-Aviv University;* b. 9 Aug. 1945, Kalinin (now Tver), Russian SFSR, USSR; s. of Abraham Kikoin and Ekaterina Sosenkova; m. Larisa Markina 1969; one s. one d.; ed Ural State Univ. (Sverdlovsk/Ekaterinburg), Physical-Tech. Inst. Moscow; Jr Scientific Researcher, Inst. of Optical-Physical Measurements, Moscow 1971–74; Sr Scientific Researcher I.V. Kurchatov Inst. of Atomic Energy, Moscow 1974–85, Leading Scientific Researcher and Vice-Head of Solid State Theory Dept 1985–96; Research Fellow, Dept of Physics, Ben Gurion Univ. of the Negev, Israel 1997–2006; Prof., School of Physics and Astronomy, Tel-Aviv Univ. 2006–; Deputy Chair. Exec. Bd Moscow Physical Soc. 1989–96, Assoc. Ed. Journal of Moscow Physical Soc. 1990–96, Journal of Experimental and Theoretical Physics 1991–; Rep. of American Inst. of Physics in Moscow 1992–94; mem. Expert Council of Supreme Attestation Cttee 1994–96; mem. Israeli Federation of Writers' Unions 2008–; Kapitza Fellowship, Royal Soc. (UK) 1995. *Publications:* three monographs, seven reviews and more than 150 papers in scientific journals, two books of collected verses. *Leisure interest:* translating poetry from Russian into English. *Address:* School of Physics and Astronomy, Tel-Aviv University, Tel-Aviv 69978, Israel (office). *E-mail:* konstk@post.tau.ac.il (office). *Website:* www.tau.ac.il (office).

KIKWETE, Lt-Col Jakaya Mrisho; Tanzanian politician and fmr head of state; b. 7 Oct. 1950, Msonga, Bagamoyo Dist; m. Salma Kikwete; five c.; ed Tengeru School, Kibaha Secondary School, Babati Secondary School, Univ. of Dar es Salaam; after graduation joined Tanzania African Nat. Union (now Chama Cha Mapinduzi (CCM) party); seconded to Tanzania People's Defence Forces as Chief Political Instructor at Monduli Cen. Mil. Acad.; commissioned as Lt and retd Col 1992; Deputy Minister, Ministries of Finance, of Water and Livestock Devt, of Energy and Minerals 1987–90, Minister 1990–94; Chair. Council of Ministers of the E African Community; Minister of Foreign Affairs and Int. Co-operation 1995–2005; Pres. of Tanzania 2005–15; Chair. African Union Ass. 2008–09; Patron Tanzania Nat. Basketball Assen; Chair. Southern African Development Community Troika on Peace, Defence and Security 2012–13; Hon. Prof., China Agricultural Univ. 2014; Hon. DIur Univ. of St Thomas) 2006, (Univ. of Dar es Salaam) 2011, (Univ. of Guelph) 2013, (Univ. of Newcastle, Australia) 2015; Hon. DHumLitt (Kenyatta Univ.) 2008; Dr hc (Univ. of Dodoma) 2010, (Nelson Mandela–AIST) 2014; AAI African Nat. Achievement Award 2007, US Doctors for Africa Award 2009, Social Good Award, UN Foundation 2011, FANRPAN Policy Leadership Award 2012. ICCF Mengha Award, International Conservation Caucus Foundation 2013, Icon of Democracy Award, The Voice Magazine (Netherlands) 2014, Leadership Excellence Award, Pan-African Youth Union 2015, African Achievers Award, Inst. for Good Governance in Africa 2015.

KİLİÇ, Serdar; Turkish government official and diplomatist; *Ambassador to USA;* b. 1958, Samsun; m.; one c.; ed Ankara Univ.; with Ministry of Tourism and Culture 1977–82; mem. Bd of Dirs, Ekşioğlu Holding 1982–84; with Eastern Europe and Asia Dept, Ministry of Foreign Affairs 1984–87, Asst Attaché, then Attaché, Embassy in Kuwait 1987–89, Attaché, then Third Sec., Consulate General in Los Angeles 1989–92, Deputy Consul-Gen., Gulf and Muslim Countries Dept, Ministry of Foreign Affairs 1992–93, Second Sec., then First Sec., Perm. Del. of Turkey to NATO 1993–97, First Sec., Deputy Gen. Directorate of NATO and Euro-Atlantic Security and Defence Affairs, Ministry of Foreign Affairs 1997–99, Chief of Section and Acting Head of Dept, Perm. Del. to NATO 1999–2003, Counsellor and Head of Dept, Deputy Gen. Directorate of Balkans and Cen. Europe, Ministry of Foreign Affairs 2003–06, Acting Deputy Gen. Dir and Minister-Plenipotentiary, then Deputy Gen. Dir, Deputy Gen. Directorate of NATO and Euro-Atlantic Security and Defence Affairs 2006–08, Amb. to Lebanon 2008–10, Sec.-Gen. Nat. Security Council 2010–12, Amb. to Japan 2012–14, to USA 2014–. *Address:* Embassy of Turkey, 2525 Massachusetts Avenue, NW, Washington, DC 20008, USA (office). *Telephone:* (202) 612-6700 (office). *Fax:* (202) 612-6744 (office). *E-mail:* embassy.washingtondc@mfa.gov.tr (office); contact@turkishembassy.org (office). *Website:* www.washington.emb.mfa.gov.tr (office).

KILLIP, Christopher David; British photographer; *Professor of Visual Studies, Harvard University;* b. 11 July 1946, Isle of Man; s. of Allen Killip and Mary Quirk; one s.; ed Douglas High School for Boys; photography in Isle of Man 1969–71; Prof. of Visual Studies, Harvard Univ. 1991–; works in many public collections including Victoria & Albert Museum, George Eastman House, USA, Stedelijk Museum, Amsterdam, Nat. Gallery of Australia, Nat. Museum, Kraków; ACGB Photography Awards 1973–74, Northern Arts Photography Fellow 1975–76, ACGB Bursary Award 1977, Henri Cartier-Bresson Award, Paris 1989. *Publications:* Isle of Man 1980, In Flagrante 1988, Fifty-five 2001, Pirelli Work 2006, Here Comes Everybody 2009, Seacoal 2011, Arbeit (Work) 2012. *Address:* Harvard University, 24 Quincy Street, Cambridge, MA 02138, USA (office). *Website:* www.chriskillip.com.

KILLY, Jean-Claude; French business executive, sports administrator and fmr Olympic skier; b. 30 Aug. 1943, St-Cloud, Seine-et-Oise; s. of Robert Killy and Madeleine de Ridder; m. Danièlle Gaubert 1973 (died 1987); one d., two step-c.; ed Ecole de Val-d'Isère, Lycées in Chambéry, Grenoble, Saint-Jean-de-Maurienne, Bourg-Saint-Maurice; French champion 1964, 1965, 1966; won three gold medals at Winter Olympics, Grenoble, France 1968; retd from competitive skiing 1968 but returned in 1972 to become professional world champion in 1973; customs officer 1965–68; Publicity Agent, Gen. Motors 1968; Marketing Consultant (concerning skiing information) United Air Lines 1969; settled in Geneva 1969 and moved into the sports clothing business with co. Veleeda-Killy; Tech. Adviser Dynamic 1981; mem. Exec. Bd Alpine Cttee of Int. Skiing Fed. 1977–94; Pres. World Sport Marketing (now Amaury Sport Org.) 1992–2000, Société du Tour de France 1992–2001; fmr Chair. Coca-Cola France, mem. Admin Bd Coca-Cola 1993, Coca-Cola Enterprises 1997; mem. Int. Olympic Cttee 1995–2013, Co-Pres. Winter Olympics, Albertville 1992, Vice-Chair. Coordination Comm. for 2002 Winter Olympic Games in Salt Lake City 1996–2002, Chair. Co-ordination Comm. for 2006 Winter Olympic Games in Turin 2000–06, Coordination Comm. for 2014 Winter Olympic Games in Sochi 2007–14; mem. Bd of Dirs Rolex SA; mem. Organizing Cttee for 2009 Alpine FIS Ski World Championships 2002–07 (resgnd); Commdr, Légion d'honneur; IOC Olympic Order; Export Oscar 1982. *Film:* Snow Job 1972. *Publications:* Skiez avec Killy 1969, Le Ski 1978. *Leisure interests:* flying, reading, cycling, walking, swimming, snowboarding. *Address:* Killy, 21 rue du pré Faucon, 74940 Annecy le Vieux, France; CIO, Château de Vidy, 1007 Lausanne; 13 chemin Bellefontaine, 1223 Cologny -GE, Switzerland. *Website:* www.killy.com.

KILMAN, Sato; Ni-Vanuatu politician; b. 30 Dec. 1957; joined British Police Force in Vanuatu as Corporal 1977, apptd Commdr of Vanuatu Mobile Force (VMP) 1984, Asst Commr 1986, Commr of Police 1992–93; pursued business interests, SK Logging Co. 1993; Minister for the Comprehensive Reform Program 1999–2001, for Agric. 2002; MP for Lakatoro, Malekula Island 2004–07, 2008–; Deputy Prime Minister and Minister of Foreign Affairs 2004–07; Leader of the Opposition 2009–10; Deputy Prime Minister and Minister of Trade and Industry 2009–10, Prime Minister 2010–13 (resgnd), 2015–16, Minister for Public Service 2010–13, Minister of Foreign Affairs, Int. Co-operation and External Trade 2014–15; currently Pres. People's Progressive Party. *Address:* c/o Prime Minister's Office, PMB 9053, Port Vila, Vanuatu (office).

KILMER, Val Edward; American actor; b. 31 Dec. 1959, Los Angeles, Calif.; m. Joanne Whalley 1988 (divorced 1996); one d.; ed Hollywood's Professional School, Juilliard; began career in theatre then film debut in 1984; f. Blessed Films (production co.). *Films include:* Top Secret 1984, Real Genius 1985, Top Gun 1986, Willow 1988, Kill Me Again 1989, The Doors 1991, Thunderheart 1991, True Romance 1993, The Real McCoy 1993, Tombstone 1993, Wings of Courage 1995, Batman Forever 1995, Heat 1995, The Saint 1996, The Island of Dr Moreau 1996, The Ghost and the Darkness 1996, Dead Girl 1996, Joe the King 1999, At First Sight 1999, Planet Red 2000, Pollock 2000, Salton Sea 2002, Run for the Money 2002, Masked and Anonymous 2003, Wonderland 2003, Spartan 2004, Blind Horizon 2004, Mindhunters 2004, Alexander 2004, Kiss, Kiss, Bang, Bang 2005, Moscow Zero 2006, 10th & Wolf 2006, Played 2006, Summer Love 2006, Deja Vu 2006, The Ten Commandments: The Musical 2006, Felon 2008, Streets of Blood 2009, Hardwired 2009, Bad Lieutenant: Port of Call New Orleans 2009, The Traveler 2010, MacGruber 2010, Gun 2010, Twixt 2011, 7 Below 2012, Riddle 2013, Palo Alto 2013, Tom Sawyer & Huckleberry Finn 2014. *Stage appearances include:* Electra and Orestes, Henry IV Part One 1981, As You Like It 1982, Slab Boys (Broadway debut) 1983, Hamlet 1988, 'Tis Pity She's A Whore 1992, The Postman Always Rings Twice (Playhouse Theatre, London) 2005. *Television includes:* The Spoils of Babylon (mini-series) 2014. *Address:* CAA, 2000 Avenue of the Stars, Los Angeles, CA 90067, USA (office).

KILPATRICK, Helen, CB, MA; British accountant and civil servant; one s. one d.; ed King's Coll., Cambridge; Grad. Trainee (Finance), Greater London Council 1982–85, Group Auditor 1985–86; Group Accountant (Housing), London Borough of Tower Hamlets 1986–87, Chief Accountant (Technical) 1987–88; Asst Borough Treasurer, London Borough of Greenwich 1988–89, Controller of Financial Services 1989–95; Deputy Chief Exec. and Dir of Resources, W Sussex County Council 1985–2000, also Treas., Sussex Police Authority; Dir-Gen. for Finance and Corp. Services, Home Office 2005–13, also acting Home Office Perm. Sec. and Accounting Officer 2012–13; Gov. of Cayman Islands 2013–18. *Address:* c/o Office of the Governor, Government Administration Building, 133 Elgin Avenue, George Town, Grand Cayman KY1-9000, Cayman Islands (office).

KILPIÄ, Maj.-Gen. Juha; Finnish army officer and UN official; b. 1953; m.; one d.; ed Finnish War Coll., NATO School, Germany, NATO Defense Coll., Italy; commissioned in Army Command Finland 1977; served in several other posts in UN peacekeeping missions including Chief of Operations UN Interim Force in Lebanon (UNIFIL) 1991, UN Disengagement Observer Force (UNDOF) 1993; Battalion Commdr NATO Operations Joint Endeavour (IFOR)/Operation Joint Forge (SFOR) 1996–97; Commdr Multinational Task Force in EU operation 2004–05; Mil. Rep. to EU and NATO, Brussels 2007–09; Chief of Staff, Army Command 2009–11; Head of Mission and Chief of Staff UN Truce Supervision Org. (UNTSO) 2011–13. *Address:* c/o Ministry of Foreign Affairs, Merikasarmi, Laivastokatu 22, POB 176, 00023 Helsinki, Finland.

KIM, Anatoly Andreyevich; Russian writer; b. 15 June 1939, S Kazakhstan; ed Literary Inst., Moscow; freelance writer 1973–; Prof. of Russian Language and Literature, Inst. of Journalism, Moscow; lecturer in S Korea 1991–95. *Publications include:* more than 20 books including novels: Gatherers of Herbs 1976, Litis 1980, Squirrel 1984, Forest-Father 1989, Onlyrya 1995, Mushroom Picking with Bach's Music 1997, The Wall 1998, Twins 2000; numerous short stories; film scripts: My Sister Lucy, Revenge, To Go Out of the Forest. *Address:* Akademika Pavlova str. 36, apt. 112, 121552 Moscow, Russia (home). *Telephone:* (495) 140-15-31 (home).

KIM, Choong-soo, BA, PhD; South Korean economist, government official, diplomatist and central banker; b. 6 June 1947; ed Seoul Nat. Univ., Univ. of Pennsylvania, USA; Research Asst, Korea Devt Inst. 1973–76, Dir, Office of Research Planning & Coordination 1988–91, Dir, Econ. Information and Educ. Center 1991–93, Pres. 2002–05; Research Assoc., Wharton Econometric Forecasting Associates Inc., USA 1976–79; Sr Research Assoc., Center for Human Resource Research, Ohio State Univ. 1979–88; Sec. to Pres. for Econ. Affairs, Office of Pres. of Repub. of Korea 1993–95, Minister and Head of OECD Office, Embassy in Paris 1995–97; Asst Minister and Special Adviser to Deputy Prime Minister, Ministry of Finance and Economy Mar–Aug. 1997; Pres., Korea Inst. of Public Finance 1997–98; Dean, Graduate School of Pan-Pacific Int. Studies, Kyung Hee Univ. 1998; Pres., Hallym Univ. 2007–08; Sr Sec. to Pres. for Econ. Affairs Feb.–June 2008; Amb. and Perm. Rep. to OECD, Paris 2008–10; Gov. Bank of Korea (central bank) and Chair. Monetary Policy Cttee 2010–14; Chair. BIS Asian Consultative Council 2012; James Joo-Jin Kim Visiting Prof. of Korean Studies, Univ. of Pennsylvania 2014–15.

KIM, Dong-jin, BS, PhD; South Korean automotive industry executive; b. 4 Dec. 1950; m.; two c.; ed Seoul Nat. Univ., Finlay Eng Coll., USA; research engineer, Korea Inst. of Science and Tech. 1972; sr research engineer, Agency for Defence Devt 1973–78; Man. Hyundai Heavy Industries Co. Ltd 1978–79, Sr Exec. Vice-Pres. Hyundai Precision & Industry Co. Ltd 1979–98, Pres. and CEO Hyundai Space & Aircraft Co. Ltd 1998–99, Pres. Hyundai Motor Co. 2000–03, then Vice-Chair. and Co-CEO, Pres. and CEO Hyundai Star Commercial Vehicle Systems, Inc., apptd Vice-Chair. Hyundai Mobis 2008; Order of Nat. Security Merit (Samil-Jang) 1985; Prize of Devotion Merit, Seoul Nat. Univ. School of Eng 1998.

KIM, Dong-yeon, LLB, MA, PhD; South Korean economist and politician; b. 1957, Eumseong, N Chungcheong Prov.; ed Kookjae Univ., Seoul Nat. Univ., Michigan Univ.; began career as officer with Econ. Planning Bd 1982; more than 20 years in govt posts, several key econ. and policy-related positions mainly in Ministry of Planning and Budget and Ministry of Finance and Economy, including Dir, Asia–Europe Meeting (ASEM) Preparatory and Planning Cttee, Ministry of Finance and Economy 1999–2002; Project Man., Int. Bank for Reconstruction and Devt (IBRD) 2002; Sr Public Sector Specialist and Project Man., World Bank 2002–05; fmr Chief Coordinator to Chief of Staff to the Pres., later Sr Sec. to the Pres. for Economy and Finance, Office of the Pres., Dir-Gen. for Strategy Planning, Ministry of Planning and Budget 2005–06, Dir-Gen. for Industrial Fiscal Planning 2006–07; Deputy Minister for Budget, Ministry of Strategy and Finance 2010–12, Second Vice Minister 2012–13; Minister for Govt Policy Coordination, Prime Minister's Office 2013–14; Deputy Prime Minister and Minister of Strategy and Finance 2017–18; Pres., Ajou Univ. 2015–; mem. Seoul Forum for Int. Affairs. *Publications:* various papers and policy reports on an extensive range of topics including budgeting, expenditure frameworks and performance management. *Address:* c/o Ministry of Strategy and Finance, Govt Complex, 477, Galmae-ro, Sejong City 30109, Republic of Korea (office).

KIM, Gye-kwan; North Korean politician and diplomatist; *First Vice-Minister, Ministry of Foreign Affairs;* b. 6 July 1943, North Pyongan; participated in Pyongyang-Washington negotiations and Geneva talks as working-level rep. of N Korea; travelled widely in Europe before 1993; served as Amb.-at-Large and maintained ties with socialist parties in Western Europe; designated Deputy Negotiator in first nuclear talks with USA, later Chief Negotiator; head of del. to four-party talks between N Korea and S Korea, China and USA to address Korean peninsula issues; Vice-Minister, Ministry of Foreign Affairs –2010, First Vice-Minister 2010–. *Address:* Ministry of Foreign Affairs, Pyongyang, Democratic People's Republic of Korea (office).

KIM, Hak-su, BA, MA, PhD; South Korean international civil servant, economist and academic; b. 27 Feb. 1938, Wonju, Kangwon; ed Yonsei Univ., Univ. of Edinburgh, UK, Univ. of S Carolina, USA; economist, Cen. Bank 1960; Sec. to Minister of Commerce and Industry 1969; London Rep., Bank of Korea 1971–73; Exec. Dir Daewoo Corpn 1977, later Pres.; Chief Planning Officer, Chief Tech. Advisor UN Dept for Tech. Co-operation and Devt 1980s; Sr Research Fellow, Korea Inst. for Int. Econ. Policy 1989–93; Pres. Hanil Banking Inst. 1993–95; Sec.-Gen. of the Colombo Plan, Sri Lanka 1995–99; Korean Amb. for Int. Econ. Affairs 1999; UN Under-Sec.-Gen. and Exec. Sec. UN ESCAP 2000–07; Distinguished Visiting Prof., Grad. School of Int. Studies, Yonsei Univ., Seoul 2007–. *Leisure interests:* classical music, trekking, walking. *Address:* Graduate School of International Studies, Yonsei University, 134 Sinchon-dong Seodamun-gu, Seoul 120-749 (office); 319-1601 Hanyong Apt, Bundang, Kyunggi, Republic of Korea (home). *Telephone:* (2) 2123-6297 (office); (2) 656-7556 (home). *E-mail:* magkim16@hotmail.com (office). *Website:* gsis.yonsei.ac.kr (office).

KIM, Hwang-sik, LLB; South Korean lawyer and politician; b. 9 Aug. 1948, Jangseong; ed Seoul Nat. Univ., Philipps-Universität Marburg, Germany; Judge, Seoul Dist Civil Court, Seoul Dist Criminal Court, Seoul High Court 1974–89, Sr Judge, Jeonju Dist Court 1989–96, Sr Judiciary Research Officer, Supreme Court 1997–2000, Chief Judge, Gwangju Dist Court 2004–05, Justice, Supreme Court 2005–08; Vice-Minister, Nat. Court Admin 2005; Chair. Bd of Audit and Inspection 2008–10; Sec.-Gen. Asian Org. of Supreme Audit Insts 2009–10; Prime Minister 2010–13. *Address:* c/o Office of the Prime Minister, 55, Sejong-no, Jongno-gu, Seoul 110-760, Republic of Korea.

KIM, Vice-Marshal (retd) Il-chol; North Korean government official (retd); b. 1933, Pyongyang; ed Mangyongdae Revolutionary School, Navy Acad., USSR; apptd Commdr East Sea Fleet 1970; mem. Party Cen. Cttee 1980–2010; Deputy in Supreme People's Ass. 1982–2010; apptd Commdr of Navy 1982; rank of Lt-Gen. 1982, Col-Gen. 1985, Gen. 1992, Vice-Marshal 1997; First Minister of the People's Armed Forces 1997–98, Minister 1998–2010; Vice-Chair. Nat. Defence Comm. 1998–2010; Kim Il Sung medal 1982, Nat. Flag Order, Nat. Hero title 1995.

KIM, Jae-ryong; North Korean party official and politician; *Premier;* briefly banished to rural farm for re-education 2015; mem. Korean Workers' Party (KWP), Chair. Chagang Prov. KWP Cttee 2015, Kangwon Prov. KWP Cttee 2016; mem. KWP Cen. Cttee 2016–, KWP Political Bureau (politburo) 2019–; mem. Supreme People's Ass. (SPA, parl.); mem. Central Mil. Comm. 2019–; Premier 2019–; visited Russia and People's Repub. of China as special envoy of Kim Jong-un. *Address:* Office of the Premier, Pyongyang, Democratic People's Republic of Korea (office).

KIM, Gen. (retd) Jang-soo, MA; South Korean fmr army officer, government official and diplomatist; b. 1948, Gwangju; m. Park Hyo-sook; one s. one d.; ed Korea Mil. Acad., Korea Nat. Defence Univ., Yonsei Univ.; served in several key posts in Army, including Chief of Operations Div., First Army, Commdg Gen., 6th Infantry Div. 1997–99, Dir, Operational Planning, Jt Chiefs of Staff 1999–2000, Dir, Operations 2000–01, Commdg Gen., VII Corps 2001–03, Chief Dir, Jt Operations, Jt Chiefs of Staff 2003–04, Deputy Commdr Korea-US Combined Forces Command and Chief Operations and Strategy Dir Jt Chiefs of Staff 2004–05, Army Chief of Staff 2005–06; Minister of Nat. Defence 2006–08; mem. Nat. Ass. (Saenuri Party) 2008–12; Chief, Nat. Security Office 2013–15; apptd Amb. to People's Repub. of China 2015.

KIM, Ji-woon; South Korean filmmaker and screenwriter; b. 6 July 1964, Seoul. *Films:* Choyonghan kajok (The Quiet Family, writer, dir) 1998, Banchikwang (The Foul King, writer, dir) 2000, Coming Out (writer, dir) 2001, Saam gaang (Three, segment 'Memories', dir, writer) 2002, Janghwa, Hongryeon (A Tale of Two Sisters, writer, dir) 2003, Dalkomhan insaeng (A Bittersweet Life, writer, dir) 2005, The Good, the Bad, the Weird 2008, I Saw the Devil 2010, The Last Stand 2013, The Age of Shadows 2016.

KIM, Jim Yong, AB, MD, PhD; American (b. South Korean) physician, university administrator and international organization official; b. 8 Dec. 1959, Seoul, South Korea; m. Younsook Lim; two s.; ed Brown Univ., Harvard Univ.; Founding Trustee, Partners in Health (Harvard-affiliated nonprofit org.) 1987, mem. Bd of Dirs 1987–2003, 2019–, Exec. Dir –2003; apptd by WHO to help lead int. response to drug-resistant tuberculosis by establishing pilot MDR TB treatment programmes and organizing effective delivery systems for antibiotics 1999; Lecturer in Social Medicine, Dept of Social Medicine, Harvard Medical School 1993–95, Instructor in Social Medicine 1995–2000, Asst Prof. of Medical Anthropology 2000–03, Asst Prof. of Medicine, Dept of Medicine 2002–03, Assoc. Prof. of Social Medicine and Assoc. Prof. of Medicine 2003–05, Assoc. Clinical Prof. of Medicine and Assoc. Clinical Prof. of Social Medicine 2005–06, François-Xavier Bagnoud Prof. of Health and Human Rights, Harvard School of Public Health 2005–09, Prof. of Medicine and Prof. of Social Medicine, Harvard Medical School 2006–09; Co-Chief Div. of Social Medicine and Health Inequalities, Brigham and Women's Hosp., Boston 2002–03; Sr Adviser to Dir-Gen. WHO 2003–06, Dir Dept of HIV/AIDS 2004–06; Pres. Dartmouth Coll. 2009–12; Pres. World Bank Group, Washington, DC 2012–19; co-Chair. World Econ. Forum Annual Meeting, Davos 2015; mem. American Anthropological Asscn 1984–, Soc. for Medical Anthropology 1986–, Soc. for Latin American Anthropology 1996–, Int. Union Against Tuberculosis and Lung Disease 1997–, Critical Anthropology of Health Working Group 1999–, Inst. of Medicine of NAS 2004–, American Acad. of Arts and Sciences 2010–; John D. and Catherine T. MacArthur Foundation Genius Fellowship 2003, Treatment Action Group "Research in Action" Award 2007, William Rogers Award for Service to Soc., Brown Univ. Alumni Asscn 2008, Distinguished Leadership Award, Korean American Coalition 2008. *Publication:* Dying for Growth: Global Inequality and the Health of the Poor (co-ed.). *Address:* c/o World Bank Group, 1818 H Street NW, Washington, DC 20433, USA (office).

KIM, Jin-pyo, MA; South Korean politician; b. 4 May 1947, Suwon, Gyeonggi Prov.; ed Gyeongbok High School, Seoul Nat. Univ., Univ. of Wisconsin, USA; Dir Consumption Tax Bureau, Ministry of Finance 1983, Dir Tax Policy Section 1988, Dir-Gen. Tax Systems Bureau 1993, Dir-Gen. Foreign Trade Affairs Bureau 1995, Asst Minister, Taxations, Ministry of Finance and Economy 1999, Vice Minister of Finance and Economy 2001; Sr Presidential Sec. for Policy and Planning Jan.–June 2002; Minister of Govt Policy Co-ordination 2002–03; Deputy Prime Minister and Minister of Finance 2003–04; Deputy Prime Minister and Minister of Educ. and Human Resources Devt –2006; mem. Nat. Ass. for Gyeonggi-do (Suwon-si Mu) 2004–, served as Democratic United Party floor leader, now mem. Minjoo Party of Korea, currently mem. National Defense Cttee, Special Cttee on Budget and Accounts, Special Cttee on Decentralization and Local Financing; Hon. Dr Public Admin (Univ. of the Cumberlands, Williamsburg, USA). *Publication:* Looking on the Bright Side: Korean Economy 2004. *Address:* National Assembly (Kuk Hoe), 1 Uisadang-daero, Yeongdeungpo-gu, Seoul 07233, Republic of Korea (office). *Telephone:* (2) 788-2001 (office). *Fax:* (2) 788-3375 (office). *E-mail:* webmaster@assembly.go.kr (office). *Website:* www.assembly.go.kr (office).

KIM, Vice-Marshal Jong Gak; North Korean army officer and politician; b. 1941, Jungsan County, South Phyongan Prov.; ed Kim Il-sung Mil. Univ.; joined Korean People's Army (KPA) Aug. 1959, attained rank of Col-Gen. 1992, Gen. 2002, Vice-Marshal 2012, First Deputy Dir KPA Gen. Political Bureau 2007–; mem. Korean Workers' Party (KWP), alt. mem. KWP Cen. Cttee 1991, alt. mem. Politburo and mem. Cen. Mil. Comm. 2010–; Vice-Minister of People's Armed Forces 1992, Minister April–Nov. 2012; mem. Supreme People's Ass. (Parl.) 1998–; mem. Nat. Defence Comm. 2009–13. *Address:* c/o Ministry of People's Armed Forces, Pyongyang, Democratic People's Republic of Korea (office).

KIM, Jong-sik, BEng, MEng; South Korean business executive; b. 4 June 1953; ed Yeungnam Univ., Kyungpook Nat. Univ.; fmr Head of Display Production and Head of Quality Control and Procurement, LG Electronics Co. Ltd, Head of Module Centre LG.Philips LCD 2006–07, Exec. Vice-Pres. LG Display Co. Ltd 2006–07, Chief Production Officer 2007–10, apptd COO 2010, apptd Pres. 2011; Pres. and CEO Hana Information and System Co. Ltd at Hana Bank; Ind. Dir STX Corpn. *Address:* c/o LG Display Company Ltd, LG Twin Tower, 128, Yeoui-daero, Yeongdeungpo-gu, Seoul 140-716, Republic of Korea. *Telephone:* (2) 3777-1010.

KIM, Marshal Jong-un; North Korean politician and army officer; *Supreme Leader;* b. 8 Jan. 1984, Pyongyang; s. of Kim Jong-il and Koh Young-hee; m. Ri Sol-ju; one d.; ed Int. School of Berne, Switzerland (disputed), Kim Il-sung Univ.; rank of Daejang (four-star Gen.) in Korean People's Army (KPA) 2010, rank of Marshal 2012, Supreme Commdr of KPA Dec. 2011–; Vice-Chair. Cen. Mil. Comm. of Korean Workers' Party (KWP) Sept. 2010–, First Sec. KWP 2012–, Chair. KWP 2016–; declared Supreme Leader, Democratic People's Repub. of Korea (following death of his father) Dec. 2011–, Chair. Nat. Defence Comm. 2012–16; Chair. State Affairs Comm. 2016–. *Leisure interests:* skiing, basketball. *Address:* Korean Workers' Party, Pyongyang, Democratic People's Republic of Korea (office). *Website:* www.rodong.rep.kp (office).

KIM, Jong-yang, BA; South Korean police officer and international organization official; *President, Interpol;* b. 30 Oct. 1961, Changwon; ed Korea Univ., Seoul Nat. Univ., Dongguk Univ.; Head, Anti-Crime Div., Pusan Nambu Police Station 1992–93, Head, Investigation Div. 1993–95; Section Chief, Intelligence Div., Korean Nat. Police Agency (KNPA) 1995–99; Chief, Gyeongnam Gosung Police Station 1999–2000; Dir, Public Security and Traffic Affairs Div., Ulsan Metropolitan Police Agency 2000–01; Chief, Ulsan Jungbu Police Station 2001–04, Seoul Seongbuk Police Station 2004–05; Asst Sec., Information and Policy Monitoring Office, Office of the Pres. 2005–07; Police Attaché, Consulate-Gen. of Repub. of Korea, Los Angeles 2007–09; Dir-Gen., Nat. Security Dept, Seoul Metropolitan Police Agency 2010–11; Dir-Gen., Foreign Affairs Bureau, KNPA 2011–12; Commr, Gyeongnam Provincial Police Agency 2012–13; Dir-Gen., Planning and Coordination Bureau, KNPA 2013–14; Head, Interpol Nat. Central Bureau, Seoul 2011–12, Del., Interpol Exec. Cttee 2012–15, Vice Pres. 2015–18, Pres. Interpol 2018–. *Address:* Interpol General Secretariat, 200, quai Charles de Gaulle, 69006 Lyons, France (office). *Telephone:* (4) 72-44-71-63 (office). *Website:* www.interpol.int (office).

KIM, Joong-kyum, BS; South Korean business executive; ed Korea Univ.; fmr Pres. Hyundai Engineering & Construction; Pres. and CEO Korea Electric Power Corpn (KEPCO) 2011–12; Chair. Korea Atomic Industrial Forum, Organizing Cttee World Energy Congress, Daegu 2013. *Address:* c/o Korea Electric Power Corporation, 411 Yeongdong-daero, Gangnam-gu, Seoul 135-791, Republic of Korea. *E-mail:* info@kepco.co.kr.

KIM, Jung-ju, MA, PhD; South Korean business executive; *Founder and CEO, Nexon Corporation;* b. 22 Feb. 1968; m. Yoo Jung Hyun; two c.; ed Korea Advanced

Inst. of Science and Tech.; Founder and CEO Nexon Corpn (online gaming co.) 1994–, also CEO NXC Corpn; Dir GS HomeShopping. *Address:* Nexon Corporation, Minerva Bldg 2/F, 694-25 Yeoksam-dong, Gangnam-gu, Seoul 135-080, Republic of Korea (office). *Telephone:* (2) 2019-8600 (office). *Website:* company .nexon.com (office).

KIM, Jung-won; South Korean business executive; b. 3 March 1948; ed Kyungnam Sr High School, Guilford Coll., New York; joined Hanil Synthetic Fiber Ind. Co. Ltd 1972, Exec. Man. Dir 1974, Vice-Pres. 1975, Pres. 1979–; Pres. Hanhyo Co. Ltd 1977, Chair. 1984–; Pres. Hanhyo Devt Co. Ltd 1978, apptd Chair. 1984; Pres. Kyungnam Woollen Textile Co. Ltd 1979; First Chair. Hanhyo Acad. 1982; Pres. Korean Amateur Volleyball Asscn 1983, Vice-Pres. Asian Volleyball Asscn 1983; awarded Saemaul Decoration 1974; First Hon. Consul Kingdom of the Netherlands 1985.

KIM, Gen. (retd) Kwan-jin; South Korean politician and fmr army officer; b. 27 Aug. 1949, Jeonju; m.; three d.; ed German Army Office Acad., Korea Mil. Acad., Seoul; commissioned as Infantry Second Lt 1972, becoming Bn Commdr and Div. G-3, 15th Infantry Div. 1983–88, Commdr, 26th Mechanics Brigade, Capital Mechanics Div. 1990–92, Chief of Mil. Strategy, J-5 Directorate, Jt Chiefs of Staff 1992–93, Asst to Pres. for Nat. Defence, Office of the Presidential Secr. 1994–96, Sec.-Gen. Staff, Army HQ 1996–98, Chief of Strategic Planning, Army HQ 1998–99, Commdg Gen., 35th Infantry Div. 1999–2000, Deputy Chief of Staff, Planning and Man., Army HQ 2000–02, Commdg Gen., 2nd Corps 2002–04, Chief Dir of Operations, Jt Chiefs of Staff 2004–05, Commdg Gen., 3rd Repub. of Korea Army 2005–06, Chair. of Jt Chiefs of Staff 2006–08; Minister of Nat. Defence 2010–14; Chief Nat. Security Office 2014–17. *Address:* c/o Ministry of National Defence, 22, Itaewon-ro, Yongsan-gu, Seoul 04383, Republic of Korea (office). *Telephone:* (2)748-1111 (office). *E-mail:* cyber@mnd.go.kr (office). *Website:* www .mnd.go.kr (office).

KIM, Oi-hyun, PhD; South Korean business executive; *President and COO, Hyundai Heavy Industries Company Limited;* b. 1 May 1954; ed Seoul Nat. Univ., Univ. of Ulsan; Sr Exec. Vice-Pres. and COO Shipbuilding Div., Hyundai Heavy Industries Co. Ltd –2011, Vice-Pres. and Co-CEO 2011–13, Vice-Chair. and Dir 2011–13, Pres. and Co-CEO 2013–14, Pres. and COO 2014–. *Address:* Hyundai Heavy Industries Co. Ltd, 1000 Bangeojinsunhwan-doro Dong-gu, Ulsan 682-792, Republic of Korea (office). *Telephone:* (52) 230-2114 (office). *Fax:* (52) 230-3470 (office). *E-mail:* ir@hhi.co.kr (office); webzine@hhi.co.kr (office). *Website:* www.hhi .co.kr (office).

KIM, Seung-youn; South Korean business executive; m.; three c.; Owner, Hanwha Eagles Professional Baseball Club 1981–; Chair. The Kyunghyang Shinmun (daily newspaper) 1986–97, Bank of Athens, Greece 1993–97, Hanwha Bank Hungary Ltd 1995–2001, Korea Life Insurance Co. Ltd 2002–05; apptd Chair. and CEO Hanwha Chemical Corpn 2008, then Chair. Hanwha Group –2014 (resgnd); mem. Bd of Dirs Overseas Contracts, Pacific Construction Co. Ltd 1977–78 (Pres. 1978–80), Korea Int. Trade Asscn 1977–78; Chair. Korea Certification Asscn for Quality and Environmental Man. 1993–97, Korea-US Exchange Council 1997, Devt Cttee, Univ. for Peace 2000, 2004–06; Chair. Ad Hoc Cttee on Corp. Restructuring, Fed. of Korean Industries 1999–2000, Cttee on Int. Co-operation 2000–04; Vice-Chair., Admin. HQ, Korea Explosives Group 1980–81, Korea Man. Asscn 1981, Fed. of Korean Industries 1985, Korea Employers' Fed. 1990, Korea-Japan Co-operation Foundation for Industry and Tech. 1996–; Pres. Korea Amateur Boxing Fed. 1980–81, 1982–96, Asian Amateur Boxing Asscn 1982–97, Gen. Asscn of the Asian Sports Feds 1983–98; Vice-Pres. Korean Olympic Cttee 1981–97 (Adviser 2006), Korea Sports Council 1992–98; Chair. Bd of Trustees, SungKongHoe (Anglican Communion and Church) Univ. 1996–2000; apptd Dir, Korean Union of Youth 1981, Korean Asscn of UN 1986 (Chair. 2006–07, 2008), Korea Bang Jung Hwan Foundation 2000–03; mem. Advisory Cttee, Korea-Japan Co-operation Council 1997–2003, World Bd of Govs, United Service Orgs Inc. 1998; Amb. for Int. Economy and Trade and Special Envoy of the Pres. of Repub. of Korea 2002–03; Amb. for Int. Exchange and Co-operation 2003–04; Chair. Foundation for Better Boxing, Int. Boxing Asscn 2009; Hon. Consul Gen. of Greece in Korea 1984–93, 2007; Hon. Pres. Gen. Asscn of the Asian Sports Feds 1991; Hon. Chair. Korea-Israel Chamber of Commerce 1994–, Korea-Greece Friendship Asscn 2009; Grand Business Founder Award, Korean Acad. of Business Historians 2009.

KIM, Soo-bong, BS, MS, PhD; South Korean particle physicist and academic; *Assistant Professor of Physics, Seoul National University;* b. 1960, Busan; ed Seoul Nat. Univ., Univ. of Pennsylvania; Research Asst Fellow, Dept of Physics, Univ. of Pennsylvania 1985–89, Postdoctoral Fellow 1989–90; Postdoctoral Fellow, Dept of Physics, Univ. of Michigan 1990–92, Research Investigator 1992–96; Research Asst Prof., Dept of Physics, Boston Univ. 1996–98; Asst Prof., Dept of Physics, Seoul National Univ. 1998–2002, currently Asst Prof.; COE Visiting Prof., High Energy Accelerator Research Org. (KEK) 1997–98; Visiting Scientist, Fermi National Accelerator Lab. 2002–03; Fellow, Korean Physical Soc. 1998–; mem. Int. Advisory Cttee, Int. Conference on Physics in Collision 1999–, IEEE NSS/MIC CIP 2000–; LG Fellowship 2001; Asahi Prize (as member of Kamiokande-II) 1988, 1999, Rossi Prize (as member of Kamiokande-II), High Energy Astrophysics Division, American Astronomical Soc. 1989, Bruno Pontecorvo Prize (shared with Wang Yifang and Kōichirō Nishikawa) 2016. *Publications:* numerous articles in scientific journals. *Address:* Gwanak Campus, Bldg 27, Room 203A, Department of Physics, Seoul National University, Shilim-dong, Kwanak-ku, Seoul 151-742, Republic of Korea (office). *Telephone:* (2) 880-5755 (office). *Fax:* (2) 884-3002 (office). *E-mail:* sbkim@phya.snu.ac.kr (office). *Website:* physics.snu.ac.kr (office).

KIM, Ssang-su, BA, BS; South Korean business executive; *President, ACE Technologies Corporation;* b. 2 Jan. 1945, Gimcheon, N Gyeongsang Prov.; m. Shin Kyung-sook; two d. one s.; ed Seongui High School, Coll. of Eng and Science, Hanyang Univ.; joined LG Electronics (fmrly named Goldstar) as engineer 1969, various sr positions include Factory Head in Refrigerator Div., Pres. of Living System Co., and Pres. of Digital Appliance Co. –2000, Vice-Chair. and CEO 2003–08; Pres. and CEO Korea Electric Power Corpn (KEPCO) 2008–11; Pres. ACE Technologies Corpn 2011–; named The Star of Asia, US Business Week 2003. *Leisure interests:* mountain-climbing, golf, reading. *Address:* ACE Technologies Corpn, 451-3 Nonhyeon-dong, Namdong-gu, Incheon 405-849, Republic of Korea (office). *Telephone:* (32) 458-1050 (office). *Fax:* (32) 458-1929 (office). *E-mail:* webmaster@aceteq.co.kr (office). *Website:* www.acetech.co.kr (office).

KIM, Suk-joon, BA; South Korean business executive; *Chairman and CEO, SsangYong Engineering and Construction Co;* b. 9 April 1955, Gyeongsang Prov.; m.; two s. one d.; ed Korea Univ., Seoul; mil. service Repub. of Korea Marine Corps 1972–75; planning office SsangYong Corpn 1977–79, NY and LA br. offices SsangYong (USA) Inc. 1979–82, Dir Planning and Project Man. Div. SsangYong Eng and Construction Co. Ltd 1982–83, CEO 1983–95, 2018–, Pres. 1983–92, Chair. 1992–95, Chair. and Co-CEO 2010, Vice-Chair. SsangYong Business Group (later SsangYong Corpn) 1991–93, 1994–95, CEO 1991–93, 1994, Chair. 1995, Chair., CEO SsangYong Motor Co. 1994–95, Chair., CEO SsangYong Cement Industrial Co. 1995; Co-Chair. Korean Party Korea-France High-Level Businessmens' Club, Korean Party Korea-Singapore Econ. Co-operation Cttee; Vice-Chair. Korea-Japan Econ. Asscn, Fed. of Korean Industries, Korean Employers' Fed.; mem. Korea Chamber of Commerce and Industries; Dir Bd of Trustees Kookmin Univ.; Baden-Powell World Fellow, World Scout Foundation; Industrial Service Merit 1986, Order of Industrial Service Merit Silver Tower 1987, Order of Industrial Service Merit Gold Tower 1991. *Address:* SsangYong Engineering and Construction Co., 9/f Daihanjedang Bldg., 7 - 23 Shincheon-Dong, Songpa-Gu, Seoul 138-240, Republic of Korea (office). *Telephone:* (2) 3433-7114 (office). *Fax:* (2) 3433-7111 (office). *E-mail:* ssyenc@ssyenc.com (office). *Website:* www.ssyenc.com (office).

KIM, Suk-soo; South Korean lawyer, politician and judge; b. 20 Nov. 1932; ed Yonsei Univ.; admitted to Korean Bar 1958; Judge Advocate, Repub. of Korea Army HQ 1960–63; judge, Masan Br., Court of Pusan Dist Court 1963–67, Pusan Dist Court 1967–69, Incheon Br., Court of Seoul Civil and Criminal Dist Court 1969–70, Seoul Criminal Dist Court 1970–71, Seoul High Court 1971–73; Research Judge, Supreme Court 1973–74; Presiding Judge, Pusan Dist Court 1974–77, Sungbook Br., Court of Seoul Dist Court 1977–79, Seoul Civil Dist Court 1979–80; Chief Judge, Incheon Br., Court of Suwon Dist Court 1980–81; Presiding Judge, Seoul High Court and Chief Judge Nambu Br., Seoul Dist Court 1981–83; Sr Presiding Judge, Seoul High Court 1983–86; Chief Judge, Pusan Dist Court 1986–88; Vice-Minister of Court Admin 1988–91; Supreme Court Justice 1991–97; Chair. Nat. Election Comm. 1993–97; Chair. Judicial Officers' Ethics Cttee of Supreme Court 1997–2001; Chair. Korea Press Ethics Comm. 2000–02; Chair. Govt Public Service Ethics Cttee 2002; Prime Minister of Repub. of Korea 2002–03; Auditor Bd of Dirs Yonsei Univ. Foundation 1997–2002; Dir Samsung Electronics Co. 1999–2001, Yonsei Law Promotion Foundation 2002; Order of Service Merit (Blue Stripes) 1997; Hon. PhD (Yonsei Univ.) 1997.

KIM, Sun-dong, MBA; South Korean petroleum industry executive; b. 1942; ed Seoul Nat. Univ.; with Korea Oil Corpn 1963–74; Man. SsangYong Cement Industrial Co. Ltd 1974–76, Dir SsangYong Corpn 1978–80; Man. Dir S-Oil Corpn 1980–84, Exec. Dir 1984–87, Vice-Pres. 1987–91, Pres. and CEO 1991–98, Vice-Chair. and CEO 1998–2000, Chair. and CEO 2000–07, apptd Chair. 2007; mem. Korea Petroleum Asscn (Chair. 1997).

KIM, Sung-hwan, BEcons; South Korean diplomatist and politician; b. 13 April 1953; m.; two d.; ed Seoul Nat. Univ., Univ. of London, UK; joined Ministry of Foreign Affairs (MOFA) 1977, becoming Vice-Consul, Consulate-Gen. in Honolulu, USA 1980, Asst Sec., Office of the Pres. 1987, First Sec., Embassy in New Delhi 1988–90, First Sec., Embassy in Moscow 1990–94, Dir E Europe Div., European Affairs Bureau, MOFA 1994–95, Aide to Minister of Foreign Affairs 1995–96, Counsellor, Embassy in Washington, DC 1996–2000, Deputy Dir-Gen., N American Affairs Bureau, Ministry of Foreign Affairs and Trade (MOFAT) 2000, Sr Aide to Minister 2000, Dir-Gen., N American Affairs Bureau 2001–02 Amb. to Uzbekistan 2002–05, Deputy Minister for Planning and Man., MOFAT 2005–06, Amb. to Austria and Perm. Rep. to Int. Orgs. in Vienna 2006–08, Vice Minister of Foreign Affairs and Trade March–June 2008, Sr Sec. to Pres. for Foreign Affairs and Nat. Security 2008–10, Minister of Foreign Affairs and Trade 2010–13. *Address:* Saenuri Party, 14-31, Yeouido-dong, Yeongdeungpo-gu, Seoul, 156-768, Republic of Korea. *Telephone:* (2) 3786-3000. *Fax:* (2) 3786-3610. *Website:* www .saenuriparty.kr.

KIM, Gen. Tae-young, BA; South Korean army officer and government official; b. 13 Jan. 1949, Seoul; m. Lee Beom-sook; one s. one d.; ed Repub. of Korea Mil. Acad., Sogang Univ., West German Mil. Acad.; commissioned as Second Lt 1973; Commdr 26th Artillery Bn 1984; Exec. Asst to Chair. of Jt Chiefs of Staff 1989–91; Commdr Artillery Regt, 8th Infantry Div. 1991–93; Vice Commdr 56th Infantry Div. 1993–95; Chief of Strategic Planning Jt Chiefs of Staff 1995–96; Exec. Defence Asst to Blue House (Office of Pres.) 1996–97; Commdr 6th Artillery Brigade 1997–98; Exec. Asst to Minister of Nat. Defence 1998–2000; Commdr 23rd Infantry Div. 2000–02; Deputy Chief of Staff for Planning and Man., Repub. of Korea Army HQ 2002–03; Dir-Gen. Policy Planning Bureau, Ministry of Nat. Defence 2003–04; Commanding Gen. Capital Defence Command 2004–05; Chief Dir for Operations, Jt Chiefs of Staff 2005–06; Commanding Gen. 1st Repub. of Korea Army 2006; Chair. Jt Chiefs of Staff 2008; Minister of Nat. Defence 2009–10 (resgnd); fmr Prof., Korean Mil. Acad. *Leisure interests:* running marathons, swimming, playing tennis.

KIM, Taek-jin, MSc; South Korean computer engineer and business executive; *Chairman and CEO, NCSoft Corporation;* m. Yoon Song-yee; one c.; ed Seoul Nat. Univ.; co-author of Hangul (Korean-language word-processing program) while at Univ. 1989; cr. Hanmesoft (computer software) 1989; staff mem. Research and Devt Centre, Hyundai Electronics Industries Co. (now Hynix) 1991–92, Head of Devt Team for Shinbiro (S Korea's first internet service provider), 1994; cr. Lineage (online fantasy computer game) 1997, expanded to Taiwan markets 2000, has signed up five million users –2002; Founder, Chair. and CEO NCSoft Corpn 1997–, est. subsidiaries and jt ventures in USA, Japan, Hong Kong and China; Regional Dir Microsoft Corpn 1998; Man of the Year, Computer Reporters Asscn 1989, New Venture Age Leader, Naeway Economic Daily 2000, Industrial Medal, Soft Expo/Digital Contents Fair 2001, Best Contrib. to Cultural Industry, Ministry of Culture and Tourism 2001. *Address:* NCSoft Corpn, 157-33 Oksan Bldg., Samsung-dong, Gangnam-gu, Seoul 135-090, Republic of Korea (office). *Telephone:* (2) 2186-3300 (office). *Website:* www.ncsoft.co.kr (office).

KIM, V. Narry, BA, MS, DPhil; South Korean biologist and academic; *Director, Centre for RNA Research, Institute for Basic Science, Seoul National University;* b. 1969; ed Seoul Nat. Univ., Univ. of Oxford, UK; Postdoctoral Fellow, Howard Hughes Medical Inst., Univ. of Pennsylvania, USA 1999–2001; Research Asst Prof., Seoul Nat. Univ. (SNU) 2001–04, Asst Prof. 2004–08, Assoc. Prof. 2008–13, Prof. 2013–, SNU Distinguished Fellow 2010–, Dir Centre for RNA Research, Inst. for Basic Science 2012–; mem. Editorial Bd, Cell 2010, EMBO Journal 2011–, Genes & Development 2012–; mem. European Molecular Biology Org. 2012; Laureate for Asia Pacific, L'Oréal-UNESCO Awards for Women in Science 2008, ranked 13th as author of High-Impact Papers in Molecular Biology & Genetics (2002–06) 2008, Ho-Am Laureate, Medicine 2009, Nat. Honour Scientist, Ministry of Educ., Science and Tech. 2010, Korea Best Scientist Award, Korean Fed. of Science and Tech. Socs 2013. *Publications:* numerous papers in professional journals. *Address:* Lab of RNomics (Narry Kim Lab), Building 504, Room 509, School of Biological Sciences, Seoul National University, 599 Gwanangno, Gwanak-gu, Seoul 151-742, Republic of Korea (office). *Telephone:* (2) 880-9120 (office); (2) 887-1343 (Lab.) (office). *Fax:* (2) 887-0244 (office). *E-mail:* narrykim@snu.ac.kr (office). *Website:* www.narrykim.org/en (office).

KIM, Vladimir, MBA, PhD; Kazakhstani mining industry executive; b. 1961; m.; three c.; ed Alma-Ata Architectural Inst.; joined Kazakhmys Group 1995, apptd Man. Dir and CEO 1995, Chair., Kazakhmys PLC 2000–13, Non-Exec. Dir 2014–; mem. Bd of Dirs KAZ Minerals PLC 2005–. *Address:* Kazakhmys PLC, 6th & 7th Floor, Cardinal Place, 100 Victoria Street, London, SW1E 5JL, England (office). *Telephone:* (20) 7901-7800 (office). *Fax:* (20) 7901-7859 (office). *Website:* www.kazakhmys.com (office).

KIM, Wan-su; North Korean government official; *Vice-Chairman, Supreme People's Assembly;* Deputy Minister of Finance –2004; Pres. Central Bank of Democratic People's Repub. of Korea 2004–09; Vice-Chair. Choe Ko In Min Hoe Ui (Supreme People's Ass.) 2009–. *Address:* Choe Ko In Min Hoe Ui, Pyongyang, Democratic People's Republic of Korea (office).

KIM, Woo-choong, BA; South Korean business executive; b. 19 Dec. 1936, Daegu; s. of Yong-ha Kim and In-hang Chun; m. Hrrja Chung 1964; four c.; ed Kyunggi High School, Seoul, Yonsei Univ.; with Econ. Devt Council; with Hansung Industrial Co. Ltd, Dir –1967 (resgnd); Founder, Daewoo Industrial Co. Ltd (textile co.) 1967, Chair. Daewoo Group, includes Daewoo Shipbldg & Heavy Machinery Ltd, Daewoo Motor Co.; Founder, Daewoo Foundation 1978; under investigation for fraud and fled 1999, returned to South Korea and arrested 2005, convicted of charges including embezzlement and accounting fraud, sentenced to 10 years in jail 2006, granted amnesty 2007; Commdr, Légion d'honneur 1996; Dr hc (Yonsei Univ., Korea Univ., George Washington Univ., USA, Univ. of South Carolina, Russian Econ. Acad., Univ. Santiago de Cali/Univ. del Valle, Colombia; numerous honours and awards including Int. Business Award, Int. Chamber of Commerce 1984. *Publications:* It's Big World and There's Lots To Be Done 1989, Every Street is Paved With Gold: The Road to Real Success.

KIM, Yo-Jong; North Korean politician; *Vice-Director of Propaganda and Agitation Department, Korean Worker's Party;* b. 26 Sept. 1988, Pyongyang; d. of Kim Jong-Il and Ko Yong-Hui; sister of Kim Jong-un; m. Choe Song 2015; ed studied in Switzerland, Kim Il-Sung Univ.; deputy Dir Propaganda and Agitation Dept, Korean Worker's Party Nov. 2014–July 2015, Vice Dir (de facto leader) 2015–, Alt. mem. of Political Bureau of Cen. Cttee, Korea Worker's Party 2017–; first mem. of ruling Kim dynasty to visit South Korea in 2018 since Korean War ended in 1953. *Address:* Korean Worker's Party, Pyongyang, The Democratic People's Republic of Korea (office). *Website:* www.rodong.rep.kp (office).

KIM, Yong-dae; North Korean government official; *Chairman, Central Committee, Korean Social Democratic Party;* Chair., Cen. Cttee, Korean Social Democratic Party (Joson Sahoeminjudang); Vice-Pres. Supreme People's Ass. (Parl.) 2009–. *Address:* Korean Social Democratic Party, Pyongyang, Democratic People's Republic of Korea (office). *Telephone:* (2) 5591323 (office). *Fax:* (2) 3814410 (office).

KIM, Yong-il; North Korean politician; b. 2 May 1944; ed Rajin Univ. of Marine Transport; served in army 1961–70; various positions in Ministry of Land and Marine Transport 1980–94, including Instructor and Deputy Dir, Minister for Marine and Land Transport 1994–2007; Premier 2007–10. *Address:* c/o Office of the Premier, Pyonyang, Democratic People's Republic of Korea (office).

KIM, Yong-nam; North Korean politician; b. 1928, North Hamgyong prov.; ed Kim Il Sung Univ., Moscow Univ.; mem. Cen. Cttee Workers' Party of Korea (WPK) 1970, Political Commissar 1977, mem. Political Bureau 1980–; Vice-Premier and Minister of Foreign Affairs 1983–98; Del. to Supreme People's Ass.; Pres. Presidium of the Supreme People's Ass. 1998–2019. *Address:* Choe ko in min hoe ui (Supreme People's Assembly), Pyongyang, Democratic People's Republic of Korea (office).

KIM, Young-se, BFA, MA, PhD; South Korean industrial designer and business executive; *CEO, Inno Design;* b. 1950, Seoul; ed Seoul Nat. Univ., Univ. of Illinois, USA; began career as designer at Mel Boldt and Assocs., Chicago and Hari and Assocs., Skokie, Ill.; fmr Design Consultant, DuPont; Asst Prof. of Industrial Design, Univ. of Illinois 1980–82; Founder and CEO Inno Design Inc., Palo Alto, Calif. 1986, Inno Design Korea 1999, Inno Design China 2004; Silver Medal, Industrial Design Excellence Awards 2005, Grand Prix, Korea Industrial Design Awards, winner of Gold, Silver and Bronze Industrial Design Awards. *Publications:* Innovator, The Trendsetter 1999, Design A to Z 2000, A Napkin Worth 12 Hundred Millions 2001, Design, Start from Love! 2001; regular contributor to The Economist. *Address:* Inno Tower, 11–13F 61-3, Nonhyun-dong, Gangnam-gu, Seoul, Republic of Korea (office). *Telephone:* (2) 344-56481 (office). *Fax:* (2) 344-75465 (office). *Website:* global.innodesign.com (office).

KIM, Young-tae; South Korean business executive; *Vice-Chairman, National Agricultural Co-operative Federation;* Vice-Pres. of Industrial Relations and Human Resources, SK Holdings Co. Ltd –2011, Pres. and Co-CEO SK Holdings Co. Ltd 2011–13; fmr CEO and Pres. of Banking & Insurance, Nat. Agricultural Co-operative Fed., currently Vice-Chair. *Address:* National Agricultural Co-operative Federation, Saemunangil 91, Chung-gu, Seoul 110-110, Republic of Korea (office).

KIM, Yu-na; South Korean figure skater (retd); b. 5 Sept. 1990, Bucheon, Gyeonggi Prov.; ed Korea Univ., Seoul; started figure skating aged seven; sr int. debut 2006; took part in torch relay for Winter Olympic Games, Turin, Italy 2006, but was too young to participate in actual competition; moved to Canada to train under Brian Orser 2007; current record holder for ladies in the short programme, the free skating and the combined total under the ISU Judging System; first female skater to surpass the 150-point free skating mark and the 200-point total mark under the ISU Judging System; retd 2014. *Medals include:* Gold Medal, S Korean Championships 2003, 2004, 2005, 2006, 2013, ISU Jr Grand Prix, Hungary 2004, Bulgaria 2005, Slovakia 2005, Gold Medal, World Jr Championships 2006, Trophée Eric Bompard 2006, 2009, ISU Grand Prix Cup of China 2007, 2008, Gold Medal, ISU Grand Prix Final 2007, 2008, 2010, ISU Grand Prix Skate America 2008, 2009, Four Continents Champion 2009, Gold Medal, World Championships 2009, 2013, Gold Medal, Winter Olympic Games, Vancouver, Canada 2010, Silver Medal, Winter Olympic Games, Sochi, Russia 2014. *Television:* host, Kim Yu-na's Kiss and Cry (SBS) 2011. *Publications include:* Kim Yu-na's Seven Minute Drama, Like Kim Yuna. *Fax:* (2) 423-80-97 (office). *Website:* www.yunakim.com (office).

KIMBALL, Warren Forbes, PhD; American historian and academic; *Robert Treat Professor Emeritus of History, Rutgers University;* b. 24 Dec. 1935, Brooklyn, NY; s. of Cyril S. Kimball and Carolyn F. Kimball; m. 1st Jacqueline Sue Nelson 1959 (died 2009); one s. two d.; m. 2nd Sally Schenck 2013; ed Villanova Univ. and Georgetown Univ.; served in USNR 1958–65; Instructor, US Naval Acad. 1961–65; Asst Prof., Georgetown Univ. 1965–67, Univ. of Georgia 1967–70; Assoc. Prof., Rutgers Univ. 1970–85, Prof. II 1985–93, Robert Treat Prof. of History 1993, now Prof. Emer.; Pitt Prof. of American History, Corpus Christi, Cambridge, UK 1988–89; Mark A. Clark Distinguished Visiting Prof. of History, The Citadel 2002–04; Historian, US Tennis Asscn 2005–; Academic Adviser, Churchill Centre; Sr Ed., Churchill journal; Farrow Award for Churchill Scholarship, Int. Churchill Soc. 1999, Arthur Link Prize, Soc. for Historians of American Foreign Relations 2001. *Publications:* 'The Most Unsordid Act': Lend-Lease, 1939–1941 1969, Swords or Ploughshares? The Morgenthau Plan 1976, Churchill and Roosevelt: The Complete Correspondence (three vols) 1984, The Juggler: Franklin Roosevelt as Wartime Statesman 1991, Forged in War: Roosevelt, Churchill and the Second World War 1997, The US Tennis Association: Raising the Game 2017. *Leisure interest* tennis. *Address:* 2540 Otter Lane, John's Island, SC 29455, USA (home). *Telephone:* (843) 768-3879 (home). *E-mail:* wkimball@rutgers.edu (office). *Website:* andromeda.rutgers.edu/~history (office).

KIMMEL, James (Jimmy) Christian; American comedian, actor, television presenter and television producer; b. 13 Nov. 1967, Brooklyn, New York; s. of James Kimmel and Joan Kimmel (née Iacono); m. 1st Gina Kimmel 1988 (divorced); two c.; m. 2nd Molly McNearney 2013; ed Univ. of Nevada-Las Vegas, Arizona State Univ.; first radio job as morning drive co-host, The Me and Him Show (KZOK-FM, Seattle) 1989; began TV career on game show Win Ben Stein's Money 1997; host, White House Correspondents' Dinner 2012, Primetime Emmy Awards 2012, 2016, Academy Awards 2017, 2018; Writers Guild Award for Best Comedy/Variety-(Including Talk) Series (co-recipient) 2012. *Television includes:* host and creator of Jimmy Kimmel Live! (ABC late-night talk show) (Writers Guild of America Award for Comedy/Variety (Music, Awards, Tributes)-Specials 2016, Critics' Choice Television Award for Best Talk Show 2017, J.D. Power Award 2018) 2003–; host, writer The Man Show (TV series) 1999–2003, host, writer, exec. producer, Crank Yankers (voice) 2002–07, writer, exec. producer The Andy Milonakis Show 2005–07, co-host, Win Ben Stein's Money (Daytime Emmy for Outstanding Game Show Host 1999, Online Film & Television Asscn Award for Best Host of a Game Show 2000) 2001–02; exec. producer: (TV films) Big Night of Stars 2008, Alligator Boots 2009, Ace in the Hole 2009, (TV series) The Adam Carolla Project 2005, Sports Show with Norm Macdonald 2011. *Films include:* as actor: Down To You 2000, Road Trip (voice) 2000, Garfield (voice) 2004, Channel 101 (TV film) 2006, The Smurfs 2 (voice) 2013, The Heyday of the Insensitive Bastards 2015, The Boss Baby (voice) 2017, Teen Titans Go! To the Movies (voice) 2018. *Address:* c/o Jimmy Kimmel Live, 6834 Hollywood Boulevard, Los Angeles, CA 90028, USA (office). *Website:* abc.go.com/shows/jimmy-kimmel-live (office).

KIMUNYA, Amos Muhinga, BA, CPA; Kenyan accountant and politician; b. 6 March 1962, Embu; ed Univ. of Nairobi; early career as accountant; fmr mem. Parl. for Kipipiri 2002–13, Minister for Lands and Settlement 2003–06, of Finance 2006–08 (resgnd), of Trade 2009–12, of Transport 2012–13; Chair. Inst. of Certified Accountants of Kenya 1999–2001; mem. Nat. Rainbow Coalition.

KIMURA, Hiroshi; Japanese business executive; b. 23 April 1953, Yamaguchi Prov.; ed Kyoto Univ.; early career with Japan Tobacco Inc. and Salt Public Corpn, fmr Exec. Vice-Pres. and Asst to CEO JT International Holding BV (subsidiary of Japan Tobacco Inc.), Dir of Business Planning and Head, Overseas Operations, Japan Tobacco Inc. 1999–2006, mem. Bd of Dirs 2005–, Rep. Dir, Pres. and CEO 2006–12, Chair. 2012–14, Exec. Corp. Adviser 2014–; Dir Asahi Glass Co. 2013–, Nomura Holdings Inc. 2015–, IHI Corpn 2016–. *Address:* Japan Tobacco Inc., 2-1, Toranomon 2-chome, Minato-ku, Tokyo, 105-8422, Japan (office). *Telephone:* (3) 3582-3111 (office). *Fax:* (3) 5572-1441 (office). *E-mail:* info@jti.com (office). *Website:* www.jti.com (office).

KIMURA, Yaichi; Japanese oil industry executive; *Representative Director and Chairman, Cosmo Oil Company Ltd;* b. 1940; joined Daikyo Oil Co. 1963, Gen. Man. Corp. Planning Dept, Cosmo Oil Co. Ltd (after merger of Daikyo Oil, Maruzen Oil and Cosmo Oil) 1988–90, Gen. Man. Finance Dept 1990–94, mem. Bd of Dirs 1993–, Dir-Gen. Corp. Planning Dept 1994–96, Man. Dir 1996–98, Sr Man. Dir 1998–2001, Exec. Vice-Pres. 2001–04, Rep. Dir, Pres. and CEO 2004–12, Rep. Dir and Chair. 2012–. *Address:* Cosmo Oil Co. Ltd, 1-1-1, Shibaura, Minato-ku, Tokyo 105-8528, Japan (office). *Telephone:* (3) 3798-3211 (office). *Fax:* (3) 3798-3841 (office). *E-mail:* info@cosmo-oil.co.jp (office). *Website:* www.cosmo-oil.co.jp (office).

KIMURA, Yasushi; Japanese oil company executive; *Chairman and Representative Director, JX Holdings Inc.;* ed Keio Univ.; fmr Exec. Dir Energy Solution Div. and Sr Vice-Pres. Nippon Oil Corpn, fmr Gen. Man. Specialities Business Co-ordination Dept, the Lubricants and Kyushu Br. Office, Pres. JX Nippon Oil & Energy Corpn 2010–, also Pres. JX Nippon Oil & Energy (Australia) Pty Ltd, mem. Bd of Dirs, JX Holdings, Inc. 2010–, Chair. and Rep. Dir 2012–; mem. Bd of Dirs,

Japan Oil Transportation Co. Ltd 2010–. *Address:* JX Holdings Inc., 2-6-3, Otemachi, Chiyoda-ku, Tokyo 100-0004, Japan (office). *Telephone:* (3) 3502-1131 (office). *Fax:* (3) 3502-9352 (office). *Website:* www.hd.jx-group.co.jp (office).

KINAKH, Col Anatoliy Kyryllovych; Ukrainian politician; b. 4 Aug. 1954, Bratuşani, Moldovan SSR; m. Marina Volodymyrivna Kinakh 1960; three d.; ed Leningrad (now St Petersburg) Vessel Construction Inst.; worked on vessel construction and in vessel repair plants in Tallinn and Nikolayev 1978–90; elected to Mykolayiv Oblast Parl. 1990; mem. Comm. on Econ. Reform and Nat. Econ. Man. 1990; Presidential Rep. in Mykolayiv Oblast, then Head of Mykolayiv Regional Admin. 1992–94; Head, Mykolayiv Regional Council of People's Deputies 1994–95; mem. Political Council People's Democratic Party of Ukraine, Deputy Chair. 1996; mem. Parl. 1992–2014; Deputy Prime Minister of Ukraine in charge of Industrial Policy 1995–96; Presidential Adviser on Industrial Policy, then Pres. Ukrainian Union of Businessmen 1996–97; mem. Higher Econ. Council at Ukrainian Presidency, Head of Co-ordination Council on Privatization of Industrial Enterprises of Strategic Importance 1997; mem. Nat. Council of Ukraine on Quality Issues 1997–2001; Head, Verkhovna Rada Cttee on Industrial Policy 1998–2001; Chair. Nat. Cttee of Int. Trade Chamber 1998–2001; First Deputy Prime Minister of Ukraine Aug.–Dec. 1999, Jan.–Sept. 2005; Prime Minister of Ukraine 2001–02; unsuccessful presidential cand. 2004; Chair. Nat. Security and Defence Council 2005–06; Minister of the Economy 2007; Chair. Party of Industrialists and Entrepreneurs of Ukraine; mem. Acad. of Cybernetics; Hon. Prof., Mykolaiv Govt Humanitarian Univ. *Leisure interest:* classical music. *Address:* Party of Industrialists and Entrepreneurs, 01203 Kyiv, vul. Sh. Rustaveli 11, Ukraine (office). *Telephone:* (44) 590-17-44 (office). *Fax:* (44) 590-17-44 (office). *E-mail:* info@uspp.org.ua (office). *Website:* www.pppu.info (office); www.kinakh.com.ua.

KINCAID, Jamaica, PhD; Antigua and Barbuda writer and academic; *Josephine Olp Weeks Chair and Professor of Literature, Claremont McKenna College;* b. (Elaine Potter Richardson), 25 May 1949, St John's; d. of Annie Richardson; m. Allen Shawn; one s. one d.; staff writer, The New Yorker 1976; apptd Visiting Lecturer on African and African American Studies and on English and American Literature and Language, Harvard Univ. 1991; Josephine Olp Weeks Chair and Prof. of Literature, Claremont McKenna Coll. 2009–; mem. American Acad. of Arts and Letters 2004–; Fellow, American Acad. of Arts and Sciences 2009–; Dr hc (Williams Coll.) 1991, (Long Island Coll.) 1991, (Amherst Coll.) 1995, (Bard Coll.) 1997, (Middlebury Coll.) 1998, (Tufts Univ.) 2011; Lila Wallace-Reader's Digest Fund Annual Writers Award 1992, Lannan Literary Award for Fiction 1999, Prix Femina Étranger 2000, Clifton Fadiman Medal, Center for Fiction 2010. *Publications include:* At the Bottom of the River (short stories; American Acad. and Inst. of Arts and Letters Morton Dauwen Zabel Award 1985) 1983, Annie John (novel) 1985, A Small Place (non-fiction) 1988, Lucy (novel) 1990, The Autobiography of My Mother (Anisfield-Wolf Book Award 1997) 1995, My Brother 1997, My Favorite Plant 1998, Poetics of Place (with Lynn Geesaman) 1998, My Garden (non-fiction) 1999, Talk Stories 2001, Mr Potter 2002, Among Flowers: A Walk in the Himalaya 2005, See Now Then 2013. *Leisure interest:* gardening. *Address:* Literature Department, Claremont McKenna College, 500 East Ninth Street, Claremont, CA 91711, USA (office). *Telephone:* (909) 607-3228 (office). *E-mail:* jamaica.kincaid@cmc.edu (office). *Website:* www.cmc.edu/lit (office).

KIND, Dieter Hans, FIEEE; German electrical engineer; *Professor Emeritus, Technical University, Braunschweig;* b. 5 Oct. 1929, Reichenberg, Bohemia (now Liberec, Czech Repub.); s. of Hans Kind and Gerta Kind; m. Waltraud Wagner 1954; three c.; ed Tech. Univ., Munich; Prof. and Dir High-Voltage Inst., Technical Univ., Braunschweig 1962–75, Prof. Emer. 1975–; Pres. Physikalisch-Technische Bundesanstalt, Braunschweig and Berlin 1975–95, Comité Int. des Poids et Mesures, Sèvres/Paris 1975–95; Ehrenring VDE 1988, Dong-Baeg Medal (Korea) 1988, Ordem do Mérito Científico (Brazil) 1995, Grosses Bundesverdienstkreuz; Hon. DrIng (Tech. Univ., Munich). *Publications include:* An Introduction to High-Voltage Experimental Technique 1978, High-Voltage Insulation Technology 1985, Herausforderung Metrologie 2002, Naturforscher und Gestalter der Technik 2006; about 50 scientific articles. *Leisure interests:* sport, literature. *Address:* Knappstrasse 4, 38116 Braunschweig, Germany (home). *Telephone:* (531) 511497 (home). *Fax:* (531) 5160239 (home). *E-mail:* dieterkind@t-online.de.

KINDELAN MESA, Mario Cesar; Cuban boxer; b. 10 Aug. 1971, Holgu; m.; ed Physical Culture and Sport, ISCFM Fasardo, Havana; began boxing aged 14 years, competed as lightweight; trained by Julian R. Gonzalez since 1990; won Pan-American Games 1999, 2003; gold medals World Championships 1999, 2001, 2003; gold medals Olympic Games 2000 (Sydney), 2004 (Athens); undefeated since winning Pan-American Games in 1999; retd after winning second Olympic gold medal 2004, returned to fight Amir Khan in a professional fight 2005 (lost on points), again retd; Best Boxer in Cuba 1999, Russell Cup for Best Boxer at World Championships 2001, Cuban Sportsman of the Year 2001.

KINDLE, Fred, MBA; Liechtenstein/Swiss business executive; *Partner, Clayton, Dubilier & Rice LLC;* b. 25 March 1959, Liechtenstein; ed Swiss Fed. Inst. of Tech., Northwestern Univ., USA; Marketing Project Man., Hilti AG, Liechtenstein 1984–86; Assoc. and Engagement Man. McKinsey & Co. (New York and Zurich) 1988–92; Head, Mass Transfer Dept Sulzer Chemtech AG, Switzerland 1992–96, Head, Product Div. 1996–99, CEO Sulzer Industries 1999–2001, CEO Sulzer Ltd 2001–04; CEO ABB Ltd 2005–08, also fmr Pres.; Partner, Clayton, Dubilier & Rice LLC, London 2008–; Chair. Exova Ltd 2008–, BCA Group 2010–; mem. Bd of Dirs VZ Holding Ltd 2002–, Zurich Financial Services and Zurich Insurance Co. Ltd 2006– (Vice-Chair. 2013–), Stadler Rail AG 2008–; mem. Swiss American Chamber of Commerce. *Address:* Clayton, Dubilier & Rice LLP, Cleveland House, 33 King Street, London, SW1Y 6RJ, England (office). *Telephone:* (20) 7747-3800 (office). *Fax:* (20) 7747-3801 (office). *E-mail:* info@www.cdr-inc.com (office). *Website:* www.cdr-inc.com (office); www.zurich.com/en/about-us/corporate-governance/fred-kindle.

KINDLER, Jeffrey B., BA, JD; American lawyer and business executive; *CEO, Centrexion Therapeutics Corporation;* b. 13 May 1955, Montclair, New Jersey; m. Sharon Sullivan; one s. one d.; ed Tufts Univ., Harvard Law School; worked at Fed. Communications Comm.; served as law clerk to US Supreme Court Justice William J. Brennan, Jr and to Judge David L. Bazelon, US Court of Appeals, DC Circuit; fmr Pnr, Williams & Connolly (law firm), Washington, DC; fmr Vice-Pres. and Sr Counsel, Litigation and Legal Policy, General Electric Co.; Sr Vice-Pres. and Gen. Counsel, McDonald's Corpn 1996–97, Exec. Vice-Pres. for Corp. Relations and Gen. Counsel 1997–2001; Chair. and CEO Boston Market Corpn –2002, Pres. Partner Brands –2002; Sr Vice-Pres. and Gen. Counsel, Pfizer Inc. 2002–04, Exec. Vice-Pres. and Gen. Counsel 2004–05, Vice-Chair. and Gen. Counsel 2005–06, CEO 2006–10 (resgnd), Chair. 2006–10, also Chair. Exec. Cttee and mem. Pfizer Exec. Leadership Team 2006–10; Man. Dir Starboard Capital Partners 2010–; Prin. and Sr Advisor, Marathon Pharmaceuticals, LLC 2012–; CEO Centrexion Corpn 2014–; Chair. GLG Inst. 2014–; Exec. Chair., vTv Therapeutics Inc. 2015–; mem. Bd of Dirs, Ronald McDonald House Charities, US-Japan Business Council, US Chamber of Commerce, Manhattan Theater Club, New York Philharmonic, Partnership for New York City, Fed. Reserve Bank of New York –2010, Nat. Center on Addiction and Substance Abuse, Columbia Univ. 2011–, Intrexon Corpn 2011–, SIGA Technologies Inc. 2013–; mem. Advisory Bd, Paragon Pharmaceuticals, LLC; mem. Bd of Trustees, Tufts Univ., John F. Kennedy Center for the Performing Arts, Business Roundtable, Manhattan Theatre Club, Council on Competitiveness, The Business Council; numerous awards, including Stephen E. Banner Award, Lawyers Div. of UJA Fed. of New York 2002. *Address:* Centrexion Therapeutics Corporation, 509 South, Exeter Street, Suite 202, Baltimore, MD 21202, USA (office). *Telephone:* (410) 522-8701 (office). *E-mail:* info@centrexion.com (office). *Website:* centrexion.com (office).

KING, Angus Stanley, Jr, BA, JD; American lawyer, broadcaster and politician; *Senator from Maine;* b. 31 March 1944; m. Mary J. Herman; four s. one d.; ed Dartmouth Coll. and Univ. of Pennsylvania; called to the Bar, Maine 1969; staff attorney, Pine Tree Legal Assistance, Skowhegan, Me 1969–72; Chief Counsel, Office of Senator William D. Hathaway, US Senate Subcttee on Alcoholism and Narcotics, Washington, DC 1972–75; fmr Pnr, Smith, Lloyd & King (law firm), Brunswick, Me; Gov. of Maine 1995–2003; Distinguished Lecturer, Bowdoin Coll. 2004–, also Bates Coll.; Of Counsel, Bernstein, Shur, Sawyer & Nelson PA, Portland 2004–; Vice-Chair. Medicaid Advisory Comm., US Dept of Health and Human Services 2005–; Senator from Maine 2013–, caucuses with the Democrats; TV host Maine Watch 1977–96; Vice-Pres. and Gen. Counsel Swift River/Hafslund Co. 1983; Prin. Independence Wind; Founder and Pres. Northeast Energy Man. Inc. 1989–94; mem. Bd of Dirs, Public Broadcasting Service 2008, Savings Bank of Maine 2010; Trustee, The Nature Conservancy in Maine; Independent; Hon. LLD (Bowdoin Coll.) 2007; John Bernotavich Award 2005. *Address:* United States Senate, Washington, DC 20510 (office); Bernstein, Shur, Sawyer & Nelson PA, 100 Middle Street, PO Box 9729, Portland, ME 04104, USA. *Telephone:* (202) 224-3121 (Senate switchboard) (office); (207) 774-1200 (Portland). *Fax:* (207) 774-1127 (Portland). *E-mail:* aking3@bowdoin.edu (office). *Website:* www.senate.gov (office); www.bernsteinshur.com.

KING, Billie Jean; American professional tennis player (retd); b. 22 Nov. 1943, Long Beach, Calif.; d. of Willard J. Moffitt; m. Larry King 1965 (divorced); ed Los Angeles State Univ.; amateur player 1958–67, turned professional 1967; Australian champion 1968; Italian champion 1970; French champion 1972; Wimbledon champion 1966, 1967, 1968, 1972, 1973, 1975; US Open champion 1967, 1971, 1972, 1974; FRG champion 1971; South African champion 1966, 1967, 1969; won record 20 Wimbledon titles (six singles, 10 doubles, four mixed) and played more than 100 matches; had won 1,046 singles victories by 1984; sports commentator, ABC-TV 1975–78; f. Women's Tennis Assn 1973; f. Women Sports magazine 1974; f. World TeamTennis 1974; Commr, US Tennis Team 1981; Capt. US Fed. Cup Team 1995–2004; Women's Olympic Tennis Coach 1996, 2000; apptd Chair. US Tennis Assn (USTA) Tennis High Performance Cttee 2005; f. Billie Jean King Leadership Initiative 2014; mem. Bd of Dirs Women's Sports Foundation, Andy Roddick Foundation, Elton John AIDS Foundation; mem. President's Council on Fitness, Sports and Nutrition; apptd Global Mentor for Gender Equality by UNESCO 2008, Nat. Amb. for AIM children's charity; Hon. Chair Tennis in the Parks Cttee, US Tennis Assn; Top Woman Athlete of the Year Award 1973, Lifetime Achievement Award, March of Dimes 1994, Sarah Palfrey Danzig Award 1995, Flo Hyman Award 1997, Arthur Ashe Courage Award 1999, Presidential Medal of Freedom 2009, NCAA President's Gerald R. Ford Award 2009, Major League Baseball's Beacon of Change Award 2010; inducted into Int. Tennis Hall of Fame 1987, Southern California Tennis Hall of Fame 2011, Nat. Gay and Lesbian Sports Hall of Fame 2013. *Achievements include:* US Tennis Assn (USTA) opened the Billie Jean King National Tennis Center 2006. *Publications:* Tennis to Win 1970, Billie Jean (with Kim Chapin) 1974, We Have Come a Long Way: The Story of Women's Tennis 1988, Pressure is a Privilege: Lessons I've Learned from Life and the Battle of the Sexes 2008. *Leisure interests:* ballet, movies.

KING, Carole; American singer and songwriter; b. 9 Feb. 1942; songwriter in partnership with Gerry Goffin; worked with artists, including Eric Clapton, Crosby and Nash, Branford Marsalis, David Sanborn; numerous concerts and tours; actress in theatre, including starring role, Mrs Johnstone, Broadway production Blood Brothers 1994; environmental activist for natural forest preservation; studied European traditional music; mem. AFTRA, AMPAS, NARAS, NAS, SAG, AFofM; Dr hc (Berklee Coll. of Music) 2013; Nat. Acad. of Songwriters Lifetime Achievement Award 1988, Grammy Awards, inducted into Songwriters Hall of Fame 1987, Rock and Roll Hall of Fame (with Gerry Goffin) 1990, Mercer Award, Songwriters Hall of Fame 2002, Trustee Award, Recording Acad. 2004, Gershwin Prize for Popular Song, US Library of Congress 2013. *Compositions include:* hit songs include: Will You Love Me Tomorrow, Take Good Care of My Baby, Go Away Little Girl, The Locomotion, Up On The Roof, Chains, One Fine Day, Hey Girl, I Feel The Earth Move, Natural Woman, Smackwater Jack, You've Got A Friend, Now and Forever (For film, A League of Their Own), soundtrack, animated film, Really Rosie. *Recordings include:* albums: The City 1968, Writer 1970, Tapestry 1971, Rhymes and Reasons 1972, Music 1972, Fantasy 1973, Wrap Around Joy 1974, Thoroughbred 1975, Really Rosie 1975, Simple Things 1977, Welcome Home 1978, Greatest Hits 1978, Touch The Sky 1979, Pearls 1980, 1994, One To One 1982, Speeding Time 1983, City Streets 1989, For Our Children 1991, A League of Their Own 1992, 'Til Their Eyes Shine 1992, Colour of Your Dreams 1993, In Concert 1994, Time Gone By 1994, A Natural Woman 1994, Carnegie Hall Concert 1996, Goin' Back 1998, Love Makes The World 2001, Beautiful: The Carole King Musical (Grammy Award for Best Musical Theater Album 2015) 2013. *Publication:* A Natural Woman: A Memoir 2012.

Address: c/o Lorna Guess, Carole King Productions, 11684 Ventura Blvd, #273, Studio City, CA 91604, USA (office). *E-mail:* messages@ckmusic.com. *Website:* www.caroleking.com.

KING, Sir David Anthony, Kt, BSc, MA, PhD, ScD, FRS, FRSC, FInstP; British academic and research scientist; *Professor Emeritus, Department of Chemistry, University of Cambridge;* b. 12 Aug. 1939, Durban, South Africa; s. of Arnold King and Patricia Vardy; m. Jane Lichtenstein 1983; three s. one d.; ed St John's Coll., Johannesburg, Univ. of Witwatersrand, Johannesburg, Imperial Coll. London; Lecturer in Chemical Physics, Univ. of East Anglia 1966–74; Brunner Prof. of Physical Chem., Univ. of Liverpool 1974–88, Head, Dept of Inorganic, Physical and Industrial Chem. 1983–88; 1920 Prof. of Physical Chem., Dept of Chem., Univ. of Cambridge 1988, Head, Dept of Chem. 1993–2000, Dir of Research, Dept of Chem. –2012, now Prof. Emer.; Fellow, St John's Coll. 1988–95, Queen's Coll. 2001–, Master of Downing Coll. 1995–2000; Chief Scientific Adviser to UK Govt and Head, Office of Science and Tech. 2000–07; Dir Smith School of Enterprise and the Environment, Univ. of Oxford 2008–12; Special Rep. for Climate Change, FCO 2013–17; Ed. Chemical Physics Letters 1990–2001; Pres. Asscn of Univ. Teachers 1976–77; Chair. British Vacuum Council 1982–85; mem. Comité de Direction, Centre Cinétique et Physique, Nancy 1974–81, Research Awards Advisory Cttee Leverhulme Trust 1980–91 (Chair. 1995–2001), Direction Cttee (Beirat) Fritz Haber Inst., Berlin 1981–93; Chair. European Science Foundation Programme 'Gas–Surface Interactions' 1991–96, Kettle's Yard Gallery, Cambridge 1989–2001; Sr Scientific Adviser to UBS; Pres. BAAS; Assoc. Fellow, Third World Acad. of Sciences 2000; Foreign mem. American Acad. of Arts and Sciences 2002; Hon. Fellow, Indian Acad. of Sciences, Downing Coll., Univ. of Cardiff 2001; Hon. Prof., Qingdao Univ., People's Repub. of China; Hon. Life Fellow, Royal Soc. of Arts 2006; Officier dans l'ordre national de la Légion d'Honneur 2009; Hon. DSc (Liverpool) 2001, (East Anglia) 2001, (Stockholm) 2003, (Genoa) 2002, (Leicester) 2002, Cardiff (2002), (Witwatersrand) 2003, (St Andrews) 2003, (York) 2004, (Oxford Brookes) 2007; Shell Scholar 1963–66, RSC Awards, Surface Chem. 1978, RSC Tilden Lecturer 1988, Medal for Research, British Vacuum Council 1991, Liversidge Lectureship and Medal 1997–98, Royal Soc. Rumford Medal 2003, Linnaeus Medal, Sweden 2007, Jawaharlal Nehru Birth Centenary Medal, Indian Nat. Science Acad. 2007, Arthur W. Adamson Award 2009, Symons Medal, Asscn of Commonwealth Univs. 2013. *Publications:* The Chemical Physics of Solid Surfaces and Heterogeneous Catalysis (seven vols) (co-ed. with D. P. Woodruff) 1980–94, The Hot Topic: How to Tackle Global Warming and Still Keep the Lights On (with Gabrielle Walker) 2008, Energy, Transport & the Environment (jtly) 2012; over 450 original publs in scientific literature. *Leisure interests:* photography, art, philosophy. *Address:* Department of Chemistry, University of Cambridge, Lensfield Road, Cambridge, CB2 1EN (office); 20 Glisson Road, Cambridge, CB1 2EW, England (home). *Telephone:* (1223) 336338 (office); (1223) 315629 (home). *Fax:* (1223) 762829 (office). *E-mail:* dak10@cam.ac.uk (office). *Website:* www.ch.cam.ac.uk (office).

KING, Don; American boxing promoter; b. 20 Aug. 1931, Cleveland; s. of Clarence King and Hattie King; m. Henrietta King; two s. one d.; convicted of manslaughter and justifiable homicide; boxing promoter 1972–; Owner, Don King Productions Inc. 1974–; fighters promoted include: Muhammad Ali, Sugar Ray Leonard (q.v.), Mike Tyson (q.v.), Ken Norton, Joe Frazier, Larry Holmes (q.v.), Roberto Durán (q.v.), Tim Witherspoon, George Foreman (q.v.), Evander Holyfield (q.v.); f. Don King Foundation and actively supports other charities including The Martin Luther King Jr Foundation; Shaker Boulevard, Cleveland renamed 'Don King Way' in his name 2016; Int. Boxing Hall of Fame 1997, Gaming Hall of Fame 2008. *Address:* c/o Don King Productions Inc., 501 Fairway Drive, Deerfield Beach, FL 33441, USA (office). *E-mail:* info@donking.com. *Website:* www.donking.com.

KING, Gayle; American journalist, editor, television presenter and actress; *Co-Host, CBS This Morning;* b. 28 Dec. 1954, Chevy Chase, Md; m. William G. Bumpus 1983 (divorced 1993); one s. one d.; ed Univ. of Maryland; spent several years of her childhood in Ankara, Turkey before returning with her family to the USA; worked at several TV stations from 1976, including WDAF-TV, Kansas City, Mo., WJZ-TV, Baltimore, Md and WTOP-TV, Washington, DC; worked as TV news anchor for CBS affiliate WFSB-TV, Hartford, Conn. 1981–99; briefly co-hosted with Robin Wagner NBC daytime talk show Cover to Cover 1991; own syndicated talk show, The Gayle King Show 1997; Ed., O, the Oprah Magazine, CBS News & Hearst 1999, now Ed.-at-Large; also worked as a special corresp. for The Oprah Winfrey Show and Good Morning America; began hosting The Gayle King Show on XM Satellite Radio 2006; hosted The Gayle King Show (live, weekday TV interview programme) on OWN: The Oprah Winfrey Network 2011–12; Co-host, with Charlie Rose and Norah O'Donnell, CBS This Morning 2012–; three Emmy Awards, American Women in Radio & Television Gracie Award for Outstanding Radio Talk Show 2008, Individual Achievement Award for Host-Entertainment/Information 2010, New York Women in Communications' Matrix Award 2010. *Film roles:* A Little Bit of Lipstick 2000, The Manchurian Candidate 2004. *Address:* CBS News, 555 West 57th Street, New York, NY 10019, USA (office). *Telephone:* (212) 975-4114 (office). *Website:* www.cbsnews.com (office).

KING, Ian; British business executive; *Chairman, Senior plc;* b. 24 April 1956; m.; one s.; began career as grad. entrant at Marconi 1976, worked in manufacturing at co.'s defence electronics manufacturing operations in Scotland and Portsmouth 1976–86, Finance Dir, Marconi Defence Systems 1986–92, Finance Dir, Marconi Electronic Systems 1992–98, apptd non-exec. Dir Canadian Marconi Co. and Dir Marconi's two Anglo/French jt ventures in Space and Sonar, first Chief Exec. Alenia Marconi Systems (jt venture between Marconi and Finmeccanica of Italy formed in Dec. 1998), Group Strategy and Planning Dir responsible for initial Strategic Business Plan for BAE Systems (following merger of British Aerospace and Marconi Nov. 1999) 1999–2001, Group Man. Dir for Customer Solutions & Support 2001–07, mem. Bd of Dirs and COO, UK and Rest of the World, BAE Systems plc 2007–17, Chief Exec. 2008–17; Dir (non-exec.), Alvis plc Jan. 2004–Aug. 2005, Rotork plc 2005–14; mem. Bd of Dirs Senior plc 2017–, Chair. 2018–; Sr Advisor Gleacher Shacklock LLP 2017–; Sr Ind. Dir Schroders plc 2018–, mem. Nominations and Remuneration Cttees. *Leisure interests:* ball sports, especially golf, football and cricket, lifetime supporter of Portsmouth Football Club. *Address:* Senior plc, 59/61 High Street, Rickmansworth, Hertfordshire WD3 1RH, England (office). *Telephone:* (1923) 775547 (office). *E-mail:* companysecretary@seniorplc.com (office). *Website:* www.seniorplc.com (office).

KING, Ivan Robert, PhD; American astronomer and academic; *Research Professor, Astronomy Department, University of Washington;* b. 25 June 1927, New York, NY; s. of Myram King and Anne King; m. 1st Alice Greene 1952 (divorced 1982); two s. two d.; m. 2nd Judith Ann Schultz 2002; ed Woodmere Acad., Hamilton Coll., Harvard Univ.; served in USNR 1952–54; Methods Analyst, US Dept of Defence 1952–56; Asst Prof., then Assoc. Prof., Univ. of Illinois 1956–64; Assoc. Prof. of Astronomy, Univ. of California, Berkeley 1964–66, Prof. 1966–93, Prof. Emer. 1993–, Chair. Astronomy Dept 1967–70; Research Prof., Astronomy Dept, Univ. of Washington 2002–; Pres. American Astronomical Soc. 1978–80; mem. AAAS, Fellow, Chair. Astronomy Section 1973; mem. NAS, American Acad. of Arts & Sciences, Int. Astronomical Union; Hon. Laurea (Univ. of Padua) 2002; Hon. ScD (Hamilton Coll.) 2005; Sec. of the Navy Commendation, USN 1954, George Darwin Lecturer, Royal Astronomical Soc. 1978. *Publications:* The Universe Unfolding 1976, The Milky Way as a Galaxy 1990; more than 200 articles in scientific journals. *Address:* Astronomy Department, University of Washington, Physics-Astronomy Bldg, B372, 3910 15th Avenue NE, Seattle, WA 98195, USA (office). *E-mail:* king@astro.washington.edu (office). *Website:* www.astro.washington.edu/king (office).

KING, John B., Jr, BA, MA, JD, EdD; American educator and government official; b. 1975, Flatlands, Brooklyn, New York; s. of John B. King, Sr and Adalinda King; m. Melissa Steel King; two c.; ed Phillips Andover School, Harvard Univ., Columbia Univ. Teachers Coll., Yale Law School; fmr high school social studies teacher in San Juan, Puerto Rico and Boston, Mass; Co-founder and Co-Dir for Curriculum and Instruction, Roxbury Preparatory Charter School 1999–2004; Man. Dir, Uncommon Schools 2005–09; Sr Deputy Commr, New York State Educ. Dept 2009–11, Commr of Educ. 2011–15, also Pres., Univ. of the State of New York 2011–; Sr Advisor, Delegated Duties of US Deputy Sec. of Educ. Jan.–Dec. 2015, Acting Sec. of Educ. Jan.–March 2016, Sec. of Educ. 2016–17; fmrly served on Dept of Educ.'s Equity and Excellence Comm.; fmr mem. Bd of Dirs New Leaders for New Schools 2005–09; James Madison Memorial Fellowship, Truman Scholar 1995, Aspen Institute-New Schools Entrepreneurial Leaders for Public Education Fellow 2008.

KING, Sir Julian, Kt, KCVO, CMG, BA; British diplomatist and EU official; *European Commissioner for the Security Union;* b. 22 Aug. 1964, West Midlands; m. Lotte Knudsen 1992; ed Univ. of Oxford, Ecole Nationale d'Admin, France; joined FCO 1985, Pvt. Sec. to Amb., Embassy in Paris 1989–90, worked on European Common Foreign and Security Policy in Luxembourg, The Hague, Lisbon (following rotating presidency) 1991–92, then in London during UK presidency 1992, then on European Defence and NATO issues in London 1993–95, Pvt. Sec. to Head of UK Diplomatic Service, Perm. Under-Sec. of State 1995–98, with UK Representation to EU, Brussels 1998, Counsellor, Head of Chancery, Perm. Mission to UN, New York 2003–04, Political and Security Cttee, UK Representation to EU, Brussels 2004, Chair. 2005, Head of Office of British Commr, Brussels 2008–09, Amb. to Ireland 2009–11; Dir-Gen. Northern Ireland Office 2011–14; Dir-Gen., Econ. & Consular, FCO 2014–16, Amb. to France Jan.–Aug. 2016; EU Commr for the Security Union 2016–. *Leisure interests:* hill walking, cooking. *Address:* European Commission, 200 rue de la Loi, 1049 Brussels, Belgium (office). *Telephone:* (2) 298-18-00 (office). *Fax:* (2) 295-01-38 (office). *Website:* ec.europa.eu/commission (office).

KING, Justin Matthew, CBE; British retail executive; *Vice-Chairman and Head of Portfolio Businesses, Terra Firma Partners Limited;* b. 17 May 1961, Stepney, London; ed Tudor Grange Grammar School (later Comprehensive School), Solihull, Solihull Sixth Form Coll., Univ. of Bath; following graduation, worked for Mars, became production shift man. on Galaxy chocolate; joined PepsiCo 1989, based in Middle East; moved to Grand Metropolitan 1990, as Man. Dir helped launch Häagen-Dazs ice-cream in UK; held various sr positions at Asda Hypermarkets in trading and human resources divs, including Retail Man. Dir 1994–2001; Dir of Food, Marks & Spencer plc 2001–04; CEO J Sainsbury plc 2004–14, also Chair. Operating Bd; Dir (non-exec.), Staples, Inc. 2007–15; Vice-Chair. and Head of Portfolio Businesses, Terra Firma Partners Ltd 2015–; mem. Bd, London Organising Cttee of the Olympic Games and Paralympic Games 2009–13; mem. Prime Minister's Business Advisory Group 2010–12; Visiting Fellow, Centre for Corporate Reputation, Univ. of Oxford; Amb. for The Scout Asscn. *Address:* c/o Dawn Tracey (PA) (office). *Telephone:* (1926) 614530 (office). *E-mail:* pa@harburyhouse.co.uk (office).

KING, Larry; American broadcaster; b. (Lawrence Harvey Zeiger), 19 Nov. 1933, Brooklyn; s. of Eddie Zeiger and Jennie Zeiger; m. 1st Frida Miller 1952; m. 2nd Alene Akins 1961 (divorced 1963, remarried 1967, divorced 1971); one d.; m. 3rd Mickey Sutphin 1993 (divorced 1993); m. 4th Sharon Lepore 1976 (divorced 1984); m. 5th Julia Alexander 1989, (divorced 1992); one s.; m. 6th Shawn Southwick 1997; two c.; disc jockey with various radio stations, Miami, Fla 1957–71; freelance writer and broadcaster 1972–75; radio personality, Station WIOD, Miami 1975–78; writer, entertainment sections of Miami Herald for seven years; host, The Larry King Show (radio talk show) 1978–94, WLA-TV Let's Talk, Washington, DC; host Larry King Live (TV) 1985–2010; host Larry King Now (web series) 2012–; columnist, USA Today, Sporting News; f. Larry King Cardiac Foundation; Dr hc (George Washington Univ.), (New England Inst. of Tech.), (Brooklyn Coll.), (Pratt Inst.); Talk Show Host of the Year, Nat. Asscn of Radio Talk Show Hosts 1993, Scopus Award, American Friends of Hebrew Univ. 1994, Golden Plate Award, American Acad. of Achievement 1996, Mahoney Award, Harvard Univ. 2000, March of Dimes' Franklin Delano Roosevelt Award 2000. *Films:* appeared as himself in films Ghostbusters 1984, Lost in America 1985, Crazy People 1990, Exorcist III 1990, Dave 1993, Spin 1995, Open Season 1996, Contact 1997, The Jackal 1997, Primary Colors 1998, Bulworth 1998, Enemy of the State 1998, The Kid 2000, The Contender 2000, America's Sweethearts 2001, John Q 2002, Marilyn's Man 2004, Shrek 2 (voice) 2004, The Stepford Wives 2004, Mr 3000 2004, Shrek the Third (voice) 2007. *Publications:* Mr King, You're Having a Heart Attack (with B. D. Colen) 1989, Larry King: Tell Me More, When You're from Brooklyn, Everything Else is Tokyo 1992, On the Line (jtly) 1993, Daddy Day, Daughter Day (jtly) 1997, My Remarkable Journey (with Cal Fussman) 2009. *Address:* c/o CNN Larry King Live, 820 1st Street, NE, Washington, DC 20002, USA (office).

KING, Mary Elizabeth, MBE; British horse rider; b. 8 June 1961, Newark-on-Trent, Notts.; d. of Lt-Commdr M. D. H. Thomson; m. David King 1995; one s. one d.; ed Manor House School, Honiton, King's Grammar School, Ottery St Mary, Evendine Court (Cordon Bleu); team gold medals 1991, 1994, 1995, 1997, 2007; rep. GB in Equestrian Eventing Team at Olympic Games in Barcelona 1992, Atlanta 1996, Sydney 2000, Athens 2004, Beijing 2008, London 2012; Team Silver Medal, Athens 2004, London 2012, Team Bronze Medal, Beijing 2008; British Open champion 1991, 1992, 1996, 2007; winner Badminton Horse Trials 1992, 2000, Burghley Horse Trials 1996; broke her neck in 2001, but made full recovery; mem. winning GBI team at Burghley Horse Trials 2001; fmr Watch Leader on 'Sir Winston Churchill' tall ship; Team Silver Medal, World Equestrian Games 2006; Team Gold and Individual Silver at European Championships, Italy 2007. *Publications:* Mary Thomson's Eventing Year 1993, All the King's Horses 1997, William and Mary 1998, Mary King: The Autobiography 2009, Mary King: My Way 2014. *Leisure interests:* tennis, snow and water skiing. *Address:* Thorn House, Salcombe Regis, Sidmouth, Devon, EX10 0JH, England (office). *Telephone:* (1395) 515842 (office). *Fax:* (1392) 258846 (office).

KING, Maurice Athelstan, QC, LLB; Barbadian lawyer, politician and diplomatist; b. 1 Jan. 1936; s. of James Cliviston King and Caroline Constance King; m. Patricia A. Williams; one s. one d.; ed Harrison Coll., Barbados, Univ. of Manchester and Gray's Inn, UK; lawyer in pvt. practice 1960–; Chair. Natural Gas Corpn 1964–76; mem. Barbados Senate 1967–75; Gen. Sec. Democratic Labour Party 1968–69; Amb. to USA and Perm. Rep. to OAS Jan.–Sept. 1976; mem. Parl. 1981–; Attorney-Gen. and Minister of Legal Affairs 1986–91, Attorney-Gen. 1991–94 and Minister of Foreign Affairs 1991–93, of Justice and CARICOM Affairs 1993–94. *Leisure interests:* music, tennis, reading, swimming. *Address:* Radstan Court, Chapman Street, St Michael, Barbados (office). *Telephone:* 426-0847 (office). *Fax:* 426-0849 (office).

KING, Phillip, CBE, MA (Cantab.); British sculptor; *Professor Emeritus, Royal College of Art;* b. 1 May 1934, Tunis, Tunisia; s. of Thomas J. King and Gabrielle Liautard; m. 1st Lilian Odelle 1957 (divorced 1987); one s. (deceased); m. 2nd Judith Corbalis 1991; ed Mill Hill School, Christ's Coll., Cambridge, St Martin's School of Art, London; Asst to Henry Moore 1957–59; taught at St Martin's School of Art 1959–74; Prof. of Sculpture, Royal Coll. of Art 1980–90, Prof. Emer. 1991–; Prof. of Sculpture, RA 1990–99, Pres. 1999–2004; Trustee, Tate Gallery 1967–69; mem. Art Panel, Arts Council 1977–79; Hon. Fellow, Christ Coll., Cambridge 2002–; 1st Prize Int. Sculpture exhbn, Piestany (Czechoslovakia) 1968, Lifetime Achievement in Contemporary Sculpture Award, Int. Sculpture Center 2010. *Leisure interest:* holidays in Corsica close to both land and sea.

KING, Ralph, BA (Hons), MPhil, PhD; Australian diplomatist; m.; two c.; fmr Middle East Analyst, Office of Nat. Assessments; now career officer with Dept of Foreign Affairs and Trade, has worked as a speechwriter and as Dir of Security Policy and Operations, and Recruitment, Performance and Forecasting Sections, postings overseas in Hanoi, Beirut and Damascus, fmr Amb. to Kuwait, Amb. to Egypt –2015, to Saudi Arabia (also accred to Bahrain, Oman and Yemen) 2015–18. *Address:* c/o Embassy of Australia, PO Box 94400, Abdullah bin Hozafa al-Sahmi Avenue, Diplomatic Quarter, Riyadh 11693, Saudi Arabia (office).

KING, Stephen Edwin, (Richard Bachman, John Swithen), BS; American writer and screenwriter; b. 21 Sept. 1947, Portland, Me; s. of Donald Edwin King and Nellie Ruth King (née Pillsbury); m. Tabitha J. Spruce 1971; two s. one d.; ed Univ. of Maine; teacher of English, Hampden Acad., Me 1971–73; Writer-in-Residence, Univ. of Maine, Orono 1978–79; mem. Authors Guild of America, Screen Artists Guild, Screen Writers of America, Writers Guild; Medal for Distinguished Contribution to American Letters, Nat. Book Foundation 2003, World Fantasy Award for Life Achievement 2004, Canadian Booksellers Asscn Lifetime Achievement Award 2007, Grand Master Award, Mystery Writers of America 2007, Nat. Medal of Arts 2015, Bram Stoker Award, World Fantasy Award, British Fantasy Soc. Award. *Television:* Kingdom Hospital. *Publications:* novels: Carrie 1974, Salem's Lot 1975, The Shining 1976, The Stand 1978, The Dead Zone 1979, Firestarter 1980, Cujo 1981, Different Seasons 1982, The Dark Tower I: The Gunslinger 1982, Christine 1983, Pet Cemetery 1983, The Talisman (with Peter Straub) 1984, It 1986, The Eyes of the Dragon 1987, Misery 1987, The Dark Tower II: The Drawing of the Three 1987, Tommyknockers 1987, The Dark Half 1989, The Dark Tower III: The Waste Lands 1991, Needful Things 1991, Gerald's Game 1992, Dolores Claiborne 1992, Insomnia 1994, Rose Madder 1995, Desperation 1996, The Green Mile (serial novel) 1996, The Dark Tower IV: Wizard and Glass 1997, Bag of Bones 1997, The Girl Who Loved Tom Gordon 1999, Hearts in Atlantis 1999, Riding the Bullet 2000, The Plant (serial novel) 2000, Dreamcatcher 2001, Black House (with Peter Straub) 2001, From a Buick 8 2002, The Dark Tower: The Gunslinger: Revised and Expanded Edition 2003, The Dark Tower V: Wolves of the Calla 2003, The Dark Tower VI: Song of Susannah 2004, The Dark Tower VII: The Dark Tower 2004, The Colorado Kid 2005, Cell 2006, Lisey's Story 2006, Blaze 2007, Duma Key 2008, Under the Dome 2009, Full Dark, No Stars (e-book) 2010, 11/22/63 2011, It: The 25th Anniversary Special Edition 2011, The Dark Tower: The Wind Through the Keyhole 2012, A Face in the Crowd (e-book) 2012, Doctor Sleep 2013, Joyland 2013, Mr. Mercedes 2014, Revival 2014, Finders Keepers: A Novel 2015, End of Watch 2016, The Outsider 2018, Castle Rock 2018, Elevation 2018; other: Night Shift (short stories) 1978, Danse Macabre (non-fiction) 1980, Different Seasons (short stories) 1982, Creepshow (comic book) 1982, Cycle of the Werewolf (illustrated novel) 1984, Skeleton Crew (short stories) 1985, Four Past Midnight (short stories) 1990, Nightmares and Dreamscapes (short stories) 1993, Head Down (story) 1993, Six Stories (short stories) 1997, Storm of the Century (screenplay) 1999, On Writing: A Memoir of the Craft (revised edn as Secret Windows) 2000, Everything's Eventual: 14 Dark Tales (short stories) 2002, Faithful (non-fiction, with Stewart O'Nan) 2005, Just After Sunset (short stories) 2008, Blockade Billy (novella) 2010, Full Dark, No Stars (short stories) 2010, 11/22/63 2011, numerous other short stories, screenplays and television plays; as Richard Bachman: Rage 1977, The Long Walk 1979, Roadwork 1981, The Running Man 1982, Thinner 1984, The Regulators 1996, Blaze 2007. *Address:* 49 Florida Avenue, Bangor, ME 04401, USA (office). *Website:* www.stephenking.com (office).

KING, Stephenson; Saint Lucia politician; *Minister of Infrastructure, Ports, Energy and Labour;* b. 13 Nov. 1958; m. Rosella Nestor 2008; MP for Castries North 2006–; Minister for Health and Labour Relations 2006–07, of Finance (including Int. Financial Services), External Affairs, Home Affairs and Nat. Security 2007–11, Prime Minister 2007–11; currently Minister for Infrastructure, Ports, Energy and Labour; mem. United Workers Party. *Address:* Ministry of Infrastructure, Ports, Energy and Labour, Union Office Complex, Castries LC04 301, Saint Lucia (office). *Telephone:* 468-4300 (office). *Fax:* 453-2769 (office). *E-mail:* psec_mincom@gosl.gov.lc (office). *Website:* infrastructure.govt.lc (office); www.govt.lc/house-of-assembly (office).

KING AKERELE, Olu Banke (Bankie), BA, MA; Liberian politician; b. 11 May 1946, granddaughter of fmr Liberian Pres. Charles D. B. King; ed Univ. of Ibadan, Nigeria, Brandeis Univ., Northeastern Univ., Colombia Univ., USA; Sr Planning Officer, Ministry of Planning and Econ. Affairs 1968–69, Deputy Dir Nat. Social Security and Welfare Corpn 1975–80; Deputy Dir UNIFEM 1982–89, Deputy Resident Rep. of UN in Senegal 1989–91, UNDP Rep. in Mauritius and the Seychelles 1991–94, Man. Dir Country Strategy and Program Devt Div., UNIDO 1994–96, Chief, E and Cen. Africa Div. Regional Bureau for Africa, UNDP 1996–97, Country Programme Advisor UNDP Africa 1998, UNDP Resident Rep. and Resident Co-ordinator UN System Operational activities for Devt in Zambia 1998–2003, Programme Co-ordinator UNDP-UNESCO Project Foundations for Africa's Future Leadership, UNESCO's Regional Officer for Educ. in Africa, 2006; Minister of Commerce and Industry 2006–07, of Foreign Affairs 2007–10; currently Chair. Angie Brooks Int. Centre for Women's Empowerment, Leadership Development, International Peace and Security; Order Distinguished Services, Second Div. (Zambia); Liberian Business Asscn Award. *Publications:* Women's Leadership in Post Conflict Liberia: My Journey 2012, Accelerating Africa's Integration through Micro-regionalism: The case of Zambia-Malawi-Mozambique Growth Triangle and its Impact (co-authored with Kojo Boafo Asiedu) 2012, The 'Growing' of Africa's Emergent Leadership 2014, The Liberian Way: Breaking the Cycle 2016. *Address:* Angie Brooks Int. Centre, Science Building, Univ. of Liberia, 3rd Floor Monrovia, Liberia (office). *Telephone:* 886545291 (office). *E-mail:* info@angiebrooksintlcentre.org (office). *Website:* www.angiebrooksintlcentre.org (office).

KING-HELE, Desmond George, MA, FRS; British writer and scientist; b. 3 Nov. 1927, Seaford, Sussex; s. of S. G. King-Hele and B. King-Hele; m. Marie Newman 1954 (separated 1992); two d.; ed Epsom Coll. and Trinity Coll., Cambridge; Royal Aircraft Establishment, Farnborough 1948–88 (research on earth's gravity field and upper atmosphere by analysis of satellite orbits), Deputy Chief Scientific Officer, Space Dept 1968–88; mem. Int. Acad. of Astronautics 1961–; Chair. British Nat. Cttee for the History of Science, Medicine and Tech. 1985–89, History of Science Grants Cttee 1990–93; Ed. Notes and Records of the Royal Soc. 1989–96; Bakerian Lecturer, Royal Soc. 1974, Wilkins Lecturer, Royal Soc. 1997; Hon. DSc (Univ. of Aston) 1979, Hon. DUniv (Univ. of Surrey) 1986; Soc. of Authors' Medical History Prize 1999; Eddington Medal, Royal Astronomical Soc. 1971, Chree Medal, Inst. of Physics 1971, Nordberg Medal, Int. Cttee on Space Research 1990. *Radio includes:* dramas: A Mind of Universal Sympathy 1973, The Lunaticks 1978. *Publications include:* Shelley: His Thought and Work 1960, Satellites and Scientific Research 1960, Erasmus Darwin 1963, Theory of Satellite Orbits in an Atmosphere 1964, Observing Earth Satellites 1966, Essential Writings of Erasmus Darwin 1968, The End of the Twentieth Century? 1970, Poems and Trixies 1972, Doctor of Revolution 1977, Letters of Erasmus Darwin 1981, Animal Spirits 1983, Erasmus Darwin and the Romantic Poets 1986, Satellite Orbits in an Atmosphere 1987, The R.A.E. Table of Earth Satellites 1957–1989, 1990, A Tapestry of Orbits 1992, John Herschel 1992, Erasmus Darwin: A Life of Unequalled Achievement 1999, Antic and Romantic 2000, Charles Darwin's The Life of Erasmus Darwin 2002, The Collected Letters of Erasmus Darwin 2006, The Shorter Poems of Erasmus Darwin (with Stuart Harris) 2012, Erasmus Darwin and Evolution 2014; more than 400 scientific or literary papers in various learned journals. *Leisure interests:* playing tennis, savouring the beauties of nature, writing verse. *Address:* 7 Hilltops Court, 65 North Lane, Buriton, Hants., GU31 5RS, England (home). *Telephone:* (1730) 261646 (home).

KING OF BOW, Baroness (Life Peer), cr. 2011, of Bow in the London Borough of Tower Hamlets; **Oona Tamsyn King,** BA (Hons); British broadcaster, journalist, writer and fmr politician; b. 22 Oct. 1967, Sheffield, S Yorks.; d. of Preston King and Murreil Hazel Stern; niece of Miriam Stoppard; m. Tiberio Santomarco 1994; four c.; ed Haverstock Comprehensive Secondary School, London, Univ. of York, Univ. of California, Berkeley, USA; worked as trade union organizer for GMB Southern Region representing low-paid workers; spent five years as a researcher at European Parl. in Brussels and Strasbourg; worked as political asst to Glyn Ford MEP, Labour Party Leader in European Parl., and later Glenys Kinnock MEP; MP for Bethnal Green & Bow 1997–2005, Parl. Pvt. Sec. to Cabinet Minister for Trade & Industry, apptd to Int. Devt Select Cttee, Urban Affairs Select Cttee; Sr Policy Adviser on Equalities and Diversity and Faith to Prime Minister Gordon Brown 2008; Founding Chair. All-Party Parl. Group on Genocide Prevention, House of Commons; Chair. Inst. for Community Cohesion (iCoCo), Rich Mix Cultural Foundation; fmr Chair. All-Party Group on Business Services; fmr Vice-Chair. British Council, London Labour MPs; fmr Treas. Friends of Islam; apptd Head of Diversity, Channel 4 TV 2009, now freelance diversity exec.; Global Dir, Diverse Marketing, YouTube 2016–; unsuccessfully challenged Ken Livingstone for Labour nomination for 2012 Mayor of London election 2010; writes for several newspapers, including The Guardian, New Statesman, Sunday Telegraph and The Observer; presenter of radio and TV documentaries; has presented parts of Open Univ. W100 course (Introduction to Law); Assoc. Fellow, Chatham House (Royal Inst. of Int. Affairs); Gov. BFI; Trustee, Tower Hamlets Youth Sports Foundation. *Television:* appearances on This Week, The Daily Politics Show, The All Star Talent Show and Have I Got News For You; hosted BBC documentary American Prophet on Martin Luther King Jr and the deep South. *Publication:* The Oona King Diaries: House Music 2007. *Leisure interests:* cinema, dance music (especially house music), cooking, history, walking in Mile End Park. *Address:* House of Lords, Westminster, London, SW1A 0PW, England. *Telephone:* (20) 7219-5353. *E-mail:* info@oonaking.com. *Website:* www.oonaking.com.

KING OF BRIDGWATER, Baron (Life Peer), cr. 2001, of Bridgwater in the County of Somerset; **Thomas (Tom) Jeremy King,** PC, CH, MA; British politician; b. 13 June 1933, Glasgow; s. of John H. King and Mollie King; m. Elizabeth J. Tilney 1960; one s. one d.; ed Rugby School and Emmanuel Coll.,

Cambridge; in packaging and printing industry 1958–70; MP for Bridgwater 1970–2001; Parl. Pvt. Sec. to Rt Hon Christopher Chataway 1970–74; Shadow Spokesman for Energy 1976–79; Minister for Local Govt 1979–83; Sec. of State for the Environment Jan.–June 1983 for Transport June–Oct. 1983, for Employment 1983–85, for NI 1985–89, for Defence 1989–92; Chair. Intelligence and Security Cttee 1994–2001; Chair. London Int. Exhbn Centre (Excel London) 1994–2007, Dir 2007–; Dir (non-exec.) Electra Investment Trust 1992–2008; mem. Nolan Cttee on Standards in Public Life 1994–97; Conservative. *Leisure interests:* cricket, skiing, forestry. *Address:* House of Lords, Westminster, London, SW1A 0PW, England (office).

KING OF LOTHBURY, Baron (Life Peer), cr. 2013, of Lothbury in the City of London; **Mervyn Allister King,** Kt, KG, GBE, BA, FBA; British economist, academic and fmr central banker; b. 30 March 1948; s. of Eric Frank King and Kathleen Alice Passingham); m. Barbara Melander 2007; ed Wolverhampton Grammar School, King's Coll. and St John's Coll., Cambridge, Harvard Univ. (Kennedy Scholar), USA; Jr Research Officer, Dept of Applied Econs, Univ. of Cambridge, mem. Cambridge Growth Project 1969–73, Research Officer 1972–76, Lecturer, Faculty of Econs 1976–77; Esmée Fairbairn Prof. of Investment, Univ. of Birmingham 1977–84; Prof. of Econs, LSE 1984–95, f. Financial Markets Group, Co-Dir 1987–91; Dir (non-exec.) Bank of England 1990–91, Exec. Dir and Chief Economist 1991–98, Deputy Gov. (Monetary Policy) 1998–2003, Gov. 2003–13, mem. Group of Thirty Consultative Group on Int. Econ. and Monetary Affairs, Inc. (G-30); Prof. of Econs and Law, New York University 2014–; School Prof. of Econs, LSE 2015–; Pres. Inst. of Fiscal Studies 1999–2003; Research Officer, Kennedy School at Harvard Univ., USA 1971–72, Visiting Prof. of Econs 1982; Visiting Prof. of Econs, MIT 1983–84; Visiting Fellow, Nuffield Coll., Oxford 2002–03; Chair. OECD's Working Party 3 (WP3) Cttee 2001–03; Man. Ed. Review of Economic Studies 1978–83; Bd mem. The Securities Asscn 1987–89; mem. Council and Exec. Cttee Royal Econ. Soc. 1981–86, 1992–97; mem. Council, European Econ. Asscn (Pres. 1993); Research Assoc., Nat. Bureau of Econ. Research; Assoc. mem. Inst. of Fiscal and Monetary Policy, Ministry of Finance, Japan 1986–91; mem. Advisory Council, London Symphony Orchestra 2001; mem. Bd of Dirs Aston Villa football club 2016 (resgnd); Pres. Chance to Shine cricket foundation; mem. Cttee, All England Lawn Tennis and Croquet Club; mem. MCC; Trustee, Nat. Gallery; Patron, Worcester Co. Cricket Club; mem. Academia Europaea 1992; Fellow, Econometric Soc. 1982; Hon. Sr Scholarship and Richards Prize, King's Coll. Cambridge 1969; Hon. Fellow, St John's Coll., Cambridge 1997, King's Coll. Cambridge 2004; Foreign Hon. Mem. American Acad. of Arts and Sciences 2000; Hon. Life Mem. Inst. for Fiscal Studies 2006, Hon. Pres. Ekenäs Cricket Club, Finland; Dr hc (London Guildhall Univ.) 2001, (Birmingham) 2002, (City Univ., London) 2002, (LSE) 2003, (Wolverhampton) 2003, (Edin.) 2005, (Helsinki) 2006; Hon. LLD (Cambridge) 2006; Wrenbury Scholarship, Univ. of Cambridge 1969, Stevenson Prize, Univ. of Cambridge 1970, Kennedy Scholarship and Harkness Fellowship 1971, Medal of Univ. of Helsinki 1982. *Publications include:* Public Policy and the Corporation 1977, The British Tax System (with J. A. Kay), Indexing for Inflation (co-ed. with T. Liesner) 1975, The Taxation of Income from Capital Growth (co-author) 1984, The End of Alchemy: Money, Banking and the Future of the Global Economy 2016; numerous articles in various journals. *Leisure interests:* cricket, Aston Villa Football Club. *Address:* House of Lords, Westminster, London, SW1A 0PW, England (office). *Telephone:* (20) 7219-5353 (office).

KINGA, Dasho Sonam, BA, MA, PhD; Bhutanese politician; b. 6 June 1973, Galing, Shongphu, Trashigan; ed Sherubtse Coll., Kyoto Univ., Japan, Lestor B. Pearson Coll., Canada; Ed. Bhutan Observer; Sr Program Officer, Save the Children US, Thimphu; Sr Research Officer, Centre for Bhutan Studies (govt think-tank), Thimphu; Publication Officer, CAPSD, Ministry of Educ.; mem. Nat. Film and TV Review Bd 1999–2003; mem. Bd of Dirs BBSC-Nat. Radio Television 2002–04; MP for Trashigang in the Nat. Council (Parl.) 2007–, Chair. House Cttee, fmr Chair. Good Governance Cttee, Deputy Chair. Nat. Council 2009–13, Chair. 2013–18; Visiting Research Fellowship, Inst. of Developing Economies (Japan) 2001; scholarship for academic excellence, Canadian Int. Devt Agency 1991, First Place, Royal Civil Service Examination 1997, Red Scarf by HM the King 2012. *Publications include:* Gaylong Sumdar Tashi (trans. of 18th century autobiographical poem from Dzongkha to English) 1998, Changes in Bhutanese Social Structure: Impact of 50 Years of Reforms 1952–2002, Flying Rocks, Speaking Statues: Writings on Bhutanese History, Myth and Culture 2004, Polity, Kingship and Democracy: A Biography of the Bhutanese State 2009; numerous articles published in Bhutan and abroad. *Address:* c/o National Council Secretariat, Langjophakha, PO Box 200, Thimphu, Bhutan (office). *Telephone:* (2) 336616 (office). *Fax:* (2) 325543 (office). *E-mail:* skinga@nationalcouncil.bt (office). *Website:* www.nationalcouncil.bt (office).

KINGMAN, Sir John Frank Charles, Kt, ScD, CStat, FRS; British mathematician, statistician and academic; b. 28 Aug. 1939, Beckenham; s. of Frank E. T. Kingman and Maud Elsie Kingman (née Harley); m. Valerie Cromwell 1964; one s. one d.; ed Christ's Coll., Finchley, London, Pembroke Coll., Cambridge; Asst Lecturer in Math., Univ. of Cambridge 1962–64, Lecturer 1964–65; Reader in Math. and Statistics, Univ. of Sussex 1965–66, Prof. 1966–69; Prof. of Math., Univ. of Oxford 1969–85; Chair. Science and Eng Research Council 1981–85; Vice-Chancellor Univ. of Bristol 1985–2001; N M Rothschild Professorship of Mathematical Sciences and Dir Isaac Newton Inst. for Mathematical Sciences, Univ. of Cambridge 2001–06; mem. Council, British Tech. Group 1984–92; mem. Bd British Council 1986–91; Pres. London Math. Society 1990–92; Chair. Statistics Comm. 2000–03; Hon. Fellow, St Anne's Coll., Oxford, Pembroke Coll., Cambridge, Univ. of Bristol; Hon. Senator Univ. of Hannover; Officier des Palmes académiques; Hon. DSc (Sussex) 1983, (Southampton) 1985, (Brunel Univ.) 2004, Hon. LLD (Bristol) 1989, (Queen's Univ., Ont.) 1999. *Publications:* Introduction to Measure and Probability (with S. J. Taylor) 1966, The Algebra of Queues 1966, Regenerative Phenomena 1972, Mathematics of Genetic Diversity 1980, Poisson Processes 1993. *Address:* c/o Isaac Newton Institute for Mathematical Sciences, 20 Clarkson Road, Cambridge, CB3 0EH, England (office).

KINGO, Lise, BA, MSc, BCom; Danish UN official; *Executive Director, United Nations Global Compact;* b. 1961; ed Univ. of Aarhus, Copenhagen Business School, Univ. of Bath, UK; Dir of Environmental Affairs, Novo Nordisk A/S 1988–99, Sr Vice-Pres. of Stakeholder Relations 1999–2002, Chief of Staff, Exec. Vice-Pres. and mem. Exec. Management 2002–14; Exec. Dir, UN Global Compact 2015–; fmr Adjunct Prof. of Sustainability and Innovation, Vrije Universiteit Amsterdam; fmr Chair., Steno Diabetes Centre; fmr mem. Bd of Dirs, GN Store Nord; fmr mem. Danish Ethics Council; Edinburgh Medal, Tomorrow Magazine Environmental Leadership Award. *Address:* United Nations Global Compact, 801 2nd Avenue, 2nd floor, New York, NY 10017, USA (office). *Telephone:* (212) 907-1301 (office). *E-mail:* info@unglobalcompact.org (office). *Website:* www.unglobalcompact.org (office).

KINGSLEY, Sir Ben; British actor; b. (Krishna Bhanji), 31 Dec. 1943, Scarborough; s. of Rahimtulla Harji Bhanji and Anna Leina Mary Bhanji; m. Daniela Lavender 2007; three s. one d. from previous relationships; ed Manchester Grammar School; with RSC 1970–80; Nat. Theatre 1977–78; Assoc. Artist, RSC; Hon. MA (Salford Univ.), Hon. DLitt (Sussex), (Hull); Padma Shri (Govt of India) 1985. *Stage appearances include:* A Midsummer Night's Dream, Occupations, The Tempest, Hamlet (title role), The Merry Wives of Windsor, Baal, Nicholas Nickleby, Volpone, The Cherry Orchard, The Country Wife, Judgement, Statements After An Arrest, Othello (title role), Caracol in Melons, Waiting for Godot. *Television appearances include:* The Love School 1974, Kean 1983, Silas Marner 1985, Lenin: The Train 1987, Murderers Amongst Us: The Simon Wiesenthal Story 1989, Sweeney Todd 1998, Anne Frank: The Whole Story (Screen Actors' Guild Award for Best Actor 2002) 2001, Mrs. Harris 2005, Tut 2015. *Films include:* Gandhi (two Hollywood Golden Globe Awards 1982, New York Film Critics' Award, two BAFTA Awards, Acad. Award, Los Angeles Film Critics' Award 1983), Betrayal 1982, Harem 1985, Turtle Diary 1985, Without A Clue 1988, Testimony 1988, Pascali's Island 1988, Bugsy 1991, Sneakers 1992, Innocent Moves 1992, Dave 1992, Schindler's List 1993, Death and the Maiden 1994, Species 1995, Twelfth Night 1996, The Assignment 1998, Weapons of Mass Destruction 1998, The Confession 1999, Parting Shots 1999, Spooky House 2000, What Planet Are You From? 2000, Rules of Engagement 2000, Sexy Beast (Best Actor, British Ind. Film Awards 2001) 2000, The Triumph of Love 2001, A.I. (voice) 2001, Tuck Everlasting 2002, House of Sand and Fog 2003, Thunderbirds 2004, Suspect Zero 2004, A Sound of Thunder 2005, Oliver Twist 2005, Lucky Number Slevin 2005, BloodRayne 2005, I Have Never Forgotten You: The Life and Legacy of Simon Wiesenthal 2006, You Kill Me 2007, The Last Legion 2007, The Ten Commandments (voice) 2007, Elegy 2007, The Wackness 2007, Transsiberian 2008, War, Inc. 2008, The Love Guru 2008, Fifty Dead Men Walking 2008, Shutter Island 2010, 1001 Inventions and the Library of Secrets 2010, Prince of Persia 2010, The Dictator 2012, Iron Man 3 (Saturn Award for Best Supporting Actor 2013) 2013, A Common Man (Madrid Int. Film Festival Award for Best Lead Actor 2013) 2013, The Boxtrolls (Voice) (Annie Award for Voice Acting in a Feature Production 2014) 2014, Exodus: Gods and Kings 2014, The Walk 2015, The Jungle Book (Voice) 2016, An Ordinary Man 2017, Backstabbing for Beginners 2018, Nomis 2018. *Address:* c/o Actors Department, Independent Talent Group Ltd, 40 Whitfield Street, London, W1T 2RH, England. *Telephone:* (20) 7636-6565. *Fax:* (20) 7323-0101. *Website:* www.independenttalent.com.

KINGSMILL, Baroness (Life Peer), cr. 2006, of Holland Park in the London Borough of Kensington and Chelsea; **Denise Patricia Byrne Kingsmill,** CBE; British lawyer; b. 24 April 1947, New Zealand; d. of Patrick Henry Byrne and Hester Jean Byrne; m. David Gordon Kingsmill 1970 (divorced 2002); one s. one d.; ed Girton Coll., Cambridge; admitted as solicitor 1980; with ICI Fibres then Int. Wool Secr. 1968–75; Robin Thompson & Partners 1979–82; Russell Jones & Walker 1982–85; Denise Kingsmill & Co. 1985–90; Partner, D.J. Freeman 1990–93; consultant, Denton Hall 1994–2000; Chair. Optimum Health Services NHS Trust 1992–99; Deputy Chair. Competition Comm. (fmrly Monopolies and Mergers Comm.) 1997–2003; apptd Head Ind. Review into Women's Employment and Pay, Dept of Trade and Industry 2001, Chair. Accounting For People Task Force –2003; Sr Adviser, Royal Bank of Scotland 2004–08; Chair. Sadler's Wells 2003–04; Deputy Chair. MFI Furniture Group 1999–2001; mem. Bd of Dirs British Airways 2004–10; Dir (non-exec.) Korn/Ferry International Ltd (executive recruiting firm), Horizon plc (IT), E.On AG Supervisory Bd; Ind. Dir (non-exec.)/Bd mem. International Consolidated Airlines Group SA (formed by merger of British Airways and Iberia), Betfair plc (gambling products and services); mem. Microsoft European Policy Council, PWC Advisory Bd (also Deputy Chair.); mem. Bd of Dirs Home Office, Rainbow UK 1993–94, Norwich and Peterborough Building Soc. 1997–2001; fmr mem. Bd of Dirs MFI Furniture Group, Telewest Communications, Manpower UK; Trustee, Design Museum 2000–10; mem. Devt Cttee, Judge Inst., Cambridge Univ. Business School 2001–06; mem. Gov. Coll. of Law 1992–2001; fmr Pro-Chancellor Brunel Univ.; mem. (Labour), House of Lords 2006–, mem. Econ. Affairs Cttee 2008–13; columnist, Management Today; Hon. Fellow, Univ. of Wales, Cardiff 2000; Hon. LLD (Brunel) 2001, (Stirling) 2003; Hon. DSc (Cranfield) 2007. *Publications:* Women's Employment and Pay Review 2001. *Leisure interests:* fly-fishing, walking. *Address:* House of Lords, Westminster, London, SW1A 0PW, England (office). *Telephone:* (20) 7219-4537 (office). *Fax:* (20) 7219-5979 (office).

KINGSOLVER, Barbara, MS; American writer; b. 8 April 1955, Annapolis, Md; m. 1st Joseph Hoffmann 1985 (separated 1992); one d.; m. 2nd Steven Hopp 1994; one d.; ed DePauw Univ., Univ. of Arizona; scientific writer, Office of Arid Land Studies, Univ. of Ariz. 1981–85; freelance journalist 1985–87, novelist 1987–; book reviewer, New York Times 1988–, Los Angeles Times 1989–, San Francisco Chronicle, The Nation, The Progressive, The Washington Post, Women's Review of Books and others; Founding mem. Rock Bottom Remainders; Woodrow Wilson Foundation/Lila Wallace Fellowship 1992; est. Bellwether Prize for Fiction: In Support of a Literature of Social Change 1997; Hon. LittD (DePauw) 1994, Hon. DHumLitt (Duke Univ.) 2008; Nat. Writers Union Andrea Egan Award 1998, Arizona Civil Liberties Union Award 1998, Nat. Humanities Medal 2000, Best American Science and Nature Writing 2001, Gov.'s Nat. Award in the Arts, Kentucky 2002, John P. McGovern Award for the Family 2002, Physicians for Social Responsibility Nat. Award 2002, Duke LEAF Award for Lifetime Environmental Achievement in the Fine Arts 2011, Richard C. Holbrooke Distinguished Achievement Award (Dayton Literary Peace Prize) 2011. *Publications include:* The Bean Trees (Enoch Pratt Library Youth-to-Youth Books Award) 1988, Holding the Line 1989, Homeland and Other Stories 1989, Animal Dreams (Edward Abbey Award for Ecofiction, PEN/USA West Fiction Award) 1990, Another America 1992, Pigs in Heaven (Mountains and Plains Booksellers Award for Fiction, Los Angeles

Times Fiction Prize) 1993, High Tide in Tucson 1995, The Poisonwood Bible (Village Voice Best Books 1998, New York Times Top Ten Books 1998, Los Angeles Times Best Books for 1998, Independence Publisher Brilliance Audio 1999, Booksense Prize 1999, Nat. Book Award (SA) 2000) 1998, Prodigal Summer 2000, Small Wonder 2002, Last Stand 2002, Animal, Vegetable, Miracle: Our Year of Seasonal Eating (American Booksellers Book of the Year Award, James Beard Foundation Award) 2007, The Lacuna (Orange Prize for Fiction 2010) 2009, Flight Behavior: A Novel 2012, Unsheltered 2018; contrib. to various anthologies, periodicals. *Leisure interests:* human rights, environmental conservation, natural history, farming. *Address:* c/o Judy Carmichael, Office of Barbara Kingsolver, PO Box 160, Meadowview, VA 24361, USA (office). *Website:* www.kingsolver.com (office).

KINGSTON, Arthur Edward, PhD, FRAS, FInstP, MRIA; British physicist and academic; *Professor Emeritus, Queen's University Belfast;* b. 18 Feb. 1936, Armagh, Northern Ireland; s. of Arthur Kingston and Henrietta Duff; m. Helen McCann 1962; one s. one d.; ed Royal School Armagh and Queen's Univ. Belfast; Research Fellow, Queen's Univ. 1959–60, Sr Research Fellow 1960–61; Asst Lecturer, Liverpool Univ. 1961–62, Lecturer 1962–63; Visiting Fellow, Univ. of Colorado, USA 1963–64; Lecturer, Queen's Univ. 1964–68, Sr Lecturer 1968–71, Reader 1971–83, Prof. of Theoretical Atomic Physics 1983–2000, Dean, Faculty of Science 1989–94, Provost for Science and Agric. 1994–98, Prof. Emer. 2000–; NASA Public Service Award. *Publications:* more than 260 papers in atomic physics and astrophysics. *Leisure interests:* gardening, reading. *Address:* Department of Applied Mathematics and Theoretical Physics, David Bates Building, The Queen's University of Belfast, University Road, Belfast, BT7 1NN (office); 25 Cadogan Park, Belfast, BT9 6HH, Northern Ireland (home). *Telephone:* (28) 9097-6040 (office); (28) 9066-9658 (home). *Fax:* (28) 9097-6061 (office). *E-mail:* a.kingston@qub.ac.uk (office). *Website:* www.qub.ac.uk/mp/amtpt (office).

KINGSTON, Maxine Hong, BA; American author and fmr academic; b. 27 Oct. 1940, Stockton, Calif.; d. of Tom Hong and Ying Lan Hong (née Chew); m. Earll Kingston 1962; one s.; ed Univ. of California, Berkeley; taught English, Sunset High School, Hayward, Calif. 1965–66, Kahuku High School, Hawaii 1967, Kahaluu Drop-In School 1968, Kailua High School 1969, Honolulu Business Coll. 1969, Mid-Pacific Inst., Honolulu 1970–77; Prof. of English and Visiting Writer, Univ. of Hawaii, Honolulu 1977; Thelma McCandless Distinguished Prof., Eastern Mich. Univ. 1986; Chancellor's Distinguished Prof., Univ. of California, Berkeley 1990–2005; Mademoiselle Magazine Award 1977, Anisfield-Wolf Book Award 1978, Stockton (Calif.) Arts Comm. Award 1981, Hawaii Award for Literature 1982, NEA Writing Fellow 1980, Guggenheim Fellow 1981, named Living Treasure of Hawaii 1980, American Acad. and Inst. Award in Literature 1990, Nat. Humanities Medal 1997, Fred Cody Lifetime Achievement Award 1998, John Dos Passos Prize for Literature 1998, Ka Palapola Po'okela Award 1999, Commonwealth Club Silver Medal 2001, California State Library Gold Medal 2002, Spirituality and Health Book Award, KPFA Peace Award 2005, Red Hen Press Lifetime Achievement Award 2006, Los Angeles Times Book Festival Lifetime Achievement Award 2007, Nat. Book Foundation Medal for Distinguished Contribs to American Letters 2008, Nat. Medal of Arts 2014, Barbary Coast Literary Legend Award 2016, Lifetime Achievement Award, Los Angeles Review of Books 2018. *Publications include:* The Woman Warrior: Memoirs of a Girlhood Among Ghosts (Nat. Book Critics Circle Award for non-fiction) 1976, China Men (Nat. Book Award) 1981, Hawaii One Summer (Ka Palapola Po'okela Award 1999) 1987, Through The Black Curtain 1988, Tripmaster Monkey: His Fake Books (PEN International USA West Award in Fiction) 1989, The Literature of California (ed.) 2001, To Be The Poet 2002; The Fifth Book of Peace 2004, Veterans of War, Veterans of Peace (ed., Northern California Book Award 2007, Pacific Justice and Reconciliation Center Peace Book Award) 2006, I Love a Broad Margin to My Life 2011; short stories, articles and poems; illustrator of Hello House by Phyllis Hoge. *Leisure interests:* gardening, yoga, tai chi, dance. *Address:* c/o Sandra Dijkstra Literary Agency (office); Department of English, University of California, Berkeley, CA 94720, USA (office). *E-mail:* elise@dijkstraagency.com (office); yinglan@berkeley.edu (office). *Website:* english.berkeley.edu (office).

KINIGI, Sylvie; Burundian civil servant, politician and UN official; b. 1952; m. (died 1993); five c.; ed Burundi Univ.; fmr exec. officer of structural adjustment programme; Prime Minister of Burundi 1993–94; fmr mem. Union pour le progrès nat. (UPRONA); fmr Sr Political Adviser and Coordinator of Programs, Special Rep. of the UN Sec.-Gen. to the Great Lakes Region in Africa; worked with Burundi Women Access Trust. *Address:* c/o Burundi Women Access Trust, c/o Women Land Access Trusts, PO Box 18968-00100, Nairobi, Kenya. *Telephone:* 77790274. *E-mail:* skinigi@yahoo.com.

KINNEAR, Greg; American actor; b. 17 June 1963, Logansport, Ind.; s. of Edward Kinnear and Suzanne Kinnear; m. Helen Labdon 1999; ed Univ. of Ariz.; began career as marketing asst, Empire Entertainment, Los Angeles; worked as reporter for MTV; creator, co-exec. producer and host Best of the Worst TV show 1990–91; Male Discovery of the Year, Golden Apple Awards 1996. *Television:* host: Best of the Worst, Talk Soup (Daytime Emmy Award (jtly) 1995), Later with Greg Kinnear; actor: Murder in Mississippi 1990, Dillinger 1991, Based on an Untrue Story 1993, Dinner with Friends 2001, The Kennedys (mini-series) 2011, Rake (series) 2014. *Films include:* Blankman 1994, Sabrina (Most Promising Actor, Chicago Film Critics Asscn Awards 1996) 1995, Dear God 1996, A Smile Like Yours 1997, As Good as It Gets (Best Supporting Actor, NBR Awards 1997, Southeastern Film Critics Asscn Awards 1998, Golden Satellite Awards 1998) 1997, You've Got Mail (Best Supporting Actor in Comedy/Romance, Blockbuster Entertainment Awards 1999) 1998, Mystery Men 1999, What Planet Are You From? 2000, Nurse Betty 2000, Loser 2000, The Gift 2000, Someone Like You 2001, We Were Soldiers 2002, Stuck On You 2003, Godsend 2004, Robots (voice) 2005, Bad News Bears 2005, The Matador 2005, Fast Food Nation 2006, Little Miss Sunshine 2006, Invincible 2006, Unknown 2006, Feast of Love 2007, Baby Mama 2008, Ghost Town 2008, Flash of Genius 2008, Green Zone 2010, The Last Song 2010, Salvation Boulevard 2011, Thin Ice 2011, I Don't Know How She Does It 2011, Stuck in Love 2012, The English Teacher 2013, Anchorman 2: The Legend Continues 2013, Heaven Is for Real 2014, Murder of a Cat 2014. *Address:* Creative Artists Agency, 2000 Avenue of the Stars, Los Angeles, CA 90067, USA (office). *Website:* www.caa.com (office).

KINNEY, Catherine R., BA; American securities industry executive; b. 1952; m.; ed Iona Coll., Harvard Graduate School of Business; joined New York Stock Exchange (NYSE) 1974, responsible for trading-floor operations and tech. 1986–95, Group Exec. Vice-Pres. 1995–2002, Pres., Co-COO, Exec. Vice-Chair. and mem. Bd of Dirs 2002–06, Pres. and Co-COO NYSE Group (after merger of NYSE and Archipelago) 2006–07, Pres. and Co-COO NYSE Euronext Inc., Paris (after acquisition of Euronext by NYSE) 2007, Group Exec. Vice-Pres. and Head of Global Listings 2007–09, also mem. Man. Bd; mem. Economic Club of New York; mem. Bd of Dirs MSCI Inc. 2009–, MetLife, Inc. 2002–04, 2009–, NetSuite, Inc. 2009–16, QTS Realty Trust, Inc. 2013–, SolarWinds Corpn 2018–, New York City Ballet, Inc., Sharegift USA; Trustee, Catholic Charities of New York; Dr hc (Georgetown Univ., Fordham Univ., Rosemont Coll.); Woman of the Year (Financial Women's Asscn) 2001, ranked by the Financial Times amongst Top 25 Businesswomen in Europe (18th) 2007.

KINNOCK, Baron (Life Peer), cr. 2005, of Bedwellty; **Neil Gordon Kinnock,** PC, BA; British politician; b. 28 March 1942, Tredegar, S Wales; s. of Gordon Kinnock and Mary Howells; m. Glenys Elizabeth Parry 1967; one s. one d.; ed Lewis School, Pengam, Univ. Coll., Cardiff; Pres. Univ. Coll., Cardiff Students' Union 1965–66; Tutor Organizer in Industrial and Trade Union Studies, Workers' Educational Asscn 1966–70; MP for Bedwellty 1970–83, for Islwyn 1983–95; mem. Welsh Hosp. Bd 1969–71; Parl. Pvt. Sec. to Sec. of State for Employment 1974–75; mem. Gen. Advisory Council BBC 1976–80; mem. Nat. Exec. Cttee, Labour Party 1978–94 (Chair. 1987–88); Leader of Labour Party 1983–92; Leader of the Opposition 1983–92; EU Commr with responsibility for Transport 1995–99, Vice-Pres. European Comm. 1999–2004; Chair. British Council 2004–09; Chair. Advisory Bd Heads of the Valleys Int. Motor Racing Circuit 2011–; Pres. Cardiff Univ. 1998–2009; Dir (non-exec.) Data Research Services 2005–12; mem. Bd of Trustees, RAND Europe 2010–; Hon. LLD (Wales) 1992; Alexis de Tocqueville Prize 2003. *Publications:* Wales and the Common Market 1971, Making Our Way 1986, Thorns and Roses 1992; contribs to newspapers, periodicals and books including The Future of Social Democracy 1999. *Leisure interests:* male voice choral music, opera, theatre, reading, grandchildren, rugby, soccer, cricket. *Address:* House of Lords, London, SW1A 0PW, England (office). *Telephone:* (20) 7219-8304 (office). *Fax:* (20) 7219-4599 (office). *E-mail:* kinnockn@parliament.uk (office). *Website:* www.parliament.uk/biographies/lords/lord-kinnock/693 (office).

KINSCH, Joseph, MSc; Luxembourg business executive; b. 2 May 1933, Esch-sur-Alzette; m. Ruth Lauxen; two s.; began career with Arbed, Burbach, Saar, Germany 1961, moved to Luxembourg HQ 1962, Dir of Accounting and Finance 1977–79, Head of Steel Processing Firms 1979–85, Group Chief Financial Officer 1985–92, apptd mem. Bd of Man. 1985, Pres. and CEO 1992–93, Chair. and CEO 1993–98, Chair. 1998–2002, Chair. Arcelor SA (following merger of Arbed, Aceralia and Usinor and now ArcelorMittal) 2002–07, now Chair. ArcelorMittal Foundation; Hon. Pres. Union of Luxembourg Enterprises, Chamber of Commerce of the Grand-Duchy of Luxembourg; Hon. Consul of Brazil in Luxembourg; Grand Officer of the Oak Crown, Officer of the Crown, Civil and Mil. Order of Adolph of Nassau, Grand Cross of Civil Merit (Spain), Grand Officer of the Order of Leopold II (Belgium), Grand Officer of the Order of Merit (Portugal), Officier, Légion d'honneur, Grand Cross of the Order of Merit of the FRG, Commdr, Cruzeiro do Sul (Brazil), Commdr, Order of the Polar Star (Sweden), Order of Industrial Merit (South Korea); Dr hc (Sacred Heart Univ., Luxembourg) 2004. *Leisure interests:* art, golf, reading. *Address:* ArcelorMittal Foundation, 19 Avenue de la Liberté, 2930 Luxembourg Ville, Luxembourg. *Telephone:* 4792-2175. *E-mail:* foundation@arcelormittal.com. *Website:* corporate.arcelormittal.com/who-we-are/arcelormittal-foundation.

KINSELLA, John; Australian poet, writer, editor and publisher; b. 1963, Perth, WA; ed Univ. of Western Australia; Writer-in-Residence, Churchill Coll., Cambridge 1997; Ed. Salt literary journal; Publr and Ed. Folio (Salt) Publishing; Richard L. Thomas Prof. of Creative Writing, Kenyon Coll., USA 2001, then Prof. of English; Adjunct Prof., Edith Cowan Univ., Western Australia, and Prin. of the Landscape and Language Centre; Consultant Ed., Westerly (journal); Int. Ed., The Kenyon Review; Fellow, Churchill Coll., Cambridge; Western Australia Premier's Award for Poetry 1993, Harri Jones Memorial Prize for Poetry, Adelaide Festival John Bray Poetry Award 1996, Sr Fellowships Literature Bd of the Australia Council, Young Australian Creative Fellowship, Grace Leven Poetry Prize, The Age Poetry Book of the Year. *Publications include:* poetry: The Frozen Sea 1983, Night Parrots 1989, The Book of Two Faces 1989, Poems 1991, Eschatologies 1991, Ultramarine (with Anthony Lawrence) 1992, Full Fathom Five 1993, Syzygy 1993, Erratum/Frame(d) 1995, Intensities of Blue (with Tracy Ryan) 1995, The Silo: A Pastoral Symphony 1995, The Radnoti Poems 1996, The Undertow: New and Selected Poems 1996, Lightning Tree 1996, Graphology (ed.) 1997, Poems: 1980–1994 1997, voice-overs (with Susan Schultz) 1997, The Hunt 1998, Kangaroo Virus (with Ron Sims) 1998, Sheep Dip 1998, Pine (with Keston Sutherland) 1998, Alterity: Poems without Tom Raworth 1998, The Benefaction (ed.) 1999, Fenland Pastorals 1999, Visitants 1999, Counter-Pastorals 1999, Wheatlands 2000, Zone 2000, Zoo (with Coral Hull) 2000, The Hierarchy of Sheep 2001, Auto 2001, Speed Factory (with Bernard Cohen, McKenzie Wark and Terri-ann White) 2002, Rivers (with Peter Porter and Sean O'Brien) 2002, Outside the Panopticon 2002, Lightning Tree 2003, Peripheral Light: New and Selected Poems (Western Australian Premier's Book Award for Poetry 2004) 2003, Four Australian Poets (with others) 2003, Doppler Effect 2004, The New Arcadia 2005, Shades of the Sublime and Beautiful 2008, Armour 2011, Jam Tree Gully 2012, The Jaguar's Dream 2012, Sack 2014, Marine (with Alan Jenkins) 2015, Drowning in Wheat: Selected Poems 2016, A Shared Wonder of Light (with John D'Alton) 2016, On the Outskirts 2017, Insomnia 2019; prose: Genre (novel) 1997, Grappling Eros (short stories) 1998, Crop Circles (play in verse) 1998, Paydirt (play), From Poetry to Politics and Back Again 2000, Divinations: Four Plays 2003, Peter Porter in Conversation with John Kinsella (with Peter Porter) 2003, The Wasps (play) 2003, Conspiracies (with Tracy Ryan) 2004, Post-colonial: A Récit (novel) 2009, In the Shade of the Shady Tree: Stories of Wheatbelt Australia (short stories) 2012, Morpheus: A Bildungsroman (novel) 2013, Lucida Intervalla 2018. *Website:* www.saltpublishing.com (office).

KINSELLA, Hon. Noël A., BA, LPh, STL, PhD, STD; Canadian human rights advocate, public servant, politician and academic; b. 28 Nov. 1939, Saint John, NB;

m. Ann Kinsella (née Conley); ed Univ. Coll., Dublin, Ireland, St Thomas Aquinas Univ. and Pontifical Lateran Univ., Rome, Italy; spent 42 years as Faculty mem. St Thomas Univ., Fredericton, NB where he taught psychology, philosophy and human rights; Assoc. Under-Sec. of State of Canada –1990; Senator 1990–14, Opposition Whip 1994–99, Deputy Leader of the Opposition 1999–2004, Leader of the Opposition 2004–06, Speaker of the Senate 2006–14, Chair. Internal Economy Cttee 2013–14, fmr mem. several Senate Standing Cttees, including Human Rights, Social Affairs, Science and Tech., and Nat. Finance; Chair. New Brunswick Human Rights Comm. 1967–88; licensed mem. Coll. of Psychologists of New Brunswick; mem. Queen's Privy Council 2015–; fmr Pres. Canadian Human Rights Foundation; mem. Advisory Council, Canadian Museum for Human Rights; mem. Bd of Govs St Thomas Univ.; Hon. Capt. (Navy); Kt, Order of Malta 1984, Order of St John 2011; Queen's Diamond Jubilee Medal 2012, Grand Cross 1st Class, Order of Merit (Germany) 2013; Dr hc (Dominican Univ. Coll., Ottawa) 2006, Hon. LLD (St Thomas Univ.) 2007, Hon. DLit (Univ. Coll. Dublin) 2011. *Publications include:* three books, several monographs and more than 50 articles on psychology and human rights.

KINSELLA, Thomas; Irish poet; b. 4 May 1928, Dublin; s. of John Paul Kinsella and Agnes Casserly Kinsella; m. Eleanor Walsh 1955; one s. two d.; with Irish Civil Service 1946–65, resgnd as Asst Prin. Officer, Dept of Finance 1965; Artist-in-Residence, Southern Illinois Univ. 1965–67, Prof. of English 1967–70; Prof. of English, Temple Univ., Philadelphia 1970–90; Dir Dolmen Press Ltd, Cuala Press Ltd, Dublin; f. Peppercanister (pvt. publishing co.) Dublin 1972; mem. Irish Acad. of Letters 1965–; Guggenheim Fellowship 1968–69, 1971–72; Hon. Sr Fellow, School of English, Univ. Coll. Dublin 2003, Hon. Freedom of City of Dublin 2007; Hon. DLitt (Nat. Univ. of Ireland) 1985, (Turin) 2005; Guinness Poetry Award 1958, Irish Arts Council Triennial Book Award 1960, Denis Devlin Memorial Award 1966, 1969, 1992, First European Poetry Award 2001, Freedom of City of Dublin 2007, Ulysses Medal, Univ. Coll. Dublin 2008. *Publications include:* Poems 1956, Another September (poems) 1958, Downstream (poems) 1962, Nightwalker and Other Poems 1966, The Táin (trans.) 1969, Notes from the Land of the Dead (poems) 1972, Butcher's Dozen (poem) 1972, New Poems 1973, Selected Poems 1956–1968 1973, Selected Poems of Austin Clarke 1976, Song of the Night and Other Poems 1978, The Messenger (poem) 1978, Fifteen Dead (poems) 1979, One and Other Poems 1979, Poems 1956–1973, Peppercanister Poems 1972–1978 1979, Poems of the Dispossessed 1600–1900 (with 100 translations from the Irish) (co-ed.) 1981, Ireland's Musical Heritage: Sean O'Riada's Radio Talks on Irish Traditional Music (ed.) 1981, Songs of the Psyche (poems) 1985, Her Vertical Smile (poem) 1985, The New Oxford Book of Irish Verse (including all new trans from the Irish) (ed.) 1986, St Catherine's Clock (poem) 1987, Out of Ireland (poems) 1987, Blood and Family (collected poems from 1978) 1988, Poems from Centre City 1990, Personal Places (poems) 1990, One Fond Embrace (poem) 1990, Madonna and other Poems 1991, Butcher's Dozen (anniversary reissue) 1992, From Centre City (collected poems from 1990) 1994, The Dual Tradition: An Essay on Poetry and Politics in Ireland 1995, Collected Poems 1956–94, The Pen Shop (poem) 1997, The Familiar (poems) 1999, Godhead (poems) 1999, Citizen of the World (poems) 2001, Marginal Economy (poems) 2006, Readings in Poetry (essays) 2006, A Dublin Documentary 2006, Man of War (poems) 2007, Belief and Unbelief (poems) 2007, Prose Occasions 1951–2006 2009, Fat Master (poems) 2012, Love Joy Peace (poems) 2012, Late Poems 2013. *Leisure interests:* history, publishing.

KINSKI, Nastassja; German actress; b. (Nastassja Nakszynski), 24 Jan. 1961, W Berlin; d. of Klaus Kinski and Ruth Brigitte Kinski; m. Ibrahim Moussa 1984 (divorced 1992); one s. one d.; one d. by Quincy Jones; film début in Falsche Bewegung 1975; Bundespreis 1983. *Films include:* Stay As You Are 1978, Tess 1978, One From The Heart 1982, Cat People 1982, Moon In The Gutter 1983, Spring Symphony 1983, Unfaithfully Yours 1984, The Hotel New Hampshire 1984, Maria's Lovers 1984, Paris, Texas 1984, Revolution 1985, Harem, Torrents of Spring 1989, On a Moonlit Night 1989, Magdalene 1989, The King's Future 1989, The Secret, Night Sun 1991, Faraway, So Close!, Terminal Velocity 1994, One Night Stand 1997, Little Boy Blue 1997, Father's Day 1997, Somebody is Waiting 1997, Sunshine 1998, Your Friends and Neighbors 1999, The Magic of Marciano 1999, The Intruder 1999, Town and Country 1999, The Lost 1999, The Claim 2000, The Day the World Ended 2001, An American Rhapsody 2001, Say Nothing 2001, Diary of a Sex Addict 2001, Beyond the City Limits 2001, .com for Murder 2002, Paradise Found 2003, A ton image 2004, Inland Empire 2006, Sugar 2013.

KINSLEY, Michael, BA, JD; American journalist; b. 9 March 1951, Detroit, Mich.; m. Patty Stonesifer; ed Cranbrook Kingswood School, Mich., Harvard Univ., Magdalen Coll., Oxford, UK and George Washington Univ.; journalist, The New Republic (magazine), Ed. 1978–95, writing 'TRB from Washington' column; editorial posts at Washington Monthly, Harper's, The Economist; Co-host Crossfire TV program (CNN) 1989–95; Founding Ed. Slate online magazine 1995–2002, columnist 2002–04; Editorial and Opinion Ed. Los Angeles Times 2004–05; columnist, Time magazine 2006–09, Politico 2009–; Ed.-at-Large, The New Republic 2013–; Contributing Ed. Vanity Fair 2014–; fmr columnist, Wall Street Journal, The Times (London), Washington Post; contrib. to New Yorker, Reader's Digest, Condé Nast Traveler; American Ed. Guardian Unlimited (London) 2006; Columbia Journalism Review Editor of the Year 1999. *Publications include:* Big Babies 1997, The Slate Diaries 2000, Please Don't Remain Calm: Provocations and Commentaries 2008, Creative Capitalism (co-ed) 2009, Old Age: A Beginner's Guide 2016. *Address:* c/o Vanity Fair, Condé Nast, 1 World Trade Center, New York, NY 10007, USA. *Website:* www.mikekinsley.com.

KINZLER, Kenneth W., PhD; American oncologist and academic; *Professor of Oncology, Johns Hopkins Oncology Center, Johns Hopkins University School of Medicine;* b. 30 Jan. 1962, Philadelphia, Pa; ed Philadelphia Coll. of Pharmacy and Science and Johns Hopkins Univ. School of Medicine (JHUSM), Baltimore, Md; Postdoctoral Fellow in Oncology, JHUSM 1988–90, Asst Prof. 1990–94, Assoc. Prof. and Co-Dir Molecular Genetics Lab. 1994–99, Prof. of Oncology 1999–, also Prof. of Oncology, McKusick-Nathans Inst. of Genetic Medicine, Johns Hopkins Univ., Dir Ludwig Center; mem. Scientific Advisory Bd, Morphotek, Inc.; mem. Founding Scientific Advisors, Personal Genome Diagnostics, Inc.; Alumni Award for Highest Average in Toxicology Curriculum, PCPS 1983, David Israel Macht Award for Excellence in Research, JHUSM 1988, Sandoz Award for Superior Academic Achievement and Contribution to Health Care, JHUSM 1988, Postdoctoral Award in Basic Science, JHUSM 1990, Young Alumnus Award, PCPS 1993, Merit Award, Nat. Cancer Inst. 2002. *Achievements include:* co-inventor of morphogenics, broad-based proprietary platform technology that regulates the ability of host organisms to repair mutations that occur during DNA replication. *Publications:* more than 220 articles in scientific journals. *Address:* Johns Hopkins Oncology Center, Room 588, Cancer Research Building, 1650 Orleans Street, Baltimore, MD 21231, USA (office). *Telephone:* (410) 955-2928 (office). *Fax:* (410) 955-0548 (office). *E-mail:* kinzlke@welch.jhu.edu (office); kinzlke@jhmi.edu (office). *Website:* www.hopkinsmedicine.org/profiles/results/directory/profile/9175399/kenneth-kinzler (office).

KIPCHOGE, Eliud; Kenyan athlete; b. 5 Nov. 1984, Kapsisiywa, nr Kapsabet, Nandi Dist, Rift Valley Prov.; m.; two s. one d.; ed Kaptel Secondary School; distance runner; based in Nijmegen, Netherlands during track season; began racing in local cross-country events 2001; won jr race in nat. cross country trials 2002 and selection to nat. team; won 5,000m at trials for World Jr Championship, but did not travel to event due to illness; won jr nat. cross country trials and world event in Lausanne 2003; broke world jr 5,000m record, Oslo 2003; Gold Medal, 5,000m, World Championships, Paris 2003 (championship record time), Marathon, Abbott World Marathon Majors, Chicago 2014, Berlin 2015, 2017, 2018, London 2015, 2016, 2018, Olympic Games, Rio de Janeiro 2016; won nat. cross country trials 2004, 2005 over 12 kilometres; won Kenya's 2004 Olympic Trials at 5,000m; Bronze Medal, 5,000m, Olympic Games, Athens 2004, World Indoor Championships, Moscow 2006; Silver Medal, 5,000m, World Championships, Osaka 2007, Olympic Games, Beijing 2008, Commonwealth Games 2010; Men's 3,000m Best Year Performance 2004–05, Head of State's Commendation 2006, IAAF Athlete of the Year 2018, Academy Exceptional Achievement Award, Laureus World Sports Awards 2019. *Address:* Athletics Kenya, Riadha House, PO Box 46722, 00100 Nairobi, Kenya. *E-mail:* athleticskenya@gt.co.ke; info@nnrunningteam.com. *Website:* www.athleticskenya.or.ke; www.nnrunningteam.com.

KIPKETER, Wilson; Kenyan/Danish professional athlete; b. 12 Dec. 1972, Kapchemoiywo, Kenya; m. Pernille Kipketer 2000; ed St Patrick's High School, Iten, Kenya; world outdoor record-holder for 800m (1 minute 41.11 seconds) 1997 and indoor record (1 minute 42.67 seconds) 1997; set new world indoor record for 1000m (2 minutes 14.96 seconds), Birmingham, UK 2000; coached by Slawomir Nowak; resident in Denmark since 1990, qualified to compete for Denmark May 1995; gold medal, World Championships 1995, 1997, 1999; gold medal, World Indoor Championships 1997; Olympic silver medal 800m, Sydney 2000; European champion 800m, Munich 2002; silver medal, World Indoor Championships 2003; unbeaten over 800m for 33 races in 1996–97; retd 2005; Amb., Int. Asscn of Athletics Fed., also Head of Int. Devt; mem. Champions for Peace club.

KIPPENHAHN, Rudolf; German astronomer; b. 24 May 1926, Bärringen, Czechoslovakia; s. of Rudolf Kippenhahn and Alma Belz; m. Johanna Rasper 1955; three d.; ed Graslitz and St Joachimsthal Schools, Univs of Halle and Erlangen; Scientific Asst, Bamberg Observatory 1951–57; staff mem., Max-Planck-Inst. für Physik und Astrophysik, Inst. für Astrophysik 1957–65, mem. of Directorate 1963, Dir 1975–91, now Prof. Emer.; Visiting Prof., Caltech, Pasadena and Princeton Univ. 1961–62; Prof., Univ. Observatory, Göttingen 1965–75; Visiting Prof., UCLA 1968, Ohio State Univ. 1979, Univ. Observatory, Hamburg 1986–87; Assoc. mem. Royal Astronomical Soc., London; mem. Bayerische Akademie der Wissenschaften, Munich; Corresp. mem. Austrian Acad. of Sciences; Hon. Prof., Univ. of Munich 1975–; Verdienstkreuz (1st Class) (FRG); Carus-Medal, Leopoldina, Halle, Carus Prize, City of Schweinfurt, Lorenz-Oken-Medal, Gesellschaft Deutscher Naturforscher und Ärzte, Eddington Medal, Royal Astronomical Soc. 2005. *Publications:* One Hundred Billion Suns: The Birth, Life and Death of the Stars 1983, Licht vom Rande der Welt 1984, Light from the Depth of Time 1987, Unheimliche Welten 1987, Stellar Structure and Evolution 1990, Der Stern von dem wir Leben 1990, Abenteuer Weltall 1991, Discovering the Secrets of the Sun 1994; and numerous articles in astronomical and astrophysical journals. *Address:* Rautenbreite 2, 37077 Göttingen, Germany. *Telephone:* (551) 24714. *Fax:* (551) 22902.

KIRALY, Charles Frederick (Karch); American professional volleyball player (retd) and volleyball coach; *Head Coach, Women's National Volleyball Team;* b. 3 Nov. 1960, Jackson, Mich.; s. of Lazlo Kiraly; m. Janna Miller; two s.; ed Univ. of California, Los Angeles; led UCLA to Nat. Collegiate Athletic Asscn championships 1979, 1981, 1982; played on nat. team, winning gold medals, Olympic Games 1984, 1988, World Championship titles 1982, 1986; won inaugural gold medal for Olympic beach volleyball (with Kent Steffes) 1996; record for most pro beach titles (148); f. Karch Kiraly Volleyball Acad., Karch Kiraly Scholarship Fund; Asst Coach, US Women's Nat. Volleyball Team 2009–12, Head Coach 2012–; Player of the Century, Fédération Internationale de Volleyball, Sportsman of the Year, Asscn of Volleyball Professionals (AVP) 1995, 1997, 1998, AVP Most Valuable Player 1990, 1992, 1993, 1994, 1995, 1998, inducted into Volleyball Hall of Fame 2001, California Sports Hall of Fame 2010. *Publications include:* co-author (with Byron Shewman) Beach Volleyball, The Sand Man (autobiog.). *Address:* USA Volleyball Headquarters, 4065 Sinton Road, Suite 200, Colorado Springs, CO 80907, USA (office). *Telephone:* (719) 228-6800 (office). *Fax:* (719) 228-6899 (office). *E-mail:* postmaster@usav.org (office). *Website:* www.teamusa.org/usa-volleyball (office).

KIRANA, Kusnan; Indonesian airline executive; *Chairman, Lion Air Group;* b. 8 Aug. 1959, brother of Rusdi Kirana; m.; two c.; began career as travel agent; co-f. (with brother) PT Lion Mentari Airlines (Lion Air) 2000, currently Chair. Lion Air Group, also includes Wings Air, Batik Air, Lion Bizjet, Malindo Air based in Malaysia, and Thai Lion Air. *Address:* PT Lion Mentari Airlines, Jl. Gajah Mada No. 7, Jakarta (office); Taman Meruya Ilir, Blok D-5 No. 3, Jakarta Barat, Indonesia (office). *Telephone:* (21) 6326039 (office). *Fax:* (21) 6348744 (office). *E-mail:* info@lionair.co.id (office). *Website:* www.lionair.co.id (office).

KIRANA, Rusdi; Indonesian airline executive and diplomatist; *Ambassador to Malaysia;* b. 1963, brother of Kusnan Kirana; m.; three c.; began career as travel agent; co-f. (with brother) PT Lion Mentari Airlines (Lion Air) 2000, Pres. Lion Air Group –2017, includes Wings Air, Batik Air, Lion Bizjet, Malindo Air based in Malaysia, and Thai Lion Air; Amb. to Malaysia 2017–. *Address:* Embassy of Indonesia, 233 Jalan Tun Razak, POB 10889, 50400, Kuala Lumpur, Malaysia (office); PT Lion Mentari Airlines, Jl. Gajah Mada No. 7, Jakarta, Indonesia (office). *Telephone:* (3) 21164016 (office); (21) 6326039 (Lion Air) (office). *Fax:* (3) 21423878; (21) 6348744 (Lion Air) (office). *E-mail:* info@kbrikualalumpur.org (office); info@lionair.co.id (office). *Website:* www.kbrikualalumpur.org (office); www.lionair.co.id (office).

KIRANANDANA, Khunying Suchada, BComm, PhD; Thai university professor; *Professor Emeritus, Chulalongkorn University;* b. Bangkok; m. Thienchay Kiranandana; two s.; ed Chulalongkorn Univ., Bangkok, Harvard Univ., USA; several positions in Faculty of Commerce and Accountancy, Chulalongkorn Univ. 1979–99, Grad. School 1999–2004, Pres. Chulalongkorn Univ. 2004–08, apptd Pres. Univ. Council 2012, now Prof. Emer.; Pres. Thai Statistical Asscn 1997–2011; mem. Sasin Advisory Bd 2004–08; mem. Test of English as a Foreign Language (TOEFL) Policy Council 1997–2000; Dir Kasikornbank PLC 2000–15 (Vice Chair. 2015–18), Serm Suk Public Co. Ltd 2008–, Dusit Thani Public Co. Ltd 2017–; apptd Chair. Phufa Shop Operations Cttee 2001; mem. Thai Red Cross Soc. Cttee 2006–, Nat. Legislature Council 2006–08; Kt, Grand Cordon (Special Class), Most Exalted Order of the White Elephant, Kt, Grand Cordon, Most Noble Order of the Crown of Thailand, Most Illustrious Order (Fourth Class) of Chula Chom Klao; Hon. DBA (Chulalongkorn Univ.). *Publications:* Inferential Statistics, an Introduction 1982, Theory of Sample Surveys 1995, Statistical Information Technology: Data in Information Systems 1998, Statistics in Everyday Life 2004. *Leisure interest:* reading. *Address:* Office of the University Council, Chulalongkorn University, 254 Phyathai Road, Patumwan, Bangkok 10330, Thailand (office). *Telephone:* (2) 218-3280 (office). *E-mail:* int.off@chula.ac.th (office). *Website:* www.chula.ac.th (office).

KIRBY, Anthony John, PhD, FRS, FRSC; British chemist, academic and research scientist; *Professor Emeritus of Bio-organic Chemistry, University of Cambridge;* b. 18 Aug. 1935, Welwyn Garden City, Herts.; s. of Samuel A. Kirby and Gladys R. Kirby (née Welch); m. Sara Nieweg 1962; one s. two d.; ed Eton Coll., Gonville and Caius Coll., Cambridge; Fellow, Gonville and Caius Coll. 1962–, Demonstrator, Lecturer in Organic Chem., Univ. of Cambridge 1968–85, Tutor 1967–75, Reader 1985–95, Prof. of Bio-organic Chem. 1995–2002, Prof. Emer. 2002–, Dir of Studies in Natural Sciences, Gonville and Caius Coll. Cambridge 1968–96; NATO Research Fellow, Brandeis Univ., Mass, USA 1963–64; Coordinator European Network on Artificial Nucleases 2000–04; Hon. DPhil (Turku) 2006; RSC Award in Organic Reaction Mechanisms 1983, RSC Tilden Lecturer 1987, RSC Ingold Lecturer 1996, Marin Drinov Medal, Bulgarian Acad. of Sciences 2003. *Publications:* The Organic Chemistry of Phosphorus (with S. G. Warren) 1967, Stereoelectronic Effects at Oxygen 1983, Stereoelectronic Effects 1996; more than 300 articles on mechanistic bio-organic chemistry. *Address:* University Chemical Laboratory, Cambridge, CB2 1EW (office); 87 Holbrook Road, Cambridge, CB1 2SX, England (home). *Telephone:* (1223) 336370 (office); (1223) 210403 (home). *Fax:* (1223) 336362 (office). *E-mail:* ajk1@cam.ac.uk (office). *Website:* www.ch.cam.ac.uk/staff/ajk.html (office).

KIRBY, Hon. Michael Donald, AC, CMG, BA, BEcons, LLM; Australian jurist; *Co-Chairman International Bar Association's Human Rights Institute;* b. 18 March 1939, Sydney, NSW; s. of Donald Kirby and Jean Kirby (née Knowles); partner Johan van Vloten 1969; ed Fort Street Boys' High School and Univ. of Sydney; Fellow, Senate, Univ. of Sydney 1964–69; mem. NSW Bar Council 1974; Deputy Pres., Australian Conciliation & Arbitration Comm. 1975–83; Chair. Australian Law Reform Comm. 1975–84, OECD Expert Group on Privacy and Int. Data Flows 1978–80, Cttee of Counsellors, Human and People's Rights UNESCO 1985, UNESCO Expert Group on the Rights of Peoples 1989; mem. Admin. Review Council of Australia 1976–84; mem. Council, Univ. of Newcastle, NSW 1977–83, Deputy Chancellor 1978–83; mem. Australian Nat. Comm. for UNESCO 1980–84 (Hon. mem. 1997–2007), Australian Inst. of Multicultural Affairs 1979–83; Judge, Fed. Court of Australia 1983–84; mem. Exec. CSIRO 1983–86; Chancellor, Macquarie Univ., Sydney 1984–93; Pres. Court of Appeal, Supreme Court of NSW 1984–96; Acting Chief Justice of NSW 1988, 1990, 1993, 1995; Admin. (Acting Gov.) NSW 1991; Justice, High Court of Australia 1996–2009; Acting Chief Justice of Australia 2007–08; Commr WHO Global Comm. on AIDS 1989–91; mem. Int. Comm. of Jurists, Geneva 1985–99, mem. Exec. Cttee 1989–95, Chair. 1992–95, Pres. 1995–98, Pres. Australian Section 1989–96; Special Rep. of Sec.-Gen. of UN on Human Rights for Cambodia 1993–96; Pres. Court of Appeal of Solomon Islands 1995–96; Pres. Australian Acad. of Forensic Sciences 1987–89; mem. Ethics Cttee of Human Genome Org. 1995–2003; Trustee, AIDS Trust of Australia 1987–93; mem. UNESCO Jury for Prize for Teaching of Human Rights 1994–96, UNESCO Int. Bioethics Cttee 1996–2006; Rapporteur, UNAIDS Global Panel on HIV/AIDS and Human Rights 2003–, Int. Group on Judicial Integrity (UNHCR) 2004–; Co-Chair. Expert Group on Bioethics and Human Rights, High Commr of Human Rights 2002–; Chair. Group of Experts, UNESCO IBC drafting of Declaration of Universal Norms in Bioethics 2004–05, Commonwealth Expert Group on Rule of Law 2011, UN Comm. of Inquiry on Democratic People's Repub. of Korea 2013–14, Expert Advisory Group on Equitable Access to Health Care 2015–16; mem. Judicial Reference Group, High Commr for Human Rights 2007–; mem. Advisory Bd Int. Human Rights Inst., De Paul Univ., Chicago, USA; Pres. Inst. of Arbitrators and Mediators 2009–10; Dir Australian Centre for Int. Commercial Arbitration 2010–; mem. Arbitration Panel CSID (World Bank) 2010–; mem. UNDP Global Comm. on HIV and Law 2010–12, Eminent Persons Group on Future of the Commonwealth of Nations 2010–11; Commr UNAIDS/Lancet Comm. on AIDS To Sustainable Health 2013–; Ed. in Chief, The Laws of Australia 2009–; mem. Global Fund, High Level Panel on Equitable Access to Health Care 2015–16, UN Sec.-Gen.'s High Level Panel on Access to Essential Healthcare 2015–16, Asia Pacific Leadership Network for Nuclear Non-Proliferation and Disarmament; Co-Chair. Int. Bar Asscn's Human Rights Inst. 2018–; Hon. Fellow, New Zealand Research Foundation, Australian Acad. of Social Sciences 1996, Acad. of Social Sciences in Australia 2004, Australian Acad. of Humanities 2006, Hon. Bencher, Inner Temple (London) 2006, Hon. mem. American Law Inst. 2000, Soc. of Legal Scholars (UK) 2007; Hon. LLD (Monash) 2015, (Queen's Univ. Ontario) 2015; numerous other hon. doctorates; Loewenthal Medal, Sydney Univ., Australian Human Rights Medal 1991, Laureate, UNESCO Prize for Human Rights Educ. 1998, Centenary Medal 2003, Australian Privacy Medal 2010, Int. Privacy Champion Award, EPIC 2010, Gruber Justice Prize 2010. *Publications include:* Industrial Index to Australian Labour Law 1978, 1984, Reform the Law 1983, The Judges 1984, A Touch of Healing 1986 (co-ed.), Through the World's Eye 2000, Judicial Activism (Hamlyn Lectures 2003) 2004, A Private Life 2011, What Would Gandhi Do? 2013, Tagore Law Lectures: Sexual Orientation & Gender Identity - A New Province of Law for India 2015. *Leisure interest:* work. *Address:* Level 7, 195 Macquarie Street, Sydney, NSW 2000, Australia (home). *Telephone:* (9) 231-5800 (office). *Fax:* (9) 231-5811 (office). *E-mail:* mail@michaelkirby.com.au (office). *Website:* www.michaelkirby.com.au.

KIRBY, Peter Maxwell, MA, MBA; Australian business executive; *Chairman, DuluxGroup Limited;* b. 2 Aug. 1947, South Africa; s. of Robert Maxwell Kirby and May Kirby; m. Erica Anne Ebden; one s.; ed Rhodes Univ., Natal Univ., Univ. of Manchester, UK, Univ. of the Witwatersrand, Harvard Business School, USA; Man. Dir Dulux Paints 1991–92; CEO ICI Paints Asia Pacific 1992–95, Chair. and CEO ICI Paints 1995–98, Exec. Bd Dir ICI PLC, Chair. DuluxGroup Ltd 2010–; Man. Dir and CEO CSR Ltd 1998–2003; Chair. Medibank Private Ltd 2004–08; mem. Bd of Dirs, Macquarie Bank Ltd 2003–; Centenary Medal 2003. *Leisure interests:* classic sports cars, boating. *Telephone:* (3) 9787-8293 (office).

KIRCHHOFF, Frank, Dr rer. nat et med. hab.; German virologist and academic; *University Professor of Virology and Director, Institute of Molecular Virology, University of Ulm;* b. 24 April 1961, Bückeburg; ed Gymnasium Adolfinum, Bückeburg, Univ. of Göttingen; Postdoctoral Fellow, Harvard Medical School 1991–94; Head of Research Group, Inst. for Clinical and Molecular Virology, Univ. of Erlangen-Nuremberg 1994–99, Lecturer 1997–99, Research Asst Prof. (C2) 1999–2001; Univ. Prof. (C3) of Virology, Faculty of Medicine, Univ. of Ulm 2001–, Dir Inst. for Molecular Virology 2009–; Professorship, Imperial Coll. London 2007; Professorships at Univs of Giessen, Basel and Göttingen 2008; Prof. and Dir Dept of Molecular Physiology, Univ. of Saarland 2009–; mem. Comm. GfV for Univ. Affairs and Int. Relations, Scientific Advisory Bd, ViroPharmaceuticals GmbH, Hanover; mem. Editorial Bd, Journal of Virology, Retrovirology, Advances in Virology, Cell 2009–, Nat. AIDS Advisory Council 2012; mem. German Nat. Acad. of Sciences Leopoldina, Soc. for Virology, American Soc. for Microbiology, Academia Europaea; Nachwuchsförderpreis, German Primate Centre 1990, German AIDS Research Award, Soc. for Infectious Diseases 1995, Thiersch Prize, Medical Faculty of Univ. Erlangen-Nuremberg 1998, Research Award, BUPA Foundation (co-recipient) 1999, Foundation Award, Univ. of Ulm 2002, German AIDS Prize, German AIDS Soc. 2003, AIDS Research Award, Heinz-Ansmann Foundation 2006, AIDS Research Award, Hector Foundation 2007, Innovation Award, German Univ. Hosps 2007, Merckle Research Prize 2007, Research Award, GlaxoSmithKline Foundation for Clinical Research 2008, Gottfried Wilhelm Leibniz Prize 2009, Advanced Grant, European Research Council 2012, Ernst Schering Prize 2013. *Publications:* numerous papers in professional journals. *Address:* Room 2.071, Building N27, Universitätsklinikum Ulm, Meyerhofstr. 1, 89081 Ulm (office); Building 48, Center for Integrative Physiology and Molecular Medicine (CIPMM), University of Saarland, D- 66421 Homburg, Germany (office). *Telephone:* (731) 50065150 (Ulm) (office); (6841) 1616440 (Saarland) (office). *Fax:* (731) 50043002 (Ulm) (office); (6841) 1616439 (Saarland) (office). *E-mail:* frank.kirchhoff@uni-ulm.de (office). *Website:* www.uni-ulm.de/en/fakultaeten/medicine.html (office); cipmm.uni-saarland.de (office); www.kirchhoff-lab.de (office).

KIRCHSCHLAGER, Angelika; Austrian singer (mezzo-soprano); b. 1965, Salzburg; m.; one s.; ed Musisches Gymnasium, Salzburg and Vienna Music Acad.; studied with Walter Berry in Vienna 1984; first performance in Die Zauberflöte, Vienna Kammeroper; concert performances in Austria, France, Germany, Italy, Czech Repub., Denmark, USA and Japan; recitals in London, Edinburgh, Amsterdam, Cologne, Frankfurt, Hohenems, Graz, Bilbao and in Scandinavia; role of Composer in Jonathan Miller production of Ariadne auf Naxos, Lausanne Opera 1998–99; sang with London Symphony Orchestra, New York Chamber Orchestra and Vienna Symphony Orchestra 1999–2000; feature broadcasts on Austrian Nat. Radio and TV (ORF); participated in film production about Hugo Wolf in role of Frieda Zerny 1992; operatic roles include appearances in Le nozze de Figaro (Schloss Schönbrunn, Vienna), Der Rosenkavalier (Geneva), Hänsel und Gretel (Graz), The Merry Widow (Vienna), Palestrina (Vienna), Don Giovanni (Ravenna and Milan), Les Contes d'Hoffmann (Paris), Ariadne auf Naxos (London), Die Dreigroschenoper (London and Paris) 2009, Die Fledermaus (Vienna) 2010–11, Pelléas et Mélisande (Helsinki) 2012; currently Prof., Mozarteum in Salzburg, Univ. of Graz; awarded title Kammersängerin (Govt of Austria) 2007; three prizes, Int. Belvedere Competition, Vienna 1991. *Recordings include:* album of Lieder by Alma Mahler, Gustav Mahler and Erich Wolfgang Korngold (solo debut) 1997; featured on recording of Mendelssohn with Claudio Abbado and Berlin Philharmonic; When Night Falls (solo recital) 1999, Handel Arias 2006, Bach Arias 2008, Hugo Wolf Songs 2009, Schumann Songs 2010, Brahms Songs Vol. 1 2010, Liszt Songs Vol. 1, Vol. 2 (BBC Music Magazine Vocal Award 2013). *Address:* c/o Phillippa Cole, Askonas Holt Ltd, 15 Fetter Lane, London, EC4A 1BW, England (office). *E-mail:* phillippa.cole@askonasholt.co.uk (office). *Website:* www.askonasholt.co.uk/artists/singers/mezzo-soprano/angelika-kirchschlager (office).

KIRIENKO, Sergey Vladilenovich; Russian economist, politician, government official and energy industry executive; *First Deputy Chief of Staff of the Presidential Administration;* b. 26 July 1962, Sukhumi; m. Maria Kirienko; one s. two d.; ed Inst. of Naval Engineers, Gorky (now Nizhy Novgorod), Acad. of Nat. Economy, Moscow; served in Soviet army 1984–86; worked as Master in Krasnoe Sormovo shipbuilding facility, Nizhy Novgorod; elected Sec. of regional Komsomol org. 1986, then Sec., Krasnoye Sormovo Komsomol Cttee, First Sec., Gorky regional Komsomol Cttee, mem. All-Union Leninist Communist Youth League (Komsomol) Central Cttee; Founder and Chair. Garantia Bank, Nizhy Novgorod 1993–96; Pres. NorSea Oil Co., Nizhy Novgorod 1996–97; First Deputy, Ministry of Fuel and Energy May–Oct. 1997, also apptd Deputy Chair. Governmental Comm. for Coordination of Implementation of Production-Sharing Agreements, Head, Interdepartmental Comm. for ind. entities' access to Gazprom's gas transportation network, also became mem. panel of state reps in Transneft; Minister of Fuel and Energy 1997–98; Prime Minister, Russian Fed. April–Aug. 1998; Founder and Co-Chair. Novaya Sila party 1998; mem. State Duma representing Right Force Alliance 1999–2000, Leader Parl. faction Union of Right Forces; Presidential Rep., Volga Fed. Dist 2000–05; Chair. State Comm. on Chemical Weapons Destruction 2001–05; Head, State Atomic Energy Corpn (Rosatom) 2005–16; First Deputy Chief of Staff of the Presidential Admin 2016–. *Address:* Office of the President,

103132 Moscow, Staraya pl. 4, Russia (office). *Telephone:* (495) 625-35-81 (office). *Fax:* (495) 606-07-66 (office). *Website:* www.kremlin.ru (office).

KIRILL I, Patriarch, CandTheol; Russian ecclesiastic; *Patriarch of Moscow and All Rus'*; b. (Vladimir Mikhailovich Gundyayev), 20 Nov. 1946, Leningrad (now St Petersburg), Russian SFSR, USSR; s. of Mikhail Gundyayev; ed Leningrad Theological Acad.; ordained as Hierodeacon 1969, Hieromonk 1969; Prof. of Dogmatic Theology and Aide to Insp., Leningrad Theological Acad. 1970; Personal Sec. to Metropolitan Nikodim, Leningrad 1970; ordained Archimandrite 1971; Rector, Leningrad Acad. and Seminary 1974; consecrated Bishop of Vyborg 1976, Archbishop 1977; Archbishop (later Metropolitan), Smolensk and Vyazma 1984–89, Archbishop, Smolensk and Kaliningrad 1989–91, Metropolitan, Smolensk and Kaliningrad 1991–2009; Patriarch of Moscow and All Rus' 2009–; Deputy Chair. Dept for External Church Relations, Moscow Patriarchate 1978–89, Chair. 1989–; Perm. mem. Holy Synod 1989–; Co-Chair. World Conf. of Religions for Peace 2006–; fmr Russian Orthodox Church Rep. to WCC, mem. WCC Cen. Cttee and Exec. Cttee 1975–; fmr Man. Patriarch's parishes, Finland; met with Pope Francis I (Head of RC Church) at José Martí Int. Airport, Havana, Cuba and signed a 30-point joint declaration on global issues, including their hope for re-establishment of full unity, the persecution of Christians in the Middle East, the Syrian Civil War and church organization in Ukraine, this was the first meeting between a pope and a Russian Orthodox patriarch since the Western and Eastern branches of Christianity split in the Great Schism of 1054 AD (although Pope Paul VI had met with Ecumenical Patriarch Athenagoras I of Constantinople in Jerusalem in 1965) 12 Feb. 2016; Hon. Citizen, Lukoyanov Dist, Nizhnii Novgorod Oblast 2000, Smolensk 2003, Rizskoye village, Vyazma Dist, Smolensk Oblast 2004, 2006, Kaliningrad Oblast of the Neman 2006, Kaliningrad 2006, Khoroshevo-Mnevniki North-Western Admin. Dist of Moscow 2006, Smolensk Oblast 2009, Kaliningrad Oblast 2009, Kemerovo Oblast 2010, Repub. of Mordoviya 2011; decorated by the Churches of Alexandria, Antioch, Jerusalem, Georgia, Serbia, Bulgaria, Greece, Poland, the Czech Lands and Slovakia, America and Finland; awarded Russian Orthodox Church Orders of St Vladimir Equal-to-the-Apostles, St Alexis the Metropolitan of Moscow, St Daniel of Moscow, St Sergius of Radonezh and St Innocent the Metropolitan of Moscow; several state decorations, including Order of the Friendship of Nations 1988, Order of Friendship 1996, Order for Services for the Motherland (Third Class) 2000, (Second Class) 2006; Order 'Honour' (Azerbaijan) 2010, Medal '65th Anniversary of Victory in the Great Patriotic War' ('Transnistrian Moldovan Rep.') 2010, Order of the Repub. (Moldova) 2011; Hon. DTheol (Theological Acad., Budapest) 1987. *Television:* host of weekly programme, ORT/Channel One 1994–. *Publication:* co-authored book on judo and sambo and their relationship to Orthodox Christianity. *Address:* Danilov Monastery DECR, MP, 115191 Moscow, ul. Danilovskii Val 22, Russia (office). *Telephone:* (495) 633-8428 (office). *Fax:* (495) 633-8428 (office). *E-mail:* cs@mospatr.ru (office). *Website:* mospat.ru/en/the_patriarch (office).

KIRK, David Edward, MBE, MB, ChB; New Zealand business executive and fmr rugby union player; *Co-founder and Partner, Bailador Investment Management*; b. 5 Oct. 1961, Wellington; ed Wanganui Collegiate School, Univ. of Otago, Univ. of Oxford, UK; played prov. rugby for Otago, toured with New Zealand Colts and first toured with All Blacks in 1983, refused to join rebel Cavaliers team on moral grounds when planned 1986 All Black tour to SA was cancelled, captained so-called Baby Blacks, was made capt. of NZ team in inaugural Rugby World Cup in 1987 and led team to victory over France in final, retd from competitive rugby aged 25 and took up Rhodes Scholarship at Worcester Coll., Oxford 1987; returned to NZ becoming coach of Wellington NPC team 1993, media commentator 1994; worked as staffer for Prime Minister Jim Bolger and as man. consultant, McKinsey & Co.; CEO Fairfax Media Ltd (publr of The Sydney Morning Herald, The Age and The Australian Financial Review in Australia, and The Dominion Post and The Christchurch Press in NZ) 2005–08 (resgnd); Co-founder and Partner, Bailador Investment Management (investment co.) 2010–. *Address:* Bailador Investment Management, Suite 4, Level 11, 6 O'Connell Street, Sydney, NSW 2000, Australia (office). *Telephone:* (2) 9223-2344 (office). *Website:* bailador.com.au (office).

KIRK, Mark Steven, BA, MS, JD; American naval officer, lawyer and politician; b. 15 Sept. 1959, Champaign, Ill.; s. of Francis Gabriel Kirk and Judith Ann Kirk (née Brady); m. Kimberly Vertolli 2001 (divorced 2009); ed New Trier High School, Blackburn Coll., Universidad Nacional Autónoma de México, Cornell Univ., London School of Econs, UK, Georgetown Univ. Law Center; commissioned as intelligence officer in US Naval Reserve 1989, holds rank of Commdr; admitted to Bar of Ill. 1992, DC 1993; Parl. aide to Julian Critchley, MP, London 1982–83; worked on staff of John Porter, fmr Rep. from Illinois 10th Congressional Dist 1984–90; campaigner, Porter for Congress, Northern Ill. 1984–90; Organizer, Bush/Quayle Campaign, Northern Ill. 1988, Dole for President 1988, various states; officer, World Bank, Washington, DC 1990; Special Asst to Asst Sec. of State for Inter-American Affairs 1991–93; Attorney, Baker & McKenzie LLP 1993–95; named as Counsel to US House Int. Relations Cttee 1995–99; mem. US House of Reps for 10th Congressional Dist of Ill. 2001–10, mem. Appropriations Cttee, House Iran Working Group, Founder and Co-Chair. House US-China Working Group, Co-Chair. Congressional Caucus on Armenian Issues, Albanian Issues Caucus in ex-Yugoslavia, mem. GOP Tuesday Group; Senator from Illinois 2010–17, mem. Appropriations Cttee, Banking, Housing and Urban Affairs Cttee, Health, Educ., Labor and Pensions, Special Cttee on Aging; mem. Bd of Dirs Population Resource Center, Princeton, NJ; mem. Navy League, Naval Reserve Asscn, New Trier Republican Org.; Republican; Navy and Marine Corps Commendation Medal, Navy Achievement Medal, Nat. Defense Service Medal, Global War on Terror Service Medal, Jt Meritorious Unit Award, Navy Unit Commendation, Navy Meritorious Unit Commendation; Kellogg Fellow, Chicago 1980, Council of Jewish Fed. Award, Washington 1988. *Publications:* contrib. of articles to various newspapers. *Leisure interests:* backpacking, skydiving.

KIRK, Paul Grattan, Jr, AB, LLB; American political official and lawyer; b. 18 Jan. 1938, Newton, Mass.; s. of Paul G. Kirk and Josephine Kirk (née O'Connell); m. Gail Loudermilk 1974; ed Harvard Univ.; Pnr, Sullivan & Worcester LLP (law firm), Boston and Washington, DC 1977–90, Counsel 1990, now Retd Pnr; Chair. Kirk & Assocs Inc. 1990–; Special Asst to Senator Edward Kennedy; Nat. Political Dir Kennedy for Pres. Cttee 1980; Treas. Democratic Nat. Cttee 1983–85, Chair. 1985–89; Interim Senator from Mass Sept. 2009–Jan. 2010; Visiting Lecturer, Mass. Continuing Legal Educ. Program, New England Law Inst., J. F. Kennedy Inst. of Politics, Harvard Univ.; Chair., Bd of Dirs J. F. Kennedy Library Foundation 1992–2009, Nominating Cttee Harvard Bd of Overseers 1993, Nat. Democratic Inst. for Int. Affairs 1992–2001; mem. Bd of Dirs ITT Corpn 1989–97, Bradley Real Estate Inc. 1992–99, The Hartford Life Insurance Co. 1995–2000, The Hartford Financial Services Group 1995–2009, 2010–, Rayonier Corpn 1993–2011, Cedar Shopping Centers Inc. 2006–; mem. Bd of Trustees, Stonehill Coll. 1984–2002, St Sebastian's School 1992–2008; Co-Chair. Comm. on Pres. Debates 1987–2009; Chair. Visiting Comm. on Harvard Athletics 2000–; Hon. LLD (Stonehill Coll.) 2002, (Southern New England School of Law) 2003; W. Averell Harriman Democracy Award 1988, Univ. of Mass Distinguished Achievement Award 2010; Hubert Humphrey Public Leadership Award 2010. *Leisure interest:* athletics. *Address:* Sullivan & Worcester LLP, One Post Office Square, Suite 2400, Boston, MA 02109, USA (office). *Telephone:* (617) 338-2987 (office). *Fax:* (617) 338-2880 (office). *E-mail:* pkirk@sandw.com (office). *Website:* www.sandw.com (office).

KIRK, Ronald (Ron), BA, JD; American lawyer, government official and fmr politician; *Senior Of Counsel, Gibson, Dunn & Crutcher*; b. 27 June 1954, Austin, Tex.; m. Matrice Kirk; two d.; ed Austin Coll., Univ. of Texas; Legis. Asst to US Senator Lloyd Bentsen, Washington, DC 1981–83; Asst City Attorney for Intergovernmental Relations and Chief Lobbyist, City of Dallas, Tex. 1983–89; shareholder, Johnson & Gibbs PC (law firm) Dallas 1990–94; Partner, Gardere Wynne Sewell LLP (law firm) 1994–2004; Sec. of State, State of Texas 1994–95; Mayor of Dallas 1995–2001; Partner, Vinson & Elkins LLP, Dallas 2005–09; US Trade Rep., Washington, DC 2009–13; currently Senior Of Counsel, Gibson, Dunn & Crutcher, also Co-Chair Int. Trade practice; mem. ABA, Nat. Bar Asscn, Tex. State Bar, JL Turner Legal Asscn, Austin Coll. Alumni Asscn, Univ. of Texas Alumni Asscn (Pres.-elect 2008–09); mem. Advisory Bd, Hart Global Leaders Forum, Southern Methodist Univ.; Hon. LHD (Austin Coll.) 2006; CB Bunkley Community Service Award, JL Turner Legal Asscn 1994, Woodrow Wilson Center Award 2000, Jurisprudence Award, Anti-Defamation League 2004, Justinian Award, Dallas Lawyers Auxiliary 2008; named one of The 50 Most Influential Minority Lawyers in America by The National Law Journal 2008. *Address:* Gibson, Dunn & Crutcher, 2100 McKinney Avenue, Suite 1100, Dallas, TX 75201-6912, USA (office). *E-mail:* rkirk@gibsondunn.com (office). *Website:* www.gibsondunn.com (office).

KIRKBY, Dame (Carolyn) Emma, DBE, OBE, MA; British singer (soprano); b. 26 Feb. 1949, Camberley, Surrey; d. of Capt. Geoffrey Kirkby and Beatrice Daphne Kirkby; one s. with Anthony Rooley; m. Howard Williams 2015; ed Sherborne School for Girls and Somerville Coll., Oxford and pvt singing lessons with Jessica Cash; specialist singer of renaissance, baroque and classical repertoire; debut London concert 1974; full-time professional singer 1975–; since mid-1970s involved in revival of performances with period instruments and the attempt to recreate the sounds the composers would have heard; performances at the Proms from 1977; freelance work with many groups and orchestras in the UK and Germany, including Consort of Musicke, Taverner Players, Acad. of Ancient Music, London Baroque, Florilegium, Freiburger Barockorchester, Fretwork, Orchestra of the Age of Enlightenment, Concerto Copenhagen, Purcell Quartet; appearances at festivals, including Bruges, Utrecht, Luzern, Mosel, Rheingau, Passau, Schleswig-Holstein, Saintes, Beaune, Ottawa, Elora, Tanglewood, Mostly Mozart (New York) and many others; Hon. DLitt (Salford) 1985; Hon. DMus (Bath) 1994, (Sheffield) 2000, (Oxford) 2008, (Newcastle) 2010; Hon. FGSM; Hon. FRAM; Hon. Fellow, Royal Coll. of Music, Trinity Coll. of Music; Handel Prize, Halle, Germany 1997, Classic FM Artist of the Year 1999, Queen's Medal for Music 2011. *Television:* subject of South Bank Show (ITV) 2008. *Recordings include:* Complete songs of John Dowland 1976–77, Messiah (Handel) 1979, 1988, Madrigals by Monteverdi, Wert, Scarlatti and other Italians, Schütz, Grabbe, Wilbye, Ward and other English composers, Monteverdi Vespers, Mass in B Minor (Bach), Handel's Athalia, Joshua, Judas Maccabaeus, Sequences by Hildegarde of Bingen (Hyperion), Arie Antiche and Songs of Maurice Greene, Dido and Aeneas, Handel's German Arias, Italian Cantatas, Songs by Arne and Handel, Stabat Mater (Pergolesi), Haydn's Creation, Mozart Motets, Mozart Concert Arias, Vivaldi Opera Arias, Handel Opera Arias, Christmas Music with Westminster Abbey Choir, Christmas Music with London Baroque, with Bell'Arte Salzburg, Bach Cantatas with Freiburger Barockorchester and with Purcell Quartet, Byrd Consort Songs with Fretwork, Handel: Sacred Contatas, Handel Gloria 2001, Lute song recitals with Anthony Rooley and with Jakob Lindberg, Bingen: A Feather On The Breath Of God 2010, Emma Kirkby – A Portrait 2011. *Website:* www.emmakirkby.com.

KIRKILAS, Gediminas; Lithuanian politician; b. 30 Aug. 1951, Vilnius; m. Liudmila Kirkilienė; one s. one d.; ed Vilnius Teachers' Training Coll., Vilnius Higher School of Politics, Vilnius Univ.; interior restorer, Monument Restoration Trust 1972–78; worked within CP 1982–90; Asst to First Sec. of Cen. Cttee of Lithuanian CP, later to Deputy of Supreme Council–Reconstituted Seimas (Parl.), Repub. of Lithuania 1989–92; Ed. and Publr Golos Litvy (The Voice of Lithuania) daily newspaper 1991–95; mem. Seimas 1992–, Deputy Speaker 2012–, fmr Chair. Cttee on Nat. Security and Defence, Cttee on Foreign Affairs, Deputy Chair. Cttee on European Affairs, Head of Seimas Del. to NATO Parl. Ass.; Elder, Group of Lithuanian Social Democratic Labour Party 1993–96; head, Presidential working group to develop nat. security strategy 1993–96; Special Rep. of Pres. for matters related to transportation between Lithuania and Kaliningrad region of Russian Fed. 2002; given rank of Amb. 2003; Minister of Nat. Defence and mem. Cttee on Nat. Security and Defence 2004–06; Prime Minister of Lithuania 2006–08; Acting Sec. of Ind. Cen. Cttee of Lithuanian CP 1990; elected Deputy Chair. Constitutive Ass. of Lithuanian Democratic Labour Party (LDLP) 1990, first Asst to the Sec. 1991–96, temporary Chair. 1993, mem. Presidium 1996–2001; following absorption of LLDP in 2001, Deputy Chair. Lithuanian Social Democratic Party (Lietuvos Socialdemokratų Partija) 2001–07, 2009–, Chair. 2007–09; Cross of Officer of the Lithuanian Grand Duke Vytautas, Order of the Cross of Vytis, Commdr Cross of the Repub. of Poland, Grand Cross of Portugal. *Publications:* Political Commentary for the Period 1995, numerous articles on policy and public life. *Leisure interests:* fishing, tennis, philosophy, literature, arts, cycling, pipe smoking. *Address:* Parliament (Seimas), Gedimino pr. 53, Vilnius 01109, Lithuania (office). *Telephone:* (5) 239-6609 (office). *E-mail:* gekirk@lrs.lt (office); Gediminas.Kirkilas@lrs.lt (office). *Website:* www.kirkilas.eu.

KIRKLAND, Gelsey; American ballet dancer and ballet teacher; b. 29 Dec. 1952, Bethlehem, Pa; d. of Jack Kirkland; m. Greg Lawrence; ed School of American Ballet; youngest mem. of New York Ballet at age 15 in 1968, Soloist 1969–72, Prin. Dancer 1972–74; with American Ballet Theater 1974–81, 1982–84, teacher, coach American Ballet Theatre 1992; Guest Dancer, Royal Ballet, London 1980–86, Stuttgart Ballet 1980; Co-founder and Co-Artistic Dir Gelsey Kirkland Acad. of Classical Ballet 2010–; fmr mem. Guest Faculty, Broadway Dance Center, New York. *Ballets include:* Firebird, The Goldberg Variations, Scherzo fantastique, An Evening's Waltzes, The Leaves are Fading, Hamlet, The Tiller in the Field, Four Bagatelles, Stravinsky Symphony in C, Song of the Nightingale Connotations, Romeo and Juliet and others. *Publications:* Dancing on My Grave (autobiog.) 1987, The Shape of Love (with Greg Lawrence) 1990, The Little Ballerina and Her Dancing Horse 1993. *Address:* Gelsey Kirkland Academy of Classical Ballet, 355 Broadway, Second Floor, New York, NY 10013, USA (office). *Telephone:* (212) 600-0047 (office). *Website:* www.gelseykirklandballet.org (office).

KIRKWOOD, Thomas (Tom) Burton Loram, CBE, BA, MSc, PhD, FMedSci, FRCPE; British medical scientist and academic; *Professor Emeritus, Newcastle University;* b. 6 July 1951; s. of Kenneth Kirkwood and Deborah Burton Kirkwood (née Collings); m. 1st Betty Rosamund Bartlett 1973 (divorced 1975); one s. one d.; m. 2nd Jane Louise Bottomley 1995; ed Dragon School, Oxford, Magdalen Coll. School, Oxford, St Catharine's Coll., Cambridge, Worcester Coll., Oxford; initially qualified as a mathematician; developed 'disposable soma' theory of ageing; Scientist, Nat. Inst. for Biological Standards and Control, London 1973–79, Staff Scientist 1979–81; Staff Scientist, Computing Lab., MRC Nat. Inst. for Medical Research, London 1981–87, Sr Staff Scientist 1987–88, Head, Lab. of Math. Biology 1988–93; Prof. of Biological Gerontology, Univ. of Manchester 1993–99 (first in GB); Prof. of Medicine and Head of Dept of Gerontology, Newcastle Univ. 1999–2004, Dir Inst. for Ageing and Health 2004–11, Assoc. Dean for Ageing 2011–15, Prof. Emer. 2016–; Sr Investigator, Nat. Inst. for Health Research 2009; Pres. Scientific Bd, AXA Research Funds 2012–; Chair. British Soc. for Research on Ageing 1992–99; Dir Jt Centre on Ageing, Univs of Manchester and Newcastle upon Tyne 1996–; Gov. Research Advisory Council, Research into Ageing 1998–2001, Chair. 1999–2000; Chair. Foresight Task Force on Health Care of Older People 1999–2001; mem. WHO Expert Advisory Panel on Biological Standardization 1985–, UK Human Genome Mapping Project Cttee 1991–93, Basic Scis Interest Group, Wellcome Trust 1992–97, Biotechnology and Biological Sciences Research Council 2001–; Specialist Adviser to House of Lords Science and Tech. Select Cttee Inquiry into Ageing 2004–06; Co-Ed. Mechanisms of Ageing and Devt 2000–; Pres. Int. Biometric Soc. (British Region) 1998–2000; European Pres. (Biology), Int. Asscn of Gerontology 2003–07; Fellow, Inst. for Advanced Study, Budapest 1997; Hon. Fellow, Faculty and Inst. of Actuaries 2002; Hon. Life mem. Royal Inst. 2002, British Soc. for Research on Ageing 2011; Hon. DSc (Hull) 2003; Heinz Karger Prize 1983, Fritz Verzár Medal 1996, British Geriatrics Soc. Dhole-Eddlestone Prize 2001, Royal Inst. Henry Dale Prize 2002, IPSEN Foundation Longevity Prize 2011. *Radio:* BBC Reith Lectures 2001. *Publications:* (co-author): Accuracy in Molecular Processes: Its Control and Relevance to Living Systems 1986, Time of Our Lives: The Science of Human Ageing 1999, Sex and Longevity: Sexuality, Gender, Reproduction, Parenthood 2001; (with C. E. Finch): Chance, Development and Aging 2000, The End of Age 2001; numerous scientific articles in learned journals. *Leisure interests:* gardening, hill-walking, pottery. *Address:* Newcastle University Institute for Ageing, Biomedical Research Building, Campus for Ageing and Vitality, Newcastle upon Tyne, NE4 5PL (office); Roughlees, Ewesley, Morpeth, Northumberland, NE61 4PH, England (home). *Telephone:* (191) 208-1103 (office). *Fax:* (191) 208-1101 (office). *E-mail:* tom.kirkwood@ncl.ac.uk (office). *Website:* www.ncl.ac.uk/camb/staff/profile/tomkirkwood.html#background (office).

KIRMANI, Tariq, MBA; Pakistani business executive; *Chairman, UBL Fund Managers Ltd;* ed Inst. of Business Admin, Karachi; spent seven years working in USA, UAE and Australia; served in oil sector in various marketing, operations and finance man. positions, first Pakistani to be elected a co. dir of a multinational oil co. 1991; Deputy Man. Dir (Marketing) Pakistan State Oil 1999–2001, Man. Dir 2001–05; Chair. and CEO Pakistan Int. Airlines 2005–07 (resgnd); Chair. UBL Fund Managers Ltd, Karachi 2010–; Chair. Nat. Acad. of Performing Arts, Greenstar Social Marketing; mem. Bd of Dirs National Bank of Pakistan (NBP), Professional Educ. Foundation, Family Educ. Services Foundation; mem. Selection Bd Inst. of Business Admin; mem. Corp. Governance Cttee Karachi Stock Exchange; Pres. Pakistan Hockey Fed. 2005–06. *Address:* Office of the Chairman, UBL Fund Managers Ltd, 5th Floor, Office Tower, Techno City, Hasrat Mohani Road, Karachi, Pakistan (office). *Telephone:* (21) 35290080 (office). *Fax:* (21) 35290070 (office). *E-mail:* info@UBLfunds.com (office). *Website:* www.ublfunds.com (office).

KIRPICHNIKOV, Mikhail Petrovich, DBiolSc; Russian politician, scientist and academic; *Dean, Faculty of Biology, Lomonosov Moscow State University;* b. 9 Nov. 1945, Moscow; m.; one d.; ed Moscow Inst. of Physics and Tech.; with Inst. of Molecular Biology 1972–89; Deputy Head, Head of Div., USSR Cttee on Science and Tech. 1989–91; Head of Div., Head of Dept, Ministry of Science and Tech. Policy 1991–93; Head, Div. of Science, Educ., High School and Tech., Russian Govt 1993–94, Head, Dept of Science and Educ. 1994–98; First Deputy Minister of Science and Tech. July–Sept. 1998, Minister 1998–2001; Prof. and Head, Protein Eng Lab., Inst. of Bio-organic Chemistry, Russian Acad. of Sciences 2000–; Pro-Rector and Head, Innovation Policy and Innovation Project Management Dept, Lomonosov Moscow State Univ. 2004–06, Dean, Faculty of Biology 2006–; Pres. Higher Attestation Comm. of Russian Fed. 2006–; mem. Russian Acad. of Sciences 1997–; Order of Honour 1998, Order of Friendship 2006; State Award in Science and Tech. 1999, Certificate of Merit, Govt of Russian Fed. 1995. *Publications:* several books and more than 300 articles and papers on biology. *Address:* Faculty of Biology, Lomonosov Moscow State University, GSP-2, Leninskie Gory 1/12, Moscow 119992 (office); Institute of Bio-organic Chemistry, Mirlukho-Maklaya str. 16/10, GSP-7 Moscow 117871, Russia (office). *Telephone:* (495) 939-27-76 (office). *E-mail:* kirpichnikov@inbox.ru (office). *Website:* www.bio.msu.ru (office).

KIRSCH, Philippe, OC, QC, LLM; Canadian judge and fmr diplomatist; b. 1 April 1947, Québec; ed Stanislas Coll., Montréal, Univ. of Montreal, Acad. of Int. Law, The Hague, The Netherlands, Int. Peace Acad., Vienna, Austria; called to the Bar, Quebec 1970; apptd QC 1988; joined diplomatic service, assignments with Bureau of Legal Affairs and US Div., Dept of Foreign Affairs and Int. Trade, Ottawa, with Embassy in Peru, Perm. Mission to the UN, New York –1985; Dir Legal Operations Div., Dept of External Affairs, Ottawa 1983–88; Amb. and Deputy Perm. Rep. to UN, New York 1988–92; Deputy Legal Adviser and Dir-Gen., Bureau of Legal Affairs, Dept of Foreign Affairs and Int. Trade 1992–94, Asst Deputy Minister for Legal and Consular Affairs 1994–96, Legal Adviser 1994–99; mem. Perm. Court of Arbitration 1995–99; Amb. to Sweden 1999–2003; Judge, Appeals Div., Int. Criminal Court (ICC), The Hague 2003–09, first Pres. ICC 2006–09; Amb. and Agent of Canada in legal disputes 1985–86, 1995–98, 1999–2003; Chair. Preparatory Comm. for ICC 1999–2002; fmr Chair. UN Comm. of Inquiry on Libya, Commr, Bahrain Ind. Comm. of Inquiry; Chair. UN Legal Ad Hoc Cttees 1993–94, 1997–99; mem. Program on Humanitarian Policy and Conflict Research Group of Professionals on Monitoring, Reporting, and Fact-finding, Harvard Humanitarian Initiative, Harvard T. H. Chan School of Public Health; mem. Advisory Bd, ABA's International Criminal Court Project; Grand Cross, Order of the Crown of Belgium, Commdr, of the Crown of Oak of the Grand Duchy of Luxembourg; Robert S. Litvack Human Rights Memorial Award 1999, Minister of Foreign Affairs Award for Foreign Policy Excellence 1999, William J. Butler Human Rights Medal 2001. *Publications:* chapters in books, articles in professional journals.

KIRSCH, Wolfgang; German banking executive; b. 19 March 1955, Bensberg; m.; two c.; ed Univ. of Cologne; banking apprenticeship at Deutsche Bank 1975–77, Corp. Customers Man. and Authorised Officer, Deutsche Bank, Düsseldorf 1981–88, Gen. Man. Deutsche Bank, Viersen 1988–93, Deputy Man. and Head of Corp. Customers Business, Deutsche Bank, Düsseldorf 1993–96, Deputy Head of Credit Line Man. for Corp. Customers Business Germany, Deutsche Bank, Frankfurt am Main 1996–98, Gen. Man. and Chief Country Officer, Deutsche Bank, Singapore 1998–2000, Man. Dir and Sr Credit Exec. of the Corporates and Real Estate Div. and CIB Corp. and Investment Bank Div., Deutsche Bank, Frankfurt am Main 2000–02; mem. Bd of Man. Dirs and Dir Risk Man. and Int. Business Devt, Deutsche Zentral-Genossenschaftsbank (DZ Bank) AG 2002–05, Deputy Chair. 2005–06, CEO 2006–18, fmr Chair. Supervisory Bd of R+V Versicherung AG, Bausparkasse Schwäbisch Hall AG, Union Asset Man. Holding AG; mem. Supervisory Bd Südzucker AG; Chair. Steering Cttee Unico Banking Group. *Address:* c/o Deutsche Zentral-Genossenschaftsbank AG, Platz der Republik, 60265 Frankfurt am Main, Germany (office).

KIRSCHNER, Marc W., PhD; American cell biologist and academic; *Professor and Chairman, Department of Systems Biology, Harvard Medical School;* ed Northwestern Univ., Univ. of California, Berkeley; postdoctoral research at Univ. of California, Berkeley and Univ. of Oxford, UK; Asst Prof. of Biochemical Sciences, Princeton Univ. 1972; Assoc. Prof. of Biochemical Sciences, Princeton Univ. 1976–78, Prof. of Biochemical Sciences 1978; Prof. of Biochemistry and Biophysics, Univ. of California, San Francisco 1978–93; Carl W. Walter Prof. and Chair. Dept of Cell Biology, Harvard Medical School 1993–2003, Founder and Chair. Dept of Systems Biology 2003–, Co-Founder Inst. for Chem. and Cell Biology, Harvard Univ. 1999; fmr Dir NIH; fmr Pres. American Soc. for Cell Biology; mem. NAS, American Acad. of Arts and Sciences; Foreign mem. Royal Soc. 1999, Academia Europaea; William C. Rose Award, American Soc. for Biochemistry and Molecular Biology 2001, Gairdner Foundation Int. Award (Canada) 2001, E.B. Wilson Medal, American Soc. for Cell Biology 2003, Dickson Prize for Science, Carnegie Mellon Univ. 2004, Harvey Prize, Technion, Israel (co-recipient) 2015. *Publication:* Cells, Embryos and Evolution (with John C. Gerhart) 1997, The Plausibility of Life: Resolving Darwin's Dilemma (with John C. Gerhart) 2005. *Address:* Department of Systems Biology, Harvard Medical School, Warren Alpert 524, 200 Longwood Avenue, Boston, MA 02115, USA (office). *Telephone:* (617) 432-2250 (office). *Fax:* (617) 432-5012 (office). *E-mail:* marc@hms.harvard.edu (office). *Website:* sysbio.med.harvard.edu/faculty/kirschner (office); kirschner.med.harvard.edu (office).

KIRSH, Nathan (Natie), BA; South African business executive; *Founder, Kirsh Holdings Group;* b. 6 Jan. 1932, Potchefstroom; m. Frances Herr; one s. two d.; ed Univ. of Witwatersrand; est. first business venture, corn milling business, in Swaziland 1958, expanded into wholesale food distribution in S Africa; f. Kirsh Holdings Group, currently Chair. Kirsh Group of Cos (interests include property holdings in Australia, S Africa, UK and USA); group cos include interests in Swazi Plaza Properties, Crest JMT Leather, Holmes Place (fitness chain), Kitec Industries (pipe maker), Abacus Property Group Ltd; property portfolio includes Tower 42 (fmrly Nat West Tower), London; Propr Jetro Holdings Inc. (operates Jetro Cash and Carry stores and Restaurant Depot warehouses in New York City); Dir Magal Security Systems, Israel 1984–2014; Trustee Eurona Foundation; Hon. DrIur (Univ. of Swaziland) 1994.

KIRSHNER, Robert Paul, AB, PhD; American astrophysicist, academic and philanthropist; *Chief Program Officer, Science, Gordon and Betty Moore Foundation;* b. 15 Aug. 1949, New Jersey; m. Jayne Loader; one s. one d.; ed Harvard Coll., California Inst. of Tech.; Postdoctoral Research Assoc., Kitt Peak Nat. Observatory 1974–76; Asst Prof., Univ. of Michigan 1976–80, Assoc. Prof. 1980–82, Prof. of Astronomy 1982–85, Dir McGraw-Hill Observatory 1980–85; Prof. of Astronomy, Harvard Univ. 1986–, Chair. of Dept 1990–97, Head of Optical and Infrared Div. of CfA 1997–2003, Co-Master of Quincy House 2001–07, Clowes Prof. of Science, 2001–15, Clowes Research Prof. of Science 2015–, Harvard Coll. Prof. 2004–09, Visiting Scientist, Kavli Inst. for Theoretical Physics 2006–07; Pres. American Astronomical Soc. 2003–05; Chief Program Officer, Science, Gordon and Betty Moore Foundation 2015–; mem. Int. Astronomical Union 1992, American Acad. of Arts and Sciences 1992, NAS 1998, American Philosophical Soc. 2005; Fellow, American Physical Soc. 1992, AAAS 1992; Hon. DSc (Univ. of Chicago) 2010; Bowdoin Prize (Useful and Polite Literature), Harvard Coll. 1970, Alfred P. Sloan Fellowship, Univ. of Michigan 1978, Henry Russel Award, Univ. of Michigan 1980, Caltech Distinguished Alumni Award 2004, Gruber Prize in Cosmology (co-recipient) 2007, Dannie Heineman Prize in Astrophysics, American Inst. of Physics 2011, James Craig Watson Medal 2014, Breakthrough Prize in Fundamental Physics (co-recipient) 2015, Wolf Prize in Physics (co-recipient) 2015. *Publications include:* The Extravagant Universe: Exploding Stars, Dark Energy, and the Accelerating Cosmos 2002; more than 300 papers in professional journals.

Address: Gordon and Betty Moore Foundation, 1661 Page Mill Road, Palo Alto, CA 94304, USA (office). *Telephone:* (650) 213-3127 (office). *E-mail:* robert.kirshner@moore.org (office). *Website:* www.cfa.harvard.edu/~rkirshner (office); www.moore.org (office).

KIRST, Michael W., MPA, PhD; American academic; *Professor Emeritus of Education and Business Administration, Stanford University;* b. 1 Aug. 1939, West Reading, Pa; s. of Russell Kirst and Marian Kirst (née Weile); m. Wendy Burdsall 1975; one s. one d.; ed Dartmouth Coll., Harvard Univ.; Assoc. Dir President's Comm. on White House Fellows, Nat. Advisory Council on Educ. of Disadvantaged Children 1966; Dir Program Planning and Evaluation, Bureau of Elementary and Secondary Educ., Office of Educ. 1967; Staff Dir Senate Sub-cttee on Manpower, Employment and Poverty 1968; Prof. of Educ. and Business Admin., Stanford Univ. 1968, now Prof. Emer., also affiliated with Stanford Center on Adolescence; Pres. California State Bd of Educ. 1977–81; Chair. Bd of International Comparative Studies in Educ., NAS 1994–; Dir Policy Analysis for California Educ.; Dir Consortium for Policy Research in Educ.; mem. Nat. Acad. of Educ., USA, International Acad. of Educ. and numerous other educ. bds, cttees, etc. *Publications include:* Contemporary Issues in Education: Perspectives from Australia and USA (with G. Hancock and D. Grossman) 1983, Who Controls Our Schools: American Values in Conflict 1984, Schools in Conflict: Political Turbulence in American Education (with F. Wirt) 1992, Political Dynamics of American Education 2001, From High School to College 2004, Remaking College: The Changing Ecology of Higher Education (with Mitchell Stevens) 2015. *Address:* School of Education, Stanford University, 485 Lasuen Mall, Stanford, CA 94305-3096, USA (office). *Telephone:* (650) 723-4412 (office). *Fax:* (650) 725-7412 (office). *E-mail:* mwk@stanford.edu (office). *Website:* www.michaelwkirst.com.

KIRSTEIN, Peter Thomas, CBE, BA, MSc, PhD, DSc, FREng, FIET, FInstP; British computer scientist and academic; *Professor, Department of Computer Science, University College London;* b. 20 June 1933, Berlin, Germany; ed Highgate School, London, Gonville and Caius Coll., Cambridge, Stanford Univ., USA; brought up in England from 1937; Lecturer in Microwave Eng, Stanford Univ. 1958; Accelerator Physicist, CERN, Geneva 1959–63, spent six months at Jt Centre for Nuclear Research, Dubna, USSR; conducted research for European Office of General Electric Corp. Research Centre, Zurich, Switzerland 1963–67, consultant 1970–95; Reader, Inst. of Computer Science, Univ. of London 1967–70, Prof. of Computer Communications Systems 1970–73; Prof., Dept of Statistics and Computer Science, Univ. Coll. London 1973–, Head of Computer Science Dept 1980–94, later Dir of Research; Sr mem. IEEE; Fellow, Royal Acad. of Eng, Inst. of Eng and Tech.; Hon. Foreign Fellow, American Acad. of Arts and Sciences 2002, Nat. Acad. of Eng (USA) 2009; Hon. Fellow, Univ. Coll. London 2006; Distinguished Fellow, British Computer Soc.; IEE Senior Award 1999, SIGCOMM Award, Asscn for Computing Machinery 1999, Postel Award, Internet Soc. 2003, Lifetime Achievement Award, Royal Acad. of Eng 2006, Internet Pioneer, Internet Soc. 2012, Marconi Prize 2015. *Achievements include:* co-authored (with Vint Cerf) early tech. paper on internet-working concept and his research group played a role in early experimental internet work. *Publications:* more than 230 papers in professional journals. *Address:* Room 7.04, Department of Computer Science, University College London, Malet Place Building, Gower Street, London, WC1E 6BT, England (office). *Telephone:* (20) 7679-7286 (office). *E-mail:* kirstein@cs.ucl.ac.uk (office). *Website:* www.cs.ucl.ac.uk (office); peterkirstein.wordpress.com (office).

KIRWAN, William E., PhD; American university administrator, academic and mathematician; *Chancellor Emeritus, University System of Maryland;* b. 14 April 1938, Louisville, Ky; s. of Albert Dennis Kirwan and Elizabeth H. Kirwan; m. Patricia Harper 1960; one s. one d.; ed Univ. of Kentucky, Rutgers Univ.; Asst Instructor, Rutgers Univ. 1963–64; Asst Prof., Dept of Math., Univ. of Maryland 1964–68; Visiting Lecturer, Royal Holloway Coll., Univ. of London, UK 1966–67; Assoc. Prof., Dept of Math., Univ. of Md at Coll. Park 1968–72, Prof. 1972–, Chair. Dept of Math. 1977–81, Vice-Chancellor for Academic Affairs 1981–88, Acting Chancellor 1982, Vice-Pres. for Academic Affairs and Provost 1986–88, Acting Pres. 1988–89, Pres. 1989–98; Pres. Ohio State Univ. 1998–2002; Chancellor Univ. System of Md 2002–14, now Chancellor Emer.; Chair. Nat. Asscn of State Univs and Land Grant Colls 1995–; currently Co-Chair. Nat. Research Council Bd of Higher Educ. and Workforce; mem. Knight Comm. on Intercollegiate Athletics (Co-Chair. 2007–); mem. Bd Dirs, Council for Higher Educ. Accreditation; Greater Baltimore Cttee, Econ. Alliance of Greater Baltimore, Md Business Roundtable for Educ., Wendy's International; Ed. Proceedings of the American Mathematical Society 1979–85; mem. Editorial Bd, Journal of Diversity in Higher Education 2007–; mem. American Math. Soc., Math. Asscn of America; American Acad. of Arts and Sciences 2002–; Officier, Order of Leopold II (Belgium) 1989; NDEA Fellow 1960–63, NSF Grants 1965–82, Hall of Distinguised Alumni, Univ. of Kentucky, Md House of Dels Speaker's Medallion 2007, Circle of Discovery Award, Coll. of Computer, Math. and Natural Sciences, Univ. of Maryland 2015. *Publications:* Advances in Complex Analysis (co-ed.) 1976; numerous published research articles and seminar talks. *Leisure interests:* classical music, tennis. *Address:* Office of the Chancellor, University System of Maryland, 3300 Metzerott Road, Adelphi, MD 20783-1690, USA (office). *Telephone:* (301) 445-1901 (office). *Fax:* (301) 445-1931 (office). *E-mail:* bkirwan@usmd.edu (office). *Website:* www.usmd.edu/usm (office).

KISELEV, Anatoly Ivanovich; Russian aviation engineer; b. 29 April 1938, Moscow; m.; one s. one d.; ed Moscow Inst. of Aviation Tech.; fmr electrician, Moscow Khrunichev Machine Construction Factory, then Eng, tester, head of lab., head of workshop, Deputy Dir 1956–72, Dir 1975–93, involved in merger of Moscow Khrunichev Machine Construction Factory and Salut Construction Bureau, Dir M.V. Khrunichev State Space Scientific Production Cen. 1993–2001; Deputy Head, then First Chief of Dept USSR Ministry of Gen. Machine Construction 1972–75; Dir-Gen. Russian-American Lokhid-Khrunichev (Int. Launch Services) 1994–2001, apptd mem. Bd Dirs 2001; Order for Service to Motherland; Lenin Prize, Hero of Socialist Labour.

KISELEV, Dmitrii Konstantinovich; Russian journalist and television broadcaster; *Head, Rossiya Segodnya (Russia Today);* b. 26 April 1954, Moscow, Russian SFSR, USSR; m. Maria Kiselev; two c. and two from previous m.; ed Leningrad State Univ.; presenter, Vesti nedeli (News of the Week) on domestic Rossiya 1 TV network; Head of official Govt-owned int. news agency Rossiya Segodnya (Russia Today) (est. to replace RIA—Novosti) 2013–, launched int. multimedia news service Sputnik 2014; Deputy Dir state TV holding co. VGTRK; placed on EU sanctions list as a result of Crimean crisis March 2014. *Address:* Rossiya Segodnya (Russia Today), 119021 Moscow, Zubovskii bulv. 4, Russia (office). *Telephone:* (495) 637-24-24 (office). *Fax:* (499) 201-45-45 (office). *E-mail:* media@sputniknews.com (office). *Website:* sputniknews.com (office).

KISELEV, Oleg Vladimirovich, CandTechSci; Russian engineer and business executive; *Deputy Chairman of the Executive Board, RUSNANO Management Company LLC;* b. 1 June 1953, Divnoye, Stavropol territory; m.; one s.; ed Moscow State Inst. of Construction; teacher Inst. of Steel and Alloys 1981–86; Deputy Dir Inst. of Chem. Physics USSR (now Russian) Acad. of Sciences 1986–88; Founder and Head Alfa-Eco co-operative, then Jt Venture Alfa-Eco, then Alfa production-finance co. including Alfa Bank and other affiliates 1988–91; Founder, Pres. and Chair. Mosexpo Co. 1992–2000, Chair. Mosexpo-Metal LLC 1999–2005; co-f. IMPEX Bank 1993, Pres. and Chair. 1993–2001; mem. Bd of Dirs Russian Bank of Reconstruction and Devt 2001–; Man. Dir and Chair. Metalloinvest (holding co.) 2001–02; CEO Media-Socium (non-profit partnership) 2002–04; Chair. Renaissance Capital 2004–05; Advisor to the CEO, Nanotechnologies State Corpn 2008–09, Dir of Business Strategy and Finance 2009–10, Deputy CEO and mem. Exec. Bd 2010; Deputy Chair. of Exec. Bd OJSC RUSNANO 2010–14, Deputy Chair. of Exec. Bd of RUSNANO Management Company LLC 2014–; Chair. Council on Foreign Econ. Relations, Ministry of Foreign Affairs 1992; mem. Govt Union on Business 1993–94, Pres. Council 1994; mem. Bd of Dirs Russian-American Foundation of Support of Business 1994, Public Council on Foreign and Defence Policy, Asscn of Russian Banks 1999. *Address:* RUSNANO Management Company LLC, Moscow 117036, 10A, Prospekt 60-letiya Oktyabrya, Russia (office). *Telephone:* (495) 988-53-88 (office). *Fax:* (495) 988-53-99 (office). *E-mail:* info@rusnano.com (office). *Website:* en.rusnano.com (office).

KISELEV, Yevgenii Alekseyevich; Russian broadcast journalist; b. 15 June 1956, Moscow; s. of Aleksei Kiselev and Anna Kiselev; m. Masha Shakhova 1974; one s.; ed Inst. of Asian and African Studies, Moscow State Univ.; teacher of Persian (Farsi) language, Higher School of KGB 1981–84; corresp., Radio Moscow Middle Eastern Dept 1984–86; TV journalist 1987–; regular host '120 Minutes' breakfast show 1987–90, staff corresp. news div. Gosteleradio (fmr USSR State Cttee for TV and radio broadcasting) 1989–90; made series of documentaries on everyday life in Israel 1989, 1990; joined newly founded Russian TV 1991, anchorman 'Vesti' late-night news programme; joined Ostankino State TV co. 1992; started 'Itogi' weekly news and current affairs programme 1992, on TNT station 2001–; Co-Founder and Vice-Pres. NTV independent broadcasting co. 1993–2000, Gen. Dir 2000–01; Co-founder, NTV-Plus Co. (direct satellite broadcasting) 1996; Gen. Dir TV-6 Independent Broadcasting Co. 2001–02; Ed.-in-Chief TVS Broadcasting 2002–03; Ed.-in-Chief Moskovskiye Novosti (Moscow News) newspaper Oct. 2003–05 (resgnd); currently radio programme presenter for Ekho Moskvy (Radio Echo of Moscow) 2005–; mem. Acad. of Russian TV; Journalist of the Year, Moscow Journalistic Union 1993, included on list of 100 most influential people in Russia, publ monthly by Nezavisimaya Gazeta 1993–; Int. Press Freedom Award, Cttee to Protect Journalists, New York 1995. *Leisure interest:* playing tennis. *Address:* Ekho Moskvy, 119019, Moscow, ul. Novyi Arbat 11, Russia (office). *Telephone:* (495) 695-92-29 (office). *Fax:* (495) 695-91-02 (office). *E-mail:* echo@echo.msk.ru (office). *Website:* echo.msk.ru (office).

KISHIDA, Fumio; Japanese politician; b. 29 July 1957; mem. House of Reps representing Hiroshima Pref. First Dist 1993–; fmr Vice-Minister for Construction, fmr Sr Vice-Minister of Educ.; Minister of State for Okinawa and Northern Territories Affairs, Quality-of-Life Policy, Science and Tech. Policy, Challenge Again, and Regulatory Reform 2007–08 (resgnd); Minister of Foreign Affairs 2012–17, of Defence July–Aug. 2017; mem. LDP (Liberal Democratic Party). *Address:* Jiyu-Minshuto (Liberal Democratic Party), 1-11-23, Nagata-cho, Chiyoda-ku, Tokyo 100-8910, Japan (office). *Telephone:* (3) 3581-6211 (office). *Fax:* (3) 3581-2667 (office). *E-mail:* koho@ldp.jimin.or.jp (office). *Website:* www.jimin.jp (office).

KISHIMOTO, Tadamitsu, MD, PhD; Japanese immunologist, academic and fmr university president; *Visiting Professor, Laboratory of Immune Regulation, Immunology Frontier Research Center, Osaka University;* b. 7 May 1939, Osaka; s. of Tadanobu Kishimoto and Yasuko Kishimoto; ed Osaka Univ. Medical School; Research Fellow, Dept of Medicine, Johns Hopkins Univ. School of Medicine, USA 1970–73, Asst Prof. 1973–74; Asst Prof., Dept of Medicine III, Osaka Univ. Medical School 1974–79, Prof. and Chair. 1991–98, Prof., Dept of Pathology and Medicine 1979–83, Prof., Inst. for Molecular and Cellular Biology 1983–91, Dean, Osaka Univ. Medical School 1995–97, Pres. Osaka Univ. 1997–2003, now Visiting Prof., Lab. of Immune Regulation, Immunology Frontier Research Center; Clemens von Pirquet Distinguished Prof., Medicine and Immunology, Univ. California, Davis, USA 2004; Chair. Seventh Int. Congress on AIDS in Asia and the Pacific 2005, 14th Int. Congress of Immunology 2010; mem. Council for Science and Tech. Policy, Cabinet Office 2004–06; fmr Pres. Int. Immunopharmacology Soc., Int. Cytokine Soc., Japanese Immunology Soc.; mem. Japan Acad. 1995, Deutsche Akad. der Naturforscher Leopoldina 2005; Foreign Assoc., NAS 1991; Foreign Assoc. mem. Inst. of Medicine, NAS 1997; Hon. Citizen, Tondabayashi City 1992; Hon. Prof., Fourth Mil. Medical Univ., Xi'an, People's Repub. of China 2002; Hon. mem. American Asscn of Immunologists 1992, American Soc. of Hematology 1997, Int. Asscn of Dental Research 2001, World Innovation Foundation 2002; Order of Culture (conferred by Emperor) 1998, Royal Decoration (Thailand) 2012; Hon. DSc (Mahidol Univ.) 2003; Dr hc (Universidad Technologica de Santiago) 2001; Behring-Kitasato Prize 1982, Osaka Science Prize 1983, Erwin von Bälz Prize 1986, Takeda Prize 1988, Asahi Prize 1988, Prize of the Japanese Medical Asscn 1990, Person of Cultural Merits, Japan 1990, Scientific Achievement Award, Int. Asscn of Allergology and Clinical Immunology 1991, Imperial Prize, Japan Acad. 1992, Sandoz Prize for Immunology, Int. Union of Immunology Soc. 1992, Avery-Landsteiner Prize, German Immunology Soc. 1996, Donald Seldin Award, Int. Soc. of Nephrology 1999, ISI Citation Laureate Award 2000, Robert Koch Gold Medal 2003, Honorary Lifetime Achievement Award, Int. Cytokine Soc. 2006, Seventh Int. Award, Japan Rheumatism Foundation 2008, Crafoord Prize, Royal Swedish Acad. of Sciences (co-recipient) 2009, Japan Prize (co-recipient) 2011. *Achieve-*

ments include: has made fundamental contribs to the understanding of cytokine functions through a series of studies on IL-6, its receptor system and transcription factors; developed anti-IL6 receptor therapy for several immune disorders, including Castleman's disease, rheumatoid arthritis and juvenile idiopathic arthritis. *Address:* Laboratory of Immune Regulation, Immunology Frontier Research Center, Osaka University, 1-3 Yamadaoka, Suita, Osaka 565-0871 (office); 3-5-31, Nankano-cho, Tondabayashi City, Osaka, Japan (home). *Telephone:* (6) 6879-4956 (office); (7) 2124-0532 (home). *Fax:* (6) 6879-4958 (office). *E-mail:* kishimot@ifrec.osaka-u.ac.jp (office). *Website:* www.ifrec.osaka-u.ac.jp/jpn/laboratory/immuneregulation (office).

KISHLANSKY, Mark Alan, MA, PhD, FRHistS; American historian and academic; *Frank Baird, Jr Professor of History, Harvard University;* b. 10 Nov. 1948, Brooklyn, NY; s. of Morris Kishlansky and Charlotte Katz; m. Jeanne Thiel 1975; two s.; ed Commack High School, State Univ. of New York at Stony Brook and Brown Univ.; Prof. of History, Univ. of Chicago 1975–91, Northwestern Univ. 1983; Prof. of History, Harvard Univ. 1991–97, Frank Baird, Jr Prof. of History 1997; Mellon Visiting Prof. of History, California Inst. of Tech. 1990; mem. Cttee on Social Thought 1990–91; Ed.-in-Chief, History Compass 2003–09; Fellow, Mass Historical Soc., Royal Historical Soc.; various research awards and other distinctions. *Publications:* The Rise of the New Model Army 1979, Parliamentary Selection: Social and Political Choice in Early Modern England, Early Modern Europe: The Crisis of Authority (co-ed. with C. M. Gray and E. Cochrane) 1987, Civilization in the West (with P. Geary and P. O'Brien) 1991, Sources of the West (ed.) 1991, Societies and Cultures in World Civilizations (with P. Geary, P. O'Brien, R. B. Worg) 1995, A Monarchy Transformed 1996. *Leisure interests:* Shakespeare, baseball, comedy. *Address:* Department of History, Robinson M-01, Harvard University, Cambridge, MA 02138, USA (office). *Telephone:* (617) 496-3427 (office). *Fax:* (617) 496-3425 (office). *E-mail:* mkishlan@fas.harvard.edu (office). *Website:* www.courses.fas.harvard.edu/~history (office).

KISIC, Lt-Gen. (retd) Jorge Raúl; Peruvian air force officer (retd) and government official; m. Maria del Rosario Caballero Bernos; ed Escuela de Oficiales de la Fuerza Aérea del Perú (EOFAP), Higher Mil. Air Acad., Madrid, Univ. de Piura; long career in Fuerza Aérea del Perú (FAP, air force), becoming FAP Operations Commdr 2001, Chief of Gen. Staff, FAP 2001–02; fmr Defence Attaché, Embassy of Peru in Ottawa; fmr Dir of Aerospace Interests and Aerial Attaché, Embassy of Peru in Bogotá; fmr Dir Mil. Police Pension Fund; Advisor, Civil Aeronautics Directorate 2010; Inspector Gen., Ministry of Defence 2011; Minister of Defence Jan.–April 2018; Pres. Federación Peruana Aerodeportiva 2002–12. *Address:* c/o Ministry of Defence, Edif. Quiñones, Avda de la Peruanidad s/n, Jesús María, Lima 1, Peru (office).

KISKA, Andrej; Slovak business executive, politician and head of state; *President;* b. 2 Feb. 1963, Poprad, Czechoslovak Socialist Repub. (now Slovakia); m. Martina Kisková; four c.; ed Slovak Tech. Univ., Bratislava; began career as designer, Naftoprojekt, Poprad; worked in USA in construction and gas stations 1990–91; f. financial services cos Triangle Group International 1992, TatraCredit 1996, Quatro 1999; f. Dobrý Anjel (Good Angel, non-profit org.), Chair. 2006–13; Pres. of Slovakia 15 June 2014–(19); Ind.; Trend Magazine Man. of the Year 2006, Krištálové krídlo (Crystal Wing Award for Philanthropy) 2011. *Address:* Office of the President, Hodžovo nám. 1, PO Box 128, 810 00 Bratislava, Slovakia (office). *Telephone:* (2) 5788-8173 (office). *Fax:* (2) 5788-8105 (office). *E-mail:* informacie@prezident.sk (office). *Website:* www.prezident.sk (office); www.andrejkiska.sk.

KISLYAK, Sergey Ivanovich; Russian diplomatist; b. 1950; m.; one d.; ed Moscow State Inst. of Eng and Tech., USSR Acad. of Foreign Trade; joined Ministry of Foreign Affairs 1977, Second Sec., Perm. Mission to UN, New York 1981–85, First Sec., Counsellor of Embassy in Washington, DC 1985–89, Deputy Dir Dept of Int. Orgs, Ministry of Foreign Affairs 1989–91, Deputy Dir Dept of Int. Scientific and Tech. Cooperation 1991–93, Dir 1993–95, Dir Dept of Security and Disarmament 1995–98, Amb. to Belgium, concurrently Perm. Rep. to NATO, Brussels 1998–2003, Deputy Minister of Foreign Affairs 2003–08, Amb. to USA and Perm. Observer, OAS, Washington, DC 2008–17; fmr mem. Coll. of Ministry of Foreign Affairs.

KISSIN, Evgeny Igorevich; British/Israeli (b. Russian) pianist; b. 10 Oct. 1971, Moscow; s. of Igor Kissin and Emilia Kissin; ed Moscow Gnessin Music School, studied piano with Anna Kantor; debut playing Mozart's D-minor concerto aged 10; appeared with Moscow Philharmonic, playing Chopin concertos 1984; tour of Japan with the Moscow Virtuosi; debut in Western Europe with the Berlin Radio orchestra 1987; British debut at the Lichfield Festival with the BBC Philharmonic 1987; London Symphony Orchestra concert 1988; concerts with the Royal Philharmonic and Yuri Temirkanov 1990; promenade concert debut with the BBC Symphony, playing Tchaikovsky's First Concerto 1990; US debut with the New York Philharmonic and a solo recital at Carnegie Hall 1990, subsequent US tour included Tanglewood 1991; Grammy Award ceremony and performances with the Chicago Symphony and Philadelphia Orchestra 1991–92; performed with the Boston Symphony; London recital debut and concert with the Philharmonia 1992–93; Prokofiev Concertos with the Berlin Philharmonic 1992–93; played Chopin and Schumann at the Royal Festival Hall, London 1997; first pianist to perform a recital at the London Proms 1997; Chopin's First Concerto at the London Proms with the Bavarian State Orchestra 1999; first concerto soloist to play in the Proms Opening concert 2000; 10th anniversary tour of recitals in the USA, including Carnegie Hall 2000–01; appearances with the Warsaw Philharmonic, Philharmonia Orchestra, Bavarian Staatskapelle, Chicago Symphony, Boston Symphony, Metropolitan Opera, Bayerische Rundfunk, and the Leipzig Gewandhaus 1999–2001; Brahms' Concerto No. 2 in B flat major at the London Proms 2002; Hon. mem. Royal Acad. of Music; Hon. DMus (Manhattan School of Music) 2001, Dr hc (Hebrew Univ. of Jerusalem) 2010; Diapason d'Or (France), Grand Prix Nobel Academie de Disque (France), Edison Klassiek Award (Netherlands) 1990, Chigiana Acad. Musician of the Year (Sienna) 1991, Musical America's Instrumentalist of the Year 1995, Triumph Award for outstanding contribution to Russia's culture 1997, Echo Award (Germany) 2002, Shostakovich Award (Moscow) 2003, Herbert von Karajan Award 2005, Arturo Benedetti Michelangeli Award 2007, Distinguished Artistic Leadership Award, Atlantic Council 2008. *Recordings include:* Tchaikovsky Concerto No.1 with Berlin Philharmonic conducted by Herbert von Karajan; live recording of Chopin Concertos with Moscow Philharmonic conducted by Dmitri Kitaenko 1984, Rachmaninov 2nd Concerto and Etudes Tableaux with the London Symphony conducted by Gergiev, Rachmaninov Concerto No. 3, Chopin Vols I and II live recital from Carnegie Hall, Prokofiev Piano Concertos 1 and 3 with Berlin Philharmonic conducted by Claudio Abbado, Haydn and Schubert Sonatas 1995, Beethoven: Moonlight Sonata, Franck: Prelude, Choral et Fugue, Brahms: Paganini Variations 1998, Chopin: 4 Ballades, Berceuse op 57, Barcarolle op 60, Scherzo No. 4 op 54 1999, Chopin recital including 24 Preludes Op. 28, Sonata No, 2 and Polonaise in A-flat, Brahms 2003, Scriabin, Medtner, Stravinsky (Grammy Award for Best Instrumental Soloist Performance, without orchestra 2006) 2005, Schubert: Piano Music for Four Hands (with James Levine) 2006, Schumann's Piano Concerto and Mozart's Piano Concerto No. 24 2007, Beethoven's Complete Piano Concertos 2008, Prokofiev Piano Concertos Nos. 2 and 3 (Grammy Award for Best Instrumental Soloist Performance with Orchestra 2010) 2009, Mozart Piano Concertos Nos. 20 and 27 2010. *Leisure interests:* friends, reading, theatre, walking. *Address:* IMG Artists, 7 West 54th Street, New York, NY 10019, USA (office). *E-mail:* lpetrikova@imgartists.com (office). *Website:* www.kissin.dk.

KISSINGER, Henry Alfred, MA, PhD; American academic, international consultant and fmr government official; *Chairman, Kissinger Associates;* b. 27 May 1923, Fuerth, Germany; s. of Louis Kissinger and Paula Stern; m. 1st Anne Fleisher 1949 (divorced 1964); one s. one d.; m. 2nd Nancy Maginnes 1974; ed George Washington High School, Harvard Coll., Harvard Univ.; went to USA 1938, naturalized US Citizen 1943; served in US Army 1943–46; joined Faculty, Harvard Univ. 1954, Dir Harvard Defense Studies Program 1958–69, mem. Faculty, Harvard Univ. Center for Int. Affairs 1960–69; Dir Study Group on Nuclear Weapons and Foreign Policy, Council of Foreign Relations 1955–56, Special Studies Project, Rockefeller Brothers Fund 1956–58; Consultant, Weapons System Evaluation Group, Joint Chiefs of Staff 1956–60, Nat. Security Council 1961–63, US Arms Control and Disarmament Agency 1961–69, Dept of State 1965–68; Asst to Pres. of USA for Nat. Security Affairs 1969–75, Sec. of State 1973–77; Trustee, Center for Strategic and Int. Studies 1977–; Chair. Kissinger Assocs Inc. (known as Kissinger McLarty Assocs Inc. 1999–2008) 1982–; mem. Pres.'s Foreign Intelligence Advisory Bd 1984–90; Chair. Nat. Bipartisan Comm. on Cen. America 1983–85; mem. Comm. on Integrated Long-Term Strategy (National Security Council and Defense Department) 1986–88; currently mem. Defense Policy Bd; fmr Chair. US Comm. investigating Sept. 11 attacks; mem. Bd of Dirs ContiGroup Cos Ltd, International Rescue Committee; Adviser to Bd of Dirs American Express, Forstmann Little & Co.; Counsellor to J. P. Morgan Chase Bank and mem. of its Int. Advisory Council; Dir Emer. Freeport McMoran Copper and Gold Inc.; Chair. Emer. Eisenhower Fellowships; mem. Exec. Cttee Trilateral Comm.; Sr Fellow, Aspen Inst.; Trustee Emer. Metropolitan Museum of Art; Chancellor The Coll. of William and Mary 2000–05; syndicated columnist, Tribune Media Services Int; Hon. KCMG 1995, Hon. Gov. Foreign Policy Asscn, Hon. Chair. World Cup USA 1994; Woodrow Wilson Book Prize 1958, American Inst. for Public Service Award 1973, Nobel Peace Prize 1973, American Legion Distinguished Service Medal 1974, Wateler Peace Prize 1974, Presidential Medal of Freedom 1977, Medal of Liberty 1986, Ewald von Kleist Award 2009, President's Medal (Israel) 2012, Henry A. Grunwald Award 2013. *Publications include:* Nuclear Weapons and Foreign Policy 1956, A World Restored: Castlereagh, Metternich and the Restoration of Peace 1812–22 1957, The Necessity for Choice: Prospects of American Foreign Policy 1961, The Troubled Partnership: A Reappraisal of the Atlantic Alliance 1965, American Foreign Policy (3 essays) 1969, White House Years 1979, For the Record 1981, Years of Upheaval 1982, Observations: Selected Speeches and Essays 1982–84 1985, Diplomacy 1994, Years of Renewal 1999, Does America Need a Foreign Policy? 2001, Ending the Vietnam War 2003, Crisis: The Anatomy of Two Major Foreign Policy Crises 2003, On China 2011, World Order 2014; and numerous articles on US foreign policy, int. affairs and diplomatic history. *Address:* Kissinger Associates, 350 Park Avenue, 26th Floor, New York, NY 10022, USA. *Telephone:* (212) 759-7919. *E-mail:* info@henryakissinger.com. *Website:* www.henryakissinger.com.

KITAGAWA, Kazuo, LLB; Japanese lawyer and politician; b. 2 March 1953; ed Faculty of Law, Soka Univ.; practised law 1981–90; licensed tax accountant 2000; mem. House of Reps for Osaka Constituency 1990–2009, 2014–, Chair. Standing Cttee on Science and Tech. 1999–2000, New Komeito Policy Research Council 2000–03, Dir Standing Cttee on Audit 1990–93, on Security 1990–93, on Finance 1994–96, on Budget 1998–99, Nat. Basic Policies 2000; Parl. Vice-Minister for Finance 1993–94; Minister of Land, Infrastructure and Transport 2004–06. *Address:* House of Representatives, 1-7-1 Nagatacho, Chiyoda-ku, Tokyo 100-0014, Japan (office). *Telephone:* (3) 3581-3111 (office). *E-mail:* webmaster@shugiin.go.jp (office). *Website:* www.shugiin.go.jp/internet/index.nsf/html/index_e.htm (office); kitagawa-sakai.jp.

KITAJENKO, Dmitriy Georgievich; Russian conductor; b. 18 Aug. 1940, Leningrad; ed Glinka School of Music, Rimsky-Korsakov Conservatory before leaving to study with Leo Ginzburg in Moscow and Hans Swarowsky and Karl Österreicher in Vienna; teacher at Moscow Conservatory 1969, Prof. 1986–90; Conductor, Nemirovich-Danchenko Theatre 1969, Prin. Conductor 1970–76; Chief Conductor, Moscow Philharmonic 1976–89; Prin. Conductor, Frankfurt Radio Orchestra 1990–95, Bergen Philharmonic Orchestra 1990–98; Conductor, Bern Symphony Orchestra 1994–2004; Prin. Conductor, KBS Symphony Orchestra, Seoul 1999–2004; Prin. Guest Conductor, Berlin Konzerthaus Orchestra 2012–, Danish Nat. Radio Symphony Orchestra; has conducted orchestras from Europe, America and Asia including Berlin Philharmonic, Leipzig Gewandhaus, Vienna Symphony, London Symphony, Gothenburg Symphony, Radio Symphony Orchestra Hamburg, Stuttgart Radio Symphony, Dresden Philharmonic, Qatar Philharmonic (Brahms cycle); Hon. Conductor, Cologne Gürzenich Orchestra 2009, Conductor of Honor, Qatar Philharmonic Orchestra 2015; USSR People's Artist 1984, RSFSR State Prize 1988, Pizzicato Excellentia and Supersonic awards, Midem Classical Award 2006, Echo Klassik Award 2006, Int. Classical Music Award for Lifetime Achievement 2015, for Opera 2016. *Recordings include:* numerous recordings, including with Moscow Philharmonic, Frankfurt RSO, Bergen Philharmonic Orchestra, Danish National Radio Symphony Orchestra, Cologne Gürzenich Orchestra; complete recordings of symphonies of Scriabin, Rachmaninov, Stravinsky, Rimsky-Korsakov, Prokofiev, Tchaikovsky and Shostakovich; also recorded works by Chopin, Gade, Grieg, Richard Strauss, Siegfried

Wagner and contemporary music. *Address:* c/o Vera van Hazebrouck, van Hazebrouck Artists, Chrysanthemenstraße 5, 41466 Neuss, Germany (office); Chalet Kalimor, 1652 Botterens, Switzerland (home). *E-mail:* vera@hazebrouck-artists.com (office). *Website:* www.kitajenko.com.

KITAJIMA, Kosuke; Japanese swimmer; b. 22 Sept. 1982, Tokyo; ed Nippon Sport Science Univ., Tokyo; fourth place in 100m breaststroke, Olympic Games, Sydney 2000; broke oldest swimming world record (200m breaststroke) at Asian Games 2002; gold medal, 100m and 200m breaststroke (set two world records), World Championships (long course), Barcelona 2003, 100m and 200m breaststroke, Olympic Games, Athens 2004, 200m breaststroke, World Championships (long course), Melbourne 2007, 100m (world record time of 58.91) and 200m breaststroke, Olympic Games, Beijing 2008, Pan Pacific Championships 2010; silver medal, 100m breaststroke, FINA World Championships (short course), Moscow 2002, 100m breaststroke, World Championships (long course), Melbourne 2007, 200m breaststroke, World Championships (long course), Shanghai 2011, 4×100m medley relay, Olympic Games, London 2012; bronze medal, 100m breaststroke, World Championships, Fukuoka 2001, 4×100m medley relay, World Championships, Barcelona 2003, 4×100m medley relay, Olympic Games, Athens 2004, 4×100m medley relay, Olympic Games, Beijing 2008, 4×100m medley relay, World Championships (long course), Barcelona 2013; set world record time of 2:07.51 for 200m breaststroke June 2008; Medal with Purple Ribbon; Most Valuable Player, Asian Games 2002, Tokyo Medal of Honour, World Pacific Rim Swimmer of the Year 2003, 2007. *Leisure interests:* fashion, driving. *Address:* c/o IMPRINT, 2-16-9-7F, Higashi, Shibuya-ku, Tokyo 150-0011, Japan (office). *Telephone:* (3) 6690-0305 (office). *Fax:* (3) 6849-4248 (office). *E-mail:* info@imprint.jp (office). *Website:* www.imprint.jp (office); www.kitajima-kosuke.com.

KITAJIMA, Yoshitoshi; Japanese business executive; *Chairman, President and CEO, Dai Nippon Printing Company Ltd;* joined The Fuji Bank Ltd 1958; joined Dai Nippon Printing Co. Ltd 1963, CEO 1970–, Chair. and Pres. 1979–, Pres. DNP IMS America Corpn 1979–; Dir Hokkaido Coca-Cola Bottling Co. Ltd 1971–, Rep. Dir and Pres. 1980–, Chair. 2007–; mem. Bd of Dirs TV Asahi Corpn, The Japan Forum; Corp. Auditor, Dai-ichi Mutual Life Insurance Co.; mem. EU-Japan Fest Cttee, Advisory Cttee Asia Pacific Univ.; Kt of the Dannebrog (Denmark), Commdr, Légion d'honneur 2007. *Address:* Dai Nippon Printing Company Ltd, 1-1 Ichigaya Kagacho 1-chome, Shinjuku-ku, Tokyo 162-8001, Japan (office). *Telephone:* (3) 3266-2111 (office). *Fax:* (3) 5225-8239 (office). *E-mail:* info@dnp.co.jp (office). *Website:* www.dnp.co.jp (office).

KITAMURA, Hiroshi, KBE; Japanese diplomatist and university administrator; b. 20 Jan. 1929, Osaka; m. Sachiko Kitamura 1953; two d.; ed Univ. of Tokyo, Fletcher School of Law and Diplomacy, Tufts Univ., Mass., USA; joined Foreign Affairs Ministry 1953, served in Washington, DC, New York, Delhi; First Sec., Embassy in London 1963–66; with Mission to OECD, Paris 1971–74; Exec. Asst to Prime Minister 1974–76; Deputy Dir-Gen. American Affairs Bureau 1977–79, Dir-Gen. 1982–84, Deputy Vice-Minister of Foreign Affairs 1984–87, Deputy Minister 1987–88; Consul-Gen. San Francisco 1979–82, Amb. to Canada 1988–90, to the UK 1991–94; Corp. Adviser, Mitsubishi Corpn 1994–99; Pres. Shumei Univ. 1998–2001; Prime Minister's Personal Rep. to Venice Summit 1987, Toronto Summit 1988; Fellow, Center for Int. Affairs, Harvard Univ. 1970; Chair. Japan–British Soc. 1994–2003; Gold and Silver Star, Order of the Rising Sun 1999; Hon. LLD (Northumbria) 1993. *Publications include:* Psychological Dimensions of US–Japanese Relations 1971, Between Friends (co-author) 1985, The UK Seen through an Ambassador's Eyes (in Japanese), Diplomacy and Food (in Japanese), An Ambassador and his Lhasa Apso (in Japanese). *Leisure interests:* Japanese classical music, food and wine, golf. *Address:* 1-15-6 Jingumae, Shibuya-ku, Tokyo, Japan (office). *Telephone:* (3) 3470-4630 (home). *Fax:* (3) 3470-4830 (home).

KITAMURA, Norio; Japanese business executive; b. 1942; ed Kagoshima Univ.; joined Toyota Motor Corpn, Pres. Toyota Motor Italia SpA 1996–2005, Chair. and CEO 2005–06; joined Japan Post Service Co. Ltd 2006, Chair. and CEO (following privatization Oct. 2007) 2007–10, CEO Japan Post Holdings Co. Ltd (Japan Post Group) 2007–10; Dir Sanrio Co. Ltd 2014–. *Address:* c/o Japan Post Service Co. Ltd, 1-3-2 Kasumigaseki, Chiyoda-ku, Tokyo 100-8798, Japan.

KITANO, Takeshi; Japanese film director, actor, comedian and screenwriter; b. 18 Jan. 1947, Tokyo; m. Mikiko Kitano; two c.; ed Meiji Univ.; Commdr, Ordre des Arts et des Lettres 2010, Officier, Ordre nat. de la Légion d'honneur 2016; Lifetime Achievement Award, Moscow Int. Film Festival 2008. *Films include:* Makoto-chan (actor) 1980, Danpu wataridori (actor) 1981, Manon (actor) 1981, Sukkari... sono ki de! (actor) 1981, Merry Christmas, Mr. Lawrence (actor) 1983, Jukkai no mosquito (actor) 1983, Kanashii kibun de joke (actor) 1985, Yasha (actor) 1985, Komikku zasshi nanka iranai! (actor) 1986, Anego (actor) 1988, Sono otoko, kyobo ni tsuki (writer, dir, actor) 1989, Hoshi tsugu mono (actor) 1990, 3-4x jugatsu (writer, dir, actor) 1990, Ano natsu, ichiban shizukana umi (writer, dir) 1991, Sakana kara daiokishin! (actor) 1992, Erotikkuna kankei (actor) 1992, Sonatine (writer, dir, actor) 1993, Kyôso tanjô (writer, actor) 1993, Minnâ-yatteruka! (writer, dir, actor) 1995, Johnny Mnemonic (actor) 1995, Gonin (actor) 1995, Kidzu ritan (writer, dir) 1996, Hana-bi (writer, dir, actor) (Venice Film Festival Golden Lion) 1997, Tokyo Eyes (actor) 1998, Kikujiro no natsu (writer, dir, actor) 1999, Gohatto (actor) 1999, Brother (writer, dir, actor) 2000, Batoru rowaiaru (Battle Royale) (actor) 2000, Dolls (writer, dir) 2002, Asakusa Kid (writer) 2002, Battle Royale II (actor) 2003, Zatôichi (writer, dir, actor) (Venice Film Festival Silver Lion) 2003, Izô: Kaosu mataha fujôri no kijin (actor) 2004, Chi to hone 2004, Takeshis' 2005, Gegege no Kitano 2007, Achilles and the Tortoise 2008, Outrage 2010, Beyond Outrage (actor, dir) 2012, Ryuzo and the Seven Henchmen (dir) 2015, Ryuzo 7 (actor) 2015, Mozu (actor) 2015, While the Women Are Sleeping (actor) 2016. *Leisure interest:* writing. *Address:* Office Kitano, 4-14 trade Akasaka Bldg. 6f, Minato-ku, Akasaka, 5-Chome, Tokyo 107-0052, Japan. *E-mail:* office@office-kitano.co.jp. *Website:* www.office-kitano.co.jp.

KITARO; Japanese musician; b. (Takahashi Masanori), 4 Feb. 1953, Toyohashi; self-taught electric guitar player; began music career during school studies; founding mem. rock band The Far East Family Band –1976; abandoned rock for new age music and released first solo album Astral Voyage 1978; composed musical score for TV documentary series Silk Road 1980–85; signed with Geffen Records 1986; first live tour of N America leading to sales of two million albums in US 1987; featured as key artist and composer in Japan's Millennium celebration event; composed soundtrack for Chinese drama The Soong Sisters 2002; performs annual televised concerts from mountain location of his Japanese home and studio base in Nagano Pref. *Albums include:* Astral Voyage 1978, Millennia 1978, Ten Kai Astral Trip 1978, Full Moon Story 1979, Ki 1979, Oasis 1979, Silk Road Suite (Vols 1–4) 1980–83, Ten Huang 1980, Queen of Millennia 1982, India 1983, Tenjiku 1983, Tenku 1986, Silver Cloud 1986, Toward the West 1986, The Light of the Spirit 1987, Kojiki (Japan Gold Disc for Fusion Instrumental 1991) 1990, Kitaro Live in America 1991, Dream 1992, Mandala 1994, Peace on Earth 1996, Cirque Ingenieux 1998, Heaven and Earth 1997, Gaia 1998, Thinking of You (Grammy Award for Best New Age Album 2001) 1999, Ancient 2001, An Ancient Journey 2002, Mizuniinorite 2002, The Soong Sisters 2002, Sacred Journey of Ku-Kai 2003, Shikoku 88 Kasho 2004, Spiritual Garden 2006, Impressions Of The West Lake 2009, Final Call 2013, Asian Café 2016. *Address:* c/o Domo Music Group Inc., 11340 West Olympic Boulevard, Suite 270, Los Angeles, CA 90064, USA (office). *Telephone:* (310) 966-4414 (office). *E-mail:* info@domomusicgroup.com (office). *Website:* www.domomusicgroup.com/kitaro (office).

KITAYAMA, Teisuke, BA; Japanese banking executive; *Chairman and Representative Director, Sumitomo Mitsui Banking Corporation;* b. 26 Oct. 1946, Tokyo; m.; one d.; ed Univ. of Tokyo; joined Mitsui Bank 1969, Gen. Man. Yokohama-Ekimae Br., Sakura Bank (fmrly Mitsui Taiyo Kobe Bank) 1992–95, Gen. Rep. in Thailand and Gen. Man. of Bangkok Br. 1995–97, Dir and Gen. Man. Planning Div. 1997–2000, Man. Dir 2000, Man. Dir Sumitomo Mitsui Banking Corpn (formed by merger of Sakura Bank and Sumitomo Bank) 2001–02, Sr Man. Dir 2002–03, Sr Man. Dir Sumitomo Mitsui Financial Group, Inc. (holding co. of Sumitomo Mitsui Banking Corpn) 2003–04, Deputy Pres. 2004–05, Pres. and Rep. Dir 2005–11, currently Chair. and Rep. Dir Sumitomo Mitsui Banking Corpn; Pres. Aspen Inst. Japan. *Address:* Sumitomo Mitsui Banking Corporation, 1-2, Yurakucho 1-Chome, Chiyoda-ku, Tokyo 100-0006, Japan (office). *Telephone:* (3) 5512-3411 (office). *Fax:* (3) 5512-4429 (office). *E-mail:* info@smbc.co.gp (office). *Website:* www.smbc.co.jp (office); www.smbcgroup.com (office).

KITAZAWA, Toshimi; Japanese politician; b. 6 March 1938, Nagano; ed Waseda Univ.; started political career as Sec. to MP; mem. Nagano Prefectural Ass. 1975–92; mem. House of Councillors for Nagano constituency 1992–, mem. Parl. Land and Transport Cttee, Fundamental Nat. Policies Cttee; mem. LDP –1993; mem. Shinshinto (New Frontier Party) 1993–98; mem. Democratic Party of Japan 1998–, fmr Vice-Pres. and Chair. Foreign Policy and Defence Cttee; Minister of Defence 2009–11. *Address:* #424, Members' Office Building, HC, Nagatacho 1-7-1, Chiyoda-ku, Tokyo, Japan (office). *Website:* kitazawa.tsukaeru.info.

KITBUNCHU, HE Cardinal Michael Michai; Thai ecclesiastic; b. 25 Jan. 1929, Samphran, Nakhon Pathom; ordained priest, Bangkok 1959; Archbishop of Bangkok 1973–2009 (retd); elevated to Cardinal, apptd Cardinal-Priest of S. Lorenzo in Panisperna 1983. *Address:* c/o Archdiocese of Bangkok, 51 Catholic Mission, Charoenkrung 40, Bangrak, Bangkok 10500, Thailand.

KITE, Thomas (Tom) O., Jr; American professional golfer; b. 9 Dec. 1949, Austin, Tex.; m. Christy Kite (deceased); two s. one d.; ed Univ. of Texas; won Walker Cup 1971; professional golfer, Professional Golfers' Asscn (PGA) 1972–2000; won Ryder Cup 1979, 1981, 1983, 1985, 1987, 1989, 1993, European Open 1980, US Open, Pebble Beach, Calif. 1992; LA Open 1993; 14 US PGA Tour wins; apptd Capt. US team for 1997 Ryder Cup, Valderrama, Spain; joined Sr PGA Tour 2000, wins include The Countryside Tradition 2000, MasterCard Championship 2002, SBC Sr Classic 2002, Napa Valley Championship 2002, 3M Championship 2004, AT&TClassic 2006, Boeing Classic 2008; currently plays on Champions Tour; spokesman for Chrysler Jr Golf Scholarship program; f. Tom Kite Design (golf course design co.); Bob Jones Award 1979, Player of the Year (Golf Writers) 1981, 1989, Vardon Trophy 1981, 1982, PGA Player of the Year 1989, elected to World Golf Hall of Fame 2004. *Leisure interest:* landscaping. *Address:* c/o PGA Tour, 112 Tpc Boulevard Ponte Vedra Beach, FL 32082, USA. *Telephone:* (512) 983-5483. *E-mail:* info@tomkitedesign.com.

KITONGA, Nzamba, LLB; Kenyan lawyer and judge; *Founder and Managing Partner, Nzamba Kitonga Advocates LLP;* b. 1956; ed Univ. of Nairobi; Prin., fmr Chair. Law Soc. of Kenya; fmr Pres. and Chair. East African Law Soc.; fmr Chair. Committee of Experts on constitutional review; fmr Vice-Chair. Goldenberg Comm. of Inquiry; apptd Judge of Appellate Div., Common Market for Eastern and Southern Africa (COMESA) Court of Justice 2005–15, Pres. Court of Justice 2005–15; currently Founder and Man. Partner Nzamba Kitonga Advocates LLP; Chair. Council for Legal Education in Kenya 2016; Jurist of the Year, 2010. *Address:* Nzamba Kitonga Advocates LLP, 209 Fortis Office Suites, Hospital Road, Upper Hill Nairobi, Kenya (office). *Telephone:* (202) 224887 (office). *Fax:* (732) 751661 (office). *E-mail:* nzamba@kit-llp.co.ke (office); info@nzambakitonga.com (office); nzambakitonga@gmail.com. *Website:* kit-llp.co.ke.

KITSIKIS, Dimitri, MA, PhD, FRSC; Canadian/French/Greek poet, historian and academic; *Professor Emeritus, Department of History, University of Ottawa;* b. 2 June 1935, Athens, Greece; s. of Nikolas Kitsikis and Beata Kitsikis (née Petychakis); m. 1st Anne Hubbard 1955 (divorced 1973); one s. one d.; m. 2nd Ada Nikolaros 1975; one s. one d.; ed American Coll. Athens, Ecole des Roches, Normandy, Lycée Lakanal and Lycée Carnot, Paris and Sorbonne, Paris; Research Assoc. Grad. Inst. of Int. Studies, Geneva 1960–62, Centre for Int. Relations, Nat. Foundation of Political Science, Paris 1962–65, Nat. Centre for Scientific Research, Paris 1965–70; Assoc. Prof. of History of Int. Relations, Univ. of Ottawa 1970–83, Prof. 1983–96, Prof. Emer. 1996–; Sr Research Scholar, Nat. Centre of Social Research, Athens 1972–74; Founder, Ed. Intermediate Region (journal) 1996–; adviser to Govts of Greece and Turkey; numerous visiting professorships, including at Univ. of Bogazici, Istanbul, Univ. of Bilkent, Ankara, Univ. of Gediz, Izmir, Sun Yat-Sen Univ., Guangzhou, and other appointments; Founder and Hon. Pres. Dimitri Kitsikis Public Foundation and Library, Athens 2008–; Study of Ataturk's Principles Award, Bogazici Univ. 1981, First Prize in Poetry, Abdi Ipekçi Peace and Friendship Prize 1992, Homo Hellenicus Award, Hellenic Evergetes Soc. 2010. *Publications include:* 37 books, including Propaganda and Pressure in International Politics 1963, The Role of the Experts at the Paris Peace Conference of 1919 1972, A Comparative History of Greece and Turkey in the 20th Century 1978, History of the Greek-Turkish Area 1981, The Ottoman Empire 1985, The

Third Ideology and Orthodoxy 1990, The Old Calendarists 1995, Turkish-Greek Empire 1996, The Byzantine Model of Government 2001, J.-J. Rousseau and the French Origins of Fascism 2006, Bektashism and Alevism 2006, A Comparative History of Greece and China 2007, The Rise of National-Bolshevism in the Balkans 2008, National Bolshevism 2010, On Heroes 2014, Greece of the Fourth of August and the Great Powers 2018; co-author of 44 other books; six vols of poetry, including Omphalos 1977, L'Orocc dans l'age de Kali 1985, Le Paradis Perdu sur les Barricades 1993, two vols of poetry and painting; hundreds of scholarly articles. *Leisure interests:* art, science fiction, study of languages. *Address:* Department of History, University of Ottawa, Ottawa, ON K1N 6N5 (office); 2104 Benjamin Avenue, Ottawa, ON K2A 1P4, Canada (home); 29 Travlantoni, Zographou, Athens 15772, Greece (home); Dimitri Kitsikis Foundation, Hagiou Ioannou Theologou 22, Zographou, Athens 15772 (office). *Telephone:* (613) 562-5735 (Ottawa) (office); (210) 778-0225 (Athens) (office); (613) 729-9814 (Ottawa) (home); (210) 777-6937 (Athens) (home); (27310) 83096 (Pikoulianika, Greece) (home); 1-40-31-32-34 (Paris) (home); (613) 842-9175 (Ottawa) (home). *Fax:* (613) 562-5995 (Ottawa) (office). *E-mail:* dimitri.kitsikis@uottawa.ca (office). *Website:* www.idkf.gr (office).

KITTEL, Charles, PhD; American physicist, academic and writer; *Professor Emeritus, Department of Physics, University of California, Berkeley;* b. 18 July 1916, New York; s. of George Paul Kittel and Helen Kittel; m. Muriel Agnes Lister 1938; two s. one d.; ed Massachusetts Inst. of Tech., Univ. of Cambridge, UK and Univ. of Wisconsin; Prof. of Physics, Univ. of California, Berkeley 1951–78, Prof. Emer. 1978–; mem. NAS, American Acad. of Arts and Sciences; Buckley Prize for Solid State Physics 1957, Berkeley Distinguished Teaching Award 1970, Oersted Medal, American Asscn of Physics Teachers 1972. *Publications include:* Quantum Theory of Solids 1963, Thermal Physics 1980, Introduction to Solid State Physics 1996, Elementary Statistical Physics 2004. *Leisure interests:* friends, wine. *Address:* Department of Physics, University of California, 559 Birge, Berkeley, CA 94720-7300, USA (office). *Telephone:* (510) 643-9473 (office). *E-mail:* kittel@berkeley.edu (office). *Website:* www.physics.berkeley.edu (office).

KITTELMANN, Udo; German arts administrator and writer; *Director, Nationalgalerie, Staatliche Museen zu Berlin;* b. 15 March 1958, Düsseldorf; began career as optician; became ind. exhbn curator for several orgs including Städtische Galerie im Lenbachhaus, Munich, Kunsthalle, Innsbruck, Austria, Salzburg Kunstverein, Austria 1987–93; Artistic Dir Kunstverein Ludwigsburg 1993–94; Dir Cologne Kunstverein 1994–2001; Commr of German Pavilion at 49th Venice Biennale 2001; Dir Museum für Moderne Kunst (MMK), Frankfurt 2002–08; Dir Nationalgalerie, Staatliche Museen zu Berlin (State Museums in Berlin) 2008–, responsible for the Alte Nationalgalerie (Old Nat. Galley), Neue Nationalgalerie (New Nat. Gallery) and the Hamburger Bahnhof, Museum für Gegenwart – Berlin (Museum for Contemporary Art), as well as the Berggruen Museum, Sammlung Scharf-Gerstenberg (Scharf-Gerstenberg Collection) and Friedrichswerdersche Kirche; curated Russian Pavilion at 55th Venice Biennale 2013. *Publications include:* Jonathan Borofsky: Dedicated to the Audience 1994, Rirkrit Tiravanija: Untitled 1996, Obsession (co-author) 1999, Gregor Schneider: Totes Haus, Biennale di Venezia 2001, World's Best New Art: Unreal Projects (co-author) 2007, Michel Majerus: If We Are Dead, So It Is 2008, Luc Tuymans: Ende 2009. *Address:* Nationalgalerie, Staatliche Museen zu Berlin, Genthiner Strasse 38, 10785 Berlin, Germany (office). *Telephone:* (30) 266424242 (office). *Website:* www.smb.museum/museen-und-einrichtungen/nationalgalerie (office).

KITTIKHOUN, Alounkèo; Laotian diplomatist; *Vice-Minister of Foreign Affairs;* b. 10 Oct. 1951, Pakse, Champasark; m. Dr Kongpadith Kittikhoun; two s.; ed Royal Inst. of Law and Admin, Vientiane, Univ. of Paris I (Panthéon-Sorbonne), Int. Inst. of Public Admin, Paris, France; joined Foreign Ministry 1977; Second Sec., then First Sec. and Counsellor, Perm. Mission to UN 1980–90, Perm. Rep. 1993–2007; Chair. Landlocked Developing Countries Group at the UN 1999–2003 and of numerous other UN bodies and cttees; Deputy Dir Dept of Int. Orgs, Foreign Ministry 1990–92, Dir 1992–93; Assistant Minister of Foreign Affairs 2007–11; currently Vice-Minister of Foreign Affairs; also Leader, Sr Officials Meetings, Asscn of Southeast Asian Nations. *Leisure interests:* golf, reading, eating, relaxing with family. *Address:* Ministry of Foreign Affairs, rue That Luang 01004, Ban Phonxay, Vientiane, Laos (office). *Telephone:* (21) 413148 (office). *Fax:* (21) 414009 (office). *E-mail:* cabinet@mofa.gov.la (office); alkktk@hotmail.com (home). *Website:* www.mofa.gov.la (office).

KITUYI, Mukhisa, BA, MPhil, PhD; Kenyan academic, politician and UN official; *Secretary-General, United Nations Conference on Trade and Development (UNCTAD);* b. 20 Oct. 1956, Bungoma Dist; s. of Jamin Kituyi and Joinah Mukasa Kituyi; m. Ling Merete (née Andersen); three s. one d.; ed Makerere Univ., Uganda, Univ. of Bergen, Norway; Researcher, Business and Econ. Research Centre, Nairobi 1982–83, Christian Michelsens Inst., Norway 1986–88; Programme Officer, Norwegian Agency for International Devt 1989–90; Programme Dir African Centre for Tech. Studies 1990–92; Exec. Dir Forum for Restoration of Democracy in Kenya 1992; MP for Kimilili constituency 1992–2007, served as Chief Opposition Whip and Chair. Defence and Foreign Affairs Cttee; Minister for Trade and Industry 2003–08, served as Chair. COMESA Council of Ministers, African Trade Ministers' Council, Council of Ministers of African, Caribbean and Pacific Group of States; Exec. Dir Kenya Inst. of Governance (think-tank), Nairobi 2008–; Under-Sec.-Gen. UN Sept. 2013–, Sec.-Gen. UNCTAD Sept. 2013–; Fellow (non-resident), Africa Growth Initiative, Brookings Inst. 2011–, Resident Scholar 2011; columnist, Sunday Nation. *Address:* United Nations Conference on Trade and Development (UNCTAD), Palais des Nations, 8–14, Avenue de la Paix, 1211 Geneva 10, Switzerland (office). *Telephone:* 229171234 (office). *Fax:* 229170057 (office). *E-mail:* sgo@unctad.org (office). *Website:* unctad.org (office).

KITZHABER, John Albert, BS, MD; American physician, academic and politician; b. 5 March 1947, Colfax, Wash.; s. of Albert Raymond Kitzhaber and Annabel Reed Kitzhaber (née Wetzel); m. 1st Sharon LaCroix 1995 (divorced 2003); one s.; partner Cylvia Hayes 2003–; ed South Eugene High School, Dartmouth Coll., Univ. of Oregon Medical School (now Oregon Health & Science Univ.); intern, Gen. Rose Memorial Hosp., Denver, Colo 1976–77; Emergency Physician, Mercy Hosp., Roseburg, Ore. 1974–75; mem. Ore. House of Reps 1979–81, Ore. Senate 1981–95, Pres. 1985, 1987, 1989, 1991; Gov. of Oregon 1995–2003, 2011–15; Pres. Estes Park Inst., Englewood, Colo 2003–, The Kitzhaber Center, Lewis and Clark Law School 2005–; Assoc. Prof., Oregon Health & Science Univ. 1989–95, now also Dir Center for Evidence Based Policy; endowed Chair on Health Care Policy, The Foundation for Medical Excellence 2003–, first recipient John Kitzhaber, MD Chair on Health Care Policy 2011–; Founder Archimedes Movt 2006–; mem. American Coll. of Emergency Physicians, Inst. of Medicine, Douglas Co. Medical Soc., Physicians for Social Responsibility, American Council of Young Political Leaders, Oregon Trout; Democrat; Neuberger Award, Oregon Environmental Council 1987, Dr Nathan Davis Award, American Medical Asscn 1992. *Address:* The Foundation for Medical Excellence, Suite 860, 1 SW Columbia Street, Portland, OR 97258, USA. *Telephone:* (503) 222-1960 (office). *E-mail:* info@tfme.org. *Website:* www.johnkitzhaber.com.

KITZINGER, Uwe, CBE, MA, MLitt; British academic; *Patron, Asylum Welcome;* b. 12 April 1928, Nuremberg, Germany; s. of Dr G. Kitzinger and Lucy Kitzinger; m. Sheila Helena Elizabeth Webster 1952 (died 2015); five d.; ed Watford Grammar School, Balliol and New Colls, Oxford; Foundation Scholar, New Coll., Oxford 1947; Pres. of Oxford Union 1950; Econ. Section, Council of Europe 1951–58; Research Fellow, Nuffield Coll., Oxford 1956–62, Official Fellow and Investment Bursar 1962–76, Emer. Fellow 1976–; Dean, European Inst. of Business Admin. (INSEAD), Fontainebleau 1976–80; Dir Oxford Centre for Man. Studies 1980–84; first Pres. Templeton Coll., Oxford 1984–91; Founding Ed., Journal of Common Market Studies 1962–; Visiting Prof. Univ. of West Indies 1964–65; Visiting Prof. of Govt and Assoc., Centre for Int. Affairs, Harvard 1969–70; Visiting Prof., Univ. of Paris VIII 1970–73; Adviser to the late Lord Soames (Vice-Pres. Comm. of the European Communities), Brussels 1973–75; Sr Research Fellow, Atlantic Council 1993–; Visiting Scholar, Harvard Univ. 1993–2003; Founding Chair. Cttee on Atlantic Studies 1967–70, Major Projects Asscn 1981–86; Pres. Int. Asscn of Macro-Eng Socs 1987–2003, Féd. Britannique des Alliances Françaises 1998–2004; Council mem. European Movt 1974–76, Royal Inst. of Int. Affairs 1976–85, Oxfam 1981–84, Fondation Jean Monnet 1990–; Chair. Oxfordshire Radio Ltd 1988, GARIWO, Sarajevo 2001–12; co-f. Lentils for Dubrovnik 1991; Trustee, Ourtree Charitable Trust 1994–; Patron, Asylum Welcome 2004–; Hon. Fellow, Templeton Coll. 2001, Green Templeton Coll. 2008; Order of the Morning Star (Croatia) 1997; Hon. LLD 1986; Tufts Univ. Jean de Meyer Award 2016. *Publications:* German Electoral Politics 1960, The Challenge of the Common Market 1961, The Politics and Economics of European Integration 1963, Britain, Europe and Beyond 1964, Commitment and Identity 1968, The Second Try 1968, Diplomacy and Persuasion 1973, Europe's Wider Horizons 1975, The 1975 Referendum (with David Butler) 1976, Macro-Engineering and the Earth (co-ed. with Ernst Frankel) 1998; broadcasts, pamphlets and articles in the European University Inst. Historical Archives, Florence. *Leisure interest:* cruising under sail (ketch Anne of Cleves). *Address:* Standlake Manor, Standlake nr Witney, Oxon., OX29 7RH, England (home); La Rivière, 11100 Bages d'Aude, France. *Telephone:* (1865) 300438 (England) (office); (1865) 300266 (England) (home); (4) 68-41-70-13 (France) (home). *E-mail:* uwe_kitzinger@yahoo.com (office); uwek@ymail.com (home). *Website:* www.eui.eu/HAEU/pdfinv/inv-uwkns.pdf.

KIVEJINJA, Kirunda, BSc; Ugandan politician; *Second Deputy Prime Minister and Minister for East African Community Affairs;* b. (Ali M. Kirunda Kivejinja), 12 June 1935; ed Busoga Coll. Mwiri, Delhi Univ., India; mem. Parl. for Bugweri; Minister of Transport and Communications –1999 (resgnd), Minister in charge of the Presidency 2003, Third Deputy Prime Minister and Minister of Information and Nat. Guidance 2006–09, Minister of Internal Affairs 2009–11; Sr Presidential Advisor for Internal Affairs to Pres. Museveni; Second Deputy Prime Minister and Minister for East African Community Affairs 2015–; Dir of External Affairs, National Resistance Movement (NRM) Secr. 1999–2003, later Head of Veterans' League; mem. East African Legis. Ass.; Dr hc (Islamic Univ. in Uganda) 2014. *Address:* Ministry of East African Community Affairs, Postel Bldg, 2nd Floor, 67/75 Yusuf Lule Road, POB 7343, Kampala, Uganda (office). *Telephone:* (41) 4340100 (office). *Fax:* (41) 4348171 (office). *E-mail:* meaca@meaca.go.ug (office). *Website:* www.meaca.go.ug (office).

KIVINIEMI, Mari Johanna; Finnish politician and international organization official; *Deputy Secretary-General, Organisation for Economic Co-operation and Development;* b. 27 Sept. 1968, Seinäjoki; m. Juha Mikael Louhivuori; two c.; ed Univ. of Helsinki; mem. Suomen Keskusta (Kesk–Finnish Centre Party), Vice-Chair. for S Ostrobothnia Region 1994–2000, Party Vice-Chair. 2003–08, Chair. 2010–12; mem. Suomen Eduskunta (Parl.) for Vaasa Co. 1995–99, for Helsinki 2007–; Special Adviser to Prime Minister Matti Vanhanen 2004–05; elected mem. Helsinki City Council 2005; Minister for Foreign Trade and Devt 2005–06, Minister of Public Admin and Local Govt 2007–10; Prime Minister 2010–11; Deputy Sec.-Gen. OECD 2014–. *Address:* Organisation for Economic Co-operation and Development (OECD), 2 rue André-Pascal, 75775 Paris Cedex 16, France (office). *Telephone:* 1-45-24-82-00 (office). *Fax:* 1-45-24-85-00 (office). *E-mail:* webmaster@oecd.org (office). *Website:* www.oecd.org (office).

KIVRIKOGLU, Gen. Huseyin; Turkish army officer; b. Dec. 1934, Bozuyuk, Bilecik; m.; one s.; ed Isiklar Mil. School, Army Acad., Army War Coll., Armed Forces Coll., NATO Defence Coll., Rome, Italy; served as platoon and battery commdr in various artillery units 1957–65, Staff Officer 9th Infantry Div. in Sarikamis 1967–70; Planning Officer, Allied Forces S Europe Operations Div., Italy 1970–72; Instructor, Army War Coll. 1972–73; Section Chief of Gen. Staff and Br. Chief of Land Forces Command; Commdr of Cadet Regt, Army Acad., Ankara 1978–80; rank of Brig.-Gen. 1980; Chief of Operations Centre, Supreme HQ Allied Powers in Europe (SHAPE), Belgium 1980–83; CO 3rd and 11th Brigades 1983–84; rank of Maj.-Gen. 1984; Chief of Staff NATO Allied Land Forces SE Europe (CLSE), Izmir 1984–86; CO 9th Infantry Div. 1986–88; rank of Lt-Gen. 1988; Asst Chief of Staff, Gen. Staff HQ; CO 5th Corps and Under-Sec. Ministry of Nat. Defence 1990–93; promoted to Four Star 1993; Commdr CLSE 1993–96, First Army, Istanbul 1996–97, Land Forces 1997–98; C-in-C Armed Forces and Chief of Gen. Staff 1998–2002; Armed Forces Distinguished Service Medal, Grand Cross and Golden Honour Medal (Turkey), Star of Romania, Order of Merit (USA), Order of Distinction Medal (Pakistan); numerous Army Acad. Badges, NATO Service Badge, Commdr Armed Forces Identification Badge.

KIWANUKA, Hon. Maria, BCom, MBA; Ugandan economist, business executive and politician; *Senior Financial Adviser to the President;* b. 12 May 1955, Kampala; d. of Alistaluko Sekagya Nsibirwa Kiwana and Margaret Ndibalekera

Lubega Kiwana; m. Mohan Kiwanuka; three c.; ed Gayaza High School, Makerere Univ., London Business School, UK; economist and financial analyst for E Asia and Southern Africa regions, World Bank Group 1980–90; worked for family businesses in pvt. sector; fmr Man. Dir Radio One and Radio Two; Minister of Finance and Economic Planning and ex-officio mem. Parl. 2011–15, Sr Financial Adviser to the Pres. 2015–; mem. Bd of Dirs, Aga Khan Foundation (East Africa), Nabagereka Devt Trust, Nkumba Univ., Uganda Devt Bank, Stanbic Bank Uganda Ltd. *Address:* c/o Ministry of Finance, Planning and Economic Development, Appollo Kaggwa Road, Plot 2-12, PO Box 8147, Kampala, Uganda.

KIYONGA, Hon. Crispus Walter Bazarrabusa, MB ChB, MHS; Ugandan physician, politician and diplomatist; *Ambassador to China;* b. 19 Sept. 1952, Kasese Dist; ed Johns Hopkins Univ., USA; medical officer 1981–83; Sr Medical Officer, Kenyatta Hosp. 1983–85; Minister for Co-operatives and Marketing 1986, for Finance 1986–92; mem. Nat. Resistance Council 1989–95; Consultant, World Bank and African Devt Bank 1992–94; elected to Constituent Ass. that drew up the 1995 Constitution of the Repub. of Uganda 1994; Minister of Internal Affairs 1994–96; mem. Parl. for Bukonjo Co. West 1996–2016; Minister of Health 1996–2001; Chair. Global Fund to Fight AIDS, TB and Malaria 2001–02; Nat. Political Commissar and Minister without Portfolio 2001–06; Minister of Defence 2006–16; Amb. to China 2017–. *Address:* Ugandan Embassy, 5 Dong Jie, San Li Tun, Beijing 100600, People's Republic of China (office). *Telephone:* (10) 65321708 (office). *Fax:* (10) 65322242 (office). *E-mail:* ugembssy@public.bta.net.cn (office).

KJAERSGAARD, Pia; Danish politician; *Speaker of the Folketing;* b. 23 Feb. 1947, Copenhagen; d. of Poul Kjærsgaard and Inge Munch Jensen; m. Henrik Thorup 1967; two c.; ed Primary School, Gentofte Folkeskole, Copenhagen School of Commerce; office asst for insurance and advertising co. 1963–67; home care asst 1978–84; mem. Folketing (Parl.) for Progress Party in Copenhagen Co. constituency 1984–87, in Funen Co. constituency 1987–95, for Danish People's Party in Funen Co. constituency 1995–98, in Copenhagen Co. constituency 1998–2007, in Zealand Greater constituency 2007–, Speaker of the Folketing 2015–; Leader of Fremskridtspartiet (Progress Party) 1985–94; mem. Ministry of Justice's Road Safety Comm. 1986–87; Chair. Parl.'s Health Cttee 1988–91; mem. Council of Reps Danmarks Nationalbank 1989–96; mem. Nordic Council 1990–94, 1998–2000, Vice-Chair. Liberal Group 1990–94; Del. to 49th, 54th and 57th UN Gen. Ass., New York 1995, 2000, 2003, 2006, 2011, 2012; mem. Defence Comm. of 1997 1997–98; Progress Party cand. in Ryvang Nomination Dist 1979–81, in Ballerup and Gladsaxe Nomination Dist 1981–84, in Hvidovre Nomination Dist 1983–84, in Middelfart Nomination Dist 1984–95; Co-founder and Chair. Danish People's Party 1995–2012; Danish People's Party cand. in Hellerup and Gentofte Nomination Dists 1997–2000, in Glostrup Nomination Dist 1997–2007, in Kalundborg Nomination Dist 2007–; Deputy Chair. Council of Foreign Affairs; mem. Bd Political Foreign Affairs and OSCE; mem. Bd of Reps Danish Arts Council 2000–11; mem. Presidium 2012; mem. Comm. of the Intelligence Service, Political-Econ. Bd; mem. Justice Comm.; mem. Man. Cttee Danish-Taiwanese Asscn 2009; Kt (First Class), Order of the Dannebrog 2002, Commdr, Order of Dannebrog 2018, Grand Cross, Order of the Falcon (Iceland) 2017, Order of the Crown (Belgium) 2017, Order of the Aztec Eagle (Mexico) 2017, Order of Merit (France) 2018, Order of Brilliant Star (China); Kosan Prize 1986, Politician of the Year 1989, Golden Post Horn, Dansk Postordre Forening (Danish Mail-Order Asscn) 1992, Medal of Honour, Friends of Overseas Chinese Asscn 1999, Special Medal of Diplomacy (Taiwan) 2003, named Politician of the Year by Landsforeningen for Erhvervsinteresser, Altinget' Ting-Prisen 2007, 2014, Nat. Asscn of Business Interests, Medal of Brilliant Star (Taiwan) 2008, Nordic Blue Berets Medal of Honour 2018. *Publications include:* ... Men Udsigten er god (... But the View is Good) 1998, Digteren og Partiformanden (co-author) 2006, Julpå Borgen II (ed.) 2012. *Leisure interests:* gardening, music, physical fitness. *Address:* Folketinget, Christiansborg, 1240 Copenhagen K, Denmark (office). *Telephone:* 33-37-51-07 (office); 33-37-55-00 (office). *E-mail:* dfpksekr@ft.dk (office); folketinget@ft.dk (office). *Website:* www.ft.dk (office); www.piadf.dk.

KJELLÉN, Bo, MPolSc; Swedish diplomatist and environment campaigner; *Senior Research Fellow, Stockholm Environment Institute;* b. 8 Feb. 1933, Stockholm; s. of John Kjellen and Elsa Kjellen; m. 1st Margareta Lindblom 1959 (died 1978); m. 2nd Gia Boyd 1980; four c.; ed Univ. of Stockholm; entered Foreign Service 1957, posted to Rio de Janeiro, Brussels, Stockholm 1959–69; Prin. Pvt. Sec. to Sec.-Gen., OECD 1969–72; Deputy Head of Mission Del. to EEC, Brussels 1972–74; Amb. to Viet Nam 1974–77; Head Multilateral Dept for Devt Co-operation, Ministry of Foreign Affairs 1977–81; Under-Sec. Admin. and Personnel 1981–85; Amb. to OECD and UNESCO 1985–91; Chief Negotiator, Ministry of Environment 1991–98; Negotiator Climate Convention 1991–2001; Chair. Swedish Research Council for Environment, Agricultural Sciences and Spatial Planning 2001–04; Visiting Fellow, Tyndall Centre, Univ. of E Anglia 2003, 2005; Sr Research Fellow, Stockholm Environment Inst. 2005–; Hon. DSc (Cranfield, UK) 1997; Hon. PhD (Gothenburg) 1999; Hon. DLaw (Stockholm) 2011; Hon. DTech (Mälardalen Univ., Sweden) 2005; Elizabeth Haub Prize for Environmental Diplomacy 1999, GEF Award for Environmental Leadership 1999. *Publications include:* A New Diplomacy for Sustainable Development: The Challenge of Global Change 2008; several articles in academic publs and in the press on environment and sustainable devt. *Address:* Stockholm Environment Institute, Kräftriket 2 B, 10691 Stockholm, Sweden (office). *Telephone:* (8) 674-74-00 (office); (18) 71-03-07 (home). *E-mail:* bo.kjellen@sei.se (office). *Website:* www.sei.se (office).

KJØNSTAD, Asbjørn, DJur; Norwegian legal scholar and academic; *Professor of Social Law, University of Oslo;* b. 6 Feb. 1943, Levanger; s. of Arne Kjønstad and Nelly Stavern Kjønstad; m. 1st Lise-Lena Stubberød 1971–81 (divorced); one d.; m. 2nd Ayala Orkan 1995 (divorced 2002); m. 3rd Ingeborg Marie Helgeland 2009; Legal Adviser, Nat. Insurance Admin. 1970–72; Research Fellow, Univ. of Oslo 1972–78, Prof. of Pvt. Law 1978–84, Head, Inst. of Pvt. Law 1983–84, Prof. of Social Law 1985–, Dean of Faculty of Law 1986–88, mem. Bd of Univ. of Oslo 1986–88, 1999–2001; Chair. Royal Comm. on Social Security Law 1982–90; Chair. Governmental Comm. on Co-ordination of Pension Schemes 1991–95, on Transfer of Pension Rights 1999–2000, on Industrial Injuries Compensation 2001–04; Guest Scholar, Boston Univ., USA 1995–96; Guest Prof., Leuven Univ., Belgium 1997; Vice-Pres. European Inst. of Social Security 1993–97; mem. Bd Nat. Council on Tobacco and Health 1972–93, 1997–2003, Head of Research Project on Tobacco Products Liability 1998–2000; Ed. Student Law Journal 1969, Norwegian Journal of Law 1991–2000, Tort Law Journal 2004–; mem. Norwegian Acad. of Science 1987–; Hon. JuD (Lund Univ., Sweden) 1996, (Copenhagen) 2012; Hon. Prize Smokefree 2004, Health Dir Karl Evang's Prize 2007. *Publications:* 40 scientific books and reports and some 300 articles on social security law, medical law, tort law, constitutional law and human rights, including: Social Security and Compensation for Personal Injuries 1977, The Industrial Injuries Insurance 1979, Constitutional Protection of Social Security 1984, Medical Law 1987, Norwegian Social Law 1987, A Simplified National Insurance Act 1990, The National Insurance Disablement Pension 1992, Health Priority and Patient's Rights (co-ed.) 1992, Law, Power and Poverty (co-ed.) 1997, Introduction to Social Security Law 1998, European Social Security Law (ed.) 1999, Social Services and the Rule of Law (co-author) 2000, Welfare Law (Vol. I, co-author) 2000, Confidentiality About Children 2001, Welfare Law II – Social Services (co-author and co-ed.) 2003, Law and Poverty (co-author and co-ed.) 2003, The Development of Tort Law 2003, Duty of Confidentiality about Children (third edn) 2009, Introduction to Social Security Law (third edn) 2009, Twelve Main Principles in Norwegian Health Law 2010, Theory Formation in Social Law 2010, Academic Freedom and Academic Manners 2010, The Right to Primary Healthcare 2011, The Rights to Specialized Healthcare 2011, Old Age Pension 2012, The Development of Patients' Rights in Norway 2012, Welfare Law I – Fundamental Rights, the Rule of Law and Coercion (fifth edn) (with Syse) 2012, Welfare Law II – Child Care and Social Law (fourth edn) (co-author with Syse and co-ed.) 2012. *Leisure interests:* outdoor exercise, skiing, jogging, mountain walking. *Address:* University of Oslo, Karl Johans gate 47, PO Box 6706, 0130 Oslo (office); Lillevannsveien 37C, 0788 Oslo, Norway (home). *Telephone:* 22-85-94-80 (office); 22-13-80-75 (home). *Fax:* 22-85-94-20 (office); 22-49-64-51 (home). *E-mail:* asbjorn.kjonstad@jus.uio.no (office). *Website:* www.jus.uio.no (office).

KLACKENBERG, Dag, LLB, MBA; Swedish business executive and politician; b. 5 Jan. 1948, Stockholm; s. of Gunnar Klackenberg and Brita Klackenberg; m.; two c.; ed Stockholm School of Econs, Stockholm Univ.; trainee, Ministry of Foreign Affairs 1974, becoming Dir-Gen. for Admin. Affairs 1993–2001; Chair. Vattenfall AB 2001–08; Man. Dir Svensk Handel (Swedish Trade Fed.) 2001–13; mem. Parl. (Moderata Samlingspartiet) for Stockholm 4 2015–; fmr Chair. Swedish Booksellers' Fed., Vattenfall AB 2001–08, Handelsbanken Regionbank Mellansverige 2003–07, Ersta Sköndal Univ. Coll., Swedish Foreign Trade Asscn, Svensk Byggtjänst, Swedish Export Credits Guarantee Bd; mem. Bd Atrium Ljungberg Gruppen AB 2004. *Address:* Sveriges Riksdag, 100 12 Stockholm, Sweden (office). *Telephone:* (8) 786-46-95 (office). *E-mail:* dag.klackenberg@riksdagen.se (office). *Website:* www.riksdagen.se (office).

KLAFTER, Joseph, BSc, MSc, PhD; Israeli chemist, academic and university administrator; *President, Tel-Aviv University;* b. 1945, Tel-Aviv; ed Bar-Ilan Univ., Tel-Aviv Univ.; post-doctoral studies in chemistry, MIT, USA; with Research and Eng Div., Exxon 1980–87; joined Raymond and Beverly Sackler School of Chem., Tel-Aviv Univ. 1987, apptd Full Prof. 1989, Gordon Chair in Chem. 1998–2003, Chair. Dept of Physical Chem. 1990–92, 1998–2002, Heineman Chair of Physical Chem. 2003–, Pres. Tel-Aviv Univ. 2009–; mem. Academic Bd, Israel Science Foundation 1996–2002, Chair. 2002–; Fellow, American Physical Soc.; Foreign mem. American Acad. of Arts and Sciences 2011; Dr hc (Wrocław Univ. of Tech.); numerous awards including Alexander von Humboldt Foundation Prize 1996, Weizmann Prize for Sciences 1999, Rothschild Prize in Chem. 2004, Israel Chemical Soc. Prize 2005. *Publications:* around 400 scientific articles; ed 18 books. *Address:* Office of the President, Tel-Aviv University, PO Box 39040, Tel-Aviv 69978, Israel (office). *Telephone:* 3-6408111 (office). *E-mail:* klafter@post.tau.ac.il (office). *Website:* www.tau.ac.il/president (office); www.tau.ac.il/~klafter1 (office).

KLAG, Michael J., BS, MD, MPH, FACP; American epidemiologist and academic; *Dean, Bloomberg School of Public Health, Johns Hopkins University;* ed Juanita Coll., Univ. of Pennsylvania, Johns Hopkins School of Hygiene and Public Health; Asst Clinical Prof., State Univ. of New York Upstate Medical Center 1982–84; Surgeon, Commissioned Corps, US Public Health Service 1982–84; joined Johns Hopkins Hosp. staff 1987, Dir Clinical Track, Preventative Medicine Residency, Johns Hopkins Univ. School of Hygiene and Public Health 1987–88, Instructor of Medicine, Jt Appointment in Epidemiology and Health Policy and Man., Johns Hopkins Univ. School of Medicine 1987–88, Asst Prof. of Medicine 1988–92, Assoc. Prof. 1992–97, Prof. 1998, Acting Dir Div. of Gen. Internal Medicine, Dept of Medicine, Johns Hopkins Univ. School of Medicine 1994–96, Dir 1996–2002, Assoc. Dir for Gen. Medicine 1996–2001, Interim Dir Dept of Medicine 2000–01, Vice-Dean for Clinical Investigation 2001–05, Interim Dir Welch Center for Prevention, Epidemiology and Clinical Research, Johns Hopkins Medical Insts 1996–97, Interim Physician-in-Chief, Johns Hopkins Hosp. 2000–01, Dean, Johns Hopkins Bloomberg School of Public Health 2005–; Visiting Prof. Univ. of Western Australia 1999; Dir Precursors Study 1988–; Trustee, Foundation Bd, The David and Lucile Packard Foundation 2015–; mem. American Heart Asscn; Fellow, American Coll. of Physicians; David M. Levine Excellence in Mentoring Award 2003, Champion of Public Health Award 2004. *Publications:* more than 120 articles. *Address:* Johns Hopkins Bloomberg School of Public Health, 615 North Wolfe Street, Baltimore, MD 21205, USA (office). *Telephone:* (410) 955-3540 (office). *Fax:* (410) 955-0121 (office). *E-mail:* mklag@jhsph.edu (office). *Website:* faculty.jhsph.edu (office).

KLAMMER, Franz; Austrian fmr skier; b. 3 Dec. 1953, Mooswald; m.; two d.; 26 World Cup race wins, including downhill titles 1975, 1976, 1977, 1978, 1983; gold medal, downhill race, Winter Olympics 1976; retd from skiing 1985; took up car racing; won European Championship Touring Car race, Nurburgring, Germany; f. Franz Klammer Foundation; UN Goodwill Amb.; mem. Laureus World Sports Acad. *Leisure interests:* golf. *Address:* Franz Klammer Foundation, Singerstrasse 27/17, 1010 Vienna, Austria. *Telephone:* 699-100-25-735. *Fax:* (1) 479-90-55. *E-mail:* charity@franzklammerfoundation.com. *Website:* www.franzklammerfoundation.com.

KLARESKOG, Lars, MD, PhD; Swedish medical scientist and academic; *Senior Professor of Reumatology and Director of Centre for Molecular Medicine, Karolinska Institutet, Karolinska Universitetssjukhuset;* b. 18 March 1945, Nässjö; s. of Jngue Klareskog and Ruth Klareskog; ed Uppsala Univ.; Research Fellow in Experimental Rheumatology, Swedish Medical Research Council 1979–82; Assoc.

Prof. in Immunology, Uppsala Univ. 1982–83, Clinical Fellow in Rheumatology and Internal Medicine (and part-time research), Uppsala Univ. Hosp. 1983–90, Prof. of Clinical Immunology and Chair. Dept of Clinical Immunology 1990–93; apptd Prof. of Rheumatology Karolinska Institutet, Karolinska Universitetssjukhuset 1993, now Sr Prof. and Dir Centre for Molecular Medicine, Chair. Dept of Medicine, 1993–99, Centre for Pharmaco-epidemiology 2005–, –fmr Chair. Rheumatology Clinic and Rheumatology Research Unit, mem. Nobel Ass./Nobel Cttee 1995–2011 (Chair. 2011); Visiting Scientist, Harvard Medical School 2004; Visiting Prof., Dept of Medicine, Univ. of Colorado, Denver, USA 2006; Visiting Prof. and Physician-in-Chief pro tempore, Hosp. for Special Surgery, Cornell Univ., USA 2007, Heraklion, Greece 2009; Visiting Prof., Imperial Coll., London (Kennedy Inst. Rheumatology) 2010; Pres. European Rheumatology Congress, Stockholm 2002; Chair. European Standing Cttee for Investigative Rheumatology 2006–08; mem. Editorial Bd, Arthritis & Rheumatism –2005, Annals of Rheumatic Diseases, Arthritis Research and Therapy, Current Opinion in Rheumatology, Rheumatology, Nature: Clinical Practice in Rheumatology; Jaan van Bremer Medal, Dutch Rheumatology Soc. Int. Prize for Rheumatology Research 2004, Haasinga Lecturer, Deutsche RheumaForschungsZentrum, Berlin/Charité 2004, First Wyeth Rheumatology Prize, Swedish Soc. for Rheumatology 2004, European League against Rheumatism Annual Meeting State of the Art Lecturer 2007, Int. Carol Nachman Prize for Rheumatoloy Research 2008, American Coll. of Rheumatology Annual Meeting State of the Art Lecturer on Rheumatoid Arthritis 2008, Söderberg Prize, Swedish Soc. for Medicine 2009–10, Sr Investigator grant, European Research Council 2010–14, Crafoord Prize, Royal Swedish Acad. of Sciences (co-recipient) 2013. *Publications:* numerous papers in professional journals. *Address:* Department of Medicine, Building D2:01, Karolinska Universitetssjukhuset, Solna, 171 76 Stockholm, Sweden (office). *Telephone:* (8) 524-800-00 (office). *Fax:* (8) 31-11-01 (office). *E-mail:* lars.klareskog@ki.se (office). *Website:* ki.se (office).

KLASSEN, Cindy; Canadian speed skater (retd); b. 12 Aug. 1979, Winnipeg, Man.; ed Mennonite Brethren Collegiate Inst., Winnipeg; began sports career as ice hockey player, played for Canadian Nat. Youth Team, switched to speed skating when she failed to be selected for Winter Olympics in 1998; bronze medal, 3000m, Winter Olympics, Salt Lake City 2002; World All-round Champion 2003; missed 2003–04 season due to serious injury; gold medal, 1500m and 3000m, World Single Distance Championships 2005; silver medal, World All-round Championships 2005; gold medal, 1500m, Winter Olympics, Turin 2006, silver medal, 1000m and Team Pursuit, bronze medal, 3000m and 5000m; World All-round Champion 2006; holder of world records at 1000m, 1500m and 3000m distances; Canada's all-time most decorated Olympian (five gold and one bronze medals); retd from speed skating 2015; named flag-bearer for closing ceremony of Winter Olympics at Turin 2006, Lou Marsh Award as Canadian Athlete of the Year, Toronto Star 2006, Bobbie Rosenfeld Award as Canadian Female Athlete of the Year 2005, 2006. *Address:* c/o Landmark Sport Group, 1 City Centre Drive, Suite 605, Mississauga, ON L5B 1M2, Canada. *E-mail:* admin@landmarksport.com. *Website:* www.cindyklassen.com.

KLASSOU, Komi Sélom, Lic. es-Lettres, DEA; Togolese politician; *Prime Minister;* b. 10 Feb. 1960, Notsè, Haho Prefecture; m.; c.; ed Univ. of Benin, Univ. de Bordeaux III, France; began career as history and geography teacher, Lycée de Tokoin, Lomé; Asst Researcher, Dept of Geography, Univ. of Benin 1989–90; fmr Lecturer, Univs of Lomé and Kara; Prefect, city of Tchaoudjo 1997–98; Minister of Culture, Youth and Sports 2000–03, of Primary and Secondary Educ. 2003–07; mem. Nat. Ass. (Parl.) for Haho Prefecture 2007–15, First Vice-Pres., Nat. Ass. 2007–15; Prime Minister 2015–; mem. ACP-EU Parl. Ass.; mem. Union pour la République; Commdr, Ordre du Mono 2006. *Address:* Office of the Prime Minister, Palais de la Primature, BP 1161, Lomé, Togo (office). *Telephone:* 22-21-15-64 (office). *Fax:* 22-21-37-53 (office). *Website:* www.primature.gouv.tg (office).

KLATTEN, Susanne, BSc, MBA; German business executive; b. 28 April 1962, Bad Homburg; d. of Herbert Quandt and Johanna Quandt; m. Jan Klatten; three c.; ed Univ. of Buckingham, UK, Int. Inst. for Man. Devt, Lausanne, Switzerland; trained as advertising exec.; man. asst Burda GmbH 1989–90; work experience in USA 1991; inherited share of BMW Group and majority of shares of Altana AG; Owner, SKion GmbH; mem. Bd of Dirs BMW Group 1997–, Byk Gulden Lomberg GmbH; Deputy Chair. Supervisory Bd SGL Carbon 2012–13, Chair. 2013–; Deputy Chair. Supervisory Bd Altana AG; Chair. Bd of Counsellors Herbert Quandt Foundation, Bad Homburg. *Address:* SKion GmbH, Herbert-Quandt-Haus, Seedammweg 55, 61352 Bad Homburg, Germany (office). *Telephone:* (6172) 404531 (office). *E-mail:* info@skion.de (office). *Website:* www.skion.de (office).

KLAUS, Václav, PhD; Czech politician, economist and fmr head of state; b. 19 June 1941, Prague; s. of Václav Klaus and Marie Klausová; m. Livia Klausová 1968; two s.; ed Prague School of Econs, Cornell Univ., Czech Acad. of Sciences; researcher, Inst. of Econs Czechoslovak Acad. of Sciences –1970; various positions Czechoslovak State Bank 1971–86; Head, Dept of Macroeconomic Policy, Inst. of Forecasting, Acad. of Sciences 1987–; f. Civic Forum Movt (Chair. 1990–91); Minister of Finance 1989–92; Chair. Civic Democratic Party 1991–2002; Deputy Prime Minister 1991–92; last Prime Minister of the Czech Socialist Repub. from July 1992 until the dissolution of Czechoslovakia in Jan. 1993; Prime Minister of the Czech Repub. 1993–97; Chair. State Defence Council 1993–97; Chair. Govt Cttee for Integration of Czech Repub. in NATO 1997; Chair. Chamber of Deputies 1998–2002; Pres. of Czech Repub. 2003–13; serves as a Nat. Centre for Policy Analysis Distinguished Leader; mem. Scientific Council, Palacký Univ., Olomouc 1997–; Distinguished Sr Fellow, Cato Inst. 2013–14 (appointment terminated); Hon. Prof., Univ. Guadalajara 1993; Hon. Chair. ODS (Civic Democratic Party) 2002–08; Kt Grand Cross, Order of the White Lion 2003, Kt Grand Cross, Order of Tomáš Garrigue Masaryk 2003, Kt Grand Cross, Order of Isabella the Catholic (Spain) 2004, Order of the White Eagle (Poland) 2007, Saxon Merit Cross 2008, Grand Cross, Order of Vytautas the Great (Lithuania) 2009, Grand Star of the Decoration for Services to the Repub. of Austria 2009, Order of the White Double Cross (Slovakia) 2013; Hon. DHumLitt (Suffolk Univ.) 1991, Dr hc (Rochester Inst. of Tech.) 1991, (Univ. Francisco Marroquín, Guatemala) 1993, (Prague School of Econs) 1994, (Belgrano Univ., Argentina) 1994, (Tufts Univ., USA) 1994, (Univ. of Aix-Marseilles) 1994, (Jacksonville, USA) 1995, (Buckingham, UK) 1996, (Tech. Univ. of Ostrava) 1997, (Toronto, Canada) 1997, (Arizona) 1997, (Dallas) 1999, (Chicago) 1999; Schumpeter Prize for Econs, Freedom Award (New York) 1990, Max Schmidheiny Freedom Prize, St Gallen 1992, Ludwig Erhard Prize, Germany 1993, Poeutinger Collegium Prize 1993, Hermann Lindrath Prize (Hanover) 1993, Konrad Adenauer Prize (Prague) 1993, Club of Europe Award 1994, Prix Transition (Fondation du Forum Universal) 1994, Adam Smith Award (Libertas, Copenhagen) 1995, Int. Democracy Medal (Center for Democracy, Washington, DC) 1995, Transatlantic Leadership Award (European Inst., Washington, DC) 1995, Prognos Award (Prognos Forum, Basel) 1995, James Madison Award (James Madison Inst., Jacksonville, USA) 1995, Karel Engliš Prize (Universitas Masarykiana Foundation, Brno) 1995, European Prize for Craftsmanship, Germany 1996, Goldwater Medal for Econ. Freedom, Phoenix, USA 1997, Bernhard Harms Medal (Kiel Inst. of World Econs) 1999, Medal of Pushkin 2007. *Publications include:* A Road to Market Economy 1991, Tomorrow's Challenge 1991, Economic Theory and Economic Reform 1991, Why am I a Conservative? 1992, Dismantling Socialism: A Road to Market Economy II 1993, The Year–How much is it in the History of the Country? 1993, The Czech Way 1994, Rebirth of a Country: Five Years After 1994, Counting Down to One 1995, Between the Past and the Future: Philosophical Reflections and Essays 1996, The Defence of Forgotten Ideas 1997, Tak pravil Václav Klaus (So Said Václav Klaus, conversations with J. Klusáková), Why I Am Not a Social Democrat 1998, Země, kde se již dva roky nevládne (The Land that has not been Governed for 2 years) 1999, Cesta z pasti (The Way Out of the Trap) 1999, From the Opposition Treaty to the Tolerance Patent 2000, Evropa pohledem politika a pohledem ekonoma (Europe, The View of the Politician and the View of the Economist) 2001, Conversations with Václav Klaus 2001, Klaus v Bruselu (Klaus in Brussels) 2001, On the Road to Democracy–The Czech Republic From Communism to Free Society 2005, Modrá, nikoli zelená planeta (Blue Planet in Green Shackles) 2007; numerous articles. *Leisure interests:* tennis, skiing, basketball, volleyball, jazz, music, reading fiction. *E-mail:* webmaster@klaus.cz. *Website:* www.klaus.cz.

KLEBANOV, Ilya Iosifovich; Russian politician and business executive; *Chairman, PAO Sovcomflot;* b. 7 May 1951, Leningrad; m. Yevgenya Yakovlevna Klebanova; one s. one d.; ed M.I. Kalinin Leningrad Polytechnical Inst.; eng electrophysicist, Electron Scientific Production Unit 1974–77; engineer, then Sr Master, Head of Construction Bureau, later Head of Div. Leningrad Optical-Mechanical Complex (LOMO) 1977–92, Dir-Gen. 1992–97; First Vice-Gov. St Petersburg 1997–98; Deputy Chair. of Russian Govt 1999–2002, Minister of Industry, Science and Tech. (Minpromnauki) 2001–03; Presidential Envoy to the Northwestern Fed. Okrug (Dist) 2003–11; Chair. OAO Sovcomflot (energy transportation co.) 2011–15, currently Chair. PAO Sovcomflot (state-owned shipping co.); apptd mem. Russian Security Council 2003. *Leisure interests:* classical music, reading, mushroom-picking. *Address:* PAO Sovcomflot, St Petersburg 191186, 3a Moyka River Embankment, Russia (office). *E-mail:* info@scf-group.ru (office). *Website:* www.scf-group.ru (office).

KLEIN, Calvin Richard; American fashion designer; b. 19 Nov. 1942, The Bronx, NY; s. of Leo Klein and Flore Klein (née Stern); m. 1st Jayne Centre 1964 (divorced 1974); one d.; m. 2nd Kelly Rector 1986 (divorced 2006); ed Fashion Inst. of Tech., New York and High School of Art and Design; started fashion business 1968; Pres./Designer, Calvin Klein Ltd 1968–2002 (co. sold to Phillips-Van Heusen Corpn); Consultant, Fashion Inst. of Tech. 1975–; mem. Council of Fashion Designers; Dr hc (Fashion Inst. of Tech.) 2003; Coty Award 1973, 1974, 1975, Coty Hall of Fame, FIT Pres.'s Award, Outstanding Design Council of Fashion Designers of America (four womenswear, two menswear). *Address:* Calvin Klein Studio, LLC, 545 West 25th Street, 18th Floor, New York, NY 10001-5501, USA. *Website:* www.calvinklein.com.

KLEIN, Étienne, DèsSc, PhD; French physicist and writer; *Director, Research Laboratory for Material Science, Commissariat à l'énergie atomique et aux énergies alternatives;* b. 1 April 1958, Paris; two c.; ed Ecole centrale, Univ. de Paris VII; physicist, Commissariat à l'énergie atomique et aux énergies alternatives 1983–, Dir Research Lab. for Material Science; Prof. of Philosophy of Science, Ecole Centrale de Paris; worked in Proton Accelerator Study Group CERN 1992–93; Officier, Ordre des Palmes académiques, Chevalier, Légion d'honneur 2010; Prix Jean Perrin 1997, Prix Grammaticakis-Neumann 2000, Prix Budget décerné 2000, Prix Jean Rostand 2004, Prix Thorel 2010. *Publications include:* Conversations avec le Sphinx: Les paradoxes en physique (Best Science Book Award 1993) 1991, Regards sur la matière: des quanta et des choses 1993, Le Temps et sa flèche (with Michel Spiro) 1994, Prédiction et probabilité 1998, La Quête de l'unité (with Marc Lachièze-Rey) 2000, L'Atome au pied du mur et autres nouvelles (Prix du meilleur livre de littérature scientifique de l'année pour) 2000, L'Unité de la physique 2000, Le Temps existe-t-il? 2002, Les Tactiques de Chronos (Prix La science se livre) 2003, La Science nous menace-t-elle? 2003, Quand la science a dit c'est bizarre! 2003, Petit voyage dans le monde des quantas (Prix Jean Rostand) 2004, Il était sept fois la Révolution: Albert Einstein et les autres... 2005, Les Atomes de l'univers 2005, Le Facteur temps ne sonne jamais deux fois 2007, Les secrets de la matière 2008, Galilée et les Indiens (Prix Thorel) 2008, Pourquoi je suis devenu chercheur scientifique 2009, Discours sur l'origine de l'univers 2010, Le Small bang des nanotechnologies 2011, Anagrammes renversantes (with Jacques Perry Salkow) 2011, Rugby quantique (with Jonny Wilkinson and Jean Iliopoulos) 2011, D'où viennent les idées 2013, En cherchant Majorana 2015, Y a-t-il eu un instant zéro? 2015. *Leisure interest:* alpinism. *Address:* Commissariat à l'énergie atomique et aux énergies alternatives/Saclay (Essonne), 91191 Gif-sur-Yvette Cédex, France (office). *Telephone:* 1-69-08-74-12 (office); 1-45-65-09-24 (home). *E-mail:* etienne.klein@cea.fr (office). *Website:* www.cea.fr (office).

KLEIN, Maj.-Gen. Jacques Paul; American (b. French) air force officer (retd) and international organization official; b. 9 Jan. 1939, Sélestat, Alsace, France; s. of Jean Paul Klein and Josephine Klein (née Wolff); m. Dr Margrete (Gretchen Siebert Klein; one s. one d.; moved with his mother to USA 1946; fmr Air Force Officer (rank of Second Lt 1963, First Lt 1965, Capt. 1967, Maj. 1973, Lt Col 1977, Col 1981, Brig. Gen. 1987, Maj.-Gen. 1992); joined Foreign Service in Operations Center of Exec. Secr. of Sec. of State 1971; Consular Officer, Consulate-Gen., Bremen; Political Officer, Office of Southern European Affairs, Dept of State; Counsellor Officer, Berlin; Political Officer, Embassy in Bonn; Man. Analysis Officer, Office of Dir-Gen. of Foreign Service; seconded to Dept of Defense as

Adviser on Int. Affairs to Sec. of Air Force with rank of Deputy Asst Sec.; Dir Office of Strategic Tech. Matters, Bureau of Politico-Mil. Affairs, Dept of State; Asst Deputy Under-Sec. of Air Force for Int. Affairs, Dept of Defense 1989–90; Prin. Adviser to Dir-Gen. Foreign Service 1990–93; Political Adviser to C-in-C, US European Command, Stuttgart 1993–96; Prin. Deputy High Rep., Bosnia and Herzegovina 1997–99; UN Transitional Admin. for Eastern Slavonia, Baranja and Western Sirmium, rank of Under-Sec.-Gen. 1996–97; Special Rep. of Sec.-Gen. to Bosnia and Herzegovina, rank of Under-Sec.-Gen. 1999–2003; UN Special Rep. for Liberia 2003–05; Visiting Lecturer in Int. Affairs and Frederick Schultz Visiting Prof. of Public and Int. Affairs, Woodrow Wilson School, Princeton Univ. 2005–06 (retd); fmr Expert, Woodrow Wilson Int. Center for Scholars; mem. Cosmos Club and Army and Navy Clubs of Washington, DC, Acad. d'Alsace, Council on Foreign Relations; Hon. Citizen, City of Vukovar 2003, City of Osijek 2013; Grand Officer, Order of the Crown (Belgium); Grand Cross of Merit (FRG); Grand Order of King Dmitar Zvonimir (Croatia); Order of King Dmitar Zvonimir with Sash and Morning Star (Croatia); Commdr, Aeronautical Order of Merit (Brazil); Commdr, Order of the Lion (Senegal); Officier, Légion d'honneur; Kt Great Band of the Humane Order of African Redemption (Nat. Transitional Govt of Liberia); Peacekeeping Medal First Class (Slovakia); Hon. LLD (Elmhurst Coll.); Hon. DHumLitt (Roosevelt Univ.); Dr hc (Jospi Juraj Strossmayer Univ.) 2011; Air Force Distinguished Service Medal, Legion of Merit (with oak leaf cluster), Bronze Star, Distinguished Honor Award, Dept of State, Defense Medal for Outstanding Public Service, Dept of the Air Force Award for Exceptional and Meritorious Civilian Service; Certificate of Appreciation and Seal of the City of Osijek 1997, The Charter of Gratitude, Pres. of Croatia 1998, Marcel Rudloff Prize, Court of Human Rights, Strasbourg 2010, Certificate of Gratitude, Asscn of Returnees of Croatia 2011, Distinguished Global Leadership Award, Evandeoski Teoloski Fakultet, Osijek, Croatia 2011.

KLEIN, Jonathan David; British/South African business executive; *Chairman, Getty Images Inc.;* b. 13 May 1960, Johannesburg, South Africa; m. Deborah Klein; three s.; with Hambros Bank Ltd, London 1983–93, Dir 1989–93; co-f. Getty Investment Holdings 1993–95; Jt Chair. Getty Communications PLC 1995–96, CEO and Dir 1996–98, Co-founder Getty Images Inc. 1998, CEO and Dir 1998–2015, Chair. 2015–; mem. Bd of Dirs Getty Images, Etsy, Squarespace, Committee to Protect Journalists, Grassroot Soccer; Chair. Bd of Friends, Global Fight Against AIDS, Tuberculosis and Malaria; Pres. Bd of Trustees of Groton School; mem. Council on Foreign Relations; Int. Center of Photography Trustee's Award (with Mark Getty) 2006, Global Business Coalition on HIV/AIDS, Tuberculosis and Malaria's Business Excellence for Innovation Award. *Leisure interests:* skiing, tennis, reading, world traveller. *Address:* Getty Images Inc., 75 Varick Street, 5th Floor, New York, NY 10013, USA (office). *Telephone:* (646) 613-3622 (office). *Fax:* (646) 613-4402 (office). *E-mail:* jonathan.klein@gettyimages.com (office). *Website:* www.gettyimages.com (office).

KLEIN, Michael L., BSc, PhD, FRS, FRSC, FInstP; British chemist, materials scientist and academic; *Laura H. Carnell Professor of Science, Department of Chemistry, Temple University;* b. 13 March 1940, London, England; m. Brenda M. Woodman; two d.; ed Univ. of Bristol; Ciba-Geigy Fellow, Univ. of Genoa, Italy 1964–65; ICI Fellow, Univ. of Bristol, Dept of Theoretical Chem. 1965–67; Research Assoc., Physics Dept, Rutgers Univ., USA 1967–68; Assoc. Research Officer, Nat. Research Council of Canada, Chem. Div., Ottawa, Canada 1968–74, Sr Research Officer 1974–85, Prin. Research Officer 1985–87; Adjunct Prof. of Physics, Univ. of Waterloo, Ont., Canada 1977–83; Prof. of Chem., McMaster Univ., Ont. 1977–88; Visiting Prof., Univ. of Amsterdam, Netherlands 1985; Néel Visiting Prof., École Normale Supérieure, Lyon, France 1988; William Smith Prof. of Chem., Univ. of Pennsylvania 1991–93, Hepburn Prof. of Physical Science 1993–2009, Dir Lab. for Research on the Structure of Matter 1993–2009, also Dir Penn Center for Molecular Modelling 1994–2009; Laura H. Carnell Prof. of Science, Dept of Chem., Temple Univ. 2009–, Dir Temple Inst. for Computational Molecular Science 2009–, Dean, Temple Coll. of Science and Tech. 2012–; mem. Editorial Bd several journals, including Journal of Physics Condensed Matter 1993–97, Molecular Physics 1993–99, Computational Materials Science 1993–, Journal of Chemical Physics 2003–, Chemical Physics Letters 2003–, Proceedings of the National Academy of Sciences 2009–; mem. RSC (Faraday Div.), ACS 1998, American Physical Soc. 1999, American Acad. of Arts and Sciences 2003, TWAS – The World Acad. of Sciences 2004, NAS 2009; Fellow, American Physical Soc. 1991; Hon. Fellow, Chemical Inst. of Canada 1979, Indian Acad. of Sciences 2005, Mongolian Acad. Sciences 2008, Chemical Research Soc. of India 2008, Jawaharlal Nehru Centre for Advanced Scientific Research, Bangalore 2015, AAAS 2015; Hon. Fellow, Trinity Coll. Cambridge 2013; Guggenheim Foundation Fellow 1989–90, Alexander von Humboldt Award, Max Planck Inst., Stuttgart 1996, Linnett Lecturer, Univ. of Cambridge 1998, ACS Phila Section Award 1998, American Physical Soc. Aneesur Rahman Prize 1999, CECAM Prize for Computational Science, European Physical Soc. 2004, CNR Rao Award, Chemical Research Soc. of India 2006, Peter Debye Award in Physical Chemistry, ACS 2008, Hinshelwood Lecturer, Univ. of Oxford 2008, RSC S. F. Boys – A Rahman Award 2011. *Publications:* four books and more than 630 papers. *Address:* Department of Chemistry, Temple University, SERC Building, Suite 704, 1925 North 12th Street, Philadelphia, PA 19122, USA (office). *Telephone:* (215) 204-4212 (office); (215) 204-1927 (office). *E-mail:* mike.klein@temple.edu (office). *Website:* icms.cst.temple.edu (office).

KLEIN, Naomi; Canadian writer, journalist and social critic; b. 1970, Montréal; syndicated columnist for The Nation, The Guardian, UK; contributing editor, Harper's; reporter, Rolling Stone; Sr Corresp., the Intercept 2017–; contrib. to numerous publs including The New York Times, The Washington Post, Newsweek, The Los Angeles Times, The Globe and Mail, El Pais, L'Espresso, The New Statesman, The New Yorker, The Boston Globe, The Guardian, London Review of Books, Le Monde; guest lecturer at Harvard Univ., Yale Univ., McGill Univ., New York Univ.; Puffin Foundation Writing Fellow, The Nation Inst.; fmr Miliband Fellow, London School of Economics; mem. Bd of Dirs 350.org; Dr hc (Univ. of King's College, Nova Scotia); Canadian Nat. Business Book Award 2001, Le Prix Médiations, France 2001, Ms. Magazine's Women of the Year Award 2001, James Aronson Award for Social Justice Journalism (for reporting from Iraq for Harper's) 2004, IPE Outstanding Activist-Scholar Award, Int. Studies Asscn 2014, Sydney Peace Prize 2016. *Publications include:* No Logo: Taking Aim at the Brand Bullies (translated into 22 languages) 2000, Fences and Windows: Dispatches from the Front Lines of the Globalization Debate 2002, The Shock Doctrine: The Rise of Disaster Capitalism (Warwick Prize for Writing 2009) 2007, This Changes Everything, Capitalism vs The Climate (Hilary Weston Writers' Trust Prize for Non-Fiction 2014) 2014, No Is Not Enough: Resisting Trump's Shock Politics and Winning the World We Need 2017. *E-mail:* klp123@gmail.com (office). *Website:* theintercept.com (office); www.naomiklein.org.

KLEINBERG, Jon M., AB, SM, PhD; American computer scientist and academic; *Professor of Computer Science, Cornell University;* ed Cornell Univ., Massachusetts Inst. of Tech.; researcher, IBM Theory and Computation Group 1995, Computer Science Principles and Methodologies Group 1996–97, mem. Visiting Faculty Program, IBM Almaden Research Center 1998–; mem. faculty, Dept of Computer Science, Cornell Univ. 1996–, currently Prof. of Computer Science; mem. Nat. Acad. of Eng, American Acad. of Arts and Sciences; NSF Career Award, Office of Naval Research Young Investigator Award, MacArthur Foundation Fellowship, Packard Foundation Fellowship, Sloan Foundation Fellowship, grants from NSF, Faculty of the Year Award, Cornell Univ. Asscn of Computer Science Undergraduates 2002, Nevanlinna Prize 2006, Harvey Prize, Technion (Israel) (co-recipient) 2013. *Achievements include:* devised the HITS algorithm for ranking Web pages. *Publications:* Algorithm Design (co-author) 2005, Networks, Crowds, and Markets: Reasoning About a Highly Connected World (co-author) 2010; numerous scientific papers in professional journals. *Address:* Computing and Information Science, Gates Hall, Cornell University, Ithaca, NY 14853, USA (office). *Telephone:* (607) 255-9197 (office); (607) 255-3600 (office); (607) 255-5331 (office). *Fax:* (607) 255-7316 (office). *E-mail:* kleinber@cs.cornell.edu (office). *Website:* www.cs.cornell.edu/home/kleinber (office).

KLEINFELD, Klaus, Dr rer. pol, Dipl.-Kfm; German business executive; b. 6 Nov. 1957, Bremen; m.; two d.; ed Georg-August Univ., Göttingen, Univ. of Würzburg; Researcher Inst. of Foundation for Empirical Social Research, Nuremberg 1982–86; Product Man. Pharmaceuticals Div., Ciba-Geigy AG, Basel 1986–87; joined Corp. Sales and Marketing Siemens AG, Advertising and Design Man. 1987, Corp. Strategies Man. 1988–94, Head, Corp. Projects 1994–95, Head, Siemens Corp. Consulting 1995–98, Head, Angiography, Fluoroscopic and Radiographic Systems Div. 1998–2000, mem. Group Exec. Man., Medical Solutions Group, COO Siemens Corpn, USA 2001–02, CEO 2002–04, mem. Man. Bd Siemens AG 2002–07, mem. Corp. Exec. Cttee 2004–07, Deputy Chair. Man. Bd 2004, Pres. and CEO 2005–07; mem. Bd of Dirs Alcoa Inc. 2003–16, Pres. and COO 2007–08, Pres. and CEO 2008–10, Chair. and CEO 2010–16; Chair. and CEO Arconic Nov. 2016–April 2017; CEO NOEM 2017–18; Adviser, Crown Prince of Saudi Arabia 2018–; mem. Supervisory Bd Bayer AG; Chair. US-Russia Business Council 2009–; mem. Bd of Trustees Brookings Inst. 2010–. *Publication:* Corporate Identity und strategische Unternehmensführung 1994. *Leisure interests:* skiing, tennis, the arts, running marathons.

KLEINROCK, Leonard, BEE, MS, PhD; American computer scientist and academic; *Distinguished Professor of Computer Science, University of California, Los Angeles;* b. 13 June 1934, New York, NY; ed Bronx High School of Science, City Coll. of New York, Massachusetts Inst. of Tech.; Prof. of Computer Science, Henry Samueli School of Eng and Applied Science, UCLA 1963, Chair. Dept 1991–95, currently Distinguished Prof. of Computer Science; Co-founder and first Pres. Linkabit Corpn; Co-founder Nomadix, Inc.; Founder and Chair. TTI/Vanguard (advanced tech. forum org.); Founding mem. Computer Science and Telecommunications Bd; mem. Nat. Acad. of Eng, American Acad. of Arts and Sciences; Fellow, IEEE, Asscn for Computing Machinery, INFORMS (Inst. For Operations Research and The Man. Sciences), Int. Electrotechnical Comm.; Founding mem. Computer Science and Telecommunications Bd of Nat. Research Council; Eminent Mem. IEEE Eta Kappa Nu 2011; hon. doctorates from around the world; Guggenheim Fellow, L.M. Ericsson Prize, NAE Charles Stark Draper Prize, Marconi Int. Fellowship Award, Okawa Prize, IEEE Internet Millennium Award, ORSA Lanchester Prize, ACM SIGCOMM Award, NEC Computer and Communications Award, Sigma Xi Monie A. Ferst Award, Townsend Harris Medal and Electrical Eng Award, City Coll. of New York, UCLA Outstanding Faculty Mem. Award, UCLA Distinguished Teaching Award, UCLA Faculty Research Lecturer, INFORMS Pres.'s Award, ICC Prize Paper Award, IEEE Leonard G. Abraham Prize Paper Award, IEEE Harry M. Goode Award, listed by Los Angeles Times amongst "50 People Who Most Influenced Business This Century" 1999, listed by Atlantic Monthly amongst 33 most influential living Americans Dec. 2006, Nat. Medal of Science 2007, Dan David Prize 2010, inducted in Internet Hall of Fame 2012, ACM SIGMOBILE Outstanding Contrib. Award 2014, Eng Lifetime Achievement Award, UCLA 2016. *Achievements include:* known as a 'father of the Internet'; developed math. theory of packet switching networks, tech. underpinning the Internet, while a grad. student at MIT 1960–62; wrote first paper and published first book on the subject; also directed transmission of first message ever sent over Internet. *Publications:* six books and more than 250 papers in professional journals on packet switching networks, packet radio networks, local area networks, broadband networks, gigabit networks, nomadic computing, performance evaluation and peer-to-peer networks. *Address:* Computer Science Department, University of California, Los Angeles, 3732G Boelter Hall, Los Angeles, CA 90095, USA (office). *Telephone:* (310) 825-2543 (office). *Fax:* (310) 825-7578 (office). *E-mail:* lk@cs.ucla.edu (office). *Website:* www.lk.cs.ucla.edu (office); www.engineer.ucla.edu (office).

KLEISTERLEE, Gerard Johannes, MA; Dutch business executive; *Chairman, Vodafone Group Plc;* b. (Gerhard Johannes Kleisterlee), 28 Sept. 1946, Germany; ed Eindhoven Tech. Univ., Netherlands; joined Royal Philips Electronics in 1974, several manufacturing and business man. positions in various divs and regions, apptd Exec. Vice-Pres. Royal Philips Electronics and mem. Bd of Man. 2000, COO Philips 2000–01, Chair. Bd of Man., Pres. and CEO Royal Philips Electronics 2001–11; Dir (non-exec.), Vodafone Group Plc April 2011–, Chair. July 2011–; mem. Supervisory Bd, De Nederlandsche Bank NV 2006–12, Daimler AG 2009–14; Dir (non-exec.), Supervisory Bd and mem. Audit Comm., Royal Dutch Shell 2010–; mem. Bd of Dirs, Dell Inc. 2010–13; mem. European Table of Industrialists 2001–11 (Vice-Chair. 2010–11); mem. Asia Business Council 2002–; Chair. Foundation of the Cancer Centre, Amsterdam 2001–12, Supervisory Bd, Eindhoven Tech. Univ. 2001–09; mem. Exec. Cttee, IMD Business School,

Lausanne 2007–11 (Chair. 2008–11); Dr hc (Catholic Univ. of Leuven) 2005. *Leisure interests:* music, reading about history. *Address:* Office of the Chairman, Vodafone Group plc, 25 Park Lane, London, W1K 1RA, England (office). *Telephone:* (1635) 33251 (Newbury) (office). *Fax:* (1635) 45713 (Newbury) (office). *E-mail:* info@vodafone.com (office). *Website:* www.vodafone.com (office).

KLEMPERER, Paul David, BA, MBA, PhD, FBA; British economist and academic; *Edgeworth Professor of Economics, University of Oxford;* b. 15 Aug. 1956; s. of Hugh G. Klemperer and Ruth Jordan; m. Margaret Meyer 1989; two s. one d.; ed King Edward's School, Birmingham, Peterhouse, Cambridge, Stanford Univ., USA; Consultant, Andersen Consulting (now Accenture) 1978–80; Harkness Fellow of Commonwealth Fund 1980–82; Lecturer in Operations Research and Math. Econs, Univ. of Oxford 1985–90, Reader in Econs 1990–95, Edgeworth Prof. of Econs 1995–, John Thomson Fellow and Tutor, St Catherine's Coll. 1985–95, Fellow, Nuffield Coll. 1995–; Visiting Lecturer, MIT 1987, Univ. of Calif., Berkeley 1991, 1993, Stanford Univ. 1991, 1993, Yale Univ. 1994, Princeton Univ. 1998; consultant to Dept of Trade and Industry 1997–2000, US Fed. Trade Comm. 1999–2001, Dept for Energy, Transport and the Regions 2000–01, Dept for the Environment, Food and Rural Affairs 2001–02, Bank of England 2007–, US Treasury 2008–09, Bank of Canada 2009; mem. UK Competition Comm. 2001–05 (consultant 2006–); Ed. RAND Journal of Economics 1993–99; Assoc. or mem. Editorial Bd Oxford Economic Papers 1986–, Review of Economic Studies 1989–97, Journal of Industrial Economics 1989–96, International Journal of Industrial Organization 1993–2000, European Economic Review 1997–2001, Review of Economic Design 1997–2000, Economic Policy 1998–99, Economic Journal 2000–04, Frontiers in Economics 2000–, Journal of Economic Analysis and Policy 2001–, Journal of Competition Law and Economics 2004–; mem. Council, Royal Econ. Soc. 2001–, Econometric Soc. 2001– (Fellow 1994), European Econ. Asscn 2002–; Hon. Fellow, ELSE 2001–, Foreign Hon. mem., American Acad. of Arts and Sciences 2005–, Argentine Econ. Asscn 2006–. *Publications include:* The Economic Theory of Auctions 1999, Auctions: Theory and Practice 2004; articles in econs journals. *Address:* Nuffield College, Oxford, OX1 1NF, England (office). *Telephone:* (1865) 278588 (office). *E-mail:* paul.klemperer@economics.ox.ac.uk (office). *Website:* www.paulklemperer.org (home).

KLEOPAS, Myrna Y.; Cypriot lawyer, diplomatist and UN official; *Rapporteur, Committee against Torture, United Nations Office of the High Commissioner for Human Rights;* b. 23 Aug. 1944; m. Yiangos P. Kleopas; practiced as lawyer 1971–79; Legal Adviser for Human Rights, Ministry of Foreign Affairs 1977–79; joined Foreign Service 1979, worked in Political Affairs Div. 1979–80, 1986–90, Dir 1996–97; Counsellor and Consul Gen., High Comm. in London 1980–86; Dir Office of Perm. Sec., Ministry of Foreign Affairs 1990–93; Amb. to China (also accred to Japan, Pakistan, Mongolia, Philippines) 1993–96, to Italy (also accred to Switzerland, Malta, San Marino) 1997–2000; High Commr to UK 2000–04 (retd); currently Rapporteur, UN Cttee against Torture, Convention against Torture and Other Cruel, Inhuman or Degrading Treatment or Punishment. *Address:* Committee against Torture, Office of the United Nations High Commissioner for Human Rights, Palais des Nations, 1211 Geneva 10, Switzerland (office). *Website:* www2 .ohchr.org/english/bodies/cat (office).

KLEPPE, Johan; Norwegian politician and veterinary surgeon; b. 29 Sept. 1928, Bjørnskinn, Andøya; s. of Jon Kleppe and Alvhild Caroliussen Kleppe; m. Inger Johansen 1961; one s. one d.; ed Veterinary Coll. of Norway; veterinary surgeon 1954–63, Dist veterinary surgeon, Andøy 1963–76, Supervisory veterinary surgeon 1966–76; Regional Veterinary Officer of N Norway 1976–94; mem. Bjørnskinn Municipal Council 1956–64; Deputy Mayor of Andøy 1964–66, Mayor 1966–68, 1975–78, mem. Exec. Cttee Andøy Municipality 1964–78; Deputy mem. of Parl. 1967; Parl. Under-Sec. of State, Ministry of Agric. 1968–69; Liberal mem. of Parl. for Nordland 1969–73, mem. lo Bd of Liberal Parl. faction 1969–73; mem. Liberal Party's Cttee on Oil Policy and EC Cttee, mem. Prin. Planning Cttee; Minister of Defence 1972–73; mem. Liberal Nat. Exec. 1966–72; Leader, Norwegian del., FAO confs, Rome and Malta 1969; Norwegian Del., UN Gen. Ass., New York 1971; fmr Bd mem. Nordland Co. Liberal Asscn; fmr Chair. Students Liberal Asscn, Oslo and Bjørnskinn and Andøy Liberal Asscn; Chair. of Bd, Directorate of State Forests 1969–77, Chair. Nat. Council on Sheep-breeding 1969–82; Chair. of Bd Nordlandsbanken A/S, 8480 Andenes 1974–90, State Veterinary Lab. for Northern Norway 1976–91, Vesteraalen Intermunicipal Planning Office 1978–88; Vice-Chair. Cttee Norwegian Veterinary Asscn 1981–84, Chair. 1984–91; Chair. of Bd Andøyposten a/s 1981–90, Troms Population Acad. Asscn 1987–94; mem. Bd Norwegian Nat. Programme for Sea Ranching 1990–94. *Publications include:* Our Security and Defense Policy 1973. *Address:* 8484 Risøyhamn, Norway (office). *Telephone:* 76-14-76-30 (office); 90-83-99-86 (home). *Fax:* 76-14-76-30 (office). *E-mail:* johankleppe@hotmail.com (home).

KLEPPNER, Daniel, PhD; American physicist and academic; *Lester Wolfe Professor Emeritus of Physics, Massachusetts Institute of Technology;* ed Williams Coll., Williamstown, Mass, Univ. of Cambridge, UK, Harvard Univ.; Fulbright Fellow, Univ. of Cambridge 1953–55; NSF Postdoctoral Fellow 1959–60; Alfred E. Sloan Foundation Fellow 1962–64; Asst Prof. of Physics, Harvard Univ. 1962–66; Assoc. Prof. of Physics, MIT 1966–73, Prof. of Physics 1974, Head, Div. of Atomic, Plasma Condensed Matter Physics, Dept of Physics 1976–79, Lester Wolfe Prof. of Physics and Assoc. Dir Research Lab. of Electronics (RLE) 1987–2000 (now Prof. Emer.), Dir NSF MIT-Harvard Center for Ultracold Atoms 2000–, Prin. Investigator, RLE Atomic, Molecular and Optical Physics Group; mem. NAS; Fellow, American Physical Soc. (APS), AAAS, American Acad. of Arts and Sciences; APS Davisson-Germer Prize 1985, APS Julius Edgar Lilienfeld Prize 1990, William F. Meggers Award, Optical Soc. of America 1990, James Rhyne Killian, Jr Faculty Achievement Award, MIT, Oersted Award, American Asscn of Physics Teachers, Wolf Prize for Physics, Wolf Foundation (Israel) 2005, Benjamin Franklin Medal in Physics 2014. *Publications:* numerous articles in scientific journals. *Address:* Room 26-237, Massachusetts Institute of Technology, 77 Massachusetts Avenue, Cambridge, MA 02139-4307, USA (office). *Telephone:* (617) 253-6811 (office). *Fax:* (617) 253-4876 (office). *E-mail:* kleppner@mit.edu (office). *Website:* www.rle.mit .edu/people/principal-investigators (office).

KLERIDES, Takis; Cypriot accountant, business consultant and fmr government official; *Chairman, Tufton Oceanic Finance Group;* b. 21 Aug. 1951, Nicosia; m. Nancy Hak 1976; one s. one d.; ed Birmingham Polytechnic, UK; joined Metaxas Loizides Syrimis & Co - KPMG, Cyprus 1977, Partner 1983–97, Sr Pnr 1997–99; Minister of Finance 1999–2003, also apptd a Gov. of IMF and EBRD 1999–2003; pvt. business consultant 2003–; mem. Monopolies Comm. 1998–99, Cyprus Olympic Cttee 1996–99; Chair. Cyprus Basketball Fed. 1988–98; currently Chair. Tufton Oceanic Finance Group; mem. Bd of Dirs Logicom Public Ltd; Fellow, Chartered Asscn of Certified Accountants; mem. Inst. of Certified Public Accountants of Cyprus (mem. Council 1991–99). *Leisure interest:* sports. *Address:* Tufton Oceanic Finance Group, 23 Kennedy Avenue, Globe House, 4th Floor, 1075 Nicosia, Cyprus (office). *Telephone:* 22460800 (office). *Fax:* 22460860 (office). *Website:* www.tuftonoceanic.com (office).

KLESSE, William (Bill) R., BS, MBA; American business executive; ed Univ. of Dayton, West Texas A&M Univ.; numerous exec. positions with Valero Energy Corpn and its predecessors for almost 40 years including Vice-Pres. of Logistics and Strategy 1982–84, then Dir of Corporate Devt, Sr Vice-Pres., Exec. Vice-Pres., Exec. Vice-Pres. Ultramar Diamond Shamrock (refining operations) 1996–99, Exec. Vice-Pres. of Operations and Chair. Shamrock Logistics LLC 1999–2001, Exec. Vice-Pres. of Refining and Commercial Operations (after merger of Ultramar Diamond Shamrock and Valero) 2001–03, Exec. Vice-Pres. and COO Valero Energy Corpn 2003–05, CEO and Vice-Chair. 2005–07, Chair. and CEO 2007–08, Chair., Pres. and CEO 2008–14, Chair. 2014; Dir Occidental Petroleum Corpn 2013–. *Address:* Occidental O.T. and Gas Corporation, 5 Greenway Plaza, Suite 110, Houston, TX 77046-0521, USA (office). *Telephone:* (713) 215-7000 (office). *Website:* www.oxy.com (office).

KLEY, Karl-Ludwig, Dr jur; German lawyer and business executive; *Chairman of the Supervisory Board, Deutsche Lufthansa AG;* b. 11 June 1951, Munich; m.; one s.; ed Ludwig-Maximilians Univ., Munich; completed industrial business apprenticeship at Siemens AG then trained as lawyer in Hamburg and Johannesburg; joined Bayer AG as Asst to Chair. of Man. Bd 1982, then Chief Financial Officer, Japan 1987–91, then numerous exec. positions in Pharmaceuticals Div., including Head, Pharmaceuticals, Italy 1994–97, then Head Corp. Finance and Investor Relations 1998; Chief Financial Officer and mem. Exec. Bd, Lufthansa AG 1998–2008; Vice-Chair. Exec. Bd, Merck KGaA 2006–07, Chair. 2007–16, also mem. Exec. Bd E. Merck OHG; Chair. Man. Bd, Baden-Badener Unternehmer Gespräche eV; Chair. Supervisory Bd, E.ON SE 2016–; Chair. Supervisory Bd, Deutsche Lufthansa AG 2017–; Vice-Chair. Business and Industry Advisory Bd and mem. Gen. Meeting, Goethe-Institut eV; mem. Supervisory Bd, BMW AG, Deutsche Lufthansa AG; mem. Bd of Dirs, Verizon Communications Inc.; Pres. German Chemical Industry Asscn (VCI); Vice-Pres. Fed. of German Industry (BDI); Hon. Prof., Otto Beisheim School of Man. 2006. *Address:* Deutsche Lufthansa AG, Von-Gablenz-Strasse 2–6, 50679 Cologne, Germany (office). *Telephone:* (69) 6960 (office). *Fax:* (69) 6966818 (office). *Website:* www.lufthansa.com (office).

KLEY, Max Dietrich; German business executive; b. 1940, Berlin; m.; three c.; ed Univs of Munich and Heidelberg; joined Legal Dept, BASF AG 1969, Head of Tax Dept 1977–82, CEO Gewerkschaft Auguste Vic., Marl 1982–87, Pres. Energy and Coal Div. 1987–90, mem. Bd of Exec. Dirs 1990–2003, Deputy Chair. 1999–2003, mem. Supervisory Bd BASF SE 2003–; Chair. Supervisory Bd Infineon Technologies AG 2002–10, Interim CEO March–Aug. 2004; Chair. Supervisory Bd SGL Group 2004–13; mem. Supervisory Bd HeidelbergCement AG (fmrly Heidelberger Zement AG) 2004–; Chair. Industrial Energy and Power Asscn 1991–97; mem. Bd of Trustees Accounting Standards Cttee Foundation 2003–; Hon. Pres. Deutsches Aktieninstitut. *Address:* c/o Supervisory Board, BASF SE, 67056 Ludwigshafen, Germany (office).

KLIBI, Chedli, BA; Tunisian politician and international organization official; b. 6 Sept. 1925, Tunis; s. of Hassouna Klibi and Habiba Bannani; m. Kalthoum Lasram 1956; one s. two d.; ed Sadiki Coll., Tunis, Sorbonne, Paris; successively high school teacher, Lecturer, Univ. of Tunis and journalist 1951–57; Dir-Gen. Tunisian Radio and TV 1958–61; Minister of Information and Cultural Affairs 1961–64, 1969–73, of Cultural Affairs 1976–78, of Information Sept. 1978; Minister, Dir Cabinet of Pres. 1974–76; Sec.-Gen. League of Arab States 1979–90; Mayor of Carthage 1963–90; currently mem. Tunisian Senat; mem. Political Bureau and Cen. Cttee, Neo Destour (Parti Socialiste Destourien); mem. Cairo Arabic Language Acad.; Grand Officier, Légion de Honneur 1972, Grand Cordon, Order of Independence and Order of Repub. (Tunisia) and several foreign decorations. *Publications include:* The Arabs and the Palestinian Question, Islam and Modernity, Culture is a Civilisational Challenge, Orient–Occident, la paix violente. *Leisure interest:* reading. *Address:* 9 rue Ibn Kaldoun, Carthage, Tunisia (home). *Telephone:* (71) 734-535 (home). *Fax:* (71) 734-820 (home).

KLICH, Bogdan Adam, MA; Polish physician, politician and academic; b. 6 May 1960, Kraków; ed Bartholomew Nowodworski High School, Kraków, Kraków Medical Acad., Jagiellonian Univ.; interned during martial law set by the communist regime 1981; physician, Kraków Medical Acad. 1986; Adviser to Chief Negotiator of Poland with EU 1989–99; doctoral studies, Dept of Historical Philosophy 1991–95; mem. Parl. 2001–04, Vice-Chair. Cttee on Foreign Affairs, mem. Cttee on Nat. Defence; Deputy Minister of Nat. Defence 1999–2000; Observer to European Parl. 2003–04; Polish Rep. and mem. Policy Cttee of Parl. Ass. of Council of Europe 2001–04; mem. European Parl. (Group of European People's Party (Christian Democrats) and European Democrats) 2004–07, Chair. Del. for Relations with Belarus 2004–07, mem. Cttee on Foreign Affairs, Human Rights, Common Security and Defence Policy 2004–07, Conf. of Del. Chairmen 2004–07; Minister of Nat. Defence 2007–11; Senator 2011–; Lecturer, Centre for European Studies, Jagiellonian Univ., Cracow Univ. of Econs 2014–; f. Inst. for Strategic Studies, Kraków; Order of Merit for Defence of Lithuania, Gold Medal of Merit, Ministry of Foreign Affairs, Slovakia. *Address:* Centre for European Studies, Jagiellonian University, ul. Garbarska 7A 31-131 Kraków, Poland (office). *Telephone:* (12) 4296207 (office). *Fax:* (12) 4296195 (office). *E-mail:* biuro@klich.pl (office); office@ces.uj.edu.pl (office). *Website:* www.ces.uj.edu.pl (office).

KLÍMA, Ivan, MA; Czech author and dramatist; b. 14 Sept. 1931, Prague; s. of Vilém Klíma and Marta Klíma; m. Helena Malá-Klímová 1958; one s. one d.; ed Charles Univ., Prague; Ed. Československy spisovatel (publishing house) 1958–63; Ed. Literární noviny 1963–67, Literární Listy 1968, Listy 1968–69; Visiting Prof., Univ. of Michigan, USA 1969–70, Univ. of California, Berkeley 1998; freelance author publishing abroad 1970–89; columnist, Lidove Noviny newspaper; mem. Council, Czech Writers 1989–, Ed.'s Council, Lidové noviny 1996–97; Exec. Pres. Czech PEN Centre 1990–93; Hostovský Award, New York 1985, George Theiner Prize (UK) 1993, Franz Kafka Prize 2002, Medal for Outstanding Service to Czech Repub. 2002, Karel Capek Prize 2010, Ferdinand Peroutka Award 2013. *Publications include:* Ship Named Hope 1968, A Summer Affair 1972, My Merry Mornings (short stories) 1979, My First Loves (short stories) 1985, Love and Garbage 1987, Judge on Trial 1987, My Golden Trades (short stories) 1992, The Island of Dead Kings 1992, The Spirit of Prague (essays) 1994, Waiting for the Dark, Waiting for the Light 1996, The Ultimate Intimacy (novel) 1997, No Saints or Angels 1999, Between Security and Insecurity: Prospects for Tomorrow 2000, Lovers for a Day: New and Collected Stories on Love 2000, Karel Capek: Life and Work 2002, The Premier and the Angel (in Czech) 2004, My Mad Century 2013; plays: The Castle 1964, The Master 1967, The Sweetshop Myriam 1968, President and the Angel, Klara and Two Men 1968, Bridegroom for Marcela 1968, The Games 1975, Kafka and Felice 1986, My Crazy Century 2009; contribs to magazines. *Leisure interests:* tennis, gathering mushrooms. *Address:* Na Dubině 5, 14700 Prague 4, Czech Republic (home); c/o Nakladatelství Academia, Václavské náměstí 34, 110 00 Prague 1, Czech Republic. *Telephone:* 73-7788981 (mobile); 221403840. *Website:* www.ivanklima.cz; www.academia.cz. *Fax:* 224223520. *E-mail:* knihy.vaclavskenam@academia.cz.

KLIMA, Viktor; Austrian politician and business executive (retd); b. 4 June 1947, Vienna; s. of Viktor Klima and Anna Varga; m. Sonja Holzinger 1995; one s. one d.; ed Vienna Tech. Univ., Univ. of Vienna; worked at Inst. for Automation and Scientific Business Consultancy; joined staff of Österreichische Mineralöl-Verwaltungs AG (ÖMV) 1970, Head Organizational Div. 1980–85, Dir Cen. Personnel Office and group's Prokuriet (holder of a gen. power of attorney) 1986, mem. Man. Bd with responsibility for finance, control, accountancy and acquisitions (subsequently also chemical div.) 1990–92; Minister of Public Economy and Transport 1992–96, of Finance 1996–97, Fed. Chancellor of Austria 1997–2000; Pres. Volkswagen Argentina 2000–12, mem. Group Bd of Man. for South America Region and Gen. Rep. of Volkswagen Aktiengesellschaft 2006–12; fmr mem. Governing Bd Fed. of Public Economy and Utility Enterprises; fmr Chair. Fed. Econ. Chamber's Petroleum Industry Labour Law Cttee, Cttee on Public and Utility Enterprises.

KLIMKIN, Pavlo A.; Ukrainian diplomatist and politician; *Minister of Foreign Affairs;* b. 25 Dec. 1967, Kursk, Russian SFSR, USSR; m. Nataliya Klimkina; two s.; ed Moscow Physical-Technical Inst.; Research Officer, E.O. Paton Electric Welding Inst., Nat. Acad. of Sciences of Ukraine 1991–93; joined Ministry of Foreign Affairs (MFA) 1993, Attaché and Second Sec., Dept of Mil. Control and Disarmament 1993–97, Third, later Second Sec., Embassy in Berlin 1997–2000, First Sec., Counsellor, MFA Econ. Co-operation Dept 2000–02, Minister-Counsellor, Embassy in London 2004–08, Dir, MFA EU Dept 2008–10, Deputy Minister of Foreign Affairs and MFA Chief of Staff 2010–12 (played central role in negotiating Ukraine–EU Asscn Agreement), Amb. to Germany 2012–14, Minister of Foreign Affairs 2014–. *Address:* Ministry of Foreign Affairs, 01018 Kyiv, pl. Mykhailivska 1, Ukraine (office). *Telephone:* (44) 238-17-48 (office). *Fax:* (44) 238-18-88 (office). *E-mail:* zsmfa@mfa.gov.ua (office). *Website:* www.mfa.gov.ua (office).

KLIMMT, Reinhard; German politician and historian; b. 16 Aug. 1942; elected mem. of Landtag 1975; Chair. SPD Landtag Party, mem. SPD Party Exec., Chair. Media Comm. of SPD Party Exec. –1998; Minister-Pres. of Saarland 1998–99; Minister of Regional Planning, Urban Devt, Construction and Transport 1999–2000; consultant to Bd of Deutsche Bahn AG 2002–. *Publications include:* überall und irgendwo: Aus der Welt der Bücher 2006, Halbe Fünf und ganze Kerle: Das Saarland der 50er Jahre 2014.

KLIMOV, Dmitri Mikhailovich; Russian mechanical engineer; b. 13 July 1933; m.; ed Moscow State Univ.; Researcher, Research Inst. of Applied Mechanics. 1958–67; Deputy Dir Inst. for Problems in Mechanics, USSR (now Russian) Acad. of Sciences 1967–89, Dir 1989, now Councillor, Corresp. mem USSR (now Russian) Acad. of Sciences 1981, mem. 1992, Academician-Sec. Div. for Problems of Machine Engineering, Mechanics and Control Processes 1996–; Deputy Chair. Scientific Council on Problems of Man. of Navigation Movt; USSR State Prize 1976, Russian State Prize 1994. *Publications include:* Inertial Navigation on the Sea 1984, Applied Methods in Oscillations Theory 1988, Methods of Computer Algebra in Problems of Mechanics 1989; numerous articles. *Leisure interest:* chess. *Address:* Institute for Problems in Mechanics, 119526 Moscow, Vernadskogo prosp. 101, block 1, Russia (office). *Telephone:* (495) 434-46-10 (office); (495) 938-14-04 (Academy). *Fax:* (495) 938-20-48 (office). *E-mail:* ipm@ipmnet.ru (office). *Website:* www.ipmnet.ru (office).

KLIMOVSKI, Savo, LLD, PhD; Macedonian politician and academic; b. 1947, Skopje; m. Radmila Klimovski; one s. one d.; ed Skopje Univ., Ljubljana Univ.; Lecturer, Asst Prof., Prof., Dean of Law Faculty, Pres., St Cyril and Methodius Univ., Skopje; mem. Exec. Council, Macedonian Ass. 1986–90; Pres. Macedonian Cttee for Educ., Culture and Physical Culture; f. Democratic Alternative (political party) 1998; mem. Govt Coalition For Changes; Speaker, Ass. of Repub. of Macedonia 1998–2000, Pres. Cttee for Constitutional Issues, Council for Inter-ethnic Relations; Pres. Repub. of Macedonia Nov.–Dec. 1999. *Publications:* Constitutional and Political System, Politics and Institutions, Political Philosophy, Parliamentary Law. *Address:* Bul. 'Patizanski odredi' nr. 3/II-19, Skopje, North Macedonia (home). *Website:* www.klimovski.com.mk.

KLIMUK, Col-Gen. Piotr Ilyich, DTechSc; Russian cosmonaut; b. 10 July 1942, Komarovka, Brest Region; m. Lilia Vladimirovna Klimuk; one s.; ed Chernigov Higher Mil. Aviation School, Air Force Acad., Lenin Mil. Political Acad.; three space flights (Soyuz 13, Soyuz 18, Soyuz 30) 1973–78; Deputy Head, then Head of Political Dept Yuriy Gagarin Centre for Cosmonauts Training 1978–91, Head of Centre 1991–2003 (retd); USSR People's Deputy 1989–91; Hero of Soviet Union 1973, 1975; Tsiolkovsky Gold Medal, USSR State Prize 1978, 1981, Gold Medal (Polish Acad. of Sciences); Order of Fatherland of the 2nd class 2002. *Publications:* Next to the Stars, Attacking Weightlessness.

KLINE, Kevin Delaney, BA; American actor and director; b. 24 Oct. 1947, St Louis; s. of Robert J. Kline and Peggy Kirk; m. Phoebe Cates 1989; one s. one d.; ed Indiana Univ. and Juilliard School; Founding mem. The Acting Co. New York 1972–76; Obie Award, Will Award for classical theatre, Joseph Papp Award 1990, John Houseman Award 1993, Gotham Award 1997. *Films include:* Sophie's Choice 1982, Pirates of Penzance 1983, The Big Chill 1983, Silverado 1985, Violets are Blue 1985, Cry Freedom 1987, A Fish Called Wanda (Acad. Award for Best Supporting Actor 1989) 1988, The January Man 1989, I Love You to Death 1989, Soapdish 1991, Grand Canyon 1991, Consenting Adults 1992, Chaplin 1992, Dave 1993, Princess Caraboo 1994, French Kiss 1995, The Hunchback of Notre Dame (voice) 1996, Fierce Creatures 1996, The Ice Storm 1997, In and Out 1997, A Midsummer Night's Dream 1999, Wild Wild West 1999, The Road to El Dorado (voice) 2000, The Anniversary Party 2001, Life as a House 2001, Orange County 2002, The Emperor's Club 2002, The Hunchback of Notre Dame II (voice) 2002, De-Lovely 2004, Pink Panther 2006, A Prairie Home Companion 2006, As You Like It 2006, Trade 2007, Definitely, Maybe 2008, The Extra Man 2010, The Conspirator 2010, Darling Companion 2012, The Last of Robin Hood 2013, Last Vegas 2013, My Old Lady 2014. *Theatre:* Broadway appearances in On the Twentieth Century 1978 (Tony Award 1978), Loose Ends 1979, Pirates of Penzance 1980 (Tony Award 1980), Arms and the Man 1985; off-Broadway appearances in Richard III 1983, Henry V 1984, Hamlet (also dir) 1986, 1990, Much Ado About Nothing 1988, Measure for Measure 1995, The Seagull 2001, Cyrano de Bergerac 2008, Darling Companion 2012, Present Laughter (Tony Award 2017) 2017. *Television includes:* Freedom: A History of Us (series) 2003, As You Like It (Outstanding Performance by a Male Actor in a Television Movie or Mini-series 2008) 2007, Bob's Burgers 2011–14. *Address:* c/o Creative Artists Agency, 2000 Avenue of the Stars, Los Angeles, CA 90067, USA.

KLINE, Lowry F., BA, JD; American lawyer and beverage industry executive; b. 1941, Louden, Tenn.; m. Jane Kline; three c.; ed Univ. of Tennessee; Partner, Miller & Martin (law firm) 1970–95; Gen. Counsel, Johnston Coca-Cola Bottling Group 1981–91; Sr Vice-Pres. and Gen. Counsel, Coca-Cola Enterprises Inc. (bottler) 1996–97, Exec. Vice-Pres. and Gen. Counsel, 1997–99, Exec. Vice-Pres. and Chief Admin. Officer 1999–2000, Dir 2000–, Vice-Chair. 2000–02, CEO 2001–04, 2005–06, Chair. 2002–08; mem. Bd of Dirs The Dixie Group, Inc., Jackson Furniture Industries, Nat. Soft Drink Asscn; mem. Bd of Trustees, Woodruff Arts Center; fmr Pres. Chattanooga Bar Asscn, Tenn. Bd of Law Examiners; fmr Chair. Tenn. Bar Foundation. *Address:* Coca-Cola Enterprises Inc., PO Box 723040, Atlanta, GA 31139-0040, USA (office). *Telephone:* (770) 989-3000 (office). *Fax:* (770) 989-3788 (office). *Website:* www.cokecce.com (office).

KLINSMANN, Jürgen; German football coach, fmr professional footballer and business executive; b. 30 July 1964, Göppingen; m. Debbie Chin 1995; one s. one d.; striker; youth player for TB Gingen 1972–74, SC Geislingen an der Steige 1974–78, Stuttgarter Kickers 1978–81; sr career with Stuttgarter Kickers 1981–84, VfB Stuttgart 1984–89 (79 goals), Inter Milan 1989–92 (won UEFA Cup 1991, Supercoppa Italiana 1989), AS Monaco 1992–94, Tottenham Hotspur 1994–95, Bayern Munich 1995–97 (won UEFA Cup 1996, Bundesliga 1997), Sampdoria 1997–98, Tottenham Hotspur (on loan) 1997–98, Orange County Blue Star 2003; won 108 caps for West Germany/Germany and scored 47 goals, mem. winning team, World Cup 1990, European Championship 1996, Capt. nat. team 1994–98, Head Coach 2004–06; Int. Amb. for FIFA World Cup, Germany 2006; Head Coach, FC Bayern Munich 2008–09; fmr Tech. Advisor, Los Angeles Galaxy (Major League Soccer); worked for RTL as 2010 FIFA World Cup Moderator; Head Coach, US men's nat. football team 2011–16; f. AGAPEDIA (children's care charity); Vice-Pres. SoccerSolutions (sports marketing and business devt consultancy); Int. Spokesman, Mastercard; West German Footballer of the Year 1988, German Footballer of the Year 1994, Football Writers' Asscn Footballer of the Year 1995, German Football Manager of the Year 2006. *Leisure interests:* travel, cinema, music, languages, family. *Address:* Soccer Solutions LLC, 744 SW Regency Place, Portland, OR 97225, USA (office). *Telephone:* (503) 297-0844 (office). *Fax:* (503) 297-0749 (office). *E-mail:* mick@soccersolutions.com (office). *Website:* www.soccersolutions.com (office).

KLOBUCHAR, Amy, BA, JD; American lawyer and politician; *Senator from Minnesota;* b. 25 May 1960, Plymouth, Minn.; d. of Jim Klobuchar and Rose Klobuchar; m. John Bessler 1993; one d.; ed Yale Univ. and Univ. of Chicago Law School; practised law in Minn. and worked closely with fmr Vice-Pres. Walter Mondale; Assoc. Pnr, Dorsey & Whitney LLP (law firm) 1985–93; Pnr, Gray Plant Mooty LLP 1993–98; Attorney and Chief Prosecutor, Hennepin Co., Minn. 1998–2007; Senator from Minnesota 2007–, Chair. Senate Democratic Steering and Outreach Cttee 2015–, mem. Jt Econ. Cttee, President's Export Council, Senate Commerce Cttee, Judiciary Subcommittee on Antitrust, Competition Policy and Consumer Rights; Pres. Minnesota Co. Attorneys Asscn 2002–03; Democrat; '40 Under 40' Award, CityBusiness, named by Minnesota Lawyer magazine Lawyer of the Year 2001. *Publication:* Uncovering the Dome 1986. *Address:* 302 Hart Senate Office Building, Washington, DC 20510, USA (office). *Telephone:* (202) 224-3244 (office). *Fax:* (202) 228-2186 (office). *Website:* klobuchar.senate.gov (office); www.amyklobuchar.com (office).

KLOPP, Jürgen Norbert; German football manager and fmr footballer; *Manager, Liverpool Football Club;* b. 16 June 1967, Stuttgart; m. Ulla Sandrock 2005; two s.; ed Johann-Wolfgang-Goethe Univ. of Frankfurt; footballer for SV Glatten and TuS Ergenzingen youth teams –1986; footballer for TuS Ergenzingen 1986–87, FC Pforzheim 1987, Eintracht Frankfurt 1987–88, FC Viktoria Sindlingen 1988–89, Rot-Weiss Frankfurt 1989–90, striker then defender for Mainz 05 team 1990–2001, team manager 2001–08; Man., Borussia Dortmund 2008–15, Liverpool FC 2015–; Deutscher Fernsehpreis for Best Sports Show 2006, German Football Manager of the Year 2011, 2012. *Television:* regular commentator, ZDF-TV 2005–08, RTL World Cup coverage 2010. *Address:* Liverpool Football Club, Anfield Road, Liverpool, L4 0TH, England (office). *Website:* www.liverpoolfc.com (office).

KLOPPERS, Marius, BE (Chem.), MBA, PhD; South African engineer and mining industry executive; b. 26 Aug. 1962; m. Carin Kloppers; three c.; ed Univ. of Pretoria, Massachusetts Inst. of Tech., USA, Institut Européen d'Admin des Affaires (INSEAD), France; early career with Sasol Ltd, S Africa; fmr man. consultant with McKinsey & Co., Netherlands; joined Billiton (BHP Billiton after 2001) 1993, held several man. positions including Gen. Man. Hillside Aluminium, COO Aluminium, CEO Samancor Manganese, Group Exec. Billiton plc, Chief Marketing Officer, apptd Chief Commercial Officer, BHP Billiton Group 2003, mem. Bd of Dirs BHP Billiton Ltd and BHP Billiton Plc 2006–13, Group Pres. Non-ferrous Materials Group –2007, Exec. Dir BHP Billiton, also CEO BHP Billiton 2007–13, Chair. Group Man. Cttee; Deputy Chair. Int. Council on Mining and Metals 2008–11, Chair. 2011–. *Address:* c/o BHP Billiton Ltd, BHP Billiton Centre, 180 Lonsdale Street, Melbourne, Vic. 3000, Australia.

KLOSE, Hans-Ulrich; German lawyer and politician; *Senior Adviser, Bosch-Stiftung;* b. 14 June 1937, Breslau; m. Anne Steinbeck-Klose; two s. two d.; ed gymnasium in Bielefeld High School, Clinton, Iowa USA and Univs of Freiburg and Hamburg; fmr lawyer in Hamburg; mem. Social Democratic Party (SPD) 1964–; mem. Public Services and Transport Workers' Union 1968; mem. Hamburgische Bürgerschaft 1970, Chair. SPD Parl. Group 1972; Senator of the Interior 1973; Mayor of Hamburg 1974–81 (resgnd); mem. (Constituency 18, Hamburg-Harburg) Bundestag 1983–2013, Chair. SPD Parl. Party 1991–94, Vice-Pres. Bundestag 1994–98, Chair. Foreign Affairs Cttee 1998–2002, Vice-Chair. 2002–13; Chair. German-American Parl. Group 2003–13; Treas. SPD 1987–91; Sr Adviser, Bosch-Stiftung; Hon. Citizen of Lima 1981; Int. Statesmanship Award, US Asscn of Former Members of Congress 2013. *Publications:* Das Altern der Gesellschaft 1993, Altern hat Zukunft 1993, Charade (poems) 1997, Charade 2 (poems) 1999, Zeitschreiben (poems) 2007. *Leisure interests:* early American cultures, art and antiques, painting, literature. *Address:* Heylstrasse 29, 10825 Berlin, Germany (office). *E-mail:* ulriklose@t-online.de (office).

KLOSSA, Guillaume, MSc, MPA; French business executive, government official and journalist; *Honorary President, EuropaNova;* ed Institut d'Études politiques, Paris, London School of Econs and Political Science, UK, École des hautes Études commerciales, Paris; Dir in charge of consulting and digital activities for Bureau Veritas group in Europe 1999–2003; Journalist Vivendi 2004–07 (co-anchor at i Television 2004 and Ed. in Chief at Bollore Média group 2005–07); adviser to French presidency of EU 2007–09, to reflection group for future of Europe at European Council 2009–10; European columnist for Metro International 2004–10; Vice-Pres. and mem. Exec. Cttee at McDonald's France 2010–12; Exec. Dir in charge of public affairs, media strategy and research, corporate strategic initiatives for European Broadcasting Union 2013–18; Special Adviser to Vice-Pres. of the EC 2018–; Pres. EuropaNova (European think-tank based in Paris and Brussels), currently Hon. Pres.; Founder 40under40 (European young leaders programme); Head of the Mission 'Innovation et production en Europe', Directorate-Gen. for Competition, Consumption and Fraud Prevention, Ministry of Economy, Industry and Employment; contrib. to Forbes magazine 2011. *Publication:* Europe, la dernière chance? (with Jean-François Jamet) 2011. *Address:* EuropaNova, 64 bis New York Avenue, 75016 Paris, France (office). *Telephone:* 1-43-42-40-90 (office). *E-mail:* contact@europanova.eu (office). *Website:* www.europanova.eu (office); www.40under40.eu.

KLUG, Gerald Rudolf, Mag.Iur; Austrian politician and fmr trade union official; b. 13 Nov. 1968, Graz; ed Acad. for Social Studies, Mödling Chamber of Labour, Karl-Franzens-Univ., Graz; began career as skilled worker (lathe operator), Siemens Mobility Co. 1987–90; mem. Pro-Ge (trade union) 1984–, Sec. 1990; Lay Judge, Graz Court of Appeal 2000; mem. Ind. Financial Tribunal of Graz Regional Financial Directorate 2001–11; Substitute mem., Gen. Ass. of Styria Prov. Health Insurance Fund 2004–05; mem. Directorate, Styria Prov. Employment Office 2003–05; mem. Bundesrat (Parl.) (Sozialdemokratische Partei Österreichs (SPÖ—Social Democratic Party of Austria) 2005–13, SPÖ Chief Whip 2010–13; Fed. Minister for Defence and Sports 2013–16, for Transport, Innovation and Tech. Jan.–May 2016. *Address:* c/o Federal Ministry of Transport, Innovation and Technology, Radetzkystr. 2, Postfach 201, 1030 Vienna, Austria (office). *Telephone:* (1) 711-62-65-0 (office). *E-mail:* kbm@bmvit.gv.at (office). *Website:* www.bmlv.gv.at (office).

KLUGE, Jürgen, Dr rer. nat, MPhys; German physicist, business executive and consultant; *Chairman, Lindau Nobel Laureate Meetings Foundation;* b. 2 Sept. 1953, Hagen; ed Univs of Cologne and Essen; with McKinsey & Co., Düsseldorf 1984–2009, German Office Man. 1999–2006; Chair. Man. Bd Franz Haniel & Cie. GmbH and Group Human Resources Man. 2010–12; Chair. Supervisory Bd Celesio AG 2010–12, Metro AG 2010–11, Schmitz Cargobull AG 2013–; Vice-Chair. TAKKT AG 2010–12; Consultant, Kluge & Partner, Düsseldorf 2012–; Sr Advisor, Bank of America Merrill Lynch 2012–; Chair. Lindau Nobel Laureate Meetings Foundation 2016–, also mem. Council Nobel Laureate Meetings; mem. Supervisory Bd SMS Holding GmbH 2010–13; Hon. Prof. of Mechanical Eng, Darmstadt Tech. Univ. 2004–, Finnish Hon. Consul, North Rhine-Westphalia and Rhineland-Palatinate 2013. *Address:* Lindau Nobel Laureate Meetings Foundation, Lennart-Bernadotte-Haus, Alfred-Nobel-Platz 1, 88131 Lindau, Germany (office). *Telephone:* (83) 82277310 (office). *Fax:* (83) 822773113 (office). *E-mail:* info@lindau-nobel.org (office). *Website:* www.lindau-nobel.org (office).

KLUM, Heidi; German/American model, fashion designer, actress, television presenter and artist and singer; b. 1 June 1973, Bergisch Gladbach, North Rhine-Westphalia, Germany; d. of Günther Klum and Erna Klum; m. 1st Ric Pipino 1997 (divorced 2002); one d. with Flavio Briatore; m. 2nd British singer Seal (divorced 2012) 2005; two s. one d.; won nat. modelling contest Model 92 1992, offered modelling contract with Metropolitan Models New York; has appeared on cover of fashion magazines, including Vogue, ELLE and Marie Claire; became known after appearing on cover of Sports Illustrated Swimsuit Issue and for work with Victoria's Secret 1997–2010; hosted Victoria's Secret Fashion Shows 2002, 2006, 2007, 2009; signed to IMG Models, New York; designer of several clothing lines, fragrances and make-up; became new face and creative adviser for European cosmetics brand Astor 2010; host, judge and exec. producer of reality show Project Runway on Bravo US cable TV channel 2004; host, judge and co-producer of Germany's Next Topmodel (German version of int. reality TV show) on German station ProSieben 2006–; judge, America's Got Talent 2013–; became Barbie's official amb. for doll's 50th anniversary 2009; naturalized American citizen 2008. *Films include:* 54 1998, Blow Dry 2001, Ella Enchanted 2004, The Life and Death of Peter Sellers 2004, The Devil Wears Prada 2006, Perfect Stranger 2007. *Music includes:* debut single Wonderland 2006. *Music videos include:* Jamiroquai's video Love Foolosophy, Kelis's Young, Fresh 'n' New 2001, video for Seal's song Secret 2010. *Television includes:* appeared in episodes of Malcolm in the Middle and Cursed; guest-starred as herself in I Get That a Lot, Spin City, Sex and the City, CSI: Miami, How I Met Your Mother, Yes, Dear, Ugly Betty, Desperate Housewives. *Address:* IMG Models, 304 Park Avenue South, New York, NY 10010, USA (office). *Telephone:* (212) 253-8884 (office). *Fax:* (212) 253-8883 (office). *E-mail:* info@imgmodels.com (office). *Website:* www.imgmodels.com (office); www.heidiklum.com.

KLUZA, Stanisław, PhD; Polish economist, government official and banking executive; *President, Bank Ochrony Srodowiska SA;* b. 2 June 1972, Warsaw; m.; ed Warsaw School of Econs, Univ. of Washington, St Louis, USA, Univ. of Glasgow, UK; early positions included working at Higher School of Int. Commerce and Finance (GSBE-HSICF and Computerland shop; worked at Unilever Polska 1994–98, McKinsey & Co. 1998–99; Fulbright Scholar, Univ. of Washington, St Louis 1999–2000, Dekaban-Liddle Scholar, Univ. of Glasgow 2001; Head, Econ. Analysis Team, Office for Strategic Planning, Bank Gospodarki Żymnościowej SA (BGŻ) 2002–03, Chief Economist and Adviser to Pres. of Man. Bd 2003–06; Second Sec. of State and Deputy Minister of Finance May–July 2006, Minister of Finance July–Sept. 2006; Chair. Komisji Nadzoru Finansowego (Polish Financial Supervision Authority) 2006–11; mem. Shadow Cabinet for Econ. Affairs, Business Centre Club 2012–16; Vice-Pres. Man. Bd Bank Ochrony Srodowiska SA 2016–, Pres. BOŚ Bank 2016–; Asst Prof., Inst. of Statistics and Demography, Warsaw School of Econs 1994–; mem. Supervisory Bd Sygnity 2006, Siarkopol 2006, Elektrownia Siersza in Trzebinia 1998–99, JSW 2012–16; mem. Panel of Experts, Związku Dużych Rodzin "Trzy Plus (Asscn of Large Families Three Plus); mem. Soc. of Polish Economists, Hon. Council of Experts of AISEC Poland, Club 01; Prime Minister's Award for Doctoral Thesis, Foundation for Polish Science Award. *Publications:* numerous articles in professional publications. *Address:* Bank Ochrony Srodowiska SA, ul. Zelazna 32, Warsaw 00-832, Poland (office). *Telephone:* (22) 8508735 (office). *Website:* www.bosbank.pl (office).

KLYCHKO, Vitaliy Volodymyrovych, CandSci, MA, PhD; Ukrainian professional boxer and politician; *Mayor of Kyiv and Head of Kyiv City State Administration;* b. 19 July 1971, Belovodskoye, Moscow Dist, Chui Oblast, Kyrgyz SSR, USSR; s. of Volodymyr Rodionovich Klychko; m. Nataliya Yegorova 1996; two s. one d.; ed Pereyaslav-Khmelnitsky State Pedagogical Univ., Taras Shevchenko Nat. Univ. of Kyiv, Nat. Acad. of Public Admin of Pres. of Ukraine; lived in different parts of the Soviet Union until his family moved to Ukraine 1984; began boxing aged 14; two-time world amateur kickboxing champion and four-time professional kickboxing champion, three-time Ukrainian boxing champion, champion of First World Mil. Championship, silver medallist at World Amateur Boxing Championship; professional boxer 1996–2013, WBO Inter-Continental Heavyweight Champion May–Oct. 1998, EBU Heavyweight Champion 1998–99, 2000–02, WBO Heavyweight Champion 1999–2000, WBA Inter-Continental Heavyweight Champion 2001–03, The Ring Heavyweight Champion 2004–05, World Boxing Council (WBC) Heavyweight Champion 2004–05, Champion Emer. 2005–08, Champion 2008–13, Champion Emer. 2013–; co-f. (with brother Volodymyr) Klitschko Brothers Foundation 2003; began political career 2006, ran simultaneously for Verkhovna Rada (Parl.) and Kyiv City Council as Head of Pora-PRP (Enough!-Party of Reforms and Order) Bloc; became bloc group leader at Kyiv City Council, group renamed UDAR of Vitaliy Klychko group 2011; Leader, Ukrainsky Demokratychny Alyans za Reformy (UDAR—Punch—Ukrainian Democratic Alliance for Reform) 2010–15; mem. Verkhovna Rada (Parl.) 2012–14, Leader of party group UDAR of Vitaliy Klychko, party merged to become Blok Petra Poroshenka 'Solidarnist' (BPP—S) 2015, Chair. Blok Petra Poroshenka 'Solidarnist' (Solidarity—Petro Poroshenko Bloc) 2015–16; a leading figure in the Euromaidan protests 2013–14; unsuccessful cand. in presidential election 2014; Mayor of Kyiv and Head of Kyiv City State Admin 2014–; agreed to carry out charitable work for UNESCO 2002; Hero of Ukraine; Bundesverdienstkreuz 2010; named by WBC as the best puncher in the history of heavyweight boxing, rated by Ring Magazine as the No. 9 pound-for-pound boxer in the world 2012, named by WBC The Eternal World Heavyweight Champion (title awarded to boxers that were undefeated as champion) 2016. *Leisure interests:* diving, music, chess. *Address:* Kyiv City State Administration, 01044 Kyiv, vul. Khreshchatyk 36, Ukraine (office). *Telephone:* (44) 1551 (office); (44) 205-73-37 (mobile) (office). *E-mail:* info@kmr.gov.ua (office); press.klichko@gmail.com. *Website:* kmr.gov.ua (office); kievcity.gov.ua (office); klichko.org.

KLYMPUSH-TSYNTSADZE, Ivanna Orestivna, BA, MA; Ukrainian research institute director, national organization official and politician; *Vice-Prime Minister, responsible for European and Euro-Atlantic Integration;* b. 5 July 1972, Kyiv, Ukrainian SSR, USSR; m.; two d.; ed M.P. Dragomanov Ukrainian State Pedagogical Univ., Inst. of Int. Relations, Taras Shevchenko Nat. Univ. of Kyiv, Montana State Univ. and Summer School at Harvard Ukrainian Research Inst., Harvard Univ., USA; began career as Project Man. at Ukrainian Centre for Ind. Political Research, Kyiv 1993, later headed Dept of Int. Relations; Project Man., Kyiv Centre of the East–West Inst. 1998–2002, Dir of the Centre for one year; Corresp., Ukrainian Service of BBC Radio in Washington, DC, USA and in the Caucasus (Tbilisi) 2002–07; Deputy Dir of Programs, later Dir Open Ukraine Foundation 2007–11; led Yalta European Strategy 2011–14; People's Deputy of Ukraine to Verkhovna Rada (Parl.) 2014–, First Deputy Chair. Cttee on Foreign Affairs, headed Perm. Del. of Verkhovna Rada to NATO Parl. Ass.; Vice-Prime Minister, responsible for European and Euro-Atlantic Integration 2016–. *Publication:* Black Sea Region: Cooperation and Security (co-author). *Address:* Office of the Cabinet of Ministers, 01008 Kyiv, vul. M. Hrushevskoho 12/2, Ukraine (office). *Telephone:* (44) 256-63-33 (office). *E-mail:* shustenko@kmu.gov.ua (office). *Website:* www.kmu.gov.ua (office).

KLYUYEV, Andriy Petrovych, PhD; Ukrainian politician and fmr mining engineer; b. 12 Sept. 1964, Donetsk; m. Zhanna Klyuyeva; three s.; ed Donetsk Polytechnic Inst. (now Donetsk Nat. Tech. Univ.); underground mine worker at Zasyadko coalmine, Donetsk 1983–86; Deputy Head of Mine Transport Dept, Bilorichenska coalmine (Voroshylovgrad Coal) 1986; fmr Eng Dir Shelf Group; fmr Pres. Promcomservice Jt Stock Co.; Dir-Gen. Ukrpidshypnyk Jt Stock Co. 1991–94; Deputy Chair. Donetsk Regional Council 1994–96, 1998, mem. Donetsk City Council 1996–2002, First Deputy Mayor of Donetsk 1996; mem. Verkhovna Rada (Supreme Council, Parl.) 2002–06, 2006–; mem. Party of the Regions, First Deputy Chair. 2001–08, Sec. of Political Council 2003–08, Deputy Chair. 2008–; Deputy Prime Minister of Ukraine 2003–04, 2006–10, First Deputy Prime Minister and Minister of Econ. Devt and Trade 2010–12; Sec. Nat. Security and

Defence Council of Ukraine 2012–14; Head of Presidential Admin Jan.–Feb. 2014 (resgnd); wanted, along with other politicians and sr army officers, for his alleged involvement in mass murder March 2014; assets frozen by EU; Order for Service of the 1st Grade 1999, 2nd Grade 2004, Diploma of Honour of the Verkhovna Rada of Ukraine 2005. *Publications:* author of 18 scientific and tech. inventions in the mining sector.

KNAIFEL, Alexander Aronovich; Russian composer; b. 28 Nov. 1943, Tashkent, Uzbekistan; s. of Aron Iosifovich Knaifel and Muza Veniaminovna Shapiro-Knaifel; m. Tatiana Ivanovna Melentieva 1965; one d.; ed Moscow and Leningrad Conservatoires; mem. Composers' Union 1968–, Cinematographers' Union 1987–; Order of Friendship 2004; DAAD Honoured Grant-Aided Composer, Berlin 1993, Honoured Art Worker of Russia 1996. *Compositions include:* Sonata on a Fairy Tale 1961, A Sling 1962, Diada 1962, Burlesca 1963, Non stop 1963, Marching and Dancing Two-voice Textures 1963, A Toast by Robert Burns 1963, Ostinati 1964, An Angel and Five Poems by Mikhail Lermontov 1964, Piano: musique militaire 1964, A Plain-air-fugue, a Fugue-interior 1964, An Anthem to Foolishness 1964, Turno a turno 1964, In via 1964, In Memory of Samuil Marshak 1964, Those Seeking the City to Come 1964–65, Passacaglia 1965, The Canterville Ghost 1965, Canterville 1965–66, Disarmament 1966, 150 000 000 1966, Lamento 1967, Salve! 1967, Petrograd Sparrows 1967, A Little White One and a Little Black One 1968, Monodia 1968, Medea 1968, Argumentum de jure 1969, Jeanne 1970–78, Baby Songs in Sleep 1972, A prima vista 1972, Appelli 1972, Status nascendi 1973–75, Two Times Two 1975, Vampampet 1975, Ainana 1978, FFPh 1978–2004, Rafferty Jazz Chorus 1980, Vera (Faith) 1980, A Call 1980, Solaris 1980, Da (Yes) 1980, A Silly Horse 1981, Accidental 1982, Nika 1983–84, Churiki 1984, Epitaphs 1984, God 1985, Agnus Dei 1985, A Kholop's Wings (A Serf's Wings) 1986, Through the Rainbow of Involuntary Tears 1987–88, Litania 1988, Notturno 1988, Shramy Marsha (Scars of Marching) 1988, Voznosheniye (The Holy Oblation) 1991, Svete Tikhiy (O Gladsome Light) 1991, Once Again on the Hypothesis 1992, Ionus – postludia 1992, Scalae Iacobis 1992, Chapter Eight 1992–93, Cantus 1993, Maranatha 1993, Butterfly 1993, In Air Clear and Unseen 1994, Alice in Wonderland 1994–2002, Amicta sole 1995, Blazhenstva 1996, Bliss 1997, With the White on the White 1997–98, Lux aeterna 1997, This Child 1997, The Tabernacle 1998, A Snowflake on a Spiderthread 1998, A Day 1999, Small Blue Feathers 2001, Petia i Dolg (Folk) 2001, A Fairy Tale of a Fisherman and a Little Fish 2002, Lukomoriye 2002–03, Confession 2003, Birth 2003, The Cherubimic Hymn 2004, Gee! 2004, Chalice 2004, Old Photos 2004, The Little Beads for Njua 2004, Of the Pope and of His Workman Balda 2004, O Spirit of Truth 2005, Tzarevna (A Tzar's Daughter) 2005, Bridge 2006–08, O Master of My Days 2007, A Mad Tea-Party 2007, For Tatianka and Annushka 2007, E.F. 2008, The Spire of Bujan 2010; incidental music for 40 films. *Publications include:* Musique militaire 1974, Diada (Two Pieces) 1975, Classical Suite 1976, The Canterville Ghost 1977, Five Poems by Mikhail Lermontov 1978, Lamento 1979, The Petrograd Sparrows 1981, A Silly Horse 1985, Medea 1989, Vera (Faith) 1990, Passacaglia 1990, Da (Yes) 1991, O Comforter 1997, Bliss 1997. *Leisure interests:* photography, shooting video films. *Address:* Skobelevski pr. 5, Apt 130, 194214 St Petersburg, Russia. *Telephone:* (812) 293-82-68. *Fax:* (812) 293-53-97. *E-mail:* knaifel@hotmail.com; knaifel@mail.ru.

KNAPP, Charles, MA, PhD; American economist, academic, fmr university administrator and fmr government official; *Distinguished Public Service Fellow, Institute of Higher Education, University of Georgia;* b. 13 Aug. 1946, Ames, Ia; s. of Albert B. Knapp and Anne Marie Knapp; m. Lynne Vickers Knapp 1967; one d.; ed Iowa State Univ. and Univ. of Wisconsin; Asst Prof. of Econs, Univ. of Texas, Austin 1972–76; Special Asst to US Sec. of Labor 1976–79; Deputy Asst Sec. of Labor for Employment Training 1979–81; Visiting Faculty, George Washington Univ. 1981–82; Sr Vice-Pres., Tulane Univ. 1982–85, Exec. Vice-Pres. 1985–87; Pres. and Prof. of Econs, Univ. of Georgia 1987–97, Pres. Emer. 2004, Distinguished Public Service Fellow, Inst. of Higher Educ. 2005–, Interim Dean, Terry Coll. of Business 2013; fmr Pres. Aspen Inst. 1997–99; mem. Bd of Trustees, Oglethorpe Univ.; Sr Fellow, Asscn of Governing Bds of Univs and Colls 1999–2000; Partner, Heidrick & Struggles Int. Inc., Atlanta 2000; Dir Aflac, Inc.; Distinguished Achievement Award, Iowa State Univ. Alumni Asscn 1994. *Publications:* A Human Capital Approach to the Burden of the Military Draft 1973, Earnings and Individual Variations in Postschool Human Investment 1976, Employment Discrimination 1978. *Address:* Institute of Higher Education, Meigs Hall, University of Georgia, Athens, Athens, GA 30602, USA (office). *Telephone:* (706) 542-0620 (office). *E-mail:* cknapp@uga.edu (office). *Website:* www.uga.edu/ihe/knapp.html (office).

KNAPP, Oscar, PhD; Swiss economist and diplomatist (retd); b. 14 Aug. 1948, Grisons; m. Elisabeth Knapp; ed Univs of St Gallen and Geneva; fmr Head of Financial, Econ. and Trade Div., Embassy in Washington, DC; Amb. to Brazil 1996–2000; Exec. mem. State Secr. of Econ. Affairs, mem. Bd of Dirs and Head, Econ. Devt Co-operation Office 2003–06; Amb. to Austria 2006–10; Head of Market Div., State Secr. for Int. Financial Affairs 2010–13; mem. Bd of Dirs SRG SSR, also Chair. SRG SSR Svizra Rumantscha. *Leisure interests:* skiing, golf, mountains. *Address:* SRG SSR, Giacomettistrasse 1, 3000 Bern, Switzerland (office). *Telephone:* (31) 350-91-11 (office). *Website:* www.srgssr.ch (office).

KNAUSGÅRD, Karl Ove; Norwegian author; b. 6 Dec. 1968, Oslo; m. 1st Tonje Aursland (divorced); two d.; m. 2nd Linda Boström Knausgård 2007; one s. one d.; ed Univ. of Bergen; published debut novel 1998; Co-Ed., Vagant literary magazine 1999–2002; consultant, new Norwegian trans. of The Bible 2009–11; wrote six autobiographical novels under series title Min kamp (My Struggle) 2009–11; Co-founder, Pelikanen publishing house 2010; NRK P2 Listeners' Prize 2009, Morgenbladet Book of the Year Prize 2010, Gyldendal Prize 2011, Welt-Literaturpreis 2015, Wall Street Journal Magazine's annual Innovator Award for literature 2015, Jerusalem Prize 2017. *Publications include:* Ute av verden (Out of the World) (Norwegian Critics Prize for Literature 2004) 1998, En tid for alt (A Time to Every Purpose Under Heaven) (P2-lytternes romanpris 2004, Southern Norway Literature Prize 2005) 2004, Min kamp 1 (My Struggle Vol. 1) (Brage Prize 2009) 2009, Min kamp 2 (My Struggle Vol. 2) 2009, Min kamp 3 (My Struggle Vol. 3) (Southern Norway Literature Prize 2010) 2009, Min kamp 4 (My Struggle Vol. 4) 2010, Min kamp 5 (My Struggle Vol. 5) 2010, Min kamp 6 (My Struggle Vol. 6) 2011, Sjelens Amerika: tekster (essays) 1996–2013 2013, Nakker (Necks) 2014, Om høsten (On autumn) 2015, Hjemme – Borte (co-author) 2015, Om vinteren (On winter) 2015, Om våren (On spring) 2016, Om sommeren (On summer) 2016. *Address:* The Wylie Agency, 17 Bedford Square, London, WC1B 3JA, England (office); c/o Forlaget Oktober AS, PO Box 6848, St. Olavs plass, 0130 Oslo, Norway (office). *Telephone:* (23) 35-46-20 (office). *Fax:* (23) 35-46-21 (office). *E-mail:* oktober@oktober.no (office). *Website:* oktober.no/nor/In-English (office).

KŇAŽKO, Milan; Slovak politician, actor and broadcast industry executive; b. 28 Aug. 1945, Horné Plachtince, Veľký Krtíš Dist; m. Eugenia Kňažková; three s.; ed Acad. of Performing Arts, Bratislava, Univ. of Nancy, France; mem. Theatre on the Promenade (drama co.), Bratislava 1970–71; actor, New Theatre, Bratislava 1971–85; mem. Slovak Nat. Theatre Drama Co. Bratislava, 1985–; Co-founder, Public Against Violence (political movt) Nov. 1989, rally speaker 1989–90; adviser to Pres. of Czechoslovakia 1989–90; Deputy Fed. Ass. 1990–92; Minister for Foreign Affairs, Govt of Slovak Repub. 1990–91; mem. and Vice-Chair. Movt for Democratic Slovakia 1991–93 (resgnd); Deputy Prime Minister, Slovak Repub. 1992–93, Minister for Foreign Affairs 1992–93; cand. in presidential election 2014; apptd Minister of Culture 1998; Chair. Govt Council of Slovak Repub. for Ethnic Groups 1992–93; Chair. Alliance of Democrats 1993–94, Ind. Deputies Club 1993–; First Deputy Chair. Democratic Union of Slovakia 1994–2000; Vice-Chair. Slovak Democratic and Christian Union (SDCHU) 2000–; Dir-Gen. Televízia JOJ (pvt. TV network) 2003–07; numerous roles on stage, in films, on TV, on radio; Merited Artist Award 1986 (returned award 1989). *Film roles include:* Nevesta hôl (The Bride of the Mountains, UK) 1972, Kohút nezaspieva 1986, Svet nic neví 1987, Maria Stuarda (TV) 1988, Dobrí holubi se vracejí 1988, Omyly tradicnej moralky (TV) 1989, Dlouhá míle (TV mini-series) 1989, Devet kruhu pekla 1989, Svedek umírajícího casu 1990, Poslední motýl (The Last Butterfly) 1991, Bel ami (TV) 2005. *Leisure interests:* family, sport, culture, theatre, golf. *Address:* c/o Televízia JOJ, PO Box 33, 830 07 Bratislava 37, Slovakia (office).

KNEALE, (Robert) Bryan (Charles), RA, RWA, FRBS; British sculptor; b. 19 June 1930, Douglas, Isle of Man; s. of William Kneale and Lilian Kewley; m. Doreen Lister 1956 (died 1998); one s. (deceased) one d.; ed Douglas High School, Douglas School of Art, Isle of Man, Royal Acad. Schools; Tutor, RCA Sculpture School 1964, Fellow, RCA 1972, Sr Tutor 1980–85, Head of Dept of Sculpture 1985–90, Prof. of Drawing 1990–95, Sr Fellow 1995; Head of Sculpture School, Hornsey 1967; Assoc. Lecturer, Chelsea School of Art 1970; Master of Sculpture RA 1982–85, Prof. 1985–90, now Trustee; mem. Fine Art Panels, Nat. Council for Art Design 1964–71, Arts Council 1971–73, CNAA 1974–82; Chair. Air and Space 1972–73; organized Sculpture '72, RA 1972, Battersea Park Silver Jubilee Sculpture 1977, Sade Exhbn, Cork 1982, Sculpture for Westminster Cathedral 1999; comms include Bronze Doors, Portsmouth Cathedral 1999, sculpture for Villa Marina Douglas and Nobles Hosp., Isle of Man 2004, Capt. Quilliam Memorial, Castletown, Isle of Man 2005, Illiam Dhone Memorial, Malew Church, Isle of Man 2006; Rome Prize 1949, Leverhulme Award 1952, Young Artist Competition Prize 1955, Arts Council Purchase Award 1978. *Address:* 10A Muswell Road, London, N10 2BG, England. *Telephone:* (20) 8444-7617. *E-mail:* bryan.kneale@googlemail.com (home).

KNELL, Gary Evan, BA, JD; American lawyer and business executive; *Chairman, National Geographic Partners;* b. 27 Feb. 1954, Sacramento, Calif.; m. Kim Larson 1981; four c.; ed Grant High School, Univ. of California, Los Angeles, Loyola Univ. School of Law; worked in Calif. State Legislature and Gov.'s Office; fmr Counsel to US Senate Judiciary and Governmental Affairs Cttees; Sr Vice-Pres. and Gen. Counsel, WNET/Channel 13, New York 1981–89; fmr Man. Dir Manager Media International (print and multimedia publishing co. in Bangkok, Hong Kong and Singapore); joined Sesame Workshop (fmrly Children's Television Workshop), producer of Sesame Street, Dragon Tales, Sagwa etc. 1989, COO 1998–2000, Chief Exec. 2000–11, responsibilities included Noggin (educational cable and online jt venture with Nickelodeon), publishing partnership with Time, Inc., and Sesame Street co-productions in S Africa, India, NI and Egypt; Pres. and CEO NPR (fmrly Nat. Public Radio) 2011–13; Pres. and CEO National Geographic Society 2014–18; Chair. Nat. Geographic Partners 2018–; mem. Council on Foreign Relations, US Nat. Comm. for UNESCO; Adviser, WFUV, public radio at Fordham Univ., Annenberg School of Communications, Univ. of Southern California, Common Sense Media; mem. Bd of Dirs Heidrick & Struggles 2007–, AARP Services, Inc., Jacob Burns Film Center, Save the Children; mem. Advisory Bd Columbia Univ.'s electronic learning venture, Fathom, Music Educators Nat. Conf., Alexandria, Center on Public Diplomacy, Univ. of Southern California; mem. Bd Smithsonian Nat. Museum of Natural History, Econ. Club of Washington, USA, Global Leadership Coalition; mem. Bd of Trustees Nat. Video Resources, Bd of Govs American Center for Children and Media, participant, Aspen Inst. Forum on Communications and Society, Columbia Univ. American Ass., UC Berkeley Grad. School of Journalism, Military Child Educ. Coalition; Dr hc (Kenyon College), (Mercy College), (Franklin University) Gordon Grand Fellow, Yale Univ., Guest Lecturer, Harvard Univ., Duke Univ., Carnegie Mellon Univ. *Address:* National Geographic Society, 1145 17th Street, NW, Washington, DC 20036-4688, USA (office). *Telephone:* (202) 857-7000 (office). *E-mail:* askngs@nationalgeographic.com (office). *Website:* www.nationalgeographic.com (office).

KNEŽEVIĆ, Goran; Serbian fmr professional basketball player and politician; *Minister of the Economy;* b. 12 May 1957, Banatski Karlovac, Autonomous Province of Vojvodina, People's Repub. of Serbia, Fed. People's Repub. of Yugoslavia; m.; four c.; ed Univ. of Belgrade; played basketball for KK Partizan, KK Vojvodina and KK Proleter; won championship of Yugoslavia, Yugoslav cup and Korać Cup with KK Partizan 1978/79; worked at Servo Mihalj Zrenjanin Plant 1983–90; Gen. Dir Servo Mihalj Tourist 1990–2000; began political career as mem. Demokratska Stranka (DS—Democratic Party); Chair. Exec. Cttee of Zrenjanin Municipality 2000; elected mem. Nat. Ass. on list of DS 2000–03; Mayor of Zrenjanin Municipality 2004–09, 2012; mem. Srpska Napredna Stranka (Serbian Progressive Party) 2010–; arrested Oct. 2008, charged with criminal conspiracy, abuse of office and bribery, detained for 13 months, released on bail Nov. 2009, acquitted Nov. 2012; Minister of Agric., Forestry and Water Man. 2012–13, of the Economy 2016–; Pres. Basketball Asscn of Serbia and Montenegro 2005–06; Mayor with Vision Award 2007. *Address:* Ministry of the Economy, 11000 Belgrade, Kneza Miloša 20, Serbia (office). *Telephone:* (11) 3642701 (office). *Fax:* (11) 3642705 (office). *E-mail:* kabinet@privreda.gov.rs (office). *Website:* www.privreda.gov.rs (office).

KNIGHT, Andrew Stephen Bower, MA; British editor and business executive; *Chairman, Times Newspaper Limited;* b. 1 Nov. 1939; s. of M. W. B. Knight and S. E. F. Knight; m. 1st Victoria Catherine Brittain 1966 (divorced); one s.; m. 2nd Begum Sabiha Rumani Malik 1975 (divorced 1991); two d.; m. 3rd Marita Georgina Phillips Crawley 2006; ed Ampleforth Coll., York, Balliol Coll., Oxford; Ed. The Economist 1974–86; Chief Exec. Daily Telegraph 1986–89, Ed.-in-Chief 1987–89; Chair. News Int. PLC 1990–94, Chair. Times Newspapers 2012–; Chair. Ballet Rambert 1984–87; Chair. Times Newspaper Holdings 1990–94; Dir News Corpn 1991–2012; Dir Rothschild Investment Trust CP 1996–2008, Chair. J. Rothschild Capital Management 2008; Chair. Shipston Home Nursing 1996–2006; Chair. Jerwood Charity 2003–06; mem. Advisory Bd Center for Econ. Policy Research, Stanford Univ., USA 1981–; Gov. mem. Council of Man. Ditchley Foundation 1982–; Founder-Trustee, Spinal Muscular Atrophy Trust; now farms in Warwicks. and Dannevirke, NZ. *Address:* Times Newspapers Limited, 1 Virginia Street, London, E98 1RL, England (office); Compton Scorpion Manor, Shipston-on-Stour, Warwicks., CV36 4PJ, England (home).

KNIGHT, Gladys Maria; American singer; b. 28 May 1944, Atlanta, Ga; d. of Merald Knight and Elizabeth Knight (née Woods); m. 2nd Barry Hankerson 1974 (divorced 1979); one s. and two c. (from previous marriage); tours with Morris Brown Choir 1950–53; formed Gladys Knight and The Pips 1953–89; mem. Lloyd Terry Jazz Ltd 1959–61; numerous tours and live appearances, TV and film appearances; solo artist 1989–; four Grammy Awards, American Music Awards 1984, 1988. *Film and TV appearances include:* Pipe Dreams 1976, Charlie & Co. (series) 1985, Desperado (TV film) 1987, An Enemy Among Us (TV film) 1987, Twenty Bucks 1993, Hollywood Homicide 2003, Unbeatable Harold 2005. *Recordings include:* albums: Letter Full of Tears 1961, Gladys Knight and The Pips 1964, Everybody Needs Love 1967, Feelin' Bluesy 1968, Silk & Soul 1968, Nitty Gritty 1969, All in a Knight's Work 1970, If I Were Your Woman 1971, Standing Ovation 1971, All I Need Is Time 1973, Imagination 1973, Help Me Make It Through The Night 1973, It Hurt Me So Bad 1973, Neither One Of Us 1973, Claudine (OST) 1974, I Feel A Song 1974, Knight Time 1974, 2nd Anniversary 1975, A Little Knight Music 1975, Bless This House 1976, Pipe Dreams 1976, Love Is Always On Your Mind 1977, Still Together 1977, Miss Gladys Knight 1978, The One And Only 1978, Gladys Knight 1979, Memories 1979, About Love 1980, Midnight Train To Georgia 1980, That Special Time of Year 1980, Teen Anguish 1981, Touch 1980, Visions 1983, Life 1985, All Our Love 1988, Christmas Album 1989, Good Woman 1991, Just For You 1994, Many Different Roads 1998, At Last 2000, Christmas Celebrations 2002, The Best Thing That Ever Happened To Me 2003, One Voice 2005, Before Me 2006, Where My Heart Belongs 2014. *Website:* www.gladysknight.com.

KNIGHT, Keith Desmond St. Aubyn, BA, QC; Jamaican lawyer and politician; b. Brompton, St Elizabeth; m.; two c.; ed Howard Univ. and Univ. of Pittsburgh, USA; admitted to Bar, Grays Inn, London, UK 1973, admitted to Inner Bar as QC 1995; entered elective politics 1989, MP for E Cen. St Catherine; Minister of Nat. Security and Justice 1989–2001, of Foreign Affairs and Foreign Trade 2001–06; Council Pres. UN Security Council Meeting concerning Afghanistan 2001; currently Opposition Senator; Co-founder and Sr Partner, Knight, Junor & Samuels, Kingston (law firm) 2006–; Exec. mem. People's Nat. Party; mem. Advocate Asscn, Jamaican Bar Asscn; Founder-Pres. Jamaica Nat. Asscn; fmr Pres. Caribbean Asscn of Students; Order of Jamaica 2014. *Address:* Knight, Junor & Samuels, 3rd Floor, 4 Duke Street, Kingston, Jamaica (office). *Telephone:* 619-2960 (office). *E-mail:* info@kjslaw.com.jm (office). *Website:* www.kjslaw.com.jm (office); www.japarliament.gov.jm (office).

KNIGHT, Malcolm D., MSc, PhD; Canadian economist and academic; *Distinguished Fellow, Centre for International Governance Innovation;* b. Windsor, Ont.; m.; three d.; ed Univ. of Toronto, London School of Econs, UK; teacher of econs, Univ. of Toronto and LSE 1971–75; joined Research Dept, IMF 1975, served successively as economist in Financial Studies Div., Chief of External Adjustment Issues, Asst Dir of Research Dept for Developing Country Studies, Deputy Dir of Middle East Dept, Monetary and Exchange Affairs Dept, European Dept; fmrly COO Bank of Canada, Sr Deputy Gov. 1999–2003, mem. Bd of Dirs; Gen. Man. BIS 2003–08; Vice-Chair. Deutsche Bank Group 2008–12; currently Distinguished Fellow, Centre for International Governance Innovation; Deputy Chair. Canadian Payments Asscn; Academic Visitor, Centre for Labour Econs, LSE 1985–86, now Visiting Prof. of Finance; fmrly Adjunct Prof., Centre for Canadian Studies, Johns Hopkins Univ. School of Advanced Int. Studies, Virginia Polytechnic and State Univ.; mem. Editorial Bd IMF Staff Papers 1987–97; mem. Bd of Dirs Global Risk Inst. in Financial Services, Swiss Re Ltd 2010–14; mem. Bd of Patrons European Asscn for Banking and Financial History, Johns Hopkins Univ. Soc. of Scholars; Trustee, Per Jacobsson Foundation, International Valuation Standards Council, Int. Accounting Standards Cttee Foundation 2003–08; mem. Financial Stability Forum (now the Financial Stability Board) 2003–08; mem. International Advisory Council, Risk Management Inst., Nat. Univ. of Singapore; Hon. Senator, Lindau Nobel Prizewinners Foundation; Dr hc (Trinity Coll., Univ. of Toronto) 2006. *Publications:* numerous publs in fields of macroeconomics, int. finance and banking. *Address:* Centre for International Governance Innovation, 67 Erb Street West, Waterloo, ON N2L 6C2, Canada (office). *Website:* www.cigionline.org (office).

KNIGHT, Sir Peter L., Kt, PhD, FRS, FInstP; British physicist and academic; *Professor Emeritus and Senior Research Investigator, Physics Department, Imperial College London;* ed Univ. of Sussex; Research Assoc., Joe Eberly group, Dept of Physics and Astronomy, Univ. of Rochester and at Physics Dept and SLAC, Stanford Univ., USA 1972–74; SRC Research Fellow, Univ. of Sussex 1974–76; Visiting Scientist, Johns Hopkins Univ., USA 1976; Jubilee Research Fellow, Royal Holloway Coll., London 1976–78, SERC Advanced Fellowship 1978–83, transferred to Imperial Coll. London 1978–79, Lecturer, Imperial Coll. London 1983–87, Reader 1987–88, Prof. 1988, now Prof. Emer., fmr mem. Imperial Coll. Man. Bd and Council, Prof. of Quantum Optics, Head of Physics Dept 2001–05, Prin. Faculty of Natural Sciences –2008, Deputy Rector (Research) –2010, Sr Research Investigator, Physics Dept 2010–; Sr Fellow in Residence, Kavli Royal Soc. Int. Centre, Chicheley Hall; Visiting Prof., Univ. of Louvain-la-Neuve; Humboldt Research Award Holder, Univ. of Konstanz; Visiting Scholar, Univ. of Texas, Univ. of Rochester; Pres. Inst. of Physics 2011–13; Past-Pres. Optical Soc. of America (OSA), mem. Bd of Dirs for seven years, Dir OSA Foundation; Co-ordinator SERC Nonlinear Optics Initiative, Past-Chair. EPS Quantum Electronics and Optics Div.; Ed. Journal of Modern Optics 1987–2006, Contemporary Physics; Chair. Defence Scientific Advisory Council, Ministry of Defence –2010, remains a Govt science adviser; Council mem. Science and Tech. Facilities Council –2012; Chief Scientific Adviser, UK Nat. Physical Lab. –2005; Chair. University Research Fellowships Ai Panel 2010–13; mem. Council of Royal Soc. 2005–07, mem. Audit Cttee and Chair. Hooke Cttee responsible for scientific meetings; Fellow, OSA; numerous prizes and awards, including the Thomas Young Medal and Glazebrook Medal of Inst. of Physics, OSA Frederic Ives Medal/Quinn Prize 2008, Royal Medal, Royal Soc. *Publications:* numerous papers in professional journals. *Address:* Quantum Optics and Laser Science Group, Department of Physics, 6M02 Huxley, Huxley Building, Imperial College, South Kensington Campus, London, SW7 2AZ, England (office). *Telephone:* (20) 7594-7727 (office). *E-mail:* p.knight@imperial.ac.uk (office). *Website:* www.lsr.ph.imperial.ac.uk/~plk (office).

KNIGHT, Philip H(ampson), MBA; American business executive; *Chairman Emeritus, Nike Inc.;* b. 24 Feb. 1938, Portland, Ore.; s. of William W. Knight and Lota Hatfield; m. Penelope Parks 1968; two s.; ed Univ. of Oregon, Stanford Univ.; First Lt, US Army 1959–60; certified public accountant, Price Waterhouse and Coopers & Lybrand –1968; Asst Prof. of Business Admin, Portland State Univ. –1968; Co-founder and Pres. Nike Inc., Beaverton, Ore. 1968–83, 1984–90, 2000–04, Chair. 1969–2016, Chair. Emer. 2016–; Dir US-Asian Business Council, Wash.; mem. American Inst. of Certified Public Accountants; Oregon Businessman of the Year 1982. *Leisure interests:* sports, reading, movies. *Address:* Nike Inc., 1 Bowerman Drive, Beaverton, OR 97005, USA (office). *Telephone:* (503) 671-3598 (office). *Fax:* (503) 644-6655 (office). *E-mail:* lisa.mckillips@nike.com (office). *Website:* www.nike.com (office).

KNÍŽÁK, Milan; Czech multimedia artist, writer, gallery director and musician; b. 19 April 1940, Plzeň; s. of Karel Knížák and Emilie Knížáková; m. 1st Soňa Švecová 1967; m., 2nd Jarka Charvátová 1970; m., 3rd Marie Geislerová 1975; ed Acad. of Fine Arts, Charles Univ., Prague; f. Aktual group; prosecuted and imprisoned on numerous occasions 1957–89 mostly for his art activities; in USA (at invitation of Fluxus group of artists) 1968–70; Rector, Acad. of Fine Arts, Prague 1990–97; Dir-Gen. Nat. Gallery Prague 1999–2011; mem. Czech TV Council 2001–03; DAAD Berlin, Barkenhoff Worpswede, Germany, Schloss Bleckede, Germany, Schloss Solitude, Germany, 5th Inter-Triennale Wrocław, Poland; Medal 1st Degree, Ministry for Educ. and Physical Training 1997, ARTeon Award for longlife art activities, Poznan 2002, Medal of Merit 2010, award for contrib. to devt of Czech culture for promoting the ideas for freedom and democracy 2015. *Films:* Concert in Holubin 1971, Stone Ceremony 1972, Material Events 1978, Kill Yourself and Fly 1982. *Albums include:* Broken Music 1979, Destroyed music 1982–83, Obřad hořící mysli (The Rite of a Burning Mind) 1991, Bossanova suita 1991, Navrhuju krysy (I Propose the Rats) 2002, Atentát na kulturu 2003, Aktual 2005, Broken Music 2005, Děti Bolševizmu 2005, Milan Knížák Life, Broken tracks 2008, Chovám v kleci bolševika 2013, Sub Rosa 2015, Necháme svět zvířatům 2017. *Plays:* Also in my Belly Grows a Tree, Heads, Adamits, Puppet play. *Television:* Kill Yourself and Fly (a film about M. Knížák) 1991. *Publications include:* Zeremonien 1971, Action as a Life Style 1986, Neo Knížák 1991, Nový ráj (New Paradise) 1996, Bez důvodu (Without Reason) 1996, Jeden z možných postojů, jak být s umění (One Way to Exist with Art) 1998, Skutečnost, že jsem se narodil, beru jako výzvu (The Fact I was Born I Take as a Challenge) 1999, Tady ve Skotsku (Here in Scotland) (with J. Lancaster) 2000, Básně 1974–2001 (Poems 1974–2001) 2001, Vedle umění (Close to the Arts) 2002, Dreams of Architecture 2012, Fashion is a Message 2014 and many others. *Leisure interests:* collecting old marionettes and scientific research on them. *Address:* Rasinovo nabrezi 1980/70, 120 00 Prague 2, Czech Republic (office); Galerie Milan Knizak, Dlouha 25, 110 00 Prague 1, Czech Republic (office). *Telephone:* (602) 321208 (office); (602) 389606 (home). *E-mail:* marie.knizakova@seznam.cz (office); hana.sauerova@centrum.cz (home). *Website:* www.milanknizak.com.

KNOBLOCH, Bernd, BBA, LLB; German business executive; b. 20 Nov. 1951, Munich; ed Ludwig-Maximilians-Universität, Munich; admitted to German Bar 1979; Man. Partner ABG Allgemeine Bautraegergesellschaft, Munich 1977–91; mem. Bd of Man. Dirs Eurohypo AG 1992–, Deputy Chair. of Man. Bd, Eurohypo AG (cr. following merger of Deutsche Hypo AG, Rheinhypo AG and Eurohypo AG 2002) 2002–04, Chair. of Man. Bd 2004–08; mem. Bd of Man. Dirs Commerzbank AG 2006–08; mem. Supervisory Bd, Hypo Real Estate Holding AG 2008–09; Dir (non-Exec.) Palatium Investment Man. Ltd 2005–; Partner and Chair. Continuum Capital GmbH & Co. KG 2009–; mem. Städel Admin, Frankfurt 2005; mem. Bd, Gemeinnuetzige Hertie-Stiftung 2006– (Chair. Man. Bd 2012–), Citycon 2012– (Deputy Chair. 2013–), Citycon, Helsinki 2012–; Pres. Bd of Trustees Friends of the Johann Wolfgang Goethe Univ., Frankfurt; mem. Supervisory Bd, BWK GmbH Unternehmensbeteiligungsgesellschaft 2015–; mem. Bd of Trustees, Schoerghuber Stiftung & Co. Holding 2009–12; mem. Advisory Bd, ULI Germany. *Address:* Opernplatz 6, 60313 Frankfurt, Germany (office). *Telephone:* (69) 77062001 (office). *Fax:* (69) 77062015 (office). *E-mail:* bernd.knobloch@palatium.com (office).

KNOLL, Wolfgang, PhD; German scientist and academic; *Scientific Managing Director, Austrian Institute of Technology;* b. 1949, Schwäbisch Hall; ed Tech. Univ. of Karlsruhe, Univ. of Konstanz; Postdoctoral Fellow, Univ. of Konstanz 1976–77, Univ. of Ulm 1977–80, Fellow, IBM Research Lab., San José, Calif., USA 1980–81; Visiting Scientist, Institut Laue-Langevin, Grenoble, France 1981; Asst Prof., Tech. Univ. of Munich 1981–86; Visiting Scientist, IBM Research Lab., San José, Calif. 1985; received Habilitation from Tech. Univ. of Munich 1986; Young Investigator/Assoc. Prof., Max Planck Inst. for Polymer Research, Mainz 1986–91, Dir 1993–2008; Visiting Scientist, Optical Sciences Center, Tucson, Ariz., USA 1988, Dept of Chem. and Nuclear Eng, Univ. of California, Santa Barbara 1990; Visiting Prof., Univ. of Erlangen 1990–91; Head of Lab. for Exotic Nano-Materials, Frontier Research Program, RIKEN Inst., Japan 1991–99; Consulting Prof., Dept of Chemical Eng, Stanford Univ., Calif. 1992–; Prof. (by Courtesy), Chem. Dept, Univ. of Florida, Gainesville 1998–; Adjunct Prof., Hanyang Univ., S Korea 1999–; Temasek Prof., Nat. Univ. of Singapore 1999–2003; Visiting Prin. Scientist, Inst. of

Materials Research and Eng, Singapore 2004–; Scientific Man. Dir AIT Austrian Inst. of Tech., Vienna 2008–; mem. Exec. Cttee Biomaterials Interfaces Group implementing biofunctional surface science into the AVS Teaching courses at Stanford Univ., Univ. of Leuwen, Belgium, Hanyang Univ., S Korea, Univ. of Florida, Gainesville, Nat. Univ. of Singapore, Univ. of Venice, Italy, Univ. of Mainz, Germany; mem. editorial bds of several int. journals; has organized several int. confs on biointerfaces and nanotechnology; Corresp. mem. Austrian Acad. of Sciences 1999; Hon. Prof., Univ. of Natural Resources and Applied Life Sciences, Vienna 2009–; Dr hc (Univ. of Twente) 2011; Heisenbergstipendium, Deutsche Forschungsgemeinschaft 1986, Merck Centennial Lecturer, Univ. of Iowa, Ames 1988, Heinrich Welker Award, Siemens/Univ. of Erlangen 1990, Eugen and Ilse Seibold Prize, Deutsche Forschungsgemeinschaft 2003, Wilhelm Exner Medal, Austrian Asscn for SME (Oesterreichischer Gewerbeverein—OGV) (jtly) 2008. *Publications:* numerous papers in professional journals on aspects of the structure/order-property/function relationships of polymeric/organic systems, in particular, in thin films and at functionalized surfaces. *Address:* AIT Austrian Institute of Technology GmbH, Donau-City-Straße 1, 1220 Vienna, Austria (office). *Telephone:* (505) 50-0 (office). *E-mail:* office@ait.ac.at (office). *Website:* www.ait.ac.at (office).

KNOPFLER, Mark, OBE, BA; British musician (guitar), singer, songwriter and record producer; b. 12 Aug. 1949, Glasgow, Scotland; s. of Erwin Knopfler and Louisa Knopfler; brother of David Knopfler; m. Lourdes Salomone 1983; two s.; ed Leeds Univ.; fmr music journalist Yorkshire Evening Post; fmr mem. bands, Brewer's Droop, Cafe Racers; f. mem., Dire Straits 1977–88, 1991–95; group toured world-wide; first-ever CD single, Brothers In Arms 1985; formed own ad hoc band, Notting Hillbillies 1989; solo artist 1984–, guest on numerous albums by other artists; Hon. DMus (Newcastle) 1993, (Leeds) 1995, (Sunderland) 2007; BPI/BRIT Awards for Best British Group 1983, 1986, Ivor Novello Awards for Outstanding British Lyric 1983, Best Film Theme 1984, Outstanding Contribution to British Music 1989, Lifetime Achievement Award 2012, Nordoff-Robbins Silver Clef Award for Outstanding Services to British Music 1985, Grammy Awards for Best Rock Vocal Group 1986, for Best Country Performance (with Chet Atkins) 1986, 1991, for Best Surround Sound Album (for Brothers in Arms) 2006, Edison Award 2003, Music Producers Guild Award for Best Studio (British Grove Studios) 2009. *Film music composition:* Local Hero 1983, Cal 1984, Comfort and Joy 1984, Alchemy Live (television) 1984, The Princess Bride 1987, Last Exit to Brooklyn 1989, Tishina 1991, Wag the Dog 1998, Hooves of Fire (television) 1999, Metroland 1999, A Shot at Glory 2001, songs for numerous other films. *Recordings include:* albums: with Dire Straits: Dire Straits 1978, Communiqué 1979, Making Movies 1980, Love Over Gold 1982, Extendedanceplay 1983, Alchemy: Dire Straits Live 1984, Brothers In Arms (BPI Award for Best British Album 1987) 1985, Money For Nothing 1988, On Every Street 1991, On The Night 1993, Live at the BBC 1995, Sultans of Swing 1998; solo: Comfort and Joy 1984, Neck and Neck (with Chet Atkins) 1990, Golden Heart 1996, Sailing To Philadelphia 2000, The Ragpicker's Dream 2002, Shangri-La 2004, All the Roadrunning (with Emmylou Harris) 2006, Kill to get Crimson 2007, Get Lucky 2009, Privateering 2012, Tracker 2015, Down the Road Wherever 2018; with Notting Hillbillies: Missing... Presumed Having a Good Time 1990. *Address:* c/o Paul Crockford Management, 10 Tottenham Mews, London W1T 4AF, England (office). *E-mail:* help@markknopfler.com. *Website:* www.markknopfler.com.

KNOT, Klaas Henderikus Willem, BEcons, DEcon; Dutch economist and central banker; *President, De Nederlandsche Bank NV;* b. 14 April 1967, Onderdendam; m.; two c.; ed Univ. of Groningen; joined De Nederlandsche Bank NV (DNB, central bank) 1995, becoming Sr Economist 1995–98, Head of Banking and Supervisory Strategies Dept 1999–2002, with Pensions and Insurance Supervisory Authority 2003–04, Dir DNB Supervisory Policy Div. 2004–09, Pres. DNB 2011–, also mem. Governing Council and Gen. Council, European Central Bank; Deputy Treas.-Gen. and Dir of Financial Markets, Ministry of Finance 2009–11; Economist, European Dept, IMF, Washington, DC 1998–99; Prof. of Econs of Central Banking, Univ. of Groningen 2005–; Vice-Chair. Financial Stability Board 2018–; mem. Bd of Dirs BIS; Chair. Koning Willem I Foundation, N.G. Pierson Foundation. *Publications:* numerous articles in leading int. journals in monetary and financial econs. *Address:* Office of the President, De Nederlandsche Bank NV, Westeinde 1, POB 98, 1000 AB Amsterdam, Netherlands (office). *Telephone:* (20) 5249111 (office). *Fax:* (20) 5242500 (office). *E-mail:* info@dnb.nl (office). *Website:* www.dnb.nl (office).

KNOTT, John Frederick, OBE, BMet, PhD, ScD, FRS, FREng, FRSA; British materials scientist and academic; *Professor of Metallurgy and Materials, University of Birmingham;* b. 9 Dec. 1938; ed Univs of Sheffield and Cambridge; Feeney Prof. of Materials and Metallurgy, Univ. of Birmingham, also Head of School of Metallurgy and Materials –1995, Dean 1995, now Prof. of Metallurgy and Materials; Pres. Int. Congress on Fracture 1993–97; Past Pres. Birmingham Metallurgical Asscn; Ed. Materials Science and Technology 2003–; mem. Governing Body and Fellow, Churchill Coll., Cambridge; Fellow, Royal Acad. of Eng 1988, Inst. of Materials, Welding Inst.; mem. Rolls-Royce Materials, Mfg and Structures Advisory Bd 1989– (Chair. 2000–); mem. Technical Advisory Group on Structural Integrity 1988– (apptd Deputy Chair. 2000, Chair. 2010); mem. TWI Research Bd 1988–, Graphite Technical Advisory Cttee 2003–, Research Programmes Group (Ministry of Defence) 2003–, Defence Nuclear Safety Cttee 2006–; Foreign mem. Acad. of Sciences of Ukraine, Japan Inst. of Metals 2005; Foreign Assoc. Nat. Acad. of Eng 2003; Foreign Fellow, Indian Nat. Acad. of Eng 2006; Hon. Prof., Beijing Univ. of Aeronautics and Astronautics, Xi'an Jiatong Univ., People's Repub. of China; Hon. DEng (Univ. of Glasgow) 2004; Dr hc (Univ. of Sheffield) 2010; Inst. of Metals Lecturer 2005, Robert Franklin Mehl Award 2005, Leverhulme Medal, Royal Soc. 2005, Brooker Medal, Welding Inst. 2008, Platinum Medal of IOM3 2009. *Publications:* numerous scientific articles in professional journals on the quantitative scientific understanding of fracture processes in metals and alloys and its eng applications. *Address:* Department of Metallurgy and Materials, School of Engineering, University of Birmingham, Elms Road, Edgbaston, Birmingham, B15 2TT (office); 5 Mildmay Close, Stratford-upon-Avon, Warwicks., CV37 9FR, England (home). *Telephone:* (121) 414-6729 (office); (1789) 261977 (home). *Fax:* (121) 414-7468 (office). *E-mail:* j.f.knott@bham.ac.uk (office). *Website:* www.eng.bham.ac.uk/metallurgy (office).

KNOWLES, Anthony (Tony) Carroll, BA; American fmr politician; b. 1 Jan. 1943, Tulsa, Okla; m. Susan Morris; two s. one d.; ed Yale Univ.; served in US Army, Viet Nam 1961–65; Owner and Man. of restaurants, The Works, Anchorage 1968, Downtown Deli, Anchorage 1978; Mayor of Anchorage 1981–87; Gov. of Alaska 1994–2002; unsuccessful cand. for US Senate 2004, for Gov. of Alaska 2006; Pres. Nat. Energy Policy Inst. 2008–; mem. Advisory Bd, Nat. Park System 2010–; mem. Citizen's Cttee for Planned Growth and Devt of Anchorage 1972, Borough Ass., Anchorage 1975–79; fmr mem. Bd of Dirs KAKM TV Station, Anchorage Chamber of Commerce; Child Advocate of the Year, American Child Welfare League 1999. *Address:* National Energy Policy Institute, PO Box 14050, Tulsa, OK 74159, USA (office). *Telephone:* (918) 631-6374 (office). *Website:* nepinstitute.org (office).

KNOWLES, Beyoncé (see BEYONCÉ).

KNOWLING, Robert E., Jr, BA, MBA; American computer engineer and business executive; *Chairman, Eagles Landing Partners;* b. 1955, Ind.; m.; four c.; ed Wabash Coll., Kellogg Grad. School of Man., Northwestern Univ.; staff mem. Indiana Bell 1970s, Head of Eng Devt Team, Ameritech 1992, later Vice-Pres. Network Operations; Exec. Vice-Pres. of Operations and Techs US West; Pres. and CEO Covad Communications, Calif. 1998–2001; Chair. and CEO Information Access Technologies Inc. 2001–03; CEO New York Leadership Acad., New York City Bd of Educ. 2003–05; CEO Vercuity Solutions, Inc. (later Telewares, Inc.) 2005–09; Chair. Eagles Landing Partners (strategic man. consulting firm) 2009–; Consultant, Grupo Salinas 2009–11; mem. Bd of Dirs, Ariba, Inc. 1999–2012, Heidrick & Struggles Int. 1998–2015, Hewlett-Packard 1999–2005, Bartech Group 2007–, Roper Industries, Inc. 2008–; mem. Advisory Bd, Ontologent, Inc., Northwestern Univ. Kellogg Grad. School of Man., Univ. of Mich. Grad. School of Business; Reginald Lewis Trailblazers Award, Wall Street Project 1999. *Leisure interest:* YMCA volunteer. *Address:* c/o Board of Directors, Ariba, Inc., 807 11th Avenue, Sunnyvale, CA 94089, USA. *E-mail:* eagleslandingpartners@gmail.com.

KNOX, Selby Albert Richard, PhD, DSc; British chemist and academic (retd); b. 24 Sept. 1944, Newcastle upon Tyne, England; s. of George H. Knox and Elsie Knox; m. Julie D. Edwards 1979; one s. two d.; ed Rutherford Grammar School, Newcastle-upon-Tyne and Univ. of Bristol; Research Fellow, UCLA 1970–71; Lecturer, Univ. of Bristol 1972–83, Reader 1983–90, Prof. of Inorganic Chem. 1990–96, Head, Dept of Chem. 1992–2001, Head, Inorganic and Materials Chem. 2001–04, Alfred Capper Pass Prof. of Chem. 1996–2004, Pro-Vice-Chancellor 2004–08; Corday-Morgan Medal and Prize 1980, RSC Award for Chem. of Noble Metals and Their Compounds 1986, RSC Tilden Lecturer 1992–93. *Publications:* more than 160 scientific papers on organometallic chem. *Leisure interests:* fly fishing, sailing, skiing, golf.

KNUDSEN, Eric Ingvald, BA, MA, PhD; American neuroscientist and academic; *Professor of Neurobiology, School of Medicine, Stanford University;* ed Univ. of California, Santa Barbara, George August Univ., Göttingen, Germany, Woods Hole Marine Biological Lab., Univ. of California, San Diego; Postdoctoral Research Fellow, California Inst. of Tech. 1976–79; Asst Prof., Dept of Neurobiology, Stanford Univ. School of Medicine 1979–85, Assoc. Prof. 1985–88, Prof. 1988–, Assoc. Chair. Dept of Neurobiology 1997–2000, Chair. 2001–05, Chair. Stanford Medical Student Scholars Program 1986–90, mem. Cttee on Courses and Curriculum 1994–96, mem. School of Medicine Appointments and Promotions Cttee 1995–98, Dir Neurosciences Grad. Program 1998–2000, mem. Research Planning Cttee Medical School Strategic Planning 2001–02, Exec. Cttee Neuroscience Inst. 2001–; Assoc. Ed. Journal of Neuroscience 1986–88, Journal of Neurophysiology 1986–89; mem. Editorial Cttee Annual Review of Neuroscience 1988–92; Co-organizer Int. Meeting: Advances in Auditory Neuroscience, San Francisco; mem. Satellite of the IUPS 1986, NSF Advisory Panel: Sensory Physiology and Perception 1986; Councillor, Int. Soc. for Neuroethology 2002–06; mem. Core research network on early experience and brain development, MacArthur Foundation 2002–05, Nat. Scientific Council on the Developing Child 2003–09; Chair. Neurosciences Grad. Admissions Cttee 2009–, Neuroscience Grad. Program Cttee 2010–; mem. NAS 2002; Fellow, American Acad. of Arts and Sciences 1996; AAAS Newcomb Cleveland Prize 1978, Young Investigator Award, Soc. for Neuroscience 1984, NAS Troland Research Award 1988, Claude Pepper Award, Nat. Inst. of Deafness and Communicative Disorders 1991, Edward C. and Amy H. Sewall Professorship, Stanford Univ. School of Medicine 1995, Givaudan-Roure Award, Asscn for Chemoreception Sciences 1996, W. Alden Spencer Award, Coll. of Physicians and Surgeons, Columbia Univ. 2002, Kuffler Lecturer, Harvard Medical School 2004, Gruber Neuroscience Prize, The Peter and Patricia Gruber Foundation 2005, Karl Spencer Lashley Award, American Philosophical Soc. 2008. *Publications:* more than 70 scientific papers, book chapters and reviews on the mechanisms of attention, learning and strategies of information processing in the central auditory system of developing and adult barn owls, using neurophysiological, pharmacological, anatomical and behavioural techniques. *Address:* Department of Neurobiology, Stanford University School of Medicine, 299 Campus Drive, Stanford, CA 94305, USA (office). *Telephone:* (650) 723-5492 (office). *E-mail:* eknudsen@stanford.edu (office). *Website:* med.stanford.edu/profiles/Eric_Knudsen (office).

KNUTH, Donald Ervin, MS, PhD; American computer scientist and author; *Professor Emeritus of The Art of Computer Programming, Stanford University;* b. 10 Jan. 1938, Milwaukee, Wis.; s. of Ervin Henry Knuth and Louise Marie Knuth (née Bohning); m. Nancy Jill Carter 1961; one s. one d.; ed Case Inst. of Tech., California Inst. of Tech.; Asst Prof. of Math., Calif. Inst. of Tech. 1963–66, Assoc. Prof. 1966–68; Prof. of Computer Science, Stanford Univ. 1968–77, Fletcher Jones Prof. of Computer Science 1977–89, Prof. of The Art of Computer Programming 1990–93, Prof. Emer. 1993–; mem. American Acad. of Arts and Sciences, NAS, Nat. Acad. of Eng, American Philosophical Soc.; Foreign mem. French, Norwegian, Bavarian, Russian Science Acads, Royal Soc. of London; 34 hon. degrees, including Paris 1986, Oxford 1988, St Petersburg 1992, Harvard 2003; Nat. Medal of Science 1979, Steele Prize, American Math. Soc. 1986, Franklin Medal, Franklin Inst. of Philadelphia 1988, Harvey Prize, Israel Inst. of Tech. 1995, John Von Neumann Medal, IEEE 1995, Kyoto Prize 1996, BBVA Award 2011 and numerous other awards. *Publications:* The Art of Computer Programming (Vol. 1) 1968, (Vol. 2) 1969, (Vol. 3) 1973, (Vol. 4A) 2011, Surreal Numbers 1974, Mariages Stables 1976, Computers and Typesetting (five Vols) 1986, Concrete Mathematics 1988, 3:16

Bible Texts Illuminated 1990, Literate Programming 1992, The Stanford GraphBase 1993, Selected Papers on Computer Science 1996, Digital Typography 1999, MMIXware 1999, Selected Papers on Analysis of Algorithms 2000, Things a Computer Scientist Rarely Talks About 2001, Selected Papers on Computer Languages 2003, Selected Papers on Discrete Mathematics 2003, Selected Papers on Design of Algorithms 2010, Selected Papers on Fun and Games 2011, Companion to the Papers of Donald Knuth 2011. *Leisure interests:* piano and organ playing, browsing in libraries. *Address:* Computer Science Department, Gates 477, Stanford University, Stanford, CA 94305, USA (office). *Telephone:* (650) 723-4367 (office). *Website:* www-cs-faculty.stanford.edu/~knuth (office).

KO, Un; South Korean novelist, essayist, critic and poet; *Poet-in-Residence and Professor, Dankook University;* b. (Ko Un-Tae), 10 April 1933, Kunsan; s. of Ko Geun-Shik and Choi Jeom-Rye; m. Lee Sang-wha 1983; one d.; teacher of Korean language and art, Kunsan Middle School 1950; served as Buddhist monk 1952–62; Sec.-Gen. Asscn of Writers for Practical Freedom 1974; arrested many times for political activities and served several prison terms; Resident Prof., Grad. School, Kyonggi Univ., Seoul 1994–98, Poet-in-Residence and Prof., Dankook Univ. 2008–; Pres. Asscn of Korean Artists 1989–90, Asscn of Writers for Nat. Literature 1992–94, Co-Pres. Nat. Trust of Korea 2000; Chair. South and North Korea Writers' Conf. 2004; Visiting Research Scholar, Yenching Inst., Harvard Univ., USA 1999, Visiting Prof., Univ. of California, Berkeley; Silver Order of Merit in Culture 2002, Bjornson Order for Literature (Norway) 2005; Dr hc (Dankook Univ.) 2010; Korean Literature Prize 1974, 1987, Manhae Prize in Literature 1989, Joong-Ang Prize for Literature 1991, Daesan Prize for Literature 1994, Manhae Grand Prize 1998, Buddhist Literature Prize 1999, Danjae Prize 2004, Unification Award 2005, Cikada Prize (Sweden) 2006, Young-Rang Poetry Award 2007, Yusim Literature Prize 2008, Lifetime Achievement Award, Griffin Fund for Excellence in Poetry (Canada) 2008, Korea Acad. of Arts Award 2008, Golden Wreath Award, Struga Poetry Evenings 2014. *Publications include:* Maninbo (Ten Thousand Lives) (poetry) 30 vols., has written numerous books of poetry, novels, non-fiction, literary criticism, travel books, biographies, translation; I, Ko Un (autobiography, three vols.) 1993, My Bronze Period (autobiography) 1995. *Address:* 173 Changmikol, Daerimdongsan Ansong, Kyonggi-do, 456–820, Republic of Korea. *Telephone:* (31) 618-1783. *Fax:* (31) 618-1781. *E-mail:* koun_poet@yahoo.co.kr. *Website:* www.koun.co.kr.

KOBAKHIDZE, Irakli, LLM, PhD; Georgian academic and politician; *Chairman, Sakartvelos Parlamenti (Georgian Parliament);* b. 25 Sept. 1978; ed Tbilisi State Univ., Inst. of State and Law of Acad. of Sciences of Georgia, Univ. of Düsseldorf, Germany; Regional Co-ordinator, USAID Public Educ. Project 2000–01; Asst Prof., then Assoc. Prof., Tbilisi State Univ. 2005–; UNDP Project Expert and Project Man. 2006–14; Assoc. Prof., Caucasus Univ. 2011–14; involved as an expert in strategic planning issues in Council of Europe Office in Georgia; fmr mem. Cttee of Experts for Human Rights and the Rule of Law Programme, Open Society–Georgia Foundation; mem. Qartuli Ocneba-Demokratiuli Sakartvelo (Georgian Dream-Democratic Georgia) 2015–, later Exec. Sec.; mem. Sakartvelos Parlamenti (Georgian Parl.) 2016–, Chair. 2016–, mem. Parl. Standing Council on Open and Transparent Govt 2017–, Head of Parl. Del. to Inter-Parl. Union 2016–; Chair. State Constitutional Comm. 2016–, Steering Comm. on NATO PA 2017–. *Address:* Room C-601, Office of the Chairman, Sakartvelos Parlamenti, 4600 Kutaisi, Abashidze 26, Georgia (office). *Telephone:* (32) 228-90-06 (office). *Fax:* (32) 299-93-86 (office). *E-mail:* ikobakhidze@parliament.ge (office). *Website:* www.parliament.ge (office).

KOBALIA, Vera; Georgian politician; *Adviser, International Business, Australia Indonesia Partnership for Economic Governance;* b. 24 Aug. 1981, Sokhumi, Abkhazia; d. of Otari Kobalia; ed King George's High School, Vancouver and British Columbia Inst. of Tech., Canada; emigrated with family to Canada 1996; Researcher, Canadian Soc. for Int. Health, Ottawa 2001–02; Producer, Global TV–Destination Funny Entertainment 2004–06; Marketing and Sales Man., Boston International 2007–08; Partner, European Breads Bakery, Vancouver 2008–10; returned to Georgia to work for Coalition for Justice (non-govt org. assisting displaced people) 2010; Minister of the Economy and Sustainable Devt 2010–12; Adviser to Pres. of Georgia 2012–13; Young Global Leader, World Econ. Forum 2012–; Managing Dir Kobalia Consulting 2013–; Adviser, Int. Business, Australia Indonesia Partnership for Econ. Governance (AIPEG) 2016–. *Address:* Australia Indonesia Partnership for Economic Governance, PO Box 8305, Metropolitan WTC, Jakarta 12083, Indonesia (office). *Telephone:* (21) 52907290 (office). *Fax:* (21) 52900143 (office). *E-mail:* info@aipeg.or.id (office). *Website:* aipeg.or.id (office).

KOBAYASHI, Akiko, PhD; Japanese chemist and academic; *Professor Emeritus, University of Tokyo;* b. 1943, Tokyo; ed Univ. of Tokyo; Research Assoc., Univ. of Tokyo 1972–93, Assoc. Prof., Dept of Chem. 1993–99, apptd Prof., Research Centre for Spectrochemistry, Grad. School of Science 1999, now Prof. Emer.; currently Prof. at Nihon Univ.; Crystallographic Society of Japan Award 1998, Complex Chemical Society Award 2006, L'ORÉAL-UNESCO Award for Women in Science (Asia-Pacific) 2009. *Achievements include:* first person to design and create single-component molecular metals. *Publications:* numerous papers in professional journals. *Address:* Research Centre for Spectrochemistry, Graduate School of Science, University of Tokyo, Hongo 7-3-1, Bunkyo-ku, Tokyo 113-0033, Japan (office). *Telephone:* (3) 5841-4417 (office). *Fax:* (3) 5841-4417 (office). *Website:* www.chem.s.u-tokyo.ac.jp (office).

KOBAYASHI, Eizo; Japanese business executive; joined ITOCHU Corpn 1972, various sr positions, including mem. Exec. Bd 2000, COO of Information Tech. and Telecommunications Div. 2001–02, Man. Dir and Chief Information Officer 2002–03, Sr Man. Dir 2003–04, Pres. and CEO 2004–10, Chair. 2010–16; Vice-Chair. Japan Foreign Council Inc.; Exec. Dir Bank of Japan 2004–. *Address:* c/o ITOCHU Corporation, 5-1 Kita-Aoyama 2-chome, Minato-ku, Tokyo 107-8077, Japan. *E-mail:* info@itochu.co.jp.

KOBAYASHI, Izumi; Japanese banking executive and international organization official; ed Seikei Univ.; joined Merrill Lynch Japan, Tokyo 1985, held several global exec. roles, Pres. and Rep. Dir Merrill Lynch Japan –2008, also served as Dir of Operations and Chief Admin. Officer; Exec. Vice-Pres. Multilateral Investment Guarantee Agency (MIGA), World Bank Group, New York, USA 2008–13; mem. Bd of Dirs ANA Holdings Inc, Suntory Holdings Limited, Mitsui & Co., Ltd; mem. Bd of Dirs Keizai Doyukai (Japanese Asscn of Corp. Execs); Business Woman of the Year Award, Veuve Clicquot 2004, featured in the Wall Street Journal's '50 Women to Watch' Oct. 2005. *Address:* ANA Holdings Inc., Shiodome-City Center, 1-5-2, Higashi-Shimbashi, Minato-ku, Tokyo, Japan (office). *Website:* www.anahd.co.jp (office).

KOBAYASHI, Ken; Japanese business executive; *Chairman, Mitsubishi Corporation;* b. 14 Feb. 1949, Tokyo; ed Faculty of Law, Tokyo Univ.; joined Mitsubishi Corpn (Ship Sales Dept), Tokyo 1971–80, Mitsubishi Corpn London Br., UK 1980–85, Ship and Rolling Stock Dept, Tokyo 1985–89, Ship and Industrial Project Dept 1989–98, Gen. Man. Ship and Industrial Project Dept 1998–2001, Gen. Man. Mitsubishi Corpn Singapore Br. 2001–03, Sr Vice-Pres., Mitsubishi Corpn and Gen. Man. Mitsubishi Corpn Singapore Br. 2003–04, Sr Vice-Pres., Div. COO, Plant Project Div., Tokyo 2004–06, Sr Vice-Pres., Div. COO, Ship, Aerospace and Transportation Systems Div. 2006–07, Exec. Vice-Pres. and Group CEO, Industrial Finance, Logistics and Devt Group April–June 2007, mem. Bd, Exec. Vice-Pres. and Group CEO, Industrial Finance, Logistics and Devt Group June 2007–08, Exec. Vice-Pres. Mitsubishi Corpn 2008–10, Sr Exec. Vice-Pres. April–June 2010, Pres. and CEO 2010–16, Chair. 2016–. *Address:* Mitsubishi Corporation, Mitsubishi Shoji Building, 3-1, Marunouchi 2-chome, Chiyoda-ku, Tokyo 100-8086, Japan (office). *Telephone:* (3) 3210-2121 (office). *Fax:* (3) 3210-8583 (office). *E-mail:* info@mitsubishicorp.com (office). *Website:* www.mitsubishicorp.com (office).

KOBAYASHI, Makoto, PhD; Japanese physicist and academic; *Professor Emeritus, High Energy Accelerator Research Organization (KEK);* b. 7 April 1944, Nagoya; ed Nagoya Univ.; Research Assoc., Kyoto Univ. 1972–79; Asst Prof., Nat. Lab. of High Energy Physics 1979–89, Prof. 1989–97, Head of Physics Div. II 1989–97; Prof., Inst. of Particle and Nuclear Science, High Energy Accelerator Research Org. (KEK) 1997–2006, Prof. Emer. 2006–, Dir Inst. of Particle and Nuclear Science 2003–06; Nishina Memorial Prize 1979, J.J.Sakurai Prize (American Physical Soc.) 1985, Japan Acad. Prize 1985, Asahi Prize 1995, Chunichi Cultural Prize 1995, Person of Cultural Merit Award 2001, Nobel Prize in Physics (jt recipient) 2008. *Address:* High Energy Accelerator Research Organization, 1-1 Oho, Tsukuba, Ibaraki 305-0801, Japan (office). *Website:* www.kek.jp (office).

KOBAYASHI, Shu, PhD; Japanese chemist and academic; *Professor, Graduate School of Pharmaceutical Sciences, University of Tokyo;* ed Univ. of Tokyo; Asst Prof., Science Univ. of Tokyo 1987–91, Lecturer, Dept of Applied Chem., Faculty of Science 1991–92, Assoc. Prof. 1992–98, Special Promoted Researcher 1997; Prof., Grad. School of Pharmaceutical Sciences, Univ. of Tokyo 1998–; Visiting Prof., Université Louis Pasteur, Strasbourg, France 1993, Kyoto Univ. 1995, Nijmegen Univ., Netherlands 1996, Philipps-Universität Marburg, Germany 1997; CREST Investigator, Japan Science and Tech. Agency, 1997–2001, SORST Investigator 2002–04, ERATO Investigator 2003–; Assoc. Ed. Journal of Combinatorial Chemistry 1999–, Advanced Synthesis and Catalysis 2000–; mem. Editorial Advisory Bd Molecules Online 1997–2000, Synthesis 1999–, Chemical Reviews 2000–; Expert Analyst, CHEMTRACTS-Organic Chemistry 1999–; Chemical Soc. of Japan Award for Young Chemists 1991, Teijin Award in Synthetic Organic Chem. 1992, New Chem. Inst. Research Award 1992, Nissan Science Foundation for Younger Generation Award 1993, Ciba-Geigy Research Foundation Award 1994, Kurata Research Foundation Award 1995, first Springer Award in Organometallic Chem. 1997, Bio-Mega/Boehrinder Ingelheim Lecturer 1999, Merck-SFC Lectureship 1999, Wyeth-Ayerst Lectureship 1999, Novartis Chem. Lectureship 2000, MIT/Wyeth-Ayerst Lectureship 2000, Nagoya Lectureship 2000, Roche Lectureship 2001, NPS Distinguished Lecturer 2001, IBM Science Award 2001, Organic Reactions Lecturer 2002, Nagoya Silver Medal 2002, Novo-Nortis Lectureship 2003, Manchester-Merck Lecturer 2004, Mitsui Chemical Catalysis Science Award 2005, JSPS Prize 205, Arthur C. Cope Scholar Award 2006, Howard Memorial Lecturer 2006. *Publications:* numerous articles in scientific journals on devt of new synthetic methods, novel catalysts, organic synthesis in water, solid-phase organic synthesis, total synthesis of biologically interesting compounds and organometallic chem. *Address:* Department of Chemistry, School of Science, University of Tokyo, Hongo, Bunkyo-ku, Tokyo 113-0033, Japan (office). *Telephone:* (3) 5841-4790 (office). *Fax:* (3) 5684-0634 (office). *E-mail:* admin@tokyo.jst.go.jp (office). *Website:* www.jst.go.jp/EN (office); utsc2.chem.s.u-tokyo.ac.jp (office).

KOBAYASHI, Takashi; Japanese particle physicist and academic; currently Assoc. Prof., Neutrino Group, 4th Physics Div., Inst. for Particle and Nuclear Studies, High Energy Accelerator Research Org. (KEK), Tsukuba; Spokesman, T2K collaboration. *Publications:* numerous articles in scientific journals on neutrino physics. *Address:* The 4th Physics Division, Institute for Particle and Nuclear Studies, High Energy Accelerator Research Organization (KEK), 1-1 Oho, Tsukuba 305-0801, Japan (office). *Telephone:* (29) 864-5414 (office). *Fax:* (29) 864-7831 (office). *E-mail:* takashi.kobayashi@kek.jp (office). *Website:* jnusrv01.kek.jp/~kobayasi (office).

KOBAYASHI, Yoshimitsu, MSc, PhD; Japanese business executive; *Representative Director, President and CEO, Mitsubishi Chemical Holdings Corporation;* b. 18 Nov. 1946, Yamanashi; ed Univ. of Tokyo, Hebrew Univ., Jerusalem; joined Mitsubishi Chemical Industry Ltd (later Mitsubishi Chemical Corpn), Tokyo 1974, Gen. Man. Information Storage Products Dept, Pres. Mitsubishi Kagaku Media 1996, CEO 2001–03, Exec. Officer, Chief Tech. Officer and Man. Exec. Officer, Mitsubishi Chemical Corpn, Man. Exec. Officer and Chief Tech. Officer –2007, Rep. Dir, Pres. and CEO 2007, Chair. 2012–17, Pres. Mitsubishi Chemical Group Science and Tech. Research Center Inc. 2005–06, mem. Bd Dirs and Rep. Dir, Mitsubishi Chemical Holdings Corpn 2006, Pres. and CEO 2007, Chair. 2015–Chair. Mitsubishi Kagaku Inst. of Life Sciences 2006, Rep. Dir, Pres. and CEO 2007–; CEO The Kaiteki Inst., Inc. 2009, mem. Bd Dirs and Chair. 2015. *Address:* Mitsubishi Chemical Holdings Corporation, 14-1 Shiba 4-chome, Minato-ku, Tokyo 108-0014, Japan (office). *Telephone:* (3) 6414-4870 (office). *Fax:* (3) 6414-3745 (office). *E-mail:* info@mitsubishichem-hd.co.jp (office). *Website:* www.mitsubishichem-hd.co.jp (office).

KÖBBEN, André J. F., PhD; Dutch professor of cultural anthropology and administrator; b. 3 April 1925, 's-Hertogenbosch; m. Agatha H. van Vessem 1953;

one s. two d.; ed Municipal Gymnasium and Univ. of Amsterdam; Prof. of Cultural Anthropology, Univ. of Amsterdam 1955–76; Visiting Prof., Univ. of Pittsburgh 1972; Cleveringa Prof., Univ. of Leiden 1980–81; Prof., Erasmus Univ. 1981–90; Dir Centre for the Study of Social Conflicts 1976–90; Curl Bequest Prize, Royal Anthropological Inst. 1952; mem. Royal Netherlands Acad. of Science 1975; Hon. mem. Anthropological Soc. 1986. *Publications include:* Le Planteur noir 1956, Van primitieven tot medeburgers 1964, Why exceptions? The logic of cross-cultural analysis 1967, Why Slavery? 1997, De Onwelkome Boodschap (The Unwelcome Message) 1999, Goldhagen Versus Browning 2002, Het Gevecht met de Engel (The Struggle with the Angel) 2003, De tijdgeest en andere ongemakken (The Spirit of the Age and other inconveniences) 2008, and numerous others. *Address:* Libellenveld 2, 2318 VG Leiden, Netherlands. *Telephone:* (71) 5215369 (home). *E-mail:* ajfkobben@planet.nl.

KOBEH GONZÁLEZ, Roberto; Mexican engineer, public servant and international organization official; ed Nat. Polytechnic Inst. of Mexico; fmr Prof. of Aeronautical Electronics, Nat. Polytechnic Inst.; 40 years of experience as public servant in Mexican Govt, occupying various posts in Civil Aeronautics Directorate, including Deputy Dir-Gen. for Admin and Air Transport, Dir-Gen. Air Navigation Services of Mexico (SENEAM) 1978–97; Rep. of Mexico on Council of ICAO, serving as First Vice-Pres., Chair. Finance Cttee, and as mem. Air Transport and Unlawful Interference Cttees 1998–2006, Pres. ICAO Council 2006–13 (retd); Emilio Carranza Medal, Award for Extraordinary Service, Fed. Aviation Admin (USA), honoured by Cen. American Corpn of Aerial Navigation Services for his contrib. to devt of aviation in Cen. America.

KOBIA, Rev. Samuel, MA, DD; Kenyan ecclesiastic and international organization official; b. 20 March 1947, Miathene, Meru; m. Ruth Kobia; two d. two s.; ed St Paul's United Theological Coll., Nairobi, McCormick Theological Seminary, Indianapolis, Ind., Christian Theological Seminary, Massachusetts Inst. of Tech., USA; ordained minister in Methodist Church, Kenya; Exec. Sec. for Urban Rural Mission, WCC 1978–84, Chair. Frontier Internship in Mission, Int. Coordination Cttee 1981–85, Vice-Moderator Comm. to Combat Racism 1984–91, Exec. Dir Justice, Peace and Creation Unit 1993–99, Dir Cluster on Issues and Themes 1999–2002, Dir and Special Rep. for Africa 2002–04, Gen. Sec. WCC 2004–10 (resgnd); Dir Church Devt Activities, Nat. Council of Churches Kenya (NCCK), 1984–87, Gen. Sec. NCCK 1987–93; helped est. Zimbabwe Christian Council 1980–81; Co-founder Nairobi Peace Group 1987, Fellowship of Councils of Churches in E and S Africa (FOCCESA) 1991; Chair. Peace Talks for Sudan 1991; Chair. Kenya Nat. Election Monitoring Unit 1992; Fellow, Centre for the Values in Public Life, Divinity School, Harvard Univ., USA 2000; Chancellor St Paul's Univ., Limuru, Kenya 2007–; currently Sr Advisor to Pres. Uhuru Kenyatta on matters of peace, cohesion, and conflict resolution; Hon. Prof., Univ. of Buenos Aires, Argentina 2004; Nat. Ecumenical Award (Kenya) 2007. *Publications include:* Origins of Squatting and Community Organization in Nairobi 1985, Together in Hope 1990, The Quest for Democracy in Africa 1993, The Courage to Hope 2003.

KOBIERACKI, Adam; Polish diplomatist; *Director, Conflict Prevention Centre, Organization for Security and Co-operation in Europe;* b. 1 June 1957, Warsaw; m.; two c.; ed Warsaw Univ., Faculty of Journalism and Political Sciences, Moscow State Inst. of Int. Relations, USSR; served in Polish Ministry of Foreign Affairs 1982–2003, Dept of Studies and Programming (security and arms control issues) 1982–89, expert in Polish Mission to the UN, Vienna 1985–86, mem. Polish Del. to the Mutual and Balanced Force Reductions Talks, Vienna 1986, to the CSCE Vienna Follow-up Meeting and Conventional Forces in Europe (CFE) Mandate Talks 1986–87, mem. and Deputy Head of Polish Del. to the CFE negotiation in Vienna 1989–90, with Dept of European Insts 1989–91, in Polish Mission to the UN (and IAEA) and the OSCE in Vienna, Counsellor and Deputy Head 1993–96, Minister Counsellor and Deputy Head of Mission and of Polish Del. to the Jt Consultative Group 1996–97, Amb. and Head of the Perm. Mission of Poland to the IAEA, UN Office and the Int. Orgs in Vienna, Head of the Mission of Poland to OSCE, Head of the Polish Del. to the Jt Consultative Group (CFE Treaty) 1997–2000, Dir Dept for European Security Policy, Ministry of Foreign Affairs 2000–01, Dir Security Policy Dept 2001–03; Asst Sec.-Gen. for Operations, NATO, Brussels 2003–07; Dir Conflict Prevention Centre, OSCE 2011–; Chief Polish negotiator at CFE adaptation talks, Vienna 1997–99; Chair. Working Group at, and Deputy Head of the Polish Del. to, the First CFE Treaty Review Conf., Vienna May 1996; Head of Polish Del. to Second CFE Treaty Review Conf., Vienna May 2001. *Publications:* contrib. to: Miedzy równowaga sil a bezpieczenstwem kooperatywnym w Europie (adaptacja rezimu CFE do nowego srodowiska miedzynarodowego) (Between the Balance of Power and Co-operative Security in Europe – The Adaptation of the CFE Regime to New International Environment) (Z. Lachowski and J. M. Nowak) 1999, Polska polityka bezpieczenstwa 1989–2000 (co-ed. R. Kuzniar) 2001, WN Scholar (Polish Security Policy 1989–2000). *Address:* Conflict Prevention Centre, OSCE Secretariat, Wallnerstrasse 6, 1010 Vienna, Austria (office). *Telephone:* (1) 514-36-6122 (office). *Fax:* (1) 514-36-6996 (office). *E-mail:* pm-cpc@osce.org (office). *Website:* www.osce.org (office).

KOBILKA, Brian Kent, MD; American molecular biologist and academic; *Professor and Chair of Molecular and Cellular Physiology, School of Medicine, Stanford University;* b. 30 May 1955, Little Falls, Minn.; s. of Franklyn A. Kobilka and Betty L. Kobilka (née Faust); m. Tong Sun Thian; two c.; ed Univ. of Minnesota-Duluth, Yale Univ.; Postdoctoral Research Fellow, Lefkowitz Lab., Duke Univ. 1984–89, Asst Prof., Duke Univ. School of Medicine 1988–89; Howard Hughes Medical Inst. Investigator 1987–2003; joined Dept of Molecular and Cellular Physiology, Stanford Univ. School of Medicine 1989, Prof. of Molecular and Cellular Physiology 2000–, also Chair of Molecular and Cellular Physiology and Helene Irwin Fagan Chair in Cardiology; Co-founder ConfometRx (biotechnology co.); mem. NAS 2011; American Soc. for Pharmacology and Experimental Therapeutics John J. Abel Award in Pharmacology 1994, Nobel Prize in Chem. (jtly with Robert Lefkowitz) 2012. *Publications include:* more than 140 publs. *Address:* Department of Molecular and Cellular Physiology and Medicine, 157 Beckman Center, 279 Campus Drive, Stanford, CA 94305-5345, USA (office). *Telephone:* (650) 723-7069 (office). *Fax:* (650) 498 5092 (office). *E-mail:* kobilka@stanford.edu (office). *Website:* med.stanford.edu/profiles/Brian_Kobilka (office); med.stanford.edu/kobilkalab/brian.html (office).

KOBLER, Martin; German diplomatist and UN official; *Ambassador to Pakistan;* b. 1953, Stuttgart; m.; three c.; ed Univ. of Bonn, Pajajaran Univ., Indonesia; served as legal practitioner 1980–83; entered foreign service 1983, Deputy Head, Balkan Task Force, Foreign Ministry 1997–98; Chief of Cabinet to fmr German Foreign Minister Joschka Fischer 2000–03, fmr Dir-Gen. for Culture and Communication, Ministry of Foreign Affairs; fmr Amb. to Egypt and Iraq 2003–07; Electoral Observer with UN missions in Haiti, Nicaragua and Cambodia, Deputy Special Rep. (Political) for Afghanistan 2010–11, Special Rep. of UN Sec.-Gen. for Iraq and Head, UN Assistance Mission for Iraq (UNAMI) 2011–13, Special Rep. of UN Sec.-Gen. for Democratic Repub. of Congo (DRC) and Head, UN Stabilization Mission in DRC (MONUSCO) 2013–15, Special Rep. of UN Sec.-Gen. and Head of UN Support Mission in Libya (UNSMIL) 2015–17, Amb. to Pakistan 2017–. *Address:* German Embassy, Diplomatic Enclave, Ramna 5, PO Box 1027, Islamabad 44000, Pakistan (office). *Telephone:* (51) 2279430 (office). *Fax:* (51) 2279436 (office). *Website:* www.pakistan.diplo.de (office).

KOBULIA, Giorgi, MD, MBA; Georgian politician; *Minister of Economy and Sustainable Development;* b. 3 Jan. 1970, Tbilisi, Georgian SSR, USSR; ed Tbilisi State Medical Inst., Emory Univ., USA; Cardiologist, Tbilisi Scientific Inst. of Cardiology 1994–96; Scientific Assoc., Merck, Sharp & Dohme, Georgia 1996–99; joined McKinsey & Co. as Consultant 2001, becoming Chief Partner, McKinsey Moscow –2018; Minister of Economy and Sustainable Devt 2018–. *Address:* Ministry of Economy and Sustainable Development, 0108 Tbilisi, Sanapiro 2, Georgia (office). *Telephone:* (32) 299-11-11 (office). *E-mail:* ministry@economy.ge (office). *Website:* www.economy.ge (office).

KOÇ, Rahmi M., BA; Turkish business executive; *Honorary Chairman, Koç Holding AŞ;* b. 1930, Ankara; divorced; three s.; ed Johns Hopkins Univ., USA; joined family business Koç Group 1958 working for Otokoç Co., Ankara, Chair. Exec. Cttee Koç Holding AŞ 1970–75, Deputy Chair. Bd of Man. 1975–80, Chair. Man. Cttee 1980, Chair. Koç Holding AŞ 1984–2003, now mem. Bd and Hon. Chair.; Pres. Rotary Club in Turkey 1976–77, Turkish Greek Business Council 1992–99, ICC 1995–96; fmr Co-Chair. Business Advisory Council for South East Europe (BAC SEE); Founder and Chair. Rahmi M. Koç Museum and Cultural Foundation, Istanbul; Chair. Bd of Trustees, Koç Univ., Bd of Vehbi Koç Foundation American Hosp.; Vice-Chair. Bd of Trustees, Vehbi Koç Foundation; Founding mem. The Turkish Marine and Environment Protection Asscn (TURMEPA), now Hon. Chair.; mem. Advisory Bd Turkish Employers Asscn, Int. Advisory Bd Council on Foreign Relations, New York, Int. Advisory Bd Allianz AG; fmr mem. JP Morgan Int. Council; Hon. Pres. Advisory Bd Turkish Industrialists' and Businessmen's Asscn; Hon. Trustee, Metropolitan Museum of Art, New York City; Hon. Fellow, Foreign Policy Asscn; Grosses Verdienstkreuz (Germany) 1982, Order of High Merit of the Italian Repub. 2001; Dr hc (Johns Hopkins) 1998, (Anadolu Üniversitesi) 1998, (Ege Üniversitesi) 1999, (Bilkent Üniversitesi) 1999, (Ovidius Univ., Romania) 2001, (Adnan Menderes Univ., Aydın) 2008; Outstanding Service Award, Pres. of Turkey 1997, Hadrian Award, World Monuments Fund 2007. *Address:* Koç Holding AŞ, Nakkaştepe Aziz Bey Sok. 1, Kuzguncuk, 34674 Istanbul, Turkey (office). *Telephone:* (216) 5310000 (office). *Fax:* (216) 5310099 (office). *E-mail:* info@koc.com.tr (office). *Website:* www.koc.com.tr (office); www.rmk-museum.org.tr (office).

KOČÁRNÍK, Ivan, CSc; Czech politician and business executive; b. 29 Nov. 1944, Třebonín, Kutna Hora Dist; m.; one s. two d.; ed Prague Inst. of Econs; worked at Research Inst. of Financial and Credit System until 1985; Dir Research Dept, Fed. Ministry of Finance 1985–89; Deputy Minister of Finance of Czechoslovakia 1990; mem. Civic Democratic Party; Vice-Premier and Minister of Finance of Czech Repub. 1992–97; Chair. Council of Econ. and Social Agreement 1992–97; Chair. Bd Czech Insurance Co. 1997–2001, Chair. Supervisory Bd 2000–07; Vice-Chair. of Supervisory Bd Unipetrol 2006; Chair. Supervisory Bd Czech Airlines (CSA) 2007–09; Adviser to Minister of Finance 2010–; Central European magazine Best Minister of Finance in 1994 1995. *Leisure interests:* tennis, skiing, hiking, music. *Address:* Letenská 15, 118 00 Prague 1, Czech Republic (office). *Telephone:* (2) 57041111 (office). *Fax:* (2) 57042788 (office). *E-mail:* podatelna@mfcr.cz (office). *Website:* www.mfcr.cz (office).

KOCH, Charles de Ganahl; American engineer, business executive and political activist; *Chairman and CEO, Koch Industries, Inc.;* b. 1 Nov. 1935, Wichita, Kan.; s. of Fred C. Koch and Mary Robinson; brother of David Hamilton Koch; m. Liz Koch; two c.; ed Massachusetts Inst. of Tech.; engineer, Arthur D. Little, Inc., Cambridge, Mass 1959–61; Vice-Pres. Koch Engineering Co., Inc. 1961–63, Pres. 1963–71, Pres. Koch Industries, Inc. 1966–74, Chair. and CEO 1967–; mem. The MIT Corpn 1977–82; supported brother, David H. Koch as Libertarian Party's cand. for Vice-Pres. 1980; funds Charles G. Koch Summer Fellow Program through Inst. for Humane Studies; Hon. Life mem. Washburn Law School Asscn; Hon. DSc (George Mason Univ.), Hon. LLD (Babson Coll.), Hon. DComm (Washburn Univ.); numerous awards including Distinguished Citizen Award, Kansas State Univ., inducted into Kansas Oil and Gas Hall of Fame, inducted into Wichita and Kansas Business Halls of Fame, Wichita State Univ. Entrepreneur in Residence, Uncommon Citizen Award, Wichita Chamber of Commerce, Recognition Award, Wichita State Univ., Distinguished Service Citation, Univ. of Kansas, Gov.'s Arts Patrons Award, Kansas Arts Comm. 1999, Dirs' Award for Global Vision in Energy, New York Mercantile Exchange 1999, Herman W. Lay Memorial Award, Asscn of Pvt. Enterprise Educ., Entrepreneurial Leadership Award, Nat. Foundation for Teaching Entrepreneurship, Adam Smith Award, American Legis. Exchange Council, Spirit of Justice Award, The Heritage Foundation, Free Enterprise Award, Council for Nat. Policy, Nat. Distinguished Service Award, The Tax Foundation 2000, Pres.'s Medal, Wichita State Univ. 2004. *Publication:* The Science of Success: How Market-Based Management Built the World's Largest Private Company 2007. *Address:* Koch Industries, Inc., PO Box 2256, Wichita, KS 67201-2256 (office); Koch Industries, Inc., 4111 East 37th Street North, Wichita, KS 67220, USA (office). *Telephone:* (316) 828-5500 (office). *Fax:* (316) 828-5739 (office). *E-mail:* info@kochind.com (office). *Website:* www.kochind.com (office).

KOCH, David Hamilton; American chemical engineer and business executive; b. 3 May 1940, Wichita, Kan.; s. of Fred C. Koch and Mary Robinson; brother of Charles de Ganahl Koch; m. Julia M. Flesher Koch; three c.; ed Deerfield Acad. prep school, Mass, Massachusetts Inst. of Tech.; began career as research engineer and process design engineer for Amicon Corpn, Cambridge, Mass; later worked for

Arthur D. Little, Inc., Cambridge, Mass, Halcon International, Inc. and its affiliate, Scientific Design Co., New York City; joined Koch Industries 1970, fmr Co-owner (with brother Charles), mem. Bd of Dirs and Exec. Vice-Pres. Koch Industries, Inc., Chair. and CEO Koch Chemical Technology Group, LLC (wholly owned subsidiary); f. David H. Koch Charitable Foundation 2000; ran on Libertarian ticket for Vice-Pres. against Carter–Mondale and Reagan–Bush 1980; Founder, fmr Chair. and donated to the free-market Citizens for a Sound Economy 1984 (separated into Americans for Prosperity Foundation and FreedomWorks 2004, continues as Chair. Americans for Prosperity Foundation); mem. Bd Cato Inst., Reason Foundation; presidential appointment to Nat. Cancer Advisory Bd of Nat. Cancer Inst. 2005; mem. Bd of Dirs The Economic Club of New York, Rockefeller Univ., American Museum of Natural History, Aspen Inst., Inst. of Human Origins, Cato Inst., The Reason Foundation; Vice-Chair. American Ballet Theatre, New York; Chair. Bd of Trustees, Americans for Prosperity Foundation, Washington, DC; Gov., New York-Presbyterian Hosp.; Life mem. MIT Corpn; mem. Bd of Visitors, M.D. Anderson Cancer Center, Houston; mem. Bd of Assocs, Whitehead Inst., Cambridge, Mass; mem. Bd of Overseers, WGBH, Channel 2, Boston; mem. James Madison Council, Library of Congress, Washington, DC; first and only Lifetime Trustee, Koch Center for Math., Science and Tech., Deerfield Acad.; mem. Bd of Trustees, Allen-Stevenson School, New York, Metropolitan Museum of Art, Memorial Sloan-Kettering Cancer Center, Hosp. for Special Surgery, New York, House Ear Inst., Los Angeles, Johns Hopkins Univ., Baltimore, Prostate Cancer Foundation, Los Angeles, Smithsonian Nat. Museum of Natural History, Washington, DC, Educational Broadcasting Corpn, Channel 13, New York; Hon. mem. Bd of Trustees, Cold Spring Harbor Lab., NY; Hon. DHumLitt (Cambridge Coll.); Entrepreneurial Leadership Award, Nat. Foundation for Teaching Entrepreneurship, Manhattan Republican Party's Business Statesman of the Year Award 2002, Corp. Citizens Award, Woodrow Wilson Int. Center for Scholars 2004, David Koch Center for Applied Research in Genitourinary Cancers est. at M.D. Anderson Cancer Center, Houston, Tex., David H. Koch Dinosaur Wing est. at American Museum of Natural History, Washington, DC 2006, David H. Koch Cancer Research Center est. at Johns Hopkins Univ.'s East Baltimore medical campus 2006, David H. Koch Inst. for Integrative Cancer Research est. at MIT 2007, New York State Theater at Lincoln Center for the Performing Arts renamed the David H. Koch Theater 2008, David H. Koch Hall of Human Origins est. at Nat. Museum of Natural History 2010, Double Helix Medal for Corp. Leadership, Cold Spring Harbor Lab. *Achievements include:* est. an MIT record in basketball by scoring an average of 21 points per game over three years, and held MIT's single-game scoring record of 41 points from 1962, when he was team capt., until broken by Jimmy Bartolotta 2009. *Address:* c/o Koch Industries, Inc., 4111 East 37th Street North, Wichita, KS 67220, USA.

KOCH, HE Cardinal Kurt, ThD; Swiss ecclesiastic; *President of the Pontifical Council for Promoting Christian Unity;* b. 15 March 1950, Emmenbrücke, canton of Lucerne; ed Ludwig-Maximilians Univ., Munich, Germany, Univ. of Lucerne; ordained priest, Diocese of Basel 1982; Bishop of Basel 1995–2010, Bishop Emer. 2010–; Pres. Swiss Episcopal Conf. 2007–10; mem. Swiss Council of Religions; Pres. of the Pontifical Council for Promoting Christian Unity 2010–13, 2013–; Archbishop (Personal Title) 2010–; mem. Congregation for the Doctrine of the Faith, Congregation for the Oriental Churches, Pontifical Council for Interreligious Dialogue 2010–, Congregation for the Causes of Saints 2011–, Congregation for Catholic Education, Congregation for Bishops 2013–; cr. Cardinal (Cardinal-Deacon of Nostra Signora del Sacro Cuore) 2010; participated in Papal Conclave 2013. *Address:* Pontifical Council for Promoting Christian Unity, Via dell'Erba 1, 00193 Rome, Italy (office). *Telephone:* (06) 69883072 (office); (06) 69884271 (office). *Fax:* (06) 69885365 (office). *Website:* www.vatican.va/roman_curia/pontifical_councils/chrstuni (office).

KOCH, Olaf G.; German business executive; *Chairman of the Management Board, METRO AG;* b. 1 June 1970, Bad Soden am Taunus; m.; three c.; ed Univ. of Co-operative Educ., Stuttgart; Man., Finance Process and Systems, Daimler Benz AG 1994–95; Founder and CEO IT-Networks GmbH 1996–98; Sr Man., Corp. War Room, DaimlerChrysler AG 1998–99, Dir, Corp. e-Business Strategy and Corp. War Room, DaimlerChrysler AG 1999–2000, Vice-Pres., Corp. e-Business 2000–02, mem. Bd of Man., Mercedes Car Group, responsible for Finance, Controlling and Strategy 2002–07; Man. Dir Operations, Permira Beteiligungsberatung GmbH 2007–09; mem. Bd of Man. METRO AG and Chief Financial Officer, responsible for Accounting, Finance Governance Centre, Planning and Controlling, Tax, Treasury, Del Credere/Collection (MIAG), Insurance (MIB) 2009–11, further responsible for CIO-Office, Information Man. and Information Tech. 2010–11, responsible for Galeria Kaufhof in Bd of Man. of METRO AG 2010–11, Chair. Man. Bd and Chief Human Resources Officer, METRO AG 2012–14, responsible for Communications, Corp. Office, CSR, Investor Relations, Internal Audit, Legal Affairs & Compliance, Projects and M&A, Public Affairs as well as Strategy, Chair. Galeria Kaufhof GmbH, mem. Advisory Bd Media-Saturn-Holding GmbH, Chair. Shareholders' Cttee, METRO Properties GmbH & Co. KG, mem. Bd of Dirs MGB Metro Group Buying HK Ltd, Hong Kong. *Address:* METRO AG, Schlüterstrasse 1, 40235 Düsseldorf, Germany (office). *Telephone:* (211) 6886-0 (office). *E-mail:* kontakt@metro.de (office). *Website:* www.metrogroup.de (office).

KOCH, Roland; German lawyer and politician; b. 24 March 1958; m.; two c.; ed Johann Wolfgang Goethe-Universität, Frankfurt am Main; co-f. Junge Union, youth org. of Christian Democratic Party (CDU) 1972, Deputy Nat. Chair. 1983–87; Town Councillor Eschborn 1997–94; Chair. CDU Main-Taunus Dist 1979–1990; mem. State Parl., Hessen 1987–2010; Fed. State Chair. CDU Hessen 1998–2010; Minister-Pres. Hessen 1999–2010 (resgnd); Chair. Bilfinger SE 2011–14; Chair. Supervisory Bd UBS Germany AG 2011–; Chair. Supervisory Bd FRAPORT AG 1999–2003, Hessische Staatsweingüter GmbH 2003–13; mem. Supervisory Bd VODAFONE Germany 2015–; Chair. Rheingau Musikfestival GmbH 2002–, Deutsche Kinder- und Jugendstiftung GmbH 2010–, Deutsche Kinder- und Jugendstiftung GmbH 2013–, Hessische Kulturstiftung 1999–2010, Flughafenstiftung Frankfurt-Rhein-Main 2005–10; Fed. Vice-Chair. CDU 2006–10; mem. Weiβer Ring charitable org.; initiator, Darmstadt Manifesto for promotion of arts and culture; active in pvt. law practice; EWS Award, European Econ. Affairs Council 2005. *Publications:* Chancengsellschaft 1996, Vision 21 1998, Aktive Bürgergesellschaft 1998, Die Zukunft der Bürgergesellschaft, Gemeinsam Chancen nutzen 2001. *Leisure interests:* cooking, art museums, tennis. *Address:* Bockenheimer Landstrasse 51-53, 60325 Frankfurt (office); Georg-August-Zinn Str. 1, 65183 Wiesbaden, Germany (home). *E-mail:* buero@roland-koch.de. *Website:* www.roland-koch.de.

KOCHARYAN, Robert Sedraki; Armenian politician and fmr head of state; b. 31 Aug. 1954, Stepanakert, Nagornyi Karabakh Autonomous Oblast, Azerbaijan SSR, USSR; s. of Sedrack S. Kocharyan and Emma A. Ohanian; m. Bella L. Kocharyan; two s. one d.; ed Yerevan Polytechnic Inst.; served in Soviet Army 1972–74; worked in different enterprises in Stepanakert and Moscow 1975–76; engineer and electrotechnician, Electro-Tech. plant, Stepanakert 1981–87; various positions at Municipal Cttee, Stepanakert town Cttee of the Komsomol Union, including post of Asst Sec. 1981–85; concurrently sec. factory CP Cttee 1987–89; Co-founder Karabakh Movt 1988; Deputy to Armenian Supreme Council 1989–94; left CP 1989; after proclamation of 'Repub. of Nagornyi Karabakh' 2 Sept. 1991 and Referendum 10 Dec. 1991 elected to Supreme Council 'Repub. of Nagornyi Karabakh', Chair. State Cttee of Defence and Leader of Repub. 1992–94; Pres. of 'Repub. of Nagornyi Karabakh' 1994–97; Prime Minister 1997–98; Pres. of Armenia 1998–2008; arrested on charge of overthrowing constitutional order of Armenia 2018. *Leisure interests:* basketball, jazz.

KOCHER, Isabelle; French business executive; *CEO, Engie SA;* b. 9 Dec. 1966, Neuilly sur Seine; m. Laurent Kocher 1989–; five c.; ed Ecole Normale Supérieure and Corps des Mines Eng School, Paris; Project Man. for the reorganization of production workshops within Soc. Européenne de Propulsion 1991–97; with Mergers and Acquisitions Dept, Compagnie Financière de Rothschild before becoming Dir of Industrial Inspection Dept at Île-de-France Regional Dept of Industry, Research and Environment Div. 1992–93; Dir Postal and Telecommunication Budgets, followed by the Defence Budget at French Budget Dept 1997–99; Industrial Affairs Advisor to the Prime Minister 1999–2002; Strategic and Devt Dept, SUEZ 2002–05, Sr Vice-Pres. in charge of Performance and Org. programmes 2005–07, COO Lyonnaise des Eaux (subsidiary of Suez Environnement) before becoming Man. Dir Lyonnaise des Eaux, as well as Exec. Vice-Pres. in charge of devt of water activities in Europe within Suez Environnement 2007–11, Exec. Vice-Pres. and Chief Financial Officer GDF SUEZ 2011–14, CEO Engie 2016–; Vice-Chair. Electrabel (Belgium); Dir, AXA, ENGIE ES, SUEZ Environnement Co. (France), International Power (UK), Engie Corp. Foundation. *Address:* Engie SA, 1 place Samuel de Champlain, 92400 Courbevoie, France (office). *Telephone:* 1-44-22-00-00 (office). *E-mail:* info@engie.com (office). *Website:* www.engie.com (office).

KOCHERGIN, Eduard Stepanovich; Russian theatrical designer; b. 22 Sept. 1937, Leningrad; s. of Stepan Kochergin and Bronislava (née Odinets) Kochergina; m. Inna Gabai 1962; one s.; ed Leningrad Theatre Art Inst., theatre production faculty (pupil of N. Akimov and T. Bruni); Chief Designer, Leningrad Drama and Comedy Theatre (now Theatre Na Liteinom) 1963–66, Komissarzhevskaya Theatre 1966–72; Chief Designer, Gorky (now Tovstonogov) Bolshoi Drama Theatre 1972–; Guest Designer at numerous Russian theatres, including Maly Theatre, Chekhov Moscow Art Theatre, Mayakovsky Theatre, Mossovet Theatre, Sovremennik, Taganka Theatre, Satira Theatre, Na Pokrovke Theatre, Novaya Opera Theatre and at theatres abroad including in Finland, Yugoslavia, Poland, Hungary, France, Germany, USA, Canada, Japan; Prof., Y.I. Repin Inst. of Painting 1983–; mem. Russian Acad. of Fine Arts 1991; Fatherland's Decoration of Merit (3rd and 4th Order), State Prize 1974, 1978; three Golden and two Silver awards, int. exhbns theatre design Novisad 1975, 1978, Prague 1975, 1979, 1987, Ind. Public Triumph Award 2008; Honoured Artist of Russia, Nicholas Roerich Prize 2013. *Publications:* Angel's Doll 2003, Baptised by Crosses 2009. *Leisure interest:* research in Russian pre-Christian culture and symbolism. *Address:* Tovstonogov Bolshoi Drama Theatre, Fontanka 65, 191023 St Petersburg, Russia (office). *Telephone:* (812) 352-89-33 (office); (812) 351-23-79 (home). *Fax:* (812) 110-47-10 (office). *E-mail:* bdt@bdt.spb.ru (office). *Website:* bdt.spb.ru (office).

KOCHHAR, Chanda D., MA, MBA; Indian banker and accountant; b. 17 Nov. 1961, Jodhpur, Rajasthan; m.; one s. one d.; ed Jai Hind Coll., Mumbai, Inst. of Cost and Works Accountants of India, Jamnalal Bajaj Inst. of Man. Studies, Mumbai; joined Project Appraisal Div., ICICI 1984, handled projects in various industries and was actively involved in bank's computerization initiatives, deputed to newly formed ICICI Bank as a part of core group for setting up and conceptualizing strategic direction for the bank 1993, served as first Head of Credit 1993–96 returned to ICICI to become part of initiatives such as infrastructure lending, structured products group and major clients group 1996–2000, Man. Dir ICICI Home Finance Ltd and ICICI Personal Financial Services 2000–01, Exec. Dir ICICI Bank Ltd 2001–06, Deputy Man. Dir 2006–07, Jt Man. Dir 2007–09, CEO and Man. Dir 2009–18, also Chair. ICICI Bank Canada Ltd, ICICI Bank UK PLC, ICICI Securities Ltd, ICICI Lombard Gen. Insurance Co. Ltd; mem. Bd of Dirs Oil and Natural Gas Corpn Ltd 2008–09; J.N. Bose Gold Medal in Cost Accountancy and Wockhardt Gold Medal for Excellence in Man. Studies, Jamnalal Bajaj Inst. of Man. Studies, Retail Banker of the Year in Asia 2004, Economic Times Award for Corporate Excellence as the Businesswoman of the Year 2005, FLO Women of Excellence Award 2009. *Leisure interest:* designing saris. *Address:* c/o ICICI Bank Ltd, ICICI Bank Towers, Bandra-Kurla Complex, Mumbai 400 051, India (office). *Telephone:* (22) 26531414 (office).

KOCIJANČIČ, Andreja; Slovenian physician and university administrator; *President, Council of Slovenian Quality Assurance Agency for Higher Education (NAKVIS);* b. 1942; m. Janez Kocijančič; one s. one d.; ed Univ. of Ljubljana; worked at Mil. Medical Acad. 1969–71; Asst Prof., Faculty of Medicine, Univ. of Ljubljana 1978–84, Assoc. Prof. 1984–89, Prof. of Medicine 1989–95, Sr Counsellor for Health 1995, Pres. Comm. for Postgraduate and Doctoral Studies 1995–2003, Rector Univ. of Ljubljana 2005–09; Deputy Dir Internal Zaloška Clinic, Clinical Centre Ljubljana 1982–87; Pres. Yugoslavia Endocrinology Asscn 1972–76; Vice-Pres. Council for Higher Educ. of the Repub. of Slovenia 1998–2002; Pres. 2002–04; Vice-Pres. Medical Chamber of Slovenia 2004–08; Pres. Council of Slovenian Quality Assurance Agency for Higher Education (NAKVIS) 2013–; Chair. Health Council of Slovenia 1982–86; mem. Exec. Cttee Int. Soc. of Endocrinology 1979–89; mem. Cen. Cttee European Fed. of Endocrine Socs 1987–95; mem. Bd of Dirs European Foundation for Osteoporosis 1995–2000. *Address:* Council of Slovenian Quality Assurance Agency for Higher Education (NAKVIS), Slovenska 9, 1000

Ljubljana, Slovenia (office). *Telephone:* (1) 4005771 (office). *E-mail:* info@nakvis.si (office). *Website:* test.nakvis.si (office).

KODEŠ, Jan, DipIng; Czech fmr tennis player and Jan Jaromir Kodeš; b. 1 March 1946, Prague; s. of Jan Kodeš and Vlasta Richterová-Kodešová; m. 1st Lenka Rösslerová-Kodešová 1967 (divorced 1988); one s. one d.; m. 2nd Martina Kodeš Schlonzová 2017; one d.; ed Univ. of Econs, Prague; first Czech national to win a Grand Slam title; Wimbledon Singles Champion 1973, French Open Singles Champion 1970, 1971, runner-up US Championships 1971, 1973, Italian Championships 1970, 1971, 1972; mem. Czechoslovak Davis Cup Team 1964–80, including 1975 (runners-up), 1980 (winners), non-playing Capt. 1982–87; Czechoslovak No. 1 player 1966–77; Bd mem. Czechoslovak Tennis Asscn 1982–98; mem. ETA Men's Cttee 1990–93; mem. ITF Davis Cup European Cttee 1997–98; Founder and Tournament Dir Czech Open, Prague 1987–98; Pres. Czech Tennis Asscn 1994–98; Dir Czechoslovak Tennis Centre 1986–92; mem. ITF/ITHF Golden Achievement Award Cttee 2006–, ITHF Enshrinee Nominating Cttee 2008–; part-owner and CEO Prague CZ Fashion sro 1994–2003; Meritorious Master of Sports 1971, State Decoration for Outstanding Work 1973, ITF Award for Services to the Game 1988, Int. Tennis Hall of Fame 1990, Czech Sport Legend (Emil Zatopek Award) 2011, ITF DC Committment Award 2012, Czech Fair Play Award 2012, USTA-IC Bill Johnston Trophy 2013. *Publications:* Tennis Was My Life (in Czech) 2006, A Journey to Glory from Behind the Iron Curtain 2010. *Leisure interests:* football, other sports, stamp and coin collecting, films, history, travelling, tennis game consulting. *Address:* Jan Kodes – PRO-TENNIS JK Consulting, Na Beránce 20, Prague 6, 160 00 Czech Republic (office). *Telephone:* (2) 33321536 (office); (2) 33321536 (home). *E-mail:* jan@kodes-tennis.com (office). *Website:* www.kodes-tennis.com (office).

KODJO, Edem; Togolese politician and administrator; *Special Envoy to Burkina Faso, African Union;* b. (Édouard Kodjovi Kodjo), 23 May 1938, Sokodé; m. 1962; two s. two d.; ed Coll. St Joseph, Univ. of Rennes, Ecole Nat. d'Admin, Paris, France; worked as admin. for Office de Radiodiffusion-Télévision Française (ORTF) 1964–67; returned to Togo 1967; Sec.-Gen., Ministry of Finance, Economy and Planning 1967–72; Admin., Banque Centrale des Etats de l'Afrique de l'Ouest 1967–76, Pres. of Admin. Council 1973–76; Dir-Gen. Soc. Nat. d'Investissement 1972–73; Minister of Finance and Economy 1973–76, of Foreign Affairs 1976–77, of Foreign Affairs and Co-operation 1977–78; Sec.-Gen. OAU 1978–83; Assoc. Prof. Sorbonne, Paris 1985–90; Prime Minister of Togo 1994–96, 2005–06; African Union Special Envoy to Burkina Faso following popular uprising that toppled Blaise Compaoré 2014–; Founder and Chair. Pan-African Inst. of Int. Relations (IPRI); Ed. Afrique 2000; mem. Rassemblement du Peuple Togolaise (RPT), RPT Political Bureau (Sec.-Gen. 1967–71); Leader Togolese Union for Democracy (UTD) –1999, Pres. Convergence patriotique panafricaine 1999–2003, then merged with several other parties to form Coalition des forces démocrates (CFD), currently Acting Chair.; mem. Club of Rome; Gov. for Togo, IMF 1973–76; fmr Chair. OAU Council of Ministers, Afro-Arab Perm. Comm. on Co-operation, OAU Cttee of Ten; Commdr, Ordre du Mono; Officier, Légion d'honneur; Dr hc (Univ. of Bordeaux I); Univ. of Sorbonne Medal. *Address:* African Union Headquarters, PO Box 3243, Roosvelt Street (Old Airport Area), W21K19, Addis Ababa, Ethiopia (office). *Telephone:* (11) 5517700 (office). *Fax:* (11) 5517844 (office). *E-mail:* dinfo@africa-union.org (office). *Website:* www.au.int (office).

KODJO, Messan Abgéyomé; Togolese politician; *President, Organisation pour bâtir dans l'union un Togo solidaire;* b. 12 Oct. 1954, Tokpli, Yoto Pref.; m.; ed Higher School of Sciences and Tech., Univ. of Benin, Univ. of Poitiers, France; fmr Sales Man. SONACOM; Minister for Youth, Sports and Culture 1988–91, for Territorial Admin and Security 1992; organized Constitutional Referendum; Gen. Man. Port Authority of Lomé 1993–99; elected Deputy 1999; Prime Minister of Togo 2000–02; Pres. Organisation pour bâtir dans l'union un Togo solidaire (OBUTS) 2008–, cand. for Pres. of Togo 2010; Pres. Groupe Afrique du Forum Francophone des Affaires; Strategic Expert, Agence des Banques Populaires pour la Coopération et le Développement. *Address:* Organisation pour bâtir dans l'union un Togo solidaire, Quartier Djidjole, 686 rue 19 Tosti, Lomé, Togo (office). *Telephone:* 251-95-95 (office). *E-mail:* info@obuts.org (office). *Website:* www.obuts .org (office).

KOEDA, Itaru, BEng; Japanese motor industry executive; *Executive Advisor and Honorary Chairman, Nissan Motor Company Limited;* b. 25 Aug. 1941; ed Univ. of Tokyo; joined Nissan Motor Co. Ltd 1965, becoming Gen. Man. of several corp. depts, fmr Vice-Pres. and Dir Nissan UK, mem. Bd of Dirs Nissan Motor Co. Ltd 1993–, Exec. Vice-Pres. –2003, Exec. Vice-Pres. and Co-Chair. 2003–08, Exec. Advisor and Hon. Chair. 2008–, Chair. Nissan Shatai Co. Ltd 2008–; mem. Bd of Dirs Renault SA 2003–08; Chair. Calsonic Kansei Corpn 2003–; Chair. JATCO Ltd 2008–; Chair. Japan Automobile Mfrs Asscn 2004–06; Chair. Japan-Mexico Econ. Cttee, Keidanren (Japan Business Fed.). *Address:* Nissan Motor Co. Ltd, 1-1, Takashima 1-chome, Nishi-ku, Yokohama 220-8686, Kanagawa, Japan (office). *Telephone:* (45) 523-5523 (office). *Website:* www.nissan-global.com (office).

KOENDERS, Albert (Bert) Gerard, BA, MA; Dutch politician and UN official; b. 28 May 1958, Arnhem; ed Free Univ., Johns Hopkins Univ., USA; personal asst to mems of House of Reps, Coordinating Foreign Policy Asst for Labour Party 1983–92; Adjunct Prof. of Int. Relations, Webster Univ., Leiden 1984–87; part-time consultant and European Dir of Parliamentarians for Global Action, New York 1987; European staff mem. and Political Adviser to Special Rep. of UN Sec.-Gen. working in Mozambique, South Africa and Mexico 1993–94; Prin. Admin., Policy Planning Staff, Directorate-Gen. for External Relations, Conflict Prevention and EU Enlargement, EC, Brussels –1997; mem. House of Reps 1997–2007; Minister for Devt Cooperation 2007–10; Special Rep. of the Sec.-Gen. and Head of the UN Operation in Côte d'Ivoire (UNOCI) 2011–13; Co-Chair. and negotiator, BUSAN Working Group on Aid Effectiveness; Special Rep. of the Sec.-Gen. and Head, UN Multidimensional Integrated Stabilization Mission in Mali (MINUSMA) 2013–14; Minister of Foreign Affairs 2014–17; Visiting Prof. for Conflict Man., Johns Hopkins Univ., Bologna 2000–02; f. Parl. Network on World Bank/IMF 2000–07; Chair. Supervisory Bd, Rutgers World Population Foundation 2011–; fmr Pres. NATO Parliamentary Ass.; fmr Deputy Chair. Netherlands Atlantic Asscn; mem. French-Dutch Cooperation Council; mem. Governing Council, Soc. for International Development; mem. Supervisory Council, Inst. for Multiparty Democracy.

KOENIGS, Tom, MBA; German politician and fmr UN official; b. 25 Jan. 1944, Frankfurt am Main; m.; three c.; ed Univ. of Berlin; co-f. (with Joschka Fischer) first Ministry for Environmental Protection of Hessen Fed. Region 1985; Head of Environmental Protection Dept, City of Frankfurt 1989–, Treas. for Frankfurt 1993–97; Co-Founder and Deputy Pres. Alliance for the Climate (int. NGO) 1990–99; Deputy Special Rep. for Civil Admin, UN Interim Admin. Mission in Kosovo (UNMIK) 1999–2002; Special Rep. of the UN Sec.-Gen. and Head, UN Verification Mission in Guatemala (MINUGUA) 2002–05; Commr for Human Rights Policy and Humanitarian Aid, Ministry of Foreign Affairs 2005; Special Rep. of the UN Sec.-Gen. for Afghanistan and Head, UN Assistance Mission in Afghanistan (UNAMA) 2006–07; apptd mem. Exec. Bd UNICEF Germany 2008; mem. Bundestag (Bündnis 90/Die Grünen—Alliance 90/Greens) 2009–. *Address:* Deutscher Bundestag, Platz der Republik 1, 11011 Berlin (office); Constituency Office, Liebigstraße 83, 35392 Gießen, Germany. *Telephone:* (30) 22773335 (office). *Fax:* (30) 22776147 (office). *E-mail:* tom.koenigs@bundestag.de (office). *Website:* www.tomkoenigs.de.

KOEPP, David; American screenwriter; b. 9 June 1963, Pewaukee, Wis.; Ian McClellan Hunter Award for Career Achievement, Writers Guild East 2013. *Film screenplays:* Apartment Zero (with Martin Donovan) 1989, Bad Influence 1990, Toy Soldiers (with Daniel Petrie, Jr) 1991, Death Becomes Her (with Martin Donovan) 1992, Jurassic Park (with Michael Crichton) 1993, Carlito's Way 1993, The Paper (with Stephen Koepp) 1994, The Shadow 1994, Suspicious 1994 (also dir), Mission: Impossible (with Robert Towne) 1996, The Trigger Effect (also dir) 1996, The Lost World: Jurassic Park 1997, Snake Eyes 1998, Stir of Echoes (also dir) 1999, Panic Room 2002, Spider-Man 2002, Secret Window (also dir) 2004, War of the Worlds 2005, Zathura: A Space Adventure (with John Kamps) 2005, Ghost Town (with John Kamps) (also dir) 2008, Indiana Jones and the Kingdom of the Crystal Skull 2008, Angels & Demons (with Akiva Goldsman) 2009, Premium Rush (with John Kamps) (also dir) 2012, Jack Ryan: Shadow Recruit (with Adam Cozad) 2014. *Address:* c/o Creative Artists Agency, 2000 Avenue of the Stars, Los Angeles, CA 90067, USA (office). *Telephone:* (424) 288-2000 (office). *Fax:* (424) 288-2900 (office). *E-mail:* info@caa.com (office). *Website:* www.caa.com (office).

KOERFER, Rolf; German lawyer and business executive; *Partner, Oppenhoff & Partner Rechtsanwälte;* m.; three c.; Partner, Oppenhoff & Rädler (law firm) 1991–2000, then at Shearman & Sterling LLP (law firm) and Allen & Overy LLP (int. law firm); Partner, Oppenhoff & Partner Rechtsanwälte 2009–; mem. Corp. Law Cttee Bundesrechtsanwaltskammer (German fed. chamber of lawyers); Chair. Supervisory Bd GLOBALE Rückversicherungs AG, Continental AG 2009–10. *Address:* Oppenhoff & Partner Rechtsanwälte, Steuerberater, Konrad-Adenauer-Ufer 23, 50668 Cologne, Germany (office). *Telephone:* (221) 2091-400 (office). *E-mail:* rolf.koerfer@oppenhoff.eu (office). *Website:* www.oppenhoff.eu (office).

KOFFI KOFFI, Paul; Côte d'Ivoirian statistician, academic and politician; *Minister-delegate to the President in charge of Defence;* b. 26 Jan. 1957, M'Bahiakro; m.; one c.; ed Ecole Nat. Supérieure de Statistique et d'Economie Appliquée, Abidjan, Int. School of Man., Paris, St John's Univ., New York; Lecturer, Ecole Nat. Supérieure des Postes et Télécommunications, Abidjan 1986–89; Lecturer in Statistics and Employment Policy, Ecole Nat. d'Admin, Abidjan 1985–89; Lecturer in Accounting, Ecole Nat. Supérieure de Statistique et d'Economie Appliquée, Abidjan 1984–89; Head of Research Dept, Ministry of Employment 1983–84, Deputy Dir of Human Resource Planning Feb.–Dec. 1984, Dir of Employment 1985–89; Sr Technical Adviser responsible for Population Planning, UN Population Fund, Conakry, Guinea 1989–94, Antananarivo, Madagascar 1995–97; Technical Adviser to Minister of Economy and Finance, responsible for monitoring econ. and financial programmes 1997–98, Deputy Chief of Staff to Minister of Economy and Finance 1998–2000, Econ. Adviser to Prime Minister 2000–03, Special Adviser to Prime Minister for financial and econ. matters and poverty reduction 2003–07, Deputy Chief of Staff to Prime Minister, responsible for crisis resolution programme 2007; Minister-Del. to Pres. in charge of Defence 2012–; Chevalier du mérite ivoirienne 2003. *Publications:* Houphouët et les mutations politiques en Côte d'Ivoire 1980–1993, Le défi du développement en Côte d'Ivoire 2008. *Leisure interests:* reading, cinema, football. *Address:* Ministry of Defence, Camp Galliéni, côté Bibliothèque Nationale, BP V241, Abidjan, Côte d'Ivoire (office). *Telephone:* 20-21-02-88 (office). *Fax:* 20-22-41-75 (office).

KOFFIGOH, Joseph Kokou; Togolese politician; b. 1948, Kpele Dafo; m.; three s. one d.; ed Univ. of Abidjan, Univ. of Poitiers, France; called to the Bar, Poitiers, France; joined Viale Chambers, Togo; f. Togo Bar Asscn 1980, Pres. 1990; Founder-mem. Observatoire panafricain de la démocratie (OPAD) 1991, Ligue togolaise des droits de l'homme 1990; Founder-mem. and Vice-Pres. FAR (Asscn for reform); Vice-Pres. Nat. Sovereign Conf.; Prime Minister of Togo 1991–94, also Minister of Defence, Minister of Foreign Affairs and Co-operation 1999–2001; apptd Minister of Regional Integration responsible for relations with Parl. 2001; Pres. Coordination nat. des forces nouvelles; Head of African Union Election Observation Mission during presidential election in Côte d'ivoire 2010. *Publications:* has published several volumes of poetry. *Leisure interests:* lawn tennis, basketball, shadow-boxing.

KOFLER, Georg; German (b. Italian) business executive; *Founder and Vice-Chairman of the Supervisory Board, Kofler Energies AG;* b. 26 April 1957, Brunico, Italy; m. José Kofler; two s.; ed Univ. of Vienna; fmrly mem. staff, Österreichischer Rundfunk (Austrian state broadcasting co.); with Eureka TV 1987–89; Co-founder (with Gerhard Ackermans and Thomas Kirch) and Chair. Pro 7 TV network 1989–2000; CEO KirchPayTV (now Premiere Fernsehen GmbH and Company KG), Munich 2002–07; f. Kofler Energies AG, Munich 2008, now Vice-Chair. Supervisory Bd. *Address:* Kofler Energies AG, Zimmerstraße 23, 10969 Berlin, Germany (home). *Telephone:* (89) 5390690 (office). *Fax:* (89) 53906969 (office). *E-mail:* info@koflerenergies.com (office). *Website:* www.koflerenergies.com (office).

KOGA, Nobuyuki; Japanese business executive; *Chairman, Nomura Holdings, Inc.;* b. 22 Aug. 1950, Fukuoka; ed Faculty of Law, Univ. of Tokyo; joined Nomura Securities Co. Ltd 1974, held numerous exec. positions including Gen. Man. of Personnel Dept, Gen. Man. of Corp. Planning Dept, Dir 1995–99, Man. Dir Nomura Holdings, Inc. 1999–2000, Exec. Vice-Pres. and COO 2000–03, Pres. and CEO 2003–08 (also of subsidiary Nomura Securities Co. Ltd, Chair. 2008–), Chair.

2011–; Exec. Officer, Olympus Corpn. *Address:* Nomura Holdings, Inc., 1-9-1, Nihonbashi, Chuo-ku, Tokyo 103-8645, Japan (office). *Telephone:* (3) 3211-1811 (office). *E-mail:* info@nomura.co.jp (office). *Website:* www.nomura.co.jp (office).

KOGAI, Masamichi; Japanese automotive industry executive; fmr Pres. AutoAlliance (Thailand) Co. Ltd; fmr Gen. Man. Hofu Plant, Mazda Motor Corpn, later Man. Exec. Officer and Gen. Man. Production Eng Div., Mazda Motor Corpn, Dir and Sr Man. Exec. Officer –2013, Rep. Dir, Pres. and CEO 2013–18.

KOGAN, Pavel; Russian violinist and conductor; *Music Director and Chief Conductor, Moscow State Symphony Orchestra;* b. 6 June 1952, Moscow; s. of Leonid Kogan and Elizaveta Gilels; m. (divorced); one s.; ed Moscow Conservatory, studied conducting in Leningrad with I. Mussin and in Moscow with Leo Ginzburg; has performed as soloist and conductor in major concert halls of Europe, USA and Asia with leading orchestras; Conductor, Bolshoi Theatre 1986–87; Music Dir Zagreb Philharmonic Orchestra 1987–90; Music Dir and Chief Conductor, Moscow State Symphony Orchestra 1989–; Prin. Guest Conductor, Utah Symphony Orchestra, USA 1997–2005; mem. Russian Acad. of Arts; Peoples' Artist of Russia 1994, Order of Friendship of the Russian Fed. 2002, Order of Merit of Russia 2007, 2014 Commdr, Ordre des Arts et des Lettres 2014; First Prize, Jean Sibelius Int. Violin Competition 1970, State Prize of the Russian Fed. 1997. *Recordings:* numerous works with the Moscow State Symphony Orchestra and other ensembles. *Address:* Moscow State Symphony Orchestra, 105082 Moscow, Spartakovskaya sq., 1/2 (office); 125009 Moscow, Brusov per. 8-10, Apt 8, Russia (home). *Telephone:* (499) 763-35-36 (office); (495) 692-13-95 (home). *Fax:* (499) 763-35-37 (office). *E-mail:* info@msso-kogan.ru (office); a.mizikaeva@msso-kogan.ru (office). *Website:* www.msso-kogan.ru (office).

KOGAN, Richard Jay, BA, MBA; American business executive; *President, Kogan Group LLC;* b. 6 June 1941, New York, NY; s. of Benjamin Kogan and Ida Kogan; m. Susan Linda Scher 1965; ed City Coll. of City Univ. of New York and Stern School of Business, New York Univ.; fmr Pres. US Pharmaceuticals Div., Ciba-Geigy Corpn; Exec. Vice-Pres. Pharmaceutical Operations, Schering-Plough Corpn 1982–86, Pres. and COO 1986–95, CEO 1996–2003 (retd); fmr Prin. Kogan Group LLC, now Pres.; Chair. Bd of Trustees, St Barnabas Medical Center 2012–, also Vice-Chair. Barnabas Health; mem. Bd Dirs, Colgate-Palmolive Co., Bank of New York Co. Inc., St Barnabas Medical Center and Corpn; mem. Council on Foreign Relations; Trustee, New York Univ.; Hon. DHumLitt; Hon. DIur (New York Univ.). *Address:* Kogan Group LLC, Suite 415, 51 JFK Parkway, Short Hills, NJ 07078-2702, USA (office). *Telephone:* (973) 379-6560 (office). *Fax:* (973) 379-7050 (office). *E-mail:* RJK@RJKogan.com (office). *Website:* www.thekogangroupllc.com (office).

KOH, Harold Hongju, AB, BA, MA, JD; American lawyer, academic, fmr university administrator and fmr government official; *Sterling Professor of International Law, Yale University Law School;* b. 8 Dec. 1954, Boston, Mass; m. Mary-Christy Fisher; one s. one d.; ed Harvard Univ., Magdalen Coll., Oxford, UK, Harvard Law School; Teaching Fellow, First-Year Legal Methods Program, Harvard Law School (Contracts and Civil Procedure) 1978–79; Clerk to Judge Malcolm Richard Wilkey, DC Circuit Court 1980–81; Clerk to Justice Harry A. Blackmun, US Supreme Court 1981–82; Assoc., Covington & Burling (pvt. law firm), Washington, DC 1982–83; Adjunct Asst Professorial Lecturer in Law, George Washington Univ. Nat. Law Center 1982–85; Attorney-Advisor, Office of Legal Counsel, US Dept of Justice 1983–85; Assoc. Prof., Yale Law School 1985–90, Prof. 1990–93, Gerard C. and Bernice Latrobe Smith Prof. of Int. Law 1993–2009, Dir Orville H. Schell, Jr Center for Int. Human Rights 1993–98, Dean, Yale Law School 2004–09, Sterling Prof. of Int. Law 2013–; Asst Sec. of State for Democracy, Human Rights and Labor, US State Dept 1998–2001; Visiting Prof. of Int. Law, Faculty of Law, Univ. of Toronto 1990, 2002; Visiting Prof., Hague Acad. of Int. Law 1993; Visiting Fellow, All Souls College and Waynflete Lecturer, Magdalen Coll., Oxford 1996–97; fmr Ed. American Journal of International Law, Foundation Press Casebook Series; mem. Bd, Harvard Univ., Brookings Inst., Nat. Democratic Inst., Human Rights First, Human Rights in China; mem. Council of the American Law Inst.; Fellow, American Acad. of Arts and Sciences, American Philosophical Soc.; Hon. Fellow, Magdalen Coll., Oxford; Dr hc (CUNY Law School); Asian American Bar Asscn of New York's Outstanding Lawyer of the Year Award 1997, Wolfgang Friedmann Award, Columbia Law School 2003, Louis B. Sohn Award, American Bar Asscn. *Publications:* has written more than 80 articles and authored or co-authored eight books, including National Security Constitution (Richard E. Neustadt Award from American Political Science Asscn as best book on American Presidency 1991) 1990, Transnational Legal Problems (with H. Steiner and D. Vagts) 1994, International Business Transactions in United States Courts 1998, Deliberative Democracy and Human Rights (with Ronald C. Slye 1999. *Address:* Yale Law School, PO Box 208215, New Haven, CT 06520, USA (office). *Telephone:* (203) 432-4932 (office). *E-mail:* harold.koh@yale.edu (office). *Website:* www.law.yale.edu (office).

KOH, Tommy Thong Bee, LLB, LLM; Singaporean international lawyer, professor of law and diplomatist; *Special Adviser, Institute of Policy Studies, Lee Kuan Yew School of Public Policy;* b. 12 Nov. 1937, Singapore; s. of Koh Han Kok and Tsai Ying; m. Siew Aing 1967; two s.; ed Univ. of Malaya in Singapore (now Nat. Univ. of Singapore), Harvard Univ., USA and Univ. of Cambridge, UK; Asst Lecturer, Univ. of Singapore 1962–64, Lecturer 1964–71, Sub-Dean, Faculty of Law, Univ. of Singapore 1965–67, Vice-Dean 1967–68, Assoc. Prof. of Law and Dean, Faculty of Law 1971–74, currently Prof. of Law; Amb. and Perm. Rep. to UN, New York 1968–71 (also accred as High Commr to Canada 1969–71), 1974–84 (also accred as High Commr to Canada and as Amb. Mexico); Amb. to USA 1984–90; Amb.-at-Large, Ministry of Foreign Affairs 1990–; Dir Inst. of Policy Studies, Lee Kuan Yew School of Public Policy 1990–97, 2000–04, Chair. 2004–09, Special Advisor 2009–; Exec. Dir Asia-Europe Foundation 1997–2000; Pres. Third UN Law of the Sea Conf. (Chair. Singapore Del. to Conf.) 1981–82; Chair. Preparatory Cttee, Chair. Main Cttee UN Conf. on Environment and Devt 1990–92; UN Sec.-Gen.'s Special Envoy to Russian Fed., Latvia, Lithuania and Estonia Aug.–Sept. 1993; Chair. Nat. Arts Council 1991–96; Chair. Nat. Heritage Bd 2002–; Chair. Centre for Int. Law, Nat. Univ. of Singapore, SymAsia Foundation of Credit Suisse; Rector, Tembusu Coll. at the Univ. Town of the Nat. Univ. of Singapore; Dir, Devt Bank of Singapore, 1994–2003, SingTel 2003–08; Commdr, Order of the Golden Ark (The Netherlands) 1993; Grand Cross, Order of Bernardo O'Higgins (Chile) 1997; Commdr, First Class, Order of the Lion of Finland 2000; Grand Officer, Order of Merit of the Grand Duchy of Luxembourg 2000; Officer, Légion d'honneur 2001; Encomienda of Isabel la Catolica (Spain) 2004; Order of Nila Utama (First Class) 2008; Order of the Rising Sun, Gold and Silver Star (Japan) 2009; Hon. LLD (Yale) 1984, (Monash); Adrian Clarke Memorial Medal 1961, Leow Chia Heng Prize 1961, Public Service Star 1971, Meritorious Service Medal 1979, Wolfgang Friedman Award 1984, Jackson H. Ralston Prize 1985, Annual Award of the Asia Soc., New York, 1985, Int. Service Award, Fletcher School of Law and Diplomacy, Tufts Univ., USA 1987, Jit Trainor Award for Distinction in Diplomacy, Georgetown Univ., USA 1987, Distinguished Service Order Award 1990, Elizabeth Haub Prize, Univ. of Brussels and Int. Council on Environmental Law 1997, Fok Ying Tung Southeast Asia Prize, Hong Kong 1998, John Curtin Medal, Curtin Univ. of Tech., WA 2000, Distinguished Service to Arts Educ., La Salle-SIA Coll. Award 2000, Peace and Commerce Award 2003, Outstanding Service Award, Nat. Univ. of Singapore 2004, Champions of the Earth, UNEP 2006, Tatler Leadership Award for Lifetime Achievement, Singapore Tatler magazine 2007, Great Negotiator Award, Harvard Law School/Harvard Kennedy School 2014. *Publications:* The United States and East Asia: Conflict and Cooperation 1995, Five Years After Rio: Some Personal Reflections 1997, The Quest for World Order: Perspectives of a Pragmatic Idealist (co-ed.) 1998, Asia and Europe: Essays and Speeches by Tommy Koh (co-eds Yeo Lay Hwee and Asad Latif) 2000, The United States-Singapore Free Trade Agreement: Highlight and Insights (co-ed.) 2004, The Little Red Dot: Reflections by Singapore's Diplomats (co-ed.) 2005, The Making of the ASEAN Charter (co-ed.) 2009, Pedra Branca: The Road to the World Court 2009, The Little Red Dot: Reflections by Singapore's Diplomats, Vol. II (co-ed.) 2009, The Tommy Koh Reader: Favourite Essays and Lectures 2013; numerous articles. *Leisure interests:* sport, reading, music. *Address:* Institute of Policy Studies, Lee Kuan Yew School of Public Policy, National University of Singapore, 469C Bukit Timah Road, Singapore 259772 (office). *Telephone:* 6516-1279 (office). *Fax:* 6762-6216 (office). *E-mail:* tommy.koh@nus.edu.sg (office). *Website:* lkyspp.nus.edu.sg/faculty/koh-tommy (office).

KOHÁK, Erazim, BA, MA, PhD; Czech philosopher, academic and author; *Senior Scholar, Centre for Global Studies, Philosophy Institute, Academy of Science of Czech Republic;* b. 21 May 1933, Prague; s. of Dr Miloslav Kohák and Dr Zdislava Koháková; m. 3rd Dorothy Koháková; three d. from 1st m.; ed Yale Univ.; exiled with parents to USA 1948; Lecturer, Boston Univ. 1960–72, Prof. 1972–90, Prof. Emer. 1995–; returned to Czechoslovakia 1990; Prof. Ordinarius, Inst. of Philosophy and Religious Studies, Charles Univ., Prague 1990–2001, Prof. Emer. 2000–; currently Sr Scholar Centre for Global Studies, Philosophy Inst., Acad. of Science of Czech Repub.; mem. American Philosophical Asscn, Husserl Circle, Ethical Panel, Nat. Public TV 2005–; mem. Czech TV Council 2001–05; Medal of Merit (Czech Repub.) 1998; Scientia et Humanitate Optimi Meritis, Acad. of Science of Czech Repub. 2009; Hlávka Medal, Czechoslavak Acad. of Science 1992, Great Gold Medal, Charles Univ. 1994, Josef Vavroušek Prize for Ecology 1997. *Publications include:* The Victors and the Vanquished 1973, Na vlastní kui 1973, Národ v nás 1978, Idea and Experience 1978, The Embers and the Stars 1984, Oheň a hvězdy (trans. by Milan Šimečka) 1985, Krize rozumu a přirozený svět 1986, Jan Patočka: His Thought and Writings (Jan Patočka: Mšlení a dílo) 1989, Dopisy přes oceán (Letters Across the Ocean) 1992, Jan Patočka: filosofický ivotopis (trans. by Josef Moural) 1993, P.S.: Psové 1993, Praské přednášky: ivot v pravě a moderní skepse (Life in Truth and Modern Scepsis) 1992, Clovek, dobro a zlo 1993, Hesla Erazima Koháka 1995, Průvodce po demokracii 1997, Pravda a pestrost 1997, Zelená svatozář: Přednášky z ekologické etiky 1998, Hesla mladých svišťů 1999, The Green Halo: Bird's Eye View of Ecological Ethics (trans. from the Czech by the author) 2000, Erazim Kohák, Poutník po hvezdách 2001, Orbis bene vivendi (Vybral a uspořádal Roman Šantora) 2001, P.S. Psové 2002, Dary noci 2003, Erazim Kohák: Zorným úhlem filosofa 2004, Svoboda, svědomí, soužití 2004, Bud' Bohu sláva za vše kropenaté 2005, Hearth and Horizon: Ethnic Identity and Global Humanity in Czech Philosophy 2008, Domov a dálava: Kulturní totonost a obecné lidství v českém myšlení 2009, Kopí dona Quijota 2010; numerous articles in professional and popular journals. *Leisure interests:* hiking, railways, ecology. *Address:* Philosophy Institute AVČR, Jilská 1, 110 00 Prague 1 (office); Babákova 2200, 148 00 Prague 414, Czech Republic (home). *Telephone:* 736-467144 (mobile) (office); (2) 72935568 (home). *E-mail:* kohak@ecn.cz (office); kohak@flu.cas.cz (office).

KOHL, Herbert H. (Herb), BA, MBA; American retail executive and politician; b. 7 Feb. 1935, Milwaukee, Wis.; ed Univ. of Wisconsin-Madison, Harvard Business School; served in Army Reserve 1958–64; worked in family-owned Kohl's grocery and dept stores, Pres. 1970–79; Chair. Wis. Democratic Party 1975–77; acquired Milwaukee Bucks professional basketball team 1985; Pres. Herb Kohl Investments; Senator from Wis. 1988–2013 (retd), Chair. Special Cttee on Aging, mem. Appropriations Cttee, Judiciary Cttee, Agric. Appropriations Sub-cttee, Judiciary Sub-cttee on Antitrust, Business Rights and Competition; f. Herb Kohl Educational Foundation Achievement Award Program 1990; Owner Milwaukee Bucks Nat. Basketball Asscn team; Democrat; Food Research and Action Center Distinguished Service Award, Wis. Farm Bureau Fed. Distinguished Service to Agric. Award, inducted into Wisconsin Athletic Hall of Fame 2007, Best of Congress Award, Working Mother Magazine and Corporate Voices for Working Families 2010.

KÖHLER, Horst, Dr rer. pol; German economist, banker, politician and fmr head of state; *Personal Envoy for Western Sahara, United Nations;* b. 22 Feb. 1943, Skierbieszow, Poland; m. Eva Luise Köhler; two c.; ed Univ. of Tübingen; began career as scientific research asst, Inst. for Applied Econ. Research, Univ. of Tübingen, 1969–76; held various positions in Ministries of Econs and Finance 1976–89, Sec. of State, Ministry of Finance, Bonn 1990–93; Pres. Deutsche Sparkassen- und Giroverband, Bonn 1993–98; Deputy Gov. IBRD and EBRD, Pres. EBRD 1998–2000; Man. Dir IMF 2000–04; Pres. of Germany 2004–10 (resgnd); Pres. European Asscn of Savings Banks 1994–97; co-f. (with wife) Eva Luise and Horst Köhler Stiftung für Menschen mit Seltenen Erkrankungen 2006; mem. Int. Advisory Bd, Kulczyk Investments SA; mem. UN Sec.-Gen.'s High-Level Panel of eminent persons on the Post-2015 Development Agenda 2012–13, Personal Envoy for Western Sahara, UN 2017–; mem. Club of Rome; Hon. Prof., Univ. of Tübingen 2003; Commdr, Ordre Grand-ducal de la Couronne de Chêne 1994; Officier, Légion d'honneur 1995, Sonderstufe des Grossen Verdienstkreuzes der Bundesrepublik Deutschland 2004; Verdienstmedaille des Landes Baden-Württemberg 2002. *Address:* MINURSO Head Quarter, Laâyoune PO Box 5846, Grand Central Station, New York, NY 10163-5846, USA. *E-mail:* minursoinformationofficer@un.org. *Website:* www.un.org/en/peacekeeping/missions/minurso.

KOHLHAUSSEN, Martin; German business executive; b. 6 Nov. 1935, Marburg/Lahn; m.; three c.; ed Univs of Frankfurt am Main, Freiburg and Marburg; bank training, Deutsche Bank, Frankfurt am Main; Man. Lloyds Bank, Frankfurt am Main 1974–76; Man. Tokyo Br. Westdeutsche Landesbank Girozentrale 1976–78, New York Br. 1979–81; mem. Bd of Man. Dirs Commerzbank AG 1982–2001, Chair. Exec. Cttee 1991–2001, Chair. Supervisory Bd 2001–10; fmr Chair. Supervisory Bd Hochtief AG, Heraeus Holding GmbH; Pres. Int. Monetary Conf. 1999, 2000; Pres. Bundesverband Deutscher Banken 1997–2000; mem. Supervisory Bd ThyssenKrupp AG, Intermediate Capital Group, Nat. Pensions Reserve Fund, Schering AG, Verlagsgruppe Georg von Holtzbrinck GmbH; mem. Bd of Dirs Bayer AG 1992–, Intermediate Capital Group 2004–; Hon. Dr rer. pol (Technische Univ., Chemnitz) 1998.

KOHLI, Om Prakash, MA; Indian academic and politician; *Governor of Gujarat;* b. 9 Aug. 1935, Delhi; s. of Manohar Lal Kohli and Shiv Devi; m. Avinash Kohli; one s. two d.; ed Punjab Univ., Univ. of Delhi; worked as Lecturer, Hansraj Coll. and Deshbandhu Coll., Univ. of Delhi for over 37 years, retd as Reader 1994; imprisoned for 19 months under Maintenance of Internal Security Act (MISA) during Nat. Emergency, Delhi, Agra and Varanasi jails; mem. Rajya Sabha (upper house of parl.) 1994–2000, Chair. Housing Cttee, mem. Standing Cttee on Urban and Rural Devt, Standing Cttee on Finance; Pres. Delhi Univ. Teachers Asscn 1973–79; Gov. of Gujarat 2014–, also of Madhya Pradesh 2016–18; mem. Bharatiya Janata Party, Pres. Delhi State BJP 1991–95, 2009–10. *Publications:* Rashtriya Suraksha Ke Morche Par, Shiksha Niti, Bhaktikal Ke Santon Ki Samajik Chetna. *Address:* Office of the Governor, Raj Bhavan, Sector 20, Gandhinagar, 382 020, India (office). *Telephone:* (79) 23243171 (office). *Fax:* (79) 23231121 (office). *E-mail:* prisec-rajbhavan@gujarat.gov.in (office). *Website:* www.rajbhavan.gujarat.gov.in (office).

KOHLI, Virat; Indian cricketer; *Captain, Indian Cricket Team;* b. 5 Nov. 1988, Delhi; s. of Prem Kohli and Saroj Kohli; m. Anushka Sharma 2017; right-handed batsman; right-arm medium pace bowler; plays for Delhi 2006–, India 2008–, Royal Challengers Bangalore 2008–; First-class debut 2006; ODI debut: India vs Sri Lanka, Dambula 18 Aug. 2008; Test debut: India vs West Indies, Kingston 20–23 June 2011; T20I debut: India vs Zimbabwe, Harare 12 June 2010; Indian Premiere League (IPL) debut: Royal Challengers Bangalore vs Kolkata Knight Riders, Bangalore 18 April 2008; played 71 tests (to Oct. 2018), scored 6147 runs (average 53.92) with 6 double-hundreds, 24 hundreds and 19 fifties, best score of 243 against Sri Lanka in Delhi 2017; played 211 ODIs (to July 2018), scored 9779 runs (average 58.20) with 35 hundreds and 48 fifties, best score of 183 against Pakistan in Dhaka 2012; played 62 T20Is (to July 2018), scored 2102 runs (average 48.88) with 18 fifties, best score of 90 against Australia in Adelaide 2016; played 103 First-Class matches (to Sept. 2018), scored 8396 runs (average 54.16) with 30 hundreds and 27 fifties, best score of 243; mem. winning Indian team of ICC Cricket World Cup 2011, of ICC Champions Trophy 2013; Capt. Indian Test Side 2014–, One-Day Int. (ODI) side 2017–, T20 Int. 2017–, Royal Challengers Bangalore 2013–; scored fastest century by an Indian against Australia, Jaipur 16 Oct. 2013, fastest batsman to 5,000 ODI runs, fastest to 10 ODI centuries; second batsman to have scored 1,000 or more ODI runs in four consecutive calendar years; highest historic ODI rating of 911 points; fastest batsman to score 24 Test hundreds (in 123 innings) since Sir Don Bradman (in 66 innings) 2018; f. Virat Kohli Foundation 2013; co-owner, FC Goa, Indian Super League 2014, UAE Royals, Int. Tennis League 2015, Bengaluru Yodhas, Pro Wrestling League 2015; launched youth fashion brand WROGN (with Universal Sportsbiz) 2014; Polly Umrigar Award for Int. Cricketer of the Year 2011–12, 2014–15, 2015–16, ICC ODI Player of the Year 2012, 2017, ICC World Cricketer of the Year 2017, Arjuna Award 2013, Wisden Leading Cricketer in the World 2016, 2017, Sir Garfield Sobers Trophy 2017, Padma Shri 2017, Rajiv Gandhi Khel Ratna Award 2018, Sir Garfield Sobers Trophy for Cricketer of the Year, ICC 2018, ICC Test Cricketer of the Year 2018, ICC ODI Cricketer of the Year 2018. *Address:* c/o Bunty Sajdeh, Cornerstone, H-1, Heliopolis, 157 A, Colaba Road, Mumbai 400005, Maharashtra, India (office); Board of Control for Cricket in India, 4th Floor, Cricket Centre, Wankhede Stadium, 'D' Road, Churchgate, Mumbai, 400020, Maharashtra, India (office). *Telephone:* (22) 22180827 (office); (22) 22898800 (office). *Fax:* (22) 22180831 (office); (22) 22898801 (office). *E-mail:* bunty@cornerstone.in (office). *Website:* www.cornerstone.in (office); www.bcci.tv (office); www.viratkohli.club.

KOHONA, Palitha T. B., LLB, LLM, PhD; Sri Lankan/Australian lawyer and diplomatist; b. Matale, Sri Lanka; ed St Thomas Coll., Mount Lavinia, Sri Lanka, Univ. of Sri Lanka, Australian Nat. Univ., Univ. of Cambridge, UK; attorney-at-law, Supreme Court of Sri Lanka; with Dept of Foreign Affairs and Trade (FAT) of Australia, led Australian del. to UNCTAD Trade and Devt Bd 1988, assigned to Uruguay Round negotiating team of Australia, in charge of Institutional Mechanisms, posted to Australian Perm. Mission, Geneva 1989, chaired UN negotiating group that developed the compliance mechanism under Montreal Protocol to Convention on Ozone Layer, mem. UN Working Group on liability mechanism under Basel Convention on Hazardous Wastes, Head of Trade and Investment Section, FAT –1995, Chief of UN Treaty Section, New York 1995–2006; initiated Annual UN Treaty Event, est. treaty training programme, oversaw computerization and on-line presentation of UN Treaty Database, oversaw preparation of UN Treaty Handbook; returned to Sri Lanka 2006; Sec.-Gen. Secr. for Coordinating the Peace Process (SCOPP) 2006–07, participated in two rounds of peace negotiations with Liberation Tigers of Tamil Eelam in Geneva and led del. to a round organized in Oslo 2006; Perm. Sec., Ministry of Foreign Affairs 2007–09; Amb. and Perm. Rep. to UN, New York 2009–15; mem. del. to UN Gen. Ass. 2006, 2008; has led official-level dels to several countries on bilateral matters, Leader of UN legal del. to North Korea at invitation of DPRK Govt 2005; Adviser, Sustainable Devt and Co-Chair. UN Working Group on Marine Biological Diversity Beyond Nat. Jurisdiction, mem. UN Advisory Panel on the Shirley Amerasinghe Prize on the Law of the Sea; Adviser, Helping Hands; Patron Renewable Energy and Int. Law, Making Art Everywhere; two merit prizes on results of First Examination in Law, Univ. of Sri Lanka, UN 21 Pin 1996, Global Citizen, Orphans International (USA). *Publications include:* The Regulation of International Trade through Law, more than 60 publs on treaty law, the environment, climate change, biological diversity, non-governmental orgs, trade and the environment, terrorism. *Leisure interests:* cricket, grass hockey, travel, music.

KOHONEN, Teuvo Kalevi, DEng, FIEEE; Finnish physicist, computer scientist and academic; *Professor, Department of Information and Computer Science, Helsinki University of Technology;* b. 11 July 1934, Lauritsala; s. of Väinö Kohonen and Tyyne E. Koivunen; m. Elvi Anneli Trast 1959; two s. two d.; ed Helsinki Univ. of Tech.; Teaching Asst in Physics, Helsinki Univ. of Tech. 1957–59, Asst Prof. in Physics 1963–65, Prof. of Tech. Physics 1965–93; currently Prof., Dept of Information and Computer Science, Aalto Univ.; Research Assoc., Finnish Atomic Energy Comm. 1959–62; Visiting Prof., Univ. of Washington, Seattle 1968–69; Research Prof., Acad. of Finland 1975–78, 1980–99, Prof. Emer. 1999–; Pres. European Neural Network Soc. 1991–92; Vice-Chair. Int. Asscn for Pattern Recognition 1982–84; mem. Acad. Scientiarum et Artium Europaea, Académie Européenne des Sciences, des Arts et des Lettres, Finnish Acad. of Sciences, Finnish Acad. of Eng Sciences; Commdr, Order of Lion of Finland, Kt, Order of White Rose of Finland; Dr hc (Univ. of York, Åbo Akademi, Univ. of Dortmund); Emil Aaltonen Prize 1983, Cultural Prize, Finnish Commercial TV (MTV) 1984, IEEE Neural Networks Pioneer Award 1991, Int. Neural Network Soc. Lifetime Achievement Award 1992, Finnish Cultural Foundation Prize 1994, Tech. Achievement Award, IEEE Signal Processing Soc. 1995, King-Sun Fu Prize, Int. Asscn for Pattern Recognition 1996, Centennial Prize, Finnish Asscn of Grad. Engineers (TEK) 1996, Medal of Finnish Acad. of Eng Sciences 1997, SEFI Leonardo da Vinci Medal, European Soc. for Eng Educ. 1998, Jubilee Prize Finnish Foundation of Tech. 1999, Italgas Prize 1999, Caianiello Int. Award 2000, Third Millennium Medal, IEEE Signal Processing Soc. 2000, Academician 2000, IEEE Frank Rosenblatt Award 2008. *Publications:* Digital Circuits and Devices 1972, Associative Memory: A System Theoretical Approach 1977, Content-Addressable Memories 1982, Self-Organization and Associative Memory 1984, Self-Organizing Maps (Springer Series in Information Sciences, Vol. 30) 1995. *Leisure interests:* philosophy of music, literature. *Address:* Department of Information and Computer Science, Aalto University, PO Box 15400, 00076 Aalto (office); Mellstenintie 9 C 2, 02170 Espoo, Finland (home). *Telephone:* (9) 4702-3268 (office). *E-mail:* teuvo.kohonen@tkk.fi (office). *Website:* www.cis.hut.fi/teuvo (office).

KOHOUT, Jan; Czech diplomatist and politician; b. 29 March 1961, Pilsen; m. (divorced); one s. one d.; ed Charles Univ., Prague; mil. service 1984–85; researcher, Inst. of Int. Relations, Prague 1985–90; Desk Officer, Int. Orgs Dept, Ministry of Foreign Affairs 1990–92, Dir UN Dept 1993–95; Deputy Head, Perm. Mission to UN, OSCE and other orgs, Vienna 1995–2000; Deputy Dir EU and Western Europe Dept, Ministry of Foreign Affairs 2000–01, apptd Political Dir 2001, apptd Deputy Minister 2002; Perm. Rep. to EU 2004–08; Deputy Minister of Foreign Affairs 2008–09; Deputy Prime Minister and Minister of Foreign Affairs 2009–10; Minister of Foreign Affairs 2013–14; mem. Czech Social Democratic Party. *Address:* c/o Ministry of Foreign Affairs, Loretánské nám. 101/5, 118 00 Prague 1, Czech Republic. *E-mail:* epodatelna@mzv.cz.

KOIKE, Yuriko, BA; Japanese politician and fmr broadcaster; *Governor of Tokyo;* b. 15 July 1952; ed Faculty of Sociology, Kwansei Gakuin Univ., Cairo Univ. and American Univ. of Cairo, Egypt; began career as interpreter and translator of Arabic 1977; Sec.-Gen. Japan–Arab Asscn 1977–78, 1990–92; interviewer and coordinator, Nippon TV Special Col Qadaffi and Yasser Arafat 1978; Anchor, Current Issues, Nippon TV 1979–88; Anchor, World Business Satellite and Top Business Execs, TV Tokyo 1988–90; elected to House of Councillors (Japan New Party) 1998; mem. House of Reps (now LDP) for Tokyo 10th District 1993–2016, Vice-Minister Man. and Coordination Agency 1992–94, Chair. Standing Cttee on Science and Tech. 1997–98, mem. Standing Cttee on Trade and Industry 1998–99, Dir Standing Cttee on Finance 1998–2000, mem. Standing Cttee on Health and Welfare 2000–03; Gov. of Tokyo 2016–; Vice-Pres. Japan New Party 1994; Founding mem. New Frontier Party 1994, Asst to Sec.-Gen. 1995–96, Dir Public Relations Bureau 1996–97; Founding mem. Liberal Party 1998, mem. Cttee on Public Relations 1999–2000; Vice-Chair. Policy Planning Cttee, Conservative Party 2000–03; Minister of Environment 2003–06; Minister of State for Okinawa and Northern Territories Affairs 2004–06, in Charge of Global Environmental Problems 2005–06; Adviser to Prime Minister on Nat. Security 2006–07; Minister of Defence (first woman) June–Aug. 2007; Visiting Prof., Chuo Univ. Grad. School 2009. *Address:* Office of Governor, 1-6-1 Nagatacho, Chiyoda-ku, Tokyo 100-8914, Japan. *E-mail:* koike@yuriko.or.jp. *Website:* www.yuriko.or.jp; www.japan.go.jp/index.html.

KOIRALA, Anuradha, BA; Nepalese activist and organization official; *Founding Chairperson, Maiti Nepal;* b. 14 April 1949; d. of Col Pratap Singh Gurung and Laxmi Gurung; one s.; ed St Xavier's Coll., Kolkata, India; fmr schoolteacher; Founder and Chair. Maiti Nepal (Mother's Home – shelter, educational facility, hospice and lobbying org. to fight domestic abuse, rape, child prostitution, child labour and trafficking of girls for sex trade) 1993–; Asst Minister for Women, Children and Social Welfare 2002–03; Distinguished Social Worker Award, Nepal 1997–98, 1999, Noted Social Worker Award, Nepal 1997–98, 100 Heroines Award 1998, Best Social Worker of the Year Award, Social Welfare Council, Nepal 1998–99, 2000, Prabal Gorkha Dakshin Bahu Medal, Nepal 1999–2000, Everest Foundation Nepal Felicitation 2000, Best Social Worker, Women's Asscn Nepal 2000, Int. Children's Award 2002, Trishaktipatta 2002, Birendra Aiswarya Padak 2002, Most Influential Woman of Nepal, BOSS magazine 2004, Amb. of Peace, Inter-religious and Int. Fed. for World Peace and Inter-religious Int. Peace Council 2005, Eurasia Reiyukai Award for outstanding contrib. in the field of social welfare, Reiyukai 2005, The Peace Abbey, Courage of Conscience Award, Sherborne, Mass, USA 2006, Queen Sofia Silver Medal (Spain) 2007, UNIFEM Prize (Germany) 2007, Shining World Peace Compassion Award, Supreme Master Ching Hai Int. Asscn 2010, CNN Hero 2010, Manhe Award (South Korea) 2011, Mother Teresa Award 2015, C10 Award, Stockholm 2015. *Leisure interests:* singing, dancing. *Address:* Maiti Nepal Central Office, 83 Maiti Marg, Pingalsthan, Gaushala, Nepal (office). *Telephone:* (1) 4492904 (office); (1) 4478401 (home). *Fax:* (1) 4489978 (office). *E-mail:* anuradha@maitinepal.org (office). *Website:* www.maitinepal.org (office).

KOIRALA, Shanker Prasad, LLB, MEcon, MA; Nepalese civil servant and government official; ed Tribhuvan Univ., Kathmandu, Centre for Research and Communications, Manila, Philippines; Section Officer, Ministry of Industry 1986–91, Section Officer, Ministry of Finance 1991–94, Asst Dir, Asian Devt Bank, Manila 1994–96, Jt Sec., Ministry of Commerce 1996–97, Jt Sec., Ministry of Culture, Tourism and Civil Aviation 1997–2007, Sec., Ministry of Information and Communication 2007–08, Sec., Ministry of Water Resources 2008, Sec., Ministry of Energy 2010–11, Sec., Ministry of Industry 2011–12, Sec., Election Comm. 2012–13; Minister of Finance, Industry, and Commerce and Supplies 2013–14. *Albums include:* Dhadkan Bhitra (solo music) 2005, Prahar (joint music album) 2007, Upamaa (Upahar – 2) (solo music) 2008. *Publications include:* Taankiko Ghans (anthology of Nepali poems) 2002, Dhadkan Bhitra (anthology of lyrics) 2005, Nirbastra Nagarimaa (anthology of poems) 2008.

KOIZUMI, Junichiro; Japanese fmr politician; b. 8 Jan. 1942, s. of Junya Koizumi; m. Kayoko Miyamoto 1978 (divorced 1982); three s.; mem. House of Reps from Kanagawa 1972–2006, Chair. House of Reps Finance Cttee; fmr Parl. Vice-Minister of Finance and of Health and Welfare; Minister of Posts and Telecommunications 1992–93; mem. Mitsuzuka Faction of LDP; Minister of Health and Welfare 1996–98; Prime Minister of Japan 2001–06; Pres. Jiyu Minshuto (Liberal-Democratic Party) 2001–06. *Address:* c/o Jiya Minshuto, 1-11-23, Nogata-che, Chiyoda-ku, Tokyo 100-8910, Japan (office).

KOIZUMI, Mitsuomi; Japanese business executive; *President and CEO, Japan Tobacco Inc.;* served successively as Sr Vice-Pres. and Head of Human Resources Group, Japan Tobacco Inc., Head of Tobacco Business Planning Div., Tobacco Business, Chief Marketing and Sales Officer, Tobacco Business and Exec. Vice-Pres. Japan Tobacco Inc., Dir 2007–, Exec. Deputy Pres. and Rep. Dir 2009–12, Pres., Rep. Dir and CEO 2012–. *Address:* Japan Tobacco Inc., 2-1, Toranomon 2-chome, Minato-ku, Tokyo, 105-8422, Japan (office). *Telephone:* (3) 3582-3111 (office). *Fax:* (3) 5572-1441 (office). *E-mail:* info@jti.com (office). *Website:* www.jti.com (office).

KOJIMA, Yorihiko, BS; Japanese business executive; *Chairman, Mitsubishi Corporation;* b. 15 Oct. 1941, Tokyo; s. of Kazuo Kojima and Sakae Kojima; ed Tokyo Metropolitan Hibiya High School, Univ. of Tokyo; joined Mitsubishi Corpn (Heavy Machinery Dept) 1965, assigned to heavy machinery section of machinery group, worked at Olayan Saudi Holdings Co. Ltd, Al-Khobar, Saudi Arabia 1978–80, with Heavy Machinery Dept, Tokyo 1980–85, with Mitsubishi International Corpn, New York, USA 1985–92, Gen. Man. Corp. Planning Office, Tokyo 1992–95, mem. Bd of Dirs Mitsubishi Corpn 1995–, Dir, Coordination, Mitsubishi Corpn 1996–97, Man. Dir, Coordination 1997–98, Man. Dir, Admin 1998–2000, Man. Dir and Group CEO New Business Initiative Group 2000–01, Exec. Vice-Pres. and Group CEO 2001, Sr Exec. Vice-Pres. and Group CEO 2001–04, Pres. and CEO Mitsubishi Corpn 2004–10, Chair. Mitsubishi Corpn 2010–; mem. Japan Asscn of Corp. Execs (Keizai Doyukai), Vice-Chair. 2003–08. *Address:* Mitsubishi Corporation, Mitsubishi Shoji Building, 3-1, Marunouchi 2-chome, Chiyoda-ku, Tokyo 100-8086, Japan (office). *Telephone:* (3) 3210-2121 (office). *Fax:* (3) 3210-8583 (office). *E-mail:* info@mitsubishicorp.com (office). *Website:* www.mitsubishicorp.com (office).

KÓKA, János, PhD; Hungarian business executive and fmr politician; *Chairman and CEO, Cellum Global Inc.;* b. 5 July 1972, Budapest; m.; two c.; ed Esztergom Pelbárt Timisoara Franciscan High School, Faculty of Gen. Medicine, Semmelweis Univ. of Medical Sciences; CEO Elender Computer Ltd (Elender Computer Kft.) 1996–2004 (and CEO of legal successors of co.); Chair. and CEO Cellum Global Inc. 2011–; European Deputy Pres. PSINet Inc. 1999–2001; Pres. Asscn of Information Tech. Enterprises 2003–; Chair. Information Tech. Program, Cttee of the Office for Nat. Research, Devt and Tech. 2004–; Minister of Economy and Transport 2004–08; mem. Parl. 2006–; mem. Szabad Demokraták Szövetsége (SzDSz—Alliance of Free Democrats), Chair. 2007–08, Leader of SzDSz Parl. Group 2007–10; IT Manager of Year Award 2000. *Leisure interests:* aviation, sailing, travel. *Address:* Cellum Global Inc., 2040 Budaörs, Távíró köz 4, Hungary (office). *Telephone:* (23) 814633 (office). *Fax:* (23) 814634 (office). *E-mail:* contact@cellum.com (office). *Website:* www.cellum.com (office).

KOKJE, Vishnu Sadashiv, LLB, MA; Indian lawyer and government official; *International President, Vishwa Hindu Parishad;* b. 6 Sept. 1939, Dahi village, Tehsil Kukshi Dist, Dhar, Madhya Pradesh (MP); m. Leena Vishnu Kokje; two d.; ed secondary educ. in Dhar MP, Holkar Coll., Indore, MP, Govt Arts and Commerce Coll., Indore, Christian Coll., Indore; practised in various legal fields, including civil law, labour and industrial law, co. matters and constitutional writs 1964–90; appeared before several Enquiry Comms and in election petitions; apptd Judge of MP High Court 1990; Pres. MP State Consumer Disputes Redressal Comm. 1992–94; Admin. Judge, Rajasthan High Court 1998–2001, Acting Chief Justice of Rajasthan High Court 2001; Sr Advocate, Supreme Court of India 2002–03; Gov. of Himachal Pradesh 2003–08; Int. Pres. Vishwa Hindu Parishad 2018–. *Leisure interests:* reading, travelling, long motor drives, computers and Internet surfing, badminton and cricket. *Address:* 201 Park Residency, 24 Bapna Compound, Race Course Road No. 2, Indore 452 003, Madhya Pradesh, India (home).

KOKOSHIN, Andrei Afanasievich, DHisSc; Russian political scientist, politician and academic; *Professor and Dean of School of World Politics, Lomonosov Moscow State University;* b. 26 Oct. 1945, Moscow; m.; two d.; ed Bauman Moscow Higher Tech. Univ.; scientific researcher, Head of Dept, Deputy Dir, Inst. of USA and Canada, Acad. of Sciences 1974–92; First Deputy Minister of Defence 1992–97; Chair. Interagency Cttee on Defence Security, Security Council of the Russian Fed. 1993–97; mem. Govt Council on Industrial Policy 1993–97; Sec., Council of Defence of Russian Fed. 1993–97; fmr Chief Military Inspector of Russian Fed.; Sec., Security Council of Russian Fed. 1997–98; mem. State Duma 1999– (mem. Otechestvo–All Russia faction –2003, United Russia faction 2003–, Deputy Chair. United Russia faction 2008–), Vice-Chair. Cttee on Industry, Construction and High Technologies 1999–2003, Chair. Cttee on CIS and Compatriot Affairs 2003–07; mem. Russian Acad. of Sciences 1987 (Acting Vice-Pres. 1998–99, Dir Inst. of Int. Security 2000–), Academician-Sec. of Social Sciences Section 2009–; mem. Russian Acad. of Social Sciences 1993, Russian Acad. of Artillery and Rocket Science and Eng 1993–, Russian Acad. of Natural Sciences; Chair. Bd High Tech. Foundation/Gorbachev Project 2001, Russian Public Bd for Educ. Devt 2001; mem. Scientific Advisory Council, Inst. for Int. Studies, Stanford Univ., USA 2000–, Gen. Council United Russia Party 2001–, Bd Dirs Nuclear Threat Initiative 2001–, Bd of Trustees Russian–American Business Council 2002, Nat. Anticorruption Comm. 2002; Dean, School of World Politics, Prof., Lomonosov Moscow State Univ. (MGU) 2003–; Hon. Chair. Russian Rugby Football League 1992–; Services for the Fatherland, Mark of Honour, Military Comradeship 1987, 1997, 2000, 2005. *Publications:* 25 books (including six as co-author) on nat. security, int. affairs, Russian nat. industrial policy and econs including Forecasting and Foreign Policy 1975, The USA in the System of International Relations in the 1980s 1984, Weapons in Space: Security Dilemma 1986, National Industrial Policy of Russia 1992, Soviet Strategic Thought 1918–1991 1999, The National Industrial Policy and the National Security of Russia (jtly) 2001, Deterrence in the Second Nuclear Age (jtly) 2001, Types and Categories of Nuclear Conflicts in the XXI Century 2003, Strategic Governance 2003, Sociology and Politology of the Military Strategy 2006, Technocrats, Neotechnocrats and Technocracy 2008, On Strategic Stability in the Past and in the Future 2009; more than 150 articles and papers. *Address:* State Duma, Okhotny Ryad 1, 103265 Moscow, Russia. *Telephone:* (495) 692-69-65 (office); (495) 938-18-92 (office). *Fax:* (495) 692-84-53 (office); (495) 938-18-93 (office). *E-mail:* kokoshin@duma.gov.ru (office).

KOKOYEV (KOKOITI), Eduard Dzhabeyevich; Georgian politician; b. 31 Oct. 1964, Tskhinvali, S Ossetian Autonomous Oblast, Georgian SSR; fmr mem. Russian nat. wrestling team; First Sec. Tskhinvali Br. of Komsomol 1989–92; business activities, Moscow 1992–2001; Rep. of 'Repub. of South Ossetia', Moscow 1997–99; Pres., 'Repub. of South Ossetia' 2001–11; mem. Kleta Partia party.

KOKUBU, Fumiya; Japanese business executive; *President and CEO, Marubeni Corporation;* joined Marubeni Corpn 1975, Corp. Vice-Pres. 2005–08, mem. Bd of Dirs 2008–, Man. Exec. Officer 2008–10, Pres. and CEO Marubeni America Corpn and Marubeni Canada Ltd, Sr Man. Exec. Officer and Regional Chief Exec. Officer for the Americas 2010–12, Chief Information Officer, Sr Exec. Vice-Pres. and COO of Global Strategy and Co-ordination Dept, Information Strategy Dept, and Research Inst. 2012–13, Pres. and CEO 2013–; Outside Statutory Auditor, Inpex Corpn. *Address:* Marubeni Corpn, 42 Ohtemachi 1-chome, Chiyoda-ku, Tokyo 100-8088, Japan (office). *Telephone:* (3) 3282-2111 (office). *Fax:* (3) 3282-4241 (office). *E-mail:* info@marubeni.com (office). *Website:* www.marubeni.com (office).

KOLA, Jukka, MSc, LicSc, PhD; Finnish agricultural scientist, academic and university administrator; *Rector, University of Helsinki;* b. 1960; ed Univ. of Arkansas, USA, Univ. of Helsinki, Univ. of Illinois, USA; Researcher/Sr Researcher, Agricultural Econs Research Inst., Helsinki 1986–92; Acting Prof., Agricultural Policy, Dept of Econs and Man., Univ. of Helsinki 1992–99, Docent, Agricultural Policy 1994, Prof. 1999–, Head of Dept of Econs and Man. 2001–03, Dean, Faculty of Agric. and Forestry 2004–06, 2007–09, Vice-Rector, Univ. of Helsinki 2010–13, Rector 2013–; Insp. of student org. Wiipurilainen osakunta 2010–13; mem. Rectors' Forum, League of European Research Univs 2013–, Bd of Dirs 2016–; mem. European Asscn of Agricultural Economists, American Agricultural Economists Asscn, Int. Asscn of Agricultural Economists, Int. Food and Agribusiness Man. Asscn, Nordic Asscn of Agricultural Scientists, Scientific Agricultural Soc. of Finland; Fulbright Scholarship, Univ. of Illinois 1989–90, Award for the best scientific article published by a younger Nordic agricultural economist in int. peer-review scientific journals 1991–94, Nordic Asscn of Agricultural Scientists, Section IX (agricultural economics), NJF-Congress 1995, Eino Kaila Award 1999, Co-operative Special Award, Pellervo-Seura, in association with UN Int. Year of Co-operatives 2012. *Publications:* numerous papers in professional journals on agricultural, food and rural economics and policy, international trade and development, new political economy, welfare economics and supply and demand analysis. *Address:* Office of the Rector, University of Helsinki, PO Box 3, Helsinki 00014, Finland (office). *Telephone:* (2) 941-22211 (office). *E-mail:* jukka.kola@helsinki.fi (office). *Website:* www.helsinki.fi/administration/rector (office).

KOLAGHASSI, Ali Hassan; Saudi Arabian business executive; currently Vice-Chair. and CEO, Saraya Holdings Ltd, also Chair. Saraya Aqaba, Saraya Bandar Jissah, Saraya Abdali (subsidiaries); Vice-Pres. Saudi Oger; Chair. Saraya Real Estate Middle East and N Africa Fund, Saraya Skies, Oger Abu Dhabi, Oger Jordan, MDI (Millennium Devt Int.), Rubicon; Dir Saudi Oger Telecom, MEDGULF-Jordan (Mediterranean and Gulf Insurance and Reinsurance Co.), Saudi Med Investment Co., AB Capital; mem. Bd of Trustees, King Hussein Cancer Foundation; Real Estate Industry Champion, Young Arab Leaders Org. 2005. *Address:* Saraya Holdings Ltd, Um Uthainah Al-Janoubi, Al-Koufeh Street, Amman, Jordan (office). *Telephone:* (6) 5505444 (office). *Fax:* (6) 5561738 (office). *E-mail:* info@sarayaholdings.com (office). *Website:* www.sarayaholdings.com (office).

KOLDING, Eivind Drachmann, MA (Law); Danish lawyer and business executive; *CEO, Novo A/S;* b. 16 Nov. 1959; ed Univ. of Copenhagen, Wharton Business School, USA; admitted to the Bar 1986; lawyer, Corp. Secr., A.P. Møller, Copenhagen 1989, later Sr Vice-Pres. and Head of Secr., Man. Dir Maersk Hong Kong Ltd 1996–98, Chief Financial Officer, A.P. Møller-Maersk A/S 1998–2006, mem. Exec. Bd and Partner, A.P. Møller-Maersk A/S and Co-CEO Container Business, A.P. Moller-Maersk A/S 2006–11, CEO Maersk Line 2006–12; mem. Bd of Dirs, Danske Bank A/S 2001–13, Vice-Chair. 2001–11, Chair. 2011–12, CEO 2012–13; CEO Novo A/S 2014–, E. Kolding Shipping ApS; Vice-Chair. Danmarks Skibskredit (Denmark Ship Finance); Chair. Safmarine Container Lines NV; mem. Bd of Dirs, Dansk Supermarked, NNIT A/S 2015–, Novo Nordisk A/S 2015–. *Address:* Novo Nordisk A/S, Novo Allé, 2880 Bagsvaerd, Denmark (office). *Telephone:* 44-44-88-88 (office). *E-mail:* webmaster@novonordisk.com (office). *Website:* www.novonordisk.com (office).

KOLESNIKOV, Borys Viktorovych, MEcons; Ukrainian business executive and politician; *Co-Chair, Opozytsiyny Blok (Opposition Bloc);* b. 25 Oct. 1962, Zhdanov (now Mariupol), Donetsk Oblast, Ukrainian SSR, USSR; m. Svitlana Kolesnikova; one s. one d.; ed Donetsk Nat. Tech. Univ., Donetsk State Univ. of Man.; employed with various commercial enterprises in Donetsk Oblast, including in steel industry, from 1980; Dir Yug Trading Co. 1991–; Vice-Pres. Shakhtar Donetsk (football club) 1998–; mem. Donetsk Oblast Council 1998–2002, Leader 2001–06; Chair. Football Fed. of Donetsk Oblast 2002; Owner and Pres. HC Donbass (ice hockey club) 2010–; mem. Verkhovna Rada (parl.) (Partiya Rehioniv—PR—Party of Regions) 2006–14; Deputy Prime Minister 2010–12, also Minister of Infrastructure; Co-Chair. Opozytsiyny Blok (Opposition Bloc) 2016–; mem. PR, Sec., PR Presidium 2014–; Order of Merit (II Degree) 2007, Honoured Economist of Ukraine, Silver Medal for Independence of Ukraine. *Address:* Opozytsiyny Blok, Kyiv, Ukraine (office). *Telephone:* (44) 223-32-12 (office). *E-mail:* pressa@opposition.org.ua (office). *Website:* opposition.org.ua (office).

KOLGA, Margus, BA, MA; Estonian diplomatist and government official; b. 1966, Tallinn; m. Maarja Maasikas; three c.; ed Tartu Univ.; Deputy Sec.-Gen., Ministry of Defence 1996–2003 (resgnd); Sr Research Fellow, Baltic Defence Coll. 2003–07; Acting Co-Chair. Defence and Mil. Terminology Comm. and mem. Mil. Educ. Bd 2004–06; Academic Dir, State Defence Course 2006–07; Dir-Gen. First Political Dept (Security Policy and Int. Orgs), Ministry of Foreign Affairs 2007–10; Amb. and Perm. Rep. to UN, New York 2010–15.

KOLLER, Arnold, Dr iur, Lic oec; Swiss politician and academic; b. 29 Aug. 1933, Appenzell; m. Erica Brauder 1972; two c.; ed Univ. of St Gallen, Freiburg Univ., Univ. of Berkeley, USA; fmr Univ. Prof. of Law, Univ. of St Gallen; mem. Swiss Parl. 1971–85; Pres. Nat. Council 1984–85; mem. Bundesrat (Fed. Council) 1986–99, Head of Fed. Mil. (Defence) Dept 1986–89; Head Fed. Dept of Justice and Police 1989–99; Pres. of Switzerland 1990, 1997; Pres. Int. Conf. on Federalism 2002; Chair. Forum of Feds 2006–10, now Fellow; Dr hc (Bern) 2002; Swiss Federalism Prize 2014. *Publications include:* Grundfragen einer Typuslehre im Gesellschaftsrecht 1967, Die unmittelbare Anwendbarkeit völkerrechtlicher Verträge und des EWG-Vertrags 1971, Für eine starke und solidarische Schweiz 1999, Zur Entstehung der neuen Bundesverfassung 2002, Aus der Werkstatt eines Bundesrates 2014. *Leisure interests:* skiing, tennis. *Address:* Steinegg, Gschwendes 8, 9050 Appenzell, Switzerland (home). *Telephone:* (71) 7872290 (home). *Fax:* (71) 7875590 (home). *E-mail:* arnold.koller@bluemail.ch (home). *Website:* www.forumfed.org (office).

KOLLER, Daphne, BSc, MSc, PhD; Israeli/American computer scientist and academic; *Chief Computing Officer, Calico Labs;* b. Jerusalem, Israel; m. Dan Avida; ed Hebrew Univ. of Jerusalem, Stanford Univ.; Postdoctoral Researcher, Computer Science Div., Univ. of California, Berkeley 1993–95; Asst Prof., Dept of Computer Science, Stanford Univ. 1995–2001, Assoc. Prof. 2001–06, Arthur G. Villard Fellow for Undergraduate Teaching 2004, Prof. 2006–14; Co-Founder Coursera (educational technology co.) 2012, Co-CEO 2012–14, Pres. 2014–16, Co-Chair. 2016–; Chief Computing Officer Calico Labs 2016–; Fellow, American Asscn for Artificial Intelligence 2004; Rothschild Grad. Fellowship 1989–90, Univ. of California Pres.'s Postdoctoral Fellowship 1993–95, Arthur L. Samuel Award for best thesis in the Computer Science Dept, Stanford Univ. 1994, Sloan Foundation Research Fellowship 1996, Office of Naval Research Young Investigator Award 1999, Presidential Early Career Award for Scientists and Engineers 1999, IJCAI Computers and Thought Award 2001, MacArthur Foundation Fellowship 2004, World Tech. Award in Information Tech. (Software), The World Tech. Network 2004, ACM/Infosys Award 2007. *Publications:* numerous scientific papers in professional journals. *Leisure interests:* reading, listening to music, hiking, travelling to exotic locations with her husband. *Address:* Calico Labs, 1170 Veterans Blvd, S San Francisco, CA 94080, USA (office). *Website:* www.calicolabs .com (office); www.coursera.org (office).

KOLLEY, Hon. Abdou, MEconSc; Gambian economist and politician; b. 1 Jan. 1970, Kembujeh; ed Univ. Jean Monnet, France (Advanced Diploma in French Language); Economist, Dept of State for Finance and Econ. Affairs 1997–2000; Sr Economist, later Prin. Economist and Dir, Gambia Divestiture Agency 2000–04; Econs Analyst, Strategic Policy Unit, UNDP, Banjul 2004–07; Minister for Trade, Employment and Industry 2007–09, Minister of Finance and Econ. Affairs 2009–10, 2010–11, 2012–13, 2015–17 (resgnd), of Trade, Regional Integration and Employment March–July 2010, 2011–12, 2013–14; fmr mem. Nat. Planning Comm. (now defunct); Insignia of Officer of Nat. Order of the Repub. of The Gambia 2010; Partner to the Private Sector Award, Gambia Chamber of Commerce and Industry 2009. *Publications include:* articles in Economic Watch magazine 2001, 2002, Cash Budgeting and PRSP/Poverty Reduction Strategies: A Review of Case Studies and Lessons for The Gambia (unpublished) 2005. *Leisure interests:* gardening, reading, public lectures. *E-mail:* abdoukolley@hotmail.com.

KOLO, Roger Christophe Laurent; Malagasy radiologist and politician; b. 3 Sept. 1943, Belo sur Tsiribihina; m. Zakia Katoun; three c.; ed Univ. of Antananarivo, Univ. of Geneva, Switzerland; lived in Switzerland for almost 30 years; Medical Asst, Geneva Univ. Clinic 1983; Head of Radiation Clinic, Hôspital cantonal de Fribourg 1987–92; Dir Inst. of Radiology, Cornavin, Geneva 1992–94; est. pvt. radiology lab., Geneva 1997; returned to Madagascar 2013, refused permission to run in presidential election due to residency requirements; Prime Minister 2014–15, also Minister of Public Health 2014–15 (resgnd); mem. Swiss Soc. of Radiology, Société Française de Radiologie. *Address:* c/o Office of the Prime Minister, BP 248, Palais d'Etat Mahazoarivo, 101 Antananarivo, Madagascar.

KOLOBOV, Yuriy Volodymyrovych; Ukrainian economist, banker and politician; b. 8 April 1973, Pavlograd, Dnipropetrovsk Region; m.; one s. one d.; ed V. Karazin Kharkiv State Univ., Kyiv Higher School of Finance, Int. Business Inst.; Head of interbank foreign exchange transactions and Deputy Dir, Kharkiv Br., PrivatBank 1995–2000; First Deputy Dir, Kyiv Br., Credit Dnepr Bank 2000–01; Deputy Chair. Bd TAS-Investbank CJSC 2001–02; Dir of Treasury, State Savings Bank of Ukraine (OshchadBank) 2003–08, Adviser to Chair. 2009–10; Chair. BTA Bank JSC June–Dec. 2008; mem. Bd and First Deputy Chair. State Export-Import Bank of Ukraine JSC 2010–12; First Deputy Chair. Nat. Bank of Ukraine 2012; Minister of Finance 2012–14. *Address:* c/o Ministry of Finance, 01008 Kyiv, vul. M. Hrushevskoho 12/2, Ukraine (office).

KOŁODKO, Grzegorz Witold, PhD; Polish economist, academic, author and politician; *Founding Director and Professor, Transformation, Integration and Globalization Economic Research;* b. 28 Jan. 1949, Tczew; m.; two d.; ed Kozminski Univ., Warsaw; Prof., Warsaw School of Econs 1972–2001, apptd Chair. of Econs 1984, Dir Inst. of Finance 1989–94; Adviser to the Gov., Nat. Bank of Poland 1982–88; Prof. of Econs, Kozminski Univ. (ALK), Warsaw 2000–; fmr consultant, World Inst. for Devt Econs Research of UN, Helsinki; IMF and World Bank expert 1991–92, 1999–2000; First Deputy Prime Minister 1994–97, 2002–03; Minister of Finance 1994–97, 2002–03; apptd Sasakawa Chair. and Distinguished Research Prof. in Devt Policy, World Inst. for Devt Econs Research, UN 1997, Research Fellow 1988, 1989, 2002; Founding Dir and Prof., Transformation, Integration and Globalization Econ. Research (TIGER) 2000–; Visiting Prof., Yale Univ., UCLA; John C. Evans Prof. in European Studies, Univ. of Rochester, NY 1998–2004; Visiting Prof., Universita di Trento, Italy 2007–, Moscow School of Econs, Lomonosov Univ. 2005–; Distinguished Prof. of Emerging Markets, Inst., Beijing Normal Univ. 2016; mem. Econ Council, Polish Govt 1989–91, Econs Cttee, Polish Acad. of Sciences 2011–15, European Acad. of Arts, Sciences and Humanities; Foreign mem. Russian Acad. of Sciences 2016; Sr Fulbright Fellow, Univ. of Illinois 1985–86; Sr Research Fellow, Inst. of Finance and Monetary Policy, Tokyo 1984; Sr Fellow, Chongyang Inst. for Financial Studies, Renmin Univ. of China; Hon. Prof., Indian Inst. of Finance 2004, Tianjin Univ., China 2005, Moscow Acad. of Econs and Law 2005, Guizhou Finance and Econs Univ., Guiyang, People's Repub. of China 2009, Alfred Nobel Univ., Dnepropetrovsk 2014; Hon. Chair. China Public Diplomacy Inst., Sanya 2016; Commdr's Medal, Order of Polonia Restituta 1997; Dr hc (Univ. of Lvov) 2003, (Univ. of Chengdu) 2004, (Finance Acad., Moscow) 2009, (Univ. of Debrecen) 2009, (Int. Inst. of Man., Kiev) 2014; numerous prizes and awards including Man of the Year Award 1994, Comandoria Restituta Medal, Poland 1997, Polish TV Best Politician Award 1997, Award of Minister for Science 2002, 2014, High Award of Polish Acad. of Sciences 2013, Special Honorary Award of Polish Economic Soc. 2015. *Publications include:* more than 400 publs in 26 languages on econ. theory and policy, including books in English: Strategy for Poland 1994, The Polish Alternative: Old Myths, Hard Facts and New Strategies in Successful Transformation of the Polish Economy 1997, From Shock to Therapy: The Political Economy of Postsocialist Transformations 2000, Post-Communist Transition: The Thorny Road 2000, Globalization and Transformation: Illusions and Reality 2001, Globalization and Catching-up in Transition Economies 2001, Emerging Market Economies: Globalization and Development 2003, Globalization and Social Stress 2005, The Polish Miracle: Lessons for Emerging Markets 2005, The World Economy and Great Post-Communist Change 2006, 20 Years of Transformation: Achievements, Problems, Prospects 2010, Truth, Errors, and Lies: Politics and Economics in a Volatile World 2011, Whither the World: The Political Economy of the Future 2014. *Leisure interests:* contemporary literature, classical music, nature, sport, marathon runner (best time 3:38), travelling (explored more than 160 countries). *Address:* Transformation, Integration and Globalization Economic Research (TIGER), 59 Jagiellonska Street, 03-301 Warsaw, Poland (office). *E-mail:* kolodko@tiger.edu.pl (office). *Website:* www.volatileworld.net (home).

KOLOKOLTSEV, Col-Gen. Vladimir Alexandrovich, DJur; Russian police officer and government official; *Minister of Internal Affairs;* b. 11 May 1961, Nizhnii Lomov, Penza Oblast, Russian SFSR, USSR; m.; one s. one d.; ed Political Coll. of VLKSM (All-Union Lenin Young Communist League—Komsomol), Ministry of Internal Affairs of the USSR; began career in police unit on guard at foreign diplomatic missions in Moscow from 1982, apptd platoon commdr of separate patrol bn of Gagarinskii Dist Exec. Cttee, Moscow 1984; entered Higher Political Coll. of Ministry of Internal Affairs, studied at Faculty of Jurisprudence, graduated 1989; returned to police service as detective of Criminal Investigation Unit of Kuntshevskii Dist Exec. Cttee, Moscow, apptd Deputy Chief of Police Station No. 20 in Moscow, later Chief of Police Station No. 8, assigned to Criminal Investigation Dept of Moscow Police Dept HQ as Sr Detective of the Second Unit 1992, apptd Chief of Police Station No. 108 in Moscow 1993–95, Chief of Criminal Investigation Div. in Cen. Dist Police Dept 1995–97; worked in Ministry of Internal Affairs and as Chief of Regional Unit No. 4, Dept on Organized Crime Prevention 1997–99, Chief of Regional Operational Search Bureau, Dept on Organized Crime Prevention for southeastern admin. region of Moscow 1999–2001, Chief of Unit No. 3, Operational Search Bureau, Ministry of Internal Affairs for Cen. Fed. Okrug 2001, later apptd Deputy Chief of this Operational Search Bureau, Chief of Police Dept in Oryol Oblast 2007–09, Deputy Chief of Criminal Investigation Dept, Ministry of Internal Affairs April–Sept. 2009, Moscow Police Commr 2009–12, rank of Militsiya Lt-Gen. 2010, Police Lt-Gen. 2011, Police Col-Gen. 2013, Maj.-Gen. of the Police 2015; Minister of Internal Affairs 2012–; Honoured Officer of Internal Affairs Authorities, several state and departmental awards. *Address:* Ministry of Internal Affairs, 119049 Moscow, ul. Zhitnaya 16, Russian Federation (office). *Telephone:* (495) 667-72-64 (office). *Fax:* (495) 667-57-33 (office). *E-mail:* mvd12@mvdrf.ru (office). *Website:* www.mvd.ru (office); en.mvd.ru/Ministry/ Minister (office); government.ru/en/gov/persons/199/events (office).

KOLOMOYSKY, Ihor Valeriyovych; Ukrainian/Cypriot/Israeli business executive; b. 13 Feb. 1963, Dnipropetrovsk, Ukrainian SSR, USSR; m. Irina Kolomoisky; one s. one d.; ed Dnipropetrovsk Metallurgical Inst.; currently Co-owner Privat Dnepropetrovsk business group; Co-f. Sentosa Ltd (oil supplier) 1991, currently mem. Bd of Dirs; Co-founder PrivatBank 1992, Chair. from 1997, currently mem. Supervisory Bd; mem. Supervisory Bd, Ukrnafta oil and gas co. 2003–, mem. Bd of Dirs, Central European Media Enterprises (CME), owns numerous other cos in other industries; Gov. Dnipropetrovsk Oblast 2014–15 (dismissed); Founder European Jewish Parl. (based in Brussels, Belgium) 2011; Pres. United Jewish Community of Ukraine 2012–, Babi Yar Foundation 2012–. *Address:* PrivatBank Head Office, 49094 Dnipropetrovsk, nab. Peremohy 50, Ukraine (office). *Telephone:* (56) 716-11-31 (office). *E-mail:* info@privatbank.ua (office). *Website:* www .privatbank.ua (office).

KOLPAKOVA, Irina; Russian ballerina (retd) and ballet teacher; *Ballet Mistress, American Ballet Theatre;* b. 22 May 1933, Leningrad (now St Petersburg); m. Vladilen Semenov 1955; one d.; ed Leningrad Choreographic School, Leningrad Conservatory; Prima Ballerina, Kirov Theatre of Opera and Ballet, Leningrad (now Mariinsky Theatre, St Petersburg) 1957–91; Ballet Mistress, American Ballet Theatre 1990–; fmr Ballet Master, Ballet Internationale, Indianapolis Ind. 1997, then Asst Artistic Dir; Prof., Vaganova Acad. of Russian Ballet, St Petersburg; Artistic Advisor and Perm. Guest Faculty, Central Wisconsin School of Ballet; Order of Lenin 1967; Merited Artist of the Russian SFSR 1957, People's Artist of the Russian SFSR 1965, Grand Prix de Ballet, Paris 1966, USSR State

Prize 1980, Hero of Socialist Labour 1983, Dance Magazine Award 2010. *Main ballet roles:* Aurora (Sleeping Beauty), Juliet (Romeo and Juliet), Desdemona (Othello), Tao Khao (The Red Poppy), Maria (Fountain of Bakhchisarai), title roles in Giselle, Cinderella, Raymonda and La Sylphide, Chopiniana (Les Sylphides), Kitri (Don Quixote), Natalie Pushkin (Pushkin), Eve (Creation of the World); cr. role of Katerina (The Stone Flower) and Shirin (Legend of Love); leading roles in Coast of Hope 1959, Ala and Lolly 1969, Creation of the World 1971. *Television:* main roles: The Lady (The Lady and the Hooligan), Woman (The House by the Roadside), Aurora (Sleeping Beauty), Raymonda (Raymonda). *Address:* American Ballet Theatre, 890 Broadway, New York, NY 10003, USA; Tolstoy House, 15-17 Rubenstein Street, St Petersburg, Russian Federation (home). *Telephone:* (212) 477-3030 (office). *E-mail:* contact@abt.org. *Website:* www.abt.org; www.cwschoolofballet.com.

KOM, Mary; Indian boxer and police officer; *Superintendent of Police (Sports), Manipur;* b. 1 March 1983; d. of Mangte Tonpa Kom and Mangte Akham Kom; m. K. Onkholer (Onler) 2005; ed Loktak Christian Mission School, St Xavier School, Adimjati School; Sub-Insp., Manipur Police 2005, Insp. 2008, Deputy Supt 2010–; Supt of Police (Sports) 2012–; East Open Boxing Championship (gold medal) 2000, World Women Boxing Championship (silver medal), Pennsylvania, USA 2001, Women Nat. Boxing Championship (gold medal), Chennai 2001, Sr Women Nat. Boxing Championship (gold medal), New Delhi 2001, Witch Cup Boxing Championship (gold medal), Hungary 2002, World Women Boxing Championship (gold medal), Turkey 2002, Nat. Games (gold medal), Hyderabad 2002, Nat. Women Sports Meet (gold medal), New Delhi 2002, Asian Women Boxing Championship (gold medal), India 2003, Sr Women Nat. Boxing Championship, (gold medal) Aizawl 2003, (gold medal) Assam 2004, (gold medal) Kerala 2004, World Women Boxing Tournament (gold medal), Norway 2004, Asian Women Boxing Championship (gold medal), Taiwan 2005, World Women Boxing Championship (gold medal), Russia 2005, Nat. Sr Women Boxing Championship (gold medal), Jamshedpur 2005, Asian Cadet Boxing Championship (gold medal), Viet Nam 2006, Vijle Women Box Tournament (gold medal), Denmark 2006, World Women Boxing Championship (gold medal), India 2006, Asian Women Boxing Championship (silver medal), India 2008, World Women Boxing Championship (gold medal), China 2008, Indo- Sweden Dual Match Boxing Tournament (gold medal), Sweden 2009, Indoor Asian Games (gold medal), Vietnam 2009, Asian Women's Boxing Championship (gold medal), Kazakhstan 2010, AIBA Women World Boxing Championship (gold medal), Barbados 2010, India Police Meet (gold medal), Pune 2010, 16th Asian Games (Bronze Medal), Guangzhou, China 2010, 12th Sr Nat. Women Boxing Championship (gold medal), Bhopal, India 2011, Asia Cup (gold medal), Haikou China 2011, 6th Asian Women's Boxing Championship (gold medal), Mongolia 2012, Olympic Games (bronze medal), London 2012, Asian Women's Boxing Championship (gold medal), Viet Nam 2017; Dr hc (Mangalayatan Univ.); Arjuna Award 2004, Padma Shri 2006, NETV People's Choice Awards 2006, People of the Year—Limca Book of Records 2007, CNN-IBN 'Real Heroes' Award 2008, Pepsi MTV Youth Icon 2008, 'Magnificent Mary', AIBA 2008, Sports Women of the year, Sahara India Pariwar 2008–09, Rajiv Gandhi Khel Ratna 2009, Amb. for Women's Boxing, Int. Boxing Asscn 2009, Param Poojaniya Shri Guruji Puruskar 2009, North East Excellence Award 2009, YFLO Women Achiever, FCCI Ladies Org. 2009–10, Sports Person of the year, Northeast, Assam Sports Journalist Asscn 2010, Sports Women of the year 2010–2011, Sahara India Pariwar, Spirit of Sports Award, NDTV India 2012, Tribal Achievers' Award, Ministry of Tribal Affairs 2012, GoI, Karmavir Purushkar Award, ICONGO 2012, Padma Bhushan (Sports) 2013. *Address:* c/o Infinity Optimal Solutions Pvt. Ltd., F-301 A, Ground Floor, Lado Sarai, New Delhi 110 030, India (office); Mary Kom Regional Boxing Foundation, National Games Village Langol, A-112, Zone-II, Imphal 795 004 (office); Samulamlan, Moirang 795 133, India (home). *Telephone:* (11) 41416161 (office); (38) 52411789 (home); 9856157822 (mobile). *Fax:* (11) 41416160 (office). *E-mail:* admin@iosindia.com (office); mcmary.kom@gmail.com; kcmarykom@yahoo.co.in. *Website:* www.iosindia.com (office); www.marykom.com.

KOMBO-YAYA, Dieudonné; Central African Republic politician and government official; *President, National Authority for Elections;* Deputy Dir OAU, later Head of Electoral Unit, Dept of Political Affairs, Africa Union (AU) 1981–2008; took part in more than 50 missions to observe elections in 30 African countries and other elections: elections in Congo (Brazzaville) 1993, Spain 1995, Madagascar 2002, Colombia 2007, presidential election in Congo 2009, presidential and parliamentary elections in Burundi 2010, constitutional referendums in Kenya and Niger 2010; mem. of mediation missions: Chad–Libya conflict 1988, Libreville agreements on the crisis in Congo (Brazzaville) 1993, Paris Agreements on the crisis in Gabon 1994, crisis between the govt and the opposition in the Comoros 1995–96, Angola–Zambia dispute 1998, crisis in the Comoros 2003, crisis in Liberia 2003, crisis in Haiti 2006; Co-initiator of project African Charter on Democracy, Elections and Governance 2002, adopted by the AU 2007; Minister of Foreign and Francophone Affairs and Regional Integration 2008–09; UN Counsellor during presidential election in Benin 2011; Pres. Nat. Authority for Elections 2013–.

KOMISARJEVSKY, Christopher, BS, MBA; American public relations executive; *Member, International Advisory Council, APCO Worldwide International;* b. 16 Feb. 1945, New Haven, Conn.; m. Reina Komisarjevsky; ed Union Coll., Univ. of Freiburg, Germany, Univ. of Connecticut School of Business, Wharton School; Capt. US Army (helicopter pilot) 1967–72, combat service in Viet Nam, 1st Cavalry Div. 1969–70; Sr Vice-Pres. Hill & Knowlton 1974–85, Deputy Man. Dir Hill & Knowlton International 1985–86, COO 1986–87, Pres. and CEO of Europe/Middle East/Africa operations 1987–88, Exec. Vice-Pres. and Man. Dir Corpn and Financial Counselling Office, USA 1990–91, Exec. Vice-Pres. and Gen. Man., New York and Eastern USA, 1991–93; Pres. and CEO Carl Byoir and Assocs 1988–90; Pres. and CEO Gavin Anderson & Co. 1993–95; Pres. and CEO Burson Marsteller, USA 1995–98, Pres. and CEO Burson Marsteller (Worldwide) 1998–2004 (retd); a.i. Harold Burson Faculty Chair, Boston Univ. Coll. of Communication 2006, currently Harold Burson Prof. and Chair in Public Relations, Boston Univ.; with APCO Worldwide, New York, mem. Advisory Council, APCO Worldwide International and Sr Counselor 2006–; Trustee, EQ Advisors Trust; mem. Univ. of Miami Rosenstiel School, Asscn for the Help of Retarded Children; mem. Arthur Page Soc.; lectured on communications and business in Spain, Switzerland and New York; Ellis Island Medal of Honor 1996. *Publications:* Peanut Butter & Jelly Management 2000 (with Reina Komisarjevsky), The Power of Reputation 2012; numerous articles on public relations topics. *Address:* APCO Worldwide, 51 Madison Avenue, Suite 2510, New York, NY 10100, USA (office). *Telephone:* (212) 300-1800 (office). *Fax:* (212) 300-1819 (office). *E-mail:* info@apcoworldwide.com (office). *Website:* www.apcoworldwide.com (office).

KOMIYAMA, Hiroshi, MEng, PhD; Japanese chemical engineer, university administrator and academic; *Chairman, Mitsubishi Research Institute, Inc.;* b. 15 Dec. 1944, Tochigi Pref., Tokyo; ed Toyama High School, Tokyo, Univ. of Tokyo; mem. staff, Univ. of Tokyo 1972–, Lecturer 1977–81, Asst Prof. 1981–88, Prof., Dept of Chemical System Eng 1988–2005, Dean, School of Eng 2000–02, Vice-Pres. Univ. of Tokyo 2003–04, Exec. Vice-Pres. 2004–05, Pres. 2005–09, Pres. Emer. 2009–; Chair. Mitsubishi Research Inst. 2009–; f. Platinum Network 2010; mem. Bd of Dirs Global Green Growth Inst. 2011–; mem. Bd of Govs Okinawa Inst. of Science and Tech.; Adviser, KAITEKI Inst., also serves as adviser to Japanese govt on issues including the environment, aging, educ. and community renovation; Councillor, Asahi Glass Foundation; Pres. Soc. of Chemical Engineers of Japan 2002–03; Best Paper of the Year, Soc. of Chemical Engineers of Japan 1979, Best Research of the Year 1992, Society Award of the Year 2003. *Publications:* Technology to Sustain the Earth 1999, Answering to the Issues of Global Warming 1999, Structuring the Knowledge 2004; numerous scientific papers in professional journals. *Address:* Office of the Chairman, Mitsubishi Research Institute, Inc., 10-3, Nagatacho 2-Chome, Chiyoda-Ku, Tokyo 100-8141, Japan (office). *Website:* www.mri.co.jp (office).

KOMMASITH, Saleumxay, MA; Laotian diplomatist; *Minister of Foreign Affairs;* b. 31 Oct. 1968, Huaphan; m. Aruni Kumamaru; two d.; ed Moscow State Univ. of International Relations, Russia, Monash Univ., Australia; has held several positions at Ministry of Foreign Affairs, including Desk Officer for Australia 1992–94, Desk Officer for USA, Europe-America Dept 1994–96, Deputy Dir Western Europe Div. 1998–2000, Second Sec., Perm. Mission to UN, New York 2000–03, Dir of UN Div., Dept of Int. Orgs, Ministry of Foreign Affairs 2003–04, Deputy Dir-Gen. Dept of Int. Orgs, Ministry of Foreign Affairs 2004–07, Dir-Gen. 2007–11, Asst Minister for Foreign Affairs 2011–12, Amb. and Perm. Rep. to UN, New York 2012–14, Deputy Minister of Foreign Affairs 2014–16, Minister of Foreign Affairs 2016–. *Leisure interests:* golf, soccer. *Address:* Ministry of Foreign Affairs, 23 rue Singha, Ban Phonxay, Vientiane, Laos (office). *Telephone:* (21) 413148 (office). *Fax:* (21) 414009 (office). *E-mail:* ict@mofa.gov.la (office). *Website:* www.mofa.gov.la (office).

KOMORI, Shigetaka, BEcons; Japanese business executive; *Chairman and CEO, Fujifilm Holdings Corporation;* ed Univ. of Tokyo; joined Fuji Photo Film Co. Ltd 1963, held various sr positions in Graphic Arts and Printing Div., Industrial Products Dept and Corp. Planning Office, Head of Fuji Photo Film Europe GmbH, Düsseldorf, Dir Fuji Photo Film Co. Ltd 1995, Man. Dir 1999, Pres. 2000–03, Rep. Dir, Pres. and CEO Fujifilm Holdings Corpn 2003–12, Chair. and CEO 2012–; Pres. Photo-Sensitized Materials Mfrs Asscn, Japan-German Soc., Japan-Netherlands Soc.; Chair. Japan Asscn of Graphic Arts Suppliers and Mfrs; Grand Cross of the Order of Merit (Germany) 2006; Medal with Blue Ribbon by HM the Emperor of Japan 2004, Leadership Award, Int. Imaging Industry Asscn (I3A) 2004, inducted into Photo Marketing Asscn Int. Hall of Fame 2006. *Address:* Fujifilm Holdings Corpn, 26–30 Nishiazabu 2-chome, Minato-ku, Tokyo 106-8620, Japan (office). *Telephone:* (3) 3406-2111 (office). *Fax:* (3) 3406-2173 (office). *E-mail:* info@fujifilm.com (office). *Website:* www.fujifilm.com (office).

KOMOROWSKI, Bronisław Maria; Polish politician and fmr head of state; b. 4 June 1952, Oborniki Śląskie, nr Wrocław; s. of Count Zygmunt Leon Komorowski and Jadwiga Komorowska (née Szalkowska); m. Anna Dembowska 1977; two s. three d.; ed Cyprian Kamil Norwid High School, Univ. of Warsaw; Ed. Słowo Powszechne 1977–80; acted as underground publr at Polish People's Repub. (PRL), co-operated with Antoni Macierewicz in monthly publ. Voice; sentenced with activists of Movt for Defence of Human and Civic Rights to one month's imprisonment for organizing demonstration of 11 Nov. 1979 1980; worked in Centre of Social Investigations of NSZZ 'Solidarity' 1980–81; a signatory of founder's declaration of Clubs in the Service of Independence 27 Sept. 1981; internee during 1980s; taught in Lower Seminar in Niepokalanów 1981–89; Man. Minister Aleksander Hall's office 1989–90; Civil Vice-Minister of Nat. Defence in govts of Tadeusz Mazowiecki, Jan Krzysztof Bielecki and Hanna Suchocka 1990–93; connected to Unia Demokratyczna (UD—Democratic Union) and Unia Wolności (UW—Freedom Union) in early 1990s, Gen. Sec. of these parties 1993–95; elected to Parl. for UD 1991, 1993; co-f. Stronnictwo Konserwatywno-Ludowe (Conservative People's Circle) 1997, joined with newly created Koło Konserwatywno-Ludowe (Conservative People's Party) and Akcji Wyborczej Solidarność (AWS—Solidarity Electoral Action); won parl. mandate as cand. of AWS 1997, Chair. Parl. Cttee of Nat. Defence 1997–2000; Minister of Nat. Defence 2000–01; became mem. of Platforma Obywatelska (PO—Civic Platform) 2001; re-elected to Sejm 2001, 2005; mem. Nat. PO Bd 2001–; Deputy Chair. Parl. Cttee of Nat. Defence and mem. Parl. Cttee of Foreign Matters, Vice-Marshal of the Sejm 2005–07, Marshal 2007–10; Acting Pres. of Poland (following death of Pres. Kaczyński in a plane crash) April–July 2010, Pres. of Poland 2010–15; The Five Class, Order of Prince Yaroslav the Wise (Ukraine) 2008, Nat. Order of Merit, Second Class (Malta) 2009, Order of the White Eagle, Grand Cross of the Order of Polonia Restituta, Royal Order of the Seraphim (Sweden) 2011, Collar of the Order of Prince Henry (Portugal) 2012, Collar Grand Cross, Order of Merit of the Italian Repub. (Italy) 2012, Grand Officer, Order of Saint Charles (Monaco) 2012, Grand Croix, Légion d'honneur 2012, Order of the Three Stars (Latvia) 2012, Kt Grand Cross, Grand Order of King Tomislav (Croatia) 2013, Grand Cross, Order of the Redeemer (Greece) 2013, Collar of the Order of the Cross of Terra Mariana (Estonia) 2014, Grand Cross (or First Class), Order of the White Double Cross (Slovakia) 2014, Grand Cross, Order of the Netherlands Lion (Netherlands) 2014; Dr hc (Mykolas Romeris Univ., Vilnius, Lithuania) 2008. *Address:* c/o Chancellery of the President, 00-902 Warsaw, ul. Wiejska 10, Poland.

KOMŠIĆ, Željko; Bosnia and Herzegovina lawyer and politician; *Member, State Presidency;* b. 20 Jan. 1964, Sarajevo; m. Sabina Komšić; one d.; ed Univ. of Sarajevo, Edmund A. Walsh School of Foreign Service, Georgetown Univ., USA; served in Army of Repub. of Bosnia and Herzegovina during Bosnian War;

embarked on political career during which he served as Deputy Mayor of Sarajevo, twice as Head of Municipal Govt of Novo Sarajevo 2000–06, and Amb. to Fed. Repub. of Yugoslavia 2001–02; mem. Socijaldemokratska Partija BiH (SDP BiH—Social Democratic Party of Bosnia and Herzegovina) 1996–2012 (Vice-Pres 2006–12); Pres Demokratska Fronta Bosne i Hercegovine (DF—Democratic Front of Bosnia and Herzegovina) 2013–; Croat mem. State Presidency 2006–14, 2018–, Chair. (Pres. of Bosnia and Herzegovina) 2007–08, 2009–10, 2011–12, 2013–14; mem. Predstavnički Dom (House of Reps) 2014–; Golden Lily, Bosnian Govt. *Address:* Office of the State Presidency, 71000 Sarajevo, Maršala Tita 16 (office); Demokratska Fronta Bosne i Hercegovine (Democratic Front of Bosnia and Herzegovina), Saliha Udžvarlića 10/III, 71000 Sarajevo, Bosnia and Herzegovina (office). *Telephone:* (33) 567510 (presidency) (office); (33) 710400 (DF) (office). *Fax:* (33) 555620 (presidency) (office); (33) 711620 (DF) (office). *E-mail:* press@predsjednistvobih.ba (office); info@zeljkokomsic.ba; info@demokratskafronta.ba (office). *Website:* www.predsjednistvobih.ba (office); www.demokratskafronta.ba (office); www.zeljkokomsic.ba.

KŌMURA, Masahiko, LLB; Japanese politician; b. 15 March 1942, Ehime Pref.; m.; two s. one d.; ed Chuo Univ.; Parl. Vice-Minister, Defence Agency 1987, for Finance 1989, for Foreign Affairs 1996; Minister of State, Dir-Gen. Econ. Planning Agency 1994–95; mem. House of Reps for Yamaguchi 1980–, Chair. Special Cttee on Disasters 1991, on Agric., Forestry and Fisheries 1991, on Prevention of Int. Terrorism and Japan's Co-operation and Support 2003, on Humanitarian Assistance for Reconstruction in Iraq 2003; Deputy Sec.-Gen. LDP, Dir Nat. Defence Div. 1991, Chair. Special Cttee on External Econ. Co-operation 2002; Minister of Foreign Affairs 1999, 2007–08, of Justice 2000–01, of Defence 2007; Pres. Japan-China Friendship Parliamentarians' Union. *Address:* Liberal-Democratic Party (LDP), 1-11-23, Nagata-cho, Chiyoda-ku, Tokyo 100-8910, Japan (office). *Telephone:* (3) 3581-6211 (office). *Fax:* (3) 5511-8855 (office). *E-mail:* koho@ldp.jimin.or.jp (office). *Website:* www.jimin.jp (office).

KONARÉ, Alpha Oumar, PhD; Malian international organization official and fmr head of state; *High Representative for South Sudan, African Union;* b. 2 Feb. 1946, Kayes; m. Adame Ba Konaré; four c.; ed Ecole nat. supérieure, Univ. of Warsaw, Poland; fmr teacher; Dir Inst. for Human Sciences, Bamako 1974, Historic and Ethnographic Div., Ministry of Culture 1975–78; Minister for Youth, Sports and Culture 1978–80 (resgnd); Research Fellow, Institut supérieur de formation et de recherche appliquée, Bamako 1980–89; consultant, UNESCO and UNDP 1981–92; f. Jamana, a cultural co-operative 1983; f. daily Les Echos, monthly for young people, Grin Grin and news service on tape cassettes for rural population 1989; Pres. of Mali 1992–2002; Chair. African Union (AU) Comm. 2003–07, Chair. AU High Level Panel for Egypt 2013–14, AU High Rep. for South Sudan 2015–; mem. ADEMA-PASJ party, Club of Madrid. *Publications:* Le Concept du pouvoir en Afrique, Bibliographie archéologique du Mali, Les grandes dates du Mali (with Adam Ba), Sikasso Tata, Les Constitutions du Mali, Les Partis politiques au Mali.

KONATÉ, Gen. Sékouba; Guinean army officer; *High Representative for the Operationalization of the African Standby Force, African Union;* b. June 1964, Kissidougou; m.; four c.; joined Guinean Army 1985, Lt 1993–2000, Capt. 2000–06, Commdr 2006–08, Lt-Col 2008–09, Gen. 2009–; Commdr, Macenta Parachute Detachment 2000–06, Deputy Commdr Guekedou Ind. Batallion 2007–08, Commdr Autonomous Air Transport Battalion (BATA) 2008–09; Minister at the Presidency, in charge of Nat. Defence 2009; Interim Pres. of Guinea 2009–10; High Rep. of the African Union for the Operationalization of the African Standby Force 2010–. *Address:* African Union, Roosevelt Street, Old Airport Area, POB 3243, Addis Ababa, Ethiopia (office). *Telephone:* (11) 5517700 (office). *Fax:* (11) 5517844 (office). *E-mail:* webmaster@africa-union.org (office). *Website:* au.int (office).

KONCHALOVSKY, Andrei Sergeyevich Mikhalkov; Russian/American theatre and film director, producer and screen writer; b. (Andron Sergeyevich Mikhalkov), 20 Aug. 1937, Moscow; s. of Sergey Mikhalkov and Natalis Konchalovskaya; brother to Nikita Sergeyevich Mikhalko; m. 1st Irina Kandat; m. 2nd Natalia Arinbasarova; one s.; m. 3rd Viviane Godet; one d.; m. 4th Irina Ivanova; two d.; m. 5th Yulia Vysotskaya; one s. one d.; ed piano studies at Moscow Conservatory, Gerasimov Inst. of Cinematography, Moscow; frequent collaborator with Andrei Tarkovsky earlier in his career; Special Silver St George for his contrib. to world cinema, 20th Moscow Int. Film Festival 1997. *Theatre includes:* numerous projects including Eugene Onegin 1985, The Queen of Spades 1990, Miss Julie 2005, King Lear 2006, One of the Last Carnival Evenings 2007, Uncle Vanya 2009, The Taming of the Shrew 2014. *Operas directed:* Our Ancient Capital (musical event to commemorate Moscow's 850th anniversary on Red Square) 1997, War and Peace 2000, Un ballo in maschera 2001, Celebrating 300 Years of St Petersburg 2003, Boris Godunov 2010. *Films include:* as actor: The Trial of Madmen 1961, Ivan's Childhood 1962, I Am Twenty 1964; as dir: The Boy and the Dove (top prize (in debutants' competition), Children and Youth Film Festival, Venice 1962) 1961, The First Teacher (Jussi Award for Best Foreign Dir, Int. Film Festival, Helsinki 1973) 1965, The Story of Asya Klyachina, Who Loved But Did Not Marry (Int. Fed. of Film Critics (FIPRESCI) Award, Hon. Mention at Berlin Int. Film Festival 1988, The Nika Award (Soviet Union) for Best Dir 1989) 1967, A Nest of Gentlefolk (Jussi Award for Best Foreign Dir, Int. Film Festival, Helsinki 1973) 1969, Uncle Vanya (Silver Seashell, San Sebastian Int. Film Festival, Spain 1971, Jussi Award for Best Foreign Dir, Int. Film Festival, Helsinki 1973) 1970, A Lover's Romance (Crystal Globe, Karlovy Vary Int. Film Festival (Czechoslovakia) 1974, Siberiade (Special Jury Prize, Cannes Int. Film Festival) 1979, Split Cherry Tree 1982, Maria's Lovers (Silver Ribbon, Italian Nat. Syndicate of Film Critics and Journalists 1985) 1984, Runaway Train 1985, Duet for One 1986, Shy People 1987, Tango and Cash 1989, Homer and Eddie (Golden Seashell (tied with La nación clandestina), San Sebastian Int. Film Festival) 1989, The Inner Circle 1992, Ryaba, My Chicken (Kinoshock Film Festival Award (Russia) 1994, Import Award, Tromsø Int. Film Festival 1995) 1994, House of Fools (Grand Jury prize, Venice Film Festival, UNICEF Award, Jury Award –Hon. mention, Bergen Int. Film Festival 2002, Gloss 2007, In the Dark (Dans le noir) (in the collective film To Each His Own Cinema (Chacun son cinéma ou Ce petit coup au coeur quand la lumiére s'éteint et que le film commence) 2007, The Nutcracker in 3D 2010, The Postman's White Nights (Silver Lion for Best Dir, Venice Film Festival) 2014. *Music videos:* Dorogie moi moskvichi (My Dear Muscovites) for Dima Bilan 2007, O Sole Mio for Dima Bilan 2007. *Television includes:* The Odyssey (mini-series) (Emmy Award for Best Dir) 1997, The Lion in Winter (mini-series) (Award for Outstanding Dir of a Mini-Series, Monte Carlo Television Festival 2004) 2003; documentaries: Sergei Prokofiev (Geniuses series) 2003, Sergei Rachmaninoff (Genuises series) 2003, Yuri Andropov (The Burden of Power series, with A. Kolesnikov) 2004, Heydar Aliyev (The Burden of Power series) 2004, Culture is Destiny (author and presenter) 2005, Alexander Scriabian (Genuises seies) 2006, Igor Stravinsky (Genuises series) 2006, Dmitri Shostakovich (Genuises series) 2007, Vladimir Sofronitsky (Genuises series) 2007, Bitva za Ukrainu 2012. *Address:* 125124 Moscow, ul. Pravda 21, str. 1, Russia. *Telephone:* (495) 255-16-17. *Website:* konchalovsky.ru; www.pc.konchalovsky.ru.

KONDIĆ, Novak, MBA, PhD; Bosnia and Herzegovina economist, academic and fmr government official; *Professor of Economics, University of Banja Luka;* b. 20 July 1952, Stratinska, Banja Luka; s. of Vlado Kondić and Gospa Kondić; m. Nevenka Predragović 1980; two s.; ed Univ. of Banja Luka; Head of Co. Accountancy Dept, Serbian Devt Bank, Banja Luka 1977–86, Head of Inspectorate Control and Information Analysis 1986–90, Dir Municipal Admin. of Public Revenues 1990–92, mem. Municipal Exec. Bd 1990–92; Deputy Dir-Gen. Payment Transaction Services for Repub. of Srpska 1992–95, for Banja Luka 1997; Minister of Finance, Repub. of Srpska 1995–97, 1998–2000; Rep. of Bosnia and Herzegovina to IMF 1998; Exec. Dir Razvojna Banka, Gen. Dir 2004–06; currently Prof. of Econs, Univ. of Banja Luka; Medal for Mil. Valour. *Leisure interests:* beekeeping, gardening, vineyard cultivation, fruit farming. *Address:* Faculty of Economics, University of Banja Luka, Trg srpskih vladara 2, 78000 Banja Luka, Bosnia and Herzegovina (office). *Telephone:* (51) 218-997 (office). *Fax:* (51) 315-694 (office). *E-mail:* info@unibl.rs (office). *Website:* unibl.org (office).

KONDO, Seiichi, BA; Japanese government official and diplomatist; m.; one d.; ed Univ. of Tokyo, St Catherine's Coll., Oxford, UK; seconded by Ministry of Foreign Affairs to Ministry of Int. Trade and Industry 1977–80, to Int. Energy Agency, OECD 1980–83, Deputy Dir OECD Desk, Ministry of Foreign Affairs 1983–86, Deputy Head of Korea Desk 1986–87, Chef de Cabinet, Vice-Minister of Foreign Affairs 1987–88, Dir Int. Press Div. 1988–90, Head of Chancery, Manila 1990–92, Counsellor for Public Affairs, Washington, DC 1992–95, Minister 1996, Head of Co-ordination and Logistics Office for G8 Summits, Asia-Pacific Econ. Co-operation and Asia-Europe Meeting 1996–97, Deputy Dir-Gen. Econ. Affairs Bureau, Ministry of Foreign Affairs 1998–99; Deputy Sec.-Gen. OECD 1999–2003; Dir-Gen. for Public Diplomacy, Ministry of Foreign Affairs 2003–06, Amb. and Perm. Del. of Japan to UNESCO, Paris 2006–08, Amb. to Denmark 2008–13; fmr Commr Japan's Agency for Cultural Affairs; Chevalier, Légion d'honneur. *Publications:* Image of Japan in the American Media 1994, The Distorted Image of Japan – The Perception Game Inside The Beltway 1997; many articles in Japanese and English-language magazines. *Leisure interests:* reading, music, tennis, golf, horse riding. *Address:* Ministry of Foreign Affairs, Kasumigaseki 2-2-1, Chiyoda-ku, Tokyo 100-8919, Japan (office); 1-11-16 Kamiosaki, Shinagawa-ku, Tokyo 141-0021, Japan (home). *Telephone:* (3) 3580-3311 (office). *Fax:* (3) 3581-2667 (office). *E-mail:* webmaster@mofa.go.jp (office). *Website:* www.mofa.go.jp (office).

KONDO, Shiro; Japanese business executive; *Representative Director and Chairman, Ricoh Company Limited;* b. 1950; joined Ricoh Co. Ltd 1973, Deputy Gen. Man. Imaging System Business Group 2000, Sr Vice-Pres. 2000–02, Exec. Vice-Pres. 2002–07, Man. Dir 2003, Gen. Man., MFP Business Group (Div. of Ricoh Co. Ltd) 2004, Exec. Vice-Pres. MFP Business Group 2005, Dir 2005–07, Rep. Dir 2007–, Pres. and CEO 2007–13, Chair. 2013–; Outside Dir Tohoku Electric Power Co., Inc., Coca-Cola Bottlers Japan, Inc., Coca-Cola W Co. Ltd, mem. Bd of Dirs Sindo Ricoh Co. Ltd. *Address:* Ricoh Company Ltd, 8-13-1 Ginza, Chuo-ku, Tokyo 104-8222, Japan (office). *Telephone:* (3) 6278-2111 (office). *Fax:* (3) 3543-9329 (office). *E-mail:* www-admin@ricoh.co.jp (office). *Website:* www.ricoh.com (office).

KONDRUSEVIC, Tadeusz Ignatyevich, DTheol; Russian ecclesiastic; *Metropolitan Archbishop of Minsk-Mohilev;* b. 3 Jan. 1946; ed Vilnius Polytech. Inst., Kaunas Ecclesiastical Seminary; with St Therese Church, Ostra Brama Church, Vilnius 1981–87; Dean Cathedral of God's mother–Angels' Tsarina, Grodno 1988–89; Titular Bishop and Apostle Admin. of Minsk, First Bishop of Belarus Catholics 1989; apptd Titular Archbishop of Hippo Diarrhytus and Apostolic Admin. for Catholics of the Latin Rite in Northern European Russia, Moscow; apptd Metropolitan Archbishop of Minsk-Mahilyow 2007, Apostolic Admin. of Pinsk 2011. *Address:* Archdiocese of Minsk-Mohilev, 220030, Minsk, Revalutsyinaya 1a, Belarus (office). *E-mail:* archdiocese@catholic.by (office).

KONÉ, Adama, MBA; Côte d'Ivoirian economist, accountant and politician; *Minister of Economy and Finance;* b. 20 Nov. 1954, Bouaflé; ed Nat. School of Admin of Ivory Coast, Adelphy Univ., Univ. of Abidjan; Auditing Officer State Socs, Dept of Investments, Ministry of Economy and Finance 1982–84, Accountant-in-charge Financial Man. and Accounting, Nat. Public Establishments 1984–89, Deputy Dir 1989–92, Dir Parapublic Accounting 1992–94; Dir Admin and Finance, Société Nouvelle de Presse et d'Edition de Côte d'Ivoire 1994–2000; Chief Auditor Insp. Treasury 2000–01, Deputy Gen. Man. Treasury and Public Accounting 2001–10, Gen. Man. 2010–16, Minister of Economy and Finance 2016–; Pres. Int. Asscn of Treasury Services 2012–; currently Chair., Nat. Comm. for Microfinance (CNM), Nat. Council of Accounting (CNC); mem. Bd of Dirs, Nat. Bank of Investment (BNI), Cotton Co. of Côte d'Ivoire (COTIVO), Cen. Bank of West African States; mem. Banking Comm., West African Monetary and Econ. Union (UEMOA); Kt Nat. Order of Côte d'Ivoire, Officer Order of Sports Merit, Commdr Order Public Service Merit. *Address:* Ministry of Economy and Finance, 16e étage, Immeuble SCIAM, ave Marchand, BP V163, Abidjan, Côte d'Ivoire (office). *Telephone:* 20-20-08-42 (office). *Fax:* 20-21-32-08 (office). *Website:* www.finances.gouv.ci (office).

KONÉ, Tiémoko Meyliet; Côte d'Ivoirian economist, politician and central banker; *Governor, Banque Centrale des Etats de l'Afrique de l'Ouest;* b. 1949, Ferkessédougou; m.; five c.; ed Banque Centrale des Etats de l'Afrique de l'Ouest Centre d'Application Technique et Professionnel, Dakar, Senegal; joined Banque Centrale des Etats de l'Afrique de l'Ouest (BCEAO) 1975, positions include Asst to Nat. Dir for Côte d'Ivoire, Central Dir for Issue and Financial Operations, BCEAO HQ, Dakar, mem. Regional and Int. Econ. Analysis Cttee, Nat. Dir for Côte d'Ivoire and Alt. Gov. at IMF 1991–98, Controller-Gen., in charge of Supervision of Operations and Inspection, Internal Audit, Control and Risk Prevention, Special Adviser and mem. BCEAO Govt, Adviser to Gov. and Dir Dept of Gen. Admin and Training, BCEAO Gov. 2011–; Head of cabinet of Côte d'Ivoire Prime Minister Guillaume Soro, with rank of Minister 2007–10; Special Adviser to Côte d'Ivoire Pres. Alassane Ouattara, in charge of Econ. and Monetary Affairs 2010–11; Minister of Construction, Urban Affairs and Habitat 2011. *Address:* Office of the Governor, Banque Centrale des Etats de l'Afrique de l'Ouest, rue Branly, BP 120, Lomé, Togo (office). *Telephone:* 22-21-25-12 (office). *Fax:* 22-21-76-02 (office). *E-mail:* ocourrier@lome.bceao.int (office). *Website:* www.bceao.int (office).

KONFOUROU, Issa; Malian diplomatist; *Permanent Representative to United Nations;* b. 1 Jan. 1970, Tienan, Circle of Macina; m.; three c.; ed Nat. School of Admin of Bamako, Univ. of Paris 1 Panthéon-Sorbonne, France; Foreign Affairs Adviser, Malian Public Service 1999, Second Counsellor Perm. Mission of Mali, New York 2000–07, Diplomatic Adviser to Prime Minister 2008–14, Technical Adviser Ministry of Foreign Affairs, Int. Cooperation and African Integration 2014–16; Perm. Rep. to UN 2016–; Chevalier de l'Ordre national du Mali 2015. *Address:* Permanent Mission of Mali, 111 E 69th Street, New York, NY 10021, USA (office). *Telephone:* (212) 737-4150 (office). *Fax:* (212) 472-3778 (office). *E-mail:* miperma@malionu.com (office). *Website:* www.un.int/mali (office).

KONG, Dan, MA; Chinese economist and business executive; b. May 1947, Beijing; s. of Kong Yuan; ed Grad. School of China Acad. of Social Sciences; Vice-Pres., later Pres., later Vice-Chair. China Everbright Group –2000, later Chair.; Vice-Chair. and Pres. China International Trust & Investment Corpn (CITIC) 2000–06, Chair. CITIC International Financial Holdings Ltd 2001–15, Dir (non-exec.) China CITIC Bank International Ltd 2001–, Chair. CITIC Group 2006–10, CITIC Resources Holdings Ltd and China CITIC Bank Corpn Ltd 2007–11. *Address:* CITIC International Financial Holdings Ltd, Suites 1801-4, Harcourt House, 39 Gloucester Road, Wanchai, Hong Kong Special Administrative Region, People's Republic of China (office). *Telephone:* 36073000 (office). *E-mail:* info@citicifh.com (office). *Website:* www.citicifh.com (office).

KONG, Jiesheng; Chinese writer and broadcaster; b. 1952, Guangzhou City, Guangdong Prov.; Vice-Chair. Guangzhou Br. of Writers' Asscn 1985; travelled to USA and co-f. literary magazine; joined Editorial bd of Today magazine 1990. *Publications include:* My Marriage 1978, On the Other side of the Stream 1979, A Life and Death Ordeal 1981, The Southern Bank 1982, The Big Jungle 1984, Story Investigations 1985.

KONG, Quan; Chinese diplomatist; *Deputy-Director, Central Foreign Affairs Office of CCP Central Committee;* b. 1955, Beijing; m.; one d.; served at Embassy in Brussels 1977–82, Attaché, Western Europe Dept, Ministry of Foreign Affairs 1982–84, Third, then Second Sec. 1985–95, Counsellor 1995–96, Counsellor, then Minister-Counsellor, Embassy in Paris 1996–99, Asst Dir-Gen. 1999–2000, Dir-Gen. of Communications 2001–06, Dir-Gen. Western Europe Dept 2006, Vice-Minister for Foreign Affairs 2006–08, Amb. to France 2008–14; mem. Perm. Cttee CCP, Tanggu Dist, Tianjin 2000–01; Deputy Dir, Cen. Foreign Affairs Office of CCP Cen. Cttee 2014–; Grand officier de la Légion d'honneur 2013. *Address:* Chinese Communist Party,No.2 Jintai Xilu, Chaoyang District, Beijing 100733, People's Republic of China (office). *Telephone:* (10) 65363691 (office). *Fax:* (10) 65368341 (office). *E-mail:* englishpd@163.com (office). *Website:* www.fmprc.gov.cn (office).

KONG NYUON, Gen. John; South Sudanese politician; b. Jonglei, Upper Nile; several years' mil. service with Sudan People's Liberation Army; fmr adviser on security affairs to Pres. of S Sudan; Minister of Defence and Veteran Affairs (first holder following independence 9 July 2011) 2011–13; apptd Gov. of Jonglei State 2013.

KONGANTIYEV, Moldomusa Tashbolotovich, LLB; Kyrgyzstani police officer and politician; b. 31 March 1958, Maili-Sai town, Osh Oblast; ed Kyrgyz State Univ.; joined Militsia (police force) as Asst, Ministry of Internal Affairs Unit, Mailisaisky Town Exec. Cttee 1979–85; mem. Road Traffic Inspectorate and Detective, Criminal Search Dept and Theft of Social Property Dept, Ministry of Internal Affairs Unit, Uzgen Dist Exec. Cttee 1985–88; Detective, Theft of Social Property Dept, Ministry of Internal Affairs Unit, Kara-Suy Dist Exec. Cttee 1988–90; Sr Detective, Theft of Social Property Dept, Ministry of Internal Affairs Unit, Bazar-Korgon Dist Exec. Cttee 1990–91; Head, Econ. Crime Dept, also Deputy Head, Ministry of Internal Affairs Unit, Jalal-Abad City 1991–95; with Directorate of Internal Affairs, Jalal-Abad Oblast 1995–99; Head, Dept of Inter-Regional Man., Ministry of Internal Affairs, Osh and Jalal-Abad Oblasts 1999–2000; Deputy Head with responsibility for Mans, Ministry of Internal Affairs, Suzak Dist, Jalal-Abad Oblast 2000–01; Head, Ministry of Internal Affairs Transport Dept, Jalal-Abad 2001–04; Head, Ministry of Internal Affairs, Rail Transport Office 2004–05; Head, Directorate of Internal Affairs, Bishkek City 2005; Deputy Minister of Internal Affairs 2005; Head, Chief Admin of Internal Affairs, Bishkek 2005–08; Minister of Internal Affairs 2008–10; Militsia rank of Gen.-Maj.

KONGO-DOUDOU, Toussaint; Central African Republic government official and fmr international organization official; ed Univ. of Wisconsin, USA; served several years with UN including as Chief of Communications and Public Information, UN Stabilization Mission in Haiti (MINUSTAH) in early 2000s, later Dir Centre d'Information des Nations-Unies (CINU), Dakar, Senegal; Minister of Foreign Affairs, African Integration and the Francophonie 2014–15. *Address:* c/o Ministry of Foreign Affairs, African Integration and the Francophonie, Bangui, Central African Republic.

KONIDARIS, Ioannis (John), DrIur; Greek professor of law; *Professor of Ecclesiastical Law, University of Athens;* b. 10 Sept. 1948, Chios; s. of Marinos Konidaris and Ioanna Konidaris; m. Ersi Mantakas 1975, one d.; ed Univs of Athens, Thessaloniki and Munich; mil. service 1971–73; mem. Bar Asscn of Athens 1974–; Asst Faculty of Law, Univ. of Frankfurt, Germany 1978–81; Lecturer in Ecclesiastical Law 1985; mem. Editorial Bd of official journal of Bar Asscn of Athens 1985–2006; Prof. of Ecclesiastical Law, Univ. of Athens 1989–; Research Scholarship, Max Planck Inst. for European History of Law, Frankfurt am Main 1989–90; Dir Research Centre for the History of Greek Law, Acad. of Athens 1994–2000, Ed. the Centre's Yearbook (Vol. 31) 1995, (Vol. 32) 1996, (Vol. 33) 1997, (Vol. 34) 1998; columnist on ecclesiastical issues, BHMA newspaper 1992–; adviser on religious subjects to Minister of Foreign Affairs 1996–99, 2001; Sec.-Gen. for Religious Affairs, Ministry of Nat. Educ. and Religious Affairs 2001–04; Founder and Ed. Nomokanonika 2002; Founder and Pres. Soc. of Ecclesiastical and Canon Law 2014–. *Publications include:* Monastic Property Law Between 9th and 12th Centuries 1979, Legal Aspects of Monastery 'Typika' 1984, 2003, Legal Theory and Praxis concerning Jehovah's Witnesses in Greece 1987, 1988, 1991, 2005, Law 1700/1987 and the Recent Crisis Between the Orthodox Church and the Greek State 1988, 1991, Issues of Byzantine and Ecclesiastical Law Vol. I 1990, Church and State in Greece 1993, The Conflict Between Law and Canon and the Establishment of Harmony Between Them 1994, Ekklesiastika Atakta 1999, Basic Legislation of State-Church Relations 1999 (third edn 2016), A Manual of Ecclesiastical Law 2000 (third edn 2016), Regulations of the Church of Greece 2001 (second edn 2015), Regulations of the Monasteries of the Church of Greece (two vols) 2002, Mount Athos Avaton 2003 (translated into Russian 2016), Issues of Byzantine and Ecclesiastical Law Vol. II 2008, Regulations of the Church of Greece, of the Church of Crete, of Mount Athos and of the Church of Cyprus 2012, Particular Ecclesiastical Regimes in Greek Territory (Ecumenical Patriarchate-Dodecanese, Mount Athos, Crete) 2013 (second edn 2017), Mount Athos Avaton 2016, Elements of Greek and Cypriot Ecclesiastical Law 2016; numerous articles on ecclesiastical law and history of law, especially Byzantine law. *Address:* University of Athens, 45 Akadimias Street, 10672 Athens (office); 107 Asklipiou Street, 11472 Athens (office); 20 Bizaniou Street, 15237 Filothei/ Athens, Greece (home). *Telephone:* (210) 3688607 (office); (210) 3630391 (pvt. office) (office); (210) 6742896 (home). *Fax:* (210) 3630391 (pvt. office) (office). *E-mail:* imkonidaris@law.uoa.gr (office). *Website:* www.law.uoa.gr (office).

KÖNIG, Johann; German gallery owner; *Owner, König Galerie, Berlin;* b. 1981; s. of Kasper König and Edda Köchl-König; f. own gallery located in fmr industrial bldg, Martin-Gropius-Bau 2002 and New Nat. Gallery since 2006, and in fmr church of St Agnes since 2013, currently represents around 30 int. artists, both young emerging and established, including Micol Assaël, Norbert Bisky, Monica Bonvicini, Claudia Comte, Elmgreen & Dragset, Tue Greenfort, Katharina Grosse, Jeppe Hein, Camille Henrot, Nathan Hylden, Annette Kelm, Kiki Kogelnik, Manfred Kuttner, Alicja Kwade, Helen Marten, Kris Martin, Justin Matherly, Michaela Meise, Natascha Sadr Haghighian, Amalia Pica, Michael Sailstorfer, Andreas Schmitten, John Seal, Jeremy Shaw, Tatiana Trouvé, Daniel Turner, Rinus Van De Velde, Jorinde Voigt, Corinne Wasmuht, Matthias Weischer, Johannes Wohnseifer, Erwin Wurm and David Zink Yi; programme includes a variety of media, including sculpture, video, sound, painting, printmaking, photography and performance; alternates solo exhbns with curated group shows and a performance-lecture series; participates in several int. art fairs, including Art Basel, Frieze Art Fair, London, FIAC, Paris and Art Basel Miami Beach; has placed works in both private and public collections, including Museum of Modern Art, New York and the Guggenheim Foundation. *Address:* König Galerie, St Agnes, Alexandrinenstr. 118–121, 10969 Berlin, Germany (office). *Telephone:* (30) 26103080 (office). *Fax:* (30) 261030811 (office). *E-mail:* info@koeniggalerie.com (office). *Website:* www.koeniggalerie.com (office).

KÖNIG, Kasper; German curator and academic; b. (Rudolf Hans König), 1943, Mettingen, Westphalia; began career as curator, Claes Oldenburg Exhbn, Moderna Museet, Stockholm, Sweden 1966; Chair. Kunst und Öffentlichkeit (Art and the Public Realm), Kunstakademie Düsseldorf 1985–88; Prof., Städelschule Frankfurt 1988–2001, Dir 1989–2001; Founding Dir Portikus Exhbn Hall, Frankfurt; Dir Ludwig Museum, Cologne 2001–12. *Exhibitions curated include:* sculpture projects, Münster 1977, 1987, 1997, 2007, 2017, Westkunst, Cologne Fair 1981, von hier aus, Düsseldorf Fair 1984, Der zerbrochene Spiegel, Vienna and Hamburg 1993, In-Between Architecture, Hanover EXPO 2000, Manifesta 10, St Petersburg, Russia 2014. *Address:* Kurfürstenstraße 13, 10785 Berlin, Germany (office). *E-mail:* office@kasperkoenig.com (office).

KONISHI, Masakazu (Mark), PhD; American (b. Japanese) neurobiologist and academic; *Bing Professor of Behavioral Biology, California Institute of Technology;* b. 17 Feb. 1933, Kyoto, Japan; ed Hokkaido Univ., Univ. of California, Berkeley; held posts at Univ. of Tubingen and Max-Planck Inst., Germany, Univ. of Wisconsin and Princeton Univ., USA; Prof. of Biology, Calif. Inst. of Tech. 1975–80, Bing Prof. of Behavioral Biology 1980–; Coues Award 1983, Dana Award 1992, inaugural Edward M. Scolnick Prize in Neuroscience Research, McGovern Inst. 2004, Gruber Prize for Neuroscience 2005, and numerous other awards. *Publications include:* The Harvey Lectures: Series 86, 1992 (The Harvey Lectures) (co-author) 1994; numerous articles in scientific journals. *Address:* Division of Biology, 156-29, California Institute of Technology, 1200 East California Boulevard, Pasadena, CA 91125, USA (office). *Telephone:* (626) 395-4951 (office). *Fax:* (626) 449-0756 (office). *E-mail:* konishim@caltech.edu (office). *Website:* biology.caltech.edu/Members/Konishi (office).

KONJANOVSKI, Zoran, BA; Macedonian engineer and politician; b. 3 March 1967, Bitola; m. Jasmina Konjanovska; two s.; ed Univ. of 'Ss Cyril and Methodius', Skopje; mechanical engineer, JP Streevo, Bitola 1999–2005; mem. Vnatrešno-Makedonska Revolucionerna Organizacija-Demokratska Partija za Makedonsko Nacionalno Edinstvo (VMRO-DPMNE—Internal Macedonian Revolutionary Org.—Democratic Party for Macedonian Nat. Unity) 1993–, mem. Exec. Cttee 2005–; Pres. Municipal Council of Bitola 2005–06; mem. Nat. Ass. 2006–; Minister of Local Govt 2006–07, of Defence 2008–11; Dir-Gen. REK (Bitola Br.) 2007–08. *Address:* c/o VMRO-DPMNE, 1000 Skopje, Makedonija 17A, North Macedonia (office). *Telephone:* (2) 3215550 (office). *Fax:* (2) 3215551 (office). *E-mail:* contact@vmro-dpmne.org.mk (office). *Website:* www.vmro-dpmne.org.mk (office).

KONJEVIĆ, Raško, BA, MA; Montenegrin economist and politician; b. 12 April 1979; ed Econs Faculty, Univ. of Montenegro, Podgorica, European Integration School; worked as journalist on daily magazine Vijesti 2000–03; Co-founder and Public Relations Man., Centre for Democratic Transition 2001–04; attended numerous specialized courses in economic science and security, organized by DCAF, as well as in public relations in co-operation with Nat. Democratic Inst., Washington, DC, USA; worked in Office of the Parl. of Montenegro 2003–06; Assoc., 'Introduction in Management', Montenegro Business School 2005–12; Assoc. Prof., School of Econs, Univ. of the Mediterranean 2006–11; mem.

Socijaldemokratska Partija Crne Gore (SDP—Social Democratic Party of Montenegro) Presidency 2007–, Vice-Pres. SDP 2009–12; Chief of Cabinet of Pres. of Parl. 2006–08; mem. Parl. 2009–12, Leader of SDP Parl. Group, mem. Security and Defence Cttee, Economy, Finances and Budget Cttee, Int. Co-operation and European Integration Cttee, EU-Montenegro Stabilization and Asscn Parl. Cttee; Pres. Capital City Ass. 2010–11; Minister of Internal Affairs 2012–16, of Finance May–Nov. 2016; mem. Bd of Dirs Budvanska rivijera 2007–11. *Address:* c/o Ministry of Finance, 81000 Podgorica, Stanka Dragojevića 2, Montenegro (office).

KONNEH, Amara Mohamed, BSc, MPA; Liberian politician; b. 7 Dec. 1972, Balla Bassa, Gbamah Dist; s. of Majumah Konneh and Mamadee Konneh; m. Hawah Konneh; four c.; ed Monrovia Coll., Drexel Univ., Pennsylvania State Univ., John F. Kennedy School of Govt, Harvard Univ., USA; refugee in Guinea aged 18; Educ. Co-ordinator for Liberian and Sierra Leonean refugee schools, Guinea Forest Region 1991–93; worked for more than ten years with devt foundations and as policy, financial systems analyst and project man. with Vanguard Group of Investment Cos, USA; returned to Liberia, becoming Deputy Chief of Staff to Pres. Ellen Johnson-Sirleaf for Policy and Communications 2005–08; Minister of Planning and Econ. Affairs 2008–11, of Finance and Devt Planning 2014–16; fmr Alt. Gov., African Devt Bank and World Bank; Chair. Mano River Union Ministerial Council; named African Finance Minister of the Year by The Banker magazine 2014. *Address:* c/o Ministry of Finance and Development Planning, Broad Street, PO Box 10-9013, 1000 Monrovia 10, Liberia (office).

KONO, Taro, BSc; Japanese politician; *Minister of Foreign Affairs;* b. 10 Jan. 1963, Hiratsuka, Odawara, Kanagawa Pref.; s. of Yohei Kono and Takeko Kono; m. Kaori Kono; one s.; ed Keio Univ., Georgetown Univ., USA; joined Int. Business Div., Fuji Xerox Co. Ltd 1986, transferred to Fuji Xerox Asia Pacific, Singapore 1991; Man. Dir, Nippon Tanshi Co. Ltd 1993; mem. House of Reps (Parl.) for Kanagawa Pref. 15th Electoral Dist 1996–, Parl. Sec. for Public Man. 2002, Chair. Foreign Affairs Cttee 2008–09; Sr Vice Minister of Justice 2005; Chair. Nat. Public Safety Comm. 2015; Minister of Admin. Reform and Nat. Public Service System Reform 2015; State Minister in Charge of Consumer Affairs, Food Safety, Regulatory Reform and Disaster Man. 2015–17; Minister of Foreign Affairs 2017–; mem. Liberal Democratic Party (LDP), Asst Sec.-Gen. 2012–. *Leisure interests:* reading, watching soccer. *Address:* Ministry of Foreign Affairs, 2-2-1, Kasumigaseki, Chiyoda-ku, Tokyo 100-8919, Japan (office). *Telephone:* (3) 3580-3311 (office). *Fax:* (3) 3581-2667 (office). *E-mail:* webmaster@mofa.go.jp (office). *Website:* www.mofa.go.jp (office).

KONO, Yohei; Japanese politician; b. 15 Jan. 1937; s. of Ichiro Kono; ed Waseda Univ., Stanford Univ., USA; began career with Marubeni Co.; elected mem. House of Reps from Kanagawa, Speaker, House of Reps 2003–09; fmr Parl. Vice-Minister of Educ., Dir-Gen. Science and Tech. Agency; Chief Cabinet Sec. (State Minister) 1992–93; Deputy Prime Minister and Minister of Foreign Affairs 1994–96, Minister of Foreign Affairs 1999–2001; Chair. LDP Research Comm. on Foreign Affairs, Pres. 1993–99; left LDP to co-found New Liberal Club (now defunct) 1976–86; mem. Miyazawa faction of LDP; Pres. Japan Asscn of Athletics Federations 1999–2013.

KONOÉ, Tadateru, BA; Japanese international organization official; b. 8 May 1939, brother of fmr Prime Minister Morihiro Hosokawa; m. Princess Yasuko of Mikasa 1966; one s.; ed Gakushuin Univ., Tokyo, London School of Econs, UK; joined Japanese Red Cross Soc. as volunteer 1964, Dir Int. Dept 1964–72, Dir-Gen. Int. Dept 1976–81, Dir Social Dept 1985–88, Dir-Gen. 1988, Vice-Pres. Japanese Red Cross Soc. 1991–2005, Pres. 2005–; seconded to Secr., Int. Fed. of Red Cross and Red Crescent Socs (IFRC), Geneva, Switzerland 1972, becoming officer, IFRC Disaster Preparedness Bureau 1972–75, Dir 1981–85, mem. IFRC Finance Comm. 1985–93, 2003–, mem. Standing Comm. 1995–2003, mem. Governing Bd 2001–05, Vice-Pres. IFRC 2005–09, Pres. 2009–17; Councillor, Japan Cttee for UNICEF; Adviser, Japan Campaign to Ban Landmines, Japan Center for Conflict Prevention; Lecturer on Micro Study on Int. Relief Orgs, Grad. School, Toyo Eiwa Univ., Tokyo 1994. *Address:* c/o International Federation of Red Cross and Red Crescent Societies, 17 Chemin des Crêts, Petit-Saconnex, PO Box 303, 1211 Geneva 19, Switzerland (office).

KONOVALOV, Aleksander Nikolayevich, MD; Russian neurosurgeon; b. 12 Dec. 1933, Moscow; s. of Nikolai Konovalov and Ekaterina Konovalova; m. Inna Konovalova 1957, one s.; ed First Moscow Medical Inst.; intern, researcher, Deputy Dir N. N. Burdenko Research Inst. of Neurosurgery 1957–75, apptd Dir 1975; mem. Russian Acad. of Medical Sciences 1992, Russian Acad. of Sciences 2000; Pres. Asscn of Neurosurgeons of Russia 2003; conducted unique operation on separation of the heads of Siamese twins 1989; Ed.-in-Chief Voprosi Neurochirurgii; Orden Druzba Narodov; USSR and Russian Fed. State Prizes. *Publications:* more than 215 works on problems of surgery. *Leisure interests:* tennis, skiing. *Address:* Novoslobodskaya str. 57/65, Apt. 33, 127057 Moscow, Russia (home). *Telephone:* (499) 978-76-18 (home).

KONOVALOV, Aleksandr Vladimirovich, PhD; Russian lawyer and government official; *Minister of Justice;* b. 19 June 1968, Leningrad (now St Petersburg), Russian SFSR, USSR; ed Law Faculty, Leningrad State Univ.; served in USSR Army 1986–88; joined St Petersburg Prosecutor's Office 1992, positions included Asst to Prosecutor of Vyborg Dist 1992, Investigator, Vyborg Dist Office 1992–94, Prosecutor, Fed. Security Law Enforcement Supervision Dept 1994–97, Deputy Prosecutor of Moscow Dist 1997–98, Prosecutor of Moscow Dist 1998–2001, First Deputy Prosecutor, St Petersburg 2001–05; Prosecutor, Repub. of Bashkortostan 2005; Presidential Envoy to Volga Fed. Okrug 2005–08; Minister of Justice 2008–; fmr mem. Security Council of Russian Fed. *Address:* Ministry of Justice, 119991 Moscow, ul. Zhitnaya 14, Russian Federation (office). *Telephone:* (495) 994-93-55 (office); (495) 955-59-99 (office). *Fax:* (495) 677-06-72 (office). *E-mail:* pst@minjust.ru (office); pr@minjust.ru (office). *Website:* minjust.ru (office); government.ru/en/gov/persons/14/events (office).

KONRÁD, György; Hungarian novelist and essayist; b. 2 April 1933, Berettyóújfalu, nr Debrecen; s. of József Konrád and Róza Klein; m. Judit Lakner; three s. two d.; ed Debrecen Reform Coll., Madách Gymnasium, Budapest, Eötvös Loránd Univ., Budapest; teacher at general gymnasium in Csepel; Ed. Életképek 1956; social worker, Budapest 7th Dist Council 1959–65; Ed. Magyar Helikon 1960–66; urban sociologist on staff of City Planning Research Inst. 1965–73; full-time writer 1973–; Pres. Akad. der Künste Berlin-Brandenburg 1997; Visiting Prof. of Comparative Literature, Colorado Springs Coll. 1988; Corresp. mem. Bayerische Akad., Munich; fmr Pres. Int. PEN; Officier, Ordre national de la Légion d'Honneur 1996, Legion of Honor Middle Cross with Star 2003, Das Grosse Verdienstkreuz des Bundesrepublik Deutschland 2003; Herder Prize, Vienna-Hamburg 1984, Charles Veillon European Essay, Zürich 1985, Fredfonden Peace Foundation, Copenhagen 1986, Fed. Critics' Prize for Novel of the Year (FRG) 1986, Maecenas Prize 1989, Manès-Sperber Prize 1990, Kossuth Prize, Friedens-Preis des Deutschen Buchhandels 1991, Karlspreis zu Aachen 2001, Franz Werfel Human Rights Award 2007. *Publications include:* novels: A látogató (The Case Worker) 1969, A városlapitó (The City Builder) 1977, A cinkos (The Loser) 1982, Kerti mulatság (Feast in the Garden) (Vol. 1 of trilogy Agenda) 1989, Kóóra (Stone Dial) (Vol. 2 of Agenda) 1995; essays: Új lakótelepek szociológiai problémái 1969, Az értelmiség utja az osztályhatalomhoz (The Intellectuals on the Road to Class Power) 1978, Az autonómia kisértése (The Temptation of Autonomy) 1980, Antipolitics 1986, Esszék 91–93 (Essays 1991–93) 1993, The Melancholy of Rebirth 1995, Várakozás (Expectation) 1995, Áramló leltár 1996, Láthatatlan hang (The Invisible Voice: Meditations on Jewish Themes) 2000, The Writer and the City 2004, The Roosters' Sorrow 2005, Figures of Wonder 2006, A Guest in My Own Country (Nat. Jewish Book Award 2008) 2007. *Website:* www.konradgyorgy.hu.

KONRÁÐSDÓTTIR, Unnur Brá; Icelandic politician and lawyer; b. 6 April 1974, Reykjavík; d. of Konráð Oscar Auðunsson and Sigrid Haraldsdóttir; three c.; ed Univ. of Iceland; Chair. Independence Kari 2003–06; lawyer, Land Registry 2004–06; Chair. Iceland League, West Nordic Council 2013–16; mem. Althingi for South Constituency 2009–17, Vice-Pres. 2009–13, Deputy Speaker 2009–13, Jan.–Feb. 2018, Feb. 2019, Pres. and Speaker 2017; mem. Welfare Cttee 2011–16, Chair. Judicial Affairs and Educ. Cttee 2013–16; mem. Economic Affairs and Trade Cttee 2014–15, Budget Cttee 2016–17; mem. Icelandic Del. to Council of Europe Parl. Ass. 2013–16, Deputy Chair. 2014–16. *Address:* Althingi, v/Austurvöll, 150 Reykjavík, Iceland (office). *Telephone:* 5630500 (office). *Fax:* 5630550 (office). *E-mail:* ubk@althingi.is (office); editor@althingi.is (office). *Website:* www.althingi.is (office).

KONROTE, Brig.-Gen. Jioji (George); Fijian politician, diplomatist, retd army officer and head of state; *President;* served in Fijian Armed Forces; Force Commdr UNFIL Peace-keeping Force, Lebanon 1999; Perm. Sec. for Home Affairs 2001; High Commr to Australia 2001–06; mem. Parl. representing Rotuman Communal Constituency 2006; Minister of State for Immigration and Ex-Servicemen 2006 (deposed following coup), for Employment Opportunities, Productivity and Industrial Relations 2014–15; mem. Parl. (FijiFirst) 2014–15; Pres. of Fiji 2015–. *Address:* Office of the President, Government House, Berkley Crescent, Government Building, POB 2513, Suva, Fiji (office). *Telephone:* 3314244 (office). *E-mail:* 3301645 (office).

KONSTANTINOV, Boris A., Dr Med.; Russian cardiac surgeon; *Director, Scientific Centre of Surgery, Russian Academy of Medical Sciences;* b. Moscow; m.; three s.; ed Moscow Sechenov Medical Inst.; Head of Div., Research Centre for Surgery (now Scientific Centre of Surgery), Russian Acad. of Medical Sciences 1968–88, Dir 1988–; mem. Presidium Pirogov Asscn of Surgeons, Inst. Soc. of Cardiovascular Surgeons, European Acad. of Cardiac Surgeons, Russian Acad. of Medical Sciences; USSR State Prize 1973, Government Prize 2001, Honored Worker of Science 2003; two Orders of Friendship of People. *Publications include:* over 300 scientific papers on heart transplants and eight monographs, including Diseases in Early Age Children 1970, Physiological and Clinical Fundamentals of Surgical Cardiology 1981. *Address:* Scientific Centre of Surgery, Russian Academy of Medical Sciences, Moscow 119879, Abrikosovsky per. 2, Russia (office). *Telephone:* (495) 246-95-63 (office). *E-mail:* admin@med.ru (office). *Website:* www.med.ru (office).

KONSTANTOPOLOU, Zoi; Greek lawyer and politician; b. 8 Dec. 1976, Athens; d. of Nikos Konstantopoulos and Lina Alexiou; ed Univ. of Athens, Paris West Univ. Nanterre La Défense and Pantheon-Sorbonne Univ., France, Columbia Univ., USA; participated in French prisoners' education programme, teaching English at Fresnes Prison 1998–2000; worked at Int. Criminal Tribunal for Fmr Yugoslavia, The Hague, Netherlands 2001; worked at office of Greek Perm. Rep. to UN, New York 2001–03; active as lawyer in Greece, focusing on penal and int. criminal law and human rights 2003–; mem. Synaspismós Rizospastikís Aristerás (SYRIZA—Coalition of the Radical Left) 2012–15; Ind. (collaboration with Popular Unity) 2015–; unsuccessful SYRIZA cand. in European elections 2009; mem. Vouli (Parl.) for Athens A 2012–, mem. Cttee on Institutions and Transparency, Cttee on Public Order and Justice, Cttee on European Affairs, Perm. Public Admin Cttee, Inter-party Cttee on German War Reparations 2012–14, Speaker of the Vouli Feb.–Oct. 2015. *Address:* Vouli, Parliament Building, Leoforos Vassilissis Sofias 2-4, 100 21 Athens, Greece (office). *Telephone:* (210) 3708011 (office). *Fax:* (210) 3232913 (office). *E-mail:* president@parliament.gr (office). *Website:* www.hellenicparliament.gr (office); www.zoikonstantopoulou.gr.

KONTSEVICH, Maxim Lvovich, PhD; Russian/French mathematician and academic; *Resident Professor, Institut des Hautes Études Scientifiques;* b. 25 Aug. 1964, Khimki, Russia; ed Moscow Univ. and Univ. of Bonn, Germany; began research at Inst. for Problems of Information Processing, Russian Acad. of Sciences, Moscow; held positions at Univ. of Bonn –1994 and Harvard Univ. and Inst. for Advanced Studies, Princeton, USA; Prof., Univ. of California, Berkeley 1993–95; Resident Prof., Institut des Hautes Études Scientifiques, Bures-sur-Yvette, France 1995–; Visiting Prof., Rutgers Univ., NJ, USA 1997–2002, Univ. of Miami, USA 2007–; mem. Editorial Bd, Compositio Mathematica 1994–, International Mathematical Research Notices 1994–, Publications Mathematiques IHES 1996–, Selecta Mathematica (New Series) 1996–, Letters in Mathematical Physics 1999–, Journal of Noncommutative Geometry 2007–, Communications in Number Theory and Physics 2007–; mem. Academia Europaea 2000, Acad. des sciences 2002; Chevalier, Légion d'honneur 2004; Otto Hahn Prize, Max-Planck Gesellschaft, Bonn 1992, Prix de la mairie de Paris 1992, Prix Iagolnitzer, Int. Asscn of Math. Physics 1997, Fields Medal, 23th Int. Congress of Mathematicians, Berlin (co-recipient) 1998, Crafoord Prize (co-recipient) 2008, Shaw Prize 2012, Fundamental Physics Prize 2012, Breakthrough Prize in Math. (co-recipient) 2015. *Publications:* more than 50 articles in math. journals on various problems in geometry and algebra, often related to string theory and quantum field theory.

Address: Institut des Hautes Études Scientifiques, 35 route de Chartres, 91440 Bures-sur-Yvette, France (office). *Telephone:* 1-60-92-66-00 (office). *Fax:* 1-60-92-66-09 (office). *E-mail:* maxim@ihes.fr (office). *Website:* www.ihes.fr/~maxim (office).

KONUMA, Michiji, DS; Japanese physicist and academic; *Professor Emeritus, Tokyo City University;* b. 25 Jan. 1931, Tokyo; s. of Haruo Konuma and Taka Konuma; m. Masae Shinohara 1960; one s. one d.; ed Musashi High School and Univ. of Tokyo; Research Assoc. Univ. of Tokyo 1958–67 (leave of absence 1963–67); Research Fellow, Consiglio Nazionale Ricerche, Italy and Visiting Prof. Scuola Normale Superiore, Pisa 1963–65; Visiting Prof., Catholic Univ. of Louvain, Belgium 1965–67; Assoc. Prof., Kyoto Univ. 1967–83; Prof., Keio Univ. 1983–96, Prof. Emer. 1996–; Prof. and Dean, Faculty of Environmental and Information Studies, Musashi Inst. of Tech. (now Tokyo City Univ.), Yokohama 1996–2001, Adviser 2001–03, Prof. Emer. 2005–; Trustee, Kanagawa Dental Coll. 2009–17; Visiting Prof., Univ. of the Air 1992–2001; Visiting Researcher, Int. Peace Research Inst., Meiji Gakuin Univ., Tokyo 2004–; Chair. Special Cttee of Nuclear Physics, Science Council of Japan 1969–72; Assoc. Ed. Progress of Theoretical Physics 1976–84; Ed. Bulletin of the Physical Society of Japan 1986–87; mem. Physics Action Council, UNESCO 1994–96; Pres. Physical Soc. of Japan 1987–88, 1991–92, Asscn of Asia Pacific Physical Socs 1994–97 (Special Adviser 2001–07), Soryushi Shogakukai Scholarship Asscn 2007–; mem. Council, Pugwash Confs on Science and World Affairs 1992–2002, Steering Cttee, Pugwash Japan 2016–; Dir Tokyu Foundation for Better Environment 2001–; Councillor, Shimonaka Memorial Foundation 2006–08, Dir 2008–; other professional appointments; Hon. mem. Roland Eötvös Physical Soc., Hungary 1997, Hungarian Acad. of Sciences 1998; Soryushi Medal for Distinguished Service 2004. *Publications:* numerous books and articles on theoretical particle physics, history of modern physics, physics educ. and 'Science and Society'. *Address:* 200-9 Kudencho, Sakaeku, Yokohama 247-0014, Japan (home). *Telephone:* (45) 891-8386 (home). *Fax:* (45) 891-8386 (home). *E-mail:* mkonuma254@m4.dion.ne.jp (home); mkonuma@keio.jp (office); konuma@tcu.ac.jp (office).

KONWAR, Devanand, BA, MA, LLB; Indian lawyer and politician; s. of Padma Kant Konwar; m. Neeva Konwar; ed Cotton Coll., Guwahati, Delhi Univ., Guwahati Univ.; student leader, Nat. Congress Party 1955, various party posts including Gen. Sec. and Vice-Pres. Assam Pradesh Congress Cttee 1982–90; elected to Assam State Ass. 1983, Minister, State Govt of Assam 1991, 2001; fmr Lecturer, English Dept, Cotton Coll., Guwahati, Assam; Marketing Man. American Standard Vacuum Oil Co. (later ESSO-Standard Oil Co.), Mumbai 1961–68; Founding Prin., Guwahati Coll. 1968; called to Guwahati High Court Bar 1969; Advocate, Supreme Court of India 1969–91, also served as Govt Advocate for states of Assam, Tripura, Arunachal Pradesh and Mizoram; elected to Lok Sabha (parl.) for Congress (I) 1978; Gov. Bihar State 2009–13, also of W Bengal Dec. 2009–Jan. 2010, of Tripura 2013–14.

KONYUKHOV, Fedor Filippovich; Russian explorer and artist; b. 12 Dec. 1951, Chkalovo, Zaporizhye Region, USSR (now Ukraine); m. Irina Konyukhov; two s. one d.; ed Odessa Navigation Coll., Leningrad Arctic Coll., Kronstadt Marine Higher School, Bobruysk School of Arts; completed solo expedition to North Pole 1989; f. School of Travellers 1991; Head, Lab. for Remote Training under Extreme Conditions, Modern Humanitarian Acad., Moscow 1998–; Plenipotentiary Rep. of UNEP (UN programme on Environmental Protection) 1997–; mem. Russian Union of Artists 1983–, Moscow Union of Artists, Graphic Arts section 1996–, Union of Journalists of Russian Fed., Union of Writers of Russian Fed.; Hon. Citizen Terni, Italy 1991, Taipei, Taiwan 1995, Nakhodka, Russia 1996; Hon. Academician of Russian Arts Acad.; Order of Friendship of Peoples, UNESCO Order; Merited Master of Sports of Russia 1989, Gold Medal of the Russian Arts Acad. *Expeditions include:* North Geographical Pole (3 times), South Geographical Pole, Pole of considerable inaccessibility in Arctic Ocean, Mt. Everest (Alpinists pole), Cape Horn (Yachtsmen pole); within program Seven Summits of the World climbed highest mountains on each continent: Elbrus (Europe/Russia) 1992, Everest (Asia) 1992, Winson Massif (Antarctica) 1996, Aconcagua (South America) 1996, Kilimanjaro (Africa) 1997, Mt. Kosciusko (Australia) 1997, Mt. McKinley (North America) 1997. *Address:* Tourism and Sports Union of Russia, Studeniy proyezd 7, 129282 Moscow, Russia. *Telephone:* (495) 478-63-02 (office). *E-mail:* oscar75@yandex.ru. *Website:* www.konyukhov.ru/eng.

KOO, Bon-joon, BS, MBA; South Korean business executive; *Inside Director, LG Electronics;* b. 1951, grandson of In-hwoi Koo, Founder of Lucky GoldStar (now LG); ed Seoul Nat. Univ., Univ. of Chicago Booth School of Business, USA; worked at GoldStar/LG Electronics in a range of business areas including planning and strategy 1986–95, held various exec. roles overseeing semiconductors, PCs, IT and chemicals, cr. and led jt venture LG.Philips LCD (became LG Display 2008) 1999–2004, Vice-Chair. and CEO LG International –2010, Vice-Chair. LG Corpn 2010–, Vice-Chair. and CEO LG Electronics 2010–15, Inside Dir 2015–; Jt Rep. Dir Koninklijke Philips Electronics NV –2007; Gen. Man. LG Twins (Korea Baseball Org.) 1990–. *Address:* LG Electronics, LG Twin Towers, 20 Yoido-dong, Youngdungpo-gu, Seoul, 150-721, Republic of Korea (office). *Telephone:* (2) 3773-1114 (office). *Fax:* (2) 3773-7813 (office). *E-mail:* info@lg.com (office). *Website:* www.lg.com (office).

KOO, John, BEcons; South Korean electronics industry executive; *Chairman, LS Group;* b. 11 Dec. 1946, Jinjoo, Namdo Prov.; ed Kyonggi High School, Princeton Univ., USA; joined LG Int. 1973, Import Section 1973–76, Man., Machinery and Electronics Div. 1976–79, Gen. Man. Hong Kong Office 1979–81, Singapore Office 1982–83, Chief, Singapore Office 1983–87, joined LG Electronics Co. Ltd (fmrly Goldstar Co. Ltd) 1987, Man. Dir Overseas Operations Div. 1987–88, Sr Man. Dir Overseas Operations Div. 1988–91, Vice-Pres. 1991–95, CEO 1994–2003, Pres. 1995–99, Vice-Chair. 1999–2003, Chair. LG Cable Ltd (now LS Cable) 2004–08, Chair. and CEO LS Group 2008–13, Chair. 2013–; Exec.-Sec., Int. Cablemakers Fed. 2007; Chair. Electronic Industries Asscn of Korea (EIAK), Industrial Design Cttee of Fed. of Korean Industries, Electronic Display Industrial Research Asscn, Subcommittee of Presidential Cttee on Green Growth 2011, Korea Invention Promotion Asscn 2014; Chair. Zenith Electronics Corpn; Vice-Chair. Korea Industrial Tech. Asscn; mem. Korea Inst. for Industrial Econs and Trade; Iron Tower Order of Industrial Service Merit 1985, Gold Tower Order of Industrial Service Merit 1995. *Address:* Office of the Chairman, LS Group, LS Tower, Hogye-dong, Dongan-gu, Anyang-si, Gyeonggi-do, 431-848, Republic of Korea (office). *Telephone:* (2) 2034-4867 (office). *Website:* www.lsholdings.com/eng (office); www.johnkoo.pe.kr.

KOOGLE, Timothy (Tim) A., BS, MS, DEng; American engineer and business executive; *Founder and CEO, Serendipity Land Holdings, LLC;* b. 1952; m. (divorced); ed Univ. of Virginia, Stanford Univ.; several years with Motorola Inc. holding various exec. positions; Pres. Intermec Corpn 1990–95, also Corp. Vice-Pres. Western Atlas Inc. (parent co.); CEO Corpn 1992–99, Chair., CEO Yahoo! Inc. 1995–2001, Vice-Chair. 2001–2003; CEO Friendster 2004, also Dir; Founder and CEO Serendipity Land Holdings LLC (pvt. land devt co.) 2004–, developer of El Banco resort, Punta de Mita, Mexico; Chair. Method Products, Inc., San Francisco 2006–14; Founder and Man. Dir The Koogle Foundation 2001–; mem. Bd of Dirs, Room to Read 2010–14, Thomas Weisel Partners Group LLC 2006–10 (also mem. Advisory Bd), Ecover 2012–, Olly Public Benefit Corpn 2014–; fmr Chair. AIM. *Leisure interests:* vintage guitars, cars. *E-mail:* tim@elbancomexico.com.mx.

KOOLHAAS, Remment (Rem); Dutch architect and academic; *Professor in Practice, Department of Architecture, Graduate School of Design, Harvard University;* b. 1944; ed Architectural Asscn, London, UK, Cornell Univ., USA; fmr journalist, Haagse Post, Amsterdam; Co-founder and Prin., Office of Metropolitan Architecture (OMA) 1975–; Prof. of Architecture, Technical Univ., Delft 1988–89; Prof. of Architecture, Rice Univ., Houston, Tex. 1991–92; Arthur Rotch Adjunct Prof. of Architecture, Grad. School of Design, Harvard Univ. 1990–95, Prof. in Practice and Urban Design 1995–, oversees Project on the City; Visiting Scholar, The Getty Center, LA 1993; f. Grosztstadt Foundation; Chevalier, Légion d'honneur 2001; Progressive Architecture Award (jtly) 1974, Le Moniteur, Prix d'Architecture 1991, Antonio Gaudi Prize 1992, Pritzker Prize 2000, Praemium Imperiale 2003, Royal Gold Medal (RIBA) 2004, European Union Prize for Contemporary Architecture 2005, Golden Lion for Lifetime Achievement, Venice Biennale 2010. *Major works include:* Casa da Música, Porto 2001–05, Netherlands Embassy, Berlin 2003, Seoul Nat. Univ. Museum of Art 2003–05, Prada Epicenter, Los Angeles 2004, Seattle Central Library 2004, Leeum Samsung Museum of Art, Seoul 2004, Wyly Theatre, Dallas 2004–09, Milstein Hall, Cornell Univ. 2006–09, Prada Transformer, Seoul, Serpentine Gallery Pavilion, London 2006, China Central Television, Beijing 2008, Riga Port City 2009, De Rotterdam Building 2009–13, Taipei Performing Arts Centre 2012–15. *Exhibitions include:* The Sparkling Metropolis, Guggenheim Museum 1978, OMA 1972–88, Architecturmuseum, Basel 1988, OMA: The First Decade, Boymans Museum, Rotterdam 1989, OMA, Museum of Modern Art, New York 1994, Light Construction, Museum of Modern Art, New York 1995. *Publications include:* Project Japan: An Oral History of Metabolism, Al Manakh, Al Manakh II, Harvard Design School Guide to Shopping, Great Leap Forward, Delirious New York: A Retroactive Manifesto for Manhattan. *Address:* OMA/AMO Rotterdam, Heer Bokelweg 149, 3032 AD Rotterdam (office); Harvard University Graduate School of Design, 48 Quincy Street, Cambridge, MA 02138, USA (office). *Telephone:* (10) 2438200 (Rotterdam) (office); (617) 495-1000 (Harvard) (office). *Fax:* (10) 2438202 (Rotterdam) (office). *E-mail:* park@oma.com (office). *Website:* www.oma.eu (office); www.gsd.harvard.edu (office).

KOOMPIROCHANA, Vikrom, BA, MA, PhD; Thai diplomatist (retd) and business executive; *Chairman, Country Group Development Public Company Ltd;* m. Sasin Monvoisin; ed Chulalongkorn Univ., Michigan State Univ. and Schiller International Univ., USA; Lecturer in History, Faculty of Arts, Chulalongkorn Univ. –1973; joined Ministry of Foreign Affairs in 1973, Amb. to Singapore 1991–95, to Malaysia 1996, to New Zealand 1997–99, Deputy Perm. Sec., Ministry of Foreign Affairs 2000–01, Amb. to Italy 2002, to UK 2003–06 (retd); Chair. Country Group Development Public Company Ltd (fmrly Dragon One PLC) 2006–; mem. Bd of Dirs Oishi Group of Cos 2006–, MFC Asset Management Public Company Ltd 2014–, Bangchak Petroleum PCL; Adviser to TCC Holding Co. Ltd, TCC Land Co. Ltd; Hon. Adviser, British Chamber of Commerce Thailand; Hon. Commr Securities and Exchange Comm. of Thailand Maha Paramabhorn (Special Grand Cordon) of the Most Exalted Order of the White Elephant; Chakrabarti Mala Medal. *Address:* Country Group Development PCL Level 20, Ploenchit Tower, 898 Ploenchit Road, Bangkok 10330, Thailand (office). *E-mail:* info@cgd.co.th (office). *Website:* www.cgd.co.th (office).

KOONS, Jeff, BFA; American artist; b. 21 Jan. 1955, York, Pa; m. 1st Ilona Staller (née La Cicciolina) 1991 (divorced 1994); one s.; m. 2nd Justine Wheeler; one s.; ed School of the Art Inst. of Chicago, Maryland Inst. Coll. of Art; fmr commodities broker, New York; Fellow, American Acad. of Arts and Sciences 2005; Hon. mem. Royal Academy, London 2010; Officier, Ordre nat. de la Légion d'honneur 2007; Hon. DFA (The Corcoran, Washington, DC) 2002; Dr hc (School of the Art Inst. of Chicago) 2008; Skowhegan Award for Sculpture 2002, inducted into Signet Soc. for Arts and Letters, Harvard Univ. 2002, Wollaston Award, Royal Acad. of Arts 2008, John Singleton Copley Award 2009, Medal of Honor, Nat. Arts Club 2009, Lotus Award of Distinction 2011, Medal of Arts, Art in Embassies, US State Dept 2012 and numerous other awards. *Address:* c/o Gagosian Gallery, 980 Madison Avenue, New York, NY 10075, USA (office). *Website:* www.gagosian.com (office); www.jeffkoons.com (office).

KOONTZ, Dean Ray, (David Axton, Brian Coffey, Deanna Dwyer, K. R. Dwyer, John Hill, Leigh Nichols, Anthony North, Richard Paige, Owen West), BS; American writer; b. 9 July 1945, Everett, Pa; s. of Raymond Koontz and Florence Logue; m. Gerda Ann Cerra 1966; ed Shippensburg Univ.; fmr teacher of English; freelance author 1969–; work includes novels, short stories, science fiction/fantasy, social commentary/phenomena and journalism; Hon. DLitt (Shippensburg) 1989. *Publications include:* Star Quest 1968, The Fall of the Dream Machine 1969, Fear That Man 1969, Anti-Man 1970, Beastchild 1970, Dark of the Woods 1970, The Dark Symphony 1970, Hell's Gate 1970, The Crimson Witch 1971, A Darkness in My Soul 1972, The Flesh in the Furnace 1972, Starblood 1972, Time Thieves 1972, Warlock 1972, A Werewolf Among Us 1973, Hanging On 1973, The Haunted Earth 1973, Demon Seed 1973, Strike Deep 1974, After the Last Race 1974, Nightmare Journey 1975, The Long Sleep 1975, Night Chills 1976, The Voice of the Night 1980, Whispers 1980, The Funhouse 1980, The Eyes of Darkness 1981, The Mask 1981, House of Thunder 1982, Phantoms 1983, Darkness Comes 1984, Twilight 1984, The Door to December 1985, Strangers 1986, Shadow Fires 1987, Watchers 1987, Twilight Eyes 1987, Oddkins 1988, Servants of Twilight 1988, Lightning

1988, Midnight 1989, The Bad Place 1990, Cold Fire 1991, Hideaway 1992, Dragon Tears 1992, Winter Moon 1993, The House of Thunder 1993, Dark Rivers of the Heart 1994, Mr Murder 1994, Fun House 1994, Strange Highways 1994, Icebound 1995, Intensity 1995, The Key to Midnight 1995, Ticktock 1996, Santa's Twin 1996, Sole Survivor 1996, Fear Nothing 1997, Seize the Night 1998, False Memory 1999, From the Corner of his Eye 2001, One Door Away From Heaven 2001, By the Light of the Moon 2002, The Face 2003, Odd Thomas 2003, Life Expectancy 2004, Frankenstein Book 1: Prodigal Son (with Kevin J. Anderson) 2004, Frankenstein Book 2: City of Night (with Ed Gorman) 2005, Forever Odd 2005, The Husband 2006, Brother Odd 2006, The Good Guy 2007, The Darkest Evening of the Year 2007, Odd Hours 2008, Bliss to You 2008, In Odd We Trust 2008, Shadowfires 2008, The Bad Place 2008, Your Heart Belongs to Me 2008, Relentless 2009, Frankenstein Book 3: Dead and Alive 2009, Breathless 2009, A Big Little Life 2009, Frankenstein Book 4: Lost Souls 2010, Odd is On Our Side 2010, Darkness Under the Sun 2010, What the Night Knows 2011, Frankenstein Book 5: The Dead Town 2011, The Moonlit Mind 2011, 77 Shadow Street 2011, House of Odd 2012, Odd Apocalypse 2012, Odd Interlude #1–#3 2012, The City 2014, The Neighbor 2014, Saint Odd 2014, Ashley Bell 2015, The Silent Corner 2017, The Whispering Room 2017, The Forbidden Door 2018, The Crooked Staircase 2018. *Address:* POB 9529, Newport Beach, CA 92658, USA (office). *E-mail:* dean@deankoontz.com (office). *Website:* www.deankoontz.com.

KOOSER, Theodore (Ted), BS, MA; American poet and writer; b. 25 April 1939, Ames, Ia; m. 1st Diana Tresslar 1962 (divorced 1969); one s.; m. 2nd Kathleen Rutledge 1977; ed Iowa State Univ., Univ. of Nebraska; Underwriter, Bankers Life Nebraska 1965–73; part-time instructor in creative writing 1970–, Sr Underwriter, Lincoln Benefit Life 1973–84, Vice-Pres. 1984–98; currently Prof., Univ. of Neb., Lincoln; Ed. and Publr, Windflower Press; Poet Laureate of the USA 2004–06; John H. Vreeland Award for Creative Writing 1964, Prairier Schooner Prizes in Poetry 1976, 1978, NEA Literary Fellowships 1976, 1984, Columbia Magazine Stanley Kunitz Poetry Prize 1984, Governor's Arts Award 1988, Mayor's Arts Award 1989, Poetry Northwest Richard Hugo Prize 1994, Nebraska Arts Council Merit Award 2000, Pushcart Prize, James Boatwright Prize. *Publications include:* Official Entry Blank 1969, Grass County 1971, A Local Habitation and a Name 1974, Shooting a Farmhouse: So This is Nebraska 1975, Not Coming to be Barked At 1976, Voyages to the Inland Sea (with Harley Elliott) 1976, Hatcher 1978, Old Marriage and New 1978, Cottonwood County (with William Kloefkorn) 1979, Windflower Home Almanac of Poetry (ed.) 1980, Sure Signs: New and Selected Poems (Soc. of Midland Authors Poetry Prize) 1980, One World at a Time 1985, As Far as I Can See: Contemporary Writers of the Middle Plains (ed.) 1989, Etudes 1992, Weather Central 1994, A Book of Things 1995, A Decade of Ted Kooser Valentines 1996, Riding with Colonel Carter 1999, Winter Morning Walks: 100 Postcards to Jim Harrison (Nebraska Book Award for poetry 2001) 2000, Local Wonders: Seasons in the Bohemian Alps (Friends of American Writers Chicago Award, ForeWord Magazine Gold Award for Autobiography, Nebraska Book Award for Nonfiction 2003) 2002, Braided Creek: A Conversation in Poetry (with Jim Harrison) 2003, Delights and Shadows (Pulitzer Prize for Poetry 2005) 2004, The Poetry Home Repair Manual 2004, Flying at Night: Poems 1965–1985 2005, Valentines 2008, House Held Up by Trees 2012; contrib. to The American Poetry Review, Antioch Review, Cream City Review, The Hudson Review, Kansas Quarterly, The Kenyon Review, Midwest Quarterly, The New Yorker, Poetry Northwest, Poetry, Prairie Schooner, Shenandoah, Tailwind. *Address:* c/o Blue Flower Arts, LLC, PO Box 1361, Millbrook, NY 12545, USA (office); 1820 Branched Oak Road, Garland, NE 68360-9303, USA (home). *Telephone:* (845) 677-8559 (office). *Fax:* (845) 677-6446 (office). *E-mail:* blueflowerarts@mac.com (office); kr84428@windstream.net. *Website:* www.blueflowerarts.com (office); www.tedkooser.net.

KOPACZ, Ewa; Polish paediatrician and politician; b. 3 Dec. 1956, Skaryszew; divorced; one d.; ed Faculty of Medicine, Medical Univ. of Lublin; Dir Dept of Health Care, Szydłowiec –2001; Councillor, Parl. of Mazowiecki 1998–2001; mem. Platforma Obywatelska (PO—Civic Platform) 2001–, Pres. Mazowieckie Voivodship br. of PO 2006–08, Vice-Pres. of PO 2010–14, Pres. 2014–16; Deputy in the Sejm (Parl.) for Radom 2001–, Chair. of Health Cttee, Marshal of the Sejm 2011–14; Minister of Health 2007–11; Prime Minister of Poland 2014–15; Grand Cross, Royal Norwegian Order of Merit 2012, Commdr, Order of St Charles (Monaco) 2012, Order of the Cross of Terra Mariana First Class (Estonia) 2014. *Address:* Platforma Obywatelska (Civic Platform), 00-490 Warsaw, ul. Wiejska 12A, Poland (office). *Telephone:* (22) 4596400 (office). *Fax:* (22) 4596431 (office). *E-mail:* biuro@platforma.org (office). *Website:* www.platforma.org (office).

KOPETZ, Hermann, PhD; Austrian physicist and academic; *Professor of Real-Time Systems, Vienna University of Technology;* ed Univ. of Vienna; fmr man. of computer process control dept at Voest Alpine, Linz; Prof. of Computer Process Control, Tech. Univ. of Berlin 1978–82; Prof. of Real-Time Systems, Vienna Univ. of Tech. 1982–; Dir Max Planck Inst., Saarbrücken, Germany 1993; Visiting Prof., Univ. of California, Irvine and Santa Barbara several times; organizer of numerous int. confs; Chair. IEEE Tech. Cttee on Fault-Tolerant Computing 1990–92, Int. Fed. for Information Processing Working Group 10.4 on Dependable Computing and Fault-Tolerance 1996–; Fellow, IEEE 1993; Wilhelm Exner Medal, Austrian Asscn for SME (Oesterreichischer Gewerbeverein—OGV) (jtly) 2005. *Achievements include:* chief architect of Time-Triggered Protocol (TTP) for distributed fault-tolerant real-time systems, which evolved out of the MARS project at Tech. Univ. of Vienna. *Publications include:* more than 100 papers and patents in the fields of real-time computing, distributed computing and fault tolerance. *Address:* Vienna University of Technology, Department of Computer Engineering, Cyber-Physical Systems Group, DE0340 Treitlstraße 3, 1040 Vienna, Austria (office). *Telephone:* (1) 58801-18230 (office). *Fax:* (1) 58801-18299 (office). *E-mail:* hermann.kopetz@tuwien.ac.at (office). *Website:* ti.tuwien.ac.at/institute (office).

KOPONEN, Harri, PhD; Finnish telecommunications industry executive; *Executive Chairman, Tecnotree OyJ;* b. 6 Dec. 1962, Lahti; s. of Onni Koponen and Aili Ikonen; m.; four c.; ed Commercial Coll. of Turku, Helsinki Univ., Helsinki School of Econs; fmr Educ. Officer, Finnish Defence Force; fmr Office Man. Oy Shell AB; fmr Head Telecom Sales, Hewlett-Packard; Global Account Exec., Ericsson, Exec. Vice-Pres. and Gen. Man. Ericsson Consumer Products in Americas, Man. Dir SonyEricsson Americas; Pres. and CEO Sonera, then Deputy CEO TeliaSonera and Head, TeliaSonera International (after merger of Swedish Telia and Sonera) 2002–04; CEO and Gen. Man. Wataniya Telecom, Kuwait 2004–08; COO Rovio Entertainment Ltd (Angry Birds) 2011–13; CEO NPTV 2013–14; CEO SSH Communications Security Corpn 2014–16, Sr Adviser 2016–; Chair. Tecnotree OyJ 2011–16, Exec. Chair. 2016–; Partner, Boardman Oy 2011–; CEO and Chair. Oy Osaka Ltd 2010–; Chair. Mobile SPA Oy; mem. Bd of Dirs Namida Diamond Factory 2013–, TLD Registry Oy 2014–, Molok Oy 2014–, Finnish Cyber Security Cluster, FISC 2015–; Baden-Powell Fellow, World Scout Foundation 2006; Defence Cross of Finland; Hon. PhD. *Achievements include:* European Champion in American Football 1985. *Leisure interests:* hockey, golf, coaching. *Address:* Tecnotree OyJ, Finnoonniitynkuja 7, PO Box 93, 02271 Espoo, Finland (office). *Telephone:* (40) 1922464 (office). *Website:* www.tecnotree.com (office).

KOPPEL, (Edward James Martin) Ted, MA; American journalist, broadcaster and writer; b. 8 Feb. 1940, Lancs., England; m. Grace A. Dorney; four c.; ed Syracuse Univ, Stanford Univ.; moved to USA 1953; news corresp. and writer, WMCA, New York 1963; joined American Broadcasting Corpn (ABC) News 1963, fmr news corresp. in Viet Nam, Chief, Miami Bureau, ABC News, Chief, Hong Kong Bureau, diplomatic corresp., Hong Kong Bureau, ABC News, Washington, anchor, ABC News Nightline 1980–2005, Man. Ed. 1980–2005; Man. Ed., Discovery Channel US 2005–08; Special Corresp., Rock Center with Brian Williams, NBC News 2011–13; co-author (with Marvin Kalb) TV special: In the National Interest (Overseas Press Club Award); columnist, New York Times, Washington Post, Wall Street Journal; contrib., NBC News, BBC America, National Public Radio; Hon. DHumLitt (Duke Univ) 1987; Hon. DIur (Univ of Southern California) 2007; 41 Emmy Awards, eight George Foster Peabody Awards, Paul White Award, Radio TV Digital News Asscn 2004, Edward R. Murrow Lifetime Achievement Award 2011. *Publications include:* The Wit and Wisdom of Adlai Stevenson 1985, In The National Interest 1977, Nightline: History In the Making and the Making of Television 1996, Off Camera: Private Thoughts Made Public 2000, Lights Out: A Cyberattack, A Nation Unprepared, Surviving the Aftermath 2015. *Address:* Janklow & Nesbit Associates, 445 Park Avenue, New York, NY 10022, USA (office).

KOPPER, Hilmar; German business executive; b. 13 March 1935, Oslanin, West Prussia; m. Brigitte Seebacher-Brandt 2003; CEO Deutsche Bank AG 1989–97, Chair. Supervisory Bd 1997–99; Chair. Supervisory Bd Daimler-Benz AG (DaimlerChrysler then Daimler AG), Stuttgart 1990–2007; Chair. Supervisory Bd Lincas GmbH, Hamburg; Chair. Supervisory Bd HSH Nordbank AG 2009–13; mem. Supervisory Bd Akzo, Arnhem, Netherlands, Bayer AG, Leverkusen, Deutsche Lufthansa AG, Cologne, Deutsche Bank, Frankfurt, Mannesmann AG, Düsseldorf, Municher Rückversicherungs-Gesellschaft, Munich, VEBA AG, Düsseldorf; Chair. Advisory Bd Brauerei Beck & Co., Bremen, Frowein GmbH & Co. KG, Wuppertal, Leopold Kostal GmbH & Co. KG, Lüdenscheid; mem. Advisory Bd Solvay & Cie SA, Brussels; fmr Deputy Chair. Morgan Grenfell Group PLC, London; Chair. Freunden und Förderern der Johann Wolfgang Goethe-Universität Frankfurt am Main eV 2001–10; Hon. Senator, Johann Wolfgang Goethe-Universität Frankfurt am Main eV 2010– Distinguished Leadership Award, International Management Development Institute 2005. *Leisure interests:* reading, collecting the wrappings that encase citrus fruits in greengrocers' shops.

KOPTEV, Yuri Nikolayevich, Cand Tech Sc; Russian engineer and manager; b. 13 March 1940, Stavropol; m.; two s.; ed Bauman Higher Tech. School; worked as engineer for Lavochkin Science-Tech. Corpn 1965–69; author of a number of space-rocket projects; Sr Engineer, Head of Dept, then Deputy Minister, Ministry of Gen. Machine Construction 1969–91; Vice-Pres. Rosobshchemash Corpn 1991–92; Dir-Gen. Russian Space Agency 1992–99, Russian Aviation and Space Agency 1999–2004; Dir Defence Industry Dept, Ministry of Industry and Energy 2004–08; Head of Advisory Group, Russian Technologies State Corpn 2008–09; apptd Chair. Science and Engineering Council 2009; Prof., Bauman Moscow State Tech. Univ.; mem. Tsiolkovsky Acad. of Cosmonautics and Presidium, Cosmonautics Fed. of Russia and Presidium, Int. Acad. of Eng; Order of the Red Banner of Labour, Order of the October Revolution, Order of Lenin, Order 'For Merit to the Fatherland' 2nd and 3rd class; numerous awards, including medals For Labour Valour', '300 Years of the Russian Navy', '100 Years of the Air Force'; Meritorious Scientist of the Russian Fed., Meritorious Worker of the Aerospace Industry of the Russian Fed.

KORALEK, Paul George, CBE, RA, RIBA; British architect (retd); b. 7 April 1933, Vienna, Austria; s. of Ernest Koralek and Alice Koralek (née Müller); m. (Audrey) Jennifer Koralek 1956; one s. two d.; ed Aldenham, Architectural Asscn; Partner and Dir Ahrends, Burton & Koralek, Architects (now ABK Architects) 1961–2009 (retd); Fellow, Royal Inst. of the Architects of Ireland; Winner Int. Competition for New Library, Trinity Coll., Dublin 1961, Competition for Nat. Gallery Extension 1982–85, Int. Competition for Devt Plan, Grenoble Univ. 1991, RIBA Architecture Award 1978, 1996, 1999, RIBA Housing Award 1977, Structural Steel Design Award 1976, 1980, 1985, Financial Times Award 1976 (Commendation 1986, 1987), Civic Trust Award 1986, 1992, Royal Inst. of the Architects of Ireland Award 1999. *Buildings include:* new British Embassy, Moscow 1999; Docklands Light Railway Extension Stations; Templeton Coll., Oxford 1969, Nebenzahl House, Jerusalem 1972, Warehouse and Showroom for Habitat, Wallingford 1974, residential bldg for Keble Coll., Oxford 1976, Arts Faculty bldg, Trinity Coll., Dublin 1979, factory for Cummins Engines, Shotts 1983, supermarket, J. Sainsbury, Canterbury 1984, Retail HQ, W.H. Smith, Swindon 1985, 1995, dept store John Lewis, Kingston 1990, St Mary's Hosp., Newport, Isle of Wight 1990, White Cliffs Heritage Centre, Dover 1991, Dublin Dental Hosp. 1998–, Techniquest Science Discovery Centre, Cardiff 1995, Insts of Tech. Tralee, Waterford, Blanchardstown 2002–, Offaly Co. Council HQ 2002, Tipperary N Riding County Offices 2000–, Convent Lands Devt Plan, Dublin 2000–, Trinity Coll. Dublin Arts Faculty extension 2002, Galway Co. Council offices extension, new library and HQ 2002, housing at Newcastle West, Co. Limerick 2004, John Wheatley Coll., Glasgow 2005. *Publications include:* Ahrends, Burton & Koralek 1991, Collaborations – The Architecture of ABK 2002. *Address:* c/o ABK Architects Dublin, 34 Lower Leeson Street, Dublin 2, Ireland (office).

KORASEV, Vladislav Borisovich; Kazakhstani politician; b. 16 Nov. 1937, Volodarskoye, Kokshetau Oblast, Kazakh SSR, USSR; ed Omsk Agricultural Institute, Higher Party School of the Central Committee of the Communist Party; joined CP of the Soviet Union 1958; worked as a tractor driver on the Borovsk state farm in Rusayevsk region of Kokshetau Oblast; served in Soviet army for three years; began working as sec. of Borovsk state farm's Komsomol (Communist Youth League) 1959–61, Sec. of Party Cttee at Michurinskiy, Volodarskiy and Chervonnyy state farms 1961–70; Instructor, Oblast Cttee 1968–70; first Sec. Kokshetau Oblast Komsomol 1970–73, first Sec. Leninskiy regional Party Cttee 1973–80; Chair. Kokshetau Oblast Union of Agricultural Workers 1980–90, Kokshetau Oblast Council of Labour Unions 1990–97; Deputy of the Majlis (Parl.) 1999–2004, Sec. Cttee on Int. Affairs, Defence and Security; Sec. Cen. Cttee, Communist People's Party of Kazakhstan (Kazakstan Kommunistik Khalyk Partiyasy) 2004. *Address:* c/o Communist People's Party of Kazakhstan (Kazakstan Kommunistik Khalyk Partiyasy), 010000 Nur-Sultan, Karasai batyr 14/7, Kazakhstan (office).

KÖRBER, Hans-Joachim; German business executive; ed Tech. Univ. of Berlin; Sr Controller, Beverages Div., R.A. Oetker 1974–80; worked for Söhnlein Rheingold 1980–85; mem. Man. Bd, Metro SB-Grossmarkle 1985–91; mem. Exec. Bd, Chair. and CEO, Metro AG 1999–2007; Chair. Air Berlin PLC 2011–, Esprit Holdings Ltd 2011–12; Dir Skandinaviska Enskilda Banken AB 2000–, Sysco Corpn; mem. Supervisory Bd Bertelsmann AG 2004; mem. Global Advisory Bd, Egon Zehnder Int.; mem. Bd of Advisors, Palamon Capital Partners 2011–. *Address:* Palamon Capital Partners, Cleveland House, 33 King Street, London, SW1Y 6RJ, England (office). *Telephone:* (20) 7766-2000 (office). *Fax:* (20) 7766-2002 (office). *E-mail:* info@palamon.com (office). *Website:* www.palamon.com (office).

KORDA, Michael Vincent, BA; American (b. British) publishing executive (retd); *Editor-in-Chief Emeritus, Simon & Schuster Inc.;* b. 8 Oct. 1933, London, England; s. of Vincent Korda and Gertrude Korda (née Musgrove); m. Carolyn Keese 1958; one s.; ed Magdalen Coll., Oxford, UK; served in RAF 1952–54; joined Simon and Schuster, New York 1958–, first as Ed., then Sr Ed., Man. Ed., Exec. Ed., Sr Vice-Pres. and Ed.-in-Chief, Ed.-in-Chief Emer. 2005–; mem. Nat. Soc. of Film Critics, American Horse Shows Asscn. *Publications include:* Male Chauvinism: How It Works 1973, Power: How to Get It, How to Use It 1975, Success! 1977, Charmed Lives 1979, Worldly Goods 1982, The Fortune 1989, Curtain 1991, Man to Man: Surviving Prostate Cancer 1997, Another Life, 2000, Making the List 2001, Country Matters 2002, Horse People 2004, Ulysses S. Grant: The Unlikely Hero 2004, Marking Time: Collecting Watches and Thinking about Time 2004, Journey to a Revolution: A Personal Memoir and History of the Hungarian Revolution of 1956 2006, Cat People (with Margaret Korda) 2006, Ike: An American Hero 2007, With Wings Like Eagles 2009, Hero: The Life and Legend of Lawrence of Arabia 2010, Clouds of Glory: The Life and Legend of Robert E. Lee 2014. *Address:* c/o Simon and Schuster, 1230 Avenue of the Americas, New York, NY 10020, USA. *Website:* authors.simonandschuster.co.uk/Michael-Korda/1487155.

KORDA, Petr; Czech professional tennis player (retd); b. 23 Jan. 1968, Prague; s. of Petr Korda and Jana Korda; m. Regina Rajchrtová 1992; two d. one s.; coached by his father until aged 18; winner Wimbledon Jr Doubles 1986; turned professional 1987; runner-up French Open 1992; winner Grand Slam Cup 1993; winner Stuttgart Open 1997, Australian Open 1998, Qatar Open 1998; mem. Czechoslovak Davis Cup Team 1988, 1996; lives in Monte Carlo; received one-year ban after testing positive for nandrolone in Wimbledon Championship 1998; retd in 1999 having won 20 professional titles (including 10 singles titles); now plays in Srs Tour; runner-up to Guy Forget 2001; won Honda Challenge 2002; Chair. Bd of Supervisors Karlštejn golf resort, Czech Repub. 2000. *Leisure interest:* golf.

KORDJE, Bedoumra, PhD; Chadian politician and fmr telecommunications engineer; ed Univ. Paul Sabatier, Toulouse, Ecole Nat. Supérieure des Télécommunications, Paris, France; engineer, Posts and Telecommunications Corpn of Chad 1981–82; engineering consultant with pvt. consultancy firm, Abidjan 1982–83; joined ADB 1983 as Telecommunications Expert, becoming Chief Telecommunications Expert –1996, Man., Infrastructure and Industry Div., N Region 1996–2002, Dir, Infrastructure Dept (North, East and South Regions) 2002–05, Dir, Water and Sanitation Dept and African Water Facility 2006–08, Sec.-Gen., ADB 2008–09, Vice Pres., Corp. Services 2009; Minister of Finance and the Budget 2013–15. *Address:* c/o Ministry of Finance and the Budget, BP 816, N'Djamena, Chad.

KORHONEN, Keijo Tero, PhD; Finnish political scientist, academic, diplomatist and fmr politician; b. 23 Feb. 1934, Paltamo; s. of Hannes Korhonen and Anna Korhonen (née Laari); m. 1st Anneli Korhonen (née Torkkila) 1958; three s.; m. 2nd Anita Korhonen (née Uggeldahl) 1990; ed Turku Univ.; Prof. of Int. Relations, Univ. of Arizona, USA from 1964, later Adjunct Prof. of Political Science; Fellow, Weatherhead Center for Int. Affairs, Harvard Univ., USA 1969–70; Deputy Dir for Political Affairs, Ministry of Foreign Affairs 1971–74; Prof. of Political History, Univ. of Helsinki 1974–77; Minister of Foreign Affairs 1976–77; Under-Sec. of State for Political Affairs, Ministry of Foreign Affairs 1977–83; Amb. and Perm. Rep. to UN, New York 1983–88; Special Adviser to the Prime Minister 1988–89; Ed.-in-Chief Kainuun Sanomat 1989–94; unsuccessful presidential cand. (ind.) 1994; fmr Deputy Chair. Paasikivi Soc.; mem. Exec. Bd Tucson Cttee on Foreign Relations. *Publications:* four books about Finnish–Soviet and Finnish–Russian relations since 1808; Finland in the Russian Political Thought of the 19th Century 1966, An Ambassador's Journal, Urho Kekkonen, the Leader and the Man, The Reverse Side of the Coin 1989, This Country Is Not For Sale 1991, An Accidental Corporal (memoir) 1999. *Leisure interests:* reading, jogging, horse riding.

KORIKI, Jojima; Japanese politician and fmr union leader; b. (Jojima Masamitsu), 1 Jan. 1947, Yanagawa City, Fukuoka Pref.; m.; one s. one d.; ed La Salle High School, Kagoshima, Univ. of Tokyo; with Cen. Research Lab., Ajinomoto Co. Inc. 1970–96, also becoming Pres., Workers' Union; mem. House of Reps (Parl.) (New Frontier Party, later DPJ) for Kanagawa 10th Dist constituency 1996–2012; mem. Democratic Party of Japan (DPJ), Chair. Policy Research Council 2010–, Acting Sec.-Gen. 2011, Chair. DPJ Diet Affairs Cttee 2012; Minister of Finance Oct.–Dec. 2012; fmr Pres. Japan Food Industry Workers' Union Council; Council mem., Japan Productivity Center for Socio-Econ. Devt. *Website:* www.jojima.net.

KORNAI, János, DrSc; Hungarian economist and academic; *Allie S. Freed Professor Emeritus of Economics, Harvard University;* b. 21 Jan. 1928, Budapest; m. Zsuzsa Dániel 1971; two s. one d.; ed Univ. of Budapest; Econ. Ed. 1947–55; Research Assoc. Inst. of Econs, Hungarian Acad. of Sciences 1955–58, Inst. of Textile Industry 1958–63; Sr Research Assoc., Computer Centre, Hungarian Acad. of Sciences 1963–67; Research Prof., Inst. of Econs, Hungarian Acad. of Sciences 1967–; Allie S. Freed Prof. of Econs, Harvard Univ. 1986–2002, Allie S. Freed Prof. Emer. 2002–; Perm. Fellow, Collegium Budapest 1992–2002, Perm. Fellow Emer. 2002–11; Distinguished Research Prof. Central European Univ. 2005–; Prof. Emer., Corvinus Univ., Budapest 2011–; Visiting Prof., LSE 1964, Univ. of Sussex 1966, Stanford Univ. 1968, Yale 1970, Princeton and Stanford 1972–73, Stockholm 1976–77, Geneva 1981, Munich 1983, Princeton 1983–84, Harvard 1984–85; Pres. Hungarian Social Science Asscn 1992, Int. Econ. Asscn 2002–05; mem. Hungarian Acad. of Sciences; Corresp. mem. British Acad.; Foreign mem. NAS, Royal Swedish Acad., Finnish Acad., Russian Acad. of Sciences, Bulgarian Acad. of Sciences; Hon. mem. American Acad. of Arts and Sciences 1972, American Econ. Asscn 1976, European Asscn for Comparative Econ. Studies 1996; Hon. Pres. Asscn of New Institutional Economists of Hungary 2004, World Interdisciplinary Network for Institutional Research 2013–; Hon. Citizen of Budapest 2005; Officier, Légion d'honneur 1997, Order of Merit, Commdr's Cross (Hungary) 2002, Order of Merit, Commdr's Cross with Star (Hungary) 2007, Leontief Medal (Russia) 2010, Grand Cross, Order of Merit (Hungary) 2010; Dr hc (Paris) 1978, (Poznań) 1978, (London) 1990, (Amsterdam), (Budapest) 1992, (Wrocław) 1993, (Turin) 1993, (Debrecen) 2001, (Stockholm) 2001, (Varna) 2003, (Veszprem) 2003, (Pecs) 2003, (Central European Univ.) 2004, (Kraków) 2008, (Pan-European Univ., Bratislava) 2013; Seidman Award 1982, Hungarian State Prize 1983, Humboldt Prize 1983, Széchenyi Prize 1994, Prima Primissima Prize 2005, Lifetime Achievement Award 2008, Hazám Award 2013, Open Soc. Prize, Central European Univ. 2018. *Publications:* Overcentralization in Economic Administration 1959, Mathematical Planning of Structural Decisions 1967, Anti-Equilibrium 1971, Rush versus Harmonic Growth 1972, Economics of Shortage 1980, Non-Price Control 1981, Growth, Shortage and Efficiency 1982, Contradictions and Dilemmas 1985, The Road to a Free Economy 1990, Vision and Reality 1990, The Socialist System 1992, Highways and Byways 1995, Struggle and Hope 1997, Welfare, Choice and Solidarity in Transition (with K. Eggleston) 2001, By Force of Thought: Irregular Memoirs of an Intellectual Journey 2006, From Socialism to Capitalism 2008, Dynamism, Rivalry and the Surplus Economy 2013. *Address:* Corvinus University of Budapest, Fővám tér 8, 1093 Budapest, Hungary (office). *Telephone:* (1) 482-5375 (office). *Fax:* (1) 482-5536 (office). *E-mail:* janos.kornai@uni-corvinus.hu (office). *Website:* www.kornai-janos.hu.

KORNBERG, Sir Hans (Leo), Kt, MA, PhD, DSc, ScD, FRS, FRSA, FRSB; British/American biochemist and academic; *University Professor and Professor of Biology, Boston University;* b. 14 Jan. 1928, Herford, Germany; s. of Max Kornberg and Margarete Kornberg (née Silberbach); m. 1st Monica M. King 1956 (died 1989); twin s. two d.; m. 2nd Donna Haber 1991; ed Queen Elizabeth Grammar School, Wakefield, England and Univs of Sheffield, Oxford and Cambridge; John Stokes Research Fellow, Univ. of Sheffield 1952–53; mem. MRC Cell Metabolism Research Unit, Univ. of Oxford 1955–61; Lecturer in Biochemistry, Worcester Coll., Oxford 1958–61; Prof. of Biochemistry, Univ. of Leicester 1961–75; Sir William Dunn Prof. of Biochemistry, Univ. of Cambridge 1975–95; Univ. Prof. and Prof. of Biology, Boston Univ., USA 1995–; Fellow, Christ's Coll., Cambridge 1975–, Master 1982–95; mem. SRC 1967–72, Chair. Science Bd 1969–72; Chair. Royal Comm. on Environmental Pollution 1976–81; mem. Agric. and Food Research Council 1980–84; mem. Priorities Bd for Research and Devt in Agric. 1984–90; Chair. Advisory Cttee on Genetic Modification 1986–95; Chair. Jt Policy Group Agric. and Environment 1986–89; mem. Bd NIREX 1986–95; Pres. Int. Union of Biochemistry and Molecular Biology 1991–94, The Biochemical Soc. 1990–95 (Hon. mem. 2001–); mem. Advisory Council for Applied Research and Devt 1982–85, Scientific Advisory Cttee, Inst. for Molecular Biology and Medicine, Monash Univ. 1987–; Commonwealth Fund Fellow, Yale Univ. and Public Health Research Inst., New York 1953–55; Vice-Pres. Inst. of Biology 1969–72; Vice-Chair. European Molecular Biological Org. 1978–81; Pres. BAAS 1984–85 (Hon. mem. 2003–); Pres. Asscn for Science Educ. 1991–92; Man. Trustee, Nuffield Foundation 1973–93; Gov. Wellcome Trust 1990–95; mem. Council, Imperial Soc. of Kts Bachelor 2005–; mem. German Acad. of Sciences Leopoldina 1982; Foreign Assoc. NAS 1986; mem. Academia Europaea 1988; Foreign mem. American Acad. of Arts and Sciences 1987, American Philosophical Soc. 1993, Accad. Nazionale dei Lincei 1997; Fellow, American Acad. of Microbiology 1992; Hon. mem. Soc. for Biological Chem., USA 1972, Japanese Biochemistry Soc. 1981; Hon. FRCP 1989; Hon. Fellow, Worcester Coll., Oxford, Brasenose Coll., Oxford, Wolfson Coll., Cambridge; Hon. FIBiol 2004, Hon. Fellow, BAAS 2005, Hon. Fellow, Foulkes Fed. 2015; Hon. ScD (Cincinnati) 1974; Hon. DSc (Warwick) 1975, (Leicester) 1979, (Sheffield) 1979, (Bath) 1980, (Strathclyde) 1985, (South Bank) 1994, (Leeds) 1995, (La Trobe) 1997; Hon. DUniv (Essex) 1979; Hon. MD (Leipzig) 1984; Hon. LLD (Dundee) 1999; Colworth Medal, Biochemical Soc. 1963, Leeuwenhoek Lecturer, Royal Soc. 1972, Warburg Medal, German Biochemical Soc. 1973. *Publications:* numerous articles in scientific journals. *Leisure interests:* conversation, cooking. *Address:* Biology Department, Boston University, 5 Cummington Mall, Boston, MA 02215 (office); 70 Carey Lane, Falmouth, MA 02540-1604, USA (home). *Telephone:* (617) 353-2440 (office); (617) 548-7632 (home). *Fax:* (617) 353-6340 (office). *E-mail:* hlk@bu.edu (office). *Website:* www.bu.edu/biology/people/faculty/kornberg (office).

KORNBERG, Roger D., BS, PhD; American biochemist and academic; *Mrs. George A. Winzer Professor of Medicine, Department of Structural Biology, School of Medicine, Stanford University;* b. 24 April 1947, St Louis, Mo.; s. of Arthur Kornberg (winner of Nobel Prize in Medicine 1959) and Sylvy Kornberg; m. Yahli Lorch; two s. one d.; ed Harvard Univ., Stanford Univ.; Postdoctoral Fellow and mem. of scientific staff, Lab. of Molecular Biology, Univ. of Cambridge, UK 1972–75; Asst Prof., Dept of Biological Chem., Harvard Medical School 1976–78; Prof., Dept of Structural Biology, School of Medicine, Stanford Univ. 1978–, now Mrs. George A. Winzer Prof. of Medicine, Dept Chair. 1984–92; Visiting Prof., Hebrew Univ. of Jerusalem 1986–; Ed. Annual Reviews of Biochemistry; Co-founder Cocrystal Pharma 2008, now Chief Scientist and Chair. Scientific Advisory Bd; mem. NAS, American Acad. of Arts and Sciences; mem. Bd of Dirs Teva Pharmaceuticals; mem. Advisory Bd Deloitte LLP, Deloitte & Touche LLP; Assoc. mem. European Molecular Biology Org.; Foreign mem. Royal Soc., London; Hon. mem. Japanese Biochemical Soc.; Dr hc (Hebrew Univ. of Jerusalem) 2001, (Univ. of Umeå) 2003, (Univ. of Regensburg) 2008, (Bar-Ilan Univ.) 2009; Eli Lilly Award 1981, Passano Award 1982, Harvey Prize 1987, Ciba-Drew Award 1990, Gairdner Int. Award (co-winner with Robert Roeder) 2000, Welch Award 2001, Gran Prix, French Acad. of Sciences 2002, Sloan Award 2005, Louisa Gross Horwitz Prize, Columbia Univ. 2006, Dickson Prize in Medicine, Univ. of Pittsburgh 2006, Nobel Prize in Chem. 2006, Aharon Katzir-Katchalsky Award, Int. Union for Pure and Applied Biophysics 2008, Ahmed Zewail Prize, Wayne State Univ. 2008, Pauling Legacy Award 2010. *Address:* Stanford University Medical School, Department of Structural Biology, Fairchild Building, 1st Floor, 299 Campus Drive, Stanford, CA 94305-5126, USA (office). *Telephone:* (650) 723-6988 (office); (650) 725-5390 (office). *E-mail:* kornberg@stanford.edu (office). *Website:* kornberg.stanford.edu (office).

KOROLOGOS, Tom Chris, BA, MS; American journalist, business executive and diplomatist (retd); *Strategic Advisor, DLA Piper;* b. 1933, Salt Lake City, Utah; s. of Chris T. Korologos and Irene M. Kolendrianos; m. 1st Joy G. Korologos (died 1997); one s. two d.; m. 2nd Ann McLaughlin; ed Univ. of Utah, Columbia Univ. Grad. School of Journalism (Grantland Rice Fellowship and Pulitzer Fellowship); officer, USAF 1956–57; journalist, New York Herald Tribune, Long Island Press, Salt Lake Tribune, Associated Press; Co-founder, Pres. and Chair. Exec. Cttee, Timmons & Co., Washington DC 1975–2003; Dir Congressional Relations for Pres. Reagan's transition 1980–81, for Nat. Bipartisan (Kissinger) Comm. for Cen. America; Sr Advisor to Senator Bob Dole during his 1996 presidential campaign; mem. Bush-Cheney transition team 2001; served in Nixon and Ford Admins as Deputy Asst to Pres. for Legis. Affairs (Senate); served for nine years under Senator Wallace F. Bennett (Republican, Utah) as his Chief of Staff in the Senate; served as a Sr Staff mem. in US Congress, as an asst to two Pres in the White House; Sr Counselor with Coalition Provisional Authority, Baghdad, Iraq May–Dec. 2003; Amb. to Belgium 2004–07; fmr mem. US Advisory Comm. on Public Diplomacy; fmr charter mem. Broadcasting Bd of Govs with jurisdiction over all non-mil. US Govt radio and TV broadcasting overseas; currently Strategic Advisor, DLA Piper; Chair. Emer. and Hon. Trustee, American Coll. of Greece. *Address:* DLA Piper LLP (US), 500 Eighth Street, NW, Washington, DC 20004, USA (office). *Telephone:* (202) 863-7275 (office). *Fax:* (202) 863-7875 (office). *E-mail:* tom.korologos@TCKorologos.net (office). *Website:* www.dlapiper.com (office).

KOROMA, Abdul G.; Sierra Leonean diplomatist and lawyer; ed King's Coll., London, UK, Kiev State Univ., USSR (now Ukraine); barrister and Hon. Bencher (Lincoln's Inn) and legal practitioner, High Court of Sierra Leone; joined Sierra Leone Govt service 1964, Int. Div., Ministry of External Affairs 1969; del. to UN Gen. Ass.; mem. Int. Law Comm. (Chair. 43rd Session); mem. of dels to 3rd UN Conf. on the Law of the Sea, UN Conf. on Succession of States in Respect of Treaties, UN Comm. on Int. Trade Law, Special Cttee on the Review of the UN Charter and on the Strengthening of the Role of the Org. Cttee on the Peaceful Uses of Outer Space; Vice-Chair. UN Charter Cttee 1978; Chair. UN Special Cttee of 24 on Self-Determination of Peoples; Deputy Perm. Rep. of Sierra Leone to the UN 1978–81, Perm. Rep. 1981–85; fmr Amb. to S Korea, to Cuba and to EEC and Perm. Del. to UNESCO; Amb. to France, Belgium, Netherlands, Luxembourg and to Ethiopia and OAU 1988; Perm. Rep. to UN –1994; Judge, Int. Court of Justice 1994–2012; fmr High Commr in Zambia, Tanzania and Kenya; Chair. UN 6th Cttee (Legal), UN Int. Law Comm.; Vice-Pres. African Soc. of Int. and Comparative Law, African Soc. of Int. Law; Pres. Henry Dunant Centre for Humanitarian Dialogue, Geneva; mem. Int. Planning Council of Int. Ocean Inst., Cttee of Experts on the Application of Conventions and Recommendations, ILO, Geneva, Institut de droit international; del. to numerous int. confs; Visiting Prof., Univ. of Bangalore, India; lecturer at numerous univs, including Stockholm, Cambridge, Columbia, Zurich, Louvain; mem. American Soc. of Int. Law, Inst. of Int. Law; Insignia of Commdr of Rokel 1991, Order of Grand Officer of Repub. of Sierra Leone 2007; Hon. LLD; Prize for the Promotion, Dissemination and Teaching of Int. Humanitarian Law, Int. Inst. of Humanitarian Law 2005. *Publications:* numerous articles on int. law. *Leisure interests:* reading, music, sports. *Address:* c/o International Court of Justice, Peace Palace, Carnegieplein, 2517 KJ The Hague, Netherlands (office).

KOROMA, Ernest Bai; Sierra Leonean politician and fmr head of state; b. 23 Oct. 1953, Makeni, Bombali Dist; m. Sia Koroma; two c.; ed Univ. of Sierra Leone; began career as teacher, St Francis Secondary School, Makeni; joined Sierra Leone Nat. Insurance Co. 1978; joined Reliance Insurance Trust Corpn 1985, Man. Dir 1988–2002; represented All People's Congress (APC) in presidential and parl. elections 2002, lost presidential vote but elected to parl. representing Bombali Dist; Leader APC 2002–, temporarily stripped of leadership due to internal party dispute 2005; Minority Leader of parl. 2005–07; Pres. of Sierra Leone 2007–18; Fellow, West African Insurance Inst.; Assoc. Inst. of Risk Man., UK; mem. Inst. of Dirs, UK. *Address:* All-People's Congress, 137h Fourah Bay Road, Freetown, Sierra Leone (office). *E-mail:* info@new-apc.org (office); info@statehouse-sl.org. *Website:* apcparty.org (office); www.statehouse.gov.sl.

KOROMA, Momodu, MSc; Sierra Leonean politician and business executive; b. 12 Sept. 1956; m.; five c.; ed Njala Univ. Coll., Univ. of Nairobi, Kenya, Univ. of Reading, UK, Int. Centre for Theoretical Physics, Trieste, Italy; govt minister 1996–, fmr Minister of Presidential Affairs; Minister of Foreign Affairs and Int. Co-operation 2002–07; mem. Sierra Leone Peoples Party (SLPP), unsuccessful cand. for Vice-Pres. of Sierra Leone 2007; currently Man. Dir Future Standards (SL) Ltd Enterprise, Freetown. *Leisure interests:* tennis, sight-seeing. *Address:* Future Standards (SL) Ltd Enterprise, 15 Main Regent Road, Freetown (office); MQ8 Spur Road, Wilberforce, Freetown, Sierra Leone (home). *Telephone:* (22) 232873 (home). *E-mail:* graceful@sierratel.se (home).

KOROTCHENYA, Ivan Mikhailovich; Belarusian politician; ed Minsk Agric. Acad.; worked as chief agronomist, then Chair. of collective farm; fmr Chair. Regional Union of Collective Farms then Chair. Viley Dist Soviet of People's Deputies; Deputy Belarus Supreme Soviet, mem. Accord faction 1994–96; mem. Presidium; Chair. Comm. on Problems of Glasnost, Mass Media and Human Rights 1990–92; elected coordinator of Workgroup at Council of Leaders of States and Leaders of Govts CIS Countries after disintegration of USSR 1992–98; Deputy Exec. Sec. CIS Secr. 1998–2001.

KOROTEEV, Anatoly Sazonovich, DTechSc; Russian physicist; *Chief Scientist, SSC Keldysh Research Centre;* b. 22 July 1936, Moscow Region; s. of Sazon Z. Koroteev and Maria P. Koroteeva; m.; one s.; ed Moscow Aviation Inst.; engineer, Sr Engineer, Head of Div., First Deputy Dir Research Inst. of Thermal Processes (now SSC Keldysh Research Centre) 1959–88, Dir 1988–2016, Chief Scientist 2016–; Corresp. mem. USSR (now Russian) Acad. of Sciences 1990, Academician 1994; Pres. Russian Acad. of Cosmonautics (named after K. Tsiolkovsky) 2005–11; mem. Int. Acad. of Astronautics, NAS; Order for Service to Fatherland Rank IV 1996, Rank III 2006; Order of Alexander Nevsky 2013; USSR State Prize 1982, Russian Acad. of Science Prize 2001, Russian Fed. Govt Prize in Science and Tech. 2001, 2012, State Prize of Russian Fed. 2002, Russian Pres.'s Prize 2005, Russian Fed. Honoured Scientist. *Publications:* Low-Temperature Plasma Generators 1966, Generator for Low-Temperature Plasma 1969, Applied Dynamics of Thermal Plasma 1975, Electric-arc Plasmotrons 1980, Plasmatrons: Structures, Characteristics, Calculation 1993, Electron-Beam Plasma 1993, Nuclear Rocket Engines 2001, Rocket Engines and Power Systems on the Basis of Nuclear Reactor 2002, Seventy Years at the Forefront of Rocket-Space Technics 2003, Gasdynamic and Thermophysical Processes in Solid Rocket Propulsion 2004, Manned Flight to Mars 2007, Advanced Energetics Technologies on Earth and in Space 2008; numerous articles on propulsion and power systems of rocket and space complexes, generation and diagnostics of low-temperature plasma, creation of electric arc plasma generators and derivation of concentrated pulse electron flows in dense environments. *Leisure interests:* history, skiing. *Address:* SSC Keldysh Research Centre, Onezhskaya str. 8, 125438 Moscow, Russia (office). *Telephone:* (495) 456-92-37 (office). *Fax:* (495) 456-82-28 (office). *E-mail:* kerc@elnet.msk.ru (office); kerc@comcor.ru (office). *Website:* www.kerc.msk.ru (home).

KOROTYCH, Vitaliy Alekseyevich; Russian/Ukrainian physician, writer and poet; b. 26 May 1936, Kiev; s. of Aleksey Korotych and Zoa Korotych; m. Zinaida Korotych 1958; two s.; ed Kiev Medical Inst.; physician 1959–66; Ed. Ukrainian literary journal Ranok 1966–77; Ed.-in-Chief Vsesvit magazine 1978–86; Ed.-in-Chief Ogonyok weekly magazine 1986–91; Sec. of Ukrainian Writers' Union 1966–69; mem. USSR Writers' Union 1981–90; USSR People's Deputy 1989–91; Prof. Boston Univ., USA 1991–98, returned to Moscow; ed. Boulevard magazine and others 1998; several Russian, Ukrainian, Polish and Bulgarian decorations and medals including two USSR State Prizes, A. Tolstoy Prize 1982, Int. Julius Fuchik Prize 1984, Wiental Prize, Georgetown Univ. (USA) 1987, Int. Ed. of the year, W P Revue (USA) 1989, Johann Wolfgang von Goethe Medallion, European Acad. of Natural Sciences 2006, Moscow Writers' Union Prize 2007. *Publications include:* Golden Hands 1961, The Smell of Heaven 1962, Cornflower Street 1963, O Canada! 1966, Poetry 1967, Metronome (novel) 1982, The Face of Enmity (novel) 1984, Memory, Bread and Love 1986, Le Visage de la haine (travel essays) 1988, Glasnost und Perestroika 1990, The Waiting Room (memoirs, Vol. I) 1991, On My Behalf (memoirs, Vol. II) 2000, Selected Poems 2005, Selected Essays 2005; many translations from English into Ukrainian and other Slavonic languages. *Address:* Trifonovskaya str. 11, Apt. 256, 127018 Moscow, Russia (home). *Telephone:* (495) 689-03-84 (home); (496) 462-67-44 (home). *Fax:* (495) 689-03-84 (home). *E-mail:* vkorotich@yandex.ru (home); vak1137@mail.ru (home).

KORS, Michael; American fashion designer; b. 9 Aug. 1959, Mineola, NY; s. of Karl Anderson and Joan L. Kors; m. Lance LePere; ed Fashion Inst. of Tech.; early career designing for Lothar's boutique, New York; f. Kors Co. (now Michael Kors Inc.) 1981, Pres. 1981–; launched women's ready-to-wear designer Celine 1997, Designer 1997–2003; launched accessories line 2001; launched Michael fragrance for women 2000, Island fragrance for men 2005 (FiFi Award for Best Bath and Body Collection 2006), Very Hollywood Michael Kors (fragrance franchise) 2009; Dupont American Original Award 1983, Elle/Cadillac Fashion Award for Excellence 1995, New York Award 1999, CFDA Award for Womenswear Designer of the Year 1999, CFDA Menswear Award 2003, Oliver R. Grace Award for Distinguished Service in Advancing Cancer Research, Cancer Research Inst. 2010, Geoffrey Beene Lifetime Achievement Award, Council of Fashion Designers of America 2010, Fragrance Foundation FiFi Award for Lifetime Achievement 2010, Couture Council Award for Artistry of Fashion 2013, McGovern–Dole Leadership Award 2016. *Publications:* articles in Vogue, The New York Times and other newspapers and magazines. *Leisure interests:* theatre, film, travel. *Address:* Corporate Headquarters, Michael Kors Inc., 11 West 42nd Street, New York, NY 10036, USA. *Website:* www.michaelkors.com.

KORTHALS ALTES, Frederik; Dutch lawyer and politician; b. 15 May 1931, Amsterdam; s. of Everhardus Joannes Korthals Altes and Mary s'Jacob; m. Henny Matthijssen; ed Leiden Univ.; practised as solicitor 1958–82; mem. First Chamber, States-Gen. 1981–82, 1991–2001; Minister of Justice 1982–89; Chair. Volkspartij voor Vrijheid en Democratie (VVD) 1975–81, Floor Leader in First Chamber, States-Gen. 1995–97, Pres. 1997–2001; Chair. Advisory Council on Int. Affairs 2002–; Pnr, Nauta Dutilh (law firm) 1990–96; Hon. Minister of State 2001–; Grand Officier, Légion d'honneur 1984, Grosses Verdienskreuz des Verdienstordens 1985, Commdr, Order of Orange-Nassau, Grand Cross Ordem do Mérito 1989, Grand Cross Ordre nat. du Mérite, Grand Cross of Sacred Treasure (Japan) 2000, Senator Gran Croce Order of San Giorgio (Parma); Prof. E.M. Meijers Medal of Law Faculty (Leiden) 1988, Nat. Police Award 1990, Molewater-De Monchy Medal, Erasmus Univ. Medical Center 2008. *Address:* 92 's-Gravenwetering, 3062 SJ, Rotterdam, Netherlands (home). *Telephone:* (10) 4526163 (home); 653-301424 (mobile) (home). *E-mail:* fka@planet.nl (home).

KORTLANDT, Frederik H. H., BA, MA, PhD; Dutch academic; *Professor of Descriptive and Comparative Linguistics, University of Leiden;* b. 19 June 1946, Utrecht; ed Univ. of Amsterdam; Asst Prof. of Slavic Linguistics, Univ. of Amsterdam 1969–72; Assoc. Prof. of Balto-Slavic Languages, Univ. of Leiden 1972–74, Prof. 1974–; Prof. of Descriptive and Comparative Linguistics 1985–; mem. Royal Netherlands Acad. 1986–; Spinoza Prize 1997. *Publications include:* Modelling the Phoneme 1972, Slavic Accentuation 1975; numerous articles on linguistics and Slavic, Baltic, Germanic, Celtic, Armenian, Japanese and other languages. *Leisure interest:* classical music. *Address:* Faculty of Letters, PO Box

9515, 2300 RA Leiden (office); Cobetstraat 24, 2313 KC Leiden, Netherlands (home). *Telephone:* (71) 527-2501 (office). *Fax:* (71) 527-7569 (office). *E-mail:* f.kortlandt@hum.leidenuniv.nl (office). *Website:* www.kortlandt.nl (office).

KORTÜM, Franz-Josef, MBA; German business executive; b. 18 Aug. 1950, Billerbeck, Coesfeld; m.; three c.; ed studies in Münster, Univ. of Regensburg; employed in family car retailing co. Billerbeck 1975; car sales exec., Bielefeld subsidiary of Daimler-Benz AG 1976; Head, Passenger Car Field Sales, Used Vehicle Sales and Truck Sales, Berlin subsidiary of Daimler-Benz AG 1979; Asst to Dir of Sales Org. Germany, Daimler-Benz AG, Stuttgart-Untertürkheim 1985; Dir Saarbrücken subsidiary of Daimler-Benz AG 1987; Dir Cen. Admin. Daimler-Benz AG 1989; Man. Dir Mercedes-Benz-owned co. Rheinische Kraftwagengesellschaft (RKW), Bonn 1990; apptd Man. Dir Webasto AG 1994, CEO 1999, Chair. 1999–2013; mem. Man. Bd Audi AG 1992, Chair. 1993–95; Federal Cross of Merit 2008.

KORTUN, Vasif; Turkish gallery curator, writer and teacher; *Director of Research and Programs, SALT;* b. 6 Nov. 1958, Istanbul; Founding Dir Museum of Center for Curatorial Studies, Bard Coll., USA 1994–97, Proje 4L, Istanbul Museum of Contemporary Art 2001–03, Platform Garanti Contemporary Art Center, Istanbul 2001–10; Co-Curator Tirana Biennial, Second Ceramics Biennial, Albisola 2003, (with ManRay Hsu) Taipei Biennial 2008, among other biennial projects; Chief Curator and Director Third Int. Istanbul Biennial 1992; Co-Dir, with Charles Esche, Ninth Int. Istanbul Biennial 2005; curated Turkish pavilions for São Paulo Biennial 1994, 1998, Venice Biennale 2007; has undertaken numerous ind. curatorial projects including exhbn of works by Cengiz Çekil at Rampa, Istanbul 2010, The Columns Held Us Up at Artists Space, New York 2009, UAE Pavilion for the Venice Biennale 2011; Ed. annual contemporary art magazine RG (in Turkish); Dir of Research and Programs, SALT, Istanbul (art centre) 2011–; mem. Bush Global Advisory Cttee of Walker Art Center, Foundation for Arts Initiatives 2009–, Tate Turner Prize Selection Cttee 2011; mem. Bd Int. Foundation Manifesta 2000–02, CIMAM 2010–13; mem. Jury of The Querini Stampalia Foundation-Furla for Art Prize, Venice 2002; Ninth Annual Award for Curatorial Excellence, Center for Curatorial Studies, Bard Coll. 2006. *Publications include:* Jahresring 51: Szene Turkei: Abseits aber Tor (with Erden Kosova) 2004; has written extensively on contemporary art and the cultural situation in Turkey for int. periodicals and publs, including Mars, NU, Flash Art, Art Asia Pacific, Art Journal, New Art Examiner, Contemporary, Crudelia, Art Fan. *Address:* SALT Beyoğlu, İstiklal Caddesi 136, Beyoğlu, 34430 Istanbul, Turkey (office). *Telephone:* (212) 3774200 (office). *Fax:* (212) 2921667 (office). *E-mail:* salt@saltonline.org (office). *Website:* www.saltonline.org (office); vasif-kortun-eng.blogspot.com (office).

KORWIN-MIKKE, Janusz Ryszard, MA; Polish politician and fmr professional contract bridge player; *Leader, Koalicja Odnowy Rzeczypospolitej Wolność i Nadzieja (KORWiN—Coalition for the Renewal of the Republic – Freedom and Hope);* b. 27 Oct. 1942, Warsaw; m. 1st Ewa Mieczkowska; m. 2nd Małgorzata Szmit; ed Faculties of Mathematics and Philosophy, Univ. of Warsaw; detained by communist authorities while studying psychology, law and sociology 1965, again arrested and expelled from univ. 1968; Researcher, Inst. of Motor Transport, then at Univ. of Warsaw 1969–74; f. Oficyna Liberałów (underground publishing house) 1978; mem. Democratic Party 1962–82; supported political strike of Szczecin Shipyard workers Aug. 1980, later an adviser of NSZZ Rzemieślników Indywidualnych 'Solidarność' (Ind. Craftsmen's Union); interned following imposition of martial law but later released; mem. Ruch Polityki Realnej (The Real Politics Movement) 1987–2009, changed name to Unia Polityki Realnej (Real Politics Union—UPR) 1989, Leader 1990–97, 1999–2003; f. Najwyższy Czas! (It's High Time!) weekly 1990; apptd by Lech Wałęsa to become a mem. of Solidarity's advisory body – Komitet Obywatelski (The Civic Cttee); mem. Sejm (Parl.) 1991–93; cand. for UPR in presidential elections 1995, 2000, 2005; Leader, Freedom and Lawfulness 2009–11, Leader, Kongres Nowej Prawicy (KNP—Congress of the New Right) (formed from it) 2011–15 (dismissed); Founder and Leader, Koalicja Odnowy Rzeczypospolitej Wolność i Nadzieja (KORWiN—Coalition for the Renewal of the Repub.– Freedom and Hope) 2015–. *Publications:* Ratujmy państwo (Let Us Save the Country) 1990, Nie tylko o Żydach (Not Only about Jews) 1991, Prowokacja? (Provocation?) 1991, Rząd rżnie głupa – czyli mowy sejmowe (Government Playing Dumb – Parliament Speeches) 1993, Wizja parlamentu w nowej konstytucji Rzeczypospolitej Polskiej (Vision of Parliament in the New Polish Constitution) 1994, Bez impasu (Without Impass), Vademecum ojca (A Father's Vade mecum) 1997, Niebezpieczne ubezpieczenia (Dangerous Insurances) 2000, Rok 2007 (Year 2007) 2001, Ekonomikka (Economics) 2001, Dekadencja (Decadence) 2002, Naprawić Polskę? No problem! (Fix Poland? No Problem!) 2004, Podatki – Czyli rzecz o grabieży (Taxes – Thing about Robbery) 2004, Kto tu dymi? (Who is Making Smoke Here?) 2007, Rusofoby w odwrocie (Russophobes in Reverse) 2009, Rząd rżnie głupa (The Government is Playing Dumb) 2013; popular book (with Andrzej Macieszczak) on contract bridge. *Leisure interests:* chess, tennis, ping pong, billiards, Go, checkers (Nat. Champion). *Address:* Koalicja Odnowy Rzeczypospolitej Wolność i Nadzieja (Coalition for the Renewal of the Republic – Freedom and Hope), Warsaw, Poland (office). *E-mail:* info@partiakorwin.pl (office). *Website:* www.partiakorwin.pl (office); korwin-mikke.pl; jkm-januszkorwinmikke.blogspot.com; korwin-mikke.blog.onet.pl.

KORZENIOWSKI, Robert Marek, (Korzeń); Polish sports coach, manager and fmr athlete; *Project Manager for Sports Medicine, LUX MED Ltd;* b. 30 July 1968, Lubaczów; m. Magdalena Kłys; two d.; ed Acad. of Physical Educ., Katowice; gold medal, 20km walk, Olympic Games, Atlanta 1996, 20km walk and 50km walk, Sydney 2000, 50km walk, Athens 2004; winner 20km walk, European Cup, La Coruña 1996; gold medal, 50km walk, World Championships, Athens 1997, Edmonton 2001, Paris 2003; gold medal, 50km walk, European Championships 1998, Munich 2002; Sport and Fair Play Amb. to European Council, Strasbourg 1997; apptd chief of sport department, Polish Public Television 2005, Gen. Man. TVP Sport (dedicated sports channel on Polish public TV 2007–09; Public Relations and Marketing Adviser, UEFA Events 2011–12; Dir Sports Business Insurance Dept, Mentor SA 2012–14; Project Man. for Sports Medicine, LUX MED Group 2014–; Pres. Sportowa Polska Foundation; organizer Int. Asscn of Athletics Feds race-walking meeting 'Na Rynek marsz!' in Kraków 1997; Hon. Citizen of Athens 2000; Officer's Cross, Order of Polonia Restituta 2000, Commdr's Cross 2004; Gold Medal for Outstanding Achievement in Sport 1996, 'Give a Hand' Ronald McDonald Foundation Award, inducted into IAAF Hall of Fame 2014. *Television:* Talks in Walk (two reportages with Hicham El Gerouj and Seghey Bubka), Dancing with the Stars (TVN). *Publication includes:* I o to chodzi (biog.). *Leisure interests:* books, cinema, cooking, history, politics. *Address:* LUX MED Ltd, Postepu 21C Street, 02-676 Warsaw, Poland (office). *Telephone:* (22) 4504500 (office). *E-mail:* sekretariat.zarzad@luxmed.pl (office). *Website:* www.luxmed.pl (office).

KORZHAKOV, Lt-Gen. (retd) Aleksander Vasilyevich; Russian army officer (retd) and politician; b. 31 Jan. 1950, Moscow; m.; two d.; ed All-Union Inst. of Law; mem. Dept 9 State Security Cttee 1970–89; personal bodyguard of First Sec., Moscow CPSU Cttee Boris Yeltsin 1986–87; Founder and Chief of Security Service of Russian Supreme Soviet 1990–91; Head of Security Service of Pres. of Russia 1991–96, Deputy Chief, Main Admin. of Bodyguards 1992–96 (discharged); elected mem. State Duma (Parl.) 1997; joined Otechestvo-All Russia faction 2000. *Publication:* Boris Yeltsin: From Dawn to Dusk (memoirs) 1997. *Leisure interest:* tennis.

KOSACHEV, Konstantin, PhD; Russian diplomatist and politician; b. 17 Sept. 1962, Moscow region; ed Moscow State Inst. of Int. Relations; Deputy Dir Ministry of Foreign Affairs, Moscow 1984; fmr Counsellor, Embassy in Stockholm; mem. State Int. Affairs Council 1998; elected Deputy, State Duma (Parl.) 1999, First Vice-Chair., Fatherland All Russia Party, State Duma 2001–12, Chair. State Duma Int. Affairs Cttee 2003–12; Chair. Russian Del., Parl. Ass. of Council of Europe (PACE) 2004–12, Vice-Pres. PACE 2005–12; Head, Russian Cooperation and Pres' Special Cttee on CIS Affairs 2012–14; currently mem. Federation Council, Chair. Foreign Affairs Cttee; mem. United Russia, currently Deputy Sec. of Presidium of the Gen. Council, mem. Editorial Bd Russia in Global Affairs; mem. Man. Bd Alexander Gorchakov Public Diplomacy Fund; mem. Russian Int. Affairs Council; Order of Friendship (Russia), Royal Order of the N Star (Sweden), Order of the Officer Cross (Hungary). *Publications include:* Restarting Russia-EU Relations 2005, Between the Past and the Future 2010. *Address:* Federation Council (Sovet Federatsii), 103426 Moscow, ul. B. Dmitrovka 26, Russia (office). *Telephone:* (495) 629-70-09 (office). *Fax:* (495) 629-67-43 (office). *E-mail:* post_sf@gov.ru (office). *Website:* www.council.gov.ru (office).

KOSAI, Akio, BA; Japanese business executive; b. 19 April 1931, Okayama; ed Univ. of Tokyo; joined Sumitomo Chemical Co., Ltd 1954, Man. Gen. Affairs Dept 1975–78, Man. Polyethylene Sales Dept, Plastic-Synthetic Rubber Div. 1978–82, Deputy Gen. Man., Osaka Works 1982–83, Dir and Gen. Man. Industrial Chemicals and Fertilizers Div. 1983; Pres. Petrochemical Corpn of Singapore (Pte) Ltd 1984–87; Man. Dir Sumitomo Chemical Co., Ltd 1987–91, Sr Man. Dir 1991–93, Pres. 1993–2000, Chair. 2000–05, Counsellor 2005–11; Deputy Chair. Nippon-Keidanren (Japan Business Fed.) and Chair. Japanese Cttee of East Asia Businessmen's Conf.; mem. Int. Advisory Council, Econ. Devt Bd (EDB) Singapore; mem. Bd of Dirs Sumitomo Bakelite Co. Ltd, Sumitomo Life Insurance Co., Inabata and Co. Ltd, Japan Fed. Employers Asscn, Japan Urea and Ammonium Sulphate Industry Asscn, Japan Soda Industry Asscn, Japan Singapore Asscn. *Address:* c/o Sumitomo Chemical Co. Ltd, 2-27-1, Shinkawa, Chuo-ku, Tokyo, 104-8260, Japan. *E-mail:* info@sumitomo-chem.co.jp.

KOSCIUSKO-MORIZET, Nathalie, MBA; French politician; b. 14 May 1973, Paris; d. of François Kosciusko-Morizet and Bénédicte Treuille; ed École nationale du génie rural, des eaux et des forêts (ENGREF), Collège des ingénieurs, Paris; Adviser, Ministry of Economy, Finance and Industry 1997–99, Man. Foreign Econ. Relations Div. 1999–2001; Head of Mission of Strategic Dir Alstom (multinational conglomerate) 2001–02; mem. Assemblée nationale (Parl.) for Essonne 2002–10; Tech. Adviser to Prime Minister on Ecology and Sustainable Devt 2002; Regional Councillor, Île-de-France 2004–10; Sec. of State for Ecology 2007–09, for Prospective Devt of the Digital Economy 2009–10, Minister for Ecology, Sustainable Devt, Transport and Housing 2010–12; spokeswoman for Nicolas Sarkozy's presidential campaign 2012; Municipal Councillor and Mayor of Longjumeau (Essonne) 2008–; mem. and Vice-Pres. Agglomeration Community Council 2008–; mem. Union pour un Mouvement Populaire (UMP). *Address:* c/o Ministry for Ecology, Sustainable Development and Energy, Grande Arche, Tour Pascal A et B, 92055 La Défense Cedex, France.

KOSHIBA, Masatoshi, PhD; Japanese physicist and academic; *Professor Emeritus, Department of Physics, University of Tokyo;* b. 19 Sept. 1926, Toyohashi City, Aichi Pref.; ed Univ. of Tokyo, Univ. of Rochester, New York, USA; Prof., Dept of Physics, Univ. of Tokyo 1970–87, now Prof. Emer., Sr Counsellor Int. Centre for Elementary Particle Physics 1987–; Prof., Tokai Univ. 1987–97; Chair., Heisel Foundation for Basic Science 2003–; Grosse Verdienstkreuz (Germany) 1985, Order of Culture 1988, Order of Cultural Merit 1997; Nishina Prize, Nishina Foundation 1987, Ashai Prize, Ashai Press 1988, 1999, Acad. Award, Acad. of Japan 1989, Fujuwara Science Foundation 1997, Wolf Prize, Govt of Israel 2000, Nobel Prize in Physics 2002. *Achievements include:* pioneer of neutrino-astronomy and cosmic-ray physics; led path-breaking experiments Kamiokande and Super-Kamiokande (massive detectors capturing neutrinos from the Sun and a distant supernova explosion 1987). *Address:* Heisel Foundation for Basic Science, Marunouchi Building, 11th Floor, Room 1109A, 2-4-1 Marunouchi, Chiyoda, Tokyo 100-6311 (office); International Centre for Elementary Particle Physics, University of Tokyo, 7-3-1 Hongo, Bunkyo-ku, Tokyo 113-0033, Japan (office). *Telephone:* (3) 3815-8384 (office). *Fax:* (3) 3814-8806 (office). *E-mail:* office@hfbs.or.jp (office). *Website:* www.hfbs.or.jp (office); www.icepp.s.u-tokyo.ac.jp (office).

KOSHIRO, Matsumoto, IX; Japanese actor; b. (Teruaki Fujima), 19 Aug. 1942; s. of Koshiro VIII; m.; one s.; debut in Kabuki (Japanese traditional theatre) when child; acted under name Kintaro, as young man Somegoro Ichikawa; became Koshiro IX 1980. *Plays include:* Kanjincho (and many other Kabuki plays), Man of La Mancha (included ten-week run on Broadway), The King and I (including six-month run in West End), Half a Sixpence, Sweeney Todd, Fiddler on the Roof, Amadeus (Salieri). *Television:* Ōgon no Hibi 1978, Sanada Maru 2016. *Films:* 13 Assassins 2010, Tenchi: The Samurai Astronomer 2012.

KOSHMAN, Col-Gen. Nikolai Pavlovich; Russian government official and association executive; *President, Russian Builders Association;* b. 5 April 1944, Mironovka, Ukraine; s. of Pavel Porfirievich Koshman and Maria Fiedoseevna

Koshman; m.; two s.; ed Mil. Acad. of Home Front and Transport; numerous posts from Commdr of team to Commdr of corps, railway armed forces 1973–91, Deputy Commdr 1991–95; mem. of Mission of Plenipotentiary Rep. of Russian Pres. to Chechen Repub.; Chair. Govt of Chechen Repub. 1996, Plenipotentiary Rep. of Russian Govt in Chechen Repub. with rank of Deputy Prime Minister 1999–2000; Deputy Minister of Transport, Russian Fed. 1997; Head Fed. Service of Special Construction Rosspetsstroy 1997–98; Adviser to the Pres. of the Russian Fed. 2001–02; Deputy Minister of Communications Jan.–Oct. 2002; apptd Chair. State Cttee of Construction (Gosstroy) 2002; currently Pres. Russian Builders Asscn. *Publication includes:* Restoration of the Economy and Social Sphere of the Chechen Republic 1999. *Leisure interests:* theatre, sports (football, tennis), hunting, travelling. *Address:* Russian Builders Association, 115093 Moscow, d.1, korp.58, str.3, Partiyniy per., Russia (office). *Telephone:* (495) 363-21-40 (office). *E-mail:* info@a-s-r.ru (office). *Website:* www.a-s-r.ru (office).

KOSKINEN, John A., BA, LLB; American business executive (retd) and government official; *Commissioner, Internal Revenue Service;* m. Patricia Koskinen; two c.; ed Duke Univ., Yale Univ. Law School, Univ. of Cambridge, UK; worked as sr exec. with Palmieri Co., including as Pres. and CEO; Deputy Dir for Man., US Office of Man. and Budget, Washington, DC 1994–97; Asst to the US Pres. and Chair. of Pres.'s Council on Year 2000 Conversion 1998–2000; Deputy Mayor and City Admin. of Washington, DC 2000–03; Pres. US Soccer Foundation 2004–08; Chair. (non-exec.) Freddie Mac (Fed. Home Loan Mortgage Corpn) Sept. 2008–March 2009, Aug. 2009–11, Interim CEO March–Aug. 2009, mem. Bd of Dirs 2008–12; Commr, Internal Revenue Service 2013–; mem. Bd of Dirs AES Corpn, American Capital Ltd, DC Education Compact; fmr Chair. Duke Univ. Bd of Trustees; Dir DC Education Compact; chaired Washington, DC Host Cttee for 1994 World Cup. *Address:* Internal Revenue Service, 1111 Constitution Avenue, NW, No. 5480, Washington, DC 20224, USA (office). *Telephone:* (202) 622-5000 (office). *Website:* www.irs.gov (office).

KOSOR, Jadranka, LLB; Croatian politician and fmr journalist; b. 1 July 1953, Pakrac; one s.; ed high school in Pakrac, Faculty of Law, Univ. of Zagreb; worked as journalist for Večernji list and Radio Zagreb 1972, radio journalist covering war topics for Croatian Radio and briefly for BBC 1991–95; mem. Parl. 1995–, apptd Vice-Pres. of Parl. 1995, Leader of the Opposition 2011–12; mem. Croatian Democratic Union (HDZ) 1995–2013, Vice-Pres. 1995–98, Deputy Pres. 2000–09, Pres. 2009–12, Ind. 2013–; Minister of Family, Veterans' Affairs and Intergenerational Solidarity 2003–09, Deputy Prime Minister of Croatia 2004–09, Prime Minister 2009–11; presidential cand. 2005; Hon. Pres. Asscn of Croatian War Veteran Invalids, Asscn of Missing Persons from the Croatian War of Independence; Hon. Vice-Pres. Deaf and Blind Asscn 'Dodir'; Hon. mem. Asscn of Parents of Deceased War Veterans; Zlatno pero Award Croatian Journalists Asscn, EC Award for Humanitarian Work, Europski krug Award of Croatian European House, Lifetime Achievement Award Ivan Šibl Croatian Nat. TV. *Publications:* two books related to the Croatian War of Independence, two books of poetry, including Koraci 1971, one children's book. *Leisure interests:* music, dancing, reading. *Address:* Parliament, 10000 Zagreb, trg sv. Marka 6, Croatia (office). *Telephone:* (1) 4553000 (office). *Fax:* (1) 4552600 (office). *E-mail:* jadranka.kosor@ymail.com (office). *Website:* jadrankakosor.eu.

KOSOVAN, Col-Gen. Alexander Davydovich; Russian construction engineer and army officer; b. 26 Oct. 1941, Akhtyrskaya, Krasnodar Territory, Russia; m.; one s. one d.; ed Novosibirsk Inst. of Eng and Construction; head of construction group, chief engineer, Deputy Head Dept of Eng Construction, Ministry of Defence 1966–84; Chief Eng, Deputy Head Construction Dept Volga Mil. Command 1984–88; Deputy Commdr Caucasus Mil. Command on construction and quartering of forces 1988–92; First Deputy Head of Dept on Construction and Quartering of Forces, Russian Ministry of Defence 1992–97, Deputy Minister of Defence in charge of military construction and housing 1997–2003; First Deputy Head Dept of City Construction Policy Making, Devt and Reconstruction of Moscow –2008, apptd Head of Dept of Urban Devt of Moscow 2008–10; Order for Service to Motherland in Armed Forces 1989, Order of Labour Red Banner 1990, Hon. Builder of Russia, Hon. Builder of Moscow, other Govt decorations. *Publications include:* numerous articles on problems of mil. construction, text-books and methodical manuals for univ. and mil. schools. *Leisure interest:* fishing.

KOSSOWSKI, Marek, BE; Polish business executive; b. 1952; ed Silesian Univ.; with Wytwórnia Sprzętu Komunikacyjnego "PZE-Kalisz" (production plant) 1971–72; clerk, Silesian Univ., Katowice 1975–76; mem. Man. Bd, then Vice-Chair., Socialist Union of Polish Students, Katowice 1976–80; Man., Regional Cttee, Polish United Workers' Party (PZPR), Katowice 1980–83; at Office of Council of Ministers, becoming Vice-Dir of Chair.'s Office 1983–86; Dir Minister's Cabinet, Ministry of Mining and Energy 1986–87; Deputy Dir-Gen., Warsaw Br., Coal Community 1988–90; Br. Dir and Mem. Man. Bd Państwowa Agencja Węgla Kamiennego SA (Govt Coal Agency) 1990–93; Dir Polski Bank Inwestycyjny SA, Warsaw 1993–94; Advisor to Pres. of Man. Bd, TUiR Warta SA (insurance co.) 1994–95, also Vice-Pres., Man. Bd Warta Vita SA; mem. Man. Bd Powszechny Bank Kredytowy SA 1995–99; Pres. Man. Bd PBK Nieruchomości SA 1999–2000; Dir, Przedsiębiorstwo Obsługi Cudzoziemców Dipservice (real estate co.) 2000–01; Under-Sec. of State, Ministry of the Economy, Labour and Social Policy 2001–03; Pres., Man. Bd, PGNiG 2003–06 (resgnd); currently Chair. EnercoNet SP.

KOSTABI, Kalev Marki (Mark); American artist and composer; b. 27 Nov. 1960, Los Angeles, Calif.; ed California State Univ., Fullerton; involved in East Village, New York art movt 1984; f. Kostabi World (studio, gallery, offices) 1988; represented in numerous perm. collections including Museum of Modern Art, New York, Metropolitan Museum of Art, New York, Guggenheim Museum, New York, Brooklyn Museum, Corcoran Gallery of Art, Washington, DC, Groninger Museum; has designed album covers including Guns 'n' Roses, Use Your Illusion, The Ramones' Adios Amigos; also designed a Swatch watch, limited-edition vases, computer accessories, Giro d'Italia pink jersey; produces weekly cable TV show The Kostabi Show; Proliferation Prize 1984. *Albums:* I Did It Steinway 1998, Songs for Sumera 2003, New Alliance 2006. *Publications include:* Sadness Because the Video Rental Store Was Closed, Kostabi: The Early Years, Conversations With Kostabi, The Rhythm of Inspiration. *E-mail:* kostabiworld@yahoo.com (office). *Website:* www.mkostabi.com (office); thekostabishow.com (office).

KOSTADINOVA, Stefka; Bulgarian high jumper (retd), government official and national organization official; *President, Bulgarian Olympic Committee;* b. 15 March 1965, Plovdiv; m. Nikolay Petrov (divorced 1999); one s.; ed Plovdiv Sports School; initially concentrated on gymnastics and swimming, later transferred to athletics; four-time European Indoor Champion: Athens 1985, Lievenne 1987, Budapest 1988, Paris 1994; European Outdoor Champion, Stuttgart 1986; set world high jump record (2.09m, still unbeaten Sept. 2005), Rome 1987; World Outdoor Champion 1987, 1995; won Silver Medal, Olympic Games, Seoul, S Korea 1988, Gold Medal, Olympic Games, Atlanta, Ga, USA 1996; five world indoor championship titles: Paris 1985, Indianapolis 1987, Budapest 1989, Toronto 1993, Paris 1997; has set altogether seven world records: three outdoors and four indoors, and has jumped over 2.00m more than 100 times, an achievement unequalled by any other athlete in the women's high jump; 1997 outdoor season curtailed due to foot injury requiring two operations, retd 1999; Vice-Pres. Bulgarian Athletics Fed. 1999–2005, Pres. 2005–; Deputy Minister of Sport and Youth 2003–05; voted Sportsperson of the Year in Bulgaria 1985, 1987, 1995, 1996, voted Sportsperson of the Year in the Balkans five times, included by IAAF in the Top 10 of the Twentieth Century Female Athletes. *Address:* Bulgarian Olympic Committee, Sofia 1040, Angel Kanchev str. 4, Bulgaria (office). *Telephone:* (2) 987-56-95 (office). *Fax:* (2) 987-03-79 (office). *E-mail:* boc@bgolympic.org (office). *Website:* www.bgolympic.org (office).

KOSTERLITZ, J(ohn) Michael (Mike), BA, MA, DPhil, FRS; American (b. British) physicist and academic; *Harrison E. Farnsworth Professor of Physics, Brown University;* b. 22 June 1942, Aberdeen, Scotland; s. of Hans Walter Kosterlitz and Hannah Gresshoener; m.; one s. two d.; ed Gonville and Caius Coll., Cambridge and Brasenose Coll., Oxford, UK; Royal Soc. Exchange Fellowship, Instituto di Fisica Teorica, Torino, Italy 1969–70; Research Fellow, Dept of Math. Physics, Univ. of Birmingham, UK 1970–73, Lecturer 1974–78, Sr Lecturer 1978–80, Reader in Math. Physics 1980–81; Postdoctoral Fellow, LASSP, Cornell Univ. 1973–74; apptd Prof. of Physics, Brown Univ. 1982, currently Harrison E. Farnsworth Prof. of Physics; Visiting Prof., Dept of Physics, Princeton Univ. 1978, Bell Labs, NJ 1978, Dept of Physics, Harvard Univ. 1978, Laboratoire de Physique des Solides, Université d'Orsay, France Jan.–May 1985, CEN, Saclay, France June 1985, Dept of Physics, McGill Univ., Canada Jan.–March 1991, Dept of Physics, Neuchatel Univ., Switzerland April–May 1991, INPE, São Jose dos Campos, São Paulo, Brazil Jan.–Feb. 1998, Dept of Physics, Univ. of Birmingham March 1998, Dept of Physics, Helsinki Univ., Finland April–June 1998, ICTP, Trieste, Italy July 1998, Dept of Physics, McGill Univ. Aug. 1999, Aug. 2000, Korea Inst. for Advanced Study, Seoul July 2004, Oct.–Dec. 2005; Fellow, American Physical Soc. 1993, American Acad. of Arts and Sciences 2007; Dr hc (Univ. of Birmingham) 2017; Maxwell Medal, Inst. of Physics (UK) 1980, Lars Onsager Prize, American Physical Soc. 2000, Nobel Prize in Physics (co-recipient with David Thouless and F. Duncan Haldane) 2016. *Publications:* four book chapters and more than 80 papers in professional journals. *Leisure interest:* travel. *Address:* Department of Physics, Brown University, Providence, RI 02912, USA (office). *Telephone:* (401) 863-3193 (office). *Fax:* (401) 863-2024 (office). *E-mail:* j_kosterlitz@brown.edu (office). *Website:* vivo.brown.edu/display/jkosterl (office).

KOSTIĆ, Branko, PhD; Montenegrin academic and fmr politician; b. 1939, Rvaši, Montenegro; s. of Vlado Kostić and Veúka Kostić (née Vukotić); m. Milica Kostić (née Pejović); two d.; ed Belgrade Univ.; joined CP 1957; Pres. Cen. Cttee of Montenegrin Youth 1963–69; Vice-Exec. and Gen. Exec. of Aluminium Combine, Titograd 1969–79; apptd Prof. of Economy, Univ. of Montenegro 1979; Vice-Pres. Montenegrin Govt 1986–89, Acting Pres. of Presidency of Montenegro 1989–90; Pres. of Presidency, SFR Yugoslavia 1991–92; Sec.-Gen. Non-Aligned Movt 1991–92; mem. Yugoslav Collective Presidency, Vice-Pres. 1991–92; Decoration, Work Achievements with Golden Wreath; Decoration, Mil. Achievements with Silver Swords; several honours and awards. *Publications include:* Aluminium and Technical Progress 1981, 1991: To Be Remembered 1996, Memoirs 2005; several publs, articles and scientific papers. *Leisure interests:* reading, writing, viniculture, gardening.

KOSTIN, Andrey Leonidovich, PhD; Russian banking executive; *Chairman of the Management Board and President, VTB Bank;* b. 1956, Moscow; m.; one s.; ed Lomonosov Moscow State Univ.; various positions with Ministry of Foreign Affairs 1979–92, including USSR Consulate Gen. in Australia 1979–82, Embassy in UK 1985–90; joined Russian Investment and Finance Co. 1992; Sr Exec. and Deputy Head of Foreign Investment Dept, Imperial Bank 1993–95; First Deputy Chair., Nat. Reserve Bank (NRB) 1995–96; Exec. Chair. Vnesheconombank (Bank for Foreign Econ. Affairs) 1996–2002; Chair. Man. Bd and Pres. VTB Bank 2002–, Chair. Supervisory Cttee VTB 24 Bank 2005–18; Prof. Graduate School of Man., St Petersburg State Univ. 2012– (also mem. Bd of Trustees 2007–); Chair. Supervisory Bd Artistic Gymnastics Fed. of Russia 2014–; mem. Bureau of Dirs Russian Union of Industrialists and Entrepreneurs 2003–; mem. Presidium, Nat. Corporate Governance Council 2011–; mem. Asscn of Banks of Russia 2017–; mem. Supervisory Bd Volleyball Fed. of Russia 2009–, Supervisory Council Pochta Bank 2017–; mem. Bd of Trustees State Academic Mariinsky Theatre 2007–, Moscow State Univ. 2007–, Finance Univ. of Russian Govt 2008–, Nat. Coordination Centre for Promoting Econ. Relations in Asia-Pacific 2014–, Russian Geographical Soc. 2017–; Orders of Merit for the Fatherland III, IVth Degree, Medal of Honour, Chevalier, Ordre nat. du Mérite. *Leisure interests:* painting, theatre, Alpine skiing. *Address:* VTB Bank, Federation Tower West 12, Presnenskaya emb. 123100 Moscow, Russia (office). *Telephone:* (495) 739-77-39 (office). *Fax:* (495) 783-19-09 (office). *E-mail:* pr@vtb.ru (office); info@vtb.ru (office). *Website:* www.vtb.ru (office).

KOSTOV, Ivan Yordanov; Bulgarian economist and politician; b. 23 Dec. 1949; m. Elena Kostova; two d.; ed Karl Marx Higher Inst. of Econs, Sofia and Kliment Ohridski Univ., Sofia; Asst Prof., Karl Marx Higher Inst. of Econs 1974; Sr Asst Prof., Scientific Communism Dept, V. Ilyich Lenin Higher Inst. of Mechanical and Electrical Eng, Sofia (now Tech. Univ.) 1979, Asst Prof. 1991; mem. Parl. 1990–2013, Chair. Econ. Affairs Cttee 1990, Deputy Floor Leader of Union of Democratic Forces—UDF Parl. Group 1993; Minister of Finance 1990–92; Prime Minister of Bulgaria 1997–2001; Chair. and Pres. Union of Democratic Forces (SDS) 1993; led group of deputies who split from UDF to form new parl. group

(United Democratic Forces) and, later, Founder and Chair. Demokrati za silna Balgarija (Democrats for a Strong Bulgaria) 2004–13.

KOŠTUNICA, Vojislav, LLB, PhD; Serbian lawyer and politician; b. 24 March 1944, Belgrade; s. of Jovan Koštunica and Radmila Arandjelovic; m. Dr Zorica Radović; ed Univ. of Belgrade; Lecturer in Law, Belgrade Univ. 1970–74; expelled for opposition to univ. admin. 1974; Sr Researcher, Inst. of Philosophy and Social Theories in Belgrade; took part in opposition movt from 1980s; Founder-mem. Democratic Party; left party to form Demokratska stranka Srbije (Democratic Party of Serbia) 1992, Chair. 1992–2014 (resgnd and left the party); remained outside mainstream politics until nominated by opposition parties to stand as a cand. against Slobodan Milošević; Pres. of the Fed. Repub. of Yugoslavia 2000–03; Prime Minister of Serbia 2004–08; Ind. *Publications include:* Political System of Capitalism and Opposition 1978, Party Pluralism or Monism (co-author) 1983, Between Force and the Law 2000, Freedom Endangered 2002, The Defence of Kosovo: Why Serbia and Not the European Union. *Address:* c/o Demokratska stranka Srbije, 11000 Belgrade, Pariska 13, Serbia. *E-mail:* info@dss.rs.

KOSTYUK, Valery V., Dr Tech.; Russian mechanical engineer; *Vice-President, Russian Academy of Sciences;* b. 26 Aug. 1940, Zaporozhye, Ukraine; ed Chelyabinsk State Polytech. Inst.; engineer, Chelyabinsk Polytechnic Inst. 1962–63; Jr, then Sr Researcher and Prof., Moscow Aviation Inst. 1963–78; Chief of Research Dept, USSR Ministry of Secondary Educ. 1978–79, Deputy Dir-Gen. of Scientific Div. 1979–84; Head of Div., USSR State Planning Comm. 1984–91; Vice-Pres., then Pres. Asscn of Int. Co-operation 1993–96; First Deputy Chair. State Cttee on Science and Tech. 1996–97; First Deputy Minister of Sciences and Tech. 1997–99; mem. Russian Acad. of Sciences, Corresp. mem. 1991–97, Chief Scientific Sec. of the Presidium 2001–13, currently Vice-Pres. Russian Acad. of Sciences, also Deputy Ed.-in-Chief, Herald of Russian Acad. of Sciences Directorate; mem. Russian Acad. of Eng and Tech.; USSR State Prize 1985. *Publications include:* numerous scientific papers on energy, thermal exchange and hydrodynamics in energy, cryogenics, rocket-space installations and nuclear reactors. *Address:* Russian Academy of Sciences, Moscow 119991, Leninsky prosp. 14, Russia (office). *Telephone:* (499) 237-81-82 (office). *E-mail:* kostyuk@pran.ru (office). *Website:* www.ras.ru (office).

KOSUMI, Bajram, DPhil; Kosovo politician and academic; *Professor, University of Pristina;* b. 20 March 1960, Tuxhec, Kamenicë; m.; four c.; ed Univ. of Priština; student movt leader, Priština 1981; sentenced to 10 years imprisonment for opposing communist govt of Yugoslavia; journalist 1991–93; mem. Alliance for Future of Kosova (AAK), Pres. Parl. Party 1994–2000, Vice-Pres. AAK 2000–10; Minister of Public Information, Interim Govt of Kosovo 1999–2000; mem. Kosovo Del., Int. Conf. for Kosovo in Rambouillet & Paris 1999; mem. Ass. of Kosovo 2001–04, 2004–07, 2007–10; Minister for Environment and Spatial Planning of Kosovo 2004–05; Prime Minister of Kosovo 2005–06 (resgnd); Prof., Univ. of Pristina 2008–, State Univ. of Tetova 2009–. *Publications:* A Concept on Sub-Policy 1995, Vocabulary of Barbarians 2000, A Concept on the New Political Thought 2001, Lyric of Fishta 2004, Literature from Prison 2006, A Decisive Year 2006. *Leisure interest:* mountain hiking. *Address:* Street Sylejman Vokshi H A, 9A Pristina (home); c/o Government Building, Assembly of Republic of Kosovo, Mother Teresa Street, N.N., Pristina, Kosovo (office). *E-mail:* bajram.kosumi@ks-gov.net (office); lamippk@yahoo.com (home).

KOSUTH, Joseph; American artist; b. 31 Jan. 1945, Toledo, Ohio; two d.; ed Toledo Museum School of Design, privately with Belgian painter Line Bloom Draper, Cleveland Inst. of Art, School of Visual Arts, New York; pioneer of conceptual art and installation art during 1960s; moved to New York 1965; f. Museum of Normal Art, New York 1967; Prof., School of Visual Arts, New York 1967–85, Hochschule für Bildende Künste, Hamburg, Germany 1988–90, Staatliche Akad. der Bildende Künste, Stuttgart 1991–97, Kunstakademie Munich 2001–06, currently at Inst. Universitario di Architettura, Venice, Italy; Visiting and Guest Lecturer, Yale Univ., Cornell Univ., New York Univ., Duke Univ., UCLA, Cal Arts, Cooper Union, Pratt Inst., Musuem of Modern Art, Art Inst. of Chicago, Royal Academy, Copenhagen, Ashmolean Museum, Oxford, Berliln Kunstakademie, RCA, London, Glasgow School of Art, Hayward Gallery, London, Univ. of Paris (Sorbonne), Sigmund Freud Museum, Vienna; co-ed. The Fox magazine 1975–76; art ed. Marxist Perspectives 1977–78; mem. Royal Belgian Acad. 2012–; Chevalier des Arts et Lettres 1993, Decoration of Honour in Gold (Austria) 2003; Dr hc (Bologna, Italy) 2001; Cassandra Foundation Grant 1968, Brandeis Univ. Creative Art Award 1990, Frederick R. Weisman Art Foundation Award 1991, Venice Biennale Menzione d'Onore 1993, 3 franc postage stamp issued in honour of his work in Figeac (France) 1999. *Publications:* Art After Philosophy and After (collected writings) 1991, Purloined (novel) 2001, Guide to Contemporary Art Special Edn 2003. *Address:* Joseph Kosuth Studios, 591 Broadway, New York, NY 10012; c/o Sean Kelly, 528 East 29th Street, New York, NY 10001, USA. *Telephone:* (212) 219-8984 (studio); (6) 68809621 (Rome) (home).

KOTAK, Uday, BCom; Indian business executive; *Executive Vice-Chairman and Managing Director, Kotak Mahindra Bank;* b. 15 March 1959; s. of Suresh Kotak and Indira Kotak; m.; two c.; ed Sydenham Coll. and Jamnalal Bajaj Inst. of Man. Studies, Bombay Univ.; Exec. Vice-Chair. and Man. Dir Kotak Mahindra Bank (fmrly Kotak Mahindra Finance Ltd) 2002–; Chair. Kotak Securities Ltd; Chair. and Dir Kotak Mahindra Primus Ltd; Dir of various subsidiary cos including Kotak Securities Ltd, Kotak Mahindra Asset Man. Co Ltd, Kotak Mahindra Capital Co Ltd, OM Kotak Mahindra Life Insurance Co Ltd; mem. Bd of Dirs Bajaj Hindustan Ltd, Dabur India Ltd, Ford Credit Kotak Mahindra Ltd, Kotak Forex Brokerage Ltd, Mahindra & Mahindra Financial Services Ltd, Hutchison Max Telecom Pvt. Ltd, Business Standard Ltd, Indiacar.com Pvt. Ltd, Blue Star Ltd –2002; mem. Advisory Cttee Nat. Stock Exchange of India Ltd; mem. Exec. Bd Indian School of Business; mem. Bd of Govs. Indian Council for Research on Int. Econ. Relations; Governing mem. Mahindra United World Coll. of India; named Global Leader of Tomorrow by the World Econ. Forum 1996, Centre for Org. Devt V. Krishnamurthy Award for Excellence 2007, named World Entrepreneur of the Year, Ernst & Young 2014. *Leisure interests:* plays sitar, cricket. *Address:* Kotak Mahindra Bank, 36–38A, Nariman Bhavan, 227 Nariman Point, Mumbai 400 021, India (office). *Telephone:* (22) 66384444 (office). *Fax:* (22) 66384455 (office). *Website:* www.kotak.com (office).

KOTANKO, Christoph, PhD; Austrian editor; b. 27 July 1953, Braunau am Inn; m. Ingrid Kotanko; one d.; ed Gymnasium, Braunau, studied Romance languages and journalism in Vienna and Paris; Domestic Ed., Wochenpresse 1979–86, Ed. news magazine profile 1986–88; Head of Domestic Policy and commentator for daily newspaper Kurier, with a special focus on European and security policy 1988–97, Deputy Ed.-in-Chief 1997–2003, Exec. Ed.-in-Chief 2003–05, Ed.-in-Chief 2005–10; Vienna corresp., OÖNachrichten 2011–; Goldenes Verdienstzeichen der Republik Österreich (für EU-Berichterstattung), Officier, Ordre nat. du Mérite 2005; Kurt-Vorhofer Prize 1999, Chief Editor of the Year 2004, 2006, 2007. *Publications include:* Eine europäische Affäre. Der Weisenbericht und die Sanktionen gegen Österreich (with Margaretha Kopeinig) 2000, Die Qual der Wahl: Die Programme der Parteien im Vergleich 2013. *Website:* www.nachrichten.at.

KOTCHEFF, Ted; Canadian/Bulgarian film and stage director; b. 7 April 1931, Toronto; m. Laifun Chung; two c.; ed Univ. of Toronto; with CBC Television 1952–57; joined ABC-TV, London 1957; f. Panoptica Productions in Canada with wife Laifun Chung 1996; granted Bulgarian citizenship 2016. *Films include:* Life At The Top 1965, Two Gentlemen Sharing 1968, Wake In Fright 1971, The Apprenticeship of Duddy Kravitz (in Canada) 1973–74, Fun with Dick and Jane 1977, Who is Killing the Great Chefs of Europe? 1978, North Dallas Forty (dir and writer) 1979, First Blood, Split Image, 1982–83, Uncommon Valour 1984, Joshua, Then and Now 1985, Switching Channels 1988, Weekend at Bernie's 1989, Winter People (dir) 1989, Folks! (actor) 1992, The Shooter 1995, Borrowed Hearts 1997. *Plays include:* Play With A Tiger, Maggie May, The Au Pair Man, Have You Any Dirty Washing, Mother Dear?. *Television includes:* The Human Voice 1966, Of Mice And Men 1968, Edna The Inebriate Woman 1971, What Are Families for? 1993, Love on the Run 1994, Family of Cops 1995, A Husband, a Wife and a Lover 1996, Borrowed Hearts 1997, Buddy Faro (series) 1998, Crime in Connecticut: The Story of Alex Kelly 1999, Law & Order: Special Victims Unit (exec. producer) 2000–12.

KOTENEV, Vladimir V.; Russian diplomatist and business executive; *Managing Director, GAZPROM Germania GmbH;* b. 1957, Moscow; m. Maria S. Koteneva; two c.; ed Moscow State Univ.; joined Foreign Service 1979, served in various positions, including Cen. Apparatus, Ministry of Foreign Affairs, becoming Adviser and Deputy Dir, Secr. of Minister of Foreign Affairs, postings abroad include Cultural Attaché, Embassy in Vienna, Amb. to Switzerland, Chargé d'affaires a.i., Embassy in Berne 1999–2001, Dir Dept for Consular Services, Ministry of Foreign Affairs 2001–04, Amb. to Germany 2004–10; Man. Dir GAZPROM Germania GmbH 2010–. *Address:* GAZPROM Germania GmbH, Corporate Communication, Markgrafenstraße 23, 10117 Berlin, Germany (office). *Telephone:* (30) 20195-0 (office). *Fax:* (30) 20195-313 (office). *E-mail:* info@gazprom-germania.de (office). *Website:* www.gazprom-germania.de (office).

KOTENKOV, Maj.-Gen. Aleksander Alekseyevich; Russian politician; b. 23 Sept. 1952, Krasnodar Territory; m.; one s.; ed Rostov-on-Don Inst. of Agric. Machine Construction, Mil.-Political Acad. by corresp.; engineer Rostov Don Factory Rubin 1974–75; army service 1975–90; People's Deputy Russian Fed. 1990–93; Deputy Chair. Cttee Supreme Soviet on Defence and Security 1991; Deputy Head, Head State Law Dept, Russian Presidency, 1992–93; Head Provincial Admin, Martial Law Zone, N Ossetia and Ingushetia 1993–95; Deputy Minister of Nat. Policy 1995–96; mem. State Duma (Parl.) 1993–96, Rep. of President in State Duma 1996–2004, apptd Rep. of President in Fed. Council 2004–13.

KOTEREC, Miloš, MSc, MBA; Slovak politician, diplomatist and UN official; *State Secretary, Ministry of Defence;* b. 11 Oct. 1962, Partizánske; m. (divorced); two c.; ed Faculty of Electrotechnical Eng and Informatics, Slovak Tech. Univ., Bratislava, Faculty of Law, Commenius Univ., Bratislava; Asst Lecturer, Faculty of Electrotechnical Eng and Informatics, Slovak Tech. Univ., Bratislava 1989–93; began career in civil service 1993, promoted to Chief of UN Section, Dept of the UN and Other Int. Orgs, Ministry of Foreign Affairs, Second Sec., Perm. Mission to UN, New York 1995–98, First Sec. and Acting Deputy Chief of Mission 1998–99, served in Dept for the OSCE, Disarmament and Council of Europe, Ministry of Foreign Affairs 1999–2000, Dir 2000–01, apptd Counsellor, Mission of Slovakia to NATO, Brussels 2001, Deputy Perm. Rep. 2001–04, Amb. and Perm. Rep. to UN, New York 2009–12, apptd Chair of First Cttee (Disarmament and International Security), UN 2010, Sr Vice-Pres. UN ECOSOC 2011–12, Pres. 2012–13; State Sec., Ministry of Defence 2012–; mem. European Parl. 2004–09. *Address:* Ministry of Defence, Kutuzovova 8, 832 47 Bratislava, Slovakia (office). *Telephone:* 960-311-740 (office). *Fax:* 960-312-642 (office). *E-mail:* press@mod.gov.sk (office). *Website:* www.mosr.sk (office).

KOTLEBA, Marian, MA, MA (Econ); Slovak politician; *Leader, Kotleba—Ľudová Strana Naše Slovensko (Kotleba—People's Party Our Slovakia);* b. 7 April 1977, Banská Bystrica; m. Frederika Pospíšilová; ed Jozef Murgas High School, Športové Gymnázium, Banská Bystrica, Matej Bel Univ.; f. Slovenská Pospolitosť (Slovak Togetherness) far-right party 2003, party banned from running and campaigning in elections 2007; cand. for Gov. of Banská Bystrica Region 2009; Gov. of Banská Bystrica Region 2013–; cand. in presidential election 2019; Leader Kotleba—Ľudová Strana Naše Slovensko (Kotleba—Our Slovakia People's Party). *Address:* Kotleba—Ľudová Strana Naše Slovensko, E.F. Scherera 4801/20, 921 01 Piešťany, Slovakia (office). *E-mail:* tajomnik@naseslovensko.net (office). *Website:* www.naseslovensko.net (office).

KOTLER, Philip, MA, PhD; American professor of marketing; *S.C. Johnson & Son Distinguished Professor of International Marketing, Kellogg School of Management, Northwestern University;* b. 27 May 1931; s. of Maurice Kotler and Betty Kotler; three d.; ed Univ. of Chicago, Massachusetts Inst. of Tech.; post-doctoral research in math., Harvard Univ., in behavioural science, Univ. of Chicago; currently S.C. Johnson & Son Distinguished Prof. of Int. Marketing, Kellogg School of Man., Northwestern Univ., Evanston, IL; consultant for IBM, Gen. Electric, AT&T, Honeywell, Bank of America, Merck; fmr Chair. Coll. of Marketing, Inst. of Man. Sciences; fmr Dir American Marketing Asscn (AMA), MAC Group; fmr mem. Yankelovivh Advisory Bd; currently mem. Bd of Govs School of Art Inst., Chicago, Advisory Bd Drucker Foundation; fmr Trustee, Marketing Science Inst.; Hon. PhD (Stockholm Univ., Univ. of Zürich, Athens

Univ. of Econs and Business, DePaul Univ., Kraków School of Business and Econs, HEC–Paris, Vienna Univ. of Econs and Business Admin, Budapest Univ. of Econ. Science and Public Admin, Catholic Univ. of Santo Domingo); Paul Converse Award, AMA 1978, Distinguished Marketing Educator Award, AMA 1985, Award for Marketing Excellence, European Asscn of Marketing Consultants and Sales Trainers, Annual Charles Coolidge Parlin Marketing Research Award 1989, Marketer of the Year, Sales and Marketing Execs Int. 1995, Marketing Educator of the Year, Acad. of Marketing Science 2002. *Publications include:* Marketing Management: Analysis, Planning, Implementation and Control 1967, Principles of Marketing, Marketing Models, Strategic Marketing for Non-Profit Organizations, The New Competition, High Visibility, Social Marketing, Marketing Places, Marketing for Congregations, Marketing for Hospitality and Tourism, The Marketing of Nations, Kotler on Marketing, Marketing Insights from A to Z 2003; over 100 articles in professional journals. *Address:* Kellogg School of Management, Northwestern University, 2001 Sheridan Road, Evanston, IL 60208, USA (office). *Telephone:* (847) 491-3522 (office). *E-mail:* taryn.tawoda@kellogg.northwestern.edu (office). *Website:* www.kellogg.northwestern.edu (office).

KOTLYAKOV, Vladimir Mikhailovich, DrGeogSc; Russian geographer and glaciologist; *Scientific Leader, Institute of Geography, Russian Academy of Sciences;* b. 6 Nov. 1931, Lobnya, Moscow Region; m. Valentina Alexeevna Bazanova; two s.; ed Moscow State Univ.; Jr Researcher, Sr Researcher, Head of Glaciology Dept, Inst. of Geography USSR (now Russian) Acad. of Sciences 1954–86, Dir 1986–2015, currently Scientific Leader; Corresp. mem., Russian Acad. of Sciences 1976, mem. 1991–; Vice-Pres. Russian Geographical Soc. 1980–2000, Hon. Pres. 2000–; People's Deputy of USSR 1989–91; mem. Academia Europaea, Earth Council 1993–2000, French Acad. of Sciences 2002–, Georgian Acad. of Sciences 1996–; Hon. mem. American, Mexican, Italian, Estonian, Ukrainian and Georgian Geographical Socs, Int. Glaciological Soc.; Chevalier, Légion d'honneur 2017; Litke Gold Medal, Russian Geographical Soc. 1985, Przhevalsky Gold Medal, Russian Geographical Soc. 1995, State Prize of Russian Fed. 2002, Russian Ind. Prize 'Triumph' 2004, Great Gold Medal, Russian Geographical Soc. 2004, Berg Gold Medal, Russian Acad. of Sciences 2005, Nobel Peace Prize 2007, Grigoriev Prize, Russian Acad. of Sciences 2009, Konstantin Medal, Russian Geographical Soc. 2011, Demidoff Prize 2012, Schmidt Prize, Russian Acad. of Sciences 2013. *Publications include:* Snow Cover of Antarctica 1961, Snow Cover of the Earth and Glaciers 1968, Glaciology Dictionary 1984, Elsevier's Dictionary of Glaciology 1990, World of Snow and Ice 1994, Science, Society, Environment 1997, World Atlas of Snow and Ice Resources 1997; Collection of Selected Works: Glaciology of Antarctica (Vol. 1) 2000, Snow Cover and Glaciers of the Earth (Vol. 2) 2004, Geography in the Changing World (Vol. 3) 2001, Ice, Love and Hypothesis (Vol. 4) 2001, In the World of Snow and Ice (Vol. 5) 2002, Science is a Life (Vol. 6) 2003, Elsevier's Dictionary of Geography 2007, Dictionary of Tourism: Nature, Culture and Travel 2013. *Leisure interest:* travelling. *Address:* Institute of Geography, Russian Academy of Sciences, Staromonetny per. 29, 119017 Moscow (office); Profsoyuznaya str. 43-1-80, 117420 Moscow, Russia (home). *Telephone:* (495) 959-00-32 (office); (495) 957-08-34 (home). *Fax:* (495) 959-00-33 (office). *E-mail:* vladkot6@gmail.com; vladkot4@gmail.com. *Website:* www.igras.com (office).

KOTROMANOVIĆ, Ante, MBA; Croatian politician and fmr army officer; b. 8 May 1968, Potravlje, Sinj; m.; one d.; ed Croatian Mil. Acad., Ban Josip Jelacic War Coll., Univ. of Zagreb; Company Commdr, Special Forces of the Croatian Armed Forces Gen. Staff 1991–92, Bn Commdr, Sinj Training Centre 1992–93, Commdr, Sinj Operations Group and 126th Sinj Brigade 1993–96, Commdr, 4th Guard Brigade Split 1996–2001, Chief of Staff of Dubrovnik Mil. Dist 2001–02, retd (rank of Col) 2002; columnist, Vecernji List (daily newspaper) 2004–05; Dir Demining Co. Zdrug Ltd 2005–06; mem. Man. Bd Urbaniko Ltd 2006–07; mem. Sabor (Parl.) 2007–11, Chair. Veterans' Cttee 2007–11; Minister of Defence 2011–16; mem. Social Democratic Party of Croatia (Socijaldemokratska partija Hrvatske) 2007–; Order of Duke Domagoj, Order of Nikola Subic Zrinski, Order of Count Jelacic; Medal for Exceptional Ventures, Memorial of Homeland War, Memorial of Homeland Gratitude. *Address:* c/o Ministry of Defence, 10000 Zagreb, Sarajevska cesta 7, Croatia (office).

KOTSCHERGA, Anatoly Ivanovich; Ukrainian singer (bass); b. 9 July 1947, Vinnitsa; s. of Ivan Kotscherga and Maria Kotscherga; m. Lina Kotscherga 1985; one d.; ed Kiev Conservatoire and studied at La Scala, Milan; soloist, Shevchenko Opera and Ballet, Kiev 1972–, also Vienna State Opera 1990–; Glinka Prize 1971, Tchaikovsky Prize 1974, USSR People's Artist 1983. *Major roles include:* Boris Godunov, Galitsky (Borodin's Prince Igor), Don Basilio (Barber of Seville), Mephistopheles (Gounod's Faust), Don Carlos (Verdi), Don Giovanni (Mozart), Khovanshchina (Mussorgsky), Dosiphey (Khovanshchina), Nilakanta (Lakmé); USSR People's Artist 1983. *Television include:* Faust 1982, Khovanshchina 1989, La guerre et la paix 2000, Lady Macbeth of Mtsensk 2002, Don Giovanni 2002, Boris Godunov 2004, Don Carlo 2008, Eugène Onéguine 2009. *Leisure interest:* tennis. *Address:* Michael Lewin International Artists' Management, c/o IAAC Kulturmanagement GmbH, Opernring 8/6, 1010 Vienna, Austria (office). *E-mail:* office@lewin-management.com (office).

KOTTO, Yaphet Fredrick; American actor; b. 15 Nov. 1944, Harlem, New York; s. of Yaphet Mangobell Kotto and Gladys M. Kotto; m. Antoinette Pettyjohn 1975; six c. *Films include:* Nothing But a Man 1963, Liberation of Lord Byron Jones 1964, Across 110th Street 1973, Live and Let Die 1974, Report to the Commissioner 1974, Sharks Treasure 1974, Monkey Hustle 1975, Drum 1976, Blue Collar 1977, Alien 1978, Brubaker 1979, Hey Good Looking 1982, Fighting Back 1982, Star Chamber 1983, Warning Sign 1985, Terminal Entry 1986, Eye of the Tiger 1986, PrettyKill 1987, The Running Man 1987, Midnight Run 1988, Nightmare of the Devil (also dir), Terminal Entry 1986, Jigsaw Murders 1988, A Whisper to a Scream 1989, Ministry of Vengeance 1989, Tripwire 1990, Hangfire 1991, Freddy's Dead 1991, Almost Blue 1992, Extreme Justice 1993, Intent to Kill 1993, The Puppet Masters 1994, Dead Badge 1995, Out-of-Sync 1995, Two If By Sea 1996, Witless Protection 2008. *Theatre includes:* Great White Hope, Blood Knot, Black Monday, In White America, A Good Place to Raise a Boy, Fences (London) 1990. *Television includes:* Raid on Entebbe 1977, Rage 1980, Women of San Quentin 1983, In Self Defense 1987, Badge of the Assassin, Harem, Desperado, Perry Mason, Prime Target, After the Shock, Chrome Soldiers, It's Nothing Personal, Extreme Justice, The American Clock, Deadline For Murder, Homicide: Life on the Street (series) 1993–99, The Defenders: Payback 1997, Homicide: The Movie 2000, The Ride 2000, Stiletto Dance 2001.

KOTZIAS, Nikolaos, MA, PhD; Greek political scientist, academic, diplomatist and politician; b. 19 Nov. 1950, Athens; ed Univ. of Athens, Univ. of Giessen, Germany; active as student in Lambrakis Democratic Youth and during mil. dictatorship in Greece; fmr mem. Communist Youth of Greece; fmr Sec. Fed. of Greek Fraternities in Germany; fmr mem. Cen. Cttee Kommounistikó Kómma Elládas (Communist Party of Greece); with Diplomatic Service, Ministry of Foreign Affairs 1993–2008, rank of Amb. 2005–; involved in negotiations on Treaty of Amsterdam, Agenda 2000, Greek–Turkish relations and European Constitution; researcher and teacher, Univs of Marburg, Oxford and Harvard; Prof. of Political Theories and Int. and European Studies, Univ. of Piraeus 2008–; Minister of Foreign Affairs Jan.–Aug. 2015, Sept. 2015–Oct. 2018 (resgnd); Ind. *Publications include:* 24 books, including EU–US Relations: Repairing the Transatlantic Rift (co-ed.) 2006, Foreign Policy of Greece in the 21st Century (in Greek) 2010, Debt Colony Greece. European Empire and German Primacy (in Greek) 2013; book chapters and articles; published works of German philosopher Jürgen Habermas in Greece; released a collection of poems. *Address:* c/o Ministry of Foreign Affairs, Odos Sofias 1, 106 71 Athens, Greece (office). *Telephone:* (210) 3681000 (office). *Fax:* (210) 3681717 (office). *E-mail:* mfa@mfa.gr (office). *Website:* www.mfa.gr (office).

KOUCHNER, Bernard, (Bernard Gridaine), KBE, DenM; French politician, physician and screenwriter; b. 1 Nov. 1939, Avignon; m. 1st Evelyne Pisier; two s. one d.; m. 2nd Christine Ockrent (q.v.); one s.; gastroenterologist, Hôpital Cochin, Paris; Co-founder and Pres. Médecins sans Frontières 1971–79; Founder, Médecins du Monde 1980; has organized and undertaken numerous humanitarian missions world-wide since 1968; mem. CP –1966, Parti socialiste 1966–2007, Ind. 2007–; Sec. of State, Ministry of Social Affairs and Employment May 1988; Sec. of State responsible for Humanitarian Action, Office of Prime Minister 1988–91, Ministry of Foreign Affairs 1991–92; Minister of Health and Humanitarian Action 1992–93, 1997–99, Minister Del., Ministry of Health 2001–02; Minister of Foreign and European Affairs 2007–10; mem. European Parl. 1994–97; UN Chief Admin., Kosovo 1999–2001; Founder, Foundation for Humanitarian Action 1993–; radio broadcaster RTL 2 1995; Founder, Malades sans Frontières 2003; fmr Prof. of Public Health and Devt, CNAM; Dr hc (Durham, Pristina, Sarajevo, Ben Gurion, Erasmus Rotterdam); Dag Hammarskjöld Prize 1979, Louis Weiss Prize (European Parl.) 1979, Athinai Prize (Alexander Onassis Foundation) 1981, Prix Europa 1984, Nobel Peace Prize (with Médecins sans Frontières) 1999, Prix de la Tolerance 2003. *Television:* as Bernard Gridaine has written scripts for series including Médecins de Nuit, Hotel de Police, Bonjour Maitre. *Publications:* La France Sauvage, Les Voraces, L'Ile de Lumière, Charité Business, Le Devoir d'Ingérence (co-author) 1988, Les Nouvelles Solidarités 1989, Le Malheur des Autres 1991, Dieu et les Hommes (co-author) 1993, Vingt idées pour l'an 2000 1995, Ce que je crois 1995, La dictature médicale 1995, Le Premier qui dit la Verité 2002, Les Guerres de la Paix 2004, Quand tu sera Président (co-author) 2004. *Address:* c/o Ministry of Foreign Affairs and International Development, 37 quai d'Orsay, 75351 Paris Cedex 07, France.

KOUDELKA, Josef; French (b. Czechoslovakian) photographer; b. 10 Jan. 1938, Boskovice; ed Technical Univ. of Prague; aeronautical engineer, Prague and Bratislava 1961–67; specialized in photography 1967–; extensive travel throughout Europe documenting lives of gypsies; exhibited in Prague 1961, 1967, MOMA, New York 1975, Amsterdam 1978, Stockholm 1980, Hayward Gallery, London 1984, numerous other venues; mem. Magnum Photos Inc. 1971–; mem. Union of Czechoslovakian artists 1965–; Chevalier des Arts et Lettres 1992; Prix Nadar 1978, Grand Prix Nat. de la Photographie (France) 1987, Hugo Erhurth Prize 1989, Prix Romanes 1989, Henri Cartier-Bresson Award 1991, Century Medal of the Royal Photographic Soc., UK, Medal of Merit 2002, and others. *Publications include:* Gypsies 1975, Photopoche Josef Koudelka 1984, Exils 1 1988, Mission Photographique Transmanche 1989, Prague 1990, Z. Fotografickeho Dila 1958–1990 1990, Divaldo Za Branou 1965–1970 1993, Black Triangle 1994, Wales Reconnaissance 1998, Chaos 1999, Lime Stone 2001, Teatro del Tempo 2003, L'épreuve totalitaire 2004, Joseph Koudelka Photofile 2007, Invasion 68 2008, Koudelka Piedmont Contrasto 2010, Roma 2011, Lime 2012, Wall 2013. *Address:* c/o Magnum Photos, 19 rue Hégesippe Moneau, 75018 Paris, France.

KOULIBALY, Mamadou, PhD; Côte d'Ivoirian economist, academic and politician; *President, Liberté et Démocratie pour la République (LIDER);* b. 21 April 1957, Azaguié, Agboville; m.; three c.; Prof. of Econ. Science, Univ. of Abidjan; Minister of Economy and Finance 2000–01; Pres. of Nat. Ass. 2001–11; acting Pres. Ivorian Popular Front (FPI) 2011; currently Pres. Liberté et Démocratie pour la République (LIDER). *Address:* Liberté et Démocratie pour la République, LIDER House, Rue des Jardins D07 Riviera Golf, 22 BP 836, Abidjan 22, Côte d'Ivoire (office). *Telephone:* 22-00-33-33 (office). *Fax:* 22-43-67-07 (office). *Website:* www.lider-ci.org (office).

KOUMBA, Bounandélé; Central African Republic politician; ed Ecole nat. des douanes de Neuilly, France; 12 years as Adviser on Int. Affairs, Communauté économique et monétaire de l'Afrique centrale (Cemac); fmr Sec. of State for Finance; Minister of Labour, Employment, Vocational Training and Social Security 2013, Minister of Finance 2014–15. *Address:* c/o Ministry of Finance and the Budget, BP 696, Bangui, Central African Republic.

KOUMI, Margaret (Maggie); British journalist; b. 15 July 1942; d. of Yiasoumis Koumi and Melexidia Paraskeva; m. Ramon Sola 1980; ed Buckingham Gate, London; sec. Thomas Cook 1957–60; sub-ed., feature and fiction writer Visual Features Ltd 1960–66; sub-ed. TV World 1966–67; Production Ed. 19 Magazine 1967–69, Ed. 1969–86, concurrently Ed. Hair Magazine; Man. Ed. Practical Parenting, Practical Health, Practical Hair and Beauty 1986–87; Jt Ed. Hello! 1988–93, Ed. 1993–2001, Consultant Ed. 2001–; Jt Ed. of the Year Award 1991. *Publications:* Beauty Care 1981, Claridges – Within The Image 2004. *Leisure interests:* reading, travel, exploring markets.

KOUMJIAN, Nicholas Henry, BA, JD, MBA; American lawyer; *International Co-Prosecutor, Extraordinary Chambers in the Courts of Cambodia;* ed Pennsylvania State Univ., Univ. of North Carolina, Univ. of Southern California; Deputy

Dist Attorney, Los Angeles County Dist Attorney's Office 1981–2000; Trial Attorney, Int. Criminal Tribunal for Fmr Yugoslavia 2000–03; Deputy Gen. Prosecutor for Serious Crimes, UN Dept of Peacekeeping Operations, Dili, Timor Leste 2003–05; 2005 to 2006 for the War Crimes Chamber of the State Court of Bosnia and Herzegovina 2005–06; Dir, MSD Colombia Human Rights program (funded by USAID) 2006–07; Prin. Trial Attorney, Special Court for Sierra Leone 2007–11, Sr Appeals Counsel (worked on trial of Charles Taylor, fmr Pres. of Liberia) 2012–13; Ind. Attorney, Int. Criminal Court, The Hague 2011–13; apptd Of Counsel, Geragos and Geragos (law firm), Los Angeles 2011; Int. Co-Prosecutor, Extraordinary Chambers in the Courts of Cambodia 2013–. *Address:* Office of the Co-Prosecutors, Extraordinary Chambers in the Courts of Cambodia, National Road 4, Chaom Chau Commune, Porsenchey District, Phnom Penh, Cambodia (office). *Telephone:* (0) 23 861 500 (office). *Fax:* (0) 23 861 555 (office). *E-mail:* info@eccc.gov.kh (office). *Website:* www.eccc.gov.kh/en/persons/mr-nicholas-koumjian (office).

KOUPAKI, Pascal Irénée, MA; Benin politician; b. 1 May 1951; ed Université Nationale du Benin, Université de Paris I, France, Centre de Formation Banque Centrale des Etats de l'Afrique de l'Ouest, Senegal; various positions with Centre de Formation Banque Centrale des Etats de l'Afrique de l'Ouest, including Dir and Asst Gov., Dakar 1979–90, Dir of Research Dept 1998–2006; Deputy Head of Cabinet of Prime Minister of Côte d'Ivoire 1990–94; with IMF 1994–96; Head of Cabinet of Prime Minister of Benin Adrien Houngbédjiego 1996–98; Minister of Devt, Economy and Finance 2006–07, Minister of State for Planning, Devt, Evaluation of Public Policy and Coordination of Govt 2007–10; Prime Minister of Benin, responsible for Co-ordination of Govt Action, Evaluation of Public Policy, Denationalization and Social Dialogue 2011–13; Leader, Union for the Devt of the New Benin (Union pour le Développement du Benin Nouveau) –2013 (resgnd); cand. in presidential election March 2015.

KOUROUMBLIS, Panagiotis (Panos); Greek politician; b. 2 Oct. 1951, Matsouki, Aetolia-Acarnania; m. Eleni Kotsopoulou; one s. one d.; blinded by explosion of a German World War II hand-grenade aged ten; took part in several student and popular struggles, later became leader of a 'social uprising' of the blind; Founding mem. World Blind Union; has worked more generally for child protection, care for the elderly and for people with disabilities; mem. Vouli (Parl.) 1996–; mem. Panellínio Socialistiko Kinima (PASOK—Panhellenic Socialist Movt) 2009–11; f. anti-austerity Enotike Metopo (Unitary Movt) 2011–12, merged into Syriza; mem. Synaspismós Rizospastikís Aristerás (SYRIZA—Coalition of the Radical Left) 2012–; Minister for Health and Social Solidarity Jan.–Aug. 2015, of the Interior and Admin. Reconstruction 2015–16, of Shipping and Island Policy 2016–18. *Address:* c/o Ministry of Shipping and Island Policy, 18510 Piraeus, Greece (office).

KOURULA, Erkki, LLL, LLM, PhD; Finnish lawyer, diplomatist and judge; *Judge, Appeals Division, International Criminal Court;* b. 12 June 1948, Lappee; m. Dr Pirkko Kourula; two c.; ed Univ. of Helsinki, Univ. of Oxford, UK; research posts at Univs of Oxford and Helsinki, Acad. of Finland, UN, Geneva 1972–82, 1984–85; Dist Judge 1979; Prof. of Int. Law, Univ. of Lapland, Rovaniemi 1982–83; Counsellor and Legal Adviser, Ministry of Foreign Affairs 1986–89, Dir Int. Law Div. 1989–91; Minister Counsellor and Legal Adviser, Perm. Mission to UN, New York 1991–95; Amb., Deputy Dir-Gen. for Legal Affairs, Ministry of Foreign Affairs 1995–98, Dir-Gen. for Legal Affairs 2002–03; Amb., Perm. Rep. to Council of Europe, Strasbourg 1998–2002; Judge, Appeals Div., Int. Criminal Court (ICC), The Hague 2003–; Head Del. to Preparatory Cttee for ICC 1994–98; Agent of Finland to European Courts of Justice and Human Rights; mem. Del. to UN Gen. Ass. 1986–90, 1995–97; mem., chair. or del. to numerous int. orgs, cttees and confs. *Publications include:* The Identification and Characteristics of Regional Arrangements for the Purpose of the United Nations Charter (doctoral thesis); contribs to publs and articles on activities of UN and ICC. *Address:* International Criminal Court, PO Box 19519, 2500 CM The Hague, The Netherlands (office). *Telephone:* (70) 515-8072 (office). *Fax:* (70) 515-8789 (office). *E-mail:* erkki.kourula@icc-cpi.int (office). *Website:* www.icc-cpi.int (office).

KOUSSA, Moussa Muhammad, BA; Libyan government official and diplomatist; b. Benghazi; ed Michigan State Univ., USA; worked as security specialist for Libyan embassies in Europe before being apptd Amb. to UK 1979–80 (expelled); Deputy Sec. for Foreign Affairs 1992–94; Head of Libyan Intelligence Agency 1994–2009; Sec. for Foreign Liaison and Int. Co-operation (Minister of Foreign Affairs) 2009–11 (fled to UK and resgnd 30 March 2011); currently lives in Qatar.

KOUTCHÉ, Komi, DESS, PhD; Benin economist and politician; b. 1977; ed Univ. d'Abomey-Calavi; held various positions in Ministry of Economy and Finance including in Cabinet of the Minister, Man., Credit Lines Dept, Dir of Operations, Fonds Nat. de la Microfinance 2007–08, Dir-Gen. 2008–13; Minister of Communication and Information Technologies 2013–15, Minister of State in charge of the Economy, Finance and Programmes of Denationalization 2014–16; mem. Ass. Nat. for 9th Dist April–June 2015 (resgnd); Officier, Ordre Nat. du mérite. *Address:* c/o Ministry of the Economy, Finance and Programmes of Denationalization, BP 302, Cotonou, Benin (office).

KÕUTS, Vice-Adm. (retd) Tarmo; Estonian naval officer (retd) and politician; b. 27 Nov. 1953, Saaremaa Island; m. Velina Kõuts; one s.; ed Tallinn Maritime Coll., Kaliningrad Tech. Inst., Nat. Defence Acad., Finland; held positions successively as officer, capt. and capt.-instructor on various ships, Estonian Shipping Co. 1973–90; Rector, Estonian Maritime Acad. 1990–93; Dir-Gen. Estonian Border Guard 1993–99; Commdr of Estonian Defence Forces 2000–06 (resgnd); mem. Riigikogu (State Ass.) 2007–11; mem. Union of Pro Patria and Res Publica (IRL—Isamaa ja Res Publica Liit); Pres. Estonian Shooting Union; Order of the Cross of Eagle (2nd Class) 1998, Royal Norwegian Order of Merit 2002, Grand Cross Order of Prince Henry the Navigator (Portugal) 2003, Order of the National Coat of Arms (2nd Class) 2005, Commdr Grand Cross of Order of Viesturs (Latvia) 2005, Distinguished Service Decoration Estonian Defence Forces. *Leisure interests:* hunting, fishing, sailing.

KOUTSOUMPAS, Dimitris; Greek lawyer and politician; *General Secretary, Kommunistiko Komma Elladas (KKE—Communist Party of Greece);* b. 10 Aug. 1955, Lamia; s. of Apostolis Koutsoumpas; ed Nat. and Kapodistrian Univ. of Athens; mem. Communist Youth of Greece, participated in Athens Polytechnic uprising against Regime of Colonels Nov. 1973; elected to Cen. Cttee, Kommunistiko Komma Elladas (KKE—Communist Party of Greece) 1987–, mem. Politburo 1996–, Dir Rizospastis (official party newspaper) 1996–2007, was also Head of Int. Relations, Gen. Sec. CP of Greece 2013–; unsuccessful cand. in parl. elections for Boeotia Pref. 2000, 2007. *Address:* Kommunistiko Komma Elladas (Communist Party of Greece), Leoforos Irakliou 145, Perissos, Nea Ionia, 142 31 Athens, Greece (office). *Telephone:* (210) 2592111 (office). *Fax:* (210) 2592298 (office). *E-mail:* cpg@int.kke.gr (office). *Website:* inter.kke.gr (office).

KOUVELIS, Fotis-Fanourios (Fotis); Greek lawyer and politician; *Minister of Shipping and Island Policy;* b. 3 Sept. 1948, Volos; m. Photeine Pallas; two d.; ed Univ. of Athens; mem. Lambrakis Youth; Founding mem. CP of KKE Interior (Greece Interior), mem. Cen. Cttee 1975–86; Founding mem. Greek Left party 1987, Gen. Sec. 1989–92; mem. Synaspismós 1992–2010; Pres. Dimokratiki Aristera (DIMAR—Democratic Left) (f. by fmr mems of Coalition of the Left of Movements and Ecology 2010) 2010–; mem. of the Vouli (Parl.) 1989–93, 1996–; Minister for Justice July–Oct. 1989, Minister of Shipping and Island Policy 2018–; Municipal Councillor, Municipality of Athens 2002–04; mem. Bd Athens Bar Assen 1975–, Chair. 1987–89; Chair. Rehabilitation Centre for Torture Victims 1991–94; mem. Peace Movements and Human Rights. *Address:* Ministry of Shipping and Island Policy, 18510 Piraeus, Greece (office). *Telephone:* (213) 1371700 (office). *Fax:* (210) 4191562 (office). *E-mail:* info@yen.gr (office). *Website:* www.yen.gr (office); www.kouvelis.gr.

KOUYATÉ, Lansana; Guinean international organization official, diplomatist and politician; b. 1950, Koba; m.; three c.; joined Foreign Service 1983, Counsellor, Embassy in Cote d'Ivoire 1983–85, Head of Africa and OAU Dept, Ministry of Foreign Affairs 1985–87, Amb. to Egypt, Sudan, Turkey, Jordan, Syria and Lebanon 1987–92, Amb. and Perm. Rep. to UN, New York 1992–97, Vice-Pres. ECOSOC 1992–93, UN Sec. Gen's Special Rep. to Somalia 1993–94, Under-Sec.-Gen. in charge of Political Affairs for Africa, Western Asia and Middle East, UN Security Council 1994–97; Exec. Sec. Econ. Community of W African States (ECOWAS) 1997–2002; Perm. Rep. to Int. Org. of Francophone Countries 2002–07; Prime Minister of Guinea 2007–08; unsuccessful cand. in presidential election 2010; Pres. Parti de l'Espoir pour le Développement National (PEDN); Commdr, Légion d'honneur, Commdr of the Mono Order (Togo), African Star (Liberia). *Publications include:* International Funding of State-owned Companies in Guinea: Problems and Prospects, The End of the Cold War and its Impact on Third-World Countries. *Address:* Parti de l'Espoir pour le Développement National (PEDN), Commune Ratoma, BP 1403, Conakry, Guinea (office). *Telephone:* 655-55-00-00 (mobile) (office). *Website:* www.pednespoir.com (office).

KOVAČ, Miro, PhD; Croatian diplomatist and politician; b. 20 Sept. 1968, Split; m.; three c.; ed Univ. of Zagreb, Univ. of Paris III: Sorbonne Nouvelle, France; Information Dept, Office of the President 1995–99, Asst Adviser for Euro-Atlantic Integration 1999–2001; Counsellor, Embassy in Brussels 2001–03, Minister-Counsellor, Embassy in Paris 2003–04, Asst Minister of Foreign Affairs 2004–06, rank of Amb. at Ministry of Foreign Affairs and European Integration 2006–08, Amb. to Germany 2008; Int. Sec., Hrvatska Demokratska Zajednica (HDZ—Croatian Democratic Union) 2014–; Campaign Chief for Kolinda Grabar-Kitarović during presidential elections 2014–15; mem. Sabor (Parl.) 2015–; Minister of Foreign and European Affairs Jan.–Oct. 2016. *Publications:* La France, la création du royaume "yougoslave" et la question croate, 1914–1929 2001, France and the Croatian Issue, 1914–1929 2005; several articles. *Address:* c/o Ministry of Foreign and European Affairs, 10000 Zagreb, trg Nikole Šubića Zrinskog 7–8, Croatia. *E-mail:* zamjenik.ministrice@mvep.hr.

KOVACEVICH, Richard (Dick) M., BEng, MEng, MBA; American banking executive; *CEO Partner, Hudson Executive Capital LP;* b. 1944; ed Stanford Univ.; Exec. Vice-Pres. Kenner Div., Gen. Mills Inc., Minneapolis 1967–72; Prin. Venture Capital 1972–75; Vice-Pres. Consumer Services Norwest Corpn, Minneapolis 1975, subsequently Sr Vice-Pres. New York banking group, Exec. Vice-Pres., Man. New York bank div., Exec. Vice-Pres., mem. Policy Cttee, Vice-Chair., COO banking group, Pres., COO, Vice-Chair., Chair. and CEO 1996–98; Pres. and CEO Wells Fargo & Co. (after merger with Norwest Corpn), San Francisco 1999–2005, Chair. and CEO 2005–06, Chair. 2006–09, now Chair. Emer.; CEO Partner, Hudson Executive Capital LP 2015–; mem. Bd of Dirs Cargill, Inc., Clearing House LLC; fmr mem. Bd of Dirs Cisco Systems, Inc., Target Corpn, PetSmart, Inc., Northern States Power Co. and ReliaStar Financial Corpn; fmr mem. Gov. Arnold Schwarzenegger's California Comm. for Jobs and Econ. Growth; Vice-Pres. and mem. Bd of Govs San Francisco Symphony; Vice-Chair. and mem. Bd of Trustees San Francisco Museum of Modern Art. *Leisure interest:* playing basketball. *Address:* Hudson Executive Capital LP, 1185 Avenue of the Americas, 32nd Floor, New York, NY 10036, USA (office). *Telephone:* (212) 521-8495 (office). *E-mail:* request@hudsonexecutive.com (office). *Website:* www.hudsonexecutive.com (office).

KOVACEVICH, Stephen; American pianist; b. 17 Oct. 1940, Los Angeles, Calif.; s. of Nicholas Kovacevich and Loreta Kovacevich (née Zuban); ed Berkeley High School, Calif., studied under Lev Shorr and Dame Myra Hess; concert debut as a pianist aged 11; moved to UK to study with Dame Myra Hess 1959; has appeared with leading world orchestras and conductors, including Colin Davis, Hans Graf, Bernard Haitink, Kurt Masur, Simon Rattle and Georg Solti; chamber music collaborations with Jacqueline du Pré, Steven Isserlis, Gautier Capuçon, Renaud Capuçon, Kyung-wha Chung, Truls Mørk, Emmanuel Pahud, Anna Larsson, Khatia Buniatishvili, Belcea Quartet, Philippe Graffin, Alina Ibragimova and Martha Argerich; Artist-in-Residence, Settimane Music Festival 2016; Kimber Award, Calif. 1959, Mozart Prize, London 1962. *Recordings include:* Beethoven's Diabelli Variations 1968, Beethoven's Sonatas No. 3 and No. 5 with Jacqueline du Pré, Brahms' Piano Concerto No. 1 (Gramophone Award) 1993, series of Schubert Sonatas, set of the 32 Beethoven Sonatas 2003, Piano Concertos of Beethoven and Brahms and Bartok's Piano Concerto No. 2 (Edison Award) with Sir Colin Davis, Beethoven's Diabelli Variations (Classic FM Gramophone Ed.'s Choice Award 2009) 2008. *Publication:* Schubert Anthology. *Leisure interests:* tennis, chess, cinema, Indian food. *Address:* c/o Claire Parker-Paphitis, International Classical Artists, Dunstan House, 14A St Cross Street, London, EC1N 8XA, England (office). *Telephone:* (20) 7902-0520 (office). *Fax:* (20) 7404-0150 (office). *E-mail:* info@icartists.co.uk (office). *Website:* www.icartists.co.uk (office).

KOVÁCS, László; Hungarian politician; b. 3 July 1939; m.; one d.; ed Coll. of Politics, Univ. of Econ. Sciences, Petrik Lajos Tech. School; chemical technician, Medicolor, Kobánya Pharmaceutical Works 1957–66; in youth and student movt 1966–75; consultant and Deputy Head, Dept for Int. Relations, Hungarian Socialist Workers' Party 1975–86; mem. Parl. 1990–2004, 2010–, mem. Foreign Affairs Cttee 1990–93 (Chair. 1993–94); mem. Presidium Hungarian Socialist Party (MSZP) 1990–2004, Head of Parl. Faction 1998–2000, Chair. 1998–2004; Deputy Minister of Foreign Affairs 1986–89, State Sec. 1989–90, Minister of Foreign Affairs 1994–98, 2002–04; EU Commr for Taxation and Customs Union 2004–10; Chair.-in-Office OSCE 1995; Vice-Chair. Socialist International 2003–08; Co-Chair. Cen. and East European Cttee 1996–2003; mem. Council of Wise Men of Council of Europe 1997–99. *Address:* National Assembly (Országgyűlés), 1055 Budapest, Kossuth tér 1–3, Hungary (office). *Telephone:* (1) 441-4000 (office). *Fax:* (1) 441-5000 (office). *Website:* www.parlament.hu (office).

KOVAL, Col-Gen. Mikhail; Ukrainian army officer and government official; served as high-ranking official in admin of Ukraine's Border Guards –2014; Interim Minister of Defence March–July 2014.

KOVALEV, Col-Gen. (retd) Nikolai Dmitriyevich; Russian security officer (retd) and politician; b. 6 Aug. 1949, Moscow; m.; one d.; ed Moscow Inst. of Electronic Machine Construction; joined KGB 1974, served for two years in Afghanistan, staff mem., Dept of Fed. Service of Counter-espionage of Moscow and Moscow Region –1994, Deputy Dir Fed. Security Service (FSB) 1994–96, Acting Dir then Dir 1996–98; mem. Security Council of Russia; mem. Comm. on Higher Mil. Titles and Posts, Council on Personnel Policy of Pres. of Russia; mem. State Duma 1999–, mem. Otechestvo-All Russia faction, currently Chair. Comm. on Monitoring the Reliability of Information Provided by State Duma Deputies on their Income, Property and Liabilities, mem. Cttee on Security and Countering Corruption, Security Budget Comm., Chair. Comm. for Struggle Against Corruption 2000–05, fmr Chair. Cttee on Veterans' Affairs; apptd OSCE Parl. Ass. Special Rep. on Anti-Terrorism 2013; Order of Merit for the Fatherland 2006, Order of Military Merit, Order of the Red Star. *Address:* State Duma, 103265 Moscow, Okhotny ryad 1, Russia. *Telephone:* (495) 292-89-19 (office). *Fax:* (495) 292-89-24 (office). *E-mail:* stateduma@duma.gov.ru (office). *Website:* www.duma.gov.ru (office).

KOVALEV, Sergey Adamovich, PhD; Russian biophysicist and politician; *Co-Chairman, Memorial;* b. 2 March 1930, Seredina-Buda, Ukraine; s. of Adam Vasil'evich Kovalev and Valentina Vasilerna Kovaleva; m. 1st Elena Viktorovna Tokareva 1949; m. 2nd Luydmila Uyr'evna Boitsova 1967; one s. two d.; ed Moscow State Univ.; worked as researcher, Moscow Univ.; participant in movt for human rights since late 1960s; assoc. of Academician A. Sakharov, Co-founder Initiative Group for Human Rights 1969; Ed., Samizdat Bulletin Chronicles of Current Events, expelled from Moscow Univ. 1969; arrested on charge of anti-Soviet propaganda 1974, sentenced to seven years' imprisonment and three years in exile 1974; lived in Kalinin, returned to Moscow 1987; mem. Project Group for Human Rights of Int. Foundation for Survival and Devt of Humanity, Engineer Inst. of Problems of Data Transmission USSR Acad. of Sciences 1987–90; People's Deputy of Russian Fed. 1990–93; Chair. Cttee for Human Rights of Supreme Soviet of Russia 1990–93; Chair. Pres.'s Cttee on Human Rights 1994–96 (resgnd); Ombudsman for Human Rights of Russian Fed. 1994–95; est. a Mission of the Commr of Human Rights in North Caucasus 1995; Co-Chair. Soviet Del. on Moscow Conf. on Human Rights 1991; Chief of Russian Del. to UN Comm. on Human Rights 1992–95; Co-founder Vybor Rossii; mem. State Duma (Parl.) 1993–95, 1999–2003; currently Co-Chair. Memorial (human rights centre), Moscow; Kt of Honour of Chkezia 1997; numerous hon. degrees; Council of Europe Human Rights Prize 1995, Olof Palme Prize 2004, Sakharov Prize For Freedom of Thought, European Parl. 2009, Lithuanian Freedom Award 2011. *Publications include:* Der Flug des weißen Raben: von Sibirien nach Tschetschenien: eine Lebensreise 1997, Russlands schwieriger Weg und sein Platz in Europa 1999, The Death Penalty 1999, World, Country, Personality 2000. *Leisure interests:* hunting, fishing. *Address:* Memorial, 127051 Moscow, M. Karetniy pereulok 12, Russia. *Telephone:* (495) 650-78-83. *E-mail:* info@memo.ru. *Website:* www.memo.ru.

KOVALEVSKY, Jean, DèsSc; French astronomer; *Astronomer, Observatoire de la Côte d'Azur;* b. 18 May 1929, Neuilly-sur-Seine; s. of Jean Kovalevsky and Hélène Pavloff; m. Jeannine Reige 1956 (died 2003); two s. one d.; ed Univ. of Paris and Ecole Normale Supérieure; Research Asst Paris Observatory 1955–59, Yale Univ. 1957–58; Head of Computing and Celestial Mechanics Service, Bureau des Longitudes 1960–71; Exec. Dir Groupe de Recherches de Geodésie Spatiale 1971–78; Founder and first Dir Centre d'Etudes et de Recherches Géodynamiques et Astronomiques 1974–82, 1988–92; astronomer, Observatoire de la Côte d'Azur, Grasse 1986–; Sec. Bureau Int. des Poids et Mesures 1991–97, Pres. 1997–2004; Pres. Bureau Nat. de Métrologie 1995–2005; mem. French Acad. of Sciences, Int. Acad. of Astronautics, Academia Europaea, Acad. of Sciences of Turin, French Acad. of Tech., Scientific Cttee European Space Agency 1979–81; Chevalier, Légion d'honneur, Commdr, Ordre du Mérite. *Publications:* Introduction to Celestial Mechanics 1967, Traité de Géodésie (with J. Levallois), Vol 4. 1971, Astrométrie moderne 1990, Modern Astronomy 1995 (reprint 2002), Fundamentals of Astrometry (with P.K. Seidelmann) 2004; about 250 scientific papers. *Leisure interests:* gardening, stamp collection. *Address:* 59 Boulevard Emile Zola, 06130 Grasse (home); Geoazur, Observatoire de la Côte d'Azur, avenue Copernic, 06130 Grasse, France (office). *Telephone:* 4-93-70-60-29 (home); 4-93-40-53-87 (office). *Fax:* 4-93-40-53-33 (office). *E-mail:* jean.kovalevsky@obs-azur.fr (office). *Website:* www.obs-nice.fr (office).

KOVANDA, Karel, MBA, PhD; Czech/British/American diplomatist (retd), consultant and business executive; *Manager, Brussels Representative Office, ČEZ Group;* b. 5 Oct. 1944, Gilsland, Cumbria, UK; s. of Oldřich Kovanda and Ivy Norman; m. Noemi Berová 1993; one s. two d.; ed Prague School of Agric., Massachusetts Inst. of Tech. and Pepperdine Univ., USA; leadership, Czech Nat. Student Union 1968–69; emigrated to USA 1970; lecturer in political science and freelance journalist 1975–80; man. positions in US pvt. sector 1980–90; returned to Czechoslovakia 1990; Czech Ministry of Foreign Affairs 1991–93, Political Dir 1993, Deputy Minister 1997–98; Perm. Rep. of Czech Repub. to UN 1993–97, to UN Security Council 1994–95, to NATO 1998–2005; Deputy Dir Gen. of External Relations, EC 2005–10; Pres. ECOSOC 1997; Gov., Asia-Europe Foundation (Singapore) 2011–13; Man., Brussels Rep. Office, ČEZ Group 2013–; Czech Order of Merit (First Class) 2003; Umurinzi – Campaign Against Genocide Medal (Rwanda) 2010. *Leisure interests:* literature, theatre, travel, stamp collecting. *Address:* Rue du Trône 60, 1050 Brussels, Belgium (office). *Telephone:* (2) 502-00-02 (office). *E-mail:* karel.kovanda01@cez.cz (office); kovankl@gmail.com (home).

KOVE, Daur Vadimovich; Georgian (Abkhaz) diplomatist and politician; *Minister of Foreign Affairs, 'Republic of Abkhazia';* b. 15 March 1979, Sukhumi; m.; two c.; ed Bashkir State Univ.; Assistant, Counsellor, Rep. Office of Abkhazia to Bashkortostan 1995–2000, Plenipotentiary Rep. of Abkhazia to Bashkortostan 2000–09; Head of Int. Dept, Ministry of Foreign Affairs 2005–06, Deputy Foreign Minister 2006–10; Head, Office of Cabinet of Ministers of Abkhazia 2010–11; Teacher of Int. Law, Sukhum Open Inst. June–Nov. 2012; Head of Legal Dept, Office for Emergency Situations of Abkhazia 2011, Adviser to Head of Dept 2013–14; Deputy Dir, Abkhazia Br. of Inst. of Eurasian Studies (Russian non-profit foundation) 2012–14; Adviser to Speaker of People's Ass. (Parl.) 2013–; Head of Protocol Dept of Pres. of 'Repub. of Abkhazia' 2014–16; Minister of Foreign Affairs, 'Repub. of Abkhazia' 2016–; For Labour Valour Medal, 20 years of 'Pridnestrovian Moldavian Repub.' Medal. *Address:* Ministry of Foreign Affairs, 384900 Sukhumi, ul. Lakoba 21, Abkhazia, Georgia (office). *Telephone:* (840) 226-70-69 (office). *E-mail:* secretariat@mfaapsny.org (office). *Website:* www.mfaapsny.org (office).

KÖVÉR, László; Hungarian politician; *Chairman, Nat. Ass. (Országgyűlés);* b. 29 Dec. 1959, Pápa; s. of László Kövér and Erzsébet Ábrahám; m. Mária Bekk 1987; three c.; ed Eötvös Loránd Univ.; Founding mem. Fidesz 1988–, Pres. 2000–01; participant in Opposition Round Table discussions as well as tripartite political negotiations 1989; mem. Parl. 1990–, Leader of Fidesz Parl. group 1994, Chair. Cttee on Nat. Security 1990–93, 2002–06; Minister without Portfolio in charge of Civil Nat. Security Services 1998–2000; Chair. (Speaker) Országgyűlés (Nat. Ass.) 2010–; Acting Pres. of Hungary following resignation of Pál Schmitt 2 April–10 May 2012; mem. Bd, Hungarian Asscn of Int. Children's Safety Service 1990– (Pres. 1994–), Hungarian Asscn for Civic Co-operation 1996–2009. *Address:* Office of the Speaker, Országgyülés, 1357 Budapest, PO Box 2 (office); Office of the Speaker, Országgyülés, 1055 Budapest, Kossuth Lajos tér 1–3, Hungary (office). *Telephone:* (1) 441-4000 (office). *Fax:* (1) 441-5000 (office). *E-mail:* info@orszaggyulesiorseg.hu (office). *Website:* www.parlament.hu (office); www.koverlaszlo.hu.

KOVIND, Ram Nath; Indian lawyer, politician and head of state; *President;* b. 1 Oct. 1945, Paraunkh Village, Kanpur Dehat Dist; m. Savita Kovind 1974; one s. one d.; private legal practice in Delhi High Court and the Supreme Court –1993; mem. Rajya Sabha (upper house of Parl.) from Uttar Pradesh 1994–2006; Gov. of Bihar 2015–17; fmr Pres. All-India Koli Samaj; mem. Bharatiya Janata Party (BJP), Pres. BJP Dalit Morcha 1998–2002, BJP nat. spokesperson 2010–12; Pres. of India 2017–; fmr mem. Man. Bd Dr B.R Ambedkar Univ., Lucknow; fmr mem. Bd of Govs, Indian Institute of Man., Calcutta. *Address:* Office of the President, Rashtrapati Bhavan, New Delhi 110 004, India (office). *Telephone:* (11) 23015321 (office). *Fax:* (11) 23017290 (office). *E-mail:* presidentofindia@rb.nic.in (office). *Website:* presidentofindia.nic.in (office).

KOVITVANIT, HE Cardinal Francis Xavier Kriengsak; Thai ecclesiastic; *Archbishop of Bangkok;* b. 27 June 1949, Ban Rak; ed St Joseph's Minor Seminary, Sam Phran, Pontifical Urbaniana Univ. and Gregorian Univ., Italy; ordained priest, Archdiocese of Bangkok 1976; Asst Priest, Nativity of Mary Church, Ban Pan, then at Epiphany Church, Koh Vai 1977–79; Vice-Rector, St Joseph's Minor Seminary, Sam Phran 1979–81; Rector, Holy Family Intermediate Seminary, Nakhon Ratchasima 1983–89; Under-Sec., Catholic Bishops' Conf. of Thailand 1989–93; Rector, Lux Mundi Nat. Major Seminary, Sam Phran 1992–2000; Parish Priest, Church of Our Lady of Lourdes, Hua Take 2000–01; Special Lecturer, Sam Phran Major Seminary 2001–03; Parish Priest, Assumption Cathedral and Sec., Council of Priests, Archdiocese of Bangkok 2003–07; consecrated Bishop of Nakhon Sawan 2007–09; Archbishop of Bangkok 2009–; cr. Cardinal (Cardinal-Priest of Santa Maria Addolorata) 2015. *Address:* 51 Catholic Mission, Charoenkrung Road 40, Bangrak, Bangkok 10500, Thailand (office). *Telephone:* (2) 2338712 (office). *Fax:* (2) 2371033 (office). *E-mail:* info@catholic.or.th (office). *Website:* www.catholic.or.th (office).

KOWALCZYK, Most Rev. Archbishop Józef, DCL; Polish ecclesiastic and diplomatist; *Archbishop Emeritus of Gniezno;* b. 28 Aug. 1938, Jadowniki Mokre; ed Hosianum Higher Ecclesiastic Seminary, Olsztyn, Catholic Univ. of Lublin, Pontifical Gregorian Univ., Rome, Roman Rota Studium; ordained priest 1962; employee, Roman Rota, Congregation for the Discipline of the Sacraments; organizer and Head of Polish Section, State Secr. 1978–89; Titular Archbishop of Heraclea and Apostolic Nuncio in Poland 1989–2010, Archbishop of Gniezno, Poland 2010–14 (retd), Archbishop Emer. 2014–; Hon. Citizen, Sandomierz 1992, Kwidzyn 1993, Chojnice 1994; Hon. mem. Soc. of Polish Canon Lawyers; Grand Order of St Zygmunt 1999; Dr hc (Agric. Acad., Kraków 1999, Cardinal S. Wyszyński Univ. 2000, Catholic Univ. of Lublin 2001); Orli Laur 2005, Outstanding Personalities Organic Work 2006. *Publications include:* Dojrzewanie czasu 1998, Na drodze konsekrowanej 1999, Służyć słowu 2000 and ed. of Karol Wojtyła's papers and Polish edition of papal teaching (14 vols). *Address:* c/o Archdiocese of Gniezno, ul. Kanclerza Jana Laskiego 7, 62-200 Gniezno, Poland.

KOWNACKI, Piotr, LLB; Polish civil servant and petroleum industry executive; b. 8 Oct. 1954, Warsaw; m. 1976; two d.; ed Univ. of Warsaw; with Inst. of Law Studies, Polish Acad. of Sciences 1979–83; Press Officer Sejm (Parl.) 1983–87; Adjudicating Counsellor, Office of the Constitutional Tribunal 1987–89; Dir Office of Govt Plenipotentiary for Reform of Local Govt Structures 1989–91; Under-Sec. of State in Office of Council of Ministers 1991; Vice-Pres. Supreme Chamber of Control 1991–99, 2001–06; Vice-Pres. Bank Ochrony Srodowiska (Bank for Environmental Protection) 1999–2001; Vice-Pres. for Auditing and Regulation, Deputy CEO and mem. Man. Bd Polski Koncern Naftowy (PKN) Orlen 2006–07, Pres. and CEO Jan.–July 2008; Chair. Supervisory Bd Unipetrol; Sec. of State and Deputy Chief of Chancellery of Pres. of Poland 2008–09, Chief of Chancellery 2008–09; convicted and fined in 2016 for transferring confidential information to journalists; Grand Cross of the Order of Merit 2008, Commdr, Cross with Star of Order of Merit 2009, Commdr, Grand Cross of Order For Merit (Lithuania) 2009.

KOYAMBOUNOU, Gabriel Jean Edouard; Central African Republic politician; b. 1947, Bangui; ed Univ. of Abidjan, École Nat. des Douanes, Françaises, Neuilly-sur-Seine, France; Prime Minister of Cen. African Repub. 1995–96; Minister of State in charge of Communication, Posts and Telecommunications, New Technologies and Francophone Affairs –2003; apptd Inspector-Gen. 2006; Second Vice-Pres. then First Vice-Pres., Mouvement pour la libération du peuple centrafricain 2006; Pres. Handball Fed.; Grand Officier, Ordre du Merite; Gold Medal in Sport. *Publication:* Mémoire sur le 'Droit Douanier'. *Leisure interest:* handball.

KOZACHENKO, Leonid Petrovich; Ukrainian engineer, economist and politician; *President, Ukrainian Agrarian Confederation;* b. 14 May 1955, Veprik, Kiev region; m.; two d.; ed Ukrainian Acad. of Agric., All-Union Acad. of Foreign Trade; worked in agric. enterprises in Fastov region 1972–86, head of collective farm in Fastiv dist 1979; party functionary CP of Ukraine 1986–88; Deputy Head of Dept, Ukrainian Ministry of Agric. 1991–2001, Dir Agroland 2000–01, Deputy Prime Minister of Agric. 2001–02; f. Ukrainian League of Businessmen 1993; Co-f. Ukrainian Asscn of Corn, Nat. Asscn of Stock Exchanges, Ukrainian Asscn for Ecology Protection; Founder and Pres. Ukrainian Agrarian Confed. 1998–; Chair. Council of Entrepreneurs, Cabinet of Ministers of Ukraine 2010–; mem. Presidential Comm. on Agric., Presidium Ukrainian Union of Businessmen; mem. Coordination Council of Businessmen at Ministry of Agrarian Policy; Charter of Honour of Verkhovna Rada; Merited Worker of Agric. of Ukraine 1998. *Leisure interests:* tennis, skiing, gliding. *Address:* Ukrainian Agrarian Confederation, Saksaganskogo str., 53/80, office 807, Kiev 01033, Ukraine (office). *Telephone:* (44) 284-32-38 (office). *E-mail:* agroconf@agroconf.org (office). *Website:* www.agroconf.org (office).

KOZAI, Toyoki, BS, MS, PhD; Japanese horticulturist, university administrator and academic; *Chief Director, Japan Plant Factory Association;* b. 25 Sept. 1943, Tokyo; m. 1967; three c.; ed Chiba Univ., Univ. of Tokyo; Research Asst, Dept of Agricultural Eng, Faculty of Agric., Univ. of Osaka Pref. 1973–77; Assoc. Prof., Dept of Horticulture, Faculty of Horticulture, Chiba Univ. 1977–90, Prof., Dept of Bioproduction Science 1990–2005, Dean Faculty of Horticulture 1999–2005, Pres. Chiba Univ. 2005–08, Prof., Centre for Environment, Health and Field Sciences 2008–09, Emer. and Visiting Prof. 2009–; Chief Dir Japan Plant Factory Asscn (non-profit org.) 2010–; Post-doctoral Fellow, Centre for Agro-Biological Research, Wageningen, Netherlands 1974–75; Visiting Researcher, Dept of Biological and Agricultural Eng, Cook Coll., Rutgers Univ., NJ, USA 1989; Prize for Academic Achievement, Soc. of Agricultural Meteorology of Japan 1982, Prize for Academic Achievement, Japanese Soc. of High Tech. in Agric. 1991, Prize for Academic Achievement, Japanese Soc. of Environment Control in Biology 1992, Prize for Academic Achievement, Japanese Acad. of Agricultural Sciences and Yomiuri Newspaper Co. 1997, Int. Scientific and Technological Award, Kunming City, People's Repub. of China 2002, Friendship Award, State Admin of Foreign Experts Affairs, People's Repub. of China 2002, Medal with Purple Ribbon, Ministry of Educ., Culture and Sports 2002, Lifetime Achievement Award, Soc. of In Vitro Biology (USA) 2009. *Publications:* numerous scientific papers in professional journals. *Address:* Centre for Environment, Health and Field Sciences, 6-2-1 Kashiwa-no-ha, Kashiwa City, Chiba 277-0822, Japan (office). *Telephone:* (471) 378114 (office). *Fax:* (471) 378114 (office). *E-mail:* kozai@faculty.chiba-u.jp (office). *Website:* www.chiba-u.ac.jp/e/education/centers/field.html (office).

KOZAK, Dmitrii Nikolayevich; Russian lawyer and politician; *Deputy Chairman of the Government;* b. 7 Nov. 1958, Bandurovo village, Hayvoron Dist, Kirovohrad Oblast, Ukrainian SSR, USSR; m.; two s.; ed Vinnytsya Polytechnical Inst., Ukrainian SSR, Leningrad (now St Petersburg) State Univ.; Asst to Prosecutor of Leningrad; on staff, Asscn of Marine Trade Ports 1985–89; on staff, Exec. Cttee, Leningrad City Council 1990–91; Head of Law Dept Office, St Petersburg 1991–94; Chair. Law Cttee, Admin. St Petersburg; mem. Govt of St Petersburg, mem. Comm. on Human Rights 1994–96; apptd Deputy Gov. St Petersburg 1998, resgnd end of year; pvt. law practice 1998–99; Deputy Head of Admin. of Russian Pres. on Legal Problems May–Aug. 1999; First Deputy Head of Govt Admin. of Russian Fed. 1999, Head 1999–2000; Deputy Head of Admin. of Russian Pres. 2000–03, First Deputy Head 2003–04; Head of Govt Admin. March–Sept. 2004; Presidential Rep. in Southern Fed. Okrug 2004–07; Minister of Regional Devt 2007–08; Deputy Chair. of Govt 2008–; Order of Merit for the Fatherland (Second Class) 2008, (First Class) 2014. *Address:* Office of the Government, 103274 Moscow, Krasnopresnenskaya nab. 2, Russia (office). *Telephone:* (495) 605-53-29 (office). *Fax:* (495) 605-52-43 (office). *E-mail:* duty_press@aprf.gov.ru (office). *Website:* government.ru/en/gov/persons/6/events (office).

KOZARIĆ, Kemal, PhD; Bosnia and Herzegovina economist, academic and fmr central banker; *Dean, Faculty of Economics, University of Sarajevo;* b. 13 Oct. 1956, Sarajevo; ed Univ. of Sarajevo; worked for 15 years in banking with Privredna Banka Sarajevo (now Central Profit Banka DD Sarajevo) as Chief of Br., Asst to Gen. Dir, City Savings Bank, Exec. Dir for Operations, Exec. Dir for Gen. Affairs, Dir, Assets and Investments Dept; Minister of Finance, Sarajevo Canton Govt 1996–2000; Deputy Gov., Central Bank of Bosnia and Herzegovina 2000–05, apptd mem. Governing Bd 2003, Gov. and Chair. Governing Bd 2005–15; apptd Chair. Governing Bd, BH Deposit Insurance Agency 2007; Dean, Faculty of Econs, Univ. of Sarajevo 2016–. *Address:* Faculty of Economic, University of Sarajevo, 71000 Sarajevo, Trg oslobođenja-Alija Izetbegović 1, Bosnia and Herzegovina (office). *Telephone:* (33) 275900 (office). *Fax:* (33) 275994 (office). *E-mail:* efsa@efsa.unsa.ba (office). *Website:* www.efsa.unsa.ba (office).

KOŽENÁ, Magdalena; Czech singer (mezzo-soprano); b. 26 May 1973, Brno; m. Sir Simon Rattle 2008; two s. one d.; ed Conservatoire, Brno, Coll. of Performing Arts, Bratislava; guest singer, Janáček Opera, Brno 1991–; debut as soloist, Vienna Volksoper 1996–97; appearances include Bach's B Minor Mass at the Queen Elizabeth Hall, London 2000, Salzburg Festival debut as Zerlina in Don Giovanni 2002, charity concerts following floods in Czech Repub. 2002, Idamante in Idomeneo at Glyndebourne 2003 and Salzburg Festival, Cherubino for Bavarian State Opera, Metropolitan Opera, Dorabella at Salzburg Easter Festival, Berlin, Varvara, Dorabella, Zerlina at Metropolitan Opera, Theatre des Champs Elysees, Covent Garden debut in La Cenerentola 2007; regular broadcasts for Czech radio and TV; tours in Europe, USA, Japan, Venezuela, Taiwan, Hong Kong, S Korea, Canada; roles include Dorabella in Così fan tutte, Isabella in Italiana in Algeri (Rossini), Venus in Dardanus (Rameau), Mercedes in Carmen, Annius in La Clemenza di Tito, Paris in Paride ed Elena, lead in Orfeo ed Eurydice (both Gluck), lead in Hermia (Britten), Poppea in L'Incoronazione di Poppea (Monteverdi), Mélisande (Debussy); Chevalier, Ordre des Arts et des Lettres 2003; First Place in Int. Scheider Competition 1992, First Place in Int. Mozart Competition, Salzburg 1995, Georg Solti Prize (France), Youngster of Arts, Europe 1996, Orphée d'Or, L'Académie du Disque Lyrique (France) 1999, Diapason d'Or (France) 2000, Echo Klassik Best New Artist (Germany) 2000, Gramophone Award (London) 2001, Gramophone Artist of the Year 2004, Person of the Year in Culture (Czech Repub.) 2002, 2003. *Recordings include:* Bach Arias (Harmony Magazine Award 1998), Johann Sebastian Bach Cantatas 2000, G.F. Handel Italian Cantatas 2000, G.F. Handel Messiah 2001, Magdalena Kožená – Le belle imagini (Echo Klassik Award 2002, Gold Record of Universal 2003) 2002, Johann Sebastian Bach Arias (Gold Record of Universal 2003, Platinum Record of Universal 2003) 2003, G.F. Handel – Giulio Cesare 2003, Magdalena Kožená – French Arias (Gramophone Award 2003) 2003, Magdalena Kožená – Songs 2004, Magdalena Kožená – Lamento 2005, Paride ed Elena 2005, La Clemenza di Tito 2006, Enchantment 2006, Mozart Arias 2006, Ah! Mio Cor 2007, Songs My Mother Taught Me 2008, Martinů's Julietta Fragments (Gramophone Award for Best Recital Recording 2009, Echo Klassik Award for Recording of the Year 2010) 2009, Ryba: Czech Christmas Mass 2009, Vivaldi Arias 2009, Des Knaben Wunderhorn 2010, Lettere Amorose 2010, Monteverdi 2016. *Leisure interests:* philosophy, music, swimming, cycling. *Address:* Central European Music Agency, Polní 6, 639 00 Brno, Czech Republic (office). *Telephone:* (5) 42213053 (office). *Fax:* (5) 42213056 (office). *E-mail:* david@cema-music.com (office). *Website:* www.cema-music.com (office); www.kozena.cz.

KOZHARA, Leonid Oleksandrovych, MA; Ukrainian diplomatist and politician; b. 14 Jan. 1963, Poltava; m.; one s.; ed Kyiv State Univ., Nat. Inst. of State and Law; Lecturer in Constitutional Law, Kyiv State Politology Inst. 1985–90; Sr Adviser to the Secr., Verkhovna Rada (Supreme Council, Parl.) 1990–92; First Sec., Embassy in Washington, DC 1994–97; various positions with Foreign Policy Dept, Admin of the Pres. 1992–94, 1997–2002; Amb. to Sweden 2002–04; Deputy Head, Admin of the Pres. 2004–05, also Head of Foreign Policy Dept, Foreign Policy Adviser to Pres. and Sec., State Council for European and Euro-Atlantic Integration 2004–05; mem. Verkhovna Rada 2006–, Deputy Chair. Int. Relations Cttee 2006–; Foreign Policy Adviser to Pres. 2010–12; Minister of Foreign Affairs 2012–14 (dismissed by parl.); Pres. Centre for Int. and Comparative Studies 2008–. *Address:* c/o Ministry of Foreign Affairs, 01018 Kyiv, pl. Mykhailivska 1, Ukraine. *E-mail:* zsmfa@mfa.gov.ua.

KOZHIN, Vladimir Igorevich; Russian business executive; *Head, Presidential Administrative Directorate;* b. 28 Feb. 1959, Troitsk, Chelyabinsk Region; m. Alla Kozhina; one s.; ed Leningrad Electrotech. Inst.; instructor, Head of Div., Petrograd Dist Comsomol Cttee; then on staff Research-Production Co. Azimuth, Dir-Gen. Russian-Polish Jt Co. Azimuth Int. Ltd 1991–93; Dir-Gen. St Petersburg Asscn of Jt Cos 1993–94; Head NW Cen. Fed. Dept of Currency and Export Control 1994–99, Head 1999–2000; Head, Office of Russian Pres. and Presidential Admin. Directorate 2000–. *Address:* Office of the President, 103132 Moscow, Nikitnikov per. 2, Russia (office). *Telephone:* (495) 606-35-63 (office). *Fax:* (495) 606-30-06 (office). *E-mail:* udprf@gov.ru (office). *Website:* www.udprf.ru (office).

KOZHOKIN, Evgeny Mikhailovich, DHist; Russian historian and academic; *Vice-Rector for Research, Moscow State Institute of International Relations (MGIMO);* b. 9 April 1954, Moscow; m.; two d.; ed Moscow State Univ.; mem. staff, Inst. of World History, USSR Acad. of Sciences 1984–90; People's Deputy of Russian Fed. 1990–93; Founder and Dir Inst. for Strategic Studies 1994–2009; Deputy Head, Fed. Agency for the CIS, Compatriots Living Abroad and Int. Human Co-operation 2009–10; Prof., Moscow State Inst. of Int. Relations (MGIMO) 2014–, Vice-Rector for Research 2015–; mem. Advisory Bd, PIR Center 2010–. *Film:* Producer and idea's author for documentary A Lonely Battalion. *Publications include:* The French Workers: From the Great French Revolution to the Revolution of 1848 1985, The State and the People: From the Fronde to the Great French Revolution 1989, The History of Poor Capitalism 2005, and more than 100 others. *Leisure interest:* swimming. *Address:* Moscow State Institute of International Relations (MGIMO), Moscow 119454, Prospekt Vernadskogo, 76, Russia (office). *Website:* mgimo.ru (office).

KOZHOKIN, Mikhail Mikhailovich, CandHist; Russian journalist and business executive; *Deputy President and Chairman, Bank VTB24;* b. 23 Feb. 1962, Moscow; ed Moscow State Univ.; Jr Researcher, Researcher, then Sr Researcher, Inst. of USA and Canada, USSR (now Russian) Acad. of Sciences 1988–92, Sr Researcher, Cen. of Econ. and Political Studies, worked with G. Yavlinsky 1992–93; Head of Information Dept ONEXIM Bank 1993–96, Deputy Chair. Exec. Cttee 1996; Asst to First Deputy Chair. of Russian Govt 1996–97, mem. Govt Comm. on Econ. Reform 1997; Ed.-in-Chief, Izvestia (newspaper) 1998–2003 (resgnd); First Vice-Pres. Public Relations Development Company CJSC 2004; Deputy Pres. and Chair. Bank VTB24 (banking services co.), Moscow 2005–; fmr Dir Holding Co. Interros on work with mass media and public relations. *Leisure interests:* travelling, water tourism. *Address:* Bank VTB24, 101000 Moscow, 35 Miasnitskaya Ul., Russia (office). *Telephone:* (495) 777-24-24 (office). *Fax:* (495) 980-46-66 (office). *Website:* www.vtb24.ru (office).

KOZLÍK, Sergej; Slovak politician; b. 27 July 1950, Bratislava; ed Univ. of Econs; clerk with Price Authority 1974–88; Head of Dept of Industrial Prices, Ministry of Finance 1988–90; Dir Exec. Dept of Antimonopoly Office 1990–92; Sec., Movt for a Democratic Slovakia (became political party 2000) 1992–; Vice-Premier, Govt of Slovakia 1993–94; Minister of Finance of Slovak Repub. 1994–97; Deputy to Nat. Council 1994–2004; mem. European Parl. (Group of the Alliance of Liberals and Democrats for Europe) 2004–, mem. Cttee on Budgets, Del. to EU-Russia Parl. Co-operation Cttee; Gov. World Bank 1994–98; Alt. Gov. IMF 1994–98. *Address:* European Parliament, Bâtiment Altiero Spinelli, 01E252, 60 rue Wiertz, 1047 Brussels, Belgium (office). *Fax:* (2) 284-92-57 (office). *E-mail:* sergej_kozlik@nrsr.sk (office). *Website:* www.europarl.europa.eu (office).

KOZLOV, Alexey Semenovich; Russian composer, saxophone player and bandleader; b. 13 Oct. 1935, Moscow; m. 1st; one s.; m. 2nd Lyalya Adburakhmanovna Absalyamova; ed Moscow Inst. of Architecture, Moscow Music Coll.; researcher, Inst. of Design 1963–76; started playing saxophone in youth clubs

1955; founder and leader of jazz quintet 1959, jazz band of café Molodezhnoye 1961–66; arranger and soloist orchestra VIO-66; teacher Moscow Experimental Studio of Jazz Music 1967–76; Founder and Music Dir jazz-rock ensemble Arsenal 1973–, festivals and tours including Delhi and Bombay 1989, Woodstock 1990, Jazz Rally, Düsseldorf 1993, Carnegie Hall 1995, Bonn 1996, with Arsenal, Chamber Soloists of Moscow, the Shostakovich String Quartet, Ars Nova Trio; master classes in towns of Russia and Oklahoma City Univ. 1994; Gen.-Man. Jazz Div., Goskoncert 1995–97; mem. Musical Cttee under Pres. of Russia 1997–; Art Dir Radio Jazz, Moscow 2001–; author of TV programmes, All That Jazz, Improvisation; composer of jazz, film and theatre music; Merited Artist of Russia; his ensemble Arsenal awarded Ovation Prize as the best jazz band in Russia 1995. *Recordings include:* Lonely Dandy 2010, Third Wind 2012, Mindstream 2013, Reconciliation 2014. *Publications:* Rock: Roots and Development 1989, Memoirs—My 20th Century, He-Goat on the Saxophone 2000; numerous articles in music journals. *Address:* Shchepkin str. 25, Apt. 28, 129090 Moscow, Russia (home). *Telephone:* (495) 688-31-56 (home); (916) 183-88-82 (home). *E-mail:* askozlov@mtu-net.ru (home); askozlov1@jandex.ru (home). *Website:* www:musiclab.ru (office).

KOZLOV, Valery Vasilyevich, DSc; Russian politician and research institute director; *Vice-President, Russian Academy of Sciences;* b. 1 Jan. 1950, Kostyly, Ryazanskaya dist; ed M.V. Lomonosov Moscow State Univ.; Sr Researcher, M.V. Lomonosov Moscow State Univ. 1972, Asst, Docent, Sr Scientist 1974–83, Prof. of Theoretical Mechanics 1983–, Deputy Dean for Science and research, Dept of Mechanics and Math. 1980–87, Vice-Rector, M.V. Lomonosov Moscow State Univ. 1989–98, Head of Dept of Math. Statistics and Random Processes 2002–; Adviser to Ministry of Gen. and Professional Educ. (later Ministry of Educ.) 1998–99, Deputy Minister 1999–2001; Founder and Ed.-in-Chief Regular and Chaotic Dynamics, Izvestiya RAN, Seriya Matematicheskaya; Assoc. Ed. Vestnik Moskovskogo Universiteta. Seriya 1. Matematika. Mekhanika; mem. Editorial Bd, Matematicheskie Zametki (Mathematical Notes), Russian Journal of Mathematical Physics; mem. Russian Nat. Cttee on Theoretical and Applied Mechanics 1955, Comm. under the Russian Fed. Pres. on awarding State Prizes of the Russian Fed.; Corresp. mem. Div. of Machine Eng, Mechanics and Control Processes Problems, Russian Acad. of Sciences 1997–2000, Full mem. (Academician) Russian Acad. of Sciences 2000–, Vice-Pres. 2001–, Head of Dept of Mechanics, Steklov Math. Inst. 2003–, Deputy Dir Steklov Math. Inst. 2004–; mem. Russian Acad. of Natural Sciences 1995; Foreign mem. Serbian Learned Soc. 2003; Lenin Komsomol Prize 1973, M.V. Lomonosov 1st Degree Prize 1986, S.A. Chaplygin Prize, Russian Acad. of Sciences 1988, State Prize of the Russian Fed. 1994, Peter The First Golden Medal, Int. Acad. of Environmental and Human Society Sciences 1995, The Breast Badge 'For Distinguished Services', Russian Acad. of Natural Sciences 1996, S.V. Kovalevskaya Prize, Russian Acad. of Sciences 2000. *Address:* Russian Academy of Sciences, 117910 Moscow, Leninsky prosp. 14, GSP-I, Russia (office). *Telephone:* (495) 237-45-32 (office). *Fax:* (495) 938-18-38 (office). *E-mail:* kozlov@pran.ru (office); vvkozlov@rcd.ru (office). *Website:* ics.org.ru (office); www.pran.ru (office).

KOZLOV, Vladimir Ivanovich; Kazakhstani politician and fmr media executive; *Leader, Alga! (Forward!);* b. 10 Aug. 1960, Aktyubinsk (now Aqtöbe), Kazakh SSR, USSR; m.; one c.; Ed. AKTiVi TV channel 1990–96; later co-founder of first pvt. television channel, Aktau-Lada; worked in advertising and PR sector 1996–98; communications specialist, Mangyshlak Nuclear Power Plant 1998; joined Democratic Choice of Kazakhstan, mem. Political Council 2003, subsequently mem. Presidium of Political Council; est. co-operation with Western politicians and non-governmental orgs 2004; Co-founder Alga! (Forward!) party after Democratic Choice of Kazakhstan party was declared illegal 2005, Leader Alga! 2007–, party denied its right to register despite being the most widely supported opposition party, activities suspended by a court May 2013; paid several visits to parls of European countries, including Polish Senate, as well as European Parl. 2006–12; campaigned in European countries against granting Kazakhstan the presidency of OSCE 2009; forbidden from participating in presidential election of 3 April 2011; arrested by staff of Nat. Security Cttee 23 Jan. 2012, went on trial in Mañğistaw Regional Court, Aktaw 16 Aug. 2012, accused of "inciting social hatred", "calling to the overthrow of the constitutional order of the state", and of "creating and managing an organised criminal group with a view to committing one or more crimes, as well as participation in such a group", sentenced to 7½ years' imprisonment in Aqtöbe with confiscation of his property Oct. 2012. *Address:* 040700 Almatı Oblast, Iliiskii Rayon, pos. Zarechnoye, Prison LA 155/14, Kazakhstan. *E-mail:* kazakhstanfree@gmail.com. *Website:* vladimirkozlov.org.

KOZLOVSKIS, Rihards; Latvian lawyer and politician; b. 26 May 1969, Rīga, Latvian SSR, USSR; ed Rīga Secondary School No. 69, Murjani Sports Gymnasium, Faculty of Law, Univ. of Latvia; teacher of Physical Educ., Latvian Acad. of Sport Educ. 1987–93; Jr Insp., 1st Police Bn, Ministry of the Interior 1991; Insp., Govt Security Agency 1991–93; Sr Insp., Dept for the Protection of Econ. Sovereignty (VESAD) 1994–96; Lt Col, Deputy Chief of the Security Police 1996–2005; Adviser and Head of Div., Security and Coordination Div. of the NATO Summit Latvia Task Force, Ministry of Defence 2005–07; lawyer, BBF Consulting Ltd 2007–11; Minister of the Interior 2011–19; mem. Zatlera Reformu Partija (Zatlers' Reform Party—subsequently renamed Reformu Partija—Reform Party) 2011–14, Vienotība (Unity) 2014–; Order of Viesturs 2006. *Address:* c/o Ministry of the Interior, Čiekurkalna 1, līnija 1, korp. 2, Rīga, 1026, Latvia (office).

KOZOL, Jonathan, BA; American writer; b. 5 Sept. 1936, Boston, Mass; s. of Harry L. Kozol and Ruth Massell Kozol; ed Harvard Coll., Magdalen Coll., Oxford, UK; Rhodes Scholar 1958; teacher in Boston area 1964–72; lecturer at numerous univs 1973–2006; Guggenheim Fellow 1972, 1984; Field Foundation Fellow 1973, 1974; Rockefeller Fellow 1978, Sr Fellow 1983; f. Education Action! (non-profit org.); mem. Editorial Bd Greater Good Magazine. *Publications include:* Death At An Early Age (Nat. Book Award in Science, Philosophy, and Religion 1968) 1967, Free Schools 1972, The Night Is Dark 1975, Children of the Revolution 1978, On Being a Teacher 1979, Prisoners of Silence 1980, Illiterate America 1985, Rachel and Her Children: Homeless Families in America (Robert F. Kennedy Book Award 1989, Conscience in Media Award, American Soc. of Journalists and Authors 1989) 1988, Savage Inequalities: Children in America's Schools (New England Book Award 1992) 1991, Amazing Grace (Anisfield-Wolf Book Award 1996) 1995, Ordinary Resurrections 2000, The Shame of the Nation: The Restoration of Apartheid Schooling in America (Nation Magazine Book Award) 2005, Letters to a Young Teacher 2007, Fire in the Ashes: Twenty-Five Years Among the Poorest Children in America 2012, The Theft of Memory: Losing My Father One Day at a Time 2015. *Address:* Education Action!, Cambridge Institute for Public Education, 16 Lowell Street, Cambridge, MA 02138, USA (office). *Telephone:* (617) 945-5568 (office). *Fax:* (617) 945-5562 (office); (978) 462-8557 (home). *E-mail:* jonathankozol@gmail.com; educationactioninfo@gmail.com. *Website:* www.jonathankozol.com.

KOZUKI, Toyohisa; Japanese diplomatist; *Ambassador to Russia;* b. 25 Oct. 1956; ed Univ. of Tokyo; joined Ministry of Foreign Affairs (MFA) 1981, Counsellor, Embassy in Moscow 1998–2000, Head of Japan–US Security Treaty, North America Dept, MFA 2000–01, Asst Minister of Foreign Affairs 2001–02, Head of Russian Dept, European Div. 2002–04, Head of Finance Dept, Secr. of Minister of Foreign Affairs 2004–06, Head of Div. and Co-ordinator of Secr., MFA 2006–08, Deputy Head of Mission, Embassy in Moscow 2008–10, Consul-Gen. in Boston 2010–11, Deputy Dir-Gen., European Dept, MFA 2011–12, Dir-Gen. 2012–14, Dir-Gen. of MFA 2014–15, Amb. to Russian Fed. 2015–. *Address:* Embassy of Japan, 129090 Moscow, Grokholskii per. 27, Russia (office). *Telephone:* (495) 229-25-50 (office). *Fax:* (495) 229-25-55 (office). *E-mail:* japan-info@japan.orc.ru (office). *Website:* www.ru.emb-japan.go.jp (office).

KOZYREV, Andrey Vladimirovich, CandHist; Russian politician; b. 27 March 1951, Brussels, Belgium; m. 2nd Elena Kozyreva; one d.; ed Moscow State Inst. of Int. Relations; worker, Kommunar factory, Moscow 1968–69; mem. staff, USSR Ministry of Foreign Affairs, various posts, to Head of Sector 1974–86, Head of Dept of Int. Orgs 1986–90; Minister of Foreign Affairs 1991–96; Deputy State Duma (Parl.) 1995–2000; mem. Bd of Dirs, Dir East European Div., ICN Pharmaceuticals 1998–; Lecturer, Moscow Inst. of Int. Relations 1996–. *Publications:* Transfiguration 1995; numerous articles on foreign policy. *Address:* International Office, MGIMO University, 76 Prospect Vernadskogo, 119454 Moscow; ICN Pharmaceuticals, Uscheva str. 24, 119048, Moscow, Russia. *Telephone:* (495) 434-9066 (MGIMO). *E-mail:* umosmgimo@gmail.com.

KPAYEDO, Kokou; Togolese administrator and diplomatist; *Permanent Representative to United Nations;* b. 27 Sept. 1961, Lome; ed L'École nationale d'administration du Togo, l'Institut International de droit du développement, l'Université du Bénin; held various positions in Ministry of Foreign Affairs and Cooperation since 1991, Chef de Cabinet 2001–03, Minister Counsellor Embassy of Togo, France 2003–09, also Perm. Del. to UNESCO, Paris 2003–09, Sec.-Gen. Ministry of Foreign Affairs and Cooperation 2009–14; Amb. to Canada 2014–16; Perm. Rep. to UN 2016–; Kt of Order of the Mono. *Address:* Permanent Mission of Togo, 112 E 40th Street, New York, NY 10016, USA (office). *Telephone:* (212) 490-3455 (office). *Fax:* (212) 983-6684 (office). *E-mail:* togo@un.int (office). *Website:* www.togodiplomatie.info (office).

KRABBÉ, Jeroen Aart; Dutch actor, artist and director; b. 5 Dec. 1944; m. Herma van Geemert; three s.; ed Acad. of Fine Arts and Toneel Drama School, Amsterdam; acted in repertory theatre and formed own acting co. within the Netherlands; Commdr, Order of the Netherlands Lion 1999; Best Actor Award, Madrid, Sorrento, Oxford 1984, Anne Frank Medal 1985, Golden Heart of Rotterdam 1986, Golden Calf Award 1996, Frans Banninick Cocq Medal 2014. *Theatre includes:* The Diary of Anne Frank, Clouds, Relatively Speaking, How the Other Half Lives, Cyrano de Bergerac, Danton's Death, Love's Labours Lost, Sleuth, A Day in the Death of Joe Egg, Sweet Bird of Youth, Love Letters, Amadeus 2005, Vaslav 2014. *Films include:* Soldier of Orange 1977, A Flight of Rainbirds 1981, The Fourth Man 1984, The Shadow of Victory 1985, Turtle Diary, No Mercy 1987, The Living Daylights, A World Apart, Crossing Delancey, Melancholia 1989, The Prince of Tides 1991, Stalin 1991, Kafka 1991, King of the Hill 1991, The Fugitive 1993, Farinelli 1994, Immortal Beloved 1994, The Disappearance of García Lorca 1995, Business for Pleasure 1996, The Honest Courtesan 1996, Cinderella 1997, Left Luggage (directorial debut; Berlin Film Festival Award 1998) 1997, Dangerous Beauty 1998, Discovery of Heaven (actor and dir, Rembrandt Best Film Award 2001) 2001, Ocean's Twelve 2004, Deuce Bigalow 2004, Man with a Camera 2004, Snuff 2006, Albert Schweitzer (title role) 2009, Transporter 3 2008, Yankee Go Home 2009, Only Decent People 2012, Tula: the Revolt 2013. *Television includes:* William of Orange (Netherlands), Miami Vice, Dynasty, One for the Dancer, Sweet Weapon, Only Love, Jesus, Stalin (all American TV), Midsomer Murders 2008, Verborgen gebreken (series) 2009, In Therapy (series) 2011, A House for Vincent (series) 2013, The Man with the Hammer (series) 2013, Snowwhite (play) 2014; host of talk shows; numerous roles in plays and series. *Publications:* The Economy Cookbook, Jeroen Krabbé: Painter, The Demise of Abraham Reiss: Nine Paintings by Jeroen Krabbé, Dum Vivimus Vivamus: 14 Paintings by Jeroen Krabbé 2013. *Telephone:* (20) 7287-0077 (Jeremy Conway, London) (office). *E-mail:* jermey@conwayvg.com (office). *Address:* Van Eeghenstraat 107, 1071 EZ Amsterdam, The Netherlands.

KRAEHE, Graham J., AO; Australian business executive; *Chairman, Bluescope Steel Ltd;* ed Adelaide Univ.; fmr Man. Dir Pacifica Ltd and WH Wylie Ltd (now Monroe); Man. Dir Southcorp Ltd 1994–2001; apptd Dir National Australian Bank Ltd 1997, Chair. 2004–05; mem. Bd of Dirs BHP Steel Ltd (now Bluescope Steel Ltd) 2002–, currently Chair.; mem. Bd of Dirs Brambles Ltd 2000–2004 (resgnd), 2005–, Deputy Chair. 2007–08, Chair. 2008–; mem. Reserve Bank of Australia Bd 2007–11; mem. Bd of Dirs Djerriwarrh Investments Ltd 2002–; mem. Prime Minister's Business Advisory Council 2013–; fmr Nat. Pres. Metal Trade Industry Assn; Chair. Australian Future Directions Forum. *Address:* Bluescope Steel Ltd, Level 11, 120 Collins Street, Melbourne, Vic. 3000, Australia (office). *Telephone:* (3) 9666-4000 (office). *Fax:* (3) 9666-4111 (office). *Website:* www.bluescopesteel.com (office).

KRAFT, Christopher Columbus, Jr., BS; American engineer and space agency administrator (retd); b. 28 Feb. 1924, Phoebus, Va; s. of Christopher Columbus Kraft and Vanda Olivia Kraft (née Suddreth); m. Elizabeth Anne Turnbull 1950; one s. one d.; ed Virginia Polytechnic Inst.; mem. Langley Aeronautical Lab., Nat. Advisory Cttee for Aeronautics 1945; selected to join Space Task Group on Project Mercury 1958; Flight Dir of all Mercury Missions: head of mission operations Gemini program; Dir of Flight Operations, Manned Spacecraft Center 1963–69; elected mem. Nat. Acad. of Eng 1970; Deputy Dir Johnson Space Center 1970–72; Dir NASA Johnson Space Center 1972–82; Fellow, American Inst. of Aeronautics and Astronautics 1966, American Astronautical Soc.; Chevalier, Légion d'honneur 1976; Hon. DEng (Indiana Inst. of Tech.) 1966, (St Louis Univ., Ill.) 1967, (Villanova) 1979; Arthur S. Fleming Award 1963, NASA Outstanding Leadership Award 1963, Spirit of St Louis Medal, American Soc. of Mechanical Engineers 1967, NASA Distinguished Service Medal (twice) 1969, Nat. Civil Service League Career Service Award 1976, W. Randolph Lovelace Award (American Astronautical Soc.) 1977, Daniel and Florence Guggenheim Award (Int. Astronautics Fed.) 1978, AAIA von Karman Lectureship Award 1979, Goddard Memorial Trophy 1979, Roger W. Jones Award 1979, inducted into Virginia Aviation Hall of Fame 1979. *Publications:* Flight: My Life in Mission Control 2001.

KRAFT, Vahur, BA; Estonian banker; *Chairman, AS Sangar;* b. 11 March 1961, Tartu; s. of Ülo Kraft and Aime Kraft; m. Anne Kraft 1990; one s.; ed Tartu Univ.; with Eesti Hoiupank (Estonian Savings Bank), rising to Head of Br. 1984–90; Vice-Chair. Bd Dirs Eesti Sotsiaalpank (Estonian Social Bank) 1990–91; Deputy Gov. Eesti Pank (Bank of Estonia) 1991–95, Gov. 1995–2005, Vice-Gov. for Estonia of IMF 1992–95, Gov. 1995–2005; New Country Man. for Nordea Bank Findland Plc (Estonia Br.) 2005–15; Chair. AS Sangar 2015–; Chair. Bd of Trustees Tartu Univ. Foundation; Chair. Supervisory Bd Estonian Deposit Guarantee Fund; mem. Supervisory Council, Financial Supervision Authority, Council of the Stabilization Reserves, Bd Centre for Strategic Initiatives; Hon. mem. Tallinn Jr Chamber of Commerce; Order of White Star, Second Class. *Address:* Sangar AS, Sopruse pst 2, 50050 Tartu, Estonia (office). *Telephone:* 730-7300 (office). *E-mail:* sangar@sangar.ee (office). *Website:* www.sangar.ee (office).

KRAGGERUD, Egil, DPhil; Norwegian classical philologist and academic; *Professor Emeritus of Classical Philology, University of Oslo;* b. 7 July 1939, S Høland, Akershus; s. of John Kraggerud and Borghild Westeren; m. Beate Sinding-Larsen 1963; three s. one d.; ed Oslo Katedralskole and Oslo Univ.; Research Fellow, Univ. of Oslo 1965–67, Lecturer in Classics 1967–68, Prof. of Classical Philology 1969–2002, Prof. Emer. 2002–; Ed. Symbolae Osloenses 1972–94; mem. Norwegian Acad. of Science and Letters, Royal Norwegian Soc. of Sciences and Letters, Acad. Europaea; Thorleif Dahl's Literary Award 1992. *Publications:* Aeneisstudien 1968, Horaz und Actium 1984, Aeneiden (seven vols) 1983–89; about 100 articles in int. journals. *Leisure interests:* skiing, concerts. *Address:* Bygdöy allé 13 A, 0257 Oslo, Norway. *Telephone:* 22-44-27-44. *E-mail:* egil.kraggerud@ifikk.uio.no. *Website:* egil.kraggerud.no.

KRAGULY, Radovan; British artist; b. 10 Sept. 1935, Prijedor, Yugoslavia (now Bosnia and Herzegovina); s. of Dragoja Kraguly and Mileva Kraguly; m. Snezana-Nena Kraguly; ed Acad. of Fine Arts, Belgrade, Cen. School of Arts and Crafts, London; Lecturer, Cambridge School of Art and Tech. –1965, Manchester Coll. of Art 1965–67, London Coll. of Printing and Design 1967–69, Ecole des Beaux Arts, Mons 1969–78, Parson School of Art and Design 1978–88; represented in perm. and major collections at Museum of Modern Art, Paris, British Museum, Victoria and Albert Museum, Museum of Modern Art, New York, Univ. of Leicester Library, Library of Congress, Washington, DC, City Art Gallery, Sarajevo, Art Council of Wales, Cardiff, Power Gallery, Sydney, Prenten Cabinet, Brussels, Nat. Museum and Gallery of Wales, Cardiff, Fond Nat. d'Art Contemporain, Paris, Manchester City Art Gallery, City Art Gallery, Banja Luka, Nat. Library of Wales, Aberystwyth, The Whitworth Art Gallery, Manchester, South London Art Gallery; mem. Acad. of Arts and Sciences, Republika Srpska; numerous prizes and awards, including Printmaking Prize (Jazu-Zagreb) 1962, Yugoslav Trienale Prize 1967, The Young Contemporary BiH, Sarajevo 1967, Printmaking Prize, April Summit, Zenica 1973, Galerija graficki kolektiv, Belgrade for Best Print of the Year 1975, Printmaking Prize, Yugoslav Art, Sarajevo 1975, 1976, Grafica Creativa, Helsinki 1975, Int. Grand Prix, Fondation Pierre Cornette de St Cyr (Paris) 1978, Major Print Prize, Biennale of Yugoslav Art, New York 1978, Grand Prix and Purchase Prize, Int. Drawing Biennale, Rijeka 1980, Major Print Prize, Salon, Dubrovnik 1980, Major Print Prize, Yugoslav Graphic Art, Zagreb 1982, Prix de Gravure, Festival d'Automne, Clermont Ferrand 1982, Major Print Prize, XVIème Salon d'Hiver, Herceg Novi 1983, Prix de Dessin, Kabinet Grafike, Zagreb 1983. *Publications include:* La Vache dans l'imaginaire 1989, The Imaginary Cow of Kraguly 1990, Kraguly – Gallery Vera Van Laer 1992, Hathor: Voies Lactées Kraguly 1995, Kraguly Hathor: VLK 1998. *Address:* 22 rue Quincampoix, 75004 Paris, France (home). *Telephone:* 1-42-74-70-47 (home). *Fax:* 1-42-74-70-47 (home). *E-mail:* kraguly@yahoo.com (home). *Website:* www.kraguly.co.uk (home).

KRÄHENBÜHL, Pierre, BA; Swiss international organization executive; *Commissioner-General, United Nations Relief and Works Agency for Palestine Refugees in the Near East (UNRWA);* b. 1966; m.; three c.; ed Univ. of Geneva; began a career in journalism and photography, but then began work at Lutheran World Fed.; joined Int. Cttee of Red Cross (ICRC) 1991, first served in field operations as del. in El Salvador and Peru, given managerial responsibilities in Afghanistan 1993–95, and subsequently in Bosnia and Herzegovina, served as Head of Operations for Cen. and South-Eastern Europe in Geneva, personal adviser to Jakob Kellenberger (Pres. ICRC) 2000–02, Dir of Operations 2002–; Commr-Gen. UNRWA 2013–. *Address:* United Nations Relief and Works Agency for Palestine Refugees in the Near East (UNRWA), Bayader Wadi Seer, POB 140157, Amman, 11814, Jordan (office). *Telephone:* (6) 5808100 (office). *Fax:* (6) 5808335 (office). *E-mail:* unrwa-pio@unrwa.org (office). *Website:* www.unrwa.org (office).

KRAJICEK, Richard Peter Stanislav; Dutch fmr professional tennis player; *Tournament Director, ABN AMRO World Tennis Tournament;* b. 6 Dec. 1971, Rotterdam; s. of Petr Krajicek and Ludmilla Krajicek; m. Daphne Dekkers 1999; one s. one d.; right-handed (one-handed backhand); began playing tennis aged three; turned professional 1989; winner, Hong Kong 1991, Los Angeles 1992, 1993, Antwerp 1992, Barcelona 1994, Rosmalen (Netherlands) 1994, 1997, Sydney 1994, Stuttgart 1995, 1998, Rotterdam 1995, 1997, Wimbledon 1996, Tokyo 1997, St Petersburg 1998, London 1999, Miami 1999; career-high singles ranking of World No. 4 March 1999; Grand Slam Singles results: semifinal, Australian Open 1992, French Open 1993, winner, Wimbledon 1996, quarterfinalist, US Open 1997, 1999, 2000; semifinal, ATP World Tour Finals 1996; won 17 singles titles and 3 doubles titles to retirement in June 2003; now competes on Masters Tour; f. Richard Krajicek Foundation 1993; Tournament Dir ABN AMRO World Tennis Tournament, Rotterdam 2004–; Dutch Sportsman of the Year 1996, ATP Arthur Ashe Humanitarian of Year Award 2000. *Publications:* Een half jaar netpost (with Tino Bakker) 2003, Naar de top (with Anja de Crom) 2005, Harde Ballen 2005, Honger naar de bal 2006, Alle ballen verzamelen 2007. *Leisure interests:* basketball, golf. *Address:* Richard Krajicek Foundation, Johan de Wittlaan 15, 2517 JR The Hague (office); ABN AMRO World Tennis Tournament, Ahoy Rotterdam NV, PO Box 5106, 3008 AC Rotterdam, The Netherlands. *Telephone:* (70) 3387445 (The Hague) (office); (10) 2933300 (Rotterdam). *E-mail:* info@krajicek.nl (office). *Website:* www.krajicek.nl (office); www.abnamrowtt.com; www.atpworldtour.com/Tennis/Players/Kr/R/Richard-Krajicek.aspx.

KRALL, Diana; Canadian singer, pianist, composer and jazz vocalist; b. 16 Nov. 1966, Nanaimo, BC; m. Elvis Costello; ed Berklee Coll., USA; began classical piano aged four; regular tours of North America, Britain, Europe and the Far East. *Film appearance:* De-Lovely 2004. *Recordings include:* albums: Steppin' Out 1993, Only Trust Your Heart 1994, All For You 1995, Love Scenes 1997, When I Look In Your Eyes (Grammy Award Best Jazz Vocal) 1999, The Look Of Love 2001, Heartdrops: Vince Benedetti Meets Diana Krall 2003, The Girl in the Other Room 2004, Christmas Songs 2005, From This Moment On (Juno Award for Vocal Jazz Album Of The Year 2007) 2006, The Very Best Of Diana Krall 2007, Quiet Nights 2009, Glad Rag Doll 2012, Wallflower 2015, Turn up the Quiet 2017, Love is Here to Stay (with Tony Bennett) 2018. *Address:* Macklam/Feldman Management, 1505 West Second Avenue, Suite 200, Vancouver, BC V6H 3Y4, Canada (office). *Telephone:* (604) 734-5945 (office). *Fax:* (604) 732-0922 (office). *E-mail:* info@mfmgt.com (office). *Website:* www.mfmgt.com (office); www.dianakrall.com.

KRALL, Hanna; Polish journalist and writer; b. 20 May 1935, Warsaw; m. Jerzy Szperkowicz; one d.; ed Univ. of Warsaw; reporter, Życie Warszawy 1955–66, Polityka 1966–, corresp. in Moscow 1966–69; corresp., Tygodnik Powszechny, Gazeta Wyborcza; freelance writer early 1980s–; Solidarity Cultural Prize 1985, Prize of Minister of Culture and Art 1989, J. Shocken Literary Prize (Germany), Kulture Foundation Award 1999, Leipzig Book Fair Award 2000, Herder Prize 2005, Ricarda Huch Award (Germany) 2008. *Publications include:* Na wschód od Arbatu (East of the Arbat) 1972, Zdążyć przed Panem Bogiem (Shielding the Flame) 1977, Sześć odcieni bieli (Six Shades of White) 1978, Sublokatorka (The Sub-tenant) 1985, Hipnoza (Hypnosis) 1989, Trudności ze wstawaniem (Difficulties Getting Up) 1990, Taniec na cudzym weselu (Dance at a Stranger's Wedding) 1993, Co się stało z naszą bajką (What's Happened to Our Fairy Tale) 1994, Dowody na istnienie (Proofs of Existence) 1996, Tam już nie ma żadnej rzeki (There is No River There Anymore) 1998, To ty jesteś Daniel (So You Are Daniel) 2001, Wyjątkowo długa linia (Incredible Long Line) 2004, Król kier znów na wylocie (King of Hearts) 2006, Różowe Strusie Pióra (Rosy Ostrich Feathers) 2009. *Address:* Stowarzyszenie Pisarzy Polskich, ul. Krakowskie Przedmieście 87/89, 00-079 Warsaw, Poland (office). *Telephone:* (22) 6433164 (home). *Fax:* (22) 6433164 (home).

KRAMAR, Marjan, BEcons; Slovenian business executive; *President of the Management Board, Nova Ljubljanska Banka d.d.;* ed Univ. of Ljubljana; began career with Helios Domzale 1982; Dir of Planning, Analyses and Business Counselling, Ljubljanska Banka Trbovlje 1983–88; mem. Man. Bd Gradbeno Podjetje SGD Beton 1988–89; Adviser to Slovenian Rep., SFRY Presidency 1989–91; Head of Prime Minister's Cabinet 1991–94; mem. Man. Bd Slovene Export Corpn 1994–2004, Pres. 1998–2004; Pres. Man. Bd Nova Ljubljanska Banka d.d. 2004–; Chair. Supervisory Bd ETI Elektroelement Izlake; fmr Vice-Chair. Supervisory Bd Revoz. *Address:* Nova Ljubljanska Banka d.d., Trg republike 2, 1520 Ljubljana, Slovenia (office). *Telephone:* (1) 4250155 (office). *Fax:* (1) 4250331 (office). *E-mail:* info@nlb.si (office). *Website:* www.nlb.si (office).

KRAMER, Daniel; American opera and theatre director; b. 15 Jan. 1977; ed Northwestern Univ., Ecole de Mime Corporeal Dramatique, UK, Int. School of Commedia dell'arte, Circus Space, UK; Assoc. Artistic Dir, Gate Theatre, Notting Hill 2004–06; Creative Assoc., Royal Shakespeare Co. 2005–06; Assoc., Young Vic 2008–12; Artistic Dir, ENO 2016–19; fmr guest artist and Prof., Harvard Univ. 2015, Brown Univ., New York Univ., Northwestern Univ., Guildhall School of Music and Drama; Fellow, NYC Drama League 1999. *Productions include:* Through the Leaves (Southwark Playhouse, Duchess Theatre, London West End) 2003, Hair, Woyzeck (Gate Theatre, Notting Hill) 2004–05, Bent (Trafalgar Studios, West End) 2006, Angels in America (Headlong, Glasgow Citizens Theatre, Lyric Hammersmith) 2007, Punch and Judy (ENO, Grand Théâtre Geneva) (South Bank Show Award for Outstanding Achievement in Opera) 2008, Bluebeard's Castle (ENO, Mariinsky and Bolshoi Theatre) (Golden Mask Award, ENO) 2009, Pictures from an Exhibition (Sadler's Wells, Young Vic) 2009, Carmen (Vlaamse Opera, Opera North) 2011, Pélleas et Mélisande (Mariinsky and Bolshoi Theatre) 2012, King Kong (Regent Theatre, Australia) 2013, The Serpent (Brown/Trinity Rep) 2014, Tristan and Isolde (ENO) 2016. *Address:* United Agents LLP, 12-26 Lexington Street, London, W1F 0LE, England (office). *Telephone:* (20) 3214–0800 (office). *Website:* www.unitedagents.co.uk/daniel-kramer (office).

KRAMER, Richard (Rich) J., BS; American business executive; *Chairman, President and CEO, Goodyear Tire & Rubber Company;* b. 30 Oct. 1963, Cleveland, Ohio; m.; four c.; ed John Carroll Univ., Ohio; certified public accountant; fmr Partner with PricewaterhouseCoopers, where he worked for 13 years; joined Goodyear Tire & Rubber Co. as Vice-Pres., Corp. Finance 2000, Vice-Pres., Finance for North American Tire 2002–03, Sr Vice-Pres., Strategic Planning and Restructuring 2003–04, Exec. Vice-Pres. and Chief Financial Officer 2004–07, Pres. North American Tire business unit 2007–10, COO Goodyear Tire & Rubber Co. 2009–10, mem Bd of Dirs Feb. 2010–, Pres. and CEO Goodyear Tire & Rubber Co. April 2010–, Chair. Oct. 2010–; mem Bd of Dirs Sherwin-Williams Co. 2012–; mem Bd of Trustees, John Carroll Univ. 2007–. *Address:* Goodyear Tire & Rubber Co., 200 Innovation Way, Akron, OH 44316-0001, USA (office). *Telephone:* (330) 796-2121 (office). *Fax:* (330) 796-2222 (office). *E-mail:* info@goodyear.com (office). *Website:* www.goodyear.com (office).

KRAMER, Baroness (Life Peer), cr. 2010, of Richmond Park in the London Borough of Richmond upon Thames; **Susan Veronica Kramer,** BA, MBA; British politician and business executive; *Minister of State for Transport;* b. 22 July 1950, Holborn, London, England; m. John Kramer (died 2006); two c.; ed St Paul's Girls' School, St Hilda's Coll., Oxford, Univ. of Illinois, USA; Pres. Oxford Union 1971; began career in finance, rose to become a Vice-Pres. of Citibank, Chicago; est. (with her husband) International Capital Partners, (advises on infrastructure projects, primarily in Cen. and Eastern Europe), currently Dir; mem. Women Liberal

Democrats Exec. 1997–2000, Liberal Democrat Fed. Exec. 2001–04, Chair. Twickenham and Richmond Liberal Democrats 2001–02; mem. London Regional Exec. 1997–2003; on Liberal Democrat party list for London constituency at European Parliament elections 1999; Liberal Democrat cand. for Mayor of London 2000; MP for Richmond Park, SW London 2005–10, apptd to Treasury Team and joined Treasury Select Cttee 2005; Liberal Democrat Shadow Int. Devt Sec. March–Dec. 2006, Shadow Trade and Industry Sec. 2006–07; Liberal Democrat Amb. to The City of London and Chair. Environmental Taxation Taskforce 2006; Shadow Transport Sec. 2007; Chancellor for the Duchy of Lancaster 2007; Shadow Minister for the Cabinet Office 2007; Families Spokesperson 2007–09; Minister of State for Transport 2013–; Trustee, Kingston Trust, Richmond Park Charitable Trust. *Publication:* contributed chapter to the Orange Book, on using market mechanisms to achieve environmental goals 2004; numerous articles. *Address:* Department for Transport, Great Minster House, 33 Horseferry Road, London, SW1P 4DR (office); House of Lords, London, SW1A 0PW, England (office). *Telephone:* (300) 330-3000 (Dept) (office); (20) 7219-1492 (House of Lords) (office). *E-mail:* kramers@parliament.uk (office). *Website:* www.gov.uk/government/organisations/department-for-transport (office); www.susankramer.co.uk.

KRAMMER, Peter Heinrich, MD; German immunologist and academic; *Head of Division of Immunogenetics, German Cancer Research Centre;* b. 2 April 1946, Rheydt; ed Univ. of Freiburg, in St Louis, USA and Lausanne, Switzerland; Internship in Internal Medicine and Pathology, Univ. of Freiburg, Univ. Hosp. and Inst. of Pathology 1971–72, Study mem., Low Molecular Weight Nuclear RNA 1972, Internship in Surgery 1972–73; mem. Basel Inst. for Immunology, Switzerland 1973–75; Assoc., German Cancer Research Centre, Inst. for Immunology and Genetics, Heidelberg 1976, Acting Head, Div. of Immunogenetics 1981–88, Head 1989–, Acting Dir 1990–, apptd Speaker, Tumorimmunology Program 1993; mem. Max-Planck Inst. for Immunology, Freiburg 1976; Visiting Prof., Dept of Microbiology, Univ. of Texas Health Science Center at Dallas, Tex., USA 1981; Visiting Scientist, Centre for Molecular Biology, Heidelberg 1984–85; Dir, Nat. Centre for Tumor Diseases 2010–; mem. German Immunological Soc. 1973, American Asscn for Cancer Research, European Molecular Biology Org. 1999, Apogenix Foundation 2000; mem. Medical Faculty, Heidelberg Univ. 1978; mem. Scientific Cttee Health Research Council; mem. Scientific Bd German Cancer Research Centre 1978–83, 1990–94, 1995–97, 1997–2000; mem. Editorial Bd Immunology Letters, Immunobiology, Cell Death and Differentiation, Cancer Research, European Journal of Immunology, Journal of Clinical Investigation, International Journal of Cancer; Order of Merit 1991; King Phillip Award for Leukemia Research 1991, Robert Koch Prize 1995, Behring Lecturer 1995, Meyenburg Prize 1996, Heinz-Ansmann Prize 1996, Kitasato-Behring Prize 1996, German Cancer Prize 1996, Cancer Research Award, Wilhelm Warner Foundation 1997, Avery Landsteiner Prize 1998, Theodor Kocher Lecture 2000, Ludwick Hirszfeld Medal, Polish Soc. for Experimental and Clinical Immunology 2000, Ernst-Jung Prize for Medicine 2000, Norman Heatley Lecturer, Univ. of Oxford, UK 2000, Annual MRC Lecturer, SOT Meeting 2001, Genius Biotech Award, Apogenix 2001, Lautenschläger Research Prize 2003, First Int. Cell Death Soc. Prize 2004, Career Award, European Cell Death Org. 2005, German Cancer Aid Prize 2011, Johann Georg Zimmermann Medal 2012. *Publications:* more than 400 articles in medical and scientific journals. *Address:* Tumorimmunology Program, Deutsches Krebsforschungszentrum, Im Neuenheimer Feld 280, 69120 Heidelberg, Germany (office). *Telephone:* (6221) 423718 (office). *Fax:* (6221) 411715 (office). *E-mail:* p.krammer@dkfz-heidelberg.de (office). *Website:* www.dkfz.de/en/immungenetik (office).

KRAMNIK, Vladimir Borisovich; Russian chess grandmaster; b. 25 June 1975, Tuapse, Krasnodar Krai, Russian SFSR, USSR; m. Marie-Laure Germon 2006; one s. one d.; started playing chess aged four; cand. for Master title 1986; Grandmaster title 1991; World Champion among young people 16–18 years of age, winner World Chess Olympiads Manila 1992, Moscow 1994, Yerevan 1996; winner major int. tournaments and matches; took part in World Championship 1993; ranked No. 1 world player (youngest holder) Jan.–June 1996, Jan.–March 2008; won match against Gary Kasparov for World Championship Oct. 2000; Classical World Chess Champion 2000–06, undisputed World Chess Champion 2006–07 (lost title to Viswanathan Anand 2007); ranked no. 3 by World Chess Fed. (FIDE) Dec 2016, apptd Continental Asst for Europe, also Councillor, Planning and Devt Comm. 2019–; retd from professional competition 2019; Chess Oscar 2000, 2006; Honoured Master of Sports of Russia. *Notable tournament victories:* Russian Championship, Kuibyshev (classical) 1990, World Championship (U18), Guarapuava (classical) 1991, Chalkidiki (classical) 1992, Overall Result PCA Intel Grand Prix 1994, Dortmund (classical) 1995, Horgen (classical) 1995, Belgrade (classical) 1995, Monaco 1996, Dos Hermanas (classical) 1996, Dortmund (classical) 1996, Dos Hermanas (classical) 1997, Dortmund (classical) 1997, Tilburg (classical) 1997, Wijk aan Zee (classical) 1998, Dortmund (classical) 1998, Monaco (blindfold and rapidplay) 1998, Monaco (blindfold and rapidplay) 1999, Linares (classical) 2000, Dortmund (classical) 2000, Match Kramnik v. Leko (rapidplay) 2001, Match Botvinnik memorial Kramnik v. Kasparov (classical) 2001, Match Botvinnik memorial Kramnik v. Kasparov (rapidplay) 2001, Monaco (blindfold and rapidplay) 2001, Match Kramnik v. Anand (rapidplay) 2001, Dortmund (classical) 2001, Match Advanced Chess Kramnik v. Anand (León) 2002, Linares (classical) 2003, Cap d'Agde (France) 2003, Handicap Simul (classical) 2004, Kramnik v. German Nat. Team 2004, Linares (classical) 2004, Monaco (overall result) 2004, Gold Medal at Turin Olympiad with overall best performance 2006, Dortmund (classical) 2006, Monaco (blindfold and rapidplay) 2007, Dortmund (classical) 2007, Tal Memorial 2007, Dortmund 2009, Zurich (rapidplay) 2009, Tal Memorial 2009, President's Cup in Baku (rapidplay) 2010, Bilbao Grand Slam Final 2010, Dortmund 2011, Hoogeveen 2011, London Chess Classic 2011, Chess World Cup 2013. *Publications:* Mikhail Tal I-III (2017 Games) 3 Chess Books 1994, Positional Play (co-author) 1996, Kramnik: My Life and Games (autobiog. with Takov Damsky) 2000, Proryv (co-author) 2000, Chess Gems: 1,000 Combinations You Should Know (with Igor Sukhin) 2007, The Zurich Chess Club, 1809–2009 (with Richard Foster) 2011. *Telephone:* (495) 495-32-72 (Moscow) (home). *Website:* www.kramnik.com.

KRAMP-KARRENBAUER, Annegret; German politician; *Chair, Christlich-Demokratische Union Deutschlands;* b. 9 Aug. 1962, Völklingen, Saarland; d. of Hans Kramp and Else Kramp; m. Helmut Karrenbauer; three c.; ed Trier Univ., Saarland Univ.; mem. Bundestag (Federal Ass., parl.) for Saarland (CDU) March–Oct. 1998; mem. Landtag (Regional Ass.) of Saarland 1999–2018; Minister-Pres. of Saarland (first female) 2011–18; mem. Christlich-Demokratische Union Deutschlands (CDU) 1981–, mem. CDU Federal Presidency 2010–, Leader, CDU in Saarland 2011–18, Gen. Sec. CDU Feb.–Dec. 2018, Chair. 2018–; mem. Konrad Adenauer Foundation; mem. Senate, Max Planck Soc. *Address:* Christlich-Demokratische Union Deutschlands, Klingelhöferstr. 8, 10785 Berlin, Germany (office). *Telephone:* (30) 220700 (office). *Fax:* (30) 22070111 (office). *E-mail:* info@cdu.de (office). *Website:* www.cdu.de (office).

KRANJEC, Marko, PhD; Slovenian economist, academic and fmr central banker; b. 12 April 1940, Novo mesto; ed Faculty of Econs, Univ. of Ljubljana; fmr Asst Prof., Faculty of Public Admin, Univ. of Ljubljana, Prof. of Public Finance 2002–06; Head, Analysis Dept, Ljubljanska Bank 1968–70; Researcher, Inst. of Int. Econ. Research 1970–76, Research Adviser 1986–90; macroeconomist, OECD, Paris –1984; economist, IBRD (World Bank), Washington, DC 1984–86; first Minister of Finance of ind. Slovenia 1990–91; Vice-Gov. Banka Slovenije (Bank of Slovenia) 1991–97, Gov. 2007–13; Amb. to the EU, Brussels 1997–2002; mem. Governing Council European Cen. Bank, Govt's Strategic Council for Econ. Devt; fmr mem. Supervisory Bd Krka, Novo mesto; Silver Order of Freedom of Repub. of Slovenia 2001. *Address:* c/o Banka Slovenije (Bank of Slovenia), 1505 Ljubljana, Slovenska 35, Slovenia (office).

KRARUP, Thorleif, BSc, BComm; Danish business executive; *Chairman, ALK-Abelló A/S;* b. 1952; Chair. Man. Bd Nykredit 1987–91; Group CEO Tryg Nykredit Holding 1991–92; Group CEO Unidanmark 1992–2000; Chair. Exec. Bd Unibank 1992–2000; Deputy CEO Nordic Baltic Holding 2000; Group CEO Nordea 2000–02, Sr Vice-Pres. 2002–04; Chair. TDC –2006; Chair. Dangaard Telecom A/S 2006; mem. Bd of Dirs ALK-Abelló A/S 2005–, Chair. 2011–; mem. Bd of Dirs Bisca A/S Exiqon A/S (Chair.), Falck A/S (Vice-Chair.), H. Lundbeck A/S, The Lundbeck Foundation. *Address:* ALK-Abelló A/S, Bøge Allé 6, 2970 Hørsholm, Denmark (office). *Website:* www.alk-abello.com (office).

KRASHENINNIKOV, Pavel Vladimirovich, DJur; Russian lawyer and politician; b. 21 June 1964, Polevskoye, Sverdlovsk Region; m. Catherine Krasheninnikov; one s. one d.; ed Sverdlovsk Inst. of Law; teacher, Sverdlovsk Inst. of Law 1991–93; Lecturer, Moscow State Univ. 1994–; Deputy Head, Chief Dept of Housing Policy, State Cttee on Construction of Russian Fed. 1993–; Head, Dept of Civil and Econ. Law, Ministry of Justice 1993–96; Deputy Chair. State Cttee on Antimonopoly Policy and Support of New Econ. Structures 1996–97; First Deputy Minister of Justice 1997–98, Acting Minister March 1998, Minister 1998–99; Co-ordinator, Pres., Comm. for Counteraction against Political Extremism in Russia 1998–99; mem. State Duma (Union of Right-Wing Forces faction) 1999–2003, Chair. Legis. Cttee 2000–03, re-elected as ind. (later joined Yedinaya Rossiya (United Russia) faction) 2003–, Chair. Cttee for Civil, Criminal, Arbitration and Remedial Legislation; Rector Russian School of Private Law 1999; State Counsellor of Justice, 1st Class 1997; Order of Friendship. *Publications:* Zhilishchnoe pravo 2006, Privatizatsiia zhil'ia: prava grazhdan do i posle privatizatsii 2006, Federal'nyi zakonotvorcheskii protsess 2009; more than 100 articles on private and public law. *Address:* State Duma, Okhotny ryad 1, 103265 Moscow, Russia (office). *Telephone:* (495) 292-92-10 (office). *Fax:* (495) 292-97-82 (office). *Website:* www.duma.gov.ru (office).

KRASIKOV, Anatoly Andreyevich, DHist; Russian journalist and academic; *Director, Center of Religious and Social Studies, Institute of Europe, Russian Academy of Sciences;* b. 3 Aug. 1931, Moscow; m.; one d.; ed Moscow Inst. of Int. Relations; mem. staff, USSR Telegraph Agency TASS 1955–92, apptd Head of French office 1966, Deputy Dir-Gen. ITAR-TASS 1978–92; Head of Presidential Press and Information Office and Exec. Sec., Council on Interaction with Religious Orgs, Office of Russian Pres. Yeltsin 1992–96; Chief Researcher, Inst. of Europe, Russian Acad. of Sciences 1996–, also Dir Center of Religious and Social Studies; Vice-Chair. USSR (later Russian) Nat. Comm. for UNESCO 1981–94; Chair. Int. Christianity Cttee 1996; Head, Centre for Studies of Problems of Religion and Soc.; Pres. Russian Chapter, Int. Religious Liberty Asscn 1997–2003, Hon. Pres. Euro-Asia Chapter 2004–; Public Policy Scholar, Woodrow Wilson Center, Washington, DC 2000; Galina Starovoitova Fellow on Human Rights and Conflict Resolution, Kennan Inst., Washington, DC 2004. *Publications include:* Church-State Relations in Russia 1998, Proselytism and Religious Liberty in Russia 1999, The Enigma of Liberty 2001, Russian Orthodoxy: Striving for Monopoly? 2004. *Leisure interests:* music, archives, tourism. *Address:* Center of Religious and Social Studies, Institute of Europe, 103873 Moscow, Mokhovaya str. 11, Bldg 3v, Russia (office). *Telephone:* (495) 692-23-04 (office). *E-mail:* ankrasikov@gmail.com. *Website:* www.ieras.ru/english/centrerel.htm (office).

KRASIN, Yury Andreyevich, DSc; Russian political scientist and academic; *Head, Department for Analysis of Socio-Political Processes, Institute of Sociology, Russian Academy of Sciences;* b. 7 June 1929, Penza; one d.; ed Leningrad State Univ., Inst. of Philosophy, Russian Acad. of Sciences; Lecturer, Asst Prof., Leningrad State Pedagogical Inst. 1952–60; Asst Prof., Inst. of Professional Skill Improvement, Moscow State Univ. 1960–63; Sr Fellow, Inst. of Philosophy USSR (now Russian) Acad. of Sciences 1963; consultant, Int. Div. CP Cen. Cttee 1963–75; Prof., Moscow Inst. of Professional Skill Improvement at Moscow State Univ. 1963–75; Prof., Head of Dept, Prorector, Acad. of Social Sciences at CPSU Cen. Cttee 1975–87; Rector Inst. of Social Sciences at CPSU Cen. Cttee 1987–91; Dir-Gen. Foundation of Social and Political Studies 1991–92; Dir Centre of Social Programmes, Int. Foundation of Social, Econ. and Politological Studies 1992–97; Head, Dept for Analysis of Socio-Political Processes, Inst. of Sociology, Russian Acad. of Sciences 1993–; Adviser, Gorbachev Foundation 1997–2011; Prof., Russian State Humanitarian Univ. 2009–; mem. Presidium Acad. of Political Science; mem. Russian Acad. of Natural Sciences; Medal for 'Labour Valour' 1961, Order 'Decoration of Esteem' 1971, Order 'Friendship of Peoples' 1979, Medal 'Veteran of Labour' 1985; Dr hc (Inst. of Sociology, Russian Acad. of Sciences) 2008; Lomonosov Prize of Moscow State Univ. 1968, USSR State Prize 1980, Pitirim Sorokin Silver Medal 2008, George Shahnasarov Medal, Russian Asscn of Political Science 2012. *Publications:* 20 books, including Dialectic of the Revolutionary Process 1972, Capitalism Today: Paradoxes of Development (co-author) 1989, Russia at the Crossroads: Authoritarianism or Democracy 1998, Russia: Quo Vadis? (with A. Galkin) 2003, Public Policy in Russia (ed.) 2005, Social Inequality and Public Policy (ed.) 2007, Metamorphoses of the Russian Reformation – Politological Subjects 2009; articles on social movts, democratic reform in Russia, civil, social and political matters. *Leisure interests:* classical music, skiing. *Address:* Institute of Sociology, Russian Academy of Sciences, 117218 Moscow, Krzhizhanovskogo str. 24/35, korp. 5 (office); 121433 Moscow, Malaya Philevskaya str. 44, Apt 11, Russia (home). *Telephone:* (495) 719-09-40 (office); (499) 144-29-83 (home). *Fax:* (495) 719-07-40 (office). *E-mail:* krasinyua@mtu-net.ru (home). *Website:* www.spbrc.nw.ru (office).

KRASNIQI, Agim; Kosovo politician; b. 3 Nov. 1964, Makoc; m.; three c.; ed Univ. of Prishtina; worked as accountant in private business 1989–2002; mem. Municipal Financing Council, Prishtina 1993–99; Financial Officer, Dept of Educ., Prishtina Regional Educ. Office Feb.–Sept. 2000; Man., Budget Dept, Central Fiscal Authority 2000–03; Dir, Budget Dept, Ministry of Finance 2003–14, Deputy Minister of Finance 2015–17, Minister of Finance 2017; mem. Lidhja Demokratike e Kosovës (LDK—Democratic League of Kosovo).

KRASNIQI, Jakup; Kosovo politician and teacher; b. 1 Jan. 1951, Negrofc/Negrovce, Drenas/Glogovac municipality; m. Sevdije (Shala) Krasniqi; one s. three d.; ed secondary school in Prishtina, Univ. of Prishtina, Univ. of Kosovo; teacher, schools in Fatos and Arllat 1972–77, in secondary school in Drenas 1976–77, in Arllat and in secondary school in Skënderaj/Srbica 1979–81, in secondary school 'Skënderbeu' in Drenas 1991–94; Chair. Educ. Council, Drenas 1995–98; clandestine political activity 1973–81, political prisoner 1981–91; Deputy of unconstituted Parl. of Kosovo 1992–98; Spokesman, HQ of Kosovo Liberation Army (KLA) 1998–99, mem. of HQ and of Political Directorate; Minister in Ministry for Reconstruction and Devt 1999–2000, in Ministry of Public Services 2002–04; Gen. Sec. Democratic Prosperity Party of Kosovo (PPDK), later Democratic Party of Kosovo (PDK) 1998–2003, re-elected Gen. Sec. 2005, currently Chair. Parl. Group of PDK; Deputy in first Legislation 2001–, Deputy, Second Mandate in Kosovo Ass. 2004, Leader of Parl. Group of PDK, Deputy, Third Mandate 2007–, Pres. Kosovo Ass. 2007–14, also Acting Pres. of Kosovo Sept. 2010–Feb. 2011, March–April 2011; mem. Presidency of Democratic League of Kosovo (LDK), Drenas br. 1991–99. *Publications include:* books: Kthesa e Madhe – Ushtria Çlirimtare e Kosovës 2006, Kosova in a Historical Context 2007, Një luftë ndryshe për Kosovën (A Different War for Kosova) 2007, Pavarësia si kompromis 2010, Lëvizja për Republikën e Kosovës 1981–1991 sipas shtypit shqiptar 2011, Pranvera e lirisë '81 2011, Flijimi për lirinë 2011, Guxo ta duash lirinë 2011, Pavarësi dhe personalitete (Në 100-vjetorin e Pavarësisë së Shqipërisë) 2012, Një histori e kontestuar (Kritikë librit të Oliver Jens Schmitt: "Kosova – histori e shkurtër e një treve qendrore ballkanike") 2013; numerous political and scientific articles published in daily papers, periodicals and scientific magazines. *Address:* Kuvendi i Kosovës/Skupština Kosova (Kosovo Assembly), 10000 Prishtina, Rruga Nënë Terezë, Kosovo (office). *Telephone:* (38) 20010004 (office); (38) 211186 (office). *Fax:* (38) 211188 (office). *E-mail:* info@assembly-kosova.org (office). *Website:* www.assembly-kosova.org (office).

KRASNOSELSKII, Vadim Nikolayevich; Russian government official, business executive and politician; *President of the 'Transnistrian Moldovan Republic';* b. 14 April 1970, Dauriya village, Transbaikal Dist, Chita Oblast (now Transbaikal Krai), Russian SFSR, USSR; m. Svetlana Krasnoselskaya, one s. two d.; ed studies in Odesa, Ukrainian SSR, mil. school in Kharkiv, Ukrainian SSR; father transferred to mil. base in Bender, Moldavian SSR 1978; joined security forces of 'Transnistrian Moldovan Republic' 1993, later became high-ranking official in Ministry of the Interior, Minister of the Interior 2007–12; began working in business 2012; mem. Supreme Council 2015–16, Speaker 2015–16; Pres. of the 'Transnistrian Moldovan Republic' 2016–. *Address:* Office of the President of the 'Transnistrian Moldovan Republic', 3300 Tiraspol, ul. Karla Marksa 187, Moldova (office). *Telephone:* (533) 6-27-20 (office); (533) 7-32-18. *Fax:* (533) 8-05-02 (office). *E-mail:* psp@president.gospmr.org (office). *Website:* president.gospmr.ru (office).

KRASTS, Guntars; Latvian economist and politician; b. 16 Oct. 1957, Rīga; m.; three s.; ed Latvian State Univ.; researcher, Inst. of Agric. Econs 1983–91; Chair. Exec. Bd RANG Ltd 1991–95; Minister of Econs 1995–97; Prime Minister of Latvia 1997–98; Vice-Prime Minister for EU Affairs 1998–99; Chair. Saeima (Parl.) Foreign Affairs Cttee 1998–2002, European Affairs Cttee 2002–04; MEP 2004–09, Vice-Chair. Cttee on Econ. and Monetary Affairs; Leader, Libertas Latvia (slate of MEP cands) 2009. *Publications include:* numerous publs in Latvia and abroad on econ. and foreign policy issues. *Leisure interests:* swimming, skiing.

KRAUSS, Alison; American country and bluegrass singer and musician (fiddle); b. 23 July 1971, Champaign, Ill.; m. Pat Bergeson (divorced 2001); one s.; singer, musician since age 14; lead singer with Union Station 1987–; Int. Bluegrass Music Asscn Awards for Female Vocalist of the Year 1990, 1991, 1993, 1995, Country Music Television Award for Independent Video of the Year (for I've Got That Old Feeling) 1991, Entertainer of the Year 1991, 1995, Country Music Asscn Awards for Female Vocalist of the Year, Single of the Year (for When You Say Nothing At All), Vocal Event of the Year (for Somewhere In The Vicinity Of The Heart, with Shenandoah), and Horizon Award 1995, Grammy Award for Female Country Vocal Performance (for Baby, Now That I've Found You) 1995, Country Music Television Award for Rising Video Star of the Year 1995, GAVIN Americana Artist of the Year 1995, Great British Country Music Award for Int. Female Vocalist of the Year 1996, for Int. Bluegrass Band of the Year 1997, 1998, 1999, 2000, Grammy Awards for Best Country Performance by a Duo or Group (for Looking In The Eyes Of Love), for Best Country Instrumental Performance (for Little Liza Jane) 1997, Gospel Music Asscn Dove Award for Bluegrass Recorded Song of the Year (for Children of the Living God, with Fernando Ortega) 1998, Canadian Country Music Award for Vocal/Instrumental Collaboration (for Get Me Through December, with Natalie MacMaster) 2000, Int. Bluegrass Music Asscn Award for Gospel Recorded Event of the Year (for I'll Fly Away, with Gillian Welch) 2001, Grammy Award for Country Performance by a Duo or Group (for The Lucky One) 2001, Grammy Award for Best Country Instrumental Performance (for Cluck Old Hen) 2003, Country Music Asscn Award for Best Video and Music Event (for Whiskey Lullaby, with Brad Paisley) 2004, Grammy Awards for Best Country Performance by a Duo or Group with Vocal (for Restless, with Union Station), for Best Country Instrumental Performance (for Unionhouse Branch with Union Station) 2006, for Best Pop Collaboration with Vocals (for Gone Gone Gone with Robert Plant) 2008, (for Rich Woman with Robert Plant) 2009, for Record of the Year (for Please Read the Letter with Robert Plant) 2009, for Best Country Collaboration with Vocals (for Killing the Blues with Robert Plant) 2009, CMA Award for Musical Event of the Year (for Gone Gone Gone with Robert Plant) 2008. *Recordings include:* albums: Different Strokes 1985, Too Late to Cry 1987, Two Highways (with Union Station) 1989, I've Got That Old Feeling (Grammy Award for Bluegrass Recording 1990, Int. Bluegrass Music Asscn Award for Album of the Year 1991) 1990, Every Time You Say Goodbye (with Union Station) (Grammy Award for Bluegrass Recording 1992, Int. Bluegrass Music Asscn Award for Album of the Year 1993) 1992, I Know Who Holds Tomorrow (with The Cox Family) (Grammy Award for Southern, Country or Bluegrass Gospel Album) 1994, Now That I've Found You: A Collection 1995, So Long So Wrong (with Union Station) (GAVIN Americana Album of the Year, Grammy Award for Best Bluegrass Album) 1997, Forget About It 1999, New Favorite (with Union Station) (Grammy Award for Best Bluegrass Album) 2001, Live (with Union Station) (Int. Bluegrass Music Asscn Awards Album of the Year, Grammy Award for Best Bluegrass Album 2003) 2002, Lonely Runs Both Ways (with Union Station) (Grammy Award for Best Country Album 2006) 2004, A Hundred Miles or More 2007, Raising Sand (with Robert Plant) (Grammy Awards for Album of the Year 2009, for Best Contemporary Folk/Americana Album 2009) 2007, Paper Airplane (with Union Station) (Grammy Award for Best Bluegrass Album 2012) 2011, Windy City 2017. *Address:* c/o Borman Entertainment, 611 Commerce Street, Nashville, TN 37203, USA (office); Union Station Land Inc., PO Box 121711, Nashville, TN 37212, USA. *Telephone:* (615) 320-3000 (office). *E-mail:* support@alisonkrauss.com. *Website:* www.alisonkrauss.com.

KRAUSZ, Ferenc, DipEng, DrTechn; Hungarian/Austrian physicist and academic; *Director, Max Planck Institute of Quantum Optics;* b. 17 May 1962, Mór, Hungary; m.; two c.; ed Eötvös Loránd Univ., Budapest, Budapest Univ. of Tech., Vienna Univ. of Tech.; Asst Prof., Vienna Univ. of Tech. 1996–98, Prof. of Electrical Eng 1999–2004; Dir Max Planck Inst. of Quantum Optics, Garching, Germany 2003–; Prof. of Physics, also Chair. of Experimental Physics, Ludwig-Maximilians-Univ., Munich 2004–; mem. Austrian Acad. of Sciences 2003–; Dr hc (Tech. Univ. Budapest) 2005; Austrian Physical Soc. Fritz Kohlrausch Award 1994, Federal Ministry of Science and Educ. START Award 1996, Ernst Abbe Foundation Carl Zeiss Award 1998, Federal Ministry of Science and Educ. Wittgenstein Award 2002, Julius Springer Award in Applied Physics (USA) 2003, Gottfried Wilhelm Leibniz Award Deutsche Forschungsgemeinschaft 2006, King Faisal Int. Prize for Science (co-recipient) 2013, Otto Hahn Prize 2013. *Publications:* one book (ed.), five book chapters and more than 100 papers on ultrashort-pulse laser physics, intense light–matter interactions, nonlinear optics, and atomic, plasma and x-ray physics. *Address:* Max Planck Institute of Quantum Optics, Hans-Kopfermann-Strasse 1, 85748 Garching (office); Lehrstuhl für Experimentalphysik, Department für Physik, Ludwig-Maximilians-University Munich, Am Coulombwall 1, 85748 Garching, Germany (office). *Telephone:* (89) 32905602 (office); (89) 28914013 (office). *Fax:* (89) 32905649 (office); (89) 28914141 (office). *E-mail:* krausz@lmu.de (office); ferenc.krausz@mpq.mpg.de (office); ferenc.krausz@physik.uni-muenchen.de. *Website:* www.attoworld.de (office); www.atto.physik.uni-muenchen.de/personen/professoren/krausz/index.html (office).

KRAUZE, Andrzej; Polish painter, illustrator and political cartoonist; b. 7 March 1947, Warsaw; m. Małgosia Krauze; three s.; ed Acad. of Fine Art, Warsaw; worked as cartoonist for periodicals Szpilki, Kultura, Solidarity Weekly 1970s; moved to London 1981; cartoonist for The Guardian, Sunday Telegraph, The Bookseller, New Society, New Statesman, Rzeczpospolita (Polish daily) and numerous other publs in UK, France and USA. *Publications include:* Nowość: Szczęście w aerozolu 1977, Lubta mnie: Wybór rysunków z lat 1976–78 1980, A year of martial law 1982, Drawings 1970–2003 2003, The Sleep of Reason... Drawings 1970–1989 2010, III wieża Babel w budowie 2011; Children's book: Zwierzęta pana Krauzego 1978, What's So Special About Today? 1984, Christopher Crocodile Cooks a Meal 1985. *E-mail:* krauze@andrzejkrauze.com. *Website:* www.andrzejkrauze.com.

KRAVCHENKO, Adm. Victor Andreyevich; Russian naval officer; b. 5 Dec. 1943, Bogdanovich, Sverdlovsk Region; m.; one d.; ed Higher Mil. Marine School, Mil. Marine Acad., Acad. of the Gen. Staff; served as Sr Asst, submarine Commdr, Head of staff, submarine div. Commdr, First Deputy Head of Staff, Black Sea Fleet 1968–91; First Deputy Commdr, Baltic Fleet 1991–96; Commdr, Black Sea Fleet 1996–98; Head of Gen. Staff, First Deputy C-in-C Russian Navy 1998–2005; Russian Acad. of Natural Sciences Hon. 'For Merits' Award; numerous other awards and decorations. *Address:* c/o General Staff of the Russian Navy, B. Kozlovsky Per. 6, 103175 Moscow, Russia.

KRAVCHUK, Leonid Makarovych, CandEconSc; Ukrainian politician and fmr head of state; b. 10 Jan. 1934, Velykyi Zhytyn (Poland, now in Rivne Oblast, Ukraine); s. of Makar Olexiyovich and Khima Ivanivna Kravchuk; m. Antonina Mikhailivna Kravchuk 1957; one s.; ed Kyiv State Univ. and Acad. of Social Sciences, Moscow; teacher of Political Economy, Chernovitsky Tech. School; party work since 1960, on staff Ukrainian CP Cen. Cttee 1970–; Head, Propaganda Dept 1980–88, Ideology Dept 1988–89, Sec., Cen. Cttee, mem. Politburo 1990; Chair. Ukrainian Supreme Soviet 1990–91; Pres. of Ukraine 1991–94; C-in-C Armed Forces of Ukraine 1991–94; mem. Verkhovna Rada (Parl.) 1994–2006; f. Mutual Understanding Movt 1994; mem. Social Democratic Party; Head, All-Ukrainian Union of Democratic Forces Zlagoda 1999–; Chair. State Cttee for Admin. Reforms 1997–99; Protector Mohyla Acad.-Nat. Univ. of Kyiv 1991; Head, Trusteeship Council, Children and Youth Activity Cen. of Ukraine 1992; Hon. Pres. East European Asscn of Businessmen; Dr hc (La Salle Univ., Phila, USA) 1992; Hero of Ukraine 2001, Order of Prince Yaroslav the Wise 2007, Order of Liberty 2014. *Publications include:* State and Authorities: Experience of Administrative Reforms 2001, We Have What We Have 2002. *Leisure interests:* chess, books, cinema. *Address:* Verkhovna Rada, 01008 Kyiv, vul. M. Hrushevskoho 5, Ukraine (office). *Telephone:* (44) 255-21-15 (office). *Fax:* (44) 253-32-17 (office). *E-mail:* umz@rada.gov.ua (office). *Website:* www.rada.gov.ua (office).

KRAVIS, Henry R., BA, MBA; American investment banker; *Co-Chairman and Co-CEO, Kohlberg Kravis Roberts & Co.;* b. 6 Jan. 1944, Tulsa, Okla; s. of Raymond Kravis and Bessie Kravis (née Roberts); m. 1st the late Diane Shulman (divorced); two c.; m. 2nd Carolyn Roehm 1985 (divorced 1993); m. 3rd Marie-Josée Drouin 1994; ed Loomis Chaffee School, Claremont McKenna Coll., Columbia Univ.; began career as Vice-Pres. Katy Industries, New York; Partner, Bear Stearns &

Co., New York 1969–76; Founding Partner, Kohlberg Kravis Roberts & Co. (investment bank), New York 1976, Sr Partner 1987, currently Co-Chair. and Co-CEO; Co-Chair. Bd of Overseers, Columbia Univ. Business School; Vice-Chair. Rockefeller Univ.; Chair. Emer. WNET, New York (public TV station); mem. Bd of Dirs Partnership for New York City (fmr Co-Chair.), Council on Foreign Relations, First Data Corpn, ICONIQ Capital, LLC, Duracell International, Inc., Safeway, Inc., AutoZone, Inc.; Founder and Chair. New York City Investment Fund; Co-founder Republican Leadership Council; mem. Business Council; Trustee, Mount Sinai Medical Center, Metropolitan Musuem of Art. *Leisure interest:* collecting art. *Address:* Kohlberg Kravis Roberts & Co., 9 West 57th Street, Suite 4200, New York, NY 10019, USA (office). *Telephone:* (212) 750-8300 (office). *Website:* www.kkr.com (office).

KRAVITZ, Lenny; American singer, musician (piano, guitar), songwriter and producer; b. 26 May 1964, New York; m. Lisa Bonet (divorced); actor, as teenager; mem. Calif. Boys Choir and Metropolitan Opera; solo artist 1989–; numerous tours world-wide, TV and live appearances; f. Kravitz Design, Miami 2005; Ordre des Arts et des Lettres 2011; BRIT Award for Best Int. Male 1994, Grammy Awards for Male Rock Vocal Performance 2000, 2001, American Music Award for Favorite Pop/Rock Male Artist 2002. *Recordings include:* albums: Let Love Rule 1989, Mama Said 1991, Are You Gonna Go My Way 1993, Circus 1995, 5 1998, Greatest Hits 2000, Lenny 2001, Baptism 2004, It Is Time For A Love Revolution 2008, Black and White America 2011, Strut 2014, Raise Vibration 2018. *Address:* Kravitz Design Inc, 13 Crosby Street, 5th Floor, New York, NY 10013, USA (office). *Telephone:* (212) 625-1644. *E-mail:* info@kravitzdesign.com. *Website:* www.kravitzdesign.com; www.lennykravitz.com.

KRAWCHECK, Sallie L., BA, MBA; American banker; b. 1965, Charleston, SC; m. Gary Appel; ed Univ. of North Carolina at Chapel Hill, Columbia Business School, New York; worked with Fortune magazine; worked for Salomon Brothers; worked for Donaldson, Lufkin & Jenrette; joined Sanford C. Bernstein stock research firm in 1994, Dir of Research 1998–2001, Chair. and CEO 2001–02; Chair. and CEO Smith Barney (div. of Citigroup) 2002–04, Chief Financial Officer and Head of Strategy 2004–07, Chair. and CEO Global Wealth Man. Div. 2007–08, mem. Man. Cttee Citigroup 2004–08; Pres. Global Wealth and Investment Man., Bank of America Corpn 2009–11, also mem. Exec. Man. Team; mem. Bd of Dirs Dell Inc., Motif Investing Inc. 2012–; mem. Advisory mem. Eurasia Group; mem. The Morehead Foundation's Cen. Selection Cttee; mem. Bd Gold Bullion International, Univ. of North Carolina at Chapel Hill Foundations, Carnegie Hall; recognized by the World Economic Forum as one of its Young Global Leaders, CNBC Business Leader of the Future Award 2007. *Address:* Motif Investing, Inc., PO Box 3548, Rancho Cordova, CA 95741, USA (office). *Telephone:* (855) 586-6843 (office). *E-mail:* service@motifinvesting.com (office). *Website:* www.motifinvesting.com (office).

KRAWIEC, Dariusz Jacek; Polish business executive; b. 23 Sept. 1967, Kołobrzeg; ed Poznań Univ. of Econs; with PEKAO SA (bank) 1992–97; Consultant, Man. Consulting Dept, Ernst & Young SA 1993; Asst, Sr Asst, Man. Asst and Man. in Corp. Finance Dept, Price Waterhouse Sp. z o.o. 1993–97; with Nomura International plc (investment bank), London, UK, responsible for Polish market 1997–2002; Pres. Man. Bd and Gen. Dir Impexmetal SA 1998–2002; Pres. Man. Bd Elektrim SA 2002; Man. Dir Sindicatum Ltd, London 2003–04; Pres. Man. Bd Action SA 2006–08; participant in PKN Orlen SA Man. Bd Mems' competition for a new term of office Feb. 2008, Vice-Pres. Man. Bd PKN Orlen SA June–Sept. 2008, Pres. Man. Bd and CEO Sept. 2008–15; Chair. Supervisory Bd Unipetrol a.s.; fmr Chair. Supervisory Bd Huta Aluminium 'Konin' SA, Metalexfrance SA, S and I SA, cemarket.com SA; mem. Supervisory Bd Impexmetal SA, Elektrim SA, PTC Sp. z o.o. (ERA GSM), Elektrim Telekomunikacja Sp. z o.o., Elektrim Magadex SA, Elektrim Volt SA, PTE AIG, Polkomtel SA.

KRAYER, Georg F., LLD; Swiss banking executive; *Honorary Chairman, Bank Sarasin & Company Ltd;* b. 30 May 1943, Basel; m. Luise Krayer; two d.; ed Univ. of Basel; joined A. Sarasin & Cie (now Bank Sarasin & Co. Ltd), Basel 1970, vocational training in Paris, France and New York, apptd Partner 1978, Chair. Bd of Admin 1997–2002, Chair. Bd of Dirs 1997–2008, Hon. Chair. 2008–; mem. Basel Stock Exchange 1978–92, Pres. 1989–92; Chair. Swiss Bankers Asscn 1992–2003; mem. Bd of Dirs Bâloise Holding Ltd 1995–2014, Vice-Chair. 2004–14; Hon. Dr rer. pol 2004. *Leisure interest:* rowing. *Address:* Bank Sarasin & Company Ltd, Elisabethenstrasse 62, 4002 Basel, Switzerland.

KREBS, Baron (Life Peer), cr. 2007, of Wytham in the County of Oxfordshire; **John Richard Krebs,** Kt, MA, DPhil, FRS, FMedSci; British zoologist and scientific administrator; *Professor Emeritus of Zoology, University of Oxford;* b. 11 April 1945, Sheffield, Yorks., England; s. of Prof. Sir Hans Adolf Krebs and Margaret Fieldhouse; two d. from previous m.; m. 2nd Sarah M. Phibbs 2013; ed City of Oxford High School, Pembroke Coll. Oxford; Departmental Demonstrator in Ornithology, Edward Grey Inst. of Field Ornithology and Oxford Lecturer in Zoology, Pembroke Coll. Oxford 1969–70, Lecturer in Zoology, Edward Grey Inst. 1976–88, E.P. Abraham Fellow in Zoology, Pembroke Coll. 1981–88, Fellow 1988–2005, Hon. Fellow 2005–; Asst Prof., Inst. of Resource Ecology, Univ. of British Columbia, Vancouver, Canada 1970–73; Lecturer in Zoology, Univ. Coll. of North Wales, Bangor 1973–74; SRC Research Officer, Animal Behaviour Research Group, Dept of Zoology, Oxford 1975–76, Fellow, Wolfson Coll. 1976–81, Royal Soc. Research Prof., Univ. of Oxford 1988–2005, Prof. Emer. of Zoology 2015–, Prin. Jesus Coll. Oxford 2005–15; Chief Exec. NERC 1994–2000; Chair. Food Standards Agency 2000–05; Dir Agric. and Food Research Council (AFRC) Unit of Ecology and Behaviour and NERC Unit of Behavioural Ecology 1989–94; Sr Scientific Consultant and Chair. Animals Research Cttee, AFRC 1991–94; External Scientific mem. Max Planck Soc. 1985; Pres. Int. Soc. of Behavioural Ecology 1988–90, Asscn for Study of Animal Behaviour 1992–94; Pres. British Science Asscn (fmrly BAAS) 2012–13; mem. (Crossbench), House of Lords 2007–, Chair. House of Lords Science and Tech. Cttee 2010–14; Chair. UK Science and Tech. Honours Cttee 2008–14, UK Climate Adaptation Cttee 2009–; Trustee, Nuffield Foundation 2007–; mem. Academia Europaea 1995; Foreign mem. American Philosophical Soc. 2000, American Acad. of Arts and Sciences 2000; Fellow, German Nat. Acad. of Sciences Leopoldina 2013; Hon. Fellow, Univ. of Cardiff 1999, Univ. Wales Inst. Cardiff 2006, Univ. Wales Bangor 2007; Hon. Fellow, German Ornithological Soc. 2003, Salters' Co. 2006, Asscn for Nutrition 2012, British Science Asscn 2012; Hon. FZS 2006; Hon. mem. British Ecological Soc. 1999; Foreign Hon. mem. NAS 2004; Hon. DSc (Sheffield) 1993, (Wales) 1997, (Birmingham) 1997, (Exeter) 1998, (Warwick) 2000, (Cranfield) 2001, (Kent) 2001, (Plymouth) 2001, (South Bank) 2003, (Heriot-Watt) 2002, (Queen's Univ., Belfast) 2002, (Lancaster) 2005, (Guelph) 2006, (Aberdeen) 2010, (Newcastle) 2012, (Western Ontario) 2015; Dr hc (Stirling) 2000; Nuffield Foundation Science Fellowship 1981, Scientific Medal, Zoological Soc. 1981, Bicentenary Medal, Linnaean Soc. 1983, Frink Medal, Zoological Soc. 1996, Elliott Coues Award, American Ornithologists' Union 1999, Asscn for Study of Animal Behaviour Medal 2000, Benjamin Ward Richardson Gold Medal, Royal Soc. for Promotion of Health 2002, Wooldridge Medal, British Veterinary Asscn 2004, Croonian Lecture and Medal, Royal Soc., London 2004, Lord Raynor Medal & Lecture, Royal Coll. of Physicians 2005, Award for Outstanding Achievement, Soc. for Food Hygiene Tech. 2005, Harben Gold Medal, Royal Inst. of Public Health 2006. *Publications:* Behavioural Ecology: An Evolutionary Aproach (co-ed.) 1978, 1984, 1991, 1997, An Introduction to Behavioural Ecology (with N. B. Davies) 1981 (revised edn 2012), Foraging Theory: Princeton Monographs in Behaviour and Ecology, No. 4 (with D. W. Stephens) 1987, Foraging Behaviour (co-ed.) 1987, Behavioural and Neural Studies of Learning and Memory (co-ed.) 1991. *Leisure interests:* gardening, music, running, walking, tennis. *Address:* Department of Zoology, University of Oxford, South Parks Road, Oxford, OX1 3PS, England (office). *Telephone:* (1865) 271295 (office). *E-mail:* john.krebs@zoo.ox.ac.uk (office). *Website:* www.zoo.ox.ac.uk/egi/members/professor-lord-krebs-kt-frs-fmedsci-ml (office); www.parliament.uk/biographies/lords/lord-krebs/3736.

KREBS, Robert Duncan, MBA; American transport industry executive (retd); b. 2 May 1942, Sacramento, Calif.; s. of Ward C. Krebs and Eleanor B. Krebs (née Duncan); m. Anne Lindstrom 1971; two s. one d.; ed Stanford and Harvard Univs; Asst Gen. Man. South Pacific Transportation Co., Houston, Tex. 1974–75, Asst Regional Operations Man. 1975–76, Asst Vice-Pres. San Francisco 1967–77, Asst to Pres. 1977–79, Gen. Man. 1979, Vice-Pres. Transportation 1979–80, Operations 1980–82, Pres. 1982–83; Dir and Pres. Santa Fe South Pacific Corpn (now Santa Fe Pacific Corpn) 1983–96, Pres., Chair. and CEO 1988–96, Pres. and CEO Burlington Northern Santa Fe Corpn 1995–2002, Chair. 2000–02; mem. Bd of Dirs Railpower Technologies Corpn 2005, Phelps Dodge Corpn –2006, UAL Corpn 2006–, Fort Worth Symphony Orchestra; Life Trustee, Ravinia Festival; Railroader of the Year (co-recipient) 1996.

KRECKLER, Luis María; Argentine sociologist and diplomatist; *Ambassador to Switzerland;* b. 16 Aug. 1954, Buenos Aires; m.; four c.; ed Univ. of Buenos Aires; joined Foreign Service 1983, Alt. Rep. to OAS 1986–90, Head, Consular Section, Embassy in Panama 1990–92, Deputy Chief, Cabinet of Señor Canciller (also Head, Unidad de Coordinación de Comitivas) 1992–96, Chief of Staff to Sec. of Foreign and Latin American Affairs 1996–98, Consul Gen. and Dir of Trade Promotion Center of Argentina, Los Angeles 1998–2005, Under-Sec. for Int. Trade, Ministry of Foreign Affairs and Worship 2005–10, rank of Amb. 2006, Sec. of Trade and Int. Econ. Relations 2010–11, Amb. to Brazil 2012–15, to Germany 2016–17, to Switzerland 2018–; Commdr, Vasco Nuñez de Balboa Order (Panama), Kt, Cross of Merit (Germany), Chevalier, Ordre nat. du Mérite, Grand Cross of the Order of Civil Merit (Spain), Great Cross, Distinguished Order of Merit (Peru) 2010, Grand Cross, Order of Merit (Chile) 2010. *Address:* Embassy of Argentina, Jungfraustr. 1, 3005 Bern, Switzerland (office). *Telephone:* 313564343 (office). *Fax:* 313564340 (office). *Website:* www.suiza.embajada-argentina.gov.ar (office).

KREMENYUK, Victor Aleksandrovich, DHist; Russian civil servant and scholar; *Deputy Director, Institute for USA and Canadian Studies, Russian Academy of Sciences;* b. 13 Dec. 1940, Odessa (now in Ukraine); m. Lyudmila Agapova; one d.; ed Moscow Inst. of Int. Relations; army service 1963–68; with Mezdunarodnaya Zhizn magazine 1968–70; with Inst. for USA and Canadian Studies, USSR (now Russian) Acad. of Sciences 1970–, Deputy Dir 1989–; expert, Cttee on Int. Problems, USSR Supreme Soviet 1989–91; expert, State Duma 1993–; worked on project Process of Int. Negotiations in Int. Inst. of Applied System Analysis Austria, lectures and seminars in USA, Germany, Austria; Chair. Expert Council of Political Sciences 1992–99; mem. Council on Higher Policy at Ministry of Foreign Affairs 1991–96; mem. Scientific Council, Russian Inst. of Strategic Studies 1995–; mem. Council of Social Sciences, Presidium of Russian Acad. of Sciences 1991–; mem. Nat. Geographical Soc., USA, Int. Asscn of Conflictology; mem. Consultative and Observation Councils Salzburg Seminar, Austria, Centre of Applied Studies on Negotiations, Switzerland; mem. Editorial Bds, magazines Econ., Politics and Ideology, Journal of Negotiations, USA 1990–2000, Journal of Peace Studies, USA; Corresp. mem. Russian Acad. of Sciences 2011; Nat. Prize for Science and Tech. (USSR) 1980, CPR Inst. for Dispute Resolution (New York) Book Award 2002, Russian Ministry for Emergencies Award for Risk Analysis. *Publications include:* more than 100 articles and 12 scientific monographs; ed. more than 50 scientific works in Russian and English. *Address:* Institute for USA and Canadian Studies, 123995 Moscow, Khlebny per. 2/3, Russia (office). *Telephone:* (495) 691-14-83 (office); (495) 430-07-95 (home). *Fax:* (495) 697-70-17 (office). *E-mail:* vkremenyuk@gmail.com (office). *Website:* www.iskran.ru (office).

KREMER, Gidon; Russian/German violinist; *Founder and Artistic Director, Kremerata Baltica;* b. 27 Feb. 1947, Riga, Latvia; ed Riga School of Music, Moscow Conservatory with David Oistrakh; recitalist and orchestral soloist worldwide 1965–; has played in most major int. festivals including Berlin, Dubrovnik, Helsinki, London, Moscow, Prague, Salzburg, Tokyo and Zürich; has played with most major int. orchestras including Berlin Philharmonic, Boston Symphony, Concertgebouw, LA Philharmonic, New York Philharmonic, Philadelphia, San Francisco Symphony, Vienna Philharmonic, London Philharmonic, Royal Philharmonic, Philharmonia, NHK Symphony of Japan and all main Soviet orchestras; has worked with Bernstein, von Karajan, Giulini, Jochum, Previn, Abbado, Levine, Maazel, Muti, Harnoncourt, Mehta and Marriner; Founder and Artistic Dir Kremerata Baltica (chamber orchestra) 1977–; Founder Lockenhaus Chamber Music Festival 1981–2011; numerous awards including Pour le Mérite for Sciences and Arts (Germany) 2016, Praemium Imperiale Award (Japan) 2016, Grosses Bundesverdienstkreuz mit Kreuz (Germany) 2017; prizewinner, Queen Elisabeth Competition, Brussels, Montreal Competition and Fourth Int. Tchaikovsky Competition (First Prize) 1970, Paganini Prize, Genoa, Grand Prix du Disque and Deutsche Schallplattenpreis, Ernst-von-Siemens Musikpreis, Premio dell' Accademia Musicale Chigiana, Frankfurter Musikpreis 1982, Triumph Prize 2000, UNESCO Prize 2001, Saeculum-Glashütte Original-Musikfestspielpreis 2007, Rolf-Schock Prize 2008, Life Achievement Prize, Istanbul Music Festival 2010, Una Vita Nella Musica – Artur Rubinstein Prize 2011. *Recordings:* more than 120 albums. *Publications:* author of five books, including Letters to a Young Pianist 2013. *Address:* Opus 3 Artists, 470 Park Avenue South, 9th Floor North, New York, NY 10016, USA (office); Kremerata Baltica, Meistaru iela 23, 1050 Riga, Latvia. *E-mail:* info@opus3artists.com (office); kristijonas@kbm.ee; kb@kremeratabaltica.lv; kristijonas@gidonkremer.net. *Website:* www.opus3artists.com/artists/gidon-kremer (office); www.kremeratabaltica.com; www.gidonkremer.net. *Telephone:* 6722-4055. *Fax:* 6721-3072.

KREMP, Herbert, DrPhil; German journalist and publicist; b. 12 Aug. 1928, Munich; s. of Johann Kremp and Elisabeth Kremp; m. Brigitte Steffal 1956; two d. (one deceased); ed Munich Univ.; reporter, Frankfurter Neue Presse 1956–57; Political Ed., Rheinische Post 1957–59; Dir Political Dept, Der Tag, Berlin 1959–61; Bonn Corresp., Rheinische Post 1961–63, Ed.-in-Chief 1963–68; Ed.-in-Chief, Die Welt 1969–77, Co-Ed. 1981, Co-Publr 1984–87, Chief Corresp. in Beijing 1977–81, Ed.-in-Chief 1981–85, apptd Chief Corresp. in Brussels 1987, Co-Ed., Springer Group newspapers 1984–87, commentator, Die Welt, Berliner Morgenpost, Welt am Sonntag, Bild, B.Z. Berlin, Hamburger Abendblatt; currently associated with Axel Springer publishing house; Bundesverdienstkreuz 1988; Konrad Adenauer Prize 1984, Theodor-Wolff Prize 1978, 2003. *Publications:* Am Ufer der Rubikon: Eine politische Anthropologie, Die Bambusbrücke: Ein asiatisches Tagebuch 1979, Wir brauchen unsere Geschichte 1988, Memoiren der Zukunft–Deutschland 2050–ein Rückblick 2003. *Address:* c/o Axel Springer Verlag AG, Axel-Springer-Str. 65, 10888 Berlin, Germany.

KRENS, Thomas, MA; American museum director; *Senior Advisor on International Affairs, Solomon R. Guggenheim Foundation;* b. 26 Dec. 1946, New York; ed Williams Coll., State Univ. of New York, Albany, Yale Univ.; Asst Prof. of Art, Williams Coll., Williamstown, Mass. 1972–80, Asst Prof. of History of Art, Grad. Program 1977–80, Adjunct Prof. of Art History 1988, Dir Williams Coll. Museum of Art 1980–88; consultant, Solomon R. Guggenheim Museum, New York 1986–88, Dir 1988, Dir Guggenheim Museums Worldwide, Dir and Trustee Solomon R. Guggenheim Foundation 1988–2008, Sr Advisor on Int. Affairs 2008–; Dir The Peggy Guggenheim Collection, Venice 1988–; mem. Asscn of Art Museum Dirs, Réunion des Musées, Council on Foreign Relations, Societé Kandinsky, Paris; Order of the Aztec Eagle (Mexico) 2006; Hon. DHumLitt (Williams Coll., Yale Univ., State Univ. of New York at Albany); Special Prize for Architectural Patronage 2000, Cultural Leadership Award, American Fed. of Arts 2007. *Publications:* Jim Dine Prints: 1970–77 1977, The Prints of Helen Frankenthaler 1980, The Drawing of Robert Morris 1982, Robert Morris: The Mind/Body Problem 1994. *Address:* Solomon R. Guggenheim Foundation, Solomon R. Guggenheim Museum, 1071 Fifth Avenue, New York, NY 10128-0173, USA (office). *Website:* www.guggenheim.org/guggenheim-foundation (office).

KRENZ, Egon; German fmr politician; b. 1937; m. Erika Krenz; ed Teacher Training Inst. Putbus and Cen. Cttee of CPSU Party Univ. Moscow; joined Freie Deutsche Jugend (FDJ) 1953, Socialist Unity Party (SED) and Confed. of Free German Trade Unions 1955; various functions within FDJ and SED 1957–64; Sec. Ernst Thälmann Pioneer Org. 1967–74, Chair. 1971–74; First Sec. FDJ Cen. Council 1974–83; mem. Nat. Council of Nat. Front 1969–; cand. mem. Cen. Cttee of SED 1971–73, mem. 1973–90, Sec. 1989–90, cand. mem. Politburo 1976–83, mem. 1983–90, Gen. Sec. 1989–90; Deputy to Volkskammer 1971–90, mem. Presidium 1971–81, Chair. FDJ Faction 1971–76; mem. Council of State 1981–84, Deputy Chair. 1984–89, Chair. (Head of State) 1989–90; stripped of membership of CP (fmrly SED); then property developer, Berlin; faced charges of manslaughter for killings of persons fleeing over Berlin Wall and other borders 1994; on trial Aug. 1995, sentenced to six and a half years' imprisonment for the deaths of those trying to cross the Berlin Wall Aug. 1997, sentence upheld on appeal Nov. 1999, released Dec. 2003, retd to Dierhagen, Mecklenburg-Vorpommern, remained on parole until end of sentence 2006; decorations include Karl Marx Orden, Banner der Arbeit, Verdienstmedaille der DDR.

KRENZ, Jan; Polish conductor and composer; b. 14 July 1926, Włocławek; s. of Otton Krenz and Eleonora Krenz; m. Alina Krenz 1958; one s.; ed Higher School of Music; conducting debut, Łódź Philharmonic Orchestra 1946; Chief Conductor, State Poznań Philharmonic Orchestra 1947–49; Chief Conductor, Polish Nat. Radio Symphony Orchestra of Katowice 1953–67; Chief Conductor, Danish Radio Orchestra, Copenhagen 1960s; Leader, Grand Opera House Orchestra (Teatr Wielki), Warsaw 1968–73; conducted Berlin Philharmonic, Staatskapelle Dresden, Leningrad Philharmonic and all the major London orchestras; Gen. Dir of Music, Bonn Orchestra 1979–82; Artistic Dir and Prin. Conductor, Kraków Philharmonic 2005–08; frequent collaboration with Yomiuri Nippon Symphony Orchestra; Diploma of Ministry of Foreign Affairs 1980; Hon. mem. Asscn of Polish Composers; Hon. Conductor, Polish Nat. Radio Symphony Orchestra of Katowice; decorations include Order of Banner of Labour (First Class), Commdr's Cross with Star of Polonia Restituta Order; State Prize 1955, 1972, City of Katowice Music Award 1957, Prize of Asscn of Polish Composers 1968, 1996, Grand Prix du Disque, France 1972, Prize of Polish Artists' and Musicians' Asscn (SPAM) Orfeusz 1974, Diamond Baton Award 1995, Gold Medal for Merit to Culture Gloria Artis 2005, Polish Music Coryphaeus Award, Inst. of Music and Dance 2011. *Compositions include:* Triptych for voice and piano 1946, Symphony No. 1 1947, Symphonic Dance for orchestra 1951, Symphony No. 2 (quasi una fantasia) 1989, Tristan in memoriam. Postludium per quartetto d'archi 1997, Aria and Perpetuum mobile for orchestra 2004, Overture for symphony orchestra 2005, Requiem for baritone solo, mixed choir and orchestra 2007. *Leisure interest:* painting. *Address:* al. J. Ch. Szucha 16, 00-582 Warsaw, Poland.

KRESAL, Katarina; Slovenian lawyer and politician; *President, European Centre of Dispute Resolution (ECDR);* b. 28 Jan. 1973, Ljubljana; ed Bezigrad High School, Faculty of Law, Univ. of Ljubljana; contractual work, Slovenian Chamber of Physiotherapists 1994–96; clerk trainee, High Court in Ljubljana 1996–98; Slovenian State Bar Exam 1999; Sr Clerk, Commercial Disputes Dept, Ljubljana Dist Court 1999–2000; Sr Consultant for Commercial and Corp. Law, Kapitalska družba d.d., Ljubljana 2000–01; mem. advisory bodies of Delo Tiskarna, BTC Terminal and Konstruktor (rep. of Kapitalska družba) 2000–01; Head of Legal Dept, Western Wireless Int. d.o.o., Ljubljana and mem. Sr Man. Team 2001–03; attorney cand., Attorneys at law Miro Senica in odvetniki, Ljubljana 2003–04, attorney at law 2004–08, Deputy Dir and Dir Econ. and Int. Affairs Dept 2005–08; Pres. Liberal Democracy of Slovenia 2007–11; Minister of Internal Affairs 2008–11 (resgnd); Founder and Pres. European Centre of Dispute Resolution (ECDR) 2012–; mem. advisory bodies of GV Zalozbe and Ius Software; mem. Asscn of Young Laywers of Slovenia, European Young Bar Asscn. *Publications include:* has published articles in foreign publs such as International Financial Review 1000 and The Guide to Mergers and Acquisitions. *Address:* European Centre of Dispute Resolution, Tomšičeva ulica 6, 1000 Ljubljana, Slovenia (office). *Telephone:* (8) 2056590 (office). *E-mail:* info@ecdr.si (office). *Website:* www.ecdr.si (office).

KRESS, Victor Melkhiorovich, Dr Econs; Russian politician; b. 16 Nov. 1948, Kostroma Region; m.; two c.; ed Novosibirsk Inst. of Agric., Russian Acad. of Man.; agronomist, agric. enterprises Tomsk Region; Deputy Chair., Agric.-Industrial complex Tomsk Region 1971–87; First Sec. Dist CP Cttee, Tomsk Region 1987–90; Chair. Tomsk Regional Soviet 1990–91, Interregional Asscn Siberian Agreement 1998–2001; Head, Admin. of Tomsk Region 1991–96, Gov. 1996–2012; mem. Federal Council of the Federation, representing Tomsk Oblast Admin. 2012–; mem. Council of Russian Fed. 1993–2000; Chair. Interregional Asscn Siberian Agreement; Order of The Sign of Respect (Znak Potcheta) 1986, Order of Merit to Russia of the IV Grade (Za Zaslugi pered Otetchestrom) 1998, Order of Merit for the Fatherland, (second class) 2008, Order of St. Sergius (first class) 2008; Medal for Working Virtue (Za Trudovya Doblest) 1976. *Publications:* Tomsk Region: Today and Tomorrow (4 vols) 1997, Russia's Hard Time: View from the Province 1998, Tomsk Region: at the Crossroads of Centuries 1999, Tomsk Region: Beginning of the 21st Century 2002. *Address:* Federal Council of the Federation, 103426 Moscow, B. Dmitrovka, 26, Russia (office). *Website:* eng.duma.tomsk.ru (office).

KRGOVIĆ, Ljubiša, MA; Montenegrin economist and fmr central banker; b. 28 Oct. 1957, Mojkovac; m. Ljiljana Krgović; three s. one d.; ed secondary school in Berane, Univ. of Montenegro, Belgrade Univ.; Researcher, Econs Inst., Univ. of Montenegro 1983–91; Dir Montenegrin Employment Bureau 1991–92; Advisor to the Prime Minister in Govt of Montenegro 1992–94; Vice-Gov. Nat. Bank of Yugoslavia 1995–99; mem. Monetary Council, Nat. Bank of Montenegro 1999–2001; Deputy Prime Minister for financial system and public spending 2000–01; Pres. Montenegro Securities Exchange 2000–02; Pres. of Council, Centralna banka Crne Gore (Cen. Bank of Montenegro) 2001–10; Owner, Winery Krgovic 2010–; mem. Bd of Dirs, Komercijalna Banka ad Budva 2012–16; mem. Man. and Supervisory Bd, NLB banka ad Beograd 2013–. *Address:* Winery Krgovic, 81000 Podgorica, Atinska 19, Montenegro (office). *Telephone:* 69-335335 (mobile) (office). *E-mail:* vinarija.krgovic@gmail.com (office). *Website:* www.winesofmontenegro.me (office).

KRICK, Gerd; German engineer and business executive; b. 8 Oct. 1938, Dresden; mil. service 1960; began career with Continental AG, Hanover 1969; moved to medium-sized enterprise in Munich 1970–75; joined Fresenius AG (now Fresenius SE), Bad Homburg 1975, mem. Bd for Research and Devt and Production and Tech. 1975–81, mem. Man. Bd 1981–91, Dir Medical Systems Div. and Deputy Chair. Man. Bd –1992, Chair. Man. Bd and CEO 1992–2003, Chair. Man. Bd and CEO Fresenius Medical Care AG 1996–97, Chair. Supervisory Bd Fresenius Medical Care AG from 1998 (until transformation of legal form to a KGaA), also Chair. Supervisory Bd Fresenius Medical Care AG & Co. KGaA, Chair. Supervisory Bd Fresenius SE 2003–18, mem. Supervisory Bd of Man. 2005–, Fresenius AG, apptd Chair. Fresenius USA Inc. 1989; mem. Bd of Dirs Gull Laboratories Inc., Adelphi Capital Europe Fund; mem. Advisory Bd HDI Haftpflichtverband der deutschen Industrie V.a.G –2008, Vereinte AG (Vereinte Krankenversicherung AG), Bd of Trustees Donau Universität Krems; Chair. Supervisory Bd Vamed AG (Austria), Fresenius Kabi AG (subsidiaries of Fresenius SE), Fresenius Kabi Austria GmbH –2004; mem. Supervisory Bd Allianz Private Krankenversicherungs-AG –2008; fmr Dir Dresdner Bank Luxembourg SA. *Address:* c/o Fresenius SE, 61346 Bad Homburg (office); Fresenius SE, Else-Kröner-Straße 1, 61352 Bad Homburg, Germany (office).

KRIELE, Martin, DJur, LLM; German legal scholar and academic; *Professor Emeritus of Philosophy and Public Law, University of Cologne;* b. 19 Jan. 1931, Opladen; s. of Dr Rudolf Kriele and Konstanze Henckels; m. 1st Christel Grothues 1960; one s. one d.; m. 2nd Alexa Michalsen; four c.; ed Univs of Freiburg, Münster, Bonn, Yale Univ., USA; admitted to the Court 1961; Prof. of Philosophy of Law and Public Law, Univ. of Cologne 1967–96, Prof. Emer. 1996–; Co-Publr, Zeitschrift für Rechtspolitik (journal); Dir Inst. for Political Philosophy and Problems of Legislation 1967; Judge, Constitutional Court of North Rhine-Westphalia 1976–88; Bundesverdienstkreuz 1988. *Publications include:* Kriterien der Gerechtigkeit 1963, Theorie der Rechtsgewinnung 1967, Einführung in die Staatslehre 1975, Legitimitätsprobleme der Bundesrepublik 1977, Die Menschenrechte zwischen Ost und West 1977, Recht und praktische Vernunft 1979, Befreiung und politische Aufklärung 1980, Nicaragua, das blutende Herz Amerikas 1985, Die Demokratische Weltrevolution 1987, Recht, Vernunft, Wirklichkeit (essays) 1990. *Leisure interest:* music (piano). *Address:* An der Winkelheide 15, 14641 Nauen OT Börnicke, Germany. *Website:* www.martinkriele.info.

KRIER, Léon; Luxembourg architect, urban planner and designer; b. 7 April 1946; ed Univ. of Stuttgart, Germany; Asst to James Stirling, London, UK 1968–70, 1973–74; project partner with J.P. Kleihues, Berlin 1971–72; in pvt. practice, London 1974–; Lecturer, Architectural Asscn School, London 1973–76, RCA, London 1977, Princeton Univ., USA 1977; Jefferson Prof. of Architecture, Univ. of Virginia, Charlottesville, USA 1982; Eero Saarinen Prof., Yale Univ. 2002, USA, Davenport Prof. 2004; Founding Trustee, New School for Traditional Architecture & Urbanism, Charleston 2002; architectural and urban design adviser to HRH The Prince of Wales; works include numerous city centre and housing redevelopment plans, schools, univs, public bldgs etc. in UK, Belgium, France, Germany, Greece, Italy, Luxembourg, Portugal, Saint Lucia, Spain, Sweden and USA; rep. of New Urbanism and New Classical Architecture; City of Berlin Architecture Prize (with Rob Krier) 1975, Jefferson Medal for Architecture 1985, European Culture Prize 1995, Silver Medal, Acad. française 1997, first recipient of Richard H. Driehaus Prize for Classical Architecture 2003, Athena Medal, Congress for the New Urbanism 2006. *Projects include:* masterplans for Poundbury 1988, 2004, furniture designs for Giorgetti, Italy 1991–, Novoli, Florence 1993, Città Nuova, Alessandria, Italy 1997, Village Hall, Windsor, Fla, USA 1997, Val d'Europe Brasserie, Agape, France 2000–03, Hardelot, France 2001, School of Architecture Auditorium, Univ. of Miami, USA 2001–04, Knokke Heuleburg Masterplan, Belgium 2001–04. *Publications include:* Buildings and Projects of James Stirling (ed.) 1974, The Reconstruction of the European City 1978, The City Within the City (ed.) 1979, Architecture and Urban Design (ed. by Richard Economakis) 1967–1992 1993, Léon Krier Drawings 1967–1980 1981, Architecture: Choice or Fate 1998 (trans. into seven languages), Drawings for Architecture 2009, The Architecture of Community (expanded US edn of Architecture: Choice or Fate) 2009, Albert Speer, Architect 2013; book chapters and articles in professional journals. *Address:* 37 rue du X Octobre, 7243 Bereldange, Luxembourg.

KRIKALEV, Sergey Konstantinovich; Russian cosmonaut and mechanical engineer; *Vice-President, S.P. Korolev Rocket and Space Corporation Energia;* b. 27 Aug. 1958, Leningrad; m.; one d.; ed Leningrad Mechanical Inst.; engineer, Research Production Co. Energia 1981–85, took part in developing new samples of space tech.; mem. Cosmonauts' team since 1985; flight engineer, Soyuz TM-7 1988, Soyuz TM-12 1991–92, STS-60 (first joint US/Russian Space Shuttle Mission) 1994, STS-88 Endeavour 1998, Expedition-1 2000–01, Commdr Expedition-11 2005; spent 310 days in orbit on Soyuz TM-12 1991–92; Vice-Pres. S. P. Korolev Rocket and Space Corpn Energia 2007–; Hon. Citizen, St Petersburg 2007; Champion of Moscow 1983, Hero of the Soviet Union 1989, Hero of the Russian Fed. 1992, NASA Space Flight Medal 1994, 1998, Medal For Merit in Space Exploration; Order of Lenin, Officier, Légion d'Honneur, Order of Friendship. *Address:* S.P. Korolev Rocket and Space Corporation Energia, 4A Lenin Street, Korolev, Moscow 141070, Russia (office). *Telephone:* (495) 513-86-55 (office). *E-mail:* post@rsce.ru (office). *Website:* www.energia.ru (office).

KRIMLY, Rayed Khalid A., BA, MA, PhD; Saudi Arabian academic and diplomatist; b. 28 Nov. 1962; m.; two d.; ed King Saud Univ., George Washington Univ., USA; Lecturer, Political Science Dept, King Saud Univ., Riyadh 1983–85, Asst Prof. 1993–2002; joined Ministry of Foreign Affairs 2002, Deputy Head of Dept of Western Countries, then Minister Plenipotentiary and Head of Dept of Western Countries 2008–10, Amb., Deputy Undersecretary for Bilateral Relations and Dir-Gen., Dept of American States 2010–12, Amb. to Greece 2012–14, to Italy 2015–18, represented Saudi Arabia in numerous confs and nat. events, including at UN, Arab League and Gulf Co-operation Council. *Publications:* several books as well as academic and journalistic articles.

KRIPKE, Saul Aaron, BA, LHD; American philosopher, logician and academic; *Distinguished Professor, Graduate Program in Philosophy and Computer Science, City University of New York;* b. 13 Nov. 1940, Bay Shore, NY; s. of Myer Samuel Kripke and Dorothy Kripke; m. Margaret P. Gilbert 1976 (divorced 1998); ed Harvard Univ.; Soc. of Fellows, Harvard Univ. 1963–66, concurrently Lecturer with rank of Asst Prof., Princeton Univ. 1964–66; Lecturer, Harvard Univ. 1966–68; Assoc. Prof., Rockefeller Univ. 1968–72, Prof. 1972–76; McCosh Prof. of Philosophy, Princeton Univ. 1977–98, now Prof. Emer.; currently Distinguished Prof., Grad. Program in Philosophy, CUNY; Fulbright Fellow 1962–63; Guggenheim Fellow 1968–69, 1977–78; Visiting Fellow, All Souls Coll., Oxford, UK 1977–78, 1989–90; Visiting Prof., The Hebrew Univ. 1998–; mem. American Philosophical Soc. 2004–; Fellow, American Acad. of Arts and Sciences; Corresp. Fellow, British Acad.; Hon. DHumLitt (Univ. of Neb. at Omaha) 1977, (Johns Hopkins Univ.) 1997, (Univ. of Haifa) 1998, (Univ. of Penn) 2005; Detur Prize 1960, Charles J. Wister Prize 1962, Howard Behrman Award 1988, Schock Prize in Logic and Philosophy 2001. *Publications:* Naming and Necessity 1980, Wittgenstein on Rules and Private Language 1982; numerous papers in professional journals and anthologies. *Address:* Graduate Program in Philosophy, CUNY Graduate Center, 365 Fifth Avenue, New York, NY 10016, USA (office). *Telephone:* (212) 817-8615 (home). *Website:* web.gc.cuny.edu/Philosophy (office); kripkecenter.commons.gc.cuny.edu.

KRISHNA, Somanahalli Mallaiah, BA, BL, MCL; Indian lawyer, politician and professor of international law; b. 1 May 1932; s. of S. C. Mallaiah and Shrimati Thayamma; m. Prema Krishna 1964; two d.; ed Maharaja's Coll. Mysore, Govt Law Coll., Bangalore, Southern Methodist Univ. Dallas, USA, George Washington Univ., USA; Fulbright Scholar, George Washington Univ. Law School, Washington, DC, later taught Int. Law; Prof. of Int. Law, Renukacharya Law Coll., Bangalore 1962–68; mem. Karnataka Legis. Ass. 1962–67, 1989–94, Speaker 1989–92; mem. Lok Sabha (Parl.) 1968–72; mem. Karnataka Legis. Council 1972–77; Minister of Commerce and Industries and Parl. Affairs 1972–77; returned to Parl. 1980; Minister of State for Industry 1983–84, for Finance 1984–85, of External Affairs 2009–12 (resgnd); Deputy Chief Minister of Karnataka 1992–94, Chief Minister 1999–2004; mem. Rajya Sabha 1996–99, 2009–14; Gov. of Maharashtra 2004–08 (resgnd); fmr mem. del. to UN, New York 1982; Pres. KPCC 1999–2000; Del. Commonwealth Parl. Seminar, Westminster, UK 1990; Global Alumni Award, Southern Methodist Univ., USA 2010. *Leisure interests:* reading, designing men's clothes, sport.

KRISHNAMURTHY, G. V. G., BA, BSc, BL; Indian election commissioner (retd) and lawyer; b. 19 Nov. 1934, Chirala, AP; s. of G.V. Subbarao and G. Rajeswaramma; m. G. Padma 1957; one s. one d.; ed Andhra Univ.; pro-independence student activist and mem. Azad Hindu Fauz Youth League 1945–47; advocate, Andhra Pradesh High Court 1958; lecturer, Law Coll. Osmania Univ. 1958, 1962; Sr Research Officer, Indian Law Inst. 1962–63; advocate, Supreme Court; Deputy Legal Adviser, Comm. of Inquiry, Cabinet Secr. 1972–73; Additional Legal Adviser, Ministry of Law and ex-officio Govt Counsel, Delhi High Court 1973–76, Supreme Court of India 1978–79; Govt Arbitrator 1979–83; Jt Sec. and Legal Adviser 1983–87; Additional Sec. Govt of India 1987–88, Special Sec. 1988–89; Sec. Law Comm. of India 1989–92; Election Commr of India 1993–99; Int. Observer Sri Lanka Pres. Elections 1999, Kazakhstan Parl. Elections 2004; Hon. LLD (Jhansi Univ.) 1996; National Citizen's Award 1990, Great Son of the Soil Award 1996, NRI Gold Int. Award 1996, Glory of India Int. Award 1998, Champion of Indian Democracy Award 2001, Pride of India Int. Award 2002. *Publications include:* Dynamics of Diplomacy 1968, Modern Diplomacy, Dialectics and Dimensions 1980; articles in legal journals. *Leisure interests:* reading, watching nature, cultural activities. *Address:* 1402 Kausumbhi, opp. Delhi Anand Vihar ISBT, Ghaziabad, India (home). *Telephone:* (120) 2778056 (home). *Fax:* (120) 2778056 (home).

KRISHNAN, Tan Sri T(atparanandam) Ananda, BA, MBA; Malaysian business executive; *CEO, Usaha Tegas Sendirian Berhad;* b. 1 April 1938, Kuala Lumpur; m.; three c.; ed Victoria Inst., Kuala Lumpur, Univ. of Melbourne, Australia, Harvard Univ., USA; f. Exoil Trading; CEO Usaha Tegas Sendirian Berhad (investment and consulting org. with interests in communications, broadcasting, media, leisure, entertainment and energy); cos in which it has an interest include Maxis Communications (took pvt. in leveraged buyout 2007), MEASAT Broadcast Network Systems, Binariang Satellites Systems, Bumi Armada, Objektif Bersatu, Celestial Pictures Ltd, Hong Kong; Man. Usaha Tegas Entertainment Systems; Head of Astro All Asia Networks PLC; developer of Petronas Twin Towers, Kuala Lumpur. *Address:* Usaha Tegas Sendirian Berhad, Level 44, Menara MAXIS, Kuala Lumpur City Centre, 50088 Kuala Lumpur (office); Maxis Communications Berhad, Level 18, Menara Maxis, KLCC Off Jalan Ampang, 50088 Kuala Lumpur, Malaysia. *Telephone:* (3) 23807788 (office); (3) 23307000. *Fax:* (3) 23806677 (office); (3) 23300008. *E-mail:* corpinfo@maxis.com.my. *Website:* www.maxis.com.my.

KRISTAN, Ivan, BA, DJur; Slovenian politician, lawyer and academic; b. 12 June 1930, Arnovo; ed Ljubljana Univ.; worked in trade unions 1956–67; Teacher, Faculty of Law, Ljubljana Univ. 1967–77, Prof. 1977–87, Dean 1983–85, Rector 1985–87, Prof. Emer.; Judge, Federal Constitutional Court 1987–91; mem. Cttee for Constitutional Reforms of the Slovenian Repub. 1970–74, 1987–90; mem. Constitutional Court of Yugoslavia 1987–91; Pres. Nat. Council of Slovenian Repub. 1992–98; Pres. of Supervising Cttee, Int. Asscn for Constitutional Law (IACL); mem. Asscn of Fighters for the Liberation of Slovenia. *Publications include:* more than 200 books, articles and scientific papers on legal problems of human rights, federalism, self-determination and sovereignty of nations, including Constitutional Law of Socialist Fed. Repub. of Yugoslavia (co-author). *E-mail:* ivan.kristan@siol.net.

KRISTEVA, Julia, DèsL; French (b. Bulgarian) psychoanalyst and writer; b. 24 June 1941, Silven, Bulgaria; m. Philippe Sollers 1967; one s.; ed Sofia Univ., Bulgaria, Ecole des Hautes Etudes en Sciences Sociales, Univ. of Paris VII; researcher in linguistics and French literature, Lab. of Social Anthropology, Ecole des Hautes Etudes en Sciences Sociales 1967–73; Prof., Univ. of Paris VII 1973–99, Prof. classe exceptionelle 1999–, Dir Ecole Doctorale Langue, Littérature, Image, civilisations et sciences humaines; Chargé de mission auprès du Pres. for the handicapped; Visiting Prof., Columbia Univ., New York 1974, Univ. of Toronto 1992; mem. Editorial Bd Telquel 1970–82; mem. Soc. psychanalytique de Paris, American Acad. of Arts and Sciences, Inst. Universitaire de France, British Acad., Acad. universelle des cultures; Chevalier, Ordre des Arts et des Lettres 1987, Chevalier, Légion d'honneur 1997, Officier, Ordre nat. du Mérite 2004, Officier de la Légion d'honneur 2008; Dr hc (Western Ontario, Canada) 1995, (Victoria, Toronto) 1997, (Harvard) 1999, (Univ. Libre de Belgique) 2000, (Bayreuth) 2000, (Toronto) 2000, (Sofia) 2002, (New School, New York) 2003; Prix Henri Hertz Chancellerie des Universités de Paris 1989, Holberg Int. Memorial Prize, Norway 2004, Grande Médaille de Vermeil de la Mairie de Paris 2005, Award of Merit, Bucknell Univ. 2006, Hannah Arendt Prize for Political Thought 2006. *Publications include:* Séméiotike: Recherches pour une sémanalyse 1969, Le Texte du roman, approche sémiologique d'une structure discursive transformationnelle 1970, La Révolution du langage poétique: l'avant-garde à la fin du XIXème siècle, Lautréamont et Mallarmé 1974, Des chinoises 1974, Polylogue 1977, Folle Vérité (with Jean Michel Ribettes) 1979, Pouvoirs de l'horreur: Essai sur l'abjection 1980, Le Langage, cet inconnu 1981, Histoires d'amour 1985, Au commencement était l'amour 1985, Soleil noir, dépression et mélancolie 1987, Etrangers à nous-mêmes (Prix Henri Hertz 1989) 1988, Les Samouraïs 1990, Lettre ouverte à Harlem Désir 1990, Le Vieil homme et les loups 1991, Les Nouvelles maladies de l'âme 1993, Le Temps sensible: Proust et l'expérience littéraire (essay) 1994, Possessions 1996, Sens et non-sens de la révolte 1996, La Révolte intime 1997, L'Avenir d'une révolte 1998, Le Génie féminin, Vol. 1: Hannah Arendt 1999, Vol. 2: Melanie Klein 2000, Colette 2002, Meurtre à Byzance 2004, La Haine et le Pardon: Pouvoirs et limites de la psychanalyse III 2005, Thérèse mon amour 2008, Leur regard perce nos ombres (with Jean Vanier) 2011, Visions capitales: Arts et rituels de la décapitation 2013, Pulsions du temps 2013, L'Horloge enchantée 2015. *Address:* Université de Paris VII, Grands Moulins, 7th Floor, bureau 777C, 5, rue Thomas Mann, 75013 Paris, France (office). *Telephone:* 1-57-27-65-25 (office). *E-mail:* julia.kristeva@univ-paris-diderot.fr (office). *Website:* www.kristeva.fr.

KRISTIANSEN, Kjeld Kirk, BSc, MBA; Danish business executive; b. 27 Dec. 1947; s. of Godtfred Kirk Christiansen and Edith Kirk Christiansen; grandson of Ole Kirk Christiansen, founder of LEGO; m. Camilla Kirk Christiansen 1974; one s. two d.; ed Århus Business School, IMD International, Lausanne, Switzerland; mem. Bd LEGO Toy Co. 1975–2019, inherited co. (majority shareholder) 1979, Vice-Chair. LEGO Group 1996–2016, Pres. and CEO 1979–2004, Chair. and Co-owner (with his three c.) LEGO A/S, Chair. and Co-owner (with sister Gunhild) KIRKBI A/S, Chair. LEGO Foundation, Ole Kirk's Foundation, Edith and Godtfred Kirk Christiansen's Foundation; Kt (1st Class), Order of the Dannebrog, Peony, Order of Civil Merit (South Korea); Freedom Prize, Max Schmidheiny Foundation 1996, Distinguished Family Business Award, Int. Inst. for Man. Devt (IMD) 1996, inducted into Nat. Toy Hall of Fame 2008. *Leisure interests:* breeding Danish horses, sports cars. *Address:* c/o LEGO Group, Aastvej 1, 7190 Billund, Denmark.

KRISTO, Vladimir, CSc, DIur; Albanian politician and judge; *Judge, Constitutional Court;* b. 8 April 1947, Korça; m.; one c.; ed Faculty of Law, Tirana Univ.; Chief of Studies' Dept, Gen. Attorney's Office 1983–92; Deputy Minister of Justice 1992–96, 2005–07; Legal Adviser to Prime Minister of Albania 1996–98; pvt. legal practice 1998–2005; mem. Constitutional Court 2007–, Pres. 2007–10, Judge 2010–; fmr mem. High Council of Justice, Co-ordination and Legal Co-operation Cttee, Council of Europe. *Publications include:* numerous articles and academic papers on law and public admin. *Address:* Constitutional Court, Bulevardi Dëshmorët e Kombit, N.26, Tirana, Albania (office). *Telephone:* (4) 228357 (office).

Fax: (4) 228357 (office). *E-mail:* vkristo@gjk.gov.al (office). *Website:* www.gjk.gov.al (office).

KRISTOFFERSON, Kris, BA, PhD; American country singer, songwriter and actor; b. (Kris Carson), 22 June 1936, Brownsville, Tex.; m. 1st; one s. one d.; m. 2nd Rita Coolidge 1973 (divorced 1980); one d.; m. 3rd Lisa Meyers 1983; four s. one d.; ed Pomona Coll. and Univ. of Oxford, UK; Capt. in US Army 1960–65; songwriter 1965–; solo recording artist 1969–; mem. of side project, The Highwaymen 1985; numerous concerts world-wide; actor 1972–; CMA Song of the Year (for Sunday Morning Coming Down) 1970, Grammy Awards for Best Country Song 1972, Best Country Vocal Performance (with Coolidge) 1973, 1976, Golden Globe for Best Actor 1976, ACM Single of the Year (for Highwayman, with The Highwaymen) 1986, two American Music Awards (with The Highwaymen) 1986, Americana Awards Free Speech Award 2003, Johnny Cash Visionary Award, CMT Music Awards 2007. *Films include:* Cisco Pike 1972, Pat Garrett and Billy the Kid 1973, Blume in Love 1973, Bring Me the Head of Alfredo Garcia 1974, Alice Doesn't Live Here Anymore 1974, The Sailor Who Fell From Grace With The Sea 1976, A Star is Born 1976, Vigilante Force 1976, Semi-Tough 1977, Convoy 1978, Heaven's Gate 1981, Rollover 1981, Welcome Home 1989, Millennium 1989, A Soldier's Daughter Never Cries 1998, Blade 1 1998, Come Dance with Me 1999, Payback 1999, Limbo 1999, Joyriders 1999, Comanche 2000, Planet of the Apes 2001, Chelsea Walls 2001, Wooly Boys 2001, D-Tox 2002, Blade II 2002, Where the Red Fern Grows 2003, Blade III 2003, The Jacket, Lives of the Saints, Where the Red Fern Grows, Dreamer 2005, Gun (voice) 2005, The Wendell Baker Story 2005, Fast Food Nation 2006, Disappearances 2006, Requiem for Billy the Kid (voice) 2006, Room 10 2006, Crossing the Heart 2007, Jump Out Boys 2008, Powder Blue 2009, He's Just Not That Into You 2009, The Last Rites of Ransom Pride 2009, Bloodworth 2010, Dolphin Tale 2011, The Greening of Whitney Brown 2011, Joyful Noise 2012, Deadfall 2012, The Motel Life 2012, Angels Sing 2013, Dolphin Tale 2 2014, 7 Minutes 2014, Lawless Range 2016, Traded 2016, The Red Maple Leaf 2016. *Television appearances include:* Freedom Road (film) 1979, The Lost Honor of Kathryn Beck (film) 1984, The Last Days of Frank and Jesse James (film) 1986, Amerika (mini-series) 1987, Christmas in Connecticut (film) 1992, Tad (film) 1995, Brothers' Destiny (film) 1995, Two for Texas (film) 1998, Perfect Murder, Perfect Town: JonBenét and the City of Boulder (film) 2000, Lives of the Saints (film) 2004, Texas Rising (mini-series) 2015, Down Dog (film) 2015. *Recordings include:* albums: Kristofferson 1970, The Silver-Tongued Devil and I 1971, Border Lord 1972, Jesus Was a Capricorn 1973, Full Moon (with Rita Coolidge) 1973, Spooky Lady's Sideshow 1974, Who's to Bless and Who's to Blame 1975, Breakaway (with Rita Coolidge) 1975, A Star Is Born (soundtrack) 1977, Surreal Thing 1976, Songs of Kristofferson 1977, Easter Island 1978, Natural Act (with Rita Coolidge) 1979, Shake Hands With The Devil (with Rita Coolidge) 1979, Help Me Make It Through The Night 1980, To The Bone 1981, The Winning Hand 1983, Music From Songwriter (with Willie Nelson) 1984, Highwayman (with The Highwaymen) 1985, Repossessed 1986, Third World Warrior 1990, Highwaymen 2 (with The Highwaymen) 1992, A Moment of Forever 1995, The Austin Sessions 1999, Broken Freedom Song: Live from San Francisco 2003, Repossessed/Third World Warrior 2004, This Old Road 2006, Closer to the Bone 2009, Please Don't Tell Me How the Story Ends 2010, Feeling Mortal 2013, Cedar Creek Sessions 2016. *Website:* www.kriskristofferson.com.

KRISTOPANS, Vilis; Latvian politician; b. 13 June 1954; m. Aija Krištopan; two s. one d.; ed Riga State Tech. Univ.; basketball player, Latvian Nat. team 1972–81; sports instructor Sports Cttee, Daugava Cen. Council 1977–83; coach, Head coach, basketball team VEF 1983–89; Chair. co-operative soc. Noster 1990; Dir-Gen. Jt Dardedze 1990–92; Vice-Pres. Interbaltija Ltd 1992–93; Minister of State Revenue 1993–94; Chair. Deutsche-Lettische Bank 1994–95; Minister of Transport Latvian Repub. 1995–98; Prime Minister of Latvia, also Minister of Agric. 1998–99; mem. Parl. (Seimas) 1993–98; mem. Bd Latvijas ceļš (Latvian Way); Pres. Latvian Basketball League 1992–97; mem. Ventspils Free Ports Bd 1994.

KRISTOVSKIS, Ģirts Valdis, LLD; Latvian politician; *Deputy Chairman, Unity;* b. 19 Feb. 1962, Ventspils; m.; two d.; ed Rīga Technical Univ., Univ. of Latvia; Sr Engineer, Ventspils Section, Inter-Collective Farm Production and Supplies Enterprise 1984–89; Deputy, Ventspils Council of People's Deputies (city govt) 1989–94; mem. Supreme Council of Latvia (fmr Parl.) 1990–93; Chief of Staff of Nat. Guard 1991–93; mem. Saeima (Parl.) 1993–2003, 2004–10, fmr Vice-Chair. Defence and Internal Affairs Cttee, mem. European Affairs Cttee; Minister of the Interior 1993–94, of Defence 1998–2004, of Foreign Affairs 2010–11; mem. European Parl. 2004–09; mem. Latvijas Tautas fronte (Popular Front of Latvia) 1988–93 (Chair. Ventspils Section 1989–90); mem. Latvijas ceļš (Latvian Way) 1993–98; mem. Tēvzemei un brīvībai/LNNK (For Fatherland and Freedom/LNNK) 1998–2008; Founder Civic Union 2008, Deputy Chair. Unity (founded as a coalition of Civic Union, New Era, and Society for a Different Politics 2010) 2010–; Pres. Track and Field Athletics Union of Latvia 2001–05, Latvian Olympic Cttee; Latvian Defence Ministry Badge of Honour 1994, Mich. Distinguished Service Medal 2000, Three Star Order (Third Class) 2000, Order of the Lithuanian Grand Duke Gediminas (Third Class) 2001, Order of Viesturs 2004, Ministry of Defence Award (Commemorative Medal for Advancing Latvia's Accession to NATO) 2004, Order of the Cross of Terra Mariana, Award of the Pres. of the Repub. of Estonia 2005. *Leisure interests:* basketball, journalism. *Address:* Unity (Vienotība), K. Barona iela 3, Rīga 1050, Latvia (office). *Telephone:* 2666-1600 (office). *E-mail:* birojs@vienotiba.lv (office). *Website:* vienotiba.lv (office).

KRIVINE, Alain; French journalist and politician; b. 10 July 1941, Paris; m. Michèle Martinet 1960; two d.; ed Lycée Condorcet and Faculté des Lettres de Paris; mem. Jeunesses communistes 1956, French CP 1958; Leader Union of Student Communists, Paris-Sorbonne Univ. 1964–65; f. Revolutionary Communist Youth 1966 (disbanded by the Govt 1968), Communist League 1969 (dissolved 1973); cand. presidential elections 1969, 1974; journalist, Rouge 1969–; mem. Political Bureau of Ligue Communiste Révolutionnaire 1974–2006; mem. European Parl. 1999–2004; mem. Secretariat UNIFI de la IVe Internationale; mem. Nouveau Parti Anticapitaliste 2009–. *Publications include:* La Farce électorale 1969, Questions sur la révolution 1973, Mais si, rebelles et repentis (with Daniel Bensaid) 1988, Ca ta passera avec l'âge 2008. *Address:* Nouveau Parti Anticapitaliste (NPA), 2 rue Richard-Lenoir, 93100 Montreuil, France. *Telephone:* 1-48-70-42-30. *Fax:* 1-48-59-23-28. *E-mail:* alain.krivine17@gmail.com.

KRIVINE, Emmanuel; French violinist and conductor; *Music Director, Orchestre National de France;* b. 7 May 1947, Grenoble; s. of Henri Krivine and Rejla Krivine (née Weisbrod); one d.; ed Conservatoire Nat. Supérieur de Musique et de Danse, Conservatoire Royal de Bruxelles, pupil of Henryk Szeryng and Yehudi Menuhin; solo violinist, Paris 1964, Brussels 1965–68; Perm. Guest Conductor, Radio-France 1976–83; Dir Lorraine-Metz Regional Orchestra 1981–83; Prin. Guest Conductor, Orchestra of Lyon 1983; Music Dir Orchestre Français des Jeunes 1984–2004; Music Dir Nat. Orchestra of Lyon 1987–2000; Co-founder and Prin. Conductor, La Chambre Philharmonique 2004–; Music Dir Orchestre Philharmonique du Luxembourg 2006–14; Prin. Guest Conductor, Barcelona Symphony Orchestra 2013, Scottish Chamber Orchestra 2015–; Music Dir Orchestre National de France 2017–; guest conductor to various int. orchestras including Berlin Philharmonic, Philadelphia Orchestra, Nat. Symphony Orchestra, Washington, London Philharmonic, Mahler Chamber Orchestra, Concertgebouw and Chamber Orchestra of Europe 1977–; Chevalier, Ordre nat. du Mérite, Officier des Arts et Lettres; Ginette-Neveu Medal 1971 and numerous other awards. *Leisure interests:* literature, philosophy. *Address:* Intermusica Artists Management Ltd, 36 Graham Street, Crystal Wharf, London, N1 8GJ, England (office). *E-mail:* mail@intermusica.co.uk (office). *Website:* intermusica.co.uk/artist/Emmanuel-Krivine (office); www.maisondelaradio.fr/concerts-classiques/orchestre-national-de-france; www.lachambrephilharmonique.com; www.sco.org.uk.

KRIVOKAPIĆ, Ranko, LLB, MA; Montenegrin lawyer and politician; *Chairman, Socijaldemokratska Partija Crne Gore (SDP—Social Democratic Party of Montenegro);* b. 17 Aug. 1961, Kotor; two c.; ed Faculty of Law, Belgrade, Atlantic Partnership Program; Founder and longtime Vice-Pres. Socijaldemokratska Partija Crne Gore (SDP—Social Democratic Party of Montenegro), Pres. 2001–; mem. (SDP), Skupština Republike Crne Gore (Ass. of Montenegro) 1989–, Pres. SDP Parl. Group 1998–2003, Pres. (Speaker) (within state union of Serbia and Montenegro) 2003–06, (sovereign state of Montenegro) 2006–16; Co-founder Democratic Forum formed with the aim of establishing a multiparty system in Montenegro 1990s; led the process of writing the Declaration of Independence of Montenegro and officially declared independence 3 June 2006; mem. Presidency of Union of Reform Forces of Montenegro 1990, Presidency of Party of European Socialists; fmr Head of Montenegrin Del. to Parl. Ass., OSCE 2003–13, Pres. Parl. Ass. 2013–14, Pres. Emer. 2014–; mem. Montenegrin Del. to the Council of Europe, Parl. Del. to NATO Parl. Ass.; Founder Cetinje Parl. Forum 2004. *Address:* Socijaldemokratska Partija Crne Gore (Social Democratic Party of Montenegro), 81000 Podgorica, Jovana Tomaševića bb, Montenegro (office). *Telephone:* (20) 248648 (office). *Fax:* (20) 248748 (office). *E-mail:* sdp@sdp.co.me (office). *Website:* sdp.co.me (office).

KRIŽANIČ, Franc, MSc, PhD; Slovenian economist, academic and government official; b. 4 Dec. 1954, Ljubljana; m.; two c.; ed Univ. of Ljubljana; apptd Assoc. Prof., Faculty of Econs, Univ. of Ljubljana 2000, Dir Law School, Econ. Inst. 2001–08; Pres. Council of Experts, Insurance Supervision Agency 2000–05; mem. Prime Minister's Strategic Council for Econ. Devt 2006–08; Pres. Supervisory Bd, Slovenian Red Cross 2007–08; mem. Parl. 2008–11; Minister of Finance 2008–11. *Publications include:* The Investment Multiplier in Slovenia 1992, The Slovenian Economy: An Econometric Study of the Periods 1986–1992–1994 1995.

KROEMER, Herbert, PhD; American scientist and academic; *Professor of Electrical and Computer Engineering, University of California, Santa Barbara;* b. 25 Aug. 1928, Weimar, Germany; ed Univ. of Göttingen; carried out pioneering work in semi-conductor research; Prof. of Electrical and Computer Eng, Univ. of Calif., Santa Barbara 1985–; Nat. Lecturer, IEEE Electron Devices Soc.; mem. NAS, Nat. Acad. of Eng, IEEE, American Physics Soc.; Dr hc (Tech. Univ., Aachen) 1985, (Lund) 1998; J. Erbers Award 1973, Heinrich Welker Medal 1982, Jack Morton Award (IEEE) 1986, Alexander von Humboldt Research Award 1994, Nobel Prize for Physics (jt recipient) 2000. *Publications:* Quantum Mechanics: For Engineering, Materials Science and Applied Physics, Thermal Physics (jt author). *Address:* ECE Department and Materials Department 2205A Engineering Science Building, Electrical and Computer Engineering Department, University of California, Santa Barbara, CA 93106-9560, USA (office). *Telephone:* (805) 893-3078 (office). *Fax:* (805) 893-7990 (office). *E-mail:* kroemer@ece.ucsb.edu (office). *Website:* www.ece.ucsb.edu/Faculty/Kroemer/default.html (office).

KROES, Neelie, MSc (Econs); Dutch economist, politician and fmr EU official; *Special Envoy for Startups, Ministry of Economic Affairs;* b. 19 July 1941, Rotterdam; ed Erasmus Univ., Rotterdam; Asst Prof. of Transport Econs, Erasmus Univ. 1965–71; mem. Rotterdam Municipal Council, Rotterdam Chamber of Commerce 1969–71; mem. Parl. 1971–77; Vice-Minister of Transport, Public Works and Telecommunication 1977–81, Minister of Transport, Public Works and Telecommunication 1982–89; Advisor to EU Commr for Transport 1989–91, Commr for Competition, EC 2004–10, Vice-Pres. and Commr for the Digital Agenda 2010–14; Special Envoy for Startups, Ministry of Econ. Affairs 2014–; Pres. Nijenrode Univ. 1991–2000; Chair. Supervisory Bd MeyerMonitor –2004, Nederlands Luchtvaart Overleg (Dutch Aviation Platform) –2004; mem. Supervisory Bd Cório, Royal P&O Nedlloyd NV, Ballast Nedam, New Skies Satellites, Lucent Technologies BV (Netherlands), Nederlandse Spoorwegen NV (Dutch Railways), Volvo Group, Thales Group –2004; Dir (non-exec.) MM02 plc –2004; mem. Bd of Trustees ProLogis International –2004; Chair. Governing Bd Delta Psychiatrical Hosp., Het Rembrandthuis Foundation, Poets of All Nations, Overlegorgaan Waterbeheer en Noordzee-aangelegenheden; fmr Chair. Nyenrode Fund, Supervisory Bd Port Support International BV, Governing Bd TBS Mental Hosp. De Kijvelanden, Governing Bd Bezinnings Groep Water, Supervisory Bd NIB Capital NV, Supervisory Bd Intis BV, Governing Bd Kunsthal; mem. Governing Bd Nelson Mandela Children Fund Member, Bd Dirs World Cancer Research Fund; fmr mem. Governing Bd Royal Trade Fair (Koninklijke Jaarbeurs), Governing Bd Stichting International Human Resources, Development VNO/NCW, Advisory Bd International Problems (AIV), Supervisory Bd of Dirs Prologis European Properties, Advisory Bd PriceWaterhouseCooper, Supervisory Bd NCM Holding NV, Bd of Dirs Brambles Industries Ltd (Australia), Supervisory Bd McDonald's, Bd of Dirs SC Johnson Wax Euro Bd, Supervisory Bd Digital Equipment BV, Supervisory Bd Groeneveld Transport Efficiency, Raad van Toezicht Veerstichting, Competitiveness Group to Chair. EC, Governing Bd Insurance Authority, Governing Bd Conservation of Nature, High Level Group on the trans-European Network; fmr adviser, Monitor Group, Arcadis (Heidemij/Grabowsky); Kt, Order of the Dutch Lion 1981, Grand Officier, Légion d'honneur 1984, Bundesverdienstkreuz 1985, Grand Officer, Order of Orange Nassau 1989, Bintang Mahaputra Adiprana Order (Indonesia) 1993; Dr hc (Hull) 1989; Woman of the Year in Infrastructure, Int. Road Fed. 1993. *Address:* Ministry of Economic Affairs, Bezuidenhoutseweg 30, POB 20401, 2500 EC The Hague, Netherlands. *Telephone:* (70) 3796868. *Website:* www.rijksoverheid.nl/ministeries/eleni.

KROGSGAARD-LARSEN, Povl, PhD, DSc; Danish scientist and academic; *Professor, Department of Drug Design and Pharmacology, University of Copenhagen;* b. 17 May 1941, Frøslev Mors; s. of Niels Saaby and Marie Saaby (née Krogsgaard) Larsen; m. Tove Krogsgaard-Larsen 1964; one s. one d.; ed Danish Univ. of Pharmaceutical Sciences; Asst Prof., Royal Danish School of Pharmacy (later Danish Univ. of Pharmaceutical Sciences, currently part of Univ. of Copenhagen) 1970–75, Assoc. Prof. 1975–86, Prof., Dept of Drug Design and Pharmacology, Faculty of Health and Medical Sciences 1986–, Rector 2001–02; mem. Royal Danish Acad. of Sciences and Letters 1986, Danish Acad. of Natural Sciences 1987, Danish Acad. of Tech. Sciences 1987; mem. Bd Dirs and Vice-Chair. Alfred Benzon Foundation 1991–2016; mem. Bd of Dirs Carlsberg Foundation 1993–2011, also Chair. 2003–11; mem. Bd of Dirs Lundbeck Foundation 2011–16, Grete Lundbeck Foundation 2013–16 (also Chair.); Chair. Carlsberg A/S 2003–12, Aūriga A/S 2002–12, Bioneer 2006–12; Kt Cross of the Order of Dannabrog (1st degree); Dr hc (Louis Pasteur), (Uppsala), (Milan); Paul Ehrlich Prize 1989, Lundbeck Foundation Prize 1989, H.C. Ørsted Award 1967, Ole Rømer Award 1983, Astra Award 1991, W. Th. Nauta Award 1996, Pharmaceutical Research Achievement Award 2004, HC. Ørsted Gold Medal 2006, Silver Medal 2011. *Film:* A Fungal Fairy Tale 2018. *Publications include:* 450 scientific articles, 80 scientific reviews, eight science books (ed.), one textbook (ed.). *Leisure interests:* history, sport. *Address:* Department of Drug Design and Pharmacology, Faculty of Health and Medical Sciences, University of Copenhagen, 2 Universitetsparken, 2100 Copenhagen (office); 25 Elmevej, Blovstrød, 3450 Allerød, Denmark (home). *Telephone:* 93-56-54-88 (office); 93-56-54-88 (home). *E-mail:* pkl@sund.ku.dk (home). *Website:* www.dfh.dk/uk (office).

KROHN DEVOLD, Kristin, MSc; Norwegian national organization official and fmr politician; *Secretary General, Den Norske Turistforening (Norwegian Trekking Association);* b. 12 Aug. 1961, Ålesund; d. of Edvard Hans A. Devold and Kristin Hoegh Krohn Devold; single; two c.; ed Univ. of Bergen, Norwegian School of Econs, Univ. of Oslo, Norwegian Nat. Defence Coll.; mem. Oslo City Parl. 1991–93; mem. Stortinget (Parl.) for Oslo 1993–97, 1997–2001, 2001–05, Sec. of the Lagting (Presidium, Stortinget) 1993–97, mem. Standing Cttee on Business and Industry 1993–97, Election Cttee 1997–2001, 2001–05, Working Procedures Cttee 1997–2001, Extended Foreign Affairs Cttee 1997–2001, Chair. Standing Cttee on Justice 1997–2001; Minister of Defence 2001–05; Substitute mem. Del. to Consultation Organ for European Econ. Area Affairs, Brussels 1993–97; Group Sec. Parl. Group, Conservative Party 1987–92, mem. Bd Party 1996, Parl. Steering Cttee 1997–2001; Sec.-Gen. Norwegian Trekking Asscn 2006–; mem. Bd Statistics Norway 1989–93, St Hanshaugen Residence for the Elderly and Nursing Home 1991–92, Main Cttee of World Handball Championship 1999, Save the Children Norway 1999–. *Address:* Den Norske Turistforening (Norwegian Trekking Association), Youngstorget 1, 0181 Oslo, Norway (office). *Telephone:* 40-00-18-68 (office). *E-mail:* info@turistforeningen.no (office). *Website:* www.turistforeningen.no (home).

KRÓL, Jan Władysław; Polish politician and economist; b. 24 June 1950, Mielec; four c.; ed Higher School of Econs, Kraków, Jagiellonian Univ., Kraków; worker, PAX Soc. 1974–81, Inco-Veritas 1982–83, Remo and Rovan cos 1983–89; mem. Solidarity Independent Self-governing Trade Union (NSZZ Solidarność) 1980–; Assoc., Dziekania Political Thought Club 1984–88; Deputy Govt Plenipotentiary for Local Govt Reform 1989–90; Deputy to the Sejm (Parl.) 1989–2001, Vice-Leader Trade and Services Comm. 1989–97, Sec. Democratic Union (UD) Parl. Caucus 1989–91, Leader, Extraordinary Cttee for consideration of bills within the State Enterprise Pact 1991–93, Vice-Marshal of Sejm 1997–2001; Co-Chair. Polish Ass. of Sejms of Poland and Lithuania 1997–2001; Co-founder and mem. Ruchu Obywatelskiego Akcja Demokratyczna (ROAD—Civic Democratic Action Movt) 1990–91, Democratic Union 1991–94; Chair. Polish-Canadian Econ. Council 1990; mem. Nat. Polish Bd of the Friends of Lithuania Club 1992; mem. Freedom Union (UW) 1994–, mem. Political Council; Chair. Programme Bd Foundation for Econ. Educ. 1999–; Deputy Pres., Council of the Bd, Foundation in Support of Local Democracy; fmr Strategic Advisor, Ernst and Young Poland; Kt's Cross and Commdr, Order of Polonia Restituta; Order of the Grand Duke Gediminas, Second Class (Lithuania). *Publications:* Świadectwo (Evidence) 1989, Przodem do przodu (Face Forward) 1993, Z notatnika posła (From Deputy Notebook) 1997, W dialogu (In Dialogue) 1999, Pułapki polskiej demokracji (Polish Democracy Traps) 2001; numerous articles. *Leisure interests:* tourism, hiking, biking, horse riding. *Address:* Biuro Krajowe, Unii Wolności, Marszałkowska 77–79, 00-683 Warsaw, Poland (office). *Telephone:* (22) 827-50-47 (office). *E-mail:* jan.krol@andersen.com (office); info@unia-wolnosci.pl (office). *Website:* www.uw.org.pl/wladze.php?id=43 (office).

KROL, John A., BS, MSc; American business executive; b. 16 Oct. 1936, Ware, Mass.; m. Janet Valley; two d.; ed Tufts Univ., Bettis Nuclear Reactor Eng School; commissioned into USN 1959, worked as nuclear engineer Bureau of Ships Naval Reactors Br.; joined E.I. du Pont de Nemours & Company as chemist, Wilmington, Del. 1963, marketing and manufacturing positions with DuPont Fibers 1965–83, Vice-Pres. 1983, Sr Vice-Pres. 1990, Group Vice-Pres., Sr Vice-Pres. DuPont Agric. Products 1986, Vice-Chair. DuPont 1992–97, Chair. 1997–98, Pres. 1995–97, CEO 1995–98 (retd); Chair. Delphi Automotive LLP 2009–15; Trustee Tufts Univ., Univ. of Del., Hagley Museum, US Council for Int. Business; mem. Nat. Agricultural Chemists Asscn, American Chemical Soc. Corp. Liaison Bd, Business Roundtable, Business Council; mem. exec. Cttee Del. Business Roundtable, Business/Public Educ. Council. *Leisure interests:* golf, tennis, squash, skiing.

KROLL, Alexander (Alex) S., BA; American advertising executive (retd); *Chairman Emeritus, Young and Rubicam Inc.;* b. 1937, Leechburg, Pa; ed Rutgers Univ.; fmr player, NY Titans, American Football League; with Young & Rubicam, Inc., New York 1962–, copywriter 1962–68, Vice-Pres. 1968–69, Sr Vice-Pres. 1969–70, Exec. Vice-Pres. and Worldwide Creative Dir 1970–75, Man. Dir Young & Rubicam USA 1975–77, Pres. 1977, Pres. and COO, Young & Rubicam, Inc. 1982, CEO 1985, then Chair. and CEO 1986, Chair. Emer. 1994–; Chair. Emer. The Advertising Council; fmr Chair. American Asscn of Advertising Agencies; fmr Partner, New York City Partnership; fmr Trustee, United States Council for Int. Business; fmr mem. Bd of Dirs Advertising Educational Foundation, Inst. for East/West Studies, NFL Alumni Board; Horatio Alger Award, Walter Camp Distinguished American Award, Nat. Human Relations Award, American Jewish Cttee, Kodak Life Achievement Award 1985, Nat. Coll. Athletic Asscn Silver Anniversary Award 1987, inducted into Coll. Football Hall of Fame 1997, Advertising Hall of Fame 1997.

KROLL, Lucien; Belgian architect, town planner, critic and writer; b. 17 March 1927, Brussels; m. Simone Marti; two d.; ed Athénée Royal de Huy, Ecole Nat. Supérieure d'Architecture de la Cambre, Institut Supérieur d'Urbanisme de la Cambre, Institut Supérieur et Int. d'Urbanisme Appliqué, Brussels; numerous works in Belgium, France, Italy, Germany, Italy and Rwanda 1953–; Founder mem. Inst. d'Esthétique Industrielle 1956; own architectural practice 1952–; environmental research, Ecolonia, Netherlands; exhbns of work in Brussels, Hanover, Utrecht, Aubervilliers, Copenhagen, Aarhus, Luxembourg, Boston; organized confs including Habiter?, Brussels 1972; visiting prof. and lecturer on urban ecology at numerous univs world-wide; mem. Acad. française d'Architecture 1985–, BDA; Academician, Int. Acad. of Architecture 1994–; Hon. mem. Bund der Deutschen Architekten; Commdr, Ordre des Arts et des Lettres; Médaille J.-F. Delarue, Acad. française d'Architecture 1980. *Publications:* CAD-Architektur 1985, Architecture of Complexity 1986, Buildings and Projects (also in German and French) 1987, Componenten 1995, Bien vieillir chez soi 1995, Enfin chez soi 1996, Eco, Bio, Psycho about Urban Ecology 1996, Tutto e paesaggio (also in French 2001), Ecologie urbane 2002, Rassegna 'Lucien Kroll'; more than 800 articles on industrial and urban architectural design and comparative architecture. *Address:* Atelier d'Urbanisme, d'Architecture et d'Informatique L. Kroll, Avenue Louis Berlaimont 20, Boîte 9, 1160 Brussels, Belgium (office). *Telephone:* (2) 673-35-39 (office). *Fax:* (2) 673-89-27 (office). *E-mail:* kroll@brutele.be (office). *Website:* homeusers.brutele.be/kroll (office).

KROLL, Sue, BA; American film industry executive; *Founder, Kroll & Co. Entertainment;* b. 1961; ed Glassboro State Univ.; began career in New York working over a seven-year period in various divs of Viacom, including Showtime Networks Inc., The Movie Channel and Viewer's Choice; relocated to Atlanta, Ga to head the Marketing Dept at Turner Network Television (TNT), then Sr Vice-Pres. and Man. Dir TNT and Cartoon Network Europe, then relocated to London, UK; joined Warner Bros. Pictures as Head of Programming and Operations for Warner Bros. International Channels 1994, Sr Vice-Pres. prior to leading the Div. (following Time Warner merger with Turner), Pres. Int. Marketing Div. 2000–07, Pres. Worldwide Marketing, Warner Bros. Pictures 2008–18; Founder Kroll & Co. Entertainment 2018–; active in numerous mentoring and volunteering orgs, including Big Brothers Big Sisters of Los Angeles, inaugural mem. Big Brothers Big Sisters' Women in Entertainment Mentorship Program; mem. Exec. Cttee Film Independent, Los Angeles; Sherry Lansing Award, Big Brothers Big Sisters of Los Angeles 2009.

KRON, Patrick; French manufacturing executive; *President, Truffle Capital;* b. 26 Sept. 1953, Paris; ed École Polytechnique, École des Mines, Paris; with Ministry of Industry 1979–84; joined Pechiney Group 1984, various operational roles, Pechiney, Greece 1984–88, various sr financial roles, Paris 1988–93, becoming Pres., Electrometallurgy Div., mem. Exec. Cttee, Pechiney Group 1993–97, Chair. Carbone Lorraine Co. 1993–95, Head, Food and Healthcare Packaging Sector, Pechiney 1995–97, and COO, American Nat. Can Co., Chicago 1995–97; CEO Imerys 1998–2002; mem. Exec. Bd Alstom 2001–16, CEO Jan. 2003–16, Chair. March 2003–16, also Chair. Alstom Resources Man. and Dir Alstom UK Holdings Ltd, apptd Chair. GE Power Service 2003, fmr Vice-Pres. (Exec.) Refractories & Abrasives, currently mem. Bd of Dirs; Pres. Truffle Capital 2016–; Chair. Finance & Audit Cttee, LafargeHolcim Ltd, mem. Bd of Dirs 2017–; mem. Bd of Dirs Bouygues 2006–, Sanofi SA 2014–, Halcor Metal Works SA 2017–, Asscn Française des Entreprises Privées, Les Arts Florissants; mem. Supervisory Bd Imerys 2003–05 (Dir 2005–06), Vivendi Universal 2005–06, Segula Technologies 2017; Chevalier, Légion d'honneur 2004, Officier, Ordre nat. du Mérite 2007. *Address:* Truffle Capital, 5 Rue de la Baume, 75008 Paris, France (office). *Telephone:* 1-82-28-46-00 (office). *Website:* truffle.com (office).

KRONKAITIS, Maj.-Gen. (retd) Jonas A., BS, MBA; Lithuanian army officer (retd); b. 1 Dec. 1935; m. Rūta Kronkaitis; one s. one d.; ed Univ. of Connecticut, Syracuse Univ., US Army War Coll., US Army Command and Gen. Staff Coll., USA; 27 years of mil. service in US Armed Forces; held positions successively as infantry platoon leader, battalion commdr, G-4 of 1st Armoured Div., Instructor in Man. Studies Ordnance School and Centre, served with 4th Armoured Corps, 2nd Armoured Cavalry Regiment and 1st Armoured Div., Germany, with 1st Cavalry Div., Viet Nam, Insp.-Gen. US Army, Jt Project Man. (Army and Navy) Guided Projectiles and Cannon Artillery Weapons Systems; Man.-Gen. Rock Island Arsenal (state-owned armament mfg co.); Dir Dept of Defence Programs, Atlantic Research Corpn (co. mfg rocket motors), USA –1997; Vice-Minister of Defence, Repub. of Lithuania 1997–99; Commdr, Lithuanian Armed Forces 1999–2004; apptd Brig.-Gen. 1999, Maj.-Gen. 2001; Co-founder Piliečių Santalka (civic group) 2006; fmr mem. AIAA, Assoc. of US Army, Lithuanian–American Community, Nat. Security Industrial Asscn, Navy League; fmr Chair. Bd Trustees Baltic Inst.; Legion of Merit; Viet Nam Cross of Gallantry, three Bronze Stars, three Meritorious Service Medals, Army Commendation Medal, Air Medal.

KROPF, Susan J., BA, MBA; American retail executive; ed St John's Univ., New York Univ.; joined Avon Products Inc. 1970, Vice-Pres. Product Devt 1990–92, Sr Vice-Pres. US Marketing 1992–93, Sr Vice-Pres. Global Product Man. 1993–94, Pres. New and Emerging Markets Div. 1994–97, Pres. Avon US 1997–98, COO for N America 1999–2001, Co. Pres. and COO 2001–07 (retd), mem. Bd of Dirs 2015–; mem. Bd of Dirs MeadWestvaco Corpn 2002–, Sherwin Williams Co. 2003–, Coach, Inc. 2006–, Kroger 2007–, Fragrance Foundation; Trustee, Wallace Foundation; mem. Cosmetic Exec. Women, Fashion Group Int; YWCA Acad. of Women Achievers Award 1997, Beautiful Apple Award, March of Dimes 2004, Lifetime Achievement Award, Cosmetic Exec. Women 2006.

KROPIWNICKI, Jerzy Janusz, DEcon; Polish politician and economist; b. 5 July 1945, Częstochowa; m.; one s.; ed Warsaw School of Econs; scientific worker, Łódź Univ. 1968–81 (dismissed); mem. Solidarity Ind. Self-governing Trade Union 1980–, Deputy Chair. Solidarity Łódź Region Br., mem. Solidarity Nat. Comm., co-organizer demonstration against martial law, arrested 13 Dec. 1981, sentenced to 6 years' imprisonment, released under amnesty July 1984; illegal activity 1984–90, co-organizer, Solidarity Regional Exec. Comm., Łódź 1984–86, co-organizer and activist, Working Group of Solidarity Nat. Comm. 1986–90; apptd scientific worker, Econ.-Sociological Faculty of Łódź Univ. 1989; Deputy to Sejm (Parl.) 1991–93 and 1997–2001; Minister of Labour and Social Policy 1991–92; Minister-Head of Cen. Office of Planning 1992–93; Minister and Head of Governmental Centre for Strategic Studies 1997–2001; Minister of Regional Devt and Construction 2000–01; Mayor of Łódź 2002–10; Advisor to Pres. Polish Nat. Bank Marek Belka 2010, mem. Monetary Policy Council 2016–; mem. Christian-Nat. Union (ZChN), mem. Presidium of ZChN Gen. Bd 1989–93, Vice-Pres. 1991–93, 2000–02, Pres. 2002–06. *Publications include:* numerous articles on econs and four books. *Leisure interests:* mountain hiking, reading (history and science-fiction).

KROTOV, Mikhail Valentinovich, Cand. Law; Russian government official; *Plenipotentiary Presidential Representative in the Constitutional Court;* b. 14 March 1963, Leningrad (now St Petersburg); ed A.A. Zhdanov Leningrad State Univ.; with St Petersburg Univ. 1986–2005, positions including Sr Lecturer, Head of Chair of Legal Protection for the Environment, Pro-Rector for Legal and Econ. Matters; First Deputy Gen. Dir Gazprom-Media 2005; Plenipotentiary Presidential Rep. in the Constitutional Court of the Russian Fed. 2005–; Order 'Of Honour', Hon. title 'Deserved Lawyer of the Russian Federation'; Educ. Prize of the Pres. of the Russian Fed. 2001, Educ. Prize of the Govt of the Russian Fed. 2007. *Publications include:* Collection of Speeches by the Plenipotentiary Presidential Representative in the Constitutional Court of the Russian Federation 2009, Civil Right 2011. *Address:* The Presidential Executive Office, Staraya Square 4, Moscow 103132, Russia (office). *Telephone:* (495) 606-44-18 (office). *Fax:* (495) 606-30-27 (office). *Website:* archive.kremlin.ru/eng/subj/97793.shtml (office).

KRSTIĆ, Lazar; Serbian economist and politician; b. 1984, Nis; ed Yale Univ., USA; Consultant, later Assoc. Prin., McKinsey & Co., New York –2013; Minister of Finance and the Economy 2013–14 (resgnd).

KRSTIČEVIĆ, Maj.-Gen. (retd) Damir; Croatian army officer (retd) and politician; *Deputy Prime Minister and Minister of Defence;* b. 1 July 1969, Vrgorac, Socialist Repub. of Croatia, Socialist Fed. Repub. of Yugoslavia; ed Army Acad., Belgrade, Univ. of Zagreb, US Army War Coll., George C. Marshall Center, European Center for Security Studies; joined Croatian Armed Forces 1991, Commdr of several divs including Scout Platoon of 4th Guards Brigade 1991, 4th Bn of 4th Guards Brigade 1991–92, 115th Brigade 1992, 113rd Brigade 1992–93, 4th Guards Brigade 1993–96, Commander, Fifth Mil. Dist 1996–97, Commdr, Training Command 1998, Deputy Chief of Gen. Staff 1998–2000 (retd); rank of Major 1992, Lt-Col 1993, Col 1993, Staff Brigadier 1995, Maj.-Gen. 1995; Chair. Supervisory Bd M SAN Grupa dd 2001–09, Deputy Chair. 2009–15; mem. Supervisory Bd KING ICT ddo 2007–15; Chair. Supervisory Bd PP Orahovica dd 2012–15; mem. Sabor (Parl.) and Head of Del. of Croatian Parl. to NATO Parl. Ass. 2015–; Deputy Prime Minister and Minister of Defence 2016–; Order of Duke Domagoj with neck badge 1995, Order of the Croatian Trefoil 1996; Memorial Medal of the Homeland War 1992, Operation Ljeto '95 Medal 1995, Operation Storm Medal 1995. *Address:* Ministry of Defence, 10000 Zagreb, trg kralja Petra Krešimira IV, Croatia (office). *Telephone:* (1) 4567111 (office). *Fax:* (1) 4568109 (office). *E-mail:* infor@morh.hr (office). *Website:* www.morh.hr (office).

KRUEGER, Anne Osborn, PhD; American economist, international organization official and academic; *Professor of International Economics, Paul H. Nitze School of Advanced International Studies, Johns Hopkins University;* b. 12 Feb. 1934, Endicott, NY; d. of Leslie A. Osborn and Dora W. Osborn; m. James Henderson 1981; one d.; ed Oberlin Coll. and Univ. of Wisconsin; Asst Prof. of Econs, Univ. of Minnesota 1959–63, Assoc. Prof. 1963–66, Prof. 1966–82; Research Assoc., Nat. Bureau of Econ. Research 1969–82; Vice-Pres. Econs and Research, IBRD 1982–86; Univ. Arts and Sciences Prof. of Econs, Duke Univ. 1987–92; Sr Fellow (non-resident), Brookings Inst. 1988–94; Herald L. and Caroline L. Ritch Prof. of Humanities and Sciences, Stanford Univ. 1993–, Dir Center for Research on Econ. Devt and Policy Reform 1996–2001; First Deputy Man. Dir IMF 2001–06, Acting Man. Dir March–May 2004, Special Adviser to the Man. Dir 2006–; Prof. of Int. Econs, Paul H. Nitze School of Advanced Int. Studies, Johns Hopkins Univ. 2007–; visiting prof. at univs in USA, Denmark, Germany, France, Australia and Sweden; mem. editorial bds of several int. econ. journals; fmr Vice-Pres. American Econ. Asscn, Pres. 1996–97; mem. NAS; Fellow, American Acad. of Arts and Sciences, Econometric Soc.; Hon. Prof., Nat. Acad. of the Economy, Moscow 2004; Dr hc (Hacettepe Univ., Ankara) 1990; Hon. DHumLitt (Georgetown) 1993; Hon. DEcons (Monash Univ., Australia) 1995; Hon. Dr of Business (Melbourne Business School) 2004; Robertson Prize, NAS 1984, Bernhard-Harms Prize, Kiel Inst. 1990; Kenan Enterprise Award, Kenan Charitable Trust 1990, Frank E. Seidman Distinguished Award in Political Economy 1993. *Publications include:* Foreign Trade Regimes and Economic Development: Turkey 1974, The Benefits and Costs of Import Substitution in India: A Microeconomic Study 1975, Trade and Development in Korea (co-ed.) 1975, Growth, Distortions and Patterns of Trade Among Many Countries 1977, The Developmental Role of the Foreign Sector and Aid: Korea 1979, Trade and Employment in Developing Countries (co-ed.) 1981, Exchange Rate Determination 1983, The Political Economy of International Trade (co-ed.) 1989, Aid and Development (co-author) 1989, Perspectives on Trade and Development 1990, Political Economy of Policy Reform in Developing Countries 1993, American Trade Policy 1995, The WTO as an International Institution (ed.) 1998, Struggling with Success: Challenges to the International Economy 2012. *Address:* Bernstein-Offit Building 574, The Paul H. Nitze School of Advanced International Studies, The Johns Hopkins University, 1717 Massachusetts Avenue NW, Washington, DC 20036, USA (office). *Telephone:* (202) 587-3238 (office). *Fax:* (202) 663-5656 (office). *E-mail:* annekrueger@jhu.edu (office). *Website:* www.sais-jhu.edu (office).

KRÜGER, Harald; German business executive; *Chairman of the Board of Management, BMW AG;* b. 13 Oct. 1965, Freiburg im Breisgau; ed Hoffmann von Fallersleben School, Braunschweig, Technical Univ. of Braunschweig, RWTH Aachen Univ.; Research Asst, Inst. of Flight System Dynamics, German Aerospace Centre (DLR), Oberpfaffenhofen 1991–92; joined BMW 1992, Traineeship, Tech. Planning/Production Div. 1992–93, Project Engineer for plant assembly at Spartanburg (USA) 1993–95, Personnel Officer for Test Vehicle Construction, Research and Innovation Centre (FIZ), Munich 1995–97, Head of Strategic Production Planning Dept, Munich 1997–2000, Head of Production Strategy and Communication 2000–03, Dir of Engine Production, Hams Hall, BMW Group UK 2003–06, Dir of Tech. Integration, Munich 2007–08, mem. Bd of Man., BMW AG, responsible for Human Resources 2008–12, for MINI, Motorrad, Rolls-Royce, Aftersales BMW Group 2012–13, for Production 2013–15, Chair. Bd of Man. 2015–. *Address:* BMW AG, 130 Petuelring, Munich 80788, Germany (office). *Telephone:* (89) 382-0 (office). *Fax:* (89) 382-258-58 (office). *E-mail:* info@bmwgroup.com (office). *Website:* www.bmwgroup.com (office); www.bmw.com (office).

KRÜGER, Hardy; German actor and writer; b. 12 April 1928, Berlin; s. of Max Krüger and Auguste Krüger (née Meier); m. 1st Renate Damrow; one d.; m. 2nd Francesca Marazzi; one s. one d.; m. 3rd Anita Park 1978; German repertory theatre 1945–56, entered films in 1943; several awards and prizes. *Films include:* Der Rest ist Schweigen 1959, Blind Date 1959, Taxi pour Tobrouk 1961, Hatari 1961, Les Dimanches de Ville d'Avray 1962, Les Quatre Verités 1962, Le Gros Coup 1963, Le Chant du Monde 1964, Flight of the Phoenix 1965, The Defector 1966, La Grande Sauterelle 1966, The Battle of Neretva 1968, The Secret of Santa Vittoria 1969, Death of A Stranger 1972, Le Solitaire 1973, Barry Lyndon 1974, Paper Tiger 1974, Potato Fritz (Best Actor Award, Cannes) 1975, A Bridge Too Far 1976, L'Autopsie d'un Monster 1976, The Wild Geese 1978. *Publications:* Ein Farm in Afrika 1970, Sawimbulu 1971, Wer stehend stirbt, lebt länger 1973, Diè Schallmauer 1978, Die Frau des Griechen 1980, Junge Unrast 1983, Sibirienfahrt, Tagebuch einer Reise 1985, Frühstück mit Theodore 1990, Weltenbummler, Reisen zu Menschen und Göttern 1992, Weltenbummler, Willkommen auf funf Kontinenten 1994, Weltenbummler, Glückliche Tage auf dem Blauen Planeten 1996, Wanderjahre 1999, Szenen eines Clowns 2001. *Address:* Maximilianstrasse 23, 80539 Munich, Germany.

KRÜGER, Manfred Paul, DPhil; German writer, academic and editor; *Lecturer, Institute for Spiritual Science and Arts;* b. 23 Feb. 1938, Köslin; s. of Paul Krüger and Hildegard Krüger; m. Christine Petersen 1962; three s. four d.; ed Oberrealschule Ansbach, Heidelberg Univ., Tübingen Univ.; Asst Prof., Erlangen Univ. 1966–73; Lecturer, Inst. for Spiritual Science and Arts, Nuremberg 1972–; Lecturer, Fachhochschule Ottersberg 1980–2010; Co-Ed. Goetheanum weekly 1984–96. *Publications include:* Gérard de Nerval 1966, Wandlungen des Tragischen 1973, Nora Ruhtenberg 1976, Bilder und Gegenbilder 1978, Wortspuren 1980, Denkbilder 1981, Literatur und Geschichte 1982, Mondland 1982, Nah ist er 1983, Meditation 1983, Rosenroman 1985, Meditation und Karma 1988, Anthroposophie und Kunst 1988, Ästhetik der Freiheit 1992, Ichgeburt 1996, Das Ich und seine Masken 1997, Die Verklärung auf dem Berge 2003. *Address:* Rieterstrasse 20, 90419 Nuremberg, Germany (home). *Telephone:* (911) 338678 (home).

KRUGMAN, Paul Robin, PhD; American economist and academic; *Professor of Economics and International Affairs, Woodrow Wilson School of Public and International Affairs, Princeton University;* b. 28 Feb. 1953, Albany, New York; s. of David Krugman and Anita Krugman; m. Robin Leslie Bergman 1983; ed Yale Univ., Massachusetts Inst. of Tech.; taught at Stanford Univ.; Asst Prof., Yale Univ. 1977–79; Asst Prof., MIT 1979–80, Assoc. Prof. 1980–82, Ford Int. Prof. of Econs 1983–2000; Sr Int. Economist for Pres.'s Council of Econ. Advisers, under Ronald Reagan 1982–83; Op-Ed Columnist, New York Times 1999–; Prof. of Econs and Int. Affairs, Woodrow Wilson School of Public and Int. Affairs, Princeton Univ. 2000–15; Prof., Grad. Center, CUNY 2015–, Distinguished Scholar, Luxembourg Income Study Center 2015–; Centenary Prof., LSE, UK; Sanjaya Lall Visiting Prof. of Business and Devt, Green Templeton Coll., Oxford Trinity Term 2014; Research Assoc., Nat. Bureau of Econ. Research; mem. Group of Thirty Consultative Group on Int. Econ. and Monetary Affairs, Inc. (G-30), Washington, DC; has served as a consultant to Fed. Reserve Bank of New York, World Bank, IMF, UN, as well as to several countries, including Portugal and the Philippines; Fellow, Econometric Soc.; Fellow, American Acad. of Arts and Sciences; Dr hc (Free Univ. of Berlin) 1998, (Universidade de Lisboa) 2012, (Universidade Técnica de Lisboa) 2012, (Universidade Nova de Lisboa) 2012, Hon. DHumLitt (Haverford Coll.) 2004, Hon. LLD (Univ. of Toronto) 2013; John Bates Clark Medal, American Econ. Asscn 1991, Adam Smith Award, Nat. Asscn for Business Econs 1995, H.C. Recktenwald Prize in Econs, Univ. of Erlangen-Nuremberg, Germany 2000, Columnist of the Year, Editor and Publisher magazine 2002, Prince of Asturias Awards in Social Sciences, Fundación Príncipe de Asturias (Spain) 2004, Nobel Memorial Prize in Econs 2008, James Joyce Award, Literary and Historical Soc., Univ. Coll., Dublin 2014. *Publications include:* author, co-author or ed. more than 33 books, including Market Structure and Foreign Trade (with E. Helpman) 1985, International Economics, Theory and Policy (with M. Obsfeld) 1988, The Age of Diminished Expectations 1990, Rethinking International Trade 1990, Geography and Trade 1991, Currencies and Crises 1992, Peddling Prosperity 1994, The Great Unravelling: From Boom to Bust in Three Short Years (New York Times best-seller) 2003, Microeconomics (with Robin Wells) 2004, Macroeconomics (with Robin Wells) 2005, The Conscience of a Liberal 2007, The Return of Depression Economics and the Crisis of 2008 2009, End This Depression Now! 2012; more than 200 professional journal articles, many of them on int. trade and finance; monthly column, The Dismal Science, for online magazine Slate, columnist for Fortune and has published articles in The New Republic, Foreign Policy, Newsweek and The New York Times Magazine. *Leisure interest:* music. *Address:* Department of Economics, 414 Robertson Hall, Princeton University, Princeton, NJ 08544-1013, USA (office). *E-mail:* pkrugman@princeton.edu (office). *Website:* www.princeton.edu/~pkrugman (office); www.princeton.edu/economics (office); www.krugmanonline.com.

KRUMMACHER, Hans-Henrik, DPhil; German academic; *Professor Emeritus, University of Mainz;* b. 24 Aug. 1931, Essen-Werden; m. Eva Wentscher 1956; one s. four d.; ed Humboldt Univ. Berlin, Univs. of Heidelberg and Tübingen; Archivist, Schiller-Nationalmuseum, Marbach a.N. 1956–58; Asst Prof., Univ. of Cologne 1958–67; Prof. of German Literature, Univ. of Mainz 1967–99, Prof. Emer. 1999–; mem. Akademie der Wissenschaften und der Literatur zu Mainz 1984; Corresp.

mem. Österreichische Akad. der Wissenschaften 1993. *Publications:* Das 'als ob' in der Lyrik 1965, Der junge Gryphius und die Tradition 1976; Ed. Eduard Mörike, Werke und Briefe 1967–, Neudrucke deutscher Literaturwerke 1975–2014, Lyra: Studien zur Theorie und Geschichte der Lyrik vom 16. bis zum 19. Jahrhundert 2013. *Address:* Am Mainzer Weg 10, 55127 Mainz-Drais, Germany (home). *Telephone:* (6131) 477550 (home).

KRUMNOW, Jürgen, Dr rer. pol; German business executive; b. 18 May 1944, Grünberg, Silesia; m. Christiane Krumnow; ed Hamburg Univ.; trainee, Deutsche Bank AG, Bremen 1964–66, Accounting Dept, Frankfurt am Main 1970–74, Exec. Secr. 1974–78, Head, Reutlingen/Tübingen Br. 1978–82, Head, Cen. Accounting and Planning Dept 1982–86, Exec. Man. 1986–88, mem. Exec. Bd 1988–99, Consultant 1999–2004; mem. Supervisory Bd TUI AG 1997–2011, Chair. 2004–11, Chair. Audit Cttee –2004; fmr mem. Supervisory Bd Volkswagen AG, Deutsche Bahn AG, Hapag Lloyd AG, Peek & Cloppenburg KG; Deputy Chair. Lenze Holding; fmr Chair. Deutsches Rechnungslegungs Standards Cttee (DRSC—German Accounting Standards Bd); mem. European Advisory Council, Air Products & Chemicals Inc., Pa, USA.

KRUPP, Fred; American lawyer, environmental activist and national organization official; *President, Environmental Defense Fund;* m. Laurie Krupp; three c.; ed Yale Univ., Univ. of Michigan Law School; spent several years in pvt. law practice in New Haven, Conn. in several firms: Cooper, Whitney, Cochran & Krupp 1984; Partner, Albis & Krupp 1978–84; Founder and Gen. Counsel, Connecticut Fund for the Environment 1978–84; Pres. Environmental Defense Fund 1984–; mem. Bd H. John Heinz III Center for Science, Econs and the Environment, John F. Kennedy School of Govt Environment Council, Leadership Council of the Yale School of Forestry and Environmental Studies; fmr mem. Pres.'s Advisory Cttee on Trade Policy and Negotiations for both Pres. Bill Clinton and Pres. George W. Bush; helped launch corp. coalition US Climate Action Partnership; Hon. DHumLitt (Haverford Coll.) 2014; Keystone Leadership in Environment Award 1999, Champion Award, Women's Council on Energy and the Environment 2002. *Achievements include:* won gold medal in FISA World Rowing Championships 2006. *Publication:* Earth: The Sequel: The Race to Reinvent Energy and Stop Global Warming (with Miriam Horn) (New York Times Best Seller) 2008. *Leisure interests:* rowing. *Address:* Environmental Defense Fund, 257 Park Avenue South, New York, NY 10010, USA (office). *Telephone:* (212) 505-2100 (office). *Fax:* (212) 505-2375 (office). *E-mail:* info@edf.org (office). *Website:* www.edf.org (office).

KRYLOV, Sergey Borisovich; Russian diplomatist and business executive; b. 26 Oct. 1949, Moscow; m.; two d.; ed Moscow State Inst. of Int. Relations, Diplomatic Acad. of Ministry of Foreign Relations; diplomatic service 1971–; translator, attaché, Embassy in Zaire 1971–76; attaché, Third, then Second Sec., Second Africa Dept, USSR Ministry of Foreign Affairs 1976–79, First Sec., Counsellor to Minister 1979–86, Asst to Deputy Minister 1986–89, Minister-Counsellor, USSR Embassy in Lisbon 1990–92, Exec. Sec., Ministry of Foreign Affairs of Russia 1992–93, Deputy Minister of Foreign Affairs 1993–96, Amb. and Perm. Rep. to UN, New York and Amb. and Perm. Rep. to other int. orgs, Geneva 1997–98, Amb. to Germany 1998–2004; Head, Int. Relations Office, Sistema Corpn 2004.

KRZAKLEWSKI, Marian, DIng; Polish politician and trade union official; b. 23 Aug. 1950, Kolbuszowa; m.; two s.; ed Silesian Tech. Univ., Gliwice 1975; scientific worker, Polish Acad. of Sciences (PAN) and Silesian Tech. Univ., Gliwice 1976–90; joined Solidarity Trade Union 1980, Chair. of Solidarity 1991–2002; apptd mem. ICFTU 1991; Co-founder and Leader, Solidarity Election Action (AWS) 1996–2001; Deputy to Sejm (Parl.) 1997–2001; Chair. Solidarity Election Action Parl. Club 1997–2001, main negotiator and jt architect of parl. and govt coalition Solidarity Election Action–Freedom Union; Co-founder and Chair. Social Movt of Solidarity Election Action (RS AWS) 1997–2000 (merged with three other parties to form Solidarity Electoral Action of the Right 2000); Hon. Chair. Social Movt of Solidarity Election Action (RS AWS) 1999; Cross of Freedom and Solidarity 2012; Man of the Year, Zycie newspaper 1996, Kisiel Prize 1997, Platinum Laurel of Skills 1998. *Publication includes:* Solidarity's Revival and Polish Politics. *Leisure interests:* family life, tourism, sport, arts, literature. *Address:* Komisja Krajowa NSZ2 Solidarnose, ul. Wały Piastowskie 24, 80-855 Gdańsk, Poland. *Telephone:* (58) 308 44 72. *Fax:* (58) 305 90 44.

KRZANICH, Brian Matthew, BS; American business executive; b. 9 May 1960, Santa Clara County, Calif.; m. Brandee Krzanich; two d.; ed San José State Univ.; began career as process engineer at Intel in NM 1982, held plant and manufacturing man. roles at several Intel factories including Manufacturing Man., Fab 12 assembly site, Chandler, Arizona 1994–96, Plant Man., Fab 5, Chandler 1996–97, Fab 17, Hudson, Mass 1997–2001, responsible for implementation of 0.13-micron logic process technology across Intel's global factory network 2001–03, oversaw integration of Digital Equipment Corpn's semiconductor manufacturing operations into Intel's manufacturing network, Head of Assembly and Test 2003–07, Head of Fab/Sort Manufacturing 2007–11, Sr Vice Pres., Intel Corpn 2010–12, Exec. Vice-Pres. and COO 2012–13, mem. Bd of Dirs and CEO Intel Corpn 2013–18; Chair. Fed. Aviation Admin Drone Advisory Cttee 2016–; mem. American Manufacturing Council Jan.–Aug. 2017; mem. Bd of Dirs Lilliputian, Semiconductor Industry Asscn (Chair. 2015), MiaSole, Inc., Deere & Co. 2016–. *Achievements include:* holds one patent for semiconductor processing.

KRZYZEWSKI, Mike, BS; American basketball coach; *Head Men's Basketball Coach, Duke University;* b. 13 Feb. 1947, Chicago, Ill.; m.; three d.; ed Weber High School, Chicago, US Mil. Acad., West Point; served as officer in US Army 1969–74; Grad. Asst Coach at Ind. Univ. 1974–75; Coach, US Mil. Acad., West Point 1976–80; Head Coach, Duke Univ. 1980–, has led Duke to Nat. Collegiate Athletic Asscn (NCAA) Championships 1991, 1992, 2001, 2010, apptd Exec.-in-Residence, Fuqua/Coach K Center on Leadership and Ethics, Fuqua School of Business; Olympic Trials Instructor 1984; coached US team in World Univ. Games 1987, World Championship Games and Goodwill Games 1990; Asst Coach, US Gold Medal Team, Olympic Games 1992; Pres. Nat. Asscn of Basketball Coaches (NABC) 1998–99; coach of Team USA 2006 World Championships, 2008 Beijing Olympics, 2014 World Championships, 2016 Rio Olympics; host, Basketball and Beyond (Sirius XM Satellite Radio show); named Nat. Coach of the Year (eight times), ACC Coach of the Year (five times), named NABC Coach of the Decade (1990s) 2000, inducted into Basketball Hall of Fame 2001, named America's Best Coach by Time magazine/CNN 2001, named Sportsman of the Year by Sports Illustrated 2011, Making History Award, Chicago History Museum 2013. *Publications include:* Leading with the Heart 2001, Beyond Basketball 2006, The Gold Standard: Building a World-Class Team 2009. *Address:* Athletic Department, Duke University, Box 90555, Durham, NC 27708, USA (office). *Telephone:* (919) 613-75005 (office). *E-mail:* gbbrown@duaa.duke.edu (office). *Website:* www.coachk.com (office).

KSEŃ, Jacek, PhD; Polish banking executive; ed Poznan School of Econs, Higher School of Planning and Statistics; Financial Markets Operator, Bank Handlowy –1978; Vice-Dir, Foreign Currency Dept, Polska Kasa Opieka SA, Paris 1978, becoming Head, Foreign Exchange Deals, Head, Foreign Bonds Team 1985–87; Commercial Rep, Bond Dept, Lyonnaise de Banque, Paris 1987–90, also Vice-Dir for Int. Financial Markets 1989–90; Ind. Sr Dealer, Int. Futures Dept, Caisse Nat. Credit Agricole 1990–96, mem. Sr Man. Team 1991–96; Pres. Man. Bd, Wielkopolski Bank Kredytowy (WBK), Poland 1996–2001, Pres. Bank Zachodni WBK (following merger) 2001–07; Chair. Supervisory Bd LOT Polish Airlines 2008–09, ARKA BZ WBK 2007–09; mem. Supervisory Bd MCI Management 2007–08; apptd mem. Supervisory Bd Sygnity SA 2007, fmr Chair.

KUBASIK, Christopher E. (Chris), BA, CPA; American business executive; *Chairman, CEO and President, L3 Technologies, Inc.;* b. 26 March 1961, Cheverly, MD; ed Univ. of Maryland, Carnegie Mellon Univ., Defense Acquisition Univ., Fort Belvoir; Partner, Ernst & Young, LLP 1996–99; joined Lockheed Martin 1999, Chief Financial Officer, Lockheed Martin Corpn 2001–07, Exec. Vice-Pres. Electronic Systems Business Area 2007–10, Pres. and COO 2010–12, Vice-Chair. June–Nov. 2012, Sr Advisor, Lockheed Martin Space Systems Co. 2012–14, Chief Exec. Lockheed Martin Aeronautics Co. –2013, fmr mem. Bd of Dirs; Pres. and CEO Seabury Group LLC 2014–15, mem. Bd of Dirs 2014; Pres. and CEO L3 Technologies, Inc. 2015–18, Chair., CEO and Pres. 2018–; Chair. Sandia Corpn (operates Sandia Nat. Labs for US Dept of Energy) 2007–10; mem. Bd of Dirs Norsk Titanium AS 2015–16, apptd Chair. 2016; serves on United Service Orgs (USO) Bd of Govs, Asscn of the United States Army Council of Trustees, Univ. of Maryland College Park Foundation Bd of Trustees; currently Operating Partner, Virgo Investment Group LLC; mem. Aerospace Industries Asscn, Air Force Asscn (AFA), Nat. Defense Industrial Asscn (NDIA), Navy League of the US, Asscn of the US Army (AUSA). *Address:* L3 Technologies, Inc., 600 Third Avenue, New York, NY 10016, USA (office). *Telephone:* (212) 697-1111 (office). *Fax:* (212) 490-0731 (office). *Website:* www.l3t.com (office).

KUBICE, Col Jan; Czech police officer and politician; b. 3 Oct. 1953; one s.; Dir Buildings of Special Importance Protection Service, Fed. Police Corps 1991–92; Dir Protection Service, Police of the Czech Repub. 1993–94, Dir Operative Documentation Unit 1994–95, Dir Organized Crime Detection Unit 1995–2008; Minister of the Interior 2011–13. *Address:* c/o Ministry of the Interior, Nad Štolou 3, PO Box 21, 170 34 Prague 7, Czech Republic. *E-mail:* public@mvcr.cz.

KUBILIUS, Andrius; Lithuanian politician; *Chairman, Tėvynės Sąjunga—Lietuvos Krikščionys Demokratai (Homeland Union—Lithuanian Christian Democrats);* b. 8 Dec. 1956, Vilnius; m. Rasa Kubilienė; two s.; ed 22nd secondary school, Vilnius, Vilnius Univ.; lab. technician, Vilnius Univ. 1979–90, then engineer, then scientific research asst; mem. Sajūdis Movt 1988–, Exec. Sec. Sajūdis Council 1990–92; mem. Seimas 1992–, First Vice-Chair. 1996–99, mem. Ass. of Elders 2000–03, 2005–, mem. Cttee on European Affairs 2004–12, Cttee of Devt of Information Society 2004–05, Cttee on Rural Affairs 2005–12, Leader of Opposition 2005–08; Prime Minister 1999–2000, 2008–12; mem. Homeland Union 1993, First Deputy Chair. 2000–03 (party absorbed Lithuanian Rightist Union Nov. 2003), Chair. Homeland Union 2003– (party merged with Lithuanian Union of Political Prisoners and Deportees Feb. 2004, merged with Lithuanian Christian Democrats May 2008); Independence Medal of Lithuania 2000, Commdr's Cross, Order of the Lithuanian Grand Duke Gediminas 2004, Third Class Order of the Cross of St Mary's Land (Estonia) 2007. *Publications include:* Kodėl krepšinis Lietuvoje gražesnis už politiką (Why Basketball is More Fascinating than Politics in Lithuania) 2004, Konservatyvioji bendruomenė (The Conservative Community) 2006. *Address:* Tėvynės Sąjunga—Lietuvos Krikščionys Demokratai (Homeland Union—Lithuanian Christian Democrats), L. Stuokos-Gucevičiaus g. 11, Vilnius 01122, Lithuania (office). *Telephone:* (5) 212-1657 (office). *Fax:* (5) 278-4722 (office). *E-mail:* sekretoriatas@tsajunga.lt (office). *Website:* www.tsajunga.lt (office); www.kubilius.lt.

KUBIŠ, Ján; Slovak diplomatist, government official and UN official; *Special Representative of the UN Secretary-General and Head of Mission, United Nations Assistance Mission for Iraq (UNAMI);* b. 12 Nov. 1952, Bratislava; m.; one d.; ed Moscow State Inst. for Int. Affairs; served in Dept of Int. Econ. Orgs, Ministry of Foreign Affairs (Czechoslovakia) 1976–80, Head of Security and Arms Control Section 1985–88, Dir-Gen. Euro-Atlantic Section 1991–92; served in Embassy in Addis Ababa 1980–85; First Sec. Embassy in Moscow 1989–90, Deputy Head and Head of Political Dept 1990–91; Chair. CSCE Cttee of Sr Officials and Amb.-at-Large 1992; Perm. Rep. (for Slovakia), UN Office, GATT and other Int. Orgs, Geneva 1993–94; Chief Negotiator (for Slovakia) for Pact for Stability in Europe 1994; Dir OSCE Conflict Prevention Centre 1994–98; Special Rep. of UN Sec.-Gen. for Tajikistan and Head, UN Mission of Mil. Observers 1998–99; Sec.-Gen. OSCE 1999–2005, Personal Rep. of Chair.-in-Office for Cen. Asia 2000; EU Special Rep. for Cen. Asia 2005–06; Minister of Foreign Affairs 2006–09; Under-Sec.-Gen. and Exec. Sec. UN Econ. Comm. for Europe 2009–12; Special Rep. of UN Sec.-Gen. for Afghanistan and Head, UN Assistance Mission in Afghanistan (UNAMA) 2012–15, Special Rep. of UN Sec.-Gen. for Iraq and Head of Mission, UN Assistance Mission for Iraq (UNAMI) 2015–; mem. UN Sec.-Gen. Sr Man. Group; OSCE Medal 1998. *Address:* United Nations Assistance Mission in Iraq (UNAMI), Diwan School-Green Zone-International Zone, Baghdad, Iraq (office). *E-mail:* unami-information@un.org (office).

KUBIV, Stepan Ivanovych; Ukrainian academic, politician and fmr central banker; *First Vice-Prime Minister and Minister of Economic Development and Trade;* b. 19 March 1962, Mshanets, Zboriv Dist, Ternopil Oblast, Ukrainian SSR, USSR; ed Lviv Polytechnic, Lviv Univ.; Researcher, Ivan Franko Univ., Lviv 1983–88; youth worker and dir, Municipality of Lviv 1988–91; Dir Student Union of Lviv 1991–94; with Western Ukrainian Commercial Bank 1994–2000, Chair.

1997–2000; Chair. JSC Kredobank 2000–08; Assoc. Prof. of Marketing and Logistics, Lviv Polytechnic 2008–; mem. Bank Supervisory Bd, Nat. Bank of Ukraine 2010–12, Gov. Feb.–June 2014; mem. Verkhovna Rada (Parl.), (Batkivshchyna—Fatherland) 2012–14 (resgnd), (Blok Petra Poroshenka—Petro Poroshenko Bloc) Nov. 2014–; commdr in House of Trade Unions, Kyiv, during mass anti-govt protests in Ukraine 2013–14; mem. Nat. Security Council Feb. 2014–; First Vice-Prime Minister and Minister of Econ. Devt and Trade 2016–; Order 'For Merits' (Third Class). *Address:* Office of the Cabinet of Ministers, 01008 Kyiv, vul. M. Hrushevskoho 12/2, Ukraine (office). *Telephone:* (44) 256-63-33 (office). *E-mail:* shustenko@kmu.gov.ua (office). *Website:* www.kmu.gov.ua (office).

KUBUABOLA, Hon. Ratu Inoke; Fijian diplomatist and politician; brother of Ratu Jone Kubuabola; m. Jiu Kubuabola; one s. two d.; worked as man. trainee and Asst Man. with New Zealand Insurance Co. Ltd, Auckland, NZ and Suva, respectively; Distribution Sec., then Gen. Sec., Bible Soc. in the Pacific 1975–87; Minister for Information in Mil. Govt 1987–88, Minister for Information, Broadcasting, Television and Telecommunication 1988–92; Chair. Cakaudrove Prov. Council 1991–2001; MP for Cakaudrove Prov. in House of Reps 1992–2001, Leader of the Opposition 1999–2000; Minister for Youth, Employment Opportunities and Sports 1992–95, for Regional Devt and Multi Ethnic Affairs 1995–97, for Works, Infrastructure and Transport 1996–97, for Information and Communication 1997–98, for Communication, Works and Energy 1998–99, Minister for Foreign Affairs and Int. Co-operation 2009–16, for Immigration, Nat. Security and Defence 2016–18; Leader of Fijian Political Party (Soqosoqo ni Vakavulewa ni Taukei, or SVT) following its defeat in 1999 election; Minister for Information and Communications in interim Cabinet formed by Laisenia Qarase 2000–01; High Commr to Papua New Guinea (also accred to Vanuatu, Solomon Islands and East Timor) 2002–06; Amb. to Japan (also accred to S Korea) 2006–09; mem. Parl. (FijiFirst) 2014–. *Address:* c/o Ministry of Immigration, National Security and Defence, PO Box 2349, Government Buildings, Suva, Fiji (office).

KUČAN, Milan; Slovenian lawyer and politician; b. 14 Jan. 1941, Križevci, Prekmurje; m. Štefka Kučan; two d.; ed Univ. of Ljubljana; joined Fed. of Communists of Slovenia 1958; mem. Cen. Cttee Fed. of Communists of Slovenia; Chair. Comm. on Educational Problems of Cen. Cttee, Youth Union of Slovenia 1963–65; Chair. Cen. Cttee 1968–69; mem. Cen. Cttee Communist Union of Slovenia 1973–78, Chair. 1986–89; Sec. Republican Conf. of Socialist Union of Slovenia 1973–78; Chair. Slovenian Skupščina (Parl.) 1978–86; Pres. of Slovenia 1990–2002; Founder and Chair. Forum 21 group of leaders who discuss Slovenian issues 2004–; mem. Club of Madrid; Grand Collar of the Order of Infante Dom Henrique (Portugal) 2000, Kt Grand Cross of the Grand Order of King Tomislav (Croatia) 2001, Order of White Double Cross 2001, Commdr Grand Cross, Chain of Order of Three Stars (Latvia) 2002, Order of the White Eagle (Poland) 2002, Order of the Cross of Terra Mariana, Kt of the Order of Elephant. *Address:* Forum 21, 1000 Ljubljana, Nazorjeva ulica 6, Slovenia (office). *E-mail:* forum@forum21.si (office). *Website:* www.forum21.si (office).

KUČERA, Jan, CSc; Czech nuclear scientist; Sr Researcher, Nuclear Physics Inst., Acad. of Sciences of the Czech Repub., Řež; mem. Nuclear Analytical Methods in the Life Sciences Int. Cttee, Chair. 2002–, Gen. Chair. Fifth Int. Conf., Prague 1993; Hevesy Medal 2006. *Publications:* Nuclear Analytical Methods in the Life Sciences (co-ed.) 1994; numerous scientific papers in professional journals. *Address:* Nuclear Physics Institute, Academy of Sciences of the Czech Republic, 25068 Řež, Czech Republic (office). *Telephone:* (2) 12241671 (office). *E-mail:* kucera@ujf.cas.cz (office). *Website:* www.ujf.cas.cz (office).

KUCHCIŃSKI, Marek Tadeusz; Polish politician; *Marshal of the Sejm;* b. 9 Aug. 1955, Przemyśl; ed Catholic Univ. of Lublin (now John Paul II Catholic Univ. of Lublin); joined Niezależny Samorządny Związek Zawodowy Rolników Indywidualnych 'Solidarność' (Solidarity Ind. Self-governing Trade Union of Individual Farmers) 1981; worked at Ogólnopolskim Komitecie Oporu Rolników (Nat. Farmers' Resistance Cttee) 1983–89; mem. Komitet Obywatelski 'Solidarność' (Solidarity Citizens' Cttee) in Przemysl Vojvodship and Nat. Solidarity Cttee of Lech Wałęsa 1989; Ed. Spojrzenia Przemyskie (Przemysl Review) monthly magazine 1989–93; instigated Strych Kulturalny ind. discussion club 1990; organized Days of Christian Culture in Przemysl 1990; Head of Przemysl Cultural Soc. 1990–2000; co-organized art exhbns 'Man-God-World' 1993–99; mem. Porozumienie Centrum (Centre Agreement) political party, including time as mem. party bd 1990–99; Second Deputy Gov., Podkarpacie Vojvodship 1991–2001; Head of Programming Bd, Polskie Radio Rzeszów (Polish Radio of Rzeszów), corresp., Radio Lwów (Radio Lviv, Ukraine), contrib. to Nowe Państwo, Rolą Katolicką and Nowy Dziennik (Polish Daily News, New York, USA) publs 1994–98; mem. Przemysl Municipal Council 1994–98; joined Porozumienie Polskich Chrześcijańskich Demokratów (Agreement of Polish Christian Democrats), mem. party bd 1999; mem. Prawo i Sprawiedliwość (PiS—Law and Justice) party, Vice-Pres. 2008–10; mem. (PiS), Sejm (Parl.) 2001–, Head of Parl. Caucus 2006–07, April–Aug. 2010, Deputy Marshal of the Sejm 2010–15, Marshal of the Sejm 2015–; Order for Service (Ukraine) 2007; Krzyż Wolności i Solidarności (Cross of Freedom and Solidarity) 2016. *Address:* Chancellery of the Sejm, 00-902 Warsaw, ul. Wiejska 4/6/8, Poland (office). *Telephone:* (22) 6942500 (office). *Fax:* (22) 6941446 (office). *E-mail:* zjablon@sejm.gov.pl (office). *Website:* www.sejm.gov.pl (office); www.marekkuchcinski.pl.

KUCHERENA, Anatoly G., Dr Jur; Russian barrister; b. 23 Aug. 1961, Mîndra, Moldova; ed Moscow Inst. of Law; f. one of the first law firms under the Moscow city bar 1995, named Kucherena & Partners Law Firm 2003–; apptd Head, Barrister and Notary Dept, Moscow State Juridical Acad. 2001; Founder and Chair. Inst. of Democracy and Cooperation 2007; Chair. Public Council, Ministry of Internal Affairs 2013–, also mem. councils for Russian District-Attorney's Office and Federal Security Service (FSB); mem. Civic Chamber; mem. Presidential Council for Civil Soc. and Human Rights, Moscow Collegium of Barristers. *Publications include:* Ball of Lawlessness, Diagnosis of a Barrister, Who Profits, One Cannot Do Without Blood; contrib. numerous publications to the press on legal problems. *Telephone:* (495) 637-34-71 (office). *E-mail:* ak@argument.ru (office). *Website:* www.kucherena.ru (office).

KUCHKAROV, Jamshid, Cand.econ.sci; Uzbekistani economist and politician; *Deputy Prime Minister and Minister of Finance;* b. 1964, Kattaqo'rg'on, Samarqand Viloyat, Uzbek SSR, USSR; ed Tashkent Inst. of Nat. Economy, Economic Inst. of the State of Colorado, USA; Sr Accountant (agricultural machinery), Kattaqo'rg'on municipality 1985; served in armed forces 1985–87; Asst Lecturer, later Sr Lecturer and Acting Assoc. Prof., Tashkent State Economic Univ. 1990–93; Deputy Head of Dept, later Head of Div., Head of Main Directorate and Dir, Central Bank of Uzbekistan 1993–95, Deputy Chair. 1996–97; Head, State Budget Dept, Ministry of Finance 1997–2005, Deputy Minister of Finance 2005–17, Minister of Finance 2017–, also Deputy Prime Minister, responsible for Macroeconomic Analysis and Forecasting, Reform of Financial and Banking Systems and Devt of Private Enterprise and Small Business 2017–. *Address:* Ministry of Finance, 100008 Tashkent, Mustaqillik maydoni 5, Uzbekistan (office). *Telephone:* (71) 239-12-52 (office). *Fax:* (71) 244-56-43 (office). *Website:* www.mf.uz (office).

KUCHMA, Leonid Danylovych, CTechSc; Ukrainian manager, politician and fmr head of state; b. 1938, Chatikine, Chernihiv Oblast; s. of Danylo Prokopovych Kuchma and Paraska Trokhymivna Kuchma; m. Ludmyla Mykolayovna Kuchma; one d.; ed Dnipropetrovsk Nat. Univ.; mem. CPSU 1960–91; engineer, constructor, Chief Constructor Research-Production, Yuzmash eng plant 1960–75, Sec. Party Cttee 1975–82, Deputy Dir-Gen. 1982–86, Dir-Gen. 1986–92; mem. Cen. Cttee CP Ukrainian SSR 1981–91; People's Deputy of Ukraine 1990–94, May-June 1994; Prime Minister of Ukraine 1992–93 (resgnd); Chair. Ukrainian Union of Industrialists and Entrepreneurs 1993–94; Pres. of Ukraine 1994–2005; charged by Ukrainian prosecutors with involvement in the murder of journalist Georgiy Gongadze March 2011, criminal charges overturned June 2012; Rep. for Ukraine at Trilateral Contact Group 2015–18; Hon. Citizen of the Donetsk Oblast 2002; numerous decorations including Kt Grand Cross with Grand Cordon, Order of Merit of the Italian Repub. 1995, Grand Cross, Order of Vytautas the Great (Lithuania) 1996, Grand Cross, Order of the Lithuanian Grand Duke Gediminas (Lithuania) 1998, Chain of the Order of Prince Henry (Portugal) 1998, Order of the Golden Eagle (Kazakhstan) 1999, Azerbaijani Istiglal Order 1999, Order of St Volodymyr (Gold) 1999, Order 'Bethlehem – 2000' (State of Palestine) 2000, Order of the Repub. (Moldova) 2003, Order of Merit for the Fatherland, First Class (Russia) 2004; Lenin Prize 1981, State Prize 1993. *Address:* Ukrainian Presidential Fund of Leonid Kuchma Charity Organization, 01024 Kyiv, vul. P. Orlyka 1/15, Ukraine (office). *Telephone:* (44) 465-93-52 (office). *E-mail:* press@ldk-fund.org.ua (office). *Website:* www.kuchma.org.ua (office).

KUČINSKIS, Māris; Latvian economist and politician; b. 28 Nov. 1961, Valmiera, Latvian SSR, USSR; m.; ed Valmiera High School No. 4, Latvian State Univ.; Economist, Finance Div., Valmiera City Council 1980–81, Chair., Valmiera City Council 1996–97, 1998–2003; Chair., Valmiera Dist Council 1998–2000; Sr Accountant, Latvia Fire-Fighting Equipment Plant 1984–87; Economist, Housing Facilities and Public Utilities of Valmiera Dist 1987–91; Deputy Dir, Apgāds Limited 1991–94, Dir 1997–98; mem. Tautas Partija (People's Party) 1998–2011, Par Labu Latviju! (For a Good Latvia!) electoral alliance; mem. 8th Saeima (Parl.) 2003–04, 9th Saeima 2006–10, 10th Saeima 2010–11, 11th Saeima July–Nov. 2014, 12th Saeima 2014–16, 13th Saeima 2018–, Chair., Sustainable Devt Cttee 2014–16, Nat. Security Cttee 2018–; Minister of Regional Devt and Local Govt 2004–06; Prime Minister of Latvia 2016–19; mem. Liepāja Partija (Liepāja Party)/Zaļo un Zemnieku Savienība (ZZS–Greens' and Farmers' Union) 2014–; Adviser, Latvian Large Cities Asscn 2010–11, Deputy Exec. Dir 2012–13, Exec. Dir 2013–16. *Address:* Latvijas Republikas Saeima, Jekaba Street 11, Rīga 1811, Latvia (office). *Telephone:* 6708-7321 (office). *E-mail:* info@saeima.lv (office). *Website:* www.saeima.lv (office).

KUCZYNSKI, Pedro Pablo, BA, MA, MPA; Peruvian economist, politician, business executive and fmr head of state; b. 1939, Lima; ed Oxford Univ., UK, Princeton Univ., USA; Loan Officer and Economist Latin America and New Zealand, World Bank 1961–66; Deputy Dir Peruvian Central Bank 1967–69; Sr Economist, IMF 1973–75; Chief Economist, Northern Latin America, World Bank 1971–72, Head of Planning Div. 1972–73; Vice-Pres. Kuhn, Loeb & Co. Int. 1973–75; Chief Economist, Int. Finance Corpn 1975–77; Pres. Halco Mining Co. 1977–80; Minister of Energy and Mines 1980–82; Man. Dir First Boston Corpn then Pres. First Boston Int. 1982–92; Pres. Westfield Capital 1992–94; Co-founder, Pres. and CEO Latin America Enterprise Fund 1994; Minister of Economy and Finance 2001–02, 2004–05; Prime Minister 2005–06; Founder and Hon. Chair. Aqualimpia (non-profit involved in water projects) 2006–; Sr Adviser and Pnr, Rohatyn Group 2007–; Chair. Supervisory Bd AMG Advanced Metallurgical Group NV 2007–; cand. in presidential elections 2011, 2016, Pres. of Peru 2016–18; fmr mem. Bd Tenaris SA, Southern Peru Copper Corpn, current mem. Comm. on Growth and Devt; mem. Peruanos Por el Kambio. *Publication:* Peruvian Democracy under Economic Stress 1977. *Address:* Aqualimpia, Calle Andrés Reyes 524 Piso 3, San Isidro, Lima 27, Peru (office); c/o Office of the President, Presidential Palace, Plaza Mayor, Lima (office); Partido Nacionalista Peruano, Avda Arequipa 3410, Lima 27, Peru (office). *Telephone:* (1) 2223605 (office). *Website:* www.agualimpia.org (office).

KUDASHEV, Nikolai Rishatovich; Russian diplomatist; *Ambassador to India;* b. 1958; m.; one d.; ed Moscow State Inst. of Int. Relations; joined diplomatic service 1981, posted to USSR (later Russian) Embassies in Singapore 1981–85, Manila 1992–96, New Delhi 1999–2002, Minister Counsellor, Embassy in New Delhi 2002–05, Amb. to Philippines (also accred to Palau, Marshall Islands and Micronesia) 2010–15; Deputy Dir, Secr. Gen. (Dept), Ministry of Foreign Affairs 2015–17; Amb. to India 2017–. *Address:* Embassy of the Russian Federation, Shanti Path, Chanakyapuri, New Delhi 110 021, India (office). *Telephone:* (11) 26873799 (office). *Fax:* (11) 26876823 (office). *E-mail:* emb@rusembindia.com (office). *Website:* rusembindia.com (office).

KUDELKA, James Alexander, OC; Canadian choreographer, dancer and fmr artistic director; *Resident Choreographer, Coleman Lemieux & Compagnie;* b. 10 Sept. 1955, Newmarket, Ont.; s. of John Kudelka and Kathleen Mary Kudelka (née Kellington); ed Nat. Ballet School of Canada; dancer, Nat. Ballet of Canada 1972–81, Artist in Residence 1992–96, Artistic Dir 1996–2005, Resident Choreographer 2005–07, continues to undertake collaborative projects; Prin. Dancer, Grand Ballets Canadiens 1981–84, Resident Choreographer 1984–90; Resident Choreographer, Coleman Lemieux & Compagnie contemporary dance co. 2008–; Isadora Duncan Dance Award 1988, Jean A. Chalmers Choreographic Award

1993, numerous Canada Council Grants. *Major works:* (for Nat. Ballet of Canada): Washington Square 1977, Pastorale 1990, Musings 1991, The Miraculous Mandarin 1993, Spring Awakening 1994, The Actress 1994, The Nutcracker (Dora Mavor Moore Award 1995–96) 1995, The Four Seasons 1997, Swan Lake 1999, The Firebird 2000, The Contract (The Pied Piper) 2002, Chacony 2004, Cinderella 2004, An Italian Straw Hat 2005; (for Grand Ballets Canadiens): In Paradisum 1983, Désir 1991; (for Toronto Dance Theatre): Fifteen Heterosexual Duets (Dora Mavor Moore Award 1991–92) 1991; (for Birmingham Royal Ballet, UK): Le Baiser de la fée 1996; (for American Ballet Theater): Cruel World 1994, States of Grace 1995; (for San Francisco Ballet): The Comfort Zone 1989, The End 1992, Terra Firma 1995, Some Women and Men 1998; (for Joffrey Ballet): The Heart of the Matter 1986. *Address:* Coleman Lemieux & Compagnie, 304 Parliament Street, Toronto, ON M5A 3A4, Canada (office). *Telephone:* (416) 364-8011 (office). *Fax:* (416) 364-8011 (office). *E-mail:* admin@colemanlemieux.com (office). *Website:* colemanlemieux.com/company/james_kudelka (office); national.ballet.ca.

KUDLOW, Lawrence (Larry) A., BA; American economist, broadcaster and fmr government official; *CEO, Kudlow and Company, LLC;* b. 20 Aug. 1947, Englewood, NJ; s. of Irving Howard and Ruth Kudlow (née Grodnick); m. 1st Susan Cullman 1981, one d.; m. 2nd Judith Pond 1987; ed Univ. of Rochester, Woodrow Wilson School of Public and Int. Affairs, Princeton Univ.; economist, Fed. Reserve Bank of New York 1973–75; Chief Economist and Corporate Vice-Pres. Paine, Webber, Jackson and Curtis, New York 1975–79; Chief Economist and Partner, Bear, Stearns and Co., New York 1979–81; Asst Dir for Econ. Policy, Office of Man. and Budget, Washington, DC 1981–82, Assoc. Dir for Econs and Planning 1982–83; Pres. and CEO Lawrence Kudlow and Assocs, Washington, DC 1983–84; Pres. and CEO Rodman & Renshaw Economics Inc. 1984–86; Chief Economist and Man. Dir Rodman and Renshaw Capital Group Inc. 1984–86; Chief Economist, Bear, Stearns & Co. 1986–94; CEO Kudlow and Co., LLC, New York 2001–; host, Kudlow and Co. (daily TV current affairs program on CNBC) and Larry Kudlow Show (weekly radio show); mem. St. Patrick's Church Parish Council; mem. Bd of Dirs Hazelden New York, Catholic Cluster School of the Diocese of Bridgeport; mem. Editorial Bd Pajamas Media; Contributing Ed. National Review magazine, columnist and econs dd. National Review Online; Hon. DrIur (Monmouth University) 2009, (University of Rochester) 2013; Extraordinary Commitment Award, St. Patrick's Church of Redding, Bishop's Humanitarian Award, Catholic Charities of Brooklyn and Queens, Humanitarian Award, Pregnancy Care Center of New Rochelle, Distinguished Communicator Award, Brooklyn Diocese, Discovery Award, Sacred Heart Univ. Visionary Award, Council for Economic Education. *Publication:* American Abundance: The New Economic and Moral Prosperity 1998. *Leisure interests:* tennis, golf. *Address:* Kudlow and Company, LLC, 301 Tahmore Drive, Fairfield, CT 06825, USA (office). *Telephone:* (203) 228-5050 (office). *Fax:* (203) 228-5040 (office). *E-mail:* svarga@kudlow.com (office). *Website:* www.kudlow.com (office).

KUDO, Yasumi; Japanese shipping industry executive; *Chairman and Chairman Corporate Officer, Nippon Yusen Kabushiki Kaisha (NYK Line);* joined Nippon Yusen Kabushiki Kaisha (NYK Line) 1975, Dir 2004–, has served as Vice-Pres. Corp. Officer, Man. of Automobile Vessel Group, Man. Dir, Corp. Officer and Sr Man. Corp. Officer, Chief Exec. of Global Logistics HQ, Pres. and Rep. Dir Nippon Yusen Kabushiki Kaisha 2009–15, Chief Exec. Bulk/Energy Resources Transportation 2010–11, Pres. Corp. Officer 2011–15, Chair. and Chair. Corp. Officer 2015–; fmr Deputy Chair. Japan Ship Owners Mutual Protection and Indemnity Asscn. *Address:* Nippon Yusen Kabushiki Kaisha, 3-2, Marunouchi 2-chome, Chiyoda-ku, Tokyo 100-0005, Japan (office). *Telephone:* (3) 3284-5151 (office). *Fax:* (3) 3284-6359 (office). *E-mail:* info@nyk.com (office). *Website:* www.nyk.com (office).

KUDRIN, Aleksei Leonidovich, CandEcon; Russian politician and academic; *Dean, Faculty of Liberal Arts and Sciences, St Petersburg State University;* b. 12 Oct. 1960, Dobele, Latvian SSR, USSR; m. 1st; one d.; m. 2nd Irina Kudrina; one s.; ed Leningrad (now St Petersburg) State Univ., Inst. of Econs, USSR Acad. of Sciences; worked as a motor mechanic and training asst at engine lab. of Acad. of Procurement and Transportation, Ministry of Defence; on staff Inst. of Social-Econ. Problems, Acad. of Sciences 1983–90; Deputy Chair. Cttee on Econ. Reform, Leningrad City Exec. Bd 1990–91; Chair. Cttee on Finance, St Petersburg Mayor's Office 1992–94; First Deputy Mayor of St Petersburg, Head Dept of Finance, Mayor's Office, St Petersburg 1994–96; Deputy Head of Admin., Head Controlling Dept at Russian Presidency 1996–97; First Deputy Minister of Finance, Russian Fed. 1997–99, concurrently Deputy Man. BRD 1997–99; First Deputy Chair. Unified Power Systems of Russia (state co.) 1999–2000; Deputy Chair. of the Govt 2000–04, 2007–11 (resgnd); Minister of Finance 2000–11 (resgnd); Chair. Bd of Trustees, European Univ. of St Petersburg 2016–; currently Dean, Faculty of Liberal Arts and Sciences, St Petersburg State Univ., also Prof., Dept of Theory and Methodology for Teaching Arts and Humanities, Hon. Prof., Dept of Econs, mem. Bd of Overseers, Arts and Humanities Programme; Merit to the Fatherland (Third Degree); World Finance Minister of the Year 2004, European Finance Minister of the Year 2004, Finance Minister of the Year, Euromoney magazine 2010. *Leisure interests:* tennis, swimming, listening to music. *Address:* St Petersburg State University, 190000 St Petersburg, 58-60 Galernaya St., Russia (office). *Telephone:* (812) 320-07-29 (office). *E-mail:* office@smolny.org (office). *Website:* www.artesliberales.spbu.ru (office).

KUDROW, Lisa, BSc; American actress; b. 30 July 1963, Encino, Calif.; m. Michael Stern; one c.; ed Vassar Coll. *Television includes:* To the Moon Alice 1990, Murder in High Places 1991, Bob (series) 1992, Friends (series) 1994–2004, The Comeback (series) 2005, Web Therapy 2008–15. *Films include:* L.A. on $5 a Day 1989, Dance with Death 1991, The Unborn 1991, In the Heat of Passion 1992, In the Heat of Passion II: Unfaithful 1994, The Crazysitter 1995, Mother 1996, Romy and Michelle's High School Reunion 1997, Clockwatchers 1997, The Opposite of Sex 1998, Analyze This 1999, Hanging Up 2000, Lucky Numbers 2000, All Over the Guy 2001, Dr. Dolittle 2 (voice) 2001, Analyze That 2002, Bark 2002, Marci X 2003, Happy Endings 2005, Kabluey 2007, P.S. I Love You 2007, Powder Blue 2009, Hotel for Dogs 2009, Paper Man 2009, Bandslam 2009, Love and Other Impossible Pursuits 2009, Easy A 2010, Neighbours 2014, Neighbours 2: Sorority Rising 2016, The Girl on the Train 2016, Table 19 2017. *Address:* c/o PMK/HBH, 700 San Vicente Boulevard, Suite G 910, West Hollywood, CA 90069; POB 36849, Los Angeles, CA 90036-0849, USA (office).

KUDRYAVTSEV, Nikolay, PhD; Russian academic; *Rector, Moscow Institute of Physics and Technology;* b. 8 May 1950, Moscow; ed Moscow Inst. of Physics and Tech.; Asst, Dept of Molecular Physics, Moscow Inst. of Physics and Tech. 1977, Deputy Dean, Faculty of Molecular and Chemical Physics 1978–87, Dean 1987–88, Head of Dept of Molecular Physics 1988, Prof. 1990, Founder mem. Lab Pulse Tech. 1991, Rector, Moscow Inst. of Physics and Tech. 1997–; Chair. Bd of Rectors of City of Moscow and Moscow Region 2012–; Vice-Pres. Russian Rectors Union 2014–; apptd Dir-Gen. JSC Phonon Defense Industry Ministry 1994; mem. Bd of Dirs Schlumberger Ltd 2007–; Corresponding mem. Russian Acad. of Sciences, Int. Acad. of Informatization; Laureate Award of the Council of Ministers 2001. *Achievements include:* holds ten patents. *Address:* Moscow Institute of Physics and Technology, 141700 Moscow, Dolgoprudny Institutskiy lane 9, Russia (office). *Telephone:* (495) 408-45-54 (office). *Fax:* (495) 408-42-54 (office). *Website:* www .mipt.ru (office).

KUDYBERDIYEV, Abibilla; Kyrgyzstani politician; Minister of Defence 2010–11, 2014–15. *Address:* c/o Ministry of Defence, 720001 Bishkek, Logvinenko 26, Kyrgyzstan (office).

KUENSSBERG, Laura Juliet; British journalist and broadcaster; *Political Editor, BBC News;* b. 1976, Italy; d. of Nick Kuenssberg and Sally Kuenssberg; m. James Kelly; ed Univ. of Edinburgh, Georgetown Univ., USA; began career with local radio and later cable TV in Glasgow; fmr reporter, Channel 4 News; joined BBC as trainee journalist in Newcastle 2000, started covering politics 2003 as Political Corresp. on programmes including Daily Politics, The Today programme, Breakfast and BBC News at Ten, becoming Chief Political Corresp., BBC 2009–11, Chief Corresp. and Presenter, Newsnight 2014–15, Political Ed., BBC News (first female) 2015–; Business Ed., ITV News 2011–14, Presenter, ITV News at Ten 2013–14; Royal TV Soc. Award for Home Affairs Reporting. *Address:* BBC News, BBC Broadcasting House, Portland Place, London, W1A 1AA, England (office). *Website:* www.bbc.co.uk/news (office).

KUFUOR, John Kofi Agyekum, KCB, MA; Ghanaian lawyer, business executive, UN official and fmr head of state; *Chancellor, George Grant University of Mines and Technology;* b. 8 Dec. 1938, Kumasi, Ashanti Region; m. Theresa Kufuor; five c.; ed Osei Tutu Boarding School, Prempeh Coll., Kumasi, Lincoln's Inn, London and Exeter Coll., Oxford, UK; called to Bar, Lincoln's Inn 1961; Clerk of Kumasi City Council; Council Rep., Constituent Ass. 1968–69; mem. Parl.; founding mem. Progress Party (PP) 1969, Popular Front Party (PFP) 1979, PFP Spokesman on Foreign Affairs 1979–82, Founding mem. New Patriotic Party (NPP) 1992–; Deputy Minister of Foreign Affairs 1969–72; arrested after mil. coup and imprisoned for 15 months 1972–73; Sec. for Local Govt 1982; returned to law practice; presidential cand. for New Patriotic Party 1996; Pres. of Ghana and C-in-C of Armed Forces 2001–09 (re-elected 2004); Chair. African Union Ass. 2007–08; apptd UN Special Envoy on Climate Change 2013; Sr Grand Warden, United Grand Lodge of England 2017–; Chancellor, George Grant University of Mines and Technology 2018–; Hon. mem. Advisory Bd of the Brazil Africa Inst. 2018, Hon. Fellow, Exeter Coll., Oxford, Liverpool John Moores Univ., UK; Grand Cordon of The Most Venerable Order of the Kts of the Pioneers (Liberia) 2008, Order of the Gold Star, World Fed. of Honorary Consuls 2008, Order of the House of Orange, state honours from several countries, including Italy, Germany and Brazil; Dr hc (Univ. of Cape Coast, Ghana); Chatham House Prize 2008, World Food Prize (co-recipient) 2011. *Leisure interests:* table tennis, reading, soccer, films. *Address:* George Grant University of Mines and Technology, Box 237, Tarkwa, Ghana (office). *Telephone:* (31) 2320324. *E-mail:* registrar@umat.edu.gh (office). *Website:* www.umat.edu.gh (office).

KUHN, Gustav, DPhil; Austrian conductor and composer; b. 28 Aug. 1945, Turrach, Styria; s. of Friedrich Kuhn and Hilde Kuhn; m. Andrea Kuhn 1971; one s. one d.; ed studied conducting with Hans Swarowsky at conservatories in Vienna and Salzburg; Univ. of Salzburg, advanced conducting studies under Bruno Maderna and Herbert von Karajan; professional conductor in Istanbul (three years), Enschede (Netherlands), Dortmund (prin. conductor) and Vienna; debut at Vienna State Opera (Elektra) 1977, Munich Nat. Theatre (Così fan tutte) 1978, Covent Garden, London 1979, Glyndebourne, Munich Opera Festival and Salzburg Festival 1980, Chicago (Fidelio) 1981, Paris Opéra 1982, La Scala, Milan 1984, Arena di Verona (Masked Ball) 1986, Rossini Opera Festival, Pesaro 1987; Gen. Music Dir in Berne, Bonn and Rome; production debut in Trieste (Fliegender Holländer) 1986; other projects include Parsifal, Naples 1988, Salome, Rome 1988, Don Carlos (French version) and Don Carlo (Italian) for 250th anniversary of Teatro Reggio, Turin 1990; Artistic Dir Neue Stimmen (New Voices) competition, Bertelsmann Foundation 1987–, Macerata Festival, Italy (productions of Così fan tutte and Don Giovanni) 1990–94, Filarmonica Marchigiana 1997–2002, Haydn Orchestra of Bolzano and Trento 2003–12, Conservatorio di Milano Philharmonic Orchestra 2004; Founder and Pres. Accad. di Montegral 1992–, Tyrolean Festival, Erl, Austria 1997–2018 (resgnd following accusations of sexual assault); Producer and Conductor, Ring Cycle, Tyrolean Festival Erl 2003, 2004, 2005, 2007; performed series of classical concerts entitled Delirium in Salzburg 2007–11; conducted two performances of Wagner's Parsifal in Beijing (first ever in China) 2013; First Prize, Int. Conducting Contest of Austrian TV and Broadcasting Corpn (ORF) 1969, Lilly Lehmann Medal (Mozarteum Foundation), Max Reinhardt Medal (Salzburg), Senator of Honour Award 'Lorenzo il Magnifico' (Florence) 1988, Artist of the Year for his contributions to music in China, Beijing Music Festival 2015. *Publications:* Aus Liebe zur Musik 1993, instrumentation of Janáček's Diary of One Who Disappeared, Opéra Nat. de Paris (released by Edition Peters). *Leisure interests:* sailing, motorcycling. *Website:* www.gustavkuhn.at.

KUHN, Michael, LLB; Kenyan/British film producer; ed Univ. of Cambridge; solicitor, Supreme Court 1974; lawyer, Denton, Hall and Burgin, London; legal adviser, Polygram UK, London 1974–78, Dir 1978–83, Gen. Counsel, Polygram Int., London 1983–87, Sr Vice-Pres. 1987–93, Pres. Polygram Filmed Entertainment, Beverly Hills, Calif. 1991–93, fmr Exec. Vice-Pres. Polygram Holding Inc., New York, mem. Man. Bd Polygram NV, Pres. and CEO Polygram Filmed Entertainment, Beverly Hills; f. Qwerty Films, London. *Films produced include:* Red Rock West 1993, Being John Malkovich 1999, Wonderous Oblivion 2003, The Order 2003, Stage Beauty 2004, Kinsey 2004, I Heart Huckabees 2004, The Moguls 2005, Alien Autopsy 2006, Severance 2006, The Duchess 2008. *Address:*

Qwerty Films, 42–44 Beak Street, London, W1F 9RH, England (office). *Telephone:* (20) 7440-5920 (office). *Fax:* (20) 7440-5959 (office).

KÜHNE, Gunther Albert Hermann, DrIur, LLM; German legal scholar and academic; *Director Emeritus, Institute for German and International Mining and Energy Law, Technical University, Clausthal;* b. 25 Aug. 1939, Gelsenkirchen; s. of Friedrich Kühne and Gertrud Kühne (née Belgard); m. Elvira Schulz 1992; ed Univ. of Cologne and Columbia Univ., New York; part-time legal adviser to German mining cos 1963–68; Research Asst Bochum Univ. Law School 1967–70; Sr Govt official, Ministry of Econs, Bonn 1971–74; Sr official, German del. OECD, Paris 1972–73; Sr Govt official, Ministry of Justice, Bonn 1974–78; Lecturer Private Law, Private Int. and Comparative Law, Bochum Univ. 1971–79; Prof. of Mining and Energy Law, Dir Inst. for German and Int. Mining and Energy Law, Tech. Univ. Clausthal 1978–2007, now Dir Emer.; Visiting Prof., Bergakademie Freiberg 1992, Tel-Aviv Univ. 1993–2003, Nanjing Univ. 2004, 2007; Ordinary mem. Braunschweig Soc. of Sciences 1994; Hon. Prof. of Law, Univ. of Göttingen 1986–. *Publications include:* numerous books and articles on aspects of law, including Die Parteiautonomie im internationalen Erbrecht 1973, IPR-Gesetz-Entwurf (Private Int. Law Reform Draft) 1980, Memorandum on the State and Reform of German International Family Law 1980, Wandel und Beharren im Bergrecht (jtly) 1992, Rechtsfragen der Aufsuchung und Gewinnung von in Steinkohleflözen beisitzendem Methangas 1994, Gegenwartsprobleme des Bergrechts (jtly) 1995, Wettbewerb, Bestandsschutz, Umweltschutz (jtly) 1997, Bestandsschutz alten Bergwerkseigentums unter besonderer Berücksichtigung des Art. 14 Grundgesetz 1998, Braunkohlenplanung und bergrechtliche Zulassungsverfahren 1999, Das deutsche Berg- und Energierecht auf dem Wege nach Europa (jtly) 2002, Das neue Energierecht in der Bewährung (co-ed.) 2002, Berg- und Energierecht im Zugriff europäischer Regulierungstendenzen (ed.) 2004, Bergrecht zwischen Tradition und Moderne (co-ed.) 2010, Das deutsche Wirtschaftsrecht unter dem Einfluss des US-amerikanischen Rechts (jtly) 2011. *Leisure interest:* Jewish history (numerous publs). *Address:* Arnold-Sommerfeld-Strasse 6, 38678 Clausthal-Zellerfeld, Germany. *Telephone:* (5323) 723025. *Fax:* (5323) 722507. *E-mail:* gunther.kuehne@iber.tu-clausthal.de (office). *Website:* www.iber.tu-clausthal.de (office).

KÜHNL, Karel, Jr, JUDr; Czech politician and diplomatist; b. 12 Sept. 1954, Prague; m. Daniela Kusínovou; one s. one d.; ed Charles Univ., Prague; freelance journalist in Australia 1978–87; ed., Radio Free Europe, Munich 1987–91; Econ. Adviser to the Premier 1991–92, to Minister of Econs 1992–93; Amb. to UK (also accred to Ireland) 1993–97; Minister of Industry and Trade 1997–98; Chief Whip of Freedom Union Party 1998–2004; Leader, Coalition Freedom Union Party–DEU, KDU–ČSL, ODA (after merger of Freedom Union Party and DEU Dec. 2001); MP (Freedom Union Party) 1998–2006, mem. Constitutional Cttee 2002, Organizing Cttee of the House 2002–04, Foreign Affairs Cttee 2003–04; Minister of Defence 2004–06; Amb. to Croatia 2007–12. *Leisure interests:* cycling, tennis. *Address:* c/o Ministry of Foreign Affairs, Loretánské nám. 101/5, 118 00 Prague 1, Czech Republic. *E-mail:* podatelna@mzv.cz.

KUHNT, Dietmar, PhD; German business executive; b. 16 Nov. 1937, Wrocław (Breslau); m. 1966; two c.; ed Univs of Cologne and Freiburg; perm. legal adviser, Rheinisch-Westfälisches Elektrizitätswerk AG (RWE) 1968, Exec. Vice-Pres. 1992–94, mem. Bd of Man. RWE Energie AG 1989, Chair. 1992–94; mem. Bd Man. RWE AG 1992–94, Chair. 1995–2003, mem. Supervisory Bd 2003–06, mem. Exec. Bd RWE Thames Water PLC, Chair. Supervisory Bd RWE Plus AG, RWE Power AG; Chair. Supervisory Bd Hochtief AG –2004, Heidelberg, Innogy Holdings PLC, Allianz Versicherungs-Aktiengesellschaft, Frankfurt am Main; mem. Supervisory Bd Hochtief AG –2008, Allianz Versicherungs AG –2008, Dresdner Bank AG –2009, GEA Group AG (fmrly MG Technologies AG) –2011, TUI AG –2011 (Chair. 2009–11), BDO Deutsche Warentreuhand AG, Hapag-Lloyd, Hapag-Lloyd Holding AG (fmrly Hapag-Lloyd AG) 2010–, GEA Group AG 2011–, Heidelberger Druckmaschinen AG (Chair. –2004), Grillo-Werke AG; mem. Int. Advisory Bd, AFK Sistema; mem. Bd of Dirs COMSTAR-United TeleSystems –2008.

KUIVASHEV, Yevgeny Vladimirovich; Russian government official; b. 16 March 1971, Khanty-Mansiysk region; m.; one s. one d.; ed Moscow Mil. Inst. of the Russian Border Guard Service, Yale Univ., USA, Tyumen State Univ.; mil. service 1989–91; various positions with Surgutneftegas 1991–97; worked in Pokovsky Town Council, Khanty-Mansiysk region 1997–2000, Head of Admin 2000–05; Lecturer in Law, Tyumen State Univ. 2000–05; Deputy Head, Federal Bailiff Service, Moscow 2005; head of Tobolsk City Admin 2005–07; Head of Tyumen City Admin 2007–11; Deputy Presidential Rep. to Urals Federal Okrug Jan.–Sept. 2011, apptd Presidential Rep. Sept. 2011; Gov. and Chair. of Presidium, Sverdlovsk Oblast 2012–17.

KUKAN, Eduard, LLD; Slovak diplomatist and politician; b. 26 Dec. 1939, Trnovec nad Váhom, W Slovakia; m. Zdenka Kukan; one s. one d.; ed Moscow Inst. of Int. Relations, Charles Univ., Prague; joined Czechoslovakian Foreign Service 1964, mem. Africa Dept 1964–68, various posts at Embassy in Zambia 1968–73, mem. Secr. of Minister for Foreign Affairs 1973–77, Minister Counsellor, Embassy in USA 1977–81, Head Dept of Sub-Saharan Africa 1981–85, Amb. to Ethiopia 1985–88, Perm. Rep. of Czechoslovakia to UN, New York 1990–93, of Slovakia 1993–94; Deputy to Nat. Council of Slovak Repub. (Parl.) 1994–98, 2006–09; Minister of Foreign Affairs March–Dec. 1994, 1998–2006; apptd mem. Exec. Cttee Democratic Union of Slovakia 1994, Chair. 1998; Vice-Chair. Slovak Democratic and Christian Union—Democratic Party 2000; UN Sec.-Gen.'s Special Envoy for the Balkans 1999–2001; Rep. to Parl. Ass., Council of Europe 2006–09; MEP 2009–; Deputy of Bratislava – Nové Mestós local self-governing bd; mem. Advisory Bd Global Panel; Hon. Prof., St Petersburg State Honorary professor of St Petersburg State University 2003; Hon. LLD (Upsala Coll., NJ, USA) 1993. *Leisure interests:* tennis, theatre. *Address:* European Parliament, Bât. Altiero Spinelli, 60 rue Wiertz, 1047 Brussels, Belgium (office); Apollo BC II, Prievozská 4, 821 05 Bratislava, Slovakia (office). *Telephone:* (2) 284-21-11 (office). *Fax:* (2) 284-69-74 (office). *E-mail:* eduard.kukan@ep.europa.eu (office). *Website:* www.europarl.europa.eu (office); www.eduardkukan.eu/en.

KUKES, Simon Grigorievich, MSc; American (b. Russian) business executive; b. 1946, Moscow; ed Moscow Chemical-Tech. Inst. (Mendeleyev Inst.), Rice Univ., Houston, Tex.; engineer, Titan Production Co. 1969–70; mem. of staff USSR Acad. of Sciences 1970–77; emigrated from USSR to Tex., USA 1977; Tech. Dir Philips Petroleum 1980s; Tech. Dir then Vice-Pres. in charge of devt in Commonwealth of Ind. States, Amoco 1991–96; Dir Planning and Devt, Yukos (largest oil refinery in Russia) 1996–98, Chair. and CEO Tyumen Oil Co. (TNK), Russia 1998–2003, helped engineer merger between TNK and BP 2002; Chair. and CEO Yukos Corpn 2003–04; CEO CJSC Samara-Nafta (exploration and production co in Volga-Urals) 2005–13 (co. acquired by NK Lukoil OAO 2013); mem. Bd of Dirs Amarin Corpn plc 2005; mem. Council of Energy, Marine Transportation and Public Policy, Columbia Univ.

KUKIZ, Paweł Piotr; Polish singer, actor and politician; *Leader, Kukiz'15;* b. 24 June 1963, Paczków; m. Małgorzata Kukiz; three d.; as singer, genres include pop, rock, pop rock and punk rock, collaborations with CDN, Hak, Aya RL, Emigranci, Piersi, Maciej Maleńczuk and Jan Borysewicz; third-placed cand. in presidential election 2015; Leader of Kukiz'15 2015–. *Films include:* Jestem przeciw 1985, Girl Guide 1995, Billboard 1998, Matki, żony i kochanki II 1998, Poniedziałek 1998, Stacja PRL 1999–2000, Dzieci Jarocina 2000, Wtorek 2001, Czwarta władza 2004, S@motność w Sieci 2006. *Recordings include:* albums: Borysewicz & Kukiz (with Jan Borysewicz) 2003, Starsi panowie (with Maciej Maleńczuk) 2010, Siła i honor 2012, Zakazane piosenki 2014. *Address:* 50-134 Warsaw, Ul. Białoskórnicza 3/1, Poland (office). *Telephone:* (69) 7374449 (office). *E-mail:* aleksandra.ziolkowska@ruchkukiza.pl (office); kontakt@ruchjow.pl. *Website:* ruchkukiza.pl (office); ruchjow.pl/#.

KULAKOV, Anatoly Vasilyevich, DPhysMathSci; Russian scientist; b. 15 July 1938; m.; one s.; ed Leningrad Polytech. Inst.; researcher, Sr Engineer, Deputy Dean, Leningrad Polytechnic Inst. 1962–79; Scientific Sec., Deputy Chair., First Deputy Chair., Council on Science and Tech., USSR Council of Ministers 1979–90; Dir-Gen. Russian Industrialists and Entrepreneurs Union from 1991; Vice-Pres. Moscow Econ. Union from 1997; mem. Bd Russian Bank of Reconstruction and Devt from 1998; Corresp. mem. USSR (now Russian) Acad. of Sciences 1984; main research in theory of electromagnetic interactions in systems of charged particles, plasma and solids. *Address:* c/o Russian Academy of Sciences, 119991 Moscow, Leninsky prosp. 32A, Russia. *Telephone:* (495) 938-03-09. *Fax:* (495) 954-33-20. *E-mail:* info@ras.ru. *Website:* www.ras.ru.

KULHÁNEK, Vratislav; Czech economist, engineer and business executive; b. 20 Nov. 1943, Plzeň; m. Marie Kulhánek 1944 (divorced); two d.; ed Univs of Prague and Pardubice; Dir Motor Jirkov, České Budějovice 1991–92, Robert Bosch, České Budějovice; Chair. Škoda Auto Mladá Boleslav 1998–2004, Chair. Supervisory Bd 2004–07; Chair. Man. Bd AAA Auto Group NV (parent co. of AAA Auto) 2007–13; with Industrial Advisors, s.r.o. 2013–; mem. Supervisory Bd, Kooperativa Insurance, Scientific Bd, Univ. of Econs, Prague; Pres. Assen of Car Industry; apptd Pres. ICC 2001; fmr Pres. Czech Inst. of Dirs, now Hon. Pres.; Dr hc Ing; Prize of Czech-German Understanding, Germany 2000, Man. for the 21st Century 2000, Alois Rasin Medal, Univ. of Econs 2003. *Leisure interests:* tennis, cars, golf. *Address:* Industrial Advisors, s.r.o., Na Ořechovce 55, 162 00 Prague 6 (office); Srubec 346, 370 06 České Budějovice, Czech Republic (home). *Fax:* (2) 24320874 (office); (2) 24324271 (office). *E-mail:* vratislav.kulhanek@industrialadvisors.cz (office). *Website:* www.industrialadvisors.cz (office); www.ciod.cz.

KULIK, Andrey B.; Russian diplomatist; *Ambassador to Republic of Korea;* b. 13 Nov. 1953; m. Marina Suanova; ed Moscow Univ. of Int. Relations, Diplomatic Acad. of the Ministry of Foreign Affairs; joined diplomatic service 1976; worked at Embassy of the USSR and the Russian Fed. to China 1976–80, 1983–89, 1993–96; Ministry of Foreign Affairs, Moscow 1980–83, 1989–93, 1996–2011, Head, Asian Dept 2012–18, Amb. to Repub. of Korea 2018–. *Address:* Embassy of the Russian Fed., 34-16, Jeong-dong, Jung-gu, Seoul 04516 Republic of Korea (office). *Telephone:* (2) 318-2116 (office). *Fax:* (2) 754-0417 (office). *E-mail:* russemb@gmail.com (office). *Website:* www.russian-embassy.org (office); korea-seoul.mid.ru (office).

KULIK, Gennady Vasilyevich; Russian politician; b. 20 Jan. 1935, Zhekomskoye, Pskov region; m.; one s.; ed Leningrad State Univ.; researcher, Head of Dept, Siberian Div. of All-Union Inst. of Agricultural Econ. 1957–65; First Deputy Head, Novosibirsk Regional Dept of Agric. 1965; Deputy Head, Chief Dept of Planning and Econs, Ministry of Agric. RSFSR 1965–86; First Deputy Chair., RSFSR State Cttee of Agric. and Industry 1986–90; First Deputy Chair., RSFSR Council of Ministers, Minister of Agric. and Food 1990–91; USSR Peoples' Deputy 1990–92; adviser to Dir, Inex-Interexport (Moscow) 1993; mem. Exec. Bd Russian Agrarian Party, Deputy Chair. Russian Agrarian Union; mem. State Duma; Deputy Chair. Cttee on Budget, Taxes, Banks and Finance 1993–98; Deputy Chair. Govt of Russian Fed. 1998–99; mem. State Duma (Parl.) (Otechestvo-All Russia faction, Yedinaya Rossiya faction) 1999–, mem. Cttee on Budget and Taxes; Merited Economist of Russia. *Publication:* 15 Years with President V.V. Putin. *Address:* State Duma, 103265 Moscow, Okhotny ryad 1, Russia. *Telephone:* (495) 292-62-23 (office). *Fax:* (495) 292-69-66 (office). *E-mail:* stateduma@duma.gov.ru (office). *Website:* www.duma.gov.ru (office).

KULIKOV, Army Gen. Anatoly Sergeyevich, DEconSc; Russian politician and military officer; b. 4 Sept. 1946, Aigursky Apanasenkovsky, Stavropol Region; m.; two s. one d.; ed Vladikavkaz Mil. Command School, USSR Ministry of Internal Affairs, M. Frunze Mil. Acad., Mil. Acad. of Gen. Staff; numerous mil. postings, including Commdr of Internal Troops 1992–95; Head of United Grouping of Fed. Troops in Chechen Repub. Jan.–July 1995; Minister of Internal Affairs 1995–98; Deputy Chair. of Russian Govt 1996–98; mem. Security Council of Russian Fed. 1995–98; mem. State Duma (Parl.) (United Russia) 1999–2007, Deputy Chair., Cttee on Security 2004–; Chair. Cen. Council Ratniki Otechestva (Warriors of the Fatherland) Movt; Chair. Council on Econ. Security, Russian Acad. of Social Sciences; Chair. World Anticriminal and Antiterrorism Forum –2001; mem. Acad. of Mil. Sciences, Acad. of Natural Sciences; Order for Services to the Fatherland (Third Degree), Order for Personal Courage, Order for Service to the Motherland in the Armed Forces of the USSR, Third Class, Order of Honour 2004; more than 30 medals. *Publications:* Chechen Node 2000, Heavy Stars 2002; numerous articles in journals and newspapers. *Leisure interests:* hunting, fishing, shooting, woodworking. *Address:* c/o Yedinaya Rossiya (United Russia), 129110 Moscow, Pereyaslavsky per. 4, Russian Federation. *Telephone:* (495) 786-82-89. *Fax:* (495) 788-44-79. *E-mail:* press@edinros.ru. *Website:* www.er.ru.

KULKA, Konstanty Andrzej; Polish violinist and academic; *Professor, Fryderyk Chopin University of Music;* b. 5 March 1947, Gdańsk; m.; two d.; ed Higher State School of Music (now the Stanisław Moniuszko Acad. of Music), Gdańsk; Prof., Acad. of Music, Warsaw (now the Fryderyk Chopin Univ. of Music) 1994–, Head of Inst. of String Instruments; numerous gramophone, radio and TV recordings; soloist with Nat. Philharmonic Orchestra, Warsaw 1984–; more than 1,500 concerts world-wide since 1967; participates in numerous int. festivals, including Lucerne, Prague, Bordeaux, Berlin, Granada, Barcelona, Brighton; concerts with Berlin Philharmonic Orchestra, Chicago Symphony Orchestra, Minneapolis Orchestra, London Symphony Orchestra, Concertgebouw Orchestra, English Chamber Orchestra, St Petersburg Philharmonic Orchestra and others; Hon. Citizen of the City of Wolbromia; Gold Cross of Merit, Commdr's Cross, Order of Polonia Restituta 2001; Diploma and Special Prize, Paganini Competition, Genoa 1964, first prize, Music Competition, Munich 1966, Minister of Culture and Arts Prize 1969, 1973, Minister of Foreign Affairs Prize 1977, Pres. of Radio and TV Cttee Prize 1978, prize winner, 33rd Grand Prix du Disque, Int. Sound Festival, Paris 1981. *Recordings include:* Antonio Vivaldi Cztery pory roku (The Four Seasons), Szymanowski: Violin Concertos Nos 1 & 2 1997, Mozart: Best of 2000, Karlowicz: Tone Poems/Violin Concerto 2002, Paderewski: Violin & Piano Works 2003, Penderecki: Violin Concertos Nos 1 & 2 2003, F. Mendelssohn's and A. Glazunov's Violin Concertos with the National Philharmonic Orchestra under Jerzy Katlewicz; Brahms's Violin Concerto with National Philharmonic Orchestra under Witold Rowicki; J. S. Bach's Sonatas for Solo Violin. *Leisure interests:* collecting gramophone records, bridge, collecting interesting kitchen recipes. *Address:* Uniwersytet Muzyczny Fryderyka Chopina, ul. Okólnik 2, 00-368 Warsaw, Poland. *Telephone:* (22) 8277241. *Fax:* (22) 8278305. *E-mail:* konstanty.kulka@wp.pl. *Website:* www.chopin.edu.pl/en/people/konstanty-andrzej-kulka.

KULLMAN, Ellen J., BSc, MA; American business executive; *Chairman and CEO, E. I. du Pont de Nemours and Co. (DuPont);* b. 22 Jan. 1956, Wilmington, Del.; d. of Joseph Jamison and Margaret Jamison; m. Michael Kullman; twin s. one d.; ed Tower Hill School, Wilmington, Tufts Univ., Northwestern Univ.; fmrly with General Electric; Marketing Man. medical imaging business, DuPont 1988, later Business Dir x-ray film business, Global Business Dir electronic imaging, Printing & Publishing, Global Business Dir White Pigment & Mineral Products 1994, Vice-Pres. and Gen. Man. 1995, Head DuPont Safety Resources 1998, Bio-Based Materials 1999, Group Vice-Pres. and Gen. Man. 2000, Head DuPont Flooring Systems and DuPont Surfaces 2001, Group Vice-Pres. Safety & Protection 2002–06, Exec. Vice-Pres. Safety & Protection, Coatings and Color, Marketing and Sales, and Safety and Sustainability 2006–08, Pres. and Dir Oct.–Dec. 2008, CEO and Dir E. I. du Pont de Nemours and Co. Jan. 2009–, Chair. Dec. 2009–; mem. Bd of Dirs United Technologies Corpn; Co-Chair. Nat. Acad. of Eng Cttee on Changing the Conversation: From Research to Action; mem. US-India CEO Forum, Exec. Cttee The Business Council 2011–12, Exec. Cttee SCI-America; mem. Bd of Trustees Tufts Univ., Bd of Overseers Tufts Univ. School of Eng; Aiming High Award 2004, Sellinger's Business Leader of the Year. *Address:* E. I. du Pont de Nemours and Co., 1007 Market Street, Wilmington, DE 19898, USA (office). *Telephone:* (302) 774-1000 (office). *Website:* www.dupont.com (office).

KULONGOSKI, Theodore (Ted) Ralph, BA, JD; American politician, lawyer and judge (retd); *Distinguished Fellow of Policy and Politics, Mark O. Hatfield School of Government, Portland State University;* b. 5 Nov. 1940, Washington Co., Mo.; m. Mary Oberst; three c.; ed Univ. of Missouri; served in US Marine Corps; fmr truck driver and steelworker; called to Bar of Ore., Mo., US Dist Court, Ore., US Court of Appeals (9th Circuit); Legal Counsel, Oregon House of Reps 1973–74, Rep. from Lane Co. 1974–77; Founding Sr Partner, Kulongoski, Durham, Drummonds & Colombo 1974–87; mem. Ore. State Senate 1978–83; Dir Oregon Dept of Insurance & Finance 1987–91; Deputy Dist Attorney, Multnomah Co. 1992; Attorney Gen., State of Oregon 1993–97; Justice, Oregon Supreme Court 1997–2001; Gov. of Ore. 2003–11; Distinguished Fellow of Policy and Politics, Mark O. Hatfield School of Govt, Portland State Univ. 2012–; Chair. Juvenile Justice Task Force 1994, Gov.'s Comm. on Organized Crime; mem. Lane Co. Bar Asscn, Missouri Bar Asscn, Oregon State Bar Asscn; Democrat. *Leisure interest:* fly-fishing. *Address:* Mark O. Hatfield School of Government, Portland State University, Portland, OR 97207, USA (office). *Telephone:* (503) 725-5856 (office). *E-mail:* trk2@pdx.edu (office). *Website:* www.pdx.edu/hatfieldschool (office).

KULOV, Feliks Sharshenbayevich; Kyrgyzstani politician; *Chairman, Ar-Namys Partiyasy (Dignity Political Party);* b. 29 Oct. 1948, Frunze (now Bishkek), Kyrgyz SSR, USSR; m. 1st Nailya Bayaliyeva; two d.; m. 2nd Fatima Kulova; three d.; ed Omsk Higher School of the Ministry of Internal Affairs of the USSR (now Omsk Judicial Inst.), Acad. of the Ministry of Internal Affairs of the USSR, Moscow; police officer in Frunze, operational platoon, Internal Affairs Bd 1966–67; Insp., Dept for Combating Narcotics, Sr Insp. in Dept A, Criminal Investigation Dept, Ministry of Internal Affairs, Kyrgyz SSR 1971–75, Head of Dept 1978–80; Deputy Head of Internal Affairs Bd, Talas Oblast Exec. Cttee 1980–84, Head of Internal Affairs Bd 1984–87; First Deputy Minister of Internal Affairs, Kyrgyz SSR 1987–91; Mil. Commdr in Frunze 1990; mem. of Presidential Council of Kyrgyz SSR 1990–91; unsuccessful cand. for Chair. of Supreme Soviet of Kyrgyz SSR Dec. 1990; resgnd party membership following coup attempt in Moscow 1991; Minister of Internal Affairs, Kyrgyz SSR/Repub. of Kyrgyzstan 1991–92; Vice-Pres. of Kyrgyzstan 1992–93; investigated on charges of corruption 1993; resgnd following scandals surrounding Seabeco Affair 1993; Gov. of Chui Oblast 1993–97; Head of State Admin (Gov.), Chui Oblast 1993–97; Minister of Nat. Security 1997–98; Acting Mayor of Bishkek April–July 1998, Mayor of Bishkek 1998–99; Founding Chair. Ar-Namys Partiyasy (Dignity Political Party) (known as Ar-Namys) 1999–; arrested on charges of abuse of office as Mayor of Bishkek 22 March 2000, found not guilty and released; sentenced to seven years' imprisonment with confiscation of property, stripped of rank of Gen.-Lt for abuse of office as Minister of Internal Affairs Jan. 2001; elected Chair. of People's Congress of Kyrgyzstan (opposition alliance) Nov. 2001; sentenced to ten years' imprisonment and prohibited from working for the Govt and for organs of local self-admin for a further three years following his release; found guilty on charges of embezzlement of state property while Gov. of Chui Oblast May 2002, freed from prison during 'Tulip Revolution'; Supreme Court annulled all charges against him April 2005; Acting First Deputy Prime Minister May 2005, Acting Prime Minister Aug. 2005, Prime Minister Sept. 2005–19 Dec. 2006 (resgnd), re-apptd Acting Prime Minister 19 Dec. 2006–29 Jan. 2007; Co-founder and Chair. United Front For A Worthy Future For Kyrgyzstan Feb. 2007–; Head of Directorate for Devt of Small and Light Energy Resources 2008–09, Dir of that Directorate at Cen. Agency for Devt, Investment and Innovation 2009–10; Head of interim Council for Social Security May 2010; Deputy of Supreme Council (Jogorku Kenesh—Parl.) 2010–; awarded title of Gen.-Maj. by Pres. of USSR 1991, awarded title of Gen.-Lt by Pres. of Kyrgyzstan 1997; Dank, 1000th Anniversary of Manas, Badge of Honour. *Publication:* Na perevale (On the Crossing—memoirs) 2009. *Address:* Ar-Namys Partiyasy (Dignity Political Party), 720033 Bishkek, Togolok Moldovan 60A, Third Floor, kom. 302, Kyrgyzstan (office). *Telephone:* (312) 32-46-01 (office). *E-mail:* ar-namys@mail.ru (office); arnamys_usa@hotmail.com (office). *Website:* www.ar-namys.org (office).

KULUKUNDIS, Sir Eddie, Kt, OBE, FRSA; British fmr business executive and theatre producer; b. 20 April 1932, London; s. of George Elias Kulukundis and Eugenie Diacakis; m. Susan Hampshire 1981; ed Collegiate School, New York, Salisbury School, Conn. and Yale Univ., USA; mem. Baltic Exchange 1959–; mem. Lloyds 1964–95, mem. Council 1983–89; Dir Rethymnis & Kulukundis Ltd 1964–, London & Overseas Freighters 1980–85, 1989–97; Chair. Knightsbridge Theatrical Productions Ltd 1970–2000; Chair. Ambassadors Theatre Group 1992–2009; Trustee, Sports Aid Trust 1986–; mem. Exec. Cttee Royal Shakespeare Theatre 1977–2003, Royal Shakespeare Theatre Trust 1969 (Vice-Chair. 1983–), Gov. Royal Shakespeare Theatre 1977–2003; Vice-Pres. Traverse Theatre Club; Dir Hampstead Theatre Ltd 1969–2004; mem. Bd of Man. Soc. of London Theatre 1973–2003, Hon. Vice-Pres. Soc. of London Theatre 2003–; Vice-Pres. UK Athletics 1998–2003, Life Pres. Ambassadors Theatre Group 2007. *London productions include:* (some jtly): Enemy 1969, The Happy Apple, Poor Horace, The Friends, How the Other Half Loves, Tea Party and the Basement (double bill), The Wild Duck 1970, After Haggerty, Hamlet, Charley's Aunt, Straight Up 1971, London Assurance, Journey's End 1972; Small Craft Warnings, A Private Matter, Dandy Dick 1973, The Waltz of the Toreadors, Life Class, Pygmalion, Play Mas, The Gentle Hook 1974, A Little Night Music, Entertaining Mr Sloane, The Gay Lord Quex, What the Butler Saw, Travesties, Lies, The Seagull, A Month in the Country, A Room with a View, Too True to be Good, The Bed Before Yesterday 1975, Dimetos, Banana Ridge, Wild Oats 1976, Candida, Man and Superman, Once a Catholic 1977, Privates on Parade, Gloo Joo 1978, Bent, Outside Edge, Last of the Red Hot Lovers 1979, Beecham, Born in the Gardens 1980, Tonight at 8.30, Steaming, Arms and the Man 1981, Steafel's Variations 1982, Messiah, Pack of Lies 1983, Of Mice and Men, The Secret Diary of Adrian Mole Aged 13¾ 1984, Camille 1985, The Cocktail Party 1986, Curtains 1987, Separation, South Pacific, Married Love, Over My Dead Body 1989, Never the Sinner 1990, The King and I, Carmen Jones 1991, Noel & Gertie, Slip of the Tongue, Shades, Annie Get Your Gun, Making it Better 1992, The Prime of Miss Jean Brodie 1994, Neville's Island 1994, The Killing of Sister George 1995. *New York productions include:* (jtly): How the Other Half Loves 1971, Sherlock Holmes, London Assurance 1974, Travesties 1975, The Merchant 1977, Once a Catholic 1979.

KULUMBEGOV, Domenti Sardionovich; Georgian civil servant and politician; b. 4 Jan. 1955, Thinala, Gori dist, Georgian SSR, USSR; ed South Ossetian State Pedagogical Inst., Modern Humanitarian Acad., North Caucasian Acad. of Public Admin, Rostov-on-Don, Russian SFSR; worked in trans-shipment base tunnel squad, Tbiltonnelstroy, Tskhinvali 1978–79; Instructor, Head of Group, Head of South Ossetian Regional Cttee of Komsomol of Georgia, Tskhinvali 1980–83; First Sec., Komsomol CC Tskhinvali 1983–85; First Sec., South Ossetian Regional Cttee of Komsomol of Georgia 1985–88; Head of South Ossetian Regional Cttee of CP Party of Georgia, Tskhinvali 1988–91; Chief Insp., Head of Dept, Deputy Dir, First Deputy Head of Migration Service of North Ossetia-Alania Vladikavkaz 1992–2000, Deputy Head of Directorate of Immigration, Ministry of Internal Affairs, Repub. of North Osetiya—Alania (Russian Fed.) Vladikavkaz 2000–06, Head of Directorate 2006; Head of Dept of Domestic Policy Admin 2006; Deputy Prime Minister, 'Republic of South Ossetia' 2009–12, Acting Prime Minister Jan.–April 2014, Prime Minister April 2014–17; Ind.; Medal 'For Valour'. *Address:* c/o Office of the Government of the 'Republic of South Ossetia', 100001 Tskhinvali, Government House, ul. Stalina 18, South Ossetia, Georgia. *E-mail:* ospress@mail.ru.

KUM, Dongwha, BS, MS, PhD; South Korean scientist, academic and research institute director; *Endowed Chair Research Scientist, Korea Institute of Science and Technology;* b. 15 Dec. 1951, Okcheon; m. Dr Eun-Ae Kim; two d.; ed Seoul Nat. Univ., Stanford Univ., USA; lab. engineer, GM Korea Incheon 1975–78; Postdoctoral Research Fellow, Stanford Univ. 1984–85; mem. staff, Korea Inst. of Science and Tech. (KIST) 1985–, Pres. KIST 2006–09, Endowed Chair Research Scientist 2009–; Council mem., Nat. Science and Tech. Council 2007, 2010; Exec. Vice-Pres., Nat. Acad. of Eng, Korea 2010–; Pres. Korean Inst. of Metals and Materials (KIMM) 2008; mem. American Soc. for Metals 1980–, Materials Research Soc. 1985–, Korea Soc. of Microscopy 1986 (Pres. 2005–06), Minerals, Metals and Materials Soc. 1990–; Lecturer, Korea Advanced Inst. of Science and Tech., Seoul Nat. Univ., Korea Univ., Yonsei Univ., Hanyang Univ., Ajou Univ., Ulsan Univ.; Science and Tech. Medal (Doyackjang) 2005; Nat. Scholarship for advanced studies in a foreign country 1978–, Prime Minister's Award 1986, Recognition for Distinguished Tech. Service, Korean Air Force 1996, Accomplishment Award (Seojungsang), KIMM 2002. *Publications:* two books (ed.), 47 scientific papers, 45 presentations in tech. meetings, seven patents, 30 R&D reports. *Address:* Korea Institute of Science and Technology, 39-1 Hawolgok-dong, Wolsong-gil 5, Seongbuk-gu, Seoul 136-791, Republic of Korea (office). *Telephone:* (2) 958-5455 (office). *Fax:* (2) 958-5449 (office). *E-mail:* dwkum@kist.re.kr (office). *Website:* www.kist.re.kr (office).

KUMA, Kengo; Japanese architect and academic; *Principal, Kengo Kuma and Associates;* b. 8 Aug. 1954, Yokohama, Kanagawa; s. of Hiroko Kuma and Toma Kuma; m.; one s.; ed Univ. of Tokyo; worked for a time at Nihon Sekkei and Toda Corpn; Visiting Scholar, Columbia Univ. and Asian Cultural Council, USA 1985–86; f. Spatial Design Studio 1987; f. Kengo Kuma and Assocs 1990; Prof.,Faculty of Environmental Information, Keio Univ. 1998–99, Prof., Faculty of Science and Technology 2001–09; Prof., Grad. School of Architecture, Univ. of Tokyo 2009–; Visiting Prof., School of Architecture, Univ. of Illinois at Urbana-Champaign, USA; Int. Fellow, Royal Inst. of British Architects 2014; Hon. Fellow, American Inst. of Architects 2014; Officier de L'Ordre des Arts et des Lettres, France 2009; Dr hc (Feng-Chia Univ., Taiwan) 2014; AIA Benedictus Award 1997, Architectural Inst. of Japan Award 1997, Int. Stone Architecture Award 2001, Togo Murano Award 2001, Spirit of Nature Wood Architecture Award, Finland 2002, Energy Performance and Architecture Award, France 2008, Bois Magazine International Wood Architecture Award (France) 2008, Mainichi Art Award 2010, Minister of Education, Culture, Sports, Science and Technology's Art Encouragement Prize 2011, Japan Information-Cultuology Soc. Award 2012, Asiagraph Award 2012, Global Award for Sustainable Architecture 2016. *Works include:* with Kengo Kuma and Assocs: M2 building 1989–91, Kiro-San observatory 1994, Kitakami Canal Museum 1994, Water/Glass, Atami 1995, Bato Hiroshige Museum 2000, Stone Museum 2000, Great (Bamboo) Wall House, Beijing 2002, Plastic House 2002, LVMH Group Japan headquarters, Osaka 2003, Lotus House 2003, Suntory's Tokyo office building Nagasaki Prefectural Art Museum 2005, Kodan apartments 2005, Water Block House 2007, The Opposite House, Beijing 2008, Nezu Museum, Minato, Tokyo 2009, Stone Roof 2010, Taikoo Li Sanlitun, Beijing 2010, Akagi Jinja and Park Court Kagurazaka 2010, Yusuhara Wooden Bridge Museum 2011, Meme Meadows Experimental House, Hokkaido 2012, Wisdom Tea House 2012, Seibu 4000 series Fifty-two Seats of Happiness tourist train refurbishment 2016, Japanese Garden Cultural Village, Portland, Oregon, USA 2017, Coeda House 2017, Seijo Kinoshita Hospital (green hospital) 2017. *Publications:* 10 Houses 1990, Introduction to Architecture – History and Ideology 1994, Catastrophe of Architectural Desire 1994, Anti Object 2000, Patterns and Layering, Japanese Spatial Culture, Nature and Architecture 2012, Plot 06 2015, Hiroba 2015, Onomatope Kenchiku (X-knowledge) 2015, L'anti oggetto Dissolvere e disintegrare l'architettura 2016, Celestial Gardens -Kyoto Imperial Palace and Villa 2017. *Address:* Kengo Kuma and Associates, 2-24-8 BY-CUBE 2F, Minamiaoyama, Minato-ku, Tokyo 107-0062 (office); 37-7-301 Yaraicho Shinjuku-ku, Tokyo 162-0805, Japan (home). *Telephone:* (3) 3401-7721 (office); (3) 3235-7784 (home). *Fax:* (3) 3401-7778 (office); (3) 3268-0928 (home). *E-mail:* kuma@ba2.so-net.ne.jp (office). *Website:* kkaa.co.jp (office).

KUMACHEVA, Eugenia, MSc, PhD, FRSC, FRS; Canadian (b. Russian) chemist and academic; *University Professor of Chemistry, University of Toronto;* b. Odessa, USSR; ed Inst. of Chemical Tech. (now Tech. Univ.), USSR, Inst. of Physical Chem., USSR (now Russian) Acad. of Sciences; joined Dept of Chem., Moscow State Univ.; Postdoctoral Fellow, Lab. of Prof. Jacob Klein, Weizmann Inst. of Science, Israel 1991–94; joined group of Prof. Mitchel Winnik, Dept of Chem., Univ. of Toronto 1995, Asst Prof. of Chem. 1996–2001, Assoc. Prof. 2001–05, Prof. 2005–13, Univ. Prof. 2013–; sabbatical leave at Harvard Univ., USA 2002; Visiting Prof., Univ. of Oxford, UK 2003, Université Louis Pasteur, Strasbourg, France 2006, Moscow State Univ. 2009, Univ. of Cambridge, UK 2010, Univ. of Bayreuth, Germany 2011; mem. Advisory Bd Max Planck Inst. for Polymer Research, Germany, Waterloo Inst. of Nanotechnology, Advanced Science Inst. (RIKEN), Japan, Brookhaven Nat. Lab., USA, Triangle Materials Science and Engineering Center, USA; Minerva Foundation Fellowship (Germany) 1992, Imperial Coll. Visiting Fellowship (UK) 1994, Premier Research Excellence Award (Canada) 1999, Int. Chorafas Foundation Award 2000, Canada Research Chair in Advanced Polymer Materials/Tier 2 2002, Schlumberger Scholarship, Univ. of Oxford 2003, Clara Benson Award (CSC) 2004, Macromolecular Science and Eng CIC Award 2005, Canada Research Chair in Advanced Polymer Materials/Tier 1 2006, E. Gordon Young Lecturer, Chemical Inst. of Canada 2007, L'ORÉAL-UNESCO Award for Women in Science (N America) 2009, Connaught Innovation Award, Connaught Foundation 2011, Humboldt Research Award, Alexander von Humboldt Foundation (Germany) 2012, Inventor of the Year, Univ. of Toronto 2012, Canada Institute of Chemistry (CIC) Medal 2017. *Publications:* numerous papers in professional journals on studies of self-assembly and non-equilibrium phenomena in polymer systems, especially polymers at surfaces and interfaces, devt of advanced polymer materials, and convection in polymeric liquids. *Address:* Room LM 627, Department of Chemistry, University of Toronto, 80 St George Street, Toronto, ON M5S 3H6, Canada (office). *Telephone:* (416) 978-3576 (office). *Fax:* (416) 978-8775 (office). *E-mail:* ekumache@chem.utoronto.ca (office). *Website:* www.chem.utoronto.ca/staff/EK (office).

KUMAKURA, Sadatake; Japanese pharmaceuticals distribution executive; *Representative Director and Chairman, Medipal Holdings Corporation;* fmr Pres. and CEO Kuraya Sanseido Inc., Rep. Dir, Pres. and CEO Mediceo Paltac Holdings Co. Ltd (name changed to Medipal Holdings Corpn following separation of prescription pharmaceutical wholesale business 2009; Kuraya Sanseido Inc. took over prescription pharmaceutical wholesale business, merged with Senshu Yakuhin Co. Ltd, Ushioda Kuraya Sanseido Inc., Yamahiro Kuraya Sanseido Inc., Heisei Yakuhin Co. Ltd and Izutsu Kuraya Sanseido Inc. and changed its corp. name to Mediceo Corpn) 2004–12, Rep. Dir and Chair. 2012–16, Hon. Chair. 2016–. *Address:* Medipal Holdings Corporation, 2-7-15, Yaesu, Chuo-ku, Tokyo 104-8461, Japan (office). *Telephone:* (3) 3517-5800 (office). *Fax:* (3) 3517-5011 (office). *E-mail:* info@medipal.co.jp (office). *Website:* www.medipal.co.jp (office).

KUMAR, Ashwani, BA, LLB, MPhil; Indian lawyer and politician; b. 26 Oct. 1952, Delhi; s. of Prabodh Chandra and Adarsh Kumari; m. Madhu Kumar 1975; one s. one d.; ed St Stephen's Coll., Delhi, Univ. of Delhi, Jawaharlal Nehru Univ., New Delhi; Sec., Gurdaspur Dist Congress Cttee, Punjab 1976; Organizing Sec., Punjab Pradesh Congress Cttee 1986; Additional Solicitor-Gen. of India 1990; fmr Sr Advocate, Supreme Court of India; mem. All-India Congress Cttee 1990–2011, Spokesperson 1999–2000; mem. Rajya Sabha (upper house of Parl.) from Punjab 2002–; Union Cabinet Minister of State for Industry 2006–09, for Planning, Parl. Affairs, Science and Tech. and Earth Science 2011–12, Minister of Law and Justice 2012–13; Gov. of Nagaland 2013–14 (resgnd), also of Manipur July–Dec. 2013; mem. Public Accounts Cttee 2009; fmr Visiting Scholar, Centre for Strategic and Int. Studies, Washington, DC; mem. numerous int. dels including to World Econ. Forum, Davos 2007 and 2012; accompanying Minister to Pres. of India on several int. state visits; Hon. LLD (Punjab Univ.) 2004. *Publications include:* Law, Ideas and Ideology in Politics: Perspectives of an Activist 2003; numerous articles in newspapers and magazines on law, econ. reforms, elections, democracy, int. affairs. *Leisure interests:* table tennis, wrestling, reading, travel, music and films. *Address:* Sewa Sadan, Opp. ITI, G.T. Road, Gurdaspur 797 001, Punjab, India (home). *Telephone:* (1874) 221808 (home). *Website:* ashwanikumar.info.

KUMAR, Meira, LLB, MA; Indian politician, lawyer and fmr diplomatist; b. 31 March 1945, Patna, Bihar; d. of Shri Jagjivan Ram, fmr Deputy Prime Minister, and Indrani Devi; m. Manjul Kumar 1968; one s. two d.; ed Indraprastha Coll., Miranda House, Delhi Univ.; joined Indian Foreign Service 1973, served at Embassy in Madrid 1976–77, Indian High Comm. in London 1977–79, Embassy in Mauritius, also served as mem. India-Mauritius Jt Comm. and at Ministry of External Affairs 1980–85; mem. eighth Lok Sabha (for Bijnor, UP) 1985–89, 11th Lok Sabha 1996–98, 12th Lok Sabha (for Karol Bagh, Delhi) 1998–99, 14th Lok Sabha (for her father's fmr constituency of Sasaram, Bihar) 2004–09, 15th Lok Sabha (Sasaram, Bihar) 2009–14, Speaker of Lok Sabha (first woman) 2009–14; mem. Consultative Cttee, Ministry of External Affairs 1986–89, 1996–98; Union Minister of Social Justice and Empowerment 2004–09; briefly inducted as mem. Cabinet as Union Minister for Water Resources 2009; Gen. Sec. All India Congress Cttee 1990–92, 1996–99, mem. Congress Working Cttee 1990–2000, 2002–04; cand. in presidential election 2017; Ed. Pavan Prasad (monthly magazine) 1980–92; mem. Court of Jawaharlal Nehru Univ. 1996–98, Court of Univ. of Delhi 1996–98, Rajghat Samadhi Cttee 1998–99; Founder and Pres. All India Samta Movt 1990; Pres. RVAKV Soc. (Inst. of Blind Girls) 1992–98, Ravidas Smarak Soc., Varanasi 2000, Jagjivan Seva Ashram, Sasaram 2002; Chair. Meera Kala Mandir, Udaipur 2000, Jagjivan Ram Sanatorium, Dehri-on-Sone 2002; Vice-Chair. Rajendra Bhawan Trust, Delhi 1987; Man. Trustee, Jagjivan Ashram Trust, Delhi 1985–2004; mem. Senate, Bihar Univ. 1969–71, Supreme Court Bar Asscn 1980, Senate, Punjab Univ. 1987–91, Governing Body, Indian Council of Cultural Relations 1987–92, Cen. Advisory Bd of Educ. 1977–90, 2004, Advisory Council, Delhi Devt Authority 1998–99, Nat. Comm. on Population, Nat. Integration Council; mem. India Int. Centre, New Delhi, India Habitat Centre, New Delhi, Nat. Sports Club of India, New Delhi. *Publications:* several poems. *Leisure interests:* keen sportswoman (holds medals for rifle shooting), equestrianism, painting, writing poetry, old monuments, Indian textiles and crafts, reading, Indian classical music. *Address:* D-1029, New Friends Colony, New Delhi 110 065, India (home). *Telephone:* (11) 26910618 (home); (98) 10630165 (mobile). *Fax:* (11) 26910618 (home). *E-mail:* meirakumar@gmail.com.

KUMAR, Mohan, MBA, PhD; Indian diplomatist; *Chairman, Research and Information System for Developing Countries, Indian Habitat Centre;* m. Mala Kumar; one s. one d.; ed Univ. of Delhi, Institut d'études politiques (Sciences Po), France; joined Foreign Service 1981, Third Sec., Perm. Mission to UN, Geneva 1981–84, Second, then First Sec., Embassies in Rabat, Morocco and Brazzaville, Congo, respectively 1984–90, Desk Officer for bilateral relations with Bangladesh, Sri Lanka and the Maldives, Ministry of External Affairs 1990–92, associated with GATT/WTO, Geneva and with Uruguay Round of Trade Negotiations 1992–2001, also lead negotiator and rep. at WTO Marrakesh Ministerial Conf. 1994, participated in WTO Ministerial Confs in Seattle, Wash. 1999 and Doha 2001, Deputy High Commr in Colombo, Sri Lanka 2001–05, Head of Div. (Jt Sec.) overseeing bilateral relations with Bangladesh, Sri Lanka, the Maldives and Myanmar, Ministry of External Affairs 2005–07, Deputy Chief of Mission, Embassy in Paris 2007–10, Amb. to Bahrain 2010–15, to France (also accred to Monaco) 2015–17; Vice-Dean and Prof., Jindal School of Int. Affairs 2017–; Chair. Research and Information System for Developing Countries, Indian Habitat Centre 2018–. *Publications:* Negotiation Dynamics of the WTO: An Insider's Account 2018. *Leisure interests:* travel, reading, cricket, tennis. *Address:* Research and Information System for Developing Countries, Core IV-B, Fourth Floor, India Habitat Centre, Lodhi Road, New Delhi 110 003, India (office). *Telephone:* (11) 24682177 (Ext. 80) (office). *Fax:* (11) 24682173 (Ext. 74) (office). *E-mail:* dgoffice@ris.org.in (office). *Website:* www.ris.org.in (office).

KUMAR, Narendra; Indian civil servant and government official; ed Delhi School of Econs, Shri Ram Coll. of Commerce, Univ. of Delhi; joined Admin. Service 1988, Officer on Special Duty to Chief Minister of Delhi 1999–2001; apptd Sec. and Commr Labour and Employment, Delhi 2001, 2004–05; apptd Excise Commr, Delhi 2002; Personal Sec. to Minister of State for Communication and Information Tech., Delhi 2003–04; Devt Commr and Div. Commr, Delhi 2006; Sec. and Commr Industries, Delhi 2006–08; fmr Sec., Industries and Commerce, Environment and Forests and Ex-officio Chair. Pondicherry Pollution Control Cttee; Devt Commr, Govt of Goa and Sec. to Gov. of Goa 2008–11; Admin. of Union Territories of Dadra and Nagar Haveli and of Daman and Diu 2011–12.

KUMAR, Nikhil, MA; Indian politician and fmr police officer; b. 15 July 1941, Hajipur Dist, Vaishali; s. of Satyendra Narayan Sinha and Kishori Sinha; m. Shyama Singh; ed St Xavier's School, Patna, Allahabad Univ.; entered civil service 1963, Indian Police Service Officer assigned to fmr Union Territory of Delhi, becoming Inspector Gen., Border Security Force 1989–91, 1992–94, Commr of Police, New Delhi 1995–97, Dir-Gen. Indo-Tibetan Border Police 1997, Special Sec. in charge of Internal Security, Ministry of Home Affairs 1997–99, Dir-Gen. Nat. Security Guards 1999–2001 (retd); mem. Nat. Security Advisory Bd 2001–03; mem. Lok Sabha (parl.) for Aurangabad constituency 2004–09, mem. Cttee on External Affairs, Jt Cttee on Salaries and Allowances of MPs, Jt Cttee on Security in Parl.; Gov. of Nagaland 2009–13, of Kerala 2013–14; Pres. Anugrah Sewa Sadan, Patna; Chair. A. N. Sinha Inst. of Social Studies, Patna; Pres. Gandhi Ashram Trust, Hajipur; mem. Indian Nat. Congress party; Police Medal for Meritorious Service 1978, Pres.'s Police Medal for Distinguished Service 1985.

KUMAR, Nitish, BSc (Eng); Indian engineer and politician; b. 1 March 1951, Bakhtiarpur, Patna, Bihar; s. of Kaviraj Ram Lakhan Singh and Parmeshwari Devi; m. Manju Kumari Sinha 1973 (died 2007); one s.; ed Bihar Coll. of Eng, Patna; involved in JP Movt led by Jayaprakash Narayan 1974–77, detained under Maintenance of Internal Security Act 1974, and during Emergency 1975; mem. Bihar Legis. Ass. 1985–89; Pres. Yuva Lok Dal 1987–88; mem. Lok Sabha 1989–; Union Minister of State, Agriculture and Co-operation April–Nov. 1990, Union Minister for Railways and for Surface Transport 1998–99 (resgnd), for Surface Transport Oct.–Nov. 1999, for Agric. Nov. 1999– March 2000, for Agric. 2000–01 (with additional charge of Railways March–July 2001), for Railways 2001–04; mem. Janata Dal (United) party, Sec.-Gen. Janata Dal, Bihar 1989, Gen. Sec. 1991–93, Deputy Leader of Janata Dal in Parl. 1991–93, apptd Leader 2004, Pres. 2016–; led Nat. Democratic Alliance to victory in Bihar Ass. elections Nov. 2005;

Chief Minister of Bihar 3–10 March 2000 (resgnd), 2005–14, 2015–18; Founder-mem. Samata Party Movt; CNN-IBN Indian of the Year (Politics) 2008, NDTV Indian of the Year (Politics) 2009, Reformer of the Year, Economics Times 2009, Polio Eradication Championship Award, Rotary Ints 2009, CNN-IBN Indian of the Year (Politics) 2010, Sir Jehangir Gandhi Medal, XLRI Jamshedpur 2011, JP Memorial Award, Manav Mandir, Nagpur 2013. *Address:* Janata Dal—United, 7 Jantar Mantar Road, New Delhi 110 001; Village Hakikatpur, PO Bakhtiarpur, Patna 800 001, India (home). *Telephone:* (11) 23368833 (Janata Dal—United) (office); (98) 68180490 (mobile); (612) 2222079 (home). *Fax:* (11) 23368138 (Janata Dal—United) (office). *E-mail:* info@janatadalunited.org (office). *Website:* www.janatadalunited.org (office).

KUMAR, Rajender, BTech, MA; Indian government official; b. 16 Dec. 1966; ed Indian Inst. of Tech., Kanpur, Asian Inst. of Man., Manila; joined Indian Admin. Service; fmr Dir (Educ.) Govt of Nat. Capital Territory of Delhi; Commr-cum-Sec. (Health/Finance), Union Territory of Andaman and Nicobar Islands –2006; Admin. of Lakshadweep 2006; Sec. (Information and Tech.), Delhi; Special Sec., Commonwealth Coordination and Public Grievances; Prin. Sec. (Power), Govt of Delhi 2007–11; apptd Chief Man. Dir Delhi Power Co. Ltd 2007; mem. Bd of Dirs Delhi Transco Ltd (apptd Chair. and Man. Dir 2007), Indraprastha Power Generation Co. Ltd (apptd Chair. 2007), Pragati Power Corpn Ltd (apptd Chair. 2007); fmr Chair. Lakshadweep Devt Corpn, SPORTS (Soc. for Promotion of Recreational Tourism and Sports); ex-officio Insp. Gen. of Police.

KUMAR, Rajnish, MSc; Indian banker; *Chairman, State Bank of India;* b. 14 Jan. 1958, Meerut, Uttar Pradesh; m. Reeta Kumar; joined State Bank of India (SBI) as Probationary Officer 1980, worked for SBI in Canada and UK, fmr Chief Gen. Man., NE Circle and Project Finance, Man. Dir and CEO, SBI Capital Markets Ltd (merchant banking div.) –2015, Man. Dir, Nat. Banking Group 2015, Chair. State Bank of India 2017–. *Leisure interests:* travel, badminton. *Address:* The Chairman, State Bank of India, State Bank Bhavan, Madam Cama Road, Mumbai 400 021, India (office). *Fax:* (22) 22742430 (office). *E-mail:* customercare@sbi.co.in (office). *Website:* www.sbi.co.in (office).

KUMAR, Shri Vijay, BE, MBA; Indian civil servant; ed Delhi Coll. of Eng, Univ. of Sydney, Australia; has served in various civil service positions under admin of Nat. Capital Territory of Delhi (GNCTD) and Daman Admin, including Sub-Div. Magistrate, East Delhi, Jt Sec., Public Works, Additional Sec. (Finance), East Delhi, Commr (Excise), Dir Dept of Educ., Sec. and Commr, Consumer Affairs, Food and Public Distribution, Civil Supplies Dept; Collector, Daman, Diu, Dadra and Nager Haveli Admin; Counsellor, Perm. Mission to WTO, Geneva 2010–13; served as CEO Delhi Jal Bd and Chair. and Man. Dir Delhi State Civil Supplies Corpn Ltd, Commr, (Value Added Tax), GNCTD Trade and Taxes Dept –2015, Admin. of Lakshadweep 2015–16; fmr Chair. and Man. Dir Delhi Transport Corpn; Golden Icon Award for Online Student Man. System, GNCTD 2006, Bronze Icon Award for Exemplary Leadership and ICT Achievement, (Professional Category) 2006, Prime Minister's Award for Excellence in Public Admin 2007, Silver Icon Award for Computer-Aided Learning, GNCTD Dept of Educ. 2007.

KUMARASWAMY, Haradanahalli Deve Gowda, BSc; Indian politician and film producer; *Chief Minister of Karnataka;* b. 16 Dec. 1959, Haradanahalli, Hassan Dist, Karnataka; s. of H. D. Deve 'Mannina Maga' Gowda and Chennamma Gowda; m. Anitha Kumaraswamy 1986; one s.; m. Radhika Kumaraswamy 2006 (bigamy); one d.; ed Basavanagudi Nat. Coll., Bangalore; began career as distributor of Kannada films in Mysore, Mandya, Hassan and Coorg dists 1990; began political career 1994, mem. Lok Sabha (Parl.) for Kanakapura 1996–98, re-elected 2009; mem. Karnataka Legis. Ass. for Ramanagaram constituency 2004–08, for Channapatna constituency 2018, mem. Cttee on Rural Devt 2009, on Food Man. in Parl. House Complex 2009, Leader of Opposition 2013; Chief Minister of Karnataka 2006–07 (resgnd), 2018–; Pres. Karnataka State Unit of Janata Dal (Secular) 2014–; Pres. Karnataka Cinema Theatre Owners Asscn 2002–; Founder and Pres. Film Producers Asscn 2003–. *Films produced include:* Surya Vamsha 1999, Galate Aliyandru 2000, Chandra Chakori 2003, Jaguar 2016. *Leisure interests:* reading, driving. *Address:* Office of the Chief Minister, Vidhana Soudha, 3rd Floor (Room 323), Bangalore 560 001 (office); No. 281, 80 ft. Road, Padmanabhanagar, Banaskankarji, IInd stage, Bangalore 560 070, India (home). *Telephone:* (80) 22253414 (office); (80) 26582230 (home). *Fax:* (80) 22281021 (office). *E-mail:* chiefminister@karnataka.gov.in (office); cm@kar.nic.in (office). *Website:* www.karnataka.gov.in.

KUMARATUNGA, Chandrika Bandaranaike, BSc; Sri Lankan politician and fmr head of state; *Chairperson, Foundation for Democracy and Justice;* b. 29 June 1945, Colombo; d. of S. W. R. D. Bandaranaike and Sirimavo R. D. Bandaranaike; m. Vijaya Kumaratunga 1978 (assassinated 1988); one s. one d.; ed St Bridget's Convent, Colombo, Institut d'Etudes Politiques de Paris (Sciences-Po), Univ. of Paris, France; mem. Exec. Cttee Women's League of SLFP 1974, Exec. Cttee and Working Cttee 1980, Cen. Cttee 1992, Deputy Leader of SLFP; Chair., Man. Dir Dinakara Sinhala (daily newspaper) 1977–85; Vice-Pres. Sri Lanka Mahajana (People's) Party (SLMP) 1984, Pres. 1988; Leader SLMP and People's Alliance; Chief Minister, Minister of Law and Order, Finance and Planning, Educ., Employment and Cultural Affairs of the Western Prov. Council 1993–94; Prime Minister Aug.–Nov. 1994, also held posts of Minister of Finance and Planning, Ethnic Affairs and Nat. Integration, of Defence, of Buddha Sasana; Exec. Pres. of Sri Lanka 1994–2005; fmrly also Minister of Defence, of Constitutional Affairs, and of Educ.; Pres. Sri Lanka Freedom Party 2000–06; Additional Prin. Dir Land Reform Comm. 1972–75; Chair. Janawasa Comm. 1975–77; Expert Consultant, FAO 1977–80; Research Fellow, Univ. of London, UK 1988–91; Guest Lecturer, Univ. of Bradford, UK 1989, Jawaharlal Nehru Univ., India 1991; Chair. Foundation for Democracy and Justice, South Asia Policy and Research Inst.; adviser on poverty alleviation to Clinton Global Initiative; Dir Club de Madrid. *Publications include:* several research papers on land reform, food policies, poverty alleviation, democracy and good governance, political violence and conflict management. *Leisure interests:* swimming, Kandyan (nat.) dance, music, reading, art and sculpture, drama, cinema. *Address:* Office of the Former President, #27 Independence Avenue, Colombo 10, Sri Lanka (office). *Telephone:* (11) 269-437-2 (office). *Fax:* (11) 267-415-9 (office). *E-mail:* officecbk@gmail.com (office). *Website:* www.presidentcbk.org (office); www.thesapri.org (office).

KUMARESAN, Jacob, MD, MPH, TM, DPH; Indian epidemiologist and international organization official; *Executive Director, World Health Organization Office, United Nations;* m. Aruna Kumaresan; ed Kilpauk Medical Coll., Univ. of Madras, Tulane Univ., New Orleans, USA; practised as surgeon in hosps around India 1978–81; Govt Medical Officer, Ministry of Health, Zimbabwe 1981, becoming Acting Provincial Medical Dir; fmr Consultant Epidemiologist, Gillis Long Hansen's Disease Center, Louisiana, USA; fmr Sr Epidemiologist, Ministry of Health, Botswana; joined WHO as Medical Officer, Global Tuberculosis Programme 1992, becoming Sr Adviser to Stop TB Initiative, Exec. Sec., Stop TB Partnership 2000, Pres. Int. Trachoma Initiative 2003–08, Co-ordinator, WHO UN Office, New York 2007, Dir WHO Centre for Health Devt (WHO Kobe Centre-WKC) 2008–11, Exec. Dir WHO Office, UN, New York 2011–; Chair. Int. Coalition for Trachoma Control; Vice-Pres. World Lung Foundation; mem. Bd of Govs Glasses for Humanity; mem. Tech. Review Panel of Global Fund to Fight AIDS, Tuberculosis and Malaria. *Address:* WHO Office at the United Nations, One Dag Hammarskjöld Plaza, 885 Second Avenue, 26th Floor, New York, NY 10017, USA (office). *Telephone:* (646) 626-6045 (office). *Fax:* (646) 626-6080 (office). *E-mail:* wun@whoun.org (office).

KUMBA, Jemma Nunu, BSc; South Sudanese politician; *Minister of Wildlife Conservation and Tourism;* m. Festo Kumba; one s. three d.; ed Univ. of Namibia; served for four years as coordinator for relief for New Sudan Council of Churches; mem. Sudan People's Liberation Movement (SPLM) 1983–, acted as SPLM peace negotiator in Machakos and Naivasha, Kenya 2002; Gender Adviser for Christian Aid, Southern Sudan Programme 2003–05; mem. Nat. Parl., Khartoum, Chair. Econ. Affairs Cttee 2005–; head of del. and mem. Pan-African Parl. 2005–, mem. Cttee for Cooperation, Int. Relations and Conflict Man. 2006–08 (Deputy Chair. 2007–08); Gov. Western Equatoria State 2009–10; Minister of Lands, Housing and Physical Planning, Govt of South Sudan 2011–13, of Electricity, Dams, Irrigation and Water Resources 2013–16, of Wildlife Conservation and Tourism 2016–; mem. Initiative for Inclusive Security. *Address:* Ministry of Wildlife, Conservation and Tourism, Ministries Complex, Juba, South Sudan (office).

KUMBLE, Anil Radhakrishna; Indian fmr professional cricketer; b. 17 Oct. 1970, Bangalore, Karnataka; s. of K N Krishna Swamy and Saroja Krishna Swamy; m. Chethana Ramatheertha 1999; one s. two d.; ed Nat. High School, Nat. Coll., Basavanagudi, Rashtreeya Vidyalaya Coll. of Eng; leg-break and googly bowler; right-handed lower order batsman; teams played for Karnataka 1989–2009, Northants. 1995, Leics. 2000, Surrey 2006, India 1990–2008 (Capt. 2007–08); First-class debut: 1989/90; Test debut: England v India, Manchester 9–14 Aug. 1990; One-Day Int. (ODI) debut: India v Sri Lanka, Sharjah, UAE 25 April 1990; India's highest-ever wicket-taker in tests and third-highest wicket-taker in tests internationally and one of only three bowlers to have taken more than 600 Test wickets; became second player, after Jim Laker of England, to capture all 10 wickets in a test innings (India v Pakistan) 7 Nov. 1999; announced retirement 2 Nov. 2008; Vice-Chair. Karnataka State Wildlife Bd 2009; Capt. Royal Challengers Bangalore, Chief Mentor 2012–13; Chair. Int. Cricket Council 2012; Chief Mentor, Mumbai Indians 2013–15; Head Coach, Indian Cricket Team 2016–17; mem. Athlete Cttee World Anti-Doping Agency 2009–; Arjuna Award, Govt of India 1995, Wisden Cricketer of the Year 1996, Padma Shri 2005; prominent intersection in M. G. Road, Bangalore named after him. *Leisure interests:* photography, wildlife. *Address:* c/o Board of Control for Cricket in India, 4th Floor, Cricket Centre, Wankhede Stadium, D Road, Churchgate, Mumbai 400020, India (office).

RAJASEKHARAN, Kummanam, BSc; Indian politician, activist and journalist; b. 23 Dec. 1952, Kummanam, Kottayam, Travancore-Cochin; s. of V. K. Ramakrishna Pillai and P. Parukkutty Amma; ed CMS Coll. Kottayam; Sub-Ed. Deepika (daily newspaper) 1974, later becoming journalist with other dailies including Rastravaartha, Kerala Desam, Kerala Bhooshanam, Kerala Dwani; Ed. Janmabhumi Daily 1989, Man. Dir 2007, Chair. 2011–; worked at Food Corpn of India 1976–87; Dist Sec., Vishva Hindu Parishad (nationalist org.), Kottayam 1979, Joint Sec. 1981; Gen. Sec. Hindu Munnani 1985, Guruvayoor Temple Action Council 1988, Sabarimala Ayyappa Sewa Samajam 2009; mem. Rashtriya Swayamsevak Sangh (nationalist volunteer org.); Gov. of Mizoram 2018–19 (resgnd); mem. Bharatiya Janata Party (BJP), Pres. Kerala BJP 2015–18; apptd Chief Patron, Aranmula Heritage Village Action Council 2012. *Address:* c/o Raj Bhawan, Aizawl, Mizoram 796001, India (office). *Website:* www.kummanamrajasekharan.in.

KUMSISHVILI, Dimitri; Georgian fmr banking executive, business executive and politician; b. 7 Sept. 1974; m.; three c.; ed V. Komarov School of Math. and Physics, Ivane Javakhishvili Tbilisi State Univ.; Leading Specialist, United Cartu Bank 1995–96, Auditor, Audit & Consulting 1996–97, Head of Treasury Dept 1997–99, First Deputy Gen. Dir, Cartu Bank 1999–2011; mem. Supervisory Bd, Tbilisi Interbank Currency Exchange 2000–11, Global Contact Consulting 2010–12; CEO Startup & Innovative Business Investment Fund 2012; Chair. Supervisory Bd, Rational Solutions 2012; Business Devt Dir, Palitra Media 2011–12; First Deputy Minister of Economy and Sustainable Devt 2012–15, Chair. Nat. Agency of State Property (LEPL) 2012–15; Chair. Cttee discussing issues concerning Rules of Expropriation of Property for Pressing Public Needs, Intergovernmental Comm. for studying cases of agreements regarding state property man., Comm. on determining property ownership of land, multi-storey residential houses and other buildings, non-residential areas, agricultural and non-agricultural lands; Deputy Mayor of Tbilisi March–Sept. 2015; First Deputy Prime Minister 2015–18, Minister of the Economy and Sustainable Devt Sept. 2015–16, 2017–18, Minister of Finance 2016–17. *Address:* c/o Ministry of Economic and Sustainable Development, 0108 Tbilisi, Chovelidzi 10A, Georgia.

KUNASEK, Mario; Austrian politician and fmr army officer; *Federal Minister of Defence;* b. 29 June 1976, Graz; m. Sabrina Koroschetz 2018; ed Graz Higher Tech. Inst.; mil. service 1995–96; joined regular Austrian Armed Forces 1996, served with Supply Regt 1, Graz; rank of Corporal 1997, of Staff Sergeant 2005; mem. Freiheitliche Partei Österreichs (FPÖ), Chair. FPÖ Gössendorf Local Br. 2005, Chair. FPÖ Graz Dist 2007, Chair. FPÖ Styria Prov. 2015; mem. Nationalrat (Nat. Council, Parl.) 2008–15, Chair. Defence Cttee 2013–15; Deputy Fed. Chair. Aktionsgemeinschaft Unabhängiger und Freiheitlicher (AUF, trade union) 2010–13; Deputy Mayor of Gössendorf 2015–17; mem. Styria Provincial Ass.

2015–17; Fed. Minister of Defence 2017–. *Address:* Federal Ministry of Defence, Rossauer Lände 1, 1090 Vienna, Austria (office). *Telephone:* (1) 502-01-0 (office). *E-mail:* presse@bmlvs.gv.at (office). *Website:* www.bundesheer.at (office).

KÜNAST, Renate; German lawyer and politician; b. 15 Dec. 1955, Recklinghausen, North-Rhine/Westphalia; ed Düsseldorf Polytechnic, Freie Universität Berlin; social worker at youth correctional facility in Berlin-Tegel 1977–79; Co-founder and mem. West Berlin Alternative List 1979, now Bündnis 90/Die Grünen MdB (Alliance 90/Greens), Chair. 1990–93, 1998–2000 (Deputy Chair. 1995–98), Chair. Nat. Exec. Cttee 2000–01; mem. Berlin Senate 1985–87, 1989–2000; mem. Bundestag (Parl.) 2002–, Co-Chair. Green Parl. party 2005–13, Chair. Legal Affairs and Consumer Protection Cttee 2014–17; Fed. Minister for Consumer Protection, Food and Agric. 2001–05, mem. Cttee on Food and Agric. 2018–; mem. Bd of Dirs Telefonseelsorge Berlin 2011–, Förderkreis politische Rhetorik und Kommunikation; mem. Nat. Campaign Cttee of No Hate Speech Movt 2017–; mem. Advisory Bd Humanist Union, Dispute Berlin; mem. Women's Business Club, Criminal Defence Lawyers Asscn, Slow Food Berlin, Dr Hauschka Community; Trustee, Berlin AIDS-Hilfe; Hon. mem. Raoul Wallenberg Foundation, Angelo Roncalli Cttee, Interessengemeinschaft für gesunde Lebensmittel; Rachel Carson Prize 2001, German-British Forum Award 2001, Michael Kay Award 2005, Eurogroup Medal 2005. *Publications:* Klasse statt Masse 2002, Die Dickmacher 2004. *Address:* Bündnis 90/Die Grünen MdB, Deutscher Bundestag, Platz der Republik 1, 11011 Berlin, Germany (office). *Telephone:* (30) 22771913 (office). *Fax:* (30) 22776913 (office). *E-mail:* renate.kuenast@bundestag.de. *Website:* www.bundestag.de/abgeordnete/biografien/K/kuenast_renate/521392 (office); www.renate-kuenast.de.

KUNCZE, Gábor, BSc, PhD; Hungarian politician and television presenter; b. 4 Nov. 1950, Pápa; m. Katalin Fellegi; ed Ybl Miklós Coll. of Tech., Budapest, Karl Marx Univ. of Econs, Budapest; fmr economist and engineer, various industrial man. roles –1983; dept head then div. chief, Industrial Mechanisation Co. 1983–85; Deputy Dir ÉPGÉPTERV Co. 1985–90; mem. Parl. 1990–2007; joined Alliance of Free Democrats (Szabad Demokraták Szövetsége—SzDSz) 1992, mem. Nat. Council 1992, Leader of Parl. Group 1993–94, 1998–2000, 2002–07, mem. Nat. Governing Cttee 1994–97, Pres. SzDSz 1997–98, 2001–07; mem. Council of Elders 1993–94, 1998–2000, 2002–; apptd Minister of the Interior and Deputy Prime Minister after his party signed coalition agreement with HSP (Magyar Szocialista Párt—MSZP) 1994–98; host for ATV television channel 2010–. *Address:* ATV, 1102 Budapest, Csoma u. 31, Hungary. *Telephone:* (1) 877-0800. *E-mail:* info@atv.hu. *Website:* www.atv.hu.

KUNDERA, Milan; French novelist; b. 1 April 1929, Brno; s. of Dr Ludvik Kundera and Milada Kunderová-Janosikova; m. Věra Hrabánková 1967; ed Film Faculty, Acad. of Music and Dramatic Arts, Prague; Asst, later Asst Prof., Film Faculty, Acad. of Music and Dramatic Arts, Prague 1958–69; Prof., Univ. of Rennes 1975–80; Prof., Ecole des hautes études en sciences sociales, Paris 1980–94; mem. Union of Czechoslovak Writers 1963–69; mem. Editorial Bd Literární noviny 1963–67, 1968; Dr hc (Michigan) 1983; Commonwealth Award 1981, Prix Europa-Littérature 1982, Jerusalem Prize 1985, Prix de la critique de l'Acad. française 1987, Nelly Sachs Preis 1987, Österreichische Staatspreis für Europäische Literatur 1988, Jaroslav-Seifert Prize (Czech Repub.) 1994, Medal of Merit (Czech Repub.) 1995, J. G. Herder Prize (Austria) 2000, Grand Prize Acad. française (for novels Slowness, Identity and Ignorance) 2001, Prix mondial Cino Del Duca 2009, Ovid Prize 2011, Prix de la Bibliothèque nationale de France 2012. *Publications include:* drama: Jacques and his master, an homage to Diderot 1971–81; short stories: Laughable Loves (Czechoslovak Writers' Publishing House Prize) 1970, The Apologizer 2015; novels: The Joke (Union of Czechoslovak Writers' Prize 1968) 1967, Life is Elsewhere (Prix Médicis) 1973, La Valse aux adieux (The Farewell Waltz) (Premio letterario Mondello 1978) 1976, Livre du rire et de l'oubli (The Book of Laughter and Forgetting) 1979, The Unbearable Lightness of Being (Los Angeles Times Prize) 1984, Immortality (The Independent Prize, UK 1991) 1989, Slowness 1995, L'Identità (Identity) 1997, La Ignorancia (Ignorance) 2000, La fête de l'insignifiance (The Festival of Insignificance) 2014; essays: The Art of the Novel 1987, Les Testaments trahis (Aujourd'hui Prize, France) 1993, Le Rideau (The Curtain) 2005, Une rencontre (The Encounter) 2009, Œuvre I and II 2011. *Address:* c/o Mr Stephen Page, Faber and Faber, Bloomsbury House, 74–77 Great Russell Street, London, WC1B 3DA, England. *Website:* www.faber.co.uk.

KUNDRA, Shri Ashish, BTech; Indian civil servant and government official; *Commissioner, Finance and Power, Government of Arunachal Pradesh;* b. 6 March 1973, Chandigarh; ed Indian Inst. of Tech., Varanasi, Banaras Hindu Univ.; joined Indian Admin. Service 1995, SDM and Land Acquisition Officer, Land Revenue Man. and Dist Admin 1998–2000, Jt Sec. (Finance and Power), Mizoram 2000–02, Dist Magistrate, Saiha, Mizoram, Land Revenue Man. and Dist Admin 2002–03, Registrar (Co-operative Soc.) 2003, Dir (Finance Dept) and Additional CEO Jal Bd, Delhi 2003–06, Additional Sec. (Public Works), Delhi Aug.–Dec. 2006, Pvt. Sec. to Minister of State for Information Broadcasting and External Affairs 2006–09, to Union Minister of Commerce and Industry 2009–14; Admin. of Daman and Diu and Dadra and Nagar Haveli 2014–16, also Chief Vigilance Officer; Commr, Finance and Power, Govt of Arunachal Pradesh 2016–; fmr Chair. Omnibus Industrial Devt Corpn, SC/ST OBC, Minority Financial Devt Corpn. *Address:* Government of Arunachal Pradesh, Naharlagun, Papum Pare 791 110, Arunachal Pradesh, India (office). *Website:* www.arunachalfinance.in (office).

KUNERT, Günter; German writer and painter; *Honorary President, PEN Centre of German-speaking Writers Abroad;* b. 6 March 1929, Berlin; s. of Adolf Kunert and Edith Warschauer; m. 1st Marianne Todten 1951; m. 2nd Erika Hinckel; ed Basic-School, Berlin; Visiting Assoc. Prof., Univ. of Texas at Austin, USA 1972; Writer-in-Residence, Univ. of Warwick, UK 1975; freelance writer 1979–; mem. Akad. der Künste (Hamburg and Mannheim), Akad. für Sprache und Dichtung, Darmstadt; Pres. PEN Centre of German-speaking Writers Abroad 2005–18; Hon. Pres. PEN Centre of German-speaking Writers Abroad 2018–; Bundesverdienstkreuz (First Class), Grosses Bundesverdienstkreuz mit Stern 2012; Dr hc (Allegheny Coll., Pa) 1988, (Juniata Coll.) 2005, (Univ. of Turin) 2005, (Dickinson Coll., Pa) 2010; Heinrich Mann Prize, Akad. der Künste (East Berlin) 1962, Becher Prize for Poetry 1973, Heinrich Heine Prize (City of Düsseldorf) 1985, Friedrich-Hölderlin Preis 1991, E.R. Curtius Prize 1991, Hans-Sahl-Preis 1996, Georg-Trakl-Preis (Austria) 1997, EU Prix Aristeion 1999, America Award for a Lifetime Contribution to Int. Writing 2009, Preis der Frankfurter Anthologie 2012. *Film:* Abschied and others. *Play:* The Time Machine (based on the novel by H. G. Wells). *TV screenplays include:* King Arthur 1990, An Obituary of the Wall 1991, Endstation: Harembar 1991 and 13 others. *Radio:* 10 radio plays. *Publications include:* Erwachsenenspiele: Erinnerungen 1997, Nachtvorstellung (poems) 1999, Die Botschaft des Hotelzimmers an den Gast 2004, Irrtum ausgeschlossen 2006, Der alte Mann spricht mit seiner Seele 2006, Auskunft für den Notfall 2008, Als das Leben umsonst war (poems) 2009, Die zweite Frau 2019; 60 volumes of poetry, prose, satire, essays, novels, short stories and lectures; Augenspiele (catalogue of exhibition of Kunert-Paintings in Hamburg with short prose). *Leisure interests:* travel, collecting tin toys. *Address:* Schulstrasse 7, 25560 Kaisborstel, Germany (home). *Telephone:* (4892) 1414 (home). *Fax:* (4892) 8403 (home).

KUNEVA, Meglena Shtilianova, LLM; Bulgarian lawyer and politician; *Chairman, Balgariya na Grazhdanite (BG—Bulgaria of Citizens);* b. 22 June 1957, Sofia; m. Andrey Pramov; one s.; ed St Clement of Ohrid Univ. of Sofia; Ed. and presenter, Bulgarian Nat. Radio 1987–91; Asst Prof., Faculty of Law, St Clement of Ohrid Univ. of Sofia 1988–89; Sr Legal Advisor Council of Ministers 1990–2001; legal consultant 1992–98; Lecturer, Free Univ. of Burgas and New Bulgarian Univ. 1992–94; legal specialist, Human Rights Inst. Turku, Finland 1993 and in Int. Relations and Environmental Law, Georgetown Univ. 1995, 1999–2000, and Environmental Law at Oxford Univ. 1996; mem. Bulgarian Del. to 4th session of UN Comm. on Sustainable Devt 1995; mem. Nat. Ass. 2001–07, Deputy Minister, Ministry of Foreign Affairs and chief negotiator with EU 2001–02, Minister of European Affairs 2002–07, Special Rep. at Convention for Future of Europe 2002; Commr for Consumer Protection, EC 2007–10; third placed presidential cand. 2011; Chair. Bulgariya na Grazhdanite (Bulgaria of Citizens) 2012–; Deputy Prime Minister for European Policy and Institutional Issues 2014–17, Minister of Educ. and Science 2016–17; mem. Berlin Conf. on European Cultural Policy; mem. Natsionalno Dvizhenie Siméon Vtori (Nat. Movt Simeon II), later Natsionalno Dvizhenie za Stabilnost i Vazkhod (Nat. Movt for Stability and Progress), Atlantic Club, Union of Bulgarian Jurists, UN Int. Council of Environmental Law, Advisory Bd Time Eco-projects Foundation; Order for Civil Merit, Spain 2002, Chevalier, Légion d'honneur 2003, Order Prince Enrique, Portugal 2004, Order of the Star of Italian Solidarity 2005, Gold Distinction of the Atlantic Club, Bulgaria 2005; Face of Bulgaria Award, Politika (newspaper) 2006. *Leisure interest:* listening to classical music. *Address:* Balgariya na Grazhdanite (Bulgaria of Citizens), Sofia 1113, Park-Hotel 'Moscow', ul. Nezabravka No. 25, 5th Floor, Bulgaria (office). *Telephone:* (2) 843-38-00 (office). *E-mail:* office@grajdani.bg (office). *Website:* grajdani.bg (office).

KUNG, Arthur Hsiang-Yun; Taiwanese business executive; fmr Vice-Pres. CPC Corpn, Chair. China American Petrochemical Co. Ltd (CAPCO) –2012, apptd Pres. CPC Corpn 2012. *Address:* c/o CPC Corporation, 2 Zuo Nan Road, Nanxun Chiu, Kaohsiung 81126, Taiwan.

KÜNG, Hans, DTheol; Swiss theologian and academic; b. 19 March 1928, Sursee, Lucerne; ed Gregorian Univ., Rome, Italy, Inst. Catholique and Univ. of Paris (Sorbonne), France; ordained priest 1954; mem. practical ministry, Lucerne Cathedral 1957–59; Scientific Asst for Dogmatic Catholic Theology, Univ. of Münster Westfalen 1959–60; Prof. of Fundamental Theology, Univ. of Tübingen 1960–63; Prof. of Dogmatic and Ecumenical Theology and Dir, Inst. Ecumenical Research 1963–80, Prof. of Ecumenical Theology, Dir Inst. of Ecumenical Research (under direct responsibility of Pres. and Senate Univ. of Tübingen) 1980–96, Prof. Emer. 1996–; Guest Prof., Univ. of Chicago 1981, of Mich. 1983, of Toronto 1985, of Rice Univ., Houston 1987; numerous guest lectures at univs worldwide; mem. PEN; Pres. Global Ethic Foundation, Germany 1995–2013, Switzerland 1997–2013, now Hon. Pres.; Co-Pres. World Conf. on Religion and Peace, New York; Founding mem. Int. Review of Theology, Concilium; Hon. Citizen City of Syracuse, Italy 2002, Tübingen, Germany 2002, Mozart Hon. Chair, European Acad. of Yuste, Spain 2004; Grosses Bundesverdienstkreuz mit Stern 2003; numerous hon. doctorates, including Hon. DD (Univ. of Wales) 1998, (Florida Int. Univ.) 2002, (Ecumenical Theological Seminary, Detroit) 2003, (Collegium Augustinianum) 2013; Hon. LHD (Ramapo Coll., NY) 1999, (Hebrew Union Coll., Cincinnati) 2000; Hon. DPhil (Genoa) 2004, (Universidad Nacional de Educación a Distancia, Madrid) 2011; Ludwig-Thoma Medal 1975, Oskar Pfister Award, American Psychiatric Asscn 1986, Karl Barth Prize, Evangelische Kirche der Union, Berlin 1992, Hirt Prize, Zürich 1993, Prize for Zivilcourage Zürich 1995, Univ. of Tübingen 1996, Theodor Heuss Prize, Stuttgart 1998, Interfaith Gold Medallion of the Int. Council of Christians and Jews 1998, Martin Luther Towns Prize 1999, Ernst-Robert-Curtius Literary Award Bonn 2001, Göttingen Peace Award 2002, Juliet Hollister Award of the Temple of Understanding 2004, Niwano Peace Prize 2005, Lev Kopelev Prize 2006, Cultural Award, German Freemasons 2007, Croatian Academic Soc. Award 2007, Steiger Award 2008, Lifetime Achievement Award, Prince Alwaleed Bin Talal Center for Muslim-Christian Understanding, Georgetown Univ. 2008, Award for Civil Courage, Freundeskreis Heinrich Heine 2008, Otto Hahn Peace Medal 2008, Abraham Geiger Award 2009, Nonino Prize 2012, Arthur Koestler Prize, Deutsche Gesellschaft für humanes Sterben (German Soc. for Dying with Dignity) 2013. *Publications include:* The Council: Reform and Reunion 1961, That the World May Believe 1963, The Council in Action 1963, Justification: The Doctrine of Karl Barth and a Catholic Reflection 1964, (with new introductory chapter and response of Karl Barth 1981), Structures of the Church 1964, (with new preface) 1982, Freedom Today 1966, The Church 1967, Truthfulness 1968, Menschwerdung Gottes 1970, Infallible? – An Inquiry 1971, Why Priests? 1972, Fehlbar? – Eine Bilanz 1973, On being a Christian 1976, Signposts for the Future 1978, The Christian Challenge 1979, Freud and the Problem of God 1979, Does God Exist? 1980, The Church – Maintained in Truth 1980, Eternal Life? 1984, Christianity and the World Religions: Paths to Dialogue with Islam, Hinduism and Buddhism (with others) 1986, The Incarnation of God 1986, Church and Change: The Irish Experience 1986, Why I am still a Christian 1987, Theology for the Third Millennium: An Ecumenical View 1988, Christianity and Chinese Religions (with Julia Ching) 1989, Paradigm Change in Theology: A Symposium for the future 1989, Reforming the Church Today 1990, Global Responsibility: In Search of a New World Ethic 1991, Judaism 1992, Credo: The Apostles' Creed Explained for Today 1993, Great Christian Thinkers 1994, Christianity 1995, A Dignified Dying: a plea for personal responsibility (with Walter Jens) 1995, Yes to a Global Ethic (ed.) 1996, A Global Ethic for Global Politics and Economics 1997, Breaking Through (with others) 1998, The Catholic Church: A Short History 2001, Women in Christianity 2001, Tracing the Way: Spiritual Dimensions of the World Religions 2002, My Struggle for Freedom (memoirs) 2003, Islam: Past, Present and Future 2006, The Beginning of all Things: Science and Religion 2006, Disputed Truth (memoirs) 2008, How to Do Good and Avoid Evil. A Global Ethic from the Sources of Judaism (with Walter Homolka) 2009, What I Believe 2010, Can We Save the Catholic Church? – We Can Save the Catholic Church! 2013, Erlebte Menschlichkeit. Erinnerungen 2013, Sieben Päpste: Wie ich sie erlebt habe 2015. *Leisure interests:* water sports, classical music. *Address:* Waldhäuserstrasse 23, 72076 Tübingen, Germany (office). *Telephone:* (7071) 62646 (office). *Fax:* (7071) 610140 (office). *E-mail:* office@weltethos.org (office). *Website:* www.weltethos.org (office).

KUNIN, Madeleine May, MA, MS; American journalist, diplomatist, academic and fmr politician; *Chairman, Institute for Sustainable Communities;* b. 28 Sept. 1933, Zürich, Switzerland; d. of Ferdinand May and Renee Bloch; m. Arthur S. Kunin 1959 (divorced 1995); three s. one d.; ed Univ. of Massachusetts, Columbia Univ. and Univ. of Vermont; moved to USA in 1940; reporter, Burlington Free Press, Vt 1957–58; Asst Producer, WCAX-TV, Burlington 1960–61; freelance writer and instructor in English, Trinity Coll., Burlington 1969–70; mem. Vermont House of Reps 1973–78; Lt.-Gov. of Vermont 1979–82, Gov. of Vermont 1985–91; Deputy Sec., US Dept of Educ., Washington, DC 1993–96; Fellow, Inst. of Politics, Kennedy School of Govt, Harvard Univ. 1983–93; Amb. to Switzerland 1996–99; Lecturer, Middlebury Coll., also fmr Scholar-in-Residence 1999–2002; Distinguised Visiting Prof., Univ. of Vermont and St Michael's Coll. 2003–, James Marsh Scholar Prof.-at-Large, Univ. of Vermont 2007–; Founder and Chair. Inst. for Sustainable Communities 1991–; Fellow, Bunting Inst., Radcliffe Coll., Cambridge, Mass. 1991–92; Democrat; more than 20 hon. degrees; Award of Excellence, International Center in New York, Foreign Language Advocacy Award, Northeast Conference on the Teaching of Foreign Languages 1995, Eleanor Roosevelt Val-Kill Medal 2009. *Publications:* The Big Green Book (with M. Stout) 1976, Living a Political Life 1995, Pearls, Politics, and Power: How Women Can Win and Lead 2008, The New Feminist Agenda: Defining the Next Revolution for Women, Work and Family 2012; articles in professional journals, magazines and newspapers. *Address:* Institute for Sustainable Communities, 535 Stone Cutters Way, Montpelier, VT 05602 (office); 9 Harbor Watch Road, Burlington, VT 05401, USA (home). *Telephone:* (802) 229-2900 (office). *Fax:* (802) 229-2919 (office). *E-mail:* isc@iscvt.org (office). *Website:* www.iscvt.org (office); www.madeleinekunin.org.

KUNITAKE, Toyoki, PhD; Japanese chemist and academic; *President, Kitakyushu Foundation for the Advancement of Industry, Science and Technology;* b. 26 Feb. 1936, Kurume, Fukuoka; ed Univ. of Pennsylvania, USA; Postdoctoral Fellow, California Inst. of Tech. 1962–63; Assoc. Prof., Faculty of Eng, Kyushu Univ. 1963–74, Prof. 1974–99; Group Dir, Spatio-Temporal Function Materials Research Group, Frontier Research System, RIKEN 1999–2007; Vice-Pres. Univ. of Kitakyushu 2001–08; Dir, NanoMembrane Technologies, Inc. 2007–; Pres. Kitakyushu Foundation for the Advancement of Industry, Science and Tech. 2009–; mem. Chemical Soc. of Japan, Eng Acad. of Japan, Soc. of Polymer Science, Japan; Medal with Purple Ribbon, Govt of Japan 1999, Person of Cultural Merit 2007, Order of the Sacred Treasure, Gold and Silver Star 2011, Order of Culture 2014; Award of the Soc. of Polymer Science, Japan (SPSJ) 1978, Award of the Chemical Soc. of Japan 1990, SPSJ Award for Outstanding Achievement in Polymer Science and Tech. 1998, Japan Acad. Prize 2001, Kyoto Prize, Inamori Foundation (co-recipient) 2015. *Publications:* numerous papers in professional journals. *Address:* Kitakyushu Foundation for the Advancement of Industry, Science and Technology, 2-1 Hibikino, Wakamatsu-ku, Kitakyushu, Fukuoka, 808-0135, Japan (office). *Telephone:* (93) 695-3111 (office). *Fax:* (93) 695-3010 (office). *E-mail:* info@ksrp.or.jp (office). *Website:* www.ksrp.or.jp/e (office).

KUNITZSCH, Paul Horst Robert, DPhil; German professor of Arabic Studies (retd); b. 14 July 1930, Neu-Krüssow; ed Free Univ. of West Berlin; Lecturer in Arabic, Univ. of Göttingen 1956–57; taught German, Cairo 1957–60; lecturer, Goethe Inst., FRG 1960–63; Special Adviser, Radio Deutsche Welle, Cologne 1963–68; Research Fellow, Deutsche Forschungsgemeinschaft 1969–75; Lecturer in Arabic, Univ. of Munich 1975–77, Prof. of Arabic Studies 1977–95; mem. Bavarian Acad. of Sciences, Acad. Int. d'Histoire des Sciences, Paris; Corresp. mem. Acad. of Arabic Language, Cairo; Göttingen Acad. of Sciences Prize 1974, Azophi Medal, Arab Union for Astronomy and Space Sciences 2014. *Publications:* Arab. Sternnamen in Europa 1959, Der Almagest 1974, The Arabs and the Stars 1989, Stars and Numbers 2004, C. Ptolemäus, Der Sternkatalog (ed.; three vols) 1986–91. *Address:* Davidstr. 17, 81927 Munich, Germany (home). *Telephone:* (89) 916280 (home). *Website:* www.naher-osten.uni-muenchen.de/personen/ehemalige/kunitzsch.

KÜNSCH, Hans Rudolf, PhD; Swiss mathematician and academic; *Professor Emeritus, Seminar für Statistik, Eidgenössische Technische Hochschule Zürich (ETH Zürich);* b. 17 Oct. 1951; ed Eidgenössische Technische Hochschule Zürich; fmr Research Student, Univ. of Tokyo, Japan; joined faculty of Eidgenössische Technische Hochschule Zürich (ETH Zürich) 1983 as Prof. of Math., Seminar für Statistik 1983–2014, now Prof. Emer., Chair., Dept of Math. 2007–09; Co-Ed. Annals of Statistics 1998–2000; Pres. Inst. of Math. Statistics 2011–14; mem. Council Inst. of Math. Statistics 2003–06. *Address:* Seminar für Statistik, ETH Zürich, LEO D1, Leonhardstr. 27, 8092 Zürich, Switzerland (office). *Telephone:* 446323416 (office). *Fax:* 446321228 (office). *E-mail:* kuensch@stat.math.ethz.ch (office). *Website:* www.ethz.ch (office); www.stat.math.ethz.ch/~kuensch (office).

KUNTJORO-JAKTI, Dorodjatun, PhD; Indonesian politician, diplomatist and business executive; *Professor Emeritus, Faculty of Economics, Universitas Indonesia;* b. 25 Nov. 1939, Rangkasbitung; ed Universitas Indonesia, Univ. of California, Berkeley, USA; Lecturer and fmr Dean of Econs, Universitas Indonesia, now Prof. Emer.; Amb. to USA 2000–01; Co-ordinating Minister for the Economy, Finance and Industry 2001–04; apptd Co-Chair. Panel 45 to formulate Indonesia's position with regard to UN reforms 2005; fmr Chair. PT Bank Tabungan Pensiunan Nasional (BTPN); mem. Bd of Govs Nat. Resilience Inst. (LEMHANNAS); Ind. Comm. American Int. Assurance/American Int. Group, Inc. (AIA/AIG), PT Hero Supermarket; Dr hc (Univ. Tech. Malaysia). *Address:* Universitas Indonesia, New Campus UI Depok, Jakarta 16424, Indonesia (office). *Telephone:* (21) 7867222 (office). *Fax:* (21) 78849060 (office). *E-mail:* io-ui@ui.ac.id (office). *Website:* www.ui.ac.id (office).

KUNWAR, Babu Ram, MA, LLM; Nepalese lawyer and government official; *Governor, Gandaki Pradesh;* b. 25 July 1960, Sandhikhark, Arghakhanchi Dist; m.; one d.; ed Nepal Law Campus; est. pvt. law practice 1988; fmr Chair. Democratic Lawyers Asscn; Attorney-Gen. 2014–15; Gov. Gandaki Pradesh 2018–. *Address:* Office of the Head of State Government, Pokhara, Gandaki Pradesh, Nepal. *Telephone:* (1) 467555 (office). *Fax:* (1) 467666 (office). *E-mail:* info@oph.p4.gov.np (office). *Website:* oph.p4.gov.np.

KUNZE, Reiner; German writer; b. 16 Aug. 1933, Oelsnitz/Erzgebirge; s. of Ernst Kunze and Martha Kunze (née Friedrich); m. Dr Elisabeth Mifka 1961; one s. one d.; ed Univ. of Leipzig; mem. Bavarian Acad. of Fine Arts, Acad. of Arts, West Berlin 1975–92, German Acad. for Languages and Literature, Darmstadt, Free Acad. of Arts Mannheim, Sächsische Akad. der Künste, Dresden; Hon. mem. Collegium Europaeum Jenense of Friedrich-Schiller-Universität Jena; Dr hc; numerous awards and prizes including Literary Prize of Bavarian Acad. of Fine Arts 1973, Georg Trakl Prize (Austria) 1977, Andreas Gryphius Prize 1977, Georg Büchner Prize 1977, Bavarian Film Prize 1979, Eichendorff Literature Prize 1984, Bayerischer Verdienstorden 1988, Grosses Verdienstkreuz der BRD 1993, Weilheimer Literaturpreis 1997, Europapreis für Poesie, Serbia 1998, Friedrich Hölderlin-Preis 1999, Hans Sahl Prize 2001, Bayerischer Maximiliansorden für Wissenschaft und Kunst 2001, Kunstpreis zur Deutsch-tschechischen Verständigung 2002, Ján Smrek Preis 2003, STAB Preis 2004, Übersetzer Preis 'Premia Bohemica' 2004, Thüringer Verdienstrorden 2008, Memminger Freiheitspreis 2009, Thüringer Literaturpreis 2009, Verdienstorden des Freistaates Sachsen 2012, Robert-Schuman-Medaille der Fraktion der EVP im Europ 2013, America Award for Lifetime Contribution to Int. Writing 2013, Südmähren-Preis 2013, Gratias Agit-Preis of Czech Repub. 2014, Hohenschönhausen-Preis 2014, Franz-Josef-Strauss-Preis 2015. *Publications include:* Sensible Wege 1969, Der Löwe Leopold 1970, Zimmerlautstärke 1972, Brief mit blauem Siegel 1973, Die wunderbaren Jahre 1976, Auf eigene Hoffnung 1981, Eines jeden einziges Leben 1986, Das weisse Gedicht 1989, Deckname 'Lyrik' 1990, Wohin der Schlaf sich schlafen legt 1991, Mensch ohne Macht 1991, Am Sonnenhang 1993, Wo Freiheit ist... 1994, Steine und Lieder 1996, Der Dichter Jan Skácel 1996, Bindewort 'deutsch' 1997, Ein Tag auf dieser Erde 1998, Die Aura der Wörter 2002, Der Kuss der Koi 2002, Wo wir zu Hause das Salz haben 2003, Die Chausseen der Dichter (with Mireille Gansel) 2004, Bleibt nur die eigene Stirn 2005, Lindennacht 2007, Mensch im Wort 2008, Die Sprache, die die Sprache spricht 2009, Was macht die Biene auf dem Meer? 2011, Wenn wieder eine Wende kommt 2011, Fern kann er nicht mehr sein 2013. *Address:* Am Sonnenhang 19, 94130 Obernzell, Germany. *Telephone:* 8591-2989 (home). *Website:* www.reiner-kunze.com.

KUNZRU, Hari Mohan Nath, BA, MA; British writer and journalist; b. 1969, Woodford Green, Essex, England; s. of Krishna Mohan Nath Kunzru and Hilary Ann David; ed Wadham Coll., Oxford, Univ. of Warwick; fmr journalist, Music Ed. Wallpaper magazine, Assoc. Ed. Wired magazine, Contrib. Ed. Mute magazine; Cullman Fellow, New York Public Library 2008; Guggenheim Fellow 2014; Somerset Maugham Award 2003, John Llewellyn Rhys Prize 2003, Granta Best of Young British Novelists 2003, Lire 50 Écrivains Pour Demain 2005, British Book Award for Decibel Writer of the Year 2005. *Publications include:* novels: The Impressionist (Observer Young Travel Writer of the Year 1999, Betty Trask Prize 2002) 2002, Transmission 2004, My Revolutions 2007, Gods Without Men 2011; other: Noise (short stories) 2006, Memory Palace (novella) 2013; contrib. to Wired, London Review of Books, Guardian, Observer, New York Times, Daily Telegraph, BBC Midnight Review. *Leisure interest:* staring out of the window. *Address:* c/o Kirsten Foster, Curtis Brown Group Ltd, Haymarket House, 28–29 Haymarket, London, SW1Y 4SP, England (office); 435 West 23rd Street, Apt 7D, New York, NY 10011, USA. *E-mail:* Kirsten.Foster@curtisbrown.co.uk (office). *Website:* www.harikunzru.com.

KUO, Way, BS, PhD, JP; American engineer, professor of engineering and university administrator; *President and University Distinguished Professor, City University of Hong Kong;* b. 5 Jan. 1951, Taipei, Taiwan; ed Kansas State Univ., USA, Nat. Tsing Hua Univ., Taiwan; with Bell Labs 1981–84; Wisenbaker Chair of Eng in Innovation, Texas A&M Univ. 1993–2003, also Exec. Assoc. Dean of Eng and Head of Dept of Industrial Eng 1993–2000; Univ. Distinguished Prof. and Dean of Eng, Univ. of Tennessee 2003–08; Pres. and Univ. Distinguished Prof., City Univ. of Hong Kong 2008–; Foreign mem. Chinese Acad. of Eng 2008; mem. US Nat. Acad. of Eng, Academia Sinica, Taiwan, Int. Acad. for Quality; Fellow, American Soc. for Quality, IEEE, Inst. for Operations Research and Man. Science, American Statistical Asscn, Inst. of Industrial Engineers; David F Baker Distinguished Research Award, Albert G Holzman Distinguished Educator Award, Award for Technical Innovation in Industrial Eng, Pan Wen-Yuan Foundation Award for Outstanding Research, IEEE Millennium Medal, Austin Bonis Award for Outstanding Achievement in the Advancement of Reliability Research. *Publications include:* author and co-author of ten textbooks on reliability and education. *Address:* Office of the President, City University of Hong Kong, Level 6, Cheng Yick-chi Building, Tat Chee Avenue, Kowloon, Hong Kong Special Administrative Region, People's Republic of China (office). *Telephone:* (852) 3442-9400 (office). *Fax:* (852) 3442-0386 (office). *E-mail:* office.president@cityu.edu.hk (office). *Website:* www.cityu.edu.hk (office).

KUOK, Khoon Hong, BBA; Singaporean (b. Malaysian) business executive; *Chairman and CEO, Wilmar International Limited;* nephew of Robert Kuok; m.; four c.; ed Univ. of Singapore; joined uncle's palm oil business PPB Oil Palms, Malaysia 1973; Gen. Man. Federal Flour Mills Bhd 1986–91; Man. Dir Kuok Oils & Grains Pte Ltd 1989–91; Co-founder, Chair. and CEO Wilmar International Ltd (palm oil producer) 1991, merged with uncle's business and head of combined group 2006–. *Address:* Wilmar International Ltd, 56 Neil Road, Singapore 088830 (office). *Telephone:* 6216-0244 (office). *Fax:* 6223-6635 (office). *E-mail:* info@wilmar.com.sg (office). *Website:* www.wilmar-international.com (office).

KUOK, Robert; Malaysian business executive; b. (Kuok Hock Nien), 6 Oct. 1923, Johor Bahru, Johor; m. twice; eight c.; ed Raffles Coll., Singapore; father arrived in

Malaya from Fujian, China early 20th century; worked in grains dept of Mitsubishi 1942–45; worked for father's food distribution co. (supplying produce for Japanese POWs in British Malaya) 1945–48, Co-founder (with other family mems) Kuok Brothers Co. (now Kuok Group) 1948, moved business to Singapore and began sugar trade 1953, built first sugar refinery in Singapore, also trading in sugar futures, palm oil, merged with Wilmar International and combined group now headed by nephew Kuok Khoon Hong 2007; built first of chain of Shangri-La hotels in Singapore early 1970s; acquired real estate in Malaysia, Singapore and China throughout the 1970s and 1980s; Head, Kerry Group (Hong Kong) –1993 (retd) with holdings in South-East Asia, People's Repub. of China, Australia and Canada; acquired holding in TV Broadcasts Ltd (Hong Kong) 1988, majority shareholding in Coca-Cola plant in China 1993, controlling share of South China Morning Post newspaper 1993 (Chair. South China Morning Post Publrs 1993–97); also owns significant shareholding in Citic Pacific, Chinese Govt's overseas conglomerate; currently Head, Kuok (Singapore) Ltd (investment holding co.), Transmile Group (air cargo outfit); est. several charitable foundations. *Address:* Kuok (Singapore) Ltd, No. 1 Kim Seng Promenade, #07-01 Great World City, Singapore 237994 (office). *Telephone:* 67333600 (office). *Fax:* 67389300 (home). *E-mail:* corporate@kuokgroup.com.sg (office). *Website:* www.kuokgroup.com.sg (office).

KURDAHI, George; Lebanese broadcaster; b. 16 Jan. 1960, Acre; s. of Gebrail Kurdahi and Lapinia Kassis; m. Ida Al Kassar; three c.; began career as journalist for Lisan ul-Hal (Lebanese daily newspaper); with Radio Monte Carlo, Paris 1979–92; Head of News, Radio Orient, Beirut 1992; fmr Gen. Man. MBC FM; currently TV presenter; Cedar Medal (Commdr rank). *Television includes:* Man sa yarbah al malyoon (Who Wants to be a Millionaire?), MBC 1, Man sa yarbah 2 malyoon 2005, 2006, Eftah Albak, LBC TV, Power of 10, Al Tahaddi, MBC 1.

KUREISHI, Hanif, CBE, BA; British writer and dramatist; b. 5 Dec. 1954, Bromley, England; m. Tracey Scoffield; three c.; ed King's Coll., London; worked as typist at Riverside Studios; Writer-in-Residence, Royal Court Theatre, London 1981, 1985–86; Chevalier des Arts et Lettres 2002; George Devine Award 1981, PEN/Pinter Prize 2010. *Plays include:* Soaking the Heat 1976, The Mother Country (Thames TV Playwright Award) 1980, The King and Me 1980, Outskirts (RSC) 1981, Cinders (after the play by Janusz Glowacki) 1981, Borderline (Royal Court) 1981, Artists and Admirers (after a play by Ostrovsky, with David Leveaux) 1981, Birds of Passage (Hampstead Theatre) 1983, Mother Courage (adaptation of a play by Brecht, RSC) 1984, Sleep With Me (Nat. Theatre) 1999, When the Night Begins (Hampstead Theatre) 2004. *Screenplays include:* My Beautiful Laundrette (Evening Standard Best Film Award 1986, New York Critics' Best Screenplay Award 1987) 1986, Sammy and Rosie Get Laid 1988, London Kills Me (also directed) 1991, My Son The Fanatic 1997, The Mother 2002, Le Week-end 2013. *Television includes:* The Buddha of Suburbia (BBC) 1993. *Publications include:* fiction: The Buddha of Suburbia (Whitbread Award for Best First Novel) 1990, The Black Album 1995, Love in a Blue Time (short stories) 1997, Intimacy 1998, Midnight All Day (short stories) 1999, Gabriel's Gift 2000, The Body 2002, Telling Tales (contrib. to charity anthology) 2004, Something to Tell You 2008, Collected Stories 2010, The Last Word 2013, The Nothing 2017; non-fiction: The Rainbow Sign (autobiography) 1986, Eight Arms to Hold You (essay) 1991, Dreaming and Scheming: Reflections on Writing and Politics (essays) 2002, My Ear at His Heart (autobiography) (Prix France Culture littérature étrangère, France 2005) 2004, The Word and The Bomb (essays) 2005; ed.: The Faber Book of Pop (co-ed.) 1995; stories in Granta, Harpers (USA), London Review of Books and The Atlantic; regular contrib. to New Statesman and Society. *Leisure interests:* jazz, cricket. *Address:* c/o Rogers, Coleridge & White Literary Agency, 20 Powis Mews, London, W11 1JN, England (office). *Telephone:* (20) 7221-3717 (office). *Fax:* (20) 7229-9084 (office). *E-mail:* info@rcwlitagency.co.uk (office). *Website:* www.rcwlitagency.co.uk (office).

KŪRIS, Egidijus, DJur; Lithuanian judge and professor of law; *Judge, European Court of Human Rights;* b. 26 Oct. 1961, Vilnius; s. of Pranas Kūris and Vanda Kūrienė; m. Andronė Kūrienė; two s. one d.; ed Vilnius Univ., Moscow State Univ., USSR; Lecturer and Assoc. Prof., Faculty of Law, Vilnius Univ. 1984–94, Assoc. Prof. then Prof., Dept of Political Theory, Inst. of Int. Relations and Political Science 1992–2013, Dir of Inst. 1992–99, Prof., Dept of Public Law, Faculty of Law 2008–, Head of Dept 2008–13; Justice of Constitutional Court 1999–2008, Pres. 2002–08; Judge, European Court of Human Rights 2013–; Great Cross of Commdr Order of Gediminas from the Grand Duke of Lithuania 2003, Grand Croix Ordre de Leopold II (Belgium) 2006, A Magyar Köztársasági Érdemrend Középkeresztje a Csillagal (Hungary) 2006, Grosse Verdienstkreuz des Verdienstordens (Germany) 2006, Ordinus Nat. 'Servinius Credencios' in gradul de Mare Cruce (Romania) 2007, Krzyż Komandorski Orderu Zasługi Rzeczypospolitej Polskiej (Poland) 2008; Medal of Ministry of Foreign Affairs 2004, Gold Medal, Yerevan Univ. (Armenia) 2005, 'Pro Merito' Medal of EC 'Democracy Through Law', Council of Europe 2007, Mykolas Romeris Award 2008, Constitution Cup 2013. *Publications include:* Self-Government, Democracy and Law, Lithuania's National Interest and Her Political System (ed.), Democracy in Lithuania: Elite and Masses (ed.), Lithuania and Her Neighbours (ed.), Lithuanian Political Parties and Party System (Vols 1–2) (ed.), Interest Groups, Power and Politics (ed.), Lithuanian Constitutional Law (co-author), Lithuanian Legal Institutions, Twenty Years of the Constitution of the Republic of Lithuania: Experience and Challenges (ed. and co-author) (all in Lithuanian), Constitutional Justice in Lithuania (co-author, in English), On Stability of the Constitution: Sources of Constitutional Law and Ostensible Omnipotence of Constitutional Courts (in Russian); more than 80 articles in Lithuanian, English, Russian, French, Polish, Latvian and Azeri. *Address:* European Court of Human Rights, 67075 Strasbourg Cedex, France (office). *Telephone:* (3) 33-88-41-26-16 (office). *E-mail:* egidijus.kuris@echr.coe.int (office). *Website:* www.echr.coe.int (office).

KURMANOV, Zainidin Karpekovich, PhD; Kyrgyzstani politician; b. 1955, Frunze (now Bishkek); m.; two c.; ed Leningrad Univ., Marshall Centre for Security Studies, Germany; fmr Prof., Interior Ministry School of Kyrgyz Repub., Kyrgyz-Russian Slavonic Univ., Arabaev Kyrgyz State Univ. 2005–07; Deputy, Supreme Council (Zhogorku Kenesh, Parl.) 2000–05, Chair., Cttee on Constitutional Legislation, State Structure, Law and Human Rights 2007, Chair. Supreme Council 2009–11; Speaker of Parl. 2009–10; mem. Bright Road People's Party (Ak Jol); Honoured Educator 2002, State Adviser of II rank. *Publications:* about 230 scientific publications, including 12 books, textbooks and booklets.

KURODA, Haruhiko, BA, MPhil; Japanese central banker and international banking official; *Governor, Bank of Japan;* b. 25 Oct. 1944; m. Kumiko Kuroda; two s.; ed Univ. of Tokyo, Univ. of Oxford, UK; joined Ministry of Finance 1967; secondment to IMF, Washington, DC 1975–78; Dir Int. Orgs Div., Int. Finance Bureau 1987–88; Sec. to Minister of Finance 1988–89; Dir of several divs, Tax Bureau 1989–92; Deputy Vice-Minister of Finance for Int. Affairs 1992–93; Commr Osaka Regional Taxation Bureau 1993–94; Deputy Dir-Gen., Int. Finance Bureau 1994–96, Dir-Gen. 1997–99; Pres. Inst. of Fiscal and Monetary Policy 1996–97; Vice-Minister of Finance for Int. Affairs 1999–2003; Special Adviser to Cabinet 2003–05; Chair. Bd of Dirs and Pres. Asian Devt Bank 2005–13 (resgnd); Gov. Bank of Japan 2013–; Prof., Grad. School of Econs, Hitotsubashi Univ. 2003–05. *Publications include:* several books on monetary policy, exchange rates, int. finance policy, int. taxation and int. negotiations. *Address:* Bank of Japan, 2-1-1, Motoishi-cho, Nihonbashi, Chuo-ku, Tokyo 103-0021 Metro Manila, Japan (office). *Telephone:* (3) 3279-1111 (office). *E-mail:* prdmail@boj.or.jp (office). *Website:* www.boj.or.jp (office).

KURODA, Reiko, PhD; Japanese chemist and academic; *Professor, Department of Life Sciences, Tokyo University of Science;* b. 7 Oct. 1947; ed Univ. of Tokyo; Prof., Dept of Life Sciences, Univ. of Tokyo, mem. Admin. Council, Univ. of Tokyo; Gov., Cambridge Crystallographic Data Centre 2006–; Vice-Pres. Int. Council for Science; mem. Science Council of Japan; Foreign mem. Royal Swedish Acad. of Sciences 2009; Laureate for Asia Pacific, L'Oréal-UNESCO Awards for Women in Science 2013. *Publications:* numerous papers in professional journals on the chirality of organic and inorganic compounds. *Address:* Department of Life Sciences, Graduate School of Arts and Sciences, University of Tokyo, 3-8-1 Komaba, Meguro-ku, Tokyo 153-8902, Japan (office). *Telephone:* (3) 5454-6600 (office). *Fax:* (3) 5454-6600 (office). *E-mail:* ckuroda@mail.ecc.u-tokyo.ac.jp (office). *Website:* bio.c.u-tokyo.ac.jp/labs/kuroda/englishpage.htm (office).

KUROKAWA, Hiroaki, LLB; Japanese computer and electronics industry executive; *Senior Executive Advisor, Fujitsu Limited;* ed Tokyo Univ.; joined Fujitsu 1967, various posts in Services, Software and Systems Engineering Depts, mem. Bd 1999–, Group Pres., Network Services Group, later Corp. Sr Vice-Pres. and Group Pres. of Software and Services Business Promotion Group 2002, Corp. Sr Exec. Vice-Pres. April–June 2003, Pres. and Rep. Dir June 2003–08, Sr Exec. Advisor 2008–, Pres. and Rep. Dir PT Fujitsu Indonesia. *Leisure interests:* mountaineering, trekking, soccer, nature, Japanese history. *Address:* Fujitsu Headquarters, Shiodome City Center, 1-5-2 Higashi-Shimbashi, Minato-ku, Tokyo 105-7123, Japan (office). *Telephone:* (3) 6252-2220 (office). *Fax:* (3) 6252-2783 (office). *E-mail:* info@fujitsu.com (office). *Website:* www.fujitsu.com (office).

KUROKI, Haru; Japanese actress; b. 14 March 1990, Osaka; New Artist Award, Nikkan Sports Film Awards 2013, New Face Award, Kinema Junpo Awards 2014, Best New Artist, Blue Ribbon Awards 2014, Best New Artist, Tokyo Sports Film Awards 2014, Best New Talent, Yokohama Film Festival 2014, Newcomer of the Year, Japan Academy Prize 2014. *Films include:* Tokyo Oasis 2011, Wolf Children (voice) 2012, A Chair on the Plains 2013, The Great Passage 2013, Flower of Shanidar 2013, The Little House (Silver Bear for Best Actress, Berlin Int. Film Festival) 2014, Silver Spoon 2014, A Stitch of Life 2015, Maku ga agaru 2015, Solomon's Perjury 2015, The Murder Case of Hana & Alice (voice) 2015, Solomon's Perjury 2 2015. *Television includes:* Jun to Ai (series) 2012, Mahoro ekimae bangaichi (series) 2013, Yo ni mo Kimyô na Monogatari: '13 Aki no Tokubetsu-hen (film) 2013, Legal High (series) 2013, Hanako & Anne (series) 2014, Gou-Gou datte Neko de aru (mini-series) 2014, Murder on the Orient Express (mini-series) 2015, The Emperor's Cook (mini-series) 2015.

KUROYANAGI, Nobuo; Japanese financial services industry executive; *Senior Advisor, Bank of Tokyo-Mitsubishi UFJ Ltd;* b. 1941; joined Mitsubishi Bank Ltd 1965, Dir Bank of Tokyo-Mitsubishi Ltd (later Bank of Tokyo-Mitsubishi UFJ Ltd) 1992–96, Man.-Dir 1996–2002, Deputy Pres. 2002–04, Prin. Exec. Officer 2004–05, Pres. 2006–08, Chair. 2008–10; Dir Mitsubishi Tokyo Financial Group Inc. 2003–, Pres. and CEO 2004–05, Pres. and CEO Mitsubishi UFJ Financial Group, Inc. (after merger with UFJ Holdings) 2005–10, Sr Advisor, Bank of Tokyo-Mitsubishi UFJ, Ltd 2014–; mem. Bd of Dirs, UnionBanCal Corpn 2008–12, MUFG Americas Holdings Corpn 2008–12, Honda Motor Co. Ltd 2009–16, Mitsubishi Research Inst. Inc. 2009–, Tokio Marine & Nichido Fire Insurance Co., Ltd 2011–, Isetan Mitsukoshi Holdings Ltd –2014; Statutory Auditor, Mitsubishi Heavy Industries Ltd, Tokyo Kaikan Co., Ltd. *Address:* Bank of Tokyo-Mitsubishi UFJ Ltd, 2-7-1, Marunouchi, Chiyoda-ku, Tokyo 100-8388, Japan (office). *Website:* www.bk.mufg.jp/global (office).

KUROYEDOV, Adm. (retd) Vladimir Ivanovich; Russian naval officer (retd); b. 5 Oct. 1944, Bamburovo, Primorsk Territory; m.; one s.; ed Pacific Higher S.O. Makarov Navy School, Navy Mil. Acad. of Gen. Staff; service in Pacific Ocean Fleet 1967–93; Head of Staff, Pacific Fleet, Commdr 1996–97; First Deputy Commdr Baltic Fleet 1993–96; First Deputy Commdr Russian Navy 1997, C-in-C of Russian Navy 1997–2005 (retd); Corresp. mem. Russian Acad. of Rocket and Artillery; numerous decorations. *Publications include:* numerous publications on mil. sciences and political problems.

KURTÁG, György; Hungarian composer; b. 19 Feb. 1926, Lugos (Lugoj, Romania); ed Franz Liszt Music Acad., Budapest and in Paris with Marianne Stein; Repetiteur, Bela Bartok Music Secondary School, Budapest 1958–63, Nat. Philharmonic 1960–68; Asst to Pal Kadosa, Franz Liszt Acad. of Music, Budapest 1967, Prof. of Chamber Music 1967–86; Composer-in-Residence, Wissenschaftskolleg zu Berlin 1993–95, Wiener Konzerthaus, Vienna 1995–96; mem. Bayerische Akad. der Schönen Künste, Munich 1987, Akad. der Künste, Berlin 1987; Hon. mem. American Acad. of Arts and Letters 2001; Merited Artist of Hungarian People's Repub. 1980, Outstanding Artist 1984, Officier des Arts et Lettres 1985; Erkel Prize 1954, 1956, 1969, Kossuth Prize 1973, 1996, Bartok-Pasztory Award 1984, Herder Prize, Freiherr vom Stein, Hamburg 1993, Feltrinelli Prize, Accad. dei Lincei, Italy 1993, Austrian State Award for European Composers 1994, Denis de Rougemont Prize 1994, Ernst von Siemens Music Prize, Munich 1998, Grawemeyer Award (for his composition ...concertante... op. 42 for violin, viola and orchestra) 2006, Gold Medal, Royal Philharmonic Soc. of London 2013, BBVA

Foundation Frontiers of Knowledge Award in the category of Contemporary Music 2014. *Compositions include:* Viola Concerto 1954, String Quartet, Op. 1 1959, Wind Quintet 1959, The Sayings of Péter Bornemissza 1963–68, Three Old Inscriptions 1967–86, Transcriptions from Machaut to Bach 1974–91, Hommage à Mihály András 1977, Omaggio a Luigi Nono 1979, Songs of Despondency and Grief 1980–94, eight Choruses 1981–82, Bagatelles 1981, Attila József Fragments 1981, Scenes from a Novel 1981–82, Requiem for the Beloved 1982–87, Kafka-Fragmente 1985–87, Rückblick (Altes und Neues für vier Spieler, Hommage à Stockhausen) 1986, Three Songs to poems by János Pilinszky 1986, Officium breve in memoriam Andreae Szervánszky 1988–89, Three in memoriam 1988–90, Ligatura–Message to Frances-Marie 1989, Messages of the late Miss R. V. Troussova, Grabstein für Stephan for guitar and Instrumentengruppen, Op. 15c (Prix de Composition Musicale, Fondation Prince Pierre de Monaco 1993) 1989, . . .quasi una fantasia. . ., Double Concerto for piano, cello and 2 chamber ensembles Op. 27.2 (Prix de Composition Musicale, Fondation Prince Pierre de Monaco 1993) 1989–90, Hommage à R. Sch. 1990, Mémoire de Laïka 1990, Ligature e Versetti for organ 1990, Layka- Emlèk for synthesizer and real sounds (co-composition with his son) 1990, Samuel Beckett: What is the Word for solo voice, voices and chamber ensemble, Op. 30b 1991, Curriculum Vitae 1992, Games, two series, Beads 1994, Inscriptions on a Grave in Cornwall 1994. *Address:* Liszt Ferenc tér 9.I.6, 1061 Budapest, Hungary.

KURTEŠ, Predrag; Bosnia and Herzegovina politician and fmr athlete; *Minister of Internal Affairs, Federation of Bosnia and Herzegovina;* b. 18 Aug. 1953, Sarajevo; m.; one c.; ed High School of Electrical Eng, School of Admin, Faculty for Business Studies, Fed. Bureau of Investigation (FBI) Acad., USA, Int. Law Enforcement Acad., Budapest, Hungary; professional athlete 1970–84; graduated as Admin. Lawyer and Grad. Economist, later Anti-Terrorism Specialist; with Ministry of Internal Affairs 1987–, held several positions, including police station investigator, several man. positions in Depts of the Criminal Police, Ministry of Internal Affairs of Sarajevo Canton, and Head of Sector of the Criminal Police with rank of Chief Inspector 2007–11; also held position of Asst Minister for Criminal Police and Acting Minister, Ministry of Internal Affairs of Sarajevo Canton; Minister of Internal Affairs, Fed. of Bosnia and Herzegovina 2011–; several nat. and int. awards and medals. *Address:* Ministry of Internal Affairs, 71000 Sarajevo, Mehmeda Spahe 7, Bosnia and Herzegovina (office). *Telephone:* (33) 590200 (office); (33) 280020 (office). *Fax:* (33) 590218 (office). *E-mail:* info@fmup.gov.ba (office); info@fbihvlada.gov.ba (office). *Website:* www.fbihvlada.gov.ba/english/ministarstva/unutrasnji_poslovi.php (office); www.fmup.gov.ba (office).

KURTI, Albin; Kosovo engineer and politician; *Chairman, Vetëvendosje! (Self-Determination!);* b. 24 March 1975, Prishtina, Socialist Autonomous Province of Kosovo, Socialist Repub. of Serbia, Socialist Fed. Repub. of Yugoslavia; Vice-Pres. UPSUP, Univ. of Prishtina Student Union 1997, organizer of nonviolent demonstrations autumn 1997, spring 1998; worked in office of Adem Demaçi when latter became political rep. of Ushtria Çlirimtare e Kosovës (Kosovo Liberation Army); arrested by Serbian forces during NATO air strikes on Yugoslavia April 1999, charged with 'jeopardizing Yugoslavia's territorial integrity and conspiring to commit an enemy activity linked to terrorism', sentenced to 15 years in prison, freed by Serbian Govt Dec. 2001; organized non-violent protests in support of families of those who disappeared in the war and in favour of Kosovo self-determination; arrested following protest Feb. 2007, detained until July, then kept under house arrest, trial not concluded; mem. Ass. of Kosovo, Chair. Cttee on Foreign Affairs; Chair. Vetëvendosje! (Self-Determination!) 2004–15, 2018–; columnist, Express, Zëri (local newspapers); voted Personality of the Year on Albanian Television Network's Top Media 2011. *Address:* Vetëvendosje!, 10000 Prishtina, Rruga Bajram Kelmendi 10/a, Kosovo (office). *Telephone:* (44) 411174 (office). *E-mail:* info@vetevendosje.org (office). *Website:* www.vetevendosje.org (office).

KURTZER, Daniel Charles, BA, PhD; American diplomatist, political scientist and academic; *Lecturer and S. Daniel Abraham Visiting Professor in Middle East Policy Studies, Woodrow Wilson School of Public and International Affairs, Princeton University;* b. June 1949, Elizabeth, NJ; s. of Nathan Kurtzer and Sylvia Kurtzer; m. Sheila Kurtzer; three s.; ed Yeshiva Univ., Columbia Univ.; joined Foreign Service 1976; Dean, Yeshiva Coll. 1977–79; Political Officer, Bureau of Int. Organizational Affairs, Embassies in Cairo and Tel-Aviv, Deputy Dir Office of Egyptian Affairs 1986–87, on Policy Planning Staff 1987–89, Deputy Asst Sec. for Near Eastern Affairs 1989–94, Prin. Deputy Asst Sec. for Intelligence and Research 1994, then Acting Asst Sec. –1997, Amb. to Egypt 1997–2001, to Israel 2001–05; Lecturer and S. Daniel Abraham Visiting Prof. in Middle East Policy Studies, Woodrow Wilson School of Public and Int. Affairs, Princeton Univ. 2005–; Commr Israel Baseball League 2007; Pres.'s Distinguished Service Award, Henrietta Szold Award by Hadassah 2005, Dir-Gen. of Foreign Service Award for Reporting. *Publications:* Negotiating Arab-Israeli Peace: American Leadership in the Middle East (co-author) 2008, Pathways to Peace: America and the Arab-Israeli Conflict (ed.) 2012, The Peace Puzzle: America's Quest for Arab-Israeli Peace, 1989–2011 (co-author) 2013. *Address:* 123A Bendheim Hall, Woodrow Wilson School, Princeton University, Princeton, NJ 08544-1013, USA (office). *Telephone:* (609) 258-9859 (office). *Fax:* (609) 258-5974 (office). *E-mail:* dkurtzer@princeton.edu (office). *Website:* wws.princeton.edu/faculty-research/faculty/dkurtzer (office).

KURZ, Sebastian; Austrian politician; *Federal Chancellor;* b. 27 Aug. 1986, Vienna; ed Univ. of Vienna; mil. service 2004–05; State Chair., Young ÖVP, Vienna 2008–11, Fed. Pres., Young ÖVP 2009, Chair. Political Acad. of ÖVP 2015–, Chair. Österreichische Volkspartei (ÖVP—Austrian People's Party) 2017–; mem. Vienna State Parl. and Municipal Council 2010–11; State Sec. for Integration (part of Ministry of Internal Affairs) 2011–13; mem. Parl. (Österreichische Volkspartei) 2013–; Fed. Minister for European and Int. Affairs 2013–14, for Europe, Integration and Foreign Affairs 2014–17; Fed. Chancellor 2017–. *Address:* Ballhauspl. 2, 1014 Vienna; Österreichische Volkspartei (ÖVP—Austrian People's Party), Lichtenfelsgaße 7 A, 1010 Vienna, Austria (office). *Telephone:* (1) 531-15-0 (office); (5) 011-50-0 (office). *Fax:* (1) 535-03-38-0 (office); (5) 011-59-0 (office). *E-mail:* post@bka.gv.at (office). *Website:* www.bka.gv.at (office); www.oevp.at (office); www.sebastian-kurz.at.

KURZWEIL, Raymond (Ray) C., BS; American computer scientist and business executive; *Director of Engineering, Google Inc.;* b. 12 Feb. 1948, Queens, NY; m. Sonya R. Kurzweil; ed Massachusetts Inst. of Tech.; built and programmed his own computer to compose original melodies aged 15; Founder and fmr CEO Kurzweil Computer Products, Inc. 1974–80, Kurzweil Music Systems, Inc. 1982–90, Kurzweil Applied Intelligence, Inc. 1982–97, Kurzweil Educational Systems, Inc. 1996; Chair. Strategy and Tech. Cttee Bd Dirs, Wang Laboratories, Inc. 1993–98; Founder, Chair. and CEO Kurzweil Technologies, Inc. 1995–, FAT KAT, Inc. 1999–, Kurzweil Cyber Art Technologies, Inc. 2000–; Founder, Pres. and CEO Medical Learning Co., Inc. and FamilyPractice.com 1997; Founder, CEO and Ed.-in-Chief www.KurzweilAI.net 2001–; Co-Founder, Chair. and Co-CEO Ray & Terry's Longevity Products, Inc. 2003; Dir of Engineering, Google Inc. 2012–; mem. Bd Dirs Medical Manager Corpn 1997–2000, Inforte 1999–, United Therapeutics 2002–; Chair. and Founder The Kurzweil Foundation; Dir Massachusetts Computer Software Council; fmr Dir Boston Computer Soc.; mem. MIT Corpn Visiting Cttee, MIT School of Humanities, MIT School of Music, Bd of Overseers, New England Conservatory of Music; Fellow, American Acad. of Arts and Sciences 2009–; Hon. Chair. for Innovation, White House Conf. on Small Business 1986; Hon. DHumLitt (Hofstra Univ.) 1982, (Misericordia Coll.) 1989, (Landmark Coll.) 2002, Worcester Polytechnic Inst. 2005; Hon. DMus (Berklee Coll. of Music) 1987; Hon. DSc (Northeastern Univ.) 1988, (Rensselaer Polytechnic Inst.) 1988, (New Jersey Inst. of Tech.) 1990, (City Univ. of New York) 1991, (Dominican Coll.) 1993; Hon. DEng (Merrimack Coll.) 1989; Dr hc in Science and Humanities (Michigan State Univ.) 2000; numerous awards including Mass's Gov.'s Award 1977, Grace Murray Hopper Award, Asscn for Computing Machinery (ACM) 1978, Nat. Award, Johns Hopkins Univ. 1981, admitted to Computer Industry Hall of Fame 1982, Pres.'s Computer Science Award 1982, The White House Award for Entrepreneurial Excellence 1986, Inventor of the Year Award, awarded by MIT, Boston Museum of Science and Boston Patent Law Asscn 1988, MIT Founders Award 1989, Engineer of the Year Award, Design News magazine 1990, Louis Braille Award, Associated Services for the Blind 1991, Massachusetts Quincentennial Award for Innovation and Discovery 1992, ACM Fellow Award 1993, Gordon Winston Award, Canadian Nat. Inst. for the Blind 1994, Dickson Prize, Carnegie Mellon Univ. 1994, Software Industry Achievement Award, Massachusetts Software Council 1996, Pres.'s Award, Asscn on Higher Educ. and Disability 1997, Stevie Wonder/SAP Vision Award for Product of the Year (for the Kurzweil 1000) 1998, Nat. Medal of Tech. 1999, Lemelson-MIT Prize 2000, inducted into Nat. Inventors' Hall of Fame, US Patent Office 2002. *Film:* The Age of Intelligent Machines (The Chris Plaque, Columbus Int. Film Festival 1987, Creative Excellence Award, US Industrial Film and Video Festival 1987, Gold Medal – Science Educ., Int. Film and TV Festival of New York 1987, CINE Golden Eagle Award 1987, Tech. Culture Award, Int. Festival of Scientific Films, Belgrade 1988, Prize of the President of the Festival, Int. Film Festival of Czechoslovakia 1988) 1987. *Achievements include:* developed first computerized Four-Way Analysis of Variance (statistical program) 1964, first computer-based Expert System for College Selection 1967, first Text-to-Speech speech synthesis 1975, first CCD Flatbed Scanner 1975, first Print-to-Speech Reading Machine for the Blind (Kurzweil Reading Machine) 1976, first Omni-Font (any-type font) Optical Character Recognition (now Xerox TextBridge) 1976, first Computer Music Keyboard capable of accurately reproducing sounds of the grand piano and other orchestral instruments (Kurzweil 250) 1984, first Knowledge Base System for Creating Medical Reports (Kurzweil VoiceMED) 1985, first commercially marketed Large Vocabulary Speech Recognition (Kurzweil Voice Report) 1987, first Speech Recognition Dictation System for Windows (Kurzweil Voice for Windows) 1994, first Continuous Speech Natural Language Command and Control Software (Kurzweil VoiceCommands) 1997, first Print-to-Speech Reading System for Persons with Reading Disabilities (Kurzweil 3000), first Virtual Performing and Recording Artist (Ramona) to perform in front of a live audience with a live band 2001, first 'host/hostess' Avatar on the Web to combine lifelike photo-realistic, moving and speaking facial image with a conversational engine 2001. *Publications include:* The Age of Intelligent Machines (MIT Press Best Seller 1991, Silicon Valley Best Seller 1991, Most Outstanding Computer Science Book of 1990 Award, Asscn of American Publishers 1991) 1990, The 10% Solution for a Healthy Life (Regional Best Seller 1993) 1993, The Age of Spiritual Machines, When Computers Exceed Human Intelligence (Nat. and Regional Best Sellers 1999, 2000, Literary Lights Prize, Boston Public Library 1999) 1999, Are We Spiritual Machines, Ray Kurzweil versus the Critics of Strong AI 2002, Fantastic Voyage: Live Long Enough to Live Forever (co-author) 2004, The Singularity is Near, When Humans Transcend Biology 2005, How to Create a Mind: The Secret of Human Thought Revealed 2014. *Address:* Kurzweil Technologies, Inc., PMB 193 733, Turnpike Street, North Andover, MA 01845 (office); Kurzweil Technologies, Inc., 15 Walnut Street, Wellesley Hills, MA 02481, USA (office). *Telephone:* (718) 263-0000 (office). *Fax:* (718) 263-9999 (office). *E-mail:* raymond@kurzweiltech.com (office). *Website:* www.KurzweilTech.com (office); www.KurzweilAI.net (office).

KUSAKA, Sumio, BL, BEcons; Japanese diplomatist; b. 1953; ed Chuo Univ., Swarthmore Coll., USA; joined diplomatic service 1978, postings have included assignments in Canberra 1981–83, Ottawa, Dar es Salaam, Boston, Washington, DC and as Consul-Gen./Deputy Chief of Mission in London, held sr econ. roles with both Ministry of Foreign Affairs (MFA) and Ministry of Finance, including as Deputy Vice-Minister for Int. Affairs and Deputy Dir-Gen., Ministry of Finance 2004–06, oversaw econ. partnership agreement negotiations with both Australia and India as Deputy Dir-Gen. for Econ. Affairs Bureau, MFA 2006–08, Amb. and Dir-Gen. for African Affairs 2010–12, Amb. and Chief of Protocol 2012–13, Amb. and Consul-Gen. in New York 2013–15, Amb. to Australia 2015–19; Fellow, Weatherhead Center for Int. Affairs, Harvard Univ. 1999–2000. *Address:* c/o Embassy of Japan, 112 Empire Circuit, Yarralumla, ACT, 2600, Australia (office).

KUSAKARI, Takao, BA; Japanese transport industry executive; *Senior Advisor, Nippon Yusen Kabushiki Kaisha (NYK Line);* b. 1940; ed Keio Univ.; joined Nippon Yusen Kabushiki Kaisha (NYK Line) 1964, Gen. Man. of Cen./S America, Africa and Specialized Cargo Div. 1990, Dir 1994–97, Man. Dir 1997–99, Sr Man. Dir 1999, Pres. 1999–2004, Chair. 2004–09, apptd Bd Counsellor and Consultant 2009, Corp. Advisor 2010–15, Sr Advisor 2015–; Corp. Auditor, Nippon Steel Corpn; fmr mem. Corp. Auditor's Bd, AOC Holdings Inc.; Pres. Japanese Shipowners' Asscn; Chair. Council for the Promotion of Regulatory Reform, Cabinet Office 2007–; Dir

Nomura Securities Co. Ltd 2011–, Outside Dir, Nomura Holdings, Inc. 2011–; Dir, Japan Productivity Centre for Socio-econ. Devt; Chair. Shipping Econs Review Cttee, Asian Shipowners' Forum; mem. Int. Advisory Council, PSA Corpn; Commdr, Ordre de la Couronne (Belgium) 2010; Official Commendation by Minister of Land, Infrastructure and Transport 2004, Medal with Blue Ribbon by Japanese Govt 2005. *Address:* Nippon Yusen Kabushiki Kaisha, 3-2, Marunouchi 2-chome, Chiyoda-ku, Tokyo 100-0005, Japan (office). *Telephone:* (3) 3284-5151 (office). *Fax:* (3) 3284-6359 (office). *E-mail:* info@nyk.com (office). *Website:* www.nyk.com (office).

KUSAMA, Saburo, BEng; Japanese manufacturing executive; b. 12 Oct. 1939, Aichi; m. Mizue Kusama; two s.; ed Univ. of Shizuoka; began work in Crystal Devices and Circuits Div., Seiko Epson Corpn 1963, various man. positions in Clocks and Tech. Design Divs, Gen. Man. Semiconductors Div. 1986, CEO Semiconductors Div. 1990, mem. Exec. Council 1990–, CEO Display and Liquid Crystals Div. 1994, Pres. Seiko Epson Corpn 2001–05, apptd CEO 2005; Outside Dir The Hachijuni Bank Ltd; Chair. Bd of Trustees, SE Gakuen (educational foundation); Akira Inoue EHS Award 2004, Medal with Blue Ribbon 2006. *Leisure interests:* golf, classical music, museums. *Address:* c/o Seiko Epson Corporation, 3-3-5 Owa Suwa, Nagano 392-8502, Japan.

KUSHERBAYEV, Krymbek Ye., DrPolSci; Kazakhstani diplomatist and politician; *Akim (Governor) of Kyzylorda Oblast;* b. 20 May 1955, Kazalinsk, Kyzylorda Oblast; ed Kazakh Polytechnic Inst.; Asst to the Deputy Prime Minister 1991–94; headed Kalinin regional Admin of Almaty 1994–95; Deputy Head of the Office and Head of Dept of Internal Policies, Office of the Cabinet 1995; Deputy Head of the Office and Head of Dept of Territorial Devt, Office of the Govt 1995–96; Press Sec. and Head of Press Service of the Pres. 1996–97; Minister of Educ., Culture and Healthcare 1997–99, of Healthcare, Educ. and Sport following reorganization of the Ministry Jan.–Oct. 1999, of Educ. and Science Oct. 1999–2000; Akim (Gov.) of West Kazakhstan Oblast 2000–03; Amb. to Russian Fed. (also accred to Finland and Armenia 2003–06; Akim (Gov.) of Mangystau Oblast 2006–11; adviser to the Pres. of Kazakhstan July–Oct. 2012; First Deputy Prime Minister and Minister of Regional Devt 2012–13; Akim (Gov.) of Kyzylorda Oblast 2013–; Parasat Medal 2003, Friendship Medal (Russian Fed.) 2006, Barys Medal, Second Degree 2009. *Address:* Kyzylorda Oblast Administration, Kyzylorda 120014, Y. Zhakhayev Str., 76, Kazakhstan (office). *Telephone:* (7242) 26-16-44 (office). *Fax:* (7242) 26-12-25 (office). *E-mail:* oblakimat@orda.gov.kz (office). *Website:* www.e-kyzylorda.gov.kz (office).

KUSHNER, Aleksandr Semyonovich; Russian poet; b. 14 Sept. 1936, Leningrad; s. of Semyon Semyonovich Kushner and Asya Aleksandrovna Kushner; m. Elena Vsevolodovna Nevzglyadova 1981; one s.; ed Leningrad Pedagogical Inst.; lecturer in literature 1959–69; Northern Palmira Award 1995, Russian Fed. State Award 1995, German Pushkin Award, Alfred Toepfer Foundation 1999, Russian Fed. Alexander Pushkin Award 2001, Nat. 'The Poet' Award 2005, Baltic Star Award 2013. *Publications include:* First Impression 1962, Night Watch 1966, Omens 1969, Letter 1974, Direct Speech 1975, Voice 1978, Canvas 1981, The Tavrichesky Garden 1984, Daydreams 1986, Poems 1986 (Selected Poems), The Hedgerow 1988, A Night Melody 1991, Apollo in the Snow (selected essays on Russian literature of the nineteenth and twentieth centuries and personal memoirs) 1991, Apollo in the Snow (selected poems trans. into English) 1991, On the Gloomy Star (State Prize) 1995, Selected Poetry 1997, The Fifth Element 1999, The Bush 2002, Cold Month of May 2005, Selected Poems 2005, Apollo in the Grass (essays on poetry) 2005, In the New Century 2006, The Time is Not to Be Chosen 2007, Clouds Opt for Anapest 2008, With Chalk and Coal 2010, Facing the Mysterious Line 2011, The Evening Light 2013, Greece and Rome in Leitmotif 2014; essays in literary journals. *Leisure interests:* reading, world painting. *Address:* Kaluzhsky pereulok No. 9, Apt 48, 193015 St Petersburg, Russia (home). *Telephone:* (812) 577-32-56 (home). *E-mail:* kushner36@yandex.ru.

KUSHNER, Anthony (Tony) Robert, BA, MFA; American playwright and screenwriter; b. 16 July 1956, New York City; s. of William Kushner and Sylvia Deutscher; m. Mark Harris 2008 (civil partner since 2003); ed Columbia Univ., New York Univ. Grad. Acting Program at the Tisch School of the Arts; family moved to Lake Charles, La 1956, moved to New York 1974; spent summers directing early original works (Masque of Owls and Incidents and Occurrences During the Travels of the Tailor Max) and plays by Shakespeare (A Midsummer Night's Dream and The Tempest) for children attending the Gov.'s Program for Gifted Children, Lake Charles, La 1978–81; Playwright-in-Residence, Juilliard School, New York 1990–92; Hon. DLitt (Purchase Coll., State Univ. of NY) 2008; Dr hc (John Jay Coll. of Criminal Justice, CUNY) 2011; Cultural Achievement Award, Nat. Foundation of Jewish Culture, Lila Wallace/Reader's Digest Fellowship, Whiting Writers' Award 1990, Tony Award for Best Play 1993, 1994, Drama Desk Award for Outstanding Play 1994, Critics' Circle Award, London Evening Standard Award, Obie Award, New York Drama Critics' Circle, American Academy of Arts and Letters Award, PEN/Laura Pels International Foundation for Theater Award for a playwright in mid-career 2002, Steinberg Distinguished Playwright Award 2008, Puffin/Nation Prize for Creative Citizenship 2011, St Louis Literary Award 2012, Nat. Medal of Arts 2012. *Screenplays:* Angels in America (HBO mini-series) (Primetime Emmy Award for Outstanding Writing for a Miniseries, Movie or a Dramatic Special 2004) 2003, Munich (with Eric Roth) 2005, Lincoln (New York Film Critics Circle Award for Best Screenplay 2012) 2012. *Television includes:* American Playhouse (series) 1993, Angels in America (film) 2004. *Publications:* Yes, Yes, No, No 1985, Actors on Acting 1986, Stella 1987, A Bright Room Called Day 1987, Hydriotaphia 1987, The Illusion 1988, The Persistence of Prejudice 1989, Widows (with Ariel Dorfman) 1991, Angels in America: A Gay Fantasia on National Themes, Part One: Millennium Approaches (Pulitzer Prize for Drama 1993, Drama Desk Award for Outstanding Play 1993) 1991, Part Two: Perestroika 1992, Slavs! 1994, Holocaust and the Liberal Imagination 1994, Thinking About the Longstanding Problems of Virtue and Happiness 1995, Homebody/Kabul 2001, Caroline, or Change (Best New Musical, Olivier Awards 2007) 2006, The Intelligent Homosexual's Guide to Capitalism and Socialism with a Key to the Scriptures 2009. *Address:* c/o Steven Barclay Agency, 12 Western Avenue, Petaluma, CA 94952, USA (office). *Telephone:* (707) 773-0654 (office). *Fax:* (707) 778-1868 (office). *E-mail:* steven@barclayagency.com (office). *Website:* www.barclayagency.com (office).

KUSHNER, Eva, OC, BA, MA, PhD, FRSC; Canadian academic; *Mary Rowell Coyne Professor, Victoria University and Professor Emerita of French and Comparative Literature, University of Toronto;* b. 18 June 1929, Prague, Czechoslovakia; d. of Josef Dubsky and Anna Dubsky-Cahill (née Kafka); m. 1st Donn J. Kushner 1949 (deceased); three s.; m. 2nd Rev. Canon Bruce Mutch 2005; ed McGill Univ., Montreal; Prof., Carleton Univ. 1961–76; Prof., McGill Univ. 1976–87, Chair. French Dept 1976–80; Prof., Pres. Vic. Univ. at Univ. of Toronto 1987–94, Dir Comparative Literature, Univ. of Toronto 1994–95, Mary Rowell Coyne Prof., Victoria Univ. 2001–, also Prof. Emer. of French and Comparative Literature; Pres. Int. Comparative Literature Asscn 1979–82; Vice-Pres. Int. Fed. for Modern Languages and Literatures 1987–93, Pres. 1996–99; Vice-Pres. RSC 1980–82, Conseil Int. de la Philosophie et des Sciences Humaines 2006–10; Visiting Prof., Princeton Univ. 2000, Univ. of Athens 2003; Hon. LitD (Acadia Univ.) 1988, Hon. DD (United Theological Coll., Montreal) 1992, Hon. DLitt (Univ. of St Michael's Coll.) 1993, (Univ. of Western Ont.) 1996, Dr hc (Szeged) 1997, Hon. Dr of Sacred Letters (Victoria Univ., Toronto) 2006; Lifetime Achievement Award, Canadian Soc. for Renaissance Studies 2002. *Publications include:* Patrice de la Tour du Pin 1961, Le Mythe d'Orphée dans la littérature française contemporaine 1961, Chants de Bohême 1963, Rina Lasnier (two edns) 1964, 1969, Saint-Denys Garneau 1967, François Mauriac 1972, L'avènement de l'esprit nouveau 1400–80 (co-author) 1988, Théorie littéraire: problèmes et perspectives (co-author) 1989, Le problématique du sujet chez Montaigne (co-author) 1995, Histoire des poétiques (co-author) 1997, Crises et essors nouveaux 1560–1610 (co-author) 2000, Pontus de Tyard et son œuvre poétique 2001, The Living Prism: Itineraries in Comparative Literature 2001, Le Dialogue à la Renaissance: Histoire et Poétique 2004, Maturations et mutations (1520–60) 2011. *Address:* Victoria University, University of Toronto, 73 Queen's Park, Toronto, ON M5S 1K7 (office); 62 Wellesley Street West, Apt. 704, Toronto, ON M5S 2X3, Canada (home). *Telephone:* (416) 585-4592 (office); (416) 538-0173 (home). *E-mail:* eva.kushner@utoronto.ca (office). *Website:* (office).

KUSHNER, Jared Corey, BA, JD, MBA; American real estate executive, publisher and government official; *Senior Advisor to the President;* b. 10 Jan. 1981, Livingston, NJ; s. of Charles Kushner and Seryl Kushner (née Stadtmauer); m. Ivanka Trump 2009; three c.; ed Harvard Coll., New York Univ.; began career as intern, office of Robert Morgenthau, Manhattan Dist Attorney, later with Paul, Weiss, Rifkind, Wharton & Garrison LLP; Publr New York Observer (Observer Media) 2006–17; CEO Kushner Companies, Inc. (real estate holding and devt co.) 2008–17; Sr Advisor to the Pres., The White House 2017–; Order of the Aztec Eagle 2018. *Address:* The White House, 1600 Pennsylvania Avenue, NW, Washington, DC 20500, USA (office). *Telephone:* (202) 456-1414 (office). *Fax:* (202) 456-2461 (office). *E-mail:* vice_president@whitehouse.gov (office). *Website:* www.whitehouse.gov (office).

KUSHNER, Robert Ellis, BA; American painter and sculptor; b. 19 Aug. 1949, Pasadena, Calif.; s. of Joseph Kushner and Dorothy Browdy; m. Ellen Saltonstall 1978; two s. one d.; ed Univ. of California, San Diego; moved to New York City and found work as a restorer and collector early 1970s; gained attention as a performance artist, using food, fabric and nudity; associated with the Pattern and Decoration movt; has participated in numerous group shows at Whitney Museum and Museum of Modern Art, New York etc.; Venice Biennale 1980, 1984; has collaborated with Master printer Bud Shark on various monotypes and lithographs since 1982; most recent installation, Scriptorium: Devout Exercises of the Heart, a group of over 1,000 drawings of flowers and plants on book pages dating from 1500 to 1920, exhibited in Desire at The Blanton Museum of Art, University of Texas, Austin 2010, travelled to Kunsthallen Brandts, Odense, Denmark, returned to USA for inaugural exhbn at DC Moore Gallery's new Chelsea location 2011, exhibited at La Jolla Athenaeum, Calif. 2012; AIA Award for Excellence in Design 1991, Benjamin Franklin Award, Publishers Marketing Asscn 1995. *Works in public collections including:* Museum of Modern Art, New York, Metropolitan Museum of Art, New York, Whitney Museum of American Art, New York, Nat. Gallery of Art, Washington, DC, Corcoran Gallery of Art, Washington, DC, Tate Gallery, London, San Francisco Museum of Modern Art, Contemporary Museum, Honolulu, Denver Art Museum, Galleria degli Ufizzi, Florence, J. Paul Getty Trust, Los Angeles, Museum Ludwig, St Petersburg, Philadelphia Museum of Art. *Performance:* Robert Kushner and Friends Eat Their Clothes, Astor Center for Food and Wine, New York 2010. *Publication:* Amy Goldin: Art in a Hairshirt (ed.) 2012. *Address:* c/o DC Moore Gallery, 535 West 22nd Street, 2nd Floor, New York, NY 10011; c/o Shark's Ink, 550 Blue Mountain Road, Lyons, CO 80540, USA. *Telephone:* (212) 247-2111 (New York); (303) 823-9190 (Lyons). *Fax:* (212) 247-2119 (New York); (303) 823-9191 (Lyons). *E-mail:* info@dcmooregallery.com; info@sharksink.com. *Website:* www.dcmooregallery.com/artists/robert-kushner; sharksink.com/artists.asp?artists=8; www.robertkushnerstudio.com.

KUSSBACH, Erich, LLM, Dr rer. pol, DrIur; Austrian academic and fmr diplomat; b. 5 May 1931; ed Eötvös Lóránd Univ., Hungary, Univ. of Vienna, Yale Univ., USA; served in Austrian Diplomatic Service 1963–96, sr positions included Head of Dept of Legal and Consular Affairs; served as legal advisor of Austrian Del. negotiating Free-Trade-Agreements with EEC; Deputy Rep. to Council of Europe and Consul Gen. in Strasbourg 1981–85; Amb. to Hungary 1993–96, also Perm. Rep. to Int. Danube Comm.; fmr Prof. of Public Int. Law and Int. Criminal Law, Catholic Pázmány Péter Univ., Budapest; Founding Pro-rector and fmr Prof. of Diplomacy, Faculty of Int. Relations, Andrássy Gyula German Speaking Univ., Budapest; apptd mem. Arbitration Panel, Nat. Fund for Victims of Nat. Socialism 2001; Hon. Prof. of Int. Humanitarian Law, Faculty of Law, Johannes Kepler Univ., Linz; Dr hc (Eoetvoes Lorand Univ.).

KUSTURICA, Emir; Bosnia and Herzegovina film director and musician (guitar); b. 24 Nov. 1954, Sarajevo; m. Maja Mandić; two c.; ed FAMU School, Prague, Czechoslovakia; teacher, Columbia Univ., New York, USA; mem. rock and roll band, No Smoking Orchestra 1986–; Advisor to Pres. of Bosnia and Herzegovina 2019–; Chair. of Jury, Cannes Film Festival 2005. *Films include:* Do You Remember Dolly Bell? (Golden Lion Award, Venice) 1981, When Father Was Away On Business (Palme d'Or, Cannes 1984) 1984, Time of the Gypsies (Best Dir, Cannes) 1988, Arizona Dream (Special Jury Prize, Berlin) 1993, Underground (Palme d'Or, Cannes) 1995, Black Cat White Cat 1998, La Veuve de Saint-Pierre 2000, Super Eight Stories 2001, Life is a Miracle 2004, Maradona (documentary)

2008, L'Affaire Farewell 2009, On the Milky Road 2016, El Pepe, Una Vida Suprema (documentary) 2018. *Recordings include:* albums with No Smoking Orchestra: Das ist Walter 1984, Dok cekaš sabah sa šejtanom 1985, Pozdrav iz zemlje Safari (Greetings from Safari Land) 1987, Male price o velikoj ljubavi (A Little Story of a Great Love) 1989, Ja nisam odavle 1997, Black Cat White Cat 1998, Unza Unza Time 2000, La Vie est un miracle (soundtrack to film) 2004, Live in Buenos Aires 2005, Time of the Gypsies 2007, Corps Diplomatique 2018. *Publications:* Smrt je neprovjerena glasina (Death is an Unverified Rumour) (autobiography) 2010, Sto jada (Hundred Pains) (novel) 2013. *Address:* c/o Yapucca Productions, 10, rue Jean Guy, 35000 Rennes France (office). *Telephone:* 2-99-67-63-31 (office). *Fax:* 2-99-31-30-83 (office). *E-mail:* yann.hamon@yapucca.com (office); office@thenosmokingorchestra.com. *Website:* www.yapucca.com (office); www.kustu.com; thenosmokingorchestra.com.

KUSUMAATMADJA, Mochtar, LLD; Indonesian politician; b. 17 April 1929, Batavia, Dutch East Indies; m. Siti Hadidjah; one s. one d.; ed Univ. of Indonesia, Yale and Harvard Law Schools and Univ. of Chicago Law School, USA; Indonesian Rep. at Law of the Sea Confs, Geneva, Colombo, Tokyo 1958–61, at UN Ass. on the Law of the Sea, Geneva and New York; Prof. and Dean, Faculty of Law, Padjadjaran Univ., London; Minister of Law and Human Rights 1973–78; Acting Foreign Minister 1977–78, then Minister of Foreign Affairs 1978–88, fmr Head of UN Comm. responsible for the demarcation of the Iraq–Kuwait Border, resgnd 1992; Indonesian Rep. at Law of the Sea Conf., Geneva and at Seabed Cttee sessions, New York; involvement in numerous int. orgs; Chair. Indonesian Chess Asscn (PERCASI) 1985. *Leisure interest:* playing chess. *Address:* c/o Ministry of Foreign Affairs, 10th Floor, Jalan Taman Pejambon 6, Jakarta Pusat 10110, Indonesia. *E-mail:* infomed@deplu.go.id.

KUSZNIEREWICZ, Mateusz Andrzej; Polish yachtsman; b. 29 April 1975, Warsaw; s. of Zbigniew Kusznierewicz and Irena Kusznierewicz; m. Agnieszka Kusznierewicz; ed Acad. of Physical Educ., Warsaw; began sailing aged nine, competed in Club Championship, Zalew Zegrzynski 1984; won first event Puchar Spojnii, Zalew Zegrzynski 1985; Polish Youth Champion, OK-Dinghy Class 1989; European Champion, OK-Dinghy Class 1991, 1994; Olympic Champion, Finn Class, Atlanta 1996, Bronze Medal, Athens 2004; World Champion, Finn Class 1998, 2000; Winner, Kieler Week Finn Class 1999, 2002; European Champion, Finn Class 2000, 2004; has also won over 20 int. regattas; apptd. Pres. Gdańsk Foundation 2013–; Sports Dir, SSL Gold Cup 2019–; mem. Yacht Klub Polski, Warsaw; Kt's Cross, Order of Polonia Restituta 1999; Sailor of the Year, Int. Sailing Fed. 1999, Most Popular Sportsman in Poland 1999. *Leisure interests:* electromechanics, other sports (especially golf, tennis and skiing). *Address:* No Limit Kusznierewicz Events, ul. Ostrobramska 75C, 04-175 Warsaw, Poland (office). *Telephone:* (22) 6117272 (office). *Fax:* (22) 6117273 (office). *E-mail:* kontakt@kusznierewicz.pl (office); mkusznierewicz@akademia.org.pl (office). *Website:* www.kusznierewicz.pl (office).

KUTARAGI, Ken, BE; Japanese computer entertainment executive and game console designer; *CEO, Cyber AI Entertainment Inc.;* b. 2 Aug. 1950, Tokyo; ed Denki Tsushin Univ.; joined Sony Corpn 1975, various positions in eng and digital research labs 1980s, worked on liquid crystal displays and digital camera projects, designed PlayStation game console 1989 and persuaded Sony to produce it after initiation of jt venture with Nintendo failed, headed team to create Sony PlayStation, released in 1994, began work on PlayStation 2 1996, released 2000, PlayStation 3 released 2006, PlayStation Vita released 2012, PlayStation 4 released 2013; apptd Chair. US Div. 1997, Pres. and CEO Sony Computer Entertainment International 1999–2006, Chair. and CEO 2006–07, Hon. Chair. 2007–11, Sr Tech. Advisor 2011–; CEO Cyber AI Entertainment Inc. 2011–; mem. Bd of Dirs Kadokawa Group Holdings, Inc. 2008–, Nojima Corpn, Rakuten, Inc. 2010–; Visiting Prof., Ritsumeikan Univ. 2009–. *Address:* Cyber AI Entertainment Inc., Setagaya-ku, Tokyo, 1-5-1 Seta, Japan. *E-mail:* info@cyber-ai-japan.com. *Website:* www.cyber-ai-japan.com.

KUTCHER, (Christopher) Ashton; American actor, producer, fmr fashion model and comedian; b. 7 Feb. 1978, Cedar Rapids, Ia; s. of Larry Kutcher and Diane Kutcher; m. Demi Moore 2005 (divorced 2013); ed Clear Creek-Amana High School, Tiffin, Ia, Univ. of Iowa; discovered by local talent scout while a biochemical engineering student at Univ. of Iowa 1997; won Fresh Faces of Iowa modelling contest 1997, pursued modelling career in New York; cr., produced and hosted Punk'd; producer and co-creator of supernatural TV programme Room 401 and reality TV programme Beauty and the Geek; co-f. Demi and Ashton Foundation 2010; Co-founder Katalyst (studio for social media); joined State Dept and sr execs from eBay and Twitter on trip to Russia to help start up a Russian Silicon Valley 2010, also part of Pres. Obama's first US-Russia Innovation Del. *Film roles:* Coming Soon 1999, Down to You 2000, Deception 2000, Dude, Where's My Car? 2000, Texas Rangers 2001, Just Married 2003, My Boss's Daughter (also co-producer) 2003, The Butterfly Effect (also exec. producer) 2004, Guess Who 2005, A Lot Like Love 2005, Bobby 2006, The Guardian 2006, Open Season (voice) 2006, What Happens in Vegas 2008, Spread (also producer) 2009, Personal Effects 2009, Valentine's Day 2010, Killers (also producer) 2010, No Strings Attached 2011, New Year's Eve 2011, Jobs 2013. *Television roles:* Just Shoot Me! (series) 2001, Grounded for Life (series) 2002, Robot Chicken (series) (voice) 2005, That '70s Show (series) 1998–2006, Miss Guided (series) 2008, Two and a Half Men (CBS series) (also writer) 2011–13, Men at Work (series) 2013. *Television produced:* exec. producer: Punk'd (series) (also writer) 2003–12, You've Got a Friend (series documentary) 2004, Beauty and the Geek (series) 2005–08, The Real Wedding Crashers (series) 2007, Adventures in Hollyhood (series documentary) 2007, Room 401 (series) 2007, Pop Fiction (series) 2008, Miss Guided (series) 2008, Opportunity Knocks (series) 2008–09, Choose Me (film) 2009, Game Show in My Head (series) 2009, The Beautiful Life: TBL (series) (also writer and co-producer) 2009, True Beauty (series) 2009–10, Numbnuts (series) 2010, Eric Finley: Comment Counselor (series) 2012, Rituals (series documentary) 2012–13, Forever Young (series) 2013. *Address:* c/o Adam Venit or Greg Siegel, WME Entertainment, 9601 Wilshire Boulevard, Beverly Hills, CA 90210, USA (office); c/o Stephanie Simon, Untitled Entertainment, 331 North Maple Drive, 3rd Floor, Beverly Hills, CA 90210, USA (office); Katalyst Films, 6430 Sunset Boulevard, Suite 1400, Los Angeles, CA 90028, USA (office). *Telephone:* (323) 785-2710 (office).

KUTELIA, Batu, PhD; Georgian politician and diplomatist; b. 16 Jan. 1974, Tbilisi; m.; one s. one d.; ed Georgian Tech. Univ., Georgian Inst. of Public Affairs, NATO Defence Coll.; Deputy Head of Mil. Cooperation Div., Mil.-Political Dept, Ministry of Foreign Affairs 1997–98, Head of Div. 1998–2000, Deputy Dir Mil.-Political Dept 2000–03; Deputy Head of Mission, Embassy in London 2003–04; Dir Political Security Dept, Nat. Security Council May–June 2004; Head of Foreign Intelligence Dept, Ministry of State Security June–Oct. 2004, Deputy Minister of State Security Oct.–Dec. 2004; Head of Foreign Intelligence Special Service 2006; Deputy Minister of Foreign Affairs Sept.–Dec. 2006; Deputy Minister of Defence 2006–07, First Deputy Minister of Defence 2007–08; Amb. to USA 2008–10; Deputy Sec., State Security Council 2010–13; Distinguished Fellow, New Westminster Coll., Canada 2014; Soros Foundation Scholarship 1994, 1995, 1996, 1997, GIPA Special Award for Academic Performance 1996, Pres. of Georgia Scholarship 1998, NATO Defence Coll. Scholarship 2000, Certificate of Appreciation of Pres. of Georgia 2000.

KUTESA, Sam Kahamba, LLB; Ugandan lawyer and politician; *Minister of Foreign Affairs;* b. 1 Feb. 1949; m. Jennifer Nankunda Kutesa; six c.; ed Makerere Univ.; in pvt. law practice with Kutesa and Co. Advocates 1973–2001; Attorney-Gen. 1985–86; mem. Parl. representing Mawogola Co. 1996; fmr Minister of State for Investment, Ministry of Finance, Planning and Econ. Devt 2001–05; Minister of Foreign Affairs 2005–11 (resgnd), 2012–14, 2015–; Chair. Regional Inter-Ministerial Cttee, Int. Conference on the Great Lakes Region 2011–14; Pres. 69th Session of UN Gen. Ass. 2014–15; mem. Nat. Resistance Movt. *Address:* Ministry of Foreign Affairs, 2A/B Apollo Kaggwa Road, POB 7048, Kampala, Uganda (office). *Telephone:* (41) 4345661 (office). *Fax:* (41) 4258722 (office). *E-mail:* info@mofa.go.ug (office). *Website:* www.mofa.go.ug (office).

KUTSYN, Lt-Gen. Mykhaylo Nikolayevich; Ukrainian army officer and fmr government official; *Chief of the General Staff and Chief of the Armed Forces;* b. 15 Aug. 1957, Svoboda, Berehove Raion, Zakarpattia Oblast; m.; two d.; ed Annunciation Higher Tank Command School, Mil. Acad. of Armoured Forces, Moscow, Operational and Strategic Nat. Defence Acad. of Ukraine; served as Tank Platoon Leader Group of Soviet Forces in Germany; commdr of a platoon and Co. Commdr of Cadets, Kharkov Higher Tank Command School 1980–87; Deputy Commdr of tank bn, then Commdr, then Deputy Chief of Staff, Tank Regt, Belarusian Mil. Dist 1990–92; enlisted in Armed Forces of Ukraine Dec. 1992; Chief of Staff and Commdr of Regt, Carpathian Mil. Dist, Army Forces of Ukraine 1992–96; Chief of Staff, Commdr of Mechanised Div., Western Operational Command 1996–99; Chief of Staff, Commdr of 13th Army Corps, Army of the Western Operational Command 2001–04; First Deputy Commdr of Western Operational Command 2004, Commdr 2004–10; Deputy Minister of Defence 2010–14; Chief of the Gen. Staff and Chief of the Armed Forces Feb. 2014–; Medal for Battle Merit (Soviet award), Medal For Mil. Service to Ukraine 1997, Order of Bohdan Khmelnytsky, Third Class 2005, Second Class 2008, Medal 'For Faultless Service', First, Second and Third Degree; numerous other medals and insignia of the Ministry of Defence. *Address:* Ministry of Defence, 01021 Kyiv, vul. M. Hrushevskoho 30/1, Ukraine (office). *Telephone:* (44) 253-11-56 (office). *Fax:* (44) 226-20-15 (office). *E-mail:* webmaster@mil.gov.ua (office). *Website:* www.mil.gov.ua (office).

KUTWA, HE Cardinal Jean-Pierre, MA, PhD; Côte d'Ivoirian ecclesiastic and composer; *Archbishop of Abidjan;* b. 22 Dec. 1945, Blockhauss; ed Minor Seminary, Bingerville, Grand Seminary, Anyama, Catholic Inst. of Occidental Africa, Pontifical Urbaniana Univ., Rome; ordained Deacon, Archdiocese of Abidjan 1970, ordained Priest 1971; Archbishop of Gagnoa 2001–06, of Abidjan 2006–; Del. of Bishops of Côte d'Ivoire to Synod of Bishops at the Vatican Oct. 2005; cr. Cardinal (Cardinal-Priest of Santa Emerenziana a Tor Fiorenza) 2014–; Pres. Bishops Comm. for Ecumenism; Vice-Pres. Regional Episcopal Conf. of Francophone West Africa. *Address:* Archevêché, avenue Jean Paul II, 01 BP 1287, Abidjan 01, Côte d'Ivoire (office). *Telephone:* 20212308 (office). *Fax:* 20214022 (office).

KUUGONGELWA-AMADHILA, Saara, MSc; Namibian politician; b. 12 Oct. 1967; m. Onesmus Amadhila; ed Univ. of London, UK, Univ. of Namibia; Dir-Gen. Nat. Planning Comm. 1997–2003; fmr Gov. African Devt Bank; Minister of Finance 2003–15; Vice Chair., Eminent Bd mem. Pan Afrikan Centre of Namibia (Pacon); mem. Swapo Party Central Cttee.

KUWAIZ, Abdullah Ibrahim el-, MA, MBA, PhD; Saudi Arabian banker, politician and diplomatist; b. 21 Aug. 1939, Dawadmi; two s. two d.; ed King Saud Univ. Saudi Arabia, Pacific Lutheran Univ. and St Louis Univ., USA; accountant, Pensions Dept, Ministry of Finance and Nat. Economy 1959–67, economist, 1967–81 (adviser 1977–81); Exec. Dir Arab Monetary Fund, Abu Dhabi 1977–80, Dir-Gen. and Chair. 1987–89; Co-Chair. Financial Co-operation Cttee, Euro-Arab Dialogue 1978–83; Asst Under-Sec. for Econ. Affairs 1981–87; Deputy Minister of Finance and Nat. Economy, Saudi Arabia 1987–2001; Amb. to Bahrain 2002–09; Chair. Saudi-Kuwait Cement Co., Saudi Arabia 1991–93; Asst Sec.-Gen. for Econ. Affairs, Co-operation Council for the Arab States of the Gulf 1981–95; mem. of Bd and mem. Exec. Cttee, Gulf Int. Bank, Bahrain 1977–90; mem. of Bd Gulf Co-operation Council's Org. for Measures and Standards 1984–95, Oxford Energy Inst., UK 1985, Int. Maritime Bureau, London 1985–88, Econ. Forum, Cairo 1994–2001, Islamic Devt Bank, Jeddah 1997–2003, Arab Fund for Econ. Devt, Kuwait 1998–2000; Gen. Man. Gulf Int. Bank, Bahrain 1997–2001; Chair. Bosna Bank Int. Sarajevo 2000; Medal of Merit for Accomplishment in Global Climate Coalition (GCC) from King Fahd Ibn Abdulaziz 1989, Lifetime Accomplishment Award Arab Bankers Association of North America (ABANA) 2003. *Publications:* numerous papers relating to banking, oil, finance and econ. devt and integration delivered at symposia in N America, Europe and the Middle East. *Leisure Interests:* hiking, swimming, reading, debating and writing. *Address:* PO Box 10866, Riyadh 11443, Saudi Arabia (home). *Telephone:* (1) 488-0882 (home). *Fax:* (1) 480-2190 (home). *E-mail:* kuwaiz@hotmail.com (home).

KUX, Barbara, MBA; Swiss business executive; b. 26 Feb. 1954, Zurich; d. of Prof. Dr Ernst Kux; m.; ed Institut Européen d'Admin des Affaires (INSEAD), France; Marketing Man., Nestlé SA, Germany 1979–84, Vice-Pres. Cen. and Eastern Europe Region, responsible for building up market leading business in Poland and Russia 1993–99; Man. Consultant, McKinsey & Co., Germany 1984–89; Vice-Pres. Asea Brown Boveri AG (ABB) responsible for entry into Cen. and Eastern Europe

1989–92, Pres. ABB Power Ventures 1989–92; Exec. Dir Ford Europe 1999–2003; Chief Procurement Office and mem. Group Man. Cttee, Royal Philips Electronics NV 2003–08; Head of Supply Chain Man. and Chief Sustainability Officer, Siemens AG 2008–13, also mem. Man. Bd; mem. Bd of Dirs Firmenich 2008–11, 2013–, Henkel AG 2013–, Umicore SA 2013–, Total SA; mem. Advisory Bd INSEAD 2003–, Max Schmidheiny-Stiftung at Univ. of St Gallen; elected Global Leader for Tomorrow, World Econ. Forum. *Leisure interests:* cultural activities, sports, spending time with friends and family.

KUZMANOVIĆ, Rajko, PhD; Bosnia and Herzegovina judge, academic and politician; *President, Academy of Sciences and Arts of Republika Srpska;* b. 1 Dec. 1931, Čelinac; s. of Nikola Kuzmanović and Vida Kuzmanović; m. Ljubica (Ladan) Kuzmanović; ed Univ. of Zagreb; fmr head of educ. service in municipality of Čelinac; fmr Speaker of Ass. in Čelinac; fmr Prin. of School of Politics, Banja Luka; fmr mem. Exec. Bd Municipality of Banja Luka; teacher, Faculty of Law, Univ. of Banja Luka 1975, External Collaborator-Asst 1975–77, Dean 1977–81, Assoc. Prof. 1981–85, Prof. of Constitutional Law 1985–, Head of Constitutional Science, Faculty of Law for 25 years, Deputy Dean 1979–81, a Dean of Faculty of Law 1983–85, 1996–2000, a Dean of Faculty of Business Economy, Deputy Rector Univ. of Banja Luka 1986–88, Rector 1988–92; fmr Deputy Rector Slavic Univ. Magen, Moscow; part-time Prof., Faculties of Law, Mostar and Prishtina, Faculty of Philosophy, Banja Luka, Coll. of Interior, Faculty of Business Economy, Banja Luka, Apeiron Pan-European Univ., Banja Luka; fmr Pres. Scientific Council Inst. for Int. Law and Int. Business Co-operation, Banja Luka, Veselin Masleša Scientific Council Centre for Political Studies and Research, Banja Luka, Council of History Inst., Asscn of Univ. Teachers and Scientific Cadre (Bosnia and Herzegovina), Community of Univs in Bosnia and Herzegovina, Community of Univs of Yugoslavia, Asscn of Lawyers in Republika Srpska; mem. Council of Educational and Pedagogy Inst. (Bosnia and Herzegovina), Council of Museums of Bosnian Krajina; mem. Parl., Ass. of Socialist Repub. of Bosnia and Herzegovina 1961–65; mem. numerous comms at Nat. Ass. of Republika Srpska 1995–2000, including Comm. for Creating and Altering the Constitution of Republika Srpska, Council of Law in the Govt of Republika Srpska; mem. League of Communists of Bosnia and Herzegovina, Cen. Cttee of League of Communists of Bosnia and Herzegovina, Republican Conf. of SSRN of Bosnia and Herzegovina; judge 1994–98, Pres. Constitutional Court of Republika Srpska 1998–2002, mem. High Prosecutor's Council; mem. Alliance of Ind. Social Democrats; Pres. of Republika Srpska 2007–10; Corresp. mem. Acad. of Sciences and Arts of Republika Srpska 1997–2004, mem. and Pres. 2004–; mem. European Acad. of Sciences and Arts, Salzburg 2009–, Russian Acad. of Natural and Social Sciences (RAEH), Moscow 2010, Spanish Royal Acad. for Economy and Finance (RACEF), Barcelona 2010, Acad. of Sciences of Higher Educ. of Ukraine, Kiev 2012; Order for Work, Order for Mil. Merits, Order for Merits for People, Pres. of Socialist Fed. of Repub. of Yugoslavia, Order of Honour Golden Rays of Republika Srpska, Peter the Great Medal of the First Order (Russian Fed.), Order of Republika Srpska 2012; Pres. of Republika Srpska Award, Medallion and Charter, Univ. of Banja Luka, Konji (Turkey), Katowice (Poland), Ostrava (Czech Repub.), Charter and Gold Coat of Arms of City of Banja Luka, Gold Medallion of Čelinac, Gold Medallion of Faculty of Law, Banja Luka, Veselin Masleša Medallion for scientific work, charters of several other cities, Higher Law Award' Femida Int. Bar Asscn (Russia), Grand Prix' Leonardo da Vinci. *Publications:* 28 textbooks, including Constitutional Law, Science of Managing Bases, Parallel Political Systems, Constitution and Civil Rights (co-author); more than 200 articles in scientific and professional journals on constitutional law and political systems, state man. and governing, educ. and schooling, and on numerous other gen. and social subjects, New Essays on Constitutionality and Statehood, The Time of Stabilisation, Hemeroteka, The Constitutional Law Topics. *Address:* Academy of Sciences and Arts of Republic of Srpska, Bana Lazarevića 1, 78000 Banja Luka, Bosnia and Herzegovina (office). *Telephone:* (51) 333702 (office); (51) 333706 (office). *Fax:* (51) 333701 (office). *E-mail:* predsjednik@anurs.org (office); medj.saradnja@anurs.org (office); anurs@blic.net (office). *Website:* www.anurs.org (office).

KUZMIN, Alexander Viktorovich; Russian architect; *President, Russian Academy of Architecture and Construction Sciences (RAACS);* b. 12 July 1951, Moscow; s. of Victor Alexandrovich Kuzmin and Antonina Alexeevna Kuzmin; m. 1996; one s. one d.; ed Moscow Inst. of Architecture; researcher, Research and Project Inst. of the Master Plan of Moscow, Dir from 1987; Deputy Head, Chief Moscow Dept of Architecture 1991, First Deputy Chair. Moscow Cttee for Architecture and Urban Devt; Chief Architect of Moscow 1996–2012, Chair. Architectural and City Planning Cttee, Moscow; Pres. and mem. Editorial Bd, Russian Acad. of Architecture and Construction Sciences (RAACS) 1998–; mem. Int. Acad. of Architecture; oversaw works to Voentorg Hotel Moscow, building forecourt, shopping malls, Theatre 'Et Cetera', Sretenskii Gate; chief architect of reconstruction of Moscow streets, cen. region of Moscow, building of Olympic village. *Leisure interest:* collecting old medals. *Address:* Russian Academy of Architecture and Building Sciences, Bolshaya Dmitrovka Street, 24, Building 1, 107031 Moscow, Russia (office). *Telephone:* (495) 625-79-67 (office). *E-mail:* raasn@raasn.ru (office). *Website:* www.raasn.ru (office).

KUZ'MUK, Col-Gen. Oleksander Ivanovich; Ukrainian military officer and politician; b. 17 April 1954, Dyatilivka, Khmelnitsk Region; m.; two c.; ed Kharkov Guards' Higher Tank School, Moscow Mil. Acad. of Armoured Forces; commdr tank platoon, Bn; Deputy Commdr Regt, Group of Soviet Troops in Germany 1975–83; Commdg posts in Leningrad, Carpathian, Odessa Mil. commands 1983–95; Commdr Nat. Guards of Ukraine 1995–96; Minister of Defence 1996–2001, 2004–05; Deputy Prime Minister 2006–07; elected MP (Party of Regions) 2012; Hon. Pistol; Order of Bohdan Khmelnytsky, 1st Class, 2nd Class, 3rd Class, Order of Danylo Halytsky, Order of Merit, 3rd Class.

KUZNETSOV, Boris Avramovich; Russian barrister and writer; b. 19 March 1944, Kirov; s. of Avram Mikhailovich Kuznetsov and Nina Aleksandrovna Ukhanova; m. 2nd Nadezhda Georgiyevna Chernaya; two c.; ed Moscow Juridical Acad., Research Inst. of USSR Ministry of Internal Affairs; mem. staff, Criminal Investigation Dept, St Petersburg and Magadan Region 1962–82; mem. Magadan Regional Bd of Lawyers 1982–85, twice expelled for disagreement with party officials; Head of Lab., Inst. of Biology Problems of the North br., USSR Acad. of Sciences, Magadan 1985–89; adviser to mems Inter-regional people's deputy 1989–91; mem. St Petersburg Bd of Lawyers 1991–95, Lawyers' Interrepublic Bd 1995–2007; fmr Head, Boris Kuznetsov and Partners Lawyer's Agency; acted in numerous high-profile criminal and human rights cases, including the families of the 118 sailors killed in the Kursk nuclear submarine, relatives of murdered journalist Anna Politkovskaya, the scientist Igor Sutyagin jailed on espionage charges, NGO dir Manana Aslamazyan; left Russia 2007, granted asylum in USA 2008; CIS Lawyer of the Year Award, Golden Sign for Defence of Russian-Speaking People and Intellectuals Outside Russia, 1998, Anatoli Koni's Medal 2001, Award Hanger from the Navy of the Russian Fed. *Publications:* Ona Utonula: Pravda O Kurske Kotoruiu Skryl Genprokuror Ustinov 2005; six other books. *Leisure interests:* pre-Revolutionary juridical literature and literature on the navy, sailing models construction.

KUZNETSOV, Lev Vladimirovich; Russian business executive and politician; *Minister of North Caucasus Affairs;* b. 25 April 1965, Moscow; ed Moscow Financial Inst.; served in Soviet Army early 1980s; Chief of Credit Man., Alfa Bank 1994; later adviser to Governing Chair. and Deputy Man. of Client Relations, International Finance Co. –1996; joined mining and metallurgical co. Norilsk Nickel 1996, held posts of Chief of Auditing Dept, Dir of Control and Auditing Activities, Deputy Gen. Dir of Norilsk Nickel, and First Deputy Gen. Dir Jt Stock Co. Norilsk Combine 1996–2002; served in various posts in Siberian local govt; Advisor on Econ. Matters to Gov. Alexander Khloponin and First Deputy Gov. of Krasnoyarsk Krai 2002–10, Acting Gov. 2010–14; Minister of North Caucasus Affairs 2014–; mem. Yedinaya Rossiya (United Russia) party. *Address:* Minister of North Caucasus Affairs, Office of the Government, 103274 Moscow, Krasnopresnenskaya nab. 2 (office); Minister of North Caucasus Affairs, 357600 Yessentuki, Stavropol Krai, Russian Federation (office). *E-mail:* duty_press@aprf.gov.ru (office). *Website:* government.ru/department/297/events (office); government.ru/en/gov/persons/324/events (office).

KUZNETSOV, Nikolai Aleksandrovich; Russian cybernetician; *Counsellor, Institute of Radioengineering and Electronics, Russian Academy of Sciences;* b. 9 March 1939, Volgogradskaya Region; m.; two c.; ed Moscow Inst. of Physics and Tech.; Jr, Sr Researcher, Deputy Dir Inst. of Problems of Man. 1965–88; Dir-Gen. of Research Production Union Moskva 1988–89; Dir Inst. for Information Transmission Problems (IPPI) 1990–2006; Counsellor, Inst. of Radioengineering and Electronics, Russian Acad. of Sciences 2006–; Corresp. mem. USSR (now Russian) Acad. of Sciences 1987, mem. 1994; mem. IEEE; research in theory of automatic man. and informatics; USSR State Prize. *Publications include:* Management of Observations in Automatic Systems 1961, Synthesis of Algorithms at Variable Criterion of Optimality 1966, Methods of Study of Stability of Dissynchronized Pulse Systems 1991. *Leisure interests:* skiing, singing. *Address:* Institute of Radioengineering and Electronics, Russian Academy of Sciences, Mokhovaya 11-7, 125009 Moscow, Russia (office). *Telephone:* (495) 629-30-05 (office). *Fax:* (495) 629-30-05 (office). *E-mail:* kuznetsov@cplire.ru (office).

KUZNETSOV, Nikolai Vasilyevich; Russian mathematician; b. 24 June 1939, Hachmas, Azerbaijan; s. of Vasilii Kuznetsov and Evdokia Gureutieva; m. Galina Pavlovna Kuznetsova 1975; two c.; ed Moscow Inst. of Physics and Tech.; jr researcher, Inst. of Math., USSR Acad. of Sciences 1965–69; jr, sr researcher, Moscow V. Lenin Pedagogical Inst. 1969–70; Head of Div., Head of Dept, Cen. Research Inst. of Information and Tech.-Econ. Studies 1970–71; Head of Div., Research Inst. of Systems of Man. and Econs 1972–73; Sr Researcher, Head of Lab. Khabarovsk Research Inst. of Complex Studies 1973–81; Deputy Dir Computer's Cen., Far East br. USSR Acad. of Sciences 1989–91; Deputy Dir Inst. of Applied Math. 1991–92; Corresp. mem. USSR (now Russian) Acad. of Sciences 1987; research in spectral theory, theory of modular and automorphic functions in math. physics. *Publications:* On Eigenfunctions of One Integral Equation 1970, Poincaré Series and Extended Lemer Hypothesis 1985; numerous articles in scientific journals. *Leisure interest:* chess. *Address:* Institute of Applied Mathematics, Far East Branch of Russian Academy of Sciences, 50 Svetlanskaya str., 690950 Vladivostok, Russia (office). *Telephone:* (4232) 22-86-30 (Vladivostok) (office); (4212) 33-46-76 (Khabarovsk) (office); (4212) 22-76-36 (home). *E-mail:* info@hq.febras.ru (office).

KUZNETSOV, Oleg Leonidovich, DTech; Russian geophysicist; *President, Russian Academy of Natural Sciences;* b. 29 Aug. 1938; m.; two c.; ed Moscow S. Ordzhonikidze Inst. of Geological Research, Moscow State Univ.; researcher, Inst. of Oil, USSR (now Russian) Acad. of Sciences 1962–70; Head of lab., All-Union Inst. of Nuclear Geophysics and Geochemistry, USSR Ministry of Geology (now State Scientific Centre of All-Russian Inst. of Geosystems) 1970–79, Dir 1979–; Prof., Moscow State Univ. 1986–; Vice-Pres. Russian Acad. of Nat. Sciences 1990–93, Pres. 1993–; Founder and Rector, Int. Univ. of Nature, Soc. and Man., Dubna 1994–2008, Pres. 2008–; Gen. Constructor, Global Information System GEOS 1985–91; mem. New York Acad. of Sciences 1994, Int. Acad. of Sciences on Nature and Soc. 1993, Int. Acad. of Higher Schooling 1995, Oriental Acad. of Oil and Gas 1994; Hon. mem. Hungarian Soc. of Geophysics, Euro-Asian Geophysical Soc.; Hon. Prospector of the USSR 1985; Hon. Worker of the Oil and Gas Industry of the USSR 1986; USSR State Prize 1982, Honoured Worker of Science and Tech. of Russian Fed. 1992, Prize of German Econ. Club 1996, A. Chizhevsky Prize 1997, Medal of Honour of the Russian Fed. 1998, Golden ROSING-2002, Gratitude of the Pres. of the Russian Fed. 2002, Honoured Worker of Science and Tech., Moscow region, Moscow Region Gov.'s Award (in Econs) 2007. *Publications:* more than 300 scientific works, including 14 monographs, four reference books, 67 inventions and more than 60 patents on geophysical processes, seismoacoustics, non-linear geophysics, geoinformatics and information tech. *Address:* Russian Academy of Natural Sciences, Varshavskoye shosse 8, 117105 Moscow, Russia (office). *Telephone:* (495) 954-53-50 (office). *Fax:* (495) 958-37-11 (office). *E-mail:* info@raen.info (office). *Website:* www.raen.info (office).

KVAMME, E(arl) Floyd, BS, MS; American engineer, computer scientist, venture capitalist and fmr government official; *Partner Emeritus, Kleiner Perkins Caufield & Byers;* b. 1938, northern Calif.; s. of Norwegian immigrant parents; ed Jefferson High School, Daly City, Univ. of California, Berkeley and Syracuse Univ.; Founder-mem. Nat. Semiconductor 1967, Gen. Man. Semiconductor Operations, Pres. Nat. Advanced Systems (subsidiary); Exec. Vice-Pres. of Sales and Marketing, Apple Computer 1982; Pnr, Kleiner Perkins Caufield & Byers 1984, now Pnr Emer.; Chair. Electronic Commerce Advisory Council for the State of Calif. 1998; Co-Chair. Pres.'s Council of Advisors on Science Tech (PCAST), Washington, DC 2001–09; Chair. Empower America; mem. Bd of Dirs, Brio Tech., Gemfire, Harmonic Lightwaves, Triquint Semiconductor, Photon Dynamics, Power Integrations; mem. Advisory Bd, Markkula Center for Applied Ethics, Santa Clara Univ., Nat. Venture Capital Asscn; mem. Exec. Cttee, The Tech. Network; fmr mem. Finance Cttee, Fong for Senate Campaign, High Tech. Advisory Cttee, Nat. Finance Cttee of the Bush for President Campaign. *Publication:* Chapter 19: How Technology Can Lead a Boom, in The 4% Solution: Unleashing the Economic Growth America Needs 2012. *Address:* Kleiner Perkins Caufield & Byers, Menlo Park, 2750 Sand Hill Road, Menlo Park, CA 94025, USA (office). *Telephone:* (650) 233-2750 (office). *Fax:* (650) 233-0300 (office). *E-mail:* plans@kpcb.com (office). *Website:* www.kpcb.com/partner/floyd-kvamme (office).

KVASHNIN, Army Gen. Anatoly Vassilyevich; Russian army officer and politician; b. 15 Aug. 1946, Ufa, Bashkir ASSR; ed Kurgan Machine Construction Inst., Acad. of Armoured Units, Acad. of Gen. Staff; army service, Commdr of regiment, div., army 1969–; Deputy, First Deputy Head, Main Operation Dept 1993–95; Commdr Allied Group of Armed Forces in Chechnya 1994–95; Commdr Armed Forces of N Caucasian Command 1995–97; Chief of Gen. Staff of Armed Forces of Russian Fed. 1997–2004; First Deputy Minister of Defence, Russian Fed. 1997–2004; Rep. of Russian Pres. to Siberian Fed. Okrug (Dist) 2004–10; Hon. Citizen of Makhachkala 2000; Hero of the Russian Fed. 1999; Order of the Holy Prince Daniel of Moscow (Russian Orthodox Church) 2000; Order of Merit for the Fatherland; Officier, Légion d'honneur 2004; Order of Courage 2005; Order of Honour 2006; Order of the Yugoslav Star (Serbia and Montenegro). *Leisure interests:* painting, sports. *Address:* Ministry of Defence, 119169 Moscow, ul. Znamenka 19, Russia (office). *Telephone:* (495) 696-71-71 (office); (495) 696-86-73 (office). *Website:* mil.ru (office).

KVIRIKASHVILI, Giorgi; Georgian politician; b. 20 July 1967, Tbilisi, Georgian SSR, USSR; m.; four c.; ed studied Medicine and Econs at Tbilisi State Medical Univ., Univ. of Illinois, USA, Georgian Tech. Univ.; Trading Operations Officer, then Deputy Dir, Credit Dept, United Georgian Bank (now VTB Bank Georgia) 1993–96; Deputy Dir-Gen. TradeInvest Bank 1996–97; Dir of Business Devt and Br. Network Man., Deputy Dir Asset-Liability Man., United Georgian Bank 1998; Exec. Man. Consultant, First Commercial Bank 2004–06; Dir-Gen. Cartu Bank 2006–11; expert in financial sector and pensions reform, Lenzie Fisher Hendry LLC March–Oct. 2012; mem. Qartuli Ocneba (Georgian Dream) 2012–, also Chair.; mem. Parl. (Axali Memarjveneebi—New Rights) 1999–2004; Minister of the Economy and Sustainable Devt Oct. 2012–15, First Deputy Prime Minister 2013–15, Minister of Foreign Affairs Sept.–Dec. 2015, Prime Minister of Georgia 2015–18 (resgnd). *Address:* c/o Chancellery of the Government, 0134 Tbilisi, P. Ingorovka 7, Georgia (office).

KVITOVÁ, Petra; Czech professional tennis player; b. 8 March 1990, Bílovec, Czechoslovakia; d. of Jiří Kvita and Pavla Kvitová; plays left-handed (two-handed backhand); trained in her hometown until age 16; turned professional 2006; played first career events on ITF (Int. Tennis Fed.) Circuit, winning two singles titles 2006; played first WTA (Women's Tennis Asscn) main draw at Stockholm 2007, won four singles titles on ITF Circuit 2007; qualified for her first WTA Tour Main Draw in Open Gaz de France 2008; winner Moorilla Hobart Int. 2009, Brisbane Int. 2011, Paris (Indoors) 2011, Mutua Madrid Open 2011, WTA Tour Championships, Istanbul 2011, Dubai Duty Free Tennis Championships 2013; Grand Slam results: fourth round, US Open 2009, 2012, quarterfinalist, Australian Open 2011, semifinalist 2012, winner, Wimbledon 2011, 2014, semifinalist, French Open 2012; quarterfinalist, Summer Olympics, London 2012; mem. Federation Cup Team for Czech Repub. 2007–, winners 2011, 2012; winner (for Czech Repub.), Hopman Cup 2012; ranked World No. 2 31 Oct. 2011; first Grand Slam event winner born in 1990s; coached by David Kotyza; WTA Newcomer of the Year 2010, WTA Player of the Year 2011, WTA Most Improved Player 2011, Karen Krantzcke Sportsmanship Award 2011, Fan Favorite Breakthrough Player 2011, ITF World Champion 2011, Czech Athlete of the Year 2011. *Website:* petrakvitova.net.

KWANKWASO, Rabiu; Nigerian politician; b. 21 Oct. 1956, Kwankwaso Village, Madobi; m.; eight c.; Exec. Gov. Kano state 1999–2003, 2011–15; Minister of Defence 2003–07; Special Presidential Envoy to Somalia and Darfur 2007; Senator (All Progressives Congress) for Kano Central 2015–; Leader, People's Democratic Party in Kano. *Address:* Senate, National Assembly Complex, 3 Arms Zones, PMB 141, Abuja, Nigeria (office). *E-mail:* repinfo@nassnig.org (office). *Website:* www.nass.gov.ng (office).

KWAŚNIEWSKA, Jolanta; Polish organization executive, lawyer and charity worker; *Founder and President, Porozumienie Bez Barier;* b. 3 June 1955, Gdansk; d. of Julian Konty and Anna Konty; m. Aleksander Kwaśniewski (Pres. of Poland 1995–2005) 1979; one d.; ed Faculty of Law, Univ. of Gdansk; began career as lawyer 1984; est. real estate agency 1991, co-dir with husband until his assumption of Presidency of Poland 1995; First Lady 1995–2005; Founder and Pres. Porozumienie Bez Barier (Communication Without Barriers Foundation, org. to help disabled people and cr. medical centre for children) 1997, est. Let's Open the World Programme (provides funds for Polish orphans to visit European countries), Help the Talented Youth Foundation; Patron Polish UNICEF, Nat. Coalition for Breast Cancer, Adults for Children Foundation; mem. UN Comité des Sages; mem. Hon. Bd Int. Centre for Missing and Exploited Children; Order of the Smile 1998, Grand Ribbon, Order of Leopold (Belgium) 1999, Grand Cross, Order of Isabella the Catholic (Spain) 2001, Grand Cross, Order of Merit (Germany) 2002, Grand Ribbon, Order of the Precious Crown (Japan) 2002, Grand Cross, Royal Norwegian Order of Merit 2003, Grand Cross, Royal Portuguese Order of Merit 2004; Woman of the Year and Warsaw Lady of the Year 1998, Dr Henryk Jordan Medal for Assistance to Children 1999, American Centre of Polish Culture in Washington Medal 1999, Medal of Merit for the Mining Industry for Aid Given to Orphaned Mining Families, For The Future of Children of Europe Award of Hungarian Asscn, Future of Europe Asscn 2002. *Leisure interests:* literature, theatre, music, fine arts, spending time with her family, travel, skiing, tennis. *Address:* Porozumienie Bez Barier, al. Przyjaciół 8 lok. 1a, 00-565 Warsaw, Poland (office). *Telephone:* (22) 8499662 (office). *Fax:* (22) 8499662 (office). *E-mail:* radafundacji@fpbb.pl (office). *Website:* www.fpbb.pl (office).

KWAŚNIEWSKI, Aleksander; Polish journalist, fmr politician and fmr head of state; b. 15 Nov. 1954, Białogard, Koszalin Prov.; s. of Zdzisław Kwaśniewski and Aleksandra Kwaśniewska; m. Jolanta Konty 1979; one d.; ed Gdańsk Univ.; fmr leader of youth movt, including Chair. Univ. Council of Polish Socialist Students' Union (SZSP) at Gdańsk Univ., Head of Culture Dept of SZSP Gen. Bd 1979–80, mem. Exec. Cttee of SZSP Chief Council 1980–81; Ed.-in-Chief Itd (student weekly newspaper), Warsaw 1981–84; Ed.-in-Chief of daily Sztandar Młodych (Banner of Youth), Warsaw 1984–85; mem. Council of Ministers 1985–89; Head, Socio-Political Cttee 1988–89; Minister for Youth Affairs 1985–87; Chair. Cttee for Youth and Physical Culture 1987–90; mem. Polish United Workers' Party (PZPR) 1977–90; mem. Social Democracy of Repub. of Poland Party (SDRP) 1990–95, Chair. 1990–95; participant in Round Table plenary debates, Co-Chair. team for trade union pluralism, mem. team for political reforms and group for asscns and territorial self-govt 1989; Co-f. Democratic Left Alliance 1991; Chair. Polish Olympic Cttee 1988–91; Deputy in Sejm (Parl.) 1991–95; Chair. Constitutional Cttee 1993–95; Supreme Commdr of Armed Forces 1995–2005; Pres. of Poland 1995–2005; Distinguished Scholar in the Practice of Global Leadership, Georgetown Univ., Washington, DC, USA 2006–, teaches in Edmund A. Walsh School of Foreign Service; Chair. European Council on Tolerance and Reconciliation 2008–; Chair. Supervisory Bd, Int. Centre for Policy Studies, Kiev, Ukraine; mem. Int. Hon. Council of the European Acad. of Diplomacy; mem. Leadership Council for Concordia 2011–; Dir, Burisma Holdings Ltd 2014–; co-leader of a European Parl. monitoring mission in Ukraine to monitor the criminal cases against Yulia Tymoshenko, Yuriy Lutsenko and Valeriy Ivaschenko 2012; mem. Bd of Trustees, Hertie School of Governance, Berlin; Hon. Citizen of Warsaw 2010; Kt, Order of White Eagle and numerous int. honours and awards, including Grand Croix, Légion d'honneur, Kt Grand Cross, Order of Bath, Kt Grand Cross, Order of St Michael and St George (GB), Grand Cross, Order of Merit (Italy) 1996, Order of Duke Gedyminas, First Class (Lithuania), Order of Leopold (Belgium), Golden Olympic Order, Int. Olympic Cttee 1998, Order of Saint Magdalena, First Degree with decorations (Polish Orthodox Church) 1998, Golden Order of Merit, Int. Amateur Athletic Fed. 1999, Order of Merit, European Olympic Cttee 2000, Order of the Repub. (Turkey) 2000, Great Order of King Tamislav with Ribbon and Great Star (Croatia) 2001, Order of Catholic Isabella with Chain (Spain) 2001, Nat. Order of Southern Cross (Brazil) 2002, Special Grand Cross of Merit (Peru) 2002, Great Banner of the Supreme Order of the Chrysanthemum (Japan) 2002, Collar of the Order of the White Lion (Czech Repub.) 2004, Grand Ribbon of the Great Order of the Chrysanthemum (Japan) 2004); Dr hc (Hebrew Univ. of Jerusalem) 2004, (Kyiv-Mohyla Acad.) 2005, (Univ. of Vilnius) 2005; Wiktor Prize 1993, 1995, 2000, Jan Karski Award 2006, Common Wealth Award of Distinguished Service 2007. *Leisure interests:* sport, literature, films. *Address:* c/o Anna Wnuk, Office of Aleksander Kwaśniewski, Aleja Przyjaciół 8/1, 00-565 Warsaw, Poland (office). *Telephone:* (22) 8487385 (office). *Fax:* (22) 6294816 (office). *E-mail:* biuro@kwasniewskialeksander.pl (office). *Website:* kwasniewskialeksander.pl (office).

KWEK, Leng Beng; Singaporean business executive; *Executive Chairman, Hong Leong Group Singapore;* s. of Kwek Hong Png; m.; two c.; father left Fujian Prov., China for Singapore and subsequently f. Hong Leong Group; joined family business in 1960s; Exec. Chair. Hong Leong Group Singapore 1990–; Chair. City Developments Ltd, Millennium & Copthorne (M&C) Hotels; mem. Bd Trustees Singapore Management Univ.; mem. INSEAD East Asia Council, Action Community of Entrepreneurship; Hon. Patron, Real Estate Developers Asscn of Singapore; Hon. DUniv (Oxford Brookes Univ.); Hon. DBA (Johnson & Wales Univ., Rhode Island); Hotelier of the Decade, Asia Pacific Hotel Investment Conference 2000, SIAS TopGun CEO Designation Award, Brendan Wood International 2012, TTG Travel Entrepreneur of the Year 2014. *Address:* Hong Leong Group Singapore, 9 Raffles Place, #36-00, Republic Plaza, Singapore 048619 (office). *Telephone:* 6438-0880 (office). *Fax:* 6534-3060 (office). *E-mail:* gerry@cdl.com.sg (office). *Website:* www.hongleong.com.sg (office).

KWIATKOWSKI, Michał; Polish business executive; b. 1947; m.; one c.; ed Silesian Tech. Univ., Gliwice; engineer, promoted to Chief Engineer KWK Sosnica coalmine 1971–90; Deputy Dir Knurów Coalmine 1990–91, Dir 1991–93; Pres. Gliwice Coal Co. 1993–98, Weglokoks Co. 1998–2001, Polish Oil and Gas Co. (PGNiG) SA 2001–03, Man. Bd EuRoPol GAZ S.a. 2003–12.

KWOK, Raymond, MA (Cantab.), MBA, JP; Hong Kong business executive; *Chairman and Managing Director, Sun Hung Kai Properties Ltd;* b. (Kwok Ping-luen), 1952, Hong Kong; s. of Kwok Tak-seng and Kwong Siu-hing; younger brother of Walter Kwok and Thomas Kwok; ed Jesus Coll., Cambridge, UK, Harvard Univ., USA; family originated from Zhongshan, Guangdong Prov., China; with Sun Hung Kai Properties Ltd (largest property developer in Hong Kong) 1979–, Vice-Chair., then Chair. and Man. Dir 2011–; Chair. SUNeVision Holdings Ltd, SmarTone Telecommunications Holdings Ltd (also non-exec. Dir; has interest in city bus operator KMB; Dir (non-exec.) Transport International Holdings Ltd, USI Holdings Ltd; Ind. Dir (non-exec.) Standard Chartered Bank (Hong Kong) Ltd; mem. Bd of Dirs Real Estate Developers Asscn of Hong Kong; mem. Gen. Cttee of Hong Kong Gen. Chamber of Commerce, Hong Kong Port Devt Council; Vice-Chair. Council of Chinese Univ. of Hong Kong; Hon. DBA (Open Univ. of Hong Kong); Hon. LLD (Chinese Univ. of Hong Kong). *Address:* Sun Hung Kai Properties Ltd, 45th Floor, Sun Hung Kai Centre, 30 Harbour Road, Wanchai, Hong Kong Special Administrative Region, People's Republic of China (office). *Telephone:* 2827-8111 (office). *Fax:* 2827-2862 (office). *E-mail:* shkp@shkp.com (office). *Website:* www.shkp.com (office).

KWOK, Thomas, BEng (Civil), MBA, JP; Hong Kong business executive; b. (Kwok Ping-kwong), 1951, Hong Kong; s. of Kwok Tak-seng and Kwong Siu-hing; brother of Walter Kwok and Raymond Kwok; ed London Business School and Imperial Coll., Univ. of London, UK; family originated from Zhongshan, Guangdong Prov., China; joined Sun Hung Kai Properties Ltd (largest property developer in Hong Kong) 1982, fmr Vice-Chair. and Man. Dir; Chair. Route 3 (CPS) Co. Ltd; Jt Chair. IFC Development Ltd; Exec. Dir SUNeVision Holdings Ltd; Ind. Dir (non-exec.) Bank of East Asia Ltd; Exec. Vice-Pres. Real Estate Developers Asscn of Hong Kong; Govt apptd mem. Provisional Construction Industry Co-ordination Bd, Council for Sustainable Devt; fmr Chair. Property Man. Cttee Building Contractors' Asscn; fmr mem. Business Advisory Group, Land & Building Advisory Cttee, Registered Contractors' Disciplinary Bd, Gen. Chamber of Commerce Industrial

Affairs Cttee, Council of Hong Kong Construction Asscn, Bd Community Chest of Hong Kong, Social Welfare Policies and Services Cttee, Council of The Open Univ. of Hong Kong; mem. Standing Cttee Ninth CPPCC Shanghai Cttee; jailed for corruption in December 2014, released on bail July 2016, pending appeal; Hon. Citizen of Guangzhou.

KWOK, Walter; Hong Kong business executive; b. (Kwok Ping-sheung), 1950, Hong Kong; s. of Kwok Tak-seng and Kwong Siu-hing; brother of Raymond Kwok and Thomas Kwok; m. 1st Lydia Ku 1982 (divorced 1982); m. 2nd Wendy Lee; family originated from Zhongshan, Guangdong Prov., China; apptd Chair. and CEO Sun Hung Kai Properties Ltd (largest property developer in Hong Kong) 1990, handed over exec. duties of SHKP to brothers while retaining title of Chair. and CEO, temporary leave of absence to visit USA and Beijing and other large cities announced 18 Feb. 2008, brought lawsuit against his brothers May 2008, resgnd 2014; Founder Empire Group Holdings 2014.

KWON, O-kyu, PhD; South Korean academic and politician; *Visiting Professor, College of Business, Korea Advanced Institute of Science and Technology (KAIST);* b. 1952, Gangneung, Gangwon Prov.; ed Seoul Nat. Univ., Univ. of Minnesota, USA, Chung-Ang Univ.; joined Ministry of Finance 1974, held various positions at now-defunct Econ. Planning Bd and at Ministry of Finance and Economy 1975–94; Researcher, World Bank 1985, 1987; Presidential Sec. 1993–98; Alt. Exec. Dir to IMF 1997–99; Dir-Gen. Econ. Policy Bureau and Deputy Minister of Finance and Economy 1999–2001; Admin. Public Procurement Service 2002; Sr Presidential Sec. for Nat. Policy 2002–04; Perm. Rep. to OECD 2004–06; Chief Econ. Policy Adviser to the Pres. 2006; Deputy Prime Minister and Minister of Finance and Economy 2006–08; currently Visiting Prof., Coll. of Business, Korea Advanced Inst. of Science and Technology (KAIST). *Address:* College of Business, Korea Advanced Institute of Science and Technology (KAIST), 335 Gwahak-ro, Yuseong-gu, Daejeon, Seoul 305-701, Republic of Korea (office). *Telephone:* (42) 958-3434 (office). *E-mail:* okwon@business.kaist.ac.kr (office). *Website:* www.kaist.ac.kr (office).

KWON, Oh-gap, BA, MA; South Korean business executive; *President and Co-CEO, Hyundai Heavy Industries;* ed Hankuk Univ. of Foreign Studies, Univ. of Ulsan Grad. School; Dir Hyundai Educational Foundation 1990–97, Exec. Vice-Pres. in charge of Gen. Affairs, Int. Trade, Public Relations and Sales Dept, Hyundai Heavy Industries, Seoul Office 1997–2006, Sr Exec. Vice-Pres. 2007–10, Pres. and CEO Hyundai Oilbank Co. Ltd 2010–14, Pres. and Co-CEO Hyundai Heavy Industries Co. Ltd 2014–; Club Leader, Ulsan Hyundai Football Club 2004–; Pres. Korea Nat. League 2009–. *Address:* Hyundai Heavy Industries Co. Ltd, 1000 Bangeojinsunhwan-doro Dong-gu, Ulsan 682-792, Republic of Korea (office). *Telephone:* (52) 230-2114 (office). *Fax:* (52) 230-3470 (office). *E-mail:* ir@hhi.co.kr (office); webzine@hhi.co.kr (office). *Website:* www.hhi.co.kr (office).

KWON, Oh-hyun, BS, MS, PhD; South Korean electronics industry executive; *Vice-Chairman and CEO, Samsung Electronics;* ed Seoul Nat. Univ., Korea Advanced Inst. of Science and Tech., Stanford Univ., USA; joined Samsung Electronics' Semiconductor Business 1985, led devt of first 64MB DRAM 1992, Vice-Pres. Memory Device Tech. 1995–98, Sr Vice-Pres. and Head of System LSI Div.'s ASIC business 1998–2000, Exec. Vice-Pres. and Head of LSI Tech. 2000–04, Pres. and Gen. Man. System LSI Div. 2004–08, Pres. Semiconductor Business 2008–11, Head of Device Solutions 2011–, Vice-Chair. Samsung Electronics Co. Ltd 2011–12, Vice-Chair. and CEO 2012–, Vice-Chair. and Head, Samsung Advanced Inst. of Tech. 2013–15. *Publications:* numerous papers at confs and symposia including ISSCC, VLSI Symposium and IEDM, has also contributed to several technical journals on semiconductor related topics. *Address:* Samsung Electronics Building, 1320-10 Seocho-2-dong, Seocho-gu, Seoul 137-857, Republic of Korea (office). *Telephone:* (2) 2255-0114 (office). *Fax:* (2) 2255-0117 (office). *E-mail:* j-npr@samsung.co.kr (office). *Website:* www.samsung.com (office).

KWON, Oh-joon, BS, PhD; South Korean business executive; *CEO, POSCO;* ed Seoul Nat. Univ., Univ. of Pittsburgh, USA; Gen. Man., Tech. Research Labs, POSCO 1986–87, Dept Man. 1996–2003, Man. Dir and Sr Vice-Pres., EU Office, POSCO 2003–06, Head of Tech. Research Labs and Exec. Vice-Pres./Sr Vice-Pres., POSCO 2007–09, Sr Exec. Vice-Pres. and Chief Tech. Officer 2011–12, Pres. and Chief Tech. Officer 2012–14, Rep. Dir and CEO 2014–; Gen. Man., Research Inst. of Industrial Science and Tech. (RIST) 1987–96, CEO 2009–11; Chair. Korea Iron & Steel Asscn 2014–, Korea–Australia Business Council 2014–, POSTECH Foundation 2015–; Vice-Chair. Fed. of Korean Industries 2014–, Korea Employers Fed. 2014–; mem. Exec. Cttee, World Steel Asscn 2014–; mem. Bd, Nat. Acad. of Eng of Korea 2015–; Order of Industrial Service Merit – Bronze Tower (Govt of South Korea) 2008; Outstanding Young Mem. Award, American Soc. for Metals 1980, IR52 Jang Young Shil Award, Korea Industrial Tech. Asscn 1996, Charles Hatchett Award, The Inst. of Materials (UK) 1997, The Best CTO Award, Korea Industrial Tech. Asscn 2013. *Address:* POSCO Head Office, 1 Goedong-dong, Nam-gu, Pohang, Kyongsangbuk-do, 790-600, Republic of Korea (office). *Telephone:* (54) 220-0114 (office). *Fax:* (54) 220-6000 (office). *E-mail:* info@posco.com (office). *Website:* www.posco.com (office).

KWON, Young-soo, BBA, MEng; South Korean business executive; *Chief Operating Officer, LG Corporation;* b. 6 Feb. 1957, Seoul; ed Seoul Nat. Univ., Korea Advanced Inst. of Science and Tech.; fmr Exec. Vice-Pres. LG Electronics Inc., later Pres. and Chief Financial Officer, also served as Head of Globalization Team at LG Electronics' HQ, Seoul as well as a financial officer at LG Electronics' overseas subsidiary in NJ, USA, CEO LG Display Co. Ltd (also known as LG.Philips LCD Co. Ltd) 2007–12, Rep. Dir, LG Display Co. Ltd and Royal Philips Electronics NV 2007–12, Head of Battery Business Div., LG Chem, Ltd 2011, Vice Chair. LG Uplus Corp –2018, COO and mem. Bd of Dirs LG Corpn 2018–. *Address:* LG Corporation, LG Twin Towers, 20, Yeouido-dong, Yeongdeungpo-gu, Seoul, Republic of Korea (office). *Telephone:* (2) 6456-4337 (office). *E-mail:* sungil.wi@lge.com (office). *Website:* www.lg.com (office).

KWONG, Most Rev. Peter K. K., MTh, DD, DSc; Hong Kong ecclesiastic; *Archbishop Emeritus of Hong Kong Sheng Kung Hui;* b. 28 Feb. 1936, Hong Kong; s. of Kwok-Kuen Kwong and Ching-lan Chan; m. Emily Ha; one s. two d.; ed Chung Chi Coll., Kenyon Coll. and Bexley Hall, Colgate Rochester; ordained priest, Anglican Church in Hong Kong 1966; Priest-in-Charge, Crown of Thorns Church, Hong Kong 1965–66; Vicar, St James's Church, Hong Kong 1967–70; Curate, St Paul's Church, Hong Kong 1971–72; mem. teaching staff, Chinese Univ. of Hong Kong 1972–79; Diocesan Gen. Sec. Anglican Diocese of Hong Kong and Macao 1979–81; Bishop of Hong Kong and Macao 1981–98, Archbishop and Primate of Hong Kong Sheng Kung Hui 1998–2006 (retd), now Archbishop Emer., Bishop of Diocese of Hong Kong Island 1998–2006, now Bishop Emer.; Sr Adviser Community Chest of Hong Kong 1999–; mem. Exec. Cttee, Consultative Cttee for Basic Law of Hong Kong 1985–90, Chair. Finance Cttee 1987–90; Adviser on Hong Kong Affairs, State Dept of People's Repub. of China 1992–97; mem. Preparatory Cttee for Special Admin. Region 1996–97, Selection Cttee 1996–97, CPPCC 1998–; Hon. Treas. Council of the Church of East Asia 1981–83, Chair. 1999–; Hon. Dir Chinese Christian Churches Union 1981–; mem. Court, Hong Kong Univ. 1981–; Vice-Pres. Church Mission Soc. 1995–; numerous appointments in health, educ., social welfare, youth orgs etc.; Gold Bauhinia Star; Hon. DD (Univ. of Hong Kong). *Address:* Bishop's House, 1 Lower Albert Road, Hong Kong Special Administrative Region, People's Republic of China (office). *Telephone:* 25265355 (office). *Fax:* 25212199 (office). *E-mail:* office1@hkskh.org (office).

KYAMBADDE, Amelia Kulubya, BBA, MBA; Ugandan politician; *Minister of Trade, Industry and Co-operatives;* b. Guildford, UK; d. of Serwano Kulubya and Mary Kafureka; m. Wilson Kyambadde 1976; six c.; ed Makerere Univ., American InterContinental Univ., UK; Sec. to Minister Yoweri Museveni 1979–81; in exile in Sweden 1983–86; Prin. Pvt. Sec. to Pres. Museveni 1986–2010; mem. Parl. (Nat. Resistance Movt) for Mawokota North 2011–; Minister of Trade, Industry and Co-operatives 2011–; mem. National Resistance Movement (NRM). *Address:* Ministry of Trade, Industry and Co-operatives, 6/8 Parliament Ave, POB 7103, Kampala, Uganda (office). *Telephone:* (41) 4314000 (office). *Fax:* (41) 4347286 (office). *E-mail:* mintrade@mtti.go.ug (office); akyambadde@parliament.go.ug (office). *Website:* www.mtti.go.ug (office).

KYAW KYAW MAUNG, BCom; Myanma banking executive and central banker; *Governor, Central Bank of Myanmar;* b. 12 April 1939; s. of U Maung and Daw Kyin Kyin; m. Daw Nyunt Nyunt Ye; four c.; ed Univ. of Mandalay; Tutor, Univ. of Mandalay 1961–62; Deputy Man., Myanmar Econ. Bank 1962–76; Deputy Man., Cen. Bank of Myanmar 1976–81, Man. 1981–86, Asst Dir 1986–87, Deputy Gov. 1992–97, Gov. 1997–2007, 2013–; mem. Bd of Govs SEACEN Centre, IMF, Asian Clearing Union. *Address:* Central Bank of Myanmar, Office 55, Nay Pyi Taw, Myanmar (office). *Telephone:* (67) 418243 (office). *Fax:* (67) 418270 (office). *E-mail:* director.admin.cbm@mptmail.net.mm (office). *Website:* www.cbm.gov.mm (office).

KYAW WIN, U, BEcons; Myanma politician; b. 1948, Labutta; ed Yangon Univ.; several years with Ministry of Nat. Planning and Finance, served in Planning Dept and later Revenue Dept –1997; Econ. Adviser to Nat. League for Democracy 1997–2015; mem. Pyithu Hluttaw (People's Ass., lower house of parl.) for Dagon Seikkan township 2015–; Minister of Finance and Revenue 2016–18.

KYDLAND, Finn K., BA, PhD; American (b. Norwegian) economist and academic; *Jeffrey Henley Professor of Economics, University of California, Santa Barbara;* b. 1 Dec. 1943; m. Judy Henley; ed Norwegian School of Econs and Business Admin, Carnegie Mellon Univ., USA; Asst Prof. of Econs, Norwegian School of Econs 1973–78; Assoc. Prof. of Econs, Carnegie-Mellon Univ. 1978–82, Prof. of Econs 1982–94, 1995–2005; Malcolm Forsman Centennial Prof. of Econs, Univ. of Texas 1994–95, Sr Research Fellow, IC^2 Inst. 1994–; Jeffrey Henley Prof. of Econs, Univ. of California, Santa Barbara 2004–, also Dir Lab. for Aggregate Econs and Finance (LAEF); Adjunct Prof., Norwegian School of Econs 1993–, Univ. of Stavanger 2007–13; Research Assoc., Nat. Bureau of Econ. Research 2008–; Research Assoc., Fed. Reserve Bank of Cleveland 1991–2008, Fed. Reserve Bank of Dallas 1994–, Fed. Reserve Bank of St Louis 1995–2007, 2010–13; mem. Scottish Council of Econ. Advisers 2007–10; mem. Editorial Bd Macroeconomic Dynamics 1996–; John Stauffer Nat. Fellow, Hoover Inst. 1982–83; Fellow, Econometric Soc. 1992–; Econ. Theory Fellow, Soc. for the Advancement of Econ. Theory 2012–; Visitante Ilustre, Universidad Nacional de Tucumán 2006; mem. Norwegian Acad. of Science and Letters 2005–, Real Academia de Ciencias Económicas y Financieras, Spain 2010–; Hon. Prof., Azerbaijan State Econ. Univ. 2011, Al-Farabi Kazakh Nat. Univ. 2011, Hunan Univ. 2013; Dr hc (Universidad Torcuato Di Tella) 2004, (Univ. of Stavanger) 2005, (Université du Québec à Montréal) 2005, (Norwegian School of Econs) 2011, (Universidad del Norte, Asunción, Paraguay 2010), Hon. DrIur (Univ. of British Columbia) 2006; Alexander Henderson Award, Carnegie Mellon Univ. 1973, Nobel Prize in Econs (jtly with Edward C. Prescott) 2004. *Publications include:* author or co-author of numerous articles in professional journals. *Address:* Department of Economics, 2014 North Hall, University of California, Santa Barbara, CA 93106, USA (office). *Telephone:* (805) 893-2258 (office). *Fax:* (805) 893-8830 (office). *E-mail:* finn.kydland@ucsb.edu (office). *Website:* econ.ucsb.edu (office); www.finnkydland.com.

KYENGE, Cécile Kashetu; Italian/Democratic Republic of the Congo politician and ophthalmologist; *Minister for International Co-operation and Integration;* b. 28 Aug. 1964, Kambove, Katanga, Democratic Repub. of the Congo; m. Domenico 1994; two d.; ed Università Cattolica del Sacro Cuore; moved to Italy 1983; became a qualified ophthalmologist in Modena, Emilia-Romagna; f. Asscn for Intercultural (DAWA) to promote mutual awareness, integration and co-operation between Italy and Africa 2002; nat. spokesperson of asscn March First, which promotes the rights of migrants in Italy 2010–; collaborates with several Italian magazines, including Combonifem and Corriere Immmigrazione; elected in dist of Modena for the Democrats of the Left 2004, later became prov. head of the Forum of Int. Co-operation and Immigration; prov. councillor in Modena for the Democratic Party (PD) 2009–13, mem. Welfare and Social Policies Cttee; also responsible for immigration policies in Emilia-Romagna for the PD; mem. Chamber of Deputies for the PD in Emilia-Romagna Feb. 2013–14; Minister (without portfolio) for Int. Co-operation and Integration April 2013–14; mem. European Parl. for NE Italy 2014–. *Address:* European Parliament, Bâtiment Altiero Spinelli, ASP 11E153, 60 rue Wiertz, 1047 Brussels, Belgium (office). *Website:* www.europarl.europa.eu (office); www.eppgroup.eu (office).

KYEREMANTEN, Alan, BEcons, LLB; Ghanaian economist, politician, diplomatist and business executive; b. 3 Oct. 1955; s. of Alexander Atta Yaw Kyerematen and Victoria Kyerematen (née Welsing); m. Patricia Christabel Kyerematen; two s.; ed Univ. of Ghana, Ghana Law School; sr corp. exec. with subsidiary of Unilever Int., Ghana –1984; Prin. Consultant to Man. Devt

Productivity Inst. 1984–90; est. Empretec Programme (promoting pvt. sector devt) 1990, expanding to 11 other countries in Africa; apptd by UNDP as first Regional Dir of Enterprise Africa 1998; Amb. to USA 2001–03; Minister of Trade, Industry and Presidential Initiatives 2003–05, of Trade and Industry 2005–07; Founding mem. New Patriotic Party—NPP, unsuccessful cand. for Pres. of Ghana 2007; apptd Special Envoy of African Union 2012; Chair. Young Exec. Forum 1992–2001; mem. Council of Govs, British Exec. Service Overseas; fmr Hubert Humphrey Fellow, Univ. of Minnesota School of Man., USA; One of Top 100 Global Leaders for a New Millennium, Time magazine 1994. *Address:* New Patriotic Party, C912/2 Duade Street, Kokomlemle, POB 3456, Accra-North, Ghana. *Telephone:* (30) 2264288. *Fax:* (30) 2229048. *E-mail:* info@newpatrioticparty.org. *Website:* www.newpatrioticparty.org.

KYL, Jon Llewellyn, BA, LLB; American lawyer and fmr politician; *Senator from Arizona;* b. 25 April 1942, Oakland, Neb.; s. of John Henry Kyl and Arlene Griffith; m. Caryll Collins 1964; one s. one d.; ed Univ. of Arizona; lawyer, Jennings, Strouss & Salmon, Phoenix, Ariz. 1966–86; legal counsel, Ariz. State Republican Party 1970–75; mem. US House of Reps, Washington, DC 1987–95; Senator from Arizona 1995–2013 (retd), 2018–Chair. Republican Steering Cttee 2001, Republican Policy Cttee 2003–07, Republican Conf. 2007, Senate Minority Whip 2007–13; Senior Of Counsel, Covington & Burling LLP, Washington, DC 2013–18; Distinguished Scholar, Sandra Day O'Connor Coll. of Law, Arizona State Univ.; Visiting Fellow, American Enterprise Inst.; Distinguished Fellow in Public Service, Coll. of Public Programs, Arizona State Univ.; Chair. Phoenix Chamber of Commerce 1984–85; Republican. *Address:* Arizona State Senate, Capitol Complex, 1700 W Washington, Phoenix, Arizona AZ 85007-2890, USA (office). *Telephone:* (602) 926-3559 (office). *Fax:* (602) 926-3429 (office). *E-mail:* webmaster@azleg.gov (office). *Website:* www.azsenate.gov (office).

KYMLICKA, Will, BA, DPhil, FRSC; Canadian philosopher and academic; *Canada Research Chair in Political Philosophy, Queen's University;* b. 22 Oct. 1962, Winnipeg, Man.; m. Sue Donaldson; ed Queen's Univ., Univ. of Oxford, UK; Lecturer, Dept of Philosophy, Queen's Univ. 1986–87, Queen's Nat. Scholar 1998–2003, Canada Research Chair in Political Philosophy 2003–; Lecturer, Dept of Philosophy, Princeton Univ., NJ 1987–88; Lecturer, Dept of Philosophy, Univ. of Toronto 1988–89, Asst Prof. 1989–90; Sr Policy Analyst, Royal Comm. on New Reproductive Technologies 1990–91; Research Dir Canadian Centre for Philosophy and Public Policy, Univ. of Ottawa 1994–98; Visiting Prof., Univ. of Ottawa 1991–93, Carleton Univ. 1994–98, Inst. for Advanced Studies, Austria 1997, Nationalism Studies Program, Cen. European Univ., Hungary 1998–, Univ. Pompeu Fabra, Spain 1998, 2003, 2012, Sciences-Po, France 2007, Wayne State Univ., USA 2009, Libera Università Internazionale degli Studi Sociali Guido Carli Univ., Italy 2010; Visiting Fellow, European Forum, European Univ. Inst., Italy 1996, Nuffield Coll., Oxford, UK 2009–11, Robert Schuman Centre for Advanced Studies, European Univ. Inst., Italy 2014–15; Pres. American Soc. for Political and Legal Philosophy 2004–06; mem. several editorial and advisory bds; Corresp. Fellow, British Acad. 2011; Dr hc (Copenhagen) 2013, (KU Leuven) 2014; Guiseppe Acerbi Prize 2001, Excellence in Research Prize, Queen's Univ. 2002, Killam Prize in Social Sciences, Canada Council 2004, North American Soc. for Social Philosophy Book Prize 2008, Premier's Discovery Award in Social Sciences, Govt of Ont. 2009, Queen's Diamond Jubilee Medal 2012, Biennial Book Prize, Canadian Philosophical Asscn 2013; several fellowships. *Publications include:* Liberalism, Community and Culture 1989, Contemporary Political Philosophy 1990, Justice in Political Philosophy (ed.) 1992, Multicultural Citizenship: A Liberal Theory of Minority Rights (Macpherson Prize, Canadian Political Science Asscn 1996, Bunche Award, American Political Science Asscn 1996) 1995, The Rights of Minority Cultures 1995, Ethnicity and Group Rights (co-ed.) 1997, States, Nations and Cultures: Spinoza Lectures 1997, Finding Our Way: Rethinking Ethnocultural Relations in Canada 1998, Citizenship in Diverse Societies (co-ed.) 2000, Politics in the Vernacular: Nationalism, Multiculturalism and Citizenship 2001, Alternative Conceptions of Civil Society (co-ed.) 2001, Can Liberal Pluralism be Exported? (co-ed.) 2001, Language Rights and Political Theory (co-ed.) 2003, Ethnicity and Democracy in Africa (co-ed.) 2004, Multiculturalism in Asia (co-ed.) 2005, Multiculturalism and the Welfare State (co-ed.) 2006, The Globalization of Ethics (co-ed.) 2007, Multicultural Odysseys: Navigating the New International Politics of Diversity 2007, The Politics of Reconciliation in Multicultural Societies (co-ed.) 2008, Identity Politics in the Public Realm: Bringing Institutions Back In (co-ed.) 2011, Zoopolis: A Political Theory of Animal Rights (co-author) 2011, Rooted Cosmopolitanism: Canada and the World (co-ed.) 2012, Multiculturalism and Minority Rights in the Arab World (co-ed.) 2014, International Approaches to Governing Ethnic Diversity (co-ed.) 2015, The Strains of Commitment: The Political Sources of Solidarity in Diverse Societies (co-ed.) 2017, Gender Parity and Multicultural Feminism: Towards a New Synthesis (co-ed.) 2018; numerous book chapters and articles in professional journals. *Leisure interest:* running marathons. *Address:* Department of Philosophy, Watson Hall 313, Queen's University, Kingston, ON K7L 3N6, Canada (office). *Fax:* (613) 533-6545 (office). *E-mail:* kymlicka@queensu.ca (office). *Website:* post.queensu.ca/~kymlicka (office).

KYNASTON, Nicolas, ARCM, FRCO; British concert organist; b. 10 Dec. 1941, Morebath, Devon; s. of Roger Tewkesbury Kynaston and Jessie Dearn Caecilia Kynaston (née Parkes); m. 1st Judith Felicity Heron 1961 (divorced 1989); two s. two d.; m. 2nd Susan Harwood Styles 1989; ed Westminster Cathedral Choir School, Downside, Accademia Musicale Chigiana, Siena, Conservatorio Santa Cecilia, Rome, Royal Coll. of Music; Westminster Cathedral Organist 1961–71; debut recital, Royal Festival Hall 1966; recording debut 1968; concert career 1971–, travelling throughout Europe, N America, Asia and Africa; Artistic Dir J. W. Walker & Sons Ltd 1978–82, Consultant 1982–83; organist, Athens Concert Hall 1995–2010; Organ Prof., RAM 2002–14; Jury mem. Grand Prix de Chartres 1971, St Albans Int. Organ Festival 1975; Pres. Inc. Asscn of Organists 1983–85; Chair. Nat. Organ Teachers Encouragement Scheme 1993–96; mem. Westminster Abbey Fabric Comm. 2000–05; consultant for various new organ projects; Hon. FRCO 1976, Hon. RAM 2010; EMI/CFP Sales Award 1974; Deutscher Schallplattenpreis 1978. *Recordings:* numerous recordings, including of Vierne's Sixth Symphony (Deutscher Schallplattenpreis). *Publication:* Transcriptions for Organ 1997. *Leisure interests:* walking, church architecture. *Address:* 28 High Park Road, Kew, Richmond-upon-Thames, Surrey, TW9 4BH, England (home). *Telephone:* (20) 8878-4455 (home).

KYPRIANOU, Markos, MA; Cypriot lawyer and politician; b. 22 Jan. 1960, Limassol; ed Univ. of Athens, Greece, Univ. of Cambridge, UK, Harvard Law School, USA; Assoc., Antis Triantafyllides & Sons 1985–91; Pnr, Kyprianou & Boyiadjis 1991–95, George L. Savvides & Co. (following merger) 1995–2003; Municipal Councillor, Nicosia 1986–91; mem. Parl. for Nicosia 1991–2003, fmr Deputy Chair. Cttee on Foreign and European Affairs, fmr mem. Cttee on Legal Affairs, Chair. House Cttee on Financial and Budgetary Affairs 1999–2003; Chair. House of Reps Del. to Parl. Ass. of OSCE; Minister of Finance 2003–04; EU Commr without Portfolio 2004, for Health and Consumer Protection 2004–06, for Health 2006–08; Minister of Foreign Affairs 2008–11; Deputy Pres. Dimokratiko Komma (Democratic Party) 2014–; Assoc. mem. ABA. *Address:* Dimokratiko Komma (Democratic Party), POB 23979, 50 Grivas Dhigenis Avenue, 1080 Nicosia, Cyprus (office). *Telephone:* 22873800 (office). *E-mail:* diko@diko.org.cy (office). *Website:* diko.org.cy (office).

KYTE, Rachel, BA, MA; British international organization official; *CEO and Special Representative of the UN Secretary General, Sustainable Energy for All;* ed Univ. of London, Fletcher School Law and Diplomacy, Tufts Univ., USA; fmr Sr Policy Adviser, Int. Women's Health Coalition; Sr Multilateral Policy Adviser, IUCN (The World Conservation Union) 1997–2000, also Sr Adviser on Gender and Rep. to EU; Prin. Specialist, Office Compliance Adviser/Ombudsman IFC/Multilateral Investment Guarantee Agency (MIGA) 2000–03; joined IFC, World Bank Group as Sr Specialist, Ombudsman, in Office of Compliance Advisor/Ombudsman 2000, Dir Environment and Social Devt Dept 2004–08, Vice-Pres. Business Advisory Services and mem. Man. Group 2008–12, Vice-Pres. and Head of Network, Sustainable Devt 2011–13, Group Vice-Pres. and Special Envoy on Climate Change 2014–15; CEO and Special Rep. of UN Sec.-Gen., Sustainable Energy for All 2016–; fmr teacher of negotiation, advocacy, public policy, Simone de Beauvoir Inst. Leadership, Mexico City; Prof. of Practice in Sustainable Devt, Fletcher School of Law and Diplomacy 2012–. *Address:* Sustainable Energy for All Initiative, United Nations Vienna International Centre, PO Box 500 F-162, 1400 Vienna, Austria (office). *Telephone:* (1) 260608-3403 (office). *E-mail:* info@se4all.org (office). *Website:* www.se4all.org (office).

KYUCHUKOV, Lyubomir Nedkov, MA; Bulgarian diplomatist, politician and business executive; b. 14 June 1955, Sofia; m.; two c.; ed English Language Secondary School, Varna, Moscow State Univ. for Int. Relations, USSR, Georgetown Univ., Washington, DC; mem. staff, Embassy in Bucharest 1981, Desk Officer, Romania and Poland, Eastern Europe Dept, Ministry of Foreign Affairs 1981–84; Political Analyst, BBSS Gallup International 1992–94; Chief Adviser, Secr. for European Integration at the Council of Ministers 1996–97; Man. consultancy co. 1997–2005; mem. Council for European and Euro-Atlantic Integration with Pres. of Bulgaria 2001–05; Deputy Minister of Foreign Affairs 2005–09, Acting Minister of Foreign Affairs May–July 2009; Amb. to UK 2009–12; participant in Nat. Round Table and Public Council on Nat. Issues 1990; Vice-Chair. Supreme Council, Bulgarian Socialist Party 1990–91, Social Democratic Political Movt 2005–07; mem. Nat. Council of Bulgarian Asscn for Support for the UN 1988–91, Exec. Council of Bulgarian Asscn for European Security and Cooperation 1989–92, Admin. Council of Devt of Civil Society Foundation 1996–97, Bd of Diplomatic Inst. 2005–09; mem. editorial staff, New Time Magazine 1992–95, Editorial Bd, International Relations Magazine 2005–; Lecturer, Japanese Agency for Int. Co-operation 1997–2000; Founder-mem. Governing Council, Inst. of Econs and Int. Relations 2003–05. *Address:* Ministry of Foreign Affairs, 1113 Sofia, ul. Al. Zhendov 2, Bulgaria (office). *Telephone:* (2) 948-29-99 (office). *Fax:* (2) 297-136-20 (office). *E-mail:* vtcherneva@mfa.bg (office). *Website:* www.mfa.bg (office).

KYUMA, Fumio; Japanese politician; b. 4 Dec. 1940; ed Univ. of Tokyo; mem. Nagasaki Prefectural Ass. 1971–80; mem. House of Reps 1980–2009, Parl. Vice-Minister of Transport 1987, Minister of State for Defence 1996–98, Dir-Gen. Defence Agency (State Minister) 1996–99; Chair. LDP Panel on Security Issues 2000, Chair. (acting) LDP Policy Research Council 2001, Acting LDP Sec.-Gen. 2002, Chair. LDP Gen. Council 2004, Minister of State for Defence 2006–07, Minister of Defence Jan.–July 2007; Grand Cordon of the Order of the Rising Sun 2013.

KYUNG-WHA CHUNG (see Chung, Kyung-wha).